Who Was Who in America

Biographical Reference Works
Published by Marquis Who's Who, Inc.

Who's Who in America

Who's Who in America/Index by Professions

Who Was Who in America

Historical Volume (1607-1896)

Volume I (1897-1942)

Volume II (1943-1950)

Volume III (1951-1960)

Volume IV (1961-1968)

Volume V (1969-1973)

Who's Who in the World

Who's Who in the East

Who's Who in the South and Southwest

Who's Who in the West

Who's Who in the Midwest

Who's Who of American Women

Who's Who in Religion

Who's Who in Finance and Industry

International Scholar's Directory

Who's Who in Government

World Who's Who in Science

Directory of Medical Specialists

Directory of Osteopathic Specialists

Marquis Who's Who Publications/
Index to all Books

Who Was Who in America®

Volume II
1943-1950
Seventh Printing-1975

A Component of
Who's Who in American History

MARQUIS
Who's Who

Marquis Who's Who, Inc.
200 East Ohio Street
Chicago, Illinois 60611 U.S.A.

Library of Congress Catalog Card Number 43-3789
ISBN 0-8379-0206-1

Distributed in the United Kingdom by
George Prior Associated Publishers
Rugby Chambers, 2 Rugby Street
London WC 1N 3 QU

Table of Contents

Preface

The appearance of this seventh printing of Volume II of WHO WAS WHO IN AMERICA became inevitable with the increased demand among biographical researchers for the books in the Who's Who in American History series. *Who's Who in America,* the major component of the series, has continued to advance the highest standards of biographical compilation throughout its more than three-quarters of a century of continuous publication. The WAS books (to use the shortened form by which they are perhaps better known) have sought to reflect the history and the genealogical heritage of America.

Basically, however, the WAS books inherited those unique characteristics that have made *Who's Who in America* both an internationally respected reference work and a household word here in the country of its origin.

Sketches in each WAS volume, for example, have not only been prepared from information supplied by the biographees themselves, but have been approved personally—and frequently revised—before being printed in a Marquis publication during the subject's lifetime. As with all WAS volumes, many of these sketches have been scrutinized and revised by relatives or legal representatives of the deceased biographee. Except for the resulting changes, and those occasional variations interjected by the compilers, the WAS biographies are printed precisely as they last appeared during the subject's lifetime. As a result, many contain personal data unavailable elsewhere. The preface to the first volume of *Who's Who in America* selected this fact as one of that volume's outstanding characteristics, and stated: "The book is autobiographical, the data having been obtained from first hand." It follows that WHO WAS WHO IN AMERICA is autobiographical to a distinctive degree. In that respect, it is unique among American biographical directories. And although condensed to the concise style that Marquis Who's Who has made famous, the sketches contain all essential facts.

There results far more than a biographical directory of some 90,000 deceased American notables within the covers of these six volumes. WHO WAS WHO IN AMERICA is a vital portion of American history from the early days of the colonies to mid-1973. It is authentic history. It is the autobiography of America.

Table of Abbreviations

The following abbreviations are frequently used in this book:

*Following a sketch signifies that the published biography could not be verified.

††Non-current sketches of WHO'S WHO IN AMERICA biographees who were born 95 or more years ago (see Preface for explanation).

A.A., Associate in Arts.
A.A.A., Agricultural Adjustment Administration; Anti-Aircraft Artillery.
A.A.A.S., American Association for the Advancement of Science.
AAC, Army Air Corps.
a.a.g., asst. adjutant general.
AAF, Army Air Forces.
A. and M., Agricultural and Mechanical.
A.A.H.P.E.R., American Association for Health, Physical Education and Recreation.
A.A.O.N.M.S., Ancient Arabic Order of the Nobles of the Mystic Shrine.
A.A.S.R., Ancient Accepted Scottish Rite (Masonic).
A.B.C.F.M., American Board of Commissioners for Foreign Missions (Congregational).
A.B. (also **B.A.**), Bachelor of Arts.
A.,B.& C. R.R., Atlanta, Birmingham & Coast R.R.
ABC, American Broadcasting Company.
AC, Air Corps.
acad., academy; academic.
A.C.L. R.R., Atlantic Coast Line R.R.
A.C.P., American College of Physicians.
A.C.S., American College of Surgeons.
actg., acting.
a.d.c., aide-de-camp.
add., additional.
adj., adjutant; adjunct.
adj. gen., adjutant general.
adm., admiral.
adminstr., administrator.
adminstrn., administration.
adminstrv., administrative.
adv., advocate; advisory.
advt., advertising.
A.E., Agricultural Engineer.
AEC, Atomic Energy Commission.
A.E. and P., Ambassador Extraordinary and Plenipotentiary.
AEF, American Expeditionary Forces.
aero., aeronautics, aeronautical.
AFB, Air Force Base.
A.F.D., Doctor of Fine Arts.
A.F. and A.M., Ancient Free and Accepted Masons.
AFL (or **A.F. of L.**), American Federation of Labor.
A.F.T.R.A., American Federation TV and Radio Artists.
agr., agriculture.
agrl., agricultural.
agt., agent.
Agy., Agency.
a.i., ad interim.
A.I.A., American Institute of architects.
AID, Agency for International Development.
A.I.M., American Institute of Management.
AK—Alaska
AL—Alabama
Ala., Alabama
A.L.A., American Library Association.
Am., American, America.
A.M. (also **M.A.**), Master of Arts.
A.M.A., American Medical Association.
A.M.E., African Methodist Episcopal.
Am. Inst. E.E., American Institute of Electrical Engineers.
Am. Soc. C.E., American Society of Civil Engineers.
Am. Soc. M.E., American Society of Mechanical Emgineers.
A.N.A., Associate National Academician.
anat., anatomical.
ann., annual.
ANTA, American National theatre and Academy.
anthrop., anthropological.
antiq., antiquarian.
A.O.H., Ancient Order of Hibernians.
A.P., Associated Press.
appmnt., appointment.
apptd., appointed.
apt., apartment.
a.q.m., assistant quartermaster.
AR—Arkansas
A.R.C., American Red Cross.
archeol., archeological.
archtl., architectural.
Ark., Arkansas
Ariz.—Arizona.
Arts D., Doctor of Arts.
arty., artillery.
AS, Air Service.
A.S.C.A.P., American Society of Composers, Authors and Publishers.
ASF, Air Service Force.
assn., association.
asso., associate; associated.
asst., assistant.
astron., astronomical.
astrophys., astrophysical.
A.T.S.C., Air Technical Service Command.
A.,T.& S.F. Ry., Atchison, Topeka & Santa Fe Ry.
Atty., attorney.
AUS, Army of the United States.
Aux., Auxiliary.
Av., Avenue.
AZ—Arizona

b., born.
B., Bachelor.
B.A. (ALSO **A.B.**), Bachelor of Arts.
B.A.A.S., British Association for the Advancement of Science.
B.Agr., Bachelor of Agriculture.
Balt., Baltimore.
Bapt., Baptist.
B.Arch., Bachelor of Architecture.
B.& A. R.R., Boston & Albany R. R.
B.A.S. (or **B.S.A.**), Bachelor of Agricultural Science.
batn., batin., batt., battalion.
B.B.A., Bachelor of Business Administration.
BBC, British Broadcasting Company.
B.C., British Columbia.
B.C.E., Bachelor of Civil Engineering.
B.Chir., Bachelor of Surgery.
B.C.L., Bachelor of Civil Law.
B.C.S., Bachelor of Commercial Scienc
bd., board.
B.D., Bachelor of Divinity.
B.Di., Bachelor of Didactics.
B.E. (or **Ed.B.**), Bachelor of Education.
B.E.E., Bachelor of Electrical Enginee ing.
BEF, British Expeditionary Force.
bet., between.
B.F.A., Bachelor of fine Arts.
bibl., bibilcal.
bibliog., bibliographical.
biog., biographical.
biol., biological.
B.J., Bachelor of Journalism.
Bklyn., Brooklyn.
B.L. (or **Litt.B.**), Bachelor of Letters.
Bldg., building.
blk., block.
B.L.S., Bachelor of Library Science.
Blvd., Boulevard.
B.& M. R.R., Boston & Marine R.R.
Bn. (or **Batn.**), Battalion.
B.O. (or **O.B.**), Bachelor of Oratory.
B.& O. R.R., Baltimore & Ohio R.R.
bot., botanical.
B.P., Bachelor of Painting.
B.P.E., Bachelor of Physical Education.
B.P.O.E., Benevolent and Protecti Order of Elks.
B.Pd. (or **Pd.B.**, or **Py.B.**), Bachelor Pedagogy.
Br., branch.
B.R.E., Bachelor of Religious Educatio
brig., brigadier, brigade.
brig. gen., brigadier general.
Brit., British; Britannica.
Bro., Brother.
B., R. & P. Ry., Buffalo, Rochester Pittsburg Ry.
B.S. (also **S.B.** or **ScB.**), Bachelor Science.
B.S. in Ry. M.E., Bachelor in Railw Mechanical Engineering.
B.S.A., Bachelor of Agricultural Scienc
B.S.D., Bachelor of Didactic Science.
B.S.T., Bachelor of Sacred Theology.
B.Th., Bachelor of Theology.
bull., bulletin.
bur., bureau.
bus., business.
B.W.I., British West Indies.

CA—California
C.A., Central America.
CAA, Civil Aeronautics Adminstrn.
CAB, Civil Aeronautics Board.
CAC, Coast Artillery Corps.
Cal., California.
Can., Canada.
Cantab., of or pertaining to Cambrid University, Eng.
capt., captain.
C. & A. R.R., Chicago & Alton R.R., no Alton Ry. Co.
Cath., Catholic.

cav., cavalry.
CBI, China - Burma - India theater of operations.
C.,B.& Q. R.R., Chicago, Burlington & Quincy R.R. Co.
CBS, Columbia Broadcasting System
CCC. Commodity Credit Corporation.
C.,C.,C.& St.L. Ry., Cleveland, Cincinnati. Chicago & St. Louis Ry.
C.E., Civil Engineer (degree), Corps of Engineers.
CEF, Canadian Expeditionary Forces.
C.& E.I. R.R., Chicago & Eastern Illinois R.R.
C.G.W. R.R., Chicago Great Western Railway.
ch., church.
Ch.D., Doctor of Chemistry.
chem., chemical.
Chem.E., Chemical Engineer.
Chgo., Chicago.
Chirurg., Chirurgical.
chmn., chairman.
chpt., chapter.
Cia, (Spanish), Company.
CIA, Central Intelligence Agency.
CIC, Counter Intelligence Corps.
C., I.&L. Ry., Chicago, indianapolis & Louisville Railway.
Cin., Cincinnati.
CIO, Congress of Industrial Organizations.
civ., civil.
Cleve., Cleveland.
climatol., climatological.
clin., clinical.
clk., clerk.
C.L.S.C., Chautauqua Literary and Scientific Circle.
C.L.U., Certified Life Underwriter.
C.M., Master in Surgery.
C. M., St.P.&P.R.R., Chicago, Milwaukee, St. Paul & Pacific R.R. Co.
C. N. Ry., Canadian Northern Ry.
C.& N.-W. Ry., Chicago & Northwestern Railway.
CO—Colorado
Co., Company;
C. of C. Chamber of Commerce.
C.O.F., Catholic Order of Foresters.
C. of Ga. Ry., Central of Georgia Ry.
col., colonel.
coll., college
Colo., Colorado
com., committee.
comd., commanded.
comdg., commanding.
comdr., commander.
comdt., commandant.
commd., commissioned.
comml., commercial.
commn., commission.
commr., commissioner.
Com. Sub., Commissary of Subsistence.
condr., conductor.
conf., conference.
confed., confederate.
Congl., Congregational; Congressional.
Conglist., Congregationalist.
CONN—Connecticut.
cons., consulting, consultant.
consol., consolidated.
constl., constitutional.
constn., constitution.
constrn., construction.
contbd., contributed.
contbg., contributing.
contbn., contribution.
contbr., contributor.
conv., convention.
coop. (or **co-op.**), cooperative.
corp., corporation.
corr., correspondent; corresponding, correspondence.
C & O. Ry., Chesapeake & Ohio Ry. Co.
C.P.A., Certified Public Accountant.
C.P.C.U., Chartered Property and Casualty Underwriter.
C.P.H., Certificate of Public Health.
cpl. (or **corpl.**), corporal.
C.P. Ry., Canadian Pacific Ry. Co.
C. R.I.& P. Ry., Chicago, Rock Island & Pacific Ry. Co.
C.R.R. of N.J., Central Railroad Co. of New Jersey.
C.S., Christian Science.
C.S. Army, Confederate State Army.
C.S.B., Bachelor of Christian Science.
C.S.D., Doctor of Christian Science.
C.S.N., Confederate States Navy.
C.& S. Ry. Co., Colorado & Southern Ry. Co.
C.,St.P.,M.&O. Ry., Chicago, St. Paul, Minneapolis & Omaha Ry. Co.
Ct., Court.
C.T., Candidate in Theology.
CT—Connecticut.
c.Vt. Ry., Central Vermont Ry.
C.& W.I. R.R., Chicago & Western Indiana R.R. Co.
CWS, Chemical Warfare Service.
cycle., cyclopedia.
C.Z., Canal Zone.

d. (also dau.), daughter.
D., Doctor.
D. Agr., Doctor of Agriculture.
D.A.R., Daughters of the American Revolution.
D.A.V., Disabled American Veterans.
D.C., District of Columbia.-D.C.
D.C.L., Doctor of Civil Law.
D.C.S., Doctor of Commercial Science
D.D., Doctor of Divinity.
D.D.S., Doctor of Dental Surgery.
DE—Delaware.
dec., deceased.
Def., Defense.
deg., degree.
Del., Delaware.
del., delegate.
Dem., Democratic.
D.Eng. (also **Dr. Engring.**, or **e.d.** Doctor of Engineering.
denom., denominational.
dep., deputy.
dept., department.
dermatol., determatological.
desc., descendant.
devel., development.
D.F.C., Distinguished Flying Cross.
D.H.L., Doctor of Hebrew Literature.
D.& H. R.R., Delaware & Hudson R.R. Co.
dir., director.
disch., discharged.
dist., district.
distbg., distributing.
distbn., distribution.
distbr., distributor.
div., division; divinity; divorce proceedings.
D.Litt., Doctor of Literature.
D.,L.& W.R.R., Delaware Lackawanna & Western R.R. co.
D.M.D., Doctor of Medical Dentistry.
D.M.S., Doctor of Medical Science.
D.O., Doctor of Osteopathy.
DPA. Defense Production Administration.
D.P.H. (also **Dr.P.H.**), Diploma in Public Health or Doctor of Public Health or Doctor of Public Hygiene.
Dr., Doctor, Drive.
D.R., Daughters of the Revolution.
D.R.E., Doctor of Religious Education.
D.& R.G.W. R.R. Co., Denver & Rio Grande Western R.R. Co.
D.Sc. (or **Sc. D.**). Doctor of Science.
D.S.C., Distinguished Service Cross.
D.S.M., Distinguished Service Medal.
D.S.T., Doctor of Sacred Theology.
D.T.M., Doctor of Tropical Medicine.
D.V.M., Doctor of Veterinary Medicine.
D.V.S., Doctor of Veterinary Surgery.

E., East.
E. AND P., Extraordinary and Plenipotentiary.
ECA, Economic Cooperation Administration.
eccles., ecclesiastical.
ecol., ecological.
econ., economic.
ECOSOC, Economic and Social Council of UN.
ed., educated.
E.D. (also **D.Eng., or Dr.Engring.**), Doctor of Engineering.
Ed.B., Bachelor of Education.
Ed.D., Doctor of Education.
edit., edition.
Ed.M. (or **M.Ed.**), Master of Education.
edn., education.
ednl., educational.
E.E., Electrical Engineer.
E.E. and M. P., Envoy Extraordinary and Minister Plenipotentiary.
Egyptol., Egyptological.
elec., electrical.
electrochem., electrochemical.
electrophys., electrophysical.
E. M., Engineer of Mines.
ency., encyclopedia.
Eng., England.
engr., engineer.
engring., engineering.
entomol., entomological.
e.s., eldest son.
E.S.M.W.T.P., Engring. Science and Management War Training Program.
ethnol., ethnological.
ETO, European Theater of Operations.
Evang., Evangelical.

exam., examination; examining.
exc., executive.
exhbn., exhibition.
expdn., expedition.
expn., exposition.
expt., experiment.
exptl., experimental.

F., Fellow.
F.A., Field Artillery.
FAA, Federal Aviation Agency.
F.A.C.P., Fellow American College of Physicians.
F.A.C.S., Fellow American College of Surgeons.
FAO, Food and Agriculture Organization.
FBI, Federal Bureau of Investigation.
FCA, Farm Credit Administration.
FCC, Federal Communications Commission.
FCDA, Federal Civil Defense Administration.
FDA, Food and Drug Administration.
FDIA, Federal Deposit Insurance Administration.
F.E., Forest Engineer.
Fed., Federal.
Fedn., Federation.
Fgn., Foreign.
FHA, Federal Housing Administration.
FL—Florida.
Fla., Florida.
FOA, Foreign Operations Administration.
Found., Foundation.
frat., fraternity.
F.R.C.P., Fellow Royal College of Physicians (England).
F.R.C.S., Fellow Royal College of Surgeons (England).
frt., Freight.
FSA, Federal Security Agency.
Ft., Fort.
FTC, Federal Trade Commission.

G.-1 (or other number), Division of General Staff.
gastroent., gastroenterological.
GA—Georgia.
Ga., Georgia.
G.A.R., Grand Army of the Republic.
GATT, General Agreement on Tariffs and Trade.
G.,C.& S.F. Ry., Gulf, Colorado & Santa Fe Ry. Co.
G.D., Graduate in Divinity.
g.d., granddaughter.
gen., general.
geneal., genealogical.
geod., geodetic.
geog., geographical; geographic.
geol., geological.
geophys., geophysical.
g.g.d., great granddaughter.
g.g.s., great grandson.
G.H.Q., General Headquarters.
G.,M.& N. R.R., Gulf, Mobile & Northern R.R. Co.
G., M.& O. R.R., Gulf, Mobile & Ohio R.R. Co.
G.N. Ry., Great Northern Ry. Co.
gov., governor.
govt., government.
govtl., governmental.
grad., graduated; graduate.
g.s., grandson.
Gt., Great.
G.T. Ry., Grand Trunk Ry. System.
GU—Guam.
G.W. Ry. of Can., Great Western Ry. of Canada.
gynecol., gynecological.

Hdqrs., Headquarters.
H.G., Home Guard.
H.H.D., Doctor of Humanities.
HHFA, Housing and Home Finance Agency.
H.I., Hawaiian Islands.
HI—Hawaii.
hist., historical.
H.M., Master of Humanics.
HOLC, Home Owners Loan Corporation.
homeo., homeopathic.
hon., honorary; honorable.
Ho. of Reps,, House of Representatives.
hort., horticultural.
hosp., hospital.
Hts., Heights.
H.Ty. (or **H.T.**), Hawaiian Territory.
Hwy., Highway.
Hydrog., hydrographic.

IA— Iowa.
Ia., Iowa.
IAEA, International Atomic Energy Agency.
IBM, International Business Machines Corporation.
ICA, International Cooperation Administration.
ICC, Interstate Commerce Commission.
I.C.R.R., Illinois Central R.R. System.
ID—Idaho.
Ida., Idaho.
I.E.E.E., Institute of Electrical and Electronics Engineers.
IFC, International Finance Corp.
I.G.N. R.R., International - Great Northern R.R.
IGY, International Geophysical Year.
IL—Illinois.
Ill., Illinois.
ILO, International Labor Organization.
Illus., Illustrated.
IMF, International Monetary Fund.
IN— Indiana.
Inc., Incorporated.
Ind., Indiana, Independent.
Indpls., Indianapolis.
Indsl., Industrial.
inf., infantry.
ins., insurance.
insp., inspector.
inst., institute.
instl., institutional.
instn., institution.
instr., instructor.
instrn., instruction.
internat., international.
intro., introduction.
I.O.B.B.,´ Independent Order of B'nai B'rith.
I.O.G.T., Independent Order of Goo Templars.
I.O.O.F., Independent Order of Odd Fellow
I.R.E., Institute of Radio Engineers.

J.B., Jurum Baccalaureus.
J.C.B., Juris Canonici Bachelor.
J.C.L., Juris Canonici Lector.
J.D., Doctor of Jurisprudence.
j.g., junior grade.
jour., journal.
jr., junior.
J.S.D., Doctor of Juristic Science.
Jud., Judicial.
J.U.D., Juris Utriusque Doctor: Doctor Both (Canon and Civil) Laws.

Kan.—Kansas.
K.C., Knight of Columbus.
K.C.C.H., Knight Commander of Court Honor.
K.P., Knight of Pythias.
K.N.S. Ry., Kansas City Southern Ry.
KS—Kansas.
KY—Kentucky.
Ky., Kentucky.

lab., laboratory.
lang., language.
laryngol., laryngological.
lectr., lecturer.
L.H.D., Doctor of Letters of Humanity.
L.I., Long Island.
lieut., lieutenant.
L.I. R.R., Long Island R.R. Co.
lit., literary; literature.
Lit. Hum., Literae Humanores (classic Oxford U., Eng.).
Litt.B. (or **B.L.**), Bachelor of Letters.
Litt.D., Doctor of Letters.
LL.B., Bachelor of Laws.
LL.D., Doctor of Laws.
LL.M. (or **ML.**). Master of Laws.
L.& N. R.R., Louisville & Nashville R.R.
L.O.M., Loyal Order of Moose.
L.R.C.P., Licentiate Royal Coll. Physicians.
L.R.C.S., Licentiate Royal Coll. Surgeons.
L.S., Library Science.
L.S.A., Licentiate Society of Apothecaries.
L.S.& M. S. Ry., Lake Shore & Michiga Southern Ry.
lt. or **(lieut.)**, lieutenant.
Ltd., Limited.
Luth., Lutheran.
L.V. R.R., Lehigh Valley R.R. co.

m., marriage ceremony.
M.A. (OR **A.M.**), Master of Arts.
mag., magazine.
M.Agr., Master of Agriculture.
maj., major.
Man., Manitoba.
M.Arch., Master in Architecture.
Mass., Massachusetts.
Math., mathematical.
M.B., Bachelor of Medicine.
M.B.A., Master of Business Administration.

MBS, Mutual Broadcasting System.
M.C., Medical Corps.
M.C.S., Master of Commercial Science.
mcht., merchant.
M.C. R.R., Michigan Central R.R.
Md., Maryland
MD—Maryland
M.D., Doctor of Medicine.
M.Di., Master of Didactics.
M.Dip., Master in Diplomacy.
mdse., merchandise.
M.D.V., Doctor of Veterinary Medicine.
Me., Maine.
ME—Maine.
M.E., Mechanical Engineer.
mech., mechanical.
M.E. Ch., Methodist Episcopal Church.
M.Ed., Master of Education.
med., medical.
Med. O.R.C., Medical Officers' Reserve Corps.
Med. R.C., Medical Reserve Corps.
M.E.E., Master of Electrical Engineering.
mem., member.
Meml. (or **Mem.**), Memorial.
merc., mercantile.
met., metropolitan.
metall., metallurgical.
Met.E., Metallurgical Engineer.
meteorol., meteorological.
Meth., Methodist.
metrol., metrological.
M.F., Master of Forestry.
M.F.A., Master of Fine Arts.
mfg., manufacturing.
mfr., manufacturer.
mgmt., management.
mgr., manager.
M.H.A., Master of Hospital Administration.
M.I., Military Intelligence.
MI—Michigan.
Mich., Michigan.
micros., microscopical.
mil., military.
Milw., Milwaukee.
Mineral., mineralogical.
Minn., Minnesota.
Miss., Mississippi.
M.-K.-I. R.R., Missouri - Kansas-Texas R.R. Co.
M.L. (or **LL. M.**), Master of Laws.
M.Litt., Master of Literature.
Mlle., Mademoiselle (Miss).
M.L.S., Master of Library Science.
Mme., Madame.
M.M.E., Master of Mechanical Engineering.
MN—Minnesota.
mng., managing.
Moblzn., Mobilization.
Mont., Montana.
M.P., Member of Parliament.
Mpls., Minneapolis.
M.P. R.R., Missouri Pacific R.R.
M.Pd., Master of Pedagogy.
M.P.E., Master of Physical Education.
M.P.L., Master of Patent Law.
M.R.C.P., Member Royal College of Physicians.
M.R.C.S., Member Royal College of Surgeons.
M.R.E., Master of Religious Education.
MS—Mississippi.
M.S. (or **M.Sc.**). Master of Science.
M.S.F., Master of Science of Forestry.
M.S.T., Master of Sacred Theology.
M.& St. L. R.R., Minneapolis & St. Louis R.R. Co.
M.,St.P.& S.S.M. Ry., Minneapolis, St. Paul & Sault Ste. Marie Ry.
M.S.W., Master of Social Work.
MT—Montana.
Mt., Mount.
mtn., mountain.
M.T.O.U.S.A., Mediterranean Theater of Operations, U.S. Army.
mus., museum; musical.
Mus.B., Bachelor of Music.
Mus.D. (or **Mus. Doc.**), Doctor of Music.
Mus. M., Master of Music.
Mut., Mutual.
M.V.M., Massachusetts Volunteer Militia.
M.W.A., Modern Woodmen of America.
mycol., mycological.

N., North.
N.A., National Academician; North America; National Army.
N.A.A.C.P., National Association for the Advancement of Colored People.
NACA, National Advisory Committee for Aeronautics.
N.A.D., National Academy of Design.
N.A.M., National Association of Manufacturers.
NASA, National Aeronautics and Space Administration.
nat., national.
NATO, North Atlantic Treaty Organization.
N.A.T.O.U.S.A., North African Theater of Operations, U.S. Army.
nav., navigation.
NB—Nebraska.
N.B., New Brunswick.
NBC, National Broadcasting Co.
NC—North Carolina.
N.,C.& St.L. Ry., Nashville, Chattanooga & St. Louis Ry.
NDCR, National Defense Research Committee.
N.E., Northeast; New England.
N.E.A., National Education Association.
Neb., Nebraska.
neurol., neurological.
Nev., Nevada.
New Eng., New England.
N.G., National Guard.
N.G.S.N.Y., National Guard State of New York.
N.H., New Hanpshire.
NH—New Hampshire.
NIH, National Institutes of Health.
N.J., New Jersey.
NJ—New Jersey
NLRB, National Labor Relations Board.
N.Ph.D., Doctor Natural Philosophy.
N.P. Ry., Northern Pacific Ry.
No., Northern.
NPA, National Production Authority.
nr., near.
NRA, National Recovery Administration.
NRC, National Research Council.
N.S., Nova Scotia.
NSC, National Security Council.
NSF, National Science Foundation.
NSRB, National Security Resources Board.
N.T., New Testament.
numis., numismatic.
N.W., Northwest
N.& W. Ry., Norfolk & Western Ry.
NV—Nevada.
N.Y., New York.
NY—New York.
N.Y.C., New York City.
N.Y. Central R.R. (or **N.Y.C. R.R.**), New York Central Railroad Company.
N.Y.,C.& St.L. R.R., New York, Chicago & St. Louis R.R. Co.
N.Y., N.H.& H. R.R., New York, New Haven & Hartford R.R. Co.
N.Y.,O.& W. Ry., New York, Ontario & Western Ry.

O—Ohio.
OAS, Organization of American States.
O.B., Bachelor of Oratory.
obs., observatory.
obstet., obstetrical.
OCDM, Office of Civil and Defense Mobilization.
ODM, Office of Defense Mobilization.
OECD, organization European Cooperation and Development.
OEEC, Organization European Economic Cooperation.
O.E.S., Order of the Eastern Star.
ofcl., Official.
OH—Ohio.
OK—Oklahoma.
Okla., Oklahoma.
Ont., Ontario.
OPA, Office of Price Administration.
opthal., ophthalmological.
OPM, Office of Production management.
OPS, Office of Price Stabilization.
O.Q.M.G., Office of Quartermaster General.
O.R.C., Officers' Reserve Corps.
orch., orchestra.
OR—Oregon.
Ore., Oregon.
orgn., organization.
ornithol., ornithological.
O.S.B., Order of Saint Benedict.
O.S.L. R.R., Oregon Short Line R.R.
OSRD, Office of Scientific Research and Development.
OSS, Office of Strategic Services.
osteo, osteopathic.
O.T., Old Testament.
O.T.C., Officers' Training Camp.
otol., otological.
O.T.S., Officers' Training School.
O.U.A.M., Order United American Mechanics.
OWI, Office of War Information.
O.-W.R.R.& N. Co., Oregon-Washington R.R. & Navigation Co.
Oxon., Of or pertaining to Oxford University, Eng.

PA—Pennsylvania
Pa., Pennsylvania
Pa. R.R., Pennsylvania R.R.
paleontol., paleontological.
pass., passenger.
path., pathological.
Pd.B. (or **B.Pd.**, or **Py.B.**), Bachelor of Pedagogy.
Pd.D., Doctor of Pedagogy.
Pd.M., master of Pedagogy.
P.E., Protestant Episcopal.
Pe.B., Bachelor of Pediatrics.
P.E.I., Prince Edward Island.
P.E.M., Poets, Playwrights, Editors, Essayists and Novelists (Internat. Assn.).
penol., penological.
pfc., private first class.
PHA, Public Housing Administration.
pharm., pharmaceutical.
Pharm.D., Doctor of Pharmacy.
Pharm.M., Master of Pharmacy.
Ph.B., Bachelor of Philosophy.
Ph.C., Pharmaceutical Chemist.
Ph.D., Doctor of Philosophy.
Ph.G., Graduate in Pharmacy.
Phila., Philadelphia.
philol., philological.
philes., philosophical.
photog., photographic.
phys., physical.
Phys. and Surg., Physicians and Surgeons (college at Columbia University).
Physiol., physiological.
P.I., Philippine Islands.
Pitts., Pittsburg.
Pkwy., Parkway.
Pl., Place.
P.& L.E. R.R., Pittsburgh & Lake Erie R.R.
P.M., Paymaster.
P.M. R.R., Pere Marquette R.R. Co.
polit., political.
poly., polytechnic.
pomol., pomological.
P.Q., Province of Quebec.
P.R., Puerto Rico.
prep., preparatory.
pres., president.
Presbyn., Presbyterian.
presdl., presidential.
prin., principal.
Proc., Proceedings.
prod., produced (play production).
prodn., production.
prof., professor.
profl. professional.
Prog., Progressive.
propr., proprietor.
pros. atty., prosecuting attorney.
pro tem, pro tempore (for the time being).
psychiat., psychiatrical; psychiatric,
psychol., psychological.
P.T.A., parent-Teacher Association.
PTO, Pacific Theatre of Operations.
pub., public; publisher; publishing; published.
publ., publication.
pvt., private.
PWA, Public Works Administration.
Py. B., Bachelor of Pedagogy.

q.m., quartermaster.
Q.M.C., Quartermaster Corps.
q.m. gen., quartermaster general.
Q.M.O.R.C., Quartermaster Officers' Reserve Corps.
quar., quarterly.
Que., Quebec (province).
q.v., quod vide (which see).

radiol., radiological.
R.A.F., Royal Air Force.
R.A.M., Royal Arch Mason.
R.C., Roman Catholic; Reserve Corps.
RCA, Radio Corporation of America.
RCAF, Royal Canadian Air Force.
R.C.S., Revenue Cutter Service.
Rd., Road.
R.D., Rural Delivery.
R.E., Reformed Episcopal.
rec., recording.
Ref., Reformed.
Regt., Regiment.
regtl., regimental.
rehab., rehabilitation.
Rep., Republican.
rep., representative.
Res., Reserve.
ret., retired.
Rev., Reverend, Review.
rev., revised.
RFC, Reconstruction Finance Corporation.
R.F.D., Rural Free Delivery.
rhinol., rhinological.
RI—Rhode Island
R.I., Rhode Island
R.N., Registered Nurse.
rontgenal., rontgenological.
R.O.S.C., Reserve Officers' Sanitary Corps.
R.O.T.C., Reserve Officers' Training Corps.
R.P., Reformed Presbyterian.
R.P.D., Rerum Politicarum Doctor (Doctor Political Science).
R.R., Railroad.
R.T.C., Reserve Training Corps.
Ry., Railway.

s., son.
S., South.
S.A., South Americe.
S.A. (Spanish) Sociedad Anonima, (French) Société Anonyme.
SAC, Strategic Air Command.
S.A.L. Ry., Seaboard Air Line Ry.
san., sanitary.
S.A.R., Sons of the Am. Revolution.
Sask., Saskatchewan.
S.A.T.C., Students' Army Training Corps.
Sat.Eve.Post, Saturday Evening Post.
Savs., Savings.
S.B. (also **B.S. or Sc.B.**), Bachelor of Science.
SC—South Carolina.
S.C., South Carolina; San. Corps.
SCAP, Supreme Command Allies Pacific.
Sc.D. (or **D.Sc.**), Doctor of Science.
S.C.D., Doctor of Commercial Science.
sch., school.
sci., science; scientific.
S.C.V., Sons of Confederate Veterans.
SD— South Dakota.

S.D., South Dakota.
S.E., Southeast.
SEATO, Southeast Asia Treaty Organization.
SEC, Securities and Exchange Commission.
sec., secretary.
sect., section.
seismol., seismological.
Sem., Seminary.
sgt. (or **sergt.**), sergeant.
SHAEF, Supreme Headquarters, Allied Expeditionary Forces.
SHAPE, Supreme Headquarters Allied Powers in Europe.
S.I., Staten Island.
S.J., Society of Jesus (Jesuit).
S.J.D., Doctor Juristic Science.
S.M., Master of Science.
So., Southern.
soc., society.
social., sociological.
sos, Services of Supply.
S. of V., Sons of Veterans.
S.P. Co., Southern Pacific Co.
spl., special.
splty., specialty.
Sq., Square.
S.R.C., Signal Reserve Corps.
sr., senior.
S.R., Sons of the Revolution.
S.S., Steamship.
SSS, Selective Service System.
St., Saint; Street.
Sta., station.
statis., statistical.
Stblzn., Stabilization.
S.T.B., Bachelor of Sacred Theology.
S.T.D., Doctor of Sacred Theology.
S.T.L., Licentiate in Sacred Theology; Lector of Sacred Theology.
St.L.-S.F. R.R., St. Louis - San Francisco Ry. Co.
supr., supervisor.
supt., superintendent.
surg., surgical.
S.W., Southwest.

T.A.P.P.I., Technical Association Pulp and Paper Industry.
T. and S., Trust and Savings.
Tb (or **TB**), tuberculosis.
Tchrs., Teachers.
tech., technical; technology.
technol., technological.
Tel.&Tel., Telephone and Telegraph.
temp., temporary.
Tenn., Tennessee.
Tex., Texas.
T.H. (or **H.T.**), Territory of Hawaii.
Th.D., Doctor of Theology.
ThM., Master of Theology.
theol., theological.
TN—Tennessee.
Tng., Training.
topog., topographical.
T.P.A., Travelers Protective Assn.
T.&P. Ry., Texas & Pacific Ry. Co.
trans., transactions; transferred.
Transl., translation; translations.
transp., transportation.

treas., treasurer.
TV, television.
TX—Texas.
TVA, Tennessee Valley Authority.
Twp., Township.
Ty. (or **Ter.**), Territory.
Typog., typographical.

U. (or **Univ.**), University.
UAR, United Arab Republic.
UAW, United Automobile Workers.
U.B., United Brethren in Christ.
U.C.V., United Confederate Veterans.
U.D.C., United Daughters of the Confederacy.
U.K., United Kingdom.
UN, United Nations.
UNESCO, United Nations Educational Scientific and Cultural Organization.
UNICEF, United Nations International Childrens Emergency Fund.
UNRRA, United Nations Relief and Rehabilitation Administration.
U.P., United Presbyterian.
U.P. R.R., Union Pacific R.R.
urol., urological.
U.S., United States.
U.S.A., United States of America.
USAAF, United States Army Air Force.
USAC, United States Air Corps.
USAF, United States Air Force.
USCG, United States Coast Guard.
U.S.C.T., U.S. Colored Troops.
USES, United States Employment Service.
USIA, United States Information Agency.
USIS, United States Information Service.
USMC, United States Marine Corps.
USMHS, United States Marine Hospital Service.
USN, United States Navy.
USNA, United States National Army.
U.S.N.G., United States National Guard.
U.S.O., United Service Organizations.
USNG, United States National Guard.
USNRF, United States Naval Reserve Force.
USPHS, United States Public Health Service.
U.S.R., U.S. Reserve.
U.S.R.C.S., U.S. Revenue Cutter Service.
U.S.S., United States Ship.
USSR, Union of Soviet Socialist Republics.
U.S.V., United States Volunteers.
UT—Utah.

v., vice.
VA—Virginia.
Va., Virginia.
VA, Veterans Administration.
vet., veteran; veterinary.
V.F.W., Veterans of Foreign Wars.
V.I., Virgin Islands.
VI—Virgin Islands.
vice pres. (or **v.p.**,), vice president.
vis., visiting.
vol., volunteer; volume.
vs., versus (against).
VT—Vermont.
Vt., Vermont.

W., West.
WA—Washington (state).
WAC, Women's Army Corps.
Wash., Washington (state).
WAVES, Womens Reserve. U.S. Naval Reserve.
W.C.T.U., Women's Christian Temperance Union.
WHO, World Health Organization.
W.I., West Indies.
WI—Wisconsin.
Wis., Wisconsin.
W.& L.E. Ry., Wheeling & Lake Erie Ry. Co.
WPA, Works Progress Administration.
WPB, War Production Board.
W.P. R.R. Co., Western Pacific R.R. Co.
WSB, Wage Stabilization Board.
WV—West Virginia.
W. Va., West Virginia.

YMCA, Young Men's Christian Association.
YMHA, Young Men's Hebrew Association.
YM and YWHA, Young Men's and Young Women's Hebrew Association.
Y.& M.V. R.R., Yazoo & Mississippi Valley R.R.
yrs., years.
YWCA, Young Women's Christian Association.

zoöl., zoölogical.

ALPHABETICAL PRACTICES

Names are arranged alphabetically according to the surnames, and under identical surnames according to the first given name. If both surname and first given name are identical, names are arranged alphabetically according to the second given name. Where full names are identical, they are arranged in order of age—those of the elder being put first.

Surnames, beginning with De, Des, Du, etc., however capitalized or spaced, are recorded with the prefix preceding the surname and arranged alphabetically under the letter D.

Surnames beginning with Mac are arranged alphabetically under M. This likewise holds for names beginning with Mc; that is, all names beginning Mc will be found in alphabetical order after those beginning Mac.

Surnames beginning with Saint or St. all appear after names that would begin Sains, and such surnames are arranged according to the second part of the name, e.g., St. Clair would come before Saint Dennis.

Surnames beginning with prefix Van are arranged alphabetically under letter V.

Surnames containing the prefix Von or von are usually arranged alphabetically under letter V; any exceptions are noted by cross references (Von Kleinsmid, Rufus Bernhard; see Kleinsmid, Rufus Bernard von).

Compound hypenated surnames are arranged according to the first member of the compound.

Compound unhyphenated surnames common in Spanish are not rearranged but are treated as hyphenated names.

Since Chinese names have the family name first, they are so arranged, but without comma between family name and given name (as Lin Yutang).

Parentheses used in connection with a name indicate which part of the full name is usually deleted in common usage. Hence Abbott, W(illiam) Lewis indicates that the usual form of the given name is W. Lewis. In alphabetizing this type, the parentheses are not considered. However if the name is recorded Abbott, (William) Lewis, signifying that the entire name William is not commonly used, the alphabetizing would be arranged as though the name were Abbott, Lewis.

VOL. 2

WHO WAS WHO

IN AMERICA

ABBOTT, Henry Pryor Almon, bishop; b. Halifax, N.S., July 11, 1881; s. Rev. John and Ella (Almon) A.; B.A., King's Coll., Windsor, N.S., 1902, M.A., 1904, D.D., 1911; studied St. Stephen's House, Oxford, England; D.D., University of the South, Sewanee, Tennessee, 1929; L.L.D., University of Kentucky, 1942; m. Rachel Gwyn, July 11, 1907; children—Henry Paul Almon, Rachel Ella Almon, Osler Almon, Faith Elizabeth, Nancy Mather Almon. Deacon, 1904, priest, 1905, Ch. of Eng.; curate St. Luke's Cathedral, Halifax, N.S., 1904-06; asst. rector Ch. of St. James the Apostle, Montreal, 1906; rector Christ Ch. Cathedral, Hamilton, Ont., 1906-14; dean of Niagara, 1910-14; dean Trinity Cathedral, Cleveland, O., 1914-19; rector Grace and St. Peter's Ch., Baltimore, Md., 1919-28; St. Chrysostom's Ch., Chicago, 1928-29; bishop of Lexington, Ky., since May 15, 1929. Del. Gen. Synod, Can., 1912, Provincial Synod, Ont., 1913, Gen. Conv., 1922-25 and 1928. Author: Help from the Hills, 1917; Pamphlet Series, 1917; The Man Outside the Church, 1918; Sparks from a Parson's Anvil, 1918; The Supreme Sacrifice, 1918; The Religion of the Tommy, 1918; (brochure) Joy Through Sorrow, 1925; Foundation Stones, 1925; Things That Matter, 1941; Comfort from Calvary, 1941. Home: Lexington, Ky. Died Apr. 4, 1945.

ABBOTT, Howard Strickland, lawyer; b. Farmington, Minn., Sept. 15, 1863; s. Rev. Abiel Howard and Mary Ellen (Strickland) A.; desc. of George Abbott, Rowley, Mass., 1642; B.L., U. of Minn., 1885; m. Mary L. Johnson, June 29, 1898; children—Emily Louise, Howard Johnson. Asst. gen. solicitor Minneapolis & St. Louis and "Soo" ry. cos., 1887-90; sec. Wis., Minn. & Pac. Ry. Co., 1888-90; atty. A.T.& S.F. Ry., at Chicago, 1890-97; spl. master in chancery, U.P. Ry. receiverships, 1897-1901, M.&St.L. R.R. receivership since 1923. Master in chancery, U.S. Dist. Court of Minn., since 1898; spl. master Minneapolis, St. Paul, Rochester & Dubuque Ry. Co., 1918-20, Electric Short Line Ry. Co., 1923-24; lecturer on public and private corps. and civil law, U. of Minn., 1897-1927. Dir. Minn. Saving Fund & Investment Co., 1888-90, Minneapolis Trust Co., 1902-20. A commr. of Am. Bar Assn. on uniform legislation for Minn., 1907-12. Mem. Minn. State Bar Assn., Delta Kappa Epsilon. Episcopalian; trustee Diocese of Minn. many yrs. Club: Minneapolis. Author: Cases on Public Corporations, 1899; Cases Private Corporations, 1899; Notes, Authorities and Deductions on Corporations, 1902, 2d edit., 1911; Municipal Corporations, 1906 (3 vols., supplemental vol., 1912); A Summary of the Law of Public Corporations, 1907; Abbott's Elliott on Private Corporations, 1909; An Elementary Treatise on the Law of Private Corporations, 1910; Abbott's Law of Public Securities, 1913. Home: 900 6th St., S.E. Office: Federal Bldg., Minneapolis, Minn. Died Jan. 7, 1944.

ABBOTT, John Jay, banker; b. N.Y. City, Mar. 11, 1871; s. John N. and Violet (Gardner) A.; ed. pub. schs.; m. Rowena Marsh, Jan. 22, 1896. Began as asst. to comptroller Chicago (now Commonwealth) Edison Co., 1892; v.p. Continental-Ill. Nat. Bank & Trust Co. and predecessors since 1904. Clubs: Chicago, Chicago Golf, Saddle and Cycle. Home: 3224 Michigan Av. Office: 231 S. La Salle St., Chicago, Ill. Died Oct. 18, 1942.

ABBOTT, Robert Sengstacke, editor, pub., b. Savannah, Ga., Nov. 24, 1870; s. Thomas and Flora (Butler) A.; ed. Beach Inst., Savannah, Claflin U., Orangeburg, S.C., and Hampton (Va.) Inst.; LL.B., Kent Law Sch., Chicago, 1898; m. Edna Rose Denison, June 1934. Founder, 1905, since editor and pub. Chicago Defender, weekly newspaper pub. in interest of colored race; pres. and treas. Robert S. Abbott Pub. Co. since 1905. Mem. Gov. Frank O. Lowden's Race Relation Commn., 1919; apptd. mem. Bd. Commrs. of Chicago Fair, 1935. Ex-pres. Hampton Alumni Assn. Mem. Art Inst. Chicago, Institut Litteraire et Artistique de Paris (France), Field Mus.; Chicago and Illinois hist. socs., Kappa Alpha Psi. Presbyterian. Mason (33°). Club: Appomattox. Author: My Trip Abroad. Home: 4742 S. Parkway, Chicago, Ill.; also Abbottsford on North Shore Drive, Benton Harbor, Mich. Office: 3435 Indiana Av., Chicago, Ill.* Died Feb. 29, 1940.

ABBOTT, W(illiam) Lewis, coll. prof.; b. Phila., Pa., June 26, 1889; s. John William and Helen Amelia (Smith) A.; grad. Friends Central Sch., Phila., 1907; B.A., U. of Pa., 1911, M.A., 1913, LL.B., 1913, Ph.D., 1920; m. Helen Shreve Reid, Sept. 29, 1917; children—Elizabeth Abbott McKeever, Marjory Reid. Asst. in sociology and econ. U. of Pa., 1911-17; prof. econs. and sociology, Hamline U., 1917-20; prof. bus. adminstrn. and banking, Colorado Coll., 1920-27; head of dept. of economics and sociology, same coll., since 1927; mem. faculty, summer schs., U. of Colo., 1931, 32, Colo. State Coll., 1936, 37, 38, 39, 40, 41, Wash. State Coll., 1936; tech. adviser U.S. Interdepartmental Com. on Labor Conditions in the growing of sugar beets, Jan.-Apr. 1934; mem. Nat. Regional Labor Bd. 14th Dist., 1934-35; speaker Colorado Springs Pub. Forum, Nov. 1936, Portland (Ore.) Pub. Forum, Feb. and Apr. 1937, Seattle Pub. Forum, Mar. 1937; mem. advisory com. State Employment Serv. (Colo.); public mem. Regional War Labor Bd., region IX, 1943-46. Pres. Colo.-Wyo. Social Science Assn., 1930-31; pres. Colo. Conf. of Social Work, 1932-33. Mem. Am. Sociol. Soc., A.A.A.S. Member Friends Society (Quaker). Author: Competition and Combination in the Wholesale Grocery Trade (pamphlet), 1920; (with B. H. Mautner) Child Labor and Farm Life in the Arkansas Valley of Colorado, 1929; also Report for Com. on Labor Conditions in the Growing of Sugar Beets, Mar. 1934. Home: 30 E. Uintah St., Colorado Springs, Colo. Died Mar. 25, 1949.

ABBOTT, William Martin, lawyer; b. San Francisco, Calif., Mar. 17, 1872; s. William and Anna Bell (Casselman) A.; LL.B., U. of Calif., 1893; m. Annie Josephine McVean, Aug. 3, 1895. Practiced at San Francisco since 1893; asst. atty. gen. of Calif., 1898-1902. V.p., gen. counsel, Market St. Ry. Co., San Francisco; pres. San Francisco & San Mateo Electric Railway Co., Sutro R.R. Co., gen. atty. United Railroads of San Francisco. Mem. Am., Calif. and San Francisco bar assns., Native Sons of Golden West. Republican. Mason (K.T., Shriner), Elk (past Grand Exalted Ruler). Clubs: Bohemian (pres. 1924-25), San Francisco Golf and Country, Rio del Mar Golf and Country, Olympic Club, Lakeside Golf and Country, Coral Casino Beach and Cabana (Santa Barbara). Address: Bohemian Club, San Francisco, Calif. Died Nov. 13, 1941.

ABDULLAH, Achmed (nom de plume of Nadir Khan-Romanoffski), b. Yalta, Crimea, May 12, 1881; s. Nicolas and Nurmahal Romanoff; ed. Eton (Eng.), Ecole Louis le Grand (Paris), Oxford, Sorbonne; m. Rosemary Dolan, May 3, 1940; 1 adopted dau., Phyllis Adams (lieut., U.S. Army Nursing Corps). Naturalized British subject. Served in British and British-Indian Army, 17 yrs., advancing from capt. to temporary rank of colonel; served in Turkish army, with rank of colonel, 1 yr.; now holds title of Kentucky Colonel. Following divorce of parents was adopted by maternal grandfather, an Afghan Moslem, which led to choice of Moslem nom de plume. Tory (British politics). Mem. 3d Order of Franciscans. Roman Catholic. Clubs: Reading Room (York Harbor, Me.); Cavalry, Poonah (Eng.); Cercle Richelieu (France). Author: Chansons Couleur Puce (Paris), 1900; A Grammar of Little Known Bantu Dialects, 1902; The Red Stain, 1915; The Blue-Eyed Manchu, 1917; Bucking the Tiger, 1917; The Honorable Gentleman and Others, 1919; The Trail of the Beast, 1919; The Man on Horseback, 1919; Wings, 1920; The Mating of the Blades, 1920; The Ten-Foot Chain, 1920; Night Drums, 1921; Alien Souls, 1922; Shackled, 1924; The Swinging Caravan, 1925; The Wild Goose of Limerick, 1926; The Year of the Wood-Dragon, 1926; Ruth's Rebellion, 1927; Steel and Jade, 1927; Lute and Scimitar (poems and ballads of Central Asia translated from several langs.), 1928; They Were So Young, 1929; (with T. C. Pakenham) Dreamers of Empire, 1929; Broadway Interlude, 1929; Black Tents, 1930; Veiled Woman, 1931; (with Faith Baldwin) Girl on the Make, 1932; Romantic Young Man, 1932; Alien Souls, 1933; Buccaneer in Spats, 1933; Cat Had Nine Lives, 1933; Love Comes to Sally, 1933; Never Without You, 1934; (with John Kenny) For Men Only (cookbook), 1937; Deliver Us From Evil, 1939; (with Fulton Oursler) Flower of the Gods, 1940; (with same) Shadow of the Master, 1941; (plays) La Carotte (Paris), 1900; Roulette (Berlin), 1913; Bucking the Tiger (with Fania Marinoff), 1919; Toto (with Leo Ditrichstein), 1920; The Grand Duke (with Lionel Atwill), 1921; Salvage (produced by David Belasco); also motion pictures: The Hatchetman, The Lives of a Bengal Lancer, British Agent, The Thief of Bagdad. Address: 533 W. 112th St., New York, N.Y. Died May 12, 1945.

ABELL, Harry Clinton, public utilities; b. of Am. parents, Winnipeg, Manitoba, Can., July 8, 1871; s. Edmund Richard and Nancy (Noel) A.; student St. John's Coll., Winnipeg; B.S. in E.E., Armour Inst. Tech., 1897, E.E., 1906; m. Fannilee Martin, June 25, 1902; 1 dau., Margaret A. Engring. apprentice Canadian Pacific Ry., 1889; with Belding Motor Co., Chicago, and Canadian Gen. Electric Co., 1892, 93; in employ Anchor Line and Internat. Navigation Co., 1898; marine engr. Spanish-Am. War, 1898; connected with Emerson McMillin & Co., later with Am. Light & Traction Co., operating pub. utilities, 1898-1921; v.p. Electric Bond & Share Co., 1921-33. Mem. Am. Soc. M.E., Am. Inst. E.E., Nat. Electric Light Assn. (dir.), Am. Gas Assn. (pres. 1925, 26), Engring. Inst. of Can. Republican. Episcopalian. Mason, Elk. Clubs: Engineers', Bankers. Address: 701 St. Louis St., New Orleans. Died Nov. 28, 1938.

ABELL, Irvin (ā'bĕl), surgeon; b. Lebanon, Ky., Sept. 13, 1876; s. Irvin and Sarah Silesia (Rogers) A.; A.M., St. Mary's Coll., St. Mary, Ky., 1894; M.D., Louisville Med. Coll., 1897; studied in U. of Berlin, Germany, 1898; Sc.D., U. of Louisville, 1937; D.Sc., Georgetown U., 1939, Manhattan Coll., N.Y. City, 1939; LL.D., Marquette U., Milwaukee, 1939; Sc. D., U. of Ky., 1942; LL.D., U. of Cincinnati, 1943; m. Carrie Harting, Oct. 19, 1907; children—Irvin, William, Rogers (dec.), Spalding. Practiced in Louisville, Ky., since 1900; prof. surgery, U. of Louisville, 1904-47; visiting surgeon, Louisville Public Hosp., St. Joseph Infirmary; cons. surgeon, Children's Free Hosp., Kosair Hosp. for Crippled Children; dir. Commonwealth Life Ins. Co., Citizens Fidelity Bank and Trust Co. Awarded Lætare medal by U. of Notre Dame, 1938. Trustee University of Louisville. Fellow American College of Surgeons, American Surgical Assn.; hon. fellow Royal College of Surgeons, Eng., 1947; member A.M.A. (pres. 1938-39), Ky. State Med. Assn. (pres. 1927), Jefferson Co. Med. Soc., Southern Med. Assn. (pres. 1933), Southern Surg. Assn. (pres. 1926), Am. Urol. Assn., Am. Gastroenterological Assn. (pres. 1939-40), Am. Coll. Surgeons (pres. 1945-46), Assn. Mil. Surgs. (pres. 1945-46), Southeastern Surg. Congress (pres. 1937), Phi Chi, Alpha Omega Alpha, Phi Kappa Phi. Catholic. Clubs: Pendennis, Louisville Country; Army and Navy Country (Washington, D.C.). Home: 1433 S. Third St., Louisville 8. Office: 321 W. Broadway, Louisville 2, Ky. Died Aug. 28, 1949.

ABERCROMBIE, Daniel Webster, academy prin.; b. Bolling Green, Ala., Nov. 25, 1853; s. Milo Bolling and Sarah Carroll (Greenleaf) A.; A.B., Harvard, 1876; studied Harvard Law Sch., 1876-77; A.M. (hon.), Brown, 1883; LL.D., Colby, 1898; Litt.D., Dartmouth, 1911; m. Emily Foote Brainerd, Dec. 23, 1878; children—Mrs. Edith A. Snow, Ralph, Mrs. Esther A. Lockwood, Daniel Webster. Tutor classics, St. Mark's Sch., Southboro, Mass., 1877-78; instr. classics, Vt. Acad., Saxtons River, Vt., 1878-82; prin. Worcester (Mass.) Acad., 1882-1918. Made various trips to Europe for study and travel; studied ednl. methods in Europe, principally in Germany and England; hon. rep. U.S. Bur. of Edn. to study ednl. methods of secondary schools of Germany. Trustee Worcester Acad., Brown U. Ex-pres. Mass. Schoolmasters' Assn., Brown Univ. Teachers' Assn., Harvard Teachers' Assn.; mem. Headmasters' Assn., Phi Beta Kappa. Republican. Clubs: Harvard (Worcester and Boston), N. E. Federated Harvard Clubs, Economic, Tatnuck, Rotary (Worcester). Author numerous published addresses and articles on edn. and school administration. Home: 8 Trowbridge Rd., Worcester, Mass. Died Sept. 26, 1935.

ABRAHAMSON, Laurentius G., clergyman, editor; b. Medåker, Sweden, Mar. 2, 1856; s. Anders G. and Britta Maria (Nelson) A.; brought to U.S., 1868; A.B., Augustana Coll., Rock Island, Ill., A.M., 1897, D.D., 1900; grad. Augustana Theol. Sem., 1880; m. Florinda M. Morris, Aug. 24 1881; children—Florinda Olivia (dec.), Ebba Valeria (Mrs. E. T. Anderson), Agnes Winnefred. Ordained ministry, 1880; pastor Altona, Ill., 1880-86; Chicago, 1886-1908; editor Augustana (official organ Luth. Augustana Synod), 1908-1940. Trustee Augustana Hosp., Chicago. Decorated Comdr. Royal Order Polar Star (Sweden). Author: Sermons (3 vols.). Compiler and editor of Jubilee Album of Lutheran Augustana Synod. Address: 3419 7th Av., Rock Island, Ill. Died Nov. 3, 1946; buried in Oak Hill Cemetery, Chicago.

ACHESON, Marcus Wilson, Jr., lawyer; b. Allegheny, Pa., Aug. 27, 1873; s. Marcus Wilson and Sophie Duff (Reiter) A.; grad. Shady Side Acad., Pittsburgh, 1890; A.B., Washington and Jefferson, 1894, A.M., 1897; m. Margaret Hawkins, June 14, 1902; children—Marcus W., Jane, William G. Hawkins, George Hawkins, David. Admitted to bar, Dec. 14, 1895, since in practice at Pittsburgh; mem. firm of Patterson, Sterrett and Acheson, 1901-13, Sterrett and Acheson, 1913-29, Sterrett, Acheson and Jones, 1929-39, Sterrett, Acheson, Childs & Barnett since 1939. Pres. Legal Aid Soc. of Pittsburgh since 1908, convening First Conf. of Legal Aid Socs., Pittsburgh, Nov. 10, 1911; pres. Nat. Alliance Legal Aid Socs., 1914-16, Nat. Assn. Legal Aid Orgns., 1931-36, Pittsburgh Housing Assn., 1928-35, Fedn. of Social Agencies of Pittsburgh and Allegheny County, 1930-34; chmn. Community Council of Pittsburgh, 1932-34; mem. bd. mgrs. Allegheny County Work House, 1930-38; mem. bd. of dirs. Public Charities Assn. of Pa.; mem. Com. on Business and Housing of President's Conf. on Home Building and Home Ownership, 1931; pres. Allegheny Cemetery; chmn. Pittsburgh Regional Labor Bd., 1935. Trustee Washington and Jefferson Coll. and Shady Side Acad. Mem. Am. Law Inst., Phi Beta Kappa. Drafted Pittsburgh Graded Tax Law, 1913; a hearing officer for Dept. of Justice in W.Pa. in conscientious objector cases since May, 1941. Home: 1060 Morewood Av. Office: Henry W. Oliver Bldg., Pittsburgh, Pa. Died May 2, 1943.

ACHRON, Isidor (äk'rŏn), pianist, composer; b. Warsaw, Nov. 24, 1892; s. Julius and Bertha (Maram) A.; grad. Conservatory of Music, Leningrad, Russia; studied piano under Annette Essipoff and Nicholas Doubasoff, composition under Anatole Liadoff; m. Lea Karina. Came to U.S., 1922, naturalized citizen, 1928. Concert pianist, playing in all parts of the world; composed first work in 1937. Composer: 1st Piano Concerto, 1937; 1st Sonnet for Violin, 1941; Valse Dramatique, 1941; 2d Sonnet for Violin; Suite Grotesque (for orchestra); Nocturne Fantasia, 1942; Gavotte Satirique for Cello, 1942; 2d Concerto for Piano and Orchestra, 1942. Served in Russian Army, 3 yrs. Club: Bohemians. Address: 45 W. 81st St., New York, N.Y.*

Died May 12, 1948.

ACHRON, Joseph (äk'rŏn), composer, violinist; b. Lozdzeye, Russia, May 1, 1886; s. Julius and Bertha (Mahram) A.; ed. private sch., Warsaw; received first violin instrn. from his father; student State Conservatory, St. Petersburg (Leningrad), 1899-1904; studied violin with Michalovich, Lotto and Auer; orchestration with Steinberg; m. Marie Rap-hoph, June 2, 1920. Came to U.S., 1925, naturalized, 1930. Appeared in first violin concert at age of 8; later appeared before family of the Czar; concert tours, Russia, 1904-07, and 1910-22; head violin and chamber music dept., Kharkov Conservatory, 1913-16; in Russian Army, 1916-18; head violin master class and chamber music dept., Leningrad Artists Union, 1918-22, also gave many concerts during this period; visited Latvia, Germany, Austria, Italy, Egypt, Palestine, France, 1922-24; composer, violinist and teacher, N.Y. City, 1925-34, Hollywood, Calif., since 1934. Has written over 80 compositions and many transcriptions for orchestra, chorus, chamber music, vocal solos, also for stage and motion pictures. Mem. Am. Musicological Soc., Pro Musica (Los Angeles), Mailamm (Los Angeles). Clubs: Bohemians (N.Y. City); Crescendo (Los Angeles). Translated Practical Manual of Harmony (by Rimsky-Korsakov). Home: 2621 N. Beachwood Drive, Hollywood, Calif.

Died Apr. 29, 1943.

ACKERMANN, Carl, coll. prof.; b. Wooster, O., Sept. 12, 1858; s. George and Dorothea (Walter) A.; A.B., Capital U., Columbus, O., 1879, A.M., 1882, Ph.D., 1901; grad. Theol. Sem. of Capital U., 1884; m. Mary Ellen Reese, Oct. 30, 1884. Ordained Luth. ministry, 1884; pastor Attica, O., 1884-90, Lithopolis, 1890-91, Fremont, 1891-92, Fostoria, O., 1892-94; pres., 1894-97, dean and prof. English, psychology and mathematics, 1897-1907, Lima (O.) Coll.; pres. Pacific Sem., Olympia, Wash., 1907-09; prof. English, Capital U., 1909-36, emeritus since 1936, sec. faculty, 1917-34. Mem. Nat. Council Teachers of English, English Teachers Assn. of Ohio, Ohio State Teachers Assn., Lutheran Hist. Soc., Shakespeare Assn. of America. Chmn. com. on Ch. Hymnal (Luth.), 1907, and of Sch. Carols (S.S. Hymnal), 1915; co-editor Luth. Ch. Year Book, 1917-19; editor Luth. Ch. Almanac and Year Book, 1920-34; statis. sec. Luth. Joint Synod of Ohio, 1916-31 and gen. sec., 1922-31. Author: The Bible in Shakespeare 1925 (enlarged edition, 1937); From the Cross, 1929; Treasured Thoughts, 1929; Higher Education of Women in the Lutheran Joint Synod of Ohio, 1937; History of Alumni Association of Capital University, 1939. Translator and editor of parts of Lenker edition of Luther's Works into English; also author and translator of several juveniles. Has traveled extensively. Home: 2315 E. Main St., Columbus, O.

Died June 7, 1943.

ADAMS, Adeline Valentine Pond, writer; b. Boston; d. George Frederick and Mary (Devine) Pond; ed. Wellesley Coll. 1 yr.; studied art, Normal Art Sch., Boston, and Paris; m. Herbert Adams, 1889. Clubs: Cosmopolitan, Women Painters and Sculptors. Author: Mary; Sylvia; John Quincy Adams Ward; The Amouretta Landscape, 1922; The Spirit of American Sculpture, 1923. Contbr. to Am. Mag., Art, Scribner's. Home: 131 W. 11th St., New York. Died July 1, 1948.

ADAMS, Alva Blanchard, U.S. Senator; b. Del Norte, Colo., Oct. 29, 1875; s. Alva and Ella (Nye) A.; Ph.B., Yale, 1896; LL.B., Columbia, 1899; m. Elizabeth Matty, Oct. 25, 1909; children—Ella (Mrs. Joseph A. Uhl), Elizabeth (Mrs. James W. Booth), Alva B., William H. Admitted to Colo. bar, 1899; began practice at Pueblo; mem. Adams & Gast; county atty. Pueblo Co., Colo., 1908-10; city atty., Pueblo, 1911-15; apptd. by gov. of Colo. mem. U.S. Senate, May 17, 1923, to fill vacancy caused by death of Samuel D. Nicholson; elected to Senate, Nov. 1932, for term 1933-39; re-elected Nov. 1938, for term 1939-45; pres. Pueblo Savings & Trust Co.; dir. Standard Fire Brick Co. Maj. J. A. Gen.'s Dept., U.S. Army, 1918-19. Democrat. Mason (33°), Elk. Home: 102 W. Orman Av., Pueblo. Office: Thatcher Bldg., Pueblo, Colo.

Died Dec. 1, 1941.

ADAMS, Andy, author; b. Whitley County, Ind., May 3, 1859; s. Andrew and Elizabeth (Elliott) A.; ed. country sch. in Ind., unmarried. Reared on farm in Ind.; went to Texas when a youth and followed occupation of a cowboy for 10 yrs.; moved to Colo. during Cripple Creek excitement; took up mining and later literature. Author: The Log of a Cowboy, 1903; A Texas Matchmaker, 1904; The Outlet, 1905; Cattle Brands, 1906; Reed Anthony, Cowman, 1907; Wells Brothers, 1911; The Ranch on the Beaver, 1927. Home: Colorado Springs, Colo. Died Sept. 26, 1935.

ADAMS, Arthur, college prof.; b. Pleasantville, N.J., May 12, 1881; s. James R. and Marietta (English) A.; A.B., Rutgers, 1902; A.M., Yale, 1903, Ph.D., 1905; B.D., Berkeley Div. School, 1910; S.T.M., Phila. Divinity Sch., 1916; m. E. Guerin Steelman, June 22, 1910; children—Esther Steelman, Richard Hancock. Instr. English, U. of Colo., 1905-06; asst. prof. English, Trinity Coll., 1906-08, asso. prof., 1908-11, prof., 1911, librarian, 1915, prof. English, U. of Me., summer session, 1912. Ordained priest, P.E. Ch., 1909. Examining chaplain, Diocese of Conn., chaplain O.R.C., U.S.A. Dir. N.J. State Commn. on Historic Sites, 1931-32. Mem. Am. Philol. Assn., Modern Lang. Assn. Am., Am. Hist. Soc., Soc. Colonial Wars (registrar gen.), Order Founders and Patriots (former gov. gen.), Saint Nicholas Soc., Conn. Hist. Soc., Phi Beta Kappa, Delta Phi; fellow Soc. of Genealogists (London), Soc. of Antiquaries (London). Clubs: Twentieth Century, Authors (New York). Mason. Author: The Syntax of the Temporal Clause in Old English Prose, 1907; A Genealogy of the Lake Family of Great Egg Harbor, New Jersey (with Sarah A. Risley), 1915. Collaborator: Concordance to the English Poems of Thomas Gray, 1908; Wordsworth Concordance, 1911. Contbr. to Dictionary American Biography and to philol. and other periodicals. Editor of Index of Ancestors and Honor Roll, Soc. Colonial Wars, 1922; General Register of the Order of Founders and Patriots, 1926. Home: 73 Vernon St. Address: Trinity College, Hartford, Conn. Died May 18, 1943.

ADAMS, Charles Clarence, univ. dean; b. West Sunbury, Pa., Jan. 15, 1883; s. John Smith and Louise (Hunt) A.; A.B., Westminster Coll., New Wilmington, Pa., 1905, D.D., 1928; grad. Pittsburgh (Pittsburgh-Xenia) Theol. Sem., 1908; spl. student Kennedy Sch. of Missions, Hartford, Conn., 1915-17; Ph.D., U. of Chicago, 1928; S.T.M., Union Theol. Sem., New York, 1936; m. Nellie B. McAuley, Nov. 26, 1908; children—Jane Louise (Mrs. Ruskin Rice), Eleanor May (Mrs. Ralph H. Bain), Ruth Robertson, John McAuley (dec.), Charles Clarence. Ordained to ministry United Presbyterian Ch., 1908; missionary to Egypt under Bd. of Fgn. Missions, U.P. Ch., 1908-39; pastor U.P. Ch., East Craftsbury, Vt., 1917-18; chmn. faculty Egyptian Evang. Theol. Sem., Cairo, Egypt, 1919-38; dean sch. of Oriental studies Am. Univ. at Cairo, Egypt, since 1939. Author: Islam and Modernism in Egypt, 1933. Contbr. articles to mags. Address: The American University at Cairo, Egypt. Home Office: Land Title Bldg., Philadelphia 10, Pa.

Died Mar. 9, 1948.

ADAMS, Charles Closson, telegraph official; b. Freeport, Pa., Aug. 15, 1858; s. Alexander Ainsworth and Isabella (Thompson) A.; ed. pub. schs., Pittsburgh, and Sharpsburg (Pa.) Acad.; m. Elizabeth K. Spillin, Feb. 15, 1896. Telegraph operator in oil regions and Pittsburgh, 1874-80; with Associated Press, Ft. Wayne, Ind.; removed to N.Y. City and entered employ of Western Union Telegraph Co.; later became mgr. Pittsburgh Office Mut. Union Telegraph Co.; apptd. mgr. Phila. office, Postal Telegraph Co., 1884, dist. supt., 1886, gen. supt. Southern div., 1902, second v.p. since 1904; v.p. Brooklyn Dist. Telegraph Co.; dir. North Am. Telegraph Co. Clubs: Rockaway Hunting (Lawrence, L.I.), Union League (New York). Home: Lawrence, L.I. Office: 253 Broadway, New York. Died Mar. 30, 1938.

ADAM, Charles Darwin, college prof.; b. Keene, N.H., Oct. 21, 1856; s. Daniel Emerson and Ellen Frances (Kingsbury) A.; A.B., Dartmouth, 1877, A.M., 1880; Andover Theol. Sem., 1879-81; Ph.D., Univ. of Kiel, 1891; Litt.D. from Dartmouth College, 1927; m. Julia A. Stevens, Aug. 24, 1881; children—David Ernest, Ellen Frances, Robert Emerson. Instr. Greek, Cushing Acad., 1881-84; prof. Greek lang., Drury Coll., 1884-93; prof. Greek lang. and lit., Dartmouth, 1893-1927. Editor The Classical Journal, 1908-13. Pres. Classical Assn. of N.E., 1906-07. Author: Demosthenes (Our Debt to Greece and Rome series), 1927. Editor: Lysias, Selected Speeches, 1906; Speeches of Æschines (Loeb Classical Library), 1919. Home: Hanover, N.H. Died May 28, 1938.

ADAMS, Charles F., business exec.; b. Newport, Vt., Oct. 19, 1876; s. Frank Weston and Elizabeth Nancy (Benoit) A.; m. Lillias Mae Woollard, June 12, 1901; 1 son, Weston Woollard. Pres. of John T. Connor Co., 1917-25; treas. Waldorf System, Inc., 1919-24; treas. First National Stores, Inc., 1925-42, now dir. and mem. exec. com.; treas. and dir. Adams-Erickson, Inc. (wholesale distributors Stromberg-Carlson radios); propr. Wedgemere Farm, Dairying and gen. farming, Framingham Center, Mass.; pres. Nat. Grocery Stores in New England; dir. Framingham Trust Co.; trustee Adams (living) Trust. Dir. Boston Nat. League Baseball Assn., 1927-35. Pioneered and developed Nat. League hockey in U.S., 1925; gov. Nat. Hockey League, 1925-37; pres. Boston Professional Hockey Assn., Inc., 1925-37, now dir.; pres., chmn. bd. and dir. Eastern Racing Assn., Inc., 1935-43. Mem. Boston Chamber of Commerce. Unitarian. Mason (Shriner, K.T.). Clubs: Down Town, University, Madison Square Garden, Republican, Bostonian Society, Paddock (Boston). Home: Salem End Rd., Framingham, Mass. Office: 55 Kilby St., Boston, Mass.* Died Oct. 1, 1946.

ADAMS, Charles Francis, banker; b. Baltimore, Md., Mar. 8, 1862; s. Orson and Annie L. (Fisher) A.; grad. Phillips Exeter Acad.; studied Yale, 1878-81; m. Mary C. H. Eichbaum, 1901; children—Anne Josephine (Mrs. Holt W. Berni), Charles F. Settled in Portland, 1890; organizer Security Savings & Trust Co., 1890, pres. since 1903; became pres. First Nat. Bank, 1927, now chmn. bd.; became dir. Ore. Mutual Life Ins. Co., 1908, treas., 1909, pres. since 1927. Republican. Mason. Office: First Nat. Bank Bldg., Portland, Ore. Died July 15, 1943.

ADAMS, Charles Partridge, landscape artist; b. Franklin, Mass., Jan. 12, 1858; s. Albert and Susan Davis (White) A.; largely self-educated; studied under Helen Chain, pupil of George Innes, Sr., and in galleries of Europe, 1914; m. Alida Reynolds Joslin, Sept. 16, 1890; children—Albert Joslin, Philip Van Ruysdael, Charles Partridge. Rep. in collections of Kansas City (Mo.) Art Assn., Denver (Colo.) Art Assn., University Club, Denver, Denver Club, Woman's Club, Denver, etc. Winner of gold medal, Nat. Mining and Indsl. Expn., Denver, 1889; gold medal, U. of Colo., 1919; hon. mention, Pan-Am. Expn., Buffalo, N.Y., 1900. Mem. Art Commn., Denver. Mem. Laguna Art Assn. Republican. Baptist. Home: 3935 Dalton Av., Los Angeles; (summer) 1745 Catalina St., Laguna Beach, Calif. Died Oct. 15, 1942.

ADAMS, Charles Ryan, clergyman; b. Switzerland Co., Ind., Jan. 5, 1874; s. Thomas Leonard and Elizabeth (Harris) A.; A.B., Hanover (Ind.) Coll., 1896, A.M., 1901; grad. study U. of Chicago, 1897-98, McCormick Theol. Sem., 1899-1901; D.D., Fargo (N.D.) Coll., 1911; m. Myra Oldfather, July 31, 1901; children—John Maxwell, Helen Miriam, Philip Rhys, Dorothy J. Ordained ministry Presbyn. Ch., 1901; pastor Kingston Ch., Greensburg, Ind., 1901-05, Fargo, 1905-11, Champaign, Ill., 1911-19; sec. New Era Movement, central dist., Gen. Assembly Presbyn. Ch., 1919-21; pastor Covenant Presbyn. Ch., Springfield, O., 1921-36, dean of chapel, Park Coll., 1936-44; pastor, Parkville Community Church (Presbyn.), Parkville, Mo., since 1944. Trustee Western Coll. for Women, Oxford, O. Moderator North Dakota Synod, 1911-12. Mem. Phi Gamma Delta. Home: Parkville, Mo.

Died July 1, 1948.

ADAMS, Clarence Henry, pres. The Internat. Trust Co.; b. Black Earth, Wis., Oct. 14, 1879; s. Frank and Emma Jane (Wilson) A.; B.A., Yale, 1902; m. Eugenia H. McFarlane, Aug. 15, 1905 (died Sept. 5, 1939); children—Clarence H., Eugene Hale. Began with Colo. Ice & Cold Storage Co., 1903, v.p., 1917-

27, pres. since 1927; mem. firm Proudfit Ormsby Commn. Co., 1905-17; pres. The Internat. Trust Co. since 1932; dir. Denver Branch of Federal Reserve Bank of Kansas City, Potash Co. of America, Denver Tramway Corp. Trustee U. of Denver. Democrat. Clubs: Denver Club, Denver Athletic, Denver Country. Home: 800 Pennsylvania St. Office: The International Trust Co., Denver, Colo.

Died Aug. 24, 1944.

ADAMS, Fred Winslow, clergyman; b. Belfast, Me., Aug. 31, 1866; s. Rev. True Page and Dorcas Ellen (Winslow) A.; Boston U., class of 1892; studied Harvard, 1893, Yale, 1901; D.D., Syracuse, 1905; S.T.D., Wesleyan U., Conn., 1916; LL.D., Am. Internat. Coll., Springfield, 1936; m. Harriet Heath, June 11, 1901; children—Winslow Heath, Vincent Taft. Asso. pastor Nostrand Av. Ch., Brooklyn, N.Y., 1896-97; pastor First Ch., Yalesville, Conn., 1897-99, Epworth Ch., New Haven, 1900-01, First Ch., Schenectady, N.Y., 1902-14; St. Andrew's Ch., New York, 1915-17; dist. supt. N.Y. Dist., 1917-18; pastor Trinity Ch., Springfield, Mass., 1918-30; minister emeritus since 1930. Editor of "The Sanctuary," New York Christian Advocate, 1913-17; professor of worship and the pastoral office, Boston U. School of Theology, 1930-40; head dept. Shakespearian drama, Curry Sch. since 1935; minister Harvard Meth. Ch., Cambridge, 1938-41; united Harvard and Epworth chs. as Harvard-Epworth Ch., 1941; minister Copley Meth. Ch., Boston, since 1941. Trustee Curry School of Expression; sec. Gen. Conf. Com. on Revision of Ritual of M.E. Ch. (adopted, 1932); mem. Gen. Conf. Com. on Orders of Worship and Revision Ritual of Meth. Ch. since 1940; mem. com. on worship, Fed. Council of Chs. of Christ; coll. preacher. Mem. Theta Delta Chi. Republican. Mason. Lecturer on literary subjects. Brought to completion in 1929, a Gothic Community Cathedral on M.E. Foundation, with community and ednl. bldgs. and Singing Tower Carillon of 61 bells, at Springfield, Mass. Author: The Christian Year; A Guide to Worship, 1937. Editor of The Christian Year Calendar, 1939, 40. Home: 4 Newport Rd., Cambridge, Mass. Address: Exeter and Newbury Sts., Boston, Mass.*

Died May 20, 1945.

ADAMS, George Heyl, newspaper man; b. Maywood, Ill., Dec. 18, 1885; s. Edward Augustus and Margaret Rosalind (Swain) A.; grad. high sch., Austin, Ill., 1903; m. Io Sublette, July 19, 1909; children—Edward Langford, Georgiana, Caroline; married 2d, Loretta M. Nevins, October 1, 1947. Reporter City Press Assn., Chicago, 1904-05, Commercial West (financial weekly), Minneapolis, 1906-07; reporter Minneapolis Journal, 1907, asst. city editor, 1908, city editor, 1909-12, mng. editor, 1912-1926; editor Minneapolis Star, 1927-35; mng. editor Minneapolis Journal, 1936-39; exec. editor Times-Tribune and Minneapolis Morning Tribune, 1939-41; editor Minneapolis Daily Times, 1941-42; writer Batten, Barton, Durstine & Osborn since 1943. Republican. Quaker. Clubs: Minneapolis Athletic, Six O'Clock Club Home: 7677 Hillside Dr., La Jolla, Calif.

Died Oct. 17, 1949.

ADAMS, Herbert, sculptor; b. Concord, Vt., 1858; s. Samuel M. and Nancy (Powers) A.; ed. Inst. of Tech., Worcester, Mass.; Mass. Normal Art Sch., and pupil of Mercié at Paris; hon. degree of M.A., Yale, 1916, Tufts, 1927; m. Adeline Valentine Pond, 1889. Awards at Chicago, Paris and St. Louis and San Francisco expns.; medal of honor, Architectural League, 1915; prize, Nat. Acad., 1916. Mem. Commn. on Fine Arts (U.S.), Nat. Academy, 1899; ex-pres. Nat. Acad. Design; mem. Am. Acad. Arts and Letters; hon. pres. Nat. Sculpture Soc.; mem. Archtl. League New York. Trustee Am. Acad. in Rome, Hispanic Soc. of America. Club: Century. Address: 131 W. 11th St., New York, N.Y.

Died May 21, 1945.

ADAMS, James Truslow, writer; b. Brooklyn, N.Y., Oct. 18, 1878; s. William Newton and Elizabeth Harber (Truslow) A.; A.B., Poly. Inst. Brooklyn, 1898; A.M., Yale U., 1900; LL.D., R.I. State Coll., 1923 Litt.D., Columbia U., 1924; L.H.D. from Wesleyan U., Conn., 1931, Lehigh U., 1933, U. of Pittsburgh, 1939; Litt. D. Princeton U., 1933, and New York U., 1937; m. Kathryn M. Seely, Jan. 18, 1927. Mem. N.Y. Stock Exchange firm until 1912; with Col. House Commn. to prepare data for Peace Conf., early in World War; later capt. Mil. Intelligence Div., Gen. Staff U.S. Army; detailed spl. duty at Peace Conf., Paris, 1919. Trustee of Bridgeport-People's Savings Bank. Mem. Am. Acad. Arts and Letters (chancellor and treas.), Nat. Inst. Arts and Letters, Mass. Hist. Soc., Am. Antiquarian Soc., Am. Hist. Assn. (exec. council 1927-28), Am. Philos. Soc.; fellow Royal Soc. of Lit. (Eng.); hon. fellow N.Y. State Hist. Soc.; hon. mem. New Eng. Hist. Geneal. Soc., N.Y. Hist. Soc. Clubs: Century (N.Y. City); Pequot Yacht (Conn.); Authors' (London, Eng.) Author: Memorials of Old Bridgehampton, 1916; History of Town of Southampton, 1918; Founding of New England, 1921 (winner Pulitzer prize of $2,000 for best book on history of U.S., 1922); Revolutionary New England, 1691-1776, 1923; New England in the Republic (1776-1850), 1926; Provincial Society (1690-1763), 1927; Hamiltonian Principles, 1928; Jeffersonian Principles, 1928; Our Business Civilization, 1929, republished in England as A Searchlight on America, 1930; The Adams Family, 1930; The Epic of America, 1931, trans. into French, German, Danish, Hungarian, Italian, Portuguese, Rumanian, Spanish, and Swedish; The Tempo of Modern Life, 1931; The March of Democracy (2 vols.), 1932-33; Henry Adams, 1933; America's Tragedy, 1935; The Record of America (with C. G. Vannest), 1935; The Living Jefferson, 1936; Building the British Empire, 1938, Empire on the Seven Seas, 1940; The American, 1943; Frontiers of American Culture, 1944; Big Business in a Democracy, 1945. Contributing editor of New Frontier Social Science Series, three volumes, 1936-37; editor in chief of Dictionary of Am. History, Six volumes, 1940; revised and enlarged J. M. Beck's Constitution of the United States, 1941; Album of American History, (vol. I, 1944, vol. II, 1945, vol. III, 1946, vol. IV, 1948). Editor in chief, The Atlas of American History, 1943. Member advisory council, Yale Review, 1926-27. By request of senators appeared before Senate Judiciary Com. in opposition to President's Supreme Court Plan, 1937. Contributor to revised Ency. Brit., Dictionary Am. Biography and leading periodicals in U.S. and England. Mem. Pulitzer prize jury in history, 1924-32, chmn., 1930-32. Awarded prize ($1,000) by Yale Rev. for article on pub. affairs of 1932. Incorporator Sons of the Middle Border and Museum, Mitchell, S.D. Inspected 30,000 miles of Am. railways, and helped open Meadows Valley, Ida., to settlement, 1908. Home: Sheffield House, Southport, Conn. Address: care Charles Scribner's Sons, 597 Fifth Av., New York, N.Y. Died May 18, 1949.

ADAMS, Jesse Earl, educator; b. Monroe City, Ind., Apr. 24, 1888; s. George Washington and Ellen (Lovelace) A.; A.B., Vincennes U., 1913; A.M., Ind. U., 1922, Ph.D., 1925; grad. study U. of Chicago; m. Esther Nicholson, Feb. 20, 1920; children—William Randolph, George Robert. Teacher rural and high schs., and prin. high schs. and consol. schs.; county supt. schs. Knox Co., Ind., 1920-21; head dept. of edn. and dir. summer session, Franklin Coll., 1922-25; prof. ednl. adminstrn., U. of Ky., since 1925; dir. of summer sessions, Univ. of Ky., 1932-40. Widely known as lecturer on ednl. subjects. Served 11 mos. in World War, as pvt. and ordnance sergt., 1917-18. Mem. N.E.A., Nat. Soc. for Study Edn., Am. Assn. Univ. Profs., Ky. Ednl. Assn., Bluegrass Sch. Executives Club, Phi Beta Kappa, Phi Delta Kappa, Kappa Delta Pi. Democrat. Baptist. Mason. Author: Equalizing Educational Opportunity in Kentucky, 1928; The Child-Centered Speller, 1930; An Introduction to Education and the Teaching Process (with W. S. Taylor), 1932; My Self-Teaching Speller, 1937; also articles in mags. Home: Summitt Drive, Montclair Subdivision, Lexington, Ky.

Died Mar. 9, 1945.

ADAMS, John Davis, social worker; b. nr. Syracuse, N.Y., Mar. 9, 1860; s. James Addison and Clara Elizabeth (Davis) A.; Litt.B., Cornell, 1882; m. Mary Cranford, Oct. 12, 1899; children—Dorothy. John Cranford, Elizabeth. Reporter, New York Tribune, 1882; reporter, telegraph editor, editorial writer, Syracuse Standard, 1883-88; editor of Time, 1888-89; editorial staff Cosmopolitan Magazine, 1890-91; asst. editor Harper's Magazine, 1891-96; pvt. sec., 1897-1902; dir. Lincoln House (neighborhood club), 1903-20, retired. Unitarian. Member Chi Phi. Home: "Wakefield," Memphis, N.Y. Died Apr. 4, 1942.

ADAMS, John Taylor, lawyer; b. LaPorte, Ind., Dec. 25, 1873; s. Thomas Leander and Nannie (Pressly) A.; prep. edn., Cutler Acad., Colorado Springs, Colo.; student U. of Neb. and U. of Denver; m. Sue E. Raber, May 29, 1902; children—John Raber, Richard Elliot. Admitted to Colo. bar, 1900; justice Supreme Court of Colo., term 1925-34 inclusive, chief justice, 1931-34; resumed law practice, 1935. Mem. Am. Bar Assn., Colo. Bar Assn., Amer. Law Inst., Phi Alpha Delta, Colo. Soc. S.A.R. (pres. 1926). Republican. Presbyterian. Mason, Odd Fellow. Home: 209 S. Gilpin St. Office: E. & C. Bldg., Denver, Colo.

Died May 13, 1942.

ADAMS, Joseph Quincy, Shakespearean scholar; b. Greenville, S.C., Mar. 23, 1881; s. Reverend Joseph Quincy (D.D.) and Mamie Fouchée (Davis) A.; A.B., Wake Forest (N.C.) College, 1900, A.M., 1901; studied U. of Chicago, 1902-03, Cornell U., 1903-04, London, 1904-05, U. of Berlin, summer of 1907; Ph.D., Cornell, 1906; Litt.D., Wake Forest Coll., 1917, Amherst Coll., 1939, U. of North Carolina, 1946; m. Helen Banks, January 29, 1931 (died 1935); 1 dau., Helen Banks. Principle Raleigh Male Acad., 1901-02; scholar in English, U. of Chicago, 1902-03; Ezra Cornell fellow in English, Cornell U., 1903-04, instr. in English, 1905, asst. prof. English literature, 1909, prof. English, 1919-31; dir. The Folger Shakespeare Library, Washington, since 1931. Member Am. Philos. Soc., Modern Lang. Assn. America (exec. council), The Shakespeare Assn. of America (hon v.p.), Grolier Club, Bibliog. Society of London, Malone Soc. of England, Washington Literary Soc., Deutsche Shakespeare Gesellschaft, Phi Beta Kappa Fraternity, Zodiac Fraternity; hon. mem. Elizabethan Club of Yale U., The Tudor and Stuart Club of Johns Hopkins U., Shakespeare Soc. of Washington. Democrat. Baptist. Club: Cosmos (Washington). Author: (with others) Studies in Language and Literature, 1910; The Conventual Buildings of Blackfriars, London, 1916; Shakespearean Playhouses, 1917; Life of William Shakespeare, 1923; (with C. S. Northup) A Register of Bibliographies of the English Language and Literature, 1925; (with J. F. Bradley) An Allusion-Book to Ben Jonson, 1922. Editor: Richard Sheridan's Rivals, 1910; John Mason's The Turke, 1913; The Dramatic Records of Sir Henry Herbert, Master of Revels, 1917; Chief Pre-Shakespearean Dramas, 1924; The Adams Shakespeare, 1929—; Titus Andronicus First Quarto, 1936; Middleton's Ghost of Lucrece, 1937; The Passionate Pilgrim, 1939; Jourdain's Discovery of the Barmudas; Oenone and Paris, 1943; The Folger Shakespeare Library Prints. Associate editor of the Materialien zur Kunde des älteren englischen Dramas; joint editor of the Cornell Studies in English; consulting editor The Shakespeare Association of America Bulletin; advisory editor, Scholars' Facsimiles and Reprints. General editor The New Variorum Shakespeare; The Publications of the Folger Shakespeare Library. Contributor philol. jours., America and Europe. Home: 2915 Foxhall Road N.W. Address: The Folger Shakespeare Library, Washington, D.C.

Died Nov. 10, 1946.

ADAMS, Karl Langdon, coll. pres.; b. Lexington, O., Sept. 5, 1888; s. Richard Otha and Ella (Langdon) A.; B.S., Ohio Univ., Athens, O., 1909; A.M., Teachers Coll., Columbia, 1929; m. Helen W. Baker, Dec. 27, 1911; children—Ruth Elizabeth, Karl Langdon. Science teacher and athletic coach, Sidney (O.) High Sch., 1910-11, Moline (Ill.) High Sch., 1911-16; asst. prin., same, 1914-16; science teacher, State Teachers Coll., St. Cloud, Minn., 1916-28; asst. to Dr. Evenden, Teachers Coll., Columbia, summer 1929; pres. Northern Ill. State Teachers Coll., DeKalb, Ill., since 1929. Drafted for service, U.S. Army, 1917. Mem. Ill. Edn. Assn. (chmn. teacher training com. since 1931), Nat. Soc. for Study of Edn. Am. Assn. Teachers Colleges, Am. Assn. Sch. Adminstrs., Phi Beta Kappa, Phi Delta Kappa, Kappa Delta Pi, Alpha Phi Omega, Pi Kappa Delta, Beta Theta Pi. Republican. Methodist. Mason. Club: Kiwanis. Home: 540 Normal Road, DeKalb, Ill.

Died Dec. 6, 1948.

ADAMS, Numa Pompilius Garfield, medical dean; b. Delaphane, Va., Feb. 26, 1885; A.B., Howard U., 1911; A.M., Columbia, 1912; M.D., Rush Med. Coll., Chicago, 1924; A.B., Dartmouth Coll., 1937; student Mass. Inst. Tech.; m. Osceola Marie Macarthy, 1915; 1 son, Charles Macarthy. Teacher of chemistry, Howard U., 1912-19; began practice of medicine at Chicago; practice in Washington, D.C., since 1929; now dean school of medicine, Howard U. Mem. bd. of dirs. Tuberculosis Assn. of D.C.; mem. advisory health council of Washington Council on Social Agencies. Fellow A.A.A.S.; mem. Nat. Med. Assn., Cook County (Ill.) Physicians Assn. Contbr. to med. jours. Home: 341 Bryant St. N.W. Office: Howard Univ., Washington, D.C.

Died Aug. 29, 1940.

ADAMS, Porter (Hartwell), educator; b. at Andover, Mass., Aug. 10, 1894; s. Charles Albert and Jeannie Hortense (Porter) A.; prep. edn. Stone Sch. and Chauncy Hall Sch., Boston; student U. of Redlands, Calif., Mass. Inst. Tech.; hon. M.Sc., Norwich U., 1933, Sc.D., 1935; m. 2d, Sue Shorter, July 27, 1931. With Cooper Aircraft Co., Bridgeport, Conn., 1915; associated with Donald Douglas on first proposed world flight, 1916; development work, 1920-22. Intelligence and communications officer, U.S. Navy, Rockland, Me., and Boston, 1917-18; aide to comdg. officer, Naval Air Sta., Chatham, Mass., 1918-19; lt. comdr. U.S.N.R., retired. Executor and trustee of various estates; pres. of Norwich U., Dec. 1933-June 1939, now pres. emeritus. Pres. Village Soc. of Thetford, Vt., since 1929; mem. Thetford Water Bd.; mem. Thetford Bd. of Selectmen, 1933-36; mem. Vt. Ho. of Reps., 1933-34; mem. Vt. Chamber of Commerce. Chmn. exec. com. Nat. Aeronautic Assn., 1922-26 and since 1928, pres. 1926-28; chmn. Municipal Air Bd., Boston, since 1922; Vt. airport supervisor for aeronautics branch, Dept. of Commerce and Civil Works Adminstrn.; dir. Miniature Aircraft Tournament under Playground Recreation Assn. America, Nat. Glider Assn.; v.p. Internat. Air Congress, Rome, Italy, 1927; tech. adviser for Am. delegation, Internat. Civil Aeronautics Conf., Washington, 1928; mem. Fed. Bd. of Maps and Surveys; mem. Am. Olympic Com., 1928; chmn. First Intercollegiate Aeronautical Conf., Yale U., 1928; chmn. aviation med. sect., First Nat. Aeronautical Safety Conf., 1928; chmn. first aviation com., Am. Legion, Dept. of Mass.; mem. advisory council on student flying activities, Mass. Inst. Tech.; mem. special com. on Aeronautical Research in Ednl. Instns. of Nat. Advisory Com. for Aeronautics; mem. New Eng. Planning Com. of Nat. Resources Bd., also chmn. aviation com.; chmn. Aero Com. of A.L. Dept., Vt., 1935; Vt. chmn. for Navy Day, 1933-40; apptd. by gov. chmn. Vt. Aviation Commn. for term, 1936-40. Mem. Vt. advisory bd. for N.Y. World's Fair. Trustee Norwich U.; elected chmn. spl. com. of trustees to administer James Jackson Cabot professorship of air traffic regulation and air transportation, and also appointed first James Jackson Cabot prof. of air traffic regulation and air transportation at Norwich Univ., Aug. 1935; trustee Thetford Acad.; v.p. Vt. Boy Scouts. Fellow A.A.A.S.; mem. Inst. of Aeronautical Sciences, Am. Soc. M.E. (exec. com., aeronautics sect.), Navy League of U.S., Soc. Automotive Engrs., Am. Acad. Air Law, Vt. Hist. Soc., Vt. Soc. Engrs., U.S. Naval Inst., Naval Order of U.S., Mil. Order of World War, Nat. Grange (7th degree), Newcomen Soc., New Eng. Railroad Club, Pi Gamma Mu, Epsilon Tau Sigma; also hon. mem. foreign aeronautical socs. Conglist. Clubs: Metropolitan, Aero (trustee), Army and Navy (Washington); St.

Botolph, Wardrcem, Engineers, Aero Club of Mass. (dir., ex-vice pres.), Aero Club of New England (dir., ex-pres.), Woodland Country (Boston); University (Boston and Northfield, Vt.); Newcomen Soc. (England). Contbr. to periodicals on subject of aviation. Inventor of aeroplane brakes, 1916, Adams type of wind tunnel balance for aerodynamical research, 1933, Adams system of combustion for steam submarines, aircraft, tanks, etc. Home: "Aero Acres," Thetford, Vt. Address: Norwich University, Northfield, Vt. Died Dec. 5, 1945.

ADAMS, Romanzo, sociologist; b. Bloomingdale, Wis., Mar. 22, 1868; s. Mighill Dustin and Catherine (Wolfe) A.; M.Di., Ia. State Teachers' Coll., Cedar Falls, Ia., 1892; Ph.B., U. of Mich., 1897, Ph.M., 1898; Ph.D., U. of Chicago, 1904; m. Nellie Cronk, Sept. 16, 1902; 1 dau., Katharine. Prin. pub schs., Ireton, Ia., 1892-94; prof. economics and sociology, Western Coll., Toledo, Ia., 1898-1900; prof. edn. and sociology, 1902-11, prof. economics and sociology, U. of Nev., 1911-20, U. of Hawaii since 1920. Mem. Inst. of Pacific Relations. Methodist. Author: Taxation in Nevada, 1918; Statistical Studies of the Japanese in Hawaii, 1923; The Peoples of Hawaii—A Statistical Study, 1925. Home: 2315 Liloa Rise, Honolulu, Hawaii. Died Sept. 10, 1942.

ADAMS, Warren Austin, prof. German; b. Skaneateles, N.Y., Sept. 14, 1861; s. Emerson H. and Annette (Austin) A.; A.B., Yale, 1886, Ph.D., 1895; studied univs. Berlin and Munich, 1887-89; grad. student New York U., Sch. of Pedagogy, 1890-91; Cornell, 1892-93; Paris, summer 1893; Yale, 1893-95; Berlin and Weimar, 1909-10, 1924-25; m. Grace Smith, Sept. 2, 1896 (died Jan. 31, 1916); children—Austin Lockwood, Henry (dec.); m. 2d, Mrs. Mary Page Billings, Sept. 13, 1926. Instr. Latin and Roman history, Kenyon Mil. Acad., Gambier, O., 1886-87; instr. German, French, Latin and Greek, Montclair (N.J.) Mil. Acad., 1889-91; instr. German, Cornell, 1891-9?, Yale, 1893-99; asst. prof. German, Dartmouth, 1899-1904, prof. since 1904, head of dept. since 1900. Mem. Modern Lang. Assn. America. Conglist. Editor Goethe's Hermann und Dorothea; Keller's Romeo und Julia auf dem Dorfe; Rogge's Der grosze Preuszenkönig. Home: Hanover, N.H. Died Aug. 25, 1944.

ADAMS, Washington Irving Lincoln, banker; b. N.Y. City, Feb. 22, 1865; s. Washington Irving and Marion L. (Briggs) A.; grad. high sch., Montclair, N.J.; m. Grace Wilson, Nov. 21, 1889. Editor The Photographic Times over 10 yrs., American Annual of Photography several yrs.; pres. Scovill & Adams Co., 1896-99; pres. Styles & Cash since 1904; chmn. Murray Hill Trust Co.; pres. The Sackett & Wilhelms Co.; treas. Montclair Holding Co.; dir. Montclair Trust Co., Bloomfield Trust Co. Maj. U.S.R. Mem. Huguenot Soc. (treas.), Soc. Colonial Wars (treas.), Founders and Patriots Am., N.J. Soc. S.A.R., Soc. War of 1812, N.E. Soc., St. Nicholas Soc. Club: Union League (v.p.). Author: The Amateur Photographer, 1893; Sunlight and Shadow, 1898; In Nature's Image, 1898; Woodland and Meadow, 1901; Personalia (verse), 1902; Photographing in Old England, 1910. Home: Montclair, N.J., and Littleton, N.H. Office: 2 W. 45th St., New York. Died Jan. 20, 1946.

ADAMSON, Robert; b. Adamson's Dist., Ga., Mar. 31, 1871; s. Augustus Pitt and Martilla Ellen (Cook) A.; ed. pub. schs. of Ga.; m. Ethel McClintock, Dec. 10, 1902. City editor Atlanta Constitution at 20, later asso. editor Atlanta Journal; polit. writer for New York World, 1899-1909; sec to Mayor William J. Gaynor, Jan., 1910, until latter's death, Sept., 1913; sec. to Mayor Kline until 1914; fire commr. N.Y. City, Jan. 1, 1914-Dec. 31, 1917. Mgr. of campaign which resulted in election of Mayor Mitchel and fusion city govt., 1914. Dir. Petroleum Heat & Power Co. Mem. exec. com. Mayor's Com. on Taxation; mem. Com. on Blighted Areas and Slums of President's Conf. on Home Building and Home Ownership; chmn. Depreciation Fund Board under Contract No. 3, Interborough Rapid Transit Co. Mem. New York Chamber of Commerce; dir. 5th Av. Assn.; chmn. ins. com. Merchants Assn. and Chamber of Commerce. Democrat. Mem. Ga. Soc. of New York, Southern Soc., Pilgrims. Clubs: Bankers, Uptown, Rumson Country. Home: 25 E. 9th St., New York; (summer) Middletown, N.J. Died Sept. 19, 1935.

ADDAMS, Clifford Isaac, painter and etcher; b. Woodbury, N.J., May 25, 1876; s. Wellington Isaac and Sarah (Neff) A.; grad. Germantown Acad., 1891; student Drexel Inst., Phila., 1894-95; Cresson traveling scholarship, Pa. Acad. of Fine Arts, 1896-99; student Whistler's Acad. Carmen, Paris, 1899-1902; apptd. apprentice to Whistler, 1901-06; m. Inez Elanor Bate, June 27, 1900; children—Dianne, James Ramage, Anthony Clifford, Martin Isaac; m. 2d, Lilian Curtis Goodhue Howard, Mar. 16, 1932. Awarded bronze medal, Panama Pacific Expn., 1915, Art Inst. Chicago, 1917; Toppan Water Color prize, 1922; Clarke prize, Nat. Acad. of Design, 1923; gold medal, Art Club, Phila., 1924; Temple gold medal, Pa. Acad. of Fine Arts, 1925; Logan silver medal, Art Inst. of Chicago, 1926. Represented by murals in Asheville (N.C.) City Hall; etchings in Met. Mus. of Art. Served in British Royal Navy, 1914-19, one of 1st 10 Americans to enter World War. Awarded Mons Star Riband by Belgium, A.W.O. by British Gov't. Fellow Royal Society of Arts; mem. Chicago, Brooklyn, and Phila. socs. of etchers. Republican. Episcopalian. Address: 64 Washington Square, New York, N.Y. Died Nov. 7, 1942.

ADDIS, Thomas, prof. medicine; b. Edinburgh, Scotland, July 27, 1881; s. Thomas Chalmers and Cornelia Beers (Campbell) A.; came to U.S., 1911, naturalized, 1917; M.B., Ch.B., U. of Edinburgh, 1905, M.D., 1908; m. Elesa Bolton Partridge, 1913; children—Elesa Campbell, Jean Thorburn. Prof. medicine Stanford U. Med. Sch. since 1911. Mem. Nat. Acad. of Science. Author: Glomerular Nephritis, 1948. Contbr. to scientific mags. Home: 1109 Alta Loma Rd., Los Angeles 46. Address: Inst. for Medical Research, 4751 Fountain Av., Los Angeles 27. Died June 4, 1949.

ADE, George (ād), author; b. Kentland, Ind., Feb. 9, 1866; s. John and Adaline (Bush) A.; B.S., Purdue U., 1887, L.H.D., 1926; LL.D., U. of Indiana, 1927; unmarried. On newspaper, Lafayette, Ind., 1887-90, Chicago Record, 1890-1900. Del. Rep. Nat. Conv., 1908. Trustee Purdue U., 1908-15. Grand consul Sigma Chi Fraternity, 1909. Promoted Ross-Ade Stadium, Purdue U., 1923-24, assisting David E. Ross. Author: Artie; Pink Marsh; Doc Horne; Fables in Slang; More Fables; The Girl Proposition, 1902; People You Knew, 1903; Breaking Into Society, 1903; True Bills, 1904; In Pastures New, 1906; The Slim Princess, 1907; Knocking the Neighbors, 1912; Ade's Fables, 1914; Hand-made Fables, 1920; Single Blessedness, 1922; The Old-Time Saloon, 1931; Thirty Fables, 1933. Plays: The Sultan of Sulu, 1902; Peggy from Paris, 1903; The County Chairman, 1903; The Sho-Gun, 1904; The College Widow, 1904; The Bad Samaritan, 1905; Just Out of College, 1905; Marse Covington, 1906; Mrs. Peckham's Carouse, 1906; Father and the Boys, 1907; The Fair Co-Ed, 1908; The Old Town, 1909; Nettie, 1914. Mem. Nat. Inst. Arts and Letters. Mem. Ind. State Council of Defense, 1917-18. Author of photoplays Our Leading Citizen, Back Home and Broke, and Woman Proof. Apptd. mem. Ind. Commn. for "Chicago World's Fair 1933." Home: Hazelden Farm, Brook, Indiana. Died May 16, 1944.

ADIE, David Craig, (ā'dē), commr. social welfare; b. Hamilton, Scotland, Sept. 3, 1888; s. Lawrence and Madeline (Cooper) A.; ed. pub. schs., Scotland; LL.D., St. Bonaventure Coll., Allegheny, N.Y., 1935; m. Ann Herr, July 31, 1916; 1 dau., Jean Cooper. Came to U.S., 1913, naturalized, 1919. Asst. sec. Minneapolis Civic and Commerce Assn., 1914-18; asso. sec. War Labor Policies Bd., 1918; impartial chmn. Men's and Boys' Clothing Industry, N.Y. City, 1919-20; campaign mgr. Am. City Bur., N.Y. City, 1921-22; sec. Charity Orgn. Soc., Buffalo, N.Y., 1922-29; sec. Council of Social Agencies, Buffalo, 1920-32; N.Y. state commr. social welfare, since 1932; professorial lecturer in sociology and social work and mem. curriculum com., U. of Buffalo; mem. faculty N.Y. Sch. Social Work (N.Y. City), Fordham U.; lecturer on social and civic questions, mem. exec. com. Nat. Council State Pub. Assistance and Welfare Adminstrn.; chairman Federal-State Adv. Com. on Welfare in defense program. Mem. White House Conf. on Children in a Democracy. Mem. bd. govs. St. Agnes Sch., Albany. Mem. Am. Assn. Social Workers, Am. Pub. Welfare Assn.; N.Y. State Assn. of Pub. Welfare Officials; Nat. Conf. of Social Work; Am. Soc. for Public Administration. Clubs: Fort Orange (Albany, N.Y.); Thursday (Buffalo). Home: Loudonville, N.Y. Office: 112 State St., Albany, N.Y. Died Feb. 23, 1943.

ADLER, Emanuel Philip, newspaper pub.; b. Chicago, Ill., Sept. 30, 1872; s. Philip Emanuel and Bertha (Blade) A.; ed. pub. schs.; m. Lena Rothschild, Feb. 5, 1902; 1 son, Philip David. Began in newspaper business at Ottumwa, Ia., 1897; now pres. Lee Syndicate Newspapers; also pres. The Times Co., The Democrat Publishing Co. (Davenport), Journal Printing Co. (Muscatine), Globe Gazette Co. (Mason City), Tribune Pub. Co. (La Crosse, Wis.), Madison (Wis.) State Journal Co., Courier Post Pub. Co. (Hannibal, Mo.), Star-Courier Pub. Co. (Kewanee, Ill.), Courier Printing Co. (Ottumwa, Ia.), Star Pub. Co. (Lincoln, Neb.). Second v.p. Associated Press, 1917-18; pres. Inland Daily Press Assn., 1917-18. Mem. and sec. Rep. State Central Com., Ia., 1910-12. Mem. B.P.O.E. Clubs: Davenport Commercial, Davenport Country. Home: 2104 Main St. Office: Times Bldg., Davenport, Ia. Died March 2, 1949.

AFFLECK, Benjamin Franklin, mfr.; b. Belleville, Ill., Mar. 1, 1869; s. James and Anna (Richardson) A.; student pub. schs.; m. Agnes H. Adams, Feb. 20, 1899; 1 dau., Mrs. Victor Spoehr; m. 2d, Irene Mansfield, Jan. 14, 1921; 1 dau., Jane Mansfield With Harrison Machine Works, 1884-89, St. L., Alton and Terre Haute R.R. (now part of I.C. R.R.), 1890-96, Ill. Steel Co., 1896-1906; sales mgr. at Chicago, Universal Atlas Cement Co., 1906-15, pres., 1915-36 (retired), now dir. Hon. mem. Portland Cement Assn. (pres. 1916-20), Am. Concrete Inst., Western Soc. Engrs.; mem. Chicago Assn. Commerce, Art Inst., Chicago, Field Museum of Natural History, Citizens Assn., Chicago (pres. 1939-40). Republican. Clubs: Engineers (hon. mem.; pres. 1916), Union League (pres. 1928), Executives (pres. 1939-40), Rotary, Arts (Chicago). Home: 800 Humboldt Av., Winnetka, Ill. Office: 208 S. La Salle St., Chicago, Ill. Died Feb. 13, 1944.

AGEE, Alva, agrl. educator; b. Cheshire, O., Oct. 1, 1858; s. Jesse Thornhill and Lydia (Mauck) A.; ed. Marietta Coll. to close of sophomore yr.; M.S., Univ. of Wooster, O.; M.S., Princeton, 1922; m. Louise Grace Hibbs, Oct. 6, 1887. Prof. in charge agrl. extension, Pa. State Coll., 1907-12; in charge agrl. extension and prof. soil fertility, Rutgers Coll., 1912-18. Asso. editor Nat. Stockman and Farmer; contbr. to agrl. periodicals since 1890; lecturer on agrl. topics since 1891. Mem. Delta Upsilon, Alpha Zeta, Phi Kappa Phi. Author: Essentials of Soil Fertility; Crops and Methods for Soil Improvement; Right Use of Lime in Soil Improvement; First Steps in Farming. Sec. Agr., N.J. State Dept. of Agr., Trenton, 1916-25. Address: 1835 Altura Pl., San Diego, Calif. Died Dec. 10, 1943.

AGG, Thomas Radford (ag), highway engring.; b. Fairfield, Ia., May 17, 1878; s. Henry and Sarah Jane (Tansey) A.; B.S. in E.E., Ia. State Coll., Ames, Ia., 1905, C.E., 1914; m. Lois Woodman, Dec. 27, 1906; children—Muriel Lois, Alice Jane. Instr. in theoretical mechanics, U. of Ill., 1905-08; road engr. Ill. Highway Dept., summers, 1906, 1907, and full time 1908-13; prof. highway engring., Ia. State Coll., 1913-30, asst. dean of engring., 1930-32, dean of engring. and dir. Engring. Expt. Sta., 1930-46; resident prof. highway engring. since July 1946, also cons. practice. Developed outstanding instrn. and research in highway engring. at Ia. State Coll. Entered Engineering Officers Training Camp, May 1917; commissioned captain, later major; served with 109th and 98th Engineers. Received George S. Bartlett award for outstanding contribution to highway progress, 1936. Member American Society Civil Engrs. (dir. Dist. 16, 1938-40); (v.p. Zone 3, 1943-44), Am. Soc. for Testing Materials, Soc. for Promotion Engring. Edn., Iowa Engring. Soc., Newcomen Soc., Tau Beta Pi, Sigma Xi, Phi Kappa Phi, Acacia. Republican. Episcopalian. Mason (32°). Mem. Rotary Internat. Author: Construction of Roads and Pavements, 1916, 5th edit., 1939; American Rural Highways, 1920; (with Dr. John E. Brindley) Highway Administration and Finance, 1927; (with W. L. Foster) Preparation of Engineering Reports, 1935; (with Anson Marston) Engineering Valuation, 1936. Home: 325 Pearson Av., Ames, Ia. Died May 7, 1947.

AHRENS, Edward Hamblin, publisher; b. Chicago, Ill., Mar. 25, 1884; s. John Paulsen and Fanny (Hamblin) A.; attended pub. schs. of Chicago; A.B., Sch. of Commerce, U. of Chicago, 1906; m. Pauline Forsyth, Dec. 18, 1912; 1 son, Dr. Edward Hamblin. Began as salesman Dodge Mfg. Co., Chicago, 1906; with A. W. Shaw Co., 1909-21; mem. advertisers service bureau, Chicago, 1909-11, advt. mgr. Factory Magazine, 1911-16, mgr. Factory Mag., 1916-17, eastern advt. dir. of the company, 1917-21; pres. and dir. Ahrens Publishing Co., New York, N.Y., since organization, 1921, also pres. and dir. 4 subsidiary cos. Mem. paper advisory com. W.P.B.; mem. Metropolitan Jr. Achievement; sec. Lawrence Park Assn. (Bronxville, N.Y.). Past pres. and dir. Associated Business Papers; dir. Nat. Publishers Assn. Mem. S.A.R. Recipient commendations for war emergency cooperation from Am. Red Cross, O.C.D., W.P.B., W.F.A., O.W.I., O.P.A., U.S. depts of agriculture, health and welfare services, War Advertising Council. Clubs: University, Psi U, Players, International Rotary (New York); Sleepy Hollow Country (Scarborough, N.Y.); Chicago (Ill.) Athletic; American Yacht (Rye, N.Y.). Home: 60 Prescott Av., Bronxville 8, N.Y. Office: 71 Vanderbilt Av., New York 17, N.Y. Died Feb. 1, 1947.

AIKEN, Alfred Lawrence (ā'kĕn), insurance; b. Norwich, Conn., July 6, 1870; s. William Appleton and Eliza Coit (Buckingham) A.; A.B., Yale U., 1891, hon. A.M., 1918; m. Elizabeth Peck Hopkins, Nov. 25, 1896. With State Mut. Life Assurance Co., 1892-94; asst. mgr. New Eng. Dept. N.Y. Life Ins. Co., 1894-99; asst. cashier State Nat. Bank, Boston, 1899-1904; pres. Worcester County Inst. for Savings, 1908-13; pres. Worcester Nat. Bank, 1913, 14; gov. Fed. Reserve Bank of Boston, 1914-17; pres. Nat. Shawmut Bank, Boston, 1918-23, chmn. bd., 1923-24; v.p. New York Life Ins. Co., 1925-36, pres., 1936-40; chmn. board, 1940-42, now director; director Fifth Avenue Bank; trustee Franklin Savings Bank. Trustee Worcester Art Mus., 1909-34, Clark U., Worcester, Mass., 1919-30, Wellesley Coll., 1919-25, Boston Symphony Orchestra, 1920-24. Mem. Mil. Order Loyal Legion, Soc. Colonial Wars, S.R., Pilgrims of U.S. Republican. Episcopalian. Clubs: Union (Boston); Links, Union, University, Union League (New York). Home: 115 E. 67th St. Address: New York Life Insurance Co., 51 Madison Av., New York, N.Y.* Died Dec. 13, 1946.

AIKEN, Wyatt, ex-congressman; b. Abbeville Co., S.C., Dec. 14, 1863; s. D. Wyatt (M.C.) and Virginia Carolina A.; ed. Cokesbury, S.C., and Washington, D.C.; m. Mary Barnwell, Apr. 27, 1892. Farmer since boyhood; served in 1st S.C. Vols. in Spanish-Am. War; battalion adj. and regimental q.-m. Official court stenographer, Abbeville, S.C., 1884-1903; mem. 58th to 64th Congresses (1903-17), 3d S.C. Dist.; Democrat. Address: Abbeville, S.C. Died Feb. 6, 1923.

AIKMAN, Walter Monteith, artist; b. New York, 1857; studied engraving in New York under Frank French and J. G. Smithwick, drawing and painting under Boulanger and Lefebvre, Paris; unmarried.

Medal for engraving, Paris Expn., 1889, and Chicago Expn., 1893; exhibited in Paris, 1900; silver medal for original engravings on wood, Buffalo Expn., 1901. Mem. Brooklyn Soc. Artists, Rockport Art Assn. Address: 133 Macon St., Brooklyn, N.Y. Died Jan. 3, 1939.

AILSHIE, James Franklin (āl'shĭ), jurist; b. Green County, Tenn., June 19, 1868; s. George W. and Martha (Knight) A.; reared on farm; ed. Mosheim (Tenn.) Coll. and Carson Coll., Jefferson City, Tenn., until 19; Ph.B., LL.B., Willamette U., Salem, Ore., 1891; LL.D., 1909; hon. LL.D., U. of Idaho, 1940; m. Lucie, d. Rev. and Mrs. J. B. Bundren, June 19, 1894; children—Mrs. Lucile McHarg, James F. (dec.), William K., Robert. Taught in pub. schs., Wash. Ty.; admitted to Ida. and Ore. bars, 1891; settled at Grangeville, Ida.; admitted to U.S. Dist. and Circuit Courts and U.S. Supreme Court, 1907; justice Supreme Court of Idaho, 1903-15 (chief justice, 1907-09, 1913-15); resigned, 1914, and resumed practice at Boise and Coeur d' Alene, Ida., 1915, specializing in corp. law and gen. trial work; elected 1934, reelected 1940, 1946; justice Supreme Court (chief justice 1939-41, 1945-46). Del. Repub. National Convention, 1900, 16, 32; defeated by 4 votes for United States Senator, 1913; member Idaho State Council of Defense, 1917-18, and since 1942. Regent, U. of Idaho, 1893-95. Mem. Idaho State Bar Assn. (pres. 1921-23, 1933-35; chmn. state com. on proc. reform); mem. Am. Bar Assn. (exec. com. 1926-29; mem. Ethics and Grievance Com., 1936; mem. gen. council, 1929-34; chmn. State Com. on Improving Adminstrn. of Justice, since 1940; mem. standing com. on state legislation, 1943); mem. Idaho Com. on Uniform State Laws, 1924-35; mem. Nat. Econ. League (v.p.), League to Enforce Peace; mem. Am. Law Inst.; nonresident lecturer on mining law and law of irrigation and water rights, Law School, U. of Ida. Presbyterian. Odd Fellow. Elk. Home: 219 E. Jefferson St. Address: State House, Boise, Ida.
Died May 27, 1947.

AILSHIE, Robert, lawyer; b. Boise, Idaho, Feb. 16, 1908; s. James Franklin and Lucie (Bundren) A.; A.B., Univ. of Idaho, 1930; Harvard Law Sch., 1930-33; unmarried. Admitted to Idaho Bar, 1933, admitted to Federal practise, 1933; asso. in practise with James F. Ailshie (father), 1934-35; asso. with James F. Ailshie Jr. (brother), 1935-38; practised alone, 1938-40; with firm of Richards & Haga, 1940-42; with firm of Langroise & Sullivan, Boise, 1942-46; attorney gen., State of Idaho since 1946. Exec. dir. for Civilian Defense, 1942, dir., 1943. Republican. Mem. Am. Bar Assn. (first chairman of the jr. section, 1934, twice on legislative com.). Home: 219 East Jefferson, Boise. Office: Attorney Generals Office, State House, Boise, Idaho. Died Nov. 16, 1947.

AINSLIE, George, mayor; b. Richmond, Va., Oct. 10, 1868; s. of George Alexander and Janet (Currie) A.; B.S., Va. Mil. Inst., Lexington, Va., 1890; LL.B., U. of Va., 1893; m. Marie Antoinette Burthe, Sept. 2, 1893. Practiced in Richmond since 1893; police commissioner, Richmond, 1903-6; mayor Sept., 1912. Organizer and first capt. of Co. B, 4th Battalion, Va. Vols. (Richmond Light Inf. Blues); resigned, 1895. Democrat. Episcopalian. Mem. Kappa Alpha (Southern). Clubs: Westmoreland, Commonwealth. Home: 1628-A W. Grace St. Office: City Hall, Richmond, Va. Died July 18, 1931.

AINSWORTH, Frank Kenley, surgeon; b. Woodstock, Vt., Oct. 23, 1856. M.D., U. of Vt., 1878; M.D., Univ. Med. Coll., New York U., 1879; unmarried. Began practice at Prescott, Ariz., 1880; moved to San Francisco, 1886; chief surgeon and mgr. hosp. dept. S.P. Co., 1886-1926 (retired). Mem. A.M.A., Calif. State Med. Soc., San Francisco Med. Soc. Republican. Universalist. Clubs: Pacific Union, Bohemian; hon. mem. California (Los Angeles). Home: 1000 Mason St., San Francisco. Died July 5, 1929.

AINSWORTH, John Churchill (āns'wûrth), financier; b. Portland, Ore., Jan. 4, 1870; s. John Commigers and Fannie (Babbit) A.; B.S., U. of Calif., 1891, M.S., 1892; m. Alice Heitshu, June 26, 1901; 1 dau., Katherine (Mrs. Abbot L. Mills, Jr.). Began with Central Bank, Oakland, Calif., 1893; elected pres. Ainsworth Nat. Bank, Portland, 1894, and continued as pres. of its successor, the U. S. Nat. Bank, chmn. bd. since 1931; formerly pres. States Steamship Co.; dir. Portland Gen. Electric Co., Pacific Power & Light Co.; dir. Federal Reserve Bank, Portland. Ex-chmn. Ore. State Highway Commn., City Planning Commn., Portland; ex-regent U. of Ore., Whitman Coll. Mem. Chi Phi. Republican. Presbyn. Mason (32°). Clubs: University, Arlington (ex-pres.), Waverly Country Club (ex-pres.). Home: 1855 S.W. Hawthorne Terrace. Office: 6th and Stark Sts., Portland, Ore.*
Died May 27, 1943.

AINSWORTH, William Newman, bishop; b. Camilla, Ga., Feb. 10, 1872; s. Rev. James Thomas and Kate (McRaeny) A.; A.B., Emory Coll., Ga., 1891, D.D., 1905; D.D., U. of Georgia, 1914; LL.D., Baylor, 1920; m. Mary A., d. Dr. Malcolm Nicholson, Oct. 11, 1893; children—William N., Malcolm D., Eloise (dec.). Ordained ministry M.E. Ch., S., 1891; pastor Grace Ch., Macon, Ga., 1892-93, Montezuma, 1894-95, Bainbridge, 1896-99, Dublin, 1900-01, Mulberry St. Ch., Macon, 1902-05, Wesley Monumental Ch., Savannah, 1906-09; pres. Wesleyan Coll., Macon, 1909-12; pastor Mulberry St. Ch., Macon, 1913-16, Wesley Monumental Ch., Savannah, 1917-18; elected bishop M.E. Ch., S., May 1918. Pres. Anti-Saloon League of America, 1935-36. Mem. Phi Beta Kappa. Home: Macon, Ga.
Died July 7, 1942.

AISHTON, Richard Henry (āsh'tŭn), railway official; b. Evanston, Ill., June 2, 1860; s. R. H. and E. A.; ed. Evanston pub. schs.; m. Rosa B. Whitbeck, Oct. 11, 1881. Entered ry. service, 1878, as axman engr. corps, C.&N.W. Ry; various duties of same ry. until 1895; asst. supt., 1895-97; div. supt., 1897-99; gen. supt., 1899-1902; asst. gen. mgr., 1902-06; gen. mgr. lines east of Mo. River, 1906-10; v.p. in charge of operation and maintenance, Oct. 20, 1900-Dec. 1914; pres. C.&N.W. Ry., May 23, 1916-Feb. 1920; dir. western div. rys., under U.S. Govt., Jan. 1918-Feb. 1920; became pres. Am. Ry. Assn., 1920; retired Oct. 1935. Became chmn. exec. com. Assn. of Ry. Executives, 1924; became gen. chmn. Presidents' Conf. Com. on Federal Valuation of Railroads in U.S., 1929. Home: 1501 Hinman Av., Evanston, Ill.
Died Oct. 3, 1946.

AITKEN, Robert (Ingersoll) (āt'kĕn), sculptor; b. San Francisco, May 8, 1878; s. Charles H. and Katherine (Higgins) A.; high sch. ed.; studied Mark Hopkins Inst. of Art, San Francisco, under Arthur F. Matthews and Douglas Tilden; m. Laure Louise Ligny, Nov. 27, 1907; children—Bruce, Lole Francine; m. 2d, Joan Louise Bruning, Apr. 14, 1934. Prof. sculpture, Mark Hopkins Inst. of Art (U. of Calif.), 1901-04; worked in Paris, 1904-07; served as instr. in sculpture, Art Students League, New York, and Nat. Acad. schs. Among important works are monuments to William McKinley, at St. Helena, Calif., 1902, Berkeley, Calif., 1902; McKinley monument Golden Gate Park, San Francisco, 1903; Hall McAllister monument, San Francisco, 1904; monument to Am. Navy, San Francisco; bronze doors, Greenhut and John W. Gates' mausoleums; "The Fountain of the Earth" and "The Four Elements," at Panama-Pacific Internat. Expn., also designs of $50 gold coin issued by U.S. Govt. in commemoration of the expn.; Missouri Centennial half dollar; San Diego Internat. Expn. half dollar; Burritt memorial, New Britain, Conn.; George Rogers Clark monument, U. of Va.; bronze group, "Light," Nela Park, Cleveland; Marine monument, Parris Island, S.C.; Alpha Delta Phi war memorial, Camp Merritt memorial, N.J.; Spanish War monument, Binghampton, N.Y.; colossal bronzes, Missisippi and Missouri rivers; fountains of the arts and sciences, Mo. State Capitol; Liberty memorial, Kansas City; Thomas Jefferson, Daniel Webster, Benjamin Franklin, Henry Clay, Hall of Fame; monument to Robert Burns, St. Louis; B. F. Jones memorial, Pittsburgh; Gen. Hann memorial, Arlington Cemetery; Pioneer Lumbermen monument, Huron Nat. Forest, Mich.; frieze on Columbus (O.) Gallery; Gen. O. O. Howard equestrian, Gettysburg National Park; Gompers monument, Washington, D.C.; West Pediment U.S. Supreme Court, Washington, D.C.; So. Penn Av. entrance Archives Bldg., Washington, D.C. Awarded Helen Foster Barnet prize, N. A. D.; Medal of Honor, Archtl. League, New York, for sculpture, 1915; silver medal for sculpture, Panama-Pacific Internat. Expn., 1915; Watrous medal for sculpture, N. A. D., 1921. Past pres. Nat. Sculpture Soc.; past vice pres. Nat. Acad. Design; mem. Archtl. League (New York), Nat. Inst. Arts and Letters (v.p.), Am. Federation of Arts, MacDowell Club, Municipal Art Soc., Union Internationale des Beaux Arts et des Lettres, Circle of Friends of the Medallion, Institut Français aux Etats-Unis. Commd. capt., U.S. Army, Aug. 8, 1917; assigned to Machine Gun Co., 306th Inf.; grad. Army and Gen. Staff Coll., A.E.F. Clubs: Bohemian (San Francisco); Lambs, Nat. Arts. Home: 44 Washington Mews. Studio: 42 Washington Mews, New York, N.Y. Died Jan. 3, 1949.

AKERMAN, Alexander (ā'kĕr-măn), judge; b. Elberton, Ga., Oct. 9, 1869; s. Amos T. and Martha Rebecca (Galloway) A.; ed. pub. schs.; m. Minnie C. Edwards, Feb. 3, 1890; children—Walter, Margaret (Mrs. Albert R. Menard), Amos T., Emory, Eugenia (Mrs. Russell B. Carson), Alexander. Admitted to Ga. bar, 1892, and began practice at Cartersville; referee in bankruptcy, 1898; asst. U.S. atty., South Dist., Ga., 1901-12, U.S. atty., 1912-14; judge, U.S. Dist. Court, Southern Dist., Fla., 1929-43. Republican. Home: 203 Phillips Pl., Orlando, Fla.*
Died Aug. 21, 1948.

AKIN, Thomas Russell, steel mfr.; b. New Bedford, Mass., Dec. 15, 1867; s. Thomas and Annie Thornton (Macomber) A.; A.B., Harvard, 1890; m. Margaret Markham, Nov. 1895 (died Mar. 1919); m. 2d, Grace Niccolls, July 24, 1920; children—William Markham, Thomas Russell. Connected with steel cos. most of time since 1890; pres. Laclede Steel Co.; dir. St. Louis Union Trust Co., First Nat. Bank in St. Louis. Dir. Am. Iron and Steel Institute. Republican. Presbyterian. Clubs: University, Noonday, Bogey, St. Louis Country. Home: 3 University Lane, St. Louis 5. Office: Arcade Bldg., St. Louis 1, Mo.
Died Aug. 8, 1945.

ALBEE, Fred Houdlett (awl'bē), surgeon; b. Alna, Me., Apr. 13, 1876; s. F. Huysen and Charlotte Mary (Houdlett) A.; A.B., Bowdoin, 1899; M.D., Harvard, 1903; traveled and studied in Europe; Sc.D., U. of Vt., 1916, Bowdoin Coll., 1917; LL.D., Colby, 1930; hon. Sc.D., Rutgers U., 1940; m. Louella May Berry, Feb. 2, 1907; 1 son, Fred H. Formerly prof. orthopedic surgery, N.Y. Post-Grad. Med. Sch. and dir. of the dept.; prof. orthopedic surgery, U. of Vt. Coll. of Medicine; cons. surgeon to 24 hospitals. Col. Med. R.C., 1917; cons. surgeon Pa. R.R. System and Seaboard Air Line; consultant in orthopedics, Byrd Antarctic Expdn.; founder and med. dir. Fla. Med. Center, Venice, Fla.; editor in chief Rehabilitation Rev.; chmn. N.J. Rehabilitation Commn.; formerly dir. U.S. Army Gen. Hosp. No. 3; mem. advisory orthopedic council to surgeon general U.S. Army. Grand Officer Crown of Roumania; Comdr. Order of Carlos P. Finlay of Cuba; Comdr. Order of Isabella Catolica (Spain); Comdr. Order of Merit (Hungary); Chevalier of the Legion of Honor (France); Cavaliere Order of the Crown (Italy); Comdr. Order of Liberatador (Venezuela); Grand Officer Order of Southern Cross (Brazil); Officer Ordem Nacional do Cruziere do Sul (Brazil). Life mem. Congressional Country Club; founding fellow and gov. Am. Coll. Surgeons; hon. fellow Royal Soc. Medicine (Great Britain); founder Internat. Soc. of Orthopedic Surgery; ex-pres. Assn. Surgeons of Pa. R.R., Am. Orthopedic Assn., Am. Acad. of Orthopedic Surgeons, Pan-Am. Med. Assn.; hon. mem. Leningrad Soc. of Orthopedic Surgeons; hon. foreign mem. Brazilian Coll. of Surgeons; mem. A. M.A., Mil. Order Foreign Wars, S.A.R., Sons of Revolution, Kappa Sigma, Phi Chi. Methodist. Clubs: International Medical, New York Athletic, Interurban Orthopedic, Harvard, Colonia Country (pres. 1914-15), Barnegat Hunting and Fishing (dir.). Author: Bone Graft Surgery, 1915; Orthopedic and Reconstructional Surgery, 1919; Injuries and Diseases of the Hip, 1937; Bone Graft Surgery in Disease, Injury and Deformity, 1940; also author numerous pamphlets on surg. subjects. Demonstrated original surg. methods of bone grafting in Germany, England and France, 1914, also in mil. hosps. of France, 1916; official rep. of Med. Corps U.S. Army, to Inter-Allied Congress, Rome, Paris and Bologna, 1919; opening address Surg. Congress of France, Paris, 1922, 29; rep. U.S. Army at Netherland Orthopedic Congress, Amsterdam, 1923; hon. Am. pres. Internat. Congress for Industrial Accidents and Diseases, Amsterdam, 1925, Budapest, 1927. Author: A Surgeon's Fight to Rebuild Men, 1943. Home: Colonia, N.J.; and Venice, Fla. Office: 57 W. 57th St., New York, N.Y.*
Died Feb. 15, 1945.

ALBERS, Homer (ăl'bĕrs), lawyer; b. Warsaw, Ill., Feb. 28, 1863; s. Claus and Rebecca (Knoop) A.; A.B., Central Wesleyan Coll., Mo., 1882, A.M., 1885, LL.D., 1922; LL.B., magna cum laude, Boston U., 1885; m. Minnie B. Martin, June 26, 1889 (died May 25, 1914); m. 2d, Katharine L. Ramsey, Sept. 2, 1916; children—Homer (dec.), Elisabeth Katharine (Mrs. Ogden Ludlow), Lt. William Edward (U.S. N.R.), Lt. (j.g.) Robert Ramsey (U.S.N.R.). Practiced, Boston, Massachusetts, since 1885; lecturer Massachusetts Institute Tech. and Boston University; prof. Boston U. Law Sch., and dean, 1912-35, now emeritus. Mem. Mass. State Ballot Law Commn., 1899-1905; declined appointment as judge Mass. Superior Court, 1903; ex-chmn. Brookline (Mass.) Sch. Com. Decorated Knight Order of Crown of Italy, 1932. Republican. Episcopalian. Ex-pres. Norfolk Co. Bar Assn.; mem. Am. Law Inst., Am., Mass. and Norfolk bar assns. Club: Brookline Country. Home: 55 Irving St., Brookline, Mass.; (summer) Marion, Mass. Died Jan 8, 1947.

ALBERT, Ernest, scene designer, landscape artist; b. Brooklyn, Aug. 15, 1857; s. Daniel Webster and Harriet Dunn (Smith) Brown; student Brooklyn Inst. Sch. of Design; m. Annie Elizabeth Bagwell, June 6, 1881 (died 1925); children—Ruby Frances, Elsie, Edith Dorothy, Ernest; m. 2d, Lissa Bell Walker, 1927. With Harley Merry, prodns. for Park and Union Square theaters; scenic artist, art dir. Pope's Theater, St. Louis; with firms Noxon, Albert & Toomey and Albert, Grover & Burridge, 1885; furnished sets for Hamlet at opening of Chicago Opera House; sets include Shakespearean prodns., Babes in the Wood, Supremacy of the Sun, Ben Hur; designed and painted stage sets for outstanding actors in N.Y., 1894-1909; landscape painter from 1909-46. A founder and 1st pres. Allied Artists of Am. Awarded Graham Art Medal, 1873. Mem. Nat. Acad. Design, Am. Water Color Soc., Chicago Art Assn., Conn. Acad. of Fine Arts, Silvermine Guild of Artists. Clubs: National Arts, Salmagundi. Died at New Canaan, Conn., Mar. 25, 1946; buried in Lakeview Cemetery, New Canaan.

ALBRIGHT, Charles Edgar, life underwriter; b. Dancyville, Tenn.; s. George Nicholas and Barbara Ellen (Thompson) A.; M.D., Rush Med. Coll., 1889; m. Laura Uihlein, Nov. 21, 1899; children—Lorraine A. Flint, Marion (Mrs. Edward S. Tallmadge), David Edgar (deceased). Intern Presbyn. Hosp., Chicago, 1889-91; asst. med. dir. Northwestern Mutual Life Ins. Co., Milwaukee, 1891-1903; travel abroad, 1903-05; life underwriter Northwestern Mutual Life Ins. Co. since 1905; leading producer for 30 consecutive yrs. in amounts varying from $1,070,500 to $3,940,000, total to June 1944, $79,273,869; dir. and mem. exec. com. Allis-Chalmers Mfg. Co., First Wis. Nat. Bank, First Wis. Trust Co.; dir. Globe Steel Tubes Co., Milwaukee Forge & Machine Co., Hoberg Paper Mills, Inc., Wis. Bankshares, Henry Uihlein Realty Co., Jos. Schlitz Brewing Co., Jos. Schlitz Realty

Corp., Majestic Realty Corp., Cuban-Am. Sugar Co., Wisconsin Securities Co., Del., Old Ben Coal Corporation. Mem. bd. govs. Marquette U.; dir. St. John's Mil. Acad. Presbyterian. Mason (32°). Clubs: Milwaukee, Wisconsin, Milwaukee Athletic, Milwaukee Country, University (Milwaukee); University (Chicago). Contbr. to journ. Home: 3534 N. Lake Drive. Office: 720 E. Wisconsin Av., Milwaukee 2, Wis.
Died June 14, 1946.

ALDEN, Ezra Hyde, railway official; b. Bridgewater, Mass., Jan. 26, 1866; s. Ezra Hyde and Mary Esther (Smith) A.; grad. high sch., Bridgewater, 1882; m. Hattie Carter Hathaway, June 28, 1892; children—Esther Hyde, Olive Hathaway (Mrs. Roy F. Larson), Philip Merriam, Margaret Wheeler, Francis Carter. With Norfolk & Western Ry. Co., since Mar., 1891, successively chief clerk to the sec., elected sec. and asst. treas., Mar. 1905, v.p. in charge of finances, 1920-36, retired on pension, Mar. 1, 1936; dir. Phila. Nat. Bank. Republican. Swedenborgian; v.p. Gen. Conv. of New Jerusalem in U.S.A. Club: Union League. Home: 6385 Woodbine Av. Office: Broad Street Station Bldg., Philadelphia. Died June 3, 1945.

ALDERSON, Victor Clifton (awl'dĕr-sŭn), cons. mining engr., educator; b. Plymouth, Mass., June 4, 1862; s. Andrew P. and Sarah P. (Sears) A.; A.B., Harvard, summa cum laude, 1885; (D.Sc., Armour Inst. of Tech., 1903, Beloit Coll., 1903; D.Eng., Colorado School of Mines, 1939; m. Harriet E. Thomas, July 3, 1888 (dec.); m. 2d, Nelle P. Bryant, July 28, 1904 (dec.). Supt. schools, Dublin, Ind., 1885-87; teacher Englewood High Sch., Chicago, 1887-93; prof. mathematics, 1893-98, dean, 1898-1900, acting pres., 1900-01, dean 1901-03, Armour Inst. of Tech., Chicago; pres. Colo. Sch. of Mines, July, 1903-13; pres. Winnemucca (Nev.) Mountain Mining Co., 1913-15; cons. mining engr., 1915-17; again pres. Colo. School of Mines, Golden, 1917-25; cons. mining engr., specialty oil shale, since 1925. Fellow A.A.A.S.; mem. Am. Inst. Mining Engrs., Am. Social Science Assn., Soc. Colonial Wars, Soc. Mayflower Descendants, Instn. Petroleum Technologists (London), Phi Beta Kappa, etc. Writer on scientific and math. subjects and tech. edn. Author: Oil Shale Industry, 1920. Home: La Jolla, Calif.
Died Feb. 25, 1946.

ALDIS, Mary Reynolds (Mrs. Arthur T. Aldis); b. Chicago, Ill., June 8, 1872; d. William Collins and Marie Antoinette (L'Hommedieu) Reynolds; ed. St. Mary's Sch., Knoxville, Ill.; m. Arthur Taylor Aldis, June 8, 1892; 1 son, Graham. A founder, 1910, of the "Aldis Playhouse" (a little theatre at her country home), where plays were presented by amateurs for many summers; founder, 1930, of Ropp Sch. of Art, Lake Forest, Ill., and Chicago. Painter of decorative water colors. Exhibited at Delphic Galleries, New York, 1932; Rollins Coll., Winter Park, Fla., 1932; Increase Robinson's Gallery, Chicago, 1933; Pataky Gallery, Orlando, Fla., 1934. Ex-pres. Chicago Visiting Nurse Assn. Author of plays, pamphlets and verse. Home: Lake Forest, Ill.; also Winter Park, Fla.
Died June 20, 1949.

ALDRED, John Edward, chmn. bd. Anglo Canadian Securities Corp.; pres. Aldred & Co., Ltd., Aldred Investment Corp. (Can.); dir. Eastern Rolling Mill Co., United Shipyards, Inc., Gladdings Inc., Industrial Corp., of Baltimore, officer or dir. many other corps. Life mem. bd. dirs. Mass. Inst. Tech. Office: 40 Wall St., New York, N.Y.*
Died Nov. 21, 1945.

ALDRICH, Charles Anderson, pediatrician; b. Plymouth, Mass., Mar. 4, 1888; s. David E. and Laura Linwood (Perkins) A.; B.S., Northwestern U., 1914, M.D., 1915; grad. student Harvard, 1921; m. Mary McCague, Oct. 3, 1916; children—Robert A., Cynthia, Stephen. Engaged in practice of medicine since 1915; intern N.Y. Nursery and Child's Hosp., 1915; intern Evanston (Ill.) Hosp., 1915-16, attending roentgenologist and jr. attending physician in medicine, 1916-21, attending pediatrist newly born service, 1930-36, asso. physician and chmn. pediatric dept., 1936-42 asst. attending physician Children's Memorial Hosp., Chicago, 1921-22, asso. attending physician, 1922-41; chief of staff, 1941-44; cons. pediatrist, Municipal Tuberculosis Sanitarium, 1925-27; cons. physician on staff Chicago Nursery and Half-Orphan Asylum, 1941-44; asso. in pediatrics, Northwestern U. Med. Sch., 1934-35, asst. prof. 1935-36, professor of pediatrics, 1941-44; prof. pediatrics, Mayo Foundation Grad. Sch., U. of Minn., since 1944; mem. sect. on pediatrics, Mayo Clinic, since 1944. Director Rochester Child Health Project, 1944. Member White House Conf. on Children in a Democracy. Mem. com. Elizabeth McCormick Child Research Grant 1941-44. Trustee Ill. Children's Home Aid Society, 1941-44. Mem. Ednl. Council, Winnetka Pub. Schs.; member Sch. Bd.; mem. bd. North Shore Country Day Sch. Mem. Northwest Pediatric Soc., Minn. Mental Hygiene Soc. (mem. bd. dirs.), National Research Council (com. on child development, etc.); member A.M.A. (mem. adv. bd. med. splty.), Am. Acad. Pediatrics (mem. com. on mental health since 1940), Am. Board Pediatrics, Inc. (sec.-treas. 1934-44, pres. 1945-47), Nat. Assn. for Nursery Edn., Soc. Research in Child Development; mem. (hon.) National Committee on Mental Hygiene, Northwest Pediatric Soc., Omaha Mid-West Clin. Soc.; sec. Am. com. Internat. Pediatric Congress in London (Eng.), 1933. Conglist. Author: Cultivating the Child's Appetite, 1927; Babies Are Human Beings (with Mary M. Aldrich), 1938 (English reprint, Understand Your Baby, 1939); Feeding Our Old Fashioned Children (with Mary M. Aldrich), 1941. Contbr. numerous professional articles and book revs. to med. periodicals. Clubs: Billings (pres.); University (Rochester). Home: 626 Fifth St., S.W. Office: Mayo Clinic, 102 Second Av. S.W., Rochester, Minn.
Died Oct. 5, 1949.

ALDRICH, Chilson Darragh, architect, writer; b. Detroit, Mich., Mar. 25, 1876; s. Charles Whipple and Julia Louesa (Saunders) A.; prep. edn., pub. schs.; spl. student U. of Minn.; m. Clara Chapline Thomas, Apr. 18, 1914. Began practice at Minneapolis, 1900; designer of residences until 1916; builder of cantonments, World War; designer and builder of log cabins, camps and vacation homes since 1918. Built replica of pioneer cabin for Minn. State Hist. Soc. Member same soc. Republican. Episcopalian. Clubs: Friars, Six O'clock, Hennepin County Sportsman's. Author: The Real Log Cabin, 1929. Contbr. to House and Garden, Country Life in America, etc. Home-Studio: 701 Kenwood Parkway, Minneapolis, Minn; (country) Pals' Cove, Grand Marais, Minn.
Died July 13, 1948.

ALDRICH, Richard S., corp. dir., ex-congressman; b. Washington, D.C., Feb. 29, 1884; s. Nelson W. and Abby (Chapman) A.; B.A., Yale, 1906; LL.B., Harvard, 1909; m. Janet Innis White, Apr. 30, 1921. Lawyer; dir. Providence Jour., Providence Nat. Bank, Providence Washington Insurance Co.; elected mem. R.I. Ho. of Rep., 1914, Senate, 1916, 68th to 72d Congresses (1923-33), 2d R.I. Dist. Republican. Office: Turks Head Bldg., Providence, R.I.
Died Dec. 25, 1941.

ALDRIDGE, Clayson Wheeler (awl'drĭj), foreign service officer; b. Rome, N.Y., Oct. 19, 1899; s. Charles Joseph and Jessie (Haskins) A.; A.B., Princeton U., 1922; Am. Scandinavian Fellowship, U. of Copenhagen, Denmark, 1923; unmarried. Apptd. foreign service officer, Mar. 1925; vice consul of career, Jerusalem, Sept. 1925; sec. in diplomatic service, Feb. 1927; 3d sec., Athens, Feb. 1927; vice consul, Aden, temp., Aug. 1927; 3d sec., Athens, June 1927, vice consul, Oct. 1929, consul, Dec. 1929; Dept. of State, Feb. 1930, resigned Nov. 1930; apptd. divisional asst. Dept. of State, Dec. 1, 1930; reinstated foreign service officer, Dec. 27, 1933, assigned to the Dept., Jan. 1934; consul, Athens, Feb. 1934, Nanking, March 1936; consul, Manila, temp., Nov. 1938; consul, Singapore, Feb. 1939, Sydney, March 1942; assigned to the Dept. of State, Nov. 1942. Home: 1006 N. George St., Rome, N.Y. Address: Dept. of State, Washington, D.C. Died Mar. 30, 1944.

ALENCASTRE, Stephen Peter (ăl'ĕn-kăs-tĕr), bishop; b. Porto Santo, Madeira, Nov. 3, 1876; s. Lucius Joseph and Augusta Leopoldina (Bayao) A.; student St. Louis Coll., Honolulu, 1890-95, Louvain, Belgium, 1895-1901. Came to Hawaii, 1883, naturalized, 1906. Ordained priest R.C. Ch., 1902; pastor Sacred Heart Ch., Honolulu, 1913-24; consecrated bishop, Aug. 24, 1924. Home: Lunalilo and Emerson Sts., Honolulu, Hawaii.*
Died Nov. 9, 1940.

ALEXANDER, Ben, pres. Masonite Corp.; b. Wausau, Wis., Oct. 6, 1894; s. Walter and Sarah (Strobridge) A.; B. Forestry, Biltmore (N.C.) Forest Sch., 1914; student U. of Wis., 1914-15; B.S., U. of Calif., 1917; m. Josephine Foster, Oct. 9, 1926; children—Foster, Sarah, Thomas, William. With Silver Falls Timber Co., Silverton, Ore., 1919-21; laborer Wausau Paper Mills Co., 1922-24; became woods supt. Walter Alexander Co., Wausau, 1922; with Masonite Corp., Chicago, since 1925, pres. since 1926; pres. Lake Superior Lumber Co., Yawkey-Alexander Lumber Co., Wausau Paper Mills Co., Northern Logging Co.; v.p. and dir. Silver Falls Timber Co., Alexander Yawkey Timber Co., Stewart and Alexander Timber Co.; asst. sec. and treas. Alexander Stewart Lumber Co.; treas. and dir. Yawkey-Bissell Lumber Co. (Wis.); sec. and dir. Walter Alexander Co. (Wis.); dir. Employers Mutual Liability Ins. Co., Marathon Paper Mills, Naval Stores Investment Co., Mont. Dakota Power Co., Mont. Dakota Utilities Co., Ontanagon Fibre Co., Tomahawk Kraft Paper Co., McCloud River Lumber Co. Served as capt. of inf., U.S. Army, during World War. Trustee Lawrence Coll., Appleton, Wis. Mem. Zeta Psi. Republican. Methodist. Mason. Clubs: Chicago, Chicago Athletic, Onwentsia Tavern (Chicago). Home: Lake Forest, Ill. Office: 111 W. Washington St., Chicago, Ill.* Died July 6, 1944.

ALEXANDER, Douglas, mfr.; b. Halifax, Yorkshire, Eng., July 4, 1864; s. Andrew and Harriet Newell (Hayward) A.; came to Can. at an early age; ed. Collegiate Inst., Hamilton, Ont.; studied law, Law Soc. of Upper Can.; Osgoode Hall, Toronto; LL.D., McMaster U.; m. Helen Hamilton Gillespie, Sept. 28, 1892. Pres. Singer Mfg. Co. since Sept. 1905. Title of baronet conferred by King of England in recognition of services of the Singer Mfg. Co. during World War, also because of personal services. Decorated Knight of Legion of Honor (French); Officer Crown of Belgium. English Ch. Home: Edgehill, Palmers Hill Rd., Stamford, Conn. Office: Singer Bldg., New York, N.Y. Died May 22, 1949.

ALEXANDER, Edward Albert, lawyer; b. Georgetown, S.C., Jan. 30, 1873; s. Isaac and Annie Josephine (Lewis) A.; B.S. with honors, Coll. of City of New York, 1892; LL.B. with honors, Columbia, 1895; m. Elise Mathylde Moeller, June 15, 1911 (now dec.); children—John Frederick, Anne Katherine; m. 2d, Estelle Kaufman, Sept. 22, 1944. Admitted to N.Y. bar, 1894, and since practiced in New York; pres. Mayal Realty Corp., Peoples Research Fedn. Apptd. del. to Conv. of Real Estate Bds. of New York, by gov. of N.Y., 1930; apptd. mem. New York George Washington Bicentennial Commn. by mayor of New York, 1931. Mem. Am. Bar Assn., N.Y. State Bar Assn., Assn. of Bar of City of New York (former mem. com. on law reform), N.Y. County Lawyers Assn. (former mem. judiciary com.), Phi Beta Kappa; former mem. of the com. on law and justice, N.Y. Bd. of Trade; chmn. executive committee of Federal Bar Association of N.Y., N.J. and Conn.; member Am. Defense Soc., Nat. Com. to Uphold Constitutional Government, New York Southern Society, Real Estate Board of New York. Democrat. Clubs: City College, Columbia University. Contributors to magazines and newspapers. Credited with having given definite start to movement for repeal of the Eighteenth Amendment, by originating and devising the State Convention method, embodied in a joint resolution introduced by the late Senator Edward I. Edwards in U.S. Senate, June 30, 1926; active in starting movement to change methods of nominating judges, and author of article entitled "Nomination and Promotion of Worthy Judges," pub. in Dec. 1928 issue of the "Panel," official organ of the Grand Jurors Assn. of N.Y. County. Author: Protect Our Investors, 1942; World Government vs. Constitution, 1944. Originated and started movement for change in legal procedure in condemnation of real property, as a result of articles written in Real Estate Mag. of the Real Estate Bd. of New York. Home: 71 W. 71st St. Office: 165 Broadway, New York, N.Y.
Died Dec. 17, 1948.

ALEXANDER, George F., judge; b. Gallatin, Mo., Apr. 20, 1882; s. Joshua W. and Roe Ann (Richardson) A.; LL.B., U. of Mo., 1905; m. Lola Mae Surface, Apr. 27, 1907; children—Lillian F. (Mrs. Dean F. Sherman), Jane, George F. Admitted to bar, 1905; city atty., Gallatin, 1907-12; removed to Ore., 1912; practiced law Portland, Ore., 1912-33; U.S. Marshal of Ore., 1917-21; U.S. dist. judge, First Div., Alaska, since 1933. Dem. nominee for circuit judge, Multnomah County, Ore., 1922. Pres. Bd. of Children's Guardians, 1st Dist. of Alaska, since 1933; chmn. Com. on Federal Relations, Western Parole and Probation Assn., 1936-38. Mem. Multnomah Co., Ore. (Portland), Bar Assn., Oregon State Bar Assn., Juneau (Alaska) Bar Assn., Sigma Chi. Democrat. Mem. Christian Ch. Mason (32°, Shriner), Elk. Mem. Juneau Shrine club (pres. 1934-39). Address: Federal Bldg., Juneau, Alaska.* Deceased.

ALEXANDER, James Patterson, judge; b. Moody, Tex., Apr. 21, 1883; s. John N. and Mary (Patterson) A.; student Baylor U., 1903; LL.B., U. of Tex., 1908; m. Elizabeth Akin, Aug. 2, 1916; children—Nancy, Betty. Admitted to Tex. bar, 1908; practiced in McGregor, 1908-11, Waco, since 1911; county judge, McLennan County, 1916-20; dist. judge 19th Judicial Dist. of Tex., 1920-24; in practice of law, Waco, 1925-30; asso. justice Court of Civil Appeals, Waco, 1931-40; chief justice Supreme Ct. of Texas, since Jan. 1, 1941; prof. civil procedure, Baylor Sch. of Law, Waco, 1920-40. Mem. Civil Judicial Council of Tex. since 1937; chmn. Nat. Conf. of Judicial Councils; mem. com. apptd. by Supreme Ct., 1940, to rewrite rules of civil procedure of State of Tex. Dir. Travis Co. chapter Am. Red Cross; mem. men's adv. council, Austin-Travis Co. Girl Scout Assn. Mem. Am. Judicature Soc., Am. Bar Assn. (vice chmn., mem. com. to gather information on reaching and preparing appellate court decisions; spl. com. on improving adminstrn. of justice; mem. council, sect. judicial adminstrn.), Tex. State (dir. 5 yrs.), Travis County bar assns., Philos. Soc. of Tex., Order of Coif, Phi Delta Phi. Democrat. Baptist. Mason (Shriner). Author of monographs on legal subjects. Home: 900 W. 17th St., Austin 21. Address: Capitol Bldg., Austin 11, Tex. Died Jan. 1 1948; buried in Texas State Cemetery, Austin.

ALEXANDER, Leigh, coll. prof.; b. Assiut, Egypt, Jan. 9, 1883; s. John R. and Carrie A. (Elder) A. (parents Am. citizens); A.B., Westminster Coll., New Wilmington, Pa., 1904; A.B., Princeton, 1905, Ph.D., 1911; B.A., Oxford U. (Eng.), 1908; m. Mary Grace Ritchie, December 30, 1914; 1 son, John Ritchie. Professor classics, Rollins College, Winter Park, Fla., 1908-09; instructor in classics, The Hill School, Pottstown, Pa., 1911-13; asst. prof. classics and ancient history, Oberlin Coll., Oberlin, O., 1913-25, asso. prof., 1925-26, prof. since 1926, head of dept. 1940-48 (Graves professorship); professor Latin, Indiana U., summer 1930; prof. Latin and ancient history, Western Reserve U., summers 1938-40. Rhodes Scholar from N.J., Oxford U., 1905-08; sec.-treas. Rhodes Scholarship com. of selection for Ohio, 1913-28. Mem. Ohio Classical Conf. (charter mem. since 1921; sec.-treas., 1930-34; pres., 1935-36; mem. exec. council, 1936-39), Classical Assn. Middle West and South, Am. Philol. Assn., Archaeological Inst. America (lecturer, 1930-32, 1938-1940); Classical Soc. of Am. Acad. in Rome, Advisory Council for Sch. of Classical Studies in Rome (since 1938), Classical Club of Greater Cleveland (vice pres., 1934-35; mem. exec. com. since 1937). Phi Beta Kappa. Ind.

Democrat. Conglist. Clubs: Social Science, Philologue (Oberlin). Author: The Kings of Lydia, 1913. Contbr. articles and reviews to professional periodicals. Home: 268 Forest St., Oberlin, O.
Died Oct. 24, 1948.

ALEXANDER, Truman Hudson, writer; b. Birmingham, Ala., Oct. 20, 1891; s. William Brooks and Nancy (Hudson) A.; ed. Howard Inst., Mt. Pleasant, Tenn., 1900-09, Vanderbilt Univ., 1909-12; m. Helen Almon, Dec. 30, 1914; children—David Almon, Truman Hudson, Helen Elizabeth. Began news reporting, 1912; wrote daily syndicated column "I Reckon So" for syndicate of Southern papers, 1922-38; syndicated as weekly feature since 1938. Mem. Newcomen Soc. (Tenn. com.), Sigma Nu. Democrat. Methodist. Mason, K.P. Club: National Press (Washington, D.C.). Author: Loot (novel), 1933. Compiled State Papers of Governor Austin Peay, 1929; contbr. to Readers' Digest and other nat. mags. Address: Route 1, Box 35, Franklin, Tenn.
Died Sep. 1, 1941.

ALEXANDER, William Albert, educator; b. Lebanon, Ind., July 25, 1875; s. John Thomas and Julia Asberine (Shirley) A.; A.B., Ind. U., 1901; m. Mary Clyde Lowder, Nov. 18, 1902; children—Julia Alice, Ellen Elizabeth. Asst. librarian, Ind. U., 1901-05; registrar, 1905-13, acting instr. history, 1907-08, dean, 1913-21, Swarthmore Coll.; librarian, Ind. U., 1921—. Dir. Ind. U. million dollar memorial fund campaign, 1921-26; acting alumni sec. Ind. U., 1935; trustee Ind. U. Foundation since 1936; mem. Advisory Com. to Acting President of Ind. U., 1937-38. Publicity dir. N.E.A., 1914-15. Mem. Assn. Colls. and Prep. Schs. of Middle States and Md., Commn. on Higher Edn. Middle States and Md., Am. Library Assn., Phi Gamma Delta. Mem. Soc. Friends. Address: Indiana University Library, Bloomington, Ind.
Died July 8, 1943; buried in Clear Creek Cemetery, Ind.

ALFORD, Leon Pratt, engineer, editor; b. Simsbury, Conn., Jan. 3, 1877; Emerson and Sarah Merriam (Pratt) A.; B.S. in Electrical Engineering, Worcester Poly. Institute, 1896, M.E., 1905, Dr. of Engineering, 1932; m. Grace A. Hutchins, January 1, 1900; 1 son, Ralph I. Shop foreman McKay Metallic Fastening Assn., Boston, 1896-97, McKay-Bigelow Heeling Assn., 1897-99; production supt. McKay Shoe Machinery Co., 1899-1902; mech. engr. United Shoe Machinery Co., Boston, 1902-07; engring. editor American Machinist, 1907-11, editor in chief, 1911-17; editor Industrial Management, 1917-20, Management Engineering, New York, 1921-23, Mfg. Industries, 1923-28; v.p. Ronald Press Co., 1928-34; asst. engr. in charge mfg. costs, Federal Communications Commn., 1935-37; prof. Administrative engring., New York Univ., since 1937. Past v.p. and mem. research coms. American Engring. Council which produced repts. on Waste in Industry, Twelve-Hour-Shift in Industry, Safety and Production in Industry and Tech. Changes in Mfg. Industries. Fellow Am. Soc. Mech. Engrs. (ex-v.p.), Inst. of Management (ex-pres.); mem. Institut Scientifique d'Organisation et de Gestion, Nat. Association Cost Accountants, Sigma Xi. Melville Gold Medalist, 1927; Gantt Gold Medalist, 1931. Methodist. Club: Engineers. Author: Bearings and Their Lubrication, 1912; Laws of Management, 1928; Life of Henry Laurence Gantt, 1934. Editor: Artillery and Artillery Ammunition, 1917; Management's Handbook, 1924; Cost and Production Handbook, 1934; Principles of Industrial Management, 1940. Home: 9 Mountain Av. N., Montclair, N.J. Office: New York University, University Heights, New York, N.Y.
Died Jan. 2, 1942.

ALFORD, Theodore Crandall, newspaper corr.; b. Lawrence, Kan., Aug. 6, 1885; s. Daniel Stillman and Susan Daphne (Savage) A.; A.B., U. of Kan., 1907; LL.B., Kansas City Sch. of Law, 1914; m. Adaline Ledbetter Harvey, June 19, 1913; children—Jane Adaline, Theodore Crandall. Began as reporter Kansas City Times, 1907; served in same capacity on various newspapers until 1928; Washington corr. Kansas City Star since 1928. Mem. Sigma Alpha Epsilon, Phi Alpha Delta. Conglist. Clubs: Nat. Press, Gridiron (Washington). Home: McLean, Va.; also 1315 35th St. N.W., Washington, D.C. Office: Albee Bldg., Washington. Died Mar. 16, 1947; buried in Rock Creek Cemetery, Washington.

ALLEE, Marjorie Hill (ăl-lē), writer; b. Carthage, Ind., June 2, 1890; d. William B. and Anna Mary (Elliott) Hill; student Earlham Coll., Richmond, Ind., 1906-08; Ph.B., Univ. of Chicago, 1911; m. Warder Clyde Allee, Sept. 4, 1912; children—Warder (dec.), Barbara Elliott, Mary Newlin. Mem. Soc. of Friends. Author: Jungle Island (with W. C. Allee), 1925; Susanna and Tristram, 1929; Judith Lankester, 1930; Jane's Island, 1931; Road to Carolina, 1932; Ann's Surprising Summer, 1933; A House of Her Own, 1934; Off to Philadelphia, 1936; The Great Tradition, 1937; The Little American Girl, 1938; Runaway Linda, 1939; The Camp at Westlands, 1941; Winter's Mischief, 1942. Home: 5537 University Av., Chicago, Ill. Died Apr. 30, 1945.

ALLEMAN, Gellert (ăl'lĕ-măn), chemist; b. Littletown, Pa., July 23, 1871; s. Monroe John and Elizabeth (Gilfillan) A.; B.S., Pa. Coll. (Gettysburg), 1893, Sc.D., 1925; Ph.D., Johns Hopkins, 1897; U. of Berlin, 1911-12; m. Katharine Constable Spencer, July 7, 1902; children—Gellert Spencer, Robert Gilfillan. Instr. chemistry, U. of Me., 1897-98, Washington U., St. Louis, 1898-1902; prof. chemistry, Swarthmore Coll. since 1902, on leave of absence since 1928, prof. emeritus since 1936. Mem. advisory board Chemical Warfare Service. Fellow Soc. of Chem. Industry (London), A.A.A.S., Chem. Soc. (London), Deutsche Chemische Gesellschaft; mem. Am. Chem. Soc., Am. Electrochem. Soc., Franklin Inst. (bd. mgrs.; v.p.). Club: Chemists (New York). Visited various European universities, 1927-28. Home: Wallingford, Pa. Died Sept. 6, 1946; buried at Media, Pa.

ALLEN, Alfred, playwright; b. Alfred, N.Y., Apr. 8, 1866; s. Rev. Jonathan A. (pres. Alfred U.); A.B., A.M., Alfred, Litt.D., 1930; studied Harvard, Johns Hopkins and Columbia univs.; spl. studies Am. Acad. Dramatic Arts, N.E. Conservatory of Music; unmarried. Prof. at Alfred U.; teacher in Baltimore, 4 yrs.; geologist state survey of N.Y.; owner of mines in Ga. and Fla., 5 yrs.; editor and pub. of "Florida," 2 yrs; editor, 2 yrs., "Dramatic Studies"; prof. De Mille and Alberti schs. and Am. Acad. Dramatic Arts; on staff Dramatic Mirror. Pres. N.Y. Johns Hopkins Alumni, 3 years. Author: (novels) The Heart of Don Vega; Judge Lynch; (plays) Chivalry (Town Topics $1,000 prize play), 1901; The Cup of Victory (with Richard Hovey); Playmates; The Earth Born, The Heart of a Star (two latter with Hughes Cornell); Br'er Rabbit and Tar Baby (with Ruth Comfort Mitchell), produced (1938) by Fed. Theater Projects. Contbr. to mags. and lecturer. Elected to Florence Nightingale Inst. of Honorables, 1931. Address: University Club, Los Angeles, Calif.
Died June 18, 1947.

ALLEN, Arthur Francis, editor; b. Warren, Ill., Dec. 15, 1867; s. Herbert W. and Cordelia (Aurand) A.; student U. of Neb., 1881-82; hon. Litt.D., Morningside Coll., 1940; m. Bernice Andrews, Oct. 4, 1899 (divorced 1919); children—Francis Aurand, Edwin Forrest. Learned printer's trade; proofreader, reporter and city editor, 1892-95, mng. editor, 1897-1922, editor since 1922, Sioux City (Ia.) Journal. Served as pvt., corpl. and sergt. 7th U.S. Inf., 1891-92, 16th Inf., 1895-97; mem. Ia. Nat. Guard, 1892-95, advancing to captain. Republican. Episcopalian. Mason (32°, K.T., Shriner). Club: National Press. Home: 704 Ninth St. Address: Sioux City Journal, Sioux City, Ia.
Died Aug. 22, 1949.

ALLEN, Calvin Francis (C. Frank), engineer; b. Roxbury (Boston), Mass., July 10, 1851; s. Calvin and Ann Priscilla (Watson) A.; grad. Roxbury Latin Sch., 1868; S.B., Massachusetts Inst. Tech., 1872; Eng. D., Northeastern Univ., 1938; m. Caroline Elizabeth Hadley, June 21, 1888; children—Mildred, Margaret, Frances (dec.). Asst. engr. water works or sewers, Providence, R.I., and Newton, Mass., 1872-78; asst. engr. A., T. & S.F.R.R., 1878-85 (except 1 yr. chief engr. water works at Las Vegas, N.M.); asst. prof. 1887, later asso. prof. and prof. railroad engring., Mass. Inst. of Tech.; retired under Carnegie Foundation, 1916 (prof. emeritus). Admitted to N.M. bar, 1885, Mass. bar, 1901; city atty., Socorro, N.M., 1886; mem. sch. com., Sharon, Mass., 1892-95 (chmn. 1893-95). Hon. mem. Boston Soc. Civ. Engrs. (ex-pres.), Am. Soc. Civil Engrs., Mass. Highway Assn. (ex-pres.), New Eng. R.R. Club (ex-pres.); mem. Am. Ry. Engring. Assn. (life), Soc. Prom. Engring. Edn. (ex-sec., ex-pres.), Technology Club (ex-sec.); mem. com. on pub. utilities Boston Chamber of Commerce (but not a mem. of the Chamber). Has been member Publ. Com., Technology Review; also of Jour. of Mass. Highway Assn. Unitarian. Republican. Author: Railroad Curves and Earthwork, 1889; Tables for Earthwork Computation, 1893; Field and Office Tables, 1903; Business Law for Engineers, 1917. Household fuel economy agent for Mass. in U.S. Fuel Administration, Sept. 1-Dec. 31, 1918. Mem. Advisory Zoning Commn. for Boston, 1922-23. Home: West Roxbury, Mass.
Died June 6, 1948.

ALLEN, Charles Morse, chemist, b. Farmington, Me., Apr. 6, 1859; s. Charles F. (D.D.) and Ruth Sibley (Morse) A.; U. of Me., 1878-9; A.B., Wesleyan U., Conn., 1882, A.M., 1886; Dresden Polytechnic and Zürich Polytechnic, 1896-1897; m. Carol Shepard, Aug. 2, 1888. Instr. chemistry, Wyoming Sem., Kingston, Pa., 1882-9; instr. chemistry, Pratt Inst., 1889-98, head of dept. of chemistry, 1898. Mem. Am. Chem. Soc., New York Chem. Teachers' Club, Phi Nu Theta, Phi Beta Kappa. Methodist. Author: Laboratory Notes on General Chemistry; Quantitative Chemical Analysis. Home: 226 Willoughby Av., Brooklyn. Died Apr. 3, 1942.

ALLEN, Charles Ricketson, vocational edn.; b. New Bedford, Mass., Aug. 6, 1862; s. John A. P. and Abbie (Chaddock) A.; B.S., Mass. Inst. Tech., 1885; studied Johns Hopkins, 1893; M.A., Harvard, 1903; D.Sc., Stout Inst., Menomonie, Wis., 1927; m. Lissa H. Hall, June 28, 1889. Teacher high sch., New Bedford, 1886-1909; in charge development of vocational training, New Bedford, 1906-11, dir. New Bedford Independent Industrial Sch. last 2 yrs.; agt. for industrial training, Mass. Bd. of Edn., 1911-17; asst. supt. training and supt. of instr. training, Emergency Fleet Corpn., 1917-18; staff Fed. Bd. Vocational Edn., Washington, Nov. 1918-19; dir. of training, C. of C., Niagara Falls, N.Y., 1920-21; spl. agt. Fed. Bd. Vocational Edn., 1921; dir. indsl. training service, Dunwoody Inst., Minneapolis, 1922-24; editor and ednl. cons. Fed. Bd. Vocational Edn. since 1924. Mem. Nat. Soc. Vocational Edn., Am. Management Assn., The Civil Legion; hon. mem. Boston Soc. Civil Engrs. Author: Laboratory Manual of Physics, 1890; The Instructor, The Man and The Job, 1919; The Foreman and His Job, 1921; (with C. A. Prosser) Vocational Education in a Democracy; Have We Kept the Faith? 1929; (with J. C. Wright) The Supervision of Vocational Education, 1926; The Administration of Vocational Education, 1927; Efficiency in Education, 1928; Efficiency in Vocational Education, 1929; (with H. A. Tiemon) Managing Minds, 1932; also a number of articles and publs. of the Federal Bd. of Vocational Education and the Dept. of the Interior. Office: Washington. Died July 6, 1938.

ALLEN, Crombie, newspaper man; b. Parker's Landing, Pa.; s. Wilson E. and Louella (Abrams) A.; A.B., Grove City (Pa.) Coll., 1895; m. Emily Patterson Lowry, June 12, 1907 (died Sept. 30, 1918); 1 dau., Jane Lowry (Mrs. Chester A. Perry). Pub. Greensburg (Pa.) Daily Tribune, 1901-11, Ontario (Calif.) Daily Report, 1911-30; traveler, writer and speaker. Mem. Calif. House of Reps., 1917-21. Ex-trustee Rotary (Internat.) Foundation. Pres. Pa. State Editorial Assn., 1911; mem. Calif. Newspaper Pubs. Assn. (pres. 1918), Press Congress of World (Calif. mem.), Sigma Delta Chi. Conglist. Clubs: University (Los Angeles), Rotary (first pres. Ontario, Calif., club 1922). Visited nearly every country in the world in interest of Rotary Internat. and Olympic Games. Founded endowments in Asia (Tokyo), Europe (Athens), N. America (Los Angeles), S. America (Buenos Aires), to advance the 4th object of Rotary Internat. world-wide peace through good-will and understanding. Gave Olympic village houses to Canberra (Australia), Cape Town (Africa), Los Angeles, Berlin and Tokyo, to become internat. houses of friendship and good-will service stations. Chmn. United Nations War Relief, topping quota 5 times; vice chmn. Publicity Com. Southern Calif. for U.S. War Bonds. Home: 617 N. Euclid Av., Ontario, Calif. Died Mar. 1, 1946.

ALLEN, Edgar, prof. anatomy; b. Canon City, Colo., 1892; s. Asa and Edith (Day) A.; Ph.B., Brown U., 1915, A.M., 1916, Arnold fellow, 1916-17, Ph.D., 1921, Sc.D., 1936; m. Marion Robins Pfeiffer, June 26, 1918; children—Frances Isabelle, Marjorie Eleanor. Asst. in biology, Brown U., 1913-15, asst. in embryology and neurology, 1915-17; investigator, U.S. Bur. Fisheries, Woods Hole, Mass., summer 1919, Fairport, Ia., summer 1922; instr. and asso. in anatomy, Washington U. Sch. of Medicine, 1919-23; prof. anatomy, Univ. of Mo. since 1923, also dean med. sch., 1929-33; prof. anatomy, Yale U. Sch. of Medicine since 1933. Served as pvt., later 2d lt. U.S. Army, May 1917-Feb. 1919. Mem. A.A.A.S., Assn. Anatomists, A.M.A., Soc. Study Internal Secretions, Soc. Zoölogists, Phi Gamma Delta, Phi Beta Pi. Contbr. to Am. Jour. Anatomy, Anat. Record, Am. Jour. Physiology, Jour. A.M.A., Endocrinology, Am. Naturalist, Biol. Bull., Embryology, etc. Home: 472 Whitney Av., New Haven, Conn.
Died Feb. 3, 1943.

ALLEN, Edwin Madison, mfr.; b. Richmond, Ind.; M.E., Purdue, 1896. Director of Mathieson Alkali Works, Inc., mfrs. soda ash, caustic soda, bicarbonate of soda, liquid chlorine, synthetic salt cake, etc., with sales offices in principal cities of U.S.; dir. Mfrs. Trust Co., Kansas City Southern R.R. Home: 7-B, 720 Park Av., New York 21, N.Y.
Died Nov. 2, 1947.

ALLEN, Eric William, univ. prof.; b. Appleton, Wis., Apr. 4, 1879; s. William Judge and Josephine Plympton (Smith) A.; A.B., U. of Wisconsin, 1901, student Milwaukee Law School, Milwaukee, Wis., m. Ida (Sally) Elliott, Jan. 1, 1906 (died April 23, 1943); children—John Eliot, Robert Kimball, Elizabeth Elliott (Mrs. Charles M. Gilbert), Eric W., Jr. Prin. high sch., La Junta, Colo., 1904; with Seattle Post-Intelligencer and other newspapers, and mgr. Seattle Engraving Co., 1905-12; initiated Dept. of Journalism, U. of Ore., 1912; now dean Sch. of Journalism, same; head Dept. of Journalism, U. of Calif., summers, 1917-26; mgr. Univ. Press, U. of Ore.; editor "Oregon Exchanges," monthly, 1916-20. At Presidio Mil. Training Camp, 1918; chief of staff, Ore. State Training Camps, 1918. Mem. Nat. Assn. Schs. and Depts. of Journalism (pres. 1923 and 1930), Am. Assn. Teachers of Journalism, Northwestern Assn. Teachers of Journalism (ex-pres.), Am. Assn. Univ. Profs., Deta Upsilon, Sigma Delta Chi (hon. nat. pres., 1925). Unitarian. Author: Printing for the Journalist. 1927. Home: Birch Lane, Fairmount, Eugene, Ore. Died Mar. 5, 1944.

ALLEN, Frank, chmn. bd. dirs. Brink's, Inc. Home: Edgewater Beach Hotel. Office: 711 W. Monroe St., Chicago. Died June 23, 1947; buried in Old Milverton Cemetery, Leamington, Eng.

ALLEN, Frank Philip, Jr., architect; b. Grand Rapids, Mich., Sept 28, 1881; s. Frank Payne and

Mary Frances (O'Connor) A.; ed. pub. and art schs. in U.S. Began practice in Grand Rapids; architect and dir. of works, Alaska-Yukon-Pacific Expn., Seattle, 1909; chief architect, dir. of works and landscape architect, Panama-Calif. Expn., San Diego, 1915-16; organizer, pres., 1917-19, Allen Shipbuilding Co., Seattle; architect of numerous bldgs. in Seattle and Southern Calif. Corpl. Co. E, 32d Mich. Vol. Inf., Spanish-Am War. Awarded Order of Rising Sun by Japanese Govt. Democrat. Mason. Home: 814 S. Alexandria Av. Office: 816 W. 5th St., Los Angeles, Calif. Died July 5, 1943.

ALLEN, Freeman Harlow, college prof.; b. Copenhagen, N.Y., Oct. 22, 1862; s. Ebenezer Allen (M.D.) and Susan (Stanton) A.; grad. State Normal School, Potsdam, N.Y., 1883-85; Ph.B., Ill. Wesleyan, 1895, A.M., 1900, Ph.D., 1910; studied Cornell, 1899, Columbia, 1908; m. Rose Lucy Priest, June 26, 1890; children—Barbara (dec.), Elizabeth Rose (dec.), Newell Priest. Prof. history, State Normal Sch., Potsdam, 1895-1909; prof. and head dept. history and politics, Colgate, 1909-34, emeritus. Instr. and lecturer N.Y. teachers' institutes 16 yrs. Traveled in U.S. during 1923-24, studying and observing departmental work in 27 colls. and univs. Y.M.C.A. sec. and lecturer, Camp Merritt, May-Sept. 1918; lecturer A.E.F. and instr. history, A.E.F. Univ., Beaune, Cote d'Or, France, Feb.-July 1919. Mem. exec. com. N.Y. State S.S. Assn.; trustee Hamilton High Sch. Mem. Am. Hist. Assn., Am. Polit. Science Assn., Am. Acad. Polit. and Social Science, Internat. Assn. of Torch Clubs, Phi Beta Kappa, Phi Delta Theta. Republican. Baptist. Mason, Forester. Author: Manual of Arithmetic Methods, 1896; (pamphlets) Studies in American History, 1899; Syllabus-Studies in European History, 1915. Prof. history and govt. with the Floating Univ. Cruise around the world, 1930-31. Home: Hamilton, N.Y. Died June, 1942.

ALLEN, Gardner Weld, physician, author; b. Bangor, Me., Jan. 19, 1856; s. Joseph Henry and Anna Minot (Weld) A.; A.B., Harvard, 1877, M.D., 1882; unmarried. Intern, Boston Lying-in Hosp., 1882, Rhode Island Hosp., Providence, 1882-83; practiced at Boston, 1884-1922; surgeon, genito-urinary dept., Boston Dispensary, 1886-1906; visiting physician, Home for Aged Women, Boston, 1889-98; surgeon, Mass. Naval Militia, 1893-1901; instr. in genito-urinary surgery, Tufts Med. Sch., 1897-1906; retired, 1922. Mem. Mass. Naval Brigade, 1890-1901; passed assistant surgeon, U.S.N., 1898; ship's surgeon, U.S. Shipping Board, 1918. Pres. Trustees of Donations for Edn. in Liberia. Mem. American Med. Assn., Mass. Med. Society, Am. Assn. Genito-Urinary Surgeons, Am. Urol. Assn., Mass. Hist. Soc., Am. Antiquarian Soc., Naval History Soc., Am. Hist. Assn., Naval Hist. Foundation, Essex Institute, Military Hist. Society of Mass., Lincoln Group of Boston. Unitarian. Clubs: Harvard and Boston City. Author: Our Navy and the Barbary Corsairs, 1905; Our Naval War With France, 1909; A Naval History of the American Revolution, 1913; Papers of Francis Gregory Dallas, U.S.N., 1917; Massachusetts Privateers of the Revolution, 1927; Papers of Isaac Hull, Commodore U.S. Navy, 1929; Our Navy and the West Indian Pirates, 1929; Papers of John Davis Long, Secretary of the Navy, 1897-1902, 1939. Contbr. chapter on Mass. in War of 1812 to Commonwealth History of Mass., and 11 naval biographies, Dictionary of Am. Biography. Home: 146 Mass. Av., Boston, Mass. Deceased.

ALLEN, Glover Morrill, naturalist; b. Walpole, N.H., Feb. 8, 1879; s. Rev. Nathaniel Glover and Harriet Ann (Schouler) A.; A.B., Harvard, 1901, A.M., 1903, Ph.D., 1904, grad. student, 1906-07; m. Sarah Moody Cushing, June 26, 1911; 1 dau., Elizabeth Cushing (Mrs. Arthur Gilman). Librarian, Boston Society Natural History, 1901-27; curator of mammals, Mus. Comparative Zoölogy, Harvard, 1907; lecturer on zoölogy, 1924, professor 1938, Harvard. Mem. expdns. to Bahama Islands, 1904, British E. Africa, 1909, Grenada, B.W.I., 1910, Sudan, 1912, Liberia, 1926, Brazil, 1929. Republican. Episcopalian. Fellow A.A.A.S., Am. Ornithologists' Union, Harvard Travelers' Club; mem. Boston Soc. of Natural History, Nuttall Ornithol. Club, Phi Beta Kappa, Sigma Xi. Author: The Birds of Massachusetts (with R. H. Howe, Jr.), 1901; Birds and Their Attributes, 1925; Bats, 1939; numerous papers chiefly on mammals and birds. Home: 25 Garden St. Office: Museum of Comparative Zoölogy, Cambridge, Mass. Died Feb. 14, 1942.

ALLEN, Henry Justin, ex-senator; b. Warren County, Pa., Sept. 11, 1868; s. John and Rebecca (Goodin) A.; ed. Baker U., and Washburn Coll. (Kan.); hon. A.M., Baker; LL.D., Washburn Coll., U. of Denver; m. Elsie J. Nuzman, Oct. 19, 1893; children—Frederick (dec.), Kathrine (dec.), Justin (dec.), Henrietta. Began as editor Manhattan Nationalist, 1894; later owned and operated several daily newspapers in smaller cities of Kan.; now chmn. bd. Wichita Daily Beacon Pub. Co.; pres. Beacon Bldg. Co.; sec. to Gov. Stanley; gov. of Kan., 1919-23; apptd. U.S. senator to succeed Vice-president Curtis, 1929; apptd. asst. to Charles G. Dawes, pres. Reconstruction Finance Corp., 1932; editor of Topeka State Journal since 1935. Dir. publicity for Rep. Nat. Com. Hoover-Curtis Campaign, 1928, 1932; pres. Great Lakes-St. Lawrence Tidewater Assn. Served as spl. advisor to State Dept. on preparation of treaty between U.S. and Canada on subject of St. Lawrence River and Great Lakes improvement for ocean navigation and power. Spl. commr. for Near East Relief to investigate work in Southern Russia, Armenia, Syria, Turkey, Greece, Palestine and Persia, 1924. In France under auspices Am. Red Cross, 1917, 1918; organized "home communication service" of Am. Red Cross in France. Pres. Kan. State Bd. Charities 5 yrs.; trustee Baker U. Independent Republican. Methodist. Mem. Delta Tau Delta. Clubs: Wichita, Kansas, Country, Kiwanis (Wichita); Cosmos (Washington, D.C.). Accompanied the first world cruise of "The University Afloat," as head of the dept. of journalism, 1926-27. As chmn. British Children's Aid of the Save the Children Federation of N.Y. City, 1941-42, organized nurseries and shelters for bombed-out British children and children of war workers. Home: 255 N. Roosevelt St., Wichita 8. Office: 513 Beacon Bldg., Wichita 20, Kan. Died Jan. 17, 1950.

ALLEN, (William) Hervey, author; b. Pittsburgh, Pa., Dec. 8, 1889; s. William Hervey and Helen Ebey (Myers) A.; U.S. Naval Acad., 1910-11; B.Sc., U. of Pittsburgh, 1915, Litt.D., 1934; studied Harvard, 1920-22; hon. Litt.D., Washington and Jefferson Coll. 1947; m. Ann Hyde Andrews, June 30, 1927; children—Marcia Andrews, Mary Ann, Richard Francis. Instr. English, Porter Mil. Acad., Charleston, S.C., 1920-21; instr. English, high sch., Charleston, 1922-24; with dept. of English, Columbia University, 1924-25; lecturer on Am. Lit., Vassar College, 1926-27; lecturer on modern poetry. Bread Loaf (Vt.) Sch. of English and Writers' Conf., 1930, 31. Midshipman U.S. Navy, 1909-10; 2d lt. 18th Pa. Inf., on Mexican border, 1916; 1st lt. 111th Inf., 28th Div., A.E.F., 1917-19, World War; wounded in action, Aug. 1918; instr. English, French Mil. Mission. Regional information rep., War Manpower Commn., consultant, 1944. Mem. bd. govs. St. Johns College, Annapolis, Md.; trustee, U. of Miami. Fellow Royal Soc. of Arts; mem. Nat. Inst. Arts and Letters, Miami Hist. Soc., Poetry Soc. America, MacDowell Colony, Poetry Soc. of South Carolina (founder), Hist. Soc. Southern Florida, Hist Soc. of Pennsylvania; Hist Soc. of Maryland, Phi Beta Kappa, Sigma Chi, Omicron Delta Kappa. Clubs: Surf (Miami Beach); Hamilton Street (Baltimore); Biscayne Bay Yacht. Author: Wampum and Old Gold, 1921; The Bride of Huitzil, 1922; Carolina Chansons (with Du Bose Heyward), 1922; The Blindman, 1923; Earth Moods, 1925; Towards the Flame, 1926; Israfel (biography of E. A. Poe), 1926; Poe's Brother (with Thomas Ollive Mabbott), 1926; New Legends, 1929; Sarah Simon, 1929; Songs for Annette, 1929; Anthony Adverse, 1933; Action at Aquila, 1937; It Was Like This, 1939; The Forest and the Fort, 1943; Bedford Village, 1944; Toward the Morning, 1948; The City in the Dawn. The City in the Dawn, 1948. Editor, Rivers of America series, since 1943. Home: The Glades Estate, Box 99, Rt. 2, Miami, Fla. Address: care Rinehart & Co., Inc., 232 Madison Av., New York, N.Y. Died Dec. 28, 1949.

ALLEN, Hubert A., army officer; b. Buchanan Co., Ia., Apr. 4, 1872; s. Joel M. and Mary Jane (McGary) A.; ed. Ia. State Coll.; m. Jessie M. Mainus, Oct. 2, 1895. Dist. comml. mgr., Ia. Telephone Co. Actively identified with Ia. N.G. about 25 yrs.; served as capt., Spanish-Am. War, 1898; apptd. brig. gen. N.A., Aug. 5, 1917; assigned Camp Cody, Deming, N.M. Mem. United Spanish War Vets. Republican. Mason, K.P. Home: 3127 3d Av., Cedar Rapids, Ia. Died May 31, 1942.

ALLEN, James Turney, philologist; b. Cleveland, O., Sept. 14, 1873; s. Robert Alfred and Martha (Turney) A.; A.B., Pomona Coll., Claremont, Calif., 1895; A.M., U. of Calif., 1896; Ph.D., Yale, 1898; traveled and studied in Germany and Greece, 1905-06; m. Amelia Sanborn, Jan. 4, 1899 (died Feb. 15, 1945); children—Dorothy (dec.), James Turney; m. 2d, Lois Hanscom, Dec. 4, 1946. Instr. Greek and classical archeology, 1898, instr. Greek, 1899, asst. prof., 1903, asso. prof., 1908, professor, 1919-43, prof. emeritus since 1943, U. of California; annual prof. Am. Sch. Classical Studies, Athens, Greece, 1924-25. Mem. Am. Philol. Assn., Philol. Assn. Pacific Coast (pres. 1914-15), Classical Assn. Pacific Coast, San Francisco Archeol. Soc. (sec., 1907-12; pres. 1939-46), Archäoligishes Institut des Deutschen Reiches, Phi Beta Kappa. Conglist. Author: First Year Greek, 1917, revised edition, 1931; The Greek Theater of the Fifth Century, B.C., 1920; The Stage Antiquities of the Greeks and Romans and Their Influence, 1927. Contributor numerous articles to philol. and archeol. jours. Home: 37 Mosswood Rd., Berkeley, Calif. Died Sep. 29, 1949.

ALLEN, John Eliot, judge; b. Claremont, N.H., June 26, 1873; s. William H. H. and Ellen E. (Joslin) A.; A.B., Dartmouth College, 1894, LL.D., 1942; LL.B., Harvard University, 1898; m. Amy L. Abbott, July 10, 1901. Admitted to New Hampshire bar, 1897, and began practice at Keene, New Hampshire, 1898; judge Probate Court, 1899-1906; asso. justice Superior Court of N.H., 1917-24; asso. justice Supreme Court of N.H., 1924-34, chief justice, 1934-43. Mason. Republican. Home: Keene, N.H. Died July 24, 1945.

ALLEN, J(ohn) Weston, lawyer; b. Newton Highlands, Mass., Apr. 19, 1872; s. Walter and Grace Mason (Weston) A.; desc. Richard Warren and George Soule, of the Mayflower; A.B., Yale, 1893; LL.B., Harvard, 1896, LL.D., 1922; m. Caroline Cheney Hills, June 12, 1901; children—Helen Spencer, Grace Weston (Mrs. William D. Hogarth), Caroline Hills (Mrs. Howard V. H. Inches). Began practice at Boston, 1896; mem. Mass. Ho. of Rep., 1915-18; atty. gen. of Mass., 1920-22; during term instituted an investigation of the fish trust, which resulted in conviction and imprisonment of the promoters; broke up powerful blackmail ring in Mass. by instituting proceedings which resulted in removal and disbarment of Dist. Attys. Tufts and Pelletier in Middlesex and Suffolk Counties; exposed silver stock swindle and secured conviction of Thomas W. Lawson and ten other operators for illegal advertising; investigated and exposed Charles Ponzi's financial operations and prosecuted him for larceny; acted in advisory capacity as atty. gen. in trial of Sacco and Vanzetti. Mem. Atty. Gen. Cummings Com. on Crime Conf., Washington, 1935; mem. Atty. General's Advisory Com. on Crime, 1935-38; apptd. spl. asst. to atty. gen. of U.S., acting as consultant to Commr. of Immigration and Naturalization on pending legislation in Congress relating to deportation of aliens, 1935-36; official rep. Dept. of Justice at 2d Internat. Congress of Comparative Law, The Hague, 1937 (v.p. of Congress); spl. asst. to Atty. Gen. of U.S. acting as consultant on pending legislation in Congress relating to Federal firearms control, 1937-38. Trustee New England Town Hall, Inc. (exec. com.). Mem. Am. Bar Assn. (v.p. 1935-36; chmn. com. on award of Am. Bar Assn. medal; chmn. com. on Semi-Centennial Fund; mem. exec. com., 1926-29; mem. com. on uniform judicial procedure, 1929-30; mem. reception com. British and French bar, 1930, council of criminal law section, 1934-39; elected to House of Delegates 1936), chmn. com. on Comparative Penal Law and Procedure, 1940-41; Nat. Crime Commn. (chmn.; mem. com. to draft criminal code; acting chmn. spl. com. on firearms regulation; chmn. com. on detection and prosecution of crime), Am. Law Inst. (charter mem.), Nat. Assn. Attorneys General, Bar Assn. City of Boston, Middlesex Bar Assn., Soc. Mayflower Descendants, Mil. Order Loyal Legion, Sons of Vets. Trustee Am. Indian Inst., 1915-29. Republican. Conglist. Clubs: Yale of Boston, Massachusetts, Old Boston (hon.); Cosmos (Washington); Century (New York). Contbr. to law jours. and current publs. Home: 219 Lake Av., Newton Highlands. Mass. Office: Tremont Bldg., Boston, Mass. Died Dec. 31, 1941.

ALLEN, Leroy, teacher; b. Wooster, O., Dec. 6, 1878; s. James H. and Emma J. (Hummer) A.; Ph.B., Coll. of Wooster, 1906; grad. Xenia Theol. Sem., 1914; A.M., U. of Chicago, 1920; Dr. Social Science, Oklahoma City U., 1930; m. Ethel J. Boyd, Aug. 19, 1914; children—Ruth Elizabeth, Janet Priscilla. Prof. economics and sociology, Cedarville (O.) Coll., 1906-22, dean, 1915-22; instr. economics and sociology, Coll. of Wooster, summers 1913-14; prof. homiletics and biblical theology, Ref. Presbyn. Theol. Sem., Cedarville, O., 1917-22; prof. economics, Southwestern Coll., 1922-25, dean Coll. of Liberal Arts and prof. Bible, 1925-39; prof. religion since 1939. Ordained U.P. ministry, 1914; pastor 2d U.P. Ch., Cincinnati, 1919-22, Presbyn. Ch., Middleton, Okla., 1923-27. Awarded Silver Cross of Societe d'Education et d'Encouragement Arts, Sciences, Lettres, Paris, Dec. 25, 1933. Fellow A.A.A.S.; mem. Nat. Assn. Biblical Instrs., Nat. Inst. of Social Sciences, Am. Assn. Univ. Profs., Am. Sociol. Soc., Societe Academique d'Histoire Internationale, Am. Inst. of Roumania; Delta Sigma Rho, Pi Kappa Delta; founder Pi Gamma Mu (nat. social science honor soc.) and pres., 1924-31, exec. sec. since 1931; corr. mem. Masaryk Sociol. Soc. Founder Social Science (quarterly mag.) and editor since 1925; hon. mem. Acad. of World Economics. Contributing editor Dictionary of the Social Sciences, 1941. Rotarian. Methodist. Home: 1414 E. 4th Av., Winfield, Kan.* Died Aug. 3, 1947.

ALLEN, Lewis George, physician and surgeon; b. Lenexa, Kan., Oct. 19, 1891; s. George and Adda May (Calvin) A.; A.B., U. of Kan., 1915, M.D., 1917; student U.S. Army Sch. of Mil. Roentgenology, 1917-18; m. Pauline Sams McLaughlin, June 2, 1920; children—Lewis George, Jr., William R. Interne, Royal Victoria Hosp., Montreal, Can., 1917; in practice as physician, specializing in radiology, Kansas City, Kan., since 1920; with Sch. of Medicine, U. of Kan., since 1924, prof. clin. roentgenology since 1938; radiologist Providence Hosp. since 1920, St. Margaret's Hosp. since 1920, Bethany Hosp. since 1927. Certified by Am. Bd. Radiology, 1934. Trustee Group Hosp. Service, Inc., Surgical Care, Inc., Boylan Research Fund, Wyandotte County Tuberculosis Assn. Fellow A.C.P., Am. Coll. Radiology (mem. commn. on education), Kansas City Academy Medicine; mem. A.M.A., Kan. and Wyandotte County med. socs., Kansas City Southwest Clin. Soc. (pres. 1939), Radiol. Soc. of N.A. (pres. 1945), Am. Roentgen Ray Soc. Home: 1051 Kimball Ave. Office: 907 N. 7th St., Kansas City, Kan. Died May 28, 1948.

ALLEN, Lucy Ellis, educator; b. Boston, Mass.; d. Nathaniel T. (founder of Allen sch. for boys) and Caroline (Bassett) A.; prep. edn. Allen Sch., West Newton, Mass., and later was a teacher there; A.B., Smith Coll. Prin. Misses Allen Sch. since 1904. Dir. Pomroy Home for Orphan Children, Newton, Mass. Mem. Am. Assn. Univ. Women. Has traveled extensively to many fgn. countries. Unitarian. Clubs: College, Smith College, Twentieth Century (Boston). Author: West Newton Half a Century Ago; Women in Art; Literary Haunts in London. Editor: Memories of My Home. Home: West Newton, Mass.* Died Nov. 12, 1943.

ALLEN, N(at) B(urtis), educator; b. Madisonville, Tex., Aug. 2, 1892; s. John Hodges and Fannie (Burtis) A.; prep. edn., Allen Acad., Bryan, Tex.; student Southwestern U., 1909-11, U. of Chicago, 1912-13; LL.D., Southwestern U., 1940; m. Pauline Yates, Nov. 4, 1916; 1 son, Nat Burtis. Teacher of mathematics, Allen Acad., 1911-22, also business mgr., 1915-22, co-prin., 1922-25, supt. since 1925, partner since 1928, owner since 1942. Democrat. Methodist. Home: Bryan, Tex. Died Mar. 16, 1946; buried at Bryan, Tex.

ALLEN, Richard Day, educator; b. Milwaukee, Wis., May 18, 1887; s. Asa A. and Edith (Day) A.; A.B., Brown U., Providence, R.I., 1910, A.M., 1912, Ph.D., 1921; m. Mary Payton Cottrell, Dec. 22, 1913; children—Gordon Cottrell, Barbara Payton, Robert Day. Teacher in high schs. at Wayne, Pa., 1910-11, Pawtucket, R.I., 1911-15, Providence, 1915-18; with Providence Bd. Edn. since 1918, asst. supt. schs. since 1926; lecturer in guidance grad. schs., Brown since 1921, Harvard, 1921-34, Boston U., 1934-40, Yale U., 1941; consultant in occupational information and vocational guidance, U.S. Office of Edn., 1938-40; mem. bd. of editors, Jr. and Sr. High Sch. Clearing House; dir. of survey of the pub. schs. of Passaic, N.J., 1941. Mem. Nat. Vocational Guidance Assn. (pres. 1929-30), N.E.A., Am. Assn. Sch. Adminstrs., Phi Gamma Delta. Baptist. Author: Common Problems in Group Guidance, 1933; Case Conference Problems in Group Guidance, 1933; Self Measurement Projects in Group Guidance, 1934; Organization and Supervision of Guidance, 1934; Manual for Class Personnel Charts, 1934; also co-author of Metropolitan Achievement Tests. Contbr. articles to ednl. jours. Home: 112 Everett Av., Providence, R.I. Died Aug. 23, 1945.

ALLEN, Robert H., army officer; b. Buchanan, Va., July 19, 1870; s. Judge John J. and Elizabeth M. A.; ed. Washington and Lee U., Lexington, Va.; hon. grad. Sch. of the Line, 1920; grad. Gen. Staff Sch., 1921; m. Stella McIntyre, June 3, 1907; 1 dau., Elizabeth A. (Mrs. John Neff). Enlisted in U.S. Army, June 8, 1893; commd. 2d lt. infantry, Oct. 31, 1895; promoted through grades to col., July 1, 1920; served as col. N.A., Aug. 5, 1917-Aug. 31, 1919; promoted chief of inf., rank of maj. gen., period of 4 yrs., beginning Mar. 28, 1925; retired with rank of maj. gen., 1929. In command of 356th Inf., 89th Division, during Meuse-Argonne offensive, 1918; with Army of Occupation in Germany until May 10, 1919. Awarded D.S.M. "for exceptionally meritorious and distinguished services" in the performance of duties of great responsibility as commanding officer, 356th Inf., 89th Div., during the Meuse-Argonne offensive, during the march into Germany, and during the occupation of enemy territory. Protestant. Home: 1048 Granada Av., San Marino 9, Calif. Died Oct. 10, 1949.

ALLEN, Rolland Craten, geologist; b. Richmond, Ind., May 24, 1881; s. George DeBolt and Florence (Brown) A.; B.A., U. of Wis., 1905 (science medal for grad. thesis), M.A., 1908; studied U. of Mich., 1909-10; D.E., Rensselaer Polytechnic Inst., 1939; m. Martha Hill, Nov. 30, 1910; children—Jean, Craten, George, Joseph, James. Teacher of science, high sch., Plymouth, Wis., 1903-04; instr. economic geology, U. of Mich., 1908-09; state geologist of Mich., 1909-19; also special lecturer in economic geology and ore deposits, U. of Mich., 1909-14; commr. mineral statistics of Mich., 1911-19, also appraiser of mines, 1913-19; adviser to Mich. Securities Commn., and valuation engr. mines, oil and gas wells, lands and timber; cons. practice; mem. Federal Excess Profits Tax Bd., 1918-19; exam. and valuation of zinc mines in Okla., 1919; resigned as state geologist of Mich., Aug. 1919; pres. Am. Inst. of Mining and Metall. Engrs., 1937; consultant for ferrous minerals and alloys, Office of Production Management, 1941; deputy chief Iron and Steel Branch, W.P.B., 1941-42, vice chairman Metals and Minerals, 1945; president Lake Superior Iron Ore Assn.; vice-pres., gen. mgr. of mines of Oglebay, Norton & Co.; pres. Reserve Mining Co., The Saginaw Dock and Terminal Co.; dir. Montreal Mining Co., Castile Mining Co., Bristol Mining Co., Brule Smokeless Coal Co., Ferro Engring. Co., Bristol Holding Co. vice-pres. and dir. Toledo, Lorain and Fairport Dock Co. Trustee Battelle Memorial Inst. Mem. A.A.A.S., Am. Assn. Economic Geologists, Am. Iron and Steel Inst., Geol. Soc. America, Mining and Metall. Soc., Sigma Xi, Alpha Chi Sigma. Republican. Mason. Club: Union (Cleveland, O.). Author of various repts., brochures and articles on geol. subjects. Home: Hudson, O. Office: Hanna Bldg., Cleveland, O. Died July 18, 1948; buried at Hudson, O.

ALLEN, Sherman, banker; b. Westford, Vt., Feb. 25, 1875; s. of George W. and Susan (Richardson) A.; m. Margaret Green Robinson, Jan. 15, 1903. On Free Press, Burlington, Vt., 1895-1901; sec. to David J. Foster, mem. Nat. Ho. of Rep., from Vt., 1901-05; pvt. sec. and chief clk. to asst. sec. of the Navy, 1905-07; Washington bureau, New York Herald, 1907-10; asst. sec. to President William H. Taft of the U.S., 1910-11; asst. Sec. of Treasury, July 1911-Oct. 1913. Treas. and mem. bd. trustees Endowment Fund of Am. Nat. Red Cross, Dec. 1912-Oct. 1913; asst. sec. and fiscal agt. Federal Resereve Bd., Sept. 1914-May 1918; treas. War Finance Corpn., May 1918-Feb. 1919; officer Nat. City Bank, New York, 1919-29, trust officer, 1926-29. Republican. Episcopalian. Club: Metropolitan (Washington). Address: The National City Bank of New York, 36 Bishopsgate, London, England. Died Dec. 30, 1938.

ALLEN, Thomas Stinson, lawyer; b. Paynes Point, Ogle County, Ill., Apr. 30, 1865; s. Benjamin Franklin and Harriet Maria (Ely) A.; A.B., U. of Neb., 1889 (class orator), LL.B., 1891; m. Mary Elizabeth Bryan (sister of William Jennings Bryan), June 28, 1898. Admitted to Neb. bar, 1891; mem. Talbot, Bryan & Allen, Lincoln, 1892-96, Talbot & Allen, 1896-1915, now Allen, Requartte & Wood; dir. Beatrice Creamery Company. Chairman Democratic State Central Committee, Nebraska, 1904-09, and 1921-32; U.S. dist. atty. for Neb. by appointment of President Wilson, Aug. 1, 1915-July 1, 1921; del. at large from Neb. to Dem. Nat. Conv., 1924, 32 and 40. Dir., treas. and gen. atty. Woodman Accident Co., pres. Comml. Mutual Surety Co. Baptist. Mason. Home: 1260 S. 20th. Office: Woodmen Accident Bldg., Lincoln, Neb. Died Oct. 29, 1945.

ALLEN, Viola, actress; b. in the South; d. C. Leslie A. and Sarah (Lyon) Allen; ed. in Boston, at Wykham Hall, Toronto, and boarding school in New York; m. Peter Duryea, 1906. Made début, Madison Sq. Theatre, New York, in Esmeralda, at age of 15; joined John McCullough Co., playing Virginia, Desdemona, Cordelia, etc. Subsequently played leading classical, Shakespearean and comedy rôles with Lawrence Barrett, Tommaso Salvini, Joseph Jefferson and William J. Florence. Leading lady at Boston Mus. for a season; also at Empire Theatre in 1893, and 4 yrs. following, creating and playing rôles in "Liberty Hall," "Sowing the Wind," "The Masqueraders," "Under the Red Robe," etc. Starred, 1898, as Gloria Quayle in "The Christian," by Hall Caine, and in 1900, produced "In the Palace of the King," by F. Marion Crawford and Lorimer Stoddard; and in 1902 as Roma in Hall Caine's "The Eternal City." In 1903, under management of her brother, began series of Shakespearean revivals, producing first "Twelfth Night," in which she played "Viola" with success; during the season of 1904-5 appeared as Hermione and Perdita in "A Winter's Tale"; 1906-7 a repertoire including "Cymbeline," "Twelfth Night," "As You Like It" and "The School for Scandal." Died May 9, 1948.

ALLEN, Walter Cleveland, mfr.; b. Farmington, Conn., Aug. 9, 1877; s. George Lewis and Albina (Marble) A.; ed. high sch., Stamford, Conn.; m. Susie C. Travis, Apr. 22, 1897; children—Mildred Louise (Mrs. Frederick L. Reid), Mary Frances (Mrs. Arthur W. Rossiter, Jr.). With Yale & Towne Mfg. Co., Stamford, until retirement Jan. 1, 1939, pres., 1915-32, chmn. bd., 1932-39; dir. First-Stamford Nat. Bank, Stamford Savings Bank. Served as maj., later lt. col., Air Service, U.S. Army, Oct. 1917-Mar. 1919. Citation for Conspicuous Service (U.S.), French Legion of Honor. Pres. Ferguson Library (Stamford). Republican. Methodist. Home: 655 Shippan Av., Stamford, Conn. Died Nov. 13, 1945.

ALLEN, William H., Jr., insurance exec.; b. Grafton, Ill., Oct. 12, 1853; s. William H. and Martha Maria (Mason) A.; ed. pub. and pvt. schs.; m. Elsie Pettijohn, Apr. 6, 1893; children—William Herbert, Ruth Parker. In banking business at Grafton, 1868-83, advancing to pres.; also actively identified with hardware, furniture and farm machinery store; settled in Calif., 1892; pres. Title Ins. & Trust Co., Los Angeles, 1895, now chmn. bd.; pres. Carmel Cattle Co., owner Muroc Clay Co.; vice-pres. Ojai Oil Co., Arrowhead Lake Co.; vice-pres. and treas. Colorado River Land Co.; formerly a director Security First National Bank of Los Angeles, and dir. and v.p. of Mortgage Guarantee Co. of Los Angeles. Republican. Home: 870 S. San Rafael Av., Pasadena, Calif. Office: Title Insurance Bldg., Los Angeles, Calif. Died June 5, 1943.

ALLING, Arthur Nathaniel (ăl'ĭng), ophthalmologist; b. New Haven, Conn., July 1, 1862; s. George and Mary (Alverson) A.; A.B., Yale, 1886; Sheffield Scientific Sch. (Yale), 1886-87; M.D., Coll. Phys. and Surg. (Columbia), 1891; m. Francella Walker, Oct. 27, 1887; 1 dau., Helen Frances. Practicing New Haven, Conn., since 1893; asst. surgeon to N.Y. Ophthalmic and Aural Hosp., 1897-1901; lecturer opthalmology, 1893-94, instr. 1894-1902, prof., 1902-38, emeritus since 1938, Yale; chief of eye clinic, New Haven Dispensary since 1896; ophthalmic surgeon, New Haven Hosp., 1905-38, cons. ophthalmic surgeon since 1938; cons. ophthalmologist, Meridian Hosp. Mem. Am. Ophthal. Soc., N.Y. Ophthal. Soc., City, County and State Med. Socs., Phi Beta Kappa, fellow N.Y. Acad. Medicine, Am. Coll. Surgeons, A.M.A. Republican. Clubs: Graduate, New Haven Lawn, Yale Faculty. Author: Diseases of the Eye, 1905; Ocular Therapeutics, 1923. Home: 190 St. Ronan St. Office: 257 Church St., New Haven Conn. Died Mar. 15, 1949.

ALLING, Paul Humiston (ăl'ĭng), foreign service; b. Hamden, Conn., July 15, 1896; s. Edson Lyman and Lulu Augusta (Harrison) A.; B.A., Trinity Coll., 1920; M.A., U. of Pa., 1924; m. Romaine Braden Loar, June 23, 1923; children—Constance Harrison, Anne Priscilla. With Nat. City Bank, N.Y. City, 1920-21; Fed. Res. Bank, Phila., 1922-24; with U.S. foreign service, Dept. of State, since 1924; v. consul, Beirut, 1924-26, Aleppo, 1926, Damascus, 1927, Beirut 1927; Dept. of State since 1928, as asst. chief, Div., Near Eastern Affairs, 1934-42; chief, 1942-44; deputy dir. Office Near East and African Affairs, 1944-45; diplomatic agent with rank of minister, Morocco, 1945-47; then consul gen., Tangier; minister to Syria, Apr. 1947. Served with Troop B, Conn. Cavalry, 1917; in France with 101st, 102d Machine Gun Batn., 3d U.S. Cavalry and Gen. Staff, G.H.Q., 1917-19. Awarded Victory medal, three stars. Mem. Delta Phi. Club: Army-Navy (Washington). Address: American Legation, Tangier, Morocco. Died Jan. 18, 1949.

ALLISON, John Maudgridge Snowden, author, educator; b. Pittsburgh, Pa., July 6, 1888; s. John Maudgridge Snowden and Margaret (Laughlin) A.; prep. edn., Lawrenceville Sch.; B.A., Princeton, 1910, M.A., 1912, Ph.D., 1914; studied U. of Paris, 1910-11; unmarried. With Yale U. most of time since 1914, instr. in history and asst. prof. until 1926, asso. prof. European history, 1926-29, became prof. European history, 1929, now Ralph W. Townsend prof. history and chmn. history dept., Yale U. Enlisted in U.S. Army, July 1917; 1st lt., adj., Mobile Hosp. No. 2, A.E.F., June 1918-Feb. 1919. Mem. Am. Hist. Assn., Psi Upsilon; fellow Institut Historique et Heraldique de France. Republican. Episcopalian. Clubs: Graduate, Lawn (New Haven); Century Assn. (New York). Author: Church and State in the Reign of Louis Philippe, 1916; Thiers and the French Monarchy, 1926; Monsieur Thiers, 1932; Malesherbes, 1938; Concerning the Education of a Prince, 1941. Address: Berkeley College, New Haven, Conn. Died Apr. 6, 1944.

ALLISON, William Henry, historiographer; b. Somerville, Mass., Aug. 17, 1870; s. George Augustus and Julia Lucinda (Powers) A.; A.B., Harvard, 1893; Newton Theol. Instn., 1896, B.D., 1902; U. of Halle, 1896-97; U. of Chicago, 1902-05, Ph.D., 1905; m. Elizabeth Lincoln Smith, Sept. 6, 1899 (died 1900); m. 2d, Emily Mills, July 31, 1905; 1 dau., Elizabeth Mills (Mrs. Albert E. Bailey, Jr.). Ordained Baptist ministry, Cambridge, Mass., May 13, 1896; pastor Penacook Ch., Concord, N.H., 1899-1902; acting prof. ch. history, Pacific Theol. Sem., 1904-05; prof. history and polit. science, Franklin (Ind.) Coll., 1905-08; head of dept. of history, Bryn Mawr Coll., Pa., 1908-10; prof. ecclesiastical history and dean Theol. Sem., Aug. 1910-15, prof. ecclesiastical history, 1910-28, Colgate U.; prof. emeritus of ch. history, Colgate-Rochester Div. Sch. since 1928. Consultant in ch. history, Library of Congress, since 1930. Prof. European history, Ohio State U., summers 1917, 19. Mem. Am. Baptist Hist. Soc. (life), Am. Hist. Assn. (life), Am. Soc. Ch. History, Phi Beta Kappa. Republican. Club: Palaver (Washington). Author: Baptist Councils in America, 1906; Inventory of Unpublished Manuscript Material relating to American Religious History (pub. by Carnegie Inst.), 1911. Contbr. numerous articles to Dictionary of American Biography, and to Dictionary of American History. Joint editor of A Guide to Historical Literature, 1931. Home: Medawisla, North Lovell, Me.; (winter) 2440 16th St., Washington, D.C. Address: Library of Congress, Washington, D.C. Died Sep. 9, 1941.

ALLSOPP, Frederick William, newspaper pub., author; b. Wolverhampton, Eng., June 25, 1867; s. William and Harriet (Dipple) A.; brought to Can. at age of 18 mos.; ed. common schs.; m. Mary F. Chapple, Sept. 7, 1891; children—William C., Frederick Reed, James Edward. Connected with Arkansas Gazette since 1884, in charge financial, business and pub. depts. since 1896; dir. Union Security Co.; sec., dir. City Market & Arcade Co.; founder Allsopp & Chapple Book Store. Trustee Donaghey Ednl. Foundation, Arkansas Museum Natural History, Little Rock Museum of Fine Arts. Mem. Ark. Press Assn. Democrat. Mason (32°). Clubs: Kiwanis, Little Rock Country. Author: Little Adventures in Newspaperdom, 1922; History of the Arkansas Press for 100 Years, 1922; Rimeries, 1926; Albert Pike (a biography), 1928; Folklore of Romantic Arkansas (2 vols.), 1931, Poets and Poetry of Arkansas. Collector of rare books. Home: 4206 Fairview Rd. Office: Arkansas Gazette, Little Rock, Ark. Died Apr. 9, 1946.

ALTHOFF, Henry (ălt'hōf), bishop; b. Aviston, Ill., Aug. 28, 1873; s. Frederick and Theresa (Poelker) A.; A.B., St. Joseph's Coll., Teutopolis, Ill.; A.M., St. Francis Solanus Coll., Quincy, Ill.; theol. studies, U. of Innsbruck, Austria. Ordained R.C. priest at Innsbruck, 1902; asst. Damiansville, 1902-03, East St. Louis, 1903-05, pastor Okawville and Nashville, Ill., 1905-14; consecrated bishop of Belleville, Feb. 24, 1914; apptd. asst. at the Pontifical Throne, Apr. 11, 1939. Home: 222 S. 3d St., Belleville, Ill. Died July 3, 1947; buried in crypt beneath St. Peters Cathedral, Belleville, Ill.

ALVORD, John Watson, engineer; b. Newton Centre, Mass., Jan. 25, 1861; s. Rev. John Watson and Myrtilla Mead (Peck) A.; ed. Howard U. Prep. Sch., 1873-74, J. W. Hunt's Normal Sch., Washington, 1874-77 (hon. C.E., U. of Wis., 1913); m. Helen C. Cornell, Sept. 4, 1889 (died 1926); m. 2d, Lucy B. Pitkin, Apr. 12, 1927. Asst. engr. constrn. Hyde Park and Lake View pumping stas., Chicago water works, 1880-84; city engr. Lake View (Chicago),

1884-88; town engr., Cicero, Ill., 1889-90; chief engr. surveys Chicago Exposition, 1890-93, medal as one of 70 designers; also chief engineer Hygeia Water Co., 1891-92; consulting engr. since 1894, to over 300 municipalities on sewerage works, water supply, sewage disposal, water power, appraisal bds., etc., among these Ill. and Mich. Canal, 1907-1901, City of Columbus, O., 1898, Dubuque Water Co., 1897, Gen. Electric Co., Des Moines, Ia., 1904, U.S. Steel Corp., Gary, Ind., 1907, City of Grand Rapids, Mich., and Des Moines (Ia.) Water Co., 1907, Milwaukee, 1910, Merriam Commn., Chicago. 1910: flood commn., Dayton, 1913, Columbus, 1913; Citizens' Terminal Plan Com., 1914, Ill. State Bd. of Natural Resources and Conservation, 1918. Supervising engr. Camp Grant (Ill.), Camp La Cruses, P.R.; cons. engr. Gt. Lakes Naval Tr. Sta. and chief engr. U.S. Housing Corp., 1917-19. Pres. Am. Water Works Assn., 1910; hon. mem. Am. Soc. C.E. (dir. 1918), Ill. Soc. Engrs. (pres. 1904-06), N.E. Water Works Association, Western Soc. Engrs. (pres. 1910; Washington award for 1929); fellow A.A.A.S.; mem. Ill. Soc. S.A.R., Soc. Mayflower Descendants. Clubs: Engineers', Union League. Author: Relief from Floods, 1918. Office: Civic Opera Bldg., Chicago, Ill. Died July 31, 1943.

ALWOOD, William Bradford, horticulturist; b. Delta, O., Aug. 11, 1859; s. David William and Ann Eliza (Bradley) A.; student Ohio State U., 1882-85, Columbian (now George Washington) U., 1886-88, Royal Pomol. Sch., Germany, 1900-01, Inst. Pasteur, Paris, 1907; m. Seffie S. Gantz, Mar. 6, 1884; children—Hubert Jackson, Helen Anna, Nellie Sarah, Mabel Seffie, William Bradford (dec.), Lewis Gantz (dec.), Esther (dec.), Richard Olney. Taught country sch., 1879-81; supt. Ohio Agrl. Expt. Sta., 1882-86; spl. agt. U.S. Dept. Agr., 1886-88; vice-dir. Va. Agrl. Expt. Sta., 1888-1904; conducted investigations in horticulture and mycology, 1888-1904; prof. horticulture and allied subjects, Va. Poly. Inst., 1891-1904; in charge investigations on fermentation of fruit products for Bur. of Chemistry, U.S. Dept. of Agr., 1900-06; enological chemist, 1907-14; fruit grower, 1914. V.p. Internat. Congress on Agrl. Edn., Paris, 1900; mem. Internat. Jury of Awards, St. Louis Expn., 1904; del. U.S. Dept. Agr. to Internat. Congress on Viticulture, France, 1907, and v.p.; pres. Internat. Congress Viticulture, San Francisco, 1915. Awarded Gold Medal and Commemorative Medal, St. Louis Expn., 1904; decorated by French Govt. with Cross, Officier du Mérite Agricole, 1907; silver medal and diploma, Nat. Ag.l. Soc., France. Fellow A.A.A.S., Royal Hort. Soc., Great Britain; mem. Permanent Internat. Commn. on Viticulture, Nat. Council of Horticulture, 1907, Société des Chemistes Experts de France; mem. nat. council Nat. Econ. League, Presbyterian. Mason. Author many pamphlets and bulls. on hort. subjects and the chem. composition of apples and grapes, and composition of wines and ciders fermented with pure yeasts. Awarded certificate Meritorious Services to Agriculture by Va. Poly. Inst., 1923. Address: Greenwood, Va. Died Apr. 13, 1946.

AMATO, Pasquale, baritone; b. Naples, Italy, 1879; ed. as civ. engr., later studied in Naples Conservatory 3 yrs. Made début at Téatro Bellini, Naples, as Germont, 1900; later toured Italy, Germany, England, Egypt and S. America; leading baritone at La Scala, Milan; first appearance in U.S. at Met. Opera House, New York, Nov. 1908; created parts of King Hadriot, in "Armide," Carlo Worms, in "Germania," Jack Rance, in "The Girl of the Golden West," etc.; has sung with marked approval in "Carmen," "Otello," "Rigoletto," "Jewels of the Madonna," etc. Died Aug. 12, 1942.

AMBERG, Emil (ăm'bĕrg), otologist; b. at Santa Fe, New Mexico, May 1, 1868; s. Jacob and Minna (Loewenbein) A.; grad. Real Gymnasium, Elberfeld, Germany, 1887, Gymnasium, Arnsberg, 1888, U. of Heidelberg, 1894; post grad. work, Berlin and Vienna; m. Cecile Siegel, Nov. 16, 1909; children—Robert Siegel, Blanche Adele (Mrs. Edward T. Kelley, Jr.). Intern Mass. Charitable Eye and Ear Infirmary, Boston, 1896-97; practiced in Detroit since 1898; med. adv. bd. North End Clinic; assistant clinical professor of rhinology, laryngology and otology, Detroit Medical College (now Wayne U. Medical Sch.), 1913-14; aurist School of the Deaf; consulting otologist Grace Hospital; cons. otologist Harper Hospital. Formerly sec. of committee on interstate reciprocity, Nat. Conf. State Med. Examining and Licensing Bds.; Fellow A.A.A.S., Am. Coll. Surgeons; mem. A.M.A., Am. Otol. Soc., Acad. Ophthalmology and Otolaryngology (life), Mich. State, Wayne County med. socs., Detroit Soc. for Better Hearing (editor official publication The Rainbow), American Hearing Society, Detroit Philos. Society, Detroit Otolaryngol. Soc., (ex-pres.), The Factfinders. Inventor of various surg. devices; extensive contbr. on med. and reform subjects. Home: 1244 Boston Blvd., W., Detroit 2, Mich. Died Apr. 12, 1948.

AMBLER, Mason Gaither, lawyer; b. Winchester, Va., Aug. 27, 1876; s. Benjamin Mason and Nannie L. (Baker) A.; grad. several schs., U. of Va., and law course same univ.; m. Isabella Brown, June 22, 1921. Admitted to W.Va. bar, 1899; mem. firm Van Winkle & Ambler, 1904-21; now mem. Ambler, McCluer & Davis. Mem. W.Va. Committee on Uniform State Laws, 1919-16. Mem. Am. Bar Assn., W. Va. Bar Assn. (chmn. exec. council 1924-25; pres. 1927-28), Delta Psi; life mem. Am. Law Inst. Democrat. Episcopalian. Home: Parkersburg, W.Va. Died Apr. 16, 1947.

AMES, Edgar, shipbuilder; b. St. Louis, Mo., Feb. 20, 1000; s. Edgar and Lucy V. (Semple) A.; A.B., Yale, 1890; m. Anne Shaw Sheldon, July 6, 1909. Engaged in harbor improvements, Seattle, 1895-1915; pres. Ames Shipbuilding & Drydock Co., 1916—, Seattle Contract Co. Built 25 steel ships (223,000 tons dead-weight), for Govt. during World War. Republican. Episcopalian. Home: 932 13th Av., N. Office: 3200 26th Av., S.W., Seattle, Wash. Died June 28, 1944.

AMES, Hobart, mfr.; b. Easton, Mass., Aug. 1865; s. Oakes Angier and Catharine (Hobart) A.; m. Julia H. Colony, June 1891. Mem. bd. dirs. Ames Shovel & Tool Co., Oliver Ames & Sons Corp., Old Colony Trust Co., Boston, Ames, Baldwin, Wyoming Shovel Co., Easton Land Co.; pres. First Nat. Bank of Easton. Clubs: Union, Tennis and Racquet, Somerset. Home: North Easton, Mass. Office: Ames Bldg., Boston. Died Apr. 22, 1945.

AMES, Joseph Sweetman, physicist; b. Manchester, Vt., July 3, 1864; s. Dr. George Lapham and Elizabeth (Bacon) A.; A.B., Johns Hopkins, 1886, fellow, 1887-88, Ph.D., 1890; LL.D., Washington Coll., 1907, U. of Pa., 1933; Johns Hopkins, 1936; m. Mrs. Mary B. (Williams) Harrison, Sept. 14, 1899 (died 1931). Asst. in physics, 1888-91, asso., 1891-93, asso. prof., 1893-99, prof. physics, 1899-1926, dir. Physical Lab., 1901-26, provost, 1926-29, pres., 1929-35, pres. emeritus since 1935, Johns Hopkins U. Hon. mem. Royal Instn. Great Britain; fellow Am. Acad. Arts and Sciences; mem. Nat. Acad. Sciences, Am. Phys. Soc. Mem. Nat. Advisory Com. for Aeronautics since 1917 (chmn. 1927-39); chairman foreign service committee of Nat. Research Council which visited France and Eng. in May and June, 1917, to study origin and development of scientific activities in connection with warfare. Home: 2 Charlcote Pl., Guilford, Baltimore, Md.* Died June 24, 1943.

ANDERSEN, Arthur Edward, accountant; b. Plano, Ill., May 30, 1885; s. John William and Mary (Aabye) A.; C.P.A., U. of Illinois, 1908; B.B.A., Northwestern U., 1917; LL.D., Luther College, 1938, Northwestern U., St. Olaf Coll. and Grinnell Coll., 1941; m. Emma Arnold, Aug. 8, 1906; children—Ethyl Bernice (Mrs. Vilas Johnson), Arthur Arnold, Dorothy Emma (Mrs. Robert E. Hornberger). Senior accountant Price Waterhouse & Co., 1907-11; comptroller Uihlein interests, Milwaukee, Wis., 1911-12; founder and senior partner Arthur Andersen & Co., accountants and auditors, since 1913; prof. accounting Northwestern U. Sch. of Commerce, 1912-22. Ex-pres. bd. trustees Northwestern U.; trustee Century of Progress, Chicago, 1933 and 1934, Chicago Sunday Evening Club. Commander of the Royal Order of St. Olav, Norway. Mem. of the American Inst. Accountants, Ill. Soc. C.P.A., Soc. Industrial Engrs., U.S. Chamber of Commerce, Art Institute Chicago, Norwegian-Am. Hist. Assn. (pres. 1936-42), Illinois State Historical Assn., Alpha Kappa Psi, Beta Gamma Sigma, Beta Alpha Psi. Clubs: Chicago, University, The Attic, and the Commercial (all located in Chicago); Glen View (Golf, Illinois); Bob O'Link Golf (Highland Park, Ill.); Milwaukee Club (Milwaukee); Broad Street (New York). Author: Complete Accounting Course, 1917; The Accounting Treatment of Overhead Construction Costs in Public Utilities, 1917; Financial and Industrial Investigations, 1924; The Major Problem Created by the Machine Age, 1931; Duties and Responsibilities of the Comptroller, 1934; The Future of Our Economic System, 1934; Present Day Problems Affecting the Presentation and Interpretation of Financial Statements, 1935; A Layman Speaks, 1941. Contbr. to tech. publs. Home: 44 Locust Rd., Winnetka, Ill. Office: 120 S. LaSalle St., Chicago, Ill. Died Jan 10, 1947.

ANDERSEN, Hendrik Christian, sculptor; b. Bergen, Norway, Apr. 17, 1872; s. Anders and Helene M.A.; brought to U.S. in infancy, settling at Newport, R.I., 1873; studied art and architecture at Boston, Paris, Naples, Rome. Author of Creation of a World Centre of Communication, containing plans for an internat. city, presented to the rulers, leading libraries and univs. of the world; 2d vol. containing the legalizing and the econ. advantages of a World Centre. Founder, World Conscience Soc. Prin. works: Fountain of Life; Fountain of Immortality; Jacob Wrestling with the Angel; Study of an Athlete; busts and medallions and portraits of Pope Benedictus XV, in Rome, etc. Address: Villa Hélène, Via P. Stanislao Mancini, Rome, Italy. Died Dec. 19, 1940.

ANDERSEN, James Roy, army officer; b. Racine, Wis., May 10, 1904; s. Niels and Inger Kerstine (Klausen) A.; B.S., U.S. Mil. Acad., 1926; M.S., Ordnance Tech. Sch. (U.S. Army), 1934; grad. Army Air Force Primary and Basic Flying Sch., 1936, Advanced Flying Sch., 1937, Tactical Sch., 1940; student special course, Columbia, 1940; m. Ester Katherine Hau, June 1, 1927; children—Nancy Jo, James Roy. Commd. 2d lt., U.S. Army, 1926, promoted through grades to brig. gen., 1945; served with ordnance dept., 1931, with air corps, 1931-45; rated air observer, air pilot, sr. air pilot. Decorated Am. Defense Medal, European Theater Medal, Asiatic-Pacific Theater Medal. Home: 100 S. Hickory St., Fond du Lac, Wis. Address: care The Adjutant General's Office, War Dept., Washington 25, D.C. Died Feb. 27, 1945.

ANDERSON, Abraham Archibald, artist; b. N.J., 1847; s. William and Sarah Louise (Ryerson) A.; early edn. Columbia Coll. Grammar Sch. and high sch. course, completing gen. studies in Europe under pvt. tutors; studied painting under Cabanel, Bonnât, Cormon, Godin and Collin; m. Elizabeth Milbank, 1887. Exhibited Paris Salon, Universal Expn., Paris, 1899, etc.; pictures: (portraits) Gen. O. O. Howard, Gov. Morgan, H. B. Claflin, Thomas A. Edison, Bishop Cleveland Coxe, Elihu Root, Charles Stewart Smith, John Wanamaker, etc., also Morning After the Ball, The Convalescent, Neither Do I Condemn Thee, etc. Address: 6th Av. and 40th St., New York. Died Apr. 27, 1940.

ANDERSON, Albert, judge; b. St. Croix Falls, Wis., Mar. 28, 1876; s. Carl and Anna Maria (Danielsdotter) A.; student Macalester Coll., St. Paul, Minn., 1896-98, Columbian U. (now George Washington U.), Washington, D.C., 1900-02; LL.B., U. of Wis., 1906; m. Mabel M. Moran, June 10, 1914; 1 son, Jerome. Admitted to Wis. bar, 1906; practiced in Hudson, Wis., 1906-09, Glendive, Mont., 1909-23, Billings, Mont., 1923-40; elected associate justice Supreme Court of Mont., 1940, to fill vacancy for term 1940-45. Mem. Mont. State Bar Assn., Am. Bar Assn. Republican. Home: 609 Holter St. Address: State Capitol, Helena, Mont.* Died Oct. 18, 1918.

ANDERSON, Alden, banker: b. Meadville, Pa., Oct. 11, 1867; s. John Z. and Sallie (Sloan) A.; student U. of Pacific, San Jose, Calif., 1880-83; m. Carrie Lois Baldwin, Mar. 2, 1892 (died 1929); 1 dau., Kathryn Baldwin (Mrs. Wm. Kenneth Potts); m. 2d, Agnes Thiele, Mar. 30, 1931. Farmer and packer, Solano Co., 1886, discontinued packing business, 1905, and entered banking; pres. Capital Nat. Bank, Capital Fed. Savings & Loan Assn. (Sacramento), Senator Hotel Corp.; chmn. bd. Calif.-Western States Life Ins. Co.; v.p. Bank of Rio Vista, Consumers Ice & Cold Storage Co.; dir. Asso. Oil Co., Natomas Co. of Calif., Tide Water Asso. Oil Co. (New York), Capital Fire Ins. Co., Sacramento, Natomas Water Co., Rice Growers Assn. of Calif. Republican. Conglist. Mason, Elk, K.P. Club: Sutter (Sacramento). Home: 1230 45th St. Office: Capital Nat. Bank, Sacramento, Calif Died Sep. 23, 1944.

ANDERSON, Alexander Pierce, botanical and chem. research; b. Red Wing, Minn., Nov. 22, 1862; s. John and Britta M. (Gustafsdotter) A.; B.S., U. of Minn., 1894, M.S., 1895; Ph.D., U. of Munich, 1897; m. Lydia Johnson, Aug. 11, 1898; children—Leonard A. (dec.), Louise A. (Mrs. R. M. Sargent), John P., Lydia Elizabeth (Mrs. R. F. Hedin), Jean M. (Mrs. F. G. Chesley). Was botanist Clemson Coll., S.C., 1896-99; asst. prof. botany, U. of Minn., 1899-1900; curator herbarium Columbia U., 1901. Made over 15,000 expts. with cereal grains and starch, 1901-36; inventor new processes of treating cereal grains and starch materials, including puffed rice, puffed wheat, Quaker Crackels and similar products. Awarded Charles Reid Barnes hon. life membership by Am. Soc. Plant Physiologists, 1937. Fellow A.A.A.S.; mem. Am. Forestry Assn., Minn. Acad. Science, Minn. Hist. Soc., Geol. Soc. Minn. Address: Laboratory, Red Wing, Minn. Died May 7, 1943.

ANDERSON, Andrew Work, coll. prof.; b. Bellaire, O., Mar. 17, 1864; s. Andrew Work and Jane (McGregor) A.; B.A., Wooster (O.) Coll., 1889, M.A., 1892; unmarried. Prof. philosophy and English, 1891-1905, philosophy and edn. since 1905, Macalester Coll., St. Paul. Teacher Wooster (O.) Summer Sch. several summers. Mem. A.A.A.S., N.E.A., Minn. Ednl. Assn. Democrat. Presbyterian. Home: 1628 Laurel Av., St. Paul. Deceased.

ANDERSON, Arch W., banker; b. Shelbyville, Ky., July 16, 1877; s. William Henry and Mary Jane (Coots) A.; grad. Central High Sch., Washington, D.C., 1895; Mo. Mil. Acad., Mexico, Mo., 1896; student Culver Mil. Acad., 1896; m. Ora Avanelle Westgate, Sept. 21, 1904; children—Mary Lewis (Mrs. R. E. Copeland), Alice Westgate (Mrs. Paul De La Vergne), Archa (Mrs. Herbert Lundahl). Clerk in wholesale house, Enid, Okla., 1897-98; clerk Bank of Enid, 1898-99; teller 4th Nat. Bank, Wichita, Kan., 1900-06; receiver Merchants and Planters Bank, Lawton, Okla., 1907-09; state bank examiner, Okla., Oklahoma City, 1909-10; cashier Central Reserve Bank, Oklahoma City, 1910-12; cashier 1st Nat. Bank, Norman, Okla., 1912; v.p. Tradesmen's State Bank, Oklahoma City, 1913-14; v.p. Stockyards Nat. Bank, Kansas City, Mo., 1914-15; sec. cashier Fed. Reserve Bank, Kansas City, 1915-19; partner Anderson-Thompson Co., bank stocks, Los Angeles, 1919-21; v.p. 1st Nat. Bank, Los Angeles, 1921-28; v.p. Security-1st Nat. Bank, Los Angeles, 1928-30; v.p. Continental Ill. Nat. Bank & Trust Co., Chicago, 1930-39; pres. Calif. Bank, Los Angeles, 1939-45; chmn. bd. since Jan. 1945; pres. Calif. Trust Co.; pres. and dir. Union Security Co.; trustee Equitable Life Ins. Co. of Ia.; dir. Southern Calif. Edison Co., Shareholders Co. Dir. Y.M.C.A., Group Corp. of Los Angeles. Treas. and trustee U. of Southern Calif. Director

Association of Reserve City Bankers. Mason (32°, Shriner). Clubs: California, Stock Exchange (dir.), San Gabriel Country (Los Angeles). Home: 1675 Rose Av., San Marino. Office: 625 S. Spring St., Los Angeles. Died Sept. 13, 1946; buried in Forest Lawn Memorial Park, Glendale, Calif.

ANDERSON, Benjamin McAlester, economist; b. Columbia, Mo., May 1, 1886; s. Benjamin McLean and Mary Frances (Bowling) A.; A.B., U. of Mo., 1906; A.M., U. of Ill., 1910; Ph.D. in Economics, Philosophy and Sociology, Columbia, 1911; m. Margaret Louise Crenshaw, May 27, 1909; children—Benjamin M., III (dec.), John Crenshaw, William Bent, Mary Louise. Prof. history, State Normal Sch., Cape Girardeau, Mo., 1905; prof. English lit. and economics, Mo. Valley Coll., Marshall, Mo., 1906; head prof. history and economics, State Teachers Coll., Springfield, Mo., 1907-11; instr. economics, Columbia, 1911-13, asst. prof., 1913; asst. prof. economics, Harvard, 1913-18; economic adviser, Nat. Bank of Commerce, New York, 1918-20; economist, Chase Nat. Bank, 1920-39; prof. economics, University of California, at Los Angeles, 1939-46, Connell professor of banking since 1946. President Economists National Com. Monetary Policy. Mem. Am. Econ. Assn., Phi Beta Kappa. Clubs: Century Assn. (New York); California Club (Los Angeles). Author: Social Value, 1911; The Value of Money, 1917; Effects of the War on Money, Credit and Banking in France and the United States, 1919; The Road Back to Full Employment (in 20th Century Fund Symposium of 6 economists), 1945. Editor and author Chase Economic Bulletin, 1920-37. Editor and author, The Economic Bulletin, Los Angeles, since 1939. Home: 306 Georgina Av., Santa Monica, Calif. Address: University of Calif., Los Angeles. Died Jan. 19, 1949; buried at Columbia, Mo.

ANDERSON, Carl Thomas, cartoonist; b. Madison, Wis., Feb. 14, 1865; s. Andrew and Mari (Eid) A.; ed. pub. schs., Janesville, Wis., and Beatrice, Neb.; student Sch. Indsl. Art, Phila., Pa., 1892-93; unmarried. Cartoonist on Phila. Times, Pittsburgh Comet, New York World, New York Journal, 1894-1906; free lance cartoonist, 1906-34, contbg. to Life, Puck, Judge, Collier's, etc.; creator cartoon of "Henry," which appeared in Saturday Evening Post, 1932-34, and now runs in 196 daily and 80 Sunday newspapers in 29 countries; syndicate cartoonist for King Features Syndicate since 1934. Non-resident mem. Nat. Arts Club of New York City. Member of Sigma Delta Chi Fraternity. His cartoons have been collected and published in Dusty—The Story of a Dog and His Adopted Boy, 1928; Henry, 1935. Author: How to Draw Cartoons Successfully, 1935. Home: 834 Prospect Place, Madison. Wis. Office: 235 E. 45th St., New York, N.Y. Died Nov. 4, 1948.

ANDERSON, Dice Robins, educator; b. Charlottesville, Va., Apr. 18, 1880; s. James Madison and Margaret Olivia (Robins) A.; prep. edn. Hoge Mil. Acad., Blackstone, Va.; A.B., Randolph-Macon Coll., Va., 1900, A.M., 1901; Ph.D., U. of Chicago, 1912; LL.D., Coll. of William and Mary, 1924; m. Ada James Ash, June 24, 1903 (now dec.); children—Dice Robins, William Dodd; m. 2d, Martha Crumpton Hardy, Dec. 24, 1932. Prof. mathematics, Central Female Coll., Lexington, Mo., 1901-02; instr. history, Randolph-Macon Acad., Bedford City, Va., 1902-03; prin. Chesapeake Acad., Irvington, Va., 1903-06; pres. Willie Halsell Coll., Vinita, Okla., 1906-07; fellow in history, U. of Chicago, 1907-08; instr. history, U. of Chicago, 1908-09; prof. history and polit. science, 1909-19, prof. economics and polit. science, and dir. Sch. of Business Administrn., 1919-20, Richmond (Va.) Coll.; pres. Randolph-Macon Woman's Coll., 1920-31; pres. Wesleyan Coll., Ga., 1931-41; prof. history and govt., Mary Washington Coll., Fredericksburg, 1941—. Lecturer, Richmond, School of Social Economy, 1917, Va. Mechanics Inst., 1919; exec. sec. Civic Assn., Richmond, 1915-20. Pres. Dept. of Colls., Va. Ednl. Conf., 1922-23; pres. Va. Assn. of Colls., 1923; mem. Va. Annual Conf. M.E. Ch., S., 7 times, 1922-29, and Conf. lay leader, Va. Conference, 1928-31; mem. Gen. Conf., M.E. Ch., S., Hot Springs, Ark., and Dallas, Tex., and of S. Ga. Conf., same, 1933, 35, 36, 37, 38; pres. Ga. Assn. of Colls., 1936-37. Mem. Am. Hist. Assn., Tau Kappa Alpha, Phi Beta Kappa, Phi Kappa Sigma. Democrat. Methodist. Club: Rotary. Author: William Branch Giles —A Study in the Politics of Virginia and the Nation (1790-1830), 1914; Edmund Randolph, Second Secretary of State (Secretaries of State series), 1927; etc. Editor Richmond College Historical Papers, 1915-17. Home: Fredericksburg, Va. Died Oct. 23, 1942.

ANDERSON, Edward Wharton, army officer; b. Manhattan, Kan., Sept. 23, 1903; A.B., Stanford U., 1928; grad. Air Corps Primary Flying Sch., 1929, Advanced Flying Sch., 1929, Tech. Sch., 1934, Tactical Sch., 1940. Apptd. 2d lt., Air Res., 1929; commd. 2d lt., Air Corps, U.S. Army, 1930, and advanced through the grades to brig. gen., 1944; comd. 41st Pursuit Squadron, 31st Pursuit Group, Jan.-Apr. 1941; group operations officer, 31st Pursuit Group, Apr.-May 1941, group exec. officer, May 1941-Mar. 1942; comdg. officer 20th Fighter Group, Mar.-Aug. 1942; became comdr. 4th Fighter Group, Sept. 1942, later becoming Fighter Wing comdr., European Theater Operations. Decorated Silver Star, Air Medal with two oak leaf clusters. Address: care The Adjutant General's Office, War Dept., Washington 25, D.C.* Deceased.

ANDERSON, Edwin Hatfield, librarian; b. at Zionsville, Ind., Sept. 27, 1861; s. Philander and Emma A. (Duzan) A.; A.B., Wabash Coll., 1883, L.H.D. (hon.), 1933; Litt.D. (hon.), Carnegie Inst. Tech., 1915; M.A., Columbia, 1916, Litt.D., 1932; Litt.D. (hon.), New York U., 1931; 1 year New York State Library Sch.; m. Frances R. Plummer, Dec. 22, 1891; children—Charlotte W. (Mrs. John W. Green, Jr.), Cecile W. (Mrs. A. James Behrendt). Cataloguer Newberry Library, Chicago, 1 year; librarian Carnegie Free Library, Braddock, Pa., 1892-95; organized, 1895, librarian, 1895-1904, Carnegie Library, Pittsburgh; engaged in zinc and lead mining in Missouri, 1905; dir. New York State Library and Library Sch., 1906-08; asst. dir., June 1908-May 1913, dir. New York Pub. Library, 1913-34, resigned Nov. 1, 1934, and retired as dir. emeritus. Pres. Keystone State Library Assn., 1901-02; mem. Pa. Public Records Commn. and Hist. Archives Commn., 1903-04; pres. N.Y. Library Assn., 1908, New York Library Club, 1910, A.L.A., 1913-14. Club: Century. Home: Dorset, Vt. Died Apr. 29, 1947.

ANDERSON, Elam Jonathan, coll. pres.; b. Chicago, Ill., Feb. 28, 1890; s. Victor C. and Hannah (Sandberg) A.; B.A., Drake U., Des Moines, Ia., 1912; M.A., Cornell U., 1915; Ph.D., U. of Chicago, 1924; LL.D., Ottawa U., 1936; L.H.D., College Osteopathic Phys. & Surg., 1942; m. Colena Michael, July 3, 1916; children—Frances Delight, Victor Charles, Elam J. Instr. pub. speaking, Cornell U., 1913-16; prof. edn. (missionary educator), U. of Shanghai, 1918-26; acting asst. prof. edn., Cornell U., 1924; prin. Shanghai Sch. for Am. Children, 1926-32; pres. Linfield (Ore.) Coll., 1932-38, U. of Redlands since 1938. Mem. Am. Co. of Shanghai Vol. Corps. Chmn. Dept. Higher Edn., Ore. State Teachers Assn., 1934-36; chmn. Program Com., Northern Baptist Conv., 1936; mem. bd. mgrs. A.B.F.M.S., Board of Education (pres. 1936); 1st v.p. Northern Baptist Conv., 1937; director California Safety Council; state chmn. Ch. Committee for China Relief, 1939; pres. Assn. of Colls. and Univs., Pacific Southwest, 1940. Member Phi Beta Kappa (president S. Calif. 1941), Phi Delta Kappa frats. Mason (32°). Clubs: Cornell (New York); Am. University, Rotary (Shanghai); (hon.) McMinnville Rotary (Redlands); University (Portland). Author: China Coll. Song Book, 1923; English Teaching Efficiency in China, 1926; Music Appreciation, Book I, 1928; Introduction to Western Music, 1929. Occasional essays on International relations. Lecturer on "International Relations in the Orient" and "Character Building in Education." Home: Redlands, Calif. Died Aug. 17, 1944.

ANDERSON, Elbridge R., lawyer; b. St. Louis, Mo., Sept. 12, 1864; s. Galusha and Mary E. (Roberts) A.; B.S., U. of Chicago, 1885; m. Elizabeth D. Harris, May 15, 1889 (dec.); 1 dau., Mary Frances (dec.); m. 2d, Blanche Webster Hobbs, Oct. 27, 1932. Began practice, 1886; mem. Bartlett & Anderson, 1889-1909, Anderson, Sweetser & Wiles, 1909-13, Anderson, Wiles & Ryder, 1913-29, Anderson, Mintz & Owen, 1929-36, Anderson & Owen, 1937, Anderson, Ham, Owen & Roberts, 1938-41; now practicing alone. Mem. Am. and Mass. bar assns., Bar Assn. City of Boston, Essex, Middlesex and Internat. bar assn. Club: Wenham College. Home: Wenham, S. Hamilton P.O., Mass. Office: 209 Washington St., Boston, Mass. Died June 22, 1944.

ANDERSON, Frederick Irving, author; b. Aurora, Ill., Nov. 14, 1877; s. Andrew and Elizabeth (Adling) Anderson; ed. pub. schs., Aurora, and special course 2 yrs. in Wharton School, U. of Pa.; m. Emma Helen de Zouche, Mar. 23, 1908. Reporter Aurora (Ill.) News, 1895-96; writer on staff New York World, 1898-1908. Mem. Authors' League America. Author: The Farmer of To-morrow, 1913; Adventures of The Infallible Godahl, 1914; Electricity for the Farm, 1915; The Notorious Sophie Lang, 1925; Book of Murder, 1930. Home: East Jamaica, Vt. Died Dec. 23, 1947.

ANDERSON, Isabel (Mrs. Larz Anderson), author; b. Boston, Mass., Mar. 29, 1876; d. Commodore George (U.S.N.) and Anna (Weld) Perkins; ed. Miss Winsor's Sch., Boston; Litt.D., George Washington U., 1918; LL.D., Boston U., 1930; m. June 10, 1897, Larz Anderson, minister to Belgium, 1911-12, ambassador to Japan, 1912-13 (died 1937). 1st comdt. District Columbia Red Cross Refreshment Corps (World War I); canteen service American Red Cross in France, 1917; served at French and Belgian front line hospitals; volunteer nurse's aide during World War II. Decorations awarded: medal of Elizabeth (Belgium); Croix de Guerre (France), and others. Elected librarian general, D.A.R., 1923; member of National Pen Women's League, Boston Authors Club, Chilton Club. Author: The Great Sea Horse, 1909; Captain Ginger Series, 1911; The Spell of Japan, 1914; The Spell of the Hawaiian Islands and the Philippines, 1916; The Spell of Belgium, 1917; Odd Corners, 1917; Zigzagging, 1918; Presidents and Pies, 1920; Topsy Turvy and the Gold Star, 1920; Polly the Pagan, 1922; The Kiss and the Queue, 1925; The Wall Paper Code, 1926; Under the Black Horse Flag, 1926; From Corsair to Riffian, 1927; Circling South America, 1928; Circling Africa, 1929; A Yacht in Mediterranean Seas, 1930; In Eastern Seas, 1934; Zigzagging the South Seas, 1936. Plays produced and published: Everyboy, 1920; The Witch in the Woods, 1925; Merry Jerry, 1928; Justice Whisker's Trial, 1929; Little Madcap's Journey, 1931; Marina, 1932; Dick Whittington, 1932-33; The Gee Whiz, 1933; King Foxy, 1933; Freedom, 1933; Robinson Crusoe, 1934; Wing, 1934; Sir Frog Goes A-Traveling, 1935; The Kiss and the Queue, 1935; Tahiti Ho, 1936; Island of the Moon, 1936; Under the Bo Tree, 1936; The Green Turban, 1937; The Gold Madonna; 1937; Fuente, The Matador, 1937; A City Built in a Night, 1937; The Red Flame, 1938; K'ung, 1938; I Hear a Call (poems), 1938. Editor: Larz Anderson: Letters and Journals of a Diplomat, 1940; General Nicholas Longworth Anderson—Letters and Journals, 1942; The Whole World Over (poems), 1944; Near and Far (poems), 1947. Home: "Weld," Brookline 46, Mass. Died Nov. 3, 1948; ashes interred in crypt of Chapel of St. Mary, National Cathedral, Mount St. Albans, Washington.

ANDERSON, James Nesbitt, educator; b. Laurens Co., S.C., Oct. 21, 1864; s. George Washington and Nancy Narcissa (Nesbitt) A.; ed. Wofford Coll. to middle of junior yr.; B.Let., U. of Va., 1886, M.A., 1887; Morgan fellow, Harvard, 1887-88; studied U. of Berlin, 1889-90, U. of Heidelberg, 1890; Ph.D., Johns Hopkins, 1894; studied U. of Paris, 1896; m. Janie Brooks Sullivan, Sept. 22, 1903; children—Ewing, James N., Mary Elizabeth, Jane Sullivan, George Washington, Angela, Hewlett Sullivan. Prof. Greek and Latin, U. of Okla., 1894-96; instr. in Latin, Vanderbilt, 1900-01; prof. Greek, Fla. State Coll., 1903-05; prof. ancient langs. and head of dept., U. of Fla., 1905, dean Coll. Arts and Sciences and head of Grad. Sch., 1910-30, dean Grad. Sch., 1930-38, now dean emeritus, head prof. emeritus of Ancient langs. Hon. mem. Conf. of Deans of Southern Grad. Schs.; mem. Chi Phi. Democrat. Author: On the Sources of Ovid's Heroides, 1896. Editor: Selections from Ovid, 1899. Home: 376 W. Magnolia St., Gainesville, Fla. Died June 16, 1945.

ANDERSON, John Edward, mayor; b. Rockingham County, N.C., Aug. 25, 1879; s. Edward Nathan and Sallie Jane Anderson; ed. Leaksville (N.C.) High Sch. and Oak Ridge (N.C.) Inst.; m. Georgia Lee Ann Sewell, Nov. 19, 1932. Railroad work, El Paso, Tex. 1902-06; real estate, El Paso, 1906-10; sec. and mgr. Elks Lodge, 1910-23; city clerk, 1923-27; city tax assessor and collector, 1927-39; mayor of El Paso since 1939; dir. El Paso Fed. Bldg. & Loan Assn. Dir. Family Welfare Assn. Mem. Brotherhood of Ry. Trainmen. Episcopalian. Mason (32°, Shriner), Jesters, Elk. Clubs: Kiwanis, Chamber of Commerce. Home: Hotel Paso del Norte. Office: City Hall, El Paso, Tex. Died Feb. 4, 1947.

ANDERSON, John George, archbishop; b. Stromness, Orkney Islands, Mar. 23, 1866; B.A., St. John's Coll., 1886, B.D., 1888; D.D., U. of Manitoba, Winnipeg, Can., LL.D.; m. Annie Violetta Kirkland, Nov., 1889; children—Cyril K., John W., Irene, Ernest R., William R., Dorothy H., Alfred, Rupert Machray (dec.). Consecrated Bishop of Moosonee, May, 1909; became archbishop of Moosonee, 1940; apptd. Metropolitan of Ontario, 1940. Dir. Lady Minto Hosp., Cochrane, Ontario, 25 yrs. Awarded King George V's Jubilee Medal, King George VI's and Queen Elizabeth's Coronation Medal. Hon. mem. Assn. of Am. Indians. One of compilers of Cree-English Dictionary, 1938; translator of a Cree Hymnal and compiler of other translations. Died June 18, 1943.

ANDERSON, John (Hargis), drama critic; b. Pensacola, Fla., Oct. 18, 1896; s. Dr. Warren Edward and Catherine Hargis A.; student Univ. Mil. Sch., Mobile, Ala., 1912-14, U. of Va., 1914-16; m. Margaret Wilber Gaines (Breuning), Dec. 24, 1920. Began as asst. critic, 1920; drama critic on N.Y. Evening Post, 1924-28, on N.Y. Evening Journal since 1928; asso. editor Arts Weekly, 1932; instr. New York U., 1928-35. Mem. Sigma Alpha Epsilon. Author: Box Office, 1929; Book of the White Mountains (with Stearns Morse), 1930; The Inspector General (adaptation of play by Gogol), 1931; The American Theatre, 1938. Wrote prefaces for plays, Spread Eagle, 1927, Accent on Youth, 1935, Wine of Choice, 1938. Contbr. of articles to Town and Country, The Stage, Saturday Review of Literature. His adaptation of Inspector General was produced in New York, 1931; The Fatal Alibi, 1932. Home: Stepney Depot, Conn. Office: N.Y. Journal-American, 1834 Broadway, New York. Died July 16, 1943.

ANDERSON, Robert van Vleck, geologist; b. Galesburg, Ill., Apr. 18, 1884; s. Melville Best (LL.D.) and Charlena (van Vleck) A.; B.A., Stanford University, 1906; married Gracella Rountree, Mar. 1923; children—Robert Playfair, Patricia Sage (Mrs. John Loveland Armstrong), Gracella Gurnee. Geological and zoölogical work, Japan, 1905; assistant in investigations of Calif. earthquake for Carnegie Inst., 1906; geologic aid, asst. geologist and geologist, U.S. Geol. Survey, 1906-13; made investigations of geol. and petroleum resources of Calif., and was member Oil Land Classification Board; as cons. geologist visited many parts of world since 1911; geologist for S. Pearson & Son, Ltd., London, Eng., 1913-18;

representative of U.S. War Trade Bd. in Sweden; Am. delegate on Inter-Allied Trade Com., Stockholm, 1918-19; dir. Whitehall Petroleum Corp., Ltd., London, 1919-23, chief geologist, 1923-26. Engaged in independent scientific work, 1927-34. Collaborateur, Service de la Carte Geologique de l'Algérie, 1930-32; research in Algeria under grant from Geol. Soc. America, 1933; with Socony Vacuum Oil Co., Inc., 1934-44; research associate, Stanford Univ., since 1945. Fellow Geological Society of America (chmn. Cordilleran sect. 1928), Calif. Acad. Sciences; mem. Paleontol. Soc. America, Assn. Am. Geographers, Soc. Econ. Geologists, Archæol. Inst. America, Am. Assn. Petroleum Geologists, Société Géologique de France, Sigma Xi. Unitarian. Author: Geology in Coastal Atlas of Western Algeria; also various reports pub. by U.S. Govt., and other scientific papers. Home: 1140 Hamilton Av., Palo Alto, Calif. Address: Dept. of Geology, Stanford University, Stanford P.O., Calif. Died June 6, 1949.

ANDERSON, Sydney, ex-congressman; b. Zumbrota, Goodhue County, Minn., Sept. 17, 1881; s. Charles B. and Anna Knudsen (Strand) A.; grad. high sch., Zumbrota, 1899; law student, Highland Park Coll., Des Moines, Ia., 1899-1900, U. of Minn., 1901-02; m. Florence Belle Douglas, June 16, 1901. Admitted to bar, 1902; practiced at Kansas City, Mo., 1903-04, Lanesboro, Minn., 1904-25; pres. Millers' Nat. Fedn., Chicago and Washington, D.C., 1925-29; v.p. Gen. Mills, Inc., Minneapolis, since 1929. Mem. 62d to 68th Congresses (1911-25), 1st Minn. Dist. chmn. Joint Commn. of Agrl. Inquiry, U.S. Congress, 1921-22. Chmn. Nat. Agrl. Conf., Washington, 1922; chmn. Nat. Wheat Conf., Chicago, 1923; was pres. Wheat Council of U.S., Chicago, and v.-chmn. Research Council, Nat. Transportation Inst., Washington. Republican. Presbyn. Served in Co. D 14th Minn. Inf. during Spanish-Am. War. Home: 2521 Pillsbury Av. Office: Chamber of Commerce Bldg., Minneapolis, Minn.* Died Oct. 8, 1948.

ANDERSON, Troyer Steele, professor history; b. Minneapolis, Minn., Apr. 28, 1900; s. Frank Maloy and Mary Gertrude (Steele); A.B., Dartmouth Coll., 1922; A.M., Harvard, 1923; B.A., Oxford, 1925, Ph.D., 1929; m. Mary F. Gerould, Sept. 11, 1926; children—Kenneth Foster, Nancy Steele. Instr. in history, Brown U., Providence, R.I., 1926-28; asst. prof. history, Swarthmore Coll., 1928-35, asso. prof., 1935-42; prof. history U. of Ia., 1942-45; prof. history Hunter Coll. since 1945; visiting lecturer, Bryn Mawr Coll., 1941. Mem. Historical Branch, G-2, War Dept. Gen. Staff (later, Hist. Div. War Dept. Special Staff), assigned to Office of Under Secretary of War, 1944-46; special consultant to sec. of war, 1946. Mem. Am. Hist. Assn., Am. Mil. Inst., Phi Beta Kappa. Democrat. Conglist. Author: The Command of the Howe Brothers during the American Revolution, 1936. Address: Department of History, Hunter College, 695 Park A., New York 21. Died Apr. 3, 1948; buried at Minneapolis.

ANDERSON, Victor Emanuel, lawyer; b. Wheaton, Minn., May 27, 1883; s. Ole and Mary Sophia (Johnson) A.; student Northwestern Coll., Fergus Falls, Minn., 1900-03; LL.B., U. of Minn., 1906; m. Annie Marie Hass, July 28, 1909; 1 son, Cyrus Victor. Admitted to Minn. bar, 1906, and began practice in 1906; county atty., Traverse County, 1909-13; mem. firm Murphy & Anderson, 1913-23; asst. atty. gen. of Minn., 1923-28; counsel for co-operative assns., 1928-33; special counsel A.A.A., U.S. Dept. Agr., 1933-35, chief field investigation sect., 1935-37; U.S. atty. for Minn. since 1937. Served as dir. Minn. Farm Bureau Fed. 8 yrs., pres. Minn. Sch. Bd. Assn. 2 terms. Dir. Minn. Council of Agr., Nat. Com. for Agr. Mem. Minn., Am. and Federal bar assns. Democrat. Lutheran. Mason. Clubs: St. Paul Athletic, Minnesota University (St. Paul). Home: 1514 Portland Av. Office: 221 Federal Bldg., St. Paul, Minn.

Died Sep. 12, 1948.

ANDERSON, William Allison, manufacturer; b. Trenton, N.J., June 4, 1870; s. Gen. Henry Reuben and Florence (Allison) A.; student Lawrenceville (N.J.) Sch., 1883-88; m. Helen S. Anderson. With John A. Roebling's Sons Co., wire mfrs., Trenton, N.J., since Nov. 1888, beginning as timekeeper, pres. since 1936; pres. John A. Roebling's Sons Co., of Chicago; dir. Otis Elevator Co., Delaware & Hudson R.R. Corp. (bd. mgrs.). Home: Princeton, N.J. Office: 640 S. Broad St., Trenton, N.J. Died Oct. 10, 1944.

ANDERSON, William Franklin, retired bishop; b. Morgantown, Va. (now W.Va.), Apr. 22, 1860; s. William and Elizabeth (Coombs) A.; student to end of jr. year, W.Va. U.; A.B., Ohio Wesleyan U., 1884; B.D., Drew Theol. Sem., 1887; A.M., New York U., 1898; D.D., Wesleyan U., Conn., 1902, Norwich U., 1920; LL.D., Ohio Wesleyan Univ., 1907, Upper Iowa U., 1907, Ohio Northern U., 1915; Litt.D., Boston Univ., 1930; m. Jennie Lulah Ketcham, June 9, 1887; children—Rev. William K., Mrs. Mary Anderson Twachtman, Ruth Teller (Mrs. Thomas Fox), Paul Charles (dec.), Lulah Virginia (Mrs. John Huntley Dupré), Katharine Livingstone (Mrs. Ashley B. Morrill), Margaret Ketchum (Mrs. J. Murray Walker). Ordained Methodist Episcopal ministry, 1887; pastor, Mott Avenue Church, New York City, 1887-89, St. James' Church, Kingston, N.Y., 1890-94, Washington Square Church, New York, 1895-98, Ossining, N.Y., 1899-1904; rec. sec. Bd. Edn. of M.E. Ch., 1898-1904, corr. sec. 1904-08; elected bishop, 1908; acting pres. Boston U., Jan. 1, 1925-Feb. 1, 1926; resident bishop, Chattanooga, Tenn., 1908-12, Cincinnati, O., 1912-24, and of Boston, 1924-32, retired; prof. history of religion, Carleton Coll. and chaplain of the college body, 1932-34. Editor The Christian Student, 1904-08. Trustee of Drew Theol. Seminary, Meharry Med. Coll., Boston U. Pres. new and enlarged Board Edn., M.E. Ch., with headquarters in Chicago, 1920-32. Visited missions of M.E. Church in North Africa, 1914; official supervision M.E. missions in Italy, France, Finland, Norway, N. Africa and Russia, 1915, 16, 17, 18. Mason (32°). As mem. for Europe of Com. of Emergency and Reconstruction of M.E. Ch. made 5 trips abroad during war, administering work in France, N. Africa, Italy, Spain, Norway, Sweden, Denmark, Finland and Russia; Army Y.M.C.A. work, spring and summer, 1918; was guest of French and Italian govts. on tours of battlefronts; del. M.E. Ch. to English Wesleyan and Irish Wesleyan confs., 1918; fraternal del. from Federal Council of Chs. of Christ in America to L'Assemblée Général du Protestantisme Francais, Lyon, France, Nov. 1919. Chevalier Legion of Honor (French), 1922. Mem. Delta Tau Delta, Phi Beta Kappa. Clubs: Masonic, University (Boston); University (Winter Park, Fla.). Author: The Compulson of Love, 1904; Hammer and Sparks, 1943. Editor: The Challenge of Today, 1915. Contbr. to religious and secular press. Spl. lecturer, 1935, on "The Modern Man and His Bible," Rollins Coll., Winter Park, Fla. Mem. faculty Tenn. Wesleyan (Junior) Coll., spring term, 1937; dept. of Bible, Fla. Southern Coll., winter terms, 1937-41. Home: 860 E. Park Av., Winter Park, Fla.; (summer) Amblewood, Puritan Rd., Buzzards Bay, Mass. Died July 22, 1944; buried in Kensico (N.Y.) Cemetery.

ANDERSON, William Gilbert, physical dir.; b. St. Joseph, Mich., Sept. 9, 1860; s. Rev. Edward and Harriet (Shumway) A.; M.D., Western Reserve, 1883; A.B., Yale, 1902, A.M., 1903, M.S., 1909; Dr. P.H., Harvard Univ., 1912; M.P.E., Springfield Training Sch., 1925; LL.D., Battle Creek Coll., 1936; studied Royal Inst. Stockholm, Univ. of Berlin, Oxford U. and U. of Calif.; m. 2d, Mrs. Alice Wheeler Hawley, July 2, 1930; 1 son, William L. (by former marriage). Teacher country sch., 1881, Adelphi Acad., Brooklyn, N.Y., 1883-92; pres. Brooklyn Normal Sch. of Physical Edn., 1885-92; asso. dir. Gymnasium, Yale, 1892-94, dir. since 1894; lecturer Yale Forestry Sch.; dean Chautauqua Sch. of Physical Edn. (summers), 1885-1904. Chmn. Conn. State Bd. of Social Hygiene 4 years. Trustee New York Normal Sch. of Gymnastics, Posse Sch., Boston. Med. examiner R.O.T.C., rank of 1st lt., World War. Mem. Am. Assn. for Advancement of Physical Edn. (organizer), Soc. of Physical Dirs. of Am. Colls., Yale Alumni Assn., Chi Psi, Sigma Xi, Sigma Delta Psi (pres. 1917-27), Alpha Kappa Kappa. Republican. Conglist. Clubs: Yale, Harvard of Conn., Harvard of New Haven. Author: Light Gymnastics, 1887; Methods of Teaching Physical Education, 1898; Manual of Physical Training (with William L. Anderson), 1913. Home: Hotel Taft, New Haven, Conn.* Died July 7, 1947.

ANDERSON, William Ketcham, clergyman; b. N.Y. City, Apr. 27, 1888; s. Bishop William Franklin and Lulah (Ketcham) A.; B.A., Wesleyan U., 1910, D.D., 1930; M.A., Columbia, 1913; B.D., Union Theol. Sem., 1914; m. Fanny E. Spencer, Dec. 19, 1916; children—Almeda Jane (Mrs. C. Dudley Ingerson), Elizabeth Cushman, William F. II, Josephine Spencer. Taught high chool, Chattanooga, Tennessee, 1910-11; pastor, Carpenter, Wyoming, 1912; ordained Meth. ministry deacon, 1915, elder, 1917; pastor Ohio State Univ., 1915-18; organizing secretary Ohio Council of Chs., 1919, and its 1st sec., 1919-20; field sec. for Ohio of Inter-Ch. World Movement, 1920; pastor Calvary Ch., Pittsburgh, Pa., 1920-26, First Ch., Butler, 1926-28, Franklin St. Ch., Johnstown, 1928-40; edn. dir. Commn. on Ministerial Training, Methodist Ch., since Oct. 1940; mem. staff, Bd. of Edn., Methodist Church. Mem. commns. on worship and music, and the ministry, Fed. Coun. of Churches. Mem. staff Ohio branch Council Nat. Defense, 1917; with Army Y.M.C.A., Camp Sherman, 1918. Trustee Wesleyan U., Wesley Foundation, Pa. State College. Del. of Pittsburgh Conf. to Gen. Conf. M.E. Ch., 1936; delegate to uniting conference of 3 Methodist bodies, 1939; delegate General Conference Methodist Church, 1940-44; N.E. Jurisdictional Conf., 1940-44. Mem. Am. Hymn Soc., Fellowship of Reconciliation, Phi Nu Theta. Mason. Club: Pocasset (Mass.) Golf. Contbr. to religious periodicals; composer of several hymn tunes and songs. Author: (chapter) Athletics at Wesleyan, 1938; (with others) A Church Membership Manual For Methodist Ministers, 1943. Editor: The Student's Handbook, 1942, 1945; Pastor and Church, 1943, 1945; The Minister and Human Relations, 1943; Protestantism, 1944; Making the Gospel Effective, 1945; Christian World Mission, 1946; Methodism, 1947. Home: 3749 Whitland Av., Nashville 5. Office: 810 Broadway, Nashville 2, Tenn. Died Feb. 7, 1947.

ANDERSON, William Thomas, editor, pub.; b. Hayneville, Houston County, Ga., Aug. 21, 1871; s. Christopher Cohen and Laura (Tooke) A.; ed. pvt. schs.; LL.D. from Mercer U., Macon, Ga., 1935; m. Elizabeth Griswold Anderson, June 21, 1898. Began with Macon Telegraph, 1888, editor and pub. since 1914. Commr. Ga. Highway Dept., 1923-25. Col. on staff of Gov. Hardman, 1926-28. Pres. bd. Sixth Dist. Agrl. and Mech. Sch., Barnesville, Ga.; mem. Bibb County Bd. of Edn. since 1908; vice chmn. Fed. Better-Housing Authority, Macon. Trustee Herty Laboratory, Savannah, Ga. Democrat. Elk, K.P. Club: Idle Hour Country. Home: Route 5, Shirley Hills. Office: 452 Cherry St., Macon, Ga.* Deceased

ANDERSON, Winslow Samuel, coll. pres.; b. Portland, Me., July 28, 1898; s. Robert Walter and Annie Frances (Lawton) A.; grad. high sch., Portland, 1916; B.S., Bates Coll., Lewiston, Me., 1921 (Phi Beta Kappa); M.S., U. of Minn., 1923; grad. study N.C. State Coll., 1923-25; LL.D., Southern College, Lakeland, Fla., 1933; Sc.D., Rollins College, Winter Park, Florida, 1942; m. Winnifred Evelyn Wilson, November 8, 1924; 1 dau., Shirley. Asst. in chemistry, Bates Coll., 1918-21; asso. prof. chemistry, Rollins Coll., 1921-22; asst. in chemistry, U. of Minn., 1922-23; instr., later asst. prof. chemistry, N.C. State Coll., 1923-25; founder Theta Kappa Nu, 1924, pres., 1924-28, exec. sec., 1925-28, treas., 1928-35, grand fraternal adviser, 1935-38 (Theta Kappa Nu now merged with Lambda Chi Alpha, of which is nat. trustee); prof. of chemistry and also dean of men, Rollins Coll., 1928, dean of the coll., 1929-42; president, Whitman College, since June 1, 1942. Served as private, U.S. Army, 1918; commd. 2d lt. Chem. Warfare Res. Trustee Webber Coll., 1939-42; mem. bd. dir. Symphony Orchestra of Central Fla., 1937-42; com. chmn. State Defense Council of Fla., 1941-42; Florida chairman Chemist Advisory Council, 1941-42; mem. Commn. on Instns. of Higher Edn. of Southern Assn. of Colls. and Secondary Schs., 1941-42; mem. Am. Chem. Soc., Am. Electrochemical Soc., S.A.R. (pres. Wash. State Soc.), Phi Beta Kappa Assn. of Central Florida (pres. 1928-33), Ohio Bates Assn. (pres. 1926-28), Fla. Bates Assn. (pres. 1930-42), Gen. Alumni Assn. of Bates Coll. (v.p. 1931-32), Am. Assn. Univ. Profs., Am. Assn. Adult Edn., Florida Acad. Sciences, Am. Legion, Archaeol. Inst. of America (pres. Walla Walla Soc. 1945-46), Walla Walla Chamber of Commerce, Assn. Academic Deans of Southern States (pres. 1934-35), Fla. Assn. Colls. and Univs. (pres. 1936-37), Assn. of Colleges of Congl. and Christian Affiliation (pres. 1938-39), Fla. Assn. Amateur Athletic Union (pres. 1929-38), Atlantic Seaboard Assn. of Amateur Athletic Union (pres. 1933-36), Southern Intercollegiate Athletic Assn. (vice-pres. 1932-34, 1938-40), Omicron Delta Kappa, Pi Kappa Delta, Pi Gamma Mu (past gov. Fla. dist.), Phi Lambda Upsilon, Gamma Sigma Epsilon; fellow A.A.A.S., Am. Inst. Chemists, Am. Geog. Soc.; hon. mem. Institut Litteraire et Artistique de France, Southern Council on Internat. Relations. Republican. Protestant. Clubs: Coll. (Bates); Big Ten University (Cleveland, O.); University (Winter Park); Round Table, Inquiry, Rotary (Walla Walla). Editor of Catalog and Directory of Theta Kappa Nu, 1926; compiler of Songs of Theta Kappa Nu, and writer of First Pledge Manual. Contbr. to ednl. jours. Address: Whitman College Walla Walla, Wash., (summer) North Bridgton, Me. Died Nov. 13, 1948.

ANDERTON, Stephen Philbin (ăn'dĕr-tŭn), lawyer; b. Greenwich, Conn., Aug. 4, 1874; s. Ralph Leigh, Jr., and Susie (Philbin) A.; student St. Louis Coll. and Coll. of City of N.Y.; LL.B., New York U. Law Sch., 1900; m. Louise Durrie, May 14, 1904 (died 1925); m. 2d, Mabelle (Harris) Patterson, June 2, 1926. Admitted to N.Y. bar, 1901; began as law clerk with Philbin & Beekman, New York, 1898, and continued with successors; became partner Beekman, Menken & Griscom, 1917, also successors, and withdrew from Beekman, Bogue, Leake, Stephens & Black, 1937; partner Anderton & Rogers, 1937-38; individual practice since 1938. Del. to Nat. Congress to Enforce Peace, N.Y. City, 1919; del. to Nat. Antinarcotic Conf., Washington, D.C., 1923; active as chmn. com. of N.Y. State Bar Assn., 1922-28, to secure N.Y. Narcotic Drug Control Law, also in formulating uniform law later adopted by National Commn. on Uniform State Laws. Mem. Am., N.Y. State bar assns., Bar Assn. of City of New York, N.Y. Law Inst., N.Y. County Lawyers Assn., Internat. Law Assn., Nat. Council of Nat. Econ. League, Economic Club of New York, Academy Polit. Science, Theta Delta Chi. Ind. Democrat. Catholic. Clubs: Metropolitan, Broad Street, Civitan, Theta Delta Chi (New York). Author: Washington's Appeal: The Foundations of Constructive Democracy, 1935. Home: Great Neck, L.I., N.Y. Office: 36 W. 44th St., New York, N.Y.* Died July 10, 1947.

ANDREWS, Adolphus, retired naval officer, business executive; born in Galveston, Texas, on October 7, 1879; son of Adolphus Rutherford and Louise Caroline (Davis) A.; ed. U. of Tex., 1896-97; grad. U.S. Naval Acad., 1901, U.S. Naval War Coll., 1920; m. Berenice Waples Platter, Sept. 16, 1914; children—Frances Waples, Adolphus. Ensign, 1901; promoted through grades to rear admiral Jan. 1934; attached to U.S.S. Dolphin as jr. naval aide to President Theodore Roosevelt, 1904-06; aide to supt. U.S. Naval Acad., 1911-14; gunnery officer U.S.S. Michigan, took part in landing at Vera Cruz, 1914; exec. officer U.S.S. Mississippi, 1917-18; comdg. U.S.S. Massachusetts, 1918; comdg. U.S.S. Mayflower, sr. naval aide to President Harding, 1922; escorted President Harding to Alaska; comdg. U.S.S. Mayflower, sr. naval aide to President Coolidge, 1923-26; naval rep. Disarmament Conf. Geneva, 1926, 27; comdg. Submarine Base, New London, Conn., 1927-29, U.S.S. Texas, 1929-31; chief of staff Naval War Coll., 1931-33; chief of staff Battle Force, 1933; chief of staff, U.S. Fleet, 1934, 35; chief of Bur. of Navigation, 1935-38; vice admiral commanding Fleet Scouting Force, 1938-41; comdt. Third Naval Dist. and comdr. North Atlantic Naval Frontier, 1941-42; vice adm. comdg. Eastern Sea Frontier, 1942-43; vice admiral retired on special duty, Navy Dept., Washington, D.C.; relieved of active duty, July 1, 1945; commr. Pacific Ocean Areas Nat. Red Cross, Honolulu, T.H., 1945-46; now president Waples-Platter Co., Fort Worth, Texas. Episcopalian. Mason. Home: Dallas, Tex. Office: Andrews Bldg., Dallas, Tex. Died June 19, 1948.

ANDRESS, James Mace, psychologist; b. Chesaning, Mich., July 30, 1881; s. James Thomas and Susan (Babion) A.; B.Pd., A.B., Mich. State Normal Coll., 1905, M.Ed., 1923; Ph.M., U. of Chicago, 1906; A.M., Harvard, 1908; Ph.D., Clark U., 1916; m. Annie Laura Turner, June 29, 1910; children—Judith, Charlotte, Philip, Ruth. Instr. history and edn., Manchester (Ind.) Coll., 1906-07; head dept. of psychology and sch. hygiene, State Normal Sch., Worcester, Mass., 1908-15; head dept. of psychology and child study, Boston Normal Sch., 1915-23. Lecturer ednl. psychology, Wheelock Kindergarten Sch., Mass., since 1917, Normal Art. Sch. since 1923; lecturer health edn. Boston U., Boston Sch. of Physical Edn., Cleveland Inst. of Sch. Hygiene; spl. agent Bur. of Edn., 1920; teacher of Chautauqua (N.Y.) Instn., 1920; etc. Mem. Corp. Walter E. Fernald State School, Mass. Soc. Mental Hygiene. Conglist. Mason. Author: Johann Gottfried Herder as an Educator, 1916; Teaching Hygiene in the Grades, 1918; Health Education in Rural Schools, 1919; Rosy Cheeks and Strong Heart, 1920; A Journey to Health Land, 1924; The Boys and Girls of Wake-up Town, 1924; Summer Fun, 1931. Collaborator: Suggestions for a Program of Health Teaching in Elementary Schools, 1921; Health and Success, 1925; Health and Good Citizenship, 1925; The Sunshine School, 1928; Health Essentials, 1928; Science and the Way to Health, 1929; Experiments in Health, 1929; Broadcasting Health, 1933; The Health School on Wheels, 1933; (with others) Canadian Health Series, 5 vols., 1937; (with others) Safe and Healthy Living, 10 vols., 1939. Editor of "Understanding the Child," 1930-35; editor of School and Health Dept., Hygeia (pub. by Am. Med. Assn.) since 1928. Home: 67 Clyde St., Newtonville, Mass. Died Feb. 5, 1942; buried at Henniker, N.H.

ANDREWS, Alexander Boyd, lawyer; b. Henderson, N.C., Feb. 2, 1873; s. Alexander B. and Julia M. (Johnston) A.; B.Litt., U. of N.C., 1893, law student, 1893-94; m. Helen M. Sharples, Nov. 5, 1908 (died 1921). Admitted to N.C. Bar, 1894, and since in practice at Raleigh; dir. Atlantic Fire Ins. Co. Dep. to Triennial Gen. Conv., Episcopal Ch., Denver, Colo., 1931, Atlantic City, N.J., 1934, Cincinnati, O., 1937, Kansas City, Mo., Cleveland, O., 1943, (chmn. com. on canons), 1940; del. to Am. Council on Edn., 1932-37. Mem. bd. of trustees U. of N.C. since 1927 (now sec.), dir. E. Carolina Teachers Coll. since 1931. Mem. Am. Bar Assn., (com. on judicial salaries, 1922-43, chmn. 1922-35), N.C. Bar Assn. (pres. 1928-29), Am. Law Inst., N.C. Soc. S.R. pres. 1931-32, sec. since 1933), American Statistical Association, Special Libraries, Sigma Alpha Epsilon. Democrat. Episcopalian. (Chancellor diocese since 1934; pres. Chancellers Assn., U.S.A. since 1943.) Mason (grand master N.C., 1916; grand comdr. K.T., 1907). Elk. Clubs: Kiwanis, Carolina Country. Wrote "Judicial Salaries in United States"; "Fifty Years Statistics of Protestant Episcopal Church, U.S.A., 1876-1930"; "Digest of Masonic Law, 1841-1926"; "Legal Education and Admission to the Bar"; "Is the Birthrate of the Episcopal Church Increasing or Decreasing?" and "Per Capita Cost of Courts." Home: 309 N. Blount St. Office: 939 Fayetteville St., Raleigh, N.C. Died Oct. 21, 1946.

ANDREWS, Annulet (Mrs. J. Kingsley Ohl), poet; b. Washington, Ga., Dec. 29, 1866; d. Dr. Henry F. and Elizabeth Koran (Morgan) Andrews; m. J. Kingsley Ohl, 1889. Contbr. poems to leading mags. and papers; syndicate and spl. corr., New York, Washington, San Francisco, London and Paris. Author: The Wife of Narcissus; Narcissus, the Near Poet (serial Saturday Evening Post). Address: Care China Bureau New York Herald, Peking, China. Died Jan. 7, 1943.

ANDREWS, Charles Henry, psychiatrist; b. Bergen, N.Y., Feb. 27, 1866; s. Robert and Julia (Beardsley) A.; M.D., U. of Buffalo, 1888; m. Myra A. French, June 11, 1889. Practiced in Buffalo since 1888; chmn. Procreation Comm. of State of N.Y. to investigate, and under certain conditions to perform surg. operations upon feeble-minded, criminal and other defective inmates of hosps., prison, etc., of the state. Home: 143 Highland Av. Office: Hotel Statler, Buffalo, N.Y. Died May 23, 1931.

ANDREWS, Charles McLean, historian; b. Wethersfield, Conn., Feb. 22, 1863; s. Rev. W. W. and Elizabeth Byrne (Williams) A.; A.B., Trinity Coll., Hartford, Conn., 1884, A.M., 1890, L.H.D., 1905; Ph.D., Johns Hopkins U., 1889; hon. A.M., Yale, 1910, Litt.D., 1935; Litt.D., Harvard (Tercentenary), 1936; LL.D., Lehigh University, 1934, Johns Hopkins University, 1939; m. Evangeline Holcombe Walker, June 19, 1895; children—Ethel (Mrs. John M. Harlan), John Williams. Associate professor history, later professor, Bryn Mawr (Pa.) College, 1889-1907; same, Johns Hopkins, 1907-10; Farnam prof. Am. history, Yale, 1910-31; dir. hist. publications, Yale U., 1931-33, emeritus since 1933; editor Yale Historical Publications, 1912-33; asso. fellow Davenport Coll., Yale; lecturer, Univ. of Helsingfors, Finland, October 1911, Univs. of Iowa, Wis., Mich., Chicago, 1919-21, William and Mary College, 1938. Mem. Am. Hist. Assn. (chmn. Winsor Prize com., 1899-1905; Public Archives Commn., 1901-15; exec. council, 1905-08; acting pres., 1924, pres., 1925), Hist. Soc. Pa., Md. Hist. Soc., Va. Hist. Soc., Conn. Hist. Soc., Am. Antiq. Soc., Am. Philos. Soc., New Haven Colony Hist. Soc., Colonial Soc. Mass.; hon. mem. Historisch Genootschap, Utrecht; corr. mem. Mass. Hist. Soc., Royal Hist. Society; fellow Am. Acad. Arts and Sciences; mem. Nat. Inst. of Arts and Letters (gold medalist 1937); mem. Am. Acad. of Arts and Letters, 1937; mem. Phi Beta Kappa. Author: The River Towns of Connecticut, 1889; The Old English Manor, 1892; The Historical Development of Modern Europe, 2 vols., 1896, 1898; Contemporary Europe, Asia and Africa, 1871-1901, 1902; A History of England (text-book), 1903; Colonial Self-Government, 1652-1689 (Vol. V of The American Nation, A History), 1904; (with Miss Davenport) Guide to the Manuscript Materials for History of U.S. to 1783 in the British Museum, etc., 1908; British Commissions, Councils and Committees, 1622-1675, 1908; A Bibliography of History (with J. Montgomery Gambrill and Lida Lee Tall); A Short History of England, 1912; Guide to the Manuscript Materials for the History of the United States to 1783 in the Public Record Office, I, The State Papers, 1912, II, Departmental and Miscellaneous, 1914; The Colonial Period of American History (Home University Library), 1912; The Boston Merchants and the Non-Importation Movement, 1917; Fathers of New England, and Colonial Folkways (Chronicles of America Series), 1919; Journal of a Lady of Quality (editor with wife), 1921, 2d edit., 1934, 3d edit., 1939; Old Houses of Connecticut (ed. with Mrs. E. P. Trowbridge), 1923; The Colonial Background of the American Revolution, 1924, 1931; Our Earliest Colonial Settlements (Anson G. Phelps Lectures on Early American History, New York U.), 1933; Colonial Period of American History, Vol. I, 1934 (Pulitzer prize 1935), Vol. II, 1936, Vol. III, 1937, Vol. IV, 1938. Editor: Dickinson's God's Protecting Providence (with wife), 1942. Contributor Chapters IX and XIV, Volume I, Cambridge History of the Brit. Empire, 1929; also many printed addresses and articles in reviews and hist. jours. Home: 424 St. Ronan St., New Haven, Conn.; (Jan.-April) Jupiter, Fla.; (June-Oct.) East Dover, Vt. Died Sept. 9, 1943.

ANDREWS, Charles Oscar, U.S. senator; b. Ponce de Leon, Fla.; s. John and Mary Angers (Yon) A.; grad. Fla. State Normal Sch., 1901; U. of Fla., 1907; honorary LL.D., Rollins Coll., Winter Park, Fla., 1941; m. Margaret Spears, Nov. 24, 1909; children—Charles, Thomas Oakley, Edgar H. Sec. of bills in Fla. State senate, 1905-09; admitted to Fla. bar, 1907; judge Criminal Court of Record, Walton Co., Fla., 1910-11; asst. atty. gen. State of Fla., 1912-19; circuit judge 17th Judicial Circuit, 1919-25; mem. Fla. House of Reps., 1927; commissioner Fla. State Supreme Court, 1929-32; mem. U.S. Senate from Fla., term 1936-41; re-elected for 6-year term Nov. 5, 1940. Served as capt. Fla. Nat. Guard, 1904-06. Mem. Fla. State bar assn. (ex-pres.), Pi Kappa Alpha; hon. mem. Phi Delta Phi. Democrat. Presbyterian. Mason, K. of P. Clubs: University (Winter Park); Rotary (Orlando). Home: Orlando, Fla. Address: Senate Office Bldg., Washington, D.C. Died Sep. 18, 1946.

ANDREWS, Frank Maxwell, army officer; b. Nashville, Tenn., Feb. 3, 1884; s. James David and Louise (Maxwell) A.; student Montgomery Bell Acad., Nashville, 1897-1901; grad. U.S. Mil. Acad., 1906; student Air Corps Tactical Sch., 1927-28, Command and Gen. Staff Sch., 1928-29; grad. Army War Coll., 1933; m. Jeannette Allen, Mar. 16, 1914; children—Josephine, Allen, Jean. Commd. 2d lt. cav., June 12, 1906; through grades to col., Aug. 1, 1935; rank of lt. gen. (temp.), Sept 19, 1941. Served in Philippine Islands, 1906-07; in Hawaii, 1911-13; served with Signal Corps (aviation sec.), 1917-20; served with Am. Forces in Germany, 1920-23; returned to U.S. as exec. officer, Kelly Field, 1923-25; mem. War Dept. Gen. Staff, 1934-35; apptd. temp. brig. gen., Air Corps, Mar. 1, 1935, temp. maj. gen., Air Corps, Dec. 27, 1935; commanding G.H.Q. Air Force, Mar. 1, 1935-Feb. 28, 1939. Apptd. brig. gen. U.S. Army, July 14, 1939; mem. War Dept. Gen. Staff, 1939-40; comdr. Panama Dept., 1942; apptd. comdr. U.S. forces in European theatre, Feb. 1943. Decorated Comdr. Order of the Crown (Italy). Clubs: Army and Navy, Metropolitan (Washington). Killed in airplane accident over Iceland, May 3, 1943.

ANDREWS, Frank Mills, architect; b. Des Moines, Ia., Jan. 28, 1867; s. Lorenzo Frank and Sophia Maxwell (Dolson) A.; studied civil engring. Ia. State Coll., Ames, Ia.; B.A. in architecture Cornell U., 1888; m. Pauline Frederick, Sept. 8, 1909. Practiced, Chicago, 1893-1898, since in New York; architect Ky. State Capitol, Mont. State Capitol, Hotel Sinton, Cincinnati; Nat. Cash Register Co. plant, Dayton, O.; United Shoe Machinery Co. plant, Beverly, Mass.; Hotel McAlpine, New York; Arlington Hotel, Washington, Claypool Hotel, Indianapolis, Ind.; Seelbach Hotel, Louisville, Ky.; New Battle House, Mobile, Ala.; organized and financed the owning co. and architect Equitable Bldg., N.Y. City; financed Hotel McAlpine deal, involving $14,000,000; pres. Greeley Sq. Hotel Co. (New York), F. M. Andrews & Co.; v.p. Arlington Hotel Co.; dir. New Haven Co. Mem. Royal Soc. of Arts (London), Alpha Delta Phi. Republican. Clubs: Pendennis (Louisville, Ky.); Queen City (Cincinnati); Lambs (New York). Read paper on American Architecture before Royal Soc. of Arts, London, May, 1911, received society's medal therefor. Home: 36 Central Park, W. Office: 1 Madison Av., New York. Died Aug. 31, 1948.

ANDREWS, Garnett, mfr.; b. Washington, Ga., Sept. 15, 1870; s. Col. Garnett (C.S.A.) and Rosalie Champe (Beirne) A.; grad. Va. Mil. Inst., 1890; student Worcester Poly. Inst., 1889; m. Elizabeth Lenoir Key, Oct. 30, 1895. Identified with mfg. business since 1896; pres. Richmond Hosiery Mills since 1900. Served as capt. Tenn. Nat. Guard, 1890; mem. War Industries Board, Employment Service, Dept. of Labor, etc., World War. Mem. Alumni Assn. Va. Mil. Inst. (bd. govs.), Tenn. Soc. S.A.R., Soc. Colonial Wars. Republican. Episcopalian. Club: Mountain City. Home: Lookout Mountain, Chattanooga, Tenn. Office: Richmond Hosiery Mills, Rossville, Ga. Died Nov. 11, 1946.

ANDREWS, James Parkhill, lawyer; b. E. Windsor, Conn., Oct. 23, 1854; s. Samuel James and Catharine Augusta (Day) A.; B.A., Yale, 1877, LL.B., 1879; m. Julia Lincoln Ray, Aug. 27, 1895. In practice at Hartford, 1879-94; reporter Supreme Court of Errors, 1894-1924; now retired. Dir. Phoenix Mutual Life Ins. Co. Mem. Am. Bar Assn., Conn. State Bar Assn., Scroll and Key (Yale); trustee Conn. Inst. for the Blind, Conn. Junior Republic, Hartford Retreat. Republican. Conglist. Clubs: University, Musical, Monday Evening; Graduate (New Haven). Author: Index Digest of Connecticut Reports, 1883; Connecticut Index Digest, 1895. Editor Index Digest Com. Repts., 1924. Contbr. Yale Law Mag., Memorial History of Hartford County. Home: 1055 Prospect Av., Hartford, Conn. Died Sept. 10, 1936.

ANDREWS, John Bertram, economist; b. South Wayne, Lafayette County, Wis., Aug. 2, 1880; s. Philo Edmund and Sarah Jane (Maddrell) A.; A.B., U. of Wis., 1904, Ph.D., 1908; A.M., Dartmouth, 1905; m. Irene Osgood, Aug. 8, 1910; 1 son, John Osgood. Asst. in economics, Dartmouth Coll., 1904-05, U. of Wis., 1905-07; founder, 1911, and editor Am. Labor Legislation Review (quarterly); sec. and mem. exec. com. Am. Assn. for Labor Legislation since 1909. Chmn. Bur. of Economics Y.M.C.A. War Work Council, 1918-19; mem. hygiene reference bd. Life Extension Inst.; mem. New York Mayor's Com. on Unemployment, 1913-14; mem. President's Unemployment Conf., 1921; mem. Pa. Unemployment Com., 1931; mem. N.Y. Com. on Workmen's Compensation, 1931; consultant Social Security Board since 1937. Tech. adviser U.S. Govt. in London and asst. sec. in Washington to first official Internat. Labor Conf. under the League of Nations, 1919; mem. govt. delegation to Geneva, 1936; special agent U.S. Dept. of Labor, 1938-39; mem. Fed. Advisory Council, U.S. Employment Service. Asso. editor Documentary History of Am. Industrial Soc.; writer of U.S. Govt. reports on occupational diseases, resulting in abolition of poisonous phosphorus match, etc. Lecturer social legislation, Columbia U., 1920, 28, 30, 39, Univ. of Calif., 1921. Mem. Am. Econ. Assn., Am. Statis. Assn. Clubs: Author's (London); Cosmos (Washington, D.C.); Gipsy Trail, Nat. Arts. Author: Labor Problems and Labor Legislation, 1922; Administrative Labor Legislation, 1936; British Factory Inspection, 1937; Labor Laws in Action, 1938; State Insurance Funds, 1939. Joint Author: (with John R. Commons) Principles of Labor Legislation, 1916; History of Labor in the U.S., 1918. Home: 15 Gramercy Park. Office: 131 E. 23d St., New York, N.Y. Died Jan. 4, 1943.

ANDREWS, Matthew Page, editor, author; b. Shepherdstown, W.Va., July 15, 1879; s. Matthew Page and Anna (Robinson) A.; A.B., Washington and Lee U., 1901, A.M., 1902, Litt.D., 1924; unmarried. Teacher pvt. schools, Winchester, Va., 1902-04, Baltimore, 1904-11; lecturer, Colonial period U.S. history; editorial adviser, Yale Univ. Press, Chronicles of America Dept., 1923; chmn. Baltimore City George Washington Bi-Centennial Commn., 1932; Chmn. Md. Tercentenary Commn. of Baltimore, 1934. Episcopalian. Mem. Delta Tau Delta, Phi Beta Kappa. Club: University. Author: A History of the U.S., 1913; A Brief History of the United States, 1916; A Heritage of Freedom, 1918; Birth of America (play), 1920; American History and Government, 1921; The Book of the American's Creed, 1921; The Biggest Book in the World, 1925; History of Maryland—Province and State, 1929; The Founding of Maryland, 1933; Soul of Maryland—Pageant of the Founding, 1934; Virginia, The Old Dominion, 1937; The Soul of a Nation, Founding of Virginia and Projection of New England, 1943; Social Planning by Frontier Thinkers, 1944; Fountain Inn Diary, George Washington's Inn Site, 1947. Home: 845 Park Ave., Baltimore, Md. Died June 20, 1947.

ANDREWS, Philip, naval officer; b. N.Y. City, Mar. 31, 1866; grad. U.S. Naval Acad., 1886; m. Clara Fuller; 1 dau., Jean Andrews (wife of C.C.

Champion, Jr., U.S.N.). Ensign, July 1, 1888; promoted through grades to rear adm., July 1, 1918. Served on Bennington during Spanish-Am. War, 1898; on duty with gen. bd., Navy Dept., 1904-06; Bur. of Navigation, 1906-07; served on Kansas, 1907-09; at Naval War Coll., Newport, R.I., 1909; aide to Sec. of Navy, 1909-11; chief Bur. of Navigation, with rank of rear adm., 1911-13; duty gen. bd., 1913; comd. Montana, 1913, Maryland, 1913-14; comdr. Naval Training Sta., San Francisco, 1915-16; Naval War Coll., Newport, R.I., 1916-17; apptd. chief of staff, 5th Naval Dist., Mar. 29, 1917; comdr. Mississippi, Jan. 1918, U.S. Naval base, Cardiff, Wales, Sept. 1918, U.S. naval forces Eastern Mediterranean, 1919-21; comdt. Navy Yard, Norfolk, Va., 1921-23; also comdt. 5th Naval Dist., Jan.-June 1923; comdr. U.S. Naval Forces, Europe, with rank of vice adm., June 1923-Oct. 10, 1925; rear adm. comdg. 1st Naval Dist and Navy Yard, Boston, 1925-30; retired Apr. 1, 1930. Address. Navy Dept., Washington. Died Dec. 19, 1945.

ANDREWS, Thomas Galphin, lawyer; b. Orangeburg, S.C., Aug. 29, 1882; s. John D. and Belle (Darby) A.; student U. of Neb., lit. and law depts. also Neb. Business Coll.; m. Adelpha M. Wolgamatt, 1904 (died 1928); 1 son, Clyde L.; m. 2d, Reba Myers, 1930; children—Thomas Clyde, William Austin, John Marshall. Admitted to Okla. bar, 1911, began practice at Stroud; city atty., Stroud, 4 yrs., Chandler, 6 yrs., county atty., 4 yrs.; justice Supreme Court of Okla., Jan. 14, 1929-Jan. 14, 1935. Mem. Am. and Okla. State bar assns., Phi Delta Phi. Mason (K.T., Shriner, 33°), Past Grand Master Grand Lodge I.O.O.F. of Okla.; rep. to Sovereign Grand Lodge I.O.O.F., 14 years; chmn. com. of three in preparation of funeral ceremony, and mem. com. of five in preparation of new rituals of Sovereign Grand Lodge I.O.O.F., chmn. Judiciary Com.; elected Deputy Grand Sire I.O.O.F., 1936, Grand Sire, 1937-38. Republican. Mem. Christian (Disciples) Ch. Clubs: Oklahoma, Men's Dinner, Lions International, Okla. Golf and Country. Author: The Jericho Road; The Mountain; A Juridical History; etc. Home: 1200 W. 20th St. Office: 905 Perrine Bldg., Oklahoma City, Okla. Died Sep. 1942.

ANDREWS, Walter Gresham, congressman; b. at Evanston, Ill., July 16, 1889; s. William Henry and Kate (Gresham) A.; grad. Lawrenceville (N.J.) Sch., 1908; LL.B., Princeton, 1913; unmarried. Head coach Princeton football team, 1913; dir. and mem. exec. com. Pratt & Lamberg, Inc. Mem. 72d to 80th Congresses (1931-49), 42d New York Dist.; chmn. armed services com. With U.S. Army, Mexican Border and France, 1916-19, advancing to rank of major, 107th Inf.; wounded in attack on Hindenburg Line, 1918. Decorated Distinguished Service Cross. Member Am. Legion. Republican. Presbyterian. Clubs: Saturn, Buffalo; Tiger Inn (Princeton); Metropolitan (Washington). Home: 172 Summer St. Office: U.S. Court House, Buffalo, N.Y. Died Mar. 5, 1949.

ANGELESCO, Constantin, diplomat; b. Bucharest, Roumania, June 4, 1869; s. Demetre and Theodora A.; grad. U. of Paris, 18:9; unmarried. Prof. clin. surgery, Bucharest U., since 1904; mem. Roumanian Parliament, 1900-18; minister pub. works and railroads, Roumania, 1914-17; prominent in sanitary orgn. of Roumanian Army; E.E. and M.P. from Roumania to U.S. since Jan. 1, 1918. Address: 1712 Connecticut Av., Washington. Died Sept. 14, 1948.

ANGELL, James Rowland, educator, psychologist; b. Burlington, Vt., May 8, 1869; s. Dr. James Burrill and Sarah Swope (Caswell) A.; bro. of Alexis Caswell Angell; A.B., U. of Mich., 1890, A.M., 1891; A.M., Harvard, 1892; Litt.D., U. of Vt., 1915; LL.D., Yale, Harvard, Princeton, Columbia, Chicago, Union, Cincinnati, McGill, Wesleyan (Conn.), Brown, Middlebury, Ill. Coll., U. of Mich., Wabash, U. of Calif., New York U., Williams Coll., Dartmouth Coll., Rutgers, University of Pennsylvania, Pennsylvania Military College, and hon. Ph.D., Rensselaer Polytech.; univs. of Berlin and Halle, 1893; traveled and studied at Vienna, Paris, Leipzig, etc.; m. Marion Isabel Watrous, Dec. 18, 1894 (died June 23, 1931); children—James Waterhouse, Marion Waterhouse, Caswell (Mrs. William Rockefeller McAlpin); m. 2d, Mrs. Katharine Cramer Woodman, Aug. 2, 1932. Instr. philosophy, Univ. of Minn., 1893; asst. prof. psychology and dir. psychol. lab., 1894-1901, asso. prof., 1901-05; prof. and head of dept., 1905-19, sr. dean, 1908-11, dean univ. faculties, 1911-19, acting pres., 1918-19, U. of Chicago; pres. Carnegie Corporation, 1920-21; president Yale University, 1921-37; ednl. counselor Nat. Broadcasting Co. since 1937. Exchange prof., The Sorbonne, Paris, 1914. Lecturer Univ. of California Wellesley Coll., Columbia U., Stanford U., etc.; Ichabod Spencer lecturer, Union U. Mem. psychology com. of Nat. Research Council; mem. com. of the adj. gen.'s office on classification of personnel in the Army, 1917-18; advisory mem. com. on edn. and spl. training, 1918; chmn. Nat. Research Council, 1919-20; dir. New York Life Ins. Co., Nat. Broadcasting Co.; vice-pres. Nat. Com. for Mental Hygiene, Internat. Com. for Mental Hygiene. Decorated Chevalier Legion of Honor, 1930, Officer, 1931; Grand Officer of the Order of the Crown of Italy, 1935; Chinese Blue Grand Cordon Order of the Jade, 1937; gold medal Nat. Inst. Social Science, 1937. Trustee Am. Museum Natural History since 1937; curator Stephens Coll., 1937; dir. Museum of Science and Industry, 1941; director Hall of Fame, 1941. Fellow American Academy Arts and Sciences; mem. American Psychological Assn. (pres. 1906), Am. Philos. Soc., Nat. Acad. Sciences, Conn. Soc. of Cincinnati, Berzelius and Aurelian socs., English-Speaking Union (nat. pres. since June 1939), Phi Beta Kappa, Sigma Xi, Delta Kappa Epsilon, Kappa Delta Pi; hon. mem. British Psychol. Soc. Clubs: Graduate (New Haven, Conn.); Yale, University (Boston); Century, Yale (New York); Cosmos (Washington, D.C.); University (Chicago). Author: Psychology (4th edit.), 1908; Chapters from Modern Psychology, 1911; Introduction to Psychology, 1913; American Education, 1937; also many articles in scientific jours. Editor of Psychological Monographs, 1912-22. Home: 155 Blake Road, Hamden, Conn. Died Mar. 3, 1949.

ANGIER, Roswell Parker (ăn'jẽr), psychologist; b. St. Paul, Minn., Oct. 21, 1874; s. Albert Edgar and Emma Frances (McNeil) A.; A.B., Harvard, 1897, A.M., 1901, Ph.D., 1903; studied at univs. of Berlin and Freiburg, Germany, 1903-06; A.M., Yale, 1917; m. Genevieve Severy, Sept. 2, 1907; children—Roswell Parker, James Severy, Philip Holt. Asst. Physiol. Lab., U. of Berlin, 1905-06; instr. psychology, Yale, 1906-08, asst. prof. 1908-17, prof., 1917-41, dir. Psychol. Lab., 1917-41, dean of freshmen, 1920-prof. of psychology and dir. of Lab. of Psychology, emeritus, since 1941. Visiting prof. Harvard, 1917, U. of Chicago, 1925. Capt. sanitary corps, U.S. Army, 1918-19. Mem. Am. Psychol. Assn., Am. Philos. Assn., Am. Physiol. Soc., Delta Upsilon, Sigma Xi. Home: R.F.D. Route 4, Box 686, Tucson, Ariz. Died June 24, 1946.

ANKENY, John D'Art, banker; b. Walla Walla, Wash., Sept. 17, 1879; s. Levi and Jennie (Nesmith) A.; ed. Shattuck Mil. Sch., Faribault, Minn., and Whitman Coll., Walla Walla; m. Mary Ridpath, July, 1906; children—Jane Ridpath (Mrs. Thos. P. Gose, Jr.), Frances Marian (Mrs. Emmett Lynch). Pres. 1st Nat. Bank of Walla Walla, Columbia Nat. Bank (Dayton, Wash.), Wahluke Investment Co. Mason, Odd Fellow, Elk. Republican. Home: 808 S. Palouse St. Office: 1st Nat. Bank, of Walla Walla, Wash. Died Oct. 1, 1942.

ANKENEY, John Sites (ăngk'nē), art educator, painter; b. Xenia, O., Apr. 21, 1870; s. John Sites and Margaret Edelia (Hutchison) A.; art edn., Art Students League, N.Y., 1889-90, 1892-93, Paris, 1893, 94, 95, 1903-04, Europe, 1905, 08, 12, Summer Sch., Harvard, 1901, 14; A.B., U. of Mo., 1906; Litt.D., Bethany Coll., 1926; m. Mrs. Lucy Gentry Tindall, Oct. 16, 1901; stepson, Richard Gentry Tindall, brig. gen., U.S. Army. Instr. in art, U. of Missouri, 1901, asst. prof., 1905, asso. prof., 1911, prof., 1913-35, on leave, 1929-35, retired, 1935; dir. and curator Dallas (Tex.) Mus. of Fine Arts, 1929-34; regional dir. for Pub. Works Art Project, Okla. and Tex., 1933-34; mem. advisory com. on decoration Post Office and Justice buildings, Washington, D.C., 1935, and Dept. of Interior Building, 1936; prof. fine arts and head of dept., La. State U., 1935-37. Rep. in collections of U. of Mo.; Lindenwood Coll., St. Charles, Mo.; Smoky River Art Club, Lindsborg, Kan.; Carl Milles Coll., Cranbrook, Mich.; Mrs. Leslie M. Maitland Coll., Estes Park, Colo., and Los Angeles; Mrs. Massey Holmes' Collection, Kansas City, Mo. Mem. Art Commn. for Central West, Panama-Pacific Expn., 1915; mem. Am. hon. com., Fontainebleau (France) Sch. Fine Arts, since 1923; leader Bureau Univ. Travel, 1929; mem. Am. advisory com., Internat. Congress Art Edn., London, 1908, mem. Am. official com., Dresden, Germany, 1912. Mem. Western Arts Assn. (treas. 1901-02; pres. 1902-03; chmn. com. on conditions of art work in colls. and univs. 1907-11), Coll. Art Assn. America (chmn. com. on orgn. 1912), Am. Assn. Univ. Profs., Am. Fedn. of Arts, Am. Artists Protective League, State Hist. Soc. of Mo., Phi Mu Alpha, Delta Phi Delta. Episcopalian. Clubs: National Arts of New York (artist mem.); University (Columbia). Contbr. papers on art history and edn. Home: 1605 East University Av., Columbia, Mo.; (summer) The Lark, High Drive, Estes Park, Colo. Died May 16, 1946.

ANSBERRY, Timothy Thomas, lawyer; b. Defiance, O., Dec. 24, 1871; s. Edward and Elizabeth (Fitzpatrick) A.; ed. pub. schs., Defiance; LL.B., U. of Notre Dame, Ind., 1893; m. Nelle Kettenring; 1 son, Peter K. Began practice in Defiance, 1893; justice of the peace, 1893-95; pros. atty., Defiance County, 1895-1903. Dem. candidate for Congress, 1904; mem. 60th to 63d Congresses (1907-15), 5th Ohio Dist.; mem. Ways and Means Com. 62d and 63d Congresses; resigned, 1915, to accept asso. judgeship Court of Appeals of Ohio; resigned 1916 and removed to Washington, D.C.; presdl. elector from Ohio, 1916. Del. Dem. Nat. Conv., 1920, 24, 28. Catholic. Clubs: Lotos (New York); Toledo (Toledo, Ohio); Chevy Chase, Metropolitan (Washington, D.C.); Bath, Indian Creek Golf (Miami Beach, Fla.). Home: 1901 Wyoming Av. Office: 1317 F St., Washington, D.C. Died July 5, 1943.

ANSPACHER, Louis Kaufman (ăns'päk-ẽr), dramatist, lecturer; b. Cincinnati, O., Mar. 1, 1878; s. Leopold Henry and Rosa (Kaufman) A.; A.B., Coll. City of New York, 1897; A.M., Columbia, 1899, LL.B., 1902; studied Post-Grad. Sch. of Philosophy, Columbia, 1902-05; m. Kathryn Kidder, actress, 1905; m. 2d, Florence Sutro Esberg, 1940. Secular lecturer at Temple Emanuel, New York, 1902-05; mem. lecture staff, League for Polit. Edn., N.Y. City, since 1906, Brooklyn Inst. Arts and Sciences since 1908; lecturer for Univ. Extension Center, N.Y. City; mem. Staff Civic Forum Lecture Bur. since its formation. Recipient Townsend Harris Award, 1945. Mem. Phi Beta Kappa. Republican. Clubs: Lotos, Players (New York). Author: (plays) Tristan and Isolde (poetical drama), 1904; Embarrassment of Riches, 1906; Anne and the Archduke John, 1907, The Woman of Impulse, 1909; The Glass House, 1912; The Washerwoman Duchess, 1913; Our Children, 1914; The Unchastened Woman, 1915; That Day, 1917; Madame Cecile, 1918; The Rape of Belgium (with Max Marcin), 1918; Daddalums, 1919; The Dancer (with Max Marcin), 1919; All the King's Horses, 1920; The New House, 1921; Dagmar, 1923; Rhapsody, 1930; Our Children, 1933; The Jazz Clown, 1933; The Intruder, 1934; This Bewildered Age, 1935; A Way of Life, 1937; Passing the Torch, 1939; The Achievement of Happiness, 1940; They Saw the Light, 1941; Slow Harvest, 1943; The Story of Liberty, 1944; Shakespeare as Poet and Lover, 1944; The Master Race Mentality, 1945; Anniversary Ode, 1946; Challenge of the Unknown, 1947. Home: Allegro, Purchase, N.Y. Died May 10, 1947.

ANTISDEL, Clarence Baumes, clergyman, educator; b. Afton, Wis., Nov. 18, 1863; s. Josiah Fuller and Mariette Baumes (Antisdel) A.; student U. of Chicago, 1883-86; B.A., U. of S. Dak., 1888, M.A., 1889, LL.D., 1922; B.D., U. of Chicago, 1892; m. Gerdena S. Vander Kolk, Oct. 27, 1896. Ordained Bapt. ministry, 1892; ednl. missionary to Congo, Africa, under Am. Bapt. Fgn. Missionary Soc., 1892-1905; missionary in Burma, 1905-13; prof. English, Benedict Coll., Columbia, S.C., 1919-21, pres. since 1921. Mem. Delta Kappa Epsilon, Phi Beta Kappa. Home: Columbia, S.C. Died Oct. 27, 1943.

ANTONIA, Sister, coll. pres. emeritus; b. Omaha, Neb., May 17, 1873; d. Patrick and Rose (Welch) McHugh; prep. edn., St. Jospeh's Acad., St. Paul, Minn., and St. Mary's Acad., Winnipeg, Man., Can.; A.B. and B.Ed., U. of Chicago, 1908, A.M., 1910; grad. study at Columbia U., U. of Minnesota and one year in Europe; LL.D., U. of Minn., 1936. Teacher St. Joseph's Acad., 1891-1904, Coll. of St. Catherine, 1904-05, 1909-14, dean, 1914-29, pres., 1917-38; now pres. emeritus. Mem. of White House Children's Conf., under President Hoover, 1929. Awarded Medal Pro Ecclesia et Pontifice by Pius XI. Mem. Am. Hist. Assn., Am. Chem. Soc., Am. Assn. Univ. Women, Phi Beta Kappa (pres. Gamma Chapter, U. of Minn., since 1938). Address: Coll. of St. Catherine, St. Paul, Minn. Died Oct. 11, 1944.

APPEL, John Wilberforce, Jr., merchant; b. Lancaster, Pa., Feb. 28, 1887; s. John and Ella Julia (Roberts) A.; A.B., Franklin and Marshall Coll., Lancaster, Pa., 1905, Harvard, 1906; grad. study New York U. and Columbia; m. Ethel M. Smith, July 2, 1910; children—Marianne Greer, Sarah Roberts, Ethel Dean, John Wilberforce. With John Wanamaker, N.Y. City, 1906; dir. Hartsdale Nat. Bank. Mem. Phi Kappa Psi. Republican. Presbyterian. Clubs: Harvard, Racquet and Tennis; Scarsdale Golf; Bedford Golf; American Yacht; Princes Tennis and Rackets, Royal Mid-Surrey Golf (London); St. Cloud Golf (Paris). U.S. amateur squash tennis champion, 1919. Home: 26 Walworth Av., Scarsdale, N.Y. Office: 184 Broadway, New York. Died Aug. 25, 1942.

APPEL, Joseph Herbert (ăp'pĕl), author and merchant; b. Lancaster, Pa., July 19, 1873; s. of Thomas Gilmore (pres. Franklin and Marshall Coll., 1878-90) and Emma Matilda (Miller) A.; A.B., Franklin and Marshall, 1892, LL.D., 1927; M.C.S., Bryant-Stratton Coll., Providence, R.I., 1931; m. Venie E. Wood, June 27, 1900; 1 son, Joseph Herbert. Admitted to Lancaster County bar, 1895, Phila. bar, 1897; with editorial dept. Phila. Times, 1896-99; with John Wanamaker since 1899, dir. adv. and publicity, Phila. store until 1912, New York store, 1912-34, exec. mgr. New York store, 1934-36, dir. 1936-40; dir. Better Business Bureau, N.Y. City, 1939-45; mem. board of trustees Franklin and Marshall Coll. Exec. chmn. loyalty com. of Mayor's Com. on Nat. Defense, New York, 1918; sec. Mayor's Com. Permanent War Memorial for N.Y. City, 1918-22; dir. Advertising Fedn. of America, 1930-38 (treas. 1930-32, now mem. adv. com.); mem. nat. adv. council Boston Conf. on Distribution. Founding mem., trustee Business History Foundation, Inc., 1947. Mem. Pa. Soc. of New York, Phi Kappa Psi. Republican. Member Reformed Church in America. Clubs: Poor Richard (Philadelphia); Advertising, New York. Author: My Own Story, 1913; Seeing America, 1916; Living the Creative Life, 1918; The Making of a Man, 1921; A World Cruise Log, 1926; John Wanamaker, a Study, 1927; Africa's White Magic, 1928; Business Biography of John Wanamaker, Founder and Builder, 1930; Man Proposes, 1933; The Whimsey Imp Goes 'Round the World Under the Southern Cross (privately circulated), 1937; Growing Up With Advertising, 1940; Home: 50 Riverside Drive, New York 24, N.Y. Died July 26, 1949.

APPLE, Henry Harbaugh, educator; b. Mercersburg, Pa., Nov. 8, 1869; s. Thomas Gilmore (pres. Franklin and Marshall Coll., 1878-90) and Emma (Miller) A.; A.B., Franklin and Marshall Coll., 1889, A.M., 1892; grad. Theol. Sem. of Reformed Church in U.S., 1892; D.D., Lafayette, 1909; LL.D., Univ. of Pa., 1913, U. of Pittsburgh, 1919, Heidelberg U., 1925, Ursinus Coll., 1934, Franklin & Marshall Coll., 1935; m.

Florence Emma Herr, Nov. 8, 1894; 1 dau., Emma (dec.). Ordained Ref. Ch. ministry, 1892; pastor St. John's Ch., Phila. 1892-98, Trinity Ch., York, Pa., 1898-1909; pres. Franklin and Marshall Coll., Lancaster, Pa., 1909-35, pres. emeritus since 1935; now serving as chmn. Draft Board, Selective Service Act. Pres. Phila. Classis, 1896, Zion Classis, 1902, Potomac Synod, 1905; mem. exec. com. Bd. Home Missions. Chaplain York City Fire Dept. (vol. dept. of 2,000 men), 1900-09; pres. Schubert Choir. Served during World War as chmn. United War Work in Lancaster County, chmn. Fed. Labor Bd. for Lancaster County.; chmn Civic Com. for War Memorial. Decorated Cross of Merit by Hungarian Govt., 1934. Mem. Coll. and Univ. Council Pa., York County Hist. Soc., Lancaster County Hist. Soc., Phi Kappa Psi, Phi Beta Kappa, Am. Acad. Polit. and Social Science, Am. Philos. Soc.; pres. Assn. of Schs., Colls. and Seminaries of Reformed Ch. in U.S.; pres. Assn. Pa. Coll. Presidents, 1920-21; pres. Lancaster Chamber of Commerce, 1928-29. Republican. Clubs: Hamilton, Country. Home: 60 N. West End Av., Lancaster Pa. Died May 19, 1943.

APPLE, Joseph Henry, educator; b. Rimersburg, Pa., Aug. 4, 1865; s. Rev. Joseph Henry and Elizabeth Ann (Geiger) A.; A.B., Franklin and Marshall Coll., 1885, A.M., 1888, hon. Ph.D., 1911; LL.D., Ursinus Coll., 1916; Temple U., 1932, Franklin and Marshall Coll., 1933; m. Mary E. Rankin, Dec. 27, 1892 (died Dec. 2. 1896); children—Miriam Rankin, Charlotte Elizabeth (dec.); m. 2d, Gertrude Harner, Nov. 23, 1898; children—Mrs. Elizabeth Apple McCain, Mrs. Emily Gertrude Payne, Joseph Henry. Prin. high sch. and prof. math., Clarion and Pittsburgh, Pa., 1885-93; pres. Hood (formerly Woman's) Coll., 1893-1934, now pres. emeritus. Dir. Frederick Hotel Co. Chmn. campaign com. for new Y.M.C.A. bldg., 1906; pres. Y.M.C.A., 1908-13. Exec. sec. Forward Movement, Reformed Ch. U.S., 1919-26; pres. Potomac Synod of Reformed Ch. in U.S., 1935-36. Chmn. campaign com. Frederick County Memorial Assn., 1926; mem. Md. Pub. Library Commn. since 1912, pres., 1917; mem. bd. of regents, Mercersburg Acad., since 1935. Mem. Frederick County Hist. Soc. (pres.); chmn. Greek War Relief Assn., Inc. (Frederick County campaign); mem. Sons of American Revolution (pres. Frederick branch; mem. nat. ednl. com.), Phi Beta Kappa (chmn. Defense Fund for dist.), Phi Kappa Psi. Mason. Clubs: Cosmos (Washington, D.C.); Rotary, Lions (Frederick). Author: Frederick in Song and Story, 1935. Lecturer and writer. Honored by community at fortieth anniversary as pres. Hood Coll., May 12, 1933, as "oldest college president in point of service." Home: 323 N. College Parkway, Frederick, Md. Died Jan. 17, 1948; buried at Frederick, Md.

APPLEBY, Troy Wilson, pres. Ohio Nat. Life Ins. Co.; b. Morrisville, Mo., Oct. 2, 1874; s. Benjamin Wilson and Susan Ellen (Hamilton) A.; A.B., Morrisville (Mo.) Coll., 1899, A.M., 1900; grad. student U. of Chicago, 1902-03; D.L.H., Union Coll., Barbourville, Ky., 1941; m. Nancy Augustia Finley, Oct. 2, 1895. Instr. in Morrisville, Coll., 1900-02; teacher in high sch., 1903-05; sec. and actuary Central Life Ins. Co. of Ill., 1905-10; sec. Federal Life Ins. Co., Chicago, 1910-14; actuary Ohio Nat. Life Ins. Co., 1914-16, sec., and actuary, 1916-22, pres. since 1922. Member board Cincinnati Street Railway Company; member bd. of dirs. Cincinnati Community Chest; member board Travelers Aid Society, Cincinnati; member board Citizenship Council (all Hamilton County); member board and executive committee Bethesda Hosp.; chmn. board Boy Rangers of Am.; state chmn. United China Relief; trustee Ohio Wesleyan U. (Del., O.), MacMurray Coll. (Jacksonville, Ill.), Union Coll. (Barbourvile, Ky.); mem. Nat. Affairs Com., Cincinnati Chamber of Commerce; trustee Y.M.C.A., Cincinnati; mem. Uniting Conf. of Methodist Chs.; trustee at large of Meth. Ch.; vice chmn. Bd. of Publs., Meth. Church. Fellow Am. Inst. of Actuaries. Methodist (trustee). Mason (32°). Clubs: Queen City, Cincinnati. Home: Grasmoor House, 2374 Madison Rd., Cincinnati; and Oaklawn Farm, Springfield, Mo. Office: 2400 Reading Rd., Cincinnati, O. Died Apr. 21, 1947.

APPLETON, Charles W., lawyer; b. Brockton, Mass., Nov. 9, 1874; s. Oliver D. and Susan A. (Hull) A.; B.S., St. Lawrence U., 1897; LL.B., New York Law Sch., 1899; LL.D. from St. Lawrence Univ., 1929; m. Harriet Russel Ferry, June 30, 1902; children—Oliver D., John R. Began practice at N.Y. City, 1899; asst. dist. atty. New York County, 1903-10, instr. Brooklyn Law Sch., 1909-18; city magistrate, New York, 1910-18; counsel Gen. Electric Co., 1918-27, v.p., 1927; dir. Electric Securities Co. Trustee St. Lawrence U., Rockefeller Inst. Med. Research; mem. Citizens Crime Commn. Mem. Am., N.Y. State and N.Y. County bar assns., Assn. Bar City of N.Y., U.S.C. of C., Merchants Assn., Am. Transit Assn., New England Soc., Acad. of Polit. Science, Alpha Tau Omega, Phi Delta Phi, Phi Beta Kappa. Democrat. Episcopalian. Clubs: Manhattan, Bankers, University, Bedford G & T, Sleepy Hollow Country. Home: 812 Park Av. Office: 570 Lexington Av., New York. Died Jan. 10, 1945.

APPLETON, William Sumner, antiquarian; b. Boston, Mass., May 29, 1874; s. William Sumner and Edith Stuart (Appleton) A.; desc. of Samuel Appleton, who came to America, 1636; A.B., Harvard, 1896; unmarried. Organizer Soc. for Preservation of New Eng. Antiquities (inc., 1910), sec. and gen. manager. Member First Corps Cadets, Mass. Vol. Militia, 3 yrs. Mem. Mass. Hist. Soc., and many others. Clubs: Harvard (Boston and New York), Union. Home: 16 Louisburg Square. Office: 141 Cambridge St., Boston, Mass. Died Nov. 24, 1947.

ARBUCKLE, Howard Bell, chemist; b. near Lewisburg, W.Va., Oct. 5, 1870; s. John Davis Arbuckle and Elizabeth (Van Lear) A.; B.A., with first honor, Hampden-Sidney Coll., 1889, M.A., 1890; spl. student in chemistry, U. of Va., 1894-95; Ph.D., in Chemistry from Johns Hopkins University, 1898; m. Ida Meginniss, June 4, 1896; children—Howard Bell, Adèle Taylor (Mrs. Donald Rohl). Fellowship at Hampden-Sidney Coll., 1889-90; prof. ancient langs., Seminary West of Suwanee (foundation for U. of Fla.), 1891-94; teacher, and prof. Agnes Scott Inst. (later coll.), Decatur, Ga., 1898-1912; prof. chemistry, Davidson (N.C.) Coll., since 1913. A founder of Continental Dorset Club for registry of pure bred Dorset sheep; contbg. editor Am. Sheep Breeder, 1900-20; founder Edgewood Stock Farm and brought over selected importation of sheep from Eng., 1901. Pres. N.C. Jersey Breeders Assn., 1930, Mem. Am. Red Poll Breeders Assn., Am. Aberdeen-Angus Breeders Assn., Continental Dorset Club (a founder), Am. Chem. Soc. (founder and ex-press. Ga. sect., ex-pres. N.C. sect.), N.C. Acad. Science (pres. 1925), Pi Kappa Alpha (councilor princeps, 1900-05; grand councilor, 1913-33), Gamma Sigma Epsilon (honorary chemical; grand chancellor 1920-28), Phi Beta Kappa, Omicron Delta Kappa, Scabbard and Blade. Presbyterian. Clubs: Kenmore Golf (founder; pres. 1925-30), Symposium (Atlanta, Ga.). Author: Redetermination of the Atomic Weight of Zinc and Cadmium, 1898; Laboratory Manual in Household Chemistry, 1912; The Life and Habits of the Honey Bee, 1925. Contbr. numerous articles to chem. lit. and agrl. jours. Researches in corn proteins and cellulose products; discovered pyrolene. Home: Davidson, N.C.; (summer) "Maplemont." Maxwelton Greenbrier County, W.Va.* Died July 19, 1945.

ARCHER, Shreve MacLaren, pres. Archer-Daniels-Midland Co.; b. Yankton, S.D., Sept. 29, 1888; s. George Alfred and Harriet Harkness (Cunningham) A.; student Hill Sch., 1904-07, Sheffield Scientific Sch. (Yale), 1907-10; m. Doris Cowley, Sept. 26, 1911; children—Helen Harriet (Mrs. Edwin J. Moles, Jr.), Georganna (Mrs. Joseph C. Uihlein, Jr.), Barbara, Doris L., Shreve M. Pres. Archer-Daniels-Midland Co.; chmn. bd., mem. executive com., Northwest Airlines, Inc.; dir. St. Paul Fire & Marine Ins. Co., First Nat. Bank (St. Paul), First Bank Stock Corp., Northwest Bancorporation, Gt. Northern Ry. Clubs: Minneapolis; Minnesota, White Bear Yacht, University (St. Paul). Home: 990 Summit Av., St. Paul, Minn. Office: 600 Roanoke Bldg., Minneapolis, Minn.* Died Nov. 10, 1947.

ARCHER, Thomas P., v.p., dir., Gen. Motors Corp.; b. Centerburg, O., Mar. 1, 1885; s. William G. and Jennie (Porter) A.; m. Frances Buell, June 30, 1933. Began as reporter, 1903; with J. V. Pilcher Mfg. Co., Louisville, Ky., and Windsor, Ont., 1906-17; became pressroom foreman Ternstedt Mfg. Co. (later div. of Gen. Motors Corp.), 1919; gen. mgr. Ternstedt Mfg. Div., 1926-29, dir. operations Fisher Body Div., 1929-43, v.p. Gen. Motors Corp., 1943, gen. mgr. Fisher Div., 1944-46, group exec. since 1946. Served U.S. Naval Air Service, 1917-19. Mem. bd. regents Gen. Motors Inst. Clubs: Detroit Athletic, Bloomfield Hills Country, Recess (Detroit), Country Club. Home: 87 Kenwood Rd., Grosse Pointe Farms 30, Mich. Office: General Motors Bldg., Detroit 2, Mich. Died Aug. 10, 1949.

ARGÜELLO, Leonardo (är-gwäl'yō), Nicaraguan physician and public man; b. Leon, 1875; s. Dr. Santiago Argüello and Carmen Barreto de Argüello; ed. U. of León (Dr. of medicine, surgery, and pharmacy, 1895); further study in Europe; m. Adela de Argüello; 8 children. Head of Municipal Council, León; Nat. deputy during various periods; pres. Nat. Congress; designated pres. of Republic; minister, pub. edn.; sec. fgn. relations; head of Nicaraguan delegation to 7th Pan-Am. Conf., Montevideo; now minister fgn. relations. Mem. Academia Nicaragüense de la Lengua correspondiente de la Española Académie Diplomatique Internationale (Paris), Sociedad Médica de Nicaragua, Real Academia Española. Author: Por el honor de un partido; El caso Nicaragua; Paz, patria y liberalismo; La política. Address: Managua, Nicaragua. Died Dec. 15, 1947.

ARKELL, Bartlett (är-kěl'), mfr. foods; b. Canajoharie, N.Y., June 10, 1862; s. James and Sarah Hall (Bartlett) A.; grad. Williston Sem., 1882; B.A., Yale Univ., 1886; m. Carrie Clark, 1886 (dec.); 1 son, William Clark; m. 2d, Louisiana Grigsby, 1900 (dec.); m. 3d, Louise Ryals, June 14, 1929. Was pres. Imperial Packing Co. at its formation and pres. Beech-Nut Packing Co., Canajoharie, N.Y., its successor, until Apr. 1941, now chmn. of bd. Clubs: Union League, University, Lotos. Home: 15 W. 10th St. Office: 10 E. 40th St., New York, N.Y. Died Oct. 12, 1946.

ARKWRIGHT, Preston Stanley (ärk'rīt), pres. Ga. Power Co.; b. Savannah, Ga., Feb. 24, 1871; s. Thomas and Martha (Stanley) A.; B.Ph., U. of Ga., 1890, LL.B., 1891; LL.D., Emory Univ., 1940; m. Dorothy Colquitt, June 2, 1896; children—Dorothy C. (wife of Glenville Giddings, M.D.), Preston S. Practiced law at Atlanta, 1891-1901; pres. Ga. Ry. & Electric Co., 1902-12, Ga. Ry. & Power Co., 1912-26, Ga. Power Co. since 1927; also pres. Atlanta Northern Ry.; dir. Commonwealth & Southern Corp. Democrat. Methodist. Home: 1585 Ponce de Leon Av. Office: 558 Electric Bldg., Atlanta, Ga.* Died Nov. 6, 1947.

ARLISS, George, actor; b. London, Eng., Apr. 10, 1868; s. William Arliss-Andrews; ed. in London; hon. M.A., Columbia, 1919; m. Florence Montgomery, of London, Sept. 16, 1899. Made first appearance on stage at Elephant and Castle Theatre, London, 1887; first tour in America with Mrs. Patrick Campbell's Co., 1901; played rôle of Zakkuri in The Darling of the Gods, with Blanche Bates, 1902; later with Mrs. Fiske; appeared as The Devil in play of that name, at Belasco Theatre, New York, 1908; toured in title rôle of Disraeli, 1911, Paganini, 1916, Hamilton, 1917; played in Green Goddess in America, 1921-23, St. James's Theatre (London), 1923-24; Old English, 1924-27; The Merchant of Venice, 1928-29; appeared in talking pictures, notably "Disraeli," "The Man Who Played God," "Voltaire," "Hamilton," "A Successful Calamity," "The Last Gentleman," "Cardinal Richelieu," "The Working Man," "The King's Vacation," "Old English," "The House of Rothschild," "The Iron Duke," "Mr. Hobo," "East Meets West," "A Man of Affairs," "Dr. Syn." Fellow Royal Soc. of Arts, 1934. Clubs: Players, Coffee House (New York); Cliff-Dwellers (Chicago); Franklin Inn (Philadelphia); Garrick, Green Room (London). Author: The Wild Rabbit, 1899; There and Back, 1900; The West End (with Sir George Dance), 1902; Widow Weeds, 1910; Hamilton (with Mrs. Hamlin), 1917; What Shall It Profit (with Brander Matthews), 1927; (autobiography) Up the Years from Bloomsbury, 1927; My Ten Years in the Studios, 1940. Home: 1 Clifton Villas, Maida Hill, London, W. 9, England. Died Feb. 5, 1946.

ARMITAGE, Paul, lawyer; b. Brooklyn, N.Y., Feb. 10, 1873; s. Herbert Grayson and Helen Harbeck (Halsted) A.; B.A., Columbia, 1894, LL.B., 1896; m. Alice Watson, May 23, 1900; children—Thomas Watson, Virginia. Practiced N.Y. City since 1896; mem. Douglas, Armitage & Halloway; dir. United Hazeltine Corp., G. R. Kinney Co., Latour Corp. Mem. Am. Bar Assn., Bar Assn. City of New York, New York County Bar Assn., Am. Inst. Mining and Metall. Engrs., Acad. Polit. Science, Psi Upsilon. Office: 30 Rockefeller Plaza, New York 20, N.Y.* Died June 28, 1949.

ARMOUR, Bernard R., pres. Heyden Chem. Corp., Am. Aniline Products, Inc.; offr. or dir. other corps. Home: 45 Gramercy Park. Office: 50 Union Sq., New York, N.Y.* Died Dec. 1, 1949.

ARMBRECHT, William Henry (ärm'brěkt), lawyer; b. Port Chester, N.Y., Feb. 9, 1874; s. Caesar and Anna Johanna (Kraft) A.; ed. pub. high sch., Knoxville, Tenn., and pvt. tutors; m. Anna Bell Paterson, Dec. 1, 1897 (dec.); children—Conrad Paterson, Mrs. Mary Bell Hale, Mrs. Elizabeth Ann Crichton, William Henry; m. 2d, Mrs. Harrison Howell, Oct. 16, 1940. Admitted to Ala. bar, 1895; atty. Mobile & Ohio R.R., 1898-99; practiced law at Mobile as mem. of various firms since 1899; U.S. atty. So. Dist. Ala., 1904, resigned, 1911; spl. asst. to U.S. atty.-gen., 1906-12 (prosecuted Honduras Lottery case, 1906; spl. counsel for govt. in civil and criminal cases, 1908-12); spl. counsel in financial matters for Mobile (city and county) 1923 and 1927; has served as trial lawyer in State and Federal Courts (including U.S. Supreme Court) for public utilities, bondholders coms. and railroads; now sr. mem. Armbrecht, Inge, Twitty & Jackson. Dir., v.p. Robinson Land & Lumber Co. of Ala. and Robinson Land & Lumber Co. of Del., 1910-40; v.p. Meridian Light & Ry. Co., 1900-10. Mem. Am., Ala. State and Mobile bar assns.; mem. Mobile Chamber of Commerce (pres. 1913). Rep. candidate for atty.-gen. of Ala., 1901; chmn. and keynote speaker Ala. Rep. convs., 1928, 32, 40; del. Rep. Nat. Conv., Phila., (Ala. mem. Com. on Resolutions); Rep. elector-at-large, State of Ala., 1940. Author of municipal bond code of Ala. and various amendments to the State constitution affecting municipalities. Episcopalian. Mason (32°). Clubs: Athelston, Mobile Country. Home: 173 S. Georgia Av. Office: Merchants Nat. Bank Bldg., Mobile, Ala. Died July 1941.

ARMS, Frank Thornton, naval officer; b. Dec. 9, 1866; entered U.S. Navy, 1892, and advanced through the grades to rear adm., 1924; retired, 1925. Home: 51 Glenwood Av., New London, Conn. Address: care Chief of Naval Personnel Navy Dept., Washington 25, D.C.* Died Apr. 18, 1948.

ARMSBY, George Newell, banker; b. Evanston, Ill., Aug. 10, 1876; s. James K. and Mary (Wyman) A.; ed. pub. and high schs., Evanston; m. Leonora Wood, Dec. 29, 1898; children—Leonora Wyman, George Newell; m. 2d, Colette Touzeau, Mar. 26, 1930. Vice pres. J. K. Armsby Co., San Francisco, 1894-1916; an organizer, 1916, v.p., dir. Calif. Packing Corp.; chmn. bd. Curtiss-Wright Corp.; dir. Capital Theatre Corp., Intercontinent Aviation, Inc., Tide Water Asso. Oil Co., Sperry Gyroscope Co., Inc., Transcontinental Air Transport Inc., Curtiss-Wright Airports Corp., Ford Instrument Co., Inc., Industrial Rayon Corp., Gen. Outdoor Adv., Moredall Realty Corp., Petroleum Corp. America, Loew's Inc., Sperry Corp., Wright Aeronautical Corp., Devon Corp., Waterbury Tool Co., Standard Gas & Electric Co., Forty Wall Street Bldg., Inc. Republican. Episcopalian. Clubs: Brook, Recess, The Creek, Turf and Field, Seawanhaka Corinthian Yacht (New York); Pacific

Union, Bohemian (San Francisco); Chicago (Chicago). Home: 14 Sutton Pl. S., New York, N.Y. Address: 40 Wall St., New York, N.Y. Died Mar. 25, 1942.

ARMSTRONG, Edward Cooke, educator; b. Winchester, Va., Aug. 24, 1871; s. James Edward and Margaret (Hickman) A.; A.B., Randolph-Macon Coll., 1890, A.M., 1894, LL.D., 1917, Ph.D., Johns Hopkins, 1897; also univs. Paris and Berlin; L.H.D., Oberlin College, 1927; L.H.D., from University of Chicago, 1941; m. Emerline Holbrook, June 8, 1905; 1 son, Percy Holbrook. Prof. French lang., 1897-1917, chmn. Romance dept., 1910-17, Johns Hopkins U.; prof. French lang., Princeton, 1917-39, prof. emeritus since 1937. Nat. recruiting sec. for the Foyer du Soldat and nat. dir. of French instrn. in the training camps, 1918; dean Am. students and lecturer in U. of Bordeaux, 1919. Trustee Am. Univ. Union in Europe, 1919-29; sec. Am. Council Learned Societies, 1925-29, chmn., 1929-35. Decorated Chevalier Legion of Honor. Mem. Modern Language Assn. America (pres. 1918, 19); fellow Medieval Acad. America, Am. Acad. Arts and Sciences, Am. Philos. Soc. Author: Syntax of the French Verb; French Shifts in Adjective Position; Taking Counsel with Candide; French Metrical Versions of Barlaam and Josaphat; Authorship of the Vengement Alixandre and of the Venjance Alixandre; Medieval French Roman d'Alexandre (with others), Vols. 1-5, 1937-43. Editor: Elliott Monographs in the Romance Langs. and Lits. (40 vols.). Co-editor: Modern Language Notes, 1911-15. Home: Princeton, N.J. Died Mar. 4, 1944.

ARMSTRONG, Helen Maitland, artist; b. Florence, Italy, Oct. 14, 1869; d. David Maitland (U.S. consul gen. to Italy) and Helena (Neilson) Armstrong; ed. at home; studied art at Art Students' League, New York, and with Rhoda Holmes Nicholls, Irving R. Wiles, William M. Chase. Designed and painted many stained glass windows, mosaics, mural decorations, etc. Prin. works: windows All Saints Ch., Biltmore, N.C.; windows in memorial chapel built by Mrs. O. H. P. Belmont; in pvt. chapel of J. C. Brady, Gladstone, N.J.; windows in Ch. of the Ascension, and St. Michael's Ch., New York; 5 windows in chancel of chapel, Sailor's Snug Harbor, Staten Island, N.Y.; 10 windows in Ch. of Our Lady of Perpetual Help, Bernardsville, N.J.; etc. Episcopalian. Address: 58 W. 10th St., New York, N.Y. Died Nov. 26, 1948.

ARMSTRONG, John Nelson, coll. pres.; b. near Gadsden, Tenn., Jan. 6, 1870; s. Robert Edgar and Elizabeth (Hathaway) A.; student Southwestern Bapt. U., Jackson, Tenn., 1891-92, Georgia Robertson Christian Coll., Henderson, Tenn., 1892-93; B.A., David Lipscomb Coll., Nashville, Tenn., 1896; M.A., Potter Bible Coll., Bowling Green, Ky., 1901-03; grad. study U. of Okla., 1917; LL.D., Central U., Indianapolis, 1930; m. Woodson Harding, June 7, 1898; children—Pattie Hathaway (Mrs. Lloyd Cline Sears), James David (adopted). Undergrad. instr. in Greek, David Lipscomb Coll., 1895-96, asst. prof., 1896-98, prof. 1898-1901; asst. prof. Greek, Potter Bible Coll., 1901-03, prof. Greek and Hebrew, 1903-05; pres. Western Bible and Literary Coll., Odessa, Mo., 1905-07; pres. Cordell (Okla.) Christian Coll., 1908-18; in evang. work, Kan., Okla., Tenn. and Ky., 1918-19; pres. Harper (Kan.) Coll., 1919-24; pres. Harding Coll., Searcy, Ark. (formerly at Morrillton, Ark.), 1924-36, pres. emeritus and dean of the Bible since 1936. Mem. Phi Beta Kappa. Mem. Ch. of Christ. Kiwanian. Writer of Undenominational Christianity, 1916; The Church, 1919. Editor Gospel Herald, 1910-22, Living Message, 1922-27. Has devoted most of summer months since 1894 to evangelistic work. Home: Searcy, Ark. Died Aug. 12, 1944.

ARMSTRONG, Lyndon King, mining engr.; b. Mukwonago, Wis., Sept. 26, 1859; s. John Adams and Laura V. (Hollenback) A.; ed. common and high schs., Fairmont, Minn.; m. Charlotte J. Grandy, 1884 (died 1890); 1 son, Halbert; m. 2d, Lulu E. Hyat, Nov. 21, 1896; children—Helen M., L. Marian. In Black Hills, later Mont., 1877-81; chemist and pharmacist in Dak. Ty., 1882-90; mining and cons. practice, Spokane, Wash., since 1890; mgr. Armstrong Syndicate. Life mem. Nat. Resources Assn. (pres. 1930-36); fellow A.A.A.S.; mem. Am. Inst. Mining and Metall. Engrs. (life), also Columbia sect. Am. Inst. Mining Engrs. (sec.-treas. 1912-39), Mineral Soc. America, Electrochem. Soc. (chmn. power com. 1934-39), Canadian Inst. Mining and Metallurgy (life); hon. mem. West Coast Mineral Assn., Asso. Engrs. of Spokane; founder and hon. mem. Northwest Mining Assn.; founder mem. Northwest Scientific Assn. (pres. 1927, trustee 1928); life mem. Eastern Wash. Hist. Soc.; asso. mem. Sigma Gamma Epsilon. Protestant. Consecutively editor, asso. editor and mem. editorial bd. Northwest Science. Home: W. 2103 17th Av. Office: Peyton Bldg., Spokane, Wash. Died June 21, 1942.

ARMSTRONG, Margaret (Neilson), author; b. New York, N.Y., Sept. 24, 1867; d. David Maitland and Helen (Neilson) Armstrong; privately educated. Writer, illustrator, painter. Dir. Assn. for Aid of Crippled Children, New York. Democrat. Episcopalian. Author: Field Book of Western Wild Flowers (J. J. Thornber), illustrated by Margaret Armstrong, 1915; Five Generations: Life and Letters of an American Family, 1930; Fanny Kemble: A Passionate Victorian, 1938; Murder in Stained Glass, 1939; Trelawny: A Man's Life, 1940; The Man with no Face, 1940; The Blue Santo Murder Mystery, 1941. Editor: Day before Yesterday—Reminiscences of a Varied Life by Maitland Armstrong, 1920. Address: 58 W. 10th St., New York, N.Y. Died July 18, 1944.

ARMSTRONG, Robert Burns, editor, publicity dir.; b. near Des Moines, Ia., Aug. 19, 1873; s. Dr. Robert B. and Sarah E. (Hardy) A.; grad. Ia. State Agrl. Coll., 1892, hon. Ph.M., 1903; m. Blanche Arline Hogin, Dec. 30, 1896; 1 son, Robert Burns. Learned printer's trade and later editor on Des Moines papers; polit. editor Chicago Record, 1896-98; in charge eastern editorial work, same, at New York, 1898-1901; had charge western office New York Herald, 1901-02; pvt. sec. to Secretary Shaw, April, 1902; asst. sec. of the Treasury, Feb. 1903-Mar. 1905; pres. Casualty Co. of America, 1905-07; removed to Pasadena, Calif.; Washington corr. Los Angeles Times, 1917-32. Nat. dir. publicity, Harding pre-convention campaign, Jan.-July, 1920; asst. dir. publicity, Coolidge campaign, 1924. Republican. Clubs: Nat. Press, Gridiron (Washington, D.C.). Address: National Press Club, Washington, D.C. Died Aug. 5, 1946.

ARMSTRONG, Samuel Treat, physician; b. St. Louis, Nov. 2, 1859; s. David Hartley and Laura Armstrong (Milligan) A.; Ph.B., St. Louis U., 1879, Ph.D., 1886; M.D., St. Louis Med. Coll. (Washington U.), 1879; m. Alice Cobin, Dec. 6, 1882; children—Mrs. Laura Lovejoy, Clairette Papin, Donald, Francis Tuttle. U.S. Marine Hospital Service Feb. 1881; resigned July 1890; maj. and brigade surgeon U.S.V., May 1898; resigned, June 1901. Companion Mil. Order Foreign Wars, Order Spanish-Am. War.; mem. A.A.A.S., N.Y. Acad. Sciences. Clubs: Army and Navy (Washington, D.C.). Contbr. med. monographs to various publs. Home: Hillbourne Farms, Katonah, N.Y. Died Aug. 31, 1944.

ARMSTRONG, William, music critic, lecturer; ed. Stuttgart and Vienna. Music critic Chicago Tribune, 1893-98; musical critic The American and Journal, New York; magazinist; lecturer on musical subjects; first American to lecture before Royal Acad. of Music, London, June 30, 1897; first London appearance, Queen's Hall, June 18, 1897. Author: Thekla; An American Nobleman; etc. Address: Hotel Belvedere, New York. Died May 18, 1942.

ARMSTRONG, William Park, theologian; b. Selma, Ala., Jan. 10, 1874; s. William Park and Alice (Isbell) A.; A.B., Princeton, 1894, A.M., 1896; grad. Princeton Theol. Sem., 1897; studied U. of Marburg, 1897, U. of Berlin, 1897-98, U. of Erlangen, 1898; grad. student, Princeton Theol. Sem., 1899; D.D., Temple U., 1915; m. Rebekah Sellers Purves, Dec. 8, 1904; children—Rebekah Purves, William Park, George Purves, Anne Elizabeth, Jane Crozier, James Isbell. Ordained Presbyn. ministry, 1900; instr. N.T. lit. 1899-1903; prof. N.T. lit. and exegesis, Princeton Theol. Sem., 1903-40; grad. prof. N.T. exegesis since 1940. Democrat. Home: Princeton, N.J. Died Mar. 25, 1944.

ARNETT, Alex Mathews (är-nĕt'), prof. history; b. nr. Sylvania, Ga., Feb. 13, 1888; s. Hamilton John and Georgia Anna (Dixon) A.; A.B., Mercer U., Macon, Ga., 1908; A.M., Columbia U., 1913; Ph.D., 1922; m. Ethel Stephens, May 30, 1916; children—Georgia Anna (Mrs. A. B. Bonds, Jr.), Dorothy Stephens. Teacher of English and history, Millen High Sch., 1908-10; teacher English, Americus (Ga.), High Sch., 1910-12; prof. history Shorter Coll., Rome, Ga., 1912-17; instr. in history, Columbia U., 1917-22; prof. history Furman U., 1922-23, Woman's Coll. of U. of N.C., since 1923. Mem. Am. Hist. Assn., Southern Hist. Assn., N.C. Hist. & Lit. Assn. Author: The Populist Movement in Georgia, 1922; Story of North Carolina (with collaboration of W. C. Jackson), 1933; Claude Kitchin and the Wilson War Policies, 1937; The South Looks at Its Past (with B. B. Kendrick), 1935. Contbr. articles and reviews. Home: 117 Kensington Rd., Greensboro, N.C. Died Aug. 7, 1945; buried at Double Heads Baptist Ch. Cemetery, Screven County, Ga.

ARNOLD, Bion Joseph, electrical engr.; b. Casnovia, near Grand Rapids, Mich., Aug. 14, 1861; s. Joseph and Geraldine (Reynolds) A.; U. of Neb., 1879-80; B.S., Hillsdale (Mich.) Coll., 1884, M.S., 1887; grad. course Cornell, 1888-89; E.E., U. of Neb., 1897; hon. M.Ph., Hillsdale, 1889, hon. diploma, 1903; D.Sc., Armour Inst., 1907; D.Eng., U. of Neb., 1911; m. Carrie Estelle Berry, Jan. 14, 1886 (dec.); m. 2d, Mrs. Margaret Latimer Fonda, Dec. 22. 1909. Chief designer, Ia. Iron Works, Dubuque; mech. engr., C.G.W. Ry.; later cons. engr. for Chicago office Gen. Electric Co.; independent cons. engr. since 1893. Designed and built Intramural Ry., Chicago Expn.; cons. elec. engr. Chicago & Milwaukee Elec. Ry., Chicago Bd. of Trade, C.,B.& Q. R.R., Grand Trunk Ry. on electrification of St. Clair tunnel; cons. engr. Wis. State Ry. Commn., 1905-07; devised plan for electrically operating trains of N.Y. Central R.R. in and out of New York, and mem. Electric Traction Commrs. engaged in carrying on the work; mem. electric traction com. Erie R.R., 1900-04; cons. engr. for city of Chicago to revise street ry. systems of city, 1902; chief engr. rebuilding Chicago traction system at cost approx. $140,000,000, and chmn. bd. supervising engrs. same since 1907; cons. engr. Pub. Service Commn., 1st Dist., N.Y., matters connected with subway and st. ry. properties, New York; chief subway engr. city of Chicago and cons. engr. on traction matters for cities of Pittsburgh, 1910, Providence, Los Angeles, San Francisco, 1911, Toronto and Cincinnati, 1912; appraised properties of Seattle Electric Co., Puget Sound Electric Ry. Co., Southern Calif. Edison Co., Los Angeles, 1911; Chicago Telephone Company's System, 1911; Internat. Ry. Co., Buffalo, N.Y., 1911; Met. St. Ry. System of Kansas City, Toronto St. Ry., and Lincoln (Neb.) Tel. & Tel. Co., 1913; Mountain States Tel. & Tel. Co., Denver, 1914; Denver Tramway Co., 1915; Brooklyn R.T. Co. surface lines, 1917-18. Chosen by the Citizens' Terminal Plan Com. of Chicago to review plans submitted by Pa. Ry. Co. and others for terminals and to recommend a comprehensive system of steam ry. terminals for city; mem. of Chicago Ry. Terminal Commn. until 1921; mem. Traction and Subway Commn., 1916-17; retained by Mass. Pub. Service Commn. to report on rys. and by Bay State Ry. Co., Boston, 1916-17; adviser to Des Moines, Omaha, Winnipeg, Sacramento, New Orleans, Detroit, Harrisburg, Rochester, Syracuse, Jersey City, Toronto, etc. Pres. The Arnold Engineering Co. Inventor of combined direct-connected machines, a magnetic clutch, storage battery improvements, and new systems and devices for elec. rys.; pioneer in alternating current, direct current and in single phase electric traction systems. Mem. Naval Consulting Board; chairman com. Am. Inst. Elec. Engrs. on Nat. Reserve Corps Civilian Engrs., 1915. Commd. maj. Engr. R.C., Jan. 23, 1917; transferred to regular army, Dec. 14, 1917, with rank lt. col., Aviation Sect., Signal Corps; assigned to equipment div. production sect. of aircraft, Washington, D.C., and continued to act in advisory capacity to Army and Navy; made 2 surveys of aircraft production, and report on aluminum situation; had control for 5 mos. previous to armistice over development and production of aerial torpedoes; hon. discharged Feb. 6, 1919; commd. maj. Aviation Sect., O.R.C., Mar. 28, 1919, col. Air Service U.S. Army, Sept. 13, 1919, col. Aux. Corps, Aug. 14, 1925; col. Inactive Reserve since 1929. Trustee Hillsdale Coll.; mem. bd. mgrs. Lewis Inst.; trustee Illinois Inst. of Technology since 1940. Pres. Am. Inst. E.E., 1903-04, elected hon. mem., 1937, was also del. for Inst. at Internat. Elec. Congress, 1900; pres. Western Soc. Engrs., 1906-07, elected hon. mem., 1927, and received Washington Award, 1929, "for devoted, unselfish and preeminent service in advancing human progress"; member A.A.A.S. (vice pres.), American Soc. Promotion Engrng. Edn.; 1st v.p. and chmn. exec. com. Internat. Elec. Congress, St. Louis, 1904; chmn. com. on award Anthony N. Brady medals of N.Y. Mus. Safety; chmn. Am. Committee on Electrolysis; mem. of Inventors Guild, Aero Club of Ill. (past pres.), N.Y. Elec. Soc., Mil. Order World War (comdr. Chicago chapter, 1932-33, state comdr. for Ill. 1937); pres. Air Bd. of Chicago, etc. Clubs: Engineers' (New York); Union League, South Shore, Commercial, Engineers, Army and Navy (pres. 1926-27). Home: 4713 Kimbark Av. Office: 231 S. La Salle St., Chicago, Ill. Died Jan. 29, 1942.

ARNOLD, Carl Franklin, lawyer, educator; b. Laramie, Wyo., May 31, 1896; s. Constantine Peter and Annie (Brockway) A.; A.B., Princeton, 1917; LL.B., Univ. of Wyo. Law Sch., 1927; J.S.D., Yale Law Sch., 1928; m. Mary Olga Moore, Dec. 21, 1928. Owned and managed cattle ranch in Millbrook, Wyo., 1919-25; admitted to Wyo. bar, 1927; mem. Arnold & Arnold; asst. prof. law and polit. science, U. of Wyo., 1928-30; visiting prof., Univ. of W.Va. Coll. of Law, summers, 1930, 31, U. of Texas Coll. of Law, 1940; dean Univ. of Wyo. Law Sch. since 1932; apptd. asst. general counsel Fed. Communications Commn., 1935-37; dean Law Sch., U. of Wyo., since 1937; apptd. attorney with U.S. Maritime Commn., 1941 (on leave from U. of Wyo.); partner Geitz & Arnold, purebred Hereford breeders. First lt. Inf., 38th Machine Gun Bn., U.S. Army, 1917-19. Mem. Am., Wyo. and Federal Communications bar assns., Phi Kappa Phi, Sigma Alpha Epsilson. Democrat. Clubs: American College Quill, Lions. Home: Laramie, Wyo. Died Sep. 13, 1941.

ARNOLD, George Stanleigh, lawyer; b. New Haven, Conn., Apr. 3, 1881; s. George Sumner and Evelyn (Thomson) A.; B.A., Yale, 1903; LL.B., Yale, 1906; m. Elizabeth Sherman Kent, Feb. 26, 1915; children—Elizabeth Sherman, Evelyn, George Stanleigh, Kent, Peter, Anthony. Instructor in rhetoric, Sheffield Scientific School (Yale), 1903-06; law examiner, United States Forest Service, 1907-09; served as counsel in the Ballinger-Pinchot controversy, 1909, for former associates in forest service; apptd. special assistant to the attorney general in oil and land litigation, 1913; asso. with William Denman in the firm of Denman & Arnold, 1911-18; pres. Pacific States Lumber Company, 1926-27. Calif. rep. of the President's Labor Mediation Commn., 1917, War Labor Policies Bd., 1918-19; spl. asst. to atty. gen. of U.S., 1934-35; chmn. President's Emergency Boards under Ry. Labor Act, 1936, 1937 and 1941. Episcopalian. Mem. Zeta Psi, Chi Delta Theta, Phi Delta Phi fraternities. Pres. Yale Alumni Assn. of Northern Calif., 1921-22. Clubs: Pacific Union, Bohemian; Meadow Club. Contbr. articles in relation to pub. lands of U.S. and development of water power thereon, etc. Home: Kentfield, Calif. Office: 41 Sutter St., San Francisco, Calif. Died Jan. 18, 1942.

ARNOLD, Henry H., army officer; b. Gladwyne, Pa., June 25, 1886; s. H. A. and Louise (Harley) A.; grad. U.S. Mil. Acad., 1907, Army Indsl. Coll., 1925, Command and Gen. Staff Sch., 1929; D. Aero. Sc., Pa. Mil. Coll., 1941; D.Sc., U. So. Calif., 1941; LL.D., Iowa Wesleyan Coll., 1942; m. Eleanor A. Pool, Sept. 10, 1913; children—Lois E., Henry H., William, David L. Commd. 2d lt. inf., 1907; and advanced through grades to gen., 1943; gen. of the Army (5-star), Dec. 1944. Detailed to Signal Corps

Aviation Sect., 1916-17; comdg. officer 7th Aero Squadron, Panama, 1917-18; dept. air service officer, San Francisco, 1919-22; comdg. officer various air fields, 1922-36; flight comdr. U.S. Alaska Flight, 1934; asst. chief Air Corps, 1936-38; became chief of Army Air Corps, 1938; apptd. dep. chief of staff for Air, 1940; became comdg. gen. Army Air Forces, 1942; now gen. of the Air Force. Awarded Distinguished Flying Cross, 1934; Clarence H. Mackay Trophy, 1912 and 1935; Distinguished Service Medal, 1942. Baptist. Mason. Clubs: Army and Navy, Columbia Country. Author: Air Men and Aircraft, 1926; Bill Bruce Series, 1928; This Flying Game (with I. C. Eaker), 1936 (rev. 1944); Winged Warfare (with I. C. Eaker), 1941; Army Flyer (with I. C. Eaker), 1942. Home: Fort Myer, Va.* Died Jan. 15, 1950.

ARNOLD, Horace David, physician; b. Boston, Nov. 4, 1862; s. George Jerome and Anna Elizabeth (Bullard) A.; A.B., Harvard, 1885, M.D., 1889; m. Ida P. Lane, June 8, 1892. House officer Boston City Hosp., Boston Lying-in Hosp., 1889-90; asst. supt. Boston Dispensary and Boston City Hosp.; instr., later prof. clin. medicine, Tufts Coll. Med. Sch., 1896-1910; dean Harvard Grad. Sch. of Medicine, 1912-16, dir. same, 1916. Mem. Nat. Bd. Med. Examiners, 1915. Major, Med. R.C., Apr. 11, 1917. Mem. A.M.A. (chmn. council on med. edn., 1917), Mass. Med. Soc., Am. Climatol. Assn., Boston Soc. for Med. Improvement, Boston Soc. Med. Sciences, etc. Mason. Clubs: Union, Harvard (Boston). Home: 427 Beacon St. Office: 520 Commonwealth Av., Boston. Died Apr., 1935.

ARNOLD, Morris Allen, retired banker; b. Mexico, Mo., May 1, 1866; s. Robert Russell and Ophelia (Morris) A.; ed. pub. schs., Mexico, Mo.; student U. of Mo., 1886; m. Georgia Moss, Oct. 11, 1893; 1 son, Lawrence M. Began as asst. cashier, 1st Nat. Bank, Mexico, Mo., 1887; clk., 3d Nat. Bank, St. Louis, Mo., 1889-91; cashier Farmers & Mchts. Bank, Centralia, Mo., 1891-97; state bank examiner, Mo., 1897-1901; v.p., 1st Nat. Bank, Billings, Mont., 1901-07; pres. 1st Nat. Bank, Seattle, 1907-29, 1st Nat. Corp., 1928-29, First Seattle Dexter Horton Nat. Bank (now Seattle-First Nat. Bank), 1929-39, chmn. bd., 1939-Sept. 1, 1940; retired. Dir. Seattle br. Fed. Res. Bank of San Francisco, 1916-33; mem. Fed. Advisory Council, 12th Fed. Reserve Dist., 1933-35; dir. and mem. exec. com. Seattle 1st Nat. Bank; dir. Fisher Flour Mills Co., Superior Portland Cement Co., Northern Life Ins. Co., Metropolitan Bldg. Co. Republican. Episcopalian. Clubs: Rainier, Seattle Golf. Home: The Highlands. Office: Seattle First Nat. Bank, Seattle, Wash. Died May 22, 1946.

ARNOLD, Oswald James, life ins. exec.; b. Rochester, N.Y., Oct. 29, 1873; s. James and Elizabeth (McKenna) A.; B.S., U. of Chicago, 1897; unmarried. Began with Ill. Life Ins. Co., Chicago, Ill., 1897, asst. sec., 1899-1901, sec. and actuary of co., 1901-25, pres. Northwestern Nat. Life Ins. Co., 1925, later chairman board. Charter mem. Am. Inst. Actuaries (pres. 1912-14; life mem. bd. govs.); mem. Am. Life Conv. (exec. com. 1925-28); mem. Minneapolis Council Social Agencies, 1931-33; mem. Minneapolis Civic Council, 1938-40, chmn. bd. dirs., 1941-45; chmn. bd. Sales Research Bur., 1935-37, exec. com., 1938; chmn. Assn. Life Ins. Pres., 1941; v.p. U.S. C. of C., 1939-40; trustee Am. Coll. Life Underwriters since 1936; dir. Minneapolis C. of C., 1930-40, Inst. Life Ins., since 1938; state chmn. Minn. War Finance Com., 1941-45; state campaign chmn. Minn. Cancer Soc., 1946. Mem. Psi Upsilon. Republican. Episcopalian. Mason (32°, K.T., Shriner). Clubs: Minneapolis, Minikahda, Lafayette, Woodhill Country (Minneapolis); Union League, University, Chicago Athletic, South Shore Country, Chicago Yacht (Chicago). Home: 1606 Mt. Curve Av. Office: 430 Oak Grove St., Minneapolis, Minn. Died June 14, 1949.

ARNOLD, Sarah Louise, college dean; b. N. Abington, Mass.; d. Jonathan and Abigail (Noyes) A.; grad. Bridgewater (Mass.) State Normal Sch.; A.M. (hon.), Tufts Coll., 1902; unmarried. Taught in Mass., Pa., Vt., N.H.; prin. training sch., Saratoga, N.Y., 2 yrs.; supervisor schs., Minneapolis, 7 yrs., Boston, 1895-1902; dean Simmons Coll. since 1902. Author: Waymarks for Teachers, 1894; Stepping Stones to Literature, 1897; Reading—How to Teach It, 1899; The Mother Tongue (with George L. Kittredge), 1900; Manual for Teachers (to accompany See and Say series) 1913; etc. Home: Newton Centre, Mass. Died Feb. 26, 1943.

ARNOLD, Waldo Robert, newspaperman; b. Kiel, Wis., May 8, 1890; s. Peter and Anna (Goettinger) A.; student U. of Wis., 1914-17; m. Mildred Marie Hussa, June 19, 1922; 1 dau., Suzanne. Asso. with Milwaukee Journal since 1917, beginning as copy reader, telegraph editor, 1919-21, news editor, 1921-36, asst. mng. editor, 1936-38, mng. editor since 1936. Served with 244th Inf., A.E.F., 1918-19. Mem. Am. Soc. Newspaper Editors, Sigma Delta Chi. Mason. Club: Milwaukee Athletic. Home: 2732 E. Beverly Rd. Office: Milwaukee Journal, Milwaukee, Wis. Died Nov. 7, 1946.

ARNOLD, William Hendrick, lawyer; b. Lisbon, Ark., Feb. 15, 1861; s. David S. and Tempie L. (Arnold) A.; ed. pub. schs. and acads.; m. Jessie Cook, Oct. 13, 1887 (died, Aug. 27, 1900); children—Jodie (Mrs. Carl Smith), Lucy (Mrs. Booker Ellis), William H., Ruth (Mrs. A. A. McCurdy), David C. (died Oct. 10, 1930); m. 2d, Kate Lewis, Mar. 17, 1903; 1 son, Richard Lewis. Admitted to Ark. bar, 1882; began practice at Prescott, Ark., 1882; practiced at Texarkana, Ark., since 1883; counsel in a number of cases in Supreme Ct. of U.S.; senior mem. Arnold & Arnold: dist. del. Dem. Nat. Conv., 1892, 1904 and 1924, del. at large, 1916; del. Ark. Constl. Conv., 1917 (chmn. com. on legislative dept. and mem. of jud. com.); mayor of Texarkana, 1892-94; mem. Sch. Bd., Texarkana, 16 yrs. (pres. 10 yrs.). Served as spl. asso. justice of Supreme Ct. of Ark. 1925-26, to decide two cases involving constl. amendments; spl. judge Circuit Ct., 8th Circuit Ark., 1929. Four-minute speaker, World War, and active in raising war funds in Liberty Loan drives; apptd. by Maj. Gen. Crowder, together with gov. and three other members, to organize and appoint legal advisory bds. and legal coms. for war work in each county in Ark.; acted in same capacity as v.p. for Ark. of Am. Bar Assn. Mem. Nat. Conf. Commrs. on Uniform State Laws. Mem. Am. Bar Assn. (gen. council for Ark. 1930-35, mem. house of delegates 1936-44), Am. Law Inst. (charter and life mem.), Ark. State Bar Assn. (ex-pres. chmn. bd. examiners for admission to Practice in U.S. Dist. Ct. for Western Dist. of Ark. since 1896), Ark. Soc. S.A.R. (ex-pres. Ark. soc. and ex-vice pres. Nat. Soc. S.A.R.—Southern Miss. Dist.). Methodist. Scottish Rite Mason. Shriner. Home: Texarkana, Ark. Died Dec. 8, 1946.

ARNY, Henry Vinecome, pharmaceutical chemist; b. Phila., Feb. 28, 1868; s. Louis Christian and Sarah (Shinn) A.; Ph.G., Phila. Coll. Pharmacy, 1889; studied U. of Berlin, 1893-94, U. of Göttingen, 1892-93, 1894-96, Ph.D., 1896; m. Katharine Moody Smith, Apr. 22, 1903; children—Robert Allen, Sarah Elizabeth, Malcolm Moody, Francis Vinacomb. Prof. pharmacy and dean Coll. of Pharmacy, Western Reserve U., Cleveland, 1897-1911; prof. chemistry, 1911-37, dean, 1930-37, Coll. of Pharmacy, Columbia Univ., now retired. Editor of The Druggists' Circular, 1914-15, Year Book, Am. Pharm. Assn., 1916-22; technical editor of American Druggist, 1928-1936. Remington medalist, 1922; Ebert medalist, 1924. Mem. com. of revision U.S. Pharmacopœia, com. of revision Nat. Formulary; pres. Am. Conf. of Pharm. Faculties, 1915-16; mem. exec. com. Am. Metric Assn., 1916-20; chmn. Nat. Conf. on Pharm. Research, 1922-29; fellow Chem. Soc. (Eng.); mem. Am. Pharm. Assn. (pres. 1923-24), Am. Chem. Soc., A.A.A.S., Franklin Inst.; hon. mem. German Pharm. Soc. (Berlin), Pharm. Soc. of Great Britain. Democrat. Episcopalian. Club: Columbia Faculty (New York). Author: Principles of Pharmacy, 1909, 4th edit., 1936. Home: 135 Watchung Av., Upper Montclair, N.J. Died Nov. 3, 1943.

ARON, Albert William (ä'rŭn), univ. prof.; b. Atkins, Ia., Feb. 28, 1886; s. John and Mary (Mohr) A.; A.B., U. of Neb., 1907, A.M., 1908; Ph.D., U. of Wis., 1913; studied at univs. of Leipzig, Berlin, 1910-11, Munich, Vienna, 1913-14; m. Margaret Schenk, September 3, 1914; children—Ilse (now deceased), Walter Arthur, Karl Frederick. Instr. of German, U. of Wis., 1911-19; prof. German, Univ. of Tex., summer, 1915; prof. economics, Elmhurst Coll., 1919-20; head German dept. Francis W. Parker Sch., Chicago, 1920-21; asst. prof. German, Oberlin (O.) Coll., 1921-23, prof. and head of dept., 1923-27; prof. German and head of dept., U. of Ill. since 1927. Mem. Modern Lang. Assn. America (sec. Germanic section, 1940, chmn. 1941; mem. executive council 1943-46), Am. Assn. Teachers German (secretary 1934, pres. 1935), Nat. Fed. of Modern Lang. Teachers (pres. 1930; exec. com. 1928-31, 1935-39), Phi Beta Kappa. Awarded Ottendorfer Memorial traveling fellowship (New York U.), 1910, Markham Memorial traveling fellowship (University of Wisconsin), 1913. Lutheran. Club: Dial. Author: Die Progressiven Formen im Mittelhochdeutschen und Frühneuhochdeutschen, 1914; Traces of Matriarchy in Germanic Hero-Lore, 1920; (with F. E. and A. E. Ross) Ich Lerne Deutsch, 1935. Asso. editor Jour. of English and Germanic Philology, 1927-32, editor (for German) since 1932; mem. editorial bd. Monatshefte für Deutschen Unterricht since 1928, German Quarterly 1942-45; editor of Drei Erzählungen von Ernst Zahn, 1929. Contbr. articles on Germanic Philology. Home: 715 W. Washington St., Urbana, Ill. Died Oct. 31, 1945.

AROSEMENA, Carlos C., diplomat; b. Panama, June 29, 1869; s. Constantine and Dolores (Icaza) A.; student Pitkins Sch., Springfield, Mass., Williston Sem., Easthampton, Mass.; C.E., B.S., Troy Poly. Inst., 1902; unmarried. Asst. and chief engr. Panama Tramway, 1st asst. and chief engr. Panama water works, and cons. engr. One of original 8 members of the "Junta" who planned separation of Panama from Colombia; came to U.S., 1903, as mem. com. to draw up Panama Canal treaty; mem. commn. that reached agreement with U.S. Govt., May, 1904, as to new monetary system for Panama; apptd. sec. of legation, 1903, E.E. and M.P., Oct. 15, 1909, Republic of Panama. Rep. Panama at inauguration of Cuban pres., Jan. 28, 1909. Roman Catholic. Mem. Theta Delta Chi. Club: Chevy Chase. Address: The Highlands, Washington. Died July 11, 1946.

ARTHUR, Joseph Charles, botanist; b. Lowville, N.Y., Jan. 11, 1850; s. Charles and Ann (Allen) A.; B.S., Ia. State Coll., 1872, M.S., 1877; student Johns Hopkins, 1879, Harvard, 1879, U. of Bonn, 1896; Sc.D., Cornell, 1886; LL.D., State U. of Ia., 1916; Sc.D., Ia. State Coll., 1920; Sc.D., Purdue, 1931; m. Emily Stiles Potter, June 12, 1901. Instr. botany, Univ. of Wis., 1879-81, U. of Minn., 1882; botanist, Expt. Sta., Geneva, N.Y., 1884-87; prof. botany, Purdue, 1887; prof. vegetable physiology and pathology, and botanist, Ind. Expt. Sta., 1888-1915; prof. emeritus, Purdue, since 1915. Speaker Internat. Congress Arts and Sciences, St. Louis, 1904; del. Internat. Bot. Congress, 1905, 10, 30. Fellow A.A.A.S. (sec. sect. F, 1886, asst. gen. sec., 1887, v.p., 1895); mem. Bot. Soc. Am. (twice pres.), Torrey Bot. Club, Deutsche Botanische Gesellschaft, Ind. Acad. Science (pres. 1902), Soc. Promotion Agrl. Science, Am. Acad. Arts and Sciences, Ia. Acad. Science, Phila. Acad. Science, Am. Philos. Soc., Am. Assn. Univ. Profs., Am. Soc. Naturalists, Mycol. Soc. Am., Am. Phytopathol. Soc. (past pres.). Author: Handbook of Plant Dissection (with C. R. Barnes and J. M. Coulter), 1886; Living Plants and Their Properties (with Daniel Trembly MacDougal), 1898; Uredinales, in N. Am. Flora, 1907-29; The Plant Rusts (with others), 1929; Manual of the Rusts in United States and Canada, 1934. Home: Lafayette, Ind. Died Apr. 30, 1942.

ASAKAWA, Kwan-Ichi (ä-sä-kä-wä), univ. prof.; b. Nihonmatsu, Japan, Dec. 20, 1873; s. Masazumi and Uta (Sugiura) A.; ed. Fukushima Middle Sch., 1888-92; Waseda U., Tokio, Japan, 1892-95; B.Litt., Dartmouth Coll., 1899, Litt.D., 1930; Ph.D., Yale, 1902; m. Miriam Dingwall, Oct. 12, 1905 (died, Feb. 4, 1913). Lecturer on history and civilization of East Asia, Dartmouth, 1902; prof. English at Waseda U., 1906-07; instr. history of Japanese civilization, 1907-10, asst. prof. of history, 1910, asso. prof., 1930, research asso. professorial rank, 1933-37, prof. history, 1937-42, prof. emeritus since 1942; curator of Japanese and Chinese collections since 1909, Yale University, asso. fellow. Saybrook College since 1935. Membre correspondent honoraire Institut Historique et Héraldique de France; member American Historical Association, Asiatic Society of Japan, Japanese Historical Association (Shigakkwai), Phi Beta Kappa, etc. Special investigations in Japan, 1906-07, 1917-19. Author: The Early Institutional Life of Japan, 1903; The Russo-Japanese Conflict—Its Causes and Issues, 1904; Ni-hon no kwa-ki, Tokyo, 1909. Translator and Editor: The Documents of Iriki, Illustrative of the Development of Japanese Feudal Institutions, 1929. Contributor chapters to "Japan," edited by Capt. F. Brinkley, 1904; editor of "Japan" in the History of Nations series, 1907; contbr. of chapters to China and the Far East, 1910, Japan and Japanese-American Relations, 1912, and to Pacific Ocean in History, 1917; also articles to Japanese, Am., English and European periodicals. Address: Yale University, New Haven, Conn. Died Aug. 11, 1948.

ASHBY, Samuel, lawyer; b. Pittsboro, Ind., Aug. 24, 1868; s. James Samuel and Jane Alexander (Watson) A.; LL.B., Ind. U., 1891; m. Ida M. Reid, Sept. 19, 1894; children—Mary Alice (Mrs. John L. H. Fuller), Sarah Elizabeth (Mrs. Earl A. Heassler), Samuel Reid. Admitted to Ind. bar, 1892, and began practice at Indianapolis; corp. counsel, Indianapolis, 1918-22, spl. counsel, Indianapolis, 1922-23; atty. for Murray Investment Co., L. S. Ayres & Co., Stout's Factory Shoe Store Co., Standard Grocery Co., Ind. World War Memorial Trustees; counsel and sec. Southwestern Ill. Coal Corp.; pres. and counsel Midland Electric Coal Corp., Snow Hill Coal Corp. Chmn. Marion County Election Commn., 1910-18. Pres., trustee and counsel Pension Fund, Disciples of Christ. Mem. Am. and Ind. State bar assns., Indianapolis Bar Assn. (pres. 1927), Indianapolis Chamber of Commerce, Indiana University Alumni Assn. Republican. Mem. Christian (Disciples) Ch. Mason. Clubs: Columbia, Kiwanis. Home: 34 E. 43d St. Office: 1309 Fletcher Trust Bldg., Indianapolis. Died Dec. 26, 1943; buried in Crown Hill Cemetery, Indianapolis.

ASHCRAFT, Leon Thomas, surgeon; b. Philadelphia, Pa., Nov. 4, 1866; s. Samuel F. and Sarah (Godshall) A.; Ph.B., Dickinson Coll., Pa., 1887; A.M., 1890; M.D., Hahnemann Med. Coll., Phila., 1890, LL.D., 1937; m. Eleida Bosler, June 18, 1908; children—Leon Thomas, John Joseph Bosler. Practiced in Phila. since 1890; prof. and head dept. urology, Hahnemann Med. Coll. and Hosp. Home: 2039 Walnut St., Philadelphia, Pa. Died Jan. 19, 1945.

ASHLEY, Clifford W(arren), marine artist; b. New Bedford, Mass., Dec. 18, 1881; s. A(biel) Davis and Caroline (Morse) A.; studied Art under Eric Pape, George Noyes and Howard Pyle; m. Sarah Rodman (Scudder) Clark, Mar. 16, 1932; children—Pauline Clark, Phoebe Warren, Jane Rodman. Work in permanent collections: New Bedford Pub. Library, and Whaling Mus., both New Bedford; Brooklyn Museum; Mass. Inst. of Tech.; Wilmington Soc. Fine Arts; Canajoharie (N.Y.) Art Museum; Mariner's Museum (Newport News, Va.). Trustee Swain Sch. of Design, New Bedford. Fellow Am. Geog. Soc.; mem. Authors' League America, Soc. for Nautical Research (London), New Bedford Port Soc. (dir.); hon. life mem. Old Dartmouth Historical Soc. (New Bedford). Clubs: New Bedford Yacht; Explorers, Century Association (N.Y.). Author: The Yankee Whaler, 1926; Whaleships of New Bedford, 1929; The Ashley Book of Knots, 1944. Home: Driftway, S. Westport, Mass. Died Sep. 18, 1947.

ASHLEY, Daniel W., pub.; b. Bath, N.H., March 15, 1894; s. William Vernon and Belle (Whitcher) A.; ed. Woodsville (N.H.) Schs.; grad. Tilton Sch., 1911; B.S., Colby Coll., 1915; m. Lillian R. Keith, June 1, 1921; 1 son, William Vernon, II. New Eng.

mgr. Woman's Home Companion, 1921-29, west. mgr., 1929-34, nat. advt. mgr., 1934-39; v.p., dir. and advt. U.S. News, 1940-46; pub. The United States News and World Report since 1947. Served as lt., U.S. Navy, World War I. Mem. Delta Kappa Epsilon. Democrat. Unitarian. Clubs: Yale (N.Y. City); Weeburn Country (Dairen, Conn.); Sunset Ridge Country (Northbrook, Ill.); Tavern (Chicago). Home: Highfield Lane, Darien, Conn. Office: 30 Rockefeller Plaza, New York 20. Died Aug. 1, 1947; buried at Milton, Vt.

ASHWORTH, John H., economist; b. Bland, Va., Oct. 19, 1879; s. William Brisindine and Martha Ellen (Compton) A.; B.A., Emory and Henry Coll., Va., 1906; Ph.D., Johns Hopkins, 1914; m. Mabel Katherine Bruce, July 31, 1907; children—Jessie Ellen, James Peery, William Bruce, Mabelle Elizabeth, Barbara Rose. Teacher rural schs., Va., 1897-1902; prin. pub. schs., Wise, Va., 1905-11; instr. economics, Pa. State Coll., 1914-15; prof. economics and polit. science, Pa. Coll., Gettysburg, 1915-18; prof. economics and sociology, Ohio Wesleyan, 1918; same, U. of Me., also head of dept., 1919-41, emeritus prof. economics, Pa. State Coll., summer, 1937. Sec. Principals' Conf. of Va. State Teachers' Assn., 1908-09, pres., 1909-10; mem. Am. Econ. Assn., Phi Beta Kappa. Conglist. Writer on econ. subjects. Home: Orono, Me. Died Sept. 30, 1942.

ASKENSTEDT, Fritz Conrad (ăs'kĕn-stĕt), physician; b. Venersborg, Sweden, Jan. 18, 1865; s. Frederik and Eleonore M. (Hjorthen) A.; ed. pvt. schs., Sweden; came to America, 1884; M.D., Pulte Med. Coll., Cincinnati, 1889; post-grad. work Charité Hosp., Berlin, Germany, and Serafimerlazarettet, Stockholm, Sweden, 1900; James Mackenzie's Inst. for Clin. Research, St. Andrews, Scotland, and Nat. Hosp. for Diseases of Heart, London, 1920; m. Lillian S. Bryan, M.D., May 10, 1904. Prof. pathology, Southwestern Homeo. Med. Coll., 1896-1910, phys. diagnosis and diseases of chest, 1899-1910, registrar, 1906-10; visiting phys., Louisville City Hosp., 1900-11. Fellow A.M.A.; mem. Am. Inst. Homeopathy, Ky. Homeo. Med. Soc. (pres. 1906-07), Ky. State Med. Assn., Falls Cities Homeo. Med. Soc. (pres., 1906-07), Southern Homeo. Assn.; hon. mem. bd. for life, Scandinavian Assn. of Louisville. Devised quantitative tests for indican and glycuronates in urine. Address: 1210 4th Av., Louisville, Ky. Died June 16, 1943.

ASKEW, Sarah Byrd (ăs'kū), librarian; b. Dayton, Ala.; d. Samuel Horton and Thyrza (Pickering) A.; ed. high sch., Atlanta, Ga.; Pratt Inst. Library Sch., 1903-04; hon. Dr. Library Science, Rutgers, 1930. Began as asst. in Cleveland Pub. Library, 1903; organizer N.J. Pub. Library Commission, 1905, and has continued with same, serving as librarian, 1913-30, sec. since 1930; reference librarian N.J. State Library, 1909-12. Library war service, 1917-19. Nat. chmn. on children's reading, Nat. Congress of Parents-Teachers, 1924-29, asso. chmn. since 1929; mem. Bd. of Edn., Trenton, since 1922. Mem. A.L.A. (vice-pres. 1938-39), N.J. Library Assn. (pres. 1939-40), Patrons of Husbandry, League for Creative Work (Ridgewood, N.J.). Presbyterian. Clubs: Contemporary, Zonta Club. Author: (brochure) The Man, the Place and the Book, 1916. Contbr. to professional mags. Home: 234 W. State St. Address: State House Annex, Trenton, N.J. Died Oct. 20, 1942.

ATCHESON, George, Jr., U.S. foreign service; b. Denver, Colo., Oct. 20, 1896; s. George and Effie Almira (Moore) A.; A.B., U. of Calif., Berkeley, 1919; M.A., Coll. of Chinese Studies, Peking, 1924; m. Mariquita de Laguna, June 28, 1922; 1 son, George, III. Newspaper and mag. work, 1913-20; language officer, U.S. Legation, Peking, 1920-23; vice consul, Changsha, 1923; Dept. of State, 1924; consul at Tientsin, Foochow, Nanking, 1928-34; 2d sec. Legation, Nanking, 1934, in charge of Legation office, Apr.-Sept. 1935; 2d sec. Embassy, Peiping, and pres. of administrative commn. of Diplomatic Quarter, 1938; Dept. of State, 1939; asst. chief, Div. of Far Eastern affairs, Apr. 1941; acting chief, Nov.-Dec. 1942 and Feb. 1943; counselor of Embassy, Dec. 4, 1942; chargé d'affaires, Chungking, China, May-September 1943, Nov.-Dec. 1944, Feb.-April 1945; assigned to Dept. of State, May 1945; U.S. rep. on Far Eastern and Pacific Sub. commn. of the United Nations War Crimes Commn., Nov. 1944-Apr. 1945; spl. duty U.N. Conf., San Francisco, 1945; minister, acting polit. advisor to supreme comdr., Allied Power, Tokyo, Aug. 1945; U.S. polit. advisor to Japan, Mar. 1946; chief diplomate sect., supreme comdr. for Allied Powers; chmn. and U.S. mem. Allied Council for Japan, Apr. 1946; ambassador, June 1946. Served with U.S. Army, 1919; instructor U.S. School of Mil. Aeronautics, Berkeley. Awarded Navy Expeditionary Medal in connection with sinking of U.S.S. Panay, on Dec. 12, 1937. Mem. Delta Upsilon, Winged Helmet, Skull and Keys, Golden Bear. Author: "Japan 1937-46" in Ten Eventful Years. Address: Dept. of State, Washington, D.C.
Died Aug. 17, 1947.

ATHERTON, Edwin Newton (ăth'ĕr-tŭn); b. Washington, D.C., Oct. 12, 1896; s. Edwin Joseph and Mary Agnes (McCarten) A.; student Georgetown U. Law Sch., 1915-16; m. Elma Catheryne Jackson, Dec. 31, 1924 (divorced, Oct. 1941); 1 son, Edwin Newton; m. 2d, Anzonetta Lloyd Collison (widow Wilson Collison, author) Oct. 16, 1942. Bank clerk, Washington, D.C., 1915; clerk Am. Foreign Service, 1916-17; vice consul Am. Foreign Service, successively at Genoa, Palermo, Trieste (Italy), Sofia (Bulgaria), Jerusalem, Vancouver, B.C., 1917-25; spl. agent Federal Bureau of Investigation, 1925-27, in charge offices at Norfolk, Va., San Francisco and Los Angeles; in private investigative work since 1927, doing business as Edwin N. Atherton & Associates, investigations and factual surveys, San Francisco and Los Angeles; directed San Francisco police graft investigation, 1935-37; investigated lobbying and corrupt practices in Calif. State Legislature, 1937-38; conducted a survey of athletic practices and conditions in Pacific Coast Intercollegiate Athletic Conf., 1938-39; commr. Pacific Coast Intercollegiate Athletic Conf. since 1940. Mem. Soc. of Former Special Agents of Fed. Bureau of Investigation (N.Y. City). Republican. Clubs: Olympic, Press (San Francisco). Home: 438 S. Camden Drive, Beverly Hills, Calif. Office: 458 S. Spring St., Los Angeles, Calif.
Died Aug. 31, 1944.

ATHERTON, Frank Cooke, financial executive; b. Honolulu, Hawaii, July 1, 1877; s. Joseph Ballard and Juliette Montague (Cooke) A.; grad. Punahou Acad., Honolulu, 1894; student Wesleyan U., Middletown, Conn., 2 years, hon. M.A., 1933; m. Eleanore Alice Simpson, June 19, 1901; children—Marjory Elizabeth, Joseph Ballard, Alexander Simpson. With Bank of Hawaii, Ltd., 1897-1904, successively clerk, receiving teller, paying teller, asst. cashier; sec. and mgr. Sugar Factors Co., Ltd., Honolulu, 1906-10; devoted several yrs. to affairs of J. B. Atherton Estate, Ltd., later joining firm of Castle & Cooke, Ltd., v.p., 1916-28, mgr., 1925-35, pres., 1928-35, chairman board since 1936; pres. Ewa Plantation Co., Waialua Agrl. Co., Ltd., Kohala Sugar Co.; vice pres. Hawaiian Trust Co., Ltd., Honolulu Star-Bulletin, Ltd.; sec. and dir. Bk. of Hawaii, Ltd.; dir. Hawaiian Pineapple Co., Ltd. Chmn. United War Work Campaign, Ty. of Hawaii, and mem. com. Liberty Loan campaigns, World War. Territorial Chairman United Service Organizations. Vice pres. Punahou Schools; chairman Territorial Com. of Y.M.C.A.; an organizer and hon. vice chmn. Inst. Pacific Relations; mem. exec. com. United Welfare Bd.; trustee Central Union (Congl.) Ch., Honolulu. Mem. Psi Upsilon. Republican. Clubs: Pacific Union (San Francisco); University, Pacific, Hawaii Polo and Racing Assn., Oahu Country. Home: 2234 Kamehemeha Avenue, Honolulu, T.H.
Died May 29, 1945.

ATHERTON, Gertrude Franklin, author; b. San Francisco, Calif., Oct. 30, 1857; d Thomas L. and Gertrude (Franklin) Horn; ed. pvt. schs. and under pvt. teachers; hon. Doctor of Letters from Mills Coll., 1935; hon. LL.D., U. of Calif., 1937; m. George H. Bowen Atherton (dec.). Has lived abroad much of time. Chevalier Legion of Honor, 1925. President of Northern California P.E.N. Center. Author: The Doomswoman, 1892; A Whirl Asunder, 1895; Patience Sparhawk and Her Times, 1897; His Fortunate Grace, 1897; The Californians, 1898; A Daughter of the Vine, 1899; The Valiant Runaways, 1899; Senator North, 1900; The Aristocrats, 1901; The Conqueror, 1902; The Splendid Idle Forties, 1902; A Few of Hamilton's Letters, 1903; Rulers of Kings, 1904; The Bell in the Fog, 1905; The Travelling Thirds, 1905; Rezanov, 1906; Ancestors, 1907; The Gorgeous Isle, 1908; Tower of Ivory, 1910; Julia France and Her Times, 1912; Perch of the Devil, 1914; California—an Intimate History, 1914; Before the Gringo Came, 1915; Mrs. Balfame, 1916; The Living Present, 1917; The White Morning, 1918; The Avalanche, 1919; Sisters in Law, 1921; Sleeping Fires, 1922; Black Oxen, 1923; The Crystal Cup, 1925; The Immortal Marriage, 1927; The Jealous Gods, 1928; Dido, 1929; The Sophisticates, 1931; The Adventures of a Novelist, 1932; The Foghorn, 1934; Golden Peacock, 1936; Can Women Be Gentlemen?; The House of Lee; The Horn of Life, 1942; Golden Gate Country, 1945; My San Francisco, a wayward biography, 1946. Address: 2280 Green St., San Francisco, Calif. Died June 14, 1948.

ATHERTON, Henry Francis, bus. exec.; b. Nashua, N.H., Aug. 3, 1883; s. Henry Bridge and Abigail (Armington) A.; A.B., Harvard, 1905, LL.B., 1909; m. Madeline W. Wesson, Feb. 8, 1913; children—Henry Francis, Walter Humphry (dec.). Admitted to New York bar, 1909; practiced law, New York, N.Y., 1909-17; sec. Nat. Aniline and Chem. Co., Inc., 1919-28; sec. Allied Chem. and Dye Corp., 1928-34, pres., 1934-46, chmn. board since 1935. Served as capt., U.S. Army, 1917-19. Mem. Assn. of Bar of City of N.Y. Club: Harvard (New York). Home: Oyster Bay, L.I., N.Y. Office: 61 Broadway, New York, N.Y. Died Feb. 10, 1949.

ATHERTON, Percy Lee, composer; b. Boston, Mass., Sept. 25, 1871; s. William and Mary Edwards (Dwight) A.; student Phillips Acad., Andover, Mass.; A.B., Harvard U., (honors in music), 1893; Royal High Sch. of Music, Munich, Bavaria, 1893-95; studied with Rheinberger, 1893-95; with O. B. Boise in Berlin, 1896; with Sgambati in Rome, 1900, and, later, with Widor in Paris; unmarried. Composer: The Heir Apparent, comic opera (text by Alfred Raymond), 1888-90; The Maharaja, Oriental opéra-comique (text by same), 1897-1900; several orchestral sketches; two sonatas, a suite and smaller pieces for violin and pianoforte; suite for flute and pianoforte; a number of pianoforte pieces; choruses, part-songs, song-cycles and about 100 songs for solo voice. Mem. Harvard Musical Assn. Clubs: St. Botolph, Harvard (Boston); Harvard, Coffee House (New York); Metropolitan, Sulgrave (Washington, D.C.). Acting-chief Music Div., Library of Congress, 1929-32. Address: Metropolitan Club, Washington, D.C. Died Mar. 8, 1944.

ATKESON, William Oscar, congressman; b. nr. Buffalo, W.Va., Aug. 24, 1854; s. Thomas and Virginia Harris (Brown) A.; Ky. U., 1873-74; grad. Fairmont (W.Va.) State Normal Sch., 1875; A.M., Pleasureville (Ky.) Normal Coll.; m. Lizzie W. Warnick, May 21, 1884 (died 1899); children—Oscar Clark (dec.), Virginia Wheat (dec.), Gladys C. (Mrs. J. W. McCreery), Floyd Warnick, Ralph Wendell, Clarence Edgar. Admitted to the Mo. bar in 1882; pros. atty. Bates Co., Mo., 1891-92; dep. labor commr., Mo., 1910-12; newspaper man; mem. 67th Congress (1921-23), 6th Mo. Dist. Republican. Odd Fellow, Woodman. Author: History of Bates County, Missouri, 1918; From the Marais des Cygnes, 1920. State warehouse commr., by apptmt. of gov. of Mo., term 1923-27. Home: Butler, Mo. Died Oct., 1932.

ATKINS, George Tyng, railroad exec.; b. Petersburg, Va., Aug. 13, 1878; s. George Tyng and Elizabeth Mayo (Harrison) A.; ed. pub. and private schs.; m. Annie Linda Evans, Aug. 31, 1904; children—Annie Linda (Mrs. Marion F. Fooshee, dec.), George Tyng, William Allen, Harriet Alford (Mrs. James S. Legg), John White (dec.), Sergeant Luther Walter, Lieutenant Dudley Townsend (killed in action, Rendova, July 4, 1943). Messenger in auditor's office, Tex. & Pacific Ry., Dallas, 1897; clerk, auditor's office, Mo., Kan. and Tex. Ry., Dallas, 1898-1901, successively file clk., rate clk., chief rate clk., gen. freight office, 1901-06; commercial agent, Mar.-Oct. 1906, chief clerk, general freight office, 1906-10; freight traffic mgr., Shreveport (La.) Chamber Commerce, 1910-18, during which time the "Shreveport Case" was filed and successfully prosecuted before Interstate Commerce Commn. Commerce Court, various state and federal courts, including U.S. Supreme Court; traffic asst., div. pub. service and accounting, U.S.R.R. Administrn., Washington, D.C., July 1918-Feb. 1919, asst. dir. div. pub. service, Feb. 1919-Mar. 1920; freight traffic mgr. M.,K&T. Lines, 1920-26; v.p. traffic M-K-T R.R. Co., 1926-35, exec. v.p. since 1935, executive vice pres. and director M-K-T R.R. Co. of Tex. and Beaver, Meade & Englewood R.R. Co.; Mo., Kan. & Tex. Transportation Co.; dir. Joplin Union Depot Co., The Union Depot Realty Co. (Joplin, Mo.), San Antonio Belt & Terminal Railway Co., Texas Central R.R. Co., Union Terminal Co. of Dallas, Wichita Falls & Northwestern Ry. Co. of Texas, Wichita Falls & Wellington Ry. Co. of Texas, Wichita Falls Ry. Co., Texas City Terminal Ry. Co. Episcopalian. Club: Noonday (St. Louis). Home: 5369 Maple Av. Office: Railway Exchange Bldg., St. Louis, Mo. Died May 3, 1945.

ATKINSON, Eleanor, author; b. Rensselaer, Ind.; d. Isaac M. and Margaret (Smith) Stackhouse; grad. Indianapolis Normal Training Sch.; m. Francis Blake Atkinson, Mar. 14, 1891. Teacher, Indianapolis and Chicago pub. schs. 4 yrs.; spl. writer Chicago Tribune, 1889-91, under pen name of Nora Marks; editor The Little Chronicle, 1909-07. Corr. mem. Chicago Hist. Soc. Author: Mamzelle Fifine (his. novel), 1903; The Boyhood of Lincoln, 1908; Lincoln's Love Story, 1909; The Story of Chicago, 1910; Greyfriars Bobby, 1912; A Loyal Love, 1912; The "How and Why" Library, 1913; Johnny Appleseed, 1915; Pictured Knowledge, 1916; Hearts Undaunted, 1917; Poilu, A Dog of Roubaix, 1918. Home: Manhasset, L.I. Died Nov., 1942.

ATKINSON, Samuel C., judge; b. Scottsboro, Ga., 1864; A.B., U. of Ga., 1884; m. Lila M. Screven; m. 2d, Lilly Slaton. Was judge City Court of Brunswick, Ga.; asso. justice Supreme Court of Ga. since Jan. 15, 1906, presiding justice since Sept. 22, 1937. Democrat. Home: Brunswick, Ga. Address: State Capitol, Atlanta, Ga. Died Oct. 5, 1942.

ATKINSON, Ralph, clergyman, educator; b. Liverpool, Eng., Oct. 1, 1871; s. John and Mary (Finnegan) A.; student Moody Inst., and McCormick Sem., Chicago; D.D., Franklin (now Muskingum) Coll., New Concord, O., 1908; D.D., Sterling Coll., 1925; m. Alice Barnett, Nov. 7, 1895; children—Barnett, Eva (Mrs. Truman Johnson), Ralph, Alice (Mrs. John Morgan Peirce). Irene (Mrs. Clarence Axtell), Clara (Mrs. Ray Gardner Brown), Gordon Campbell. Came to U.S., 1890, naturalized, 1899. Ordained ministry U.P. Ch., 1894; missionary to Ireland, 1889; associated with Dwight L. Moody in evangelical work, 1893; pastor Fifth Ch., Chicago, 1894-1902, First Ch., Sparta, Ill., 1902-07; evangelist, U.S. and Great Britain, 1907-09; pastor First Ch., Seattle, Wash., 1909-16; evangelist, 1916-18; with Dr. R. A. Torrey, in China, Japan and Korea, 1919; teacher of homiletics and evangelism and asso. dean Bible Inst., Los Angeles, 1918-29; Bible conference speaker and evangelist since 1929. Supt. missions U. P. Ch., Chicago, 1900-01; moderator of Presbytery, Chicago and Southern Ill.; del. to Gen. Assembly U. P. Ch., Philadelphia, Pa., 1899, Washington, Pa., 1911, Loveland, Colo., 1915, Cambridge, O., 1922, Washington, D.C., 1927, Pan Presbyn. Alliance, Cardiff, Wales, 1925, Conf. on Faith and Order, Lausanne, Switzerland, 1027. Dir. Music, Joint Gen. Assemblies of Presbyn. Chs., Atlanta, Ga., 1913; chmn. com. of evangelism, Fedn. of Chs., Seattle. Wash., 1911-14; del. World Conf. on Stewardship and Ch. Finance (Edinburgh), 1081; supt. missions Synod of Calif., 1934-39; moderator Gen. Assembly U.P. Ch. of North America,

1938-39. Mem. Pi Gamma Mu. Visited mission fields on trip around world, 1933. Home: 1023 Fremont Av., South Pasadena, Calif. Died June 21,

ATTERIDGE, Harold Richard, playwright; b. Lake Forest, Ill., July 9, 1886; s. Richard H. and Anna T. (O'Neill) A.; Ph.B., U. of Chicago, 1907; m. Mary Teresa Corless, Feb. 1, 1923. Began playwriting in 1905. Mem. Phi Kappa Psi. Club: Authors' (London). Author: A Winning Miss; The Girl in the Kimono (prod., Chicago, 1907); Vera Violetta; The Whirl of Society; Broadway to Paris (with George Bronson-Howard); The Honeymoon Express; The Passing Show of 1912 (with George Bronson-Howard); The Passing Show of 1913; Two Little Brides; The Man with Three Wives; The Whirl of the World; The Passing Show of 1914; Dancing Around; Maid in America; The Peasant Girl; The Passing Show of 1915; A World of Pleasure; Passing Show of 1916; Robinson Crusoe, Jr.; Passing Show of 1917; Show of Wonders; Doing Our Bit; Sinbad; Passing Show of 1918; Monte Cristo, Jr.; Passing Show of 1919; The Little Blue Devil; The Passing Show of 1921; The Last Waltz; Bombo; The Rose of Stamboul; Make It Snappy; Passing Show of 1922; Passing Show of 1923; The Dancing Girl; The Passing Show of 1925; Big Boy; Artists and Models, Paris Edition; Gay Paree; Everybody's Welcome; also talking picture scenarios (in collaboration) Artists and Models; The Courtesan; The Dream Girl; Marjorie; The Ritz Revue; Sky High; Princess Flavia; Night in Paris; Night in Spain; Ziegfeld Follies of 1927; Collette; New Gay Paree of 1927; The Greenwich Village Follies; Night in Spain; Night in Venice; Pleasure Bound; Broadway Nights; Duchess of Chicago; New Ziegfeld Follies, 1933; Thumbs Up. Active in radio work for several years, writing outstanding programs. Club: Fraternity. Home: Lynbrook, L.I., N.Y.* Died Jan. 16, 1938.

ATWATER, David Hay, corp. official; b. Fall River, Mass., Nov. 9, 1898; s. William Cutler and Ida Wilson (Hay) A.; ed. pvt. schs.; student Phillips Andover Acad., 1915-17; m. Eleanor Bartlett, Aug. 10, 1918; children—David Hay, Damaris Sayre, Sally Anne, Eleanor Bartlett, Nathaniel Bartlett. Clk. with Elkhorn Coal Co., 1918-22; v.p. and gen. mgr. Wm. C. Atwater & Co., Inc. (Fall River, Mass.), 1922-30, president and general manager since 1930; also president Atwater Steamship Company, Atwacoal Transportation Co., Old Colony Machine Works Co., Fall River Nav. Co.; dir. Durfee Trust Co. Served in A.E.F., U.S. Army, World War. Trustee Union Hosp. Protestant. Mason (32°). Clubs: Lions, Quequechan (Fall River); Fall River Yacht (Tiverton, R.I.); Cruising of America. Office: 150 S. Main St., Fall River, Mass.* Died Sep. 25, 1944.

ATWATER, Helen Woodard, home economist; b. Somerville, Mass., May 29, 1876; d. Wilbur Olin (prof. chemistry, Wesleyan U., Conn.) and Marcia (Woodard) A.; B.L., Smith Coll., 1897, D.Sc., 1943. Was editorial asst. to father, an investigator in problems of human nutrition; mem. scientific staff Office of Home Economics, Dept. of Agr., 1909-23; editor Jour. of Home Economics, 1923-41. Executive chmn. dept. of food prodn. and home economics of Woman's Com. Council of Nat. Defense; chmn. Women's Joint Congressional Com., 1926-28. Fellow A.A.A.S.; mem. Am. Home Econ. Assn.. Am. Public Health Assn. (mem. com. on hygiene of housing 1942-46), Am. Assn. Univ. Women, Omicron Nu, Health Assn. (chmn. com. on hygiene of housing since 1942), Am. Assn. Univ. Women, Omicron Nu, Phi Upsilon Omicron. Club: Women's Nat. Press (Washington, D.C.). Author of U.S. Dept. Agr. bulls., mag. articles and other publs. on nutrition and home economics. Home: 3133 Connecticut Av. N.W., Washington, D.C. Died June 26, 1947.

ATWILL, Lionel, actor; b. Croydon, Eng., Mar. 1, 1885; s. Alfred and Ada Emily (Dace) A.; ed. under pvt. tutor and at Mercer's Sch., London; m. Elsie Mackay, of Australia, 1920; m. 2d, Mrs. Louise Cromwell MacArthur, June 1930 (divorced); 1 son, John Anthony; m. 3d, Mrs. Paula Pruter Shelstone, July 1944. Began as architect; first appearance in The Walls of Jericho, at Garrick Theatre, London, 1905; toured in plays of Shakespeare, Shaw, Pinero, Galsworthy, Ibsen, and several current successes; in Australia, 1910; returned to London, 1912—played in Milestones, Poor Little Rich Girl, Little Minister, Years of Discretion; came with Mrs. Langtry to U.S., 1915, and toured as Dick Marsden in Mrs. Thompson; played in New York in The Lodger, Eve's Daughter, L'Elevation, Wild Duck, Hedda Gabler, Doll's House, Tiger! Tiger!!; starred by Belasco in Deburau, The Grand Duke, The Comedian; appeared season of 1923-24 in The Heart of Cellini, later in The Outsider, and in Cæsar and Cleopatra, 1925, in Beau Gallant, 1926; directed The Squall, Lady Alone, The Adventurer, The Thief, and played in same, 1926-27; played Napoleon in play of same name, also played in revival of The Outsider, season 1927-28; in The Silent Witness, 1931; in motion pictures, 1932-33, in Silent Witness, Dr. X, Wax Museum, Song of Songs, Nana, The Devil is a Woman, Captain Blood, The High Command (England), Three Comrades, The Great Waltz, Son of Frankenstein, Hound of the Baskervilles, The Sun Never Sets, etc. Clubs: British Commonwealth; Green Room (London); Maryland Yacht, Baltimore Country. Address: White Lodge, Pacific Palisades, Calif. Died Apr. 22, 1946.

ATWOOD, Frank Ely, lawyer; b. Carrollton, Mo., Oct. 5, 1878; s. Jacob Smith and Nancy (Goodson) A.; student U. of Mo., 1898; A.B., William Jewell Coll., Liberty, Mo., 1902, A.M., 1912, LL.D., 1930; read law in office of Lozier & Morris, Carrollton; m. Agnes Rea Luscombe, Oct. 22, 1908. Admitted to Mo. bar, 1904; mem. Lozier, Morris & Atwood, Carrollton, 1905-11; sr. mem. Atwood & Atwood; mayor of Carrollton, 1914-15; pros. atty. Carroll County, Mo., 1915-19; legal adviser Draft Board, Carroll County, 1917-18; mem. Mo. Constl. Conv., 1922 (chmn. com. on suffrage and elections); asst. gen. counsel Mo. Pub. Service Commn., 1923-24; judge Supreme Court of Mo., 1925-35; resumed practice. Del. Rep. Nat. Conv., 1936; mem. Rep. Program Com., 1938-40. Trustee William Jewell Coll. Mem. Am. Bar Assn. (chmn. spl. com. on law lists, 1937-39), Mo. State Bar Assn. (pres. 1934-35), Am. Law Inst., Am. Judicature Soc. (pres. 1938), Mo. Inst. for Adminstrn. of Justice (dir.), Phi Gamma Delta, Phi Delta Phi, Order of the Coif. Republican. Baptist. Mason. Home: 1008 Fairmount Blvd. Office: Central Trust Bldg., Jefferson City, Mo. Died Mar. 5, 1943.

ATWOOD, Hinckley Gardner, mfr.; b. Northwood, Ia., July 14, 1871; s. Gardner Hinckley and Martha (Dunning) A.; B.S., Cedar Valley Sem., Osage, Ia., 1889; m. Cecyl Conway, Nov. 27, 1900; children—Harry G., Guy D. Pres. Atwood-Stone Co. (grain commn.), Minneapolis, Minn., 1900-10; pres. Am. Milling Co., Peoria, Ill., since 1910; chmn. bd., pres., Allied Mills, Inc.; pres. Century Distilling Co.; dir. Pabst Brewing Co., C.,B.& Q. Ry. Co. Mem. Chicago Board of Trade. Clubs: Creve, Cœur, Country (Peoria); Union League (Chicago). Home: 505 Parkside Dr., Peoria, Ill. Office: Board of Trade Bldg., Chicago, Ill. Died June 27, 1941.

ATWOOD, J(ames) Arthur, banker, mfr.; b. Wauregan, Conn., May 18, 1864; s. James S. and Julia A. M. (Haskell) A.; Ph.B., Yale, 1885; m. Helen Louise Mathewson, Dec. 11, 1888 (dec.); children—James Arthur (dec.), Dorothy; m. 2d, Elsie Hopkins Young, Nov. 4, 1926. Agent for the Wauregan Co., 1889-1908, Quinebaug Co., Danielson, Conn., 1897-1908, gen. mgr. both, 1908-17, treas., 1917-32; gen. mgr. Lockwood Co., Waterville, Me., 1908-11; pres. Williamsville (Conn.) Mfg. Co., 1890-1902, Windham County Nat. Bank, 1904-14; treas. Ponemah Mills, 1909-32, now president; pres. Brooklyn (Conn.) Savings Bank, Wauregan Mills, Incoroprated; dir. Am. Mut. Liability Ins. Co., Firemen's Mut. Ins. Co., R.I. Hosp. Trust, Union Mut. Fire Ins. Co., Lorraine Mfg. Co., Pawtucket, R.I. Mem. Delta Psi. Republican. Clubs: St. Anthony (New York); Misquamicut Golf (Watch Hill, R.I.). Home: Wauregan, Conn. Died Sep. 26, 1949.

ATWOOD, Julius Walter, bishop; b. Salisbury, Vt., June 27, 1857; s. Frank Carley and Sarah M. (Thomas) A.; A.B., Middlebury (Vt.) Coll., 1878, A.M., 1882; student, Gen. Theol. Sem., New York, 1878-79; B.D., Episcopal Theol. Sch., 1882, D.D., 1913; m. Anna Richmond, Nov. 13, 1895 (died 1907); two daughters—Mrs. Elizabeth Duer Curtin and Mrs. Ellen Ives. Ordained deacon, 1832, priest, 1883, P.E. Church; rector Ch. of the Ascension, Ipswich, Trinity, Columbus, Ohio, 1894-1906, Trinity, Phoenix, Ariz., 1906-11; consecrated bishop of Ariz., Jan. 18, 1911, resigned, 1925; asst. to bishop of Md., 1926, to bishop of Pa., 1927-30; to bishop of Mass., 1930, Conn. and Western Mass., 1931; spl. preacher in English and Am. cathedrals and chs. Archdeacon, Diocese of Ariz., 1907-11; deputy to Gen. Conv., 1910; founder, and pres. St. Luke's Homes, Phoenix, Tucson and Prescott. Spl. lecturer on ch. history, U. of the South and Kenyon Coll. Mem. Essex Inst., Ohio Hist. Soc., Am. Geog. Soc., S.A.R. (chaplain-gen., 1904-07). Clubs: Century (New York); Cosmos (Washington); Authors' (London). Author: The Spiritual Influence of John Greenleaf Whittier, 1893; also sermons and addresses. Home: Phoenix, Ariz. and Cosmos Club, Washington, D.C. Office: Church Missions House, 281 4th Av., New York, N.Y. Died Apr. 10, 1945.

ATWOOD, Millard V., newspaper editor; b. Groton, N.Y., Aug. 6, 1886; s. Frank R. and Minnie A. (Van Marter) A.; A.B., Cornell U., 1910; m. Grace Doughty, Dec. 14, 1911; children—Ruth, Martha, Susan. Began as reporter, 1904; telegraph editor Ithaca (N.Y.) News, 1910-11; publisher weeklies in central N.Y., 1911-24; mem. extension staff, N.Y. State Coll. of Agr., Cornell U., 1918-24, prof. of extension teaching, 1923-24; mng. editor Utica Observer-Dispatch, 1924-27; mng. editor Rochester Times-Union, 1927-29; asso. editor The Gannett Newspapers since 1929. Mem. Am. Assn. of Agrl. Coll. Editors (sec. 1921-22, pres. 1922-23), Am. Soc. Newspaper Editors (sec. 1934 30; v.p. since 1940), Frank E. Gannett Newspaper Foundation (dir.), Phi Beta Kappa, Sigma Delta Chi. Presbyterian. Mason. Clubs: Cornell, City (Rochester). Author: The Country Newspaper, 1923; (with Amy H. Croughton) Shepard's Pie, 1933; Grace in Thine Eyes, 1935; Some Other Power, 1937; Sawdust in His Shoes, 1940. Home: 566 Arnett Blvd. Office: Times-Union Bldg., Rochester, N.Y. Died Nov. 3, 1941.

ATWOOD, Wallace Walter, geographer, geologist; b. Chicago, Ill., Oct. 1, 1872; s. Thomas Green and Adalaide Adelia (Richards) A.; B.S., U. of Chicago, 1897, Ph.D., 1903 D.Sc., Worcester Polytechnic Institute, 1943; LL.D., Clark University, Worcester, Mass., 1946; married Harriet Towle Bradley, Sept. 22, 1900; children—Rollin Salisbury, Wallace Walter, Jr., Mrs. Harriet Olmsted, Mrs. Mary Hedge. Asst. geologist, N.J. Geol. Survey, 1897, Wis. Natural History Survey, 1898-99; instr., Lewis Inst., Chicago, 1897-99, Chicago Inst., 1900-01; fellow asst. and asso., 1899-1903, instr. and asst. prof. physiography and gen. geology, 1903-10, asso. prof., 1910-13, U. of Chicago; prof. physiography, Harvard, 1913-20; president Clark Univ., Sept. 1920-1946, president emeritus since 1946; dir. Clark School of Geography, 1920-46. Asst. geologist, U.S. Geological Survey, 1901-09, geologist since 1909; geologist, Ill. Geol. Survey since 1906. Recipient, distinguished service award, U. of Chgo. 1945, distinguished service medal, Chgo. Geog. Soc., 1948. Pres. Nat. Parks Assn., 1929-33. Fellow Geol. Soc. Am., Am. Acad. Arts and Sciences, Am. Antiquarian Soc.; mem. Assn. Am. Geographers (ex-pres.), Chicago Geog. Soc., Ill. Acad. Sciences, Chicago Museum and Library Extension Council, Nat. Council Geography Teachers, Delta Kappa Epsilon; pres. Pan-Am. Inst. of Geography and History, 1932-35, now hon. pres.; mem. Commn. Internationale de l'Atlas des Formes du Relief Terrestre; hon. member National Academy of Science of Mexico, Mexican Society of Geography and Statistics. Capt., Harvard R.O.T.C., 1917. Author: Physical Geography of the Devils Lake Region (with R.D. Salisbury), 1899; Physical Geography of the Evanston-Waukegan Region of Ill. (with J. W. Goldthwait), 1908; Interpretation of Topographic Maps, 1908; Glaciation of the Uinta and Wasatch Mountains, 1909; Mineral Resources of Southwestern Alaska, 1910; Geology and Mineral Resources of the Alaska Peninsula, 1911; New Geography, Book II, 1920; Home Life in Far Away Lands, 1928; The Americas, 1929; Nations Beyond the Seas, 1930; The United States Among the Nations, 1930; The World at Work, 1931; Physiography and Quaternary Geology of the San Juan Mountains, Colorado, 1932; The Growth of Nations, 1936; Physiographic Provinces of North America, 1940; The Protection of Nature in the Americas (publ. No. 50, Pan-Am. Institute of Geog. and History), 1941; The United States in the Western World, 1944; The Rocky Mountains, 1945; co-author (with Ruth E. Pitt) Our Economic World, 1948; also numerous sci., and ednl. papers. Founder and editor of Economic Geography, 1925. Clubs: Worcester, Worcester Economic; Tatnuck Country; Cosmos (Washington, D.C.); University (Boston and New York). Home: 21 Otsego Road, Worcester 5, Mass. Died July 24, 1949.

AUCHINCLOSS, Gordon (aw'chin-clŏs), lawyer; b. N.Y. City, June 15, 1886; s. Edgar Stirling and Maria La Grange (Sloan) A.; grad. Groton (Mass.) Sch., 1904; A.B., Yale, 1908; LL.B., Harvard, 1911; m. Janet, d. Col. Edward M. House, Sept. 14, 1912; children—Louise, Edward House. Began practice in New York, 1911; asst. U.S. atty., Southern Dist. N.Y., 1913-15; spl. asst. to atty. gen. of U.S. in charge certain tax litigation, 1915-17; asst. treas. Dem. Nat. Com., 1916; apptd. asst. to the counselor of Dept. of State, May 1917; sec. Am. War Mission to Eng. and France, Nov. 1917; sec. to Col. Edward M. House during negotiations of Armistice, Paris, Nov. 1918 and during Peace Conf., Paris, 1919. Mem. law firm Auchincloss, Alley & Duncan, New York; dir. Chase Nat. Bank of City of N.Y., Internat. Paper & Power Co., The Crosse & Blackwell Co., Societe Financiere de Transports et d'Entreprises Industrielles (Brussels), Solvay Am. Corp., Compania Hispano Americana de Electricidad (Barcelona). Mem. N.Y. State Bar Assn., Assn. Bar City of N.Y., Psi Upsilon, Scroll and Key (Yale). Presbyterian. Clubs: Links, Broad Street (New York); Piping Rock (Locust Valley). Home: Locust Valley, L.I., N.Y. Office: 50 Broadway, New York, N.Y. Died Apr. 16, 1943.

AUER, John, pharmacologist, physiologist; b. Rochester, N.Y., Mar. 30, 1875; s. Henry and Luise (Hummel) A.; S.B., U. of Mich., 1898; M.D., Johns Hopkins Med. Sch., 1902; m. Clara Meltzer, Oct. 1, 1903; children—James, Helen, John. Med. house officer, Johns Hopkins Hosp., 1902-03; fellow, asst., asso. and asso. mem. Rockefeller Inst. for Med. Research, 1903-06 and 1907-21; instructor in physiology, Harvard Medical Sch., 1906-07; prof. pharmacology and dir. Dept., St. Louis U. Sch. of Medicine, since 1921; pharmacologist, St. Mary's group of hosps., since 1924. Mem. Am. Assn. for Advancement of Science, Am. Physiological Society, Am. Society for Pharmacology and Exptl. Therapeutics (sec. 1912-16; pres., 1924-27), Soc. for Exptl. Biology and Medicine (v.p. 1917-19), Assn. Am. Physicians, Harvey Soc., St. Louis Acad. Sciences, St. Louis Med. Soc. Maj. Med. Officers' Reserve Corps, 1917-22. Contbr. researches: Investigations on Digestion; Respiration; Heart; Physiological Action of Various Drugs; Functional Disturbances Caused by Anaphylaxis; Studies on War Gas, Tetanus, Reflexes, Connective Tissue, Liver, Gall-bladder. Home: 1936 McCausland Av., St. Louis 17. Office: 1402 S. Grand Av., St. Louis 4, Mo. Died Aug. 30, 1948.

AUERBACH, Herbert S., merchant; b. Salt Lake City, Utah, Oct. 4, 1882; s. Samuel H. and Eveline (Brooks) A.; student Fresenius Labs. and J. J. Meier Sch., Wiesbaden, Germany, 1897-99; Lausanne Tech. Sch., Lausanne, Switzerland, 1901; Mining Engr., Columbia University Sch. of Mines; M.A., Columbia University, Electro Metallurgy; unmarried. Mining engr. in charge properties in Ida. and Colo., 1906-10; engaged in real estate, building and mercantile bus., Salt Lake City, since 1911; pres. and mgr. Auerbach Co. Dept. Store; pres. Auerbach Realty Co., Brooks Co.; chmn. bd. dirs. Federal Reserve Bank (Salt Lake City branch, Dist. 12). Major, Ordnance sect. U.S. Army, 1918. Mem. Army Ordnance Assn., Washington (1918-43). Pres. Utah State Hist. Soc. Mem. Am. Soc. of Composers, Authors and Publishers. Clubs: Rotary, Sons of Pioneers, Timpanogos (Salt Lake City). Home: 368 S. State St. Office: Broadway at State St., Salt Lake City, Utah. Died Mar. 19, 1945.

AUERBACH, Joseph S., lawyer, author; s. Dr. Julius and Alice (Cornell) A.; A.B., New York U., 1875, LL.B., 1877, A.M., 1891 (Litt.D., 1918); m. Katharine Hone, 1881; children—John Hone, Helen D. (Mrs. Herman LeRoy Emmet). Practiced in New York since 1879; now mem. Davies, Auerbach, Cornell & Hardy; dir. City & Suburban Homes Co. Mem. New York and George Washington U. Councils. Mem. Am. and N.Y. State bar assns., Assn. Bar of City of New York, Met. Museum of Art, etc. Trustee of the Mutual Life Ins. Co. Clubs: Union, University, Authors, Delta Phi, etc. Author: The Lesson of Bishop Potter's Life, 1912; Essays and Miscellanies (3 vols.), 1914-23; The Bible and Modern Life, 1914; "A Club," 1915; DeLancy Nicoll—an Appreciation; The Bar of Other Days, 1940. Home: University Club, 1 W. 54th St. Office: 1 Wall St., New York, N.Y. Died Sep. 16, 1944.

AUF DER HEIDE, Oscar Louis, ex-congressman; b. N.Y. City, Dec. 8, 1874; s. Carl F. and Louise A.; ed. pub. schs.; m. Mary Andras, Aug. 18, 1895; children—Carl F., Mrs. May M. Johnsen, Oscar L. In real estate business, West New York; mem. Town Council, 1899-1902; pres. Bd. of Edn., 1903-04; mem. N.J. State Assembly, 1908-11, inclusive; mem. Bd. of Assessors, West New York, 1912, 13; mayor of West New York, 1914-17; mem. Bd. Freeholders of Hudson County, N.J., 1915-24; mem. 69th to 72d Congresses (1925-33), 11th N.J. Dist., and 73d Congress (1933-35), 14th N.J. Dist. Democrat. Home: West New York, N.J. Democrat. Home: West New York, N.J. Died March 29, 1945.

AUGUSTINE, William Franklin, banker; b. Richmond, Va., Nov. 16, 1885; s. John Anthony and Elizabeth Olivia (Hamill) A.; educated pub. schs., Richmond; student in law, Richmond Coll. (now U. of Richmond); m. Carrie Pace Neal, Mar. 27, 1912; 1 dau., Carrie Neal (Mrs. Frank A. Pickard). Began bus. career with Merchants Nat. Bank, Richmond, Va., 1902, asst. cashier, 1912-18, vice-pres., 1918-26; v.p. First and Merchants Nat. Bank, 1926; vice-pres. Nat. Shawmut Bank of Boston since Jan. 1, 1927; vice pres. Hingham (Mass.) Trust Co.; dir. Melrose (Mass.) Trust Co.; trustee Franklin Savings Bank, Boston. Chmn. Bankers Com. of New England Council. Treas. Va. Bankers Assn., 1914-19, sec. 1919-26; treas. Mass. Bankers Assn., 1933-34, mem. Ins. com., 1934-38. Mem. Am. Bankers Assn. (treas. 1941-43; pres. state sec. sect., 1924-25; pres. clearing house sect. 1928-29; pres. nat. bank div. 1936-37; mem. exec. council 1924-25, 1927-29, 1931-32, 1935-39, 1941-43, 1945-47), Assn. Res. City Bankers (pres. 1929), Jamestown Soc., Soc. Colonial Wars, S.R., Phi Kappa Sigma. Mason. Episcopalian. Clubs: Country (Brookline); Commonwealth (Richmond). Home: 800 High St., Dedham, Mass. Died Feb. 9, 1947; buried at Richmond, Va.

AUGUSTYN, Godfrey William, chmn. bd. Marine Nat. Exchange Bank; b. Milwaukee, Wis., Jan. 3, 1872; s. Jacob V. A. and Sya (Krueger) A.; ed. pub. schs.; m. Catharine DeBlaey, May 8, 1894. Began with Nat. Exchange Bank, Milwaukee, as messenger, 1890, became asst. cashier, 1913, cashier, 1922, dir., 1924, v.p., 1925, pres., 1929; Nat. Exchange Bank and Marine Nat. Bank consolidated July 31, 1930, and became pres. Marine Nat. Exchange Bank, chmn. bd. since Jan. 1942; treas. Colby Besemer Iron Co.; dir. Leader Card Works. Mem. Milwaukee Bd. of Edn., 20 yrs., pres., 2 terms. Trustee Milwaukee Public Library and Museum. Home: 1116 W. Wright St. Office: 625 N. Water St., Milwaukee, Wis. Died Sep. 10, 1944.

AUSTIN, Albert E., ex-congressman; b. Medway, Mass., Nov. 15, 1877; A.B., Amherst Coll., 1899, A.M., 1904; M.D., Jefferson Med. Coll., 1905. Consulting internist Greenwich Hosp., Conn.; pres. and mem. of bd., Trust Co. of Old Greenwich, since 1925. Mem. 76th Congress (1939-41), 4th Conn. Dist. Home: Lucas Point, Old Greenwich, Conn. Died Jan. 26, 1942.

AUSTIN, Richard Loper, banker; b. Phila., Pa., Mar. 28, 1859; s. John Brander and Sarah (Bell) A.; ed. Phila. High Sch.; m. Lorraine Fleming, Dec. 9, 1886 (died 1912); 1 dau., Lucylle. Began as clk. Central Nat. Bank, Phila., 1876; cashier Independence Nat. Bank, 1885-89, pres., 1889-1901; v.p. Girard Nat. Bank, 1901-14, pres., 1914; an organizer Fed. Reserve Bank, Phila., Nov. 1914, and fed. reserve agent and chmn. of bd., 1914-38. Mem. bd. trustees Gen. Assembly of Presbyn. Ch., Presser Foundation. Club: Union League. Home: Union League Club, Philadelphia, Pa. Died Sep. 10, 1948.

AUSTIN, William Lane, statistician; b. "Hurricane Farm," Scott County, Miss., Jan. 25, 1871; s. Richmond Pearson (M.D.) and Sue D. (Lane) A.; Harperville (Miss.) Coll., 1886-91; Ph.B., U. of Miss., 1897, LL.B., 1898; m. Eley D. Campbell, Dec. 29, 1903 (died Nov. 1, 1939). With U.S. Bur. of Census since 1900, statistician in charge census of plantations, 1910, chief clk., 1913-17; chief statistician div. agr., 1917-32, also chief statistician div. of cotton and tobacco statistics, 1917-29, in charge 14th decennial census of agr., irrigation and drainage; 1919-22, of 1925 census of agr., 1924-26, and of 15th decennial census of agr., horticulture, irrigation and drainage, 1930-32; asst. dir. Bur. of Census, 1933, dir. 1933-41; retired 1941. Mem. Am. Statis. Assn., Internat. Statis. Inst., Inter-Am. Statis. Inst., Phi Kappa Psi. Mason. Democrat. Methodist. Home: Eastland Plantation, Doddsville, Miss. Died Oct. 10, 1949.

AUTEN, James Ernest (aw't'n), corporation executive; b. Berlin Township, Knox County, Ohio, July 8, 1883; s. William A. and Ida (Steele) A.; ed. pub. schs. and mech. engring. course Internat. Corr. Sch.; m. Bertha J. Harre, Dec. 17, 1908 (died July 1936); m. 2d, Mary J. Dillon, Nov. 21, 1942; children —Hudson W., Richard L., James William, Mary Steele. Employe Goodrich Rubber Co., Akron, O., 1898; bookkeeper and cashier J. Parker Alexander Brick Co., Akron, 1901-03; draftsman Sterling Boiler Co., 1903-04; developing and designing pumping and elec. machinery in engring. depts., successively with Wellman, Seaver Morgan Co., and White Motor Co., Cleveland, O.; H. H. Bridgewater Machine Company, Akron, O.; Sandusky Foundry Machine Company, Rice Barton & Fails Co., Worcester, Mass., Barber Coleman Co., Rockford, Ill., Western Electric Co., Chicago, 1908-09; master mechanic Indiana Harbor (Ind.) Works, Am. Steel Foundries, 1909-11; engr. of constrn. Firestone Tire & Rubber Co., Akron, 1911-14; charge of designing new plant, later asst. to pres. Cadillac Motor Car Co., 1914-18; asst. to pres. Sampson Tractor Co., 1918-20; with Lafayette Motor Co., later gen. mgr. Nash Motor Co., Milwaukee, Wis., 1920-33; asso. with Universal Winding Co., Providence, R.I., 1933-36; pres. and dir. Gen. Asphalt Co. (now Barber Asphalt Corp.), 1936-41; also during period 1936-41, inclusive, was mng. dir. Trinidad Lake Asphalt Operating Co., Ltd.; dep. chmn. and dir. Trinidad Lake Petroleum Co., Ltd., Petroleum Development Co., Ltd., Trinidad Lake Asphalt Co., Ltd., Trinidad Lake Asphalt (Overseas), Ltd., and pres. and dir. Uinta Ry Co. (Mack, Colo.); with W.P.B., Washington, D.C., 1942-45. Clubs: Racquet (Phila.); Rumson (N.J.) Country. Mason. Pioneer designer, constructor and operator Am. built comml. electric steel melting furnace. Home: 880 Judson Pl., Stratford, Conn. Died Oct. 1, 1947.

AVERS, Henry Godfrey (ā'vērs), mathematician; b. Elmore, O., Mar. 6, 1886; s. John H. H. and Elizabeth (Nieman) A.; Ohio Northern U., 1906-08; A.B., George Washington U., 1913; m. Helen Nelson, May 24, 1924. With U.S. Coast and Geodetic Survey since 1908, chief mathematician Div. of Geodesy since 1924. Mem. Math. Assn. America, Philos. Soc. Washington, Washington Soc. Engrs., Washington Acad. Sciences, A.A.A.S., Am. Soc. C.E. (sec. div. of surveying and mapping), Am. Geophysical Union (chmn. sect. of geodesy, 1932-35), Am. Astron. Society, American Congress on Surveying and Mapping. Mem. National Geog. Society Committee of Experts which determined that Comdr. Byrd reached North Pole by airplane, 1926 and the South Pole in 1929. Lutheran. Mason (32°, Shriner). Club: Cosmos. Author: Fourth General Adjustment of the Precise Level Net in the United States and the Resulting Standard Elevations (with William Bowie), 1914; Precise Leveling from Reno to Las Vegas, Nev., and from Tonopah Junction, Nev., to Laws, Calif. (with George D. Cowie), 1916; Precise Leveling in Texas, 1922; Precise Leveling in Georgia, 1923; Manual of First-Order Leveling, 1928; Triangulation in Utah, 1937. Home: 4109 38th St. N.W., Washington, D.C. Died Jan. 19, 1947.

AVERY, Clarence Willard, corp. official; b. Dansville, Mich., Feb. 15, 1882; s. Delvino Cortez and Elmina (Remington) A.; student Ferris Inst., 1901, U. of Mich., 1901-03, hon. D. Eng., 1947; m Lura Warner, Jan. 5, 1905; children—Eloise (Mrs. Harvey B. Greene), Anabel (Mrs. Robert V. Baxley). Manual training teacher and supervisor, 1903-12; successively foreman, supt., chief development engr., Ford Motor Co., 1912-27; mfg. mgr. and chief engr., Murray Corp. of America, 1927-28, pres., 1928-49, chmn. bd. since 1930. Pres. Detroit Board of Commerce, 1940-42; dir. Federal Reserve Bank of Chicago 1942-48, chmn. bd. and Fed. Res. agent 1947-48; dir. Kalamazoo Vegetable Parchment Co., Mich. Bell Telephone Co. since 1944. Clubs: Detroit Athletic, Detroit Club, Detroit Golf (Detroit), The Chicago (Chicago). Home: 1560 Wellesley Dr., 3. Office: Murray Corp. of America 7700 Russell St., Detroit 11, Mich. Died May 13, 1949.

AVERY, George True, educator; b. Georgetown, Colo., Apr. 17, 1880; s. George Washington and Cleora Francelle (Smith) A.; A.B., U. of Colo., 1915; A.M., Harvard, 1917; Ph.D., Stanford U., 1924; m. Wilma Clyde Ellsworth, July 11, 1907; children—Wilma Lanore, George Ellsworth. Teacher in rural sch., Colo., 1900-01; in business, 1903-13; teacher of English, Greeley (Colo) High Sch., 1915-16; asst. prof. psychology and edn., Colo. State Coll., 1916-19, asso. prof., 1919-33, dir. of summer sessions since 1919, prof. and head dept. rural and vocational edn. since 1933, dean, summer session, since 1940; on leave as acting supervisor of education, Moore Dry Dock, and United States Navy Yard, 1943; now dir. of training Joshua Hendy Iron Works and United States Maritime Commission, Sunnyvale, Calif.; acting prof. psychology and edn., San Jose State Coll., 1923-24. Mem. Colo. State Bd. for Vocational Edn. (pres. 1937), Colo. Classroom Teachers Assn. (pres. 1934-36, v.p. 1927-28, 1937-38), Colo. Edn. Assn. (pres. 1933, v.p. 1934), N.E.A. (v.p. 1935-36, chmn. com. on resolutions 1934-35), Am. Psychol. Assn. (pres. Rocky Mt. Br. 1934, exec. sec. 1938), Colo. Wesley Foundation (pres. 1933-34), Colo. Epworth League (pres. 1911), Colo.-Wyo. Acad. Science, Nat. Soc. for Study of Edn., Colo. Agrl. Coll. Scientific Soc. (pres. 1925, sec. 1922) Colo. Schoolmasters Club, Colo. Soc. for Mental Hygiene (dir.), Colo. Child Study Sect. (pres. 1929), Phi Beta Kappa, Sigma Xi, Phi Delta Kappa, Tau Psi Epsilon, Alpha Tau Alpha, Iota Lambda Sigma. Methodist. Mason. Author of monograph and articles to jours. Address: 651 Homer Av., Palo Alto, Calif. Died Dec. 26, 1944; buried in Alta Mesa Cemetery, Palo Alto.

AVERY, Moses Nathan, banker; b. Washtenaw County, Mich., Dec. 27, 1855; s. Nathan and Matilda (Rockwell) A.; student Eastman Business Coll., 1876; M.D., U. of Mich. Med. Sch., 1881; m. Sarah Elizabeth Gorton, 1880 (now deceased); children—Lena Ethel (dec.), Florence Lucile, Lewis Gorton. Practiced medicine at Niles, Mich., 1881-89; organized German Am. Savings Bank, Los Angeles, 1890 (original cashier, elected president, 1899), title was changed to Guaranty Trust & Savings Bank, 1917; v.p. and chmn. exec. com. Security Trust & Savings Bank, into which the Guaranty Trust & Savings Bank was merged, 1921; now mem. exec. and trust coms. and chmn. real estate mortgage loan com., Security-First Nat. Bank of Los Angeles (formed by merger of Security and First Nat. trust and savings banks); dir. Security-First Co., Washington Blvd. Beach Co. Mem. Los Angeles Chamber of Commerce. Republican. Presbyn. Clubs: California, Los Angeles Country. Home: 5930 Franklin Av., Hollywood, Los Angeles. Address: Security-First Nat. Bank of Los Angeles, Los Angeles, Calif.* Died Sep. 9, 1942.

AVERY, Nathan Prentice, lawyer; b. Norwich, Conn., May 13, 1869; s. Edwin P. and Adelaide L. (Smith) A.; A.B., Amherst Coll., 1891; studied law in office Hon. C. A. Hitchcock, Syracuse, N.Y., and with Hon. E. W. Chapin, Holyoke, Mass., 1891-95; post grad. study, Clark Univ., Worcester, 1895-96; m. Katharine Van Valkenburgh, July 7, 1897; children—Adelaide (Mrs. Frank E. Button), Katharine (Mrs. Carlos E. Allen). Served as prin. Yates High Sch., Chittenango, N.Y., 1891-95; admitted to Mass. bar, 1896, and since engaged in gen. practice at Holyoke; city solicitor, 1899-1904, mayor of Holyoke, Mass., 1904-10; mem. Constl. Conv. of Mass., 1917-18; mem. Bd. Referees, Met. Dist. Water Com.; mem. Avery, Healy & Button; trustee and clk. Mechanics Savings Bank; v.p., dir. J. and W. Jolly, Inc. Mem. Sch. Bd., Holyoke, Mass. Pres. Holyoke Pub. Library and Museum. Mem. Am. Bar Assn. (ho. del. from Mass.), Mass. State Bar Assn. (pres. 1932-35), Hampden County Bar Assn. (past pres.), Phi Beta Kappa, Theta Delta Chi. Apptd. by governor mem. Judicial Council of Mass. for term of 4 years. Congl.-Christian. Mason, Odd Fellow, Elk. Awarded, Amherst medal "for eminent service," 1941. Home: 1150 Northampton St. Office: 56 Suffolk St., Holyoke, Mass. Died Apr. 12, 1947.

AVES, Dreda, soprano; b. Norwalk, O.; d. Rev. Charles S. and Jessie Olivia (Hughes) Aves; ed. U. of Tex, 1913-14, Columbia, 1916; studied Damrosch Inst. of Musical Art, New York, 2 yrs, Début in Carmen, Baltimore, 1922; began with Metropolitan Opera Co., 1927; guest artist Dresden Opera Co., 1928, Phila. Civic Opera Co., 1927; has appeared in concerts with Friends of Music (New York), Detroit Symphony Orchestra, Cleveland Symphony Orchestra, etc.; toured with San Carlo Opera Co., 1924 and 1925. Address: San Carlo Opera Co., 1697 Broadway, New York. Died Apr. 17, 1942.

AVINOFF, Andrey (ă-vēn'ŏf), dir. emeritus Carnegie Museum; born Tulchin, Russia, February 14, 1884; s. Gen. Nicholas and Alexandra (Lukianovitch) A.; LL.M., U. of Moscow, 1905; Sc.D., U. of Pittsburgh, 1927; L.H.D., Washington and Jefferson Coll., 1934; unmarried. Specialized in entomology, and exhibited paintings since 1904; owned a noted collection of butterflies of Asia before the Revolution in Russia; served with Red Cross, World War I; came to U.S., 1917; asso. curator entomology, Carnegie Mus., 1924-26, dir. 1926-45. Adv. prof. zoology and adv. prof. fine arts, U. of Pittsburgh, 1928-45; v.p., Am. Assn. of Museums since 1944. Mem. Museum Assn. of England, also various learned socs. of Am. and of nine European countries, including Spanish Nat. Acad. of Sciences, Sigma Xi, Phi Sigma, Omicron Delta Kappa, Scabbard and Blade. Trustee Am. Mus. of Natural History. Mem. Russian Orthodox Ch. Clubs: Century Assn., Grolier. Address: 952 5th Av., New York, N.Y. Died July 16, 1949.

AVIS, John Boyd (ā'vis), judge; b. Deerfield, Cumberland Co., N.J., July 11, 1875; s. John H. and Sallie (Barker) A.; ed. pub. sch., Deerfield; hon. LL.D., South Jersey Law Sch., of Camden, 1938; m. Minnie Genung Anderson, Sept. 27, 1899 (dec.). Admitted to N.J. bar, 1898, and practiced at Woodbury until 1929; dir. Woodbury Trust Co. Judge U.S. Dist. Court, N.J. Dist., since 1929. Mem. N.J. Gen. Assembly, 1902-05 (speaker 1904-05); mem. N.J. State Senate, 1906-08; del. to Rep. Nat. Conv., 1912; Rep. presdl. elector, N.J., 1928. Presbyterian. Mason, Odd Fellow, Moose, Forester, Red Man; mem. Grange. Home: 48 Newton Av., Woodbury, N.J. Chambers: U.S. Court House, Camden, N.J. Died Feb. 1944.

AYER, Joseph Cullen, clergyman; b. Newton, Mass., Jan. 7, 1866; s. Joseph Cullen and Caroline Eliza (Roberts) A.; ed. Harvard, Berlin, Halle and Leipzig; B.D., Episcopal Theol. Sch., Cambridge, Mass., 1887; fellow Johns Hopkins, 1899-1900; A.M., Ph.D., Leipzig, 1893; hon. S.T.D., U. of the South, 1917; D.D. from Episcopal Theol. School, Cambridge, Mass., 1931; D.C.L., Divinity School of P.E. Church, Philadelphia; m. Cora Julia Whittaker, Jan. 11, 1894; children—

Caroline Elizabeth, Richard Gordon Lawrence. Deacon, 1887, priest, 1890, P.E. Ch.; asst. Charlestown, Mass., 1887; rector S. Groveland, Mass., 1888-90, Keene, N.H., 1893-95, Nantucket, Mass., 1895-99; lecturer on canon law, Episcopal Theol. Sch., Cambridge, Mass., 1901-05; prof. ecclesiastical history, P.E. Div. Sch., Phila., 1905-36; lecturer on History of Religions, Univ. of Pa., 1927-36; rector St. Philip's Ch., Phila., 1929-36; retired. Mem. Am. Ch. Historical Society, Oriental Club. Editor: The World's Orators (G. C. Lee, Editor-in-chief), vol. 2, vol. 3 (collaboration), and vol. 4, 1900. Author: Die Ethik Joseph Butlers, 1893; The Rise and Development of Christian Architecture, 1902; A Source Book for Ancient Church History, 1913. Also articles in revs. on canon law, music and painting. Home: 200 St. Mark's Sq., Philadelphia, Pa. Died Apr. 15, 1944.

AYNESWORTH, Kenneth Hazen (āns'wûrth), surgeon; b. Florence, Tex., Feb. 9, 1873; s. George Levin and Sarah Ellen (Hickman) A.; student at Baylor U., 1892-93, and 1893-94; M.D., U. of Tex., 1899; post-grad. work, Friederik Wilhelm U., Berlin, 1902, Johns Hopkins, 1909; LL.D., Baylor U., 1933; m. Maude Brian, Dec. 31, 1902; children—Kenneth Hazen, Morgan Brian, Edna Maude (wife of Dr. R. Wilson Crosthwait), Nancy Milling (Mrs. Thomas Clifton Mann). Became house surgeon John Sealy Hosp., Galveston, Tex., 1900; was demonstrator in anatomy, U. of Tex., 1901; in practice of surgery, Waco, since 1903; cons. surgeon M.K.&T. Ry. since 1906; on surg. staff Providence Sanitarium, Waco. Mem. Waco Sch. Bd. and Bd. of Health, 1906-16; chmn. Waco City Planning and Zoning Commn. since 1930; regent U. of Tex. since 1933, vice-chmn. bd. regents since 1941; chairman Baylor Centennial Foundation, Baylor University; commissioner Housing Authority of the City of Waco, Texas, since 1938. Fellow American College Surgeons, Texas Surg. Society (founder, ex-president), Southern Surg. Assn., American Board of Surgery, Texas Philos. Soc.; pres. McLennan County Med. Soc., 1939; mem. Am., Tex. State and County med. socs., Central Tex. Archeol. Soc., Tex. Acad. Science, Tex. State Hist. Assn., West Tex. Archeol. and Paleontol. Soc., Alpha Mu Pi Omega, Alpha Omega Alpha, etc. Donated large library on history of Tex. and Southwest to Baylor U., large med. library to Providence Sanitarium, Waco; also donated to Baylor U. thousands of specimens of Indian archeology. Democrat. Baptist. Mason. Club: Fish and Boating. Contbr. of articles to various surg. jours., also articles on higher edn. to various publs. Home: 415 Mt. Lookout Av. Office: 601 Franklin Av., Waco, Tex. Died Oct. 30, 1944.

AYRES, Albert Douglass (ârz), lawyer; b. Fort Bidwell, Calif., June 25, 1874; s. Irvin and Annie Laura (Poore) A.; student Oakland (Calif.) High Sch., 1889-93; U. of Calif., 1893-95; m. Emma McCormick (dec.); children—Albert Douglass, Irvin Leathe; m. 2d, Enola Sims (divorced). Admitted to Calif. bar, 1896; practiced at Oakland, 1897, San Francisco, 1899, Reno, Nev., 1900; now mem. Ayres, Gardiner & Pike. Dep. dist. atty. at Reno, 1908; mem. Nev. legislature, 1911-13. Mem. Am., Nev. State, Washoe County (Nev.), N.Y. County, City of New York bar assns. Formerly chmn. bd. of bar examiners of Nevada; formerly mem. Nat. Conf. Commrs. on Uniform State Laws. Mem. Sons Am. Revolution. Mason. K.P. Elk. Republican. Presbyterian. Home: 936 S. Virginia St. Office: 15 E. First St., Reno, Nev. Died Oct. 3, 1944.

AYRES, Harry Morgan, univ. prof.; b. Montclair Heights, N.J., Oct. 6, 1881; s. Morgan Willcox and Sarah Ella (Roe) A.; A.B., Harvard, 1902; Ph.D., 1908; m. Amy Wentworth Sawyer, June 6, 1905; children—Ann Wentworth (Mrs. Donald B. Hart), Mary Willcox (Mrs. John W. Draper, Jr.). Asst. in English, Harvard, 1904-05; lecturer in English, 1908-09, instr., 1909-10, asst. prof., 1910-19, asso. prof. 1919-28, prof. since 1928, dir. summer session since 1939; dir. Casa Italiana since 1940; acting dir. Univ. Extension, Columbia, 1942-46, dir. since 1946. Chmn. Westport (Conn.) Sch. Com., 1920-23; selectman, 1923-24; mem. Conn. Ho. of Rep., 1923-25. Mem. Modern Lang. Assn. America, Am. Dialect Society, Phi Beta Kappa. Clubs: Century, Harvard (New York). Translator: An Ingenious Play of Esmoreit, 1924; A Marvelous History of Mary of Nimmegen, 1924; Beowulf, 1933. Author: Carroll's Alice, 1936. Editor: (with others) The Modern Student's Book of English Literature, 1924; A School Dictionary of the English Language, 1925. Home: Woodbury, Conn. Office: Columbia University, New York 27, N.Y. Died Nov. 20, 1948.

AYRES, Leonard Porter, statistician; b. Niantic, Conn., Sept. 15, 1879; s. Milan Church and Georgiana (Gall) A.; Ph.B., Boston U., 1902, A.M., 1909, Ph.D., 1910, hon. Doc. Commercial Science, 1923; Teachers Coll. (Columbia), 1907-09; LL.D., from U. of Rochester, 1930; Litt.D. from Portia Law School, 1938; unmarried. Teacher in Puerto Rico, 1902; supt. schools, dist. of Caguas, 1903-04; city supt. schs., San Juan, 1904-06; gen. supt. schs., P.R., and chief div. statistics, 1906-08; dir. depts. edn. and statistics, Russell Sage Foundation, 1908-20; vice-pres. Cleveland Trust Co. since 1920, also dir. railroads including C. & O. Ry. Co. During World War dir. div. of statistics of War Industries Board, Priorities Bd., Council Nat. Defense, and Allies Purchasing Commn. Col., Gen. Staff and chief statis. officer U.S. Army; chief statistician A.E.F.; chief statis. officer Am. Commn. to Negotiate Peace; econ. adviser to Dawes Plan com., 1924; col. O.R.C., U.S. Army, and mem. Gen. Staff Eligibility List; returned to active duty, Oct. 1940; brig. gen., July 1941; retired 1942. Chairman, 1932-41 and since 1944, Economic Policy Commn. of American Bankers Association, chairman Research Council same since 1937; member Cleveland Foundation Distribution Com., 1922-40, also mem. S. P. Fenn Distbn. Com. Fellow Am. Statis. Assn. (pres. 1926), A.A.A.S. (v.p. 1919 and 1930); mem. Am. Econ. Assn. (v.p. 1934), N.E.A., Phi Beta Kappa, Beta Theta Pi. Author: Course of Study for Schools of San Juan, 1905; Medical Inspection of Schools (co-author), 1908, revised 1912; Laggards in Our Schools, 1909; Open Air Schools, 1910; Seven Great Foundations, 1911; The Public Schools of Springfield, Ill., 1914; The Measurement of Spelling Ability, 1915; School Buildings and Equipment, 1915; Health Work in the Public Schools, 1915; Child Accounting in the Public Schools, 1915; Organization and Administration, 1915; Summary of the School Survey of Cleveland, O., 1916; The War with Germany, 1919; Index Numbers for State School Systems, 1920; Price Changes and Business Prospects, 1921; The Automobile Industry and Its Future, 1921; Business Recovery Following Depression, 1922; The Nature and Status of Business Research, 1922; The Prospects for Building Construction in American Cities, 1922; Economics of Recovery, 1933; The Chief Cause of This and Other Depressions, 1935; Inflation, 1936; Turning Points in Business Cycles, 1939. Home: 2061 E. 96th St. Office: Cleveland Trust Co., Cleveland. Died Oct. 29, 1946; buried in Arlington National Cemetery.

AYRES, Louis, architect; b. Bergen Point, N.J., Aug. 25, 1874; s. Chester Derby and Mary Caroline (Ostrom) A.; B.S., Rutgers Coll., New Brunswick, N.J., 1896, L.H.D., 1926; studied architecture in the office of McKim, Mead & White, and office of York & Sawyer; m. Mrs. Edith M. (Donald) Twining, Nov. 28, 1928. Mem. firm York & Sawyer since 1910; firm architects for Federal Reserve Bank of N.Y., Bowery Savings Bank Bldg., Greenwich Savings Bank, Guggenheim Dental Clinic, N.Y. Acad. of Medicine, St. Luke's Hosp., Nurses' Residence, N.Y. City Hosp. for Chronic Diseases (all New York); First Nat. Bank of Boston; The Royal Bank of Canada (Montreal); Allegheny Gen. Hosp. (Pittsburgh); Legal Research Buildings of U. of Mich.; gymnasium and dormitories for Rutgers U.; U.S. Memorial Chapel, Meuse-Argonne Cemetery (France); U.S. Dept. of Commerce Bldg. (Washington). Member Federal Fine Arts Commn., 1921-25; member Smithsonian Fine Arts Commission, 1939. Fellow A.I.A.; member of National Academy of Design, National Institute of Arts and Letters. Clubs: Century, University (New York); Cosmos (Washington, D.C.). Home: 149 E. 73d St. Office: 101 Park Av., New York, N.Y. Died Nov. 30, 1947.

AYRES, Samuel Gardiner, educator; b. Peru, N.Y., Apr. 25, 1865; s. Rev. David Clough and Katharine C. (Moore) A.; grad. Burlington (Vt.) High Sch., 1885; Drew Theol. Sem., 1888; B.D., 1893; D.D., Garrett Biblical Inst., 1931; m. Olive Reynolds, Apr. 25, 1889. Asst. librarian, 1888-92, librarian, 1892-Sept. 1, 1911, Drew Theol. Sem.; pres. Correspondence Sch. of Theology, Madison, N.J., Sept. 1, 1911-Mar. 1, 1912; librarian with title asst. Garrett Bibl. Inst., 1912-24, asso. librarian, 1924-29, librarian, 1929-31, now emeritus. Mem. Troy Conf., Meth. Ch. Mem. A.L.A., N.J. Library Assn. (pres. 1902), Life mem. Ill. Library Assn., Meth. Hist. Soc. of N.Y.; hon. mem. New Eng. Meth. Hist. Soc., Browning Soc., N.Y.; mem. Am. Soc. of Church History. Author: Drew Theological Seminary Record, 1895; Fifty Literary Evenings, 1897 (2d series, 1904); History of the English Bible (with Charles Fremont Sitterly), 1899; Index to the Expositor's Bible, 1905; Alumni Record of Drew Theol. Sem., 1867-1905, 06; Jesus Christ Our Lord, An English Bibliography of Christology, 1907; A Calendar of Christian Thought, serial, 1909; Words of Comfort (feature), 1915-17; Methodist Heroes of Other Days, 1916; Asbury and His Helpers, 1916; In the Highlands (feature), 1917-20; The Troy Conference Centennial Pageant, 1932. Assisted in the revision of McClintock and Strong's Ency.; contbr. articles, Hymnology and many biog. articles to New Internat. Ency., 1903-05, 1914-16; articles in The Americana, 1918-19; contbr. to S.S. Cyclo., 1913, Dictionary of American Biography, 1931, and to religious periodicals. Since retirement has engaged in research into the history of churches of the Troy Conf. Meth. Ch. and its ministry; has furnished 69 churches with historical material for anniversaries. Address: 71 South Willard St., Burlington, Vt. Died Dec. 29, 1942.

B

BABB, Max Wellington, pres. Allis-Chalmers Mfg. Co.; b. Mt. Pleasant, Ia., July 28, 1874; s. Washington Irving and Alice (Bird) B.; A.B., Ia. Wesleyan Coll., Mt. Pleasant, 1895; LL.B., U. of Mich., 1897; m. Vida Kemble, Oct. 23, 1900; children—Winifred, Irving T., Max Wellington. Admitted to bar, 1897, and practiced at Mt. Pleasant in firm Babb & Babb; apptd. atty. Allis-Chalmers Co., 1904, and moved to Chicago, Ill., and later moved to Milwaukee, Wis.; vice-pres. and general attorney same, 1913-32, pres. since 1932; dir. Fed. Reserve Bank of Chicago, Allis-Chalmers Mfg. Co., Cutler-Hammer, Inc., Wis. Telephone Co.; trustee and mem. exec. com. Northwestern Mutual Life Ins. Co.; trustee Milwaukee-Downer Coll. Was dir. Chamber of Commerce U.S.A. Mem. Beta Theta Pi. Republican. Methodist. Clubs: Milwaukee, University, Milwaukee Country. Home: 6440 N. Lake Drive. Office: Allis-Chalmers Mfg. Co., Milwaukee, Wis. Died Mar. 13, 1943.

BABCOCK, Samuel Gavitt, bishop; b. Newport, R.I., Oct. 8, 1851; s. Stanton and Sarah J. B.; took spl. courses in coll.; grad. Episcopal Theol. Sch., Cambridge, Mass., 1891, B.D., 1897; (D.D., Brown U., 1915); m. Abbie G. Miller, 1875 (died 1922); m. 2d, Mary K. Davey, 1923. Deacon, 1877, priest, 1891, P. E. Ch.; asst. pastor Grace Ch., Providence, R.I., 1891-92, rector Christ Ch., Hyde Park, Mass., 1892-1903; archdeacon of New Bedford, 1899-1903; archdeacon of Mass., 1903-13; elected bishop P.E. Ch., Apr. 10, 1913, retired, Jan. 1, 1938. Clubs: Twenty, Clerical, Clericus. Home: 12 Washington Sq., Marblehead, Mass. Office: 1 Joy St., Boston, Mass. Died June 20, 1942.

BABCOCK, Warren La Verne, hosp. dir.; b. Eden, Erie County, N.Y., Mar. 14, 1873; s. David H. and Eliza C. (Belknap) B.; desc. James Babcock, Mass., 1642; M.D., Coll. Physicians and Surgeons, Baltimore, Md., 1893; m. Helen M. Wood, Dec. 30, 1896; children—Warren Wood (M.D.), Lyndon Ross, Kenneth Belknap (M.D.), Mrs. Margaret Carter Lovell. Mem. med. staff, Md. State Hosp., Catonsville, Md., 1893-94; Binghamton State Hosp., 1894-95, St. Lawrence (N.Y.) State Hosp., 1895-1902; chief surg. N.Y. State Soldiers' and Sailors' Home, Bath, N.Y., 1902-04; dir. Grace Hosp., Detroit, 1904-37, treas. and trustee since 1937. Commd. mem. Med. Corps U.S. Army, May 1917; served as comdg. officer Am. Red Cross Hosp. No. 3, Paris, later comdg. officer Base Hosp. No. 6, Bordeaux; hon. disch. as col., Feb. 1919. Officer Legion of Honor (France), 1919. Treas. and trustee Mich. Hosp. Service; mem. A.M.A., Mich. State Med. Assn., Wayne Co. Med. Assn. (ex-pres.), Am. Hosp. Assn. (ex-sec. and ex-pres.), Detroit Philatelic Soc. (ex-pres.). Baptist. Mason. Home: 245 Willis Av. E., Detroit, Mich.; (winter) 2945 6th Av. N., St. Petersburg, Fla. Died Dec. 27, 1942.

BABLER, Jacob L., b. Monroe, Wis., May 3, 1872; s. Henry J. and Saloma (Luchsinger) B.; ed. pub. schs.; student law dept. Washington U. Entered life ins. business, 1902; apptd. mgr. New York Life office, New Haven, Conn., 1904; trans. to Buffalo, 1905; mgr. territory west of Mo. River for N. Am. Life Ins. Co., 1907-09; organized Internat. Life Ins. Co. of St. Louis. Mem. Rep. State Central Com., Mo., and Rep. Nat. Com., 1916-24. Methodist. K. of P., Elk. Office: Metropolitan Bldg., St. Louis. Died May 31, 1945.

BACHE, Jules Semon (bāch), banker; b. N.Y. City, Nov. 9, 1861; s. Semon and Elizabeth (Van Praag) B.; ed. Charlier Inst. (now La Salle Sch.), New York; m. Florence R. Scheftel, May 23, 1892. Began as cashier Leopold Cahn & Co., bankers, 1880, head of firm since 1892, when name was changed to J. S. Bache & Co.; dir. Ann Arbor R.R. Co., Am. Indemnity Co. (Baltimore), Cuba Distilling Co., Empire Trust Co., New Amsterdam Casualty Co., New River Collieries Co., U.S. Indsl. Alcohol Co., Tenn. Corp., Chrysler Corp. (v.p.), Dome Mines Co., Ltd. (pres.), Motor Products Corp., Julius Kayser & Co. (mem. exec. com.), Tenn. Copper & Chem. Corp. (mem. exec. com.); trustee U.S. Casualty Co. Mem. Met. Museum Art, Am. Museum Natural History N.Y. Zoöl. Soc. Clubs: Pilgrims, Economic (New York); Bath and Tennis, Seminole Golf (Palm Beach, Fla.). Home: 814 5th Av., New York, N.Y.; (summer) Camp Wenonah, on Upper Saranac Lake, N.Y. Office: 36 Wall St., New York, N.Y. Died Mar. 24, 1944.

BACHE, Louise Franklin (bāch), exec. sec.; b. Washington, D.C.; d. George Mifflin (comdr. U.S.N.) and Harriet (DuBois) Bache; A.B., George Washington U., 1919; M.S., Simmons Coll., 1923; unmarried. Dir. health edn., Milbank Memorial Fund, Syracuse, N.Y., 1923-28; dir. pub. relations, Nat. Probation Assn., 1928-31, Nat. Community Chests and Councils, New York, N.Y., 1931-35; exec. sec. Nat. Fedn. Bus. and Professional Women's Clubs, Inc., since 1935. Mem. exec. bd. Women's Action Com. on Victory and Lasting Peace, Com. on Participation of Women in Post War Planning. Presbyterian. Author: Health in an American City, 1934. Home: 47 Wild Cliff Road, New Rochelle, N.Y. Office: Nat. Federation of Business and Professional Women's Clubs, Inc., 1819 Broadway, New York 23, N.Y. Died July 31, 1948.

BACKUS, Standish, pres. Burroughs Adding Machine Co.; b. Detroit, Mich., Jan. 12, 1875; s. Charles Kellogg and Evelyn (Standish) B.; grad. high sch., Detroit, 1895; A.B., U. of Mich., 1898; LL.B., Detroit Coll. of Law, 1901; m. Lotta E. Boyer, Jan. 16, 1907; children—Standish, Barbara Boyer (Mrs. Edward H. Jewett, II), Charles Kellogg II, Dorothy Evelyn (Mrs. Edmund P. Lunken), Virginia Standish. Admitted to Mich. bar, 1901; began practice in office of Earl D. Babst (now chmn. bd. Am. Sugar Refining Co.); associated with Hon. Otto Kirchner, 1902-13; mem. firm Stevenson, Carpenter, Butzel & Backus, 1913-20; sec. Gen. Motors Corp., 1911-17, gen. counsel, 1917-20; pres. Burroughs Adding Machine Co. since Jan. 16, 1920; dir. James S. Holden Co.; formerly a dir. Detroit Edison Co., Detroit Trust Co.,

Mich. Savings Bank, Standard Accident Ins. Co., Frederick Stearns and Co., First Nat. Co. of Detroit and Sattley Co. Mem. Detroit Bd. of Estimates, 1909-17 (pres. 1912); mem. Legal Advisory Bd. under Selective Draft Law, 1917; mem. Bd. of Supervisors Wayne County, 1920; trustee Village Grosse Pointe Shores. Trustee Harper Hosp., Rackham Engring. Foundation. Hon. life mem. Detroit Engring. Soc., Cranbrook Inst. of Science; life mem. The Essex Inst., Salem, Mass., U. of Mich. Union, Ann Arbor, Mich.; mem. Am. and Mich. State bar assns., Mediaeval Acad. America, Psi Upsilon. Republican. Baptist. Clubs: Detroit, University, Yondotega, Detroit Country, Detroit Boat, Grosse Pointe, Grosse Pointe Hunt, Grosse Pointe Yacht, Bloomfield Hills Country, Witenagemote; University, Grolier (N.Y.); Essex County, Singing Beach (Manchester, Mass.); Olympia Skating (pres.). Hon. mem. Officers Mess, The Essex Scottish, Windsor, Ont. Home: 725 Lake Shore Road, Grosse Pointe Shores, Mich. Office: Burroughs Adding Machine Co., Detroit, Mich. Died July 13, 1943.

BACKUS, Wilson Marvin, clergyman; b. Prairie du Chien, Wis., Feb. 11, 1865; s. Edwin Eli and Clarissa Jeanette (Brainard) B.; ed. Ia. State Coll., Cornell Coll., Mt. Vernon, Ia., and Cambridge U., Eng.; m. Mary Day, Sept. 2, 1890; children—Edwin Burdette, Hugh Day. Ordained Unitarian ministry, 1888; pastor successively, Alton, Ill., Chicago, Minneapolis, Minn., and at Lawrence, Kan., since 1923. Pres. Southwestern Federation of Religious Liberals since 1928. Author of various monographs on religious subjects. Home: 1115 Louisiana St., Lawrence, Kan. Died Sept. 4, 1945.

BACON, Charles Sumner, obstetrician; b. Spring Prairie, Wis., July 30, 1856; s. John Jr. and Chloe Ann (Thompson) B.; Ph.B., Beloit Coll., 1878, D.Sc., 1925; M.D., Northwestern U., 1884; post-grad. study in Germany and Austria, 1891, 1894-95; m. Marie von Rosthorn, Aug. 17, 1895; children—Alfons Rosthorn, Ernst Lecher, Charles Sumner, Maria Helene. Practiced, Chicago, since 1884; formerly interne of Cook County Hosp. and asst. surgeon Alexian Bros. Hosp.; prof. obstetrics, Chicago Policlinic, 1895-1917; prof. obstetrics, head Dept. Obstetrics and Gynecology, U. of Illinois Medical Sch., 1903-26, now emeritus; consulting obstetrician Chicago Municipal Tuberculosis Sanitarium, Grant Hospital; chief of staff Salvation Army Hospital. Fellow Am. Coll. Surgeons, Am. Assn. of Obstetrics, Gynecology and Abdominal Surgery, A.M.A., A.A.A.S.; mem. Ill. Med. Soc., Chicago Med. Soc. (pres. 1905-06), Chicago Gynecol. Soc. (pres. 1902-03, 1923-24), Chicago Pathol. Soc., Inst. of Medicine (Chicago), Chicago Society of Med. History, Chicago Acad. Science, Citizens School Com. of Chicago (vice-pres.), Phi Beta Kappa. Author: Synopsis of Lectures on Obstetrics, 1913; Obstetrical Nursing, 1915; also numerous papers on gynecol. and obstet. subjects. Clubs: University, City. Home: 2333 Cleveland Av., Chicago. Died July 10, 1947; buried at Spring Prairie, Wis.

BACON, Clara Latimer, mathematician; b. Hills Grove, Ill., Aug. 13, 1866; d. Larkin Crouch and Louisa (Latimer) Bacon; Ph.B., Hedding Coll., Ill.; A.B., Wellesley Coll., 1890; A.M., U. of Chicago, 1904; Ph.D., Johns Hopkins, 1911. Prin. pvt. schs., Dover, Kan., and Litchfield, Ky., until 1891; prof. mathematics, Hedding Coll., 1891-93; prin. high sch., Abingdon, 1893-95; prof. mathematics, Grand Prairie Sem., Onarga, Ill., 1895-97; instr. mathematics, 1897-1904, asso. prof., 1904-14, prof. since 1914, Goucher Coll. Mem. Am. Math. Soc., Math. Assn. Am., Am. Assn. Univ. Profs., Equal Suffrage League of Baltimore. Methodist. Club: College. Home: 2316 N. Calvert St., Baltimore. Died Apr. 14, 1948.

BACON, Edwin Munroe, journalist, author; b. Providence, R. I., Oct. 20, 1844; A.M., Dartmouth, 1879. At age of 19 became reporter on Boston Advertiser; editor Illustrated Chicago News; on New York Times, 1868-72; on staff of Boston Advertiser, 1872-73; editor-in-chief Boston Globe, 1873-78; mng. editor Advertiser, 1878-84; and editor-in-chief, 1884-86; 1886-91, editor-in-chief Boston Post; editor Time and the Hour, 1897-1900. Author and editor of various hist. works relating to Boston and N. E., including Boston Illustrated; Bacon's Dictionary of Boston; Boston of To-day; Walks and Rides in the Country Round About Boston; Historic Pilgrimages in New England; Literary Pilgrimages in New England; Boston: A guide Book; The Connecticut River and the Valley of the Connecticut. Address: 16 Pinckney St., Boston. Died Feb. 24, 1916

BACON, Frank Rogers, mfr.; b. Milwaukee, Wis., Sept. 28, 1872; s. Edward Payson and Emma (Rogers) B.; ed. Lake Forest Acad., high sch., Milwaukee; Princeton U. 1 yr.; m. Ellen Alsted, Nov. 14, 1895; children—Edward Alsted, Elizabeth, Frank Rogers. Organized Am. Rheostat Co. (Wis. corp.), 1896, and became its pres.; organized 1899 the Cutler-Hammer Mfg. Co. (Wis. corp.) which absorbed Am. Rheostat Co. and Cutler-Hammer Mfg. Co. of Ill., pres. of consolidated company until 1924, chairman board, 1924-31; chmn. and president, 1931-45, now chmn.; mem. finance and exec. coms. and trustee Northwestern Mut. Life Ins. Co.; dir. Marine Nat. Exch. Bank (Milwaukee), Bucyrus-Erie Co. With Ordnance Dept. of U.S. Army, 1917-19; asst. ordnance dist. chief Chicago, and mem. Ordnance Claims Bd. for adjustment of war contracts, Aug. 1918-Mar. 1919. Mem. Adv. Bd. Chicago Ordnance Dist. U.S. Army since 1918; mem. bd. dirs. Army Ordinance Assn., Milwaukee Post. Mem. Am. Inst. Elec. Engrs., Calif. Inst. Assn., Pasadena, Calif. V.p. Columbia Hosp; Republican. Presbyterian. Clubs: Milwaukee, Milwaukee Press, University, Country, Engineers', Electric Mfrs. (New York); Press (Chicago). Died Oct. 6, 1949.

BACON, Gaspar Griswold, lawyer; b. Jamaica Plain, Mass., Mar. 7, 1886; s. Robert and Martha (Cowdin) B.; grad. Groton Sch., Mass., 1904; A.B., Harvard, 1908, LL.B., 1912; m. Priscilla Toland, July 16, 1910; children—William Benjamin, Gaspar Griswold, Robert. Admitted to Mass. bar, 1912, since practiced in Boston. Mem. Mass. State Senate, 1925-32 (pres. 1929-32); lieut. gov. of Mass., 1933-34; now prof. govt., Boston U. Served in World War as capt. and maj. F.A., Aug. 1917-Feb. 1919; with 81st Div., School of Fire, Ft. Sill, Okla., and 16th Div.; now col., chief of staff, Mass. State Guard; commd. maj. Air Corps, A.U.S., March 1942; attached to 8th Air Force, E.T.D., 1942; 3d Army, 1943-44; commd. lt. col., Oct. 1944. Awarded Croix de Guerre with silver star (Fr.); Am. Service Medal; European-African-Middle Eastern Service Medal; Legion of Honor. Vis. prof. of govt. (by invitation), U. of N.C., 1947; completed 20 yrs. Gaspar G. Bacon Lectureship on Constitution of U.S., Boston U., 1947. Pres. Franco-American Review. Mem. Am. Bar Assn., Mass. Hist. Soc., Phi Beta Kappa. Republican. Episcopalian. Mason (K.T., 32°), K.P.. Elk. Moose. Clubs: Republican, Roosevelt, Somerset, Tennis and Racquet, Harvard, Middlesex (Boston); Norfolk Hunt (Mass.); Harvard, Racquet and Tennis (New York). Author: The Constitution of the United States, 1928; Government and the Voter, 1931; Individual Rights and the Public Welfare, 1935. Home: 222 Prince St., Jamaica Plain, Mass. Address: Boston U., 688 Boylston St., Boston. Died Dec. 25, 1947.

BACON, Selden, lawyer; b. New Haven, Conn., Sept. 28, 1861; s. Leonard Woolsey and Susan (Bacon) B.; student Yale, 1878-81; A.B., Carleton Coll., 1882, A.M., 1885; LL.B., U. of Wis., 1884; m. Sarah Blair Fairchild, Oct. 24, 1894; children—Frances Fairchild (Mrs. George E. Gary), Lee Fairchild, Lucius Fairchild (dec.); m. 2d, Josephine Dodge Daskam, July 25, 1903; children—Anne (Mrs. Roger Pryor Dodge), Deborah, Selden Daskam. In practice of law at Minneapolis, 1884-94; prof. law, U. of Minn., 1888-94; in practice at N.Y. City since 1894; mem. Duer, Strong & Whitehead since 1914. Rep. of provost marshal gen. on local draft bd., 1917. Mem. Am. Bar Assn., New York County Lawyers Assn. (dir.), Archæol. Inst. America, Am. Geog. Soc. Clubs: Yale, New York Yacht. Author: Equity Pleading and Procedure, 1891. Home: Pleasantville, Westchester County, N.Y. Office: 43 Exchange Pl., New York. Died June 25, 1946.

BADING, Gerhard Adolph, diplomat; b. Milwaukee, Wis., Aug. 31, 1870; s. of John and Dorothea (Ehlers) B.; student Northwestern U., Watertown, Wis.; M.D., Rush Med. Coll., Chicago, 1896; m. Carol Royal Clemmer, Dec. 15, 1895. House physician, Milwaukee Hosp., 1896-97; instr. surg. pathology Milwaukee Med. Coll., 1897-1901; asso. in surgery, 1901-05, prof. operative surgery, 1905-07, Wis. Coll Phys. & Surg.; surgeon Johnston Emergency Hosp., 7 yrs.; cons. surgeon Milwaukee County Hosp., 4 yrs. Commr. of health, Milwaukee, 1906-10; mayor of Milwaukee 2 terms, 1912-16; E.E. and M.P. to Ecuador, by appmt. President Harding, 1922; apptd. A.E. on special mission by President Coolidge, 1925; A.E. on special mission by President Hoover, 1929; resigned from the diplomatic service, 1930. U.S. examining surgeon for pensions, 1897-1912. Mem. Light Horse Squadron, W.N.G., 1890-93; served as lt. col. N.G., P.I.; 1st lt. M.O.R.C., 1917, capt. 1917, maj. 1919; served at Fort Riley, Kans., 4 months, 34th Div., Camp Cody, N.M., 7 months, P.I., 9 months, China expedition, Tientsin, 3 months; hon. discharge, Camp Grant, Ill., July 1919. Decorated Al Merito primera classe, Ecuador. Regent Marquette Univ., Milwaukee. Lutheran. Mem. A.M.A., Am. Pub. Health Assn., Wis. State, Milwaukee Co. and Milwaukee med. socs., Am. Legion, Phi Rho Sigma. Clubs: Town, City. Home: 2711 N. Hackett Av., Milwaukee. Died Apr. 11, 1946.

BADLEY, Brenton Thoburn, retired bishop; born Gonda, U.P., India, May 29, 1876; s. Brenton Hamline and Margaret Mary Anne (Scott) B. (Am. missionaries); student Simpson Coll., Ia.; B.A., Ohio Wesleyan U., 1897, D.D., 1922; M.A., Columbia, 1899; LL.D., Simpson College, 1926; m. Mary Putnam Stearns April 29, 1903 (deceased); children—Brenton Hamline (deceased), Mary Esther (Mrs. S. R. Burgoyne), Luther Stearns. Prof. English lit. Lucknow Christian Coll. (founded by his father), in 1900-10; gen. sec. Epworth League for India and Burma, 1910-17; asso. sec. Bd. of Foreign Missions M.E. Ch., 1917-19; exec. sec. Centenary Movement in India, 1919-23; elected bishop of M.E. Church, 1924. Fellow Am. Geog. Soc.; mem. Phi Beta Kappa, Sigma Alpha Epsilon. Republican. Methodist. Author: The Making of a Christian College in India, 1906; also (booklet) The New American-Indian, 1904; God's Heroes, Our Examples, 1914; New Etchings of Old India, 1918; India, Beloved of Heaven (with O. M. Buck and J. J. Kingham), 1918; Hindustan's Horizons, 1923; Indian Church Problems, 1929; The Solitary Throne—Some Beliefs of Mahatma Ghandi, 1931, 4th edit., 1935; Visions and Victories in Hindustan, 1931; Warne of India, 1932; Faith, 1938; The Making of a Bishop, 1943; Stories and Illustrations, 1949. Address: Mirzapore, U.P., India. Died Feb. 1, 1949.

BAEHR, William Alfred (bâr), public utilities; b. Oshkosh, Wis., Sept. 15, 1873, s. Alfred Frederick and Harriet (Klotsch) B.; B.S., U. of Wis., 1894; m. Mabel Scott Christie, June 1, 1899; children—William Byron, Mabel Irene. Pres. North Continent Utilities Corp., Great Falls Gas Co., Great Northern Utilities Co., Elk River Power & Light Co., Denver Ice & Cold Storage Co., Western Railways Ice Co., North Shore Coke & Chemical Co., North Shore Gas Co., The S. W. Shattuck Chemical Co., North Continent Mines, Inc.; also officer or dir. many other corps. Mem. Beta Theta Pi. Republican. Episcopalian. Mason. Clubs: Chicago Athletic Assn., Union League, Mid-Day, Skokie Country. Home: 360 Palos Rd., Glencoe, Ill. Office: 231 S. LaSalle St., Chicago, Ill. Died Feb. 18, 1943.

BAEKELAND, Leo Hendrik, chemist; b. Ghent, Belgium, Nov. 14, 1863; s. Karel L. and Rosalia (Merchie) B.; B.S., U. of Ghent, 1882, D. Nat. Sc., maxima cum laude, 1884; laureate of the 4 Belgian universities, 1887; hon. D.Ch., U. of Pittsburgh, 1916; hon. D.Sc., Columbia, 1929; hon. D.A.Sc., U. of Brussels, Belgium, 1934; hon. LL.D., U. of Edinburgh, 1937; m. Celine Swarts, Aug. 8, 1889; children—Jenny (dec.), George W., Mrs. Nina Baekeland Wyman. Asst., later asso. prof. chem., U. of Ghent, 1882-89; prof. chem. and physics, Govt. Higher Normal Sch. Science, Bruges, Belgium, 1885-87; came to America in 1889; founded 1893, and conducted until 1899, Nepera Chem. Co., mfg. photographic papers (Velox paper, etc.) of his invention; sold to Eastman Kodak Co., 1899, and since in research chem. work. Consulting chemist and helped develop Townsend electrolytic cell for Hooker Electrochem. Co., Niagara Falls, 1905; pres. Bakelite Corp., 1910-39, mfg. Bakelite (a chem. synthesis from phenol and formaldehyde, replacing hard rubber and amber for uses in electricity and industrial arts where former plastics are unsuited). Mem. U.S. Naval Consulting Board since 1915; mem. U.S. Nitrate Supply Com., 1917, and chmn. com. on patents of Nat. Research Council, 1917; trustee of Inst. of Internat. Education since 1919; mem. advisory bd. Chem. Div. U.S. Dept. of Commerce since 1925. Awarded Nichols Medal, American Chemical Society, 1909; John Scott Medal, Franklin Institute, 1910; Willard Gibbs Medal, Am. Chem. Soc., Chicago sect., 1913; Chandler Medal (first award), Columbia U., 1914; Perkin Medal for industrial chemical research, 1916; grand prize, Panama-Pacific Exposition, 1915; Pioneer trophy, Chemical Foundation, 1936; scroll of hon. Nat. Inst., of Immigrant Welfare, 1937; Messel medal, Soc. of Chem. Industry, London, 1938; Franklin medal, Franklin Inst., 1940. Decorated Officer Legion of Honor (France); Order of Crown of Belgium; Comdr. Order of Leopold (Belgium). First Chandler lecturer, Columbia U., on occasion of 50th anniversary of Sch. of Mines, 1914; hon. prof. chem. engring., Columbia U., since 1917. U.S. del. Internat. Congress Chemistry, 1909. Pres. Inventors' Guild, 1914; pres. sect. plastics, Internat. Congress Chemistry, 1912. Hon. mem. Electro-chem. Soc. (pres. 1909); mem. Am. Chem. Soc. (pres. 1924), Am. Inst. Chem. Engrs. (pres. 1912), Belgian-Am. Ednl. Foundation, Deutsche Chem. Ges., Soc. Chem. Industry of London (v.p. 1905), Nat. Acad. Sciences, Am. Inst. City N.Y., Phi Lambda Epsilon (hon.), Tau Beta Pi, Sigma Xi; life mem. Am. Philos. Soc., A.A.A.S., Franklin Inst., Royal Soc. of Arts (London), Société Chimique de France, Société de Chimie Industrielle of Paris (hon.); hon. mem. Royal Soc. of Edinburgh, Soc. Belge des Electriciens, Am. Inst. Chemists. Clubs: Chemists' (honorary member; pres. 1904), University, Columbia Faculty (N.Y.); Cosmos (Washington); Engineers of Dayton (hon.); Cruising Club of America (N.Y.); Biscayne Bay Yacht (Fla.). Many patents U.S. and abroad, on the subjects of organic chemistry, elec. insulation, synthetic resins, plastics, etc. Contbr. numerous publications on photo-chemistry, electro-chemistry, organic chemistry, chem. industries, patent reform, social and philos. subjects, etc. Home: Coconut Grove, Fla.; and Yonkers, N.Y. Office: 30 E. 42nd St., New York, N.Y. Died Feb. 23, 1944.

BAETJER, Edwin G. (bät'jĕr), lawyer; b. Baltimore, Md., June 25, 1868; s. John G. and Mary A. B., LL.B., U. of Md., 1890; unmarried. Admitted to Md. bar, 1890, and practiced since at Baltimore. Mem. Venable Baetjer and Howard; dir. Safe Deposit & Trust Co. of Baltimore, Mercantile Trust Co. of Baltimore, Baltimore Transit Co., Dun-Bradstreet, Inc. Chmn. Draft Appeals Bd. and federal food adminstr. for Md., World War; chmn. City Service Commn., Baltimore. Mem. Md. Natural Resources Conservation Commn. Trustee Johns Hopkins U., McDonogh Sch. Clubs: Maryland, University (Baltimore); Links (New York). Home: 16 W. Madison St., Carlisle, Md. Office: Mercantile Trust Bldg., Baltimore, Md. Died July 20, 1945.

BAGGS, Arthur Eugene, ceramist; b. Alfred, N.Y., Oct. 27, 1886; s. Vernon André and Mary (Green) B.; ed. Alfred (N.Y.) Acad., 1900-03, N.Y. State Coll. of Ceramics, Alfred U., 1903-05 and 1910-11; student Art Students League, New York, 1912-13; hon. L.H. D., Alfred U., 1936; m. Helen Dorothy French, Nov. 11, 1915 (died Apr. 2, 1919); children—Arthur Eugene, Hartwell French (dec.); m. 2d. Laura Esther Trowbridge, Sept. 29, 1921; 1 dau., Mary Trowbridge. Dir. pottery dept., The Handcraft Shops, Marblehead, Mass., 1905-08; dir. Marblehead Potteries, 1908-15, owner and dir. since 1915; part time instr. ceramics, Ethical Culture Sch. and Sch. of Design and Liberal Arts, N.Y. City, 1913-20; asso. ceramist Cowan Pottery Studio, Rocky River, O., 1925-28; master in ceramics, Cleveland Sch. of Art, 1927-28; prof. ceramic art, Ohio State U., since 1928. Received hon. mention Boston Soc. Arts and Crafts Spl. Exhbn., 1907; awarded Mrs. J. Ogden Armour prize for pottery, Art Inst. Chicago, 1915; Boston Arts and Crafts Soc. medal, 1925; Charles F. Binns medal, 1928; first prize for pottery, Cleveland Museum of Art, 1928; first prize for pottery, Robineau Memorial Exhbn., Syracuse Museum of Fine Arts, 1933; first prize for pottery Nat. Ceramic Exhbn., Syracuse, N.Y., 1938. Works on exhbn. Met. Museum (New York), Museum of Fine Arts (Boston), Columbus Gallery of Fine Arts, Newark Art Museum, etc. Fellow Am. Ceramic Soc.; mem. Soc. Arts and Crafts (Boston), Columbus Art League, Keramos, Tau Sigma Delta. Contbr. on ceramics to var. mags. Home: 4549 N. High St. (2). Address: Ohio State University, Columbus, O. Died Feb. 15, 1947.

BAGLEY, William C(handler), prof., editor; b. Detroit, Mar. 15, 1874; s. William Chase and Ruth (Walker) B.; B.S., Mich. State Coll., 1895, LL.D., 1940; M.S., U. of Wis., 1898; Ph.D., Cornell U., 1900; Ed.D., R.I. State Coll., 1919; m. Florence MacLean Winger, Aug. 14, 1901; children—Ruth W., Joseph W. (dec.), William C., Florence W. (dec.). Teacher pub. and normal schs., 1895-97, 1901-08; prof. edn., U. of Ill., 1908-17, Teachers Coll. (Columbia), 1917-40, emeritus since 1940. Fellow A.A.A.S.; mem. N.E.A. (editor Journal, 1920-25; pres. nat. council of edn., 1931-37), Nat. Soc. for Study of Edn. (pres., 1911-12), Soc. Coll. Teachers of Edn. (pres., 1918-19), Sigma Xi, Kappa Delta Pi, Phi Delta Theta. Author: The Educative Process, 1905; Classroom Management, 1907; Craftsmanship in Teaching, 1911; Educational Values, 1911; Human Behavior (with S. S. Colvin), 1913; School Discipline, 1915; History of the American People (with C. A. Beard), 1918; The Preparation of Teachers (with W. S. Learned), 1919; The Nation and the Schools (with J. A. H. Keith), 1920; A First Book in American History (with C. A. Beard), 1920; Our Old World Background (with same), 1922; An Introduction to Teaching (with J. A. H. Keith), 1924; Determinism in Education, 1925; The California Curriculum Study (with G. C. Kyte), 1926; The Mastery Spellers (with J. H. Smith), 1928; Education, Crime and Social Progress, 1931; Standard Practices in Teaching (with M. E. MacDonald), 1932; Education and Emergent Man, 1934; Reading to Learn (with G. A. Yoakam and P. A. Knowlton), 1935, 38; A Century of the Universal School, 1937; The Teacher of the Social Studies (with T. Alexander), 1937; America, Yesterday and Today (with R. F. Nichols and C. A. Beard), 1938. Editor, School and Society, since 1939. Home: Southfield Point, Stamford, Conn. Office: 15 Amsterdam Av., New York 23, N.Y. Died July 1, 1946.

BAGLEY, Willis Gaylord Clark, treas. State of Iowa; b. Magnolia, Wis., Oct. 29, 1873; s. Shepherd Stephen and Louisa (Cain) B.; ed. Mason City (Ia.) pub. schs.; m. Winifred Bogardus, May 15, 1895; children—Margaret Louise, Burton Bogardus, Robert Willis. Began as messenger for First Nat. Bank of Mason City, Ia., 1890, successively bookkeeper, teller, asst. cashier, cashier and v.p., pres. 1928-38; treas. State of Iowa since 1939; dir. Northwestern States Portland Cement Co.; dir. Midland Investment Co., Mason City Globe Gazette Co.; trustee Masonic Building Co., Mason City Cemetery Assn.; Pres. Mason City Bd. of Edn., 16 yrs.; pres. C. of C.; treasurer Iowa Bankers Assn., 1911; president 1930; mem. exec. council Am. Bankers Assn., 1928-30, v.p. for Ia., 1934-35. Republican. Methodist. Mason, Elk, Odd Fellow, Maccabee, Ben Hur, Woodman, Moose. Home: Mason City, Ia. Address: Des Moines, Ia. Died Oct. 20, 1943.

BAILEY, Benjamin Franklin, elec. engr.; b. Sheridan, Mich., Aug. 7, 1875; s. William Martin and Lucy (Stead) B.; B.S. in Elec. Engring., U. of Mich., 1898, A.M., 1900, Ph.D., 1907; m. Elsie Marion Eggeman, Dec. 30, 1902; 1 son, Benjamin Franklin, Jr. Designer Edison Illuminating Co., Detroit, 1898; in testing dept., Gen. Electric Co., Schenectady, N.Y., 1898-99; instr. in electrotherapeutics, 1900-01, instr. in elec. engring., 1901-06, asst. prof., 1906-10, jr. prof., 1910-13, prof. since 1913, U. of Mich., also head Dept. of Elec. Engring. since 1925. Chief engr. Fairbanks-Morse Elec. Mfg. Co., 1908-09, cons. engr. Fairbanks-Morse Elec. Mfg. Co. and of Howell Elec. Motors Co.; inventor Bailey elec. lighting, starting and ignition system, also inventor of single-phase condenser motor; dir. Bailey Elec. Co., Howell Electric Motor Co.; v.p., dir. Fremont Motor Corp. Republican. Episcopalian. Fellow Am. Inst. E.E. (life); mem. Soc. Automotive Engrs., Sigma Xi, Tau Beta Pi, Eta Kappa Nu. Honored by Nat. Assn. Mfrs. as a modern pioneer. Clubs: Faculty, Michigan Union, Barton Hills Country, Ann Arbor Golf. Author: Induction Coils, 1903; Induction Motors, 1911; Elementary Electrical Engineering, 1913; Principles of Dynamo Electric Machinery, 1915; Alternating Current Machinery, 1934. Home: Ann Arbor, Mich. Died Oct. 31, 1944.

BAILEY, Carl Edward, ex-governor; b. Bernie, Mo., Oct. 8, 1894; s. William Edward and Margaret Elmyra (McCorkle) B.; grad. Campbell (Mo.) High Sch., 1912; student Chillicothe Business College, 1915; Litt.D. from Subiaco College, 1935; LL.D. from Arkansas State College, Jonesboro, Arkansas, 1938; m. Margaret Bristol, Oct. 10, 1915; divorced April 16, 1942; children—Carl Edward, Frank Albert, Reginald Eugene, Elizabeth Dixon, Alfred Bristol, Richard Robert; m. 2d, Marjorie Compton, Oct. 27, 1943. Began as school teacher 1913; has been laborer, farmer, bookkeeper and accountant; asst. secretary Arkansas Cotton Growers Coop. Assn., 1923-24; in practice law, 1924-35; dept. pros. atty., 6th Judicial Dist. of Ark., 1927-31, pros. atty., 1931-35; atty. gen. State of Ark., 1935-37; gov. of Ark., 2 terms, 1937-41; now senior partner of the law firm Bailey & Warren; president of The Carl Bailey Company, Inc., with stores at North Little Rock, Conway and England, Ark.; also operates large farm. Mem. Am. and Ark. State bar assns. Democrat. Mem. Christian (Disciples) Ch. Mason. Clubs: Little Rock, Quapaw, Big Lake. Home: Capitol Hill Apts., Little Rock. Office: Union Life Bldg., Little Rock, Ark. Died Oct. 23, 1948.

BAILEY, Charles Justin, army officer; b. Tamaqua, Pa., June 21, 1859; s. Milton and Fanny L. (Andruss) B.; B.S., U.S. Mil. Acad., 1880; grad. Arty. Sch., 1888; M.A., U. of Vermont, 1898; LL.D., St. Johns Coll., 1922; m. Mary M. Dodge, Nov. 4, 1885 (died May 16, 1923); children—Mrs. Omira Chilton, Mrs. Merry Alden Gandy; m. 2d, Mrs. Elizabeth Hegeman Bailey, Dec. 27, 1924. Commd. 2d lt. 1st Arty., June 12, 1880; 1st lt., Jan. 14, 1888; capt., Mar. 2, 1899; maj., June 11, 1905; lt. col. Coast Arty. Corps, Sept. 1, 1908; col., Mar. 11, 1911; brig.-gen., Oct. 10, 1913; maj. gen., Nat. Army, Aug. 5, 1917; maj. gen., regular army, Oct. 5, 1921; comdg. Philippine Dept., Apr. 15-Aug. 15, 1918; comdg. 81st Div. Nat. Army, Camp Jackson, Columbia, S.C., Aug. 1918; comdg. 81st Div., A.E.F. in France, Aug. 1918-May 1919 and in U.S. until demobilized June 19, 1919; comdg. Middle Atlantic Coast Arty. Dist., July 1919; apptd. comdr. 3d Corps Area, Aug. 16, 1921; retired Dec. 1, 1922. Distinguished Service Medal (U.S.); comdr., Order of Leopold (Belgium); Officer Legion of Honor (France); Croix de Guerre with Palm (France). Trustee Chautauqua Instn. Club: Army and Navy (Washington). Home: 153 S. Main St., Jamestown, N.Y. Died Sep. 21, 1946.

BAILEY, Edward Monroe, chemist; b. New London, Conn., Aug. 27, 1879; s. Edward Monroe and Louise Maria (Hagan) B.; Ph.B., Yale, 1902, M.S., 1905, Ph.D., 1910; m. Myrtle Mix Studley, June 11, 1906; 1 son, Irving Monroe. Asst. chemist Conn. Agrl. Expt. Sta., 1902-17, chemist in charge since 1917; state chemist, Conn., since 1919. Mem. Joint Com. on Definitions and Standards for Food Products, U.S. Dept. Agr., 1922-38; consultant Council Pharmacy and Chemistry, 1920-30; mem. Council Pharmacy and Chemistry and Council on Foods, A.M.A., 1930-38. Mem. Am. Chem. Soc., Assn. Official Agrl. Chemists, Assn. Feed Control Officials, Assn. Dairy, Food and Drug Control Officials, Sigma Xi. Club: Graduate. Contbr. numerous articles on chemistry and biochemistry of foods, drugs and agrl. products in scientific jours. and station repts. Home: 854 Edgewood Av., New Haven, Conn. Died Apr. 13, 1948.

BAILEY, Florence Augusta Merriam, author; b. Locust Grove, N.Y., Aug. 8, 1863; d. Hon. Clinton L. and Caroline (Hart) Merriam; sister of Clinton Hart Merriam; A.B., Smith Coll., 1886; LL.D., U. of New Mexico, 1933; m. Vernon Bailey, Dec. 16, 1899 (died Apr. 20, 1943). Interested in ornithology. Fellow Am. Ornithologists' Union; mem. Cooper Ornith. Club (life), Nat. Audubon Soc. (emeritus, 1934), Biol. Soc. Washington. Awarded Brewster medal, Am. Ornithologists' Union, 1931. Author: Birds Through an Opera Glass, 1889; My Summer in a Mormon Village, 1895; A-Birding on a Bronco, 1896; Birds of Village and Field, 1898; Handbook of Birds of Western United States, 1902; Birds of the Santa Rita Mountains in Southern Arizona, 1923; Birds of New Mexico, 1928; Birds, in Vernon Bailey's Wild Animals of Glacier National Park, 1918, and Cave Life in Kentucky, 1933; Among the Birds in the Grand Canyon Country, 1939. Contbr. about 100 papers on birds. Address: 1834 Kalorama Rd. N.W., Washington, D.C. Now deceased.

BAILEY, Joseph Weldon, Jr., ex-congressman; b. Gainesville, Tex., Dec. 15, 1892; s. Joseph Weldon and Ellen (Murray) B.; B.S., Princeton, 1915; B.L., U. of Va., 1919; m. Roberta Lewis, Nov. 6, 1924; 1 son, Joseph Weldon. Admitted to Texas bar, 1920; member firm Bailey & Shaeffer; mem. 73d Congress (1933-35) Texas at large. Served as 1st lt., 314th Field Arty. Regt., World War I; enlisted World War II, commd. capt. U.S. Marine Corps Res. Democrat. Presbyterian. Club: Brook Hollow Golf. Home: 4217 Versailles St. Office: Kirby Bldg., Dallas. Died in service July 17, 1943.

BAILEY, Josiah William, senator; b. Warrenton, N.C., Sept. 14, 1873; s. Christopher Thomas and Annie Sarah (Bailey) B.; A.B., Wake Forest (N.C.) Coll., 1893, LL.D., 1931; law study under S. F. Mordecai, also Trinity Coll. (now Duke U.) and Wake Forest Law Sch., 1907-08; LL.D., Colby College, 1938; D.Litt., Elon Coll. North Carolina, 1939; LL.D., Duke Univ., 1941; m. Edith Pou, Aug. 16, 1916; children—James Hinton Pou, Annie Elizabeth, Josiah William, Edith Pou, Sally. Editor Biblical Recorder, 1893-1907; admitted to N.C. bar, 1908, and began practice at Raleigh; U.S. collector internal revenue, N.C., 1913-21. Presdl. elector at large, N.C., 1908; mem. Constl. Commn. of N.C., 1913-14; U.S. senator from N.C. for terms, 1931-37, 1937-43 and 1943-49. U.S. del. to Internat. Aviation Conf., Chicago, 1944; chmn. com. Air Commerce U.S. Senate since 1938. Hon. mem. Omicron Delta Kappa. Democrat. Baptist. Home: 513 N. Blount St., Raleigh, N.C. Died Dec. 15, 1946; buried in Oakwood Cemetery, Raleigh, N.C.

BAILEY, Thomas L., gov. of Miss.; b. Maben, Miss., Jan. 6, 1888; s. Anderson Bean and Rosa (Powell) B.; A.B., Milsaps Coll., Jackson, Miss., 1909, LL.B., 1912; m. Nellah Massey, Aug. 23, 1917; children—Harold Melby, Nellah Pope. Admitted to Miss. bar, 1913, and since practiced in Meridian, mem. firm of Bailey & Gillespie; mem. Miss. Legislature, 1916-40, speaker, 1924-36; gov. of Miss., term 1944-48; dir. Meridian Bldg. & Loan Assn., Meridian, Miss.; dir. and v.p. Miss. City Lines (operating in cities of Meridian, Laurel and Hattiesburg, Miss.). Mem. Miss. Bldg. Commn., 1932-36; pres. Nat. Exchange Club, 1925-27; mem. Miss. Hosp. Commn., 1936-40. Mem. Miss. State Bar Assn., Lauderdale County bar Assn., Kappa Sigma. Mem. Knights of Pythias. Mason (Shriner). Methodist. Mem. Exchange Club. Home: 2406 24th Av., Meridian, Miss. Address: New Capitol Bldg., Jackson, Miss.* Died Nov. 2, 1946.

BAILEY, Thomas Pearce, prof. ethology; b. Georgetown, S.C., Aug. 18, 1867; s. Thomas Pearce (M.D.) and Maria Laval (Williams) B.; A.B., South Carolina Coll., 1887; A.M., U. of South Carolina, 1889, Ph.D., 1891; fellow in psychology, Clark U., 1892-93; m. Charlotte R. Burckmyer, Mar. 20, 1893 (died Sept. 16, 1893); m. 2d, Minneola Davis, Aug. 1, 1895 (died Sept. 18, 1931); children—Thomas Laval, James Preston, Minneola, Mary Belin; m. 3d Carol Purse Oppenheimer, Sept. 12, 1935. Principal graded sch., Georgetown, S.C., 1887-88; tutor English and history, 1888-89, sec., 1889-91, adj. prof. biology, 1891-92, U. of South Carolina; prin. graded schs., Marion, S.C., 1893-94; asst. prof. edn., 1894-98, asso. prof. edn., 1898-1900, U. of Calif; asst. prof. edn. in univ. extension div., U. of Chicago, 1900-03; prof. psychology and applied psychology, 1903-05, prof. psychology and edn., 1905-08, psychology and secondary edn., 1908-09, dean dept. of edn., 1905-09, U. of Miss.; supt. city schs., Memphis, Tenn., 1909-10; investigator for N.Y. Bur. of Municipal Research, 1910-11; dean of All Saints' Episcopal Coll., Vicksburg, Miss., 1911-12; coöperative lecturer, Miss. schs. and colls., 1912-14; prof. philosophy and psychology, U. of the South, 1914-26; cons. psychologist, Miss. State Insane Hosp., summers, 1924-25; prof. philosophy, psychology, ethology, and cons. psychologist, Rollins Coll., 1926-44; prof. emeritus since 1944. Mem. Phi Beta Kappa. Episcopalian. Democrat. Author: Love and Law, 1890; Race Orthodoxy in the South, 1914. Contbr. to Proc. N.E.A. and to ednl. and psychol. jours. Home: 351 E. Comstock Av., Winter Park, Fla. Died Feb. 7, 1949.

BAILEY, Vernon, biologist; b. Manchester, Mich., June 21, 1864; s. Hiram and Emily B.; student U. of Mich., 1893, Columbian (now George Washington) U., 1894-95; m. Florence Augusta Merriam, Dec. 16, 1899. Served as chief field naturalist, U. S. Biol. Survey; retired July 31, 1933. Fellow A.A.A.S.; mem. Am. Ornithologists' Union, Cooper Ornithol. Club, Am. Forestry Assn., Washington Acad. Sciences, Biol. Soc. Washington. Author: Spermophiles of the Mississippi Valley, 1893; Pocket Gophers of Mississippi Valley, 1895; Revision of Voles of the Genera Evotomys and Microtus, 1897; Mammals of District of Columbia, 1900, 1923; Biological Survey of Texas, 1905; Life Zones and Crop Zones of New Mexico, 1913; Revision of the Pocket Gophers of the Genus Thomomys, 1915; Wild Animals of Glacier National Park (mammals); Beaver Habits and Beaver Farming, 1923; Biological Survey of North Dakota, 1927; Animal Life of Carlsbad Cavern, 1928; Animal Life of Yellowstone National Park, 1930; Mammals of New Mexico, 1931; Mammals of Oregon, 1936; Cave Life of Kentucky. Home: 1834 Kalorama Road, Washington. Died Feb. 14, 1942.

BAIN, Ferdinand R., public utilities; b. Chatham, N.Y., May 3, 1861; s. Milton and Charlotte M. (Nash) B.; ed. Bishop's Prep. Sch., Poughkeepsie, N.Y.; m. Mrs. Elizabeth S. Fisher, Mar. 27, 1925. Chmn. bd. Southern Counties Gas Co.; pres. Santa Monica Savings Bank. Republican. Clubs: California, Los Angeles Country, California Country, Beach (Los Angeles); Rainier (Seattle, Wash.); Lotos (New York). Home: Palms, Calif. Office: 810 S. Flower St., Los Angeles. Died Aug. 13, 1945.

BAIN, H(arry) Foster, mining engr.; b. Seymour, Ind., Nov. 2, 1872; s. William M. and Radie (Foster) B.; B.S., Moores Hill College, 1890; post-grad. study, Johns Hopkins Univ., 1891-93; PhD. from Univ. of Chicago, 1897; m. Mary Wright, Dec. 1, 1902; 1 dau., Margaret. Asst. Ia. Geol. Survey, 1893-95; asst. state geologist, Iowa, 1895-1900; mgr. mines, Ida. Springs and Cripple Creek, Colo., 1901-03; geologist, U. S. Geol. Survey, 1903-06; dir. Ill. Geol. Survey, 1905-09; editor Mining and Scientific Press, San Francisco, Apr., 1909-15; editor Mining Mag., London, 1915-16; explorations in Far East, 1916-17, 19-20; asst. dir., U. S. Bur. of Mines, Apr. 1918-19, dir., 1921-24; cons. engr. Argentine, 1924-25, Columbia, 1929. Mem. Commn. for Relief in Belgium, 1915-16. Lecturer on econ. geology, Univ. of Ia., 1897, U. of Chicago, 1903-04. Fellow Geol. Soc., Am.; mem. Am. Inst. Mining and Metall. Engrs. (sec. since 1925), Mining and Metall. Soc. America, Canadian Mining Inst., Inst. of Mining and Metallurgy. Clubs: University (Urbana, Ill.); Engineers' (San Francisco and New York); Cosmos (Washington, D.C.). Home: 38 E. 53d St. Office: 29 W. 39th St., New York. Died March 9, 1948.

BAINBRIDGE, William Seaman, surgeon; b. Providence, R.I.; s. Rev. William Folwell and Lucy Elizabeth (Seaman) B.; grad. Mohegan Lake School, Peekskill, N.Y., 1888; student Columbia; M.D., Coll. of Physicians and Surgeons (Columbia), 1893; grad. Presbyn. Hosp., 1895, Sloane Maternity Hosp., 1896; post-grad. Coll. Phys. and Surg., 1896; abroad 2 yrs.; hon. A.M., Shurtleff Coll., Ill., 1899; M.S., Washington and Jefferson Coll., 1902; Sc.D., Western U. of Pa., 1907; LL.D., Lincoln Memorial U., and Coe College; Litt.D., Lincoln Memorial U., 1923; Dr. Honoris Causa, U. of San Marcos, Peru, 1941; m. June Ellen Wheeler, Sept. 9, 1911; children—Elizabeth (dec.), William Wheeler, John Seaman, Barbara (Mrs. Angus McIntosh). Professor operative gynecology, New York Post-graduate Medical School, 1900-06; professor surgery, New York. Poly. Med. Sch. and Hosp., 1906-18; surgeon, N.Y. Skin and Cancer Hosp., 1903-18; surg. dir. N.Y. City Children's Hosps. and Schs., Manhattan State Hosp., Ward's Island; cons. surg. or gynecologist to 16 metropolitan and suburban hosps.; hon. prof. med. faculty, Univ. Santo Domingo, Dominican Republic. Dir. Equitable Life Assur. Soc. of U.S., The Americas Foundation. Member Reserve Corps United States Navy, 1913-17; since Apr. 6, 1917 served as lieut. comdr., comdr. and capt. (med. dir.), M.C., U.S. N.R.; during World War operating surgeon on U.S.S. George Washington; med. observer for U.S. with allied armies in the field, later attached to surgeon general's office to write report; cons. surgeon and chief, Physiotherapeutic Division, U.S. Naval Hospital, Brooklyn, New York; made consulting surgeon 3rd Naval Dist.; now cons. surgeon 3d Naval Dist. and attending specialist in surgery, U.S. Pub. Health Service, N.Y. City and vicinity. Official rep. of U.S. Govt. since 1921 at internat. congresses mil. medicine, surgery and sanitation; pres. 8th session Internat. office Medico-Military Documentation, Luxemburg, 1938, chmn. 9th session, Washington and New York, 1939. On official mission to all republics of Central and South America for Navy Dept. and State Dept., 1941. Decorated U.S. Naval Reserve Medal; Conspicuous Service Cross (N.Y. State); Officer, later Comdr. Legion of Honor (French); Officer Order of Leopold and Military Cross, 1st Class (Belgian); Commander, later Grand Officer Order of Crown of Italy, Vittorio-Veneto Commemorative Cross (Italian); Médaille Commémorative, Médaille Reconnaissance (French); Silver Medal of Merit (Italian R.C.); Officer, later Comdr. Order Polonia Restituta; Comdr. Order of White Lion (Czechoslovakia); Grand Officer Order of Crown (Rumania); Officer Orden del Libertador (Venezuela); Order of Gediminas (Lithuania); Cross of Merit (Hungary); Gold Cross of Merit (Poland); Comdr. Order of the Crown (Belgium); Comdr. Order of the Crown, Medal of Red Cross (Jugoslavia); Cruz de la Orden del Merito Naval (Spain); Comdr. Order of Saints Mauritius and Lazarus (Italy); Comdr. Order of the Sun (Peru); Comdr. of The Oak Leaved Crown (Luxemburg); Order of Merit, first class, Knight, Order of White Rose (Finland); Gold Medal Order of Distinguished Auxiliary Service, Salvation Army. Hon. mem. Royal Acad. Medicine of Belgium, Royal Acad. Medicine Rome, Soc. of Surgeons of Poland, Soc. of Surgeons of Paris, Assn. Mil. Surgeons of Mexico, Union Medicale Latine, Assn. Mil. Surgeons of Hungary, Acad. of Surgery of Peru, Nat. Acad. Medicine Mexico, Acad. Sciences and Arts, Mexico, Nat. Acad. Med. Venezuela, French Gynecol. Soc., Nat. Acad. of Medicine of Spain; fellow Am. Assn. Obstet., Gynecol. and Abdominal Surgeons, Internat. Coll. Surgeons (internat. treas., 1935-46; surg. regent, New York State; chairman board trustees of U.S. chapter), American Geriatrics Society (hon.), International College Anesthetists, Royal Institute Pub. Health (life), fellow Royal Soc. Medicine (Eng.), A.M.A., N.Y. Acad. Medicine; mem. N.Y. State Med. Soc., Greater N.Y. Med. Assn., Assn. Mil. Surgeons of U.S. (pres. 1935), Internat. Med. Club of New York (pres. 3 terms, 1934-38), Am. Acad. Physical Medicine (pres. since 1941), St. Andrews Soc., Soc. Colonial Wars, S.R., S.A.R., Huguenot Soc., Soc. of Cincinnati (hon.), Mil. Order Foreign Wars (comdr. gen. Nat. Comdry., 1926-32), Military Order World War, Society Legion of Honor, Am. Soc. French Legion of Honor, St. Nicholas Society, Soc. of Am. Wars, Am. Legion (comdr. Tiger Post 1932-35), Delta Upsilon, The Newcomen Soc., various foreign societies. Clubs: Authors, Columbia University, Pilgrims of United States, Quill (pres. 1938-39), Foreign Students Cosmopolitan, Union League, Nat. Arts, Rotary (pres. N.Y., Rotary 1933), Army and Navy of America (New York); Inter-allied Officers (London and Paris); Union Interalliée (Paris). Author: A Compend of Operative Gynecology, 1906; Life's Day Guide-Posts and Danger Signals in Health, 1909; The Cancer Problem, 1914 (French, Italian, Spanish, Polish, Arabic edits.); also brochures, med. papers and repts. Address: 34 Gramercy Park, New York, N.Y. Died Sept. 22, 1947.

BAIRD, Joseph Edward, congressman; b. Perrysburg, O., Nov. 12, 1865; LL.B., U. of Mich., 1893; m. Ida Graham; children—Edward G., Florence E., Richard K. Admitted to Ohio bar, 1893, and practiced at Bowling Green; mem. 71st Congress (1929-31) 13th Ohio Dist. Republican. Home: Bowling Green, O. Died June 14, 1942.

BAIRD, Lucius Olmsted; b. Chicago, June 15, 1863; s. Lyman and Elizabeth (Warner) B.; B.A., Yale, 1885; student Chicago Law Sch., 1887-88; B.D., Yale Div. Sch., 1890; D.D., Drury Coll., 1910; D.D., Whitman Coll., 1926; m. Jeannette Stuart Woods, Sept. 19, 1895; children—Elizabeth (Mrs. Frederick A. Burwell), Jean (Mrs. Richard L. Frayn), Harriet (dec.). Ordained Congl. ministry, 1890; pastor Pullman, Wash. (as mem. "Yale Band"), 1890-94, Ottawa, Ill., 1895-1905, St. Mary's Av. Ch., Omaha, Neb., 1905-10; western sec. Am. Missionary Assn., Chicago, 1910-17; Congl. missionary supt., Wash., Ida. and Alaska, at Seattle, Wash., 1917-33; supt. Congl. Extension Soc. of Seattle, 1929-36. Pres. Congl. Summer Assembly, 1912-15. Mem. Psi Upsilon. Home: 5026 16th Av. N.E., Seattle. Died Dec. 18, 1948.

BAKER, Albert, lawyer; b. Evansville, Ind., Nov. 22, 1851; s. Conrad and Matilda E. (Sommers) B.; prep. edn. City Acad., Indianapolis, Ind.; grad. Wabash Coll., Crawfordsville, Ind., 1874, LL.D., 1932; m. Anna S. Campbell, Oct. 19, 1876; children—Ellen Sommers (Mrs. John Chandler Dallam), Conrad Campbell, Gertrude Johnston, Rosemary Campbell. Admitted to Ind. bar, 1876, and practiced since at Indianapolis; mem. firm Baker, Hord & Hendricks, 1876-88, Winter, Baker & Daniels, 1888-89, Baker & Daniels, 1889-1940, now Baker, Daniels, Wallace and Seagle. Chmn. Draft Bd., Indianapolis, 1917-19. Mem. Am., Indianapolis and Indiana bar assns., Art Assn. of Indianapolis. Republican. Presbyn. Home: 1416 N. Penn St. Office: Fletcher Trust Bldg., Indianapolis, Ind. Died Oct. 29, 1942.

BAKER, Benedict J., bus. exec. pres. and dir. B. J. Baker & Co., Inc.; chmn. bd. and dir. Gamewell Co., Consolidated Machine Tool Corp., Eagle Signal Corp., Everlastik, Inc., Rockwood Sprinkler Co. of Mass.; dir. Rockwood Corp., Worcester Fire Extinguisher Co. Home: Jerusalem Rd., North Cohasset, Mass. Office: 209 Washington St., Boston, Mass.* Died Nov. 18, 1948.

BAKER, Bertha Kunz, lecturer, dramatic reader; b. Erie, Pa.; d. Jacob and Caroline (Weiss) Kunz; grad. Erie High Sch., 1880, followed by pvt. study and foreign travel; m. Dr. L. B. Baker, Oct. 5, 1892 (died, Feb., 1907). Teacher langs. and lit., Erie High Sch., 1883-92. Since 1890 engaged as lecturer and dramatic reader, at Chautauqua Assembly and in colls., univs. and lyceum courses throughout U.S.; especially interpretive recitals of masterpieces of classics and modern literature; lecturer and reader at Brooklyn Inst. of Arts and Sciences, U. of Chicago, Phila. Soc. for Univ. Extension, etc. Author: Art in Education of the Emotions; Practical Problems in Literary Interpretation; Studies in Emotional Expression. Home: 21 31st St., New York. Died Oct. 11, 1943.

BAKER, Ellis Crain, engineer; b. Brandon, Miss., Feb. 1, 1889; B.S., Miss. State Coll., 1911; M.S. in M.E., Ia. State Coll., 1930; m. Emma Pearson Davis, June 29, 1915; children—James Oliver, Ellis Crain. Efficiency Engr., Meridian (Miss.) Lt. & Ry. Co., 1911-12; instr. mech. engring., Miss State Coll., 1912-13, asst. prof., 1913-14; prof. Okla. Sch. Mines and Metallurgy, Wilburton, Okla., 1914-17; asst. prof. mech. engrg., Texas A. and M. Coll., Coll. Station, Tex., 1917-19; chief engr., asst. supt. boiler plant, Internat. Shipbldg. Co., Houston, Tex., 1919-21; asst. prof. mech. engrg., Okla. A. and M. Coll., 1921-23, asso. prof. 1923-30, prof. and head mech. engring. dept. since 1930. Mem. Am. Soc. Mech. Engrs., Am. Assn. Univ. Profs., Am. Soc. for Engring. Edn., Okla. Soc. Prof. Engrs., Pi Tau Sigma, Sigma Tau. Registered professional engr., Okla. Home: 801 Monroe St. Office: Okla. A. and M. Coll., Stillwater, Okla. Died Feb. 22, 1949.

BAKER, Frank Collins, zoölogist; b. Warren, R.I., Dec. 14, 1867; s. Francis Edwin and Anna Collins (Thurber) B.; ed. Brown U., 1888; Jessup scholar, Acad. Natural Sciences, Phila., 1889-90; B.S., Chicago Sch. of Science, 1896; m. Lillian May Hall, June 16, 1892 (died Aug. 9, 1934). Was a member of Mexican exploring expdn. sent out by Acad. of Natural Sciences, 1890; invertebrate zoölogist, Ward's Natural Sciences Establishment and sec. Rochester Acad. Sciences, 1891-92; curator zoölogy, Field Columbian Mus., Chicago, 1894; curator Chicago Acad. of Sciences, 1894-1915 (life mem.); zoöl. investigator N.Y. State Coll. of Forestry, Syracuse U., 1915-17; curator Natural History Mus., U. of Ill., 1917-39; curator emeritus since 1939; consultant on Invertebrate Pleistocene Paleontology, Ill. Geol. Survey. V.-pres. Audubon Soc., 1900-15. Fellow A.A.A.S., Geol. Soc. America, Paleontol. Soc. America; mem. Am. Assn. Museums, Ill. Acad. Sciences (vice-pres. 1931), Museums Assn. (British), Ecol. Soc. America, Am. Malacological Union (pres. 1942), Limnological Soc. America, Sigma Xi; corr. mem. Zoöl. Soc., London. Clubs: University, Kiwanis. Author: A Naturalist in Mexico, 1895; Mollusca of the Chicago Area, 1898-1902; Shells of Land and Water, 1903; The Lymnæidæ of North and Middle America, 1911; Relation of Mollusks to Fish in Oneida Lake, 1916; Life of the Pleistocene, 1920; Mollusca of Big Vermilion River (in relation to sewage pollution), 1922; Fresh Water Mollusca of Wisconsin, 1928; The Mollusca of the Shell Heaps or Escargotieres of Northern Algeria, 1939; Fieldbrook of Illinois Land Mollusca, 1939; Use of Animal Life by the Mound-Builders of Illinois. Contbr. to zoöl. and geol. jours., principally on mollusca. Field zoölogist Wis. Geol. and Natural History Survey, 1920-22, Ill. Natural Hist. Survey, 1931-32. Home: Urbana, Ill. Died May 7, 1942.

BAKER, Franklin Thomas, college prof.; b. Hagerstown, Md., Sept. 12, 1864; s. John Henry and Julia (McCoy) B.; A.B., Dickinson Coll., 1885, A.M., 1889, Litt.D., 1908; A.M., Columbia, 1900; m. Emilie Addoms Kip, Sept. 15, 1896. Instr. high sch. and sem., 1885-87; instr. Dickinson Prep. Sch., 1887-92; instr. English, 1892-93, prof. English, 1893-1933. Teachers Coll., Columbia Univ., emeritus prof. English, 1933. Lecturer, Brooklyn Inst., 1890-1906, Univ. of Ill., summers, 1909, 17, Univ. of Ind., summers, 1916, 17; Univ. of Calif., 1924, Univ. of Wyoming, summers, 1928, 31. Club: Century. Editor: DeQuincey's Revolt of the Tartars, 1896; The DeCoverley Papers, 1899; Browning's Shorter Poems, 1899; Tennyson's The Princess, 1902; Macauley's Poems, 1904; Cranford, 1905; Stevenson's Treasure Island, 1909; Tennyson's Idylls, 1914. Author: Course Study in English (Teachers Coll. Record), 1900; The Teaching of English, 1903; Language Reader Series (with G. R. Carpenter and others), 1905; English Composition (with H. V. Abbott), 1908; Bibliography of Children's Reading, 1908; Every Day English (with A. H. Thorndike), 1913; Every Day Classics, 1917; "Studies in English" to Class Room Teacher, 1927; Good Companion Series of Readers (with A. I. Gates and C. Peardon), 1936-37; also articles in ednl. jours. Home: Park Hill, Yonkers, N.Y. Died Feb. 3, 1949.

BAKER, George Barr; b. Wyandotte, Mich., Apr. 1, 1870; s. George Payson and Celestia Barr (Hibbard) B.; m. Laura Pike, May 10, 1910. Reporter, Detroit Tribune, 1895-96, Detroit Journal, 1897-99; European corr., Detroit Journal, 1900-01, McClure's Magazine (English office), 1902; art critic "Academy and Literature" (Eng.), 1903; Am. corr. London Daily Express and Paris Matin, 1904-05; journalist sec. to Joseph Pulitzer, 1906; asso. editor Everybody's Mag., 1907-10; lit. editor Delineator, 1911-14. Dir. Am. Relief Administration, exec. com. Commn. for Relief in Belgium Ednl. Foundation; mem. exec. com. Am. Relief Administration Children's Fund; dir. Am. Child Health Assn.; chmn. Internat. Conf. between Authors and Motion Picture Producers, 1923-24; mem. council Authors' League America. Ship's writer U.S.S. Yosemite through Spanish-Am. War; mem. Commn. for Relief in Belgium, 1916; comdr. U.S.N.R.F.; exec. officer U.S. Naval Cable Censorship, 3d Naval Dist., 1917; attached to force comdr. in European waters, 1918; attached to dir.-gen. of relief under Supreme Economic Council, Paris, during Peace Conf., 1919. Dir. publicity Coolidge presidential campaign, 1924, head of naturalized citizens organizations for Rep. Nat. Com. in Hoover campaign, 1928; general consultant, White House Conference on Child Health and Protection, 1930-31; now retired. Officer Crown of Belgium; Comdr. Order of Leopold (Belgium); Order of the White Rose of Finland, Order of Restituta (Poland). Republican. Mem. Soc. Colonial Wars, S.R. Clubs: Players, Dutch Treat, Brook (New York); National Press (Washington, D.C.); Burlingame (Calif.); Bohemian (San Francisco); West Indian (London, Eng.). Home: Burlingame, Calif. Office: Graybar Bldg., New York, N.Y. Died July 29, 1948.

BAKER, George Randolph; b. Randolph, N.B., Can., Dec. 20, 1871; s. Charles Parker and Hannah Amanda (Shaw) B.; prep. edn., Horton Acad. and Acadia Coll.; A.B., Cornell U., 1896; grad. Rochester Theol. Sem., 1899; D.D., Lake Forest U., 1922, Acadia U., 1925, Denison U., 1934; m. Kate Hopper, Feb. 20, 1895; children—Ruth Ada (dec.), Kathrine (dec.), Charles Parker. Came to U.S., 1891, naturalized citizen, 1910. Ordained Bapt. ministry, 1896; successively pastor Ft. Plain, N.Y., Leominster, Mass., and Ithaca, N.Y., until 1920; asso. sec. Bd. of Edn., Northern Bapt. Conv., 1920-39. Trustee Keystone Junior Coll.; corporator Peddie School. Mem. bd. of mgrs. of Bd. of Edn. of Northern Bapt. Conv. Republican. Club: Clergy (New York). Home: 527 Riverside Drive. Office: 152 Madison Av., New York, New York.* Died May 2, 1941.

BAKER, J(ames) Norment, surgeon, state health officer; b. Abingdon, Va., Apr. 11, 1876; s. James Biscoe and Sallie Claiborne (Barksdale) B.; A.B., U. of Va., 1895, M.D., 1898; post-grad. courses Johns Hopkins Hosp., Baltimore, and Mass. Gen. Hosp., Boston; m. Marguerite Rice, Apr. 29, 1908; children—Samuel Rice, J. Norment (dec.). Interne, St. Vincent's Hosp., Norfolk, Va., 1898-99; surgeon in charge Plant System hosps., Waycross, Ga., 1899, Montgomery, 1900-01; practice of gen. surgery and female urology, Montgomery, Ala., since 1918; surgeon for Atlantic Coast Line and Central of Ga. R.R., U.S. Employees Compensation Commn., Southern Bell Telephone Co.; visiting surgeon Memorial Hosp. and Highland Park Sanitarium; state health officer of Ala. since 1930. Maj. Med. Corps, World War. Sec. State Bd. of Med. Examiners of Ala.; mem. Nat. Bd. Med. Examiners of U.S.; pres. (1940-41) Conf. of State and Provincial Health Authorities of N.A.; ex-pres. Fed. of State Med. Boards of U.S. Fellow Am. Pub. Health Assn. (pres. Southern Branch); Am. Coll. Surgeons; mem. Am. and Southern med. assns. (ex-chmn. pub. health sect.), Southern Surg. Assn. (v.p. 1921), Phi Kappa Psi, Pi Mu. Democrat. Episcopalian. Club: Country (Montgomery). Home: 602 S. Perry St. Office: 519 Dexter Av., Montgomery, Ala. Died Nov. 9, 1941.

BAKER, Joseph Richardson, lawyer; b. New Hartford, N.Y., Feb. 11, 1872; s. Alonzo E. and Cordelia (Richardson) B.; A.B., Hamilton Coll., Clinton, N.Y., 1893; m. Florilla G. Richmond, Feb. 21, 1928. Admitted to N.Y. bar, 1896; law clerk Commn. to Five Civilized Tribes, Dept. of Interior, 1902-03; with Post Office Dept., 1903-06, Dept. of State, 1906-16;

special agent Dept. of State in Samoa, and vice and dep. consul at Apia, 1911; asst. solicitor Dept. of State, 1916-42, when retired; acted as agent for the Department of State, in Panama, 1917. Member U.S.-Panama Commission to negotiate a treaty, 1924; commissioner U.S. General Claims Commission, U.S., and Mexico, 1924; del. of U.S. to Paris Conf. on Air Navigation, 1929; tech. adviser to U.S. delegation at Geneva Conf. on Red Cross and Prisoners of War, 1929; agent Dept. of State in Germany, 1929; commr. U.S. Gen. Claims Commn., U.S. and Panama, 1933; agent of Dept. of State in Mexico, 1935; in Can., 1940, 41; tech. adv. to U.S. delegation at Buenos Aires Conf. on Maintenance of Peace, 1936. Mem. Am. Soc. Internat. Law, also Sigma Phi and Phi Beta Kappa fraternities. Republican. Presbyterian. Collaborator: Commercial Laws of the World; The Laws of Maritime Warfare; The Laws of Land Warfare; Selected Topics connected with The Laws of Warfare. Prepared: The Laws of Neutrality. Clubs: Arts. Home: 41 Baltimore St., Kensington, Md. Died Jan. 5, 1946.

BAKER, Josephine Turck, editor, author; b. Milwaukee, Wis.; d. James Byron and Sarah (Ashby) Turck; B.A., Milwaukee-Downer Coll.; hon. Ph.D., Chicago Law Sch., 1917; m. Frederick Sherman Baker, Nov. 10, 1888. Founder, 1899, and editor Correct English Magazine; pres. and founder, Internat. Soc. for Universal English; pres. and treas. Correct English Pub. Co. Author: Correct English; Correct English Complete Grammar and Drill Book; Correct English in the School; Correct English in the Home; Correct Social Letter Writing; The Art of Conversation; How Can I Increase My Vocabulary; The Correct Word; The Correct Preposition; Correct Business Letter Writing; Correct Standardized Pronunciation; The Literary Work Shop; Your Everyday Vocabulary; Correct Synonyms and Antonyms; (novel) The Burden of the Strong, 1915; (drama) Madame de Staël, 1927; (poems) Songs of Triumph, 1933; also wrote four plays. Home: 1742 Asbury Av., Evanston, Ill. Died May 30, 1942.

BAKER, Oliver Edwin, economic and sociological geographer; b. Tiffin, Ohio, Sept. 10, 1883; s. Edwin and Martha (Thomas) B.; B.Sc., Heidelberg Coll., Ohio, 1903, M.Sc., 1904; M.A., in Polit. Scince, Columbia, 1905; studied forestry, Yale U., 1907-08, agr., U of Wis., 1908-12, economics, 1919-21, Ph.D., 1921; hon. D.Sc., Heidelberg (O.) College and Ph.D., Goettingen (Germany), 1937; m. Alice H. Crew, 1925; children—Helen Thomas, Sabra Z., Edwin Crew, Mildred Coale. With Wis. Agrl. Expt. Sta., 1910-12; U.S. Dept. Agr. since 1912; employed in research on farm population and on rural youth surveys, 1930-42; in charge of preparation, and editor of Atlas of Am. Agr., issued in sects., 1914-36; professor of geography, U. of Md. since 1942, also in charge preparation of Econ. Atlas of World. Mem. Assn. Am. Geographers (pres. 1931), Am. Meterol. Soc., Farm Economic Assn., American Sociol. Society. Author: (with A. R. Whitson) The Climate of Wisconsin and Its Relation to Agriculture, 1912; (with V. C. Finch) Geography of the World's Agriculture, 1917; (with M. L. Wilson and Ralph Borsodi) Agriculture and Modern Life, 1939; also, with others, of sections of Atlas Am. Agr. Contbr. to U.S. Dept. Agr. Year Books, 1915-38, and to geographic publs. Home: College Park, Md. Office: University of Maryland, College Park, Md. Died Dec. 2, 1949.

BAKER, Ray Stannard ("David Grayson") author; b. Lansing, Mich., Apr. 17, 1870; s. Maj. Joseph Stannard and Alice (Potter) B.; B.S., Mich. State Coll., 1889; LL.D., 1917; partial law course and studies in lit., U. of Mich.; Litt.D., Amherst Coll., 1925; Litt.D., Duke Univ., 1938; m. Jessie I., d. Prof. William James Beal, Jan. 2, 1896; children—Alice Beal (Mrs. Alice B. Hyde), James Stannard, Roger Denio, Rachel Moore (Mrs. Robert Napier). Reporter and sub-editor of Chicago Record, 1892-97; managing editor McClure's Syndicate, 1897-98; asso. editor McClure's Magazine, 1899-1905; one of editors American Mag., 1906-15. Spl. commr. Dept. of State in Great Britain, France and Italy, 1918; dir. Press Bur. of Am. Commn. to Negotiate Peace, at Paris, 1919. Dem. presdl. elector State of Mass., 1928. Technical adviser during production by the 20th Century Fox Company of the moving picture, "Wilson" 1943-44. Trustee Jones Library of Amherst, Mass. Director Woodrow Wilson Foundation of New York City. Mem. National Instructor Arts and Letters, Society of American Historians, Phi Beta Kappa. Clubs: Century (New York). Author: Numerous books including—Seen in Germany, 1901; Following the Color Line, 1908; The Spiritual Unrest, 1910; What Wilson Did at Paris, 1919; The New Industrial Unrest, 1920; Woodrow Wilson and World Settlement, a History of the Peace Conference (3 vols.), 1922. Edited (with Prof. W. E. Dodd): The Public Papers of Woodrow Wilson (6 vols.), 1925-26; Woodrow Wilson—Life and Letters (authorized biography), first 2 vols., 1927, second 2 vols., 1931, fifth vol., 1935, sixth vol., 1937, seventh and eighth vols. (final), 1939. Native American; The Book of My Youth, 1942. American Chronicle (autobiography), 1945. Pulitzer prize for biography, 1940. Also under pseudonym of "David Grayson"; Adventures in Contentment, 1907; Adventures in Friendship, 1910; The Friendly Road, 1913; Hempfield, 1915; Great Possessions, 1917; Adventures in Understanding, 1925; Adventures in Solitude, 1931; The Countryman's Year, 1936; Under My Elm, 1942; (with J. B. Baker) American Pioneer in Science (life of William James Beal). 1925. Home: Amherst, Mass. Died July 12, 1946.

BAKER, S. Josephine, M.D.; b. Poughkeepsie, N.Y., Nov. 15, 1873; d. Orlando D. M. and Jennie Harwood (Brown) B.; M.D., Woman's Med. Coll., New York Infirmary, 1898; interne New Eng. Hosp., Boston, 1898-99; Dr.P.H., Bellevue Med. Coll. (New York U.), 1917; unmarried. Asst. to commr. of health, N.Y. City, 1907-08; dir. Bur. Child Hygiene, Dept. of Health, 1908-23; former consultant U.S. P.H.S., and various other orgns.; consultant Children's Bur. of U.S. Dept. Labor; mem. State Bd. Health, N.J., mem. bd. and cons. pediatrician, Clinton (N.J.) Reformatory for Women. Former mem. from U.S. of Health Com. League of Nations. Organized 1st bur. of child hygiene under govt control, N.Y. City, leading to lowest baby death rate of any large city in America or Europe. Hon. pres. Children's Welfare Fedn. Trustee N.Y. Infirmary for Women and Children. Fellow A.M.A., Am. Pub. Health Assn., New York Acad. Medicine; mem. Am. Child Health Assn. (ex-pres.), N.Y. State and N.Y. County med. socs., Am. Women's Med. Assn. (past pres.); assso. mem. Am. Acad. Pediatrics, hon. mem. N.J. State Med. Soc. Democrat. Unitarian. Clubs: Cosmopolitan, Women's City, Present Day (pres.; Princeton, N.J.). Author: Healthy Mothers, 1923; Healthy Babies, 1923; Healthy Children, 1923; Child Hygiene, 1925; Fighting for Life, 1939. Formerly lecturer on child hygiene, Columbia and New York univs. Home: Trevenna Farm, Belle Mead, N.J. Died Feb. 22, 1945.

BAKER, Stephen, banker; b. Poughkeepsie, N.Y., Aug. 12, 1859; s. Stephen and Anna Mary (Greene) B.; ed. pvt. and pub. schs.; m. Mary Dabney Payson, Oct. 28, 1890. Began with Bank of Manhattan, 1891, pres., 1893-1927, now hon. chmn. bd.; dir. N.Y. Clearing House Bldg. Co.; trustee Bowery Savings Bank. Mem. bd. of mgrs. St. Luke's Hosp. Republican. Episcopalian. Clubs: Union, Union League, Down Town Assn. Home: 160 E. 72d St. Office: 40 Wall St., New York, N.Y. Died Dec. 30, 1946.

BAKER, Walter Hudson, business exec.; b. Washington County, Pa., Aug. 28, 1879; s. N. R. and Mary (Perrin) B.; A.B., Washington and Jefferson Coll., 1898; m. Amy Patterson Duncan, April 7, 1909 (dec. Nov., 1942); 1 dau., Anna (Mrs. David Palmer Weimer, Jr.); m. 2d, Wilma Sinclair (Le Van). Pres. Universal Cyclops Steel Corp., Bridgeville, Pa.; dir. Union Nat. Bank, Pittsburgh, Pa., Citizens Nat. Bank, Washington, Pa. Trustee Washington and Jefferson Coll. Mem. Phi Delta Theta. Republican. Methodist. Mason. Clubs: Bath, Indian Creek Golf (Miami Beach); University, Duquesne (Pittsburgh); Engineers (New York); Oakmont Country (Oakmont, Pa.). Home: Washington, Pa. Office: Universal Cyclops Corp., Bridgeville, Pa. Deceased.

BAKER, William Gideon, Jr., investment banking; b. Frederick County, Md., Dec. 21, 1874; s. William G. and Susan Ellen (Jones) B.; A.B., Western Md. Coll., 1894; A.B., Yale, 1896; LL.B., U. of Md., 1899; m. Mary Drake Sawyers, Feb. 1, 1911. Associated with Sewell S. Watts (now deceased) in firm of Baker, Watts & Co., investment bankers, Baltimore, 1900, and the firm has since continued under same title, retired as active partner in firm, Oct. 1, 1942, but is still a limited partner; dir. Standard Lime & Stone Co., Chesapeake & Potomac Telephone Co. of Baltimore. Mem. N.Y. Stock Exchange. Chairman sales committee, Liberty Loan, Baltimore district, World War I. Formerly vice president Community Fund. President Investment Bankers Assn. of Am., 1918-19. Trustee Buckingham Sch. for Boys. Mem. Phi Beta Kappa. Mason. Ind. Democrat. Clubs: Maryland, University, Elkridge. Home: "Wyndon," Towson, Baltimore County. Office: Calvert and Redwood Streets, Baltimore 3, Md. Died Dec. 27, 1948.

BALCH, Allan Christopher (bălch), elec. engr.; b. Valley Falls, N.Y., Mar. 13, 1864; s. Ebenezer Atwood and Hannah (Hoag) B.; M.E. in E.E., Cornell U., 1889; hon. LL.D. from Claremont Coll.; m. Janet Jacks, Apr. 29, 1891. Began practice, Seattle, Wash., 1889; removed to Los Angeles, Calif., 1896; pres. Greenwich Investment Corp., Lerdo Land Co., Summit Lake Investment Co.; also pres. Meridian Limited; dir. Southern Calif. Gas Co. Pres. bd. trustees and mem. Obs. Council of Calif. Inst. Tech.; pres. Good Hope Hosp. Assn.; dir. Southern Calif. Symphony Assn.; mem. bd. govs. of the Los Angeles Museum; mem. advisory com. of the Huntington Library, Pasadena. Mem. Hollywood Bowl Assn., Alpha Delta Phi. Mason (32°, K.T., Shriner). Republican. Clubs: California (Los Angeles); Bel Air Bay Club; Bohemian Club. Home: Hotel Biltmore. Office: Union Bank Bldg., Los Angeles, Calif. Died Apr. 30, 1943.

BALCH, William Monroe, clergyman, educator; b. Monroe, Wis., Nov. 25, 1871; s. Rev. Manning Brown and Harriet Lucy (Monroe) B.; B.L., U. of Wis., 1891, M.L., 1894; studied law, same univ., 1891-92; Ph.D., U. of Wooster, 1900; m. Beulah Genevieve Richards, June 27, 1893; children—Mary Monroe, Robert Manning, Mrs. Elizabeth East, Mrs. Esther Sarah McIntyre. Ordained ministry of M.E. Ch., 1892; pastor successively Mineral Point, Wis., St. Louis, Mo., Lincoln, Neb., Dover, N.H., Topeka, Kan., etc., until 1919; gen. sec. Meth. Fedn. for Social Service, 1909-12; prof. sociology, Baker U., 1919-32, prof. history since 1932; dir. summer sessions, same univ., 1923-26. Del. Gen. Conf. M.E. Ch., 1904, 08; mem. Seminar on Mexican Relations, City of Mexico, 1927; vice-chmn. Kans. State Commn. for Crippled Children since 1931. Mem. Kan. State Committee on U.S. Defense Bonds. Mem. Am. Sociol. Soc., Am. Hist. Assn., Phi Delta Phi, Sigma Phi Epsilon. Author: Theories of Industrial Liberty, 1900; Christianity and the Labor Movement, 1912; The State and the Kingdom, 1926. Contbr. to American Mercury, Christian Advocate, Meth. Rev., Homiletic Rev., Jour. of Social Philosophy, etc. Home: Baldwin, Kan. Died Nov. 17, 1941.

BALDOMIR, Alfredo (văl'dō-mēr), former President of Uruguay; b. Montevideo, Uruguay, Aug. 27, 1884; s. Francisco Baldomir and Eugenia Ferrari; student at military sch. and of architecture. Completed military sch. and entered army, rising to mem. of Gen. Staff and, 1917, became head of a division; became prof. engring., Military Sch., 1923; successively chief of military constrns. (Gen. Staff), 1925; chief of police, Montevideo, 1931; sec. of Ministry of Nat. Defense, 1934, minister of nat. defense, 1935; President of Uruguay, 1938-42. Address: Montevideo, Uruguay.* Died Feb. 25,1948.

BALDRIDGE, H. Clarence, ex-gov.; b. Carlock, Ill., Nov. 24, 1868; s. William John and Caroline (Wright) B.; student Ill. Wesleyan U., Bloomington, Ill., 1890-93; m. Cora A. McCreight, Feb. 1, 1893; children—Marion Claire, Lela Gail. Settled at Parma, Ida., 1904, and engaged in merc. business and farming; pres. First Nat. Bank, 1916-27. Mem. Ida. Ho. of Rep., 1911-13, Senate, 1913-15; lt. gov. of Ida., 1923-27; gov. of Ida. 2 terms, 1927-31; retired from mercantile business, 1942. Trustee Coll. of Idaho. Mem. Phi Gamma Delta. Republican. Presbyterian. Mason. Home: 1003 Fort St., Boise, Idaho. Died June 7, 1947.

BALDWIN, Asa Columbus, civil engr.; b. Austinburg, O., June 21, 1887; s. Adelbert Mortimer and Florilla (Williams) B.; B.A., Western Reserve U., Cleveland, O., 1908; student evenings law dept. George Washington Univ., 1910-13; m. Louise Smith, Dec. 8, 1917 (died May 6, 1933); children—Mortimer Wells, Frances Louise, Sylvia; m. 2d, Mrs. Marguerite Holliday, Dec. 12, 1935. Joined U.S. Coast and Geodetic Survey, 1909; was field officer Internat. Boundary Commn., establishing Alaska-Can. boundary, Mt. St. Elias to Arctic Ocean, 1909-13; leader in ascent of Mt. St. Elias, 1913. Pvt. engring. practice in Alaska, 1914-17, and in Seattle and Alaska since 1920; West Coast rep. Schlumberger Electrical Prospecting Methods of Paris since 1928; pres. Yellow Band Gold Mines, Inc., since 1938; mng. engr. Indianola Land Company, 1928-33. Geodetic engineer for International Boundary Commn. under NRA, 1933-34. Enlisted in Alaska for World War; entered O.T.C., Presidio, San Francisco, Aug. 27, 1917; 1st lt. Inf., Nov. 27, 1917; trans. to Engr. Corps and assigned to 29th Engrs., U.S. Army; sent overseas, June 1918; attached to G.H.Q., A.E.F., orientation officer for arty., Argonne-Meuse battle; hon. disch. Apr. 26, 1919. Mem. bar D.C. and Alaska; mem. Am. Soc. C.E., Beta Theta Pi. Lecturer on Alaska, seasons of 1926-27, making 2 transcontinental tours. Home: 3514 Wallingford Av. Office: Alaska Bldg., Seattle, Wash. Died Sep. 18, 1942.

BALDWIN, Benjamin James, retired physician; b. in Bullock Co., Ala., Nov. 16, 1856; s. Benjamin James and Martha (Barnett) B.; ed. Randolph-Macon Coll., Ashland, Va.; grad. Bellevue Med. Coll., New York, 1877; m. Hulit Morris, 1884 (died 1894); m. 2d, Kate Sistrunk, July, 1896. Began practice of medicine, 1878; now retired; ex-pres. Med. Assn. of State of Ala.; ex-mem. Ala. State Bd. Health; ex-pres. Montgomery Gas Co., Elyton Land Co. (Birmingham, Ala.); ex-chmn. exec. com. of Birmingham (Ala.) Water Works Co., and former dir. Birmingham Trust & Savings Co.; now v.p. Montgomery Hotel Co., and dir. North and South Ala. Div., Louisville & Nashville R.R. Pres. bd. edn., City of Montgomery, since 1894; sec. Conf. for Edn. in the South. Democrat. Episcopalian. Address: Montgomery, Ala. Died July 10, 1932.

BALDWIN, Edward Robinson, physician; b. Bethel, Conn., Sept. 8, 1864; s. Rev. Elijah C. and Frances Marsh (Hutchinson) B.; brother of Albertus Hutchinson B.; M.D., Yale Med. Sch., 1890; hon. M.A., Yale, 1914; Sc.D., Dartmouth, 1937; m. Mary Caroline Ives, June 1, 1895; 1 son, Henry Ives. Began practice at Cromwell, Conn., 1891; at Saranac Lake, N.Y., since 1893. Specializes in lung and throat diseases; researches in lab. since 1892; trustee Reception and Gen. hosps., Trudeau Sanatorium. Mem. Saranac Lake Sch. Bd., 1895; pres. Saranac Lake Bd. of Health, 1899-1901. Mem. Assn. Am. Physicians, A.M.A., Nat. Tuberculosis Assn. (pres. 1916-17), Am. Climatol. Assn., Assn. Am. Pathologists and Bacteriologists. Republican. Presbyterian. Home: Saranac Lake, N.Y. Died May 6, 1947.

BALDWIN, Frank Conger, architect; b. Galesburg, Ill., June 13, 1869; s. Charles Edward and Alta (Conger) B.; graduate St. Paul's School, Concord, New Hampshire, 1887; student in architecture, Mass. Inst. Tech., 1887-90; m. Lilian E. Edson, June 24, 1896 (died Oct. 23, 1922); m. 2d, Alice Matthews Storrs, Sept. 12, 1926. Formerly mem. firm of Stratton and Baldwin; practiced at Detroit, Mich., 1893-1911, then moved to Washington, D.C., and retired; pres. Farmers Creamery Co. of Fredericksburg, Va. Fellow Am. Inst. Architects; v.p. same, 1911-14; mem. Phi Gamma Delta. Mayor of Grosse Pointe, Mich., 1903; pres. Detroit Sch. of Design, 1909-11. Mem. Architectural League, New York. Episcopalian. Clubs:

Cosmos, Arts (Washington); Detroit Boat; Nantucket Golf, Nantucket (Mass.) Yacht Club: Century (New York). Author: Baldwin's Specification Index, 1904; also articles on exploration and big game hunting. Home: 2122 Bancroft Pl. N.W., Washington, D.C.; (summer) "The Crossways," Nantucket, Mass.
Died Nov. 25, 1945.

BALDWIN, Henry Alexander, sugar planter; b. Paliuli, Maui, T.H., Jan. 12, 1871; s. Henry Perrine and Emily (Alexander) B.; prep. edn., Haiku Sch., Maui, 1884-86, Punahou Sch., Honolulu, H.T., 1886-87, Phillips Acad., Andover, Mass., 1888-89; student Mass. Inst. Tech., 1890-94; m. Ethel Frances Smith, of Honolulu, July 19, 1897; children—Leslie Alexander (dec.), Jared Smith (dec.), Frances Hobron (Mrs. James Walter Cameron). Mgr. Haiku Sugar Co., 1897-1904; mgr. Maui Agrl. Co. since 1904, now pres.; pres. Baldwin Packers, Haleakala Ranch, East Maui Irrigation Co., Haleakala Pineapple Co., Maui Pineapple Co.; v.p. Alexander & Baldwin, Ltd.; dir. Bishop First Nat. Bank, Bishop Trust Co. Mem. Hawaii Ty. Senate, 1913-21; territorial del. to 67th Congress (1921-23); chmn. Maui Co. Rep. Com., 1912-44; mem. Ty. Accountancy Commn.; mem. Hawaii Ho. of Rep., 1933, Senate, 1934-36; president Hawaii Senate, 1937 session. Trustee Maunaloa Seninary (chairman), Maui Aid Assn., Fred Baldwin Memorial Home; chmn. bd. mgrs. Kula Farm and Sanitarium, 1923-33. Mem. Chi Phi. Clubs: Maui Fair and Racing Assn., Maui Country; University, Pacific, Ad, Commercial (Honolulu); Pacific Union, Bohemian, Transportation (San Francisco). Home: Makawao, Maui, H.T. Office: Paia, Maui, T.H. Died Oct. 8, 1946.

BALDWIN, Henry de Forest, lawyer; b. Clinton, Ia., Nov. 7, 1862; s. Simeon and Mary Sarah (Marvin) B.; A.B., Yale, 1885; LL.B., Columbia, 1887; grad. work Berlin and Heidelberg Univs., 1887-88; m. Jessie Pinney, Sept. 4, 1890 (died Jan. 30, 1932); children—Dorothea (Mrs. Parker McCollester), Marian (Mrs. Perry Dunlap Smith), Sherman, Eleanor de Forest. Admitted to N.Y. state bar, 1887, and practiced N.Y. City since 1888; asst. corp. counsel N.Y. City, 1895-98; mem. firm Lord, Day & Lord since 1900; pres. Queens Co. Water Co., 1908-25. Mem. com. Police Problem, 1905-08; fusion cand. Justice Supreme Ct., 1911; chmn. N.Y. Charter Commn., 1922, art commn. N.Y. City, 1929-31; chmn. bd. trustees Peoples' Inst., 1911-34; trustee N.Y. Botan. Garden since 1921 (v. pres. since 1928); treas. Nat. Probation Assn., since 1927; trustee Am. Acad. in Rome 1932-44; vice president Civil Service Reform Assn. Mem. N.Y City bar assn. (mem. exec. com., 1913-15, v.p., 1932-33), Council on Fgn. Relations Democrat. Clubs: Reform (trustee-sec., 1889-97), Century treasurer, 1916-44), University, Coffee House, Down Town Assn., Cruising. Home: 320 East 72nd St. Office: 25 Broadway, New York, N.Y. Died May 18, 1947.

BALDWIN, Lewis Warrington, railway official; b. Waterbury, Anne Arundel County, Md., Feb. 26, 1875; s. Richard and Sophronia Jane (Furlong) B.; B.S., St. John's Coll., Annapolis, Md., 1893; C.E., Lehigh U., Bethlehem, Pa., 1896, hon. Dr. Engring., 1938; m. Marye Dodge, Dec. 1903; children—Richard, Roccena, L. Warrington. Entered service engring. dept. I.C. R.R., July 20, 1896; successively supt., engr. maintenance of way, and gen. supt., I.C. and Yazoo & Miss. Valley rys., 1906-15; gen. mgr., and v.p. and gen. mgr., Central of Ga. Ry., Savannah, Ga., 1915-18; asst. regional dir. U.S.R.R. Adminstrn., Southern Region, Atlanta, Ga., Feb.-June 1918; similar position, Allegheny Region, Phila., Pa., 1918-19; regional dir. Allegheny Region, Oct. 1, 1919-Feb. 29, 1920; v.p. in charge operating dept. I.C. R.R., Mar. 1, 1920-Mar. 31, 1923; pres. and mem. exec. com. and chief exec. officer Mo. Pacific R.R. Co., Gulf Coast Lines, Internat.-Great Northern R.R. Co., and subsidiary cos. since 1923; chmn. exec. com. and mem. mng. com. Denver & Rio Grande Western R.R. Co. Past pres. St. Louis Symphony Soc., St. Louis Chapter S.A.R. Director, St. Luke's Hospital, St. Louis, Mo.; chairman Region 8, Boy Scouts of America. Mem. American Society C.E. (past pres.), Am. Ry. Engring. Assn., Beta Theta Pi. Episcopalian. Clubs: Chicago (Chicago) Bankers (N.Y. City); Noonday, Racquet, St. Louis Country, Log Cabin (St. Louis). Home: 23 Westmoreland Pl. Office: Missouri Pacific Bldg., 13th and Olive Sts., St. Louis, Mo.
Died May 14, 1946.

BALDWIN, Roger Sherman, lawyer; b. N.Y. City, Nov. 26, 1873; s. Simeon and Mary Sarah (Marvin) B.; ed. Morse's School, N.Y. City; Real Gymnasium, Braunschweig, Germany; A.B., Yale, 1895, LL.B., 1897; M.L., New York U., 1900; m. Mary Catherine Vail, Aug. 23, 1904; 1 dau., Catherine Vail (Mrs. Donald C. Blanke). Admitted to N.Y. bar, 1897. Conn. bar, 1919; began practice at N.Y. City; now mem. Baldwin, Todd & Lefferts. Former mem. Squadron A., N.Y. N.G. Chmn. Fuel Com.; sec. Exeption Bd. of Greenwich; mem. Fed. Food Adminstrn., Washington, D.C., World War I. Mem. Greenwich Defense Council; mem. Board of Estimate and Taxation, Greenwich; former dir. Greenwich Chamber Commerce; trustee Fairfield State Hospital; former mem. Conn. State Highway Safety Commn.; mem. Conn. Special Tax Commn., 1933-34; mem. State Evacuation com. (Conn.). Mem. Am., N.Y. and Greenwich bar assns., Assn. of Bar City of N.Y., N.Y. County Lawyers Assn., Conn. Soc. S.A.R., Descendants of Signers of Declaration of Independence. Psi Upsilon. Clubs: University, Century, Yale, Bankers, Down Town Assn. (N.Y. City); Yale Graduates (New Haven); Field, Round Hill (Greenwich); Manursing Island (Rye, N.Y.); Woodstock (Vt.) Country. Home: Round Hill Road, Greenwich, Conn. Office: 120 Broadway, N.Y. City. Died Mar. 23, 1949.

BALDWIN, William Ayer, railway official; b. Elmira, N.Y., July 26, 1876; s. Charles H. and Florence E. (Ayer) B.; prep. edn., Elmira Acad.; E.E., Cornell Univ., 1896. Chainman Erie R.R. Co., 1896, and continued with the company and its subsidiaries as rodman and asst. engr., 1899-1902, trainmaster, 1902-03, div. engr., 1903-09, again trainmaster, 1909-10, supt. Chicago and Lima div., 1910-12, Del. and Jeffersons divs., 1912-14, gen. supt. lines, east of Salamanca, 1914-17, lines west of Salamanca, 1917-18; gen. mgr., Erie System, 1918-1920; mgr. Ohio region Erie R.R. Co., 1920-22; v.p. with hdqrs. in N.Y. City, 1922-28; dir. N.Y., Susquehanna & Western R.R., Chicago & Erie R.R., N. J. & N. Y. R.R. and 34 other corps., mostly subsidiaries of the Erie R.R. Co.; retired, 1928. Mem. Delta Kappa Epsilon. Clubs: Elmira City; Arizona Club, Phoenix Country. Home: Phoenix, Ariz. Died Dec. 15, 1945.

BALDWIN, William Wright, railway official; b. Keosauqua, Ia., Sept. 28, 1845; s. Charles and Rachel (Wright) B.; B.S., Ia. State U., 1866; LL.B., Ia. Law Sch., 1867; m. Alice Tuttle, Sept. 13, 1870; children—Martin Tuttle, Rachel, William Wright, Jr. (killed in battle in France, July 1918), Roger Allan. Enlisted as pvt., Co. D, 44th Ia. Inf., May 1864. Admitted to bar, 1868; land commr. C. B. & Q. Ry. for Ia. and Neb., 1879-91, asst. to pres., 1891-1909, v.p. since 1909, fed. treas., 1918-20. Office: 547 W. Jackson Blvd., Chicago. Died July 17, 1936.

BALDY, John Montgomery, gynecologist; b. Danville, Pa., June 16, 1860; s. Edward Hurley and Henrietta Cooper (Montgomery) B.; prep. edn. St. Paul's Sch., Concord, N.H.; M.D., U. of Pa. Dr. of Medicine, 1884; m. Edith Lyndsey, Aug. 5, 1896; m. 2d, Helen M. Constien, May 1919. Practiced, Scranton, Pa., 1885-91, and subsequently at Phila.; retired 1923. Home: Devon, Pa. Died Dec. 13, 1934.

BALKE, Clarence William, chemist; b. Auburn, O., Mar. 29, 1880; s. William Frederick and Clara Jacobena (Class) B.; A.B., Oberlin (O.) Coll., 1902; Ph.D., U. of Pa., 1905; m. Minnie Maude Coddington, Apr. 21, 1905; children—Claire Coddington, Roger Redfield, Barbara, Hildegarde, Abigail Strader. Acting prof. physics and chemistry, Kenyon Coll., Gambier, O., 1903-04; instr. in chemistry, Oberlin Coll., summer 1903; instr. in chemistry, U. of Pa., 1906-07; asso. in chemistry, U. of Ill., 1907-10; asst. prof. inorganic chemistry, 1910-13, prof., 1913-16; chem. dir. Fansteel Products Co., North Chicago, Ill., since 1916. Mem. Am. Chem. Soc., Sigma Xi, Phi Eta, Phi Lambda. Club: Bonnie Brook Golf (Waukegan, Ill.). Contbr. papers on rare metals to Jour. Am. Chem. Soc., Chem. Bull., Chem. Age, etc. Discoverer of new methods of dehydrating, amalgamating, welding and processing; also methods for the mfr. of tantalum and columbium. Home: 40 Deere Park Drive, S., Highland Park. Office: Fansteel Products Co., North Chicago, Ill. Died July 8, 1948.

BALL, Caroline Peddle, sculptor; b. Terre Haute, Ind., Nov. 11, 1869; d. Charles Rugan and Mary Elizabeth (Ball) Peddle; pupil of Augustus St. Gaudens and Kenyon Cox, New York; m. Bertrand E. Ball, Oct. 14, 1902; 1 dau., Mary Aseneth. Hon. mention Paris Expn., 1900; sculptor of figure of Victory in quadriga on the U.S. bldg., at Paris Expn., 1900; memorial corbels, Grace Ch., Brooklyn; memorial fountain, Auburn, N.Y. Home: Harwinton, Conn. Died Oct. 1, 1938.

BALL, Elmer Darwin, entomologist; b. Athens, Vt., Sept. 21, 1870; s. Leroy A. and Mary A. (Mansfield) B.; B.S., Ia. State Coll., 1895, M.Sc., 1898; Ph.D., Ohio State U., 1907; m. Mildred R. Norvell, June 14, 1899. Asst. in zoölogy and entomology, Ia. State Coll., 1895-97; asso. prof. same, Colo. Agrl. Coll., 1898-1902; prof. zoölogy and entomology, Utah Agrl. Coll., 1902-07; dir. Expt. Sta. and Sch. of Agr., Utah Agrl. Coll., 1907-16; state entomologist of Wis., 1916-18; prof. zoölogy and entomology, Ia. State Coll., and state entomologist of Ia., 1918-21, on leave as asst. sec. agr., June 12, 1920-Oct. 1, 1921; dir. scientific work, U.S. Dept. Agr., 1921-25; in charge of celery insect investigations, Fla. State Plant Bd., Sanford, Fla., 1925-28; dean of Coll. Agr. and dir. Agrl. Expt. Sta., Univ. of Ariz., 1928-31, now prof. zoölogy and entomology (on leave). Fellow A.A.A.S., Entomol. Soc. America, Utah Acad. Science (pres., 1910), Ia. Acad. Science; mem. Washington Acad. Science, Biol. and Entomol. socs. Washington, Am. Assn. Econ. Entomologists (pres. 1918), Pacific Slope Assn. Econ. Entomologists (pres., 1915-16), Ecol. Soc. America, Sigma Xi, Phi Kappa Phi, Gamma Sigma Delta (nat. pres. 1921-22). Author of systematic and life-history studies of Membracidæ, Cercopidæ, Jassidæ and Fulgoridæ, economic studies of codling moth, grasshoppers and leaf hoppers, causing "curly leaf" of sugar beets and "hopper burn" of potatoes, biol. studies of celery tyer, also studies of poultry breeding. Address: University of Arizona, Tucson, Ariz. Died Oct. 5, 1943.

BALL, Francis Kingsley, editor; b. Mercer County, Pa., Nov. 29, 1863; s. Francis Asbury and Fanny Ann (Johnston) B.; A.B., Drury, 1887, LL.D., 1920; Oberlin Theol. Sem., 1887-88; Harvard, 1888-1894, A.B., 1890, A.M., 1891, Ph.D., 1894; travel and study abroad, 1897-99 (winter of 1898-99 at U. of Berlin); m. Janet Nettleton, July 21, 1891. Teacher of English composition, Oberlin Acad., 1887-88; instr. in Latin, Harvard, 1892-93; prof. Greek, U. of N.C., 1894-97; instr. Greek and German, Phillips Exeter Acad., 1899-1910; instr. German, The Browne and Nichols Sch., Cambridge, Mass., 1910-12; editor Ginn & Co., pubs., Boston, 1912-38; retired. Mem. Am. Philol. Assn. Author: The Elements of Greek, 1902; Hero Stories from American History (with A. F. Blaisdell), 1903; A German Drill Book, 1904; Short Stories from American History (with same), 1904; A German Grammar, 1907; Introductory Sketch to Homer's Iliad, the World's Greatest Poem, 1909; The American History Story-Book (with same), 1911; The English History Story-Book (with same), 1912; The Child's Book of American History (with same), 1913; Heroic Deeds of American Sailors (with same), 1915; Am. History for Little Folks (with same), 1917; Pioneers of America (with same), 1919; Log Cabin Days (with same), 1921; Constructive English—A Handbook of Speaking and Writing, 1923; Building with Words—Elementary Grammar and Composition, 1926. Translator of several poems of Heinrich Heine, 1909; The Epochs of German Agrarian History and Agrarian Policy (from Dr. Carl Johannes Fuchs's inaugural address at U. of Freiberg), appearing in Prof. Thomas Nixon Carver's Selected Readings in Rural Economics, 1916. Home: 1217 Beacon St., Brookline, Mass. Died June 8, 1940.

BALL, Frank Clayton, mfr.; b. Greensburg, O., Nov. 24, 1857; s. Lucius Stiles and Maria P. (Bingham) B.; ed. pub. schs. and Canandaigua (N.Y.) Acad.; LL.D. from Indiana U., 1929; m. Elizabeth Wolfe Brady, 1893; children—Edmund Arthur, Mrs. Lucina Owsley, Mrs. Margaret Petty, Frank Elliott (dec.), Mrs. Rosemary Wright Bracken. Began mfg. business with 4 brothers (3 now deceased), at Buffalo, 1880, moved to Muncie, Ind., 1888, and is pres. Ball Bros. Co., main offices at Muncie, and factories in Tex., Ill., Okla., W.Va. and Ind.; also pres. Muncie & Western Railroad Co.; dir. Borg Warner Corp., Chicago. Ball Bros. donated $7,000,000 or more to ednl. and welfare work including: bldgs. for Y.M.C.A. and Y.W.C.A. at Muncie, also Ball Memorial Hosp. and Masonic Auditorium; James Whitcomb Riley Children's Hosp., Indianapolis; Hillsdale Coll., Mich.; Keuka Coll., N.Y.; etc. Dir. Ball Memorial Hosp., Y.M.C.A., Ball State Teachers Coll. (Muncie). Republican. Presbyterian. Mason (32°). Clubs: Rotary, Athletic, Columbia. Home: Muncie, Ind.
Died Mar. 19, 1943.

BALL, Fred Samuel, lawyer; b. Portsmouth, O., Feb. 14, 1866; s. William Henry and Jane (St. Clair) B.; Ph.B., Ohio State U., 1888; m. Florence Corinne, d. Rev. Simon Peter Richardson, of Ga., Oct. 4, 1893 (died 1933); children—Fred St. Clair, Charles Arthur, Richard Arledge. Admitted to bar, 1891, since practiced at Montgomery, Ala.; mem. Ball & Ball (self and 3 sons). Counsel in case of Alonzo Bailey, in which Supreme Court of U.S. held invalid Ala. statute giving right to an employer or landlord to hold a laborer or tenant under a written contract, and compel him to perform services under pain of criminal prosecution. Dir. Cudady Packing Co. Ala., Tennille Furniture Co., Ala.-Ga. Syrup Co. (Montgomery), etc. Trustee and dir. Montgomery Y.M.C.A. Sec. Ala. Child Labor Com., 1902-12; mem. Nat. Council and Internat. Com., Y.M.C.A. (Nat. Board, 1924-27 and since 1933). Mem. Am. and Ala. State bar assns., League to Enforce Peace, Chamber of Commerce, Phi Delta Theta (treas. gen. council, 1894-98); pres. Montgomery Bar Assn., 1917-18; trustee and ex-pres. Children's Protective Assn. Ind. Democrat. Methodist. Clubs: Commercial (pres., 1909-10), Country. Home: 1504 S. Perry St. Office: First Nat. Bank Bldg., Montgomery, Ala. Died July 3, 1942.

BALL, Henry Price, engineer; b. Phila., Pa., Jan. 8, 1868; s. Joseph and Sarah (Price) B.; B.S., U. of Pa., 1887, M.E., 1888; m. Anna Crosby Daily, May 30, 1891 (died April 23, 1934); 1 dau., Mabel; m. 2d, Miss Margaret A. Capeliss, April 3, 1937. With United Edison Mfg. Co., 1888-93, and designed and patented many devices for distribution of electricity for lighting, ry. and marine work; with Ward-Leonard Electric Co., 1893-1900, designed and patented complete line of rheostat theater dimmers and circuit breakers for control of electric current; chief engr. Gen. Incandescent and Arc Light Co., designed and patented apparatus for distbn. of high tension currents and automatic safety devices for control of same, large central sta. equipment, remote control switches and switchboard apparatus used by Commonwealth Edison Co., Chicago and Brooklyn, N.Y. Edison Co., etc.; cons. engr. Gen. Electric Co., 1903-08, designed and patented automatic machinery for reproduction of music played on piano and for mfr. of music rolls for use in piano players; engr. heating dept. Gen. Electric Co., Pittsfield, Mass., 1908-14, designed and patented complete line of electric heating devices for domestic and indsl. use; mem. firm, chief engr. and factory mgr. S. Sternan & Co., Brooklyn, 1914-17; supt. enamel factory of Lalande & Grosjean Co., Woodhaven, L.I., 1917-20; cons. engr. since 1920. Has taken out over 100 patents in U.S. and fgn. countries. Mem. Am. Inst. Elec. Engrs., Edison Pioneers, Beta Theta Pi. Republican. Home: 295 Parkside Av., Brooklyn, N.Y. Office: 141 5th Av., New York, N.Y. Died May 1, 1941.

BALL, Louise Charlotte, oral surgeon; b. N.Y. City, May 28, 1887; d. Robert Jemison and Louise S.M. (Hansen) B.; A.B., Hunter Coll., N.Y. City; Hunter Coll. faculty, 1906-17; D.D.S., Coll. Dental and Oral Surgery, now Columbia U. Sch. of Dentistry, 1915; m. John B. Bundren, June 20, 1917. Associated with Prof. W. J. Gies as dental investigator, Columbia U. Sch. of Medicine, 1914; dental clinician apptd. to Bellevue Hosp. and Neponsit Hosp. for Children, N. Y., 1915-16; founder, 1916, and dean New York Sch. Dental Hygiene, Hunter Coll.; founder 1916, dir. 1916-19, courses in oral hygiene, Columbia U.; asst. to dir. of extension courses, Columbia U., 1916-18; expert examiner in dental hygiene and dentistry, Municipal Civil Service Commn., City of N.Y., 1917-19; dir. courses in gen. and dental roentgenology, War Service Training Sch., N.Y. City, 1917-18; dir. Yorkville Dist. Dispensary for Oral Hygiene and Dental Diagnosis, 1918; mem. adv. council Dept. of Health, N.Y. City, 1918; founder, 1923, chmn., 1923-29, Dental Council of N.Y. State, Nat. Women's Party; founder, 1923, chmn., 1926, Dental Research Club of Women Dentists; founder, 1920, hon. pres. since 1920, Internat. Dental Health Foundn. for Children, Inc. Conducted free ednl. dental clinics in 7 South Am. countries, 1923, and preventive dentistry campaign for sch. children in S. Africa, 1927; pvt. practice of dentistry, N.Y. City, since 1915. Conducts 3 annual essay contests on subject of public dental health and nutrition open to student dental hygienists and dentists and members of N.Y. Dietetic Assn. Trustee Howard U. Mem. Am. Dental Assn., 1st Dist. Dental Soc. of N.Y., Am. Assn. Women Dentists, Assn. of Alumni of Sch. Dental and Oral Surgery (Columbia), Biochem. Soc. of Coll. Physicians and Surgeons of Columbia Univ. (ex-v.p.), Kimberly Dental Soc. of Union of S. Africa (hon. founder mem.), Am. Assn. Univ. Women, Soc. of Va. Women in N.Y. (pres. 1937-39), Internat. Council of Women at Brussels (v.p. Internat. Press Com. 1936-38), Westchester County Hist. Soc., Congress of States Soc. (v.p. 1937-39), Nat. Council of Women of U.S., United Daughters of the Confederacy, D.A.R., Civil Legion, English-Speaking Union, Nat. Woman's Party (founder), N.Y. League of Business and Professional Women (past v.p.), Amateur Cinema League; hon. charter mem. Nat. Chinese Women's Assn.; charter mem. Old Town of Mamaroneck Hist. Soc.; hon. mem. Am. Internat. Acad. (Washington, D.C., chapter). Episcopalian. Clubs: Soroptimist of N.Y. (pres. 1934-36), Engineering Women's, Dixie (N.Y. City). Author of bull. Denticuring—Home Care of the Teeth and Nutrition (2 million copies printed in several langs.), Dental Riddlegrams, and many articles on dental hygiene and diet in mags. Producer of Say It with Pearls, motion picture on dental health and nutrition. Home: (country) 733 Stuart Av., Mamaroneck, N.Y. Office: 130 East End Ave., New York. Died June, 1946.

BALL, Michael Valentine, M.D., surgeon; b. Warren, Pa., Feb. 14, 1868; s. George and Mary (Cohn) B.; high sch., Warren, Pa.; M.D., Jefferson Med. Coll., Phila., 1889; post grad. work, U. of Berlin, 1889-90; m. Grace Paterson, 1905; children—Mary, John George, Jean, William Lincoln. Began as interne German Hosp., Phila., then resident physician Eastern State Penitentiary, 1892-95; instr. in bacteriology, Polyclinic, Phila., 1896-97; pres. Bd. of Health, Warren, 1901-07; prof. clin. pathology, New York Med. Coll. for Women, 1916-17; specializes in diseases of eye and ear. Mem. A.M.A., Acad. Nat. and Oto-Laryngology, A.A.A.S. Mason (32°, Shriner). Club: Shakespeare (Warren). Author: Essentials of Bacteriology, 1891. Home: Warren, Pa. Died May 26, 1945.

BALL, Oscar Melville, biologist; b. Miami, Mo., Aug. 25, 1868; s. William Henry and Eliza Anne (Braden) B.; B.A., U. of Va., 1897; fellow in botany, U. of Va., 1898; student U. of Bonn, 1900, Leipzig, 1900-03; M.A., Ph.D., Leipzig, 1903; m. Mary B. Moon, June 16, 1900; 1 dau., Julia B. (wife of Lt. Robert M. Lee). Instr. in biology, U. of Va., 1896-97; prof. chemistry, Miller Sch., Va., 1897-1900; prof. botany and mycology, 1903-09, botany and zoology, 1909-11, biology, since June 1, 1911, Agrl. and Mech. Coll. of Texas. Mem. Deutsche Botanische Gesellschaft; fellow Tex. Acad. Science (v.p.); mem. A.A.A.S., Am. Econ. Soc., Nat. Inst. Soc. Sciences, Paleontol. Soc. Am., etc. Democrat. Mason (K.T., Shriner). Author of various papers on plant physiology, soil bacteriology and palaeobotany. Research in fossil flora of the Eocene. Address: College Station, Texas. Died Nov. 11, 1942.

BALL, Sydney Hobart, mining engr.; b. Chicago, Ill., Dec. 11, 1877; s. Farlin Q. and Elizabeth (Hall) B.; A.B., U. of Wis., 1901, Ph.D., 1910; m. Mary Ainslie, Dec. 8, 1913; 1 dau., Mary Virginia. Geologist, Mo. Bur. Mines and Geology, 1901-02; instr. geology, U. of Wis., 1902-03; asst. geologist, U.S. Geol. Survey, 1903-07; in charge expdn. exploring for minerals in Belgian Congo for Ryan-Guggenheim group, 1907-09; gen. practice in Europe, Asia, Africa, American and Greenland since 1909; cons. mineralogist U.S. Bur. of Mines; mining consultant War Production Bd., 1942-44. Mem. American Inst. Mining and Metall. Engrs. (dir. 1924-27), Geol. Soc. Am., Soc. of Econ. Geologists (pres. 1930), Mining and Metall. Soc. America (v.p. 1925-27; pres. 1933-34), Geol. Soc. of Belgium, Gemol. Inst. Am. (adv. bd., hon. mem.) C.R.B. Ednl. Fund (dir.), Psi Upsilon; hon. mem. Chem. Metall. and Mining Co. of South Africa. Officer Ordre Royal du Lion (Belgian). Republican. Clubs: Engineers', Explorers', (ex-gov.), Mining (pres. 1944-46). Author: Geology of Miller Co. (Mo. Bur. Mines), 1903; Geologic Reconnaissance in Southwestern Nevada and Eastern Calif., 1907; Geology of Clear Creek Quadrangle (U.S. Geol. Survey), 1906; annual chapter "Gemstones" in Minerals Yearbook; also pamphlets and tech. and geol. articles particularly on precious stones. Home: 829 Park Av. Office: 26 Beaver St., New York, N.Y. Died Apr. 8, 1949; buried Nantucket Island, Mass.

BALL, Thomas Henry, ex-congressman; b. at Huntsville, Tex., Jan. 14, 1859; ed. in pvt. sch. and Austin Coll., Huntsville; later pursued farming and mercantile business; served 3 terms as mayor of Huntsville; retired to practice law; attended law lectures, U. of Virginia. Was chmn. Dem. exec. com. Walker County, Tex., 12 yrs., of 1st Supreme jud. dist., Tex., 3 terms; del. to every State Dem. Conv. since 1886, Dem. Nat. Convs., 1892, 1896, del.-at-large, 1900; mem. 56th to 59th Congresses (1897-1905), 1st Tex. Dist. Address: Houston, Tex. Died May 7, 1944.

BALL, Thomas Raymond, ex-congressman, architect; b. New York, N.Y., Feb. 12, 1896; s. Thomas Watson and Alice L. (Raymond) B.; student Anglo-Saxon Sch., Paris, France, Heathcote Sch., Harrison, N.Y., Art Students League, N.Y. City; studied drawing with Speicher, Du Mond, composition under Miller, design under father, Thomas Watson Ball; m. Elvira Urisarri de Polo, Dec. 18, 1934; 1 dau., Diana Willoughby Urisarri. Designer in 1916; after World War engaged in profession of architecture; designed many residences in eastern Conn., new chancel for Seabury Memorial, Groton, Conn., and (with Ernest Sibley) Old Lyme Sch. Served with Depot Batt. 7th N.Y. Inf. guarding N.Y. City Aqueduct, 1917; overseas with Camouflage Sect., 40th U.S. Engrs., 1918-19. Mem. Conn. Ho. of Rep., 1927-37, author of law establishing Conn. Archtl. Examining Bd.; mem. 76th Congress (1939-41), 2d Conn. Dist. Mem. Old Lyme Bd. Edn., 1926-38. Co-ordinator of transportation and rationing officer, Electric Boat Co., Groton, Conn., since 1942. Mem. Am. Inst. Architects, Conn. Hist. Soc., New Eng. Historic-Geneal. Soc., Antiquarian and Landmark Soc. of Conn., S.A.R., Soc. for Preservation of New Eng. Antiquities, Soc. of Founders of Norwich, Naval Hist. Foundation, Soc. of Colonial Wars, Order of Founders and Patriots of America, American Legion, Old Lyme Chamber of Commerce. Republican. Episcopalian. Mason (32°), I.O.O.F., Elk, Grange. Clubs: Town Hall, Church (New York); Thames (New London); Old Lyme Beach. Home: Old Lyme, Conn. Died June 16, 1943.

BALL, Willis Manville, editor; b. Tallahassee, Fla., Aug. 25, 1859; s. Glover Alling and Christina Elizabeth (Hackett) B.; ed. pub. sch. and under private tutor; student West of Suwannee Sem. (now U. of Fla.); LL.D., U. of Fla., 1942; m. Fannie Earner Leverette, July 2, 1879 (died Feb. 5, 1905); m. 2d, Jessie Atkinson McGriff, Apr. 10, 1924; children—Philip Manville and (adopted) Vida, Patricia. Editor Fla. Times-Union since 1902; chmn. bd. Fla. Pub. Co.; v.p. Morris Plan Co. Mem. Chamber Commerce, Jacksonville. Democrat. Episcopalian. Odd Fellow. Home: 1855 Powell Pl. Office: Times-Union Bldg., Jacksonville, Fla. Died Sept. 12, 1947.

BALLAGH, James Curtis (băl'ĕr), univ. prof.; b. Brownsburg, Va.; s. Rev. Dr. James H. and Margaret Tate (Kinnear) B.; grad. Washington and Lee U., 1884, U. of Va., 1888; A.B. (extra ordinem), Johns Hopkins, 1894, Ph.D., 1895; LL.D., U. of Ala., 1906; m. Josephine Jackson, July 6, 1897 (died June 19, 1921); children—James Curtis Jackson, Dorothy Vaughan, Thomas Carter, Josephine de Hanmere; m. 2d, Jane Lee Moffitt, Aug. 24, 1925. Prof. of mathematics, Cox Coll., Ga., 1889; asst. prof. biology, Tulane U., 1891; asst. instr., and asso. in history, 1895-1905, asso. prof. Am. history, 1905-11, prof., 1911-13, Johns Hopkins; asst. prof. and prof. polit. science, U. of Pa., since 1913; visiting prof. history, polit. science and foreign relations, Md. State Normal Coll., summer 1916, N.Y. City Pub Sch. Com., winters 1919-21; also summers, history, New York U., 1921; polit. science, U. of Mich., 1925, W.Va. Univ., 1929; lecturer U. of Va. Inst. Pub. Affairs, 1935; lecturer polit. science, U. of Pa., summers 1920-36. Author: White Servitude in the Colony of Virginia, 1895; A History of Slavery in Virginia (John Marshall prize essay), 1902; American Foreign Policy in the Orient, 1915; America's International Diplomacy, 1918. Also numerous articles in revs., encys. and biog. dictionaries. Editor: Southern Economic History, 1607-1909 (Vols. V and VI of The South in the Building of the Nation), 1910; The Letters of Richard Henry Lee, Vol. I, 1762-78, Vol. II, 1779-94, 1911-13; sometime co-editor Johns Hopkins Studies in Hist. and Polit. Science, and of Annals of Am. Acad. of Polit. and Social Science. Traveled investigating politics and education in Japan, China, India and Europe, 1890. Won C. Morton Stewart prize Johns Hopkins U., 1895. Mem. Delta Psi. Home: 5864 Woodbine Av. Address: 5864 Woodbine Av., Overbrook, Philadelphia, Pa. Died Sep. 28, 1944.

BALLANTINE, Stuart, radio engr.; b. Germantown, Pa., Sept. 22, 1897; s. Charles Mansfield and Mary Stuart (Beverland) B.; ed. Grad. Sch. Harvard U., 1920-21, 1923-24; m. Virginia Gregory Orbison, June 18, 1927. With Marconi Co., 1914-15; bacteriol. lab., H. K. Mulford Co., 1916; research engr., Radio Frequency Labs., 1922-23; engaged in private research, 1924-27; dir. research Radio Frequency Labs., 1927-29; pres. Boonton Research Corp., 1929-34; pres. Ballantine Labs., Inc., elec. communication apparatus, Boonton, N.J., since 1935. Served as expert radio aide, U.S. Navy, 1917-20. Fellow Am. Phys. Soc., Acoustical Soc. Am., Inst. Radio Engrs. (pres. 1935); mem. Radio Club of Am., Franklin Inst. (mem. com. on science and the arts since 1935). Award for development of Navy radio compass, U.S. Navy, 1921; Morris Liebmann Memorial award by Inst. Radio Engrs., 1931; Elliott Cresson medal by Franklin Inst., 1934; John Tyndall fellow at Harvard, 1923-24. Mem. Ref. Episcopal Ch. Clubs: Harvard (Phila.); Rockaway River (Denville); Knoll (Boonton). Author: Radio Telephony for Amateurs, 1922. Contbr. about 40 articles on elec. communication. Home: 200 Overlook Av., Boonton, N.J. Died May 4, 1944.

BALLANTYNE, John business exec.; b. Philadelphia, Pa.; Mar. 20, 1900; s. Walter and Hattie (Todd) B.; B.S., U. of Pa., 1921; m. Alberta Fern Baker, Mar. 20, 1935; children—John Williams, Dolores Marie. With Weigner, Rockey and Co., Philadephia 1921-29; partner Mathieson, Aitken & Co., C.P.A., 1929-34; treas. Philco Corp., 1940-41, vice pres. in charge of operations, 1941-43, pres. since April, 1943. Mem. Phila. Chamber of Commerce (dir.), Radio Mfrs. Assn. (dir.). Clubs: Union League (Philadelphia), Huntingdon Valley Country, Seaview Country, Cedarbrook Country. Home: Mill and Coates Rds., Meadowbrook, Pa. Died June 10, 1949. Buried Ivy Hill Cemetery, Germantown, Pa.

BALLARD, Sumner, fire insurance; b. N.Y. City, Nov. 4, 1865; s. Frank Wade and Anna Judson (Marten) B.; unmarried. Began in ins., N.Y. City, 1881; pres. Internat. Ins. Co. since 1908; pres. Reinsurers Underwriting Corp. since 1923; U.S. mgr. Skandinavia Ins. Co. of Copenhagen; dir. U.S. Fire Ins. Co., Niagara Fire Ins. Co., Nat. Liberty Ins. Co., Baltimore Am. Ins. Co., Sanborn Map Co. (v.p.), Nat. Bd. Fire Underwriters Bldg. Corp., Fire Companies' Adjustment Bur., Jour. of Commerce. Fellow Ins. Inst. of America; mem. Nat. Bd. of Fire Underwriters (sec.), Soc. Mayflower Descendants, Soc. Colonial War, S.R., St. Nicholas Soc.; mem. Museum City of New York (life). Republican. Clubs: Metropolitan, Down Town, Turf and Field, Seawanhaka-Corinthian Yacht, Pilgrims. Home: 10 E. 79th St. Office: 80 John St., New York, N.Y. Died 1941.

BALLIET, Thomas M., college prof.; b. Mar. 1, 1852; s. Nathan and Sarah B.; A.B., Franklin and Marshall Coll., 1876, A.M., 1879, Ph.D., 1887, LL.D., 1927; student Yale and Leipzig; m. Elizabeth Stearns, Aug. 2, 1898. Supt. schs., Springfield, Mass., 1887-1904; prof. science of edn. and dean Sch. of Edn., New York U., 1904-19. Has written several monographs. Home: 15 Claremont Ave., New York. Died Feb. 18, 1942.

BALLOCH, Edward Arthur, surgeon; b. Somersworth, N. H., Jan. 2, 1857; s. George Williamson and Martha J. (Palmer) B.; A.B., Princeton, 1877; A.M., 1891; M.D., Howard U., Washington, 1879; m. Lillian F. McGrew, June 8, 1886; 1 dau., Agnes M. In practice of surgery at Washington, 1879; prof. surgery, 1904, dean med. dept., 1909, Howard U. Attending surgeon and chmn. adv. staff, Freedmen's Hosp. Republican. Presbyterian. Fellow Am. Coll. of Surgeons, So. Surg. and Gynecol. Assn.; mem. A.M.A., Med. Soc. D.C. (ex-pres.), Washington Gynecol. and Obstet. Soc., Washington Surg. Soc., S.A.R. Club: Cosmos. Address: The Wyoming, Washington. Died March 2, 1948.

BALLOU, Hosea Starr, investment banker; b. N. Orange, Mass., Feb. 9, 1857; s. Rev. Levi and Elvira Bliss (Goodell) B.; ed. Harvard, 1877-79; U. of Berlin, Germany, 1880-81; Sorbonne and College de France, Paris, 1881-82; m. Mary Farwell, June 1, 1885; children—Luther F., H. Starr. Mem. H. S. Ballou & Co. since 1884. Mem. Am. Hist. Assn., N.E. Hist.-Geneal. Soc., Am. Acad. Polit. and Social Science, Mass. Soc. Colonial Wars, Bunker Hill Monument Assn., Universalist Hist. Soc. (pres.), Ballou Family Assn. of Am. (ex-pres.), Starr Family Assn. (pres. emeritus), Westfield Normal Alumni Assn. of Eastern Mass. (ex-pres.). Author: Life of Hosea Ballou, 2d, 1896. Home: Winthrop Rd., Brookline, Mass. Office: 53 State St., Boston. Died Dec. 6, 1943.

BALLOU, William Hosea, mycologist, ichthyologist; b. Hannibal, Oswego County, N.Y., Sept. 30, 1857; s. Rev. Ransome R. and Mary Abigail (Green) B.; student Northwestern, 1877-81, U. of Pa., 1896; spl. studies in natural science; hon. Sc.D., Ft. Worth (Tex.) U., 1911; Litt.D., Chicago Law Sch., 1920; LL.D., Coll. of Oskaloosa, Ia., 1921; unmarried. Recorder U.S. Lake Survey, 1875-77; U.S. scientific survey of Niagara Falls, 1876; asst. engr. U.S. Yellowstone River Survey, 1878; govt. naturalist and representative of Harper's Weekly, Greely Relief Expdn., 1884; conducted crusade making animals safe in transport at sea (thanked by Queen Victoria and made perm. hon. commr. of U.S. by Sec. of Agr. Wilson), and other like crusades, 1892-95; editor New York Despatch (weekly), 1895-98; sec. Greater New York Pub. Co., 1895-96; founder, sec. Westchester Free Hosp., 1892-95; Pres. Pocantico Water Works Co., 1893-96; v.p. New York & Westchester Water Co., 1891-98, etc.; owner and editor Science News Service. Hon. commr. U.S. Dept. Agr., del. of Davenport (Ia.) Acad. Natural Sciences, rep. of Am. Mus. Natural History and Popular Science Monthly at 7th Internat. Geol. Congress, St. Petersburg, 1897; conducted govt. war propaganda to catch and eat more fish, under Herbert Hoover, 1917-18. Advocate of Louis Agassiz's theory of multiple origin of man, and species of animal and plant life. Discoverer of many species of fungi new to science, a number of which have been named in his honor; has listed over 1,000 species growing in Greater N.Y. City; founder nat. movement to conserve wild mushrooms, 1908. Mem. Nat. Inst. Social Sciences, Am. Soc. Ichthyologists and Herpetologists, American Soc. Mammalogists, Alumni Assn. of Northwestern Univ., Soc. Am. Military Engineers, Civic Forum, Alumni and Economic clubs (New York); fellow Société Académique d'Histoire Internationale, France, which decorated him with the Sovereign's Grand Cross and Grand gold medal "for services to humanity"; also awarded hon. chair of French Royal U., and of Paevia Sch. of Langs., Italy, for advocacy of Agassiz' theory of multiple origin of man and associated animals. Fellow Geopractic Soc. of Am. (adv. editor for same). Life founder mem. Civil Legion of War Workers; awarded Civil Legion of Honor, 1931. Republican. Author: (novels) A Ride on a Cyclone, 1889; The Bachelor Girl, 1890; The Upper Ten, 1891; An Automatic Wife, 1891; Spectacular Romances, 1892; and over 300 poems. Donor of large collections of natural history to Northwestern U., and of fungi to State Museum, at Albany, N.Y., New York Bot. Garden, and Lloyd Inst., Cincinnati. Made geol. survey of Central Kans., discovering fossils of pre-fish, preamphibia, pre-reptiles with associated bivalves, and first plants in Devonian and Carboniferous Rock strata, and Upper Cretaceous marsupial, 1923; discovered fossil brachiopods in Silurian rocks, West Virginia, by which Prof. Edward Drinker Cope and Dr. James Hall fixed geological age of the Appalachian System of mountains as Silurian, 1889; discovered cancer on tail of a boa constrictor in Honduras, 1890; first to define cancer as a fungus, originating in reptiles and fish and breeding by infinitely small spores, later investing entire reptile or fish and communicated to man by the drinking of infected water; scheduled 300 snakes and iguanas killed by cancer. Wrote poem, "The Unknown Soldier," for memorial service at Arlington, Nov. 11, 1921. Adv. editor Northwestern U. Alumni News and Living Age. Contbr. on popular science to Hearst syndicates; etc. Home: Closter, Bergen County, N.J. Died Nov. 30, 1937.

BAMBERGER, Louis, merchant, philanthropist; b. Baltimore, Maryland, May 15, 1855; s. Elkan and Theresa (Hutzler) B.; hon. D.Sc., Newark Coll. Engring., hon. M.A., Rutgers; hon. LL.D., Newark U.; unmarried. Noted for his philanthropies; with his sister, Mrs. Felix Fuld, widow of his late partner, donated as an initial endowment, $5,000,000 for the establishment of Inst. for Advanced Study at Princeton, now under direction of Dr. Frank Aydelotte; upon retirement from business distributed over $1,000,000 among employes; donor of Newark Museum Bldg. (about $750,000). Home: 602 Center St., South Orange, N.J. Office: 131 Market St., Newark, N.J. Died March 11, 1944.

BANCROFT, Frederic, historian; b. Galesburg, Ill., Oct. 30, 1860; s. Addison N. and Catherine (Blair) B.; A.B., Amherst, 1882; Ph.D., Columbia, 1885; studied at Göttingen, 1883, Berlin, Freiburg (Baden) and Ecole des Sciences Politiques, Paris, 1885-87; LL.D., Knox Coll., Galesburg, Ill., 1900; L.H.D., Amherst, 1932. Librarian Dept. of State, 1888-92. Lecturer polit. history of Civil War and reconstruction, Amherst, 1888; on polit. and diplomatic history U.S., 1889-97, and on European diplomatic history, 1898-99, Columbia; has also lectured at Johns Hopkins and U. of Chicago, on polit. history U.S.; at Lowell Inst., Boston, 1902-03, on Life in the South. Long on lit. staff New York Nation. Del. Congress of Historians, Paris, 1900. Author: The Negro in Politics, 1885; Life of William H. Seward, 2 vols., 1900; (with William A. Dunning) The Public Life of Carl Schurz, 1908; Calhoun and the Nullification Movement in South Carolina, 1928; Slave-Trading in the Old South, 1931. Editor: Speeches, Correspondence and Public Papers of Carl Schurz, 6 vols., 1913; The Mission of America, and other War Time Speeches of Edgar A. Bancroft, 1927. Contbr. to revs. and mags. Address Metropolitan Club, Washington, D.C. Deceased.

BANCROFT, Milton H., painter; born Newton, Mass., Jan. 1, 1866; s. William H. and Martha (Varney) B.; prep. edn. Newton pub. schs.; student Mass. State Normal Art Sch., 1883-86; prof. in tech. studies, Swarthmore Coll., Pa., 1886-92, but continued studies irregularly, Pa. Acad. Fine Arts; supt. schs. and instr. in Pa. Academy Fine Arts, 1892-94; studied in Colorossi, Delacluse and Julien acads., Paris, 1894-99; m. Margaret Corliss Moore, 1894; children—John Townsend, Anna Moore, Thomas Leggett. Exhibited in Société des Artistes Francais, and in all large exhibitions of New York, Phila., Boston, Washington and Chicago; specialty portraits; executed mural decorations for Court of the Seasons, Panama-Pacific Expn., San Francisco. Experimented with various techniques in landscape studies, 1920-45. Served with A.R.C. in Europe, World War I. Instr. Mechanics Inst., New York, Salmagundi Club. Home: Sandy Spring, Md. Died Dec. 13, 1947; buried in Friends Cemetery, Sandy Springs, Md.

BANKER, Howard James, biologist; b. Schaghticoke, N.Y., Apr. 19, 1866; s. Amos Bryan and Frances Alcena (Welling) B.; A.B., Syracuse U., 1892; A.M., Columbia, 1900, Ph.D., 1906; m. Mary Eugenia Wright, Aug. 23, 1894. Teacher, Troy Conf. Acad., Poultney, Vt., 1892-95 (vice prin., 1895); ordained deacon, 1894, elder, 1896, M.E. Ch.; pastor Union Ch., Proctor, Vt., 1895-98; teacher mathematics, Dickinson Sem., Williamsport, Pa., 1900-01; teacher biology, Southwestern State Normal Sch., Calif., Pa., 1901-04; prof. biology, DePauw U., Greencastle, Ind., 1904-14; investigator, Eugenics Record Office, Cold Spring Harbor, L.I., 1914-33 (acting supt. 1915-16; acting asst.-dir., 1920-21, 23); exec. com. and sec. sect. 2, 2d Internat. Congress of Eugenics. Fellow A.A.A.S.; mem. Phi Beta Kappa, Sigma Xi, Delta Upsilon. Author: The Hydnacæ of North America, 1906; The Bancker or Banker Families of America, 1909. Editor The Underwood Families of America, 1913. Contbr. to scientific jours. of papers on mycology and eugenics. Address: 14 Myrtle Av., Huntington, L.I. Died Sept. 23, 1943.

BANKHEAD, John Hollis, U.S. senator; b. Lamar, Ala., July 8, 1872; s. John Hollis and Tallulah (Brockman) B.; A.B., U. of Ala., 1891; LL.B., Georgetown U., 1893; LL.D., Ala. Poly-technic Inst., U. of Ala.; m. Musa Harkins, Dec. 26, 1894; children—Marion (Mrs. Charles B. Crow), Walter Will, Louise (Mrs. H. M. Davis). Admitted to Ala. bar, 1893, and began practice at Jasper; mem. firm Bankhead & Bankhead, of Jasper and Birmingham; pres. Bankhead Coal Co., 1911-25; U.S. senator, 3 terms, 1931-49. Maj., Ala. N.G., 1901-03. Mem. Ala. Ho. of Rep., 1903 (author of Ala. election law). Delegate-at-large, Dem. Nat. Conv., 1936, 1940; received 98 votes at 1944 Democratic National Convention for Vice President of United States. Chairman Red Cross drive, Walker County, Alabama, World War. Trustee U. of Ala. Mem. Sigma Alpha Epsilon, Phi Beta Kappa. Democrat. Methodist. Clubs: Southern (Birmingham); Golf (Jasper). Home: Jasper, Ala. Died June 12, 1946.

BANKS, Alexander French, retired ry. pres.; b. Crawford County Ind., Jan. 31, 1861; s. Henry Bartlett and Julia C. (French) B; ed. pub. schs.; m. Blanche Nichelson, November 13, 1883 (died Sept. 20, 1934); children—Duke N., Mrs. Blanche B. Alexander, Charles A. Began business career with St. Louis & Southeastern Railway Company, 1877, contracting agent, at Evansville, 1878-80; traveling agent and gen. agent, Continental Fast Freight Line, 1880-88; gen. agent Ia. Central Ry., Peoria, Ill, Jan.-Sept. 1888; gen. frt. agent, 1888-89, gen. frt. and pass. agt., 1889-90, traffic mgr., 1890-93, Ia. Central Ry.; traffic mgr., 1893-1901, pres, 1901-31. Elgin, Joliet & Eastern Ry. Club: Glenview Home: 1821 Brae Burn Rd., Altadena, Calif. Died Nov. 7, 1948.

BANNING, Kendall, editor, author; b. New York, Sept. 20, 1879; s. William Calvin and Helen Josephine (Mellen) B.; A.B., Dartmouth, 1902; m. Hedwig v. Briesen, May 19, 1906 (died July 7, 1912); 1 daughter, Barbara (Mrs. Harrison Tweed); m. 2d, Dorothy Carter Sanders, November 15, 1915; 1 son, William Calvin. Managing and associate editor, System, 1903-17; managing editor, Hearst's Mag., Cosmopolitan, 1919-21; editor, Popular Radio, 1922-28; editorial dir. New Fiction Pub. Corp., also of Leslie-Judge Co., 1923-27; vice pres. New Fiction Pub. Corp., Leslie-Judge Co., Popular Radio, Inc., 1922-28; editorial dir. Pub. Utilities Fortnightly, 1929-34. Officer N.Y. and Ohio N.G., 1902-09; capt. 1st Aero Squadron (provisional), N.Y., 1913-14; maj. Signal Corps, U.S. Army, 1917; dir. div. of pictures, Com. on Public Information, Washington, 1917. Maj., Gen. Staff, U.S. Army, 1918-19; officer in charge of compilation of pictorial record and history of the war; lt. col. Signal Reserve since 1922; with Office of Chief of Ordnance since 1943; chief historian Army Ordnance Dept., 1943-44. Member Society 1812, Order Founders and Patriots America, Veteran Corps Arty., Phi Delta Theta. Clubs: The Players (New York); Army and Navy Club (Washington, D.C.). Editor: Songs of the Hill Winds, 1902 (Dartmouth anthology); Songs for a Wedding Day, 1907; How to Build Your Own Radio Receiver (with L. M. Cockaday), 1924. Author: Flotsam, 1903; Bookplates, 1906; Songs of the Love Unending, 1912; The Squire's Recipes, 1912; The Sun Dial (song cycle, with Gena Branscombe), 1912; Bypaths in Arcady, 1914; Pirates, 1916; Mon Ami Pierrot, 1916; Songs of the Unafraid (song cycle, with Gena Branscombe), 1918; Phantom Caravan, 1920; The Great Adventure, 1925; Mother Goose Rhymes, Censored, 1930; Drum Beats (1936 Kaleidograph Book award), 1937; West Point Today, 1937; Annapolis Today, 1938; The Fleet Today, 1940; Submarine! The Story of Undersea Fighters, 1942; Our Army Today, 1943 "Copy," one-act play, prod. by Edmund Breese, 1911 12; The Garden of Punchinello, pantomime, prod with Mlle. Dazie, 1917; A Garden Fate, pantomime prod. 1919; and miscellaneous songs. Contbr. to mags. Address: Old Lyme, Conn. Died Dec. 27, 1944; buried in Arlington National Cemetery.

BANTA, Arthur Mangun (bän'tȧ), zoölogist; b. near Greenwood, Ind., Dec. 31, 1877; s. James Henry and Mary (Mangun) B.; B.S., Central Normal Coll., Ind., 1898; A.B., Ind. U., 1903, A.M., 1904; Edward-Austin fellow, Harvard, 1905-06, Ph.D., 1907; m. Mary Charlotte Slack, July 26, 1906; children—James Jerry, Ruth, Leah Margaret. Instr. in pub. schs., Ind., 1895-97; prin. high sch., 1899-1901, Johnson County Normal Sch., summer, 1901; asst. in zoology, Ind. U., 1903-05; instr. Ind. U. Biol. Sta., summers, 1903, 1904; asst. in zoölogy, Harvard, 1905-06, teaching fellow, 1906-07; with the U.S. Fish Commn., Woods Hole, Mass., summers, 1906, 09; prof. biology, Marietta Coll., Ohio, 1907-09; resident investigator, Sta. for Exptl. Evolution of the Carnegie Instn., Cold Spring Harbor, N.Y., 1909-30; professorial lecturer in genetics, U. of Minn., 2d semester, 1927; visiting professor experimental zoölogy, Brown U., 1929-30, research prof. biology, 1930-45, prof. emeritus since June, 1945; associate Carnegie Instn. of Washington, 1930-32 and 1936-37. Mem. Nat. Research Council Board of Fellowships in the Biol. Sciences, 1933-37. Fellow A.A.A.S.; mem. Am. Soc. Zoölogists, Am. Soc. Naturalists (sec. 1935-37), Genetics Soc. of America, Limnological Soc. of America, Soc. Exptl. Biology and Medicine, Ecol. Soc. America, Sigma Xi. Investigator of effects of changed environment on cave animals; heredity, development, longevity and sex determination in lower organisms, sex intergrades, etc. Author: The Fauna of Mayfield's Cave, 1907; Selection in Cladocera on the Basis of a Physiological Character, 1921; Studies on the Physiology, Genetics, and Evolution of some Cladocera, 1939. Contbr. to biol. jours. Home: 168 Medway St., Providence, R.I. Died Jan. 2, 1946.

BARBER, Charles Williams, army officer; b. Gloucester Co., N.J., Sept. 21, 1872; s. George W. and Ellen (Taggart) B.; ed. pub. schs. and business coll.; studied law in office of Hon. H. S. Grey, atty. gen. of N.J., 1899; m. Katherine Runge, Mar. 8, 1894; 1 son, Russell George. Commd. 2d lt. 4th N.J. Inf., Spanish-Am. War, July 16, 1898; 1st lt., Sept. 27, 1898; capt., Mar. 3, 1899; hon. mustered out, Apr. 6, 1899; 1st lt. 28th U.S. Inf., July 5, 1899; hon. mustered out vol. service, May 1, 1901; commd. 2d lt. 2d Inf. U.S. Army, Feb. 2, 1901; 1st lt., Nov. 11, 1901; capt. 4th Inf., Mar. 11, 1911; assigned to 3d Inf., Jan. 1, 1915; retired as maj., Sept. 1, 1916; brig. gen., N.A., July 25, 1917. Served in Philippines, 1899-1901, 1902-03, 1906-08; duty with Isthmian Canal Commn., Panama, 1908-15; Mexican border service, 1916; apptd. brig. gen. and adj. gen. of N.J., Dec. 5, 1916; in charge orgn. state troops for war, registration and selection of drafted men, etc.; comdg. 29th Div., July 28-Aug. 25, 1917; comdg. 57th Infantry Brigade, Camp McClellan, Anniston, Ala., Sept. 11, 1917; in command 57th Inf. Brig. in front line sectors and as chief of staff, Base Sect. No. 2, Bordeaux (gen. staff officer A.E.F.), June 1918-July 1919; returned to status of retired officer, Aug. 1919; brig. gen. retired, June 21, 1930. Special representative Atlantic Refining Co. in Mexico, 1920; gen. mgr. Antilles Molasses Co., 1920-21; pres. and dir. Charles W. Barber & Son, Inc., investment bankers, New York; chmn. bd. and dir. Thermoid Co., Trenton, N.J.; dir. Southern Asbestos Co., Charlotte, N.C., Brager-Eisenberg, Inc., Baltimore. Officer Legion of Honor (France); D.S.M. (U.S.); D.S.M. (State of N.J.). Mem. Mil. Order Carabao. Republican. Methodist. Mason. Clubs: Army and Navy (Manila and Washington), Bankers (New York). Home: Short Hills, N.J. Office: 111 Broadway, New York, N.Y. Died Jan. 7, 1943.

BARBER, George Garfield, pres. Nat. Maté Corp.; b. Mar. 24, 1883; s. George and Christine (Miler) B.; ed. high sch., Pittsburgh; m. Isabel Davison Fox, June 8, 1907; children—Marian Louise, George Fox, Isabel Anne, Christine Miller, Dobert Speer. With Carnegie Steel Co., to 1905, Ward-Mackey Co., 1905-07; with Ward-Corby Co., 1907-10, sec. and treas.; with Ward Baking Co., 1910-15, sec. and treas.; with Ward Motor Vehicle Co., 1915-17, sec. and treas.; with United Bakeries Corp., 1917-23, sec. and treas.; with Continental Bakeries Co., 1923-27, was chmn. bd.; pres. Columbia Baking Co., 1930-32; dir. Nat. Boston Montana Mining Co.; now pres. Nat. Maté Corp. Formerly mem. bd. of pensions, Presbyn. Ch., U.S.A. Trustee Milligan Coll. (Tenn.), Coll. of Ozarks, Union Theol. Sem., Harvard-Yenching Inst. (Cambridge, Mass.); pres. bd. trustees Yenching U. Republican. Presbyn. Clubs: Army and Navy (New York); Bald Peek Country (N.H.). Home: 20 Lyncroft Rd., New Rochelle, N.Y. Office: 551 5th Av., New York, N.Y.* Died July 10, 1943.

BARBOUR, Henry Ellsworth, lawyer; b. Ogdensburg, St. Lawrence County, N.Y., Mar. 8, 1877; s. William J. and Mary M. (Houston) B.; student Union Coll., Schenectady, N.Y., 1898, law dept., George Washington U.; m. Mary D. Meux, Oct. 29, 1907; children—John M., Richard H. Began practice at Fresno, 1902; mem. 66th to 72d Congresses (1919-33), 7th Calif. Dist. Republican. Presbyterian. Mem. Fresno County and Calif. State bar assns., Sigma Phi. Club: Sierra (hon.). Home: Fresno, Calif. Died Mar. 21, 1945.

BARBOUR, Henry Gray, pharmacologist; b. Hartford, Conn., Mar. 28, 1886; s. John Humphrey and Annie (Gray) B.; A.B., Trinity Coll., Hartford, 1906; M.D., Johns Hopkins, 1910, fellow, 1910-11; research, Freiburg, 1911, Vienna, 1912, London, 1913; m. Lilla Millard Chittenden, Sept. 15, 1909; children—Henry Chittenden, Dorothy Gray (Mrs. John D. Hersey), Russell Chittenden. Asst. prof. pharmacology, Yale, 1912-21; prof. pharmacology, McGill U., 1921-23; prof. physiology and pharmacology, U. of Louisville, 1923-31; asso. prof. pharmacology, Yale U., 1931-37, research asso. and chmn. pharmacology and toxicology since 1937. U.S. gas investigations, 1917-18. Fellow Internat. Coll. Anesthetists; mem. A.M.A., Am. Physiol. Soc., Soc. Pharmacology and Exptl. Therapeutics, Am. Soc. Biol. Chemists, Soc.

Exptl. Biology and Medicine, Central Soc. for Clin. Research, Am. Soc. Anesthetists (hon.), Phi Beta Kappa, Sigma Xi, Alpha Omega Alpha, Nu Sigma Nu, Delta Phi. Republican. Episcopalian. Clubs: Pithotomists, Innominate (hon.), Graduate, New Haven County, Yale (New York). Author: Experimental Pharmacology and Toxicology. Contbr. to Am. Jour. Physiology, Jour. Pharmacology and Exptl. Therapeutics, Jour. Biol. Chemistry, and article Heat Regulation and Fever, in Blumer's Practitioner's Library. Asso. editor Archives Internat. de Pharmacodynamie et de Therapie. Home: 656 Prospect St., New Haven, Conn. Died Sept. 23, 1943.

BARBOUR, Percy E., cons. mining engr.; b. Portland, Me., Aug. 1, 1875; s. Clifford S. and Clara A. (Ford) B.; Mayflower desc. on paternal side; B.S., Worcester Poly. Inst., 1896, C.E., 1908; m. Viola Grace Hackward, Mar. 21, 1909. Mgr. Mass. Fan Co., ventilating engrs., Boston, 1897-1900; engr. with Bingham Consol. Copper Co., Utah and Boston, 1900-03; engr. at smelter, Tenn. Copper Co., 1904; gen. mgr. Navaho Gold Mining Co., Bland, N.M., 1905-06; cons. mining engr., Goldfield, Nev., 1907-08; dep. sheriff Esmerelda County, Nev., 1907; engineer with Am. Smelting & Refining Co. and U.S. Smelting Co., Salt Lake City, Utah, 1909-10; gen. supt. Salt Lake Copper Co. (Ore. and Ida.), and lessee copper mine at Tecoma, Nev., 1910-11; gen. mgr. Uwarra Mining Co., Candor, N.C., 1911-14; editorial staff and mng. editor Engineering and Mining Journal, New York, 1915-17; asst. sec. Am. Inst. Mining and Metall. Engrs., New York, founder and editor Mining and Metallurgy, 1919-25; asst. to mgr. exploration dept., St. Joseph Lead Co., 1925-27; cons. mining engineer since 1927. Mem. N.Y. State Bd. for Licensing Professional Engrs. and Land Surveyors, 1920-29, chmn. bd., 1922-23 and 1927-28; sec. and treas. Mining and Metall. Soc. of America, 1925-29, asst. sec. and treas., 1929-30, sec. and treas. since 1931. Mem. Mass. Naval Brigade, 1898-1900; lt. Me. Coast Arty., 1914-16; service on Mexican border with 22d Regt., N.Y. Engrs., as lt. 1916-17; first dept. supt. and asst. organizer N.Y. State Troopers, Dept. State Police, 1917-18; capt. engrs., U.S. Army, 1918-19; hon. disch., 1919; maj. Engr. Res., 1919-22, lt. col. Engr. Res., 342d Engrs., exec. officer, 1922-33; comdg. 363d Engrs., 1933-39; promoted col., 1934, col. (inactive), 1939. Mem. N.Y. County Grand Jury, 1928-38. Mem. Am. Inst. Mining and Metall. Engrs., Mining and Metall. Soc. America; charter mem., sec., treas. and ex-dir. Soc. Am. Mil. Engrs. (gold medalist). Republican. Conglist. Mason, K.T. Club: Mining (New York). Author "Secondary Copper" and tech. articles and papers; internationally regarded as an authority on economics of copper, gold and silver. Speaker on Gold at Norman Waite Harris Memorial Foundation, U. of Chicago, 1932, and People's Inst. of Pub. Affairs, U. of Va., 1932, and various associations and societies. Home: 540 Prospect Av., Mamaroneck, N.Y. Office: 90 Broad St., New York, N.Y. Died May 4, 1943.

BARBOUR, Philip Foster, pediatrist; b. Danville, Ky., Feb. 24, 1867; s. Lewis Green and Elizabeth Anne (Ford) B.; A.B., Central U. of Ky., 1884, A.M., 1899; M.D., Hosp. Coll. of Medicine, Louisville, Ky., 1890; m. Jessie Lemont, Oct. 29, 1891; children—Mrs. Ruth Lamb, Philip Lemont; m. 2d, Elizabeth Akin, Jan. 6, 1909; 1 dau., Mrs. Catherine Akin Maxson. Practiced at Louisville since 1892; practice limited to diseases of children. Prof. chemistry, 1895-98, prof. diseases of children, 1898-1907, Hosp. Coll. of Medicine; same, Louisville Coll. of Medicine, 1907-08; clin. prof. diseases of children and head dept. pediatrics, Med. Dept., U. of Louisville, 1908-40; retired from practice, 1940; formerly visiting pediatrist, Louisville City Hosp.; formerly mem. staff, Crippled Children's Hosp.; consultant pediatrist Ky. State Dept. Health, Ky. State Bapt. Orphan Asylum, Children's Free Hosp. Fellow Am. Coll. Physicians, Am. Acad. Pediatrics (state chmn.); mem. A.M.A., Assn. Am. Teachers of Diseases of Children, Southern Med. Assn., Ky. State Med. Soc. (pres.); ex-pres. Ky. Alumni Assn. of Delta Kappa Epsilon; ex-pres. Conf. of Social Workers; pres. Ky. State Pediatric Soc., Louisville Soc. for Mental Hygiene; med. chmn. Ky. White House Conf.; ex-pres. Louisville Council of Chs. Trustee Centre Coll. Elder 2d Presbyn. Ch. Clubs: Rotary, Executives. Home: 1304 S. 6th St. Office: 620 S. Third St., Louisville, Ky. Died Nov. 1, 1944.

BARBOUR, Ralph Henry ("Richard Stillman Powell"), author; b. at Cambridge, Mass., Nov. 13, 1870; s. of James Henry and Elizabeth Middleton (Morgan) B.; ed. New Ch. Sch., Waltham, and Highland Mil. Acad., Worcester, Mass. Author of numerous books for boys, also many short stories in magazines for boys. Address: 1401 El Rado, Coral Gables, Fla. Died Feb. 19, 1944.

BARBOUR, Thomas, naturalist; b. Martha's Vineyard, Mass., Aug. 19, 1884; s. William and Julia Adelaide (Sprague) B.; A.B., Harvard University, 1906, A.M., 1908, Ph.D., 1910, hon. Sc.D., 1940; Sc.D., Havana University, 1930, Dartmouth, 1935; Sc.D., University of Florida, 1944; m. Rosamond Pierce, Oct. 1, 1906; children—Martha Higginson (dec.), Mary Bigelow, William (dec.), Julia Adelaide, Louisa Bowditch, Rosamond (dec.). Made zoöl. explorations in East and West Indies, India, Burma, China, Japan, South and Central America, for Museum Comparative Zoölogy, Cambridge; student especially of geog. distribution of reptiles and amphibians; now dir. of Harvard Univ. Museum and Museum Comparative Zoölogy; prof. of zoölogy; mem. faculty, Peabody Museum, Harvard; custodian Harvard Biol. Station and Bot. Garden, Soledad, Cuba, since 1927; exec. officier in charge of Barro Colorado Island Lab., Gatun Lake, Panama, 1923-45. Del. Harvard U. to 1st Pan-Am. Scientific Congress, Santiago, Chile, Dec. 1907-Jan. 1908; del. at founding Nat. U. of Mexico, City of Mexico, 1910. Fellow Royal Geog. Soc. (London), Royal Asiatic Soc. (Straits br.), A.A.A.S., Am. Acad. of Arts and Sciences, Nat. Acad. Science, N.Y. Zoöl. Soc.; hon. fellow Acad. Sciences, Havana, Cuba; corr. mem. Hispanic Soc. America; mem. Am. Soc. Zoölogists, Am. Philos. Soc., Mass. Hist. Soc., Am. Antiquarian Soc., Washington Acad. Science (v.p.), Acad. Natural Sciences of Phila., Phi Beta Kappa and Sigma Xi fraternities; foreign mem. Zoöl. Soc., London; Linnaean Soc., London; corr. mem. Nederlandesche Dierkundige Vereliningung, Amsterdam; hon. mem. Zoöl. Soc. Phila.; pres. Boston Soc. Natural History, 1924-27 and since 1940. Clubs: Somerset, Harvard, Tavern (Boston); Century, Harvard, Boone and Crockett (New York); Cosmos (Washington, D.C.). Author scientific papers in relation to reptiles and fishes, their systematic classification and geog. distribution. Home: 278 Clarendon St., Boston, Mass. Died Jan. 8, 1946.

BARBOUR, W. Warren, U.S. senator; b. Monmouth Beach, N.J.; s. William and J. Adelaide (Sprague) B.; grad. Browning Sch., N.Y. City, 1906; m. Elysabeth C. Carrere, Dec. 1, 1921; children—Elysabeth C., Warren, Sharon. Appointed member U.S. Senate, Dec. 1, 1931, to fill vacancy caused by death of Dwight Morrow and elected to Senate, Nov. 1932, for term expiring 1937; elected, Nov. 1938, to fill vacancy for term ending Jan. 3, 1941; re-elected, Nov. 5, 1940, for term expiring Jan. 1, 1948. Mem. N.G. N.Y. 10 yrs. Republican. Presbyn. Clubs: Union League, Racquet and Tennis; Rumson (N.J.) Country; Metropolitan, Chevy Chase Country (Washington, D.C.). Home: Locust, N.J. Died Nov. 22, 1943.

BARCLAY, McClelland, artist and illustrator; b. St. Louis, Mo., May 9, 1891; s. Robert and Minnie G. (Hamilton) B.; prep. edn., Central High Sch., St. Louis, and Western High Sch., Washington, D.C.; studied art, Corcoran Sch. of Art, Washington, 1909-12, Art Students' League, New York, 1912-14, Art Inst., Chicago, 1919-22; awarded perpetual life scholarship, St. Louis Mus. Fine Arts. Began as advertising illustrator, 1912, also known for sculpture and portrait painting. Awarded 1st prize, World War I, for recruiting poster, by Conf. Com. on Nat. Preparedness, 1917; 1st prize for poster "Fill the Breach," for 2d Red Cross drive; 1st prize, "The Human Cross," Marine Corps Recruiting Poster, 1918; 1st prize for "At the Front of the Front," Chicago Assn. Commerce, 1920; etc. Creator of the "Fisher Body Girl"; designer of covers for Ladies' Home Jour., Pictorial Rev., Saturday Evening Post, illustrations for Cosmopolitan, etc. Naval camoufleur, 1918, also made posters for Am. Protective League. Appointed lieut. U.S.N.R., June 13, 1938, lieut. comdr., May 21, 1942; called to active duty, Oct. 19, 1940; transferred to Class D, Sept. 1942. Reported missing in action while passenger on ship torpedoed in Solomon Sea, July 18, 1943. Awarded Purple Heart posthumously August 26, 1944. A founder Artists' Guild of Chicago; mem. Artists' Guild New York, Art Inst., Chicago. Democrat. Episcopalian. Mason. Clubs: Players, New York Athletic, Lotos (N.Y.) Maidstone (East Hampton, N.Y.). Address: 36 W. 59th St., New York. Died July 19, 1943.

BARDWELL, Winfield William, judge; b. Excelsior, Minn., July 18, 1872; s. William E. and Araminta (Hamblet) B.; prep. edn., Excelsior Acad.; LL.B., U. of Minn., 1893, LL.M., 1904; m. Edith May Champlin, Feb. 1894 (died May 6, 1929); children—Mildred (Mrs. Roy W. Hall), Marian Araminta (Mrs. Chauncy Beebe), Charles C.; m. 2d, Mrs. Grace E. Finch, June 21, 1930; children—Grace Finch (Mrs. John Clark Wells), Ruth Finch (Mrs. Henry Gilman Lykken, Jr.). Admitted to Minn. bar, 1893, and began practice at Minneapolis; presiding judge, Dist. Ct., Minn., since 1919; pres. Minneapolis College of Law since 1924; member faculty University of Minnesota many years; president Hennepin County Law Library. Mem. Minnesota House of Rep., 1903, 05. Mem. State Dist. Judges Assn. (pres.), Theta Delta Chi, Delta Chi. Republican. Conglist. Mason, Elk. Clubs: Minneapolis Athletic, Interlachen Country, Minneapolis Auto. Home: 2901 Brookwood Terrace, Minneapolis, Minn. Died Dec. 22, 1946.

BARKER, Albert Winslow, artist and lecturer; b. Chicago, Ill., June 1, 1874; s. Albert Sampson and Julia (Beam) Winslow Barker; student Pa. Acad. of Fine Arts, 1890-95; A.B., Haverford Coll., 1917; A.M., U. of Pa., 1920, Ph.D., 1921; studied lithography under Bolton Brown, 1927; m. Agnes McMakin, April 20, 1904; 1 dau., Agnes Susan (Mrs. H. Walter Davis); m. 2d, Anna Ellis Roberts, 1910; 1 dau., Elizabeth Roberts; m. 3d, Alice Paxson, July 30, 1926. Instr. Sch. of Industrial Art, Phila., Pa., 1903-13, summer sch. U. of Pa., 1921-23; dir. of art edn., Wilmington (Del.) pub. schs., 1921-29. Represented by lithographic prints in Library of Congress, New York Public Library, Baltimore Museum, Pa. Museum, Los Angeles Museum, Boston Museum of Fine Arts, Smithsonian Instn., Corcoran Gallery (Washington, D.C.), Uffizi Gallery (Florence, Italy), Honolulu Gallery of Art, Fogg Museum. Awarded gold medal Internat. Print Makers Expn. by Print Makers Soc., of Calif., 1935. Mem. Phi Beta Kappa. Contbr. of articles to scientific mags. Research-work in chemistry of lithographic technique. Address: Moylan, Pa. Died Dec. 5, 1947.

BARKER, Frederick William, patent attorney; b. London, Eng., Dec. 18, 1864; s. Walter and Amelia Elizabeth (Bonney) B.; ed. Whitgift Sch., Croydon, Eng.; m. Constance Beatrice Reynolds, Oct. 31, 1888; children—Confred Walter, Mark Stanley, Dorothea Beatrice, Edythe Constance, Amy Blanche Frances; m. 2d, Mabel Mary Parker, Feb. 21, 1928. Began practice in Eng.; was an atty. of Henry Ford in the Selden suit; dir. and treas. V. J. Burnelli Airplanes, Inc.; director Central Aircraft Corp. Editor Aero World, 1916. Member of Aeronautical Society of America (dir., ex-pres.), N.Y. Patent Law Assn., St. George's Soc. Clubs: British Schs. and Univs., British Luncheon, Inc. (past pres.). Author: Epitome of the World's Patent Laws, 1890; Contentment, 1895; Inventor is Central Figure in Aeronautics, 1922. Contbr. to periodicals Home: Red Bank, N.J. Died July 8, 1948.

BARKER, Lewellys Franklin, M.D.; b. Norwich, Ont., Can., Sept. 16, 1867; s. James F. and Sarah Jane (Taylor) B.; ed. Pickering Coll., Ont., 1881-84; M.B., U. of Toronto, 1890; student U. of Leipzig, 1895, univs. of Munich and Berlin, 1904; hon. M.D., U. of Toronto, 1905; LL.D., Queen's Univ., Kingston, Can., 1908, McGill Univ., Montreal, Can., 1911; Univ. of Glasgow, Scotland, 1930; m. Lilian H. Halsey, Oct. 1903; children—John Hewetson, William Halsey, Margaret Taylor. Asso. in anatomy, 1894-97, Johns Hopkins U.; resident pathologist, Johns Hopkins Hosp., 1894-99; asso. prof. anatomy, 1897-99, pathology, 1899-1900, Johns Hopkins U.; prof. and head dept. anatomy, Rush Med. Coll. (U. of Chicago), 1900-05; prof. medicine, Johns Hopkins U. and chief physician Johns Hopkins Hosp., 1905-13; now emeritus prof. medicine Johns Hopkins and visiting phys. Johns Hopkins Hosp.; Johns Hopkins med. commr. to P.I., 1899; mem. special commn. apptd. by sec. of treasury to determine existence of non-existence of plague in San Francisco, 1901. Corr. mem. Budapest Royal Soc. Physicians, Medico-Chirurg. Soc. of Edinburgh, Gesellschaft für Innere Medizin und Kinderheilkunde in Wien; mem. Swedish Med. Soc.; chmn. bd. scientific dirs. Wistar Inst. of Anatomy; pres. Nat. Com. for Mental Hygiene, 1909-18, Assn. Am. Physicians, 1913, Am. Neurol. Assn., 1916, Southern Med. Assn., 1919, Assn. for Study of Internal Secretions, 1919, med. and chirurg. faculty of Md., 1923; vice-pres. A.M.A., 1917; v.p. Am. Soc. for the Control of Cancer; chmn. advisory bd. Federal Industrial Inst. for Women, Alderson, W.Va., and of Med. Council U.S. Veterans Bureau. Mem. Phi Beta Kappa. Clubs: Maryland, Johns Hopkins (Baltimore); Century and Charaka (New York). Author: The Nervous System and Its Constituent Neurones, 1899; Translation of Wernre Spalteholz's Hand Atlas of Human Anatomy, 1900; Laboratory Manual of Human Anatomy (with Dean De Witt Lewis and D. G. Revell), 1904; The Clinical Diagnosis of Internal Diseases, 1916; Tuesday Clinics at Johns Hopkins Hospital, 1922; Blood Pressure (with N. B. Cole), 1924; The Young Man and Medicine, 1927; Psychotherapy, 1940. Co-Editor: Endocrinology and Metabolism, 1922. Also numerous med. papers and addresses. Home: 208 Stratford Rd. Office: 1035 N. Calvert St., Baltimore, Md. Died July 13, 1943.

BARKER, M. Herbert, physician; b. Villisca, Ia., Aug. 20, 1899; s. William Asa and Bessie May (Kimel) B.; student U. of Minn., 1919-21; B.S., U. of S.D., 1923; M.D., Rush Med. Coll. (U. of Chicago), 1925; M.S., Northwestern U., 1931; m. Nancy Maes Henderson, Mar. 3, 1928; 1 dau., Nancy Marion; m. 2d, Marjorie Leigh, Feb. 15, 1945; Intern Wesley Memorial Hospital, Chicago, 1925, and 1926; research in cardio-renal disease at Harvard Medical Sch. and Peter Bent Brigham Hosp., 1927-29; resident in medicine, Passavant Memorial Hosp., Chicago, 1930-31, now asst. prof. medicine, Northwestern U. Med. Sch.; attending physician Memorial Hosp.; expert consultant to U.S. Surgeon Gen.; former cons. in cardio-renal disease, Vets. Diagnostic Center, Edward Hines Hosp. Served with U.S. Marines, 1918-19. Col. U.S. Army, Medical Corps, World War II. Mem. Com. on Hypertension for America and Great Britain; mem. advisory counsel Ill. State Pneumonia Control Commn.; chmn. Com. for Nomenclature of Renal-vascular Disease; mem. Central Clin. Research Club. Fellow Central Society Clinical Research (peripheral cardio disease, vascular sect.), American College Physicians; mem. Society Medical History, A.M.A., Sigma Nu, Phi Chi, Sigma Xi, Pi Kappa Epsilon. Received citation, Legion of Merit, 1944. Clubs: Saddle and Cycle, Chicago Yacht, Racquet (Chicago). Contbr. numerous articles to med. jours. and papers to med. meetings. Home: 411 Wrightwood Av. Office: 720 N. Michigan Av., Chicago 11, Ill. Died Aug. 14, 1947.

BARKER, Reginald Charles, author; b. Brighton, Sussex, Eng., May 15, 1881; s. Reginald and Mimmie (Magnese) B.; ed. pvt. sch., Eng.; m. Edith Maude Granger, Aug. 11, 1911; children—Rudyard Charles (dec.), Thor, Kenneth. Came to U.S., 1900, naturalized citizen, 1923. Worked as sailor, cowboy, miner, trapper and lumberman. Republican. Clubs: Olympia Yacht; Boise Writers'. Author: Grizzly Gallagher, 1927; Wild Horse Ranch, 1927; Gentleman Grizzly, 1928; Hair-Trigger Brand, 1929. Contbr. to Blue Book, Complete Stories, Western Story Mag. Home: Hollywood, Calif. Died Oct. 21, 1937.

BARKHORN, Henry Charles, physician; b. Newark, N.J., Dec. 2, 1885; s. Charles Henry and Jennie

(Hodson) B.; M.D., Cornell U. Med. Sch., 1907; m. Mariette Louise Gless, Sept. 9, 1914; children—Henry Charles, Jr., Janet Louise, Richard Edward, Mariette Amie. In practice of medicine and surgery at Newark, N.J., since 1909, specializing in diseases of ear, nose and throat since 1917. Fellow American Coll. Surgeons; mem. Am. Med. Assn., N.J. State and Essex County (ex-pres.) med. socs., Soc. of Surgeons of N.J., Acad. of Medicine of Northern N.J. (pres. 1937-39), Practitioners Club (pres. 1931-32), Doctors Club (pres. 1921-22), Essex County Tuberculosis League (v.p. since 1937), Cornell Med. Alumni Assn. (pres. 1928-30), St. Benedicts Prep. Alumni (pres. 1931-32). Democrat. Roman Catholic. Home: 45 Johnson Av., Newark, N.J. Died July 27, 1949.

BARKLEY, William Elliot, banker; b. New Point, Ind., Oct. 18, 1863; s. William Elliot and Nancy (Hart) B.; student Northern Ind. Normal Sch., 1880-82, Northwest Mo. Normal Sch., 1882-87; m. Edna McDowell, Nov. 24, 1898. Asst. treas. Lincoln (Neb.) Savings Bank and Safe Deposit Co., 1892-94; sec., treas. Lincoln Safe Deposit and Trust Co., 1898-1912, pres. Lincoln Trust & Safe Deposit Co., 1912-20; pres. Lincoln Joint Stock Land Bank and v.p. Freemont Joint Stock Land Bank since 1920; also pres. Union Bank, Union Nat. Life Ins. Co. (both of Lincoln). Republican. Club: University. Home: 2829 S 24th St. Office: Barkley Bldg., Lincoln, Neb. Died Apr. 4, 1944.

BARKSDALE, Joseph Downs, lawyer; b. Arcadia, La., June 6, 1874; s. Allen and Eliza (Copeland) B.; A.B., Ruston (La.) Coll., 1892; student Tulane U., 1892-93; read law in father's office; m. Olive Standifer, Nov. 28, 1900; m. 2d, Rosa Colvin, Nov. 7, 1915. Admitted to La. bar, 1897, and practiced in Ruston until 1917, then moved to New Orleans; organized Hodge Ship Co., Moss Point, Miss., and was exec. sec. for 2 yrs.; moved to Shreveport, La., 1922, and resumed practice of law, sr. mem. Barksdale, Bullock, Clark & Van Hook, Shreveport (firm dissolved Jan. 1942), and Barksdale & Barksdale, Ruston; removed to Ruston, 1942, to practice as member firm of Barksdale & Barksdale. Mem. Constitutional Convention of La., 1921. Member Am. Bar Assn., La. State Bar Assn. (pres. 1932-33), Kappa Sigma. Author of pamphlet, "A Country Lawyer in a Wood Ship Yard." Address: Ruston, La. Died Jan. 9, 1944.

BARLOW, Arthur J., exec. v.p. and dir. Kingsport Press; b. New York, N.Y., 1893. Mason. Home: 50 Woodside Dr., Greenwich, Conn. Office: Kinsport Press, 1 E. 57th St., New York. Died Nov. 9, 1949.

BARLOW, De Witt Dukes, civil engr.; b. Phila., Pa., Oct. 4, 1880; s. Thomas Arnold and Elizabeth (Dukes) B.; B.S., Phila. High Sch., 1898; B.S. in C.E., U. of Pa., 1901; m. Elizabeth Hail Moody, May 16, 1905; children—Anne May, Esther Moody, Elizabeth Hail, De Witt D., Carlton Montague, Jean Lewis. Began practice at Phila., 1901; pres. Atlantic, Gulf & Pacific Co. since 1921; also pres. North Atlantic Dredging Co. Asso. chief of Dredging Sect., War Industries Bd., 1918-19; chmn. Dredge Owners' Protective Orgn. since 1920; chmn. Nat. Assn. River & Harbor Contractors. Mem. Alien Enemy Hearing Bd., Dist. of N.J. Mem. Common Council, Plainfield, N.J., 1922-23; mem. Bd. of Health, 1923-24; pres. Bd. of Edn., 1924-37; pres. Plainfield Symphony Soc.; mayor of City of Plainfield, 1937-38. Mem. bd. dirs., Metropolitan Popular Season, Inc. Chmn. N.J. Citizens Com. for the Princeton Local Govt. Survey. Chairman Plainfield and North Plainfield Chapter of The American Red Cross. Mem. Am. Soc. C.E., Sigma Xi. Republican. Presbyterian. Clubs: Engineers, U. of Pa. (New York); Plainfield Engrs., Plainfield Country. Home: 930 Woodland Av., Plainfield, N.J. Office: 15 Park Row, New York 7 N.Y. Died Sep. 23, 1945.

BARLOW, Elmer Elbert (bär'lō), judge; b. Arcadia, Wis., May 18, 1887; s. Robert and Elizabeth (Niclai) B.; LL.B., U. of Wis., 1909; m. Kate Clausen, Nov. 4, 1913 (died 1930); children—Elizabeth (Mrs. Fred Daft), Robert C.; m. 2d, Anna Wohlgenant, Oct. 5, 1937. Admitted to Wis. bar, 1909; in gen. practice, 1909-39; legal counsel to gov. of Wis., 1939; tax commr. of Wis., 1940-42; justice Supreme Court of Wis. since Dec. 1942. Served as mem. Officers Reserve Corps, 1925-35. Mem. Wis. State and Tri-County bar assns., Phi Alpha Delta. Republican. Mason. Club: Madison. Home: 116 Pearl St., Arcadia, Wis. Office: State Capitol, Madison, Wis. Died June 26, 1948.

BARLOW, John, educator; b. Amenia, N.Y., Nov. 28, 1872; s. Henry and Helen Cythera (Benton) B.; B.S., Middlebury (Vt.) Coll., 1895, D.Sc., 1933; A.M., Brown U., 1896; student Cornell U., Summer Sch., 3 yrs.; D.Sc., Rhode Island State College, 1943. Teacher Rhode Island State College, 1897, Fairmont Coll. (now Municipal U.), Wichita, Kan., 1898-1902; prof. zoölogy, R.I. State Coll. since 1902, dean Sch. Sciences and Business, 1924, acting pres., 1930-31 and 1940-41, became v.p., 1931. Fellow A.A.A.S.; charter mem. Am. Entomol. Soc.; mem. Phi Beta Kappa, Phi Kappa Phi. Home: Kingston, R.I. Died Nov. 26, 1944.

BARNARD, Charles Inman, newspaper man; b. Boston, Mar. 15, 1850; s. George Middleton and Susan (Tilden) B.; ed. Boston Latin Sch., 1862-6; Mass. Inst. Tech., 1869-71; LL.B., Harvard, 1874; m. Anna Santrüchek, July 29, 1879 (died Nov. 30, 1906). Mil. sec. to Gen. Stone Pasha, chief of staff to Khedive of Egypt, 1875-9; employed on various missions to Constantinople, Khartoum and Massawa to Abyssinia, 1876; chief of Soudan bur. of Gen. Charles E. Gordon, gov.-gen. of Soudan, 1877-8; tutor to Prince Mahmoud Helmy Pasha, son of Ismail Pasha, Khedive of Egypt, 1879-81; mem. Superior Council Pub. Instrn. of Egyptian Govt., 1881-2; war corr. New York Herald and London, in Egypt, 1882-3; corr. New York Herald with spl. missions in Paris, London, Berlin, Vienna, St. Petersburg, Constantinople, Brussels, The Hague, Copenhagen, etc.; Paris corr. New York Tribune since 1897. Knight Legion of Honor, France; comdr. Imperial Turkish Order of the Osmanieh, 1882; officer Imperial Turkish Order of Medjidieh, 1882, conferred by the Khedive Tewfik for services rendered to Egyptian Govt.; Egyptian war medal, battle of Tel-el-Kebir, 1882. Mil. corr. New York Tribune in Paris, Aug. 1, 1914-Sept. 1, 1915; present in French trenches and arty. observation stas. at Albert, Ribécourt, etc.; associated with internat. law firm of S. G. Archibald, Paris. Pres. Am. Foreign Press Assn., Paris, 1909-15. Clubs: American (v.p.), Harvard (exec. com.) (both of Paris). Author: Paris War Days, 1914. Address: 8 Rue Théodule-Ribot, Paris, France. Died May 11, 1942.

BARNARD, George M. (bär'närd), commr. Interstate Commerce Commn.; b. New Castle, Ind., June 6, 1881; s. William O. and Mary V. (Ballenger) B.; B.L., U. of Mich., 1903; m. Marion H. Dingee, Oct. 4, 1911; children—Mary (Mrs. James W. Forgie), Margaret (Mrs. Andrew J. Sordoni, Jr.), Julia (Mrs. Raymond W. Steele), Ruth (Mrs. William Halloway III), William O., George M. Admitted to bar, 1903; prosecuting atty., Henry County, Ind., 1906-10; mayor, City of New Castle, Ind., 1910-14; engaged in practice of law, New Castle, Ind., 1914-21; apptd. to public service commn. for Ind., 1921, commd. for 4 yrs., resigned 1921; became partner in firm Ralston, Gates, Lairy, Van Huys & Barnard, Indianapolis, Ind., 1922; apptd. to pub. service commn. for Ind., 2-yr. term, 1941, reapptd. for 4-yr. term, 1943; apptd. by Pres. Roosevelt as mem. Interstate Commerce Commn. for term 1944-50. Mem. Henry County, Indianapolis and Ind. State bar assns. Republican. Quaker. Clubs: Columbia (Indianapolis); Westward Country (New Castle). Address: Interstate Commerce Commission, 12th St. and Constitution Av., Washington, D.C. Died Jan. 2, 1949.

BARNARD, Harry Everett, chemist; b. Dunbarton, N.H., Nov. 14, 1874; s. Nelson H. and Celestia A. (Rider) B.; B.S., N.H. College of Agrl. and Mechanic Arts, 1899; Ph.D., Hanover (Ind.) College, 1913; D.Sc. from Univ. of N.H., 1928; m. Marion Harvie, June 20, 1901. Asst. chemist, N.H. Expt. Sta., 1899, U.S. Smokeless Powder Factory, Indian Head, Md., 1900-01; chemist, N.H. State Bd. of Health, 1901-05; Ind. State Bd. of Health, 1905-19; state food and drug commn. of Ind., 1907-19; state commr. of weights and measures of Ind., 1911-19; food and drug inspn. chemist, U.S. Dept. Agr., 1907-19; pres. H. E. Barnard, Inc. Pres. Ind. Sanitary and Water Supply Assn.; dir. Am. Chem. Soc. (founder and 1st pres. Ind. Sect.); mem. Am. Inst. Chem. Engrs., Soc. Official Agrl. Chemists, Nat. Assn. State Food Commrs., Federal Food Standards Com., Indianapolis Technical Soc.; president Lake Michigan Water Commission; secretary Indiana Branch National Conservation Assn.; mem. exec. com. Nat. Conservation Congress, 1912. Federal Food Administrator for Ind., 1917-19. Pres. Am. Inst. of Baking, 1919, 27; sec. Am. Bakers' Assn., 1921-25; dir. White House Conf. on Child Health and Protection, 1929-31, Corn Industries Research Foundation, 1931-34; dir. research Nat. Farm Chemurgic Council, 1935-40, professional specialist in chemistry, War Manpower Commn., since 1941; with Fed. Economics Assn., 1945. Trustee New Hampshire Coll., 1903-06. Mem. Sigma Alpha Epsilon, Alpha Chi Sigma, Phi Kappa Phi. Clubs: Irvington Athenæum, Indianapolis Literary; City, Chemists (Chicago); University (Evanston, Ill.); Cosmos (Washington, D.C.); Chemists' (New York). Author of N.H. and Ind. bd. of health reports and papers and addresses on subjects of food, drugs, water, sanitation, nutrition, child welfare, chemurgy, etc. Home: 5050 Pleasant Run Parkway, Indianapolis, Ind. Office: Cosmos Club, Washington. Died Dec. 31, 1946; buried in Washington Park Mausoleum, Indianapolis.

BARNARD, J(ames) Lynn, educator; b. Milford, Otsego County, N.Y., Aug. 9, 1867; s. James Taylor and Cora Ophelia (Smith) B.; grad. Cooperstown (N.Y.) High Sch., 1886; B.S., Syracuse U., 1892; Ph.D., U. of Pa., 1897; m. Jessie May Cummings, Sept. 6, 1893; children—Grover (dec.), Margaret, Frances Cummings. Prof. history and polit. science, Ursinus Coll., Collegeville, Pa., 1897-1904; field agt., New York and Phila. charity orgn. socs., 1904-06; prof. history and govt., Phila. Sch. of Pedagogy, 1906-20; dir. social studies Pa., Dept. Pub. Instrn., 1920-27; prof. polit. science and dir. social studies for teachers, Ursinus Coll., 1927; mem. faculty, Mass. State Normal Sch., Hyannis, summer, 1914, Teachers Coll. (Columbia), 1916, U. of Pittsburgh, 1917, 18, Harvard, 1919, 20, Pa. State College, 1923-32, Univ. of Pa., 1935, Western State Teachers Coll., Kalamazoo, Mich., 1937. Mem. Am. Acad. Polit. and Social Science, Am. Polit. Science Assn., Phi Kappa Psi, Phi Beta Kappa, Kappa Phi Kappa. Methodist. Author: Factory Legislation in Pennsylvania, 1906. Co-author: The Teaching of Community Civics (U.S. Bureau Edn.), 1915; Citizenship in Philadelphia, 1918; Our Community Life, 1926; Epochs of World Progress, 1927; Civics Readers, 3 vols., 1938. Editor and compiler: Getting a Living, 1921. Contbr. to periodicals. Home: Collegeville, Pa. Died Aug. 10, 1941.

BARNARD, William Nichols, educator; b. Canton, Ill., Apr. 24, 1875; s. William Stebbins and Mary (Nichols) B.; M.E., Cornell U., 1897; m. Edith Nourse Robinson, Apr. 17, 1919. Instr. in machine design, Cornell U., 1897-99; engine designing, with Russel Engine Co., 1899-1903; asst. prof. of machine design and steam engring., Cornell U., 1903-07, prof. of steam engring., 1907-15, sec. of Sibley Coll. of Mech. Engring., 1910-15, prof. of heat power engring., 1915-38; dir. of Sibley Sch. of Mech. Engring. since 1938; coordinator of civilian pilot training, Cornell U. Served as pres. of academic bd. of U.S. Army Sch. of Mil. Aeronautics, Cornell U., 1917-19. Registered Professional Engr., N.Y. Mem. Am. Soc. Mech. Engrs., Soc. for Promotion Engring. Edn., Cornell Soc. Engrs., Sigma Xi, Tau Beta Pi, Phi Kappa Phi, Atmos. Republican. Author: Valve Gears, 1907; Elements of Heat-Power Engineering (with C. F. Hirschfeld), 1912; Heat-Power Engineering (with F. O. Ellenwood and C. F. Hirshfeld), Part 1, 1926, Parts 2 and 3, 1933. Home: 201 Bryant Av., Ithaca, N.Y. Died Apr. 3, 1947.

BARNASON, Charles Frederick (bär'nä-s'n), univ. prof.; b. Reykjavik, Iceland, Feb. 28, 1886; s. Sigurdur and Thorbjörg (Benónýsdóttir) B.; came to U.S., 1900, naturalized, 1926; A.B., Coll. City of N.Y., 1915; A.M., Cornell U., 1917; Ph.D., Harvard, 1936; student univs. of Wisconsin, Grenoble, Paris and Berlin; m. Gudrun Thomasson, Aug. 29, 1918. Teacher of French, Lakewood (O.) High Sch., 1918-21; prof. Romance languages, Waynesburg (Pa.) Coll., 1925-27; asst. prof. modern langs., Marietta (O.), 1927-29; instr. in German, Harvard, 1930-37; prof. modern langs. and chmn. dept., Northeastern U., Boston, Mass., since 1937. Recipient Ward Medal, Coll. City of N.Y., 1915. Univ. fellow Cornell, 1916-17; fellow U. of Wis., 1917-18. Mem. Mediaeval Acad. America, Modern Lang. Assn. Am., New England Modern Lang. Assn. Club: Harvard (Hingham, Mass.). Author: The Revival of Old Norse Literature, 1600-1750, 1938; Early Danish and Swedish Writers on Native History (in Studies in Honor of John A. Walz, Lancaster), 1941. Home: 122 Downer Av., Hingham, Mass. Office: 360 Huntington Av., Boston, Mass. Died Dec. 23, 1949.

BARNES, Alfred Victor, chmn. bd. American Book Co.; b. Brooklyn, N.Y., July 25, 1870; s. Alfred Cutler and Josephine (Richardson) B.; student Brooklyn Poly., Brooklyn Latin Sch., Yale, 1891; m. Martha E. Sitt, Sept. 6, 1923. Served as chief of mfg. Am. Book Co., dir. since 1907, later vice-pres., chmn. bd. since 1931. During World War served as lieut. col., U.S.A. Ordnance Dept., and dist. chief, Baltimore Dist. Clubs: Society of Colonial Wars, Yale, St. Anthony, New Canaan Country, Woodway Country. Home: New Canaan, Conn. Office: 88 Lexington Av., New York, N.Y. Deceased

BARNES, Clifford Webster, educator, capitalist; b. Corry, Pa., Oct. 8, 1864; s. Joseph and Anna (Webster) B.; A.B., Yale, 1889, B.D., 1892; A.M., U. of Chicago, 1893; LL.D., Lake Forest Univ., 1913, Ill. Coll., 1925; m. Alice Reid, May 5, 1898 (died May 12, 1938); 1 dau., Lilace Reid. Resident worker, Hull House Social Settlement, Chicago, 1893-94; pastor in Chicago, 1894-97; student at Oxford, Eng., 1898; dir. Student Christian Movement, Paris, France, 1898-99; acting pres., American Art Association, Paris, 1898-99; instr. sociology and dir. Univ. Settlement Work, U. of Chicago, 1899-1900; pres. and prof. sociology, Ill. Coll., 1900-05; gen. sec. Religious Edn. Assn. of America, 1905-06; special commr. to Europe to investigate moral and religious training in schs., 1906-07; hon. sec. and chmn. exec. com. Internat. Com. on Moral Training since 1907; chmn. executive com. Legislative Voters League, 1907-24, pres., 1909-24; pres. founder, Chicago Sunday Evening Club since 1908; founder Com. of 15, 1908, pres. 1908-16, mem. exec. com., 1909, pres., 1935-39, chmn. bd. since 1939; chmn. Chicago Community Trust since 1915; pres. Chicago Ch. Fed., 1925-27; v.p. Chicago Assn. Commerce, 1927-31, dir. mem. exec. com. since 1931; trustee Chicago Y.W.C.A. since 1929; v.p. exec. and budget com., Joint Emergency Relief Fund of Cook County, 1931-34; mem. bd. dirs. Grenfell Assn. since 1936; mem. Chicago Plan Commn., 1936, Chicago Recreation Commn., 1937; v.p. World Alliance for Internat. Friendship, 1927-35; del. triennial internat. meeting, same, Cambridge, 1931; del. World Conf. on Faith and Order, Lausanne, 1927; mem. exec. com. Com. of 1000; mem. advisory com. Federal Council Chs. of Christ in America; pres. War Recreation Bd. of Ill., 1917-23; pres. War Camp Community Service Chicago, 1917-19; mem. Navy Commn. on Training Camp Activities, 1917-19; major and department commissioner American Red Cross Commission to Greece, 1918-19; v.p. Chicago Community Fund since 1934; dir. Chicago Council of Social Agencies since 1919; mem. of corp. Lake Forest Acad. since 1934. Decorated Medal of Military Merit, with silver palm (Greece), 1918; Knight Order of Golden Cross (Greece), 1919; Alumni Medal for Distinguished Service, U. of Chicago, 1941. Trustee Estate of Simon Reid. Clubs: Chicago, University, City, Union League (Chicago); Onwentsia (Lake Forest, Ill.); Yale (New York); Annandale Country (Pasadena, Calif.). Home: Lake Forest, Ill. Office: 10 S. La Salle St., Chicago, Ill. Died Sep. 18, 1944.

BARNES, George Emerson, clergyman; b. Hersey, Mich., May 26, 1882; s. Joseph Asa and Ella Minerva (Bennett) B.; Olivet (Mich.) Coll., 1899-1901; B. A., U. of Mont., 1902; Rhodes scholar at Oxford U., England, 1904-07 (M.A.); B.A., Christ Ch. Coll., 1907 (first honors in theology); D.D., Alma (Mich.) Coll., 1916; m. Myrtle Kendall Montague, Aug. 4, 1908; children—Kendall Montague, Allan Campbell, Robert Gaylord, Margaret Elizabeth. Ordained Presbyn. ministry, 1907; pastor Coldwater, Mich., 1907-12, 1st Ch., Battle Creek, 1912-18, 1st Ch., Flint, 1918-22, Overbrook Presbyn. Ch., Phila., Pa., since 1922. Chmn. Presbyn. War Service Commn. for Mich. and Wis., 1918; camp pastor, Camp Custer, Mich., 1918. Moderator Synod of Mich., 1915-16; mem. Home Missions Council Presbyn. Church U.S.A., 1913-16. Gov. 9th Dist. Rotary Clubs, 1921-22, Sec. Assn. Am. Rhodes Scholars; bus. mgr. Am. Oxonian; pres. Phila. Federation of Churches, 1939-41; mem. adv. bd. World Alliance for Friendship; vice pres. Presbyn. Minister's Fund; moderator Presbytery of Phila., 1936-38; chmn. Com. on Arrangements for Sesquicentennial Gen. Assembly, 1938; mem. Supervisory Com. on Social Edn. and Action of Presbyn. Ch., 1936-38; del. to World Confs. at Oxford and Edinburgh, 1937. Mem. Gen. Council Presbyn. Ch., U.S.A., 1938-44, chmn. com. of united promotion; exec. chmn. Presbyn. War Time Service Commn.; chmn. Presbyn. Restoration Commn.; chmn. bd. dirs. Church World Service, Inc.; pres. Phila. Council Churches, 1946-47; Com. for World Council of Churches; v.p. Presbyn. Hospital. Del. to meeting World Council of Churches in Amsterdam, Aug. 1948. Republican. Mason. Clubs: Contemporary (pres. 1945-47), Union League, Rotary of Phila. (pres. 1928-29); Gull Lake (Mich.) Country. Writer on religious subjects. Home: 6376 City Line Av., Philadelphia 31, Pa. Died Dec. 29, 1948.

BARNES, George O., public official; b. Sugar Run, Pa., Oct. 6, 1878; s. Oscar O. and Frances E. (Wright) B.; studied Valparaiso (Ind.) U., Georgetown U. Law Sch. 1 yr., Am. Inst. Banking 1 yr., accountancy 1 yr.; m. Joanna L. Kane, Sept. 2, 1908; children—George Anthony, Mary Elizabeth, Edward Oscar, Eugene Kane, Joanne. With Nat. Bank Redemption Agency, U.S. Treasury Dept., Washington, 1902-29, supt., 1920-29; asst. treas. of U.S., 1929-33; exec. asst. to treas. of U.S., 1933-40; asst. to treas. of U.S. since July 1, 1940. Republican. Catholic. Home: 608 Rolling Road, Chevy Chase, Md. Office: Treasury Dept., Washington, D.C.
Died Sep. 19, 1944.

BARNES, Gilbert Hobbs, prof. economics; b. Lincoln, Neb., Mar. 30, 1889; s. Gilbert M. and Harriet Ross (Hobbs) B.; student O. Wesleyan U., 1908-10; A.B., U. of Mich., 1912, A.M., 1913, Ph.D., 1929; grad. student U. of Pa., 1913-15; m. Ruth Holt, Sept. 24, 1912 (died Nov. 27, 1918); 1 son, Gilbert Holt; m. 2d, Elizabeth Booton, July 2, 1929. Instr. history, U. of Mich., 1911-13; Harrison fellow, history, U. of Pa., 1913-15; instr., asst. prof. economics, Carnegie Inst. Tech., 1915-17, prof. and head of dept. social sciences, 1917-20; prof. and head of dept. economics, Ohio Wesleyan U., since 1920; visiting prof. economics, Swarthmore (Pa.) Coll., 1934-35. Mem. Am. Econ. Assn., Kappa Sigma, Phi Beta Kappa. Methodist. Author: The Antislavery Impulse (1830-44), 1933. Editor: (with D. L. Dumond) Letters of Theodore Dwight Weld, Angelina Grimké Weld and Sarah Grimké, 1934. Contbr. biog. articles. Home: 477 W. Central Av., Delaware, Ohio. Died Aug. 12, 1945.

BARNES, Harlan Ward, newpaper pub.; b. Fedora, S.D., Dec. 4, 1883; s. Arthur Herman and Sarah Elizabeth (Raymond) B.; A.B., Ia. State Univ., 1907; m. Maude Morford, Dec. 4, 1909; children—Arthur Morford, Mary (Mrs. William P. Baxter). Teacher Cedar Rapids and Burlington, Ia., 1907-09; partner with father as pubs., The Eagle, Eagle Grove, Ia., 1909-18, sole owner 1918, consolidated with 2 other papers, 1924-27; editor-publisher Eagle Grove Eagle. Del. to Rep. Nat. Conv., Philadelphia, 1940; del. to state and county Rep. convs. since 1926; campaign mgr. for Gov. R. D. Blue of Ia., 1944, 46. Dir. Security Savings Bank. Selected as Master editor-pub. by Ia. Press Assn., 1938. Mem. Nat. Editorial Assn. (N.E.A. mem. U.S. Nat. Commn. for UNESCO, 1946, 47), Ia. Press Assn. (past pres., dir.), Chamber of Commerce (past pres., dir.). Conglist. Mem. Woodmen of World, Odd Fellow, Mason (past master); Sigma Delta Chi, Delta Sigma Rho, Za Ga Zig Shrine. Club: Rotary (past pres.). Home: 703 W. Broadway. Office: 116 W. Broadway, Eagle Grove, Ia. Died March 15, 1947.

BARNES, Mary Clark (Mrs. Lemuel Call Barnes), author; b. Warsaw, Pa., Feb. 14, 1851; d. Nathaniel and Maria (Hanford) Clark; B.Ph., Kalamazoo (Mich.) Coll., 1875, M.Ph., 1878; m. Lemuel Call Barnes, Jan. 2, 1879. Teacher English lit. and history Kalamazoo Coll., 1875-79; organized Neighbors League of Am., Inc., 1917, for work among non-English-speaking residents of America; organized and conducted Sch. of Americanization, at Chautauqua Assembly, N.Y., summer, 1919; nat. dir. Americanization Dept. for Nat. W.C.T.U., May 1919-Nov. 1920. Mem. Authors' Guild of Authors' League of Am., Am. Assn. Univ. Women. Baptist. Author: Athanasia, 1907; Early Stories and Songs for New Students of English, 1912; The New America (with husband), 1913; Neighboring New Americans, 1920; (with husband) Pioneers of Light (100 yrs. of Am. Bapt. Publn. Soc.), 1924; Life Exultant, 1925; We, the People and Our Constitution, 1927; How Came Our Constitution?, 1930; John Smith, Usher, 1933. Contbr. to periodical press. Address: 3260 Henry Hudson Parkway, New York 63, N.Y. Deceased.

BARNES, Raymond F(latt), church exec.; b. Rahway, N.J., Apr. 7, 1877; s. James Thomas and Adelaide Mary (Flatt) B.; ed. Pingry Sch., Elizabeth, N.J., and Rutgers Prep. Sch., New Brunswick, N.J.; LL.D., Hobart Coll., 1937; m. Grace Adline Weeber, Nov. 4, 1903; 1 dau., Phyllis. Mem. Boyce & Barnes, contractors, Astoria, L.I., 1901-07; confidential advisor to Hoople & Nichols, N.Y., 1907-09; sec. and treas. U.S. Wood Preserving Co., New York, 1909-11; pres. Oak Ridge Co., New York, 1911-16; pres. Mountain Lakes Co., N.J., 1911-16; mem. Barnes Mfg. Co., Jersey City, 1916-25; trustee and mem. finance com. South Brooklyn Savings Bk.; dir. and mem. exec. com. First Nat. Bank, Jersey City, N.J.; treas. Gen. Conv. P.E. Ch. since 1925 (mem. budget and program com.); treas. of Diocese, Diocesan Council, Archdeaconries of Brooklyn, Queens and Nassau, and Suffolk of Diocese of L.I.; treas. Trustees of the Estate Belonging to Diocese of L.I., Aged and Infirm Clergy Fund, Episcopal Fund, Group Life Ins. Fund, Diocesan Ch. Extension Fund; agt. Ch. Properties Fire Ins. Corp.; trustee Am. Ch. Bldg. Fund Com. of P.E. Ch. Del. Gen. Conv. P.E. Ch. since 1922. Mem. Soc. Mayflower Descs., The Pilgrim John Howland Soc., Soc. of Colonial Wars, St. Nicholas Soc. of the City of New York, St. Nicholas Soc. of Nassau Island; life mem. Sons of Revolution, Society of the War of 1812, Vet. Corps of Artillery (World War Cantonment div.). Mason. Club: Brooklyn (Brooklyn). Traveled extensively among missionary fields of Protestant Episcopal Church in U.S. and abroad. Contbr. to church periodicals. Home: 42A Monroe Pl. Office: 170 Remsen St., Brooklyn, N.Y. Died Aug. 9, 1949.

BARNES, Roswell Parkhurst, church exec.; b. Council Bluffs, Ia., July 10, 1901; s. William Smith and Mary Agnes (Bigham) B.; grad. Wyoming Sem., Kingston, Pa., 1920; A.B., Lafayette Coll., Easton, Pa., 1924, A.M., 1926, D.D., 1941; grad. student at Columbia Univ., 1929. Union Theol. Sem., New York, 1930; m. Helen Ackley Bosworth, June 29, 1926; children—Margaret Agnes, Roswell Parkhurst. Teacher of English, Blair Acad., 1924-26; exec. sec. Com. on Militarism in Edn., 1926-28; asso. minister Park Av. Presbyn. Ch., N.Y. City, 1928-32; ordained to ministry of Presbyn. Ch., 1932; pastor Univ. Heights Presbyn. Ch., N.Y. City, 1932-37; asso. sec. dept. internat. justice and good will, Fed. Council of Chs., 1937-40; asso. gen. sec. Fed. Council of Chs. of Christ in Am. since Jan. 1940. Sec. of conf. on internat. affairs, Provisional Com. of World Council of Chs., 1939; dir. War Prisoners' Aid; dir. United China Relief; mem. Am. Com. for World Council of churches. Mem. Phi Beta Kappa, Tau Kappa Alpha, Kappa Phi Kappa. Author: A Christian Imperative. Editor: Federal Council Bulletin. Contbg. editor: The Presbyn. Tribune. Contbr. to religious jours. Office: 297 4th Av., New York 10. Died Aug. 9, 1949.

BARNES, William Preston, banker; b. Ashley County, Ark., July 28, 1866; s. William Wilson and Irene Jane (Dean) B.; student country schools; m. Loula Hughes, Sept. 22, 1891; m. 2d, Hannah Denmead Warren, Apr. 5, 1917; 1 son, William Preston. Began as clerk gen. mdse. store, then traveling salesman, 1892-1902; organized firm of Holmes and Barnes, Ltd., wholesale grocers, Baton Rouge, La., 1901, and active until 1932; chmn. bd. La. Nat. Bank, Jan. 1, 1920-Feb. 18, 1932, when was made pres.; pres. Holmes and Barnes, Ltd.; dir. La. Fire Ins. Co., Louisiana Underwriters Agency. Home: 620 Convention. Office: Third St., Baton Rouge, La.*
Died Mar. 6, 1944.

BARNETT, Frank Willis, editor; b. Glennville, Ala., Oct. 23, 1865; s. Augustus William and Celeste (Treutlen) B.; studied U. of Ala., Vanderbilt U., The Sorbonne, Paris, U. of Vienna, U. of Berlin, New York Law Sch., Southern Baptist Theol. Sem.; LL.D., Howard Coll., 1918; Litt.D., U. of Ala., 1924; m. Maud Proctor, July 21, 1900; children—Frank Willis, Proctor Hawthorne. Practiced law successively at Birmingham, Ala., New York, N.Y., and Atlanta, Ga., until 1895; ordained Bapt. ministry, 1895; pastor Johnson City, Tenn., 1895; asst. pastor, First Ch., Nashville, 1897, Forsyth, Ga., 1898-1900; owner and editor Ala. Baptist, 1902-17; asso. editor Age-Herald, Birmingham, Ala., 1917-21; on editorial staff Birmingham News from 1921; now retired. Democrat. Mem. Kappa Alpha. Mason. Home: 3900 10th Av. S., Birmingham, Ala. Died June 29, 1941.

BARNETT, John T., lawyer; b. Potsdam, N.Y., June 22, 1869; s. John and Katherine B.; grad. State Normal and Training Sch., Potsdam, N.Y., 1891; LL.B., Chicago Coll. of Law, 1896; m. Sue Sayre Nash, Jan. 24, 1906 (died 1911); m. 2d, Emily Louise Schlesiner, Mar. 7, 1917 (died Oct. 1926); m. 3d, Maybelle Fuller, Feb. 3, 1932. Was prin. pub. schs. of Silverton, Colo., 1891-93; also owner and editor Silverton Miner; admitted to Ill. bar, 1896, and practiced in Chicago; removed to Colo., 1897; asso. in practice with James H. Teller (former chief justice Colo. Supreme Court), 1911-13, with Judge John Campbell (also former chief justice same court), 1913-20; atty. Ouray Co., Colo., 1898-1910; atty. gen. of Colo., 1909, 10. Pres. Mountain Producers Corp. since 1920. Sec. Dem. State Central Com., 1912-16; mem. Dem. Nat. Com. for Colo., 1913-28. Catholic. Clubs: University, Denver Country, Denver, Cherry Hills. Home: 4100 South Clarkson St., Englewood, Colo. Office: First Nat. Bank Bldg., Denver, Colo.
Died Feb. 1, 1942.

BARNETT, Otto Raymond, patent lawyer; b. Washington, D.C., Sept. 21, 1868; s. Theodore J. and Eugenia M. (Hodge) B.; LL.B. Northwestern U., 1888; m. Mabel D. Rowley, June 18, 1895; children—Lawrence Theodore, Sherman Rowley; m. 2d, Katharine C. McNeil, Mar. 23, 1934. Admitted to Ill. bar, 1889, to U.S. Supreme Court, 1897; entered office of James H. Raymond, 1887, mem. Raymond & Barnett until 1907, Barnett & Truman since 1912; prof. patent law, Northwestern U., 1902-04, 1910, 1928-29; gen. counsel Vapor Car Heating Co. Mem. Am. Patent Law Assn. (ex-pres.), Chicago Patent Law Assn. (ex-pres.), Am. Bar Assn., Illinois State Bar Assn., Chicago Bar Assn., Am. Law Inst. Former mem. Park Bd., Plan Commn. and Bd. of Edn., Glencoe, Illinois; pres. Library Bd., Glencoe, 1910-33; chmn., trustees' sect. and legislative com., Ill. Library Assn.; mem. New Trier High Sch. Bd. Republican. Mem. Glencoe Union Ch. Mason (32°). Clubs: Union League, Law, Skokie Country (Chicago); etc. Author: Patent, Property and Anti-Monopoly Laws. Contbr. to Yale Law Jour., Mich. Law Rev., Ill. Law Rev., etc. Home: 684 Greenleaf Av., Glencoe, Ill. Office: 2300 Board of Trade Bldg., Chicago, Ill.
Died Mar. 27, 1945.

BARNHARDT, Jesse Homer (bärn'härt), clergyman; b. Cabarrus County, N.C., Feb. 22, 1873; s. Jacob Rufus and Mary Elizabeth (Smith) B.; student N.C. Coll., Mt. Pleasant, 1892-94; A.B., Duke U., 1899; D.D., Ky. Wesleyan Coll., Winchester, 1926; m. Hattie Misenheimer, May 1, 1900; children—Mary Bess (Mrs. W. Banks Wilson), Max Lloyd, Margaret Reamy; m. 2d, Bertha Reinhardt, Feb. 25, 1928. Ordained ministry M.E. Ch., S., 1899; pastor successively High Point, Asheville, Greensboro, and Charlotte—all N.C., until 1925; pastor at Salisbury, N.C., 1929-31, Reidsville, N.C., 1931-33, Grace Ch., Wilmington, 1933-35. Pres. Conf. Bd. Ch. Extension and mem. bd. edn., Western N.C. Conf.; M.E. Church, S.; mem. Gen. Conf. M.E. Ch., S., Atlanta, Ga., 1918, Hot Springs, Ark., 1922, Chattanooga, Tenn., 1924, Memphis, Tenn., 1926, Birmingham, Ala., 1938; presiding elder Greensboro and Winston-Salem districts; later presiding elder Raleigh District; now pastor Rockingham (N.C.) Meth. Ch.; attended Ecumenical Conf. of Methodism, London, 1921. Mem. Duke Univ. Commn., Interchurch Commn. Trustee Emory U., Duke U., Davenport Coll., Lenoir, N.C. Mason, Odd Fellow, K.P. Author: Looking Them Over, 1931. Home: Rockingham, N.C.* Died Jan. 21, 1945.

BARNHILL, John Finch, surgeon, author; b. Flora, Ill., Jan. 2, 1865; s. Robert and Angeline (Shirts) B.; M.D., LL.D., Central Coll. Phys. and Surg., Indianapolis; studied New York Eye and Ear Infirmary, New York Polyclinic, Central London Ear, Nose and Throat Hosp., ear dept. U. of Vienna, ear and throat dept., U. Berlin; LL.D. from Indiana U. in 1929; m. Celeste Terrell, Feb. 13, 1889. In practice at Indianapolis since 1888; specialist in surgery of the head and neck; formerly prof. oto-laryngology, Ind. U. Sch. of Medicine, later prof. surgery head and neck. Fellow Am. Coll. Surgeons; sec. ear and throat sect. A.M.A., 1901-03, chmn. same, 1904; v.p. Am. Ear, Throat and Nose Assn., 1908; pres. Am. Acad. Ophthalmology and Otolaryngology, 1931; member Am. Laryngol. Soc. (pres. 1938), Am. Otol. Soc., Am. Laryngol., Rhinol. and Otol. Soc. (pres. 1927-28), Am. Acad. Ophthalmology and Otolaryngology (pres. 1932), Ind. State Med. Assn.; fellow Am. Coll. Surgeons; mem. Sigma Xi, Nu Sigma Nu. Republican. Methodist. Mason (32°). Author: Text Book on Ear, Nose and Throat, 1928; (stories) Not Speaking of Operations. Co-Author: Barnhill and Wales Modern Otology, 1907; Diseases Ear, Nose and Throat, 1927; Surgical Anatomy of the Head and Neck, 1937; Hatching the American Eagle, A Narrative of the American Revolution, 1937. Home: Casa Rio Vista, 5369 Pine Tree Drive, Miami Beach, Fla. or at home, 5369 Pine Tree Drive, Miami Beach. Died Mar. 10, 1943.

BARNUM, Dana Dwight; b. Bethel, Conn., Aug. 15, 1872; s. William H. and Lydia (Alvord) B.; M.E., Stevens Inst. Tech., Hoboken, N.J., 1895; m. Mary Caroline Munroe, Oct. 23, 1900. Draftsman, E. W. Bliss & Co., Brooklyn, N.Y., 1895; chemist, Worcester Gas Light Co., 1895-96; supt. of distribution, same co., 1896-1902, supt., 1902-09, gen. mgr., 1909-12, pres., 1915; began with Boston Consol. Gas Co., 1917, president, 1921-37; now associated with War Dept. Price Adjustment Board, Washington, D.C. Mem. N.E. Assn. Gas Engrs., Am. Gas Assn., Am. Standards Assn. (pres., 1936-37 and 1938), Soc. of Gas Lighting (New York), Beta Theta Pi, Theta Nu Epsilon. Republican. Episcopalian. Home: Brighton Hotel, 2123 California St., Washington, D.C. Died March 19, 1947.

BARNUM, Malvern-Hill, army officer; b. Syracuse, N.Y., Sept. 3, 1863; s. Gen. Henry A. and Luvina (King) B.; grad. U.S. Mil. Acad., 1886; distinguished grad. Inf. and Cav. Sch., 1893; grad. Army War Coll., 1915; grad. Gen. Staff Coll., 1920; m. Martha Maginness, Oct. 24, 1889; children—Frances (Mrs. F. E. Davis), Malvern-Hill (dec.). Commd. 2d lt. 3d Cav., July 1, 1886; promoted through grades to col., July 1, 1916; brig. gen. N.A., Oct. 31, 1917; brig. gen. regular army, Mar. 2, 1923. Duty Rock Island (Ill.) Arsenal, 1893-94; adj. of 10th Cav. during Santiago

Campaign, 1898; wounded at San Juan Hill, July 2, 1898 (awarded citation for bravery); duty U.S. Mil. Acad., 1899-1902; a.d.c. to Maj. Gen. J. F. Weston, P.I., 1905-09; insp. small arms practice, Philippine Div., 1908-09; adj. 8th Cav., 1910-11; duty Gen. Staff, 1915-17; apptd. comdr. 183d Brigade Inf., 92d Div., Oct. 31, 1917; arrived in France, June 19, 1918; chief of Am. Sect. Inter-Allied Armistice Commn., Dec. 1918-July 1919. Comdr. U.S. Disciplinary Barracks, Ft. Leavenworth, Kan., Sept. 1920-Mar. 1923; brig. gen. U.S. Army, Feb. 9, 1923, comdg. 18th Inf. Brigade, 1923; maj. gen., June 13, 1927; retired, Sept. 3, 1927. Awarded D.S.M., order of the Purple Heart (U.S.). Commander Legion of Honor (French); Comdr. Order of the Bath (British); Comdr. Order of Leopold, and Croix de Guerre (Belgium); Order St. Maurice and St. Lazarus (Italian), Comdr. Mass. Commandery Loyal Legion (also comdr. nat. orgn.). Naval and Mil. Order Spanish-Am. War; mem. S.R., Phi Gamma Delta. Episcopalian. Clubs: Army and Navy (Washington, D.C., Manila, Boston); Phi Gamma Delta (New York); Algonquin; Sankaty Head Golf. Home: 194 St. Paul St., Brookline, Mass. Address: care War Dept., Washington, D.C. Died Feb. 18, 1942.

BARR, George Andrew, lawyer; b. Manhattan, Ill., May 25, 1873; s. George and Jane (McGrath) B.; A.B., U. of Ill., 1897; m. Mary Worrell Speer, Oct. 16, 1902; children—James Worrell, Joseph Milton. In practice of law at Joliet, Ill., mem. Barr & Barr, since 1899; state's atty., Will County, Ill., 1908-12; dir. United Printers & Publishers, Inc., James G. Heggie Mfg. Co., Joliet Wrought Washer Co. Dir. Dept. Trade and Commerce, State of Ill., 1920-22. Chmn. Will County Rep. Central Com., 1912-24; del. to Ill. State Constl. Conv., 1920-22. Trustee Medical Center Commission of Ill. since 1941. Mem. U. of Ill., 1924-36, pres. board, 1930-31. Mem. Am. and Ill. State bar assns., Joliet Chamber Commerce (pres. 1917-19), Shield and Trident, Phi Delta Theta. Presbyterian. Mason (K.T., Shriner), Odd Fellow, K.P., Elk. Clubs: Union League (Chicago); Joliet Country. Home: 106 3d Av. Office: 416 Rialto Sq. Bldg., Joliet, Ill. Died Jan. 26, 1945.

BARR, Robert, author; b. Glasgow, Scotland, Sept. 16, 1850; ed. Normal School, Toronto, Ont.; taught school until 1876, after that on editorial staff Detroit Free Press; writing under pen name, "Luke Sharp"; in England since 1881. Was made chief by an Iroquois tribe in Canada. Author: In a Steamer Chair; From Whose Bourn; The Face and the Mask; Revenge; In the Midst of Alarms; A Woman Intervenes; The Mutable Many; also numerous short stories in Am. and English mags. Address: Hillhead, Woldringham, Surrey, England. Died Oct. 22, 1912.

BARRÈRE, Georges (bär-âr), musician; b. Bordeaux, France, Oct. 31, 1876; s. Gabriel Francois and Marie Périne (Courtet) B.; student Conservatoire Nation of Music, Paris, France (1st prize 1895); m. Cecile Elise Allombert, July 6, 1917; children—Claude and Gabriel Paul (by 1st marriage), Jean Clement (by 2d marriage). Came to U.S., 1905, naturalized citizen, 1931. Began as flutist, 1893; flutist Colonne Orchestra, Paris, 1900-05, Opera National, Paris, 1900-05; teacher Schola Cantorum, Paris, 1899-1905; flutist N.Y. Symphony Orchestra, 1905-28; teacher Inst. of Musical Art, N.Y. City, since 1905, Juilliard Sch. of Music since 1930. Decorated Legion of Honor (French). Club: Century Assn. Home: 54 Riverside Dr. Address: care Arthur Judson, 113 W. 57th St., New York, N.Y. Died June 14, 1944.

BARRETT, Charles D., marine officer; b. Henderson, Ky., Aug. 16, 1885; s. Robert South and Kate (Waller) B.; student Episcopal High Sch., Alexandria, Va., 1901-03; attended field officers course, Marine Corps Schs., Quantico, Va., 1932-33; brevet etat maj., École Supérieure de Guerre, Paris, 1929; m. Emily Hawley Beach Johnson, Mar. 2, 1918; children—Charles Dodson, Constance Cardigan. Commd. 2d lt., U.S. Marine Corps., 1909, 1st lt., 1916, capt., 1916, maj., 1918, lt. col., 1934, col., 1937, brig. general, 1942, major general, Oct. 1943. Received Mexican Service medal, 1914; Victory medal (with Meuse-Argonne clasp), 1918; Expeditionary medal, 1922. Mem. U.S. Naval Inst. (former dir.). Home: 213 S. Pitt St., Alexandria, Va. Office: Headquarters, U.S. Marine Corps, Washington, D.C. Died Oct. 1943.

BARRETT, Darwin Sherwood, Jr., ry. official; b. Cleveland, O., Oct. 16, 1891; s. Darwin Sherwood and May (Twitchell) B.; ed. pub. schs. Cleveland, O.; m. Edna Dueringer, Dec. 4, 1912; children—Darwin Sherwood III, Phyllis Edna, Janet Emily. Began as private sec. to O. P. and M. J. Van Sweringen, 1913, later asst., then asso. and dir. in many cos., including railroad and real estate, owned and controlled by them; v.p. C.&O. Ry. Co., Cleveland, O., since 1938. Home: 2691 Wadsworth Rd. Office: C.&O. Ry. Co., 3500 Terminal Tower, Cleveland, O. Died Feb. 7, 1943.

BARRETT, Don Carlos, economist; b. Spring Valley, O., Apr. 22, 1868; s. I. Merritt and Mary (Evans) B.; A.B., Earlham Coll., Richmond, Ind., 1889, A.M., 1893; A.M., Harvard, 1897, Ph.D., 1901; studied at univs. of Göttingen and Berlin, 1903-04; m. Marcia Frances Moore, Aug. 3, 1892. Prin. in secondary schs., 1889-92; instructor in history and economics, Earlham Coll., 1892-93; instr. in economics, Harvard, 1896-97; instr., later asst. prof. economics, Haverford (Pa.) Coll., 1897-1907, prof., 1907-34, dean of coll., 1904-08, prof. emeritus since 1934; visiting prof. economics, Stanford, 1924, Princeton, 1917-18, 1926-28. Mem. Economists' Nat. Com. on Monetary Policy, Am. Econ. Assn., Am. Acad. Polit. and Social Science, Am. Assn. Univ. Profs., Phi Beta Kappa. Mem. Soc. of Friends. Author: The Greenbacks and Resumption of Specie Payments, 1931. Contbr. to econ. mags. Address: Route 7, Box 490, Indianapolis, Ind. Died Jan. 19, 1943.

BARRETT, John Ignatius, educator; b. Baltimore, Md., Apr. 13, 1884; A.B., Loyola Coll., Baltimore, 1905, A.M., 1915, Ph.D., 1923; A.B., St. Mary's Sem., Baltimore, 1907, S.T.B., 1910; J.C.B., Catholic Univ., 1911, J.C.L., 1912; LL.D., Gonzaga U. 1923. Dir. of Catholic education, Archdiocese of Baltimore, since 1922. Home: 1114 Poplar Grove, Baltimore, Md.* Died June 10, 1944.

BARRETT, Leonard Andrew, clergyman, lecturer; b. Covington, Ky., Nov. 1, 1874; s. Andrew and May (Unsicker) B.; A.B., Centre Coll., Danville, Ky., 1898, D.D., 1921; grad. McCormick Theol. Sem., 1900; m. Nelie Ihrig, of Wooster, O., Oct. 31, 1900; children—Leonard Ihrig, Mrs. Elizabeth May Gould. Ordained Presbyterian ministry, 1900; asst. minister 3d Ch., Chicago, 1900-03; minister Eells Memorial Ch., Cleveland O., 1903-11, First Ch., Ann Arbor, Mich., 1911-24; writing and lecturing since 1924; stated supply 2d Presbyn. Ch., Oak Park, Ill., since 1931-43. Mem. Beta Theta Pi, Alpha Kappa Lambda. Republican. Rotarian. Clubs: Century, Literary (Wooster); University (Chicago and Cleveland). Author: The Essence of Christianity, 1927; also syndicated editorials since 1926. Lectures: The Spirit of Youth; The Soul of a City; Mankind in the Making; The Message of Victor Hugo to the Twentieth Century. Home: 1706 Beall Av., Wooster, O. Died Feb. 27, 1945.

BARRETT, Richard Warren, lawyer; b. Hillsboro, O., July 11, 1872; s. Richard C. and Abi (Johnson) B.; A.B., Earlham Coll., Richmond, Ind., 1897; LL.B., U. of Pa., 1905; unmarried. Admitted to bar, 1905, and began practice at Phila., Pa. Asst. counsel Com. of Seventy, 1905-07; lecturer in Wharton Sch., U. of Pa., 1906-10; police magistrate, Phila., 1909-11; resigned and became connected with Lehigh Valley R.R. as attorney, 1911, asst. gen. solicitor, 1913-20, gen. solicitor, 1920-26, v.p. and gen. counsel, 1927-44, now retired. Republican. Quaker. Clubs: University (Phila.); University, Railroad, Ardsley (New York); Cosmos (Washington, D.C.). Home: 42 W. 58th St. Office: 143 Liberty St., New York, N.Y. Died Sep. 15, 1946.

BARRON, George Davis, mining engr.; b. St. Louis, Mo., Jan. 20, 1860; s. of Samuel and Mary Ann (Williamson) B.; ed. Washington U., St. Louis, Mo.; m. Mrs. Josephine L. (Macy) Chamberlin, Oct. 29, 1918. Mining engr. since 1886; operated and owned important mines and metall. plants in Mexico, principally between 1898 and 1910; now retired. Trustee Village of Rye, 1903-04, United Hosp. of Rye since 1909 (pres. 1911-21); dir. Engring. Foundation of N.Y. Fellow A.A.A.S.; member Am. Inst. Mining and Metallurgical Engineers (treas. 1918-22). Republican. Protestant. Clubs: Union League, Engineers', Apawamis Golf, Blind Brook, American Yacht, Clove Valley Rod and Gun, Onteora, Lake Placid. Home and Office: Rye, N.Y.* Died Apr. 1, 1947.

BARROWS, Edwin Armington, public utility official; b. Providence, R.I., Oct. 8, 1869; s. Edwin and Harriet E. (Armington) B.; A.B., Brown U., 1891; m. Theodora L. Colt, Jan. 17, 1900 (div. 1930); children—Theodora (dec.), Edwin Armington, Barbara DeWolf (dec.); m. 2d, Mrs. Beatrice Binney Richmond, Oct. 7, 1933. With R.I. Hosp. Trust Co., Providence, 1891-1902; nat. bank exam., 1902-04; sec. and treas. Narragansett Electric Lighting Co., 1904-16, pres., 1916-27, v.p., 1927-28, chmn. bd., 1928-35. Now with Littlefield & Co., investment securities. Mem. Psi Upsilon. Republican. Clubs: Agawam, Turks Head. Home: 4 John St., Providence 6. Office: Hospital Trust Bldg., Providence 3, R.I. Died Apr. 18, 1948.

BARROWS, Nat(haniel) A(lbert), newspaperman; b. Rochester, Mass., Mar. 14, 1905; s. Hiram and Lucy (Dunham) B.; grad. Boston English High Sch., 1923; student Harvard, 1929-31; m. Dorothea Whittier, Sept. 23, 1939; 1 son, Richard Nathaniel Whittier. Reporter, rewrite man, feature writer, Latin Am. writer, Boston Globe, 1925-41; joined Chicago Daily News Fgn. Service, Dec. 1941, assigned to Northern Latin Am. and Caribbean, 1941-42, Britain, 1942-43, Sweden and Finland, 1943-45; covered Potsdam Conf., Berlin, 1945; postwar fgn. corr. in Holland, France, Germany, Britain, Scandanavia, Middle East; U.N. corr. since Jan. 1946. Wounded by German dive-bombers at Finnish front in Lapland, 1944. Recipient Sigma Delta Chi award for distinguished service in fgn. correspondence, 1949. Mem. U.N. Correspondents Assn. (sec. 1948-49). Ind. Republican. Episcopalian. Club: Overseas Press of Am. Author: Blow All Ballast, the Story of the Squalus, 1940. Home: 29-65 162d St., Flushing, L.I., N.Y. Died in plane crash, India, July 1949.

BARROWS, Stanley Hill, mfr. chemicals and refractories; b. Chicago, Ill., Aug. 11, 1883; s. George Groves and Martha Wayne (Thompson) B.; ed. grammar schs. and business coll.; m. Frances Stehlin, Apr. 26, 1904; children—Louise Hill, Marcia Josephine, George Groves, II. Lumber buyer, 1902-06, pres. Park Ridge (Ill.) Lumber & Coal Co., 1906-14, Park Ridge State Bank, 1908-26, Barrows Lumber Co. (East St. Louis, Ill.), 1918-26; chmn. bd. Nat. Kellastone Co.; pres. Calif. Chem. Corp., Sierra Magnesite Co., Industrial Chem. Corp. of Del., Industrial Chem. Co. of Calif., Chem. Reduction Co.; dir. Lake Shore Trust & Savings Bank (Chicago), Great Northern Ins. Co. Clubs: Bohemian, San Francisco Golf, San Francisco Yacht, St. Francis Yacht; Alverada Gun (Calif.); La Cumbre Country (Santa Barbara); Grand Island Lodge (Bath, Ill.); Chicago Athletic Assn. Home: Pinebrook Acres, Carson City, Nev. Address: Calif. Chemical Co., Newark, Calif.; and Chrysler Bldg., New York, N.Y. Died 1949.

BARROWS, William Morton, zoölogy; b. Rochester, N.Y., Apr. 7, 1883; s. Walter Bradford and Lizzie Maud (Withall) B.; B.S., Mich. State Coll., 1903; B.S., Harvard, 1905, M.S., 1906, Sc.D., 1920; m. Eleanor S. Burton, June 25, 1908; children—William Morton, Arthur Burton. Prof. science, Manchester Coll., North Manchester, Ind., 1906-07; instr. in zoölogy, N.H. State Coll., Durham, 1907-09; with Ohio State U., since 1909, prof. zoölogy and entomology since 1923. Mem. A.A.A.S., Am. Soc. Zoölogists. Author: Science of Animal Life, 1927; Laboratory Exercises in Zoölogy, 1930. Contbr. many articles to scientific publs. Home: 123 Clinton St., Columbus, O. Died Feb. 24, 1946.

BARRY, Herbert, lawyer; b. Wilmington, N.C., Feb. 25, 1867; s. Maj. (U.S. Army) Robert Peabody and Julia Kean (Neilson) B.; prep. edn. various private schs.; B.L., U. of Va., 1888; m. Ethel M. Dawson, Feb. 16, 1898; children—Herbert, Eleanor, Stuyvesant. Admitted to Va. bar, 1888, N.Y. bar, 1890; mem. firm Davies, Auerbach, Cornell & Barry, 1897-1913; sr. partner, Barry, Wainwright, Thacher & Symmers since 1913. Mem. Troop A, later Squadron A, N.G.N.Y., 1891-1908; capt., 1900-08, and mem. Gov. Hughes' staff; maj. Squadron A Cav., N.Y.G., Dec. 1917; commd. maj. inf. U.S. Army, May 1918; served overseas, May 1918-June 1919; hon. discharged, July 1919; subsequently commd. lt. col. 302d Regiment Cav., O.R.C., 1923, retired, 1931, with rank of col. Pres. Bd. of Edn., West Orange, for many yrs. Mem. Am. Bar Assn., Assn. Bar City of New York, New York County Bar Assn., N.Y. State Bar Assn., S.R., Soc. Colonial Wars, and other patriotic and civic bodies; former gov. The Virginians of N.Y. City; former pres. Ex-members Assn. of Squadron A. Republican. Episcopalian. Clubs: University, Downtown, Rock Spring Club. Contributed to Virginia Law Review, papers on many subjects published in each year, 1923-37, later compiled under title Viewed with Detachment; also articles to mags. Compiled History of First Fifty Years of Squadron A (pub. by Assn. of Ex-Mems. of Squadron A). Home: Llewellyn Park, West Orange, N.J. Office: 72 Wall St., New York, N.Y. Died June 19, 1947.

BARRY, John Daniel, journalist, author; b. Boston, Dec. 31, 1866; A.B., Harvard, 1888. Devoted to journalism, writing novels and plays and lecturing on social and lit. subjects; wrote daily essay for San Francisco Bulletin, 1910-18, for San Francisco Call, 1918-26, for San Francisco News since 1926. Author: The Princess Margarethe; The Intriguers; Mademoiselle Blanche; A Daughter of Thespis; The Congressman's Wife; Our Best Society; Intimations (essays); Outlines (short stories); The City of Domes (an illustrated description of the Panama-Pacific Expn.); The Meaning of the Exposition; The Palace of Fine Arts and the French and Italian Pavilions; Reactions (essays); The Dilemma (drama). Contbr. to mags. Address: The News, San Francisco, Calif. Died Nov. 3, 1942.

BARRY, Philip, dramatist; b. Rochester, N.Y., June 18, 1896; s. James Corbett and Mary Agnes (Quinn) B.; A.B., Yale, 1919; Harvard, 1919-22; m. Ellen Semple, July 15, 1922; children—Philip Semple, Jonathan Peter. With Code Dept., Am. Embassy, London, England, May 1918-Feb. 1919. Mem. Nat. Institute Arts and Letters, Philadelphia Art Alliance, American Soc. Dramatists, Authors League America, Dramatists Guild, Alpha Delta Phi. Clubs: Yale, University, Century, Coffee House, River (New York City); National Golf (Southampton); Maidstone (East Hampton). Roman Catholic. Author: You and I (3-act comedy), 1922; The Youngest (3-act comedy), 1924; In a Garden (3-act play), 1925; White Wings (3-act comedy), 1926; John (5-act play), 1927; Paris Bound (3-act comedy), 1927; Cock Robin (3-act play in collaboration with Elmer L. Rice), 1928; Holiday (3-act comedy), 1929; Hotel Universe (1-act play), 1930; Tomorrow and Tomorrow (3-act play), 1931; The Animal Kingdom (3-act comedy), 1932; The Joyous Season (3-act comedy), 1933; Bright Star (3-act play), 1935; Here Come the Clowns (2-act play), 1938; Spring Dance (3-act comedy), 1936; War in Heaven (book), 1938; The Philadelphia Story (3-act play), 1939; Liberty Jones (3-act play), 1940; Without Love (3-act play), 1942; Foolish Notion (3-act play), 1944. Home: Jupiter Island, Hobe Sound, Fla.; (summer) "Still Pond," East Hampton, L.I., N.Y. Died Nov. 3, 1949.

BARRY, William Bernard, congressman; b. Ireland, 1902; s. Thomas J. and Catherine J. (Hennelly) B.; B.C.S., N.Y. Univ., 1925, LL.B., 1929; m. Emily B. La Mude, Feb. 7, 1934; children—Jane, Brian. Came to U.S., 1907, naturalized through father becoming citizen, 1912. Admitted to N.Y. bar, 1929, and practiced in N.Y. City; law clk., 1926-30; partner Keith, Wilson & Barry, 1930-32; asst. dist. atty. Queens County, N.Y., 1932-33; spl. U.S. atty. for Dept. of Justice, 1933-35; elected to 74th Congress, Nov. 5, 1935, 2d N.Y. Dist., to fill vacancy caused by resignation of W. F. Brunner, reelected 75th to 78th Congresses (1937-45), 2d N.Y. Dist. Mem. Queens County Dem. Exec. Com., 1930-36. Mem. Delta Phi Epsilon, Theta Chi. Catholic. Elk. Home: St. Albans, L.I., N.Y. Office: 163-18 Jamaica Av., Jamaica, L.I., N.Y.* Died Oct. 20, 1946.

BARRYMORE, John, actor; b. Feb. 15, 1882; s. late Maurice Barrymore (Herbert Blythe) and Georgiana (Drew) B.; m. Katherine Corri Harris, 1910; m. 2d, Mrs. Leonard M. Thomas, Aug. 5, 1920; 1 dau., Diana; m. 3d, Dolores Costello, Nov. 24, 1928 (div.); children—Dolores Ethel Mae, John Blythe, Jr.; m. 4th, Elaine Barrie Jacobs, Nov. 9, 1936 (div. Nov. 1940). Début as Max, in "Magda," Chicago, Oct. 1903; and in New York, as Corley, in "Glad of It," December following; played in London in "The Dictator," 1905, and later in Australia, in the company of William Collier; toured in "The Boys of Company B"; played Lord Meadows in "Toddles," 1908; appeared at Chicago as Mac, in "A Stubborn Cinderella," and later at Broadway Theatre, New York, in same part; played Nathaniel Duncan, in "The Fortune Hunter," Robert Hudson, in "Uncle Sam," Pete, in "Princess Zim Zim"; starred in "Are You a Mason?", "Half a Husband," "Thief in the Night," "Peter Ibbetsen," "My Dear Children," etc.; as co-star with brother Lionel, scored great success in "The Jest"; appeared as Richard III, 1920. A leading man in moving pictures, among them "The Dictator," "Sherlock Holmes," "The Test of Honor," etc.; played "Hamlet" in New York and London, 1924-25; recently starred in motion pictures, The Sea Beast, Beau Brummel, Don Juan, Bill of Divorcement, Reunion in Vienna, Counsellor-at-Law, etc. Home: 6 Tower Rd., Beverly Hills, Calif. Died May 29, 1942.

BARSTOW, William Slocum, elec. engr.; b. Brooklyn, N.Y., Feb. 15, 1866; s. Frank D. and Mary (Slocum) B.; A.B., Columbia, 1887; hon. Dr. Engring., Stevens Inst. Tech.; hon. Dr.Sc., Columbia; m. Françoise M. Duclos, Oct. 4, 1894; 1 son, Frederic D. With Edison Machine Works, Schenectady, N.Y., Paterson, N.J., New York and Brooklyn, 1887-89; asst. supt., 1889-90, gen. supt. and chief engr., 1890-97, gen. mgr., 1897-1901, Edison Electric Illuminating Co., Brooklyn; cons. elec. engr., 1901-06; practiced as W. S. Barstow & Co., Inc., 1906-12; organizer, 1912, Gen. Gas & Electric Corp. and pres. until 1929; now senior partner Barstow, Campbell & Co.; pres. Thomas Alva Edison Foundation, Inc. Trustee Stevens Inst. Tech. Fellow Am. Inst. Elec. Engineers; mem. Elec. Soc. (ex-pres.), Illuminating Engring. Soc., Edison Pioneers (pres. 8 yrs., then hon. pres.), Am. Electro-chemists Soc., United Engring. Societies (library bd.; mem. exec. com.). Clubs: Columbia University, Lawyers, Engineers, University, Delta Upsilon, N. Hempstead Country, Manhasset Bay Yacht, New York Yacht; Everglades, Boca Raton, Seminole, Sailfish Club of Florida, Hobe Sound Yacht (commodore). Home: Great Neck, N.Y. Office: 70 Pine St., New York. Died Dec. 26, 1942.

BARTH, Charles H., Jr., Army officer; born Kan., Oct. 1, 1903; B.S., U.S. Mil. Acad., 1925; grad. Civil Engring. Cornell U., 1927; commd. 2d lt. Corps of Engrs., 1925, and advanced to brig. gen., 1943; served as chief of staff to comdg. gen. U.S. Forces in Iceland, 1943; killed in airplane crash, Iceland, May 3, 1943.

BARTHOLOMEW, Charles L. ("Bart") (bär-thŏl′ ŏ-mū), cartoonist; b. Chariton, Ia., Feb. 10, 1869; s. Col. O. A. and Mary (Smith) B.; B.S., Ia. State Coll., Ames, 1888; m. Ella L. Henderson, June 17, 1890. Reporter on editorial staff and cartoonist for Minnesota newspapers and nat. syndicates, 1888-1940; now dean School of Illustrating and Cartooning, Art Instruction, Incorporated, Minneapolis, Minn. Cartoons have been extensively used in magazines and reviews in America and in Europe. Illustrator of Children's books; Bandit Mouse, Paddle Fleet People, Alphabetic Mother Goose, Natural History Stories, Funny Adventures of Captain Pipp et al, Gopher Calendar, Pirate Frog, Puggery Wee, 1900-10; Bart's Cartoons (10 vols.), 1894-1905. Author of Bart Chalk Talk System, and Crayon Presentation. Editor of 12 textbooks on illustrating and cartooning; creative artist lecturer U. of Minn. and Assn. Am. Agrl. Coll. Editors; cartoon headings on farm data for Cornell U. and univs. of Minn., N.C., W.Va., etc. Home: 6600 Irving Av. S. Office: 500 S. 4th St., Minneapolis 15, Minn. Died Feb. 15, 1949.

BARTHOLOMEW, Edward Fry, college prof.; b. Sunbury, Pa., Mar. 24, 1846; s. William and Susanna Elizabeth (Wolf) B.; A.B., Pa. Coll., Gettysburg, Pa., 1871, A.M., 1882; U. of Berlin, 1894-95; Ph.D., Augustana Coll., 1896; L.H.D., Carthage College, 1911, and D.D., 1888; also LL.D. from Carthage College, 1930; m. Catherine L. Fasold, July 11, 1872; children—Mrs. Netta Cordelia Anderson, Frank Rollin (dec.), Cotta, George Edward, Paul Fasold. Ordained Lutheran ministry, 1875; prin. Kahoka High Sch., Mo., 1872-73; prof. natural sciences, Carthage Coll., 1874-83; prof. English lit., Mt. Morris Coll., Ill., 1883-84; pres. Carthage Coll., Ill., 1884-88; prof. English lit. and philosophy, Augustana Coll., since 1888. V.p. Augustana Coll. and Theol. Sem., 1911-19. Editor The Musical Profession, 1905. Pres. Internat. Soc. Pianoforte Teachers and Players, 1901-05. Author: Outlines of English Literature, 1897; The Relation of Psychology to Music, 1899; Christ the Discoverer of the Individual, 1902; Head, Heart and Hand, 1903; The Economy of Power, 1904; Rational Musical Pedagogy, 1905; Psychology of Prayer, 1922; Biblical Pedagogy, 1927. Contbr. to mags. on lit., philos. and mus. subjects. Home: Rock Island, Ill. Died June 11, 1946.

BARTHOLOMEW, William Henry, educator; b. Louisville, Ky., July 26, 1840; s. Peter Hiawatha and Rebecca (Coons) B.; ed. pub. and pvt. schs., Louisville; LL.D., State U. of Ky., 1902; m. Susan Agnes Johnston, Mar. 20, 1862 (died Oct. 27, 1918); children—Benjamin Gray, Mrs. Mildred Tingley Ramsey, William Henry, Susan Mills. Began as teacher in pub. schs., Louisville, 1858, continuing as teacher and prin. 53 yrs.; prin. Girls' High Sch., 1881-1911. Ex-pres. So. Ednl. Assn., Ky. Ednl. Assn., Louisville Ednl. Assn.; made life mem. N.E.A. by teachers of Louisville, 1877, and now serving 4th term (24 yrs.) as mem. Nat. Council same. Mem. bd. Free Pub. Library, Ky., Inst. for the Blind. Pres. dirs. Christian Ch. Widows and Orphans' Home of Ky.; life mem. Ky. Exec. Com. S. S. Assn.; elder Broadway Christian Ch., Louisville. Mason (33°). Past Comdr. De Molay Commandery, K.T.; Past Grand Patron Grand Chapter Order Eastern Star of Ky.; editor O.E.S. column, Masonic Home Journal; Past Patriarch, I.O.O.F. Clubs: University, Filson. Speaker and writer on lit., scientific and ethical subjects. Mem. State Bd. of Edn. of Ky. for 20 consecutive yrs.; ordained minister of Christian Ch. Author: History of De Molay Commandery No. 12, K.T. and History of the Broadway Christian Church. Home: 426 E. Gray St. Office: City Comptroller's Office, Louisville. Died Jan. 19, 1927.

BARTLETT, Frederic Huntington, physician; b. Fayetteville, N.Y., July 3, 1872; s. Delancey and Almeria (Farnham) B.; A.B., Harvard, 1895; A.M., Columbia, 1899, M.D., 1905; m. Eleanor Pearson, June 1902; children—Phyllis Brooks (Mrs. John Pollard), Frederic Pearson; m. 2d, Isabelle Reid Woolley, Sept. 11, 1923. Teacher of English, Pomfret (Conn.) Sch., 1895-97, Belmont Sch., 1899-1900, Stanford U., 1900-01; engaged in practice of medicine since 1907; associated with Dr. L. Emmett Holt, 1907-11; attending physician, Babies Hosp., New York, N.Y., 1909-23; chief of pediatrics, Fifth Av. Hosp., 1923-34, attending physician Babies Hosp., since 1934. Served as major, Med. Corps, U.S. Army, 1917-19; medical chief, base hospital, Camp Jackson, S.C. Mem. Am. Pediatric Soc., N.Y. Acad. of Medicine, Am. Med. Assn., N.Y. State and County med. socs. Clubs: Harvard, Century Association (New York). Author: Treatment of Internal Diseases (translation of Nicholas Ortner), 1908; Infants and Children: Their Care and Feeding, 1933. Home: 26 Jones St. Office: 115 E. 82d St., New York, N.Y. Died Oct. 19, 1948.

BARTLETT, George True, army officer; b. N.H., Apr. 29, 1856; s. Thomas and Elizabeth W. (Titcomb) B.; student U. of Kans.; B.S., U.S. Mil. Acad., 1881; grad. Arty. Sch., 1890; m. Cornelia Terrell, Sept. 18, 1884 (died Feb. 14, 1888); children—Charles Terrell, Geoffrey; m. 2d, Helen Walton, Nov. 28, 1893 (died Dec. 26, 1940). Commd. 2d lt. 3d Arty., June 11, 1881, advanced through grades to maj. gen., 1917; 1st lt., Dec. 10, 1889; maj. commissary of subsistence, vols., June 3, 1898; hon. discharged vols., June 13, 1899; capt. arty., Mar. 2, 1899; maj. Arty. Corps, Mar. 26, 1906; lt. col. Coast Arty. Corps, Dec. 4, 1909; col., Dec. 5, 1911; brig. gen., May 15, 1917; maj. gen. N.A., Aug. 5, 1917; Prof. mil. science and tactics, Pa. Mil. Coll., 1885-88, and Agrl. and Mech. Coll., Tex., 1894-98; chief commissary, Dept. of Santiago, Cuba, 1898; adj. Arty. Sch., Ft. Monroe, Va., 1903-06; mem. bd. to revise drill regulations for Coast Arty., 1902-06; mem. Gen. Staff Corps, Dec. 10, 1909-Dec. 20, 1911, and July 10, 1916-June 22, 1917; hon. discharged from N.A. Mar. 26, 1918; retired at his own request after more than 40 years' service, Sept. 25, 1918. Served in World War as comdr. brigade Railroad Arty., A.E.F., July 12-Sept. 8, 1917; comdr. Base Sect. No. 3, A.E.F., in France, Oct. 7, 1917-Mar. 22, 1918. Mem. Interallied Mil. Commn., in Greece, Apr. 21, 1917-Nov. 8, 1918; mil. attaché at Athens, Mar. 22-Oct 21, 1918; retired 1918. Republican. Episcopalian. Home: Terrell Rd., San Antonio, Tex. Died March 11, 1949.

BARTLETT, John Pomeroy, patent lawyer; b. Collinsville (Canton), Conn., June 4, 1858; s. John N. and Ellen Root (Strong) B.; Ph.B., Sheffield Scientific Sch. (Yale), 1878; LL.B., Yale Law Sch., 1881; m. Eleanor Pauline Fitch, May 19, 1885; children—Margaret K. (Mrs. Robert McArdle), Eleanor (Mrs. Wm. C. Skinner). Gen. practice, New Britain, Conn.; then specialized in patents, trademarks and copyrights, firm of Mitchell, Hungerford & Bartlett; corp. counsel New Britain, 1896-97; removed to New York, 1897; firm of Mitchell, Bartlett & Brownell, now Bartlett, Eyre, Keel & Weymouth. Mem. Am. Bar Assn., A.A.A.S., New York Bar Assn., New York County Bar Assn., Bar of U.S. Supreme Court, New York Patent Law Assn. (pres. 1926-27), Am. Patent Law Assn. (pres.), Berzelius Soc. (Yale), N.E. Soc., Empire State br. S.A.R. Republican. Episcopalian. Clubs: University, Yale, Cosmos (Washington, D.C.). Home: 42 W. 58th St. Office: 36 W. 44th St., New York, N.Y. Died March 3, 1948.

BARTLETT, John Thomas, author; b. Raymond, N.H., Jan. 15, 1892; s. John Thomas and Emma Louise (Tucker) B.; direct desc. Govs. John Winthrop and Thomas Dudley; grad. Pinkerton Acad., Derry, 1910; student Middlebury (Vt.) Coll., 1910-11; m. Margaret M. Abbott, Sept. 7, 1912; children—Forrest Abbott, John Thomas, Richard Adams, Margaret Emily. Began as reporter News-Advertiser, Vancouver, B.C., 1912; investigator and writer for agrl. press, New Eng., 1915-17, Colo., 1917-19; business research since 1919; editor Bartlett Service (nat. editorial service for business papers, conducted in partnership with wife, Margaret A. Bartlett) since 1921; co-publisher The Author and Journalist, Denver, since 1928; co-publisher Boulder Daily Doings since 1930. Sec. Mountain States compliance com., Retail Farm Equipment Code, 1934-35; Rep. congl. chmn., 2d Dist. of Colorado, 1940-46; delegate to 1944 Republican National Convention. Mem. Boulder C. of C. (president 1939), Colorado Authors' League (pres. 1936), Mountain States Hardware and Implement Assn. (sec. since 1930). Republican. Conglist. Clubs: Rotary, Town and Gown. Author: (with Charles M. Reed) Retail Credit Practice, 1928; (with same) Credit Department Salesmanship, 1932; (with same) Methods of Instalment Selling and Collection, 1934. Has specialized in legislative, tax and public relations problems of Am., business, contbg. several hundred articles to nat. business mags. Home: 637 Pine St., Boulder, Colo. Died Jan. 23, 1947.

BARTLETT, Maitland, clergyman; b. Milwaukee, Wis., Nov. 8, 1869; s. Francis Wayland and Mary Jane (Stewart) B.; prep. edn., Macalester Prep. Sch., 1888; A.B., Princeton U., 1891, A.M., 1895; student Princeton Theol. Sem., 1895, Erlanger U., 1896; Berlin U., 1897; unmarried. Ordained ministry Presbyn. Ch. in U.S.A., 1896; pastor Stella Ch., Wilkes-Barre, Pa., 1896-99; asst. Pastor First Ch., Princeton, N.J., 1899-1900; stated supply First Ch., Princeton, N.J., 1900-06, Laurel Springs, N.J., 1906-07; pastor Beck Memorial Ch., N.Y. City, 1906-29; travel in Europe, 1929-32; stated clerk Presbytery of New York, 1932. Served with Y.M.C.A. in France during World War, 1917-18. Director or trustee many coms. and ch. orgns. Republican. Clubs: Princeton Club, Century, Listeners. Home: 77 Christopher St. Office: 156 Fifth Av., New York. Died Jan., 1944.

BARTLETT, Murray, college pres.; b. Poughkeepsie, N.Y., Mar. 29, 1871; s. Stanley and Lida Carolina (Simpson) B.; B.A., Harvard, 1892, M.A., 1893; grad. Gen. Theol. Sem., 1896; D.D., U. of Rochester, 1908; LL.D., Trinity Coll., 1922; S.T.D., Gen. Theol. Sem., 1926; Columbia, 1928; L.H.D., Hobart, 1937; m. Blanchard Howard, Apr. 15, 1903; 1 dau., Blanchard. Curate Grace Ch., N.Y. City, 1896-97; rector St. Paul's Ch., Rochester, N.Y., 1897-1908; dean, Cathedral of St. Mary and St. John, Manila, 1908-11; mem. bd. regents U. of Philippines; 1st pres., and organizer U. of Philippines, 1911-15 (1200 students and 7 schs.); founder of the Grad. Sch. of Tropical Medicine and Public Health; pres. Hobart and William Smith colls., Geneva, N.Y., 1919-36; trustee Geneva Savings Bank. Mem. Selective Service Board 518, Geneva, N.Y., since 1940. Rep. P.E. Ch. War Commn., Camp Kearney, Calif., 1917; overseas sec. Y.M.C.A., 1917; apptd. hon. chaplain 18th Inf., 1918, serving until Mar. 1919; wounded in Marne-Aisne offensive, July 22, 1918; maj. Chaplains Reserve, Nov. 28, 1922, lt. col., Aug. 1, 1931. Awarded D.S.C. (U.S.); Croix de Guerre and Chevalier Legion of Honor (French). Pres. Middle States Assn. of Colls. and Prep. Schs., 1930-31. Fellow A.A.A.S.; member Acad. Political Science, N.Y. State Hist. Soc., Soc. 1st Div. A.E.F. (life), Phi Beta Kappa. Democrat. Mason (33°). Harvard (New York); University, Seneca Yacht (Geneva, N.Y.). Home: 90 Jay St., Geneva, N.Y. Died Nov. 13, 1949.

BARTLETT, Robert Abram, explorer; b. Brigus, Newfoundland, Aug. 15, 1875; s. William James and Mary J. (Leamon) B.; ed. Brigus High Sch., and Meth. Coll., St. Johns, Newfoundland; passed exam. for Master of British Ships, Halifax, N.S., 1905; hon. A.M., Bowdoin Coll., 1920; unmarried. Began explorations wintering with R. E. Peary, at Cape D'Urville, Kane Basin, 1897-98; on a hunting expdn., Hudson Strait and Bay, 1901; capt. of a sealer off Newfoundland coast, 1901-05; comd. the Roosevelt, 1905-09, taking active part in Peary's expdn. to the pole, reaching 88th parallel; comd. ship on pvt. hunting expdn. to Kane Basin, 1910; with Can. Govt. Arctic Expedition, 1913-14, as captain of the C.G.S. Karluk, which was crushed by ice, Jan. 1914; with 17 persons reached Wrangel Island; leaving 15 persons on island, with one Eskimo crossed ice to Siberia and returned with rescuing party, reaching Wrangel Island in Sept. 1914, and Sept. 12, 1915, reached Nome, Alaska, with 13 survivors. Cmdr. 3d Crocker Land Relief Expdn. to N. Greenland, returning with party, 1917; marine supt. Army Transport Service, New York, since Oct. 1917. Was sent, 1925, by Nat. Geog. Soc. to locate bases for aircraft, N.W. Alaska, and shores Arctic Ocean, also recording times and currents and dredging for flora and fauna. Expdn. to North Greenland and Ellesmere Land, 1926, to Fox Basin and West Shores Baffin Land, 1927, to Siberia, 1928, to Labrador, summer 1929, head of expdn. to N.E. coast of Greenland for Mus. of Am. Indian and Mus. of Natural History of Phila., 1930, expdn. to Greenland for Am. Mus. Natural History, Bot. Gardens of N.Y. City and Smithsonian Instn. (Washington), 1931, to N.W. Greenland (erecting monument in memory of Admiral R. E. Peary), 1932, to Baffin Land, 1933, to N.W. Greenland, Ellesmere and Baffin Lands, under auspices of Acad. of Natural Sciences of Phila., 1934, to N.W. Greenland under auspices of Field Scientific research in Eastern Arctic, 1936-41; in government service, Hudson Bay, Baffin Land and Greenland (on own schooner Morrissey), 1942-44. Awarded Hubbard gold medal, National Geographic Society, 1909; Hudson-Fulton silver medal, 1909; silver medal, English Geog. Soc., 1910; Kane medal, Phila. Geog. Soc., 1910; silver medal, Italian Geog. Soc., 1910; gold medal, Harvard Travelers Club, 1915; awarded the Back Grant, Royal Geog. Soc., 1918, "in recognition of splendid leadership after the 'Karluk' was lost"; gold medal Am. Geog. Soc. Hon. mem. "Society of Dorset Men in London," England, Boy Scouts of America; life mem. Am. Mus. Natural History; mem. Marine Soc. (New York), Am. Geophys. Union, Am. Legion, Vets. Fgn. Wars, New York Garrison 194, Army and Navy Union of U.S.A.; corr. mem. Am. Geog. Soc. Confirmed rank of lt. comdr. U.S. N.R.F., 1920. Mason. Clubs: City, Travelers' (Boston); Ends of the Earth, Explorers', Travel, Aero of America, Cruising of America, Coffee House (New York); Wilderness, Boone and Crockett. Author: Last Voyage of the Karluk, 1916; The Log of Bob Bartlett, 1928; Sails over Ice, 1934. Home: Brigus, Newfoundland. Address: Explorers' Club, 10 W. 72d St., New York, N.Y. Died Apr. 28, 1946.

BARTON, Arthur James, minister, publicist; b. nr. Jonesboro, Ark., Feb. 2, 1867; s. William H. and Eliza M. (Morgan) B.; ed. Southwestern Bapt. U. (now Union U.), Jackson, Tenn., 1886-91, A.B. (conferred later), D.D., 1897; D.D., Baylor, 1903; LL.D., from Union, 1927; m. Georgia May Jones, Dec. 27, 1893; 5 children—Landis (Mrs. Jno. D. Freeman), Rev. W. Henderson, 3 died in infancy. Ordained Baptist ministry, 1888; prin. Gadsden (Tennessee) Male and Female Academy, 1891-92; pres. Lexington (Tenn.) Baptist Coll., 1892-94; pastor village chs. to 1894, Edgefield Ch., Nashville, Tenn., 1894-96; asst. corr. sec. Foreign Mission Board Southern Bapt. Convention and editor Foreign Mission Jour., 1896-99; corr. sec. Mission Bd., Ark. Bapt. State Conv., 1900-02; a founder and editor Bapt. Advance, Little Rock, 1902-04; field sec. Home Mission Bd., Southern Bapt. Conv., 1904-05; pastor Beech St. Ch., Texarkana, Ark., 1906-07, 1st Ch., Waco, Tex., 1907-09; corr. sec. Edn. Bd., Bapt. Gen. Conv. of Tex., 1909-14; pastor Emmanuel Ch., Alexandria, La., Oct. 1918-21; founder and pastor Cavalry Ch., Alexandria, 1921-24; supt. Mo. Bapt. Gen. Assn., 1924-26; gen. dir. Cooperative Program Southern Bapt. Conv., 1926-27; v.p. Southern Bapt. Conv., 1932; chmn. exec. com. Nat. Conf., Washington, Dec. 1911, which framed Sheppard-Kenyon Bill as to inter-state shipments of liquor (same in substance as Webb Bill) and pres. 2d Nat. Conf. to promote this legislation; official del. U.S. Govt. to Internat. Conf. Against Alcoholism, Milan, Italy, Sept. 1913; chmn. Nat. Conf. Washington, July 1915, on wording of Sheppard-Hobson Resolution for Prohibition Amendment to Fed. Constn., and chmn. Nat. Prohibition Constl. Commn. Mem. Southern Sociol. Congress (com. on race econ. progress); official del. U.S. Govt. to 16th Internat. Congress Against Alcoholism, Lausanne, Switzerland, Aug. 22-27, 1921; supt. Anti-Saloon League of Tex. and editor Home and State, 1915-18; chmn. Commn. on Social Service of Southern Bapt. Conv.; member Nat. Exec. Com. and Nat. Legislative Com. Anti-Saloon League America since 1913 (chmn. Nat. Exec. Com. 1924-34), pres. Nat. Conf. of Orgns. Supporting the Eighteenth Amendment, 1929-32; mem. exec. com. Nat. Temperance Council; mem. Nat. Council Boy Scouts of America; mem. Clergymen's Advisory Bd. of World Alliance for Internat. Friendship Through the Chs.; supt. dept. ch. extension, Home Mission Bd., Southern Bapt. Conv., 1927-30; pastor Temple Bapt. Ch., Wilmington, N.C., since 1930. Address: 1810 Market St., Wilmington, N.C. Died July 19, 1942.

BARTON, George Aaron, univ. prof., author, clergyman; b. Farnham, Province of Quebec, Can., Nov. 12, 1859; s. Daniel and Mary Stevens (Bull) B.; A.B., Haverford Coll., 1882, A.M., 1885; A.M., Harvard, 1890, Ph.D., 1891; LL.D., Haverford Coll., 1914; S.T.D., Trinity, 1924; m. Caroline Brewer Danforth, June 26, 1884 (died May 30, 1930); 1 dau., Rhoda Caroline (adopted); m. 2d, Katherine Blye Hagy, June 6, 1931. Teacher, mathematics and classics, Friends' Sch., Providence, 1884-89; lecturer Haverford Coll., 1891-95; prof. Bibl. lit. and Semitic langs., Bryn Mawr Coll., 1891-1922; prof., Semitic langs., and history of religion, Univ. of Pa., 1922-32, prof. emeritus since 1932; prof., N. Test. lit. and lang., Divinity Sch., P.E. Ch., Phila., 1921-37, prof. emeritus since 1937. Acknowledged minister, Soc. of Friends (Orthodox), 1879-1918; deacon, 1918; priest, 1919, P.E. Ch. Dir. Am. Sch. Oriental Research in Baghdad, 1921-34; sec. and treas., Am. Schools of Oriental Research, 1918-34. President Society Bibl. Literature and Exegesis, 1913-14; president American Oriental Society, 1916-17; pres., Phila. Soc. Archæol. Inst. of America, 1916-25. Mem. Am. Philos. Soc., Phi Beta Kappa. Asso. Victoria Inst. of Great Britain. Fellow Society of Arts, London; fellow Mitglied der Orient Gesellschaft, Mitglied der deutsche Morganlanden Gesellschaft, Berlin; also fellow A.A.A.S.; mem. Harvard Bibl. Club; Phila. Oriental Club. Author: A Sketch of Semitic Origins, Social and Religious, 1902; Roots of Christian Teaching as Found in the Old Testament, 1902; A Year's Wandering in Bible Lands, 1904, The Haverford Library Collection of Cuneiform Tablets, or Documents from the Temple Archives of Telloh, Part I, 1905, Part II, 1909, Part III, 1914; Ecclesiastes in the International Critical Commentary, 1908; The Heart of the Christian Message, 1910, 2d edit., 1912; Commentary on Job in the Bible for Home and School, 1911; The Origin and Development of Babylonian Writing, 1913; Sumerian Business and Administrative Documents from the Earliest Times to the Dynasty of Agade, 1915; Archæology and the Bible, 1916, 7th edit., 1937; Religions of the World, 1917, 4th edit., 1937; Miscellaneous Babylonian Inscriptions, Part I, Sumerian Religious Texts, 1918; The Religion of Israel, 1918, 2d edit., 1928; Jesus of Nazareth, a Biography, 1922; (translations in Japanese and Korean, 1938); Hittite Studies No. 1, 1928, No. 2, 1932; Studies in New Testament Christianity, 1928; The Royal Inscriptions of Sumer and Akkad, 1929; A History of the Hebrew People, 1930; Semitic and Hamitic Origins, Social and Religious, 1934; Christ and Evolution, 1934; The Apostolic Age and the New Testament, 1936. Contbr. various articles to learned journals; also to Ency. of Religion and Ethics, Jewish Ency., Dictionary of Am. Biography. Home: (winter) 3610 Royal Palm Av., Coconut Grove, Fla.; (summer) Weston, Mass. Died June 28, 1942.

BARTON, Ralph Martin, golf architect; b. Newport, N.H., July 21, 1875; s. Charles Wilson and Ida Eldora (Walker) B.; prep. edn., Phillips Andover Acad., 1892-96; A.B., Dartmouth Coll., 1904; grad. work Harvard, 1907-08, U. of Chicago, 1910-12; m. Verna C. Cate, Sept. 1899; 1 dau., Ruth Verna (Mrs. Kenneth R. Spaulding); m. 2d, Elizabeth E. Spofford, July 1908; m. 3d, Anna Niergarth, June 1935. Instr. in mathematics, later asst. prof., Dartmouth Coll., 1903-12; dean of civil engring. and prof. of mathematics, U. of N.M., 1912-13; prof. of mathematics, later dean and acting pres. Lombard Coll., 1913-16; asst. prof. in mathematics, U. of Minn., 1916-21; golf architect since 1921; supervising architect and supt. of constrn. Furness Withy Co., Bermuda, 1921-22, Yale Univ. Athletic Assn., 1924-25; also architect Laconia, McKenzie, Lancaster, Pecketts, Greenfield, Dartmouth Coll., Giant Valley, Wilmington, Concord, Babson Park, Newport, Plymouth, Ammonoosuc, Waumbek, Mountain View, North Conway country clubs. Mem. Am. Math. Soc., Circolo Matematico, Alpha Delta Phi, Sphinx (Dartmouth). Republican. Conglist. Address: Jefferson, N.H. Died Nov. 14, 1941.

BARTON, William Henry, Jr., engr., curator; b. Baltimore, Md., July 7, 1893; s. William Henry and Helen E. (Pritchett) B.; B.S. in C.E., U. of Pa., 1917, C.E., 1921, M.S., 1923; m. Celia Mason, Aug. 19, 1920. Engring. work U.S. Bur. Public Roads, 1917-Jan. 1918 and Jan. 1919-Aug. 1920; teacher civil engring., U. of Pa., Sept. 1920-June 1930, Pa. Military College, September 1930-June 1935; lecturer curator of astronomy Hayden Planetarium since Sept. 1935. Corpl. then sergt. San Corps, U.S. Army, 1918-19; reserve, 5 yrs.; mem. Brit. Astron. Assn., Am. Assn. of Museums, N.Y. Acad. Sciences, Am. Astron. Soc., Royal Astron. Soc. of Canada, Tau Beta Pi, Sigma Xi. Author: (with L. H. Doane) Sampling and Testing Highway Materials, 1925; (with S. G. Barton) Guide to the Constellations 1928; (with J. M. Joseph) Starcraft, 1935; An Introduction to Celestial Navigation, 1942; Stereopix, 1943. Contbr. articles to Sky mag. Home: 875 W. 181st St. Address: American Museum of Natural History, New York. Died July 7, 1944.

BARTOW, Francis Dwight, banker; b. Annapolis, Md., Nov. 13, 1881; s. Jacob Field and Anna Key (Steele) B.; ed. Rectory Sch., New Milford, Conn.; m. Sabina Redmond Martin, May 8, 1906; children—Clarence Whittemore, Francis Dwight, Philip Key. Began with 1st Nat. Bank, N.Y. City, 1902; partner J. P. Morgan & Co., 1926, later becoming vice-pres., now dir. Republican. Episcopalian. Clubs: Recess, Nat. Golf Links, The Links, New York Yacht, Jekyll Island. Home: 57 E. 66th St., New York, N.Y.; Lattingtown Rd., Glen Cove, L.I., N.Y. Office: 23 Wall St., New York, N.Y.* Died Sep. 24, 1945.

BARUTH, Ralph Howard, business exec.; b. New York, N.Y., June 2, 1888; s. David and Helen (Rosenthal) B.; ed. New York pub. schs.; m. Estelle Hirsch, June 6, 1911; children—Gladys (Mrs. Paul Gretsch), Lila (Mrs. H. Gordon Pelton). Entire career with Julius Kayser Co., New York, N.Y., floor salesman, 1909-12, traveling salesman, 1913-15, mgr. hosiery dept. 1916-28, sales mgr. and dir., 1929, vice pres. and dir. since 1930, 1st vice pres. and dir. since 1942. Home: 411 W. End Av., New York 24. Office: 500 Fifth Av., New York 18, N.Y. Died Nov. 1947.

BASCOM, Florence (băs'kŭm), geologist; b. Williamstown, Mass.; d. John and Emma (Curtiss) Bascom; A.B., B.L., U. of Wis., 1882, B.S., 1884, A.M., 1887; Ph.D., Johns Hopkins, 1893. Instr. geology and petrography, Ohio State U., 1893-95; lecturer and asso. prof., Bryn Mawr Coll., 1895-1906, prof. geology, 1906-28, prof. emeritus since 1928; geol. asst., U.S. Geol. Survey, 1896-1901, asst. geologist, 1901-09, geologist, 1909-36. Asso. editor Am. Geologist, 1896-1905. Fellow Geol. Soc. America (councilor 1924-26; 2d v.p. 1930), A.A.A.S.; mem. Phila. Acad. Natural Sciences, Geog. Soc. Phila., Washington Acad. Sciences, Seismological Soc. Am., Soc. of Women Geographers, Div. Geology and Geography of Nat. Research Council, Mineral. Soc. Am., Inst. Mineralogy and Meteorology, England, Geol. Soc. Washington, Pick and Hammer Club, Am. Geog. Soc., Petrologist Club, Phi Beta Kappa, Sigma Xi. Joint author and author geologic folios; also bulletins and numerous papers in tech. jours. Address: Williamstown, Mass. Died June 18, 1945.

BASQUIN, Olin Hanson (băs'kwĭn), physicist; b. Dows, Ia., Jan. 30, 1869; s. Oliver William and Hannah (Valentine) B.; A.B., Ohio Wesleyan U., 1892; A.B., Harvard, 1894; A.M., Northwestern Univ., 1895, Ph.D., 1901, D.Sc., 1930; m. Jessie C. Guthrie (died 1907); m. 2d, Anna Stuart, Sept. 12, 1908; children—Harold G., Maurice H. Chief engr., Luxfer Prism companies, at Chicago, 1897, at London, 1898, at Berlin, 1899; asst. prof. physics, 1901-09, prof. applied mechanics, 1909-26, Northwestern U.; with Haskelite Mfg. Corp. since 1926, now v.p. in charge of engineering. Editor: Luxfer Prism Pocket Book, 1898; Luxfer Prism Hand Book (translation into German and French), 1899; also papers on experimental work in physics and in strength of materials. Chanute Medal, 1915, by Western Soc. Engrs. for best paper in civ. engring. Republican. Methodist. Mem. Western Soc. Engrs., Sigma Xi, Delta Tau Delta. Asso. engr.-physicist as specialist on study of tests of steel columns, U.S. Bur. Standards, summer, 1916; in charge exptl. investigations on steel for Navy Dept., summer 1917; investigations of engring. properties of plywood for use in mil. airplanes, 1918. Author: Tangent Modulus and the Strength of Steel Columns in Tests (Bur. of Standards), 1924. Home: 225 Kedzie St., Evanston, Ill. Office: 135 S. La Salle St., Chicago, Ill. Died Mar. 30, 1946.

BASSETT, Charles Nebeker, banker; b. Clinton, Ind., Oct. 8, 1880; s. Oscar Thomas and Myrtle (Nebeker) B.; A.B., Wabash Coll., Crawfordsville, Ind., 1901; m. Myra Giles Powers, July 14, 1915; children—Myra Hathaway (Mrs. H. M. Daugherty, Jr.) Barbara Giles, Elizabeth Avery. Pres. O. T. Bassett & Co., El Paso, Tex., 1902-20; v.p. State Nat. Bank, El Paso, 1910-21, pres. since 1921. Mem. Beta Theta Pi. Republican. Presbyterian. Mason (K.T., 32°, K.C.C.H.). Club: El Paso Country. Home: 226 Pennsylvania Av. Address: State National Bank, El Paso, Tex. Died June 10, 1944.

BASSETT, Edward Murray, ex-congressman; b. Brooklyn, Feb. 7, 1863; s. Charles R. and Elvira (Rogers) B.; A.B., Amherst Coll., 1884; LL.B., Columbia U., 1886; (hon.) A.M., Hamilton Coll., 1903, and Harvard U., 1927; m. Annie R. Preston, May 14, 1890; children— Preston R., Marion P. (Mrs. James Luitweiler), Isabel D. (Mrs. Theron Wasson), Howard M., Helen P. (Mrs. Alfred H. Hauser). Practiced law, Buffalo, 1886-92; mem. Bassett, Thompson & Gilpatric, New York, 1902-42; mem. firm Bassett & Bassett, New York, since 1942. Mem. Brooklyn Bd. Edn., 1899-1901; chmn. Sch. Bd., 38th Dist., 1901-03; mem. 58th Congress (1903-05), 5th N.Y. Dist.; mem. Pub. Service Commn., N.Y., 1907-11; chmn. Heights of Bldgs. Commn., N.Y. City, 1913-15; chmn. Zoning Commn., N.Y. City, 1916-17; apptd. by Sec. Hoover as mem. adv. com. on zoning, Dept. of Commerce, 1922; pres. Nat. Conf. on City Planning, 1928-30. Writer on bankruptcy, eminent domain and police power; author, "Zoning, the Laws, Administration and Court Decisions During the First 20 Years," "Master Plan," Russell Sage Foundn., N.Y. Mem. Phi Beta Kappa. Home: 1716 Newkirk Av., Brooklyn. Office: 233 Broadway, New York. Died Oct. 27, 1948; buried at Ashfield, Mass.

BATCHELDER, Charles Clarence, lecturer, publicist; b. Boston, Mass., Aug. 15, 1867; s. Charles Clarence and Annie M. (Leatherbee) B.; grad. Boston Latin Sch., 1885; B.A., magna cum laude, Harvard, 1889; studied at Sorbonne (Paris) and Harvard Grad. Sch. of Business Administration; unmarried. Editor Harvard Daily Crimson, 1885-89; treas. Boston Lumber Co., 1891-1914; under sec. of interior of the Philippines, 1914-16; econ. investigator for the Philippines in China, Japan, Sumatra, etc., 1916; field dir. for Am. Red Cross, 1917; rep. of War Trade Bd., in charge comml. and financial subjects in Seattle, New York and Washington, D.C., 1918-19; acting comml. attaché, Dept. of Commerce, in Pekin, China, and trade commr. in Siberia, 1919-20; trade commr. in India, 1920-21; acting chief Far Eastern Div., Bur. Foreign and Domestic Commerce, 1921-22; trade commr. in India, 1922-23; lecturer on internat. relations, New York U., 1923-26, also lecturer Brown U., Baroda (India), Georgetown U., U. of Philippines, Harvard Grad. Sch. of Bus. Adminstrn., Williamstown Inst. Politics, U. S. War Coll., Inst. Pacific Relations, etc. Author various Govt. publs. and articles on internat. relations in mags. Home: 449 Park Av., New York. Died May 4, 1946.

BATCHELDER, Roger, newspaper man, author; b. Washington, D.C., June 5, 1897; s. Frank Roe and Mabel Caroline (Streeter) B.; A.B., from Harvard U., 1918; m. Florence May Holt, Apr. 26, 1920; children—Austin (dec.), Carol. Contributor full page Sunday feature articles to the Boston Herald, 1917-

18, Essex Market Court column, New York Evening World, 1919-20; "New Yorkers for a Day or Two" column, 1921; real estate editor, 1924-25; New York corr. Boston Globe, 1925-34; writer "Skylines of New York," and "Footlights of Broadway," weekly columns for North American Newspaper Alliance, 1932-33. Served as private 8th Mass. Inf. on Mexican border 5 mos., 1916; commd. 2d lt. Inf. U.S. Army, Jan. 15, 1919; commd. 1st lt. Inf. O.R.C., June, 1923; captain Inf. O.R.C., 1929-41; on active duty Mitchel Field, L.I. Captain A.U.S., 1941-42. Member Kappa Gamma Chi. Republican. Conglist. Mason. Club: Harvard (New York). Author: Watching and Waiting on the Border, 1917; Camp Devens, 1917; Camp Upton, 1918; Camp Dix, 1918; Camp Lee, 1918; Sweethearts for Three (newspaper serial), 1920; novelization of motion picture, Secrets, 1924; also the Book of Fort Dix, The Book of Fort Devens, The Book of Camp Edwards, The Book of Camp Claiborne, The Book of Camp Livingston, 1941. Address: 1215 S.E. First St., Evansville, Indiana. Died Dec. 13, 1947.

BATEMAN, George F., dean sch. of engrng., prof. mech. engrng. and head dept., Cooper Union Inst. of Tech. Address: Cooper Union, Cooper Square, New York, N.Y. Died Jan. 29, 1948.

BATEMAN, Harry, researcher; b. Manchester, Eng., May 29, 1882; s. Samuel and Marnie Elizabeth (Bond) B.; B.A., Trinity Coll., Cambridge, 1903, M.A., 1906; studied Göttingen and Paris, 1905-06; came to U.S., 1910; Ph.D., Johns Hopkins, 1913; m. Ethel Horner Dodd, July 11, 1912; children—Harry Graham (dec.), Joan Margaret. Prof. mathematics, theoretical physics and aeronautics, Calif. Inst. Tech., Sept. 1917—. Mem. American Physical Society, American Math. Soc., London Math. Soc., Brit. Assn. Adv. Science, Am. Philos. Soc., Am. Acoustical Soc., Nat. Acad. of Science; fellow Royal Soc. (London). Episcopalian. Author: Electrical and Optical Wave Motion, 1915; Differential Equations, 1918; Partial Differential Equations of Mathematical Physics, 1931, second edition, 1944. Home: 1107 San Pasqual St., Pasadena, Calif. Died Jan. 21, 1946.

BATEMAN, Robert Johnston, clergyman; b. Plymouth, N.C., Oct. 27, 1879; s. Robert Johnston and Mollie Winifred (Darden) B.; ed. Bethel Hill Inst., Wake Forest (N.C.) Coll., Southern Bapt. Theol. Sem., Louisville, Ky.; D.D., Howard Coll., Birmingham; LL.D., Union U., Jackson, Tenn.; m. Mae Ford, Nov. 16, 1904; children—Robert Johnston, William Carey. Ordained Bapt. ministry, 1895; successively pastor Fayetteville St. Ch., Raleigh, N.C., Park Pl. Ch., Norfolk, Va., First Ch., Troy, Ala., First Ch., Meridian, Miss., First Ch., Asheville, N.C., First Ch., Tulsa, Okla.; now pastor First Ch., Memphis, Tenn. Mem. exec. com. Bapt. State Conv. Trustee Tenn. Coll., Murfreesboro, and Union U., Jackson, Tenn. In charge religion of Com. of Miss. River Discovery, Memphis Chamber of Commerce. Contbr. weekly articles to Mirror (ch. paper); also articles to newspapers and mags. Home: 252 N. McLean St., Memphis, Tenn. Died Apr. 18, 1943.

BATEN, Anderson Monroe, author, publisher; b. Brenham, Texas, Jan. 14, 1888; s. Rev. Anderson Edith (pres. Howard Payne Coll.) and Clara Kate (Williams) B.; mother desc. of Roger Williams and Seth Williams, major gen. of Union forces, 1864; grad. Howard Payne Coll., 1910; student Baylor U., 1910-11; student dept. of law, Am. Extension U., Los Angeles, 1927-30; m. Deulah Gertrude Golden, Feb. 28, 1912. Laborer on ranch, 1912, on railroad section gang, 1913; railroad clerk, 1913-18; real estate and ins., 1918-29; Div. of Finance, Work Projects Adminstrn. since 1938. Mem. Shakespeare Assn. of America; hon. life mem. Barrington Fiction Club (Dallas, Tex.); mem. Co-operative Club Internat.; hon. mem. Eugene Field Soc.; charter mem. Freethinkers of America; mem. Exchange Club, Dallas. Baptist. Mason. Democrat. Author: The Philosophy of Life, 1930; Slang from Shakespeare, Together with Literary Expressions (transcribed into Braille, by Library of Congress, and Am. Red Cross, 1940), 1931; Why Are You Standing Still (transcribed into Braille, by Am. Red Cross, 1935), 1934; Do You Believe in Yourself, 1935; The Philosophy of Success, 1936; The Philosophy of Shakespeare, 1937; The Language of Life, 1938; (pamphlets): Monthly Income Insurance, 1925; On the Five-Yard Line, 1930; Will Rogers, 1935; Sketch of Dallas, 1936; (essays): Lord Byron —A Spring Storm; Ludwig Beethoven. Contbg. editor to Baptist Standard, Dallas Life Mag. Address: 401 Allen Bldg., Dallas, Tex. Died May 1943.

BATES, Blanche, actress; b. Portland, Ore., 1873; d. F. M. Bates, removed to San Francisco with parents, 1876; ed. San Francisco pub. schs.; m. Lt. Milton F. Davis, U.S.A.; 2d, George Creel, Nov. 28, 1912. First appearance on stage, Stockwell's Theatre, San Francisco, 1894; starred as Mrs. Hillary, in "The Senator," 1895; played leading parts in various comedies, 1896-98; appeared in Shakespearean rôles in Augustin Daly's Co., 1898; later starred in "The Great Ruby," "The Musketeers," "Madame Butterfly"; created title rôle of Cigarette in "Under Two Flags," Princess Yo-San, in "The Darling of the Gods," the Girl in "The Girl of the Golden West"; with Henry Miller in "The Changelings." Died Dec. 25, 1941.

BATES, George Joseph, congressman; b. Salem, Mass., Feb. 25, 1891; s. Thomas F. and Annie (Burns) B.; ed. pub. schs., Salem; m. Nora Jennings, Oct. 31, 1911; children—Thomas (dec.), Mary, Catherine, William, Margaret (dec.), George, Raymond, Carolyn, Francis. Mem. Mass. Legislature, 1918-24; mayor Salem, 1924-37; mem. 75th and 78th to 80th Congresses (1937-49), 6th Mass. Dist. Republican. Home: Salem, Mass.* Died Nov. 1, 1949.

BATES, Harry Cole, lawyer; b. Detroit, Mich., Aug. 9, 1891; s. Harry Cole and Fannie F. (Barry) B.; Ph.B., Hamilton Coll., Clinton, N.Y., 1912, Ph.M., 1915, hon. A.M., 1931; LL.B., N.Y. Law Sch., 1915; m. Helen Morris Turner, Sept. 29, 1928; children—Robert Phillips Turner (adopted), Harry Cole III, Charles Turner, David Field. Law clk. with Everett, Clarke & Benedict, N.Y. City, 1912-16; atty. asso. with Britton & Gray, Washington, D.C., 1916-17; atty. Met. Life Ins. Co., 1917-27, asst. gen. counsel, 1927-36, gen. counsel since 1936. Served as 2d lt., field arty., U.S. Army, 1917-18, 1st lt., 1918-19, with A.E.F., 1918-19. Trustee of Hamilton Coll. Member Assn. Life Ins. Counsel (sec.-treas., 1925-41, vice pres., 1941-45, pres., 1945-46), Sigma Phi, Phi Beta Kappa, Phi Delta Phi. Republican. Contbr. to Proceedings of Assn. Life Ins. Counsel. Home: Sunnyside Lane, Irvington-on-Hudson, N.Y. Office: 1 Madison Av., New York, N.Y. Died Feb. 14, 1948.

BATES, Henry Moore, emeritus prof. of law and dean; b. Chicago, Ill., Mar. 30, 1869; s. George Chapman and Alice E. B.; Ph.B., U. of Mich., 1890 LL.D., 1941; LL.B., Northwestern, 1892; LL.D., Kalamazoo Coll., 1925, Wayne U., 1940; m. Clara A. Belfield, Sept. 4, 1894; 1 dau., Helen Belfield Van Tyne. Practiced law, Chicago, 1892-1903, member of firm Harlan & Bates; Tappan prof. law, U. of Mich., 1903-39, dean Law School, 1910-39, emeritus since 1939; prof. of law, Harvard Law Sch., 1917-18. Pres. Assn. Am. Law Schs., 1912-13; mem. exec. com. Am. Inst. Criminal Law, 1911-14; pres. Order of the Coif (legal scholarship soc.), 1913-16; commr. on uniform state laws, 1921-33; mem. Am. Bar Assn., Am. Polit. Science Assn., Chicago Law Inst., Am. Judicature Soc. (mem. bd. dirs.), Social Science Research Council, Detroit Committee on Foreign Affairs, Phi Beta Kappa, Alpha Delta Phi, Phi Delta Phi; charter mem. Am. Law Inst. (mem. council, 1924-29); fellow Am. Acad. Arts and Sciences. Clubs: University, Chicago Literary (Chicago); Detroit, Economic (Detroit). Home: 1921 Cambridge Rd. Office: Legal Research Bldg., Ann Arbor, Mich. Died April 15, 1949.

BATES, John Lewis, ex-governor; b. N. Easton, Mass., Sept. 18, 1859; s. Rev. Lewis Benton and Louisa D. (Field) B.; A.B., Boston U., 1882, LL.B., 1885; LL.D., Wesleyan, Conn., 1903; m. Clara Elizabeth Smith, July 12, 1887; children—Lewis Benton (dec.), John Harold, Dorothy. Practiced at Boston since 1885. Mem. Boston Common Council, 1891-92; mem. Mass. House of Representatives, 1894-99 (speaker, 1897-99); lt.-gov. Mass., 1900-02; gov. Mass., 1903-04. Pres. Mass. Constl. Conv., 1917, 18. 19. Republican. Pres. bd. trustees Boston U., 1907-27. Mason (33°). Home: 148 Strathmore Road. Office: 10 Tremont St., Boston. Deceased.

BATES, William Nickerson, univ. prof.; b. Cambridge, Mass., Dec. 8, 1867; s. Charles and Anna Pamela (Nickerson) B.; grad. Cambridge Latin Sch., 1886; A.B., with honors, Harvard, 1890, A.M., 1891, Ph.D., 1893; student Am. Sch. Classical Studies, Athens, Greece, 1897-98; hon. L.H.D., U. of Pa., 1940; m. Edith Newell Richardson, Dec. 28, 1901 (died Feb. 27, 1926); children—William Nickerson, Robert Hicks. Instr. Greek, Harvard, 1893-95; with U. of Pa. since 1895, as instr. Greek, asst. prof. and prof. Greek language and literature, also head dept., 1910-39, emeritus prof. since 1939. Editor Transactions of Univ. Museum, 1904-07; editor Am. Jour. Archæology, 1908-20, editor-in-chief, 1920-24. Incorporator, 1902, recorder, 1903-09, Archæol. Inst. America; mem. mng. com. Am. Sch. Classical Studies in Athens since 1902, prof. Greek lang. and lit. and acting dir., 1905-06. Del. Internat. Congress for History of Religions, Leyden, 1912. Mem. governing bd. Am. Foundation in France for Prehistoric Studies (now Am. Sch. Prehistoric Research), 1921-25. Fellow Am. Acad. Arts and Sciences; mem. Am. Philol. Assn., Oriental Club, Classical Club, Hellenic Soc. (London), Archæol. Club (Boston), Founders and Patriots America (gov. Pa. Society of the Order, 1943-45), Phi Beta Kappa (pres. Philadelphia Association of the Society, 1941-43). Republican. Unitarian. Clubs: Harvard (Philadelphia); Harvard (Boston). Editor Iphigenia in Tauris (of Euripides), 1904, Chinese edition, 1936. Reviser: Hertzberg's History of Greece, 1905. Author: Date of Lycophron, 1895; Notes on the Theseum at Athens, 1901; The Old Athena Temple on the Acropolis, 1901; Etruscan Inscriptions, 1905; New Inscriptions from the Asclepieum at Athens, 1907; Five Red-Figured Cylices, 1908; Two Labors of Heracles on a Geometric Fibula, 1911; Euripides, a Student of Human Nature, 1930; Sophocles, Poet and Dramatist, 1940; etc.; also numerous articles in archeol. and philol. jours. Home: winter: Harvard Club, Boston, Mass., summer: Ogunquit, Me. Died June 10, 1949.

BATTLE, George Gordon, lawyer; b. Cool Spring Plantation, Edgecombe County, N.C., Oct. 26, 1868; s. Turner Westray and Lavinia (Bassett-Daniel) B.; U. of N.C., 1882-83, U. of Va., 1886-89; m. Martha, d. Dr. George W. Bagby, of Richmond, Va., Apr. 12, 1898. Admitted to bar, 1891, and since practiced at New York; asst. dist. atty., New York County, 1892-97; Dem. candidate for dist. atty., New York County, 1909; mem. Battle & Marshall, 1901-11, now of Battle, Levy, Fowler & Neaman. Mem. Assn. Bar City of N.Y., Southern Soc., N C. Soc. of N.Y., The Virginians. Clubs: Down Town, Metropolitan, Manhattan, Church, Nat. Democratic. Home: 20 E. 76th St. Office: 30 Broad St., New York, N.Y. Died Apr. 29, 1949.

BAUER, Charles Christian (bou'ĕr); b. Springfield, O., Nov. 17, 1881; s. William F. and Catharine (Shackelford) B.; grad. high sch., Springfield, 1898; m. Shirley Erskine Neal, of Hamilton, O., June 29, 1905; children—Neal (Mrs. J. D. Elliott), Shackelford (deceased). Engaged in advertising until 1922; with Hamilton Holt and Everett Colby, organized League of Nations Assn., 1922, exec. dir., 1922-23, 1925-29; mem. exec. com., Geneva Inst. of Internatl. Relations since 1924; vice chmn. council, League of Nations Assn. since 1929; exec. vice chmn. Com. for Consideration of Inter-Governmental Debts since 1932; exec. dir. and secretary, Tax Foundation since July 1942. Mem. exec. com. Nat. World Court Com. since 1932; dir. financial development Nat. Com. for Mental Hygiene, 1936. Member executive committee, American Friends of Czechoslovakia; served as pres. Community Councils, N.Y. City, 1919-25. Mem. Council on Foreign Relations, Acad. of Polit. Science, Am. Economic Assn., Governmental Research Assn. Episcopalian. Mason. Clubs: Westchester Country (Rye, N.Y.); Sachem of Yale Univ. (hon.). Home: 65 E. 96th St. Office: 30 Rockefeller Plaza, New York, N.Y. Died Mar. 15, 1947.

BAUSCH, Edward (boush), mfr.; b. Rochester, N.Y., Sept. 26, 1854; s. John J. and Barbara B.; student Cornell U., 1871-74, LL.D.; A.M., U. of Rochester, 1908; m. Matilda G. Morell, October 31, 1878 (died July 14, 1940). Chairman board Bausch & Lomb Optical Company; vice-president Monroe County Savings Bank; dir. Lincoln-Alliance Bank and Trust Co. of Rochester, Taylor Instrument Cos. Fellow Rochester Museum of Arts and Sciences. Dir. Rochester Gen. Hosp., Rochester Community Chest; 1st v.p. Rochester Sch. for Deaf; trustee and 1st vice-chmn. Bur. of Municipal Research of Rochester. Awarded gold medal of honor, Am. Soc. Mech. Engrs., 1936. Fellow A.A.A.S., Am. Micros. Soc. (hon. mem.), Royal Micros. Soc.; mem. Rochester Acad. Science. Author: Manipulation of the Microscope. Inventor various scientific devices. Home: 663 East Av. Office: 635 St. Paul St., Rochester, N.Y. Died July 30, 1944.

BAUSCH, William, vice-pres. Bausch & Lomb Optical Co.; b. Rochester, N.Y., Mar. 25, 1861; s. John Jacob and Barbara (Zimmerman) B.; student Rochester pub. schs., Collegiate Inst., Rochester, and Hale's Prep. Sch.; m. Kate Zimmer, Oct. 1, 1891. Began in father's factory, 1875, and became interested in mfr. of eye-glasses; sec. Bausch & Lomb Optical Co., 1909-35, v.p. since 1935; trustee East Side Savings Bank, Rochester. Pres. and trustee Rochester Dental Dispensary. Republican. Clubs: Rochester, Genesee Valley, Oak Hill Country, Country (Rochester). Home: 1063 St. Paul St. Office: 635 St. Paul St., Rochester, N.Y.* Died Oct. 19, 1944.

BAWDEN, Samuel Day, missionary; b. Elyria, O., Dec. 2, 1868; s. Rev. H. H. and Harriet Newell (Day) B.; B.Sc. in M.E., U. of Ill., 1890; grad. Rochester Theol. Sem., 1897- LL.D., Linfield Coll., 1931; D.D., Denison Univ., 1931; m. Minnie L. Cotton, June 23, 1896; children—Herbert Newton, Dorothea Caroline. Chaplain, State Industrial Sch., Rochester, N.Y., 1895-1904; sent to India by Am. Bapt. Fgn. Missionary Soc., 1904; mgr. Indsl. Expt. Sta., Ongole, 1907-12, Erukala Indsl. Settlement, Kavali, 1914-33. now grown to four settlements; treas. South India Mission and pastorVepery Bapt. Ch., Madras, 1933-38; retired, 1938. Mem. Madras Rep. Council of Missions, Nat. Missionary Council of India, Madras Ednl. Council. Awarded silver Kaisar-i-Hind medal by British Govt., 1919. "for distinguished service in India," in investigation of social and economic problems of the native population, replaced by gold medal, 1930. Home: 331 E. Main St., Kent, Ohio. Died Aug. 3, 1946.

BAXTER, Bruce Richard, bishop; b. Rock Run, O., Aug. 18, 1892; s. John Matthew and Nina K. (Bartleson) B.; A.B., Oberlin, 1915; M.A., Oberlin, Grad. Sch., 1916; S.T.B., Boston U. Sch. of Theology, 1917; D.D., Coll. of Pacific, 1925; LL.D., Chapman Coll., Los Angeles, 1932, Whitman Coll., 1936; L.H.D., Los Angeles Coll. Osteopathic Physicians and Surgeons, 1940; S.T.D., Coll. Puget Sound, 1943; Litt.D., Willamette U., 1943; m. Martha Harrold, Sept. 2, 1924. Ordained M.E. ministry, 1918; field sec. M.E. Centenary Movement, 1918, Interchurch World Movement, 1919; prof. English Bible, Mt. Union Coll., 1920-24; prof. homiletics and chaplain, U. of Southern Calif., 1924-30, asst. to pres. of univ., 1930-34, dean Sch. of Religion, 1931-34; pres. Willamette U., Salem, Ore., 1934-40, acting pres., 1940-41; bishop of Meth. Church since 1940; assigned to Portland area, comprising Oregon, Washington, Idaho and Alaska. Delegate to M.E. Ecumenical Conference, London, Eng., 1921, Meth. Gen. Conf., 1940; preacher at Highbury Quadrant Congl. Ch., London, summer 1925; Matthew Simpson foundation lecturer De Pauw U., 1932. Mem. War Work Council, Y.M.C.A., 1917-18; dir. Y.M.C.A., Salem; trustee Pacific School of Religion, Berkeley, Willamette U., Salem, College of Puget Sound, Tacoma, Iliff School of Theology, Denver, Colorado; former member board of directors Symphonies under the Stars Foundation (Hollywood Bowl); mem. Bd. and Nat. Council of Student Christian Assn.; head Chaplains Corp. of Civilian Defense, Portland. Mem. Meth. Commn. on Army and Navy Chaplains; mem. bd. edn., Missions and Ch. Extension (home div.), Evangelism, Hosp. and Homes, Meth. Ch.; mem. Federal Council of Chs. of Christ in Am.; mem. Nat. Council Christians and Jews; mem. bd. Good Will Industries. Fellow Pacific Geog. Soc. Bibl. Lit., Exegesis, Ore. Tuberculosis Association, Phi Beta Kappa, Alpha Tau Omega, Phi Chi Phi; v.p. Ore. Amateur Ath. Union; pres. Oregon Assn. Independent Colls. (1939-40). Republican. Mason (K.T., 32°). Clubs: Rotary (pres. Salem Rotary Club 1940); Breakfast (Los Angeles); Rotary, University, Portland City (Portland, Ore.). Lecturer and contbr. numerous articles to ch. and ednl. periodicals. Travelled extensively in Far East, Africa and South Seas. Home: Ambassador Apts., 1209 S.W. Sixth St., Portland 4. Office: 1219 S.W. Taylor, Portland 5, Oregon. Died June 20, 1947.

BAXTER, John Babington Macaulay, chief justice of New Brunswick; b. Saint John, N.B., Feb. 16, 1868; s. William and Margaret (MacAuley) B.; B.C.L., King's Coll. Law Sch.; hon. D.C.L., King's Coll.; LL.D., St. Josephs Coll.; LL.D., Univ. of N.B.; m. Grace Winnifred Coster, Jan. 14, 1924; children—John Babington Macaulay, Jr., Eleanor Cowden, Frederick Coster Noel, Mary Faith. Began as atty. at law, Oct. 16, 1890; barrister, 1891, King's counsel, 1909; atty. gen. of N.B., 1916-17; premier of N.B., 1925-31. Mem. Parliament (Can.), 1921-25; mem. Provincial Parliament, N.B., 1911-21, 1925-31; judge Supreme Court, N.B., 1931-35, chief justice since 1935. Served as lt. col., 3d N.B. Regt. of Arty., 1907-12. Alderman, St. John, 1892-94 1899-1902, 1904-09. Mason (33°). Clubs: Cliff (St. John); City (Fredericton, N.B.). Author: New Brunswick Regiment of Artillery, 1793-1896, pub. 1896; Simon Baxter, His Ancestry and Descendants, 1944. Home: 34 Dufferin Row. Office: Provincial Bldg., St. John, N.B., Can. Died Dec. 27, 1946.

BAYARD, Thomas Francis, ex-senator; b. Wilmington, Del., June 4, 1868; s. Thomas Francis (U.S. senator) and Louisa (Lee) B.; A.B., Yale, 1890; student law dept., Yale, 1890-1901, and in father's office, 1891-93; m. Elizabeth Bradford, d. Dr. Alexis I. du Pont, of Wilmington, Oct. 3, 1908. Admitted to Del. bar, 1893; moved to N.Y. City, 1897, and was apptd. asst. corp. counsel; returned to Wilmington, 1901. Chmn. Dem. State Com., 1906-16; city solicitor, Wilmington, 1917-19; elected to U.S. Senate from Del., Nov. 1922, to fill vacancy for unexpired term ending Mar. 4, 1923, and re-elected for term ending Mar. 4, 1929; was the 5th mem. of family to occupy senatorial chair from Del. Episcopalian. Home: Wilmington, Del. Died July 12, 1942.

BAYLIS, Robert Nelson, engineer; b. Englewood, N.J., Mar. 16, 1867; s. Robert and Martha N. (Smith) B.; M.E., Stevens Inst. Tech., 1887; m. Lilian Burt, Aug. 4, 1913. Draftsman, engr., chief engr. and factory mgr. C. & C. Electric Motor Co., New York, 1890-93; chief elec. engr. Walker Co., at Cleveland, O., 1893-97; pres. Baylis Co., engrs. and mfrs., Bloomfield, N.J., 1897. Pres. common council, Englewood, N.J., 1906-09. Mem. Am. Soc. Mech. Engrs., Am. Inst. Elec. Engrs., Nat. Geographic Soc., Delta Tau Delta. Home: Caldwell, N.J. Office: Bloomfield, N.J. Died Sept. 5, 1942.

BEACH, Amy Marcy Cheney (Mrs. H. H. A. Beach); b. Henniker, N.H., Sept. 5, 1867; d. Charles Abbott and Clara Imogene (Marcy) Cheney; early edn. by mother; piano and harmony under Junius W. Hill, Ernest Perabo and Carl Baermann; studied fugue, form, counterpoint and instrumentation alone with text books; m. Henry Harris Aubrey Beach, Dec. 2, 1885 (died 1910). Played in concerts and recitals from 1883; since 1885, devoted time to playing and composition. Hon. mem. Boston Browning Soc., in recognition of music written to Browning's poetry. Compositions: Mass in E flat (sung by Boston Handel and Haydn Soc., 1892); The Rose of Avontown, cantata for female voices; Gaelic Symphony; Festival Jubilate, for mixed voices; The Minstrel and the King, ballad for male voices; Sylvania, wedding cantata for mixed voices; Help Us, O God, motet for mixed voices, unaccompanied: Concerto for piano and orchestra (played by Boston Symphony Orchestra); Aria, Jephthah's Daughter; cantatas, The Sea-Fairies and the Chambered Nautilus; Quintet for piano and strings; Service in A; also many songs, etc. Home: Hillsboro, N.H. Died Dec. 27, 1944.

BEACH, Daniel Magee, lawyer; b. Watkins, N.Y., May 24, 1873; s. Daniel Beach and Angelica Church (Magee) B.; B.L., Hobart Coll., Geneva, N.Y., 1892; student Univ. of Göttingen, Germany, 1893-94, Columbia Law Sch., 1894-95; N.Y. Law Sch., LL.B., 1896; m. Marion H. Lindsay, Oct. 31, 1901; children—Daniel M., Lindsay (Mrs. George E. Norton), Alexander, Marion (Mrs. John E. Moreton). Admitted to N.Y. bar, 1897; mem. Harris, Beach, Keating, Wilcox & Dale. Home: 50 Barrington St. Office: 5 S. Fitzhugh St., Rochester, N.Y. Died July 22, 1948.

BEACH, George Corwin, Jr., army officer; b. Topeka, Kan., Oct. 28, 1888; s. George Corwin and Laura (Rosseau) B.; M.D., Kansas City U. Med. Coll., 1911; grad. Army Med. Sch., 1917; m. Jessie Spencer, Nov. 16, 1914. Interne University Hosp. of Kansas City, 1911-12; asst. surgeon Soldiers Home, Hampton, Va., 1912-14; commd. 1st lt., Med. Corps, U.S. Army, 1914; promoted through grades to brig. gen., 1943; asst. surg. gen., Army Med. Center, Washington, D.C. Awarded D.S.M., World War I. Second v.p. United Services Automobile Assn. Fellow Am. Coll. Physicians, A.M.A.; diplomate Am. Bd. Internal Medicine; mem. Assn. Mil. Surgeons, Phi Beta Pi; hon. mem. Tex. Internists Soc. Episcopalian. Club: San Antonio Country. Home: 204 Artillery Post, Fort Sam Houston, Tex. Address: care War Dept., Washington, D.C. Died Nov. 18, 1948.

BEACH, H(arry) Prescott, lawyer; b. Hamden, Conn., Feb. 23, 1871; s. Lt. Dennis and Josephine (Jackson) B.; LL.B., Columbia, 1891; m. Laura Dolbear, Nov. 27, 1895; children—George A. H. (dec.), Prescott, Louis Dolbear, Laura Lancaster (wife of Dr. Leopold Edward Thron), Robert Treat. Began reading law in office of Joseph H. Choate, N.Y. City, Sept. 1, 1891; in gen. practice, 1895-1932; gen. counsel and v.p., Chale Realty Co., 1927-32; dir. and mem. exec. and finance coms. Morris Plan Industrial Bank of New York. Mem. Merchants Assn. of N.Y. City, 1914-32. Official arbitrator Am. Arbitration Assn.; pres. N.Y. State Bd. of Commrs. of License since 1914; pres. Seamen's Christian Assn. (N.Y. City) since 1914; vice-chmn., dir., Seamen's House of Y.M.C.A.; dir. and mem. finance com. Y.M.C.A. of N.Y. City; mem. N.J. State, N.Y. City and Montclair Town, George Washington bicentennial coms.; mem. N.Y. City Park Assn. Pres. and trustee The Revolutionary Memorial Soc. of N.J.; mem. Nat. Soc. Sons Am. Revolution (past v.p. gen. nat. soc., nat. trustee and past pres. N.J. soc.), N.Y. Soc. Colonial Wars, New Jersey Society Colonial Wars, American Friends of Lafayette, Anglo-Am. Records Foundation, Vet. Artillery Corps and Mil. Soc. of War of 1812, Nat. Geneal. Soc., Inst. of Am. Genealogy (fellow), N.Y. Geneal. and Biog. Soc. (mem. publication bd.), Geneal. Soc. of N.J. (v.p. and trustee), N.J. Archæol. Soc., Hist. Congress of N.J. (pres.), N.J. Numismatic Soc. (ex-president and mem. executive committee), Phi Gamma Delta Fraternity, etc. Democrat. Episcopalian (formerly mem. vestry Christ Church, Glen Ridge, N.J.). Clubs: Phi Gamma Delta, University (New York); Down Town (Newark); Church Club of N.J. Author: (with others) The Story of Montclair, 1930. Contbr. on hist. and biog. topics, also short stories and poems. Home: 376 Upper Mountain Av., Montclair, N.J. Office: 550 W. 20th St., New York, N.Y. Died July 18, 1943.

BEACH, Lansing Hoskins, army officer; b. Dubuque, Ia., June 18, 1860; s. Myron Hawley and Helen Mary (Hoskins) B.; grad. U.S. Mil. Acad., 1882; m. Anna May Dillon, June 18, 1890; 1 son, Lansing Dillon. Commd. additional 2d lt. engrs., June 13, 1882; promoted through grades to col., Feb. 27, 1913. Commr. on part of U.S. in determining boundary between Tex. and Indian Terr., 1886; engr. commr. of D.C., 1898-1901; while in that position initiated the improvement of Rock Creek Park and obtained first appropriation from Congress for the purpose; secured abolition of railroad grade crossings in Washington and originated the plan for removal of Pa. R.R. from the Mall and establishment of a union station; personally selected names now borne by streets in street extension plan of D.C. Div. engr. Gulf Div. embracing all states touching the Gulf of Mexico, 1908-15; mem. Miss. River Commn., 1913-20; div. engr. Central Div. embracing Ohio River basin, 1915-20; sent by U.S. to Europe, 1911, to study and report upon conditions of navigation there; advanced maj. gen. and chief of engrs., Jan. 9, 1920; retired, June 18, 1924. Mem. U.S. Commn. to confer with Mexican Commn. to determine equitable div. of waters of Rio Grande and Colorado rivers. Mem. Am. Soc. C.E., Am. Soc. Mil. Engrs. (ex-pres.). Clubs: Army and Navy (Washington, D.C.); Los Angeles (Calif.) Athletic; Twilight (Pasadena). Address: 690 Bradford St., Pasadena, Calif. Died Apr. 2, 1945.

BEACH, Rex (Ellingwood), author; b. Atwood, Mich., Sept. 1, 1877; s. Henry Walter and Eva Eunice (Canfield) B.; ed. Rollins Coll., Winter Park, Fla., 1891-96, Chicago Coll. Law, 1896-97, Kent Coll. Law, 1899-1900; m. Edith Crater, 1907 (died Apr. 15, 1947). Pres. Authors' League Am., 1917-21. Clubs: Chicago Athletic (sec. 1905-06), Press (Chicago); Players, Lambs, New York Athletic, Coffee House (New York); Sleepy Hollow Country, St. Andrews Golf Club, Ardsley Club. Author: Pardners, 1905; The Spoilers, 1906; The Barrier, 1907; The Silver Horde, 1909; Going Some, 1910; The Ne'er-do-Well, 1911; The Net, 1912; The Iron Trail, 1913; The Auction Block, 1914; Heart of the Sunset, 1915; Rainbow's End, 1916; The Crimson Gardenia, 1916; Laughing Bill Hyde, 1917; The Winds of Chance, 1918; Oh, Shoot, 1921; Flowing Gold, 1922; Big Brother, 1923; The Goose Woman, 1925; Padlocked, 1926; The Mating Call, 1927; Don Careless, 1928; Son of the Gods, 1929; Money Mad; (plays) Going Some (with Paul Armstrong); The Spoilers (with James McArthur); Men of the Outer Islands, 1932; Beyond Control, 1932; Alaskan Adventures, 1933; Hands of Dr. Locke, 1934; Masked Women, 1934; Wild Pastures, 1935; Jungle Gold, 1935; Personal Exposures, 1941; The World in His Arms, 1946 (motion picture rights purchased by Internat. Pictures). Died Dec. 7, 1949.

BEACH, Walter Greenwood, emeritus prof., b. Granville, O., May 20, 1868; s. David Edwards and Alice (Allen) B.; A.B., Marietta Coll., O., 1888; A.B., Harvard, 1891, A.M., 1892; Stanford, 1897-98; m. Flora Victoria Warner, Dec. 28, 1892 (died Oct. 22, 1938); children—Susan Elizabeth, Walter Edwards, Rachel Julia, Allen Warner. Professor philosophy and history, Marietta (O.) College for Women, 1893-97; successively asst. prof., prof. and head dept. of econ. science and history, State Coll. of Wash., 1898-1910; prof. social science, U. of Wash., 1910-17; dean Coll. of Sciences and Arts, State Coll. of Wash., Aug. 1917-20; prof. social science, Stanford U., 1920-33, emeritus prof. since 1933. Mem. Phi Beta Kappa and Delta Upsilon fraternities. Conglist. Author: Introduction to Sociology and Social Problems, 1925; Social Aims in a Changing World, 1932; Oriental Crime in California, 1932; American Democracy and Social Change (with others), 1936; Social Problems and Social Welfare (with others), 1937; Growth of Social Thought, 1939; The Government of the U.S. (with others), 1941; Democracy and Social Policy (with others), 1945. Home: 1899 N. Raymond Av., Pasadena, Calif. Died Oct. 6, 1948.

BEACH, William Mulholland, surgeon; b. Stoneboro, Pa., Sept. 15, 1859; s. Oliver and Ann Elizabeth (Mulholland) B.; A.B., Waynesburg (Pa.) Coll., 1882, A.M., 1885; M.D., Jefferson Med. Coll., 1889; m. Lucy Lazear Miller, 1882. Prof. Latin and Greek, Ozark (Mo.) Coll., 1882-85; pres. Odessa (Mo.) Coll., 1885-87; an organizer and surgeon Presbyn. Hosp., Pittsburgh, 1895-1914; proctologist South Side Hosp., 1906-11; examining surgeon for pensions, 1893-97. First lt. Med. Corps, N.G. Pa., 1894-97. Fellow Am. Coll. Surgeons, A.M.A. (chmn. sect. gastroenterology, 1918-19); mem. Am. Proctologic Soc. (sec., 1899-1903, pres., 1903-04), Am. Acad. Medicine, Med. Soc. State of Pa., Allegheny County Med. Soc. Mem. bd. trustees, Waynesburg Coll. Democrat. Presbyterian. Mason. Clubs: Union, Americus, Pittsburgh, Athletic Association. Contbr. 2 chapters in Cook's Diseases of the Rectum and Colon. Inventor of proctoscope and colostomy supporter. Home: Bellefield Dwellings. Office: Bessemer Bldg., Pittsburgh. Died Oct. 23, 1930.

BEAKES, Crosby Jordan (bēks), lawyer; b. Glenwood, N.J., Dec. 13, 1876; s. George E. and Hannah Norris (Jordan) B.; attended Unadilla Acad., 1890-93; A.B., Hamilton Coll., 1897, A.M., 1898; LL.B., New York Law Sch., 1899; m. Gertrude A. Hulse, June 2, 1905; children—Barbara, Norris. Clk. in law office, 1898-1902; employed by Title Guarantee & Trust Co., 1902-05; entered law dept. N.Y.C. R.R., 1905, gen. counsel same since 1933, also gen. counsel various subsidiaries; dir. Cambria & Indiana R.R. Co., N.Y. & Harlem R.R. Co., Cleveland, Cincinnati, Chicago & St. Louis Railway Co., Chicago & Harrisburg Coal Co., Clearfield Bituminous Coal Corporation, Merchants Despatch Transportation Corporation, Despatch Shops, Inc., Michigan Central R.R. Co., Michigan Air Line R.R. Co., West Shore R.R. Co., N.Y. State Realty and Terminal Co., Northern Refrigerator Line, Inc., Realty Hotels, Inc. Mem. Delta Kappa Epsilon, Phi Beta Kappa. Republican. Clubs: Union League (N.Y. City); Scarsdale Golf (Scarsdale, N.Y.). Home: 18 Colonial Rd., White Plains, N.Y. Died May 18, 1948.

BEAL, Carl H. (bēl), petroleum geologist and engineer; b. in Kansas, July 16, 1889; s. William Harvey and Anna (Erwin) B.; A.B., Stanford U., 1913, M.A., 1915, E.M., 1919; m. Cynthia Hardy Anderson, Jan. 30, 1929; children—Carlton H., Thomas E. Engaged in oil production in Coalinga, Calif., 1913; geologist in Calif. and Canada, 1914; oil and gas inspector, Okla., 1915; petroleum technologist U.S. Bur. of Mines and valuation expert U.S. Bur. of Internal Revenue, 1916-19; cons. petroleum geologist and engr., Calif. and Mexico, 1919-25; v.p. Marland Oil Co., 1922-28; cons. petroleum geologist and engr. since 1928; pres. Northern Resources, Ltd., West Coast Royalty Co., Ltd.; dir. Tide Water Asso. Oil Co. Mem. Am. Assn. of Petroleum Geologists, Am. Inst. of Mining and Metall. Engrs., Soc. of Econ. Geologists. Sigma Xi. Clubs: California, Bel-Air Country, Burlingame Country, Midwick Country, Uplifters' Polo, San Mateo-Burlingame Polo, Riviera Country, Bel-Air Bay Club. Contbr. tech. articles and bulls. on oil production, seismology, etc., for official governmental and institutional pubs. Died Sept. 7, 1946.

BEAL, Harry, clergyman; b. Oneida, N.Y., May 26, 1885; s. Joseph and Helen Clymena (Clark) B.; prep. edn., Colgate Acad., Hamilton, N.Y.; A.B., Yale, 1906; B.D., Episcopal Theol. Sch., Cambridge, Mass., 1911; D.D., Ch. Div. Sch. of the Pacific, 1929; D.D., U. of Southern Calif., 1936; m. Marjorie Berry Clements, June 18, 1913; 1 dau., Louise Marjorie. Master at St. Paul's Sch., Concord, N.H., 1906-08; deacon, 1911, priest, 1912, P.E. Ch.; minister in charge, Constableville, Port Leyden and Greig, N.Y., 1911-14; rector Ch. of the Messiah, West Newton and Auburndale, Mass., 1914-17, Grace Ch., New Bedford, Mass., 1917-23; dean of Holy Trinity Cathedral, Havana, Cuba, 1923-26, St. Paul's Cathedral, Los Angeles, Calif., 1926-37; declined election as bishop of Honolulu, 1929; consecrated bishop of Panama C.Z., Jan. 13, 1937. Deputy Gen. Conv. of P.E. Ch., 1928, 31, 34; pres. Los Angeles Council of Social Agencies, 1933-35. Chaplain Soc. Colonial Wars in State of Calif., 1934-36. Mem. S.A.R., Colonial Wars, Phi Beta Kappa, Psi Upsilon. Republican. Kiwanian. Home: Bishop's House, 334 Gorgas Road. Address: Box 1441, Ancon, C.Z. Died Nov. 22, 1944; buried at Ancon, C.Z.

BEAL, James Hartley, pharm. chemist; b. New Phila., O., Sept. 23, 1861; s. Jesse and Mary B.; student Buchtel Coll. (now Akron), and U. of Mich.; B.Sc., Scio (Ohio) Coll., 1884; A.B., 1888; LL.B., Cincinnati Law Sch., 1886; Ph.G. Ohio Med. Univ., 1894; Sc.D., Mt. Union Coll., 1895; Pharm.D., U. of Pittsburgh. 1902; Pharm.M., Phila. Coll. Pharmacy, 1913; m. Fannie Snyder Young, Sept. 29, 1886; children—George Denton. Nannie Esther. Dean dept. pharmacy and prof. chemistry and pharmacy, 1887-1907, acting pres. 1902-04, Scio (O.) Coll.; dir. era course in pharmacy, New York. 1889-1909; professor chemistry, metallurgy and microscopy, Pittsburgh Dental College, 1896-1904; prof. theory and practice of pharmacy, U. of Pittsburgh, 1903-11; gen. sec. and editor Jour. of the Am. Pharmaceutical Assn., 1911-14; dir. pharmacy research. U. of Ill., 1914-17. Mem. Ohio Ho. of Rep., 1901. Editor Midland Druggist and Pharmaceutical Review, 1908; chmn. com. on uniformity of legislation, methods of analysis and marking of food products, Nat. Pure Food and Drug Congress, 1898. Trustee U.S. Pharmacopoeial Conv., 1900 (pres. bd. trustees, 1910, 1940); pres. Am. Pharm. Assn., 1904-05. Ohio State Pharm. Assn., 1898, Am. Conf. Pharm. Faculties, 1907-08, Am. Druggists Fire Ins. Co., 1939-45; nat. councilor U.S. Chamber of Commerce, 1917-18; pharm. expert, War Industries Bd., 1918; pres. Nat. Drug Trade Conf., 1918-20. Remington medalist, 1919. Author: Notes on Equation Writing and Chemical and Pharmaceutical Arithmetic, 3d edition, 1903; Pharmaceutical Interrogations, 1896; Interrogations in Dental Metallurgy, 1900; Practical Pharmacy, 1907; Prescription Practice and General Dispensing, 1908; Principles of Theory and Practice of Pharmacy (5 vols.), 1910 Contbr. to pharm. jours. Now retired. Home: Fort Walton, Fla. Died Sept. 20, 1945.

BEAL, Junius Emery, publisher; b. Port Huron, Mich., Feb. 23, 1860; s. Rice A. and Phebe (Beers) B.; grad. Ann Arbor High Sch., 1878; B.L., U. of Mich., 1882; m. Ella Travis, 1889; children—Travis Field (dec.), Loretta. Editor and pub. Ann Arbor Courier (weekly), Times (daily), 1882-1904; pub. Dr. Chase's Recipe Book. Pres. Ann Arbor & Ypsilanti St. Ry. Co., 1891-96; sec., treas. Ann Arbor Electric Co., 1894-1902; mem. bd. dirs. Ann Arbor Savings and Commercial Bank, Detroit Fire & Marine Ins. Co.; v.p. Peninsular Paper Co. Rep. presdl. elector, Mich., 1888; pres. Rep. League of Mich., 1889; mem. Mich. Ho. of Reps., 1905-06; trustee Old People's Home (Chelsea); mem. Ann Arbor Sch. Bd., 1884-1904. Dir. Forest Hills Cemetery. Pres. Mich. Press Assn., 1893. Del. Gen. Conf. M.E. Ch., 1912-16, 28; gov. Mich. Soc. Colonial Wars; mem. Wesleyan Guild (U. of Mich.), Beta Theta Pi, Phi Beta Kappa. Methodist. Clubs: University, Mich. Union, Ann Arbor Golf, Huron Hills, Rotary. Home: Ann Arbor, Mich. Died June 24, 1942.

BEAL, Thomas Andrew, univ. dean; b. Ephraim, Utah, July 20, 1874; s. Henry and Stena (Byergo) B.; A.B., U. of Utah, 1906; A.M., Columbia, 1910, M.S. in Business, 1919, grad. student, 1926; student U. of Heidelberg, Germany, 1925, U. of Berlin, 1925-26; m. Ida Peterson, June 19, 1901. Teacher, Snow Coll., Ephraim, Utah, 1898-1914; prof. business and economics, U. of Utah, since 1914, dean Sch. of Business, 1917-41; dean emeritus, School of Business, professor emeritus Economics and Business since 1941: director of Bank Ephraim, 1912-14. Member Board Regents, Univ. of Utah, 1912-14. Mem. Am. Econ. Assn., Nat. Tax Assn., Am. Assn. Univ. Profs., Phi Kappa Phi. Republican. Mem. Ch. of Latter Day Saints. Club: Rotary (Salt Lake City) Home: 944 Military Drive, Salt Lake City, Utah. Deceased.

BEAL, Walter Henry, Agrl. research; b. nr. Old Church, Va., Dec. 9, 1867; s. John and Charlotte Columbia (Ellett) B.; A.B., Va. Poly. Inst., 1886, M.E., 1886; m. Eleanor Gilliss Ashby, Apr. 27, 1910; children—Major Walter Henry, Jr., Mrs. Elizabeth B. Devlin, Anne Ashby, Ensign William Ashby. Assistant chemist, Massachusetts Agrl. Experimental Sta., 1887-91; specialist in agrl. meteorology, soils and fertilizers, editor, and asso. in expt. sta. administration. Office of Experiment Stations, U.S. Dept. Agriculture, 1891-1938. Democrat. Episcopalian. Author various papers on scientific agriculture; contbr. to Experiment Station Record, International Ency., Internat. Year Book, Webster's Internat. Dictionary, Ency. Americana. Fellow A.A.A.S.; mem. Agrl Hist. Soc., Va. Hist Soc. Club: Cosmos. Home: 1852 Park Road N.W., Washington, D.C. Died Jan. 1, 1946.

BEALE, Charles Hallock, clergyman; b. Patchogue, N.Y., Aug. 20, 1854; s. David Brainard and Esther (Hallock) B.; ed. Hillside Sem., Northport, N.Y.; (D.D., Olivet Coll., Mich.; m. Lucy M. Reeve, Aug. 22, 1886; 1 son, Arthur Stanley. Ordained Congl. ministry, 1878; pastorates: Cadillac, Mich., 1882-86; Lansing, Mich., 1886-94; Boston, 1894-1904; Grand Av. Ch., Milwaukee, 1904-24. Editor Central Congregationalist, 1888-93. Author: Harmony of Gospels, 1892. Home: West Boothbay Harbor, Me. Died Nov. 1, 1939.

BEALE, Joseph Henry, lawyer; b. Dorchester, Mass., Oct. 12, 1861; s. Joseph H. and Frances E. (Messinger) B.; A.B., Harvard, 1882, A.M., LL.B., 1887; LL.D., U. of Wis. and U. of Chicago, 1904, Cambridge Univ., 1921, Harvard, 1927, Boston Coll., 1932, U. of Mich., 1933; m. Elizabeth C. Day, Dec. 23, 1891; children—Elizabeth Chadwick (Mrs. B. D. Edwards), Joseph Henry, Alice. In practice, Boston, 1887-92; lecturer, Harvard, 1890-92, asst. prof. law, 1892-97, prof., 1897-1908, Carter prof. gen. jurisprudence, 1908-12, Royall prof. law, 1912-37, retired 1937; prof. law and dean law sch., U. of Chicago, 1902-04. Mem. Mass. State Commn. for Simplifying Criminal Pleadings, 1900; reporter for conflict of laws, Am. Law Inst. Fellow Am. Acad. Arts and Sciences. Author: Cases on Criminal Law, 4th edit., 1927; Cases on Damages, 2d edit., 1909; Cases on Carriers, 2d edit., 1909; Criminal Pleading and Practice, 1899; Cases on the Conflict of Laws, 2d edit., 1927; Foreign Corporations, 1904; Innkeepers, 1906; Railroad Rate Regulation (with Bruce Wyman), 1906; Cases on Municipal Corporations, 1911; Cases on Liability; Cases on Taxation; A Treatise on the Conflict of Laws. Home: 29 Chauncy St., Cambridge, Mass. Died Jan. 20, 1943.

BEAMAN, Alexander Gaylord Emmons, insurance; b. West Hartford, Conn., June 23, 1885; s. Alexander Franklin and Anna Maria (Gabel) E., stepson of George Crichton Beaman; grad. high sch., Joliet, Ill., 1901; grad. Gregg Sch., Chicago, 1902; m. Adelaide Bereman Walton, Apr. 10, 1926; 1 son, Gaylord Walton. Head of comml. dept., high schs., Green Bay, Wis., 1902; teacher of shorthand, Gregg Sch., Chicago, 1903; sec. to pres., later gen. mgr.'s asst., A.T.&S.F. Ry., Chicago, 1903-08, Los Angeles, 1908-22; disbursing officer, Pacific Southwest Trust & Savings Bank, 1922-23; mng. editor Masonic Digest, 1923-25; sec. Masonic Periodicals Corp., 1923-25; dir. and officer various finance corps.; organized, 1929, and heads A. G. Beaman Agency, Ltd., gen. ins.; exec. sec., war price and rationing board, 1942-43; pres. Fire-Police Pension Commn., City of Los Angeles; dir. and sometime sec.-treas. Midnight Mission Inc.; dir. and treas. Travelers' Aid Society; trustee and sec. Calif. Coll. in China Foundation; v.p. and dir. Hollywood Acad. of Fine Arts; sec.-treas. and dir. Foundation for Med. Research, Educational Foundation, Inc.; sec. Coll. of Chinese Studies (Peking). Chmn. Com. for Care Homeless Men in Southern Calif., and of Com. of Council Social Agencies Los Angeles for care of Transients, 1934-35. Fellow Royal Geog. Soc., Am. Geog. Soc., Pacific Geog. Soc., Philalethes Soc.; mem. Soc. Colonial Wars, S.A.R., Hist. Soc. Southern Calif., Am. Inst. Graphic Arts, Bibliog. Soc. America, The Bookfellows Soc. (Chicago), Inst. of Pacific Relations, Am. Soc. Social and Political Science. Republican. Conglist. Mason (32°, K.C.C.H., K.T., Council, Shriner). Clubs: Scribes (past pres.), Authors' (asst. sec.), Book Club of Calif., Uplifters (past sec.), Zamorano (past gov.), Barlow Society; Doric (hon.), Santa Fe Masonic (hon.), Hollywood Shrine (hon.), Town Hall of Los Angeles (founder; dir.). Editor Los Angeles Consistory Bulletin since 1912. Author: A Doctor's Odyssey, 1935; History of Masonry in Los Angeles County, 1935; Pigeoneer, 1939. Research work along linguistic lines among Mayan writings, Ancient Chinese, Southwestern Indians, Alaskan tribes, etc. Home: 2284 Moreno Drive. Office: 904 Financial Center Bldg., Los Angeles, Calif. Died Oct. 22, 1943.

BEAMAN, Bartlett, army officer; b. Princeton, Mass., July 20, 1891; s. A.B., Harvard, 1913. Flying cadet, 2d Air Interceptor Command, Tours, France, 1917; commd. 1st lt., 1918, later served with 3d Air Command and with 5th Air Depot; participated in Meuse-Argonne Offensive; with 12th Aero Squadron, Am. Forces in Germany; disch., 1919; commd. 1st lt., aviation section Signal Res., 1919, and advanced through the grades to brig. gen., 1944; on active duty since 1941; assigned with inelligence div. Office Chief of Air Corps, Washington, D.C., Feb-July 1941, chief, evaluation unit, July 1941-Jan. 1942; became wing exec. officer, Hdqrs. 1st Bombardment Wing, European Theatre of Operations, 1942; chief of staff, 1st Bombardment Div., 1943-45. Decorated Legion of Merit, Bronze Star, Air Medal, Distinguished Service Medal. French Croix de Guerre and Legion of Honor. Home: 3700 Massachusetts Av. N.W., Washington 16. Died Nov. 14, 1947.

BEAMISH, Richard Joseph, lawyer, writer; b. Scranton, Pa., Nov. 6, 1869; s. Francis Allen and Mary (Loftus) B.; ed. high sch. and Sch. of the Lackawanna, Scranton; m. 3d, Maud Weatherly, Aug. 14, 1909; children—Dorothy (Mrs. John J. Madigan), Ella (Sister M. Amator), Richard J., Elsa. Admitted to Pa. bar, 1890 and began practice at Scranton; asst. dist. atty. Lackawanna County, 1890-93; mng. editor Scranton Free Press, 1893-97, Carbondale (Pa.) Anthracite; directing editor Philadelphia Press, 1911-20; special writer, Philadelphia Inquirer; polit. editor Philadelphia Record; became sec. Commonwealth of Pa., Jan. 20, 1931; chief counsel Pa. Pub. Service Commn., 1935-37; mem. Pa. Pub. Utility Commn. since 1937. Managed the presidential campaign of Judge George Gray of Delaware for Dem. nomination, 1908. Mem. Pub. Service Commn., Pa., 1926. Mem. Aero Club of Pa. Clubs: Art, Friendly Sons of St. Patrick (Phila.); National Press (Washington). Author: History of the World War (with F. A. March), 1918; America's Part in the World War (with same), 1919; Lindbergh—the Lone Eagle, 1927, Contbr. of articles to Tariff Review, etc. Writer of 20 articles on industrial conditions in Europe, many reprinted by Rep. Nat. Com. in presdl. campaign, 1928; mem. Latin-Am. tour of President-elect Hoover, winter 1928-29. Home: Riverview Manor Apts., Front and Harris Sts., Harrisburg, Pa. Died Oct. 1, 1945.

BEAN, R(obert) Bennett, college prof.; b. Gala, Botetourt County, Va., Mar. 24, 1874; s. William Bennett and Ariana Williamson (Carper) B.; B.S., Va. Poly. Inst., 1900; M.D., Johns Hopkins, 1904; m. Adelaide Leiper Martin, May 22, 1907; children—Mary Archer, William Bennett, Helen Holmes, George Martin. Asst. in anatomy, Johns Hopkins, 1904-05; instr. anatomy, U. of Mich., 1905-07; dir. anat. lab., Philippine Med. Sch., Manila, 1907-10; asso. prof. and prof. anatomy, Tulane U., 1910-16; prof. anatomy, U. of Va., since 1916. Pres. New Orleans Acad. Sciences. Fellow A.A.A.S.; mem. Am. Anat. Assn., Am. Anthrop. Assn., Sigma Xi; corr. mem. Soc. Romana Antropologia. Author: The Racial Anatomy of the Philippine Islanders, 1910; The Races of Man, 1932; The Peopling of Virginia; also many papers pertaining to anatomy. Home: University, Va. Died Sep. 3. 1944.

BEAN, William Smith, physician; b. Sumter County, S.C., Sept. 9, 1890; s. William Smith and Katherine (Fleming) B.; B.A., Presbyterian Coll. of S.C., 1909; M.D., U. of Va., 1914; m. Sophie Willis Carlisle, Apr. 9, 1918; children—William S., III, Howard Carlisle, George Adam, Joseph Sanborn. Commd. officer, U.S. Pub. Health Service, 1915, served in various capacities as surgeon; med. officer in charge Marine Hosp., Mobile, Ala., 1928-34, Pittsburgh, 1934-38, Norfolk, Va., 1934-42, Baltimore since Sept. 1942. Mem. A.M.A., Assn. Mil. Surgeons, Pi Kappa Alpha, Phi Beta Kappa. Democrat. Presbyterian. Address: U.S. Marine Hosp., Baltimore, Md.* Deceased.

BEARD, Charles Austin, author; b. nr. Knightstown, Ind., Nov. 27. 1874; s. William Henry and Mary (Payne) B.; Ph.B., DePauw U., 1898; LL.D., 1917; Oxford U., Eng., 1898-99; Cornell U., 1899-1900; Columbia, 1902-04, A.M., 1903, Ph.D., 1904; m. Mary Ritter, of Indianapolis, Mar. 8, 1900; children—Miriam, William. Adjunct prof. of politics, 1907-10, asso. prof., 1910-15, prof. politics, 1915-17, Columbia University; dir. Training Sch. for Public Service, N.Y. City, 1917-22; adviser Inst. Municipal Research, Tokyo, 1922; adviser to Viscount Geto, Japanese minister of home affairs, after earthquake in 1923. Mem. Am. Hist. Assn. (pres. 1933), Am. Polit. Science Assn. (pres. 1926), Nat. Assn. for Adult Edn. (pres. 1936). Phi Beta Kappa, Phi Gamma Delta. Author: The Office of Justice of the Peace, 1904; Introduction to the English Historians, 1906; Development of Modern Europe (with J. H. Robinson), 2 vols., 1907; Readings in Modern European History (with same), 2 vols., 1908-09; Readings in American Government, 1909; American Government and Politics, 1910; American City Government, 1912; Economic Interpretation of the Constitution, 1913; Contemporary American History, 1914; Economic Origins of Jeffersonian Democracy, 1915; History of the American People (with W. C. Bagley), 1918; Our Old World Background (with same), 1922; History of the United States (with wife), 1921; Cross Currents in Europe To-day, 1922; Economic Basis of Politics, 1922; Administration and Politics of Tokyo, 1923; Rise of American Civilization (with wife), 1927; American Party Battle, 1928; The Balkan Pivot—Yugoslavia (with George Radin), 1929. Editor: Whither Mankind, 1928; Toward Civilization, 1930; American Leviathan (with son), 1930. Editor: America Faces the Future, 1932; The Nature of the Social Sciences, 1934; The Future Comes (with G. H. E. Smith), 1934; The Idea of National Interest, 1934; The Open Door At Home, 1934; The Discussion of Human Affairs, 1936; America in Midpassage (with wife), 1939; The American Spirit (with wife), 1942; The Republic, 1943; A Basic History of The U.S., (with wife), 1944; American Foreign Policy in the Making, 1932-41, 1946; President Roosevelt and the Coming of the War 1941, 1947. Home: New Milford, Conn. Died Sept. 1, 1948; buried in Ferncliff Cemetery, Hartsdale, N.Y.

BEARD, James Thom, mining engr.; b. Brooklyn, Oct. 19, 1855; s. Ira and Isabella O. B.; grad. Adelphia Acad., Brooklyn, 1874; C.E., E.M., Columbia Sch. of Mines, 1877; m. Amelia E. Lawson, May 9, 1887; children—James Thom, Howard Iranæus, Amelia Elizabeth. Asst. engr. Brooklyn Bridge, 1877-79; resident div. engr. C.,B.& Q.R.R., 1880-83; U.S. dept. mineral surveyor, Colo., 1883-85; mining engr. Ottumwa Fuel Co., 1885-91; propr. Iowa Coal Exchange, 1891-96; asso. editor Mines and Minerals and prin. Sch. of Mines, Internat. Corr. Sch., Scranton, Pa., 1896-1911; sr. asso. editor Coal Age, New York, 1911. Sec. Ia. State Mine Examining Bd., 1888-94. Inventor: Beard-Mackie Sight Indicator for testing gas; Beard deputy safety lamp; Beard-Stine centrifugal mine fan. Republican. Mem. North Engring. Inst. Mining and Mech. Engrs., Am. Inst. Mining and Metall. Engrs.; founder, editor in chief Mine Inspectors' Inst. U.S.A.; fellow A.A.A.S.; etc. Author: The Ventilation of Mines, 1894; Design of Centrifugal Ventilators, 1899, Mine Gases and Explosions, 1908; Coal Age Pocket Book, 1916; Mine Gases and Ventilation, 1919. Compiler: Mine Examination Questions and Answers (3 vols.), 1923. Contbr. to mining jours. Home: 58 Washington Av., Danbury, Conn. Died Dec. 26, 1941.

BEARD, John Grover, univ. dean; b. Kernersville, N.C., Apr. 5, 1888; s. James William Asbury and Susan Jane (Phillips) B.; Ph.G., Sch. of Pharmacy, U. of N.C., 1909; Ph.M.; Phila. Coll. of Pharmacy and Sci., 1930; m. Mary Polk McGehee, Apr. 22, 1913 (died 1930); 1 son, Lt. Comdr. John Grover; m. 2d, Gladys Helen Angel, Dec. 27, 1932. With Univ. of

N.C. since 1909, exec. sec., 1922-31, dean Sch. of Pharmacy since 1931. Founder and mng. editor Carolina Jour. of Pharmacy until 1940. Sec.-treas. N.C. Pharm. Assn., 1912-40; vice chmn. House of Delegates, Am. Pharm. Assn., 1920-21; local sec. Am. Pharm. Assn., 1923; mem. Nat. Pharm. Syllabus Com., 1924, chmn. and editor, 1928-38; chmn. sect. of edn. and legislation, Am. Pharm. Assn., 1924, 1st v.p., 1931-32, mem. of council, 1943-44; vice-president American Association of Colleges of Pharmacy, 1925-26, pres., 1929-30, mem. executive com., 1930-31 and 1939-40; sec. Nat. Com. for Study of Pharmacy, 1929-34; pres. Nat. Assn. Pharm. Assn. Secs., 1930-31. Mem. Elisha Mitchell Scientific Soc. (pres. 1917-19), A.A.A.S., Kappa Sigma, Kappa Psi. Democrat. Methodist. Author: Therapeutic Terms and Common Diseases, 1916; Latin for Pharmacists, 1942. Editor and compiler National Pharmaceutical Syllabus, 4th edit. Editor Carolina Jour. of Pharmacy. 1915-40. Home: Chapel Hill, N.C. Died Apr. 23, 1946.

BEARD, Mary, nurse; b. Dover, N.H., Nov. 14, 1876; d. Ithamar Warren and Marcy (Foster) B.; grad. N.Y. Hosp. School of Nursing, 1903; hon. Dr. of Humanities, Univ. of N.H., 1934; unmarried. Began as visiting nurse, Waterbury, Conn., 1904; dir. Instructive Dist. Nursing Assn., Boston, 1912-22; dir. Community Health Assn., Boston, 1922-24; asso. dir. Internat. Health Div., Rockefeller Foundation, N.Y. City, 1924-38; dir. of nursing service, Am. Nat. Red Cross, Washington, D.C., 1938-44, retired. Hon. mem. Florence Nightingale Internat. Foundation, Assn. of Collegiate Schs. of Nursing; mem. Nat. Orgn. for Pub. Health Nursing, Nat. League of Nursing Edn., Am. Nurses Assn. Episcopalian. Club: Cosmopolitan (N.Y. City). Author: The Nurse in Public Health, 1929. Home: Westport, Conn. Office: American Red Cross, Washington, D.C. Died Dec. 4, 1946.

BEARD, Reuben Alview, clergyman; b. Marysville, O., Aug. 30, 1851; s. of Philander Charles and Lucinda (Howard) B.; prep. edn. Sparta (O.) Acad.; admitted to bar, 1872, and practiced law until 1876; grad. Oberlin Theol. Sem., 1879; D.D., Whitman Coll., Wash., 1891; m. Lucinda E. Barton, June 26, 1870 (died Jan. 7, 1875); m. 2d, Mary Emma Smith, Mar. 6, 1879; children—Marguerite Lucile, Ralph Finney, Hubert Kingsley. Ordained Congl. ministry, 1879; pastor Brainerd, Minn., 1879-82, Fargo, Dak. Terr., 1882-88; supt. Home Missions, Wash., 1888-91; pres., Fargo Coll., 1891-94; pastor: Nashua, N.H., 1894-97; Cambridge, Mass., 1897-1903; N.E. sec. Congl. Home Missionary Soc., 1903-06; pastor 1st Ch., Fargo, 1906-30. Mem. N.D. Bd. of Am. Red Cross. Mason (32°). Clubs: Commercial, Kiwanis, Red River Congregational. Home: 713 Third Av., S., Fargo, N.D. Died July 14, 1941.

BEARDSLEY, Arthur Lehman (bērdz'lē), pres. Miles Laboratories, Inc.; b. Buchanan, Mich., Dec. 27, 1869; s. Solomon Lehman and Martha (Foster) B.; ed. pub. schs., Kalamazoo, Mich.; m. Stella Huggett, June 16, 1896; children—Olive Maude (Mrs. Robert Jerome Earl), Edward Huggett. With Edwards & Chamberlain Hardware Co., Kalamazoo, 1889-1900, Ocmulgee Lumber Co., Lumber City, Ga., 1901-02; asso. with Cleveland Twist Drill Co., 1902-20; with Miles Labs., Inc., mfrs. proprietary medicine, Elkhart, Ind., since 1920, successively as purchasing agent, plant mgr., treas. and gen. mgr., now pres. and treas.; dir. First Nat. Bank of Elkhart. Republican. Presbyterian. Mason (K.T., 32°). Clubs: Chicago Athletic, Rotary, City, Christiana Country (Elkhart). Home: 302 E. Bearsley Av. Office: Myrtle and McNaughton Sts., Elkhart, Ind. Died Jan. 4, 1944.

BEARDSLEY, James Wallace, engineer; b. Coventry, Chenango County, N.Y., Sept. 11, 1860; s. William Hurd and Catherine Tremper (Phillips) B.; grad. State Normal Sch., Cortland, N.Y., 1884; C.E., Cornell, 1891; m. Ellen J. Pearne, Sept. 7, 1893; 1 son, Wallace Pearne. Asst. engr. with Sanitary Dist. of Chicago, in charge constrn., 1892-98; with U.S. Bd. Engrs., on deep waterways, in charge St. Lawrence River surveys, 1898-1900; with U.S. Corps of Engrs., in charge harbor work, 1900-02; in P.I., as cons. engr. to Philippine Commn., 1902-03; chief Bur. of Engring., 1903-05, dir. Pub. Works, P.I., 1905-08; cons. engr. investigating irrigation in Java, India and Egypt, 1908-09; irrigation engr. with J. G. White & Co., New York, 1909-10; chief engr. Puerto Rico Irrigation Service, 1910-16; private cons. practice, 1916-18; cons. engr. in ordnance, 1918; asst. chief engr. grand canal surveys of China, 1918-19; chief engr. and mem. Junta Central de Caminos, Panama, 1920-21; cons. engr., 1922-25; with Obras Publicas, Santo Domingo, R.D., 1926-29; private cons. practice since 1930. Mem. Am. Soc. C.E., Western Soc. Engrs., Delta Phi, Sphinx Head (Cornell). Republican. Methodist. Club: Technology (Syracuse). Home: 141 Franklin St., Auburn, N.Y. Died May 15, 1944.

BEARDSLEY, William Agur, clergyman; b. Monroe, Conn., May 5, 1865; s. Agur and Elizabeth Ann (Lewis) B.; B.A., Trinity Coll., Conn., 1887, M.A., 1890, D.D., 1922; grad. Berkeley Div. Sch., Conn., 1890, D.D., 1920; m. Alletta H. Warwick, June 23, 1897 (died Dec. 27, 1935); 1 son, Warwick. Deacon, 1890, priest, 1891, P.E. Ch.; asst. St. Thomas Ch., New Haven, 1890-92, rector, 1892-1934, rector emeritus since 1934. Examining chaplain Diocese of Conn., 1910-32, also sec. bd., 1918-32; dep. Gen. Conv. P.E. Ch., 1916, mem. Standing Com. 1917-39, sec. of com., 1932-34, pres., 1934-39; registrar Diocese since 1917; hon. canon Christ Ch. Cathedral. Trustee Berkeley Divinity School, 1915-35 and since 1941, secretary of the board, 1931-35; trustee and secretary of the board Episcopal Academy, Connecticut. Mem. and dir. New Haven Colony Hist. Soc. (pres. 1913-22), Conn. Soc. Colonial Wars, Am. Hist. Assn., Church Hist. Soc., Phi Beta Kappa, Psi Upsilon. Author: An Old New Haven Engraver and His Work—Amos Doolittle, 1914. Editor General Catalogue of Officers, Teachers and Alumni of the Episcopal Acad. of Conn., 1796-1916, 1916. Compiler: Notes on some of the Warwicks of Virginia, 1937; History of St. Thomas' Church, New Haven, 1940. Contbr. Dictionary Am. Biography. Author of monograph on Bishop Chauncey B. Brewster, 1942; numerous historical sermons on Connecticut parishes. Home: 70 Elm St., New Haven, Conn. Died Dec. 28, 1946.

BEATON, Ralph Hastings (bā'tŭn), pres. Winifrede Co.; b. Indianapolis, Ind., Apr. 28, 1876; s. Thomas Augustas and Laura Adelia (Smith) B.; ed. Ohio State U.; m. Eleanor Kurtz, Oct. 19, 1904; 1 dau., Mrs. Eleanor Ione Krumm. Pres. Winifrede Co., Kokomo (Ind.) Gas & Fuel Co., Richmond (Ind.) Gas Corp., Exact Weight Scale Co. Trustee Columbus Gallery of Fine Arts. Mem. Archæol. and Hist. Soc. Ohio. Republican. Club: Columbus. Home: 260 N. Columbia Av. Office: 50 W. Broad St., Columbus, O. Died July 3, 1943.

BEATTIE, Robert Brewster, clergyman; b. Middletown, N.Y., Sept. 19, 1875; s. Rev. Charles (D.D.) and Harriet Harris (Tobias) B.; prep. edn., Wallkill Acad., Middletown; B.A., Union Coll., Schenectady, N.Y., 1896, D.D., 1917; grad. Princeton Theol. Sem., 1899; m. Cecilia Dolson, Nov. 2, 1899 (deceased); 1 son, Charles Robert. Ordained ministry Presbyn. Ch., 1899; pastor Broad Av. Presbyn. Ch., Altoona, Pa., 1899-1903, First Ch., Franklin, 1903-12, First Presbyn. Ch., East Orange, N.J., 1912-42. Trustee Bloomfield Sem., Home for Aged Presbyterians (Belvidere, N.J.). Mem. Beta Theta Pi. Clubs: Essex County Country, Rock Spring Country, Rumson Country. Home: Rumson, N.J. Died Oct. 9, 1946.

BEATTY, Arthur (bē'tē), prof. English; b. St. Marys, Can., Mar. 6, 1869; s. Robert and Susan (Cherry) B.; B.A., U. of Toronto, 1893; studied at Cornell U.; Ph.D., Columbia, 1897; univs. of Oxford and Paris; m. Carlotta J. K. McCutcheon, June 29, 1899; 1 son, Arthur Hamilton McCutcheon. Instr. rhetoric, 1896-1902, instr. English, later prof., U. of Wis. Decorated Officier d'Academie (France), 1919. Life mem. Wis. Acad. Sciences, Arts and Letters, Wisconsin Archæological Society; mem. Modern Lang. Association of America. Republican. Congregationalist. Clubs: University (Madison); Authors' (London). Author: William Wordsworth—His Doctrine and Art in Their Historical Relations, 1st edit., 1922, second edition, 1927. Translator: Brunetière's Art and Morality, 1899. Editor: De Quincey's Opium Eater, 1900; Tennyson's Idylls of the King, 1904, 1928; Swinburne's Selected Poems, 1906; Swinburne's Selected Dramas, 1909; Macaulay's Lays of Ancient Rome, 1911; Romantic Poets of the Nineteenth Century, 1927; Representative Poems of William Wordsworth, 1937. Home: Madison, Wis. Died Feb. 27, 1943.

BEATTY, Bessie (bēt'tī), radio commentator; b. Los Angeles, Jan. 27, 1886; d. Thomas Edward and Jane Mary (Boxwell) Beatty; ed. Girls' Collegiate School, and Occidental College; m. William Sauter (actor), Aug. 15, 1926. Began as reporter Los Angeles Herald, 1904, dramatic editor, 1905-06; went to San Francisco to edit special edition of the Bulletin, 1908, and continued on editorial staff until 1917; organized social service dept. of the Bulletin, edited daily feature page, and acted as special correspondent in Washington, D.C., Alaska, the Orient, etc.; spent 8 mos. in Russia, 1917, and later contributed articles to leading magazines; became editor McCall's Magazine Aug. 15, 1918, and later special corr. in Russia, Hearst's Magazine and Good Housekeeping. Organized, and conducted for 6 years, "Happyland," summer camp for boys and girls of San Francisco poor; wrote and spoke for equal suffrage in Calif. and Nev. campaigns. Mem. Internat. P.E.N., N.Y. League of Women Voters, N.Y. State Dem. Women, World Center for Women's Archives (director), Museum of Costume Art, Phi Delta Gamma (hon.). Clubs: Women's City, Nat. Arts, Pen and Brush, Actors' Dinner (pres. 1933-35), San Francisco Center. Author: Political Primer for the New Voter, 1912; The Red Heart of Russia, 1918. Lecturer on Russia and Feminism. Contbr. of short stories to mags. Co-author plays "Salt Chunk Mary," 1927, Jamboree, 1932. Former dir. of edn. Nat. Campaign, NRA Garment-Label; former dir. Nat. Label Council. Conducts daily 45-minute radio program, WOR, N.Y. City. Home: 142 E. 19th St., New York, N.Y Died Apr. 6, 1947.

BEATTY, Sir Edward (bē'tī), railway official; b. Thorold, Ont., Oct. 16, 1877; s. Henry and Harriet M. (Powell) B.; B.A., U. of Toronto; hon. degrees, McGill U., 1925, U. of Toronto, 1925, Bishop's U., 1927, McMaster U., 1930, U. of Western Ontario, 1935, New York U., 1936, U. of New Brunswick, 1936, Queen's U., 1937, U. of Alberta, 1938, Dartmouth Coll., 1938; unmarried. Began with law firm, McCarthy, Osler, Hoskin & Creelman, Toronto, 1898; admitted to Ont. bar, 1901; with Canadian Pacific Ry. since 1901, as asst. in law dept., 1901-05, asst. solicitor, 1905-10, gen. solicitor, 1910-13, gen. counsel, 1913, v.p. and gen. counsel, 1914-18, dir. since 1916, pres. since 1918, also chmn. bd. since 1924; chmn. Canadian Pacific Steamships, Consol. Mining and Smelting Co., West Kootenay Power & Light Co.; pres. Quebec Salvage & Wrecking Co.; alternately pres. and v.p. Northern Alberta Rys. and Toronto Terminal Ry. Co.; dir. Bank of Montreal, Royal Trust Co., Canadian Industries, Ltd., Sun Life Assurance Co., Royal Exchange Assurance Co., Waldorf-Astoria Hotel Corp., M.,St.Paul&S.S.M. R.R., Canadian Investment Fund, Henry Gardner Co. (London), Amalgamated Metals, Ltd. (London), Toronto, Hamilton & Buffalo Ry. Chancellor McGill U.; chmn. Rhodes Scholarship Selection Com. for the Province of Quebec; mem. of Corp. of Bishop's U.; pres. The Boy Scouts Assn. of Canada; pres. Shawbridge Boys' Farm and Training Sch.; pres. Nat. Com. for Mental Hygiene (Canada); v.p. and trustee Royal Victoria Hosp.; pres. Montreal Orchestra; pres. British Empire Games Assn.; hon. pres. St. John Ambulance Assn., Canadian Nat. Inst. for the Blind, Montreal Boys' Assn., mem. advisory bd. Montreal Gen. Hosp.; gov. Canadian Corp. of Commissionaires; freeman, Vancouver, B.C., London, Ont., Saint John, N.B., Cranbrook, N.B.; hon. capt. Royal Canadian Naval Vol. Reserve. Decorated Knight Grand Cross Order of the British Empire, 1935; Hon. Bencher of the Middle Temple (London), 1935; Knight of Grace Order of the Hosp. of St. John of Jerusalem, 1934; Knight Comdr. first class, Order of St. Olaf (Norway), 1924. Clubs: Mount Royal, St. James's, University, Montreal Hunt, Forest and Stream, St. George's (Montreal); York (Toronto); Rideau, Country (Ottawa); Century (N.Y. City); Ranelagh, Marlborough (London, Eng.). Home: 1266 Pine Av., W. Office: Windsor St. Station, Montreal, Quebec, Can.
Died Mar. 23, 1943.

BEATTYS, George Davis (bā'tēs), lawyer; b. Poughkeepsie, N.Y., July 20, 1862; s. George Hubbell and Mary Elizabeth (Davis) B.; A.B., Wesleyan U., Conn., 1885, A.M., 1888; LL.B., Columbia, 1887; m. Jessie L. McDermut, Oct. 22, 1890 (died Feb. 20, 1932); children—Frank L., Mrs. Adele M. Beatty, Mrs. Madeleine Dobbrow, Mrs. Jessie Rogers. Practiced in N.Y. City since 1887; gen. counsel Æolian Co., Mutual Bond & Mortgage Corp.; asst. corp. counsel, Brooklyn, 1906. Mem. 7th Regt. N.Y.N.G., 5 yrs.; prize commr. E. Dist., N.Y., Spanish-Am. War. Mem. bd. mgrs. Methodist Hosp., Am. Bible Soc.; trustee John St. M.E. Ch. Trust Fund Soc. (pres.). Trustee Wesleyan U., Conn., 1905-35. Mem. Gen. Conf. of Meth. Ch., 1936. Member American Bar Assn., N.Y. State Bar Assn., Assn. Bar City of N.Y., Phi Nu Theta, Phi Beta Kappa (Wesleyan). Republican. Methodist. Mason. Home: 177 Harrison Av., Westfield, N.J. Office: 27 W. 57th St., New York, N.Y. Died Sep. 28, 1945.

BEAUMONT, John Colt (bō'mŏnt), officer Marine Corps; b. Washington, D.C., Oct. 7, 1878; s. John Colt and Frances Sayer (King) B.; student St. John's Coll., Annapolis, 1895-96, Fordham U., 1897-99; grad. Naval War Coll., 1930, Army War Coll., 1931; m. May Lansing Gates 1906 (died 1916); 1 dau., Natalie; m. 2d, Helen Ferguson Tucker, April 3, 1937. Commd. 2d lt. U.S.M.C., 1900, and promoted through grades to Col., apptd. brig. gen., July 25, 1935; served in the Philippines, 1902-04, Nicaraguan Revolution, 1912, Vera Cruz occupation, 1914, Haitian Revolution, 1915, World War, 1917-18; on staff comdr.-in-chief U.S. fleet, 1923-25, and 1927-29; comdr. of U.S. Marine Corps Forces in China, 1933-36; comdr. of 2d Brigade Marines, Shanghai, during China-Japan hostilities Sept. 1937-Feb. 18, 1938. Awarded Order de Merite by President of Nicaragua; Navy Cross, World War. Catholic. Clubs: Army and Navy (Washington); University (Phila.); Chevy Chase (Md.). Address: Navy Dept., Washington, D.C. Died Apr. 12, 1942.

BEAUX, Cecilia (bō), artist; b. Phila.; d. John Adolphe and Cecilia Kent (Leavitt) Beaux; pupil of Wm. Sartain, the Julian School and the Lazar School, Paris; LL.D., U. of Pa., 1908, M.A., Yale, 1912. Awarded gold medal of Phila. Art Club; Dodge prize, Nat. Acad. of Design; bronze and gold medals, Carnegie Inst.; gold medal of honor and the Temple gold medal of Pa. Acad. of Fine Arts; also gold medal at Paris Expn., 1900; Saltus gold medal, Nat. Acad. Design, 1913; medal of honor, Panama, 1915; gold medal, Art Inst. Chicago, 1921; gold medal, Am. Acad. Arts and Letters, 1926; gold medal, National Achievement Award, 1934. Represented at Pa. Acad. Fine Arts; Toledo Art Museum; Met. Museum, New York; Brooks Memorial Gallery, Memphis; John Herron Art Inst., Indianapolis; Boston Art Museum; Art Inst. Chicago; Corcoran Gallery, Washington, D.C.; Luxembourg Gallery, Paris; Gallery of the Uffizi, Florence, Italy. Exhibited at Champs de Mars, 1896. N.A., 1902; Sociétaire des Beaux Arts; mem. Nat. Inst. Arts and Letters, Am. Acad. of Arts and Letters. Address: (May-Dec.) Gloucester, Mass.; (Dec.-May) 132 E. 19th St., New York, N.Y.
Died Sep. 17, 1942.

BEAVEN, Albert William (běv'ĕn), clergyman; b. Moscow, Ida., Oct. 21, 1882; s. Rev. Samuel William and Lizzie Josephine (Baker) B.; B.A., Shurtleff Coll., Alton, Ill., 1906; grad. Rochester Theol. Sem., 1909, B.D., 1930; D.D., Shurtleff, 1919, U. of Rochester, 1920, McMaster Univ., 1931; Colby Coll., 1940; LL.D., Hillsdale Coll., Hillsdale, Mich., 1930; hon. L.H.D., Alfred U., 1939; m. Grace Hunter Haddow, June 23, 1909 (died April 15, 1938); children—

Winifred Elizabeth (dec.), Mary-Jean (Mrs. Bradford Sherman Abernethy), Robert Haddow, Margaret Helen; m. 2d, Marion Harrison Barbour, May 27, 1939. Ordained Bapt. min., 1908; pastor Lake Av. Ch., Rochester, N.Y., 1909-29; developed "Three Period Session Plan" of religious edn.; "Wednesday Night Club" idea for the midweek service; "Church Service Corps" form of parish organization; pres. and prof. practical theology, Colgate-Rochester Divinity Sch. since July 1, 1929. Lecturer on "Church Management" at Rochester Theological Sem., 1923, 29; at Summer Conf. Union Theological Sem., 1924. Convention preacher Northern Bapt. Conv., 1922; 1st v.p. same 1924-25 and 1928-29, pres., 1930-31; served as univ. preacher, Cornell U., Mt. Holyoke, U. of Chicago, Duke, Columbia, Wesleyan University, Pa. State College; lecturer, Chautauqua, N.Y., 1927 and 1929; Cole lecturer Vanderbilt Univ., 1939. Y.M.C.A. work, Camp Wadsworth, S.C., 1917; secretary Y.M.C.A., in U.S., France and Germany, World War. Pres. bd. mgrs. Newark (N.Y.) Custodia Asylum, 1915-18; pres. bd. trustees Rochester Theol. Sem., 1922-28, Colgate-Rochester Div. Sch., 1928-29; pres. N.Y. State Council of Churches, 1932; pres. Fed. Chs. of Rochester and Monroe County, 1932-33. Mem. Bd. of Edn. of Northern Bapt. Conv.; chmn. bd. mgrs. Am. Bapt. Home Mission Soc., 1932-41; pres. N.Y. State Bapt. Conv., 1926-29, Federal Council Chs. of Christ in America, 1932-34; member at large Asso. Boards for Christian Colls. in China; v.p., Bapt. World Alliance, 1934-39; mem. bd. mgrs. Internat. Soc. of Christian Endeavor; mem. bd. mgrs. Rochester Pub. Library; mem. editorial board of Religion in Life; member bd. dirs. Rochester Civic Music Assn. since 1931; pres. Conf. of Theol. Seminaries of U.S. and Can.; mem. bd. dirs. Rochester Community Chest; trustee Westminster Choir School (Princeton, N.J.); pres. bd. of trustees of Shaw University Raleigh, North Carolina. Member Chamber Commerce (Rochester), Pi Gamma Mu, Theta Phi, Alpha Chi. Republican. Mason. Hon. mem. Rochester Rotary Club. Author: Fine Art of Living Together; Putting the Church on a Full Time Basis; Sermons for Every Day Living; Fireside Talks with the Family Circle; The Lift of a Far View; The Local Church—Its Purpose and Program; Remaking Life. Contbr. to ch. periodicals; also chapters in various vols. on religion. Home: 1122 S. Goodman St., Rochester, N.Y. Died Jan. 24, 1943.

BEAVER, Harry C., mfr. pumps and machinery; b McAlisterville, Pa., Aug. 13, 1876; s. Spencer F. and Minerva (Beasor) B.; ed. Juniata Coll., Huntingdon, Pa., Martin's Business Sch., Pittsburgh, Marquette U. Law Sch.; m. Jane Carvel, Jan. 17, 1901; children—Paul F., Winifred (Mrs. A. N. Clifton), Harry C. Began with Pa. R.R., 1896; successively with U.P. R.R., Westinghouse Electric and Mfg. Co., Allis-Chalmers Mfg. Co. (Milwaukee), Stevens-Duryea Co. and Rolls-Royce Co. of America (both of Springfield, Mass.), until 1930; pres. Worthington Pump and Machinery Corp., Harrison, N.J., 1931-45; vice chmn. bd. since Jan. 1945. Conglist. Home: Longmeadow, Mass. Address: Worthington Pump and Machinery Corp., 2 Park Av., New York. Died Apr. 2, 1947; buried at Longmeadow, Mass.

BEAZELL, William Preston (bē-zĕl'), writer; b. St. Clairsville, O., June 21, 1877; s. Rev. B. F. and Mary (Welling) B.; B.A., Allegheny Coll., 1897, Litt.D., 1928; m. Isabel Howe, 1909. Reporter Pittsburgh Leader, 1897-98; reporter and night city editor, Pittsburgh Commercial Gazette, 1898-1903; political and editorial writer, Pittsburgh Times, 1903-06; night editor, Pittsburgh Post, 1906-07; editor, Pittsburgh Index and Pittsburgh Bulletin, 1907-10; joined staff of The World, New York, 1910, day mng. editor, 1921-30; asso. in journalism, Sch. of Journalism, Columbia, 1923-32; asst. editor of Today (mag.), 1934; mng. dir. Saratoga Springs Authority, 1935-44. Sec. and exec. dir. Citizens Com. on Control of Crime in New York, 1936-41. Pub. relations adviser to Com. on Costs of Med. Care, Real Estate Bondholders Protective Com., Nat. Transportation Com., Am. Inst. of Consulting Engrs., President's Com. on Mobilization of Relief Resources, 1931; exec. sec. N.Y. State NRA Com., 1933. Trustee and past pres. Gen. Alumni Assn. of Allegheny Coll.; pres. Soc. of Meth. Preachers Sons. Mem. Phi Delta Theta, Sigma Delta Chi (hon. nat. pres., 1929), Am. Soc. Newspaper Editors (dir. 1929), N.Y. State Hist. Assn., Long Island Hist. Soc., Bucks County Hist. Soc., A.A.A.S., Pennsylvania Acad. Sci. Made first lay survey of development of Air Service, U.S. Army, for which received official commendation, 1918; covered whole series of successful and attempted transatlantic flights, Newfoundland, 1919. Clubs: Players, Dutch Treat (New York); Nat. Press (Washington, D.C.). Author: The Great Boz Ball. Contbr. numerous nature essays in Atlantic Monthly, etc. Home: Greenriggin, Tinicum, Pa. Died Mar. 12, 1946.

BEBB, Charles Herbert, architect; b. West Hall, Mortlake, Surrey, Eng., Apr. 10, 1856; s. Henry Charles Lewis and Jessie (Green) B.; grad. high sch., Kensington, London; student King's Coll., London, Yverdun and U. of Lausanne, Switzerland, and Sch. of Mines, London; m. Virginia Rutter Burns, Nov. 22, 1882 (died Dec. 6, 1926); 1 son, Joseph Crispia. Came to U.S., 1880; naturalized citizen, 1915. Began practice, Chicago, Ill., 1886; moved to Seattle, Wash., 1893; mem. Bebb and Gould, Seattle, 1912-39, now Bebb and Jones; firm architects of buildings for U. of Washington, residences and comml. buildings, Bellingham, Everett, Mt. Vernon, Yakima, etc.; personally in charge as supervising architect of Wash. State Capitol since 1911, and has served as architect for county, city, sch. and park bds. and as chmn. Bd. of Appeals. Fellow Am. Inst. Architects, 1911, Royal Soc. Arts, London; mem. Wash. State Chapter A.I.A (pres. 3 terms). Republican. Mason (32°, Shriner). Clubs: University, Rainier, Ranch, Seattle Golf, Olympic Golf, Kalso Gun. Home: University Club. Office: Hoge Bldg., Seattle. Died June 21, 1942.

BECK, Edward Scott, newspaper man; b. Bainbridge, Ind., Dec. 12, 1868; s. Moses Milton and Mary Hamilton (Scott) B.; A.B., U. of Mich., 1893; m. Cora Frances Reilly, 1896 (died 1899); m. 2d, Grace Kennicott Redfield, Aug. 23, 1911 (died Dec. 2, 1928); m. 3d, Clare Florence Beebe, May 2, 1931. With Chicago Tribune since 1893 as reporter, copy-reader, night city editor, city editor and mng. editor, and as asst. editor-in-chief since 1936; also 2d v.p. Chicago Tribune Co. Mem. Beta Theta Pi, Loyal Legion. Clubs: University, Chicago, Tavern, Glenview Golf, Casino; Everglades, Seminole, Bath and Tennis (Palm Beach). Home: "The Grove," Glenview, Ill.; and Fairways, Palm Beach, Fla. Office: Chicago Tribune, Chicago, Ill. Died Dec. 25, 1942.

BECK, Jean-Baptiste, prof. Romanic langs. and history of music; b. Guebwiller, Alsace, Aug. 14, 1881; s. Jean-Baptiste and Barbara (LaWurlin) B.; ed. Ecole Alsacienne, Paris, U. of Strasbourg, Sorbonne and Ecole des Hautes Etudes, Paris; Ph.D., history music; b. Guebwiller, Ht.-Rhin, Fr., Aug. 14, U. of Strasbourg, 1907; m. Louise Goebel, June 15, 1912; children—Jean-Marie Baumont, Marie-Louise. Prof. Latin, Ecole Alsacienne, 1900-02; French exchange prof., U. of Vienna, 1910; prof. Romanic langs., U. of Ill., 1911-14, Bryn Mawr Coll., 1914-20, U. of Pa. since 1920; prof. history of music, Yvette Guilbert Sch., 1916-18, Columbia and Inst. Mus. Art, 1919-20, Curtis Inst. Music, 1924-38. Organist, St. Léger, 1899, St. Gervais, Paris, 1900-02. Fellow Am. Mediæval Acad., Am. Geog. Soc.; mem. Am. Inst. Polit. Science, Am. Musicol. Soc. (exec. bd.), Council of Learned Socs. (com. on musicology); rep. of Curtis Inst. of Music at Beethoven Centennial, Vienna, 1927. Catholic. Author: Die Melodien der Troubadours, 1908; La Musique des Troubadours, 1909; Corpus Cantilenarum Medii Aevi: le Manuscript Cangé, 1927; Le Manuscript du Roi (in collaboration with Madame Louise Beck), 1938. Discoverer of key to translation of medieval music. Home: 125 Radnor St., Bryn Mawr, Pa. Died June 23, 1943; buried Sleepy Hollow Cemetery, Tarrytown, N.Y.

BECK, Marcus Wayland, judge; b. Harris County, Ga., Apr. 28, 1860; s. Rev. James W. and Margaret Wells B.; A.B., U. of Ga., 1881, LL.B., 1882; m. Carrie R. Ellis, 1888; children—Mrs. C. S. Moeckel, Mrs. M. B. Batterton, Marcus W. (died in battle, Belleau Woods, France, June 14, 1918) and 1 son died in infancy. Mem. Ga. Senate, 1890; solicitor-general, 1892-94; judge Superior courts, Flint Circuit, 1894-98; resigned as judge to become major 3d Ga. Infantry during Spanish-Am. War; justice Supreme Ct. of Ga. since 1905 (presiding justice since Oct. 1, 1917). Mem. bd. of consulting editors Am. and English Ency. Law and Practice. Mem. Phi Beta Kappa. Baptist. Democrat. Home: Stratford Rd. Office: State Capitol, Atlanta, Ga. Died Jan. 21, 1943.

BECKER, Alfred Le Roy, lawyer; b. Buffalo, N.Y., Mar. 22, 1878; s. Tracy Chatfield and Minnie Alfredena (Le Roy) B.; A.B., Harvard, 1900; LL.B., U. of Buffalo, 1902; m. Eulabee Dix, Dec. 22, 1910; children—Philip Dix, Joan L. A.; m. 2d, Mary Cecelia Hawkins, Nov. 5, 1933; adopted son, George Vincent. With Roberts, Becker, Messer & Groat, Buffalo, 1902-07; lecturer on contracts, U. of Buffalo Law Sch., 1902-06; with Hoyt & Spratt, 1907-14; deputy attorney general State of N.Y., 1915-19; member firm Franc & Becker, 1919-27; practiced alone from 1928-39; associated in practice with Charles P. Franchot, 1939-44; practicing alone since May 1944. Member of advisory board of Selective Service System, 1941-43. Became nationally prominent on account of investigation and exposure of German plots and propaganda, 1917-19. Republican. Mason. Author: Mr Adriaen van der Donck, 1902; Medical Jurisprudence, Forensic Medicine and Toxicology, 1910; Forged Checks and Drafts, 1927; Franchot Ancestry, 1941. Contbr. of articles on hist. and geneal. topics. Home: 2121 Cedar Av. Office: 60 E. 42d St., New York, N.Y. Died July 12, 1948.

BECKER, Arthur Dow, osteopathic physician; b. Austin, Minn., Aug. 20, 1878; s. Marcus and Sarah Growden (Blair) B.; D.O., S. S. Still Coll. Osteopathy and Surgery, Des Moines, Ia., 1903; D.O., Kirksville Sch. Osteopathy, Kirksville, Mo., 1910; B.S., Kirksville Coll. of Osteopathy and Surgery, 1925; hon. D.Sc. in Osteopathy from same, 1938; D.Sc. (hon.), College of Osteopathic Physicians and Surgeons, Los Angeles, Calif., 1944; m. Mabel Rollins, Oct. 17, 1906; children—Rollin Edward, Alan Robert. Practiced at Preston, Minn., 1903-08, 1911-15, Minneapolis, 1915-22, Seattle, Wash., 1926-28; mem. faculty and dean Kirksville Coll. Osteopathy and Surgery, 1922-26; mem. faculty and vice pres., 1928-35; pres. Des Moines Still Coll. of Osteopathy, 1935-42; sr. consultant, Detroit Osteopathic Hosp. since 1944. Pres. Am. Coll. Osteopathic Internists since 1944; pres. Am. Osteopathic Assn., 1931-32, trustee, 1913-16, 1927-30, 1933-39; pres. Associated Colleges of Osteopathy, 1938-39; twice pres. Minn. State Osteopathic Assn. Member Minn. State Board Osteopathic Examiners 9½ years. Received Distinguished Service Certificate from the American Osteopathic Assn., 1941. Republican. Mason, Rotarian. Contbr. to various osteopathic publs. Office: 517-27 Florida National Bank Bldg., St. Petersburg 5, Fla. Died May 16, 1947; buried at Austin, Minn.

BECKER, Carl Lotus, college prof.; b. Lincoln Twp., Blackhawk County, Ia., Sept. 7, 1873; s. Charles DeWitt and Almeda (Sarvay) B.; ed. Cornell Coll., Mt. Vernon, Ia., 1892-93; B.Litt., U. of Wis., 1896, grad. student, 1896-97, fellow, 1897-98, Ph.D., same univ., 1907; fellow constl. law, Columbia, 1898-99; Litt.D., Yale, 1932, Rochester, 1938; Columbia, 1939; m. Maude H. Ranney, June 16, 1901. Instr. in history and polit. science, Pa. State Coll., 1899-1901; instr. in history, Dartmouth, 1901-02; asst. prof. in European history, 1902-07; asso. prof., 1907-08, prof., 1908-16, U. of Kan.; prof. U. of Minn., 1916-17, Cornell U. since 1917. Mem. Am. Hist. Assn., Am. Acad. Arts and Sciences, Am. Philos. Soc., Inst. of Arts and Letters, Am. Antiquarian Soc. Author: Political Parties in the Province of New York from 1760-75, 1908; Beginnings of the American People, 1915; Eve of the Revolution, 1918; Our Great Experiment in Democracy, 1924; The Declaration of Independence—A Study in the History of Political Ideas, 1922; The Spirit of '76 (with G. M. Clark and W. E. Dodd), 1926; Modern History, 1931; The Heavenly City of the Eighteenth Century Philosophers, 1932; Every Man His Own Historian, 1935; Progress and Power, 1936; Story of Civilization (with Frederic Duncalf), 1938; Modern Democracy, 1941; New Liberties for Old, 1942; The Founding of Cornell University, 1943; How New Will The Better World Be?, 1943; also various essays on hist. subjects. Home: 109 W. Upland Rd., Ithaca, N.Y. Died Apr. 10, 1945.

BECKER, William Dee, mayor; b. East St. Louis, Ill.; s. John Philip and Anna A. (Cammann) B.; student Smith Acad., St. Louis; A.B., Harvard U.; LL.B., Washington U., 1901; m. Margaret Louise McIntosh, June 10, 1902; children—Alan Dee, Anne Louise (Mrs. Lawrence H. Stern). Admitted to Mo. bar, 1901, and began practice of law; judge St. Louis Court of Appeals, 1916-40; mayor, St. Louis, 1941-43. Mem. Am., Mo. State and St. Louis bar assns., St. Louis Chamber of Commerce, Lawyers' Assn. of St. Louis, Washington U. Alumni Assn. Republican. Clubs: University, Noonday, Harvard. Home: 5374 Delmar Blvd. Office: City Hall, St. Louis, Mo. Died Aug. 1, 1943.

BECKERS, William Gerard, mfg. chemist; b. Kempen, Rhein, Germany, Feb. 12, 1874; s. Gerard and Maria Magdalena (Frantzen) B.; student Poly Inst., Aix la Chapelle; Ph.D., U. of Freiburg, 1897; m. Marie Antoinette Pothen; children—William Kurt, Elsa M. Served as 1st lt. German Army; asst. prof. chemistry Royal Dye Sch., Crefeld, 1898-1900; became connected with Bayer Co., mfrs. dyestuffs and chemicals, Elberfeld, 1900, and came to U.S., 1902, in charge tech. depts. of Am. br., same co.; founder, 1911, Beckers' Aniline & Chem. Works, of which was pres. and chmn. bd.; company consolidated with other cos., 1917, as Nat. Aniline & Chem. Co., Inc., of which is dir. and vice pres.; also dir. of Allied Chemical & Dye Corporation, Murray Hill Trust Co. (New York), Bolton Nat. Bank, Aviation Corp. (Del.), Canadian Colonial Airways, Inc. Naturalized citizen of U.S., 1911. Trustee Polytechnic Inst., Brooklyn. Mem. Am. Chem. Soc., Soc. Chem. Industries (Eng.). Republican. Clubs: Chemists, Lawyers' (New York); Montauk, Riding and Driving (Brooklyn, N.Y.); Country, Sagamore Golf (Lake George, N.Y.); Aviation Country Club, L.I. Home: 1067 5th Av., New York; (summer) Beckersville, N.Y. Office: 61 Broadway, New York. Died Nov. 3, 1948.

BECKET, Frederick Mark, chemist, metallurgist; b. Montreal, Can., Jan. 11, 1875; s. Robert Anderson and Anne (Wilson) B.; B.A.Sc., McGill U., 1895; LL.D., McGill U., 1934; A.M., Columbia U., 1899, grad. study, 1900-02, Sc.D., 1929; m. Geraldine McBride, Oct. 8, 1908; children—Ethelwynne (Mrs. Paul H. Folwell), Ruth Alene (Mrs. Ruth Becket Trauter). Came to U.S., 1895, naturalized citizen, 1918. With Westinghouse Electric & Mfg. Co., East Pittsburgh, Pa., 1895-96, Acker Process Co., at Jersey City, N.J., 1896-98, at Niagara Falls, N.Y., 1899-1900, Ampere Electrochem. Co., 1902-03, Niagara Research Labs., 1903-06; with Electro Metall. Co. and Union Carbide Co. since 1906; consultant Union Carbide & Carbon Corp. Fellow A.A.A.S.; mem. Am. Inst. of City of New York, N.Y. Acad. of Science, Am. Inst. Mining and Metall. Engrs. (pres. 1933), Electrochem. Soc. (pres. 1925-26, hon. mem. 1936), Mining and Metall. Soc. America, Am. Soc. for Metals, Iron and Steel Inst. of London. Awarded Perkin medal, 1924, Acheson medal, 1937; Elliott Cresson medal, 1940; Howe Memorial lecturer, 1938. Clubs: Chemists' (pres. 1939), Engineers', Mining, Niagara (Niagara Falls). Contbr. to tech. publs. Home: 625 Park Av. Office: 30 E. 42d St., New York, N.Y. Died Dec. 1, 1942.

BECKMAN, Francis Joseph, archbishop; b. Cincinnati, O., Oct. 25, 1875; s. Francis and Elizabeth C. (Fenker) B.; grad., maxima cum laude, St. Gregory Prep. Sem., 1897; grad. in philosophy and theology, Mt. St. Mary's Sem., Cincinnati, O., 1902; studied at Louvain U., Belgium, 1904-05, Gregorian U. of Rome, Italy (Jesuits), 1905-08, S.T.B., 1906, S.T.L.,

1907, S.T.D., 1908. Ordained priest R.C. Ch., 1902; prof. philosophy, Mt. St. Mary's Sem., 1908-12; rector (pres.) Mt. St. Mary's Theol. Sem., 1912-24, also prof. of dogmatic theology; served as censor librorum, Archdiocese of Cincinnati, counselor of Archdiocese, synodal examiner, etc.; apptd. bishop of Lincoln, Neb., Dec. 23, 1924, consecrated, May 1, 1925; apostolic administrator Diocese of Omaha, 1926-28; apptd. asst. at papal throne with title Roman Count, 1928; archbishop of Dubuque, Ia., Jan. 1930-46; retired since 1946; apptd. Titular Archbishop of Phulla. Founder, CYO-Civic Orchestra, Dubuque, 1937; Dubuque Symphony Orchestra, 1938; Columbia Museum, Dubuque; Nat. Antiquarian Soc. Organizer, dir. and chmn. Catholic Students, Mission Crusade (1,000,000 members), 1918-40; spiritual director of Confraternity of Pilgrims (headquarters in St. Paul, Minn.). Author of pastoral letters and radio addresses. Address: care Mt. St. Agnes, Dubuque, Ia. Died Oct. 17, 1948.

BECKWITH, Isbon Thaddeus, theologian; b. Old Lyme, Conn., 1843; s. William and Carolina (Champion) B.; A.B., Yale, 1868, Ph.D., 1872; student univs. of Göttingen and Leipzig, 1872-74; D.D., Trinity Coll., Hartford, 1898; unmarried. Instr. Greek, U. of Tenn., 1868-70, Yale, 1870-72 and 1874-79; deacon, P.E. Ch., 1875, priest, 1876; prof. Greek, Trinity Coll., 1879-98; prof. interpretation of the N.T., Gen. Theol. Sem., 1898-1906. Mem. Archæol. Inst. Am., Am. Philol. Assn., Soc. Bibl. Lit. and Exegesis. Editor: Bacchantes of Euripides (in College Series of Greek Authors). Author: Critical and Exegetical Commentary on the Apocalypse of John, 1919. Address: Galen Hall, Atlantic City, N.J. Died Sept. 9, 1936.

BECKWITH, Theodore Day, bacteriologist; b. Utica, N.Y., Dec. 8, 1879; s. Theodore George and Jane (Day) B.; B.S., Hamilton Coll., 1904, M.S., 1907; Ph.D., U. of Calif., 1920; m. Cornelia Lyon, June 14, 1910; children—Josephine Day, Jane Crosby, Stephen Lyon, Theodore Day. Algologist, U.S. Dept. Agr., 1904-05, scientific asst., 1905-07; asst. prof. bacteriology and plant pathology, N.D. Coll., 1907-10, prof., 1910-11, asst. botanist, N.D. Expt. Sta., 1907-11; head dept. bacteriology, Ore. State Coll., and bacteriologist Expt. Sta., 1911-20; asso. prof. of bacteriology, U. of Calif., and mem. Calif. Stomatological Research group, 1920-32; asso. prof. bacteriology, U. of Calif. at Los Angeles, 1932-33, prof. since 1933, head dept. since 1934; research asso. Calif. Expt. Sta., 1934-35; cooperated with Huntington Library in research dealing with foxing of paper, 1933-39; consultant for pulp and paper industry. Capt. Sanitary Corps, U.S. Army, 1918-19. Fellow A.A. A.S., Calif. Acad. Sciences; mem. Soc. Exptl. Biology and Medicine (sec. Pacific Coast sect., 1925-32; chmn. Southern Calif. sect., 1935-36; council mem., 1935-36), Soc. Am. Bacteriologists (chmn. Southern Calif. sect.; council mem., 1936-37), Am. Pub. Health Assn., Southern Calif. Pub. Health Assn. (exec. com. 1938-1942); pres., 1941-42 Western Soc. Naturalists, Inst. Food Technology, Southern Calif. Dental Assn. (hon.), Phi Beta Kappa, Sigma Xi, Alpha Zeta, Gamma Alpha, Kappa Psi, Delta Upsilon, Delta Omega. Presbyterian. Mason. Author: Causes and Prevention of Foxing in Books (with T. M. Iiams), 1937. Contbr. many articles on water supply, sewage germicides, metabolism, paper faults, medical and dental bacteriology. Home: 333 - 19th St., Santa Monica, Calif. Died July 18, 1946.

BEDAUX, Charles E. (bĕ-dō'), chmn. bd. Internat. Bedaux Co.; also officer or dir. many other corps. Address: 20 E. 40th St., New York, N.Y.* Died Feb. 19, 1944.

BEDE, J. Adam (bēd), ex-congressman; b. on farm, Lorain County, O., 1856; ed. public school, Ohio, and Tabor Coll., Iowa; learned printers' trade; taught school; did work as reporter on newspapers West and South; edited weekly and daily papers, studied law. Originally Republican, but supported Cleveland in 1884, 88, 92; U.S. marshal Dist. of Minn., 1 yr. (resigned); returned to Republican party on financial issue, 1896; mem. 58th to 60th Congresses (1903-09), 8th Minn. Dist.; served on Rivers and Harbors Com. and was advocate of internal developments; lifetime advocate of St. Lawrence Seaway; mem. Minn. Legislature, 1931-33. Supported Franklin Roosevelt in elections of 1932, 36, 40. Engaged in farming, lecturing and editorial work. Home: 2901 Lake Av., S. Office: Exchange Bldg., Duluth, Minn. Died Apr. 11, 1942.

BEDFORD-JONES, Henry James O'Brien (John Wycliffe, pseud.), author; b. Napanee, Ont., Can., Apr. 29, 1887; s. William John Wicliff and Henrietta Louise (Roblin) B.; m. 2d, Mary Bernardin, of Chicago. Clubs: Cliff Dwellers (Chicago, Ill.); Authors' (London). Author: Son of Cincinnati, 1925; Rodomont, 1925; King's Passport, 1927; D'Artagnan, 1929; Centaur to Cross, 1929; This Fiction Business, 1929; Cyrano, 1930; D'Artagnan's Letter, 1931; Drums of Dambala, 1932; King's Pardon, 1933; Mission and the Man; the Story of San Juan Capistrano, 1939; also many juvenile books, novels, poems, translations, etc. Home: Conway, Mich.* Died May 12, 1949.

BEEBE, Murray Charles, elec. engineer; b. Racine, Wis., Feb. 25, 1876; s. Charles Seth and Selma Barsena (Eastman) B.; B.S., U. of Wis., 1897; m. Ethel Fairmont Snyder, Jan. 13, 1922. Instr. elec. engring., U. of Wis., 1897-1900; development work for George Westinghouse, 1900-02; tech. supt., Nernst Lamp Co., Pittsburgh, 1902-04; asso. prof. elec. engring., 1905-07, prof. 1907-18, U. of Wis.; engr. Western Electric Co., New York, 1918-20; chief engr., Wadsworth Watch Case Co., Dayton, Ky., 1920-25; dir. mfg. lab. Scovill Mfg. Co., Waterbury, Conn., 1925-42; chief of research, Lea Mfg. Co., Waterbury, Conn., since 1942. Fellow Am. Inst. E.E., Am. Chem. Soc., Chi Psi, Tau Beta Pi, Eta Kappa Nu. Club: Chemists (New York). Home: Mt. Carmel, Conn. Died Nov. 28, 1943.

BEEDE, Herbert Gould, mfr. machinery; b. Providence, R.I., Nov. 26, 1870; s. Charles Gould and Ida Emma (Jenks) B.; grad. English and Classical Sch., Providence, 1889; A.B., Brown U., 1893; m. Agnes Newman, May 26, 1897; children—Frederic Newman, Robert Jenks. Began as draftsman Fales & Jenks Machine Co., Pawtucket, 1893, sec. and gen. mgr., 1909-30; pres. Standard Engring. Works, 1910-29; pres. Ft. Dummer Mill, Brattleboro, Vt., 1912-28; pres. Woonsocket Machine and Press Co., 1919-30; pres. Rheabat Corp., 1923-26; v.p. Pantex Pressing Machine, Inc., of Ill., Tex., and Ga., 1926-30, pres. and chmn. bd. since 1930; pres. Pantex Machinery Co., Ltd. of Can.; dir. Berkshire Fine Spinning Associates since 1928; agt. Fales & Jenks div. Whitin Machine Works, 1930-39; dir. and mem. exec. com., Blackstone and Merchants Mut. Fire Ins. Cos.; mem. R. I. advisory bd. Liberty Mutual Ins. Co. of Boston; dir. Industrial Trust Co. (Providence), 1922-34, Colonial Finance Trust since 1929 (mem. exec. bd. 1932-40), Westminster Bank, 1921-27, Pawtucket Safety Deposit Co.; trustee Pawtucket Instn. for Savings (mem. board of investment); commr. of Sinking Fund City of Pawtucket, 1927-33. Mem. Nat. Assn. Cotton Mfrs., Southern New Eng. Textile Club, R.I. Hist. Soc., Mayflower Soc., Soc. Colonial Wars. Hereditary Order of Descendants of Colonial Govs. Former mem. Royal Soc. for Encouragement of Arts, Mfrs. and Commerce, London, Eng. Republican. Universalist. Mason. Home: 21 Blaisdell Av., Pawtucket. Office: 521 Roosevelt Av., Central Falls, R.I. Died March 5, 1943; buried Swan Point Cemetery, Providence.

BEEDY, Carroll Linwood, ex-congressman, lawyer; b. Phillips, Me., Aug. 3, 1880; s. Clarence Edgar and Myra Mildred (Page) B.; A.B., Bates Coll., 1903, LL.D., 1933; LL.B., Yale, 1906. Began practice at Portland, Me., 1907; pros. atty. Cumberland County, Me., 2 terms, 1917-21; mem. 67th to 73d Congresses (1921-35), First Maine Dist. Engaged in the practice of law in Washington, D.C., since 1935. Republican. Mem. Phi Beta Kappa, Alpha Delta Phi, Phi Delta Phi, Delta Sigma Rho. Mason. Home: 10 Oakdale St., Portland, Me.; and 1025 Connecticut Av., Washington. Died Sept. 30, 1947.

BEELER, John A(llen), cons. engr.; b. Towanda, Ill., June 28, 1867; s. John and Emma Walker (Mead) B.; ed. pub. schs.; m. Fannie Mary Gillette, Feb. 14, 1895 (died Nov. 19, 1908); children—Horace Gillette (dec.), Mrs. Dorothy Long; m. 2d, Amanda Rosini Gall, July 17, 1913; children—Betty Malvina, Esther Lois, Rosemary Virginia. Asst. engr. constrn. cable rys., Cincinnati and Denver, Colo., 1885-90; chief engr. Denver Contractors' Assn., 1889-90, Met. St. Ry. Co., Denver, 1891-92, Denver Tramway Co., 1890-1902; v.p. and gen. mgr, same, 1902-15; v.p. and gen. supt. D. & N.W. Ry. Co. (electric), 1903-15; dir. in charge operations, Denver & Intermountain R.R. Co. (electrified steam line), 1913-15; cons. practice since 1915. Cons. engr. on transit and other pub. utility problems for cities of New York, Boston, Washington, D.C., Kansas City, New Orleans, Richmond (Va.), Dallas, Houston, Atlanta, Louisville, Cincinnati, St. Louis, Toronto, Cleveland, Seattle; consulting traffic expert, New York Transit Commn., 1921-26; councillor and member advisory comm. of Eno Foundation for Highway Traffic Control; director The Beeler Organization, Transit Planners. Mem. American Soc. C.E. Baptist. Club: Scarsdale Golf (New York). Home: Scarsdale, N.Y. Office: 155 E. 44th St., New York, N.Y. Died July 11, 1945.

BEERS, Clifford Whittingham, sec. Am. Foundations for Mental Hygiene; b. New Haven, Conn., Mar. 30, 1876; s. Robert Anthony and Ida (Cooke) B.; Ph.B., Sheffield Scientific Sch. (Yale), 1897, hon. M.A., 1922; m. Clara Louise Jepson, 1912. In business N.Y. City, 1898-1900, 1904-06. Founder, 1908, Conn. Soc. for Mental Hygiene (first orgn. of its kind, since which similar ones have been founded in many states); founder, 1909, and sec. Nat. Com. for Mental Hygiene; visited Great Britain, France and Belgium, 1923, in interests of internat. mental hygiene movement; had private audiences with King Albert and Cardinal Mercier and interviews with other leaders abroad; founder, 1928, and since sec. Am. Foundations for Mental Hygiene; organized and became sec.-gen. 1st Internat. Congress on Mental Hygiene, held in U.S., 1930; founder, 1930, and gen. sec. Internat. Com. for Mental Hygiene; founder, 1931, and sec. Internat. Foundation for Mental Hygiene. Mem. Nat. Inst. Social Sciences; hon. mem. Am. Psychiatric Assn., Am. Orthopsychiatric Assn. and British Nat. Council for Mental Hygiene, and other mental hygiene societies. Awarded (1933) Cross of Chevalier of Legion of Honor by French Govt. in recognition of international work in mental hygiene; awarded (1933) the gold medal of Nat. Inst. Social Sciences for "distinguished services for the benefit of mankind"; honored (1934) by publication of presentation edition of "Twenty-five Years After —Sidelights on the Mental Hygiene Movement and Its Founder," containing about 500 25th anniversary tributes, collected by the late Dr. William H. Welch, chmn. of the Tribute Com., apptd. by Nat. Com. for Mental Hygiene in connection with the anniversary celebration. Clubs: Graduate, Berzelius (New Haven); Yale (New York). Author: A Mind That Found Itself (autobiography), 1908, 24th edit., 1939; also articles on the mental hygiene movement. Home: 171 Sherwood Place, Englewood, N.J. Office: 1790 Broadway, New York, N.Y. Died July 9, 1943.

BEERS, George Emerson, lawyer; b. Bridgeport, Conn., Oct. 7, 1865; s. Rev. John Samuel and Maria Josephine (Wakeman) B.; B.A., with honors, Trinity Coll., Hartford, Conn., 1886, M.A., 1889; LL.B., magna cum laude, Yale, 1889, M.L., 1890; m. Margaret Lowry, Aug. 17, 1892; children—Mrs. Margaret Lowry Chittenden, Henry Samuel, William Leslie, Josephine Wakeman. Practiced in Tenn., 1889-92, at New Haven since 1892. Compensation commr. 3rd Congressional Dist., 1913-23, Conn. commr. on Nat. Commn. Uniform State Laws, 1916-40, vice pres., 1933-34; mem. firm Beers & Beers. Mem. Bd. of Fellows, Trinity, 1908-14. Mem. Am. Bar Assn. (regional v.p. 1932-33; chmn. sect. on Real Property, Probate and Trust Law, 1938-40), Conn. State Bar Assn., Am. Law Inst., Delta Psi, Phi Beta Kappa. Episcopalian. Clubs: Graduates (New Haven); Appalachian Mountain Club. Editor: Baldwin's Digest of Connecticut Reports (revision), 1900; Stephen's Digest of Law of Evidence (N.E. edit.), 1901; Wills on Circumstantial Evidence (Am. edit.), 1905. A consulting editor American and English Encyclopedia of Law and Practice, 1911-13. Has contributed largely to legal encys. and periodicals. Home: Guilford, Conn. Office: 205 Church St. New Haven, Conn. Died Dec. 25, 1947; buried in Oak Lawn Cemetery, Fairfield, Conn.

BEERS, Lucius Hart, lawyer; b. New York, N.Y., Nov. 28, 1859; s. Henry Newell and Martha (Hart) B.; A.B., Columbia, 1881; LL.B., Columbia Law School, 1883; married. Practiced New York, 1883; mem. firm of Lord, Day & Lord; dir. Lawyers Trust Co., 25 Broadway Corp., West Bay Co., Eastern Offices Co. Mem. Bar Assn. of City of New York, N.Y. State Bar Assn., Am. Bar Assn., S.R., Psi Upsilon. Trustee Barnard Coll. Clubs: University, Century Assn., Down Town Assn., St. Nicholas. Home: Westhampton Beach, L.I., N.Y.; and 131 E. 62d St., New York, N.Y. Office: 25 Broadway, New York, N.Y. Died Oct. 1, 1948.

BEERS, William Harmon, architect; b. Greensburg, Ind., May 26, 1881; s. William Harmon and Caroline Ryder (Gately) B.; student U. of Gottingen, 1897, U. of Dresden, 1898; B.S., Columbia, 1903; architect diploma of the French Government, Ecole des Beaux Arts, Paris, France, 1910; married Elizabeth Lee Dodge, April 23, 1927; 1 daughter Elizabeth Lee (Mrs. Marvin Stephens). Draftsman, Welles Bosworth, 1909-12; in practice of architecture, New York, N.Y., since 1912; partner firm Beers & Farley; architecture editor New York Herald Tribune, 1928-33. Served as capt., U.S. Army, World War I; overseas 1½ yrs.; commnd. major, U.S. Army, 1942, promoted lieut. col., 1943, col., 1945; served in England, North Africa, Italy and France. Received citation from Gen. Pershing, World War I; decorated Bronze Star (World War II); Croix de Guerre, 1944; 5 battle stars. Fellow Am. Inst. Architects (past chmn. pub. information committee; past vice pres. and past sec. New York chapter); mem. Columbia School of Architects, Soc. of Architects, given diploma by French Govt. Clubs: Racquet and Tennis, Century Association (New York); Bedford (N.Y.) Country. Home: Bedford Village, N.Y. Office: 238 E. 49th St., New York, N.Y. Died July 1, 1949; buried at Newton, Conn.

BEERY, Wallace, actor; born Kansas City, Mo., April 1, 1886; s. Noah and Margaret Beery, student Chase Sch., Kansas City; 1 adopted daughter, Carol Ann. Ran away from home to join a circus and became an elephant trainer; first identified with films as a female impersonator; notable for character roles in "Big House," "Hell Divers," "The Champ," "Grand Hotel," "The Good Old Soak," "Bad Man of Brimstone," "Stable Mates," "Sergeant Madden," etc. Awarded gold medal as "world's best movie actor," Internat. Motion Picture Expn., Venice, Italy, 1934. Mem. advisory bd. Bank of America, Hollywood, Calif. Mason (32°, Shriner). Home: Beverly Hills, Calif. Died April 25, 1949.

BEESON, Charles Henry, univ. prof.; b. Columbia City, Ind., Oct. 2, 1870; s. Henry Norris and Magdalena (Wekerle) B.; A.B., Ind. U., 1893, A.M., 1895, studied U. of Chicago, 1896-97, 1901-03; U. of Munich, 1903-05, 1906-07, Ph.D., 1907; LL.D., Indiana U., 1939; m. Mabel Banta, 1897. Tutor and instr. Latin, Indiana U., 1893-96; instr. Latin, U. of Chicago, 1906, Univ. High Sch., 1907-08; instr. Latin, 1908; asst. prof., 1909, asso. prof., 1911, prof. since 1918, U. of Chicago; annual prof. Am. Acad. in Rome, 1930-31. Capt. Mil. Intelligence Div., Gen. Staff, U.S. Army, 1918-19; capt. O.R.C., 1919. Fellow Mediæval Acad. America (pres. 1936-39), Am. Acad. Arts and Sciences, Am. Philos. Soc.; mem. American Philological Assn., Classical Assn. Middle West and South, Phi Beta Kappa, Phi Kappa Psi. Asso. editor Classical Philology (mng. editor 1936-38); asso. editor Archivum Latinitatis Medii Aevi (Bulletin Du Cange). Club: Quadrangle. Author: Second Latin Book (with F. J. Miller), 1901; Hegemonius Acta Archelai, herausgegeben im Auftrage der

Kirchenväter-Commission der königl. Preussischen Akademie der Wissenschaften, 1906; Isidor-Studien, Quellen und Untersuchungen zur lateinischen Philologie des Mittelalters, begründet von Ludwig Traube, 1913; New Second Latin Book (with H. F. Scott), 1916; Third Latin Book (with F. W. Sanford and H. F. Scott), 1923; Primer of Medieval Latin, 1925; Lupus of Ferrières, as Scribe and Text Critic 1930. Home: 1228 E. 56th St., Chicago, Ill. Died Dec. 1949.

BEESON, Jasper Luther, educator; b. Keener, Ala., Aug. 31, 1867; s. Capt. W. B. and Mary A. (Sibert) B.; A.B., U. of Ala., 1889, A.M., 1890, LL.D., 1929; Ph.D., Johns Hopkins U., 1893; m. Leola Selman, 1894; 1 dau., Catherine Selman. Instr. physics, U. of Ala., 1888-89, also chemist Ala. Geol. Survey; research chemist La. Expt. Sta. and prof. chemistry, La. Sch. of Sugar, 1893-97; prof. nat. science, 1897-1911, prof. chemistry and physics, 1911-14, prof. chemistry since 1914, acting pres., 1922-23 and 1927-28, dean Coll. Arts and Sciences, 1925, also chmn. faculty, 1909-27, pres., 1928-34 (pres. emeritus), Ga. State Coll. for Women. Fellow A.A.A.S.; mem. Am. Chem. Soc., Pi Gamma Mu, S.A.R. (past pres. Ga. Soc.); corr. mem. Académie Latine des Sciences, Arts et Belles Lettres (Paris). Democrat. Presbyterian elder. Author of Beeson Genealogy. Writer on tech. subjects; deviser of scientific apparatus. Home: 202 N. Columbia St., Milledgeville, Ga. Died Jan. 10, 1943.

BEETS, Henry, clergyman; b. Koedyk, near Alkmaar, Netherlands, Jan. 5, 1869; s. Jasper and Margaret (Smit) B.; came to America, 1886; grad. Calvin Coll. and Sem., Grand Rapids, Mich., 1895; LL.D., Muskingum Coll., 1911; m. Clara Poel, 1895 (died, 1946); children—Henry Nicholas, Abel Jasper, William Clarence. Ordained ministry Christian Reformed Church, 1895; pastor Sioux Center, Ia., 1895-99, LaGrave Av. Ch., Grand Rapids, 1899-1915; Burton Heights, Grand Rapids, 1915-20; sec. and dir. of Missions, Christian Reformed Church, 1920-39; stated clerk Christian Reformed Church, 1902-42; mem. joint com. Am. and Canadian chs. to revise Metrical Version of the Psalms, 1902-09; del. Gen Synod Reformed Chs. of Netherlands, 1902, 11, 23, 33, 39; pres Grand Rapids Ministers' Conf., 1930-31; mem. Maatschappy der Ned. Letterkunde. Asso. editor Gereformeerde Amerikaan (Dutch monthly), 1898-1916; editor in chief The Banner, 1904-29; editor and pub. Reformed Review and Heidenwereld since 1915. Republican. Club: Rotary. Author: Life of President McKinley (Dutch), 1901; Life and Times of Abraham Lincoln (Dutch), 1909; Triumphs of the Cross (Dutch), 1909, 1914; Compendium of the Christian Religion Explained, 1915, 19, 24; History Christian Reformed Church (Dutch), 1918; The Christian Reformed Church—Its History, Work and Principles, 1923; "Student's Compendium of the Heidelberg Catechism," 1925-29; The Reformed Confession Explained, 1929; Bible History, Book by Book, 1934; The Man of Sorrows, 1935; Johanna of Nigeria, 1937; Toiling and Trusting, for Indians and Chinese, 50 Years of Christian Reformed Mission Work, 1940. Edited and prefaced 2d edit., Dr. A. Kuyper's "Stone Lectures on Calvinism," 1931; Van het groote Goed (Holland-Am. sermons), 1934; The Christian Reform Church, its Roots, History, Schools and Mission Work, 1946. Contbr. Christian Encyclopedia and Michigan Encyclopedia. Member Grand Rapids Art and Museum Com. since 1933. Contbr. to Knickerbocker Weekly and Hollanders Who Help Build America. Knight Order of Orange-Nassau (Netherlands). 1934 Home: 737 Madison Av. S.E., Grand Rapids 3, Mich. Died Oct. 29, 1947.

BEGIEN, Ralph Norman (bē-gēn'), railway official; b. Somerville, Mass., Mar. 15, 1875; s. Henry M. and Louisa Florence (Thayer) B.; grad. high sch. Medford, Mass.; student Harvard, 1893-95; m. Ida Davenport, Rozzelle, Dec. 11, 1900; children—Ralph Norman, John Thayer, Jeanne Marie. Instrument man, draftsman and jr. asst. engr. with U.S. Nicaragua Canal Commn. and Isthmian Canal Commn., surveys across Nicaragua, 1897-1900; asst. engr. bridges and location, Guayaquil & Quito R.R. in Ecuador, S.A., 1900; mathematician in office of surveyor, Washington, D.C., 1901; with B. & O. R.R., 1902-23; successively asst. engr. until 1908, div. engr. Phila. div., 1908-09, acting engr. maintenance of way, Main Line System, 1909, asst. to chief engr., 1910, asst. to gen. mgr., 1910-11, asst. gen. supt., 1912; gen. supt. B.&O., S.W. R.R., 1913-16, chief engr. B.&O. System and C.,H.&D. Ry., under receivers, 1916-17; gen. mgr. Eastern Lines, B.&O. R.R., 1917; asst. to federal mgr. B.&O. Lines East, Western Md., Cumberland Valley, Cumberland & Pa., Coke & Coal and Wheeling Terminal rys., 1918; federal mgr. under U.S. R.R. Administration, B.&O. Western Lines, Dayton & Union R.R. and Dayton Union R.R., 1919; gen. mgr. B.&O. R.R., Lines West since 1933; v.p. C.&O. and Hocking Valley rys., in charge of maintenance of way, equipment and operation since 1932; v.p. Chesapeake & Ohio R.R., advisory. Mem. Am. Soc. C.E., Am. Ry. Assn., Harvard Engring. Assn. Episcopalian. Home: 2610 Monument Av. Office: First & Merchants Bank Bldg., Richmond, Va.* Died Feb. 27, 1944.

BEHREND, Ernst Richard, paper mfr.; b. Coeslin, Germany, Mar. 29, 1869; s. Moritz and Rebecca (Wolf) B.; ed. Dresden and Charlottenburg; m. Mary Brownell, June 1, 1907; 1 d., Harriet Ellen. Came to U.S., 1896, naturalized, 1901. Engr. with Pusey & Jones Co., Wilmington, Del., later with Nekoosa Paper Co.; rep. of Am. paper mill machinery mfrs. in Eng., France, Germany and Scandinavia, 1897; founder 1898, and pres. Hammermill Paper Co., Erie, Pa. Home: East Lake Rd., Erie, and Newport, R.I. Address: Hammermill Paper Co., Erie, Pa. Died Sept. 22, 1940.

BEHRENDT, Walter Curt (bē'rĕnt), architect; b. Metz, December 16, 1884; s. Alfred and Henriette B.; student Technische Hochschule of Charlottenburg, and of Munich, univs. of Berlin and Munich; Dr. Engring. in architecture, Technische Hochschule, Dresden; m. Lydia Hoffmann, pianist, Apr. 15, 1913. Came to U.S. 1934. Civil Service Prussian Ministry Pub. Works, 1912-16, Dept. Housing, 1919-26, archtl. adviser to minister of finance, Dept. Pub. Bldgs., 1927-33; tech. dir. City Planning Assn., Buffalo, N.Y., since 1937; prof. city planning and housing, U. of Buffalo, 1937-41; spl. lecturer, Dartmouth Coll., 1934-37, prof. city planning and housing since 1941. Served as pvt. German army, in World War, 1916-18. Author: Modern Building, 1937; and several books in German published in Berlin. Editor of German publs. published in Berlin, 1919-25. Home: McKenna Rd., Norwich, Vt. Died Apr. 26, 1945.

BEHRENS, Herman Albert (bâr'ĕnz), insurance; b. Hamburg, Germany, Sept. 29, 1883; s. Ralph H. and Johanna (Lowenstein) B.; brought to U.S., 1889; ed. pub. schs. San Francisco, Calif.; student U. of Calif., 1897-1901; m. Grace G. Galbraith, Nov. 17, 1907; 1 dau., Barbara Louise. Asst. sec. Pacific Mutual Life Ins. Co. of California, 1903-12; came to Chicago 1907; v.p. and mgr. Continental Casualty Co. of Chicago, 1912-28, pres., 1928-37, chmn. bd. since 1937; pres. Continental Assurance Co. since 1928. Served as dep. commr. Bur. of War Risk, U.S. Govt., 1917-18. Republican. Christian Scientist. Mason (32°, Shriner). Clubs: Attic, Drug and Chemical, Stock Exchange Lunch, San Francisco Yacht (San Francisco); Meadow (Tamalpais, Calif.). Home: Wayne, Ill.; (summer) Belvedere, Calif. Office: 910 S. Michigan Av., Chicago, Ill. Died Mar. 13, 1945.

BEHYMER, Lynden Ellsworth ("Bee") (bē-hī'mēr), impresario and mgr. world-celebrities on the Pacific Coast; b. New Palestine, O., Nov. 5, 1862; s. Aaron S. and Nancy Moyer (Leach) B.; grad. Shelbyville (Ill.) High Sch., 1881; hon. Mus. D.; hon.LT.D., m. Menettie Sparkes, Jan. 3, 1886. Pub. and ed. of mag. of celebrities; became theatrical and musical mgr. shortly after settling in Los Angeles, 1886. Founder Philharmonic Artists Courses in West; mgr. concerts, opera companies, ballet, lectures, theater, touring attractions. Presented "La Boheme" first time in America, Oct. 14, 1897, in Los Angeles; in 1898, formed and managed for 20 years, Los Angeles Symphony Orchestra; formed for W. A. Clark, Jr., present Philharmonic Orchestra, 1918, mgr. 4 years. Presented Metropolitan Opera Co. on Pacific Coast, 1901, 02, 04, 06, Boston Opera Co., 1910, 12, Chicago Opera Co., 1914, 16, 18. Rep. Columbia Concerts Corp. and Nat. Concert and Artists Corp. and S. Hurok Attractions on Pacific Coast. For 50 yrs. promoted a cultural Los Angeles and Southwest; brought to the West Coast for tour Sarah Bernhardt, Eleanora Duse, Enrico Caruso, Sir Henry Irving, Edwin Booth, Paderewski, Rabindranath Tagore, Jacob Riis, Feodor Chaliapin; presented first time in concert Lawrence Tibbett, Maud Allan, Isadora Duncan, etc.; Pacific Coast representative of many famous concert artists. Trustee University Southern Calif., 1939. Decorated Palms of France, 1908; Redeemer of Greece, 1912; St. Stanislas of Russia, 1912; Crown of Italy, 1914; Crown of Leopold of Belgium, 1916; Orange-Nassau of Holland, 1932; Crown of Charlemagne, 1939; Order of St. Lazarus of Jerusalem, 1940; Order of the White Lion of Czechoslovakia, 1947; also by other countries in recognition of their national artists brought to West. Scottish Rite Mason; Knights Templar, Shriner; B.P.O. Elk; and many other local organizations. President Gamut Club. Grand trouper of Troupers, Inc. Home: 439 S. Kingsley Drive. Address: Philharmonic Auditorium, Los Angeles 13, Calif. Died Dec. 16, 1947.

BEK, William Godfrey (bĕk), coll. dean; b. near Washington, Mo., Nov. 20, 1873; s. Wilhelm Friedrich and Annette (Michalsky) B.; grad. State Normal Sch., Warrensburg, Mo., 1897; A.B., U. of Mo., 1903, A.M., 1905; Harrison fellow in Germanics, U. of Pennsylvania, 1905-1907, Ph.D., 1907; D.Litt., University of Missouri, 1948; m. Ada Springgate, September 1, 1909; 1 daughter, Ellen Heatherly (Mrs. Albert G. Selke). Teacher in Missouri, 1895-1900; instructor in German, University of Missouri, 1907-11; asst. prof. German, U. of N. Dak., 1911-12, prof. since 1912; jr. dean Coll. Liberal Arts, same univ., 1923, acting dean, 1926-27, dean, 1930. Mem. Modern Lang. Assn. America, Phi Beta Kappa, Phi Mu Alpha. Mem. Congregational Ch. Club: Lions (pres. 1922-24); Gov. Lions Internat. Dist. Five, 1926-27. Author: German Settlement Society of Philadelphia and its Colony, Hermann, Missouri, 1907; The Followers of Duden—Early German Immigration in Missouri, 1923; also brochures relating to German settlements in U.S. Translator of Duden's Amerikanische Reise; Paul Wilhelm's Duke of Wuerttemberg's Erste Reise nach dem nördlichen Amerika; Heinrich Boernstein's Fuenfundsiebzig Jahre in der Alten und Neuen Welt; E. D. Kargau's St. Louis in fruheren Jahren; John T. Buegel's Tagebuch-Erfahrungen im amerikanicshen Buergerkreig; Nicholas Hesse's Das Westliche Nord Amerika. Address: Box 66, University Station, Grand Forks, N.D. Died Aug. 14, 1948.

BELDING, Frederick Norton, retired silk mfr.; b. Rockville, Conn., April 1, 1887; s. of Alvah Norton and Lizzie Smith (Merrick) B.; ed. St. Paul's Sch., Concord, N.H.; A.B., Princeton, 1910; m. Helen Maxwell, June 11, 1921 (died 1930); children—Maxwell Merrick, Virginia. Began as workman with Belding Bros. & Co., Rockville, 1910, asst. mill mgr., 1912-16, v.p. and gen. mgr., 1916-26; v.p. Hockanum Mills Co., Rockville, 1927-34; pres. Belding Land and Improvement Co.; v.p. Peoples Savings Bank (Rockville); trustee Hartford Conn. Trust Co.; dir. Avery Rock Salt Mining Co., Detroit Rock Salt Co., Retsof Mining Co., Internat. Salt Co. (N.J.), Nat. Fire Ins. Co. (Hartford), Travelers Ins. Co., Travelers Indemnity Co., Travelers Fire Ins. Co., Charter Oak Fire Ins. Co., United Nat. Indemnity Co., Mechanics & Traders Ins. Co. Trustee Rockville City Hosp., Rockville Pub. Library, Milo M. Belding Library (Ashfield, Mass.). Republican. Episcopalian. Mason (32°, Shriner), Odd Fellow, Elk. Clubs: Union League, Bankers (New York); Hartford (Conn.); Country (Farmington, Conn.); Longmeadow (Mass.) Country. Home: 54 Talcott Av., Rockville, Conn.; (summer) Eastern Point Groton, Conn. Died Nov. 12, 1945.

BELL, Alphonzo Edward, real estate, farmer; b. Los Angeles, Calif., Sept. 29, 1875; s. James George and Susan Abiah (Hollenbeck) B.; grad. Occidental Coll. Acad., 1891; A.B., Occidental Coll., 1895; student San Francisco Theol. Sem., 1895-97; m. Minnewa Shoemaker, Dec. 25, 1902; children—Elizabeth Hollenbeck (Mrs. Ralph Joseph Tingle; now dec.), Minnewa Shoemaker (wife of Dr. Rex Lewis Ross), Alphonzo Edward. Began career as farmer, land developer and subdivider, near Santa Fe Springs, Calif.; then oil wells were developed on farm lands owned by him; organized Alphonzo E. Bell Corp., 1922, and developed residential subdivision, Bel-Air, in West Los Angeles; also subdivided other acreages between Bel-Air and Pacific Ocean; interested in ranching, citrus and grape cultivation in Coachella Valley near Palm Springs, Calif.; has been interested in oil bus. throughout career, having substantial developments of crude oil in Santa Maria Valley; pres. Alphonzo E. Bell Corp.; mem. bd. of trustees Occidental Coll., Church Fedn. of Los Angeles, mem. bd. of church extension, Los Angeles Presbytery. Mem. Phi Gamma Delta. Presbyterian (elder). Clubs: Bel-Air Country, University, California (Los Angeles), Bel-Air Bay (Pacific Palisades). Home: 850 Linda Flora Drive, Bel-Air. Office: 801 Moraga Drive, Bel-Air, Los Angeles, 24, Calif. Died Dec. 27, 1947.

BELL, Brian, newspaperman; b. York, S.C., Mar. 30, 1890; s. James B. and Nancy (Watson) B.; ed. Presbyn. Coll. of S.C., Davidson Coll. and Washington and Lee U.; hon. Litt.D., Washington and Lee U., 1937; m. Alberta Harris, June 9, 1917; children—Jane Brian (Mrs. J. William Magee), Brian. With The State, Columbia, S.C., as reporter, sports editor, news editor, 1909-24; with Associated Press since 1924, as staff mem., Atlanta, Ga., 1924, chief New Orleans Bureau, 1925, gen. staff, New York, 1926-30, chief Los Angeles Bureau, 1930-36, news editor Western Div., San Francisco, 1936-39, chief Washington Bureau since Jan. 1, 1939. Mem. Pi Kappa Alpha, Omicron Delta Kappa, Sigma Delta Chi. Presbyterian. Mason (32°, Shriner). Clubs: Washington Golf and Country, National Press, Gridiron (Washington, D.C.). Home: 4641 Rock Spring Road, Arlington, Va. Office: 330 Star Bldg., Washington, D.C. Died June 8, 1942.

BELL, Charles S., judge; b. Carthage, Cincinnati, O., Oct. 8, 1880; s. Samuel Walter and Mary Alice (Logan) B.; LL.B., McDonald's Inst. of Law, 1908; unmarried. Admitted to Ohio bar, 1910; asst. solicitor of Carthage, 1910-11; solicitor of Elmwood Place, 1912-16; first asst. county prosecutor, 1919-23, pros. atty., 1923-27, judge of the Court of Common Pleas of Hamilton County, O., 1927-42; judge of the Supreme Court of Ohio since Dec. 1, 1942. Life mem. of the Hamilton County Rep. Club; pres. of the Samuel W. Bell Home for the Blind; div. leader of the Community Chest and War Chest. Mem. Hamilton County and Ohio State bar assns. Mason (Shriner), Moose, Elk, Eagle. Clubs: Courier Press, Cincinnati, Western Hills Country (Cincinnati). Home: 914 Ludlow Av., Cincinnati, O. Office: Judiciary Bldg., Columbus, O.* Died Aug. 22, 1945.

BELL, Charles Webster, congressman; b. Albany, N.Y., June 11, 1857; s. Matthew and Elizabeth Emma B.; ed. pub. and pvt. schs.; m. Elizabeth May Dillman, June 1, 1894. Removed to Calif., 1877; engaged in fruit farming, later real estate business; county clk., Los Angeles County, 1899-03; mem. State Senate, Calif., 1907-12, when elected mem. 63d Congress, 9th Calif. Dist. Progressive. Presbyterian. Mason. Home: Pasadena. Died April 19, 1927.

BELL, Edward Price, journalist, author, lecturer; b. Parke Co., Ind., Mar. 1, 1869; s. Addison William and Elizabeth Nancy (Price) B.; Wabash College, Ind., 1894-97, hon. A.M., 1900, D.Litt., 1919; LL.D., Northwestern U., 1928; m. Mary Alice Mills, Dec. 21, 1897; children—Alice Elizabeth Price, Edward Price, John Addison Price. Entered newspaper work at Terre Haute, Ind.; reported Chippewa outbreak in Northern Minn., 1898, and race riots in N.C., same yr.; exposed, in The Chicago Record, jury bribing in Cook County, Ill., and legislative corruption at Springfield; London corr. Chicago Daily News, 1900-23, covering all great events in Eng. during that time; interviewed 5 British Cabinet ministers on German-World War;

first corr. who ever interviewed a British sec. of state for foreign affairs; extensive experience with British fleet, armies, and flying services. Lectured widely to boys of pub. schs. in Eng., on importance of Anglo-Am. unity for preservation of free instns., and throughout the Middle West, on the duty of America to participate resolutely in the effort to organize a stable world peace. Devoted 1924 and 1925 to interviewing leading men of various countries, including President Coolidge, Marx, Mussolini, Poincare, Ramsay MacDonald, Mackenzie King, Kato, Shidehara, Tang-Shao-yi, Gov. Gen. Wood, Senator Osmena, Senator Quezon, and others, on internat. and interracial problems, especially those centering in the Pacific Ocean. Accompanied Herbert Hoover on his Latin-Am. good-will tour, 1928-29; attacked British-Am. bickering in the English and Am. press and originated the idea of a conf. in Washington of the heads of English-speaking states (Premier Ramsay MacDonald and President Herbert Hoover) to lay foundations of permanent peace in the English-speaking world, 1929; toured world (1934-35) for Literary Digest, interviewing at length premiers and foreign ministers of principal countries of Asia and Europe, also Pope Pius XI, on problem of world peace; political editor, Saturday Spectator, Terre Haute, Ind., since 1941. Served as pres. Assn. Am. Correspondents in London; hon. mem. Phi Beta Kappa, Pi Gamma Mu; mem. Delta Tau Delta, Sigma Delta Chi. Presbyn. Author: World Chancelleries, 1925; Europe's Economic Sunrise, 1927; Primary Diplomacy, 1933; Let Us Go Seaward, 1937; Studies of Great Political Personalities, 1938; Seventy Years Deep, 1940; also many short stories, chief of which are "Zory's Race," and "Billy's Wife," appearing mainly in the Strand Mag., London. Clubs: Pilgrims, American, American Luncheon (London). Home: Merrywood, Gulfport, Miss. Died Sep. 23, 1943.

BELL, Enoch Frye, editorial sec. A.B.C.F.M.; b. N. Hadley, Mass., May 26, 1874; s. Rev. James Madison (D.D.) and Susan (Frye) B.; B.A., Yale, 1898; grad. Auburn Theol. Sem., 1902; S.T.B., Andover Theol. Sem., 1906; D.D., Middlebury (Vt.) Coll., 1925; m. Anna Elizabeth Bowman, Sept. 11, 1901; 1 son, John Frye. Ordained Congl. ministry, 1902; missionary to Japan, 1902-05; asst. foreign sec. A.B.C.F.M., 1906-10, asso. foreign section, 1910-19, editorial sec. and editor missionary Herald, 1920-42; now librarian and historian A.B.C.F.M. Mem. Phi Beta Kappa. Republican. Home: Brookline, Mass. Office: 14 Beacon St., Boston. Died June 10, 1945; buried at Leominster, Mass.

BELL, Frank Breckenridge, steel mfr.; b. Mercer, Pa., Sept. 24, 1876; s. John W. and Hester Martin (Davitt) B.; student Grove City (Pa.) Coll., 1893; M.E., Lehigh U., 1897; m. Mary Ewing Stranahan, June 16, 1904; children—Davitt Stranahan, James Alexander, Elizabeth Ewing. Began with Clairton (Pa.) Steel Co., 1904; various positions in steel works, 1904-09; supt. Inter-Ocean Steel Co., Chicago Heights, Ill., 1909-16; pres. Kennedy-Stroh Corp., Pittsburgh, Pa.; 1916; pres. Edgewater Steel Co., Pittsburgh, 1916-42, chmn. bd. since 1942; dir. Fidelity Trust Co. (Pittsburgh). District chief Pittsburgh Ordnance Dist. Mem. Iron and Steel Institute, American Soc. for Testing Materials, Am. Soc. M.E. Republican. Presbyterian. Clubs: University, Duquesne, Oakmont Country, Longue Vue Country. Home: 808 Devonshire St. Address: Box 478, Pittsburgh, Pa. Died May 6, 1949.

BELL, Frederic Somers, lumberman; b. Webster City, Ia., Mar. 19, 1859; s. Jairus Moffat and Helen Eliza (Somers) B.; Ph.B., U. of Mich., 1879; m. Frances Bradley Laird, June 22, 1882; 1 son, Laird. Admitted to Minn. bar, 1880; in lumber bus. since 1881; chmn. bd. Weyerhaeuser Timber Co., Tacoma, Wash.; dir. Potlatch Forests, Inc.; pres. Laird, Norton Co., Winona, Minn. Mem. Minn. State Highway Commn., 1912-15. Pres. bd. trustees Carleton Coll., Minn. State Hist. Soc. Mason. Republican. Clubs: Arlington Country (Winona); Minnesota (St. Paul); Minneapolis (Minneapolis); University (Chicago). Home: Briarcombe, Winona, Minn. Died March 13, 1938.

BELL, Howard James, Jr., coll. pres.; b. Washington, D.C., Jan. 22, 1914; s. Howard James and Frances Potter (Howland) B.; ed. Episcopal Acad. A.B., Lafayette Coll., 1934; A.M., Princeton, 1936 Ph.D., 1937; student (summer) Syracuse U., 1937, Columbia, 1945; m. Ruth Adelaide Haines, July 17, 1937; children—Peter Howland, Elizabeth Haines Instr. English, Beaver Coll., 1936-38; instr. English and journalism, Bradley U., Peoria, Ill., 1937-39, asst. prof., 1939-41, asso. prof., 1941-45, ednl. dir., Army specialized training program, 1943-44, asst. to pres., 1944-46; pres., Jamestown Coll., Jamestown, N.D., since 1946. Member Modern Language Assn., American Association University Profs., N.E.A., N.D. Edn. Assn., Peoria Council of Churches (pres., 1942-44); Peoria Citizens Forum (mem. bd. dirs., 1944-46), Phi Beta Kappa, Phi Delta Epsilon, Theta Delta Chi. Republican. Presbyterian (elder). Contbr. articles to scholarly jours. Address: Jamestown Coll., Jamestown, N.D. Died Dec. 6, 1948.

BELL, J(ames) Carleton, psychologist; b. Mt. Vernon, O., Dec. 11, 1872; s. Edwin Willis and Mary Angeline (Campbell) B.; A.B., Denison U., Granville, O., 1896; U. of Berlin, 1900-01; U. of Leipzig, 1901-02; A.M., Harvard, 1903, Ph.D., 1904; m. Rhoda P. Serra 1906; children—Rosamond, Elizabeth Louise, James Carleton. Instr. Greek, Denison U., 1895-96; instr. Latin, Girls' Home Sch., Berlin, 1896-98, Boys' Latin Sch., Boston, 1904-05; instr. exptl. psychology, Wellesley Coll., 1905-07; lecturer on abnormal psychology, Harvard, 1905-06; dir. Psychol. Lab., Brooklyn Training Sch. for Teachers, 1907-12; prof. art of teaching and dir. Sch. of Art of Teaching, U. of Tex., 1912-16; teacher, psychology and edn., Brooklyn Training Sch. for Teachers, 1916-24; prof. edn. Coll. of City of New York, since 1924; dir. Townsend Harris Hall High Sch., 1926-29. Lecturer ednl. psychology, Cornell, summer session, 1909, Brooklyn Inst. Arts and Sciences, 1911, New York U. summers, 1912, 19, 26, Summer Sch. of the South, 1915: lecturer in education, N.Y. Univ., 1919-26. Organizer of N.Y. Society for Exptl. Study of Edn. Fellow A.A.A.S.; mem. N.Y. Acad. Pub. Edn., Am. Psychol. Assn., N.E.A., Nat. Soc. for Study of Edn., Phi Beta Kappa, Phi Delta Kappa, Beta Theta Pi. Founder Jour. Ednl. Psychology. Editor: Contributions to Education, vols. I and II. Republican. Baptist. Home: 1032A Sterling Pl., Brooklyn, N.Y. Died Feb. 28, 1946.

BELL, Marcus Lafayette, lawyer; b. Pine Bluff, Ark., Jan. 11, 1880; s. Marcus Lafayette and Cynthia Ellen (Vanderwerker) B.; A.B., U. of Ark., 1898, LL.D., 1922; law student U. of Chicago, 1903; m. Ruth Van Doren, d. George M. Bogue, Nov. 8, 1906; children—Marcus Lafayette, Robert Bogue, Ruth Juliet, Katherine Van Doren. Practiced at Pine Bluff, 1902-04; entered law department C.,R.I.&P. Ry. Co., New York, 1904; became assistant attorney, same road, Chicago, 1905, local attorney, 1906, assistant general attorney, 1909, general attorney, 1910, gen. solicitor in charge of all legal affairs of the company, May 1, 1914; also gen. solicitor under receivership, in charge all legal matters, from Apr. 20, 1915, and gen. counsel of reorganized co. since June 28, 1917, v.p. and dir. since July 10, 1918; dir. and mem. exec. com. Pere Marquette R.R. Co., 1924-29; mem. Moore & Bell, New York, 1921-34. Vice-pres. Nat. Assn. of Travelers Aid Socs. Resided Chicago until Jan. 1, 1919, since at New York City. Mem. Phi Beta Kappa. Episcopalian. Mem. various clubs New York City and Chicago, Ill. Home: Noroton, Conn. Office: La Salle Station, Chicago, and 25 Broad St., New York. Died June 15, 1945; buried in Bellwood Cemetery, Pine Bluff, Ark.

BELL, Miller Stephens, banker; b. Milledgeville, Ga., Mar. 19, 1874; s. Matthew Raiford and Susan (Edwards) B.; ed. Georgia Mil. Coll., Milledgeville; m. Olive West, June 30, 1897 (died Oct. 7, 1924); children—Mrs. Olive Bell Davis, Miller Raiford, Frank West; m. 2d, Leone Bonner Youmans. Left college in junior year to become connected with Milledgeville Banking Co., of which is now pres.; dir. Milledgeville Brick Works Co. Apptd., 1914, 17, mem. Annual Assay Commn. to test weight and fineness of gold and silver in the U.S. mints. Mayor of Milledgeville, 1907-23; mem. State Dem. Exec. Com.; mem. bd. regents Univ. System of Ga.; chmn. bd. trustees Wesley Memorial (Atlanta); trustee Wesleyan Coll. (Macon, Ga.), Normal and Industrial Coll., Ga. Mil. Coll.; dir. Ga. State Coll. for Women, 1908-31. Pres. Ga. Bankers' Assn., 1905; 1st v.p. Mayors' Conv. of Ga.; chmn. Baldwin County NRA; mem. Georgia Bicentennial Commn. Lay del. General Conf. M.E. Ch. S. six times, chmn. lay delegation, 1934. Pres. Milledgeville Chamber Commerce, Tax Revision Assn. of Ga. Democrat. Past Grand Chancellor, K.P. of Ga., and Supreme Rep. from Ga. to Supreme Lodge, 1915-44; Mason, etc. Lt. col. on staff of Gov. Dorsey. State treas. Kiwanis Dist. of Ga., 1921-26. Home: Milledgeville, Ga. Deceased.

BELL, William Bonar, biologist; b. Milton, Ia., June 2, 1877; s. Robert Pollock and Isabel (Bonar) B.; M. Didactics, Ia. State Teachers Coll., Cedar Falls, 1899; A.B., State U. of Ia., 1902, M.S., 1903, Ph.D., 1905; m. Clara Carlton Preston, Sept. 5, 1906; children—Julia Carlton, David Bonar. Asst. prof. biology, later prof. zoölogy and physiology, N.D. Agrl. Coll., 1905-16; biol. Fish and Wildlife Service, U.S. Department Interior, Washington, D.C., since 1916, title chief div. of wild life research. Retired Aug. 1, 1944. Fellow A.A.A.S.; mem. Am. Soc. Mammalogists, Soc. of Am. Foresters, Am. Forestry Assn., Am. Ornithologists Union, Washington Biol. Soc., Wash. Acad. Sci., Sigma Alpha Epsilon, Sigma Xi, Alpha Zeta. Episcopalian. Mason. Author of govt. reports and bulls. Home: 803 Rittenhouse St. N.W., Washington 11, D.C. Died March 30, 1949.

BELLAIRE, Robert Thomas, foreign corr., writer, lecturer; b. Le Mars, Ia., Oct. 20, 1914; s. Louis and Vivian (Gallagher) B.; grad. Sioux City High Sch., 1931; post grad. student, Bronxville (N.Y.) High Sch., 1 yr.; student Columbia, 1933, 35, 36; m. Mona Marie Badgerow, Dec. 7, 1937; children—Judith Mona, Robert Gordon, Thomas Martin. Before leaving college began to write, doing free lance work on Baltimore Sun and Toronto Star, also tutored in English and assisted in dept. of government at Columbia. Started on trip around world, 1936; joined United Press, Shanghai, 1936, handling general news coverage; later headed night desk and covered daytime war news breaks; day desk, 1937; bureau mgr. in Shanghai, 1938; Tokio bureau mgr., 1941; six months interned in Tokio concentration camp; returned to U.S. on Gripsholm, 1942, with first repatriated Americans. Had 48-hour world-wide exclusive dispatches for United Press with first news to come out of Japan after attack on Pearl Harbor, filed from Lorenzo Marques, Portuguese East Africa, July 1942. Temporary duty, U.S. Army Air Forces, 1943-45. Mem. Writers War Board, Sigma Delta Chi. Roman Catholic. Clubs: American (Shanghai; Tokio); Jr. C. of C.; Overseas Press, Lambs (New York). Contbr. of articles to nationally known mags. In Shanghai during Japanese air raids, had narrow escapes from death while at work. During internment in Tokio withstood all pressure brought to persuade him to become Japan's radio voice directing propaganda at U.S. Home: 19 Brookridge Drive, Greenwich, Conn. Address: United Press Assn., New York, N.Y. Died Sep. 29, 1945.

BELLAMANN, Henry, author, musician; b. Fulton, Mo., Apr. 28, 1882; s. George Heinrich and Caroline (Krähenbühle) B.; student Westminster Coll., Fulton, Mo., 1897-98, U. of Denver, 1898-1900; spl. studies in London, Paris, New York; pupil of Isidor Philipp, Charles M. Widor; Mus. Doc., De Pauw U., 1926; m. Katherine Jones, Sept. 3, 1907. Dean Sch. of Fine Arts, Chicora Coll. for Women, Columbia, S.C., 1907-24. Pianist and lecturer on modern French music; chairman of Examining Board Juilliard Music Foundation, 1924-26, Rockefeller Foundation, Vassar College, 1928-29; dean Curtis Institute of Music, 1931-32. Member American Soc. French Legion of Honor, Nat. Assn. Music Teachers, S.C. Assn. Music Teachers (pres. 1920-23), Babcock Soc. of Psychol. Research (pres.), Internat. Musical Soc., Am. Philatelic Soc., Beethoven Assn., Authors' League of Am., P.E.N., N.Y. Acad Science (psychology div.). Decorated Officier de l'Instruction Publique (France), 1924; Chevalier Legion of Honor (France), 1931. Author: A Music Teacher's Note Book, 1920; Cups of Illusion (verse), 1923; Petenera's Daughter (novel), 1926; The Upward Pass (verse), 1927; Crescendo (novel), 1928; The Richest Woman in Town (novel), 1932; The Gray Man Walks (novel), 1936; Kings Row (novel), 1940; Floods of Spring (novel), 1942; Victoria Grandolet (novel), 1944; Red Shoes Run Faster (novelette), 1944; Doctor Mitchell of Kings Row (2d novel of Kings Row trilogy, in collaboration with Katherine Bellamann), released as Parris Mitchell of Kings Row, 1947. Translator of Dante's Divine Comedy; da Sacra rappresentazione di Abramo e d'Isaac, Feo Belcare. Editor of Overtones (music mag. of Curtis Inst. of Music); lit. editor The State, Columbia, S.C., 1923-33. Contbr. critical articles to mags.; translator of Brahm's Songs. All later novels translated into various foreign langs. and made into motion pictures. Address: 2 East 88th St., New York, N.Y. Died June 16, 1945.

BELLAMY, John Dillard, congressman; b. Wilmington, N.C., March 24, 1854; grad. Davidson Coll., N.C., 1873; B.L., Univ. of Va., 1875; m. Emma M. Hargrove, Dec. 6, 1876; city atty., Wilmington, 1881; mem. State senate, 1891; delegate Nat. Conv., 1892; mem. Congress, 1899-1903, 6th N.C. dist. Democrat. Home: Wilmington, N.C. Died Dec. 25, 1942.

BELLINGER, William Whaley, clergyman; b. Richland Ponds, Barnwell Dist., S.C., Dec. 25, 1863; s. Amos Northrop and Maria Louisa (Whaley) B.; A.B., Union Coll., N.Y., 1883; B.D., Gen. Theol. Sem., 1888; M.A., Trinity Coll., Conn., 1889; D.D., Hobart, 1901; L.H.D., Union, 1909; D.C.L., Syracuse U., 1920; m. Catharine Carr Miles, Dec. 29, 1886 (died Mar. 3, 1939); children—Mrs. Katharine Polhemus, William Hart, John B., Northrop Terry (dec.). Made deacon, 1886, ordained priest, 1887, P.E. Ch.; minister in charge Grace Ch., Albany, N.Y., 1886; rector Trinity Ch., Wethersfield, Conn., 1886-89; asst. minister St. Mary's Ch., Brooklyn, N.Y., 1889-90, rector same, 1890-99; rector Grace Ch., Utica, N.Y., 1899-1908; vicar St. Agnes' Chapel, Trinity Parish, New York, since 1908. Trustee New York P.E. Pub. Sch. and mem. of Sch. Com.; pres. St. Luke's Home for Aged Women; v.p. Corps for Relief of Widows and Orphans of Clergy of P.E. Ch. in State of N.Y. Del. to Gen. Conv. P.E. Ch., 1904-07. Mem. Soc. for Promotion of Religion and Learning in State of N.Y. (v.p.), N.Y. Bible and Prayer Book Soc., Psi Upsilon, Theta Nu Epsilon. Clubs: Union League, University. Home: 115 W. 91st St., New York, N.Y. Died Apr. 6, 1943.

BELLOWS, Johnson McClure, impresario, musical and dramatic critic; b. New York, N.Y., Mar. 19, 1870; s. George Gates and Mary (McClure) B.; grad. General Theol. Sem., 1893. Ordained ministry Protestant Episcopal Ch., 1893; asst. rector St. James Ch., New York, 1894-95; rector Grace Ch., Norwalk, Conn., 1895-1901; apptd. chaplain U.S. Navy, by Theodore Roosevelt, 1902; served with rank of jr. lt., 1902-08; resigned from Navy and ch., 1908, to take up profession of music. Pupil of Sargent and Bissell. Music critic on Hartford Globe and Times, 1908-11; same, St. Paul Dispatch and Pioneer Press, 1911-15; for several years manager of Chicago Office, Columbia Concerts Corp., of Columbia Broadcasting System; retired. Mem. Soc. Colonial Wars, New York. Address: Care Bankers Trust Co., 529 5th Av., New York, N.Y. Died Apr. 8, 1949.

BELMONT, Perry; b. N.Y. City, Dec. 28, 1850; e. s. late August and Caroline Slidell (Perry) B.; A.B., Harvard, 1872; studied civil law, U. of Berlin; LL.B., Columbia, 1876; m. Jessie Robbins, 1899. Admitted to bar, 1876; in practice, 1876-81; mem. 47th to 50th Congresses (1881-89), chmn. Com. on Foreign Affairs, 1885-89; E.E. and M.P. to Spain, 1888-89; del. Dem. Nat. Conv., 1890, 96, 1900, 04, 12; maj. insp. gen. 1st Div., 2d Army Corps, U.S.V., 1898. Commd. capt. U.S. Q.-M. Corps, U.S. Army, May 1917. Mem.

advisory bd. Am. Defense Soc. Mem. S.R., Soc. of the Cincinnati. Comdr. Legion of Honor of France; Sacred Mirror (Japan). Clubs: Metropolitan (New York and Washington, D.C.); Knickerbocker, Brook, New York Yacht, Army and Navy, Union, Harvard, Jockey, Turf and Field (pres.), United Hunts Assn. (pres.), Coaching, Democratic, Manhattan, Newport Reading Room. Author: National Isolation an Illusion, 1924; Survival of the Democratic Principle, 1926; Return to Secret Party Funds, 1927; Political Equality, Religious Toleration, 1928; An American Democrat, 1940. Home: Newport, R.I. Died May 25, 1947.

BENCHLEY, Robert Charles, writer; b. Worcester, Mass., Sept. 15, 1889; s. Charles Henry and Jane (Moran) B.; A.B., Harvard, 1912; m. Gertrude Darling, June 6, 1914; children—Nathaniel Goddard and Robert, Jr. With adv. dept. Curtis Pub. Co., Phila., 1912-14; industrial personnel work, Boston, 1914-15; asso. editor New York Tribune Sunday Mag., 1916-17; editor New York Tribune Graphic, 1917; sec. to Aircraft Bd., Washington, D.C., 1917-18; mng. editor Vanity Fair, 1919-20; condr. "Books and Other Things" column, New York World, 1920-21; dramatic editor "Life," 1920-29, "New Yorker," 1929-40; with Music Box Revue, 1923-24; made movietone "shorts" for Fox Film Co., 1929, for MGM, 1937-39, for Paramount, 1941; appeared in occasional feature pictures since 1935. Clubs: Century, Coffee House, Harvard, Players. Author: Of All Things, 1921; Love Conquers All, 1922; Pluck and Luck, 1925; The Early Worm, 1927; 20,000 Leagues Under the Sea, or David Copperfield, 1928; The Treasurer's Report, 1930; No Poems, 1932; From Bed to Worse, 1934; My Ten Years in a Quandary, 1936. After 1903, What?, 1938; Inside Benchley, 1942; Benchley Beside Himself, 1943; One Minute Please, 1945; posthumously, Benchley —Or Else, 1947; Chips Off the Old Benchley, 1949. Occasional radio work since 1937. Home: 2 Lynwood Rd., Scarsdale, N.Y. Died Nov. 21, 1945; buried Prospect Hill Cemetery, Nantucket, Mass.

BENDA, Wladyslaw Theodor (bĕn'dȧ), illustrator, painter; b. Poznan, Poland; s. Jan S. (pianist and composer) and Ksawera (Sikorska) B.; educated school of tech., and Academy of Art, Cracow; art schs. in Vienna, San Francisco, and New York; m. Romola Campfield, 1919; children—Eleonora, Basia. Came to U.S., 1899; naturalized citizen, 1911; has made illustrations for Century Mag., Scribner's, Cosmopolitan, McClure's, Collier's, etc., and many books; also decorative painter. Creator of a new type of masks used on stage under name Benda masks. Author: Masks, 1945; wrote article on modern masks in Ency. Brit.; lectures on masks, and gives stage demonstrations of his masks. Mem. Soc. of Illustrators. Clubs: Coffee House, Dutch Treat. Decorated Chevalier Order Polonia Restituta (Poland). Studio and home: 2 W. 67th St., New York 23, N.Y. Died Nov. 30, 1948.

BENDIX, Max, conductor; b. Detroit, Mar. 28, 1866; studied violin; became concert-meister in Van der Stucken's orchestra, New York, 1885; concert meister Theodore Thomas Orchestra, 1886-96, asst. condr., 1891-96. Conducted series of orchestra concerts for 6 weeks, Chicago, 1892; asst. conductor and, after Mr. Thomas' resignation, sole condr. Expn. Orchestra of 114 selected artists at Chicago Expn. Organized and for several seasons directed Max Bendix String Quartet; condr. official orchestra, St. Louis Expn., 1904; specially engaged as concert meister for Wagnerian operas, Met. Opera House, New York, 1905; concert meister and condr. Hammerstein's Manhattan Opera, 1906; concert and recital tour throughout U.S., 1907, and in Europe, 1908; condr. Met. Opera, New York, 1909-10, Nat. Symphony Orchestra, Chicago, 1914; official condr. San Francisco Expn., 1915. Est. Bendix Music Bur., New York; mus. dir. Met. Opera House; dir. for Henry W. Savage, 1916-17; Gallo-English Opera and Commonwealth Opera, 1918-19, Royal English Opera, 1920, St. Louis Municipal Opera, 1920; apptd. mus. dir. Chicago World's Fair 1933, after winning contest sponsored by Chicago Daily News to select the band master and dir.; verdict of jury unanimous with band of 60 to make tour of world in behalf of Expn. Composer of music Jane Cowl prodn., Romeo and Juliet, Fokine Ballet in Johannes Kreisler, G. V. Hobart's allegorical play, Experience. Clubs: Lotos, Lambs, Bohemian. Died Dec. 6, 1945.

BENDIX, Vincent, engr., inventor, industrialist; b. Moline, Illinois, 1882; son of Rev. John Bendix; mechanical, engineering and general education; m. Elizabeth Channon, Apr. 6, 1922 (divorced). Early pioneer in design and building of automobiles; inventor Bendix drive which made automobile self starting practicable, has been used on more than 65 million cars; introduced in U.S. first volume production 4-wheel brakes for automobiles; organized and chmn. bd. Bendix Aviation Corp., comprising allied group mfgs. here and abroad of automotive, aviation, marine and industrial apparatus until retired in 1942; instrumental in development and formation corp. for manufacture Bendix Home Laundry; dir. Pioneer Instrument Co., Bendix Eclipse of Can., Bendix Home Appliances, Jaeger Watch Co. Founder and sponsor Bendix Transcontinental Air Race and donor Bendix Trophy; sponsor Internat. Glider Meet, Elmira, N.Y., and donor of Bendix Glider Trophy. Past pres. Soc. Automotive Engrs.; dir. Swedish Chamber of Commerce (New York). Clubs: Engineers (N.Y.); Metropolitan, Cloud, Economic, Lotos (New York); Bath and Tennis, Seminole (Palm Beach); Woodmount Rod and Gun Club (Berkley Springs, W.Va.); Havana Country (Cuba). Office: 401 Bendix Drive, South Bend, Ind.; also 30 Rockefeller Plaza, New York, N.Y. Died Mar. 27, 1945.

BENEDICT, James Everard, naturalist; b. Norwalk, Conn., Jan. 5, 1854; s. James B.; A.B., Union Coll., 1880, A.M., 1884, Ph. D., 1892; m. Elizabeth M. Junken, Nov. 23, 1883; children—James Everard, Charles Junken, Elizabeth Jennie, Ruth. Resident naturalist U.S. Fish Commn. str. Albatross, 1883-86, during its stay on the Atlantic, and subsequently asst. curator div. of marine invertebrates. U.S. Nat. Mus., and chief of the exhibits of biology; retired 1930. Contbr. many papers on natural history subjects. Home: 1013 Highland Drive, Silver Spring, Md. Died 1940.

BENEDICT, Ruth Fulton, anthropologist; b. New York, N.Y., June 5, 1887; d. Frederick S. and Beatrice J. (Shattuck) Fulton; A.B., Vassar Coll., 1909; Ph.D., Columbia U., 1923; m. Stanley R. Benedict, June 18, 1914 (died Dec. 21, 1936). Lecturer in anthropology, Columbia U., 1923-30, asst. prof., 1930-36, asso. prof., 1936-48, prof., 1948; field trips to Am. Indian tribes, 1922-39; on leave with Bureau of Overseas Intelligence, O.W.I., 1943-46. Author: Patterns of Culture, 1934; Zuni Mythology (2 vols.), 1935; Race: Science and Policies, 1940; The Chrysanthemum and the Sword: Patterns of Japanese Culture, 1946. Home: 448 Central Park West, New York 25. Office: Dept. of Anthropology, Columbia University, New York, N.Y. Died Sept. 17, 1948.

BENES, Eduard (bĕ'nĕsh), president of Czechoslovakia; b. Kozlany, Bohemia, May 28, 1884; s. Matej and Anna (Benes) B.; ed. Univs. of Prague, Paris, Dijon; received hon. degrees from many colls. and univs. including Columbia, Colorado, Princeton, Yale and Trinity Coll. in U.S.A., 1939; m. Anna Vlcek, 1909. Began diplomatic career in Paris working for cause of Czechoslovakian liberation in close collaboration with Thomas Masaryk, 1915; gen. sec. Czechoslovak Nat. Council, Paris, 1917; minister for foreign affairs, Czechoslovakia, 1918-35, premier, 1921-22, pres., 1935-38. Prof. Prague Univ., from 1921. Rapporteur gen. of Disarmament Conf.; mem. Council of League of Nations, 1923-27, pres. of Council several times, pres. of Assembly of the League, 1935; one of the drafters Geneva Protocol; leading figure in Little Entente; resigned presidency of Czechoslovakia after "Munich Agreement," going to London; came to U.S., Feb. 1939, as visiting prof. under Charles Walgreen Foundation, U. of Chicago; became full prof., U. of Chicago, July 1939. Recognized by Great Britain and United States as president of Czechoslovakia, July 1941; re-elected pres. Czechoslovakia, June 19, 1946. Mem. Institut de France, Académie des Sciences Morales et Politiques. Author: My War Memories (tr. from Czech by Paul Selver), 1928; Problem of Central Europe and the Austrian Question, 1934; Problem of Czechoslovakia, 1936; Struggle for Collective Security and the Italo-Abyssinian War, 1935; Democracy—Today and Tomorrow, 1939; President Benes on War and Peace, 1943; Six Years in Exile, 1946. Home: Praha-Hrad, Czechoslovakia. Address: 1775 Broadway, New York, N.Y. Died Sept. 3, 1948.

BENÉT, Laurence Vincent, mech. engr.; b. West Point, N.Y., Jan. 12, 1863; s. Brig. Gen. Stephen V. and Laura (Walker) B.; prep. edn., Emerson Inst., Washington; Ph.B., Yale, 1884; m. Margaret Cox, Dec. 20, 1899 (died July 20, 1941). With La Société Hotchkiss & Cie., Paris, since 1885; now hon. pres. Ensign U.S. Navy, Spanish-Am. War, 1898; with Am. Ambulance and Hosp. Service, Aug. 1914-1917, rank of comdt.; mem. advisory com. Purchasing Bd., A.E.F., Sept. 1917-Jan. 1918. Past pres. and gold medalist Am. Chamber Commerce in France, Am. Aid Soc. Decorated Grand Officer Legion of Honor, Medal of Honor, 1st Class (France); Comdr. Mil. Order of Christ (Portugal); Comdr. Order of Crown of Rumania; Officer of Osmania (Turkey); Am. Field Service, First Class, etc. Mem. Am. Soc Mech. Engrs., Yale Engring. Assn., Nat. councillor Chamber Commerce of the U.S., Ingénieurs Civiles de France, U.S. Naval Inst., S.R., S.A.R., Loyal Legion, Mil. Order of Foreign Wars of the U.S., U.S. Army Ordnance Assn., United Vets. of Spanish-Am. War; fellow Am. Geog. Soc., St. Augustine's Hist. Soc. Republican. Episcopalian. Clubs: Metropolitan, Army and Navy (Washington); University (New York); Cercle Interallié. American (Paris). Home: 2101 Connecticut Av., Washington, D.C. Died May 21, 1948; buried in Arlington Nat. Cemetery.

BENÉT, Stephen Vincent, author; b. Bethlehem, Pa., July 22, 1898; s. James Walker (col. U.S. Army) and Frances Neill (Rose) B.; B.A., Yale, 1919, M.A., 1920, Litt.D., 1937; m. Rosemary Carr, Nov. 26, 1921; children—Stephanie Jane, Thomas Carr, Rachel. Awarded gold medal by Roosevelt Memorial Assn., 1933. Mem. Alpha Delta Phi, Chi Delta Theta, Wolf's Head, Am. Academy of Arts and Letters. Episcopalian. Clubs: Elizabethan (New Haven, Conn.); Coffee House, Century (New York). Author: Five Men and Pompey, 1915; Young Adventure, 1918; Heavens and Earth, 1920; The Beginning of Wisdom, 1921; Jean Huguenot, 1923; Tiger Joy, 1925; Spanish Bayonet, 1926; John Brown's Body (Pulitzer prize for best vol. of verse), 1928; Ballads and Poems, 1931; James Shore's Daughter, 1934; Burning City, 1936; The Devil and Daniel Webster, 1937; Thirteen O'Clock, 1937; Johnny Pye and the Fool-Killer, 1938; Tales Before Midnight, 1939; Selected Works of Stephen Vincent Benet, 1942; Western Star, 1943 (awarded Pulitzer Prize for Verse); America, 1944; We Stand United, 1945; The Last Circle, 1946 (last four published posthumously). Address: care Brandt and Brandt, 101 Park Av., New York. Died March 13, 1943.

BENJAMIN, Gilbert Giddings, prof. history; b. Fond du Lac, Wis., Dec. 6, 1874; s. Gilbert Lyman and Clara (Lyon) B.; Ph.B. magna cum laude, Syracuse U., 1899; M.A., Yale, 1904, Ph.D., 1907; m. Laura Goundrey, October 16, 1912; children—Mary Barnes, Gilbert Giddings. Vice prin. Silver Creek (N.Y.) High Sch., 1899-1901; univ. scholar in history, Yale, 1901-02, fellow in history, 1902-05, asst., 1902-06, also instr. New Haven High Sch.; head dept. history, 4 summers, Syracuse U.; instr. history, Coll. City of N.Y., 1907-11; prof. and head dept. history, Allegheny Coll., 1911-13; acting head dept. U. of Pittsburgh, 1913-14; prof. history, State U. of Ia., 1915-28; prof. European history U. of Southern Calif. since 1928. Prof. history, summer sessions, U. of Chicago, 1924, Univ. of Tex., 1925, Univ. of Southern Calif., 1926-27, Northwestern U., 1931; lecturer on history Palisades Summer Sch. and Assembly, Santa Monica, Calif., 1926. Resident, University Settlement, N.Y. City, 1907-10. Four-minute speaker, World War.; rep. of U.S. Com. of Pub. Information at Camp Dodge, Ia., 1918. Mem. Am. Hist. Assn. (exec. council Pacific coast br. 1928-29 and 1934-35), Ia. State Hist. Assn., Ia. Social Science Assn. (pres. 1916-17), Am. Assn. Univ. Profs. (pres. U. of Southern Calif. br. 1933-34), Syracuse Alumni Assn., Economic History Soc. of Gt. Britain, Académique D'Histoire Internationale, Pacific Geog. Soc. (life fellow), Phi Beta Kappa (pres. Ia. Chapter, 1917-18), Phi Kappa Psi, Phi Delta Kappa, Alpha Pi Zeta (pres. U. of Southern Calif. Chapter, 1930-31), Phi Alpha Theta, Pi Gamma Mu; fellow Royal Hist. Soc. of Great Britain. Congregationalist. Clubs: Faculty (U. of Southern Calif.); Yale, Twenty Club of Southern Calif. (pres. 1935-36). Author: The Germans in Texas—a Study in Immigration, 1910; Modern and Contemporary European Civilization (with H. G. Plum), 1923. Contbr. to polit. and hist. jours. Home: 2297 W. 23d St., Los Angeles, Calif. Died, May 28, 1941.

BENNETT, Andrew Carl, naval officer; b. Goodland, Kan.; s. Andrew Pierce and Harriet Winefred (Kirkpatrick) B.; grad. U.S. Naval Acad., 1912; post grad. student various service schools; m. Jessie Crawford Biggam, Oct. 16, 1920; children—Betty Duff (wife of Lt. Donald Francis Banker, U.S.N.), Anne Douglas (wife of Lt. Charles Francis Helme, Jr., U.S.N.). Commd. ensign, U.S. Navy, 1912, advancing to rear adm., 1942; comd. submarines and submarine units, 24 yrs. also served in battleships and cruisers; comd. U.S.S. Savannah (light cruiser), 1940-42; unit comdr., Oran, Algeria, area of invasion of North Africa, Nov. 8, 1942; comdt. 8th Naval Dist., hdqrs. in New Orleans, La., since 1943. Decorated Navy Cross, also 6 campaign medals (U.S.); Legion of Honor (France). Mason (32°, Scottish Rite, Shriner). Clubs: Army-Navy Country (Washington, D.C.); Boston (New Orleans, La.). Deceased.

BENNETT, Arthur Ellsworth, clergyman; b. Elgin, Ill., Dec. 5, 1865; s. Charles Wesley and Sarah Jane (Clark) B.; B.S., Kan. Normal Coll., 1889, A.B., 1890; Pd.M., Normal Sch. of N.M., 1898; Pd.D., New York Univ., 1905; LL.D., Upper Iowa U., 1936; m. Mary Ann Steeley, Sept. 1, 1891; 1 son, Rev. A. Vincent. Prin. public schools, Wheatland, N.D., 1885-88; supt. schs., Lisbon, N.D., 1891-92; supervisor of teacher training, Kan. Normal Coll., 1892-95; v.p. Normal Sch. of N.M., 1895-99; dean Sch. of Edn., Upper Ia. U., 1899-1913; dean Highland Park Coll., 1913-16, Des Moines Coll., 1917-18; prof. ednl. psychology and dir. extension div. Sch. Religious Edn., Boston U., 1918-25; dean education, Des. Moines Univ., 1925-31; pres. Upper Iowa U., 1931-36; pastor Immanuel Meth. Ch., Des Moines, since 1936. Lecturer and conductor teachers inst.; commencement orator. Fellow Am. Genetic Society; mem. N.E.A., Pi Kappa Delta, Sigma Nu. Republican. Methodist. Mason, Odd Fellow. Author: The Rational Method in Geography, 1917; Laboratory Method in the History of Education, 1908; The Training of Teachers for the Rural Schools, 1912; Bible Study Credit, 1914. Address: 2824 49th St., Des Moines, Ia.

BENNETT, Henry Eastman, prof. edn.; b. Buffalo, N.Y., Feb. 6, 1873; s. William Morris and Georgia Ann (Eastman) B.; student Florida Agrl. Coll.; grad. Peabody Normal Coll., Nashville, Tenn., 1896; A.B., U. of Chicago, 1907, M.A. 1922; Ph.D. (Chicago), 1925; m. Daisy Green, Sept. 15, 1897; children—Gladys Elizabeth, Loren Eastman. Teacher pub. schs. Okahumpka, Fla., 1891-93; prin. high sch., Fernandina, Fla., 1896-97; teacher, State Normal Sch., Defuniak Springs, Fla., 1897-1900; chief clk. State Dept. Edn., Fla., 1900-03; pres., State Normal Sch., Fla., 1903-05; dean Normal Dept., U. of Fla., 1905-06; prof. philosophy and edn., 1907-12, prof. edn., 1912-25, Coll. of William and Mary; now research adviser Am. Seating Co. Y.M.C.A. ednl. dir. with A.E.F. in France, Jan. 1918-May 1919. Mem. N.E.A., Phi Beta Kappa, Phi Delta Kappa. Democrat. Presbyterian. Author: School Efficiency, 1917; Psychology and Self Development, 1923. Co-Author: Brevard and Bennett's History and Government of Florida, 1904. Home: 7111 S. Shore Drive. Office: 14 E. Jackson Blvd., Chicago. Died 1941.

BENNETT, Horace Wilson, realtor, author; b. Hamburg, Mich., Sept. 4, 1862; s. Horace Alderman and Sarah (Wilson) B.; ed. pub. schs.; m. Julie Riche, Feb. 17, 1897; children—Mark John, Mrs. Marguerite Bennett Cobb, Gladys (Mrs. Archibald F. MacNichol), Virginia (Mrs. Charles Crocker). Organizer Horace W. Bennett & Co., 1918, successor to Bennett & Myers, orgn. 1884; one of the original owners and developers of Cripple Creek, Colo.; pres. Ritz-Carlton Realty Co., The Bennett and Myers Investment Co., Bi-Metallic Investment Co., Home Public Market Co.; dir. 15th St. Investment Co., Denver Tramway Corp. Republican. Episcopalian. Clubs: Denver Athletic, Colorado Motor, Denver Country, Cherry Hills Country, Denver (Denver); Everglades (Palm Beach, Fla.). Author: Bright Yellow Gold; Silver Crown of Glory; A Modern Prince from an Ancient House. Home: Wolhurst, Littleton, Colo. Office: 210 Tabor Bldg., Denver, Colo. Died June 9, 1941.

BENNETT, Louis L., coast guard officer; b. Baltimore, Md., June 16, 1886; s. Louis and Marie (Hopban) B.; ed. pvt. and pub. schs., Baltimore and Annapolis, Md.; grad. U.S. Coast Guard Acad., 1909; married, Feb. 14, 1910. Commd. ensign, U.S. Coast Guard, 1909, and advanced through grades to commodore, 1945; sea duty included three cruises to Bering Sea, 1916-22; attached to office Chief of Naval Operations, 1935-36; constructed and commanded Coast Guard Training Sta., Groton, Conn.; now comdr. 11th Coast Guard Dist., Long Beach, Calif. Awarded Navy Commendation Ribbon, Victory Medal (World War I), Am. Defense, Am. Theater and World War II medals. Mem. U.S. Naval Inst. Clubs: Propeller of U.S. (Los Angeles); Pacific Coast (Long Beach). Home: 214 East Ocean Blvd. Office: 11th Coast Guard Dist., Long Beach, Calif. Died Oct. 13, 1949.

BENNETT, Michael John, endocrinologist; b. Phila., Pa., Jan. 13, 1905; s. Michael Smith (D.D.S.) and Lucy Aquilla (Stump) B.; student U. of Pa., 1923-24, U. of the South, 1924-25; M.D., Hahnemann Med. Coll., 1929; postgrad. study, U. of Pa., 1930-31; m. Mary Cornelia Hunsicker, June 7, 1929; children—Mary Gay, Anne Louise (dec.), Michael John, Merle Joyce. Interne Montreal Homeopathic Hosp., 1929-30; instr. gynecology, Hahnemann Hosp., 1930-36; attending gynecologist Broad St. Hosp., 1939-41; endocrinologist Doctor's Hosp., 1941; dir. Endocrin Research Clinic, 1939, Mem. A.M.A., Pa. State Med. Soc., Phila. County Med. Soc. (chmn. sect. on endocrinology, 1941), Am. Inst. Homeopathy, Southern Homeopathic Med. Assn., Phi Gamma Delta, Phi Alpha Gamma. Republican. Presbyterian. Mason. Asso. editor of Medical World; editor of Jour. of the Am. Inst. of Homeopathy. Home: Welsh Road, Huntingdon Valley, Pa. Office: 269 S. 19th St., Philadelphia, Pa. Deceased.

BENNETT, Philip Allen, congressman; b. on farm Dallas County, Mo., Mar. 5, 1881; s. Marion F. and Mary (O'Bannon) B.; ed. Buffalo High Sch. and Springfield (Mo.) Normal and Business Coll.; m. Bertha Tinsley, May 16, 1912; children—Marion Tinsley, Mary Edith. Began as sch. teacher, 1899; editor and pub. Buffalo (Mo.) Reflex, 1904-21; state senator, 19th Mo. Dist., 1921-25; lt. gov. of Mo., 1925-29; mem. 77th Congress (1941-43), 6th Mo. Dist.; dir. O'Bannon Banking Co., 1918-36. Served as county chmn., 8 yrs., Congl. chmn., 2 yrs., state committeeman, 2 yrs.; del. Rep. Nat. Conv., 1912. Republican. Elder South St. Christian Ch., Springfield. Mason, Odd Fellow. Past dept. comdr. Sons of Union Vets of Civil War. Home: 507 S. Main Av. Office: 216½ S. Jefferson, Springfield, Mo. Died Dec. 7, 1942; buried Hazelwood Cemetery, Springfield, Mo.

BENNETT, Richard, actor, manager; b. Bennett's Mill, Cass Co., Ind., May 21, 1872; s. George W. and Eliza L. (Hoffman) B.; ed. Kokomo High Sch., Logansport Normal Sch.; m. Mable Morrison, Nov. 8, 1903; children—Barbara, Constance, Joan. Played in "Charley's Aunt," "Jane," "Royal Family," "What Every Woman Knows," "The Barker," etc.; prepared Brieux's play, "Damaged Goods," for Am. stage and appeared as George Dupont, also as Doctor; prod. Brieux's "Maternity," at Princess Theatre, New York, Jan. 16, 1915. Associated with Charles Frohman in producing plays 1896-1908. Episcopalian. Mason, Elk. Died Oct. 22, 1944.

BENNY, Allan, congressman, lawyer; b. Brooklyn, July 12, 1867; s. Robert and Agnes B.; ed. pub. sch. Bayonne, N.J., 1873-82; m. Catherine W. Warren, Nov. 29, 1888. Admitted to N.J. bar, Feb., 1889; mem. Bayonne common council, 1892-94; N.J. legislature, 1897-99; city atty., Bayonne, 1900-03, resigned; mem. Congress, 9th N.J. dist., 1903-05. Democrat. In contest Hudson circuit court for membership in Bayonne common council, 1894, declared by Justice Lippincott of N.J. Supreme Court, to be not a citizen of U.S., because at time of his birth his father was a Scotchman not naturalized in U.S.; decision unanimously reversed by N.J. Supreme Court on appeal. Address: Bayonne, N.J. Died Nov. 7, 1942.

BENSON, Philip Adolphus, banker; b. N.Y. City, Dec. 17, 1881; s. Edward Adolphus and Georgianna (Whann) B.; B.C.S., New York U., 1911; certified pub. accountant, N.Y., 1911; m. Louise A. Melville, Sept. 23, 1911; children—William Melville, Robert Elliot, Philip Adolphus, Evelyn. Began as office boy Phenix Ins. Co. of Brooklyn, 1895; with Mutual Life Ins. Co. of New York, 1896-1906, Realty Associates of Brooklyn, 1906-17; with The Dime Savings Bk. of Brooklyn as asst. sec., later sec. and treas. until 1932, pres. since 1932; trustee Title Guarantee & Trust Co., Kings Co. Trust Co., Atlantic Mutual Insurance Co.; director Abraham & Straus, Inc., Commonwealth Ins. Co. of N.Y., North Brit. & Mercantile Ins. Co., Brooklyn Garden Apts. (treas.), Savings Bank Trust Co., Institutional Securities Corp.; past pres. Am. Bankers Assn.; trustee Provident Loan Society of N.Y. Dir. Brooklyn and Queens Y.M.C.A.; trustee Y.W.C.A.; mem. board mgrs. Seamen's Branch Y.M.C.A.; pres. Railroad Security Owners Assn. Trustee Long Island Coll. of Medicine, Brooklyn Inst. of Arts and Sciences; mem. Council New York U., Nat. Assn. Mutual Savings Banks (pres. 1933-34), Brooklyn Chamber of Commerce (dir.); pres. bd. dirs. Adelphi Acad. of Brooklyn; dir. Stony Brook Assembly (Stony Brook School); chmn. Appeal Bd. Selective Service, 1941-46. Member of Banking Board of the State of New York, New York State Society of C.P.A., Chamber of Commerce of State of N.Y., Downtown Brooklyn Assn. (v.p.), Holland Soc., Sons of the Revolution, Delta Sigma Pi. Republican. Mem. Reformed Ch. Clubs: Bankers, Montauk (Brooklyn), Sea Cliff Yacht; Manhasset Bay Yacht. Author: Real Estate Principles and Practices (with Nelson L. North), 1922. Home: 280 Prospect Av., Sea Cliff, L.I., N.Y. Office: 9 De Kalb Av., Brooklyn, N.Y. Died Oct. 16, 1946.

BENSON, Stuart, editor; b. Detroit, Mich., Jan. 3, 1877; s. George Stewart and Martha (Bennett) B.; student U. of Mich., 1896-98; Detroit School of Art; m. Mary Helen Duggett, 1921. Began as illustrator, 1900, later advt. writer, publicity mgr., art editor, Collier's Weekly, 1910-13; prodn. mgr. Erickson Co., 1913-17; syndicate mgr.; mem. New York Stock Exchange firm, Morgan, Livermore & Co., 1919-24; art editor Collier's Weekly, since 1924. Served overseas as capt. and maj. inf., 1917-19. Decorated Légion d'Honneur, Étoile Noire and Croix de Guerre (France). Clubs: Players, Dutch Treat, Westport Country. Author: (play) Find Cynthia (prod. by Kilbourn Gordon, Inc., 1922). Contbr. short stories and spl. articles. Home: Weston, Conn. Office: 250 Park Av., New York. Died Oct. 19, 1949.

BENT, Silas, writer; b. Millersburg, Ky., May 9, 1882; s. Rev. Dr. James McClelland and Sallie (Burnam) B.; A.B., Ogden Coll., Bowling Green, Ky., 1902; m. Elizabeth Chism Sims, Oct. 3, 1916. Staff writer Louisville and St. Louis newspapers, 1902-11, except 1908, when occupied chair in Sch. of Journalism, U. of Mo.; engaged in publicity work (promotion of sound banking system) for Nat. Citizens' League, 1912-13, later newspaper work, N.Y. City; dramatic reviewer for Reedy's Mirror, St. Louis, 1917-20, and on editorial staff New York Times, 1918-20; in charge of mag. and newspaper publicity, Dem. Nat. Com., 1920; asso. editor The Nation's Business, Washington, 1920-22; free-lance writer since 1922. Lectured on metropolitan journalism, at New Sch. for Social Research, New York, 1927. Club: Nat. Press (Washington). Author: Ballyhoo—The Voice of the Press, 1927; Strange Bedfellows, 1928; Machine Made Man, 1929; Justice Oliver Wendell Holmes, A Biography, 1932; Buchanan of The Press (novel), 1932; Slaves by the Billion, 1938; Newspaper Crusaders: A Neglected Story, 1939; Home: The Log Cabin, Old Greenwich, Conn. Died July 30, 1945; buried Fairview Cemetery, Bowling Green, Ky.

BENTLEY, Arthur, pres. Miehle Printing Press & Mfg. Co.; b. Manchester, Eng., Dec. 14, 1876; s. Thomas Potter and Ellen (Croxall) B.; ed. pub. schs., Eng.; C.P.A., U. of Ill., 1903; m. Cherry Ford, Nov. 7, 1906; children—Ford, Barbara, Joan. Came to U.S., 1902, naturalized, 1909. In chartered accountant's office, Eng., 1893-1902; with Price, Waterhouse & Co., pub. accountants, Chicago, 1902-05; comptroller Am. Steel Foundries, 1905-10; 1st v.p. Miehle Printing Press & Mfg. Co., 1910-24, pres. since 1924; dir. Miehle Printing Press & Mfg. Co., Ltd. (London), Am. Steel Foundries, Dexter Folder Co. Clubs: Chicago, Glen View. Office: 14th St. and Damen Av., Chicago, Ill. Died Apr. 3, 1946.

BENTON, Alva Hartley, agrl. economist; b. Mendon, O., Jan. 26, 1886; s. Chester Elias and Addie Caldwell (Snodgrass) B.; B.S., Ohio State U., 1912; M.S., Pa. State Coll., 1913; Ph.D., U. of Wis., 1921; grad. study, U. of Minn., 1915, Harvard, 1930; m. Sarah Alice Mitchamore, Aug. 5, 1913; children—Robert Hartley, Elizabeth Louise (wife of Dr. Leon Orris Jacobson). Asst. prof. farm management, U. of Minn., 1913-18; prof. rural economics, U. of Manitoba (Can.), 1918-22; head dept. marketing and rural orgns., N.D. Agr. Coll. and Expt. Station, Fargo, 1922-33; prin. agrl. economist and prin. social scientist, U.S. Dept. Agr., since 1933, now asst. head div. of program study and discussion, Bureau of Agrl. Economics. Mem. Am. Farm Econ. Assn., Am. Econ. Assn., Am. Soc. Agrl. Sciences, Pi Kappa Alpha. Author: Introduction to the Marketing of Farm Products; also number of agrl. expt. station bulletins. Home: 1529 W. Falkland Lane, Silver Spring, Md. Office: South Bldg., Dept. of Agriculture, Washington, D.C. Died Nov. 23, 1945; buried in Cedar Hill Cemetery, Washington.

BENTON, Elbert Jay, prof. history; b. Dubuque, Ia., Mar. 23, 1871; s. Oliver Dustin and Sarah (Proctor) B.; A.B., Kansas City U. (Campbell Coll.), 1895; post-grad. work in history, U. of Chicago; fellow in history, Johns Hopkins, 1902-03, Ph.D., 1903; m. Emma Kaul, June 1895 (died May 1925); m. 2d, Irene J. Kaul, June 20, 1927. Prin. High Sch., Holton, Kan., 1895-97; teacher hist., Lafayette (Ind.) High Sch., 1898-1901; instr. history, 1903-06, asst. prof., 1906-09, prof., 1909-41, dean Grad. Sch., 1925-41, now emeritus, Western Reserve U.; Albert Shaw lecturer, Johns Hopkins, 1907. Sec. and dir. Western Reserve Hist. Soc. Author: History of Taxation in Kansas, 1900; The Wabash Trade Route, 1903; International Law and Diplomacy of the Spanish-American War, 1908; Peace Without Victory, 1918; A Short History of the Western Reserve Hist. Soc., 1942; The Cultural History of Cleveland, Part I, 1943, Part II, 1944, Part III, 1946. Joint Author (with H. E. Bourne); Introductory American History, 1912; History of the U.S., 1913; Story of America and Great Americans, 1923; American History, 1925; (with W. A. Hamm and H. E. Bourne) A Unit History of the United States, 1932; A History of the National City Bank, Cleveland, 1845-1945, 1945. Contbr. to reviews and hist. publs. Home: 2856 Woodbury Rd., Shaker Heights, Cleveland, O. Died March 28, 1946.

BENTON, Elma Hixson, teacher; b. Burlington, Ia., Feb. 18, 1874; d. Daniel W. and Helen (Orr) Hixson; A.B., U. of Minn., 1910; A.M., Columbia, 1918; m. Charles W. Benton, May 29, 1899 (died 1913). Began teaching, 1890; county supt. schs., Otter Tail County, Minn., 1898; mem. staff, Teachers' Coll., N.Y. City, 1917-19; prin. Hosmer Hall, prep. sch. for girls, St. Louis, since 1919. Mem. D.A.R., Phi Beta Kappa. Conglist. Clubs: College, Wednesday. Address: Hosmer Hall, St. Louis. Died Oct. 6, 1942.

BENTON, J(ames) Webb, diplomatist; b. Ft. Meyer, Virginia, July 9, 1892; s. James Watson and Sarah (Henry) B.; B.A., Cambridge U. (England), 1914, M.A., 1920; unmarried. With Foreign Service since 1920; 3d sec. Embassy, Rio de Janeiro, 1921-22; 2d sec., Montevideo, 1922-24; chargé d'affaires, Caracas, 1924; 2d sec., Lisbon, 1925-27; sec. of Legation, Warsaw, 1927-29; 2d sec., Embassy Madrid, 1929-32; chargé d'affaires Legation, Prague, 1933-34, 1st sec. 1935; consul, Bremen, 1936; 1st sec., Legation The Hague, 1937-39; 1st sec. Legation, Bucharest, 1939-41; consul gen., Marseille, France (interned). Del. 8th Internat. Road Congress, 1942, The Hague, 1938; 1st sec. Legation, Bern, 1942; consul general, Leopoldville, 1944; counselor Am. Embassy near the Netherlands Govt., London, 1944; counselor Embassy, The Hague, 1945. Served as 1st lt. U.S. Army, 1917-19. Decorated with Order of the Sacred Treasure (Japan), 1919. Address: Care American Embassy, The Hague, The Netherlands. Died Oct. 23, 1947.

BENTON, John Edwin, lawyer; b. Maidstone, Vt., May 14, 1875; s. Josiah Henry and Harriet Buxton (Niles) B.; student Phillips Exeter Acad., 1893-96; LL.B., Boston Univ. Sch. of Law, 1898; m. Kate Lanmon Nims, Sept. 4, 1907 (died Sept. 12, 1927); m. 2d, Janet Benton Whidden (Mrs. C. T. Whidden), Aug. 7, 1929; 1 dau. (adopted), Jean Elizabeth (Whidden). Admitted to Mass. bar, 1898; admitted to practice in N.H., 1901; became mem. of firm of Cain & Benton, Keene, N.H., 1903; formed firm of Benton & Pickard, 1911-18; gen. solicitor of the Interstate Commerce Commn., Bureau of Valuation, 1918-19; general solicitor of the National Association of Railroad and Utilities Commrs., 1919-44, advisory counsel since 1944. Mem. N.H. House of Reps., 1907-08; mayor of Keene, N.H., 1910; mem. Public Service Commn. of N.H., 1911-15. Mem. Am. Bar Assn., I.C.C. Bar Assn., Communications Commn. Bar Assn., Am. Judicature Soc.; pres. N.H. Assn. of Washington, D.C., 1940-41; pres. Southern Alumni Assn. of Phillips Exeter Acad., 1942-43. Episcopalian. Clubs: Cosmos, National Press (Washington, D.C.). Home: 711 Elm St., Chevy Chase, Md. Office: 7413 New Post Office Bldg., Washington, D.C. Died June 21, 1948.

BERESFORD, Harry, actor; b. London, Eng., Nov. 4, 1867; s. Harry Morgan and Sara (Christie) B.; left college for the stage at 17; m. Edith Wylie, June 19, 1913. Joined Gaiety Theatre Co., London; came to U.S. with Henry E. Dixey Co., 1886, and has since played in America; starred at head of own co., 10 yrs., touring South and West; in vaudeville 6 yrs.; appeared at Belmont Theatre, New York, in "Boys Will Be Boys" two seasons; joined Henry W. Savage Co., in "Shavings," 1920, created part Clem Hawley, in "The Old Soak," 1922; appeared in "Stolen Fruit," 1925-26; in "Shavings," London, 1926-27, later in one-act playlet of "Old Soak"; played in "The Perfect Alibi," New York, season 1928-29, in "Michael and Mary," New York, 1929-30; with Paramount Studios, Hollywood, since 1930. Naturalized citizen of U.S., 1902. Clubs: Lambs, Players (New York); Masquers, Lakeside Golf (Hollywood). Home: Toluca Lake, Calif. Died Oct. 4, 1944.

BERETTA, John King, banker; b. Ft. Smith, Ark., Nov. 5, 1861; s. Alexander and Jane (Staggs) B.; ed. St. Mary's Coll., San Antonio, Tex.; m. Sally Mills Ward, Dec. 9, 1896; 1 son, John Ward. Founder Laredo Nat. Bank, 1895, pres. until 1912; pres. until 1946, Loredo Bridge Co., which built and operated Internat. Bridge at Laredo, Tex.; pres., chmn. Nat. Bank of Commerce, San Antonio, 1912-46; chmn. First Nat. Bank of San Antonio, Texas, Kleberg First Nat. Bank of Kingsville, Texas. Member San Antonio Board of Edn., 4 yrs.; mem. Commn. of Control for Tex. Centennial Celebrations, 1936-39. Mason (32°, Shriner). Democrat. Episcopalian. Kiwanian. Home: 404 W. French Pl. Office: First National Bank, San Antonio, Tex. Died June 21, 1948.

BERG, John Dani•, chief executive officer; b. Pittsburgh, Pa., Dec. 17, 1882; s. Daniel P. and Sarah Jane (Turney) B.; M.E., Lehigh U., 1905, Dr. Engring. (hon.), 1947; m. Martha Moody Biggert, October 10, 1911; children—Perker, D. R., R. T., P. J., Martha Berg Stout. Vice-pres. Dravo-Doyle Co., 1906-23, pres. 1923-34; chmn. bd. Dravo Corp., 1934-46, chief exec. officer since 1946; dir. Dravo-Doyle Co., Union Barge Line Corp., Fullerton-Portsmouth Bridge Co., Consol. Natural Gas Co., Trustee, Lehigh Univ. Mason (32°, Shriner). Clubs: Duquesne (Pittsburgh); Edgeworth (Pa.); Allegheny Country (Sewickley); Union League (New York); Eastward Ho Country (Chatham). Home: R.D., Chatham, Mass. Office: Neville Island, Pittsburgh. Died June 29, 1949.

BERGEN, John Tallmadge, clergyman; b. Bergen Island (now Bergen Beach), Kings County, N.Y., Sept. 21, 1860; s. John C. and Mary Tallmadge (Brower) B.; desc. of Hans Hansen van Bergen; A.B., Rutgers Coll., New Brunswick, N.J., 1883, A.M., 1894, D.D., 1903; diploma Union Theol. Sem., 1886; post-grad. work same, 1893; m. Ellen Grace Dean, 1883 (dec.); children—Dean (dec.), Hansen, Cornelius, Edwin Hope (dec.), Willis, Baldwin (dec.), Tallmadge; m. 2d, Eliza Grace Updegraff, May 17, 1906; 1 dau., Grace Updegraff. Ordained Ref. Ch. (Dutch) ministry, 1886; pastor Shokan, N.Y., 1886-89, Hope Church, Holland, Mich., 1889-1892, S. Brooklyn, 1892-95; prof. ethics and evidences, Hope Coll., Holland, Mich., 1895-1905, also chair Bible and missions same, 1895-1906; pastor Hope Ch., Holland, Mich., 1900-06; Westminster Presbyn. Ch., Dubuque, Ia., 1906-11; pres. Albert Lea (Minn.) Coll., 1911-13; pastor 1st Presbyn. Ch., Minneapolis, 1913-30, Homewood Presbyn. Ch., Minneapolis, Oct. 1, 1930; ret. Sept. 1947. Instr. in N. T. Greek and Apologetics, Northwestern Evang. Theol. Sem. since 1937, instr. Bibl. philosophy and psychology, 1938-39. Pres. Fed. Minneapolis Ministers, 1917-18; mem. Fed. Council Chs. of Christ in Am.; mem. S.R., S.A.R., Mil. Order Fgn. Wars (state comdr., 1924), Phi Beta Kappa. Mem. Minn. Home Guard, Apr. 1917-Mar. 1918; commd. 1st lt., Minn. brig. staff, Mar. 18, 1918; recruiting and publicity work in Minn.; sworn into federal service Aug. 29, and commd. 1st lt. Air Service, U.S. Army, Oct. 29, 1918, duty Vancouver (Wash.) Cantonment; hon. discharged, Dec. 11, 1918; retained as 1st lt. Minn. brigade staff; hon. discharged Dec. 31, 1920; commd. civ. aide to U.S. sec. of war for Minn., 1925-33; commd. capt. (aux), U.S. Army, Oct. 25, 1929; commd. capt. (inactive) U.S. Army chaplain, 1929, 1934, 1939; chaplain, vol. emergency duty, 1942-44; now chaplain Post No. 1, Am. Legion; department chaplain Minn., American Legion, 1933; chaplain Minnesota D.R., 1933. Hon. chaplain, Great Lakes Command Canadian Legion, (cap.) Nov. 11, 1918; reinstalled Mar., 1945; sworn in for emergency duty, U.S. Army, Oct. 29, 1942; Author: (textbook) Evidence of Christianity, 1902, 3d edit., 1923, 4th edit., 1937; From the Word to the World, 1927, 2d and 3d edits., 1933; Atonement and the Atonement, 1938; Aristotle Looks into Evolution, 1940; college song, Take My Love to Rosalie; table songs. Morning Hymn and Evening Praise; hymn folio What Did You Say? and At Bethany, 1937; also numerous articles on religious topics. Home: 1711 N. Xerxes Av., Minneapolis, Minn. Died Aug. 18, 1948.

BERGER, Charles L., ex-chmn. bd. Eastern Malleable Iron Co.; b. Branford, Conn., Nov. 9, 1870; s. Anthony Andrew and Pauline (Stengel) B.; grad. high sch., Branford, and New Haven Business Coll.; m. Maud Isbell, Nov. 15, 1893; children—Sherwood, Dorothy. Pres. Eastern Malleable Iron Co., 1924-34, chmn. bd., 1935-36; retired; chmn. bd. and vice-pres. Corley Co.; chmn. bd. Naugatuck Savings Bank; director Colonial Trust Co.; trustee Naugatuck Savings Bank. Republican. Conglist. Clubs: Waterbury (Conn.); Naugatuck Golf. Home: 45 Rockwell Av., Naugatuck, Conn. Died June 14, 1948.

BERGIN, Alfred, clergyman; b. Väster Biterna, Västergötland, Sweden, Apr. 24, 1866; s. Johannes and Maja Stina (Anderson) B.; came to U.S., 1883; A.B., Gustavus Adolphus Coll., St. Peter, Minn., 1892; B.D., Augustana Coll. and Theol. Sem., 1894, D.D. from same, 1919; A.M., U. of Minn., 1899, Ph.D., 1904; m. Anna Hult, June 13, 1894; children—Mrs. Adelia Maria Hulda Ingeborg Stone, Carl Alfred Emanuel (dec.), Mrs. Ruth Alfrida Elizabeth Engberg, Esther Gudrun Linnea, Ada Mathilda Victoria (dec.), Valdemar Justinus Emanuel (dec.). Editor of Gustaviana, St. Peter, 1891-92. Ordained Swedish Lutheran ministry, 1894; pastor, Sanborn, N.D., 1894-95, Warren, Minn., 1895-97, Cambridge, Minn., 1897-1904, Bethany Ch., Lindsborg, Kan., since Nov. 24, 1904; also prof. ethics, Bethany Coll., 1912-1920. Vice-pres. Kan. Conf. of Augustana Synod, 1907-11, pres., 1918-22; trustee Gustavus Adolphus College, 1889-1905, Bethany College, 1905-1935, Augustana Book Concern, 1915-20; president board Home for Aged, Lindsborg, Kansas, since 1912. Member foreign mission board, Augustana Synod, 1921-1930; asst. editor Theol. Quarterly, 1921-1927; chmn. McPherson Chapter A, Am. Red Cross since 1927; pres. Nat. Am. Assn. of Westgoths since 1932; commr. from the State of Kansas to Tercentenary at Wilmington and Phila., 1938. Author: Någraord i vigtiga frågor, 1898; Minneskrift från Fyrtioårsfesten i Cambridge, Minn., 1904; The Laws of the Westgoths, from MSS. of Aeskil, 1200 A.D., 1905; Lindsborg, a History of Central Kansas, 1909; The Swedish Settlement in Kansas, 1910; Faith and Life, 1912; Under Pines and Palms, 1916; Call to Lutheran Rallying, 1917; Lindsborg after Fifty Years, 1919; Up to Jerusalem, 1925; The Story of Lindsborg, 1929. Contbr. to several publs. Traveled in Europe, 1914, 37, around Mediterranean, 1924. Attended Ecumenical Conf. on Faith and Order, Edinburgh, Scotland, 1937. Home: Lindsborg, Kan. Died Mar. 26, 1944.

BERGIN, John William, univ. pres.; b. Houston, Tex., Apr. 25, 1872; s. John William and Rebecca (Smallwood) B.; Ph.B., Southwestern Univ., 1897, D.D., 1919; LL.D., 1942; m. Lena L. Lyons, September 21, 1898; children—Joe Lyons, John Williams, Robert G., David, James Carroll. Ordained to ministry Meth. Ch., 1897; pastor in Texas, successively at Marshall, Corsicana and Ft. Worth; dist. supt. successively of Waco, Waxahachie and Georgetown districts; now district superintendent Waco District; pres. Southwestern Univ. since Oct. 1935. Pres. Bd. Edn., Central Tex. Conf.; sec. same, Tex. Conf.; mem. 5 gen. confs.; trustee and chmn. exec. com. Southwestern U.; pres. of Council of Church Related Colls. in Tex.; mem. Inst. of Pub. Affairs 1939. Club: University. Address: 2104 Gorman Av., Waco, Tex. Died June 10, 1947.

BERGLUND, Abraham, prof. commerce; b. San Francisco, Calif., Dec. 10, 1875; s. Hans and Anna Christina B.; A.B., U. of Chicago, 1904; Ph.D., Columbia, 1907; m. Edna M. Glass, Aug. 21, 1907. Instr. in economics, Wash. State Coll., 1907-09; spl. agt. Bur. of Corps., Washington, D.C., 1909-13; asst. prof. economics, U. of Wash., 1913-17, asso. prof., 1917-18; spl. expert, U.S. Tariff Commn., 1918-22; asso. prof. commerce, U. of Va., 1922-26, prof. since 1926. Economic adviser to Interdepartmental Com. on Shipping Policy, 1934-35. Mem. Am. Econ. Assn., A.A.A.S., Va. Social Science Assn., Am. Acad. Polit. and Social Science, Acad. of World Economics, Am. Assn. Univ. Profs. Episcopalian. Author: The United States Steel Corporation, 1907; The Principles of Ocean Transportation, 1931. Joint Author: The Tariff on Iron and Steel, 1929; Labor in the Industrial South, 1930. Contbr. to Am. Econ. Review, Quarterly Jour. Economics, Jour. Polit. Economy, Harvard Business Review, Ency. of the Social Sciences, etc. Home: Charlottesville (University Station), Va. Died May 28, 1942.

BERGSON, Henri (Louis), philosopher, writer; b. Paris, France, Oct. 18, 1859; s. Michael and Kate B.; ed. Lycée Condorcet and Ecole Normale. Prof. philosophy, Lycée d'Angers, 1881-83, Lycée de Clermont, 1883-88; prof. Coll. Rollin, 1888-89, Lycée Henri IV, 1889-97, Ecole Normale supérieure, 1897-1900, Coll. of France, 1900-21; Gifford lecturer, U. of Edinburgh, 1912. Awarded Nobel prize for literature, 1927. Decorated Grand Cross Legion of Honour, Officier de l'Instruction Publique. Author: Laughter, 1911; Creative Evolution, 1911; Introduction to Metaphysics, 1912; Matter and Memory, 1912; Time and Free Will, 1913; Dreams, 1914; Mind-Energy, 1920; Chevalier, 1928; The Two Sources of Morality and Religion, 1935.* Died 1943.

BERL, Ernst, research prof.; b. Freudenthal (formerly Austria), July 7, 1877; s. Max and Agnes B.; student chem. engring., Tech. U. of Vienna, 1894-98; Ph.D., U. of Zurich, 1901; m. Margaret Karplus, Mar. 28, 1912; children—Herbert, Walter George. Came to U.S., 1933, naturalized, 1938. Asst. U. and Tech. U. of Zurich, 1901, asst. prof., 1904-10; chief chemist rayon factory, Tubize, Belgium, 1910-14; chief chemist Austrian War Ministry, 1914-19; prof. chem. technology and electro-chemistry, Tech. U. of Darmstadt, 1919-33; research prof. Carnegie Inst. Tech. since 1933. Mem. Am. Chem. Soc., Am. Inst. Chem. Engrs., Faraday Soc., Soc. Am. Mil. Engrs., Army Ordnance Assn., N.Y. and Pa., Acad. of Sciences, Am. Inst. of Chemists, Sigma Xi. Mem. U.S. Explosives Adv. Com. Home: Schenley Apts., Pittsburgh. Died Feb. 16, 1946; buried at Washington.

BERMAN, Louis, M.D.; b. N.Y. City, Mar. 15, 1893; s. Nathan and Dora (Rothfeld) B.; student Coll. City of New York, 1909-11; M.D., Coll. Physicians and Surgeons (Columbia), 1915; studied in Paris, Berlin and Vienna, 1922-23; B.S., Columbia, 1924; unmarried. Began practice in N.Y. City, 1915; asso. in biol. chemistry, Sch. of Medicine, Columbia, 1921-28, and engaged in research on the glands of internal secretion; also in active med. practice, specializing in internal glandular conditions; visiting endocrinologist Central Neurological Hospital, 1934, asso. visiting neurologist, 1937. Mem. Crime Prevention Com. of City Club of N.Y., sub-com. Case Studies of Crime Prevention, 1936-37; mem. bd. dirs. Nat. Crime Prevention Inst., 1936-37; apptd. exam. physician of Rehabilitation, Selective Service System, July 21, 1943. Fellow N.Y. Acad. of Sciences; mem. Am. Ethnol. Assn., A.M.A., Assn. for study of Internal Secretions, A.A.A.S., Am. Genetic Assn., Med. Soc. County of N.Y., Am. Therapeutic Soc., Central Med. Soc. of N.Y. City; the founder and sec. N.Y. Endocrinol. Soc. Club: Authors. Author: The Glands Regulating Personality, 1921, revised edit., 1928; The Personal Equation, 1925; The Religion Called Behaviorism, 1927; Food and Character, 1932; Study of Relation of Ductless Glands to Homosexuality, 1933; New Creations in Human Beings, 1938; Behind the Universe of a Doctor's Religion, 1943. Also many technical articles published in medical journals on nutrition, metabolism, diet and endocrine glands. Discovery of the internal secretion of the parathyroid glands, 1924, also relation of the internal secretion of the ovaries to cholesterol metabolism, 1927; discovery of curative value of ovarian residue for certain breast tumors, 1929; discovery of value of adrenal cortex in treatment of Paget's Disease, 1930; discovery of ameliorative action of benzedrine on oculogyric crises of Parkinsonism, 1935; special study of the endocrine glands in relation to criminology, at Sing Sing Prison, New York, 1932 (pamphlet published on Crime and the Endocrine Glands). Lectures on Psycho-Endocrinology: The Relations of the Psyche and the Internal Secretions, 1940; Discovery of Mode of Action of Insulin in Treatment of Insanity, 1942. Editor dept. of endocrinology Journal of Medical Practice, 1935, 36. Books "Glands Regulating Personality" and "Food and Character" selected for micro-filming for the Crypt of Civilization, 1938. Lecturer American Institute of New York on the Endocrine Glands in War and Peace at Am. Inst. of N.Y., 1942; chmn. All Nations Com. for World Unity, 1942-43. Address: 1050 Park Av., New York, N.Y. Died May 16, 1946.

BERMAN, Morris, army officer; born N.Y., Aug. 10, 1891; grad. Air Service Pilots School, Bombardment Sch.; commd. 2d lt. Inf., 1917; transferred to Air Service and advanced to brig. gen., Sept. 1942.† Died Nov. 11, 1945.

BERNADOTTE FOLKE, Count (bĕr-nā-dôt' fôl-kĕ), Swedish diplomat; B. Jan. 2, 1895. Stockholm, Sweden; s. Prince Oscar Carl August and Ebba Henriette (Munck) B.F.; student Officers' Mil. Sch. of Karlberg (Swedish West Point); Mil. Riding Sch. (Stromsholm); LL.D. (hon.), Univs. Copenhagen and Uppsala; m. Estelle Romaine Manville, Dec. 1, 1928; 2 sons. Has been good will ambassador to U.S. several times; rep. Sweden at Chicago's Century of Progress, 1933; commr. gen. Swedish Pavilion, N.Y. World's Fair, 1939-40; chmn. bd. of Det Bästa, Swedish edit. of Reader's Digest. Served as head of an orgn. similar to Am. U.S.O. during 2d World War. As pres. Sveriges Scoutförbund (Boy Scouts) closely linked this youth group with Sweden's defensive measures; vice chmn. Swedish Red Cross, aided in exchange of disabled German and Brit. war prisoners; arranged for transfer of Danish and Norwegian polit. prisoners, held in several German prison camps, to single camp operated under supervision of Swedish Y.M.C.A., 1945. On Apr. 24, 1945 received proposal by Himmler, Gestapo chief for complete German surrender to England and U.S. with condition that Germany be allowed to continue the resistance to Russia's armies in East. Stockholm Fgn. Office relayed terms to Brit. and Am. ministers in Sweden; acquainted Himmler with Allied rejection of terms, Apr. 27, Flensburg, Germany. Pres. Swedish Red Cross since Jan. 1, 1946. Decorated Grand Cross of the Order of St. Olav (Norway); received book containing names of 7000 men and women he saved from Nazi concentration camps; comdr. French Legion of Honor. Home: Dragongården, Djurgården. Stockholm, Sweden. Died Sept. 17, 1948.

BERNHEIMER, Charles L., merchant; b. Ulm, Germany, July 18, 1864; s. Leopold M. and Amalie (Bing) B.; ed. Thudichum's Coll., Geneva, Switzerland, 1880; m. Clara Silbermann, 1893 (dec.); children—Mrs. Hellen B. Halle, Alice M. (Mrs. Henri Pallain). Began as office boy, 1881, with firm of Adolph Bernheimer, wholesale dry goods, New York, continued with its successors, Bernheimer & Walter, and Bear Mill Mfg. Co., Inc.; pres. of latter, 1907-29, now chmn. bd.; trustee East River Savings Bank. One of three who originated the fusion movement which resulted, 1913, in the election of John Purroy Mitchel as mayor of Greater New York; in this campaign he was treas. of the Citizens' Municipal Com., the so-called "Committee of 107," and ran the campaign without a deficit. Largely instrumental in opening up the desert country between the Colo. River and Navajo Mt. in northern Ariz. and southern Utah, also discovered many heretofore unknown natural bridges, cliff ruins and dinosaur tracks, which latter have been pronounced by Am. Mus. Natural History and other scientific bodies as the most perfect specimens ever discovered. Chairman com. on arbitration New York Chamber of Commerce since 1911 (mem. exec. com.). Director American Arbitration Assn., New York. Mem. American Chamber of Commerce in London, Internat. Law Assn., Safety First League (v.p.), New York Bd. of Trade (dir., hon. v.p.), Am. Geog. Soc., Museum Natural History (patron); mem. advisory com. Sch. of Business, Columbia. Trustee Baron de Hirsch Fund, Valeria Home. Club: Nat. Republican. Author numerous mag. articles and publication entitled Rainbow Bridge. Home: 1200 5th Av. Office: 8470 4th Av., care Bear Mill Mfg. Co., New York, N.Y., and 659 5th Av., New York, N.Y. Died July 1, 1944.

BERNIE, Ben, orchestra leader, radio entertainer; b. Bayonne, N.J., May 31, 1893; studied engring.; became a violin salesman; began in vaudeville, 1910; teamed with Phil Baker, 1914-17; orchestra leader N.Y. City, 1923-28; later in London; master of ceremonies on many radio shows. Address: Beverly Hills, Calif. Died Oct. 20, 1943.

BERNSTEIN, Charles, neurologist; b. Carlisle, N.Y., Dec. 21, 1872; M.D., Albany Med. Coll., 1894; m. Lillian Stebbins, Jan. 3, 1904. Began practice in Albany, 1894; supt. Rome State Sch., Rome, N.Y., since 1902. Member A.M.A., Am. Assn. for Study of Feeble Minded (pres. 1915 and 1916), Am. Forestry Assn., N.Y. State Agrl. Soc. Mason, Elk. Clubs;

Rome, Masonic, Rome Country. Author ann. reports and various articles in med. jours. Address: Rome State School, Rome, N.Y. Died June 13, 1942.

BERNSTEIN, David, vice-pres., treas. and dir. Loews, Inc.; also officer or dir. many other theatrical enterprises. Office: 1540 Broadway, New York, N.Y.* Died Nov. 10, 1945.

BEROLZHEIMER, Edwin Michael, chmn. Eagle Pencil Co.; b. N.Y. City, Jan. 16, 1887; s. Emil and Gella (Goldsmith) B.; student Phillips Exeter Acad.; Harvard; m. Myra Bessie Cohn, Jan. 26, 1911; children—Emile Albert Berol, Margaret Gella (Mrs. Frank B. Craig). Supt. Eagle Pencil Co., New York City, 1919, vice pres., 1921, pres., 1925-46, chmn. bd. since 1946; chmn. bd. Hudson Lumber Co.; v.p. and dir. Blaisdell Pencil Co.; mem. adv. bd. Chemical Bank & Trust Co.; owner Cloister Kennels. Served as capt., Ordnance, U.S. Army, World War I. Mem. Nat. Panel of Arbitrators of Am. Arbitration Assn.; perpetual mem. N.Y. Soc. Mil. and Naval Officers of World Wars. Trustee Mt. Sinai Hosp., N.Y. City, 1928-41. Vice pres. Irish Setter Club of America. Republican. Clubs: Harvard, Anglers, Armor and Arms. Home: The Cloisters, Tarrytown, N.Y.; also Davant Plantation, Ridgeland, S.C. Office: 710 E. 14th St., New York 9, N.Y. Died Mar. 15, 1949.

BERRY, Edward Wilber, paleontologist; b. Newark, N.J., Feb. 10, 1875; s. Abijah Conger and Anna (Wilber) B.; educated privately; m. Mary Willard, Apr. 12, 1898; children—Edward Willard, Charles Thompson. Pres., treas. and mgr. Daily News, Passaic, N.J., 1897-1905; asst. in paleobotany Johns Hopkins U., 1907-08, instr., 1908-11, asso. 1911-13, asso. prof. of paleontology, 1913-17, prof. since 1917, dean, 1929-42, provost, 1935-42; sr. geologist U.S. Geological Survey since 1910; asst. state geologist of Md., 1917-42. Fellow Paleontol. Soc. America (pres. 1924). Geol. Soc. America (pres. 1945); Am. Acad. Arts and Sciences, A.A.A.S., Am. Soc. Naturalists; mem. Am. Philos. Soc., Nat. Acad. Sciences, Washington Acad. Sciences, Torrey Bot. Club, Société Géologique de France, Academia Nacional de Ciencias en Cordoba, Argentina, Sociedad Geologica del Peru. Awarded Walker prize, Boston Society of Natural History, 1901. Conglist. Club: Hopkins. Wrote: Lower Cretaceous of Maryland (Md. Geol. Survey), 1911; Upper Cretaceous of Maryland (same), 1916; Eocene Floras of Southeastern North America (U.S. Geol. Survey), 1916; Tree Ancestors, 1923; Paleontology, 1929; also over 500 articles on paleontol., geol. and biol. subjects in Am. and foreign scientific periodicals. Has specialized on classification and evolution of plants, particularly in Southeastern N. America, equatorial America and South America. Home: 19 Elmwood Road, Baltimore, Md. Died Sep. 20, 1945.

BERRY, George Leonard, union official; b. Lee Valley Tenn., Sept. 12, 1882; s. Thomas Jefferson and Cornelia (Trent) B.; ed. common schs., Hawkins County, Tenn.; m. Marie Gehres, Aug. 7, 1907. Began work at age of 9½ yrs. with Jackson (Miss.) Evening News; held every position in printing office in various cities, including St. Louis, Omaha, Denver, San Francisco; joined Press Assistants Union at St. Louis, 1899; pres. Internat. Pressmen and Assistants Union of N.A. since 1907; organized movement and built Pressmen's Home, Tenn.; mem. Labor Advisory Bd. of Cotton Textile Nat. Indsl. Relations Bd., NRA; mem. mediation bd. for steel and coal industries, Nat. Labor Bd., NRA; apptd. divisional adminstr. NRA; apptd. coördinator for Indsl. Coöperation, 1935; apptd. U.S. senator from Tenn., May 7, 1937, to fill unexpired term of Nathan L. Bachman (dec.). Pvt. 3d Miss. Regt., Spanish-Am. War; maj. engring. div., A.E.F., World War; labor adviser on Am. Commn. to Negotiate Peace, 1919. Decorated Victory medal; citations from Maj. Gen. Black, Engrs. Corps, and President Wilson. Del. representing A.F. of L. to Brit. Trades Union Congress, Newport, Wales, 1912; del. Internat. Econ. Congress, Zurich, 1912, Internat. Printers' Congress, Stuttgart, Germany, 1912; hon. mem. Nat. Soc. Operative Printers and Assts. of England, Printing Machine Mgrs. Soc. of Gt. Britain; mem. Am. Soc. Mil. Engrs., French Legion of Honor; one of founders of Am. Legion (past nat. vice comdr.). Democrat; defeated by 3 votes for Vice Presidential nomination, 1924, declined to have name submitted to conv., 1928; chmn. Labor Div., Dem. Nat. Conv., 1928 campaign. Baptist. Mason (32°, K.T., Shriner); hon. mem. St. Brides Masonic Lodge of England; mem. Printing Trades Council Masonic Assn., Chicago; life mem. Elks, Moose, Eagles, Odd Fellows, Rotary Internat. Club: Press (Seattle). Author: Labor Conditions Abroad, 1912; also many pub. reports, pamphlets, etc. Speaker for U.S. Govt. before House of Commons, England, and Chamber of Deputies, France, during World War I. Address: Pressmen's Home, Tenn. Died Dec. 4, 1948.

BERRY, George Ricker, theological prof.; b. W. Sumner, Me., Oct. 15, 1865; s. William Drake and Joann Floyd (Lawrence) B.; A.B., Colby Coll., 1885, D.D., 1904; graduated Newton Theol. Instn., 1889; Ph.D., U. of Chicago, 1895; m. 1st, Carrie Loeia Clough, Aug. 16, 1893 (died 1909); children—Hilda Marion (Mrs. York W. Brennan), Miriam Clough, Lawrence W. (dec.); m. 2d, Edith Van Wagner, July 1, 1913 (died Dec. 13, 1926). Ordained Bapt. ministry, 1889; pastor Liberty, Me., 1889-92; grad. student, 1892-95, fellow in Semitics, 1893-94, asst. in Semitics, 1895-96, U. of Chicago; instr. Semitic langs., 1896-98, prof. Semitic langs., 1898-1916, prof. hermeneutics and O.T. history and theology, 1916-18, prof. O.T. interpretation and Semitic langs., 1918-28, Colgate U.; prof. Semitic langs. and lit., Colgate-Rochester Div. Sch., 1928-34 (emeritus). Hon. lecturer Am. Sch. of Oriental Research, Jerusalem, 1929-30, annual prof., 1933-34, hon. lecturer, 1935-36. Mem. Nat. Ins., Social Sciences, Delta Upsilon, Phi Beta Kappa. Baptist. Republican. Author: The Letters of the Rm. 2 Collection in the British Museum, 1896; New Old Testament, 1897; New Lexicon of the New Testament, 1897; The Book of Proverbs (in Am. Commentary on the Old Testament), 1904; The Old Testament Among the Semitic Religions, 1910; Premillennialism and Old Testament Prediction, 1929; The Book of Psalms (in Am. Commentary on the Old Testament), 1934; Higher Criticism and the Old Testament, 1937; Old and New in Palestine, 1939; The Old Testament—A Liability or an Asset, 1941. Editor gen. catalogue Colgate Univ., 1905, 13, 19, Colgate-Rochester Div. Sch., 1930. Contbr. to cyclopedias and to theol. jours. Home: Hamilton, N.Y.; (winter) 2 Prescott St., Cambridge, Mass. Died May 24, 1945.

BERRY, Martha McChesney, philanthropist; b. nr. Rome, Ga., Oct. 7, 1866; d. Capt. Thomas and Frances (Rhea) Berry; ed. Edgeworth Sch. (Mme. Le Fevbre), Baltimore; European travel; Pd.D., Univ. of Ga., 1920; LL.D., Univ. of N.C., 1930; Dr. of Humanities, Berry Coll., 1933; LL.D., Bates Coll., 1933; LL.D., Duke U., 1935; Dr. of Pub. Service, Oglethorpe U., 1935; D.Litt., Oberlin, 1936; LL.D., U. of Wis., 1937; unmarried. Founded, in 1902, and dir. the Berry Schools (for mountain boys and girls), also founder, 1926 Berry Coll., both at Mount Berry, Ga. Mem. Colonial Dames America, D.A.R.; v.p. Am. Forestry Assn. Voted "distinguished citizen" by Ga. legislature, 1924; awarded Roosevelt Medal for services to the nation, 1925; Pictorial Review award of $5,000 for outstanding service, 1927; voted one of 12 greatest Am. women in nation-wide poll, 1931; gold medal, Town Hall Club of New York, for accomplishment of lasting merit, 1931; apptd. only woman mem. bd. of regents of Univ. System of Ga., 1932; biennial medal of Soc. Colonial Dames for eminent patriotic service, 1933; received at Court of St. James by King and Queen, 1934; apptd. mem. Nat. Com. Celebrating 400th Anniversary of First Printed English Bible, 1935; apptd. only woman mem. Ga. State Planning Commn., 1937. Awarded gold medal Nat. Inst. Social Sciences, 1939. Voted Southern Woman of year, 1939, Progressive Farmer poll. Given annual humanitarian award of Variety Clubs of America, 1940. Hon. mem. Kappa Delta Pi. Episcopalian. Clubs: Woman's, Town, Cosmopolitan (New York); Atlanta (Ga.) Woman's; Garden Club of America. Lecturer and contbr. to mags. on Southern mountaineers. Publisher, Southern Highlander and Mt. Berry News. Home: Mount Berry, Ga. Died Feb. 27, 1942; buried beside Mount Berry Chapel, Mount Berry, Ga.

BERRYMAN, Clifford Kennedy, cartoonist; b. Versailles, Ky., Apr. 2, 1869; s. James T. and Sallie C. B.; grad. Prof. Henry's Sch. for Boys, Versailles, 1886; self-taught in drawing; hon. A.M., George Washington U., 1921; m. Kate G. Durfee, July 5, 1893; children—Mary Belle (dec.), Florence Seville, James Thomas. Draftsman in U.S. Patent Office, 1886; gen. illustrator, 1891-96, cartoonist, 1896-1907, Washington Post; cartoonist, Washington Evening Star, since Feb. 1, 1907; originator of "Teddy Bear." Winner of Pulitzer Prize, 1943. Mem. Lit. Soc. of Washington, Am. Federation of Arts, D.C., Soc. S.A.R., Soc. Colonial Wars, Sons of Colonial Wars. Mason (K.T., Shriner). Clubs: Nat. Press, University, Washington Arts, Torch, Landscape, Chevy Chase, Gridiron (pres. 1926), Alfalfa. Author: Berryman's Cartoons of the 58th House (probably the only cartoonist who has cartooned every mem. of any one Congress). Address: 2114 Bancroft Pl., N.W. Office: Washington Evening Star, Washington, D.C.* Died Dec. 11, 1949.

BERRYMAN, John Brondgeest, chmn. Crane Co.; b. Toronto, Can.; ed. pvt. schs.; widower; children—Paul, Ruth. Became connected with the Crane Co., 1892, and has held various official positions, 1st v.p., 1914-31, pres. 1932-35, now chmn., also chmn. Crane, Ltd. (Montreal, Can.). Mem. Art Inst. Chicago. Republican. Clubs: Union League, Chicago Yacht. Home: Box 118, Downers Grove, Ill. Office: 836 S. Michigan Av., Chicago, Ill.* Died Aug. 11, 1945.

BESLER, William George, ry. chmn.; b. Galesburg, Ill., Mar. 30, 1864; s. John D. and Anna (Chapin) B.; student Mass. Inst. Tech., 1884-86; m. Effie B. Lewis, Oct. 10, 1888. Began as trainmaster's clk., C.,B.&Q. Ry., at Galesburg, 1880, and advanced to div. supt.; supt. and gen. supt. Phila. & Reading Ry., 1899-1902; gen. mgr., 1902-03, v.p. and gen. mgr., 1903-14, pres. and gen. mgr., 1914-26, chmn. bd. since Nov. 1926, Central R.R. of N.J. Clubs: Railroad, Engineers', Technology (New York). Home: Plainfield, N.J. Office: 143 Liberty St., New York, N.Y. Died May 20, 1942.

BESLEY, Frederic Atwood (bĕz'lē), surgeon; b. Waukegan, Ill., Apr. 19, 1868; s. William and Sylvia (Jocelyn) Besley; M.D., Northwestern University, 1894; married Mrs. Myra E. Busey, October 6, 1910. Began practice Chicago, 1894; prof. surgery, Northwestern U. Med. Sch.; mem. staff Victory Memorial Hosp., Waukegan, Ill. Commd. maj. Med. R.C., 1917, later col. Med. Corps U.S. Army, and on duty in France. Fellow Am. Coll. Surgeons (sec.; pres. 1937); mem. Am. Surg. Assn., A.M.A., Lake County Med. Soc., Chicago Surg. Soc. Clubs: University. Home: 1505 N. Sheridan Rd., Waukegan, Ill. Died Aug. 16, 1944.

BESSON, Harlan, lawyer; b. Hoboken, N.J., July 1, 1887; s. Samuel Austin and Arabella (Roseberry) B.; student Rutgers Coll., 1903-06; LL.B., N.Y. Law Sch., 1908; m. Addie Case, May 14, 1913; 1 dau., Roberta. Admitted to New Jersey bar, 1909; now mem. firm Besson and Pellet. Town atty., Secausus, N.J., 1914-22; asst. U.S. atty., 1922-29; 1st asst. prosecutor Hudson County, N.J., 1929-32; U.S. dist. atty., N.J., 1932-35; now engaged in practice as mem. firm Besson & Pellet; prof. N.J. pleading and practice and federal practice and procedure, John Marshall Law Coll., Jersey City, N.J. Served as lt. inf., Mexican border, 1916; capt. U.S. Army, World War; lt. col. Inf. Res.; active duty since Sept. 1941; lt. col., comdg. officer, 2d Service Command Tactical School, 1942-45; dir. State Guard Section, Fort Dix, N.J., July 1945-Feb. 1946; promoted to full col. and retired for physical disability, Nov. 10, 1946. Awarded Army Commendation Ribbon, 1946. Pres. Dept. N.J., Res. Officers Assn. of America, 1939-40. Mem. Sons of the Revolution, Delta Upsilon. Republican. Presbyterian Mason. Home: 201 Harrison St., Frenchtown. Office: 84 Washington St., Hoboken, N.J. Died Jan. 10, 1949.

BEST, Gertrude Delprat (Mrs. James Burt Best), newspaper pub.; b. Faribault, Minn.; d. George Richard and Mary Louise (Beane) Delprat; ed. pub. and pvt. schs.; m. James Burt Best, Oct. 1890 (died 1922); children—Richard Delprat (dec.), Stanley (dec.), Robert Delprat. Owner and pub. Everett Daily Herald from decease of husband, 1922-39. Republican. Episcopalian. Author: The Yankee Doodle Book for Young America, 1912. Contbr. articles under nom de plume of Gertrude D. Optimus. Home: 1310 Rucker Av., Everett, Wash. Died Sept. 26, 1947.

BESTOR, Arthur Eugene, pres. Chautauqua Instn.; b. Dixon, Ill., May 19, 1879; s. Orson Porter and Laura Ellen (Moore) B.; A.B., U. of Chicago, 1901; LL.D., Colgate U., 1919; Colby Coll., 1930; m. Jeanette Louise Lemon, Mar. 24, 1905; children—Arthur Eugene, Mary Frances (Mrs. Ambrose Lanfear Cram, Jr.), Charles Lemon. Prof. of history and polit. science, Franklin Coll., 1901-03; lecturer polit. science. Extension Div., U. of Chicago, 1904-12; asst. dir., Chautauqua Instn., 1905-07, dir., 1907-15, pres. since 1915. Chmn. com. on lectures and entertainments in training camps of Nat. War Work Council Y.M.C.A., May-Sept. 1917; dir. speaking div. of Com. on Pub. Information, Sept. 1917-Sept. 1918. Am. mem. council World Assn. for Adult Edn. Mem. advisory com. to U.S. commr. of edn. on emergency edn. program, 1933-34. Trustee Chautauqua Instn., Town Hall, Incorporated (chairman board, 1935-43), Lake Placid Club Educational Foundation (president), Near East Relief (chairman board), Near East Foundation, Sofia (Bulgaria) Am. Sch. (exec. com.). Member American Assn. Adult Education; member Commission to Study the Organization of Peace; member American Platform Guild (chmn. War Bd.), Delta Upsilon, Phi Beta Kappa. Clubs: City, Town Hall, Lake Placid, Chautauqua Golf. Home: 435 Riverside Drive, New York, N.Y. Office: 521 5th Av., New York, N.Y., and Chautauqua, N.Y. Died Feb. 3, 1944.

BETTEN, Francis Salesius, prof. history; b. Wocklum, Germany, Apr. 16, 1863; s. Francis Salerius and Clara (Mertens) B.; ed. Germany. Entered Soc. of Jesus; began teaching in Austria; came to America, 1898; prof. history, Canisius Coll., Buffalo, N.Y., 1898-1908, St. Louis U., 1908-09, St. Ignatius Coll. (now John Carroll U.), Cleveland, O., 1909-28, Marquette U., Milwaukee, Wis., since 1928. Mem. Am. Catholic Hist. Assn., Catholic Central Verein, Am. Numismatic Assn., Société Académique D'Histoire Internationale. Author: Ancient World (text-book), 1917; (with Rev. A. Kaufmann) Modern World (text-book), 1919; Historical Terms and Facts, 1924; (brochure) St. Boniface and St. Virgil (two supposed conflicts between them), 1927; Ancient and Medieval History (text-book), 1928; also various pamphlets. Collaborator: Life of St. Boniface by Kurth (translation); From Many Centuries. Home: 1131 W. Wisconsin Av., Milwaukee. Died Dec. 8, 1942; buried Calvary Cemetery, Milwaukee.

BETTMAN, Alfred, lawyer; b. Cincinnati, O., Aug. 26, 1873; s. Louis and Rebecca (Bloom) B.; A.B., Harvard, 1894, A.M., LL.B., 1898; m. Lillian Wyler, June 20, 1904. Practiced at Cincinnati since 1898; asst. pros. atty. Hamilton County, O., 1909-11; city solicitor, Cincinnati, 1912-13; atty. for trustees Cincinnati Southern Ry., 1915-17; spl. asst. to atty. gen. of U.S., War Div., 1917-19; in charge div. of prosecution in Cleveland (O.) Foundation Survey of Administration of Criminal Justice, 1921, and wrote the report on that subject; now mem. Moulinier, Bettman & Hunt; dir., gen. counsel Title Guarantee & Trust Co. of Cincinnati. Adviser on prosecution to Nat. Conf. Law Observance and Enforcement, author report "Survey Analysis." Active in municipal reform, city planning, housing, municipal financing, etc.; chmn. City Planning Commn. of Cincinnati, Am. Bar Assn.'s Com. on City Planning and Zoning, and vice chmn. Regional Planning Commn. of Hamilton County, O. Mem. adv. com. on housing and zoning, U.S. Dept. Commerce, mem. com. on city planning of President Hoover's Conf. on Home Building and Home Ownership; consultant National Resources Planning Board.

Mem. American, Ohio, and Cincinnati bar assns., Am. City Planning Inst. (dir.), Am. Soc. of Planning Officials, British Town Planning Institute, Am. Sociol. Society, Am. Polit. Science Assn., Nat. Municipal League, Am. Planning and Civic Assn., etc. Democrat. Jewish religion. Author of numerous articles, reports on city planning law, and city, state, regional planning statutes. Mem. 1923 to 1939 of Judicial Council of Ohio (to reorganize the judicial system of the state). Home: 684 Stanley Av. Office: First Nat. Bank Bldg., Cincinnati, O. Died Jan. 21, 1945.

BETTMAN, Gilbert, judge; b. Cincinnati, O., Oct. 31, 1881; s. Louis and Rebecca (Bloom) B.; prep. edn., Hughes High Sch., Cincinnati; A.B., Harvard, 1903, A.M., 1904, LL.B., cum laude, 1907; m. Iphigene Molony, June 30, 1916; children—Gilbert, Carol Helen, Alfred II. Admitted to Ohio bar, 1907, and since practiced at Cincinnati; elected vice mayor of Cincinnati, Nov. 1921; mem. City Survey Com. and Citizens' Traction Com., City of Cincinnati, 1922-25; temp. and permanent chmn. Rep. State Conv., Ohio, 1924; dean Y.M.C.A. Law Sch., Cincinnati, 1919-30; atty. general of Ohio, 2 terms, 1929-33; elected justice Supreme Court of Ohio, 1941. Capt. M.I.D., Gen. Staff, 1918-19; chmn. nat. legislative com. Am. Legion, 1921; comdr. Am. Legion, Dept. of Ohio, 1922. Mem. Legal Aid Soc. (v.p.). Mem. Am., Ohio State and Cincinnati bar assns. Rep. candidate for U.S. Senate, 1932. Jewish religion. Clubs: University, Harvard. Home: 14 Elmhurst Pl., Cincinnati, O. Office: State House, Columbus, Ohio. Died July 17, 1942.

BETTS, Edward C., army officer; b. Ala., June 9, 1890; LL.B., U. of Alabama, 1911; grad. Inf. Sch., 1925. Commd. capt., inf., U.S. Army, 1917, and advanced through the grades to brig. gen., 1943; prof. of law, U.S. Mil. Acad., 1938-42; theater judge advocate, European Theater of Operations, U.S. Army, since Apr. 1942. Address: care Judge Advocate General's Office, War Dept Washington 25, D.C. Died May 6, 1946.

BETTS, Philander, III, engineer; b. Nyack, N.Y., May 28, 1868; s. Philander, Jr., and Sarah Taulman (Demarest) B.; B.S., Rutgers Coll., N.J., 1891, M.S., 1895; E.E., Columbian (now George Washington) U., 1903, Ph.D., 1914, hon. Dr. Engring., 1932; m. Nancy Bell Hammer, Nov. 19, 1896 (deceased Nov. 22, 1938); 1 son, Philander Hammer; m. 2d, Mrs. Nelle Campbell Allen (widow of Lyman W. Allen), June 18, 1940. Constructing engr. Field Engring. Co., New York, directing constrn. of some of the earliest electric lines in Newark, N.J., and Phila., 1890-93; with Westinghouse Elec. & Mfg. Co., 1893-95; elec. engr., Washington Navy Yard, 1895-1901; instr. in mech. and elec. engring., Corcoran Scientific Sch., Washington, 1901-05; asst. prof., George Washington U., head of elec. engring. dept. and in charge of all mech. and elec. engring. labs., 1905-10; chief engr. Pub. Utilities Commn., N.J., 1910-34. Has served as consulting engr. in many important elec. light and power projects. Fellow Am. Inst. Elec. Engrs.; mem. Am. Soc. Mech. Engrs., Illuminating Engring. Soc., Am. Electric Ry. Assn., S.A.R. (past pres. N.J. Soc.), Beta Theta Pi. Mason (33°). Republican. Mem. Dutch Reformed Church. Maj. Engr. Res. Corps, July 14, 1917; lt. col. Q.M. Corps, Mar. 18, 1918; active duty, War Dept., Washington; hon. discharged, May 31, 1919; citation of sec. of war "for efficient service in the Construction Division of the Army"; col. Engr. Res. Corps, comdr. 373d Engrs. Sr. past comdr., North Jersey Chapter Mil. Order of World War, also past comdr. N.Y. Chapter; v.p. and mem. gen. staff N.J. State Reserve Officers Assn. (hon. v.p. for life); mem. Am. Legion, Sojourners (ex-pres. Manhattan Chapter). Compiler and editor of the hist. records in connection with all War Dept. construction in this country. Prominent in field of pub. service regulation, valuation and rate-making. Home: 100 Tenth Av., Belmar, N.J. Died Feb. 5, 1945.

BEVAN, Arthur Dean, surgeon; b. Chicago, Ill., Aug. 9, 1861; s. Thomas and Sarah (Ramsey) B.; ed. Sheffield Scientific Sch. (Yale), 1878-79; M.D., Rush Med. Coll., Chicago, 1883; hon. A.M., Yale, 1916; m. Anna L. Barber, Feb. 1896. U.S. Marine Hosp. Service, 1883-87; prof. anatomy, Ore. State U., 1886-87; prof. anatomy, 1887-99, asso. prof. surgery, 1899-1902, apptd. prof. surgery, 1902, head of surg. dept., Rush Med. Coll., 1907. Has served as professorial lecturer on surgery, Univ. of Chicago, since 1901; surgeon Presbyn. Hosp. (ex-pres.). Fellow Am. Surg. Assn. (pres. 1932); mem. A.M.A. (pres. 1917-18), Chicago Med. Soc. (pres. 1898-99), etc. Served as surgeon and maj., Ore. N.G.; dir. gen. surgery, surg. div. of Surgeon Gen. Gorgas' office, Washington, D.C., World War. Officer Legion of Honor (France) in recognition of services as pres. of Am. Medical Assn., 1918. Clubs: Chicago, Old Elm, University. Editor: American Edition of Lexer's General Surgery. Compiler: Text-book of Anatomy by American Authors; Text-book of Surgery by American Authors. Home: 1550 N. State St., Chicago; and Lake Forest, Ill. Office: 122 S. Michigan Av., Chicago, Ill. Died June 10, 1943.

BEVEN, John Lansing, ry. official; b. McComb, Miss., Feb. 17, 1887; s. William and Genevieve (Delaney) B.; ed. grammar sch. and business coll., New Orleans, La.; m. Charlotte LaNoue, July 22, 1914; children—Louise Adele (Mrs. Wm. J. O'Brien, Jr.), John L., Jr., Charlotte LaNoue. With I.C. R.R. since 1900, messenger, freight office, and yard clk., to 1904, chief clk. to supt., 1905-10, chief clk to gen. supt., 1911-14, trainmaster, 1915-16, supt., 1917, special asst. to regional dir., Atlanta and Phila., 1918, asst. to fed. mgr., Ill. Central, 1919, asst. to senior v.p., 1920-23, asst. to pres., 1924, v.p., 1925-30, senior v.p., 1931-38; pres. Ill. Central System since Dec. 1938; chmn. bd. Madison Coal Corp., Peoria and Pekin Union Ry.; pres. Chicago & Ill. Western R.R.; dir. Central of Georgia Ry. and the Terminal R.R. Assn. of St. Louis. Republican. Catholic. Clubs: Chicago, Commercial, Economic, Traffic, Western Railway, South Shore Country (Chicago); New Orleans Country, Boston (New Orleans). Home: 5120 Hyde Park Blvd. Office: 135 E. Eleventh Place, Chicago, Ill. Died Jan. 3, 1945.

BEVIER, Isabel, college prof.; b. Plymouth, O., Nov. 14, 1860; d. Caleb and Cornelia (Brinkerhoff) B.; Ph.B., U. of Wooster, 1885; Ph.M., 1888; Case Sch. Applied Science, summers, 1888-89; Harvard Summer Sch., 1891; Prof. Atwater's laboratory, summer, 1894; Mass. Inst. of Tech., 1897-98; hon. D.Sc., State Coll. of Iowa, 1920, Wooster Coll., 1936; unmarried. Prin. high school, Shelby, Ohio, 1885-87; instr. high sch., Mt. Vernon, O., 1887-88; prof. natural science, Pa. Coll. for Women, 1888-97; prof. chemistry, Lake Erie Coll., Painesville, O., 1898-99; prof. household science and dir. of courses, U. of Ill., 1900-21; chmn. dept. of home economics, U. of Calif., Southern Br., 1921-23; now prof. emeritus, U. of Ill. Lecturer on home economics, U. of Ariz., 1st semester, 1925-26. Asst. in nutrition investigations, Dept. of Agr., 1894-99. Fellow A.A.A.S.; mem. Am. Home Econ. Assn. (ex-pres.), N.E.A. (v.p. sect. manual training and house economics), Am. Chem. Soc., Pub. Health Assn. Mem. bd. editors Home Econ. Jour.; mem. Jury of Awards, Chicago Expn., 1893. Chmn. dept. of conservation woman's com. Ill. div. Council Nat. Defense; home economics dir., food adminstrn. for Ill.; mem. subcom. on human nutrition. Nat. Research Council, 1919. Presbyterian. Author: Home Economics Movement (with Susanna Usher), 1906; Food and Nutrition (with Susanna P. Usher), 1906, 08, 15; Selection and Preparation of Food (with Anna R. Van Meter), 1906, 10, 15; The House—Plan, Decoration and Care, 1907; Some Points in the Making and Judging of Bread (U. of Ill. Bull., Vol. X, No. 25), 1913; Planning of Meals (U. of Ill. Bull.), 1914; Home Economics in Education, 1923, revised edit., 1928; also mag. articles. Home: 605 Lincoln Av., Urbana, Ill. Died March 17, 1942.

BEWLEY, Edwin Elmore (bū'lē), banker and miller; b. Ft. Worth, Tex., Oct. 2, 1881; s. Murray Percival and Hallie (Samuell) B.; B.S., U. of Tex., 1902, M.A., 1903; m. Martha Jennings, Oct. 26, 1913; 1 son, Edwin Elmore. Began as flour miller, 1902, and since in milling and grain business; identified with banking since 1925; chmn. bd. Ft. Worth Nat. Bank, Tex. Nat. Mut. Fire Ins. Co.; chmn. Bewley Mills; pres. State Reserve Life Ins. Co.; v.p. Millers Mut. Fire Ins. Co.; dir. Chicago, Rock Island & Gulf Ry. Dir. Tarrant County Water Control and Improvement Dist. No. 1, Fort Worth & Denver City Ry. Co., Nash Hardware Co. Mem. Beta Theta Pi. Mason (Shriner), Elk. Democrat. Mem. Christian Ch. Clubs: Ft. Worth, Rivercrest Country, Exchange, Colonial. Home: Rivercrast, Fort Worth. Office: Ft. Worth Nat. Bank, Fort Worth, Tex. Died Dec. 21, 1946.

BEXELL, John Andrew, educator; b. Sweden, June 8, 1867; s. Swan Johnson and Kristina (Anderson) B.; came to America, 1882; B.S., Augustana Coll., Rock Island, Ill., 1895, M.A., 1901; post grad. work, U. of Chicago, and U. of Minn.; m. Dena Dahn, May 12, 1897. Instr. in commerce, 1893-98, asst. prof. mathematics, 1898-1903, Augustana Coll.; prof. commerce, 1903-08, financial sec., 1904-08, Utah Agrl. Coll.; dean Sch. of Commerce, Ore. Agrl. Coll., since 1908, bus. mgr., 1908-10. Dir. Ore. Statis. Bur., 1912. Conducted agrl. survey of Ore., 1912. Collaborator U.S. Bur. of Markets, 1915-20. Mem. C. of C. (Corvallis), Am. Econ. Assn., Pacific Coast Econ. Assn. (pres.), Phi Kappa Phi, Alpha Kappa Psi, Beta Alpha Psi, Lambda Chi Alpha. Republican. Presbyterian. Home: Corvallis, Ore. Died Feb. 6, 1938.

BEYER, Otto Sternoff (bī'ēr), cons. engineer; b. Woodridge, N.J., Sept. 18, 1886; s. Otto Sternoff and Marie (Clobus) B; M.E., Stevens Inst. Tech., 1907; grad. study U. of N.Y. and U. of Pa., 1907-10; m. Clara Mortenson, July 30, 1920; children—Morten, Donald, Richard. Engr. apprentice E. W. Bliss Co. and Midvale Steel Co., 1907-08; motive power engr. Erie R.R., 1908-12; gen. foreman C.,R.I.&P. Ry. Shops, Horton, Kan., 1912-16; cons. engr. in development labor-management coöperative programs with several ry. systems and industrial cos., 1920-33; dir. sect. labor relations, Federal Coördinator of Transportation, 1933-35; mem. Nat. Mediation Board, Jan. 1936-Jan. 1942, chmn. 1937, 1940, on leave of absence, Jan. 1942-Feb. 1943, resigned Feb. 1943; dir. div. transport personnel Office of Defense Transportation, Jan. 1942-June 1944, representing transportation on War Manpower Commission. Consultant, T.V.A. Bonneville Power Administration, U.S. Maritime Commission, The Alaska Railroad, U.S. Department of Interior. Special lecturer, George Washington University. Served in organization U.S. Army Sch. Aeronautics, Urbana, Ill., 1917; capt. U.S Army, 1918-19, organizing and training tech. personnel for ry. and heavy arty. maintenance, later directing all training of ordnance personnel; after the war dir. arsenal orders sect. Army Ordnance Dept. Club: Cosmos. Pres. Baltic-American Soc. of Washington, D.C. Democrat. Author reports and bulls.; contbr. numerous professional articles. Home: Spring Hill, McLean, Va. Office: Albee Bldg., Washington. Died Dec. 8, 1948; buried in Arlington National Cemetery.

BIANCHI, Martha Dickinson, author; b. Amherst, Mass.; d. William Austin and Susan Huntington (Gilbert) Dickinson; ed. by tutors from Amherst Coll. and at Miss Porter's Sch., Farmington, Conn.; studied music at Smith Coll. Sch. of Music and with Agnes Morgan in New York; Litt.D., Amherst Coll., 1931; m. Col. Alexander Bianchi, July 19, 1903. Hon mem. Zeta Chapter of Phi Delta Gamma. Conglist. Clubs: National Arts (New York); Authors (Boston). Author: Within the Hedge, 1899; The Cathedral, 1901; A Modern Prometheus, 1908; The Cuckoo's Nest, 1909; A Cossack Lover, 1911; The Sin of Angels, 1912; Gabrielle and Other Poems, 1913; The Kiss of Apollo, 1915; The Point of View, 1918; The Wandering Eros, 1925; Emily Dickinson, Face to Face, 1932. Editor and translator: Russian Lyrics and Cossack Songs, 1910. Editor: The Single Hound with Preface (poems by Emily Dickinson), 1914; Life and Letters of Emily Dickinson, 1924; Complete Poems of Emily Dickinson with Preface, 1924 (the two preceding books named in 100 best books of the century by Am. women, at Century of Progress, Chicago, 1933); The Further Poems of Emily Dickinson with Preface (with Alfred Leete Hampson), 1929; Poems of Emily Dickinson, Centenary Edit., with Preface (with Alfred Leete Hampson), 1930; Unpublished Poems of Emily Dickinson (with Alfred Leete Hampson), 1935. Editor with Alfred Leete Hampson, The Poems of Emily Dickinson (Collected), 1937. Contbr. to mags. Mem. original com. of 13 for orgn. of Keats-Shelley Memorial at Rome. Address: (summer) "The Evergreens," Amherst, Mass.; (winter) care Brown Shipley, 123 Pall Mall, London, Eng. Died Dec. 21, 1943.

BICKLEY, Howard Lee, judge; b. Mexico, Mo., May 3, 1871; s. Samuel W. and Alice Perrin (Dobyns) B.; ed. pub. schs.; studied law U. of Mo.; m. Ruth K. Phillips, 1897; children—Frances Alice, Samuel P. (dec.). Admitted to Mo. bar, 1895, and began practice at Mexico; served as pros. atty. Audrain County, Mo.; moved to Raton; now justice Supreme Court of New Mexico. Regent U. of N.M. Mem. Am. Bar Assn., Nat. Econ. League, N.M. Hist. Soc. Democrat. Mem. Christian Ch. Mason (32°), K.P., Elk, Kiwanian. Home: 173 Federal Pl. Address: Supreme Court Bldg., Santa Fe, N.M. Died Mar. 4, 1947.

BICKNELL, Frank Alfred, landscape painter; b. Augusta, Me., Feb. 17, 1866; s. James Austin and Clara Smith (Peterson) B.; studied under Albion H. Bicknell, Boston; at the Académie Julian, Paris; under Bouguereau, Tony Fleury, Ferrier, Bramtot and others; unmarried. Represented by works in the Nat. Gallery, Washington; Montclair Museum, N.J.; Lotos Club and Nat. Arts Club, New York; Boston Art Club; Art Club of Denver, Colo.; also in numerous pvt. collections, including that of President Woodrow Wilson. Mem. Chicago Water Color Soc.; associate Nat. Acad. Asso. prof. Coll. of Fine Arts, Carnegie Inst. Tech., Pittsburgh, since 1919. Clubs: Lotos (life), Nat. Arts (life), Salmagundi, MacDowell. Home: Old Lyme, Conn. Died Apr. 7, 1943.

BIDDLE, Andrew Porter, physician; b. Detroit, Mich., Feb. 25, 1862; s. William S. and Susan Dayton (Ogden) B.; midshipman U.S. Naval Acad., 1880-83; M.D., Detroit Coll. Medicine, 1886; hon. D.Sc., Coll. of the City of Detroit, 1929; hon. M.A., University of Michigan, 1935; m. Grace Wilkins, October 20, 1892 (died January 12, 1941); 1 dau., Beatrice Bradish (dec.). Practiced at Detroit, Michigan, since 1886; prof. dermatology and head dept., Wayne U. Coll. of Medicine, 1902-18; cons. dermatologist St. Mary's Hosp., Children's Hosp. of Mich., City of Detroit Receiving Hosp., Woman's Hosp., Protestant Children's Home. Mem. Mich. State Bd. of Health, 1913-19; mem. Detroit Bd. Edn., 1917-25 (pres. 1918-19); mem. Detroit Library Commn. since 1926 (pres. 1931 and 1943). Major surgeon, 31st Michigan Volunteer Infantry, Spanish-American War, 1898. Fellow American College of Physicians; mem. American Dermatol. Assn. (pres. 1925-26), A.M.A., Mich. State Med. Soc. (pres., 1916-18), Wayne County Med. Soc., Detroit Acad. Medicine (ex-pres.), Detroit Dermatol. Soc. (ex-pres.), Mich. Commandery Naval and Mil. Order Spanish-Am. War (commander, 1927). Episcopalian. Home: 791 Seminole Av. Office: David Whitney Bldg., Detroit, Mich. Died Aug. 2, 1944.

BIDDLE, A(nthony) J(oseph) Drexel, author, explorer, lecturer; b. W. Phila., Pa., Oct. 1, 1874; s. Edward and Emily (Drexel) B.; ed. pvt. sch., Phila., and Heidelberg, Germany; m. Cordelia Rundell Bradley, June 11, 1895. Lived in Madeira Islands, studying conditions there, returning to U.S., 1891; joined staff of Phila. Public Ledger, also contbd. to mags. and humorous jours.; revived Phila. Sunday Graphic, 1895, and became its editor; head pub. house of Drexel Biddle, 1897-1904; founder of movement known as Athletic Christianity; founder, 1907, and pres. Drexel Biddle Bible Classes (200,000 members) in U.S., England, Ireland, Scotland, W.I., W. Africa, S. Australia and Canada. Prof. on faculty of Bureau of Investigation, Training School of Dept. of Justice. Served in France as captain U.S. Marine Corps, 1918; now colonel in U.S. Marine Corps Reserve. Commanded U.S. Marine Corps Combat Team, exhibiting at Phila. Sesqui-Centennial; instr. of individual combat, U.S. Marine Corps. Fellow Royal Geographical Society; corr. mem. Société Archéologique de France. Amateur boxing champion. Author: A Dual Rôle, 1894; All Around Athletics, 1894; An Allegory and Three Essays, 1894; The Froggy Fairy Book, 1896; The Second Froggy Fairy Book, 1897; Shantytown Sketches, 1898; Word for Word and Letter for Letter, 1898; The Flowers of Life, 1898; The Madeira Islands (2 vols.), 1900; The Land of the Wine (2 vols.), 1901; Do or Die, Military Manual of Advanced Science in Individual Combat (pub. by U.S. Marine Corps), 1937. Office: 112 Drexel Bldg., Philadelphia, Pa. Died May 27, 1948.

BIDDLE, Ward Gray, univ. adminstr.; b. Madison County, Ind., Mar. 23, 1891; s. Charles W. and Nellie (Gray) B.; student Winona Coll. (Winona Lake, Ind.), 1910 (summer); A.B., U. of Ind., 1916, post grad. work; m. Dona Ruth Roberts, June 3, 1917; children—Elizabeth Ruth, Nancy Ward. Pub. sch. teacher, Madison County, 1909-14; teaching asst., Ind. U., 1915-16, mgr. bookstore, 1923-36, dir. Ind. Union, 1932-36, comptroller, 1936-42, sec. bd. trustees, 1937-42, v.p., treas. since 1942; asst. sec.-treas., Pendleton (Ind.) Trust Co., 1916-19; asst. cashier, Anderson (Ind.) Banking Co., 1919-21; cashier and dir., Middletown (Ind.) State Bank, 1921-23. Mem. Ho. of Reps., Ind., 1931-32, of Senate, 1933-37; dir. Bloomington C. of C.; treas. and dir. Alumni Council (Ind. U. Alumni Assn.); dir. bd. govs., James Whitcomb Riley Memorial Assn.; v.p. Hoosier Art Salon Patrons Association; regent Sigma Nu; pres. Assn. U. and Coll. Bus. Officers, Ind., 1941-42; dir. Ind. U. Foundation; ex-pres. and life mem., Nat. Assn. Coll. Stores; life mem., Nat. Assn. Coll. Unions. Mem. Nat. Assn. Coll. and U. Bus. Officers, Beta Gamma Sigma, Alpha Phi Omega, Daubers Club, Nat. Soc. Scabbard and Blade, Theta Alpha Phi. Received Sigma Delta Chi leather medal, 1939, for "most outstanding service to Ind. U. by a member of the Staff." Presbyterian. Mason, 33°, K.T., Shrine, Grand Master Royal and Select Masters of Ind., 1939. Clubs: Columbia (Indianapolis), Indiana Society of Pioneers, Indiana Historical Society, Kiwanis (ex-pres.) (all of Bloomington). Home: 601 S. Park Av. Office: Administration Bldg., Indiana University, Bloomington, Ind. Died May 28, 1946.

BIEGLER, Philip Sheridan (bĭg'lẽr), prof. elec. engring.; b. St. Paul, Minn., Jan. 30, 1880; s. Charles Augustus and Mary Elizabeth (McClung) B.; B.S., U. of Wis., 1905, E.E., 1915; M.S., U. of Ill., 1916; m. Martha Irene Shipman, Dec. 29, 1909; children—Winifred Pearle, Shipman Sheridan. With Chicago Edison Co., 1905-06; instr. and asst. prof. elect. engring., State U. of Ia., 1906-09; with Washington Water Power Co., 1909-10; asst. prof. elec. engring., Purdue, 1910-11; prof. same, U. of Mont., 1911-13; asst. prof., U. of Ill., 1913-18; asso. editor Electrical World, N.Y. City, 1918-21 asso. prof. elec. engring., State Coll. of Washington, 1921-23; prof. elec. engring., U. of Southern Calif., since 1923, also dean coll. of engring., 1928-40. Instr. U.S. Ground Sch. of Aviation, U. of Ill., 1917. Fellow Am. Inst. E.E. (past chmn. Los Angeles sect.); mem. Soc. Promotion Engring. Edn. (past chmn. Pacific Southwest Sect.), Los Angeles Council Engring. Socs., Sigma Xi, Phi Kappa Phi, Tau Beta Pi, Eta Kappa Nu, Sigma Tau, Sigma Phi Delta, Lambda Chi Alpha. Republican. Unitarian. Home: 5470 Bradna Dr., Los Angeles, Calif. Died Jan. 13, 1948.

BIERBAUM, Christopher Henry, (bẽr'boum), cons. engr.; b. Garnavillo, Ia., Feb. 14, 1864; B.S., Northern Illinois Normal School, 1886; M.E., Cornell U., 1891; unmarried. Instr. in exptl. engring., Cornell U., 1892-96; cons. engr. Am. Stoker Co., Dayton, O., 1896-98; mem. Bierbaum & Merrick, engrs., Cincinnati, 1898, Buffalo, N.Y., 1901; founder, v.p. and consulting engineer in charge of research Lumen Bearing Co. since 1901; private consulting office, Buffalo, 1903-28; Am. Soc. of Mechanical Engrs. Rep. on the Adv. Com. for Metall. Research in the U.S. Bur. of Standards. Fellow A.A.A.S., Am. Soc. Mech. Engrs. (formerly chairman bearings metals research committee); member American Institute Mining and Metall. Engring., Am. Soc. for Metals, Am. Microscopical Soc., Sigma Xi. Contbr. many articles to tech. jours. and to engring. handbooks. Inventor of microcharacter, a device for studying physical properties of the microscopic constituents of metals, also determining the relative hardness of rolled metal sheets of less than two thousandths of an inch in thickness. Originator and patentee of phosphor nickel bearing bronzes. Pioneer in studies of corrosive effect of oxidized mineral lubricating oils. Home: 113 Florence Av., Buffalo 14. Office: 197 Lathrop St., Buffalo 12, N.Y. Died June 15, 1947.

BIERD, William Grant, railway official; b. Baltimore, Md., May 24, 1864; s. Obediah and Mary B.; ed. pub. schs.; m. Maude Chapman, Feb. 25, 1891 (died Jan. 6, 1927). Began at 17 as bridge gang laborer C.&N.W. Ry.; resigned after 5 yrs.; successively overseer of constrn., C.,B.&Q.Ry.Co., yardmaster U.P. R.R. (Cheyenne, Wyo.), trainmaster Norfolk & Western R.R. (Roanoke, Va.), Lehigh Valley Rd. (Buffalo, N.Y.), until 1902; trainmaster and div. supt., 1902-04. asst. to the gen. mgr., 1904-05, C.,R.I.&P. Ry.; gen. supt. and gen. mgr. Panama R.R. & Steamship Co., Colon, Panama, 1905-07; gen. supt., N.Y., N.H.&H.R.R., 1907-09; v.p. and gen. mgr., M.&St.L. R.R., 1910-14; pres., later receiver, C.&A.R.R., 1914-31, now corporate adviser. Democrat. Clubs: Chicago, Chicago Golf. Home: 1320 N. State Parkway. Office: 340 W. Harrison St., Chicago. Died Feb. 21, 1944.

BIGELOW, Frederic Russell, insurance exec.; b. St. Paul, Minn., Mar. 31, 1870; s. Charles H. and Alida (Lyman) B.; A.B., Williams Coll., 1891; m. 2d, Virginia Dousman, Oct. 24, 1932. With St. Paul Fire & Marine Ins. Co. since 1891, pres., 1911-38, now chmn. bd. Republican. Presbyterian. Mem. Chi Psi. Home: 493 Portland Av. Office: 5th and Washington Sts., St. Paul. Died Sept. 8, 1946; buried in Oakland Cemetery, St. Paul.

BIGELOW, Harry Augustus, educator; b. Norwood, Mass., Sept. 22, 1874; s. Erwin A. and Amy (Fisher) B.; A.B., Harvard, 1896, LL.B., 1899; m. Mary Parker, Apr. 12, 1902 (died Jan. 15, 1920). Instr. criminal law, Harvard Law Sch., 1899-1900; engaged in practice of law in Honolulu, H.T., 1900-03; asst. prof. law, 1904-06, asso. prof., 1906-09, prof. since 1909, dean of Law Sch., U. of Chicago, 1929-39, emeritus. Mem. Am. Law Inst. (advisor on law of property and conflict of laws), Am., Ill. State and Chicago bar assns., Acad. of Arts and Sciences, Phi Beta Kappa, Phi Alpha Delta, Order of the Coif. Democrat. Clubs: Tavern, University, Quadrangle, Lake Zurich Country. Editor: 3d edit. May's Criminal Law, 1905; Bigelow's Cases on the Law of Personal Property, 1917, 30, 42; Cases on the Law of Rights in Land, 1919, 33, 45. Co-ed. (with Ralph W. Aigler and Richard R. Powell) Cases on the Law of Property, 1942. Author: The Introduction to the Law of Real Property, 1919, 33, 45; Conservation of Family Estates, 1942; also legal treatises and articles. Took part in first expdn. to cross unexplored country west of Lake Edward, in Belgian Congo, 1924-25. Apptd. trustee in bankruptcy Insull Utility Investments, Inc., 1933. Home: 1225 E. 56th St., Chicago 37, Ill. Died Jan. 8, 1950.

BIGELOW, S(amuel) Lawrence, chemist; b. Boston, Feb. 23, 1870; s. Samuel Augustus and Ella Harriet (Brown) B.; A.B., Harvard, 1891; B.S., Mass. Inst. of Tech., 1895; Ph.D., U. of Leipzig, 1898; m. Mary Crawford Barry, May 10, 1892; children—John Lawrence, Robert Barry, Anne Harrison. Instr. gen. chemistry, 1898-1901, asst. prof. and acting dir. lab. of gen. chemistry, 1901-04, jr. prof. 1904-05, jr. prof. gen. and phys. chemistry, 1905-07, prof. from 1907, U. of Mich.; now emeritus. Episcopalian. Fellow A.A.A.S.; mem. Am. Chem. Soc., Am. Electrochem. Soc., Mich. Acad. Sciences, Franklin Inst., Phila., Sigma Xi. Author: Theoretical and Physical Chemistry, 1912. Home: 39 Highland St., West Hartford 7, Conn. Died Dec. 3, 1947; buried at Ann Arbor, Mich.

BIGGAR, Oliver Mowat, lawyer; born in Toronto, Ontario, October 11, 1876; son of Charles Robert Webster and Jane Helen (Mowat) B.; student Upper Canada Coll., 1894; B.A., Univ. Coll., Toronto, 1898 Osgoode Hall, 1901; King's Counsel, Alberta, 1913, Canada, 1920, Ontario, 1934; m. Muriel Elizabeth Whitney, Apr. 30, 1908; daughter—Sally Vernon Called to Bar of Ontario, 1901, N.W. Terr. 1903 Alta. and Sask., 1906; practised with Biggar & Burton, Toronto, 1901-02, Short Cross & Biggar, Edmonton, 1903-15; counsel for Woods, Sherry, Collison & Field, Edmonton, 1915-20; Smart & Biggar, since 1927. Mem. Mil. Service Council, 1917, Canadian Del to Peace Conf., 1919; Chief Electoral Officer, 1920-27 dir. Canadian Geog. Soc., 1931, chmn. Canadian Sec tion Permanent Joint Bd. on Defense, 1940-45; dir of censorship, 1942-44. Clubs: Rideau (Ottawa) Country (Ottawa). Author: Biggar on Patents Burroughs & Co. (Eastern), Ltd., Toronto, Ont. 1927. Decorated Companion St. Michael and St George, Commander, Legion of Merit (U.S.). Home: 197 Clemow Av. Office: 609 Victoria Bldg., Ottawa, Ont. Died Sept. 4, 1948; buried at Toronto, Ont., Can.

BIGGIN, Frederic Child, college dean; b. Middletown, N.Y., Oct. 12, 1869; s. Samuel and Louise (Hart) B.; grad. McDonogh Sch., Md., 1886, Md. Inst. of Art and Design, 1888; B.S. in architecture, Cornell, 1892; M.S., Lehigh, 1913; m. Mabel Augusta Desh, June 19, 1894; children—Harold Lyle, Beverly Basset, Dorothea Child, Mrs. Mabelle Groves. Instr. in architecture, Lehigh, 1892-97; practicing architect, 1897-1911; head prof. architectural engring., Okla. A. and M. Coll., Stillwater, 1911-16; head prof. architecture, Ala. Poly. Inst. since 1916, dean Sch. of Architecture and Allied Arts since 1927. Served as architect in Construction Div., U.S. Army, 1918. Mem. Ala. State Bd. for Registration of Architects. Fellow Am. Inst. Architects; mem. Scarab, Theta Chi. Democrat. Episcopalian. Home: 300 N. College St., Auburn, Ala.* Died Oct. 14, 1943.

BILBO, Theodore Gilmore (bĭl'bō), senator; b. Juniper Grove, Miss., Oct. 13, 1877; s. James Oliver and Beedy (Wallace) B.; U. of Nashville, 1897-1900, Vanderbilt U. Law Dept., 1905-07, U. of Mich., 1908; m. Lillian S. Herrington, May 25, 1898; 1 daughter, Jessie Forress; m. 2d, Linda R. Gaddy, Jan. 27, 1903; 1 son, Lt. Col. Theodore Gilmore. Teacher in dist. and high schs., Miss., 6 yrs.; admitted to Tenn. bar, 1908; mem. Bilbo & Shipman, Poplarville, Miss., 1913-16. Mem. Miss. Senate, 1908-12; lt. gov. of Miss., 1912-16; gov. of Miss., 1916-20 and 1928-32; U.S. senator from Miss., term 1935-41, re-elected for terms 1941-47 and 1947-53. Democrat. Baptist. Mason (32°). Home: Poplarville, Miss. Died Aug. 21, 1947.

BILL, E(arl) Gordon, college dean; b. Billtown, N.S., June 23, 1884; s. Caleb Rand and Margaret Ann (Bligh) B.; A.B., Acadia U., 1902; A.B., Yale, 1905, A.M., 1906, Ph.D., 1908; hon. D.C.L., Acadia U., 1935; grad. work, U. of Bonn, Germany, 1910-11; m. Lucy Ethel Van Wart, Aug. 15, 1906; children—Betty Lou (dec.), Andrew Phillips, Margaret, John Caleb. Instr. mathematics, Yale, 1908-10, Purdue U., 1911-12; asst. prof. mathematics, Dartmouth Coll., 1912-19, prof. since 1919, dean of freshmen and dir. admissions, 1921-33, dean of the faculty since 1933. Asst. dir. and dir. Military Service Br., Dept. of Justice, Ottawa, Can., in charge Can. Selective Draft, Apr. 1918-Oct. 1919. Mem. Coll. Entrance Exam. Bd. Mem. New Eng. Assn. Colls. and Secondary Schs., Phi Beta Kappa, Sigma Xi, Zeta Psi. Conglist. Home: 32 Occom Ridge, Hanover, N.H. Died Nov. 28, 1947.

BILLOW, Clayton Oscar, cons.; b. Shelby, O., June 14, 1860; s. David and Susan (Tressler) B.; grad. high sch., 1879; m. Helen Parker, Nov. 24, 1887; children—Robert (dec.), Virginia. Various occupations until 1883; with Champion City Oil Co., 1884-88, and carried on experiments with crude oil for fuel; gen. western mgr. Pasteur-Chamberlain Filter Co., St. Louis, Mo., 1888-89; organized, with E. E. Billow, the Nat. Supply Co., furnaces, forges, kilns, etc., and appliances for the storing, controlling and burning of fuel oil, Chicago, 1890, and sec. and treas. same; asst. mech. engr. Chicago Expn., 1892-93, and designed and operated fuel oil appliances connected with the power plant. Mem. Am. Soc. Mech. Engrs., Western Soc. Engineers, Franklin Inst., Society Am. Mil. Engrs., A.A.A.S., S.A.R., Ohio Soc. (ex-pres.). Republican. Lutheran. Mason (33°, K.T.). Grand Sovereign, Grand Imperial Council of the Red Cross of Constantine for the U.S. of America and its possessions, 1938-39. Decorated Knight Grand Cross; admitted mem. Chapter Gen., Knight Grand Cross, 1938. Clubs: Union League, Engineers'. Pioneer in the development of the art of oil burning industrially and inventor of many appliances incidental thereto. Home: 1212 Ashland Av., Wilmette, Ill.* Died Mar. 19, 1945.

BILMANIS, Alfred (bĕl'mŭn-Is), Latvian minister to U.S.; b. Riga, Latvia, Feb. 2, 1887; degree of Ph.D. Was newspaper editor; became chief of press in Ministry of Foreign Affairs, 1920; sub.-del. to League of Nations, 1930; E.E. and M.P. to Russia, 1932-35, to U.S. since Oct. 1, 1935. Professor associate in polit. history, Commerce Inst. of Riga. Mem. Latvian Press Soc. (hon.). A founder Rotary and Pen Club of Riga. Author: History of Sweden; History of Poland; Agrarian Question in Latvia; Latvian Press; Latvia in the Making; The Baltic States and the Baltic Sea; Baltic Essays; Law and Courts in Latvia; Latvia as an Independent State. Contributor to Ency. Brit. Home: 4704 17th St. N.W., Washington, D.C. Died July 26, 1948.

BINGHAM, Eugene Cook, chemist; b. Cornwall, Vt., Dec. 8, 1878; s. W. Harrison and Mary Lucina (Cook) B.; B.A., Middlebury (Vt.) Coll., 1899, D.Sc., 1936; Ph.D., Johns Hopkins Univ., 1905; student univs. of Leipzig, Berlin and Cambridge, 1905-06; m. Edith Irene Snell, June 18, 1907. Prof. chemistry, Richmond (Va.) Coll., 1906-15; asst. physicist, U.S. Bureau of Standards, 1915-16; prof. chemistry, Lafayette Coll., since Aug. 1916. Chemist, U.S. Bureau of Standards, 1918-19, on lubrication investigation. Was awarded certificate of merit by Franklin Inst. for improved form of variable pressure viscometer, 1921. Chem. com. on plasticity Am. Soc. Testing Materials. Mem. Am. Chem. Soc., Soc. of Rheology, A.A.A.S., Am. Assn. Univ. Profs., Am. Inst. Chem. Engrs., Delta Kappa Epsilon, Phi Beta Kappa, Tau Beta Pi, Alpha Chi Sigma; hon. mem. Va. Chemists Club; sec. the Bingham Assn. Republican. Conglist. Club: Blue Mountain Club of Pa. (pres.). Author: Laboratory Manual of Inorganic Chemistry, 1911; Fluidity and Plasticity, 1921; also numerous papers pub. in Am., English and German scientific periodicals. Editor: Rheological Memoirs, 1940. Inventor: Improved laboratory hood, machine for ruling with waterproof inks, encased cement columns, self-lighting and non-glare surface for highways, instruments for the precise measurement of viscosity and plasticity. Home: 602 Clinton Terrace, Easton, Pa. Died Nov. 6, 1945.

BINGHAM, Robert F(ry), lawyer; b. Sidney, O., July 3, 1891; s. Evan William and Lizzie Anna (Fry) B.; A.B. cum laude, Miami U., 1913; LL.B., Western Reserve U., 1916; m. Edna May Koppenhafer, July 3, 1917; children—Robert Evan, Elizabeth Ann. With Thompson, Hine & Flory, attys., Cleveland, since 1914, partner since 1924; dir. National City Bank of Cleveland, J. A. Wigmore Land Co. (N.Y.), Leader Building Co., Hodell Chain Co., Pontiac Improvement Company, Cleveland Ignition Company, Warner & Swazey Co. (Cleveland); vice-pres., treas. Freehold Co. Mem. Shaker Heights Bd. Edn., 1936-40; mem. Charter Commn.; govt. appeal agt. Selective Service Bd. 38, Cleveland Heights; chmn. Mayor's Joint Com. on Hosps.; pres. St. Lukes Hosp.; trustee Cleveland Hosp. Service Assn., Fenn Coll. (Cleveland), Y.M.C.A., Am. Allergy Fund; trustee and v.p. Med. Mutual of Cleveland, Inc.; Hiram House; trustee, board of managers of the Elisabeth Severance Prentiss Foundation; trustee Air Foundation. Mem. Am., Ohio State, Cleveland bar assns., Phi Beta Kappa, Delta Kappa Epsilon, Phi Delta Phi, Order of the Coif. Republican. Presbyn. Mason. Clubs: Union, Mayfield Country, D.K.E. (N.Y.).

Co-author: City Growth and Values; City Growth Essentials, 1928: Financing Real Estate, 1924. Home: 2891 Paxton Rd., Shaker Heights, O. Office: 1122 Guardian Bldg., Cleveland, O. Died Sept. 5, 1947.

BINYON, Robert Laurence, author; b. Lancaster, Eng., Aug. 10, 1869; s. Frederick and Mary (Dockray) B.; St. Paul's Sch., London, 1881-88; B.A., Trinity Coll., Oxford, 1892; LL.D., Glasgow U., 1915; D.Litt., Oxford; m. Cicely Margaret Powell, 1904; m. Helen Francesca Mary, Agatha Margaret Eden (Mrs. Humphrey Higgens), Nicolette Mary (Mrs. Basil Gray). Asst. in dept. of printed books, British Museum, 1893-95, asst. in dept. prints and drawings, 1895-1909, deputy keeper, 1909-32, keeper, 1932-33; retired, 1933; Norton prof. poetry, Harvard U., 1933-34; Byron prof., Athens U., 1940. Decorated Companion of Honour, Chevalier de la Legion d'Honneur. Club: Athenaeum (London). Author: Painting in the Far East, 1908; Collected Poems, 2 vols., 1931; Akbar, 1932; Dante's Inferno (translated), 1933; The Spirit of Man in Asian Art, 1935; Dante's Purgatorio (translated), 1938; The North Star (poems), 1941. Editor: Golden Treasury of Modern Lyrics, 1924; Poems of Blake, 1931. Plays produced: Attila; Arthur. Home: Westridge Farm House, Streatley, Berkshire, England. Died Mar. 10, 1943.

BIRCH, Reginald Bathurst, artist; b. London, Eng., May 2, 1856; s. William Alexander and Isabella (Hoggins) B.; ed. Royal Acad. Munich; 1 son, Rodney Bathurst (by 2d marriage). For many years with St. Nicholas, Harper's, Century, Life, etc.; illustrator of Little Lord Fauntleroy and many other works of fiction. Club: Players. Home: 113 E. 17th St., New York. Died June 17, 1943.

BIRD, Philip Smead, clergyman; b. Newtonville, Mass., Nov. 9, 1886; s. Joseph Edward and Gertrude Hubbard (Smead) B.; A.B., Pomona Coll., Claremont, Calif., 1909; M.Litt., U. of Calif., 1910; grad. Union Theol. Sem., 1913; D.D., Hamilton Coll., Clinton, N.Y., 1924, Western Reserve U., 1928; LL.D., Coll. of Ozarks, Clarksville, Ark., 1933; m. Margaret Hubbell Kincaid, July 11, 1922; 1 dau., Margaret Elizabeth. Student asst., Madison Av. Presbyn. Ch., N.Y. City, 1911-13; ordained ministry, Presbyn. Ch., 1913; asst. pastor Claremont, Calif., 1913-14, asso. pastor, 1914-15; also lecturer in bibl. lit., Pomona Coll., 1913-15; pastor Dobbs Ferry, N.Y., 1915-20; also instr. in bibl. lit., The Masters Sch., 1917-20; pastor 1st Presbyn. Ch., Utica, N.Y., 1920-28. Ch. of the Covenant, Cleveland, O., since 1928. Chmn. Ch. Extension Com. of Presbytery of Cleveland, 1929-33; pres. Federated Chs. of Greater Cleveland, 1931-33; dir. religious work and camp speaker, Nat. War Work Council, Y.M.C.A., 1917-19; hon. trustee Schauffler Coll. of Religious and Social Work; trustee Cleveland Y.M.C.A., The Masters Sch. (Dobbs Ferry-on-Hudson, N.Y.), Western Reserve U. (Cleveland), Phillis Wheatley Assn. of Cleveland, Coll. of the Ozarks, Neighborhood Association of Cleveland, Westminster Foundations of Ohio, 1943; chairman Cleveland Peace Committee. Moderator, Presbytery of Cleveland, 1942-43. Mem. New Eng. Soc. of Cleveland and the Western Reserve, Soc. Mayflower Descendants, Nat. Chapter of Internat. Soc. of Theta Phi, Phi Beta Kappa. Clubs: Union, Alathian, Rowfant, Rotary. Home: 1689 E. 115th St., Cleveland 6. Office: 11205 Euclid Av., Cleveland 6, Ohio. Died June 10, 1948.

BIRKHOFF, George David (bûr'kŏf), mathematician; b. Overisel, Mich., Mar. 21, 1884; s. David and Jane Gertrude (Droppers) B.; student Lewis Inst., Chicago, 1896-1902, U. of Chicago, 1902-03; A.B., Harvard, 1905, A.M., 1906; Ph.D., U. of Chicago, 1907; hon. Sc.D., Brown, 1923, U. of Wis., 1927, Harvard, 1933, U. of Pa., 1938, Sofia, 1939; LL.D., St. Andrews, 1938; hon. Dr., Poitiers, 1933, Paris, 1936, Athens, 1937, University of Buenos Aires, 1942; hon. mem. faculty, San Marcos, Lima, 1942; University of Chile, 1942; m. Margaret Elizabeth Grafius, Sept. 2, 1908; children—Barbara (Mrs. Robert Treat Paine, Jr.), Garrett, Rodney. Instr. in mathematics, U. of Wis., 1907-09; asst. prof. mathematics, 1909-11, Princeton U., prof., 1911-12; asst. prof. mathematics, Harvard, 1912-19, prof., 1919-33, Perkins prof. since 1933, dean faculty of arts and sciences, 1935-39; lecturer Collège de France, 1930. Decorated Officier French Legion of Honor. Editor of Annals of Mathematics, 1911-13; editor Trans. of Am. Math. Soc., 1920-25; editor Am. Journal of Mathematics since 1943. Mem. Nat. Acad. (pres. 1936-37), Nat. Acad. Sciences of Argentina, Circolo Matematico di Palermo, Royal Danish Acad. Sciences and Letters, Göttingen Acad. Sciences, Inst. of France, Lima Acad. of Sciences, Royal Acad. of the Lincei, Royal Inst. of Bologna, Pontifical Acad. of Sciences; Royal Irish Acad., Royal Soc., Edinburgh; honorary member Edinburgh Mathematical Society, London Mathematical Soc., Peruvian Philosophic Society, Scientific Society of Argentina; member Sigma Alpha Epsilon, Phi Beta Kappa, Sigma Xi. Awarded Querini-Stampalia prize, 1918, Royal Inst. Science, Letters and Arts, of Venice, Bôcher prize of Am. Math. Soc., 1923, for researches in dynamics, and prize awarded by A.A.A.S., 1926; biennial prize of Pontifical Acad. of Sciences, Vatican City, 1933, for research on systems of differential equations. Club: Century (N.Y. City). Author: Relativity and Modern Physics, 1923; The Origin, Nature and Influence of Relativity, 1925; Dynamical Systems, 1928; Aesthetic Measure, 1933; Basic Geometry (with Ralph Beatley), 1941. Contbr. to math. jours. Home: 987 Memorial Dr., Cambridge, Mass. Died Nov. 12, 1944.

BIRNIE, Rogers, army officer; b. Glen Burn farm, Carroll Co., Md., Apr. 5, 1851; s. Rogers and Amelia Knode (Harry) B.; grad. U.S. Mil. Acad. No. 1 in class, 1872; m. Helen Gunn, Dec. 30, 1879. Second lt. 13th Inf., June 14, 1872; advanced through grades to col., Oct. 10, 1907. Regimental q.m., Feb. 1874; served at Camp Douglas, Utah, 1872-74; in engr. service with U.S. Geog. Survey, W. of 100th meridian, 1874-79; attended maneuvers of the 9th Corps d'Armée in France, 1880; served in the 7th Army Corps and in Havana during Spanish-Am. War; formerly inspector West Point Foundry, Cold Spring, N. Y.; acting chief of ordnance U.S.A., Oct. 1912-July 1913; pres. Ordnance Bd., July 3, 1913-15; retired Apr. 5, 1915. Chevalier Légion d'Honneur, France. Home: 530 Fifth Av., New York. Died Sept. 25, 1939.

BISBEE, William Henry, brigadier-gen. U.S. Army, retired; b. in R.I., Jan. 28, 1840. Pvt. and 1st sergt. Co. A, and sergt.-maj. 2d Battalion 18th Inf., Sept. 2, 1861-July 11, 1862; 2d lt. 18th Inf., June 9, 1862; 1st lt., Dec. 31, 1862; bvtd. capt., Dec. 31, 1862, "for gallant and meritorious services in battle of Murfreesboro, Tenn."; and capt., Sept. 1, 1864, for same during Atlanta campaign and in battle of Jonesboro, Ga.; promoted through grades to rank of brig.-gen., Oct. 2, 1901. Served in campaigns and many battles under Gens. Thomas, Buell, Halleck, Rosecrans, Sherman; wounded at Hoover's Gap, Tenn., June 26, 1863, at siege of Atlanta, Aug. 1864; long service on western frontier; built Ft. Phil Kearny, Dak., 1866, participating in frequent engagements with Sioux Indians; adj.-gen. U.S. troops in Chicago riots, 1877; engaged in suppressing Cœur d'Alene miners' outbreaks, 1892; comd. U.S. troops, Ogden, Utah, and Pocatello, Ida., in Debs riots and Commonwealers' outbreaks, 1893-94; comd. battalion at Jackson's Hole in Bannock Indian disturbances, 1895; comd. regt. through Santiago campaign; with Capron's battery at battles of El Caney and San Juan, Cuba; had charge of payment of $3,000,000 appropriation to Cuban army; served in Philippines, 1899-1902; comd. sub-dist. embracing 19 native towns in provinces of Pangasinan and Nueva Ecija, Luzon; comdg. all troops north of Manila on Island of Luzon; retired Oct. 1, 1902. Mem. Loyal Legion (hon. comdr. in chief), S.A.R., Army of the Cumberland, Soc. Santiago de Cuba. Home: 30 Babcock, S. Brookline, Mass. Address: Care Adj.-Gen. U.S. Army, Washington, D.C. Died June 11, 1942.

BISHOP, Arthur Giles (bĭsh'ŭp), banker; b. Flint, Mich.; s. Russell and Mary (Thomson) B.; B.A., U. of Mich., 1873; m. Carrie E. Spencer, Sept. 24, 1879; children—R. Spencer, Mrs. Katharine Miner. Chmn. bd. Genesee County (Mich.) Savings Bank; dir. Gen. Motors Corp., Union Commerce Investment Co. (Detroit). Republican. Episcopalian. Clubs: Detroit Club, Detroit Golf, Detroit Athletic. Home: 606 E. Kearsley St. Office: Genesee County Savings Bank, Flint, Mich. Died Jan. 22, 1944.

BISHOP, Charles McTyeire, theological prof.; b. Jefferson, Ashe County, N.C., Feb. 2, 1862; s. Benjamin W. S. and Julia Anne (Goodykoontz) B.; A.B., Emory and Henry Coll., Emory, Va., 1884, A.M., 1886; D.D., Central Coll., Mo., 1899; LL.D., Baylor U., 1920, Southwestern U., 1923; m. Phoebe Eleanor Jones, June 3, 1889; children—Phoebe Eleanor, Mary Martha, Eugene Hendrix, Dorothea Frances, Rose Boddie. Ordained to ministry of M.E. Ch., S., 1889; pastor, Asheville, N.C., 1887-89, in Mo. (Kansas City, St. Joseph, Columbia, etc.), 1889-1910; pres. Southwestern U., Georgetown, Tex., 1911-22; resigned and now pres. emeritus; pastor St. Paul's M.E. Ch., Houston, Tex., 1921-24; prof. and head dept. N.T., Sch. of Theology, Southern Meth. U., 1925-34, now emeritus. Mem. Gen. Conf. M.E. Ch., S., 1906, 1910; mem. Gen. Bd. of Missions, same, 1906-10; mem. Commn. on Unification of M.E., and M.E. Ch., S. Traveled in Europe, 1900; Cole lecturer Vanderbilt U., 1909; lecturer in summer schs. First pres. Ednl. Assn. of the M.E. Ch., S., 1918-19; first pres. Southwestern Soc. Biblical Study and Research. Founder of Alpha Chi, college scholarship society, with chapters in 30 institutions. Mem. Pi Gamma Mu, Sigma Alpha Epsilon, Internat. Soc. of Theta Phi. Author: Jesus the Worker, 1910; Characteristics of the Christian Life, 1925. Contbr. to theol. and ednl. jours. Home: 2102 Commonwealth Av., Houston 6, Tex. Died Nov. 30, 1949.

BISHOP, Eben Faxon, sugar factor; b. Naperville, Ill., Oct. 27, 1863; s. Linus Dewey and Frances (Hulbert) B.; ed. pub. schs. and bus. coll.; m. Annie S. Walker, July 21, 1891. With C. Brewer & Co., factors and sugar commn., Honolulu, since 1883, now chmn. bd., dir. Hilo Sugar Co., Onomea Sugar Co., Pepeekeo Sugar Co., Honomu Sugar Co., Waimanalo Sugar Co., Matson Navigation Co. Trustee B. P. Bishop Mus. Polynesian Ethnology. Republican. Episcopalian. Mason. Home: 2345 Nuuanu Av. Office: 827 Fort St., Honolulu, H.T.* Died Feb. 11, 1943.

BISHOP, Edwin Whitney, clergyman; b. Norwich, Conn., May 12, 1869; s. Sherman B. and Ellen L. (Webber) B.; B.A., Williams, 1892; grad. Hartford Theol. Sem., 1897; studied U. of Berlin, 1897-98; D.D., Dartmouth, 1905; m. Rachel Rand, June 11, 1903; children—David Rand, Helen, Ruth. Instr. natural science, Whitman Coll., Wash., 1893-94; ordained Congl. ministry, 1898; pastor Stafford Springs, Conn., 1898-1900, Concord, N.H., 1900-07, Oak Park, Ill., 1908-09, Grand Rapids, Mich., 1909-15, Brockton, Mass., 1915-18; pastor Plymouth Congl. Ch., Lansing, 1918-39, pastor emeritus since 1939. Served as moderator Mich. Congl. Chs., chmn. American Red Cross, pres. Social Service Bureau, etc. First lecturer, W. F. Ayers Foundation on The Evolution of the Soul. Mem. Theta Delta Chi, Phi Beta Kappa, Theta Phi. Republican. Mason (32°, K.T.). Author of many printed sermons; contbr. to mags. Home: 213 W. Allegan St., Lansing, Mich. Died Jan. 19, 1942; buried Deepdale Cemetery, Lansing.

BISHOP, Frederic Lendall, physicist; b. St Johnsbury, Vt.; s. Lendall and Ellen (Bishop) B.; B.S., Mass. Inst. Tech., 1898; Ph.D., University of Chicago, 1905; Sc.D., University of Pittsburgh, 1938; m. Lelia Prior, Aug. 9, 1899 (died Feb 26, 1925); 1 son, Frederic Lendall; m. 2d, Marie Thorne, Aug. 14, 1928; children—Ann Thorne, Ellen Marie. Prof. physics, U. of Pittsburgh since 1909, dean Sch. of Engring., 1909-27, Sch. of Mines, 1920-27; cons. engr., Am. Window Glass Co., Window Glass Machine Co. Editor Engineering Education. Fellow A.A.A.S.; mem. Am. Phys. Soc., Am. Inst. E.E., Soc. Promotion Engring. Edn. (sec.). Clubs: University, Field (Pittsburgh); Cosmos (Washington). Contbr. papers on engring. education, thermal conductivity, heat of dilution, electric furnaces, viscosity, mechanical mfr. of glass, etc. Home: Fox Chapel Manor, Fox Chapel Borough, Pittsburgh, Pa. Died 1948.

BISHOP, John Peale, author; b. Charles Town, W.Va., May 21, 1892; s. Jonathan Peale and Margaret Miller (Cochran) B.; Litt.B., Princeton, 1917; m. Margaret Grosvenor Hutchins, June 17, 1922; children—Jonathan Peale, Robert Grosvenor, Christopher. Mng. editor Vanity Fair, 1920-22. Director of Publications Program, 1941-42, later spl. consultant, Office of Coordinator of Inter-Am. Affairs. Served as 1st lt. Inf. U.S. Army, 1917-19, with Hdqrs. Troop, 84th Div., A.E.F. Mem. Phi Beta Kappa. Club: Princeton Quadrangle. Editor (with Allen Tate): American Harvest: Twenty Years of Creative Writing in the United States, 1942. Author: Green Fruit (poems), 1917; Undertaker's Garland (poems, with Edmund Wilson), 1922; Many Thousands Gone (stories), 1931; Now with His Love (poems), 1933; Act of Darkness (novel), 1935; Minute Particulars (poems), 1936; Selected Poems, 1941. Contbr. articles, verse, fiction to mags. Home: Sea Change, South Chatham, Mass. Died Apr. 4, 1944.

BISHOP, William Samuel, theologian; b. Northampton, Mass., Aug. 26, 1865; s. George Sayles and Hannah More (Williston) B.; A.B., Rutgers Coll., New Brunswick, N.J., 1887, A.M., 1891; New Brunswick Theol. Sem., Princeton Theol. Sem., Gen. Theol. Sem., B.D., 1894, D.D., 1905; studied Oxford U., Eng., 1903; m. Mary Eliza Luttrell, June 17, 1907. Deacon, 1891, priest, 1891, P.E. Ch.; in charge Christ (now St. Barnabas') Ch., Denver, 1891-92, St. Barnabas' Ch., Glenwood Springs, Colo., 1892-94; curate St. John's Chapel, Trinity Parish, N.Y. City, 1894-1902; prof. dogmatic theology and philosophy, U. of South, Sewanee, Tenn., 1902-13; rector's asst. Grace Ch., Orange N.J.; vicar St. Thomas Church, Washington, D.C., 1929-35, vicar emeritus since 1935. Chaplain of the Nat. Cathedral Sch. for Girls, 1921-23; examining chaplain Diocese of Washington, 1923-35; dir. Soc. for Home Study of Holy Scripture, 1929-36, pres., 1939-43. Secretary Sewanee Summer School of Theology, 1904-06; lecturer dogmatic theology, Gen. Theol. Sem., 1908; lecturer Coll. of Preachers, Washington, 1932-33. Mem. Phi Beta Kappa, 1886, Delta Phi, S.A.R., Soc. Descendants of Colonial Govs. Republican. Author: The Development of Trinitarian Doctrine in the Nicene and Athanasian Creeds, 1910; Spirit and Personality, 1923; The Theology of Personality, 1926; The Gospel of Divine Personality, 1928; Christ and the Spirit, 1941. Address: 1912 Belmont Rd., Washington 9, D.C. Died Mar. 14, 1944.

BISSELL, E. Perot, architect. Fellow Am. Inst. Architects. Address: 410 W Chelton Av., Philadelphia, Pa. Died July 3, 1944.

BISSELL, Pelham St. George, jurist; b. N.Y. City, Apr. 11, 1887; s. Rev. Pelham St. George and Helen Alsop (French) B.; student at Cutler School, N.Y. City; A.B., Columbia, 1909, A.M., 1910, LL.B., 1912; LL.D., Hobart and William Smith Colls., 1943; m. Mary Valentine Yale Bissell, Nov. 10, 1910; children—Helen Alsop (Mrs. Charles Hecker Stout), Pelham St. George III, Mary Sackett (Mrs. James J. Christie), Nancy Wemple (Mrs. David Lawrence), Ruth Mason (Mrs. Joseph M. Schwartz), Ophelia Louise (Mrs. William W. Molla), George Henry, Elizabeth Goodwin (dec.). Began the practice of law in N.Y. City, 1912; special attorney U.S. Dept. of Justice, Customs Div., 1921-24; counsel to U.S. appraiser Port of N.Y., 1922-24; dep. asst. atty. gen. State of N.Y., 1929; justice Municipal Court, New York, since Jan. 1, 1931 (re-elected 1940), designated acting pres. justice, 1934, pres. justice since June 7, 1934, (redesignated, 1939, 41). Chmn. Mayor's Board of Survey, settling N.Y. City Building Service Employees strike, 1936; instituted small claims parts of Municipal Court in each of five boroughs of City, 1934; centralized jury cases in Brooklyn, Bronx and Queens and non-jury cases over $100 in Manhattan with centralized motion calendar. Sponsored and instituted Government Project whereby lawyers in needy circumstances are assigned by Municipal Court as trial counsel for indigent litigants, 1935. Rep.-Fusion-Independent Progressive candidate for justice Supreme Court, First Dist., New York, 1938. Awarded Columbia U. medal for service at bar and on bench,

1940. Commd. 2d lt. Inf. R.C., U.S. Army, May 11, 1917; 1st lt. Inf., N.A., Dec. 31, 1917; capt. inf., U.S. Army, Mar. 26, 1919; maj. Inf. Reserve, June 9, 1922, lt. col. Inf. Res., Dec. 10, 1930; overseas with 77th Div., participated in Baccarat and Vesle sectors, Oise-Aisne and Meuse-Argonne offensives; commended in Argonne by comdg. gen. 77th Div.; awarded Conspicuous Service Cross by State of N.Y. Mem. City Advancement Com. Boy Scouts of America. Mem. Am. Bar Assn., Assn. Bar City New York, N.Y. County Lawyers Assn., St. Nicholas Soc., The Pilgrims, Soc. Colonial Wars (council), S.R. (past pres.), Soc. War of 1812, Mil. Order World War (past N.Y. State comdr.), Mil. Order Foreign Wars (past national commander general), Soc. Am. Wars (past comdr. gen.), La Société des 40 Hommes et 8 Chevaux (past nat. pres.), Am. Legion (past comdr.), N.Y. Soc. Mil. and Naval Officers of World War, Res. Officers Assn. (state exec. com.), Vets. Foreign Wars (past judge advocate), N.Y. Hist. Soc., Columbia Alumni Fed. (dir.), Grant Monument Assn. (trustee), Grand Street Boys Assn., Ends of Earth Club, Junior O.U.A.M., Phi Delta Phi, Free Sons of Israel, Foresters of America, Phi Sigma Omega; fellow Inst. Am. Genealogy. Republican. Episcopalian. Mason (32°), Elk, Sojourners (past pres. Manhattan chapter). Clubs: Union League, Military and Naval (v.p.), Church, Columbia Univ., Nat. Republican (New York), Army and Navy (Washington, D.C.). Home: 270 Park Av. Chambers: 8 Reade St., New York, N.Y. Died Sept. 8, 1943.

BITTNER, Van Amburg, labor official; b. Bridgeport, Pa., Mar. 20, 1885; s. Charles and Emma Ann (Henck) B.; m. Bertha May Walters; 1 dau., Anna Mary (Mrs. James Wohler). Labor representative since 1908; rep. United Mine Workers of America, 1908-42; rep. steelworkers organizing com. from formation (1936) until meeting of constitutional convention (1942) when it became United Steelworkers of America, C.I.O., now v.p.; labor rep. on Nat. War Labor Bd. since 1943. Mason. Home: 56 Lincoln Av., Crafton. Office: Commonwealth Bldg., Pittsburgh, Pa. **Died July 20, 1949.**

BIXLER, James Wilson, clergyman; b. Hanover, Pa., Feb. 28, 1861; s. David D. and Almira (Wilson) B.; A.B., Amherst, 1882, A.M., 1887; B.D., Yale, 1887; Hooker fellow Yale Div. Sch., 1888-89; D.D., Roanoke, 1903; m. Clara M. Burleigh, Oct. 15, 1921; children—(by 1st marriage), Julius S.; (by 2d marriage), Elizabeth S., James W., Herbert E. Ordained Congl. ministry, 1889; pastor North Ch., Haverhill, Mass., 1889-91, 2d Ch., New London, Conn., 1891-1916; prof. Bibl. and Christian theology, Atlanta Theol. Sem., 1916-18; pastor Congl. Ch., Exeter, N.H., 1918-36, pastor emeritus since 1936; pulpit supply Brentwood (N.H.) Congl. Ch. since 1937. Mem. N.H. House of Rep. 1925-29 (chmn. Indsl. Schs. Com.; chmn. N.H. State Hosp. Com., 1927-29); mem. N.H. State Senate, 1933-35 (chmn. edn. com.); corporate mem. A.B.C.F.M.; overseer Charitable Fund, Amherst Coll.; mem. Exeter Eventide Home for Aged. Pres. Assn. of Ministers of Exeter and vicinity. Mem. Phi Beta Kappa, Psi Upsilon. Republican. Mason, Odd Fellow. Home: 15 Lincoln St., Exeter, N.H. Died Aug. 22, 1943.

BIZZELL, James Adrian, soil technologist; b. Glenwood, N.C., Apr. 13, 1876; s. Hannibal Newton and Mary Catherine (Underwood) B.; B.Sc., State Coll. Agr. and Engring., Raleigh, N.C., 1895, M.Sc., 1900; Ph.D., Cornell U., 1903; m. Elizabeth Tillotison Peters, April 15, 1924; children—Mary Catherine, James Royal. Asst. chemist N.C. Expt. Sta., 1895-1901; fellow in chemistry, Cornell U., 1901-02; asst. chemist Cornell U. Expt. Sta., 1903-08; asst. prof. soil technology, N.Y. State Coll. Agr., 1908-12, prof. since 1912. Mem. Am. Soc. Agronomy, Sigma Xi, Alpha Chi Sigma, Gamma Alpha, Acacia. Presbyterian. Mason (K.T., Shriner). Home: Forest Home, Ithaca, N.Y. Died Nov. 1, 1944.

BIZZELL, William Bennett (bĭ-zĕl'), educator; b. Independence, Tex., Oct. 14, 1876; s. George McDuffie and Sarah Elizabeth (Wade) B.; B.S., Baylor U., Waco, Tex., 1898, Ph.B., 1900; LL.M., Ill. Coll. of Law, Chicago, 1911, D.C.L., 1912; A.M., U. of Chicago, 1913; LL.D., Baylor, Tex., 1919; Ph.D., Columbia, 1921; m. Carrie Wray Sangster, Aug. 16, 1900. Supt. pub. schs., Navasota, 1900-10; pres. Coll. of Industrial Arts, Denton, 1910-14; pres. Agrl. and Mech. Coll. of Tex., 1914-25; pres. U. of Okla., 1925-41, pres. emeritus and head department of sociology since 1941. Fellow A.A.A.S., Royal Economic Soc. of Eng.; mem. Am. Sociol. Soc., Am. Polit. Science Assn., Am. Economics Assn., Phi Delta Kappa, Sigma Tau Delta, Phi Beta Kappa, Acacia. Democrat. Baptist. Mason (K.T., Shriner). Author: Austinean Theory of Sovereignty, 1912; Judicial Interpretation of Political Theory, 1914; The Social Teaching of the Jewish Prophets, 1916; Farm Tenantry in the United States, 1921; Rural Texas, 1923; The Green Rising, 1927; The Relations of Learning, 1934. Home: 830 S. Elm St., Norman, Okla. Died May 13, 1944; interred at Rose Hill Mausoleum, Oklahoma City, Okla.

BLACK, Benjamin Warren, physician and medical administrator; b. Fillmore, Utah; s. George Warren and Birdie Susannah (Robison) B.; student University of Utah, 1909-10, Brigham Young U., 1911, U. of Chicago, 1911-12; M.D., Medico-Chirurgical Coll., U. of Pa., 1916; m. Jean Blackburn, Sept. 15, 1909; children—Dr. Benjamin Marden, Margaret Susannah. Teacher and prin., pub. schs., Utah, 1904-09; interne, Dr. W. H. Groves, L.D.S. Hosp., Salt Lake City, Southern Pacific R.R. Hosp., 1916-17; acting asst. surgeon to senior surgeon, U.S.P.H.S., 1920-24; exec. officer U.S. Vets. Bur., 1924-26, med. dir., 1926-28; med. dir. Alameda County (Calif.), Oakland, since 1928. Served in M.R., U.S. Army, 1917-19, advancing from 1st lt. to lt. col.; now lt. col., Med. Res. Pres. Oakland Forum, 1940-42; member exec. com. Oakland Community Chest. Charter fellow Am. Coll. of Hosp. Adminstrs. (regent); fellow Am. Coll. Phys., Assn. of Mil. Surgeons, Am. Psychiat. Assn., A.A.A.S., A.M.A.; mem. Am. Hosp. Assn. (pres. 1940-41; mem. council on edn.), Kiwanis Internat. (past dist. gov., Calif.-Nev. District; now internat. trustee), Western Inst. for Hospitals. (dir. 1938-40), Western Hosp. Assn. (pres. 1931-33), Calif. Med. Assn., Alameda County Med. Assn., Phi Rho Sigma. Mason (32°; K.C.C.H. past master Lodge of Perfection). Clubs: Commonwealth, Claremont Country (Oakland). Author: Medical Policies and Procedures, 1936; also author articles in Hospitals, Modern Hosp., Hosp. Management, etc. Home: 250 Tunnel Rd., Berkeley, Calif. Office: 2701 Fourteenth Av., Oakland, Calif. Died Dec. 1, 1945; buried in Mountain View Cemetery, Oakland.

BLACK, Charles Clarke, judge; b. Mt. Holly, N.J., July 29, 1858; s. John, Jr., and Mary Anna (Clarke) B.; A.B., Princeton, 1878, A.M., 1881; student law dept. U. of Mich., 1879-80; m. Alice Greenleaf Hazen, Feb. 12, 1890 (died Mar. 21, 1915); m. 2d, Helen Newbold, July 6, 1918. Admitted to the bar, 1881, and engaged in practice at Jersey City, N.J. Member State Bds. Taxation and Equalization, 1891-1908, N.J. Tax Commrs., 1896, 1904; Dem. candidate for gov. of N.J., 1904; judge Circuit Court of N.J., 1908-14; justice Supreme Court of N.J., 1914-30. Mem. bd. mgrs. Provident Inst. for Savings, Jersey City, N.J. Author: Proof and Pleadings in Accident Cases, 1886; New Jersey Law of Taxation, 5th edit., 1940; Law and Practice in Accident Cases, 1900. Home: 80 Gifford Av. Office: 15 Exchange Pl., Jersey City, N.J. Died Dec. 23, 1947.

BLACK, Ernest Bateman, cons. engr.; b. Mt. Sterling, Ill., Jan. 13, 1882; s. Moses and Mary Ella (Winslow) B.; B.S., U. of Kan., 1906, C.E., 1924; m. Faye Irene Bunyan, June 16, 1914; children—Robert Winslow, Mary Helen, Patricia Ann, John Bunyan. Masonry insp., A.,T.&S.F. Ry., 1906-07; asst. engr. Riggs & Sherman Co., Toledo, O., 1907-09; jr. partner J. S. Worley Co. and Worley & Black, 1909-14; sr. partner Black & Veatch, cons. engrs., since 1915. Served as capt. and maj. Air Service, Air Craft Prodn. U.S. Army, 1917-18, also chief engr. War Credits Bd. and engr. Sect. B, Constn. Div. of Army; consultant-chief Water Supply Unit, Civil Engr. Branch, Constrn. Div. Q.M.C., U.S. Army, 1941. Pres. Kansas City Area Boy Scouts of Am., 1940, 41, 42, 43. Mem. Nat. exec. bd. Boy Scouts of America, 1944-46, chmn. region VIII, 1946. Pres. U. of Kansas Gen. Alumni Assn., 1928-29. Mem. American Institute Consulting Engineers, American Society Civil Engrs. (president 1942), Society of Am. Mil. Engrs. Director, 1943, 44, 45, Am. and New England water works assns., Kansas Engineering Soc., Sigma Xi, Tau Beta Pi. Republican. Presbyterian. Mason (Shriner). Clubs: University, Mission Hills Country, Kansas City Engrs. (Kansas City, Mo.). Contbr. articles on engring. to tech. jours. Home: 824 W. 62d St. Office: 4706 Broadway, Kansas City, Mo. Died July 4, 1949.

BLACK, Forrest Revere, prof. law; b. Tiffin, O., Nov. 3, 1894; s. Albert Freeman and Electa May (Walton) B.; B.A., U. of Wis., 1916, M.A., Columbia, 1919; LL.B., Ohio State U., 1920; Ph.D., Robert Brookings Grad. Sch. of Govt., 1925; scholarships at Columbia U. Law Sch., Robert Brookings Grad. Sch. of Govt. and Social Science Research Council; m. Adelaide Abbott Hodgson, June 18, 1926; 1 son, Forrest Revere. Admitted to the Ohio bar, 1920, and practiced at Tiffin, 1920-21; instr. in polit. science, U. of Minn., 1921-22; asst. prof. polit. science, Washington U., 1922-23, asso. prof., 1923-24; asso. prof. polit. science, State U. of Ia., 1925-27; prof. law, U. of Ky., 1927-34; mem. Ky. Liquor Commn., 1933-34; chief atty. AAA, Washington, D.C., 1934-36; prof. law, George Washington University, 1936; special atty. U.S. Dept. of Justice, 1937; special asst. to atty. gen., Office of Chief Counsel, Bureau of Internal Revenue, 1938-43; college debator and orator. Served at Great Lakes Naval Training Sta., 1918. Speaker 5 presdl. campaigns, 1920-36; Dem. candidate for Congress, 13th Dist. of Ohio, 1936. Mem. Ohio and Ky. bar assns., Am. Assn. Law Teachers, Am. Polit. Science Assn., Delta Theta Phi, Order of Coif. Author: Should Trade Unions and Employers Associations Be Made Legally Responsible? ($1,000 prize monograph), 1920; Ill-Starred Prohibition Cases, 1931; War and the Constitution—A Study of Civil Liberty in War Time, 1932; Judicial Mileposts on the Road to Absolutism, 1933; The Crisis in Democracy, 1936. Contbr. of articles to New Republic, The Nation, Vanity Fair, Plain Talk and more than 60 legal articles in leading law reviews. Made Ky. Col. by Gov. of State. Home: 6406 Beechwood Dr., Chevy Chase, Md. Office: Bureau of Internal Revenue, Washington, D.C. Died Sept. 21, 1943.

BLACK, Norman David, newspaper pub.; b. Merrill, Wis., Jan. 20, 1887; s. Norman B. and Jenny (Christenson) B.; grad. high sch., Marinette, Wis., 1904; m. Cora Powers, Apr. 20, 1912; children—Norman D., Margaret. Began with Grand Forks Times as printer, 1906, and continued after consolidation with Grand Forks Herald, advancing to supt.; with others, purchased control in The Fargo Forum, 1917, becoming gen. mgr., pub. since 1931, also v.p., treas. of corp.; pres. Dakota Photo Engraving Co.; dir., sec. and treas. WDAY, Inc. Republican. Presbyn. Clubs: Rotary (pres. 1931-32); Minneapolis Athletic; Riviera Country (Pacific Palisades, Calif.). Home: 1122 8th St. Office: Fargo Forum, Fargo, N.D. Died Aug. 3, 1944.

BLACK, William Wesley, prof. edn.; b. Michigantown, Ind., July 23, 1859; s. Jonathan and Mary Ann (Wayt) B.; grad. Ind. State Normal Sch., Terre Haute, Ind., 1892; A.B., U. of Ill., 1898, A.M., 1899 m. Anna Eliza Stockton, Apr. 10, 1883; 1 son, Okla Karl (dec.); m. 2d, Mary Jane Daily, Aug. 5, 1925. Teacher, rural and town schs.; supt. schs., Paris, Ill., 1894-96; instr. science and art of instrn.; Ill. State Normal Sch., Normal, Ill., 1900-01; prof. science and art of instrn., Chicago Teachers' Coll., 1901-06; supervising prin., Washington, D.C., 1906-08; prof. edn., Ind. U., 1908-25; retired as prof. emeritus. Mem. N.E.A., Nat. Supts.' Assn., Phi Delta Kappa, etc. Home: Bloomington, Ind. Deceased.

BLACKALL, Clarence Howard, architect; b. N.Y. City, Feb. 3, 1857; s. Rev. Christopher Rubey and Eliza (Davis) B.; B.S., U. of Ill., 1877; A.M.. École des Beaux Arts, Paris, 1878-80; m. Emma Murray, Dec. 5, 1883; children—Marian (Mrs. H. W. Miller), R. M. Practiced, New York, 1880-82, Colorado Springs, Colo., 1882, Boston since 1882; designed and erected 1st steel frame bldg., Boston, 1892; architect for Tremont Temple, Colonial Theatre, etc., Boston, and other notable structures. Trustee Charlestown Five Cents Savings Bank; pres. 245 Tremont St. Inc., 50 Stuart St. Inc. Mem. Boston and Cambridge bldg. law commns. First holder Rotch Traveling Scholarship, Boston, 1884-86 (sec. since 1891, trustee). Fellow A.I.A.; mem. Archtl. League America, New York Archtl. League (1st sec. 1880), Boston Archtl. Club (1st pres. 1889-93). Boston Soc. Architects (sec. 1905). Cambridge Municipal Art Soc. (sec 1905, chmn. bd. of appeal). Sch. house commr., Boston, 1923-26. Author: Builders' Hardware, 1890. Editorial writer, The Brickbuilder, Boston, since Jan. 1895; contbr. to tech. jours. Home: 88 Main St., Concord, Mass. Office: 31 West St., Boston. Died March 5, 1942.

BLACKBURN, William J., physician; b. Hamilton, O., Sept. 17, 1872; s. Robert and Mary J. (Martin) B.; student Ohio Northern U., 1890-93; M.D., Pulte Med. Coll., Cincinnati, and Ohio State U., 1900; M.D., U. of Mich., 1915; m. Mary A. Lane, June 30, 1896; 1 dau., Catharine (Mrs. Richard C. Sharp). Teacher, high sch., Lockington, O., 1894-97. In practice at Dayton, O.; specialist on diseases of eye, ear, nose and throat; mem. staff Miami Valley Hosp., lecturer in Training Sch. Pres. Sanito Chem. Co., Inc.; dir. Dayton Bldg. & Loan Assn. Trustee Miami Valley Hosp. Fellow Am. Coll. Surgeons; mem. Am. Medical Association, Ohio State Medical Association, Montgomery County Tuberculosis Association (v.p.), Montgomery County Med. Soc., Dayton Acad. Ophthalmology and Otolaryngology (past pres.), Theta Kappa Psi. Republican. Mem. U.B. Ch. Mason (K.T., Scottish Rite, Shriner; past illustrious potentate of Antioch, Dayton; past master). Clubs: Exchange, Arabic, Executives, Triangle (pres.), The Presidents Club (vice-pres.), Miami Valley Golf. Contbr. to professional publs. Home: 58 E. Dixon Av., Oakwood, Dayton. Office: Reibold Bldg., Dayton, O. Deceased.

BLACKERBY, Philip Earle, pub. health physician; b. Berlin, Ky., July 8, 1881; s. Philip and Carrie Blanche (McDonald) B.; M.D., Louisville (Ky.) Univ., 1904; student New York Postgrad. Med. Sch. and Hosp.; m. Helen Clara Young, June 20, 1906; children—Philip E., Mary (Mrs. Leonard S. May). Private practice, Erlanger, Ky., 1906-15; field clinician, Ky. State Bd. Health, 1915-17, state registrar, Bur. Vital Statistics, 1917-21; dir. county health work, 1921-43, asst. state health commr. and asst. sec. State Bd. Health, 1925-43, State Health Commr., sec. State Bd. Health since Aug. 1943; dean sch. lab. technicians of State Bd. of Health. Served as capt., Med. Res. Corps, World War I; state chmn. procurement and assignment physicians of Ky., World War II. Fellow A.M.A., Am. Pub. Health Assn. (also mem. Southern br.). Mem. med. adv. com. to State Welfare Instns.; mem. bd. trustees Frontier Nursing Service (ex-officio mem.). Mem. Southern, Ky. State (sec.), Jefferson County Med. Assn., Conf. State and Provincial Health Authorities of N. Am. State and Territory Health Officers. Mem. Am. Legion. Methodist. Club: Executive (Louisville). Home: 559 Sunny Side Dr., Louisville 6. Office: 620 S. Third St., Louisville 2, Ky. Died June 24. 1948.

BLACKFORD, Staige D(avis), physician; b. Alexandria, Va., Dec. 28, 1898; s. Launcelot Minor and Eliza Chew (Ambler) B.; student Episcopal High Sch., Alexandria, 1908-17; B.S., U. of Va., 1923, M.D., 1925; m. Lydia H. Fishburne, Aug. 20, 1927; children—Staige D., Linda H. Interne, Mass. Gen. Hosp., Boston, 1925-27, student physician and instr. in medicine, 1927-28; asst. prof. of practice of medicine, U. of Va., 1938-40, asso. prof., 1940-46, prof. since 1946; pvt. practice of medicine, specialist in internal medicine, Charlottesville, Va., since 1927 connected with U. of Va. Hosp. Served as pvt., 1st class, U.S.A.A.C., U.S. Army, 1917-19; overseas,

France; lt. col., M.C., U.S. Army, 1942-45; overseas, Italy; mem. selective service bd. of appeal No. 4, Va., 1940-42. Certified Am. Bd. Internal Medicine, 1937. Diplomate Nat. Bd. Med. Examiners, 1927. Awarded Croix de Guerre (France, 1917); Legion of Merit (U.S. 1945); Croce di Guerra (Italy 1945). Mem. bd. trustees Episcopal High Sch. Fellow A.C.P.; mem. Am. Clin. and Climatologic Assn., A.M.A., Delta Kappa Epsilon, Phi Rho Sigma, Alpha Omega Alpha, Sigma Xi. Democrat. Episcopalian. Home: 1403 Hilltop Rd. Office: Univ Hosp., Charlottesville, Va. Died July 17, 1949.

BLACKMAN, William Waldo, physician; b. Bridgewater, Oneida County, N.Y., May 25, 1856; s. William Wise and Sarah Angeline (Waldo) B.; ed. Waterville Union Sch. and Acad.; M.D., New York Homeo. Med. Coll., 1877; m. Lora C. Jackson, Sept. 14, 1887. Resident physician Brooklyn Maternity Hosp., 2 yrs.; in practice as homeo. physician, Brooklyn, since 1877; asst. prof. anatomy, 1883-88, prof., 1888-96, New York Homeo. Med. Coll.; attending physician to Brooklyn Homeo. Hosp., 1888-94; surgeon to Cumberland St. Hosp., Brooklyn, 1894-1907; also cons. surgeon to Prospect Heights Hosp., Brooklyn Nursery; med. dir. Prospect Heights Hosp. Member New York State Homeo. Med. Soc. (pres. 1929), Am. Inst. Homeopathy, Kings County Homeo. Med. Soc. (pres. 1907); pres. Alumni Assn. of New York Homeo. Med. Coll., 1904-05; mem. Soc. Mayflower Descendants. Trustee New York Homeo. Med. Coll. and Hosp. since 1905. Republican. Unitarian. Mason, Shriner. Address: 519 Clinton Av., Brooklyn, N.Y. Died Oct. 20, 1943.

BLACKMORE, George Augustus, business exec.; b. Wilkinsburg, Pa., Jan. 7, 1884; s. George H. and Elizabeth (Bealafeld) B.; ed. pub. schs., Wilkinsburg, and night study at colls. and corr. schs.; m. Mary Suckling Stengle, Feb. 16, 1935; children (by former marriage)—Thelma Phynetta (Mrs. Thelma B. Neff), Helen Elizabeth (Mrs. W. W. Priest), George Stewart. Began as office boy, Union Switch & Signal Co., Swissvale, Pa., 1896, later stenographer gen. mgr.'s office, became chief clerk engring. dept., 1900, same in N.Y. office, 1904, asst. to Eastern mgr., 1909, Eastern mgr. in charge N.Y., Atlanta and Montreal offices, 1911, gen. sales mgr., Swissvale, 1916, 2d v.p., 1917, 1st v.p. and gen mgr., 1922, pres., 1929, chmn. and pres., 1940-46; v. pres. and gen. mgr. Westinghouse Air Brake Co., Wilmerding, Pa., 1932-36, became pres., July 1936, now chmn., chief exec. officer; chmn., Duff-Norton Mfg. Co., 1940, dir. Westinghouse Air Brake Co., Union Switch & Signal Co., Union Switch & Signal Construction Co. A. M. Byers Co., Duff-Norton Mfg. Co., Mellon Nat. Bank and Trust Company, Westinghouse Electric Corporation, Canadian Westinghouse Co., Hamilton, Can., Pittsburgh Screw and Bolt Corp., Flannery Bolt Co., Bendix-Westinghouse Automotive Air Brake Company, Cardwell-Westinghouse Co., Westinghouse Brake & Signal Co., Ltd. (London). Republican. Presbyterian. Mason. Clubs: Engineers, Railroad, Railroad-Machinery (New York); Racquet (Phila.); Pittsburgh, Duquesne, Pittsburgh Athletic, Oakmont Country, Longue Vue Country, Railway (Pittsburgh); Allegheny Country (Sewickley, Pa.); Rolling Rock Club (Ligonier, Pa.); Chicago (Chicago). Home: Perrysville, Pa. Office: Union Switch & Signal Co., Swissvale, Pa.; Westinghouse Air Brake Co., Wilmerding, Pa. Died Oct. 2, 1948.

BLAFFER, Robert Lee (bläf'ĕr), oil refining; b. New Orleans, La., Aug. 5, 1876; s. John Augustus and Clementine A. (Schneider) B.; prep. edn., T. W. Dwyer Pvt. Sch., New Orleans; student Tulane U., 1892-94; m. Sarah Jane Campbell, Apr. 22, 1909; children—John Hepburn, Sarah Jane, Cecil Amelia, Joyce Campbell. Began with Monongahela Consol. Coal & Coke Co., New Orleans, 1894; in oil business Spindletop, Tex., 1902; mem. firm Blaffer & Farish, 1903-17; v.p. and treas., Humble Oil & Refining Co., 1917-33, pres. and treas., 1933-37, chmn. bd. and treas., 1937-41; chmn. bd. South Texas Commercial Nat. Bank. Area coordinator Div. of Contract Distribution, Office of Production Management. Chmn. bd. of trustees Kinkaid Sch., Houston; trustee Rice Inst., Houston. Episcopalian. Mason. Clubs: Bayou, Houston, Tejas, Houston Country (Houston); Boston (New Orleans). Home: 6 Sunset Rd. Office: 1201 Commerce Bldg., Houston, Tex. Died Oct. 22, 1942.

BLAIR, David H., ex-commr. internal revenue; b. High Point, N.C., Jan. 13, 1868; s. Solomon and Abigail (Hunt) B.; student Guilford Coll., 1886-87; A.B., Haverford, 1891; studied law, U. of N.C., 1897-98; m. Adelaide Cannon Douglass, Nov. 27, 1917; 1 son, David H. Admitted to N.C. bar, 1897, and began practice at Winston-Salem; commr. internal revenue, May 27, 1921-June 1, 1929; now engaged in practice of law; partner Blair & Korner. Mem. Phi Beta Kappa. Republican. Quaker. Clubs: Nat. Press (Washington, D.C.); Chevy Chase. Home: Wardman Park Hotel. Office: Transportation Bldg., Washington, D.C. Died Sep. 12, 1944.

BLAIR, Francis Grant, supt. public instrn.; b. Nashville, Ill., Oct. 30, 1864; s. William and Mary J. (Crane) B.; grad. Ill. State Normal Univ., 1892 B.S., Swarthmore Coll., Pa., 1897; fellow, Columbia, 1899; LL.D., Colgate, 1913, Ill. Wesleyan, 1916; Dr. of Edn., R.I. State Coll., 1926; m. Lillian Caton, 1898. Taught country schs., 1884-86; prin. schs., Malden, Ill., 1886-89, Leroy, Ill., 1892-95, Franklin Sch., Buffalo, N.Y., 1897-99; supt. training dept. Eastern Ill. Normal Sch., 1899-1906; state supt. pub. instrn., Ill., 1906-35. Pres. N.E.A., 1926-27. Author: Schulykill River Anthology; Song Bird Pageant; Wreath of Wild Flowers; Liberty Bell Pageant; Light Bearers' Pageant; also vol. of ednl. addresses. Home: Abraham Lincoln Hotel. Office: 440 E. Canedy St., Springfield, Ill. Died Jan. 26, 1942.

BLAIR, Henry Patterson, lawyer; b. Plymouth, N.H., Dec. 8, 1867; s. Hon. Henry William and Eliza Ann (Nelson) B.; A.B., Dartmouth, 1889; LL.B., Columbian (now George Washington) U., 1892. Practiced in Washington, D.C., since 1892; mem. Blair & Thom, 1896-1909; prof. law, George Washington U., 1901-09; 1st asst. corp. counsel, Washington, D.C., 1905-09. Mem. Bd. of Edn., Washington, D.C., 1910-16 (pres. 1913-16). Mem. Alpha Delta Phi, Phi Beta Kappa. Republican. Episcopalian. Club: University. Office: Colorado Bldg., Washington, D.C. Died Oct. 3, 1948.

BLAIR, James Thomas, lawyer; b. Loudon, Tenn., Nov. 11, 1871; s. Samuel Tate and Louise (Osborne) B.; A.B., Cumberland U., 1892, LL.B., 1895, LL.D. from same Univ., 1928; LL.D., Missouri Valley Coll.; m. Grace E. Ray, June 19, 1901; children—Capt. James T., Capt. Samuel C., Grace Mary (Mrs. C. Turner), Margaret Ray (Mrs. L. M. Eurcy), Ensign William Clark. Prin., Dover High Sch., 1892-93; prof., Ozark College, 1893; began practice of law, 1896; pres. Obion (Tenn.) College, 1895, 96; mem. Mo. Ho. of Rep., 1899-1901; mem. com. to revise statutes of Mo., 1899-1900; asst. atty. gen. of Mo., 1909-11; mem. commn. to aid the Supreme Court, 1911-15; judge Supreme Court of Mo., term 1915-25 (chief justice, 1921-22); practicing law since Jan. 2, 1925; now mem. law firm Cox & Blair; elected March 1941, mem. of the Appellate Judicial Commn. of Mo. for term ending Dec. 31, 1945. Mem. Am., Mo. State and St. Louis bar assns., Tenn. Soc., Lawyers Assn. Democrat. Presbyterian. Mason. Club: Triple A. Home: Hotel York. Office: Title Guaranty Bldg., St. Louis, Mo. Died Apr. 12, 1944.

BLAIR, Joseph Paxton, lawyer; b. Columbus, Miss., Dec. 5, 1859; s. David Paxton and Elizabeth Armstead (Pope) B.; M.A., U. of Va., 1881; m. Eugenie Kruttschnitt, Apr. 16, 1890; 1 son, Paxton. Asst. prof. mathematics, U. of La., 1881-83; admitted to La. bar, 1883, and practiced at New Orleans; mem. Leovy & Blair until 1895, Denégre & Blair, 1895-1913; gen. counsel S.P. Co., at N.Y. City, 1913-29, retired. Mem. S.A.R., Phi Beta Kappa. Episcopalian. Clubs: University, Century, Church. Home: 555 Park Av., New York, N.Y. Died Nov. 15, 1942.

BLAIR, William Allen, banker, lawyer; b. High Point, N.C., June 4, 1859; s. Solomon I. and Abigail P. (Hunt) B.; A.B., Haverford, 1881; A.B., Harvard, 1882; Johns Hopkins, 1885-86; admitted to bar, 1894; A.M., Duke U. (formerly Trinity), N.C., 1889; LL.D., U. of N.C., 1947; m. Mary Eleanor Fries, Nov. 20, 1895; children—Mrs. Margaret A. McCuiston, Marian H., John Fries. Prin. high schs. and supt. schs., High Point and Winston, N.C., 1885-87; lecturer on pedagogy, Swarthmore, 1886; supt. State Normal Sch., 1887-89; was v.p., later pres. and chmn. bd. People's Nat. Bank of Winston-Salem for over 40 years; pres. Midas Mines, Orange Crush Bottling Co., Gross Mining Co., etc. Pres. State Board Charities and Public Welfare since 1904; editor The School-Teacher, 1887-89; N.C. commr. to Paris Expn., 1889; v.p. Sound Money League for N.C. since 1896; pres. N.C. Bankers' Assn., 1898; mem. exec. com. and treas. Conf. for Edn. in the South; mem. U.S. Assay Commn., 1905; chmn. State Bd., Allotments and Appeals; trustee Peabody Coll. for Teachers, 1909, Salem Coll., Winston Salem State Teachers Coll.; dir. Conf. of Social Service since 1930; dir. Gen. Research Council since 1931; commr. Sesquicentennial Battle of Guilford since 1931; mem. advisory com. Nat. Conf. Jews and Christians; mem. Council Yenching U., China; v.p. Court of Honor, Boy Scouts (received Silver Beaver award). Mem. Am. Bankers Assn. (v.p. for N.C., 1919), Mexican Chamber of Commerce, Am. Palestine Society, Southern Hist. Soc., Southern Lit. Soc., Wachovia Hist. Soc., Audubon Soc. (life), Phi Beta Kappa (Haverford); hon. mem. Eugene Field Soc. Clubs: Cosmos, Shakespeare, N.C. Harvard (exec. com. and v.p.). Author of articles in ednl. and other jours.; also sundry lectures, addresses, poems, etc. During war speaker for all activities. Mem. board counselors Federal Writers Project of Works Progress Adminstrn. Contbr. chapters to Ashe's Biographical History of North Carolina, Knox's History of Banking, Smith's Western North Carolina, etc. Received from Grand Lodge of Masons gold button for "50 years outstanding service," 1940; citation from gov. and council of state for 53 yrs. service on State Bd. of Public Welfare. Home: 210 S. Cherry St., Winston-Salem 3, N.C. Died Mar. 2, 1948; buried Moravian Graveyard, Winston-Salem, N.C.

BLAIR, W(illiam) Reid, zoölogist; b. Phila., Pa., Jan. 27, 1875; s. William Reid and Jeannette (Houston) B.; D.V.S., McGill U., Montreal, Can., 1902, LL.D. from same univ. in 1928; m. Mildred Myrtle Kelly, Oct. 29, 1896. Veterinarian and pathologist, N.Y. Zoöl. Park, 1902-22; prof. comparative pathology, Vet. Dept. New York U., 1905-17; cons. veterinarian, N.Y. State Dept. Agr. Asst. dir. N.Y. Zoöl. Park, 1922-26, dir., 1926-40; exec. sec. Am. Com. Internat. Wild Life Protection since 1938. Pres. Vet. Med. Soc., 1922-23; v.p. and trustee Bronx Soc. of Arts and Sciences; life mem., fellow N.Y. Zoöl. Soc.; fellow A.A.A.S., Am. Geog. Soc.; life mem. Quebec Zoöl. Soc.; mem. council N.Y. Acad. Sciences; corr. mem. Royal Zoöl. Soc. of Ireland, Zoöl. Soc. of London, Internat. Soc. for Preservation of European Bison; life mem. Soc. for Preservation of Fauna of the Empire; trustee Am. Soc. of Mammalogists; sr. fellow Am. Inst. of Park Execs.; mem. Nat. Inst. of Social Sciences, Am. Vet. Med. Assn., N.Y. Graduates Soc. of McGill U., Phi Beta Zeta. Commd. maj., Veterinary Corps, U.S. Army, 1917; served in France and Germany as chief vet. 4th Army Corps, 1918-19; hon. discharged, June 1919; col. Res. Corps. U.S. Army, 1923. Received Citation of Merit, Park Assn. of N.Y. City, 1940. Active in wild life conservation of birds and mammals. Clubs: Century, Authors, Boone and Crockett. Author: Diseases of Wild Animals in Confinement (pub. N.Y. Zoöl. Soc.), 1911; In the Zoo, 1929. Also contbr. scientific publs. on comparative medicine. Home: 271 College Road, Riverdale, New York, N.Y. Died Mar. 1, 1949.

BLAISDELL, Thomas Charles (blāz'dĕl'), educator; born Oil City, Pa., Aug. 29, 1867; son John William and Harriet Irene (Morse) B.; Allegheny Coll.; A.B., Syracuse U., 1888, A.M., 1891; U. of Neb., 1896-97; U. of Pittsburgh, 1901-04, Ph.D., 1904; LL.D., Alma (Mich.) Coll., 1916; m. Kate Christy, May 18, 1893; children—Mrs. Mary Dawson, Thomas Charles, Donald Christy, William Morse. Prof. English, Allegheny (Pa.) High Sch., 1890-96; prof. English and pedagogy, City Normal Sch., Pittsburgh, 1897-1906; prof. English lit., Mich. Agrl. Coll., 1906-12; pres. Alma Coll., 1912-15; dean Sch. Liberal Arts, Pa. State Coll., 1915-20; prof. teaching of English, State Teachers Coll., Slippery Rock, Pa., 1920-35; prof. teaching of English, Florida Southern Coll.; retired 1940. Popular and educational lecturer. Mem. N.E.A., Nat. Council Teachers of English (pres. 1923-24), Shakespeare Assn. America, Nat. Soc. Study of Edn., Phi Delta Theta, Phi Kappa Phi. Conglist. Mason (32°). Author: Steps in English, Book I and Book II (co-author), 1903; English in the Grades, 1905; Composition-Rhetoric, 1906; A Teacher's Handbook, 1912; How to Teach English, 1924; Ways to Teach English, 1930; Ways to Write English, 1941. Editor: Macbeth, 1917; Julius Cæsar, 1917; Merchant of Venice, 1918; As You Like It, 1919; Hamlet, 1919. Supervising editor The Instructor Literature Series. Chautauqua speaker, summers 1917-20. Spent 13 months, 1924-25, in trip around the world; studied conditions in Russia, summer 1932; studied schs. of Puerto Rico and Virgin Islands, winter 1938-39; studied conditions in Hawaii, Sept.-July 1939-40. Home: 111 West Sixth St., Sanford, Fla. Died Dec. 11, 1948.

BLAKE, Chauncey Etheridge, lawyer; b. Rockford, Ill., June 15, 1881; s. George Mathew and Carrie (Brown) B.; LL.B., Univ. of Wis., 1904; m. Katharine Wentworth Sanborn, Oct. 18, 1905; children—George Golder, Alice (Mrs. Frank D. Crane). Admitted to Wis. bar, 1904, and since in practice before U.S. and Wis. Cts.; sr. partner Sanborn, Blake & Aberg, Madison, Wis. Republican. Quaker. Mason (K.T.). Clubs: Madison, Psi Upsilon and Phi Delta Phi. Home: 1016 Sherman Av. Office: 16 N. Carroll St., Madison. Wis. Deceased.

BLAKE, Clinton Hamlin, lawyer and author; b. Englewood, N.J., July 26, 1883; s. Clinton Hamlin and Mary Gibson (Parsons) B.; A.B., Columbia U., 1904 (class sec.), A.M. in Polit. Science, 1905, LL.B., 1906; m. Margaret Duryee Coe, June 10, 1908; children—Margaret Coe (Mrs. Theodore W. Oppel), Marion Stanley (Mrs. William G. Cullimore). Dorothy Dexter (Mrs. George H. Macy), Clinton Hamlin, Jr. Admitted to N.Y. bar, 1906, later to bars of United States Circuit and Dist. courts, Ct. of Appeals, D.C., United States Patent Office, and Supreme Ct. of U.S.; member Blake, Voorhees & Stewart, N.Y. City; specializes in laws relating to corporations, architecture and building, and unfair competition; president and director Harper-Gow Corp.; dir. and vice pres. Citizens Nat. Bank & Trust Co., Englewood, 1925-36; chmn. of Bd., 1936-41; dir. Pond's Extract Co., Penn Sugar Co.; dir., mem. exec. com., v.p. and gen. counsel Nat. Sugar Refining Co. Special lecturer on law of architecture and bldg., Mass. Inst. Tech., 1921-22, 25, Columbia U., 1928, New York U., 1933, and on same subject before various archtl. societies; instr. in architecture New York U., 1928. Councilman at large, pres. Common Council, Englewood, 1914-16; mayor of Englewood, 2 terms, 1916-18; resigned to enter Army. Mem. N.J. State Council of Defense, 1917-18; chmn. War Draft Bd. No. 5, Bergen County, N.J., 1917-18; capt. Signal Corps, U.S. Army, 1918-19. Former mem. exec. com. N.J. div. Am. Liberty League; former dir. and mem. exec. com. N.J. div. Assn. Against Prohibition Amendment; charter member com. on Food, Drug and Cosmetic Law. Trustee The Barrington School. Mem. Am. Bar Assn., New York State Bar Assn., Assn. of the Bar of the City of New York, Beta Theta Pi. Republican. Clubs: University, Down Town Assn., Beta Theta Pi (New York) Wyantenuck Golf (Great Barrington). Author: The Law of Architecture and Building, 1916-25; The Architect's Law Manual, 1924; Acquiring The Home, 1925; special report to 14th Internat. Congress of Architects, Paris, 1937; also many serial and special articles in mags. since 1915. Editor legal dept. Am. Architect, 1921-27 and 1934-36. Runner-up New Jersey golf champ., 1904. Home: Seekonk Road, Great Barrington, Mass.; (summer) Sugar Hill, N.H. Office: 20 Exchange Place, New York, N.Y. Died Jan. 25, 1947.

BLAKE, Edgar, bishop; b. Gorham, Me., Dec. 8, 1869; s. Charles H. and Abigail (Redlon) B.; ed. common schs. of Me.; grad. Boston U. Sch. Theology, 1898; D.D., Neb. Wesleyan U., 1909, Wesleyan U., Middletown, Conn.; 1915; LL.D., DePauw U., Greencastle, Ind., 1929; m. Charlotte Woodman, Feb. 4, 1891; (died Mar. 19, 1925); children—Edgar, Everett, Mrs. Charlotte McConnell, Mrs. Rachel Hamilton; m. 2d, Mary Jane Eaton, Jan. 28, 1930. Ordained M.E. ministry, 1899; pastor Salem, N.H., 1895-99, Lebanon, N.H., 1899-1903, Manchester, N.H., 1903-08; asst. sec., 1908-12, corr. sec. Bd. of Sunday Schs. of M.E. Ch., 1912-20; bishop since May 18, 1920. Mem. Phi Beta Kappa. Republican. Mason. (K.T.). Address: 1242 S. Greenway Drive, Coral Gables, Fla. Died May 26, 1943.

BLAKE, Edgar, Jr., hosp. supt.; b. Hartford, Conn.; s. Edgar and Charlotte (Woodman) B.; grad. Evanston Acad., 1912; B.A., Wesleyan U., 1916; m. Margaret Hingeley, May 22, 1919; children—Edgar, John Hingeley, Suzanne, Charlotte, Joseph Hingeley. Dir. Boys Farm and Trade Sch., Charvieu Isere, France, 1920-30; supt. Meth. Hosp., Gary, Ind., 1931-41; supt. Wesley Memorial Hosp., Chicago, since 1941. Served as ensign, U.S. Navy Res. Force, World War I. Pres. Ind. Hosp. Assn., 1937; pres. Civil Service Commn., Gary, Ind., 1939-41; pres. Am. Protestant Hosp. Assn., 1942. Trustee, Northwestern Univ. Mem. Am. Coll. of Hosp. Administr., Alpha Chi Rho. Methodist. Home: 201 E. Delaware Place. Chicago, Ill. Died March 28, 1947.

BLAKE, Edward Everett, nat. chairman Prohibition party; b. Burr Oak, Kan., May 14, 1875; s. Edward Everett and Sarah Elizabeth (Kenyon) B.; student pub. schs., Chicago, Ill.; m. Hilda Belle Walker, Dec. 27, 1910. Office boy, later advt. auditor Price Baking Powder Co., Chicago, Ill., 1890-99; advt. auditor Royal Baking Powder Co., N.Y. City, 1899-1902; business mgr. New Voice, Chicago, 1902-03; owner, pub. and editor Home Defender, 1905-09; traveling rep. various concerns, 1909-12; mail order mgr. P. A. Stark Piano Co., 1912-18; advt. mgr. Melville Clark Piano Co., 1918-20; advt. mgr. Apollo Piano Co., 1920-22; est. piano business, 1922; editor Nat. Prohibitionist since 1933. Nat. chmn. Prohibition party since 1932. Baptist. Home: 330 N. Austin Blvd., Oak Park, Ill. Office: 82 W. Washington St., Chicago 2, Ill. Died Sept. 9, 1947.

BLAKE, Theodore Evernghim, architect; b. Brooklyn, N.Y., Oct. 11, 1869; s. Clarence Alexander and Elizabeth Duncan (Mason) B.; student Poly. Inst., Brooklyn, N.Y., 1882-88; Ecole des Beaux-Arts, Paris, France, 1892-95; unmarried. Draftsman with Carrere & Hastings, 1888-91; associate of Correre & Hastings, 1895-1927. Prin. works include House and Senate Office Bldgs., Washington, D.C.; Manhattan Bridge No. 3, N.Y. City; New York Public Library, N.Y. City. In practice in own name since 1927. Principal works include Mount Hope Bridge, Providence, R.I.; Christian Science Church, Phila.; Second Church of Christ Scientist, N.Y. City; Craige Colony State Inst. of N.Y.; Harbeck Chapel, Woodlawn Cemetery, N.Y. City; Rosemary School Group, Greenwich, Conn. Mem. 23rd Regt., Brooklyn, 106 Inf., N.Y. Nat. Guard, 1889-98. Fellow A.I.A., mem. Beaux-Arts Inst. of Design. Clubs: Century Assn., St. Nicholas Soc., Coffee House (New York City), Field (Greenwich, Conn.), Cosmos (Washington, D. C.) Home: 17 LaFayette Pl., Greenwich. Conn. Address: 32 E. 57th St., New York 22, N.Y. Died July 3, 1949. Buried Putnam Cemetery, Greenwich, Conn.

BLAKE, Tiffany, editorial writer; b. Chicago, Ill., Nov. 19, 1870; s. Samuel Coleman and Adaline (Jones) B.; prep. edn., Lake View High Sch., Chicago; LL.B., Northwestern U., 1893; m. Margaret Pynchon Day, Oct. 7, 1905. Dramatic and music editor Chicago Journal, 1900-02; lit. editor Chicago Evening Post, 1902-05, chief editorial writer, 1905-08; chief editorial writer Chicago Tribune, 1908-39, retired. Republican. Home: 1301 Astor St. Office: Tribune Tower, Chicago, Ill. Died Sept. 28 1943.

BLAKELEY, George Henry (blāk'lē), engineer; b. Livingston, N.J., Apr. 19, 1865; s. Joseph and Mary A. (Gibson) B.; B.S., Rutgers Coll., 1884, C.E., 1894, ScD., 1924; m. Grace Delia Bogart, Apr. 12, 1893; 1 son, George Bogart. Private engineering practice 1884-1888; bridge eng. Erie R.R., 1888-90; chief engr. Passaic Steel Co., 1890-1902, mgr. of sales, 1902-05; structural engr., Bethlehem Steel Co., 1906-08, mgr. structural steel dept., 1908-27, v.p. since 1927; pres. Bethlehem Steel Bridge Corp., 1916-23; pres. McClintic-Marshall Corp., 1931-35; dir. Bethlehem Steel Corp., Bethlehem Steel Co., Bethlehem Shipbuilding Corp., Bethlehem Steel Export Corp. Actively identified with constrn. of many important bridges and bldgs., among which are Delaware River Bridge (Phila.), Peace Bridge, Niagara River (Buffalo, N.Y.), Golden Gate Bridge (San Francisco), Merchandise Mart (Chicago), Chase Nat. Bldg. (New York), Field Museum (Chicago); expert in devising and developing improvements in mfr. and uses of structural steel, the most important of which are broad flange structural steel sections, introduced by Bethlehem Steel Co. in 1908, and which are in gen. use in steel construction. Life trustee Rutgers Univ. Mem. Am. Soc. C.E., Am. Soc. Mech. Engrs., Am. Iron and Steel Inst., Chi Psi, Tau Beta Pi, Phi Beta Kappa; fellow Am. Geog. Soc. Republican. Episcopalian. Clubs: University, Lawyers, Whitehall, Chi Psi, New York Yacht (New York); Art (Phila.); Manhasset Bay Yacht (L.I.); Saucon Valley Country (Bethlehem). Home: Fountain Hill, Bethlehem, Pa. Died Dec. 25, 1942.

BLAKELY, John Russell Young, naval officer; b. Phila., Pa., July 17, 1872; grad. U.S. Naval Acad., 1892. Commd. ensign, 1894 promoted through grades to rear adm. U.S. Navy, June 4, 1926. Served on Yankee, Merrimac and New Orleans, Spanish-Am. War; on Paducah, 1906-07; exec. officer Wolverine, 1907; navigator Maine, 1909, Washington, 1909-11; duty Bur. of Navigation, Washington, D.C., 1911-14; comdr. Des Moines, 1914-17, and later comdr. Seattle, World War; comdr. Arizona, 1922-24; comdr. light cruiser div., Asiatic Fleet, 1927-29; comdt. 15th Naval Dist., 1929-30; mem. Gen. Bd., 1930-32; retired, June 1, 1932. Address: Navy Dept., Washington. Died Mar. 28, 1942; buried in Arlington National Cemetery.

BLAKESLEE, Francis Durbin, educator, lecturer, newspaper corr.; b. Vestal, Broome County, N.Y., Feb. 1, 1846; s. Rev. George H. and Hester A. (Cargill) B.; A.B., Syracuse U., 1872, A.M., 1875; D.D., Wesleyan U., Conn., 1889; Litt.D., Ia. Wesleyan, 1905; m. Augusta Mirenda Hubbard, Sept. 9, 1869 (died Oct. 24, 1911); children—George Hubbard, Albert Francis, Theodora Louise; m. 2d, Harriet B. Badeau, Dec. 28, 1918. Q.-m.'s clerk, 50th N.Y. Engrs., Rappahannock Sta., Va., winter, 1863-64; clerk in q.-m.-gen.'s office, Washington, D.C., Feb. 1864-July 1865; ordained M.E. ministry, 1870, pastor, Canisteo, N.Y., Jan.-Aug. 1868; prin. Whitney's Point (N.Y.) Union Sch., 1869-70; pastor, East Groveland, N.Y., 1871-73; prin. East Greenwich (R.I.) Acad., 1873-84; traveled in Europe 1884-85, 1889; pastor Thames St. Ch., Newport, R.I., 1886-87; prin., E. Greenwich Acad., 1887-99; pres., Ia. Wesleyan U., Mt. Pleasant, Ia., 1899-1900, Cazenovia (N.Y.) Sem., 1900-08; supt. Binghamton (N.Y.) Dist. Anti-Saloon League, 1908-15, field sec., 1915-18; again pres. East Greenwich Acad., 1918-20; traveled extensively in the Orient and Europe, 1921-25; lecturer Victorian (Australia) Anti-Liquor League, 1922-24. Del. Gen. Conf. M.E. Ch., 1892; pres. R.I. State Sunday Sch. Assn., 1894-95. Ex-pres. Syracuse Univ. Alumni Assn. of Southern Calif., Lovers of Shakespeare Club of Los Angeles; pres. Proximo Club of Los Angeles, 1930, 32, Retired Meth. Ministers' Assn. of Southern Calif., 1930-31; nat. chaplain Abraham Lincoln Fellowship; chaplain and lecturer Lincoln Fellowship, Southern Calif. Mem. Delta Kappa Epsilon, Phi Beta Kappa. Mem. Central N.Y. Conf. of M.E. Ch. Republican. Wrote: (brochure) How My Father Obtained Lincoln's Autograph; (pamphlet) Personal Recollections of Abraham Lincoln (mag. articles); The Grand Review at the Close of the Civil War. Home: 2702 S. Hobart Blvd., Los Angeles, Calif. Died Sep. 12, 1942.

BLAKESLEE, Fred Gilbert, author; b. Hartford, Conn., June 17, 1868; s. Capt. Henry E. and Helen E. (Butler) B.; pub. sch. edn.; unmarried. With the Ætna Ins. Co., 1884-1931, retired. Served in U.S. Navy, Spanish-Am. War; capt. Governor's Horse Guard, 1910; mil. instr. West Middle Sch. Dist. (Hartford), 1904-19. Mem. Spanish War Vets., S.A.R., Soc. for Army Hist. Research (London), Am. Military Inst. Clubs: The Masquers (Hollywood); Authors' (London); Armor and Arms (New York). Author: Sword Play for Actors, 1905; Army Uniforms of the World, 1919; Uniforms of the World, 1929; Police Uniforms of the World, 1934; Eastern Costume, 1935; Postal Uniforms of the World, 1937; Transportation Uniforms of the World, 1939. Also writer on fencing, the sword and military insignia of rank in Ency. Americana and contbr. mag. articles. Hon. maj. of inf., Nat. Chinese Army in recognition of service to Chinese students in U.S. Traveled in the East for purpose of costume research, 1931-32 and 1936. Home: 3746 Vantage Av., North Hollywood, Calif. Died Oct. 3, 1942.

BLANCHARD, Frederic Thomas, prof. English; b. Harvard, Mass., Sept. 24, 1878; s. Frederick George and Elizabeth Lucindy (Seaver) B.; B.L., U. of Calif., 1904; Calif. fellow at Yale, 1906-08, M.A., 1908, Ph.D., 1922; m. Mary Helen Webster, Dec. 21, 1912 (died Sept. 22, 1945). Instr. Latin and French, Berkeley preparatory School, 1904-06; assistant in rhetoric, Yale, 1906-08; instructor, English, University of Calif., 1908-15; asst. prof. English, Rice Inst., Houston, Tex., 1915-19; asso. prof. English and asst. dir. extension div., U. of Calif., 1919-20; chmn. dept. of English, U. of Calif., at Los Angeles, 1920-36, asso. prof. 1920-23, prof. since 1923; prof. English, summer sessions, Berkeley, Los Angeles, Columbia. Fellow A.A.A.S., Royal Soc. of Arts (London); mem. Modern Lang. Assn. America, Philol. Assn. Pacific Coast, Am. Assn. Univ. Profs. (former councillor), Phi Beta Kappa Alumni Assn. of Southern Calif. (past councillor), English-Speaking Union, Phi Beta Kappa (ex-pres. Eta Chapter of California). Psi Upsilon, Mu Lambda; honorary member Stevenson Soc., Pi Delta Phi, Pi Gamma Mu; hon. corr. mem. Institut Littéraire et Artistique de France. Clubs: Athenian (Oakland, California); University (Los Angeles); Lotos (New York); Authors (London). Author: Essays in Exposition (with others), 1914; Fielding, the Novelist, 1926; Perspective Criticism, 1930; The Art of Composition, 1934; The Art of the Novel, 1938 (awarded silver medal by Royal Society of Arts, London). Contributor to Dictionary of World Literature, The Structure of English. various periodicals. European travel and study, 1931-32 and 1938-39 Home: 4440 Cromwell Av., Los Angeles 27. Calif. Died Feb. 3, 1947.

BLANCHARD, Grace, author; b. Dunleith, Ill.; d. George Augustus and Frances (Sargent) Blanchard; A.B., Smith Coll., 1882. City librarian, Concord, N.H., 1895-1935. Clubs: Woman's, College, Shakespeare. Author: Phil's Happy Girlhood; Phillida's Glad Year; The Island Cure. Contbr. to mags. Home: 14 Blake St., Concord, N.H. Died Jan. 9, 1944.

BLANCHARD, William Martin, prof. chemistry; b. Perguimans County, N.C., Aug. 25, 1874; s. William Stewart and Artemecia (Towe) B.; A.B., Randolph-Macon Coll., Ashland, Va., 1894, A.M., 1897; Ph.D., Johns Hopkins, 1900; Sc.D., Simpson Coll., Indianola, Ia., 1937; traveled and studied in Europe, 1912-13; m. Hattie Godwin, Sept. 10, 1901; 1 son, Wm. Godwin; m. 2d, Vera Worth, Aug. 9, 1933. Fellow in chemistry, Johns Hopkins U., 1899-1900; instr. chemistry Rose Poly. Inst., Terre Haute, Ind., 1900-01; prof. chemistry, De Pauw U., 1901-39, dean College of Liberal Arts, 1927-41; retired 1941; prof. chemistry, U. of Southern Calif., Los Angeles, summer 1936. Sec.-treas. Ind. Intercollegiate Conf., 1926-39. Fellow A.A.A.S., Chem. Soc. (London), Ind. Acad. Science; mem. Am. Chem. Soc., Deutsche Chemische Gesellschaft, Phi Beta Kappa. Del. Gen. Conf. M.E. Ch., 1920, 24, 32. Author: Laboratory Exercises in General Chemistry, 1909, 2d edit., 1918; An Introduction to General Chemistry, 1928; Laboratory Manual in General Chemistry, 1928. Contbr. to scientific periodicals. Home: Greencastle, Ind. Died Dec. 21, 1942.

BLANEY, Dwight, artist; b. Brookline, Mass., Jan. 24, 1865; s. Henry and Mary F. (Wood) B.; exhibited at Carnegie Inst., Pa. Acad. of Fine Arts, Corcoran Gallery, Cincinnati Mus. Mem. Boston Soc. Water Color Painters, Copley Soc. of Boston, Guild of Boston Artists. Clubs: Tavern, Odd Volumes. Home: 82 Mt. Vernon St., Boston, Mass. Died Feb. 2, 1944.

BLANKENBURG, Lucretia Longshore (Mrs. Rudolph Blankenburg), club woman; b. New Lisbon, O.; d. T. Elwood and Hannah E. (Myers) Longshore; ed. Friends' Central Sch., Phila.; m. Rudolph Blankenburg, April 18, 1867. Pres. Pa. State Suffrage Assn., 1892-1908; 1st v.p. Gen. Fedn. Women's Clubs, 1912-14 (hon. v.p.). Mem. New Century Club, Working Woman's Guild, Civic Club. Author: The Blankenburgs of Philadelphia, 1928. Address: Bellevue Stratford Hotel, Philadelphia. Died March 28, 1937.

BLANTON, Annie Webb, educator; b. Houston, Tex.; d. Thomas Lindsay and Eugenia (Webb) Blanton; B.Litt., U. of Tex., 1899, M.A., 1923; grad. work, U. of Tex., U. of Chicago and Cornell U.; Ph.D., Cornell, 1927. Teacher high sch., Austin, Tex., 1890-91; asso. prof. English, N. Tex. State Normal Coll., Denton, Tex., 1891-1918; state supt. pub. instrn., Tex., 1919-23; adjunct prof. ednl. administration, U. of Tex., 1923-26, asso. prof. and head of the rural edn. dept., 1927-28, asso. prof. ednl. adminstrn., 1928-32, prof. ednl. adminstrn. since 1933. Mem. Tex. State Teachers' Assn. (pres. 1917-18), Nat. Edn. Assn. (vice-pres., 1917, 19, 21), Am. Assn. Univ. Women, Am. Assn. Univ. Profs.; mem. Federated Business and Professional Women's Club; Eugene Field Soc. (hon.), D.A.R. (pres. of Chapter 1938), United Daughters of Confederacy, Daughters of Republic of Tex., Phi Beta Kappa, (hon), Kappa Delta Pi, Pi Lamba Theta, Pi Gamma Mu, Delta Kappa Gamma (natl. pres. 1929-33; national exec. sec. since 1933; editor Delta Kappa Gamma Bulletin since 1934). Democrat. Methodist. Member Woman's Benefit Association. Club: Denton Shakespeare (ex-president). Author: Grammar Outline, 1908; Supplementary Exercises in Punctuation and Composition; Hand Book of Information on Education in Texas; Advanced English Grammar, 1927, 28; A Study of the Salaries of Texas College Teachers; Child of the Texas One-Teacher School, 1935. Home: Rural Route 2. Office: 804 Littlefield Bldg., Austin, Tex.

BLAUVELT, Lillian Evans, prima donna soprano; b. Brooklyn, Mar. 16, 1874; d. Peter I. and Elizabeth Augusta Blauvelt; ed. pub. schs.; began mus. edn. at 5, violin study at 7; began vocal edn. at Nat. Conservatory of Music, New York, 1889; studied under M. Jacques Bouhy in New York, and Paris. Sang in concerts in France and Belgium, later in Moscow, with Philharmonic Soc.; made début in opera at Théâtre de la Monnaie, Brussels, in Mirelle; returned to U.S., singing in concerts, oratorios and recitals under Seidl, Thomas, Damrosch, etc.; sang before Queen Margherita in Italy. 1898; before Queen Victoria, June, 1899; at Handel Festival, Crystal Palace, London, June, 1900; annual tours in Europe and America since 1898. Received decoration of Order of St. Cecilia at Rome, Apr. 7, 1901 (only woman ever so honored). Sang the Coronation Ode by spl. command at Albert Hall, London, receiving the coronation medal from King Edward VII. Appeared at Royal Covent Garden, London, 1903; toured Great Britain and Ireland, 1904, Germany and Russia, 1905; starred in Rose of Alhambra (opera comique), 1906-07; toured Europe, 1908, 1909, received decorations and honors from England, Germany, France and Russia. Address: 2604 Bedford Av., Brooklyn, N.Y. Died Aug. 29, 1947.

BLAXTER, Henry Vaughan, lawyer; b. Derby, Eng., June 29, 1882; s. George Henry and Mary Louisa (Bishop) B.; came to U.S., 1885, naturalized, 1904; student St. Pauls Sch., Concord, N.H., 1898-1901; A.B., Harvard, 1905; LL.B., U. of Pittsburgh, 1907; m. Isabell Sloan Kennedy, December 16, 1908 (died July 3, 1944); children—Henry Vaughan, Dorothy Bonbright (Mrs. Richard H. Reiber), George Harold. Admitted to Pa. bar, 1907; partner in firm Lazear & Blaxter until 1917; mem. Blaxter & O'Neill, 1926-36, Blaxter, O'Neill & Houston since 1936; chmn. bd. Mackintosh-Hemphill Company; mem. board of dirs. Bareco Oil Company, Pittsburgh Business Properties, Inc., Pittsburgh Hotels, Inc., Union Nat. Bank of Pittsburgh, Universal-Cyclops Steel Corp. Served as chmn. sub-com. on lower courts of justice of Pittsburgh Civic Assn., 1913. Trustee and v.p., Children's Hosp. (Pittsburgh); Trustee Shadyside Acad.; dir Legal Aid Soc. of Pittsburgh; dir. and v.p. Pittsburgh Civic-Business Council. Regional v.p. Eastern Dist., Associated Harvard Clubs, 1935-36. Mem. Am., Pa. State and Allegheny bar assns ; asso mem Am. Iron & Steel Inst. Republican. Episcopalian. Clubs: Harvard-Yale-Princeton, Duquesne, Oakmont Country Pittsburgh Golf, Fox Chapel Golf (Pittsburgh); Harvard (New York); Rolling Rock (Ligonier, Pa.). Home: 1414 Bennington Av. Office: Oliver Bldg., Pittsburgh, Pa. Died Oct. 30, 1948.

BLEASE, Coleman Livingston, ex-senator; b. Newberry County, S.C., Oct. 8, 1868; s. Henry Horatio and Mary A. (Livingston) B.; LL.B., Georgetown U., 1889; m. Lillie B. Summers, S.C., Feb. 1890 (died 1934). Admitted to bar, 1889, and began practice with brother, Harry H., at Newberry; sr. mem. firm Blease & Dominick (Hon. Fred H.), and sr. mem. Blease & Blease. Mem. S.C. Ho. of Rep., 1890-98 (speaker pro tem, 1891-92); Dem. presdl. elector, 1896, 1900; city atty., Newberry, 1901-02; mem. S.C. Senate, 1904-08 (pres. pro tem, 1907-08); mayor of Newberry, 1910; gov. of S.C., terms 1911-13, 1913-15 (resigned, Jan. 1915 and resumed practice in Columbia, S.C.); mem. U. S. Senate, term 1925-31. Served as chmn. Dem. party, Newberry County; del. to state convs. of Dem. party many yrs. and mem. Dem. state exec. com., S.C., 18 yrs.; pres. of State Democratic Conv., 1926; del. to Dem. Nat. Conv., 1928 (com. on platform). Mem. Am., S.C. State, Newberry Co. and Richland County bar assns. Methodist. I.O.O.F. (past Grand Master and past Grand Rep.; Grand Patriarch Grand Encampment, of S.C. and rep. to Sovereign Grand Lodge); past Great Sachem, past Great Rep. Improved Order Red Men (resigned as chmn. judiciary com. and as mem. same, 1920); Great Rep. to Great Council U.S., I.O.R.M.; Moose (past Dictator Loyal Order of Moose; chmn. Com. on Resolutions at 32d Am. Conv. Supreme Lodge of the World, Mooseheart, Ill., June 1920). Past Chancellor Comdr., K. of P.; Elk; W.O.W.. Home: Columbia, S.C. Died Jan. 9, 1942.

BLEININGER, Albert Victor (blīn'ing-ẽr), chemist; b. Polling, Bavaria, July 9, 1873; s. Francis and Lina (Pfeifer) B.; prep. edn., Munich, Germany; came to U.S., 1887; shop experience in clay industries, 1889-96; B.S. in Chemistry, Ohio State U., 1901, Ceramic Engr., 1931, Lamme medal from the same univ., 1932; D.Sc., Alfred University, 1933; m. Hulda Gertrude Thomson, June 7, 1907 (died July 27, 1938); children—Edward Orton, Alice Vivien; m. 2d, Helen Thomson, Aug. 31, 1940. Instr. in ceramics, 1901-05, asst. prof., 1905-06, asso. prof., 1906-07, Ohio State U.; asst. prof. ceramics, U. of Ill., 1907-08; chief, clay products sect. U.S. Geol. Survey, 1908-10, U.S. Bureau of Standards, 1910-11; prof. and dir. dept. ceramics, U. of Ill., 1910-12; in charge of ceramics div., Nat. Bureau of Standards, Pittsburgh, 1912-20; chemist Homer Laughlin China Co. since 1920. Asst., Ohio Geol. Survey, 1900-04. Chmn. sub-com. on ceramic chemistry Nat. Research Council; chmn., research com. U.S. Potters' Assn. Mem. Sigma Xi, Acacia, Alpha Chi Sigma; fellow A.A.A.S.; mem. Am. Chem. Soc. (asst. editor Abstract Jour.), Am. Ceramic Soc. (pres. 1908; editor Trans., 1905-07). Author: The Manufacture of Hydraulic Cements, 1904. Editor Collected Works of H. A. Seger, 1903. Contbr. to periodicals on the silicate industries. Home: Newell, W.Va. Died May 19, 1946.

BLETHEN, Clarence Brettun, newspaper man; b. Portland, Me., Feb. 1, 1879; s. Alden J. and Rose A. (Hunter) B.; m. Rae Kingsley, Aug. 10, 1909; five sons. Connected with Seattle Times in various capacities since 1900, succeeding father, who died July 12, 1915, as editor and pub.; pres. Seattle Times Co. since 1921; also pres. Blethen Corp. Mustered into federal service as col. coast arty., U.S. Army, July 25, 1917; at close of war commanded 24th Arty.; brig. gen. U.S. Army, Res., 1924. Inventor and patentee of various newspaper printing processes. Home: Olympic Hotel, Seattle; and Sunnyview Farm, Medina, Wash. Died Oct. 30, 1941.

BLICHFELDT, Hans Frederik (blĭk'fĕlt), prof. emeritus; b. Denmark, Jan. 9, 1873; s. Erhard Christoffer Laurentius and Nielsine Maria (Scholer) B.; came to U.S., 1888; A.B., Stanford, 1896, A.M., 1897; Ph.D., U. of Leipzig, 1898; unmarried. Instr. in mathematics, Stanford, 1898-1901, asst. prof., 1901-06, asso. prof. 1906-13, prof., 1913-38, now emeritus. Asso. prof. Univ. of Chicago, summer, 1911; prof. Columbia Univ., summer quarters, 1924, 25. Mem. Nat. Research Council, 1924-27. Mem. A.A.A.S., Am. Math. Soc., Math. Assn. America, Nat. Acad. Sciences. Decorated Knight of Order of Dannebrog (Denmark), 1939. Author: (joint) Theory and Application of Finite Groups, 1916; Finite Collineation Groups, 1917. Contbr. to Trans. Am. Math. Soc., etc. Home: 520 W. Crescent Drive, Palo Alto, Calif. Died Nov. 16, 1945.

BLINN, Randolph, writer, editor; b. Richmond, Va., Sept. 7, 1887; s. Hobart and Amanda Randolph (Ross) B.; Ph.B., U. of Va., 1908; m. Ethel Powelson Hueston. Staff of N.Y. World, 1909-10; asso. editor Ladies' Home Jour., 1910-11; editor Stageland (weekly mag.), 1911-12; travel gathering material, 1913-14; foreign corr. Internat. News Service, 1914-16; officer in U.S. Army, 1917-20; foreign corr. Hearst publications, 1921-27; editorial writer Portland (Me.) News, 1927-28; asso. editor King Features, 1928-31; freelance writer 1931-32; Capitol staff Washington Times, 1934-35; foreign commerce officer, Shanghai, China, 1935; asst. to dir. Bureau of Foreign and Domestic Commerce, Washington, D.C., 1936-39; tech. adviser to Com. on Commerce, U.S. Senate, 1937-38; asso. dir. of pub. relations, New York World's Fair, 1939-40; Washington Corr. Baltimore News-Post since 1940. Democratic nominee for N.J. Assembly, 1941. Mem. Soc. of Colonial Wars, Sons of the Revolution, Descendants of the Signers of the Declaration of Independence, Soc. Native Virginians. Episcopalian. Clubs: National Press (Washington, D.C.); Bankers (N.Y.); Automobile (Paris). Address: 3100 Connecticut Av., Washington, D.C. Died Feb. 4, 1943.

BLISS, Collins Pechin, educator; b. Carlisle, Pa., Apr. 28, 1866; s. John Collins and Mary Newton (Pechin) B.; B.A., Princeton, 1888, M.A., 1891; Ph.B. in Arch., Columbia, 1891; spl. work, Cornell U., 1896; hon. Dr. Engring., Stevens Inst. of Tech., 1936; m. Jessamine Coon, of Cleveland, Ohio, 1898. With Gregory Furnace Co., Phila., 1891-93, Globe Iron Works (shipbuilding), Cleveland, O., 1893-96; instr. and asst. prof. mech. engring., 1896-1902, prof., 1902-30, dean of Coll. of Engring., 1930-36, dean emeritus since 1936, New York U.; pres. Engring. Index, Inc., cons. engr. in constrn., 1902-12. Trustee Robert Coll., Istambul. Mem. Am. Soc. M.E. (com. on standardization), Soc. Promotion Engring. Edn., Princeton Engring. Soc., Iota Alpha, Tau Beta Pi, Sigma Xi. Republican. Presbyterian. Clubs: Princeton, Faculty. Home: Eton Hall, Scarsdale, N.Y. Died Dec. 27, 1946.

BLISS, Cornelius Newton; b. at New York City, 1874; s. Cornelius N. (ex-sec. of interior) and Elizabeth M. (Plumer) B.; A.B., Harvard, 1897; m. Zaidee C. Cobb, Apr. 26, 1906; children—Elizabeth Addison, Cornelius N., Anthony Addison. Dir. Bankers Trust Co., New York Life Ins. Co.; trustee Met. Museum of Art; incorporator of Am. Red Cross; mem. bd. govs. (hon.), N.Y. Hosp.; dir. Milbank Memorial Fund. Dir. Met. Opera Assn., Inc. Home: Westbury, L.I., N.Y. Office: 1 Wall St., New York, N.Y. Died Apr. 5, 1949.

BLISS, Elmer Jared, shoe mfr.; b. Wrentham, Mass., Aug. 11, 1867; s. Leonard Carpenter and Eliza Crocker (Fisher) B.; student Edgartown High Sch.; m. Lina Harding, Apr. 24, 1901 (died Dec. 31, 1924); children—E. Jared, Muriel Harding. Founded Regal Shoe Co., Sept. 1, 1893 (retail stores in principal cities of U.S. and factories at Whitman, Mass.); dir. Am. Mutual Liability Ins. Co., Am. Policyholders Ins. Co., Regal Shoe Co. Mem. Two Hundred Fifty Associates, Harvard Business School; mem. advisory group of Business and Engring. Administration, Mass. Inst. Technology. D.S.M. for services in U.S. and France, World War. Republican. Episcopolian. Clubs: Edgartown Yacht, Algonquin, Norfolk Hunt. Holds 87 patents on shoe mfg. machinery, etc. Home: "Dunroving Ranch," Chilmark, Mass. Office: 10 High St., Boston, Mass. Died July 1, 1945.

BLOCK, Philip Dee, steel mfr.; b. Cincinnati, O., Feb. 16, 1871; s. Joseph and Rose (Cahn) B.; grad. Hughes High Sch., Cincinnati, 1888; m. Celia F. Leopold, June 1, 1899; children—Madeline Babette (Mrs. H. H. Straus), Philip Dee. With Block-Pollak Iron Co., Chicago and Cincinnati, 1888-93; made v.p. and treas. Inland Steel Co., 1893, now chmn. exec. com.; dir. Buffalo Steel Co., Red Top Steel Post Co., First Nat. Bank, Chicago. Mem. Art. Inst., Chicago. Clubs: Mid-Day, Standard, Lake Shore Country. Home: 1525 Astor St. Office: First Nat. Bank Bldg., Chicago, Ill. Died June 29, 1942.

BLOCKER, William Preston, consul general; b. Hondo, Medina County, Texas, Sept. 30, 1892; s. Vincular Harwood and Daisy D. B.; ed. public schs., prep. schs., and normal course; studied law under law firm; m. Joy Ovada, Feb. 29, 1916; 1 son, William Johnston. Pub. sch. teacher and traveling salesman until 1912; apptd. vice and dept. consul at Ciudad Porfirio Diaz, Mex., July 18, 1913; vice consul and consul at Piedras Negras, 1915-23; consul at Guaymas, 1923-24; apptd. foreign service officer, July 1, 1924; consul at Mazatlan, 1925-29, at Juárez, 1929-35, at Santiago de Cuba, 1935-36; consul at Monterrey, 1936; 1st sec. at Mexico City, Aug.-Nov. 1936, and Aug.-Oct. 1937; consul Tampico, Apr. 1938, at Monterrey, May 1938, consul gen. Cuidad Juárez, since 1938; del. Inter-Am. Travel Congress, Mexico City, 1941. Democrat. Episcopalian. Mason. Address: U.S. Consulate. Ciudad Juárez, Mexico. Died Feb. 28, 1947.

BLOOD, Henry Hooper, governor; b. Kaysville, Utah, Oct. 1, 1872; s. William and Jane Wilkie (Hooper) B.; student Brigham Young U., Provo, U.; m. Minnie A. Barnes, June 4, 1896; children—Russell H., Mrs. David J. Ellison, Alan B., Evelyn (Mrs. Robert B. Sims). Began as clerk in Kaysville Cooperative Mercantile Instn.; mem. faculty Brigham Young Coll., Logan, Utah, 1904-05; became mgr. Kaysville Milling Co., 1905; pres. Kaysville-Layton Milling Co., Kaysville Canning Corp.; dir. Layton Sugar Co., John R. Barnes Co., Kaysville Coöperative; city recorder, Kaysville, 1893; county treas. Davis County, 1896-1900; mem. Pub. Utilities Commn. of Utah, 1917-21, Utah State Rd. Commn., 1922-32 (chmn. 1925-32); gov. of Utah since 1932. Chmn. Davis County Bd. Edn., 1911-18; pres. Western Assn. State Highway Officials, 1927-31, Am. Assn. State Highway Officials, 1930-31; chairman executive committee Western Govs. Conf. Pres. North Davis Stake, 1915-37; pres. Calif. Mission since 1941. Mem. Salt Lake City Chamber of Commerce. Democrat. Mem. Ch. of Latter Day Saints (bishop Kaysville Ward, 1907-15). Clubs: Rotary, Lions, Timpanogos, Alta. Home: Kaysville, Utah. Address: State Capitol, Salt Lake City, Utah. Died June 19, 1942.

BLOOM, Charles James, pediatrician; b. New Orleans, La., October 23, 1886; Albert and Rose B.; B.Sc., Tulane University, New Orleans, 1908, M.D., 1912; grad. study, Harvard, 1914-16; m. Gladys Marie Reiss, Jan. 9, 1919; children—Charles James, Albert Reiss, Gladys Marie. Instr. zoölogy, Tulane U., 1907, lecturer biology, 1908; interne Touro Infirmary, New Orleans, 1912-14; pathol. interne Floating Hosp. for Children, also Infants' Hosp., Boston, 1914-16; instr. undergrad. med. dept., Tulane U., 1916-20, prof. pediatrics and in charge post-grad. med. dept., 1916-37; prof. pediatrics and head dept., post-grad. med. dept., La. State U., 1937-39. Formerly senior pediatrician Presbyterian Hosp., Lying-In Hosp., New Orleans Dispensary for Women and Children, also physician in charge at St. Vincent's Orphanage, 7th St. Protestant Orphans' Home, sr. pediatrician Hotel Dieu, visiting pediatrician Episcopal Home for Girls, examining pediatrician Jewish Fed. Camp; now sr. visiting pediatrist Charity Hosp.; pediatrician in charge 7th St. Protestant Orphans' Home; sr. pediatrician, dept. of pediatrics, Touro Infirmary, since 1914, mem. exec. com. and sec. of staff since 1943; co-chief dept. pediatrics Mercy Hosp.; cons. pediatrist Memorial Home, French Hosp., Flint Goodrich Hosp.; physician in charge Metairie Park Country Day School; mem. faculty Southern Pediatric Seminar, Saluda, N.C.; founder and gen. chmn. Magnolia School. Commd. 1st lt. Med. Res. Corps, World War. Mem. bd. Pure Milk Soc., New Orleans. Mem. A.M.A., La. State Med. Soc., La Salle Parish Med. Soc., 6th Dist. Med. Soc., Southern Med. Assn., La. State Pediatric Soc. (pres. 1935), Am. Coll. Physicians, Am. Acad. Pediatrics, Mental Hygiene Soc. (dir.), Tulane Alumni Association (exec. com. since 1943), Beta Theta Pi, Nu Sigma Nu, Kappa Delta Phi, Alpha Omega Alpha, Stars and Bars. Democrat. Catholic. Author: Care and Feeding of Babies in Warm Climates, 1922, revised, 1937. Contbr. many professional articles to mags. Home: 36 Versailles Blvd. Office: 3439 Prytania St., New Orleans, La.* Died Aug. 29, 1947.

BLOOM, Sol, congressman; b. Pekin, Ill., Mar. 9, 1870; s. Garrison and Sara B.; moved with family to San Francisco, Calif., in infancy; ed. pub. schs.; m. Evelyn Hechheimer, 1897; 1 dau., Vera. Successively in newspaper, theatrical and music pub. business; supt. constrn. Midway Plaisance, Chicago Expn., 1893; settled in N.Y. City, 1903, and engaged in real estate and constrn. business; capt. N.Y. Reserves, 1917; mem. 68th to 81st Congresses (1923-51), 20th N.Y. Dist., Chmn. Com. on Foreign Affairs; dir. U.S. George Washington Bicentennial Com.; dir. gen. U.S. Constitution Sesquicentennial Com.; chmn. Com. on Celebration of 150th Anniversary U.S. Supreme Court. U.S del. UNRRA Conf., Atlantic City, U.N. Confs. at San Francisco, London, N.Y. City; signer of U.N. Charter; del. Inter-Am. Conf., Rio de Janeiro, 1947; 1947; dir., U.S. commr. New York World's Fair, 1939. Hon. mem. Vets. Foreign Wars, Mason (32°, Shriner). Home: 310 Riverside Drive, N.Y.; 1930 Columbia Rd. N.W., Washington, D.C. Office: New House Office Bldg., Washington, D.C. Died Mar. 7, 1949.

BLOOMFIELD, Leonard, linguist; b. Chicago, Ill., Apr. 1, 1887; s. of Sigmund and Carola (Buber) B.; A.B., Harvard, 1906; post-grad. work, U. of Wis., 1906-08, U. of Chicago, 1908-09, U. of Leipzig, 1913-14, U. of Göttingen, 1914; Ph.D., U. of Chicago, 1909; m. Alice Sayers, Mar. 18, 1909; children—Roger Montour, James Sheldon. Asst. in German, U. of Wis., 1906-08, U. of Chicago, 1908-09; instr. in German, U. of Cincinnati, 1909-10, Univ. of Ill. 1910-13; asst. prof. comparative philology and German, U. of Ill., 1913-21; prof. German and linguistics, Ohio State U., 1921-27; prof. Germanic philology, U. of Chicago, 1927-40; Sterling prof. of linguistics, Yale U., since 1940 Asst ethnologist, Canadian Department of Mines, summer 1925. Mem. American Assn. for Advancement of Science, Linguistic Soc. of America, Royal Danish Acad. of Scis., others. Author: Introduction to the Study of Language, 1914; Tagalog Texts with Grammatical Analysis, 1917; First German Book, 1923, 1928; Menomini Texts, 1928; Sacred Stories of the Sweet Grass Cree, 1930; Language, 1933; Plains Cree Texts, 1934; Linguistic Aspects of Science, 1939; various lang. manuals for the Armed Forces. Contbr to philol. jours. Address: Yale University. New Haven, Conn. Died Apri. 18, 1949.

BLOOMINGDALE, Charles, writer; b. Phila., Mar. 16, 1868; s. Charles and Caroline Cadette (Elfelt) B.; A.B., U. of Pa., 1887; m. Katherine Fleck, 1898. Printer, advertiser, and newspaper man, since 1892. Wrote daily articles for Philadelphia Press from Atlantic City for 4 yrs. under pen-name "Karl," also edited dept. entitled "Up the Street and Down Again." Contbr. vers de société for Puck, Judge, Saturday Evening Post, and many other papers under pen-name "Karl"; owned and edited Footlights and Stageland. Clubs: Pen and Pencil, Press. Author: Mr., Miss and Mrs., 1899; A Failure, 1904. Home: 5221 Pine St. Office: Welsbach Co., Broad and Arch Sts., Philadelphia. Died Feb. 24, 1942.

BLOW, Allmand M., vice-pres. Amerada Petroleum Corp.; b. Leadville, Colo., Oct. 9, 1891; s. A.A. and Jennie (Goodell) B.; student Va. Mil. Inst., 1906-10, Met.E., Columbia Sch. of Mines, 1913; m. Dorothy Deneen, Apr. 20, 1918; 1 dau., Frances D. With the Amerada Petroleum Corp., Tulsa, Okla., since 1920, v.p. since 1928. Mem. Am. Inst. Mining Engrs., Am. Petroleum Inst., Midcontinent Oil & Gas Assn., Soc. of the Cincinnati. Home: 2101 E. 25th Pl. Office: Beacon Bldg., Tulsa, Okla. Died March 21, 1948; buried in Hollywood Cemetery Richmond, Va.

BLUE, Burdette, pres. Indian Territory Illuminating Oil Co.; b. Pleasanton, Kan., Jan. 3, 1886; s. George Frederick and Mattie (Gibson) B.; LL.B., U. of Kan., 1905; m. Violet Catherine Kroenert, Oct. 12, 1911; children—David Burdette, John Frederick (dec.). Admitted to Okla. bar, 1907; practiced in Bartlesville, Okla., until 1917, also served as city atty. 9 yrs.; apptd. gen. counsel Indian Territory Illuminating Oil Co., 1917, v.p. and gen. counsel, 1919, v.p. and gen. mgr., 1926, pres. and gen. mgr., 1935-41; now in gen. practice law. Chmn. Oil Production Mid-Continent Area under NRA. Mem. Am. and Okla. State bar assns., Phi Kappa Psi. Mason (32°). Clubs: Kansas City, Tulsa, Oklahoma, Hillcrest Country. Home: Sophian Plaza Apts. Office: Nat. Bank of Tulsa Bldg., Tulsa, Okla. Died May 17, 1943.

BLUE, Rupert, sanitarian; b. Richmond County, N.C., May 30, 1868; s. John G. and Annie M. (Evans) B.; U. of Va., 1889-90; M.D., U. of Md., 1892, D.Sc., 1909; grad. London School Tropical Medicine, 1910; D.Sc., U. of Wis., 1913; Dr. Pub. Health, U. of Mich., 1913; unmarried. Interne, 1892, asst. surgeon, 1893, passed asst. surgeon, 1897, surgeon, 1909, surgeon-gen., 1912-20, U.S. Pub. Health Service. Was in charge of operations in eradication of bubonic plague in San Francisco, 1903-04; served through the epidemic of yellow fever in New Orleans, 1905; dir. sanitation of Jamestown Expn., 1907; dir. 2d campaign against bubonic plague, San Francisco, 1907-08. U.S. del. Internat. Med. Congress, Buenos Aires, Argentina, 1910; U.S. del. Internat. Office Public Hygiene, Paris, France, 1920-23, for the revision of the Internat. Sanitary conv. of 1912; U.S. del. to 3d Decennial Revision of Internat. Nomenclature of Diseases; advisor to U.S. Mission Lausanne Peace Conf., 1922-23; Am. del. Opium Conf., League of Nations, Geneva, 1923. In charge activities of U.S. Pub. Health Service in Europe, 1920-23. Fellow A.M.A. (pres. 1916), Am. Pub. Health Assn.; hon. fellow Am. Coll. Surgeons; mem. Assn. Mil. Surgeons of U.S. (pres. 1915-17), San Francisco County Med. Soc. (hon.), Am. Soc. Tropical Medicine, Nat. Soc. Social Sciences, Med. Vets. World War, S.R., Soc. of War of 1812, Phi Beta Kappa (Va.). Chmn. com. on sanitation, Gen. Med. Bd., Council Nat. Defense, 1917-19. Chevalier Legion of Honor (France). Clubs: Army and Navy, Chevy Chase (Washington, D.C.). Home: 1808 I St. N.W., Washington, D.C. Died Apr. 12, 1948.

BLUM, Edward Charles, merchant; b. N.Y. City, Feb. 24, 1863; s. Adolphe and Ida (Deutsch) B.; ed. pvt. schs. and lycées, France; m. Florence Abraham, June 12, 1894; children—Mrs. Alice B. Taliaferro, Robert E. Chmn. bd. Abraham & Straus, Inc.; v.p. Abrast Realty Co.; pres. Federated Dept. Stores, Inc.; dir. Equitable Life Assurance Soc. of U.S., New York Worlds Fair, 1939; trustee Dime Savings Bank, Kings County Trust Co. Chmn. bd. Brooklyn Inst. Arts and Sciences; ex-pres. Jewish Hosp.; vice chmn. N.Y. State Probation Commn.; chmn. Municipal Art Commn. Mem. Nat. Econ. League (nat council), French Inst. in U.S.A., France-America Soc., N.Y. State Chamber of Commerce, Brooklyn Chamber Commerce (3d v.p.), Nat. Inst. Social Sciences. Decorated Chevalier of the Legion of Honor (France); Officer of the Order of Leopold II (Belgium); Great Silver Cross (Austria). Clubs: Rembrandt, Unity, Brooklyn, Montauk, Bay Shore Yacht, 20th Century, National Republican. Office: 422 Fulton St., Brooklyn, N.Y. Died Nov. 20, 1946; buried in Salem Fields Cemetery, Brooklyn.

BLUMENTHAL, Sidney, chmn. bd. Sidney Blumenthal & Co.; b. New York, N.Y., June 17, 1863; s. August and Bertha B.; ed. Quaker sch., New York, 3 yrs., pvt. sch., Germany, 6 yrs., Packard Commercial Sch., New York, 6 months; m. Lucy A. Picard, Apr. 1903; children—Andre, Mrs. Doris Stein, Yvonne L. Mem. firm A. & S. Blumenthal, 1882-99; pres. Sidney Blumenthal & Co., 1899-1934, chmn. bd. since 1934. Mem. N.Y. State Chamber of Commerce, Commerce and Industry Assn. of N.Y., Ednl. Alliance of N.Y. (hon. dir.), Acad. of Polit. Science, Met. Mus. of Art, Am. Mus. of Natural History, Mus. of Modern Art, N.Y. Zool. Soc., N.Y. Bot. Gardens, Am. Inst., Am. Fed. of Arts, The Navy League. Clubs: Advertising, Nat. Republican. Home: Florival Farm, Peekskill, N.Y. Office: 1 Park Av., New York, N.Y. Died Jan. 5, 1948.

BLY, John Marius, college dean; born of naturalized Am. parents, Ullensvang, Hardanger, Norway, Nov. 11, 1885; s. Haldor and Ingeleiv (Sexe) B.; brought to U.S., 1887; B.A., St. Olaf Coll., Northfield, Minn., 1912; student U. of Minn., 1912-14 and 1927-28; grad. Luther Sem., St. Paul, 1915; student in Coll. of Chinese Studies, Peking, China, 1915-16; M.A., Columbia, 1924; student Harvard, summer 1931; m. Minnie Saboe, June 26, 1918; children—Marjorie Ingeleiv, Chauncey Goodrich, Theodore Saboe, Haldor Marius, James (dec.), Patricia (dec.). Missionary to China, 1915-27; educational director Lutheran United Mission and supt. Boys' High Sch., Sinyang, China, 1916-27; exec. sec. Honan (China) Christian Ednl. Assn., 1918-27; prof. of psychology, St. Olaf Coll., 1927-39, prof. history of East Asia since 1940, regisrar 1935-46; dean of academic adminstrn. since 1946. Mem. Am. Assn. Collegiate Registrars, N. Central Assn. Coll. Registrars (pres.), Assn. Minn. Colls. (sec.), Fgn. Policy Assn., Minn. Acad. of Science, Am. Psychol. Assn., Phi Delta Kappa. Lutheran. Home: Northfield, Minn. Died Feb. 6, 1947.

BLYTHE, Samuel George, writer; b. Geneseo, N.Y., May 19, 1868; s. Samuel H. and Catherine (Houston) B.; ed. Geneseo State Normal Sch.; m. Carolyn Hamilton Oakes, Sept. 19, 1888; one son, Stuart Oakes (q.v.). Served as mng. editor, Buffalo Express, 1893-96; editor in chief, Buffalo Courier and Enquirer, 1897-98; mng. editor Cosmopolitan Magazine, 1899; chief Washington corr. New York World, 1900-07; chmn. standing com. of corrs., 1906-07; staff writer Saturday Evening Post since 1907. Clubs: National Press, Gridiron of Washington, D.C. (pres. 1907), Bohemian, Family (San Francisco, Calif.). Author: We Have With Us Tonight, 1909; Cutting It Out, 1912; Fun of Getting Thin, 1912; The Making of a Newspaper Man, 1912; The Price of Place, 1913; The Old Game, 1914; The Fakers, 1915; Western Warwick, 1916; Hunkins, 1919; The Manikin Makers, 1921; Keeping Fit at Fifty, 1923; A Calm Review of a Calm Man, 1923; The Revolt of Peter Purdy, 1926; The Bootleggers, 1928; Reformers, Ltd., 1928; Get Rid of That Fat, 1929. Editorial supervisor, "Cavalcade of the Golden West," 1939, and "America—Cavalcade of a Nation," 1940, produced at the San Francisco Internat. Expn., 1939, 1940. Address: Box 550, Monterey, Calif. Died July 17, 1947.

BOARDMAN, Mabel Thorp, American Red Cross; b. Cleveland, O.; d. William Jarvis and Florence (Sheffield) Boardman; ed. pvt. schs., Cleveland and New York, and in Europe; hon. A.M., Yale, 1911; LL.D., Western Reserve U., Smith Coll., George Washington U.; L.H.D., Converse Coll. Formerly mem. Central committee and secretary American Red Cross; now mem. bd. incorporators. U.S. delegate 8th, 9th, 15th, 16th, Internat. Red Cross confs., London, Washington, Tokyo, London. Decorated by King of Sweden with personal Order of Merit, 1909; gold crown, Italy, 1909; decorated by Emperor of Japan with Fifth Order of Crown, 1912; Medal of Merit, 1st Class (French); Red Cross decorations from Portugal, Serbia, Chile; Legion of Honor (France), 1935; Hon. Auxiliary Commandos, British St. John's Ambulance Assn. Episcopalian. Clubs: Chevy Chase, Sulgrave (Washington); Colony (New York), Murray Bay (Can.). Author: Under The Red Cross Flag, 1915. Home: 1801 P St., Washington. Died Mar. 17, 1946; buried in Cathedral of St. Peter and St. Paul, Mount Saint Albans, Washington.

BOAS, Franz, anthropologist; b. Minden, Westphalia, July 9, 1858; s. M. and Sophie (Meyer) B.; univs. of Heidelberg, Bonn and Kiel, 1877-81; Ph.D., Univ. of Kiel, Germany, 1881, M.D., honoris causa; LL.D., Sc.D., Oxford U., Clark U., Howard U. and Columbia Univ.; hon. citizen, honoris causa, Univ. of Bonn, Graz; m. Marie A. E. Krackowizer, 1887; children—Mrs. Helene Marie Yampolski, Ernst P., Mrs. Marie Franziska Michelson. Explored Baffin Land, 1883-84; asst. Royal Ethnog. Museum, Berlin, and docent of geography, Univ. of Berlin, 1885-86; investigations in N.A., Mexico, Porto Rico, 1886-1931; docent anthropology, Clark U., 1888-92; chief asst. dept. of anthropology, Chicago Expn., 1892-95; lecturer physical anthropology, Columbia U., 1896-99, prof. anthropology, 1899-1937, prof. emeritus since 1937; asst. curator, 1896; curator, 1901-05, dept. anthropology Am. Mus. Natural History; hon. philologist, Bureau Am. Ethnology, 1901-19. In Mexico, 1910-12; hon. prof. Nat. Mus. of Archeology, Mexico; corr. sec. Germanistic Soc. America, 1914; pres. Emergency Soc. German and Austrian Science, 1927; nat. chmn. Com. for Democracy and Intellectual Freedom, 1939-40, hon. chmn. since 1940; mem. Nat. Acad. Sciences, Am. Philos. Soc., Am. Antiq. Soc., Am. Folklore Soc. (editor 1908-25, pres. 1931); fellow A.A.A.S. (v.p. 1895, 1907; pres. 1931), N.Y. Acad. Sciences (pres. 1910), Am. Anthrop. Soc. (pres. 1907, 1908), Am. Acad. Arts and Sciences; honorary mem. Anthropology Soc. Vienna, Société des Américanistes, Paris, Senckenbergische Gesellschaft, Frankfort, Geog. Soc. Göteborg, Geographical Soc. Hamburg, Geographical Society of Würzburg; honorary fellow Anthropol. Inst. of Great Britain and Ireland, Folk Lore Soc. of London; cor. mem. Inst. for History of Civilization (Oslo), Anthrop. socs. of Berlin (until 1939), Brussels, Florence, Moscow, Paris, Rome, Stockholm, Washington, and of Am. Numis. Soc., German Anthropol. Soc., Prussian, Munich, Danish, Vienna Acad. Sciences, Leopoldina Acad. Halle, Soc. for Oriental Lang., Frankfort; senator Deutsche Akademie, Munich. Author: The Growth of Children, 1896, 1904; Changes in Form of Body of Descendants of Immigrants, 1911; The Mind of Primitive Man, 1911, 1938; Kultur und Rasse, 1913; Primitive Art, 1927; Anthrop. and Modern Life, 1928-38; General Anthropology (with others), 1938; Race, Language and Culture, 1940; Dakota Grammar (with Ella Deloria), 1941; also publs. on anthropometry, linguistics and anthropology of North America. Editor Jesup N. Pacific Expdn., Internat. Jour. Am. Linguistics, etc. Home: Grantwood, Bergen County, N.J. Address: Columbia Univ., New York, N.Y. Died Dec. 21, 1942.

BOCK, Otto, judge; b. Milwaukee, Wis., Feb. 21, 1881; s. William and Wilhelmina (Koehler) B.; LL.B., John Marshall Law Sch., Chicago, 1908; m. Hilda Schabarum, Aug. 24, 1911; children—William Karl, Richard Walter, Paul Kenneth, Edward James, Thomas Frederick. Admitted to Colo. bar, 1909, bar of U.S. Supreme Court, 1930, Interstate Commerce Commn., 1930; began practice in Denver; asst. U.S. atty. for Colo., 1914-21; mem. Pub. Utilities Commn. of Colo., 1924-31 (chmn. 4 yrs.); judge 2d Judicial Dist. of Colo., 1933-38; mem. Supreme Court of Colo. since Jan. 1939; lecturer on public utility law, Westminster Law Sch., Denver; public rep. Mountain States Regional Labor Bd. Mem. Dem. Exec. Com., City and County of Denver, 1922-28; mem. Dem. State Exec. Com. of Colo., 1928-30; candidate for mayor of Denver, 1931. Mem. Am., Colo. and Denver bar assns., Colo. Hist. Soc.; hon. mem. Phi Alpha Delta. Democrat. Lutheran. Clubs: Law (past pres.), Denver Athletic, City. Home: 3059 W. 34th Av. Address: State Capitol Bldg., Denver, Colo. Died Aug. 14, 1942.

BÖCKMAN, Marcus Olaus (bŭk′măn), theologian; b. Langesund, Norway, Jan. 9, 1849; s. Frederik and Nicoline (Bodom) B.; grad. Christiania U., Norway, 1867 (passed examen philosophicum, 1868); theol. dept., 1875; D.D., Muhlenberg Coll., Pa., 1900; LL.D., St. Olaf Coll., Northfield, Minn., 1925; Litt.D., Luther Coll., Decorah, Ia., 1930; m. Leonharda Holby, 1875 (died 1888); m. 2d, Inga Holby, 1896 (died 1937). Ordained Luth. ministry, Christiania, 1875; pastor Goodhue County, Minn., 1875-86; prof. theology, Luthersk Presteskole, Northfield, Minn., 1886-90; one of editors Lutherske Vidnesbyrd, 1888-90; at Augsburg Sem., Minneapolis, 1890-93; pres. and prof. theology, Sem. of United Norwegian Luth. Ch., St. Paul, 1893-1917; pastor Wartburg Congregation, St. Anthony Park, Minn., 1902-15; pres. Luth. Theol. Sem., 1917-30, pres. emeritus and prof. theology, 1930-36. Knight Commander Order of St. Olaf, Norway, 1912. Address: 1415 W. Grantham St., St. Paul, Minn. Died July 21, 1942.

BOE, Lars Wilhelm (bō), coll. pres.; b. Calumet, Mich., Dec. 27, 1875; s. Rev. Nils E. and Anna D. (Reque) B.; A.B., St. Olaf Coll., Northfield, Minn., 1898; grad. United Luth. Ch. Sem., Minneapolis, 1901; D.D., Roanoke Coll., Salem, Va., 1921; LL.D., Wittenberg Coll., Springfield, O., 1924; m. Helga L. Jacobson, 1909; children—Esther Vivikke, Edel Ruth Margaret. Ordained Lutheran ministry, 1901; pastor Chickasaw County, Iowa, 1901-04, Forest City, Ia., 1904-15; pres. Waldorf Coll. (prep. sch.), Forest City, 1904-15; gen. sec. bd. trustees and bd. regents, United Norwegian Luth. Ch., 1915-17; gen. sec. bd. trustees and bd. edn., Norwegian Luth. Ch., 1917-18; pres. St. Olaf Coll., Northfield, Minn., since Sept. 1, 1918. Mem. Nat. Luth. Council; mem. Continuation Com. Luth. World Conv. Mem. Ho. of Rep., Ia., 1909-11, Senate, 1913-15. Decorated Order of St. Olaf, by King of Norway, 1926; apptd. Commander, 1940. Pres. State Council of Minn. Colls. since 1937; vice-pres. Norwegian Am. Hist. Assn. since 1939. Home: Northfield, Minn. Died Dec. 27, 1942.

BOETTCHER, Charles (bĕch′ẽr), capitalist; b. Cellada, Germany, Apr. 8, 1852; ed. in Germany; m. Fannie A. Cowan; children—Claude K., Ruth (Mrs. A. E. Humphreys, Jr.). Came to U.S., 1869, and engaged in hardware business at Cheyenne, Wyo.; in mercantile business at Greeley, Ft. Collins and Boulder, Colo., 1872-74; mining, banking and mercantile business, Leadville, Colo., 1879-90; settled in Denver, 1890, and associated, 1900, with C. S. Morey and others in organizing Great Western Sugar Co.; also an organizer Western Packing Co., Colo. Cement Co., Ideal Cement Co.; now pres. Ideal Cement Co., chmn. bd. Denver Tramway Co.; v.p. Great Western Sugar Co., Cache La Poudre Co. Clubs: Denver, Denver Athletic, Denver Country. Office: Ideal Cement Co., Denver, Colorado. Died July 2, 1948.

BOFINGER, D. T., pres. The Great Atlantic & Pacific Tea Co. of America. Address: 420 Lexington Av., N.Y. City. Deceased.

BOGERT, George H., artist; b. New York, 1864; s. Henry and Helen Anderson (Evans) B.; first studied art under Thomas Eakins; went to France, 1884, and studied under Raphael Collins, Aimé Morot and Puvis de Chavannes. Webb prize, 1898; 1st Hallgarten prize, Nat. Acad. Design, 1899; bronze medal, Paris Expn., 1900; hon. mention, Pa. Acad. Fine Arts, 1892, A.N.A.; mem. Soc. Landscape Painters, New York, Pa. Aca. Fine Arts. Address: Lotos Club, New York, N.Y. Died Dec. 12, 1944.

BOGUSLAWSKI, Moissaye (bō-gōō-slăf′skē), pianist; b. Nov. 1, 1887; s. Frank (flutist), and Anna (Niemkowski) B.; ed. grammar schools of Chicago;

languages self-taught, studied piano with Rudolph Ganz; hon. Mus. Doc., Chicago Coll. of Music, 1931; m. Edna Rena Good (pianiste), Dec. 1907 (died May 31, 1925); 1 son, Myron Good; m. 2d, Lillian Stumbaugh, pianiste, 1926. Director piano dept., Kansas City (Mo.) Conservatory, 1909-19; prof. piano, Bush Conservatory, Chicago, 1919-21; head prof. piano, Chicago Mus. Coll., since Sept. 27, 1921; organizer, 1931, since pres. Boguslawski Coll. of Music. Co-editor University Course of Music Study. Toured principal cities of U.S. as piano soloist; appeared with Met. Opera House Orchestra, at Carnegie Hall, New York, May 24, 1919, also with Detroit and Minneapolis Symphony orchestras. Has developed a method of musical therapeutics as a mind restorative for insanity. Author: "Piano-Play" Books (10 vols. for child piano study). Editor: Moderne Edition (piano music). Lecturer on "Musical Classics for the Masses." Home: 210 E. Pearson St. Office: 323 S. Wabash Av., Chicago, Ill. Died Aug. 30, 1944.

BOHLEN, Francis Hermann (bō'lĕn), lawyer, educator; b. Chestnut Hill, Pa., July 31, 1868; s. John and Priscilla (Murray) B.; grad. St. Paul's Sch., Concord, N.H., 1884; LL.B., U. of Pa., 1892, LL.D., 1930; m. Margaret Tiers Woodville, Oct. 17, 1892; children—Priscilla (Mrs. Stephen Bonsall Brooks), Francis Hermann, Mary Ellen (Mrs. Richard Tilghman); m. 2d, Ingrid Kleen, June 23, 1913; 1 son, John. W. A. fellow U. of Pa. Law Sch., 1893-95, lecturer, 1898-1901, asst. prof. law, 1901-05, prof. of law, 1905-14. Algernon Sydney Biddle prof., 1914-25, 1928-38, prof. emeritus since 1938; Langdell prof. law, Harvard, 1925-28. Sec. Industrial Accident Com. State of Pa., 1911-15; counsel to Workmen's Compensation Bd., Pa., 1915-22, and to State Workmen's Ins. Fund, 1915-23; former dir. Pa. Wire Glass Co. Dir. Assn. against Prohibition Amendment, 1931. Mem. Delta Psi. Author: Cases on Torts, 1915; Studies in the Law of Torts; also essays on Evidence and Workmen's Compensation. Reporter Law of Torts for Am. Law Institute, 1923. Address: 1301 Montgomery Av., Wynnewood, Pa. Died Dec. 9, 1942.

BOHN, W(illiam) Frederick (bōn), ednl. exec.; b. St. Louis, Mo., Aug. 24, 1878; s. William Ferrel and Ellen (Frisbie) B.; A.B., Oberlin Coll., 1900, A.M., 1908; D.B., Oberlin Grad. Sch. of Theology, 1905; D.D., Bates Coll., 1921; m. Eva Beardsley, Nov. 28, 1901. Ordained Congl. ministry, 1902; sec. to pres. Oberlin Coll., 1905-13, sec. bureau of appmts., 1906-15, asst. to pres., 1913-44, asst. emeritus, since 1944. Director Oberlin Savings Bank Co. Chmn. bd. trustees Oberlin-Shansi Memorial Assn. Decorated L'Ordre du Jade, for promoting international friendship, Republic of China, 1936. Member Ohio Society of New York, Sons of Am. Revolution. Independent Republican. Clubs: Exchange, Oberlin Golf. Home: 285 Oak St., Oberlin, O. Died Dec. 21, 1947.

BOISSEVAIN, Charles Hercules (bwäs-văn), physician; b. Amsterdam, Holland, Oct. 18, 1893; s. Charles Ernest Henri and Maria Barbera (Pijnappel) B.; grad. Gymnasium, Amsterdam, 1911; M.D., U. of Amsterdam, 1919; m. Countess Marie Theresa Zwetana von Hartenan, 1925; m. 2d, Ruth Davis Dangler, 1928; children—Menso, Maria Barbera. Came to U.S. 1923, naturalized, 1930. Research asso. Institut Pasteur de Brabant, Brussels, 1921-23; visiting research prof., Colo. Coll., Colorado Springs, since 1924; lab. dir. Colo. Foundation for Research in Tuberculosis since 1924; capt. Sanitary Corps, U.S. Army. Serving as maj., U.S. Army Med. Corps; overseas since 1944. Mem. A.M.A., Soc. for exptl. Biol. and Medicine. Clubs: Cheyenne Mountain Country (Colorado Springs); University (Chicago). Home: 16 Fifth St., Broadmoor, Colorado Springs, Colo. Died Oct. 18, 1946.

BOLAND, Patrick J., congressman; b. Scranton, Pa.; s. Christopher T. and Frances (Biglin) B.; ed. St. Thomas Coll., Scranton; m. Sarah Jennings, Nov. 24, 1908; children—Francis Joseph, John Jennings, Lenore, Christopher, Eileen; m. 2d, Veronica Barrett, Oct. 27, 1931; children—Patrick J., Eugene. Began work as a carpenter; now mem. firm of Boland Bros., gen. contractors. Mem. 72d to 77th Congresses (1931-43), 11th Pa. Dist. Former mem. City Council, Scranton, and county commr., Lackawanna County, Pa. Democrat. Mem. Knights of Columbus, Knights of St. George, Lackawanna Bowling Assn., B.P.O. Elks. Club: Good Fellowship. Home: 734 Clay Av., Scranton, Pa. Died May 18, 1942.

BOLDT, Hermann Johannes (bōlt), gynecologist; b. nr. Berlin, Germany, June 24, 1856; s. Hermann and Amalie (Krüger) B.; came to U.S., 1865; ed. public grammar and high schs.; studied and practiced pharmacy; M.D., Univ. Med. Coll. (New York U.), 1879; m. Hedwig Krüger, 1891. In practice since 1879; since 1891 has confined practice to gynecology; prof. gynecology, N.Y. Post-Grad. Med. Sch. and Hosp. (now post-grad. dept. of Columbia U.), 1890-1923; now prof. emeritus; was cons. gynecologist, Stuyvesant Polyclinic, Post Graduate, Beth Israel, St. Vincent's and Union hosps.; retired, 1929. Extensive investigator into physiol. action of cocaine and gynecol. pathology. Inventor of various gynecol. instruments and an operating table for abdominal surgery which received medal at Paris Expn., 1900, and also a modern examining table for office work. Fellow Am. Coll. Surgeons (founder mem. and former mem. bd. govs.); hon. mem. Am. Gynecol. Soc., Am. Gynecol. Club, Westchester Surg. Soc.; mem. Nat. Soc. of Sciences, N.Y. Acad. Sciences, Internat. Gynecol. Soc. and Obstet. Soc. (ex-pres.), N.Y. Acad. Medicine (ex-chmn. gynecol. sect.), Southern Surg. Soc., Mil. Surgeons U.S.A., Royal Soc. of Medicine (London), Gynecol. Soc. of Germany; hon. mem., ex-pres. German Med. Soc. (New York); hon. mem. Gynecol. Soc. of Great Britain, Gynecol. Soc. of Germany. His only child, Hermann J., Jr., 1st lt. 102d Inf., was killed in France, July 20, 1918, while on vol. duty on hazardous mission as aerial observer attached to 1st Am. Escadrille; was awarded citation and Croix de Guerre with palm by order of General Petain. Home: (winter) Hotel Albemarle, St. Petersburg, Fla. Address: 29 Greenridge Av., White Plains, N.Y. Died Jan. 12, 1943.

BOLSTER, Wilfred, judge; b. Roxbury, Mass., Sept. 13, 1866; s. Solomon Alonzo and Sarah Jane (Gardner) B.; A.B., Harvard U., 1888, A.M., 1891, LL.B., 1891; m. Jeanie Tolman Pond, Oct. 4, 1893; children—Philip Wilfred, Robert Pond, Gardner Thurston. Began practice of law, Boston, 1891; mem. Boston Sch. Bd., 1901-03; spl. justice Municipal Court of Boston, 1904-06, chief justice, 1906-39, retired; chmn. Central and Boston legal advisory bds., 1917-18; mem. Mass. Judicial Council since 1930; chmn. Mass. Ballot Law Commn., 1940. Fellow Am. Acad. Arts and Sciences. Republican. Clubs: Union of Boston. Home: 44 Audubon Rd., Wellesley, Mass. Died May 3, 1947.

BOLTON, Reginald Pelham, engring. expert; b. London, Eng., Oct. 5, 1856; s. Rev. James and Lydia Louisa (Pym) B.; ed. pvt. schs.; m. Kate Alice Behenna, May 4, 1878; children—Ivy, Guy; m. 2d, Ethelind Huyck, Sept. 3, 1892. Came to America, 1879. In cons. practice and traveling in Europe, designing and erecting machinery for mines, shipyards, marine engines, to 1894, since in New York; cons. engr. to Dept. of Water Supply, N.Y., Plant System, R. H. Macy Co., N.Y. Central Terminal, etc., also in connection with erection of numerous tall bldgs.; pres. Electric Meter Corp. Mem. Am. Scenic and Historic Preservation Soc.; trustee Dyckman Inst., City Hist. Club; sec. Washington Heights Taxpayers Assn., 1904-27; mem. Am. Soc. C.E., Am. Inst. Cons. Engrs., Am. Soc. M.E., Am. Soc. Heating and Ventilating Engrs. (pres. 1911); hon. life mem. N.Y. Hist. Soc.; asso. mem. Instn. Civil Engineers, England (Telford gold medal, 1902). Club: National Arts. Author: Motive Powers, 1895; The Assault of Mt. Washington, 1776, 1901; Elevator Service, 1908; The Indians of Washington Heights, 1909; Building for Profit, 1911, 15, 22; Power for Profit, 1915; An Expensive Experiment, 1913, 17; A Municipal Experiment, 1917; New York City in Indian Possession, 1920; Indian Paths in the Great Metropolis, 1922; Washington Heights—Its Eventful Past, 1924; Indian Life of Long Ago in the City of New York, 1934. Home: 638 W. 158th St. Office: Bolton Bldg., 116 E. 19th St., New York, N.Y. Died Feb. 18, 1942.

BOLTON, Thaddeus Lincoln, psychologist; b. Sonora, Ill., July 27, 1865; s. William and Amelia Sophia Charlotte (Dort) B.; A.B., U. of Mich., 1889, Ph.D., Clark U., 1894; m. Martha Louise Busse, Sept. 6, 1921; 1 son, Peter Oughtred (dec.). Instr., later prof. psychology, U. of Neb., 1900-10; prof. psychology, Tempe (Ariz.) Normal Sch., 1910-13, U. of Mont., 1913-17, Temple U., Phila., 1917-37, prof. emeritus since 1938. Trustee Sch. of Occupational Therapy. Fellow A.A.A.S., mem. Am. Psychol. Assn., Sigma Xi, Alpha Tau Omega, Tau Psi Xi. Republican. Conglist. Was editor Univ. of Neb. Studies; founder, and for 3 yrs. editor Ariz. Jour. Edn.; contbr. to Am. Jour. Psychology, Psychol. Rev., Jour. of Philosophy, Kraepelin's Psychologische Arbeiten, Jour. of Vocational Psychology. Conducted extensive research upon value of sugar as a food. Home: 231 Wayne Av., Narberth, Pa. Died Jan. 3, 1948.

BOND, Albert Richmond, clergyman, editor; b. Wilson County, Tenn., Mar. 9, 1874; s. James Houston and Mary Catherine (Cason) B.; A.B., A.M., U. of Nashville, Tenn., 1895; Th.M., Southern Bapt. Theol. Sem., 1898; D.D., U. of Florence (Ala.), 1911; m. Ruth Pugh, Dec. 20, 1898 (died June 6, 1914); 1 son, Richmond Pugh; m. 2d, Catherine Elizabeth Walmsley, Oct. 7, 1925. Ordained Bapt. ministry, 1895; pastor Magnolia and Brookhaven, Miss., 1899-1901, Pembroke, Ky., 1901-03, Price Hill, Cincinnati, 1903-05, West Point, Ga., 1905-08, Marietta, 1908-11, Clarksdale, Miss., 1912-13, Aberdeen, 1913-14, Franklin, Tenn., 1915-17; editor Baptist and Reflector, 1917-20; editorial sec. edn. bd., Southern Baptist Conv., 1920-27; pres. Montezuma (N.Mex.) Bapt. Coll., 1926; sec. Southern Bapt. Edn. Assn., 1915-27, 1930-31; sec. Council Ch. Schs. of the South, 1924-27; asst. mgr. Birmingham Independent, 1931; editor Southern Radio News, 1932-33, Life Underwriter, 1933-36; engaged in original research in N. T. Greek, and special writer for periodicals since 1936. Democrat. Mason (K.T.). Author: The Master Preacher—a Study of the Homiletics of Jesus, 1911; also various ednl. surveys. Home: 1605 12th Av. S., Birmingham, Ala. Died Dec. 19, 1944.

BOND, Carrie Jacobs, composer; b. Janesville, Wis., Aug. 11, 1862; d. Hannibal (M.D.) and Emma (Davis) Jacobs; ed. pub. schs.; m. Frank L. Bond (M.D.), June 1887 (died 1895); 1 son, Fred Jacobs Smith (dec.). Pres. C. J. Bond & Son, pubs. Episcopalian. Mem. Am. Assn. Pen Women; hon. mem. Kappa Beta Gamma. Clubs: Woman's Press, Amateur Musical, etc. Composer of 175 songs, among them: "Just A-weary-in' for you"; "I Love You Truly"; "A Perfect Day"; "Life's Garden" (words by her son); "Lovely Hour"; also greeting cards and mottoes. Author: The Roads of Melody (autobiography), 1927; (for children) Tales of Little Cats; Tales of Little Dogs; Animal Stories; (collection of writings) The End of the Road, 1941. Home: 2042 Pinehurst Rd., Hollywood, Calif. Died Dec. 28, 1946; buried in Memorial Court of Honor, Forest Lawn Memorial Park, Glendale, Calif.

BOND, Carroll Taney, judge; b. Baltimore, Md., June 13, 1873; s. James and Elizabeth (Lyon) B.; grad. Phillips Acad., Exeter, N.H., 1890; A.B., Harvard, 1894; LL.B. U. of Md., 1896; LL.D., Johns Hopkins, 1929; unmarried. Admitted to Md. bar, 1896, and practiced at Baltimore until 1911; asso. judge Supreme Bench, Baltimore City, 1911-24; appointed to fill vacancy as asso. judge Court of Appeals, of Md., Apr. 1924, until election 1926, chief judge Nov. 1924; elected Nov. 1926, for full term, 1926-41, and designated chief judge, reapptd. chief judge for term expiring Nov. 1942. Served as corpl. and 1st sergt. 5th Md. Regt., U.S. Vols., Spanish-Am. War. Trustee Peabody Inst., Provident Hosp. (colored); mem. Littleton-Griswold Fund Com. of Am. Hist. Assn.; dir. Legal History Soc. Mem. Phi Beta Kappa. Democrat. Protestant. Clubs: Maryland, Gibson Island. Home: 3507 N. Charles St., Baltimore, Md. Died Jan. 18, 1943.

BOND, Thomas Emerson, retired railroad exec.; b. Toledo, O., Nov. 2, 1876; s. William Morris and Nannie (Evans) B.; student Lewis Acad., Wichita, Kans., 1891-92; m. Kathryn Lancaster Ten Eyck, Aug. 7, 1920. Clk. traffic dept. D.&R.G. R.R., Denver, Colo., 1900-05; rate clerk Colo. Fuel & Iron Co., Denver, 1905-08; with Elgin, Joliet Eastern Ry., Chicago, Ill., since 1908, as clerk traffic dept., 1908-14, chief of tariff bureau, 1914-18, asst. traffic mgr., 1920-23, traffic mgr., 1923-32, vice pres., 1932-41, pres. 1941-46; retired, 1946. Assigned to U.S. Food Administration as asst. western traffic mgr. at Chicago, 1918-19; assigned to Western Freight Traffic Com., U.S. R.R. Administration, Chicago, 1919-20. Mem. Nat. Freight Traffic Golf Assn., Am. Assn. of Freight Traffic Officers, Town and Country Equestrian Assn. (dir.). Clubs: Union League (pres., 1944); Traffic Club of Chicago, Mid-Day, Executives, Western Railway (Chicago); Traffic (Milwaukee, Wis.). Republican. Episcopalian. Home: 848 Ainslie St. Office: 208 S. La Salle St., Chicago, Ill. Died Dec. 9, 1949.

BONE, Winstead Paine, educator; b. at Douglass, Tex., Nov. 23, 1861; s. Robert Donnell and Minerva Griselda (Burk) B.; A.B., Trinity U., Tex., 1883, A.M., 1894, D.D., 1907; B.D., Cumberland U., Lebanon, Tenn., 1886, LL.D., 1932; grad. Union Theol. Sem., New York, 1888; U. of Berlin, 1889-90; Div. Sch., U. of Chicago, 1894; m. Martha Ready Williamson, Sept. 29, 1897. Ordained Cumberland Presbyn. ministry, 1883; pastor, Greenville, Tex., 1886-87, Nashville, Tenn., 1888-89, Athens, Ala., 1890-91, Dallas, Tex., 1891-94; prof. N.T. Greek and interpretation, 1894-1909, pres. June 1909-14, prof. Bibl. lit. and ethics since June 1914, Cumberland U., also dean Theol. Sch., 1906-09. Writer S.S. lesson comments, 1894-1906. Democrat. Presbyterian. Mason. Mem. Nat. Assn. Bible Instrs., Beta Theta Pi; gen. sec. Alumni Assn. of Cumberland U. and editor Cumberland Alumnus, 1920-29. Author: History of Cumberland University, 1935. Home: 420 W. Main St., Lebanon, Tenn. Died Feb. 12, 1942.

BONHAM, Milledge Lipscomb (bŏn'ăm), judge; b. Edgefield, S.C., Oct. 16, 1854; s. Milledge Luke and Ann Patience (Griffin) B.; student Sachtleben's Acad., Columbia, S.C., 1863-64, Edgefield Acad., 1866-72, Carolina Mil. Inst., Charlotte, N.C., 1875-76; LL.D. from U. of South Carolina, 1935; m. Daisy Aldrich, Oct. 24, 1878; children—Milledge Louis, Proctor Aldrich, Martha Ann; m. 2d, Lillian L. Carter, Mar. 2, 1925. Began practice of law at Ninety Six, S.C., 1877; master in equity, Abbeville County, S.C., 1881-85; adj. gen. of S.C., 1885-90; judge 10th Jud. Circuit, S.C., 1924-31; asso. justice Supreme Court, S.C., 1931-40, chief justice since Jan. 10, 1940. Pres. Univ. South Carolina Soc., 1937. Mem. S.C. State Bar Assn. (pres.), Anderson County Bar Assn. (pres.), Soc. of the Cincinnati of New Jersey, S.A.R., S.C.V., Aztec Club 1847, Civil Legion. Democrat. Episcopalian. K.P. Clubs: Lions, Anderson Country. Address: 248 Greenville St., Anderson, S.C. Died June 23, 1943.

BONILLAS, Ygnacio, mining engr., diplomat; b. San Ygnacio, Sonora, Mex., Feb. 1, 1858; s. Gervasio and Dolores (Fraijo) B.; S.B., Mass. Inst. Tech., 1884; m. Mary Borton, June 29, 1885. Mining insp., State of Sonora, 1911-13; sec. in first Carranza Cabinet, 1884-88, of Nogales, Mex., 1896-98; prefect of Magdalena Dist., 1890-92; mem. 23d Congress, State of Sonora, 1911-13; sec. in first Carranza Cabinet, 1913-17; A.E. and P. from Mexico to U.S. since Mar. 1917. Mem. commn. to settle difficulties arising from Villa's attack on Columbus, N.M., and Pershing Expdn., 1916-17. Mem. Am. Inst. Mining Engrs., Am. Acad. Polit. and Social Science, Alumni Assn. Mass. Inst. Tech. Mason. Address: Mexican Embassy, Washington. Died Jan. 31, 1944.

BONNER, Albert Sydney, mfr.; b. New York, N.Y., Aug. 20, 1891; s. Sydney Noyes and Maud (Barnett) B.; B.C.E., Princeton U., 1913; m. Evelyn B. Coulter, Sept. 23, 1916; children—Joyce K., Albert S., Jr. Employed by Thompson-Starrett Co., Chicago, 1913-

15, Clark Equipment Co., Buchanan, Mich., since 1915, pres. since 1942; dir. First Nat. Bank of Niles (Mich.), Associates Investment Co., South Bend, Ind., Clark Equipment Co., Buchanan, Mich. Republican. Episcopalian. Clubs: University, Tavern (Chicago); Bankers (N.Y. City). Home: 109 N. Detroit St. Office: Clark Equipment Company, Buchanan, Mich. Died Feb. 8, 1945.

BONNER, John Joseph, diocesan supt. schs.; b. Phila., Pa., Nov. 2, 1890; s. Hugh A. and Susan M. (Fleming) B.; grad. Roman Catholic High Sch., Phila., 1908, grad. St. Charles Sem., Overbrook, Pa., 1912; A.B. and Th.D., U. of Propaganda, Rome, Italy; LL.D., Villanova Coll., 1929. Ordained priest R.C. Ch., 1917; served as chaplain, U.S. Army, World War, 1918-19; asst. prin. and teacher, Roman Catholic High Sch., Phila., 1919-23; pastor St. Bernard's Ch., Easton, Pa., 1923-24; dean and teacher, Immaculata Coll., 1924-26; diocesan supt. schools, Phila., since 1926. Pres. Catholic Ednl. Assn. of Pa.; treas. gen. of Nat. Catholic Ednl. Assn. Home: St. Bridget's Rectory, 3667 Midvale Av., Phila. 29. Office: 19th and Wood Sts., Philadelphia 3, Pa. Died Nov. 1945.

BONNER, Robert Johnson, prof. Greek; b. Oxford County, Ont., Can., Oct. 24, 1868; s. John and Nancy (Turnbull) B.; B.A., U. of Toronto, 1890, Litt.D., 1927; grad. Ont. Law Sch., 1893; Ph.D., U. of Chicago, 1904; Litt.D., U. of Dublin, 1937; m. Annie Willson (B.A.), Dec. 25, 1894; children—Gordon Willson, Brant, Patricia. Prof. Latin, John B. Stetson U. De Land, Fla., 1900-03; asso. instr. in Greek, 1905, prof. Greek, 1913-37, prof. emeritus since 1937, chmn. dept., 1927-34, University of Chicago; Sather professor classical literature, University of California, 1932. Asso. editor Classical Philology. Corr. mem. Acad. of Athens; mem. Am. Philol. Assn., Classical Assn. of Middle West and South, Phi Beta Kappa (hon. 1934); fellow Am. Acad. Arts and Sciences, 1935. Author: Greek Composition, 1903; Elementary Greek (with T. C. Burgess), 1907; Evidence in Athenian Courts, 1905; Lawyers and Litigants in Ancient Athens, 1927; Administration of Justice from Homer to Aristotle (with Gertrude Smith), Vol. I, 1930, Vol. II, 1938; Aspects of Athenian Democracy, 1933. Address: University of Chicago, Chicago. Died Jan. 23, 1946; buried at Ridgetown, Ont., Can.

BONNEY, Sherman Grant, physician; b. Cornish, Me., July 15, 1864; s. Dr. Calvin Fairbanks and Harriott O. (Cheney) B.; A.B., Bates Coll., Me., 1886, A.M., 1889; M.D., Harvard, 1889; m. Nancy Brooks Little, Nov. 23, 1886; m. 2d, Mrs. Jessie Elwood Ray, Dec. 1, 1915. Began practice at Lewiston, Me., 1889; removed to Denver, 1891; formerly prof. medicine and dean, Med. Dept. U. of Denver; ex-pres. trustees Denver and Gross Coll. of Medicine (Med. Dept. U. of Denver); was prof. medicine, U. of Colo., now prof. emeritus; formerly visiting phys. St. Luke's Hosp. emeritus physician, St. Joseph's Hosp. Retired from active practice 1930. Fellow Am. Coll. Physicians; mem. Am. Climatol. Assn., A.M.A., Colo. State Med. Soc., Denver Clin. and Pathol. Soc. (ex-pres.); formerly mem. Nat. Assn. Study and Prevention of Tuberculosis, Am. Soc. Tropical Medicine. Author: Pulmonary Tuberculosis and Its Complications, 1908, 2d edit., 1910. Donor of Bonney Memorial Library in Cornish, 1929, named in honor of his parents. Home: 320 High St., Denver, Colo. Died Nov. 19, 1942.

BONTE, George Willard (bŏn'tē), writer, illustrator, designer; b. Cincinnati, O., May 16, 1873; s. Charles Edgar and Mary E. (Butterfield) B.; ed. Cincinnati Sch. of Tech., Cincinnati Art Sch. and Art Students' League, New York; m. Marie Louise Quarles, June 25, 1902. Joined staff Cincinnati Tribune, 1894; Outing Mag., New York, 1896; with New York Herald, 1900-20, art dir., 1906-20, Sunday editor, 1912-13; v.p. James Gordon Bennett Memorial Fund for New York Journalists; art mgr. for publicity and advertising depts. of Selznick Pictures Corp., 1920-23; art mgr. Warner Bros. Motion Pictures, 1923-31. Republican. Universalist. Chmn. bd. reps. News Photographic Agencies of U.S. to handle official photographs during World War I. Mem. Ohio Soc. of N.Y. Author: America Marches Past, a pictorial review of America through the years, 1936. Home: 310 W. 99th St., New York, N.Y.
Died Mar. 13, 1946.

BOOK, William Henry, clergyman; b. Craig County, Va., July 4, 1863; s. Henry L. and Mary E. (Elmore) B.; father killed in Pickett's charge, Gettysburg, Pa.; ed. Milligan Coll., Tenn.; m. Kate McKenzie; children Abbott, Lois, Howard, Elizabeth (Mrs. William Sugden), Katherine, William, Sheldon, Dorothy, Mary V., m. 2d, Mary Davis, July 18, 1906; 1 son, Morris. Ordained ministry Ch. of Christ, 1882; three pastorates in Va., and evangelistic work at Washington, D.C., Baltimore, Richmond and other cities; pastor Tabernacle Ch. of Christ, Columbus, Ind., 1905-25; now gen. evangelist for the Churches of Christ. Trustee Butler Coll.; also trustee Mountain Mission Sch., Grundy, Va.; dir. McGarvey Bible Sem., also of the Home Finding Assn., Louisville. Hon. mem. Eugene Fields Literary Society. Mason, K.P., Red Man. Author: Real Life and Original Sayings, 1899; Tabernacle Sermons, 1909; Indiana Pulpit, 1911; Sermons for the People, 1918. Regular contbr. to The Lookout (weekly). Author of I Am the Bible, which has been translated into Turkish. Guest speaker, Piedmont Assn., Gordonsville, Va., 20 seasons; extensive writer for periodicals. Home: Columbus, Ind. Died July 10, 1946.

BOOMER, Lucius Messenger, hotel man; b. Poughkeepsie, N.Y., Aug. 22, 1878; s. Lucius S. and Bertha (Sterling) B.; student U. of Chicago; m. Jorgine Slettede, September 11, 1920. Began with the Flagler System, Fla.; in charge Hotel McAlpin, New York, 1912-22; regarded as the pioneer in scientific operation of large hotels; now chairman of board, Hotel Waldorf-Astoria Corporation; president The Savarins, Incorporated, Louis Sherry, Incorporated. Served in Am. Red Cross in World War; organized and operated Hotel du Louvre, Paris, for army of- ficers. Mem. Soc. Mayflower Descendants. Protestant. Clubs: Lambs, Cincinnati Society, Bohemian. Author: Hotel Management, 1925. Office: 301 Park Av., New York 22, N.Y. Died June 26, 1947.

BOONE, Daniel, life insurance; b. Brooklyn, N.Y., Sept. 7, 1879; s. Daniel and Mary Bell (Lusk) B.; student Mo. Mil. Acad., 1894-96, Culver Mil. Acad., 1896-97; m. Katherine Hockin, 1920 (died 1934). Clerk N.Y. Life Ins. Co., St. Louis office, 1898-99, agt. same company in Mo. and Kan., 1899-1905, agency instr. in Ind. and Ill., 1905-07; mgr Columbian Nat. Life Ins. Co., Kansas City and San Francisco, 1907-09; with father organized Midland Life Ins. Co., Kansas City, Mo., 1909, sec., 1909-16, v.p. and agency mgr., 1916-20, pres. since 1920; co. merged with Kansas City Life Ins. Co., Aug. 1941, and since v.p. and dir. of latter company. Pres. Am. Life Conv., 1932-33. Mem. bd. visitors Culver Mil. Acad. Democrat. Club: Mission Hills Country (Kansas City, Mo.). Home: 1248 Stratford Rd. Office: 3520 Broadway, Kansas City, Mo.
Died Nov. 26, 1944.

BOOTH, Ballington, reformer; b. Brighouse, Eng., July 28, 1859; s. Rev. William (founder Salvation Army) and Catherine B.; m. Maud Charlesworth, Sept. 16, 1886; formerly comdr. Salvation Army in Australia and U.S.; founded Vols. of America (inc. Nov. 6, 1896), a religious reform and benevolent orgn., of which has since been gen. in chief and pres. Ordained presbyter, Chicago, Aug., 1896. Writer, public speaker. Home: Blue Point, N.Y. Address: 34 W. 28th St., New York. Died Oct. 5, 1940.

BOOTH, Charles Gordon, writer; b. Manchester, Eng., Feb. 12, 1896; s. William and Emily Ada (Hill) B.; ed. grammar schs., Manchester and Toronto and Winnipeg, Can.; m. Lillian Lind, Sept. 25, 1937; 1 son, Charles Rockwell. Came to U.S., 1922, naturalized, 1930. Enlisted with Canadian E.F., 1916. Mem. Screen Writers Guild, Acad. Motion Picture Arts and Scis., Mystery Writer of America. Author: Sinister House, 1926, 27; Gold Bullets, 1929; Murder at High Tide, 1930; Seven Alibis, 1932; The Cat and the Clock, 1935; The General Died at Dawn, 1937; Mr. Angel Comes Aboard, 1944; Murder Strikes Thrice, 1946; (moton pictures) The General Died at Dawn; The Magnificent Fraud; Hurricane Smith; The Traitor Within; Johnny Angel, 1945; The House on 92nd Street (Academy Award); Fury at Furnace Creek, 1948. Contbr. to leading mags. Home: 162 N. Rexford Dr., Beverly Hills, Calif. Office: Goldstone-Willner Agency, 9121 Sunset Blvd., Hollywood 26, Calif. Died May 22, 1949.

BOOTH, Ewing E., army officer; b. Bower Mills, Mo., Feb. 28, 1870; s. Nathaniel and Martha B.; honor graduate Infantry and Cavalry Schools, 1903; graduate Army Staff College, 1905; married (wife died Jan. 1943); 1 dau. Gladys (Mrs. P. L. Thomas). Captain 1st Colorado Volunteer Infantry, May 1, 1898; hon. discharge, July 14, 1899; capt. 36th U.S. Inf., July 5, 1899; hon. mustered out, Mar. 16, 1901; 1st lt. 7th Cav., U.S. Army, Feb. 2, 1901; capt. 10th Cav., Aug. 22, 1904; trans. to 7th Cav., May 11, 1905; a.d.c. to Maj. Gen. J. F. Bell, 1912-15; assigned to 1st Cav., Oct. 4, 1915; maj., May 15, 1917; lt. col, N.A., Aug. 5, 1917; col. N.A., Feb. 3, 1917; brig. gen. N.A., June 26, 1918; col. cav, U.S. Army, July 1, 1920; brig. gen., July 21, 1924; major gen., Dec. 23, 1929. Served as chief of staff Eastern Dept., June-Aug. 1917; chief of staff 77th N.A. Div., Aug. 5, 1917-June 25, 1918; commanded 8th Brigade, 4th Div. of regular army, June 25, 1918-January 10, 1919. Participated in French sector activities, May, June and July, 1918; 2d Marne offensive, July and Aug. 1918; St. Mihiel salient offensive, Sept. 1918; Meuse-Argonne offensive, Sept. and Oct. 1918; with Army of Occupation, Germany, Nov. 18, 1918-Jan. 10, 1919; asst. chief of staff, G 1, Service of Supply, Jan. 15-June 20, 1919; chief of staff S.O.S., and chief of staff Am. Forces in France, June 21, 1919-Jan. 8, 1920; dep. Allied high commr. to Armenia, Jan. 5-June 30, 1920; asst. comdt. Gen. Service Sch., Aug. 1, 1920-June 30, 1921; dir. Gen. Service Schs., 1921-23; instr. War Coll., 1923-24; comd. 4th Cav. and 1st Cav. Brigade on Mexican border, 1924-25; comdt. Cav. Sch., Ft. Riley, Kan., 1925-27; asst. chief of staff, G-4, War Dept., 1927-30; deputy chief of staff, Oct. 12-Dec. 21, 1930; comdg. 1st Cavalry Div., Apr. 27, 1931-Jan. 31, 1932; comdg. Philippines Dept., P.I., Apr. 9, 1932-Sept. 7, 1933; retired, Feb. 28, 1934. Commended for action on the Vesle; cited with 7th and 8th brigades for service in the Bois de Fays; decorated D.S.M. (U.S.); Croix de Guerre and Legion of Honor (French); Philippine Congressional medal; Spanish-Am. War medal; Philippine Insurrection medal; Cuban Occupation medal; Mexican border medal; World War with 4 stars; also by Panama. Address: 4707 Harrison St., Chevy Chase, Md. Died Feb. 19, 1949; buried Arlington Nat. Cemetery, Washington.

BOOTH, Fenton Whitlock, judge; b. Marshall, Ill., May 12, 1869; s. Lyman and Fayette A. (Whitlock) B.; student DePauw U., 3 yrs.; LL.B., U. of Mich., 1892, LL.D., 1940; LL.D., Howard, 1923; m. Anna Harlow, 1893 (died 1895); 1 dau., Mrs. Donald B. Jameson; m. 2d, Mabel Dana, 1897; children—Virginia, Mrs. Le Roy B. Miller, Mrs. Louise B. Moyer (dec.). Admitted to bar, 1892, practiced at Marshall, Ill., 1892-1905; mem. 40th Gen. Assembly, Ill.; candidate for judge Circuit Court, 1897; del. Rep. Nat. Conv., 1904; apptd. asso. justice U.S. Court of Claims, Mar. 17, 1905, and apptd. chief justice by President Coolidge, Apr. 23, 1928; retired June 15, 1939. Mem. faculty, Nat. Univ. Law Sch. Mem. Delta Upsilon, Phi Delta Phi, National Press Club. Home: 4825 Washington Blvd., Indianapolis, Ind. Died July 26, 1947.

BOOTH, George Gough, newspaper pub.; b. Toronto, Can., Sept. 24, 1864; s. Henry Wood and Clara L. (Gagnier) B.; pub. sch. education; hon. M.A., U. of Mich., 1925; m. Ellen Warren Scripps, June 1, 1887- (died Jan. 24, 1948). In mfg. business, 1883-88; became mgr. Detroit Evening News, 1888; pres. Evening News Assn. (pub. Detroit News), 1906-29, dir. to 1949; established Evening Press, Grand Rapids, 1893; founded Booth Newspapers, Inc., pubs. 8 Mich. daily newspapers, Grand Rapids Press, Flint Jour., Kalamazoo Gazette, Saginaw News, Jackson Citizen Patroit, Muskegon Chronicle, Bay City Times, and Ann Arbor News, being chmn. bd. dirs. or pres. or both, 1914-36, dir. to 1949; v.p. and dir. James E. Scripps Corp. Mem. Soc. Arts and Crafts, Founders Soc. Detroit Inst. of Arts, Am. Fedn. Arts, Art Alliance America, A.I.A. (Mich. chapter). Episcopalian. Clubs: Detroit; Bloomfield Hills Country. Established, with wife, Cranbrook Found. and the following instns. on country estate at "Cranbrook," Bloomfield Hills, Mich.: Christ Ch. Cranbrook (Episcopal), Cranbrook Acad. Art, Cranbrook Inst. Sci., Cranbrook School (boys), Kingswood School Cranbrook (girls), Brookside Sch. Cranbrook (young children). Home: "Cranbrook," Lone Pine Rd., Bloomfield Hills, Mich. Office: Buhl Bldg., Detroit 26. Died Apr. 11, 1949; buried Birmingham, Mich.

BOOTH, Henry Kendall, clergyman; b. Peru, Ill., Apr. 19, 1876; s. Sanford Samuel and Ella (Kendall) B.; A.B., Hamilton Coll., 1898, A.M., 1901, D.D., 1929; B.D., Chicago Theol. Sem., 1901, D.D., 1918; m. Olive Mears, Oct. 17, 1900 (died Jan. 3, 1921); m. 2d, Leona Hays, Nov. 6, 1922; children—Henry Kendall, Helen Louise. Ordained Congl. ministry, 1901; pastor Michigan City, Ind., 1901-02, Tucson, Ariz., 1902-04, Sacramento, Calif., 1904-07, Berkeley, 1907-09, Long Beach since 1909. Mem. Long Beach Bd. of Edn. Mem. Phi Beta Kappa, Alpha Delta Phi. Republican. Author: The Religion of an Evolutionist, 1918; New Testament History and Literature, 1919; The Philosophy of Prayer, 1921; Religion for Today, 1923; The Background of the Bible, 1928; The Bridge Between the Testaments, 1929; The World of Jesus, 1933; The Great Galilean Returns, 1936. Office: 241 Cedar Av., Long Beach, Calif.*
Died Oct. 16, 1942.

BOOTH, Maud Ballington, reformer; b. Limpsfield, Surrey, Eng., Sept. 13, 1865; d. Rev. Samuel and Maria Charlesworth; ed. at Belstead, Eng., and in Switzerland; m. Ballington Booth, September 16, 1886 (died October 5, 1940). Landed in America, Apr. 16, 1887; engaged with her husband in reform and relief work in connection with the Salavation Army, 1887-96, and after leaving that movement, in the Volunteers of America, which he founded, 1896, and upon death of husband became comdr.-in-chief; in charge of extensive prison work throughout U.S. Served with Y.M.C.A. during World War in France and Germany. One of the founders of Parent-Teachers Assn. (hon. vice pres. since 1943). Author: Branded, 1897; Look Up and Hope; Sleepy Time Stories, 1889; Lights of Childland, 1901; After Prison—What?; The Curse of Septic Soul Treatment; Wanted—Antiseptic Christians; Twilight Fairy Tales, 1906; Was It Murder? Home: Blue Point, N.Y. Address: 34 W. 28th St., New York, N.Y. Died Aug. 26, 1948.

BOOTH, Robert Asbury, lumberman; b. Yamhill County, Ore., May 15, 1858; s. Robert and Mary (Minor) B.; grad. Umpqua Acad., Wilbur, Douglas County, Ore., 1875; Healds Business Coll., San Francisco, 1879; LL.D., Coll. of Pudget Sound, Tacoma, Wash., 1922, Williamette U., 1923; hon. M.A. in Public Service, U. of Oregon, 1929; m. Clintona A. La Raut, May 15, 1881 (now deceased); children—Echo V. (dec.), Robert Roy, Floyd Wilson (dec.), Barbara Wenzorl. Mercantile business, 1880-85; principal Ore. State Normal Sch., Drain, Ore., 1886-87; organized First Nat. Bank, Grants Pass, Ore., 1889, and served as cashier, later pres. until 1905; v.p. Grants Pass Banking & Trust Co., 2 yrs.; pres. Douglas Nat. Bank, Roseburg, 5 yrs.; organized Booth-Kelly Lumber Company, 1897, and was manager; organized Ore. Land & Live Stock Co., now pres.; organized Ochoco Timber Company, 1923. Delegate from Oregon to Rep. Nat. Conv., St. Louis, 1896; del. to Rep. State Conv. 20 yrs. continuously; mem. Ore. Senate, 1900-08; mem. Bd. Highway Commrs. of Ore., 5 yrs., chmn., 3 yrs., expending $50,000,000 for good roads. Trustee Willamette U., 35 yrs.; mem. bd. dirs. Ore. Tuberculosis Soc.; founder Student Loan Fund at U. of Ore., Ore. Agrl. Coll., Reed Coll., Willamette U. and Pacific Coll., Newberg, Ore.; mem. State Park

Commn. Presented to State of Ore. heroic bronge equestrian statue, representing pioneer clergyman, 1923. Methodist. Rotarian. Clubs: Commercial (Portland, Ore.); Commercial (Eugene). Address: The Booth-Kelly Lbr. Co., Eugene, Ore. Died Apr. 28, 1944.

BORDEN, William Cline, surgeon; b. Watertown, N.Y., May 19, 1858; s. Daniel J. and Mary L. (Cline) B.; ed. Adams (N.Y.) Collegiate Inst; M.D., Columbian (now George Washington) U., 1883, Sc.D., 1931; m. Jennie E. Adams, Oct. 27, 1883; children—Daniel Le Ray, William Ayres. Apptd. 1st lt. asst. surgeon U.S.A., Dec. 3, 1883, capt., Dec. 3, 1888; maj. brigade surgeon vols., June 4, 1898-Mar. 31, 1899; maj. surgeon, Feb. 2, 1901; lt. col. and retired, 1909. Comd. Gen. Hosp., Key West, Fla., during Spanish-Am. War; Gen. Hosp., Washington, 1898-1907; also prof. mil. surgery, Army Med. Sch., and prof. surg. pathology and mil. surgery, Georgetown U., 1898-1907; comd. div. hosp., Manila, 1908; prof. surgery and dean med. dept., George Washington U. and surgeon in chief George Washington U. Hosp., 1909-June 1931. Returned to active service for war as chief of surg. service Walter Reed Army Gen. Hosp., 1917-19. Mem. Med. Soc., Surg. Soc., Med. Hist. Soc. D.C., A.M.A., S.A.R. (N.Y. chap.); a founder and fellow American Coll. Surgeons. Clubs: Chevy Chase, Army and Navy (Washington); Crescent Yacht (Watertown, N.Y.). Author: Use of the Röntgen Ray by the Medical Department of the United States in the War with Spain, 1898 (published by joint resolution of Congress). 1900. Also several secs. in standard surg. works and many med. monographs and articles. Home: 2306 Tracy Pl., Washington. Died Sept. 29, 1934.

BORG, Carl Oscar (bôrg), artist; b. Grinstad, Sweden, Mar. 3, 1879; s. Gustaf and Kristina (Borg) B.; ed. pub. schs., Sweden; m. Madeline Carriel, August 15, 1918 (divorced August 18, 1937); m. 2d, Anna Lilly Lindstrand, October 3, 1938. Came to U.S. 1901; self-taught in art; has painted in Central and S. America, Spain, Morocco, Valley of the Nile and Italy; specializes in desert and Indian subjects. First prize, Painters' Club, Los Angeles, Calif., 1909; hon. mention, Vichy, 1913; silver medal, Versailles, 1914, San Diego, 1915, San Francisco Expn., 1915; gold medal, San Diego Expn., 1916; 1st prize, Phoenix, Ariz., 1916; 2d Black prize, Los Angeles, 1918; Maybury prize, Los Angeles, 1920; silver medal, Société des Artistes Français, 1920; hon. mention Calif. Water Color Soc., 1923; Huntington prize, Calif. Art Club, 1923; 2d prize, Painters of the West, Los Angeles, 1924, gold medal, Painters of the West, 1928; silver medal, Long Beach, Calif., 1928; 1st prize, Sacramento, Calif., 1929; Elizabeth Fisher prize, Ebell Club, Los Angeles, 1930; honorable mention Laguna Beach Art Assn., 1935; The Linné Medal, Royal Acad. of Science (Stockholm, Sweden), 1945. Represented in U. of Calif., municipal collection Phoenix, Ariz., Los Angeles Mus., Calif. State Library, Sacramento, M. H. de Young Memorial Mus., San Francisco, Los Angeles Pub. Library, Hearst Free Library, Anaconda, Mills Coll., Calif., Oakland Mus., Milwaukee Art Inst., Montclair (N.J.) Mus., Bibliothèque Nationale, Paris, France, Gothenburg (Sweden) Mus., Univ. of Lund (Sweden); Vänersborg's Mus. (Sweden); Nat. Mus., Statens Etnografiska Mus., Royal Library (Stockholm); Am. Swedish Hist. Mus., Phila. Mem. Am. Fedn. Arts, San Francisco Art Assn., San Francisco Soc. Etchers, Calif. Watercolor Soc., Print-Makers Soc. of Calif., Laguna Beach, Art Assn., Am. Artists Professional League, Société Internationale des Beaux Arts et des Lettres (Paris). Asso. National Academy, 1938; corr. mem. Sociedade de Geographia, Lisbon, Portugal. Clubs: California Art, Salmagundi (New York). Address: 226 E. Padre St., Santa Barbara, Calif. Died May 8, 1946.

BORIE, Charles Louis (bô'rē), architect; b. Phila., Pa., June 9, 1870; s. Beauveau and Patty Duffield (Neill) B.; student St. Paul's Sch., Concord, N.H., 1884-88; B.S., U. of Pa., 1892; m. Helen Sewell, Oct. 1892 (died Nov. 1928); children—C. Louis, 3d, W. J. Sewell, Henry Peter, Beauveau, 3d; m. 2d, Carrie Tyson Drayton, June 1934. Began practice in 1904; now mem. of firm Zantzinger & Borie, Phila. Prin. works: Masonic Homes, Elizabethtown, Pa.; Valley Forge (Pa.) Chapel; Phila. Divinity Sch.; dormitories at Princeton and Sheffield Scientific Sch. (Yale); dormitories and Adminstrn. Bldg. of U. of Chicago; St. Paul's Ch., Chestnut Hill, Pa.; Pa. Museum of Art; Dept. of Justice Bldg., Washington, D.C. Trustee Library Co. of Phila., University Museum of Phila., U. of Pa.; chmn. Council of Am. Acad. in Rome, Smithsonian Gallery of Art Commn. (Washington, D.C.). Fellow A.I.A.; mem. Am. Acad. Arts and Letters, Nat. Inst. of Arts and Letters. Episcopalian. Home: Rydal, Pa. Office: Architects Bldg., Philadelphia, Pa. Died May 11, 1943.

BOSCHEN, Frederick Wegener (bō'shĕn), army officer; b. Brooklyn, N.Y., May 9, 1876; s. Charles Nicholas and Caroline Augusta (Wegener) B.; ed. Browne's Coll., Brooklyn; m. Vida Gotthelf, Sept. 25, 1912; children—Frederick W., 2d (dec.), Betty. Entered U.S. Army as pvt. 47th N.Y. Inf., 1898; commd. 2d lt., 1903, advanced through grades to maj. gen., Apr. 23, 1936; served in Hosp. Corps during Spanish-Am. War; successively maj., lt.-col., col. during World War; chief of finances U.S. Army from 1936 until retired. Commr. U.S. Soldier's Home, Washington, D.C.; fiscal agent Civilian Conservation Corps. Chevalier Legion of Honor; Croix de Guerre (with palms and gold star); Belgium Mil. Medal; special legislative medal, N.Y.; etc. Conglist. Mason. Clubs: Army and Navy, Army and Navy Country (Washington, D.C.); Bohemian (San Francisco), Polo (Manila, P.I.). Home: Wardman Park Hotel, Washington, D.C. Died Apr. 1, 1942.

BOSLEY, Frederick Andrew (bŏs'lē), artist; b. Lebanon, N.H., Feb. 24, 1881; s. Andrew and Jennie May (Hill) B.; prep. edn., Murdock Sch., Winchendon, Mass., 1896-1900; student Sch. Mus. Fine Arts, Boston, Mass., under Tarbell and Benson, 1900-06, Paige traveling scholarship, Europe, 2 yrs.; m. Emily Linzee Sohier, Sept. 10, 1908; children—Edward Sohier, Elizabeth Brimmer de Vermandois, Ermengarde de Vermandois (dec.). Instr. of painting, Sch. Museum of Fine Arts, Boston, 1913-31. Represented in collections of Boston Museum Fine Arts, Locust Club, Phila., Pa., and in private collections. Awarded bronze medal, Pan-Am. Expdn., San Francisco, Calif., 1915; 1st hon. mention, Internat. Exhbn., Carnegie Inst., Pittsburgh, Pa., 1920; hon. mention, Concord (Mass.) Art Assn., 1920; Locust Club gold medal, Pa. Acad. Fine Arts, Phila., 1925. Mem. Guild of Boston Artists, Copley Soc., Am. Fed. Arts, Concord Art Assn. (dir.). Associate Nat. Acad., 1931. Republican. Unitarian. Club: St. Botolph. Home: 127 Main St., Concord, Mass.; (summer) Piermont, N.H. Died March 22, 1942; buried in Sleepy Hollow Cemetery, Concord, Mass.

BOSS, Andrew, prof. agr.; b. Wabasha, Minn., June 3, 1867; s. Andrew and Janet (Nesbit) B.; grad. Sch. of Agr., U. of Minn., 1891; D.Sc., Kan. State Agrl. Coll., 1927; m. Evalina LaMont, Dec. 15, 1891; children—Hazel Vivian, Elna Violet, Mabel Evelyn, Kenneth Andrew, Wallace LaMont. With Sch. and Coll. of Agr., U. of Minn., since 1895; chief div. agr. and animal husbandry, same, 1905-09, chief div. of agronomy and farm management since 1909, vice dir. expt. sta. since 1917. Fellow A.A.A.S.; mem. Am. Soc. Agronomy, Am. Farm Econ. Assn., Sigma Xi, Gamma Sigma Delta, Alpha Zeta. Conglist. Author: Farm Management, 1914. Home: 1443 Raymond Av., St. Paul. Died Jan. 13, 1947.

BOSSANGE, Edward Raymond (bŭs-änzh'), architect, educator; b. Enghien, France, June 6, 1871; s. Gustave Pierre and Marie (Coindreau) B.; brought to U.S., 1880; Ph.B. in architecture, Columbia, 1893; studied Beaux Arts Ateliers, N.Y. City, 1893-97; student under Garnier and Vermare, Rome, 1900-01; m. Maud Everett, May 17, 1913; children—Edward Raymond, Hector. Began practice in N.Y. City, 1898, was with Ernest Flagg, Carrere & Hastings and Warren & Witmore, architects; independent practice, 1900-05; mem. firm Bossange & Newton, 1905-08; asso. with Butler & Rodman, 1908-10; prof. architecture Cornell U., 1913-15; dir. and dean coll. of fine arts, 1915-23, Carnegie Inst. Tech.; prof. architecture and dir. Sch. of Architecture, Princeton, 1923-26; chmn. dept. of architecture, New York U., 1926-30, dean coll. of fine arts, 1930-35, dean school of architecture, 1935-41, dean emeritus, 1941. Mem. 7th Regt. N.Y. Nat. Guard, 1898-1905. Formerly fellow A.I.A.; mem. Psi Upsilon; past mem. Architectural League, Beaux-Arts Soc. Episcopalian. Address: San Anselmo, Marin County, Calif. Died Nov. 16, 1947.

BOSTWICK, Arthur Elmore, librarian; b. Litchfield, Conn., Mar. 8, 1860; s Dr. David Elmore and Adelaide (McKinley) B.; A.B., Yale, 1881, Ph.D., 1883, grad. fellow phys. science, 1881-84; LL.D., Washington U., 1932; m. Lucy Sawyer, June 23, 1885 (died Aug. 31, 1930); children—Andrew Linn (died Nov. 17, 1939), Esther, Elmore McNeil. Instr. and proctor, Yale, 1883-84; teacher high sch., Montclair, N.J., 1884-86; on staff Appleton's Cyclopedia of American Biography, 1886-88; lit. work, 1888-90; asst. editor The Forum, 1890-92; asso. editor Standard Dictionary and office expert in physics, 1892-94; chief librarian New York Free Circulating Library, 1895-99; librarian Brooklyn Pub. Library, 1899-1901; chief of circulation dept. New York Pub. Library, 1901-09; librarian St. Louis Pub. Library, 1909-38, now asso. librarian; editor science dept., Literary Digest, 1891-1933. Pres. N.Y. Library Club, 1897-99, New York State Library Assn., 1902-03, Mo. Library Assn., 1917; pres. A.L.A., 1907-08 (mem. war service com. 1917, pub. bd. 1909-21, pres. 1918-21; chmn. library survey com., 1922-29); pres. Assn. of Am. Library Schs., 1933; mem. Univ. Council, N.Y. State U., 1904; fellow Am. Library Inst., 1906 (pres., 1909-12, 1925-27); del. Copyright Conf., 1905-06; pres. Mo. Library Commn., 1911-17; pres. New England Society of St. Louis, 1911; president St. Louis Archeol. Soc., 1915; mem. Municipal Art Commn., 1917; pres. of the St. Louis Art League, 1920; pres. St. Louis br. League of Nations Non-Partisan Assn., 1924-33; pres. Mo. Welfare League, 1926-36; pres. St. Louis branch Foreign Policy Assn., 1927; hon. dir. Library Assn. of China since 1925. Visited China, 1925, by invitation Chinese Assn. for Advancement of Edn., to inspect Chinese libraries. Mem. Phi Beta Kappa. Clubs: Authors (N.Y. City); Artists' Guild, Town and Gown, Church Club (pres. 1914), Round Table Club. Author: Young Folks, Cyclopedia of Games and Sports (with J. D. Champlin), 1890; The American Public Library, 1910, rev. edits., 1917, 23, 29; The Different West, 1913; Earmarks of Literature, 1914; The Making of an American's Library, 1915; Library Essays, 1920; A Librarian's Open Shelf, 1920; A Life with Men and Books, 1939. Editor: Classics of Am. Librarianship (vols. I-VIII), 1915-29; The Popular Library Throughout the World, 1933. Wrote many sketches in Appleton's Cyclo. of Am. Biography, 1888, Standard Dictionary, 1894; also numerous articles Appleton's Annual Cyclo., including yearly rev. of progress of physics; contbr. on phys. science, lit. and library economy. Home: 5475 Cabanne Av. Address: Public Library, St. Louis, Mo. Died Feb. 13, 1942.

BOSTWICK, Frank Matteson, naval officer; b. Janesville, Wis., Apr. 13, 1857; s. Joseph Morton and Harriet Maria (Allen) B.; grad. U.S. Naval Acad., 1877; m. Elvira (Gregg) Hartwell, Aug. 14, 1879. Promoted through the various grades to capt., 1909; retired at own request, with rank of commodore, June 30, 1910. Served on Pacific sta. and Navy Yard, Mare Island, Cal., 1877-86, 1889-98; Asiatic sta., 1886-89; on bd. U.S.S. Charleston during Spanish-Am. War, 1898; on Charleston, Bennington and Marietta, Philippine sta., 1898-1901; navigator and later 1st lt., Oregon Mar.-Oct., 1901; comd. Nipsic, Oct., 1901-May 1904, Philadelphia, May-Aug., 1904, Eagle, Sept. 1904-Sept. 1906; lighthouse insp., 10th dist., Sept. 1906-June, 1908; comd. Buffalo, June, 1908-Apr., 1909; capt. of yard, Navy Yard, Portsmouth, N.H., June, 1909-July, 1910. Received Spanish and Philippine campaign medals. Episcopalian. Club: University (Buffalo). Address: Care Franklin Nat. Bank, Philadelphia. Died Dec. 20, 1945.

BOSTWICK, Roy Grier, lawyer; b. Du Bois, Pa., June 18, 1883; s. Charles Edgar and Elizabeth Rebecca (Grier) B.; A.B., and A.M., Bucknell U., Lewisburg, Pa., 1905; LL.B., University of Pittsburgh Law School, 1908; LL.D., Bucknell University, 1944; m. Marie Louise Leiser, November 28, 1912. Admitted to Pa. bar, 1908 and since engaged in gen. practice at Pittsburgh; mem. Brown, Stewart and Bostwick, 1909-21, Thorp, Bostwick, Reed & Armstrong, Pittsburgh, since 1921; v.p. and dir. Wilkinsburg Bank; pres. and dir. Arcade Land Co.; sec. and dir. Wilkinsburg Hotel Co.; director Bankers Lithographing Company. Served as chief Div. of Analysis and chief Div. of Complaints, Nat. War Labor Board, Washington, D.C., during World War I. Chairman bd. trustees Bucknell U. Pres. and trustee Family Soc. of Allegheny County; dir. Federation Social Agencies, of Public Charities Assn. of Pa.; v.p. East Boroughs Council Boy Scouts; secretary Law Library Committee of Allegheny County. Fellow Am. Geog. Soc. (New York). Mem. Allegheny County Bd. of Pub. Assistance; director Pittsburgh Chapter Am. Red Cross; dir. Council Chs. Pittsburgh; chmn. Pittsburgh Round Table, Nat. Conf. Christians and Jews. Mem. chambers of commerce of Pittsburgh and Wilkinsburg. Mem. Am., Pa. and Allegheny County bar assns., Am. Law Inst., Am. Judicature Soc., Am. Museum of Nat. Hist., Fgn. Policy Assn. (Pittsburgh), Acad. Polit. Sci., Council on Foreign Relations, Inc. (New York), Pennsylvania Society (N.Y.), Navy League, National Aeronautic Association of U.S.A., Western Pennsylvania Historical Society, Phi Beta Kappa, Kappa Sigma, Theta Delta Tau, Omicron Delta Kappa, Phi Beta Kappa Associates (N.Y.). Republican. Presbyterian. Mason (K.T., 32°, Shriner). Clubs: Civic of Allegheny County, Duquesne, University, Amen Corner, Harvard-Yale-Princeton (Pittsburgh); Longue Vue Country (Verona, Pa.); Pittsburgh Field (Aspinwall, Pa.); Wilmas (Wilkinsburg, Pa.); Union League (New York). Home: 120 Ruskin Av., Pittsburgh; (summer) Lewisburg, Pa. Office: 2812 Grant Bldg., Pittsburgh, Pa. Died May 23, 1947.

BOSWORTH, Francke Huntington, Jr., architect; b. N.Y. City, Nov. 29, 1875; s. Francke Huntington and Mary Hildreth (Putnam) B.; A.B., Yale, 1897; Ecole des Beaux Arts, Paris, France, 1897-1901; m. Fanny Foote, Apr. 30, 1902; children—Mary H., Isabel C. Practiced at New York, 1902-18; with Am. Red Cross in France, 1918-19; prof. and dean Coll. of Architecture, Cornell U., 1920-28, prof. since 1928, prof. emeritus since 1940. Past mem N.Y. State Bd. of Examiners for Architects; past pres. Assn. Collegiate Schools of Architecture. Fellow Am. Inst. Architects, 1926; mem. Soc. Beaux Arts Architects, Phi Kappa Phi, Tau Beta Pi, Psi Upsilon. Clubs: University, Century (N.Y.). Home. 916 Stewart Av., Ithaca, N.R. Died Apr. 28, 1949.

BOSWORTH, Hobart Van Zandt, actor; b. Marietta, O., Aug. 11, 1867; s. Daniel Perkins and Clara Mumford (Van Zandt) B.; m. Cecile Kibre, Dec. 22, 1920; 1 son, George Hobart. With McKee-Rankin Stock Co., San Francisco, 1885, later with Mrs. D. P. Bowers & Co.; in Mexico with Hermann, the magician, and for 10 yrs. with the Augustin Daly Stock Co., New York; spent 9 yrs., in Colo. and the Southwest; became identified with motion pictures, 1909, as actor, later writer of scenarios and dir.; pres. Bosworth Co., which made a specialty of Jack London's stories; produced tabloid version of London's Sea Wolf, in vaudeville, 1917. Screen plays; Behind the Door; His Own Law; The Cup of Life; Foolish Wives; Blind Hearts; The Eternal Three; Captain January; Hearts of Oak; Winds of Chance; My Son; Far Cry, etc.; in sound pictures and the radio. Republican. Clubs: The Players (New York); Olympic (San Francisco). Address: Le Cañada, Calif. Died Dec. 20, 1943.

BOUCK, Zeh (bouk), writer; b. N.Y. City, Apr. 3, 1901; s. John A. and Alice (White) Schmidt (Zeh Bouck, pen and legal name); grad. Townsend Harris High Sch., New York, 1920; m. Charlotte Bosse, Sept. 15, 1928; children—Myrl (dec.), Paul Alfred. Radio columnist N.Y. Sun (formerly Globe) since 1922;

research engr. Daven Radio Corp., 1922-24; contbg. editor Radio Broadcast, 1923-28; radio editor Boys Life, 1924-26; chief engr. Amsco Products, 1925-27, Dejur Amsco, 1927-29; cons. engr., 1930-32; consultant consumer orgns.; cons. engr. Harco Steel Constn Co. 1944; engr. in charge aeronautics Pilot Radio Tube Co., 1927-30; advt. mgr. Arcturus Radio Tube Co., 1928-30; mng. editor Aero News and Mechanics, 1928-30; mng. editor CQ magazine, 1944; contbg. editor Radio Engineering, 1926-27, Radio News, 1928-37, All-Wave Radio, 1936-38; columnist Cincinnati Enquirer, 1927-30; pres. Zeh Bouck Labs., 1931-32; cons. engr., program consultant, publicity since 1922; specializing in radio scripts, fiction and in popular scientific articles since 1939. Organized and accompanied as radio engineer first flight, United States to Bermuda, 1930, first land plane circumnavigatory flight of S.A., 1930. Fellow Radio Club of America; mem. Inst. Radio Engrs. Author: Making a Living in Radio, 1936. Home: Middleburg, N.Y. Died Aug. 26, 1946.

BOUDINOT, Truman Everett (bōōd′nō), army officer; b. Hamilton, Ia., Sept. 2, 1895; s. George Arthur and Eva Margaret (Tower) B.; grad. Cav. Sch. troop officers course, 1920, Inf. Sch. advanced course, 1928, Command and Gen. Staff Sch., 1937; m. Lolita Margaret Sargent, June 1, 1922; children—Truman Everett (cadet U.S. Mil. Acad.), Burton Sargent. Commd. 2d lt., U.S. Army, 1917, advancing through the grades to brig. gen., 1944; serving in European Theater of Operation since 1943; comdg. C. C. B., 3d Armored Div., in Normandy, France, Belgium and Germany, since July 1944. Decorated Mexican Service Medal (1918), World War I and Defense service medals, European Theater Service Medal with 3 bronze stars, Legion of Merit, Silver Star with 2 oak leaf clusters, Distinguished Service Medal (posthumously) (U.S.), Chevalier Legion of Honor, Croix de Guerre with palms (France). Mem. Heroes of '76, Theta Xi. Mason, Sojourner. Home: 308 South Doheny Dr., Beverly Hills, Calif. Address: care The Adjutant General's Office, War Dept., Washington 25. Died Dec. 21, 1945; buried in Arlington National Cemetery.

BOUGHTON, Willis, author; b. Victor, N.Y., Apr. 17, 1854; s. Myron and Jane M. (Farnam) B.; A.B., U. of Mich., 1881; higher diploma, Teachers Coll. (Columbia), 1902; A.M. (hon.), Dickinson Coll., 1891; Ph.D., Ohio U., 1900; m. Martha Elizabeth Arnold, July 8, 1884 (died May 18, 1928); children—Willis Arnold, Paul N. Editor Ann Arbor Courier, 1881-82; in bus. Ann Arbor, 1882-86; teacher, Cincinnati, 1889; prof. history and English, Ohio U., 1890-91, rhetoric and English lit., 1892-99; Phila. sec. Am. Soc. for Extension of Univ. Teaching, and lecturer on English, U. of Pa., 1891-92; asst., dept. English, Erasmus Hall High Sch., Brooklyn, 1899-1924, chmn. dept., 1900-03, retired 1924. Lecturer: Brooklyn Teachers' Assn., 1904-07, and since 1913; English lit., Adelphi Coll., 1906-07; English poetry and poets, in public lecture system of New York Bd. of Edn., 1903-16; lecturer, Brooklyn Inst., 1909-28, pres. dept. of philology, 1913-30; teacher of English Colby Acad., 1927-28. Lecturer in English, extramural div., New York U., 1913-18. Mem. Beta Theta Pi. Mason. Author: Mythology in Art, 1890; History of Ancient Peoples, 1896; Ode to Learning, 1912; English Literature in Outline, 1913; American Literature in Outline, 1913; (joint author) Allen's History of Civilization, 1888. Editor: Irving's Life of Goldsmith, 1903; Tennyson's Idylls, 1904, enlarged edit., 1913; Milton's Minor Poems, 1909. Joint editor Journal of Pedagogy, 1890-92; Chronicle of Erasmus Hall Academy, 1906. Wrote: Chronicles of St. Mark's Church; words to songs United States, America, Christmas Carol, 1917 and Song of the People, 1938. Home: 280 E. 21st St., Brooklyn, N.Y. Died June 16, 1942.

BOULT, William Thomas (bōlt); b. Ballyshannon, Ireland, Feb. 14, 1886, of American parents; s. Rev. Samuel and Elizabeth (Patterson) B.; student Colgate Acad., Hamilton, N.Y., and Lafayette Coll., Easton, Pa.; grad. Union Theol. Sem., 1913; m. Iola Slator, Aug. 19, 1907; children—Iola Slator (Mrs. Chester O. French, Jr.), Myrtle Matilda (Mrs. George H. Heuger, Jr.). Ordained to ministry of Congregational Church, 1908; pastor Spring Valley, New York, 1908-13; pastor Bound Brook, New Jersey, 1913-20; with J. H. Brooks & Company, investment bankers, Scranton, Pa., 1920-22; pastor Bedford Park Ch., N.Y. City, 1923-26; since 1923 treas. Corp. Gen. Council of Congl. and Christian Chs., Annuity Fund for Congl. Ministers, Bd. of Home Missions of Congl. and Christian Chs. and ten other affiliated corps. During World War served overseas with Y.M. C.A., and as speaker for Nat. Service Sect. of U.S. Shipping Bd. Trustee, Talladega (Ala.) Coll., Am. Coll. (Madura, India), Piedmont Coll. (Demorest, Ga.), Tougaloo (Miss.) Coll., Le Moyne College (Tenn.). Mem. Phi Delta Theta. Independent Republican. Clubs: Clergy, Lake Placid. Home: 16 Sycamore Av., Mt. Vernon, N.Y. Office: 287 4th Ave., New York, N.Y. Died Mar. 19, 1943.

BOURLAND, Benjamin Parsons (bōōr′lănd), b. Peoria, Ill., May 2, 1870; s. Benjamin L. T. and Clara Elizabeth (Parsons) B.; early edn. in France, Switzerland, Germany (Royal Gymnasia, Wiesbaden), 1882-85; A.B., U. of Mich., 1889, A.M., 1890; U. of Vienna, 1895-97, Ph.D., 1897; m. Gertrude L. Thayer, June 18, 1902. Instr. in French, U. of Mich., 1892-95; student in Vienna, Paris, Florence, Madrid, Rome, 1895-98; instr. in Romance langs., 1898-99, asst. prof., 1899-1901, U. of Mich.; asso. prof. Romance langs., Adelbert Coll. and Western Reserve U., 1901-03, prof., 1903-40, in Grad. Sch., 1927-40, Romance philology, 1937-40; retired June 1940. Was dir. of junior membership, 1917-18, asso. dir. bur. personnel, 1918, dir. dept. of development, 1918-19, mem. advisory com., 1919-20, Lake Div. of Am. Red Cross. Mem. Modern Lang. Assn. America, Am. Philol. Assn., Am. Linguistic Soc., Hispanic Soc. of America, Mediæval Acad. of America, Alpha Delta Phi, Phi Beta Kappa; associé de l'Institut Phonétique, Paris. Unitarian. Club: Rowfant (president 1927-29). Editor: Téllez's Don Gil de las Calzas Verdes, 1902; Alarcón's El Sombrero de Tres Picos, 1907; The Rimed Chronicle of the Cid, 1912; Cyrano de Bergerac, Satyrical Letters, 1915. Home: Marshfield, Mass. Died Jan. 12, 1943; buried in Mt. Hope Cemetery, Boston.

BOURNE, Henry Eldridge (bōrn), coll. prof.; b. E. Hamburg, N.Y., Apr. 13, 1862; s. James R. and Isabella G. (Staples) B.; A.B., Yale, 1883, B.D., 1887, Hooker fellow, same, 1887-88; L.H.D., Marietta (Ohio) Coll., 1910; LL.D., Western Reserve U., 1935; widower; children—Margaret Gibbs, Richard Mason. Asst. editor The Congregationalist, Boston, 1888-89; teacher of history and psychology, Norwich (Conn.) Free Acad., 1889-92; prof. history Western Reserve, 1892-1930, registrar, Coll. for Women, 1893-1901, prof. history, Grad. Sch., 1926-30, prof. emeritus since 1930. Consultant in European history, Library of Congress, 1929-36. Lecturer summer sessions, U. of Chicago, 1911, 20, 22, Ohio State U., 1914, U. of Ore., 1918, U. of Tex., 1921, Columbia, 1926, Cornell, 1928. Fellow Royal Hist. Soc.; mem. Soc. d'Histoire Moderne, Am. Hist. Assn., Mississippi Valley Hist. Assn., Phi Beta Kappa. Author: The Teaching of History and Civics, 1902, 2d edition, 1910; Mediæval and Modern History, 1905; Revolutionary Period in Europe, 1914. Joint author: Introductory American History, 1912; History of the United States, 1913; Story of America and Great Americans, 1923; American History, 1925. Editor: Lecky's French Revolution, 1904. Compiler: Catalogue of Autographs Relating to the French Revolution (John Boyd Thacher Collection, vol. 3), 1931. Contbr. to revs. Mem. bd. of editors, Am. Hist. Rev., 1926-36, mng. editor, 1929-36. Home: 2504 Derbyshire Rd., Cleveland Heights, Ohio. Died June 19, 1946.

BOUSFIELD, M(idian) O(thello) (bōōs′fēld), physician; b. Tipton, Mo., Aug. 22, 1885; s. Willard Haymen and Cornelia Catherine (Gilbert) B.; A.B., U. of Kan., 1907; M.D., Northwestern U., 1909; m. Maudelle Tanner Brown, Sept. 9, 1914; 1 dau., Maudelle. Interne Freedmen's Hosp., Washington, D.C.; began practice in Kansas City, Mo., then in Chicago, 1914; sec. Ry. Men's Internat. Benevolent and Indsl. Assn. (pioneer Negro labor orgn.), 1915-19; 1st v.p. and med. dir. Liberty Life Ins. Co., Chicago, 1919-25, pres., 1925-29; 1st v.p. and med. dir. Supreme Liberty Life Ins. Co. (succ. to Liberty Life Ins. Co. since 1929, chmn. exec. com., 1929-23; dir. Negro health, Julius Rosenwald Fund, Chicago, 1933-June 1942; cons. to U.S. Children's Bur., Chicago Bd. of Health. Pres. Chicago Urban League, 1935-39, now dir.; mem. exec. com Nat. Urban League; formerly mem. advisory schools com., Chicago Board of Education, mem. Bd. of Education, Oct. 1939-June 1942 (resigned); chmn. health and housing Conf. on Negro and Negro Youth, 1937-39; mem. advisory com. U.S. Children's Bur.; mem. exec. com. Children's Bur. Commn. on Children in Wartime, 1942-43; mem. planning com. White House Conf. on Children in Democracy, 1939; sec. Nat. Citizens Com., 1940-42; sr. warden St. Edmund's P.E. Ch. since Sept. 1940. Fellow Am. Pub. Health Assn., A.M.A.; Inst. of Med. of Chicago; mem. Nat. Med. Assn. (pres. 1933-34; chmn. commn. on hosps. and med. edn. since 1934), Nat. Hosp. Assn., Nat. Conf. on Social Work, American Trudeau Soc., Ill. Med. Soc., Chicago Med. Soc., U.S. del. to Pan-Am. Child Health Conf. Tech. dir. Provident Medical Associates since 1946. Awarded U. of Kan. alumni citation for distinguished service, 1941. Served as col. Med. Corps, Army of the U.S., comdg. officer, Station Hosp. 1, Ft. Huachuca, Ariz., 1942-45. Awarded Legion of Merit, U.S. Army, 1946. Author: Economics of a Tuberculosis Case Finding Program; Hospitals Internships and Residences for Negro Physicians; Reaching the Negro Community; Health Education in the Home; Physicians of Color in the U.S. Home: 9323 S. Michigan Av. Office: 3501 S. Parkway, Chicago, Ill. Died Feb. 16, 1948.

BOUTON, Archibald Lewis (bou′tŭn), prof. English; b. Cortland, N.Y., Sept. 1, 1872; s. Lewis and Emily (Lamont) B.; graduate State Normal Sch., Courtland, N.Y., 1892; A.B., Amherst, 1896; M.A., Columbia, 1900; research studies in English, U. of Edinburgh, 1907-08, 10, Harvard (sabbatical leave), 1916-17, Huntington Library, Calif., 1923-24; hon. D.Litt., Albion, 1922; m. Caroline Jessup MacNair, June 12, 1901; 1 dau., Margaret MacNair. Greek master, Rutgers Grammar Sch., 1896-98; instr. English, New York U., 1898-1901, asst. prof. English, 1901-05, prof., 1905, head of dept., 1914-36, dean Univ. Coll., of Arts and Pure Science, at University Heights, 1914-36, acting dean Grad. Sch., 1925-27; lecturer summers, U. of Calif., 1925, U. of Colo., 1927-30. Mem. Modern Lang. Assn. America, English Assn. Great Britain, Modern Humanities Research Assn., Phi Beta Kappa, Delta Kappa Epsilon. Editor: Lincoln and Douglas Debates, 1905; The Poetry and Prose of Matthew Arnold, 1927. Club: Century. Home: 2107 Oakdale St., Pasadena, Calif. Died Apr. 18, 1941.

BOUVE, Clement L(incoln) (bō-vā′), register of copyrights, lawyer; b. Hingham, Mass., May 27, 1878; s. Edward Tracy and Delphine (Dolores) B.; prep. edn. pvt. schs., Germany and Switzerland, 1886-90, Roxbury (Mass.) Latin Sch., 1891-95; A.B., Harvard 1899; Harvard Law Sch., 1900-02; m. Mary McLean, Sept. 10, 1906; children—Margaret, Warren Lincoln, Mary Elizabeth. Admitted to Mass. bar, 1903; sec. to Edward H. Strobel, adviser to Siamese Govt., 1903-04; asst. dist. atty., city and dist. of Manila, P.I., 1905-08; in practice of internat. and of federal law, Washington, D. C., 1909-36, register of copyrights since Aug. 1, 1936. Commr. for U.S. on Mixed Claims Commn., U.S. and Panama, 1916-17; asst. agt. for U.S., Gen. and Spl. Claims Commns., U.S. and Mexico, 1924-25, agt. 1926-31; tech. adviser, Internat. Aeronautic Conf., Washington, Dec. 1928; mem. bd. advisers, Harvard Research in Internat. Law, 1928, 29. Served as captain, later major, Field Artillery, U.S. Army, Am. Expeditionary Force, 1917-19. Mem. Am. Bar Association, Am. Soc. of Internat. Law, Society of Colonial Wars, Loyal Legion, American Legion. Republican. Unitarian. Clubs: Cosmos, Harvard, Chevy Chase (Washington); St. Botolph (Boston). Author: Laws Governing the Exclusion and Expulsion of Aliens from the United States, 1912; also numerous articles on internat. and aviation law. Home: 109 Shepherd St., Chevy Chase, Md. Office: Copyright Office, Library of Congress, Washington, D.C. Died Jan. 14, 1944.

BOW, Warren E., (bou), supt. of schools, univ. pres.; b. Detroit, Mich., June 2, 1891; s. Sandy and Anna (Cushing) B.; B.S., U. of Ill., 1914; A.M., U. of Mich., 1923; LL.D., Battle Creek Coll., 1931; m. Marian Flaherty, Nov. 7, 1929; children—Nancy Ann (dec.), Warren James. Teacher and prin., grade and high schs., 1915-22; asst. dean Detroit Teachers Coll., 1922-25, acting dean, 1925-26, dean, 1926-30; asst. supt. Detroit Schs., 1930-39, first asst. supt., 1939-41, dep. supt., 1941-42, supt. since 1942; pres. Wayne U., Detroit since 1942. Served as capt., maj., Field Arty., 32d Div., A.E.F. Mem. The Citizens' Housing and Planning Council of Detroit (v.p. 1941-43), Detroit Bd. of Commerce. Mem. N.E.A., Mich. Edn. Assn., Detroit Teachers Assn., Am. Vocational Assn., Mich. Indsl. Edn. Soc., Engring. Soc. of Detroit, Am. Legion, Phi Delta Kappa, Kappa Delta Pi, Mu Sigma Pi, Sigma Pi. Mason (K.T., Consistory, Shriner). Clubs: Detroit Athletic, Economic, Northwest Kiwanis (pres. 1927), Ridgevale Rod and Gun, St. Andrews Soc., Noontide, University of Michigan (Detroit, Mich.). Home: 18318 Birchcrest Drive. Office: 1354 Broadway, Detroit. Died May 12, 1945; buried in Evergreen Cemetery, Detroit.

BOWDEN, Aberdeen Orlando (bou′dĕn), educator, anthropologist; b. Fulton, Ky., Dec. 13, 1881; s. Isaiah and Malenda Agnes (Emerson) B.; A.B., State U. of Ky., 1908, A.M., 1910; A.M., Harvard, 1912; studied U. of Chicago, 1 yr.; Ph.D., Columbia U., 1929; m. Katharine Kennan Marsh, Aug. 21, 1913; children—Gordon Townely, Anne Emerson. Prin. high sch., Maysville, 1908-09, Henry County High Sch., Paris, Tenn., 1909-11, high sch., Laurel, Mont., 1913-14, Huron, S.D., 1914-18, Huron Jr.-Sr. High Sch., 1918-20; supt. city schs., Huron, 1920; head of dept. and prof. edn. and philosophy, Baylor Coll., Belton, Tex., 1920-22; pres. N.M. State Teachers' Coll., 1922-34; head of dept. of anthropology, U. of Southern Calif., and dir. Calif. branch of Sch. of Am. Research, since Sept. 1934; adviser Veterans Rehabilitation, Sawtelle, Calif.; dir. Jemez Field Sch. of Archeology, summer 1935; field work in anthropology in S.A., 1 semester. Was pres. N.M. Ednl. Council; mem. board of control, Sch. of Am. Research; mem. Nat. Illiteracy Commn., Geographical Board of N.M. Fellow A.A.A.S., American Geographic Society; mem. American Men of Science, N.E.A. (com. on tenure), Save Our Schools Com. (nat.), Am. Acad. of Polit. and Social Science, Am. Sociol. Soc., Am. Anthropol. Assn., Nat. Economic Council, Nat. Soc. for Study of Ednl. Sociology, N.M. Endl. Assn. (pres. 1928-29), School Master's Club of N.M. (pres. 1932-33), Phi Beta Kappa, Phi Delta Kappa, Kappa Delta Pi, Phi Sigma Pi, Pi Gamma Mu, Mu Alpha Nu, Sigma Xi; del. of N.E.A. to World Federation of Edn. Assns., Geneva, Switzerland, 1929; pres. N.M. Science Commn., 1931-32; pres. N.M. Assn. for Science, 1930-31; pres. N.M. Coll., Presidents' Assn.; pres. Southwestern Archeol. Soc., 1937-38. Baptist. Mason. Rotarian (gov. 42d dist. 1932-33). Author: Consumers' Uses of Arithmetic, 1929; Tomorrow's Americans (with Ida Clyde Clarke), 1930; Social Psychology of Education, 1937; Man and Civilization, 1938; The American Scene, 1942; Preface to Human Nature; The Day Before Yesterday in America. Compiler of Bibliographies in Education Sociology (with others), 1928. Chmn. N.M. Elementary Course of Study, 1930. Contbr. to scientific and ednl. press. Winner various awards for scholarship. Home: 4815 Angeles Vista Blvd., Los Angeles 43, Calif. Died Feb. 10, 1946.

BOWDEN, Garfield Arthur (bō′dĕn), chem. research; b. Dec. 19, 1880; s. John and Agnes (Lukey) B.; grad. Normal Sch., Platteville, Wis., 1901; B.S., U. of Chicago, 1913; grad. work, U. of Chicago and University of Cincinnati; m. Lucy E. Bell, September 10, 1902 (deceased June 9, 1942); children—Paul Webster, Isabel Agnes. Principal of the State Graded Sch., Revere, Minn., 1901-02, high sch., Pepin, Wis., 1902-06; in charge science and math. depts., high sch., Winona, Minn., 1906-08; head of science dept. Twp. High Sch., Waukegan, Ill., 1908-11, asst. prin., 1915-17; asst. prof. methods of science teaching, Teachers Coll., Normal (Ill.) U., 1917-18; head of science dept. University Sch., Cincinnati, 1918-37; head of chem. research and ednl. depts. A. S. Boyle & Co., Inc., Cincinnati, O., and Jersey City, N.J., and for Am. Home Products, Jersey City, N.J.; asst. prof. methods of science teaching, N.C. State Teachers Coll., Raleigh summers 1924-27. Fellow of Royal Soc. of Arts (London); mem. Acad. Polit. Science, A.A.A.S., Central Assn. Science Teachers, Am. Chem. Soc., Schoolmasters Club (Cincinnati), Cincinnati Astron. Soc., Cincinnati City Beautiful Assn., Torch Club, Phi Delta Kappa. Presbyterian. Author: Gen. Science, 1923; Foundations of Science, 1931. Home: 139 N. Arlington Av., East Orange, N.J. Office: 1934 Dana Av., Cincinnati, O.; and 257 Cornelison Av., Jersey City, N.J. Deceased.

BOWDEN, Laurens Reeve, insurance exec.; b. New York, N.Y., Mar. 12, 1879; s. Joseph B. and Alice Mitchell (Jaggar) B.; LL.B., Yale, 1899; m. Cary L. Wade, Sept. 15, 1927. With Pacific Fire Ins. Co., Bankers & Shippers Ins. Co. and Jersey Ins. Co. of New York, since 1902; started as jr. clerk, now vice chmn. and dir. Mem. S.A.R. Clubs: Yale, Downtown Assn. Home: 65 E. 55th St. Office: 12 Gold St., New York, N.Y. Died June 16, 1948.

BOWEN, Ezra, prof. economics; b. Bethlehem, Pa., Jan. 11, 1891; s. Franklin Haylander and Lena (Babcock) B.; B.S., Lehigh Univ., 1913, M.S., 1916; Ph.D. from Columbia, 1931; m. Catherine Drinker, Mar. 19, 1919; children—Catherine Drinker, Ezra, Was instr., asst. prof. and asso. prof. economics, Lehigh U., 1914-20; prof. and head dept. of economics, Lafayette Coll., since 1920. Pres. Civil Service Commn., City of Easton. Mem. Am. Econ. Assn., Am. Assn. for Labor Legislation, Am. Acad. Polit. and Social Science, Psi Upsilon. Democrat. Presbyterian. Club: Psi Upsilon (Phila.). Author: Social Economy, 1929; An Hypothesis of Population Growth, 1931. Home: Easton, Pa. Dec. 26, 1945.

BOWEN, Harry; chmn. of bd. Pocahontas Fuel Co. Address: Pocahontas, Va.* Died 1942.

BOWERMAN, Guy Emerson, banker; b. Coldwater, Mich., Oct. 8, 1866; s. Thomas Henry and Elizabeth (Daken) B.; ed. high sch.; m. Susanne Eugena Wilson, Sept. 18, 1888; 1 son, Guy Emerson. Began banking in S.D., 1884; St. Anthony, Ida., 1899; prominently identified with development of Southeastern Ida. Mem. Ida. Ho. of Rep., 1913-14; 1st com. of finance, under new commn. form of govt., State of Ida., 1919; served as col. on staff of Gov. Davis of Ida. Mem. Am. Bankers' Assn. (exec. mgr. N. Y. City, 1920-21; pres. state bank div., 1927). Organized Arlington Heights State Bank, Los Angeles, sold same; now retired. Pres. Ida. State Bankers' Assn., 1911. Republican. Mason. Clubs: Los Angeles Country, The Beach (Los Angeles). Home: 628 N. Maple Drive, Beverly Hills, Calif. Died March 15, 1940.

BOWERS, William Gray, coll. prof.; b. nr. Franklin, W.Va., June 16, 1879; s. Josephus and Emily (Bond) B.; B.Sc., Ohio Wesleyan U., 1905; A.M., Ind. U., 1911; spl. student U. of Calif., 1915; Ph.D., Ohio State U., 1919; m. Ollie Quitera Smith, 1901; children—Emily Margaret, John Edward. Began teaching at 16; taught in pub. sch. of W.Va., 5 yrs.; asst. in Zoölogy, Ohio Wesleyan U., 1904; prin. ward sch., Urbana, O., 1905; prin. high sch., Aspen, Colo., 1906; supt. schs., Leesburg, O., 1907; science teacher summer, Ind. Normal Sch., Muncie, Ind., 1907; phys. science teacher, State Normal and Indsl. Sch., Ellendale, N.D., 1908-18; v.p. same, 1914, 16; prof. food chemistry, and head of lab. of State Food Commn., Agrl. Coll., N.D., 1918-20; head of chem. dept. Colo. State Teachers Coll. 1920. Mem. Am. Chem. Soc., Colo. Ednl. Assn., N.E.A., Colo. Science Club. Republican. Methodist. Wrote: The Nutrition Value of the Soy Bean; Laboratory Instruction in Elementary Chemistry; also articles on food adulteration, on methods in teaching of chemistry, etc. Commencement speaker and institute instr. Home: 1117 19th St., Greeley, Colo. Died May 29, 1945.

BOWES, Edward (Major) (bōz), radio programs; b. San Francisco, Calif.; s. John M. and Amelia (Ford) B.; ed. public schools, San Francisco, and private tutors; hon. LL.D., Villanova Coll., 1939; m. Margaret Illington (deceased). Began radio career with Capitol Family Hour, 1925; originated Major Bowes Amateur Hour, 1934, voted most popular on air, 1935; mng. dir. Capitol Theatre, New York, until May 1941; v.p. and dir. Mordall Realty Corp.; exec. dir. Major Bowes Enterprises, Tyro Productions, Inc. Consultant Office of War Information. Hon. mem. Soc. of California Pioneers. Decorated Knight of Malta. Clubs: The Lambs, Cloud, Sleepy Hollow Country, Catholic, Monmouth Beach, Officers of Army and Navy; (yacht clubs): Mobile; Buccaneer (Mobile, Ala.); Norris (Knoxville, Tenn.); Austin (Tex.); Inlet Yachting Center Fleet (Atlantic City); Fairhaven (N.J.); Green Bay (Wis.); Sarnia (Mich.); Port Huron, St. Clair River Yachting Assn. (Port Huron, Mich.); Erie (Pa.); Racine (Wis.); New Bedford (Mass.); Galveston Yacht Basin (Tex.); Pontiac, Oakland Country Boat (Pontiac, Mich.); Gull Lake Yacht (Battle Creek, Mich.); Saginaw (Bay City, Mich.); Corinthian (Tiburon, Calif.); St. Paul (Minn.); Lorain (O.); Oshkosh (Wis.); Everett (Wash.); Duluth (Minn.). Author of Verses I Like (poems). Home: Rumson, N.J. Office: 1697 Broadway, New York. Died June 13, 1946; buried in Sleepy Hollow Cemetery, New York.

BOWIE, Edward Hall, meteoroligist; b. Annapolis Junction, Md., Mar. 29, 1874; s. Thomas John and Susanna Hall (Anderson) B.; M.S., St. John's Coll., Annapolis, Md., 1920; m. Florence C. Hatch, Dec. 12, 1895; children—Mrs. Helen McKinstry Prentiss, Mrs. Margaret Lowndes Wallace, Mrs. Susanna Anderson Lindquist. Entered service U.S. Weather Bur., Dec. 1891; asst. observer at Memphis, 1891-95, Montgomery, Ala., 1896-98; observer, Dubuque, Ia., 1898-1901; section dir., Galveston, Tex., 1901-03; local forecaster, St. Louis, 1903-09; chief forecast div. U.S. Weather Bur., 1910-12, nat. forecaster, 1909-24, prin. meteorologist and dist. forecaster, Pacific States, since 1924. Commd. maj. Signal Corps, July 9, 1917, and ordered to France for meteorol. forecasts for A.E.F.; resigned and returned to Weather Bur., Dec. 1918. Mem. coms. meteorology and scientific hydrology, Am. Geophys. Union. Fellow Am. Meteorol. Soc., Calif. Acad. Sciences; mem. Philos. Soc. Washington, Washington Acad. Sciences. Mason. Clubs: Faculty (Berkeley, Calif.); Family (San Francisco, Calif.). Home: 844 Contra Costa Av., Berkeley, Calif. Office: U.S. Weather Bur., San Francisco, Calif. Died July 29, 1943.

BOWLEY, Albert Jesse (bō'lē), army officer; b. Westminster, Calif., Nov. 24, 1875; s. Freeman S. and Flora E. (Pepper) B.; grad. U.S. Mil. Acad., 1897; m. Elsie Ball Wright, Sept. 12, 1931. Commd. 2d lt. 4th Arty., June 11, 1897; promoted through grades to col., May 15, 1917; brig. gen. N.A., June 26, 1918; brig. gen. regular army, Apr. 29, 1921; major gen., Feb. 20, 1931; lieut. gen., Aug. 5, 1939. Participated in Siege of Santiago, Cuba, July 1898; in Philippines, 1899-1901; participated in General Lawton's campaign in Northern Luzon; instr. in chemistry, mineralogy, geology and electricity, and senior instr. arty. tactics, U.S. Mil. Acad., 1901-05; a.d.c. to Maj. Gen. F. D. Grant, at Governor's Island, N.Y., 1906-08, at Chicago, 1908-10; in Philippines, 1910-11; mil. attaché to China, 1911-14; duty Fort Sill and Mexican border, 1915-17; organized 17th F.A., 1917, and went to France as its head, Dec. 1917; service Troyon sector, Chateau-Thierry, Belleau Woods, Soissons offensive, Marbache sector, St. Mihiel offensive, Blanc Mont offensive, Meuse-Argonne offensive, Moselle sector; apptd. comdr. 2d F.A. Brigade, 2d Div., A.E.F., June 26, 1918; apptd. chief of arty, 6th Corps, Nov. 6, 1918; at Gen. Staff Coll., 1919-20; mem. Gen. Staff Corps, 1920-21; apptd. comdr. Ft. Bragg, N.C., July 1921; in command 8th Corps Area, June-Dec. 1928, 2d Div., 1928-29; asst. Chief of Staff (G1), Washington, D.C., 1929-31; in command Hawaiian Div., Schofield Barracks, T.H., 1931-34, 5th Corps Area, 1934-35, 3d Corps Area (headquarters at Baltimore), 1935-38, 9th Corps Area, and 4th Army, 1938-39; retired from active service, Nov. 30, 1939. Medals Spanish-Am. War. Cuban Occupation, Philippine Insurrection, Mexican Border, Victory, also Distinguished Service Medal; Officer Legion of Honor, and Croix de Guerre, 4 palms and 1 silver star (France); Order of Chi Hua (Plentiful Rice), by Chinese Govt.; Order of Solididad (Republic of Panama); Order of White Elephant (Siam); Royal Order of St. Olav (Norway); Gen. Staff Medal, War Dept. (U.S.). Club: Army and Navy (Washington, D.C.). Home: 2819 McGill Terrace, Washington 8, D.C. Died May 22, 1945.

BOWLING, William Bismarck, judge; b. Calhoun County, Ala., Sept. 24, 1870; s. William E. and Sarah (Elston) B.; grad. State Teachers Coll., Jacksonville, Ala., 1892; m. Frances Collins, June 2, 1896; children—George Randolph, Marion Elston (Mrs. G. L. Jenkins), Sarah Frances (Mrs. John Thomas Frazer), Elizabeth Craig (dec.). Teacher city schs., Montgomery, Ala., and Columbus, Ga., 7 yrs.; admitted to Ala. bar, 1900, and began practice at Lafayette; pros. atty. 5th Jud. Circuit of Ala., 1904-20 (resigned); elected to 66th Congress for an unexpired term (1920-21), and 67th to 70th Congresses (1921-29), 5th Ala. Dist.; resigned to accept appointment as judge 5th Judicial Circuit, Ala., reëlected judge, 1934 and 1940 Chmn. Board of Education, Dadeville, Ala., 12 yrs.; 1st vice-president and president, 1941-43, Alabama Baptist State Convention. President Ala. Assn. of Circuit Judges, 1940-41; mem. bd. trustees, Alabama Polytechnic Inst., Auburn. Hon. mem. Omicron Delta Kappa; mem. Iota Circle, U. of Ala. Democrat. Mason (Shriner), K.P. Home: Lafayette, Ala. Died Dec. 1946.

BOWMAN, Harold Martin, prof. law; b. Des Moines, Ia., Jan. 17, 1876; s. Martin T. V. and Josephine (Webber) B.; LL.B., U. of Mich., 1899, B.Litt., 1900, A.M., 1901; Ph.D., Columbia, 1903; Columbia U. fellow in administrative law, 1902-03; m. Mary Catherine Kauffman, June 19, 1907; children—Mary Jean (Mrs. C. Arnold Anderson), Nancy Ray. Admitted to bar, Michigan and Iowa, 1899, and practiced in Des Moines and New York; became instructor in political science, 1903-04, assistant professor, 1904-06, Dartmouth, also instructor law, Tuck School of Administration and Finance, 1903-06; spl. expert Interstate Commerce Commn., 1904; expert U.S. Senate com. on interstate commerce, 1905; editorial writer, N.Y. Globe, 1906-10; lecturer, 1910-14, prof. of law, since 1914, Boston U. Sch. of Law, also dir. curriculum, 1935-44; in charge of division of law and govt. of Boston U. Coll. of Liberal Arts, 1933-36. Mem. S.A.R., Am. Bar Assn., Am. Polit. Science Assn. mem. exec. council, 1918, A.A.A.S., Phi Beta Kappa, Chi Psi, Phi Delta Phi. Republican. Protestant. Clubs: University (Boston), Appalachian Mt. Author: The Administration of Iowa, 1903. Compiled a Twelve-year Survey of State R.R. Taxation (Interstate Commerce Commn.), 1903. Home: 97 Annawan Rd., Waban. Mass. Office: 11 Ashburton Pl., Boston, Mass. Died Nov. 21, 1949.

BOWMAN, Isaiah, univ. pres.; b. Waterloo, Ont., Can., Dec. 26, 1878; s. Samuel Cressman and Emily (Shantz) B.; grad. State Normal Coll., Ypsilanti, Mich., 1902; B.Sc., Harvard, 1905; Ph.D., Yale University 1909; hon. M.A., 1921; hon. M.Ed., Mich. State Coll., 1927; hon. Sc.D., Bowdoin Coll., 1931, universities of Cuzco and Arequipa, Peru, 1941; LL.D., Dartmouth, Charleston, Dickinson and U. of Pennsylvania, 1935, U. of Wisconsin and Harvard U., 1936, Queen's U. and U. of Western Ontario, 1937, Washington College, 1940; m. Cora Olive Goldthwait, June 28, 1909; children—Walter Parker, Robert Goldthwait, Olive. Assistant in physiography, Harvard, 1904-05; instructor in geography, State Normal College, Ypsilanti, 1903-04; instructor in geography, 1905-09, assistant professor, 1909-15, Yale University; director American Geog. Soc., N.Y., 1915-35; president Johns Hopkins University since July 1, 1935; member board directors American Telephone & Telegraph Company. Leader first Yale South American Expedition, 1907; geographer and geologist, Yale Peruvian Expedition, 1911; leader expdn. to Central Andes, under auspices Am. Geog. Soc., 1913. Chmn. Nat. Research Council, 1933-35. vice chmn. Science Advisory Board, 1933-35. Chief territorial specialist Am. Commn. to Negotiate Peace, 1918-19; and mem. various territorial commns. of the Peace Conf., Paris, 1919; physiographer U.S. Dept. Justice in Red River boundary dispute; Am. member Permanent Internat. Commission, China and U.S., since 1940; member of the London Mission of the Department of State, April 1944; chairman of the territorial committee, Department of State, 1942-43; vice chairman post-war advisory council, Dept. of State, 1943-1944; spl. adviser to Sec. of State, 1943-45; mem. American delegation Dumbarton Oaks Conf., August-September, 1944; adviser to U.S. delegation United Nations Conf., San Francisco, 1945. Mem. board dirs., Council on Foreign Relations, Woods Hole Oceanographic Instn., American Geographical Soc. of N.Y. (Councilor 1935); president International Geographical Union, 1931-34; mem. Am. Philos. Soc. (council 1935), Assn. Am. Geographers (pres. 1931), Nat. Acad. of Sciences (vice pres. 1941-45); mem. A.A.A.S. (pres. 1943); associate mem. Nat. Acad. of Sciences, Peru, hon. corr. mem. Geog. Society La Paz, Bolivia, Hispanic Soc. America, Royal Geog. Soc., London, Swedish Soc. Anthropology and Geography (for. mem., 1939), geog. socs. of Phila., Berlin, Finland, Jugoslavia, Rome, Colombia, etc.; corr. mem. Soc. Chilena de Hist. y Geogr.; fellow American Acad. Arts and Sciences. Mem. Phi Beta Kappa. Livingstone gold medal, Royal Scottish Geog. Soc., 1928; Bonaparte-Wyse gold medal of Geog. Soc. of Paris, 1917, for explorations in and publs. on S. America; gold medal, Geog. Soc., Chicago, 1927; Civjic medal, Geog. Soc. of Belgrade, 1935; Henry Grier Bryant gold medal, Geog. Soc. of Phila., 1937; Patron's medal, Royal Geog. Soc. (London), 1941. Clubs: Explorers (ex-sec. and ex-v.p.), Century (New York); Cosmos (Washington, D.C.). Author: Forest Physiography, 1911; South America, 1915; The Andes of Southern Peru, 1916; The New World—Problems in Political Geography, 1921; Desert Trails of Atacama, 1923; An American Boundary Dispute, 1923; The Mohammedan World, 1924; International Relations, 1930; The Pioneer Fringe, 1931; Geography in Relation to the Social Sciences, 1934; Design for Scholarship, 1936; Graduate School in American Democracy, 1939. Co-editor and part author of Human Geography; editor and collaborator for Limits of Land Settlement, 1937. Home: 108 West 39 St., Baltimore 10. Office: Johns Hopkins University, Baltimore 18, Md. Died Jan. 6, 1950.

BOYCE, William D., publisher; b. Allegheny County, Pa., June 16, 1860; s. David and Margaret J. B.; ed. U. of Wooster, O.; m. Mary Jane Deacon, 1883. Began bus. career as adv. solicitor, Chicago, 1881; became newspaper pub. in Dak.; organizer and mgr., bur. of correspondence, rep. 1,200 newspapers, New Orleans Cotton Expn., 1884; est. "patent inside" house. Chicago, and Winfield, Kan.; assisted in establishing Saturday Blade, Chicago, became owner; bought Chicago Ledger and other publs. now pub. by W. D. Boyce Co. (pres.); pres. Marseilles (Ill.) Land & Water Power Co. Owner of Boyce Bldg., Chicago. Republican. Clubs: Union League, Chicago Athletic. Address: 112 Dearborn St., Chicago. Died Nov. 17, 1923.

BOYD, D. Knickerbacker, architect, structural standardist; b. Phila., Jan. 5, 1872; s. David, Jr., and Alida Visscher (Knickerbacker) B.; ed. Friends' Central Sch., Rugby Acad., Phila., Pa. Acad. Fine Arts, Spring Garden Inst., Phila., and U. of Pa.; m. Elizabeth Hörnli Mifflin, Sept. 10, 1896; children—Barbara Mifflin (Mrs. Lawrence C. Murdoch), Lysbeth Knickerbacker (Mrs. Henry P. Borie). Practiced Phila. since 1892; designer Carnegie Library Bldg., Phila., chs., factories, apartment bldgs., schs. and suburban homes. Lecturer and writer on constrn. economics, archtl. adviser Structural Service Bur.; consultant on bldg. codes, zoning, production and application of bldg. materials and on informational publications. During World War, chief materials information sect., U.S. Housing Corp., U.S. Dept. of Labor and rep. on War Industries Board. Editor Structural Service Book, Jour. A.I.A. Mem. correlating com. on legislation and administration of President's Conf. on Home Building and Home Ownership. Fellow Am. Inst. Architects (ex-sec., ex-v.p.); mem. coms. on building regulations and on pub. information and civilian defense of Phila. chapter A.I.A.;

ex-pres. Pa. State Assn. A.I.A., Phila. chapter A.I.A.; ex-pres. Phila. Building Congress; v.p. Am. Constrn. Council (coms. on apprenticeship and better building); mem. Phila. com. Better Homes in America; mem. exec. com. Zoning Fed. of Phila.; mem. Archtl. League of New York, Am. Federation of Arts (ex-dir.), N.E.A., Phila. Housing Assn., Regional Plan of Phila. (advisory com.), Com. to Revise Building Code of Philadelphia, Civil Legion, War Industries Bd. Assn., S.R. (chmn. com. on protection of historic bldgs.), Independence Hall Association (exec. sec.), Netherlands Society, Society of Cincinnati of Pennsylvania; honorary member N. Texas Chapter, A.I.A. Pa.; state archtl. advisor Home Owners Loan Corp.; administrative asst. Pa., Works Progress Administrn.; co-ordinator of exhibits, N.Y. State Worlds Fair Commn.; advisor on building industry relations, Russell Sage Foundation; consultant on housing and labor relations, U.S. Housing Administration; consultant Federal Committee on Apprenticeship. Contributing editor Pencil Points, N.Y. City. Episcopalian. Club: T Square (Phila.). Home: 320 W. Springfield Av., Phila., and 53 W. 33d St., New York, N.Y. Office: 1 S. 15th St., Philadelphia, Pa. Died Feb. 21, 1944.

BOYD, Ernest, author; b. Dublin, Ireland, June 28, 1887; s. James Robert and Rosa (Kempston) B.; ed. pvtly. and passed competitive examination for British consular service. Mem. editorial staff Irish Times, 1910; entered consular service 1913; v. consul at Baltimore (Md.), Barcelona (Spain), and Copenhagen (Denmark); resigned and settled in N.Y. City, 1920; editorial staff Evening Post, 1920-22; reader and adviser on foreign lit. for Alfred A. Knopf, publisher, 1922-23. Associate mem. Irish Acad. of Letters. Author: Ireland's Literary Renaissance, 1922; Contemporary Drama of Ireland, 1917; Appreciations and Depreciations, 1917; Portraits—Real and Imaginary, 1924; Studies in Ten Literatures, 1925; H. L. Mencken, 1925; Guy de Maupassant—A Biographical Study, 1926; Literary Blasphemies, 1927; (with Madeline Davidson) After the Fireworks—a Comedy, 1930; The Pretty Lady, 1934. Also translator: Opium, by Jean Cocteau; L'Image, by Denys Amiel; Il Problema Centrale, by Arnaldo Fraccaroli; Les Propos d'Anatole France; Der Untertan, by Heinrich Mann; Une Belle Journée, by Henri Céard; Ranke Viljer, by Gustav Wied; Droll Stories, by H. de Balzac; Sword in the Soul, by R. Chauviré; Rabelais, by A. France; Maya, by S. Gantillon; 88 Short Stories, by G. de Maupassant. Editor and translator of Collected Novels and Stories of Guy de Maupassant. 18 vols. Home: 151 E. 19th St., New York, N.Y. Died Dec. 30, 1946.

BOYD, James, author; b. Dauphin Co., Pa., July 2, 1888; s. John Yeomans and Eleanor Gilmore (Herr) B.; grad. Hill Sch., Pottstown, Pa., 1906; A.B., Princeton, 1910; Trinity Coll., Cambridge U., 1912; m. Katharine Lamont, Dec. 15, 1917; children—James, Daniel Lamont, Nancy. 1st lt. U.S. Army, with A.E.F., in France, World War; participated in action at St. Mihiel, 1st and 2d Meuse-Argonne offensives. Mem. Soc. of Cincinnati. Club: Coffee House (New York). Author: Drums, 1925; Marching On, 1927; Long Hunt, 1930; Roll River, 1935; Bitter Creek, 1939. Home: Southern Pines, N.C.* Died Feb. 25, 1944.

BOYD, James Harrington, lawyer; b. Keene, Coshocton County, O., Dec. 7, 1862; s. James and Mary (Ross) B.; student Wooster (O.) U., 1881-83; B.A., Princeton, 1886, M.A., 1888, D.Sc., 1892; student mathematics and physics, U. of Göttingen, 1890-93; LL.B., Harvard, 1903; m. Susan Adams, Mar. 25, 1896; children—Helen, Mary, James. Prof. mathematics, U. of Chicago, 1893-1902; admitted to Ohio bar, 1904, and since practiced at Toledo. Served as chmn. Employees' Liability Commn., under Gov. Harmon of Ohio, 1910-11, and is author of Ohio Workmen's Compensation Act providing for compulsory industrial insurance, adopted in Ohio and other states. Apptd., Dec. 1, 1934, legal consultant Federal Emergency Relief Administrn., to write a brief for Com. on Economic Security on constitutionality of a model compulsory state unemployment insurance act provided for in Federal Security Act; spl. atty. U.S. Dept. of Justice for Toledo Housing and Slum Clearance Project. Mem. Ohio Bar Assn., Phi Beta Kappa. Democrat. Presbyn. Author: A Treatise on the Law of Compensation for Injuries to Workmen Under Modern Industrial Statutes (2 vols.), 1913; College Algebra. Contbr. articles on legal subjects to Yale, U. of Mich. and U. of Calif. law journals and to Am. Jour. of Sociology. Home: 2124 Robinwood Av. Office: Nicholas Bldg., Toledo, O. Died Jan. 2, 1946.

BOYD, James Oscar, clergyman; b. Ranway, N.J., Oct. 17, 1874; s. Oscar Endly and Mary Elizabeth (French) B.; B.A., New York U., 1895, M.A., 1897, D.D., 1915; student Erlangen U., Germany, 1895-96; B.D., Princeton Theol. Sem., 1899; Ph.D., Princeton, 1905; m. Bertha Work McManigal, May 22, 1901 (died Aug. 6, 1938); children—Alden Work, Elizabeth French, Anna Laughlin (dec.), Mary Florence. Traveling fellow New York U., 1895-96; teaching fellow Princeton Theol. Sem., 1899-1900; instr. in O.T., 1900-07, asst. prof. Orient. & O. T. lit., Princeton Theol. Sem., 1907-15; pastor of the Church of the Redeemer (Presbyn.), Paterson, N.J., 1915-21; sec. Am. Bible Society for the Levant, 1921-37; asst. sec. American Bible Society, 1937-42; sec. for Versions since 1942. Educational secretary of International Com. Y.M.C.A., lecturing to British and Anzac troops in Egypt, Palestine, Syria and Cilicia, 1918-19 (on leave absence). Mem. Phi Beta Kappa, Psi Upsilon. Author: The Text of the Ethiopic Octateuch, 1905; Ezekiel and the Modern Dating of the Pentateuch (brochure), 1908; Sin and Grace in the Koran (in Centennial Vol. of Princeton Sem.), 1912; Brief History of the O.T., 1917. Editor: The Octateuch in Ethiopic, Vol. I—Genesis, 1909, Vol. II—Exodus and Leviticus, 1911; Glimpses of High Politics (by N. V. Tcharykow), 1931; Maps of Bible Lands, 1939. Contbr. critical articles on O.T. and Semitic subjects in Princeton Theol. Rev., encys., etc. Stone lecturer, Princeton Theol. Sem., Oct. 1921. Home: 178 George St., New Brunswick, N.J. Office: American Bible Society, 450 Park Av., New York 22, N.Y. Died Aug. 13, 1947.

BOYD, William, architect; b. Glasgow, Scotland, Aug. 24, 1882; s. William and Mary Jane (Binnie) B.; brought to U.S., 1888; B.S., U. of Pa.; m. Catherine McCutcheon, Jan. 6, 1914; children—William, Elizabeth Collier. Began as draftsman, 1909; partner, Ingham & Boyd, Architects, since May 1, 1911. Fellow A.I.A.; mem. Sigma Xi, Delta Kappa Epsilon. Mason. Home: Poia Rd., Sewickley, Pa. Office: Empire Bldg., Pittsburgh, Pa. Died March 1, 1947.

BOYD, William H., lawyer; b. Fairview, O., Aug. 11, 1864; s. George W. and Mary A. (Campbell) B.; m. Anna M. Judkins, Sept. 7, 1892; children—Mildred A. (dec.), Mary Gertrude (Mrs. R. E. Le Lievre). Admitted to Ohio bar and now in practice at Cleveland; pres. firm Boyd, Brooks and Wickham. Candidate for mayor of Cleveland, 1905; pres. Ohio Electoral Coll., 1920. Mem. Am., Ohio State and Cuyahoga County bar assns., Cleveland Chamber Commerce. Republican. Mason, K.P., Elk. Club: Cleveland Athletic. Home: 3233 Chadbourne Rd., Shaker Height 20. Office: Terminal Tower, Cleveland, O. Died Oct. 15, 1947.

BOYD, William Waddell, college pres.; b. Allegheny, Pa., Mar. 8, 1862; s. Joseph Reed and Martha J. (McGonagle) B.; student Muskingum Coll., New Concord, Ohio, 1 yr.; A.B., Marietta Coll., 1884, M.A., 1887, Ped.D., 1911; LL.D., Miami U., 1933; studied in Europe 9 summers; m. Mary A. Gates, Sept. 1, 1887; children—Randolph King (dec.), Marion Margaret (Mrs. Walter Havighurst). Teacher pub. schs., Cambridge, O., 1884-85; teacher Crawfis Inst., Lancaster, 1885-90; prin. high sch., Marietta, 1890-91; supt. schs., Marietta, 1891-98, Painesville, 1898-1902; high sch. insp., Ohio State U., 1902-07; dean Coll. of Edn., same, 1907-14; pres. Western Coll. for Women, Oxford, O., 1914-31, now emeritus. Mem. Ohio State Bd. Sch. Examiners, 1898-1903; trustee Ohio Sunday Sch. Assn., Marietta Coll.; coll. counsellor Ohio Dept. of Edn. Mem. N.E.A., Ohio State Teachers Assn., North Central Assn. Colls. and Secondary Schs., Phi Beta Kappa, Alpha Sigma Phi. Pres. North Central Assn., 1925, Ohio Coll. Assn., 1923. Republican. Presbyterian; vice-moderator Gen. Assembly of Presbyn. Ch., 1920. Clubs: Cincinnati Business Men's; Cincinnati Schoolmasters' (Columbus). Author: The Government and Civil Institutions of Ohio, 1906. Trustee Western Reserve Acad., Hudson, O. Cruise travel lecturer. Home: 1170 E. Broad St., Columbus, O.* Died Feb. 2, 1944.

BOYNTON, George Rufus, painter; b. Pleasant Grove, Wis.; s. David and Julia (Hancock) B.; ed. high sch. and normal coll. in Minn.; began drawing while at sch.; student Nat. Acad. Design (medalist) and Art Students' League, and under Walter Shirlaw, C. Y. Turner and J. G. Brown; m. Mary Ellicott Junius, July 8, 1906. Portraits in Union League Club, 7th Regt. Armory, 71st Regt. Armory, West Point, New York Univ., Yale Coll., Columbia Univ., Union Coll., Coll. of the City of New York, New York Yacht Club, Larchmont Yacht Club, also the U.S. Dist. Court, etc. Has painted portraits of Gen. F. D. Grant, Gen. Alexander S. Webb, Gen. Stewart L. Woodford, Gen. James Grant Wilson, Rear Admirals Charles D. Sigsbee and Coghlan, Dr. William Temple Hornaday, Melville E. Stone, Edwin Markham, U.S. Senator Royal S. Copeland, Charles Evans Hughes, Elihu Root, Victor Lawson, Chancellor Elmer Ellsworth Brown, Gov. Herbert Lehman; portraits in numerous pvt. collections. Has been called painter laureate of army and navy life. Mem. Artists' Fund; life mem. N.Y. Geneal. and Biog. Soc., N.Y. Hist. Soc. Clubs: MacDowell, Lotos (life), Barnard. Republican. Unitarian. Address: Gainsborough Studios, 222 Central Park South, New York, N.Y.; (summer) Elizabethtown, Essex Co., N.Y.* Died Jan. 5, 1945.

BOYNTON, Melbourne Parker, clergyman; b. Lynn, Mass., Nov. 6, 1867; s. of Benjamin Skinner and Mary Elizabeth (Croscup) B.; Calif. Coll., Oakland; Div. Sch., U. of Chicago; (D.D., Des Moines Coll., Ia., 1911); m. Hattie Wells, Sept. 8, 1892; children—Melbourne Wells, Ben Lynn. Ordained Bapt. ministry, Sept. 8, 1892; consecutively asst., acting and pastor First Ch., San Francisco, 1894-07; became pastor Lexington Av. Ch. (now Woodlawn Bapt.), Chicago, Aug. 1897, erected new edifice and dedicated it Oct. 26, 1902, dedicated $100,000 church house, 1924, retired Feb. 7, 1937, now pastor emeritus for life. President of Ill. Anti-Saloon League; was twice pres. Chicago Ch. Fed. Council; 1st pres. Ill. Vigilance Assn. (4 terms). Candidate for Congress in Rep. primaries, 1916, 2d Congressional Dist. Ill. Pres. nat. bd. dirs. and mem. administrative com., Anti-Saloon League of America; chmn. advisory bd. of Bur. of Food, Farm Products and Markets; City of Chicago. Dir. Better Govt. Assn.; twice pres. Ill. Bapt. Pastoral Union, also of Bapt. Ministers' Conf., twice moderator Chicago Bapt. Assn.; occasional lecturer, Bapt. Missionary Training School and Northern Bapt. Theol. Sem., both Chicago; pres. Night Church of Chicago; chmn. Interdenom. Commn. Chicago Bapt. Assn.; chmn. Commn. on Coöperation and Fellowship of Ill. Bapt. State Conv.; pres. Ernest A. Bell Memorial Assn., dir. Central Howard Assn., Chicago Tract Soc.; ex-pres. Little Point Sable Assn. of Mich.; pres. Alumni of Div. Sch. of Univ. of Chicago; hon. mem. Woodlawn Business Men's Assn.; hon. pres. Anti-Saloon League of Ill. Clubs: City, Hamilton (Chicago), Kiwanis Club of Woodlawn (hon.), T Club (hon., life). Candidate against ratification at special election for or against ratification of 21st Amendment, 1933. Address: Shelby, Mich. Died June 16, 1942.

BOYNTON, Percy Holmes, prof. English; b. Newark, N.J., Oct. 30, 1875; s. George Mills and Julia Hoyt (Holmes) B.; A.B., Amherst, 1897; A.M., Harvard 1898; hon. Litt.D., Amherst Coll., 1939; grad. student U. Chicago, 1902-03; m. Lois Damon, Oct. 11, 1902 (died July 6, 1939), children—Holmes, Damon; m. 2d, Florence Brinkman Rice, February 28, 1941. Instr. in English, Smith Acad., St. Louis, 1898-1902; reader in English, U. of Chicago, 1902-03, asso. in English, 1903-05, instr., 1905-09; asst. prof., 1909-14, asso. prof., 1914-23, prof. 1923-41; retired; also dean in Colls. of Arts, Literature and Science, 1912-23, U. of Chicago. Sec. of Instruction, Chautauqua Instn., 1903-14; prin. summer schools, same, 1914-17. Visiting professor California Inst. of Technology, winter 1942; and at Univ. of Puerto Rico, 1944-45. Member Psi Upsilon Fraternity. Author: London in English Literature, 1913; Principles of Composition, 1915; History of American Literature (coll. text book), 1919; History of American Literature (sch. text book), 1923; Some Contemporary Americans, 1924; More Contemporary Americans, 1927; The Rediscovery of the Frontier, 1931; The Challenge of Modern Criticism, 1931; Literature and American Life, 1936; The American Scene in Contemporary Fiction, 1940. Joint author of First View of English and American Literature, 1909. Editor: A Book of American Poetry, 1918; Mark Twain's Tom Sawyer, 1920; Milestones in American Literature, 1923; Franklin's Autobiography, 1925; Cooper's The Spy, 1927. Dir. and chmn. operating com. Marine Hist. Assn. of Mystic, Conn. Home: Mystic, Conn.; (winter) Winter Park, Fla. Died July 8, 1946.

BOYNTON, Thomas Jefferson, lawyer; b. Westfield, Vt., Dec. 30, 1856; s. David F. and Lydia (Roberts) B.; ed. State Normal Sch., Johnson, Vt.; m. Hattie L. Story, Dec. 27, 1879. Admitted to Vt. bar, 1881; postoffice insp. in charge, at Boston, 1887-89 and 1893-97; mem. Vt. Ho. of Rep., 1892; mem. City Council, Everett, Mass., 1898; city solicitor, 1900, 1901; mayor, Everett, 1904, 1906, 1907; atty.-gen. of Mass., 1914; U.S. dist. atty., Dist. of Mass., 1917-June 1920; chmn. bd. of trustees Suffolk University. Mem. Middlesex Bar Assn., Vt. Assn. of Boston. Democrat. Unitarian. Mason. Club: Boston City. Pres. bd. trustees Suffolk U. Home: 19 Adams St., Arlington, Mass. Office: 453 Broadway, Everett, Mass.* Died Mar. 12, 1945.

BOZELL, Leo B., advertising; b. Mitchell County, Kan., Oct. 13, 1886; s. Oscar F. and Clarinda J. (Wallis) B.; A.B., U. of Kan., 1910; m. Mildred Cooper, June 20, 1917 (died 1918); m. 2d, Lois Robbins, Aug. 20, 1921; children—John Oscar, Leo Brent, Patricia Wyman. Reporter, then city editor, Omaha Daily News, 1912-17; later exec. sec. Omaha Real Estate Bd., 1919-26; now partner Bozell & Jacobs, advertising agency, Omaha; pres. Bozell & Jacobs, Inc., Chicago, Bozell & Jacobs, Inc., Indianapolis; treas. Bozell & Jacobs, Houston. Served in U.S. Army, Oct.-Nov. 1918. President Omaha Chamber of Commerce, 1943. Mem. Delta Upsilon. Democrat. Episcopalian. Clubs: Omaha, Omaha Country (Omaha); University (Chicago); Indianapolis Athletic. Home: 96th and Dodge Road, Benson Station, Omaha, Neb. Office: Electric Bldg., Omaha, Neb. Died Mar. 24, 1946.

BRACELEN, Charles Michael (brās'lĕn), lawyer; b. Humboldt, Neb., Jan. 11, 1878; s. Thomas and Sarah A. (Donahue) B.; A.B., U. of Neb., 1902; student Coll. of Law, U. of Neb., 1902-03, Creighton U., Omaha, 1904-06; m. Mary Ellen Thornton, Aug. 20, 1900 (died 1924); 1 dau. Mrs. Ellen Bracelen Flood. Admitted to Minn. bar, 1907, and began practice of law at Minneapolis; moved to N.Y. City, 1918, and apptd. atty. Am. Telephone & Telegraph Co.; spl. counsel postmaster gen. during govt. operation of telephone and telegraph systems as war measure, 1918-19; gen. solicitor Am. Telephone & Telegraph Co., 1922-26, v.p. and gen. counsel since 1926. Mem. Am. Bar Assn., Bar Assn. City of New York, Phi Beta Kappa. Democrat. Catholic. Club: University. Home: 1120 Park Av. Office: 195 Broadway, New York, N.Y. Died Oct. 8, 1942.

BRACH, Emil J., business exec.; b. Schoenwald, Germany, 1859. Pres. and dir. E. J. Brach & Sons. Address: 4656 W. Kinzie St., Chicago 44, Ill. Died Oct. 29, 1947.

BRACKETT, Elliott Gray, surgeon; b. Newton, Mass., Apr. 6, 1860; s. Nathaniel and Abigail (Wilder) B.; grad. Newton High Sch., 1878; M.D., Harvard, 1886; m. Katherine F. Pedrick, Jan. 17, 1901. Formerly chief of service, orthopedic dept. Mass. Gen. Hosp.; dir. orthopedic surgery, U.S. Army, since Aug.

1917; col. M.C. U.S. Army. Fellow Am. Coll. Surgeons; mem. Am. Orthopedic Assn., Mass. Med. Soc. Clubs: University, Harvard. Home: 160 Newbury St., Boston, Mass. Died Dec. 29, 1942.

BRACKETT, William Oliver, clergyman; b. Sherman, Tex., Apr. 5, 1901; s. William Oliver and Elizabath Wilson (Moore) B.; A.B., U. of Mo., 1924; Th.B., Princeton Theological Seminary, 1928; Ph.D., U. of Edinburgh, Scotland, 1935; D.D., Missouri Valley College, 1941; m. Nancy Alexis Thomson, June 24, 1931; children—Joanna Elizabeth, Thomas Oliver, Sarah Evershed. Asst. minister St. George's West Ch., Edinburgh, 1928-30; asso. minister Westport Presbyn. Ch., Kansas City, Mo., 1930-34; minister-in-charge Collegiate Ch. of St. Nicholas, N.Y. City, 1935-36; minister First Presbyn. Ch., Lake Forest, Ill., since 1936. Trustee Ferry Hall, Lake Forest, Ill., Princeton Theol. Sem., Presbytery of Chicago. Fellow Corp. Lake Forest (Ill.) Acad. Mem. advisory council of Sunday Evening Club, Chicago. Mem. Ch. Extension Bd., Presbytery of Chicago. Mem. Phi Delta Theta, Chicago Cleric. Republican. Clubs: Onwentsia, Winter (Lake Forest); University (Chicago). Contbr. articles to religious jours. Home: 588 E. Deer Path, Lake Forest, Ill. Died July 26, 1945.

BRADBURY, Robert Hart, chemist; b. Phila., Pa., Sept. 25, 1870; s. Robert and Margaret C. (Hart) B.; A.B., Central High Sch., Phila., 1887; Ph.D., U. of Pa., 1893; m. Mabel Bradner, June 27, 1901; children—Robert Hart, Mabel Campbell. Asst. chemist, Cambria Iron Co., 1889; chemist S. P. Wetherill Paint Co., 1891-92; prof. chemistry, Central Manual Training Sch., Phila., 1893-1907; head dept. of science, Southern High Sch., Phila., 1907-30; retired. Consulting chemist, Am. Chem. Paint Co. Lecturer on phys. chemistry, dept. of philosophy, U. of Pa., 1894-95. Mem. Am. Chem. Soc., Franklin Inst. Author: An Elementary Chemistry, 1903; A Laboratory Manual of Chemistry, 1903; An Inductive Chemistry, 1912; Laboratory Studies in Chemistry, 1912; A First Book in Chemistry, 1922, 3d edit. revised, 1938; New Laboratory Studies in Chemistry, 1923; Looseleaf Work-book for the Chemistry Laboratory, 1934. Home: 2114 Chestnut Av., Ardmore, Pa. Died March 27, 1949.

BRADBURY, Samuel, physician; b. Germantown, Phila., Pa., Apr. 30, 1883; s. Samuel and Martha Washington (Chapman) B.; Northeast Manual Training Sch., Phila.; M.D., U. of Pa., 1905; m. Althea Norris Johnson, Sept. 26, 1914; children—Samuel, Emily Carey (Mrs. Alfred Vail), Althea Norris (Mrs. David Loshak), Wilmer Johnson. With Germantown and Pennsylvania Hosps., Phila., until 1911; assistant visiting physician City Hospital, New York, 1912-17, visiting physician, 1917-24; asst. visiting physician Belleville Hosp., 1924-27; chief in medicine, Cornell Clinic, and asst. prof. clin. medicine, Cornell U. Med. Coll., New York, 1921-27; cons. phys. N.Y. Infirmary for Women and Children, 1924-27; dir. Out Patient Dept., Pa. Hosp., Phila., since 1927; dir. service and coordinator dept. med., Germantown Hosp. Commd. 1st lt. Med. Res. Corps, Mar. 1916; captain Med. Corps, U.S. Army, Oct. 1918; served in France, July 1917-Apr. 1919; former maj. U.S. Med. Reserve Corps, Diplomate Am. Bd. Int. Med. Mem. A.M.A. Med. Soc. State of Pa., Phila. County Med. Soc., Coll. of Physicians of Phila., Am. Climatol. and Clinical Association, Acad. Medicine of New York, Am. Assn. Advancement of Science, Harvey Society. Republican Club: Mask and Wig (Phila.). Author: Internal Mediciine—Treatment, 1923; (monograph) What Constitutes Adequate Medical Service? (pub. 1927, by The Com. on Dispensary Development of the United Hosp. Fund of New York); also contbr. to Cyclopedia of Medicine and Text Book of Medicine by Am. Authors, Adequate Medical Care, 1937. Home and Office: 151 W Coulter St., Philadelphia 44, Pa. Died Aug. 30, 1947.

BRADEN, William, mining engr.; b. Indianapolis, Mar. 24, 1871; s. William and Martha (Burford) B.; ed. pvt. schs. and Mass. Inst. Tech.; m. Mary Kimball, June 6, 1893; 1 child, Spruille. Asst. to chief engr., Montana Co., Marysville, Mont., 1889; surveyor Elkhorn Mining Co. and Anaconda Co.; chemist and assayer, later asst. supt., Ark. Valley Smelter, Leadville, Colo., to 1893; engr. and rep. in British Columbia, for Omaha and Grant Smelting & Refining Co., also examination of mines in North and South America, 1893-98; expert engr. for Boston and Mont. and Butte and Boston interests in litigation with F. Aug. Heinze, at Butte, 1898-1901; gen. manager Velardeña Mines, Mexico, Bruce Mines, Ontario, Can., and mine examinations in the U.S. and Mexico, 1901-03; organizer and gen. mgr. Braden Copper Co., Chile; with Anaconda Copper Mining Co. and directing operations of Andes Exploration Co. in S.A., 1913-18; cons. and mining examinations, 1919-30; mining explorations in N. and S. America, 1931-39. Mem. Am. Inst. Mining and Metall. Engrs., Club de la Union, Santiago, Chile. Home: Monarch Hotel. Office: 730 Van Nuys Bldg., Los Angeles, Calif. Died July 18, 1942.

BRADFORD, George Henry, lecturer; b. nr. Morrisville, Ill., Nov. 20, 1871; s. James and Kate (Bartlett) B.; A.B., Mo. Wesleyan Col., 1897; S.T.B., Iliff Sch. of Theology (U. of Denver), 1898; B.O., U. of Denver, 1898; D.D., Carrollton, 1900; married. Ordained M.E. ministry, 1897; pastor Wesley Ch., St. Joseph, Mo., 1898-1901; Oakley Ch., Kansas City, Mo., 1901-05; chancellor Epworth U., Oklahoma City, 1905-11 (1st successful attempt at organic union of M.E. Ch. and M.E. Ch., S.); became chancellor Methodist U. of Okla., Guthrie (amalgamation of Ft. Worth U., Tex. and Epworth U., Oklahoma City), 1911; apptd. by City of Miami, dir. Civic Forum and Bayfront Park Auditorium, 1933. Chmn. Okla. Conf. delegation to Gen. Conf. M.E. Ch., Baltimore, 1908-12. Mem. Beta Theta Pi. Republican. Mason (32°). Clubs: Men's Dinner, Golf Country. Lyceum and Chautauqua lecturer. Address: 158 N.E. 4 St., Miami, Fla. Died Jan. 30, 1945.

BRADFORD, Roark, author; b. Lauderdale County, Tenn., Aug. 21, 1896; s. Richard Clarence and Patricia Adelaide (Tillman) B.; ed. pub. schs.; arty. schs. U.S. Army, 1917-19; m. Mary Rose (Sciarra) Himler; 1 son, Richard Roark. Reporter Atlanta Georgian, 1920-22, Macon (Ga.) Telegraph, 1923, Lafayette (La.) Daily Advertiser, 1923; night city editor, later Sunday editor New Orleans Times Picayune, 1924-26; has devoted all time to writing since 1926. Served as 1st lt. Arty. Reserve, U.S. Army, 1917-20. Coast defense of Balboa, C.Z., World War. Served as lt., United States Naval Reserve, 1942-45; assigned to Bureau of Aeronautics Training Lit. Division, Navy Department, Washington, D.C. Member Officers Reserve Corps Association; member National Institute of Arts and Letters. Awarded 1st prize, O. Henry Memorial Award, 1927. Democrat. Club: Players (New York). Author: Old Man Adam and His Chillun, 1928 (play The Green Pastures based on this work); This Side of Jordan, 1929; Ol' King David and the Philistine Boys, 1930; How Come Christmas, 1930; John Henry, 1931; Kingdom Coming, 1933; Let the Band Play Dixie (short stories), 1934; The Three-Headed Angel, 1937; (play) John Henry (music by Jacques Wolfe), 1940; The Green Roller (publ. posthumously), 1949. Contbr. short stories to Collier's, Saturday Evening Post, Harper's, etc. Address: 719 Toulouse St., New Orleans. Died Nov. 13, 1948.

BRADLEE, Henry G., engineer; b. Boston, Mass., Jan. 25, 1871; s. John Tisdale and Sarah E. (Goddard) B.; S.B., Mass. Inst. Tech., 1891; m. Marion Chamberlin, Nov. 9, 1898; children—Mrs. Elizabeth Perry, Henry G. With Stone & Webster, engineers and mgrs. pub. service corps. since June 1, 1891, and mem. firm 1907-20; now vice president, chmn. executive committee and director, Stone & Webster, Inc.; dir. numerous traction, light, power and other cos. Clubs: Union, Country, Downtown. Home: Brookline, Mass. Office: 49 Federal St., Boston, Mass. Died Sept. 3, 1947.

BRADLEY, Alice, home economist; b. Bradford, Mass., June 28, 1875; d. Albert Emerson and Kate Evelyn (Cole) Bradley; grad. high sch., Hyde Park, Mass., 1893, Boston Cooking Sch., 1897; spl. courses, Mass. Inst. Tech., Teachers Coll. (Columbia). Teacher of cooking, Ottawa and Montreal, Can., 3 yrs.; dietitian, Mass. Homeo. Hosp., 3 yrs.; teacher, Miss Farmer's Sch. of Cookery, Boston, 9 yrs., New York Cooking Sch., 2 yrs.; owner and prin. Miss Farmer's School of Cookery, 1915-44; cooking editor Woman's Home Companion, 1916-36. Mem. Am. and Eastern Mass. home economics assns., Mass. Hort. Society, National Travel Club, Universal Cookery and Food Assn., London. Methodist. Clubs: Zonta, Hyde Park Current Events. Author: Food Values, Economical Menus, 1917; The Candy Cook Book, 1917; Cooking for Profit, 1921; For Luncheon and Supper Guests, 1922; Desserts, 1930; Six Hundred Suggestions for Serving Meat, 1935; The Alice Bradley Menu-Cookbooks, 1936 and 1937; War Time Cookery, 1943. Contbr. to mags. Lecturer on subjects relating to foods, food values, and cookery. Home: 11 Dell Av., Hyde Park, Mass. Died Nov. 27, 1946.

BRADLEY, Charles Leininger, railway exec.; b. Cleveland, O.; s. Morris Alva and Ann (Leininger) B.; grad. University School, Cleveland; A.B., Cornell U., 1908; m. Gertrude Baker, Apr. 28, 1912; children—Mary Agnes, Alva II. Chmn. bd. Erie R.R. Co. since 1928; chmn. bd. Cleveland Ry. Co., 1929-37; pres. The Higbee Co. Civilian mem. Cleveland Dist. Ordnance Bd. Republican. Episcopalian. Clubs: Union, Tavern, Pepper Pike, Country. Home: 2301 Coventry Rd., Cleveland Heights, O. Office: The Higbee Co., Cleveland, O. Died Dec. 18, 1943.

BRADLEY, Frederick Van Ness, congressman; b. Chicago, Ill., Apr. 12, 1898; s. Carl D. and Emily (Jessup) B.; prep. edn. Rogers City (Mich.) High Sch., 1912-14, Montclair (N.J.) Acad., 1914-16; A.B., Cornell U., 1921; m. Marcia Marie Hillidge, Nov. 20, 1922; 1 son, Carl D., II (dec.). Salesman Mich. Limestone & Chem. Co., Buffalo, 1921-23, purchasing agent, 1928-38; purchasing agent Bradley Transportation Co., Rogers City, Mich., 1924-38; mem. 76th to 80th Congresses (1939-49), 11th Mich. District. Served in S.A.T.C., 1918. Mem. Delta Chi. Republican. Presbyterian. Clubs: Congressional Country, Kiwanis. Home: 4121 Argyle Terrace N.W., Washington, D.C., and Rogers City, Mich. Died May 24, 1947.

BRADLEY, John Jewsbury, army officer, lawyer; b. Chicago, Ill., Apr. 20, 1869; s. Timothy M. and Emma (Cookson) B.; B.S., U.S. Mil. Acad., 1891; grad. Army Sch. of Line, 1912, Army Staff Coll., 1913; m. Caroline Sladen, Sept. 14, 1893; children—Frances Sladen (Mrs. William Elbridge Chickering), John Jewsbury, Jr., Joseph Sladen. Commd. 2d lt., 14th Inf., U.S. Army, 1891, advancing through the grades to brig. gen., 1926, retired, 1929; admitted to New York bar, 1928, Washington (state) bar, 1908; now engaged in practice of law, N.Y. City. Served overseas in Philippines, China, France. Decorated Distinguished Service Medal, Silver Star, Purple Heart (U.S.), Officer Legion d'Honneur (France), Comdr. Order of Crown (Italy), Companion of St. Michael and St. George (England). Trustee Disabled Am. Vets. Service Foundation. Mem. Mil. Order of World Wars, S.R., N.Y. State, West Point Soc. Hon. mem. Guards Club (London), 1918. Clubs: Military and Naval, University (New York); Army and Navy (Washington, D.C.). Home: 57 W. 58th St., New York 19. Office: 475 Fifth Av., New York 17, N.Y. Died May 21, 1948; buried at U.S. Military Academy, West Point, N.Y.

BRADLEY, Lee Carrington, lawyer; b. Birmingham, Ala., Nov. 12, 1871; s. Richard Carrington and Sarah (Gurley) B.; A.B., Southern Univ. (now Birmingham Southern Coll.), 1890, A.M., 1891; m. Eleanor Lyons, June 24, 1896; children—Lee C., Thomas Lyons (dec.). Practiced at Birmingham since 1892; asst. solicitor Jefferson County, Ala., 1893-95, solicitor, 1896; counsel to Bradley, Baldwin, All & White; gen. counsel of alien property custodian (U.S.), 1918; receiver Birmingham Ry., Light & Power Co., 1919-24. Mem. Am., Ala. State and Birmingham bar assns., Alpha Tau Omega; asso. mem. Assn. Bar City of N.Y. Democrat. Methodist. Club: Birmingham Country. Home: 640 Idlewild Circle. Office: Comer Bldg., Birmingham, Ala. Died May 31, 1942.

BRADLEY, Luke C.; pres. Consolidated Electric & Gas Co., also officer or dir. many other pub. utility companies. Home: 130 East End Av., New York, N.Y. Office: 26 Exchange Place, Jersey City, N.J.* Died May 12, 1944.

BRADLEY, Philip Read, mining engr.; b. Georgetown, Calif., Oct. 12, 1875; s. Henry Sewell and Virginia (Shearer) B.; B.S. in Mining, U. of Calif., 1896; m. Mabel Harland, Feb. 13, 1903; children—Philip Read, Henry Harland, Ruth, Frances. Former mining supt. and mgr.; cons. engr. since 1897; pres. Alaska Juneau Gold Mining Co., Treadwell Yukon Co.; v.p. Pacific Mining Co., Atolia Mining Co., Bunker Hill and Sullivan Mining and Conc. Co. Mem. Am. Inst. Mining Engrs., Mining and Metall. Soc. Protestant. Clubs: Engineers, Bohemian, Press. Home: 506 Linden Av., Grass Valley, Calif. Office: Crocker Bldg., San Francisco, Calif. Died Dec. 31, 1948.

BRADLEY, Robert L., M.D.; b. Middleton, Tenn., June 30, 1866; s. Thomas F. and Margret (Waters) B.; Savoy (Tex.) Coll., 1884; M.D., U. of Louisville, 1890; post-grad. work New Orleans Polyclinic, 1895, New York Polyclinic Med. Sch. and Hosp., 1902, 06, 10, also laboratory work at Chicago, Ill., 1923; m. Mary E. Boxley, Dec. 2, 1891; children—Palmer, Margaret Frances and Mary Roberta. Practiced in Tioga, Tex., 1890-99, Roswell, N.M., since 1899; pres. Roswell Nat. Bank, 1905; 1st v.p. First State Bank & Trust Co., 1911-14. Served as capt. Med. Corps, U.S. Army, 1918-19. Mayor of Roswell; mem. N.M. State Bd. Med. Examiners. Fellow Am. Coll. Surgeons; mem. N.M. Med. Soc. (pres. 1912), Pecos Valley Dist. Med. Soc. (pres. 1909-15 and since 1927), Chaves County Med. Soc., North Tex. Med. Soc. Democrat. Methodist. Club: Roswell Country. Home: Roswell, N.M.* Died June 19, 1943.

BRADLEY, Samuel Stewart, aeronautics; b. Medina, O., June 27, 1869; s. John Albro and Eleanor (Stewart) B.; grad. high sch., Ann Arbor, Mich.; student civ. engring., U. of Mich., 1887-89; hon. M.S., U. of Mich., 1937; m. Genevieve Cornwell, Dec. 17, 1901. Engaged in civ. engring., 1889-91; sec. and gen. mgr. New Duluth Co., 1891-97; treas. Atlas Iron & Brass Works, 1893-97; originated and perfected practical improvements in business systems, including perpetual stock inventory and constant balanced ledgers, 1898-1904; pres. Patterson, Gottfried & Hunter, Ltd., 1901-11, Young Machine & Tool Co., 1905-11, Frasse Co., 1906-09, supt. Brooklyn (N.Y.) Park Dept., 1914-17, gen. mgr. Mfrs. Aircraft Assn., 1917-36, chmn. bd. since 1937; v.p. and gen. mgr. Aeronautical Expns. Corp., 1927-29; dir. Wilcox & Gibbs Sewing Machine Co. Mem. council Aeronautical Chamber of Commerce of America (v.p. and gen. mgr. 1921-29). Mem. and sec. Am. Aviation Mission to Europe, 1919; mem. various sub coms. of Nat. Advisory Com. for Aeronautics, 1918-20; mem. Inst. of Aeronautical Sciences. Republican. Episcopalian. Clubs: University of Michigan, Psi Upsilon, Union League (New York); "M" (Ann Arbor); Union Interallies (Paris). Ed. annual edits. of Aircraft Year Book, 1920-29; pub. Airplane Patent Digest (bimonthly), 1929-36. Home: 45 Park Av. Office: 30 Rockefeller Plaza, New York, N.Y. Died April 10, 1947.

BRADLEY, William Clark, banker, mfr.; b. Oswichee, Russell County, Ala., June 28, 1863; s. Forbes and Theresa Ann (Clark) B.; ed. James J. Slade High Sch., Columbus, Ga., and Agrl. and Mech Coll., Auburn, Ala.; m. Sarah M. Hall, Apr. 27, 1887; 1 dau., Elizabeth B. (Mrs. D. A. Turner). Chmn. bd. Columbus Mfg. Co., Bradley Realty & Investment Co., Eagle & Phenix Mills, Columbus Iron Works (all Columbus); pres. Columbus Bank & Trust Co., Gate City Cotton Mills (Atlanta, Ga.), W. C. Bradley Co. (Columbus); dir. Central of Ga. Ry. Co., Citizens & Southern Nat. Bank (Atlanta),

Bibb Mfg. Co. (Macon, Ga.), Coca-Cola Co., Coca-Cola Internat. Corp. Republican. Protestant. Clubs: Muscogee, Columbus Country; Capital City (Atlanta); Merchants (New York). Home: 1951 Wynnton Rd. Address: Box 100, Columbus, Ga. Died July 26, 1947.

BRADSHAW, John Hammond, surgeon; b. Boston, Mass., Oct. 6, 1860; s. Franklin Emmons and Ann Lovisa (Hammond) B.; student Ripon (Wis.) Coll., 1876-80; M.D., Coll. Physicians and Surgeons, N.Y. City, 1884; m. Lena Swasey Patterson, Sept. 3, 1894 (died 1928); 1 son, John Hammond. House physician Orange Memorial Hosp., 1883-90, attending surgeon, 1890-1920, cons. surgeon since 1920; cons. surgeon Jersey City Med. Center since 1933. Fellow Am. Coll. Surgeons; mem. A.M.A., N.J. Med. Soc., Essex Co. Med. Soc., Orange Med. Soc., N.J. Soc. Surgeons, Clin. Soc. Republican. Presbyterian. Club: Shongon (Dover, N.J.). Contbr. articles on med. history of N.J. and many articles on med. ethics to med. jours. Home: 27 High St., Orange, N.J. Died Jan. 20, 1943.

BRADY, Thomas, Jr., lawyer; b. Prentiss, Miss., Sept. 20, 1870; s. Pickens and Margaret (Burrow) B.; prep. edn., Blountville Academy, Miss.; student lit. dept. and law sch. of U. of Miss.; LL.B. cum laude, U. of Mississippi, 1894 (editor-in-chief of University magazine); m. Jane Tullia Smith, Nov. 16, 1901; children—Thomas Pickens, Tullius, Dalton Burrow. Admitted to Miss. bar, 1894, and began practice at Brookhaven; formerly gen. counsel Miss. Central R.R. Co.; atty. Ill. Central R.R. Co.; gen. counsel Pearl River Valley R.R. Co.; chmn. bd. Brookhaven Bank & Trust Co. Apptd. spl. U.S. pros. atty., White Cap cases, 1902; del. to Dem. Nat. Conv., 1916, 1932. Chmn. adv. bd. Lincoln County, Miss., World War; named as eligible World War Railroad Dept., rank of maj., just before peace declared; mem. President's Emergency Com. for Employment; mem. Com. of 15, to confer with Miss. State Senate and Ho. of Reps. on legislation del. to annual conf. A.L.A., Los Angeles, 1930; mem. Research Commn. State of Miss.; chmn. for Miss. of United States Soc. (mem. advisory counsel); mem. Com. Revising Banking Laws of Miss.; pres. County Commn., Archives and History, State of Miss.; apptd. by Railroad Commn. of State of Miss. to serve on Com. of Asso. Motor Carriers of Miss.; mem. Bar Commn. of State of Miss. Formerly chairman board trustees Brookhaven schools. Invitee Newcomen Society. County chairman Finnish Relief Fund Committee. Mem. Am. Acad. Polit. and Social Science, Am. and Miss. State bar assns., Lincoln Scholarship Fund, Stable Money Assn., Abraham Lincoln Assn., Thrift Security Foundation, Inc., Nat. Econ. League, Phi Kappa Psi (mem. Hall of Fame), Phi Delta Phi. Associated with Phi Beta Kappa in cultural development of Am. Democrat. Clubs: New Orleans Athletic, Boston (New Orleans); Lotus (New York); Sumner Club of Yale University (New Haven, Conn.). Mem. advisory council of Living Age (mag.). Author of pub. articles. Home: Natchez Rd. Office: Brookhaven Bank & Trust Bldg., Brookhaven, Miss.

Died Mar. 6, 1944.

BRADY, William A., theatrical mgr.; b. San Francisco, June 19, 1863; s. Terence A. and Catherine B.; pub. sch. edn.; m. Marie Rene (dec.); 1 dau., Alice (dec.); m. 2d, Grace George (actress), Jan. 8, 1899; 1 son, William A. (dec.). Began career, San Francisco, 1882; produced many popular plays since 1888; lessee Manhattan Theatre, New York, 1896, until its demolition; now owner The Playhouse, New York City. Built William A. Brady's Playhouse, 1910, and the Forty-eighth St. Theatre, 1912; appointed by President Wilson, 1917, chmn. of com. to organize motion picture industry to coöperate with Com. on Public Information; pres. Nat. Assn. Motion Picture Industry, 1915-20. Was exec. head World Film Co. Has produced many plays and managed many stars, such as Grace George, Alice Brady, Robert Mantell, Holbrook Blinn, Wilton Lackaye, Douglas Fairbanks, Tallulah Bankhead, Laurette Taylor, Florence Reed; produced over 250 plays in N.Y. City; managed sport champions, including James J. Corbett and James J. Jeffries. Home: 510 Park Av. Office: 137 W. 48th St., New York, N.Y.* Died Jan. 6, 1950.

BRAGDON, Claude (brăg'dŭn), architect, artist, author, lecturer; b. Oberlin, O., Aug. 1, 1866; s. George Chandler and Catherine Elmina (Shipherd) B.; M.Arch., U. of Mich.; m. Charlotte Coffyn Wilkinson, Nov. 3, 1902; children—Henry Wilkinson, Chandler; m. 2d, Eugenie Macaulay Julier, July 13, 1912. Began as architect in Rochester, N.Y.; built N.Y.C. R.R. Sta. and Rochester C. of C.; art dir. for Walter Hampden's prodns. of Cyrano, Hamlet, Macbeth, Othello, Merchant of Venice and others; delivered Scammon lectures at Chicago Art Inst., 1915; exhibited paintings at Ferargil Galleries, N.Y., 1941. Three time winner of President's Medal of Archtl. League of N.Y. Fellow A.I.A.; mem. Theosophical Soc. of Am. Author: The Golden Person in the Heart, 1898; The Beautiful Necessity, 1910; Episodes from an Unwritten History, 1912; A Primer of Higher Space, 1913; Projective Ornament, 1913; Four-Dimensional Vistas, 1916; Architecture and Democracy, 1918; Oracle, 1921; Old Lamps for New, 1925; The New Image, 1928; Merely Players, 1929; The Eternal Poles, 1931; The Frozen Fountain, 1932; An Introduction to Yoga, 1933; Delphic Woman, 1936; More Lives Than One (autobiography), 1938; The Arch Lectures, 1942; Yoga for You, 1943; co-translator (with Nicholas Bessaraboff) and publisher of Ouspensky's Tertium Organum, 1920. Home: Shelton Hotel, Lexington Av., at 49th St., New York, N.Y. Died Sep. 17, 1946.

BRAINARD, David Legge (brān'ērd), army officer; b. Norway, N.Y., Dec. 21, 1856; s. Alanson and Maria C. (Legge) B.; ed. State Normal Sch., Cortland, N.Y.; m. Sara H. Guthrie, June 1917. Pvt., corporal and sergt. Troop L, 2d Cav., Sept. 18, 1876-July 31, 1884; sergt. Signal Corps, Aug. 1, 1884-Oct. 21, 1886; commd. 2d lt. 2d Cav., Oct. 22, 1886; brig. gen., N.A., Oct. 2, 1917; brig. gen. U.S. Army, July 25, 1918; retired July 27, 1918. Participated in Sioux, Nez Perce and Bannock campaigns, 1877-78; wounded in face and right hand; detailed for duty with Howgate Arctic exploring expdn., 1880; with Lady Franklin Bay Arctic Expdn., under Lt. Greely, 1881-84; associated with Lt. Lockwood in exploring interior of Grinnell Land and the northwest coast of Greenland; on May 13, 1882, reached the then highest point North ever attained, 83° 24′ 30″; was one of 7 survivors rescued by Comdr. W. S. Schley, June 1884; commd. 2d lt. 2d Cav. "for distinguished and meritorious services in connection with the Arctic Expdn., 1881-84." Awarded the Back Grant of Royal Geog. Soc., 1885, for spl. services in connection with his work of exploration in Arctic regions; Charles P. Daly gold medal, 1926, by Am. Geog. Soc., for Arctic explorations; explorer's medal, Explorers Club, N.Y. City, 1929; Purple Heart, 1933. Fellow Am. Geog. Soc.; mem. Nat. Geog. Soc. Clubs: Explorers, Military-Naval (New York); Army and Navy (Washington). Author: Outpost of the Lost (Arctic Journal), 1929; Six Came Back, Aug. 1940. The only survivor of the Greely Arctic Expedition. Address: Army and Navy Club, Washington. Died Mar. 22 1946; buried in Arlington National Cemetery.

BRAINERD, Eleanor Hoyt, author; b. Iowa City, Iowa, 1868; d. Walter and Louisa (Smith) Hoyt; A.M., Cincinnati Wesleyan Coll.; m. Charles Chisholm Brainerd, June 1904. Taught in Cincinnati Wesleyan Coll. and Gardner School for Girls, New York. Author: The Misdemeanors of Nancy, 1902; Nancy's Country Christmas and Other Stories, 1904; Concerning Belinda, 1905; In Vanity Fair, 1907; Bettina, 1907; The Personal Conduct of Belinda, 1910; For Love of Mary Ellen, 1912; Pegeen, 1914; How Could You, Jean? 1917; Our Little Old Lady, 1919. Home: 1080 S. El Molino Av., Pasadena, Calif. Died Mar. 18, 1942.

BRAISLIN, William C. (brāz'lĭn), otologist; b. Burlington, N.J., July 1, 1865; s. John and Elizabeth (Webber) B.; grad. Peddie Inst., 1885; student Princeton, 1885-87; M.D., Coll. Phys. and Surg. (Columbia), 1890; spl. courses in anatomy of the ear, human and comparative, under Drs. Huntington and Blake, 1901-02; m. Alice Cameron, Oct. 19, 1892 (died Sept. 30, 1927); children—William Donald (dec.), John Cameron, Gordon Stuart, Alice Cameron (Mrs. Robert Hadley Bennet). Began practice, Brooklyn, 1890; with Brooklyn Eye and Ear Hosp. since 1892, attending otologist and oto-laryngol. surgeon since 1903; sec. exec. com. bd. of dirs., same, 1904-21, now lecturer to graduates in medicine and mem. bd. trustees; lecturer to undergraduates, L.I. Coll. Hosp., 1919-24, clin. prof. otology since 1920. Mem. advisory bd. (Norwegian Hosp. group) Federal Draft Com., World War. Mem. Am., N.Y. State and Kings County med. socs., Am. Otol. Soc., Am. Oto-Laryngol. Soc. Episcopalian. Author: Relief of Deafness by Medication of Eustachian Tubes; (brochure) Study of Some Casts of the Infantile Pharynx, 1909; also abt. 90 papers, mostly on treatment of deafness. Home-Office: 425 Clinton Av., Brooklyn, N.Y.* Died Dec. 3, 1948.

BRAMER, Samuel Eugene; b. Phila., Pa., July 4, 1885; s. Hirsch and Cecile (Mandel) B.; student pub. schs.; m. Beatrice Brown, June 25, 1933; 1 dau., Mrs. Cecile Kahn. With Copperweld Steel Co. since 1915, now pres. and gen. mgr. Home: Pasadena Dr., Aspinwall, Pa. Office: Glassport, Pa.* Deceased.

BRAMHAM, William Gibbons (brăm'ŭm); b. Hopkinsville, Ky., July 13, 1874; s. James Goss and Rosa Mason (Cooke) B.; studied law at U. of N.C.; m. Ninnon Marie Umstead, Oct. 20, 1897; 1 son, Winfrey Peyton. Admitted to N.C. bar, 1905, and began practice at Durham, N.C. Mem. Rep. State Exec. Com., N.C., 1918-29; Rep. state chmn., 1922-26; del. at large to Rep. Nat. Conv., 1924 (mem. com. to notify President Coolidge of nomination), 1928 (chmn. N.C. delegation); pres.-treas. of B-1 Distributing Corporation. Pres.-treas. of Nat. Assn. Professional Baseball Leagues, 1933-46, consultant to president (of National Association) since 1946; mem. nat. bd. arbitration, Professional Baseball Clubs, 1920-29; pres. South Atlantic Assn. Professional Baseball Clubs, 1923-30, Piedmont League Professional Baseball Clubs, 1915-31, Eastern Carolina League Professional Baseball Clubs, 1928-29, Va. League Professional Baseball Clubs, 1924-28. Mem. Am., N.C. State and Durham bar assns., N.C. Sons of Am. Revolution. Presbyn. Mason (Shriner), K.P., Woodman of the World, Knights of the Most Noble Order of the Garter. Clubs: Durham Shrine, Hope Valley Country, Hillandale Country, Princess Ann Country, Virginia Seniors Golf Assn. Home: 114 Buchanan Rd. Office: 111 Corcoran St. Durham, N.C. Died July 8, 1947.

BRAMMER, George Edward (brăm'mẽr), lawyer; b. Dedham, Ia., March 4, 1886; s. William Harrison and Martha (Edwards) B.; LL.B., Drake U., 1908, LL.M., 1911; LL.D., Central Univ. of Iowa (Central Coll.), 1943; m. Mary Frances Gilliland, June 21, 1911; children—Mary Carolyn (Mrs. John P. Harper), James William. Admitted to Iowa bar, 1908, and since in practice at Des Moines (except in 1922); mem. firm Brammer, Brody, Charlton, Parker & Roberts; judge 9th Judicial Dist. (Iowa), 1922. Chmn. board dirs. Dutton-Lainson Co., Hastings, Neb.; dir. Cent. Nat. Bank & Trust Co., Des Moines. Mem. Am., Ia. State and Polk County bar assns. Trustee Drake Univ. (chmn. Law Sch. com.). Served as Rep. from Polk County in 36th Gen. Assembly, 1915. Mem. Sigma Alpha Epsilon, Delta Theta Phi. Republican. Mem. University Christian Ch. Mason (Shriner). Clubs: Des Moines, Wakonda. Home: 1085 44th St. Office: Empire Bldg., Des Moines, Ia. Died May 9, 1948.

BRAND, Charles John, agriculturist, economist; b. Lac Qui Parle County, Minn., Oct. 24, 1879; s. Charles and Mary (Buri) B.; B.A., U. of Minn., 1902; m. Mary E. Vining, Dec. 24, 1903. Asst. curator of Botany, Field Museum, Chicago, 1902-03; with U.S. Dept. Agr., 1903-19. In charge clover and alfalfa investigations, 1903-09, paper plant investigation, 1909-14, cotton handling and marketing, 1912-19, and chief of Bur. of Markets, May 15, 1913-July 1, 1919 (as such enforced presidential proclamation governing stockyards and concerns dealing in live stock, and supervised wartime purchase and distbn. of nitrate of soda for agrl. use). V.p. and gen. mgr. Am. Fruit Growers, Inc., Pittsburgh, 1919-22; cons. specialist in marketing, U.S. Dept. Agr., 1922-25; exec. sec. and treas. Nat. Fertilizer Assn., 1925-45; exec. dir. Fertilizer Code Authority, 1933-35; dir. 1661 Crescent Pl. N.W., Inc., Washington, since 1926; pres., 1928-31, treas. since 1943; Co-administrator of Agrl. Adjustment Act, May-October, 1933. Del. 1st Pan-Am. Financial Conf., 1915; del. 2d Pan-Am. Scientific Congress, 1915-16; as mem. War Emergency Agr. Conf., St. Louis, 1917, drew up program for regulation of storage and distributing agencies, which substantially was embodied in the Food Control and Production Acts of Aug. 1917; mem. joint price fixing com. and cotton compression com. Council of Nat. Defense, 1917-18; chmn. com. on cotton distbn., mem. wool section, War Industries Board, and by exec. order in charge of liquidation wool sect. after dissolution of board and until June 30, 1919; mem. com. on trade assns., Chamber of Commerce of U.S., 1922-23; agrl. commr. to Europe, 1923; del. Internat. Congresses, Chambers Commerce, 2d, Rome, 1923, 5th, Amsterdam, 1929, 6th, Washington, 1931, 9th, Berlin, 1937; del. 4th Internat. Grassland Conf., Aberystwyth, Wales, and 5th Internat. Tech. and Chem. Congress Agrl. Industries, Scheveningen, Holland, 1937; del. 1st Internat. Congress on Chem. Fertilizers, Rome, 1938; del. and agrl. program chmn. 7th Internat. Management Congress, 1938; chmn. Am. Com. on Internat. Inst. of Agr., Rome, Italy, since April 1937; del. Pan-Am. Commercial Congress, 1927; inspected agrl. and indsl. conditions in Brazil, Argentina, Chile, Peru, 1942, also nitrate industry, Chile; rep. at 100th anniversary of U. of Chile, 1942. Mem. bd. trustees, Santiago (Chile) Coll. Former dir. Am. Trade Assn. Executives; 2d pres. Washington Trade Assn. Execs.; chmn. National Manufacturing Trade Group, Nat. Industrial Council, 1943-44; mem. Agrl. and Indsl. Relations com., Western Regional Res. Lab., U.S. Dept. Agr., Albany, Calif., since 1942. Decorated Comendador, Orden Al Merito, Republic of Chile, 1944. Fellow A.A.A.S.; mem. Washington Acad. Sciences, Am. Economic Association, Academy Political Science, Agricultural History Soc. (pres., 1945-46), Am. Soybean Assn. (life), Fla. Plant Food Assn. (asso.), Am. Marketing Assn., Farm Economic Assn., Am. Trade Assn. Executives, Nat. Aeronautic Assn., Am. Acad. Polit. and Soc. Sci., Sigma Xi, Trustee Nat. Presbyn. Church and Covenant-First, Washington. Clubs: Chevy Chase, Cosmos, Nat. Press (Washington); Lake Placid (Essex County, N.Y.). Author: What Economic System for America, 1945, and numerous bills, addresses and papers on agrl. and fertilizer economics, production, marketing and distribution. Home: 1661 Crescent Pl., N.W., Washington 9. Office: Investment Bldg., Washington 5. Died June 29, 1949; buried in Rock Creek Cemetery, Washington.

BRANDE, Dorothea (Thompson), Mrs. Seward Collins, writer; b. Chicago, Ill., Jan. 12, 1893; d. Frederic Shepard and Alice (Prescott) Thompson; ed. privately and at Mrs. Starrett's Sch. for Girls, U. of Chicago, Lewis Inst., U. of Mich.; m. 2d, Seward Collins, 1936; 1 son, Justin Herbert Brande (by 1st marriage). Circulation mgr, Am. Mercury, 1923-26; asso. editor The Bookman, 1927-32; asso. editor Am. Review, 1933-34, now mem. editorial staff. Author: Becoming a Writer 1934; Most Beautiful Lady, 1935; Wake Up and Live, 1936; Letters to Philippa, 1937; My Invincible Aunt, 1938. Home: New Canaan, Conn. Address: The American Review, 231 W. 58th St., New York, N.Y.* Died Dec. 17, 1948.

BRANDEN, Paul Maerker, author, translator; b. Berlin, Germany, Feb. 27, 1888; s. George Leopold and Sophie (Wiener) B.; Ph.D., U. of Berlin, 1912; m. Elsa Weinberg, Nov. 14, 1924. Came to U.S., 1912, naturalized, 1919. Reporter N.Y. German Herold, 1912, later asst. and actg. mng. editor until 1918; free lance writer; editor American Monthly, 1925-32; with Metro-Goldwyn-Mayer, Hollywood, Calif., 1930; freelancing in Hollywood, Calif., and lecturing in Pacific Coast states since 1937; propaganda analyst and staff editorialist, News Research Service, Inc., Los Angeles, Calif., since 1939. With Foreign Lang. Div. Liberty Loan Orgn. and contbr. George Creel's Com. on Pub. Information, World War. Author: Her Majesty Elizabeth (with wife and Countess Larisch),

1934; The Patient's Dilemma (with S. A. Tannenbaum), 1935; My Royal Relatives (with wife and Countess Larisch), 1936. Translator: P. Kammerer's Inheritance of Acquired Characteristics, 1924; S. Freund's Problem of Lay-Analysis, 1927; As They Saw Us (co-author), 1929; E. Koch-Weser's Germany in the Post-War World, 1930; P. Freuchen's Eskimo (with wife), 1931; Mohammed Essad-Bey's Nicholas II, and His Reza Shah (with wife), 1936. Contbr. to Hearst's March of Events, also many articles to nat. mags. Home: 1843 N Cherokee Av., Hollywood, Calif. Died Jan. 3, 1942.

BRANDON, Edmund John, lawyer; b. Cambridge, Mass., May 24, 1894; s. Edward John and Mary A. (Corcoran) B.; A.B., Boston Coll., 1915; LL.B., Boston U., 1919; m. Anna Coleman McCarthy, July 20, 1925. Admitted to Mass. bar, 1910, United States District Court, 1921, Supreme Court of the U.S.; United States attorney, District of Massachusetts since 1939; regional adminstr. in N.E. for U.S. Securities and Exchange Commn., 1935-36; receiver Atlantic Nat. Bank of Boston, 1936-39. Pres. Commonwealth Charitable Corp.; trustee Commonwealth Charitable Trust. Served as lt., U.S. Navy, 1917-19. Mem. Am. Bar Assn., Bar Assn. City of Boston, Federal Bar Assn. (pres. Boston Chapter). Democrat. Catholic. K. of C. (former state dep. supreme knight). Knight, Sovereign Mil. Order of Malta. Clubs: Boston Yacht, Cohasset Yacht, Clover, Algonquin, Corinthian Yacht; Bankers Club of New York. Home: 150 Beacon St., Chestnut Hill, Boston; (summer) Cohasset, Mass. Office: 10 Post Office Sq., Boston. Died Nov. 1, 1946; buried in Holyhood Cemetery, Chestnut Hill, Mass.

BRANDT, John Lincoln, clergyman, lecturer; b. Somerset, O., Oct. 26, 1860; s. Isaac and Elizabeth (Loveberry) B.; acad. edn.; LL.D.; m. Nina E. Marquis, Dec. 25, 1882; children—James M., Mrs. Virginia Berg, John L.; m. 2d, Grace Lee Crutcher, Dec. 18, 1907; children—Bonnie Bell, Pauline, Joseph B. Ordained minister Christian (Disciples) Ch.; pastorates, Denver, Terre Haute, Toledo, Valparaiso, St. Louis, Muskogee, Okla., Cathedral Ch. of Christ, Melbourne, Australia, N. Berendo Christian Ch., Los Angeles; gen. evangelist, 2 yrs.; now retired from active ministry; lyceum lecturer; extensive traveler. Mason. Clubs: Lyons, Papyrus. Author: Lord's Supper, 1888; Turning Points in Life, 1890; Marriage and the Home, 1892; The False and the True, 1893; Soul Saving Sermons, 1895; Anglo-Saxon Supremacy, 1915; Great Bible Questions, 1926; Finding Christ, 1930. Writer for mags. and religious jours. Address: 842 N. Mariposa Av., Los Angeles 27. Died March 27, 1946; buried at Forest Lawn, Los Angeles.

BRANN, Donald W., army officer; b. Rushville, Ind., Sept. 26, 1895; s. Oliver Canby and Dorothy B.; student Purdue U., 1913-14, U. of Mich., 1914-15; grad. company officers training course, Inf. Sch., 1931, Command and Gen. Staff Sch., 1935; Army War Coll., 1938; m. Dorothy Teel, Dec. 27, 1922; 1 dau., Dorothy Ballard (wife of Lt. Col. Dorsey E. McCrory). Entered U.S. Army as 2d lt., inf., 1917, advancing through the grades to maj. gen., 1944. Decorated Distinguished Service Medal with oak leaf cluster, Legion of Merit (U.S.); Chevalier Legion of Honor, Croix de Guerre with palm, (France) Italian Order of the Crown, Silver Star (Italy); Hon. Comdr. Order British Empire; Polish Gold Cross of Merit with Swords; Czechoslovakian War Cross; War Medal, Order of Military Merit, National Order of Southern Cross (Brazil). Mem. Phi Delta Theta. Office: care The Adjutant General, U.S. Army, Washington. Died Dec. 29, 1945; buried in U.S. Military Cemetery, Castel Fiorentino, near Florence, Italy.

BRANN, Louis Jefferson, ex-gov.; b. at Madison, Me., July 8, 1876; s. Charles M. and Nancy (Lancaster) B.; student U. of Me., 1894-98; m. Martha Cobb, Mar. 8, 1902; children—Dorothy Lee (Mrs. Albert McLennan), Marjorie Eveleth (Mrs. William H. Dougherty), Nancy Elizabeth. Began practice, 1902; city solicitor, Lewiston, 1906-08; collector of taxes, Lewiston, 1908; register of probate, Androscoggin County, Me., 1909-13; judge Lewiston Municipal Court, 1913-15; mayor of Lewiston, 1915-16 and 1923-24; mem. Ho. of Rep., Me., 1917; gov. of Me., 2 terms, 1933-37; now mem. Brann, Isaacson & Lessard. Mem. Me. State and Androscoggin County bar assns., Beta Theta Pi. Democrat. Christian Scientist. Mem. K.P., Elks, Grange. Club: Lions Internat.; hon. mem. Bangor Lions Club. Home: 14 Mountain Av. Office: 133 Lisbon St., Lewiston, Me.* Died Feb. 3, 1948.

BRANNIGAN, Gladys (brăn'ĭ-găn), artist; b. Hingham, Mass., June 14, 1882; d. Preston Adams and Eve (Knox) Ames; B.A., George Washington U., 1903, M.A., 1904; studied art, Corcoran Art Sch., Washington, D.C., Nat. Acad. Design, and Art Students League, New York; m. Robert Alan Brannigan, Sept. 7, 1905 (died 1933). Formerly artist on Washington Star. Represented by work in Woman's University Club, Pen and Brush Club and American Museum of Natural History—all New York; Public Library, Portsmouth, N.H.; George Washington Univ., Washington, D.C.; reredos in St. John's Church, Massena, N.Y.; historical paintings, Parker Hall, Keene, N.H.; Municipal Bldg., Dover, N.H.; U. of N.H., Durham. Spl. award Ariz. Art Exhbn., 1925; hon. mention, New Haven Paint and Clay Club Exhbn., 1928, Greenwich Soc. of Artists, 1930, Ogunquit Art Centre, 1932; painting selected by the Governor's Com. to represent N.H. in Nat. Exhbn. of American Art, 1937 and 1938; represented N.H. in N.Y. World's Fair, 1939 and 1940. Served on Mayor's Com. of Women, N.Y. City, at beginning of World War, also on Board for Registration of Military Resources, State of N.Y., and with Col. House's Commn. as translator and compiler. Mem. Allied Artists America, Southern States Art League, Nat. Arts Club of New York, New York Painters, Am. Water Color Soc., etc. Author of numerous articles for Welles Pub. Co. and World Horizons. Address: 140 W. 57th St., New York, N.Y.* Deceased.

BRANSHAW, Charles E., army officer; born Vt., Aug. 6, 1895; grad. Air Corps Tactical Sch., 1935; rated pilot, combat observer, tech. observer, aircraft observer. Began as private, F.A., Colo. Nat. Guard, 1916; commd. 1st lt. Aviation Sect., 1917, and advanced through the grades to maj. gen., June 1943; retired as maj. general for disability incident to the service on Dec. 31, 1944. Served as 1st lt. Aviation Sect., World War I. Awarded Distinguished Service Medal, Legion of Merit. Address: Concan, Texas. Died May 8, 1949. Buried Concan, Tex.

BRASHEAR, Peter Cominges (brā-shēr), executive; b. Stephensport, Ky., Jan. 20, 1867; s. Joseph David and Anna (Scott) B.; desc. Benois de Brassier, French Huguenot, who settled in Va., 1653; ed. Hanover (Ind.) Coll.; m. Rida Cronly Payne, June 8, 1904; 1 dau., Mrs. Zalmon G. Simmons, Jr. With First Nat. Bank, Owensboro, Ky., 1886-94; U.S. internal revenue officer, 1894-98; auditor Provident Savings Life Ins. Co., N.Y. City, 1900-09; with Ft. Orange Paper Co., Castleton on Hudson, since 1910, successively v.p. and treas., pres., and chmn. bd., 1929-35, pres. since 1935, chmn. bd. since 1936; pres. Castleton Building Savings & Loan Assn., Castleton Corp.; mem. Constitutional Conv., N.Y., 1933. Served as 1st lt. and q.m. 4th Ky. Inf., U.S. Vols., Spanish-Am. War; chmn. 5 Liberty Loan drives, World War. Mem. Huguenot Soc. America, Sigma Chi. Republican. Presbyterian. Mason. Clubs: Union League (New York); Fort Orange, Albany Country, Schuyler Meadows Country (Albany, N.Y.); Cannes Country (Mougins, France). Col. on staffs of Gov. Sampson and Gov. Laffoon of Ky. Home: "Brashear Place," Castleton on Hudson, N.Y. Office: Castleton on Hudson, N.Y.; also 475 5th Av., New York, N.Y. Died Apr. 19, 1943.

BRATTON, Theodore DuBose, bishop; b. Winnsboro, S.C., Nov. 11, 1862; s. John and Elizabeth Porcher (DuBose) B.; B.D., U. of the South, 1887, D.D., 1902; LL.D., U. of Miss., 1911; m. Lucy Beverly Randolph, July 17, 1888 (died Jan. 1905); m. 2d, Mrs. Ivy Perrin Gass, Aug. 15, 1906; children—William DuBose, John, Randolph, Marion, Mary Means, Isabel. Deacon, 1887, priest, 1888, P.E. Ch.; rector of Ch. of the Advent, Spartanburg, S.C., 1888-99, St. Mary's Sch. for Young Women, 1899-1903; consecrated bishop of Miss., Sept. 29, 1903. Prof. history, Converse Coll., 1890-99; pres. Synod of Sewanee, 1923-26; chancellor Univ. of the South, 1935-38, retired Nov. 1938. Democrat. Served with Y.M.C.A. in France, 1918-19. Acting chaplain of the Port, Brest, France, 1918. Mem. Phi Beta Kappa. Author: Wanted Leaders—A Study in Negro Development; Sermons and Essays; A Prophet of Reality, The Life and Works of the Rev. Dr. William Porcher DuBose, Chaplain gen. United Confederate Veterans, 1930. Home: 1541 W. Capitol, Jackson, Miss. Died June 26, 1944.

BRATTON, Walter Andrew, educator; b. Stamford, Vt., June 22, 1874; s. Wheeler C. and Nancy (Barber) B.; A.B., Williams, 1895, post-grad. work, 1898-99, Sc.D., 1928; LL.D., Whitman College, Walla Walla, Wash., 1942; U. of Berlin, 1903-04; student Columbia U., 1927-28; m. Clarice Winship Colton, 1901; children—Robert, Jean. Prof. mathematics, Whitman Coll., Walla Walla, Wash., since 1895, dean of science group, 1909-34, of coll., 1934-35, acting pres., 1936-38, pres., 1938-42, retired 1942. Asso. prof. edn., Stanford U., summer 1932. Red Cross dir. for Eastern Wash., Eastern Ore. and Ida., World War. Trustee St. Paul's School, Walla Walla. Mem. American Mathematical Society, Mathematical Assn. America, A.A.A.S., Am. Assn. Univ. Profs., Inland Empire Teachers' Assn., Archeol. Inst. of America, Chamber of Commerce, Phi Beta Kappa. Democrat. Episcopalian. Clubs: Inquiry, Country, Rotary. Elected First Citizen of Walla Walla, 1942-43. Home: 570 Boyer Av., Walla Walla, Wash. Died Nov. 23, 1943.

BRAUCHER, Howard S. (brou'kēr), recreation worker; b. Royalton, Niagara County, N.Y., July 19, 1881; s. Solomon A. and Emma (Alberty) B.; A.B., Cornell U., 1903; Union Theol. Sem., 1903-05; Teachers Coll. (Columbia), 1904-05; New York Sch. of Philanthropy, 1904; hon. M.P.E., Internat. Y.M.C.A. Coll., 1931; m. Edna Vaughan Fisher, Jan. 18, 1912; children—Robert, Jane. Worker Ch. of the Covenant, New York, 1903-04; worker Madison Sq. Ch. House, New York, 1904-05; sec. Asso. Charities, Portland, Me., 1905-09; sec. Nat. Recreation Assn. (formerly Playground and Recreation Assn. America) May 14, 1909-June 11, 1941, president since June 1941. Editor of Recreation (formerly The Playground) since 1910; sec. War Camp Community Service, 1917-18; chmn. Nat. Social Work Council, Apr. 20, 1922-June 7, 1940; mem. bd. dirs. Nat. Information Bureau, 1918-Feb. 27, 1940; mem. N.Y. City Com. on Use of Leisure Time, 1933; mem. advisory com. National Youth Adminstrn., 1935-43; mem. Conf. Committee on Urban Problems under the U.S. ference Committee on Urbans Problems under the U.S. Chamber of Commerce, 1942. Mem. Nat. Council Boy Scouts of America. Fellow Am. Physical Edn. Assn.; Nat. Conf. Social Work, N.E.A., Am. Assn. Social Workers, Foreign Policy Association, American Academy of Physical Education, American Planning and Civic Assn., Am. Assn. for Adult Edn., Acad. Polit. Science, Soc. of Recreation Workers of Am., Museum of Modern Art, Phi Beta Kappa. Clubs: Nat. Arts, Town Hall. Home: Massapequa, L.I., N.Y. Office: 315 Fourth Av., New York, N.Y. Died May 22, 1949.

BRAUN, Maurice, artist; b. Nagy Bittse, Hungary, Oct. 1, 1877; s. Ferdinand and Charlotte (Leimdorfer) B.; brought by parents to U.S., 1881; art edn., Nat. Acad. Design, N.Y. City, 5 yrs., Chase Sch. of Art, 1 yr.; m. Hazel Boyer, Jan. 30, 1919; children—Charlotte LeClere, Ernest Boyer. Represented in permanent collections of San Diego (Calif.) Mus., San Diego Fine Arts Gallery, Wichita (Kan.) Art Assn., San Antonio (Tex.) Art Assn., Waco (Tex.) Art Gallery, Phoenix (Ariz.) Municipal Collection, Bloomington (Ill.) Art Assn., Oklahoma City (Okla.) Art Assn., etc. Awarded Hallgarten prize, Nat. Acad. Design, 1900; gold medal, Panama-Pacific Expn., 1915; gold medal, Panama, Calif. Expn., 1916; Tex. landscape prize of $2,000, 1929; bronze medal, Painters of the West, 1929; Gardena high sch. purchase prize, 1929. Republican. Theosophist. Clubs: California Art, San Diego Fine Arts Society, San Diego Art Guild; Salmagundi (New York). Studio: 61 Silvergate Pl., Point Loma, Calif. Died Nov. 7, 1941.

BRAUNER, Olaf Martinius (broun'ēr), artist; b. Christiania, Norway, Feb. 9, 1869; s. Julius F. and Andrea M. (Holter) B.; grad. Mass. Normal Art Sch., Boston, 1892, Sch. of Drawing and Painting, Museum Fine Arts, Boston, 1895; m. Nikoline B. Berntsen, June 26, 1895 (died July 22, 1925); children—Gertrude Nikoline, Karen Andrea (Mrs. Paul F. Rhines), Erling Bernhard, Olaf Arnliot, Arnliot Roald; m. 2d, Inga Lohne, Oct. 23, 1926; children—Inga Holter, Erik Torfinn. Has exhibited at Pennsylvania Academy of Fine Arts, Worcester Academy of Fine Arts, Boston Art Club, Phila. Art Club, Cincinnati Art Museum, St. Louis Museum, Detroit Museum, Corcoran Gallery, Brooklyn Inst., Nat. Acad. Design, Internat. Exhbn. Am. Numismatic Soc., Internat. Exhbn. of Ghent, Chicago Norske Klub; has painted portraits of many prominent persons in America and in foreign countries; prof. of painting, Cornell U. since 1900. Hon. mem. Central N.Y. Chapter A.I.A.; mem. Gargoyle Soc., Cornell Chapter of Phi Kappa Phi. Pi Kappa Alpha. Republican. Presbyn. Club: Cornell U. (N.Y.). Represented by works in Amherst Coll., Cornell U., U. of Mich., Kimball Library, Vt., and other schools and instns. Works include a large altar picture in the Luth. Evang. Church, Oak Park, Ill.; picture in Vanderpoel Memorial Gallery, Chicago; designed Gindell memorial medal for the Chicago Architectural Club, and the Clifton B. Brown memorial medal for the Coll. of Architecture, Cornell U.; War Memorial, Kappa Sigma; also Dane memorial bronze relief in the Walnut Hill Cemetery, Boston; has modeled fountains for private gardens. Awards in exhibitions at Chicago Norske Klub. Home: 414 E. Buffalo St., Ithaca, N.Y. Died Jan. 3, 1947.

BRAY, Frank Chapin, editor; b. Salineville, O., May 7, 1866; s. Rev. James Madison and Wilhelmina (Chapin) B.; Ph.B., Wesleyan U., Conn., 1890; m. Gertrude McMillan, June 18, 1901 (dec.); 1 dau. Martha Wilhelmina (Mrs. J. F. Jenkisson). Apprenticed to printer, 1878; worked at case and reporting to get through coll.; proofreader Hartford (Conn.) Courant, 1890) city editor, Middletown (Conn.) Herald, 1891; mng. editor Erie (Pa.) Morning Dispatch, 1892-94; editor "Topics of the Day" dept. of the Literary Digest, New York, 1894-99, editing also in 1898-99 the Phi Kappa Psi Shield, and depts. in Werner's Magazine, New York, and The Chautauquan; editor The Chautauquan, 1899, editor in chief, 1902, editor-mgr., 1906-14, the Chautauqua Press (Chautauqua Literary and Scientific Circle Books, The Chautauquan Magazine, Chautauqua Special Courses for Home Study); Chautauqua editor The Independent; asso. editor Current Opinion, 1914-16; editorial sec. The World's Court League and editor League of Nations Mag., 1919; editorial staff, Literary Digest, 1920-33; editor Canadian Border Contact Survey, 1933; editor information dept. Near East Relief, 1922; mem. staff of New Standard Encyclopedia, 1931. Clubs: National Arts (New York); Chicago Literary. Author: Reading Journey Through Chautauqua, 1905; The World of Myths, A Dictionary of Universal Mythology, 1935; Headlines in American History, 1937; New Internationale—a Better World, 1945. Lectures on cultural and international topics. Editor National Arts Broadcast; chairman thirty-day Annual Arts Club Exhibit of 2,000 new books-of-the-year from all leading publishers, with authors' night programs and honor luncheons to guest authors, 1935-45. Pres. Nat. Summer Book Fair, Chautauqua, N.Y., 1941. Sr. adviser to juniors, curator Nat. Arts Club (elected honorary life member, 1946). Address: 15 Gramercy Park, New York 3, N.Y. Died Mar. 24, 1949.

BRAY, William Crowell, chemist; b. Wingham, Ont., Can., Sept. 2, 1879; s. William Thomas and Sarah Jane (Willson) B.; B.A., U. of Toronto, 1902; Ph.D., U. of Leipzig, Germany, 1905; m. Nora

Thomas, June 30, 1914. Research asso., 1905-10, asst. prof. physico-chem. research, 1910-12, Mass. Inst. Tech.; asst. prof. chemistry, 1912-16, asso. professor, 1916-18, prof. since 1918, University of Calif. Chmn. dept. chemistry, 1943-June 1945. Am. U. Experiment Sta., Washington, D.C., 1918; asso. dir. Fixed Nitrogen Research Lab., Washington, 1919. Fellow Am. Acad. Arts and Sciences; mem. Nat. Acad. Sciences, Am. Chem. Soc., Am. Electrochem. Soc. Contbr. papers on inorganic and phys. chem. in Jour. Am. Chem. Soc. Home: 2708 Virginia St., Berkeley 4, Calif. Died Feb. 24, 1946.

BRAYTON, Aaron Martin, editor, pub.; b. La Crescent, Minn., Nov. 30, 1872; s. Aaron Harry and Elizabeth Knox (Orr) B.; LL.B., U. of Wis., 1896; m. Inez Eugenia Cooley, Jan. 19, 1898; children—Inez Almira, Richard Knox, Potter Burnell. Admitted to Wis. bar; in practice at Spokane, Wash., 1897-1899; city editor La Crosse (Wis.) Daily Press, 1901-02; mng. editor La Crosse Morning Chronicle, 1902-04; editor and pub. La Crosse Tribune, 1904-19, Wis. State Jour., Madison, 1919-42, publisher emeritus since 1942; sec. Wis. State Jour. Pub. Co.; v.p. Badger Broadcasting Co. Life mem. Wis. State Hist. Soc. Republican. Presbyterian. Clubs: Madison; La Crosse. Address: 678 S. Lafayette Park Pl., Los Angeles 5, Calif. Died Jan. 18, 1949.

BREADON, Sam, baseball exec.; b. New York, N.Y., July 26, 1876; s. William and Jane (Wilson) B.; ed. pub. schs. of New York City; m. Josephine Christian, 1905; 1 dau., Frances (Hedges); m. 2d, Rachel Wilson, June 25, 1912; 1 dau., Janet. Formed retail automobile company under the name of Western Automobile Co., 1903, sold company and retired from automobile bus. 1936; pres. Western Automobile (name changed to Sam Breadon Automobile Co. 1935) since 1905. Pres. St. Louis Nat. Baseball Club since Jan. 1920. Episcopalian. Home: 22 Washington Terrace, St. Louis 12. Office: 3623 Dodier St., Sportsmans Park, St. Louis 7, Mo. Died May 10, 1949.

BRECKINRIDGE, James Carson, maj. gen. U.S. Marine Corps.; b. in Tenn., Sept. 13, 1877; advanced through grades to maj. gen., Feb. 1, 1935; now comdr. Marine Barracks, Quantico, Va. Address: Navy Dept., Washington, D.C. Died Mar. 2, 1942.

BRECKINRIDGE, Sophonisba Preston, social worker, educator; b. Lexington, Ky., 1866; d. William Campbell Preston and Issa (Desha) Breckinridge; S.B., Wellesley, 1888; Ph.D., U. of Chicago, 1901; J.D., 1904; LL.D., Oberlin Coll., 1919, U. of Ky., 1925, Tulane U., 1939. Mem. Ky. Bar. Mem. faculty Chicago U. since 1902; resident of Hull House, 1908-20; instr. then prof. household adminstrn., 1902-25; prof. social economy, 1925-29, Samuel Deutsch prof. pub. welfare adminstrn., 1929. Delegate: Women's Peace Cong., The Hague, 1915; Pan Am. Child Cong., Lima, Peru, 1930; Pan Am. Cong., Montevideo, 1933. Interested in civic and philanthropic work; sec. Immigrants' Protective League; dean Chicago Sch. of Civics and Philanthropy; pres. Am. Assn. Schools of Social Work, 1934-35; v.p. Nat. Am. Woman's Suffrage Assn., 1911; pres. Ill. Welfare Assn. 1930; pres. Chicago chap. Assn. Social Workers; pres. Chicago Woman's City Club. Mem. Order of Coif, Phi Beta Kappa. Author: Legal Tender, A Study in Am. Monetary History, 1901; (with Edith Abbott) The Delinquent Child and the Home, 1912; (with Marion Talbot) The Modern Household, 1912; (with Edith Abbott) Truancy, 1917; New Homes for Old, 1921; Madeline McDowell Breckinridge, a Leader in the New South, 1921; Family Welfare Work in a Metropolitan Community, 1924; Public Welfare Administration, 1927; The Family and the State, 1934; Social Work and the Courts, 1934; The Illinois Poor Law and its Administration, 1939. Home: 5544 Woodlawn Av., Chicago 37. Office: 1313 E. 59th St., Chicago. Died July 30, 1948.

BREHM, John S., publisher; b. Newville, Pa., Dec. 28, 1874; s. Samuel Henry and Rebecca (Wogan) B.; ed. high sch.; m. Sadie P. Dewey, July 3, 1901. Circulation dir. Chicago Record & Daily News, 1896-1914; circulation dir. The Crowell-Collier Pub. Co., Co., N.Y. City, since 1914, now also v.p. Protestant. Clubs: N.Y. Athletic; Westchester (N.Y.) Country. Home: 17 W. 54th St. Office: The Crowell-Collier Pub. Co., 250 Park Av., New York, N.Y.* Died Nov. 2, 1946.

BRELSFORD, Millard (brĕls'fōrd), clergyman; Bowlusville, O., Aug. 17, 1873; s. Charles and Mary Ellen (Hanback) B.; A.B., Denison U., 1897; D.D., 1917; B.D., Rochester Theol. Sem. (now Colgate-Rochester Div. Sch.), 1900; m. Gertrude Maude Carhartt, May 16, 1900 (died Aug. 21, 1933); children—Ernest Carhartt, Charles Millard; m. 2d, Nelle C. Frye, Aug. 19, 1937. Ordained to ministry Bapt. Ch., June 9, 1900; pastor First Ch., Urbana, O., 1900-1905, East Cleveland Ch., Cleveland, O., 1905-13, First Ch., Granville, O., 1913-19, East Cleveland Ch., 1919-33; travel in Holy Land, 1934; sec. Bd. of Trustees, Denison U., since 1914, full time sec. since 1934, also treas. since 1938. Trustee Denison U., 1902-45; trustee Ohio Bapt. Conv., 1901-38, and since 1939; pres. Ohio Bapt. Conv., 1930-35. Republican. Mason. Mem. Phi Beta Kappa, Phi Gamma Delta, Rotary. Home: 122 S. Prospect St. Office: Denison University, Granville, O. Died Mar. 20, 1946.

BRENGLE, Henry Gaw (brĕng'l), banker; b. Baltimore, Md., Feb. 25, 1866; s. James Shriver and Millicent Anne (Gaw) B.; A.B., Harvard, 1887; unmarried. Began in banking business with H. L. Gaw & Co., Phila., 1887; pres. Phila. Trust Co., 1918-26; pres. Fidelity-Phila. Trust Co., 1926-37. Clubs: Philadelphia Rittenhouse (Phila.); University (New York). Home: Radnor, Pa. Office: Broad and Walnut Sts., Philadelphia, Pa. Died Nov. 10, 1943.

BRENNAN, Martin S., clergyman; b. St. Louis, July 23, 1845; s. William C. and Margaret (Hackett) B.; A.B., Christian Brothers Coll., St. Louis, 1865, A.M., 1869; Sc.D., 1896. Ordained priest, R.C. Ch., 1869; pastor St. Lawrence O'Toole Parish, St. Louis, 1892-1910, Sts. Mary and Joseph Parish, Jan. 1910; prof. astronomy and geology, Kendrick Sem., St. Louis, since 1892. Lecturer on science at Catholic schs. Apptd. domestic prelate by Pope Pius XI, May 27, 1923. Fellow A.A.A.S., Am. Geog. Soc.; Mem. British Astron. Assn., Astron. Soc. of the Pacific, Astron. and Astrophys. Soc. Am., Am. Math. Soc., St. Louis Acad. Science. Author: Electricity and Its Discoverers; What Catholics Have Done for Science; Astronomy, New and Old; Science of the Bible. Contbr. scientific articles to mags. Address: 6304 Minnesota Av., St. Louis. Died Oct. 3, 1927.

BRENNEMANN, Joseph (brĕn'nĕ-măn), pediatrist; b. Peru, Ill., Sept. 25, 1872; s. Joseph and Mary (Schaefer) B.; Ph.B., U. of Mich., 1895; M.D., Northwestern U., 1900; St. Luke's Hosp., 1900-02; m. Bessie D. Daniels, Jan. 2, 1905; children—Mary Elizabeth, Barbara, Deborah. Chief of staff, Children's Memorial Hosp., prof. Pediatrics, U. of Chicago, 1921-41; medical dir. Children's Hosp., Los Angeles, prof. Pediatrics, U. of S. Calif. Med. Sch., 1941-43; Am. Pediatric Soc., Chicago Pediatric Soc., Am. Acad. Pediatrics, Inst. of Medicine Chicago, Soc. for Pediatric Research (hon.), Chicago Medical Soc., British Pediatric Soc. (corr. mem.), Nu Sigma Nu. Contbr. to pediatric literature. Editor of Brennemann's Practice of Pediatrics. Home: Reading, Vt. Died July 2, 1944.

BRENTANO, Arthur (brĕn-tä'nō), bookselling; b. Hoboken, N.J., Apr. 20, 1858; s. Emil and Sara (Loewenthal) B.; ed. pub. schs., Evansville, Ind., and Cincinnati, O.; m. Rowena M. L. LanFranco, Jan. 30, 1890 (dec.); children—Rowena LanFranco, Emily (Mrs. Edward A. Hermann), Arthur, Marion (Mrs. Franklyn Kingsland Oakes). Began with Brentano's, Inc. (now Brentano's Book Stores, Inc.), N.Y. City, 1873, pres. since 1915. Pres. Brentano's Société Anonyme, Paris; one of founders Am. Canoe Assn. Republican. Home: 224 Midland Av., East Orange, N.J. Office: 586 Fifth Av., New York, N.Y. Died Jan. 28, 1944.

BRESNAHAN, William H., corp. official; b. Lynn, Mass.; s. Maurice V. and Mary (Sheehan) B.; ed. Lynn (Mass.) pub. and high schs.; m. Mary E. Thompson, Oct. 28, 1914. Chmn. bd. Compo Shoe Machinery Corp. Home: 145 Puritan Rd., Swampscott, Mass. Office: 150 Causeway, Boston, Mass.* Died May 6, 1947.

BRESSLER, Raymond George, state dir. agrl. and conservation; b. Halifax, Pa., Mar. 9, 1887; s. Ryan Andrew and Ellen (Etzweiler) B.; Shippensburg Normal Sch., 1904; A.B., Valparaiso U., 1908; A.M., Wofford Coll., Spartanburg, S.C., 1910; B.S., Tex. Agrl. and Mech. Coll., 1917; M.S., U. of Wis., 1918; student Columbia U., 1925-26 and 1930; LL.D., Northeastern U., Boston, 1932; Ed.D., R.I. Coll. of Edn., Providence, 1932; Sc.D., R.I. Coll. of Pharmacy and Allied Sciences, 1933; m. Sara Lebo, Feb. 4, 1910; children—Raymond George, Angelin, Elaine, Sara Hope, Ryan Andrew II. Teacher in rural sch., 1904-05; prin. grammar sch., Halifax, Pa., 1905-06; coach and dir. physical edn., Wofford Coll., 1908-10; asst. prof. English and pub. speaking, Texas Agrl. and Mech. Coll., 1910-15; dir. inter-scholastic athletics and head dept. rural edn. extension, U. of Tex., 1915-17; asst. dir. of vocational edn., Tex. State Dept. of Pub. Instruction, 1917-18; prof. rural economics and sociology, Pa. State Coll., 1918-22, vice dean and dir. of instrn. in Sch. of Agr., 1922-27; dep. sec. of agr. for state of Pa., 1927-31; treas. Pa. Farm Show, 1927-31; dir., 1930-31; pres. R.I. State Coll., 1931-40; dir. Agrl. and Conservation for Rhode Island, since Mar. 5, 1941. Mem. exec. com. R.I. Agrl. Conference; chmn. R.I. Milk Control Bd.; chmn. agrl. com., State Civilian Defense; mem. exec. com. Atlantic Marine Fisheries Commn.; mem. State Planning Board, Safety Council. Member Atlantic States Market Officials (pres), Phi Kappa Phi, Alpha Zeta, Tau Kappa Epsilon, Scabbard and Blade, Keystone Farmer. Conglist. Mason. Clubs: British Empire (Providence); Pennsylvania (Harrisburg). Co-Author: Questions on Century Readings in English Literature, 1915; Jolly Games and Fun Makers, 1927. Home: East Greenwich, R.I. Office: 310 State House, Providence, R.I. Died May 9, 1948.

BREWER, Earl LeRoy, ex-governor; b. Carroll County, Miss., Aug. 11, 1869; s. Ratcliff Rodney and Mary Elizabeth (McEachern) B.; LL.B., U. of Miss., 1892; m. Minnie Marion Block, 1897; children—Minnie, Earlene, Claudia. Practiced with Julian C. Wilson, at Water Valley, 1892-1901; mem. Miss. Senate, 1895-99; dist. atty. 11th Jud. Dist., 1902-06 (resigned); candidate for gov. of Miss., 1906; gov. of Miss., 1912-16; now mem. firm Brewer & Hewitt. Democrat. Presbyn. Mason, K.P. Home: Jackson, Miss.* Died Mar. 10, 1942.

BREWER, Nicholas Richard, artist and writer; b. High Forest, Olmsted County, Minn., June 11, 1857; s. Peter and Mary Ann (Russell) B.; ed. dist. sch. to 15; studied art after marriage, under D. W. Tryon and Charles Noel Flagg, New York; m. Rose Mary Koempel, May 20, 1879. Exhibited at Nat. Acad. Design, N.Y., 1885, later in Newport, R.I., Boston, Chicago, Indianapolis, Milwaukee, Pittsburgh, St. Louis and many other cities, won 2d prize Minn. State Art Soc., 1912. Awarded 1st prize Minn. Inst. of Arts and Sciences, St. Paul, Minn., 1915; 1st prize, Illinois State Art Exhibition, 1917; Municipal Art League purchase prize, Art Inst. Chicago, 1921; Edgar B. Davis purchase prize ($1250), Tex. Wildflower Exhibit, Witte Museum, San Antonio, 1929. Rep. in collections of governors' portraits as follows—William Sprague (R.I.), John A. Johnson and W. S. Hammond (Minn.), James McGovern (Wis.), Norbeck and Edmunds (S.D.), C. H. Brough (Ark.), Dan Moody (Tex.), Frank White (N.D.), also W. H. Holmes—in Nat. Gallery (Washington), Art Institute Chicago, Hackley Gallery (Muskegon), University of Minn., Univ. of Texas, Univ. of Oklahoma, Univ. of Nebraska. Has also done portraits of Mr. and Mrs. F. M. Hall, Henry Ward Beecher, Ulysses S. Grant, Joseph Jefferson, Ignace Paderewski, Maude Powell, Margaret Anglin, Ruth Bryan Owen, George M. Reynolds, Cardinal Mundelein, Most Rev. John Ireland, Rt. Rev. James Hugh Ryan, Justices Pierce Butler, Willis Van DeVanter and George Sutherland (U.S. Supreme Ct.), Frederic A. Delano, Pres. F. D. Roosevelt, Vice-Pres. J. N. Garner, Senator J. T. Robinson, Speaker Rainey, Sec. of Navy Swanson. Was prof. art, Coll. of St. Thomas, of St. Paul, 1894-97. Author: "Trails of a Paintbrush"; also short stories. Roman Catholic. Mem. Am. Fedn. of Arts, Salmagundi Club (New York), Arts Club (Washington), Nat. Arts Club (New York), Chicago Soc. Artists, Southern States Art League. Address: 468 Glenham Av., St. Paul, Minn.* Died Feb. 15, 1949.

BREWER, Robert Du Bois, banker; b. Melrose, Mass., Feb. 18, 1881; s. Frank Crocker and Sarah Mulford (Du Bois) B.; B.L., Dartmouth, 1904; LL.B., Harvard, 1907; m. Margaretta McCandless, Jan. 6, 1916; children—Robert D., Sarah, Ruth Anne. Admitted to bar, 1907; began practice at Boston; with food adminstrn., Washington, 1918; again practiced, 1919-21; asst. to treas. Provident Instn. for Savings in Town of Boston, 1921-24, treas., 1925-29, now trustee, vice pres. and mem. bd. of investments; pres. Merchants Nat. Bank of Boston, 1929-42, now chmn. of bd.; trustee William Underwood Co.; treasurer Widows Soc. in Boston; dir. N. E. Mutual Life Ins. Co. Club: Union (Boston). Home: Hingham, Mass. Office: 28 State St., Boston, Mass. Died Jan. 9, 1949.

BREWSTER, André Walker (brōō'stēr), army officer; b. in N.J., Dec. 9, 1862; grad. Army War Coll., 1907. Commd. 2d lt. 10th Inf., Jan. 19, 1885; 1st lt. 22d Inf., Dec. 17, 1891; trans. to 9th Inf., Feb. 9, 1892; capt. a.q.m. vols., Oct. 15, 1898; hon. discharge vols., May 12, 1899; capt. U.S. Army, Mar. 2, 1899; trans. to 25th Inf., Jan. 29, 1908; maj. 19th Inf., Mar. 15, 1908; insp. gen., 1909-13; lt. col. inf., Dec. 2, 1913; col., July 1, 1916; brig. gen. N.A., 1917; maj. gen. N.A., Nov. 28, 1917; maj. gen. U.S. Army, Dec. 1, 1922; retired Dec. 9, 1925. Address: War Dept., Washington, D.C.* Died Mar. 27, 1942.

BREWSTER, David Lukens, marine corps officer; b. Washington, D.C., Dec. 31, 1887; s. Robert John Walker and Leila (Shoemaker) B.; grad. Tech. High Sch., Washington, D.C., 1904-08, Service Staff and Command Schs., 1923 and 1938; m. Mercer B. Taliaferro, Feb. 26, 1919; children—David Andre, Austin (Mrs. Charles D. Barrett, Jr). Commd. 2d lt., U.S. Marine Corps, 1910, and advanced through the grades to brig. gen.; naval aviator, 1917-22; chief of staff, 1st Marine Div., 1938-40; administrative deputy, 1st Marine Amphibious Corps, 1943-44. Decorated Legion of Merit, Distinguished Marksman (U.S.); Portuguese Grand Order of Aviation; Nicaraguan Order of Merit. Home: 1437 44th St. N.W., (7). Address: care The Advocate General's Office, Navy Dept., Washington 25, D.C. Died July 10, 1945.

BREWSTER, Elisha Hume, judge; b. Worthington, Mass., Sept. 10, 1871; s. Charles K. and Celina S. (Baldwin) B.; grad. Williston Sem., Easthampton, Mass., 1893; LL.B., Boston U., 1896; m. Alice M. Thompson, June 20, 1900 (died June 6, 1904); m. 2d, Jessie W. Cook, June 28, 1906. Began practice at Springfield, 1896; mem. Mass. Ho. of Rep., 1902-04; judge U.S. Dist. Court, Dist. of Mass., by apptmt. of President Harding, 1922. Mem. S.A.R. Republican. Conglist. Mason. Clubs: Colony (Springfield); Worthington (Mass.) Golf. Home: 240 Washington Blvd., Springfield 8. Office: Post Office Bldg., Springfield, Mass. Died Apr. 29, 1946.

BREWSTER, Ethel Hampson, coll. prof.; b. Chester, Pa., July 3, 1886; d. Joseph Fergus and Emma Jane (Hampson) B.; A.B., Swarthmore Coll., 1907; A.M., U. of Pa., 1911, Bennett fellow in classics, 1912-14, Ph.D., 1915; student Sch. of Classical Studies, Am. Acad. in Rome, 1926-27; unmarried. Instr. in Latin, French and English, high sch., Chester, Pa., 1907-09; head of dept. classics, high sch., West Chester, Pa., 1909-12; instr. in Latin, Vassar Coll., 1914-16; asst. prof. Greek and Latin, Swarthmore Coll., 1916-24, also dean of women, 1921-28, asso. prof., 1924-28, prof. and chmn. of dept. classics since 1928, acting dean of the coll., 1932-33. Mem.

Am. Philol. Assn., Archeol. Inst. America, American Hist. Assn., Am. Assn. Univ. Profs., Am. Assn. Univ. Women, Phi Beta Kappa. Democrat. Contbr. to philol. and ednl. jours. Home: West House, Swarthmore, Pa. Died Aug. 19, 1947.

BREWSTER, George Thomas, sculptor; b. Kingston, Mass., Feb. 24, 1862; s. Altheus and Mary S. (Cushman) B.; pub. sch. edn., Stoughton, Mass.; student Mass. State Normal Art Sch., 3½ yrs., Ecole des Beaux Arts, Paris, 3 yrs.; m. 2d, Lina A. G. Totten, July 11, 1918; children—Thomas I., Eleanor C., George A. (dec.). Engaged professionally as sculptor since 1884; founder modeling class, Art Students' League, New York, 1886; instr. R.I. State School of Design, 1893-94, All-Arts Studios, Greenwich, Conn., 1933, 34 and 35, Cooper Union, New York, 1900-33. Mem. Nat. Sculpture Soc., Architectural League, Municipal Art Soc., Am. Federation of Arts. Clubs: Nat. Arts; Washington Arts (Washington, D.C.). Home: 595 Steamboat Rd., Greenwich, Conn. Died Mar. 6, 1943.

BREWSTER, R(eginald) R., lawyer; b. White Cloud, Kan., Oct. 23, 1876; s. Arthur S. and Anna (Byard) B.; ed. U. of Kan.; m. Grace A. Sloane, Dec. 29, 1898; children—Robert R., William B., Elizabeth G., Phillip S. Admitted to Kan. bar, 1899; in practice Kansas City, Mo., 1900; asst. pros. atty., Jackson County, Mo., 1902; mem. firm Brewster, Brewster & Brewster; active in politics. Chmn. bd. trustees Children's Mercy Hosp Rep candidate for U S Senate, 1922 Home: 235 W 53d St. Office: Federal Reserve Bank Bldg., Kansas City, Mo. Died June 3, 1946.

BREZING, Herman, educator; b. Heidelberg, Ont., Can., Apr. 30, 1877; s. Jacob and Elizabeth (Hauff) B.; came to U.S., 1888, citizen, 1893; student Wagner Coll., Rochester, N.Y., 1890-94, Mt. Airy Theol. Sem., Phila., 1894-97; D.D., Hartwick Sem., Oneonta, N.Y., 1929; m. Harriet Richman, Aug. 11, 1915; children—Herman Jacob, Robert Albert. Ordained ministry Lutheran Ch., 1898; pastor Holy Trinity Ch., Jamestown, N.Y., 1898-1900, St. Matthew's Ch., Toledo, O., 1900-04, Zion Lutheran Ch., Niagara Falls, N.Y., 1904-31; pres. Wagner Coll., Staten Island, N.Y., 1931-34; resident dir. Wartburg Orphans' Farm Sch., Mt. Vernon, N.Y., since 1934. Dir. Inner Mission Bd., United Luth. Ch. in America. Democrat. Rotarian. Address: Wartburg School, Mt. Vernon, N.Y. Died July 1, 1945.

BRIAN, Donald, actor, singer; b. Feb. 17, 1875, St. Johns Newfoundland; s. Denis Francis and Margaret (Silvey) B.; educated at English High Sch., Boston; m. Florence Meagher Gleason, Mar. 1, 1910; m. 2d, Virginia OBrien, November 27, 1926; 1 daughter, Denise Madeleine. Made his first appearance on the stage as Hardie Grant, in Shannon of the Sixth, 1896; subsequently played in Three Little Lambs, Florodora, Silver Slipper, Little Johnny Jones, Forty-five Minutes from Broadway, The Merry Widow, The Dollar Princess; The Marriage Market, 1914; The Girl from Utah, 1915; star of Charles Frohman's The Siren Co., 1913; co-star with Julia Sanderson and Joseph Cawthorn, 1916-17; starred in Her Regiment 1917-18; The Girl Behind the Gun, 1918-19, with Peggy Wood in Buddies, 1919-21, and in revival of The Chocolate Soldier, 1921-22; with Up She Goes, Barnum Was Right, and Rolling Home—all 1923; costar with Alys Delysia in The Courtesan, 1923-24; costar with Vivian Martin in Just Married (tour of Keith vaudeville), 1924-25; co-star with Julia Sanderson in No, No, Nanette special company, 1925-26; with Castles in the Air, Yes, Yes, Yvette, 1927; co-star with Edna Leedom, in Breakfast in the Sun, 1927-28; toured in vaudeville and guest star in stock, radio broadcasting and talking pictures, 1928-29; starred in Hows Your Health, Candlelight, revival of Merry Widow and Private Lives, 1930-31, Reunion in Vienna, 1933, Music in the Air, 1934, and Fly Away Home, 1935. In motion pictures, 1936-37; teacher of light opera, New Eng. Conservatory of Music, 1938; teacher dramatic Sch., Great Neck, N.Y., since 1939; played in Very Warm for May (New York), 1939; Mornings at Seven, 1940; co-star with Luella Grear in The Vinegar Tree, summer 1942. Clubs: The Lambs, Players. Home: Windsor Apts., Great Neck, N.Y. Address: The Lambs, 130 W. 44th St., New York, N.Y. Died Dec. 22, 1948.

BRICE, John A., newspaperman; b. Woodward, S.C., June 28, 1876; s. Joseph Clarence and Margaret (Adams) B.; A.B., Erskine Coll., 1896; unmarried. Began as clerk, 1896; sec. and treas. The Atlanta Journal, 1901-34, v.p. and gen. mgr., 1934-39, pres. since 1939. Democrat. Presbyterian. Mason (Shriner), Elk. Clubs: Capital City, Piedmont Driving, Rotary. Home: Capital City Club. Office: Atlanta Journal Bldg., Atlanta, Ga. Died Jan. 9, 1946.

BRICKER, Luther Otterbein, clergyman; b. Rockingham County, Va., May 15, 1874; s. John Wesley and Mary Jane (Hawes) B.; ed. Shenandoah Coll., Dayton, Va., U. of Va., and Union Theol. Sem., New York; D.D., Western Coll., Toledo, Ia.; m. Kathryn Acker, Nov. 5, 1901 (dec.); 1 dau., Eileen Ruth (dec.); m. 2d, Louanna Rhodes, July 23, 1924. Ordained ministry Christian (Disciples) Ch. 1900; pastor Staunton, Va., 1900-03, Cedar Rapids, Ia., 1903-07, Maryville, Mo., 1907-10; pastor First Christian Ch., Atlanta, Ga., 1910-24; founded, 1924, and since pastor, Peachtree Ch., and in 1928, dedicated one of most beautiful Gothic chs. in America. Mem. Com. of 100, Miami Beach. Trustee U. Sch. of Religion, Disciples Foundation, Vanderbilt U. Mem. Soc. of Virginians. Mem. Com. on Worship, Fed. Council Chs. of Christ in Am. Official rep. Disciples of Christ in Am. on Commn. on Ways of Worship in the World Council of Chs. Clubs: Friars, Capital City, Ansley Park Golf, Indian Creek Club, Surf (Miami Beach, Fla.). Author: The Christian Life, 1914; The Voice of the Deep, 1926; Cultivate Your Own Garden, 1935; The Windows of Peachtree Church, 1938; The Altar, 1940. Home: 4731 Pine Tree Drive, Miami Beach, Fla. Died Aug. 13, 1942; buried in Westview Cemetery, Atlanta.

BRIDGES, Charles Higbee, army officer; b. Whitehall, Ill., Mar. 1, 1873; s. Jehoshaphat and Annette (Cheney) B.; grad U.S. Mil. Acad., 1897, Army Sch. of the Line, 1908, Army Signal Sch., 1909, Army War Coll., 1920; m. Mrs. Sadie Awl, 1914. Commissioned 2d lt., U.S. Army, June 11, 1897; promoted through grades to colonel, July 1,1920; colonel (temp.) World War. Served in Santiago Campaign, War with Spain, 1898; in Philippine Insurrection, 1899-1902; custodian of Aguinaldo, Sept. 1901-Jan. 1902; insp. gen. 2d Div., A.E.F., France, Nov. 1917-Feb. 1918; asst. chief of staff 2d Div., to July 25, 1918; asst. chief of staff 6th Army Corps, France, Mar. 9-Nov. 11, 1918; insp. gen. 5th Div., June-Sept. 1920; insp. 5th Corps Area to July 1921; chief of staff 5th Corps Area to Oct. 28, 1922; brig. gen., asst. adj. gen., July 2, 1927-Feb. 1, 1929; became maj. gen., The Adj. Gen., Feb. 1, 1929; now retired. Clubs: Army and Navy, Chevy Chase. Home: 1870 Wyoming Av., N.W., Washington, D.C. Died Sept. 11, 1948.

BRIDGES, H(edley) Francis G(regory), govt. official; b. Fredericton, N.B., Can., Apr. 7, 1902; s. Hedley Vicars Burpee and Mabel Eloise Fulton (Gregory) B.; A.B. of New Brunswick, 1922, LL.D. (hon.), 1946; unmarried. Prin. Hillsboro High Sch., 1922-23, Campbellton High Sch., 1923-27; called to Bar, 1927; practiced law, Campbellton, N.B., 1927-42; mem. Campbellton Town Council, 1929; elected to N.B. Legislature, 1935, speaker, 1936-38; elected to Fed. House of Commons for York-Sunbury, 1945; Minister of Fisheries since 1945; head Can. del. meeting at St. John's Newfoundland Air Bases, 1946, signed fisheries treaty with U.S. establishing Internat. Fisheries com., 1946. Served as major, 2d Can. Corps in Can., Eng., northwest Europe, 1944-45. Selected for tour of British Isles as guest of Lord Beaverbrook, 1926. Created King's Counsel, 1946. Liberal. Mem. Anglican Ch. Mason. Elk. Clubs: Campbellton Gyro, Fredericton Curling, Restigouche Golf and Country, Rideau of Ottawa. Home: Chateau Laurier. Office: House of Commons, Ottawa, Ont., Can. Died Aug. 10, 1947.

BRIDGES, Thomas Reed, clergyman; b. Ghent, Ky., Jan. 13, 1868; s. David Matthew and Mary Ann (Reed) B.; A.B., Hanover (Ind.) Coll., 1887, A.M., 1890, D.D., 1904; B.D., Union Theol. Sem., 1891; unmarried. Deacon and priest P.E. Ch., 1915; pastor Second Presbyn. Ch., Newark, N.J., 1895-1905, South Ref. Ch., New York, 1905-14; curate Ch. of the Incarnation, New York, 1915-18; rector All Saints Ch., Mobile, Ala., 1919-41; retired from active service. Home: Metuchen, N.Y. Died June 7, 1943.

BRIGGS, Asa Gilbert, lawyer; b. Arcadia, Wis., Dec. 20, 1862; s. Isaac Austin and Elizabeth B.; B.S., U. of Wis., 1885, LL.B., 1887; m. Jessica Pierce, Oct. 21, 1891; children—Allan, Paul Austin, Mary Elizabeth. Admitted to Minn. bar, 1887; in practice, St. Paul, 1887-1901; gen. counsel C.G.W. Ry., 1901-09; gen. practice since 1908. Vice pres. for Minn. of Gt. Lakes St. Lawrence Tidewater Assn., 1928-39; trustee St. Paul Bur. of Municipal Research (ex-pres.); pres. St. Paul Assn. Commerce, 1925 and 1927; dir. St. Paul Chamber of Commerce, 1921-30; director U.S. Chamber of Commerce, 1930-34; dir. nat. bd. Camp Fire Girls, 1931-39. Mem. Am. Interprofessional Inst., Am. Acad. Polit. and Social Science, Am. Peace Soc., U. of Wis. Alumni Assn. (pres., dir. for life). Republican. Methodist. Mason (Shriner). Clubs: Minnesota, St. Paul Athletic, Informal, Town and Country. Home: 793 Fairmount Av. Office: First Nat. Bank Bldg., St. Paul, Minn. Died Aug. 31, 1945.

BRIGGS, George Isaac, headmaster; b. Nashville, Tenn., May 10, 1886; s. George Isaac and Matilda (Harrison) B.; student Battle Ground Acad., Franklin, Tenn., 1899-1903; A.B., Southwestern Presbyn. U., Clarksville, Tenn., 1907; m. Susie Lee Roberts, Dec. 29, 1910; children—Jane, Sarah Ewing. Teacher Latin and Bible, McCallie Sch., Chattanooga, 1907-13; headmaster Darlington Sch. for Boys, Rome, Ga., 1914-17; teacher Baylor Sch., Chattanooga, 1919-24; headmaster Battle Ground Acad. since 1925. Served as 1st lt. inf., World War I. Sec. Mid-South Assn. Pvt. Schs.; mem. Sigma Alpha Epsilon. Democrat. Methodist. Mason. Home: Franklin, Tenn. Died May 3, 1944.

BRIGGS, Warren Richard, architect; b. Malden, Mass., June 6, 1850; s. Evans E. and Mary Georgianna B.; ed. pvt. schs.; tech. edn. École des Beaux Arts, Paris; m. Eliza H. Beach, Feb. 7, 1882; children—Marjory B., Roger B. Engaged in archtl. practice since 1869. Principal works: Fairfield County Court House, Bridgeport, Conn., Bridgeport Orphan Asylum, N.Y.N.H. & H. R.R. Station, Bridgeport, etc. Fellow Am. Inst. Architects (ex-pres. Conn. chapter), Archtl. League New York, Société Anciens Élèves du Jules André. Republican. Clubs: University, Seaside, Seaside Outing, Brooklawn Country (Bridgeport), Housatonic (Stratford), Metabetchouan Fishing and Game (Canada). Author: Modern American School Buildings. Home: 947 Broad St., Stratford, Conn. Died May 30, 1933.

BRIGHAM, Carl Campbell (brig'ŭm), prof. psychology; b. Marlboro, Mass., May 4, 1890; s. Charles Francis and Ida (Campbell) B.; grad. Marlboro High Sch., 1908; Litt.B., Princeton, 1912, A.M., 1913, Ph.D., 1916; m. Elizabeth Duffield, Feb. 10, 1923; 1 dau., Elizabeth Hollister. Began as coll. instr., 1916; asst. to chief, Federal Bd. for Vocational Edn., 1919-20; asst. prof. psychology, Princeton, 1920-24, asso. prof., 1924-27, prof. since 1928. Adviser Canadian Mil. Hosps., 1917; 1st lt. Tank Corps. 1917-18. Mem. A.A.A.S., Am. Psychol. Assn. Clubs: Nassau, Quadrangle (Princeton); Princeton, University (New York). Author: Two Studies in Mental Tests, 1917; Study of American Intelligence, 1923; Study of Error, 1932. Contbr. to scientific publs. Home: 114 Mercer St., Princeton, N.J. Died Jan. 24, 1943.

BRIGHT, John, dist. judge; b. Middletown, N.Y., May 23, 1884; s. Frank and Ellen (Higham) B.; ed. Middletown High School and Ramsdell's Bus. Sch., 1901, and legal edn. in office Thomas Watts; m. Cornelia Denton, May 24, 1909; 1 son, John Denton. Admitted to N.Y. bar, Jan. 26, 1906; corp. counsel, City of Middletown, 1910 and 1917; dir. Orange County Trust Co. since 1914; U.S. Dist. judge Southern Dist. of N.Y. since 1941. Mem. Bd. of Edn., Middletown, N.Y., 1910. Mem. N.Y. State, Orange County, Middletown Bar assns., Assn Bar City of New York. Episcopalian (jr. warden, Grace Ch., Middletown). Mason, past master and past dist. deputy. Club: Orange County Golf (Middletown, N.Y.). Home: 78 Highland Av., Middletown, N.Y. Address: United States District Court, Foley Square, New York, N.Y. Died Mar. 24, 1948.

BRIGHTMAN, Horace Irving, lawyer; b. N.Y. City, Jan. 29, 1872; s. Horace and Julie (Willson) B.; A.B., Columbia, 1892; LL.B., New York Law Sch., 1893; m. Florence Church Mead, Nov. 10, 1904 (dec.). Admitted to N.Y. bar, 1894, and practiced since at N.Y. City. Mem. Phi Gamma Delta. Republican. Clubs: Phi Gamma Delta (New York); Waccabuc Country (Lake Waccabuc). Home: Lake Waccabuc, N.Y. Office: 299 Madison Av., New York. Died April 3, 1940.

BRILL, Abraham Arden, psychiatrist; b. Austria, Oct. 12, 1874; s. Philip and Esther B.; Ph.B., New York U., 1901; M.D., Coll. Phys. and Surg. (Columbia), 1903; m. K. Rose Owen, May 21, 1908; children—Gioia Bernheim, Edmund. Formerly asst. phys. Central Islip State Hosp., and in clinic of psychiatry, of Zurich, Switzerland; formerly chief of clinic in psychiatry, Columbia U., and lecturer on psychoanalysis and abnormal psychology, New York Univ.; was asst. prof. psychiatry, Post-grad. Med. Sch.; now lecturer on psychoanalysis and psychosexual sciences, Columbia Univ.; clinical professor psychiatry, New York Univ. Member New York State and N.Y. Co. med. socs., N.Y. Neurol. Soc., Am. Psychopathol. Assn., Am. Psychoanalytic Assn., A.M.A., New York Acad. Medicine, New York Soc. for Clin. Psychiatry, New York Psychiat. Soc., Am. Psychiatric Assn., Am. Therapeutic Assn., A.A.A.S., Anthropol. Ethnol. Soc. Clubs: City, Lotos. Author: Psychoanalysis—Its Theories and Practical Application; Fundamental Conceptions of Psychoanalysis, 1921, 1922; Freud's Contribution to Psychiatry, 1944; Lectures on Psychoanalytic Psychiatry, 1946; also numerous pamphlets on Psychiatric subjects. Translator: Jung's Psychology of Dementia Præcox, 1909, 1936; Freud's Selected Papers on Hysteria, 1909; Three Contributions to the Theory of Sex (Freud), 1910, 30; Freud's Interpretation of Dreams, 1913, 1932; Psychopathology of Everyday Life, 1914; Wit and Its Relations to the Unconscious, 1916; Leonardo da Vinci, 1916; The History of the Psychoanalytic Movement, 1917; Totem and Taboo, 1918; Reflections on War and Death, 1918; Psychoanalysis—Exploring the Hidden Recesses of the Mind, 1924. Editor: English edition of Bleuler's Text Book of Psychiatry, 1925; Breuer and Freud—Studies in Hysteria, 1936; The Basic Writings of Sigmund Freud, 1938 Home: 15 W. 70th St. Office: 88 Central Park West, New York, N.Y. Died Mar. 2, 1948.

BRINCKERHOFF, Henry Morton, elec. engr.; b. Fishkill-on-Hudson, N.Y., Apr. 20, 1868; s. Peter Remsen and Helen (Morton) B.; grad. Stevens Inst. of Tech., 1890; m. Florence L. Fay, Jan. 20, 1903. Constrn. work Thomson-Houston Co. on West End Street Ry., Boston; asst. engr. in power house Utica Belt Line Street Ry., 1891-92; foreman in charge car equipment, Gen. Elec. Co., Boston, Coney Island and Brooklyn Ry.; asst. elec. engr. Intramural Ry., World's Columbian Expn., Chicago, 1893, first 3d rail elevated road of U.S.; elec. engr. Met. West Side Elevated Ry., Chicago, first large elevated road for city transportation equipped with electricity, Aug. 1, 1894, asst. gen. mgr. and gen. mgr. 1898-1906; elec. asso. of William Barclay Parsons since 1906. Mem. Am. Soc. Elec. Engrs., Western Soc. Engrs. Residence: 3 W. 8th St. Office: 60 Wall St., New York. Died Oct. 13, 1949.

BRINSER, Harry Lerch, naval officer; b. Middletown, Pa., Nov. 11, 1876; s. Christian and Mary (Lerch) B.; student Harrisburg Acad., 1893-95; grad. U.S. Naval Acad., 1899; m. Natalie Meylert Bulkley,

Nov. 1, 1919; 1 son, Harry Meylert. Became ensign U.S. Navy, June 1899; advanced through grades to rear adm., Oct. 1, 1932. Served in Battle of Santiago, Philippine Insurrection, Boxer Rebellion; comdg. U.S.S. Columbia, World War; became dir. of Navy Yards, 1932; later comdr. Cruiser Div. 4; mem. Gen. Board, Navy Dept.; retired, Dec. 1, 1940. Awarded Navy Cross, 1924.†* Died Dec. 9, 1945.

BRINSTAD, Charles William (brĭn′städ), church official; b. La Crosse County, Wis., July 17, 1864; s. Ole P. and Caroline (Olson) B.; prep. edn., Wayland Acad., Beaver Dam, Wis.; B.A., U. of S. Dak., 1888, M.A., 1890; B.D., Div. Sch. U. of Chicago, 1893; D.D., Berkeley Bapt. Div. Sch., 1921; m. Lillie May Bower, May 27, 1893; 1 son, Paul Edward. Left home at 17 and worked way through acad., coll. and theol. sem.; ordained Bapt. ministry, 1889; pastor successively St. Paul, Minn., Marshall, Mich., and Fremont Neb., until 1900; exec. sec. Neb. Bapt. State Conv., 1900-06, Northern Calif. Bapt. Conv., 1906-33; retired for further research in anthropology; organized 82 chs. and raised over $3,000,000 for religious and educational purposes. Organized and directed religious and ednl. work for Calif. Indians, Chinese, Hindus, Japanese, Mexicans, Negroes and Russians. Chancellor of California Coll., Oakland, Calif., 1909, 10. Dir. and treas. Am. Nat. Building and Loan Assn. Trustee U. of Redlands, Berkeley Bapt. Div. Sch.; dir. Mexican Bapt. Theol. Sem. (Los Angeles), Bapt. Bd. of Missionary Coöperation. Mem. Delta Kappa Epsilon. Republican. Clubs: Commonwealth, Devonshire Country. Edited 6 vols. Neb. Baptist Annuals and 27 vols. Northern Calif. Baptist Annuals. Author: "Group Life Insurance for Ministers and Missionaries," "Harmonizing Capital and Labor." Home: 187 Stanyan St., San Francisco, Calif. Died Aug. 17, 1942.

BRINTON, Christian, art critic, lecturer; b. Homestead Farm, W. Chester, Pa., Sept. 17, 1870; s. Joseph Hill and Mary (Herr) B.; B.A., Haverford (Pa.) Coll. (Phi Beta Kappa), 1892, M.A., 1906, Litt.D., Haverford Coll., 1914; studied U. of Heidelberg and Paris, and Ecole du Louvre. Asso. editor The Critic, 1900-04; advisory editor Art in America, 1915. Mem. Kunsthistorisches Institut, Florence. Asso. of Am. Scandinavian Foundation; trustee Am. Swedish Hist. Museum; mem. Am.-Russian Inst., Phila. Fellow Phila. Museum of Art; mem. Internat. Jury of Awards, Dept. of Fine Arts, San Francisco Expn., 1915. Decorated by King Gustav V, of Sweden, Knight of the Royal Order of Vasa, 1917; by King Albert of Belgium, Officer of Order of the Crown, 1931. Mem. of the Belgian League of Honor. Dir. foreign art, Sesquicentennial Internat. Expn., Phila., 1926. Clubs: The Players (New York); The Centaur (London). Author: Modern Artists, 1908; Catalogue, the Ignacio Zuloaga Exhibition, 1909; Die Entwicklung der Amerikanischen Malerei (Berlin), 1910; Masterpieces of American Painting (Berlin, Germany, and New York City), 1910; Catalogue, The Walter Greaves Exhibition, 1912; Catalogue, The Scandinavian Exhibition, 1912; La Peinture Américaine (Paris), 1913; Catalogue, The Constantin Meunier Exhibition, 1913; Introduction to History of Russian Painting, 1916; Catalogue, The Swedish Exhibition, 1916; Impressions of the Art at the Panama-Pacific Exposition, 1916; Catalogue, The Ignacio Zuloaga Exhibition, 1916; Catalogue, The Boris Anisfeld Exhibition, 1918; Catalogue, The Official Exhibition of War Paintings and Drawings by British Artists, 1919; Catalogue, Nicholas Roerich Exhibition, 1920; Introduction to History of Scandinavian Art, 1922; Catalogue, the Russian Exhibition, 1923; Catalogue, The Ivan Mestrovic Exhibition, 1924; Catalogue, The Italian Exhibition, 1926; Catalogue, Soviet Russian Art Exhibition, New York, 1929; Catalogue, The Belgian Exhibition, 1930; The Face of Soviet Art, 1934; Catalogue, The Soviet Art Exhibition, 1934; The Poster in Time and Space, 1937; Gustavus Hesselius, 1938; Mary Cassatt, 1939; Russian Culture in America, 1940; Catalogue, Collection of International Art, Philadelphia Museum of Art, 1941. Contributor to Iconographic Dictionary of Art; articles on art to International Studio, Art in America, L'Art et les Artistes, La Renaissance, Magazine of Art, Vanity Fair, Scandinavian Review, etc. Home: Quarry House, West Chester, Pa. Died July 14, 1942.

BRISCO, Norris Arthur (brĭs′kō), college prof.; b. Napanee, Ont., July 23, 1875; s. Robert McIntyre and Mary (Ham) B.; A.B., Queen's U., Kingston, Ont., 1898 (honors in history), A.M., 1900 (in polit. science); Ph.D., Columbia, 1907; fellow Royal Hist. Soc., 1909-14; m. May Bartlett, June 29, 1907; children—Norris B., Ruth, Margaret. Tutor in history, Coll. City of N.Y., 1905-07, instr. in economics, 1907-15; prof. polit. economy and sociology and head of dept., State U. of Iowa, 1915, prof. commerce and head dept., 1916, dir. Sch. of Commerce, 1917-20; prof. of merchandising and dir. New York U. Sch. of Retailing, since 1920, dean since 1928. Mem. Am. Econ. Assn., Eta Mu Pi (hon. mem.), Eastern Commercial Teachers Assn., Artus, Delta Sigma Pi; pres. N.Y. Society of Queen's Univ. Republican. Episcopalian. Mason. Club: Authors (London); Canadian Club of N.Y. (hon. mem.). Author: The Economic Policy of Robert Walpole, 1907; Economics of Business, 1913; Economics of Efficiency, 1914; Fundamentals of Salesmanship, 1916; Retail Salesmanship, 1920; Retail Salesmanship Source Book, 1920; (with John W. Wingate) Retail Buying, 1925; Retail Receiving Practice (with same), 1925; Principles of Retailing (with others), 1927; Retail Credit Procedure (with others), 1929; Store Salesmanship (with O. P. Robinson and Grace Griffith); Store Management, 1931; Retail Accounting (with Dr. C. K. Lyons), 1934; Retailing, 1935; (with John W. Wingate) Buying for Retail Stores, 1937; (with John W. Wingate) Elements of Retail Merchandising, 1938; (with Rudolph Severa) Retail Credit, 1943; (with Leon Arnowitt) Introduction to Modern Retailing, 1942. Editor of Retailing Series, 1925; editor of Canada sect., Book of Knowledge, 1911-14; editor Efficiency Soc. Jour., 1915-17. Contbr. to scientific and business publs. Home: 18 East Lane, Short Hills, N.J. Died May 9, 1944

BRISTOL, Arthur LeRoy, naval officer; b. Charleston, S.C., July 15, 1886; s. Arthur LeRoy and Alice Marion (Blodgett) B.; student Coll. of Charleston, 1901-02; grad. U. S. Naval Acad., 1906; unmarried. Comd. ensign U.S. Navy, 1906; advanced through grades; commd. rear adm., July 1939. Decorated Navy Cross; Distinguished Service Medal; World War medal; Mexican Campaign medal; Russian Order of Stanislaus. Clubs: Army and Navy (Washington); Chevy Chase (Md.); New York Yacht. Home: Charleston, S.C. Address: care Navy Dept., Washington, D.C. Died Apr. 20, 1942.

BRISTOL, Edward Newell, book publisher; b. Morris, Conn., Apr. 22, 1860; s. Alva Myron and Mary (Judd) B.; ed. Williston Sem., Easthampton, Mass., and under pvt. tutors; m. Minna Baumgarten, Dec. 29, 1885 (died 1929); children—Arthur Edward, Lucy Friederike (Mrs. Edward N. Goodwin), Herbert Greene, Ralph Buffum. Began as agt. for Henry Holt & Co., New York, 1882, dir. and sec. same, 1903-18, v.p. and gen. mgr., 1918-26, chmn., 1926; v.p. Glen Ridge (N.J.) Realty Co. Mem. Borough Council, Bd. of Edn. and trustee Pub. Library (all of Glen Ridge). Mem. Am. Hist. Assn., Metropolitan Mus. of Art., Am. Polit. Science Assn. Conglist. Clubs: City, Players (New York); Glen Ridge Country. Home: 64 Melrose Pl., Montclair. N.J. Office: 257 Fourth Av., New York. N.Y. Died Mar. 2, 1946.

BRISTOW, Joseph Little, ex-senator; b. in Wolfe County, Ky., July 22, 1861; s. William and Savannah (Little) B.; A.B., Baker U., Kan., 1886 (LL.D., 1909); m. Margaret A. Hendrix, Nov. 11, 1879; children—William H. Bristow (dec.), Bertha May (dec.), Joseph Quayle, Frank Baker, Edwin McKinley (dec.). Clerk Dist. Ct., Douglas Co., Kan., 1886-90; owner and editor Salina Daily Republican, 1890-95, Ottawa (Kan.) Herald, 1895-1905, Salina Daily Republican-Journal, 1903-25. Pvt. sec. to Gov. Morrill, 1895-97; 4th asst. postmaster gen., 1897-1905; sec. Rep. State Com., 1894-98; had charge of invesigation of Cuban postal frauds and reorganization of Cuban postal service, 1900; conducted the postal investigation under Roosevelt adminstrn., 1903; spl. commr. Panama R.R., 1905; U.S. senator, 1909-15; chmn. Kan. Utilities Commn., 1915-18; now in charge of large estate nr. Fairfax, Va. Mem. bd. trustees Baker U., Baldwin, Kan. for 40 years. Home: Salina, Kan. Address: Fairfax, Va. Died July 14, 1944.

BRITTAIN, Charles Mercer, church official; b. Conyers, Ga., Dec. 16, 1873; s. Jabez Mercer (D.D.) and Ida (Callaway) B.; ed. Emery Coll., Oxford, Ga., 1 yr.; A.B., Mercer U., 1898; studied Southern Bapt. Theol. Sem., 1904-05; D.D., Columbia Coll., Lake City, Fla., 1917; m. Susie Marie Moore, June 27, 1900; children—Kingman Mercer, Charles Colquitt, Milner Callaway, Nathaniel Henry, Carson. Ordained ministry Southern Bapt. Ch., 1900; pastor McDonough, Ga., and Kissimmee, Fla., until 1907; editor Fla. Bapt. Witness, 1907-08; pastor First Ch., Columbia, Ala., 1912-13; head of history and psychology depts., also business mgr., Columbia Coll., Lake City, Fla., 1913-18; pastor First Ch., Ocala, Fla., 1919; treas. Fla. Bapt. Assemblies, 1912-25; asst. sec. Bapt. Bd. of Missions, 1919-25, secretary and executive officer, 1925-41, sec. emeritus for life since 1941; director Florida Baptist Assemblies. Y.M.C.A. sec. with U.S. Army in Cuba, 1898; Fla. del. World Bapt. Alliance, Toronto, 1928, Berlin, 1934. Trustee Stetson U. Mem. Southern Bapt. Hist. Soc., Am. Bapt. Hist. Soc. (fellow), Kappa Alpha. Democrat. Home (summer): Ridgecrest, N.C. Office: 210 Rogers Bldg., Jacksonville, Fla. Died Jan. 12, 1943; buried in Riverside Memorial Park, Jacksonville.

BRITTEN, Fred Albert, ex-congressman; b. Chicago, Nov. 18, 1871; s. Michael and Eva (Fey) B.; ed. pub. schs. and bus. coll.; m. Alma Hand, Mar. 4, 1907. In gen. bldg. constrn. bus. since 1894; pres. Overseas Industries, Inc. Alderman 23d Ward, Chicago, 1908-12; chmn. Civil Service Commn., 1909; mem. 63d to 73d Congresses (1913-35), 9th Ill. Dist. Republican. Clubs: Army and Navy (Washington); Chicago Athletic, South Shore Country, Germania, Hamilton (Chicago); National Capital Skeet (pres.). Home: Belden-Stratford Hotel, Chicago; and 2253 Sheridan Circle, Washington, D.C. Office: 431 S. Dearborn St., Chicago. Died May 4, 1946.

BROCK, George William, normal sch. pres.; b. Etowah County, Ala., Feb. 18, 1864; s. Josiah and Louisa (Riggs) B.; grad. State Normal Sch., Florence, Ala., 1893; A.B., U. of Ala., 1900, LL.D., 1920; studied Summer Sch. of the South LL.D., Howard Coll., Birmingham, Ala., 1917; m. Carrie L. Luttrell, July 6, 1899; m. 2d, Mary A. Boyd, Aug. 30, 1910. Supt. schs., Opelika, Ala., 1902-07; instr. University Summer Sch., Tuscaloosa, Ala., 1905-08; chmn. faculty, State Normal Sch., Livingston, Ala., 1907-10, pres. since 1910. Democrat. Baptist. Home: Livingston, Ala. Died May 20, 1941.

BROCKHAGEN, Carl Homer (brŏk′hä-gĕn); b. Prairie City, Ia., Oct. 26, 1877; s. George Henry and Elizabeth Mary B.; ed. St. Benedict's Coll., Atchison, Kan.; m. Gertrude Ayres Camp, Feb. 13, 1926; children—Robert Homer (dec.), Marian Camp. Newspaper work since 1898; formerly pres. and publisher The Portland Telegram, Inc., Sacramento Union, San Francisco Bulletin and part owner Oakland Enquirer, now controlling owner Cesana and Associates Advertising Agency, San Francisco. Mem. Sigma Delta Chi. Republican. Catholic. K.C. Club: Fraternity. Home: 683 Twelfth Av. Office: Monadnock Bldg., San Francisco, Calif. Died Dec. 2, 1941.

BROCKIE, Arthur H., architect; b. Phila., Pa., Jan. 17, 1875; s. William and Anna Peniston (Howell) B.; B.S. in Arch., U. of Pa., 1895; student Am. Acad. in Rome (John Stewardson traveling scholar), 1899-1900; m. Frances Fox, Oct. 25, 1905. With Cope & Stewardson, Architects, Phila., 1895-99; architect in own name since 1900. Served as corpl., Battery A, Pa. Vols., Spanish Am. War, Porto Rican campaign, 1898. Fellow A.I.A.; (past pres. Phila. chapter); mem. Zeta Psi. Club: T-Square Club (Phila., Pa.). Home: Stenton Av. above Joshua Rd., Whitemarsh, Chestnut Hill, Pa. Address: 1700 Walnut St., Philadelphia, Pa. Died Sep. 23, 1946.

BROCKMAN, Fletcher Sims; b. Amherst County, Va., Nov. 18, 1867; s. Willis Allen and Rosa Emory (Wood) B.; A.B., Vanderbilt U., 1891; LL.D., Colgate U., 1929; Master of Humanics, Internat. Y.M.C.A. Coll., Springfield, Mass., 1930; m. Mary Buford Clark, Nov. 21, 1895; children—Allen Clark (dec.), Washington Clark, Emory Wood, Julia (dec.). Student sec. Internat. Com. Y.M.C. Assns. for the 13 Southern States, 1891-97; traveling sec. Student Vol. Movement for Foreign Missions, 1897-98; went to Nanking, China, 1898, as foreign sec. Internat. Com. Y.M.C. Assns.; gen. sec. Nat. Com. Y.M.C. Assns. of China, 1901-15; asso. gen. sec. Internat. Com. Y.M.C.A., 1915-24; administrative sec. Nat. Council, Y.M.C. Assns. of U.S., for Far East, 1924-29; now sec. Com. for Promotion of Friendship between American and Far East. Ex-chmn. Am. Intersem. Missionary Alliance; actg. chmn. Student Vol. Movement; asso. gen. sec. Nat. War Work Council Y.M.C.A. of the U.S.; mem. exec. com. Nat. Christian Council of China, Nat. Com. Am.-Japanese Relations, Foreign Policy Assn., Commn. on Interracial Coöperation, Foreign Com. of Y.M.C.A. of U.S. and Can.; mem. bd. dirs. of China Famine Relief of U.S.A.; mem. Nat. Advisory Council of Lingnan U.; mem. N. Am. Council of Coll. of Chinese Studies, Associated Bds. of Christian Colleges in China, Nat. Conf. of Jews and Christians (advisory com.), Internat. Com. Y.M.C.A., S. C. Council, Am. Oriental Soc., Inst. of Pacific Relations, Phi Beta Kappa, Phi Delta Theta. Decorated Order of the Bountiful Crop (Chinese), 1921, and Order of the Jade (Chinese), 1937. Mem. Meth. Ch. Author: I Discover the Orient, 1935; (brochures) How to Hold English-Speaking Chinese in the Church, 1906; The Programme of Reform, 1908; The Future of China. 1911. etc. Home: Silver Dune, Columbia, S.C. Died Nov. 11, 1944.

BRODEK, Charles Adrian (brō′dĕk), lawyer; b. New York, N.Y., Jan. 20, 1872; s. Solomon and Fredericka (Schattman) B.; B.S., Coll. City of N.Y., 1890; A.M., Columbia, 1891; student Sch. of Law, Columbia, 1890-93; m. Hortense Josephy, Oct. 25, 1899; children—Edith Joyce (Mrs. Jack Marqusee), Catherine M. (Mrs. E. J. Marx, Jr.), Frances J. Began practice with Wilcox, Barkley & Brodek, 1893, changed name to Wilcox & Brodek, 1897; practiced alone, 1905-20; now mem. of Brodek & Eisner. Dir. Baker, Smith & Co., E. J. Realty Corpn., Mademoiselle, Inc., Asbestos Constrn. Co., Nat. Paper & Type Co., E. Day Co., Far Rockaway Securities Co., Lake Garfield Groves, Inc., Mulford Realty Corp., Josephy-Spero Realty Corp., Plaza Stores, Ltd., Rosenthal Co., Somac, Inc., Tre-O-Ripe Groves, Inc., South Shore Finance Corpn., Wissahickon Groves, Inc. Mem. Am. and N.Y. State bar assns., Assn. Bar City of N.Y., New York County Lawyers Assn. Democrat. Jewish religion. Mason. Clubs: Bankers (New York); Inwood Country (L.I.); Beach (Atlantic Beach, L.I.). Home: 419 E. 57 St. Office: 72 Wall St., New York, N.Y. Died Sep. 19, 1944.

BROEDEL, Max, educator; b. Leipzig, Ger., June 8, 1870; s. Louis and Henrietta (Frenzel) B.; ed. Acad. Fine Arts, Leipzig; U. of Leipzig, 1886-90; came to U.S., 1894; m. Ruth Marian Huntington, Dec. 31, 1902; children—Elizabeth, Ruth (dec.), Carl, Elsa. Med. illustrator, anatomy and physiology, Leipzig, until 1893; Johns Hopkins Hosp., Baltimore, until 1911; instr., Johns Hopkins, 1907-11, asso. prof. of art as applied to medicine since 1911, also head of dept. Evang. Lutheran. Home: 320 Suffolk Rd., Guilford, Baltimore. Died Oct. 26, 1941.

BRODERICK, Bonaventure Finnbarr, bishop; b. Hartford, Conn., Dec. 25, 1868; s. John Harris and Margaret (Healy) B.; A.B., St. Charles Coll., Md., 1891; Ph.D., U. of the Propaganda (Urban Coll.), Rome, 1893, D.D., 1897; grad. N. Am. Coll., Rome, 1897; grad. course in history and archæology under Prof. Marucchi and other masters, 1897-98. Ordained R.C. priest, 1896; prof. history, English grammar and Italian lit., Diocesan Sem., Hartford, 1898-1900; acting pastor Branford, Conn., 1898, Westport, Conn., 1900; apptd. Am. sec. to Mons. Sbaretti, Havana, Cuba, 1900, and carried on negotiations between church and state to successful settlement, 1905;

created private chamberlain by Pope Leo XIII, 1901; apptd. Am. sec. to Apostolic del. to P.I., 1901, resigned upon apptmt. of Taft Commn., 1902; represented R. C. Ch. at inauguration of Cuban Republic, May 20, 1902; apptd. titular bishop of Juliopolis, Sept., and consecrated, Oct. 28, 1903; auxiliary bishop of Havana, 1903-Mar. 1, 1905. Apptd. gen. commr. of the Pope for collection of Peter's Pence, 1904. Engaged in literary and editorial work, 1910-40. Editor Millbrook (N.Y.) Round Table since 1936. Mem. The Arcadia (Rome), being first American so honored; mem. Collegium Cultorum Martyrum, Rome. Author: The Jewish Catacombs in Rome, 1900; Italian Settlement in the United States, 1905; The So-called Altar of Calvinus, 1930; The Lapis Niger, 1931; The Forum Stele, 1931. Address: Frances Schervier Hosp., New York, N.Y. Died Nov. 18, 1943.

BRONK, Isabelle, college prof.; b. Duanesburg, N.Y.; d. Abram and Cynthia (Brewster) Bronk; ed. Brockport (N.Y.) State Normal Sch., Wellesley, 1878-81, Germany and France, 1883-84, U. of Leipzig, Sorbonne, and College de France, 1889-91; Ph.B., Ill. Wesleyan U., 1893; Ph.D., U. of Chicago, 1900; studied summers at Bibliothèque Nationale and U. of Grenoble, and in Paris and Madrid, 1910-11. Fellow in Romance langs., U. of Chicago, 1898-1900, asst. in Romance langs. and lits. and head of Beecher House, U. of Chicago, 1900-01; asst. prof. French lang. and lit., 1901-02, prof. and head of Romance dept., Swarthmore Coll., 1902-27, prof. emeritus since 1927. Interested in the work of Women's Internat. League for Peace. Mem. modern lang. assns. of Am., Middle States, Md., and Pa., Am. Assn. Univ. Profs., Am. Assn. Univ. Women, Colonial Dames Am., Phi Beta Kappa. Author: Paris Memories, 1927. Editor of Poésies diverses, by Antoine Furetière, 1908. Contbr. to Modern Lang. Notes, Modern Lang. Jour., Nation, New York Evening Post, Education, School and Society, etc. Home: Swarthmore, Pa. Died Jan. 10, 1943.

BRONSON, Dillon, clergyman; b. Wyoming, Ia., Aug. 27, 1863; s. James Anson and Jennie (Van Benschoten) B.; A.B., Cornell Coll., Ia., 1884; A.M., 1887, D.D., 1900; S.T.B., Boston U., 1888; studied U. of Berlin, 1890-91; m. Susan Hall Peirce, Nov. 21, 1894 (died 1932); m. 2d, Pauline Harris. Ordained M.E. ministry, 1892; pastor, Newton, Mass., 1892-97, Salem, 1897-1900, St. Mark's Ch., Brookline, 1900-06; supt. Boston Missionary and Ch. Extension Soc., 1906-10; supt. Boston District M.E. Ch., 1911-17; with Church of all Nations, Boston, 1917-20; pulpit supply 5 leading Meth. chs. in Calif. since 1927. Del. Gen. Conf., M.E. Ch., 1908, 12. Trustee Boston U. Fellow Sch. of Philosophy, U. of Southern Calif.; mem. Phi Beta Kappa. Mason. Traveled extensively in Europe, Alaska, Labrador, Spitzbergen and Iceland, and visited mission fields in Asia, Palestine, Egypt, S. Africa and S. America; made 3d journey around the world, 1927. Home: Alhambra, Calif. Died Jan. 4, 1943.

BRONSON, Harrison Arthur, judge; b. Nunica, Mich., Nov. 19, 1873; s. Charles Henry and Clementine (Fowler) B.; B.A., U. of N.D., 1894, M.A., 1895; LL.B., U. of Minn., 1901; m. Alice LaChance, June 18, 1901; 1 dau., Mrs. Clementine Fowler Johnson. Admitted to N.D. bar, 1901, and practiced at East Grand Forks and Grand Forks; lecturer on real property law, Law Coll., U. of N.D., 1902-17; mem. N.D. Senate, 1913-17 (led fight for equal suffrage and against judicial recall); 1st asst. atty. gen. N.D., 1917-18; asso. and chief justice Supreme Court, N.D., term Dec. 1, 1918-Jan. 6, 1925; resigned Dec. 1921; gen. counsel for N.D. doing business as N.D. Mill & Elevator Assn., 1925-28, 1933-34 and 1937-39; gen. counsel N.D. Terminal Exchange since 1924; gen. counsel N.D. Bd. of Med. Examiners, 1933-43, Northern Packing Co. Mem. State Bd. of Bar Examiners, 1911-18; counsel N.D. State Council of Defense, 1917-18; Defense Savings Com. State of N.Dak.; life mem. Commrs. on Uniform State Laws. Mem. Am. Bar Assn., since 1908, N.D. Bar Assn. (pres. 1941-42), Law Alumni U. of N.D. (pres. 1937-40), Order of the Coif, Phi Beta Kappa, Phi Delta Phi, The Civil Legion. Republican. Presbyterian. Clubs: Grand Forks Country, Lions (hon.), Fortnightly (pres. 1931), Cavaliers. Author: Bronson's Recitals in Municipal Bonds, 1901; Law of Fixtures, 1905; Analysis, Notes Real Property, 1906; Real Property Law (lands), 1914; North Dakota Practice and Procedure, 1945. Home: Grand Forks, N.D. Died April 22, 1947.

BROOKE, (Charles Frederick) Tucker, author, educator; b. Morgantown, W.Va., June 4, 1883; s. St. George Tucker and Mary Harrison (Brown) B.; A.B., U. of W.Va., 1901, M.A., 1902; fellow in German, U. of Chicago, 1903-04; first Rhodes Scholar from W.Va., Oxford U., 1904-07, B.A., first class honors, 1906, B.Litt., 1907; D.Litt., Lawrence Coll., Appleton, Wis., 1935; m. Grace Drakeford of Hertfordshire, Eng., July 27, 1909; children—Elizabeth, St. George, Alfred (dec.). Instr. in English, Cornell U., 1909; instr. in English, Yale, 1909-13, prof., since 1920, now Sterling prof. and fellow of Calhoun Coll., exchange prof., U. of London, 1920. Research asso. Huntington Library, 1928-29. Member American Philos. Society, Conn. Academy of Arts and Sciences, Modern Language Assn. of America, Bibliog. Soc. of London, Kappa Alpha (Southern), Phi Beta Kappa. Democrat. Episcopalian. Clubs: Elizabethan, Graduate (New Haven); Yale (New York). Author: The Shakespeare Apocrypha, 1908; The Works of Christopher Marlowe, 1910; The Tudor Drama, 1911; Shakespeare's Sonnets, 1936; etc. Gen. editor The Yale Shakespeare. Home: Calhoun College, New Haven, Conn. Died June 22, 1946; buried in Church Yard, Zion Ch., Charlestown, Jefferson County, W.Va.

BROOKHART, Smith W., ex-senator; b. Scotland County, Mo., Feb. 2, 1869; s. Abram Colar and Cynthia (Wildman) B.; ed. country schs. and ½ yr. in high sch. and Southern Ia. Normal Sch., Bloomfield, Ia.; studied law in offices of Payne & Sowers, Bloomfield, and Wherry & Walker, Keosauqua, Ia.; m. Jennie Hearne, of Keosauqua, June 22, 1897; children—Charles E., John R., Smith W., Florence H., Edith A., Joseph W. Teacher, country and high schs., 5 yrs.; admitted to bar, 1892, and practiced at Washington, Ia.; county atty. Washington County, 1895-1901; mem. firm S. W. & J. L. Brookhart, farmers; elected to U.S. Senate to fill vacancy occasioned by resignation of William S. Kenyon, and took seat Dec. 2, 1922, for term ending March 3, 1925, reëlected for term 1925-31, but election was contested and Dem. opponent was seated by Senate, Apr. 12, 1926; again elected Nov. 2, 1926 for term ending 1933. Spl. advisor to Agrl. Adjustment Administration, U.S. Dept. of Agr., Washington, D.C., 1933-35. Progressive Republican; chmn. Rep. State Conv., Ia., 1912. Mem. Farmers' Union, Farm Bur., Am. Legion, Spanish-Am. War Vets., Nat. Rifle Assn. K.P. Author: Rifle Training in War, 1918; Rifle Training for War, 1920. Club: Commercial. Home: Washington, Ia. Died Nov. 14, 1944.

BROOKS, Arthur Alford, clergyman; b. Mt. Pleasant, O., Jan. 25, 1879; s. Leonidas Culver and Lina (Alford) B.; Cornell Coll., Mt. Vernon, Ia., 1902; A.B., Baker U., Baldwin, Kan., 1908; student U. of Chicago, summer 1913; D.D., Neb. Wesleyan U., 1918; m. Clara B. Mason, Jan. 12, 1910; children—Arthur Alford, Lee Culver, Theodore Lincoln. Ordained ministry M.E. Ch., 1906; successively pastor Superior and Hastings, Neb., Ft. Dodge, Ia., Lincoln, Neb., and Des Moines, Ia., until 1930, St. Paul's Ch., Cedar Rapids, Ia., 1930-38, First Church, Omaha, Neb., 1938-45; dist. supt., Omaha dist. Neb. Conf. Methodist Ch., since 1945. Del. to Ecumenical Conf. on Methodism, London, 1921, Atlanta, Ga., 1931; del. to Gen. Conf. M.E. Ch., Columbus, 1936; pres. Neb. Council of Churches; pres. bd. trustees Methodist Hospital, Omaha; pres. bd. trustees, Crowell Memorial Home, Blair. Trustee Cornell College (Mt. Vernon, Ia.). Nat. chaplain T.P.A. Mem. Delta Tau Delta. Omaha Chamber of Commerce. Republican. Mason (K.T., 32°, Shriner; grand prelate Grand Commandery, K.T. of Neb.). Clubs: Rotary, Ad-Sell, High Twelve (Omaha). Home: 526 S. 51st St. Office: Grain Exchange Bldg., Omaha, Neb. Died March 22, 1947.

BROOKS, Arthur Thomas, clergyman; b. Brighton, Eng., Jan. 21, 1881; s. Charles Jonas and Cordelia Francis (Seney) B.; ed. New York Univ., 1905-06, Union Theol. Sem., 1906-07, N.Y. Sch. of Philanthropy, 1911-12; D.D., Northern Bapt. Theol. Sem., Chicago, 1934; m. Olive King Sullivan; children—Olive King, Anna Francis. Brought to U.S., 1889, naturalized citizen, 1903. Began as builder and architect, 1898; pastor Grace Bapt. Ch., N.Y. City, 1905-10, First Ch., Tarrytown, 1910-15; field sec. Judson Memorial Fund, 1915-17; religious work dir. Y.M.C.A., World War, 1917-19; pastor Dudley Street Church, Boston, 1921-46; retired from ministry, 1946. Trustee Gordon Coll. of Theology and Missions, Boston, Mass. Fellow Royal Geographical Society; mem. Phi Gamma Delta. Republican. Mason, chaplain Washington Lodge. Club: Boston City. Author: The Practical and Profitable in Church Administration, 1930. Home: 60 Waverly St., Roxbury, Mass. Died Aug. 15, 1947.

BROOKS, Arthur Wolfort, bishop; b. Uniontown, Ky., Mar. 15, 1889; s. George Henry and Eva (Wolverton) B.; ed. U. of Louisville Theol. Sem., 1907-11, Gen. Theol. Sem., N.Y. City, 1917; also studied theology under private tutor; hon. B.D., and D.D., conferred by Episcopate of Eastern Ch. (Alexandria); m. Jane Nagle, Apr. 18, 1927; 1 dau., Margaret Ellen. Began as student pastor in mission churches, 1908; ordained deacon Protestant Episcopal Ch., 1915, priest, 1916; asst. curate St. Thomas' Ch., N.Y. City, 1917, Ch. of the Messiah, Brooklyn, N.Y., 1919-21, St. George's Ch., Astoria, L.I., N.Y., and prof. in Greek Theol. Sem., 1921-24; ednl. staff Lord's Day Alliance of New York, 1924-26; on staff Brooklyn Fedn. of Churches, 1926-27, bishop (Apostolic Episcopal Ch.) since May 4, 1925; pastor-adminstr. and bishop Christ's Ch. By-The-Sea, Broad Channel, L.I., N.Y. Pres. St. John's Soc. for Welfare and Social Service; pres. Epiphany Guild of America, Inc.; pres. Jamaica Bay Parkway Community Assn. Decorated Knight Order of St. James the Apostle; Knight Grand Chaplain. Became the Presiding Bishop of the Old Catholic Orthodox Ch. in the United Kingdom of Great Britain and Northern Ireland, Oct. 8, 1941, and was enthroned by title Bishop Titular of Sardis, in the Oratory Chapel of St. Vincent, Deacon and Martyr, Northampton, Eng., on Palm Sunday, 1942. Now mem. Holy Governing Synod, Western Orthodox Cath. Ch.; apptd. Legate of Patriarch of Antioch, Archbishop Titular of Ebbsfleet, in communion with Patriarchate and See of Glastonbury. Home: 9148 193d St., Hollis, L.I., N.Y. Died July 7, 1948.

BROOKS, Bryant Butler, ex-governor; b. Bernardston, Mass., Feb. 5, 1861; s. Silas Newton and Malissa Minerva (Burrows) B.; ed. Powers Inst., Bernardston, and high sch., Chicago; m. Mary Naomi Willard, Mar. 10, 1886. Live stock grower in Wyo. since 1882; now pres. Consol. Royalty Oil Co., and Wyoming Nat. Bank. Mem. Wyo. legislature, 1892; del. Rep. Nat. Conv. St. Louis, 1896; presidential elector, 1900; gov. of Wyoming, 1905-11. Republican. Mason (33°). Home: Casper, Wyo. Died Dec. 7, 1944.

BROOKS, Eugene Clyde, educator; b. Greene Co., N.C., Dec. 3, 1871; s. Edward Jones and Martha Eleanor (Brooks) B.; A.B., Trinity Coll., Durham, N.C., 1894; research work, Columbia U., 1913-14; Litt.D., Davidson Coll., 1918; LL.D., Trinity, 1919, U. of N.C., 1920; m. Ida Myrtle Sapp, Dec. 19, 1900; children—Martha Eleanor, Eugene Clyde, Sarah Voss. Prin., Kinston (N.C.) city schs., 1900; supt., Monroe (N.C.) schs., 1900-03; sec. ednl. campaign com. and supervisor rural pub. sch. libraries and loan fund for bldg. sch. houses, Raleigh, N.C., 1903-04; supt., Goldsboro (N.C.) schs., 1904-07; prof. history and science of edn., Trinity Coll., N.C., 1907-19; state supt. pub. instrn., N.C., 1919-23; pres. N.C. State Coll. Agr. and Engring., 1923-34, now emeritus; ednl. research since 1934. Editor North Carolina Education (state teachers' mag.), 1906-23; pres. N.C. Teachers' Assembly, 1912. Mem. N.E.A., Ednl. Finance Inquiry of Am. Council Edn., Chmn. County Govt. Adv. Commn., 1927-31; chairman Legislative Commn. on Distbn. of Public Sch. Equalization Fund, 1925-26; mem. N.C. Park Commn.; pres. Assn. of So. Agrl. Workers, 1931-32, N.C. Coll. Conf., 1931-32; mem. ednl. survey com. of the Textile Foundn. for Improvement of Textile Edn., and spl. rep. to report on textile edn. in European schs., 1933. Democrat. Methodist. Author: History in the Public Schools, 1907; The Story of Cotton and the Development of the Cotton States, 1911; The Story of Corn and the Westward Migration, 1913; Woodrow Wilson as President, 1916; Education for Democracy, 1919; Stories of South America, 1922; Our Dual Government, 1924. Contbr. Braxton Craven and Trinity College (series in Trinity Register), 1917. Editor vol. North Carolina Poems, 1912. Home: Raleigh, N.C. Died Oct. 18, 1947.

BROOKS, Joshua Loring, pres. Brooks Bank Note Co.; born Brookline, Mass., Jan. 19, 1868; son Lyman B. and Maria Cordelia (Loring) B.; student Boston U., 1886-90; m. Margaret Robinson, June 6, 1894; children—Lawrence, Robert Pearmain, Joshua Loring, John Dudley. Founder, 1889, and since pres. and treas. Brooks Bank Note Co., Springfield, Mass.; dir. Springfield Street Ry. Co., Third Nat. Bank & Trust Co. (Springfield); owner Newagen (Me.) Inn and Cottages. Active in war service during World War. Founder Eastern States Expn., Springfield, 1914 (pres. 25 years); incorporator Springfield Hosp., dir., and former chairman New England Council; mem. Springfield Y.M.C.A.; incorporator Springfield (internat. Y.M.C.A.) Coll., Springfield; member and on original exec. com. in founding, Asso. Industries of Mass.; del. Rep. Nat. Conv., Chicago, 1932. Mem. National Lithographers Association, Maine Hotel Association, Society Mayflower Descendants, S.A.R., Theta Delta Chi. Republican. Conglist. Club: Colony (Springfield). Awarded William Pynchon Medal, 1916, 'for distinguished public service;" Mass. State Medal, 1929, "for outstanding service to agr." Home: 27 Mulberry St. Office: 140 Wilbraham Av., Springfield, Mass. Died Feb. 16, 1949; interred Hillcrest Mausoleum, Springfield, Mass.

BROOKS, Morgan, electrical engr.; b. Boston, Mar. 12, 1861; s. Francis A. and Frances (Butler) B.; Ph.B., Brown U., 1881; M.E., Stevens Inst. of Tech., Hoboken, N.J., 1883; m. Frona Marie Brooks, Apr. 24, 1888; children—Henry M., Charles F., Frances (Mrs. Lincoln Colcord), Frederick A., Roger, Edith, Mrs. Frona B. Hughes, Dorothy Prescott (Mrs. Joseph M. Thomas). With Am. Bell Telephone Co., Boston, 1884-86; sec.-treas. St. Paul Gas Light Co., 1887-90; organizer Elec. Engring. Co. of Minneapolis; prof. elec. engring., U. of Neb., 1898-1901, U. of Ill., 1901-29, emeritus. Patented automatic telephone system, 1896. Fellow Am. Inst. Elec. Engrs. (dir. 1907-10, v.p. 1910-12); mem. Am. Soc. Mech. Engrs. (life), Illuminating Engring. Soc., Western Soc. Engrs., Delta Kappa Epsilon, Sigma Xi, Tau Beta Pi. Pres. Western Unitarian Conf., Chicago, 1917-22. Contbr. to engring. mags. Home: 907 W. Oregon St., Urbana, Ill. Died Apr. 25, 1947.

BROOKS, Peter Anthony, univ. pres.; b. Watertown, Wis., Jan. 14, 1893; s. Joseph and Maria (McDonough) B.; A.B., Marquette U., 1921; M.A., St. Louis U., 1924. Admitted to Society of Jesus; ordained priest, Roman Catholic Ch., 1931; pres. Campion high sch., Prairie du Chien, Wis., 1934-37; provincial, Missouri Province, Society of Jesus, 1937-43; pres. of Marquette U., 1944. Served as 2d lieut., U.S. Coast Guard Artillery, 1918-19. Home: 1131 West Wisconsin Av. Office: Marquette University, Milwaukee 3, Wis. Died May 16, 1948.

BROOKS, Raymond Cummings, educator; b. Tabor, Ia., Sept. 26, 1869; s. Rev. William Myron (D.D.) and Adelia Sophia (Jones) B.; A.B., Tabor Coll., Ia., 1891; post-grad. work, Oberlin, 1891-92; B.D., Yale Div. Sch., 1895; D.D., Tabor, 1905, Whitman Coll., 1913; m. Sylvia Mabel Drake, June 18, 1896. Instr. in philosophy, Tabor Col., 1895-96; ordained Congl. ministry, 1896; pastor 1st Ch., Eugene, Ore., 1896-1900, Pilgrim Ch., Oakland, Calif., 1900-08, and

Mills Coll., Oakland, 1901-08; 1st Ch. Walla Walla, Wash., 1908-13; asso. prof. philosophy of religion, Whitman, Coll., Walla Walla, 1910-13; pastor 1st Ch. Berkeley, Calif., 1913-21; prof. homiletics, Pacific Sch. of Religion, Berkeley, 1913-19; head Dept. of Religion, Pomona Coll., Claremont, Calif., 1921-35, now emeritus; pres. Cumnock Schools, Los Angeles, 1935-42 Pres. Pilgrim Place in Claremont since 1921. Home: 489 W. 6th St., Claremont, Calif. Died May 14, 1944.

BROOKS, Robert M(ary), univ. prof.; b. Galveston, Tex., Sept. 12, 1877; s. Robert and Nellie Antoinette (Derham) B.; A.B., Coll. of Immaculate Conception, 1894; student St. Stanislaus Coll., Macon, Ga., 1894-97, 1900-1901, St. Charles Coll., Grand Coteau, La., 1897-1900; St. Louis University, 1907-11; A.M., St. Louis University, 1911. Joined Society of Jesus, 1894, ordained priest, 1910. Teacher Spring Hill, Ala., High School, 1901-07; prof. of classics and philosophy, Loyola Univ., New Orleans, St. Charles Coll., Grand Coteau, La., 1911-12 and 1913-21; prin. Jesuit High Sch., Galveston, 1921-22; prof. of classics, Loyola Univ., New Orleans, 1925-29; prin. Jesuit High Sch., Shreveport, La., 1929-32; prof. of classics, Loyola Univ., since 1934. Mem. Classical Assn. of Middle West and South. Democrat. Home: 6363 St. Charles Av., New Orleans, La. Died Aug. 13, 1945.

BROOKS, Stewart; b. at Mobile, Ala., Oct. 25, 1867; s. Leslie Everitt and Elizabeth Fontaine (Stewart) B.; B.S., Vanderbilt U., 1888, LL.B., 1890; m. Emma Conner, Sept. 16, 1896 (died 1902); children—Olive, Elizabeth (Mrs. Henry DuBarry Knower). Admitted to Ala. bar, 1890, and practiced at Mobile until 1924; pres. Title Ins. Co., 1915-27, Stonewall Ins. Co., 1923-27, Peoples Bank of Mobile, 1924-27; statistician Ala. State Docks and Terminals, 1939. Solicitor 13th Judicial Circuit, Alabama, 1896-1900; mem. Bd. Public Works, Mobile, 1900-09 (pres. 1906-09; pres. Mobile Bar Assn., 1915-16, Mobile Library Bd., 1920-34. Mem. Phi Delta Theta. Democrat. Methodist. Club: Round Table. Tome: 201 Rapier Av., Mobile, Ala. Died Feb. 20, 1942.

BROOKS, Stratton Duluth, educator; b. Everett, Mo., Sept. 10, 1869; s. Charles Myers and Marian (McClure) B.; grad. Mich. State Normal Coll., 1890, B.Pd., 1892, M.Pd., 1899; A.B., U. of Mich., 1896; A.M., Harvard, 1904; LL.D., Colby College, 1912, Kingfisher (Okla.) College, 1920, and Drury College, Springfield, Mo., 1929; m. Marcia Stuart, Sept. 3, 1890; children—Helen Marcia, Marian Stuart, Dorothy, Elizabeth Ann. Principal high school, Danville, Ill., 1890-92, Adrian, Mich., 1896-98, La Salle, Ill., 1898-99; v.p. Mt. Pleasant (Mich.) Normal Sch., 1893; asst. prof. edn. and high sch. insp., U. of Ill., 1899-1902; asst. supt. schs., Boston, 1902-06; supt. of schs., Cleveland, Jan.-Mar. 1906; supt. of schs., Boston, 1906-12; pres. U. of Okla., 1912-23; pres. U. of Mo., 1923-31; ednl. dir. Order of De Molay since 1931. Federal food adminstr. for Okla., 1917-18. Mem. N.E.A. (nat. council), Nat. Soc. for Scientific Study of Edn., Nat Council Boy Scouts, Phi Beta Kappa. Author: Brooks's Readers; Composition-Rhetoric (with Marietta Hubbard), 1906; English Composition, Book 1, 1911, Book 2, 1912. Home: 17 E. 65 Terrace, Kansas City 5. Office: 201 E. Armour Blvd., Kansas City 2, Mo. Died Jan. 18, 1949.

BROOMFIELD, John Calvin, clergyman; b. Eyemouth, Scotland, July 4, 1872; s. James and Christina (Mason) B.; ed. Adrian (Mich.) Coll., 1892-93; Geneva Coll., 1893-96; D.D., Kansas City U., 1910, Geneva College, 1930; hon. LL.D., Adrian College, 1930, Central Coll., 1940; m. Moselle Mar Donaldson, Oct. 6, 1898. Came to U.S., 1892, naturalized citizen, 1899. Ordained M.P. ministry, 1896; pastor First Ch., Uniontown, Pa., 1896-98, Fourth Ch., Pittsburgh, 1898-1905, M.P. Temple, Fairmont, W.Va., 1905-24, and 1937-39; traveling pres. Pittsburgh Conf. M.P. Ch., 1924-28, Gen. Conf., 1928-37; consecrated bishop in the Meth. Church at Uniting Conf. Kansas City, Mo., Apr. 30, 1939, assigned to Mo. Area. Mem. Oxford Conf., July 1937, and Edinburgh Conf., August 1937. Surveyed educational, medical and evangelistic work of the church in Japan, China and India, also served on many confs. in U.S., Europe and the Orient; mem. administrative com. Federal Council Chs. of Christ in America. Religious work dir. and dir. United War Work Campaign, World War. Contbr. to ch. periodicals. Home: St. Louis, Mo. Died Jan. 8, 1950.

BROUGHTON, Joseph Melville, senator; born Raleigh, N.C., Nov. 17, 1888; s. Joseph Melville and Sallie (Harris) B.; grad. Hugh Morson Acad., 1906; A.B., Wake Forest (N.C.) Coll., 1910; student Harvard Law Sch., 1912-13; m. Alice Harper Willson, Dec. 14, 1916; children—Alice Willson, Joseph Melville, Robert Bain, Woodson Harris. Teacher, Bunn, N.C., 1910-12; reporter Winston-Salem (N.C.) Journal, 1912; acting supt. pub. instrn., Wake County, N.C., 1914; admitted to N.C. bar, 1914, and in practice at Raleigh; governor of N.C. for term 1941-45; elected Democratic U.S. senator from N.C. on November 2, 1948, sworn in office, December 31, 1948; elected for regular term beginning Jan. 1949. Former pres. Raleigh Chamber Commerce and Raleigh Community Chest. Mem. N.C. State Senate, 1927, 29; temporary chmn. and keynote speaker N.C. Dem. Conv., 1936; Dem. elector at large, 1936. Trustee Wake Forest Coll., Olivia Raney Pub. Library; former mem. Raleigh Sch. Com. Mem. N.C. Bar Assn. (pres. 1936), Wake County Bar Assn., Am. Bar Assn. Democrat. Baptist. Mason. Jr. Order, Modern Woodmen of World. Clubs: Watauga, Carolina Country, Raleigh Country (all Raleigh). Author of pamphlets: The Legal Status of Women in North Carolina; The Language of the Law (N.C. Bar Assn. 1936); Social and Economic Aspects of Trusts (Am Bar Assn. 1937). Home: Wardman Park Hotel. Office: Senate Office Bldg., Washington, D.C. Died Mar. 6, 1949.

BROUGHTON, Levin Bowland (brou'tŭn), coll. dean; b. Pocomoke City, Md., Mar. 29, 1886; s. William Thomas and Alice Mary (Bowland) B.; B.S., U. of Md., 1908, M.S., 1911; Ph.D., Ohio State U., 1926; m. Laurise McDonnell, Dec. 27, 1911; children—Elinor C., Levin Barnett. Asst. chemist Md. Agrl. Expt. Station, 1908-11; asst. prof. chemistry, U. of Md., 1911-14, asso. prof., 1914-18, prof. agrl. chemistry, 1918-29, prof. chemistry and state chemist since 1929, dean Coll. of Arts and Sciences since 1938. Mem. Am. Chem. Soc. (councillor 1937-38), Assn. Official Agrl. Chemists (v.p. 1939; mem. Com. B, since 1936, chmn. 1939), Phi Kappa Phi, Sigma Xi, Alpha Chi Sigma, Kappa Alpha. Club: Rotary. Address: College Park, Md.* Died Dec. 1943.

BROUSSARD, James Francis (broos-särd'), univ. prof.; b. St. Martinville, La., May 22, 1881; s. Theodore Laizaire and Blanche Alice (Bienvenu de la Guérinière) B.; A.B., La. State U., 1902, A.M., 1903; grad. student U. of Paris, 1909-10; docteur ès lettres, U. of Montreal, 1940; docteur honoris causa, U. of Toulouse, 1935; m. Nora Mary Dougherty, June 4, 1924; 1 son, Frederick Dougherty. Prin. St. Martinville High Sch., 1903; prof. Romance langs., La. State U., 1904-16; asso. prof., U.S. Naval Acad., 1916-22; prof. Romance Langs., La. State U., 1922-31, dean of adminstrn., 1931-36, head dept. Romance langs. since 1937; lecturer on French phonetics, Middlebury Coll., Vt., summer 1924; lecturer on La. French culture, U. of Bordeaux, U. of Toulouse, 1936. Officier d'Académie de France, 1923; Chevalier of the French Legion of Honor, 1935; Knight Commd. of the Order of the Crown of Italy, 1937; Médaille d'argent, Bordeaux. Mem. La. State U. Alumni Fed. (pres. 1926), Southeastern Conf. (v.p. 1928), Comité Permanent de la Survivance Française en Amérique, Kappa Sigma, Phi Sigma Iota, Sigma Delta Pi, Phi Kappa Phi, Omicron Delta Kappa. Democrat. Author: Contes Choises de Daudet, 1917; Elements of French Pronunciation, 1918; Pour Parler Français, 1920; Le Créole Louisianais, 1940. Contbr. Modern Lang. Jour. Address: La. State University, University, La. Died Nov. 2, 1942.

BROWN, Alexander, banker; b. Baltimore, Oct. 25, 1858; s. George S. Brown; grad. Princeton, 1878. While at Princeton won 1st prize in gymnasium, also hurdle race, breaking Princeton record. Entered business with father, 1880, and on latter's death, 1890, became head of Alex. Brown & Sons, oldest banking house in America; retired 1923. Home: Mondawmin, Baltimore. Died 1949.

BROWN, Alice, author; b. Hampton Falls, N.H., Dec. 5, 1857; d. Levi and Elizabeth (Lucas) Brown; grad. Robinson Sem., Exeter, N.H., 1876. Author: Fools of Nature; Meadow-Grass (New England stories); By Oak and Thorn (English travels); Life of Mercy Otis Warren; The Road to Castaly (poems); The Day of His Youth (a story); Robert Louis Stevenson—a Study (with Louise Imogen Guiney); Tiverton Tales (stories); King's End, 1901; Margaret Warrener, 1901; The Mannerings; High Noon; Paradise; The County Road, 1906; The Court of Love, 1906; Rose MacLeod, 1908; The Story of Thyrza, 1909; Country Neighbors (stories), 1910; John Winterbourne's Family, 1910; The One-Footed Fairy, 1911; The Secret of the Clan, 1912; Vanishing Points (stories), 1913; Robin Hood's Barn, 1913; My Love and I, 1913; Children of Earth (Winthrop Ames' $10,000 prize play), 1915; The Prisoner, 1916; Bromley Neighborhood, 1917; The Flying Teuton, 1918; The Black Drop, 1919; The Wind Between the Worlds, 1920; Homespun and Gold, 1920; One-Act Plays, 1921; Louise Imogen Guiney—A Study, 1921; Old Crow, 1922; Ellen Prior, 1923; The Mysteries of Ann, 1925; Dear Old Templeton, 1927; The Golden Ball, 1929; The Marriage Feast, 1931; The Kingdom in the Sky, 1932; The Diary of a Dryad (pvtly. printed), 1932; Jeremy Hamlin, 1934; The Willoughbys, 1935; Fable and Song (privately printed), 1939; Pilgrim's Progress (play, privately printed), 1944. Home: 11 Pinckney St., Boston 14, Mass. Died June 21, 1948.

BROWN, Alice Van Vechten, college prof.; b. Hanover, N.H., June 7, 1862; d. pres. Samuel Gilman and Sarah (Van Vechten) Brown; ed. pvt. tutors and schs., Clinton and Utica, N.Y.; studied at Art Students' League, New York, 1881-85; later with various artists, and traveled abroad; unmarried. Asst. dir., Norwich (Conn.) Art Sch., 1891-94; dir., 1894-97; prof. art, Wellesley Coll., Mass., since 1897. Mem. Art Students' League, Coll. Art Assn. (mem. com. on standards), Copley Soc. of Boston, League of Women Voters, League of Nations Non-Partisan Assn., Archæol. Inst. America (com. on mediæval and renaissance studies.). Clubs: Cosmopolitan (New York); Mayflower (Boston); Lyceum (London). Author: (with William Rankin) Short History of Italian Painting, 1914, 21. Home: Wellesley, Mass. Died Oct. 16, 1949.

BROWN, Ames, writer; b. Greenville, N.C., Jan. 21, 1892; s. William Benjamin and Nancy Lee (Ames) B.; A.B., Univ. of N.C., 1910, A.M., 1911; m. Carolyn M. Harriss, Nov. 23, 1931; 1 son, Ames. Began on local staff, Baltimore Sun, 1911; Washington corr. Raleigh (N.C.) News and Observer, Nashville Tennesseean, etc., 1912-13; White House rep. New York Sun, 1913-16; corr. Phila. Record, 1915-17; dir. of publicity, Com. on Public Information, Washington, D.C., 1917; capt. U.S. Army, 1918; chief intelligence officer, U.S. Shipping Bd.; 1st v.p. and treas. Thos. F. Logan, Inc., Adv., New York, 1919-26; 1st v.p. Lord & Thomas and Logan, 1926-28, pres., 1928-31; asst. to mgr. Alaska Div. Pan Am. Airways 1942; asst. director public information 1944. Contbr. to North Am. Review, Atlantic Monthly, Review of Reviews. World's Work, etc. Episcopalian. Democrat. Clubs: Sleepy Hollow, Wings. Home: Croton-on-Hudson, N.Y. Died May 25, 1947.

BROWN, Arthur Charles Lewis, univ. prof.; b. Avon, N.Y., Aug. 18, 1869; s. Rev. Fortune Charles and Sarah (Lewis) B.; A.B., Hobart Coll., Geneva, N.Y., 1893, Litt.D., 1937; A.B., Harvard, 1894, A.M., 1895, Ph.D., 1900; Rogers traveling fellow of Harvard at univs. of Paris and Freiburg, 1900-01; m. Octavia Crenshaw, June 15, 1907; children—Morris Pemberton, Barbara Lewis, Arthur Charles Lewis. Instr. English, Haverford Coll., 1896-98; instr. and asst. prof. English, Univ. of Wis., 1901-06; prof. English, Northwestern U., 1906; lecturer on Irish lit., U. of Cincinnati, 1909; Northwestern U., 1941-42; lecturer in English, U. of Chicago, summers, 1902, 09, Columbia Univ., summers 1913, 15, 24; specialist in Celtic romance. Fellow Newberry Library. Fellow Mediæval Acad. of America; mem. Modern Lang. Assn. of America, Am. Irish Hist. Soc., Phi Beta Kappa. Democrat. Episcopalian. Club: Cliff Dwellers (Chicago). Author: Iwain, A Study in the Origins of Arthurian Romance, 1903; The Origin of the Grail Legend, 1943. Editor: Macbeth (in the Tudor Shakespeare), 1911. Contbr. to philol. jours. Home: 625 Colfax St., Evanston, Ill. Died June 28, 1946.

BROWN, Arthur Voorhees, banker; b. New Bethel, nr. Indianapolis, Ind., Mar. 17, 1863; s. Samuel Miller and Mahala (Brady) B.; Ph.B., Butler Coll., 1885, LL.D., 1938; m. Katharine Malott, Jan. 8, 1896; children—Volney Malott, Arthur Voorhees, Katharine Malott. Read law in office of Harrison, Miller & Elam (Harrison, Pres. of U.S.); admitted to Ind. bar, 1886, began practice at Indianapolis; dep. pros. atty., Marion County, 1888-90; county atty., Marion Co., 1890-95; vice pres. Union Trust Co. (Indianapolis), 1915-16, pres. 1916-42, chmn. bd. since 1942; pres. Ind. Nat. Bank, Indianapolis, 1932-42, chmn. bd. since 1942; former pres. Indiana Hotel Co; dir. Indianapolis Power & Light Co., Real Silk Hosiery Mills. Pres. Indianapolis Clearing Ho. Assn. 7 yrs., Indianapolis Community Fund, 1932-33, Indiana Methodist Hosp., 20 yrs., now hon. trustee. Treas. Riley Hosp, Butler Foundation; trustee Butler U.; former treas. Indianapolis Chapter Am. Red Cross, now treas. emeritus; mem. adv. bd., Salvation Army. Life mem. American Hist. Assn.; mem. Indiana State and Indianapolis bar assns., Indiana Pioneer Soc., Sigma Chi. Methodist. Mason (33°). Clubs: University, Columbia, Woodstock, Indianapolis Athletic, Dramatic, Contemporary. Home: 3172 N. Meridian St. Office: Union Trust Co., 120 E. Market St., Indianapolis, Ind. Died Apr. 15, 1949.

BROWN, Ashmun (Norris), newspaper corr.; b. Seattle, Wash., Dec. 6, 1872; s. Beriah and Jennie (McHugh) B.; ed. private schs., Wash. (state) and California; m. Elizabeth Jewett, Oct. 7, 1903 (died Aug. 12, 1908; m. 2d, Florence Coleman, Oct. 22, 1913. Newspaper reporter, Seattle, Tacoma, San Francisco and Victoria, B.C., 1890-96; city editor Spokane Spokesman-Review, 1896-99; city editor and Sunday editor Anaconda (Mont.) Standard, 1899-1902; city editor Butte Inter-Mountain, 1902-04, Seattle Post-Intelligencer, 1904; news editor, 1907-09, and Washington corr., same, 1909-10; syndicate and mag. writer, also asso. editor Arms and the Man, Washington, D.C., 1911-14; Wash. corr. Seattle Post-Intelligencer, 1914-21; Wash. corr. Providence Journal, 1920-42. Served as pvt., 1st lt., maj., N.G. State of Wash., pvt. sec. to gov. of Wash., 1905-07; to sec. of Interior, Washington, D.C., 1910-11. Mem. bd. visitors U.S. Naval Acad., 1931. Republican. Episcopalian. Clubs: Gridiron (pres., 1927), Nat. Press (Washington, D.C.). Author: A Study of the Cotton Industry, 1923; Canada—Our Most Agreeable Neighbor, 1925. Pulitzer hon. mention, 1936, for Washington correspondence. Home: 3809 Kanawha St. N.W., Washington 15, D.C. Died Jan. 30, 1948; buried in Glenwood Cemetery, Washington, D.C.

BROWN, Benjamin Beuhring, lawyer; b. Charleston, W.Va., March 14, 1893; s. James Frederick and Jennie Morgan (Woodbridge) B.; A.B., Princeton, 1914; LL.B., Harvard Law Sch., 1917; m. Hester Moulton Newhall, Aug. 22, 1917; children—Gertrude Woodbridge, James Frederick, Benjamin Beuhring, Elizabeth Newhall. Admitted to W.Va. bar, 1919, since in practice at Charleston; member Brown, Jackson & Knight, 1919-46; president Lewis Land & Coal Co.; dir. Kanawha Valley Bank, Central Trust Co., W.Va. Building & Loan Assn., Slab Fork Coal Company, Scotia Coal & Coke Company, Eagle Land Company. Trustee Charleston Masonic Temple, Kanawha Presbyterian Church. Mem. American, West Virginia State bar assns., Bar Assn. City of Charleston. Served with 5th and 6th regt. Marines, A.E.F., 1 yr.; commd. 1st lt. inf., O.R.C., 1918, serving in Sommedieu and Marbache sectors, Chateau-Thierry,

Aisne defensive and Marne-Aisne offensive; 1st lt. W.Va. Nat. Guard, 1921-22. Rep. State legislature, 1925 (mem. judiciary com., com. on railroads; chmn. mil. affairs com.). Democrat. Presbyterian. Mason (K.T.). Clubs: Cloister Inn, Acacia, Edgewood Country. Home: 127 Alderson St. Office: Kanawha Valley Bldg., Charleston, W.Va. Died July 8, 1949.

BROWN, Calvin Smith, univ. prof.; b. Obion County, Tenn., Feb. 13, 1866; s. Calvin Smith and Margaret A. (Martin) B.; B.S., Vanderbilt, 1888, M.S., 1891, D.Sc., 1892; univs. of Paris and Leipzig, 1894-95; Ph.D., Univ. of Colorado, 1899; Spain, Italy, Greece, 1903-04; m. Maud Morrow, 1905; children—Edith, Robert Venable, Calvin Smith, III. Instructor or asst. prof. English, comparative lit., or modern langs., Vanderbilt U., U. of Colo., and U. of Mo., 1889-1905; prof. Romance langs., 1905-09, prof. German lang., 1908-13, prof. modern langs. since 1913, U. of Miss. Archæologist, Miss. Geol. Survey. Fellow A.A.A.S. Mem. Phi Beta Kappa. Editor: Tennyson's Enoch Arden and the two Locksley Hall poems, 1897; The Later English Drama, 1898; Latin Songs with Music, 1914. Author: The Lignite of Mississippi, 1907; Archeology of Mississippi, 1926; Botany of Tishomingo Park, Miss., 1936. Home: University, Mississippi.* Died Sep. 10, 1945.

BROWN, Charles Carroll, cons. civil engr.; b. Austinburg, Ohio, Oct. 4, 1856; s. George Pliny and Mary Louise (Seymour) B.; studied engring. Cornell University, 1874-75; C.E., U. of Mich., 1879, hon. A.M., 1913; m. Cora Stanton, Sept. 10, 1878 (dec.); children—Edith Stanton (dec.), Edwin Stanton (dec.); m. 2d, Eileen Finkle, Jan. 2, 1930. Prof. of civil engring., Rose Poly. Institute, 1883-86, Union College, 1886-93; consulting engr. N.Y. State Bd. Health, 1888-93; city engr., Indianapolis, 1894-95. Editor Municipal Engring., 1896-1917; in Ill. Div. of Highways, 1918-19; prof. engring., Valparaiso U., 1919-21; engr., Dept. Pub. Works, St. Petersburg, Fla., 1921-23; city engr., Lakeland, Fla., 1923-27; prof. civil engring., U. of Fla., 1927-33; also cons. engr.; ex-chmn. Gainesville City Plan Board; cons. engr. Fla. Mapping Project. Fellow Fla. Engrs. Soc. (ex-pres.); mem. Am. Soc. C.E. (life), Am. Pub. Works Assn. (ex-pres., sec.), Am. Assn. Engrs. (ex-pres. Fla. Chapter), Sigma Xi (2d nat. pres.), Sigma Tau, Phi Delta Theta. Author: Report on Croton Water Shed of the City of New York, 1889; Directory of American Cement Industries (5 edits.), 1901-09; Handbook for Cement Users (3 edits.), 1901-05. Home: 848 Orange Park Av., Lakeland, Fla. Died Nov. 26, 1949.

BROWN, Charles Edward, museum dir.; b. Milwaukee, Wis., Oct. 24, 1872; s. Theodore Dewitt and Elizabeth Charlotte Brown; hon. M.A., U. of Wis., 1931; m. Bertha Rose Stredy, 1902; children—Theodore Taggart, Lorraine Charlotte; m. 2d, Dorothy Moulding Miller, 1937; 1 dau., Priscilla D. Asst. Milwaukee Public Museum, 1900-04; curator U.S. Philippine Expn., St. Louis, 1904; dir. Wis. State Hist. Mus., Madison, 1908-44; editor The Wis. Archæologist, 1901-41; faculty of Wis., 1915-44; retired since 1944; pub. Scenic and Hist. Wis. and Wis. Folklore booklets. Mem. Wis. N.G., 1893-96. Pres. Lake Monona Wild Life Sanctuary; sec. Wis. Archæol. Soc. 1901-41; mem. Am. Anthrop. Assn. (ex-pres. central sect.); vice-pres. Midwest Museum Conf., 1941 pres. Wis. Museum Conf., 1941. Awarded La. Purchase Exposition medal, 1904, Lapham medal for anthropol. research, 1926; medal for achæological research, Ill. Academy of Science, 1941. Republican. Episcopalian. State dir. Federal Writers Projects under Works Progress Adminstrn., 1935-38; mem. advisory board, Nat. Gallery of the Am. Indian, 1939; pres. Paul Bunyan's Trusty Recorders. Address: 1934 Monroe St., Madison, Wis. Died Feb. 15, 1946.

BROWN, (A.) Curtis, pres. Curtis Brown, Ltd., Internat. Publishing Bureau; b. Lisle, N.Y., Oct. 30, 1866; s. Lewis H. and Ellen (Curtis) B.; ed. pub. schs.; m. Caroline Louise Lord, Aug. 25, 1890; children—Marshall Curtis, Beatrice Curtis, Spencer Curtis. In editorial work, Buffalo Express, 1884-94; Sunday editor New York Press, 1894-98; London rep. of New York Press, Chicago Tribune and many other Am. papers, 1898-1916; established Internat. Pub. Bureau, Curtis Brown, Ltd., London and New York, 1899, and continues as pres. of the London Company. Club: Devonshire. Author: Contacts. Home: 27 Cheyne Walk, London, England. Office: 6 Henrietta St., Covent Garden, London, Eng.; also 347 Madison Av., New York, N.Y. Died Sep. 23, 1945.

BROWN, David Chester, surgeon; b. Norfolk, Va., Nov. 16, 1863; s. Orlando and Martha P. (Whittlesey) B.; M.D., Yale, 1884; post-grad. work, Hartford (Conn.) Hosp., univs. of Berlin and Prague; m. Catharine Cobden, June 19, 1889. Practiced at Danbury, Conn., since 1886; surgeon Danbury Hosp.; med. aide to gov. of Conn.; chmn. med. sect. State Com. (Conn.) Nat. Council of Defense. Commd. capt. Med. Corps, U.S. Army, July 23, 1917; maj., med. sect. Provost Marshal General's Office, Washington, D.C., July 28, 1918. Fellow A.C.S.; mem. A.M.A. (trustee); chmn. bd. trustees Fairfield County Med. Soc. (past pres.); past pres. Conn. State and Danbury medical societies, New York Acad. Medicine. Mem. Mayflower Soc. Republican. Conglist. Mason (K.T., Shriner). Home: 330 Main St., Danbury, Conn. Died May 12, 1943.

BROWN, Demetra Vaka, author; b. a Byzantine Greek, on Island of Bouyouk-Ada (Prinkipo) in the Sea of Marmora; came to America at age of 17. Was on editorial staff of a Greek newspaper in New York, then teacher of French at Comstock Sch. till her marriage to Kenneth Brown, Apr. 21, 1904. Traveled extensively in youth, through the Balkans and Asia Minor; with husband to Greece and Saloniki when Grecian situation was most critical, World War I, and interviewed King Constantine, Venizelos, and others; wrote series of articles appearing first in Collier's Weekly, 1918, under title "In the Heart of the German Intrigue"; went to Constantinople and Asia Minor, 1921, for Asia Magazine, to study the polit. and social conditions of the country; met polit. leaders of the Sultan as well as those of Mustafa Kemal, just beginning his rise to power. Since Italy attacked Greece (Oct. 1940) has been actively speaking and broadcasting, both in English and Greek, for the Greek War Relief, of which is director. Chairman Mercy Corps for Greece, American Hellenic Association for Rehabilitation of Maimed Soldiers of Greece. Author: The First Secretary (with Kenneth Brown), 1907; Haremlik, 1909; The Duke's Price (with Mr. Brown), 1910; Finella in Fairyland, 1910; In the Shadow of Islam (with Mr. Brown), 1911; A Child of the Orient, 1914; In the Grasp of the Sultan, 1916; In the Heart of the Balkans, 1917; In the Heart of the German Intrigue, 1918; A Pawn to a Throne (with Mr. Brown), 1919; The Unveiled Ladies of Stamboul, 1923; Delarah, 1943. Writes mostly under name of Demetra Vaka. Lecturer. Home: "Glimpsewood," Dublin, N.H. Address: (winter) 817 N. Dearborn St., Chicago, Ill. Died Dec. 17, 1946.

BROWN, Edna Adelaide, author, librarian; b. Providence, R.I., Mar. 7, 1875; d. Joseph Farnum and Adelaide Victoria (Ballou) Brown; student Brown U., 1894-96; B.L.S., N.Y. State Library Sch., 1898. Formerly with Providence Pub. Library and Rosenberg Library, Galveston, Tex.; librarian Memorial Hall Library, Andover, Mass., 1906-39. Mem. Am. Library Assn., New York State Library Sch. Assn., Mass. Library Club. Republican. Episcopalian. Clubs: November (Andover); Woman's City (Boston). Author: Four Gordons, 1911; Uncle David's Boys, 1913; When Max Came, 1914; Arnold's Little Brother, 1915; Archer and the "Prophet," 1916; The Spanish Chest, 1917; At the Butterfly House, 1918; Rainbow Island, 1919; That Affair at St. Peter's, 1920; Journey's End, 1921; The Silver Bear, 1921; The Chinese Kitten, 1922; Whistling Rock, 1923; Robin Hollow, 1924; Three Gates, 1928; Polly's Shop, 1931; How Many Miles to Babylon?, 1941; also juvenile plays. Home: Andover, Mass. Died June 23, 1944; buried in Christ Ch. Cemetery, Andover.

BROWN, Edward Scott ("T. Brown"), cartoonist; b. Stillwater, Minn., Sept. 14, 1876; s. George Sylvester and Ida (Rogers) B.; ed. Central High Sch., Minneapolis, Minn.; m. Amelia Otis, Sept. 12, 1905; children—Edward Scott, Phil Rogers, Gordon George, Claire Elin. Began as comic strip artist, Chicago Daily News, 1904; cartoonist, same 1917-25; cartoonist New York Herald Tribune since 1925. Mem. Arctic Brotherhood. Alaska. Clubs: Adventurers' (Chicago). Home: 35 East Av., Norwalk, Conn. Died Dec. 28, 1942; buried at Lakeview, New Canaan, Conn.

BROWN, Eli Huston, Jr., lawyer; b. Owensboro, Ky., May 3, 1875; s. Eli Huston and Nancy Washington (Dorsey) B.; B.A., Ky. U. (now Transylvania U.), 1895; student Law Dept., U. of Va., 1896; m. Rose McKnight Crittenden, Dec. 17, 1902; children—Virginia Crittenden, Eli Huston, Dorsey Washington. Admitted to practice, Owensboro, Ky., 1897; mem. Brown & Brown (Eli Huston, Jr., Eli Huston, III, and Dorsey Washington Brown). Officer or dir. many companies, mem. Ky. Ho. of Rep., 1899-1906, speaker, 1904-06; chmn. State Bd. of Prison Commnrs., 1906-12; atty. Ky. Ins. Rating Bd., 1916-19. Democrat. Mem. Am. Ky. State and Louisville Bar assns., Am. Prison Assn., Kappa Alpha. Clubs: Pendennis, Louisville Country, Sleepy Hollow, Big Spring Golf, Furniture Club of America. Home: 1428 St. James Court. Office: Bd. of Trade Bldg., 301 W. Main St., Louisville. Died Oct. 13, 1945; buried in Family Graveyard, Bloomfield, Ky.

BROWN, Everett J., lawyer; b. of American parents, Yokohama, Japan, Dec. 14, 1876; s. John W. and Matilda (Delger) B.; Ph.B., U. of Calif., 1898; LL.B., Hastings Coll. of Law (U. of Calif.), 1901; m. Winifred Osborne, June 28, 1905; children—Winifred (Mrs. Harmon Chase Bell), Everett J., Jr., Jean McLaren (Mrs. Cameron Wolfe). Admitted to Calif. bar, 1901, and in practice of law at Oakland, Calif.; dept. dist. atty. Alameda County, 1903-07, dist. atty., 1907-08; judge of Superior Court, 1908 20; partner Snook & Brown, 1920-26, Brown & Ledwich, 1926-30, Brown, Ledwich & Rosson, 1930-35, Brown & Rosson, 1936-42; partner Brown, Rosson & Gillis since 1943. Director Peralta Hospital, Inc.; trustee Mountain View Cemetery Assn. Mem. Am. Calif. State and Alameda County bar assns. Republican. Clubs: Claremont Country, Athenian Nile. Home: 300 Sheridan Av., Piedmont, Calif. Office: Central Bank Bldg., Oakland, Calif. Died Jan. 12, 1947; buried in Mountain View Cemetery, Oakland.

BROWN, Frank Chouteau, architect; b. Minneapolis, Jan. 1876; s. Frank Buckman and Emma Clara (Hollidge) B.; studied Minneapolis Sch. Fine Arts, Boston Art Club, and in Europe; m. Mabel Stowell Franklin, Nov. 20, 1912 (died Sept. 1935); m. 2d, Ruth Krieger, June 1939. Located in Boston, 1895; specializes in residence and suburban architecture, including gardens and country estates; has written extensively for mags. upon architectural and kindred subjects; editor The Architectural Review, 1907-19; designer of book plates, book covers and stage settings for plays since 1916; lecturer on Architecture, Boston U. Summer Sch. and Teachers' Classes since 1921; lecturer on theatre and stage settings, Emerson Coll. of Oratory, 1931; instr. in architecture, Mass. State Sch. of Art; archtl. consultant, Boston City Planning Bd.; Nat. Park Service, Branch Plans and Design, Dept. Interior. Dist. adminstr. Fed. Historic Am. Bldgs. Survey, Mass. and New England, since 1934; instr. architecture, history of theatre and scenic design, Mass. Univ. Extension, 1935-40. Contbg. editor The Architectural Record, 1921-26. Fellow Boston Soc. Architects, Am. Inst. Architects; mem. American Soc. of Architectural Historians, Boston Archtl. Club, Studio Club (Minneapolis); dir. Drama League America, Am. Pageant Assn. Club: Twentieth Century. Author: Letters and Lettering, 1902; The Orders of Architecture (with F. A. Bourne), 1904; Book Plate Designs, 1905; New England Colonial Houses, 1915; The Brick House, 1919; Modern English Churches, 1917, 1923; Modern English Country Houses, 1923; Architectural Design and Lettering (with Herman Ritow), 1928. Contbr. to Pencil Points and The Monograph Series—Records of Early American Architecture. Asso. editor: Monograph Series since 1937. Editor: Old-Time New England, since 1945. Home: 25 S. Russell St., Beacon Hill, Boston; (summer) "Little Pond," Marblehead Neck, Mass: Office: Care Soc. for Preservation of N.E. Antiquities, 141 Cambridge St., Boston 14, Mass. Died Nov. 18, 1947.

BROWN, Frank Clyde, prof. English; b. Harrisonburg, Va., Oct. 16, 1870; s. John Michael and Emma Catherine (Liskie) B.; A.B., U. of Nashville, 1893; A.M., U. of Chicago, 1902, Ph.D., 1908; m. Ola Marguerite Hollis, 1893; m. 2d, Mrs. Mary Henkel Wadsworth, 1932. Began teaching, 1893; prof. English and chmn. dept. Trinity Coll. (now Duke U.), Durham, N.C., since 1909. Organizer, 1913, and sec.-treas. N.C. Folk-Lore Soc.; mem. Modern Lang. Assn. America, Am. Folk-Lore Soc., Folk-Lore Soc. (of England), English Folk-Song Soc., Scottish Folk-Song Soc., Irish Folk-Song Soc., Welsh Folk-Song Soc., Phi Beta Kappa, Omicron Delta Kappa (nat. pres. 1931-33), Sigma Upsilon, Phi Delta Theta. Democrat. Methodist. Club: Hope Valley Country. Author: Elkanah Dettle—His Life and Works, 1910. Editor: North Carolina Folk-Lore, 1915; Outlines of English Literature, 1931. Home: 410 Buchanan Road, Durham, N.C. Died June 2, 1943.

BROWN, George Marion; b. Milledgeville, Ga., Oct. 5, 1865; s. Joseph E. (gov. Ga., 1857-65) and Elizabeth (Grisham) B.; ed. U. of Ga., Moore's Bus. U., Atlanta, Ga.; m. Corrie Hoyt, Feb. 10, 1887; children—Corrie Hoyt, Mary (dec.), George M., Jr. (dec.). Southeastern agt., 1884-87, asst. to traffic mgr., 1887-92, Western & Atlantic R.R.; fire ins. agt., Atlanta, 1892-90; organized Ga. Savings Bank & Trust Co., Atlanta, 1899, since pres.; organizer and first pres. Miller Union Stock Yards, Atlanta, Ga.; pres. Grisham Investment Co. Mem. Bd. Sinking Fund Commn. City of Atlanta, 1903-26; mem. adv. com. R.F.C. for Ga. since orgn., 1932-40. Moderator Atlanta Assn. Bapt. Chs., 1911-13; trustee Vet. Ministers' Fund (pension) of Atlanta Assn. Bapt. Chs., Ga. Bapt. Hosp. (1st chmn. exec. com. 3 yrs.); mem. Home Mission Bd., Southern Bapt. Conv., 12 yrs. Hon. mem. Am. Ry. Accounting Officers' Assn. Mem. Chamber of Commerce (Atlanta), Am. Poultry Assn., Chi Phi, Soc. Colonial Wars. Chmn. bd. deacons Ponce de Leon Av. Baptist Ch., 15 yrs. Club: Capital City. Home: 40 Muscogee Av. Office: Georgia Savings Bank Bldg., Atlanta, Ga. Died May 16, 1942.

BROWN, George Samson, lawyer; b. Brooklyn, N.Y., Nov. 26, 1865; s. Thomas Edwin (D.D.) and Elizabeth Campbell (Samson) B.; A.B., Brown, 1888; grad. student Columbia Law Sch., 1888-90; m. 2d, Elizabeth Plummer Foster, Apr. 30, 1895; children—Philip Foster, Margaret Campbell (Mrs. Christopher A. Connor), George Samson (dec.). Admitted to bars of New York State and State of Wash., 1890, in practice of law in latter state until 1897; admitted to Nev. bar, 1897; dist. judge Fourth Nev. Jud. Dist., 1903-11; mem. Brown & Belford, Reno, since 1911. Mem. bd. regents U. of Nev. since 1929. Mem. Am. and Nev. bar assns., Alpha Delta Phi, Phi Beta Kappa, Phi Delta Phi. Democrat. Episcopalian (chancellor missionary dist. Nev. since 1910). Home: 737 Humboldt St. Office: First Nat. Bank Bldg., Reno, Nev. Died Aug. 9, 1943.

BROWN, George Stewart, judge; b. Baltimore, Aug. 15, 1871; s. Stewart and Anne (Gill) B.; B.A., Johns Hopkins, 1893; LL.B., U. of Md., 1895; m. Susan Morton, June, 1, 1904; 1 son, Stewart. Began practice in Baltimore, 1895; mem. Brown & Brune, 1900-13. Mem. City Council, Baltimore, 1899-1907; judge U.S. Customs Court by apptmt. of President Wilson, since 1913. Mem. Alpha Delta Phi. Democrat. Presbyterian. Clubs: University (Baltimore); University (New York). Author: Judicial Review in Customs Taxation, 1918. Home: 15 Clark St., Brooklyn. Office; 201 Varick St., New York. Died Oct. 1, 1934.

BROWN, George Van Ingen, surgeon; b. St. Paul, Jan. 15, 1862; s. Matthew Wilson and Emily (Lynch) B.; ed. at home, high sch., St. Paul, and under pvt. tutor; D.D.S., Pa. Coll. Dental Surgery, Phila., 1881; M.D., Milwaukee Med. Coll., 1895, C.M. (Master of Surgery), 1895; A.B., Northern Ill. Coll., Easton,

1898; M.D., Marquette U., Milwaukee, 1909; m. Elizabeth Kathleen Selby Jones, Sept. 22, 1884; 1 son, Selby Van Ingen. Practiced oral surgery and dentistry, St. Paul and Duluth, Minn., 1881-98; splst plastic surgery, Milwaukee, since 1898. Prof. operative dentistry and oral surgery, dean dental dept, Milwaukee Med. Coll., 1898-1902; spl. lecturer on oral surgery, dental dept., U. of Ill., 1902-03, State U. of Ia., 1903-04, U. of Tenn., 1904, Vanderbilt U., 1905, Southern Dental Coll., Atlanta, Ga., 1909-15; prof. oral surgery and oral pathology, State Univ. of Iowa, 1904-10; apptd. by U.S. Senate del. to Internat. Med. Congress, Madrid, Spain, 1903; apptd. to make report on harelip and cleft palate before the Internat. Med. Congress, Budapest, 1911; chief of staff St. Mary's Hosp., 1936; on surg. staff Columbia Hosp. and St. Mary's Hosp., of Milwaukee; plastic surgeon State of Wis. Gen. Hosp., at U of Wis., and also at Wis. Orthopedic Hospital, Madison; cons. staff Milwaukee Children's Hosp., Wis. Meth. Hosp. and Madison Gen. Hosp., Madison, Wis.; attending mem. on surg. staff, Milwaukee County Hosp., Wauwatosa, Wis. Served as 1st lt., capt., maj., lt. col., Med. R.C., 1915-19; col., Officers Reserve Corps, U.S. Army, 1923; pres. bd. examiners for applicants for apptmt. to Med. R.C., at Milwaukee; later at Office Surgeon Gen., Washington, D.C., in charge sect. of plastic and oral surgery of head surg. div.; organized sch. of plastic and oral surgery, at Ft. Oglethorpe, Ga., 1918; in charge plastic and oral surg. operative reconstruction work for returned soldiers with disfigured faces and jaws, at U.S. Army Gen. Hosp. No. 11, Cape May, N.J., and later chief of maxillo-faciale service, Walter Reed Hosp., Takoma Park, D.C.; apptd. surgeon U.S.P.H.S., 1919; with Bur. War Risk Ins. as consultant in plastic surgery, at Milwaukee, 1919; consultant plastic surgery Vets. Adminstrn.; medical consultant, Veterans Service Exchange; professor of oral and plastic surgery, U. of Wis., 1920-37, now emeritus. Fellow Am. Coll. Surgeons, Tri-State Med. Soc. (pres. 1920-21); member A.M.A. and affiliated assns., Wis. State, and Milwaukee County med. socs., Milwaukee Acad. Medicine (honorary mem.), Companion Mil. Order World War, State Hist. Soc. of Wis., Société Scientifique Française de Chirurgie Réparatrice, Plastique et Esthétique (Paris, France), Pan-American Med. Assn., The American Society of Plastic and Reconstructive Surgery, Am. Board of Plastic Surgery, Pi Gamma Mu, Delta Sigma Delta, Alpha Kappa Kappa and many other professional orgns., U.S. and Europe; hon. fellow Internat. Coll. of Surgeons (Geneva, Switzerland). Speaker Interstate Post-Grad. Med. Assn. of North America, 1920-35. trustee since 1920. Awarded Jarvie medal by N.Y. State Dental Society. Episcopalian (senior warden of St. Paul's Church). Mason. Clubs: University, Rotary, Army and Navy (Washington, D.C.); Authors' (London). Author: The Surgery of Oral and Facial Diseases and Malformations, 4th edit., 1938; chapter in Ochsner's Surgical Diagnosis and Treatment, chapter in Sajous' Cyclopedia of Practical Medicine, also monographs, papers and occasional poems. Mem. advisory council Living Age (mag.). Home: 7152 North Beach Dr., Fox Point, Milwaukee, Wis. Office: 759 N. Milwaukee St., Milwaukee, Wis. Died Apr. 2, 1948.

BROWN, George William, clergyman; b. Harrisville, Pa., Mar. 10, 1888; s. Robert Leech and Clara Emma (Wick) B.; grad. Mercer (Pa.) Acad., 1905; B.A., Washington and Jefferson Coll., 1910, M.A., 1914; grad. McCormick Theol. Sem., Chicago, 1914; D.D., Maryville (Tenn.) Coll., 1933; m. Ruth M. McAfee, Oct. 15, 1914; children—George William (dec.), Robert McAfee, Harriet McAfee, Ruth Elizabeth. Ordained ministry Presbyn. Church, U.S.A., 1914; pastor successively at Marengo, Ill., Independence, Ia., Carthage, Ill., Carnegie and Ben Avon, Pa., until 1928; gen. sec. Am. Bible Soc., 1928-38; pastor West Presbyn. Ch., Binghamton, N.Y., 1938-1944. Chaplain with A.E.F., 1918-19. Commr. to Gen. Assembly of Presbyn. Church, U.S.A., 1927, 33, 38; chmn. Com. on Social Edn. and Action of Binghamton Presbytery. Mem. Phi Delta Theta. Contbr. on religious subjects. Home: 84 Nassau St., Princeton, N.J. Died Mar. 28, 1947.

BROWN, Harry Fletcher, chemist; b. Natick, Mass., July 10, 1867; s. William H. and Maria F. (Osgood) B.; A.B., Harvard Univ., 1890, A.M., 1892; hon. D.Sc., U. of Delaware, 1930; m. Florence M. Hammett, Oct. 26, 1897. Chief chemist at U.S. Naval Torpedo Sta., Newport, R.I., 1893-1900; engaged in the investigation and development of smokeless powder in the Navy Dept.; gen. supt. Internat. Smokeless Powder & Chem. Co., 1900-04; dir. of mfr. smokeless powder, E. I. du Pont de Nemours & Co., 1904-15, v.p. in charge smokeless powder dept., 1915-19, now v.p. and dir. E. I. du Pont de Nemours & Co.; also v.p. and dir. Christiana Securities Co. Trustee U. of Del. Mem. Am. Chem. Soc., Nat. Edn. Assn. Home: 1010 Broome St. Office: Du Pont Bldg., Wilmington, Del. Died Feb. 28, 1944.

BROWN, Harry Winfield, newspaper editor; b. N.Y. City; s. Winfield and Mary (Morey) B.; ed. New York U. Reporter New York Sun, 1896-98; city editor Cincinnati Post, 1898-1900; editor Kentucky Post, Covington, Ky., 1900-06; editor in chief Cincinnati Post, 1906-14; editorial staff N.Y. Times, 1914-19; pres. and gen. mgr. Cincinnati Commercial Tribune, 1919-30, paper sold to Cincinnati Enquirer and suspended publication; editorial staff Cincinnati Enquirer since 1931. Life mem. bd. trustees, Cincinnati Southern Ry. Republican. Episcopalian. Mason (32°). Clubs: Queen City, Country, Riding, Cuvier Press (pres.), Cincinnati Club, Automobile (Cincinnati); Phi Gamma Delta (New York); Nat. Press (Washington, D.C.). Home: Queen City Club. Office: 617 Vine St., Cincinnati, O. Died Feb. 13, 1945.

BROWN, Helen Gilman (Mrs. William Adams Brown); b. New York, Oct. 12, 1867; d. Daniel Rogers and Helen (Gilman) Noyes; ed. Miss Porter's Sch., Farmington, Conn.; m. William Adams Brown, D.D., Mar. 30, 1892; children—John Crosby II, William Adams, Winthrop Gilman, Helen Adams (dec.). Known for philanthropic and religious activities; hon. chmn. women's com. Washington Cathedral; chmn. advisory com. Nat. Soc. Colonial Dames of State of N.Y.; mem. women's advisory com. Federal Council of Chs. in Am.; mem. exec. com. Washington Cathedral Com., N.Y. Former nat. pres. Women's Land Army; nat. chmn. finance dept. Y.W.C.A., also of Sulgrave Manor Endowment; pres. Colonial Dames Soc. State of N.Y.; v.p. Nat. Soc. Colonial Dames of America and of Nat. War Work Council Y.W.C.A.; was founder and chmn. Women's Auxiliary Union Settlement Assn., etc. Mem. English-Speaking Union (hosp. com.), Order of Colonial Lords of the Manor. Republican. Episcopalian. Clubs: Colony Cosmopolitan of New York (charter member; ex-president); Albemarle (London). Author: Story of a New England Schoolmaster, 1900. Home: 1105 Park Av., New York, N.Y.; also "The Tree-Tops," Seal Harbor, Me. Died Dec. 12, 1942.

BROWN, Herbert J., pres. and dir. Brown Co., mfrs. of cellulose paper, etc.; b. Portland, Me., 1861; ed. Williams Coll. Home: 125 State St. Office: 404 Commercial St., Portland, Me.* Died Apr. 16, 1945.

BROWN, John Albert, petroleum producer; b. Hampton, Pa., July 28, 1885; s. John and Viola (Albert) B.; ed. Girard Coll.; m. Ella Marie Mathisen, Sept. 22, 1916. Mgr. of Mexican business of Standard Oil Co. (N.J.), 1916-26; traveling for foreign production of same co., 1926-28; became pres. Gen. Petroleum Corp. of Calif., 1929; now pres. and chmn. exec. com. Socony-Vacuum Oil Co., Inc., dir. Socony-Vacuum Oil Co., Inc., South Am. Gulf Oil Co., Colombian Petroleum Co., Am. Petroleum Inst., Chase Nat. Bank. Republican. Clubs: Blind Brook, Metropolitan, St. Andrews Golf. Office: 26 Broadway, New York. Died Sept. 9, 1944; buried in Sleepy Hollow Cemetery, Tarrytown, N.Y.

BROWN, John Griest, lawyer; b. Edina, Mo., Oct. 29, 1879; s. Edwin James and Amelia X. (Sever) B.; student Kirksville (Mo.) Normal Sch. (now Teachers' Coll.), 1896-99; LL.B., Mo. State U., 1902; LL.B., Yale, 1903; LL.D., Polytechnic Intermountain College, 1941; m. Cordelia Ashlock, May 3, 1901; children—John Griest, Jr., William Ashlock. Admitted to Mont. bar, 1903, and began practice at Butte; legal dept. F. Augustus Heinze, mining companies, Butte, Mont., 1904-07; asst. atty. gen. of Mont., preparing first rule of practice for Mont. R.R. Commn., 1907; asso. with William Wallace, Jr. as asst. div. counsel Northern Pacific Ry., 1907-12; asso. in gen. practice with William Wallace, Jr., and T. B. Weir, Helena, Mont., 1913-20; asso. with former Gov. S. V. Stewart, Helena, 1920-32; asso. with son, William A. Helena, since 1934; counsel for Mont. Bankers Assn., 21 yrs. Mem. Mont. Bar Book and Gavel, Phi Alpha Delta, Sigma Alpha Epsilon, Phi Delta Phi, Phi Lambda Epsilon. Republican. Baptist. Mason, K.T. (past grand comdr.: mem. jurisprudence com. Grand Encampment), 33°, Scottish Rite, Southern Jurisdiction, Life mem. Elks. Club: Montana (Helena). Author of several brochures, including "Bozeman Trail," "Incidents of Lewis and Clark Journey," "Life of Father DeSmet." With pres. of Mont. Fed. of Labor wrote and secured pasage of first Am. Act on workmen's compensation. Pub. speaker; active in Rep. politics. Home: 432 Dearborn Av. Office: Holter Block, Helena, Mont. Died Aug. 5, 1941.

BROWN, John Jacob, officer corps.; b. Tyler, Tex., Jan. 19, 1873; s. John A. and Emma A. (Sanford) B.; ed. pvt. schs.; M. Mary Katherine McCoole, 1922. Constrn. engr. for Concol. Compress Co., Tex., 1895; later associated with Henry R. Worthington Pump Co. of New York as specialist on development of hydraulic equipment for compressing cotton; when latter became part of Internat. Steam Pump Co., made gen. Western mgr., headquarters at Chicago; became v.p. Wheeler Condenser and Engring. Co., New York, 1907, elected pres. 1918; during World War I, acted as chmn. Condenser Com., War Industry Board and a mem. Nonferrous Metals Com.; upon consolidation of Wheeler Condenser and Engring. Co. and Power Specialty Co. as Foster Wheeler Corp., became chmn. bd. of the latter; chmn. bd. Foster Wheeler, Ltd., Canada; director Fidelity Union Trust Co., Cranford Trust Co., Foundation Foreign, Liberty Mutual Inc. Co. Mem. Am. Soc. Mech. Engrs., Soc. Naval Architects and Marine Engrs., New York Southern Soc. Clubs: Engineers, Bankers, Recess, Baltusrol Golf, Abenakee, Boca Raton. Home: Cranford, N.J.; also Biddeford Pool, Me. Office: 165 Broadway, New York. Died Feb. 15, 1946; buried in Fairview Cemetery, Westfield, N.J.

BROWN, Joseph Clifton, educator; b. Piqua, O., Apr. 5, 1879; s. Joseph Arthur and Effie (Hunter) B.; B.S., Hanover (Ind.) Coll., 1901; student U. of Chicago (2 summers) M.A., Teachers Coll., Columbia, 1914; m. Celia Frances Fisher, June 19, 1905; children—Helen Anne, Edgar William. Teacher, high school, Noblesville, Ind., 1901-03; supt. schs., Paoli, Ind., 1903-04; teacher mathematics dept. Normal Sch., Charleston, Ill., 1905-11; head mathematics dept. Horace Mann Sch., N.Y. City, 1911-15; teacher mathematics, summer sessions Teachers Coll., Columbia, 1913, 14; mem. dept. of edn. U. of Ill., 1915-16; pres. State Teachers Coll., St. Cloud, Minn., 1916-27, State Teachers Coll., DeKalb, Ill., since 1927. Mem. N.E.A., Nat. Soc. Study of Edn. (pres., 1919-20), Beta Theta Pi, Phi Delta Kappa. Republican. Presbyterian. Author: How to Teach Arithmetic (Brown and Coffman), 1914; Mathematical Curricula of Various Countries (Bur. of Edn.), 1914; Modern Business Arithmetic (Finney and Brown), 1916; Junior High School Mathematics (Wentworth, Smith and Brown), 1918; The Brown-Eldredge Arithmetics, 1924. Address: DeKalb, Ill. Died Jan. 16, 1945.

BROWN, Marshall Stewart, univ. prof.; b. Keene, N.H., Nov. 6, 1870; s. George A. and Ida (Stewart) B.; Ph B., Brown U., 1892, A.M., 1893; U. of Heidelberg, 1895-96; L.H.D., New York University, 1932; LL.D., Brown University, 1941; m. Margaret, daughter Professor Henry M. Baird, of New York, June 12, 1900; children—Susan B., Marshall S., Robert B., Margaret C., Julia B.; m. 2d, Josephine Switzer, d. W. M. Marshall, of New York, July 6, 1935. Instr. English, Brown, 1892-93; instructor history, U. of Mich., 1893-94; acting prof. history and polit. science, 1894-99, prof. 1899-1940, acting dean Coll. of Arts and Pure Science, 1916-17, dean of the faculties 1917-40, dean emeritus since 1940, New York U.; also chmn. Committee on Administration, 1923, and Commission on Graduate Work, 1926-40; in charge of N.Y. University S.A.T.C., 1918-19. History examiner of Coll. Entrance Exam. Bd., 1905-09; mem. bd. of edn., City of Yonkers, 1908-18. Mem. Am. Hist. Assn., History Teachers' Assn. of Middle States and Md., Zeta Psi, Phi Beta Kappa. Mem. mayor's publ. com. of records of N.Y. City Council; chmn. War Issues Course, New York U., War Dept., 1918-19. Club: Zeta Psi of New York. Author: Epoch making Papers in United States History, 1903; History of the Zeta Psi Fraternity, 1899. Address: New York Univ., University Heights, New York, N.Y. Died Sept. 18, 1948.

BROWN, Nathaniel Smith, lawyer; b. Barry, Ill., Aug. 28, 1872; s. James C. and Mary Sophia (Smith) B.; A.B., Central Coll., Danville, Ind., 1898; LL.B., U. of Mo., 1901; m. Nora B. Gentry, Oct. 7, 1905. Admitted to bar, 1901, and since in practice at St. Louis. Asst. counsel, La. Purchase Expn. Co., 1901-06; apptd. asst. atty. Wabash Ry. Co., 1907, later v.p. and gen. solicitor, then gen. counsel to receivers; now v.p. of law, Wabash R.R. Mem. Am., Mo. State and St. Louis bar assns., Law Library Assn. Republican. Home: 49 Vandeventer Pl. Office: Railway Exchange Bldg., St. Louis, Mo. Died Sep. 17, 1943.

BROWN, Orville Harry, physician; b. Sabetha, Kan., July 18, 1875; s. Edward Matthew and Sarah Katherine (Hull) B.; student Ottawa (Kan.) U., 1897-99; A.B., U. of Kan., 1901; Ph.D., U. of Chicago, 1905; M.D., St. Louis U., 1905; grad. work, Marine Biol. Lab., Woods Hole, Mass., summers, 1902, 05; studied Vienna and London, 1906; m. Margaret Paisley, Oct. 16, 1907; 1 dau., Paisley. Asst. in physiology, U. of Kan., 1901-02; fellow and asst. in physiology, U. of Chicago, 1902-04; asst. prof. pharmacology, St. Louis U., 1904-07; phys. in chief, later supt., Mo. State Sanatorium, 1907-09; asst. prof. medicine, St. Louis U., 1910-16; removed to Phoenix, Ariz., 1917. First lt. Med. R.C.; state supt. public health of Ariz., 1918. Fellow A.M.A., Am. Coll. Physicians, Royal Soc. Medicine (London); mem. Am. Assn. Biol. Chemists, State and local med. socs., Alpha Tau Omega, Alpha Kappa Kappa, Sigma Xi, Alpha Omega Alpha. Democrat. Presbyterian. Author: Laboratory Physiology, 1905; Asthma, 1916. Formerly editor Southwestern Medicine. Contbr. articles in med. jours. on physiology and clin. medicine. Home: Arcadia, Calif. Died July 25, 1943.

BROWN, Parke, newspaper man; b. Detroit, Minn., Feb. 1, 1883; s. John T. and Nellie (Pierson) B.; B.L., Northwestern U., 1904; m. Mrs. May Fletcher Van Wormer, Apr. 22, 1936. With Chicago Tribune since 1904; corr. with A.E.F., 1917-18, at Berlin, Germany, 1918-21, corr. in Orient and tropics, 1926-27, now polit. editor. Address: Tribune, Chicago, Ill. Died Sep. 30, 1943.

BROWN, Philip King, physician; b. Napa, Cal., June 24, 1869; s. Henry Adams and Charlotte Amanda (Blake) B.; A.B., Harvard, 1890, M.D., 1893; U. of Berlin, 1895-96, Göttingen, 1896; m. Helen Adelaide Hillyar, Mar. 7, 1900; children—Hillyar Blake, Harrison Cabot, Phoebe Hearst, Bruce Worcester. In practice of medicine, San Francisco since 1893; asst. in nervous diseases, U. of Calif., 1894, asso. prof. clin. medicine, 1896-98, instr. animal pathology, 1896-99; vis. physician, 1896-97, later cons. physician, Mt. Zion Hosp., San Francisco; cons. pathologist French Hosp., 1896-1901; asso. in medicine and instr. clin. pathology, Cooper Med. Coll., 1899-1902; instr. clin. pathology and exptl. medicine, U. of Calif.; med. dir. So Pacific Hosp.; attending physician, City and County Hosp., 1905-17; founder, med. dir. Arequipa Sanatorium (for tuberculous wage-earning women), Manor, Calif. Mem. Assn. Am. Physicians, Am. Climatol. and Clin. Assn., A.M.A., Boylston Med. Soc., Calif. Acad. Medicine, Calif. State Med. Soc., Soc. Colonial Wars, Soc. Am. Wars, S.A.R., Royal Legion. One of organizers San Francisco Settlement Assn. and San Francisco Boys' Club. Democrat. Mem.

Gov. Olsen's Com. on Health Ins., 1939. Clubs: Burlingame, Commonwealth. Contbr. on animal pathology, heart and lung diseases, leprosy, social problems in medicine, etc. Home: 1 25th Av., N. Office: 909 Hyde St., San Francisco. Died Oct. 1940

BROWN, Preston, army officer; b. Lexington, Ky., Jan. 2, 1872; s. Col. John Mason B.; A.B., Yale, 1892, M.A., 1920; honor grad. Army Sch., of the Line, 1913; grad. Army Staff College, 1914, Army War College, 1920; LL.D., Trinity Coll., Hartford, 1926; m. Susan Ford Dorrance, of Wilkes-Barre, Pa., Feb. 8, 1905; 1 son, Dorrance (died June 1936). Served as private and corpl. Battery A, 5th Arty., Sept. 1894-Mar. 26, 1897; commd. 2d lt. 2d Inf., Mar. 2, 1897; promoted through grades to maj. gen., Dec. 10, 1925; chief of staff, 2d Div., near Verdun, at Chateau-Thierry, Soissons and St. Mihiel, Apr.-Sept. 1918; chief of staff, 4th Army Corps in front of Metz, Sept., 1918; comdg. gen. 3d Div., Battle of the Meuse-Argonne, Oct. 1918; asst. chief of staff, A.E.F., at advanced Gen. Hdqrs. in occupied German territory, Nov. 1918; instr., dir. and acting comdt. Army War Coll., Washington, 1919-21. Awarded D.S.M. for exceptionally meritorious and distinguished services. As chief of staff 2d Div. directed the details of the battles near Chateau-Thierry, Soissons and at the St. Mihiel salient; also, in comd. of 3d Div. in the Meuse-Argonne offensive, at a critical time, through his judgment and energetic action, div. was able to carry to a successful conclusion the operations at Claire-Chenes and Hill 294. Comdg. gen. 3d Inf. Brigade, 1921, 2d Div., 1924, 1st Div., 1925, 1st Corps Area, 1926-30; deputy chief of staff, U.S. Army, Mar. 9-Oct. 10, 1930; comdg. gen. Panama Canal Dept., Nov. 24, 1930-Nov. 14, 1933; comdg. gen. 2d Army and 6th Corps Area, 1933-34, retired, Nov. 30, 1934. Comdr. Legion of Honor (France); Comdr. Order of the Crown (Belgium). Mem. Soc. of the Cincinnati. Clubs: University (New York) Graduate (New Haven, Conn.); University (Denver) Home: Vineyard Haven, Mass. Died June 30, 1948.

BROWN, R. Lewis, judge; b. Philipsburg, Mont., May 25, 1892; s. Wingfield Ludwell and Sally (Perkins) B.; LL.D., State Univ. of Mont., 1916; m. Gay Elise Neu, July 24, 1922; children—Robert Lewis, Gay Elise. Admitted to Mont. state bar 1916; county atty., Granite County, 1916-18; pvt. law practice, Butte, Mont., 1925-45; asst. county atty., Silverbow County, 1932-34; asst. U.S. dist. atty. for Mont., 1934-45; judge, U.S. Dist. Court of Mont. since 1945. Mem. State and County bar assns. Democrat. Elk. Club: Country. Home: 1109 Diamond St. Office: Federal Bldg., Butte, Mont. Deceased.

BROWN, Ralph Hall, univ. prof.; b. Ayer, Mass., Jan. 12, 1898; s. William and Nellie (Leavitt) B.; student Massachusetts State Coll., 1915-17; B.S., U. of Pennsylvania, 1921; Ph.D., U. of Wisconsin, 1925; m. Eunice Rasmussen, Mar. 21, 1924; children—George Burton, Nancy Eleanor, Laura Leavitt. Asst., dept. of geography, U. of Wisconsin, 1921-25; instr. geography, U. of Colorado, 1925-27, asst. prof., 1927-29; assistant professor geography, University of Minnesota, 1929-38, associate professor, 1938-45, professor since 1945; teacher summers, Iowa State Teachers College, 1922 and 1923, George Peabody College for Teachers, 1924 and 1925, Pennsylvania State Coll., 1937. Recipient of research grants, including Social Sci. Research Council, 1937-38. Mem. Nat. Council Geography Teachers, Am. Geog. Soc., Minn. Hist. Soc., A.A.A.S., Assn. Am. Geographers (sec. 1942-46, editor Annals since 1947), Sigma Xi. Chmn. St. Anthony Park Library Assn. Author: Mirror for Americans; Likeness of the Eastern Seaboard, 1810 (spl. publ. Am. Geog. Soc.), 1943; Historical Georgraphy of the United States, 1948. Home: 1454 Chelmsford St., St. Paul 8, Minn. Office: University of Minnesota, Minneapolis 14, Minn. Died Feb. 23, 1948; buried Sunset Memorial Park, Minneapolis.

BROWN, Ray, illustrator; b. Groton, Conn., July 16, 1865; s. Samuel W. and Marianna (Ward) B.; ed. pvt. sch., S. Hadley, Mass., high sch., and Worcester (Mass.) Poly. Inst. to sr. yr.; m. Gertrude Foster, Sept. 14, 1893. Began newspaper work in Chicago as artist and writer; later in charge art dept. Chicago Times, Chicago Times-Herald, New York Evening Journal, and New York Morning Journal; art dir. Everybody's Magazine, 1904-10, Everybody's Magazine and the Butterick Pub. Co., and treas. and dir. Ridgway Pub. Co., 1910-15 (resigned); formerly v.p. Hawley Advertising Co. (retired). Has illustrated several books. Author: How It Feels to be the Husband of a Suffragette, 1915; Uncle Bill's Letters to His Niece, 1917. Home: 55 E. 76th St., New York, N.Y. Died Apr. 30, 1944.

BROWN, Robert K., dentistry; b. Sharpsburg, Pa., Sept. 22, 1893; s. William Richard and Bella Jane (Dyer) B.; student Indiana State Normal Sch. of Pa., 1908-11, U. of Mich., 1912-14; D.D.S., U. of Mich., 1919, M.S., 1928; m. 2d, Inez Fredrica Rieger, Sept. 14, 1938; children—(1st marriage) Robert Benaway, Patricia Ann. Teacher in Pa. public schools, 1911-12; practiced dentistry in Cleveland, O., 1919-21; instr. operative dentistry, Sch. of Dentistry, U. of Mich., 1921-23, asst. prof., 1923-28, prof. and dir. operative clinic, 1928-35; full time practice of dentistry, Ann Arbor, Mich., since 1935; lecturer and research worker in dentistry. Served as mem. enlisted Med. Reserve Corps, U.S. Army, 1917-19. Trustee Pierre Fauchard Acad. Fellow Am. Coll. Dentists; mem. Am. Dental Assn., Mich. State and Washtenaw dental socs., Sigma Phi Epsilon, Delta Sigma Delta, Omicron Kappa Upsilon. Episcopalian. Club: University. Mem. publ. com. The Dental Survey; contbg. editor Jour. of Mich. State Dental Soc.; contbr. articles to dental jours. Home: 504 E. Ann St. Office: Campus Bldg., Ann Arbor, Mich. Died Mar. 28, 1944.

BROWN, Robert Sater, editor; b. Ross, O., Jan. 15, 1900; s. William and Daisy (Sater) B.; B.S., Ohio State U., 1922; m. Leona Wilby Brayshaw, Sept. 22, 1927; children—Barbara Lee, Martin. Served as reporter and desk man on Ohio, Ind., and Fla. newspapers, 1922-28; news editor, Cleveland Times, 1926-27; mng. editor Toledo News-Bee, 1929-31, editor, 1932-33; Sunday and mng. editor Toledo Times, 1931-32; with Wash. bur. Scripps-Howard Newspapers as corr. for Cleveland Press, Cincinnati Post, Columbus Citizen and other Ohio Scripps-Howard papers, 1934-37; editor Columbus Citizen since 1937; now on military leave. Served as private in U.S. Army, World War I. Serving as major, Army Service Corps, Washington, D.C. Member Alpha Gamma Rho, Pi Delta Epsilon, Sigma Delta Chi. Presbyterian. Club: National Press (Washington); Columbus Athletic, Columbus Country. Home: 2347 Bexley Park Road. Office: 34 N. Third St., Columbus, O. Died July 31, 1944.

BROWN, Roscoe Conkling Ensign, newspaper man b. Scottsville, N.Y., Aug. 23, 1867; s. Dyer D. S. and Mary Ann (Ensign) B.; brother of Selden Stanley B.; A.B., U. of Rochester, 1889, M.A., 1904, Litt.D., 1925; m. Bertha Backus, Feb. 11, 1897; children—Grosvenor (deceased), Helen Ensign (Mrs. Robert M. Winslow), Elizabeth Grosvenor (Mrs. Lyndon B. Hardwick), Lawrence Roscoe, Truman Backus, Mary Stanley (Mrs. Alfred M. P. Amey), Bertha Raymond (deceased). Was with New York Tribune, 1889-1913, editorial writer, 1895-1906, mng. editor, 1906-12, asst. editor, 1912-13; asso. in journalism, 1914, asst. prof., 1917, prof. journalism, 1919-36, emeritus, 1936—, Columbia. Mem. N.Y. State Civil Service Commn., 1905-11; mem. Council Nat. Civil Service Reform League; trustee Brooklyn Public Library. Mem. Phi Beta Kappa. Clubs: Union League, Century (New York). Author: (with W. F. Johnson) Political and Governmental History of the State of New York. Home: 200 Hicks St., Brooklyn 2, N.Y. Died Dec. 13, 1946.

BROWN, Wade Hampton, medical research; b. Sparta, Ga., Oct. 18, 1878; s. George Rives and Laura Virginia (Brown) B.; B.S., U. of Nashville, 1899; grad. student U. of Chicago, 1902-03; M.D., Johns Hopkins, 1907; m. Beth Gillies, Oct. 29, 1908; children—Wade Gillies, Elspeth, Wade Hampton. Instr. pathology, U. of Va., 1907-08; instr. same, U. of Wis., 1908-10, asst. prof., 1910-11; prof. pathology, U. of N.C., 1911-13; with Rockefeller Inst. since 1913, asso. mem., 1914-22, mem. scientific staff for medical research since 1922. Mem. Assn. Am. Physicians, Am. Soc. Pathologists and Bacteriologists, Am. Soc. for Exptl. Pathology, Am. Soc. for Pharm. and Exptl. Therapeutics, Soc. for Exptl. Biology and Medicine, A.A.A.S., Sigma Xi, Nu Sigma Nu. Democrat. Presbyterian. Contbr. of more than 75 papers in med. procs. and jours.; has specialized in study of biology of syphilitic infections, constitutional factors and physical environment in relation to heredity and disease. Home: 34 Westcott Rd., Princeton, N.J. Died Aug. 4, 1942.

BROWN, William Adams, theologian; b. New York, N.Y. Dec. 29, 1865; s. John Crosby and Mary E. (Adams) B.; prep. edn., St. Paul's Sch., Concord, N.H.; A.B., Yale, 1886, A.M., 1888, Ph.D., 1901; grad. Union Theol. Sem., 1890; U. of Berlin, 1890-92; D.D., Union Coll., 1903, Yale, 1907, U. of St. Andrews, Scotland, 1922, Oxford U., England, 1937; S.T.D., Columbia University, 1937; m. Helen Gilman Noyes, March 30, 1892 (she died December 15, 1942); 3 sons, 1 daughter (deceased). Ordained to Presbyterian ministry, 1893; instructor, 1892-95, provisional prof., 1895-98, Roosevelt prof. systematic theology, 1898-1930, research professor in applied theology, 1930-36, now emeritus, Union Theol. Sem. Mem. Yale Corp., 1917-34; chmn. Com. on Ednl. Policy of Yale U., 1919-30; acting provost Yale Univ., 1919-20; pres. Religious Edn. Assn., 1928-31; sec. Gen. War-Time Commn. of the Chs., 1917-19; chmn. Com. on the War and the Religious Outlook; mem. Com. of Fourteen (chmn. 1916-18); mem. administrative com., and chmn. dept. research and edn., Federal Council Chs. of Christ in America since 1924, chairman dept. of relations with chs. abroad since 1936, mem. advisory council since 1934; mem. Bd. of Home Missions of Presbyn. Ch., 1910-23; mem. continuation com. Universal Christian Council for Life and Work; chmn. administrn. com. same, 1932-38, pres. Am. sect. since 1936; mem. continuation com. and exec. com., World Conf. on Faith and Order; v.p. Constantinople Woman's Coll., 1927-30, pres. bd. trustees since 1930; pres. Near East Coll. Assn. since 1936; mem. Commn. on Higher Edn., India, 1930-31; dir. N.Y. Inst. for Deaf and Dumb; a founder, 1907, and dir. Grenfell Assn. of America. Mem. Soc. Bibl. Lit. and Exegesis, Am. Philos. Soc., A.A.A.S.; patron Met. Museum of Art. Mem. Phi Beta Kappa. Clubs: Century, Yale, American Alpine, Authors; Royal and Ancient St. Andrews (Scotland); Authors' (London). Author: Musical Instruments and Their Homes, 1888; The Essence of Christianity, 1902; Christian Theology in Outline, 1906; Life of Morris K. Jesup, 1910; The Christian Hope, 1912; Modern Theology and the Preaching of the Gospel, 1914; Is Christianity Practicable?, 1916; Modern Missions in the Far East, 1917; The Church in America, 1922; Imperialistic Religion and the Religion of Democracy, 1923; The Creative Experience, 1923; The Life of Prayer in a World of Science, 1926; The Quiet Hour, 1926; Beliefs that Matter, 1928; Pathways to Certainty, 1930; God at Work, 1933; Ministerial Education in America, Vol. 1, 1934; The Church, Catholic and Protestant, 1935; Finding God in a New World, 1935; Church and State in Contemporary America, 1936; The Minister—His World and His Work, 1937; The Case for Theology in the University, 1938; A Teacher and His Times, 1940; A Creed for Free Men, 1941; The New Order in the Church, 1943. Contributor to Hastings' Dictionary of the Bible, Hastings' Encyclopedia of Religion and Ethics, Political Science Quarterly, etc. Member editorial board, Constructive Quarterly; editorial board Review of the Churches, Religion in Life. Review of Religion; American editor The International Library since 1934. As rep. of Fed. Council of Churches in U.S. attended by invitation enthronement of Archbishop of Canterbury, Apr. 23, 1942. Home: 1105 Park Av. Office: Union Theol. Seminary, Broadway and 120th St., New York, N.Y. Died Dec. 15, 1943.

BROWN, William Perry, author; b. in Indian Ty., 1847; s. Gen. Philip Perry and Sarah (Jackson) B.; ed. Madison (now Colgate) U.; m. Emma E. Hayes, Sept. 3, 1890. Engaged in newspaper work, 1884-86; contbr. serials, short stories, poems, etc., to mags. and periodicals, since 1886. Author: A Sea Island Romance, 1888; Roraima, 1896; Ralph Granger's Fortunes, 1902; Sea Island Boys, 1903; Vance Sevier, 1903; Florida Lads, 1903; The Easterners, 1910; Nick Carter's Persistence, 1911; Who Was Milton Marr, 1912; The Luck of Vance Sevier, 1912; At the End of the World, 1912; Forbidden Fruit, 1913; Passion Paramount, 1913. Also series of juvenile war books (under nom de plume of Capt. William B. Perry): Our Sammies in the Trenches, Our Jackies with the Fleet, Our Pilots in the Air (all 1918). Address: Glenville, W.Va. Died Sept. 4, 1923.

BROWN, Wrisley, lawyer; b. Washington, July 22, 1883; s. Charles Albert and Mary Louise (Wrisley) B.; student, Columbian (now George Washington) U., 1901-02; studied under pvt. teachers, 1903-04; LL.B., Nat. U., Washington, D.C., 1907, LL.M., with honors, 1908; m. Mrs. Mozelle Price Whitford, 1920. Apptd. to classified civil service from Me., Feb. 13, 1905, and assigned to Treas. Dept.; law clerk to comptroller of the treas., 1907-09; examiner, Dept. of Justice, Mar. 15-Oct. 8, 1909; spl. asst. to the atty. gen. U.S., 1909-18; also consulting atty., Bureau of Investigation, 1910-Jan. 7, 1918. Conducted the investigation that resulted in impeachment, on July 11, 1912, of Robert W. Archbald, U.S. circuit judge; was counsel for the mgrs. on the part of Ho. of Rep. in the trial before the Senate, culminating in conviction. Represented U.S. before an English commn., at London, June and July 1914, in litigation under the Nat. Banking Laws. Republican. English Lutheran. Commd. 2d lt. D.C.N.G., July 2, 1902; 1st lt., July 15, 1903; resigned, Dec. 4, 1904; commd. maj. Signal Res. Corps, Dec. 17, 1917; transferred to Air Service, Oct. 18, 1918; commd. lt. col. U.S. Army, July 3, 1919; resigned Sept. 28, 1920. Pres. Potomac Freight Terminals Co.; pres. and gen. counsel, Terminal Refrigerating & Warehousing Corp., Consol. Terminal Corp.; dir. Nat. Bank of Washington, Norfolk & Washington Steamboat Co. Mem. Am. Bar Assn., Am. Acad. Polit. and Social Science, Archeol. Inst. America (pres.), Am. Inst. of Refrigeration, Chamber of Commerce of U.S. (nat. councillor), Washington Board of Trade, English-Speaking Union (dir.), Am. Legion, Mil. Service Legion. Clubs: Bankers of America (New York); University Club, Army and Navy Club, Nat. Press Club, Rotary Internat., Seigniory of Canada. Author of "The Impeachment of the Federal Judiciary," pub. as a public document pursuant to a resolution of the U.S. Senate, Jan. 13, 1914. Address: 2319 Wyoming Av. N.W., Washington, D.C.; (country) "Hollowtree," Sandy Spring, Md. Died Mar. 19, 1943.

BROWNE, Arthur Wesley (broun), educator; b. Brooklyn, N.Y., Nov. 24, 1877; s. Henry Bewley and Kate Matilda (Day) B.; B.S., summa cum laude, Wesleyan U., 1900, M.S., 1901; Ph.D., Cornell U., 1903; Sc.D. from Wesleyan U., 1933; m. Helen Elizabeth Westgate, Feb. 20, 1904; children—Arthur Westgate, Robert Lewis, Ruth Westgate (dec.), Helen Westgate, Catherine Day. Asst. chemist, S.S. White Dental Mfg. Co., Prince Bay, N.Y., 1895-97; grad. scholar in chemistry, 1901-02, instr., 1903-06, asst. prof. inorganic and analytic chemistry, 1906-10, prof. same, 1910-22, prof. inorganic chemistry since 1922, actg. head dept. chemistry (2d semester), 1924-25, Cornell; visiting prof. chemistry, U. of Chicago, summer 1931. Served as consultant during World War, chem. expert Ordnance Dept. at large. Mem. Alpha Delta Phi, Omega Upsilon Phi, Gamma Alpha, Alpha Chi Sigma, Phi Beta Kappa, Sigma Xi, Aldjebar, Phi Kappa Phi, Tau Beta Pi. Independent Republican. Conglist. Contbr. articles to Am. Year Book, 1910-19; also numerous professional articles on original researches in Am. and European chem. jours. Home: 216 Dearborn Place, Ithaca, N.Y. Died Dec. 15, 1945.

BROWNE, Charles, physician; b. Phila., Pa., Sept. 28, 1875; s. William Hardcastle and Alice (Beaver) B.; A.B., Coll. of N.J. (now Princeton U.), 1896, A.M., 1899; M.D., U. of Pa., 1900; U. of Berlin, 1902-03; m. Georgeanna Gibbs, April 30, 1913; children—Colston Hardcastle, Anthony DeHooges, Archibald Ayres, Charles Brown. Began practice at Princeton, N.J., 1906; overseer of poor, Princeton, 1913-16; mayor of Princeton, 4 terms, 1916-23; pres. bd. trustees Princeton Hosp., 1919-28; mem. 68th Congress (1923-25), 4th N.J. Dist.; mem. bd. Pub. Utility Commrs., N.J., since Mar., 1925. Dir. 1st Nat. Bank (Princeton), Del. & Bound Brook R.R. Co. Mem. Borough Council, Princeton, N.J., 1933-35; mem. N.J. House of Assembly, 1936-39, 1941-42. Assistant to surgeon Old Point Comfort Army Hospital, Spanish-Am. War, 1898; student Plattsburg Camps, 1915-16; commd. 1st. lt. Med. Corps, U.S. Army, 1917; capt., Sept., 1918; comdt. U.S. Army Convalescent Hosp. No. 1 at Lawrenceville, N.J. Mem. bd. mgrs. N.J. State Home for Women; mem. Grad. Council Princeton U. Mem. Am. Inst. of Polit. and Social Science. Democrat. Presbyterian. Author: Gun Club Cook Book, 1930; Gun Club Drink Book, 1939. Clubs: University, Princeton, Racquet and Tennis (New York); University, Racquet, Princeton (Phila.). Home: Princeton, N.J. Died Aug. 16. 1947

BROWNE, Charles Albert, chemist; b. North Adams, Mass., Aug. 12, 1870; s. Charles Albert and Susan (MacCallum) B.; B.A., Williams, 1892; M.A., 1896; M.A. and Ph.D., U. of Göttingen, Germany, 1902; hon. D.Sc., Williams, 1924, Stevens Inst. Tech., 1925; m. Louise McDanell (A.B., Stanford, A.M., Columbia, Ph.D., Yale), Feb. 9, 1918; 1 dau., Caroline Louise. Engaged as chemist, New York, 1892-94; instr. in chemistry, Pa. State Coll., 1895-96; asst. chemist, Pa. Expt. Sta., 1896-1902; studied sugar chemistry in Germany, 1900-02; research chemist, La. Sugar Expt. Sta., New Orleans, 1902-06; chief sugar lab., U.S. Bur. Chemistry, Washington, D.C., 1906-07; chemist in charge of N.Y. Sugar Trade Lab., Inc., 1907-23; chief, Bur. of Chemistry, U.S. Dept. Agr., 1923-27; acting chief Bur. of Chemistry and Soils, 1927, chief of chem. and technol. research, 1927-35, supervisor chem. research, 1935-40, retired as collaborator, Bur. Agrl. and Indsl. Chemistry, 1940. U.S. del. 6th Internat. Congress of Applied Chemistry, Rome, 1906, Internat. Soc. of Sugar Cane Technologists, Brisbane, 1935. Fellow A.A.A.S. (v.p. chemistry sect., 1931, sec. history sect. 1941); mem. Am. Chem. Soc. (bd. of editors, 1911-22; chmn. N.Y. sect., 1923; chmn. sugar sect., 1919-21; chmn. history of chemistry sect., 1922-23; editor, Golden Jubilee number, "A Half-Century of Chemistry in America," 1926), Assn. Official Agrl. Chemists (pres. 1924-25), Washington Acad. Sciences, History of Science Soc. (recording sec. 1926-28; president 1935-36), Agrl. History Soc., S.A.R., Nat. Geog. Soc., Phi Beta Kappa, Sigma Xi, Phi Lambda Upsilon; hon. mem. Am. Oil Chem. Soc.; hon. fellow Sugar Technol. Assn. of India. Historian, American Chemical Society since 1945. Gold and silver medals for sugar exhibits, St. Louis Expn., 1904; award of distinction, Associate Grocery Manufacturers of America for applications of science to food manufacturing, 1935. Nicholas Appert Medal for outstanding achievement in food tech., 1944. Unitarian. Mason (32°). Club: Cosmos (Washington, D.C.). Author: Handbook of Sugar Analysis, 1912; Sugar Tables for Laboratory Use, 1912; (with F. W. Zerban) Physical and Chemical Methods of Sugar Analysis, 1941; Source Book of Agricultural Chemistry, 1943; Thomas Jefferson and the Scientific Trends of His Time, 1943; also numerous bulletins and papers. Contbr. to Ency. Britannica, 13th and 14th edits., to Ency. Americana, 1941 edit., and to Dictionary of Am. Biography. Advisory editor Chemistry in Agriculture, 1926; co-editor, Wiley's Principles and Practices of Agricultural Analysis, 3d edit. Home: 3408 Lowell St. N.W. Office: U.S. Bureau of Agrl. and Industrial Chemistry, Washington 25, D.C. Died Feb. 3, 1947.

BROWNE, Edward E(verts), ex-congressman; b. Waupaca, Wis., Feb. 16, 1868; s. Edward L. and Mary (Parish) B.; B.Litt., U. of Wis., 1890, LL.B., 1892; m. Rose C. Cleveland, 1893; children—Katherine B. (Mrs. William B. Camlin), Mrs. Marcus Hobart, Edward L., Thomas. Admitted to Wisconsin bar, 1892, and since in practice at Waupaca; now senior member of law firm of Browne & Browne (established 1852). District attorney Waupaca County, 3 terms, 1898-1905; member Wisconsin Senate 2 terms; mem. 63rd to 71st Congresses (1913-31) 8th Wisconsin Dist.; mem. Foreign Affairs Com. 8 yrs., Highway Com., Labor and Civil Service coms.; mem. State Conservation Commn. of Wis. Mem. Bd. Regents U. of Wis. Pres. Bar Assn. of 7th Judicial Circuit of Wis., 1937; curator of Wis. Hist. Soc. While mem. Wis. Senate drafted the first state aid road law and law providing for a system of extensive pub. parks. Mem. American Bar Assn., Wisconsin State Bar Assn., English-Speaking Union, Mayflower Soc. Republican. Episcopalian (sr. warden St. Marks Ch., 1908-13, 31, 42, 43). Mason (32°). Clubs: Congressional Country (dir.), Waupaca Golf (charter mem.); University (Winter Park, Fla.). Home: Waupaca, Wis. Died Nov. 23, 1945.

BROWNE, George Elmer, artist; b. Gloucester, Mass., May 6, 1871; s. Josiah Hill and Katherine (Cowan) B.; ed. pub. schs., Salem, Mass.; studied art at Sch. of Drawing and Painting, Mus. of Fine Arts, and Cowles Art Sch., Boston; Acad. Julian, Paris, under Jules Lefebvre and Tony Robert Fleury; m. Lillian B. Putnam, Nov. 2, 1893; 1 son, Harold. Awarded medal, Mechanics Fair, Boston, 1895; Book Plate Prize, Salmagundi Club, New York, 1898; George Inness, Jr. Prize, Salmagundi Club, 1901. Regular exhibitor at Paris Salon, also Munich, Berlin, Rome, London, and in leading cities of U.S. Rep. in following collections: Nat. Collection of Fine Arts, Washington, D.C.; Montclair (N.J.) Mus.; Erie (Pa.) Art Club; Omaha Pub. Library; Art Inst., Chicago; Milwaukee Art Inst.; Toledo (O.) Mus.; Union League Club, Chicago; University Club, Milwaukee; Salmagundi Club, New York; Art Collection, Lawrence, Kan.; Luxembourg Gallery, Paris, 1922; Harrison Collection, Los Angeles Museum, 1923. Painting "Bait Sellers of Cape Cod," purchased by French Govt. from Paris Salon, 1904; painting purchased by Art. Mus., Atlanta, Ga., 1922, Ranger Fund of Nat. Acad. Design, 1929, and Birmingham (Ala.) Public Library; rep. in Art Museums, Montpelier and Cahors, France, also in collection at U. of Wis., Madison. Awarded Isidor prize, Salmagundi Club, 1916, 18; Vezan prize, 1919; $1,000 Shaw prize, 1920; Trumbell prize, 1921; Tuthill prize, Art Inst. Chicago, 1923; water color prize, Baltimore Art Club, 1926; Shaw water color prize, Salmagundi Club, 1927; gold medal, Allied Artists of America, 1928; Rodney Wilcox Jones prize, Nat. Arts Club, 1931; Gregg prize, National Arts Club, 1932; Altman $500 prize Nat. Acad. Design, 1934; gold medal of honor, Allied Artists America, 1934; Carrington prize, Salmagundi Club, 1937; William Church Osborn prize Am. Water Color Soc., 1936; Layman's prize Salmagundi Club, 1938, 40, 43; Adolph and Clara Obrig prize Am. Water Color Soc., 1938; Nat. Arts Club prize, 1938. Dir. and instr. Browne Art Class, Provincetown, Mass.; instructor Grand Central Sch. Art, 1942-43; prof. and teacher of painting, Mary Washington Coll., Fredericksburg, Va., since Sept. 1944; former instr. Met. Art School, N.Y.; conducted classes abroad, 1922, 25, 27 and 29. Decorated Officier de l'Instruction Publique (French), 1925; Chevalier de lá Legion D'Honneur, 1936. N.A., 1928; mem. council of Nat. Acad. Design, 1933-35; mem. Nat. Inst. Arts and Letters, Allied Artists of Am. (pres. 1930-35), National Commn. to Advance American Art, Artists Professional League, Am. Fine Arts Foundation, Conn. Acad. Fine Arts, Grand Central Art Gallery (New York), Archtl. League of New York, Painter Gravers America, Group of American Artists, Artists' Fund Soc., New York Water Color Soc., Allied Artists' Assn. (New York), Am. Water Color Soc., Am. Soc. of Etchers, Municipal Art. Soc. (New York), Provincetown Art Assn. (v.p.), Am. Art. Assn. (Paris). Clubs: Lotos (life), Nat. Arts (life), Salmagundi (pres. 1935, 36; life mem.), Century (New York); Beachcombers of Provincetown, Mass. (ex-pres.). Home: (summer) Provincetown, Mass. Studio: (winter) Hotel des Artistes, 1 W. 67th St., New York, N.Y. Died July 12, 1946.

BROWNE, Herbert Wheildon Cotton, architect; b. Boston, Mass., Nov. 22, 1860; s. Thomas Quincy and Juliet Frances (Wheildon) B.; ed. Noble's Private Sch. (Boston), Boston Museum of Fine Arts, Mass. Inst. Tech., Julian's Studio (Paris); studied painting with Fabio Fabii, Florence, Italy, 1883; unmarried Student in office of Andrews and Jaques, architects, 1888-90; partner in firm Little and Browne, architects, Boston, Mass., 1890-1939; retired since 1939. Fellow Am. Inst. Architects; mem. Mediaeval Acad. America (life), Navy League of U.S.A. (life), Soc. Preservation New England Antiquities (life mem.); trustee 1912-15, 1916-19, 1920-23 and 1936-39). Boston Soc. Architects. Home: 66 Beacon St., Boston 8, Mass. Died Apr. 29, 1946; buried in Sleepy Hollow Cemetery, Concord, Mass.

BROWNE, Lewis, author; b. London, Eng., June 24, 1897; s. Harry Abrahim and Stessa (Fiesca) B.; came to U.S., 1912; B.A., U. of Cincinnati, 1919; B.H., Hebrew Union Coll., Rabbinical Sem., 1920; post-grad. work, Yale, 1920-22; m. Myna Eisner Lissner, 1930 (divorced, 1941). Rabbi, Temple Israel, Waterbury, Conn., 1920-23; free lance writer, 1923-24; rabbi Free Synagogue of Newark, N.J. (asso. with Rabbi Stephen S. Wise), 1924-26; organizer and pres. Newark Labor Coll., 1925; resigned rabbinate, 1926, to devote time to writing and lecturing. Visiting prof., summers, Pa. State Coll., 1928, U. of Calif. at Los Angeles, 1932, 33, University of Hawaii, 1937, 39; extension div. lecturer on History of Civilization, University of Calif., 1934-39, Columbia University (1938-43). Author: Congregational Prayer Service, 1925; Stranger Than Fiction, 1925—English edit. of same under title of The Story of the Jews, 1926; This Believing World, 1926; That Man Heine (with Elsa Weihl), 1927; The Graphic Bible, 1928; The Final Stanza, 1929; Why Are Jews Like That?, 1929; Since Calvary, 1931; Blessed Spinoza, 1932; How Odd of God, 1934; All Things Are Possible, 1935; Oh, Say, Can You See!, 1937; Something Went Wrong, 1942; See What I Mean?, 1943; The Wisdom of Israel, 1945; The World's Great Scriptures, (illustrated by author), 1946. Radio commentator, lecturer, world traveler. Civilian lecturer on orientation for War Dept., 1942-49. Home: Uplifters Ranch, Santa Monica, Calif. Died Jan. 3, 1949.

BROWNING, George Landon, judge; s. John Armistead and Mary Lewis (Willis) B.; LL.B., Georgetown U.; m. Eva Byrd Hill Ransom, Feb. 28, 1906; children—Armistead Willis, George Landon II, Francis Henry Hill. Was messenger, U.S. Ho. of Rep.; later in practice with Hon. James Hay, Madison, Va.; practiced with John G. Williams, Orange, Va., after 1911, later with A. T. Browning and S. M. Nottingham; now justice Supreme Court of Va. Mem. Bd. of Visitors Virginia Mil. Inst. 3 terms. Mem. Pi Kappa Alpha. Democrat; long active in campaigns, nat. and state. Episcopalian. Mason (32°, K.T.). Home: Old Manse Orange, Va. Address: Supreme Court of Appeals, Richmond, Va. Died Aug. 26, 1947

BROWNING, Webster E., missionary sec., retired; b. Sweet Springs, Mo., Apr. 14, 1869; s. Caleb and Frances (Akers) B.; B.A., Park Coll., Mo., 1891, M.A., 1893, D.D., 1912, LL.D., 1933; grad. study, U. of Calif., 1891-93; grad. San Francisco Theol. Sem., 1893; B.A., Princeton, 1894; Ph.D., Coll. of Emporia, 1895; D.Litt., U. of San Marcos, Lima, Peru, 1920; m. Hallie May Riley, June 6, 1895; children—Alice Davidson (dec.), Elsie Elizabeth (Mrs. Basil W. Berg). Instr. dept. of classics, Princeton U., 1894-95; ordained Presbyn. ministry, 1895; pastor Garden City, Kan., 1895-96; apptd missionary to Chile, 1896; prof. Instituto Inglés, Santiago, 1896-98, prin., 1898-1916; ednl. sec. Com. on Cooperation in Latin America, 1916-27; students' lecturer on missions, Princeton Theol. Sem., 1919; exec. sec. Com. on Cooperation in River Plate Republics, 1927-36; acting sec. Presbyn. Bd. of Foreign Missions, New York, Apr.-Oct. 1933, sec. 1936-1940, retired June, 1940. Del. of Princeton U. to Pan Am. Scientific Congress, Santiago, Chile, 1910, of U.S. Govt. to Congress on Child Welfare, Montevideo, 1919, of Presbyn. Bd. to Mexico Mission, 1919, to Colombia and Venezuela, 1922-23; commr. of the Presbytery of Chile to Gen. Assembly of Presbyn. Ch., 1903, 37. Chmn. bd. mgrs. Ward Coll., Buenos Aires, 1926-36; mem. bd. of trustees MacKenzie Coll., S. Paolo, Brasil. Mem. Chi Alpha. Author: The Republic of Ecuador, 1920; The Republic of Paraguay, 1920; Roman Christianity in Latin America, 1924; New Days in Latin America, 1925; Modern Missions on the Spanish Main (with W. R. Wheeler), 1925; The River Plate Republics, 1928; The West Coast Republics of South America (co-author), 1930; Joseph Lancaster, James Thomson and the Lancasterian System in Latin America, 1936. Also various other writings relating to Latin America. Translator: The Invisible Christ (by Dr. Ricardo Rojas), 1931; and many Spanish works. Home: 433 Bloomington Av., Wooster, O. Died Apr. 16, 1942.

BROWNSON, Carleton Lewis, coll. prof.; b. New Canaan, Conn., Jan. 19, 1866; s. Dr. William Greene and Caroline Louisa (Barstow), B.; A.B., Yale, 1887, post-grad. student, 1887-90, Ph.D., 1897; univs. of Berlin and Munich, and Am. Sch. Classical Studies at Athens, 1890-92; m. Emma Josephine Potter, Dec. 28, 1892; 1 dau., Katherine (dec.). Instr. Greek, Yale, 1889-90, 1892-97; asst. prof. Greek, 1897-1904; asso. prof., 1904-15, prof., 1915-17, and prof. classical langs., 1917-36, dean, 1909-26, acting pres. Dec. 1918-June 1919, prof. emeritus since 1936, Coll. City of N.Y. Mem. Am. Philol. Assn., Archeological Inst. of Am., Phi Beta Kappa, Delta Kappa Epsilon. Conglist. Author: A Shorter History of Greece, 1896; Plato's Studies and Criticisms of the Poets, 1920. Translator and Editor: Xenophon's Hellenica, 1908; Xenophon's Historical Works, 3 vols., 1917-23. Home: 228 W. 71st St., New York, N.Y. Died Sept. 28, 1948.

BROY, Charles Clinton, foreign service officer; b. Sperryville, Va., July 26, 1887; s. James Ennis and Susan Belle (Hite) B.; A.B., Roanoke Coll., 1906, A.M., 1907; A.M., Princeton, 1908; m. Mrs. Cecil Norton Sisson, April 9, 1925; children—Anne Norton, James William, Beverly Hite. Apptd. as consular assistant, 1909; consul, 1916; serving at Boma (Congo), Milan, Dublin, Queenstown (Cobh), Cherbourg, Dept. of State, Nassau (Bahamas), London, and Brussels. Mem. Am. Foreign Service Assn. Mason. Address: care Dept. of State, Washington, D.C. Died Sep. 1943.

BROYLES, Joseph Warren (broilz), coll. pres.; b. Chuckey, Tenn., Mar. 9, 1901; s. Sidney Hiram and Daisy Florence (Bailey) B.; student U. of Chattanooga, 1917-19; A.B., Tusculum Coll., Greeneville, Tenn., 1921, D.D., 1934; S.T.B., Boston U. Sch. of Theology, 1924; student Harvard, 1923; M.A., Drew U., Madison, N.J., 1930, Ph.D., 1932; m. Edith Verna Allen, June 10, 1924; children—Joseph Warren, Jr., John Allen. Ordained to ministry, Meth. Ch., 1924; pastor First Ch., Newport, Tenn., 1924-26, First Ch., Maryville, Tenn., 1926-29, First Ch., Johnson City, Tenn., 1931-35, First Ch., Knoxville, Tenn., 1935; prof. philosophy and social ethics, Hamline U., St. Paul, Minn., 1936-39; pres. Snead Jr. Coll., Boaz, Ala., 1939-42; pres. and mem. bd. trustees, W.Va. Wesleyan Coll., Buckhannon, since 1942. Mem. Rotary. Home: 66 Kanawha St., Buckhannon, W.Va.* Died Sep. 29, 1945.

BRUCE, Edward, artist, lawyer; b. Dover Plains, N.Y., Apr. 13, 1879; s. James M. and Mary (Bright) B.; A.B., Columbia, 1901, LL.B., 1904; Dr. of Arts, Harvard U., 1938; m. Margaret Stow, 1909. Practiced law in N.Y. City and Manila; engaged in foreign trade and banking in Far East. Began painting landscapes at 14; made collection of early Chinese paintings, now in Fogg Museum, Cambridge, Mass.; resided in Anticoli Corrado and Florence, Italy, 1923-29, later in Calif.; rep. of Pacific Coast and Far East interests at Washington, D.C., 1931-33; Chief of Sect. of Fine Arts of the Treasury Department, Washington, since 1933. Paintings on exhbn. in Whitney Museum of Am. Art, New York; Phillips Memorial Gallery, Washington, D.C.; Los Angeles Museum; San Francisco Museum of Art; etc. A.N.A.; mem. Alpha Delta Phi. Awards: Friedsam Fellowship gold medal award, 1938; Columbia U. medal for excellence, 1937. Member Commission of Fine Arts, Jan. 18, 1940. Clubs: Century, India House (New York); Cosmos (Washington, D.C.). Home: 2900 Connecticut Av. Address: Procurement Div., Treasury Dept., Washington, D.C. Died Jan. 27, 1943.

BRUCE, Frank M., Sr., pub.; b. Milwaukee, Wis., Dec. 25, 1885; s. William George and Monica (Moehring) B.; B.A., Marquette Univ., 1905, M.A., 1910; B.A., Univ. of Wis., 1906; m. Alma Müeller, Nov. 24, 1910; children—William George, Frank, Alice Mary (Mrs. James Gaunt), Jane, Robert C. Entire career with The Bruce Pub. Co., pubs. ednl. mags., Milwaukee; started as office boy, 1906 and advanced through ranks to pub., sec.-treas. of co. Recipient Alumni award of Merit, Marquette Univ., 1946. Mem. Nat. Sch. Service Inst. (sec.), Internat. Serra (past pres.), Marquette Univ. Alumni Assn. (past pres.), Rural Life Conf. (sec.), St. Vincent de Paul Soc. (met. pres.), Religious Pubs. Assn., Ch. Goods Dealers and Cath. Book Pubs. Assn., Cath. Press Assn., Holy Name Soc., Roman Catholic. K.C. Clubs: Rotary (past pres.), Milwaukee Athletic, University, Milwaukee Adventurers. Home: 1113 S. Third St., Office: 540 W. Milwaukee St., Milwaukee 1, Wis. Died Aug. 1949.

BRUCE, Henry William, univ. adminstr.; b. Amherst, O., Feb. 1, 1897; s. William and Anna (Flowers) B.; A.B., U. of Southern Calif., 1924, J.D., 1929; m. Margaret Strause, June 30, 1922. Grad. mgr. athletics, U. of Southern Calif., 1922, purchasing agt., asst. comptroller, comptroller, v.p. since 1922. Mem. Bd. Park Commrs., Los Angeles, 1932-41. Mem. State and Los Angeles bar assns., (hon.) Purchasing Agts. Assn. Los Angeles, Kappa Alpha, Alpha Kappa Psi, Blue Key, Skull and Dagger. Republican. Methodist. Mason. Club: University (Los Angeles). Home: 4003 Olympiad Drive, Los Angeles 43, Calif. Died Mar. 11, 1945.

BRUCE, James Deacon, physician; b. Blackstock, Ont. Can., Oct. 4, 1872; s. John and Mary (Deacon) B.; M.D., Detroit Coll. Medicine and Surgery, 1896; m. Grace A. Campbell, May 25, 1904. Came to U.S., 1892, naturalized, 1896. In gen. practive, Michigan, 1896-1904, 1906-16, and 1919-25; asst. in internal medicine, U. of Mich., 1904-05, dir. internal medicine, Univ. of Mich., and chief med. service of Univ Hosp., 1925-28 dir. post-grad. medicine, 1925-42, consultant to Univ. med. service, 1925-42; mem. exec. com., Univ. Med. Sch., 1930-42, vice pres. in charge univ. relations, 1931-42, chmn. div. health sciences, 1935-42, also chmn. div. extramural services, 1936-42; vice-pres. emeritus, 1942, Univ. of Mich. Mem. Med. Advisory com., Nat. Com. on Econ. Security, 1934; mem. Nat. Research Council, Div. Med. Sciences, (com on medicine, 1940-42); mem. Nat. Com. on Grad. Med. Edn., 1937-40; chmn., Asso. States Postgrad. Com., 1937-41; mem. Mich. Tuberculosis Sanatorium Commn., 1932-46; pres. Mich. Council on Adult Education, 1941-46; mem. Mich. Com. on Juvenile Delinquency, 1943-46; mem. Mich. Adult Edn. Advisory Com., 1944-46. Served as capt., M.C., Canadian Army, later maj., M.C., U.S. Army, overseas, 1916-19, World War I. Fellow, Am. Coll. Surgeons, Am. Coll. Physicians (gov. for Mich., 1930-36, regent since 1936, pres., 1940-41, regent 1941-46; member Mich. State Med. Soc., (councillor, 1923-34), Washtenaw County Med. Soc., A.M.A., Alpha Omega Alpha, Phi Kappa Phi, Delta Omega, Phi Rho Sigma. Conglist. Mason. Clubs: Crystal Downs Country, University, Barton Hills Country, University of Michigan. Home: 631 Oxford Rd. Address: University Hospital, Ann Arbor, Mich. Died Sept. 5, 1946.

BRUCE, Robert Glenn, pres. E. L. Bruce Co.; b. Kansas City, Mo., Dec. 11, 1885; s. Edwin L. and Eva (Glenn) B.; student pub. schs.; m. Ruby Partee, Nov. 3, 1915; 1 dau., Beverley Sue. Pres. E. L. Bruce Co., Memphis, Tenn., since 1913; also pres. M.&S.V. R.R. Co. since 1921, E. L. Bruce, Inc., since 1925, E. L. Bruce, Ltd., since 1925. Home: 1508 Goodbar Pl. Office: E. L. Bruce Co., Memphis.* Died July 23, 1945.

BRUCE, W(illiam) Cabell, ex-senator; b. Staunton Hill, Charlotte County, Va., Mar. 12, 1860; s. Charles and Sarah (Seddon) B.; Norwood (Va.) High Sch. and Coll., 1875-78); U. of Va., 1879-80; LL.B., U. of Md.; LL.D., Hampden-Sydney Coll., Va.; LL.D., Loyola Coll., Baltimore, Md., 1930; m. Louise E., d. of Judge William A. Fisher, Oct. 15, 1887; children—James, David K.E. Mem. law firm Fisher, Bruce & Fisher, Baltimore, 1887-1903, 1908-10. Mem. of Md. Senate, 1894-96 (pres. 1896); head of Baltimore Law Dept., 1903-08 (resigned); mem. Baltimore Charter Commn., 1910; gen. counsel Public Service Commn. of Md., 1910-22, and for term 1929-35; mem. U.S. Senate, term 1923-29. Democrat. Episcopalian. Author: Benjamin Franklin, Self-Revealed, 1918 (awarded Pulitzer prize, as best biography of year); Below the James, 1918; John Randolph of Roanoke, 1923; Seven Great Baltimore Lawyers, 1931; Recollections, 1931; Imaginary Conversations with Franklin, 1933; The Inn of Existence, 1941; also 3 compilations of essays and addresses. While at University of Virginia, in competition with Woodrow Wilson and others, was awarded medal as best debater of Jefferson Lit. Soc., and medal for best essay; was co-editor U. of Va. Mag. Home: Ruxton, Md. Died May 9, 1946; buried in St. Thomas Churchyard, Garrison Forest, Md.

BRUCE, William George, publisher; b. Milwaukee, Wis., Mar. 17, 1856; s. Augustus F. and Appolonia (Becker) B.; LL.D., Mount Mary College, 1939; educated in public schools and by private instruction; m. Monica Moehring, May 4, 1880 (she died Jan. 4, 1938); children—William Conrad, Frank Milton, Monica Marie. Founded, 1891, and since pub. Am. Sch. Bd. Jour.; founded Industrial Arts Magazine, 1914, Hospital Progress, 1919; acquired Catholic School Journal, 1929. Member Milwaukee Sch. Bd., 1889-94; mgr. Milwaukee ednl. exhibits at Chicago Expn., 1893, as chmn. sch. bd. com.; mgr. Wis. ednl. exhibits at St. Louis Expn., 1904, as chmn. Wis. Ednl. Com. Chmn. Dem. City and County Com., Milwaukee, 1896-1906; tax commr. Milwaukee, 1904-06; pres. Auditorium Bd., 1912-14, 1936-45; pres. Milwaukee Harbor Commn., 1913-45, Nat. Assn. of Comml. Secretaries, 1915-16, Great Lakes Harbors Assn.; mem. Wis. Deep Waterway Commn., 1919-35; pres. Am. State Bank. Served as del. Wis. Constl. Conv. for Repeal of Eighteenth Amendment, 1933; mem. Federal Emergency Board of Public Works for Wisconsin, 1933. Awarded Laetare Medal for outstanding service, U. of Notre Dame, 1947. Clubs: Athletic, Old Settlers, Jefferson (pres. 1892-95). Author: Bruce's Sch. Architecture, 1904; Man. on School Adminstrn., 1904; Commercial Organizations, 1920; History of Milwaukee, 1921; Commercial Secretaries, 1922. Also pamphlets on taxation, immigration, 1915, community progress, pride and patriotism, 1916, social ins., 1918, Jewish problem, 1928. Home: 1137 S. 3d St. Office: 540 N. Milwaukee St., Milwaukee 1. Died Aug. 13, 1949; buried in Holy Trinity Cemetery, Milwaukee.

BRUCE, William Herschel, college pres.; b. Troup County Ga., Apr. 8, 1856; s. Hilery Sanford (M.D.) and Catherine Rebecca (Pruitt) B.; A.B., Ala., Poly. Inst., Auburn, 1883; A.M., Baylor Univ., Waco, Tex., 1886; Ph.D., Mercer Univ., Macon, Ga., 1890; LL.D., Trinity U., Waxahachie, Tex., 1917; m. Lillie O. Hart, Nov. 6, 1879; children—Lilian Maud, Byron Sanford, Ralph Thomas, Homer Lindsey. Supt. schs., Blanco, Tex., 1884-93, Marble Falls, Tex., 1893-96, Athens, 1896-99; pres. John Tarleton Coll., Stephenville, Tex., 1899-1900; prof. mathematics, N. Tex. State Teachers Coll., Denton, 1901-06, pres. 1906-23, pres. emeritus, since 1923. Instr. mathematics, 3 summer sessions, U. of Tex.; condr. summer schs., San Marcos, San Antonio, Port Lavaca, Tex., 1893-1901; chmn. Tex State Bd. Examiners, 1906-10. Pres. Tex. State Teachers' Assn., 1905; fellow Tex. Acad. Science; mem. N.E.A., A.A.A.S., Am. Assn. Teachers' Colleges, Kiwanis Club, Alpha Tau Omega, Kappa Delta Pi. Democrat. Baptist. Mason (32°, K.T., Shriner). Author: Bruce's Plane and Solid Geometry; Principles and Processes of Education; Some Noteworthy Properties of the Triangle and its Circles; The Nine Circles of the Triangle; The Charms of Solitude (verse). Co-author Sutton and Bruce's Arithmetics. Lecturer on edn., teachers' institutes. Home: Denton, Tex. Died Dec. 30, 1943.

BRUMLEY, Oscar Victor (brŭm'lē), veterinary medicine; b. Leipsic, O., Mar. 9, 1876; s. Joseph and Phillipina (Leffler) B.; D.V.M., Ohio State, 1897; post-grad. work, Royal Vet. Coll., Berlin, Germany, 1901-02; m. Annabell Tawney, Nov. 26, 1906. With Ohio State U. since 1898, prof. vet. surgery and dir. vet. clinics since 1910, sec. Coll. Vet. Medicine since 1912, dean same since 1929. Pres. Bd. of Health, Columbus. Member of Upper Arlington Board of Health, 1942-43. Mem. Am. Vet. Med. Assn. (pres. 1938; chmn. exec. bd. and bd. of govs. 1941-44), A.A.A.S., Ohio State and Northwestern Ohio vet. medical associations, U.S. Live Stock Sanitary Assn., Chamber Commerce, Columbus, Sigma Xi, Phi Zeta, Omega Tau Sigma, Alpha Psi, Acacia. Maj. Vet. O.R.C. Republican. Methodist. Mason. Club: Faculty. Author: Posology and Prescriptions, 1912, 20; Diseases of the Small Domestic Animals, 1921, 31, 37, 43. Contbr. vet. subjects. Home: 2185 Cambridge Blvd., Columbus, O. Died Jan. 13, 1945; buried at Leipsic, O.

BRUN, Constantin (brōōn), diplomat; b. Copenhagen, Denmark, Oct. 5, 1860; s. Maj. Gen. A. and Ella Amalie (Bluhme) B.; grad. Coll. of Herlufsholm, 1878; LL.D., U. of Copenhagen, 1883. Second lt. Hussars of the Guard, 1885; asst. in Ministry of Foreign Affairs, 1885; sec. Legation at Berlin, 1887, at Paris, 1891; E.E. and M.P. to U.S., 1895-1908, to Eng., 1908-12, again to U.S., 1912-30, retired; now hon. counselor to Danish Legation. Del. from Denmark at Peace Conf., The Hague, 1907; signed treaty ceding the Danish West Indies (Virgin Islands) to the U.S., 1916. Knight Order of Dannebrog, 1894, Grand Cross, 1911; Chamberlain to King of Denmark, 1897. Home: 1605 22d St. N.W. Address: Danish Legation, Washington, D.C. Died Dec. 23, 1945.

BRUNER, Henry Lane (brōōn'ẽr), zoölogist; b. Knox County, Ill., Jan. 10, 1861; s. Frances Marion and Esther (Lane) B.; A.B., Abingdon (Ill.) Coll. (united with Eureka Coll., 1884), 1880; Yale, 1880-81; Ph.D., U. of Frieburg, Baden, 1896; D.Sc., Butler U., 1932; m. Carolyn Aumock, Sept. 10, 1890 (died 1894); 1 son, Harold Aumock; m. 2d, Emma Pfeiffer, June 15, 1897; children—Margaret Emilie (Mrs. H. W. Hudson), Henry Pfeiffer. Taught natural sciences various colleges, 1881-86; prof. biology and geology, Drake University, 1891-92, Butler University, 1892-1919, professor zoölogy, 1919-38, head of dept., 1892-38, dir. grad. studies 1932-38, prof. emeritus since 1938. Fellow A.A.A.S., Ind. Acad. of Science (pres. 1919), Ia. Acad. of Science (emeritus); mem. Am. Soc. Zoölogists, Eugenics Soc., Am. Assn. Univ. Profs. (emeritus), New York Acad. Sciences (asso.), S.A.R., Phi Kappa Phi. Republican. Mem. Disciples Church. Club: Professional Men's Forum. Author: Laboratory Directions in College Zoölogy, 3d edit., 1942; contbr. to Anatomy and Physiology of Vertebrates. Home. 324 S. Ritter Av., Indianapolis. Died March 17, 1945; buried in Crown Hill Cemetery, Indianapolis.

BRUNS, Henry Frederick, naval officer; b. Nov. 24, 1889; entered U.S. Navy, 1914; advanced in Civil Engr. Corps to rear admiral, June 1943.*† Died Jan. 20, 1947.

BRUNSWIG, Lucien Napoleon (brün'swig), pres. Brunswig Drug Co.; b. France, Aug. 10, 1854; s. Charles and Rosalie (de Lehault) de B.; B.S., Coll. of Etain, Meuse, France, 1871; m. Annie Mercer, Apr. 12, 1878 (died May 5, 1892); children—Aimée (Mrs. Alexander Field), Etta (Mrs. T. S. Sholars), Annie B. (Mrs. Marshall J. Wellborn), Walter M.; m. 2d, Marguerite Wogan, July 2, 1898; 1 dau., Marguerite (Mrs. Elmer Victor Staude, Jr.). Came to U.S., 1871, naturalized, 1888. Partner Finley & Brunswig, New Orleans, 1881-95; police commr., New Orleans, 1895-99; pres. Brunswig Drug Co., wholesale druggists, Los Angeles, Calif., since 1904. Pres. Pacific Coast and Inter-mountain Independent Wholesale Druggists since 1928; mem. Kappa Psi, Rho Chi, Officer Legion of Honor (France). Mem. Knights of Columbus. Republican. Clubs: California, University, Army and Navy, Westport Beach (Los Angeles). Home: 3528 W. Adams St. Office: 501 N. Main St., Los Angeles, Calif.* Died July 17, 1943.

BRUSH, Louis Herbert, newspaper publisher; b. in Alliance, Ohio, January 24, 1872; s. James Alpheus and Amelia (McCall) B.; A.B., Mt. Union College, Alliance, O., 1890, hon. LL.D., 1938; m. Maude Stewart, Sept. 18, 1895; 1 son, Thomas Stewart (dec.). Circulation manager the Alliance (O.) Review, 1890-93, circulation manager the Youngstown (O.) Sun, 1893-94; purchased the Salem (O.) News, 1897, E. Liverpool (O.) Review, 1901; purchased with others Marion (O.) Star, 1923, Steubenville Herald-Star, 1926, Canton Repository, 1927, Portsmouth Times, 1930; purchased half interest in Ironton (O.) Tribune, 1930; organized Brush-Moore Newspapers, Inc., and pres. since 1927; v.p. Ohio Mut. Ins. Co.; v.p. First Nat. Bank. Trustee, treas. Mt. Union Coll.; trustee Harding Memorial Assn., McKinley Memorial Assn. Mem. Ohio Soc. of N.Y., Soc. Mayflower Descs., Sigma Alpha Epsilon. Republican. Methodist. Mason (32°), Shriner, Elk. Clubs: Union, The Country (Cleveland); Canton (Canton, O.); Committee of One Hundred, Surf, Indian Creek (Miami Beach, Fla.). Home: 663 S. Lincoln Av Office: 624 E. State St., Salem, O. Died June 24, 1948.

BRUST, Peter, architect; b. Milwaukee County, Wis., Nov. 4, 1869; s. Christopher and Catherine (Biever) B.; student Pio Nono High Sch., St. Francis, Wis., 2 yrs.; m. Olga Greulich, June 5, 1902; children—Paul C., Catherine (Mrs. Floyd Haboeck), John J. Engaged in practice of architecture, Milwaukee, Wis., since 1906; asso. with Richard Philipp as senior partner, firm of Brust & Philipp, 1906-27; practiced individually, 1927-37; asso. with sons as senior partner, firm Brust & Brust since 1937. Co-architect for Kohler Co. plant and Kohler Village; other works include many institutional, comml. and indusl. buildings in middle west. Mem. Art. Commn., City of Milwaukee, 10 yrs.; mem. Metropolitan Park Com. of Milwaukee during its life of 10 yrs. (now discontinued); mem. mayor's adv. council, 5 yrs.; mem. bd. of appeals on zoning, Milwaukee, 20 yrs.; mem. Wis. Building Code Adv. Com., 25 yrs., chmn. 12 yrs. Mem. bd. examiners of architects and professional engrs. for State of Wis. Fellow Am. Inst. Architects (mem. bd. dirs. 1940-43; pres. Wis. chapter 2 terms). Office: Brust & Brust, 135 W. Wells St., Milwaukee 3, Wis. Died June 22, 1946.

BRYAN, Charles Wayland, ex-gov. and mayor; b. Salem, Ill., Feb. 10, 1867; s. Judge Silas Lilliard and Mariah Elizabeth (Jennings) B.; ed. U. of Chicago and Illinois Coll. (non-graduate); m. Bessie Louise Brokaw, Nov. 29, 1892; children—Silas Millard, Virginia (dec.), Mrs. Mary Louise Harnsberger. Settled in Lincoln, 1891; mem. governor's staff, rank of col., 1897-1902; pub. and asso. editor The Commoner, 1901-23; editor and propr. American Homestead 5 yrs.; engaged in farming and wholesale coal business; mayor of Lincoln, 1915-17; city commr., 1921-22; served as chmn. Park Bd., Municipal Ownership League, etc.; gov. of Neb., 1923-25, 1931-33 and 1933-35; served as mayor of Lincoln, 1935-37. Democratic candidate for vice-pres. of U.S., 1924, for gov. of Neb., 1926, 28; ind. candidate by petition for gov. of Neb., 1938. Political sec. and business agent of his brother, William Jennings Bryan, 1897-1925. Established municipal coal yard, municipal employment bur., legal aid dept., in Lincoln, and state gasoline filling stas.; owner and operator, State Coal Co. (non-profit orgn. to regulate price of coal). Mem. Lincoln Chamber Commerce. Odd Fellow. Woodman. Elk. Clubs: Kiwanis, University Club. Home: Lincoln, Neb. Died Mar. 4, 1945.

BRYAN, Enoch Albert, educator; b. Bloomington, Ind., 1855; s. Rev. John and Eliza Jane (Philips) B.; A.B., Ind. U., 1878, A.M., 1885, LL.D., 1920; A. M., Harvard, 1893; LL.D., Monmouth, 1902, Mich. Agrl. Coll., 1907, Washington State Coll., 1929; m. Hattie E. Williams, 1881; children—Arthur W., Mrs. Eliza May Kulzer, Mrs. Gertrude Hayes. Supt. pub. schs., Grayville, Ill., 1878-82; pres. Vincennes (Ind.) U., 1882-93, Wash. Agrl. Coll., and Sch. of Sciences (now State Coll. of Wash.), 1893-1916; commr. of edn. State of Ida., 1917-23; research prof. economics and econ. history, State Coll. of Wash., 1923-39 (pres. emeritus). Author: The Mark in Europe and America; History of State College of Washington, 1928; Orient Meets Occident or The Advent of the Railways into the Pacific Northwest, 1935. Home: Pullman, Wash. Died Nov. 6, 1941.

BRYAN, George Sands, editor, writer; b. Matteawan, Dutchess County, N.Y., Sept. 6, 1879; s. George James and Rachel Anne (Hendrickson) B.; B.A., Amherst, 1900; m. Alice Rhoda Hancock, Sept. 27, 1922. On editorial staff Internat. Year Book, 1900, New Internat. Ency., 1900-03, Ency. Americana, 1903-04; editor, later adv. mgr. and vice-pres. The University Soc.; on advt. staff Ency. Britannica, 1915-16; later chiefly engaged in research and editorial work. Member of the Phi Beta Kappa Fraternity. Author: Sam Houston, 1917; (brochure) Notes on Early New England Eating, 1920; (brochure) Pioneers of the Great West, 1920; Yankee Notions (verse), 1922; The Ghost in the Attic, and Other Verses, 1926; Edison: The Man and His Work, 1926 (which has been translated into German, Italian, Czech and Hebrew languages); The Great American Myth: The True Story of Lincoln's Murder, 1940; Mystery Ship: The Mary Celeste in Fancy and in Fact, 1942; The Spy in America, 1943. Compiler: The Camper's Own Book, 1912; The Camper's Own Book (2d issue), 1913; Poems of Country Life, A Modern Anthology, 1912, 16. Translator: The Eleventh Elegy of Book V of Sextus Propertius, 1900; The Assumption of Hannele (from the German of Gerhart Hauptmann), 1911. Editor: Useful Knowledge Books, 1923-34; Struggles and Triumphs: or The Life of P. T. Barnum (2 volumes, with introduction and notes), 1927; also sets of educational works. With poem Blue-Bonnet won prize for lyric of a Texas state song; contbr. over signature "G.S.B." of New England verses to N.Y. Tribune, World, etc. Phi Beta Kappa poet, Hunter Coll., 1922. Wrote foreword to the Limited Editions Club's Snow-Bound. Contbr. Dictionary of Am. Biography, Dictionary Am. History. Staff contbr. to The Volume Library, 1939. Home: 16 Young Av., Pelham, N.Y. Died Dec. 22, 1943.

BRYAN, John Stewart, pres. and pub. newspapers; b. "Brook Hill," Henrico County, Va., Oct. 23, 1871; s. Joseph and Isobel Lamont (Stewart) B.; A.B., A.M., U. of Va., 1893; LL.B., Harvard, 1897; Litt.D., Washington and Lee U., 1911; LL.D., U. of Richmond, Coll. of Charleston, Ohio U., Dartmouth Coll., U. of Pa., Syracuse U., Coll. of William and Mary; m. Anne Eliza Tennant, June 4, 1903; children—Mrs. Amanda B. Kane, David Tennant, Stewart. Admitted to bar, 1897; practiced law, Richmond, 1898-1900; in newspaper bus. with father on Richmond Times-Dispatch, 1900-1915; became pres. and pub., Richmond News Leader, Nov. 1909; pres. and pub. Richmond Times-Dispatch and News Leader since 1940; pres. and pub. Richmond Newspapers, Inc.; mem. bd. dirs. Southern Ry. Co. Vice rector bd. of visitors, Coll. of William and Mary, 1926-34, pres. 1934-42, now chancellor. Pres. Richmond Community Fund, 1926, 27, Community Chests and Councils, Inc., 1933 (now v.p.). Originator and editor in chief Trench and Camp, issued in over 30 camps, 1917-18; mem. war work council of Y.M.C.A., World War; later lt. comdr. Intelligence Dept., Naval Res. Corps. Decorated Royal Order of St. Olav in Norway. Rector, Bd. of Visitors, U. of Va., 1920-22; mem. bd. overseers Harvard University, 1937-43; chairman 5th Federal Reserve District Committee for Post-War Economic Development. Member Volunteer Participation Committee of 3d Civilian Defense Area. Chairman Richmond Pub. Library Bd.; pres. Richmond Council Boy Scouts of America, 1914-28, now hon. pres.; awarded Silver Beaver; trustee U. of Richmond and Episcopal High Sch., Alexandria, Va. One of founders and v.p. Va. Museum of Fine Arts. Pres. Am. Newspaper Pubs. Assn., 1926-28; v.p. Nat. Inst. Social Sciences; mem. Va. Hist. Soc. (pres. 1935-38), Va. Soc. of the Cincinnati, S.A.R., S.R., Soc. Colonial Wars, Assn. for Preservation Va. Antiquities, Confederate Memorial Lit. Soc., Mass. Hist. Soc., Washington Nat. Monument Soc., Va. Sesqui-centennial Commn., Yorktown Sesqui-centennial Assn. (v.p.), New England Hist. and Geneal. Soc., Delta Psi, Phi Beta Kappa, Omicron Delta Kappa. Mem. Nat. Council P.E. Ch. in America, 1919-28. Democrat. Episcopalian. Clubs: Commonwealth, Country (Richmond); University (New York). Author: Joseph Bryan: His Times, His Family, His Friends, 1935; Diary of John Randolph Bryan, Midshipman U.S.N. 1823-29, 1941 (both published for pvt. distribution). Address: Richmond Newspapers, Inc., Richmond, Va.
Died Oct. 16, 1944.

BRYAN, William Alanson, ornithologist, zoölogist; b. nr. New Sharon, Ia., Dec. 23, 1875; s. William A. and Catherine M. (Pearson) B.; B.S., Ia. State Coll., 1896; m. Ruth M. Goss, June 20, 1900; m. 2d, Elizabeth Jane Letson, Mar. 16, 1909 (died 1919); m. 3d, Maud M. Robinson, June 21, 1921. Asst. dept. zoölogy in charge Ia. State Coll. Museum, 1893; on expdn. to Big Stone Lake, 1894; spl. lecturer on museum methods, U. of Minn., Ind. U., U. of Chicago, Purdue U., Ia. Coll. and Drake U., 1895-97; asst. curator in charge dept. ornithology, Field Columbian Museum, 1898-99; apptd. rep. U.S. Dept. Agr. to investigate fauna of H.I., 1899; traveled extensively in Europe and America, studying museum adminstrn., 1900; curator, Bishop Museum of Ethnology and Natural History, Honolulu, 1900-07; organized, and was made pres. Pacific Scientific Instn., 1907; prof. zoölogy and geology, U. of Hawaii, 1909-19; scientific expdn., Latin America, 1919-20; dir. Los Angeles Museum History, Science and Art, 1921-40 (retired). Presented pvt. collection, 10,000 natural history specimens, to New Sharon (Ia.) High Sch., 1903; hon. curator Pacific ornithology, Minn. Acad. Natural Sciences, 1904. Fellow A.A.A.S.; mem. Am. Orinthologists' Union, Cooper Ornith. Club, Am. Fisheries Soc., Am. Mus. Assn., Southern Calif. Acad. Natural Science (pres. 1925), Hawaiian Hist. Soc. (v.p.); mem. 4th Internat. Ornith. Congress. Author: Key to Birds of Hawaiian Group, 1901; Natural History of Hawaii, 1915; also monographs of Marcus Island, and various scientific papers. Home: 142 S. Hayworth Av., Los Angeles, Calif. Died June 18, 1942.

BRYANT, Frederick Howard, judge; b. Lincoln, Vt., July 25, 1877; s. Lester A. and Mary A. (Delphy) B.; A.B., Middlebury (Vt.) Coll., 1900; LL.D., Syracuse University, 1936, LL.D., Middlebury Coll., 1940; m. Florence B. Boyce, Oct. 22, 1907; children—Frederick Boyce, Robert Boyce. Admitted to N.Y. bar, 1903, and began practice at Malone. Apptd. judge U.S. Dist. Court, Northern Dist. of N.Y., 1927. Mem. Chi Psi. Republican. Episcopalian. Mason. Home: Malone, N.Y. Died Sep. 4, 1945.

BRYSON, Charles Lee, author, editor; b. Dade Co., Mo., Mar. 10, 1868; s. James Neil and Margaret Ann (Hargis) Bryson; Central Normal Coll., Indiana; married Georgia DePue; 1 daughter, Minnetta. Served on staff of the Denver (Colo.) Post, 1901-12; was on staff Chicago Examiner 4 yrs.; on staff Central Div. of Am. Red Cross, Apr. 1917-Nov. 1918; two years city editor Chicago Jour. of Commerce; later on Herald and Examiner, Chicago; editor Lions' Club Mag. since 1923. Broadcaster of stories for children. Past pres. Press Club and editor of official mag., The Scoop. Author: Tan and Teckle, 1908: Woodsy Neighbors of Tan and Teckle, 1911; Double Trouble, 1944; also many mag. stories. Joint author: Chicago and Its Makers, 1929. Home: 521 Forest Av., Glen Ellyn, Ill. Office: 332 S. Michigan Av., Chicago, Ill. Died Apr. 18, 1949.

BRYSON, Joseph Montgomery, lawyer; b. Pittsburgh, Mar. 26, 1867; s. John Campbell and Nancy (Chambers) B.; B.S.D., State Teachers' Coll., Warrensburg; studied law under James Hagerman, Kansas City, Mo. Admitted to bar, 1889; gen. counsel M., K.&T. Ry. Co. since 1910. Mem. Am., Mo. State and St. Louis bar assns. Republican. Presbyterian. Clubs: Noonday, Sunset Hill, Bellerive Country. Home: 5570 Chamberlain Av. Office: Railway Exchange Bldg., St. Louis. Died Oct. 1938.

BUCH, Joseph Godfrey (bŭk), hotel exec., state ofcl.; b. Trenton, N.J., Aug. 7, 1881; s. Adam and Katherine (Prieth) B.; ed. parochial and pub. schs., Trenton, also Stewart Coll. hon. degree Doctor of Humane Letters, Rider Coll., Trenton, 1940; hon. LL.D., John Marshall Coll., 1941; unmarried. Mgr. and propr. hotels, Trenton, N.J., since 1906; v.p. Trenton Hotel Co. since Sept. 1940; dir. Chambersburg Trust Co. Apptd. by Gov. A. Harry Moore mem. and elected chmn. N.J. State Crippled Children's Temporary Commn., 1926, chmn. and dir. permanent commn. since 1931; mem. N.J. Rehabilitation Commn., 1928 and 1931; mem. Unemployement Compensation Commn., 1937, now chmn.; mem. N.J. Council Nat. Youth Administrn. (advisory com.); pres. N.J. State Hotel Assn. (chmn. legislative com.); mem. Am. Hotel Assn. (chmn. protective com.), N.Y. State Hotel Assn.; bd. dirs. Internat. Soc. for Crippled Children (extension com.-at-large; second regional conf. and ednl. publicity coms.; advisory com. for U.S.); chmn. bd. N.J. State Elks Assn. (gen. chmn. crippled children's com.); mem. Hotel Greeters of Am., Inter-State Fair Assn. (dir.), Trenton Chamber of Commerce, Kiwanis (vocational guidance and placement com.), B.P.O.E. (treas. Trenton Lodge No. 105; chmn. Bd. Grand Trustees, 1939; Grand Exalted Ruler, 1941). Awarded Trenton Times Civic Cup, 1928, as "the outstanding citizen of Trenton for the year." Clubs: Elks, Republican, Kiwanis, Weasel, Circus Saints and Sinners, Tadpole, Trenton Country, Yardley Country; Tavern (N.Y. City). Home: 26 Charles St. Office: 732 Broad Street Bank Bldg., Trenton, N.J.* Died June 21, 1945.

BUCHER, John Calvin, educator; b. Dillsburg, Pa., Aug. 31, 1865; s. Joseph and Mary Ann (McClure) B.; prep. edn., York (Pa.) Collegiate Inst., 1884-86; A.B., Princeton, 1890, A.M., 1894; m. Florence Katherine Van Dyck, Feb. 3, 1898 (died 1908); children—Julius Van Dyck, Alan T., Florence Katrine Van Dyck; m. 2d, Mrs. Frances Hodges White, Apr. 5, 1924. Asst. prin., later prin. prep. dept. Am. U. of Beyrout, 1890-94; master of English, Mohegan Lake (N.Y.) Sch., 1895-1903; prin., Peekskill (N.Y.) Mil. Acad. since 1903. Mem. Phi Beta Kappa. Progressive candidate for Congress, 1912. Republican. Presbyterian. Home: Oak Hill St., Peekskill, N.Y. Died March 27, 1945.

BUCK, Clarence Frank; b. Monmouth, Ill., June 6, 1870; s. Cyrus L. and Julia Ann (Bake) B.; B.S., Monmouth (Ill.) Coll., 1890; m. Lena Staat, June 9, 1898; children—Mrs. Dorothy Ettl, Mrs. Mildred Ebersole, Henry Staat, Mrs. Julia A. Bardens, Cordelia Meloy. Farmer and stock raiser, Ill. and Mont.; pub. Monmouth Daily Atlas, 1892-1910. Chief of Monmouth Fire Dept., 1896-1905; postmaster, Monmouth, 1899-1915; mem. Ill. Senate, 1917-21; dir. finance U.S. Shipping Bd., 1923-24; collector of customs, Chicago, 1924-25; dir. of agriculture for State of Ill., 1929-30; Rep. candidate for state treas., 1930, 36. Chmn. Warren County Rep. Com., 1890-98; sec. and pres. Ill. League Rep. Clubs, 1900-04; mem. Rep. State Central Com., 1906-12; del. Rep. Nat. Conventions, 1928-40. Pres. Warren County Crop Improvement Assn. and v.p. Warren County Farmers' Inst., 1915-16; treas. Ill. State Firemen's Assn. Trustee Monmouth Coll.; pres. Monmouth Hosp., 1007-17. Presbyn. Odd Fellow, K.P., Elk, Modern Woodman. Clubs: Rotary (local), Monmouth Country. Home: Monmouth, Ill. Died Sep. 2, 1944.

BUCK, Frank Henry, congressman; b. on farm nr. Vacaville, Calif., Sept. 23, 1887; s. Frank Henry and Annie Elizabeth (Stevenson) B.; B.L., U. of Calif., 1908; LL.B., Harvard, 1911; m. Zayda Zabriskie, Apr. 18, 1911; children—Frank H., Margaret Anne, Brevoort, Edward Zabriskie; m. 2d, Eva M. Benson, Jan. 23, 1926; children—William, Carol. Admitted to the Calif. bar in 1911; in practice of law, 1911-17; pres. Frank H. Buck Co. (fruit and farming), 1916-32; v.p. Belridge Oil Co.; dir. Booth Kelley Lumber Co., Mem. 73d to 77th Congresses (1933-43), Calif. Dist. Mem. exec. com. Calif. Dem. State Com., 1928-32; chmn. Dem. State Convs., 1932, 36, 38; delegate Dem. Nat. Conventions, 1928, 36. Vice-pres. Am. Fruit and Vegetable Shippers Assn., 1926-36; nat. councilor U.S. Chamber of Commerce, 1932. Mem. Calif. Hist. Soc., Theta Delta Chi. Democrat. Presbyterian. Elk, Eagle. Clubs: Pacific Union (San Francisco); Claremont Country (Oakland); Sutter (Sacramento). Home: Vacaville, Calif. Died Sep. 17, 1942.

BUCK, Phillip Earl, lawyer; b. Prince Frederick, Md., Mar. 1, 1897; s. James Emory and Eva M. (Williams) B.; ed. pub. and private schs., Md., and business coll.; LL.B., John B. Stetson U., 1923; m. Frederica Lane, Feb. 24, 1924; children—Carolyn Virginia, Elizabeth Williams, Phillip Edwards. Admitted to Fla. bar, 1923, and began practice at DeLand; counsel city of DeLand and other municipalities; dir. of litigation under Nat. Industrial Recovery Act in cooperation with Dept. of Justice and Federal Trade Commn., Washington, D.C., 1935-1941; now engaged in private practice of law; counsel for NRA in Schecter Case before United States Supreme Court, 1935; mem. Fair Trade Practice Bd. of Federal Trade Commn., 1935; gen. counsel Federal Alcohol Adminstrn. Div., U.S. Treasury Dept., 1935-39; conducted many industrial hearings and confs.; in charge of formulation of standards for production, trade practices and advertising of intoxicating beverages; counsel for Federal Trade Commn. in investigation of whiskey industry before Temporary Nat. Com. (monopoly com.) of Congress, 1939. Served in 350th Squadron, Aviation Corps, U.S. Army, 1918-19. Mem. Am. Legion (past comdr. DeLand Post), Federal Bar Assn., Sigma Nu Phi. Home: Deland, Fla. Died Jan. 14, 1947; buried in Arlington National Cemetery.

BUCKHAM, John Wright (bŭk'ăm), theologian; b. Burlington, Vt., Nov. 5, 1864; s. Matthew Henry and Elizabeth (Wright) B.; B.A., U. of Vt., 1885; grad. Andover Theol. Sem., 1888; D.D., U. of Vt., 1904; m. Helen E. Willard, Jan. 1, 1889; children—Margaret, Willard Bayard, Sidney Hickok. Ordained Congl. ministry, 1888; pastor Conway, N.H., 1888-90, Salem, Mass., 1890-1903; prof. Christian Theology, Pacific Sch. of Religion, 1903-37, emeritus since 1937. N.W. Taylor lecturer, Yale, 1914. Chmn. commn. on theology of Internat. Congl. Council, 1920. Pres. John Muir Assn. since 1938. Mem. Am. Philos. Assn., British Inst. of Philosophy, Phi Beta Kappa, Sigma Phi. Club: Berkeley. Author: Whence Cometh Help, 1902; Christ and the Eternal Order, 1906; Personality and the Christian Ideal, 1909; John Knox McLean, a Biography, 1914; Mysticism and Modern Life, 1915; Progressive Religious Thought in America, 1919; Religion as Experience, 1922; Personality and Psychology, 1924; The Humanity of God, 1928; Christianity and Personality, 1935; The Inner World, 1941. Co-editor of George Holmes Horrison, 1934. Contbr. to religious mags. Lecturer Am. Sch. of Religion, Athens, Greece. 1927. Home: 101 Tamalpais Rd., Berkeley, Calif. Died Mar. 30, 1945.

BUCKLEY, John Peter, dental educator; b. Lowell, Lake County, Ind., Dec. 20, 1873; s. William and Nancy Elizabeth (Darst) B.; grad. teachers' course, Valparaiso U., 1894, Ph.G., 1896; D.D.S., Chicago Coll. Dental Surgery, 1898; m. Jennie M. Snyder, Sept. 25, 1898; 1 son, Clarence Elmore. Dir. chem. lab., Chicago Coll. Dental Surgery, 1896-1903; prof. materia medica and therapeutics, Coll. of Dentistry (U. of Ill.), 1903-04; same, Chicago Coll. Dental Surgery, 1904, 27; prof. dental history and economics, Coll. of Dentistry (U. of Southern Calif.), 1919-26. Pres. Hollywood Y.M.C.A. since 1926; foreman of Los Angeles County Grand Jury, 1934; mem. Las Angeles Police Commn. since 1938. Fellow Am., Coll. Dentists. Mem. Am. Dental Assn. (pres. 1923), Ill. State Dental Soc. (pres. 1916), Alumni Assn. Chicago Coll. Dental Surgery (pres. 1902), Odontographic Soc. Chicago (pres. 1904), Delta Sigma Delta (supreme grand master 1929). Republican. Presbyterian. Mason (K.T., Shriner). Clubs: Hollywood Athletic, Masonic (Hollywood); Los Angeles Country. Author: Modern Dental Materia Medica, Pharmacology and Therapeutics, 1909; Handbook on Dental Therapeutics, 1911; etc. Pres. Buckley Pharmacal Co. Home: 7056 Los Tilos Rd., Hollywood, Calif. Died May 14, 1942.

BUCKNER, Mortimer Norton, banker; b. New Orleans, La., Mar. 10, 1873; s. Newton and Pamela (Norton) B.; B.A., Yale, 1895, M.A., 1928; LL.D., Colgate, 1932; m. Paula Kellerman, 1908; children—Caroline, Newton. Pres. New York Trust Co., 1916-

21, chmn. bd. since 1921; chmn. board, The New York Trust Co., v.p. Houbigant, Inc., Cheramy, Inc.; dir. Am. Canadian Properties Corp., Carolina, Clinchfield & Ohio Ry. Co., C.,M.&St.Paul Ry. Co., Carolina Clinchfield & Ohio Ry. of S.C., Clinchfield Northern Ry. of Ky., Columbia Graphophone Factories Corp., City of N.Y. Insurance Co., New York Life Ins. Co., Safe Deposit Co. of the N.Y. Trust Co., Pa. Water & Power Co., Roseton Brick Co., Provident Loan Society of the City of N.Y., Home Ins. Co., J. P. Maguire & Co., Nat. Distillers Products Corp., Internat. Power Securities Corp., Pres. Nat. Credit Corp. ($500,000,000 bankers pool), 1931. Vice-pres. Dodge Memorial Fund; treas. State Charities Aid Assn.; trustee The Boys' Club of New York, Miriam Osborn Memorial Home Assn., Ednl. & Development Farmers Fedn. Fund, Asheville, N.C.; dir. and chmn. exec. com. New York Worlds Fair 1939, Inc. Clubs: University, Yale, Racquet and Tennis, Links, City Midday, Recess, Jekyll Island, Madison Square Garden, Fishers Island, New York Yacht, Nat. Golf Links, Garden City Golf, Southside Sportsmen's, Links Golf. Home: Fishers Island, N.Y. Office: 100 Broadway, New York, N.Y. Died Feb. 25, 1942.

BUCKNER, Simon Bolivar, Jr., army officer; b. Munfordville, Ky., July 18, 1886; s. Simon Bolivar (lt. gen. C.S.A.) and Delia Hayes (Claiborne) B.; student Va. Mil. Inst., 1902-04; B.S., U.S. Mil. Acad., 1908; grad. advanced course, Inf. Sch., Fort Benning, Ga., 1924, Command and Gen. Staff Sch., Fort Leavenworth, Kan., 1925, Army War Coll., Washington, D.C., 1929; m. Adele Blanc, Dec. 30, 1916; children—Simon Bolivar III, Mary Blanc, William Claiborne. Commd. 2d lt. inf., U.S. Army, 1908, advanced through grades to lieut. gen. (temp.), 1943; served as maj. aviation sect., Signal Corps, comdr. training brigs., World War; instr. inf. tactics, U.S. Mil. Acad., 1919-23; instr. Command and Gen. Staff Sch., 1925-28; exec. officer, Army War Coll., 1929-32; asst. comdt. cadets U.S. Mil. Acad., 1932, comdt., 1933-36; comdr. 66th Inf. (light tanks), 1937-38, 22nd Inf., 1938-39; chief of staff 6th div., 1939-40; comdg. gen. Alaska Defense Force, July 1940; comdg. gen., Okinawa, 1945. Mem. S.A.R., Aztec Club of 1847, Ends of the Earth Club. Democrat. Protestant. Clubs: Army and Navy, Army, Navy and Marine Corps Country (Washington, D.C.). Address: Hdqrs. A.D.C., care Postmaster, Seattle, Wash. Killed in action, Okinawa, June 18, 1945.

BUCKNER, Thomas Aylette, insurance; b. Bloomingdale, Ill., Jan. 18, 1865; s. Walker and Margaret (Tully) B.; ed. Woodland Coll., Independence, Mo.; m. Myrtie Lewis; children—Thomas Aylette, Mrs. Mary Buckner Washburn. Began as office boy with New York Life Ins. Co., pres., 1931-36, chmn. bd. 1936-40. Mem. Southern Kansas Soc., New England Soc. Home: Riverdale-on-Hudson, N.Y. Office: 51 Madison Ave., New York, N.Y. Died Aug. 8, 1942.

BUCKWALTER, Tracy V., consultant Timken Roller Bearing Co.; b. Jersey Shore, Pa., Apr. 28, 1880; s. David B. and Ellen Virginia (Harmen) B.; grad. Woodward Township High Sch., Houtzdale, Pa., 1895; m. Hattie Mae Emmons, Oct. 22, 1902 (died May 21, 1941); children—Lawrence E., Emory T., Theodore J., Eugene P., Norman R., Tracy V.; m. 2d, Sara Porter Gregory, Nov. 18, 1941. Began as apprentice with elec. contractor, Phila., 1896; with Pa. R.R., Altoona, Pa., as machinist, 1900, asst. foreman, 1901, draftsman, 1906, foreman motive power engring. dept., 1911; with Timken Roller Bearing Co., Canton, O., as chief engr., 1916-22, vice president, 1922-46; dir. Spun Steel Corp., developed electric trucks, gas-electric locomotives, while at Altoona roller bearing steel mills, roller bearing machine tools Timken locomotive, inexpensive bearing for automotive vehicles, etc.; has supervised tests of locomotive and railroad car axles under auspices Assn. Am. Railroads since 1933, steam locomotive balancing since 1936. Mem. Soc. Automotive Engrs., Am. Soc. Mech. Engrs., Am. Welding Soc., A.A.A.S., Am. Geog. Soc., Ohio Forestry, Am. Museum Natural History, Ohio Chamber of Commerce, Princeton Engring. Assn. (Bracket mem), Awarded Modern Pioneer by Nat. Assn. Mfrs., 1939; Henderson Medal by Franklin Inst. for transportation of roller bearings, 1946. Presbyterian. Clubs: Canton, Brookside Country (Canton); Catawba Cliffs Beach, Catawba Cliffs Yacht (Lakeside, O.); Coral Ridge Yacht (Ft. Lauderdale); and railway clubs in N.Y. City, Pittsburgh, Buffalo, Toronto, Montreal, Chicago, Atlanta. Author of several technical booklets on axle testing, roller bearings, locomotives, automotive equipment, etc. Author: The Railroad. Home: 2301 Del Mar Place, Ft. Lauderdale, Fla. Died March 14, 1948; buried in Lauderdale Memorial Park, Ft. Lauderdale.

BUDD, Edward G., mfr.; pres. Edward G. Budd Mfg. Co., Budd Wheel Co., Budd International Corp. (dir. several other cos.). Home: 157 Pelham Rd., Germantown, Pa. Office: 25th St. and Hunting Park Av., Philadelphia, Pa.* Died Nov. 30, 1946.

BUDGE, David Clare, surgeon, corp. exec.; b. Paris, Ida., Sept. 27, 1873; s. William and Ann (Hyer) B.; Brigham Young Coll., 1892-94; D.D.S., Chicago Coll. Dental Surgery, 1898; M.D., Rush Med. Coll. (U. of Chicago), 1900; m. Retta Bowen, Apr. 29, 1903; children—Rush C., Ruth Ann. Began practice at Logan, Utah, 1900; established William Budge Memorial Hosp., 1903, now med. dir.; est. Budge Clinic, 1905, formerly chief of staff; med. and chief surgeon both instns.; formerly surgeon Amalgamated Sugar Co., Ore. Shortline R.R. Co., Utah-Ida., Central R.R. Co.; pres. D.C. Budge Co., Consolidated Investment Co., Budge Holding Co., Budge Land & Livestock Co., Budge Holding Co., Consolidated Investment Co., dir. First Security Corp. of Ogden (chain of 35 banks); chmn. advisory bd. First Security Bank of Logan. President Utah State Bd. Med. Examiners, 1903-18. Fellow Am. Coll. Surgeons, Am. Coll. Dentists; mem. A.M.A., Utah State Med. Assn. (pres. 1934-35), Sigma Nu. Republican. Mem. Ch. of the Latter Day Saints. Rotarian. Traveled around world, through 21 countries, 1932. Home: 69 East 1st N. Office: 3 N. Main St., Logan, Utah. Died June 22, 1947; buried in Logan Cemetery, Logan, Utah.

BUEHLER, Henry Andrew (bū'lĕr), geologist; b. Monroe, Wis., May 27, 1876; s. Andrew and Katherine (Bleiler) B.; A.B., U. of Wis., 1901; hon. D.Sc., U. of Mo., 1925; unmarried. Asst. state geologist, Mo., 1901-07; mining geologist, 1907-08; state geologist, Mo., since 1908, also dir. Mo. Bur. Geology and Mines. Mem. Am. Geol. Soc., Am. Inst. Mining and Metall. Engrs. (pres. 1935), Soc. Econ. Geologists, Am. Assn. Petroleum Geologists, A.A.A.S., St. Louis Acad. Science, Wis. Acad. Sciences, Arts and Letters Tau Beta Pi. Clubs: Noonday (St. Louis); Cosmos (Washington, D.C.). Home: Rolla, Mo. Died Mar. 14, 1944.

BUELL, Raymond Leslie, publicist; b. at Chicago, Ill., July 13, 1896; s. Rev. Henry Charles and Laura May (Mohler) B.; A.B., Occidental Coll., Los Angeles, Calif., 1918; student U. of Grenoble, Isère, France, 1919; M.A., Princeton, 1920, Ph.D., 1923; LL.D., Miami U., 1936, Occidental Coll., 1937; m. Frances March Dwight, June 26, 1928; children—Elizabeth Winslow, Henry Dwight. Asst. prof. history and economics, Occidental Coll., 1920-21; instr. in govt., Harvard, 1922-25, asst. prof., 1926-27; lecturer in colonial govt., Columbia; lecturer in govt., U. of Calif., summer 1922; visiting prof. in internat. relations, Yale, 1930-31; lecturer, Sch. of Pub. and Internat. Affairs, Princeton, 1931-32; lecturer, New Sch. of Social Research, N.Y. City, 1932; visiting lecturer in internat. relations, Harvard, 1933-34; special lecturer in internat. politics, Fletcher Sch. of Law and Diplomacy, since 1938; adviser on foreign affairs Time, Incorporated. Served with A.E.F., 1918-19. Investigated political conditions in Africa under auspices of Bureau of International Research, Harvard and Radcliffe, 1925-26; research dir., of Foreign Policy Assn., 1927-33; rep. of Foreign Policy Assn. at Pan-American Conf., Havana, 1928; pres. Foreign Policy Assn., 1933-39; lecturer Williamstown Inst. of Politics, 1928, 32; lecturer Oberlin Peace Inst.; chmn. Commn. on Cuban Affairs, 1934; dir. Geneva Research Center, 1935-36; chmn. Pub. Affairs Com., 1936-38; mem. Wendell Willkie's campaign staff, 1940. Unsuccessful candidate, Rep. congressional primary, 1st Mass. dist., 1942. Mem. Am. Polit. Science Assn., Am. Soc. Internat. Law, Council on Foreign Relations, Phi Beta Kappa, Am. Legion. Presbyn. Republican. Clubs: University (New York); Cosmos (Washington). Author: Contemporary French Politics, 1920; The Washington Conference, 1922; International Relations, 1925, revised edit., 1929; The Native Problem in Africa (2 vols.), 1928; Europe—A History of Ten Years (with aid of Foreign Policy Assn. staff), 1928; Poland: Key to Europe, 1939; Isolated America, 1940. Editor and co-author: New Governments in Europe, 1934, revised edit., 1937; Democratic Governments in Europe, 1935; Liberia: A Century of Survival, 1945. Home: Richmond, Mass. Office: Time and Life Bldg., New York. Died Feb. 20, 1946; buried at Richmond, Mass.

BUENGER, Theodore, college pres.; b. Chicago, Apr. 29, 1860; s. Theodore E. and Martha (Loeber) B.; A.B., Concordia Coll., Ft. Wayne, Ind., 1879; grad. Concordia Theol. Sem., St. Louis, 1882, D.D., 1923; m. Ottilie Meier, Apr. 8, 1885. Ordained Evang. Luth. ministry, 1882; minister to 31 settlements in Northwestern Wis., 1882-84; pastor in Cook County, Ill., 1884-91; pres. Concordia Coll., St. Paul, Minn., since it was founded, 1893. Republican. Address: Concordia College, St. Paul. Died 1943.

BUFFINGTON, Joseph, judge; b. Kittanning, Pa., Sept. 5, 1855; s. Ephrain and Margaret Chambers (Orr) B.; B.A., Trinty Coll., Conn., 1875; LL.D., Lafayette Coll., 1915, also Trinty, U. of Pittsburgh, Princeton, Washington and Jefferson Coll., Grove City Coll., Pa., Mil. Coll., Dickinson Coll.; D.C.L., Mt. St. Mary's Coll.; m. Mary Alice Simonton, Jan. 29, 1885; 1 son, Joseph. Admitted to bar, 1878; practiced at Kittanning, Pa., 1878-92; U.S. dist. judge, Western Dist. Pa., 1892-1904; U.S. circuit judge, 3d Circuit, since Sept. 21, 1906; sr. and presiding judge U.S. Circuit Court of Appeals. Decorated Chevalier Order of the Golden Crown (Italian); Order of the White Lion (Czechoslovakia). Sr. trustee Trinity (Conn.) Coll.; chmn. Henry C. Frick Ednl. Commn. for endowment of pub. schs.; mem. Carnegie Hero Commn. Mem. Psi Upsilon, Phi Beta Kappa. Republican. Episcopalian. Address: U.S. Court House, Philadelphia, Pa.* Died Oct. 21, 1947.

BUGBEE, Henry Greenwood, urologist; b. Waterbury, Conn., 1881; s. Walter T. and Flora (Greenwood) B.; M.D., Columbia U. Coll. of Physicians and Surgeons, 1903; m. Della Searles, 1906; children—Dorothy B. Kelsey, Eleanor Clift, Henry G., Jr. Surgeon-in-chief, Vassar Brothers Hosp., 1906-10; urologist, Woman's and Lawrence hosps. (pres. med. bd.); urologist, St. Luke's Hosp., New York; consulting urologist Vassar Bros. Hosp. (Poughkeepsie), Muhlenberg Hosp. (Plainfield), Mountainside Hosp. (Montclair), Mather Hosp. (Port Jefferson). Fellow Am. Coll. Surgeons; mem. Alumni of St. Luke's Hosp. (ex-pres.), N.Y. Acad. of Medicine, A.M.A. (former chmn. sect. of urology), Am. Urol. Assn. (ex-pres.), Am. Assn. of Genito-Urinary Surgeons (ex-pres., ex-sec.), Am. Bd. Urology, N.Y. Urol. Assn. (ex-pres.), Clin. Soc. of Genito-Urinary Surgeons (sec., pres.), Quiz Med. Soc., Royal Med. Soc. (Budapest), Société d'Urologie Française, Société Internationale d'Urologie (del. for U.S.; pres. of Congress 1939). Clubs: Hospital Graduates (ex-pres.), Charaka, University, Century. Author of 80 articles on urological subjects, also sect. in Lewis' Surgery. Mem. editorial bd. Jour. of Urology. Home: 124 E. 38th St. Office: 2 E. 54th St., New York, N.Y. Died Jan. 17, 1945.

BUGBEE, Lucius Hatfield, clergyman, editor; b. Glendale, O., Apr. 29, 1874; s. Lucius Halen and Emily Jane (Fish) B.; A.B., Boston U., 1897, S.T.B., 1899; M.A., U. of Chicago, 1901; D.D., Grove City Coll., 1906; S.T.D., Syracuse, 1930; m. Georgia M. Scofield, July 1, 1903; children—Robert Earl, Lucius Hatfield, Warren Albert, Elizabeth, Georgia Anna. Ordained M.E. ministry 1898; pastor Bemus Point, N.Y., 1899-1900, Stone Ch., Meadville, Pa., 1901-07, St. Mark's, Brookline, Mass., 1907-11, Centre Ch., Malden, Mass., 1911-16, Christ Ch., Pittsburgh, Pa., 1916-20, Hennepin Av. Ch., Minneapolis, Minn., 1920-30; editor ch. sch. publs. of M.E. Ch. since 1930; editor and exec. sec. of editorial division Board of Edn. of the Meth. Church since 1940. Retired, 1945. Served at mil. camps under Y.M.C.A., World War I. Mem. Phi Beta Kappa, Beta Theta Pi. Club: University. Author: Flutes of Silence, 1920; Living Leaders, 1923; Christ Today, 1926; The Divine Presence, 1930; The Sanctuary, 1947. Home: 90 Lakeside Dr., Bemis Point, N.Y. Died Feb. 22, 1948.

BUGGE, Sven Brun (bōō'gȧ), engineer, business exec.; b. Larvik, Norway, Jan. 9, 1878; s. Sven Brun and Henriette (Corneliussen) B.; grad. Horten (Norway) Tech. Sch., 1898; m. Doris Charnock, Nov. 22, 1911. Formerly connected with Jensen & Dahl, Oslo, Norway; Lubecker Machinenbau Gesellschaft, Germany; La Compagnie de pulp de Chicoutimi, and Brompton Pulp and Paper Co. (both Prov. of Quebec), Conn. Valley Timber Co., McIndoes, Vt.; engineered plant at Mosinee, Wis., 1910-11; built board mill, Bogalusa, La., and Kraft mill at Ocean Falls, B.C.; built plant of Tomahawk (Wis.) Kraft Paper Co., became vice pres. and gen. mgr., 1924, later pres. and gen. mgr. until retirement, 1946; pres. Bradley Bank since 1929 Life mem. Am. Soc. M.E., Am. Forestry Assoc. Republican. Episcopalian. Home: Tomahawk, Wisconsin. Died Aug. 9, 1949.

BUIST, Archibald Johnston (bū'ist), surgeon, gynecologist; b. Charleston, S.C., Feb. 7, 1872; s. John Somers and Margaret Sinclair (Johnston) B.; grad. Lawrenceville (N.J.) Sch., 1889; A.B., Princeton U., 1893; M.D., Med. Coll. State of S.C., 1896; m. Alice Stock Mitchell, 1899; 1 son, Archibald Johnston; m. 2d, Elizabeth Roller Gestefeld, 1916. Began practice at Charleston, 1896; prof. gen. surgery, Med. Coll. State of S.C., 1904-10, prof. abdominal surgery and gynecology, 1910-12, prof. gynecology, 1912-39, emeritus prof. of gynecology since 1939; visiting gynecologist Roper Hosp. Mem. Am. Bd. of Surgery. Dir. Francis Marion Hotel (Charleston). Formerly surgeon gen. S.C. State Militia; served as chmn. 3d Dist. Med. Advisory Bd. of S.C., draft period, World War, and chmn. local chapter Am. Red Cross. Pres. bd. trustees Charleston Museum; trustee Enston Home. Fellow Am. Coll. Surgeons, Southern Surg. Soc., Southeastern Surg. Congress; mem. Am. and Southern med. assns., Cap and Gown (Princeton). Mason, K.P. Episcopalian. Home: 132 Tradd St. Office: 279 Meeting St., Charleston, S.C. Died Sep. 12, 1943.

BUIST, Henry (bŭst), lawyer; b. Charleston, S.C., Mar. 3, 1863; s. George Lamb and Martha Allston (White) B.; grad. Episcopal Acad. of Conn., Cheshire, 1880; A.B., Yale, 1884; law, U. of Va., 1885; m. Frances Gualdo Ravenel, Oct. 20, 1887; children—George Lamb, Harriott Ravenel (Mrs. Augustine T. Smythe), Frances Gualdo Ravenel (Mrs. George E. Grimball), Henry. Admitted to S.C. bar, 1886, and began practice at Charleston, mem. Buist & Buist, now sr. mem.; counsel for Carolina Savings Bank (dir.), S.A.L. Ry., Standard Oil Co. of N.J., Metropolitan Life Ins. Co., Atlantic Life Ins. Co., Armour Fertilizer Works, Am. Agrl. Chem. Co., New Amsterdam Casualty Co., Standard Shipping Co., dir. Eagle & Phoenix Mills. Capt., Palmetto Guard. Mem. Am. and S.C. State bar assns., Psi Upsilon. Episcopalian. Clubs: Charleston, Country of Charleston (Charleston); University (New York). Home: 37 King St. Office: 30 Broad St., Charleston, S.C. Died Nov. 7, 1946.

BULKELEY, Harry Clough, former v.p. Rotary. Internat.; b. Leavenworth, Kan., May 29, 1878; s. Martin Luther and Mary Rebecca (Clough) B.; ed. pub. schs., Leavenworth; m. Irene Calnen, Feb. 20, 1906; children—Kenneth Calnen, Gerald Clough, Eugene Chester, Mary Cathryne (Mrs. Richard Beverly Eyre), Irene Carolyn (Mrs. Charles Walter Reeder), Philip Curtis. Clk., later salesman, W. B. Young Supply Co., Kansas City, Mo., 1898-1901; dept. mgr. Crane Co., 1901-05; gen. mgr. Crampton-Farley Brass Co., 1905-13; sales mgr. Am. Sanitary Mfg. Co., 1913-18, pres.

since 1918; president Reliable Agency, Incorporated; director Abingdon Bank and Trust Company. Mayor, Abingdon, 1917-19. Pres. Abingdon Sch. Bd., 1923-25; trustee Hedding Coll., 1937-40; trustee Illinois Wesleyan Univ., Bloomington, Ill. Pres. Tubular Plumbing Goods Assn.; v.p. Rotary Internat., 1943-44. Republican. Methodist. Mason (32°, Shriner). Clubs: Rotary, Galesburg, Chicago Athletic. Home: 510 W. Adams. Office: 308 E. Latimer, Abingdon, Ill Died Nov. 3, 1948.

BULKLEY, Harry Conant, lawyer; b. Monroe, Mich., Mar. 7, 1870; s. John McClelland and Mary Disbrow (Cole) B.; A.B., U. of Mich., 1892, LL.B., 1895, hon. M.A., 1921, LL.D., 1930; m. Cora Buhl Strong, Aug. 23, 1899. Engaged in law practice, Detroit, since 1895; mem. Bulkley, Ledyard, Dickinson & Wright. Ex-regent U. of Mich. Mem. Am. and Mich. bar assns., Bar Assn. City of Detroit, Am. Law Inst., Delta Kappa Epsilon. Republican. Presbyterian. Clubs: Detroit, University, Yondotega, Grosse Pointe Club. Home: 749 Seminole Av. Office: Union Guardian Bldg., Detroit, Mich. Died Feb. 17, 1943.

BULL, Ernest M., pres. steamship lines; b. Elizabeth, N.J., Oct. 2, 1875; s. Archibald Hilton and Evelyn (Vandeventer) B.; B.S., Cornell U., 1898; m. Edith Upham, Oct. 3, 1899; children—Dorothy (Mrs. Edward B. Wright), Carolyn, E. Myron, Edith Arlyn (Mrs. C. Archer Sterling). Began with A. H. Bull Steamship Company, New York City, 1898, president since 1920; president A. H. Bull & Company, Inc., Bull Insular Line, Inc., Baltimore Insular Line, Inc., Bull Steamship Line, Forty West Street Realty Corp., Ericsson Line, Economical Homes Assn.; dir. Corn Exchange Bank & Trust Co. Mem. Psi Upsilon. Republican. Episcopalian. Clubs: Union League (New York); Montclair (N.J.) Golf. Home: 33 Prospect Av., Montclair, N.J.; also P.O. 317, Monroe, N.Y. Office: 115 Broad St., New York, N.Y. Died Oct. 6, 1943.

BULLARD, Robert Lee, army officer; b. Youngsboro, Ala., Jan. 15, 1861; s. Daniel and Susan (Mizell) B.; ed. Agrl. and Mech. Coll. of Ala.; B.S., U.S. Mil. Acad., 1885; LL.D., Columbia U. and Ala. Poly. Inst.; D.M.S., Pa. Military Coll.; m. Rose D. Brabson; children—Robert Lee, Peter C., Rose, Keith; m. 2d, Mrs. Ella R. Wall, Aug. 1927. Commd. 2d lt., U.S. Army, June 14, 1885; advanced through grades to col., Mar. 11, 1911; brig. gen., June 16, 1917; maj. gen., Nov. 27, 1918; retired Jan. 15, 1925. Served in United States with regiment during Spanish-Am. War, and in P.I. during period of insurrection; built Iligan-Lanao mil. rd. and gov. of Lanao Moros, Mindanao, 1902-04; spl. aid and investigator for the U.S. provisional gov. of Cuba, 1907; supervisor (sec.) of pub. instrn. and fine arts, Cuba, 1908. Comdg. regt., dist. and nat. guard brigade in Mexican Border bandit raids, and nat. guard mobilization on border, 1915-16; comdr. O.T.C., Ark., May, 1917; brig. gen. U.S. Army, June 14, 1917; comdg. 2d Brigade, 1st Div., A.E.F. in France, June, July, Aug. 1917; maj. gen. N.A., Aug. 5, 1917; establishing and condg. various inf. officers' schs. in France, to Dec. 14, 1918; condg. 1st Div. A.E.F., in training maneuvers, trenches and open field in all its engagements and operations against Germans, Dec. 14, 1917-July 14, 1918, 3d Corps, July 14-Oct. 11, 1918; lt. gen., Oct. 16, 1918; maj. gen. (regular army), Nov. 1918; comdg. 2d. Army A.E.F. in all its operations and engagements, training, occupation of enemy territory in France and in Luxembourg, Oct. 11, 1918-Apr. 15, 1919; retired, Jan. 15, 1925, with rank of lieutenant general; president of the National Security League since 1925. Wrote the famous message at the opening of the 2d Battle of the Marne, July 1918, which marked the turning point of the war, concluding with the words, "We are going to counter-attack." Awarded D.S.M., 1918; decorations from France, Belgium and Italy. Author of numerous articles in magazines, newspapers and military journals. Home: 2 E. 86th St., New York, N.Y. Died Sept. 11, 1947; buried U.S. Military Academy Cemetery, West Point, N.Y.

BULLARD, W(ashington) Irving, banker, textile manufacturer and inventor; born in Waltham, Mass.; son of George E. and Mary E. (Green) Bullard; student Boston University, 1905; m. Annie E. Jacobs, Oct. 28, 1903; children—Barbara Anita, Charlotte Frances, Edward Jacobs (major Air Corps); m. 2d, Eleanor Gaither Clark, May 16, 1931; children—Mary Ann, Sarah Clark. Was newspaper reporter, editor bond market dept. Wall St. Jour.; now pres. and owner E. H. Jacobs Mfg. Co., Danielson, Conn.; pres. E. H. Jacobs Mfg. Corp., Charlotte, N.C.; Danielson, Conn.; v.p. McClain Distributing Co., Charlotte, N.C.; dir. and v.p. Wauregan Cotton Mills; treas. Williamsville Buff Mfg. Co.; organizer and 1st pres. Colonial Air Transport; pres. Vineyard Theatres, Inc.; formerly v.p. Merchants Nat. Bank (Boston) and Central Trust Co. (Chicago); was dir. Federal Mutual Fire Ins. Co., Danielson Building & Loan Assn., Federal Mutual Liability Ins. Co. Served in U.S. Navy, World War 1; naval intelligence, U.S. Navy, 1939-42, World War II. Mayor of Danielson 3 terms; mem. city council of Charlotte, 1943-45. Formerly treas. and dir. Nat. Assn. of Cotton Mfrs., 10 yrs., vice pres. and treas. Asso. Industries of Mass., 4 yrs., vice pres. Boston C. of C., 4 yrs., treasurer Boston Music School, Settlement. American treasurer World Cotton Conference; dir. Am. Internat. Chamber. of Commerce; chmn. com. on aeronautics, Chamber of Commerce of U.S.; chmn. com. on aviation, Chicago Assn. Commerce; mem. Chicago Aero Commn. Mem. Beta Theta Pi. Republican. Episcopalian. Clubs: Union League (N.Y. City); University (Boston); Charlotte (N.C.) Country; Union Interalliée (Paris). Author: Textile Mill Stocks as Investments, 1910; Women's Work in War Time, 1917; Whirl of the World, 1921. Lecturer and writer on economic, financial and industrial subjects. Home: 2208 Sherwood Av., Charlotte, N.C. Died June 28, 1948.

BULLINGTON, John P., lawyer; b. Palisade, Colo., April 12, 1899; s. Stephen Davis and Maude (Gilliland) B.; LL.B., Univ. of Tex., 1925, Certificat, Law School Univ. of Paris, 1926, J.S.D., Yale, 1927; m. Frankie Maude Carroll, Dec. 26, 1926; children—Kate, John. Asso. Baker, Botts, Parker & Garwood, 1927-35; partner Baker, Botts, Andrews and Walne, since 1935; dir. Texas and New Orleans R.R. Co., Texas Town Lot Co., Southern Pacific Building Co., Southern Pacific Terminal Co., Van Vleck Co., Union Nat. Bank of Houston; mem. exec. com., dir., Schlumberger Well Surveying Corp.; chairman bd., Electro-Mechanical Research, Inc. Sterling Research Fellow, Yale Law Sch., 1926-27. Mem. Museum of Fine Arts of Houston (pres., bd. of trustees), Inter-Am. Bar Assn (mem. of council), Am. Bar Assn., Am. Law Inst., Am. Soc. of Internat. Law, Am.-Foreign Law Assn., Académie Diplomatique Internationale, Phi Delta Phi, Phi Kappa Psi. Clubs: Tejas, Houston Country, River Oaks Country, Eagle Lake Rod & Gun (Houston), Bankers (New York). Home: 3023 Del Monte Drive. Office: Esperson Bldg., Houston, Tex. Died Jan. 12, 1948.

BULLOCK, Calvin, investment banker; b. Toledo, O., July 26, 1867; s. Calvin and Mary Edgell (Miller) B.; grad. Worcester Academy, 1888; A.B., Williams College, 1892; m. Alice Katherine Mallory, Dec. 28, 1892; children—Calvin Mallory (dec.), Hugh, Katherine Seymour (Mrs. Henry Puryear Cole). Has been in investment banking business since 1894; pres. Nation-Wide Securities Co., U.S. Electric Light & Power Shares, Inc., Carriers & General Corp., Bullock Fund, Ltd., Dividend Shares, Inc., Canadian Investment Fund, Ltd. Mem. Chi Psi. Republican. Episcopalian. Clubs: Bankers, Recess, Union, University, Williams, Piping Rock, Racquet and Tennis, Century, Bond, Pilgrims (New York); Denver; Everglades (Palm Beach); Boca Raton (Boca Raton, Fla.); Lenox (Lenox, Mass.); Mount Royal (Montreal). Home: 720 Park Av. Office: 1 Wall St., New York, N.Y. Died June 22, 1944.

BULLOWA, Jesse G. M. (bŏŏl'ō-wȧ), physician; b. New York, N.Y., Oct. 19, 1879; s. Moritz and Mary (Grunhut) B.; A.B., Coll. City of N.Y., 1899; M.D., Coll. Phys. and Surg. (Columbia), 1903; m. Sadie Nones, Sept. 24, 1907; children—Margaret, James, Elizabeth, Jean, Anne. Visiting physician Harlem and Willard Parker hospitals; clin. professor of medicine, New York Univ. Coll. of Medicine, since 1928; cons. physician N.Y. Infirmary for Women and Children and Norwalk Gen. Hosp., Norwalk, Conn.; cons. Serologist at Long Beach Hosp., Long Beach, N.Y. Trustee Littauer Foundation, Inc. Fellow N.Y. Acad. of Medicine, A.A.A.S., N.Y. Acad of Sciences; mem. Am. Med. Assn., N.Y. Pathol. Soc., Soc. for Exptl. Biology and Medicine, Assn. for Study of Internal Secretions, Nat. Tuberculosis Assn., Am. Assn. Immunologists, American Trudeau Society; also Alpha Omega Alpha and Phi Beta Kappa fraternities. Democrat. Jewish religion. Mason. Translator: Bechold's Colloids in Biology and Medicine, 1919. Author: The Management of the Pneumonias, 1937; The Specific Therapy of the Pneumonias, 1939. Contbr. articles to med. jours. Address: 400 E. 58th St., New York, N.Y. Died Nov. 10, 1943.

BUMPUS, Hermon Carey, educator; b. Buckfield, Me., May 5, 1862; s. Laurin A. and Abbie Ann (Eaton) B.; Ph.B., Brown U., 1884; Ph.D., Clark U., 1891; Sc.D., Tufts, 1905, Brown, 1905; LL.D., Clark, 1909; m. L. Ella Nightingale, Dec. 28, 1886; children—Hermon Carey, Laurin Dudley. Prof. biology, Olivet Coll., 1886-89; fellow Clark U., 1889-90; asst. prof. zoölogy, Brown U., 1890-91, asso. prof. zoölogy, 1891-92, prof. comparative anatomy, 1892-1901; asst. dir. Marine Biol. Lab., 1893-95; dir. biol. lab. U.S. Fish Commn., Woods Hole, 1898-1901; asst. to pres. and curator dept. invertebrates, 1901-02, dir., 1902-11, Am. Museum Natural History, New York; business mgr. U. of Wis., 1911-14; pres. Tufts Coll., 1914-19; sec. Corp. Brown U., 1924-39; consulting dir. Buffalo Museum of Science, 1925-30; mem. Bd. Fellows, Brown U., since 1905; mem. faculty of pure science Columbia U., 1905-11. Trustee R.I. Hosp., 1895-1901, Home for Feeble Minded, Waverly, Mass., 1915-19, Somerville Pub. Library, 1915-18, Children's Museum, Boston, 1915-19; trustee Marine Biol. Lab., Woods Hole, since 1900; trustee Am. Sch. of Prehistoric Research since 1918; trustee Mt. Desert Biol. Lab. since 1924; mem. Bd. Edn., New Rochelle, N.Y., 1908-11; chmn. Mass. Security League, 1919. Awarded Pugsley Medal by Am. Scenic and Historic Preservation Society, 1941; Am. Assn. of Museums diploma, 1941. Pres. American Morphol. Society, 1902, Am. Soc. Zoölogists, 1903, R.I. Audubon Soc., 1899, 1902, Am. Assn. of Museums, 1906, Fourth Internat. Fishery Congress, Washington, 1908; mem. Am. Soc. Naturalists (sec. 1895-98, v.p. 1899), Nat. Assn. Audubon Socs., Peary Arctic Club, Am. Philos. Soc.; fellow A.A.A.S., N.Y. Acad. of Sciences (rec. sec. 1905, corr. sec. 1909); hon. mem. R.I. Med. Soc., K. K. Oesterreichische Fischerei-Gesellschaft, Vienna; hon. fellow Met. Museum of Art; corr. mem. Senckenbergische Naturforschende Gesellschaft, Frankfurt a M; chmn. Com. on Museums in Nat. Parks; chmn. advisory bd. Nat. Park Service, 1936-40. Mem. Phi Beta Kappa. Author: A Laboratory Course in Invertebrate Zoölogy, 1893. Also numerous monographs and articles on biol. and ednl. subjects. Home: Duxbury, Mass. Died June 21, 1943.

BUNKER, Frank Forest, educator, author; b. El Dara, Ill., Jan. 17, 1873; s. Theodore C. and Clara (Wood) B.; diploma State Normal Sch., Los Angeles, Calif., 1893; Ph.B., U. of Calif., 1901; Ph.D., New York U., 1913; m. Isabel Ball, 1899 (died 1906); m. 2d, Gertrude Deane, Dec. 1908. Prin. elementary schs., Calif., until 1898; prin. high sch., Santa Rosa, 1898-1900; instr. pedagogy and psychology, State Normal Sch., San Francisco, 1901-06; asst. supt. schs., Seattle, Wash., 1906-07, Los Angeles, 1907-08; supt. schs., Berkeley, 1908-12; mgr. oil corp., La., 1912-18; chief of city sch. div. U.S. Bur. Edn., Washington, D.C., 1918-21; exec. sec. Pan Pacific Union, Honolulu, T.H., 1921-24; editor Carnegie Instn. of Washington, 1926-39. Christian Sci. Com. on Publ. for Dist. of Columbia, 1939—. Dir. edn. surveys of Columbia, S.C., Memphis, Tenn., Wilmington, Del., and Hawaii. Author: Reorganization of the American School System (Bur. of Edn. publ.), 1918; Hawaii and the Philippines, 1928; China and Japan, 1928; The Junior High School Movement—Its Beginnings, 1935; also many govt. reports, bulls., and mag. articles. Initiated Junior High Sch. movement, now nation-wide, by reorganizing pub. sch. system, Berkeley, Calif., 1909. Home: 1736 Columbia Rd. N.W., Washington, D.C. Died Sep. 25, 1944.

BURBANK, Elbridge Ayer, artist; b. Harvard, Ill., 1858; s. A. J. and Annie M. B.; pupil Acad. Design, Chicago; later studied under Paul Navin and Frederick Fehr at Munich. Awards: Yerkes 1st prize, Chicago, 1893; medal and hon. mention, Atlanta Expn., 1895. Exhibited at Paris Expn., 1900. Began painting of N.Am. Indians, 1897, has since made portraits of 125 different types; rep. in collections of Field Mus. and Newberry Library, Chicago, Smithsonian Instn., Washington, and elsewhere. Home: 602 Emporia St., Muskogee, Okla. Died 1949.

BURCH, Edward Parris, cons. engr.; b. Menomonie, Wis., Aug. 1870; s. Newell and Susan (Parris) B.; E.E., U. of Minn., 1892; m. Harriet Jackson; 1 dau., Mrs. Imogene Wolcott. Elec. engr. Twin City Rapid Transit Co., 1892-99, in charge of installing 10,000-horsepower plant for utilizing the water power of St. Anthony's Falls for operating the electric rys. of Minneapolis and St. Paul; consulting engr., specializing in water power and elec. power work since 1900; dir. Minneapolis, Northfield & Southern Ry. Lecturer on electric railroading, 1902-10, prof. ry. elec. engring., 1913-14, U. of Minn. Consulting engr. Detroit Electric Ry. Commn., 1914-15; mem. research com. Minn. Com. Pub. Safety, 1917; ry. and power valuations, 1921-26; receiver Minneapolis, Anoka & Cuyuna Range Ry., 1926-29; cons. engr., Burch & McWethy, 1930-36; mem. Mayor's Survey Commn., Minneapolis, 1930. Mem. Am. Inst. E.E., Geol. Soc. of Minn. (pres. 1938), Phi Gamma Delta. Presbyterian. Author: Electric Traction for Railway Trains, 1911, Telephone Rates in Detroit, 1916-20. Home: 1729 James Av. S., Minneapolis, Minn. Died May 4, 1945.

BURCHARD, Edward Lawver (bûr'chärd), civic worker; b. Freeport, Ill., Sept. 5, 1867; s. Horatio Chapin and Jane (Lawver) B.; Ph.B., Beloit (Wis.) Coll., 1891; spl. studies, U. of Chicago, 1894; m. Alice Barton, Oct. 4, 1893; 1 dau., Marion B. (Mrs. R. P. Bradish); first man resident of Hull House, Chicago, 1891-92; chief clk., mines dept., World's Fair, Chicago, 1892-93; recorder and librarian, Field Museum Natural History, 1894-98; chief of library and archives division, U.S. Coast and Geodetic Survey, Washington, D.C., 1898-1903; chief of div., Library of Congress, 1903-06; sec. Civic League, Freeport, Ill., 1908-09; sec. Chicago School of Civics and Philanthropy and later dir. of its Extension Dept. (now Sch. of Social Service Adminstrn., U. of Chicago), 1909-14; dir. various City Club civic exhibits, with field trip to Europe, 1912-15; sec. Civics Extension Com., Chicago, 1914-16; sec. Chicago Community Center Conf., 1916; sec. Nat. Community Center Assn., 1917-20; asst. to U.S. Food Adminstrn. and aid to Council of Nat. Defense on community councils, 1917, Washington, D.C.; asso. editor The Community Center (mag.), 1920-24; exec. sec. Chicago Youth Week, 1927-35; sec. Supt. of Schools Advisory Council, Chicago, 1926-34; sec. Education Club (adminstrs. in Chicago Regional Area), 1928-36; chief of Div. of Ednl. Tours, Century of Progress Expn., 1934; exec. sec. Chicago Recreation Commn., 1935-40, now actg. executive; mem. Society of Recreation Workers of America, Nat. Edn. Assn., Business Men's Research Foundation, Coördinating Councils (nat. incorporation), Beta Theta Pi. Club: Chicago Rotary No. 1. Author and compiler of various publs. of the Chicago School of Civics and Philanthropy, Chicago City Club, Edn. Dept. of Chicago Public Schools; also author, "Early Trails and Tides of Travel to the Blackhawk Country" (issued by Ill. Hist. Soc.); Genealogy of the Shellenberger Family, 1939. Contbr. to jours. Home: Woodmere Hotel, Chicago, and 1042 Lincoln Av., Freeport, Ill. Address: 1630 Burnham Bldg., Chicago, Ill. Died Nov. 29, 1944.

BURCHFIELD, Albert Horne, mcht.; m. Clara A. Dicken; 1 son, Albert Horne. Chmn. of bd. Joseph Horne Co., dept. store, Pittsburgh, Pa. Clubs: Duquesne, Pittsburgh Athletic, Longue Vue, Shannopin Country. Home: 210 Tennyson Av. Office: Penn Av. and Stanwix St., Pittsburgh, Pa. Died Feb. 17, 1942.

BURDELL, William Frederick, chmn. bd. Huntington Nat. Bank of Columbus; b. Columbus, O., Dec. 22, 1857; s. William and Dorothy B.; ed. pub. schs., Columbus; married, Nov. 10, 1880; children—Fred W., Robert K., Dorothy, Edwin S. Chmn. bd. Huntington Nat. Bank of Columbus. Home: 665 E. Broad St. Office: 17 S. High St., Columbus, O. Died Nov. 10, 1945.

BURDEN, Oliver D., lawyer; b. Nelson, N.Y., Mar. 15, 1873; s. James H. and Lucia (Groesbeck) B.; Ph.B., Cornell U., 1896; LL.B., 1897; m. Irene de Tamble, June 26, 1905; children—Oliver D., Natalie, Mary de T. Admitted to the New York bar, 1898, and began practice at Syracuse; chmn. Draft Bd., 22 mos., 1917-18; became U.S. dist. atty., Northern Dist. of N.Y., 1923. Atty. for Theodore Roosevelt in libel case of Wm. Barnes vs. Roosevelt. Mem. Am., N.Y. State and Onondaga County bar assns., Commercial Law League, Delta Chi, Sigma Tau, Quill and Dagger. Republican. Presbyterian. Mason (Shriner), Odd Fellow, K.P. Clubs: Syracuse Century, Onondaga Golf. Home: 509 University Pl. Office: University Bldg., Syracuse, N.Y. Died Nov. 10, 1947.

BURDETT, William Carter, foreign service officer; b. Nashville, Tenn., Feb. 3, 1884; s. William Potter and Serafina (Carter) B.; educated at University of Tennessee; m. Elizabeth Hardwick Burke, Jan 18, 1918; children—William Carter, Edward Burke, Agnes Elizabeth, Mary Elizabeth. Mining engineer and mine operator, South America, 1903-06, Greenville, Tenn., 1906-17; U.S. consul, Ensenada, Mexico, 1919-22, Seville, Spain, 1922-25, Brussels, Belgium, 1925-30; consul gen., Lima, Peru, 1930-32; sec. of Embassy, Lima, 1932; sec. of Legation, Panama, 1933-35; consul gen. Buenos Aires, Argentina, 1935-37; consul gen. Rio de Janeiro, Brazil, 1937-39; counselor of Embassy, Rio de Janeiro, 1939-41; dir. Foreign Service Officers Training Sch., 1941-42; mem. Foreign Service Sch. Bd. since 1941. Served in U.S. Army, Philippine Insurrection, 1900-03; capt. inf., U.S. Army, World War; wounded at battle of Blanc Mont; maj. O.R.C. Awarded D.S.C. (U.S.); Croix de Guerre (France); Purple Heart (U.S.). Mem. S.A.R. Office: (U.S.) care Hermitage Cement Co., Knoxville, Tenn. Address: State Dept., Washington, D.C.* Died Jan. 14, 1944.

BURDICK, Charles Kellogg, prof. law; b. Utica, N.Y., Feb. 7, 1883; s. Francis M. and Sarah Underhill (Kellogg) B.; B.A., Princeton, 1904; LL.B., Columbia, 1908; m. Ruth Nutting, May 26, 1909. Practiced with law firm Wilmer, Canfield & Stone, New York, 1908-09, prof. law, Tulane U., 1909-12, U. of Mo., 1912-14, Cornell U., since 1914, acting dean, 1923-24, 1925-26, dean, 1926-36; prof. law, summer sessions, Columbia Univ., 1912, 13, 14, 16, Univ. of Chicago, 1925, Stanford Univ., 1928; asso. mem. All Souls Coll., Oxford, Eng., 1930. Asso. dir. Bur. of Information Service, Dept. of Civilian Relief, Am. Red Cross Hdqrs., 1918. Mem. N.Y. State Commn. to Investigate Adminstrn. of Justice, 1931-39. Mem. N.Y. State Judicial Council, 1934; chmn. N.Y. State Law Revision Commn., 1934. Counsel to Gov. Lehman of New York in Geoghan removal proceedings, 1936. Mem. Am. and N.Y. State bar associations, Acad. Polit. Science, Am. Law Inst., Internat. Law Assn., Am. Soc. Internat. Law, Am. Judicature Soc., Adv. Com. of Research in Internat. Law, Cap and Gown (Princeton), Phi Delta Phi (Columbia), Phi Kappa Phi, Order of the Coif. Unitarian. Club: Century (New York). Author: The Law of the American Constitution; Burdick's Cases on the Law of Public Service and Carriers (2d edit.); Model Draft of an Extradition Convention, with Comment; also numerous law revs. and mag. articles. Co-author of article on Law and Jurisprudence in Am. Year Book, 1918; editor 4th edit. Burdick's Law of Torts and 4th edit. Burdick's Cases on Torts. Home: Myron Taylor Tower, Ithaca, N.Y. Died June 22, 1940.

BURDICK, Clark, ex-congressman; b. Newport, R.I., January 13, 1868; s. J. Truman and Emily F. (Sherman) B.; student Harvard Law Sch., 1893-94; m. Elizabeth L. Peckham, Feb. 9, 1898. Practiced at Newport since 1894; city solicitor 2 yrs.; mem. R.I. Ho. of Rep., 1906-08, Senate, 1915-16; mayor of Newport, 1917-18; mem. 66th to 72d Congresses (1919-33), 1st R.I. Dist. Republican. Episcopalian. Mason (32°). Club: Miantonomi (ex-pres.). Home: Newport, R.I. Died Aug. 27, 1948.

BURDICK, William Livesey, prof. law; b. East Greenwich, R.I., Mar. 22, 1860; s. Daniel and Annie (Potter) B.; desc. of Robert Burdick, who came from Eng. to Newport, R.I., in 1651; A.B., Wesleyan U., Conn., 1882, A.M., 1885, LL.D., 1937; Ph.D., Chattanooga U., 1884; Harvard Grad. Sch., 1888-89; LL.B., Yale, 1898; m. Nellie D. Gates, June 29, 1882 (died 1926); children—Harry S. (dec.), Harold D. (dec.), William Leroy, Helen (Mrs. J. K. Laughlin); m. 2d, Elizabeth Pettengill, Nov. 21, 1927. Admitted to Conn. bar, 1886, Kan. bar, 1899; prin. Fargo (N.D.) Coll., 1891-92; instr. U. of Colo., 1892-95; prof. law, Univ. of Kan., 1898, vice-pres., 1916, acting dean School of Law, 1919-22, became dean, 1935, now emeritus. Commr. on Uniform State Laws; civil service commr. of Kan., 1915-21; reviser U.S. statutes, 1919-24. Republican. Conglist. Mem. Phi Beta Kappa, Am. Bar Assn., Kansas Bar Assn., S.A.R., Psi Upsilon, Phi Delta Phi. Mason (33°); grand master, Kan., 1915. Author: Elements of Sales, 1901; Case-Book on Sales, 1907; Real Property, 1914; New Trials and Appeals in Kansas and Oklahoma, 1906. Contbr. of Husband and Wife (Cyclo. of Law), 1906; Appeals (cyclo. of Procedure), 1911; Roman Law, 1938; Bench and Bar of Other Lands, 1939; The Law of Crimes, 1945. Toured the world for special study of foreign legal systems, 1932-33. Contbr. many articles to various encyclopædias of law. Home: Lawrence, Kan.: and Martha's Vineyard, Mass. Died June 11, 1946.

BURFORD, Archie Dean, deputy commr. Bureau Internal Revenue; b. Big Springs, Nebraska, Feb. 5, 1892; s. Wader McKim and Lenora Elizabeth (Ramsey) B.; student Neb. State Teachers Coll., 1911-13; A.B., U. of Wyoming, 1916, grad. work, 1921-23; graduate work, Am. Univ., 1938; m. Carolyn May Russell, Aug. 22, 1914; children—Archie Dean, Benton, Lucille Kathryn (Mrs. L. E. Ofenstein), Eleanor Josephine. High school teacher, prin., dist. supt., Wyo., and instr. summers, U. of Wyo., 1913-24; with U.S. Bureau of Internal Revenue since 1924, as special agent, San Francisco and Seattle, 1924-27, special agent in charge, San Francisco, Memphis, Dallas Divs., 1927-42, acting head unjust enrichment div., 1938-41, dep. commr. since Nov. 1942. Mem. University Club. Mason (Shriner). Home: 2901 Stanford St., Dallas, Tex. Office: 2509 Internal Revenue Bldg., Washington, D.C. Deceased.

BURGE, Flippen D. (bûrj), architect; b. Corinth, Miss., Dec. 6, 1894; s. John David and Decie (Flippen) B.; prep. edn., Montgomery Bell Acad., Nashville, Tenn.; B.S., Ga. Sch. of Tech., 1916; m. Tyler Daniel, Nov. 6, 1917; 1 son, Charles Daniel. Began as draftsman Arthur Tufts Co., Atlanta, 1916; in gen. practice architecture since 1919; now mem. Burge & Stevens. Firm architects for Techwood Homes (1st fed. slum clearance project), Atlanta; also 3 other such projects; architects and engrs., airports, Savannah, Ga., Meridian, Miss., Bainbridge, Ga., Ozark, Ala., Sylvania, Ga., govt. hospitals at Augusta and Atlanta, Ga. Served in U.S. Navy, World War. Mem. Am. Inst. Architects (former sec. for Ga. Chapter), Beta Theta Pi. Club: Piedmont Driving (Atlanta). Architects for Dunkler Hotels, American Bakeries and Beigel Cotton Mills. Baptist. Home: 240 Nacoochee Drive N.W. Office: Palmer Bldg., Atlanta, Ga. Died Apr. 22, 1946; buried in West View Cemetery, Atlanta.

BURGER, John D., pres. Lorr Laboratories; b. Chicago, Ill., Dec. 8, 1887; s. Nathan John and Mary (Reiss) B.; student Chicago Latin Sch., 1902-07, U. of Chicago, 1907-08; m. Kathryn Reynolds, June 12, 1915. Began as salesman for smoker's articles, Chicago, 1912; purchased Kaywoodie Co., New York, 1925; formed Civic Premier Pipe Co., New York, 1920; took over pipe dept. United Cigar Stores Co., 1925; organized Lorr Laboratories, Paterson, N.J., 1933, and since pres.; chmn. bd. Kaywoodie Co. Mason. Clubs: River, Rockefeller Center, Manhattan (New York); Westchester Country (Rye, N.Y.); Turf and Field (Long Island, N.Y.); Augusta National (Augusta, Ga.); Everglades, Bath and Tennis (Palm Beach, Fla.); Boca Raton (Boca Raton, Fla.); The Gatineau Fish and Game Club (Point Comfort, Quebec, Canada). Composer: The Waltz of Memory, 1941; Dreamy Like Music, 1943. Guest on program "We the People" broadcast Feb. 3, 1942, over WABC. Home: 464 Winthrop Rd., West Englewood, N.J.; also "Burgerville" Burgerville, Quebec, Canada. Office: Lorr Laboratories, Paterson, N.J. Died October 31, 1943.

BURGES, Richard Fenner (bûr'jĕs), lawyer; b. Seguin, Tex., Jan. 7, 1873; s. William H. and Bettie (Rust) B.; ed. in pub. schs.; m. Ethel Petrie Shelton, Dec. 7, 1898 (died 1912); 1 dau., Jane Rust (Mrs. Preston R. Perrenot). Admitted to Tex. bar, 1894; city atty., El Paso, 1905-07; mem. Tex. Ho. of Rep., 2 terms, 1913, 17; asso. counsel for U.S. in Chamizal Arbitration with Mexico, 1910-11; pres. Internat. Irrigation Congress, 1915-16; counsel for Tex. interests in negotiations between Tex. and New Mexico on division of waters of Pecos River, 1923; special counsel for Tex., Rio Grande Compact Commn., Colo., N.M. and Tex., apptd. commr. for Tex. on same commn. to execute 1929 compact; gen. counsel, El Paso County Water Improvement Dist.; special atty. Dept. of Justice in regard rectification of channel of the Rio Grande, 1935-40. Served as capt. and major 141st Inf., U.S. Army, during active operations in France, World War. Cited by Marshal Petain; awarded Croix de Guerre with gilt star (French). Mem. Am. Bar Assn., Tex. Bar Assn., Am. Forestry Assn., Tex. Forestry Assn. (pres. 1921-23), Tex. Hist. and Library, Commn., Tex. Hist. Assn., Va. Hist. Soc. Democrat. Author of El Paso Commission Charter, and of Texas Irrigation Code, and Forestry Act. Partially explored and published first account of Carlsbad (N.M.) Cavern which has since been made a nat. park. Special counsel for Tex. in case of Tex. vs. N.M. in U.S. Supreme Court. Home: 603 W. Yandell Blvd. Office: First Nat. Bank Bldg., El Paso, Tex. Died Jan. 13, 1945.

BURGES, William Henry, lawyer; b. Seguin, Tex., Nov. 12, 1867; s. William Henry and Bettie (Rust) B.; LL.B., U. of Tex., 1889; m. Anna Pollard, Sept. 23, 1896. Admitted to bar, 1889; city atty., El Paso, Tex., 1893-96; mem. firm Turney & Burges, El Paso, Tex., 1897-1917, of Gregory, Burges & McNab, Chicago, Mar. 1917-Nov. 1918, of Turney, Burges, Culwell & Pollard, El Paso, Tex., 1918-38, Burges, Burges & Scott, El Paso, 1938-40, Burges, Burges, Scott, Rasberry & Hulse since 1941. Chief counsel, all copper cos. and other defendants in civil and criminal cases arising out of deportation of I.W.W.'s from Bisbee, Ariz., 1917; special asst. to U.S. atty. gen. in charge postal fraud prosecutions, Northern Dist. Tex., 1924. Regent U. of Tex., 1911-14. Mem. Am. Bar Assn. (exec. com. 1912-15), Tex. Bar Assn. (pres. 1909-10), Phi Beta Kappa, Order of Coif; del. to Universal Congress Lawyers and Jurists, St. Louis, 1904. Office: First Nat. Bank Bldg., El Paso, Tex. Died May 11, 1946.

BURGESS, Charles Frederick, chemical engr.; b. Oshkosh, Wis., Jan. 5, 1873; s. Frederick and Anna A. (Heckman) B.; B.S., U. of Wis., 1895, E.E., 1897, Ph.D., 1926; Dr. Engrg., Ill. Inst. Technology, 1944; m. Ida M. Jackson, June 25, 1903; children—Betty, Jackson. Instr. and asst. prof. elec. engring., 1895-1900, prof. applied electro-chemistry and chem. engineering, 1900-13, U. of Wis. Engr. for Wis. R.R. Commn., 1908-13. Pres., chmn. of bd., C. F. Burgess Lab.; dir. Burgess-Parr Co. and Burgess-Manning Co. Inventor process for electrolytic purification of iron; also inventor of various iron alloys, improvement in dry cells, etc.; has taken out over 400 patents covering various products and processes. Awarded Octave Chanute medal by Western Society Engrs., 1911; Perkin medal of Chemical Societies, 1932; Edward Goodrich Acheson award, 1942. Member District Draft Bd. for Southern Wisconsin, 1917-18. Mem. Internat. Jury of Awards, St. Louis Expn., 1904. Mem. Am. Electrochem. Soc. (ex-pres.), Soc. Chem. Industry, Am. Chem. Soc. Am. Gas Inst., Western Soc. Engrs., Am. Electroplaters' Soc., Royal Institution of Gt. Britain, Beta Theta Pi, Tau Beta Pi, Alpha Chi Sigma. Clubs: University, Union League, Lake Shore (Chicago); Chemists' (New York); Niagara (N.Y.). Author sci. and tech. papers dealing with chem. engrg. subjects. Home: Bokeelia, Fla. Address: 180 North Wabash Av, Chicago, Ill. Died Feb. 13, 1945.

BURGESS, Elizabeth Chamberlain, prof. emeritus; b. Bath, Me., 1877; d. George Henry and Marcia Hill (Woodbury) Burgess; diploma Roosevelt Hosp. Nursing School, 1904, Teachers Coll., 1911; B.S., Columbia U., 1923, A.M., 1925; unmarried. Asst. dir. and instr. nursing schools, 1905-12; dir. nursing sch. and supt. nurses, Michael Reese Hosp., Chicago, 1912-16; insp. nursing schs., 1916-20; sec. to Bd. Nurse Examiners, N.Y. State Dept. Edn., 1920-22; lecturer, instr., asst. prof., asso. prof., Teachers Coll., Columbia U., 1920-35, prof. nursing edn., 1935-47. Asst. insp. nursing service, Office Surgeon-Gen. U.S. Army, during World War I. Pres. Nat. League Nursing Edn., 1929-33 and mem. bd. dirs., 1933-41; mem. many coms.; rep. on com. on the grading of nursing schs.; chmn. com. for adminstrn. of accrediting of nursing Schools 1939-48. Episcopalian. Republican. Contbr. articles to profesional jours. Home: 520 W. 114th St., New York, N.Y.; (summer) West Cornwall, Conn. Died July 22, 1949.

BURGESS, Ellis Beaver, clergyman; b. Fort Loudon, Pa., Nov. 19, 1869; s. Andrew and Sarah Catherine (Beaver) B.; A.B., Mercersburg (Pa.) Coll., 1886; A.M., Gettysburg Coll., 1905; grad. Gettysburg Theol. Sem., 1893; D.D., Gettysburg Coll., 1915; LL.D., Thiel Coll., 1930; m. Fannie Louise Brinkerhoff, June 13, 1893; children—Ellis Shields, Milton Valentine. Ordained ministry Luth. Ch., 1893; pastor Avonmore (Pa.) Parish, 1893-95, Connellsville Parish, 1895-1920. Pres. Pittsburgh Synod of Gen. Synod, 1901-02; statis. sec. Gen. Synod, Luth. Ch., 1905-18; pres. Pittsburgh Synod United Luth. Ch., 1919-30; missionary supt. United Luth, Synod of N.Y., 1930-32; church extension rep. Bd. of Am. Missions, 1932; president United Lutheran Synod of N.Y., 1934-39. Presiding officer, U.L.C.A., 1922; mem. exec. bd. U.L.C.A., 1922-30 and 1932-40; mem. exec. com. Nat. Luth. Council, 1930-41, pres. 1937-41, mem. bd. of Protestant Deaconesses, 1920-30. Author: The General Synod in Western Pennsylvania, 1904; Memorial History of the Pittsburgh Synod, 1926. Editor of Centennial History of the Borough of Connellsville; Ministerial Register of The United Lutheran Synod of New York; The Lutherans of Western Pennsylvania. Home: 73 Haldane St., Crafton, Pittsburgh 5, Pa. Died Dec. 20, 1947.

BURGESS, W(illiam) Starling, naval architect and engr.; b. Boston, Dec. 25, 1878; s. Edward and Caroline Louisa (Sullivant) B.; A.B., Harvard, 1901; m. Helene Adams Willard, October, 1901 (died 1902); m. 2d, Rosamond Tudor, Oct. 13, 1904; children—Edward (dec.), Frederick Tudor, Starling; m. 3d, Elsie Janet Foos, Nov. 1925; children—Ann, Diana. Established W. Starling Burgess Co., builders of yachts and commercial vessels, 1904; established Burgess Co. and Curtis, aeroplane builders, Marblehead, Mass., 1910; entered firm Burgess & Morgan, Ltd., naval architects, New York, 1926; mem. Burgess & Donaldson, Inc., since 1931. Designed "Enterprise," defender America's cup against Sir Thomas Lipton's "Shamrock V," 1930; also designer exptl. aluminum ship, 1935. Served as gunner's mate, U.S.S. Prairie, Spanish-Am. War; lt. comdr. Constrn. Corps, U.S.N., World War. Awarded Collier prize, 1915, for greatest progress in aviation during preceding year. Died March 19, 1947.

BURGHALTER, Daniel (bûrg'hăl-tĕr), church official; b. Geneva, Ind., Oct. 16, 1867; s. Christian and Mary (Hartman) B.; prep. edn., Mission House Coll., Plymouth, Wis., 1886-87; A.B., Heidelberg Coll.,

Tiffin, O., 1892, D.D., 1915; grad. Heidelberg Theol. Sem., Tiffin, 1895; m. Paulina T. Miller, June 19, 1895; children—Calvin Miller (dec.), Joel Miller. Ordained ministry Ref. Ch. in U.S., 1895; home missionary, Lima, O., 1895-96; pastor Germantown, O., 1896-98, Dayton, 1898-1901; editor Christian World, 1901-03; pastor Galion, O., 1903-11; field sec. Bd. of Foreign Missions Ref. Ch. in U.S., at Phila., since 1911; prof. missions, Heidelberg Coll., 1916-24; made inspection trip to Japan and China, 1910-20. Retired from active ministry, 1935. Member Interdenominational Laymen's Movement, speakers' bur., O., Pa., and W.Va., 1913-15, and on speakers' team of same at 12 nat. convs.; del. Nat. Laymen's Congress, Washington, 1916; etc. Republican. Author: The History of The First Reformed Church of Galion, O., 1910; Dawning and Turning in Japan and China, 1923; The History of Central Ohio Classics, 1939. Home: 272 E. Market St., Tiffin, O. Died June 21, 1947; buried in Greenlawn Cemetery, Tiffin, O

BURGIN, William Olin, congressman; b. Marion, N.C.; s. Merritt and Mary Elizabeth (Smith) B.; ed. Rutherfordton Mil. Inst., 1890-93; U. of N.C. Law Sch., 1912-13; m. Edith Leigh Greer, Dec. 12, 1912. Began as clerk in general store, 1893, later traveling salesman and merchant; admitted to N.C. bar and began practice in Lexington; pres. and atty. Industrial Bank of Lexington; pres. Carolina Panel Co.; dir. and atty. Commercial Bank of Lexington; dir. United Furniture Co., Industrial Bldg. & Loan Assn. Mem. 76th and 78th Congresses (1939-45), 8th N.C. Dist. Mayor Thomasville, N.C., 1910-12; mem. N.C. Gen. Assembly, 1901, N.C. Senate, 1903. Democrat. Methodist. Mason. K.P. Home: Lexington, N.C.* Died Apr. 11, 1946.

BURK, Joseph Edwill, educator; b. Galveston, Tex., Apr. 9, 1893; s. Joseph Edward and Marie (de Loche) B.; A.B., Southwestern U., 1914; A.M., Southern Meth. U., 1926; Ph. D., New York U., 1930; m. Isabelle Foster, June 28, 1917; children—Jean Marie, Margaret Alice. Teacher, high schools, Tex., 1914-17; teacher of English, Southwest Tex. State Teachers Coll., 1917-18, North Tex. State Teachers Coll., 1923-28; instr. of English, New York U., 1928-30; dean, Ward-Belmont Sch., 1930-39, pres., June 1939; dean, Meredith Coll., Raleigh, N.C., 1945-46. Mem. Tenn. Assn. of Colleges (pres. 1944), Jr. Coll. Assn. of So. Colleges (chmn.), Phi Delta Kappa. Democrat. Methodist. Mason. Club: Kiwanis (pres. 1939). Contbr. to Jr. Coll. Jour. Address: Ward-Belmont School, Nashville, Tenn. Died Oct. 6, 1946; buried at Williamsburg, O.

BURKE, Charles Henry, ex-commr. Indian affairs; b. Genesee County, N.Y., Apr. 1, 1861; s. Walter and Sarah B.; m. Caroline Schlosser, Jan. 14, 1886. Admitted to bar, 1886, but engaged in real estate and investment business. Mem. S.D. Ho. of Rep., 1895-97; mem. 56th to 59th Congresses (1899-1907) and 61st and 62d Congresses (1909-13), S.D. at large, and 63d Congress (1913-15), 2d S.D. Dist.; commr. Indian affairs, 1921-29 (resigned). Commr. to Internat. Colonial and Overseas Expn., Paris, France, 1930-31. Republican. Home: Pierre, S.D. Address: 1870 Wyoming Av., Washington. Died Apr. 7, 1944.

BURKE, Kendall Edwards, educator, clergyman; b. Loveland, Colo., Oct. 23, 1893; s. John J. and Nettie (Clark) B.; A.B., Eugene (Ore.) Bible U., 1919; B.S., Ore. State Coll., 1932, M.S., 1934; D.D., Butler U., 1941; m. Edna Lawrence, Sept. 10, 1917; children—Donald Paul, Hermon Edwin. Ordained to ministry Disciples of Christ Ch., 1916; pastor, Junction City, Ore., 1917-19; asst. pastor Univ. Christian Ch., Seattle, Wash., 1920-21; pastor Ballard Ch., Seattle, 1921-24; pastor, Moscow, Ida., 1924-25, Ellensburg, Wash., 1925-30, Dallas, Ore., 1930-36; prof., Northwest Christian Coll., Eugene, Ore., 1936-39, pres. since 1939. Mem. Kappa Delta Pi. Home: 1192 Jefferson St., Eugene, Ore. Died Mar. 21, 1943.

BURKE, Stephen Patrick, cons. engr.; b. N.Y. City, Mar. 18, 1897; s. Patrick Joseph and Ada May (Finney) B.; B.S., Columbia U., 1917, Chem. Engr., School of Mines, Engring. and Chemistry (Columbia), 1920, Ph.D., Columbia, 1922; m. Catharine Regis Moran, Oct. 1, 1924; children—Stephen Patrick, Joan, William Dennis. Research chemist Combustion Utilities Corp., N.Y. City, 1922-23, research dir., 1923-30; chmn. grad. council and dir. indsl. science div., W.Va. U., 1930-36; tech., consultant Federal Emergency Relief Adminstrn. also of W.Va. State Planning Bd.; econ. and financial adviser to Governor and W.Va. legislature, 1932-36; research dir., Consolidation Coal Company, 1936-39; cons. engr. since 1936, visiting prof. chem. engring., Columbia, 1939-41, prof. chem. engring. since 1941. Mem. Tech. Bd. of Arbitration on the Value Correlation of Coals, 1934; tech. adviser Northern W.Va. Subdivisional Code Authority, 1934; same Northern W.Va. Coal Assn., 1935; tech. adviser Joint Legislative Com. on Social Security, 1935-36; chmn. advisory bd., W.Va. Dept. of Public Assistance, 1936-37, member same, 1937-38; president, Fairmont Coal, Incorporated, 1939-42; mem. A.A.A.S., Am. Inst. Chem. Engrs., Am. Inst. Mining Engrs., Am. Gas Assn., Am. Chem. Soc., Tau Beta Pi, Sigma Gamma Epsilon, Phi Lambda Upsilon, Sigma Xi, Phi Beta Kappa. Catholic. Clubs: Columbia Univ., Chemists, Catholic (New York); Torch (Washington, D.C.). Home: 435 Riverside Dr. (25). Office: 301 Havemeyer Hall, Broadway and 118th St., New York, N.Y. Died Mar. 10, 1945.

BURKHART, Harvey Jacob, dentist; b. Cleveland, Aug. 14, 1861; s. Jacob and Biena (Buckholtz) B.; Dansville (N.Y.) Sem.; D.D.S., Baltimore Coll. Dental Surgery, 1890 (1st honors); LL.D., U. of Rochester, 1920; m. Jane Hingston, Nov. 6, 1890; 1 son, Richard Hingston; m. 2d, Lou Mercereau Davenport, Nov. 24, 1917. Practiced in Batavia, N.Y., 1890-1916; now dir. Rochester Dental Dispensers. Mayor of Batavia, 1902-04, 1915-16. Mem. Nat. Dental Assn. (pres. 1899), N.Y. State Dental Soc. (pres. 3 yrs.), 8th Dist. Dental Soc. (ex-pres.); chmn. com. to organize 4th Internat. Dental Congress, St. Louis, 1904. Republican. Episcopalian. K.T. Clubs: Batavia, Rochester, Monroe. Rep. of George Eastman of Rochester, N.Y., in establishment of Children's Dental Clinics in London, Rome, Stockholm, Paris and Brussels. Home: 76 Barrington St., Rochester, N.Y. Died Sept. 1946.

BURLEIGH, Harry T., singer, composer. Baritone soloist St. George's P.E. Ch., 44 yrs.; has toured U.S. and many foreign countries appearing before many distinguished audiences. Composed or arranged numerous negro spirituals. Address: care St. George's P.E. Ch., New York, N.Y. Died Sep. 12, 1949.

BURLEW, Ebert Keiser (bur-loo'); asst. secretary Interior (retired); b. Sunbury, Pa., Dec. 27, 1885; s. John Raker and Lillie Cecelia (Gemberling) B.; ed. at pub. high sch., business coll. and by pvt. tutor; LL.B., Washington Coll. of Law, 1921; m. Marion K. Swalm, 1907 (died 1915); 1 son, John Swalm; m. 2d, Lydia J. Cherot, Apr. 30, 1917. Sec. to pres. of Grit Publishing Company, Williamsport, Pa., 1908-09; with P. F. Collier & Sons, 1909-10; office of Adj. Gen., War Dept., 1910-14; in Post Office Dept., 1914-23, sec. to 3d asst. postmaster gen., 1917-22, confidential clk. to postmaster gen., 1921; private sec. to postmaster gen., 1922-23; administrative asst. Dept. of Interior, 1923-38; 1st asst. sec. of the Interior, 1938-43, resigned; admitted to Dist. of Columbia bar, 1921; bar of Supreme Court of U.S., 1925. Baptist. Mason. Club: University. Address: 740 N.E. 90th St., Miami, Fla. Died Oct. 20, 1945.

BURLINGHAM, Louis Herbert, hospital adminstrn.; b. Willimantic, Connecticut, Feb. 18, 1880; s. William Herbert and Maria J. (Stoughton) B.; A.B., Yale, 1902; M.D., Johns Hopkins, 1906; m. Grace Semple, Sept. 19, 1921. House Officer Mass. Gen. Hosp., Boston, 1906-07, asst. resident physician and asst. adminstr., 1907-12; asst. supt. Peter Bent Brigham Hosp., Boston, 1912-17; administrator St. Louis Children's Hosp., 1917-25; supt. Barnes Hosp., St. Louis, 1917-39; lecturer on hosp. adminstrn., Washington U. Med. Sch., 1917-39; formerly asso. editor Modern Hospital. Mem. Med. Council U.S. Vets. Bur.; formerly trustee St. Louis Community Fund; formerly dir. Bur. for Homeless Men. Mem. American College of Hospital Administrators, Am. Hosp. Assn. (trustee 1919-24; pres. 1928), Mo. Hosp. Assn. (former pres.), Phi Beta Pi; hon. mem. Am. Dietetic Assn. Republican. Methodist. Club: Med. Superintendents. Home: Congress Hotel, 275 Union Blvd., St. Louis, Mo. Died June 24, 1946.

BURNAM, Curtis Field, surgeon, radiologist; b. Richmond, Ky., Jan. 17, 1877; s. Anthony Rollins and Margaret (Summers) B.; A.B., Central U., Ky., 1895; M.D., Johns Hopkins, 1900; m. Florence Overall, Oct. 10, 1908; 1 dau., Mary (Mrs. Howard C. Smith). Resident gynecologist, Johns Hopkins Hosp., 1900-05, later asso. gynecologist, Johns Hopkins Hosp., and asso. in gynecology Johns Hopkins Med. Sch. until 1912; surg. and radiologist Howard A. Kelly Hosp., Baltimore; visiting physician in ray therapy, Johns Hopkins Hosp. and asso. prof. surgery, Johns Hopkins Med. Sch. Fellow Am. Coll. Surgeons; member A.M.A., Med. and Chirur. Faculty of Md., Am. Gynecol. Soc., Am. Urol. Assn., Southern Surg. Assn., Southern Med. Assn., Am. Radium Soc. (Janeway medal 1936), Am. Coll. Radiology. Presbyterian. Club: Elkridge Hunt. Author: (with Howard Atwood Kelly) Diseases of the Kidneys, Ureters and Bladder, 1914, and of many med. papers, including those relating to work with Dr. Samuel Crowe of Johns Hopkins relating to prevention and cure of deafness. Office: 1418 Eutaw Pl., Baltimore, Md. Died Nov. 29, 1947; buried in Druid Ridge Cemetery, Baltimore.

BURNETT, Charles Theodore (bûr-nět'), professor psychology, emeritus; b. Springfield, Massachusetts, June 24, 1873; s. Charles Martin and Alice (Munyan) B.; A.B., Amherst, 1895, L.H.D., 1930; Bowdoin L.H.D., 1944; Ph.D., Harvard, 1903; m. Sue Winchell, Dec. 16, 1914; children—David Winchell, Bettina and Audrey (twins). Began as instr. in psychology, Bowdoin Coll., 1904, prof. psychology since 1909. Fellow A.A.A.S.; mem. Am. Psychol. Assn., Psi Upsilon, Phi Beta Kappa. Democrat. Conglist. Author: Splitting the Mind, 1925; Hyde of Bowdoin, 1931. Home: Brunswick, Me. Died Jan. 31, 1946.

BURNETT, Edmund Cody, historical research; b. Henry Co., Ala., Nov. 29, 1864; s. Jesse Montreville Lafayette and Henrietta Sarah (Cody) B.; A.B., Carson (now Carson and Newman) College, Tenn., 1888; A.B., Brown U., Providence, R.I., 1890, A.M., 1895, Ph.D., 1897, Litt.D., 1938; m. Susan Elizabeth Susong, Oct. 6, 1914; children—Edmund Cody, Elizabeth Susong, Sue Stokely, Thomas Jesse McCormick. Asst. prof. mathematics, 1890-91, prof. Greek and modern langs., 1891-94, Carson and Newman Coll.; instr. in Greek, 1894-95, instr. in history, 1895-99, Brown U.; prof. of English, Bethel Coll., Russellville, Ky., 1899-1900; prof. of history, Mercer U., Macon, Ga., 1900-05; mem. Staff Dept. Hist. Research, Carnegie Instn., 1907-36. Mem. Am Hist. Assn., Southern Hist. Assn., Tenn. Hist. Soc., East Tenn. Hist. Soc., Am. Polit. Sci. Assn.; Am. Geog. Soc., The Author's Guild, Phi Beta Kappa. Clubs: Palaver, Cosmos. Author: The Government of Federal Territories in Europe, 1897; The Committee of the States, 1784, 1913; Ciphers of the Revolutionary Period, 1917; The Name 'United States of America', 1925; Perquisites of the Presidents of the Continental Congress, 1929; Who was the First President of the United States?, 1932; Our Union of States in the Making, 1935; Southern Statesmen and the Confederation, 1937; 'The More Perfect Union': The Continental Congress Seeks a Formula, 1937; The Catholic Signers of the Constitution, 1938; The Continental Congress (Loubat Prize 1943), 1941. Editor: Papers relating to Bourbon County, Ga., 1910; Letters of Members of the Continental Congress, Vols. 1 to 8, 1921-36; Letters of Barnett Hardeman Cody and Others, 1861-64, 1939; Letters of Three Lightfoot Brothers, 1861-64, 1942; Letters of a Confederate Surgeon: Dr. Abner Embry McGarity, 1862-65, 1946; The Economics of the French Broad Region, 1946-49; also articles in Agrl. History, etc. Contributor to Cyclopedia of American Government, Am. Hist. Review, Dictionary of Am. Biography, Co-operative History of the State of New York, Dictionary of American History, World Affairs, etc. Home: Del Rio, Tenn., and 1204 Newton St. N.E., Washington 17. Died Jan. 10, 1949; buried in Union Cemetery, Newport, Tenn.

BURNETT, Paul Moreton, life ins.; b. Baltimore, Md., Jan. 18, 1867; s. William Thomas and Amelia (Chapman) B.; ed. Baltimore City Coll. and U. of Md.; m. Elisabeth Jackson, Nov. 12, 1895; 1 dau., Ellinor (wife of Dr. Stewart H. Clifford). In practice of law at Baltimore with Charles J. Bonapart, 1885-1920; counsel Mut. Life Ins. Co. of Baltimore, 1898-1920, dir. since 1900, v.p. 1915-20, chmn. bd. 1920-22, became pres. 1922; now chmn. bd. Monumental Life Insurance Company. Maj. infantry, Maryland N.G., until 1916. Treas. Burmont Hosp. for Crippled Children; dir. Md. Gen. Hosp., Md. League for Crippled Children. Presbyn. Mason (32°). Contbr. to art and archtl. mags. Home: Charles St. and Blythewood Rd. Office: Charles and Chase Sts., Baltimore, Md. Died Oct. 30, 1944.

BURNHAM, Frederick Russell, explorer; b. Tivoli, Minn., May 11, 1861; s. Rev. Edwin O. and Rebecca (Russell) B.; family removed to Los Angeles, 1870; ed. Clinton High Sch.; was cowboy, scout, guide, miner, dep. sheriff, etc., in West; m. Blanche Blick, 1884 (died, Dec. 22, 1939); m. 2d, Ilo K. Willits, Oct. 28, 1943. Went to Africa, 1893; scout in Matabele War in Rhodesia, and for services there the govt. presented him with the campaign medal, and jointly with his two companions was given 300 square miles of land in Rhodesia in recognition of exceptional service. Discovered in the granite ruins of an ancient civilization of Rhodesia a buried treasure of gold and gold ornaments dating before Christian era; led expdn. to explore Barotzeland preparatory to the bldg. of the Cape to Cairo Ry.; took active part in 2d Matabele War on staff of Sir Frederick Carrington; was commd. to capture or kill the Matabele God M'Limo and succeeded in entering his cave in the Matopa Mts. and killing him; operated gold mines in Klondike and Alaska, 1898-1900; was sent for by Lord Roberts, Jan. 1900, to go to S. Africa for service in the Boer War, and was made chief of scouts of the British Army in the field; wounded, June 2, 1901, while on scouting duty (destroying the enemy's ry. base) and invalided home; for services there was commd. maj. in British Army, presented with large sum of money and received personal letter of thanks from Lord Roberts; on arrival in England was comd. to dine with Queen Victoria, spending the night at Osborne House, and was created mem. Distinguished Service Order by King Edward, who also presented him with S. African medal with 5 bars and the cross of the D.S.O.; made surveys of the Volta River, W. Africa, 1902, exploring parts of French Nigeria Hinterland of Gold Coast Colony, and took active part in native troubles of that time; comd. an exploration of magnitude from Lake Rudolph to German E. Africa, covering a vast region along Congo basin and head of the Nile, 1903-04; discovered a lake of 49 sq. miles composed almost entirely of pure carbonate of soda of unknown depth; made archæol. discovery of Maya civilization extending into the Yaqui country, as shown by stone carvings and writings, 1908. Engaged with John Hays Hammond in diverting the Yaqui River through a system of canals into the delta containing 700 sq. miles of land. Vice pres. Dominguez Oilfields Co. Mem. Calif. State Park Commn.; mem. Save the Redwoods League; mem. exec. council, Boy Scouts of Am. Clubs: Boone and Crockett (New York); Sunset (Los Angeles). Author: Scouting on Two Continents; Taking Chances. Home: P.O. Box 518, Santa Barbara, Calif. Office: Union Oil Bldg., Los Angeles. Died Sept. 1, 1947; buried at Three Rivers, Tulare County, Calif.

BURNHAM, Smith, prof. history; b. Charleston, Mich., Aug. 20, 1866; s. Orsemus and Margaret Elizabeth (Smith) B.; Ph.B., Albion (Mich.) Coll., 1892, A.M., 1896, LL.D., 1932; grad. study, U. of Chicago, 1896, U. of Pa., 1899-1900; m. Ella Lillian Caster, Aug. 31, 1893; 1 dau., Margaret Elizabeth. Teacher, pub. schs. Vicksburg, 1884-86; sch. prin., Climax, Mich., 1888-89; instr. history, Albion Coll., 1892-96, prof., 1896-98; prof. history, State Normal Sch., West Chester, Pa., 1898-1919; prof. history and chmn. dept. of social science, Western State Teachers Coll., Kalamazoo, Mich., since 1919; dir. Fidelity Bldg. & Loan Assn. Trustee Albion Coll. Mem. Am. Hist. Assn., Miss. Valley Hist. Assn., Mich. Ednl. Assn., N.E.A., Sigma Chi. Republican. Methodist. Rotarian. Author: Short History of Pennsylvania, 1912; Our Beginnings in Europe and America, 1918; The Making of Our Country, 1920; Hero Tales from History, 1922; (with T. H. Jack, the following) The Beginnings of Our Country, 1932; The Growth of Our Country, 1933; America Our Country, 1934. Lecturer before ednl. groups. Home: 131 S. Prairie Av., Kalamazoo, Mich. Died Dec. 14, 1947.

BURNS, Frank, ex-mem. Rep. Nat. Com.; b. Chicago, Ill., June 4, 1885; s. John Alexander and Catherine (MacPherson) B.; student high schs., Chicago, 1899-1903; m. Katherine Gertrude Nutt, June 28, 1919; children—Barbara, James Allen. Began as ins. agent, 1903; mgr. ins. office, Chicago, 1916-22; v.p. and mgr. Lumberman's Indemnity & Exchange Mut. Ins., Seattle, Wash., 1922-24; pres. Frank Burns, Inc., internat. reinsurance brokers, since 1924; mem. Wash. State Legislature, 1932-34; mem. Rep. Nat. Com. for Wash., 1933-37; Rep. candidate for governor of State of Washington, 1940. Episcopalian. Mason. Clubs: Rainier, Broadmoor, Washington Athletic (Seattle). Author: Reciprocal Insurance, 1925. Home: 1818 Broadmoor Drive. Office: White-Henry-Stuart Bldg., Seattle, Wash. Died Dec. 27, 1945; interment Mausoleum Acacia Memorial Park, Seattle.

BURQUE, Henri Alphonse (bûrk), judge; b. Nashua, N.H., Sept. 20, 1879; s. Alphonse and Marie Louise (Dutilly) B.; student Coll. Ste. Marie de Monnoir, Marieville, P.Q., 1893-97; A.B., Laval U. Sem. of Philosophy, St. Sulspice, Montreal, 1899; J.B., Boston U. Law Sch., 1903; m. Mabel M. Budro, Aug. 23, 1906; children—Lucille Yvonne (Mrs. Russell J. Nash), Eloise Jessie. Admitted to N.H. bar, 1903, in practice at Nashua, 1903-24; city solicitor, Nashua, 1911-14; clk. N.H. Senate, 1913; mayor of Nashua, 1920-24; became justice Superior Court of N.H., 1924, chief justice, 1937-41; justice Supreme Court of N.H. since Apr. 1, 1941. Dir., mem. exec. and trust investment coms., Indian Head Nat. Bank; referee, Nat. R.R. Adjust. Bd., 1942-44; mem. emergency bds., R.R. employees disputes, 1945-46; referee, Nat. R.R. Adjustment Bd., 1942-44; mem. emergency bds., R.R. employees disputes, 1945-46; trustee Nashua Pub. Library, Daniel Webster Council Boy Scout Trust Fund; chmn. Nashua chapter Am. Red Cross, 1943-44. Mem. N.H., Hillsborough County and Nashua bar assns. Democrat. Roman Catholic, K.C., Elk, Catholic Order of Foresters, St. Jean Baptiste of Nashua and of America. Club: Country. Home: 353 Main St., Nashua, N.H. Died Feb. 9, 1947; buried in Woodlawn Cemetery, Nashua.

BURR, Allston; b. Newton, Mass., July 3, 1866; s. Isaac Tucker and Ann Frances (Hardon) B.; A.B., Harvard, 1889, hon. A.M., 1931; m. Elisabeth Jenks Randolph, June 11, 1898 (died Sept. 1939). With Thompson-Houston Electric Co., Boston, 1889-93; treas. United Electric Securities Co., 1893-98; mem. firm Perry, Coffin & Burr, securities, 1898-1916; dir. of Coffin & Burr, Inc. Served as alderman of Newton, Mass., 1905-10. Chmn. Boston Chapter Am. Red Cross, 1916-21, now dir. Overseer Harvard, term 1931-37; trustee Boston Athenaeum; dir. Boston Provident Association; also member of council Radcliffe College. Unitarian. Clubs: Harvard, Somerset, Tavern, Union, Union Boat (Boston); Harvard, University (New York); Faculty (Cambridge, Mass.); Alpine (London); also Am., Canadian, French and Swiss Alpine Clubs. Home: Chestnut Hill, Mass. Office: 60 State St., Boston, Mass. Died Jan. 18, 1949.

BURR, Karl Edward, lawyer; b. Columbus, O., Mar. 6, 1877; s. Charles Edward and Elizabeth (Palmer) B.; A.B., Princeton, 1900; LL.B., Ohio State U. Coll. of Law, 1903; m. Louise C. Gwynne, July 7, 1903. Practiced in Columbus since 1903; mem. Burr, Porter, Stanley & Treffinger; gen. counsel Ohio Bell Telephone Co., Columbus & Southern O. Electric Co., solicitor Pa. R.R. Co.; atty. Postal Telegraph-Cable Co., Ry. Express Agency, etc.; dir. Ohio Bell Telephone Co., Columbus & Southern O. Electric Co., State Industrial Bk., Am. Nat. Fire Ins. Co. Republican. Episcopalian. Clubs: Union Club (Cleveland); Columbus Country, Rocky Fork Hunt and Country (Columbus); Nassau, Ivy (Princeton). Home: 180 N. Drexel Av., Bexley (Columbus). Office: 50 W. Broad St., Columbus, O. Died July 9, 1945.

BURRIS, William Paxton, univ. prof.; b. near Knightstown, Ind., Nov. 15, 1863; s. Elwood and Ruth Abigail (Paxton) B.; Ph.B., De Pauw U., 1891, L.H.D., 1911; A.M., Harvard, 1901; scholar, Teachers Coll., Columbia, 1901-02, Master's Diploma, 1902, fellow, 1903; m. Harriet Ferguson Clearwaters, Dec. 28, 1891 (died Jan. 4, 1934); children—Ruth (dec.), Elizabeth; m. 2d, Della Malone Roberts, Oct. 3, 1936. Supt. pub. schs., Bluffton, Ind., 1891-97, Salem, O., 1897-1900; prin. Teachers' Training Sch., Albany, N.Y., 1902-05; prof. history and principles of edn. and dean, Coll. for Teachers, U. of Cincinnati, 1905-22, prof. history and philosophy of edn., Grad. Sch., 1922-28; retired. Mem. Soc. Coll. Teachers of Edn., A.A.A.S., Kappa Delta Pi, Beta Theta Pi, Phi Delta Kappa. Originator of Case Method for study of teaching; opponent of nationalization of Am. education and state monopoly in establishment of schs. Home: 123 S. Edinburgh Av., Los Angeles. Died Nov. 8, 1946.

BURROUGHS, Harry Ernest, lawyer; b. April 15, 1890, Kashoffka, Russia; s. Nathan and Hannah Burroughs; LL.B., L.H.D., Suffolk Law School, LL.M., Boston U. Law Sch.; m. Hannah R. Sonnabend, June 21, 1922; children—Warren Herbert, Jean, Harry E. Admitted to Mass. bar, 1912; in private practice of law in Boston since 1912. Founder and pres. Burroughs Newsboys Foundation (a charitable organization for the benefit of newsboys, shoeblacks, etc.), 1927, and Agassiz Village of the Burroughs Newsboys Foundation, 1935. Mem. Mass. Recruiting Com., during World War I, Four Minute Men and mem. Plattsburg Training Camp. Mem. Nat. Youth Adminstrn. Am. Bar Assn., Mass. State Bar Assn.; Bar Assn. of City of Boston; Law Soc. of Mass. (chmn. of bd.), Bigelow Assn., Boston University Alumni Assn. Mason (32°), Elk. Clubs: Twentieth Century, Boston City, Puddingstone. Author: Tale of a Vanished Land, 1930; Boys in Men's Shoes, 1944. Home: 131 Kilsyth Road, Brookline. Office: 18 Tremont St., Boston. Mass. Died Dec. 18, 1946.

BURROUGHS, Prince Emmanuel, clergyman; b. Caldwell County, Tex., Dec. Dec. 31, 1871; s. of Hardy Marshall and Virginia (Duval) B.; A.B., Baylor U., 1891, D.D., 1907, Hardin Simmons U., 1906; Th. M., S. Bapt. Theol. Sem., 1896; m. Corinne G. Alexander, Apr. 4, 1898; m. 2d, Corinne G. Riley, Aug. 24, 1937. Ordained to Baptist ministry, Sept. 2, 1891; pastor in Tex. and Ky. until 1902, 1st Ch., Temple, Tex., 1902-06; Broadway Ch., Fort Worth, Tex., 1906-10; ednl. sec. Bapt. Sunday Sch. Bd., Nashville, 1910-42. Member board trustees Baylor Coll. for Women, Belton, Tex., 1902-10; mem. and sec. bd. trustees Southwestern Bapt. Theol. Sem., Fort Worth, Tex., 1907-10. Author: Bible Division, Convention Normal Manual, 1913; Winning to Christ, 1914; Old Testament Studies, 1915; The Present-Day Sunday School, 1917; Church and Sunday School Buildings, 1917; Building a Successful Sunday Sch., 1921; A Complete Guide to Church Building, 1923; How to Plan Church Buildings, 1925; Growing a Church, 1927; The Functioning Church, 1928; Our Lord and Ours, 1928; Our Church and Ours, 1928; Honoring the Deaconship, 1929; The Baptist People, from the First to the Twentieth Century, 1934; The Grace of Giving, 1934; Let Us Build, 1938; Fifty Fruitful Years, The Story of the Sunday School Board of the Southern Baptist Convention, 1941; The Spiri-
buried in Alta Vista Cemetery, Gainesville, Ga.
tual Conquest of the Second Frontier, 1942. Home: 635 Green St., Gainesville, Ga. Died May 22, 1948;

BURROWS, Montrose Thomas, surgeon; b. Halstead, Kan., Oct. 31, 1884; s. Thomas Forbes and Carolina Melvina (Richards) B.; grad. high sch., Halstead, 1901; A.B., University of Kansas, 1905; M.D., Johns Hopkins University, 1909; m. Flora Barbara Hege, Sept. 4, 1918; children—Bette Burrows Tanner, Helen Eugenia Ferrey, Zelta Reynolds, Loy Montrose. Fellow and asst. Rockefeller Inst. Medical Research, 1909-11; instructor in anatomy, Cornell U. Med. Sch., 1911-15; asso. in pathology and resident pathologist Johns Hopkins Med. Sch. and Hosp., 1915-17; acting prof. pathology, Washington U., 1917-20; asso. prof. surgery, same, and dir. research labs. Barnard Free Skin and Cancer Hosp., St. Louis, Mo., 1920-28; now specializing in cancer treatment and research, Pasadena, Calif. Served as 1st lt. Med. Corps, U.S. Army, 1916-19. Mem. A.M.A., A.A.A.S., Am. Assn. Anatomists, Am. Soc. Exptl. Pathology, Soc. Experimental Biology and Medicine, Sigma Nu, Nu Sigma Nu, Sigma Xi. Republican. Methodist. Contributor to biological reviews. Research in tissue culture, vitamin theory of cancer, heart muscle contraction, poliomyelitis, cancer, focal infections, etc. Home: 5202 Maywood Av., Los Angeles, Calif. Office: 201 N. El Molino Av., Pasadena, Calif. Died Aug. 21, 1947.

BURROWS, Robert Jay, v.p. Clark Equipment Co.; b. Youngstown, O., Nov. 28, 1882; s. George and Caroline (Zedaker) B.; B.S. in E.E., Clarkson Coll. of Technology, 1906; m. Grace Willis, Dec. 21, 1904; 1 son, Willis Jerome. Engr. Weston-Mott, Utica, N.Y., 1906-10; employed by Lee & Porter Mfg. Co., Buchanan, Mich., mfrs. of automobile axles, 1910-13; with Clark Equipment Co., Buchanan, Mich., since 1913, beginning as engr., v.p. since 1917. Member Am. Soc. M. E., Soc. Automotive Engrs., Omicron Pi Omicron (Sigma Alpha Epsilon chapter). Presbyterian. Clubs: South Bend Country (South Bend, Ind.); Orchard Hills Country (Buchanan, Mich.); Del Mar (Santa Monica, Calif.). Home: 105 N. Detroit St., Buchanan, Mich. Office: Clark Equipment Co., Battle Creek, Mich.* Died Jan. 12, 1947.

BURRUSS, Julian Ashby (bûr'ŭs), college pres.; b. Richmond, Va., Aug. 16, 1876; s. Woodson Cheadle and Cora Emmett (McDowell) B.; B.S. in C.E., Va. Poly. Inst., Blacksburg, Va., 1898; studied Richmond Coll., Harvard U.; A.M., Columbia, 1906; Ph.D., magna cum laude, U. of Chicago, 1921; LL.D., Hampden-Sydney College, 1937; scholar, 1905-06, fellow in edn., 1906-07, Columbia; m. Rachel Cleveland Ebbert, June 18, 1907; children—Julian Ashby, Jean McDowell. Instr., Normal Coll., Waleska, Ga., 1899-1900, Searcy (Ark.) Female Inst., and Speers-Langford Mil. Acad., 1900-01; prin. Leigh Sch., Richmond, Va., 1901-04; dir. manual arts, pub. schs., Richmond, 1904-05, 1907-08; pres. State Normal Sch. for Women, Harrisonburg, Va., 1908-19; taught in summer quarters, U. of Chicago, 1919, 20, 21; pres. Va. Agrl. and Mech. Coll. and Poly. Inst. since July 1, 1919. Chmn. State Agrl. Commn.; chmn. Com. on Industrial Development of State Chamber of Commerce; gov. 56th Dist. of Rotary International; pres. Assn. Land Grant Colls. and Univs. Presbyterian. Mason. Mem. State Board of Agriculture, Virginia Truck Expt. Sta. Board, Commn. on Med. Edn. in Va., Commn. on Simplification and Economy of State and Local Govt. in Va., Va. State Teachers' Assn. (pres. 1912-13), Va. Assn. of Colls. and Schs. for Girls (pres. 1912-13), N.E.A., Appalachian Forest Research Council, Commn. on Rural Electrification in Va., Va. Acad. of Science, Va. Social Science Assn., Newcomen Soc., Phi Beta Kappa; Omicron Delta Kappa, Alpha Zeta, Phi Kappa Phi, Pi Gamma Mu, Pi Delta Epsilon, S.A.R.; fellow A.A.A.S. Trustee Mary Baldwin College. Club: University (Blacksburg). Author: The Business Administration of Colleges, 1921. Home: Blackburg, Va.* Died Jan. 4, 1947.

BURT, David Allan, mfr.; b. Wheeling, W.Va., Dec. 24, 1876; s. John Lukens and Martha (McKelvey) B.; grad. Wheeling High Sch., 1892; m. Elizabeth McLain, Oct. 16, 1901; children—David A., Martha S., Elizabeth M. (dec.), William L. Office boy, clk., paymaster, Whitaker Iron Co., Wheeling, 1892-98; chief clk. Ætna Standard Iron & Steel Co., 1899-1903; auditor, treas., pres. La Belle Iron Works, 1904-20; v.p. Wheeling Steel Corp., 1921-23, now dir.; formed partnership with H. C. Hazlett under name Hazlett & Burt, investment bankers and brokers, 1923; president Jefferson Co.; dir. Woodward Iron Co., Wheeling Steel Corp., Chesapeake & Potomac Telephone Co., Continental Roll & Steel Foundry Co. Chmn. W.Va. State Tax Commn., 1926-27; v.p. bd. govs., W.Va. U. Mem. Acad. Polit. Science, Am. Iron & Steel Inst. Republican. Presbyn. Mason. Clubs: Duquesne (Pittsburgh); Fort Henry (Wheeling). Home: Echo Point, Wheeling. Office: Wheeling Steel Corporation Bldg., Wheeling, W.Va. Died July 28, 1948.

BURT, Frank Henry, pres. Y.M.C.A. Coll.; b. Galva, Ill., Feb. 3, 1863; s. George Preston and Frances (Willard) B.; B.S., Knox Coll., 1886, LL.D., 1911; M.H., Internat. Y.M.C.A. Coll., 1910; m. Lola Maddox, May 5, 1896. Asst. State sec. Ill. Y.M.C.A., 1889-1900; state sec. Mo. Y.M.C.A., 1900-03; dir. secretarial training, Y.M.C.A. Coll., Chicago, 1903-05, pres. since 1905. Republican. Baptist. Club: Union League. Home: 5338 Woodlawn Av. Address: 5315 Drexel Av., Chicago. Died Apr. 23, 1942.

BURTON, Harry Edward, astronomer; b. Onawa, Ia., June 11, 1878; s. William and Sarah Martha (Van Dorn) B.; A.B., U. of Ia., 1901, M.S., 1903; fellow in mathematics, State U. of Ia., 1902-03; m. Ina Burroughs Robinson, Aug. 22, 1911. Apptd. computer, U.S. Naval Obs., Feb. 1, 1909; advanced through the grades to prin. astronomer; head of equatorial div. since July 1, 1929. Mem. Am. Astron. Soc., Internat. Astron. Union, Sigma Xi. Discovered, May 8, 1915, the separation of Comet Mellish (1915a) into 2 components; derived new elements of orbits of satellites of Mars and redetermined position of equator of Mars in 1929 (A.J. 929). Wrote introduction to Observations of Double Stars, 1928-44. Received letter of commendation from Sec. of Navy, 1935. Coauthor of Publications, U.S. Naval Observatory, Second Series, Vol. XII. Editor Manual of Field Astronomy, for Naval Officers detailed to Hydrographic Surveys. Contbr. to Astronomical Journal. Address: U.S. Naval Observatory, Washington 25, D.C. Died July 19, 1948.

BURTON, Harry Edwin, coll. prof.; b. Boston, Mass., May 29, 1868; s. Edwin Scott and Sarah Jane (Sedgberg) B.; A.B., Harvard, 1890, A.M., 1893, Ph.D., 1895; student Am. Sch. Classical Studies, Rome, 1895-96, 1897-98; m. May Grace Harvey, June 20, 1895; 1 son, Harvey. Classical teacher, Peekskill (N.Y.) Mil. Acad., 1890-92; instr. Latin, 1896-97, asst. prof., 1898-1903, prof., 1903-16, Daniel Webster prof. Latin lang. and lit. 1916-38; emeritus since 1938, Dartmouth. Instr. in Grad. Sch., Harvard (on leave of absence), 1903. Justice Municipal Court of Hanover, N.H., 1911-38; moderator town of Hanover, 1920-38. Pres. N.E. Classical Assn., 1939-40. Republican. Conglist. Author: Latin Grammar, 1911; Aspects of College and University Administration (monograph), 1916; The Discovery of the Ancient World, 1932. Editor: Selections from Livy, 1905; The Aeneid of Virgil, 1919; Latin Fourth Year (with R. M. Gummere), 1931. Ann. prof., Am. Acad. in Rome, 1927-28. Home: Hanover, N.H. Died Mar. 20, 1944.

BURWELL, Arthur Warner, chemist; b. Rock Island, Ill., Aug. 26, 1867; s. Charles A. and Cornelia P. (Bonnell) B.; student Kaiser Wilhelm Univ., Strassburg, Germany (Ph D.); m. Bertha Schade, Dec. 22, 1898; children—Richard Bonnell, Oliver Peckham, Cornelia. Chemist Standard Oil Co., 1893-98; consulting chemist to 1922; research in oxidation of petroleum hydrocarbons, 1922-26; practical oxidation of petroleum hydrocarbons since 1926; v.p. and tech. dir. Alox Corp., Niagara Falls, N.Y. Awarded gold medal by Western N.Y. Sec. of Am. Chem. Soc. for "work in producing and utilizing fatty acids and other chemicals from petroleum," 1941. Mem. Am. Chem. Soc., German Chem. Soc., Automotive Engrs., Am. Soc. Testing Materials, Electrochem. Soc., Am. Petroleum Inst., Am. Inst. Chemistry. Republican. Mason (32°, Shriner). Clubs: Rotary, Torch. Author: Oiliness, 1935; also many articles to tech. jours. on decomposition of petroleum hydrocarbons, lubricants, etc. Holds many patents in mfr. of lubricants, etc. Home: Crescent Drive, Tuscorora Park, Wilson, N.Y. Office: Alox Corp., 3943 Buffalo Av., Niagara Falls, N.Y. Died May 24, 1946.

BUSCH, Adolphus, III, pres. Anheuser-Busch, Inc.; b. St. Louis, Mo., Feb. 10, 1891; s. August A. and Alice (Zisemann) B.; ed. Smith Acad.; m. Mrs. Florence Parker Lambert, June 21, 1913; m. 2d, Mrs. Catherine Milliken Bowen, Sept. 13, 1930. Pres. Anheuser-Busch, Inc., St. Louis, Mo., Dallas Hotel Co. (Hotel Adolphus), Dallas, Tex.; chmn. bd. Mfrs. Bank & Trust Co., St. Louis, Mo., Busch-Sulzer Bros. Diesel Engine Co., Mfrs. Railway Co., St. Louis & O'Fallon Ry. Co., St. Louis Refrigerator Car Co. Clubs: Racquet, Noonday, University. Home: Huntleigh Village, St. Louis County. Office: 9th and Pestalozzi Sts., St. Louis, Mo. Died Aug. 29, 1946.

BUSCHMAN, S. L., pres. and dir. Nat. Can Corp.; dir. Can Mfrs. Inst. Home: 336 West End Av. Office: care National Can Corp. 110 E. 42d St., New York, N.Y.* Died Sep. 1945.

BUSH, Henry Tatnall, banker; b. Wilmington, Del., Nov. 24, 1880; s. Walter Danforth and Rebecca Gibbons (Tatnall) B.; ed. Friends' Sch., Wilmington; m. Lydia Moore, Apr. 14, 1906 (dec.); 1 son, Henry Tatnall; m. 2d, Marjorie L. Dingee (mother of Mrs. Anne D. Haden), May 25, 1929. Began as clerk with Harlan & Hollingsworth Corp., Wilmington, 1897; pres. Farmers' Bank since 1927; dir. Wilmington Savings Fund Soc., Farmers Mut. Fire Ins. Co., Wilson Line, Inc., Farmers Bank of State of Del. Vice-pres. Woodlawn Trustees, Inc. Trustee Wilmington Free Library; dir. Wilmington Gen. Hosp., Wilmington Music Sch. Served on Selective Service Bd. No. 4; state chmn. Del. War Finance Com. Pres. Wilmington C. of C., 1927. Mem. Soc. of Colonial Wars, Wilmington Soc. Fine Arts. Republican. Club: Wilmington. Home: Beaver Valley, Wilmington. Office: Farmers' Bank, Wilmington, Del. Died May 7, 1945.

BUSH, Irving T., terminal exec.; b. Ridgeway, Mich., July 12, 1869; s. Rufus T. and Sarah M. (Hall) B.; acad. edn. Hill Sch., Pottstown, Pa.; m. Belle Barlow, Feb. 2, 1891; m. 2d, Maud (Howard) Beard (widow of Francis D. Beard), Apr. 20, 1907; m. 3d, Marian Spore, June 9, 1930. Traveled around world in father's yacht, "Coronet," 1888-89, and has been many times abroad. At 19 entered Bush & Denslow Mfg. Co., of which his father was pres., becoming sec. a yr. later; early became interested in relieving congestion of business and traffic in New York; began establishing warehouses, 1895, under title of The Bush Co., Ltd.; founded Bush Terminal Co., 1902, and has created the Bush Terminal, with 125 warehouses, 8 piers, 18 model loft or industrial bldgs., and facilities for receiving, shipping, storing, selling and mfg. goods, covering about 30 city blocks (200 acres) in South Brooklyn, N.Y., attracting over 300 mfg. and wholesale establishments. Also established the 30-story Sales Bldg., 42d St., N.Y. City. Pres. Bush Terminal Company and Bush Terminal R.R. Co. Mem. Chamber of Commerce of State of N.Y. (pres. 1922-24, v.p. 1924-28). Recipient of French Legion of Honor. Mem. The Pilgrims of the U.S., Sons of the Revolution, France-America Soc., Inc., Metropolitan Museum of Art and Am. Museum of Natural History, Am. Soc. of the French Legion of Honor, Inc. Conglist. Clubs: New York Yacht, India House, National Arts. Home: 280 Park Av. Office: 100 Broad St., New York 4, N.Y. Died Oct. 21, 1948.

BUSHFIELD, Harlan J., U.S. senator; b. Atlantic, Ia., Aug. 6, 1882; s. John A. and Cora (Pearson) B.; student Dakota Wesleyan U., Mitchell, S.D., 1899-1901, LL.D., 1939; LL.B., U. of Minn., 1904; m. Vera Cahalan, Apr. 15, 1912; children—Janith (wife of Dr. John L. Work), John P., Harlan J. Admitted to S.D. bar, 1904, and began practice in Miller; gov. of S.D., 1938-42; U.S. senator from S.D. since 1943. Mem. S.D. and American bar assns. Republican. Presbyterian. Mason. Home: Miller, S.D. Address: Senate Office Bldg., Washington, D.C. Died Sept. 27, 1948; buried in D.A.R. Cemetery, Miller, S.D.

BUSHNELL, Edward, lawyer; b. Fremont, O., May 18, 1865; s. Ebenezer and Cornelia K. (Woodruff) B.; A.B., Western Reserve U., 1887; m. Maude Sherwin, April 20, 1892; children—Elisabeth (dec.), Nelson Sherwin. Admitted to Ohio bar, 1891, and since in practice of law at Cleveland; mem. firm Bushnell, Burgess & Fulton, Cleveland; pres. West 9th Co., Auditorium Co.; treas. Prospect Realty Co.; dir. Liberty Savings & Loan Co. Mem. Bd. Edn., Cleveland, 1914-17 (pres. 1916 and 1917); mem. Cleveland Bar Assn. (pres. 1933-34). Republican. Presbyterian. Clubs: Tavern, Delta Kappa Epsilon. Home: 1900 E. 81st St. Office: Terminal Tower Bldg., Cleveland, O.* Died Nov. 17, 1944.

BUSHNELL, Herbert Martin, banker; b. Lincoln, Neb., July 1, 1893; s. Herbert Martin and Elsie N. (Campbell) B.; LL.B., Coll. of Law; U. of Neb.; m. R. Barbara Harney, Feb. 11, 1931. Joined U.S. Nat. Bank, 1919, dir. since 1928; dir. Chicago, Burlington and Quincy R.R. since 1944; dir. Nat. Security Ins. Co. Gov. of Ak-Sar-Ben. Mem. exec. com. Asso. of Omaha Taxpayers. Home: 111 S. 49th St. Office: U.S. National Bank, Omaha, Neb. Deceased.

BUSHNELL, Robert T., lawyer; b. New York, N.Y., July 9, 1896; s. Robert Stowe and Mary Rockland (Tyng) B.; prep. edn. Phillips Andover Acad., 1912-15; A.B., Harvard U., 1919; LL.B., Harvard Law Sch., 1921; m. Sylvia P. Folsom, June 30, 1924; children—Frederic Folsom, Priscilla Alden. Admitted to Mass. bar, 1921; asst. dist. atty., Middlesex County, 1923-27, dist. atty., 1927-31; private practice of law, specializing in trial of cases, 1931-41; attorney general of Massachusetts, 1941-45. Served as pvt., sergeant and 2d lt., U.S. Infantry, World War. Mem. Am., Mass., Boston and Middlesex bar assns., Mass. Law Soc. Mem. Union Church of Waban, Mass. Mason, Odd Fellow. Club: Harvard. Home: 193 Fuller St., West Newton, Mass. Office: 31 State St., Boston 9, Mass. Died Oct. 22, 1949.

BUSSEWITZ, Maxillian Alfred (bŭs'sĕ-witz), prof. physiology; b. Posen, Prussia, Mar. 4, 1867; s. Charles S. and Pauline (Cunard) B.; came to U.S., 1880; student Milwaukee State Normal Sch., 1892-93; A.B., Ripon (Wis.) Coll., 1899; A.M., U. of Wis., 1900; M.D., Wis. Coll. Physicians and Surgeons, 1907; m. Hattie S. Studley, 1893 (died 1937); children—Beatrice (Mrs. A. J. Schinner), Lucille (Mrs. L. E. Thomson), Beulah (dec.). m. 2d, Mary A. Beineke, 1939. Teacher, prin. and supt. schs. until 1898; asst. state supt. schs., Wis., 1901-02; prof. physiology, Marquette U., since 1907, also prof. emeritus same, Milwaukee State Teachers Coll.; chmn. bd. State Bank of Mayville; treas. Bussewitz Realty Co. Mem. Battery C, Wis. Nat. Guard, 1892-94; lt. col. O.R.C., U.S. Army. Mem. Am., Wis. State and Milwaukee County med. assns., N.E.A., Wis. State Teachers Assn., Acad. Arts and Sciences, Horace Mann League, School Masters' Club. Republican. Conglist. Mason (32°, Shriner). Wrote: (monograph) Evolution of Ideals in Secondary Education, 1902. Home: 2129 E. Kenwood Blvd., Milwaukee. Died Sept. 20, 1942.

BUTLER, Burridge Davenal, publisher; b. Louisville, Ky., Feb. 5, 1868; s. Rev. Thomas Davenal and Marie Burridge (Radcliffe) B.; LL.D., Blackburn U.; m. Winifred Whitfield (died 1904); m. Ina Hamilton Busey, July 30, 1906. In editorial work, Grand Rapids, 1885-93; advt. mgr. at Chicago, 1894-99; founded Omaha Daily News (v.p.), 1899, St. Paul Daily News (v.p.), 1900, Minneapolis Daily News (pres.), 1903; sold newspaper properties and returned to Chicago, 1909; was also interested in Kansas City World, Des Moines News, and other newspapers; owner and publisher The Prairie Farmer (founded 1841) since 1909; pres. Prairie Farmer Pub. Co.; pres. Prairie Farmers' Protective Assn. since 1916; pres. WLS Agrl. Broadcasting Co., Chicago; chmn. bd. of dirs. Salt River Valley Broadcasting Co. (KOY), Phoenix, Ariz., 1936; chmn. bd. (KTUC) Tucson (Ariz.) Broadcasting Co.; chmn. bd. Arizona Farmer Pub. Co., Phoenix. Served as state dir. U.S. Boys' Working Reserve, World War; mem. Nat. Council Boy Scouts of America; chmn. Western div., Nat. Federation of Boys' Clubs; pres. Union League Foundation for Boys' Clubs, 1929-30. Trustee Blackburn U. Mem. Agrl. Pubs.' Assn. (ex-pres.), Chicago Hist. Soc., Art Inst. Chicago; associate mem. Field Museum, Chicago. Mem. Christian (Disciples) Ch. Mason. Clubs: Union League; Phoenix Club, Country (Phoenix, Ariz.); Old Pueblo (Tucson, Ariz.). Owns art collection, also owner of experimental farm. Interested in work of underprivileged boys. Rep. of agrl. publs. Audit Bur. of Circulation, dir. 2 yrs. Home: Hinsdale, Ill.; and R. No. 1, Phoenix, Ariz. (Nov. to May). Office: 1230 Washington Blvd., Chicago, Ill. Died Mar. 30, 1948.

BUTLER, Charles C., lawyer; b. Milwaukee, Wis., Feb. 6, 1865; s. Washington Irving and Henrietta (Comstock) B.; LL.B., U. of Mich., 1891; LL.D., U. of Denver, 1925, U. of Colo., 1937; m. Emma Allen, June 5, 1901. Admitted to Colo. bar, 1891, and began practice at Denver; dep. dist. atty., Arapahoe County, Colo., 1892, Teller County, Colo., 1904; judge, Dist. Court, Colo., 1913-27; justice, Supreme Court, Colorado, term 1927-37; (chief justice part of that time); assistant district attorney, 1937-38. Mem. Colo. Bar Assn. (1st v.p. 1912-13, 1923-24). Denver Bar Assn. (pres. 1925-26); pres. Teller County Bar Assn., 1900. Republican. Mason. Home: 1138 Downing St., Denver, Colo. Died Nov. 16, 1946.

BUTLER, Charles St. John, M.D.; b. Bristol, Tenn., Mar. 1, 1875; s. Matthew Moore and Mary Taylor (Dulaney) B.; student King Coll.; A.B., Emory and Henry College, 1895, LL.D., 1932; M.D., University of Virginia, 1897; m. Ingeborg Maria Nordqvist, July 4, 1899; children—Maria Nordqvist (wife of Harry L. Brockmann, M.D.), Martha Amanda (Mrs. Erik W. Ehn), Ruth Elizabeth. Began practice at Bristol, 1899; entered Med. Corps, U.S. Navy, as lt., j.g., 1900, and advanced through grades to rear admiral, 1935; retired Apr. 1, 1939. Instr. in bacteriology and tropical medicine, various times, U.S. Naval Med. Sch., 1907-21; occasional lecturer at George Washington U., Jefferson Med. College, 1923-24; commanding officer Naval Med. Sch., Washington, D.C., 1921-24, and 1927-32; comdg. officer U.S. Naval Hosp., Brooklyn, 1932-35; dir. gen. of pub. health of Republic of Haiti, 1924-27; comdg. officer U.S. Naval Med. Supply Depot, Brooklyn, N.Y., 1935-36, U.S. Navy Med. Center, Washington, D.C., 1936-38. Mem. med. bd. Nat. Research Council, 1924-26. Fellow Am. Med. Assn., Am. Coll. Surgeons, Am. Coll. Physicians, N.Y. Acad. Medicine; diplomate Am. Bd. of Internal Medicine; mem. A.A.A.S., Am. Acad. Tropical Medicine (pres. 1940), N.Y. Soc. Tropical Medicine (pres. 1935), Washington Acad. Sciences, Am. Soc. Tropical Medicine (pres. 1927), Am. Soc. Clin. Pathologists, Mil. Surgeons of U.S., Sigma Alpha Epsilon, Alpha Omega Alpha; hon. mem. Soc. of Medicine of Haiti. Decorated Medal of Honor and Merit (Haiti); letter of commendation from U.S. Navy Dept. for service in World War I. Democrat. Club: Army and Navy (Washington). Author: Syphilis Sive Morbus Humanus, 1936, coll. edit. (2d), 1939; also author of numerous papers dealing with tropical medicine, seasickness, etc. Home: 848 Anderson St., Bristol, Tenn. Died Oct. 7, 1944.

BUTLER, George Harrison, Jr., lawyer; b. Smithdale, Amite County, Miss., Oct. 15, 1877; s. George Harrison and Mary Elizabeth (Tarver) B.; LL.B., U. of Miss., 1901; m. Mamie Imogene Gardner, Apr. 1, 1904; children—Mary Lyneille (Mrs. John Countiss, Jr.), George Harrison, Jr. Admitted to Miss. bar, 1901, and began practice at McComb City; asst. atty. gen. of Miss., 1907-10; practiced at Jackson, Miss., 1910-12; with R. Walter Moore's Orgn., Washington, D.C., 1912-13, representing railroads in the southeast in interstate commerce matters; mem. Butler, Easterling & Potter, Jackson, 1913-14; sr. mem. firm Butler & Snow since 1926; firm attys. for Southern Bell Telephone & Telegraph Co., Am. Telephone & Telegraph Co., also many ins., oil and other cos. Mem. Research Commn., Miss., 1930-32. Trustee State Insane Hosp., Miss., 1914-17, State Blind Inst., 1919-26. Mem. Am. Law Inst., Am. Bar Assn., Miss. Bar Assn. (ex-pres.), Hinds County Bar Assn., (ex-pres.). Mason (K.T., Shriner). Democrat. Methodist. Home: 819 North State St. Office: Deposit Guaranty Bank Bldg., Jackson, Misss. Died Nov. 27, 1948; buried in Cedarlawn Cemetery, Jackson.

BUTLER, James Joseph, ex-congressman; b. St. Louis, Aug. 29, 1862; s. Edward and Ellen (O'Neill) B.; B.S., St. Louis U., 1881; m. Rose Mary Lancaster, Aug. 11, 1896. Admitted to bar, 1884, and since in practice at St. Louis; pres. Empire Circuit Co., Cincinnati. Mem. Bd. Edn., 1882-83; city atty., 1886-94; mem. 57th and 58th Congresses (1901-05), 12th Mo. Dist. Democrat. Was twice elected to 57th Congress and twice unseated by party vote; the second unseating bringing about the longest and bitterest filibuster in the history of the Ho. of Reps. Del. Dem. nat. convs. 1904, 08. Home: 3711 W. Pine Blvd. Office: Navarre Bldg., St. Louis. Died May 31, 1917.

BUTLER, Mary, artist; b. Chester County, Pa.; d. James and Rachel M. (James) Butler; ed. Darlington Sem., West Chester, Pa.; art edn., Philadelphia Sch. Design for Women (Horstmann fellowship), Pa. Acad. Fine Arts; pupil of William M. Chase, Robert Henri, Edward W. Redfield, Cecelia Beaux, of Phila., Gustave Courtois, Prinet, Ingelbert, Girardot, in Paris. Has specialized on mountain and sea pictures. Represented at Pennsylvania Academy of Fine Arts, Philadelphia Museum of Art, West Chester State Teachers College, Teachers College and Art Museum, Springfield, Mo., Art-Museum, Peoria, Ill., Edmonton (Can.) Art Museum, etc.; one man exhibitions, Pa. Acad. Fine Arts, 1942. Awarded honorable mention, Buffalo Soc. Artists, 1913, 14; gold medal, Plastic Club, Philadelphia, 1918; Mary Smith prize, Pa. Acad. Fine Arts, 1925; spl. award of honor, Nat. Art Exhbn., Springville, Utah, 1926, 27; 2d prize, water colors, Plastic Club, 1929; hon. mention Eloise Egan prize, Nat. Assn. Women Painters and Sculptors. Life mem. Pa. Acad. Fine Arts; mem. Fellowship Pa. Acad. Fine Arts (hon. pres.), hon. mem. Phila. Branch of International Altrusa, Phila. Water Color Club, Alumnæ Phila. Sch. Design for Women, Plastic Club, Com. of 1926 of Pa., Fairmount Park Art Assn., Print Club of Philadelphia, Am. Fed. of Arts, Am. Artists Professional League, Phila. Art Alliance; mem. Council for Preservation of Natural Beauty in Pa. Presbyterian. Clubs: New Century (hon.), Contemporary (Phila.). Home: 2127 Green St., Philadelphia, Pa.; (summer) Uwchland, Pa. Died Mar. 16, 1946.

BUTLER, Nicholas Murray, university pres., emeritus; b. Elizabeth, N.J., Apr. 2, 1862; s. Henry L. and Mary J. (Murray) B.; A.B., Columbia, 1882, A.M., 1883, Ph.D., 1884; univ. fellow in philosophy, 1882-85; student at Berlin and Paris, 1884-85; hon. degrees conferred by Yale, Harvard, Princeton, Johns Hopkins, U. of Chicago, Toronto, St. Andrews, Manchester, Oxford, Cambridge, Glasgow, Paris, Strassburg, Nancy, Louvain, Rome, Prague, Breslau, Budapest, Szeged (Hungary), Edinburgh, Syracuse, Univ. of Pennsylvania, Williams, Dartmouth, Brown, Amherst, Fordham Univ., Univ. of Calif., Univ. of State of N.Y., Univ. of King's Coll., N.S., Univ. of Santo Domingo, University of Puerto Rico, Univ. of Lyon, Tulane, Wesleyan, Charles IV (Prague), Sofia (Bulgaria); m. Susanna Edwards Schuyler, 1887 (died January 10, 1903); 1 daughter, Sarah Schuyler (wife of Captain Neville Lawrence, London; died February 21, 1947); married 2d, Kate La Montagne, March 5, 1907. Assistant in philosophy, Columbia, 1885-86, tutor, 1886-89, adj. professor, 1899-90, dean faculty philosophy, and prof. philosophy and edn., 1890, president, 1901-45, president emeritus since 1945; pres. Barnard Coll. and Teachers Coll., 1901-45; Coll. Pharmacy, 1904-45; president Bard College, 1928-44, N.Y. Post-Grad. Med. School, 1931-45. First pres. N.Y. Coll. for Training of Teachers (now Teachers College), 1886-91; mem. N.J. State Bd. Edn., 1887-95; organized Coll. Entrance Exam. Bd., 1893, chmn. 1901-04; pres. Paterson, (N.J.) Bd. Edn., 1892-93. N.J. commr. Paris Expn., 1889; del. Rep. Nat. Conv., 1888, and 8 times since 1904; chmn.

N.Y. Rep. Conv., 1912; received Rep. electoral vote for vice pres. of U.S., 1913. Received 69½ votes from N.Y. as candidate for pres. of U.S., Rep. Nat. Conv., 1920. Chmn. administrative bd. Internat. Congress of Arts and Sciences, St. Louis Expn., 1904; chmn. Lake Mohonk Conf. on Internat. Arbitration, 1907, 09, 10, 11, 12. Watson prof. of Am. history and instns. at British univs., 1923; chmn. Nat. Com. on Reconstruction of U. of Louvain, 1915-25; pres. Am. br. of Conciliation Internationale, and editor 1907, editor Paris branch, 1906-37; pres. Rogers Memorial Library, Southampton, N.Y., since 1932; trustee Carnegie Foundation Advancement of Teaching since 1905, Carnegie Endowment for Internat. Peace, 1910 (pres. 1925-45; pres. emeritus since 1946), Carnegie Corp., 1925-45 (chmn. 1937-45), Cathedral of St. John the Divine since 1914, American-Slav. Inst. Prague (pres. since 1924), dir. N.Y. Life Ins. Co.; trustee Barnard Coll., Teachers Coll., Columbia University Press; vice president Congress Royal Institute for Public Health (London, England), 1920; member Commission on Reorganization of Government of State of N.Y., 1925-26; vice chmn. Mayor's N.Y. City Com. on Plan and Development, 1926-27; pres. Citizens Budget Com. (N.Y.), 1936-46, honorary pres. since 1946. Membre de l'Institut de France since 1923; member of American Academy of Arts and Letters since 1911 (chancellor, 1924-28; president, 1928-41), The Pilgrims (v.p., 1913-28; president 1928-46), Am. Philos. Soc. since 1901, Am. Psychol. Assn., N.E.A. (pres. 1895; life mem.), Am. Hist. Assn., N.Y. Hist. Soc. since 1905, Germanistic Soc. (pres. 1906, 07; dir. 1908-17; hon. v.p. since 1930), Am. Scandinavian Soc. (1st pres. 1908-11), Am. Acad. in Rome (since 1905), Univ. Settlement Soc. (pres. 1905-14), France-America Soc. (pres. 1914-24), Am. Red Cross, N.Y. Chamber Commerce (hon. mem.), adv. bd. Lycee Francaise de New York since 1939, Am. Hellenic Soc. (pres. since 1917), Italy America Soc. (pres. bd. trustees 1929-35), American Society French Legion of Honor, Inc. (hon. pres. since 1944), Bricklayers, Masons and Plasterers International Union of America (since 1923), Philos. Soc. (since 1938), Nat. Inst. Soc. Sci. (since 1937), N.Y. Acad. Pub. Edn. (since 1938), Psi Upsilon, Phi Beta Kappa; hon. adviser of Amigos Mexicanos del Pueblo de Norteamerica (Mexican Friends of the Am. People); corr. mem. Associazione Internazionale per gli Studi Mediterranei, Rome, 1930; v.p. Stresemann Memorial Friedens-Stiftung, Berlin, since 1931; hon. pres., Panamerican Soc. of Santiago, Cuba, 1939; mem. bd. govs. Pan American Trade Com., 1939; life mem. and hon. v.p. Internat. Benjamin Franklin Soc., Inc., 1939; hon. mem. Institut des Hautes Etudes Internationales (Sofia, Bulgaria), 1939, German American Writers Association, 1939, Inst. Journalists (British); foreign or honorary member various societies; corr. mem. Instituto de Investigaciones Historicas, Dominican Republic (since 1936); fellow N.Y. Geneal. and Biog. Soc., 1929. Awarded one-half of Nobel peace prize 1931; awarded diploma of honor by La Academia Mexicana correspondiente de la Espanola, 1939; decorated by govts. of France, Germany, Greece, Jugo-Slavia, Belgium, Poland, Italy, Rumania, Czechoslovakia, Austria, Hungary, Holland, Cuba, Chile, etc.; Grand white Cordon with red borders of Order of Jade by govt. of China, 1938. Awarded Erasmus medal, 1937; Mark Twain medal, 1936; Union Federale des Combattants medal (France), 1936; Insignia Order of Merit (Dominican Republic), 1937; Nat. Hist. Order of Merit of "Carlos Manuel de Cespedes," Republic of Cuba, 1940; New York Acad. of Pub. Edn. medal, 1938; honorary. Citizen of Trujillo City, Dominican Republic, 1937; Grand Cross Legion of Honor (France), 1937; Alexander Hamilton Medal for public service, 1947. Clubs: Union, Century, Metropolitan, University, Round Table, Columbia University, National Golf, Garden City Golf, Lawyers (hon.), Lotos (president 1923-34), Links Golf, Englewood Golf; University (Washington, D.C.); Bohemian (San Francisco); Athenæum, Reform (hon.; both of London); Southampton (pres. since 1932), Beach of Southampton; Am. Club of Paris (hon.); hon. mem. Brit. Schools and Univs. club of New York, 1937. Editor: Ednl. Rev., 1889-1920; The Great Educators Series, 1892-1901; The Teachers' Professional Library, 1894-1929; Bibliothek d. Amerikanischen Culturgeschichte (Berlin), 1912; Columbia University Contributions to Philosophy and Education, 1888-1902; co-editor: International Padagogische Bibliothek. Author: The Meaning of Education, 1898, revised edit., 1915; True and False Democracy, 1907; The American as He Is, 1908; (translation: L'Americain Tel Qu'il Est, 1938); Education in the United States, 1910; Philosophy, 1911; Why Should We Change Our Form of Government?, 1912; The International Mind, 1913; A World in Ferment, 1918; Is America Worth Saving?, 1920; Scholarship and Service, 1921; Building the American Nation, 1923; The Faith of a Liberal, 1924; The Path to Peace, 1930; Looking Forward, 1932; Between Two Worlds, 1934; The Family of Nations, 1938; Across the Busy Years, 1939; Why War?, 1940; Liberty, Equality, Fraternity, 1942; The World Today, 1946; also many published essays and addresses. Home: 60 Morningside Drive, New York, N.Y. Died Dec. 7, 1947.

BUTLER, William John, veterinary surgeon; b. Bowling, Scotland, May 31, 1881; s. Hugh and Isabella (Fenwick) B.; brought to U.S., 1889; grad. Manual Training High Sch., Brooklyn, N.Y., 1899; D.V.S., New York Univ., 1903; m. J. Ozella Cato, May 24, 1921; children—Hugh Cato, Cato Kay. Began practice in Mont., 1903, also live stock insp. and rancher; mining in Mexico, 1910-13, also rep. Am. stock men, at Mazatlan; state vet. surgeon of Mont. since 1913; dir. labs. Mont. Live Stock Sanitary Bd.; adminstr. of relief, Montana, 1934-35. Student O.T.C., Ft. Douglas, Utah, 1916; maj. Mont. N.G., 1917-18; enlisted in U.S. Army and detailed Sept. 1918 to F.A., Central O.T.S., Camp Zachary Taylor, Ky.; hon. disch. Dec. 1918. Del. from U.S. to the 13th Internat. Congress of Veterinary Medicine, Zurich, Switzerland, 1938. Dir., mem. Vet. Bd. Internat. Live Stock Expn., Chicago; dir. Mont. State Fair; president Montana Stallion Registry Board; chairman Montana Milk Control Board since 1935; mem. U.S. Live Stock Sanitary Assn. (pres. 1922-23), Mont. Vet. Med. Assn. (pres. 1938-39), Mont. Bd. of Entomology, Am. Vet. Med. Assn., Western States L.S.S. Assn. (pres. 1924-25), Am. Pub. Health Assn., Internat. Assn. Dairy and Milk Inspectors, A.A.A.S. Democrat. Presbyn. Mason. Club: Montana (pres. 1923). Author of pamphlets and articles on diagnosis and control of disease in domestic and wild animal life, production of clean milk and its care, and range conditions affecting live stock. Home: 704 Stuart St. Address: Capitol Station, Helena, Mont. Died Oct. 29, 1948.

BUTLER, William Mill, editor, author; b. Rochester, N.Y., June 21, 1857; s. Theophilus and Mary (Miller) B.; ed. common schs. and Hyde Park Commercial Coll., Scranton, Pa.; m. Helen J. Perrine, Nov. 24, 1880 (died Dec. 7, 1932). Began career on Scranton Daily Times, in 1876; apptd. city editor of Wilkes-Barre Daily Record, same year, but broke down from overwork; editor of Reformer, Galt, Ont., 1877-78; then reporter, city editor and editor in chief Rochester Post-Express, 1879-86; also served as city editor and associate editor Rochester Democrat and Chronicle; editor Home Mag., Binghamton, 1896-97; chief foreign corr. dept., Phila. Commercial Mus., 1899-1900; vice-consul and acting consul gen. for Paraguay, at Phila., 1899-1902; pub. trade jours., N.Y. City, 1905-25; in chem. business, 1925-27. Active in urging humane treatment and sanitary care of dead on battlefields during World War I (address on subject before the House Com. on Mil. Affairs officially pub.). Historian of Soc. of the Genesee, N.Y., since 1913. Mem. A.A.A.S., Rochester Hist. Soc., N.Y. Zoöl. Soc. (life). Ind. Republican. Mason (32°, Shriner), K.P., Knight Golden Eagle. Author: Pantaletta (a satire on the woman's rights question), 1882; The Whist Reference Book, 1898; History of Paraguay, 1900 (awarded vote of thanks by Congress of Paraguay and $500 (gold) for this history); Democracy and Other Poems, 1920 (Democracy reprinted in 6,000 daily and weekly newspapers and set to music, in competition, by 12 Am. composers); The Sea-Serpent (comic opera), 1920; (monograph) The Human Eye Color, 1934; Rough-Riding on Olympus, A Bully Biography of Theodore Roosevelt, 1937; The Moonlight Oracle, 1939; Victory Song, Anglo-American War-Song (set to music by Clifford W. Walsh, composer), 1941; Tabloid History of Greatest Rochester, 1942; The Amazon (female) Minstrels, a Satire, 1943. Contributor to Centennial History of Rochester and Dictionary of Am. Biography. Visited South America and reported to State Dept. of U.S. a tentative offer of subsidy for a direct steamship line to Paraguay; trapped a jaguar (said to be the largest ever brought to this country) and presented it for display in New York Zoöl. Park, 1901. In 1934, N.Y. Supreme Court declared him sole and exclusive owner of Necrosan, of which U.S. Govt. had used $150,000 worth while bringing home soldier dead from Europe; still retains one-third interest. Address: Boyden and Elmwood Avs., Maplewood, N.J. Died May 13, 1946.

BUTTFIELD, W. J., pres., gen. mgr. and dir. Vulcan Detinning Co. Dir. Continental Can Co., Inc., Marco Chemicals, Inc. Home: Plainfield, N.J. Office: Vulcan. Detinning Co., Sewaren, N.J. Died Dec. 30, 1948.

BUTZEL, Fred M. (bŭt'zĕl), lawyer; b. Detroit, Mich., Aug 25, 1877; s. Magnus and Henrietta (Hess) B.; Ph.B., U. of Mich., 1897; LL.D., Wayne U., 1935; unmarried. Admitted to Mich bar, 1899, and since practiced at Detroit. Pres. Parkside Hosp., chairman exec. com. Detroit Jewish Welfare Fedn.; vice president Detroit Community Fund, Service Men's Bureau, Detroit Chapter American Red Cross, Legal Aid Bureau of Detroit Bar Association. Jewish religion. Clubs: Social Workers, Detroit Yacht, Franklin Hills. Home: 299 Mack Avenue. Office: National Bank Building, Detroit, Mich. Died May 20, 1948.

BUXTON, G. Edward; b. Kansas City, Mo., May 13, 1880; s. G. Edward and Sarah Amelia (Harrington) B.; prep. edn., Highland Mil. Acad., Worcester, Mass., 1895-98; Ph.B., Brown U., 1902, LL.D., 1948; LL.B., Harvard, 1906; m. Aline H. Armstrong, Jan. 19, 1910; 1 son, Coburn Allen. Reporter Providence (R.I.) Journal, 1902-03; mgr. Title Guarantee Co. of R.I., 1906-11; admitted to R.I. bar, 1907; asst. to trustee John Carter Brown estate, 1911; treas. Providence Journal Co., 1912-20, war corr., France, Germany and Belgium, Aug. 1914-Feb. 1915; vice pres. B.B.&R. Knight, Inc., 1920-26; pres. B.B.&R. Knight Corp., 1926-35; pres. Androscoggin Mills, Bates Mfg. Co., Edward Mfg. Co., Hill Mfg. Co., York Mfg. Co. (all 5 cos., 1932-40); chairman of bd. Panhandle Production and Refining Co., Inc., since 1946; dir. Fruit of the Loom, Inc. Served as asst. dir. Office of Strategic Services, Washington, resigned June 30, 1945. Member Cotton Textile Industry Commission of NRA; v.p. Cotton Textile Inst., Inc., 1933-34. Mem. R.I.N.G., 1900-03, 1906-16, advanced from 2d lt. to major; served as maj. and lt. col., infantry, U.S. Army, 1917-19; participated engagements St. Mihiel and Meuse-Argonne; 3 citations; col., U.S. Res. Decorated Medal for Merit, Purple Heart (U.S.). Hon. Comdr. Mil. Div. Order Brit. Empire. Polonia Restituta (Poland). Del. to Rep. Nat. Conv., Kansas City, Mo., 1928, and to Rep. Nat. Conv., Cleveland, O., 1936. Republican Nat. Committeeman for Rhode Island, 1940-41; chmn. Brown Univ. Housing and Development Campaign. One of founders R.I. Boy Scouts. Mem. 82d Div. Nat. Assn. (pres. 1929-30), Am. Legion (one of founders in France), Soc. of the Cincinnati, S.A.R., Phi Delta Theta, Republican. Mason, Elk. Clubs: Hope, Art (Providence); Army and Navy (Washington); Knickerbocker. Merchants (New York). Author: Official History 82d Division A.E.F., 1920. Home: 85 Power St., Providence, R.I. Died Mar. 15, 1949.

BUZBEE, Thomas Stephen (bŭz'bē), lawyer; b. Little Rock, Ark., Sept. 6, 1875; s. John S. and Emma (Speer) B.; ed. pub. schs.; m. Minnie Lee Wooldridge, Oct. 9, 1895; children—Alvin Stephen, Martha Emma (Mrs. Durbin Bond). Admitted to Ark. bar, 1900, and since practiced at Little Rock; asst. to gen. solicitor Choctaw, Okla. & Gulf Ry. Co., 1900-04; atty. C., R.I.&P. Ry. Co. for states of Ark. and La. since 1906; now mem. Buzbee, Harrison & Wright. Democrat. Mem. Meth. Ch., S. Club: Country. Home: 300 N. Woodrow St. Office: 1025 Pyramid Bldg., Little Rock, Ark. Died Dec. 29, 1948.

BYAS, Hugh (bī'ás), author, newspaper corr.; born and educated in Scotland; married. Foreign service in South Africa; joined the Times, London, 1910; mng. editor Japan Advertiser, Tokyo, principal Am. daily in Far East, 1914-22; newspaper work, England, 1922-26; chief corr. for the London Times in Japan, 1926-41; staff corr. in Japan for N.Y. Times, 1927-41; left Japan, May 1941, arriving in N.Y. City; recorded the movement in the Jap. army which led through the Manchurian "incident" and the China "affair" to the present war in the Pacific; covered the period in which the Jap. army gained control of the govt. Author: The Japanese Enemy: His Power and Vulnerability, 1942; Government by Assassination, a Study of Modern Japan, 1942; also chapter on Far East in We Saw It Happen. Contbr. articles on Japan to mags. Lecturer Yale U., 1943-44. Home: 2 Livingston St., New Haven, Conn. Address: care Alfred A. Knopf, Inc., New York, N.Y. Died Mar. 6, 1945.

BYERS, John Frederic, mfr.; b. Edgeworth, Pa., Aug. 6, 1881; s. Alexander MacBurney and Martha (Fleming) B.; grad. St. Paul's Sch., Concord, N.H., 1900; B.A., from Yale U., 1904; m. Caroline Mitchell Morris, Dec. 6, 1905 (died Nov. 13, 1934); children—Alexander M. III, John Frederic, Nancy Lee, Buckley Morris; m. 2d, Jeannine Decroix Schley, Dec. 1, 1937; 1 dau., Marie Maude. Chmn. bd. A. M. Byers Co.; dir. Mellan National Bank & Trust Co. (Pittsburgh), Westinghouse Air Brake Co., Union Switch & Signal Co., Western Allegheny R.R. Co. Trustee Carnegie Inst., Carnegie Inst. of Technology and Carnegie Library (all of Pittsburgh). Republican. Presbyterian. Clubs: Pittsburgh, Duquesne, Allegheny Country (Pittsburgh); Racquet and Tennis, Brook, Links (New York); Nat. Golf Links, Deepdale Golf. Home: Sewickley, Pa. Died June 11, 1949.

BYINGTON, Edwin Hallock, (bi'ing-tun), prof. homiletics and liturgics; b. Adrianople, Turkey, Dec. 15, 1861; s. Rev. Theodore Linn and Margaret Esther (Hallock) B.; came to America, 1867, and later returned to Turkey; ed. Robert Coll., Constantinople, 1874-78; grad. Phillips Acad., Andover, Mass., 1879; A.B., Amherst, 1883, D.D., 1928; studied Hartford Theol. Sem., 1884-85; grad. Auburn (N.Y.) Theol. Sem., 1887; m. Sophia Weston Janes, Sept. 2, 1891 (died Dec. 22, 1906); m. 2d, Helen Prince Foster, June 28, 1910. Ordained Congl. ministry, 1887; pastor Springfield, Mass., 1887-91; asst. to late Rev. R. S. Storrs, pastor Ch. of the Pilgrims, Brooklyn, 1891-1900; pastor Beverly, Mass., 1900-09, West Roxbury, Mass., 1909-27; instr. in homiletics and liturgics, Gordon Coll. Theology and Missions and Div. Sch., Boston, 1918-27, prof. since 1927. Mem. Phi Beta Kappa. Author: Open Air Preaching, 1892; Byington's Chart of Jewish National History (map and booklet), 1895; The Children's Pulpit, 1910; The City of the Second Life, 1918; Pulpit Mirrors, 1927; The Quest for Experience in Worship, 1929; The Minister's Week-Day Challenge, 1931. Contbr. to Great Themes of the Christian Faith (edited by Charles W. Ferguson), 1930. Address: Needham, Mass. Died Jan. 25, 1944.

BYRAM, Harry E., ry. official; b. Galesburg, Ill., Nov. 28, 1865; s. Maynard and Cornelia B.; common sch. edn.; m. Estella Berquist, May 26, 1891 (died June 1909); m. 2d, Mrs. L. T. Morrison, Oct. 1910 (died Sept. 1934); m. 3d, Mrs. Helen J. Williams, Feb. 16, 1935. Began as call boy C.,B.&Q.R.R.Co. at Galesburg, at 16; was stenographer and clerk at Chicago until 1889; clerk in gen. mgr.'s office and chief clerk in v.p.'s office G. N. Ry., St. Paul, 1894-98; asst. gen. supt. Mont. Central Ry., Great Falls, Mont., Mar. 1898-Oct. 1899; supt. Cascade div. G. N. Ry., Everett, Wash., 1899-1902; asst. to 1st and later to 4th v.p. C.,R.I.&P. Ry. Chicago, 1902-04; gen. supt. Southwestern dist. C.,R.I.&P., Topeka, Kan., Feb.-July 1904; gen. supt. Neb. dist. C.,B.&Q.R.R., Sept. 1904-May 15, 1909, asst. to the 2d v.p., May

15, 1909-Feb. 1, 1910, v.p., Feb. 1, 1910-Oct. 1, 1917, C.,B.&Q.R.R.Co.; pres. C.,M.&St.P.Ry., Oct. 1, 1917, later receiver, chmn. bd. since reorganization, 1927. Home: Fairfield, Conn. Office: 52 Wall St., New York, N.Y. Died Nov. 11, 1941.

BYRNE, James, lawyer; b. Springfield, Mass., Jan. 16, 1857; s. Michael and Ellen (Buckley) B.; A.B., Harvard, 1877, LL.B., 1882; LL.D., New York U., 1917, Harvard, 1927; m. Helen Macgregor, Apr. 21, 1896. Practiced law, New York, since 1883. Regent U. of State of N.Y., 1916-37, vice chancellor, 1929-33, chancellor, 1933-37. Mem. exec. com. Council of Am. Law Inst., 1923-34, v.p., 1928-34; pres. Harvard Law Sch. Assn. of N.Y. City, 1915, Assn. Bar City of N.Y., 1921-23, Harvard Alumni Assn., 1920, Harvard Club of New York, 1922-24; mem. Harvard Corp., 1920-26. Mem. Am. Red Cross Com. to Italy, 1917-19. Decorated Officer Crown of Italy, 1918; Commendatore of Crown of Italy, 1921; Chevalier Legion of Honor (France), 1921. Catholic. Mem. Phi Beta Kappa. Clubs: Century, Union, University, Harvard, Downtown, Piping Rock. Home: 1088 Park Av. Office: 598 Madison Av., New York, N.Y. Died Nov. 4, 1942.

BYRNE, Joseph (J. Grandson), M.D.; b. Ireland, Mar. 21, 1870; s. Patrick and Margaret (O'Neill) B.; B.A., Carlow Coll. (Royal U., Ireland), 1890; M.A., St. Francis Xavier's Coll., N.Y., 1893; M.D., Coll. Phys. and Surg. (Columbia), 1895; LL.B., N.Y. Law School, 1900; LL.D., Fordham University, 1921; fellow American College Physicians, 1927. Came to the United States, 1891, naturalized, 1897. Practiced at New York since 1897; dean Fordham U. Medical School, 1917-21; pres. med. bd. Central and Neurol. Hosp., Welfare Island, N.Y.; consulting neurologist, City, Fordham, and Neurological Hosps. Has served as mem. of advisory board, Health Dept., N.Y. City; capt. 69th Vol. Regt., Spanish-Am. War, 1898. Fellow N.Y. Acad. Medicine; mem. Royal Coll. of Surgeons (Eng.), Soc. for Exptl. Study of Biology and Medicine, New York Neurol. Soc., Alumni Assn. Coll. Phys. and Surg. (Columbia). Author: Physiology of the Semi-circular Canals, and Their Relation to Seasickness, 1912; Seasickness and Health, 1912; The Mechanism of Pain, 1918; Sensory-Psychic Integration, 1924; The Pupils in Visceral and Somatic Disorders, 1926; Studies on the Physiology of the Eye, Still Reaction, Sleep, Dreams, Hibernation, Repression, Hypnosis, Narcosis, Coma, and Allied Conditions, 1933; Clinical Studies on the Physiology of the Eye, 1934; Studies on the Physiology of the Middle Ear, 1938; The Effect of Stimulation of the Cortex Cerebri Upon the Mechanisms which Mediate Movements of the Iris and the Membrana Tympani, 1937; The Mechanism of Sensation and Emotion, 1941; The Physiological Basis of Perception, 1941. Has made extensive studies, experimental and clinical, on the mechanism of sensation, and contributed numerous articles on that and kindred subjects. Home: 600 W. 161st St., New York, N.Y. Died May 13, 1945.

BYRNES, Timothy Edward, lawyer, corp. official; b. Bellows Falls, Vt., Nov. 22, 1853; s. Daniel and Hanora (Clifford) B.; B.S., U. of Minn., 1879; Columbia Law Sch., New York, 1881; m. Clara Mar Goodrich, May 15, 1883; children—George Goodrich, Clifford Hamilton, Frederick Edward. Practiced law, Minneapolis, 1881-1900; chief appointment div., Treas. Dept., Washington, 1889-91; counsel G.N. Ry., N.P. Ry., 1894-1904; pres. Vt. Asbestos Corp.; former pres. Montpelier & Wells River R.R., Barre R.R., Nantucket Steamboat Co., Industrial Finance Co.; v.p. N.Y.,N.H.&H. R.R., B.&M. R.R., N.E. Navigation Co., 1904-13; dir. Merchants Nat. Bank, 1908-16. Clubs: Union, Algonquin, Beacon, Commercial, Merchants, Exchange, Traffic (Boston); Country (Brookline); Union League (New York). Home: 236 17th Av. N.E., St. Petersburg, Fla.; (summer) Hyde Park, Vt. Died March 19, 1944; buried in Royal Palm Cemetery, St. Petersburg Fla.

C

CABELL, Robert Hervey; b. Brunswick, Mo., Dec. 1, 1867; s. Dr. Robert Hervey and Alice (Oliver) C.; grad. high sch., June 1886, N.Y. Commercial Coll., 1890; m. Eva Patterson, Oct. 1897; children—Robert Hervey, Jr., Charles Egner, Helen (Comtesse Jacques de Lailhacar) Joseph Patterson. Began as salesman with Armour & Co., 1892, promoted dept. mgr., 1898, mng. dir. European interests with hdqrs. in London, 1913-34, gen. mgr., Chicago, 1934, pres., 1935-40; retired Jan. 1940. Mem. British Meat and Allied Trades Com., 1914-18. Mem. Internat. C. of C., Pilgrims of U.S., Newcomen Society, S.A.R., Am. C. of C. of London (a founder). Democrat. Presbyterian. Mason. Clubs: American (a founder), Royal Automobile (London); Chiabirta (Biarritz); Bankers (New York); Ridgewood (N.J.) Country. Home: 212 Sunset Av., Ridgewood, N.J. Died Dec. 12, 1947; buried Hollenback Cemetery, Wilkes Barre, Pa.

CABLE, Frank T. (kā'b'l), torpedo boat expert; b. New Milford, Conn., June 19, 1863; s. Abijah and Olive L. (Taylor) C.; ed. Claverack (N.Y.) Coll.; m. Nettie A. Hungerford, May 29, 1892. Engaged in elec. and engring. work in minor capacities, 1890-97; supt. Holland Submarine Boat Co., 1897-1901, and as elec. engr. developed the original Holland boat, commanding her on every trip until she was sold to the U.S. Govt., 1900; conducted trials of the first submarine built by the English Govt., and trained crew to operate same, 1902; also conducted trials of Adder class of submarines for U.S. Govt., 1903; of first Holland submarine bought by the Russian Govt., and trained the crew, 1904; of 5 submarines for the Japanese Govt. and trained crews for same, 1905; consulting engineer, Electric Boat Co.; organizer, 1910, New London Ship & Engine Co., Groton, Conn. Pres. New London Building & Loan Assn.; trustee New London Savings Bank. Member Soc. Naval Architects. Republican. Conglist. Clubs: Thames, Harbour (New London); Transportation (New York) Home: New London, Conn. Office: Groton, Conn. Died May 21, 1945.

CABOT, George E., trustee; b. Brookline, Mass., Feb. 22, 1861; s. Edward C. and Martha Eunice (Robinson) C.; student G.W.C. Noble's Sch. and Mass. Inst. Tech.; m. Eliza Tileston Hemenway; children—George (dec.), Edward C. Spent early yrs. in elec. industry; mgr. telephone co., Brookline, Mass.; supt. Western Electric Light Co., Boston; treas. and gen. mgr. Holtzer-Cabot Electric Co. until 1892; since in carereal estate and trustee under wills; now pres. Cabot, Cabot & Forbes, Inc., Boston; v.p. Mass. Hosp. Life Co.; pres. Boston Athenæum; dir. Boylston Market Assn.; trustee Mass. Building Trust, Fenway Studios Trust, State Street Associates, Kensington Real Estate Trust, Boston Museum Fine Arts; member Mass. Hist. Society. Clubs: Somerset, Country, Essex County. Home: 169 Marlborough St., Boston, Mass.; (summer) Manchester, Mass. Office: 60 State St., Boston, Mass. Died Apr. 18, 1946.

CABOT, Hugh, surgeon; b. Beverly Farms, Mass., Aug. 11, 1872; s. James Elliot and Elizabeth (Dwight) C.; A.B., Harvard, 1894, M.D., 1898; LL.D., Queen's U., Belfast, 1925; m. Mary Anderson Boit, Sept. 1902 (now deceased); children—Hugh Cabot, Mary Anderson (dec.), John Boit, Arthur Tracy; m. 2d, Elizabeth Cole Amory, Oct. 1938. Began practice, Boston, Mass., 1900; asst. surgeon and surgeon, Mass. Gen. Hosp., 1902-19; surgeon Bapt. Hosp., 1900-19; asst. prof. surgery, Harvard Med. Sch., 1910-18, clin. prof., 1919; prof. surgery, U. of Mich., 1919-30, dean Med. Sch., 1921-30; prof. surgery, Grad. Sch., U. of Minn., 1930-39; surgeon Mayo Clinic, 1930-39. Honorary lt. col. Royal Army Med. Corps (British), 1916-19; mentioned 4 times in dispatches; decorated Companion Order St. Michael and St. George. Fellow Am. Coll. Surgeons; hon. fellow The Royal Society of Medicine (London); mem. Am. Surg. Assn., A.M.A., Am. Assn. Genito-Urinary Surgeons, Assn. Français d'Urologie, Société Internationale d'Urologie, Phi Beta Kappa, Alpha Omega Alpha, Sigma Xi. Overseer Harvard Coll., 1929-35. Republican. Clubs: Harvard (Boston, Mass.); Boone and Crockett (New York). Author: Surgical Nursing, 4 edits., 1924, 30, 37, 40; The Doctor's Bill, 1936; The Patient's Dilemma, 1940. Editor: Modern Urology, 1918, 3d edit., 1936. Contbr. articles in med. jours. since 1900. Home: 465 Warren St., Needham, Mass. Died Aug. 14, 1945.

CABOT, William Brooks, engr.; b. Brattleboro, Vt., Feb. 2, 1858; s. Norman F. and Lucy T. (Brooks) C.; student Sheffield Scientific Sch. (Yale); C.E., Rensselaer Poly. Inst., 1881; m. Elisabeth Lyman Parker, May 29, 1886. Began in civ. engring. dept. U.P. Ry., in the West, later in iron mfg., Everett, Pa.; v.p. Holbrook, Cabot & Rollins Corp., Boston and New York, 1895-1907. Mem. Am. Antiquarian Soc., Am. Acad. Arts and Sciences, Royal Geog. Soc. (London). Episcopalian. Clubs: Explorers', Boone and Crockett (New York); Harvard Travelers, St. Botolph (Boston). Author: Labrador, 1920. Home: 447 Marlboro St., Boston, Mass.* Died Jan. 30, 1949.

CADMAN, Charles Wakefield, composer; b. Johnstown, Pa., Dec. 24, 1881; s. William C. and Caroline (Wakefield) C.; studied with Leo Oehmler (harmony), W. K. Steiner (organ playing), orchestration under Luigi Von Kunits, all of Pittsburgh, Pa.; hon. degree Mus.D., Wolcott Conservatory of Music, Denver, Colo., 1924; hon. degree Mus.D., U. of Southern Calif., 1926; unmarried. Formerly music critic, Pittsburgh Dispatch; organist Pittsburgh churches and Pittsburgh Male Chorus. First published organ pieces and ballads, 1904; later became interested in Indian music; first Indian songs were rejected five times by pubs. before finding acceptance; visited the Omaha Indian reservation, 1909, and secured phonographic records of Indian songs and flute pieces. Mem. Nat. Inst. Arts and Letters, Am. Composers and Conductors Assn., Am. Soc. of Composers, Authors and Pubs.; chmn. Congress of Am. Music which led to festival at Los Angeles, Calif., June 1915. Clubs: Jonathan (honorary), Uplifters' (Los Angeles); Soc. of N. & S. Am. Composers. Composer: Four American Indian Songs; Sayonara; Three Songs to Odysseus; The Vision of Sir Launfal (cantata for male voices); song cycles, White Enchantment and The Morning of the Year (for mixed voices); chamber music includes—piano sonata in A Major; violin sonata in G; trio in D. Major; quintet for piano and strings in G Minor; A Mad Empress Remembers (for violincello and orchestra); orchestral works, symphony in E Minor (Pennsylvania); Aurora Borealis (fantasy for piano and orchestra); Oriental Rhapsody; American suite for strings; Dark Dancers of the Mardi Gras (piano solo part); Thunderbird suite; Trail Pictures; From Hollywood (suite for piano); The Sunset Trail (operatic cantata); school operettas, Lelawala Hollywood Extra, The Ghost of Lollypop Bay, The Golden Trail, The Belle of Havana, The Bells of Capistrano; (high school cantatas) The House of Joy, The Far Horizon; also the Garden of Mystery, grand opera in 1 act (prod. New York, Mar. 18, 1925); Shanewis (The Robin Woman), grand opera on an Am. subject, 2 scenes, prod. Met. Opera House, 1918, and 1919; the first Am. opera to live beyond one season at this instn.; Indian opera in 3 acts; A Witch of Salem (opera in 2 acts), prod. Chicago Civic Opera Co., Dec. 8, 1926. One of founders and mem. bd. dirs. Hollywood Bowl. Contbr. to music jours. Address: Los Angeles. Died Dec. 30, 1946; buried in Forest Lawn Cemetery, Glendale, Calif.

CADMAN, Paul Fletcher, economist; b. Oakland, Calif., Nov. 4, 1889; s. Charles Keeney and Ella Elizabeth (Fletcher) C.; B.A., U. of Calif., Berkeley, 1915; student Gen. Theol. Sem., N.Y. City, 1916; D. en D., Univ. of Paris, France, 1922; m. Ethel Frances Mills, Dec. 25, 1919. Asso. prof. economics U. of Calif., 1927-28, dean of men, 1928; exec. sec. San Francisco Stock Exchange, 1930-32; asso. prof. economics and asst. to pres. U. of Calif., 1933-35; pres. Am. Research Foundation, San Francisco, 1936-40; economist Am. Bankers Assn., N.Y. City, 1940-44; assistant to president and dir. of Research, Henry J. Kaiser Co., 1944. Served as comdt.-adj., Sect. 133, Am. Ambulance, 1916; capt. F.A., 2nd Div., A.E.F., 1917. Decorated Croix de Guerre, Fourragère de la Croix de Guerre, Chevalier de l'Ordre National de la Légion d'Honneur (France). Trustee and chairman of the board of trustees, American Field Service Fellowships for French Universities, Inc. Fellow Royal Econ. Soc.; mem. Nat. Inst. Social Sciences, Am. Inst. Banking, Am. Acad. Polit. and Social Sci., Am. Econ. Assn., Acad. Polit. Science, Foreign Policy Assn., Am. Museum Natural History, National Probation Association, National Geographic Soc., Inst. for Pacific Relations, English-Speaking Union, The Newcomen Society, Phi Delta Theta, Beta Gamma Sigma, Alpha Kappa Psi, Omicron Delta Gamma, Pi Delta Phi. Republican. Episcopalian. Clubs: Bohemian (San Francisco); St. Moritz Figure Skating (Berkeley); Athenian-Nile. Author: National Income and Deficit Financing, 1939; Economics of Discontent, 1940; also numerous monographs on Franco-Am. history. Home: R.F.D. 1, Box 103, Happy Valley Rd., Lafayette, Calif. Office: 1522 Latham Square Bldg., Oakland 12, Calif.; also 314 British Empire Bldg., 620 Fifth Av., New York, N.Y. Died Nov. 11, 1946.

CADY, Hamilton Perkins, chemist; b. Camden, Kan., May 2, 1874; s. Perkins E. and Ella M. (Falkenbury) C.; Carleton Coll., Northfield, Minn.; A.B., U. of Kan., 1897, Ph.D., 1903; grad. work Cornell, 1897-99; m. Stella C. Gallup, June 5, 1900; children—Ruth Caroline, George Hamilton, Helen Frances. Asst. prof. chemistry, 1899-1905, asso. prof., 1905-11, prof. chemistry since 1911, U. of Kan., also chmn. chem. dept. until 1940. Fellow A.A.A.S.; mem. Am. Chem. Soc., Kan. Acad. Science, Sigma Xi, Alpha Chi Sigma. Conglist. Author: (with Edgar Henry Summerfield Bailey) A Laboratory Guide to the Study of Qualitative Analysis, 1901; The Principles of Inorganic Chemistry, 1912; General Chemistry, 1916. Home: Lawrence, Kan. Died May 26, 1943.

CADY, Samuel Howard, lawyer; b. Excelsior, Sauk County, Wis., Feb. 4, 1870; s. William Curtis and Emogene (Huntington) C.; B.A., U. of Wis., 1895, LL.B., 1897; m. Helen Baker, May 11, 1899; children—Helen B. (Mrs. L. S. Griffith), Jessie S. (Mrs. Gordon M. Conklin), Alice H. (Mrs. J. L. Pickering). Admitted to Wis. bar, 1897; practiced law at Green Bay, Wis., 1897-1921; Wisconsin atty. C.&N.W. Ry. Co., at Milwaukee, 1921-24; asst. gen. solicitor some co., Chicago, 1924-25, gen. solicitor, 1925-33, v.p. and gen. counsel since Feb. 1933. Mem. Delta Upsilon. Republican. Conglist. Clubs: Milwaukee (Milwaukee); Union League (Chicago). Home: 2915 Grant St., Evanston, Ill. Office: 400 W. Madison St., Chicago, Ill. Died Oct. 3, 1942.

CAHILL, Bernard J. S., architect; b. London, Eng., Jan. 30, 1866; s. James Alban and Elizabeth (Smith) C.; ed. Ratcliffe Coll. (U. of London), 1884; S. Kensington Sch. of Art, London, 1887; came to U.S., 1888; m. Lida Boardman Hall, Mar 5, 1897 (now dec.); m. 2d, Laura Georgiana McCune, June 26, 1907; 1 son, Bernard James Alban. Practicing architecture at San Francisco, 1891, Vancouver, B.C., Portland, Ore., and Oakland, Calif.; specialist in mausoleum design and mortuary architecture. Editor, Am. Builders Review, 1906. Inventor of the "Butterfly Map" or Octahedral System of Projection, 1899-1935, suited for internat. meteorology, geography and geophysics, including aviation and radio, adopted by Pacific div. of Pan-Am. Airways 1939, by Alameda School Board, 1940; featured by N.Y. Times and Associated Press as the standard world map of the future). Author pamphlet, On Thinking Federally and other pamphlets on architecture, cartography, etc. Original plans for The Civic Center made in 1904, finally adopted by the City of San Francisco, Jan. 1912. Planned Multnomah Hotel, Portland, Ore.; Magnavox factories, Oakland; Diamond Head Memorial Park, Honolulu; Catacombs and Columbarium Cypress Lawn, San Francisco; St. Mary's Mausoleum, Sacramento; etc. Home: 1834 Clinton Av., Alameda, Calif. Died Oct. 4, 1944.

CAHILL, Isaac Jasper, clergyman; b. Richwood, O., Aug. 1, 1868; s. Uriah and Isabelle (Warbs) C.; B.A., Central Ohio Coll., East Liberty, 1887; B.A., Hiram (Ohio) Coll., 1889, M.A., 1892; studied U. of Chicago; m. Lillian M. Skidmore, Aug. 9, 1887; children—Paul Trester, Vaughan Dabney, Helen Lillian, Sarah Louise. Ordained ministry Disciples of Christ, 1889; pastor North Fairfield, O., 1889-92, Kenton, 1892-96, Dayton, 1896-1909; gen. sec. Ohio Christian Missionary Soc., 1910-31; campaign sec. Men and Millions Movement, 1918; 1st v.p. United Christian Missionary Soc., 1931-36; mem. commn. on the ministry, Disciples of Christ, 1924-28; mem. exec. com. Ohio Council of Chs., 1921-25; trustee Pension Fund, Disciples of Christ, 1928-30; sec. Nat. Evangelistic Assn., Disciples of Christ, 1932-36; head of mission of Disciples of Christ in Jamaica, B.W.I., 1937-38; pastor Crawford Rd. Christian Ch., Cleveland, O., 1939-40; acting pastor First Christian Ch., Athens, O., 1940-41, Bellefontaine, O., 1941; Evansville, Ind., 1941, Steubenville, O., 1942, Roanoke, Va., 1942, New Philadelphia, O., 1943-44; acting pastor First Christian Church, Birmingham, Ala., since Oct. 1944. Editor of Ohio Work (monthly), 1910-31. Contbr. to Christian Evangelist World Call. Home: 1628 Marlowe Av., Lakewood, O. Died Jan. 10, 1945.

CAHILL, James Christopher, lawyer, publisher, educator; b. St. Paul, Minn., June 2, 1885; s. Patrick and Marie (Fleming) C.; Ph.B., Loyola U., Chicago, 1926; LL.B., St. Paul Coll. of Law, 1905; m. Harriet M. Gould, Apr. 26, 1911; children—Richard Gould, Harriet Marie (Mrs. John Shields). Admitted to Minn. bar, 1906, practicing at St. Paul until 1911, sec. to mayor of St. Paul, 1908-10; editor in chief Callaghan & Co., pubs., Chicago, 1913-27, v.p., 1924-39, gen. mgr., 1927-39; prof. law, Loyola U., 1926; chmn. of bd., Foundation Press, Chicago; exec. West Publishing Co., St. Paul. Mem. Chicago Bar Assn., Chicago Law Inst., Chicago Literary Soc., Medievalists. Clubs: Lake Shore Athletic (Chicago); Minnesota (St. Paul). Editor: Cahill's Illinois Statutes (8 edits.), 1921-33; Ill. St. Bar Assn. Statutes, 1935; Cahill's Consolidated Laws of N.Y. (2 edits.) 1923, 1930; Cahill's N.Y. Civil Practice (7 editions), 1924-37; Cahill's New York Criminal Code, 1928; Cahill's New York Practice Series, 1927; Cahill's Mich. Compiled Laws, 1922; Cyclopedic Law Dictionary, 1922; Callaghan's Iowa Digest, 1921; Callaghan's Illinois Statutes Annotated, 1924; Volumes 165-243 Illinois Appellate Court Reports, 1914-27. Editor in chief Fletcher's Cyclopedia of Corp., 1st edit., 1917. Co-author. Nichols Cahill New York Practice and Forms, (16 vols.), 1938-39. Home: 265 Mount Curve Bvld. Office: 50 W. Kellog Blvd., St. Paul, Minn.* Died Apr. 5, 1946.

CAILLOUET, Adrian Joseph (kī-whĕt'), judge; b. Thibodaux, La., Feb. 19, 1883; s. Judge L. Philip and Marie Adele (Lagarde) C.; A.B., St. Mary's (Ky.) Coll., 1902, A.M., 1921; m. Effie Amelia Briggs, Sept. 29, 1909; children—L. Philip, Raymond Anthony (dec.), Bernard Joseph, Adrian Joseph, Jr. Admitted to La. bar, 1913, and began practice at Houma; judge, U.S. Dist. Court, Eastern Dist. of La., since 1940. Mem. American and Louisana bar associations, Holy Name Society, St. Vincent dePaul Society, Knights of Columbus, Catholic Knights of America. Democrat. Home: 2300 Dublin St. Office: 205 U.S. Post Office Bldg., New Orleans 18, La. Died Dec. 19, 1946.

CAIN, Rolly Morton, pres. and gen. mgr. Abbott Labs.; b. Davies County, Ind., Jan. 14, 1882; s. Charles L. and Emma Edith (Swan) C.; ed. Ind. pub. schs.; m. Dersie A. Myers, Apr. 9, 1909 (died Nov. 30, 1934); children—George R., Ruth (Mrs. Rudy L. Ruggles); m. 2d, Charlotte Fisher Lorndale, Sept. 12, 1937. Pres. Swan-Myers Co., Indianapolis, Ind., 1913-30; when company merged with Abbott Labs., North Chicago, Ill. (mfg. and distbn. pharms. and distbn. pharms. and chems.), 1930, became vice pres. and dir.; exec. vice pres., asst. gen. mgr., chmn. exec. com. and dir. Abbott Labs. 1933-Mar. 46; pres. and dir. Abbott Labs. Internat. Co., and Abbott Labs. Export Corp., 1943-Mar. 1946; pres. and gen. mgr. Abbott Labs. since Mar. 1946. Republican. Presbyterian. Mason. Clubs: Chicago Athletic; Glen View (Ill.); Onwentsia (Lake Forest, Ill.). Home: 3240 Lake Shore Drive, Chicago, Ill. Office: Abbott Laboratories, North Chicago, Ill. Died Feb. 21, 1947.

CAIRNS, Frederick Irvan, mining engr.; b. Susquehanna, Pa., Mar. 6, 1865; s. Rev. John and Magdelena (Hardie) C.; A.B., Hamilton Coll., N.Y., 1887, A.M., 1891; Met. E., Columbia, 1890; m. Marie Budd, Apr. 16, 1895; 1 son, Samuel Budd. Supt. Mich. Smelting Co. Mem. Am. Inst. Mining Engrs., 1897. Republican. Presbyterian. Home: Houghton, Mich. Died Apr. 14, 1944.

CALDER, A(lexander) Stirling, sculptor; b. Phila., Jan. 11, 1870; s. Alexander Milne and Margaret (Stirling) C.; pupil Pa. Acad. Fine Arts and Chapu and Flaguière, Paris, France; m. Nanette Lederer, Feb. 22, 1895; children—Margaret, Alexander. Curator of sculpture, Pa. Mus., 1905. Awarded gold medal, Phila. Art Club, 1893; hon. mention, Buffalo Expn., 1901; silver medal, St. Louis Expn., 1904; spl. Walter Lippincott prize, 100th Anniversary Exhbn., Pa. Acad. of Fine Arts, 1905; grand prize Alaska-Yukon Expn.; designer's medal, San Francisco Expn., 1915 gold medal of honor Archtl. League, N.Y. City, 1932 McClees prize, Pa. Acad., 1932; Maida Kregg memorial prize, Nat. Arts Club, N.Y. City, 1933, sculpture prize, 1934. Represented in permanent collection Pa. Acad., and in Fairmount Park and Franklin Inn Club, Phila.; statute in Smithsonian grounds, Washington; Art Museum St. Louis; John Herron Art Inst., Indianapolis, Metropolitan Museum, New York; Telfair Art Acad., Atlanta. Acting chief, dept. of sculpture, San Francisco Expn., 1915; mem. Internat. Jury of Awards, 1915. Associate Nat. Acad., 1906; Nat. Academician, 1913. Mem. Nat. Inst. Arts and Letters, Nat. Sculpture Soc., Pub. Art League U.S., Municipal Art Soc. N.Y., Archtl. League New York, Art Club Phila., Fellowship Pa. Acad. Fine Arts, Fairmount Park Art Assn., Phila.; charter mem. League of N.Y. Artists, New Soc. of Artists. Clubs: Century, The Players, Nat. Arts. Studio: 252 Fulton St., Brooklyn, N.Y. Died Jan. 6, 1945.

CALDER, William M., ex-senator; b. Brooklyn, N.Y., Mar. 3, 1869; ed. public schs., New York; LL.D., George Washington U., 1920, Syracuse (N.Y.) U., 1921, Fordham U. and Gonzales Coll., 1922; m. Catherine E. Harloe, 1893. Engaged as builder and erected over 4,000 houses at Brooklyn; bldg. commr., Brooklyn, 1902-03; mem. 59th to 63rd Congresses (1905-15), 6th N.Y. Dist.; del. Rep. Nat. Conv., 9 times to 1940; mem. U.S. Senate, 1917-23. Home: 551 1st St. Office: 3041 Av. U., Brooklyn, N.Y. Died Mar. 3, 1945.

CALDERWOOD, Alva John (kăl'dēr-wŏŏd), coll. dean; b. New Bedford, Pa., Feb. 14, 1873; s. William and Esther Ellen (Cowden) C.; A.B., A.M., Grove City (Pa.) Coll., 1896, Ph.D., 1908, Litt.D., 1921; A.B., Harvard, 1899; m. Leonora Neal, July 2, 1900; children—Helen Frances (Mrs. Rev. J. Stanley Harker), Esther Rebekah (dec.), Lt. John Neal (U.S. N.R.). Prof. English and mathematics, Grove City Coll., 1896-99, prof. Latin since 1899, dean since 1914. Sec. Selective Service Bd. No. 1, Mercer Co., Pa., since Oct. 1940. Mem. Midwestern Ednl. Assn. of Pa. (pres. 1936), Classical Assn. of Middle Atlantic States. Republican. United Presbyn. (ruling elder). Clubs: Grove City, Commercial, Grove City Country. Public speaker. Home: 310 Poplar, Grove City, Pa. Died Dec. 11, 1940

CALDWELL, James E., banker; b. Memphis, Tenn. Sept. 18, 1854; s. Alexander Samuel and Matilda Watson (Sheppard) C.; ed. pvt. schs. and business coll.; m. May Winston, Oct. 12, 1875; children—James E. (dec.), Elsie (Mrs. Daniel F. Carter Buntin), Charles Winston, William Underwood (dec.), Shirley (dec.), Margaret (dec.), May Winston (dec.). Rogers Clarke, Meredith, Dandridge (dec.). Propr. James E. Caldwell, gen. ins., 1876-96; pres. Cumberland Telephone & Telegraph Co., 1890-1913, chmn. bd., 1913-25; pres. First and Fourth Nat. Bank, Nashville, since 1912; pres. Nashville Trust Co.; chmn. bd. Southern Bell Telephone Co.; dir. Mo. State Life Ins. Co., St. Louis, Mo. Chmn. bd. trustees Peabody Coll. Democrat in Tenn. matters, Republican nationally. Presbyterian. Author: Recollections of a Life Time, 1923. Home: Longview, Franklin Pike, Nashville. Office: First and Fourth National Bank, Nashville, Tenn. Died Sept. 26, 1944.

CALDWELL, Otis William, scientist; b. Lebanon, Ind., Dec. 18, 1869; s. Theodore Robert and Belle C.; B.S., Franklin (Ind.) Coll., 1894, Ph.D. from University of Chicago, 1898; LL.D., Franklin Coll., 1917; m. Cora Burke, Aug. 25, 1897. Prof. biology, Eastern Ill. State Normal Sch., 1899-1907; asso. prof. botany, 1907-13, prof. botany and dean Univ. College, 1913-17, U. of Chicago; prof. edn. in Teachers' Coll. (Columbia U.), and dir. Lincoln Exptl. Sch., 1917-27; dir. Div. of School Experimentation of Inst. of Ednl. Research, 1920-27; dir. Inst. of Sch. Experimentation, 1927-35; retired as emeritus prof. Gen. sec. A.A.A.S. 1933-47; prof. botany, U. of Ind. Summer School of Biology, 1904; visiting prof., U. of Calif., 1931, Atlanta U., 1937-38. Fellow A.A.A.S. (chmn. com. on the place of science in education, 1924-40. Author: Laboratory and Field Manual of Botany, 1901; Plant Morphology, 1903; Practical Botany (with J. Y. Bergen), 1911; Introduction to Botany, 1914; Elements of General Science, 1914; Laboratory Manual of General Science (with others), 1915; Then and Now in Education, 1923; Biology in the Public Press, 1923; Open Doors to Science, 1925; Introduction to Science (with F. D. Curtis), 1929; Biological Foundations of Education (with C. C. Skinner and J. W. Tietz), 1931; Biology for Today (with F. D. Curtis and N. H. Sherman), 1933; Do You Believe It (with G. E. Lundeen), 1934; Everyday Biology (with F. D. Curtis and N. H. Sherman), 1940; Everyday Science (with F. D. Curtis), 1943. Editor: Science Remaking the World (with E. E. Slosson), 1923. Contbr. to science and ednl. jours. Home: New Milford, Conn. Office: Boyce Thompson Inst., Yonkers, New York. Died July 5, 1947

CALDWELL, William E(dgar), obstetrician, univ. prof.; b. Northfield, O., Feb. 23, 1880; s. Milton Etsil and Susanna Adams C.; M.D., N.Y. Univ. and Bellevue Hosp. Med. Sch., 1904; unmarried. Interne N.Y. Lying-In Hosp., 1904-05, 3d. surg. div. Bellevue Hosp., 1905-08; resident obstetrician Manhattan Maternity Hosp., 1908-09; adjunct asst. attending physician, Bellevue Hosp., and instr. in obstetrics, N.Y. Univ. Med. Sch., 1909-14, asst. prof. and asst. attending physician Bellevue Hosp. Obstet. Service, 1914-20; asso. prof. and asso. dir. Sloane Hosp., Columbia U., 1920-27, prof. clin. obstetrics and gynecology and asso. dir. Sloane Hosp., Columbia U., since 1927. Served as capt. of Med. Corps, U.S. Army, 1918. Fellow Am. Coll. Surgeons; mem. A.M.A., Med. Soc. of State of N.Y., Med. Soc. of County N.Y., N.Y. Obstet. Soc., N.Y. Acad. Medicine, Am. Gynecol. Soc., Am. Gynecol. Club, Sigma Xi, Nu Sigma Nu. Republican. Presbyterian. Clubs: Century Assn., N.Y. Athletic, Ohio Soc. of N.Y.; Silver Springs Country (Ridgefield, Conn.). Contbr. many professional articles to Am. Jour. Obstetrics and Gynecology and other jours. Home: 875 Park Av., New York, N.Y. Died Apr. 1, 1943.

CALHOUN, George Miller, prof. Greek; b. Lincoln, Neb., Jan. 29, 1886; s. James Duncan and Odus (Alderman) C.; A.B., Stetson U., Deland, Fla., 1906; A.B., U. of Chicago, 1907, Ph.D., 1911; m. Elinor McKay Miller, Dec. 18, 1913; children—James Duncan (dec.), John Archibald. Instr. Greek, later adj. prof., U. of Tex., 1911-17; asst. and asso. prof. Greek, U. of Calif., 1917-26, prof. since 1926; Barbara Weinstock lecturer, U. of Calif., 1925; visiting Carnegie prof. of internat. relations, univs. of Copenhagen, Oslo and Stockholm, Sept.-Nov. 1928; prof., univs. of Chicago, Tex., Calif., and Stanford U., summers since 1912; mgr. U. of Calif. Press, 1924-33. Mem. Am. Philol. Assn. (pres. 1940-41), Philol. Assn. of Pacific Coast (pres. 1934-35), Am. Association Univ. Profs., Am. Hist. Assn., Soc. Roman Studics, Soc. Hellenic Studies, Classical Assn. England and Wales, Assn. Guillaume Budé (comité américain), Phi Beta Kappa (hon.), Delta Sigma Phi. Democrat. Episcopalian. Club: Faculty. Author: Athenian Clubs in Politics and Litigation, 1913; The Business Life of Ancient Athens, 1926; The Ancient Greeks and the Evolution of Standards in Business, 1926 (Japanese transl.); The Growth of Criminal Law in Ancient Greece, 1927; A Working Bibliography of Greek Law (with Catherine Delamere), 1927. Contbr. to philol. and hist. jours., law revs., etc. Mem. editorial bd. Jour. of Economic and Business History, 1931-32; asso. editor Classical Philology; joint editor Sather Classical Lectures. Home: 571 Euclid Av., Berkeley, Calif. Died June 16, 1942.

CALHOUN, John William, educator; b. Manchester, Tenn., Oct. 24, 1871; s. George Washington and Maria Frances (Glasgow) C.; student Winchester (Tenn.) Normal Coll., 1896-97; A.B., U. of Tex., 1905; A.M., Harvard, 1908; LL.D. Abilene Christian Coll., 1938; m. Evelyn Scott, Aug. 22, 1910; 1 dau., Evelyn Elizabeth (Mrs. William Kay Miller). Teacher rural schs., Tenn., 1890-97, Tex., 1897-1901; tutor in pure mathematics, U. of Tex., 1905-09, instr., 1909-13, adjunct prof., 1913-17, asso. prof., 1917-19, asso. prof. applied mathematics, 1919-23, prof. since 1923, comptroller, 1925-37, and 1939-40, pres., ad interim, 1937-39. Austin scholar Harvard Univ., 1907-08. Fellow Texas Academy of Science; mem. Texas State Teachers Association, Phi Beta Kappa, Delta Kappa Epsilon. Democrat. Clubs: University, Town and Gown (Austin, Texas). Author: Unified Mathematics (with Karpinski and Benedict), 1918; Algebra for Junior and Senior High Schools (with White and Simpson), 1930; The Short and Simple Annals of the Poor, 1944. Home: 2805 Rio Grande St., Austin 21, Tex. Died July 7, 1947.

CALHOUN, Patrick, lawyer; b. Fort Hill, S.C., Mar. 21, 1856; s. Andrew Pickens and Margaret Maria (Green) C.; ed. in pvt. schs.; m. Sarah Porter, Nov. 4, 1885. Admitted to Ga. bar, 1875, Mo. bar, 1876; practiced at Atlanta, 1878-94; prominent in consolidation of ry. and traction interests, notably Central R.R. of Ga., Richmond & Danville, and Richmond & West Point Terminal Ry. and Warehouse Co. for all of which was counsel, 1889-92; devoted attention to consolidation and development of st. rys., taking active part in the consolidation of st. ry. systems in Pittsburgh, St. Louis, Baltimore and San Francisco. Dir. Phila. Co., United Rys. of Pittsburg, Houston Oil Co. of Tex., Calhoun Falls Investment Co., Calhoun Mills; owner Euclid Heights, Cleveland O. (dir. Euclid Heights Realty Co.), largely interested in real estate in S.C., Ga. and Texas. Home: Charlston, S.C., Euclid Heights, Cleveland, O., and 9 E. 88th St., New York. Address: 30 Broad St., New York. Died June 16, 1943.

CALISCH, Edward N. (kă'lish), clergyman; b. Toledo, O., June 23, 1865; s. Harry and Rebecca (Van Noorden) C.; grad. Hughes High Sch., Cincinnati, 1883; B.L., U. of Cincinnati, 1887; rabbi, Hebrew Union Coll., 1887, hon. D.H.L., 1928; M.A., U. of Va., 1904; Ph.D., 1908; hon. LL.D., U. of Richmond, 1940; m. Gisela Woolner, Jan. 22, 1890; children—Harold Edward, Mildred G. (dec.), A. Woolner, Edward N. II; m. 2d, Mrs. Essie S. Labenberg, July 17, 1927. Rabbi, Peoria, 1887-91, Richmond, Va., 1891-45, rabbi emeritus since 1945 (50th anniversary May, 1941); mem. Central Conf. Am. Rabbis (pres. 1921-23; mem. exec. bd.); mem. exec. com. Am. Jewish Com., Joint Distbn. Com., Jewish Welfare Bd.; pres. Richmond Rabbinic Council. Mem. State Council Defense, Va., and 4-minute man, World War I. Mem. Va. War History Commn. Mem. Non-Partisan Assn. League of Nations (v.p.); Soc. for Prevention Cruelty to Animals, Eng.-Speaking Union (treas.), Alumni Assn. Hebrew Union Coll., Raven Soc. of U. of Va., Phi Beta Kappa (pres. Richmond Chapter, 1940), B'nai B'rith. Mem. exec. com. Richmond Chapter American Red Cross; mem. bd. of United Service Organizations; mem. Economic League of America. Mason, Elk. Clubs: Jefferson, Rotary, Richmond Ember (pres.), Lakeside Country. Author: A

Child's Bible, 1890; A Book of Prayer, 1893; The Jew in English Literature, 1908; Method of Teaching Biblical History, Jr. Grade, 1914; Methods of Teaching Sr. Grade, 1914; Beth Ahabah Bulletin (homiletical addresses), quarterly since 1921; Collected Addresses, 1930 Home: Hotel Jefferson, Richmond, Va. Died Jan. 7, 1946.

CALKINS, Gary Nathan, zoölogist; b. Valparaiso, Ind., Jan. 18, 1869; s. John W. and Emma F. (Smith) C.; S.B., Mass. Inst. Tech., 1890; Ph.D., Columbia, 1897, Sc.D., 1929; m. Anne Marshall Smith, June 28, 1894; m. 2d, Helen Richards Colton, 1909; children—Gary Nathan, Samuel Williston. Asst. biologist, Mass. State Bd. Health, and lecturer in biology, Mass. Inst. Tech., 1890-93; tutor biology, 1894-96, zoölogy, 1896-99, instr., 1899-1903, adj. prof., 1903-04, adj. prof. invertebrate zoölogy, 1904, prof., 1904-06, professor of protozoölogy, 1906-39, prof. emeritus since 1939, Columbia Univ. Biologist New York State Cancer Lab., 1904-08; clk. of corp., Marine Biol. Lab. Fellow A.A.A.S., New York Zoöl. Soc.; mem. Am. Soc. Naturalists, Am. Morphol. Soc., Soc. Exptl. Biology and Medicine, Nat. Acad. Sciences. Pres. Am. Soc. Cancer Research, 1913-14, Soc. Exptl. Biology and Medicine, 1919-21. Dir. Am. Univ. Union, Paris, France, 1926-27. Author: The Protozoa (Vol. VI, Columbia U. Biol. Series), 1901; Protozoölogy, 1908; Biology, 1914; Biology of the Protozoa; 1926. Also numerous scientific papers. Home: Scarsdale, N.Y. Died Jan. 4, 1943.

CALKINS, Truesdel Peck, coll. pres.; b. Brownville, N.Y., Oct. 7, 1877; s. John and Julia (Allen) C.; studied Ives Sem., Cazenovia Sem. and Hudson River Inst.; A.B., Ohio Northern U., 1898, M.S., 1905, Pd.D., 1931; m. Harriet Cooke, Oct. 21, 1905; children—Marjorie Starr, Virginia Louise. Supt. of schs., Catskill, N.Y., 1905-12, Ridgefield Park, N.J., 1912-15, Hempstead, L.I., N.Y., 1915-32; dir. Bur. of Appointments and asst. prof. edn., New York U., 1932-37; asso. prof. edn. and dir. Div. of Edn., Hofstra Coll., 1937-39, pres. of Coll. since 1939. Dir. Second Nat. Bank, Central Nassua, Inc., pres. and dir. Franklin Shops, Inc., Hempstead Apt. Co. (all of Hempstead, N.Y.). Trustee Hempstead Pub. Sch. System. Mem. Pi Gamma Mu, Kappa Delta Pi. Republican. Episcopalian. Mason. Clubs: Hempstead (N.Y.) Golf; Nat. Republican (New York). Home: 167 Fulton Av., Hempstead, N.Y. Died June 8, 1942.

CALL, Arthur Deerin, editor of World Affairs, sec. Am. Peace Soc., permanent exec. sec. U.S. Group of Inter-parliamentary Union; b. Fabius, N.Y., Sept. 27, 1869; s. Charles E. and Jennie (Aylworth) C.; studied law, 1888-90; grad. State Normal Sch., Cortland, 1892; Ph.B., Brown U., 1896, A.M., 1905; grad. student philosophy, edn. and science, Yale, 1903-04; LL.D., Howard U., 1926; m. Mabel Winter Soule, June 29, 1897; children—Alden Aylworth (dec.), Margaret Farrar (Mrs. Richard S. Ladd), Benjamin Winslow (dec.). Dir. schs. under Z. R. Brockway, at N.Y. State Reformatory, Elmira, 1896-97; prin. schs., Elmira, 1897-99; supt. schs., Holliston, Medway and Sherborn, Mass., 1899-1902, Ansonia, Conn., 1902-04; supt. schs., etc., Hartford, Conn., July 1904-12; exec. dir. Am. Peace Soc., 1912-15; sec. Am. Peace Soc. and editor of World Affairs, continuing Advocate of Peace Through Justice, since 1915; permanent exec. sec. of the Am. Group of Inter-parliamentary Union since 1920; lecturer on edn. and philosophy, George Washington U., 1913-18; attended many internat. congresses abroad; pres. Conn. Peace Soc., 1906-12; pres. N.E. Assn. Sch. Supts., 1911-12; mem. N.E.A. (sec. dept. superintendence, 1910-11), Am. Acad. Polit. and Social Science, Am. Soc. Internat. Law, Delta Kappa Epsilon, Brown Alumni Assn. D.C. and Md. (pres. 1914-18). Dir. Conn. Prison Assn., 1908-12; chmn. Dist. Family Welfare Assn., Washington, 1914-19, mem. bd. mgrs., 1930-38. Conglist. Rep. of Am. Peace Soc. 5 mos. at Paris, Peace Conf., 1918-19; dir. Internat. Peace Bureau, at Berne, 1915-30; dir. 23d Conf. Inter-parliamentary Union (41 parliaments), Washington, 1925. Chevalier Cross Legion of Honor (French), 1926. Clubs: Cosmos, Palaver, Monday Evening (pres. 1921-22). Author of Federal Convention 1787, an International Conference Adequate to Its Purpose; Our Country and World Peace, 1926, etc. Joint Author: Metcalf and Call Readers, 1911; Fisher and Call's Text for Foreigners. Wrote pamphlets: The Will to End War; The Patriotic Duty Facing the Americas; Some Recent Developments of the Organized Peace Movement in America; Estimate of the Situation; Cumber and Entanglements; The Inter-parliamentary Union; If George Washington Were with Us Today; Force and World Peace; Three Views of Collective Security; Ralph Waldo Emerson, Realist; Education for World Peace; Christ of the Andes; James Madison; William Ladd; Ninety Percent of Us Believe; The Vitality of the Parliamentary System; etc. Home: 8815 Reading Rd., Silver Spring, Md. Office: 734 Jackson Pl., Washington, D.C. Died Oct. 23, 1941.

CALLANDER, Cyrus N., surgeon; b. 1865; M.D., Trinity Med. Coll., Ontario, Can., 1897. Practiced at Fargo, N.D., since 1899; staff surgeon St. John's and St. Luke's hosps.; orthopedic surgeon Fargo Clinic. Fellow Am. Coll. Surgeons; mem. Am. and N.D. State med. assns. Home: Fargo, N.D. Died Sept. 20, 1930.

CALLES, Plutarco Elías, Mexican statesman; b. Guaymas, Sonora, Sept. 25, 1877; s. Plutarco Elías Lucero and Jesus Calles; ed. Colegio de Don Benigno Lopez y Sierra; m. Natalia Chacón (dec.); m. 2d, Leonor Llorente. Began as teacher in public schools, became inspector of schools, Guaymas; then prof., Colegio de la Moneda; joined forces of Medero, 1910, becoming gen. in revolutionary army, 1914; gov. and mil. comdr., Sonora, 1915-19; sec. of industry, commerce and labor, 1919; founded an industrial school in Sonora; head of campaign for Gen. Obregon; served as sec. of war; sec. of interior, 1920-23; President of Mexico, 1924-28 (noteworthy for highway construction, founding Bank of Mexico, amortization of public debt).* Died Oct. 19, 1945.

CALVE, Emma, operatic singer; b. France, 1866; m. Alnor Gaspari, Mar. 1910. Début 1882, at Théâtre de la Monnale, Brussels (Massenet's "Herodiade"), 1882; first appeared in Paris in "Aben Hamet," 1884; as Carmen and as Santuzza, in "Cavalleria Rusticana," at the Opera Comique; Covent Garden, London, 1892; came to Met. Opera Co., New York, 1893; retired from stage, 1910. Home: Chateau de Cabrieres, Aguessac, Aveyron, France. Died Jan. 6, 1942.

CALVERY, Herbert Orion, pharmacologist; b. Eddy, Tex., Dec. 9, 1897; s. Luther and Theresa Irene (Marricle) C.; ed. Peniel Coll.; B.S., Greenville Coll., Ill., 1919; A.B., U. of Ill., 1921, M.S., 1923, Ph.D., 1924; m. Gertrude V. Lane, June 2, 1925; children—Catherine Ann, George Herbert. Teacher, 1919; asst. chemistry, U. of Ill., 1920-22, fellowship, 1922-24; asst. prof. U. of Louisville, 1924-25; instr. Johns Hopkins Med. Sch., 1925-27; asst. prof. physiol. chemistry, University of Michigan Medical School, 1927-35; senior pharmacologist Food and Drug Administrn. 1935-36, chief div. pharmacology since 1936. Fellow A.A.A.S., John Simon Guggenheim Memorial Foundation Fellow in Europe in 1932-33 mem. Am. Chem. Soc. (chmn. biol. div. 1939-40), Am. Soc. Biol. Chemists, Am. Soc. Pharmacology and Exptl. Therapeutics, Soc. Exptl. Biology and Medicine, Am. Pub. Health Assn., Sigma Xi, Alpha Chi Sigma, Phi Lambda Upsilon, Phi Sigma. Dem. Contbr. to jours., texts, encys. on biochemistry and toxicology. Home: 47 W. Baltimore St., Kensington, Md. Died Sep. 23, 1945.

CAMDEN, Harry Poole, sculptor; b. Parkersburg, W.Va., Mar. 10, 1900. Fellow Am. Acad. in Rome; elected associate mem. Nat. Acad. Design. 1942. Address: 281 Rye Beach, Rye, N.Y.* Died July 29, 1943.

CAMDEN, Johnson Newlon; b. Parkersburg, W.Va., Jan. 5, 1865; s. Hon. Johnson Newlon (ex-U.S. senator) and Ann (Thompson) C.; ed. Va. Mil. Inst., Lexington, Va.; studied law Columbia U. Sch., of Law, and Summer Law Sch., U. of Va.; m. Susanna Preston Hart, Oct. 16, 1888. Farmer and breeder of fine cattle and horses at Spring Hill Farm, nr. Versailles, Ky., since 1896; actively identified with opening and development of coal mines in eastern Ky.; apptd. by Gov. James B. McCreary as U.S. senator from Ky., June 16, 1914, to fill vacancy, and elected in Nov. following, for unexpired term ending Mar. 4, 1915. Democrat. Episcopalian. Clubs: Lexington, Country (Lexington, Ky.); Metropolitan University (Washington, D.C.). Home: Bersailles, Ky. Died Aug. 16, 1942.

CAMERON, A(rnold) Guyot, editor; b. Princeton, N.J., Mar. 4, 1864; s. Henry Clay and Mina (Chollet) C.; A.B., Princeton, 1886, A.M., 1888, Ph.D., 1891; abroad, 1887-88; m. Anne Wood Finley, June 21, 1899; children—Constance Guyot (Mrs. Townsend Ludington), Arnold Guyot, David Pierre Guyot, Nicholas Guyot, Stéphanie Guyot (dec.), Gerard Guyot, Yvonne Guyot. Prof. French and German langs. and their lits., Miami U., 1888-91; asst. prof. French (in charge of dept.), Sheffield Scientific Sch. (Yale), 1891-97; prof. French, John C. Green Sch. of Science, Princeton, 1897-1900; Woodhull prof. French, Princeton, 1900-05; prof. Summer Sch. of New York U., 1909; on staff Wall Street Journal, 1912-16. War preparedness service, 1917; speaking mission to France, 1918; govt. service, 1919. Mem. exec. bd., All-America Standards Council; a founder Soc. of Friends of de Grasse; mem. Am. Friends of Lafayette; hon. mem. Berzelius (Yale), Colonial and Cannon clubs (Princeton). Mem. Soc. Acad. d'Histoire Internationale, Civil Legion, S.R., S.A.R., Mil. Soc. War of 1812, Vet. Corps Arty. State of New York, Phi Beta Kappa. Republican. Presbyterian. Author: The Torrens System—Its Simplicity, Serviceability and Success. Editor of textbooks; contbg. editor All-America since 1928. Contbr. to financial and econ. publs. Home: Princeton, N.J. Died July 29, 1947.

CAMERON, Edgar Spier, painter; b. Ottawa, Ill., May 26, 1862; s. John Rush and Emily (Spier) C.; ed. pub. schools, Chicago Acad. Design, Art Students' League, New York, Académie Julian and École des Beaux Arts, Paris; m. Marie Gelon, 1890. Art critic, Chicago Tribune, 1891-1900; exhibitor Paris Salon; hon. mention, Yerkes Prize Competition, 1892; worked on decoration for Chicago Expn., 1893; mem. Internat. Jury, Paris Expn., 1900; silver medal, Paris, 1909. Most important works "Dreamland" and group of paintings awarded M.A.L. prize and later exhibited in spl. Am. exhbn. at Royal Acad., Berlin; works include figure, landscape and decorative paintings, and painting "Cabaret Breton," purchased by Friends of Am. Art for permanent collection of Art Inst., Chicago, 1917; represented in Chicago Hist. Soc., Union League, Arché and Woman's Aid clubs, Chicago and Ft. Sheridan; mural decorations Supreme Court Library, Springfield, Ill.; decorations for Genesee County Court House, Flint, Mich.; mural decorations First Nat. Bank & Trust Bldg., Oklahoma City, Okla.; "The Rain Dance," "Youth and Moonlight" purchased by Commn. for the Encouragement of Local Art of Chicago; "Noctourne" purchased by Municipal Art League, 1926 (on exhibition with the League's collection at Union League Club). Awarded Butler prize, Art Institute of Chicago, 1913, Clyde Carr and Rosenwald prizes, 1917. One of founders Municipal Art League, Chicago. Clubs: Cliff Dwellers, Green Room (hon. mem.). Decorated Officier de l'Instruction Publique by Ministry of Fine Arts, France. 1920. Address: 10 E. Ohio St., Chicago, Ill. Died Nov. 5, 1944.

CAMERON, George Hamilton, army officer; b. Ottawa, Ill., Jan. 8, 1861; s. Dwight Foster and Fanny Elizabeth (Norris) C.; student Northwestern U., 1878-79; grad. U.S. Mil. Acad., 1883; m. Nina Dean, d. Lt. Col. J. G. Tilford, U.S. Army, May 22, 1888; children—Douglas Tilford, lt. U.S. Army, killed in action in France, Nov. 3, 1918, Nina Tilford (wife Brig. Gen. John B. Thompson), Margaret Hughes (wife Lt. Col. Buckner M. Creel). Commd. 2d lt. 7th Cav., June 13, 1883; promoted through grades to col., July 1, 1916; brig.-gen. N.A., Aug. 5, 1917; maj. gen. U.S. Army, Nov. 28, 1917. Served in Dak. and Kan., 1883-88; duty as instr. and asst. prof., dept. of drawing, U.S. Mil. Acad., 1888-95; duty in Wash. and Calif., 1895-98; equipped first U.S. horse transport Tacoma, and sailed for Manila, P.I., Aug. 5, 1898; participated in Lawton's northern campaign and Schwan's southern campaign in Luzon; sec. Sch. of Application for Cav. and Field Arty., Ft. Riley, Kan., 1901-06; at Camp Overton, Mindanao, P.I., 1906; sec. and asst. comdt., Mounted Service Sch., 1907-10; at Camp Stotsenburg, P.I., 1910-12; comdg. Big Bend Dist., Tex., to Aug. 1913; at Army War Coll., 1913-14; Gen. Staff, to Dec. 10, 1916; comdg. 5th and 25th Cav., to Aug. 25th, 1917; comdg. 80th Inf. Brigade, N.G., Camp Kearny, Cal., to Dec. 4, 1917; comdg. 4th Div. Regular Army at Camp Greene, Charlotte, N.C., and in France to Aug. 16, 1918, participating in offensive from Marne to Vesle; comdg. 5th Corps A.E.F., to Oct. 12, 1918, in St. Mihiel and Argonne-Meuse offensives; comdr. Camp Gordon, Ga., to May 1, 1919; comdt. Cavalry Sch., Fort Riley, Kan., to Sept. 1, 1921; chief of staff, 76th Div. Org. Res., Hartford, Conn., to July 31, 1924; retired after 45 yrs. service. Home: Fishers Island, N.Y. Died Jan. 28, 1944.

CAMERON, Norman W., educator; b. Zion, Md., Sept. 27, 1876; s. Levi Oldham and Mary Ellla (Wilson) C.; A.B. magna cum laude, Washington Coll., Chestertown, Md., 1895, A.M., 1897; Ph.D., U. of Pa., 1912; grad. student Columbia, 1916, Johns Hopkins, 1917; m. Louise Marguerite Sehrt, Aug. 11, 1920; children—Norman, Caroline May. Prin. pvt. acad., 1895-96; prin. high sch., 1897-98; and supt. of schs., Blacksburg, S.C., 1898-1901; teacher and administrative officer in ednl. system, P.I., 1901-04; supervising prin., Lewes, Del., 1905-07, Elkton, Md., 1907-09; head dept. of psychology, State Normal Sch., West Chester, Pa., 1909-13; head dept. of psychology and edn., Western State Teachers Coll., Kalamazoo, Mich., 1913-16; dir. of teacher training and prin. City Normal Sch., Baltimore, Md., 1916-24; supt. of schs., Pottstown, Pa., 1924-26, Chester, Pa., 1926-28; pres. State Teachers Coll., West Chester, Pa., 1928-35; supt. of schs., Garfield, N.J., 1936-39; lecturer, writer. Mem. Garfield (N.J.) Bd. of Trade. Fellow A.A.A.S., mem. N.E.A., Nat. Assn. Sch. Adminstrs., Progressive Edn. Assn., Nat. Soc. for Study of Edn. Acad. of Polit. and Social Science; English-Speaking Union, Pa. Acad. of Science, Bergen County C. of C., Chester County Hist. Soc., Pi Gamma Mu; pres. Md. State Teachers Assn., 1919; pres. Baltimore Public Sch. Prins. Assn., 1918-23. Republican. Mason. Clubs: West Chester Golf and Country; hon. life mem. Chester (Pa.) Kiwanis Club. Home: 314 E. Joppa Road, Towson 4, Md. Died Nov. 25, 1947.

CAMERON, Shelton Thomas, lawyer; b. Richview, Ill., Aug. 14, 1857; s. John William and Rachel Catherine (Barber) C.; ed. Emerson Inst., 1876-78; LL.B., LL.M., George Washington Law Sch., 1880; m. Roberta A. Freeland, Aug. 17, 1883; children—Breta Eleanor (dec.), Thomas William (dec.), Myrle (Mrs. John F. Oberlin), Leslie (Mrs. B. K. Molecamp), Mildred (Mrs. F. Bascom Smith). Admitted to Minn. bar, 1881; in practice at Minneapolis, 1881-84; asst. county atty., Butler County, Kan., 1885; asst. examiner U.S. Patent Office, 1888; practiced patent law in U.S. courts, 1896; mem. Cameron, Kerkam & Sutton, Washington, D.C., since 1927. Mem. Am. Patent Law Assn. Republican. Mason. Club: Civitan. Home: 4901 16th St. N.W. Office: 700 10th St. N.W.. Washington, D.C. Died Dec. 1, 1944.

CAMP, John Spencer, composer, organist; b. Middletown, Conn., Jan. 30, 1858; s. John Newton and Mary (Gleason) C.; A.B., Wesleyan U., 1878, A.M., 1880, Mus.D., 1933; studied law a yr.; then music with E. A. Parsons, Shelley, Dudley Buck and Dvorak; Mus.D., Trinity Coll., Hartford, 1921; m. Susie Virginia Healy, 1885. Formerly served as organist and choirmaster First Ch. of Christ (Congl.), Hartford, resigned May 1, 1918. Trustee Hartford Municipal Auditorium, Soc. for Savings, Wesleyan University, Middletown, Conn.; mem. Conn. Civil Service Reform Assn., Municipal Art Soc., Nat. Guild Organists (a founder), S.A.R., Nat. Municipal League and Delta Kappa Epsilon Fraternity. Clubs:

St. Wilfred's (New York); Hartford, Hartford Golf, 20th Century, University, Congregational (Hartford, Connecticut). Composer: 46th Psalm (for chorus, solos and orchestra); Song of the Winds (ballad for soprano solo, chorus and orchestra); The Prince of Peace (cantata); The Morning Star (Christmas cantata); also anthems, songs and works for orchestra, string quartette, organ and piano; also The Prince of Life (Easter cantata); 5 songs to words of Sidney Lanier; Suite for Orchestra, Pilgrim Suite —in three movements; Petite Suite for Violin and Piano, 4 movements; overture for orchestra, The Time Spirit; Lex et Veritas, composition for male choruses, piano and organ. Was conductor Hartford Philharmonic Orchestra, 1902-12. Home: 38 Willard St., Hartford, Conn. Died Feb. 1, 1946.

CAMP, Lawrence Sabyllia, lawyer; b. Fairburn, Ga., Nov. 20, 1898; s. William Rudicil and Eugenia Sabyllia (Smith) C.; LL.B., Atlanta Law Sch., 1916, hon. LL.D., 1938; m. Rubye Tanner, June 25, 1918; 1 son, William Lawrence. Admitted to Ga. bar, 1916, and in practice at Fairburn, 1916-24; city attorney Fairburn, Ga., and atty. for Campbell Co., 1918-20; mem. Ga. State Legislature, 1920-25; atty. gen. of Ga., 1932; U.S. dist. atty. Northern Dist. of Ga., Feb. 1, 1934-July 1, 1942; now mem. firm of Howard, Camp & Tiller. Chmn. Dem. State Com., 1930-32. Mem. Am., Ga. State and Atlanta bar assns. Democrat. Baptist. Mason. Home: 1625 Sussex Rd. N.E. Address: Hurt Bldg., Atlanta, Ga. Died May 6, 1947.

CAMPBELL, Charles Macfie (kăm'bĕl), M.D.; b. Edinburgh, Scotland, Sept. 8, 1876; s. Daniel and Eliza (McLaren) C.; student George Watson's Coll., Edinburgh; M.A., Edinburgh U., 1897, B.Sc., 1900, M.B., Ch.B., 1902, M.D., 1911; also student Paris, Heidelberg; m. Jessie Deans Rankin, June 3, 1908; children—Annie McNicol, Edith Storer, Charles Macfie, Katherine Rankin. Came to U.S., 1904, naturalized citizen, 1918. Asst. phys., Psychiatric Inst., Ward's Island, N.Y., later asst. phys. at Bloomingdale Hosp., White Plains, N.Y., until 1913; asso. prof. psychiatry, Johns Hopkins, 1913-20; prof. psychiatry, Harvard Med. Sch., since 1920. Dir. Boston Psychopathic Hosp. Mem. Am. Psychiatric Assn., Am. Neurol. Assn., Am. Sch. Hygiene Assn., etc. Home: 58 Lake View Av., Cambridge, Mass. Office: 74 Fenwood Rd., Boston, Mass. Died Aug. 7, 1943.

CAMPBELL, Donald J., corp. official; pres. Campbell, Wyant & Cannon Foundry Co.; pres. Ordnance Steel Foundry Co., C.W.C. Crankshaft Corp., Campbell, Wyant & Cannon Engineering Co.; dir. Nat. Motor Castings Co., Automotive Parts Co. Home: Spring Lake, Mich. Office: Muskegon Heights, Mich. Died Oct. 11, 1943.

CAMPBELL, Donald Malcolm (Don M. Campbell), M.D.; b. Wardsville, Ont., Can., Dec. 12, 1864; s. George and Fannie H. C.; M.D., Detroit Coll. Medicine, 1885; studied at U. of Edinburgh, also at London, Dublin, N.Y. City, and Chicago; Licentiate Royal Coll. Surgeons, Edinburgh, 1886; hon. D.Sc., Colls. of City of Detroit (now Wayne U.), 1931; m. Olive Douglas, June 1894. Specializes in treatment of eye, ear, nose and throat; emeritus prof. ophthalmology, Detroit Coll. Medicine (now Wayne U.) since 1892; cons. oculist and aurist, Harper Hosp.; sr. mem. firm Drs. Campbell, Campbell, Summers & Pittman. Fellow Am. Coll. Surgeons; mem. A.M.A., Mich. State and Wayne County med. socs., Am. Otol. Soc., Am. Acad. Ophthalmology and Oto-Laryngology, Detroit Ophthal. and Otol. Club. Republican. Presbyterian. Mason. Clubs: Detroit, Detroit Athletic, Cannes Golf (France). Home: Book Cadillac Hotel. Office: David Whitney Bldg., Detroit, Mich. Died Aug. 25, 1942.

CAMPBELL, George Alexander, clergyman; b. Morpeth, Kent County, Ontario, Can., Jan. 27, 1869; s. Peter and Isabella (McLarty) C.; B.D., Drake U., Des Moines, Ia., 1892, A.B., 1896, D.D., 1931; B.D., U. of Chicago, 1898; D.D., Culver-Stockton Coll., 1916; m. Luna May Jameson, Dec. 20, 1892 (died Mar. 10, 1940); children—Rosabelle (Mrs. C. E. McCartney), Edward Jameson, Georgia May (Mrs. Edward W. Lollis), Robert Alexander, Mary Evalyn (Mrs. James Auer). Ordained to ministry Disciples of Christ, 1890; pastor, Chicago, 1895-1910, Hannibal, Mo., 1910-18, Union Av. Christian Ch., St. Louis, Feb. 1, 1918-Jan. 31, 1938. Editor Christian Oracle, 1898-1900, and successor, The Christian Century, 1900. Pres. Ill. Christian Missionary Conv., 1905; Mo. Christian Missionary Conv., 1915; mem. exec. com. United Christian Missionary Soc.; chmn. bd. mgrs. same, 1921-22; pres. Bd. Church Extension, 1921-29; ex-pres. St. Louis Ch. Fedn., also of St. Louis Ministerial Alliance; del. to Universal Christian Conf. on Life and Work, Stockholm, Sweden, 1925; del. from Internat. Conv. Disciples of Christ to Conf. Chs. of Christ of Gt. Britain and Ireland, Leeds, Eng., 1930; pres. Internat. Conv. Disciples of Christ, Pittsburgh, 1933. Trustee or dir. Drake U., William Woods Coll., Culver-Stockton Coll., Christian Bd. of Publication; mem. exec. com. Christian Board of Publication, St. Louis; mem. Central Exec. Bd. of Nat. Benevolent Assn. Mem. Phi Beta Kappa. Mason, Scottish Rite. Author: Chores and the Altar, 1931. Co-editor: My Dad—Preacher, Pastor, Person. Acting editor The Christian Evangelist, 1938-40; pastor emeritus, Union Av. Christian Church, St. Louis. Served on joint com. of Bapts. and Disciples in publishing "Christian Worship, A Hymnal," 1941. Home: 7728 Delmar Blvd., St. Louis, Mo.; (summer) Pentwater, Mich. Died Aug. 17, 1943.

CAMPBELL, Harold George (kămp'bĕl), supt. schs.; b. Fraserburgh, Aberdeenshire, Scotland, Jan. 13, 1884; s. George and Eleanor (Anderson) C.; came to U.S. with parents, 1888; grad. Maxwell Training Sch. for Teachers, 1902; A.B., Polytechnic Inst., Brooklyn, 1908; A.M., New York Univ., 1910, L.H.D., 1935; studied Cornell and Columbia; LL.D., Fordham U.; LL.D., University of State of New York, 1941; m. May Hazelwood, 1908 (died Feb. 28, 1935); 1 dau., Hazel (Mrs. Robert Walker); m. 2d, Mildred Freygang, 1938. Taught in all grades, elementary schs., and in evening elementary schs.; apptd. teacher history Eastern Dist. High Sch., Brooklyn, 1910, administrative asst. same dist., 1920, also prin. Flushing High Sch., 1920; elected asso. supt. schs., N.Y. City, 1924, dept. supt. 1929, supt. schs. N.Y. City since 1934. Apptd. mem. President Roosevelt's Com. on Use of Leisure Time; mem. com. reporting on Nat. Outlook on Education, etc. Mem. or officer Brooklyn Teachers Assn., High Sch. Principals Assn., New York Schoolmasters Club, Brooklyn and Queens Men's Teachers Assn., Acad. of Edn., Dept. of Superintendence of N.E.A., Am. Vocational Assn., Scholia Club, St. Andrews Soc. Clubs: City, Canadian (asso. mem). Author of textbooks and numerous articles on ednl. subjects; widely known as public speaker. Home: 33-52 81st St., Jackson Heights, New York, N.Y. Died June 17, 1942.

CAMPBELL, James Alexander, oculist, aurist; b. Platteville, Wis., Jan. 12, 1847; s. Dr. James C. and Permelia C. (Oliver) C.; M.D., Homœ. Med. Coll. of Mo., 1869; post-grad. course, St. Louis U.; at Berlin, Vienna, Paris, 1872-73, 78, 92; m. Eva B. Burden, Sept. 15, 1880; children—Roy Alexander, Marjorie Evelyn, Ralph Burden. Practiced, St. Louis, since 1869; later practice limited to eye and ear; prof. chemistry, Homœ. Med. Coll. of Mo., 1869-72, prof. ophthalmology and otology, 1878-1908, pres., 1898-1908; oculist and aurist, St. Louis Children's Hosp., 1879-1910, Good Samaritan Hosp., 1878-98, Christian Brothers' College; oculist to Girls' Industrial Home. Fellow Am. Coll. Surgeons; mem. Am. Inst. Homœopathy, Nat. Homœ. Ophthal., Otol. and Laryngol. Assn., Mo. Inst. Homœopthay, Acad. Science, St. Louis, Am. Bd. of Ophthalmic Examination, Mo. Soc. Prevention Blindness, Mo. Hist. Soc., S.R. Mason (K.T.). Home: 4920 McPherson Av. Office: 613 Locust St., St. Louis. Died June 3, 1933.

CAMPBELL, James LeRoy, physician; b. Fulton County, Georgia, July 15, 1870; s. Thomas Jefferson II, and Mary Jane (Brown) C.; M.D., Atlanta Med. Coll.; m. Mary Jones, Sept. 20, 1899; children—Lula Grove (Mrs. George M. Ivey), James LeRoy, Jr. Prof. surg. anatomy, clinical surgery, Emory U. Sch. of Medicine, 1905-20; prof. clinical surgery, 1920-40; chief, surg. service, Emory U. Div. of Grady Hosp., 1921-30; emeritus prof. clinical surgery, Emory U. Sch. of Medicine, since 1940. Author of present Ga. state law for control of cancer; established state aid cancer clinics for treatment of indigent cancer victims in Ga.; secured amendment to constitution of Ga., exempting ednl. institutions from taxation, 1918. Ga. state chmn. Am. Soc. for Control of Cancer, 1920-29; chmn. cancer commn. of Med. Assn. of Ga., since 1918; chmn. exec. com. Ga. Div. of Women's Field Army of Am. Soc. for Control of Cancer, 1937-47; member board of dirs. Am. Soc. for Control of Cancer, 1939-46. Fellow A.M.A., Am. Coll. of Surgeons; mem. Southern Med. Assn., Fulton Co. Med. Soc., Med. Assn. of Ga., Omicron Delta Kappa, Phi Beta Kappa, Alpha Omega Alpha. Democrat. Methodist. Author of numerous articles in professional journals. Home: 1315 Fairview Rd. N.E. Office: 478 Peachtree St., Atlanta 3, Ga. Died June 11, 1948.

CAMPBELL, James Mann, clergyman; b. Scotland, May 5, 1840; s. John and Janet (Nicol) C.; ed. in schs. of Dumbartonshire, Scotland, and at Glasgow and Edinburgh universities; D.D., Gale Coll., Wis., 1899, Pomona Coll., Calif., 1914; m. Euphemia K. Brotchie, Jan. 24, 1868. Ordained Congl. ministry, 1866; came to U.S., 1874; pastorates: Streator, Ill., Abingdon, Ill., Watertown, Wis., Morgan Park, Ill., Lombard, Ill. Author: Unto the Uttermost, 1889; The Indwelling Christ, 1895; After Pentecost, What? 1897; The Teachings of the Books, 1899; Clerical Types, 1900; Bible Questions, 1900; Typical Elders and Deacons, 1903; Paul the Mystic, 1907; The Heart of the Gospel, 1907; Grow Old Along With Me, 1911; The Presence, 1911; The Place of Prayer in the Christian Religion, 1914; Prayer in its Present Day Aspects, 1916; New Thought Christianized, 1917; The Place of Prayer in God's Plan of World Conquest, 1918; The Second Coming of Christ, 1919; What Christian Science Means and What We Can Learn From It, 1920; Heaven Opened, A Book of Comfort and Hope, 1924; Life's Highest Loyalty, 1925. Contbr. to religious periodicals. Home: Claremont, Calif. Died May 7, 1926.

CAMPBELL, J(ames) Phil(ander); b. Dallas, Paulding County, Ga., Mar. 2, 1878; s. Daniel F. and Sarah McGrayer C.; spl. course N. Ga. Agrl. Coll.; grad. Ga. State Normal Sch.; B.S.A., State Coll. of Agr. of U. of Ga.; m. Loraine Montez Proctor, Jan. 1, 1907; children—Elizabeth, Virginia, Proctor, Montez, Phil, Douglas, Mary Lois. Reared on a farm; began teaching at 17; helped to secure legislation for agriculture in rural schs.; organized a pvt. agrl. sch., 1906; spent 6 mos., 1907, in traveling over state advocating dist. agrl. schs. and a state coll. of agr.; first extension supervisor S.E. States, 1908-10; state agent U.S. Dept. of Agr. and member staff Ga. State Coll. Agr., 1910-34. Organized, 1913, in Ga., 10,000 boys, in corn clubs; 2,500 girls, in canning clubs; 5,000 adult farmers, in farm demonstration work. Dir. extension work in agr. and home economics of Ga., since July 1, 1915; leave of absence from state work, 1933-34, to assist Agrl. Adjustment Adminstrn. in cotton belt crop replenishment div.; chief Agrl. Rehabilitation Sect., Agrl. Adjustment Adminstrn., 1934-35; now asst. chief Soil Conservation Service. Conservation dir. for Ga. Food Adminstrn. during World War I. Mem. Ga. State Bd. Forestry, 1926-32; sec.-treas., later v.p., pres. and mem. exec. com. Assn. Southern Agrl. Workers, 1929-35. Cooperated with various State Legislatures on legislation authorizing orgn. of Soil Conservation Dists. Baptist. Mem. Epsilon Sigma Phi. Homes: Athens, Ga. Addresss: Soil Conservation Service, Washington; also Box 832, Athens, Ga. Died. Dec. 11, 1944.

CAMPBELL, Lucien Quitman, prof. English, dean; b. Evergreen, La., Jan. 18, 1893; s. Daniel Quitman and Anna Clark (Tillman) C.; A.B., Tulane U., 1915; A.M., U. of Tex., 1924; student summers, George Washington U., 1934, George Peabody Coll., 1936, U. of Colo., 1937; m. Mary Cornelia Tanner, Dec. 24, 1919; 1 dau., Mary Anna. Instr. in English and pub. speaking, U. of Okla., 1915-17; prof. of English, Simmons Coll., 1917-26; dean and prof. English, Miss. Woman's Coll., 1926-36; prof. of English, Hardin-Simmons U., since 1936, also asst. dean, 1936-38, acting dean, 1938-43, dean since Mar. 1943. Mem. Phi Beta Kappa, Kappa Delta Phi, Delta Sigma Rho. Club: Rotary. Democrat. Home: 1701 Sandefer St., Abilene, Tex. Died Sep. 7, 1945.

CAMPBELL, Luther, A., judge; b. Bergen County, N.J., Nov. 28, 1872; s. Abraham D. Campbell; ed. pub. schs.; read law in office of father. Admitted to N.J. bar, 1894; and practiced with father until 1896; counsel to Hackensack, N. J., 12 yrs.; apptd. judge Circuit Court of N.J., 1914; apptd. judge Supreme Court of N.J., 1923. reaptd., 1924, 31, resigned, 1932, becoming chancellor Court of Chancery of N.J. Democrat. Address: 1 Exchange Place, Jersey City, N.J. Died Dec. 28, 1947.

CAMPBELL, Marcus B., judge U.S. Dist. Court, Eastern Dist. N.Y. since 1923. Address: U.S. District Court, P.O. Bldg., Brooklyn, N.Y.* Died Aug. 31, 1944.

CAMPBELL, Robert Fishburne, clergyman; b. Lexington, Va., Dec. 12, 1858; s. John Lyle (LL.D.) and Harriet Hatch (Bailey) C.; A.M., Washington and Lee U., 1879; grad. Union Theol. Sem., Hampden-Sidney, Va. (now of Richmond, Va.), 1885; D.D., Davidson (N.C.) Coll., 1893; m. Sarah Montgomery Ruffner, Oct. 8, 1885 (died 1917); 1 son, Ruffner Campbell; m. 2d, Julia T. Berryman, June 18, 1919; 1 son, Robert Fishburne. Ordained ministry Presbyn. Ch. in U.S., 1885; pastor successively Millboro and Windy Cove schs., Bath County, Va., Davidson Coll. Ch. and Buena Vista, Va., until 1892; pastor First Presbyn. Ch., Asheville, N.C., 1892-38, pastor emeritus since 1938; appointed James Sprunt lecturer for 1930, Union Theol. Sem. Founder Good Samaritan Mission, Asheville; chmn. Home Missions Com. of Asheville Presbytery since organization, 1896; moderator General Assembly Presbyn. Ch. in U.S., 1927. Mem. bd. Union Theol. Sem., King Coll., Bristol, Tenn., Montreat (N.C.) Coll. Chmn. Inter-racial Commn., Asheville. Mem. Delta Kappa Epsilon, Phi Beta Kappa. Club: Pen and Plate. Wrote: (brochures) The Race Problem in the South; Classification of the Mountain Whites; Sunday Laws and Liberty; Freedom and Restraint (lectures); also numerous published addresses. Home: 6 Pearson Drive, Asheville, N.C. Died Apr. 3, 1947.

CAMPBELL, Robert Willis, lawyer; b. Frankfort, Clinton County, Ind., July 30, 1874; s. Joseph C. and Lena (Nicoll) C.; A.B., Leland Stanford Jr. U., 1896; Hastings Coll. of Law, San Francisco, 1897-98; read law in offices of Reddy, Campbell & Metson (father a partner), San Francisco, Calif.; LL.D., Northwestern U., 1936; m. Bertha Gary, Sept. 10, 1901; 1 dau., Elizabeth (Mrs. Edward S. Clark). Admitted to Calif. bar, 1899; removed to Chicago, 1904; mem. firm Knapp & Campbell to 1930; now counsel Knapp, Cushing, Hershburger, Stevenson, Chicago, Ill.; also mem. firm Campbell, Smith & Campbell, Pasadena. Republican. Methodist. Mason (K.T.). Clubs: Annandale (Calif.); California (Los Angeles); University (Pasadena). Home: 1000 S. San Rafael Av., Pasadena 2. Office: First Trust Bldg., Pasadena 1, Calif. Died Feb. 16, 1947.

CAMPBELL, Ross Turner, college pres.; b. Clifton, O., Dec. 1, 1863; s. William A. and Mary A. (Turner) C.; A.B., Westminster Coll., Pa., 1886, A.M., 1903; grad. Xenia (O.) Theol. Sem., 1891; D.D., Westminster, 1904; m. Margaret Swartwood, July 21, 1892. Ordained in U.P. ministry, 1892; pastor Hanover, Ill., 1892-94; prin. Pawnee Acad., Pawnee City, Neb., 1894-1904; pres. Amity Coll., 1904-10; pres. Sterling (Kan.) Coll., 1910-33. Author: Studies in Old Testament; Class-Room Lectures on The Apostles' Creed and The Shepherd Psalm. Home: McDonald, Pa. Died 1940.

CAMPBELL, Rowland, merchant; b. Cross Hill, S.C., Dec. 27, 1894; s. Thomas Atkinson and Sudie Marie (Carter) C.; grad. U. High Sch. (U. of Chicago), 1916; student U. of Chicago, 1916-19; m. Evelyn Kimmel, Jan. 9, 1930; children—Nancy, Jane. Pres. Campbell, Inc., Chicago, 1922-37; v.p. Neumode Hosiery Co., Chicago, 1926-27; pres. Campbell's Dollar Stores, Inc., since 1927; partner Jas. F. Shea & Co., 1937-38; chmn. bd. Reo Motor Car Co., 1937-39, pres. and gen. mgr., 1938-39; exec. v.p. Paine Lumber Co., Ltd., Oshkosh, Wis., 1939-40. Served as private, French Army, World War. Mem. Delta Kappa Epsilon. Conglist. Home: 1515 S. Alicia Drive, Appleton, Wis. Office: 214 W. College Av., Appleton, Wis. Died Oct. 20, 1943.

CAMPBELL, Thomas Edward, ex-governor; b. Prescott, Ariz., Jan. 18, 1878; s. Daniel and Eliza (O'Flynn) C.; ed. public schs., and St. Mary's Coll., Oakland, Calif., 1 yr.; m. Eleanor Gayle Allen, June 18, 1900; children—Thomas Allen, Alex Brodie. County assessor, Yavapai County, Ariz., 1907-11, 1912-15; Rep. candidate for Congress, 1914; state tax commr., 1915-16; elected gov. of Ariz. on face of returns, Nov. 1916, and assumed the office, but relinquished it Dec. 25, 1917, after recount of votes showed plurality of 43 for George W. P. Hunt; elected gov. for term Jan. 1919-Jan. 1921; reelected gov. term Jan. 1921-23. Pres. Contaro Farms Co., Marana, Ariz. Mgr. The Employers Council, Tucson, Ariz. National councillor National Highways Assn.; president League of Southwest since 1920; chairman Committee of Western Governors, Colorado River Basin Project, 1921; chmn. Fact Finding Commn. on Federal Reclamation, 1923-24; chmn. Bd. of Survey and Adjustments Federal Reclamation Projects, 1925; mem. Rep. Nat. Com., 1924-28; commr. gen. of U.S. Internat. Expn., Seville, Spain; pres. U.S. Civil Service Commn., 1930-33; Rep. candidate for gov., 1936. Clubs: Arizona (Phoenix); Old Pueblo (Tucson, Ariz.). Author: Centralized Authority in Taxation, 1912. Home: Tucson, Ariz. Died Mar. 1, 1944.

CAMPBELL, Thomas Huffman, clergyman; b. Eaton, O., Aug. 6, 1863; s. Jehu Bennett and Alzina (Huffman) C.; B.A., Ohio Wesleyan U., 1885, M.A., 1891, S.T.D., 1898; B.D., Drew Theol. Sem., 1895; m. Luella Stafford, Mar. 23, 1886; children—Hurst Vincent (dec.), Kenyon Stafford, Harold Huffman (dec.), Dorothy. Entered M.E. ministry, 1885; pastor successively in Ohio at York Centre, Agosta, Napoleon, Hicksville, Kenton, Bellefontaine, St. Paul's Ch., Toledo, until 1905; supt. Bellefontaine Dist., 1905-06; pastor Trinity Ch., Lima, 1906-11, King Av. Ch., Columbus, 1911-18; supt. Columbus District, 1918-24; pastor North Broadway Church, Columbus, 1924-29; asso. pastor Central M.E. Ch., Columbus, 1929-30; retired from active ministry, 1931. Dir. religious work Y.M.C.A., Camp Funston, Kan., summer, 1918. Organizer, 1914, and trustee Wesley Foundation, Ohio State U., 1914-26. Mem. bd. mgrs. Foreign Missions M.E. Ch., 1920-32; del. to Gen. Conf. M.E. Ch. 5 times; chmn. hdqrs. com. Ohio Anti-Saloon League, 1919-31. Trustee Ohio Wesleyan U., 1899-1936, now trustee emeritus; trustee Ohio Meth. Children's Home, 1920-37, Home for Aged (Cincinnati) since 1920, Ohio Annual Conf., 1920-39. Mem. Ohio State Archeol. and Hist. Soc., S.A.R., Phi Gamma Delta, Phi Beta Kappa, Pi Gamma Mu, Odevene Club. Republican. Mason (32°). Home: 3655 Medbrook Way, Columbus, O. Died Sep. 29, 1944.

CAMPBELL, William James, theol. sem. pres.; b. Carlton, Prince Edward Island, Can., Sept. 28, 1877; s. Donald and Mary Ann (McPherson) C.; Ohio Northern U., 1896-98; Bangor Theol. Sem., 1900-03; A.B., Dartmouth, 1905, D.D., 1924; S.T.B., Harvard, 1907, M.A., 1908, LL.D., Marietta Coll., Marietta, O., 1937; became an American citizen 1919; m. Clara Smythe Green, Jan. 1906; 1 dau., Louise Grace. Ordained Presbyterian ministry, 1905; joined Congregational Church; asso. pastor First Congl. Ch., Detroit, 1908-10; pastor First Ch., Port Huron, Mich., 1910-13, First Ch., Kalamazoo, 1913-15, Williston, Ch., Portland, Me., 1915-21, Youngstown, O., 1921-28; pres. Atlanta Theol. Sem. Foundation (Vanderbilt U.) 1929-1948: prof. of practical theology, Vanderbilt U., 1934-48; pastor First Congl. Ch., Boothbay Harbor, Me., since 1948. Mem. Am. Acad. Polit. and Social Science, Am. Soc. of Church History. Mason (K.T., 32°, Shriner). Clubs: University, Executives. Home: Boothbay Harbor, Me. Died Mar. 2, 1949. Buried Mt. Hope Cemetery, Bangor, Me.

CAMPBELL, William Neal (kăm'ĕl) woolen mfr.; b. Galveston, Tex., Nov. 8, 1893; s. Judge John W. and Mary Virginia (Stowe) C.; LL.B., Cumberland U., 1915; m. Mildred Goodall, June 9, 1920; children—Constance Virginia, Barbara Louise, William Neal. Employed as pvt. sec. to Clay Stone Briggs, mem. Congress from Tex.; mem. firm Campbell & Ward, wool mchts., Boston, 1922-30; former pres. and treas. Goodall Worsted Co. and Palm Beach Mills 1930-44. At 1st Officers Training Camp, Leon Springs, Tex., 1917; U.S. Navy, Harvard Radio Sch., 1917; 1st lt., 7th Cav., Tex. N.G., U.S. Army, 1917-18. Trustee Nasson Jr. Coll., Springvale, Me. Past comdr. Am. Legion, Sanford, Me. Republican. Unitarian. Clubs: Westchester Country (New York); Algonquin, University, Brae Burn County (Boston); The Country (Brookline). Home: Fairfields, Kennebunkport, Me. Died Sep. 8, 1947.

CANADA, John Walter, lawyer; b. Memphis, Tenn., Dec. 27, 1876; s. W. W. and Sallie T. (Brewster) C.; grad Memphis Inst., 1895; student Millsaps Coll., Jackson, Miss., 1895-97; m. 2d, Virginia Broaddus, Mar. 16, 1934. Admitted to Tenn. bar, 1897; gen. atty. M.P.R.R.; v.p. and gen. counsel Union Railway Co. since 1905; gen. counsel and mem. exec. com. and bd. of dirs. Union Planters Nat. Bank & Trust Co., Plough, Inc., gen. counsel Ark. & Memphis Ry., Bridge & Terminal Co., Memphis Union Station Co.; counsel for Tenn. and Miss. for St.L.&S.L. R.R.; gen. atty. for Tenn. M.P.R.R.; atty, St. Louis Southwestern Ry. Co. Served in Cuba as capt. 4th Tenn. Vols., Spanish-Am. War; retired at Col. Tenn. Nat Guards. Mem. Kappa Alpha. Democrat. Episcopalian. Clubs: University, Tennessee, Memphis Country (Memphis). Home: Adanac Lodge, Memphis. Office: 2910 Sterick Bldg., Memphis, Tenn. Died June 11, 1944.

CANARUTTO, Angelo (kä-nä-rōō'tō), orchestra condr.; b. Trieste, Italy, July 31, 1909; s. Dante and Alice (Camerini) C.; student Royal Conservatory of Music, Trieste, 1914-28; m. Mary Mickita, Jan. 20, 1934. Came to U.S., 1928. Asst. condr. Verdi Theatre, Trieste, 1923-27; chorus master Pa. Grand Opera Co., Phila., 1928-29; asst. condr. San Carlo Opera Co., 1933; condr. Podrecca's Teatro del Piccoli, on world tour, 1933-35; condr. Cincinnati Summer Opera Co., 1936-38; became condr. Chicago Civic Opera, 1935; asst. condr. Metropolitan Opera Assn., New York, since 1941. Home: 24-03 41 Av., Long Island City, N.Y. Died Aug. 29, 1944.

CANDEE, Helen Churchill, author; b. New York; d. Henry and Mary C. (Churchill) Hungerford; ed. various private schs. in New Haven and Norwalk, Conn.; married; 1 dau., Edith (Mrs. Harold C. Mathews). Lecturer on the liberal arts and the Orient. Decorated by French Indo-China govt., 1929. Mem. India Soc. (London); Les Amis de l'Orient (Paris). Author: Susan Truslow, 1900; An Oklahoma Romance, 1901; How Women May Earn a Living, 1900; Decorative Styles and Periods, 1906; The Tapestry Book, 1912; Angkor, the Magnificent, 1924; New Journeys In Old Asia, 1927; Weaves and Draperies, 1931. Contbr. to mags. Home: 1049 Park Av., New York. Died Aug. 23, 1949.

CANDEE, Lyman, fire insurance; b. N.Y. City, Dec. 19, 1865; s. Joseph Russell and Sarah Ann (Shepherd) C.; ed. pub. schs.; m. Clara Louise Simmons, Nov. 8, 1893. First v.p. Globe and Rutgers Fire Insurance Co., N.Y. City; pres. Golden Hill Bldg. Co. Mem. Ins. Soc. of New York (v.p.), Soc. Colonial Wars, S.R., Huguenot Soc. Episcopalian. Clubs: Bankers, Drug and Chemical, Church, Westchester Country. Home: The Park Lane, 299 Park Av., New York, and Dobbs Ferry, N. Y. Office: 111 William St., New York. Died Mar. 1, 1943.

CANDLER, Ezekiel Samuel, Jr., ex-congressman; b. Belleville, Hamilton County, Fla., Jan. 18, 1862; s. E. S. and Julia (Bevill) C.; removed with parents when 8 yrs. old to Tishomingo County, Miss.; LL.B., Univ. of Miss., 1881; m. Nancy Priscilla Hazlewood, Apr. 26, 1883 (died April 17, 1921); children—Julia Bevill (Mrs. W. Miller Garnsey), Susan Hazlewood (Mrs. P. M. Egerton), Lucy Alice (Mrs. Charles Roy Wiselogle); m. 2d, Mrs. Effie Merrill Newhardt, Jan. 14, 1924 (died Feb. 15, 1930); m. 3d, Mrs. Ottie Doan Hardenstein, June 21, 1933. Admitted to bar at 19; in practice at Iuka, Miss., 1881-87, Corinth, Miss., since 1887; mem. Candler & Candler, since 1881, Mayor of Corinth, 1934-38. Chmn. Democratic County Exec. Com., 1884; presidential elector, 1888, 1932; mem. 57th to 66th Congresses (1901-21), 1st Miss. Dist. Moderator Tishomingo Bapt. Assn., 1896-1905; represented same in Southern Bapt. Conv. several times. Home: Corinth, Miss. Died Dec. 19, 1944.

CANDLER, John Slaughter, lawyer; b. Villa Rica, Ga., Oct. 22, 1861; s. Samuel Charles and Martha (Beall) C.; A.B., Emory Coll., 1880, A.M., 1883, LL.D., 1924; m. Lula Garnier, January 16, 1884 (now deceased); children—Asa Warren (dec.), Allie Garnier (Mrs. J. Sam), Guy; m. 2d, Florida George Anderson, August 1, 1906 (died Oct. 7, 1935); m. 3d, Martha Erwin, Dec. 31, 1936. Admitted Ga. bar, 1882; solicitor gen., 1887-96; judge Stone Mountain Jud. Circuit of Ga. Superior Courts, 1896-1902; asso. justice Supreme Court, Georgia, 1902-06, resigned to resume law practice. Alderman, City of Atlanta, 1909-14; mayor pro tem. and pres. Gen. Council, 1911, 12, 14. A.-d.-c. on staff Gov. Alexander H. Stephens, with rank of lt.-col.; mil. judge advocate gen. Ga., 1886-93; col. 5th Inf. Ga. N.G., 1893-1901; col. 3d Ga. Vol. Inf., in Spanish-Am. War, 1898. Mem. Gen. Conf. M.E. Ch., S., 5 times between 1890 and 1934; mem. Commn. on Unification of the two branches of the denomination; pres. Bd. of Edn., North Ga. Conf.; mem. S.R., Kappa Alpha, Phi Beta Kappa, Phi Delta Phi, Omicron Delta Kappa. Democrat. Mason (32°, Shriner). Home: 199 Tuxedo Road. Office: 410 Palmer Bldg., Atlanta, Ga.* Died Dec. 9, 1941.

CANDY, Albert Luther, univ. prof.; b. Grant County, Ind., Mar. 12, 1857; s. Jacob and Hannah (Schaeffer) C.; A.B., U. of Kan., 1892, A.M., 1893; Ph.D., U. of Neb., 1898; m. Eda L. McCain, Aug. 24, 1886 (died Apr. 23, 1893); 1 son, Albert McCain; m. 2d, Ella Van Brunt, June 27, 1895. Prof. mathematics and civil engring., Campbell U., Holton, Kan., 1886-91, Fremont (Neb.) Normal School, 1892-93; with U. of Neb. since 1893, as prof. mathematics, and chmn. dept., also acting dean coll. of arts and sciences, 1922-23, 1924-25, prof. emeritus since 1935. Alderman, City of Lincoln, 1909-13. Republican. Presbyterian. Fellow A.A.A.S.; mem. Math. Assn. America, Am. Math. Soc., Am. Assn. Univ. Profs., Sigma Xi. Author: Analytic Geometry, 1900-09; Construction, Classification and Census of Magic Squares of an Even Order, 1937; Construction, Classification and Census of Magic Squares of Order Five, 1938, rev., 1939. Pandiagonal Magic Squares of Prime Order, 1940; Pandiagonal Magic Squares of Composite Order, 1941; Supplement to Pandiagonal Magic Squares of Prime Order, 1942. Home: 1003 H St., Lincoln, Neb. Deceased.

CANFIELD, Arthur Graves, college prof.; b. Sunderland, Vt., Mar. 27, 1859, s. Malcolm and Harriett Augusta (Graves) C.; A.B., William Coll., 1878, A.M., 1881, L.H.D., 1920; m. Jeannette Platt Sayre, June 6, 1895; children—Ellen, Ruth. Instr. modern langs., U. of Kan., 1883-87, prof. Romance langs., 1887-1900; prof. Romance langs., U. of Mich., since 1900. Mem. Modern Lang. Assn. Am., Am. Dialect Soc., Am. Folk Lore Soc., Société des anciens textes français, Société d'histoire littéraire de la France, Société de Linguistique Romane. Author: French Lyrics, 1899; Poems of Victor Hugo, 1906. Home: Ann Arbor, Mich. Died Dec. 5, 1947.

CANFIELD, Harry C., manufacturer; b. Moores Hill, Ind., Nov. 22, 1875; s. Elias C. and Martha E. C.; ed. Moores Hill (Ind.) Coll., Central Normal Coll.; m. Kathryn E. Elder, Oct. 4, 1899; children—Vyola E., Harry M. Teacher pub. schs., 1896-98; began as bookkeeper Western Furniture Co., Batesville, Ind., 1899, salesman, later sales mgr., purchased the plant, pres., treas. and gen. mgr., since 1922; also head Harry C. Canfield Co., wholesale furniture, sales commn. business; pres. bd. Batesville State Bank. Mem. 68th to 72d Congresses (1923-33), 4th Ind. Dist. Trustee Batesville Memorial. Democrat. Baptist. Mason, Odd Fellow, Eagle. Home: Batesville, Ind. Died Feb. 9, 1945.

CANN, James Ferris, lawyer; b. Savannah, Ga., Dec. 11, 1868; s. James Ferris and Anna Sophia (Turner) C.; ed. pub. schs. Savannah and Ga. Mil. Acad.; studied law summers, U. of Va.; m. Eliza Chisholm, Oct. 10, 1916; 1 son, James Ferris. Admitted ot Ga. bar, 1889, and since practiced in Savannah; partner G. T. and J. F. Cann and successors, now Anderson, Cann & Dunn; state senator, 1900-02; mem. Ga. Ho. of Rep., 1902-05; pres., dir. Industrial Savings & Loan Co., Tybee Beach Co., Savannah Ware house & Compress Co., Chatham Fertilizer Co., Blum Corp.; v.p., dir. Cann Estate; former chmn. council Savannah Beach Tybee Island since 1920; judge adv. gen. of Ga., 1910-16. Pres. Savannah Benevolent Assn. Member Savannah Cotton Exchange. Served as capt. Co. C, Savannah Vol. Guards, 1896-1903; capt. Co. K, 2d Ga. Inf. Vols. Spanish-Am. War, 1898; maj., div. judge adv. Nat. Army, World War, 1917. Mem. Am., Ga. State and Savannah bar assns., Ga. Hist. Soc., Telfair Acad. Arts and Sciences, Am. Legion, Spanish Am. War Veterans, Naval Mil. Order Spanish Am. War, Sons of Revolution, Sigma Alpha Epsilon. Democrat. Episcopalian (vestryman St. John's Church in Savannah). Clubs: Oglethorpe (ex-pres.), Savannah Golf (ex-pres.), Savannah Yacht (ex-commodore). Home: 111 E. 54th St. Office: Blun Bldg., Savannah, Ga. Died Feb. 14, 1944.

CANNON, James, Jr., bishop; b. at Salisbury, Md., Nov. 13, 1864; s. James and Lydia Robertson (Primrose) C.; A.B., Randolph-Macon Coll., 1884; A.M., Princeton, 1889; B.D., Princeton Theol. Sem., 1888; D.D., Randolph-Macon, 1903; m. Lura Virginia Bennett, Aug. 1, 1888 (died 1928); children: 3 daus., 6 sons; m. 2d, Mrs. Helen Hawley McCallum, July 15, 1930. Entered ministry in Virginia Conference M.E. Church, South Portsmouth, Virginia., 1888; pres. Blackstone Coll. for Girls, 1894-1918, also editor Christian Advocate, 1904-18; superintendent Anti-Saloon League of Virginia, 1910-19; elected bishop Methodist Episcopal Church, South, May 1918. Supt. Anti-Saloon League of Va., 1910-19; gen. supt. Southern Assembly, 1911-19; mem. Gen. Conf. M.E. Ch., S., 5 times; mem. exec. com. Anti-Saloon League of America since 1902, of administrative com. since 1927, chmn. nat. legislative com. since 1914; del. World's Missionary Conf., Edinburgh, 1910; chmn. bd. Temperance and Social Service, M.E. Ch., S., 1918-34; chmn. exec. com. World League Against Alcoholism since 1919; visited Europe 10 times, in connection with war problems, 1918-22, yearly as mem. various commns., 1918-37; del. and mem. continuation coms. of Universal Conf. on Life and Work and Faith and Order, Geneva, 1920-37, Lausanne, 1927, Life and Work, Stockholm, 1925; del. to Meth. Ecumenical Confs., London, 1921, Atlanta, 1931; chmn. Ednl. Campaign Commn. M.E. Ch., S., 1919-22; chmn. Southern Commn. Unification of Methodism, 1918-26; mem. exec. and adminstr. com. Fed. Council of Chs. since 1918; chmn. Federal Council Commission on Relation with Religious Bodies in Europe, 1920-24, chmn. Commn. on Marriage and the Home, 1922-30; bishop in charge of mission work of M.E. Ch., S., in Mexico, Belgian Congo, Cuba and Brazil, 1918-34, of Ala., 1920-22, of Pacific Coast work, 1934-38; chmn. com. Southern Anti-Smith Democrats, 1928; trustee Ch. Peace Union since 1924; mem. Spl. Survey Com. Near East; chmn. Com. on Near East Relief for M.E. Ch., S.; delegate World Conf. on Life and Work, Oxford, July 1937, World Conf. on Faith and Order, Edinburgh, Aug. 1937, World Peace Conf., Geneva, Sept. 1937. Mem. Phi Beta Kappa. Independent Democrat. Recipient of first Am. award "for distinguished religious service," by Christian Herald, 1928. Contbr. to religious and secular press since 1891. Address: 24 N. Allen Av., Richmond, Va.; (legal residence, Blackstone, Va.). Died Sep. 6, 1944.

CANNON, Sylvester Quayle, ch. official, cons. engr.; b. Salt Lake City, June 10, 1877; s. George Quayle and Elizabeth (Hoagland) C.; student Latter Day Saints Coll., Salt Lake City, 1889-93, U. of Utah, 1894-95; B.S. in Mining Engring., Mass. Inst. Tech., 1899; m. Winnifred Saville, June 15, 1904; children—Julian Saville, Elinor, Winfield Quayle, Sylvia, Lawrence Saville, Lucile, Donald James. Began as mining and civil engr., 1899; traveled abroad, 1899-1902 and 1907-09; cons. engr., 1902-07 and since 1909; in charge Weber River Hydrog. Survey for state engr. of Utah., 1905-07; water supply engr., Salt Lake City, 1912-13, city engr. in charge of improvements costing $11,000,000, 1913-25; cons. engr., 1925-26; cons. engr. U.S. Reclamation Service, American Falls Project, Ida., 1923; mem., State Advisory Bd., Pub. Works Adminstrn., 1933-34. Presiding Bishop, Latter Day Saints Ch., 1925-38, financial affairs supervision 1,000 bishops, 9,000 Aaronic Priesthood mems. Asso. Council of Twelve Apostles, Ch. of Jesus Christ of Latter Day Saints (Mormon), 1938-39 (mem. to date). Pres. Deseret News Pub. Co., Cannon Investment Co.; dir. Amalgamated Sugar Co., Hotel Utah Co., U.S. Fuel Co., Zion's Coöp. Merc. Instn., Zion's Savings Bank. Pres. McCune Sch. of Music and Art; chmn. bd. Deseret Gymnasium. Mem. Am. Soc. C.E. Republican. Clubs: Commercial, Timpanogos. Home: 1334 Second Av. Office: 47 E.S. Temple, Salt Lake City, Utah. Died May 29, 1943.

CANNON, Walter Bradford, physiologist; b. Prairie du Chien, Wis., Oct. 19, 1871; s. Colbert Hanchett and Wilma (Denio) C.; A.B., Harvard U., 1896, A.M., 1897, M.D., 1900, Sc.D., 1937; Sc.D., Yale Univ., 1923; LL.D., Wittenberg Coll., 1927, Boston Univ., 1929; Washington Univ.; Doctor, honoris causa, Univs. of Liege and Strasbourg, 1930, Paris, 1931, Madrid, 1938, Barcelona, 1939. Catholic Univ. of Chile, 1944. Baly medalist, Royal College Physicians, London, 1931. National Institute Social Science, 1934; m. Cornelia James, June 25, 1901; children—Bradford, Wilma Denio, Linda, Marian, Helen. Instructor zoölogy, 1899-1900, instr. physiology, 1900-02, asst prof., 1902-06, George Higginson prof., Sept. 1, 1906-Aug. 31, 1942, emeritus prof. since Sept. 1, 1942. Harvard. Croonian lecturer, Royal Soc., London, 1918; Harvard exchange prof. to France, 1929 30; Linacre lecturer, Cambridge U., 1930; Herter lecturer, New York, 1932; Beaumont lecturer, Detroit, 1933; Kober lecturer, Assn. Am. Physicians, 1934; Caldwell lecturer, Am. Röntgen Ray Soc., 1934; Newbold lecturer, Phila. College of Physicians, 1934; Hughlings Jackson lecturer, McGill University, 1939; visiting prof. Peiping Union Med. Sch., 1935; hon. fellow Stanford U., 1941. Fellow A.A.A.S. (pres. 1939), Am. Acad. Arts and Sciences; mem. Nat. Acad. Sciences (fgn. sec.), Acad. of Sciences of U.S.S.R. (hon.), Am. Philos. Soc., Am. Physiol. Soc., Assn. Am. Physicians, Soc. Exptl. Biology and Medicine, A.M.A., Mass. Med. Soc., Phi Beta Kappa, Alpha Omega Alpha; corr. mem. Société de Biologie (Paris), R. Academia delle Scienze, Bologna, Sociedad de Biologia, Buenos Aires, Société Belge de Biologie (Brussels), Royal Soc. Medicine (Budapest); fgn. mem. Royal Soc. London, Royal Swedish Acad. of Science; hon. mem. Academic Nacionale de Medicina (Spain), Royal Soc. Edinburgh, British Physiol. Soc., Academia de Medicina (Barcelona), Académie Royale de Medecine de Belgique (Belgium), Nat. Acad. of Medicine (Mexico). Pres. Med. Research Soc. of Am. Red Cross, France, 1917-18. Awarded Friedenwald medal by the Am. Gastroenterological Assn., 1941. Lieut. colonel, Med. Corps, U.S. Army, 1918. Decorated Companion of the Bath (British), 1919; D.S.M. (U.S.) Author: A Laboratory Course in Physiology, 1910; The Mechanical Factors of Digestion, 1911; Bodily Changes in Pain, Hunger, Fear and Rage, 1915, revised edit., 1929; Traumatic Shock, 1923; The Wisdom of the Body, 1932, revised edition was published in 1939; Digestion and Health, 1936; Autonomic Neuro-effector Systems (with A. Rosenblueth), 1937; The Way of an Investigator, 1945. Contributor of articles describing movements of stomach and intestines, effects of emotional excitement, organic stabilization, chem. mediation of nerve impulses, etc., and papers on med. edn. and in the defense of med. research. Club: Faculty (Cambridge). Home: 20 Prescott St., Cambridge, Mass. Died Oct. 1, 1945.

CANTWELL, John Joseph, archbishop; b. Limerick, Ireland, Dec. 1, 1874; s. Patrick and Ellen (O'Donnell) C.; Sacred Heart Coll., Crescent, Limerick, St. Patrick's College, Thurles, Ireland. Ordained priest R.C. Ch., 1899; came to U.S., 1899; curate, Berkeley, Calif., 1899-1904; sec. to archbishop of San Francisco, 1904-14; vicar gen. San Francisco Diocese, 1914-17; consecrated bishop, Diocese of Monterey and Los Angeles, Dec. 5, 1917, of Los Angeles and San Diego, Dec. 3, 1922; appointed archbishop of Los Angeles, July 11, 1936; installed Dec. 3, 1936; appointed bishop-asst. to Papal Throne, 1929. Founder Newman Club, U. of Calif. Awarded Golden Rose of Tepeyac, 1930; Knight Comdr. Holy Sepulchre, 1931; Distinguished Medal, Republic of Lebanon, 1937. Home: 100 Fremont Pl. Address: 714 W. Olympic Blvd., Los Angeles. Died Oct. 30, 1947.

CAPERS, William Theodotus (kā-pẽrs), bishop; b. Greenville, S.C., August 9, 1867; s. late Rt. Rev. Ellison and Charlotte (Palmer) C.; S.C. Coll., 1885-86; Furman U., S.C., 1886-87; grad. Theol. Sem. of Va., 1894; M.A., State U. of Ky., Lexington, 1911; D.D., U. of South, 1914, Va. Theol. Sem., 1914; m. Rebecca Holt, d. late Gen. Goode Bryan, of Augusta, Ga., Jan 30, 1889 (died May 11, 1931); children—George Bryan (dec.), Ellison Howe, William Theodotus, Samuel Orr; m. 2d, Mrs. Louis (Cash) Myers, June 3, 1936. In business, 1887-90; deacon, 1894, priest, 1895, P.E.Ch.; rector, Grace Ch., Anderson, S.C., 1895-1901, Holy Trinity Ch., Vicksburg, Miss., 1901-03, Trinity Ch., Asheville, N.C., 1903-05; dean Christ Ch. Cathedral, Lexington, Ky., 1905-12; Ch. Holy Apostles, Phila., 1912-13; elected bishop of missionary dist. of Spokane, Oct. 1913, but declined; bishop co-adjutor, Diocese of W. Tex., Dec. 1913-16; bishop of West Tex. since Oct. 16, 1916; pres. Eccles. Province of the Southwest, 1926-35. Mem. Gen. Bd. of Missions, P.E. Ch., 1910-13; mem. Army and Navy Commn. P.E. Ch. Mem. Huguenot Soc. of S.C., Rotary Internat. Mason (32°), K.P. Author published sermons and addresses. Home: 108 W. French Pl., San Antonio, Tex. Died Mar. 29, 1943.

CAPES, William Parr, author; b. Clinton, N.Y., Jan. 4, 1881; s. Robert and Emma (Cherry) C.; ed. Clinton (N.Y.) Mil. Sch. and Clinton High Sch.; Hamilton Coll., 1903; m. Regina Marion Dufft, Nov. 11, 1922; 1 son, Robert Parr. Editor Evening Star, Schenectady, N.Y., 1903-10; sec. to mayor of Schenectady, 1904-06, 1910-11; asst. to dir. N.Y. Assn. for Improving Condition of the Poor, N.Y. City, 1910-15; organizer and dir. N.Y. State Bur. Municipal Information since 1915. In charge water waste study for U.S. Fuel Adminstrn. during World War; sec. N.Y. State Conf. of Mayors and Other City Officials since 1910; dir. N.Y. State Municipal Training Inst., 1940; mem. advisory com. N.Y. State Fuel Commn., 1922. Mem. N.Y. State Local Finance Commn. since 1941; mem. N.Y. State Municipal Revenue Commn. since 1943. Episcopalian. Mason (32°, K.T., Shriner). Author: Municipal Housecleaning (with Jeanne D. Carpenter), 1918; Modern City and Its Government, 1922. Home: 85 College St., Clinton, N.Y. Office: 6 Elk St., Albany N.Y. Died Aug. 21, 1946

CAPPS, Stephen Reid, geologist; b. Jacksonville, Ill., Oct. 15, 1881; s. Stephen Reid and Rhoda (Tomlin) C.; student Ill. Coll., Jacksonville, 1899-1901; A.B., U. of Chicago, 1903, fellow in Geology, 1906-07, Ph.D., 1907; m. Julia Isabelle Webster, Nov. 21, 1911; children—Louise C. Scranton, Stephen Reid, Mary Capps Stelle, Webster. Began as instructor Univ. High School, Chicago, 1904; geologist with U.S. Geological Survey since 1907, assistant chief geologist, 1942-44; geologist Military Geology Unit, 1944-45; engaged in areal study and economic studies in Alaska, 1908-36, of gold placers in Idaho and Colo. and of Manganese deposits in Brazil since 1936. Grant memorial lecturer, Northwestern U., 1936. Mem. Geological Society of America, American Geophysical Union, Geological Soc. of Washington, Washington Acad. Sciences, Alpha Delta Phi, Sigma Xi. Club: Cosmos. Spent 2 yrs. in Near East in petroleum exploration for Standard Oil Co. of N.Y. Author of "The Southern Alaska Range," "Geology of the Alaska Railroad Belt," and many bulletins and articles on geol. subjects. Home: 3308 35th St. N.W. Washington, D.C. Died Jan. 19, 1949.

CAPT, James Clyde, govt. official; b. Tex., June 12. 1888; s. Felix W. and Carrie (Bell) C.; ed. pub. schools, San Antonio, Tex., and Baylor U., Waco, Tex.; divorced; children—Thelma (Mrs. Milton L. Conner), Berlette (Mrs. Robert S. Swain); m. 2d. Katherine Gordon Parker, Dec. 14, 1946. Has been engaged in business successively as railroad employee, small businessman, owner and operator system of dairy products plants, field rep. for Tex. Relief Commn., exec. officer Work Projects Adminstrn.; asst. to director of Bureau of the Census, 1939-41, dir. since Mar. 25, 1941. Served as capt. U.S. Army, with A.E.F., 1917-18. Home: The Westchester, Cathedral Av. N.W., Washington 16; 510 E. Quincy St., San Antonio, Tex. Office: Bureau of the Census, Dept. of Commerce, Washington 25. Died Aug. 30, 1949; buried Arlington (Va.) Nat. Cemetery.

CARDEN, George Alexander, lawyer; born in Dalton, Ga., Nov. 23, 1865; s. Moses White and Salena (Dunn) C.; A.B., Agrl. and Mech. Coll., Auburn, Ala., 1882; Union Coll. of Law (Northwestern U.), 1884, 85; m. Carrie Burns Shumard, June 26, 1890 (died Nov. 2, 1899); children—Isabel (Mrs. William V. Griffin), Salena (Mrs. Garnet Hulings), Carrie (Mrs. Gerald C. Maxwell); m. 2d, Rose Porter, Feb. 17, 1903; children—Mrs. Elizabeth Carden Ingersoll, Dr. George A. Admitted to the Tex. bar, 1889; asst. dist. atty. and acting dist. atty., Dallas, 1897, 98; purchased a number of ships and surrendered them to U.S. Govt. when needed by it, during World War, at sacrifice of several million dollars. Formerly mem. and chmn. Dem. State Exec. Com. of Tex. Mem. Am. Bar Assn., Alpha Tau Omega. Episcopalian. Clubs: University (New York). Home: Washington Hotel, Washington, D.C. Died June 3, 1946.

CAREW, Harold David, writer, editor; b. North Attleborough, Mass., Mar. 10, 1890; s. Harry D. and Ella (Walsh) C.; ed. high sch., Peterborough, N.H., and Suffolk Law Sch., Boston, Mass.; m. Laura Judson Wright, July 1, 1920. Reporter, feature, polit. and editorial writer on newspapers, Boston, New York and Washington, 1907-13; spl. writer Boston Common, 1912-13; editor Cambridge (Mass.) Gridiron, 1913-15; mng. editor Salem (Mass.) Evening Mail, 1915-17; Sunday feature writer Boston Advertiser, 1919; mem. editorial staff Boston Evening Record, 1920, Insurance Journal, 1921-22; mem. book review staff Boston Transcript, 1912-22; lit. editor Pasadena (Calif.) Star-News since 1923. Served with 73d Arty., C.A.C., U.S.A., A.E.F., 1917-19. Clubs: University, Cauldron (hon.); Authors' (Hollywood). Author: Shots from the Notebook of a Gunner, 1919; History of Pasadena and the San Gabriel Valley, California, 1930; Gypsy Caravan (verse), 1931. Contbr. verse, essays, etc., to The Bookman, etc. Home: Sierra Madre, Calif. Office: The Star-News Pasadena, Calif. Died June 25, 1943.

CAREY, Eben James, physician, educator; b. Chicago, Ill., July 31, 1889; s. Frank White and Mary Anne (Curran) C.; pre-med. studies, U. of Calif., 1909-11; 1st and 2d yrs. in medicine, 1911-13; B.S., Creighton U., Omaha, Neb., 1916, M.S., 1918, D.Sc., 1920; M.D., Rush Med. Coll., Chicago, 1925; m. Helene Lichnovsky, Sept. 3, 1919; 1 dau., Mary Anne. Instr. and asst. prof. anatomy, Creighton U., 1914-20; prof. and dir. dept. of anatomy, Marquette U. Sch. of Medicine, Milwaukee, 1920-26, also dean med. students, 1921-26, acting dean, 1926, dean and prof. of anatomy since Aug., 1933; med. dir. Marquette Free Dispensary, 1924; chief of staff Marquette U. Hosp., 1926. Commd. 1st lt. R.O.T.C.; now lt. col. State Staff, Wis. Nat. Guard. Chmn. Scientific Exhbn., Inter-State Postgrad. Med. Assembly, Milwaukee, 1931; in charge med sect., dept. exhibits, Chicago World's Fair, 1933-34; dir. med. science exhibits, Museum of Science and Industry, Chicago, since 1934. Mem. advisory com. med. exhibits, Tex. Centennial, Dallas, 1935-36, Golden Gate Internat. Expn., 1939; mem. scientific com. A.M.A., 1935-41. Chmn. program com. Council on Scientific Work, Med. Soc. of Wis. Silver medal for exhibit illustrating original investigation on intrinsic wave mechanics of the nervous and muscular systems, convention of A.M.A., Atlantic City, June, 1937. Hon. fellowship Am. Coll. of Dentistry, 1939. Fellow A.A.A.S., A.M.A., N.Y. Acad. Sciences; mem. Wis. State and Milwaukee County (pres. 1942) med. socs., Milwaukee Acad. Medicine (pres. 1939-40), Chicago Inst. Medicine, Newcomen Soc. Eng., Alpha Omega Alpha, Pi Kappa Epsilon, Phi Chi (chmn. exec. trustees, editor Quarterly since 1932). Democrat. Catholic. Fourth degree, K.C. Author: Studies in Anatomy, 1924; also many tech. articles. Silver medal for scientific exhibit on exptl. bone origin and pathology, at A.M.A. Conv., Minneapolis, Minn., 1928; citation of merit for scientific exhibit of continued exptl. studies on bone origin at A.M.A. Conv., Portland, Ore., July, 1929; citation of merit, A.M.A. Conv., Detroit, 1930, Philadelphia, 1931; gold medal for studies on origin of muscle and bone, Radiol. Soc. of N.A., 1933; gold medal for exhibit on motor nerve endings, A.M.A. meeting, Atlantic City, June 1942. Clubs: Rotary, University (Milwaukee); Rotary (Chicago). Home: 6119 W. Wisconsin Av., Wauwatosa, Wis. Office: 561 N. 15th St., Milwaukee, Wis. Died June 5, 1947.

CAREY, Francis King, lawyer; b. Baltimore, Md., July 1, 1858; s. James and Susan B. Carey; A.B., Haverford Coll., 1878, A.M., 1881; LL.B., U. of Md., 1880; m. Anne Galbraith Hall, Apr. 27, 1886; children—Louise (Mrs. Carey Rosett), Francis J., Margaret T. (Mrs. Percy C. Madiera, Jr.), Eleanor I. (dec.), Andrew G., Reginald S. In practice of law at Baltimore, Md., since 1880; pres. Charleston (S.C.), Ry., Gas & Electric Co., 1901-03; former mem. law firms of Steele, Semmes & Carey, and Carey, Piper & Hall; former pres., now chairman. bd. dirs. Nat. Sugar Manufacturing Co.; pres. Nat. Sugar Securities Co. Chmn. Md. Tax Revision Commn., 1922-24; mem. Municipal Exec. Com. after Baltimore fire of 1904; chmn. Baltimore Bar Assn. Com. for Corp. Law, 1908; chmn. City Plan Com. constructing Fallsway Blvd. During World War served as mgr. Red Cross War Fund Campaign for Md. and mgr. Hoover Food Conservation Campaign for Md. Mem. exec. com. League of Nations Assn. (Md. branch); mem. exec. com. (Md. sect.) com. to Defend America by Aiding the Allies; mem. adv. bd. Fight for Freedom Com. (Md. branch). Democrat. Episcopalian. Clubs: Maryland (Baltimore, Md.). Author: Municipal Ownership of Natural Monopolies, 1901; Law of Husband and Wife (Stewart and Carey), 1881; Carey's Forms and Precedents, 1885. Home: 8 West Read St. Office: Calvert Bldg., Baltimore, Md. Died Oct. 3, 1944.

CAREY, Peter Bernard, grain broker; b. Chicago, Nov. 3, 1886; s. Simon and Mary (O'Brien) C.; grad. De La Salle Inst., Chicago, 1903; m. Mary Frances Angsten, Feb. 12, 1916, children—Bernard, Philip, Mary, Charles. In grain business since 1903; mem. Chicago Bd. of Trade (pres. 1932-35). Democrat. Roman Catholic. Clubs: Chicago Athletic, Midland, Four Seasons, Beverly Country. Home: 9640 Winchester Av. Office: 208 S. La Salle St., Chicago. Died Oct. 31, 1943.

CAREY, William Gibson, Jr., mfg. exec.; b. Schenectady, N.Y., July 3, 1896; s. W. Gibson and Eleanor Mackubin (Calvert) C., both from Md.; B.S. from Union College, 1918; m. Eleanor Towne, June 16, 1923; children—Eleanor Calvert, William Gibson, III. Engaged in pulp and paper business, New York, 1919-23; sec. and treas. Phila. Paper Mfg. Co., 1923-26; gen. mgr. Phila. div. Container Corp. of America, 1926-29; asst. to pres. Yale & Towne Mfg. Co., 1929, then v.p. and treas., pres. since 1932; dir. Irving

Trust Co., Colgate-Palmolive-Peet Co., New York Telephone Co., Armstrong Cork Co., Research Corp. Trustee Consol. Edison Co., Mutual Life Ins. Co., New York. Served as lt. and capt., 307th F.A., U.S. Army, in France, World War I. Pres. China-America Council of Commerce and Industry, 1941 45, dir. of that organization, 1944-47. President U.S. C. of C., 1939-40; mem. sr. council, 1940 to 1947; vice chmn. Business Adv. Council Dept. Commerce, 1944, grad. mem., 1944 to 1947; chmn. Nat. Industrial Conference Board, 1947; mem. board directors Commerce and Industry Assn. of New York, Am. Arbitration Assn. Life trustee Union Coll. (Schenectady); gov. New York Hosp.; mem. Vestry of Parish of Trinity Ch. (N.Y. City), vestry of St. Mark's Parish, Mt. Kisco, N.Y. Mem. Newcomen Soc. of England, Alpha Delta Phi. Clubs: Alpha Delta Phi, University, Uptown (New York); Field (Greenwich, Conn.); Bedford Golf and Tennis. Home: Greenwich, Conn. Office: 405 Lexington Av., New York 17, N.Y. Died Oct. 4, 1947.

CARHARTT, John Ernest (kär'härt), clergyman; b. Roscoe, O., May 18, 1884; s. John Mossman and Emily Cornelia (Taylor) C.; student Denison U., Granville, O., 1900, Western Reserve U., Cleveland, 1910-12; B.A., Kenyon Coll., Gambier, O., 1914; grad. Bexley Hall Theol. Sem., Gambier, 1915; D.D., Denison U., 1933; Kenyon Coll., 1939; unmarried. Ordained deacon, 1915, priest, 1916, P.E. Ch.; sec. to Bishop DuMoulin and rector St. Andrew's Ch., Toledo, 1915-19; sr. curate in charge Trinity Cathedral Cleveland, 1919-21; rector St. Alban's Ch., Cleveland Heights, 1921-29; field rep. and lecturer, Washington (D.C.) Cathedral, 1930-31; rector St. Peter's Ch., Ashtabula, O., since 1931. Mem. Diocesan Council of Ohio, 1927-35, Diocesan Dept. of Religious Education, 1927-37, Diocesan Commn. Forward Movement since 1934; provincial dep. to Gen. Conv. P.E. Ch., 1931, 34; del. to Provincial Synod, 1934; historiographer and registrar of Diocese of Ohio since 1939; chmn. publicity dept. and editor Church Life, 1928-31; First lt. chaplain, U.S. Army, World War, 1918; chaplain U.S. Army Res. since 1919; mem. Chaplain's Assn. of U.S., Res. Officers Assn.; nat. chaplain Army and Navy Union of U.S. since 1940; chmn. Youth Edn. in Americanism of 2d Dist., 9th Div. of Am. Legion of Ohio. Trustee Smith Home for Aged Women, Ashtabula Chmn. advisory board, Selective Service, Ashtabula; pres. Ashtabula Board of Health; mem. Nat. Sojourners, Exchange Club, Phi Gamma Delta, O.E.S. Republican. Mason (32°); Grand Chaplain, Grand Lodge of O., 1936-37; Eminent Comdr. of Columbian Commandery K.T., Ashtabula, 1936-37. Home: 252 W. 49th St., Ashtabula, O. Died Jan. 25, 1943.

CARLIN, George Andrew, editor; b. Brooklyn, N.Y., Nov. 30, 1890; s. Frederick William and Joan (Driscoll) C.; attended Amherst Coll., 1908-10; LL.B. Fordham, 1917; m. Mary Carr, Apr. 26, 1922; children—Joan (Mrs. John Alden), George, William, Julia, Michael. Teacher, Puerto Rico, 1910-11; reporter, Brooklyn Daily Eagle, 1911-12; Brooklyn Standard Union, 1912-16; New York Sun, 1916-19; London corr., Edward Marshall Syndicate, 1920-21; New York Herald, 1921-22; Metro Pictures, 1922-25; Warner Brothers, 1925-28; editor, Metropolitan Newspaper Service, 1928-30; editor, United Feature Syndicate, since 1930, general mgr. since 1936. Has syndicated columns by Raymond Clapper, Ernie Pyle, Drew Pearson, Mrs. Roosevelt, Westbrook Pegler, Heywood Broun, Marquis Childs, Thomas L. Stokes, Public Papers of Pres. Roosevelt; also Bill Mauldin's cartoons, "Li'l Abner," "Tarzan," "Nancy," etc. Served with first Army headquarters regt., A.E.F., 1917-19. Mem. Nat. Press, Dutch Treat, Cherry Valley, Coffee House, Delta Kappa Epsilon. Democrat. Catholic. Home: 44 Hilton Av., Garden City. Office: 220 E. 42nd St., New York. Died Nov. 28, 1945; buried in Holy Rood Cemetery, Westbury, L.I.

CARLISLE, Floyd Leslie, pub. utility; b. Watertown, N.Y., Mar. 5, 1881; s. Wm. S. and Catherine (Burdick) C.; A.B., Cornell U., 1903 (pres. sr. class); m. Edna Rogers, Nov. 21, 1912; children—Adele, John, Floyd L., Kathryn. Practiced law at Watertown, 1903-10; organizer, and pres. Northern N.Y. Trust Co., 1910-22, chmn. bd. till 1925; pres. St. Regis Paper Co. of Can.; chmn. bd. Northern N.Y. Utilities, 1921; moved to N.Y. City, 1922, as head of F. L. Carlisle & Co., investment bankers; now pres. Michabo Corp.; chmn. bd. Niagara Hudson Power Co., Consol. Edison Co. of N.Y., Inc., Frontier Corp., St. Regis Paper Co. (pres. 1916-37); dir. St. Regis Paper Co. of Canada, Taggart Corp., Valve Bag Co., Brooklyn Edison Co., Consol. Telegraph & Elec. Subway Co., Long Island R.R. Co., N.Y. & Queens Electric Light & Power Co., New York Steam Corp., Westchester Lighting Co., Yonkers Electric Light & Power Co. Trustee Cornell University. Mem. Am. and N.Y. State bar assns. Democrat. Episcopalian. Clubs: University, Cornell, Engineers, Piping Rock, Broad St., Manhattan, City, Economic, Seawanakha-Corinthian Yacht, Eastern Yacht, New York Yacht, Creek (New York); Manhassett Bay Yacht. Home: Locust Valley, L.I. Office: 4 Irving Pl., New York, N.Y. Died Nov. 9, 1942.

CARLSON, Evans Fordyce, Marine Corps officer; b. Sidney, N.Y., Feb. 26, 1896; s. Thomas Alpine and Joetta (Evans) C.; student George Washington Univ.; spl. student internat. law and politics, 1935-36, 37; m. Peggy Tatum; children—Evans Charles (officer U.S.M.C.), Anthony John. Entered U.S. Army, 1912; served in Philippine Islands, Hawaii, Mexican Border; commd. capt., F.A., 1917; in France and Germany, 1917-19; asst. adj. gen., 87th Div., mem. staff of Gen. John Pershing, and with Army of Occupation; returned to civilian life, 1920-21; entered U.S. Marine Corps, 1922; served in West Indies, with Battle Fleet and in Nicaragua; observer with Chinese armies, 1937-38; joined Chinese guerrilla forces in penetrations behind Japanese lines; resigned U.S.M.C. to lecture and write, 1939; reentered Marine Corps, 1941, becoming comdr. 2d Marine Raider Bn. (Carlson's Raiders) with rank of lt. col., and advanced through the grades to brig. gen.; retired, 1946, as result of wounds in action. Decorated Navy Cross (3), Legion of Merit, Purple Heart (2), Presidential Unit Citation (3), Mexican Border Medal (World War I), German Occupation, Marine Corps Expeditionary, Yangtze Service, Nicaraguan Campaign, Asiatic-Pacific Theater (with 6 stars) and Am. Theater medals (U.S.); Italian War Cross; Presidential Medal of Merit, Medal of Distinction (Nicaragua). Mem. Inst. Pacific Relations, Inst. Ethnic Relations; consultant Nat. Inst. Social Relations. Mason (Scottish Rite). Club: Army and Navy (Washington, D.C.). Author: Twin Stars of China, 1940; The Chinese Army, 1940. Home: Brightwood, Ore. Died May 27, 1947.

CARLSON, John Fabian, landscape painter; b. Province of Smaland, Sweden, May 4, 1875; s. Carl Wilhelm Theodore and Clara Mathilda (Fridorf) C.; came to America, 1886; ed. pub. schs., Art Students' League, Buffalo and New York; m. Margaret Goddard, Apr. 19, 1913; children—David, Robert Eric, Peter Worth. Was head instr. landscape painting, Art Students' League, New York. Represented in Corcoran Gallery, Washington, Toledo (O.) Museum, Oberlin (O.) Collection, Dallas (Tex.) Pub. Art Gallery, Brooks Memorial Gallery, Memphis, Tenn.; Lincoln (Neb.) Art Soc. Collection; Randolph Macon Women's Coll. Collection, Lynchburg, Va.; Baltimore Museum of Fine Arts, Baltimore, Md.; Montclair Museum of Fine Arts, Montclair, N.J.; Virginia Museum of Fine Arts, Richmond, Va.; Carnegie Institute, Pittsburgh, Pa. Silver medal, Soc. Washington Artists, 1913; first Isidor prize and Vezin prize, both Salmagundi Club, 1912; first prize, Swedish-Am. exhbn., Chicago, 1911, 13; silver medal, San Francisco Expn., 1915; Carnegie prize, Nat. Acad., 1918; Shaw water-color prize, Salmagundi Club, 1923; Ranger Fund purchase prize, Nat. Acad., 1923; Isidor prize, Am. Oil Exhibition, Salmagundi Club, 1925; medal of award, Montclair (N.J.) Art Mus., 1933; First Altman prize, Nat. Acad.; 1936. Founder John F. Carlson Sch. of Landscape Painting, Woodstock, 1923. Mem. adv. bd. (art) Oberlin Coll.; N.A., 1926; mem. Am. Water Color Soc., N.Y. Water Color Club; founder mem. Painters and Sculptors Gallery Assn., New York, Am. Artists Professional League. Clubs: Salmagundi, Nat. Arts (life). Author: Elementary Principles of Landscape Painting, 1928. Home: Woodstock, N.Y. Died Mar. 20, 1945.

CARLSTROM, Oscar E., lawyer; b. New Boston, Ill., July 16, 1878; s. Charles A. and Clara Carolina (Spang) C.; ed. high sch., New Boston; studied law with Bassett & Bassett, Aledo; m. Alma C. Nissen, Dec. 30, 1903; children—Charles Henry, Marilyn Lucille. Admitted to Ill. bar, 1903, began practice at Aledo; mem. Bassett & Carlstrom, 1903-04; practiced alone until 1913; city atty., Aledo, 4 yrs.; mem. Graham & Carlstrom, 1913-15; state's atty., Mercer County, Ill., 1916-20; mem. Carlstrom & Hebel, 1919-22; del. State Constl. Conv., 1920; mem. State Tax Commn., 1921-25; attorney gen. of Ill., 2 terms, 1925-33; county judge, Mercer County, Ill., 1943-48. Mem. Co. D, 39th U.S. Vol. Inf., Aug. 26, 1899-May 6, 1901, Spanish-Am. War, serving in Philippines 16½ mos.; capt. 6th Ill. Inf., later 123d F.A., Mar. 26, 1917-June 7, 1919, overseas 1 yr., World War I. Mem. Veterans of Foreign Wars (dept. comdr. for Ill., 1944); United Spanish War Veterans (nat. comdr., 1921-22. Republican. Presbyterian. Mason (K.T., 32°, Shriner). Clubs: Aledo, Kiwanis, Oak View Country (Aledo); Svithiod Singing (Chicago). Home: Aledo, Ill. Died March 5, 1948.

CARLTON, William Newnham Chattin, librarian; b. Gillingham, Kent County, Eng., June 29, 1873; s. William Thomas Chattin and Alice Isabel (Newnham) C.; came to Am. 1882; ed. Mt. Hermon Sch., Mass., 1890-91; pvt. study, under Rev. Samuel Hart, D.C.L., 1893-99; hon. M.A., Trinity Coll., Conn., 1902, L.H.D., 1915; m. Sara Hayden, June 24, 1903; children—Sara Newnham, Patricia Hayden. Asst. Pub. Library, Holyoke, Mass., 1887-90; asst. librarian, Watkinson Library of Reference, Hartford, Conn., 1892-99; librarian, Trinity Coll., Hartford, 1899-1909, instr. in English, 1901-03; librarian, Newberry Library, Chicago, July 1, 1909-Dec. 31, 1919; dir. Am. Library in Paris, Inc., 1920-21; acting librarian, Public Library, Hamilton, Ont., Can., 1921-22; librarian, Williams Coll., Feb. 1922-June 30, 1938. Mem. Am. Library Inst. (pres. 1919-20), N.Y. Hist. Soc. Episcopalian. Publications: A reissue in fascsimile of Short Catechism Drawn Out of the Word of God (by Samuel Stone), with intro., 1899; Relation of the Pequot Warres (written in 1660 by Lt. Lion Gardener), printed from the original manuscript, with hist. intro., 1901; Charles Jeremy Hoadly, LL.D., A Memoir, 1902; Bibliography of the Official Publications of Trinity College, 1824-1905, 1905; Poems and Letters of Lord Byron, 1911; Origin and Character of the Icelandic Sagas, 1912; Unique or a Description of a Proof Copy of R. L. Stevenson's Beach of Falesá, 1914; Notes on the Bridgewater House Library, 1918; Reading with a Purpose—English Literature, 1925; Pauline—Favorite Sister of Napoleon, 1930. Contributor to The Library Journal, Encyclopedia Americana, Educational Review, Modern Language Notes, Bibliographical Society Papers, The Bookman, N.Y. Evening Post Lit. Rev., N.Y. Herald Tribune "Books." Editor The American Collector, 1927-28. Clubs: Wayfarers (Chicago); Players (New York). Home: 17 E. 98th St., New York. Died Feb. 3, 1943.

CARMAN, George Noble, educator; b. Walworth, N.Y., July 18, 1856; s. John and Electa (Camburn) C.; A.B., U. of Mich., 1881, hon. A.M., 1906; m. Ada J. MacVicar, July 25, 1883. Prin., Ypsilanti (Mich.) High Sch., 1880-82; supt., schs., Union City, Mich., 1882-85; prin., Grammar Sch. No. 15, Brooklyn, 1885-89, high school, St. Paul, Minn., 1889-93; dean, Morgan Park Acad. of U. of Chicago, 1893-95; dir. Lewis Inst., Chicago, 1895-1935, emeritus since 1935. Clubs: Chicago Literary, Union League, City. Address: Fenville, Mich. Died June 24, 1941.

CARMELIA, Francis Albion (kär-mĕl'ē-ä), U.S. Public Health Service; b. Montgomery County, Pa., 1889; s. Francis A. and Lida (Ware) C.; M.D., Jefferson Medical College, 1911; m. Sara Ellis Brownback, 1913. Commd. U.S.P.H.S., 1913; asst. surg. general, 1926-36; supervisor Dist. 5 (Rocky Mt. and Pacific Coast states, Alaska and Hawaii), 1936-40; med. dir. (retired), 1940; consulting public health practice since 1940. Address: 1503 Riverview Blvd., Norristown, Pa. Died Dec. 15, 1947.

CARMICHAEL, Thomas Harrison, prof. pharmaceutics; b. Phila., Jan. 27, 1858; s. William and Julia Baker (Hunter) C.; A.B., Central High Sch., Phila.; M.D., Hahnemann Med. Coll., Phila., 1887; m. Emily H. Leonard, Nov. 23, 1897; 1 son, Leonard. Interne Ward's Island Hosp., New York, 1886-87; lecturer on pharmaceutics, 1897-1908, prof. of pharmacodynamics, 1908-13, asso. prof. materia medica, 1913-19, Hahnemann Med. Coll. Mem. Am. Inst. Homeopathy (1st v.p., 1908, pres., 1911-12, trustee, 1912-13), Homeo. Med. Soc. Co. of Phila. (pres. 1908, 1917, trustee since 1912); ex-pres. Allen Lane Sch. Assn.; chmn. Com. on Homeo. Pharmacopoeia, 1907, 08, 09, 10, 12, and since 1933; chmn. Com. on Revision Homeo. Pharmacopoeia of U.S., 1935; censor Sr. Mil. Med. Assn., 1917. Vice-pres. Pan.-Am. Homeopathic Congress, 1941. Dir. and chmn. Auxiliary Com. Germantown and Chestnut Hill Improvement Assn. Mem. Germantown Hist. Soc., Pi Gamma Mu. Episcopalian; vestryman Christ Ch., and St. Michael's Ch., Germantown for 18 yrs. Club: Oxford Medical. Address: President's House, Tufts College, Mass.Died Oct. 9, 1942.

CARMICHAEL, William Perrin, civil engineer; b. Warren County, Ind., Apr. 14, 1858; s. Ralph Erskine and Rebecca (Dill-Kent) C.; A.B., Wabash Coll., Ind., 1879, A.M., 1886; m. Alice Norris, Mar. 2, 1887; 1 dau., Katherine Norris. Exec. sec. Ind. Engring. Soc., 1891-93; mgr. Williamsport (Ind.) Stone Co., 1893-98; pres. Wm. P. Marmichael Co., Williamsport, Ind., St. Louis, Mo., Mexico City, Mex., engring. contractors, 1898-1910; v.p. and gen. mgr. Unit Constrn. Co., St. Louis, 1910-14; pres. Carmichael-Cryder Co., Inc., St. Louis, 1914-29; pres. The Carmichael Gravel Co., Williamsport, Ind., and St. Louis, 1914-25; v.p. and treas. Midwest Consol. Utilities, 1931-36; retired. Pres. of Winona Lake Instns., 1918-39; now pres. Nowata County Gas Co. Republican. Presbyterian. Mem. Am. Soc. Engring. Contractors, S.A.R. Clubs: City, Mo. Athletic. Home: 7749 Delmar Blvd., St. Louis, Mo.; (summer) Winona Lake, Ind. Died Dec. 17, 1944.

CARMODY, Terence Francis, lawyer; b. Watkins, N.Y., July 1, 1871; s. Thomas and Margaret (Lawlor) C.; grad. high sch., Waterbury, Conn., 1890; LL.B., Yale, 1895; m. Lauretta Ryan, June 30, 1903; children—Edward, John (dec.), Francis, Guerin, Marie-Louise, Paul (dec.). Practiced at Waterbury since 1895, sr. mem. firm Carmody, Larkin & Torrance; state's attorney, 1917-24; dir. Colonial Trust Co., Watertown Trust Co. Pres. Waterbury Chamber of Commerce, 1921-25. Trustee Taft School Corp., Canterbury Sch., Inc. Mem. Am. Bar Assn., Conn. Bar Assn. (pres. 1926-28). Catholic. Club: Waterbury. Home: 265 Cutler St., Watertown, Conn. Office: 111 W. Main St., Waterbury, Conn. Died July 3, 1943.

CARMODY, Thomas Edward, surgeon; b. Shiawassee County, Mich., May 22, 1875; s. Thomas and Mary Ann (Gorman) C.; D.D.S., Dental Sch., U. of Mich., 1897, D.D.Sc., 1898; grad. Sch. of Medicine, U. of Colo., 1903; m. Mary Jane McBride, Nov. 7, 1899; children—David, Ruth P. (Mrs. William G. Summers), Mary Alice (Mrs. Howard D. Cobb). In practice as physician and surgeon since 1903, specializing in otorhinolaryngology, bronchoesophagology, oral and plastic surgery; prof. bacteriology and histology, Dental Coll., U. of Denver, 1898-1905, prof. oral surgery and rhinology, 1905-32; asst. in laryngology and otology, Med. Sch., U. of Colo., 1905-33; chief of otolaryngology, child research council, research dept., U. of Colo., 1928-36. Surgeon general of Colo., 1909-11. Served as 1st lt., Med. Res. Corps, U.S. Army, 1917; major, Med. Corps, U.S. Army, 1918-19. Fellow Am. Coll. Surgeons, Am. Coll. Dentists, Internat. Coll. Surgeons. Mem. Denver County Med. Soc. (sec., 1904, pres., 1923), Denver Dental Soc. (pres., 1907), Colorado Otolaryngol. Soc. (1st pres.), Col. Soc. for Crippled Children (1st pres.), Am. Acad. of Opthal. and Otolaryn. (pres.,

1923), Am. Bronchoesophagological Soc., Am. Laryn., Rhenol. and Otol. Soc. (pres., 1936), Am. Laryn. Assn. (pres., 1941), Am. Otol. Assn., Am. Soc. of Oral and Plastic Surgs., Am. Soc. of Plastic and Reconstructive Surgery, Am. Med. Assn. (chmn. otolaryn. sec., 1931); mem. 1st Internat. Otolaryn. Congress, Copenhagen, Denmark, 1929; mem. bd. dirs. Nat. Soc. for Crippled Children. Home: 1901 Hudson St. Office: 227 16th St., Denver, Colo. Died Aug. 30, 1946.

CARNEGIE, Louise Whitfield; b. New York, N.Y., Mar. 7, 1857; d. John W. and Fannie M. (Davis) Whitfield; attended Miss Haines' Sch., New York, 1864-76; M.H.L., New York U., 1921; LL.D., St. Andrews U., Scotland, 1935; m. Andrew Carnegie, Apr. 22, 1887 (died Aug. 11, 1919); 1 dau., Margaret (Mrs. Roswell Miller). Received Freedom of City of Dunfermline, Scotland, 1907, Edinburgh, Scotland, 1935; Pa. Soc. medal, 1934. Mem. National Society of Colonial Dames of America, Huguenot Society of America. Member Daughters of the Cincinnati. Republican. Presbyterian. Clubs: International Garden (New York); Sulgrave (Washington). Home: 2 E. 91st St., New York, N.Y.; and Skibo Castle, Dornoch, Scotland. Died June 24, 1946; buried in Sleepy Hollow Cemetery, N. Tarrytown, N.Y.

CARNEY, Thomas J(oseph), pres. Sears, Roebuck & Co.; b. Chicago, Ill., Apr. 7, 1886; s. Thomas and Mary (Morris) C.; ed. pub. schs.; m. Margret Coughlan, Feb. 5, 1920; children—Thomas Joseph, Mel Coughlan, Marcia Ellyn. With Sears, Roebuck & Co., mail order house, since 1903, successively exec. in Chicago store, gen. supt. at Dallas, Tex., and gen. mgr. eastern territory, v.p., 1930-39, pres. since Jan. 1939. Home: 1155 Mohawk Rd., Wilmette, Ill. Office: 925 S. Homan Av., Chicago, Ill. Died June 29, 1942.

CARPENTER, Allen Fuller, prof. mathematics; b. Marengo, Ia., June 12, 1880; s. Henry Merritt and Sophronia Allen (Fuller) C.; A.B., Hastings Coll., Hastings, Neb., 1901, D.Sc., 1937; A.M., U. of Nebraska, 1909; Ph.D., U. of Chicago, 1915; m. Margaret Anna Daily, Aug. 30, 1905; children—Richard Henry (dec.), Eleanor Jane (Mrs. Robert William MacKay). Instr. in mathematics, Hastings Coll., 1901-08, U. of Nebraska, 1908-09; instr. in mathematics, U. of Washington, Seattle, Wash., 1909-15, asst. prof., 1915-19, asso. prof., 1919-26, prof. since 1926, exec. officer, dept. of mathematics since 1936; asso. prof. mathematics U. of Chicago, summer 1923. Served as pvt., Presidio Regt., S.A.T.C., July-Sept. 1918. Chmn. Seattle Civil Service Pension Commn., 1928. Fellow A.A.A.S.; mem. Am. Math. Soc., Am. Assn. Univ. Profs., Sigma Xi, Theta Chi. Club: Faculty Men's (U. of Wash). Home: 6202 51st St. N.E., Seattle 5, Wash. Died Oct. 16, 1949.

CARPENTER, Charles Ernest, prof. law; b. Olin, Ia., Oct. 31, 1878; s. Asa E. and Lelia L. (Littlefield) C.; A.B., U. of Kan., 1903, A.M., 1904; LL.B., Harvard University, 1908; married Jessie Bird Bennett, August 31, 1905 (died August 1936); adopted children—Corinne Lillian (Mrs. E. C. Walker), Marguerite Roberts (Mrs. B. B. Busselle); married second, Mildred Struble, 1940. Teacher country school, 1896-98; principal high school, Eureka, Kan., 1904-05; admitted to Massachusetts bar, 1908; member Ropes, Gray & Gorham, Boston, 1908-09; asst. prof. and prof. law, U. of N.D., 1909-14; asst. prof. law, U. of Ill., 1914-18; Y.M.C.A. sec., A.E.F., 1918-19; dean Washburn Coll. of Law, Topeka, Kan., 1919-22; prof. law, U. of Ore., 1922-31, also dean Law Sch., 1927-31; prof. law, U. of Southern Calif., since 1931. Mem. Phi Beta Kappa, Phi Alpha Delta, Order of Coif. Mason. Conglist. Author: Treatise on Suretyship and Guaranty, 1912; A Real New Deal, 1936; Workable Rules for Proximate Cause, 1932, Private Enterprise and Democracy, 1940; also many articles in law publs. and revs. Home: 100 So. Van Ness Av., Los Angeles. Died June 16, 1948.

CARPENTER, Clinton E., coll. pres.; b. Seekonk, Mass., June 3, 1892; s. H. Miles and Alice (L.) Carpenter; student Bridgewater Normal Sch., 1913-15; B.Sc. in Edn., Boston Univ., 1929, M.Ed., 1932; student Univ. of Clermont-Ferrand, France, 1920, Harvard U., 1922-23; m. Beatrice Upham, Oct. 4, 1917. Teacher, Seekonk, Mass., 1911-13; teacher and prin. Taunton, Mass., 1915-22; dir. of training, State Normal Sch., North Adams, Mass., 1922-28, State Teachers Coll., Fitchburg, Mass., 1928-40, pres. State Teachers Coll., Worcester, Mass., since 1940. Served with A.E.F., 1919-20. Edited: The Problems of Childhood (Angelo Patri, author). Home: 381 May St. Office: Teachers Coll., Worcester, Mass. Died June 1948.

CARPENTER, Elbert Lawrence, lumber mfr.; b. Rochelle, Ill., Mar. 6, 1862; s. Judson E. and Olivia (Detwiler) C.; ed. high school, Clinton, Iowa and Lake Forest (Ill.) Acad.; hon. Doctor of Music, U. of Minn., 1935; m. Florence Isabelle Welles, June 4, 1890. In lumber business at Minneapolis since 1887; asso. with Thomas H. Shevlin and Hovey C. Clark; organized Shevlin-Carpenter Co. in 1892; chmn. bd. Shevlin, Carpenter & Clarke Co., a management corp.; also officer or dir. in the various corps. under its management; retired in 1937 from all exec. positions in the lumber business; dir. First Nat. Bank and Trust Co., Minneapolis, St. Paul and Sault Ste. Marie Ry., Northwestern Nat. Life Ins. Co.; trustee Farmers & Mechanics Savings Bank. Pres. Nat. Lumber Mfrs. Assn.; pres. Orchestral Assn. of Minneapolis since its organization in 1903. Trustee Westminster Presbyn. Ch. Clubs: Minneapolis, Woodhill. Home: 314 Clifton Av. Office: 900, First National-Soo Line Bldg., Minneapolis, Minn.* Died Jan. 29, 1945.

CARPENTER, Ford Ashman, meteorologist, aeronaut; b. Chicago, Ill., Mar. 25, 1868; s. Lebbaeus Ross and Charlotte (Eaton) C.; ed. Dilworth Acad.; Carson Astronomical Obs.; U.S. Balloon and Airship Schs., etc.; LL.D., Whittier (Calif.) Coll., 1913; Sc.D., Occidental Coll., Los Angeles, Calif., 1921. With U.S. Weather Service various stations, 1888-1919; special observer, 1940-41; mgr. dept. meteorology and aeronautics, Los Angeles Chamber of Commerce, 1919-41. Hon. lecturer, summer sessions U. of Calif. 1914-16, 1939-41; lecturer, U.S. Army Aviation School, San Diego, 1915, Monterey Mil. Encampment, 1916-17; mem. faculty (lecturer meteorology) Southern br. U. of Calif., 1919-30; lecturer on meteorology, Air Service, War Dept., 1915-44, Babson Inst., 1921-35, Columbia, Cornell, and Northwestern, 1923-38, New York U., West Point Mil. Acad., Annapolis Naval Acad., Poly. Inst. Brooklyn, Carnegie Inst. Pittsburgh, Field Mus., 1925-38, Goodyear-Zeppelin Co., 1926-29, War Coll. (Washington), etc., Meteorological adviser Palos Verdes Estates, 1914-20, Pauba Rancho, 1921-31, TWA, 1927-30, Santa Fe Ry. Co., 1922-35, American Airways, TWA, United Airlines, 1927-38, Los Angeles Municipal Airport, 1927, Hollywood Bowl, 1928, Amer.-Hawaiian Steamship Co., 1934-40. Climatol. adviser to Frank A. Vanderlip, 1927-37. Selected and surveyed L.A. Municipal Airport, 1927. Served as pvt., Signal Corps, U.S. Army, 1888; lt. U.S.N.R., class 5, 1920-21; lt. col. Inactive Res., U.S. Army aide, 9th Civilian Defense Area. Meteorol. in defense, World War I; in Intelligence, World War II, lecturing to pre-aviation cadets, 1943-44. Meteorol. observer of aerial bombing of former German battleships, 1921. Radio broadcaster over Stations KFI, KFAC, and KMTR, 1923-41. International balloon pilot No. 913, Fédération Aeronautique Internationale since 1921. Meteorological and aeronautic adviser to naval affairs com. of 72d Congress, 1930; nat. councilor U.S. Chamber of Commerce, Washington, 1933-38. Mem. 8th Internat. Geog. Congress, Washington, D.C., 1904, Internat. Congress Tuberculosis, Washington, D.C., 1908; mem. photographic com. standards, U.S. Dept. Agr., 1908. Climatol. commr. Seattle Expn. (gold medal for meteorol. exhibit), 1909; first photographed red snow in natural colors, 1911; asst. in U.S. Weather Bur. meteorograph ascents into stratosphere, alt. 108,000 ft., 1913; mem. Pan Am. Med. Congress, 1915, 1st International Aero Congress (v.p.), Omaha, 1921. Past fellow A.A.A.S., Royal Meteorol. and Geog. Socs. (London), Am. Seismol. Soc., Am. Assn. Univ. Profs., S.A.R.; fellow San Diego Soc. Nat. History, Southern Calif. Acad. Science (pres. 1929-31, v.p. 1932-39), Nat. Assn. Balloon Corps Vets., Los Angeles Mus. (gov. 1920-40), Am. Climatol. and Clin. Assn., Nat. Aero. Assn., Assn. Mil. Engrs., Sigma Xi, Phi Beta Kappa. Republican. Episcopalian. Mason (32°, Shriner). Clubs: University, Sunset, Scribes (Los Angeles, Calif.); Sojourners, Army and Navy (Washington, D.C.). Author of monographs, pamphlets, articles, etc., including the following: Climate and Weather of San Diego; Influence of the College Spirit; Aviator and Weather Bureau; Meteorological Methods; Aerial Pathways; Roadbeds of the Air; Weather and Flight; Aids to Air Pilots; Climatic Comparisons; Old Probabilities mate; Commercial Climatology; Gen. "Billy" Mitchell As I Knew Him; Sailing Around America's Shores of Two Oceans; Climatology of a Block of Ice, 1945. Contbr. Atlantic Monthly, Scientific Am., Nation's Business, etc. Editor, Meteorology and Aeronautics, 1919-41. Inventor of anemometric scale, hythergraph, televentscope and ventograph. Home: University Club. Office: 108 W. 6th St., Los Angeles 14. Died Nov. 1947.

CARPENTER, George Albert, ex-judge; b. Chicago, Ill., Oct. 20, 1867; s. George B. and Elizabeth Curtis (Greene) C.; A.B., Harvard, 1888; LL.B., 1891; m. Harriet Isham, May 10, 1894; children—Katherine Snow (Mrs. Ed J. Birmingham, II), George Benjamin, Isham (dec.). Admitted to bar, 1890; elected judge Circuit Court of Cook County, Ill., 1906, and reelected, 1909; apptd. judge U.S. Dist. Court, Northern Dist. of Ill., Dec. 1909, confirmed, Jan. 1910; resigned, June 30, 1933; now associated as counsel with Tenney, Sherman & Rogers, & Guthrie, Chicago. (New York and Boston). Home: Drake Towers, 179 Lake Shore Drive. Office: 120 S. La Salle St., Chicago. Died Sept. 13, 1944; buried in Rosehill Cemetery, Chicago.

CARPENTER, Hubert Vinton, electrical engr.; b. near Thomson, Ill., Jan. 29, 1875; s. Charles Higley and Mary Elizabeth (Burge) C.; B.S. in E.E., U. of Ill., 1897; M.S. in mathematics and physics, 1899; LL.D., State Coll. of Washington, 1938; m. Maggie Edith Staley, June 19, 1899; children—Charles B., Florence Edith, William Harold, Arthur C. Instr. physics, U. of Ill., 1897-1901; asst. prof. physics and elec. engring., State Coll. of Wash., 1901-03, head dept. of mech. and elec. engring. since 1903, dean coll. Mech. arts and engring. since June 1917; consultant Nat. Resources Planning Bd. Fellow Am. Inst. E.E.; mem. Am. Soc. M.E., Soc. Promotion Engring. Edn., Tau Beta Pi, Sigma Tau, Phi Kappa Phi, Sigma Xi, Theta Xi. Methodist. Home: Pullman, Wash. Died Nov. 15, 1941.

CARPENTER, Robert Ruliph Morgan, director of E. I. du Pont de Nemours & Co.; b. Wilkes-Barre, Pa., July 30, 1877; s. Walter Samuel and Belle (Morgan) C.; prep. edn., Hillman Acad., Wilkes-Barre, Pa.; special study Mass. Inst. Tech.; m. Margaretta L. du Pont, Dec. 18, 1906; children—Louisa d'A., Renee du Pont, Robert Ruliph Morgan, William K. du Pont. Began as engr., E. I. du Pont de Nemours & Co., Wilmington, 1904, successively purchasing agent, dir. development dept., vice pres., mem. exec. com., mem. finance com., gen. mgr., cellulose dept.; mgr. pyralin dept.; mem. exec. com., retired 1931; now dir., mem. salary and bonus com. Dir. Phila. Nat. League Base Ball Club, Christiana Securities Co. Trustee Acad. Natural Sciences of Phila., American Wildlife Foundation. Dir. Delaware Chapter Am. Red Cross; dir., pres. Memorial Hosp., Wilmington Park, Inc. Mem. Phi Beta Epsilon. Repub. Clubs: Wilmington, Wilmington Whist, Wilmington Country, Vicmead Hunt, Wilderness, Boone and Crockett; Midday (Phila.); Explorers, Campfire, Am. Pioneer Trails. Author: Game Trails, Alaska to Africa. Home: Montchanin, Del. Office: E. I. du Pont de Nemours & Co., Wilmington, Del. Died June 11, 1949.

CARR, Alexander, actor; b. Rumni, Russia, 1880; brought to U. S. when a child. Début in music hall, St. Paul, Minn.; played in "The Stroke of Twelve," Nashville, Louisville and Buffalo; "Toplitsky, or The End of the World," Palace Theatre, London, 1909; "The Sweetest Girl in Paris," 1910; "Louisiana Lou," 1911-12; "Business before Pleasure," 1918-19, etc. Died Sept. 20, 1946.

CARR, Floyd LeVerne, church official; b. Alfred, N.Y., Jan. 24, 1880; s. Adelbert John and Alice F. (Green) C.; prep. edn., high sch., Hornell, N.Y., 1897; Ph.B., Brown U., 1901; B.D., Newton Theol. Instn., 1906; m. Florence Newell Lawton, June 13, 1906; 1 dau., Dorothy May. Ordained Bapt. ministry, 1906; pastor successively North Uxbridge, Mass., Roslindale Ch., Boston, First Ch., Lynn, Mass., and Wilkinsburg, Pa., until 1923; field sec. Bd. of Missionary Coöperation, Northern Bapt. Conv., 1923-24; field sec. Dept. of Missionary Edn., Northern Bapt. Conv. 1924-45. Author: Survey for Baptist Pastors, 1920; (booklets) Missionary Heroes Courses, 1925; Missionary Anniversary Programs for Sunday Schools, 1926. Founder of a chain of 30 boys' camps to train boys for church leadership; now retired. Home: 83 Merriam St., Lexington 73, Mass. Died May 23, 1948.

CARR, James Ozborn, lawyer; b. Duplin County, N.C., Sept. 6, 1869; s. Joseph H. and Mary Susan (Dickson) C.; Ph.B., cum laude, U. of N.C., 1895; studied law, same univ., 1896; m. Susan Parsley, June 18, 1907. Admitted to N C. bar, 1896, and began practice at Kenansville, 1897; moved to Wilmington, 1899; became mem. Rountree & Carr, 1899; now mem. Carr, James & Carr. Chmn. Board of Edn., New Hanover Co., 1909-16 and 1927-31; U.S. atty., Eastern Dist. of N.C., 1916-19 and since Feb. 16, 1934; mem. platform com. Dem. Nat. Conv., 1920; chmn. State Ednl. Commn., 1925-27; mem. N.C. Judicial Conf. since 1925; mem. State Sch. Commn., 1933-34. Mem. Phi Beta Kappa. Presbyn. Home: Masonburo Sound. Office: 609 Murchison Bldg., Wilmington, N.C.* Died Mar. 7, 1949.

CARR, Reid Langdon, lawyer; b. Cornwall, Vt., Oct. 20, 1880; s. Anson K. and M. Louise (Langdon) C.; A.B., Middlebury (Vt.) Coll., 1901; LL.B., New York Law School, 1903; LL.D., Middlebury College, 1944; married Eleanora Fredericksen, Feb. 5, 1916. Instructor in New York Law School, 1903-16; member firm Morgan & Seabury, 1905-07, Morgan, Morgan & Carr, 1907-21, Clark, Carr & Ellis, 1921-40; president and director Columbian Carbon Co., Columbian Fuel Corp., Coltexo Corp., Southern Gas Line, Inc., Southern Carbon Co., Pineville Gas Co., Magnetic Pigment Co.; dir. Ark., La. & Mo. R.R. Co., Irving Trust Co., Frederick H. Levey Co., Peerless Carbon Black Co., Carbon Black Export, Inc., Interstate Natural Gas Co., Columbian-Phillips Co., D. Appleton Century Co.; Miss. River Fuel Co. Trustee Middlebury Coll. Mem. N.Y. Bar Assn., Assn. Bar City of N.Y., Chamber of Commerce, N.Y. State, S.R., Society Colonial Wars, Phi Beta Kappa, Delta Kappa Epsilon. Republican. Episcopalian. Clubs: Union, Metropolitan, Union League, Uptown, Church; Creek (Locust Valley, N.Y.); Nat. Golf Links of Am., Bald Peak Country (N.H.). Home: 925 5th Av. Office: 41 E. 42d St., New York, N.Y. Died Oct. 7, 1948.

CARR, Robert Franklin, pres. Dearborn Chemical Co.; b. Argenta, Ill., Nov. 1871; s. Robert F. (M.D.) and Emily A. (Smick) C.; B.S., Univ. of Ill., 1893, LL.D., 1929; m. Louise B. Smiley, 1906 (died Sept. 7, 1925); children—Louise (Mrs. W. P. Hodgkins), Florence (Mrs. Edgar L. Marston, II), Robert Franklin. With Dearborn Chemical Co., Chicago, since 1894, pres. since 1907; director Wilson & Co., Continental Illinois Bank and Trust Co., Peoples Gas Light & Coke Co. (all of Chicago); director Chicago & Eastern Illinois Railroad. Served as major General Staff, U.S. Army, Purchase, Storage and Traffic Division under General Goethals, July 1918-Jan. 1, 1919. Pres. Home for Destitute Crippled Children (Chicago), 1921-33; trustee U. of Ill., term 1915-21, pres. of bd., 1920, 21 (donor of fellowship in chemistry); trustee Northwestern Mut. Life Ins. Co., Milwaukee; chmn. U. of Illinois Memorial Stadium Com. ($1,850,000 stadium completed Oct. 1924, funds all raised among alumni, faculty and students; dedicated to 180 U. of Ill. men who lost lives in World War); chmn. com. to finance and build Illinois Students Union. Mem. Bd. of Edn., Chicago, 1931-33; director general Analine and Film Corporation; trustee Century of Progress Expn., Chicago; trustee Passavant Hospital. Member American Chemical Society, Art Inst. Chicago (life), Chicago Historical Soc., Field Mus. of Chicago (life), Kappa Sigma. Democrat. Episcopalian. Clubs: University (ex-president), Chicago, Commercial, Old Elm, Onwentsia, Shoreacres, Casino, Saddle & Cycle (Chicago); Seigniory (Quebec); Everglades (Palm Beach, Fla.). Home: 545 Deerpath Av., Lake Forest. Ill. Office: 310 S. Michigan Av., Chicago, Ill.* Died Jan. 22, 1945.

CARR, Wilbur John, asst. sec. of state; b. near Hillsboro, O., Oct. 31, 1870; s. Edward Livingston and Catharine (Fender) C.; grad. Commercial Coll. of Ky. U., Lexington, 1889; LL.B., Georgetown U., 1894; LL.M., Columbian (now George Washington) U., 1899; LL.D., George Washington U., 1925, Hillsdale Coll., 1927; m. 2d, Edith Adele Koon, Jan. 20, 1917. Clerk of Dept. of State, 1892-1902; chief, Consular Bur., Dept. of State, 1902-07; chief clerk, Dept. of State, 1907-09; mem. of Bd. of Examiners for the Consular Service; mem. of board to formulate plan for the examination of candidates for the consular service, 1905; chmn. Com. on Business Methods, Dept. of State, since 1907; dir. consular service, Nov. 30, 1909-24; vice chmn. Div. of Foreign Relations and rep. of the Dept. of State on the Div. of Federal Relations, Nat. Research Council, 1920; budget officer, Dept. of State, 1921; mem., 1924-28, and chmn., 1928-37, Bd. of Foreign Service Personnel, Board of Examiners for the Foreign Service, and Foreign Service School Bd.; U.S. rep. Permanent Internat. Com. of Permanent Assn. of Road Congresses, 1927-33; asst. sec. of state, 1924-37; E.E. and M.P. to Czechoslovakia, 1937; special rep. of the President of U.S. at the funeral of ex-President Masaryk of Czechoslovakia, Sept. 1937; retired, 1939. Honored by John Carroll Acad. of Diplomacy, Georgetown U.; representative of Dept. of State on U.S. Bd. of Jamestown Expn., 1907, Internat. Congress Tuberculosis, 1908, Seattle Expn., 1909, etc. Mem. Am. Soc. Internat. Law, Council on Fgn. Relations, Ohio Soc. Trustee, George Washington University; Garfield Hosp. Clubs: Metropolitan, Cosmos, Nat. Press, Lake Placid, Gamma Eta Gamma. Contbr. Ency. Americana, Am. Jour. Internat. Law, etc. Address: 2300 Wyoming Av., Washington, D.C. Died June 26, 1942.

CARREL, Alexis (kăr'rĕl), surgeon; b. Sainte Foy les Lyon, France, June 28, 1873; s. Alexis and Anne (Ricard) C.; L.B., U. of Lyon, France, 1890, M.D., 1900; Sc.B., U. of Dijon, France, 1891; M.D., Belfast, 1919; Sc.D., Columbia U., 1913, Brown and Princeton Univs., 1920, U. of the State of N.Y., 1937, Manhattan Coll., 1938; LL.D., U. of Calif., 1936; m. Anne de la Motte, 1913. Interne hôpitaux de Lyon, 1896-1900; prosector, U. of Lyon, 1900-02, came to America, 1904; U. of Chicago Physiol. Labs., 1905-06; staff Rockefeller Inst. for Med. Research, 1906-12, mem. 1912-39, mem. emeritus since 1939. Winner of Nobel prize, 1912, for success in suturing blood vessels and transplantation of organs; winner of Nordhoff-Jung Cancer prize, 1931; Newman Foundation award, U. of Ill., 1937; Phi Beta Kappa, Dartmouth, 1937; Rotary Club of New York Service medal, 1939. Served as maj. French Army Med. Corps, 1914-19. Special mission for French Ministry of Pub. Health, 1939-40. Decorated Comdr. Legion of Honour, France; Comdr. Order of Leopold; D.S.M.; C.M.G.; Orders of Northern Star of Sweden, Isabella of Spain. Sr. fellow Am. Surg. Assn.; mem. Am. Philos. Soc., Am. Coll. Surgeons, Am. Soc. Physiology; asso. mem. A.M.A.; Soc. Clin. Surgery (sr. mem.) Accademico Pontificio, Pontificia Accademia delle Scienze; hon. fellow Royal Soc. of Med.; foreign asso. Societa Italiana delle Scienze, corr. mem. various foreign academies. Club: Century (N.Y. City). Catholic. Author: Treatment of Infected Wounds (with Georges Dehelly), 1917; Man, the Unknown, 1935; The Culture of Organs (with Charles A. Lindbergh), 1938. Contbr. on biol. and surg. subjects. Address: Rockefeller Institute, 66th St. and York Av., New York. Died Nov. 5, 1944; buried Ile St. Gildas, Penvenan, Côtes-du-Nord, France.

CARRELL, William Beall, orthopedic surgeon; b. Lawrenceburg, Tenn., 1883; s. Charles A. and Virginia L. C.; B.S., Southwestern U., 1905, M.D., 1908; m. Beulah Stewart, Sept. 20, 1905; children—W. Brandon, Mary Stewart, John Robert. House Surgeon, St. Paul's Sanitarium, Dallas, 1909-10; prof. orthopedic surgery, Baylor Med. School; chief surgeon to Tex. Scottish Rite Hosp. for Crippled Children; orthopedic surgeon, Baylor Hosp., Parkland Hosp., Methodist Hosp. Served as capt., later maj. Med. Corps, U.S. Army. Fellow Am. Coll. Surgeons; mem. American and Southern med. assns., State Med. Assn. of Tex., Am. Orthopedic Assn., Dallas County Med. Soc., Tex. State Surg. Soc., Central States Orthopedic Soc., Internat. Orthopedic Society. Democrat. Methodist. Mason (33°, I.G.H.). Clubs: University, Dallas Athletic, Dallas Country. Given Dallas Service Award, 1926. Home: 3612 Overbrook Drive. Office: 3701 Maple Av., Dallas, Tex. Died Feb. 23, 1944.

CARRICO, Joseph Leonard (kăr'ĭ-kō), educator; b. Raywick, Marion Co., Ky., Dec. 27, 1881; s. William and Mary Elizabeth (Hardesty) C.; A.B., St. Mary's Coll., St. Mary, Ky., 1902, A.M., 1921; Litt.B., U. of Notre Dame, Ind., 1903; Ph.D., Catholic U. of America, 1908. Joined Congregation of the Holy Cross, 1902; ordained priest R.C. Ch., 1908; began teaching at U. of Notre Dame, 1908; dean Coll. of Arts and Letters, 1919-23, head Dept. of English, 1923-30, dir. of studies since 1930. Democrat. Address: University of Notre Dame, Notre Dame, Ind. Died Nov. 21, 1944.

CARRIGAN, Edward, clergyman, univ. prof.; b. Hancock, Mich., Jan. 13, 1892; s. Samuel and Margaret (Ryan) C.; student St. Mary's Coll., Kan., 1912-14; A.B., St. Louis, U., 1918, M.A., 1921, divinity student, 1924-28; student Gonzaga U., 1918-19. Joined Soc. of Jesus (Jesuits), 1914; ordained priest R.C. Ch., 1927; instr. English, John Carroll U., Cleveland, 1921-23; prof. of English, Xavier U., Cincinnati, 1928-29, dean Coll. Liberal Arts, 1930-38; prof. English Loyola U., Chicago, since 1938. Mem. Modern Lang. Assn. America, Nat. Council Teachers of English, English Assn. (London). Democrat. Home: 6525 Sheridan Road, Chicago, Ill. Died May 9, 1944.

CARRINGTON, Gordon de L., army officer; b. Evansville, Ind., Nov. 15, 1894; s. Dr. Paul (U.S. P.H.S.) and Belle (Gordon) C.; student San Diego Jr. Coll., 1914-15, U. of Calif., 1915-16; grad. Coast Arty. Sch., 1922, Command and Gen. Staff Sch., 1932, Army War Coll., 1936; m. Jeannie Garnham, June 10, 1917; children—George Baker, William Miles, Virginia Fairholm. Commd. 2 lt., Coast Arty., U.S. Army, 1916, and advanced through the grades to brig. gen. (temp.), 1942. Mem. Theta Xi.†
Died Aug. 21, 1944.

CARRINGTON, William J(ohn), gynecologist; b. Jefferson City, Mo., Feb. 4, 1884; s. William T. and Mary (Holloway) C.; ed. Warrensburg (Mo.) Normal Sch., 1898-1900; A.B., U. of Mo., 1904; M.D., Jefferson Med. Coll., Phila., 1908; m. Lucy Grier, Jan. 10, 1910; children—William, Lucy, Mary Catherine, Elizabeth, Emily, Jane Randolph. Interne Jefferson Hosp., Phila., 1908-09; engaged in practice of medicine at Atlantic City, N.J., since 1910, specializing in gynecology and obstetrics since 1920; now lt. col. Med. Corps, chief of Surgical Services and chief of Women's and Obstetric Sections, Schick Gen. Hosp., Clinton, Ia.; attending gynecologist, Atlantic City Hospital, Pine Rest, Atlantic County Hospital for Mental Diseases, Atlantic City Municipal Hospital; director Guarantee Trust Co. President School Board, Ventnor, New Jersey, 1928-29; past president Atlantic Council Boy Scouts. Fellow Am. Coll. Surgeons, Internat. Coll. Surgeons (Geneva); diplomate Am. Bd. Gynecology and Obstetrics. Mem. A.M.A. (past vice pres.), Med. Soc. of N.J. (ex-pres.), N.J. Sanitation Assn., N.J. Surgical Society, Phila. Obstet. and Pathol. Socs., Atlantic County Med. Soc. (past pres.), Eugene Field Soc., Nat. Physicians Committee, Jefferson Alumni Assn. (past pres.), Kappa Sigma. Congregationalist. Clubs: Kiwanis International (past internat. pres.), Atlantic City Country, Haddon Hall Racquets. Contbr. to med. jours. Author: Safe Convoy. Address: 1601 Harrison Dr., Clinton, Ia. Died July 25, 1947.

CARROLL, Ben, vice-pres., treas., Liggett & Myers Tobacco Co. Address: 630 Fifth Av., New York, N.Y. Died June 6, 1945.

CARROLL, Charles Eden, clergyman; b. Waitsfield, Vt., June 25, 1877; s. George Eden and Emily (Stackhouse) C.; A.B., Morningside Coll., Ia., 1905; A.M., U. of Neb., 1912; Ph.D., U. of Denver, 1914; m. Blanche Elsie Kingery, Feb. 12, 1906; children—Dorothy Helen, Donald Kingery. Ordained M.E. ministry, 1909; pastor Lincoln, Neb., 1910-13. Denver, Colo., 1913-17; with bureau of surveys of Bd. of Home Missions and Ch. Extension of M.E. Ch., Phila., 1917-19; prof. social sciences, Sch. of Religious Edn. and Social Service, Boston U., 1919-27; pastor chs. in Greater Boston, 1927-31, Bryan Memorial M.E. Ch., Miami, Fla., 1931-33, Tarpon Springs, 1933-34, Grace Church, St. Petersburg, 1934-38, Coronado Beach-New Smyrna, 1938-39, Hastings 1939-40; Parrish St. Meth. Ch., Wilkes-Barre, Pa., 1940-45. Retired. Republican. Mason. Author: Political Parties and Our Presidents (pamphlet); Equitable Apportionments and Adequate Ministerial Support (brochure); The Community Survey in Relation to Church Efficiency, 3 edits. Home: 515 W. Amelia Av., Orlando, Fla. Died Oct. 27, 1946.

CARROLL, Earl, theatrical dir. and producer; b. Pittsburgh, Pa., Sept. 16, 1893; s. James and Elizabeth (Wills) C.; attended grammar schs. until age of 10; m. Marcelle Hontabat, Oct. 25, 1916 (dec.). Program boy, various Pittsburgh theatres, 1903-09; assistant treasurer in boxoffice Nixon Theatre, Pittsburgh, Pa., 1910; worked his way around the world at age 16; held various positions in Manila, Hongkong, Shanghai, etc.; song writer, 1912-17; collaborator of over 400 songs, wrote music and lyrics for "So Long Letty," "Canary Cottage" and many others. Became independent mgr., N.Y. City, 1919; built first Earl Carroll Theatre, 1922; wrote book, lyrics and music for 1st and 2nd Earl Carroll Vanities, 1922 (15 Vanities production, 2 Sketch Book Revues, 1923-36); has produced 60 legitimate stage productions including "White Cargo" and others, dramas, musical comedies, revues, etc., built second Earl Carroll Theatre, New York, 1931; built present Earl Carroll Theatre, Hollywood, Calif., 1938; produced 12 major revues in Hollywood. Pictures: "Murder at the Vanities," "Night at Earl Carroll's"; latest pictures, "Vanities," "Sketch Book"; "Earl Carroll Vanities," Earl Carroll Theatre, Hollywood, Calif., opened December 25, 1946. Served as pilot, United States Army Air Corps, World War I. Founder mem. A.S.C.A.P. Clubs: Lotos, Lambs, Friars (N.Y. City). Home: 1114 Schuyler Road, Beverly Hills, Calif. Office: 6230 Sunset Blvd., Hollywood, Calif. Died June 17, 1948.

CARROLL, Edward Ambrose, Dem. Nat. committeeman; b. Mulfords, Minn., Jan. 11, 1888; s. Edward James and Bridget Ann (Gannon) C.; ed. pub. schs. and bus. coll., Minneapolis, Minn.; m. Adele Miller, June 1, 1911; children—Helen Kathleen, Mary Adele. Took homestead in Big Bend, Wash., 1906; wheat grower in Big Bend, Douglas County, Wash., 1906-23; bank cashier, Bridgeport, Wash., 1906-16; organized Commercial Bank, Mansfield, Wash., 1917; pub. The Journal, East Wenatchee, Wash., since 1936; dir. State Parks, Olympia, Wash., since Oct. 1941; mayor Bridgeport, Wash., 1910-14. Mem. Dem. State Com. since 1906, Dem. Nat. Com. since 1936. Catholic. K.C., Elk, Eagle. Home: Olympia, Wash.*
Died June 28, 1946.

CARROLL, Frederick Aloysius, banker; b. Worcester, Mass., May 13, 1887; s. Peter T. and Catherine (Mackin) C.; grad. Classical High Sch., Worcester, Mass., 1905; student Clark Coll., Worcester, 1905-06; A.B., Dartmouth Coll., 1909; LL.B., Harvard, 1912; m. Mary Elizabeth Sheehan, Sept. 16, 1915; children—Robert Mackin (officer submarine service U.S.N.R.), Ruth Alice, Marion Elizabeth (Mrs. Florin J. Hailer, Jr.), Nancy Jane, Cathleen, Mary Louise. Admitted to Mass. bar, 1912; engaged in gen. practice of law, Worcester, Mass., 1912-14; atty., Am. Steel & Wire Co., Worcester, 1914-16; gen. atty., Liberty Mutual Ins. Co., Boston, 1916-24; with Nat. Shawmut Bank of Boston since 1924, vice pres. and trust officer, having direct supervision of trust, transfer and real estate depts., head of legal dept. and counsel since 1935; trustee Home Savings Bank; v.p. Shawmut Assn. of Boston, Shawmut Bank Investment Trust; dir. United Mutual Fire Insurance Company; National Association of Investment Companies since 1944; Shawmut Corp. of Boston, Devonshire Financial Service Corp. Dir. Boston Better Bus. Bureau. Gen. vice chmn. Emergency Relief Campaign, 1933, chmn. eastern Middlesex dist. United War Fund, 1942; chmn. war economy div., region 5, Mass. Com. on Pub. Safety since 1942; asst. dir., div. services and supplies Mass. Com. on Public Safety, 1942. Mem. Am. Bankers assn. (mem. exec. com., trust div., 1934-37, chmn. 1942-43; v.p. trust div., 1943-44, pres. since 1944); chmn. sub-com. on bankruptcy 1937-40; mem. exec. council, 1943-44; mem. administrative com., 1944; mem. conf. com. under code of ethics for trust bus. since 1930, Corporate Fiduciaries Assn. of Boston (pres. 1932-34; mem. exec. com. since 1934), Am. Bar Assn. (mem. com. on effect of Fed. legislation and regulations on real property since 1943; mem. com. on trust and probate decisions since 1943). Mem. advisory com. Boston Coll. Sch. of Bus. Adminis. Pres. Dartmouth Alumni Assn. of Boston; mem. Dragon Senior Soc., Kappa Kappa Kappa. Clubs: Oakley Country, Hatherly Country, Algonquin; Harvard (N.Y. City); Beacon Society, Clover (Boston). Lecturer on trusts and banking, Amos Tuck Sch. of Finance and Bus. Adminstrn., Dartmouth Coll., and Am. Inst. of Banking. Contbr. of numerous articles on trusts and banking to various publs. Home: 53 Shattuck Rd., Watertown, Mass. Office: 40 Water St., Boston, Mass. Died Oct. 17, 1945.

CARROLL, Raymond G., writer; b. at Buffalo, N.Y.; s. Andrew W. and Sarah A. (Gondre) C.; married Madame Grace Fjorde, (contralto opera singer). Reporter on newspapers in Ill., Ohio, Mo. and N.Y.; on staff Evening World, New York, 1900-12, later Paris corr. New York World. Traveling corr., visiting Egypt, India and European countries, several yrs.; in Mexico, 1915, S. America, 1916; accredited war corr. with A.E.F. in France, June 1917 until close of war; spl. corr. with Am. Battle Fleet, Apr.-June 1917; corr. Phila. Public Ledger and London Times with A.E.F.; was at Peace Conf., Paris; London corr. Phila. Public Ledger, 1918-20; chief corr. same, in New York, 1920-24; Paris corr. Public Ledger and New York Evening Post, 1924-26; in charge Washington Bur. for same, 1926-28, Paris corr., 1928-34. Regular contbr. to Saturday Evening Post, 1934-37; Washington corr. Syracuse (N.Y.) Herald-Journal and other U.S. newspapers since 1941; also Washington corr. St. Thomas Times-Journal (Ont.) and other Canadian newspapers, and contbr. to various Am. periodicals since 1937. Policy consultant of Nat. Seaway Council and Great Lakes Harbors Assn. Creator of "A plan to establish and protect the future of an American Merchant Marine; assure permanent foreign markets for American agriculture and industry products and rehabilitate the financial structure of America's trunk line railroads." Member Psi Upsilon. Clubs: National Press (Washington, D.C.); Psi Upsilon (New York). Author: Paris, the Real, as Seen Today; Cash and Carry On; Station U.S.A.; The Prairie Patriarch; Washingtonia. Contbr. serials, short stories and syndicated articles to newspapers and mags. (under nom de plume of "Arnold Garrycolm"). Home: 4000 Cathedral Av., Washington, D.C.
Died June 25, 1945.

CARRYL, Charles Edward, author; b. New York, Dec. 30, 1841. Officer and dir. in various railways, 1863-72. Mem. New York Stock Exchange. Club:

Union. Author: Davy and the Goblin, 1884; The Admiral's Caravan, 1891; The River Syndicate and Other Stories, 1899. Office: 50 Exchange Pl., New York. Died 1920.

CARSON, Charles Clifton, clergyman; b. Rogersville, Tenn., Jan. 2, 1870; s. John Milton and Marietta Mariah (Wells) C.; A.B., Sweetwater (Tenn.) Coll., 1889; special course Southwestern Presbyn. U., Clarksville, Tenn., 1890; grad. Auburn (N.Y.) Theol. Sem., 1892; D.D., Davidson (N.C.) Coll., 1905; U. of Ga., 1905; LL.D., King Coll., Bristol, Tenn., 1917, Litt.D., 1927; m. Mollie Netherland Stamps, Jan. 4, 1893 (dec.); 1 dau., Mollie Stamps (Mrs. Almond Gray); m. 2d, Mamie Cassels, Nov. 3, 1897; children—Elizabeth, Charles Clifton, Mary Cassels. Ordained ministry of the Presbyn. Ch. in U.S., 1892; pastor Flemington and Blackshear, Ga., 1892-98, Valdosta, Ga., 1899-1908, Bristol, Tenn., 1908-27; Gen. Assembly evangelist since 1927; built 2 chs. Trustee King Coll., Louisville Theol. Sem. Moderator of 3 synods of Presbyn. Ch. in U.S. Mem. Am. Red Cross (ex-chmn. Bristol chapter), Y.M.C.A., Sigma Alpha Epsilon. Democrat. Kiwanian. Author: The Glorious Gospel, 1926. Home: 9 The Prado, Atlanta, Ga. Died May 18, 1944.

CARSON, Harry Roberts, bishop; b. Norristown, Montgomery County, Pa., Dec. 8, 1869; s. Henry Samuel and Mary (Thomas) C.; student U. of the South, Sewanee, Tenn., 1893-95, D.D., 1923; m. Zoe Theotiste Garig, Feb. 21, 1900; 1 son, Harry R., U.S. Navy. Deacon, 1895, priest, 1896, P.E. Ch.; gen. missionary Diocese of La., 1895-98; chaplain 2d La. Vol. Inf., Spanish-Am. War, 1898-99; rector St. Mary's Ch., Franklin, La., 1899-1904, Grace Ch., Monroe, 1904-10; archdeacon Northern La., 1910-12; chaplain Ancon Hosp., C.Z., 1913-22, also archdeacon of Panama; bishop of Haiti since Jan. 10, 1923, also in charge of Dominican Republic, Jan. 1, 1928-43; now retired. Mem. S.A.R., Kappa Sigma. Democrat. Mason. Decorated Comdr. Nat. Order of Honneur et Merite (Haiti) for eminent services rendered to the Republic, 1933. Address: Port au Prince, Haiti; also 281 Fourth Av., New York, N.Y. Died July 13, 1948; buried in Cathedral of Holy Trinity, Port au Prince, Haiti.

CARSON, James Oliver, surgeon; b. Warren County, Ky., Dec. 30, 1855; s. Oliver Cromwell and Mary Elizabeth (Collins) C.; A.B., Warren Coll., Bowling Green, Ky., 1876; M.D., U. of Louisville, 1878; post-grad. study, eye, ear, nose and throat, Polyclinic Post-Grad. Sch. of Medicine and Surgery, New York, 1887-88; m. Margaret Poindexter, Oct. 25, 1893; children—Louise Porter (wife of Dr. W. P. Drake), James Oliver (dec.), Elizabeth (wife of Lt. Col. W. O. Sibert; now dec.), Margaret (Mrs. R. N. Kolm; now dec.), Alice Lorraine, William Oliver, M.D. Has been specialist in the treatment of eye, ear, nose and throat at Bowling Green, Ky., since 1878; mem. of the staff City Hosp., Bowling Green Quarantine Officer for Ky. State Bd. of Health, Ky.-Tenn. state line, yellow fever epidemic, 1879; U.S. pension examiner since 1887. Former mem. Ky. N.G.; mem. Bd. for Med. Examiners of doctors for Med. Corps, U.S. Army, World War. Fellow Am. Coll. Surgeons; mem. Am., Ky. State and Warren County med. assns. Democrat. Mason (Royal Arch and K.T.), Elk. Clubs: Rotary (ex-pres.; hon. mem.), XV Club, Bowling Green Country. Made survey and report on dysentery epidemic, mountains of southeastern Ky., for State Bd. of Health, 1885, same on trachoma conditions in Green River sect., 1914-15. Home: 1133 State St. Office: 442½ Main St., Bowling Green, Ky. Died Mar. 15, 1943.

CARSON, William E.; chmn. State Conservation and Development Commn. of Va., 1926-34; a leader in establishing Shenandoah Nat. Park, the Colonial Nat. Hist. Park and system of state parks in Va.; a leader in movement by which the Va. State Historic Dept. was established and in the development of historic markers System along roadsides of Virginia; reorganized the State Forestry and Geol. depts.; also active in creation of Federal Reserve System; wrote the water power laws of Va.; est. Rapidan Camp and Skyline Drive through Shenandoah Nat. Park; presented recreation park to town of Front Royal; pres. Riverton Lime & Stone Co.; was pres. Nat. Lime Assn. 15 yrs.; v.p. Nat. Conf. on State Parks. Home: "Killahevlin," Riverton, Va. Died Mar. 25, 1942.

CARSTARPHEN, William Turner (kär-stär'fĕn), physician; b. Garysburg, N.C., Aug. 25, 1875; s. John R. and Willie E. (Turner) C.; A.B., Wake Forest (N.C.) Coll., 1897; M.D., Jefferson Med. Coll., Phila., 1904; grad. work, same coll., 1910. Began practice Garysburg, N.C., 1904, removed to Kittrell, 1908; prof. physiology, later prof. pharmacology, bio-chemistry and prof. ednl. hygiene, Wake Forest Coll., 1910-17, splty. gastroenterology; chief med. sect., Works Progress Administration, N.Y. City. Apptd. by War Relocation Authority chief med. officer, Rohwer, Ark., 1942, Granada, Colo., 1943. Commissioned capt. Med. R.C., May 1917; major Med. Corps, U.S. Army, Feb. 1918; lieut. col., March 4, 1919; hon. discharged, Aug. 26, 1919. Served as special insp. and instr. at Camp Pike, Ark., sanitary insp. 87th Div. in England, area insp. in France, in comd. 5th Sanitary Train, 5th Div., Luxembourg, and post surgeon, Foreign Office, Paris. Fellow A.M.A.; mem. N.Y. County, N.Y. State med. socs., Union County Med. Soc., Southern Sociol. Congress, Sigma Phi Epsilon, etc. Democrat. Baptist. Mason. Home: Westport, Conn. Died Nov. 2, 1947.

CARTER, Benjamin Estes, jurist; b. Texarkana, Ark., Nov. 1, 1894; s. Jacob Monroe and Nellie Haywood (Estes) C.; ed. Phillips Exeter Academy, 1910-12; A.B., Harvard, 1916, LL.B., 1922; m. Hilda Arnoldson, Sept. 26, 1923; 1 dau., Lydia Estes. Admitted to Ark. bar, 1922; city atty. Texarkana, Ark., 1924-28; rep. from Miller County in Ark legislature, 1933-37; chmn. of Ark. Dept. of Pub. Utilities, 1941-42; asso. justice of Ark. Supreme Court since 1943. Officer of F.A., 1916-19; with A.E.F. 16 months. Mem. officers res. corps, 1921 36, Ark. Nat. Guards, 1936-41, Texarkana Sch. Bd., 1937-40. Mem. Kappa Sigma. Mason. Club: Texarkana Country. Home: Forrest Road, Texarkana, Ark. Address: 210 State Capitol, Little Rock, Ark. Died Apr. 11, 1943.

CARTER, Boake, radio news commentator; b. Baku, S. Russia, Sept. 1898; s. Thomas and Edith Harwood-Yarred C.; ed. Christ's Coll., Cambridge, Eng.; m. Beatrice Olive Richter, 1924; children—Michael Boake, Gwladys Sheleagh Boake. Came to America, 1920, naturalized citizen, 1933. Began as newspaper reporter, Daily Mail, London; in oil business in Mexico and Central America, 1920-23; with Tulsa (Okla.) World, Mexico City Excelsior, Phila. Evening Bulletin, Daily News, Phila., and other newspapers, until 1932; then with Philco Radio & Television Corp., Phila.; news commentator over Mutual Network. Served in British Royal Air Force, World War, 1918. Clubs: Sketch, British Officers, Gibson Island Yacht, Torresdale, Delaware River Yacht. Author: Black Shirts—Black Skin, 1935; Johnnie "Q" Public; I Talk as I Like; This is Life; Why Meddle in the Orient? Why Meddle in Europe? Address: 1440 Broadway, New York, N.Y.* Died Nov. 16, 1944.

CARTER, Edwin A.; b. Springfield, Mass., Feb. 20, 1863; s. Edwin Y. and Rebecca L. (Dickinson) C.; student Springfield High Sch., 1877-79; m. Nina M. Goodwin, Oct. 9, 1895; 1 son, Charles Goodwin. Began as bank clk., Sept. 9, 1879; dir. Chapman Valve Mfg. Co. since 1897, chmn. bd. since 1931; dir. Union Trust Co., Springfield Instn. for Savings, Torrington Co., Springfield Fire and Marine Ins. Co., Western Mass. Cos., United Electric Light Co., Bowles Lunch, Inc., Wico Elec. Co. Trustee Springfield Hosp. Republican. Conglist. Mason (Shriner), I.O.O.F. Clubs: Colony, Springfield Country (Springfield); Union League (New York); Algonquin (Boston); Longmeadow Country. Home: 238 Maple St. Office: 25 Harrison Av., Springfield, Mass. Died May 31, 1943.

CARTER, Fred Afton, manufacturer; b. Sweetwater, Tenn., Oct. 14, 1870; s. Matthew and Mary (Brown) C.; B.S., Sweetwater Coll., 1886; m. Josephine King, Nov. 14, 1895; children—Josephine Rankin (Mrs. M. P. Kilpatrick), Mary Craig (Mrs. Paul B. Carter; now dec.); m. 2d, Belle Jones, June 14, 1905. Laborer in flour mill, 1886; clerk retail dry goods store, 1887-90; bookkeeper Sweetwater Woolen Mills, 1890-92, sec., treas., 1892-1906; sec., treas., Am. Textile Woolen Co., 1906-10, pres. and gen. mgr. since 1910; dir. Burkhart Schier Chemical Co., Chattanooga, Signal Mountain Portland Cement Co., Chattanooga, Sweetwater Hosiery Mills. Trustee Hiwasse Coll. (Madisonville, Tenn.), Tennessee Wesleyan College, Athens, Tennessee, Bob Jones College (Cleveland, Tenn.); president emeritus board directors Holston Orphanage (Greenville, Tenn.); mem. Tenn. State Com. Y.M.C.A. Methodist; supt. of Sunday sch. 40 yrs. Mason (32°, Shriner), I.O.O.F., Woodmen of World, Jr. Order United Am. Mechanics. Club: Kiwanis. Home: Sweetwater, Tenn. Died Feb. 17, 1948.

CARTER, George Henry, former pub. printer of U.S.; b. Mineral Point, Wis., Sept. 10, 1874; s. George and Mary Ann Battin (Lanyon) C.; Ph.B., U. of Ia., 1898; LL.B., George Washington U., 1920; m. Madge E. Penny, Sept. 1, 1904; 1 dau., Mrs. Madge Carter Goolsby; m. 2d, Lydia Althouse Goedecke, Dec. 1, 1938. Newspaper and printing work, Le Mars, Ia., 1890-94; state news editor, Sioux City Tribune, 1898-99; reporter, The Nonpareil, Council Bluffs, 1899-1900; clerk, U.S. Census Office (Washington, D.C.), 1900-01; city editor The Nonpareil, Council Bluffs, 1901-05; polit. writer The Capital, Des Moines, 1905-07; asst. tel. editor, The Washington Post, 1907-09; Washington corr., 1909-10; sec. Printing Investigation Commn., Washington, 1910-11; clerk Joint Com. on Printing, U.S. Congress, 1911-21, originator and sec., U.S. paper specifications com., 1910-21; pub. printer of U.S., Apr. 5, 1921-July 2, 1934; asst. to pres. Lanston Monotype Machine Co., Phila., 1935-42; spl. asst., U.S. Senate Sergt.-at-Arms, 1942; printing consultant and engr., N.Y., since 1942. Chmn. U.S. Conference on Printing, 1921-33; hon. mem., mech. com., Am. Newspaper Pub's. Assn., 1932-34; U.S. del. to First Internat. Congress of Master Printers, Gothenburg, Sweden, 1923, Third Internat. Congress, London, Eng., 1929. Mem. bar of U.S., D.C., and Iowa supreme courts. Hon. life mem. Internat. Printing Pressmen and Assistants' Union, United Typothetæ of America; hon. mem. Printing House Craftsmen (Washington, D.C.). Mem. Am. Inst. Graphic Arts (N.Y.), 1922-42, Typog. Union No. 101 (Washington, D.C.), 1927-42, Am. Soc. Mech. Engineers, 1930-42, Soc. Am. Mil. Engineers, Phi Kappa Psi; 1st hon. mem. British Printing Industry Research Assn. Republican. Episcopalian. Mason (33°, K.T., Shriner, Royal Order of Scotland), Eagle. Clubs: Nat. Press, Alfalfa (Washington, D.C.); Metropolitan Mus. of Art. Author of Congressional editon of Declaration of Independence and Constitution of United States, with Notes, 1934; Baron von Steuben's Statute Proceedings; Congressional Printing Handbook; also various reports and articles. Mem. N.Y. Board of Commercial Arbitration for Graphic Arts; mem. Advisory Com. for Dobbins Vocational Printing School (Phila.), 1938-42. As pub. printer, 1924, drafted and secured enactment by Congress of first law establishing collective bargaining and arbitration of wages for employees of U.S. Govt. Printing Office. Traveled in 16 European countries, Russia, and Vatican City, 1923, 26, 27, 29, 30, and 31, on official business as Public Printer for U.S. Govt. Printing Office to study printing methods, equipment and research. Address: 137 E. 38th St., New York 16, N.Y., or care Wright & Kistle, Council Bluffs, Ia. Died Oct. 23, 1948.

CARTER, James, clergyman; b. N.Y., Oct. 1, 1853; s. Walter and Eliza Ann (Thomson) C.; A.B., Columbia, 1882; grad. Union Theol. Sem., 1885; D.D., Franklin and Marshall Coll., 1921; m. Emma Amelia Smuller, Sept. 30, 1885 (died October 16, 1928). Ordained to the ministry of the Presbyterian Church, 1885; stated supply and pastor Mendham, N.J., 1885-89; pastor Ch. of the Covenant, Williamsport, Pa., 1889-1905; prof. church history and sociology, Lincoln U., 1905-22; prof. homiletics and church history, 1922-28; also stated supply, Mendham, N.J., 1917-18. Asst. editor Carmina Sanctorum, 1886; mem. synodical com. on home missions and sustentation, 1890-97; traveled in Europe, 1870, 1902, and in Europe and the Orient, 1904, 1907; tour of historic study in Europe 8 months, 1911. Collaborated with Joint Com. on Organic Union of Presbyn. Ch. U.S.A. and United Presbyn. Ch. Mem. Com. on Penal Affairs of Pa., Am. Nat. Red Cross. Mem. Am. Humane Assn., Am. Bible Soc. Presbyn. Ministers Social Union (Phila.), Phi Beta Kappa, Phila. Chapter of Alumni Assn. of Columbia U., The League of Faith, Indian Rights Assn., Chester County Tuberculosis Soc. Author: Songs of Work and Worship, 1899; Walter Carter, Autobiography and Reminiscences, 1901; John Huss, the Man and the Martyr, 1915; A Century of Service, 1924; The Gospel Message in Great Pictures, 1929. Article, "Socialism," in New Schaff-Herzog Ency., 1911. Contbr. to periodicals. Club: Automobile (Phila.). Address: Lincoln University, Chester County, Pa. Died Apr. 9, 1944.

CARTER, Jesse Francis, judge; b. Lodge, S.C., Sept. 12, 1873; s. Miles McMillan and Janie Irene (Kinard) C.; student Peabody Coll., Nashville, Tenn., 1897-1901; A.B., U. of Nashville, 1903; LL.B., Univ. of S.C., 1905; special student U. of Chicago, 1908; m. Lydia Belle Jenkins, Oct. 3, 1911; children—Lydia Frances, Janey Beth (Mrs. F. B. Kirkland), Martha Jaudon. Admitted to S.C. bar, 1905, and practiced in Bamberg, 1905-27; elected asso. justice Supreme Court of S.C., 1927, re-elected, 1930, 40. Mem. State Senate, 1925-27. Served as mem. State Council of Defense, atty. for local draft bd. and 4 minute speaker, World War. Mason, K.P. Club: Bamberg Lions. Home: Bamberg, S.C. Died Nov. 5, 1943.

CARTER, John Ridgely; b. Baltimore, Nov. 28, 1864; s. Bernard and Mary B. (Ridgely) C.; B.A., Trinity Coll., Conn., 1883, M.A., 1885, LL.D., 1911; Leipzig, 1884; LL.B., Univ. of Md., 1887; Harvard Law Sch., 1888; m. Alice Morgan, May 24, 1887 (died Jan. 30, 1933). Admitted to bar, 1889. Sec. to Am. ambassador at London, 1894-96; 2d sec. Am. Embassy, London, 1896-1905, sec., 1905-09, chargé d'affaires, 1897; E.E. and M.P. to Roumania, Servia and Bulgaria, 1909-10; accredited as M.P. in temporary charge of embassy at Constantinople, Oct. 5, 1910-June 4, 1911; apptd. E.E. and M.P. to Argentine Republic, Aug. 12, 1911, but declined. Entered J. P. Morgan & Co., Feb. 15, 1912; partner Morgan, Harjes & Co., Paris, Sept. 21, 1914. Asso. sec. Alaska Boundary Tribunal, 1903. Clubs: Metropolitan (Washington); Knickerbocker (New York); Marlborough, Turf, Bachelors', St. James' Prince's, Beefsteak (London); Cercle de l'Union, Travellers, Cercle Interallié (Paris). Treas. Am. Red Cross in Europe; grand officier Légion d'Honneur and Médaille de la réconnaissance (France). Address: 14 Place Vendôme, Paris, France. Died June 3, 1944.

CARTER, Oberlin Montgomery, capt. corps in engrs., U.S.A.; b. in Ohio, 1856; entered Mil. Acad. from Ohio, apptd. by Pres. Grant, June 14, 1876; 2d lt. engrs., 1880; 1st lt., June 15, 1882; capt., Dec. 14, 1891. Mem. Am. Soc. C.E.'s. Address: War Dept., Washington. Died July 1944.

CARTER, Richard Burrage, ink mfr.; b. West Newton, Mass., Apr. 8, 1877; s. John W. and Helen (Burrage) C.; A.B., Harvard, 1898, A.M., 1899; m. Annie I. Waterhouse, June 28, 1906, (died Sept. 4, 1908); m. 2d, Elsie Hobart, Dec. 28, 1914. Began with The Carter's Ink Co., 1900, pres. since 1903. Mem. Boston Chamber Commerce. Republican. Swedenborgian. Phi Beta Kappa. Clubs: Harvard, Brae Burn Country; Newton Boat; Harvard (New York). Home: 11 Forest Av., West Newton 65, Mass. Office: 239 First St., Cambridge, Mass. Died June 8, 1949.

CARTER, William, clergyman; b. Pittington, England, May 22, 1868; s. Joseph and Thomasina (Whitford) C.; came to U.S., 1883; B.A., Parsons Coll., Ia., 1891, M.A., 1894; grad. McCormick Theol. Sem., 1894; D.D., Knox College, 1907; LL.D., Parsons College, 1925; m. Alice Kellogg, May 17, 1893; children—Mrs. Florence Carter Snow, Mrs. Louis A.

Cerf, Jr., William K., Whitford van Dyke. Ordained to ministry of Presby. Ch., 1893; pastor 1st Ch., Sterling, Ill., 1894-99, 1st Ch., Kansas City, Mo., 1899-1906, Madison Av. Ref. Ch., N.Y. City, 1906-12; sec. Internat. Peace Forum, 1912-14; pres. Ch. and Sch. Social Service Bur., New York, 1914-16; pastor Throop Av. Presbyn. Ch., Brooklyn, 1915-33. Chmn. of Interdenominational Fellowship of the Spirit since 1933. Am. corr. for Christian Herald, Messina Earthquake, 1908; special corr. for Brooklyn Eagle in Far East, 1922. Chaplain Junior Plattsburg (N.Y.) Camp, 1917; Y.M.C.A. traveling chaplain through southern camps, 1918; lieut. col. chaplain U.S. Res. (past nat. and N.Y. state chaplain); sr. chaplain 77th Div., 2d Corps Area, Reserve. Lecturer N.Y. City Board of Edn., 1909-19. Special tariff speaker for Rep. Nat. Com., following Woodrow Wilson through New England, 1912; speaker for Rep. Nat. Com., 9th Congl. Dist., Va., 1912, 14. Republican. Presbyterian. Clubs: Chi Alpha, Sigma Chi, Union League (New York); Authors' (London); Army and Navy (Washington, D.C.). Mem. Institut Litteraire et Artistique de France. Author: The Gates of Janus (epic story of the World War), 1919; The Other Side of the Door, 1927; A Nation's Sire, 1931; World Poetry, Its Origins and Developments, 1943; (brochures) Milton and His Masterpiece; Studies in the Pentateuch. Extensive traveler, and lecturer on history, literature and current events. Home: 25 E. 99th St., New York, N.Y. Died July 26, 1949.

CARTER, William Spencer, educator; b. Warren Co., N.J., Apr. 11, 1869; s. William and Ann (Stewart) C.; M.D., U. of Pa., 1890; m. Lillian V. McCleavy, Oct. 1894; children—Margaret Stewart (Mrs. R. M. Wilkinson), Mary Taylor (Mrs. H. C. Emery). Asst. demonstrator of pathology, U. of Pa., 1891-94, asst. prof. comp. physiology, 1894-97, demonstrator of physiology, 1896-97; prof. physiology, U. of Tex., 1897-1922, dean of med. faculty, 1903-22; asso. dir. med. science div. Rockefeller Foundation, 1922-1934; dean of med. faculty, U. of Tex., 1935-38. Former mem. Nat. Bd. of Med. Examiners. Mem. Am. Med. Assn., Am. Physiological Soc. Awarded Boylston prize, 1892; Alvarenga prize, 1903. Author: Notes on Pathology and Bacteriology (with David Riesman), 1895; Laboratory Exercises in Physiology, 1916. Address: 151 Day St., Auburndale, Mass. Died May 12, 1944.

CARTER, Winthrop Lakey, paper mfr.; b. West Newton, Mass., Feb. 19, 1885; s. James Richard and Carrie (Giles) C.; A.B., Yale, 1907; m. Elizabeth Barton, Sept. 14, 1909; children—Katharine, Sydney H., Barton, Winthrop L. Began in paper mfg., Nashua, New Hampshire, 1907; pres. Nashua Gummed and Coated Paper Company, Nashua Package Sealing Co., Canadian Nashua Paper Co.; dir. Carter, Rice & Co., Berwin Paper Corp., Mutual Boiler Ins. Company of Boston, The Liberty Mutual Insurance Company, Second National Bank of Boston, Gummed Paper Manufacturing Company, Ltd., Leicester, Eng.; mem. Indsl. Loan Com., Fed. Reserve Bank, 1st Dist. Lt., U.S.N.R., 1918-22. Pres. New England Council, 1935-36; mem. Am. Waxed Paper Assn. (pres. 1924-25), N.H. Mfrs. Assn. (pres. 1915-17), Beacon Soc., Alpha Delta Phi. Republican. Clubs: Nashua Country, Yale, Union (Boston); The Country (Brookline); Yale (New York); American (London). Home: Hollis, N.H.; and 326 Hammond St., Chestnut Hill, Mass. Office: 44 Franklin St., Nashua, N.H. Died Feb. 22, 1944.

CARTOTTO, Ercole (kär-tŏt'tō), portrait painter; b. Valle Mosso, Piemonte, Italy, Jan. 26, 1889; s. Joseph and Tersilla (Quazza) C.; came to U.S., 1905; art edn., Sch. of Mus. of Fine Arts, Boston, Mass., 1909-16; m. Elena Tortorella, Jan. 26, 1922; children—Beatrice Catherine, Joan Therese. Instr. in drawing and artistic anatomy, Sch. of Mus. of Fine Arts, 1914-16. Enlisted in U.S. Army, 1918. Rep. by portraits at Met. Mus. of Art, New York, the Vatican, Rome, Fine Arts Galleries, San Diego, Calif., Cleveland (O.) Mus. of Art, Pratt Inst., Brooklyn, N.Y., Columbia U., N.Y. State Hist. Mus., Ticonderoga, N.Y.; Smith Coll. Mus. of Art, Amherst Coll., Forbes Library, Northampton, Mass., Newark (N.J.) Museum, Fordham Univ., Harvard Univ., Univ. of Newark, N.J., Converse Coll., Spartanburg, S.C., Internat. Y.M.C.A. Coll., Springfield, Mass., State House, Montpelier, Vt., State House, Trenton, N.J. Mansion Museum Pioneer Memorial State Park, Harrodsburg, Ky.; Phi Gamma Delta, N.Y. City; Jones Library, Alpha Delta Phi, Amherst, Mass.; U.S. Dept. of Justice, Washington, D.C.; collection of 21 drawings in all medias, Amherst Coll., John Hopkins U., Baltimore, Md. Painted portraits of Calvin Coolidge, Mrs. Calvin Coolidge, Judge William H. Moore, Lady Isabella Howard, Dr. Edward Hitchcock, Prof. John Mason Tyler, Atty. Gen. John G. Sargent, Chief Justice Harlan F. Stone, Dwight W. Morrow, Mr. and Mrs. Geo. D. Pratt, Percival Lowell, Chas. M. Pratt, Stanley King, Dr. John H. Finley, Prof. Frederick J. E. Woodbridge, Arthur F. Egner, Miss Beatrice Winser, John Cotton Dana, Robert Frost, Gov. Chas. Edison, Vice Chancellor Malcolm G. Buchanan; Prof. Alfred V. Churchill, Mrs. John Sherman Hoyt, Lt. Comdr. James A. Farrell, Jr., and Mrs. Farrell, Mrs. Helen Hines Tison, Master MacFarlane Cates. Now specializing in portraits of women and children. Exhibited groups of pictures at Toledo Art Mus., Corcoran Gallery of Art, Boston Mus. Fine Arts, Pa. Acad. Fine Arts. Awarded The Master's Studio, 1914-16, Sch. Mus. Fine Arts, Boston; Hallgarten prize, Nat. Acad. Design, New York, 1919; Brooks Jones prize, Baltimore Water Color Club, 1924; Diploma with Cross of Merit, also gold medal, Bologna, Italy, 1931. Mem. Am. Fed. Arts, Alumni Sch. Mus. of Fine Arts, Soc. of Four Arts of Palm Beach. Clubs: Nat. Arts (New York); Cosmos (Washington); Tokeneke. Home: Tokeneke Park, Darien, Conn. Died Oct. 3, 1946.

CARVALHO, Solomon Solis (kär-väl'-ō), newspaper man; b. Baltimore, 1856; s. Solomon N. (artist) and Sarah (Solis) C.; A.B., Coll. City of N.Y., 1877; m. Helen Cusack, May 1895. On staff N.Y. Sun, 1878-87; N.Y. World, 1887-96; gen. mgr. of all of W. R. Hearst's newspapers, 1897-1917, subsequently advisory counsel; now exec. of Hearst Enterprises, Inc. Address: 959 8th Av., New York, N.Y. Died Apr. 12, 1942.

CARVER, George Washington, educator; b. of slave parents, on farm near Diamond Grove, Mo., about 1864; in infancy lost father, and was stolen and carried into Ark. with mother, who was never heard of again; was bought from captors for a race horse valued at $300, and returned to former home in Mo.; worked way through high sch., Minneapolis, Kan., and later through coll.; B.S.Agr., Iowa State Coll. Agrl. and Mechanic Arts, 1894, M.S. Agr. 1896; D.Sc., Simpson Coll., Indianola, Ia., 1928; unmarried. Elected me. faculty, Ia. State Coll. Agrl. and Mechanic Arts, and placed in charge greenhouse, devoting spl. attention to bacterial lab. work in systematic botany; teacher Tuskegee Inst. since 1896, now dir. Dept. of Agrl. Research. Apptd., Aug. 1, 1935, collaborator in Bur. of Plant Industry, U.S. Dept. Agr., div. of mycology and disease survey. Mem. Royal Soc. of Arts, London, 1917. Awarded Spingarn medal, 1923, Roosevelt medal, 1939. Home: Tuskegee Institute, Ala. Died Jan. 5, 1943.

CARVER, Jay Ward, lawyer; b. Calais, Vt., Feb. 19, 1881; ed. Goddard Sem. Admitted to Vt. bar, 1905, and began practice at Barre; state's atty. Washington County, Vt., 1910-14; mem. Vt. Senate, 1915; later atty. gen. of Vt. Universalist. Home: Barre, Vt. Died July 23, 1942.

CARVETH, Hector Russell, electrochemist; b. Port Hope, Ont., Can., Jan. 23, 1873; s. Joseph and Martha Ann (Butterfield) C.; student Victoria U., 1892-96; A.B., U. of Toronto, 1896; fellow in chemistry, Cornell U., 1896-98, Ph.D., 1898; m. Josephine McCollum, Dec. 22, 1915; children—Florence Camille, Nancy Page, Marie Josephine, Hector Russell, Stephen Melhuish, Daniel Butterfield, Rodney Penrhyn. Came to U.S., 1896, naturalized, 1907. Lecturer in phys. chemistry, Cornell U., 1898-1905; chemist, Internat. Acheson Graphite, 1905-06; works mgr., Niagara Electro Chem. Co., 1906-17, pres., 1932; vice pres. The Roessler & Hasslacher Chem. Co., 1917-28, pres. 1928-32; dir. E. I. du Pont de Nemours, 1930-32; retired, 1932. Mem. Am. Chem. Soc., Am. Electrochem. Soc., D.U. Mason. Clubs: Republican. Chemists, Drug and Chemical, New York Athletic (New York); Empire State, Niagara, Rotary, Niagara Falls Country, Annisquam Yacht. Research in metallic chromium and production, properties, reactions and uses of sodium and other alkali metals. Home: 352 Buffalo Av., Niagara Falls, N.Y. Died Sept. 17, 1942.

CARY, George, architect; b. Buffalo, N.Y.; s. Walter (M.D.) and Julia (Love) C.; Ph.B., Columbia, 1885; B.S., Harvard, 1883; Ecole des Beaux Arts, Paris, 1886-89; m. Allithea Birge, of Buffalo, Dec. 31, 1908; children—Marion Love (dec.), George, Allithea, Maria Love, Charles II. Practiced Buffalo since 1891; architect Buffalo Gen. Hosp., U. of Buffalo, Buffalo Improvement scheme, Buffalo Hist. Bldg., and many other pub. and pvt. bldgs., Buffalo and elsewhere; mem. bd. of architects, Buffalo Expn., 1901. Fellow Am. Inst. Architects since 1892. Author: (book) Grouping of Public Buildings and Gardens, with adjoining Water Front Excursion Docks and Union Station, for City of Buffalo, 1905. Home: 460 Franklin St. Office: 101 W. Huron St. Buffalo, N.Y.* Died May 5, 1945.

CARY, George Foster, banker; b. East Machias, Me., Mar. 16, 1867; s. Charles and Mary Elizabeth (Cary) C.; grad. Washington Acad., East Machias, 1884; A.B., Bowdoin Coll., Brunswick, Me., 1888, A.M., 1928; m. Charlotte Coleman, May 18, 1889; 1 son, Charles Austin. Cashier Machias Bank, 1889-1902; bank inc. as Machias Banking Co., pres. same, 1902-12; treas. Machias Savings Bank, 1897-1912 (resigned); treas., dir. Union Safe Deposit & Trust Co., Portland, Me., 1912-24; pres. Casco Mercantile Trust Co., 1924-30, chmn. bd., 1930-34. Overseer of Bowdoin Coll., 1899-1938. Mem. Delta Kappa Epsilon, Phi Beta Kappa. Republican. Conglist. Home: Mt. Dora, Fla. Died Aug. 26, 1943.

CARY, Melbert Brinckerhoff, lawyer; b. Racine, Wis., July 23, 1852; s. John Watson and Isabel (Brinckerhoff) C.; A.B., Princeton, 1872; m. Julia Metcalf, Apr. 28, 1880; children—Julia Madeleine (Mrs. Ronald E. Curtis), Isabel Frances (Mrs. Henry A. Stone), Caroline Tileston Metcalf (dec.), Melbert B. Admitted to Wis. bar, 1874, and practiced at Milwaukee; removed to New York, 1883; now mem. Cary, Miller & McEwen; asst. gen. counsel C.,M.&St.P. Ry. Co. Chmn. Dem. State Central Com., Conn., 1898-1900; Dem. candidate for gov. of Conn., 1902 (defeated). Pres. bd. trustees New York Homœ. Coll. and Flower Hosp. Mem. Phi Beta Kappa, University Club. Author: The Connecticut Constitution; The Woman Without a Country. Pub. of Lalors Cyclopedia of Political Science, Political Economy and U.S. Hist. Home: 2 W. 55th St., New York, N.Y.* Died Mar. 17, 1946.

CASE, Arthur Ellicott, univ. prof.; b. Trenton, N.J., Apr. 11, 1894; s. Charles Blackwell and Florence N. (Case) C.; ed. N.J. State Model Sch., Trenton, 1901-10; A.B., Yale U., 1914, Ph. D., 1923; LL.B., Harvard U., 1917; m. Grace Robbins Lewis, June 16, 1927; children—Richard Stockton, Daniel Fairfield. Asso. with law firm Rawle & Henderson, Phila., 1917-18 and 1919-20; instr. in English, Yale, 1923-26, asst. prof., 1926-30; prof. English, Northwestern U., since 1930. Served as pvt., later 1st lt., Chem. Warfare Service, U.S. Army, World War; capt. U.S. Res., 1919-29. Mem. Modern Lang. Assn. America, Bibliog. Soc. (London), Beta Theta Pi. Methodist. Club: University (Evanston). Author: A Bibliography of English Poetical Miscellanies (1521-1750), 1935; Four Essays on Gulliver's Travels, 1945; also articles for mags. Editor: All's Well That Ends Well, 1926; Gulliver's Travels, 1938; British Drama from Dryden to Sheridan (with G. H. Nettleton), 1939. Home: 713 Ingleside Pl., Evanston, Ill. Died Jan. 19, 1946.

CASE, Clarence Marsh, prof. sociology; b. Indianapolis, Ind., Jan. 18, 1874; s. Elon Ervin and Pamelia (Marsh) C.; B.A., Earlham Coll., 1905; M.A., Brown U., 1908; studied Harvard Grad. Sch., 1908-09; Ph.D., U. of Wis., 1915; m. Catharine Moore, Aug. 15, 1899. Teacher and ward prin., pub. schs., Noblesville, 1896-1904; pastor S. 8th St. Meeting of Friends, Richmond, Ind., 1904-07; resident minister Moses Brown Sch., Providence, R.I., 1907-10; prof. and head dept. history and social sciences, Penn Coll., Oskaloosa, Ia., 1910-17; asso. prof. sociology, State U. of Ia., 1917-23; prof. sociology, U. of Southern Calif., since 1923; visiting prof. sociology and anthropology, Stanford U., summer 1930; visiting prof. sociology, Harvard summer 1935; asso. editor Jour. Applied Sociology; mem. advisory editorial board Am. Jour. of Sociology. Mem. Am. Sociol. Soc. Pacific Sociol. Soc. Author: The Banner of the White Horse—A Tale of the Saxon Conquest, 1917; Non-violent Coercion—A Study in Methods of Social Pressure, 1923; Outlines of Introductory Sociology, 1924; Social Process and Human Progress, 1931; Studies in Social Values, 1944. Home: 1260 Leighton Av., Los Angeles, Calif. Died July 20, 1946.

CASE, Howard Gregory, surgeon; b. Fulton, N.Y., Nov. 13, 1880; s. William and Louisa (Appenzeller) C.; M.D., Syracuse U. Coll. of Medicine, 1903; m. Harriet T. Edgerton, July 26, 1900 (died 1920); m. 2d, Addie F. B. Brown, Nov. 3, 1921; 1 dau., Carol Ruth. Demonstrator of anatomy, Syracuse U. Coll. of Medicine, 1903-06, instr. in anatomy, 1907-10, in surg. anatomy and clinical surgery, 1911-23, asso. prof. surgery, 1924-34; clinical surg. asst., Syracuse Free Dispensary, 1903-08, asst. surgeon, 1909-13 surgeon, 1914-23, anesthetist Hosp. of Good Shepherd, 1905-08, asst. surgeon, 1909-13, adj. surgeon, 1914-22; attending surgeon, Univ. (Syracuse) Hospital, 1923-34. Pres. Bd. Trustees, Cazenovia (N.Y.) Sem.; mem. Founders Group of Am. Board of Surgery. Mem. A.M.A., Onondaga County Med. Soc., Syracuse Acad. of Medicine, Phi Delta Theta, Nu Sigma Nu. Republican. Presbyterian. Club: Lake Placid (N.Y.). Licensed air pilot. Home: 1372 S. Salina St., Syracuse, N.Y. Died Aug. 4 1943.

CASE, Shirley Jackson, educator; b. Hatfield Point, N.B., Can., Sept. 28, 1872; s. George F. and Maria (Jackson) C.; A.B., Acadia U., 1893, A.M., 1896, D.C.L., 1928; B.D., Yale, 1904, Ph.D., 1906, D.D., 1917; studied U. of Marburg, 1910; m. Evelyn Hill, June 29, 1899. Teacher mathematics, St. Martin's (N.B.) Sem., 1893-95, Horton Collegiate Acad., Wolfville, 1895-97; teacher of Greek, New Hampton (N.H.) Lit. Instn., 1897-1901; instr. in N.T. Greek, Yale, 1905-06; prof. history and philosophy of religion, Bates Coll., Lewiston, Me., 1906-08; asst. prof. N.T. interpretation, 1908-13, asso. prof., 1913-15, prof., 1915-17, prof. early ch. history and N.T. interpretation, 1917-25, prof. history of early Christianity since 1925, chmn. dept. of church history since 1923, dean Divinity Sch., 1933-38, dean emeritus since 1938, U. of Chicago; prof. religion and dean Sch. of Religion, Lakeland, Fla., since 1939. Chmn. Church History Deputation to Orient, 1931-32; Rauschenbusch lecturer Colgate-Rochester Divinity Sch., 1933, Lowell Inst. lecturer, 1936. Mng. editor Am. Jour. of Theology, 1912-20; editor Jour. of Religion, 1927-39; editor Religion in the Making since 1940. Mem. Soc. Bibl. Lit. and Exegesis (pres. 1926), Am. Soc. Ch. History (pres. 1924-25). Baptist. Author: The Historicity of Jesus, 1912, 2d edit., 1928; The Evolution of Early Christianity, 1914; The Millennial Hope, 1918; The Revelation of John, 1919; The Social Origins of Christianity, 1923; Jesus—A New Biography, 1927; Studies in Early Christianity (with others), 1928; Experience with the Supernatural in Early Christian Times, 1929; Jesus Through the Centuries, 1931; The Social Triumph of the Ancient Church, 1933; Makers of Christianity from Jesus to Charlemagne, 1934; Highways of Christian Doctrine, 1936; Christianity in a Changing World, 1941; The Christian Philosophy of History, 1943; The Origins of Christian Supernaturalism, 1946; part author and editor of Bibliographical Guide to the History of Christianity, 1931. Contbr. to Hastings' Dictionary of the Apostolic Church, Hastings' Ency. of Religion and Ethics, G. B. Smith's A Guide to the Study of the Christian Religion; Mathews and Smith, A Dictionary of Religion and Ethics; Ferm, Encyclopedia of Religion; also to religious mags. and revs. Home: 102 E. Belvedere St., Lakeland, Fla. Died Dec. 5, 1947.

CASEY, Charles Clinton, coll. pres.; b. Mt. Vernon, Ill., Dec. 5, 1881; s. Thomas Alexander and Charity Ann (Lane) C.; A.B., Ark. Conf. Coll., 1904; A.M., U. of Denver, 1906, LL.D., 1934; student Teachers Coll. (Columbia), 1924 and 1929; m. Pearle Rosencrans, Sept. 3, 1907; children—Ronald Victor (dec.), Gerald Rosencrans (dec.), Theodore Alan, Kenneth (dec.). Head of dept. of mathematics and dean, Ark. Conf. Coll., 1904-09; prin. high sch., Longmont, Colo., 1909-14, supt. of schs., Longmont, 1914-30; pres. Western State Coll. of Colo., Gunnison, since 1930. Mem. Chamber of Commerce, Gunnison. Mem. N.E.A., Am. Assn. Sch. of Adminstrs., Colo. Edn. Assn., Colo. Soc. for Mental Hygiene; Southwestern Colo. Archæol. Soc., Colo. Schoolmasters Club (pres. 1935-36), Scholia Club, Kappa Delta Pi, Phi Delta Kappa, Izaak Walton League. Republican. Methodist. Mason (32°), I.O.O.F. Clubs: Rotary, Golf, College Hiking and Outing. Home: College Campus, Gunnison, Colo. Died July 31, 1946.

CASEY, John Francis, contractor; b. Ontario, Can., May 28, 1872; s. John and Agnes (McKinley) C.; ed. Holy Ghost Coll.; m. Mary Ethel Lee, Oct. 14, 1896; children—Marjorie, John, Kathleen, Sam B., Rosemary, William. Chmn. bd. Swindell Dressler Corp., Railway Maintenance Corp., John F. Casey Company, New Castle Refractories Co., John Lee Estate, Inc., Elastic Stop Nut Company, American Gas Accumulator Company, Agaloy Tubing Company; dir. Forbes Nat. Bank, Western Allegheny R.R., Pressed Steel Car Co. Trustee Carnegie Inst. of Tech. and U. of Pittsburgh. Dir. Tuberculosis League of Pittsburgh, Pittsburgh Hosp. and Community Fund. Republican. Roman Catholic. Clubs: Duquesne, Fox Chapel, Rolling Rock, Long Vue, Field (Pittsburgh); Chicago; Union (Cleveland); Metropolitan, Grolier (N.Y. City). Home: 718 Devonshire St., Pittsburgh. Died Nov. 7, 1948.

CASEY, John Schuyler, pres. M. H. Treadwell Co., Inc.; b. N.Y. City, Sept. 3, 1880; s. Patrick Joseph and Sarah (Rhoads) C.; ed. Coll. City of N.Y.; m. Rosemarie Meehan, Feb. 18, 1914; children—Mrs. J. H. Roach, Mrs. P. F. MacGuire, Mrs. H. J. McCarty, Jr. With M. J. Drummond Co., 1898-1902; Glamorgan Pipe & Foundry Co., Lynchburg, Va., 1902-04; Dept. of Water Supply, Gas and Electricity, New York, 1903-05; pres. M. H. Treadwell Co., Inc., N.Y. City, since 1935; Treadwell Construction Co., Treadwell Engineering Co., Midland (Pa.) Barge Co. Clubs: New York Athletic (gov.), Downtown Athletic, Manhattan (New York City); Duquesne (Pittsburgh); Blind Brook (Port Chester, N.Y.); Saranac Inn Golf; Winged Foot Golf. Home: 784 Park Av. Office: 140 Cedar St., N.Y. City. Died Dec. 1, 1948.

CASH, Wilbur Joseph, writer, editor; b. Gaffney, S.C., May 2, 1901; s. John William and Nannie Lutitia (Hamrick) C.; student Wofford Coll., Spartanburg, S.C., 1918-19; A.B., Wake Forest (N.C.) Coll., 1922; student Wake Forest Coll. Law Sch., 1922-23; m. Mary B. Ross Northrop, 1940. Mem. staff Charlotte (N.C.) Observer, 1923; instr. English, Georgetown (Ky.) Coll., 1923-24; instr. English and French, Blue Ridge Sch. for Boys, Hendersonville, N.C., 1924-25; mem. staff Chicago Post, 1924; free-lance newspaper work, Chicago, 1925; mem. staff Charlotte News, 1926-27; traveled in Europe, 1927; editor Cleveland Press, Shelby, N.C., 1928; free-lance writer and journalist, 1929-37; asso. editor Charlotte News, 1937-41; Guggenheim fellow (for writing of novel in Mexico), 1941-42. Mem. S.A.T.C., Wofford Coll., 1918. Democrat. Baptist. Author: The Mind of the South, 1941; also series of articles syndicated by South. Newspaper Syndicate, Dallas, Tex. Contbr. to Am. Mercury, Nation, etc. Home: Mexico, D.F., Mexico. Address: care Alfred A. Knopf, Inc., 501 Madison Av., New York, N.Y. Deceased.

CASPARI, Charles Edward (kăs-pär'ī), cons. chemist; b. Baltimore, Md., Apr. 9, 1875; s. Charles and Leslie Virginia (Heinichen) C.; A.B., Johns Hopkins U., 1896, Ph.D., 1900; m. Emilie Ganz (b. in Paris, France), Mar. 4, 1903; children—Florence L. (Mrs. Oliver Abel, Jr.), Charles Edward, Emilie C. (Mrs. M. E. Gilderbloom, Jr.). Instr. organic chemistry, Columbia U., 1900-01; research chemist Mallinckrodt Chem. Works, St. Louis, 1901-03; prof. chemistry, St. Louis Coll. Pharmacy, 1903-30, prof. emeritus since 1930, dean since 1926; mem. Revision Com. U.S. Pharmacopœia, 1910-40. Fellow A.A.A.S.; mem. Am. Chem. Soc., Am. Pharm. Soc., Franklin Inst., Phi Beta Kappa. Democrat. Unitarian. Clubs: Noonday, University, Missouri Athletic, Bellerive Country (St. Louis); Chemists (N.Y. City). Contbr. to Proceedings Am. Pharm. Assn. Home: 6951 Kingsbury Blvd. Office: 4588 Parkview Place, St. Louis, Mo. Died June 9, 1942.

CASSELS, Edwin Henry, lawyer; b. Tomah, Wis., Oct. 6, 1874; s. William Beveridge and Mary (Wilson) C.; A.B., U. of Wis., 1895; A.M., Harvard, 1900; Harvard Law Sch.; m. May van Steenwyk, Nov. 25, 1903; children—Mariette van Steenwyk, Edwin Henry, Jr., Elizabeth Starr. Admitted to Wis. bar and began practice at La Crosse, 1901; removed to Chicago, 1903; asst. corp. counsel, Chicago, 1907-08; spl. counsel to Chicago City Council Com. on Harbors, Wharves and Bridges, 1909-10; mem. Wilkerson, Cassels & Potter until 1922; special counsel in Europe Bureau of the Budget, 1922; mem. Cassels, Potter & Bentley since July 1923. Director American Arbitration Association; director and treasurer World Citizens Association. Served in United States Field Artillery, 1918. Trustee Antioch College; trustee Library of Internat. Relations; director International Relations Center; former pres. Bd. of Edn., Glencoe; general counsel, National Association Marble Dealers; general counsel of the New Orient Society of America. Member Am., Ill. State, Chicago and N.Y. bar assns., Law Club, Legal Club, Delta Upsilon. Republican. Presbyterian. Clubs: Chicago, University, City, Attic, Harvard (Chicago), Skokie Country (Glencoe), Century, Harvard (New York). Home: Glencoe, Ill. Office: 209 S. La Salle St., Chicago. Died July July 8, 1947.

CASSIDY, Lewis Cochran, lawyer; b. Philadelphia, Pa., Oct. 29, 1898; s. H(ugh) Gilbert and Mary Dorothea (Fagan) C.; A.B., Mt. St. Mary's Coll., Emmitsburg, Md., 1919, A.M., 1921; grad. study, Harvard Law Sch., 1919-20, Pugsley scholar, 1929-30, S.J.D., 1930, faculty research fellow, 1936-37; LL.B., Georgetown U., 1922, LL.M., 1923, Ph.D. cum laude, 1923; Academie de Droit International de la Haye, 1931, 33; Carnegie scholar, 1933; U. of Leiden, 1933; U. of Mich., 1934, 36; m. Clara L. McGrew, Sept. 14, 1929; children—Lewis C. 4th, Isabelle, Truman Hugh, John Walsh; m. 2d, Mrs. Juanita Newton Harris, 1943; stepsons—Everett Grant, Jr., Charles Giles, Newton Nolan. Admitted to D.C. bar, 1922, Pa. bar, 1923, Mass. bar, 1937, Tenn. bar, 1938; to bar of Supreme Court of U.S., 1937; practicing in Phila., 1923-28 and since 1937; prof. law, Creighton U., 1928-29, Georgetown U., 1930-34; dean, U. of San Francisco Law School, 1934-36; prof. law, Cumberland U., Lebanon, Tenn., 1937-39, National U. since 1939; special asst. to atty.-gen. since 1939. Apptd. consul ad honorem by Republic of Panama, 1938. Served as pvt. inf., U.S. Army, 1918; capt. U.S. Marine Corps Reserve. Now lt., U.S. Coast Guard, legal assistance officer, 8th Naval Dist., 1943-44. Del. at large Democratic National Convention, 1924; candidate for Democratic nomination for U.S. senator, 1932. Member American Bar Association, Am. Soc. Internat. Law, S.A.R., Gamma Eta Gamma, Pi Sigma Alpha; corr. mem. Ancien Institut Historique et Heraldique de France. Club: Harvard. Contbr. to New York U. Law Quarterly Review, Georgetown Law Jour., Miss. Law Review, Lahore (India) Law Coll. Jour., Juridical Review (Scotland), etc. Address: 6535 Germantown Av., Philadelphia, Pa.; and 3137 Key Blvd., Arlington, Va. Died Feb. 6, 1949.

CASTILLO, Ramon S. (käs-tē'yō), Argentine statesman; b. Catamarca, Argentina, Nov. 20, 1873; s. Rafael and Maria B. Castillo; student Nat. Univ. of Buenos Aires, 1891-96; hon. Dr. Univs. of Heidelberg and Rio de Janeiro; m. Delia Luzuriaga; 4 sons, 1 dau. Became sec. of Comml. Court of City of Buenos Aires, 1893; judge of Criminal Court of Buenos Aires, 1903-05; mem. Civil and Comml. Bd., Province of Buenos Aires, 1905-07; judge of comml. law, Buenos Aires, 1907-10; prof. law, Nat. Univ. of Buenos Aires, 1907-12, prof. comml. law, 1912; summer session prof., U. of La Plata, 1910; mem. Criminal Court of Appeals, Buenos Aires, 1910-13; mem. Comml. Court of Appeals, Buenos Aires, 1913-18; mem. Advisory Bd., Nat. Univ. of Buenos Aires, 1915-28, also del. to Supreme Advisory Bd., dean of univ., 1923-28; requested to replace gov. of Tucuman, North Central Argentina, 1930; senator for Catamarca, 1932-35; minister of public instruction, 1936; minister of interior, 1936-37; became v.p. of Argentina, 1938; appointed acting pres. of Argentina, Aug. 1940, upon resignation of Roberto M. Ortiz. Vice-pres. Argentine Com. for Pan-Am. Comml. Arbitration; mem. Spanish Acad. (soc. which establishes language laws for all Spanish-speaking countries); mem. Nat. Coalition Party. Author articles on law, commerce, cultural subjects; contbr. articles to many mags. Address: Viamonte 1701, Buenos Aires, Argentina. Died Oct. 12, 1944.

CASTLES, Alfred Guido Rudolph (surname adopted), capitalist; b. Chicago, Apr. 19, 1851; s. Rudolph and Amalia (Hoffmann) Schloesser; student Concordia Coll., Ft. Wayne, Ind.; M.D., Rush Med. Coll., Chicago, 1871; post-grad. work in Europe; m. Emma M. R. MacDonell, Nov. 19, 1874; children—Amelia Jeanette (Mrs. J. G. Barnett), Frances Helen Imogene (Mrs. Carl Thomsen), Alexander Rudolph, Amalia Angela Aloysia (Mrs. Eric Earl Eastman). Asst. physician, Imperial Royal Hosp., Vienna; practiced as dermatologist and laryngologist, Chicago, several yrs.; acquired mining property, Lassen County, Calif., 1894, developed same; engaged in investment business, Los Angeles, 1909; resumed practice, specializing in glandular therapy (endocrinology); licensed to practice in Ill. and Calif. Republican. Episcopalian. Mason (K.T., Shriner). Clubs: Jonathan, Gamut, Hollywood. Address: Castle Sans Souci, 1851 Argyle Av., Hollywood, Calif. Died Dec. 2, 1933.

CERF, Barry, college prof.; b. San Luis Obispo, Calif., Sept. 4, 1881; s. Ernest and Babbette (Hirsch) C.; A.B., U. of Calif., 1902, A.M., 1903; studied in Paris, France, and Florence, Italy; Ph.D., Harvard, 1908; m. Emily Pratt Owen, Sept. 20, 1912; children—Barbara, Edward Owen, Cornelia. Instr. Romance langs., U. of Wis., 1908-10, asst. prof., 1910-12, asso. prof., 1912-21; prof. comparative lit., Reed Coll., 1921. Capt., Chem. Warfare Service, A.E.F., 1918-19. Democrat. Author: Alsace-Lorraine since 1870, 1919; Anatole France, 1926. Contbr. to Modern Philology, Romanic Review, Publs. of Modern Lang. Assn., etc. Home: 1351 E. 32d St., Portland, Ore. Died 1948.

CASTNER, Joseph Compton, army officer; b. N.J., Nov. 18, 1869; B.Sc., Rutgers Coll., 1891, M.S., 1916; grad. Inf. and Cav. Sch., 1895, Army War Coll., 1915 and 1921, Gen. Staff Sch., 1920. Commd. 2d lt. 4th Inf., Aug. 1, 1891; 1st lt., Apr. 26, 1898; capt. squadron Philippine cav., Apr. 3, 1900; hon. mustered out service, June 30, 1901; capt. U.S. Army, Feb. 2, 1901; q.m. Feb. 26, 1908; promoted through grades to brig. gen., Nov. 14, 1921; served as brig. gen. N.A., with A.E.F., World War; retired, Nov. 30, 1933; later advanced to rank of major gen. Received 3 silver star citations, two for gallantry against insurgent forces, Philippine Islands, 1899, one for gallantry in action during World War, and Distinguished Service Medal during World War I. Mem. Phi Beta Kappa. Home: 360 Euclid Av., Oakland, Calif. Died July 8, 1946.

CATHCART, Arthur Martin, prof. law; b. Attica, Ia., Feb. 2, 1873; s. Daniel Pierson and Isabelle (Swain) C.; A.B., Leland Stanford Univ., 1896; Harvard Law Sch., 1896-97; m. Edna Emma Wallace, June 28, 1905; children—Wallace Daniel, Robert Samuel, Arthur James. Admitted to bar, 1903; in practice of law, Colorado Springs, Colo., 1903-04; instr. law, Stanford U., 1904-06, asst. prof., 1906-07, asso. prof., 1907-09, prof., 1909-38; prof. law, Duke Univ., 1938-39; mem. faculty, Hastings Coll. of The Law, 1939-49; lecturer in law, U. of Calif., summer, 1909; prof. law, U. of Chicago, summers, 1911, 22, 1927-28. Mayor of Palo Alto, 1920-24. Mem. State Bar of Calif., Delta Upsilon, Delta Chi, Phi Beta Kappa, Order of the Coif. Conglist. Club: Commonwealth (San Francisco). Home: 710 Alvarado Row, Stanford University, Palo Alto, Calif. Died Nov. 1, 1949; buried at Palo Alto, Calif.

CATHCART, Charles Sanderson, chemist; b. New Brunswick, N.J., Jan. 2, 1865; B.Sc., Rutgers, 1886, M.Sc., 1889. Asst. chemist to Austin & Wilber, chemists, 1886-89; asst. chemist N.J. Agrl. Coll. Expt. Sta., 1889-93; chief chemist Lister's Agrl. Chem. Works, Newark, N.J., 1893-1907; chief chemist N.J. Agrl. Expt. Sta. since 1907; state chemist since 1912. Fellow A.A.A.S.; mem. Am. Chem. Soc. Home: New Brunswick, N.J. Died Dec. 9, 1945.

CATHCART, Robert Spann, surgeon; b. Columbia, S.C., Sept. 25, 1871; s. William Richard and Mary Eliza (Kelly) C.; Ph.G., U. of S.C., 1890; M.D., Med. Coll. State of S.C., 1893; m. Katherine Julia Morrow, Jan. 5, 1898; children—Mary Frances (Mrs. William Smith Stevens), Katherine Morrow (Mrs. William G. Hamm), Robert S., Hugh. Began practice at Charleston, South Carolina, 1893; professor of surgery, Emeritus, Medical College of State of S.C.; surgeon A.C.L. R.R., S.A.L. Ry., South Carolina Power Co., The Citadel (mil. coll.). Commd. 1st lt., Med. R.C., 1917; maj. chief of surg. service, Camp Wadsworth, Spartanburg, S.C., later Camp Sevier, Greenville, S.C., and Gen. Army Hosp., Parkview, Pa., 1917-18; commd. lt. col. Med. Reserve Corps, June 4, 1924 (inactive); col. on Citadel staff, 1934. Diplomate Am. Bd. of Surgery (founder's group). Fellow Am. Coll. Surg; mem. Am., Southern Tri-State (past pres.), S.C. State med. assns., Southern Surg. Assn., (past pres.), Medical Society of South Carolina (past president), St. George's Society, S.C. Society. Democrat. Episcopalian. Mason (K.T., Shriner). Home: 2 Water St. Office: 75 Hasell St., Charleston 8, S.C. Died Apr. 29, 1949.

CATHER, David Clark (kăth'ẽr), naval med. officer; b. Clearbrook, Va., Dec. 19, 1879; s. Clark and Cordelia (Shaull) C.; ed. Shenandoah Valley Acad., Winchester, Va., 1893-97; M.D., U. of Pa., 1903; m. May Haynes Sumpter, Aug. 20, 1915 (died Feb. 16, 1940). Commd. lt., j.g., Med. Corps, U.S. Navy, July 28, 1904, and advanced through the grades to rear adm., Nov. 1, 1939; retired Dec. 1, 1942. Fellow Am. Coll. Surgeons; mem. A.M.A. Mason. Clubs: Army and Navy (Washington, D.C.); Jonathan (Los Angeles, Calif.). Home: Jonathan Club, 545 S. Figueroa St., Los Angeles, Calif. Died June 25, 1944.

CATHER, Willa (Sibert) (kăth'ẽr), author; b. Winchester, Va., Dec. 7, 1876; d. Charles F. and Mary Virginia (Boak) Cather; B.A., U. of Neb., 1895, Litt.D., 1917; Litt.D., U. of Mich., 1924, Columbia, 1928, Yale, 1930, Princeton, 1931; LL.D., U. of Calif., 1931; unmarried. On staff newspaper, 1898-1901; asso. editor McClure's Mag., 1906-12. Author: April Twilights, 1903; The Troll Garden, 1905; Alexander's Bridge, 1912; O Pioneers, 1913; The Song of the Lark, 1915; My Antonia, 1918; Youth and the Bright Medusa, 1920; One of Ours (Pulitzer prize novel), 1922; A Lost Lady, 1923; The Professor's House, 1925; My Mortal Enemy, 1926; Death Comes for the Archbishop, 1927; Shadows on the Rock, 1931; Obscure Destinies, 1932; Lucy Gayheart, 1935; Not Under Forty, 1936; Sapphira and the Slave Girl, 1940. Awarded Prix Femina Americaine, 1933, "for distinguished literary accomplishment." Mem. Am. Acad. Arts and Letters. Address: care A. A. Knopf, 501 Madison Av., New York, N.Y. Died Apr. 24, 1947.

CATT, Carrie Chapman, lecturer; b. Ripon, Wis., Jan. 9, 1859; d. Lucius and Maria (Clinton) Lane;

ed. State Coll. of Ia., took spl. course in law; was prin. high sch. and gen. supt. of schs., Mason City, Ia.; m. Leo Chapman, 1885 (died 1886); m. 2d, George William Catt, 1890 (died 1905). State lecturer and organizer Ia. Woman Suffrage Assn., 1887-90; since then in service of Nat. Am. Woman Suffrage Assn., of which was pres., 1900-04, and since 1915; pres. Internat. Woman Suffrage Alliance, 1904-23; worked for suffrage in successful campaigns in all the woman suffrage states; leader in campaign to submit suffrage amendment to Federal Constn., bill successfully passed in Ho. of Rep., May 1919 and Senate, June 1919, ratified Aug. 24, 1920, proclaimed Aug. 26, 1920. Mem. woman's com. Council Nat. Defense; founder, 1919 and since hon. pres. Nat. League of Women Voters; organizer and chairman Nat. Com. on the Cause and Cure of War, 1925-1932, hon. chairman since 1932. Decorated Order of White Rose (Finland), 1942. Awarded: (for services to woman suffrage, human rights and peace) Pictorial Review Prize of $5000, 1930; Am. Hebrew Medal, 1933; Turkish Govt. postage stamp, 1935; Am. Women's Assn., 1940; Gen. Fedn. of Women's Clubs, 1940; Nat. Inst. Soc. Sci., 1941; Chi Omega, 1941; citation of honor by Pres. F. D. Roosevelt, 1936. Address: 120 Paine Av., New Rochelle, N.Y. Died Mar. 9, 1947.

CATTELL, J(ames) McKeen (kȧ-tĕl'), psychologist; b. Easton, Pa., May 25, 1860; s. Rev. William C. (pres. Lafayette Coll.) and Elizabeth (McKeen) C.; A.B., Lafayette, 1880, A.M., 1883; student Göttingen, Leipzig, Paris, Geneva, 1880-82; fellow Johns Hopkins, 1882-83; student and asst. U. of Leipzig, 1883-86, Ph. D., 1886; LL.D., Lafayette, 1907; Sc.D., U. of Ariz., 1924; D.H.L., Wittenberg Coll., 1928; m. Josephine Owen, Dec. 11, 1888; children—Eleth (dec.), McKeen, Psyche, Owen (dec.), Quinta, Ware, Jaques. Lecturer U. of Pa. and Bryn Mawr Coll., 1887, U. of Cambridge, 1888; prof. psychology and exec. head of dept., U. of Pa., 1888-91, Columbia, 1891-1917; also head dept. anthropology, 1896-1902, dept. philosophy, 1902-05, Columbia. Chmn. bd. Psychol. Corp.; pres. 9th Internat. Congress of Psychology, 1929. Fellow A.A.A.S. (v.p. 1898, 1913, pres. 1924), Am. Acad. of Arts and Sciences, N.Y. Acad. Sciences (pres. 1902); mem. Nat. Acad. Sciences, Am. Psychol. Assn. (pres. 1895), British Psychol. Soc. (hon. mem.), Am. Soc. of Naturalists (pres. 1902), Am. Philos. Soc., Am. Physiol. Soc., Washington Acad. Science (v.p. 1921), Eugenics Research Assn. (pres. 1914), Am. Edn. Research Assn. (hon.), Delta Kappa Phi, Soc. Sigma Xi (pres. 1913-15); Phi Beta Kappa. Editor of The Psychological Review, 1894-1904, Science since 1894, The Scientific Monthly since 1900, School and Society 1915-39, The American Naturalist, 1907-38, American Men of Science since 1906, Leaders in Education since 1932. Pres. Science Press Printing Co.; pres. Science Service, 1928-37, trustee since 1920. Author of researches on psychol. measurements, individual differences, the applications of psychology, etc.; also numerous publications on psychology, scientific organizations and education. Decorated Comdr. Legion of Honor (France), 1937. Home: Garrison, N.Y. Office: The Science Press, Lancaster, Pa. Died Jan. 20, 1944.

CAVINS, Lorimer Victor (kăv'ĭns), educator; b. nr. Mattoon, Ill., May 21, 1880; s. Joseph and Malissa Elizabeth (Ferguson) C.; grad. Ill. State Normal U., 1903; A.B., U. of Ill., 1906; A.M., Harvard, 1910; Ph.D., U. of Chicago, 1924; m. Neva Julia Adams, Oct. 2, 1913; children—Lawrence Everrett (dec.), Helen Irene, Arnold (dec.), Marjorie Mae, Virginia Lee. Supt. schs., Hinckley, Ill., 1903-05; head of English dept., East St. Louis, Ill., 1906-09; Stevens Point Normal Sch., Wis., 1910-12; Joliet (Ill.) Township High Sch. and Jr. Coll., 1913-17; prof. edn., W.Va. U., 1919-25; vis. prof., U. of N.D., summer, 1925; U. of Akron, summer, 1932; conducted surveys for ednl. instrn.; dir. ednl. research, State Dept. Edn., W.Va., since 1925; owner of Harvard Plantation, Yazoo Valley, Miss. Pres. Ill. State English Assn., 1917; dir. Bur. Ednl. Research; dir. state survey of edn., W.Va.; chmn. bur. of research, state depts. edn., N.E.A.; tech. adviser edn. in govt. survey of Okla., by Brookings Instn., 1934; ednl. specialist Md. Youth Study by Am. Council on Education, 1936-37. Mem. Phi Delta Kappa. Republican. Methodist. Author: Financing Education in West Virginia, 1925; Organization, Administration and Finance (Vol. I, Survey of Edn. in W.Va.) and Education Achievement (Vol. II), 1928; Standardization of American Poetry for School Purposes, 1928. Now editor in chief Am. Educator Encyclopedia and The Wonderland of Knowledge. Home: 1716 Franklin Av. Office: State Dept. of Education, State House, Charleston, W.Va. Died Jan. 28, 1945; buried at Mattoon, Ill.

CAWTHORN, Joseph (Bridger), actor; b. N.Y. City, Mar. 29, 1868; s. Alfred and Sarah E. (Willett) C.; ed. by mother at home; m. Queenie Vassar, June 1, 1901. First appeared on stage as a child. Principal comedian in "Nature," Acad. of Music, New York City; Alice Neilsen Opera Co., America, London; "The Beauty and the Beast," "Mother Goose," "Little Nemo," "Girlies"; starred "In Tammany Hall," K. & E., "The Hoyden," "The Slim Princess," "The Sunshine Girl," "The Girl From Utah," "Sybil," "The Rambler Rose," "The Half Moon," "The Bunch and Judy," "The Blue Kitten," "Light Wines and Beer," "Sunny," etc.; appeared in motion pictures since 1926. Home: 721 Linden Drive, Beverly Hills, Calif. Died Jan. 21, 1949.

CHAFFEE, Jerome Stuart (chăf'ē), physician and surgeon; b. Amenia, N.Y., Nov. 11, 1873; s. James Stuart and Lydia Ann (Judd) C.; grad. Wilbraham Acad., 1891; Ph.B., Yale, 1894; M.D., U. of Pa., 1897; grad. Army Med. Sch., 1902; m. Grace Dutcher Ketcham, Nov. 7, 1900. Interne, St. Christopher Hosp., Phila., Pa., 1897-98, Cooper Hosp., Camden, N.J., 1898; practiced, Sharon, Conn., since 1903; founder and dir., Sharon Hosp., since 1909, 40 beds, non-profit instn., approved by Am. Coll. Surgeons, (pres. bd. trustees); surgeon, N.Y.C.R.R., health officer and med. examiner since 1905. Served as asst. surgeon med. corps, U.S. Navy, 1898-99, stationed at U.S. Navy Hosp., New York, and with Asiatic fleet under Admiral Dewey, resigned 1899; 1st lt. and asst. surgeon, med. dept., U.S. Army, 1899-1903, stationed Columbus, O., later United States Army Med. Sch., (studying under Reed and Carroll), Army-Navy Hosp., Hot Springs, Ark., Plattsburg, N.Y., Ft. Porter, Buffalo, N.Y., resigned 1903; capt., Conn. Nat. Guard, 1917-19. Fellow Am. Coll. Surgeons. Mem. Mil. Order Fgn. Wars, Nu Sigma Nu. Republican. Mem. Presbyterian Ch. Clubs: Yale (New York), Amrita, Poughkeepsie, Sharon Country, Litchfield County, University. Address: Sharon, Conn. Died Nov. 26, 1947.

CHALMERS, Thomas Mitchell, missionary; b. nr. Monmouth, Ill., Dec. 6, 1858; s. James Adams and Hannah (Cunningham) C.; student Kan. State Normal Sch., 1878-79, Monmouth (Ill.) Coll., 1881-85, United Presbyn. Theol. Sem., Xenia, O., 1885-86, 1887-88, United Presbyn. Theol. Sem., Allegheny, Pa., 1886-87; D.D., Evangelical Theol. Coll., Dallas, Tex.; m. Anna Magdalene von Gunten, Aug. 20, 1895; 1 dau., Ruth Deborah. Ordained to ministry U.P. Ch., 1889; pastor Mundale, N.Y., 1889-1890; lecturer on reform and prophecy, 1892-94; missionary to the Jews, Chicago, 1894-1901, Pittsburgh, 1902-03; studied in Europe, 1904-06; founder N.Y. Jewish Evangelization Soc., dir. and sec. since 1908; editor Jewish Missionary Mag. and its predecessors since 1911; pastor E. 187th St. U.P. Ch., New York, 1913-19. Republican. Author: (booklet) Present Condition of Israel in the Light of Prophecy, 1923; Israel in Covenant and History, 1925; (pamphlet) The Earth, the Eternal Seed Plot of the Universe, 1925; Under the Olive Trees, 1931. Home: 2654 Marion Av., New York. Died Jan. 29, 1937.

CHAMBERLAIN, Arthur Henry, educator; b. Oak Lawn, Ill., Oct. 3, 1872; s. James Adams and Sarah Elma (Leavitt) C.; brother of James Franklin C.; grad. Cook County (Ill.) Normal Sch., 1892, Throop Polytechnic Inst. (now Calif. Inst. of Technology), Pasadena, Calif., 1896; diplomas, Leipzig, Germany, and Nääs, Sweden, 1899; Master's Diploma, Teachers' Coll. (Columbia), 1903; B.S., Columbia, 1903, A.M., 1904; grad. student, U. of Calif., 1910-11; unmarried. Dir. of dept., 1896-1900, prof. edn. and prin. Normal Sch., 1900-09, dir. summer session, 1900-04, dean, 1903-09, acting pres., 1907-08, Throop Poly. Inst. Instr. summer session, U. of Calif., 1911. Dept. pres., 1903-05, 1915-18, 19; state dir. for Calif., 1905-07, 15, 19; treas., exec. com. and dir., 1907-10, N.E.A.; chmn. Nat. Com. on Thrift Edn.; mem. County Bd. of Edn. (Los Angeles), 1910-12; state com. Nat. Soc. for Promotion Industrial Edn.; mem. Nat. Council Edn. Independent Republican. Universalist. Woodman. Mason (32°, Shriner). Clubs: Twilight, Commonwealth, University, Sequoia. Author: Educative Hand Work Manuals, 2 vols., 1901, 05; Bibliography of the Manual Arts, 1902, 11; The Conditions and Tendencies of Technical Education in Germany, 1908; Standards in Education, with Some Consideration of Their Relation to Industrial Training, 1908; N. America (with James Franklin Chamberlain), 1911; Europe, 1912; Asia, 1913; South America, 1913; Africa, 1914; Australia and Islands, 1915; The Growth of Responsibility and Enlargement of Power of the City School Superintendent, 1913; Ideals and Democracy, 1913; Thrift and Conservation (with James Franklin Chamberlain), 1919; Interpreting Education, 1933. Editor Thrift Text Series. Mng. editor Sierra Educational News and sec. Calif. Teachers' Assn. and Calif. Council of Edn., 1912-28. Contbr. to mags.; lecturer on tech. and ednl. topics. Ednl. dir. Am. Soc. for Thrift; sec. Calif. Assn. for Thrift and Conservation; chmn. bd. League of Western Writers. Publisher Overland Monthly and Out West Magazine; also pres. Overland-Outwest Publs.; dir. of edn. for Calif., Panama-Pacific Internat. Expn., 1915. Chief of occupational direction, Army Ednl. Corps, A.E.F., 1919. Dir. Forums and Speakers' Bureau, San Francisco. Home: 1546 Rose Villa, Pasadena, Calif. Office: 230 Eddy St., San Francisco, Calif. Died Oct. 30, 1942.

CHAMBERLAIN, Charles Joseph, botanist; b. Sullivan, O., Feb. 23, 1863; s. Esdell W. and Mary (Spencer) C.; A.B., Oberlin Coll., 1888, A.M., 1894, D.Sc., 1923; Ph.D., U. of Chicago, 1897; research at Bonn, 1900-01; m. Mary E. Life, July 30, 1888 (died Feb. 27, 1931); 1 dau., Mrs. Mabel Allsopp; m. 2d, Martha Stanley Lathrop, Oct. 30, 1938. Prin. Crookston (Minn.) High School., 1889-93; student U. of Chicago, 1893-96; asst. and asso. in botany, 1897-1901, instr. 1901-07, asst. prof. morphology and cytology, 1908-11, asso. prof., 1911-15, prof., 1915-29, now emeritus, U. of Chicago. Am. editor cytology in Botanisches Centrallblatt since 1902. Mem. Bot. Soc. Am. (pres. 1931-32), Assn. Internationale des Botanistes, Kaiserlich Deutsche Akademie der Naturforscher, Deutsche Botanische Gesellschaft; fellow A.A.A.S., Naturforscher Gesellschaft an der K. Universität zu Kiew (hon.), Correspondant Société de Genève; Botanical Soc. of India (corr. mem.). Author: Methods in Plant Histology, 1901, 5 edits. to 1932; The Morphology of Gymnosperms (with Prof. John M. Coulter), 1901, 17; The Morphology of Angiosperms (with same), 1903; The Living Cycads, 1919; Elements of Plant Science, 1930; Gymnosperms, Structure and Evolution, 1935. Contbr. to Bot. Gazette since 1895. Has collected Cycadaceæ in Mexico, Cuba, Australia and Africa, and has pub. numerous researches upon this family. Clubs: Quadrangle, Chaos. Home: 6127 Greenwood Av., Chicago. Died Jan. 5, 1943.

CHAMBERLAIN, Clark Wells, coll. pres.; b. Litchfield, O., Oct. 29, 1870; s. Wells Alexander and Cynthia Amanda (Aldrich) C.; A.B., Denison U., Ohio, 1894; grad. student and fellow U. of Chicago, 1897-1900. Columbia, 1909-11, Ph.D., 1910; LL.D., Linfield Coll., 1922; m. Jessie Isabel Husted, of Norwalk, O., Dec. 27, 1900; children—Mary Husted (dec.), John Husted, Margaret Aldrich, Stuart Hay, Elizabeth Clark. Instr. physics and mathematics, Western Reserve Acad., Ohio, 1894-97; prof. physics and astronomy, Colby Coll., 1900-01; prof. physics, Denison U., 1901-08; prof. physics, Vassar Coll., 1908-13; prof. physics and pres. Denison U., 1913-25; with Cavendish Lab., Cambridge U., 1925-27; asso. prof. of physics, Mich. State Coll., 1927. Pres. Am. Bapt. Ednl. Soc., 1917-20, Bd. of Edn. of Northern Bapt. Conv., 1920-22, Ohio Bapt. Edn. Soc., since 1913, Assn. Am. Colls., 1921. Fellow A.A.A.S., Am. Phys. Soc.; mem. Nat. Inst. Social Sciences. Address: Michigan State College, Lansing, Mich. Died Oct. 13, 1948.

CHAMBERLAIN, James Franklin, educator; b. Centreville, Utah, 1869; s. James Adams and Sarah Elma (Leavitt) C.; grad. Cook Co. (Ill.) Normal Sch., 1890; Ed.B. and S.B., U. of Chicago, 1904; m. Mary Agnes Scobey, Aug. 1900. Taught in Chicago schs., 1890-94; prof. geography, State Normal Sch., Los Angeles, 1895-1919; asst. prof. geography, Southern Br. U. of Calif., 1919-20; pres. N.M. State Normal Sch., 1921-22. Fellow Am. Geog. Soc.; mem. Assn. Am. Geographers, Assn. Pacific Coast Geographers, Am. Geog. Soc., Phi Delta Kappa. Republican. Christian Scientist. Author: How We Are Fed, 1902; Field and Laboratory Exercises in Physical Geography, 1902; How We Are Clothed, 1904; How We Are Sheltered, 1906; How We Travel, 1908; Geography—Physical, Economic, Regional, 1921; Problems in Geography, 1928; Canada, Land of the Maple Leaf, 1934; Geography and Society, 1938; (with Arthur Henry Chamberlain) North America, 1911; Europe, 1912; Asia, 1913; South America, 1913; Africa, 1914; Oceania, 1916; Thrift and Conservation, 1919. Home: 5146 Rose Villa, Pasadena, Calif. Died March 31, 1943.

CHAMBERLAIN, John Loomis, army officer; b. New York, Jan. 20, 1858; s. Jabez Lewis and Charity (Hart) C.; prep. edn. Geneseo State Normal Sch., 1872-76; apptd. from N.Y., and grad. U.S. Mil. Acad., 1880; m. Carolyn Marrow, Sept. 9, 1896 (died Feb. 9, 1947); children—John Loomis, Mary Carolyn. Commissioned second lieutenant First Artillery, June 12, 1880; promoted through grades to major general, March 28, 1921. Instructor U.S. Mil. Acad., 1884-88; grad. Arty. Sch., 1890; spl. field officer's course, Army Service Sch., 1912; army War Coll., 1912-13; in campaign against Sioux Indians, 1890-91; chief ordnance officer dept. of Mo., 1891-93; instr. mil. science and tactics, Peekskill Mil. Acad., 1895-96; mil. attaché, Vienna, 1897-98; with U.S. siege train and 7th Army Corps, U.S. Volunteers, 1898-99; insp.-gen. Calif. and P.I., 1901-05, and in campaign against Moros, Apr. 1903; insp.-gen. Pacific Div., Dec. 1906-June 30, 1907, Dept. of the East, Aug. 13, 1907-June 30, 1909, Philippine Div., Sept. 1, 1909-Sept. 15, 1911, Western Div., Nov. 11, 1911-Aug. 15, 1912, Western Dept., Aug. 1, 1913-Sept. 1914; dept. insp., Eastern Dept., 1914; insp.-gen. U.S. Army, with rank of brig. gen., Feb. 21, 1917; promoted to maj. gen., I.G., Oct. 6, 1917. Tour of inspection A.E.F. in France, July 10-Sept. 20, 1918; retired Nov. 6, 1921; tour of inspection of all activities under the War Dept. in Great Britain and Europe July, Aug., and Sept. 1920; four months tour of Europe, the Near East and Africa July, Aug., Sept. and Nov. 1921. Awarded D.S.M., 1919, "for exceptionally meritorious service to U.S. Govt." Club: Army and Navy. Home: 1319-30th St. N.W., Washington. Died Nov. 14, 1948; buried in Arlington Nat. Cemetery.

CHAMBERLIN, Frederick, historian; b. N. Abington, Mass., May 21, 1870; s. Edward and Sarah C.; grad. Phillips Exeter Acad., 1891; LL.B., Harvard, 1894; studied polit. economy and history at Collège de France, Paris, 1894-95; dramatic history and playwriting, Harvard Grad. Sch., and 16th Century English history at Univ. Coll., London; m. Frances M. Harvey, of Charlestown, Mass., June 22, 1894. Harvard corr. for Boston papers, 1891-94; Paris corr. several Am. jours., 1894-95; practiced law in Boston, 1895-1912; lit. work in Europe since 1912. Rep. campaign speaker. Spl. mission for U.S. Govt. to P.I., 1904; v. consul, Palma de Mallorca, 1920. Served as pvt. 1st lt., batln. adj. and insp. rifle practice, 5th Mass. Inf., 1900-04. Fellow Royal Hist. Soc., Soc. of Antiquaries. Clubs: P.E.N., Pilgrims. Author: The Blow from Behind, 1903; In the Shoe String Country, 1906; Around the World in Ninety Days, 1906; The Girl from Home (comedy, prod. Boston, 1910); The Philippine Problem, 1913; The Private Character of Queen Elizabeth, 1921; The Sayings of Queen Elizabeth, 1923; The Wit and Wisdom of Queen Bess, 1925; Chamberlin's Guide to Majorca, 1925; The

Balearics and their Peoples, 1927; The Private Character of Henry VIII, 1931; Elizabeth and Leycester, 1939. Made the complete survey, 1926-27, in the Island of Minorca, in Mediterranean Sea, of the megalithic monuments, over two hundred in number; discovered the 9th known taula (gigantic prehistoric altar), at Biniac Vey, Apr. 23, 1926, also found the taula at Bella-Ventura, one at San Angladó and one at Torraubet Vey. Address: The King's Library, British Museum, London, Eng. Died Sept. 20, 1943.

CHAMBERLAIN, William W.; b. Johnstown, N.Y., May 22, 1876; s. David W. and Katherine (Sutliff) C.; ed. grammar and night schs.; m. Estella E. Forbes, Nov. 22, 1898; children—Everett J., Kenneth B. Began as newsboy at 10; apprenticed printer's trade at 13; ins. and real estate business since 1899; head firm of W. W. Chamberlain; dir. and treas. Cady Real Estate Co.; partner Baker & Chamberlain steamship business; dir. Johnstown Bank, Johnstown Community Hotel. Mayor City of Johnstown, 1920. Mem. Mayors' Conf. State of N.Y. (was treas., later v.p. and life mem. advisory bd.); del. Rep. State Conv. several times; treas. Fulton County Rep. Com.; mem. Fulton County Rep. Advisory Bd.; mem. Rep. Senatorial Com. Del. Gen. Conf. M.E. Ch., Saratoga Springs, N.Y., 1916; v.p. Laymen's Assn. Troy Conf. M.E. Ch.; v.p. and mem. bd. mgrs. Johnstown Hist. Soc.; pres. Sir William Johnson Council of Boy Scouts; mem. Board of Stewards, of the Finance Commn. and of the Sustentation Commn. of Troy Conf.; dir. Johnstown Community Chest; mem. administrative bd. N.Y. State Council of Chs.; pres. bd. dirs. Johnstown Y.M.C.A. Pres. Fulton County (N.Y.) Humane Soc.; v.p. N.Y. State Humane Soc.; mem. advisory bd. Salvation Army. Pres. Mohawk Valley Towns Assn. Mem. Bishops Com. on Catholic Youth Orgn. of Albany Diocese; mem. Nat. Com. on Jewish Emergency. Mem. Nat. Boy Scout Council; mem. unemployment com. for Fulton Co. Selective Service System of U.S.; chmn. Com. for County of Fulton on the Hard Fuel System. Mem. N.Y. Tax Assn., N.Y. State Hist. Soc., Mohawk Valley Hist. Soc. (pres.). Trustee Syracuse U. Odd Fellow, Eagle, Moose. Clubs: Colonial, Rotary (pres.). Home: 17 N. William St. Office: 16 N. Market St., Johnstown, N.Y. Died Nov. 25, 1945.

CHAMBERLIN, Harry Dwight, army officer; b. Elgin, Ill., May 20, 1887; s. Dwight Allen and Corinne Leona (Orth) C.; student Elgin Acad., 1905-06; B.A., U.S.M.A., 1910; distinguished grad. French Cavalry Sch., Saumur, France, 1923, Italian Cavalry Sch., Tor di Quinto, Italy, 1924; grad. Command and Gen. Staff Sch., Ft. Leavenworth, 1928, Army War Coll., 1933; m. Sally Garlington, June 24, 1912; m. 2d, Helen Bradman, Aug. 13, 1933; children—Lydia, Frederica Dwight. Commd. 2d lt., U.S. Cavalry, June 15, 1910; advanced through grades to brig. gen., Apr. 1941; chief of Staff 1st Cavalry Div., 1938-39; comd. 2d U.S. Cavalry (oldest cav. regt. in U.S.), Fort Riley, Kan., 1939-41; comd. task force of Army, Navy, Marines and Air Corps which occupied New Hebrides Islands, Apr. 1942; returned to U.S. for major operation, June 1942; comd. Southwestern Security Dist., La Jolla, Calif., March 1943; comd. Fort Ord, Calif., Sept. 1943. Decorated Mexican Campaign medal, World War Campaign medal (2 stars), Belgian Mil. Cross. Episcopalian. Club: Army and Navy (Washington). Mem. Equitation Team in Inter-Allied Games, Paris, 1919; 2d individual place, 1920; mem. Olympic Team, Antwerp, Belgium, 1922; capt. Army polo team, 1926; won Nat. 12-Goal and Nat. 20-Goal championships, 1926-27; mem. U.S. Olympic Equestrian Team, Amsterdam, 1929; capt. Army Equestrian Team, Germany, Ireland and Poland, 1928; captain United States Olympic Equestrian Team, Los Angeles, Calif., 1932, won first Individual place in 3-day event, won second place in Prix des Nations. Author: Riding and Schooling Horses, 1934; Training Hunters, Jumpers and Hacks, 1937; also many articles. Home: Presidio of Monterey, Calif. Died Sept. 29, 1944; buried in Nat. Cemetery, Presidio of Monterey, Calif.

CHAMBERLIN, Rollin Thomas, geologist; b. Beloit, Wis., Oct. 20, 1881; s. Thomas Chrowder and Alma Isabel (Wilson) C.; student univs. of Geneva and Zürich, Switzerland, 1899-1900; S.B., Univ. of Chicago, 1903, Ph.D. from same, 1907; Sc.D., Beloit Coll., 1929; m. Dorothy Ingalls Smith, Nov. 11, 1922; children—Frances Dresser, Isabel Chrowder, Louise Ingalls. Mem. U.S. Geol. Survey, 1907-08; with U. of Chicago Oriental Ednl. Investigation Commn. to China, 1909; research asso., U. of Chicago, 1909-11; investigation of Brazilian iron ore resources, 1911-12; instr. in geology, 1912-14, asst. prof., 1914-18, asso. professor, 1918-23, prof. since 1923, U. of Chicago, Carnegie Institution Expedition to Samoa, 1920. Mng. editor Jour. of Geology, 1922-28, editor since 1928. Fellow Geol. Soc. America (v.p. 1933), A.A.A.S. (v.p. 1933), British A.A.S., Am. Geophys. Union, Seismological Soc. of America; mem. Nat. Acad. Sciences, Am. Philosophical Soc., Phi Gamma Delta, Phi Beta Kappa, Sigma Xi, Gamma Alpha; v.-chmn. div. geology and geography, Nat. Research Council, 1922-23. Republican. Episcopalian. Clubs: University, Quadrangle, South Shore Country, Am. Alpine. Contbr. numerous scientific articles. Home: 9300 Pleasant Av., Chicago 20, Ill. Died Mar. 6, 1948.

CHAMBERS, Charles Edward, artist; b. Ottumwa, Ia.; s. Horatio Cox and Rosa (Lee) C.; grad. high sch., Ottumwa; student Art Inst. Chicago, Art Students' League, New York; m. Fanny Munsell (artist), (who died Aug. 27, 1920); one son, Richard Munsell; m. 2d, Pauline B. True, 1934. Has specialized in black and white and full-color oil paintings for magazines and magazine covers, also paintings for advertising, among them a series of portraits and paintings of musicians for Steinway & Sons, and a series of paintings for Chesterfield Billboards which ran for 5 years; illustrated "Get Rich Quick Wallingford" stories, which ran for 9 yrs. in Cosmopolitan Mag., as well as Chinese stories, by Pearl S. Buck, in same mag.; many frontispieces for Harper's Mag.; illustrator of serial and short stories for Woman's Home Companion, Ladies' Home Jour., McCall's Mag., etc. Mem. Soc. Illustrators, Am. Artists Professional League, Allied Artists of America, Artists Guild (pres.). Awarded scholarship at Art Students' League; Shaw prize for illustrations. Club: Salmagundi. Winner 2d Altman prize, Nat. Acad. Design, 1931. Died Nov. 5, 1941.

CHAMBERS, Robert Foster, prof. chemistry; b. Providence, R.I., Oct. 8, 1887; s. William Spicer and Annie Andrews (Foster) Chambers; Ph.B., Brown Univ., 1909, M.S., 1910, Ph.D., 1912; m. Helen Newman Peirson, 1915 (deceased); 1 daughter, Frances C. Wesson; m. 2d, Nettie Mildred Sumner, of Attleboro, Mass., 1930. Instr. in chemistry, Brown Univ., 1915, asst. prof., 1916-22, asso. prof., 1922-32, prof. since 1932. Mem. Am. Chem. Soc., Providence Engring. Soc., Rhode Island Hist. Soc., Delta Phi, Phi Beta Kappa, Sigma Xi. Mason. Clubs: University Art (Providence). Home: 254 Irving Av., Providence 6, R.I. Died Nov. 17, 1947.

CHAMBERS, Walter Boughton, architect; b. Brooklyn, Sept. 15, 1866; s. William P. and Caroline (Boughton) C.; A.B., Yale, 1887; entered École des Beaux Arts, Paris, France, 1889; pupil of Blondel; m. Ethel Notman, June 9, 1897 (died July 19, 1898); m. 2d, Elizabeth M. Ferguson, Apr. 23, 1901. Fellow Am. Inst. Architects (also New York chapter); mem. Soc. Beaux Arts Architects. Clubs: Century, University. Home: 137 E. 66th St. Office: 111 E. 40th St., New York. Died Apr. 19, 1945.

CHAMBERS, Will Grant, college dean; b. Pleasant Unity, Westmoreland County, Pa., Apr. 26, 1867; s. Joseph Harold and Susan Brinker (Jamison) C.; grad. Central State Normal Sch., Lock Haven, Pa., 1887; A.B., Lafayette Coll., 1894, A.M., 1897; grad. scholar, Clark U., 1897-98, U. of Chicago, 1899-1901; Litt.D., Lafayette Coll., 1917; Sc.D., Gettysburg Coll., 1934; m. Claudia May Orcutt, July 19, 1894 (died Mar. 19, 1896); 1 dau., Mrs. Claudia Orcutt Miller; m. 2d, Sunshine Foulke, June 27, 1901. Teacher pub. schs., Mt. Pleasant, Pa., 1887-88; instr. Central State Normal Sch., 1888-90, 1892; prof. mathematics, Indiana Normal Sch., Pa., 1894-97, 1899, 1900; prof. psychology and edn., Moorhead (Minn.) State Normal Sch., 1901-04; prof. psychology and child study, Colo. State Normal Sch., 1904-09; prof. edn., U. of Pittsburgh, 1909-21, dean sch. of edn., 1910-21; dean summer session, Pa. State Coll., 1921-37, dean sch. of edn., same, 1923-37; retired 1937. Republican. Protestant. Fellow A.A.A.S.; mem. N.E.A. (pres. dept. of child study, 1909-10), Am. Psychological Assn., Soc. Coll. Teachers of Edn. (pres. 1916-17), Simplified Spelling Bd. (advisory council), Pa. State Ednl. Assn. (pres. 1920), Pa. Schoolmasters' Club, Nat. Soc. for Study of Edn.; chemn. Sect. V, 4th Internat. Congress on Home Edn. Dist. dir. War and Navy Depts. Commn. on Training Camp Activities, Honolulu, 1918-19. Mem. Theta Delta Chi, Phi Beta Kappa, Phi Delta Kappa, Phi Kappa Phi, Kappa Phi Kappa (nat. pres. 1931-33), Kappa Delta Pi, Pi Gamma Mu. Contbr. to ednl. mags. and revs. Home: 333 W. Park Av., State College, Pa.* Died Apr. 16, 1949.

CHAMBERS, William Nesbitt, missionary; b. N. Norwich, Ont., Can., Feb. 22, 1853; s. Robert and Catherine Lucas (Nesbitt) C.; student Queen's U., Ont., Can., 1871-73; B.A., Princeton, 1876, M.A., 1879; D.D., Queen's, 1911, Princeton, 1911; m. Cornelia Pond Williams, May 7, 1884; children—Ralph Gordon (dec.), Talcott, Williams (dec.), Kate Ethel, Dorothea Nesbitt. Missionary A.B.C.F.M. to Turkey since 1879. Conducted relief work in Erzerum Province, relieving 50,000 or 60,000 persons; moved to Adana, 1899, made pres. Internat. Relief Commn.; served as govtl. (Turkish) commr. of industries for women of Adana Vilayet; now retired. Author: Yoljuluk. Address: Care American Mission, Beirut, Syria. Died Aug. 7, 1934.

CHAMBLISS, Alexander Wilds (chăm'blĭs), judge; b. Greenville, S.C., Sept. 10, 1864; s. John Alexander and Mary (Mauldin) C.; ed. prep. and high schs. and under private tutors; studied law under Augustine T. Smythe, Charleston, S.C., and Gen. William H. Payne, Warrenton, Va.; m. Lillian Carter Nelson, Apr. 26, 1886 (died December 1931); children—John Alexander II, Lillian Nelson; m. 2d, Agnes Shalliday, July 1933 (died Nov. 15, 1946). Admitted to Virginia State bar, 1884; began practice at Chattanooga, Tenn., 1886; mem. firm Chambliss & Chambliss until 1911, Sizer, Chambliss & Chambliss, 1911-23; vice-pres. Provident Life & Accident Ins. Co. Mem. State Senate, Tenn., 1899-1900; mayor of Chattanooga, 2 terms, 1901-05; judge State Court of Civil Appeals, 1917-18; mayor of Chattanooga, 1919-23, and re-elected for 2d term of 4 yrs. (resigned); apptd. asso. justice Supreme Court of Tenn., by gov. Oct. 1923, and elected to same office Aug. 1924; chief justice State Supreme Court since Feb. 1, 1947. Mem. Am., Tenn. State, and Chattanooga Law Library bar assns., Sons Confederate Vets., etc. Mason, K.P. Democrat. Baptist. Clubs: Civitan (hon.), Kiwanis (hon.), Mountain City, Fairyland Country. Home: Lookout Mountain, Tenn. Address: Supreme Court Bldg., Nashville, Tenn. Died Sept. 30, 1947.

CHAMBLISS, Hardee, educator; b. Selma, Ala., Dec. 4, 1872; s. Nathaniel Rives and Anna Dummett (Hardee) C.; grad. Va. Mil. Inst., 1894; M.S. Vanderbilt U., 1899; Ph.D., Johns Hopkins, 1900; m. Julita McLane Sturdy, 1903 (died 1916); children—Joseph Hardee, John Lockwood, Hardee C., Allan McLane Francis; m. 2d, Emma Marie Henne, June 27, 1918. Instr., Columbia U., 1900-01; research chemist Moore Electric Co., Newark, N.J., 1901-03; Gen. Chem. Co., New York, 1903-09; prof. in charge chemistry, Oklahoma Coll., Stillwater, 1909-15; asst. commr. of health, Okla., 1915-16; chem. dir. Commercial Acid Co., St. Louis, Mo., 1916-17. Commd. maj. O.R.C., Aug. 1917; called to active duty, Dec. 7, 1917, and assigned to Gun Div., Ordnance Dept.; trans. to Nitrate Div. of Ordnance, Feb. 3, 1918, and directed researches, N.Y. City, conducted by War Dept. in coöperation with Gen. Chem. Co.; later put in charge all research work of Ordnance Dept., Nitrate Div., in New York and vicinity; detailed as comdg. officer U.S. Nitrate Plant No. 1, Sheffield, Ala., Feb. 1919; promoted lt. col., July 1919; hon. discharged, Nov. 29, 1920, and apptd. plant mgr, U.S. Nitrate Plant 1, resigned Sept. 1, 1921; prof. chemistry, Catholic U. of Am., 1921, dean Sch. of Science, 1925-30, dean Sch. of Engring.. 1930-34; retired; now cons. chemist. Promoted col. O.R.C., 1929. Fellow A.A.A.S.; mem. Am. Chem. Soc., Sigma Alpha Epsilon. K.C. (4°). Democrat. Home: 1715 Varnum St. N.W., Washington. Died June 1, 1947.

CHANCEY, Robert Edward Lee, lawyer; b. Pierce County, Ga., December 16, 1880; s. Lewis William and Isabel (Bennett) C.; attended Ga. Normal Coll., Athens, Ga., 1898-99, Ga. Normal College, Abbeville, Ga., 1899-1900; LL.B., Mercer U. Law Sch., Macon, Ga., 1902; m. Jennie Emma Cortino, Oct. 10, 1906; children—Robert Edward Lee (dec.), William Bennett. Admitted to Ga. bar, 1902, Fla. bar, 1903; elected and apptd. county solicitor Hillsborough County, Fla. (1916-20 and 1925-29); elected mayor of Tampa, Fla., 1931, for 4-yr. term, reelected in 1935 and 1939. Formerly mem. advisory commn. State Defense Council of Fla. Mem. Hillsborough County Bar Assn. (ex-pres.), ex-member U.S. Conference of Mayors (advisory council); mem. advisory committee Atlantic and Gulf Canal Assn.; dir. Fla. State Chamber of Commerce, Community Chest, Tampa (ex-dir.), Fair and Gasparilla Assn.; mem. Fla. State Game and Fish Assn. (ex-pres.), Tampa Civic Art Commn. (ex-pres.). K.P., Elk. Home: Odessa, Fla., Route 1. Address: 706 Stovall Office Bldg., Tampa, Fla. Died June 1, 1948.

CHANDLER, Bert D., judge; b. Lenawee County, Mich., Mar. 19, 1874; s. Spencer G. and Viola (Doolittle) C.; student Hudson (Mich.) High Sch.; m. Carolyn Fitch, Aug. 10, 1910. Admitted to Mich. bar, 1895; mem. firm Fellows & Chandler, 1895-1916; elected circuit judge, 1914; elected asso. justice, Mich. Supreme Court, 1936. Democrat. Mason, Elk, K. of P. Home: Hudson, Mich. Address: Capitol Bldg., Lansing, Mich. Died Dec. 13, 1947.

CHANDLER, Charles Quarles, banker; b. Rocheport, Mo., Aug. 18, 1864; s. Charles Quarles and Ann Elizabeth (Woods) C.; ed. pub. schs.; m. Olive Frances Thayer, June 22, 1898; children—Margaret, Charles Jerome, William Woods, Elizabeth; m. 2d, Alice Throckmorton, Sept. 5, 1917; children—Olive, George Throckmorton, Anderson Woods. In banking business, Kan., since 1883; now chmn. bd. 1st Nat. Bank in Wichita. Trustee Northwestern Mutual Life Ins. Co.; dir. Kan. Bankers Surety Co., Chandler Nat. Bank, Lyons, Kan. Trustee Ottawa U. Republican. Baptist. Rotarian. Home: 200 Clifton St. Office: 1st Nat. Bank in Wichita, Wichita, Kan. Died Dec. 19, 1943.

CHANDLER, Frank Wadleigh, college prof.; b. Brooklyn, June 16, 1873; s. Frank Hilton and Narcissa (Davis) C.; A.B., Brooklyn Poly. Inst., 1894; A.M., Columbia, 1896, Ph.D., 1899; University of Cincinnati, Litt.D., 1944; traveled and studied in Europe, Africa, Asia, South and Central America, various times; married, Adele Walton, November 26, 1901. Instr., 1899, asst. prof. lit. and history, 1900-01, prof., 1901-07, prof. English, 1907-10, Brooklyn Poly. Inst., professor English and comparative literature, University of Cincinnati, since Sept., 1910, and dean of college of liberal arts, 1913-28; professor emeritus since 1943; lecturer comparative lit., Columbia, 1901-04, and at nineteen summer sessions. Mem. of Modern Language Assn. America, Phi Beta Kappa. Author: Romances of Roguery, an Episode in the History of the Novel, 1899; The Literature of Roguery (in the Types of Literature Series), 1907; Aspects of Modern Drama, 1914; The Contemporary Drama of France, 1920; Modern Continental Playwrights, 1931. Editor of texts in Tudor Shakespeare, Modern Students' Library and Modern Readers' Series, also of Twentieth Century Plays, 1935. Contbr. to reviews and to Library of World's Best Literature, New Ency. Americana, Columbia Course in Literature. Home: 323 Warren Av., Cincinnati, O. Died June 13, 1947.

CHANDLER, George Brinton; b. Fryeburg, Me., Oct. 21, 1865; s. James Everett and Henrietta N. (Sanborn) C.; A.B., Bowdoin, 1890; m. Mabel Ayers, June 5, 1895; children—Mrs. Ruth Moore, Fielding, Mrs. Faith Jeffries. Prin. high schs., Franklin and

Milford, Mass., successively, 1890-91 and 1891-92; asso. with Ginn & Co., Boston, 1892-1905; Am. Book Co., New York, 1905-16. Speaker in nat., state and local campaigns since 1896; mem. Conn. Ho. of Rep., sessions 1909 and 1911 (chmn. coms. on railroads, labor, spl. investigating com.); specialized on social and indsl. problems; apptd. by President Taft mem. Nat. Commn. on Indsl. Relations, 1912; mem. Compensation Commn. of 1st Congressional Dist. of Conn., 1913-24; pres. Hartford Get-Together Club, 1910-11. Chmn. com. on publicity Conn. State Council of Defense, May, 1917-Nov. 12, 1918; mem. Mil. Census Commn. State of Conn., Mar.-May, 1917; exec. v.p. Conn. Chamber of Commerce 1919-26; sec. Ohio Chamber Commerce, Mar. 1, 1926 to Nov. 16, 1939, since exec. vice pres. Served as chmn. Chambers of Commerce Com. N.E. Shippers Advisory Bd. and as sec. Organizing Com. of N.E. Conf.; sec.-treas. Nat. Assn. of State Chambers of Commerce, 1929. Lecturer Summer Sch. for Comml. and Trade Execs., Northwestern U., 1927; also lecturer before civic, ednl. and indsl. socs. Mem. S.A.R. (Conn.), Theta Delta Chi. Republican. Conglist. Clubs: Athletic, Columbus (Columbus); Cincinnati (Cincinnati). Author: Industrial History of Connecticut, 1925. Home: 167 S. Drexel Av. Office: Hoster Building, Broad at Fourth Sts., Columbus, O. Died Nov. 24, 1943; buried at Rocky Hill, Conn.

CHANDLER, Harry, newspaper pub.; b. Landaff, N.H., May 17, 1864; s. Moses Knight and Emma Jane (Little) C.; ed. high sch., Lisbon, N.H.; m.; children—(1st wife) Franceska (dec.), Alice May; (2d wife) Constance, Ruth, Norman, Harrison Gray, Helen, Philip. Began as clk. circulation dept., Los Angeles Times; chmn. bd. Times-Mirror Co., pub. The Times. Organized syndicate, purchased 862,000 acres of land in Lower Calif., 1899, and made pres. Calif.-Mexico Land & Cattle Co., the property producing $18,000,000 worth of cotton in 1919; purchased 47,000 acres of land adjoining Los Angeles, 1909, and organized Los Angeles Suburban Home Co., entire area sold in 7 yrs.; organized syndicate, 1912, and purchased Tejon Ranch, 281,000 acres in Los Angeles and Kern counties, Calif., now maintaining thereon about 11,500 head of live stock; in 1927 helped organize the Vermejo Club and purchased Bartlett Ranch in Colo., famous the country over as a sportsman's paradise, consists of 340,000 acres; officer or dir. in many Calif. corps., including banking, land, transportation, oil, irrigation and manufacturing companies. Trustee California Institute of Technology. Member American Newspaper Publishers Assn. (pres. 1930-31). Republican. Mason (33°, Shriner). Clubs: Athletic, Automobile Club of Southern Calif. Presented gold watch by Los Angeles Realty Bd. as the most useful citizen of Los Angeles for the year 1921. Office: Times Bldg., Los Angeles, Calif.
Died Sep. 23, 1944.

CHANDLER, Jefferson Paul, lawyer; b. St. Joseph, Mo., Jan. 6, 1872; s. Jefferson and Catherine (O'Toole) C.; B.A., Princeton, 1893; Columbian Law Sch., Washington, D.C., 1893-94; m. Elizabeth Shankland, June 1, 1904. Admitted to Calif. bar, 1895, and began practice at Los Angeles; partner Shankland & Chandler, 1904-14; sr. mem. Chandler & Wright; dir. Calif. Trust. Co., Calif. Portland Cement Co., Pacific Mutual Life Ins. Co. Mem. Am. Bar Assn., State Bar of Calif., Los Angeles County Bar Assn. (ex-pres.). Democrat. Catholic. Clubs: California, Los Angeles Athletic, Los Angeles Country. Home: 715 W. 28th St. Office: 210 W. 7th St., Los Angeles, Calif. Died Feb. 4, 1948; buried at San Gabriel, Calif.

CHANDLER, Lloyd Horwitz, naval officer; b. Washington, D.C., Aug. 17, 1869; grad. U.S. Naval Acad., 1888. Commd. ensign, U.S. Navy, 1890, and advanced through the grades to rear adm., 1930; retired, 1921; served on U.S.S. San Francisco, Spanish-Am. War, 1898, U.S.S. Connecticut, 1906-07; comd. U.S.S. Salem, 1911-12, Illinois, 1912, Nebraska, 1912, Illinois, 1912-13, New Hampshire, 1916-18; chief of staff, Battleship Force One, Atlantic Fleet, 1918-19. Decorated Navy Cross. Address: Navy Department, Washington 25. Died Jan. 17, 1947; buried in Glenwood Cemetery, Washington.

CHANDLER, Percy Milton, corp. official; b. Philadelphia, Pa., Feb. 6, 1873; s. John Walter and Almira (Taylor) C.; ed. Friends' Central Sch., Phila.; m. Emma B. Mendenhall, Oct. 20, 1897; m. 2d, Nancy Louise Krebs, Nov. 1, 1917; m. 3d, Marie Leonard Langtree, Oct. 7, 1926. Pres. and director Chandler & Company, Inc., Brandywine Farms Corp., Pennfar Realty Company; chairman and director of P. H. Butler Co.; director Phila. Dairy Products Co., Nat. Food Products Corp. Mem. numerous clubs. Mem. Soc. of Friends. Home: 280 Park Av., New York, N.Y.; and "Brandywine Lodge," Pocopson, Pa. Office: 30 Rockefeller Plaza, New York, N.Y.; and 1500 Walnut St., Philadelphia, Pa. Died Oct. 14, 1944.

CHANDLER, Theodore Edson, naval officer; b. Annapolis, Md., Dec. 26, 1894; s. Lloyd Horwitz and Agatha Buford (Edson) C.; B.S., U.S. Naval Acad., 1915, post-grad. work in explosives, 1921, M.S. in Chem. Engring., Univ. of Mich., 1922, Army Indsl. Coll., 1931; m. Beatrice Bowen Fairfax, Apr. 28, 1919; children—Theodora Edson (Mrs. John James Green). Commd. ensign 1915, and advanced through the grades to rear admiral (temp.) 1942; during World War I served on U.S.S. Conner, a destroyer basing at Brest, France; commanded U.S.S. Pope on the Asiatic Station, 1929-30, U.S.S. Buchanan in the Battle Force, 1934-35 and U.S.S. Omaha, 1941-43; asst. naval attaché at Paris, Madrid, Lisbon, 1935-38; comdr. of All Forces, Aruba-Curacao, 1943-44; comdr. Assault Group Allied Invasion Southern France, 1944; comdr. Battleship Div. 2, Philippine Invasion and Battle of Leyte Gulf, 1944; comdr. Cruiser Div. 4, Invasion of Lingayen Gulf, Philippines, 1945. Decorated: Navy Cross, Distinguished Service Medal (Army), Silver Star Medal, Legion of Merit, Gold Star in lieu 2d Legion of Merit (Combat V), Purple Heart Medal, Victory Medal with Destroyer Clasp, World War I, Yangtze Service Medal, Am. Defense Medal with bronze A, Am. Campaign Medal, European-African-Middle Eastern Campaign Medal with bronze star, Asiatic-Pacific Medal with 3 bronze stars, World War II Victory Medal, Philippine Liberation Medal with 2 bronze stars; Officer Legion of Honor (France); Nat. Order of Cruzeviodo Sul (officer), War Service Medal with Diploma and Citation (Brazil); Hon. Companion of Distinguished Service Order (Great Britain); Order of Orange Nassau (Netherlands). Recipient letter of commendation from Sec. of Navy. Clubs: New York Yacht, Chevy Chase, Army-Navy Country, Army-Navy (Washington). Home: 2811 Albemarle St., Washington. Killed in action, Jan. 6, 1945.

CHANLER, Lewis Stuyvesant, lawyer; b. Newport, R.I., Sept. 24, 1869; s. Hon. John Winthrop and Margaret Astor (Ward) C.; ed. pvt. tutors and at Cambridge, Eng.; LL.B., Columbia, 1891; m. Alice Chamberlain, 1890. In law practice, New York, since 1891; lt.-gov. N.Y., 1906-08; Dem. nominee for gov., 1908. Mem. N.Y. Canal Bd.; former mem. bd. mgrs. Hudson River State Hosp. and House of Refuge, Randall's Island. Home: Tuxedo Park, N.Y. Office: 346 Broadway, New York. Died Feb. 28, 1942.

CHANNING, J(ohn) Parke, mining engr.; b. New York, Mar. 24, 1863; s. Roscoe H. and Susan (Thompson) Channing; E.M., Columbia, 1883, M.S., 1914; unmarried. Engr. and supt. iron and copper mines, Lake Superior Mining Dist., 1885-94; deputy commr. mineral statistics, Mich., 1884; insp. mines, Gogebic Co., Mich., 1897-1900; made several trips to Mexico and C.A. to examine and report on properties; asst. mgr. Calumet & Hecla Mining Co., 1893-94; with old Boston & Mont. Consolidated Mining Co. (now part of Anaconda Copper Co.), 1895-96; consulting engr., New York, 1896; developed and equipped mines and reduction works of Tenn. Copper Co., also pres., 1903-08; made original report on Nev. Consolidated Mine; organized Gen. Development Co., 1905, which found and developed properties of Miami Copper Co., one of porphyry coppers; dir. Tenn. Corp., Kerr Lake Mines, Ltd., San Cayetano Mines, Ltd., Miami Copper Co.; retired 1926. Democrat. Unitarian. Mem. Mining and Metall. Soc. Am. (pres. 1910-12), Am. Inst. Mining and Metall. Engrs., Lake Superior Mining Inst., Am. Geog. Soc., Instn. of Mining and Metallurgy (England). Author numerous tech. articles for mining socs., engring. and scientific mags., etc.; delivered course of lectures on mine plants at Columbia and various addresses elsewhere. Address: 61 Broadway, New York. Died Oct. 11, 1942.

CHAPIN, Arthur Beebe (chā'pĭn); b. Chicopee, Mass., Nov. 17, 1868; s. Judge Edward W. and Mary Lavinia (Beebe) C.; grad. Phillips Acad., Andover, Mass., 1887; A.B., Amherst, 1891; m. Tirzah L. Sherwood, Nov. 25, 1896 (died Dec. 22, 1901); m. 2d, Marion S. Murlless, Dec. 18, 1907. Admitted to Mass. bar, 1896; in practice with father at Holyoke, Mass., 1897-1904; city solicitor, Holyoke, 1896; mayor of Holyoke, 1899-1904; treas. Commonwealth of Mass., 1905-09; bank commr., Mass., 1909-12; v.p., later pres. Am. Trust Co., Boston, 1912-29; gen. mgr. N.Y. office of Whiting Paper Co., 1929-31; treas. R.R. Credit Corp., Washington, D.C., 1932-37; now pres. Farr Alpaca Co. (in receivership); dir. Holyoke & Westfield R.R.. Asst. treas., later treas., Andover Theol. Sem., 1910-32. Chmn. Holyoke Com. of British War Relief Soc. Del. to Rep. Nat. Conv., 1924; former mem. Mass. Bd. Tax Appeals; mem. of commnr. to revise tax laws of Mass. Mem. S.A.R. (former treas. Mass. chapter), S.R.; ex-pres. Mass. Bankers Assn., Mass. Trust Co. Associates. Republican. Conglist. Mason (K.T.). Club: University (Boston). Home: 210 Oak St., Holyoke, Mass.
Died Mar. 19, 1943.

CHAPIN, Henry Dwight, physician, author; b. Steubenville, O., Feb. 4, 1857; s. Henry Barton and Harriet Ann (Smith) Chapin; A.B., Princeton, 1877, A.M., 1885; M.D., Coll. Phys. and Surg. (Columbia), 1881; m. Alice Delafield, June 1, 1907. Prof. emeritus, diseases of children, N.Y. Post-Grad. Med. Sch. and Hosp. Former pres. Hosp. Social Service Assn. of New York; dir. Havens Relief Fund Soc., Life Saving Benevolent Assn., N.Y. Post-Grad. Med. Sch. and Hosp., Working Women's Protective Union, Children's Welfare Fedn. Mem. Am. Pediatric Soc. (pres. 1910-11), N.Y. Acad. Medicine, N.Y. County Med. Soc., Soc. of Mayflower Descendants, Soc. Colonial Wars, S.R. Club: Century. Author: Theory and Practice of Infant Feeding, 1902 (3 edits.); Vital Questions, 1905; A General Treatise on Diseases of Children, 1909 (6 edits.); Health First—The Fine Art of Living, 1917; Heredity and Child Culture, 1922. Also sociol. and med. articles in various mags. Chmn. pub. health div. of N.Y. State Reconstruction Commn. Awarded Columbia U. medal for "outstanding contributions to problems relating to the care of children and as a pioneer in hospital social service," 1933. Home: Lawrence Park W., Bronxville, N.Y. Died June 27, 1942.

CHAPMAN, Charles C(larke), business exec.; b. Macomb, Ill., July 2, 1853; s. Sidney S. and Rebecca Jane (Clarke) C.; ed. common schs.; m. Lizzie Pearson, Oct. 23, 1884 (died Sept. 19, 1894); children—Ethel Marguerite (wife of Dr. Wm. Harold Wickett), Charles Stanley; m. 2d, Clara Irvin, Sept. 3, 1898; 1 son, Irvin. Supt. erection of bldgs. in Chicago, 1871-73; in mercantile business, 1873-76; found pub. business, Galesburg, 1878, in partnership with brother as Chapman Bros., Chicago, 1880; orange grower, Calif., since 1894, developed several large ranches; chmn. bd. Bank of America, Fullerton branch; pres. Chapman Bros. Co., Chas. C. and S. J. Chapman Co., Chapman Orchards Co., Southern Meat Co., Community Hotel Co.; dir. Bank of America, San Francisco. Pres. bd. trustees Calif. Christian Coll., Los Angeles. Republican. Mem. Disciples of Christ Ch. Mason (32°, K.T., Shriner). Builder of hospital at Nantungchow, China. Home: Fullerton, Calif. Died Apr. 5, 1944.

CHAPMAN, Charles Edward, college prof.; b. Franklin, N.H., June 3, 1880; s. Frank Hilton and Ella Frances (James) C.; Princeton, 1898-1900; A.B., Tufts Coll., 1902; LL.B., Harvard, 1905; A.M., U. of Calif., 1909, Ph.D., 1915; U. of Seville, Spain, 1912-13; m. Elizabeth Adams Russell, June 29, 1907; 1 son, Seville Dudley; m. 2d, Alice Aimee Fleming, Jan. 31, 1929. Admitted to bar, Mass. and Calif., 1906; with United Rys., 1906-07, Western Electric Co., 1907-08; teacher history, Riverside (Calif.) High Sch., 1909-10; asst. in history, U. of Calif., 1910-12; Native Sons traveling fellow, research work, archives of Spain, 1912-14; instr. in history, U. of Calif., 1914-15, asst. prof., 1915-19, asso. prof., 1919-27, prof. since 1927; U.S. exchange prof. to Chile for 1920; Pacific coast scout St. Louis Nat. Base Ball Club, 1921-32, Cincinnati Club since 1932. Mem. board editors Hispanic-Am. Hist. Rev., 1917-19; advisory editor Hispanic-Am. Hist. Rev. since 1922. Member advisory council Latin-American Organization for Continental Solidarity. Rep. of State of Calif. and U. of California at exercises in honor 2d centenary birth of Father Serra, held at Petra, Majorca, 1913; rep. U. of Calif. at Am. Congress of Bibliography and History, Buenos Aires, 1916. Mem. Am. Hist. Assn. (pres. Pacific Coast br., 1933), Am. Congress Bibliography and History (permanent com.), Am. Assn. Univ. Profs., Phi Sigma Kappa, Phi Beta Kappa (Tufts); mem. advisory bd. Calif. History Commn.; fellow Tex. State Hist. Soc., Royal Hist. Soc.; corr. mem. Hispanic Soc. America; hon. mem. Am. Library of Univ. of Sanitago de Compostela, Buenos Aires. Club: Orinda Country. Author: The Founding of Spanish California, 1916; A Californian in South America, 1917; A History of Spain, 1918; Catalogue of Materials in the Archivo General de Indias for the History of the Pacific Coast and the American Southwest, 1919; A History of California—the Spanish Period, 1921; A History of the Cuban Republic, 1927; Colonial Hispanic America—A History, 1933; Republican Hispanic America—A History, 1937; Play Ball! Advice for Young Ball Players (with Henry L. Severeid), 1941; also numerous articles on the history of Spanish Calif. and Hispanic America. Has traveled widely in Europe, Asia, Africa and N. and S. America. Awarded Mitre medal of Hispanic Soc. of America for achievement in field of Hispanic Am. studies; also Portales medal of Republic of Chile, and De Hostos medal of Puerto Rico. Home: 12 Via Farallon, Orinda, Calif. Address: Box 17, Library, Univ. of California, Berkeley, Calif. Died Nov. 18, 1941.

CHAPMAN, Emmanuel, educator; b. Chicago, Ill., Feb. 7, 1905; s. Harry and Clara (Skoor) C.; ed. U. of Chicago, 1921-24; A.B., Loyola U., Chicago, 1930-31; A.M., Ph.D., U. of Toronto, 1931-34; m. Shulamith Aboulafia, June 26, 1939. Instr. in philosophy, U. of Toronto, 1931-34, U. of Notre Dame, 1934-36; asso. prof. of philosophy, Grad. Sch. and Sch. of Edn., Fordham Univ., 1936-44; dept. psychology and philosophy, Hunter College, N.Y. City. Founder of Committee of Catholics for Human Rights and The Voice for Human Rights. Founding member Conference on Science, Philosophy and Religion; member Council for Democracy (national board of dirs.); bd. dirs. Greater N.Y. com. for Japanese Americans; mem. nat. adv. bd., Commn. on Law and Social Action; mem. exec. com., N.Y. State Commn. against Discrimination in Edn. Mem. panel on Labor Arbitration, radio station WMCA; mem. advisory council, station WEVD, N.Y. Mem. editorial adv. bd., One People; annual contbr., Encylopedia Americana; contributing editor of The Commonweal, Philosophic Abstracts, Dictionary of Philosophy, Who's Who in Philosophy, Dictionary of the Arts, Journal of Aesthetics and Art Criticism. Mem. Am. Philos. Assn., Am. Cath. Philos. Assn., Am. Assn. Univ. Profs. Democrat. Roman Catholic. Home: 7 West 92d St. Office: 695 Park Av., New York, N.Y. Died Apr. 17, 1948.

CHAPMAN, Frank Michler, ornithologist; b. Englewood, N.J., June 12, 1864; s. Lebbeus and Mary A. (Parkhurst) C.; acad. edn. (Sc.D., Brown, 1913); m. Fannie Bates Embury, 1898; 1 son, Frank Michler. Asso. curator ornithology and mammalogy, Am. Museum Natural History, 1888-1908, curator ornithology since 1908; originator there of the habitat of bird groups and seasonal bird exhibits. Zoölogical explorations in temperate and tropical America since 1887. Dir. Bureau of Publications Am. Red Cross, 1917-18;

commr. Am. Red Cross to Latin America, 1918-19. Pres. Linnæan Soc., New York, elected 1897; pres. Burroughs Memorial Assn., 1921-25; fellow Am. Ornithologists' Union (pres. 1911); v.p. Explorers Club, 1910-18; hon. mem. N.Y. Zool. Soc., British Ornithologists' Union, Sociedad Ornithologica del Plata, Deutschen Ornithologischen Gesellschaft; mem. Nat. Academy of Sciences, Am. Phil. Soc., Soc. Colonial Wars. Awarded first Linnæan medal by Linnæan Soc. of New York, 1912; first Elliot medal by Nat. Acad. of Sciences, 1918; medal Roosevelt Memorial Asso. 1928; awarded medal, Burroughs Memorial Assn., 1929. Clubs: Explorers, Century (New York). Author: Handbook of Birds of Eastern North America, 1895; Bird-Life, a Guide to the Study of Our Common Birds, 1897; Bird Studies with a Camera, 1900; A Color Key to North American Birds, 1903; The Economic Value of Birds to the State, 1903; The Warblers of North America, 1907; Camps and Cruises of an Ornithologist, 1908; The Travels of Birds, 1916; The Distribution of Bird-Life in Colombia, 1917; Our Winter Birds, 1918; What Bird Is That?, 1920; Birds of Urubamba Valley, Jeru, 1921; The Distribution of Bird-Life in Ecuador, 1926; My Tropical Air Castle, 1929; Autobiography of a Bird-Lover, 1933; Life in an Air Castle, 1938; The Post-Glacial History of Zonotrichia capensis; Birds and Man; also numerous papers on birds and mammals. Editor and founder Bird-Lore. Office: American Museum Natural History, New York, N.Y.* Died Nov. 15, 1945.

CHAPMAN, Howard Rufus, clergyman; b. Rockford, Ill., Sept. 10, 1868; s. Darius H. and Lucy Savage (White) C.; B.A., Shurtleff Coll., Alton, Ill., 1894, M.A., 1897, D.D., 1912; grad. Rochester Theol. Sem., 1897; grad. work U. of Mich.; m. Mary Octavia Carr, June 9, 1897; children—Richard Carr, Donald Harding. Ordained ministry Bapt. Ch., 1897; pastor Genessee St. Ch., 1896-1900; Michigan Av. Ch., Saginaw, Mich., 1900-10, First Ch., Lincoln, Neb., 1910-18, Atchison, Kan., 1918; Bapt. univ. pastor at U. of Mich., 1919-39; rep. Northern Bapt. bd. of edn., in summer assemblies and confs. in many states as speaker and instructor in missions and religious edn., 1921-35. Lecturer on missions and religious edn. Mem. Mich. Acad. of Science, Arts and Letters. Pastor First Ch., Northville, Mich., since 1939. Mason. Clubs: Exchange, Mich. Ministers. Home: 217 N. Wing St., Northville, Mich. Died Dec. 7, 1942.

CHAPMAN, James Blaine, church exec.; b. Yale, Ill., Aug., 1884; s. Thomas Smith and Ruth Catherine (Roberts) C.; B.D., Peniel Coll., 1915, D.D., 1918; D.D., Pasadena Coll., 1927; m. Maud Frederick, Feb., 1903 (dec.); children—Lois Catherine, James Blaine (dec.), Grace Bess, Frederick Harold, George Brilhart (dec.), Paul Benton, Gertrude Edwina; m. 2d, Louise Robinson, June 1942. Ordained to ministry, 1903; evangelist and pastor, 1900-11; president Peniel (Texas) College, 1912-18; editor Herald of Holiness, 1920-28; general supt. Church of the Nazarene since 1928. Has traveled in South Amer., Africa, China, India, Japan, Palestin, Egypt, Italy, Great Britain in interest of the church. Author: Some Estimates of Life; History of the Church of the Nazarene; Thirty Thousand Miles of Missionary Travel; What it Means to be a Christian; Christ and the Bible; Your Life, Make the Most of it; Singing in the Shadows; Christian Men in a Modern World; Bud Robinson, A Brother Beloved; The Touch of Jesus; Ask Dr. Chapman; The Divine Response; Religion and Everyday Life; Outlines and Illustrations; The Preaching Ministry; The Terminology of Bible Holiness; A Day in the Lord's Court; The Nazarene Primer. Home: Indian Lake, Vicksburg, Mich. Address: 2923 Troost Av., Kansas City, Mo. Died July 30, 1947.

CHAPMAN, James Wilkinson, Jr., lawyer; b. Chestertown, Kent Co., Md., Sept. 30, 1871; s. James Wilkinson and Mary Amanda (Webb) C.; A.B., Washington Coll., Chestertown, 1892, M.A., Ph.D., Johns Hopkins, 1896; LL.B., U. of Md., 1897; m. Julia Clare Vannort, Nov. 11, 1903; children—Samuel Vannort, Mary Clare. Practiced in Baltimore since 1897; U.S. commr., 4th Jud. Circuit, 1936. Pres. Sch. Bd., Baltimore, 1915-20. Mem. Board of Visitors and Govs. of Washington Coll.; mem. bd. dirs. Y.M.C.A., Baltimore; mem. Am. Br. Assn., Md. State Bar Assn., (sec.; pres. 1930-31), Baltimore City Bar Assn., Eastern Shore Soc. of Baltimore (pres. 1927-28). Democrat. Clubs: University, John Hopkins. Author: State Tax Commissions in the United States, 1897; also (address) Maryland Laid the Cornerstone of Our Federal Union, 1931. Home: Northway Apts. Office: Mercantile Trust Bldg., Baltimore, Md. Died Dec. 13, 1943.

CHAPMAN, Joseph, corp. official; b. Dubuque, Ia., Oct. 17, 1871; s. Joseph and Katharine C. (Cassiday) C.; ed. Central High Sch., Minneapolis, Coll. of Law, U. of Minn.; m. Elizabeth G. Mayhew, Dec., 1896. Began in banking business, 1888; cashier Northwestern Nat. Bank, Minneapolis, 1904-07; v.p. same until Oct., 1919; dir. N.W. Nat. Bank & Trust Co., 1903-34; v.p., dir. N.W. Nat. Bank Bldg., 1928-36; pres. L. S. Donaldson Co., 1919-29; pres., dir. Donaldson Realty Co., 1924-39; receiver Public Utilities Consolidated Corp., 1929-35; co-trustee Soo Line Ry.; dir. Soo Line Ry.; pres. Citizens Utilities Co., 1935-46; trustee Farmers and Mechanics Bank; vice pres. and dir. Nicolet Hotel; sec. and dir. Shawmut Co.; dir. Maryland Casualty Co., Baltimore. Trustee Dunwoody Industrial Inst. Pres. Hennepin County Good Roads Assn. (pres. 1908-09), Minn. Bankers' Assn. (sec. 1899-1906), Phi Delta Phi. Republican. Methodist. Mason. Clubs: Minneapolis, Lafayette. Home: Orono, Lake Minnetonka, Wayzata, Minn. Office: Northwestern Bank Bldg., Minneapolis. Died May 11, 1948.

CHAPMAN, Ross McClure, M.D., psychiatrist; b. Belleville, N.Y., July 13, 1881; s. Eugene A. and Agnes (McClure) C.; grad. Union Acad., Belleville, 1898; student Syracuse U., 1898-1901; M.D., U. of Mich., 1905; m. Marion E. Clapp, Dec. 29, 1908; 1 dau., Mary Harris (dec.). Began practice, Watertown, N.Y., 1905; interne Utica State Hosp., 1906-07; sr. asst. physician Binghamton State Hosp., 1908-16; 1st asst. St. Elizabeth's Hosp., Washington, D.C., 1916-20, also instr. psychiatry, George Washington U., 1916-20; med. supt. Sheppard and Enoch Pratt Hosp. since 1920; asso. prof. psychiatry, U. of Md., 1920-23, prof. since 1923. Commd. maj. Med. Corps, U.S. Army, 1918; div. psychiatrist, 6th Div., with Army of Occupation in Germany, as asst. consulting neuro-psychiatrist. Mem. A.M.A., Md. Med. Assn., Baltimore County Med. Soc., Southern Med. Assn., Am. Psychiatric Assn. (pres. 1937-38), Am. Psychopathol. Assn. (pres. 1928), Am. Psychoanalytic Assn., Nu Sigma Nu, Phi Kappa Psi. Republican. Presbyn. Mason. Clubs: Maryland (Baltimore); Army and Navy (Washington). Home: Towson, Md. Died Sept. 24, 1948; buried Druid Ridge Cemetery, Baltimore.

CHAPMAN, Theodore S., lawyer; b. Jerseyville, Ill., Sept. 27, 1877; s. Theodore S. and Sarah (Landon) C.; grad. pub. grammar and high schs., Jerseyville; read law in office of James C. Hutchins, Chicago, and was admitted to the Ill. bar, 1900; unmarried. In legal dept. of Ill. Trust & Savings Bank, 1900-04; in active practice on own account for 1 yr.; gen. counsel Harris Trust & Savings Bank since 1907; also in gen. practice since 1913; senior mem. firm Chapman and Cutler. In Red Cross service in France, 1918. Pres. and trustee Chicago Home for Incurables; trustee Monticello Coll. (Godfrey, Ill.), of Gads Hill Center (Chicago). Mem. Am., Ill. State and Chicago bar assns., Assn. Bar, City New York. Republican. Baptist. Clubs: Chicago, Union League, Mid-Day, Attic, Tavern (Chicago); Metropolitan, Recess (New York). Home: 1242 Lake Shore Drive. Office: 111 W. Monroe St., Chicago, Ill. Died June 1, 1943.

CHAPMAN, William Gerard, author; b. Peekskill, N.Y., May 26, 1877; s. William G. and Emmeline (Welch) C.; ed. pub. and pvt. schs., Brooklyn, N.Y.; m. Florence E. Chapman, Jan. 8, 1910; children—Gerard, Ralph, Florence. Formerly connected with Judge, Leslie's Weekly; Wall St. reporter Brock's Commercial Agency, 1900-01; western business mgr., N.Y. Commercial, 1901-03; est. and propr. International Press Bureau, 1903. Mem. Authors' League America, Soc. Midland Authors, S.A.R. Club: Cliff Dwellers. Author: Green Timber Trails, 1919. Contbr. short stories to mags. and newspapers. Home: Hinsdale, Ill. Office: 100 W. Monroe St., Chicago. Died June 11, 1945.

CHAPPELL, Will H., lawyer; b. Georgetown, Ind., July 24, 1866; s. Jesse and Sarah E. (Chappell) C.; ed. Gates Acad., and Okla. Bapt. U., Shawnee; m. P. M. Turner, Oct. 27, 1887; children—Elwood B., Florence, M. Ellen, Evelyne. Admitted to bar, 1890, and began practice Lincoln, Neb.; judge, Municipal Court, Guthrie, Okla., 1909-11; became judge, Criminal Court of Appeals, Okla., 1928; now in practice of law. Mem. Okla. Ho. of Rep., 1907-08 (minority leader). Vice chmn. Okla. Rep. State Com., 1903-13; pres. Young Men's Rep. Clubs of Neb., 1895; speaker Nat. Rep. Bureau. Baptist. Home: 615 S.E. 48th St., Oklahoma City, Okla. Died Nov. 28, 1947.

CHAPPELLE, Benjamin Franklin (shăp-pĕl), univ. prof.; b. Phila., Pa., Oct. 5, 1885; s. Sassman Smith and Candace (Reeser) C.; A.B., Dickinson Coll., Carlisle, Pa., 1908, A.M., 1911; studied univs. of Berlin, Heidelberg, Lausanne, Poitiers, U. of Calif. and U. of Pa.; Ph.D., U. of Pa., 1917; m. Frances Arcadia Willoughby St. John, July 29, 1925 (died Sept. 6, 1936); 1 dau., Caroline Willoughby. Asst. prof. Romance languages, Gettysburg Coll., 1911-16, U. of Pa., 1918-21; prof. modern langs. and head of dept., U. of Nev., 1921-38, of foreign langs. since 1938. Mem. Nev. State Parks Commn., term 1940-50. Awarded "Palmes Académiques" with title Officier d'Académie (France), 1934. Mem. Nat. Fed., Modern Lang. Teachers, Am. Assn. Teachers of Spanish and Portuguese, Am. Anthropol. Assn., Am. Ethnol. Soc., A.A.A.S., Am. Assn. Teachers of Italian, Am. Association Teachers of French, American Assn. Univ. Profs., Inter-Am. Soc. of Anthropology and Geography, Washoe Horseman's Assn.; fellow A.A.A.S.; mem. Philologisch-Historische Verbindung, "Cimbria" (Heidelberg), Alpha Chi Rho, Phi Kappa Phi, Pi Gamma Mu, Phi Beta Kappa. Republican. Mem. Ref. Ch. of America. Odd Fellow, K.P., Elk. Author: The German Element in Brazil (monograph), 1917. Home: 576 Ridge St., Reno, Nev. Died Dec. 23, 1948.

CHARLS, George Herbert, steel exec.; b. Cincinnati, O., May 27, 1878; s. George Henry and Elizabeth (Luckey) C.; ed. U. of Cincinnati; m. Juanita Cargill. Vice pres. Am. Rolling Mill Co., 1901-18; v.p. and gen. mgr. Berger Mfg. Co. and Stark Rolling Mill Co., 1918-21; pres. and gen. mgr. United Alloy Steel Corp., 1921-28; pres. and treas. Metro Coal & Limestone, Inc.; dir. Metropolitan Paving Brick Co. Commr. Hot Rolled Strip Steel Inst., 1927-28; pres. Nat. Assn. Flat Rolled Steel Mfrs., 1928-31; sec. Am. Iron and Steel Inst., 1932-33. Home: 11455 Juniper Rd., Cleveland. Died Sept. 11, 1944.

CHASE, Adelaide Cole, artist; b. Boston; d. J. Foxcroft and Irma (de Pelgrom) Cole; studied with Tarbell, of the Art Mus. Sch., Boston, and Carolus Duran, Paris; m. William Chester Chase, June 27, 1892. Painter of portraits; silver medal, St. Louis Expn., 1904, Panama P.I. Expn., 1915. A.N.A. Address: 8 Marlboro St., Boston, Mass.* Died Sep. 4, 1944.

CHASE, Arthur Minturn, pub., author; b. N.Y. City, June 3, 1873; s. Edward Payson and Marion (Moffat) C.; A.B., Harvard, 1896; m. Myra Olive Chase, June 29, 1907 (dec.); children—Arthur Minturn (dec.), Louise Weld (Mrs. John I. H. Baur). With Dodd, Mead & Company, New York City, 1898-1947. Democrat. Episcopalian. Clubs: Harvard Club and The Players Club (New York). Author: The Party at the Penthouse, 1932; Danger in the Dark, 1933; Murder of a Missing Man, 1934; Twenty Minutes to Kill, 1936; No Outlet, 1940; Peril at the Spy Nest, 1943. Home: 65 Laurel Pl., New Rochelle, N.Y. Died Sept. 7, 1947.

CHASE, Frederic Hathaway, lawyer; b. Concord, Mass., July 27, 1870; s. Abial Hathaway and Martha Frances (Simpson) C.; A.B., Harvard, 1892; LL.B., Harvard Law Sch., 1894; m. Theodora Kyle, Aug. 17, 1898; children—Martha F., Frederic H., Theodore. Admitted to Mass. bar, 1894; asst. dist. atty. Suffolk Dist. (Boston), 1903-06; justice Superior Court of Mass., 1911-20; resigned and resumed practice; member firm of Stewart, Chase and Baldwin, 1920-43, Palmer, Dodge, Chase & Davis, since 1943; president Bar Assn., City of Boston, 1939-41; trustee Crabtree Estate. Special asst. to U.S. atty gen., 1941, Dept. Justice Conscientious Objectors Hearing Officer for Mass. Author: Life of Lemuel Shaw, Chief Justice 1918. Club: Union (Boston). Home: Concord, Mass. Office: 53 State St., Boston, Mass. Died June 17, 1948.

CHASE, Frederick Starkweather, mfr. brass goods b. Waterbury, Conn., July 2, 1862; s. Augustus Sabin and Martha (Starkweather) C.; grad. Phillips Acad., Andover, Mass.; 1883; A.B., Yale, 1887; m. Elsie Rowland, Feb. 17, 1890; children—Ethel Rowland (Mrs. Gordon B. Hurlbut), Helen Starkweather (Mrs. Rufus R. Rand), Augustus Sabin, Edmund Rowland, Fredrika (Mrs. D. K. Brent, Jr.), Justine Whittemore (Mrs. G. E. Haight). Began with Waterbury Mfg. Co., 1887, sec., 1895-1900; treas. Chase Rolling Mill Co., 1900-11; treas. Chase Metal Works, 1911-18; pres. Chase Companies, Inc., mfrs. of brass goods from 1918, now retired; pres. Chase Brass & Copper Co., Inc., from 1927; dir. Citizens & Mfrs., Nat. Bank, Kennecott Copper Corp., Hope & What-Cheer Mut. Fire Ins. Co., Factory Mut. Liability Ins. Co., Automobile Mut. Ins. Co. of Am., Veeder-Root, Inc. Former pres. Waterbury Hosp. Mem. Delta Kappa Epsilon, Scroll and Key. Independent Republican. Episcopalian. Clubs: Waterbury, Waterbury Country, Graduate, Elizabethan (New Haven); Yale (New York). Home: Middlebury, Conn. Died Dec. 5, 1947.

CHASE, George Davis, college prof.; b. Dighton, Mass., Oct. 27, 1867; s. Whitman and Mehitable Doane (Kelley) C.; A.B., Harvard, 1889; A.M., 1895, Ph.D., 1897; U. of Leipzig, 1897-98; LL.D., Univ. of Maine, Orono, 1927; m. Alice Elizabeth Guild, July 13, 1897; children—Elizabeth Miller, George Davis, Margaret Taft. Teacher, Bristol Acad., Taunton, Mass., 1889-94, Lawrenceville (N.J.) Sch., 1898-99; asst. prof. comparative philology, Cornell U., 1899-1901; instr. Latin, Wesleyan U., 1901-02, asso. prof., 1902-05; prof. Latin, U. of Me., 1905-38, dean of grad. study, 1923-38, prof. of classics emeritus and dean of grad. study emeritus since 1938. Mem. Classical Assn. of New England, Am. Dialect Soc., Phi Beta Kappa, Phi Kappa Phi. Mason. Author: Selected Lives of Nepos; also papers in Harvard Classical Studies and proc. Am. Philol. Assn., Am. Dialect Notes. Home: Orono, Me. Died May 7, 1948.

CHASE, Joshua Coffin, citrus grower and shipper; b. Germantown, Pa., Sept. 23, 1858; s. Edwin Theodore and Lucia Toppan (Coffin) C.; A.B., Central High Sch. of Phila., 1878; m. Sarah Jane Whitner, Feb. 24, 1892 (died 1894); children—Franklin Whitner (dec.), Joshua Coffin (dec.); m. 2d, Mary C. Justice Lee, May 24, 1904) 1 dau., Cecilia Justice (Mrs. R. C. Lasbury, Jr). Accountant and salesman, Phila. and N.Y. City, 1878-84; one of the founders Chase & Company, Sanford, Fla., 1884; in Calif., 1897-1904, mng. dir. Earl Fruit Co., car lot distributors California fruits and vegetables; in 1907 filed complaints resulting in Interstate Commerce Commission decision reducing rates on Florida fruits and vegetables; incorporated Chase & Company, 1914, president until 1925, now chairman of the board; pres. Fla. Citrus Exchange, 1930-31; pres. Chase Investment Co., Chase & Co. Coöp.; director Growers & Shippers League of Florida, Realty Trust Co., Barnett Nat. Bank, Fla. Bank & Trust Co. at Winter Park. Awarded Silver Beaver, Boy Scouts of America, Rollins College decoration of honor, 1935; honorary trustee Rollins. Served on Liberty Loan coms., Jacksonville, Fla., World War I; mgr. Hoover Jacksonville European Relief Campaign. Secured for city of Jacksonville site for Memorial Park. Dir. Children's Home

Soc. of Fla. Member Newcomen Soc., Florida Hist. Soc. (pres. 1936, 37, 38, 39), Order Founders and Patriots of Am., S.A.R. Presbyterian. Mason. Clubs: Rotary (Orlando, Fla.); Megunticook Golf, Camden Yacht (Camden, Me.); University (Winter Park, Fla.). Home: 950 Palmer Av., Winter Park, Florida; (summer) Camden, Me. Office: Sanford, Fla. Died Jan. 7. 1948; buried at Sanford, Fla.

CHASE, Ray P., lawyer; b. Anoka, Minn., Mar. 12, 1880; s. Charles Edwin and Lena May (Giddings) C.; A.B., U. of Minn., 1903; student U. of Minn. Law Sch., 1904-05; B.L., St. Paul Coll. of Law, 1919; m. Lois McGaffey, Nov. 30, 1910; children—Lora Lee (Mrs. C. M. Watson), Phyllis Patricia (Mrs. S. J. Jablonski). Engaged in printing and pub. business, 1904-15; state auditor and land commr. of Minn., 1921-31; Rep. nominee for gov. of Minn., 1930; mem. 73d Congress (1933-35), Minn. at large. Head Ray P. Chase Research Bureau with offices in Chicago, Minneapolis, St. Paul and Washington; elected Railroad and Warehouse Commr. of Minn. November 7, 1944. Mem. Alpha Delta Phi, Delta Sigma Rho. Republican. Methodist. Has written several books and various tracts on tax, economic and political subjects. Home: Anoka, Minn. Died Sep. 18, 1948.

CHASSAIGNAC, Charles Louis, physician; b. New Orleans, Jan. 25, 1862; s. Eugene and Elvire (Porche) C.; M.D., U. of La., 1883; m. Jennie Morris, 1899; children—Elizabeth, Morris (dec.); m. 2d, Mathilde Labry, Oct. 10, 1906; children—Charles Louis, Peter Edward, Stanton Paul, Arthur W., Marie Elvire. Dean and prof. genito-urinary diseases, New Orleans Polyclinic (Grad. Sch. of Medicine, Tulane U.), 1889-1915; editor New Orleans Med. and Surg. Jour., 1896-1922; one of founders and pres. New Orleans Sanitarium and Training Sch. for Nurses; cons. surgeon Charity Hosp.; retired from active practice; supt. Eye, Ear, Nose and Throat Hosp. since 1922. Pres. Orleans Parish Med. Soc. for 3 yrs.; ex-pres. La. State Med. Soc. Author: Yellow Fever (trans. from Touatre), 1898. Contbr. to med. jours. Home: 1213 Marengo St., New Orleans. Died Apr. 1, 1936.

CHATFIELD-TAYLOR, Hobart C., author; b. Chicago, Mar. 24, 1865; s. Henry Hobart and Adelaide (Chatfield) Taylor; B.S., Cornell U., 1886; (Litt.D., Lake Forest [Ill.] Coll., 1913); m. Rose, d. late Senator Charles B. Farwell, of Ill., June 19, 1890 (died Apr. 5, 1918); m. 2d, Estelle Barbour Stillman, June 23, 1920. Editor America, 1888-90; consul of Spain at Chicago, 1892-94; Commander of the Order of Merit, Ecuador; Chevalier of the Legion of Honor and Officier de l'Instruction Publique, France; Chevalier Order of Saints Maurice and Lazarus and Chevalier Order of the Crown, Italy; Chevalier Order of Isabella the Catholic, Spain; Officer Order of the Crown, Belgium; Chevalier Order of St. James (for artistic, lit. and scientific merit), Portugal; Officer of the Bust of the Liberator, Venezuela. Fellow Royal Geog. Soc., Eng.; hon. pres. Soc. of Midland Authors; mem. Nat. Inst. Arts and Letters, New Hampshire Soc. of the Cincinnati, N.Y. Soc. of Colonial Wars, Kappa Alpha. Clubs: Union, Century, Coffee House (N.Y. City); Orleans (London); University (Chicago); Santa Barbara Club. Author: With Edge-Tools, 1891; An American Peeress, 1893; Two Women and a Fool, 1895; The Land of the Castanet, 1896; The Vice of Fools, 1898; The Idle Born, 1900; The Crimson Wing, 1902; Molière, a Biography, 1906; Fame's Pathway, 1909; Goldoni, a Biography, 1913; Chicago, 1917; Cities of Many Men, 1925; Tawny Spain, 1927; Charmed Circles—A Pageant of the Ages from Aspasia's Day to Ours, 1935. Contbr. to mags. and periodicals. Home: "Far Afield," 900 Hot Springs Road, Santa Barbara, Calif. Died Jan. 16, 1945.

CHEATHAM, Joseph J., naval officer; b. Tenn., Feb. 11, 1872. Entered Supply Corps, U.S. Navy, Sept. 6, 1894; promoted through grades to capt., July 1, 1917; apptd. paymaster gen., Apr., 1929, with rank of rear adm.; retired Mar. 1, 1936. Address Navy Dept., Washington, D.C. Died Sep. 8, 1942.

CHEATHAM, B. Frank, army officer; b. Beech Grove, Tenn., May 20, 1867; s. Gen. Benjamin Franklin and Anna Bell (Robertson) C.; student U. of the South, Sewanee, Tenn.; grad. Gen. Staff Sch., 1920, Army War Coll., 1921; m. Mary Warren Denman, Dec. 7, 1901; children—B. F. III, William D., Virginia. Served as maj., Tenn. Vol. Inf., Spanish-Am. War; commd. capt., Q.M. Corps, U.S.A., Feb. 2, 1901, and advanced through grades to col., July 1, 1920; q.m. gen., rank of maj. gen., 1926-30, retired. Served in P.I., Spanish-Am. War, in France, World War. Mem. Sigma Alpha Epsilon. Awarded D.S.M. (U.S.); decorated Comdr. Legion of Honor (France). Clubs: Army and Navy, Chevy Chase. Home: 2101 Connecticut Ave., N.W. Address: War Dept., Washington. Died Dec. 2, 1944.

CHELEY, Frank Howbert (che'le), boy worker; b. Colorado Springs, Colo., Feb. 10, 1889; s. Robert Austin and Agnes (Scott) C.; prep. edn. high sch., Colorado Springs; student Colo. Coll., 1908-11; m. Eva Belle Willson, of Colorado Springs, Apr. 26, 1911; children—Virginia Rose, Jack Austin. Dir. boys' work, Y.M.C.A., South Bend, Ind., 1907-15 metropolitan dir. boys' work, St. Louis, Mo., 1915-18; western rep. Internat. Com. Y.M.C.A.'s, Denver, Colo., 1918-21; gen. editor Modern Boy Activity, 20 vol. library devoted to boy training, 1921-24 owner and manager of the Cheley Colorado Camps since 1921; also owner and manager Boy Stuff Publications, Denver, since 1924; lecturer on boy problems. Member Phi Delta Theta. Author: Buffalo Roost, 1909; Three Rivers Kids, 1910; Told by the Campfire, 1911; Camp and Outing Activity (with G. C. Baker), 1912; Overland for Gold, 1914; Stories for Talks to Boys, 1918; Little Leads to Leadership, 1920; Scouting for Leadership, 1920; Campfire Yarns, 1921; The Job of Beinig a Dad, 1923; Mystery of Chimney Rock, 1924; Climbing Manward, 1924; Boy's Book of Campfires, 1926; Boy Riders of the Rockies, 1928; Take It From Dad, 1930; Bettering Boyhood, 1931; The Will to Win, 1931; Marked Trails for Boys, 1931; After All It's Up to You; Boy Days and Boy Ways, 1935; Our Social Assets, 1936; Our Leisure Time, 1936; The Business of Living, 1936; By Emberglow, 1937; These Boys of Ours, 1938; Yourself Inc., 1939. Contbr. to boys' mags. Home: 601 Steele St., Denver Colo. Died Dec. 18, 1941.

CHENEY, Charles, silk mfr.; b. Hartford, Conn., June 7, 1866; s. Frank Woodbridge and Mary (Bushnell) C.; prep. edn., St. Paul's Sch., Concord, N.H., 1882-85; student Mass. Inst. Tech., 1886; m. Mary Brainard, 1893; children—Marion (Mrs. Rodney G. Dennis), Ward; m. 2d, Mary Bell, 1901; children—Barbara (Mrs. Harry A. Watkins), Maribel (Mrs. John H. Humpstone), Sylvia (dec.). Began as apprentice Cheney Bros., silk mfrs., South Manchester, Conn., 1887, and advanced to chmn. bd.; retired, 1932. Pres. Silk Assn. America 8 yrs.; chmn. Nat. Industrial Conf. Bd., 3 yrs. Republican. Home: South Manchester, Conn. Died Apr. 11, 1942.

CHENEY, Charles Henry, city planner; b. of Am. parents, Rome, Italy, Feb. 11, 1884; s. (Lemuel) Warren and May Lucretia (Shepard) C.; A.B. in Architecture and Engring., U. of Calif., 1905; student Ecole des Beaux Arts, Paris, France, 1907-10; studied principal cities of France, Italy, Spain and Eng.; m. Cora B. Barnhart, Nov. 9, 1906; children—Warren Dewitt, Mrs. Charlotte Elizabeth Bosserman, Mrs. Frances Sasman. Worked in N.Y. City, with Charles A. Platt and others, 1910-12; consulting architect Berkeley Sch. Bd., 1913-20; consultant to Calif. State Commn. of Immigration and Housing, 1914, 1932-36; sec. Calif. Conf. on City Planning, 1914-28, v.p. 1929. Tech. consultant in city planning to Riverside, Santa Barbara, Monterey, Long Beach, Alameda, Berkeley, Fresno, Palo Alto and other Calif. cities; also Chandler, Ariz., Portland, Ore., Spokane, Wash., and for townsite and subdivision development at Cerritos Park and Atlantic Village in Long Beach, Palos Verdes Estates, Rancho Santa Fe, etc., in Calif., and for Classen Co., Oaklahoma City, Okla. Technical Consultant Housing Authority of Los Angeles County, 1928-29. Mem. bd. 3 engrs. which prepared major traffic street plan adopted by people of Los Angeles, Nov. 1924. Mem. Palos Verdes Art Jury, 1923-40; pres. bd. trustees Palos Verdes Library and Art Gallery. Mem. Am. Inst. of Planners, San Francisco Art Assn. (life), Alpha Delta Phi. Episcopalian. Author of Major Traffic Street Plan, Boulevard and Park System of Portland, Ore., 1920, Santa Barbara, 1925, Riverside, 1928; and of numerous city planning, housing, and zoning laws and ordinances adopted in Calif., Ore., and other states. Home and Office: Palos Verdes Estates, Calif. Died May 8, 1943.

CHENEY, Clarence Orion, psychiatrist; b. Poughkeepsie, N.Y., 1887; s. Albert Orion and Caroline (Adriance) C.; A.B., Columbia, 1908; M.D., Coll. Physicians and Surgeons, Columbia, 1911; m. Josephine Scott, June 7, 1915; 1 son, Robert Scott. Intern Manhattan State Hosp., 1911; asst. physician and pathologist, same, 1912-17; asst. dir. N.Y. State Psychiatric Inst., 1917-22; asst. supt. Utica State Hosp., 1922-26; supt. Hudson River State Hosp., Poughkeepsie, 1926-31; dir. N.Y. State Psychiatric Institute and Hosp., 1931-36; dir. New York Hospital, Westchester Div., 1936-46, emeritus since 1946; instructor in psychiatry, Cornell Med. Sch., 1917-22; lecturer in psychiatry, Syracuse Med. Sch., 1922-26; prof. clin. psychiatry, Columbia U., 1931-33, prof. psychiatry, 1933-36; prof. clin. psychiatry, Cornell Med. Sch., since 1936. Fellow Am. Psychiatric Assn. (sec.-treas. 1928-33; chmn. bd. examiners 1933-38; pres. 1935-36); mem. New York Psychiatric Soc. (pres. 1943-44), N.Y. Soc. for Clinical Psychiatry (pres. 1934-35), N.Y. Neurological Society, A.M.A., New York State Med. Soc. (ex-chmn. sect. on neurology and psychiatry), Westchester County Med. Soc., Assn. for Research in Nervous and Mental Diseases, Royal Medico-Psychol. Assn. England (corr. mem.), U. Council of Columbia U. (mem. 1935-36), Alpha Chi Rho, Alpha Omega Alpha, Sigma Xi; fellow N.Y. Acad. Medicine, American College of Physicians. Clubs: Kiwanis of Utica (pres. 1925-26); Rotary, University (White Plains). Editor: Outlines of Psychiatric Examinations, 1934. Asso. editor of Psychiatric Quarterly and Am. Jour. of Psychiatry. Address: 11 Burling Av., White Plains, New York Died Nov. 4, 1947.

CHENEY, Clifford D., mfr.; b. Manchester, Conn., Jan. 3, 1877; s. Knight D. and Ednah D. (Smith) Cheney; grad. Yale, 1898; m. Elizabeth Cheney, May 25, 1904. Chmn. Cheney Bros., silk mfg., South Manchester, Conn.; sec. and dir. Pioneer Parachute Co., Inc.; dir. Hartford Gas Co. Republican. Office: Cheney Bros., Manchester, Conn. Died Sept. 6, 1948.

CHENEY, Louis Richmond, capitalist; b. S. Manchester, Conn., Apr. 27, 1859; s. George Wells and Harriet K. (Richmond) C.; ed. pvt. and pub. schs., Manchester, and Hartford (Conn.) High School; m. Mary A. Robinson, 1890; m. 2d, Mrs. Margaret Crain, 1933. Began in silk mfg., 1879, and retired, 1893. Former pres. Hartford Chamber Commerce; pres. Hartford Hospital. Col. q.-m.-gen., Conn. Nat. Guard, 1895-97; maj. comdg. 1st Governor's Foot Guard, Hartford, 1898-1903, 1906-08. Councilman and alderman, City of Hartford, 1896-1902, mayor, 1912-14; state senator, 1915. Republican. Clubs: Hartford, Hartford Golf, Country (Hartford); Wellsway; Mountain Lake, Florida. Home: 40 Woodland St. Office: 36 Pearl St., Hartford, Conn. Died 1944.

CHENEY, Russell, artist; b. S. Manchester, Conn., Oct. 16, 1881; s. Knight Dexter and Ednah Dow (Smith) C.; grad. high sch., Hartford, Conn., 1899; A.B., Yale, 1904; art study, Art Students League, N.Y. City, 1904-07, Julian Academy, Paris, 1907-09; unmarried. Represented in collections of Palace of Fine Arts, San Francisco, Calif.; Newark (N.J.) Art Museum; Morgan Memorial, Hartford, Conn.; Boston Museum Fine Arts, Portland (Me.) Art Museum, Museum of New Mexico, Santa Fe. Pres. Art Students League, 1910-11. Mem. Psi Upsilon, Skull and Bones (Yale). Home: Kittery, Me. Died July 12, 1945.

CHENEY, Sherwood Alfred, army officer (ret.) b. S. Manchester, Conn., Aug. 24, 1873; s. John S. Cheney; grad. U.S. Mil. Acad., 1897, Army War Coll., 1907, Gen. Staff Coll., 1921; m. Louise Delano, Sept. 10, 1921 (died 1923); m. 2d, Charlotte S. Hopkins, Nov. 23, 1925. Comd. additional 2d lieut. engrs., June 11, 1897; 2d lieut., July 5, 1898; advanced through the grades to brig. gen., (temp.), Oct. 1, 1918; brig. gen. U.S. Army, Apr. 1, 1933. In field in Cuba, May-Sept., 1988; in Philippines, 1899-1901; participated in operations about San Fabian, later in Cavite Province and in expdn. to Nueva Caceres, and chief engr. officer Dept. of Southern Luzon; a.-d.-c. to Maj. Gen. J. C. Bates, at Chicago and St. Louis, 1903-05; duty with Gen. Staff, 1907-11; dir. Army Field Engr. Sch., 1914-15; on Mexican border, 1915-17; went to France on special commn., June 1917; comdr. 110th Regt. Engrs., 1918; rep. of chief of engrs. at Gen. Hdqrs., A.E.F., 1918; dir. Army Transport Service, later dir. gen. transportation, 1919; Am. mem. Inter-Allied Mil. Mission to Baltic Provinces, Nov. 1919-Jan. 1920, in Baltic States and Germany; mem. Gen. Staff Corps, 1921-24; military attaché to China, 1921-24 retired Aug. 24, 1937. Awarded D.S.M. "for services in organization of engineer units and repatriation of A.E.F. from France." Clubs: Hartford (Hartford, Conn.); Army and Navy (Washington). Home: 34 Park St., Manchester, Conn. Died March 13, 1949.

CHENEY, Thomas Perkins, lawyer; b. Ashland, N.H., Aug. 17, 1891; s. Dr. Jonathan Morrison and Lucy Ashland (Hughes) C.; student Holderness Sch. for Boys, Plymouth, N.H., 1907-09, Worcester (Mass.) Acad., 1909-12, Norwich U., Northfield, Vt., 1912; LL.B., Boston U., 1916; m. Ella Mills Wardner, Sept. 6, 1917; 1 son, Thomas Perkins. Admitted to N.H. bar, 1916; asst. in office of atty. gen. of N.H., 1916-17; mem. Young & Cheney, Laconia, N.H., 1919-25; practice alone, Laconia, 1925-35; mem. Cheney, Nighswander & Lord, Laconia, since 1935; county solicitor, Belknap Co., 1920-25; atty. gen. of N.H., 1935-40; v.p. and trustee Laconia Savings Bank; dir. Peoples Nat. Bank, Laconia. Served in U.S. Army, 1917-18; former maj. Judge Advocate General Department, New Hampshire National Guard. Rep. floor leader N.H. Ho. of Reps., 1927; chmn. Rep. State Com., 1926-28, 1934-35; del. at large Rep. Nat. Conv., 1928, 1936. Trustee Worcester (Mass.) Acad. Mem. N.H. Bar Assn. (past pres.), N.H. Bankers Assn. (past pres.), N.H. Savings Banks Assn. (past pres.), Am. Law. Inst. (life), N.H. Vets. Assn. (past pres.), Am. Legion (1st comdr. Frank W. Willains Post No. 1), Grange. Republican. Conglist. Mason, Elk, K. of P. Home: 16 Gale Av. Office: 507 Main St., Laconia, N.H. Died June 11, 1942.

CHERINGTON, Paul Terry, marketing expert; b. Ottawa, Kan., Oct. 31, 1876; s. Fletcher Bailey and Caroline E. (Reed) C.; Ohio Wesleyan U., 1893-97; B.S., U. of Pa., 1902, A.M., 1908; m. Marie Louise Richards, Aug. 16, 1911; children—Charles Richards, Paul Whiton. Asst. editor The Manufacturer (pub. by Mfrs.' Club, Phila.), 1897-1902; editor Publs. of Phila. Commercial Museum, 1902-08; instr., 1908-13, asst. prof., 1913-18, prof. marketing, 1918-19, Graduate Sch. of Business Adminstrn. (Harvard); with textile sect. div. of planning and statistics, U.S. Shipping Bd., Washington, D.C., 1918; sec.-treas. Nat. Assn. Wool Mfrs., Boston, 1919-22; editor Quarterly Bull. of Nat. Assn. of Wool Mfrs., 1919-22; dir. research, J. Walter Thompson Co., advt. agency, 1922-31; prof. marketing and distribution, Grad. Sch. of Business, Stanford U., 1928-29; distbn. consultant service, 1931-39; lecturer on marketing, Univ. of Chicago, 1914, New York U., 1932-35; partner McKinsey & Co., management consultants, New York, since Nov. 1939. Chmn. com. on maintenance of resale prices Chamber of Commerce U.S.A., 1914-16; chairman sub. committee on the Census of Distribution, Chamber Commerce U.S.A., conducting distribution census in 11 cities, mem. Advisory Com. of U.S. Bur. of the Census. Chmn. Census Com. on Met. Dist., 1933-40. Mem. Am. Econ. Assn., Am. Statis. Assn. (v.p. 1936), Am. Marketing Assn. (pres. 1931-32), Nat. Assn. Teachers of Marketing and Advertising (past pres.), Soc. for Advancement of Management (pres. of N.Y. chapter 1937), Market Research

Council (past pres.), Alpha Tau Omega, Alpha Delta Sigma. Republican. Conglist. Clubs: Bankers, Harvard, Town Hall (New York). Author: Advertising as a Business Force, 1912, (brochure) The Boston Market Situation, 1915; The First Advertising Book, 1916; The Wool Industry, 1917; (brochure) The Port of Boston—Its Problems, 1917; The Elements of Marketing, 1920; (brochure) Some Commercial Aspects of Styles and Fashion, 1924; (brochure) College Education for Business, 1925; Retail Shopping Areas of Walter Thompson Co., 1927; The Consumer Looks at Advertising, 1928; Commercial Problems of the Woolen and Worsted Industries, 1932; People's Wants and How to Satisfy Them, 1935. Editor: Population and Its Distribution, fifth edit., 1931. Home: 35 Claremont Av. Office: 60 E. 42d St., New York, N.Y. Died Apr. 1943.

CHERRIE, George Kruck, field naturalist; b. Knoxville, Ia., Aug. 22, 1865; s. Martin and Agnes (Breckenridge) C.; ed. Knoxville, Ia., and State Agrl. Coll., 1880; m. Stella M. Bruere, Dec. 1, 1895; m. 2d, Esther Atwell, Jan. 12, 1934. Asst. taxidermist, U.S. Nat. Museum, 1888, accepting position in Am. Museum, New York later; appointed taxidermist and curator of birds, mammals and reptiles, Nat. Museum, Costa Rica, 1889; asst. curator ornithology, in charge of dept., Field Museum of Natural History, Chicago, 1894-97; conducted explorations in Valley of the Orinoco for Lord Rothschild, 1897-99; ornithol. explorations, for Tring Museum, in French Guiana, 1902-03; explorations in Trinidad and Valley of Orinoco, for Brooklyn Inst. Museum, 1905 and 1907; curator ornithology and mammalogy, Brooklyn Inst. Arts and Sciences, 1899-1911; mem. Am. Museum expdn. to Colombia, S.A., valley of the Magdalena River and the high interior, 1913; rep. Am. Museum Natural History on Roosevelt expdn. through So. Am., 1913-14; naturalist Collins-Day S. Am. expdn., 1914-15; dir. Cherrie-Roosevelt South American expdn. for Am. Museum Natural History, 1916-17; South Am. service for U.S. Bur. Naval Intelligence, 1918-19; a leader Anthony-Cherrie expdn. to Ecuador for Am. Museum Natural History, 1920-21; Cherrie expdn. to Ecuador for same, 1921; Mazaroni River diamond fields, British Guiana, 1922; expdn. to Central Brazil, 1924; naturalist Roosevelt-Simpson Asiatic expdn. for Field Museum, Chinese Turkestan, 1925-26; leader Marshall Field Brazilian expdn., 1926. Mem. Am. Ornithologists' Union; hon. fellow Am. Museum Natural History, 1921; Boone and Crocket Club, New York; Explorers Club, New York; Ends of the Earth Club, New York; Camp Fire Club of Chicago; hon. Boy Scout Field Museum, 1926. Wrote on Central American Birds with descriptions of new species, etc., in The Auk and Proc. U.S. Nat. Museum, 1890-96; also The Ornithology of Santo Domingo (Publs. Field Museum of Natural History, Chicago), 1896; New Birds of the Orinoco Region and of Trinidad, 1909; Dark Trails, Adventures of a Naturalist, 1930. Home: Newfane, Vt. Died Jan. 20, 1948.

CHERRY, C. Waldo, clergyman; b. Pittsburgh, Pa., May 17, 1873; s. John D. and Katherine (Stebbins) C.; B.A., Princeton, 1894; B.D., Western Theol. Sem., Pittsburgh, 1897; D.D., U. of Rochester, 1921; LL.D., Beaver College, Jenkintown, Pa., 1933; m. Sarah Ann Fleming, June 30, 1898; children—Walter F., Katherine F. (Mrs. J. Harold Thomson), Ralph Waldo. Pastor, Natrona (Pa.) Presbyn. Ch., 1897-1901, Parnassus, Pa., 1901-03, Second Presbyn. Ch., Troy, N.Y., 1903-14, Central Presbyn. Ch., Rochester, N.Y., 1914-22, Pine St. Presbyn. Ch., Harrisburg, Pa., 1922-39. Chaplain Co. 23, N.Y.N.G., Troy, 1903-14; Y.M.C.A. chaplain, Camp Dix, Wrightstown, N.J., 1917. Trustee Gen. Assembly Presbyn. Ch. U.S.A.; mem. Bd. Foreign Missions, same. Republican. Mason (32°). Clubs: Torch, Eclectic, Country (Harrisburg); Juniata (Mt. Union, Pa.). Home: 300 Parkway Road, Harrisburg, Pa. Died Oct. 10, 1944.

CHERRY, James William, judge; b. Hancock County, Ill., Apr. 5, 1872; s. Alfred Newton and Mary Ellen (Banks) C.; grad. high sch., Anthony, Kan., 1892; studied law in father's office, 1890-93; m. Louise Keller, June 21, 1898; children—Alfred Keller, Winona, Louise, Mary Ellen, James William, Keller Banks. Admitted to Utah bar, 1893, and practiced at Salt Lake City 2 yrs.; practiced in Manti, Utah, 1895-1900, La Grande, Ore., 1900-02, Mt. Pleasant, Utah, 1902-23; dist. atty. 7th Jud. Dist. of Utah, 1912-16; justice Supreme Court of Utah, term 1923-32. Republican. Unitarian. Grand Master of Masons, of Utah, 1914. Home: 46 W. 2d St., Mesa, Ariz. Died March 23, 1949; buried at Mesa, Ariz.

CHERRY, Ulysses Simpson Grant, lawyer; b. Lewistown, O., Dec. 2, 1863; s. Amos and Elizabeth (Smith) C.; grad. Ohio Normal U., Ada, 1885; read law in offices of William H. West, Bellefontaine, O., until Sept. 1886; LL.B., Law Dept., Columbian (now George Washington) U., Washington, D.C., 1887 (first prize in contest on legal essays); m. S. Winnifred Clyde, Sept. 12, 1888 (died May 16, 1900); children—Ulysses S. G., M. Lucile, S. Genevieve, R. Winnifred; m. 2d, Louie A. Palmer, Feb. 6, 1906; 1 dau., Annis V. Practiced at Sioux Falls, S.D., 1887—; spl. asst. counsel 3 atty.-gens. of S.D.; represented the state in noteworthy case, in re McClellan estate, in U.S. Supreme Court, U.S. Circuit Court Appeals, State Supreme, Circuit and County courts, covering period of 18 yrs. Practice has extended to state and federal courts in 20 western states. Mem. Dem. State Central and Campaign coms., 1896; nominee for U.S. senator, 1920, 24, 32. Episcopalian. Mem. Am. Bar Assn. (ex-mem. gen. counsel and exec. com.), S.D. State Bar Assn. Supreme representative from S.D. to Supreme Lodge, K. of P., for 16 yrs. Mem. S.D. State Council Defense, World War; founder and organizer of Atlantic, Yellowstone & Pacific Highway. Clubs: Dakota, Elks (Sioux Falls). Home: 1504 S. Main Av. Office: 1st Nat. Bank Bldg., Sioux Falls, S.D. Died Mar. 22, 1943.

CHERRY, Walter L., dairy machinery; b. Troy Mills, Ia., Jan. 9, 1874; s. John George and Mary Ann (Miles) C.; student Coe Coll., Cedar Rapids, Ia., 1 yr.; m. Laura Fox White, Dec. 14, 1905; children—Virginia (Mrs. David J. Luick), Isabelle (now deceased), Walter L. Began with his father, 1891, in the manufacture of dairy machinery and supplies, inc., 1898, as J. G. Cherry Co., of which was sec. until 1901, pres., 1901-28; pres. Cherry-Burrell Corp., 1928-44, chmn. exec. com. since Jan. 1944. Trustee Coe Coll. Dir. Nat. Dairy Assn., Nat. Dairy Council, American Dairy Federation; member Chamber Commerce U.S.A. (ex-director). Ia. Conservation League, Ia. State Hist. Soc. Republican. Presbyn. Clubs: Union League, Indian Hill, Electric (Chicago); Cedar Rapids Country. Home: 80 Indian Hill Road, Winnetka, Ill. Office: 427 W. Randolph St., Chicago, Ill. Died Feb. 5, 1946.

CHESNEY, Cummings C., elec. engr.; b. Selinsgrove, Pa., Oct. 28, 1863; s. John C. and Jane (McFall) C.; B.S., Pa. State Coll., 1885; taught mathematics and chemistry, Doylestown Sem. and Pa. State Coll., 1885-88; m. Elizabeth Cutler, 1891; children—Malcolm M., Elizabeth, Margaret, Katherine, Barbara. Joined William Stanley's laboratory force, Great Barrington, Mass., 1888; with U.S. Elec. Lighting Co., Newark, 1889-90; one of incorporators, 1890, Stanley Elec. Mfg. Co., Pittsfield, Mass.; 1st v.p. and chief engr. Stanley Electric Mfg. Co., 1904; was 1st v.p. and chief engr. Stanley-G. I. Electric Mfg. Co.; mgr. Pittsfield works of Gen. Electric Co., 1906-27; v.p. and chmn. mfg. com., Gen. Electric Co.; pres. Berkshire Morris Plan Bank, 1931-35, Berkshire Trust Co., 1934-39; pres. Pittsfield Coal Gas Co.; hon. v.p. Gen. Electric Co.; dir. G.E. Employees Securities Corp., Mass. Mut. Life Ins. Co., Agrl. Nat. Bank, Pittsfield, Springfield Fire and Marine Insurance Co., N.E. Fire Ins. Co., Sentinel Fire Ins. Co., Boston & Albany R.R. Co. Pioneer in many elec. improvements; laid out first polyphase power transmission plant to be put into successful operation in America; also pioneer in designing alternating current generators for high voltages, and many other developments. Pres. Am. Inst. E.E., 1926-27; mem. Soc. of Arts, London. Awarded Edison medal by Am. Inst. E.E., 1922. Home: 74 Dawes Av., Pittsfield, Mass. Died Nov. 27, 1947.

CHESNUT, James Lyons, clergyman; b. Coulterville, Ill., July 11, 1897; s. James Lyons and Jane (Wallace) C.; A.B., Cedarville (O) Coll., 1918, A.M., 1919, D.D., 1927; B.D., Princeton Theol. Sem.; m. Irene Wright, Oct. 19, 1920; children—James Lyons, III, Donald Blair. Ordained to ministry of Presbyn. Ch., U.S.A.; pastor successively at Covington, Ohio, Fort Wayne, Ind., Richmond, Ind., First Presbyn. Ch., Fairmont, W.Va., now pastor Bellevue Presbyn. Ch., Pittsburgh, Pa. Trustee Cedarville Coll., Davis and Elkins Coll., Elkins, W.Va. Mason (32°). Home: 25 N. Howard Av., Bellevue, Pittsburgh, Pa. Deceased.

CHESTER, Frederick Dixon, bacteriologist; b. San Domingo, Hayti, Oct. 8, 1861; s. Edwin Smith and Elizabeth (Walthall) C.; B.S., Cornell, 1882, M.S., 1885; m. Emma L. Sherwood, June, 1883. Prof. geology and botany, Del. Coll., 1882-9; mycologist and bacteriologist, Del. Agrl. Expt. Sta., and bacteriologist, in charge of the State bacteriol. and pathol. lab., 1899-1906; in business since 1906. Fellow A.A.A.S.; mem. Am. Geol. Soc., Soc. for the Promotion of Agrl. Science, Am. Bacteriol. Soc. Author: Manual of Determinative Bacteriology, 1901. Also monographs on the geology of Del. and Eastern Md., and papers and reports on mycology and bacteriology. Address: Chester Springs, Pa. Died Jan. 1, 1943.

CHESTER, Wayland Morgan, zoölogist; b. Noank, Conn., Mar. 10, 1870; s. Charles I. and Harriet (Morgan) C.; A.B., Colgate, 1894, A.M., 1896; student Harvard U., 1909-10; Sc.D., Hillsdale (Mich.) Coll., 1926; m. Laura Davis, Aug. 30, 1897; children—Morgan Elliott, Harry Wilbur, Margaret Ashbey, Albert Brigham. Asst. in geology and natural history, 1894-96, instr. biology, Colgate U., 1896-1900, prof. since 1900. Republican. Baptist. Fellow A.A.A.S.; mem. Am. Soc. Zoölogists, Am. Micros. Soc., Am. Assn. Univ. Profs., Phi Beta Kappa, Beta Theta Pi. Contbr. papers on Cœlenterata. Home: Hamilton, N.Y. Died Feb. 7, 1945.

CHEW, Oswald, lawyer, trustee; b. Philadelphia, May 24, 1880; s. Samuel and Mary Johnson (Brown) C.; student William Penn Charter Sch., 1893-95; grad. St. Paul's Sch., Concord, N.H., 1898; B.A., Harvard, 1903; studied law at Harvard and U. of Pa., 1903-05; m. Ada Knowlton, June 3, 1908. Admitted to Pa. bar, 1907, and practiced in Phila.; dir. Food Gardens Assn., Inc. (for the unemployed), Phila., since 1932; pres. Mfrs. Land & Improvement Co. since 1933; pres. Radnor Realty Co., pres. Gloucester Land Co. Attended Camp Plattsburg, N.Y., 1915-16; mem. Commn. for Relief in Belgium, 1916 (awarded Commn.'s medal); volunteer ambulance driver, France, 1916-17; with Am. Field Service in Argonne and Verdun sectors; civilian interpreter, G.H.Q., A.E.F., 1917; commd. lt. and assigned to liaison service, 1918; hon. disch., St. Aignan, France, 1919; capt. cav. U.S. Army Res., 1928. Awarded Croix de Guerre (France), 1917; field service medal by French Ministry of War, 1919; Medaille Commemorative de la Grande Guerre, 1922; French Victory medal, 1924; Chevalier French Legion of Honor, 1925; promoted Officer same. (vice-pres. Fed. Alliance Française for Eastern States), Am. Legion, Hist. Soc. of Pa.; founder mem. "France Forever." Rep. Episcopalian. Clubs: Philadelphia, Automobile of Phila., Harvard (New York); Franklin Inn. Editor: France, Courageous and Indomitable, 1925; Stroke of the Moment, 1926. Author: For a Better World Tomorrow. Home: Radnor, Pa.; (summer) Marion, Mass. Office: Commercial Trust Bldg., Philadelphia, Pa. Died Dec. 6, 1949.

CHEYDLEUR, Frederic D(aniel) (shād-lûr'), professor French; b. Ballston Spa, N.Y., Jan. 30, 1879; s. John Baptist and Genevieve Catherine (L'Espérance) C.; A.B., Williams, 1905; Docteur d'Université, Univ. of Grenoble, France, 1914; m. Minnie Ashley Payne, June 17, 1911; children—Benjamin Frederic, Eleanor Payne, Raymond Dudley. Head of modern lang. dept., Peekskill (N.Y.) Mil. Acad., 1905-07, Worcester (Mass.) Acad., 1907-12; instr. in French, Williams, 1914-18; asst. prof. French, W.Va. U., 1918-19; asst. prof. French, U. of Wis., 1919-21, asso. prof., 1921-30, professor since 1930, also director of placement and attainment examinations, since 1935; teacher or lecturer, summer sessions, Cornell University, 1917, New York State College for Teachers, 1918, W.Va. U., 1919, U. of Ill., 1921, 23, 25, U. of Wash. and Colo. State Teachers Coll., 1929, U. of Chicago, 1930. Mem. Modern Lang. Assn. America, Am. Assn. Univ. Profs., Nat. Fedn. Modern Lang. Teachers, Wis Assn. Modern Fgn. Lang. Teachers (pres. 1933-34), Wis. State Teachers Assn., Am. Assn. Teachers of French (v.p. 1934-37; pres. 1937-38), Société des Amis de la Bibliothèque Nationale et des Grandes Bibliotheques de France, Phi Delta Kappa Fraternity. Presbyterian. Mason (32°). Author: Essai sur l'Evolution des Doctrines de M. Georges Sorel, 1914; The American Council French Grammar Test-Selection Type, 1927; French Idiom List, 1929. Co-author of Am. Council on Edn., French Reading Tests, 1937-39. Contbr. lit. and research articles to N.Y. Herald-Tribune Books, Philosophical Review, Modern Lang. Jour., North Am. Review, Saturday Review of Literature, French Review, Publs. of Modern Lang. Assn. Am., Publs. Modern Foreign Lang. Study, Jour. Ednl. Research, etc. Contbr. to A Commemorative Volume by The Inst. for Research in English Teaching, Tokyo, 1933. Collaborator in Experiments and Studies in Modern Language Teaching, 1934. Editor of Ball, Meylan, Ball's Introduction to French Grammar, 1938; Placement Tests in Foreign Language, Univ. of Wis., 1930-43; Criteria of Effective Teaching in Basic French Courses at the U. of Wis., 1945. Home: 2109 Rowley Av., Madison, Wis. Died June 11, 1949; buried at Forest Hill Cemetary, Madison, Wis.

CHEYNEY, Edward Gheen (chān'ē), forester; b. Washington, D.C., Nov. 24, 1878; s. Rufus Taylor and Lucie Marie Brunin (de Bolmar) C.; A.B., Cornell U., 1900; studied Yale Forest Sch., 1904-05; m. Harriet Frances Porter, Sept. 11, 1907; children—Virginia Brunin, Lucie Marie. With U.S. Forest Service, 1903-04; assistant, University of Minnesota College of Forestry, 1905, assistant professor, 1907, professor and dir., 1910-25, prof., 1925-47, retired. Fellow Soc. Am. Foresters; mem. Sigma Xi, Alpha Zeta, Gamma Sigma Delta, Xi Simga Pi. Episcopalian. Club: Campus. Author: The Farm Woodlot (with J. P. Wentling), 1914; Scott Burton, Forester, 1917; Scott Burton on the Range, 1920; Scott Burton and the Lumber Thieves, 1922; Scott Burton—Logger, 1923; Scott Burton in the Blue Ridge, 1924; Scott Burton's Claim, 1926; What Tree Is That?, 1927; Matu, the Iroquois, 1928; Sylvics, 1929; This is Our Land (with T. S. Hansen), 1940; American Silvics and Silviculture, 1941. Home: Apalachicola, Fla. Deceased.

CHEYNEY, Edward Potts, univ. prof.; b. Wallingford, Pa., Jan. 17, 1861; s. Waldron J. and Fannie (Potts) C.; A.B., U. of Pa., 1883, A.M., 1884, LL.D., 1911; student vis. German univs. and student in British Mus.; m. Gertrude Squires, June 10, 1886. Now prof. history emeritus, U. of Pa. Author: Social Changes in England in the 16th Century, 1896; Social and Industrial History of England, 1901; Short History of England, 1904; European Background of American History, 1904; Readings in English History, 1908; History of England from the Defeat of the Armada to the Death of Elizabeth, 1913. Also monographs and rev. articles on hist. and economic subjects. Home: R.D. 3, Media, Pa. Died Feb. 1, 1947.

CHILD, Clarence Griffin, univ. prof.; b. Newport, R.I., Mar. 22, 1864; s. Rev. William Spencer (S.T.D.) and Jessie Isabella (Davis) C.; A.B., Trinity Coll., Hartford, 1886, A.M., 1891; U. of Munich, 1891-92, Johns Hopkins, 1892-95, Ph.D., 1895; L.H.D., Trinity Coll., 1902; LL.D., Washington Coll., Md., 1916; m. Elizabeth Reynolds, June 20, 1899; children—Elizabeth Reynolds, William Spencer. Coll. prep. teacher, 1881-90; instr. English and mathematics, Trinity Coll., 1890-91; asst. editor, New Worcester's Dictionary, 1895-1903; instr. English, 1896-1901, asst. prof., 1901-06, prof. since 1906, dean Grad. Sch.,

Univ. of Pa., 1904-07. Non-resident lecturer in Anglo-Saxon, Bryn Mawr Coll., 1900-01. Mem. Modern Lang. Assn. Am., Am. Dialect Soc., Psi Upsilon. Independent Republican. Episcopalian. Author: John Lyly and Euphuism, 1894; Palatal Diphthongization of Stem Vowels in the Old English Dialects, 1903. Editor: Malory's Merlin and Sir Balin, 1904, etc. Translator: Beowulf, 1904, etc. Contbr. tech. articles, stories, etc., to periodicals. Home: Merion, Pa. Died Sept. 20, 1948.

CHILD, Eleanor Dodge, educator; b. Newburyport, Mass., Nov. 13, 1902; d. Robert Gray and Alice (Childs) Dodge; student Winsor Sch., Boston, 1912-20; A.B., Vassar Coll., Poughkeepsie, N.Y., 1925; student, Columbia U. Teachers Coll., 1929-30; m. Josiah Humphrey Child, Mar. 27, 1941; 1 son, Edwin Dodge, 1941. Teacher, Winsor Sch., Boston, 1925-29, Brearley Sch., New York City, 1930-31; warden, Vassar Coll., 1931-40, trustee since 1942. Mem. Board Y.W.C.A. (Boston). Home: 33 W. Cedar St., Boston. Died Apr. 5, 1948.

CHILDERS, Sylvester Earl, clergyman; b. Palo Pinto County, Texas, May 28, 1886; s. Thomas Lazarus and Mary Elizabeth (Russell) C.; A.B., Eugene (Ore.) Bible U., 1910, B.D. and B.O., 1911, D.D., 1925; A.B., U. of Ore., 1912; m. Velma Dale Inman, July 12, 1911; children— Rowena Dale, Earl Gerald, Donald Thomas, Milton Edward. Ordained ministry Disciples of Christ Ch., 1912; pastor Dean Av. Ch., Spokane, 1912-13; supt. missions, Inland Empire (western U.S.), 1913-15; pastor Fruitville Ch., Oakland, Calif., 15-17 Albany, Ore., 1917-18; prof. N.T. exegesis and archeology, Eugene Bible U., 1918-29, pres., 1929-34; pastor First Christian Ch., Eugene, since 1928; now doing special lecture and stewardship work in evangelistic field. Pastor of Garfield Park Christian Church, Santa Cruz, Calif., 1943; dean Bible Dept., Milligan (Tenn.) Coll., 1945-46. Author: Bible Messages for the Modern Mind, 1927; also series of lectures entitled "The Story of the Church"; contbr. on religious subjects, writer of Bible-school lesson material. Address: 45 Errett Circle, Santa Cruz, Calif. Died March 29, 1948; buried at Portland, Ore.

CHILDRESS, L(evi) Wade (chil'drĕs); b. in Murfreesboro, Tenn., Mar. 20, 1876; s. William Sumner and Inez (Wade) C.; student pub. schs., Murfreesboro, 1882-92; m. Lucy Marshall Turner Oct. 7, 1903; children—Wade Turner, Fielding Turner, Lila Marshall (Mrs. Kenneth B. Wick, Jr.). Clerk St. Louis Drayage Co., 1893-94; with various railroads, 1894-1902; with Columbia Terminals Co. since 1902, now chmn. bd.; organized Miss. Valley Barge line 1929, pres. 1929-47, chmn. bd. since 1947; dir. of Mercantile Commerce Bank & Trust Co., Mercantile Commerce Nat. Bank; pres. Laclede Gas Light Co. Former pres. St. Louis Community Fund; dir. Y.M.C.A.; chmn. bd. Govtl. Research Inst., trustee Central Inst. for the Deaf Presbyn. Orphanage of Mo. Mem. St. Louis Chamber of Commerce. Independent. Presbyterian. Mason (32°). Clubs: Noonday, Round Table, Racquet, St. Louis Country (St. Louis). Home: 9030 Clayton Rd., Clayton, Mo. Office: 1017 Olive St., St. Louis, Mo. Died Jan. 31, 1950.

CHILDS, Ross Renfroe, agronomist; b. Wayside, Ga., Jan 22, 1888; s. William Simpson and Nancy Antonette (Walker) C.; B.S.A., U. of Ga., 1912, M.S.A., 1913; m. Claudia Lamb, Nov. 29, 1923. Instr. agronomy, Ga. State Coll. Agr., 1913-14; scientific asst., Office of Creal Investigations, U.S. Dept. Agr., 1914-18; prof. agronomy, in charge cotton industry, U. of Ga. State Coll. Agr., May 1919-July 1934, exec. sec. cotton adjustment, under Agrl. Adjustment Administrn., 1934-39; extension agronomist, Ga. Agr. Extension Service, since 1939. Served as 2d lt. Air Service, U.A. Army, 1918-19. Fellow A.A.A.S.; mem. Am. Soc. Agronomy. Am. Genetic Assn., Ga. Acad. Science, Phi Kappa Phi. Democrat. Baptist. Mason (32°, Shriner). Home: 175 University Drive, Athens, Ga. Died Feb. 20, 1942.

CHILES, Harry Linden (chīlz), osteopathic physician; b. Louisa, Va., July 1, 1867; s. Henry and Isabella Pottie (Hunter) C.; student Louisa Acad., 1884-90; D.O., Am. Sch. of Osteopathy (pres. grad. class), 1901; m. Anne Clare, Dec. 20, 1894; children—Henry, Ellen Clare (Mrs. J. H. R. Pickett). Editor and pub. local newspaper and teacher pub. schs., 1887-90; business mgr. and editor Roanoke (Va.) Evening World, 1894-95; supt. Fanning Sch. for Girls, Nashville, Tenn., 1895-99; studied law and admitted to Va. bar, 1889; sec.-treas. Old Dominion Investment Co., Roanoke, Va., 1890-94; removed to Auburn, N.Y., 1901 and began practice of osteopathy; asso. editor Jour. of Osteopathy (1st osteopathic pub.), 1900-01; sec., exec. officer and editor Jour. of Am. Osteopathic Assn. and Osteopathic Mag., 1903-23. Mem. Am. Osteopathic Assn. (sec. since 1901), New Jersey State and Essex County osteopathic societies; N.Y. State Osteopathic Soc. (sec.-trustee, 1902-04). Active in founding A. T. Still Research Inst. and Osteopathic Foundation, 1907. Member Sigma Sigma Phi (honorary fraternity). Author many addresses and professional articles; contbr. of "Osteopathy" in Reference Handbook of the Medical Sciences; and chapters in volume, The Lengthening Shadow of Dr. A. T. Still, by Dr. A. G. Hildreth, 1938. Awarded Distinguished Service certificate by Am. Osteopathic Assn., 1929. Democrat. Disciple of Christ. Mason. Clubs: Atlas, Rotary (since 1916). Home: Crozet, Va. Died July 17, 1945.

CHILTON, Robert S.; b. Washington, D.C., June 19, 1861; s. Robert S. and Mary Virginia (Brent) C.; ed. pub. schs., Niagara Falls, Ont., and by private instruction; m. Mary E. Dooly, Oct. 12, 1898 (died May 25, 1926); children—Robert Brent (dec.), Virginia, Maurice. Clerk Dept. State, 1877-80; pvt. sec. to V.P. Levi P. Morton, 1889-93; chief clk. Dept. State, 1893; chief of Consular Bur., Dept. State, 1895-1902; made tour of inspection of Am. consulates throughout the world, 1897-98; consul at Toronto, Can., 1905-Oct. 1913, resigned. Mem. Consular Reorganization Bd., 1906. Clubs: Metropolitan, Arts, Chevy Chase (Washington, D.C.); Toronto (Toronto). Home: Washington, D.C. Address: Hotel Cecil, San Francisco, Calif. Died Apr. 3, 1947.

CHITTENDEN, Kate S., musician; b. of American parents, Hamilton, Ont., Can., Apr. 17, 1856; d. Curtis Strong and Caroline Young (Peterson) Chittenden; ed. Helmuth Coll., London, Ont., Can., 1870-73; unmarried. Teacher of piano and organist, Helmuth Coll., 1874-76; taught pvtly. in N.Y. since 1876; organist and choir dir. Calvary Bapt. Ch., New York, 1879-1906; lecturer New York Bd. of Edn., 1892-1919; in charge of music, Catherine Aiken School, Stamford, Conn., 1890-1924; mem. staff Metropolitan Coll. of Music, 1892-1900; dean of faculty of Am. Inst. of Applied Music (successor to the Metropolitan Coll. of Music), 1900-33; head of piano dept. Vassar Coll., Poughkeepsie, N.Y., 1899-1930; lecturer on musical subjects. Co-founder Am. Guild of Organists; founder and hon. dir. Hartley House Settlement Music Sch. ending 74 years of piano teaching; hon. mem. Sorosis Club. Episcopalian. Composer for piano. Home: 853 7th Av., New York 19, N.Y. Died Sep. 16, 1949.

CHITTENDEN, Russell Henry, univ. prof. and dir.; b. New Haven, Conn., Feb. 18, 1856; s. Horace Horatio and Emily Eliza (Doane) C.; Ph. B., Sheffield Scientific Sch. (Yale) 1875, Ph.D., 1880; student Heidelberg U., 1878-79; LL.D., U. of Toronto, 1903, U. of Birmingham, 1911, Wash. U., 1915, Yale, 1922; Sc.D., U. of Pa., 1904; m. Gertrude Louise Baldwin, June 20, 1877; children—Edith Russell, Alfred Knight (dec.), Lilla Millard (Mrs. Harry Gray Barbour). Asst. 1874-77, inst., 1877-78, 1879-82, prof. physiol. chemistry, 1882-1922 (emeritus), dir. Sheffield Scientific Sch., 1898-1922, all of Yale; lecturer physiol. chemistry, Columbia, 1898-1903. Mem. referee bd. of consulting scientific experts to Sec. of Agr. Hon. M.D., Conn. State Med. Society, 1934. Mem. Nat. Acad. Sciences, Am. Philos. Soc., Société des Sciences Médicales et Naturelles dé Bruxelles; corr. mem. Société de Biologie, Paris; pres. Am. Soc. of Naturalists, 1893, Am. Physiol. Soc., 1895-1904, Am. Soc. Biol. Chemists, 1907. Fellow Am. Acad. Arts and Sciences; hon. fellow N.Y. Acad. of Medicine, 1930. Mem. advisory com. on food utilization; mem. exec. com. Nat. Research Council, 1917; U.S. rep. on Inter-Allied Scientific Food Commn. at London, Paris and Rome, 1918. Clubs: Graduate (New Haven); Yale (New York). Editor: Studies in Physiological Chemistry, 4 vols., 1884, 1901. Author: Digestive Proteolysis, 1895; Physiological Economy in Nutrition, 1905; Nutrition of Man, 1907; History of the Sheffield Scientific School (2 vols.), 1928; Development of Physiological Chemistry in the United States, 1930; also many papers on physiol. subjects in Am. and foreign jours. Home: 83 Trumbull St., New Haven, Conn. Died Dec. 26, 1943.

CHRESTMAN, Marion Nelson, lawyer; b. Vanzandt County, Tex., Sept. 29, 1877; s. Larkin Marion and Louise Malone (Allen) C.; student law dept., Valparaiso (Ind.) Coll., 1903 to 1904; m. Mary Elizabeth Wathen, Apr. 15, 1909. Taught sch., 1900-04; law apprentice Burgess & Burgess, 1904-07; mem. firm Burgess, Burgess & Chrestman (now Chrestman, Brundidge, Fountain, Elliott & Bateman), Dallas, Tex., since 1908. Pres. Tex. Civil Judicial Council (16 yrs.), 1929-41; mem. Tex. Relief Com. (ex-officio mem.); mem. advisory com. to Supreme Court of Tex. to write procedural civil statutes into rules and rewrite rules of procedure; chmn. City Plan Com. of Dallas, 1939; mem. Bd. of Edn., Dallas, 1918-22; v.-chmn. Civil Service Bd. of Dallas, 1931-33. Mem. Dallas Bar Assn. (pres. 1926-27), Am. and State of Tex. and Am. bar assns., Internat. Assn. of Ins. Counsels (pres. 1936-37). Democrat. Baptist. Mason (32°; Blue Lodge; Scottish Rite; Shriner). Club: Lakewood Country (Dallas). Author: Annual Law Reports of State of Texas since 1929. Home: 6703 Country Club Circle. Office: 2003 Republican Bank Bldg., Dallas, Tex. Died May 20, 1948.

CHRISTENSON, John August, surgeon; b. Sweden, July 6, 1872; s. Nils and Elenore (Christenson); A.B., Augustana Coll., Rock Island, Ill., 1900; postgrad. study, State U. of Ia., 1901, and in med. schs. of Europe; M.D., Coll. Phys. and Surg. (Univ. of Ill.), 1905; LL.D., Augustana Coll., Rock Island, Ill., 1945; m. Selma Rundquist, Sept. 14, 1905; 1 dau., Eunice Elizabeth. Came to U.S. with parents in 1879. Practiced medicine since 1905; attending surgeon Augustana Hosp., Chicago, since 1911, v.p. med. staff. Pres. bd. dirs. Augustana Coll., Rock Island, Ill. Pres. Central Bldg. Loan Assn.; dir. bd. Old Republic Credit Life Ins. Co. Former pres. Am. Fedn. of Luth. Brotherhood, Augustana Luth. Brotherhood. Mem. A.M.A., Ill. State and Chicago med. socs., Scandinavian Med. Soc., Med. Alumni Assn. U. of Ill., (pres. 1945). Republican. Clubs: Swedish (past pres.), Nordic Country. Home: 421 Melrose St. Office: 3179 N. Clark St., Chicago, Ill. Died Sept. 13, 1948.

CHRISTIAN, Andrew Dunscomb, lawyer; b. Richmond, Va., July 8, 1892; s. Andrew Henry Jr. and Frances Williamson (Archer) C.; B.L., U. of Va., 1913; m. Nellie Rennolds, Sept. 9, 1918; children—Nellie Rennolds, Andrew Henry, Archer. Admitted to Va. bar, June 18, 1913; in practice at Richmond, 1913-42; mem. Christian, Barton & Parker, Richmond, since 1926; director The Tredegar Company. Served as major, field artillery, United States Army, during World War. Major, U.S. Army Air Forces July 24, 1942, Feb. 9, 1945; served with 14th Air Force, active duty in China. Mem. Bar Assn. of City of Richmond (pres. 1938-39), Am. and Va. State bar assns.; mem. (legal section) Am. Life Conv. (chmn. 1926-27); mem. Assn. of Life Ins. Counsel, Alumni Assn. of U. of Va. (v.p. 1940-42; Soc. of the Cincinnati in State of Va. (v.p. since 1939), Delta Psi. Democrat. Episcopalian. Clubs: Commonwealth and Country of Va. (Richmond). Home: 1643 Monument Av. Office: 909 E. Main St., Richmond, Va. Died Jan. 3, 1946.

CHRISTIAN, George Eastland, lawyer; b. Burnet, Tex., Jan. 17, 1888; s. George and Juliet (Johnson) C.; student Southwestern U., Georgetown, Tex., 1906-07; B.A., U. of Texas, 1911; studied law, U. of Tex.; m. Ruby Scott, June 13, 1923; children—Juliet Elizabeth, George Eastland, Martha Josephine. Admitted to Tex. bar, 1912; practiced at Burnet, Tex., 1915-17 and 1919-25; dist. atty. 33d Jud. Dist., Tex. 1919-25; asst. atty. gen. Tex., 1925-27; mem. Bd. Pardon Advisers, Tex., 1927; judge of Commn. in Aid of Court of Criminal Appeals, Tex., since 1927. Grad. First O.T.C., Leon Springs, Tex.; commd. 2d lt.; served in A.E.F., participating in Meuse and Argonne offensives; hon. disch. as 1st lt., 344th Machine Gun Batt., 90th Div. Mem. Am. Bar Assn., Tex. Bar Assn., Sigma Nu. Democrat. Methodist. Mason. Home: 3108 Wheeler St. Address: State Capitol, Austin, Tex. Died April 15, 1941; buried in State Cemetery, Austin, Tex.

CHRISTIAN, Palmer, organist; b. Kankakee, Ill., May 3, 1885; s. David Warren and Cora (Palmer) C.; ed. high sch., Kankakee; studied music, Cosmopolitan Sch. of Music, Chicago; studied organ with Clarence Dickinson, and theory with Olaf Andersen at Am. Conservatory, Chicago; studied organ at Royal Conservatory of Music, Leipzig, with Karl Straube, and theory with Gustav Shreck; private study with Alexandre Guilmant, Paris; hon. Mus.D., Am. Conservatory of Music, 1939; m. Mary Lois Wilkinson, Nov. 21, 1911. Formerly concert organist with hdqrs. in Chicago; made 6 transcontinental tours, also played in larger cities of Europe, and with leading orchestras of U.S.; municipal organist, Denver, 2 yrs.; prof. of organ and university organist, U. of Mich., since Jan. 1924. Mem. Am. Guild Organists, Phi Mu Alpha. Served as Am. rep. at Internat. Organ-Orchestra Concert, Wanamaker Auditorium, New York, 1925. Republican. Club: Cliff Dwellers (Chicago). Home: Ann Arbor, Mich. Died Feb. 19, 1947.

CHRISTIAN, William Peter, bag mfr.; b. Minneapolis, Minn., Nov. 30, 1875; s. Peter Bonesteel and Mary Catharine (Howe) C.; student Central High Sch., Minneapolis, 1890-91; m. Mary Eleanor Turner, Sept. 16, 1903; children—William Turner, George Henry, Harvey Gordon. Clerk in various establishments, Minneapolis, 1891-98; with Hardwood Mfg. Co. (later Northern Bag Co.), 1899-1936, sec., treas., 1904-18, v.p., 1918-28, pres., 1928-36; sec., treas. and dir. Hewitt & Brown, Inc., 1920-38; dir. Chase Bag Co., Hancock-Nelson Mercantile Co., O. B. McClintock Co., Minneapolis Savings & Loan Assn., Shevlin, Carpenter, Hixon Lumber Co.; partner Cameron and Christian Insurance Agency. Served in Spanish-American War, 1898-99. Trustee Citizens Club for Boys' (treas.), Citizen's Aid Society of Minneapolis (sec. and treas.), Breck Sch. for Boys (treas.); treas. and mem. exec. com. Hennepin County Tuberculosis Assn.; dir. Asso. Industries of Minneapolis, 1935-38, Wells Memorial House, 1912-38; dir. Minneapolis Y.M.C.A., Union City Mission (treas. 1939). Republican. Episcopalian. Clubs: Lions, Minneapolis, Athletic, Citizens, Minnetonka Country. Home: Howards Point, Lake Minnetonka, Excelsior, Minn. Office: 430 Rand Tower, Minneapolis, Minn. Died Feb. 5, 1945.

CHRISTIANSON, Theodore, former gov. of Minn.; b. Lac qui Parle Township, Lac qui Parle County, Minn., Sept. 12, 1883; s. Robert and Emma (Ronning) C.; A.B., U. of Minn., 1906, LL.B., 1909; LL.D., Hamline Univ., 1929; L.H.D., Augustana Coll., 1930; LL.D., Macalester Coll., 1938; m. Ruth E. Donaldson, June 4, 1907 (died 1944); children—Robert James, Paul Theodore; m. 2d, Mayme B. Bundy (Mrs. Corydon DeKalb Bundy), '46. Admtd. to Minnesota bar, 1909, and began practice at Dawson; publisher Dawson Sentinel, 1909-25; member Minnesota House of Representatives, 1915-25 (chairman com. on appropriations 4 terms); gov. of Minn., 3 terms, 1925-31; mem. 73d Congress (1933-35), Minn. at large and 74th Congress (1935-37), 5th Minn. Dist.; mgr. Nat. Assn. Retail Grocers, 1937-39; pub. relations counsel Nat. Assn. Retail Druggists, 1939-48. Mem. Phi Beta Kappa, Delta Sigma Rho, Theta Chi, Delta Theta Phi. Republican. Presbyterian. Mason. Author: Minnesota, A History of the State and Its People; also numerous mag. and newspaper articles. Editor, National Assn. Retail Druggists Journal. Home: Lac qui Parle Acres, Dawson, Minn. Died Dec. 10, 1948; interred Sunset Memorial Mausoleum, Minneapolis.

CHRISTMAN, Henry Jacob (krĭst′mȧn), theologian; b. Massillon, O., June 2, 1869; s. William and Lovina (Felger) C.; A.B., Heidelberg Coll., Tiffin, O., 1893; grad. Heidelberg Theol. Sem., 1896; S.T.D., Ursinus Coll., Collegeville, Pa., 1905; LL.D., Catawba College, Salisbury, N.C., 1934; m. Mary M. Poorman, June 18, 1896; 1 dau., Clara Lucile. Ordained ministry Ref. Ch. in U.S., 1896; pastorates, Uniontown, O., 1896-1901, Dayton, O., 1901-02. Prof. Central Theol. Sem., 1902-34, pres., 1912-34; prof. Eden Theol. Sem., 1934-38, prof. emeritus since 1938. Pres. Gen. Synod of Ref. Ch. in U.S., 1932-34. Home: 210 Hedges St., Tiffin, O. Died June 13, 1945.

CHRISTIAN, Sanders Lewis, U.S. Pub. Health Service; b. Mooringsport, La., Dec. 2, 1888; s. Early Clayton and Carrie Bell (Bickham) C.; student La. State U., 1906; M.D., Tulane U., New Orleans, 1912; m. Jeanne Vitter, Nov. 7, 1911; 1 dau. Carolyn Yvonne. Commd. asst. surgeon U.S. Pub. Health Service, Dec. 31, 1914, passed asst. surgeon, Nov. 8, 1919, surgeon, Jan. 13, 1923, asst. surgeon-gen., 1934; med. dir., Jan. 8, 1941; U.S. Marine Hosp., New Orleans, 1915-17; relief sta., Norfolk, Va., 1917-19; med. officer in charge Marine Hosp., Savannah, Ga., 1919-20; Mt. Alto Hosp., Washington, D.C., 1920-22; immigration duty, Antwerp, 1922-24, London, 1924-25; chief surg. service U.S. Marine Hosp., Stapleton, N.Y., 1925-28; med. officer in charge Marine Hosp., Norfolk, Va., 1928-33; asst. surgeon gen. in charge hosp. div., U.S.P.H.S., Washington, D.C., 1933-40; med. officer in charge, Marine Hospital, San Francisco, Calif., since July 1, 1940. Fellow Am. Coll. Surgeons; mem. A.M.A., Phi Chi. Address: U.S. Marine Hospital, San Francisco, Calif.* Deceased.

CHRISTMAN, Warren Ursinus, newspaperman; b. Minersville, Pa., Oct. 9, 1882; s. Rev. David Miller and Myra (Weidner) C.; attended high sch., Bellvue, O., 1899; student Heidelberg U., Tiffin, O., 1900-02; m. Florna Jane Whittaker, Dec. 19, 1910; 1 dau., Lurline. Newspaper work on Tiffin Tribune, Canton (O.) News, Cincinnati Enquirer, Toledo Blade, Cleveland Leader, and other newspapers, 1905-10; with Pittsburgh Post since 1910, as reporter, 1910-14, mng. editor since 1914. Home: 1009 Cochran Road, Mt. Lebanon, Pittsburgh. Office: Grant St., Pittsburgh, Pa. Died May 27, 1944.

CHRITTON, George Alvah (krĭt′tŭn), lawyer; b. Fountain County, Ind., June 4, 1870; s. John W. and Sarah Ann (Brown) C.; ed. dist. schs., Fountain County, Ind., and Sedgwick County, Kan.; Wichita (Kan.) Business Coll.; State Normal Sch., Emporia, Kan.; LL.B., Kent Coll. of Law, Chicago, 1896; LL.B., Chicago Coll. of Law (Lake Forest U.), 1897; m. Laura Fair, Feb. 24, 1897 (died Jan. 17, 1938); children—Ernest Fairfax, George Alvah, Jr.; m. 2d, Mrs. Horace Wright Cook (mother of Marion Claire, opera and radio singer and wife of Henry Weber, WGN Orchestra condr.), Feb. 22, 1941. In law dept. of Met. Elevated R.R. Co., 1894-1904; mem. Dyrenforth, Lee, Chritton & Wiles (now Chritton, Schroeder, Merriam & Hofgren) since 1905, sr. partner since 1937; member of faculty of John Marshall Law School; formerly secretary Fair-Chritton Lumber Company, Chritton, Mississippi; director of and counsel Columbian Bank Note Co. Mem. Am. Bar Assn., Ill. State Bar Assn. (bd. mgrs. 7 yrs.), Chicago Bar Assn. (chmn. legal edn. com. 5 yrs.), Chicago Patent Law Assn. (pres. 1930-31), Chicago Law Inst. Pres. Oak Park Sch. Bd., 1907-18; ex-pres. Chicago Bapt. Social Union, Chicago Bapt. Assn.; pres. Chicago Foundlings' Home, Bapt. Old People's Home; mem. bd. trustees Divinity School University of Chicago, Chicago Baptist Association, Chicago Church Federation; moderator several years of First Baptist Church of Oak Park, Ill. Republican. Mem. Sons Am. Rev. Mason. Clubs: Union League, Oak Park Country. Home: 940 Bonnie Brae, River Forest, Ill. Office: 2800 Board of Trade Bldg., Chicago, Ill. Died Jan. 15, 1948.

CHURCH, Samuel Harden, pres. of the Carnegie Institute; b. Caldwell County, Mo., Jan. 24, 1858; s. William and Emily (Scott) C.; Litt.D., Western U. of Pa., 1895; A.M., Bethany, 1896, Yale, 1897; LL.D., U. of Pittsburgh, 1909; m. Bertha Jean Reinhart, Mar. 15, 1898. Was col. on staff Gov. Hoadly of Ohio, and presented with sword by gov. and staff for conduct in handling troops for suppression of riots in Cincinnati, 1884; Republican speaker in nat. campaigns in various parts of U.S. since 1896; del. Rep. Nat. Conv., 1904. Was supt. transportation, then became vice-pres. of Pennsylvania Railroad at Pittsburgh. President Carnegie Institute, Pittsburgh, Pa., trustee Carnegie Corp. of New York. Mem. Am. Mission to Morocco, 1923. Officer Legion of Honor, France (returned to Vichy government upon it collaboration with Hitler). Clubs: Duquesne, Athletic, Pittsburgh Golf, Allegheny, University, Junta, Rolling Rock, Fox Chapel (Pittsburgh); Authors (New York); National Liberal (London); American (Paris). Author: Oliver Cromwell, a History, 1894; John Marmaduke, 1897; Beowulf (poem), 1901; Corporate History of the Pennsylvania Railroad Lines West of Pittsburgh, 15 vols., 1898-1920; Penruddock of the White Lambs, 1907; A Short History of Pittsburgh, 1908; The American Verdict on the War, 1915; Flames of Faith, 1924; The Liberal Party in America, 1931. Also plays, The Unknown Soldier, The Road Home. Contbr. to mags. Home: 4781 Wallingford St. Address: Carnegie Institute, Pittsburgh, Pa. Died Oct. 11, 1943.

CHURCHILL, Alfred Vance, artist, teacher; b Oberlin, O., Aug. 14, 1864; s. Charles Henry and Henrietta (Vance) C.; Oberlin Coll., 1881-87, A.M., 1898; student Berlin, Leipzig, and Académie Julian, Paris, 1887-90, U. of Paris, 1904-06; m. Marie Marschall; 1 son, Lewis Nelson, Dir. art dept. and prof. fine arts, Ia. (now Grinnell) Coll., 1891-93; instr. secondary and normal schs., St. Louis, Mo., 1893-97; prof. fine arts and dir. art dept, Teachers Coll. (Columbia), 1897-1905; prof. art history and interpretation, Smith Coll., since 1906, and dir. Smith Coll. Mus. Art, 1920. Lecturer, Johns Hopkins, 1902, University of Chicago, 1914, 16, 17. Vice pres. Coll. Art Assn. America. Home: 38 Franklin St., Northampton, Mass. Died Dec. 29, 1949.

CHURCHILL, Frank Edwin, composer; b. Ridlandville, Maine, Oct. 20, 1901; s. Andrew Jackson and Clara Estelle (Curtis) C.; student Los Angeles pub. and high schs., U. of Calif. at Los Angeles, 1921-23; m. Carolyn Kay Shafer, June 10, 1933. Began as atmosphere pianist for silent pictures, 1923; on radio sta. KNX, 1924-29; musical composer for Walt Disney Productions, Ltd., Burbank, Calif., since 1930. Mem. Am. Soc. Composers, Authors and Pubs., Musicians Union (Los Angeles). Club: Hollywood (Calif.) Athletic. Composer: songs Who's Afraid of the Big Bad Wolf, Whistle While You Work, Heigh-Ho, Some Day My Prince Will Come, One Song, I'm Wishing, With a Smile and a Song, Look Out for Mister Stork, Baby Mine, Casey Junior, The Song of the Roustabouts, Put Your Heart in a Song, Happy As A Lark, Galloping On Our Way, Tea Time At Four O'Clock; also complete scores for Disney animated cartoons. Home: Paradise Ranch, Castaic, Calif. Office: Disney Studios, Burbank, Calif. Died May 14, 1942.

CHURCHILL, Marlborough, army officer; b. Andover, Mass., Aug. 11, 1878; s. John Wesley and Mary (Donald) C.; A. B., Harvard, 1900; m. Mary Smith, Oct. 7, 1904. Comd. 2d lt. Arty. Corps, July 16, 1901; 1st lt., Jan. 25, 1907; assigned to 3d Field Arty., June 6, 1907; trans. to 1st Field Arty., Aug. 2, 1910; capt., Apr. 13, 1911; trans. to 5th Field Arty, Jan. 8, 1912; maj., May 15, 1917; lt. N. A., Aug. 5, 1917; col. N. A., June 12, 1918; brig. gen. N. A., Aug. 8, 1918. Instr., Sch. of Fire for Field Arty., 1912-14; insp.-instr., Field Arty. of Organized Militia of Va., Pa. and D. C., 1914-16; editor Field Artillery Jour., July 1914-Jan. 1916; mil. observer with French Armies in the field, Jan. 1916-Apr. 1917; exec. officer Am. Mil. Mission, Paris, Apr.-June 1917; gen. staff, A. E. F., Aug. 1917-Jan. 1918; acting chief of staff, Army Arty., 1st Army, A. E. F., Jan.-May 1918; returned to U. S., June 1918; gen. staff, U. S. Army, since June 6, 1918, as chief, mil. intelligence br., June-Aug. 1918, asst. chief of staff and dir. of mil. intelligence, since Aug. 1918; spl. duty, Am. Commn. to Negotiate Peace, Dec. 1918-Apr. 1919; hon. discharged from temporary commn, as brig gen., June 30, 1920. Decorated D. S. M.; Officer Legion of Honor (France); Companion of the Bath (Eng.); Comdr. Order of the Crown (Italy); Comdr. Order of Leopold (Belgium). Clubs: Army and Navy (Manila and Washington); Harvard (N. Y. City), Metropolitan, Racquet (Washington). Home: 2301 Connecticut Av. Address: Care War Dept., Washington. Died July 9, 1942.

CHURCHILL, Winston, author; b. St. Louis, Nov. 10, 1871; s. Edward Spaulding and Emma Bell (Blaine) C.; grad. U.S. Naval Acad., 1894; m. Mabel H. Hall, Oct. 22, 1895. Author: The Celebrity, 1898; Richard Carvel, 1899; The Crisis, 1901; The Crossing, 1904; Coniston, 1906; Mr. Crewe's Career, 1908; A Modern Chronicle, 1910; The Inside of the Cup, 1913; A Far Country, 1915; The Dwelling Place of Light, 1917; The Uncharted Way, 1941. Home: Plainfield, N.H. Died Mar. 12, 1947; buried at Plainfield, N.H.

CLABAUGH, Hinton Graves, industrial engineer; b. Talladega, Alabama; s. John Henry and Martha Hinton (Graves) Clabaugh; m. Mary Louise Farson, August 16, 1909 (died 1937); children—Louise Farson, Hinton Graves, George Francis; m. 2d, Mary Elizabeth Law, Mar. 22, 1939 (div.). Confidential investigator United States Senate Comm., 1909: entered United States Government service as special agent Department of Justice, May 1910, asst. supt. at Chicago, 1911, 12, in charge in Cincinnati, 1913; asst. supt. N.Y. City, 1914, div. supt. at Chicago, Sept. 1914-Dec. 1918; asst. to pres. Peabody Coal Co. and pvt. practice as industrial engr., Dec. 1918-22; represented U.S. Govt. and Chicago and Ill. bar assns. in special cases; identified with Commonwealth Edison Co., Public Service Co. of Northern Illinois, Peoples Gas Light & Coke Co. and other utilities since 1922. Lieut. United States Naval Reserve, 1917-21, lt. commander, 1926-39, comdr since July 1939. Chmn. Ill. Pardon and Parole Bds., 1926-29. Mem. Ry. Spl. Agts. Assn., Am. Gas Assn., Am. Electric Ry. Assn., Am. Legion, Mil. Order World War, Reserve Officers Assn. of U.S., Sojourners. Republican. Mason. Clubs: Lake Shore, Electric, Army and Navy. Home: 153 Bertling Lane, Winnetka, Ill. Office: 79 W. Monroe St., Chicago, Ill. Died May 31, 1946.

CLAIR, Matthew Wesley, bishop; b. Union, W.Va., Oct. 21, 1865; s. Anthony and Ollie (Green) C.; grad. classics and theology, Morgan Coll., Baltimore, Md., 1889; Ph.B., Bennett Coll., Greensboro, N.C., 1897, Ph.D., 1901; D.D., Howard, 1911, Morgan, 1918, LL.D., 1920; LL.D. Wilberforce U., 1928; m. Fannie M. Walker, Nov. 12, 1889 (died Feb. 27, 1925); m. 2d, Eva F. Wilson, Nov. 2, 1926. Ordained M.E. ministry, 1889; pastor, Harpers Ferry, W.Va., 1889-93, Stuanton, Va., 1893-96, Ebenezer Ch., Washington, D.C., 1896-97; presiding elder of Washington Dist., 1897-1902; pastor Asbury Ch., Washington, 1902-19 (built $80,000 ch. edifice); dist. supt., Washington, 1919-20; elected bishop, 1920, and was assigned to Monrovia, Liberia. Former mem. Am. advisory com. Booker Washington Agrl. and Industrial Inst., Liberia; former mem. Board of Edn., Republic of Liberia, apptd. by President C.D.B. King; mem. Fed. Council of Chs.; mem. Gen. Conf. M.E. Ch., 1904, 16, 20; trustee Morgan Coll., Philander Smith Coll. Mem. Am. Geog. Soc., Alpha Phi Alpha, Pi Gamma Mu. Republican. Mason, Odd Fellow. Home: 1040 Russell Av., Covington, Ky. Died June 28, 1943.

CLAPP, Augustus Wilson, lawyer; b. Hudson, Wis., Feb. 9, 1877; s. Newel Harvey and Sarah Elizabeth (Jones) C.; B.A., Yale, 1898; m. Lucy Sargent Sanborn, June 6, 1902; children—Dorothy, Augustus Wilson; m. 2d, Rosina Kraft, June 17, 1922; m. 3d, Gladys Hays, Mar. 2, 1935. Admitted to Minn. bar, 1901; mem. Clapp & Macartney, St. Paul, 1901-06; chief law officer to commr. to Five Civilized Tribes, Muskogee, Okla., 1906-07; mem. Rodgers & Clapp, Muskogee, 1907-12; mem. Clapp & Macartney, St. Paul, and successors since 1912 (sr. mem. Clapp, Briggs, Gilbert & Macartney, 1922-40); v.p., gen. counsel, dir. and mem. exec. com. Weyerhaeuser Timber Co. of Tacoma since 1932; moved to Tacoma 1940. Chief labor sect., priorities div., War Indus. Bd., 1918. Mem. exec. com. Lumber Code Authority, under NRA, 1933-34. Mem. Am. and Wash. bar assns., Phi Beta Kappa. Republican. Clubs: Minnesota (St. Paul); Bohemian (San Francisco); Tacoma, Tacoma Country and Golf; Rainier (Seattle). Home: Tacoma Country and Golf Club. Office: 802-7 Tacoma Bldg., Tacoma, Wash. Died Aug. 5, 1946.

CLAPP, Clift Rogers, lawyer; b. Boston, Mass., Feb. 10, 1861; s. Howard and Abigail Frances (Rogers) C.; A.B., Harvard, 1884; LL.B., 1887; m. Gertrude Blanchard, Oct. 6, 1892; children—Howard Rogers (dec.), Mrs. Emily Blanchard Gleason, Mrs. Elizabeth Brewer Penney. Began practice in Boston, 1887; now retired. Mem. Bar Assn. City of Boston, Mass., Middlesex and American bar assns. Republican. Unitarian. Clubs: Harvard (Boston); Brae Burn (West Newton); Tuesday (Newton). Home: 49 Temple St., West Newton, Mass. Office: 50 Federal St., Boston, Mass. Died Mar. 19, 1945.

CLAPP, Franklin Halsted, clergyman; b. N.Y. City, Aug. 11, 1871; s. Henry Bennett and Sarah (Halsted) C.; grad. Centenary Collegiate Inst., Hackettstown, N.J., 1897; A.B., Wesleyan U., Middletown, Conn., 1901; B.D., Drew Theol. Sem., 1903; D.D., Albion (Mich.) Coll., 1921; grad. study Mansfield Coll., Oxford, 1922; Drew Theol. Sem. and Columbia Teachers Coll., 1926; Th.M., Drew Theol. Sem., 1926; m. Marie Wolcott Welles, July 9, 1903; children—Clayton Welles (dec.), Halsted Welles. Ordained ministry M.E. Ch., 1903; successively pastor Jackson, Alma, Niles, Manistee, Grand Rapids, Battle Creek, Reed City, Traverse City (all of Mich.); supt. Albion dist., 1919-25; endowment sec. Drew Theol. Sem., 1926-28; pres. Gammon Theol. Sem., Atlanta, Ga., 1928-32; made trip around world visiting missions, 1936; mem. staff Bd. of Foreign Missions, M.E. Ch., lecturing widely in interest of world friendship since 1937; prof. psychology, Martin Coll., Pulaski, Tenn., since 1942. Formerly sec. bd. trustees Albion Coll.; trustee Gammon Theol. Sem. Mem. Psi Upsilon. Republican. Home: (summer) Rapid City, Mich.; (winter) Pulaski, Tenn. Died May 21, 1944; buried in Woodlawn Cemetery, New York City.

CLAPP, Frederick Gardner, cons. geologist; b. Boston, July 20, 1879; s. Edward Blake and Mary Frances (Jones) C.; S.B. in Geology, Mass. Inst. Tech., 1901; m. Helen Drew Ripley, Dec. 28, 1908; children—Clara Frances, Edward Gardner, Priscilla. Instr. in geology, Mass. Inst. Tech., 1901-03; geologist with U.S. Geol. Survey, 1902-08; consulting geologist and petroleum engr., specializing in reports on oil and gas properties since 1908; mng. geologist, The Associated Geol. Engrs., 1912-18; chief geologist, The Associated Petroleum Engrs. since 1919; also petroleum and natural gas expert, Canadian Dept. of Mines, 1911-15; in charge geol. explorations in China, 1913-15; in charge investigations in Australia and New Zealand, 1923-25; petroleum adviser Imperial Govt. of Iran, 1927, 28, 33; explorations in Iran and Afghanistan, 1934-38; Oklahoma oil operations, 1939-43; special lecturer on oil geology, Harvard, 1921; reported to committee of United States Senate in Teapot Dome Case, 1923. Christian Scientist. Fellow Geol. Society America, A.A.A.S., Am. Geog. Society, Royal Geog. Soc.; mem. Am. Inst. Mining and Metall. Engrs., Geol. Soc. Washington, Am. Asiatic Assn., Am. Geophys. Union, Am. Petroleum Inst., Am. Assn. Petroleum Geologists, Inst. of Petroleum (London), Soc. Economic Geologists, Royal Central Asian Soc., Am. Inst. for Iranian Art and Archeology, Société Géologique de France; hon. mem. Sociedad des Ingerieros del Peru. Clubs: Explorers (New York); Teheran (Iran). Author of books and papers on travel, geology, petroleum, natural gas, geography and water supply. Home: 91 Warwick Rd., Bronxville, N.Y. Office: 50 Church St., New York, N.Y. Died Feb. 18, 1944.

CLAPPER, Raymond, newspaper corr.; b. Linn County, Kan., May 30, 1892; s. John William and Julia (Crow) C.; student U. of Kan., 1913-16; m. Olive Ewing, March 31, 1913; children—Janet, Peter.

Began as reporter Kansas City (Missouri) Star, 1916; with United Press Assns., 1916-33, in Chicago, Milwaukee, St. Paul, New York and Washington offices, night mgr. and chief polit. writer. Washington bur., 1923-28, mgr. Washington bur., 1929-33; spl. writer Washington Post, 1934-35; polit. commentator Scripps-Howard Newspapers since Jan. 1936 Dir. Nat. Press Bldg. Corpn. Mem. Sigma Delta Chi (hon. nat. pres., 1939). Clubs Gridiron (pres. 1939), Overseas Writers, National Press. Author: Racketeering in Washington. Home: 3125 Chain Bridge Rd., Office: 1013 13th St., Washington, D.C. Died Feb. 1944.

CLARK, Allen Culling; b. Phila., Pa., Feb. 23, 1858; s. Appleton Prentiss and Elizabeth C. (Woodman) C.; ed. pub. schs., Washington, D.C.; LL.B., National U., D.C., 1878; m. Sarah Pearce, Nov. 21, 1882 (died 1910); children—Mary R. (Mrs. Robert L. Graveley), Elizabeth G., Henry W., Dorothy C. (Mrs. William H. Winchcole). Sec., trustee Equitable Life Ins. Co. of D.C., since 1885; trustee Lincoln Hall Assn.; dir. Nat. Capital Bank; trustee Columbia Title Ins. Co. Mem. Columbia Hist. Soc. (pres.) Washington Acad. Sciences (manager). Md. Historical Society, Miss. Valley Hist. Assn., Virginia Historical Soc. Author: Greenleaf and Law in the Federal City, 1901; William Duane, 1905; Life and Letters of Dolly Madison, 1914; Dr. and Mrs. William Thornton, 1914; Life of Daniel Carroll of Duddington, 1921; Abraham Lincoln in the National Capital, 1925; Abraham Lincoln—the Merciful President, 1927; Origin of the Federal City, 1927; George Washington—Places Associated with His Presence in Maryland, Virginia and District of Columbia, 1932; Robert Mills, Architect and Engineer, 1935; The Trollopes, 1935; Zalmon Richards, Educator, 1935; James Barry, 1935; Commodores James Barron, Stephen Decatur, 1939; Suter Tavern; also series of biographies of mayors of the City of Washington; also numerous hist. essays, chiefly local in character. Baptist. Home: 2020 O St. Office; 816 14th St. N.W., Washington, D.C. Died May 16, 1943.

CLARK, Alson Skinner, painter; b. Chicago, Mar. 25, 1876; s. Alson Ellis and Sarah Morse (Skinner) C.; ed. Art Inst., Chicago, 1898; Chase Art Sch., New York, 1898-99; Whistler and Mucha schs., Paris, 1900-01; m. Atta Medora McMullin, Sept. 30, 1902; 1 son, Alson. Principal works: "The Coffee House," "The Bridge Builders," "The Song of the Nightingale." Bronze medal, St. Louis Expn., 1904; Martin Cahn prize, Art Inst., Chicago, 1906; bronze medal, San Francisco Expn., 1915; hon. mention, Calif. Club, 1922, Los Angeles Museum Art; museum grand prize, Southwest Museum, Los Angeles, 1923; Huntington prize, Los Angeles Museum, 1925; prize Calif. State Exhbn., Pasadena Art Inst., 1930; Mrs. McBride prize, Pasadena Art Inst., 1933. Represented in Albert and Victoria Museum, London; San Diego Fine Arts Gallery; Calif. State Library; Art Inst. Chicago; Addison Gallery of Art, Andover, Mass.; also curtains in Pasadena Community Playhouse and Pasadena Junior College; murals in Carthay Circle Theatre, Los Angeles, also murals in many public buildings. Mem. Allied Artists America, Chicago Soc. Artists, Print-makers of Los Angeles. Joined U.S. Naval Reserve, 1917, and sent as interpreter, rank of ensign to France; promoted lt. Naval Aviation Forces. Home: 1149 Wotkyns Drive, Pasadena, Calif. Died March 22, 1949.

CLARK, Arthur Bridgman, college prof.; b East Onondaga, N.Y., Aug. 11, 1866; s. George Brown and Caroline Delano (Bridgman) C.; B.Arch., Syracuse U., 1888, M.Arch., 1891; student New York Sch. of Art, under William Chase, 1898; studied with Whistler, Paris, 1899, John Twachtman, 1903; m. Hannah Grace Birge, Sept. 1, 1891; children—Birge Malcolm, Esther Bridgman, Donald Eastman, David Bridgman. Began as instr. architecture, Syracuse U., 1889; with Stanford U., 1892-1931, prof. of edn. in graphic art, 1916-31. Mem. City Planning Commn., Palo Alto, Calif. Mem. San Francisco Art Assn. (dir.), Pacific Arts Assn., Delta Upsilon. Progressive Rep. Unitarian. Author: Observing and Drawing Geometrical Models, 1895; Design, 1915; Art Principles in House Furniture and Village Building, 1921. Home: Stanford University, Calif. Died May 15, 1948.

CLARK, Arthur Bryan, chmn. Asso. Seed Growers, Inc.; b. Orange, Conn., May 25, 1880; s. Everett Bryan and Charlotte (Woodruff) C.; A.B., Yale, 1902; m. Glenna Hostetter, June 30, 1902; children—Arthur Bryan, Glenna Marie Crafts, Gordon Hostetter. Began as treas. Everett B. Clark Seed Co. (Milford, Conn.), 1902, pres. and treas., 1907-28; president and treasurer Associated Seed Growers, Incorporated (succeeding Clark Seed Co.), New Haven, 1928-42, chairman of the board since 1942; pres. Milford Trust Co., 1911-33; director Union & New Haven Trust Co., New Haven Savings Bank. Director New Haven Hospital; trustee New Haven Y.M.C.A., 1935-46, pres. State Y.M.C.A., 1927-29; pres- Died Dec. 3, 1947.

CLARK, Barzilla Worth, ex-gov.; b. Hadley, Ind., Dec. 22, 1881; s. Joseph Addison and Eunice (Hadley) C.; student Terre Haute (Ind.) High Sch., 1895-99; m. Ethel S. Peck, Oct. 26, 1905; children—Ferris Hadley, Mary Elizabeth (Mrs. Fred M. Laidlaw), Alice Salome (Mrs. Edwin Springer), Lois Frances (Mrs. Merlin S. Young). Began in bus. as farmer and stock buyer, 1900; held Idaho license as civil engineer and was associated with reservoir and water power developments, 1905-37; mem. City Council, Idaho Falls, 1908-12, mayor, 1913-15 and 1926-36; gov. of Ida., 1937-39. Democrat. Methodist. Address: 1083 S. Boulevard, Idaho Falls, Ida. Died Sept. 21, 1943.

CLARK, Calvin Montague, theologian; b. Hartford, Wis., Jan. 30, 1862; s. Anson and Mary Lanman (Hooker) C.; A.B., Williams Coll., 1884, D.D., 1914; grad. Andover Theol. Sem., 1888; U. of Berlin, Germany, 1888-90; m. Helen Munson Cobb, June 29, 1893; children—Cornelius Edwards, Charlotte Rowe, Katharine Hooker, Ruth Huntington. Ordained Congl. ministry, Dec. 30, 1890; pastor First Ch., Wolfboro, N.H., 1890-93, Centre Ch., Haverhill, Mass., 1893-1906; prof. eccles. history, Bangor Theol. Sem., 1906-36, since emeritus; corp. mem. A.B.C.F.M. Mem. Soc. Bibl. Lit. and Exegesis, Am. Soc. Ch. History, Phi Beta Kappa, Delta Upsilon. Author: Seventy-Five Years of Centre Church; History of Bangor Theological Seminary, 1916; History of the Congregational Churches of Maine (Vol. 1), 1926, (Vol. II), 1935; American Slavery and Maine Congregationalists, 1940. Home: 306 Union St., Bangor, Me. Died Mar. 1, 1947; buried Mount Hope Cemetery, Bangor.

CLARK, Edward Gay, ry. official; b. Howell, Mich., May 2, 1872; s. Malcolm and Emma B. (Taylor) C.; ed. Central High Sch., Minneapolis; m. Olive G. Pacey, Mar. 12, 1895; 1 son, Edward Gay. Stenographer and clerk Western Transit Co., Minneapolis and Duluth, 1893-97; clk. Wisconsin Central Ry., Minneapolis, May-Sept. 1897, sec. to gen. freight agent, Milwaukee, 1897-98, chief clerk gen. freight office, Milwaukee, 1898-99, New England agent, Boston, 1899-1901, gen. agt., Milwaukee, 1901-02, 2d asst. gen. frt. agt., 1902-06, 1st asst. gen. frt. agt., Chicago, 1906-09; asst. gen. frt. agt., M.,St.P.& S.Ste.M. Ry. Co., Minneapolis, 1909-16, gen. frt. agt., 1916-28, frt. traffic mgr., 1928-38, gen. traffic mgr. since Jan. 1938; dir. M.,St.P.&S.Ste.M. Ry. Co., Wis. Central Ry. Co. Mem. Minneapolis Civic and Commerce Assn. Republican. Methodist. Mason (Shriner). Clubs: Union League, Chicago Traffic (Chicago); Minneapolis Athletic, Minneapolis Traffic; New York Athletic. Home: 2301 Humboldt Av. S. Office: 1619 Soo Line Bldg., Minneapolis, Minn.* Died Apr. 30, 1947.

CLARK, Edward Hardy, mining; b. St. Louis, Mo., Nov. 19, 1864; s. Austin Whitmire and Angeline (Whitley) C.; ed. Salem (Mo.) Acad.; m. Eva Turner, Jan. 30, 1895; children—Edward Hardy and Helen Tarleton (Mrs. H. C. Park). Business mgr. Estate of U.S. Senator George Hearst, 1896-1919; executor Estate of Mrs. Phoebe A. Hearst; vice-pres. Cerro de Pasco Copper Corp., 1901-29, pres. 1929-42, now dir. and chmn. of bd.; pres. and dir. Homestake Mining Co. of Calif. (properties in Black Hills, S.D.) since 1914; dir. Cerro de Pasco Ry. Co. of N.J.; mem. bd. dirs. Am. Metal Co., Ltd., Am. Trust Co., Babicora Development Co., Calif. Pacific Title Ins. Co., Consol. Cigar Co., Eureka Mining Co. of Chichuahua, Guanacevi Mining Co., Irving Trust Co., San Luis Mining Co., Santa Eulalia Mining Co. Mem. Am. Inst. Mining Engrs. Clubs: Pacific Union, Commonwealth, San Francisco Golf, Burlingame Country (San Francisco); Metropolitan (New York). Home: 950 Mason St., San Francisco, Calif. Office: 40 Wall St., New York, N.Y.; Hearst Bldg., San Francisco, Calif. Died Dec. 16, 1945; buried in Cypress Lawn Cemetery, San Francisco.

CLARK, Edward W., mem. Dem. Nat. Com.; b. San Jose, Calif.; s. Jacob Austin and Julia (Reardon) C.; ed. elementary schools and business coll., Salt Lake City; unmarried. In cattle, sheep, mining and mercantile business; pres. Southern Nev. Power Co., Southern Nev. Telephone Co. Mem. Dem Nat. Com. for Nev. since 1934. Chmn. Co. Council of Defense, 1917-18. Mem. Nev.-Colo. River Commn. Catholic. Home: 429 S. Main St., Las Vegas, Nev.* Died Apr. 15, 1946.

CLARK, Ellery Harding, lawyer, author; b. W. Roxbury, Mass., Mar. 13, 1874; s. Benjamin Cutler and Adeline Kinnicutt (Weld) C.; A.B., Harvard, 1896, LL.B., 1899; m. Victoria Maddalena, 1904; 1 son, Ellery Harding. Practiced at Boston since 1900; physical dir. Browne & Nichols Sch., Cambridge, Mass., 1918-28. Mem. Boston Sch. Com., 1902, 03, 04; Bd. of Aldermen, 1908. Mem. Harvard track team 4 years; U.S. rep. at Olympic Games, at Athens, Greece, 1896, and won high and broad jump there; all-around athletic champion of N.E., 1896, 97, 1909, 10; all-around athletic champion of America, 1897, 1903. Sec. Humane Soc. of Mass. Mem. Boston Bar Assn. Republican. Episcopalian. Clubs: Union, Boston Athletic. Author: Massachusetts Street Railway Accident Law, 1902; United States Street Railway Accident Law, 1904; Practical Track and Field Athletics (with John Graham), 1904; Loaded Dice, 1909; The Carleton Case, 1910; Dick Randall, The Young Athlete, 1910; Reminiscences of an Athlete, 1911; The Camp at Sea Duck Cove, 1912; Pharos, 1913; Uncle Ebenezer's Millions, 1915; Track Athletics Up-To-Date, 1920; The Money Gods, 1922; Putting It Over, 1923; Daughters of Eve, 1924; Carib Gold, 1925; The Lost Galleon, 1927; The Strength of the Hills, 1929; This World and the Next, 1934. Poems: Kingdom of God; Andrew Jackson; The Sacrifice, Pub. "Poet Lore," 1944-49. Home: Cohasset, Mass. Office: Ames Bldg., Boston, Mass. Died July 27, 1949. Buried Forest Hills, Mass.

CLARK, Eugene Bradley, engineer, mfr.; b. Washington, D.C., July 27, 1873; s. Ezra W. and Sylvia Anne (Nodine) C.; M.E., Cornell U., 1894; m. Laura Wolfe, Oct. 28, 1899 (died 1917); children—Helen Cecil (Mrs. Leo Wolman), Eugene B., John M.; m. 2d, Mrs. Luella M. Coon, 1919. Began as elec. engr. for Westinghouse Electric & Mfg. Co., Pittsburgh, 1894; elec. engr., later asst. mgr. Ill. Steel Co., South Chicago, 1896-1906; pres. Am. Sintering Co. since 1906; pres. Clark Equipment Co., Am. Ore Reclamation Co., Buffalo Sintering Corp. Mem. Soc. Automotive Engrs., Art Inst. Chicago, Field Museum of Natural History, Oriental Inst. Clubs: Chicago, University, Bob O'Link Golf, Tavern (Chicago); South Bend (Ind.) Country; Detroit Athletic; India House (New York); Surf, Indian Creek (Miami, Fla.). Home: Buchanan, Mich.; and Chicago, Ill. Offices: Buchanan. Mich.; and 310 S. Michigan Av., Chicago, Ill. Died July 29, 1942.

CLARK, Ezra W(estcote), industrialist; b. Washington, D.C.; s. Maj. Ezra W. and Sylvia Ann (Nodine) C.; U. of Pa., 1905; post grad. course, U. of Ohio; m. Ruth Hill, April 17, 1929. Began as city editor Chicago Inter-Ocean; successively automobile editor, Memphis News-Scimitar; bus. mgr. Mobile Item; formerly v.p. Clark Equipment Co., Buchanan, Mich.; gen. mgr. Clark Truc-Tractor Div., Battle Creek, Mich.; dir. Clark Equipment Co., Buffalo Sintering Co.; v.p. Central Nat. Bank (Battle Creek, Mich.). Lt., U.S. Army Air Force, World War I; special advisor to Army and Navy on material handling problems in European Theatre Operations for Sec. of War, 1942-43. Awarded War Dept. citation for overseas services. Past pres. Battle Creek Chamber of Commerce. Clubs: Bankers, Salmagundi (New York); National Press (Washington, D.C.); Detroit (Mich.); Battle Creek (Mich.) Country; Tavern (Chicago). Author: The Unit Package Method of Material Handling, 1937; also numerous articles and pamphlets on indusl. problems. Home: 35 Elizabeth St. Office: Post Building, Battle Creek, Mich. Deceased.

CLARK, Frank William, newspaper editor; b. Brooklyn, N.Y., Dec. 10, 1875; s. William and Frances (Scott) C.; ed. high sch., Greene, N.Y., and Riley (now Commercial) Coll., Binghamton; m. Mary Valerie Stuart MacLeod, 1901. Began as reporter, Binghamton Republican, 1893; reporter Binghamton, N.Y. City and Chicago, 1894-1900; city and Sunday editor Buffalo (N.Y.) Courier, 1900-03; editor Binghamton Press, 1904; mng. editor Cleveland World-News, 1905; N.Y. City corr. for Cleveland, Chicago and Milwaukee newspapers, night editor Publishers' Press, N.Y. City, 1905-06; mng. editor Newark (N.J.) Star, 1907-08; copy editor, spl. writer N.Y. Evening World, N.Y. Evening Telegram, N.Y. Herald, 1909; editor Niagara Falls (N.Y.) Cataract Journal, 1910; mng. editor Knickerbocker Press, Albany, 1911-15; with N.Y. World, 1916; Sunday editor Syracuse Herald, 1917-18; editor Binghamton Press, 1918; mng. editor Syracuse Herald, 1919-21; editor The Knickerbocker Press and Albany Evening News, 1922-25; asso. editor Syracuse Herald, 1926; editor Binghamton Press, 1926-29; mng. editor Syracuse Herald, 1929-39, Syracuse Herald-Journal and Syracuse Herald-American, July 1939-Mar. 1945; now retired. Member N.Y. Nat. Guard, 1893-98. Episcopalian. Elk. Home: Hotel Syracuse, Syracuse, N.Y. Deceased.

CLARK, Fred Emerson, professor of marketing; b. Parma Township, Jackson County, Mich., August 26, 1890; s. Guy Eugene and Ida Amelia (Leonard) C.; B.A., Albion (Mich.) Coll., 1912; M.A., Univ. of Ill., 1913, Ph.D., 1916; m. Carrie Patton, Aug. 17, 1915; 1 son, Frederick Eugene. Scholar in economics, 1912-13, fellow in economics, 1913-14. Univ. of Ill.; instr. economics, Univ. of Ariz., 1914-15; fellow in economics, Univ. of Ill., 1915-16; instr. commerce and industry, Univ. of Mich., 1916-17; prof. business adminstrn., Delaware Coll., 1917-18; asst. prof. economics, Univ. of Mich., 1918-19; visiting prof. marketing, Univ. of Chicago, summer 1921, Columbia University, summer 1922, University of Wisconsin, summer 1934; asso. professor economics and marketing, Northwestern Univ., 1919-23, prof. since 1923, head of dept. of marketing and orgn., 1927-39, chmn. dept. of marketing, 1939-47, dir. Grad. Div. School of Commerce, 1937-47; chmn. Ph.D. Com.; School of Commerce, since 1942; Morrison professor of marketing since 1945. Chmn. economics sub-committee of marketing committee of Com. for Economic Development, 1944-46. Member of American Econ. Assn., Am. Assn. Univ. Profs., Nat. Assn. Teachers of Marketing and Advertising (pres. 1929), Am. Management Assn., Am. Marketing Soc., Am. Marketing Assn. (pres. 1938), Am. Farm Econ. Assn., Midwest. Marketing Soc., Delta Sigma Rho, Alpha Pi Zeta, Delta Tau Delta, Phi Eta, Alpha Kappa Psi, Beta Gamma Sigma, Phi Beta Kappa. Methodist. Club: University. Author: The Purposes of the Indebtedness of American Cities (1880-1912), 1916; Principles of Marketing, 1922, revised, 1932, 42 (with Carrie Patton Clark); Marketing of Agricultural Products in the United States (with L. D. H. Weld), 1932. Editor: Readings in Marketing, 1924, revised, 1933; article on marketing, Winston's Loose-Leaf Business Ency., 1931; Co-author various articles in Ency. Britannica, Ten Eventful Years, 1936-46, and in Britt. Book of the Year, 1946. Home: 1907 Orrington Av., Evanston, Ill. Died Nov. 26, 1948.

CLARK, George Ramsey, naval officer; b. Monroe O., Mar. 20, 1857; s. Peter Williamson and Louisa Jane (Boyd) C.; grad. U.S. Naval Acad., 1878; m. Mary Winchell Brown, Oct. 29, 1889. Commd. ensign, U.S. Navy, 1884, and advanced through the grades to rear admiral, 1918; retired, 1921; served in Spanish-Am. War, Philippine Insurrection, Boxer Rebellion; apptd. judge advocate general, 1918. Decorated Navy Cross, Distinguished Service Medal. Author: (with others) The Navy, 1775-1909, 2 vols., 1910; Short History of U.S. Navy, 1911. Address: Navy Dept., Washington 25, D.C. Died Dec. 14, 1945.

CLARK, Henry W., lawyer; b. Castleton, Vt., July 27, 1874; s. Henry L. and Lora (Holt) C.; A.B., U. of Vt., 1897, LL.D., 1922; LL.B., New York Law Sch., 1899; admitted N.Y. bar, 1899; m. Marion C. Logan, Dec. 31, 1904 (died 1936). Gen. counsel and v.p. U.P. R.R. System, and mem. Clark, Carr & Ellis. Mem. Phi Beta Kappa, Soc. of Mayflower Descendants. Home: 280 Park Av. Office: 120 Broadway, New York, N.Y. Died July 17, 1942.

CLARK, Hubert Lyman, zoölogist; b. Amherst, Mass., Jan. 9, 1870; s. William Smith (pres. Mass. Agrl. Coll.) and Harriet Kapuolani Richards (Williston) C.; A.B., Amherst Coll., 1892; Ph.D., Johns Hopkins U., 1897; hon. Sc.D., Olivet (Mich.) Coll., 1927; m. Fannie Lee Snell, Apr. 4, 1899; children—William Smith, Stirrat (dec.), Janet Stirrat, Edith. Prof. biology, Olivet Coll., 1899-1905; asst. Museum Comparative Zoölogy, Harvard, 1905-12, curator of echinoderms, 1912-27, became curator of marine invertebrates, and asso. prof. zoölogy, 1927, emeritus prof., also curator; acting prof., Williams Coll., 1920-21; acting asso. prof., Stanford U., 1936; research associate Hancock Foundation, University of So. Calif., 1946-47. Received Clarke Memorial Medal, Royal Soc. of New South Wales, Australia, for research in Australian sci., 1947. Sci. investigations in Jamaica (5 visits), Tobago, Bermuda, Galapagos Islands and Australia (3 visits). Chmn. bd. visitors Andover-Newton Theol. Sem. 1930-40. Republican. Conglist. Author of numerous sci. papers, including 3 monographs on Austrian Echinoderms, 1921, 38, 46 Home: 97 Lakeview Av., Cambridge 38, Mass. Died July 31, 1947; buried in West Cemetery, Amherst, Mass.

CLARK, James Edwin, editor; b. Clinton, Oneida County, N.Y., Aug. 30, 1871; s. John J. and Annie T. (Sheridan) C.; grad. Utica (N.Y.) Free Acad., 1892; m. Ella Talcott, Feb. 12, 1895; children—H. Mildred, Edwin C., James T. On editorial staff Utica Daily Press, 1893-94, Utica Observer, 1894-1911; editor Am. Motorist, New York, 1912-13; dir. and sec. Conf. Com. on Nat. Preparedness, Inc., 1915, 16, 17; dir. and mgr. League for Preservation of Am. Independence, Inc., 1918-20 (now dir.); editor Am. Bankers Assn. Journal, 1921-32; v.p., dir. Royalty Depositor Corp., New York. A pioneer in advocating preparedness, also in organizing movement to prevent ratification of covenant of League of Nations. Author numerous econ. articles, inspirational editorials. Home: 17 Huguenot Drive, Larchmont, N.Y. Office: 21 West St., New York. Died Apr. 23, 1945.

CLARK, John Brittan, clergyman; b. Brooklyn, N.Y., Sept. 2, 1864; s. Richard P. and Maria (Charles) C.; A.B., Amherst, 1886 (Phi Beta Kappa); grad. Union Theol. Sem., 1889; D.D., Alma (Mich.) Coll., 1913; m. Irene Woodbridge, Feb. 16, 1892; children—Dorothy (dec.), Elisabeth Woodbridge (dec.), David Cartwright. Ordained Congl. ministry, 1889; pastor Pilgrim Chapel, Brooklyn, 1890-92, Lee Av. Congl. Ch., Brooklyn, 1892-98, then Westminster Presbyn. Ch., Detroit, later 1st Ch., Washington, D.C., then Erskine Memorial Ch., Tryon, N.C. Moderator of Synod of Baltimore, Congl. Conf. of Carolinas. Certified Braille transcriber (5 vols. in Braille have been accepted for circulation by the Library of Congress, Washington, D.C.). Author: Guide Posts Along the Way, 1926; The Challenging Christ, 1929; The Future Life, 1931; Things That Trouble People. Home: Cumberland, Md.; (summer) Middlefield, Mass.; (winter) St. Augustine, Fla. Died Oct. 30, 1944.

CLARK, John Cheesman, lawyer; b. Plattsburg, N.Y., Mar. 24, 1863; s. George Lafayette and J. Ann (Walling) C.; A.B., Wesleyan U., Conn., 1886, M.A., 1889; LL.B., Columbia Law Sch., 1889; LL.D., Grinnell Coll., Ia., 1915, Wesleyan U., Conn., 1920; m. Addie Perry Burr, Jan. 24, 1894; 1 dau., Jane P. Practiced, New York, since 1889., sec. commns. that revised sch. laws of New York, 1894-96 inclusive; 1st sec. Citizens' Union, 1897; asst. corp. counsel, assigned to office of Mayor Low, 1902-03; mem. Olin, Clark & Murphy; justice Supreme Ct. of N.Y., 1916; pres. N.Y. State Civil Service Commn., 1917-19, 1921-22. President trustees Wesleyan Univ., 1912-20; chairman of board of trustees New York Y.M.C.A.; trustee International Committee Y.M.C.A.; governor Lake Champlain Association. Mem. Am. Bar Assn., Assn. Bar City of New York, Psi Upsilon, Phi Beta Kappa. Republican. Methodist. Clubs: Metropolitan, Down Town, Psi Upsilon. Home: 825 Fifth Av. Office: 120 Broadway, New York, N.Y. Died June 27, 1946.

CLARK, Lucius Charles, president emeritus; b. Grundy County, Ia., June 4, 1869; s. Albert and Mary (Troutman) C.; A.B., Cornell Coll., Ia., 1893; S.T.B., Boston U. Sch. of Theology, 1897; D.D., Upper Ia. U., 1904; grad. student, Glasgow, Scotland, 1910-11; LL.D., American Univ., Washington, D.C., 1943; m. Hattie E. Young, June 21, 1894. Ordained M.E. ministry, 1893; pastor Beaman, Ia., 1894, Tama, 1895-96, Eldora, 1897-1900, Belle Plaine, 1901-03, Osage, 1904-05, Iowa City, 1905-09, Mason City, 1910-13, Washington, D.C., 1913-20, Washington Fed. of Chs., 1920-21; chancellor Am. Univ., 1922-33, dean, Grad. School and dir. School of Polit. Sciences, 1933-34, now chancellor emeritus. Mem. Phi Beta Kappa, Theta Sigma. Republican. Author: The Worshipping Congregation, 1893. Home: 3031 Sedgwick St. N.W., Washington. Died March 27, 1949; buried in Rock Creek Cemetery, Washington.

CLARK, Roy Wallace, ry. official; b. Petoskey, Mich., Oct. 4, 1880; s. George and Annie (Stacey) C.; grad. high sch., Kalamazoo, Mich., 1898; student Detroit (Mich.) Bus. U., 1900-01; m. Margaret Caroline Haines, Oct. 26, 1904 (died June 12, 1938); children—George Evans, Edward Stacey, Margaret Caroline (Mrs. Lewis C. Stone). With N.P. Ry. Co. since 1902, stenographer to chief engr., 1902, stenographer in pres.' office, 1903-04, chief clk. same, 1904-07, asst. to pres., 1907-18, asst. to federal mgr., 1918-20, asst. to pres., 1920-27, gen. traffic mgr., 1927-38, v.p. of traffic dept. since 1938. Republican. Presbyn. Mason (32°). Clubs: Minnesota, Athletic, Town and Country Golf (St. Paul); Minneapolis; Union League (Chicago). Home: 1118 Summit Av. Office: Northern Pacific Ry. Co., St. Paul, Minn. Died Oct. 3, 1948.

CLARK, Taliaferro, med. dir.; b. The Plains, Fauquier County, Va., May 14, 1867; s. Edwin Parsons and Judith Ann (Taliaferro) C.; A.B., Emory and Henry Coll., 1886; M.D., U. of Va., 1890; m. Margaret Wolforth, Oct. 7, 1897; children—Judith Madison, William T., David S., Charles E., Richard H., Fitzhugh T. Interne, Randall's Island Hosp., N.Y. City, 1890-92; in practice, Washington, D.C., 1892-97; asst. surgeon, U.S. Pub. Health Service, 1897-1902, passed asst. surgeon, 1902-12, surgeon, 1912-25, sr. surgeon, 1925-30, med. dir., 1930, asst. surgeon gen. and chief Div. of Veneral Diseases, 1930-33; in supervisory charge U.S.P.H.S. activities—immigration, quarantine, etc., British Isles and continental Europe, 1926-29; retired. Dir. child hygiene investigation, 1915; dir. bureau sanitary service, Am. Red Cross, 1917-19. Mem. Internat. Sanitary Conf., Paris, 1926; del. to Internat. Conf. Tropical Medicine, Cairo, Egypt, 1928. Am. mem. Office Internat. d'Hygiène Publique. Cons. in health, Julius Rosenwald Fund. Mem. Sigma Alpha Epsilon. Contbr. many health bulletins and other papers. Home: Germantown, Md. Died July 3, 1948.

CLARK, Virginius E., aeronautical engr.; b. in Pa., Feb. 27, 1886; grad. U.S. Naval Acad., 1907; mil. aviator, 1913; post grad. course in aeronautical engring., Mass. Inst. Tech., 1914; chief aero engr. U.S. Army, 1915-20; mem. Nat. Advisory Com. for Aeronautics, 1917-18; mem. Joint Army and Navy Bd. for Aeronautics, 1917-20; mem. Bolling Aero Mission to Europe, 1917; comdg. Army Exptl. Sta., McCook Field, Dayton, O., 1917; chief engr. Dayton-Wright Co., 1920-23; v.p. and chief engr. Consolidated Aircraft Corp., 1923-27; gen. mgr. and chief engr. Am. Airplane & Engring. Corp., 1931-32. Fellow Inst. of Aeronautical Sciences. Mem. Nat. Aeronautical Safety Code Com.; 1920-24; v.p. Soc. Automotive Engrs., 1922-23. Address: 1067 Corsica Drive, Pacific Palisades, Calif.* Died Jan. 30, 1948.

CLARK, Wallace, consulting engr.; b. Wyoming, Cincinnati, O., July 27, 1880; s. William Allen and Mary (Rankin) C.; A.B., U. of Cincinnati, 1902; hon. deg. D.Eng., Stevens Inst. Technology, 1943; m. Pearl Franklin, May 11, 1922. With Remington Typewriter Co., 1907-17; staff engr. H. L. Gantt, 1917-20; head of scheduling div., U.S. Shipping Bd., 1918; cons. management engr.; head Wallace Clark & Co. since 1920; engineer member Kemmerer Finance Commission to Poland, 1926; Am. representative, committee on scientific management, International Labor Office, Geneva, Switzerland. Fellow American Society M.E.; mem. Am. Management Assn., Soc. for the Advancement of Management, Association Consulting Management Engineers, Civil Engineers of France, Masaryk Acad., also other foreign management insts. Decorated Comdr. Cross Poland Restored; Gantt medallist, 1934. Clubs: Engineers, University (N.Y. City); Cosmos (Washington); Interalliée (Paris, France). Author: The Gantt Chart, 1922; Shop and Office Forms, 1925; The Foreman and His Job, 1926. Address: 521 Fifth Av., New York 17, N.Y. Died July 4, 1948.

CLARK, Washington A., banker; b. James Island, S.C., Feb. 22, 1842; s. Ephraim Mikell and Susan Jane C.; ed. Mt. Zion Coll. and S.C. Coll. (now U. of S. C.); m. Esther Virginia Melton, Dec. 26, 1866. Admitted to S.C. bar, 1871, and began practice at Columbia; mem. Melton & Clark; later associated in practice with Judge Samuel W. Melton; became pres. Carolina Nat. Bank, 1881, now chmn. bd. Entered army of C.S.A., Apr. 1861; organized Signal Corps. at Charleston, S.C., continuing until surrender of Johnson's Army at Greensboro, Apr. 26, 1865. Democrat. Home: Columbia, S.C. Died March 7, 1931.

CLARKE, Arthur Edward, banker; b. N.Y., Feb. 26, 1872; s. John and Ann (Smith) C.; ed. pub. schs., New York; m. Bessie Vollmer, Sept. 4, 1901. With New York Life Ins. Co., at home office, New York, and London, Eng., 1886-1903; moved to Lewiston, Ida., 1903; now pres. First Nat. Bank of Lewiston, State Bank of Clarkston, First Bank of Culdesac, Vollmer Security Co., Vollmer-Clearwater Co.; dir. Erb Hardware Co.; mem. advisory bd. Spokane (Wash.) agency Reconstruction Finance Co. since 1932. Republican. Episcopalian. Home: Lewiston, Idaho. Deceased.

CLARKE, Edwin Leavitt, sociologist; b. Westboro, Mass., May 21, 1888; s. Edwin Augustus and Edith (Leavitt) C.; A.B., Clark Coll., 1909, A.M., Clark U., 1911; student Columbia U., 1911-14, Ph.D., 1916; m. Elisabeth Bodfish, Jan. 1, 1918 (died Feb. 8, 1920); m. 2d, Marguerite Walters, June 1, 1921; children—Margaret Jean, Winifred Dorothy. Teacher, South Canon City (Colo.) High Sch., 1909-10; asst. prof. sociology, Hamilton Coll., 1914-18; instr. and asst. prof. sociology, Ohio State U., 1919-23; asst. prof. sociology U. of Minn., 1923-27; prof. sociology Oberlin Coll., 1927-30; prof. sociology Rollins Coll., since 1930; visiting prof., summer sessions, Atlanta University, 1932, George Peabody Coll., 1936. Secretary Florida Voters League since 1944. Served as pvt., Base Hosp. No. 48, 1918, 2d lt., Sanitary Corps, U.S. Army General Hospital No. 8, 1918-19. Active in work for race cooperation. Mem. American Esperanto Academy, Am. Sociological Society, Southern Sociol. Soc., Phi Beta Kappa, Pi Gamma Mu. Socialist. Unitarian. Author: American Men of Letters: Their Nature and Nurture, 1916; The Art of Straight Thinking; And Your Neighbor: The Social Teachings of Jesus and Life Problems, 1947. Home: 1470 Glencoe Av. Address: Rollins Coll., Winter Park, Fla. Died Sept. 15, 1948.

CLARKE, Ernest Swope; b. Falmouth, Ky., Nov. 25, 1872; s. Asahel Rawlings and Martha Ann (Swope) C.; A.B., Bethany Coll., W. Va., 1892; m. Mary Virginia Oldham, June 12, 1900; children—George Oldham, Ernest S. Began practice of law at Falmouth, 1894; county atty., Pendleton Co., Ky., 1897-1904; county treas., 1905-07, county judge, 1909-15; became justice Ky. Court of Appeals, Dec. 1915, chief justice, Sept. 1, 1925, resigned 1926; dir. First Nat. Bank and Ky. Trust Co., Louisville, since 1926, v.p., trust officer, 1926-46. Trustee U. of Louisville, Am. Printing House for the Blind, Kentucky Female Orphans' School. Mem. Beta Theta Pi. Democrat. Mem. Disciples of Christ. Mason. Clubs: Pendennis, Conversation, Lawyers, Louisville Country. Home: Louisville, Ky. Office: 5th and Court Pl., Louisville, Ky. Died Sept. 20, 1948.

CLARKE, Herbert Lincoln, cornetist, band dir.; b. Woburn, Mass., Sept. 12, 1867; s. William Horatio and Eliza Tufts (Richardson) C.; ed. pub. schs., Indianapolis, Ind., Somerville, Mass., and Toronto, Ont.; hon. Mus.D., Phillips U., Enid, Okla., 1939; m. Lillian Bell Hause, Feb. 7, 1896; children—Ruby Bell, Ralph Hamilton, Herbert Lincoln. Was cornet soloist with Queen's Own Rifle Regt. Band of Canada, then with Gilmore's Band until death of P. S. Gilmore, later in F. N. Innes' Band, Victor Herbert's 22d Regt. Band and 7th Regt. Band, New York, and with John P. Sousa for 4 European tours; cornet soloist and asst. conductor Sousa's Band, 1904-17; dir. Anglo Canadian Concert Band of Huntsville, Ont., 1918-23; dir. Municipal Band, Long Beach, Calif., 1923-43; now retired. Played at great world expns. in Paris, Glasgow, Chicago, San Francisco, Buffalo, Pittsburgh, St. Louis, etc.; toured the world, 1911, as asst. conductor and soloist of Sousa's Band. Past pres. Am. Bandmasters Assn.; mem. Am. Soc. Composers, Authors and Publishers; mem. Sons of American Revolution. Wrote: Elementary Studies for the Cornet, 1911; Technical and Characteristic Studies. Composer of cornet solos and compositions for piano, band and orchestra. Home: R. 1, Box 561-B2, Garden Grove, Calif. Died Jan 30, 1945; buried in Congressional Cemetery, Washington.

CLARKE, Hermann Frederick, investment banker; b. Newton, Mass., Mar. 29, 1882; s. Arthur French and Mary Rice (Leslie) C.; grad. Boston Latin Sch., 1901; A.B., Harvard University, 1905; m. Dorothy Locke Johnson, June 10, 1914; children—Barbara Locke (wife of Doctor Nelson Hastings), Mary Elizabeth (Mrs. Arthur E. Beane, Jr.), Arthur French, Dorothea Leslie. Clerk, New England Mut. Life Ins. Co., 1905-07; with S.D. Loring & Son, 1907-09; with Estabrook & Co. since Jan. 1, 1909, becoming partner, 1922; dir Bigelow & Dowse Co., O.S. Walker Co.; Vitrified Wheel Co. Pres. and trustee, Home for Aged Couples; treas. and member bd. trustees, Children's Hosp. (Boston); trustee Brookline Pub. Library; mem. Mass. Charitable Fire Soc. Dir. Bostonian Society. Town meeting member of Town of Brookline. Mem. Mass. Hist. Soc., Am. Antiquarian Soc., Colonial Society of Massachusetts, Essex Institute. Clubs: Odd Volumes (Boston); The Country (Brookline). Author: John Coney, Silversmith, 1932; Jeremiah Dummer; Colonial Craftsman and Merchant, 1935; John Hull, A Builder of the Bay Colony, 1940; also various papers on hist. subjects. Home: 420 Warren St., Brookline. Office: 15 State St., Boston, Mass. Died Oct. 29, 1947.

CLARKE, James Frederic, surgeon; b. Fairfield, Ia., Feb. 23, 1864; s. Charles Shipman and Sarah Louisa (Wadsworth) C.; student Parsons College, Fairfield, Ia., 1881, 82, Sc.D., 1933; B.S., State Univ. of Ia., 1886, A.M., 1889; M.D., Univ. of Pa., 1889; studied Johns Hopkins Univ. and Univ. of Göttingen, Germany; m. Melinda Eliza Clapp, Oct. 13, 1891. Interne Phila. Gen. Hosp. 2 yrs.; practiced at Fairfield since 1889; lecturer on hygiene, U. of Ia., 3 yrs.; lecturer on fungi and bacteria, Parsons Coll., Fairfield. Maj., surgeon 49th Ia. Inf., U.S. Army, Spanish-Am. War, in Cuba, and introduced trained nurses to U.S. Army; lt. col. M.C., World War, in

France; organizer and comdr. Hosp. Unit R; built second county hosp. in Ia. at Fairfield; developed cretin children by thyroid feeding. Served as mayor of Fairfield; mem. Ia. Ho. of Rep., 1906-07. Fellow Am. Coll. Surgeons; mem. Am. and Ia. State med. socs., etc., Delta Tau Delta. Democrat. Conglist. Mason (K.T., Shriner). Club: Fairfield Rotary (organizer and pres. 1st 3 years). Home: Fairfield, Ia. Died Apr. 12, 1942.

CLARKE, John Hessin; b. at Lisbon, O., Sept. 18, 1857; s. John and Melissa (Hessin) C.; A.B., Western Reserve U., 1877, A.M., 1880, LL.D., 1916; LL.D., Brown U., 1924; unmarried. Admitted to Ohio bar, 1878; practiced at Lisbon, 1878-80, Youngstown, 1880-97, at Cleveland, 1897-1914; gen. counsel N.Y., C.&St.L. R.R. 13 yrs.; U.S. dist. judge, Northern Dist. of Ohio, 1914-16; asso. justice Supreme Court of U.S., July 14, 1916-Sept. 1922; resigned in order to give his entire time to cultivating public opinion favorable to world peace. Pres. League of Nations Non-Partisan Assn. of U.S., 1922-30. Trustee World Peace Foundation (Boston), 1923-31; hon. life trustee Youngstown Pub. Library; trustee Cleveland Pub. Library, 1903-06. Mem. Phi Beta Kappa. Clubs: City (Cleveland); Cuyamaca, University (San Diego). Home: Hotel El Cortez, San Diego, Calif. Died Mar. 22, 1945.

CLARKE, Lorenzo Mason, clergyman; b. Canandaigua, N.Y., 1859; s. Dr. Noah T. and Laura Mason (Merrill) C.; A.B., Amherst, 1880, D.D., 1900; grad. Auburn Theol. Sem., 1885; m. Maude Fowler, 1885. Ordained Presbyn. ministry, 1885; pastor First Ch., Wolcott, N.Y., 1885-89, Park Central Ch., Syracuse, N.Y., 1889-97. First Ch., Brooklyn, since 1897. Trustee Union Theol. Sem.; dir. Packer Inst., Brooklyn, L.I., Hist. Soc. Author: Our Feast of Tabernacles; Concerning the Life Beyond; The Church Glorious; The Law of Rest; also other works. Address: 128 Henry St., Brooklyn. Died Nov. 6, 1944.

CLARKE, Walter James, physician; b. St. Andrews, N.B., Can., Dec. 25, 1864; s. Nelson and Mary Jane (Martin) C.; B.A., U. of New Brunswick, Fredericton, N.B., 1885; M.D., Coll. Phys. and Surg., Columbia, 1889; m. Annie Waite Knight, Oct. 27, 1897. Practiced in N.Y. City since 1889; pres. Orleans Real Estate Co. Mem. New York County Med. Soc. Episcopalian. Home: 224 W. 72d St., New York. Died May 22, 1937.

CLARKSON, Heriot, judge; b. Kingville, Richland County, S.C., Aug. 21, 1863; s. Maj. William and Margaret S. (Simons) C.; desc. Benjamin Simons, from France to S.C. about 1685, also of Esther Marion, only sister of Gen. Francis Marion; ed. Carolina Mil. Inst., Charlotte, N.C.; law study U. of N.C., 1884, LL.D., 1928; m. Mary Lloyd Osborne, Dec. 10, 1889; children—Francis Osborne, Edwin Osborne, Thomas Simons, Margaret Fullarton (Mrs. John Garland Pollard, Jr.). Was admitted to N.C. bar, 1884, and began practice of law at Charlotte; asso. in practice with Judge Charles H. Duls, 1888-1913, later sr. mem. Clarkson, Taliaferro & Clarkson. Mem. N.C. Ho. of Rep,, 1899; city atty., Charlotte, 1901-05; solicitor 12th Jud. Dist. of N.C., 1904-10; apptd., by Gov. Cameron Morrison, asso. justice Supreme Court of N.C., May 26, 1923, and elected to same office Nov. 1924, and re-elected Nov. 1926 and Nov. 1934 for terms of 8 yrs.; General Assembly of 1935 unanimously passed an act applicable alone to himself allowing retirement on ⅔ pay. Mem. N.C. Hist. Commn. Mem. N.C. Society of the Cincinnati, S.R., Sigma Alpha Epsilon, Gamma Eta Gamma. Democrat. Episcopalian. Pres. Anti-Saloon League, 1908, when N.C. voted out the distillery and saloon by a majority of 44,196; was chmn. Com. on Good Roads that drew the bill practically adopted by the legislature of N.C., 1921, that provided for the good road system of N.C. Promoter and developer of Little Switzerland, N.C.; organized united dry forces of N.C. and state voted, Nov. 1933, against repeal of prohibition by 184,572 majority; pres. Interstate Y.M.C.A. of the Carolinas. Address: Supreme Court, Raleigh, N.C. Died Jan. 7, 1942.

CLARKSON, Wright, radiologist; b. Center Cross, Va., Dec. 9, 1889; s. Julian Wright and Margaret Lemuel (Clarkson) C.; grad. Randolph Macon Acad., Bedford City, Va., 1908; M.D., Med. Coll. of Va., Richmond, 1912; grad. U.S. Army Med. Sch., Washington, D.C., 1918; m. Caroline Robinson Davis, Oct. 28, 1919; 1 son, Julian Wright. In pvt. practice, Hardy, Ky., 1913-15, Mt. Solon, Va., 1915-18, Petersburg, Va., since 1920; specialized in radiology and oncology since 1918. Lt. M.C., U.S. Army, during World War; chief X-Ray Service Gen. Hosp. 41, Staten Island, N.Y., 1920; lt. comdr. M.C., U.S.N.R. Trustee Southern Coll., Petersburg. Founder, Va. Radiol. Soc., Fourth District Medical Society of Va., Va. Cancer Foundation. Member A.M.A., Am. Coll. of Radiology, Am. Roentgen Ray Soc., Radiol. Soc. of N.A., Am. Soc. for Study of Neoplastic Diseases (ex-pres.), Tri-State Med. Assn., Med. Society of Va., Petersburg Med. Faculty, Phi Beta Pi. Democrat. Episcopalian. Clubs: Commonwealth (Richmond); Country. Radiol. editor of Southern Medicine and Surgery. Home: 205 S. Sycamore St., Petersburg, Va. Died Oct. 18, 1943.

CLAUSEN, Frederick Harold, mfr.; b. Fox Lake, Wis., Oct. 22, 1875; s. Henry and Nicolina (Christenson) C.; B.L., U. of Wis., 1897, LL.B., 1899; m. Eleanor Bliss, Sept. 19, 1900; children—Margaret (wife of Dr. Clarence Manning), Catherine Martha (wife Dr. John H. Karsten), Elna Mary (Mrs. Raymond Hadley). With Van Brunt Mfg. Co. since 1900, factory mgr., 1913-19, pres. since 1919; chmn. board of dirs. Holeproof Hosiery Co.; vice-president National Founders Association, Horicon State Bank; dir. Deere & Co., Wis. Power & Light Co. Dir. code activities of farm machinery industry. Rep. nominee for U.S. Senator from Wis., 1940. Has served as pres. sch. bd., city atty. and alderman, Horicon, and mem. county bd. of Dodge County. Pres. bd. regents U. of Wis., 1933-35; trustee Milwaukee-Downer Coll. Mem. Chamber of Commerce of U.S. (dir.), Wis. Mfg. Assn. (ex-pres.; now mem. exec. com.), Phi Gamma Delta. Republican. Episcopalian. Mason (32°), Odd Fellow. Clubs: Rotary (Horicon); Tuscumbia Golf (Green Lake). Home: Horicon, Wis. Died Oct. 20, 1944.

CLAUSSEN, George, lawyer; b. Clinton, Ia., Aug. 6, 1882; s. John and Wiebke (Banderob) C.; ed. pub. schs.; student Coll. of Law, State Univ. of Ia., 1901-03; m. Luella Fahr, Mar. 18, 1920; 1 son, Robert George. Admitted to Ia. bar, 1912, and practiced in Clinton, 1912-15; county atty., 1915-18; judge Municipal Court, Clinton, 1918; resumed law practice, 1919-32; partner Wolfe, Wolfe & Claussen; apptd. judge Supreme Court of Iowa, 1932, chief justice, 1934; resumed practice at Clinton, partner Miller & Claussen, 1935; apptd. judge Dist. Court of Ia., 7th Dist., June 1941. Mem. Am., Ia. State and Clinton County bar assns. Republican. Mason. Home: 710 2d Av. Address: Court House, Clinton, Ia.* Died Dec. 18, 1948.

CLAWSON, Rudger; b. Salt Lake City, Utah, Mar. 12, 1857; s. Hyrum Bradley and Margaret Gay (Judd) C.; ed. private schs. and U. of Deseret (now U. of Utah); m. Florence Ann Dinwoodey, Aug. 12, 1882 (div.); 1 son, Rudger Elmo; m. 2d, Lydia Spencer, Mar. 29, 1883; children—Remus Rudger, Hiram Bradley, Margaret Gay, Daniel Spencer, Vera Mary, Samuel George, Lorenzo Snow, Marion, Lydia. Born in the Church of Jesus Christ of Latter-day Saints; president Box Elder Stake, 1888-98, mem. Council of 12 Apostles since 1898 (pres. since 1921), mem. Gen. Bd. Young Men's Mutual Improvement Assn., 1900-20, mem. and 1st pres. of Ch., 1901, mem. Gen. Bd. of Edn. since 1905, pres. European Mission, 1910-13. Trustee Brigham Young U. since 1939. Home: 51 Canyon Rd. Office: 47 E. South Temple St., Salt Lake City, Utah. Died June 21, 1943.

CLAYTON, Henry Helm, meteorologist; b. Murfreesboro, Tenn., Mar. 12, 1861; s. Dr. Henry Holmes and Maria L. (Helm) C.; ed. pvt. schs., 1869-77; m. Frances Fawn Coman, Sept. 21, 1892; children—Henry Comyn (deceased), Lawrence Locke, Frances Lindley Asst., Astron. Obs., Ann Arbor, Mich., 1884-85; asst., Harvard Astronomical Obs., 1885-86; observer, Blue Hill Meteorol. Obs., 1886-91; local forecast official U.S. Weather Bur., 1891-93; meteorologist, Blue Hill Meteorol. Obs., 1894-1909; dean Sch. of Aeronautics Assn. Inst., Boston, 1909-10. Employed by Oficina Meteorologica Argentina to study methods of weather forecasting in the Argentine Republic and also to inaugurate near Cordoba a sta. for exploring the upper air by means of kites, Mar.-Oct. 1910; engaged in business, 1911-12; forecast official, Oficina Meteorologica Argentina, Buenos Aires, 1913-22; researches, in coöperation with the Smithsonian Instn., in regard to the relation of world weather changes to observe conditions on the sun, 1923-25; pvt. weather service and cons. meteorologist for business orgns., 1925-42; research associate, Harvard University, 1943-44. In charge, 1905, of Tiesseren de Bort-Rotch expdn. for exploring the atmosphere over the Atlantic ocean with kites and sounding balloons; accompanied Oscar Erbsloh in the German balloon Pommern, Oct. 1907, when record-making balloon voyage was made from St. Louis to Asbury Park, N.J. Inaugurated a new system of weather forecasting, based on solar heat changes in Argentina, 1918. Cons. expert in Cloud Atlas prepared for Hydrographic Office, under Capt. Sigsbee, U.S. Navy; invented attachment for anemometers, Blue Hill box kite, etc. Del. Pan-Am. Scientific Congress, Washington, D.C., 1915; del. Argentine Weather Service to 6th Internat. Meteorol. Conf., Holland, 1923. Fellow Am. Acad. Arts and Sciences. Author: World Weather, 1923; World Weather Records (pub. by Smithsonian Instn.), 1927 and 1934; Solar Relations to Weather, 1943; also numerous papers on meteorol. subjects (1939-41); studies of periodic changes in solar activity pub. by Smithsonian Institution and in Jour. of Atmosphere, Electricity and Terrestrial Magnetism of Carnegie Institution. Home: Canton, Mass. Died Oct. 27, 1946.

CLAYTON, Lawrence, govt. official; b. Salt Lake City, Utah, Mar. 1, 1891; s. Nephi Willard and Sybella White (Johnson) C.; student U. of Mich., 1911-13, U. of Utah, summer 1913; A.B., Stanford, 1914; LL.B., Harvard, 1917; m. Ruth Dunn, July 22, 1921; children—Sybella, Lawrence, Barbara. Vice pres. and mgr. Clayton Investment Co., Salt Lake City, 1920-23; with First Nat. Bank, Ogden, Utah, 1924-34, asst. cashier, 1924-28, asst. vice president 1928-31, v.p., 1931-34; asst. to chmn. Fed. Res. Bd., 1934-45; pres. Clayton Securities Corp., Boston, Mass., 1945-47; mem. bd. govs., Fed. Res. System, Washington, D.C., since Feb. 1947. Served with U.S. Army, 1917-19; lt. field arty., 1917, advancing through grades to major, 1919; with 102d F.A., 26th (Yankee) Div., 1918; asst. dir. mil. affairs, Transportation Corps, Tours, France, Jan.-July 1919; participated in campaigns, Second Marne, St. Mihiel, Meuse-Argonne; maj., F.A. Res., 1919, promoted lt. col., 1928, col. since 1939; on inactive duty. Mem. Phi Beta Kappa, Alpha Sigma Phi. Clubs: Burning Tree (Washington); Hatherly Country (North Scituate, Mass.); Algonquin (Boston). Mem. Ch. of Jesus Christ of the Latter-day Saints. Home: 3 Gannett Rd., North Scituate, Mass. Office: Federal Reserve Bldg., Washington 25, D.C. Died Dec. 4, 1949.

CLEARY, Michael Joseph (klēr'ĭ), life ins. exec.; b. Iowa County, Wis., Sept. 23, 1876; s. Michael and Bridget (Ducey) C.; LL.B., U. of Wis., 1901; m. Bonnie Blanchard, Nov. 15, 1915; children—Catherine B., Mary E., James Thomas. Admitted to Wis. bar, 1901, and practiced at Blanchardville as mem. firm Chandler & Cleary, 1901-15; exec. counsel to Gov. Philipp, Jan.-July 1915; commr. of ins., Wis., 1915-19; v.p. Northwestern Mut. Life Ins. Co., 1919-32, pres., 1932-47; dir. Wis. Tel. Co.; Regent U. Wis.; mem. bd. govs. Marquette Univ. Republican. Catholic. Clubs: University, Milwaukee, Milwaukee Country. Home: 3032 Summit Av. Office: 720 E. Wisconsin Av., Milwaukee, Wis. Died Feb. 22, 1947.

CLEAVELAND, Harry Hayes, insurance; b. Rock Island, Ill., Aug. 13, 1869; s. Henry Clay and Olivia Sophia (Hayes) C.; grad. high sch., Rock Island, 1887; B.S., Knox Coll., Galesburg, Ill., 1890; LL.D., Knox Coll., 1940; m. Olive Cox, Oct. 25, 1892; children—Eleanor Maude (Mrs. David James McCredie), Olive Marion (dec.), Harry Hayes II, Dorothy (Mrs. Frederic B. White), Ann Cox (Mrs. W. Stewart McDonald). Organizer H. H. Cleaveland Agency, ins., Rock Island, Ill., 1890; dir. Ins. Fedn. of Ill.; chmn. bd. and pres. Bituminous Casualty Corp.; pres. Fort Armstrong Co., Memorial Park Development Co.; v.p. Streckfus Steamers, Inc.; dir. Black Hawk Federal Bldg. & Loan Assn. Director state dept. pub. works and bldgs., Ill., 1929-33; pres. Bd. of Edn., Rock Island, 1910-19; v.p. Ill. Chamber Commerce, 1925-27. Trustee Knox Coll., 1944. Republican. Mason (33°, grand comdr. Ill. K.T., 1910-11), Elk. Clubs: (Rock Island Arsenal Golf, Treadway Rod and Gun (Rock Island); Union League (Chicago); Fairchild Tropical Garden, Dinner Call (Miami, Fla.), Century. Home: 56 Hawthorne Rd. Office: Cleaveland Bldg., Rock Island, Illinois. Died May 24, 1946.

CLEMENT, John Addison (klĕm'ĕnt), prof. education; b. Alliance, O., May 19, 1875; s. John Aime and Emaline (Bowman) C.; student Ohio Normal U., Mt. Union Coll.; A.B., McPherson (Kan.) Coll., 1902; A.M., U. of Kan., 1910; Ph.D., magna cum laude, U. of Chicago, 1911; m. Clara Caroline Wheeler, Sept. 21, 1905. Prof. edn. and psychology, McPherson Coll., 1903-05; research scholar in edn., U. of Chicago, 1905-06; asst. prof. edn., U. of Kan., 1909-10; fellow in edn., U. of Chicago, 1910-11; pres. McPherson Coll., 1911-13; lecturer and asst. prof. edn., Northwestern U., 1913-16; head of dept. edn. and psychology, De Pauw U., 1916-20; asso. prof. secondary edn., Northwestern U., 1920-23, prof., 1923-24; prof. edn., U. of Ill., summer 1923-44; asst. county supt. schools, Champaign Co., Ill., since 1944; prof. education, U. of Washington, summers 1917-20, Univ. of Pa., summer 1927. Member National Soc. Study of Edn., N. Central Assn. Secondary Schs. and Colls., Phi Delta Kappa, Alpha Tau Omega. Republican. Methodist. Mason (K.T.). Author: The Standardization of the Schools of Kansas, 1911; Curriculum Making in Secondary Schools, 1923; Principles and Practices of Secondary Education, 1925; Coöperative Supervision in Grades Seven to Twelve, 1930. Joint editor of High School Curriculum Reorganization, 1933; Educational Significance of Analysis, Appraisal and Use of Textbooks, 1939; Manual for Analyzing and Selecting Textbooks, 1942. Address: Gregory Hall, Urbana, Ill. Died Nov. 1, 1947.

CLEMENTS, Berthold A., business exec.; b. Indianapolis, Ind., 1877. Pres. and dir. American Arch Co., Diamond Fire Brick Co. Dir. Harbison-Walker Refractories Co., G. M. Basford Co., Lima Locomotive Works, Inc., Gen. Railway Signal Co. Home: 115 Central Park West. Office: American Arch Co., 60 E. 42d St., New York, N.Y. Died Nov. 23, 1949.

CLEMENTS, Colin (Campbell), playwright; b. Omaha, Neb., Feb. 25, 1894; s. William George and Ada (von Swanback) C.; A.B., U. of Wash., 1917; student Carnegie Inst. Tech., 1918, 47 workshop, Harvard, 1922-23; m. Florence Ryerson, 1927. Play reader, actor and stage mgr. for Portmanteau Theatre, N.Y. City, 1918; traveled abroad, 1919-21; master in English, Lawrenceville Sch., 1921-22. Student Military O.T.S., 1917; in U.S. Army, 1918. Awarded Near East Relief Medal. Mem. Authors' League America, Sigma Chi, Sigma Upsilon. Episcopalian. Author: The Touchstone and Other Plays, 1919; Seven Plays of Old Japan, 1920; Job—A Drama, 1922; A Book of Prayers for Boys, 1922; Plays for a Folding Theatre, 1923; Plays for Pagans, 1924; Wreckage (with Mary Heaton Vorse), 1924; Curtain, 1925; The Boy Through the Window, 1928; (following with wife) All On a Summer's Day, 1928; Seven Suspects, 1930; This Awful Age, 1930; Fear of Fear, 1931; Diana Laughs, 1932; Mild Oats, 1933; Blind Man's Buff, 1933; Shadows, 1934; The Borgia Blade, 1937; Ladies Alone—Eight Comedies, 1937; First Person Singular—a book of monologues, 1937; Angels Don't Marry and Other One-Act Plays, 1938; Isn't Nature Wonderful (monologues), 1938; June Mad (comedy), 1939; Through the Night (play), 1940;

Winnie Weeks (monologues), 1940; Glamour Preferred (comedy), 1941; Ever Since Eve (comedy), 1941; Harriet (with Florence Ryerson; star Helen Hayes), 1943; Spring Green (comedy) 1944; The Divine Flora (comedy), 1947; Oh! Susanna (comedy with music), 1947; Strange Bedfellows (with Florence Ryerson), 1948. Writer motion pictures. Editor: Sea Plays, 1925; They Do Not!, 1926. Dramatized Rip Van Winkle for the Roumanian Theatre, and Queen Marie's Ilderim (with Ion Paretz, formerly dir. Nat. Theatre of Roumania). Contbr. to Mags. Address: 939 Stone Canyon Rd., Bel-Air, Los Angeles 24, Calif. Died Jan. 29, 1948.

CLEMENTS, Frederic Edward, ecologist; b. Lincoln, Neb., Sept. 16, 1874; s. Ephraim G. and Mary (Scoggin) C.; B.Sc., U. of Neb. 1894, M.A., 1896, Ph.D., 1898, LL.D., 1940; m. Edith Schwartz, May 30, 1899. Instr. and asso. prof. botany, 1894-1906, prof. plant physiology, 1906-07, U. of Neb.; prof. and head of dept. of botany, U. of Minn., 1907-17; State botanist, dir. bot. survey of Minn.; in charge ecol. research, Carnegie Instn., Washington, 1917-41, retired; in charge Lab. Ecol. Research since 1941; collaborator U.S. Soil Conservation Service since 1934; cons. National Highway Research Bd., 1935. Fellow A.A.A.S., (gen. sec., 1910); mem. Neb. Acad. of Science, Am. Microscop. Soc., Bot. Soc. of Am (v.p. 1905; councillor, 1906-10), Am. Geographers Assn., Am. Nomenclature Commn., Internat. Nomenclature Commn., Internat. Cong. of Science, Am. Nature Study Soc. (dir. 1905), Am. Breeders Assn., St. Paul Inst., Minn. Mycol. Soc. (pres. 1908), Minn. Garden Club (pres. 1910), Ecol. Soc. of Am., Paleontol. Soc., Soc. Am. Foresters, Am. Meteorol. Soc., Am. Soc. Mammologists, Am. Soc. of Naturalists, Am. Soc. Plant Physiologists, Brit. Ecol. Soc., Societas Phytogeographica Suecana of Sweden (hon.), Reale Academia Agricultura of Italy (hon.), Sigma Xi, Phi Beta Kappa. Author: The Phytogeography of Nebraska (with Dr. Pound), 1898, 2d edit., 1900; Histogenesis of Caryophyllales, 1899; Greek and Latin in Biological Nomenclature, 1902; Herbaria Formationum Coloradensium, 1902; Development and Structure of Vegetation, 1904; Research Methods in Ecology, 1905; Plant Physiology and Ecology, 1907; Cryptogamæ Formationum Coloradensium, 1908; Genera of Fungi, 1909; Minnesota Mushrooms, 1910; Rocky Mountain Flowers, 1913 (with Dr. Edith Clements); Plant Succession, 1916; Plant Indicators, 1920; Aeration and Air-Content, 1921; The Phylogenetic Method in Taxonomy (with Dr. Hall), 1923; Experimental Pollination (with Dr. Long), 1923; Experimental Vegetation (with Dr. Weaver), 1924; Phytometer Method in Ecology (with Dr. Goldsmith), 1924; Plant Succession and Indicators, 1928; Flower Families and Ancestors (with Dr. Edith Clements), 1928; Plant mer) Manitou, Colo. (Alpine Lab.). Died July 26, 1945.

CLEMMONS, Joe Rainey, physician; born Longview, Tex., Sept. 4, 1896; s. Joe Rainey and Livina Feraby (McKay) C.; student Simmons Coll., 1913-17; M.D., U. of Tenn., 1924. Interne Mason Hosp., Ga., 1924-26; supt., Macon Hosp., Macon, Ga., 1926-29; asst. dir. Strong Memorial Hosp., U. of Rochester (N.Y.) Sch. Med. and Dentistry, 1930-37; med. dir. Roosevelt Hosp., New York City, 1937-46, exec. vice pres. and med. dir. since 1946. Co-chmn. on insurance coverage, council on administrative practice, Am. Hosp. Assn., 1938-40; state chmn. Procurement and Assignment Service for Physicians, War Manpower Commn., 1942-46.Hosp. cons. Am. Hosp. Assn., Am. Dietetic Assn., 1939-44, Am. Assn. Nurse Anesthetists, 1942-44; mem. com. National League Nursing Education on Accreditation, 1941-44. Member board trustees, Miriam Osborn Memorial Home, Harrison, New York, 1945-48. Member Greater New York Hosp. Assn. (vice pres. 1944, pres. 1945; mem. council on professional practice, 1938-44). Fellow, Am. Coll. Hosp. Adminstrs., Am. Med. Assn.; mem Am. Public Health Assn., Westchester Co. Med. Soc., N.Y. State Med. Soc., N.Y. Co. Med. Soc., N.Y. Acad. Med., N.Y. State Hosp. Assn., Med. Supts. Club, Hosp. Soc. of N.Y., Phi Chi. Mason. Clubs: University (New York). Home: Cambridge House, Scarsdale, N.Y. Office: 428 W. 59th St., New York 19, N.Y. Died Apr. 2, 1949.

CLENDENING, Logan, physician; b. Kansas City, Mo., May 25, 1884; s. Edwin McKaig and Lide (Logan) C.; student U. of Mich., 1903-05; M.D., U. of Kan., 1907; m. Dorothy Hixon, July 22, 1914. Began practice at Kansas City, 1909; instr. in internal medicine, Med. Dept., U. of Kan., 1910-17, asso. prof. medicine, 1920-28, prof. clin. medicine since 1928; pres. St. Luke's Hosp. staff, 1922-23. Major Med. Corps, chief of med. service Base Hosp., Fort Sam Houston, 1917-19. Fellow Am. Coll. Physicians (bd. govs., 1926-30; bd. regents 1931), Am. Therapeutic Soc., Am. Climatol. and Clin. Assn. Free Thinker. Clubs: Kansas City, University, Kansas City Country (Kansas City); Grolier (New York); Valley (Montecito, Calif.); Santa Barbara (Santa Barbara, Calif.). Author: Modern Methods of Treatment, 1924; The Human Body, 1927; The Care and Feeding of Adults, 1931; Behind the Doctor, 1933; Source Book of Medical History, 1942; Methods of Diagnosis (published Posthumously). Home: 1247 W. 56th St. Office: Univ. of Kansas Medical School, Kansas City, Kan. Died Jan. 31, 1945.

CLEOPHAS, Mother Mary, coll. pres.; b. Philadelphia, Pa., July 12, 1880; d. Charles T. and Katherine (Delaney) Foy; A.B., Catbolic U. of America, 1919; M.A., Fordham U., 1921; grad. study, U. of Pa., 1919-20. Began as teacher in New York, 1904; prin. St. Leonard's Acad., Philadelphia, 1914-18, St. Walburga's Acad., New York, 1919-23; dean, Rosemont Coll., 1924-36, v.p., 1936-39, pres. since 1939. Address: Rosemont Coll., Rosemont, Pa. Died Jan. 6, 1946.

CLERK, Ira (clärk), banker; born at Ingham, Australia, June 21, 1885; s. Arthur Temple and Alice Maud May (Cunningham) C.; student Boys Normal Sch., Brisbane, 1898-1900, Toowoomba Grammar Sch. (prep. sch.), Jan.-Dec. 1901; m. Winifred Mastick, Dec. 27, 1913; children—George Temple, Franklyn, Douglas, Norman. Came to U.S., 1905, naturalized citizen, 1914. Clerk New Zealand Loan & Mercantile Agency Co., Brisbane, Australia, 1902-05; Sanger (Calif.) Lumber Co., 1905; Canadian Bank of Commerce, San Francisco and elsewhere, 1906-12, Bank of Italy, San Francisco, 1913-14; with Federal Res. Bank of San Francisco since Nov. 1914. beginning as acting asst. cashier, 1st v.p. since 1936. Episcopalian. Clubs: Bohemian, Commonwealth, San Francisco Flycasting (San Francisco); Encinal Yacht (Alameda). Home: 1209 Bay St., Alameda, Calif. Office: 400 Sansome St., San Francisco 20, Calif. Died Sep. 28, 1946.

CLEVELAND, Frederick Albert, economist; b. Sterling, Ill., Mar. 17, 1865; s. William A. and Mary T. (Humaston) C.; Ph.B., De Pauw U., 1890; studied law, 1889-91; fellow Univ. of Chicago, 1897-99; Ph.D., Univ. of Penn. 1900; m. Jessica England Lindsay, July 17, 1902; 1 son, Lindsay; married 2d, Jane Van Buren (Salisbury) Hugo, 1927, Practiced law, 1891-96; instr. in finance, Univ. of Pa., 1900-03; prof. finance, Sch. of Commerce, New York Univ., 1903-05; mem. comm. appointed by Mayor McClellan to investigate finances of New York, 1905; mem. com. on hosp. finances and needs, New York, 1906; com. on phys. welfare of sch. children, 1906; dir. Bur. of Municipal Research, N. Y. 1907-17. Mem. com. for revision of accounts and methods, N.Y., 1908-10; in charge of President's inquiry into methods of bus. of U.S. Govt., 1910; chmn. President Taft's Commn. on Economy and Efficiency, 1911-13; in charge of staff inquiry into methods of U.S. Customs Service, at New York, 1913; in charge of U.S. Senate com. inquiry into adminstrn. of Indian affairs, 1914; engaged in inquiries into state and municipal govts., 1915; dir. of studies in adminstrn. pub. by Inst. Govt. Research, 1916-17; sec. Indsl. Service & Equipment Co., 1917-18; spl. staff, war work, 1918; chair U.S. citizenship, Maxwell Found., Boston U., 1919-29; mem. Commn. of Financial Advisory to Chinese Nat. Govt., 1929-30; advisor to Legislation of Yuan, 1931-32; chief inspector of salt revenue, China, 1931-35, hdqrs. Shanghai. Decorated Emblem of Order of Blue Jade, 1935. Author: Growth of Democracy in the U.S., 1898; Funds and Their Uses, 1902; ednl. edit. same, First Lessons in Finance 1903, 23; The Bank and Treasury, 1905; Railroad Promotion and Capitalization, 1912; Railroad Finance (with F. W. Powell), 1913; Chapters in Municipal Administration and Accounting, 1909; Handbook Municipal Accounting, 1913; Organized Democracy, 1913; Democracy in Reconstruction (with Joseph Schafer), 1919; The Budget and Responsible Government (with A.E. Buck), 1920; American Citizenship, 1927; Modern Scientific Knowledge, 1929. Home: 12 Vernon St., Norwood, Mass. Died Jan. 26, 1946.

CLEWIS, Alonzo Charles (kloo'is), banker; b. Dooly County, Ga., Dec. 25, 1864; s. Richard and Jane (Roberts) C.; ed. pub. schs. of Ga.; m. Amelia Munro, Dec. 18, 1889 (now dec.); children—Mary (Mrs. George B. Howell), Alonzo Charles. In banking and related lines of business since 1890; chmn. bd. Exchange Nat. Bank, Tampa, Fla.; pres. First Savings and Trust Co., Tampa; dir. Tampa Abstract and Title Ins. Co. Mem. State Planning Bd. Independent Democrat. Episcopalian. Elk. Home: 2509 Bayshore Blvd. Office: 512 Franklin St., Tampa, Fla. Died Feb. 15, 1944.

CLIFTON, Albert Turner, mfr.; b. Waco, Tex., May 8, 1879; s. William Ridley and Birtie (Henry) C.; student Baylor U. and Horners Mil. Sch., Oxford, N.C.; grad. Philadelphia (Pa.) Textile Sch., 1899; student Toby Bus. Coll., Waco; m. Mary Lacy, Aug. 31, 1904; children—Albert Lacy, Mary B., William Lacy. Employed in cotton mill, Gastonia, N.C., 1899-1901; operator West & Hillsboro Mills, 1900-08; pres. Clifton Mfg. Co., mfrs. tents, awnings, etc., Waco, since 1909; chmn. bd. Tex. Textile Mills, Dallas Textile Mills, First National Bank (Waco), Behrens Drug Co., Mid-Tex. Motors, Inc.; vice pres. Clifton-Simpson Hardware Co., Miller Co., Inc., dir. M-K-T R.R. Co., Texas Central R.R. Co., Brazos Valley Cotton Mills, Dr. Pepper Co. Dir. and mem. advisory com. Dallas Loan Agency, Reconstruction Finance Company; v.p. Employees Council of Tex.; dir. Tex. Employers Ins., Southern States Industrial Council (Nashville). Democrat. Presbyn. Mason (Shriner). Clubs: Texas (Dallas) (dir.), Shrine, Lake Waco Country. Home: 2600 Austin Av. Office: Clifton Mfg. Co., Waco, Tex. Died Oct. 31, 1948.

CLINE, Pierce, college pres.; b. Waleska, Ga., Feb. 17, 1890; s. John Wesley and Lula Columbus (Sharp) C.; student Reinhardt Coll., Waleska, Ga., 1910-12; Ph.B., Emory U., Atlanta, 1916, A.M., 1917; postgrad. study, U. of Chicago and Columbia; m. Mary Dowdell, Aug. 14, 1923; children—James Hill, Louise Dowdell, Pierce. Instr. in history, Emory Coll., 1917-18; prof. history, Birmingham (Ala.) Southern Coll., 1919; pres. Robert E. Lee Inst., Thomaston, Ga., 1919-20; prof. history Centenary Coll. of La., Shreveport, since 1920, now pres. Centenary Coll.; also lecturer. Mem. Am. Hist. Assn., Pi Kappa Delta, Phi Beta Kappa. Democrat. Methodist. Mason. Home: Centenary Campus, Shreveport, La. Died Oct. 25, 1943.

CLINTON, Marshall, surgeon; b. Buffalo. N.Y., July 22, 1873; s. Spencer and Sarah (Riley) C.; M.D., U. of Buffalo, 1895; m. Alethe Evans, Dec. 12, 1900 (divorced); children—DeWitt II, Karl, Geoffrey (dec.), Marcia, Marshall; m. 2d, Virginia Shepherd, M.D. Practiced, Buffalo, 1895-Dec. 1940; prof. surgery U. of Buffalo, later emeritus attending surgeon Buffalo Gen. Hosp.; retired 1938. Asst. surgeon 202d N.Y. Regt., Spanish-Am. War, 1898; chief surgeon consultant, 2d Army, A.E.F., World War I, commd. maj. Med. R.C., June 12, 1917; lt. col., June 6, 1918; dir. Buffalo Base Hosp. No. 23, 1917-19. Fellow Am. Coll. Surgeons, Am. Surg. Assn.; mem. Buffalo Acad. Medicine, etc. Republican. Episcopalian. Home: Bluff City, Tenn. Died Sept. 3, 1943; buried Morning View Cemetery, Bluff City.

CLIPPINGER, Walter Gillan, college pres.; b. Lurgan, Franklin County, Pa., Mar. 1, 1873; s. Harry R. and Harriet Rebecca (Gillan) C.; B.A., Lebanon Valley Coll., Pa., 1899, D.D., 1912, LL.D., 1927; B.D., Bonebrake Theol. Sem., 1903; student U. of Chicago, 1907-09; LL.D., Otterbein Coll., 1922, L.H.D., 1940; m. Sara A. Roop, May 19, 1903; children—Donald R., Walter G., Charlotte L. (Mrs. John Cummins). Salesman Dodd, Mead and Co., pubs., New York, 1899-1900; with U. B. Pub. House, Dayton, 1903-05; prof. religious edn., Bonebrake Theol. Sem., 1905-09; pres. Otterbein Coll., 1909-39, now pres. emeritus. Mem. bd. trustees Internat. Council Religious Edn., 1935-40; pres. Ohio Anti-Saloon League, 1936-43; Torch (pres. 1938-39), Westerville Lions, Schoolmasters of Central Ohio. Wrote: Student Relationships. Home: Westerville, O. Died Sept. 30, 1948.

CLOCK, Ralph H., lawyer; b. Geneva, Ia., Sept. 3, 1878; s. Henry and Susan (Reeve) C.; student Hampton (Ia.) High Sch., 1894-98, U. of Minn., 1901-03; LL.B., Drake U., Des Moines, Ia., 1904; m. Maude E. Harriman, Nov. 7, 1906; 1 son, Henry Harriman. Admitted to Iowa bar, 1904, to Calif. bar, 1910; practiced in Long Beach, Calif., since 1910; partner Clock, Waestman & Clock; judge superior court, Los Angeles County, 1923-25; director Western Trust & Savings Bank, Long Beach. Member American, Calif. State, Los Angeles County and Long Beach bar assns., Alpha Tau Omega. Republican. Mason, K.P., Elk. Clubs: Pacific Coast, Virginia Country. Home: 2767 E. Ocean Av. Office: Jergins Trust Bldg., Long Beach, Calif. Died May 29, 1944; interned Sunnyside Mausoleum, Long Beach, Calif.

CLOPTON, Malvern Bryan, surgeon; b. St. Louis, Mo., Oct. 8, 1875; s. William H. and Belle (Bryan) C.; prep. edn., St. Louis High Sch.; student U. of Va., classical course, 1893-95, M.D., 1897; m. Mrs. James T. Walker, 1909 (died 1911); m. 2d, Mrs. Rachel Lowe Lambert, 1934. Began practice at St. Louis, 1897; interne Johns Hopkins Hosp., 1898-1900; clin. prof. surgery, Washington U. Sch. of Medicine; asst. surgeon Barnes Hosp.; asso. surgeon St. Louis Children's Hosp.; chief of staff St. Luke's Hosp., 1933-37; consulting surgeon Jewish Hosp. Lt. col. Med. Corps, U.S. Army, 1917-19; with Base Hosp. No. 21 and C.O. Mobile Hosp. No. 4, A.E.F. Fellow Am. Coll. Surgeons; mem. A.M.A., Am. Southern and Western surg. assns., St. Louis Surg. Soc., Soc. Clin. Surgery. Member board directors Washington Univ. Democrat. Episcopalian. Clubs: University, Racquet, St. Louis Country, Log Cabin Club, Round Table. Contbr. to med. jours. Home: Clarksville, Mo. Office: Beaumont Medical Bldg., St. Louis, Mo. Died Apr. 21, 1947; buried in Bellefontaine Cemetery, St. Louis.

CLOSE, Ralph William, diplomat; b. Cape Town, S. Africa, Oct. 27, 1867; s. George and Jane C.; ed. S. African Coll., 1887; B.A., LL.B., Univ. Cape of Good Hope; m. Florence Agnes Mills, Dec. 16, 1897; 1 dau., Heather Edith (wife of Comdr. Wilfred Stanley Mann, Brit. Navy). In civil service of Govt. of Cape Colony, South Africa, 1887-94; practiced as barrister, 1894-1933; apptd. King's counsel, 1912; mem. S. African Parliament, 1915-33; E.E. and M.P. from S. Africa to U.S. since 1934. Hon. mem. Metropolitan, Chevy Chase, Cosmos and University Clubs—all Washington, D.C. Mem. Ch. of Province of S. Africa (Anglican). Clubs: Civil Service, University and Owl (Cape Town, S. Africa). Address: Legation of the Union of South Africa. 3101 Massachusetts Av., Washington, D.C. Died Mar. 1945.

CLOTHIER, Morris Lewis (klōth'yĕr), merchant; b. Phila., July 24, 1868; s. Isaac Hallowell and Mary Clapp (Jackson) C.; B.S., Swarthmore Coll., 1890; hon. A.M., U. of Pa., 1910; LL.D., Villa Nova, 1912, and Pa. Coll., 1919, Lafayette, 1920, Swarthmore, 1921, Ursinus, Franklin and Marshall, Washington colleges, 1923; Litt.D., Pa. Military Coll., Chester, Pa., 1926; L.H.D., Dickinson College, 1937; m. Lydia May Earnshaw, April 26, 1900. Entered employ of Strawbridge & Clothier, June 30, 1890, admitted to partnership, 1895, became sr. and mng. partner, 1903, now chmn. bd.; dir. Phila. Nat. Bank, Penn Mut. Life Ins. Co., Lehigh Valley R.R. Co.; mem. bd.

mgrs. Girard Trust Co.; dir. Union Passenger Ry. Co., Pa. Fire Ins. Co., Guarantee Co. of N. America. Mem. bd. mgrs. Mem. Pa. Commn. to St. Louis Expn., 1904; Rep. presdl. elector at large for Pa., 1908. Trustee U. of Pa. Mem. Phi Kappa Psi, Phi Beta Kappa; hon. mem. sr. soc. Book and Key. Mem. Soc. of Friends, Mason (33°). Clubs: Rittenhouse, University, Art, Union League, Racquet (Phila.); University (New York). Home: Villa Nova, Pa. Office: 801 Market St., Philadelphia, Pa. Died Sept. 8, 1947.

CLOUD, Charles H., clergyman, univ. pres.; b. Cincinnati, O., Feb. 20, 1879; s. Francis H. Cloud and Julia C. (Schierburg) C.; educated St. Xavier Coll., Cincinnati, O.; A.B., St. Louis U., St. Louis, Mo., 1903, A.M., 1904; Creighton U., Omaha, Neb.; Ph.D., Gregorian U., Rome, Italy, 1913. Entered Society of Jesus at Florissant, Mo., 1897; ordained priest R.C. Ch., 1912. Assistant prof. physics and mathematics, St. Louis Univ., 1904-09, prof. of ethics, 1915-18, regent schs. of dentistry and medicine, St. Louis Univ., 1918-24, pres. same univ., 1924-30; provincial Chicago Province of the Society of Jesus, 1930-36; dean Sch. of Philosophy, West Baden Coll., West Baden Springs, Ind., 1938-39; pres. U. of Detroit, 1939-44; became pres., Milford Novitiate of the Society of Jesus, Chicago Province, Sept. 1944. Address: Milford Novitiate, Milford, O. Died Oct. 6, 1944; buried in Milford Novitiate Cemetery.

.d. late Daniel (banker) and Maria Louisa (Woodward) Cloud; ed. pvt. schs., Baltimore; unmarried. Writer by profession, since 1893. Lit. editor Baltimore News, 1906-14. Mem. Woman's Literary Club. Author: (collected ballads) Down Durley Lane, 1898 (Am. and English edits.); (collected poems A Reed by the River, 1902; also 19 connected tales of Colonial and Revolutionary periods; character studies of women, now republished in various collections of readings, including, Mrs. Chick (translated into German), novelettes, A Woman, a Spaniel and a Walnut Tree, The Other Thing, From a Little Red Book, Concerning Mr. Dick Daggart, Birthright. Also The Witch, The Ballad of Sweet P, and The Matrimonial Opportunities of Maria Pratt, used by inpersonators; The O'Tara stories, pub. in Harper's Weekly and Uncle Remus's Home Magazine; several songs, music and words, pub. in collections; critical articles,

CLOUSE, Wynne F. (klouz), lawyer; b. Goffton, Tenn., Aug. 29, 1883; s. Thomas Jefferson and Eunetta C.; LL.B., Cumberland U., 1912; m. Linnie Alice Dowell, Dec. 24, 1907; 1 dau., Geneva Eunetta (Mrs. H. H. Mayberry, Jr.). Mem. 67th Congress (1921-23), 4th Tenn. Dist.; special asst. U.S. atty. gen.; receiver Tenn. Central R.R.; referee in bankruptcy for Nashville and Columbia divs. of Middle Dist. of Tenn. since 1924. Widely known in the South as an orator and atty. Home: "Wynnewood," Franklin, Tenn. Died Feb. 19, 1944.

CLYCE, Thomas Stone (klīs), clergyman, educator; b. Kingsport, Tenn., Sept. 12, 1863; s. William Henry and Elizabeth (Hagy) C.; A.B., King Coll., Bristol, Tenn., 1887; B.D., Columbia (S.C.) Theol. Sem., 1890; B.D., Louisville, Theol. Sem., 1894; D.D., Southwestern Presbyn. U., 1900; LL.D., King Coll. (Bristol, Tenn.), 1912, Baylor U., 1920, Austin Coll., 1925; m. May De Perrin, Oct. 5, 1892; children—Wallace Perrin, Dorothy (Mrs. Allan G. Smith), Elizabeth. Ordained ministry Presbyn. Ch. in U.S., 1890; pastor Decatur, Ala., 1890-91, Woodland Ch., Louisville, 1891-96, Jackson, Ala., 1896-1900, also pres. Jackson Agrl. Coll., 1896-1900; pres. Austin Coll., Sherman, Tex., 1900-30, pres. emeritus since 1930, prof. philosophy since 1931. Moderator Gen. Assembly Presbyn. Ch. in U.S. since 1912. Mem. Philos. Soc. of Texas. Democrat. Mason. Club: Rotary Internat. Home: 1023 N. Grand Av. Address: Austin College, Sherman, Tex. Died Mar. 6, 1946.

COALE, James Johnson (kōl), clergyman; b. Arch Spring, Pa., May 25, 1879; s. Rev. James Johnson and Arabela (Parker) C.; B.S., Princeton, 1901; grad. Union Theol. Sem., 1905; m. Nellie Ansley Johnson, July 15, 1908; children—Virginia Bonham (Mrs. Bernard Fisher), James Johnson, III, Ansley Johnson. Ordained Presbyterian ministry, 1905; assistant minister, Rutgers Church, New York City, 1904-06; pastor White Sulphur Springs, Montana, 1906-08, Belden Avenue Church, Chicago, 1909-11, Lackawana, N.Y., 1912-17; exec. sec. Presbyn. Federated Council of Baltimore, Md., 1917-24; supt. Ch. Extension Com., Presbyn. Union, Presbytery of Cleveland, 1924-27; asso. pastor and dir. student work, First Ch., Annapolis, Md., 1928-32, pastor since 1932; mem. Presbyn. Bd. Nat. Missions, New York. Mason. Chautauqua lecturer. Writer of articles on social and religious topics in Yale Rev. and other periodicals. Retired No. 15, 1943. Home: 800 32nd Av. N., St. Petersburg, Florida. Died Sept. 22, 1947.

COBB, Florence Etheridge, lawyer, suffragist; b. Bridgeport, Conn., Sept. 20, 1878; d. of Samuel W. and Emma A. (Nichols) Etheridge; ed. Columbian U., Washington, D.C.; LL.B., Washington Coll. of Law, Washington, 1910, LL.M., 1911; m. T. S. Cobb, Mar. 25, 1921. Prof. sales, Washington Coll. of Law, 1915-18. Originator of Inaugural Suffrage Parade, held Mar. 3, 1913. Treas. Fed. Employees Union, 1916, 17; 4th v.p. Nat. Fedn. of Federal Employees, 1917-21; U.S. probate atty., U.S. Indian Service, 1918-21; municipal judge City of Wewoka, 1934-37; justice of the peace, Wewoka, since 1940. Chmn. for Okla. of Nat. Woman's Party since 1922; organized conv. of Govt. Workers' Council of Nat. Woman's Party, Washington, D.C., 1924. Editor, The Gossip (weekly mag.); contbr. verse to Harlow's Weekly and other mags. Home: Wewoka, Okla. Deceased.

COBB, Henry Evertson, clergyman; b. Hopewell, Dutchess County, N.Y., Mar. 25, 1863; s. Rev. Oliver Ellsworth and Cornelia Whitney (Polhemus) C.; Flushing (N.Y.) Inst., 1872-80; New York U., 1880-82; A.B., Rutgers, 1884, D.D., 1901, New York U., 1901; grad. Princeton Theol. Sem., 1888; S.T.D., Columbia, 1930; m. Elizabeth Colgate Penrose, Feb. 3, 1891; children—Dorothy Penrose (Mrs. Fred'k Lewis Allen, dec.), Oliver Ellsworth (dec.), Emily Linnard (Mrs. L. F. Holmes), Clement Biddle Penrose (M.D.). Was ordained to the ministry of Reformed Church, June 1888; minister, West Troy, N.Y., 1888-1902, West End Collegiate Ch., New York, Jan. 1903-31, now senior minister of the Collegiate Church of N.Y. City. Pres. Riverside Day Nursery; trustee Vassar Coll. (chmn. bd., 1919-29), 1909-29, Rutgers Coll., Leake and Watts Orphan Asylum (pres. bd.); mem. bd. mgrs. Presbyn. Hosp.; dir. Union Theol. Sem., Lake Placid Edn. Foundation, Utica (Miss.) Normal and Indsl. Inst. (pres. bd.); pres. Am. and Foreign Christian Union; acting pres. Gen. Synod Ref. Ch. America, 1923-24; del. Ref. Ch. to Queen Wilhelmina's Jubilee, 1923; del. Internat. Missionary Conf., Oxford, 1923; pres. Bd. Foreign Missions, Ref. Ch. America, 1915-33. Mem. Psi Upsilon, St. Nicholas Soc. (chaplain). Clubs: Century, Rutgers, Clergy, Lake Placid. Author: The Victories of Youth, 1900; The Ships of Tarshish, 1909. Contbr. to mags. Home: Hotel Gramatan, Bronxville, N.Y. Address: Rm. 510, 52 Vanderbilt Av., New York, N.Y. Died Aug. 14, 1943.

COBB, Irvin S(hrewsbury), author; b. Paducah, Ky., June 23, 1876; s. Joshua Clark and Manie (Saunders) C.; LL.D., University of Georgia, 1918, Dartmouth College, 1919, University of Kentucky, 1942; m. Laura Spencer Baker, June 12, 1900; 1 dau., Mrs. Elisabeth Rogers. Shorthand reporter, contbr. of comic drawings, reporter on local paper up to 17; editor Paducah Daily News at 19; staff corr. and writer "Sour Mash" column, Louisville (Ky.) Evening Post, 1898-1901; mng. editor Paducah News Democrat, 1901-04; spl. writer and editor humor section, New York Evening Sun, 1904-05; staff humorist and spl. writer New York Evening World and Sunday World, 1905-11; staff contbr. to Saturday Evening Post, 1911-22; staff contbr. to Cosmopolitan Mag., 1922-32; represented Saturday Evening Post as war corr. in Europe, 1914-15, 1917-18; lectured through U.S. Apptd. col. on staff comdr. in chief U.C.V., 1917, and on staffs govs. of Ky., 1918-21. Chevalier Legion Honor (France), 1918; major O.R.C., U.S. Army, 1922. Democrat. Mem. Southern Soc. of New York, The Kentuckians, National Sons of Confederate Veterans. Elk. Clubs: Lambs (New York City); Bohemian, Family (San Francisco). Author: (plays) Funabashi (musical comedy), produced 1907; Mr. Busybody (musical skit), 1908; Back Home (comedy), with Bayard Veiller, prod. 1915; Sergeant Bagby (1-act play), with Bozeman Bulger, prod. 1913; Guilty As Charged (one-act play), with Harry Burke, prod. 1915; Under Sentence (drama), in collaboration with Roi Cooper Megrue, prod. 1916; Happy New Year (sketch), 1928; (books) Back Home, 1912; Cobb's Anatomy, 1912; The Escape of Mr. Trimm, 1913; Cobb's Bill of Fare, 1913; Roughing It De Luxe, 1914; Europe Revised, 1914; Paths of Glory, 1915; Old Judge Priest, 1915; Fibble, D.D., 1916; Speaking of Operations—, 1916; Local Color, 1916; Speaking of Prussians—, 1917; Those Times and These, 1917; The Glory of the Coming, 1918; The Thunders of Silence, 1918; The Life of the Party, 1919; From Place to Place, 1919; Oh, Well, You Know How Women Are!, 1919; The Abandoned Farmers, 1920; A Plea for Old Cap Collier, 1921; Jeff Poindexter, 1922; One Third Off, 1921; Sundry Accounts, 1922; Stickfuls, Snake Doctor, A Laugh a Day, 1923; Goin' on Fourteen, 1924; Alias Ben Alibi, 1924; Here Comes the Bride, 1925; More Laughs for More Days, 1925; On an Island That Cost Twenty-four Dollars, 1926; Some United States, 1927; Prose & Cons., 1926; Chivalry Peak, 1927; Ladies and Gentlemen, 1927; All Aboard, 1928; This Man's World, 1929; Irvin Cobb at His Best, 1929; Red Likker, 1929; To Be Taken Before Sailing, 1930; Both Sides of the Street, 1930; Incredible Truth, 1931; Down Yonder, 1932; One Way to Stop a Panic, 1933; Murder Day by Day, 1933; Faith, Hope and Charity, 1934; Judge Priest Turns Detective, 1936; Azam, 1937; Four Useful Pups, 1939; Exit Laughing, 1941; Glory, Glory, Hallelujah, 1941; Roll Call, 1942; Curtain Call, 1944. Wrote: New York Through Funny Glasses series; The Hotel Clerk series; Live Talks with Dead Ones; Making Peace at Portsmouth; The Belled Buzzard; Twixt the Bluff and the Sound; Shakespeare's Seven Ages and Mine; The Island of Adventure; etc. Contbr. to mags. and syndicates. Winner of first prize of O. Henry Award Commn. for best short story pub. in 1922. Filled many radio engagements, 1930-36; starred or featured in various moving pictures, 1934, 35, 36; wrote numerous stories for screen use, 1932-42. Home: Santa Monica, Calif. Died Mar. 10, 1944.

COBB, Randell (Smith), lawyer; b. Gainesville, Tex., July 8, 1897; s. Thomas S. and Lillian L. (Smith) C.; LL.B., Okla. Univ., 1919; m. Mary E. Burke, June 9, 1920; 1 dau., Betty Jane (Mrs. William J. Harris). Admitted to Okla. bar, 1919, gen. practice of law, Oklahoma City, Okla., 1919-20; asst. atty. gen. Okla., 1920-33; first asst. atty. gen., Okla., 1933-43; atty. gen. of Okla., 1943-46; sr. mem. law firm, Cobb, Hill, Godfrey and Hoyt, Oklahoma City, Okla. since Feb. 1946. Served as 2d lt. U.S. Army, 1918-19. Dept. comdr. Am. Legion of Okla., 1940-41. Mem. Am. Bar Assn., Phi Delta Phi. Democrat. Methodist. Mason. Home: 2124 N. Stonewall. Oklahoma City, Okla. Died May 13, 1948.

COBURN, Nelson Francis, educator; b. Lowell, Mass., May 2, 1889; s. Charles Francis and Fanny Marsh Johnston (Lane) C.; A.B., Harvard U., 1911, A.M., 1912; student U. of Grenoble (France), 1911-13, Inst. of Burgos (Spain) and U. of Madrid (Spain), 1913-14; m. Vera Turnbull Marzouk, June 12, 1920; children—Ralph Maurice Hazelton, Eleanor Frances. Instr. in French and Spanish, U. of Neb., 1914-15; instr. French, Spanish and Italian, U. of Minn., 1915-17, 1921-24; newspaper corr. for Paris edition Chicago Tribune, Rome, Italy, 1920-21; asso. prof. and head modern foreign lang. dept., St. John's Coll., 1924-25; headmaster, Miami Shores Sch., Fla., 1925; headmaster Coburn Sch., Miami Beach, Fla., since 1926. Commd. 2d lt., 352d U.S. Inf., 1917; demobilized 1st lt., detached duty, Gièvres, France, 1919. Mem. Am. Assn. Univ. Profs., Pi Eta (Harvard). Unitarian. Mason. Home: 1010 Bay Drive. Office: 1000 Bay Drive, Miami Beach, Fla. Died Sep. 14, 1944.

COCHEU, Frank Sherwood, army officer; b. Brooklyn, N.Y., Nov. 22, 1871; s. Theodore and Catharine Elizabeth (Benson) C.; grad. U.S. Mil. Acad., 1894; Army War Coll., 1908, 21, Gen. Staff Coll., 1919, Gen. Staff Sch., 1920; m. Kathleen Lacey, Aug. 4, 1897. Commd. 2d lt. inf., U.S.A., June 12, 1894; advanced through grades to maj. gen. of the line, Mar. 1934; col. N.A., brig. gen. U.S.A., World War. Participated in Santiago Campaign, 1898, Philippine Insurrection, 1899-1902; in France, 1918-19, battles Artois Sector, St. Mihiel and Meuse-Argonne offensives. Mem. Gen. Staff Corps, 1907-11, 1914-17, 1921-25; asst. dir. Army War Coll., 1908-11; asst. comdt. Int. Sch., 1925-27; retired, Nov. 30, 1935. Awarded D.S.M. (U.S.); Conspicuous Service Medal (N.Y. State). Mason (K.T.). Home: The Highlands, Washington. Address: War Dept., Washington. Died July 11, 1940.

COCHRAN, George Ira, lawyer; b. Oshawa, Ont., Can., July 1, 1863; s. George and Catherine Lynch (Davidson) C.; ed. Toronto Coll. Inst., U. of Toronto, Osgoode Hall, Law Society; m. Isabelle May McClung, Apr. 3, 1907. Came to U.S., 1888, naturalized 1893. Admitted to Calif. bar, 1888; pres. Pacific Mutual Life Ins. Co. of California., 1906-36 and since 1945; atty. for Los Angeles Clearing House, 1893-94; assisted in organization of United Electric, Gas and Power Co.; dir. Central Investment Corp., Grand Central Garage, Artesian Water Co., Rosedale Cemetery Assn., Long Beach Bath House and Amusement Co., Seaside Water Co. Regent U. of California, University of Southern California (trustee). Mem. Calif. and Los Angeles bar assns. Clubs: Bohemian (San Francisco); California, Athletic, Wilshire Country (Los Angeles); Westport Beach Club. Home: 2249 S. Harvard Blvd., Los Angeles. 7. Died June 27, 1949.

COCHRAN, John Joseph, congressman; b. St. Louis County, Mo., Aug. 11, 1880; s. James and Elizabeth (Hamilton) C.; ed. pub. schs.; m. Jeanette Brown, Jan. 11, 1912 (dec.). Studied law in Washington, D.C.; admitted to Mo. bar; served as sec. to Congressman William L. Igoe, 1912-18, and to Harry B. Hawes and Senator William J. Stone; elected to fill unexpired term as mem. of Congress, at gen. election, Nov. 2, 1926; mem. 70th to 72d Congresses (1927-33), 11th Mo. dist.; mem. 73d Congress (1933-35), Mo. at-large; mem. 74th to 79th Congresses (1935-47), 13th Mo. Dist.; chmn. com. on accounts. Democrat. Roman Catholic. Clubs: National Press, Elks. Address: Boatmens Bank Bldg., St. Louis, Mo. Died Mar. 6, 1947.

COCHRANE, Aaron Van Schaick (kŏk'rān), judge; b. Coxsackie, N.Y., Mar. 14, 1858; s. Francis and Barbara C.; A.B., Yale, 1879; m. Margaret M. Hawyer, Oct. 10, 1882; children—Mrs. Margaret C. Ferriss, Francis A. Admitted to bar, 1881, and practiced at Hudson, N.Y., 1881-1901; police justice, Hudson, 1887-88; dist. atty. Columbia County, N.Y., 1889-92; mem. 55th and 56th Congresses (1897-1901), 19th N.Y. Dist.; justice Supreme Court of N.Y., 3d Dist., for terms 1901-15, 1916-29; designated presiding justice Appellate Div., 3d Dept.; now official referee State of N.Y. Trustee Hudson Savings Bank; pres. Farmers Nat. Bank of Hudson. Mem. Phi Beta Kappa. Home: Hudson, N.Y. Died Sep. 7, 1943.

COCKAYNE, Charles Alexander, university pres.; b. Bellaire, O., Feb. 4, 1879; s. Benjamin Franklin and Sarah Julia (Brockman) C.; A.B., Heidelberg U., Tiffin, O., 1901, A.M., 1903; A.M., Yale, 1906, Ph.D., 1908; unmarried. Prin. High Sch., Wadsworth, O., 1901-03; Martins Ferry, 1903-05; fellow and asst. in philosophy, Yale, 1906-08; assisted in compilation of 2d edit., American Men of Science, 1908-09; prof. philosophy and edn., Toledo U., 1909-10, pres. and prof. philosophy since 1910. Mem. A.A.A.S., Nat.

Geog. Soc. Address: 26 19th St., Toledo, O. Died Feb. 28, 1949.

COCKE, Charles Hartwell, physician; b. Columbus, Miss., Dec. 1, 1881; s. Charles Hartwell and Rowena Lockhart (Hudson) C.; grad. Episcopal High Sch. of Va., 1899; B.A., U. of Va., 1902; M.D., Cornell U., 1905; grad. student U. of Vienna, 1908; m. Amy Grace Plank, Nov. 12, 1914. Practiced in Birmingham, Ala., 1909, Asheville, N.C., since 1913; practice limited to internal medicine with special attention to tuberculosis; attending physician Asheville Mission Hosp., Biltmore Hosp.; cons. physician Patton Memorial Hosp. (Hendersonville, N.C.). Mem. Asheville Chamber of Commerce. Served as secretary and heart and lung consultant Medical Advisory Board during World War. Fellow American Coll. Physicians (1st vice-pres. 1942, 43, 44), American College Chest Physicians, A.M.A.; mem. North Carolina State and Buncombe County med. socs., Am. Clin. and Climatol. Assn., Nat. Tuberculosis Assn., Am. Trudeau Soc., Southern Med. Assn., Southern Interurban Clin. Club, Am. Assn. of History of Medicine, Internat. Union against Tuberculosis (corr. mem), Phi Kappa Psi, Nu Sigma Nu. Democrat. Episcopalian. Club: Biltmore Forest Country (Asheville). Contbr. many papers to med. jours. Home: 230 Pearson Dr. Office: Flat Iron Bldg., Asheville, N.C. Died Aug. 3, 1944.

COCKERELL, Theodore Dru Alison, naturalist; b. Norwood, Eng., Aug. 22, 1866; s. Sydney John and Alice Elizabeth (Bennett) C.; ed. at pvt. schs. in Eng. and Middlesex Hosp Med. Sch.; m. Annie S. Fenn, 1891 (died 1893); children—Austin (dec.), Martin (dec.); m. 2d, Wilmatte Porter, 1900. Resided in Colo., 1887-90, studying entomology, botany, etc.; curator pub. mus., Kingston, Jamaica, 1891-93; prof. entomology, N.M. Agrl. Coll., 1893-96, and 1898-1900; entomologist, N.M. Agrl. Expt. Sta., 1893-1901; cons. entomologist, Ariz. Agrl. Expt. Sta., 1900-09; teacher of biology, N.M. Normal U., 1900-03; curator Colo. Coll. Mus., 1903-04; lecturer on biology, Colo. State Prep. Sch., 1904-1927; lecturer on entomology, Univ. of Colo., 1904-06, professor systematic zoölogy, 1906-12; professor of zoölogy, 1912-34, professor emeritus since 1934. Author: Zoölogy; Zoölogy of Colorado; also of over 3,000 articles and notes in scientific publs., principally on mollusca, insects, fishes, palæontology and subjects connected with evolution. Fellow A.A.A.S., Am. Mus. Natural History (hon.); corr. mem. Phila. Acad. Natural Sciences, Am. Entomol. Soc.; mem. Am. Philos. Soc. Has made scientific explorations in Siberia, Japan, South America, Madeira Islands, Russia, Australia, Morocco, Central and South Africa, etc. Home: Boulder, Colo. Died Jan. 26, 1948.

CODY, Frank (kō'dĭ), educator, Detroit councilman; b. Belleville, Mich., Dec. 31, 1870; s. Timothy M. and Clarissa (Kipp) C.; grad. Mich. State Normal Coll., Ypsilanti, Mich., 1891, M.Pd., 1912; M.A., U. of Mich, 1924; LL.D., from U. of Detroit, 1933; m. Frances Youngblood, 1901 (died 1902); m. 2d, Louise Burns, 1905 (died July 27, 1921); children—Louise, Burns, Frederick, Frances. Supt. of schs., Delray, Mich., 1891-1906; prin. McMillan High Sch., Detroit, 1906-13; gen. supervisor pub. schs., Detroit, 1913-14; asst. sup. schs., Detroit, 1914-19; acting supt. schs., Detroit, Mar. 15, 1919, supt. July 1, 1919-July 1, 1942; mem. Detroit City Council since Nov. 1942. Pres. Wayne Univ., 1933-42. Mem. State Bd. of Edn., Mich., 1914-42. Republican. Episcopalian. Mason. Clubs: Detroit, Rotary, Detroit Athletic. Home: 725 Burlingame Av. Office: City Hall, Detroit, Mich. Died Apr. 8, 1946.

CODY, Rev. Hiram Alfred, author; b. Cody's, N.B., Can., July 3, 1872; s. George Redmond and Loretta A. C.; ed. King's Coll., N.S.; m. Jessie F. Flewelling, Sept. 19, 1905; children—Douglas Flewelling, Kenneth White, Norman Redmond, George Albert, Frances Margaret Lilian. Author: Apostle of the North (memoirs of Rt. Rev. William Carpenter Bompas), 1908; The Frontiersman—A Tale of the Yukon, 1910; The Fourth Watch, 1911; On Trail and Rapid by Dog-Sled and Canoe, 1910; The Long Patrol, 1912; The Chief of the Ranges, 1913; If Any Man Sin, 1915; Rod of the Lone Patrol, 1916; Under Sealed Orders, 1917; The Touch of Abner, 1919; Glen of the High North, 1920; Jess of the Rebel Trail, 1921; The King's Arrow, 1922; The Trail of the Golden Horn, 1923; The Master Revenge, 1924; Songs of a Bluenose, 1925. Address: Care George H. Doran Co., 244 Madison Av., New York. Died Feb. 9, 1948.

COE, Frank Winston, army officer; b. Kan., Nov. 27, 1870; grad. U.S. Mil. Acad., 1892, Arty. Sch., 1896; m. 1895, Anne Chamberlaine; 1 son, William Chamberlaine; m. 2d, 1923, Martha Pratt Donnellan. Commissioned add. 2d lt. 1st Artillery, June 11, 1892; promoted through grades to colonel, May 15, 1917; brig. gen., U.S. Army, Aug. 5, 1917; maj. gen. and chief of Coast Arty., May 24, 1918; retired, Mar. 1926. Instr. mathematics, U.S. Mil. Acad., 1898-1902; adjutant U.S. Mil. Acad., 1903-07; asst. to Chief Coast Arty., Washington, 1908-09; apptd. dir. Coast Arty. Sch., Monroe, Va., 1909; chief of staff, Western Dept., San Francisco, 1916; chief of staff, First Div., A.E.F., June-Aug. 1917; comdr. 30th Brigade, Heavy Arty., A.E.F., Sept. 1917-May 1918. D.S.M., 1919. Address: War Dept., Washington, D.C.* Died May 25, 1947.

COE, John Allen, mfr.; b. Bethany, Conn., Aug. 23, 1868; s. John A. and Cornelia A. (Wakelee) C.; ed. pub. schs.; m. Jessie M. Boice, May 25, 1892; children—Helen Boice (Mrs. Allen H. Boardman), John Allen. Began with Osborne & Cheesman Co., Ansonia, Conn., 1885; with Guild & Garrison, Brooklyn, N.Y., 1887-92, Birmingham Brass Co., Shelton, Conn., 1892-1903; with Am. Brass Co., since 1903, now chmn.; pres. Waterbury Savings Bank, Anaconda Am. Brass Co., Ltd., New Toronto, Ont.; dir. Colonial Trust Co. (Waterbury), Torrington Printing Co., Hendey Machine Co. (Torrington), Anaconda Copper Mining Co. of N.Y. City, Mutual Fire Insurance Company of Boston, Mass. Trustee Methodist Hospital, Brooklyn; director Waterbury Hosp.; president Silas Bronson (pub.) Library, Waterbury. Life mem. Soc. Colonial Wars, S.A.R. Republican. Methodist. Mason. Clubs: Waterbury, Country (Waterbury); Union League, Recess (New York). Home: 493 Willow St. Office: 414 Meadow St., Waterbury, Conn. Died Aug. 4, 1948.

COFER, Leland Eggleston, industrial hygiene; b. Richmond, Va., Nov. 16, 1869; s. Nathan Pliny and Effie (Mountcastle) C.; student Richmond (Va.) Coll., 1884-87; M.D., Richmond Med. Coll., 1889; m. Clara Drake-Smith, Aug. 25, 1893 (died 1906); m. 2d, Luisita Leland, Oct. 15, 1919. Served in U.S. Marine hosps. at Boston, Buffalo, Norfolk, Savannah, Mobile, San Diego and San Francisco, 1889-1900; organized campaign for the eradication of plague from Seattle, Wash., and the northwest; chief quarantine officer H. I., 1900-08; organized quarantine system there and served as president Hawaiian Board of Health, having charge of Leprosy Station; appointed asst. surgeon gen. U.S. P.H.S., Sept. 5, 1908, in charge div. of maritime quarantine of U.S. and its possessions and dependencies, also of med. function of immigration; loaned by Govt. as health officer, Port of New York, Apr. 23, 1916; dir. indsl. Hygiene, State of N.Y. Mem. A.M.A., Am. Assn. Mil. Surgeons, Am. Assn. Tropical Medicine. Clubs: Union, National Golf Links (New York); Metropolitan (Washington, D.C.). Home: 141 Barton Av., Palm Beach, Fla. Died Feb. 17, 1948.

COFFEY, Walter Bernard, surgeon; b. 1868; M.D., Cooper Med. Coll. (now Stanford Med. Dept.), San Francisco, 1889; LL.D., St. Mary's Coll., Oakland, Calif.; m. Laura E. Terry, 1902. Chief surgeon and mgr. Hosp. Dept., S.P. Co. Mem. bd. St. Francis Hosp. Fellow Am. Coll. Surgeons; mem. A.M.A., Calif. Med. Soc., etc. Home: 2340 Vallejo St. Office: Medical Bldg., Bush and Hyde Sts., San Francisco. Died March 25, 1944.

COFFIN, John Lambert, physician; b. Boston, Feb. 20, 1852; s. Abel Hale and Julia Ann (Holland) C.; A.B., Tufts Coll., 1871; A.M., 1874; M.D., Boston U. Sch. of Medicine, 1876; post-grad. course, New York Med Coll. and New York Polyclinic; m. Annie Weeman Jones, Nov. 8, 1880; children—Louisa Wendtè and Julia May (twins), Bartlett (dec.), Holland. Began practice at West Medford, Mass., 1876, later practiced in Boston; became lecturer and prof. dermatology, Boston U. Sch. of Medicine, 1885, now prof. emeritus. Ex-chmn. trustees State Insane Hosp., Westborough, Mass.; trustee Pub. Library, Northborough; mem. Sch. Com. and Bd. of Health, Medford. Ex-pres. Mass. Homœ. Soc., Boston Homœ. Med. Soc.; mem. Am. Inst. Homœopathy, Me. State Homœ. Soc. (hon.). Mason. Unitarian. Home: Northborough, Mass. Office: 220 Clarendon St., Boston. Died May 18, 1935.

COFFIN, William Carey, engr., architect; b. Pittsburgh, Sept. 7, 1862; s. William Carey and Jane McCormick (Osborne) C.; C.E., Western U. of Pa. (now U. of Pittsburgh), 1883; D.Sc., U. of Pittsburgh, 1936; m. Vida Hurst, 1889. With Keystone Bridge Co., 1883; chief engr. Fort Pitt Boiler Works 1883-85; with Riter-Conley Mfg. Co., 1885-1908, v.p. from incorporation, 1898; asst. gen. sales agent Jones & Laughlin Steel Co., 1909-15; v.p. Blaw-Knox Co., 1915-23; engr. and architect, 1923-27, is now retired. Designed and built some of the largest blast furnaces, steel plants and oil refineries in U.S. and Can. and secured many large contracts in U.S. and foreign countries, including electric power houses in Dublin, Ireland, Glasgow, Scotland, and Bristol, England; later designed and built several residences at Miami Beach, Fla. Mem. council Nat. Civil Service Reform Assn., 1908-18; mem. Fed. Trades Com. of Chamber of Commerce U.S.A., 1913-18; proponent codes of fair trade practice to Congress, 1913, 35; president of board of trustees University of Miami. Mem. American Iron and Steel Inst., Pittsburgh Chamber of Commerce. Republican. Presbyterian. Mason (32°). Author: Governmental Regulation of Cooperation in Trade, Seeds of Progress and Success, New Approach to Spiritual Revival, The Place of Big Business in a Democracy, Enduring Faith; also studies of social economic conditions in Europe, and S. America. Tech. consultant War Manpower Commn. Home: 238 E. San Marino Dr., Miami Beach, Fla.; also 5731 Bartlett St., Pittsburgh, Pa. Died Dec. 4, 1944.

COFFMAN, L. Dale, lawyer, educator; b. Delta, Ia., Aug. 28, 1905; s. Ralph Gideon and Georgia (Green) C.; B.A., State U. of Iowa, 1926, J.D., 1928; LL.M., Harvard, 1929, S.J.D., 1935; m. Helen Crouch, Dec. 31, 1925; 1 dau., Georganne. Practiced law with Sargent Gamble & Read, Des Moines, Ia., 1928-31; prof. law, U. of Nebraska, 1931-37; counsel Gen. Electric Co., Schenectady, N.Y., 1937-46; dean Sch. of Law, Vanderbilt U. since 1946. Mem. Phi Delta Phi, Phi Beta Kappa, Kappa Sigma, Order of Coif. Mason. Editor: Cases on Nebraska Trial Practice. 1933. Contbr. articles to law publs. since 1928. Home: 1301 24th Av. S., Nashville 5, Tenn. Died Sept. 1949.

COGGESHALL, George Whiteley (kŏgs'hawl), chemist; b. Des Moines, Ia., Dec. 21, 1867; s. John M. and Mary J. (Whiteley) C.; B.S., Grinnell (Ia.) Coll., 1890; grad. work, Harvard, 1891-92; Ph.D., Leipzig, 1895; m. Anna Torrey, Sept. 6, 1900; children—Elizabeth (Mrs. John C. West), Mary (Mrs. John H. Hollands), Dorothy (Mrs. Walter P. Wilson). Instr. in physical chemistry, Harvard, 1895-97; developing new chem. products, 1898-1910; chief chem. engr., Inst. Industrial Research, Washington, D.C., 1911-23; dir. Industrial Research Laboratories, 1923-29; dir. research, S. D. Warren Co., 1925-40. In charge surfacing concrete vessels, Emergency Fleet Corp., 1918. Fellow A.A.A.S., Am. Acad. Arts and Sciences; mem. Am. Chem. Soc., Am. Electrochem. Soc., Am. Inst. Mining and Metall. Engrs., Soc. Chem. Industry, Am. Inst. Chem. Engrs., Washington Acad. Sciences, American Genetic Association, American Geographical Soc. Clubs: Cosmos (Washington); St. Botolph (Boston); Cumberland (Portland); Faculty (Cambridge). Contbr. papers on standard calomel, electrodes, titanium mordants, potash from feldspathic rocks, etc. Developed various chem. processes, including Portland cement, rare metal compounds, gasoline from heavy oils, phosphates, paper pulp, paper specialties, etc. Home: Princes Point, Yarmouth, Me. Died Nov. 18, 1944.

COHEN, George Harry, lawyer; b. Lowell, Mass., Feb. 5, 1892; s. Abraham L. and Sarah (Grodjiensky) C.; A.B., Trinity Coll., 1911; A.M., Yale, 1912, Ph.D., 1914, LL.B., 1917; m. Pauline Kaufman, Aug. 25, 1931. Admitted to Conn. bar, 1917; mem. Cohen and Cohen; special asst. U.S. atty., 1919-21, and 1936; asst. U.S. atty., 1921-34, and 1934-36; U.S. atty., 1934. Editor and pub. Conn. Hebrew Record, English weekly, 1920-23; editor Conn. State Bar Journal 1935-44. Entered U.S. Army as pvt., 1917; discharged as first lt., 1918. Mem. Com. to draft Civil Rules Conn. Fed. Ct. Mem. Am., Conn. State and Hartford County bar assns., Conn. Hist. Soc., Am. Numismatic Assn., Alpha Mu Sigma, Phi Beta Kappa. Republican. Jewish religion. B'nai B'rith. Mason. Home: 258 N. Oxford St. Office: 750 Main St., Hartford, Conn. Died Feb. 23, 1949.

COHEN, Louis, cons. engr.; b. Kiev, Russia, Dec. 16, 1876; s. Abraham and Nattie (Resnik) C.; B.Sc., Armour Inst. Tech., 1901; student U. of Chicago, 1902; Ph.D., Columbia, 1905; m. Ethel Slavin, Jan. 3, 1904; 1 dau., Mrs. Louis P. Sissman. With scientific staff, Bur. of Standards, Washington, 1905-09; with Elec. Signaling Co., 1909-12; cons. practice since 1913; prof. elec. engring., George Washington U., 1916-29; cons. engr., War Dept., 1920-24; lecturer Bur. of Standards, Washington since 1928; U.S. del. Provisional Tech. Com. Internat. Conf. on Elec. Communication, Paris, France, 1921; mem. advisory tech. bd., Conf. on Limitation of Armament, Washington, 1921-22; technical expert German-Austrian claim commn., 1929-31. Fellow A.A.A.S., Am. Inst. E.E., Am. Inst. Radio Engrs., Am. Physical Soc. Author: Formulæ and Tables for Calculation of Alternating Current Problems, 1913; Heaviside's Electrical Circuit Theory, 1928; also many papers in scientific and tech. jours. Inventor of many devices in radio and cable telegraphy. Home: 303 Roosevelt St., Bethesda, Md. Died Sept. 28, 1948.

COHEN, Morris Raphael, prof. philosophy; b. Minsk, Russia, July 25, 1880; s. Abraham Mordecai and Bessie (Farfel) C.; brought to U.S., 1892; B.S., College of the City of New York, 1900; Ph.D., Harvard University, 1906; m. Mary Ryshpan, June 13, 1906 (died June 11, 1942); children—Felix S., Leonora D., Victor W. Teacher of history, Ednl. Alliance, New York, 1899-1900, Davidson Collegiate Inst., 1900-01; teacher pub. schs., N.Y. City, 1901-02; teacher mathematics, Coll. City of New York, 1902-04, 1906-12; prof. philosophy, same coll., 1912-38, now emeritus; prof. of philosophy, U. of Chicago since 1938; asst. dept. of philosophy, Harvard, 1905-06; lecturer on philosophy, Columbia, 1906-07, 1914-15, summer 1918, Johns Hopkins, 1921, 25, U. of Chicago, summer 1923, New School of Social Research, 1923-38, Columbia Law Sch., summer 1927, Law Sch. of St. John's Coll., 1928-31; visiting prof. Yale, 1929-31, Stanford U., 1937, Harvard U., 1938-39. Mem. exec. com. Internat. Congress of Philosophy, 1926. Fellow A.A.A.S. (v.p.; chmn. sect. hist. and philologic scis.); mem. Am. Assn. Univ. Profs. (council 1918-21), Am. Philos. Assn. (pres. 1929, Carus Lecturer 1941), Thomas Davidson Soc. (pres. 1899, 1901-02, 1906-08). Organizer Conf. on Legal and Social Philosophy, 1913, Conf. on Jewish Relations (pres. 1933-41; hon pres. since 1941); president Jewish Occupational Council since 1939. Author: Reason and Nature, 1931; Law and the Social Order, 1933; Preface to Logic, 1944; Faith of a Liberal, 1945. Co-Author: Cambridge History of American Literature, Vol. 3, 1922; Contemporary American Philosophy, Vol. 1, 1930; An Introduction to Logic and Scientific Method (with E. Nagel), 1934. Editor Modern Legal Philosophy Series, Chance, Love and Logic: Philosophic Essays by C. S. Peirce (1923); Jewish Social Studies; asso. editor Jour. of History of Ideas. Contbr. to Encyclopedia of Social Sciences, and various periodicals. Home: 2617 39 St. N.W., Washington, D.C. Died Jan. 29, 1947.

COHILL, Edmund Pendleton (kō'hĭl), fruit grower; b. Elmira, N.Y., Dec. 3, 1855; s. Andrew Arnold and Mary Jane (Mapes) C.; grad. Harrisburg (Pa.) Commercial Coll., 1874; m. Mary Ellen Rinehart, Oct. 23, 1876; children—Marie Agnes (dec.), Louise Elizabeth (dec.), Samuel Rinehart, Leo Aloysius, William Joseph (dec.), James Andrew, Marguerite Cecelia (dec.), Suella; m. 2d, Emma M. Glover, Sept. 4, 1923. Private secretary to George M. Ball, gen. mgr. Empire Transportation Co., Phila., 1875; cashier same co., Baltimore, 1876-77; began fruit culture, 1886, which grew into Tonoloway Orchard Co., having 980 acres in apples; was an organizer and pres. Hancock Bank, and organizer and v.p. First Nat. Bank; pres. and treas. Tonoloway Orchard Co.; v.p. Russell Creek Coal Co., Corona Orchard Co.; dir. Baltimore br. Fed. Reserve Bank of Richmond since 1924. Dir. Am. Angora Goat Breeders' Assn.; v.p. Md. State Hort. Soc. (pres. 1905-06); mem. exec. com. Eastern Apple Growers' Assn., Am. Apple Congress; exec. bd. Nat. Apple Growers' Assn., 1917-18; pres. Md. Agrl. Soc. since 1918; pres. Md. State Farm Bur. since 1923; v.p. Nat. Pecan Groves Co.; mem. exec. com. Southern region, Am. Farm Bur. Fed., 1924-26, now dir. for Southern Region. Sch. commr. Washington County, Md., 1900-12. Democrat. Home: Hancock, Md. Died Mar. 5, 1943.

COHN, Charles Mittendorff, pub. utilities; b. Baltimore, Md., Apr. 25, 1873; s. Moritz Gustav and Emily Caroline (Stoll) C.; LL.B., U. of Md., 1895; A.B., Loyola Coll., Baltimore, 1897, A.M., 1899, LL.D., 1942; unmarried. Began as jr. clerk Consol. Gas Co., 1885; sec. Consol. Gas Electric Light & Power Co., 1906-10, gen. mgr., 1910, v.p., 1910-31, exec. v.p., 1931-42; pres., 1942, chmn. bd., pres. since 1943; dir. and mem. exec. com. Industrial Bldg. Co.; dir. and mem. exec. com. Fidelity Trust Co. Democrat. Presbyn. Mason (33°). Clubs: Maryland, Baltimore Country. Home: 2941 N. Charles St. Office: Lexington Bldg., Baltimore, Md. Died Dec. 5, 1946.

COIT, Alfred (koit), lawyer, banker; b. New London, Conn., Nov. 4, 1863; s. Alfred and Ellen (Hobron) C.; A.B., Yale, 1887, LL.B., 1889; m. Gertrude Barker, June 4, 1890 (died Dec. 12, 1926); 1 dau., Gertrude. Judge of probate ct., New London, 1892 to 1910; president and attorney Union Bank & Trust Co.; 1st vice-pres. and attorney Savings Bank of New London. Trustee Lawrence and Memorial Asso. hospitals; sec. and treas. Chapman Tech. High Sch.; pres. New London Library; past pres. New London Y.M.C.A. Mem. Conn. State Bar Assn., S.A.R. Republican. Conglist. Mason, Elk. Club: Thames. Home: 146 Huntington St. Office: Manwaring Bldg., New London, Conn. Died May 30, 1947.

COIT, Ruth, educator; b. Phila., Pa., June 9, 1868; d. Edward Woolsey and Caroline Mattocks (Moore) Coit; ed. Mrs. Comegy's and Miss Bell's Sch., Chestnut Hill, Phila., and Miss Agnes Irwin's Sch., Phila.; spl. instrn. under Dr. Joseph Howland Coit, St. Paul's Sch., Concord, N.H.; unmarried. Teacher, St. Louis, Mo., 1894-97, Cambridge, Mass., 1902-05; asst. to Arthur Gilman, 1902-07; headmistress The Cambridge Sch. for Girls, 1907-18; exec. sec. northeastern field com. of National Bd. Y.W. C.A., 1918; spl. study and travel in Europe, 1921-23; headmistress St. Mary's Hall (name changed to The Ruth Coit School, 1937), San Antonio, Tex., 1924-37. Commr. Bexar County Council of Girl Scouts. Formerly dir. Pan-American Round Table of San Antonio; mem. budget sub-com. San Antonio Community Chest; mem. New Eng. Soc. for Preservation Antiquities, Women's National Republican Club, English Speaking Union; President San Antonio Art League, Delta Kappa Gamma; mem. Soc. of Mayflower Descendants in Texas. Awarded Irwin decoration, 1934. Episcopalian. Address: 424 East Ashby Place, San Antonio 2, Tex. Died Nov. 3, 1946.

COLBRON, Grace Isabel (kōl'brŭn), writer; b. at New York, N.Y.; d. W. T. and Isabel (de Forest) Colbron; educated in private schs., New York, Summit, N.J., and Berlin; unmarried. Lived in Germany for many yrs. as journalist, critic and translator, and as theatrical agt., representing Elizabeth Marbury and Heinrich Conried; specialty translating, book reviewing and critic of writings relating to German and Scandinavian life and lit.; lecturer on economic and literary subjects. Mem. Women's Trade Union League. Henry George Foundation of America, Silvermine Guild of Artists. Clubs: Gamut, Women's City, Town Hall (New York). Author: (with Clayton Hamilton) The Love That Blinds (play); with (Augusta Groner) Joe Müller—Detective; The Club Car Mystery. Translator: The Reckoning (German play, "Liebelei," by Arthur Schnitzler); Comtesse Coquette (Italian play "Infidele," by Robert Braceo); A Marriage, by Björnstjerne Björnson (Norwegian play); The Man with the Black Cord (by Augusta Groner); Mene Tekel (by Augusta Groner); The Lady in Blue (by Augusta Groner); The Third Sex (by Ernst von Wolzogen); Anatol and Other Plays (by Arthur Schnitzler), 1917; The Guardsman, by Ferenzc Molnar (Hungarian play); Shadows that Pass, by Otto Rung (Danish novel); The Teddy Expedition, by Kai Dahl (Danish); Venture's End, by Karin Michaelis (novel); Birds Around the Light, from the Danish of Jacob Paludan; The Brand of the Sea, from the Danish of Knud Andersen; Surf, from the Danish of same; The Red House, from the German of Elsa Jerusalem (under pseud. of R. J. Marchant). Editor and translator of German and Scandinavian sect. of Library of World's Best Mystery and Detective Stories. Dramaturgic asst. to Hans Bartsch, play broker. Contbr. to revs. Home: New Canaan Conn. Died Sept. 8, 1943.

COLBY, Everett, lawyer; Ph.B., Brown, 1897, hon. A.M.; m. Edith Hyde, June 30, 1903; children—Elizabeth (deceased), Edith Hyde, Anne Gordon, Everett, Chas. L. (deceased). Member Barry, Wainwright, Thacher and Symmers. Member New Jersey Board of Education, 1902-04; mem. New Jersey Gen. Assembly, 1903-05, Senate, 1906-09. Served as aide to gov. of N.J., 1903-04, and as adj. Nat. Guard N.J. Progressive candidate for gov. of N.J., 1913; mem. Rep. Nat. Campaign Com., 1916; chmn. exec. com. League of Nations Non-Partisan Com. from organization to 1930; chmn. exec. com. Nat. World Court Com.; mem. N.J. Rep. State Com., 1934-39. Trustee Brown U., 1905-40. Served in U.S. Food Administration, 1917. Maj. O.R.C., 1918. Mem. Phi Beta Kappa (hon.). Home: Llewellyn Park, W. Orange, N.J. Office: 72 Wall St., New York, N.Y. Died June 19, 1943.

COLBY, Mrs. Nathalie Sedgwick, author; b. N.Y. City, Feb. 4, 1875; d. William Tucker and Katherine (Sedgwick) Washburn; ed. pvt. schs.; m. Bainbridge Colby, June 22, 1895 (divorced 1929); children—Katherine Sedgwick (Mrs. Frederick Delafield, 2d), Nathalie Sedgwick, Frances Bainbridge (Mrs. Robert Cameron Rogers). Author: Green Forest, 1927; Black Stream, 1927; A Man Can Build a House, 1928; For Life, 1936; Glass Houses (a story), 1937; Remembering, 1938; also short stories, essays and verse in mags. Clubs: Cosmopolitan, P.E.N. Home: 169 E. 78th St., New York, N.Y. Died June 10, 1942.

COLCORD, Lincoln (Ross) (kōl'kŭd), author; born at sea off Cape Horn, Aug. 14, 1883; s. Lincoln Alden and Jane French (Sweetser) Colcord; descended from a family of seafarers extending back five generations; graduated Searsport (Maine) High Sch., 1900; student U. of Me., intermittently, 1900-06; leaving coll. middle of junior yr.; hon. M.A., 1922 (Phi Beta Kappa, 1924); m. Blanche T. Nickels, May 4, 1910; 1 dau., Inez Nickels; m. 2d, Loomis Logan, Feb. 16, 1928 (divorced Jan. 7, 1929); m. 3d, Frances Brooks, July 23, 1929; 1 son, Brooks. Spent his boyhood to age of 14 at sea with father, mostly on voyages to China and trading on China Sea; civil engineer with Bangor and Aroostook R.R., in Me. woods, 1906-09; began writing short stories, 1909. Sec. Penobscot Marine Mus., Searsport, Me., since 1936; asso. editor American Neptune, Salem, since 1941. Democrat. Member Kappa Sigma. Mason. Clubs: The Players, Cruising Club of America, Colonial Society of N.E. Author: The Drifting Diamond, 1912; The Game of Life and Death, 1914; Vision of War, 1915; An Instrument of the Gods, 1922. Co-Author: (with George Wasson) Sailing Days on the Penobscot, 1932. Staff corr. Phila. Public Ledger, Washington Bureau, 1917-18; asso. editor The Nation, N.Y., 1919-20. Co-translator with author (O. E. Rölvaag) Giants in the Earth, 1927. Home: Searsport, Me. Died Nov. 16, 1947.

COLE, Ernest E., univ. pres., lawyer; b. Savona, N.Y., Nov. 18, 1871; s. Aaron and Elmina (Orcutt) C.; grad. Haverling Acad., Bath, N.Y., 1892; LL.B., Cornell U., 1895; Pd.D., N.Y. State Coll. for Teachers, 1927; LL.D., from Alfred U., 1930, Colgate U., 1942, Univ. State of New York, 1942; m. Minnie M. Pierce, Dec. 31, 1896; children—Robert Ernest, William Sterling, James Pierce. Admitted to N.Y. bar, 1895; successively prin. pub. schs., Greenwood, Painted Post and Addison, N.Y., 1895-1916; began practice at Bath, 1916; mem. Cole & Knapp, 1916; counsel N.Y. State Edn. Dept. and U. of State of N.Y., 1926-28; deputy commr. of edn. and counsel, 1928-40; pres. U. of State of N.Y. and commr. of edn., 1940-42. Mem. New York Assembly, 1920-22, Senate, 1923-26 (chmn. com. on pub. edn.). Republican. Presbyterian. Mason (32°). Home: 109 E. Steuben St., Bath, N.Y. Office: 100 State St., Albany, N.Y. Died Nov. 19, 1949.

COLE, Lawrence Wooster, psychologist; b. Toledo, O., May 15, 1870; s. Irving and Josephine (Webb) C.; A.B., U. of Okla., 1899; A.M., Harvard, 1904, Ph.D., 1910; m. Fannie B. Cooksey, June 28, 1900; children—Elizabeth J., Margaret, Mary Louise. Supt. schs., El Reno, Okla., 1897-1900; instr. and asso. prof. psychology, 1900-04, prof., 1904-08, U. of Okla.; instr. exptl. psychology, Wellesley Coll., 1908-09; professor psychology and edn., University of Colorado, 1910-38, professor emeritus since 1938; regent Univ. of Colorado, 1939-45. Director School of Social Serv., U. of Colo., 1911-20. Mem. Bd. Edn., Norman, Okla., 1901-04, 1905-07, Boulder, Colo., 1915-27. Fellow A.A.A.S.; mem. Am. Psychol. Assn., Sigma Xi, Sigma Nu, Phi Beta Kappa. Contbr. various reports of experimental investigation in comparative and human psychology. Capt. Sanitary Corps U.S. Army, Sept. 6, 1918-June 22, 1919; served as psychol. examiner. Author: Factors of Human Psychology. Translator of Duprat's Psychologie Sociale. Home: 845 14th St., Boulder, Colo. Died Mar. 19, 1946; buried in Green Mountain Cemetery, Boulder.

COLE, Leon J(acob); b. Allegany, N.Y., June 1, 1877; s. Elisha Kelley and Helen Marion (Newton) C.; student Mich. Agrl. Coll., 1894-95, 1897-98; A.B., Univ. of Mich., 1901; Ph.D., Harvard, 1906; Sc.D., Michigan State College, 1945; married Margaret Belcher Goodenow, August 28, 1906; children—Margaret Valeria, Edward Goodenow. Asst. in zoölogy, U. of Mich., 1898-1902, teaching fellow, Harvard U., 1902-06, chief of Div. of Animal Breeding and Pathology, Agrl. Expt. Sta., R.I., 1906-07; instr. in zoölogy, Sheffield Scientific Sch. (Yale), 1907-10; asso. prof. exptl. breeding, U. of Wis., Apr. 1910-14, prof., 1914-18, prof. genetics, 1918 47; on leave as chief Animal Husbandry Div., Bur Animal Industry, U.S. Dept. Agr., 1923-24; chmn. Div. Biology and Agr., Nat. Research Council, 1926-27. Mem. Harriman Alaska Expdn., 1899; zoöl. expdn. to Yucatan, 1904. Investigator, U.S. Bur. of Fisheries, summers, 1901-06. Fellow A.A.A.S. (v.p. Sect. F., 1940); Poultry Science Assn.; mem. Am. Soc. Zoölogists, Am. Genetic Assn., Genetic Soc. of America (vice-president 1937, president 1940), Eugenics Soc., Am. Soc. Naturalists (v.p. 1917; sec. 1927-31), Am. Ornithologists' Union, Am. Soc. Mammalogists, Soc. Animal Production, Board Biol. Fellowships of Nat. Research Council (1928-36), Wis. Acad. Science (pres. 1924-27), Sigma Xi (pres. Wis. Chapter 1917-18; nat. exec. com. 1932-34), Phi Kappa Phi, Gamma Sigma Delta, Phi Sigma (hon. nat. pres., 1940-46); corr. mem. Czechoslovak Acad. Agr. Contbr. on zoölogy, animal behavior, genetics and animal breeding. Organizer Am. Bird Banding Assn., 1909. Home: 312 N. Prospect Av., Madison 5, Wis. Died Feb. 17, 1948.

COLEBAUGH, Charles Henry (kōl'baw), editor; b. Phila. Pa., Dec. 7, 1892; s. Henry Hires and Mary Elizabeth (Wright) C.; ed. pub. schs., Phila.; m. Georgette Jeanne Herbert, July 15, 1922. Began with R. A. Foley Adv. Agency, Phila.; joined Collier's in 1917, mgr. adv. promotion, 1919; mgr. adv. promotion for Crowell Pub. Co., 1921; asso. editor Collier's Weekly, 1924, mng. editor, 1926, editor since 1943. Home: Colebrook, Conn.; and Clearwater, Fla. Office: 250 Park Av., New York, N.Y. Died May 10, 1944.

COLEMAN, Christopher Bush, historian; b. Springfield, Ill., Apr. 24, 1875; s. Louis Harrison and Jenny Bush (Logan) C.; A.B., Yale, 1896; B.D., U. of Chicago, 1899; U. of Berlin, 1904-05; Ph.D., Columbia, 1914; m. Juliet Brown, June 25, 1901; children—Ruth (dec.), Constance (Mrs. E. P. Richardson), Martha Julian (Mrs. E. C. Bray). Acting professor history, 1900, professor, 1901-19, vice-president, 1912-19, Butler College; head of department of history and political science, Allegheny College, 1920-24; director Hist. Bureau of State of Ind. since 1924, also sec. Indiana Historical Soc.; dir. State Library, 1936-42. Mem. George Rogers Clark Memorial Commn. of Ind., 1927-40; exec. sec. George Rogers Clark Sesquicentennial Commn., 1928-35; sec. Conf. of Hist. Socs., 1926-38. Mem. Am. and Miss. Valley historical associations, Phi Beta Kappa, Delta Kappa Epsilon. Club: Indianapolis Literary. Author: Church History in the Modern Sunday School, 1910; Constantine the Great, Historical, Legendary and Spurious, 1914; Memoirs of Louis Harrison Coleman, 1920; Indiana (1779-1929), 1929; The United States at War, 1943. Editor of Lorenzo Valla on the Donation of Constantine, 1922. Director Indiana Historical Collections since 1924. Contbr. to hist. mags. Home: 4314 Central Av. Address: State Library and Historical Bldg., Indianapolis, Ind. Died June 25, 1944.

County, Va., July 21, 1879; s. Henry Frank and Jane (Patrick) C.; student William and Mary Coll., 1894-97; M.D., Med. Coll. of Va., 1903; student N.Y. Polyclinic Postgraduate Med. Sch., 1906; m. Julia Langhorne Cone, Apr. 28, 1917; children—Anne Putney, Julia Langhorne, Claude C., Jane Patrick; m. 2d, Ruth Threadcraft Putney, June 16, 1931. Began practice at Richmond, 1910; prof. principles of surgery, Med. Coll. of Va., 1912-13, prof. neurol. surgery since 1924; clin. prof. neurol. surgery, U. of Va., 1937-1941. Served as maj. Med. Corps, U.S. Army, during World War; dir. Sch. of Brain Surgery, U.S. Army, Ft. Oglethorpe, 1918; civilian consultant in neurol. surgery to surgeon general, World War II; neurosurgical consultant Special Medical Advisory Board Veterans' Administration. Member board of visitors Coll. of William and Mary. Fellow Am. Coll. Surgeons; mem. Soc. Neurol. Surgeons (pres. 1926). Southern Surgical Assn., A.M.A., Kappa Alpha, Phi Beta Kappa. Democrat. Clubs: Country Club of Va.; Gloucester Country. Author: Medical Department U.S. Army in the World War, vol. 2 (with others), 1924; section on the nervous system in Horsley and Bigger's Operative Surgery, 4th edit., 1937; sect. on Peripheral Nerves in Bancroft's Surgery, 1945. Contbr. surgical

COLEMAN, Frederick W. B., diplomat; b. Detroit, May 17, 1874; s. Silas B. and Rebecca (Backus) C.; A.B., U. of Mich., 1896; LL.B., 1899; unmarried. Am. minister to Estonia, Latvia and Lithuania, 1922-31; Am. Minister to Denmark, Nov. 1, 1931-May 1, 1933; engaged in political-economic survey in U.S., 1935-38. Served in U.S. Army, 1917-19. Address: Sanford, N.C. Died Apr. 2, 1947.

COLEMAN, Frederick William, army officer; b. Baltimore, Md., July 16, 1878; s. Frederick William and Clara Pauline (Adams) C.; B.A., Rock Hill (Md.) Coll., 1897; grad. Command and Gen. Staff Sch., 1904, Army War Coll., 1922; m. Blanche Lippincott Forbes, Dec. 8, 1902; children—Emilie Tyler (dec.), Frederick William III. Apptd. 2d lt. inf., U.S. Army, Sept. 9, 1898; and advanced through grades to col., Apr. 27, 1921; maj. gen., chief of finance, U.S. Army, 1932-36; retired from active service, Sept. 30, 1936. Gov. U.S. Soldiers' Home, Washington, D.C., since May 1, 1936. Served in

Spanish-Am. War, Philippine Insurrection, on Mexican border: lt. col. and col., asst. chief of staff, 91st Div., World War. Awarded D.S.M.; Silver Star with Oak Leaf Cluster (U.S.). Mason. Clubs: Army and Navy Country, Chevy Chase, Alfalfa. Address: U.S. Soldiers' Home, Washington. Died Jan. 5, 1945; buried in Arlington National Cemetery.

COLEMAN, George Preston, civil engr., banker; b. Williamsburg, Va., May 4, 1870; s. Charles Washington and Cynthia Beverley (Tucker) C.; m. Mary Haldane Begg, Feb. 21, 1900; children—Janet Haldane (Mrs. Raymond de Witt Kimbrough), Cynthia Beverley Tucker (Mrs. Singleton P. Morehead). City engr., Winona, Minn., 1901-06; asst. Va. state highway commr. 1906-11, commr., 1911-23; pres. Peninsula Bank & Trust Co., Williamsburg, Va., since 1927; also pres. Williamsburg Finance Corp., Jamestown Corp., Williamsburg Inn, Inc., Williamsburg Gazette, Noting First Mortgage, South Atlantic Corp., Richmond; dir. Am. Gas Accumulator Co. and Signal Service (Elizabeth, N.J.), Argaloy Tubing Co. (Springfield, O.). Mayor of Williamsburg, 1929-34. Organizer Va. Good Road Association (president three terms); member committee to formulate Va. State Highway System. Member American Assn. of State Highway Officials (organizer, past pres. and past chmn.; as chmn. of legislative com. wrote 1st Federal aid road bill, Bankhead Bill, which made possible the participation of the Nat. Gov. in constrn. of comprehensive road system); Am. Road Builders Assn. (past pres.), Appalachian Highway Assn. (v.p.), Va. Hist. Soc., Southern Soc. of New York, S.R., Sons of Confederacy, Soc. of the Cincinnati of Va., Colonial Wars, Jamestown Soc., Kappa Sigma, Phi Beta Kappa. Democrat. Episcopalian. Clubs: Commonwealth (Richmond), Flat Hat. Awarded medal by French Govt. for services connected with Sesquicentennial celebration. Home: Williamsburg, Va. Died June 17, 1948.

COLEMAN, John Francis, cons. engr.; b. Jefferson County, Miss., Nov. 23, 1866; s. James Wood and Elizabeth Treeby (Chaffe) C.; hon. Dr. of Engring., Tulane U., 1935; m. Annie Hunter, Nov. 12, 1890; 1 son, Eugene Hunter (dec.). Rodman, Guatemala Northern R.R., 1884-85; levelman, later resident engr., Kansas City, Memphis & Birmingham R.R., 1885-88; asst. engr. Phila. Smelting & Refining Co., Pueblo, Colo., 1888-89; asst. U.S. engr., Miss. River, 1889-90; asst. engr. Tex. & Pacific Ry., 1890-93; contractor, New Orleans, 1893-94; div. engr. New Orleans & Western R.R., 1894-96; prin. asst. city engr., New Orleans, 1896-99; cons. civ. engr. since 1900; chief engr. New Orleans Great Northern R.R., 1905-07. Cons. engr. Bd. Commrs. Port of New Orleans, 1901-30; also formerly cons. engr. for ports of Corpus Christi, Freeport, Houston, Beaumont (all in Tex.), Lake Charles, La., Mobile, Ala., Jacksonville, Fla., Charleston, S.C., Richmond, Va.; builder of ship yard at Mobile for U.S. Steel Corp., Nov. 1917-Nov. 1919; now sr. partner J. F. Coleman Engring. Co., cons. engrs. Mem. Engrs. Advisory Bd., Reconstruction Finance Corporation, 1932-33, adv. engr. since 1938. Trustee Eye, Ear, Nose and Throat Hosp., New Orleans. Hon. mem. Am. Soc. C.E. (ex-pres.); mem. Am. Inst. Cons. Engrs. (ex-pres.), Am. Ry. Engring. Assn., Am. Shore and Beach Preservation Association, Am. Assn. Port Authorities, La. Engring. Soc. (ex-pres.; hon. mem.), Am. Engring. Council (pres. 1934-35). Democrat. Episcopalian. Home: 3116 Prytania St. Office: Carondelet Bldg., New Orleans, La. Died June 3, 1944.

COLEMAN, Warren, M.D.; b. Augusta, Ga., Jan. 19, 1869; s. John Scott and Hetty Kennedy (McEwen) C.; A.B., Transylvania U., Lexington, Ky., 1888; grad. work Johns Hopkins, 1888-89; M.D., Univ. Med. Coll., New York, 1891; hon. M.A., Transylvania, 1899; m. Mrs. Bertie A. Twiggs, March 18, 1946. Practiced New York, 1891-1938; physician City (Charity) Hospital, 1896-99; instructor pathology, University Med. Coll., 1891-98; asst. curator, Bellevue Hosp., 1892-98, asst. visiting phys., 1899, visiting physician, 1908-27, cons. physician since 1927; prof. clin. medicine and applied pharmacology, Cornell U. Med. Coll., New York, 1909-17; asst. prof. medicine, Univ. and Bellevue Hosp. Med. Coll (now N.Y. Univ. Coll. of Medicine), 1918-31, prof. clinical medicine, 1932-33, now emeritus; prof. clin. medicine, U. of Ga. Sch. of Medicine, since 1938; cons. physician Lenox Hill Hosp. (N.Y. City); formerly cons. physician Monmouth (N.J.) Memorial Hosp., Med. Center of Jersey City (N.J.). Fellow Am. Coll. Physicians, A.M.A.; mem. Assn. American Physicians, American Board of Internal Medicine, New York Academy of Sciences, Georgia Academy of Science, Am. Nat. Red Cross, N.Y. Pathol. Soc., N.Y. Med. and Surg. Soc. (hon.), Society American Bacteriologists, American Gastroenterological Assn., A.A.A.S., Richmond County (Ga.) Med. Society (hon.), Assn. Military Surgeons, Sons of Revolution in State of Ga., Soc. of the Cincinnati in the State of Ga., Phi Alpha Sigma, etc.; non-resident fellow New York Acad. Medicine, retired member New York State Med. Soc., New York County Med. Soc., formerly member Am. Genetic Assn., Soc. Exptl. Biology and Medicine, Assn. for Study of Internal Secretions, Am. Bible Soc., Harvey Soc. Democrat. Mem. Christian (Disciples) Ch. Clubs: Century Assn., Pilgrims, Camp-Fire of America. Writer on med. subjects. Home: 2749 Hillcrest Av., Augusta, Ga. Died Feb. 13, 1948.

COLES, Alfred Porter (kōlz), banker; b. Wilson County, Tenn., July 5, 1861; s. J. F. and Susan (Hunt) C.; ed. Cumberland U. Prep. Sch. and Vanderbilt U.; m. Nellye Bell, Jan. 18, 1893. Formerly pres. Am. Nat. Bank, El Paso; organizer and pres. El Paso Cotton Mills Co.; chmn. bd. El Paso br. Fed. Reserve Bank; pres. El Paso Real Estate Co.; head of firm of A. P. Coles & Bros., real estate and mortgage loans; also head of Coles Bros. & Saunders Co.; farmer and live stock raiser. Active in war work and in spl. duty by apptmt. of sec. of war. Methodist. Mason, K.P. Clubs: Toltec, El Paso Country, La Cumbre Golf (Santa Barbara, Calif.). Home: 800 Magoffin Av., El Paso, Tex., and "Boscobel," Montecito, Santa Barbara, Calif. Office: 204 N. Oregon St., El Paso, Tex. Died July 29, 1941.

COLEY, Edward Huntington (kō'lē), bishop; b. Westville, New Haven, Conn., Aug. 22, 1861; s. James Edward and Mary Gray (Huntington) C.; B.A., Yale, 1884; grad. Berkeley Div. Sch., 1887; S.T.D., Syracuse University, 1912; D.D., Berkeley Divinity School, 1924; D.D., Hamilton College 1942; married Julia Seely Covell, October 23, 1889; children—Marjory Covell (widow of Rev. Edmund Jayne Gates), Elizabeth Huntington (Mrs. John Futhey Fox), Mary Huntington. Deacon, 1887, priest, 1888, P.E. Ch.; curate St. John's Ch., Stamford, Conn., 1887-88; minister in charge Christ Ch., Savannah, Ga., 1888-89; rector St. Mary's Ch., South Manchester, Conn., 1889-93; asst. rector St. John's Ch., Stamford, 1893-97; rector Calvary Ch., Utica, N.Y., 1897-1924; elected suffragan bishop of Diocese of Central N.Y., May 14, 1924; consecrated bishop Oct. 7, 1924; elected bishop of Diocese of Central N.Y., May 6, 1936, retired July 1st, 1942. Member Standing Committee of the Diocese of Central New York, 1905-22 (sec. 1906-17, pres. 1917-22); president board trustees Munson-Williams-Proctor Inst.; mem. bd. mgrs. Utica State Hosp. for Insane (sec.); trustee Home for Homeless; mem. Oneida County Com. of State Charities Aid Assn. Mem. Oneida Hist. Soc. Republican. Home: Waterville, N.Y. Died June 6, 1949.

COLGATE, James Colby, broker; b. Yonkers, N.Y., May 23, 1863; s. James Boorman and Susan F. (Colby) C.; A.B., Colgate U., 1884, LL.D., 1922; LL.B., Columbia, 1887; m. Hope H. Conkling, June 4, 1890; children—Susan E. (Mrs. Mather Cleveland), Margaret W. (Mrs. James S. Dennis), Hope H. (Mrs. William T. Jerome, Jr.), Mary Evelyn (dec.). Admitted to bar, 1887, and practiced at New York, 1887-90; broker since 1891; sr. mem. Jas. B. Colgate & Co. until dissolution of the firm, Dec. 31, 1941; trustee Mutual Life Insurance Co., New York Trust Co. Mem. Corp. of Colgate U. since 1888 (sec. 1892-1921, pres. 1921-35). Mem. Assn. Bar City of New York, Phi Beta Kappa, Delta Kappa Epsilon. Clubs: University, Metropolitan, Down Town Assn. Home: Bennington, Vt. Office: 44 Wall St., New York, N.Y. Died Feb. 26, 1944.

COLLADAY, Samuel Rakestraw, clergyman; b. N.Y. City, Sept. 16, 1868; s. William R. and Elizabeth D. (Wiltberger) C.; A.B., U. of Pa., 1891; Phila. Divinity Sch., 1891-92; Berkeley Divinity Sch., 1892-94, B.D., 1901, D.D., 1919; m. Marie L. Hill, Apr. 23, 1895; children—Charles Rittenhouse, Elizabeth Wiltberger, Montgomery Hill. Deacon, 1894, priest, 1895, P.E. Ch.; rector's asst. St. James's Ch., Phila., 1894-96; rector Ch. of Messiah, Phila., 1896-1900, Christ Ch., Middle Haddam, Conn., 1902-06; prof. lit. and N.T. interpretation, Berkeley Divinity Sch., 1900-09; dean St. Mark's Cathedral, Salt Lake City, Utah, 1909-16; rector St. James Ch., West Hartford, Conn., 1916-17; rector Christ Ch., Hartford, 1917-19; dean Christ Ch. Cathedral, 1919-36, dean emeritus since Oct. 1, 1936. Del. to Gen. Conv. P.E. Ch., 1919, 22, 25, 28, 34. Mem. Phi Beta Kappa. Home: 52 Meadowbrook Road, West Hartford, Conn. Died March 21, 1945.

COLLETT, George Richard, pres. Kansas City Stock Yards Co.; b. Hartford, Mich., Jan. 6, 1872; s. George Few and Sarah (Phillips) C.; ed. pub. schs., Hartford; student Kent Coll. of Law, Chicago; m. Florence Marsden Herendeen, 1901, (died 1908); 1 dau., Florence Herendeen (Mrs. Robert Moss Ayres); m. 2d, Mollie E. Switzer, 1915; 1 son, George Richard, Jr. In employ Chicago & W. Mich. R.R. and Ind., Ill. & Ia. R.R., 6 yrs.; with Armour & Co., packers, Chicago and Ft. Worth, Tex., 1896-1905; gen. mgr. Milwaukee (Wis.) Stock Yards, 1905-07; vice-pres. St. Louis Nat. Stock Yards, 1907-13; v.p. Kansas City Stock Yards Co., 1913-18; v.p. Morris & Co., packers, Chicago, 1918-21; pres. Kansas City Stock Yards Co., since 1921; pres. Kansas City Connecting R.R. St. Louis Nat. Stock Yards, E. St. Louis Junction R.R.; v.p. Am. Stock Yards Assn.; dir. Okla. Nat. Stock Yards Co., Nat. Stock Yards Nat. Bank (Nat. Stock Yards, Illinois), Inter-State Nat. Bank, Kansas City, Oklahoma City Junction Ry. trustee Kansas City U., Kansas City Conservatory of Music; dir. St. Luke's Hosp. Republican. Episcopalian. Mason (32°, K.T., Shriner). Clubs: Kansas City, Kansas City Country; Mo. Athletic (St. Louis). Home: 1020 W. 53d St. Terrace. Office: Live Stock Exchange Bldg., Kansas City, Mo. Died July 4, 1942.

COLLIER, Frank Wilbur (kŏl'yẽr), clergyman, educator; b. Ellicott's Mills, Md., Jan. 5, 1870; s. of Frank M. and Drucilla Talbot (Harden) C.; A.B., Johns Hopkins, 1896; S.T.B., Boston U., 1899, Ph.D., 1910; m. Rose Lee Carlisle, Dec. 21, 1896. Ordained M.E. ministry, 1897; pastor Barre, Mass., 1897-1901, Gleasondale, 1901-02, Malden, 1902-06; instr. in N.E. Deaconess Training School, 1907-08; pastor Stoneham, 1909-12, First Ch., Boston, 1912-13; dir. of research and prof. philosophy, Am. Univ., 1914-36, now emeritus, dean Sch. Arts and Sciences, 1920-27, dir. of research merged with deanship, 1925, also head dept. of philosophy. Mem. N.E. Conf. M.E. Ch., N.E. Meth. Hist. Soc., John Hopkins Alumni Assn., Boston U. Alumni Assn., A.A.A.S., British Inst. Philos. Studies, Sixth Internat. Congress of Philosophy, Southern Soc. for Philosophy and Psychology, Am. Assn. of Univ. Profs., Chi Psi Omega, Pi Gamma Mu. Mason. Clubs: Cosmos, Nat. Travel. Author: Back to Wesley, 1924; John Wesley Among the Scientists, 1927. Frequent contbr. to newspapers and mags. Editor: The Word and Life, 1912. Lecturer psychology, School of Religious Edn., Y.M.C.A., and School of Business, Washington Y.M.C.A., 1919-20; lecturer on social psychology, U. of Md., 1921-24. Mem. advisory council Living Age. Home: Florence Court West. Office: American University, Washington, D.C. Deceased.

COLLIER, William, comedian; b. Nov. 12, 1866; s. Edmund (actor) and Henrietta (Engel) C.; m. Louise Allen (died Nov. 1909); m. 2d, Paula Marr. Appeared in many minor parts in various comedies until 1901; starred in "On the Quiet," New York, 1901-02, London, 1903-04; starred in "Caught in the Rain," 1906-07; "Who's Who," 1913-14, etc. Address: Lambs' Club, 130 W. 44th St., New York. Died Jan. 13, 1944.

COLLINS, Albert Hamilton, educator; b. Covin, Ala., Nov. 13, 1894; s. Hosea Dean and Mavis Obera (Harkins) C.; B.S., Ala. Poly. Inst., 1921, LL.D., 1938; M.A., Columbia, 1927; L.H.D., Birmingham-Southern Coll., 1937; LL.D., University of Alabama, 1938; D.Ped., Oglethorpe University, 1940; married Julia Clara Higgins, July 11, 1923; children—Mavis Carline (dec.), Julia Clara, Elizabeth Ann, Alberta. Teacher rural schs., Ala., 1913-15, high schs. of Ala., 1921-23; prin. Montgomery County High Sch., Ramer, Ala., 1923-27; supervisor high schs., State Dept. of Edn., and prof. secondary edn., Ala. Poly. Inst., 1928-35; state commr. of public welfare, Ala., 1935-37; state supt. of edn., Ala., 1937-42; state dir. Office of Price Adminstrn. since Sept. 1942. Mem. Ala. Text Book Commn., 1935; mem. Am. Council on Edn.; mem. Ala. State Pub. Welfare Bd. since 1937; sec. and exec. officer Ala. State Bd. of Edn. Trustee Ala. Coll., Ala. Poly. Inst., U. of Ala. (1937-42). Ensign U.S. Navy during World War. Mem. Alpha Gamma Rho, Gamma Sigma Delta, Omicron Delta Kappa, Phi Kappa Delta, Kappa Delta Pi. Democrat. Baptist. Mason. Club: Kiwanis (Montgomery). Contbr. to ednl. jours. Home: Lowndesboro, Ala. Office: Bell Building, Montgomery, Ala. Died June 24, 1945; buried at Loundesboro, Ala.

COLLINS, Clifford Ulysses, surgeon; b. Batavia, O., Dec. 17, 1867; s. John Dalton and Martha (Cox) C.; M.D., Marion Sims Coll. of Medicine (now St. Louis U.), 1892; m. Belle Henry, Jan. 2, 1890; 1 dau., Constance (Mrs. Alvin Anderson). In practice of medicine at Vandalia, Ill., 1891-93; in Peoria since 1893; specialized in surgery since 1904; became mem. staff St. Francis Hosp., 1898, now hon. mem. staff; organized Collins Clinic, 1916; chmn. Bd. of Pub. Health Advisors, Dept. of Pub. Health, State of Ill., since 1929; hon. mem. staff Methodist Hosp. Fellow Am. Coll. Surgeons; mem. A.M.A., Am. Bd. Surgery, Peoria Med. Soc. (past pres.), Western Surg. Assn., Interstate Post Grad. Med. Assn. (trustee; past pres.), Peoria Assn. of Commerce (pres. 1912-13). Republican. Mem. Christian (Disciples) Ch. Mason (32°). Clubs: Rotary (pres. 1931) University, Creve Coeur. Home: 553 Moss Av. Office: Jefferson Bldg., Peoria, Ill. Died June 12, 1943.

COLLINS, Franklin Wallace (born Collings; changed to Collins when entered college), editor, publisher; b. Pompey Hill, Onondaga Co., N.Y.; Virgil (N.Y.) common sch., Drydren Union Sch. and Acad., N.Y.; Syracuse U., 1878-79, hon. D.C.L., 1910; hon. D.Litt., John Brown U., Siloam Springs, Ark., 1942; m. Mary Deborah Brown, Sept. 4, 1885 (now deceased); children—Charles Franklin, Rex Abraham, Kenneth Brown (deceased); m. 2d, Sunnyve Carlsen, Mar. 2, 1916 (died April 2, 1927; 1 dau., Sunny Louise (died Dec. 18, 1926); m. 3d, Edith Kent, Apr. 3, 1928. Admitted to Pa. bar, 1882, and practiced in Sayre, Pa., and Waverly, N.Y., 1882-83, Duluth, Minn., 1883-86, Lincoln, Neb., 1886-97; dep. county atty., Lincoln, Neb., 1893; asst. to U.S. Atty. Gen., 1897-1913; editor Paramount Issue, prohibition paper, Billings, Montana, 1916-17; editor and publisher San Marino (Calif.) Tribune, 1920-43. President Young Men's Rep. Club, Lincoln, 1892-93; pres. State League of Republican Clubs, Nebraska, 1894-96; Chautauqua lecturer, 1892-96; speaker for Nat. Rep. Com., 1896-1912; exec. of McKinley for Pres. campaign in Neb., 1896; founder and sec. Alexander Hamilton Nat. Memorial Assn., which planned and built the memorial on south front of U.S. Treasury Bldg., Washington, D.C.; one of principals in founding and financing John Brown U., 1919-25, also trustee; religious extension dir., Y.M.C.A., Camp Lewis, 1918. Awarded bronze trophy by citizens of San Marino for distinguished service, Apr. 1941. Mem. Calif. Newspaper Pubs. Assn., Delta Kappa Epsilon. Mason, Odd Fellow. Protestant. Clubs: Rotary, San Marino City. Author: Pepigrams and Jingles, 1924; Rizal, the Patriot and Martyr of the Philippines, 1930; also (under name of Frank Collins) syndicated paragraphs to newspapers, entitled: Frankinsense and Myrth, and Jingles in Pure Jinglish. Home: 120 W. Huntington Place, Arcadia, Calif. Office: San Marino Tribune, San Marino, Calif. Died Oct. 24, 1943; buried at San Gabriel, Calif.

COLLINS, J(ames) Franklin, botanist; b. N. Anson, Me., Dec. 29, 1863; s. James H. and Josephine (Witherell) C.; ed. pub. schs. N. Anson and Providence, R.I.; hon. Ph.B., Brown Univ., 1896; unmarried. Art metal worker, Providence, 1879-99; became interested in botany in 1883 (pvt. study); curator, Brown U. Herbarium, 1894-1911 and 1924-38; instr. in botany, Brown U., 1899-1905, asst. prof., 1905-11, head dept., 1906-11, demonstrator, 1913-25, lecturer, 1925-38, pathologist, U.S. Dept. Agr., 1911-33, retired. Mem. N.E. Bot. Club (crypto. curator, 1918-36; asso. editor 1929-36), Josseyln Bot. Soc., R.I. Hort. Soc., R.I. Field Naturalists' Club (ex-pres.), R.I. Bot. Club (ex-pres.), Sullivant Moss Soc., Sigma Xi. Author: Illustrated Key to the Trees of Northeastern North America (with H. W. Preston), 1912; also many bulls. on tree surgery and tree diseases. Contbr. Bull. Torrey Bot. Club, Rhodora, Bryologist, and U.S. Govt. publs., 1893—, Rhode Island Arbor Day Programs, 1910-11; also illustrations in "Botanizing," 1899, and 200 illustrations in Gray's Manual (7th edit.), 1908. Club: Faculty. Home: 37 Circuit Drive, Edgewood, R.I. Died Nov. 29, 1940.

COLLINS, Joseph Victor, educator; b. Wooster, O., Dec. 26, 1858; s. Henry Franks and Lydia C. Beall (Wasson) C.; Ph.B., U. of Wooster, 1879, Ph.D., 1886; grad. student Johns Hopkins, 1880-83; m. Jeannette M. Gasche, Dec. 30, 1886; children—Paul Fiske, Helen Jeannette MacElwee. Tutor in mathematics, U. of Wooster, 1879-80; prof. mathematics, Hastings Coll., Neb., 1883-88; prof. mathematics and astronomy, Miami U., 1888-93; head dept. of mathematics State Teachers Coll., Stevens Point, Wis., 1894-1937, emeritus prof. of mathematics since 1937. Presbyterian. Author: Text-book of Algebra, 1893; Practical Elementary Algebra, 1908; Practical Algebra, First Year Course, 1910; Second Course, 1911; Advanced Algebra, 1913; A Course in Bible Reading, 1923; Home Reading Course on Bible, 1932; (r, x) Coördinates, 1934; The Money Problem, 1935; English Words of Latin and Greek Origin, 1939. Contbr. articles to mags on metric system, language, prohibition, ednl. and polit. reforms, etc. Alumnus Phi Beta Kappa, Kappa of Ohio, 1927. Home: Stevens Point, Wis. Died Mar. 3, 1943.

COLLINS, Philip Sheridan, magazine publisher; b. Phila., Pa., Oct. 28, 1864; s. James C. and Lucinda B. (Copeland) C.; ed. pub. schs., Pierce Coll.; m. Anna M. Steffan, Nov. 14, 1894 (died Apr. 1, 1910); children—James S., Alan C.; m. 2d, Mary F. Schell, Oct. 20, 1913. Reporter on Pub. Ledger, Phila., 1886-90; with Curtis Pub. Co., 1890-1937, circulation mgr., 1892-1937, dir. since 1909, gen. business mgr., 1916-27, treas. and business mgr., 1927, v.p. and treas., 1928-37; retired; also dir. Castanea Paper Co., Tradesmen's Nat. Bank & Trust Co.; pres. Am. Foundation; v.p. Curtis Inst. of Music. Mem. Soc. Mayflower Descendants. Republican. Presbyterian. Clubs: Penn Athletic, Philadelphia Print, Philobiblon (Philadelphia); Congressional Country (Washington, D.C.); Huntingdon Valley Country. Home: Wyncote, Pa. Office: 744 Public Ledger Bldg., Philadelphia, Pa. Died Sept. 29, 1943.

COLLINS, Stewart G., army officer; b. Minn., Oct. 29, 1880; B.S., U. of Minn., 1904; commd. capt. Inf., Minn. Nat. Guard, Nov. 1918; maj. F.A., June 1919, advanced to brig. gen., Dec. 1940; Fed. Service, Feb. 1941; command of 68th Inf. Brigade, 34th div., in training, Camp Claiborne, La., since 1941. Address: Camp Claiborne, La.* Deceased.

COLLINS, Winifred, social work; b. Knoxville, Ill.; d. Thomas and Sarah (Kersey) Collins; prep. edn. St. Mary's Episcopal Sch. for Girls, Knoxville; A.A., Lewis Inst.; Ed.B. and B.S., U. of Chicago; grad. study Chicago Sch. of Civics and Philanthropy. Supervisor of home economics and dir. of neighborhood works and summer outing at Chicago Commons Settlement House, Chicago, 1907-17; during that period also served as sec. Chicago Westside United Charities Advisory Com., friendly visitor for Westside United Charities, mem. Chicago Municipal Markets Com. (apptd. by mayor); chmn. foods and markets com., Chicago Woman's City Club; pres. Teachers' Assn. of Chicago Housekeeping Centers and Chicago Home Economics Club; v.p. Chicago Westside Juvenile Protective League; v.p. Chicago Housing Assn.; supt. dept. social science, Tenn. Coal, Iron & R.R. Co., Birmingham, 1917-37, supt. bureau of community service since 1937. Chmn. recreation div. Southeastern Council; chmn. finance com., mem. exec. bd. dirs., Girl Scouts of Jefferson County, Ala.; sec. Dixie Region Girl Scouts. Mem. Nat. Conf. of Social Workers, Am. Assn. of Social Workers (pres. Ala. chapter 1934-36), Ala. Conf. of Social Workers, Nat. Amateur Athletics Fedn., Am. Assn. of Univ. Women (mem. bd. Birmingham br.; chmn. ednl. com. Ala. chapter; mem. nat. com. on econ. and legal status of women), Inst. of Social Work for Southern Executives (mem. exec. bd.). Episcopalian. Clubs: Music Study, Little Theatre, Birmingham Social Workers, Birmingham Country, Cadmian Circle. Home: 2250 Highland Av., Birmingham, Ala. Died Nov. 5, 1941.

COLLITZ, Klara Hechtenberg (kŏl'lĭts), author; b. Rheydt (Rhineland); grad. Höhere Lehrerinnen-Bildungsanstalt, Neuwied am Rhein, 1881; studied Lausanne, 1882-83; U. of London, Eng., Latin and French philology, 1889-92; 1st class honors, Oxford U., 1895, U. of Chicago, 1897, U. of Bonn, 1898; Ph.D., U. of Heidelberg, 1901; grad. work Bryn Mawr Coll., 1904-07, Johns Hopkins U., 1908-11; m. Hermann Collitz (prof. Germanic philology), Aug. 13, 1904 (died May 13, 1935). Lecturer in French philology, Victoria Coll., Belfast, Ireland, 1895-96; in charge of Germanic philology, Smith Coll., Mass., 1897-99; lecturer in Germanic philology, for women students, Oxford U., 1901-04. Mem. Linguistic Soc. of America, British Fedn. Univ. Women (London, Eng.), Oxford Society (Oxford, Eng.), Old Students' Assn. (Oxford, Eng.), Alumni Assn. Johns Hopkins Univ., Am. Assn. of Univ. Women, Oxford Soc., Goethe Soc., Congrès International pour les Sciences Phonétiques (Gand, Belgium), Phi Beta Kappa. Clubs: College (Bryn Mawr Coll.); Johns Hopkins U. Women's Faculty. Author: Das Fremdwort bei Grimmelshausen, 1901; Der Briefstil im 17 Jahrhundert, 1903; Fremdwörterbuch des 17 Jahrhunderts, 1904; Verbs of Motion in Their Semantic Divergence, 1931; The History of Alliteratives in German, 1933; Clipped Appellatives in German, 1936; Verba Dicendi, 1937. Compiler: Selections from Early German Literature, 1910; Selections from Classical German Literature, 1914; Index to Paul & Braune's Beiträge (vols. 1-50), 1926; Biographical Sketch of Hermann Collitz and Bibliography of Prof. Collitz' Writings, 1930; Bibliography of the Writings of Klara H. Collitz, 1938; also contbr. to philol. jours. Home: 1027 N. Calvert St., Baltimore, Md. Died Nov. 23, 1944.

COLPITTS, Edwin Henry, electrical engr.; b. Point de Bute, N.B., Can., Jan. 19, 1872; s. James Wallace and Celia Eliza (Trueman) C.; A.B., Mt. Allison U., Sackville, N.B., 1893, LL.D. (hon.), 1926; A.B., Harvard, 1896, A.M., 1897; m. Annie Dove Penney, Aug. 17, 1899; 1 son, Donald Bethune. Came to U.S., 1895, naturalized 1920. Asst. in physics, Harvard, 1897-99; telephone engr. Am. Telephone & Telegraph Co., Boston, 1899-1907; research engr. Western Electric Co., New York, 1907-17, asst. chief engr., 1917-24; asst. v.p. dept. of development and research, Am. Telephone & Telegraph Co., 1924-34; v.p. Bell Telephone Laboratories, 1933-37; retired. Iwadare lecturer, Japan, 1937. Served with U.S. Signal Corps on staff Gen. Edgar Russel, 1917-18. Fellow Am. Inst. E.E., Inst. Radio Engrs., Am. Phys. Soc., Acoustical Soc. of Am., A.A.A.S.; mem. Am. Chem. Soc., Harvard Engring. Soc. of New York, Telephone Pioneers of Am. Republican. Presbyterian. Club: Canoe Brook Country. Home: 309 Lawn Ridge Rd., Orange, N.J. Died March 6, 1949.

COLTER, Fred(erick) Tuttle, cattleman, irrigation reclamation; b. Neutrioso, Ariz., Feb. 2, 1879; s. James H. G. and Rosa (Rudd) C.; parental grandmother was a Tuttle, a direct descendant of the family of Tuttles who came from Tuttlefield, England, on the Good Ship Planter in 1627, founded New Haven, Conn., and gave of their homestead for site of Yale College; grad. high sch. and business college; m. Dorothy Burton, Aug. 20, 1927. Began cattle business at 12 as hired hand; had charge of outfit at 19; was pres. Cross Bar Land & Cattle Co., Colter-Greer Sheep Co., Colter Construction Co.; pres. Colter Live Stock & Agricultural Co., pres. Northern Ariz. Land Co., 1921; dir. Lyman Reservoir Co.; vice-pres. Stockman's State Bank, St. Johns, Ariz. Formerly vice-president Arizona Cattlemens Assn., and a director of National Livestock Assn.; was mem. Constl. Convention, Ariz.; mem. Arizona Senate, 8 terms; State Fair commissioner, Ariz., 5 yrs.; mem. Bd. Supervisors, Apache County, 5 yrs.; chmn. Dem. Central Com., Apache County; mem. Dem. Nat. Com., 1916-20; del. Dem. Nat. Conv., New York, 1924 (platform com.); Dem. nominee for gov. of Ariz., 1918 (defeated in gen. election by 300 votes); road commr. Apache County; rep. of gov. and State of Ariz., with Los Angeles Chamber of Commerce, before the U.S. Senate Irrigation and Reclamation Com., Oct. 1925, and before Congress and President of U.S. 1926, 27, 28, 37, 38, in relation to Colorado River irrigation; pres. since 1923, Ariz. Highline Reclamation Assn. (non-profit orgn.), to defeat Colorado River compact and build dams and High Line Canal, irrigating 4 million acres of land, developing 5 million electric H.P. Now pres. Colter, Ariz., Water Filing and Reclamation Assn. Trustee for Ariz. of major future water resources, filing on them in behalf of State, since 1923. Candidate for gov. of Ariz., 1930; mem. Ariz. House of Reps., 1934 and 1940-41. First pres. of Ariz. White Mountain Game and Fish Assn. Mem. advisory board Am. Hist. Soc.; mem. Correspondence Com. of Guards of Washington. Filed Pub. Works Adminstrn. loan application as Ariz. water trustee for $350,000,000 for construction of the Grand-Canyon-Glen-Bridge-Verde-Highline Project, Nov. 1933, and renewed application, May 1935, of which sec. of interior has approved $173,000,000. Pub. of "Highline" (book regarding Colo. River), 1934; "Colter's Reclaimer" (mag.); wrote book "Diligence in Protection and Development of Arizona Water Resources." Mem. advisory bd. Nat. Rivers and Harbors Congress; governor's rep. on Colo. River matters before legislature and congress; expert and adviser to Colo. River Commn. of Ariz. Candidate for Congress, 1942. Elk. Home: Colter, Springerville, Ariz. Office: 210-212 S. Third Av., Phoenix, Ariz.* Deceased.

COLTON, Arthur (Willis), author; b. Washington, Conn., May 22, 1868; s. Willis S. and Lucy P. (Gibson) C.; A.B., Yale, 1890, Ph.D., 1893; m. Amy Richards, Sept. 1917. Instr. English literature, Yale, 1893-95. Librarian Univ. Club, New York, 1906-1929. Author: Bennie Ben Cree, 1900; The Delectable Mountains, 1901; The Debatable Land, 1901; Tioba, 1903; The Belted Seas, 1905; The Cruise of the Violetta, 1906; Harps Hung Up in Babylon, 1907. Contbr. to mags. Address: Palisades, N.Y. Died Dec. 28, 1943.

COMERFORD, Frank Dowd (kŭm'ēr-fôrd), pub. service exec.; b. Worcester, Mass., July 31, 1893; s. Patrick and Mary Jane (Dowd) C.; A.B., Holy Cross Coll., Worcester, 1914, LL.D., 1934; LL.B., Harvard, 1917; m. Mary Margaret McLoughlin, June 17, 1929; children—Frank D., Mary, John. Admitted to Mass. bar, 1917, practiced with Ropes, Gray, Boyden & Perkins, 1917-27, mem. firm, 1925-27; pres. N.E. Power Assn., 1927-35, chmn. bd., 1935-1941; pres. Boston Edison Co. since 1935, now also mem. exec. com.; dir. 1st Nat. Bank of Boston, John Hancock Mutual Life Ins. Co., Liberty Mutual Ins. Co., Children's Hosp. (Boston); mem. exec. com. Asso. Edison Illuminating Cos; trustee Framingham Union Hospital; member corporation Massachusetts General Hospital. Mem. Bar Assn. City Boston, Boston Chamber Commerce. Catholic. Clubs: Exchange, Engineers, University (Boston); Algonquin, Framingham Country, Eastern Yacht, Boston Yacht, New Bedford Yacht. Home: Salem End Rd., Framingham, Mass. Died Nov. 24, 1941.

COMMONS, John Rogers, economist; b. Hollandsburg, Darke County, O., Oct. 13, 1862; s. John and Clara (Rogers) C.; A.B., Oberlin, 1888, A.M., 1890, LL.D., 1915; Johns Hopkins U., 1888-90; LL.D., U. of Wis., 1931; m. Ella Brown Downey). (A.B., Oberlin, 1888), Dec. 25, 1890. Instr. polit. economy, Wesleyan U., 1890; prof. sociology, Oberlin Coll., 1892, Ind. U., 1893-95, Syracuse Univ., 1895-99; expert Indsl. Commn., 1901; asst. sec. Nat. Civic Fedn., 1902; prof. economics, U. of Wis., 1904-32, prof. emeritus since 1932. Mem. Industrial Commn. of Wis., 1911-13; mem. Federal Commn. Industrial Relations, 1913-15; mem. Wis. Minimum Wage Bd. since 1919; asso. dir. Nat. Bur. Econ. Research, 1920-28; chmn. Unemployment Insurance Bd., Chicago Clothing Trades, 1923-25; mem. Am. Econ. Assn. (pres. 1917), Nat. Monetary Assn. (pres. 1922-23), Nat. Consumers' League (pres. 1923-35); mem. Am. Philos. Soc. since 1937. Author: The Distribution of Wealth; Social Reform and the Church; Proportional Representation; Regulation and Restriction of Output by Employers and Unions; Trade Unionism and Labor Problems; Races and Immigrants in America; Labor and Administration; Labor Legislation (with John B. Andrews); History of Labor in the United States (with others); asso. editor Documentary History of American Industrial Society; War Book of the Univ. of Wisconsin; Industrial Goodwill, Industrial Government (with others); Legal Foundations of Capitalism; (with others) Can Business Prevent Unemployment?; Institutional Economics; Myself (an autobiography). Contbr. to reviews and periodicals. Home; Madison, Wis. Address: Fort Lauderdale, Fla. Died May 11, 1944; buried in Forest Hills Cemetery, Madison, Wis.

COMPTON, Alfred Donaldson, coll. prof.; b. New York, N.Y., July 19, 1876; s. Alfred G. and Frances E. (Feeks) C.; B.S., City Coll., Coll. City of New York, 1897; student Columbia, 1898-1906; m. Elizabeth C. Roberts, June 17, 1909; children—Alfred D., George C. Began as tutor in English, City Coll., 1897, advancing through various teaching positions, prof. of English, ret. 1946. Pres. Students Aid Assn. (City Coll.). Mem. Am. Assn. Univ. Profs., Am. Dialect Soc., Phi Beta Kappa, Delta Kappa Epsilon. Author: First Aid in English, 1934; A Brief Anthology of English Literature, 1933. Home: 501 W. 138th St., New York, N.Y. Died Jan. 28, 1949.

COMPTON, Lewis; b. Perth Amboy, N.J., Nov. 7, 1892; s. James Lewis and Emma (DeBow) C.; ed. public schools of Perth Amboy and Phillips Exeter Acad., 1910-13; m. Beatrice Camille Vincent, Sept. 12, 1923; children—Camille Emma, James Vincent. Served as ensign, U.S. Navy, World War; asso. with Minwax Waterproofing Co., 1913, later with Compton Auto Sales Co.; mem. Compton Brothers, gen insurance; state dir. N.J. Emergency Relief Adminstrn., 1934-36; asst. adminstr. for N.J., Works Progress Adminstrn., 1936; asst. to pres. Thomas A. Edison, Inc., West Orange, N.J., 1936-40; asst. sec. of the Navy, Feb. 1940-41, resigned to accept appointment as commr. of finance for the State of New Jersey. Mem. Council, Borough of Metuchen, N.J.; dir. Bd. of Chosen Freeholders, Middlesex County, N.J.; Port Raritan Dist. Commn. Mem. Am. Legion, Mil. Order of World War, S.A.R. Democrat. Presbyterian. Elk. Club: Army and Navy (Washington, D.C.); Raritan Yacht. Home: 303 Alabama Av., Alexandria, Va. Office: Navy Dept., Washington, D.C. Died Oct. 24, 1942.

COMSTOCK, Clarence Elmer, author; b. Galesburg, Ill., May 5, 1866; s. Milton Lemmon and Cornelia Ann (Churchill) C.; A.B., Knox Coll., 1888, A.M., 1891, Sc.D., 1938; student Johns Hopkins U., 1892-93, 1894-95, U. of Chicago, 1895-96; m. Lucia Gary Driggs, Dec. 27, 1900; children—Robert Milton (dec.), Harold Elmer, George Churchill. Teacher mathematics, Blackburn U., Carlinville, Ill., 1888-89, Knox Coll., 1889-92, 1893-94, Princeton-Yale Sch., Chicago, 1896-97; prof. mathematics, Bradley Poly. Inst., Peoria, Ill., 1897-1939, emeritus, 1939. Mem. Am. Math. Soc., Math. Assn. America, Central Assn. Science and Math. Teachers (ex-pres.), A.A.A.S., Math. Assn.

(Eng.) Pi Gamma Mu. Republican. Presbyterian. Club: University. Author: Elementary Algebra, 1907; Plane and Solid Geometry, 1912; Plane Geometry (Sykes-Comstock), 1918; Beginners' Algebra (same), 1922; Solid Geometry (same), 1922; Second Course in Algebra (same), 1923; Plane and Solid Geometry (Sykes-Comstock-Austin), 1933. Home: 203 Fredonia Av., Peoria, Ill. Died Apr. 4, 1948.

COMSTOCK, F. Ray, theatrical producer; b. Buffalo, N.Y., 1880; s. David B. and Emma (Dean) C.; ed. pub. schs.; unmarried. Began as theatrical producer, 1900; sec. Frand Theatre Co. Producer of "Very Good Eddie," "Oh Boy," "Oh, Lady Lady," "Oh, My Dear," "Nobody Home," "Rose of China," "Leave It to Jane," "Sitting Pretty," "Let Us Be Gay," "Polly Preferred," "Adam and Eva," "Chu Chin Chow," "Mecca"; (with Morris Gest) "The Miracle," etc.; brought to U.S. Balieff's "Chauve-Souris," The Moscow Art Theatre and The Moscow Art Theatre Musical Studios; presented Mme. Eleanora Duse for her last tour of America. Mason (Shriner). Clubs: Lambs, Columbia Yacht, Maryland Jockey, Hialeah, Paddock. Address: Lambs Club, 128 W. 44th St., New York, N.Y. Died Oct. 15, 1949.

COMSTOCK, William Alfred, real estate broker; b. Alpena, Mich., July 2, 1877; s. William B. and Myra (Rapelji) C.; Ph.B., U. of Mich., 1899; m. Josephine White, Apr. 22, 1919; children—Kirke White (adopted), William III. Engaged in electric railroad constrn., 1899-1909, electric railroad operation, 1909-22; pres. State Savings Bank, Alpena, Mich., 1906-09; dir. First State Bank, Detroit, 1922-29; also engaged with several mfg. interests, 1910-31; in real estate business since 1924; vice-president Gale Manufacturing Company, Albion, Mich., since 1926. Member of Detroit City Council since 1942. Served as private 1st O.T.C., Fort Sheridan, Ill., 1917 (hon. disch., defective vision). Alderman, Alpena, 1911-12, mayor, 1913-14; Dem. state chmn., Mich., 1920-24; mem. Dem. Nat. Com., 1924-28; governor of Mich., 1933-34; mem. Civil Service Com., Michigan, 1939-40. Regent, U. of Mich., 1914-16. Mem. Zeta Psi. Democrat. Episcopalian. Mason, Elk, Eagle. Clubs: Detroit, University (Detroit); Ridgevale Rod and Gun (Alpena County, Mich.). Home: Tuller Hotel. Office: 672 Penobscot Bldg., Detroit 26, Mich. Died June 16, 1949.

CONBOY, Martin, lawyer; b. N.Y. City, Aug. 28, 1878; s. Martin and Bridget (Harlow) C.; A.B., Gonzaga Coll., Washington, D.C., 1898, A.M., 1899; LL.B., Georgetown U., 1898, LL.M. 1899, Ph.D., 1915, LL.D., 1920; also LL.D. from Gonzaga Coll., 1921, Duquesne U., Pittsburgh, 1933; m. Bertha L. Mason, July 31, 1912; children—Catherine (Mrs. John F. Dailey, Jr.), Constance (Mrs. John T. Kelley) and Marion. Director of Selective Service for New York City, World War, 1918; co-ordinating advisor to Selective Service Headquarters, New York State since 1940; U.S. atty., Southern Dist. New York, Dec. 26, 1933-May 15, 1935; mem. law firm Conboy, Hewitt, O'Brien & Boardman, N.Y. City. Mem. bd. regents Georgetown U. Mem. Am. Law Inst., Am. Bar Assn., N.Y. State Bar Assn., Assn. Bar City of New York, N.Y. County Lawyers Assn., Canadian Bar Assn. (hon.); pres. Nat. Alumni Soc., Georgetown Univ.; mem. Phi Delta Phi (hon.). Decorated Knight Commander St. Gregory the Great; Knight of Malta; Grand Officer Equestrian Order of Holy Sepulchre. Democrat. Clubs: Links, Manhattan, Catholic (pres. 1922-27), Lawyers, India House, New York Yacht, Sleepy Hollow Country, Hudson River Country, Long Island Country. Home: Riverdale-on-Hudson, N.Y. Office: 39 Broadway, New York. Died March 5, 1944; buried in Gate of Heaven Cemetery.

CONE, Frederick Preston, ex-gov.; b. Benton, Fla., Sept. 28, 1871; s. William Henry and Sarah Emily (Branch) C.; student Florida Agrl. Coll., Jasper Normal Coll.; m. 2d, Mildred Thompson, Aug. 1930; 1 dau. by 1st marriage, Jessie (Mrs. Mark Byron, 3d). Admitted to Fla. bar, 1892; served in Fla. State Senate, 1907-13 (pres. of Senate, 1911); gov. of Fla., 1937-41; now mem. Cone & Chapman. Pres. Columbia County Bank. Del. to Dem. Nat. Convs. since 1912. Baptist. Mason, Shriner, Elk. Clubs: Lake City, Rotary. Home: Lake City, Fla. Died July 28, 1948.

CONE, Helen Gray, college prof.; b. New York, Mar. 8, 1859; d. John C. and Julia D. (Gray) C.; grad. N.Y. City Normal Coll., 1876; L.H.M., New York U., 1908; Litt.D., Hunter Coll., 1920. Prof. English, New York City Normal Coll. (now Hunter Coll.), 1899-1926. Assisted Jeannette L. Gilder in editing Pen Portraits of Literary Women, 1887. Author: Oberon and Puck, Verses Grave and Gay, 1885; The Ride to the Lady, and Other Poems, 1891; Soldiers of the Light, 1910; A Chant of Love for England, and Other Poems, 1915; The Coat Without a Seam, 1919. Home: 550 W. 157th St., New York. Died Jan. 31, 1934.

CONKLIN, Edmund Smith, prof. psychology; b. New Britain, Conn., Apr. 19, 1884; s. Edmund Sidney and Catherine Annette (Smith) C.; B.H., Springfield (Mass.) Y.M.C.A. Coll., 1908; M.A., Clark U., 1909; fellow in psychology, 1909-11, Ph.D., 1911; Sc.D., Clark U., 1939; m. Helen Corey Holbrook, June 27, 1915; children—Marietta Muir, Edmund Holbrook. Asst. professor psychology and acting heat of dept., U. of Ore., 1911-13, prof. and head of dept., 1913-29, prof. and chmn. dept., 1929-34, acting dean of grad. sch., 1922-23; prof. and head dept. psychology, Ind. U., since 1934; visiting prof., U. of Chicago Divinity Sch., winter 1931 and during the summer terms of 1930 to 1933. Mem. editorial bd. Jour. Genetic Psychology, Genetic Psychology Monographs, Psychological Record. Fellow A.A.A.S.; mem. Am. Psychol. Assn., Am. Assn. Univ. Profs., Midwestern Psychol. Assn. (pres. 1938-39), Sigma Xi, Phi Gamma Delta. Rep. of Am. Psychol. Assn. on Nat. Research Council, 1939-1941. Author: Principles of Abnormal Psychology, 1927 (rev. edit. 1935); Psychology of Religious Adjustment, 1929. Principles of Adolescent Psychology, 1935; (with F. S. Freeman) Introductory Psychology for Students of Education, 1939. Home: 904 S. Hawthorne Dr., Bloomington, Ind. Died Oct. 6, 1942.

CONLAND, Henry H., pub. Hartford Courant; b. Brattleboro, Vt., May 11, 1882; s. James and Matilda (McGuirk) C.; ed. pub. schs.; m. Caroline Mathilde Henschel, Feb. 11, 1909; children—Henry James, Charles Henschel, Stephen, Mary Elizabeth. Began as reporter Hartford (Conn.) Courant, 1904, treas., 1915-29, pub. since 1926; pres. and dir. Hartford Retreat; dir. Hartford Courant Co., Conn. Mut. Life Ins. Co., Phoenix Ins. Co., Veeder-Root, Inc., Greenfield Recorder Pub. Co., Conn. Fire Ins. Co., Holo-Krome Screw Corp., Aetna Life Ins. Co., Aetna Casualty & Surety Co., Automobile Ins. Co. of Hartford. Chairman Hartford Bridge Commn.; mem. Flood Commn. of the City of Hartford; mem. bd. Hartford Police Commr. Dir. bur. of advertising, Am. Newspaper Publishers Assn. Republican. Episcopalian. Club: Hartford. Home: 285 N. Oxford St. Office: 64 State St., Hartford, Conn. Died Apr. 15, 1944; buried in Fairview Cemetery, West Hartford, Conn.

CONNELL, Albert James, educator; b. New York, N.Y., Mar. 17, 1882; s. Edward J. and Emma Augusta (McGean) C.; ed. St. Ursla's Acad., New York grade and high schools, Cooper Union; unmarried. Clerk N.Y.C. R.R., 1900-02; with Joseph P. McHugh & Co., New York City, 1902-03, Tiffany Studios, and Schmit Bros., N.Y. City, 1903-10; U.S. Forest Service, 1910-17; with Los Alamos Ranch Sch., private prep. school for boys, since 1917, dir. since 1918. Roman Catholic. Home: 544 Canyon Rd., Santa Fe, N.M. Died Feb. 11, 1941.

CONNELL, Carl W., army officer; born Ala., Mar. 16, 1890; grad. Air Service Engring. Sch., 1921, Air Corps Tactical Sch., 1929, Command and Gen. Staff Sch., 1931, Army War Coll., 1937; rated command pilot, combat observer, tech. observer. Began as sergt. Signal Corps June 1917; commd. 1st lt. Aviation Sect., Signal Corps, June 1917, and advanced through the grades to brig. gen., June 1942; served as capt. Signal Corps, World War I. Address: Air Corps, A.P.O. 501, care Postmaster, San Francisco, Calif.* Died Jan. 7, 1946.

CONNELL, Richard, author; b. Poughkeepsie, N.Y., Oct. 17, 1893; s. Richard Edward and Mary Elizabeth (Miller) C.; student Georgetown U., 1911-12; A.B., Harvard, 1915; m. Louise Herrick Fox, Nov. 8, 1919. Reporter, New York American, 1915-16; adv. writer J. Walter Thompson Co., New York, 1916-17; editor "Gas Attack," 27th Div. magazine, 1917-18; asst. adv. mgr. Am. Piano Co., 1919-20. Served as pvt. 27th Div., U.S. Army, 2 yrs.; in France with A.E.F. 1 yr. Club: Harvard (New York). Author: The Sin of Monsieur Pettipon, 1922; Apes and Angels, 1924; Variety, 1925; The Mad Lover, 1927; Murder at Sea, 1929; Ironies, 1930; Playboy, 1936; What Ho!, 1937; also numerous stories, screen plays, and original stories for motion pictures. Home: 505 N. Arden Dr., Beverly Hills, Calif. Died Nov. 22, 1949.

CONNELL, William Henry, civil engr.; b. N.Y. City, Jan. 12, 1878; s. Edward J. and Emma Augusta (McGean) C.; ed. De La Salle Inst., New York; m. E. Nena Watters, Apr. 23, 1913. Civ. engring. work, various depts., N.Y. City, 1908-1912, including topog. surveys, water supply, highway and bridge dept. service, dept. commr. pub works assisting boro pres. in reorganization of engring depts., also built service test roadway and installed modern methods of highway maintenance and constrn.; chief engr. Bur. Highways and Street Cleaning, Phila., modernizing highway and street cleaning work and built service test rd., 1912-17; engring. exec. with Day & Zimmerman, placing a number of large orgns. in the field for war work, 1917-19; spl. staff engr. Phila. Rapid Transit Co., 1919-23; chief exec., dept. sec. and engring. exec. Pa. Dept. of Highways, in charge of constrn. and maintenance of state highway system, comprising 11,500 miles of rd., 1923-27; in cons. practice, 1927-29; exec. dir. Regional Planning Federation of Phila. Tri-State Dist., 1929-40; civil works adminstr. Phila. County, 1933-34; dir. local work division Federal Emergency Relief Adminstrn., Phila. County, 1934-35; consulting engineer. Mem. Nat. Highway Research Council, Am. Roadbuilders Assn. (ex-pres.), Am. Assn. State Highway Officials, Am. Soc. C.E.; hon. mem. Street and Road Assn. of England. Clubs: Engineers, Racquet. Address: 112 S. Oxford Av., Ventnor, N.J. Died Aug. 3, 1943.

CONNELLY, Edward Michael, lawyer; b. Bellingham, Wash., Sept. 8, 1892; s. Patrick Edward and Elizabeth (Murphy) C.; B.A., Gonzaga Univ., Spokane, Wash., 1912, M.A. 1914, LL.B. 1915; m. Grace Ellsworth, Olympia, Wash., Apr. 5, 1920; children—Ellsworth Irving, James Patrick. Admitted to Wash. bar, 1917; admitted to bar of U.S. Dist. Courts of Wash., Ida., Ore., and Circuit Court of Appeals, 9th Circuit; sec. to J. Stanley Webster, judge Supreme Court of Wash., Jan.-July 1917; deputy prosecuting atty., Pacific County, Washington, 1920; chief asst. prosecuting atty. Spokane County, 1924-28; U.S. atty. for Eastern Dist., Wash., since Apr. 17, 1942. Democrat. Roman Catholic. Mem. Knights of Columbus, Elks. Clubs: Early Birds (Spokane), Athletic Round Table, Press Club. Home: 2314 S. Jefferson St., Spokane, Wash. Died Aug. 31, 1947.

CONNESS, Leland Stanford, newspaper corr.; b. Boston, Mass., Mar. 29, 1880; s. John and Mary Russell (Davis) C.; father U.S. senator from Calif., 1863-69; grad. Boston Latin Sch., 1898; m. Rosalie Thornton, Mar. 30, 1913. Began as reporter in Seattle, Wash., later at North Yakima and Honolulu; editor Hawaii Herald, 1909-12; with New York World Bur., 1913-14; in charge publicity, Woodrow Wilson Independent League, campaign of 1916; served with Dem. Nat. Com., 1932 campaign. Club: Nat. Press. Home: Cumberland Apt. Address: National Press Club, Washington, D.C. Died Apr. 8, 1942.

CONNICK, Charles Jay, artist in stained glass; b. Springboro, Pa., Sept. 27, 1875; s. George Herbert and Mina Mirilla (Trainer) C.; ed. pub. schs.; studied life drawing in night classes, Pittsburgh, 1895-1900; student Boston Art Club and Copley Soc., 1900-09; research and study of old glass, England and France, 1910, 22, 25, 28, 31, 35; M.F.A., Princeton U., 1932; A.F.D., Boston U., 1938; m. Mabel R. Coombs, July 1920. Employed as designer in Pittsburgh, New York and Boston, 1895-1911; entered business on own account, 1913. Important windows designed and made: western windows, including the great rose, nave windows in Arts and Education Bays, and windows in Saint Martin's Chapel, Cathedral of Saint John the Divine, chancel and east transept windows, St. Patrick's Cathedral, N.Y. City; east window to "Christian Brotherhood" and four great choir windows symbolizing the Christian Epics—Dante's "Divine Comedy," Bunyan's "Pilgrim's Progress," Milton's "Paradise Lost," and Malory's "Morte d' Arthur" in the Chapel of Princeton U.; all windows in U. of Pittsburgh Chapel and nearby Stephen Foster Shrine. 10 great clerestory windows symbolizing Old and New Testament subjects in the East Liberty Presbyn Ch., Pittsburgh; all windows, including Nettie Fowler McCormick Memorial over entrance, in Fourth Presbyterian Church, Chicago; great north and south transept rose windows, including the 5 lancets beneath each, aisle window next to south transept, two clerestory windows in east side of south transept, and window in each side of the lower north transept, as well as all the windows in The Chapel of Grace, Grace Cathedral, San Francisco; other important windows are in The First Baptist Church, Malden, Church of Our Saviour and All Saints' Ch. (Brookline), Jessie Woodrow Sayre Memorial, Chapel of Reformatory for Women (Framingham), St. Peter's Episcopal Ch. (Cambridge), Chapel of Mass. Gen. Hospital, Emmanuel Ch., Ch. of St. John the Baptist and Boston U. Chapel (Boston), Chapel of the Holderness Sch. (Plymouth, N.H.), also many other New England chs., Ch. of Saint Vincent Ferrer, Saint James, Saint Michael and Saint Peter's chs. (N.Y. City), Westminster Presbyn. Ch. (Buffalo), Saint Agatha's Ch. and St. Clement's Ch. (Phila.), Calvary Ch. (Pittsburgh), Ch. of the Covenant (Erie), Pine St. Presbyn. Ch., Great South Window (Harrisburg), The Hill School Chapel (Pottstown, Pa.), Trinity College Chapel and National Shrine (Washington, D.C.), Franklin St. Presbyn. Ch. (Baltimore), St. Charles Coll. Chapel, Catonsville, Maryland; Saint Paul's Cathedral and Chapel of Little Flower (Detroit), Saint Chrysostom's Ch. (Chicago), Ch. of the Holy Spirit (Lake Forest), First M.E. Ch. (Evanston, Ill.), Christ Ch., and Fenwick Club, Chapel of the Holy Spirit (Cincinnati), Chapel at Dillon Hall, Notre Dame Univ., Notre Dame, Ind.; House of Hope Presbyn. Ch., Cathedral and Nazareth Hall Chapel (Saint Paul's), St. Mark's and Hennepin Av. Ch. (Minneapolis), Saint Dominic's Ch. and Star of Sea Ch. (San Francisco), Forest Lawn Memorial Park, Glendale, Calif., Am. Ch. (Paris, France), St. John's Cathedral (Denver), Art Museum (Univ. of Kan.), Two Chapels, U.S. Aviation Station, Jacksonville, Fla.; Chapel at U.S. Submarine Base, New London, Conn.; St. Cecilia's Cathedral and Church of St. Margaret Mary, Omaha; Father Flanagan's Home, Boystown, Nebraska; Church Street Church, Knoxville, Tenn., etc. Author of "Adventures in Light and Color," an introduction, history and appraisal of ancient and modern stained glass, 1937; series of articles entitled "Windows of Old France," for International Studio, 1923-24; also articles for numerous art, architectural and ecclesiastical publications. Mem. Poetry Soc. (New York), Arts and Crafts Soc. (pres. 1934-39), Copley Soc. Mediæval Acad. of America, Stained Glass Assn. of America (pres., 1931-39); hon. mem. Am. Inst. of Architects, Soc. of Architects; fellow Am. Acad. of Arts and Sciences. Awarded gold medal, San Francisco Exposition, 1915; Logan medal, Chicago, 1917-21; Arts and Crafts medal, Boston, 1920; American Inst. of Architects craftsmanship medal, 1925. Del. Am. Commn. to study French Expn., 1925. Clubs: Examiner Club, Boston City Art, Early Am. Glass Club, Architectural, Boston Author's (Boston); Century (New York). Home: 70 Hull St., Newtonville, Mass. Studio: 9 Harcourt St., Boston, Mass. Died Dec. 28, 1945.

CONNING, John Stuart, church official; b. Whithorn, Scotland, June 4, 1862; s. James and Marian

(McKeand) C.; student Oberlin (O.) Coll. and U. of Toronto; B.D., Knox Coll., Toronto, 1890; D.D., St. John's Coll., Annapolis, Md., 1919; m. Margaret Alison, Jan. 1, 1890; children—Norman Elmer, Gordon Russell, Margaret Helen, John Keith Gardner. Came to U.S., 1897, naturalized citizen, 1918. Ordained ministry Presbyn. Ch., Canada, 1890, pastor successively Caledonia, Ont., Can., Knox Ch., Walkerton, Ont., Reid Memorial, Walbrook and Westminster chs., Baltimore, Md., until 1919; pres. Presbyn. Training Sch., Baltimore, 1898-1919; sec. Bd. Nat. Missions Presbyn. Ch., U.S.A., 1919-32. Mem. com. on Hebrews of Internat. Missionary Council and sec. joint department of Coöperating Boards, Home Missions Council. Author: Our Jewish Neighbors, 1928; Leila Adler, 1929; The Jew in the Modern World, 1931. Contbr. Missionary Rev. of World, Internat. Missionary Rev., Presbyn. Mag., etc. Home: 1 Highland Terrace, Upper Montclair, N.J. Office: 156 Fifth Av., New York, N.Y. Died June 20, 1946.

CONNOLLY, Joseph Peter, coll. pres.; b. Cleveland, Nov. 15, 1890; s. Peter Albert and Bertha Elizabeth (Orwig) C.; A.B., Oberlin (O.) Coll., 1912; A.M., U. of Mo., 1915; A.M., Harvard, 1916, Ph.D., 1927; spl. studies in geology, Mass. Inst. Tech., 1917; m. Anna Ruth Lewis, Dec. 22, 1924; children—Lewis Peter, Thomas Joseph. Geol. fieldworker, Mo. State Bur. Mines and Geology, 1914-15; instr. in geology, U. of Mo., 1919; prof. mineralogy and petrography, S.D. State Sch. Mines, since 1919, also v.p., 1926-35, pres. since 1935; editor Black Hills Engineer since 1935; cons. geologist. Served as pvt., later 2d lt., Motor Transport Corps, U.S. Army, 1917-18. Leader Nat. Geog. Society, S.D. Sch. of Mines, Joint Paleontological Expdn., 1940. Fellow Geol. Soc. America, Mineralogical Society, America, A.A.A.S.; mem. Soc. Econ. Geologists, Am. Institute Mining and Metallurgical Engrs., Mining and Metall. Society of Am., Am. Society for Engineering Edn., Newcomen Society of England, Sigma Xi, Gamma Alpha, Sigma Gamma Epsilon fraternities; honorary member Sigma Tau, Triangle. Republican. Episcopalian. Writer of bulletins on mineralogy and econ. geology of Black Hills for S.D. State Sch. Mines; contbr. to National Geographic Mag., Jour. of Geology, Proc. S.D. Acad. Science, Black Hills Engr., etc. Home: 1804 W. Boulevard, Rapid City, S.D. Died Oct. 7, 1947.

CONNOLLY, Joseph Vincent, editor; b. New Haven, Conn., Feb. 7, 1895; s. Joseph and Ellen Teresa (Reynolds) C.; student high sch., New Haven, 1908-11; m. Marguerite Stanford, Jan. 2, 1919; children—Joseph, Mary Jacqueline. Reporter, New Haven Union, 1912-18, New York Sun, 1919-20; with King Features Syndicate since 1920, now pres.; pres. Internat. News Service, Central Press Assn., Internat. News Photos. Served as lt. U.S. Army, World War. Democrat. Catholic. Clubs: Westchester Country (Rye, N.Y.); Pelham (N.Y.) Country; 100,000 Mile Club. Home: 25 Benedict Pl., Pelham, N.Y. Office: 235 E. 45th St., New York. Died Apr. 18, 1945; buried in St. Lawrence Cemetery, New Haven, Conn.

CONNOR, Guy Leartus, neurologist; b. Detroit, Mich., Oct. 10, 1874; s. Leartus (M.D.) and Anna Amelia (Dame) C.; A.B., Williams, 1897; M.D., Johns Hopkins, 1901; m. Daisy Wicks, Nov. 14, 1901. Practiced in Detroit since 1901; formerly asst. clin. prof. neurology, psychiatry and preventive medicine, Detroit Coll. of Medicine; was also neurologist St. Mary's Hosp., Children's Free Hosp.; med. dir. Bd. Edn., Detroit, 1914-36; mem. Mich. State Bd. of Registration in Medicine, 1917-29, sec., 1924-29. Mem. Fedn. State Med. Bds. (pres. 1928). Mem. Am. Coll. of Physicians, Am. Med. Assn., Mich. State Med. Soc. (pres. 1923-24), Wayne Co. Med. Soc., Detroit Acad. Medicine (pres. 1917), Zeta Psi. Republican. Presbyterian. Clubs: Detroit Athletic, Detroit Boat. Home: 8120 E. Jefferson Av., Detroit, Mich. Died Apr. 19, 1943.

CONRAD, Frank L., utilities exec.; b. Cincinnati, O., Sept. 15, 1886; s. Benjamin Franklin and Emma (Eberle) C.; m. Miriam Leonhardt, Apr. 21, 1908; 1 dau., Miriam Frances. Engr. Sandersen & Porter, N.Y. City, 1908-19; mem. engring. firm Wm. G. Woolfolk & Co., Chicago, 1919-29; cons. engr., N.Y. City; 1929-38; pres. and dir. United Light & Rys. Co., Am. Light & Traction Co., Continental Gas & Electric Corp., United Light & Railways Service Co.; dir. Iowa-Ill. Gas & Electric Co. (Rock Island, Ill.), Detroit (Mich.) Edison Co., Iowa Power & Light Co. (Des Moines, Ia.), Milwaukee (Wis.) Solvay Coke Co., Milwaukee (Wis.) Gas Light Co., Madison (Wis.) Gas & Electric Co. Mem. Am. Soc. E.E. Episcopalian. Mason. Clubs: Detroit (Detroit); Union League (Chicago), Chicago (Chicago); Recess (New York). Home: Hotel Ambassador East. Office: 105 W. Adams St., Chicago, Ill. Died Oct. 22, 1949.

CONRADI, Edward (kŏn(rä-dē), coll. pres. emeritus; b. New Bremen, O., Feb. 20, 1869; s. Charles F. and Gertrude (Bruetsch) C.; A.B., Univ. of Ind., 1897, A.M., 1898; fellow Clark Univ., 1902-05, Ph.D., 1904, hon. fellow, 1904-05; LL.D., Rollins Coll., Winter Park, Florida, 1933, Univ. of Florida, 1939, University of Indiana, 1942; married Augusta D. E. Grothaus, Aug. 24, 1898; children—Elizabeth Lillian, Louisa May Ruth. Supt. schs., Carlisle, Ind., 1898-1902; prin. Normal and Industrial Sch., St. Petersburg, Fla., 1905-09; pres. Fla. State Coll. for Women, July 1909-Oct. 1941. Mem. N.E.A., Assn. Colls. and Secondary Schs. of Southern States, Fla. Acad. of Sci., Soc. for Scientific Study of Edn., Fla. Hist. Soc., Fla. State Chamber of Commerce, Phi Beta Kappa, Phi Kappa Phi. Presbyterian. Contbr. to mags., chiefly on pedagogical and ethl. topics. Home: 458 W. College Av. Address: State College for Women, Tallahassee, Fla. Died Dec. 1, 1944.

CONRY, Thomas, coll. pres.; b. Manchester, Ia., Jan. 27, 1869; s. John and Mary (Whalen) C.; A.B., St. Joseph's Coll., Dubuque, Ia., 1895, LL.D., 1939. Ordained priest R.C. Ch., 1898; asst. pastor St. Raphael's Cathedral, Dubuque, 1899-1900; head of English Dept., Columbia Coll., Dubuque, 1901-24, pres emeritus, 1939; domestic prelate, 1926; vicar gen. archdiocese of Dubuque, 1934-44; prothonotary apostolic, 1934. Supervising editor of The Witness, official organ Archdiocese of Dubuque. Address: Loras College, Dubuque, Ia. Died June 29, 1947; buried Mount Olivet Cemetery, Dubuque, Ia.

CONS, Louis (kôns), prof. French lit.; b. Lyons, France, May 26, 1879; s. Claude Joseph and Henriette (Gauthier) C.; A.B., Lycée Ampère, 1896; grad. study Lycée Henry IV, Paris; Licence ès Lettres, Sorbonne, 1899; grad. study Collège de France, Ecole des Hautes Etudes, Paris, 1901-04; m. Jeannette Curtis, Sept. 16, 1909. Came to U.S., 1910. French tutor, Royal Court of Prussia, 1905-08; editor, Hachette's Pub. House, Paris, 1908-10; asso. prof. French lit., Bryn Mawr (Pa.) Coll., 1910-14; asso. prof. French lit., Princeton, 1919-27; prof. French lit., U. of Ill., 1927-29; prof. French lit. and head of dept., Swarthmore Coll., 1929-31; prof. French lit., Columbia Univ., 1931-37; prof. French lit., Harvard U. since 1937. Served as pvt., corpl. and lt. infantry, French Army, 1914-18. Mem. Modern Lang. Assn., America, Société des Anciens Textes français, Pi Delta Phi, Phi Kappa Epsilon. Decorated Officier d'Académie; Croix de Guerre; Chevalier Legion of Honor. Club: University. Author: De Goethe à Bismarck, 1909; De Washington à Roosevelt, 1910; L'Auteur de la Farce de Pathelin (discoverer of identity of author of this farce), 1926; Anthology of French Renaissance, 1931; François Villon, 1936. Home: 56 Fayerweather St. Address: Widener Library, Harvard University, Cambridge, Mass. Died Apr. 19, 1942.

CONWAY, Barret, ry. official; b. St. Louis, Mo., Nov. 14, 1878; s. Edmund Virgil and Cora Bailey (Barret) C.; ed. public schools (St. Louis), Carleton Coll. (Farmington, Mo.) and Westminster Coll. (Fulton, Mo.) until 1898; m. Louise Shoenberger, June 1, 1909; children—Louise Reynolds, Robert Barret, Elizabeth Barret. Began as clerk and stenographer in office of gen. supt. C.&A. Ry. Co., Chicago, 1900; with C.&N.W. Ry. Co. since July, 1900, successively clerk and stenographer, 1900-02, sec. to pres., 1902-10, asst. sec., C.&N.W. Ry. Co., 1910-28, asst. sec. and asst. treas., 1928-33, vice-pres. and sec. since Feb. 15, 1933; also sec. C.St.P.M.&O. Ry. Co. since Feb., 1933 and v.p. since 1940. Mem. Beta Theta Pi. Conglist. Club: Indian Hill (Winnetka), Union League (Chicago). Home: 387 Linden St., Winnetka, Ill. Office: 400 W. Madison St., Chicago, Ill. Died Dec. 7, 1949.

CONWAY, Joseph W., lawyer; b. Salt Lake City, Utah, Dec. 3, 1898; s. John and Katherine (Ward) C.; student Tempe (Ariz.) State Teachers Coll., 1915-18; LL.B., U. of Ariz., 1924; m. Gertrude Fuqua, Sept. 3, 1932; 1 dau., Sara Dana. Began in mining, 1917, became smelter craneman, 1918, advertising sales and copywriter Tucson Citizen, 1921; admitted to Ariz. bar, 1924, and began practice in Ariz.; now atty. gen. for State of Ariz. Served in U.S. Army, 1918. Address: Capitol Bldg., Phoenix, Ariz. Deceased.

CONWELL, Walter Lewis; b. Covington, Ky., Jan. 25, 1877; s. Lewis A. and Fannie (Danby) C.; grad. Manual Training High Sch., Phila.; engring. dept., U. of Pa., 1894-98; m. Josephine Whetstone, Jan. 1901; m. 2d Lillian P. Denkman, 1937. With Tennis Construction Co., ry. contractors, advancing to chief engr., 1898-1901; salesman Westinghouse Electric & Mfg. Co., 1901-11, pres. Transportation Utilities Co. ry. supplies, 1911-16; asst. to pres. Safety Car Heating & Lighting Co. (Pintsch system), 1916-19, pres., since 1919; chmn. bd. Pintsch Compressing Co.; chmn. of board Vapor Car Heating Co.; dir. Carrier Corp., Seatrain Lines, Wicolator Co. Mem. Am. Inst. E.E. Clubs: Downtown Athletic, Montclair Golf; Rolling Rock (Pittsburgh); Chicago (Chicago); Cloud. Home: 80 Lloyd Rd., Montclair, N.J. Office: 230 Park Av., New York, N.Y. Died May 27, 1948.

CONYNGHAM, William Hillard (kŏn'ing-hăm), banking; b. Wilkes-Barre, Pa., June 7, 1868; s. William Lord and Olivia (Hillard) C.; grad. Wilkes-Barre Acad., 1884; Ph.B., Yale, 1889; m. Mae Turner, 1897 (died 1902); m. 2d, Jessie Guthrie, 1918; children— William Lord 2d, George Guthrie, John Nesbitt, 3d. Began in wholesale mines supply and hardware business, 1889; now pres. Eastern Pennsylvania Supply Co.; pres. First Nat. Bank of Wilkes-Barre; chmn. bd. dirs. Lehigh Valley Coal Co.; dir. Lehigh Valley Coal Corp., Morris Run Coal Mining Co. Republican. Clubs: Westmoreland, North Mountain (Wilkes-Barre); Rittenhouse (Philadelphia); University (New York); Saddle and Sirloin (Chicago); Graduate (New Haven, Conn.); Bankers of America (New York City). Home 130 S. River St. Office: 1232 Minces Nat. Bank Bldg., Wilkes-Barre, Pa. Died Apr. 25, 1943.

COOK, Alfred A., lawyer; A.B., Coll. of City of N.Y., 1892; A.M., Columbia, 1894, LL.B., 1895; mem. firm Cook, Nathan, Lehman & Greenman. Mem. Am. Bar Assn., Assn. of Bar of City of N.Y. (chmn. judiciary com.). Home: 630 Park Av. Office: 20 Pine St., New York, N.Y.* Died Jan. 2, 1950.

COOK, Chauncey (William), banker; s. William Wallace and Clara E. (Dearborn) C.; student University of Michigan, 1906-08; m. Keziah Birely, December 23, 1919. Construction engineer and contractor, 1908-14; mining engineer and superintendent, Mexico, 1914-15; supt. steel plant, Hamilton, Ont., 1915-17; gen. dir. constrn. work, France, 1919-21; asst. to pres. steel plant, Hamilton, 1921-22; supt. construction, N.Y. City, 1922-24; sec.-treas. By-Products Coke Plant, Troy, N.Y., 1924-29; v.p. and gen. mgr., 1929-35; pres. and dir. Mfrs. Nat. Bank, Troy, N.Y. since 1935; dir. Marine Midland Group, Inc.; director Ludlow Valve Co., Wm. H. Frear & Co. Served as capt., later major engineers, U.S. Army, with A.E.F., 1917-19. Trustee Russell Sage Coll., dir. Samaritan Hospital (both Troy). Clubs: Troy, Country (Troy); Fort Orange (Albany, N.Y.). Home: 34 Myrtle Av. Office: Manufacturers National Bank, Troy, N.Y. Died Aug. 4, 1949.

COOK, Fannie, author; b. St. Charles, Mo., Oct. 4, 1893; d. Julius and Jennie (Michael) Frank; A.B., U. of Mo., 1914; M.A., Washington U., 1916; m. Dr. Jerome E. Cook, Oct. 28, 1915; children—Robert Jerome, Howard Frank. Part time lecturer English, Washington U., 1918-35; civic worker since 1924; editor Missouri Bulletin, League of Women Voters, 1931-35; chmn. Mo. Com. for Rehabilitation of The Sharecropper, Inc., since 1910; mem. St. Louis Mayor's Race Relations Commn., 1943-46; lecturer in midwest on inter-racial, legislative and literary subjects; exhibited water-color portraits, St. Louis Artists Guild, 1946. Awarded $1000 prize in Reader's Digest article contest for new writers, 1936; citation of merit for work among sharecroppers, St. Louis Urban League, 1944; trophy for outstanding contbn. to inter-racial welfare, St. Louis Argus, 1946; George Washington Carver Memorial Award, 1946 ($2,500 given by Doubleday & Co.), for novel showing importance of Negro to life of America. Author: The Hill Grows Steeper, 1938; Boot-Heel Doctor, 1941; Mrs. Palmer's Honey, 1946. Contbr. short stories, articles and reviews to mags. and newspapers. Address: 400 Purdue Av., St. Louis 5, Mo. Died Aug. 25, 1949.

COOK, Frank Gaylord, lawyer; b. Arcade, N.Y., May 13, 1859; s. Ebenezer W. and Delphia E. (Chaddock) C.; A.B., Harvard, 1882, LL.B., 1885; m. Alice Burr Sterling, June 30, 1896. Began practice at Boston, 1886. Commr. of Union Conf. of Congl. Chs. of Boston and Vicinity, 1903-08; trustee and clerk, Andover Theol. Sem., 1907-08. Mem. Cambridge Hist. Soc. (sec. 1905-10, v.p.), Delta Upsilon (charter mem. Harvard chapter, chmn. board of trustees and pres. of corp. until 1928), Phi Beta Kappa. Chmn. provisional com. Nat. Council Congl. Chs. of U.S., 1910-13. Author articles on Oliver Ellsworth and Theophilus Parsons in Great American Lawyers; extensive writer on legal, polit., hist. and social subjects; contbr. to Atlantic Monthly, N. Am. Review, Review of Reviews, etc. Clubs: Harvard Union, Harvard Faculty, Boston Congregational (pres. 1908); Authors' (London, Eng.). Tours around the world, 1924-25 and 1931. Retired since Mar. 1946. Address: Harvard Faculty Club, Cambridge, Mass. Died March 3, 1948.

COOK, James Henry, naturalist; b. Kalamazoo, Mich., Aug. 26, 1858; s. Henry and Elizabeth (Shaw) C.; ed. pub. schs.; m. Kate Graham Cook, Sept. 28, 1886; children—Harold James, John Graham (dec.). Mgr. WS Ranch, Socorro County, N.M., 1882-87; owner Agate Springs Ranch, Agate, Sioux County, Neb., since 1887. Discovered Agate Springs Fossil Quarries, from which many valuable prehistoric specimens have been secured; maintains with Harold J. Cook, a free mus. of natural history, at Agate. Guide and scout with Texas Rangers in early 70's; Scout for U.S. cav. in Geronimo Indian Campaign, 1885, 86. Mem. Am. Inst. Social Sci., Nebraska State Hist. Soc., Nat. Indian War Vets.; hon. mem. Boy Scouts America; asso. mem. Order Indian Wars of U.S. Republican. Protestant. Author: Fifty Years on the Old Frontier, 1923; also stories of adventure. Lecturer on geology, evolution, etc. Home: Agate, Neb. Died Jan. 26, 1942.

COOK, R(obert) Harvey, physician; b. Eaton, O., 1870; s. George Frederick and Sallie J. (Pryor) C.; A.B., Miami U., 1891, A.M., 1894; M.D., Med. Coll. of Ohio, 1894; post-grad. work in New York and abroad; m. Besse Orr, Dec. 18, 1895; children—George Harvey, M. O. Specializes in nervous diseases. Became Supt. of Oxford Retreat, a pvt. hosp., 1910, now retired. Mem. A.M.A., Am. Psychol. Assn., Ohio State Med. Soc., Cincinnati Acad. Medicine, Beta Theta Pi. Republican. Presbyterian Mason (32°). Home: Oxford, O. Died Nov. 24, 1949.

COOK, Sidney Albert, prof. psychology; b. New Haven, Conn., July 2, 1892; s. Albert Stanburrough and Emily (Chamberlain) C.; A.B., Yale U., 1915 ed. Cornell U., 1915-16; A.M., Yale U., 1921; Ph.D. Columbia U., 1928; m. Alison Loomis Cook, Sept. 4 1920; children—Paul 2d, James Carey, Andrew Beveridge, Philip Sidney. Engaged as instr. psychology, Rutgers Coll., 1922-26, asst. prof., 1926-28; asso. prof. psychology, N.J. Coll. for Women, Rutgers U., 1929-31, prof. psychology since 1931, head of dept. philosophy and psychology since 1929; psychol. clinician, New Brunswick School System, 1922-32. Lecturer, Middlesex Gen. Hosp., 1925-30. Mem. Twp. Bd. Edn., 1937. Served as ambulance driver, Am. Ambulance Field Service in the French Army (1916-17); 2d lt., 1st lt., motor truck supply train, and A.S., U.S. Army, 1917-19, with A.E.F. in France. Officer 7th Regt., New York State Guard, 1942-43. Fellow A.A.A.S. Mem. Am. Genetic Assn., Am. Acad. Polit. and Social Science, Am. Psychol. Assn., N.Y. Acad. Sci., N.J. State Teachers Assn. (pres. mental hygiene dept., 1933), Sigma Xi, Phi Delta Kappa, Pi Gamma Mu, Psi Chi, Lambda Chi Alpha. Republican. Episcopalian. Home: Hillcrest, River Rd., New Brunswick, N.J. Died Feb. 4, 1944.

COOK, Walter Wheeler, prof. law; b. Columbus, O., June 4, 1873; s. E. H. and Clara Wing (Coburn) C.; A.B., Columbia, 1894, A.M., 1899, LL.M., 1901; LL.D., Univ. of Wis., 1929; as John Tyndall fellow of Columbia U., studied at univs. of Jena, Leipzig and Berlin, 1895-97; m. Helen Newman, Nov. 14, 1899; children—Mrs. Helen Coburn Law, Mrs. Dorothy Newman Breland, Edith Newman, Mrs. Mary Newman Hall; m. 2d, Elizabeth Stabler Iddings, Sept. 23, 1931. Asst. in mathematics, Columbia Univ., 1894-95. 1897-1900; instr. jurisprudence and pub. law, 1901-02, asst. prof. pub. law, 1902-03, prof. law, 1903-04, U. of Neb.; prof. law, U. of Mo., 1904-06, U. of Wis., 1906-10, U. of Chicago, 1910-16, Yale U., 1916-19, Columbia U., 1919-22; prof. law, Yale, 1922-28; prof. of law, Johns Hopkins, 1928-33; prof. of law, Northwestern Univ., 1935-43. Visiting prof. of jurisprudence, Johns Hopkins, 1926-28. Sec.-treas. Assn. Am. Law Schs., 1912-15, and pres., 1915-16; nat. sec.-treas. Order of Coif, 1912-26; nat. pres., 1926-29; pres. Am. Assn. Univ. Profs., 1931-33, gen. sec., 1933-35; chmn. Com. on Enrollment and Disbarment, U.S. Treasury, 1934-35, mem. of same com. since 1935. Mem. Delta Kappa Epsilon, Phi Beta Kappa, Phi Delta Phi, Cosmos Club (Washington). Author: The Logical and Legal Bases of the Conflict of Laws; Cases on Equity; Cases on Pleading (with E. W. Hinton); Readings on the Forms of Action at Common Law; The Powers of Courts of Equity; also articles on equity, trusts, municipal corps., and quasi-contracts in Am. Law and Procedure; contbr. to legal periodicals. Address: 357 E. Chicago Av., Chicago, Ill. Died Nov. 7, 1943.

COOK, William Locke, judge; b. Bon Aqua, Hickman, County, Tenn., Dec. 6, 1869; s. William and Elizabeth (Weems) C.; ed. under mother and Prof. G. T. Abernathy, Montgomery County, Tenn.; studied law, Vanderbilt U., 1 yr., later in office of Col. Thomas C. Morris, of Charlotte, Tenn.; m. Nancy Clements Collier, Nov. 28, 1897; children—William Collier, Louise, Mary Baxter. Admitted to Tenn. bar, 1892, and began practice at Charlotte; mem. 50th Gen. Assembly of Tenn., 1897-98; elected judge Circuit Court, 9th Jud. Dist. of Tenn., for unexpired term, 1908, reelected, 1910, 1918; resigned Apr. 15, 1923, to fill vacancy on Supreme Court of Tenn., by apptmt. of Gov. Peay; elected to same office for 3 terms, 1926-42. Mem. S.C.V. Democrat. Methodist. Mason. Home: 2011 Belmont Blvd., Nashville, Tenn. Died Mar. 5, 1942.

COOK, Willis Clifford; b. Gratiot, Wis., Oct. 5, 1874; s. Alfred and Sarah (Cole) C.; LL.B., U. of Wis., 1895; m. Mary Butler Miller, 1899; 1 son, Alfred L. Began practice at Plankinton, S.D., 1899; county judge, Aurora County, S.D., 1900-02; mem. S.D. Senate 2 terms, 1905-09; chmn. Rep. State Central Com., 1906-12; mem. Rep. Nat. Com. for S.D., term 1916-24; E.E. and M.P. to Venezuela, 1921-29. Past pres. S.D. Soc. S.A.R. Mem. Am. Acad. Polit. and Social Science, Am. Soc. Internat. Law, Acad. of Polit. Science. Home: Sioux Falls, S.D. Died Jan. 5, 1942.

COOKE, (Alexander) Bennett, surgeon; b. Bowling Green, Ky., 1867; s. William Alexander and Nancy (Burnam) C.; B.A., Ogden Coll., Bowling Green, Ky., 1886, A.M., 1892; M.D., Vanderbilt U., 1891; post-grad. work New York, Chicago, London, Berne, Vienna; m. Dorothy Daisy Soden, Louisville, Ky., July 10, 1894; dau., Dorothy Soden C. (Mrs. Raymond Tremaine). Began practice, Nashville, Tenn., 1895; removed to Los Angeles, Calif., 1913; prof. of anatomy, med. dept., U. of Nashville, 1897-1900; prof. of anatomy and clinical surgery, med. dept., Vanderbilt U., 1900-03; sr. attending surgeon Los Angeles County Hosp. since 1911; prof. of surgery, Coll. of Medical Evangelists, Los Angeles. Fellow Am. Med. Assn. (judicial council, 1913-17); fellow Am. Coll. of Surgeons since organization; mem. Sons of Revolution. Pres. Tenn. State Med. Assn., 1907. Author: Diseases of the Rectum and Anus, 1914; Life—What Is It? Contbr. to med. journals. Address: 402 S. Manhattan Pl., Los Angeles, Calif. Died Dec. 9, 1946.

COOKE, C(harles) Montague, Jr., zoölogist; b. Honolulu, T.H., Dec. 20, 1874; s. Charles Montague and Anna Charlotte (Rice) C.; A.B., Yale U., 1897, Ph.D., 1901; Sc.D., University of Hawaii, 1936; m. Eliza Lefferts, Apr. 25, 1901; children—Carolene Alexander, Charles Montague. Has studied nearly all the large collections of Hawaiian land shells in museums of Europe and America; malacologist with Bishop Museum, Honolulu, T.H. Trustee Honolulu Acad. Arts, Bishop Museum. Mem. Washington Acad. Sciences, Acad. Natural Sciences, Phila., Malacological Soc., London. Republican. Conglist. Club: Pacific (Honolulu). Home: 2859 Manoa Rd., Honolulu, T.H. Died Oct. 29, 1948.

COOKE, Clarence Hyde, banker; b. Honolulu, T.H., Apr. 17, 1876; s. Charles M. and Anna C. (Rice) C.; prep. edn. Punchon Acad.; matriculated at Yale, 1897; m. Lily Love, Aug. 11, 1898 (died Jan. 28, 1933); m. 2d, Elnora Sturgeon, July 10, 1936. In banking business, Honolulu, since 1897; became pres. Bank of Hawaii, 1909, now chmn. bd.; chairman bd. Cooke Trust Co., Ltd.; chmn. bd. Hawaiian Electric Co.; v.p. Hawaiian Agricultural Co., Wailuku Sugar Co., Ewa Plantation Co., Waialua Agrl. Co.; dir. Mutual Telephone Co., Hilo Sugar Co., Olokele Sugar Co., etc.; treas. Molokai Ranch, Ltd. Mem. Hawaiian Ho. of Rep., many terms since 1913 (speaker of House, 1923, 27); mem. Hawaiian Senate, 1929-31. Republican. Conglist. Home: 3860 Old Pali Rd. Address: Bank of Hawaii, Honolulu, T.H. Died Aug. 23, 1944.

COOKE, Douglas H., publisher; b. Hinsdale, Ill., Oct. 28, 1886; s. Henry H. and Mary Melissa C.; ed. Phillips Acad., Andover, Mass.; m. Theodora Walcott, Apr. 2, 1909; children—Drusilla (Mrs. Howard E. Gregg), Eloise (Mrs. Edward Mitchell Taylor), Elizabeth Walcott. Former editor and pub. Judge and Leslie's Weekly; pres. and treas. New Fiction Pub. Corp., Popular Radio, Inc.; dir. Speak-O-Phone, Inc. Presbyterian. Clubs: Salmagundi, Uptown (New York); Arts (Washington, D.C.); Milton Point Casino (gov.); Green Meadow Country (Rye). Author: Building Industrial Morale, 1919; The Ear in Education, 1930; The New Force in Education, 1931. Home: 12 E. 86th St. Office: 250 W. 54th St., New York. Died Feb. 18, 1948.

COOKE, Hereward Lester, physicist; b. Montreal, Can., Mar. 26, 1879; s. Miles Woodifield and Clara Maude (Eager) C.; B.A., McGill, 1900, M.A., 1903; studied Emmanual Coll., Cavendish Lab., Cambridge U., 1903-06; m. Olive Lois MacCallum, 1911; children—Margaret Priscilla, Hereward Lester. With Princeton U. since 1906, prof. physics since 1919. Researches in radioactivity, thermionics, 1903-13; surveying with aeroplane photographs since 1919; theatre acoustics since 1928. Served as capt. Royal Engrs., B.E.F., in France, 1916-19. Mem. Am. Physical Soc., Acoustical Soc. America, Am. Soc. Photogrammetry, Optical Soc. of America. Clubs: Princeton (New York); Nassau Club, Princeton, N.J. Home: 37 Palmer Square, Princeton, N.J. Died Sep. 30, 1946.

COOKSEY, George Robert; b. Washington, D.C.; s. Charles E. and Sarah Virginia (Smith) C.; ed. pub. schs.; m. Annie C. Colliflower, Oct. 14, 1907 (died 1921); children—George Robert, Jr., Annie Catherine Virginia, Charles Thurman, Harry Joseph, Joseph Edward, Mary Audrey. With Washington office of Associated Press, 1898-1913; pvt. sec. to Sec. of the Treasury McAdoo, 1913-17; asst. to secretaries of the Treasury, McAdoo, Glass, Houston, and Mellon, Mar. 6, 1917-Oct. 8, 1921; dir. War Finance Corp., 1920-29; mem. liquidating com. of War Finance Corp., 1929-32, chmn. May 11, 1929-Mar. 7, 1932; mem. Federal Farm Loan Bd., May 10, 1927-Mar. 7, 1932; sec. Reconstruction Finance Corp. since Feb. 2, 1932; mem. bd. trustees Electric Home and Farm Authority since Aug. 1, 1935, and v.p. since Aug. 21, 1935; sec. Disaster Loan Corp. since Feb. 15, 1937; sec. Metals Reserve Co. since June, 1940; sec. and mem. board dirs. Rubber Reserve Co. since June, 1940 (sec. rubber buying com. since July, 1940); mem. board dirs. Defense Supplies Corp. since Aug., 1940. Catholic. Club: Nat. Press. Home: 4211 16th St. N.W. Office: 811 Vermont Av. N.W., Washington, D.C. Died July 25, 1941.

COOLEY, Frederick Boyden, mfr.; b. Deerfield, Mass., Nov., 1875; s. Alfred Allen and Charlotte (Clapp) C.; grad. Deerfield Acad., 1893; A.B., Harvard, 1897; m. Florence Adsit, 1902; children—Esther Boyden, Katrina Adsit, Robert Adsit, Roger Greenwood. Advanced from clk. to supt. N.Y. Car Wheel Co., 1899-1903; pres. Lancaster Malleable Iron Works, 1903-05; dist. mgr. Nat. Car Wheel Co., Sayre, Pa., 1905-07; gen. mgr. Buffalo Car Wheel & Foundry Co., 1907-13; president New York Car Wheel Co., 1913-41; chairman board of directors since 1941. Organizer, 1919, pres. until 1922, Internat. Metal Hose Co., Cleveland, O.; pres. until 1926, New York Car Wheel Co. of Ind.; dir. and mem. exec. com. Mfrs. & Traders Trust Co., Buffalo; dir. Fed. Reserve Bank (Buffalo), 1924-33. Pres. Millard Fillmore Hosp., Buffalo; v.p. Buffalo City Cemetery Assn.; mem. exec. com. and dir. Assn. Mfrs. Chilled Car Wheels; mem. Am. Soc. for Testing Materials (com. on cast iron). Republican. Presbyterian. Clubs: Saturn; Turkey Point Country Shooting (Long Point, Ont.); Turtle Lake Fish and Game (Quebec). Home: 561 Franklin St. Office: 15 Forest Av., Buffalo, N.Y. Died Oct. 12, 1944.

COOLEY, Mortimer Elwyn, engr.; b. Canandaigua, N.Y., Mar. 28, 1855; s. Albert Blake and Achsah (Griswold) C.; ed. Canandaigua Acad.; grad. U.S. Naval Acad., 1878; hon. M.E., U. of Mich., 1885; LL.D., Mich. Agrl. Coll., 1907; Eng. D., U. of Neb., 1911; Sc.D., Armour Inst. Tech., 1923; Eng. D., University of Michigan, 1929; B.Sc. from U.S. Naval Academy, 1938; m. Carolyn Elizabeth Moseley, December 25, 1879; children—Lucy Alliance (Mrs. Wm. O. Houston), Hollis Moseley, Anne Elizabeth (Mrs. E. C. Howe), Margaret Achsah (Mrs. Harvey F. Cornwell). Professor mechanical engineering, 1881-1928, dean College Engineering, 1904-28, and dean College of Architecture, 1913-28, University of Michigan, now dean emeritus, Colleges Engineering and Architecture. In navy on cruise in Mediterranean, 1879, Atlantic Coast, 1880, Bureau Steam Engineering, 1881; chief engineer U.S. Navy, 1898-99, serving on U.S.S. Yosemite during Spanish-American War and at League Island Navy Yard; chief engr. officer Mich. Naval Brigade, 1895-1911. Dist. ednl. dir. S.A.T.C., 7th dist. (Mich., Wis., Ill.), 1918. Mem. Bd. of Public Works, Ann Arbor, 1888-90; pres. common council, two terms, 1890-91; Dem. candidate for U.S. senator, Mich., 1924. Appraised rolling stock and power plants Detroit st. rys., 1899; in charge appraisal of Mich. rys., telegraphs, telephones, etc., 1900-01; assisted in appraisal mech. equipment, Newfoundland rys., 1902; cons. engr., Wis. railroad appraisal, 1903; in charge reappraisal of Mich. rys., 1903-04-05; mem. traction valuation com. Chicago, 1906; appraised Mich. telephone properties, 1907; in charge appraisal of hydro and steam electric cos. and rys. for Mich. R.R. and Utilities Commn., 1910-21; spl. investigation public utility properties in Minneapolis, Milwaukee, Cleveland, St. Louis, Boston, New York, Sault Ste. Marie, Red Wing, Buffalo, Evansville, Washington, D.C., N.J., etc., since 1906. State engr. for Mich. under Federal Pub. Works Adminstr., 1933-34, becoming director, 1935; chmn. Mich. State Highway Advisory Bd. since 1934. Mech. expert in patent causes, 1893-1925. Chmn. Block Signal and Train Control Board, Interstate Commerce Commn., 1907-12. Mem. Engring. Com., Chicago Expn., 1893; com. on awards, Pan-Am. Expn., Buffalo, 1901; mem. advisory council Joint Commn. on Postal Service, 1920-23; pres. Am. Engring. Council, 1921-23. Mem. Gilbert Wilkes Camp No. 17, Spanish Am. War. Awarded navy service medal, Sampson, Detroit Naval Res. medal; recipient Washington Award of Western Society of Engineers. Mem. Internat. Board of Judges, Fisher Body Craftsmen's Guild. Hon. citizen, Boys Town; hon. mem. Nat. Council, Boy Scouts of America. Mem. National Committee on Independent Courts, 1937; member council National Economics League. Past mem. Am. Inst. Cons. Engrs.; fellow Am. Geog. Soc., Inst. of Am. Genealogy, Royal Soc. of Arts (London); past fellow A.A.A.S. (v.p. sect. D, 1898); hon. mem. Am. Soc. M.E. (v.p. 1902-03, pres. 1919, chmn. Detroit sect. 1916-17), Am. Soc. C.E. (dir. 1913-16), Franklin Inst., Soc. Promotion Engring. Edn. (pres. 1920-21), Mich. Engring. Soc. (pres. 1903), Nat. Assn. Power Engrs.; mem. Detroit Engring. Soc., Cooley Family Association of America (founder; pres. 1936-38), Griswold Family Assn. of America, Soc. of Descendants of Henry Wolcott, Sigma Phi, Tau Beta Pi, Sigma Xi, Phi Kappa Phi, Iota Alpha, Acacia, Aero. Soc., Vulcans, Michigamua, Scabbard and Blade, Sigma Rho Tau. Clubs: Army and Navy (Washington); Sigma Phi (New York); Detroit, Yondotega, Prismatic, Witenagemote (Detroit); University, Scientific, Town and Gown (Ann Arbor); hon. life mem. Heart O'Nature Club. Author: Cooley Genealogy. The Mortimer E. Cooley Foundation at U. of Mich. named in his honor. Home: 1405 Hill St., Ann Arbor, Mich. Died Aug. 25, 1944.

COOLEY, Thomas Benton, pediatrist; b. Ann Arbor, Mich., June 23, 1871; s. Thomas McIntyre and Mary Elizabeth (Horton) C.; A.B., U. of Mich., 1891, M.D., 1895; D.Sc., 1940; grad. study, Harvard, 1895-96, Germany, 1900-01; m. Abigail Hubbard, Dec. 21, 1903; children—Emily Holland, Thomas McIntyre. Interne Boston (Mass.) City Hosp., 1895-97; instr., med. dept., U. of Mich., 1898-1900; resident physician Boston City Hosp., 1902-03; asst. prof. hygiene, U. of Mich., 1903-05; in pvt. practice, specializing in diseases of children, Detroit, since 1905; maj. and asst. chief Children's Bur. Am. Red Cross, in France, 1918-19; chief of pediatric service and chmn. staff, Children's Hosp. of Mich., 1921-41; prof. and head dept. of pediatrics, Wayne U. Coll. of Medicine, 1936-41, emeritus prof. since 1941. Member Am. Inst. of Nutrition, Soc. for Research in Child Development, Soc. for Pediatric Research, Mich. State and Wayne Co. med. socs., Am. Acad. Pediatrics (ex-pres.), Am. Pediatric Soc. (ex-pres.), Detroit Acad. Medicine, Delta Kappa Epsilon, Nu Sigma Nu, Sigma Xi. Awarded Cross of Legion of Honor (France), 1924. Club: University. Contbr. to Abt's Pediatrics, Am. Jour. Diseases of Children, Brennemann's Pediatrics, Jour. of Pediatrics. Home: 7840 Van Dyke Pl., Detroit 14, Mich.; (summer) Sorrento, Me. Died Oct. 13, 1945.

COOLIDGE, Emelyn Lincoln, pediatrist; b. Boston, Mass., Aug. 9, 1873; d. George A. and Harriet Abbot (Lincoln) Coolidge; ed. pub. and pvt. schs., Boston, New York and Washington, Woman's Med. Coll., New York, and Cornell U. Med. Coll., M.D., 1900; unmarried. Engaged in practice as children's specialist since June 1900, asst. supt. Babies' Hosp., New York, 1892-1900, acting supt., 1900-01, res. phys., 1902, visiting phys. out-patients dept. same, 1903-05; pediatrist to Soc. of the Lying-in Hosp., New York, 1903-32. Conducted The Baby's Page, Ladies Home Journal, 1902-21; became editor Babies' Dept., Pictorial Review, 1921, resigned 1937; also occasional contbr. to other papers. Mem. Cornell Alumnæ, Am. Child Health Assn., Authors' League, Com. of One Hundred, etc. Unitarian. Author: How to Feed the Baby from Birth to Three, 1902: The Mother's Manual, 1904; First Aid in Nursery Ailments, 1910; The Home Care of Sick Children, 1916; The Young Mother's Guide, 1916. Home: 220 W. 98th St., New York 25, N.Y.; (summer) 29 Virginia Av., Long Beach L.I. N.Y. Died Apr. 14, 1949.

COOLIDGE, Marcus Allen, ex-senator; b. Westminster, Mass., Oct. 6, 1865; s. Frederick Spaulding and Ellen Drusilla (Allen) C.; ed. pub. schs.; m. Ethel Louise Warren, October 1, 1898; children—Louise (Mrs. Donald Fell Carpenter), Judith (Mrs. Gordon Hughes), Helen (Mrs. Harry H. Woodring). Began in chair and rattan business with father; gen. contractor, building street rys., water works, bridges, etc., 1883-1905; became pres. Fitchburg Machine Works, 1905; now pres. Seneca Falls (New York) Machine Co., mfrs. machine tools. Chmn. and treas. Wilson Advisory Com., 1916; apptd. by President Wilson spl. envoy to Poland, representing the Peace Commn.; mayor of Fitchburg, 1916; chmn. Dem. State Conv., Mass., 1920; del. Dem. Nat. Conv., 1920, 24; mem. and treas. Dem. State Com.; mem. Dem. Electoral Coll., Mass., 1929; mem. U.S. Senate, term 1931-37. Trustee and president Cushing Academy, Ashburnham, Mass. Universalist. Home: 164 Blossom St., Fitchburg, Mass. Died Jan. 23, 1947.

COOLIDGE, Mary (Elizabeth Burroughs) Roberts, writer; b. Kingsbury, Ind., Oct. 28, 1860; d. Prof. Isaac Phillips and Margaret Jane (Marr) Roberts; Ph.B., Cornell, 1880, M.S., 1882; Ph.D., Stanford U., 1896; Litt.D., Mills College, 1927; m. Albert W. Smith, Aug. 28, 1890; m. 2d, Dane Coolidge, July 30, 1906. On staff of the Rural New Yorker, 1880-81; teacher of history, Washington (D.C.) High Sch., 1882-84; prin. and teacher history Miss Nourse and Miss Roberts' pvt. sch., Cincinnati, O., 1884-86; instr. of history and economics, 1886-90, sec. bd. examiners, 1888-90, Wellesley Coll.; asst. and asso. prof. of sociology, Stanford U., 1896-1903; research assistant to Carnegie Instn., Washington, 1904-08; head worker South Park Settlement, San Francisco, 1905-06; research work, San Francisco Relief Survey, 1909; prof. sociology, Mills Coll., 1918-27. Republican. Unitarian. Pres. Calif. Civic League, 1915-17; trustee of Pacific Colony for the Feebleminded, 1917-20; mem. Calif. State Bd. of Edn., term 1928-32; mem. San Francisco br. of Am. Indian Defense Assns. Mem. Am. Assn. Univ. Profs., Nat. League of Women Voters, Am. Assn. of Univ. Women. Clubs: Calif. Writers (pres. 1932-35), College Women's. Author: Chinese Immigration, 1909; Why Women Are So, 1912; The Rain Makers, Indians of Arizona and New Mexico, 1929; The Navajo Indians (with Dane Coolidge), 1930; The Last of The Seris (with Dane Coolidge), 1939. Reviser Warner's American Charities, 1908 and 1918. Contbr. of sociol. and econ. articles to mags. Home: Dwight Way End, Berkeley, Calif. Died Apr. 13, 1945.

COOMARASWAMY, Ananda Kentish (kōō-mä'rā-swä'mi), b. Colombo, Ceylon, Aug. 22, 1877; s. Sir Mutu and Elizabeth (Clay) C.; D.Sc., U. of London (Eng.), 1904; m. D. Luisa Runstein; 1 son, Rama Ponnambalam. Dir. Mineral Survey of Ceylon, 1906; initiated movement in India for national edn.; in charge art sect. United Provinces Exhbn., at Allahabad, 1910-11; fellow for research in Indian, Persian and Muhammadan Art, Museum Fine Arts, Boston, since 1917. Author: Rajput Painting, 1916; Indian Drawings (2 vols.), 1910-12; Myths of the Hindus and Buddhists (with Sister Nivedita), 1913; Buddha and the Gospel of Buddhism, 1916; The Dance of Siva, 1918, 25; History of Indian and Indonesian Art, 1927; Yaksas, parts I and II, 1929, 31; A New Approach to the Vedas, 1933; The Transformation of Nature in Art, 2d edit., 1935; Elements of Buddhist. Iconography, 1935; Rg Veda as Land-Náma-Bók, 1935; La Sculpture de Bodhgaya, 1935; Patron and Artist, 1936; Mirror of Gesture, 2d edit., 1936; Spiritual Authority and Temporal Power in the Indian Theory of Government, 1942; Why Exhibit Works of Art?, 1943; Hinduism and Buddhism, 1943; Figures of Speech of Figures of Thought, 1946; Am I My Brother's Keeper?, 1947; Time and Eternity, 1947; Gotama the Buddha, 1948. Home: 649 South St., Needham, Mass. Address: Museum of Fine Arts, Boston, Mass. Died Sept. 9, 1947.

COOMBS, George Holden (kōōmz), physician; b. Brunswick, Me., Jan. 7, 1863; s. David Edwin and Annie (Lee) C.; M.D., New York Univ., 1886; m. Gertrude Farnsworth Willett, June 6, 1889 (died Aug. 24, 1928); 1 dau., Jessie Willett (Mrs. Parker Burroughs Stinson); m. 2d, Elizabeth E. Fossett, Oct. 31, 1929. General practice Brunswick, Me., 1880-90, Toledo, O., 1890-91, Waldoboro, Me., 1891-1920, 1928-32 and since 1939; epidemiologist and social hygiene div. of State Dept. of Health, 1921-28; dir. State Bur. Health, 1932-39. Mem. Knox County and Me. State med. assns. Soc. Alumni Internes Bellevue Hosp. Home: Waldoboro, Me. Died Nov. 20, 1948.

COOMBS, Zelotes Wood, prof. English; b. Wrentham, Mass., June 8, 1865; s. George Weston and Ellen Adams (Wood) C.; A.B., Amherst, 1888, A.M., 1895; U. of Va. Law Sch., 1889-90, U. of Berlin, 1894-95, Paris, summer 1901; m. Elizabeth Maury Haynes, Sept. 1, 1908. Inst., Brooklyn Poly. Inst., 1888-89, U. of Va., 1889-90; began with Worcester Poly. Inst., 1890, prof. English, 1913-37, sec. faculty and dean of admissions, 1935-37, now prof. and dean emeritus. Mem. Alpha Delta Phi. Republican. Episcopalian. Clubs: Worcester, Tatnuck Country. Address: Worcester Poly. Institute, Worcester, Mass. Died 1948.

COON, Owen L., executive; b. Le Roy, Ill., July 1, 1894; s. James S. and Rose O. (Rike) C.; B.A., Northwestern U., 1915, LL.B., 1919; m. Louise Dowdell, March 22, 1930; children—Eleanor Rose (Mrs. Wm. Briggs), Harry H., Owen L. Admitted to Illinois bar, 1918, practiced law, 1919-25; pres., Motor Acceptance Co., Evanston, Ill., 1925-34; pres., Gen. Finance Corp., 1934-39, chmn. bd. since 1939. Chmn. Terminal Nat. Bank, Climax Industries, Inc., Mid-States Ins. Co. (chmn. bd.), The Wacker Corp., GFC Loan Co. Trustee of Northwestern U. Past pres. Evanston War Chest. Treas. War Memorial Com. (Evanston); mem. City Planning Commn. of Evanston. Chmn. city div., Community and War Fund of Chicago, 1944, hon. chmn. 1945; chmn. suburban div. Community and War Fund of Metropolitan Chicago, 1943; director of Goodwill Industries of Chicago, (pres. 1946). President Am. Finance Conf., 1937-38. Methodist. Mem. Phi Beta Kappa, Delta Sigma Rho, Order of the Coif, Phi Gamma Delta, Delta Theta Phi. Clubs: Chicago, Chicago Athletic, Mid-Day (Chicago); Westmoreland Country (Wilmette); Univ. (Evanston). Home: 1201 Sheridan Road, Evanston. Office: 184 W. Lake St., Chicago, Ill. Died Aug. 21, 1948.

COONS, Leroy Wilson, church official; b. Arcanum, O., Aug. 23, 1872; s. Philip and Almira (Fouts) C.; student St. Lawrence U., Canton, N.Y., 1895; A.B., Bowdoin, 1907, A.M., 1908; D.D., St. Lawrence, 1915; m. E. Loraine Thomas, Aug. 25, 1897; 1 son, Quentin Leroy. Ordained ministry Universalist Ch., 1895; pastor successively Hallowell, Pittsfield and Augusta, Me., until 1914, Haverhill, Mass., 1914-22; supt. Universalist Chs. in Mass., 1922-42. Mem. Alpha Delta Phi, Phi Beta Kappa. Mason (K.T.). Clubs: University, Bowdoin Coll. (Boston). Home: 204 Clark Rd., Brookline, Mass. Died Aug. 25, 1948.

COOPER, Elisha Hilliard, mfr.; b. Rockport, Mass., Oct. 2, 1869; s. James Wesley and Ellen (Hilliard) C.; B.A., Yale, 1892; m. Margaret Miller, 1901; children—Stanley M., Ford H., Richard F. Chmn. Fafnir Bearing Co., New Britain, Conn., since 1926; dir. Stanley Works, Hart & Cooley Co., Inc., New Britain Trust Co. Republican. Conglist. Home: 169 Vine St., New Britain, Conn. Died Jan. 4, 1947.

COOPER, Frank, judge; b. Glenville, N.Y., Oct. 1869; A.B., Union U., 1893, A.M., 1896; m. Mabel Rice Gannon, 1908. Admitted to N.Y. bar, 1895, and practiced at Schenectady; corp. counsel, Schenectady, 1910-13, 1916, 17, 20; U.S. dist. judge for Northern District of N.Y., 1920-41; retired. V.p. N.Y. State Council of Chs. Mem. N.Y. State Bar Assn., Schenectady County Bar Assn. (pres. 1918, 19), Chi Psi. Democrat. Clubs: Union, Alumni, Chi Psi (N.Y.). Home: 537 Western Av., Albany, N.Y.* Died July 16, 1946.

COPELAND, Charles, artist; b. Thomaston, Me., Sept. 10, 1858; s. George and Mary F. (Monroe) C.; ed. pub. sch., Thomaston; m. Eda O. Mills, Oct. 27, 1886. Engaged as illustrator and painter in water color; exhibited at Soc. Am. Artists, Pa. Acad. Fine Arts, Boston Art Club, etc. Mem. Boston Art Club, Boston Soc. Water Color Painters (pres.). Home: Newton Center, Mass. Died Mar. 7, 1945.

COPLEY, Ira Clifton (kŏp'lē), publisher; born in Knox County, Ill., Oct. 25, 1864; s. Ira Birdsell and Ellen (Whiting) C.; A.B., Yale; LL.B., Union Coll. Law, Chicago, 1889; m. Edith Strohn, Mar. 3, 1892 (died Oct. 25, 1929); m. 2d, Mrs. Chloe Davidson Worley, Apr. 27, 1931. Became mgr. Aurora (Ill.) Gas Light Co., 1889; consol. several gas cos. under name of Western United Gas and Electric Co., 1905, and of allied interests, 1921, under name of Western United Corporation, of which was pres. until 1926; publisher the Aurora Beacon News since 1905, Elgin (Ill.) Courier since 1909, Joliet Herald News since 1913, Illinois State Journal since 1927, also Illinois State Register since Apr. 1942; president, later chmn. The Copley Press, Incorporated, Aurora, 1928-42, now chmn. corp.; owner San Diego (Calif.) Union and Tribune since Feb. 1928; San Diego Sun since Nov. 1939, and of papers now comprising the Southern California Associated Newspapers, Los Angeles, since January 1928. Lt. colonel and inspector rifle practice, Ill. Nat. Guards, 1894-98; on staff Gov. C. S. Deneen, Ill., 1905; served as commr. to build new penitentiary for state; mem. park and pub. library bds., Aurora; mem. 62d to 67th Congresses (1911-23), 11th Ill. Dist. Republican. Mason, K.P., Elk. Donor of site, building fund and $1,000,000 endowment to Aurora Hosp., renamed Copley Memorial Hosp. Home: Aurora, Ill. Died Nov. 2, 1947; buried in Spring Lake Cemetery, Aurora, Ill.

CORBETT, Lamert Seymour, educator; b. Jamaica Plain, Mass., Feb. 11, 1887; s. Albert and Eliza A. (Fulmer) C.; B.S., Mass. Agrl. Coll., 1909; B.S.A., Boston U., 1909; M.S., U. of Ky., 1913; m. Mabel A. Campbell, Sept. 20, 1913; children—Alan Campbell, Barbara. Asso. with United Fruit Co., Bocas Del Foro, Panama, 1909-10; teacher Sue Bennett Memorial Sch., London, Ky., 1911-12; asst. prof. Ky. Agrl. Expt. Sta., 1912-13; prof. of animal industry, U. of Me., since 1913, dean of men since 1929. Fellow A.A.A.S.; mem. Am. Soc. of Animal Production, Am. Genetic Assn., Am. Dairy Science Assn., Am. Dairy Cattle Club (mem. advisory council), Am. Soc. of Univ. Profs., Alpha Zeta, Phi Kappa Phi. Methodist. Mason. Home: Orono, Me. Died Feb. 8, 1945.

CORBIN, William Herbert, mfr.; b. Union, Conn., July 20, 1864; s. William M. and Josephine (Walker) C.; A.B., Yale, 1889, M.A., 1914; m. Mary Williams, July 16, 1890; children—Walker Williams, Elinor (Mrs. C. Wardell St. John). Instr., Westminster Sch., Dobbs Ferry, N.Y., 1889-92; head master, Pingry Sch., Elizabeth, N.J., 1892-97; treas. Central Woolen Co., Stafford Springs, Conn., 1897-1906; sec. and treas., William H. Wiley & Son Co., 1900-16, and of its successor, The Wiley, Bickford, Sweet Co., 1916-22, v.p., 1922-26; v.p., treas. and dir. Ballard Oil Co. of Hartford, 1932-33; exec. v.p. Hartford Chamber Commerce, 1926-29, pres., 1929-30; dir. Hartford Better Business Bur., 3 yrs. Mem. Hartford Common Council 3 years, alderman 2 years; tax commr., Conn., 1907-20; apptd. by Conn. legislature, 1909, mem. special com. to investigate oyster properties of the state and method of taxation; apptd. by Gov. Simeon E. Baldwin mem. special com. to investigate taxation of pub. service and financial corps. of state, Nov. 1911. Chmn. W. Middle Dist. Sch. Committee, 19 yrs.; pres. Hartford Public Library; vice-pres. Health Associates, Inc., since 1939; trustee Horace Bushnell Memorial, Watkinson Library. Mem. S.A.R., Psi Upsilon, Skull and Bones (Yale). Clubs: University, Twentieth Century, Twilight. Author of various reports, papers read at confs. and mag. articles. Nat. Tax Assn. Republican. Conglist. Home: 172 Collins St., Hartford, Conn. Died Apr. 14, 1945.

CORBITT, James Howard, lawyer; b. Boykins, Southampton County, Va., Apr. 29, 1869; s. James Madison and Martha Ann (Whitney) C.; student Richmond (Va.) Coll. (now U. of Richmond), 1886-88; B.A., B.Ph., U. of Va., 1892, M.A., 1893, student Law Dept., 1897-98; m. Roberta Clifford Ansley, Nov. 26, 1902; children—Roberta Ansley (Mrs. Tomlin Braxton Horsley), Anne Middleton (Mrs. Lamar Wight Little), Harriet Whitney. Instr. in natural philosophy, U. of Va., 1891-97; admitted to Va. bar, 1898, Ga. bar, 1899; practiced in Atlanta, Ga., 1899-1900, Suffolk, Va., since 1900; div. counsel Virginian Ry. Co.; asst. div. counsel Southern Ry. Co.; dist. counsel S.A.L. Ry., counsel N.&W. Ry., A.C.L. R.R. Co.; Served as chairman Legal Advisory Board for Nansemond County, Va., 1917-18; organized Nansemond Chapter Am. Red Cross, Nov. 1917. Mem. Alumni Bd. Trustees, U. of Va.; mem. bd. of visitors, U. of Va., since 1934. Mem. Va. State Bar Assn. (pres. 1927-28), Am. Bar Assn. (bd. govs. 1936-38; del. 1st Inter-Am. Bar Assn. Conf., Havana, 1941), Am. Law Inst., Am. Judicature Soc., Va. Hist. Soc., New England Hist. Geneal. Soc., Soc. Colonial Wars, N.Y. Southern Soc., Alpha Tau Omega, Lambda Pi, Phi Delta Phi, Phi Beta Kappa, Tilka Soc. (U. of Va.). Democrat. Clubs: Virginia (Norfolk); Princess Anne Country (Virginia Beach); Commonwealth (Richmond); Colonnade (U. of Va.); Farmington Country (Charlottesville, Va.); University, Cosmos (Washington, D.C.). Home: 117 S. Broad St. Office: National Bank of Suffolk Bldg., Suffolk, Va. Died June 21, 1945; buried in Hollywood Cemetery, Richmond, Va.

CORCORAN, Sanford William, clergyman; b. Ont., Can., Feb. 25, 1876; s. John Sanford and Ann Jane (Highfield) C.; A.B., Ohio Wesleyan U., 1904, D.D., 1924; S.T.B., Boston U., 1906, grad. student, 1906-07; m. Anne Kunes, July 1909; children—Sanford William, John. Came to U.S., 1898, naturalized, 1903. Asst. pastor Christ Ch., Pittsburgh, 1907-09; pastor Walton Ch., Pittsburgh, 1909-11, Ben Avon Ch., Pittsburgh, 1911-17, 1st M.E. Ch., Beaver, Pa., 1917-22; supt. Washington Dist., Pittsburgh Conf., 1922-24, Allegheny Dist., 1924-26; gen. supt. M.E. Ch. Union (now Methodist Church Union), Pittsburgh, since 1926. Member General Conference M.E. Church, 1928, 32, 36, 40 (judiciary committee 1936 conference), Board Edn. of M.E. Ch., 1928-36, 6th Ecumenical Methodist Conf., 1931, Pittsburgh Council of Churches of Christ (exec. com.), Pa. Council of Churches, Budget Com. of Community Fund of Pittsburgh, Fed. Council of Churches of Christ in America, 1928-32; mem. exec. com. Bd. of Home Missions and Ch. Extension of M.E. Ch., 1936-40; del. to Uniting Conf., 1939. First Reserve of Judicial Council of Meth. Ch. Home: 3218 Latonia Av., Dormont. Office: Smithfield St. and 7th Av., Pittsburgh. Died Mar. 17, 1946; buried in South Side Cemetery, Pittsburgh.

CORIAT, Isador Henry (kôr'ĭ-ät), psychiatrist, neurologist; b. Phila., Pa., Dec. 10, 1875; s. Harry and Clara (Einstein) C.; prep. edn., high sch., Boston; M.D., Tufts Coll. Med. Sch., 1900; spl. student in philosophy, Harvard, 1909-10; m. Etta Dann, Feb. 1, 1904. Asst. and 1st asst. phys., Worcester Insane Hosp., 1900-05; neurol. staff Boston City Hosp., 1905-19; neurologist, Mt. Sinai Hosp., 1905-14; cons. neurologist Chelsea Memorial and Beth-Israel hosps., 1919-28; neuropsychiatrist Forsyth Dental Infirmary, 1913-29; instr. neurology, Tufts Coll. Med. Sch., 1914-16. Instructor; mem. training com. and training analyst, Boston Psychoanalytic Inst. Neurologist Med. Advisory Bd., World War; contract surgeon in neuropsychiatry, U.S. Army, 1917. Fellow A.M.A., Mass. Med. Soc., Boston Med. Library, Am. Psychiatric Assn.; mem. Am. Psycho-Pathol. Assn. (v.p. 1931-32), N.E. Soc. Psychiatry, Internat. Psychoanalytic Assn. (v.p. 1936-37), Boston Med. History

Club, Mass. Psychiatric Soc., Am. Psychoanalytic Assn. (pres. 1924-25 and 1936-37; v.p. 1935-36), Boston Soc. Neurology and Psychiatry, Boston Psychoanalytic Soc. (pres. 1930-32 and 1941-42), Jewish Acad. of Arts and Sciences, Am. Bd. Psychiatry and Neurology; hon. mem. Tau Epsilon Phi. Collaborating editor Journal of Abnormal Psychology, 1906-26; now same Psychoanalytic Review; collaborator for psychoanalytic terms for Dictionary of Psychology. Republican. Mason. Author: A Laboratory Manual of Clinical and Physiological Chemistry (with Dr. A. E. Austin), 1898; Religion and Medicine (with Drs. Worcester and McComb), 1908; Abnormal Psychology, 1910, 2d edit., 1914; The Hysteria of Lady Macbeth, 1912, 2d edit., 1919; The Meaning of Dreams, 1915; What Is Psychoanalysis?, 1917; Repressed Emotions, 1920; Stammering, 1928; also monographs and articles on nervous and mental diseases, psychopathology and psychoanalysis. Address: 416 Marlboro St., Boston, Mass. Died May 26, 1943.

CORLETT, William Thomas, physician; b. Orange, O., Apr. 15, 1854; s. William and Ann (Avery) C.; ed. Oberlin Coll., 1870-73; M.D., Wooster Univ., 1877; student and intern London Hosp., 1879-81, Hôpital St. Louis, Paris, France, 1881; diploma Royal Coll. Phys., London, 1881; later studied in Vienna, Berlin and Breslau; m. Amanda Marie Leisy, June 26, 1895; children—Christine L. (Mrs. Horace F. Henriques), Ann E. (Mrs. Daniel B. Ford), Helen A., Edward L. Prof. diseases of the skin and genitourinary diseases, Wooster U., 1883-85; prof. dermatology and syphilology, Western Reserve U., 1885-1914, sr. prof., 1914-24, emeritus prof. since 1924. Fellow Royal Soc. of Medicine (Great Britain), A.A.A.S., A.M.A.; mem. Am. Dermatol. Assn. (hon. mem., pres. 1905), Am. Acad. Dermatology and Syphilology (hon.); corr. mem. British Assn. Dermatology and Syphilology. Clubs: Union, Kirtland. Author: Treatise on the Acute Infectious Exanthemata, 1901; The American Tropics, 1908; The People of Orrisdale and Others, 1918; Early Reminiscences, 1920. Wrote: The Scaly Diseases of the Skin (Vol. III, Morrow's System of Dermatology, etc.), 1894; The Vegetable Parasitic Diseases of the Skin (in Bangs and Hardaway's American Text-Book of Genito-Urinary Diseases, etc.), 1898; Purpura, Pompholyx and Pellagra, in Reference Handbook of the Medical Sciences, 1903; also on Lichen, Lentigo, Granuloma, Annulare in 1915 edition; The Medicine-Man of the American Indian and His Cultural Background, 1935. Also articles on diseases of the skin in leading Am. and foreign jours. Home: 11015 East Blvd, Cleveland. Died June 11, 1948.

CORLEY, Jesse Lee, church official; b. Duxbury, Mass., Feb. 23, 1877; s. Joseph Edmund and Ida Champ (Ferris) C.; student Ia. Wesleyan Coll., Mt. Pleasant, 1892-96, Ia. Coll., Grinnell, 1896-98; A.B., Ohio Wesleyan U., 1901, D.D., 1926; S.T.B., Boston U. Sch. Theology, 1904; D.D., U. of Southern Calif., 1925; m. Mary Elizabeth Davies, Jan. 1, 1907; children—Mary Elizabeth, William Edmund (dec.), Dorothy Lee. Ordained ministry M.E. Ch., 1906; asst. pastor Morgan Memorial Ch., Boston, Mass., 1902-03; pastor Bond Hill, Cincinnati, O., 1904-06, Norwood, O., 1907-11, St. Paul's Ch., Dayton, O., 1911-15, Van Wert, O., 1915-19; originator Van Wert plan religious edn., 1917; dir. religious edn., Southern Calif. Conf. M. E. Ch., since 1919; exec. sec., Conf. Bd. Edn., since 1928; exec. sec. Interdenominational Conf. on Christian Way of Life, 1927-30; representative of World's Sunday School Assn. on special deputation to China, 1930-31. Mem. Bd. Foreign Missions, M.E. Ch., 1936-40; dir. Calif. Church Council; mem. exec. bd. Municipal League of Los Angeles, 1937-39; Served as private, inf., U.S. Vols., in Philippines, Spanish-Am. War., 1898-99. Trustee Southern Calif. Council of Religious Edn., also trustee University Religious Conf., Univ. of Calif. at Los Angeles; del. Gen. Conf. of M.E. Ch., Columbus, O., 1936; del. at large, Uniting Conf. Meth. Ch., 1939; reserve del., Gen. Conf., Meth. Ch., 1940; del. to Jurisdictional Conf., Meth. Ch., 1940; mem. exec. council of Church Fedn. of Los Angeles; mem. bd. mgrs. Goodwill Industries, Los Angeles; Mem. Religious Edn. Assn., Phi Delta Theta. Mason (K.T.). Correspondent Zion's Herald. Home: 1125 Brent Av., S. Pasadena, Calif. Office: 125 E. Sunset Blvd., Los Angeles, Calif. Died Feb. 8, 1943.

CORNBROOKS, Thomas Mullan, naval architect; b. Wilmington, Del., Oct. 26, 1876; s. William Henry and Elizabeth Ellis (Mullan) C.; grad. Wilmington High Sch., 1892; course in naval architecture with pvt. tutor; m. Harriet Boulden Walters, June 12, 1900; children—Charles W., Thomas E., William H., Harriet W., Elizabeth M. Apprenticeship with The Harlem and Hollingsworth Co., Wilmington, 1892-97; asst. chief draftsman with same co., 1897-98; naval architect Md. Steel Co., 1898-1912, chief engr., 1912-14; asst. mgr. Md. Shipbuilding Plant of Bethlehem Steel Co., 1914-17; became supt. contracts and sales, Bethlehem Shipbuilding Corp., Ltd., 1917; pres. Merrill-Stevens Shipbuilding Corp., Louisiana Shipbuilding Corp., S. Jacksonville Realty Corp., 1918-19; asst. mgr. New York Shipbuilding Corp., 1919-21; asst. to sr. v.p. N.Y. Shipbuilding Corp., 1921-24; pres. Camden (N.J.) Motors Co., Security Fuel Oil Burner Corp., Camden, 1924-25; dir. marine sales Pusey & Jones Corp.; Pres. T. M. Cornbrooks Co., marine consultants, since 1939. Tech. agt. Isherwood System of Ship Constrn. Commr. Borough of Collingswood, 1925-29. Chairman standardization com. Bethlehem Steel and subsidiary cos.; chmn. advisory com. and dir. Camden Dealers' Used Car Exchange, 1925. Mem. and sec. freeboard com. U.S. Govt.; mem. subcom. on electric spot welding of Council National Defense; mem. sub-com. on standard ships U.S. Govt.; mem. tech. com. Am. Bur. Shipping. Mem. Soc. Naval Architects and Marine Engrs., Instn. Naval Architects, London; asso. mem. Inst. Naval Engrs., Washington, D.C. Republican. Methodist. Mason. Address: 609 Tatem Av., Collingswood, N.J. Died Apr. 18, 1944; buried in Harleigh Cemetery, Camden, N.J.

CORNICK, Howard, lawyer; b. Knoxville, Tenn., June 10, 1874; s. Tully Robinson and Sophia Kennedy (Boyd) C.; LL.B., U. of Tenn., 1895; m. Lillian Kathleen Waring, Oct. 29, 1901; children—Howard Waring, Evelyn Lillian. Admitted to Tenn. bar, 1895, and began practice at Knoxville; moved to Prescott, Ariz., 1918; mem. law firm Cornick & Carr. Mem. Ariz. State Senate, 1923-24. Pres. bd. trustees Prescott Schs., 1926-27. Mem. Am. and Ariz. State bar assns., Sigma Alpha Epsilon. Democrat. Episcopalian. Mason. Clubs: Rotary, Hassayampa Country. Home: Sunset Park, Prescott, Ariz.; and 21 W. Vernon, Phoenix, Ariz. Office: Union Block, Prescott, Ariz.; and Title and Trust Bldg., Phoenix, Ariz. Deceased.

CORNISH, Louis Craig, clergyman; b. New Bedford, Mass., Apr. 18, 1870; s. Aaron and Frances V. (Hawkins) C.: student Harvard, 1889-91, 1892-93; A.B., Stanford U., 1894; Harvard Div. Sch., 1898-99; A.M., Harvard, 1899; D.D. from St. Lawrence and Meadville, 1922; D.D., Independent Church of Philippines, 1930; D. Polit. Science, U. of Szeged, Hungary, 1931; S.T.D., Pacific Unitarian Sch. for the Ministry, 1939; m. Frances Eliot Foote, June 14, 1906. Asst. in ethical dept., Stanford U., 1894; sec. to Episcopal bishop of Mass., 1894-98; ordained Unitarian ministry, 1899; minister First Parish, Hingham, Mass., 1900-15; sec. at large Am. Unitarian Assn., 1915-16; sec. 1916-25, administrative v.p. 1925-27, pres., 1927-37. Chmn. Anglo-Am. Ch. Commissions to Rumania, 1922, 24; Unitarian commr. to the Philippines, 1937; hon. pres. Independent Ch. of the Philippines, 1939. Home: (winter) Winter Park, Fla.; (summer) Harvard, Mass. Died Jan. 6, 1950.

CORREGAN, Charles Hunter, printer; b. Oswego, N.Y., Dec. 11, 1860; s. William H. and Susannah (Gilmore) C.; grad. Oswego High Sch., 1879; studied law, 1879-81; m. Margaret Watson, May 3, 1890. Reporter on Oswego Times, 1881-84; foreman of Auburn Dispatch, 1887-88, Syracuse Standard, 1889-92; mgr. New York Labor News Co., 1902-04; foreman New York Daily People, 1904; now with Syracuse Journal. Pres. Central Trades and Labor Assembly of Syracuse, 1892; v.p. State Fedn. of Labor of N.Y., 1893; candidate of Socialist Labor Party for gov. of N.Y., 1900, for President of the U.S., 1904. Episcopalian. Home: 315 Temple St., Syracuse, N.Y. Died June 19, 1946.

CORRIGAN, Jones Irwin Joseph, clergyman, educator; b. Chelsea, Mass., Dec. 30, 1878; s. Thomas and Mary (Irwin) C.; student Boston Coll., 1893-97; A.B., Woodstock (Md.) Coll., 1905, A.M., 1906; theol. studies at Jesuit House of Studies, Woodstock. Joined Soc. of Jesus (Jesuits), 1897; ordained priest R.C. Ch., 1912; teacher philosophy and ethics at Woodstock Coll., Loyola Coll. (Baltimore, Md.), and since 1916 at Boston Coll. Lecturer on war aims; S.A.T.C., Boston Coll., 1917-19; speaker for Nat. Open Forum Speakers' Bur. Mem. N.E. Assn. Colls. and Secondary Schs. Dir. R.C. Clergy Retreats in Dioceses of Eastern U.S. Home: Chestnut Hill, Mass. Died Sept. 9, 1936.

CORRIGAN, Joseph Moran, univ. rector; b. Phila., Pa., May 18, 1879; s. Daniel David and Mary (Moran) C.; prep. edn., Phila. Cathedral Sch., La Salle Coll. Prep. Sch.; student Overbrook Sem., 1894-97; Ph.B., Pontifical Coll. of N. America, Rome, Italy, 1898, and in 1903; S.T.D. from same; LL.D., Villanova Coll., 1926; Litt.D., Duquesne U., 1929; LL.D., U. of Notre Dame, 1938; LL.D., LaSalle Coll., 1938; D.S.S. (hon.) Georgetown U., 1939; hon. LL.D., St. John's, 1940, Fordham U., 1940; D.Pol.Sc., Catholic U. of the Sacred Heart, Milan, Italy, 1941. Ordained priest R.C. Ch., 1903; asst. rector, successively, Our Lady of Rosary, St. Agatha's and St. Columba's chs. (all Phila.), and supt. Catholic Missionary Soc.; served as diocesan dir. of charities (Phila.), moderator of priests' conferences and later as dir. laymen's retreats; was prof. dogmatic theology St. Charles Sem., Overbrook, Pa., and apptd. rector of the seminary, 1925; rector Catholic U. of America, by apptmt. of Pope Pius XI, since Mar. 1936. Apptd. prelate of Papal Household, with title of Rt. Rev. Monsignor, Dec. 1929; apptd. Prothonotary Apostolic, Apr. 8, 1937; titular bishop of Bilta, 1940. Address: Catholic University of America, Washington, D.C. Died June 9, 1942.

CORROON, Richard Aloysius, insurance chmn.; b. Brooklyn, N.Y., Feb. 18, 1882; began with S. A. Coykendall, ins. brokers, 1898; organized firm of R. A. Corroon & Co., 1905; elected president American Equitable Assurance Co. of New York, 1918, and New York Fire Ins. Co., 1925; chmn. of the bd. and dir. Merchants & Mfrs. Ins. Co. of New York, Central Fire Agency, Inc., R. A. Corroon & Co., Inc.; pres. and dir. Globe & Republic Ins. Co. of America, Corroon & Reynolds, Inc., Corroon & Reynolds Corp. Home: Massapequa, L.I., N.Y. Office: 92 William St., New York 7, N.Y. Died Nov. 14, 1946.

CORSE, William Malcolm (kôrs), metall. and chem. engr.; b. Malden, Mass., May 25, 1878; s. William Alexander and Genevieve Hancock (Alexander) C.; grad. high sch., Medford, Mass., 1895; S.B., Mass. Inst. Tech., 1899; m. Edith Wright Bell, June 4, 1902 (died 1923); 1 dau., Margaret Bell (Mrs. Richard Southwick Burr); m. 2d, Ruth Winifred Albert, Sept. 20, 1924. Began as chemist for William S. Merrell Chemical Co., Cincinnati, O., 1899; with Detroit (Mich.) White Lead Works, 1900-02; chemist, foundry supt. and asst. supt., Detroit Lubricator Co., 1902-06; asst. gen. mgr. Mich. Smelting & Refining Co., Detroit, 1907; works mgr. Lumen Bearing Co., Buffalo, N.Y., 1908-12; gen. mgr. Empire Smelting Co., Depew, N.Y., 1913, and for Titanium Bronze Co., Niagara Falls, 1914-18; mfg. supt. Ohio Brass Co., Mansfield, O., 1918; gen. mgr. Monel Products Co., Bayonne, N.J., 1919-22; with Nat. Research Council, Washington, D.C., 1922-24; cons. metallurgist, Washington, since 1925. Special duty and brass foundry practice, at Portsmouth (N.H.) Navy Yard, 1918. Sec. Am. Institute of Metals (A.I.M.E.) for 25 years, treas. 30 yrs., and ex-pres. sec. trustees Internat. Critical Tables; sec. Advisory Com. on Non-Ferrous Alloys to Bur. of Standards 21 yrs.; mem. Am. Inst. Mining and Metall. Engrs., Am. Inst. Chem. Engrs., Am. Chem. Soc., Am. Soc. for Metals, Am. Soc. for Naval Engrs., Electrochem. Soc., Soc. Am. Mil. Engrs., Army Ordnance Assn., U.S. Naval Inst., Washington Acad. Sciences, S.A.R., Soc. Colonial Wars; hon. corr. mem. on Council of Inst. of Metals of Gt. Britain. Republican. Conglist. Clubs: Cosmos, Arts, Burning Tree (Washington); Rotary (Keene, N.H.); Chemists (New York); Lake Placid (Lake Placid, N.Y.). Author: Bearing Metals and Bearings. Home: Westmoreland, N.H. Office: 810 18th St. N.W., Washington. Died June 3, 1944; buried in Woodlawn Cemetery, Everett, Mass.

CORTISSOZ, Royal (kôr-tē'sōz), journalist; b. Brooklyn, New York, 1869; D.H.L., Wesleyan Univ. and Bowdoin Coll.; m. Ellen Mackay Hutchinson (died Aug. 13, 1933). Art editor New York Herald-Tribune since 1891, literary editor, 1897-1913. Chevalier Order of Leopold (Belgium). Mem. Am. Acad. Arts and Letters; hon. fellow Am. Inst. Architects, Met. Mus. of Art, Architectural League, Nat. Sculpture Soc., Soc. American Etchers, trustee American Academy in Rome, Hispanic Soc. Am. Clubs: Century, Players, Coffee House, Garden City Golf. Author: Augustus St. Gaudens, 1907; John La Farge, 1911; Art and Common Sense, 1913; Life of Whitelaw Reid, 1921; Nine Holes of Golf, 1922; The New York Tribune, 1923; American Artists, 1923; Personalities in Art, 1925; The Painter's Craft, 1930; An Introduction to the Mellon Collection, 1937. Editor: Don Quixote; The Autobiography of Benvenuto Cellini; Whitelaw Reid's American and English Studies. Home: 167 E. 82d St. Office: 230 W. 41st St., New York, N.Y. Died Oct. 17, 1948.

CORWIN, Robert Nelson, prof. German; b. Baiting Hollow, L.I., N.Y., Oct. 6, 1865; s. Josiah Frank and Jane Amanda (Norton) C.; B.A., Yale, 1887; Ph.D., Heidelberg U., 1893; m. Margaret Wardell Bacon, Oct. 6, 1888; children—Margaret Trumbull, Wallace Graham, Leonard Bacon. Instr. in German, Yale, 1892-97, asst. prof., 1897-99, became prof., 1899, now emeritus, asso. fellow of Pierson Coll., Yale. Mem. Modern Lang. Assn. (v.p.), N.E. Assn. of Colls. and Secondary Schs., Elizabethan Club, Graduates Club, Assn. New England Deans; life mem. College Entrance Examination Bd. (chmn. 1916-19). Editor: Paul Heyse's Vetter Gabriel, 1911; Theodor Storm's Auf der Universität, 1912; Gottfried Keller's Romeo und Julia auf dem Dorfe, 1913. Contbr. to periodical lt. on edn. Sec.-treas. and historian Class of 1887, Yale Univ. Home: 247 St. Ronan St., New Haven, Conn. Died Oct. 14, 1944.

CORSON, William Russell Cone, insurance; b. New York, N.Y., Feb. 18, 1870; s. Adam Clark and Henrietta Hequemberg (Cone) C.; B.A., Yale, 1891; m. Marion Fay Lyles, June 25, 1891; children—Dorothy Lyles (Mrs. John M. Ellis), Mildred Cone (Mrs. John R. Cook). Began in shop of Eddy Elec. Mfg. Co., Windsor, Conn., 1891, supt., later sec. until 1902; practiced as cons. engr., Hartford, 1902-07; asst. engr. Hartford Steam Boiler Inspection & Ins. Co., 1907-09, asst. sec., 1909-16, sec. and treas., 1916-21, v.p. and treas., 1921-27, pres. since 1927, chmn. bd. since Feb. 1942; dir. Standard Surety & Casualty Co., Standard Ins. Co. of N.Y., Piedmont Fire Ins. Co., Aetna Ins. Co., Aetna Life Ins. Co., Aetna Casualty & Surety Co., Conn. Mutual Life Ins. Co., World Fire & Marine Ins. Co., Automobile Ins. Co. of Hartford, Hartford County Mutual Fire Ins. Co., Society for Savings, Century Indemnity Co., Arrow-Hart and Hegeman Electric Co. Conservation engr., Conn., for U.S. Fuel Adminstrn., 1918; mem. bd. Water Commrs., Hartford, 1921-24; chmn. Hartford Sewerage Disposal Commn., 1927; pres. Hartford Community Chest, 1924-25; trustee American School for the Deaf, Wadsworth Atheneum and The Watkinson Library. Mem. American Institute Electrical Engrs., Zeta Psi. Republican. Episcopalian. Clubs: Hartford, Engineers. Home: 40 N. Beacon St. Office: 56 Prospect St., Hartford, Conn. Died Oct. 1945.

COSGRAVE, George (kŏz'grāv), judge; b. Calaveras County, Calif., Feb. 20, 1870; s. Michael and Margaret (Pyne) C.; ed. San Jose State Normal Sch., 1887-89; m. Irene Copeland, June 1, 1904; 1 dau., Margaret Sowers. Admitted to Calif. bar, 1895, and began practice at Fresno; judge U.S. Dist. Court,

Southern Dist. of Calif., since 1930; retired from active service, 1940. Trustee Fresno State College. Republican. Mason. Clubs: Sierra (San Francisco); University Sequoia, Sunnyside Country (Fresno). Home: 1644 Van Ness Av., Fresno, Calif. Died Aug. 4, 1945.

COSGRAVE, Jessica Garretson, educator; b. New York; d. Rev. Ferdinand Van Devere and Helen (Philbrook) Garretson; A.B., Barnard Coll., 1893; LL.B., New York U., 1898; m. John O'Hara Cosgrave, Jan. 4, 1913. Organized, 1900, and principal of The Finch School (now Finch Junior College), pres. of latter. Lecturer on modern politics, history, philosophy, economics. Mem. Kappa Kappa Gamma. Club: Colony (charter mem.). Presbyterian. Author: Gardens, 1925; Mothers and Daughters, 1925; Psychology of Youth, 1929. Home: Ridgefield, Conn.; and 39 E. 79th St., New York. Office: 52 E. 78th St., New York, N.Y. Died Oct. 31, 1949.

COSGRAVE, John O'Hara, editor; b. Melbourne, Australia, July 11, 1864; s. John and Mary (Kirby) C.; ed. at Auckland, New Zealand, in Ch. of England Grammar Sch., and Auckland Coll. and Grammar Sch.; m. 2d, Jessica Garretson Finch, 1913. On San Francisco Alta Californian, 1886; reporter San Francisco Call, 1887-90; editor and pub. The Wave, San Francisco, 1890-1900; mng. editor Everybody's Magazine, under Doubleday, Page & Co., Dec. 1900, and editor same, 1903-11, for Ridgway Co.; mng. editor Collier's Weekly, Oct. 1911-12; Sunday editor New York World, 1912-27. Clubs: The Players, Dutch Treat (New York). Author: The Academy for Souls, 1931; Man: A Citizen of the Universe. Address: Ridgefield, Conn.; and 39 E. 79th St., New York, N.Y. Died Sept. 19, 1947.

COSS, John J., univ. prof.; A.B., Wabash Coll., 1906; A.M., Columbia, 1908; Litt.D., 1929; B.D., Union Theol. Sem., 1909. Formerly instr. philosophy, Columbia U., now collegiate prof. and dir. summer session. Address: Columbia University, New York. Died Apr. 28, 1940.

COSTIKYAN, S. Kent (kŏs'tĭk-yăn), merchant; b. Marsovan, Asia Minor, Jan. 23, 1867; s. Simeon and Turvanda C.; student Colgate U., 1884-86; Dr. of Commercial Law, Lincoln Memorial U., 1926; m. Mary Ransom Kent, Jan. 15, 1895; children—Kent Ransom, Alexandra Kent (Mrs. Theodore C. Jewett), Clarke Warren, Granger Kent. Came to U.S., 1884, naturalized, 1891. Organized firm of Costikyan Freres, importers, Rochester, N.Y., 1886; reorganized as Kent-Costikyan, Inc., N.Y. City, 1900, and pres. of same since 1900. Served as chmn. Montclair (N.J.) Com. for Near East Relief World War; maintained sch. for orphans and needy children at Marsovan, Asia Minor, 1900-15. Mem. Organization Com. of 100 of Chicago World's Fair, 1893; trustee Lincoln Memorial U., 1925-36. Decorated by Shah of Persia for promoting commercial relations between Persia and U.S., 1907. Ind. Republican. Conglist. Mason, Elk, Moose. Clubs: Montclair Golf. Home: Rockliffe Apts., Montclair, N.J. Office: 307 East 63d St., New York 21, N.Y. Died July 3, 1949.

COTHRAN, Frank Harrison (kŏth'răn), cons. engr.; b. Millway, S.C., Aug. 28, 1878; s. Wade Elephare and Sara Elizabeth (Chiles) C.; m. Blanche Clardy, June 15, 1910; children—Frank Harrison, James Clardy, Samuel Alexander. Surveying with ry. and land surveys, 1899-1900; primary levelman U.S. Geol. Survey, 1901; asst. mining engr. Cranes Nest Coal Co., Toms Creek, Va., 1902; res. engr. South & Western Ry. (now Carolina, Clinchfield & Ohio Ry.), in charge location and constrn. in Breaks of Sandy, 1902-03, locating engr., 1905-06, asst. engr. in charge locating parties, 1906-07; in charge constrn. plant and equipment, Va.-Pocahontas Coal Co., Coalwood, W. Va., 1903; asst. locating engr. Coal and Coke Ry., W.Va., 1903-04; resident engr. Clover Fork (W.Va.) Tunnel, 1904-05; locating engr. proposed Bristol & Kingsport Ry., 1907-08; mem. Cothran and Cothran, engrs. and contractors, Greenwood, S.C., 1908-10; locating engr. Coal & Coke Ry., 1910, also Atlanta N.E. Ry., 1910-11; reconnaissance engr., Va.-Carolina Ry., 1910; engr. Ga. Granite Co., Atlanta, Ga., 1911; locating engr. Piedmont & Northern Ry., 1911-12, div. engr., 1912-14: in charge field surveys Quebec (Canada) Development Company, 1914-15, Southern Power Co., Charlotte, N.C., 1915-16; resident engineer in charge Bridgewater Development, Western Carolina Power Co., 1916-20; resident engr. in charge additions, Lookout Shoals Dam, Southern Power Co., 1916; division engr. for Southern Power Co., Bridgewater, N.C., 1920-22; v.p. and gen. mgr. Alma & Jonquiere Ry., Duke-Price Power Co., Ltd., also v.p. Quebec (Can.) Development Co., 1923-27; chief engr. Piedmont & Northern Ry., 1927-29; v.p., gen. mgr. and chief engr. Beauharnois Constrn. Co., 1929-33; cons. engr. from 1933; pres. Durham & Southern Ry. and Piedmont & Northern Ry. since Mar. 1937, also cons. engr. Sergt. 1st South Carolina Volunteer Infantry, Spanish-Am. War. Mem. Am. Soc. C.E., Am. Ry. Engring. Assn., Inst. Engrs. of Canada, Corp. Professional Engrs. of Que. (Can.). Mason. Clubs: Charlotte Country (Charlotte, N.C.); Poinsett (Greenville, S.C.); Traffic (New York); Biltmore (N.C.) Forest Country. Home: 917 Queens Rd. Office: Power Bldg., Charlotte, N.C. Died Sept. 1, 1948.

COTTAM, Gilbert (Geoffrey) (kŏt'tăm), public health official; b. Manchester, England, August 2, 1873; s. Rev. Henry (M.A.) and Eliza Mary (Warburton) C.; came to the United States at the age of 16 years; M.D., St. Louis University, 1893; m. F. May Isham Ruddick, June 16, 1896; 1 son, Dr. Geoffrey Isham Warburton; m. 2d, Grace Elizabeth Pulley, June 21, 1930 (she died on September 24, 1945). Interne, St. Louis (Missouri) Female Hospital, 1893-94; engaged in practice, Rock Rapids, Ia., 1894-1910, Sioux Falls, South Dakota, 1910-30 and 1940-43; Minneapolis, Minnesota, 1930-40; mem. staff Sioux Valley Hosp.; chief of staff, McKennan Hosp., 1943; supt. S.D. State Bd. of Health since 1943. Commissioned captain medical section Officers Reserve Corps, U.S. Army, May 28, 1918, and began active service at Camp Dodge, Iowa; went overseas with Base Hosp. 88, Sept. 1918, and was made chief of surg. service of same, in France; maj., May 19, 1919; chief of surg. service, Ft. Riley, Kan., until discharged, Oct. 9, 1919; col. (inactive) Medical Reserve, U.S. Army. Chief of Emergency Medical Service, Office of Civilian Defense, Sioux Falls, S.D., 1943. Licentiate (founders' group) American Board of Surgery, 1937. Fellow American College Surgeons (bd. govs. 1925), A.M.A.; mem. Western Surg. Assn. (life), State Med. Assn. S. Dak. (pres. 1922-23), Minn. Path. Soc., Minneapolis Surg. Soc., Sioux Valley Med. Assn. (pres. 1927-28), Am. Public Health Assn., and various other medical societies. Mem. Alpha Omega Alpha. Republican. Episcopalian. Mason. Clubs: Minneapolis Professional Men's (pres. 1940; life member). Contbr. to surg. publs. Mem. editorial bd. Journal Lancet, 1931-37 and since 1940; asso. editor Minnesota Medicine, 1937-40. Home: St. Charles Hotel. Office: State Capitol, Pierre, S.D. Died Mar. 4, 1949.

COTTINGHAM, Claybrook, college pres.; b. Ottoman, Va., May 4, 1881; s. George and Virginia Louise (Palmer) C.; A.B., Richmond Coll. (now U. of Richmond), 1899; M.A., 1900; LL.D., Baylor U., 1920; m. Myrtle Baker, June 8, 1904; children—Mary Virginia, Margaret Drew, Claybrook Baker. Asst. prin. Chesapeake Acad., Irvington, Va., 1900-02; prof. Greek and philosophy, Mt. Lebanon Coll., 1902-05, pres., 1905, 06; prof. Greek and philosophy, Louisiana Coll., 1906-10, pres., 1910-41; pres. Louisiana Poly. Inst., 1941-49. Was president La. Baptist Conv.; pres. Southern Bapt. Edn. Assn.; mem. Internat. Rotary Club (pres. Alexandria sect., 1927; gov. 17th dist., 1928-29; internat. dir., 1930-31). Mem. La. Teachers' Association (pres. coll. section, 1923-24, 1936-37); vice-pres. Southern Intercollegiate Athletic Assn., 1926-27. Mem. Phi Beta Kappa, Omicron Delta Kappa, Alpha Phi Omega. Democrat. Home: Pineville, La. Died Aug. 17, 1949; buried in Pineville, La.

COTTINGHAM, George W., editor; b. Houston, Tex., May 17, 1894; s. George R. and Harriet Mary (Williams) C.; Ph.B., U. of Chicago, 1915; m. Mary Lee MacKenzie, Sept. 29, 1926; children—Charles Heath, George Wallace, Jr., Mary Lee. With The Houston Chronicle since 1915, as reporter, city editor, news editor, mng. editor; editor since 1935. Mem. Public Safety Commn. of the State of Tex. Home: 3412 Piping Rock Lane. Office: The Houston Chronicle, Houston, Tex. Died Apr. 12, 1948.

COTTRELL, Frederick Gardner, chemist; b. Oakland, Calif., Jan. 10, 1877; s. Henry and Cynthia L. (Durfee) C.; B.S., U. of Calif., 1896; U. of Berlin, 1901; Ph.D., U. of Leipzig, 1902; hon. LL.D., U. of Calif., 1927; m. Jessie M. Fulton, Jan. 1, 1904; two children (both dec.). Le Conte fellow U. of Calif., 1896-97; chem. teacher Oakland High Sch., 1897-1900; instr. phys. chemistry, 1902-06; asst. prof., 1906-11; U. of Calif.; consulting chemist, June-Aug. 1911, chief phys. chemist (field duty), 1911-14, chief chemist, 1914-15, chief metallurgist, 1916-19, asst. dir., 1919, 20, dir., June 2-Dec. 31, 1920, U.S. Bur. Mines; chmn. div. chemistry and chem. technology, Nat. Research Council, 1921-22; dir. Fixed Nitrogen Research Lab., U.S. Dept. Agr. 1922-27; chief div. fertilizer and fixed nitrogen investigation, Bur. Chemistry and Soils, U.S. Dept. Agr., 1927-30; cons. chemist Bur. Chemistry and Soils, 1930-40, Bur. Plant Industry, U.S. Dept. Agr., July 1940-Aug. 1943; pres. Research Associates, Inc., 1935-38; technical consultant Smithsonian Institution, 1928-29, and same, Research Corp., N.Y. City, since 1930. Mem. Am. Chemical Soc., Am. Inst. Mining Engrs., Am. Electrochem. Soc., Nat. Acad of Sciences, Am. Philos. Society, Société de Chimie Industrielle (hon.), Sigma Xi, Phi Beta Kappa, Alpha Xi Sigma. Home: 1557 Waverley St., Palo Alto, Calif. Died Nov. 16, 1948.

COTTRELL, Jesse Samuel; b. Knoxville, Tenn., Oct. 23, 1878; s. Samuel Houston and Telitha Anne (Simpson) C.; student U. of Tenn. several yrs., LL.B., 1906; LL.B., Chattanooga Law Sch., 1909, Georgetown (D.C.) Law Sch., 1914; m. Lucile A. Wilcox, January 14, 1918 (divorced 1929); 1 dau., Betty Anne; m. 2d, Mary Elisabeth James, Oct. 15, 1938. Connected with newspapers at Knoxville, Chattanooga, Nashville and Tucson, Ariz.; sec. to U.S. Senator Newell Sanders, of Tenn., 1910-11; Washington corr. Charlotte (N.C.) Observer, Anderson (S.C.) Mail and Independent, Nashville (Tenn.) Banner; Union and Leader, Manchester, N.H., Troy (N.Y.) Record and Watertown (N.Y.) Daily Times. Mem. Tennessee legislature, 1907-09; mem. Tennessee N.G. 4 yrs.; captain U.S. Army, World War, 1917-19, and while in army was assigned to M.I.D., Phila.; E.E. and M.P. to Bolivia, by apptmt. of President Harding, Oct. 19, 1921-28, spl. ambassador by apptmt. of President Coolidge, to Bolivian Centennial, Aug. 5-30, 1925; spl. ambassador to inauguration of President Siles, Jan. 10, 1926; resigned from diplomatic service, Feb. 23, 1928; mng. editor Tucson Citizen, 1928-32. Decorated High Order of The Condor, Bolivian Govt. Pres. Ariz. Press Club, 1930-31. Independent Republican. Baptist. Elk. Club: Nat. Press (Washington, D.C.; mem. bd. govs., 1943-46). Author: From Ocean to Ocean, Through Peru, Bolivia and the Argentine. Home: 2509 N. Powhatan St., Arlington, Va. Address: National Press Bldg., Washington, D.C. Died Nov. 24, 1944.

COUCH, Benjamin Warren (kōōch), lawyer; b. Concord, N.H., Aug. 19, 1873; s. Benjamin Warren and Susan Cornell (Woodward) C.; B.S., Dartmouth Coll., 1896; student Harvard Law Sch., 1897-98; m. Gertrude A. Underhill, Nov. 8, 1900. Admitted to N.H. bar, 1889, and since practiced in Concord; pres. and dir. Northern R.R., Concord & Portsmouth R.R., Ford & Kimball; v.p. and dir. Mfrs. & Merchants Mutual Ins. Co., United Life & Accident Ins. Co.; treas. and dir. Concord Gas Co.; trust officer and dir. Mechanicks Nat. Bank; dir. Eagle & Phoenix Hotel Co., N.H. Fire Ins. Co., Merchants Mutual Casualty Co., Buffalo; trustee Merrimack County Savings Bank. Pres. and trustee Margaret Pillsbury Gen. Hosp., and Rolfe & Rumford Home. Mem. Am. Bar Assn., N.H. Bar Assn., Sigma Chi. Republican. Unitarian. Mason, Odd Fellow. Clubs: Snowshoe, Wonolancet, Bow Brook, Concord Country. Home: 7 Merrimack St. Office: 4 School St., Concord, N.H.* Died Nov. 4, 1945.

COULTER, John Stanley, physician; b. Phila., Pa., Sept. 27, 1885; s. Levi and Clara (Kinnier) C.; grad. Central High Sch., Phila., 1905; M.D., Univ. of Pa. Med. Sch., 1909; grad. Army Med. Sch., Washington, D.C., 1911; grad. Univ. of Philippines Med. Sch., 1916; m. Margaret Noyes; 1 son (by previous marriage), John Alfred. Settled in Chicago, 1920; prof. in charge physical therapy depts. of Northwestern Univ. Med. Sch., Ill. Central, St. Luke's, Alexian Brothers, Passavant and Wesley hospitals. Chairman council on physical medicine of American Medical Association. Served with Medical Corps, U.S. Army, as 1st lt., capt., maj. and lt. col., 1910-20. Fellow Am. Coll. Surgeons; mem. Am. Med. Assn., Ill. State and Chicago med. socs., Am. Rheumatism Assn., Am. Congress Physical Medicine, Soc. Phys. Medicine, Inst. of Medicine, Chicago. Democrat. Presbyterian. Asso. editor: Principles and Practice Phys. Therapy, 1934, Medical Cyclopedia Service, Vols. 1935, 36, 37, 38, 39, 40, 41, 42, 43, 44, 45, also 2d edition, 1940. Asst. editor: Archives of Physical Therapy and Acta Americana. Contbr. to Reimann's Treatment in General Medicine, 1939, and Barr's Modern Medical Therapy in General Practice, 1940. Glasser's Medical Physics, 1943. Author: History Physical Therapy, 1933. Home: Westville, Ind. Office: 122 S. Michigan Av., Chicago, Ill. Died Dec. 16, 1949.

COULTER, Stanley, biologist; b. Ningpo, China, June 2, 1853; s. Moses Stanley and Caroline E. (Crowe) C.; brother of John Merle C.; A.B., Hanover Coll., 1871, A.M., 1874; Ph.D., 1889, LL.D., in 1907; Sc.D., Purdue Univ., 1931; Sc.D. from Wabash Coll., 1933; m. Lucy E. Post, June 21, 1877. Prof. biology and dir. Biol. Lab., 1887-1926, dean Sch. of Science, 1907-26, and dean of men, 1919-26, acting chmn. of faculty, 1921, Purdue Univ., now emeritus. Mem. State Bd. of Forestry, 1902-16. Mem. Conservation Commn. of Ind., since 1916 (chmn., 1925-33). Fellow A.A.A.S., Ind. Acad. of Science, Western Soc. Naturalists, Bot. Soc. of Am., Am. Genetic Assn.; pres. Indiana Tuberculosis Assn., 1927. Author: Forest Trees of Indiana, pamphlet, 1892; Flora of Indiana, 1890; Pharmacology of Remedies in Common Use; also 11 pamphlets upon nature study; 45 pamphlets of scientific studies and reports, and 70 other titles, book reviews, biog. sketches, etc. Address: Eli Lilly & Co., Indianapolis. Died June 26, 1943.

COUNCIL, Walter Wooten, health commr. Alaska; b. Councils, N.C.; s. John Pickett and Johnnie (Wooten) C.; student U. of N.C., 1899-1902, M.D., U. of Va., 1905; m. Virginia Scurry, 1907 (dec.); children—Nancy, Mary Lee; m. 2d, June Murry, 1927 (dec.); m. 3d, Ruby Alleine Apland, 1934. Began as surgeon Ellamar Mining Co., 1906; surgeon Copper River Ry. and Kennicott Copper Corp., Cordova, Alaska, 1911-27; asst. surgeon U.S. Public Health Service, 1916-27; now health commr. Ter. of Alaska, Juneau. Formerly mayor of Cordova, Alaska; ex-pres. Juneau Chamber of Commerce. Mem. Am. com. Internat. Congress of Industrial Accidents and Diseases. Mem. Am. Med. Assn., Alaska Territorial Assn., Am. Child Health Assn. Democrat. Episcopalian. Elk, K.P., Moose. Address: 109 Front St., Juneau, Alaska.* Deceased.

COUNCILOR, James Allan, certified pub. accountant; b. Marlette, Mich., Nov. 28, 1884; s. John Wesley and Ella Frances (Gates) C.; student George Washington U., 1907-09, Washington Sch. of Accountancy, Washington, D.C., 1912-14; hon. M.C.S., Benj. Franklin U., 1928; m. Vesta Nora Crane, Dec. 6, 1909; 1 son, James Allan. Stenographer Ill. Central R.R., Waterloo, Ia., 1904-05; U.S. Dept. of Interior, Washington, D.C., 1906-13; U.S. Treasury, 1914-15; U.S. Bur. of Efficiency, 1916-18; Internal Revenue Bur., 1919-20; pub. accounting since 1921; sr. partner James A. Councilor & Co., certified pub. accountants, Washington, D.C.; dir. Security Savings & Commercial Bank, Washington, D.C. Mem. Bd. Pub. Welfare, Washington, D.C.; mem. Washington Bd. of Trade,

Washington Building Congress, War Hospitality Com.; dir. and comptroller Recreation Services, Inc.; dir. and mem. exec. com. Community War Fund of Washington; dir. Boys Club of Metropolitan Police; dir. Pres. Cup Regatta Assn. Mem. advisory board Internat. Accountants Soc., Am. Inst. Accountants, Am. Soc. of C.P.A. (past pres.), D.C. Inst. of C.P.A. (past pres.), Beta Alpha Psi (hon. accounting fraternity). Republican. Baptist. Mason (32°, K.T., Shriner, Royal Order of Jesters). Clubs: University, National Press, Columbia Country, Congressional Country. Home: 1701 Kalmia Rd. N.W. Office: Tower Bldg., Washington, D.C.; and First National Bank Bldg., Chicago. Died Feb. 14, 1945; buried in Rock Creek Cemetery, Washington.

COVERDALE, William Hugh (kŭv'ĕr-dāl), cons. engr.; b. Kingston, Ont., Can., Jan. 27, 1871; s. William Miles and Fannie (O'Neill) C.; prep. edn., Collegiate Inst., Kingston; B.A., Geneva Coll., Beaver Falls, Pa., 1891, Dr. Sci., 1914; LL.D., Queen's U., 1922; m. Harriet E. Hinchliff, June 30, 1911; children—William Hugh, Mary, Harriet Hinchliff, Miles. With engring. dept. Pa. Lines West of Pittsburgh, 1891-1900; engring. practice, N.Y. City, since 1900, except 1 yr. traveling in Europe; mem. firm Coverdale & Colpitts, cons. engrs. since 1913; chmn. bd. and pres. Am. Export Lines; pres., mng. dir. Canada Steamship Lines, Ltd., Century Coal Co., Davie Shipbuilding & Repairing Co., Canadian Shipbuilding & Engineering, Ltd.; pres. and dir. 1020 Fifth Av. Corp.; dir., mem. exec. com., Gen. Airline and Film Corp., Republic Steel Corp., Seaboard Air Line R.R. Co.; Georgia & Florida Railroad, Anglo-Newfoundland Development Co., Montreal Trust Co., Richmond, Fredericksburg & Potomac R.R. Co., Richmond-Washington Co., Tenn., Ala. & Ga. Ry. Co., Comml. Nat. Bank, Canadian Car and Foundry Co., Ltd., dir. Schenley Industries, Inc. trustee Atlantic Mutual Ins. Co., Alantic Mut. Indemnity Co. Dir. American Arbitration Association. Member American Soc. Civil Engrs., Am. Inst. Cons. Engrs. Clubs: Metropolitan, University, Engineers, Recess, Mt. Royal, Mt. Bruno Country, St. James, Beaconsfield Golf (Montreal); Kingston Yacht, Cataraqui Golf and Country (Kingston Can.). Home: 1020 5th Av., New York, N.Y.; (summer) Le Moine's Point Farm, Portsmouth, Ont., Can. Office: 120 Wall St., New York, N.Y. Died Aug. 10, 1949.

COWAN, Frank Irving (kou'ăn), lawyer; b. Palmyra, Me., May 20, 1888; s. Lewville A. and Fannie Evelyn (Woodworth) C.; A.B., Bowdoin Coll., 1913; LL.B., U. of Me., 1918; m. Helen Anna Caspar, Oct. 11, 1913; children—Caspar Frank, Frederick Walter, Douglas Reinhard, Cynthia. Teacher, Plymouth (Me.) High Sch., 1908-09, Newton (Mass.) Tech. High Sch., 1913-14, Calais (Me.) Acad., 1914-15; admitted to Me. bar, 1917, to practice in Fed. Courts, 1921, to practice in U.S. Supreme Court, Apr. 9, 1942; practiced in Bangor, Me., 1917-18, Portland since Feb. 1918; associated with Woodman & Whitehouse, Portland, 1918-21; practiced alone, 1921-25 and 1929-40; associated with brother, Walter A., 1925-29, with son, Caspar F., since 1940; sec.-treas. Cumberland Nat. Farm Loan Assn., 1918-28; disclosure commr., Cumberland County, 1924-40; dir. Fed. Land Bank of Springfield, 1932-35; pres. State Mutual Fire Ins. Co., 1935-40, and since 1942; dir. Aroostock Mut. Fire Ins. Co.; dir. Aroostock Patrons Mut. Fire Ins. Co.; instr. in property law, Peabody Law Sch., 1936-41; atty. general of Maine, 1941-45. Founded Cumberland Legal Aid Bureau under auspices Cumberland Bar Assn., 1939; sec. for State of Me. for New Eng. Legal Aid Council and Nat. Assn. Legal Aid Orgns.; chmn. legal aid com. Cumberland Bar Assn. since 1939; mem. Baxter State Park Authority, 1941-45; member Portland City Council, 1920-21, president 1921; recorder Portland Municipal Court, 1927-31; mem. Me. State Legislature, 1939-40. Conducted investigation and audit of State Trust Funds, 1931 (resulted in restoration of funds). Mem. Am., Me. State and Cumberland County bar assns., Nat. Assn. Attys. Gen., Grange, Delta Upsilon, Phi Kappa Phi. Mason. Clubs: Bowdoin, Woodfords, Kiwanis, Penguin Ski, Cumberland Fish and Game Assn., Lincoln, Eastern States Mountain. Compiled and donated to the State an index of Private and Special Laws of Maine from 1820 to 1944. Home: 10 Orkney St., Portland, Me. Died Feb. 23, 1948.

COWING, Hugh Alvin (kō'wĭng), physician and surgeon; b. nr. Muncie, Ind., July 28, 1860; s. Granville and Lucy (Moran) C.; grad. high sch., 1882; taught sch. 8 yrs.; M.D., Miami Med. Coll., 1890; Chicago Policlinic, 1899; m. Alice E. Frey, June 23, 1892 (died 1942); children—Kemper Frey, Mrs. Rachel Wilson (deceased). Practiced at Muncie, Indiana, since 1890; mem. Muncie Board of Health, 1892, president since 1939; secretary Delaware County (Ind.) Bd. of Health 23 yrs.; v.p. State Bd. of Health, Ind., 1917-18, 1921-22, pres., 1919-20, 1923-25; mem. staff of Ball Memorial Hosp., v.p. of staff, 1932-33. Pres. Del. County Children's Home Assn. 25 yrs., Del. County Bd. Guardians 15 yrs.; dir. Muncie Y.M.C.A., 27 yrs., pres. same, 1881 and 1936-43. Mem. board Muncie Peoples Savings and Loan Assn. (now Muncie Federal Savings and Loan Assn.), v.p. 1939-43. Mem. A.M.A., Ind. State Med. Assn., Delaware County Medical Society (sec. 1896, pres. 1906); member Indiana State Com. Internat. Congress on Tuberculosis, 1908; mem. Volunteer Med. Service Corps, Council Nat. Defense, 1918. Republican. Methodist. Mason. Author: A Meandering Hoosier, 1937, also numerous professional papers and lectures read before nat., state and county med. assns. and articles in med. jours., also many poems and sketches. Home: 206 S. High St., Muncie, Ind.* Deceased.

COWLES, Gardner (kōlz), newspaper pub.; b. Oskaloosa, Iowa, February 28, 1861; s. William Fletcher and Maria Elizabeth (LaMonte) C.; A.B., Ia. Wesleyan Coll., 1882, A.M., 1885; LL.D., Drake U., 1931; m. Florence M. Call, Dec. 3, 1884; children—Helen (Mrs. James D. Le Cron), Russell, Bertha C. Quarton, Florence (Mrs. David S. Kruidenier), John, Gardner. In newspaper business since 1903; chairman of board, treas., publisher The Register and Tribune Co., Des Moines, Ia., pubs. of Des Moines Register, Sunday Register, Des Moines Tribune. Mem. Ia. Ho. of Rep. 2 terms, 1899-1903; apptd. by President Hoover, mem. Commn. on Conservation and Administration. of Public Domain, 1929; dir. Reconstruction Finance Corp., July 1932-Apr. 1933. Independent Republican. Clubs: Des Moines, Prairie. Home: 100 W 37th St. Address: Register and Tribune, Des Moines, Ia. Died Feb. 28, 1946.

COWLES, Cheney, editor; b. Spokane, Wash., Sept. 7, 1908; s. William Hutchinson and Harriet Bowen (Cheney) C.; student Thacher School, Ojai, California, 1922-26; B.A., Yale University, 1930; married to Sarah E. Ferris, June 14, 1939; children—Phoebe, Frank Cheney. Began as circulation solicitor, 1930; held various positions in newspaper work, business and news, 1930-36; financial editor Spokane Daily Chronicle, 1936; city editor Spokane Spokesman-Review, 1937, exec. editor, 1938; mng. editor Spokane Daily Chronicle, 1939-41. First lt., F.A. Res. since 1938, 2d lt., 1930; ordered to active duty on staff of Maj. Gen. John F. Curry, comdr. Second Air Force, May 1, 1941, at Fort George Wright, Spokane, Wash., promoted capt., maj., 1942; asst. chief of staff, A-2 (Intelligence), on staff of comdg. gen., Second Air Support Command, Colorado Springs, Colo., entire command transferred to Shreveport, La., 1943. Received Spokane Jr. C. of C. distinguished service award, 1937. Republican. Clubs: Spokane City, Spokane Ski, Cheyenne Mountain Country. Home: 2602 W. Second Av. Office: Spokane Daily Chronicle, Spokane, Wash. Died May 1943; buried in Greenwood Cemetery, Spokane.

COWLES, William Hutchinson, newspaper publisher; b. Evanston, Ill., Aug. 14, 1866; s. Alfred and Sarah Frances (Hutchinson) C.; B.A., Yale, 1887, LL.B., 1889; m. Harriet Bowen Cheney, Feb. 12, 1896; children—Harriet, William Hutchinson, Cheney. Began newspaper work as reporter at Chicago, 1889; publisher of the Spokane Spokesman-Review since 1893. Dir. Associated Press, 1912-44. Republican. Unitarian. Hon. mem. Phi Beta Kappa. Clubs: University (New York) and (Chicago); University, Spokane Country, Spokane City; Santa Barbara (Calif.) City. Home: 2602 W. 2d Av. Office: Morning Spokesman-Review, Spokane, Wash. Died Jan. 15, 1946; buried in Greenwood Cemetery, Spokane.

COUPER, William, sculptor; b. Norfolk, Va., Sept. 20, 1853; s. John D. and Euphania M. (Cowling) C.; began art studies in Cooper Inst., New York: entered Royal Acad., Munich, 1874, for study of drawing and anatomy; went to Florence, 1875; entered studio of Thomas Ball; m. Eliza Chickering Ball, May 9, 1878. Lived in Italy 22 yrs.; settled at New York, 1897; splty. ideal works, portrait statues, busts and bas-reliefs. Mem. jury for acceptance of works of art sent from Italy to Chicago Expn., 1893, and other expns. in this country; now retired. Home: 105 Upper Mountain Av., Montclair, N.J. Died June 26, 1942.

COUNTY, Albert John, ry. official; b. Dublin, Ireland, Aug. 1, 1871; s. Thomas and Katharine Stackpole (Smith) C.; B.S. in economics, U. of Pa., 1908; m. Hester Caven Fraley, Sept. 2, 1902; children—William F., John O. Clk., purchasing dept. Gt. Southern & Western Ry. Co., Ireland, 1885-90; clk. in secretary's dept. Pa.R.R., Phila., 1890-98, chief clk., 1898-1900, asst. to sec. Pa.R.R.Co., 1900-01, asst. sec. Pa.R.R.Co. and important subsidiary cos., and Supt. Employes' Saving Fund, 1901-06, asst. to v.p., 1906-13, and 1913-16, spl. asst. to pres. Pa.R.R. Co. and nearly all subsidiary cos. in Pa. System East of Pittsburgh, apptd. v.p. in charge of accounting, Mar. 8, 1916, apptd. v.p. in charge accounting and corporate work, May 1, 1923, v.p. in charge of treasury and accounting depts. and corporate work, 1925, and v.p. in charge of finance and corporate relations, 1929-38, retired Dec. 1, 1938, also former pres. and dir. of most of branch lines of Pa. R.R.; dir. Norfolk & Western Ry., Phila. Nat. Bank. Reporter for N. Am. to Internat. Ry. Congress on Ry. Accounts and Statistics, 1910. Mem. Am. Acad. Polit. and Social Science. Clubs: Union League, St. David's Golf (Phila.); Economic, Bankers' (New York). Home: St. Davids, Pa. Died Aug. 20, 1944.

COWAN, Robert Ernest (kou'ăn), librarian, bibliographer; b. Toronto, Ont., Can., July 2, 1862; s. Robert Hawke and Lydia Rebecca (Peer) C.; came with parents to U.S., 1870; student U. of Calif., 1882-84; hon. A.M., U. of Southern Calif., 1929; m. Marie Margaret Fleissner, Nov. 7, 1894; 1 son, Robert Granniss. Engaged in book-selling in San Francisco, 1895-1920; librarian, William Andrews Clark, Jr., Library, Los Angeles, Calif., 1919-33. Mem. Am. Hist. Assn., Calif. Library Assn., Calif. Hist. Soc.; hon. mem. Soc. Calif. Pioneers. Clubs: Grolier, Zamorano, Book Club of Calif. Author: (with Boutwell, Dunlap) Bibliography of the Chinese Question in the United States, 1909; Bibliography of the History of Calif. and the Pacific West, 1914; The Bibliography of the Spanish Press in Calif., 1919; (with Robert Granniss Cowan) Bibliography of California, 1510-1930, 1933; Bibliographical Notes on Certain of the Earliest Editions of Bret Harte's "Heathen Chinee," 1934; The Forgotten Characters of Old San Francisco, 1937; Robert Browning, 1812-1889 (an essay), 1941; also many brochures on Calif. history. Home: 2151 W. 20th St., Los Angeles, Calif. Died May 29, 1942.

COX, Benjamin, clergyman; b. Wellingboro, Eng., Dec. 19, 1866; s. John and Deborah (Watts) C.; came to America, 1880; student Southern Bapt. Theol. Sem., Louisville, Ky., 1896-97; U. of Chicago, 1898-1901; D.D., Union Univ., Jackson, Tenn., 1930; m. Jennie Dunlap, Feb. 26, 1890. Ordained Bapt. ministry, 1894; pastor Carlisle and Brinkley, 1895-96, Argenta, Ark., 1894-95, 1st Ch., Little Rock, 1897-1913, Central Ch., Memphis, 1913-33; apptd. first probation officer of Federal Court, Memphis, Oct. 5, 1925; supt. Open Door Mission, Memphis. Pres. Cox-Garrett Soc. of Memphis, Tenn., and Dallas, Tex. Pres. Bapt. Advance Pub. Co., Little Rock, for many yrs.; ex-pres. Bd. Bapt. Schs. and Colls., Ark.; ex-pres. bd. trustees Central Bapt. Coll., Conway, Ark.; sec. bd. trustees Bapt. Memorial Hosp., Memphis; mem. State Bapt. Mission Board; trustee Union Univ., Jackson, Tenn.; dir. Memphis Salv. Army, Nat. No-Tobacco League. Founder of Memphis Noon Prayer Meeting, Jan. 19, 1914, held every week day since, without collection, members in every state, and many foreign countries; supt. Open Door Mission (formerly Noon Prayer Meeting), Memphis; founder of Strand Bible Class, Feb., 1921; city organizer Memphis Ann. Bible Conf., 1920. Author of a book of verse, a booklet entitled An Army Y.M.C.A. Parson; also pamphlets and published sermons. Address: 1823 Walker, Memphis, Tenn. Died 1944.

COX, George Clarke, investment counsel, writer; b. Columbus, O., May 17, 1865; s. Edward Wesley and Mary Hollingsworth (Clarke) C.; A.B., Kenyon Coll., Gambier, O., 1886 (Phi Beta Kappa), A.M., 1900; studied U. of Geneva, Switzerland, 1899-1902; A.M., Harvard, 1908, Ph.D., 1910; m. Alice Maude Chapman, Aug. 23, 1893. Clergyman of P.E. Ch., 1888-1908; resigned ministry, 1908, because of change in theol. views. Asst. in philosophy, Harvard, 1908-11; asst. prof. philosophy, Dartmouth, 1911-15; practice as expert ins. adviser, N.Y. City, 1915-20; econ. analyst since 1920. Co-founder firm Cox and Trainer, investment counsel, 1924-30; head of Cox & Jordan, afterwards Cox, Van Cleef & Jordan, 1930-32; since doing business under own name. Mem. Am. Philos. Assn., Am. Econ. Assn., Acad. Polit. Science. Club: Harvard (New York). Contbr. to Jour. of Philosophy, N.Y. Times Annalist, Barron's Weekly, also to newspapers and mags. on philos., economic and political topics; public addresses on such topics. Author: The Public Conscience, 1922. Founder, 1938, and former editor The Gold Barometer. Home: 320 E. 42d St. (Tudor City), New York, N.Y. Office: 29 Broadway, New York, N.Y. Died Dec. 17, 1943.

COX, George Howland, Jr., writer, lecturer; b. New Bedford, Mass., Feb. 8, 1883; s. George Howland and Ella Parkhurst (Whittemore) C.; student Cambridge High and Latin Sch., 1892-97, Powder Point Sch. (Duxbury, Mass.), 1897-98, St. John's Mil. Sch. (Manlius, N.Y.), 1898-1900, Harvard, 1904-06; m. Mabel Holroyd, 1920 (died 1921); 1 dau., Priscilla Howland (died 1922); m. 2d, Elizabeth Bull Prudden, 1931 (she died in 1946). Entered business career as a bank clerk, also bond salesman, in Cincinnati, O., 1906-09; bond salesman Ernest Smith, Inc., Boston, 1910-12; asst. sec. Mass. Trust Co., Boston, 1913-17; bond salesman White, Weld & Co., Boston, 1919-21; mem. Whitney, Cox & Co., investments, 1921-22; with accounting dept. United Fruit Co., Guatemala, 1922-29; corr. for Christian Science Monitor, 1930-34; dir. Inter-Am. Center and lecturer on Hispanic Am. history, George Washington U., 1934-46. Served as 2d lt., Air Corps., U.S. Army, Kelly Field, San Antonio, Tex., and Wilbur Wright Field, Fairfield, O., and mil. police officer at Dayton and Springfield, O., World War; capt. 101st Engrs. Mass. Nat. Guard, 1919-22; govt. appeal agent, Selective Service, Washington, D.C., 1941-46; radio commentator WGY, Schenectady, N.Y., 1937-42; lecturer U.S. Army, Bolling Field, Washington, D.C.; Latin American news commentator, WWDC, Washington, 1941. Pres. Back Bay Board of Trade, Boston, 1913-14. Awarded Medal of Merit by Republic of Ecuador, 1936, 43. Mem. Pan-Am. Soc., Acad. Polit. Sci., Mil. Order World Wars. Mason. Club: Cosmos (Washington). Author: (short stories) My Friend Chico, 1930; (musical play) The Wanderer, 1906; music and lyrics of Look Out for Squalls, 1943. Asso. editor of The World Affairs Magazine 1936-38. Deceased.

COX, George James; prof. of art and chmn. dept. of art, U. of Calif. at Los Angeles. Author: Pottery for Artists and Students, 1914; Art for Amateurs and Students, 1924; Art and the Life, 1933. Address: Univ. of Calif. at Los Angeles, Los Angeles, Calif.* Died May 3, 1946.

COX, Harvey Warren, univ. pres.; b. Birmingham, Ill., Feb. 19, 1875; s. Christopher Columbus and

Salisa (Richardson) C.; Ph.B., Neb. Wesleyan U., 1902; A.M., U. of Neb., 1906; A.M., Harvard, 1910, Ph.D., 1911; LL.D., U. of Florida, 1920; Dr. Humanities, Boston U., 1938; m. Daisy Esther Frisbie, Aug. 26, 1903; children—Warren Edward, Ruth Esther, Albert Frisbie. Prof. philosophy, Neb. Wesleyan U., 1902-09; asst. in philosophy, Harvard, 1910-11; prof. philosophy, 1911-20, dean Teacher's Coll., 1916-20, U. of Florida; pres. Emory University, Aug. 1920-42, chancellor since 1942. Dist. supervisor personnel methods S.A.T.C., Southeastern District, 1918. Pres. Educational Assn. of M.E. Ch.,' S., 1929-30; lay leader, North Ga. Conf., M.E. Ch., S., 1926-30; del. Gen. Conf. (Quadrennial) M.E. Ch., S., 1930, 1934, 1938; del. Uniting Conf. Meth. Church, 1939, vice chairman Atlanta Regional Labor Board, 1934-35; chmn. coll. sect. Edn. Assn. of M.E. Ch., South, 1936; mem. General Board of Education of the Methodist Church (chmn. finance com.). Mem. Phi Beta Kappa, Kappa Alpha, Phi Kappa Phi, Omicron Delta Kappa, Kappa Phi Kappa, Tau Kappa Alpha. Methodist. Mason. Clubs: Atlanta, Friars, Kiwanis. Home: 1265 Ridgewood Dr. N.E., Atlanta, Ga. Office: Emory University, Ga. Died July 27, 1944.

COX, James Monroe, college pres.; b. Fredonia, Ala., Feb. 26, 1860; s. John Wesley and Martha C.; A.B., Clark U., Atlanta, 1884; grad. Gammon Theol. Sem., Atlanta, 1886 (D.D., 1898); m. Hattie W. Robinson, Sept. 20, 1887. Mem. Little Rock Conf. M.E. Ch.; pres. Philander Smith Coll., Little Rock, Ark., since 1896. Rep. Little Rock Conf. in 5 Gen. Confs. M.E. Ch.; now mem. Univ. Senate, M.E. Ch. Republican. Address: 912 W. 11th St., Little Rock, Ark. Died Jan. 2, 1948.

COX, Leonard Martin, naval officer; b. New Liberty, Ky., Mar. 21, 1870; s. Attilla and Kate Ware (Martin) C.; C.E., Rensselaer Poly. Inst., 1892; m. Jane Torbitt Castleman, Oct. 16, 1895; 1 dau., Katharine Castleman. Engring. work, Louisville & Nashville Railroad, until 1899; commd. lt. jr. grade, Corps of Civ. Engrs., U.S. Navy, Feb. 23, 1899; lt., Apr. 16, 1907; lt. comdr., Oct. 9, 1909; comdr., Aug. 29, 1916, capt., 1921. Made first American survey of Island of Guam, together with report on island conditions, 1901-03; in charge constrn. floating dry dock Dewey, 1903-06; chief engr. Louisville, Henderson & St. Louis R.R., 1906-07; mem. Alaskan R.R. Commn. by presdl. appointment, 1912-13 (commn. made first report on which appropriation for Alaskan railroads was based). During World War pub. works officer, Navy Yard, New York, until Sept. 1917; in charge of all pub. works 12th Naval Dist., South of San Francisco Bay, including constrn. air station and marine expeditionary base, San Diego, until Nov. 1918; asst. mgr. Div. of Shipyard Plants, Emergency Fleet Corp., U.S. Shipping Bd., 1918-19; transferred to Mare Island Navy Yard as public works officer of 12th Naval Dist., June 1919; retired for physical disability, May 31, 1923. Mem. Am. Soc. Civil Engrs. (Norman medal, 1907), Naval Inst., A.A.A.S., Engring. Inst. of Canada, Theta Delta Chi. Republican. Episcopalian. Clubs: Army and Navy (Washington, D.C.); Commercial, Engineers', Commonwealth (San Francisco). Home: Malvern Woods, St. Helena, Calif. Died Dec. 12, 1943.

COX, Louise Howland King, painter; b. San Francisco, June 23, 1865; pupil Nat. Acad. Design, Art Students' League and Kenyon Cox; m. Kenyon Cox, June 30, 1892 (died Mar. 17, 1919). Awards: 3d Hallgarten prize, Nat. Acad. Design, 1896; bronze medal, Paris Expn., 1900; silver medals Buffalo Expn., 1901, St. Louis Expn., 1904. Represented in Nat. Gallery of Art, Washington (Evans gift). A.N.A., 1902. Address: Mt. Kisco, N.Y. Died Dec. 10, 1945.

COX, Theodore Sullivan, educator; b. "Emery Place," D.C., Aug. 17, 1894; s. William Van Zandt and Juliet Hazeltine (Emery) C.; A.B., U. of Mich., 1917; LL.B., U. of Va., 1922; m. Christiana Osborne Jones, June 20, 1931. Admitted to Va. bar, 1921; instr. law, U. of Va., 1922-24; engaged in research in history, politics and pub. law, Stanford U., 1925-26, Johns Hopkins U., 1926-27, and in Washington, D.C., 1927-30; prof. jurisprudence since 1930, dean Sch. of Jurisprudence since 1932, Coll. of William and Mary. Served as 1st lt., 314th F.A., U.S. Army; capt., 125th F.A., A.E.F., World War 1; capt., Provost Marshall Gen.'s Dept., 1942; maj., later lt. col., Gen. Staff Corps, 1944-46; with 15th Army Group, 7th Army, 8th (British) Army, 6th Army Group, 1st (French) Army, and S.H.A.E.F. and U.S. Forces European Theater; participated in engagements in Sicily, Naples-Foggia, Rome-Arno, Northern France, The Rhine, Ardennes, Central Europe. Decorated Bronze Star Medal. Del. Internat. Congress Comparative Law, The Hague, 1932, 37; dir. Tidewater Automobile Assn. of Va. since 1935; member Williamsburg Planning and Zoning Commn., 1933-43; pres. Williamsburg Chamber of Commerce, 1940-42. Member of American and Virginia bar associations, American Historical Assn., Am. Law Inst., American Judicature Soc., Mil. Order of World War, Soc. Colonial Wars, S.R., Order of Coif, Phi Beta Kappa, Phi Alpha Delta, Omicron Delta Kappa, Phi Kappa Phi. Independent Democrat. Episcopalian. Clubs: Army and Navy, Corinthian Yacht (Washington); Farmington Country (Charlottesville, Va.); Colonnade (University, Va.). Contbr. to Dictionary of Am. Biography and to legal and other periodicals. Home: Jamestown Road at Chandler Court, Williamsburg, Va. Died May 10, 1947; buried in Arlington Cemetery.

CRABBS, George Dent, director, Philip Carey Mfg. Co.; vice-pres. Cincinnati Union Terminal Co.; dir. Federal Reserve Bank of Cleveland, Procter & Gamble Co., Cincinnati Street Railway Company, Cincinnati, New Orleans & Texas Pacific Ry. Co., Carthage Mills, Inc., Wheeling Steel Corp., Robert A. Keasbey Co., Cincinnati Gas & Elec. Co., Del. Floor Products, Inc. Home: 352 Lafayette Av., Cincinnati. Office: First Nat. Bank Bldg., Cincinnati, O Died Sept. 29, 1948.

CRABITÈS, Pierre (krä-bĕ-tēz'), ex-judge; b. New Orleans, La., Feb. 17, 1877; s. Pierre and Martha (Patton) C.; A.M., Coll. Immaculate Conception, New Orleans, 1895; LL.B., Tulane U., 1898; LL.D., Loyola Univ., New Orleans, 1918; grad. study U. of Paris; married; 1 son, Henry. Admitted to La. bar, 1900, and practiced at New Orleans until 1911; Am. judge, Mixed Tribunal, Cairo, Egypt, 1911-36; spl. lecturer La. State U. Law Sch. Spl. asst. U.S. minister, Cairo, Egypt, Apr. 1, 1942-Apr. 30, 1943; special assistant United States minister, Baghdad, Iraq, since May 1943. Appointed American mat. commissioner under provisions of Egypto-Am. Arbitration Treaty, 1929, by President Roosevelt, Apr. 3, 1939. Catholic. Author: Gordon, The Sudan and Slavery, 1933; Ismail, the Maligned, 1933; The Winning of the Sudan, 1934; American Officers in the Egyptian Army, 1938; Benes, Statesman of Central Europe, 1935; Ibrahim of Egypt, 1935; Clement VII and Henry VIII, 1936; Unhappy Spain, 1937; Victoria—Guardian Angel, 1937; The Spohatim of Suez, 1940. Died Oct. 9, 1943.

CRABTREE, Ernest Granville, surgeon; b. Zanesville, O., Nov. 23, 1883; s. Charles Carroll and Laura (Bunting) C.; Ph.B., Wooster Coll., 1906; M.D., Harvard, 1914; m. Edith Reese, 1914; children—Charlotte Elizabeth, James Carroll, Edward Melvin. Prof. chemistry, Huron Coll., 1906-08; interne Mass. Gen. Hosp., 1911-13, resident urologist, 1913-16, visiting urologist, 1919-28; teaching fellow, Harvard, 1915-16, instr. urology since 1919; urologist Boston Lying-in Hosp., Beth Israel Hosp. and N.E. Bapt. Hosp., Boston, Newton (Mass.) Hosp.; cons. urologist hosps., Bangor, Me., Peterborough, N.H., Exeter, N.H., Gloucester, Mass., Gardiner, Mass. Served as maj. Hosp. Unit 22, B.E.F., 1917-19, surgeon in charge surg. div., 1917-18. Decorated Officer Mil. Div. Order of the Brit. Empire, 1919. Fellow Am. Coll. of Surgeons; mem. A.M.A., Mass. Med. Soc., Internat. Urol. Assn., Am. Urol. Assn. (president-elect; pres. N.E. br., 1939-40), Am. Assn. Genito-Urinary Surgeons, N.E. Surg. Socs., Boston Obstet. Soc., Am. Soc. for Social Hygiene (dir. 1936-1939), Mass. Soc. for Social Hygiene (pres. 1935-38). Republican. Clubs: Harvard (Boston); St. Botolph. U.S. collaborator Italian Urol. Jour. Author: Urological Diseases of Pregnancy, 1942. Home: 85 Dean Rd., Brookline, Mass. Office: 99 Commonwealth Av., Boston, Mass. Died May 30, 1947.

CRABTREE, James William, sec. emeritus Nat. Edn. Assn.; b. Crabtree (P.O.), Scioto Co., O., Apr. 18, 1864; s. Peter and Sarah Catherine (Williams) C.; grad. State Normal Sch., Peru, Neb., 1887; B.S., Bloomfield Scientific Inst., 1890; B.A. and M.A., U. of Neb., 1908; LL.D. from the same univ., 1935; abroad, 1907; m. Donna A. Wilson, July 6, 1899; children—Eunice Katherine, Donna Lu Verne, Mary Elizabeth. Taught in rural schools, 6 yrs.; supt. schs., Ashland, Neb., 1889-95; asst. teacher mathematics, U. of Neb., 1895-96; prin. Beatrice (Neb.) High Sch., 1896-97; state high sch. insp. for U. of Neb., 1897-1904; pres. Peru State Normal Sch., 1904-10; state supt. pub. instrn. of Neb., 1910-11; pres. River Falls (Wis.) State Teachers Coll., 1911-17; sec. Nat. Education Assn., 1917-35 (membership increased from 7,300 to 216,000 since 1917), sec. emeritus, 1935; acting sec. gen. World Federation of Edn. Assns., 1935-38. Pres. Neb. State Teachers Assn., 1897-98; treas. N.E.A., 1904; mem. Nat. Council Education; mem. Neb. Acad. Science, North Central Assn. Secondary Schs. and Colls.; sec. Central Assn. State Normal School Presidents, 1908; sec. President Hoover's Advisory Com. on Edn., 1931-32. Republican. Campbellite (Christian). Author: Roll of Honor Word Book, 1899; The Crabtree Speller, 1908; The Canvasser and His Victims (pamphlet); What Counted Most (an autobiography); also edni. pamphlets and many reports. Address: 1304 Euclid St. N.W., Washington. Died June 9, 1945; buried in Rock Creek Cemetery, Washington.

CRAIG, Malin, army officer; b. St. Joseph, Mo., Aug. 5, 1875; s. Maj. Louis Aleck and Georgie (Malin) C.; grad. U.S. Mil. Acad., Apr. 26, 1898; honor grad. Inf. and Cav. Sch., 1904; grad. Army Staff Coll., 1905; Army War Coll., 1910; m. Genevieve Woodruff, Apr. 29, 1901; 1 son, Malin. Commd. 2d lt. 4th Inf., Apr. 26, 1898; trans. to 4th Cav., June 23, 1898; promoted through grades to brig. gen., Apr. 28, 1921; maj. gen., July 24, 1924; general, Oct. 2, 1935; served as lieut. colonel, colonel and brig. gen., World War. In Santiago Campaign from June 12, 1898, China Relief Expdn., June-Oct. 1900; a.d.c. to Brig. Gen. Barry, in Philippines, 1900-01, to Gen. Bell, 1902-04; again in Philippines, 1907-09; duty Gen. Staff Corps, 1910-12, 1917-19; arrived in France, Oct. 5, 1917; apptd. comdr. 166th Brigade Inf., 83d Div., 4th Army Corps, A.E.F., July 20, 1918; chief of staff 41st Div., Aug. 25, 1917-Jan. 19, 1918, chief of staff 1st Corps, Jan. 20, 1918-Nov. 12, 1918; chief of staff 3d Army, Nov. 13, 1918-July 2, 1919; apptd. dir. Gen. Staff Coll., Washington, D.C., 1919; comdg. Dist. of Ariz., 1920-21, comdt. Cav. Sch., Ft. Riley, Kan., Sept. 1, 1921-July 1, 1923; comdg. Coast Defenses, Manila and Subig Bay, Sept. 17, 1923-July 10, 1924; maj.-gen., chief of cav., July 24, 1925; asst. chief of staff U.S. Army, Mar. 21, 1926; comdg. 4th Corps Area, Apr. 2-Oct. 5, 1927; comdg. Panama Canal Div., Oct. 13, 1927-Mar. 31, 1928; comdg. Panama Canal Dept., Apr. 1, 1928-Aug. 10, 1930; comdg. 9th Corps Area, Oct. 13, 1930-Jan. 24, 1935, 4th Army, Oct. 3, 1933-Jan. 24, 1935; comdg. Army War Coll., Feb. 3, 1935-Oct. 1, 1935; chief of staff, U.S. Army, Oct. 2, 1935-Aug. 31, 1939, retiring with rank of general. Decorated with D.S.M.; with oak leaf cluster (United States); Commander of Legion of Honor, Croix de Guerre with 2 Palms (French); Companion of Bath (British); Comdr. La Couronne (Belgian); Crown of Italy; Estrellá de Abdon Calderon, 1st Class (Ecuador). Home: 2126 Connecticut Av. Address: care of Adj. General, War Dept., Washington, D.C. Died July 25, 1945.

CRAIGE (Francis) Burton (krāg), lawyer; b. Salisbury, N.C., Dec. 23, 1875; s. Kerr and Josephine (Branch) C.; desc. Archibald Craige, a Scot who settled at Trading Ford, Anson (now Rowan County), N.C., about 1750, and was one of the founders of Salisbury, N.C.; prep. edn. Davis Mil. Sch., Winston-Salem, 1890-91, Horner Mil. Sch., Oxford, N.C., 1891-93; A.B., with honors, U. of N.C., 1897; student U. of N.C. Law Sch., 1900-01, hon. LL.D., 1939; m. Jane Caroline Henderson Boyden, Nov. 9, 1911; children—Francis Burton, IV (dec.), Jane Boyden (Mrs. Gordon Gray), Archibald. Newspaper reporter, 1897, prin. Church High Sch., Salisbury, 1897-98; instr. Horner Mil. Sch., 1898-1900, meanwhile studying law; admitted to N.C. bar, 1901; asso. with father and brother in firm of Craige & Craige (est. 1832), Salisbury, 1901-11; moved to Winston-Salem, 1911, as counsel of R. J. Reynolds Tobacco Co.; after a breakdown in 1916 and recovery in 1917, declined further exclusive employment and re-entered general law practice as senior partner of Craige & Craige, at Salisbury and Winston-Salem; director Wachovia Bank & Trust Co.; member N.C. Constl. Commn., 1932-33; Trustee Univ. of N.C. (est. 1776) and Salem Coll. (est. 1772); a founder and trustee Rowan Memorial Hosp., Salisbury. Member Am. Bar Assn., N.C. Bar Assn., Am. Historical Soc., N.C. Historical Soc., Soc. of the Cincinnati (N.C. Chapter), Phi Beta Kappa (pres.), Sigma Nu, Democrat, Episcopalian. Clubs: Twin City, Old Town, and Forsyth Country Clubs; Chevy Chase (Washington, D.C.); Princess Anne Country (Virginia Beach, Va.). Author: North Carolina in the Federal Convention of 1787, with sketches and biographies of delegates. Has endowed professorship of jurisprudence at Univ. of N.C. Homes: 134 Cascade Av., Winston-Salem, N.C.; 329 Bank St., Salisbury, N.C.; Cavalier Shores, Virginia Beach, Va. Died Jan. 11, 1945.

CRAM, Harold E(dgerly), newspaper editor; b. Portland, Me., 1890; s. Henry Osbourne and Frances Ellen (Bibber) C.; grad. Portland High School; student Eric Pape School of Art, Boston, 3 years; m. Berniece Nina Banks (newspaperwoman), June 3, 1937. Illustrator and newspaper artist, 1910-18; began writing short stories and became free lance writer for newspapers and mags.; with Evening Express, Portland, Me., 1919-25, successively as reporter, exchange and asst. state editor, financial editor; with Portland Telegram since 1925, as automobile editor, 1925-28, asst. editor, 1928-37, editor since 1937. Served 3 years in Me. Nat. Guard. Episcopalian. Contbr. fiction to mags.; illustrates his own stories. Home: Shore Acres, Cape Elizabeth, Portland, Me. Office: 177 Federal St., Portland, Me. Died Nov. 21, 1948.

CRAM, Ralph Adams, architect, author; b. Hampton Falls, N.H., Dec. 16, 1863; s. Rev. William Augustine and Sarah Elizabeth (Blake) C.; ed. Augusta, Me., Westford, Mass., and Exeter, N.H.; Litt.D., Princeton, 1910, Williams, 1928; LL.D., Yale, 1915, Notre Dame, 1924; hon. Phi Beta Kappa, Harvard, 1921; m. Elizabeth Carrington, d. Capt. Clement Carrington Read, C.S.A., of Va., Sept. 20, 1900; children—Mary Carrington (Mrs. Edward Nicholas), Ralph Wentworth, Elizabeth Strudwick. Architect since 1889; supervising architect Princeton U., 1907-29; cons. architect Bryn Mawr and Wellesley colleges. A.N.A.; fellow Am. Acad. Arts and Sciences, A.I.A., Royal Soc. of Arts, Royal Geog. Soc. (London); mem. Am. Acad. of Arts and Letters, Nat. Inst. Arts and Letters, Mediæval Acad. America, Boston Soc. Architects (ex-pres.), Am. Federation Arts, Architectural Assn. (London); hon. corr. mem. Royal Inst. British Architects. Clubs: Century (New York); Art (Phila.). Author: The Decadent, Black Spirits and White, Church Building, 1901; The Ruined Abbeys of Great Britain, 1906; Impressions of Japanese Architecture and the Allied Arts, 1906; The Gothic Quest, 1907; Excalibur, 1908; The Ministry of Art, 1914; Heart of Europe, 1915; The Substance of Gothic, 1917; The Nemesis of Mediocrity, 1918; The Great Thousand Years, 1918; The Sins of the Fathers, 1919; Walled Towns, 1919; Gold, Frankincense and Myrrh, 1919; Towards the Great Peace, 1922; The Catholic Church and Art, 1929; The Cathedral of Palma de Mallorca, 1933; Convictions and Controversies, 1935; My Life in Architecture, 1936; The End of Democracy, 1937. Home: "Whitehall," Sudbury, Mass. Office: 248 Boylston St., Boston, Mass. Died Sep. 22, 1942.

CRAMER, William (krā'mẽr), pathologist; b. Brandenburg, Germany, June 2, 1878; s. Siegmund and Olga (Harff) C.; student chemistry Munich U., 1896-97, Berlin U., 1897-1900; D.Sc., Edinburgh U., 1903; M.R.C.S. and L.R.C.P., Ohio Coll., London, 1915-17; m. Belle Klauber, of New York, 1906; children—Ian William David, Michael William Valentine. Naturalized British subject, 1914; came to U.S., 1939. Research chemist and asst. to prof. pharmacology, U. of Berlin, 1900; jr. mem. scientific staff Imperial Cancer Research Fund, London, 1903-05; lecturer chem. physiology, U. of Edinburgh, 1905-14; sr. mem. scientific staff, Imperial Cancer Research Fund, London, 1915-39; research asso., Barnard Free Skin and Cancer Hosp., St. Louis, Mo., since 1940; mem. med. faculty, Washington U., St. Louis, since 1940; Middleton Goldsmith lecturer Pathol. Soc. of New York, 1940; lecturer British Med. Assn. and German Soc. for Cancer Research. British del. Council of Internat. Union against Cancer (mem. statis. com.), Internat. Cancer Congress, Madrid, 1933, Brussels, 1936, Atlantic City, 1939. Awarded Ellis prize in physiology, 1906. Mem. Pathol. Club (Edinburgh), Biochem. Soc., Physiol. Soc. and Pathol. Soc. (England), Royal Soc. Medicine (London), Leewenhoek Vereeniging (Amsterdam), Am. Assn. for Cancer Research; mem. British Med. Assn. Com. on Radium Beam Therapy. Author: Practical Course in Chemical Physiology, 3d edit., 1918; Fever, Heat Regulation, Climate and the Thyroid Adrenal Apparatus, 1928; also chapters in various text books. Editor Cancer Review; mem. editorial com. Acta of Internat. Union Against Cancer. Home: 5364 Cabanne Av. Office: Barnard Free Skin and Cancer Hosp., St. Louis, Mo. Died Aug. 10, 1945.

CRANDALL, Bruce Verne (krăn'd'l), editor, author; b. Hillsdale, Mich., Oct. 16, 1873; s. Lathan Augustus and Mary (Nichols) C.; student Western Reserve U., 1891-92; m. Minnie Smith, Dec. 9, 1898; children—Bruce Nichols, Willard Smith, Mary Elizabeth, Margaret Louise. Began as office boy with Franklin MacVeagh & Co., Chicago, 1892; with Railway Review, 1896-1900; pub. Railway Master Mechanic, 1900-08; pres. Bruce V. Crandall Service, Inc., 1908-22; editor Iron Trail, 1921-22; editor Northwestery Ry. System Magazine, 1922-24; owner and editor Railway Review, 1924-26; asso. editor South Coast News, 1930-31; editor Venice-Nokomis News, Venice, Fla., 1938-39. Chmn. Greater Orange County Com., 1931. Sec.-treas. Western Ry. Club, Inc., 1920-27; sec. Vets. Assn. of C.&N.W. Ry., 1924-27; pres. Descendants of First Families of America; sec. Crandall, Mount, and Nichols societies; mem. Delta Tau Delta. Club: Three Lakes Rod and Gun. Author: Autocrat at the Lunch Table, 1915; Carman's Helper, 1917; Locomotive Terminal Cost Data, 1918; Track Labor Cost Data, 1919; After Forty Years, 1925; Railroading On the Rails and Off, 1927; Reveries of an Editor, 1932; Is This the Armageddon?, 1942. Home: Rod and Gun Club, Three Lakes, Wis. Died Nov. 19, 1945.

CRANE, Albert Sears, hydraulic engr.; b. Addison, N. Y., May 30, 1868; s. Albert Gallatin and Julia Ayrault (Holden) C.; grad. Addison Union Sch., 1884; C.E., Cornell U., 1891; unmarried. Asst. engr., Newton, Mass., 1891-95; asst. engr. dept. of sewers, Brooklyn, N.Y., 1895-98; chief asst. engr. Mich. Lake Superior Power Co., Sault Ste. Marie, Mich., 1898-1900; chief engr. The Lake Superior Power Co., Sault Ste. Marie, Ont., Can., 1900-02; prin. asst. engr. Chicago Drainage Canal, 1902-05; hydraulic engr. J. G. White & Co., New York, 1905-13, vice-pres., 1913-28; cons. hydraulic engr. since 1928. Mem. Am. Soc. C.E., Am. Inst. E.E., Western Soc. Engrs., Boston Soc. C.E., Chi Psi. Republican. Presbyterian. Clubs: Engineers, Cornell, Lawyers (New York). Has engaged in constrn. of 30 large earth dams, 60 masonry dams, 40 hydroelectric stations, 6 irrigation projects, etc. Home: 32 W. 40th St. Office: 80 Broad St., New York. Died Aug. 25, 1946; buried at Addison, N.Y

CRANE, Frederick Evan, retired chief judge; LL.B., Columbia, 1889, LL.D., 1923; LL.D., St. Lawrence U., 1921, St. John's Coll., 1930, New York Univ., 1931, Union Coll., 1935, Fordham U., 1936; married; children—Dorothy B. (Mrs. Russell Marston), Frederick Ralph. Admitted to bar, 1890; practiced at Brooklyn, 1890-1901; co. judge, Kings Co., N.Y., 1901-06; Justice Supreme Court of N.Y., 2d Dist., term Jan. 1, 1907-Dec. 31, 1920; apptd. judge Court of Appeals, Jan. 1917, and unanimously elected by all parties to same office, 1920, for term ending, 1940, unanimously elected chief judge, 1934. Republican. Address: 25 Nassau Blvd., Garden City, L.I., N.Y.* Died Nov. 21, 1947.

CRANE, Frederick Lea, newspaper publisher; b. Elizabeth, N.J., Feb. 12, 1888; s. Augustus Stout and Minerva Carlisle (Lea) C.; M.E., Stevens Inst. Tech., Hoboken, N.J., 1910; m. Gwendolen Kershner, January 20, 1917; children—Dorothy Jean (deceased), Marian Lea (Mrs. Robert Edward Graef) and Robert Clark. Became cadet engr. Westinghouse Machine Co., 1910; later appraisal engr. West Penn Traction Co., statistician West Penn Power Co., and constrn. engr. United Gas Improvement Co., with Elizabeth (N.J.) Daily Journal since 1920, chmn. bd. Union Co. Savings Bank; dir. Elizabethport Banking Co.; v.p., trustee, Evergreen Cemetery, Elizabeth Y.M.C.A. (past pres.). Mem. Am. Newspaper Pubs. Assn., Asso. Press, Tau Beta Pi. Republican. Presbyterian (ruling elder and clerk of session). Mason. (32°), Elk. Clubs: Rotary, Suburban Golf (Elizabeth). Home: 11 English Village 1-A, Cranford, N.J. Died Aug. 16, 1949; buried at Evergreen Cemetary, Elizabeth, N.J.

CRANE, Jason George, pres. Telephone Bond & Share Co.; b. Seymour, Ind., Mar. 22, 1880; s. Allen S. and Bell (Campbell) C.; B.S. and E.E., Purdue U.; m. Margaret Frances Sheron, Sept. 21, 1905; children—Allen S., Margaret Lucille. Became supt. of maintenance Pioneer Telephone Co. of Okla., 1907; v.p. Theodore Gary & Co. since 1920; pres. Telephone Bond & Share Co., 1925-30 and since 1936; also officer or dir. many other telephone companies. Office: Telephone Bldg., Kansas City, Mo. Died June 18, 1942.

CRANE, Martin McNulty, lawyer; b. Grafton, W. Va., Nov. 17, 1855; s. Martin and Mary (McNulty) C.; early orphaned; ed. pub. and pvt. schs., Texas, nearly completing usual coll. course; taught sch. 4 years; m. Eula O. Taylor, Jan. 22, 1879. Admitted to bar, 1877; practiced at Cleburne, 1877-95, at Dallas since 1899; sr. mem. Crane & Crane; pros. atty. Johnson County, 1878-82; mem. Tex. Ho. of Rep., 1885 (declined renomination); senate, 1890-92; lt. gov., 1892-94; atty. gen., 1895-99. Democrat. Chief counsel for bd. of mgrs. in impeachment of Gov. James E. Ferguson, of Tex., 1917. Del. at large Dem. Nat. Conv., Baltimore, 1912, San Francisco, 1920. Chairman of the Anti-Ku Klux committee to prevent the election of Ku Klux candidate for governor. Clubs: Critics, Dallas Golf and Country. Home: 4005 Gaston Av. Office: Republic Bank Bldg., Dallas, Texas.* Died Aug. 3, 1943.

CRANFILL, James Britton, physician, editor; b. Parker County, Tex., Sept. 12, 1858; s. Eaton and Martha Jane (Galloway) C.; ed. common schs. of Gonzales County, Tex.; M.D., Tex. Med. Bd., 1879; LL.D., Simmons Coll., 1900, Baylor U., Waco, Tex., 1920; m. Ollie Allen, Sept. 1, 1878. Practiced medicine, 1879-82; editor of the Turnersville Effort, 1881-82; editor of Gatesvile Advance, 1882-86, Waco Advance, 1886-88; financial sec. Baylor U., 1888-89; supt. Bapt. mission work of Tex., 1889-92; ordained Bapt. minister, 1890; founder, and editor Texas Baptist Standard, 1892-1904; editor Baptist Tribune, 1905-07; editorial writer Asso. Prohibition Press; editor Baptist Bookman, 1917-18; joint editor The Pilot, 1925; editor The Advance, 1928. Vice-pres. B.Y.P.U., 1891-93. Prohibition candidate for v.p. of U.S., 1892; stated lecturer S. W. Bapt. Theol. Sem., 1921. Mem. exec. bd. Ministers' Relief Bd. of Southern Bapt. Conv.; v.p. Bapt. Gen. Conv. Tex., 1928-29 and 1936-37; trustee S.W. Bapt. Theol. Sem., Bishop Coll. Hon. mem. Philomathesian Soc. (Baylor U.); mem. Am. Sociol. Assn., Old Trail Drivers' Assn. Author: Courage and Comfort, 1890; Cranfill's Heart Talks, 1906; R. C. Buckner's Life of Faith and Works (joint author), 1914; Dr. J. B. Cranfill's Chronicle, 1916; Dr. J. B. Cranfill's Joke Book, 1917; From Nature to Grace, 1925; From Memory, 1937. Also pub. Riley's History of Texas Baptists, 1907. Editor and compiler: Carroll's Sermons, 1895; Interpretation of the English Bible (13 vols.), Baptists and Their Doctrines, Evangelistic Sermons, The River of Life, Inspiration of the Bible, The Day of the Lord, Jesus the Christ, Revival Messages, The Holy Spirit, Ambitious Dreams of Youth, The Faith That Saves, Christ and His Church, The Providence of God, The Way of the Cross, Messages on Prayer, Saved to Serve; We Would See Jesus, A Quest for Souls, God's Call to America, by George W. Truett. Editor: Golden Years (an autobiography by Mrs. W. L. Williams), 1921; Carroll's History of Texas Baptists, 1923. Home: 5619 Swiss Av. Office: Kirby Bldg., Dallas. Died Dec. 28, 1942; buried in Grove Hill Cemetery, Dallas.

CRANSTON, Claudia, author; b. Denton, Tex., Nov. 10, 1886; d. Christopher and Esther Ann (Baker) Cranston; student Denton Coll. Staff editor on Vogue Mag.; asso. editor Good Housekeeping. Democrat. Author: Ready to Wear, 1933; How to Entertain, 1933; The Murder on Fifth Avenue, 1934; Murder Maritime, 1935; Sky Gypsy, 1936; I've Been Around, 1937. Contbr. articles, fiction, verse to various mags. Address: Box 253, Winnsboro, Tex. Died June 24, 1947.

CRASSWELLER, Frank, lawyer; b. London, Eng., Jan. 4, 1856; s. Christopher and Sarah (Halifax) C.; student pvt. sch., Eng., 1861-69, pub. sch., Goderich, Ont., Can., 1879, Toronto (Can.) Normal Sch., 1884; m. Alison Moffett Douglas, 1885 (died 1930); children—Harold D., Frank H., Elsie I. (Mrs. Roy W. Deetz), Mark, Allan; came to Can., 1869, to U.S., 1888, naturalized citizen U.S., 1893. Woodsman, Muskoka, Can., 1869-79; teacher, Huron County, Ont., 1879-88; admitted to bar, 1889, and since in practice law; partner Crassweller & Crassweller, Duluth, Minn., since 1897; pres. Hugo Mfg. Co. since 19.., also several other small corps. Mem. and pres. Duluth City Council, 1897-1900; mem. City Planning Commn., Duluth, since 1922 (from orgn.); mem. Minn. State Bd. Law Examiners, 1921-29 (pres. 1927-29), Duluth Bd. of Edn., 1918-23, since 1935 (pres. 1920-23); mem. Minn. State Bar Assn. (pres. 1916-17), Duluth Comml. Club (pres. 1906-07). Elected to Duluth Hall of Fame 1942. Presbyterian. Mason (Blue Lodge, Scottish Rite, Shriner), Kiwanis. Home: 4701 Cooke St. Office: Suite 312, Exchange Bldg., Duluth, Minn. Deceased.

CRATHORNE, Arthur Robert (krā'thôrn), mathematics; b. Scarborough, Eng., Oct. 26, 1873; s. Francis and Ann (Harrison) C.; B.S., Univ. of Ill., 1898; U. of Wis., 1900-02; Ph.D., Goettingen U., 1907; m. Charlotte Pengra, 1904 (died 1915); children—Mary Preston (Mrs. Laurence Coughlin), Anne Harrison (Mrs. Carter L. Loth), Arthur Robert (died in service, 1943); married 2d, Katherine Layton, 1917. Tutor in mathematics, University of Maine, 1898-1900; instructor in mathematics, University of Wis., 1901-04, with U. of Ill. since 1907, successively as instructor, asso., asst. prof., asso. prof., and prof. since 1935. Mem. Nat. Com. on Math. Requirements, Nat. Research Council Com. on Statistics; fellow A.A.A.S., Royal Statis. Soc., Inst. of Math. Statistics, Am. Statis. Assn. (v.p.); mem. Am. Math. Soc., Math. Assn. America, Econometric Soc., Phi Kappa Sigma, Sigma Xi, Phi Kappa Phi and Pi Mu Epsilon. Episcopalian. Club: University. Author: College Algebra (with H. L. Rietz), 1909, 4th edit., 1939; School Algebra (with H. L. Rietz and E. H. Taylor), Vols. 1 and 2, 1915; Mathematics of Finance (with H. L. and J. C. Rietz), 1921; Introductory College Algebra (with H. L. Rietz), 1923, 3d edit., 1943; Handbook of Mathematical Statistics (with others), 1924; Trigonometry (with E. B. Lytle), 1930, 2d edit., 1938; Brief Trigonometry (with G. E. Moore), 1941; Intermediate Algebra (with H. L. Rietz and L. J. Adams), 1942. Math. editor Nelson's Loose Leaf Ency. Contributor to math. and statis. jours. Home: 802 Pennsylvania Av., Urbana, Ill. Died Mar. 7, 1946; buried in Mount Hope Cemetery, Urbana.

CRAVEN, Frank, actor; born in Boston. Known for many yrs. for successful delineation of a wide range of characters: has appeared in the principal theatres in U.S., and in London, Eng.; scored with marked success in "Bought and Paid For," "Two Many Cooks" (of which was the author), "This Way Out," "New Brooms," and many other plays. Author: Too Many Cooks; This Way Out; The First Year; Spite Corner; New Brooms; Money from Home; The 19th Hole; That's Gratitude; The Girl from Home; The New Dictator (musical book and lyrics). Co-author: Pigs; Salt Water. Directed "Salt Water," in addition to "Riddle Me This," "Bridle Wise," "Whistling in the Dark," "A Touch of Brimstone." Vaudeville sketches are "The Little Stranger," "Honor Among Thieves," "April Showers," "Nothing to Wear." Appeared in motion pictures: "City for Conquest," "The Girl from Cheyenne," "The Richest Man in Town," "Girl Trouble," "Through Different Eyes," "Keeper of the Flame," "Half Pint Kid," "Pittsburg," "Destiny," 1942. Played Stage Manager in "Our Town," N.Y. City, 1938, also in motion picture version; played Judge Peabody in "Village Green," N.Y. City, 1941. Clubs: The Lambs, Players, Century, Coffee House.* Died Sep. 1, 1945.

CRAVEN, James Braxton, clergyman; b. Trinity, North Carolina, May 8, 1879; s. James Lucius (M.D.) and Nannie (Bulla) C.; educated Trinity College and Vanderbilt University; D.D., Duke University, 1938; m. Katherine Covington, June 22, 1905 (died Nov. 21, 1943); children—Katherine Covington (deceased), James Braxton. Entered ministry Western N.C. Conference, 1900; ordained M.E. Ch. South, 1902; pastor Hot Springs, N.C., 1900, Cooleemee, N.C., 1901-04. Holmes Memorial Ch., Salisbury, 1905, Bethel Ch., Asheville, 1905-07, Main St. Ch., Salisbury, 1908-09; prof. Science Davenport Coll., Lenoir, N.C., 1909-10, pres., 1910-22; presiding elder Charlotte Dist., 1921-25, Greensboro Dist., 1925-29; pastor Main St. Ch., Gastonia, N.C., 1929-33; presiding elder Charlotte Dist., 1933-37; pastor W. Market St. Ch., Greensboro, 1937-44; district superintendent Charlotte Dist., 1944-45, retired, 1946. Trustee Duke U. Mem. Gen. Conf. M.E. Ch.S., 1926, 34, 38, Uniting Conf., Meth. Ch., 1939, Gen. Conf. Meth. Ch., 1940. Address: 500 W. Union St., Morganton, N.C. Died Apr. 13, 1947.

CRAWFORD, Eben G., business executive; pres. Cleveland Electric Illuminating Co., dir. Nat. City Bank, North American Co., Cleveland Cliffs Iron Co. Home: 2864 Eaton Rd., Shaker Heights, O. Office: 75 Public Square, Cleveland, O. Died Apr. 17, 1945.

CRAWFORD, Morris Barker, physicist; b. Sing Sing (now Ossining), N.Y., Sept. 26, 1852; s. Morris D'Camp and Charlotte (Holmes) C.; A.B., Wesleyan U., Conn., 1874, A.M., 1877; univs. of Leipzig and Berlin, 1877-80; m. Caroline L. Rice, Dec. 25, 1883; children—Holmes (dec), Frederick North (dec.), Margaret. Tutor mathematics, Wesleyan U., 1874-77, instr. physics, 1880-81, asso. prof., 1881-84, prof., 1884-1921, prof. emeritus since 1921. Fellow A.A.A.S.; mem. Am. Physical Soc. Home: Middletown, Conn. Died Oct. 9, 1940.

CRAWFORD, Porter James, pub. health; b. Seville, O., May 29, 1895; s. Porter W. and Ella Gertrude (Foskett) C.; B.S., Buchtel Coll., 1916; M.D., Western Reserve U., 1920; M.P.H., Johns Hopkins U., 1935; m. Ruth Elizabeth Frisbie, Aug. 30, 1919; children—James Telfer, Porter Foskett, Elizabeth Craig. Interne Lakeside Hospital, Cleveland, 1920-21; in private practice of medicine, 1921-23; with pub. health adminstrn., O., 1924-27; mem. staff Internat. Health Div. of The Rockefeller Foundation since 1928, engaging in yellow fever studies and control, Brazil, 1928-34, malaria studies, Panama, 1935-38, regional dir. for the Caribbean since 1939; consultant in pub. health to Republic of Panama, 1936-40. Officer Cuban Pub. Health Assn. Fellow A.M.A., Am. Pub. Health Assn., Royal Soc. Hygiene and Tropical Medicine; mem. Am. Soc. Tropical Medicine, A.A.A.S., Isthmian Med. Soc., Delta Omega. Independent Republican. Served U.S. Army, 1 mo., 1917. Enlisted Med. Res. Corps, 1917-18. Clubs: Union (Panama); American (Havana). Contbr. to Higiene y Sanidad (Mag.), Panama. Decorated by Cuban government, Dec. 2, 1940, Order of Merit, "Carlos J. Finlay." Home: Apartado 1710, Habana, Cuba. Address: Room 5500, 49 W. 49th St., New York, N.Y. Died Dec. 27, 1946.

CRAWFORD, William Henry, educator; b. Wilton Center, Ill., Oct. 6, 1855; s. John and Lucy Jane C.; A.B., Northwestern U., 1884, A.M., 1887; B.D., Garrett Bibl. Inst., Evanston, Ill., 1884; D.D., Northwestern, 1893; LL.D., Dickinson, 1902, Northwestern, 1912, Colorado, 1917, Muhlenburg, 1918, U. of Pittsburgh, 1918, Allegheny, 1920; m. Jennie M. Foote, July 24, 1884; children—John Raymond (dec.), Lucy Pearl (dec.). Ordained M.E. ministry, 1884; pastor Ravenswood, Chicago, 1884-86, Fulton St. Church, Chicago, 1886-89; prof. hist. theology, Gammon Theol. Seminary, 1889-93; pres. Allegheny Coll., 1893-1920, now emeritus. Nat. War Work Council sec. of Y.M.C.A., World War I, in France Dec. 1917-May 1918. One of the judges to select names for Hall of Fame; trustee Carnegie Foundn. for the Advancement of Teaching. Mem. Fedn. for Social Service, Am. Hist. Assn., Phi Beta Kappa, Phi Kappa Psi. Mason (33°). Author: Life of Savonarola, 1906; The Church and the Slum, 1908; Thoburn and India, 1909. Editor: The American College, 1915. Home: Meadville, Pa. Died March 6, 1944.

CRAWLEY, David Ephraim, Dem. nat. committeeman; b. Center, Miss., Feb. 11, 1886; s. Dr. James T. and Lucy (Dickin) C.; LL.B., U. of Miss., 1911; m. Emma Newell, Oct. 13, 1917; children—David Ephraim, Emma Shirley. Admitted to Miss. bar, 1911, and since practiced law, Kosciusko, Miss.; dist. atty., 1920-32; state senator, 1916-20 and 1940-44. Nat. Dem. exec. committeeman since 1944. Served as capt., 334th F.A., U.S. Army, World War I. Mem. Miss. State Bar Assn. (pres. 1937), Am. Legion (dept. comdr. Miss. 1943-44), Kosciusko Chamber of Commerce. Mason (Shriner). Home: 118 Brantley St. Office: Crawley Bldg., Kosciusko, Miss. Died Nov. 29, 1946.

CREAGER, John Oscar (krē'gẽr), educator; b. South Whitley, Ind., Sept. 3, 1872; s. John Reuben and Julia Anne (Banfil) C.; Ohio State U., 1893-94; Lebanon U., 1894-96; B.A., Yale, 1897, M.A., 1809; Harvard, 1899-1900; grad. student Stanford, summer, 1922; Ph.D., New York U., 1925; m. Leoti Fudge, of Eaton, O., Dec. 17, 1899; 1 son, Joe Tyler (dec.). Pres. Lebanon U., 1900-07; traveled in Europe, studying systems of training of teachers, 1907-08; head Dept. of English, Univ. Sch. for Boys, Cleveland, 1908-10; prin. State Normal Sch, Wyo., and prof. edn., 1910-17, dean Coll. of Edn., 1913-17, U. of Wyo.; commr. of edn. for Wyo., 1917-19; pres. Northern Ariz. Normal Sch., Flagstaff, 1919-20; dir. Sch. of Edn., U. of Ariz., 1920, dean Coll. of Edn. and dir. summer sessions, 1922-26; prof. of Coll. edn. New York U., 1926-27; dean Coll. of Edn., U. of Ark., 1927-29; prof. of coll. and univ. edn., New York U., since 1929. Spl. instr. Stanford, summer, 1922, U. of Hawaii, summer, 1933. Was pres. Wyo. State Bd. Died Jan. 5, 1943.

CREAL, Edward Wester (krēl), congressman; b. LaRue County, Ky., Nov. 20, 1883; s. Edward Calvin and Ruth Jennie (Bryant) C.; student Southern Normal Sch., Bowling Green, Ky., East Lynn Coll., Buffalo, Ky.; B.S. and LL.B., Centre Coll., Danville, Ky.; m. Alice Beatrice Crady, Aug. 14, 1909; children—Dolph Edward, James Crady. Admitted to Ky. bar and practiced in Hodgenville; co. supt. schs., 1910-18; co. atty., 1918-28; dist. atty., 1929-36; elected to 74th Congress, Nov. 5, 1935, 4th Ky. Dist., to fill vacancy caused by death of C. R. Carden; re-elected to 75th to 78th Congresses (1937-45), same dist.; mem. Judiciary Com.; owner Herald News, weekly newspaper, since 1920. Mem. State Dem. Com., 15 yrs. Mem. Ky. State Bar Assn., Ky. State Press Assn., Commonwealth Attys. Assn. of Ky. (ex-pres.). Baptist. Mason. Home: Hodgenville, Ky. Died Oct. 13, 1943.

CREE, Arch(ibald) C(unningham), denominational exec., clergyman; b. Innerleithen, Peebleshire, Scotland, Mar. 9, 1872; s. Archibald and Agnes (Walker) C.; came to U.S., 1888; M.A., Wake Forest Coll., 1898; Th.M., Southern Bapt. Theol. Sem., Louisville, Ky., 1900, Th.D., 1905; LL.D., Mercer U., Macon, Ga., 1920; m. Virginia Carroll, Oct. 15, 1901; children—Mary Carroll (Mrs. J. M. McLaughlin), Virginia Carroll (Mrs. J. M. Snyder), Agnes Walker (Mrs. Larry Rogers). Ordained ministry of Missionary Baptist Ch., 1894; pastor, Gaffney, S.C., 1900-03, Louisville, Ky., 1903-05, Nashville, Tenn., 1905-08, Moultrie, Ga., 1909-12; enlistment sec. Home Missionary Bd. Southern Bapt. Conv., 1912-15; exec. sec. of Exec. Bd. Ga. Bapt. Conv., 1915-30; exec. sec.-treas. Home Mission Bd., Southern Bapt. Conv., 1928-29; pastor First Bapt. Ch., Salisbury, N.C., 1930-41. Vice-pres. Southern Baptist Conv., 1931, N.C. Bapt. Convention, 1932-34. Trustee Sunday Sch. Bd., Nashville, Tenn., Bapt. Bible Inst., New Orleans, La.; trustee Bd. Ministerial Relief and Annuities, Dallas, Tex.; southern pres. The British-American Fraternal. State dir. in securing over $10,000,000 subscriptions in Ga. for the Southern Bapt. $75,000,000 campaign in 1919. Treas. Christian Index (weekly). Democrat. Mason. Rotarian. Toured 25 foreign lands. Address: 427 Lincolnton Rd., Salisbury, N.C. Died Dec. 15, 1944.

CREECH, Harris (krēch), banker; b. Cleveland, O., Feb. 26, 1874; s. James and Clarabelle (Simmons) C.; ed. high sch.; m. Carlotta Pope, 1903; children—Florence, James Pope. Began with Garfield Savings Bank, Cleveland, 1892; asst. sec. and treas. same, 1898-1901, sec. and treas., 1901-10, v.p., 1910-16, pres., 1916-23; pres. The Cleveland Trust Co. since Apr. 9, 1923; dir. Sherwin Williams Co., Ajax Mfg. Co., Ohio Bell Telephone Co., Firestone Tire & Rubber Co., The Cleveland-Cliffs Iron Co. Trustee Cleveland Community Funds. Republican. Clubs: Union, Mayfield, Kirtland, Rowfant. Home: 2572 Stratford Rd., Cleveland Heights, O. Office: Cleveland Trust Co., Cleveland, O. Died May 18, 1941.

CREEL, Enrique C., diplomat; b. Chihuahua, Mex., Aug. 31, 1854; s. Reuben W. (of Ky.) and Paz (Cuilty) C.; self ed.; m. Angela Terrazas, Sept. 12, 1880. Mcht., sch. teacher, newspaper man, tanner, farmer, miner, banker, ry. official, financier; mem. city council, Chihuahua, 1876-80; mem. Mex. Nat. Congress, 1898-1904; speaker of House, 1892; gov. State of Chihuahua, 1903-06; A.E. and M.P. of Mex. to U.S., since 1906. Pres. Banco Central Mexicano; v.p. Chihuahua & Pacific R.R., Kansas City, Mex. & Orient R.R.; dir. several banking and ins. cos.; interested in other mfg. enterprises in Mex. Home: Chihuahua, Mex. Address: Mexican Embassy, Washington. Died Aug. 7, 1931.

CREIGHTON, Frank W(hittington), bishop; b. Phila., Pa., Dec. 3, 1879; s. Thomas and Elizabeth (Whittington) C.; ed. Northeast Manual Training High Sch. and Brown's Coll. Prep. Sch., Phila.; S.T.B., Phila. Div. Sch., 1915, S.T.D., 1926; D.D., Kenyon Coll., 1940; m. Maude R. Hawk, Aug. 15, 1903; children—Thomas Hawk, William Forman. Engaged in business, Phila., 1898 to 1912; lay reader, St. Bartholomew's Ch., Wissinoming, Phila., 1906-13; vicar Ch. of the Redeemer, Andalusia, Pa., 1913-16; deacon, 1914, priest, 1915, P.E. Ch.; examining chaplain, rector, St. Andrew's Parish, Albany, N.Y., 1916-23; rector, St. Ann's Ch., Brooklyn, N.Y., 1923-26; missionary bishop of Mexico, 1926-33; exec. sec. Dept. of Domestic Missions, P.E. Ch., 1930-33; suffragan bishop of Long Island and archdeacon of Queens and Nassau, 1933-37; bishop coadjutor of Michigan, 1937-39, bishop of Mich. since 1940. Mem. Patriotic Order Sons of America. Democrat. Clubs: Detroit, Economic Club of Detroit. Author of "Our Heritage," "Mexico," Christianity Is Life. Contbr. to various mags. Home: 4000 Cathedral Av., Washington. Died Dec 23, 1948

CRELLIN, Edward Webster, civil engr.; b. Carroll County, O., May 15, 1863; s. Edward Mortimer and Sarah Jane (Simmons) C.; C.E., State U. of Ia., 1890; m. Amy Hutchison, June 10, 1896. Founder Des Moines Bridge and Iron Works (later named Pittsburgh, Des Moines Co.), being pres. of both cos. until retirement, 1921. Mem. Am. Soc. C. E., A.A.A.S., Calif. Inst. Assos., Sigma Xi, Tau Beta Pi. Republican. Methodist. Address: 1550 San Pasqual St., Pasadena 4, Calif. Died May 16, 1948.

CRENIER, Henri (krĕn-nyā), sculptor; b. Paris, France, Dec. 17, 1873; s. Henri August and Josephine (Bouteillé) C.; Ecole des Beaux Arts, Paris; pupil of Falquiere; m. Lucy Adler, Sept. 11, 1899; children—Pierre, Camille. Came to U.S., 1902, naturalized citizen, 1911; has specialized in portrait busts and statues; principal works, pediments and caryatids on City Hall, San Francisco, Calif.; "Spirit of the Garden," home of Charles M. Schwab, Loretto, Pa.; "Boy and Turtle," Met. Mus., New York, and Mt. Vernon Pl., Baltimore; "Playmates," bronze fountain for Charles M. Schwab; Fenimore Cooper memorial, Scarsdale, N.Y.; four groups "Ocean, Earth, Fire, Wind," in marble, also "Achievement," gilded bronze fountain, for Alfred I. du Pont; group fountain, in marble, "Water Lilies," for W. T. Pratt; Christopher Columbus memorial, bronze bas-relief, Mamaroneck, N.Y.; cast stone bas-relief, for Oak Hill (W.Va.) Post Office. "The Mail Rider." Served as pvt. French Army, 1894. Mem. Nat. Sculpture Soc., Archtl. League, New York. Catholic. Home: 350 E. 54th St., New York, N.Y. Died Oct. 1, 1948.

CRESAP, Mark Winfield (krĕs'ăp), clothing mfr. b. Pleasant Grove, Minn., Nov. 15, 1872; s. Charles W. and Angie (Wood) C.; student Northwestern U., 1898; m. Jessie Cope, June 12, 1900; children—Helen Ames (Mrs. Samuel N. Comly), Mark Winfield. With editorial dept. Chicago Record-Herald, 1899-1903; with Hart, Schaffner & Marx, wholesale clothiers, since 1903, now chmn. of the bd.; chmn. Men's Clothing Code Authority, 1933-35; dir. First Nat. Bank, United Air Lines. Mem. War Com. Union League Club, 1917-18. Pres. Clothing Mfrs. Assn. of U.S.; v.p. bd. trustees Northwestern U., 1930-35, pres. of bd., 1935-37. Awarded Alumni medal, Northwestern U. Mem. S.A.R., Delta Mu Delta, Delta Upsilon (awarded shield for service to Alma Mater), Delta Sigma Pi. Republican. Clubs: Chicago, Mid-Day, Commercial (pres. 1934-35), Caxton, Tavern, Indian Hill; 100,000 Mile (United Air Lines). Passenger on first flight of Pan-Am. Clipper, New York to Marseilles and return, June 28-July 4, 1939. Home: Woodley Rd., Winnetka, Ill. Office: 36 S. Franklin St., Chicago, Ill. Died May 30, 1942.

CRESSWELL, Robert, newspaper pub.; b. Phila., Pa., May 29, 1897; s. Charles Thomson and Bell C. (Catherwood) C.; grad. St. Paul's Sch., Concord, N.H., 1915; A.B., Princeton U., 1919; m. Catharine R. Henriques, May 28, 1921 (divorced); children—Robert, Henry. With N.Y. Herald Trib., 1922-40, successively as reporter, copy reader, circulation mgr., treas. and dir.; pres., dir. and pub. Phila. Evening Public Ledger Jan. 1, 1941-Jan. 5, 1942; with Office of Strategic Services, Washington, D.C., to Mar. 9, 1942. Commd. lt. col. Army of U.S., Mar. 29, 1943. Trustee St. John's Guild. Republican. Episcopalian. Clubs: Century Assn. University (N.Y. City); Philadelphia, Sunnybrook Golf, Franklin Inn (Phila.); Ivy (Princeton). Home: 15 W. Bell's Mills Road, Philadelphia, Pa. Died Sept. 1943.

CRET, Paul Philippe (krā), architect; b. Lyons, France, Oct. 23, 1876; s. Paul Adolphe and Anna Caroline (Durand) C.; ed. Lycée of Bourg, École des Beaux Arts, Lyons, École des Beaux Arts, Paris; architecte diplômé du gouvernement français, 1903; Sc.D., U. of Pa., 1913; M.A., Brown, 1929; Dr. Arts, Harvard University, 1940; m. Marguerite Lahalle, Aug. 1905. Prof. design, U. of Pa., 1903-37, prof. emeritus since 1937, now associate trustee. Paris prize, 1896, Rougevin prize, 1901, and grand medal of emulation, École des Beaux Arts, Paris, 1901; gold medal, Salon des Champs Elysées, Paris, 1903; medal of honor, Architectural League of New York; Phila. award (Bok prize), 1931; distinguished award Washington Soc. Architects; gold medalist of A.I.A.; gold medal Pan.-Am. Expn.; grand prize, Paris, 1937; Prize of Honor, 5th Pan-Am. Congress of Architects, Montevideo, 1940; Award of Merit, U. of Pa. Alumni Soc., 1940. Architect (with Albert Kelsey) of Pan-American Union (Washington, D.C.); Valley Forge memorial arch, Rittenhouse Square, Phila.; Indianapolis Pub. Library (with Zantzinger, Borie and Medary); Detroit Inst. of Arts (with Zantzinger, Borie and Medary); Hartford County Bldg. (with Smith & Bassette, Hartford, Conn.); Folger Shakespeare Library (Washington, D.C.); Hall of Science at Century of Progress Expn., Chicago, 1933; Federal Reserve Bank and Delaware River Bridge, Phila.; war memorials at Varennes, Fismes (France); memorials at Chateau Thierry, Bony, Waereghem and Gibraltar for Am. Battle Monuments Commn.; Central Heating Plant, Washington; new bldgs. U. of Tex.; Federal Res. Bd. Bldg., Washington; Calvert St. Bridge; new buildings U.S. Military Academy; new buildings U.S. Naval Academy; designer for Budd Co. streamlined trains since 1933; Philadelphia Zoo, new bldgs.; concealment projects for U.S. Army; Naval Medical center, Bethesda. Nat. Academician; mem. Philos. Soc. N.Y. Acad. Arts and Letters, pres. Art Jury, City of Phila.; mem. Pa. State Art Commn., Nat. Commn. of Fine Arts. Mem. Société architectes diplômés, Soc. Beaux Arts Architects, T-Square Club (hon. pres.); fellow A.I.A.; mem. Phi Beta Kappa, Sigma Xi; hon. corr. mem. Royal Inst. Brit. Architects; hon. mem. Acad. d'Architecture Lyon, Mich. Soc. Architects. Trustee Phila. Museum. Consultant bd. of design N.Y. Expn., 1939; consultant U.S. Navy Dept. since 1938. Consultant U.S. Engineers, and Pub. Roads Adminstrn. Served in French Army and with 1st Div., A.E.F., 1914-19. Decorated Officer Legion of Honor, and Croix de Guerre (France). Mem. Archtl. Commn., Chicago World's Fair Centennial Celebration 1933; consulting architect Am. Battle Monuments Commn., also Brown Univ. and univs. of Texas, Pennsylvania and Wisconsin. Clubs: Racquet, Art Alliance (Phila.); Century (N.Y.); Cosmos (Washington, D.C.). Home: 516 Woodland Terrace. Office: 1518 Walnut St., Philadelphia 2, Pa. Died Sep. 8, 1945.

CRILE, George (Washington), surgeon; b. Chili, O., Nov. 11, 1864; s. Michael and Margaret (Dietz) C.; B.S., Ohio Northern U., 1885, A.M., 1888; M.D., Wooster U. (now Western Reserve U.), 1887, A.M., 1894; student Vienna, 1893, London, 1895, Paris, 1897; hon. Ph.D., Hiram Coll., 1901; LL.D., Wooster U., 1916; M.Ch., U. of Dublin, 1925; LL.D., U. of Glasgow, 1928; Doctor honoris causa, U. of Guatemala, 1939; m. Grace McBride, Feb. 7, 1900; children—Margaret (Mrs. Hiram Garretson), Elisabeth (Mrs. J. A. Crisler, Jr.), George Jr., Robert. Lecturer and demonstrator histology, 1889-90, prof. physiology, 1890-93, prof. principles and practice of surgery, 1893-1900, Wooster U.; prof. clin. surgery, 1900-11, surgery, 1911-24, Western Reserve U.; visiting surgeon Lakeside Hosp., 1911-24; one of founders Cleveland Clinic Foundation, now dir. research. Brigade surgeon vols., maj., Cuba and Porto Rico, 1898; maj. Med. O.R.C. and professional dir. of U.S. Army Base Hosp. No. 4, Lakeside Unit (B.E.F., No. 9), in service in France, May 1917-May 1918; sr. consultant in surg. research, May 1918-Jan. 1919; lt. col., June 1918, col., Nov. 1918, brig. gen. Med. O.R.C., 1921; brig. general Auxiliary R.C., since 1929. Awarded D.S.M. (U.S.), 1919; hon. mem. Military Div., 3rd Class, Companion of Bath (British), 1919; Chevalier Legion of Honor (French), 1922. Alvarenga prize, Coll. Phys., Phila., 1901; Cartwright prize, Columbia, 1897 and 1903; Senn prize, A.M.A., 1898; Am. med. medal for service to humanity, 1914; Nat. Inst. Soc. Sciences medal, 1917; Trimble Lecture medal, 1921; 3d laureate of Lannelongue Foundation (Lannelongue Internat. medal of surgery presented by Société Internationale de Chirurgie de Paris), 1925; Cleveland medal for public service, 1931; Distinguished Service Gold Key, American Congress of Physical Therapy, 1940. Fellow American Assn. Anatomists, A.A.A.S., American Surgical Association (president 1923), Am. Coll. Surgeons (pres. 1916; mem. bd. regents since 1913; chmn. bd. regents 1917-39), A.M.A., Am. Physiol. Soc., Am. Assn. Obstetricians, Gynecologists and Abdominal Surgeons, Southern Surg. Assn., Southern Med. Assn., Am. Philos. Soc.; mem. Assn. Am. Pathologists and Bacteriologists, Am. Soc. Clin.

Surgery, Soc. Exptl. Biology and Medicine, Nat. Inst. Social Sciences, National Research Council, Assn. Study Internal Secretions, Am. Heart Assn., Am. Med. Editors' Assn., Ohio State Medical Assn., Cleveland Acad. Medicine, Cleveland Med. Library Assn.; Interstate Post Grad. Med. Assn. of N. America (chmn. program com.); hon. or corr. fellow or mem. many Am. and European societies. Clubs: Union (Cleveland); 100,000 Mile Club. Author: Surgical Shock, 1897; Surgery of Respiratory System, 1899; Certain Problems Relating to Surgical Operations, 1901; On the Blood Pressure in Surgery, 1903; Hemorrhage and Transfusion, 1909; Anemia and Resuscitation, 1914; Anoci-Association (with Lower), 1914, 2d edit., title, Surgical Shock and the Shockless Operation through Anoci-Association, 1920; Origin and Nature of the Emotions, 1915; A Mechanistic View of War and Peace, 1915; Man, An Adaptive Mechanism, 1916; The Kinetic Drive, 1916; The Fallacy of the German State Philosophy, 1918; A Physical Interpretation of Shock Exhaustion and Restoration, 1921; The Thyroid Gland (with others), 1922; Notes on Military Surgery, 1924; A Bipolar Theory of Living Processes, 1926; Problems in Surgery, 1928; Diagnosis and Treatment of Diseases of the Thyroid Gland (with others), 1932; Diseases Peculiar to Civilized Man, 1934; The Phenomena of Life, 1936; The Surgical Treatment of Hypertension, 1938; Intelligence Power and Personality, 1941. Home: 2620 Derbyshire Rd. Office: Cleveland Clinic, Euclid Av. at E. 93d St., Cleveland, O. Died Jan. 7, 1943.

CRIMONT, Joseph Raphael (krī'mŏnt), bishop; b. Ferrières, nr. Amiens, France, Feb. 2, 1858; s. Joseph and Alexandrine (Niquet) C.; student Coll. La Providence, Amiens, 1869-75; Coll. of St. Louis, St. Helier, Jersey Island, 1883-86; D.D., Woodstock (Md.) College, 1890; Ph.D., Seattle College, 1942. Came to U.S., 1886, became naturalized citizen, 1893. Ordained R.C. priest, 1888; missionary Crow Reservation, Mont., 1890-93, in Alaska, 1894-97; superior Holy Cross Mission, Yukon River, 1897; pres. Gonzaga Coll., Spokane, Wash., 1901-04; prefect apostolic of Cath. Alaska Missions, 1904-17; bishop since 1917. Mem. Catholic Soc. of Alaska (pres.). Democrat. Mem. K.C. Address: Juneau, Alaska. Died May 20, 1945; buried in Shrine of St. Therese, Juneau, Alaska.

CRISSEY, Forrest (krĭs'sē), writer; b. Stockton, Chautauqua County, N.Y., June 1, 1864; s. Merrill and Eunice (Tracy) C.; ed. pub. schs., N.Y. and Ill.; m. Kate D. Shurtleff, July 14, 1887; 1 son, Paul L. Began as country corr. Chicago Times, at Marengo; first fiction story, written at age of 20, accepted by Ballou's Monthly, Boston; went to Geneva, Ill., on the Patrol (a county newspaper), to Chicago, 1893, and was connected with the Chicago Times and other newspapers; reporter Chicago Evening Post, 1895, special editorial and feature writer, same, 1896-1900; became special editorial rep. Phila. Saturday Evening Post, 1900, and almost ever since identified with that publ. Author: The Country Boy, 1897; (poems) In Thompson's Woods, 1901; Tattlings of a Retired Politician, 1904; Hand-Book of Modern Business Correspondence, 1908; Where Opportunity Knocks Twice, 1914; The Story of Foods, 1917; Romance of Moving Money, 1934; Progress in the Probate Court, 1935; Life and Times of Senator Theodore E. Burton, 1936; Biography of Alexander Legge, 1936; Montgomery Ward; Founder of Mail Order Selling—the Man and the System, 1939. Contbr. to Country Gentleman, Harper's, etc.; specialist in institutional biographies. Home: Geneva, Kane County, Ill Died Nov. 5, 1943.

CRISSINGER, Daniel Richard, gov. Fed. Res. Bd.; b. Tully Twp., Marion County, O., Dec. 10, 1860; s. John and Margaret (Ganshorn) C.; B.S., Buchtel Coll., Akron, O., 1885, LL.B., U. of Cincinnati, 1886; m. Ella Frances Scranton, 1888. Began law practice at Marion, O., 1886; served as pros. atty., Marion, 2 terms; city solicitor, 3 terms; gen. counsel Marion Steam Shovel Co., 22 yrs.; owner of several farms in Marion County; had supervision of City Nat. Bank of Marion, name changed to Nat. City Bank & Trust Co., became pres., Sept. 5, 1920. Comptroller of Currency, 1921-23; gov. Fed. Res. Bd., May 1, 1923-Sept. 15, 1927 (resigned); chmn. exec. com. The F. H. Smith Co., Washington, since 1927. Republican. Mason (K.T., Shriner), Elk. Club: Metropolitan (Washington). Home: 1801 16th St. N.W. Office: 815 15th St. N.W., Washington. Died July 12, 1942.

CRIST, Harris McCabe, editor; b. Sparlan, Ill., Aug. 25, 1874; s. Phillip A. and Mary (Fowler) C.; pub. sch. edn.; m. Addie Slack, Apr. 28, 1911. Began as page in U.S. Senate; Washington corr. Brooklyn Eagle, 1905-10, asst. mng. editor and news editor, 1911-16, mng. editor since 1916, v.p. since 1932; trustee Fulton Savings Bank; mem. adv. bd. Mfrs. Trust Co. Home: Vineyard Haven, Mass. Office: Brooklyn Eagle, Brooklyn, N.Y. Died Jan. 19, 1946.

CRIST, Raymond Fowler (krĭst), b. El Paso, Ill., Aug. 7, 1871; s. Philip Abright and Mary Alice (Fowler) C.; student Columbian (now George Washington) U., 1889-91; D.D.S., Howard U., 1897; LL.B., Washington Coll. of Law, 1917; m. Genevieve Wetmore, May 14, 1896; children— Marian Brownell (Mrs. Edward G. Lippitt), Ernest Wetmore (dec.), Fowler Raymond (dec.), Genevieve Rider (Mrs. Harry A. Bolles), Hazel Harris (Mrs. Samuel Carter Barnett), Raymond Fowler (lt. col. U.S.M.C.). Messenger boy, U.S. Govt. Printing Office, 1884; promoted to clk., 1895; cashier, Dept. of Commerce and Labor, 1903-04; pvt. sec. to Sec. Commerce and Labor, 1904-05; commercial agt. to Japan, China and Africa, 1905-07; asst. chief, Div. of Naturalization, 1907-13; dep. commr. of naturalization, Dept. of Labor, 1913-19, dir. of citizenship, 1919-22, commr. of naturalization, 1923-33, exec. official in charge of laws governing naturalization of aliens, of counsel for U.S. in State and Federal Cts. of highest original jurisdiction and U.S. Supreme Ct., also supervisor of citizenship edn. in U.S. pub. schs.; retired Aug. 10, 1933; in law practice before U.S. Govt., 1933-42; chief of employee relations to employees in War Production Bd., 1942-43. Mem. Council of Nat. Defense, 1917-18; mem. Federal Council on Citizenship Training, 1923, sec. 1925. Pres. Bible Truth Seekers Foundation, Inc., since 1937. Author of ednl. books used in Americanization classes of U.S. pub. schs.; reports on edn. in citizenship responsibilities; Bible studies and interpretations. Methodist. Home: 3025 Newark St., Washington, D.C.* Died Aug. 5, 1944.

CRISTY, Albert Moses (krĭs'tē), judge; b. Hudson, O., Feb. 13, 1889; s. Rev. Albert Barnes and Mary Wilhelmina (Linsley) C.; A.B., Brown U., 1909; LL.B., cum laude, Harvard, 1914; m. Jessamine J. Bowman, Sept. 28, 1915; children—Carol Linsley, Jessamine Prentice, Albert Bowman, George Frederick. Teacher, Williston Sem., Easthampton, Mass., 1909-11; admitted to H.T. bar, 1914, and began practice at Honolulu; mem. Brown, Cristy & Davis, 1919-26. First dep. city atty., Honolulu, 1915-19; mem. H.T. Ho. of Rep., 1921; judge, Circuit Court 1st circuit, T.H., since 1926. Commissioner to compile R.L. of Hawaii 1935 and 1945. Mem. Bar Assn. Hawaii (sec. 1915-21), Phi Beta Kappa, Phi Gamma Delta. Republican. Conglist. Home: 2120 Kamehameha Av. Chambers: Judiciary Bldg., Honolulu, T.H. Died July 11, 1949.

CRITTENDEN, Walter Hayden, lawyer, art patron; b. Cleveland, O., Feb. 8, 1859; s. Seth Whitmore and Cornelia Goldthwaite (Bacon) C.; A.B., Amherst Coll., 1881; m. Lillian M. Haines, Nov. 4, 1897 (dec.). Admitted to N.Y. bar, and engaged in gen. practice since 1883; patron of the arts and leader in civic affairs; dir. Bucyrus-Erie Co. Trustee Brooklyn Savings Bank, Storm King School, Packer Collegiate Institute; v.p. Brooklyn Inst. of Arts & Sciences; chmn. governing comm. Brooklyn Mus.; dir. Brooklyn Children's Aid Society. Member French Legion of Honor. S.A.R., Alpha Delta Phi. Ind. Republican. Presbyterian. Clubs: Rembrandt, Storm King Golf. Home: Cornwall, N.Y. Deceased.

CROCKER, Bosworth (maiden name Mary Arnold Crocker), author; b. London, England; d. John Bosworth and Mary (Arnold) Crocker; brought to U.S. in childhood; ed. pub. and pvt. schs. and spl. student Ohio State U.; m. Henry Arnoux Childs (now dec.); children—Marion L. (Mrs. H. D. Kingsbury), Harold F. Childs, Helen L. (Mrs. John Balsam), Edith Winifred (Mrs. Oakley Wiseman); m. 2d, Ludwig Lewisohn, author, at Charleston, S.C., 1906, and at Newark, N.J., 1910 (divorced 1937; legalized pen name). Mem. Soc. Am. Dramatists, Authors' League America (charter mem.), P.E.N. Internat. Literary Assn., Poetry Society, English-Speaking Union, Shakespeare Society. Club: Town Hall. Author: The Dog, produced by Bryden Road Players, 1915; The Last Straw, prod. by Washington Square Players, 1917; Pawns of War (foreword by John Galsworthy), 1918; The Baby Carriage, prod. by Provincetown Players, 1919; Humble Folk (collection one-act plays, foreword by Ludwig Lewisohn), 1923; Heritage, four-act play selected from 57 mss. submitted by Soc. Am. Dramatists and prod. by Pasadena Community Players, 1925; Cost of a Hat, prod. Cellar Players, 1925; Reprisal, 3 act play, radio production, 1926; Iseult of The White Hands (poetic drama), 1927; Josephine, 1927; Cocotte, 1929; The Tragic Three, 1931; Harmony, 1931; Great Loves (1-act plays); radio prods. Nat. Broadcasting Co.; Child of the Waters (biblical drama), 1935; Coquine, 1937. Dramatic critic, Town Topics, 1919-24. Contbr. poems and facetious verse, lit. and dramatic criticism to jours. Engaged in editorial work for Columbia Univ. Press, 1932-33. Home: 175 Claremont Av. Address: Town Hall Club, 123 W. 43rd St., New York, N.Y. Died Apr. 8, 1946.

CROCKER, Frank Longfellow, lawyer; b. Portland, Me., May 28, 1876; s. Ira and Emily (Longfellow) C.; student Harvard, 1894-96; grad. New York Law Sch., 1898; m. Katharine Wood, Oct. 9, 1901; children—Elizabeth, Faith, Charity. With Henry D. 1905, now practicing alone. Mem. Am. Bar Assn. Hotchkiss, atty., N.Y. City, 1898-1903, Rollins & Rollins, 1903-05; became mem. firm Crocker & Wickes, Address: 247 Park Av., New York. Died June 26, 1945.

CROCKER, Templeton, scientific research; b. San Francisco, Calif., Sept. 2, 1884; s. Charles Frederick and Jennie (Easton) C.; grad. Westminster Sch., Simsbury, Conn., 1903; A.B., Yale, 1908; unmarried. Research in South Seas, Galapagos Islands, for Calif. Acad. Sciences, 1932; Solomon Islands for Bishop Museum, Honolulu, 1933, Eastern Polynesia, Pitcairn and Easter Islands for Am. Museum of Natural History, 1934-35, Lower Calif. and west coast of Gulf of Calif. for Dr. William Beebe, New York Zoölogical Society, 1936, Hawaii, Tongareva, Samoa for American Museum Natural History, 1936-37. Decorated Chevalier Legion of Honor (France). Fellow Royal Geographical Soc.; mem. Am. Museum Natural History, N.Y. Zoöl. Soc., Field Museum, Calif. Acad. Sciences, S.A.R., Native Sons of the Golden West, Soc. Mayflower Descendants. Republican. Episcopalian. Clubs: Pacific Union, Bohemian (San Francisco); The Brook (N.Y. City); St. James', Royal Automobile, Authors (London). Author: The Cruise of the Zaca, 1933. Author of libretto of opera Fay-Yen-Fah. Home: 945 Green St. Office: Shreve Bldg., San Francisco, Calif. Died Dec. 12, 1948.

CROCKER, Theodore D., business exec.; b. Elyria, O., Oct. 8, 1878; s. Otis Doane and Dora R. (Hartshorn) C.; E.E., Ohio State U., 1904; m. Hilda Laurier Weber, Sept. 14, 1907; children—Jean Laurier (Mrs. Emerson Gissel Wulling), Thomas Doane. Employed by Lincoln Electric Co., Cleveland, O., 1898-1900; power plant operation, constrn. and sales, Milwaukee (Wis.) Electric Railway and Light Co., 1904-12; asst. to v.p. and gen. mgr. Northern States Power Co., Minneapolis, Minn., 1912-18, asst. v.p. in charge operation, 1918-23, asst. gen. mgr., 1923-31, v.p. and dir. 1931-42, v.p. and gen. mgr., 1942-43, pres. and dir. since 1943. Trustee William Hood Dunwoody Indsl. Inst., Minneapolis, Minn. Mem. Am. Inst. E.E., Minn. Resources Commn., Sigma Alpha Epsilon. Clubs: Engineers, Minneapolis, Minnesota. Home: 4735 Fremont Av. S., Minneapolis 9. Office: 15 S. 5th St., Minneapolis 2, Minn. Died June 29, 1947.

CROCKER, Walter James, veterinarian; b. Ada, Minn., Nov. 20, 1885; s. Walter Joseph and Helen (Wiley) C.; B.S.A., Utah Agrl. Coll., 1909; V.M.D., U. of Pa., 1911; m. Rosa Binder, Feb. 6, 1915; 1 dau., Helen Marie. Lecturer and instr., Vet. Sch., U. of Pa., 1911-13, asst. prof. vet. pathology, 1913-14, asst. prof. vet. pathology and bacteriology, 1914-16, prof. vet. pathology since Apr. 1916; asst. dir. Wistar Inst. of Anatomy and Biology, U. of Pa., 1920-21; dist. mgr. J. Lee Nicholson Inst., 1921; gen. mgr. Globe Labs., 1922-24; dir. Globe Labs., Globe Livestock Co. and Cleo Ranch Co., 1923-25; clin. pathologist, Phila. Gen. Hosp., since 1925. Mem. Am., Pa. State and Keystone vet. med. socs., Phila. Pathol. Soc., Internat. Assn. Vet. Med. Museums, Dallas and Fort Worth Vet. Med. Assn., Tex. Vet. Med. Assn., Pa. Fish and Game Protect. Assn., Sigma Xi, Sigma Alpha, Alpha Psi. Republican. Episcopalian. Mason (33°, Shriner). Clubs: University, Norristown Rifle. Author: Veterinary Post Mortem Technic, 1917. Translator: Mastitis of the Cow and Its Treatment (by Sven Wall), 1918. Contbr. numerous scientific articles on hematology; hemography in diagnosis, prognosis and treatment; hemography in the diagnosis of appendicitis; nonspecific immune-transfusion in treatment septicemia and typhoid fever. Home: 5909 Christian St., West Philadelphia, Pa. Deceased.

CROFT, Harry William, refractories; b. Allegheny City, Pa., Dec. 12, 1865; s. William and Abigail Jane (Goehring) C.; ed. pub. schs., Allegheny City, and Iron City Coll., Pittsburgh; m. Mary Augusta Graham, Dec. 14, 1892; children— Florence Graham (Mrs. William F. Bickel), Richard Graham, Winifred Graham (Mrs. William S. Wilson), Eleanor Graham (Mrs. J. Henry O'Neill). With Livingston & Co., Allegheny, 1881-87; began with Harbison-Walker Refractories Co., mfrs., 1887, later becoming chmn. bd.; dir., General Ry. Signal Co. Republican. Presbyterian. Mason. Clubs: Oakmont Country (Pittsburgh); Round Hill Country (Greenwich, Conn.); Blind Brook (Port Chester, N.Y.). Home: Clapboard Ridge Rd. Office: Smith Bldg., Greenwich, Conn. Died Feb. 25, 1947.

CROISSANT, De Witt Clinton (krol-sänt'), prof. English; b. Evanston, Ill., Aug. 23, 1876; s. John Dempster and Sarah (Sands) C.; A.B., Princeton, 1899, Charles Scribner fellow in English, 1902-03, Ph.D., 1911; student U. of Chicago, 1899-1901, Munich, 1903-04; m. Elizabeth Troutman, June 16, 1903; 1 dau., Dorothy. Inst. in English, U. of Colo., 1901-02; same, George Washington, U., 1905-06; asst. prof., 1906-10; asst. prof. English, 1911-13, asso. prof., 1913-15, dir. univ. extension, 1913-14, U. of Kan.; prof. Summer Sch. U. of Okla. since 1912; gen. field agent, Simplified Spelling Bd., 1915-16; prof. English, George Washington U., since Sept. 1916; visiting prof. English, Mass. Inst. Tech., 1919-20. Special investigator, U.S. Bur. Efficiency, 1918-19. Mem. Simplified Spelling Bd. Pres. Community Drama Guild, Washington, 1928-31. Mem. Modern Lang. Assn. America, S.A.R., Sigma Chi, Am. Assn. of Univ. Profs. Presbyn. Clubs: Federal Schoolmen's, Cosmos, Arts (Washington). Author: Studies in the Work of Colley Cibber, 1913. Home: 1717 Q St. N.W., Washington, D.C. Died Aug. 15, 1941.

CROLL, Morris William, univ. prof.; b. Gettysburg, Pa., Apr. 16, 1872; s. Luther Henry and Jane Crawford (Smyth) C.; A.B., Gettysburg (Pa.) Coll., 1889, hon. Litt.D., 1932; A.B., Harvard, 1894, A.M., 1895; Ph.D., U. of Pa., 1901; unmarried. Teacher, University Sch., Cleveland, O., 1895-99; asso. editor Lippincott Worcester Dictionary, 1901-05; instr. in English Literature, Princeton U., 1905-06, asst. prof., 1906-18, asso. prof., 1918-23, prof., 1923-32, prof. emeritus since 1932. Mem. Modern Lang. Assn. America, Am. Acad. Arts and Sciences. Democrat. Lutheran. Club: Princeton (New York). Editor: Lyly's Euphues (with H. L. Clemons), 1916. Contbr. articles on English prose style of 16th and 17th Centuries to professional jours. Home: 40 Bayard Lane, Princeton, N.J. Died Aug. 17, 1947.

CROMWELL, William Nelson, lawyer; b. 1854; s. Col. John Nelson C.; LL.B., Columbia, 1876; LL.D., Kenyon Coll., 1904. Now sr. of law firm of Sullivan & Cromwell; specialty is internat. and corp. law; organized, 1899, Nat. Tube Co., Am. Cotton Oil Co., since then many other corps.; apptd. assignee and reorganized Decker, Howell & Co., 1890, N.P.R.R. Co., and later many others, and put all on a paying basis; was one of organizers U.S. Steel Corp.; gen. counsel New Panama Canal Co. of France and carried through the transfer of the Panama Canal to the U.S.; reorganized Brazil ry. system abroad during World War I. Officer or dir. many corps. Awarded Grand Croix de la Légion d'Honneur (France), Comdr. Grand Cross Order of the Crown (Rumania). Home: 12 W. 49th St. Office: 48 Wall St., New York, N.Y. Died July 19, 1948.

CROOKS, Ezra Breckenridge, univ. prof.; b. Clinton, Ky., Oct. 6, 1874; s. James David and Mary Elizabeth (Bugg) C.; B.A., Central Coll., Fayette, Mo., 1899; M.A., Vanderbilt, 1901; S.T.B., Harvard, 1908, M.A., 1909, Ph.D., 1910; m. Mary Elizabeth Groves, Sept. 10, 1902 (died 1906); m. 2d, Mary Lasher, Sept. 8, 1909; children—Anna Elizabeth, James Lasher. Editor St. Louis Christian Advocate, 1901; ednl. missionary M.E. Ch., S., Brazil, 1902-06; asst. in depts. philosophy and history, Harvard, 1910-11; asst. prof. philosophy, Northwestern U., 1911-13; head dept. philosophy and edn., Randolph-Macon Woman's Coll., Lynchburg, Va., 1913-22; head dept. philosophy and social sciences, U. of Del., since 1922; also editor Delaware Notes (yearly publ. by members of faculty U. of Del.). Dir. publicity U.S. Food Adminstrn. in Va., 1917-18; went to France under Y.M.C.A., with Portuguese Troops, British 5th Army. Decorated officer Mil. Order of Christ (Portuguese); two citations from the field. Fellow A.A.A.S.; mem. Am. Philos. Assn., Am. Sociol. Soc., Eastern Sociol. Soc., N.E.A., Am. Assn. Univ. Profs., Sigma Alpha Epsilon, Phi Kappa Phi. Democrat. Methodist. Clubs: University (Newark); Lions (Lynchburg); Harvard (Wilmington); Torch of Delaware. Home: Newark, Del. Died March 8, 1941.

CROOK, William McKissack, lawyer; b. Kedron, Tenn., Dec. 24, 1875; s. Wiley Jarmon and Jennie Thompson (Parham) C.; student Vanderbilt U., 1895-96; LL.B., Columbian (now George Washington) U., 1897; m. Jennie Maude Helsel, June 9, 1897; children—Theo Helsel, Philip Godbey, William McKissack, Jr., also 3 who died in infancy. Practiced at Beaumont, Tex., from 1899. Legal adviser to local Exemption Bd., World War I; chmn. Bd. of Appeal 5, Tex. Selective Service, World War II. Mem. American Bar Assn., Texas Bar Assn. (pres. 1928-29), Jefferson County Bar Assn., Am. Law Inst. (life), Am. Maritime Law Assn., Nat. Conf. Commrs. on Uniform State Laws (chmn. Tex. bd. since 1909), Jefferson County Judicial Commn., Bars of Supreme Courts of U.S. and Texas and the Treasury Dept. of U.S. V.p., dir. Tex. Law Rev., Beaumont Iron Works Co., Sabine-Neches Automobile Assn. Democrat (independent in nat. politics). Methodist. Mason (32°, K.T., Shriner). Club: Beaumont Country. Registered patent atty. Now retired. Home: 3715 Tangley St., Houston, Tex. Died April 19, 1949.

CROPPER, Walter V., clergyman, educator; b. Lewis County, Ky., May 11, 1886; s. William Henry and Laura Ann (Adams) C.; A.B., Ky. Wesleyan Coll., Winchester, 1909; B.D., Vanderbilt, 1915; D.D., Ky. Wesleyan Coll., 1929; m. Angela Gray McConnell, Nov. 24, 1915; children—Walter Vincent, Myra Gray, Alice Katharine; m. 2d, Mary Elizabeth Chinn, Apr. 24, 1933; 1 dau., Ann Petry. Ordained ministry M.E. Ch., S., 1912; pastor successively Hazard, Campbellsburg and Middlesboro, Ky., 1909-18; mission. sec. Ky. Conf. M.E. Ch., S., 1918-20; pastor Shelbyville and Ft. Thomas, Ky., 1920-28; acting pres. Ky. Wesleyan Coll., 1928, sec. of edn., 1929; pastor Centenary M.E. Church, Shelbyville, 1930-34; presiding elder Shelbyville Dist. to 1934, Lexington Dist., M.E. Ch., S., 1934-37; pastor Frankfort, Ky., 1937-38. Vice-pres. Bd. of Ch. Extension, M.E. Ch., S., 1934-38; sec. Bd. of Ch. Extension, Meth. Ch., since 1938; exec. sec. Div. Home Missions and Ch. Extension, Bd. of Missions and Ch. Extension of Methodist Ch. since Jan. 1, 1943; pres. Ky. Rural Ch. Council, 1935-38. Mason (K.T.), K.P. Home: 1115 Fourth St., Louisville, Ky. Died Feb. 18, 1949.

CROSBY, Evan, artist; b. Newark, N.J., Jan. 8, 1898; s. James Junius and Martha Gaunt (Woodward) A.; student Kingsley Sch., Essex Fells, N.J., 1914-17, N.Y. Sch. of Fine and Applied Arts, 1921-22, Nat. Acad. Design, 1922-24 (pupil of G. W. Maynard, C. Hawthorne, G. E. Browne, A. W. Woelfle). Studio manager Am. Desatype Co., New York City, 1919. Served in 302d Field Signal Batt., A.E.F., 1917-19. Represented by Metropolis, Montclair (N.J.) Art Mus.; A Memory, Summit (N.J.) High Sch.; Old N.Y. Post Office, Met. Museum of Art; also in State Teacher's Coll., Trenton, N.J.; Gould Acad., Bethel, Me. Awarded bronze medal, Plainfield (N.J.) Art Assn.; medal of award, Montclair Art Assn.; same, Am. Artists' Professional League; 3d Hallgarten prize, Nat. Acad. Design; lay members' prize, also Annual Oil prize, Salmagundi Club (New York), 1939, 41, 44; first prize, N.J. Gallery; Thomas Burnham Enders, M.D., Memorial prize for marine painting, Allied Artists of Am., 1943; hon. mention, New Rochelle (N.Y.) Art Assn., Nat. Academician since 1941; mem. Artists Professional League, Grand Central Art Galleries, Audubon Artists, Allied Artists of Am. Salmagundi Club (v.p.), Montclair Arts Assn., Summit Art Assn. (hon.). Home and studio: 355 Sixth Av., New York 14, N.Y. Died Jan. 12, 1943.

CROSBY, Franklin Muzzy, flour mfr.; b. Bangor, Me., Jan. 16, 1875; s. John and Olive (Muzzy) C.; grad. Phillips Acad., Andover, Mass., 1893; B.A., Yale, 1897; m. Harriett McKnight, Apr. 10, 1901. Engaged in manufacturing of flour at Minneapolis since 1898; vice-president General Mills, Inc.; vice-president S. T. McKnight Co.; dir. First Nat. Bank, Minneapolis. Trustee William Hood Dunwoody Industrial Inst., The Blake Sch. (both of Minneapolis). Presbyterian. Clubs: Minneapolis (Minneapolis); University (Chicago). Home: Ferndale, Wayzata, Minn. Address: General Mills, Inc., 400 Second Av. S., Minneapolis, Minn. Died June 29, 1947.

CROSBY, Oscar Terry; b. Ponchatoula, La., Apr. 21, 1861; s. George L. and Elizabeth (Terry) C.; grad. U.S. Mil. Acad., 1882; LL.D.; m. Jeanne Bouligny, 1886; children—Miriam (Countess Caracciolo), Elizabeth (dec.), Juliette (Mrs. Arthur Hornblow, Jr.), Celeste. Resigned from army as 1st lt. engrs., 1887; was gen. supt. Sprague Electric Ry. & Motor Co.; gen. mgr. ry. dept. Gen. Electric Co.; experimenter in and author on elec. subjects, 1887-96; was pres. local electric ry. and lighting cos., Washington, D.C., and several pub. utility corpn., Wilmington, Del., Chester, Pa., and Trenton, N.J. Explored portions of Abyssinia and Soudan, 1900, and portions of Turkestan and Tibet, 1903; made expedition to Borneo, 1915, to S.W. Africa, 1927. Dir. Commn. for Relief in Belgium, having immediate charge of all work in Belgium and Northern France, 1915. Asst. sec. of Treasury in charge fiscal bureaus, 1917; in Europe as pres. Inter-Ally Council on War Purchases and Finance, Nov. 1917-Mar. 1919. Comdr. League of Honor (France); awarded Order of the Crown (Italy), Order of the Crown (Belgium). Mem. Royal Geog. Soc. (London); pres. World's Federation League, New York. Clubs: Metropolitan, Cosmos (Washington, D.C.); University (New York). Author: Tibet and Turkestan; How to Strike—Why to Strike, 1910; International War, Its Causes and Its Cure, 1919; Electrical Railway in Theory and Practice; Adam and Eve, 1926. Writer and speaker on polit., philos. and financial subjects. Home: "View Tree," Warrenton, Va. Died Jan. 2, 1947.

CROSBY, Raymond Moreau, artist; b. Grand Rapids, Mich., 1874; s. Moreau Stephen and Mary (Moseley) C.; B.A., Yale, 1898; studied art in Italy and France; m. Edith T. Ames, June 25, 1900. Artist on staff of Life (New York). Member Soc. of Illustrators. Clubs: Yale, St. Botolph (Boston); Players, Century (New York); Graduate (New Haven, Conn.). Home: (summer) Yarmouthport, Mass. Studio: 252 Boylston St., Boston. Died Dec. 13, 1945.

CROSBY, Walter Wilson, cons. civil engr.; b. Brooklyn, N.Y., Sept. 2, 1872; s. Wilson and Hannah A. (Seaver) C.; B.C.E., Me. State Coll., 1893, C.E., 1896; D.Sc., Maryland State Coll., 1912; D. Engring. U. of Maine, 1926; m. Florance Lapham Fletcher, 1921. Ry. and gen. engring. work, 1893-97; res. engr. for Mass. Highway Commn., 1897-1901; roads engr., Baltimore County, Md., 1901-04; gen. supt. Bd. of Park Commrs., Baltimore, 1904-05; chief engr Md. Geol. and Econ. Survey, 1905-17; chief engr. State Roads Commn. of Md., 1908-12; capt. and maj. N.G. Md., 1904-17; maj. and asst. chief of staff 15th Div., U.S. Army, 1916-17; maj. Engr. O.R.C., U.S. Army, Aug. 31, 1917, lt. col. 104th Engrs., 29th Div., A.E.F., Sept. 8, 1917-June 30, 1919; lt. col. U.S. Army, retired, 1928. Awarded Order of Purple Heart (U.S.). With U.S. Nat. Park Service, 1921; supt. Grand Canyon Nat. Park, 1922-24; location engineer Highway Dept. of Pa., 1924-26. Chmn. Coronado City Planning Commn., 1928-45. Del. 1st Internat. Road Congress, Paris, 1908; v.p. 2d Congress, Brussels, 1910, 3d Congress, London, 1913, 4th Congress, Seville, 1923, 5th Congress, Milan, Italy, 1926; fellow A.A.A.S., American Geog. Soc.; mem. American Society Civil Engineers (life), Internat. Assn. Road Congresses (life), American Fisheries Soc., Izaak Walton League, Maine Soc. S.A.R., Md. Soc. S.R., Mil. Order Foreign Wars, Mil Order World War, Am. Legion, Beta Theta Pi, Phi Kappa Phi. Unitarian. Clubs: Coronado Riding, Engineers (Baltimore, Maryland; hon. life mem.). Author: Some Western Fishing; Notes on Highway Location and Surveying (with G. E. Goodwin), 1929. Wrote 3 sects. of Am. Highway Engineers' Handbook; also many official reports and tech. articles. Home: 1040 Adella Av., Coronado, Calif. Deceased.

CROSMAN, Henrietta, actress; b. Wheeling, W.Va., Sept. 2, 1870; d. Maj. G. H. (U.S.A.) and Mary (Wick) Crosman; ed. Moravian Sem., Bethlehem, Pa.; m. Maurice Campbell, 1897. With Bartley Campbell's stage Co. in "White Slave," 1889, later played leads with Robert Downing; mem. Daly's Co., 1890; Daniel Frohman's Stock Co., 1891-92; Chas. Frohman's leading woman, 1892-94; stock star engagements, 1898-99; starred by Jacob Litt., Apr. 16, 1900; began career as star under management Maurice Campbell in "One of Our Girls," by Bronson Howard; produced "Mistress Nell," by Geo. C. Hazelton, Bijou Theater, New York, Oct. 9, 1900; played Jess Loraine in the "Real Thing," 1911; etc. Died Oct. 3, 1941.

CROSS, Anson Kent, art educator; b. Lawrence, Mass., Dec. 6, 1862; s. George O. and Abigail (Brown) C.; ed. pub. schs., Lawrence, Mass.; grad. Mass. Normal Art Sch., Boston, 1883; m. Mrs. Sarah Martin, July 27, 1903; m. 2d, Gertrude E. Whipple, July 14, 1913. Taught free hand and mech. drawing, evening drawing schs., Lawrence, Mass., 1879-81; mem. faculty Normal Art Sch., 1882-1921; instr. evening drawing schs., Boston, 1883-86; prin. same, 1886-1900; instr. in Art Mus. Sch. of Drawing and Painting, 1891-1926; dir. univ. extension, Art Dept. of Columbia U., 1926-36; dir. Anson K. Cross Art Sch., Inc., (summers) Boothbay Harbor, Me., (winters) St. Petersburg, Fla. Invented rotary snowplow when pupil in high sch. and has taken out 23 patents since 1887. Patented Vermeer's camera, 1934. Bronze medals, Mass. Charitable Mechanics Assn., Boston, 1887; Paris Expn., 1899, for artists' easels; bronze medal, Mass. Charitable Mechanics Assn., 1892, for landscape painting; patented the Cross drawing glass, 1912, for which was awarded bronze medal, Panama P.I. Expn., 1915; patented drawing and painting glass, 1921. Hon. mem. Copley Soc.; artist mem. Boston Art Club. Author: Free-Hand Drawing, Light and Shade, and Free-Hand Perspective, 1892; Drawing in Public Schools, 1893; Mechanical Drawing, 1895; Color Study, 1896; Free-Hand Drawing, 1896; Primary Lessons, 1896; Grammar Lessons, 1896; National Drawing Cards, 1896; National Drawing Books, 1896; Light and Shade, 1897; Drawing and Painting Self Taught, 1922. Apptd. mem. advisory council The Living Age, 1933. Home: Boothbay Harbor, Me. (May to Nov.); St. Petersburg, Fla. (Nov. to May). Died June 17, 1944.

CROSS, Earle Bennett, clergyman, educator; b. Rangoon, Burma, Asia, Nov. 27, 1883; s. Benjamin Putnam and Susane Agnes (Brock) C.; grad. Classical High Sch., Providence, R.I., 1901; B.A., Brown U., 1905, M.A., 1907, Ph.D., 1909; B.D., Newton Theol. Instn., 1910; m. Beatrice Irving Bodwell, Sept. 1, 1910; 1 dau., Jean Florence. Ordained Bapt. ministry, 1910; pastor successively Meshanticut Park, Lime Rock and Crompton, R.I., until 1910, Central Av. Ch., Dover, N.H., 1910-15; acting asso. prof. Bibl. lit. Brown U., 1912-13; instr. O.T., Newton Theol. Instn., 1913-14; pastor First Ch. New Britain, Conn., 1916-18; sec. Nat. Com. Northern Bapt. Laymen, Jan.-Aug., 1919; sec. statis. dept. Inter-Ch. World Movement, 1919-20; sec. Boys' Work Div. Internat. Com. Y.M.C.A., 1920-21; asst. sec. Am. Bapt. Foreign Mission Soc., 1921-23; Hoyt prof. Hebrew lang. and lit., Rochester Theol. Sem., 1923-28; Hoyt prof. Old Testament interpretation, Colgate-Rochester Div. Sch., since 1928. Mem. Soc. Bibl. Lit. and Exegesis, Am. Inst. Archeology, Oriental Soc., Nat. Assn. of Teachers of Speech, Delta Tau Delta, Phi Beta Kappa. Author: The Hebrew Family—A Study in Sociology, 1927; Proverbs, in Abingdon Bible Commentary, 1929; Modern Worship and the Psalter, 1932; The Ideal of a Home, 1934. Home: 76 Dartmouth St., Rochester, N.Y. Died Nov. 29, 1946.

CROSS, Judson Lewis, coll. pres.; b. Colorado Springs, Colo., Nov. 10, 1878; s. Rev. Roselle Theodore (D.D.) and Emma Asenath (Bridgman) C.; A.B., Colorado Coll., 1901; B.D., Yale, 1904; m. Florence Emily Isham, Sept. 13, 1904; children—Margaret Isham (wife of Dr. Vernon William Lippard), Elizabeth Murdock (Mrs. Charles Ruggles Langmuir), Judson Bridgman. Ordained to ministry of Congregational Ch., 1904; pastor Congregational Ch., Trumbull, Conn., 1904-08, Pilgrim Ch., Schenectady, N.Y., 1908-14, Rollstone Ch., Fitchburg, Mass., 1914-27; New England sec. Am. Missionary Assn., also for Commn. on Missions, Congl. Chs., 1927-35; president Tougaloo (Miss.) Coll., 1935-47. Mem. religious and educational mission with A.E.F. under auspices of Y.M.C.A. following armistice, 1919. Moderator, Middlesex Union of Congl. Chs.; dir. Congl. educational and publishing societies of Congl. Chs. Dir., vice pres. and pres. Fitchburg (Mass.) Welfare Assn. Trustee Alice Freeman Palmer Inst., Sedalia, N.C. Club: City (Boston, Mass.). Address: care Judson B. Cross, Webster Hall, Exeter Academy, Exeter, N.H., and Georgetown, Me. Died Oct. 20, 1947; buried at New Haven, Conn.

CROSS, Roy, chemist; b. Ellis, Kan., Jan. 13, 1884; s. George Washington and Ada (Pendleton) C.; A.B., U. of Kan., 1905; M.D., U. Med. Coll., Kansas City, 1908; m. Mary Forbes, Oct. 1, 1917. Teaching fellow chemistry, U. of Kan., 1905-06; teacher chemistry Univ. Med. Coll., Kansas City, 1906-12; mgr. or pres. Kansas City Testing Lab. since 1908; v.p. and consultant Gasoline Products Co., 1922-26; pres. Silica Products Co., 1924-35; v.p. Cross Development Co., 1924-35; pres. Cross Engring. Co., Cross Development Corp., Cross Labs.; cons. chemist. Trustee, Midwest Research Inst., Kan. City Museum Assn., Kan. City Art Institute, Kansas Univ. Research Foundation, Kansas Univ. Endowment Assn. Fellow A.A.A.S.; mem. Am. Inst. Chem. Engring., Am. Chem. Soc., Am. Concrete Inst., Am. Petroleum Inst., Am. Soc. for Testing Materials, Kansas City Engrs., Am. Forestry Assn., Phi Beta Kappa, Sigma Xi. Co-inventor of Cross cracking process and designer of approximately 200 refining plants for gasoline. Holder of about 100 U.S. patents. Republican. Clubs: University, Mission Hills Country, Kansas City Farmer's (Kansas City, Mo.). Author: Handbook of Petroleum, Asphalt and Natural Gas, 1931; Handbook of Bentonite, 1935; Random Recollections of a Chemist, 1941; From A Chemist's Diary, 1943; also bulletins on mineral waters, air conditioning, etc. Home: 4511 Holmes St. Office: 700 Baltimore Av., Kansas City, Mo. Died Mar 21, 1947.

CROSS, Samuel Hazzard, educator; b. Westerly, R.I., July 1, 1891; s. Samuel Hazzard and Jessie (Kerr) C.; prep. edn., high sch., New Bedford, Mass.; A.B., Harvard, 1912, A.M., 1915, Ph.D., 1916; studied at univs. of Gratz, Freiburg, Berlin and Leningrad; m. Constance Curtis, June 28, 1918 (div., 1944); children—Caroline Lee, Anne Louise, Ricarda. Instr. Western Reserve U., 1916-17; commd. service with U.S. Army, 1917-20; detailed with Am. Commn. to Negotiate Peace, 1919-20; trade commr. U.S. Dept. Commerce, 1920; commercial attaché Am. Embassy, Brussels, Belgium, 1921-25; with Am. Legation. The Hague, 1923-25; chief of European Div., U.S. Dept. Commerce, 1925-26. Lecturer on European trade and economics, Georgetown U., 1925-26; lecturer in history, Harvard, 1927; instr. German, Harvard and Tufts Coll., 1928-30; prof. Slavic langs. and lit., Harvard, since 1930, chmn. dept. Germanic langs. and lits., 1935-39. Editor, Speculum, Am. Slavonic Review, Byzantian; consulting editor, Journal of Central European Affairs. Fellow American Academy of Arts and Sciences, Mediæval Academy of America; delegate America Council Learned Societies (chmn. com. on Slavic Studies); mem. Seminarium Kondakovianum (Belgrade); Institut des Etudes Slaves (Univ. of Paris), Slavonic Inst. (Prague), Sch. of Slavonic Studies (Univ. of London), Académie Diplomatique Internationale (Paris), Cercle Gaulois (Brussels), Phi Beta Kappa, Iroquois, Signet. Episcopalian. Clubs: Harvard (Boston, Harvard (New York); Harvard Faculty (Cambridge). Home: G-22 Lowell House. Office: 545 Widener Library, Cambridge, Mass. Died Oct. 14, 1946; buried in Mount Auburn Cemetery, Cambridge.

CROSS (Charles) Whitman, geologist; b. Amherst, Mass., Sept. 1, 1854; s. Rev. Moses Kimball and Maria (Mason) C.; B.S., Amherst, 1875; Ph.D., U. of Leipzig, 1880; D.Sc., Amherst, 1925; m. Virginia Stevens. Asst. geologist U.S. Geol. Survey, 1880-88, geologist, 1888-1925; retired account of age limit; chief sect. petrology, 1903-06. Mem. Nat. Acad. Sciences (treas. 1911-19), Geol. Soc. America (pres. 1918), Washington Acad. Sciences, Am. Philos. Soc.; hon. corr. Acad. Nat. Sc. Phila., 1924; foreign mem. Geol. Soc. London. Mem. Nat. Research Council, 1918-22 (treas. 1918-19, vice chmn. division of geology and geography 1918). Author of geol. reports and maps published by U.S. Geol. Survey, and of many papers in periodicals, on geol., petrographical or mineral subjects. Part author: Quantitatime Classification of Igneous Rocks, 1903. Engaged in rose cultivation and cross-breeding since retirement. Home: 3901 Connecticut Av., Washington 8, D.C. Died Apr. 20, 1949.

CROSS, Wilbur Lucius, ex-gov.; b. Mansfield, Conn., Apr. 10, 1862; s. Samuel and Harriet M. (Gurley) C.; A.B., Yale, 1885, Ph.D., 1889; Litt.D., Univ. of S.C., Columbia, U. of Mich., Yale, Brown; also LL.D., Wesleyan, Harvard, Rochester, and Southern California Universities and Trinity, Union and Yeshiva colleges; married Helen B. Avery, July 17, 1889 (deceased); children—Wilbur Lucius, Samuel Avery, Elizabeth Baldwin (deceased), Arthur William (deceased). Instructor 1894-97, assistant professor, 1897-1902, prof. English, 1902-21, Sheffield Scientific School (Yale); dean Grad. School, Yale, 1916-30, and Sterling prof. English, 1921-30, acting provost, 1922-23. Gov. of Conn., 4 terms, 1931-39. Editor Yale Review; lecturer Columbia, 1903. Trustee Conn. Coll. for Women. Ex-chancellor Am. Acad. Arts and Letters; ex-pres. Nat. Inst. Arts and Letters; mem. Am. Philos. Soc., Soc. of the Cincinnati, Soc. Mayflower Descendants, Soc. Colonial Wars, Soc. Colonial Govs. S.A.R. Chevalier Legion of Honor (France) Phi Beta Kappa. Clubs: Graduate (pres. 1922-26), Elizabethan (pres. 1927-29), Authors of New York. Author: Development of the English Novel, 1899; Life and Times of Laurence Sterne, 1909, rev. edit. 1925, 3d edit., 1929; History of Henry Fielding, 1918; An Outline of Biography, 1924; Modern English Novel, 1929; Four Contemporary Novelists, 1930; Connecticut Yankee, an Autobiography, 1943. Editor: (with notes and essays) Macbeth, 1900; Ivanhoe, 1903; Silas Marner, 1903; Works of Laurence Sterne and Fitzgerald's Life of Sterne, 1904; Stevenson's Inland Voyage and Travels with a Donkey, 1909; Defoe's Robinson Crusoe, 1911; Sterne's Political Romance, 1914; Lounsbury's Life and Times of Tennyson, 1915; Love's Labour's Lost, 1925; Tristram Shandy, 1925; Sentimental Journey, 1926. Editor dept. of English lit. in New Internat. Ency., 1901-03. Gen. editor of novel in Belles Lettres Series, and of English Readings for Schools. Contbr. lit. criticisms to mags. Editor of the Yale Shakespeare. Home: 24 Edgehill Rd., New Haven, Conn. Died Oct. 5, 1948.

CROSSE, Charles Washburn, naval officer; b. Sun Prairie, Wis., Apr. 1, 1885; ed. high school, Stoughton, Wis.; grad. U.S. Naval Acad., 1907. Commd. ensign, U.S. Navy, 1909, and advanced through the grades to rear adm.,1942; served in U.S. Ships Virginia, Ohio, Maryland, Denver, Missouri, Milwaukee, Charleston, Selfridge, Rigel, Seattle, Gold Star, Marblehead, Argonne; assigned to sea duty, 1941. Decorated Victory Medal with escort clasp, Am. Defense Service Medal with fleet clasp, Nicaraguan Campaign and Asiatic-Pacific Campaign medals. Home: 513 N. Page St., Stoughton. Wis. Address: Navy Dept., Washington 25, D.C. Died Apr. 20, 1949.

CROUSE, George N(ellis) (krous), merchant; b. Syracuse, N.Y., Oct. 15, 1877; s. Col. George N. and Florence J. (Marlette) C.; grad. Phillips Acad., Andover, Mass., 1896; Ph.B., Yale, 1901; grad. study, Med. Sch., Yale; m. Janette Clara Ten Eyck, Apr. 22, 1924. Bought out C. E. Crouse & Co., wholesale grocers, Syracuse, 1903; pres. Crouse Grocery Corp. (Syracuse), 1903-39; pres. Benedict Mfg. Co. (E. Syracuse). Pres. Common Council, Syracuse, 1916-21; park commr., Syracuse, 1914-15. Four minute speaker, Nat. Civil Legion. Mem. Syracuse C. of C. (chmn. aviation com.), Nat. Aeronautic Association, Berzelius Soc., Sons Am. Revolution, Nu Sigma Nu, Delta Iota Epsilon, Chi Eta Sigma. Republican. Presbyterian. Mason (past master, 32°—Past Thrice Potent Master, K.T., Past Comdr., Shriner, Past High Priest of Chapter); ex-mem. adv. council Order of De Molay, Odd Fellow, Elk (Past Exalted Ruler, ex-pres. State Assn.). Clubs: Liederkranz, Turn Verein, Republican Escort (ex-pres.). Owns and pilots own airplane, made 3 trans-atlantic flights in Graf Zeppelin and one in DO-X. Chmn. Elks Nat. Defense Com., Syracuse, N.Y. Address: 185 Robineau Road, Syracuse 4, N.Y. Died July 7, 1945.

CROW (Herbert) Carl, author; b. Highland, Mo., Sept. 26, 1883; s. George Washington and Elvira Jane (Sharrock) C.; student Carleton Coll., Farmington, Mo., 1900-01, U. of Mo., 1906-07; m. Helen Marie Hanniger, Apr. 1, 1925. Began as printer's apprentice, 1898; mem. editorial staff Ft. Worth Star-Telegram, 1906-11; asso. city editor China Press, Shanghai, 1911-13; business mgr. Japan Advertiser, Tokyo, 1913-14; Far Eastern rep. Comm. on Pub. Information, 1916-18, World War; propr. advertising agency, Shanghai, 1919-37. Spl. asst. to dir. Office of War Information, 1941-43. Mem. Phi Delta Theta. Clubs: Columbia Country, American, Shanghai (Shanghai); Advertising, Players (New York). Author: Handbook for China, 1912; America and the Philippines, 1913; Japan and America, 1915; 400 Million Customers (pub. in English, French, German, Swedish, Danish, Spanish, Dutch, Polish), 1937; Master Kung (pub. in German, Swedish), 1938; I Speak for the Chinese (pub. in London, also Burmese transl.), 1938; He Opened the Door of Japan (also pub. in London as Harris of Japan), 1939; The Chinese Are Like That (pub. in London as My Friends the Chinese; also in French), 1939; Foreign Devils in the Flowery Kingdom, 1940; America in Stamps, 1940; Meet the South Americans, 1941; Japan's Dream of World Empire, 1942; The Great American Customer, 1943; China Takes Her Place, 1944; The City of Flint Grows Up, 1945; also mag. articles principally about the Far East. Home: 82 Washington Pl., New York, N.Y. Died June 1945.

CROW, Charles Langley, college prof.; b. Norfolk, Va., Nov. 16, 1866; s. George Lemuel and Virginia Caroline (Simmons) C.; M.A., Washington and Lee U., 1888; Ph.D., U. of Göttingen, Germany, 1892; studied Collège Colonial Paris, France, 1901. Nat. U. of Mexico, 1922-24, Centro de Estudios Históricos, Madrid, Spain, 1932; m. Cornelia Mead Seabury, June 12, 1906. Teacher Latin, French and German, Charlotte Hall (Md.) Mil. Acad., 1888-89; teacher Old English, Sauveur Summer Sch., Rockford, Ill., 1893; asst. prin., Norfolk (Va.) High Sch., 1894-95; in charge modern langs., Weatherford (Tex.) Coll., 1894-95, also sec. of faculty; in charge modern langs., Washington and Lee U., 1899-1905; prof. modern langs., U. of Fla., 1905-24, prof. German and Spanish, 1924-33, prof. emeritus since 1933, also sec. of faculty, 1905-29. Mem. Am. Assn. Univ. Profs., Franklin Soc. (Zurich, Switzerland—internat.), Florida Hist. Soc., Pi Kappa Alpha, Phi Kappa Phi, Alpha Phi Epsilon. Democrat. Presbyterian. Author: Das Kurze Reimpaar in Mittelenglischen, 1892; Ultimo, 1908. Editor: Maldon and Brunnanburh, 1897. Home: Gainesville, Fla. Died March 16, 1942.

CROWE, Francis Trenholm, civil engr.; b. Trenholmville, Quebec, Can. (parents Am. citizens), Oct. 12, 1882; s. John and Emma Jane (Wilkinson) C.; grad. Dummer Acad., South Byfield, Mass., 1901; B.S.; U. of Me., 1905, Dr. Engring., 1935; m. Linnie Korts, Dec. 9, 1913; children—Patricia, Betty. Began as civil engr., 1905; construction engr. Jackson Lake, McDonald Lake, Tieton dams; asst. gen. supt. Arrowrock Dam; gen. supt. Guernsey, Combie, Deadwood, Parker, Gene Wash, Copper Basin dams, 1931-37; gen. supt. of constrn. in charge of constrn. Boulder Dam for Six Companies, Inc., since 1938; gen. supt. constrn. Shasta Dam, for Pacific Constructors, Inc. Mem. Am. Soc. Civil Engineers, Sigma Alpha Epsilon, Tau Beta Pi. Republican. Episcopalian. Mason (32°, Shriner), Elk, Rotarian. Home: 1658 Orange St., Redding, Calif. Died Feb. 26, 1946.

CROWELL, Henry Parsons, philanthropist, mfr.; b. Cleveland, O., Jan. 27, 1855; s. Henry L. and Anna (Parsons) C.; ed. Greylock Inst., S. Williamstown, Mass.; m. Lillie Augusta Wick; 1 d., Mrs. Frederick G. Herrick; m. 2d, Susan Coleman, July 10, 1888; 1 son, Henry Coleman. Pres. Quaker Mill Co., Ravenna, O., 1881, until it was sold to Am. Cereal Co., of Akron, O., 1891; v.p. and gen. mgr. of latter company, 1891-98, pres. since 1898; pres. the Quaker Oats Co., chmn. bd., 1922-42, hon. chmn. since 1942; chmn. bd. Perfection Stove Co., Cleveland. Pres. bd. trustees Moody Bible Inst., Chicago, 1902-45; owner Wyoming Hereford Ranch, Cheyenne, Wyoming. Presbyterian. Clubs: Union League, Chicago. Home: 770 Humboldt Av., Winnetka, Ill.; (winter) Green Court, Augusta, Ga. Died Oct. 23, 1944; buried Lakeview Cemetery, Cleveland.

CROWLEY, Karl Allen (krō'lē), lawyer; b. Smithville, Tenn., Apr. 1, 1894; s. Pleasant Campbell and Alva (Nesmith) C.; LL.B., Cumberland U., 1914; m. Annie Lee Frazier, May 30, 1917; children—Anne Frazier, Karl Allen; m. 2d, Matt Swaim; 1 son, William James. Admitted to Tennessee bar; in practice of law at Smithville, Tenn., until 1917; attorney Office of Alien Property Custodian, 1917-19; in law practice Ft. Worth, Tex., 1919-33; solicitor Post Office Dept., Washington, D.C., 1933-38. Del. Dem. Nat. Conv., Houston, 1928, Chicago, 1932, Phila., 1936, Chicago, 1940, Chicago, 1944. Mem. Delta Sigma Phi. Mason, K.P. Mem. Christian Ch. Address: Fort Worth Nat. Bank Bldg., Fort Worth, Tex. Died Mar. 30, 1948.

CROWN, James Evans, editor; b. Catlett, Fauquier Co., Va., Aug. 11, 1873; s. Rev. James Henry and Hannah Eliza (Stone) C.; ed. Forest Hill Acad., Standardsville, Va., 1882-86, Randolph Macon Coll., Ashland, Va., 1887-88 and 1891-94, Chesapeake Acad., Irvington, Va., 1889-90, Randolph Macon Acad., Beford, Va. (orator's medal), 1890-91; m. Nellie Mae Schumacher, Dec. 4, 1906. Read law in office of Hunton, Payne & Meridith, 1895-97; reporter Washington Times, 1898, New York World, Washington Bur., 1899-1901; city editor Richmond News, 1901-02, Chicago Inter Ocean, 1903-05, Chicago Tribune, 1905-07, Chicago Herald Examiner, 1907-10, Denver Republican, 1910, New York Evening World, 1910-11, New Orleans Item, 1911-13, Chicago Herald Examiner, 1913-16; city editor New Orleans States, 1916-36, editor since 1936; secretary pro-tem. Times-Picayune Publishing Company. Awarded silver plaque for civic leadership and performance by Young Men's Business Club, 1940, also made hon. mem.; received Sigma Delta Chi award for "courage in journalism." Democrat. Methodist. Has spoken before various publishers' orgns. and at many colls. Contbr. to Harper's Weekly, New York Times and Chicago Tribune. Home: 1203 Soniat St. Office: 615 North St., New Orleans. Died Jan. 10, 1945; buried at Coldwater, Mich.

CROWNFIELD, Gertrude, author; b. Baltimore, Md.; d. Herman Frederic and Sophia Henrietta (Ring) Crownfield; ed. pub. schs., under pvt. tutelage and course of nursing in New York Post-Grad. Hosp.; unmarried. Teacher primary grades, pvt. and pub. schs., Urbana, Ohio, and Marinette, Wis., 10 yrs.; sec. to nerve specialist, 1906-27. Author: The Little Tailor of the Winding Way, 1917; Princess White Flame, 1920; The Shadow Witch, 1922; The Blue Swordsman, 1924; Time in Rime (and other juveniles), 1925; Alison Blair, 1927; The Feast of Noël, 1928; Joscelyn of the Forts, 1929; Freedom's Daughter, 1930; Heralds of the King, 1931; Katharine Gordon—Patriot, 1932; Mistress Margaret, 1933; Where Glory Waits, 1934; Traitor's Torch, 1935; Conquering Kitty, 1935; King's Pardon, 1937; The Decree, 1937; Strong Hearts and Bold, 1938; Cristina of Old New York, 1939; Diantha's Signet Ring, 1939; Lone Star Rising, 1940; Angelique, 1941; Proud Lady, 1942. Home: Hotel Bedford, 118 E. 42nd St., New York, N.Y. Address: care J. B. Lippincott Co., Washington Sq., Philadelphia, Pa. Died June 2, 1945.

CROWNHART, Jesse George, editor; b. Superior, Wis., Oct. 8, 1896; s. Charles Henry and Jessie Elizabeth (Evans) C.; grad. high sch., Madison, Wis., 1915; A.B., U. of Wis., 1921; m. Hildegarde Lucretia Wooll, Oct. 30, 1926; children—Elizabeth Ann, George William. Legislative corr., Madison, for Holmes News Service (dir.), Milwaukee Sentinel, Madison Capitol Times, Superior Telegram, 1921-23; sec. Wis. State Med. Soc. and editor Wis. Med. Jour. since 1923; sec. Wis. Hosp. Assn., 1930-37. Mem. Governor's Com. on Pub. Welfare, 1936-37. Bayonet instr., Ordnance Dept., U.S. Army, later attended O.T.S., Camp Gordon, Ga., Feb.-Dec. 1918; capt., Wis. N.G., 1919-21, maj., ordnance officer, 1921-26. Mem. Wis. Hist. Soc., Am. Hosp. Assn., Wis. Press Assn., Nat. Collegiate Players, Phi Kappa Phi, Pi Epsilon Delta, Chi Phi, White Spades. Republican. Conglist. Elk, Rotarian. Clubs: Madison; University (Milwaukee). Joint Author: Who's Who at Wisconsin, 1920; Medical Blue Book of Wisconsin, 1928, 29; Sickness Insurance in Europe, 1938. Home: 1904 Jefferson St. Office: Tenney Bldg., Madison, Wis. Died June 5, 1941.

CROWNINSHIELD, Bowdoin Bradlee (kroun'in-shēld), naval architect; b. New York, N.Y., Oct. 13, 1867; s. Benjamin W. and Katherine M. Crowninshield; A.B., Harvard Univ., 1890; m. Priscilla Janet MacPhail, May 12, 1901 (died Oct. 6, 1915); m. 2d, Laura Widlar, Oct. 12, 1916. In practice as naval architect since 1897; was architect of Thomas W. Lawson's yacht "Independence" and the largest sailing vessel, the seven-masted schooner "Thos. W. Lawson." Pres. and gen. mgr. Crowninshield Shipbuilding Co., Fall River, Mass., Sept. 1, 1917-1926; resumed practice, firm of Crowninshield & Burbank, Jan. 1926; inspector of hulls building for U.S. Navy at Manchester, Ipswich, and Amesbury, Mass., since Jan. 15, 1943. Served with Am. Vol. Motor Ambulance Corps in Northwestern France, Jan.-July 1916; present at Battle of Verdun 20 days. Author: Wooden Sailing Ships, Fore and Afters. Address: The Orchard, Bradlee Rd., Marblehead, Mass. Died Aug. 12, 1948.

CROWNINSHIELD, Frank (Francis Welch Crowninshield) ("Arthur Loring Bruce"), editor; b. Paris, France, June 24, 1872; s. Frederic (artist) and Helen S. (Fairbanks) C.; ed. under tutelage abroad, and at Lyon's Acad., New York; unmarried. Pub. of The Bookman, 1895-1900; asst. editor Metropolitan Magazine, 1900-02, Munsey's Magazine, 1903-07; literary agt. in London, 1908-09; art editor Century Magazine, 1910-13; editor Vanity Fair, 1914-35; now editorial advisor to the Condé Nast Publications. Formerly sec. The Museum of Modern Art. Clubs: Knickerbocker, The Coffee House, Links, Dutch Treat, The Cavendish Artists and Writers, Illustrators, Links Golf. Author: Manners for the Metropolis, 1908; The Bridge Fiend, 1909. Contbr. satirical and critical articles to many mags. Home: 333 E. 68th St. Office: Graybar Bldg., 43d St. and Lexington Av., New York, N.Y. Died Dec. 28, 1947; buried in Mt. Auburn Cemetery, Cambridge, Mass.

CROWNOVER, Arthur, Sr. (kroun'ō-vēr), presiding judge; b. Alto, Franklin County, Tenn., Nov. 16, 1874; s. William and Laura (Montgomery) C.; ed. U. of South Sewanee, Tenn., LL.B., 1895, D.C.L., 1938, Phi Beta Kappa; m. Emma Sims, Apr. 25, 1906; children—Arthur Jr., Emma (Mrs. G. Harwood Koppel), Robert Nicholls Sims, Marguerite Héloise (Mrs. Héloise C. Mader). Admitted to Tenn. bar, 1895, and began practice at Winchester, mem. Billingsley & Crownover 1897-98, Crownover & Crabtree, 1900-10, Estill & Crownover, 1912-23; Crownover & Hickerson, 1923; lecturer on med. jurisprudence, U. of South, 1900-04. First county atty., Franklin County, Tenn., 1900-04; first chmn. Tenn. State Highway Comm., 1914-18; justice, Court of Appeals, Tenn., since 1923, elected presiding judge of that court, Feb. 22, 1941. Mgr. state campaign of Gov. Austin Peay, Tenn., 1922. Member board of trustees Univ. of the South. Mem. Am. and Tenn. State bar assns., Delta Theta Phi. Democrat. Episcopalian. Mason, K.P. Clubs: Civitan (internat. pres. 1935-36), Freolac (literary). Joint Author: Decisions of Tenn. Court of Appeals (25 vols.), 1925-42. Home: 2212 State St., Nashville, Tenn. Died June 16, 1942; buried in Mount Olivet Cemetery, Nashville.

CROWTHER, James Edwin, clergyman, missionary; b. Burnley, Lancashire, Eng., May 10, 1877; s. Thomas and Elizabeth (Rowbotham) C.; came to U.S., 1901; B.A., Dak. Wesleyan U., 1908, M.A., 1911 (D.D., 1915); B.D., Garrett Bibl. Inst., Evanston, Ill., 1910; m. Mary Stanworth-Crowther, Sept. 4, 1897. Pastor M.E. Ch., in S.Dak., 1901-06; field sec. Anti-Saloon League, S.Dak., 1906-07; missionary sec., Dak. Conf., 1907-08; spl. sec. Africa Jubilee Campaign, Chicago, 1908-09; western field sec., Missionary Edn. Movement, Chicago, 1909-12; sec. Dept. of Income, Bd. of Foreign Missions of M.E. Ch., N.Y. City, 1912-16; pastor 1st Ch., Seattle, Wash., 1916-21, Arch St. Ch., Phila., 1921-23, University Temple, Seattle, 1923-29, Grace M.E. Ch., St. Louis, Mo., 1929-32, Trinity Ch., Denver, Colo., 1932-36, First Church, San Jose, Calif., 1936-40; pastor The Church of the Wayfarer, Carmel-by-the-Sea, Calif., since 1940. Pres. Seattle Council of Churches, 1924-25, Met. Ch. Fedn. of St. Louis, 1930-31. Mem. Sherwood Eddy European Seminar, 1934. Mem. African Society (London), Pi Kappa Delta, Phi Kappa Phi, Pi Gamma Mu. Made tour of the missions of the M.E. Ch. in Africa by authority of the Bd. of Foreign Missions, 1915; del. to Gen. Conf. M.E. Ch., 1920, to Inst. of Pacific Relations, Honolulu, 1925; host to Inst. of Internat. Relations, Seattle, 1928. Mason (32°, K.T., Shriner). Author of pageant, The Wayfarer. Address: P. O. Box 1175, Carmel-by-the-Sea, Calif. Died Mar. 13, 1947; buried at Glendale, Calif.

CROWTHER, Samuel, writer, farmer; b. Phila., Pa.; s. Samuel and Catherine (Orr) C.; Friends Select School; B.S., U. of Pa., 1901, LL.B., 1904; m. Mary M. Owens, Nov. 21, 1914; children—Samuel Crowther, 3d, Deirdre, John (died July 1935). Newspaper corr. in Balkan States, 1905; corr. N.Y. Tribune and System Magazine, in Eng. and Germany, 1918-19; special corr. Collier's Weekly, Europe, 1923; mem. of Com. for Promotion of Wealth and Income of People of N.H. 1937. Del. N.H. Constl. Conv., 1938, 41. Rep. Conf. of N.E. Govs. before Ways and Means Com., 1940. Mem. Am. Acad. Polit. and Social Science, Acad. of Polit. Science. Author: American Rowing, 1905; Common Sense and Labour, 1920; Why Men Strike, 1920; The Book of Business, 1920; My Life and Work (with Henry Ford), 1922; The First Million the Hardest (with A. B. Farquhar), 1922; Life of John H. Patterson, 1923; Today and Tomorrow (with Henry Ford), 1926; Men and Rubber (with Harvey S. Firestone), 1926; The Presidency vs. Hoover, 1928; The Romance and Rise of the American Tropics, 1929; Money, 1929; Prohibition and Prosperity, 1930; Edison as I Know Him (with Henry Ford), 1930; Moving Forward (with Henry Ford), 1930; Your Money (pamphlet), 1932; A Basis for Stability, 1932; America Self-Contained, 1933; A Primer (pamphlet), 1934; A Second Primer (pamphlet), 1935; Why Quit Our Own (with George N. Peek), 1936; What We Earn—What We Owe, 1939; Time to Inquire, 1942; Series of signed editorials for Hearst Newspapers on Bretton Woods Monetary Conf., 1944, U.N. Conf., San Francisco, 1945. Contbr. mags., newspapers. Home: Stagecoach Road Farm, Sunapee, N.H. Died Oct. 27, 1947.

CROZIER, William (krō'zhūr), retired army officer; b. Carrollton, O., Feb. 19, 1855; s. Judge Robert and Margaret (Atkinson) C.; B.S., U.S. Mil. Acad., 1876; Dr. of Engring., U. of Mich., 1923; m. Mary Hoyt Williams, Oct. 31, 1913. Commd. 2d lt. 4th Arty., June 15, 1876; 1st lt. ordnance, July 11, 1881; capt. (14 yrs. service), June 14, 1890; maj. insp.-gen. vols., May 17, 1898; hon. discharged from vol. service, Nov. 30, 1898; apptd. prof. natural and exptl. philosophy, U.S. Mil. Acad., Feb. 23, 1901 (declined); brig. gen. chief of ordnance U.S. Army, Nov. 22, 1901; maj. gen. chief of ordnance U.S. Army, Oct. 6, 1917; maj. gen. U.S. Army, July 12, 1918; retired from active service, Jan. 1, 1919. Served in Powder River campaign against the Sioux Indians, winter of 1876-77; in campaign against the Bannocks, 1878. With Gen. Buffington, invented the Buffington-Crozier disappearing gun carriage; invented a wire gun. Del. Internat. Peace Conf. at The Hague, 1899; staff officer in field in Philippine insurrection, 1900; chief ordnance officer of Peking relief expdn., 1900; pres. Army War Coll., 1912-13. Served as brig. gen., chief of ordnance, U.S. Army, Nov. 22, 1901-July 1918; maj. gen., July 12, 1918-Jan. 1, 1919; retired; mem. War Council, Dec. 1917-June 1918, in which capacity in theatre of war in France and Italy, Jan.-May 1918; comd. Northeastern Dept. U.S. Army, July-Dec. 1918. Decorated Legion of Honor (French), S.S. Maurizio e Lazzaro (Italian), Polonia Restituta (Poland). Mem. A.A.A.S., Am. Geog. Soc. Clubs: University (New York); Metropolitan, Army and Navy, Chevy Chase (Washington). Home: 1735 Massachusetts Av., Washington. Died Nov. 10, 1942; buried in Arlington National Cemetery.

CRUIKSHANK, William Mackey (krŏŏk'shănk), army officer; b. Washington, D.C., Nov. 7, 1870; s. John C. and Euphrasia (Antisell) C.; grad. U.S. Mil. Acad., 1893, Sch. of Submarine Defense, 1903, Army War Coll., 1920; m. Cornelia B. Holabird, Apr. 30, 1904; 1 dau., Mary Holabird. Commd. 2d lt. Arty., June 12, 1893; promoted through grades to col. May 15, 1917; brig. gen. N.A., July 12, 1918; hon. discharged as brig. gen., temp., Aug. 31, 1919; brigadier general regular army, Sept. 1, 1925; retired November 30, 1934. Instr. mathematics, U.S. Mil. Acad., 1895-98 and 1898-99; in Santiago Campaign, July 22-Aug. 30, 1898; dist. and post arty. engr. at Ft. Howard, Md., 1904-07; adj. 5th F.A. in Philippines, 1907-09; arrived in France with 1st Div., June 26, 1917; apptd. comdr. 3d Brigade Field Arty., 3d Div., 3d Army Corps, A.E.F., May 22, 1918, chief of arty., 4th Corps, Oct. 30, 1918-Jan. 1, 1919; with Army of Occupation in Germany, Nov. 17, 1918-Jan. 1, 1919, and Apr. 22, 1919-Aug. 5, 1919; General Staff Corps, Aug. 1920-24; comdt. F.A. Sch., Fort Sill, Okla., 1930-34; retired, Nov. 30, 1934. D.S.M. (U.S.); Officer Legion of Honor (French). Episcopalian. Mem. Mil. Order Loyal Legion. Clubs: Army and Navy. Home: 2126 Connecticut Av., Washington, D.C. Died Feb. 23, 1943.

CRUMLEY, Thomas Ralston, elec. engr.; b. Wayne, Pa., Sept. 20, 1878; s. David and Mary (Coleman) C.; B.S., Pa. State Coll., 1901; m. Nancy Bartlett, 1908. Constrn. engr., Hudson River Water Power Co., 1901-04; asst. supt. Phila. and Westchester Traction Co., 1904-08; elec. engr. Evansville & Ind. Ry. Co., 1908-15; chief engr. Gen. Engring. & Management Corp., 1915-21, pres., 1921-27; v.p. Nat. Pub. Service Corp., 1925-27; v.p. Jersey Central Power & Light Co., 1925-28, pres. and gen. mgr. since 1928. Mem. Am. Inst. E.E. Republican. Episcopalian. Mason. Club: Deal Golf. Home: Eatontown, N.J. Office: 501 Grand Av., Asbury Park, N.J.* Died Oct. 5, 1944.

CRUMP, Walter Gray, surgeon; b. Pittsford, N.Y., Aug. 6, 1869; s. Samuel and Susan Gray (Cutting) C.; grad. biol. courses Princeton, 1892; M.D., New York Homœpathic Medical College (now New York Medical College), 1895; D.Sc., Albright College, Reading, Pa., 1934; m. Eudora L. Wright, 1900; 1 son, Walter Gray, II. Surgeon to Fifth Avenue Hospital; cons. prof. surgery N.Y. Polyclinic Med. Sch. and Hosp.; surgeon New York Ophthalmic, Yonkers, Port Chester, Jamaica, Mt. Vernon, Tarrytown, Dobbs Ferry, South Side (Bayshore), Fitkin Memorial, (Asbury Park), Middletown State, Evang. Deaconess (Brooklyn), Prospect Heights (Brooklyn) hospitals; consulting Surgeon, Harlem Hospital. Emeritus professor surgery, N.Y. Med. Coll. Trustee Howard U., Washington, D.C., Tuskegee Inst. Fellow and gov. Am. Coll. Surgeons; mem. A.M.A., Acad. Path. Science, N.Y. Co. Med. Soc.; hon. mem. N.J. State Med. Soc.; mem. Nat. Assn. Am. Coll. Profs. (vice-pres.), Alpha Sigma (founder). Mason (32°). Clubs: Dunham, Alpha. Home: 837 Madison Av., New York. Died May 1, 1945; buried at Pittsford, N.Y.

CRUNELLE, Leonard (krū-nĕl), sculptor; b. Lens, Pas-de-Calais, France, July 8, 1872; s. Alberic and Marie (Strady) C.; pupil of Lorado Taft and Art Ins. Chicago; m. Augusta Waughop, Sept. 1893; children—Marguerite, Jean W., Lawrence D., Lucille, Leonard, Alice Yvonne (dec.). Sculptor in Chicago since 1901. Principal works: status of Gov. Richard Oglesby, Lincoln Park, Chicago; status of Gov. John M. Palmer, Springfield, Ill.; Negro war memorial, Chicago; statue of Abraham Lincoln, Freeport, Ill.; statue of Abraham Lincoln as captain in Blackhawk War, Dixon, Ill.; 2 Lincoln figures in Lincoln Tomb, Springfield, Ill.; monument to Maj. Gen. Artemas Ward, Washington, D.C.; monument of Dr. Mayo, Rochester, Minn.; George Washington, Robert Morris, Haym Salomon Monument, Chicago, Ill. Mem. Soc. Western Artists, Chicago Soc. Artists. Club: Cliff Dwellers. Home: 2034 E. 73d St. Studio: 6016 Ingleside Av., Chicago, Ill. Died Sep. 10, 1944.

CRUSE, Thomas, army officer; b. Owensboro, Ky., Dec. 29, 1857; s. James Barnhill and Mildred Davis (King) C.; Center Coll., Ky., 1874-75; grad. U.S. Mil. Acad., 1879; honor grad. Inf. and Cav. Sch., Ft. Leavenworth, Kan., 1891; grad. Army War Coll., 1916; m. Beatrice Cottrell, Feb. 14, 1882; children—Fred Taylor, James Thomas (dec.). Commd. 2d lt. 6th Cav., in Ariz., June 13, 1879; 1st lt., Sept. 28, 1887; captain, a.-q.-m., December 1, 1896; major q.-m. U.S. Vols., May 12, 1898; hon. discharged from vol. service, May 1, 1901; maj. q. m., July 5, 1902; lt. col., dep. q.-m. gen., Feb. 17, 1910; col. Q.-M. Corps, Feb. 1, 1913; brig. gen., Jan. 9, 1917; retired Jan. 1918. Awarded Medal of Honor, "for distinguished gallantry in action with hostile Indians," Aug. 1882; also Indian Campaign Medal, Philippine Campaign Medal. Democrat. Baptist. Mason. Clubs: Army and Navy (Washington and Manila); University (St. Louis). Home: Longport, N.J. Address: War Dept., Washington. Died June 8, 1943.

CRUTTENDEN, Walter Barnes, chmn. bd. Springfield Fire & Marine Ins. Co.; b. Madison, Conn., Jan. 27, 1873; s. Samuel Dudley and Roda (Chittenden) C.; B.A., Yale, 1894, LL.B., 1896, M.L., 1897; m. Marie Hinsdale, June 15, 1904. Admitted to Conn. bar, 1896; engaged in practice of law, 1896-1900; examiner and special agent Nat. Fire Ins. Co., Hartford, Conn., 1900-12; special agent Springfield (Mass.) Fire & Marine Ins. Co., 1912-19, asst. sec., 1919-24, v.p. since 1924, dir. since 1926; v.p. and dir. Sentinel Fire Ins. Co., Springfield, Mass., since 1926; v.p., dir. New Eng. Fire Ins. Co., Springfield, Mass., since 1927; v.p. and dir. Mich. Fire & Marine Ins. Co., Detroit, since 1927; v.p., dir., N.E. Casualty Ins. Co., Springfield, Mass., since 1939, pres., 1940-46; now chairman board for each insurance co.; director Underwriters Salvage Co., Van Norman County, Springfield Street Railway Co., Alfa Finance Corp., Holyoke Water Power Company, Fire Companies Adjustment Bureau, Incorporated; director and member executive com. Third Nat. Bank and Trust Co.; trustee and mem. bd. of investment Springfield Instn. for Savings; mem. exec. com., chmn. com. on conf. Nat. Bd. of Fire Underwriters; trustee Am. Foreign Ins. Assn., Ins. Executive Assn. Trustee, incorporator, Springfield Hosp.; incorporator Wesson Mem. Hosp. Member Insurance Inst. of America (fellow). Republican. Congregationalist. Mason (32°). Clubs: Country (Longmeadow, Mass.), Colony (Springfield, Mass.). Home: 32 Overbrook Lane, Longmeadow, Mass. Office: 195 State St., Springfield, Mass. Died Sep. 5, 1949.

CRUZE, James, motion picture dir.; b. Utah; ed. pub. schs.; m. Betty Compson, 1 dau., Julia. Dir. of films: The Covered Wagon; Old Ironsides; Old Homestead; Hollywood; The Fighting Coward; One Glorious Day; also hero in the motion picture serial The Million Dollar Mystery. Home: Flintridge, Pasadena. Address: Hollywood, Calif. Died Aug. 4, 1942.

CUDAHY, John, ambassador; b. Milwaukee, Wis., Dec. 10, 1887; s. Patrick and Anna (Madden) C.; A.B., Harvard, 1910; LL.B., U. of Wis., 1913; LL.D., Carroll Coll., 1935; m. Katharine Reed, Aug. 2, 1913; children—Toulgas, Michael. Admitted to Wis. bar, 1913; in practice, 1913-17; ranching in Mexico, 1920-23; in real estate business, 1923-33; A.E. and P.P. to Poland, 1933-37; served as minister to Ireland, 1937-39; ambassador to Belgium, 1939-40. Capt., U.S. Army, World War. Democrat. Catholic. Author: Archangel—The American War with Russia, 1920; Mañana Land, 1925; African Horizons, 1929. Home: Granville, Wis. Died Sep. 6, 1943.

CUDAHY, Joseph M.; b. Chicago, Ill., Sept. 12, 1878; s. Michael and Catherine (Sullivan) C.; m. Jean Morton. With packing industry from beginning of career to 1916; dir. Morton Salt Co. Home: 830 N. Green Bay Road, Lake Forest, Ill. Office: Room 406, 310 S. Michigan Av., Chicago, Ill. Died Oct. 25, 1947.

CULKIN, Francis D., congressman; b. Oswego, N.Y., Nov. 10, 1874; s. Anthony and Brigid (Dugan) C.; ed. pub. schs., Oswego and Rochester, N.Y.; m. Louise Hosmer, June 30, 1914; children—Francis Hosmer, Josephine Louise. Began as newspaper reporter, Rochester, 1894; admitted to N.Y. bar, 1902, and began practice at Oswego. Served as pvt., N.Y. Vols., Spanish-Am. War; capt., N.G.N.Y., 1901-08. Dist. atty., Oswego County, N.Y., 1911-21; county judge, Oswego County, 1921-28; mem. 70th (elected to fill vacancy, Nov. 6, 1928) and 71st to 77th Congresses (1928-43, 32d N.Y. Dist. Trustee Oswego City Library, Oswego City Hosp. Mem. Am. Bar Assn. Republican. Catholic. Club: Oswego Yacht (trustee). Home: 60 W. Cayuga St. Office: Grant Block, Oswego, N.Y. Died Aug. 4, 1943.

CULLEN, Countee, author, teacher; b. N.Y. City, May 30, 1903; s. Frederick Asbury and Carolyn Belle (Mitchell) C.; A.B., N.Y. U., 1925; A.M., Harvard, 1926; m. Ida Mae Roberson, Sept. 27, 1940. Teacher Frederick Douglass Junior high school, N.Y. City, since 1934. Methodist. Awarded Guggenheim fellowship, 1928. Editor: Caroling Dusk (anthology of verse by Negro poets), 1928. Author: Color, 1925; Copper Sun, 1927; Ballad of the Brown Girl, 1928; The Black Christ, 1930; One Way to Heaven, 1932; The Medea, 1935; The Lost Zoo, 1940; My Lives and How I Lost Them, 1942; St. Louis Woman (a musical in collaboration with Anna Bontempo, produced on Broadway), 1946; (poetry) On These I Stand (published posthumously), 1947. Mem. Phi Beta Kappa. Address: care Harper & Bros., New York. Died Jan 9, 1946; buried in Woodlawn Cemetery, New York.

CULLEN, Richard J., chmn. of corp. and dir. Internat. Paper Co. Pres. and dir. Internat. Envelope

Corp.; dir. Canadian Internat. Paper Co., Ariz. Chem. Co. Address: International Paper Co., 220 E. 42d St., New York 17. Died Nov. 13, 1948; buried at Hamilton, Ont., Can.

CULLEN, Thomas H., congressman; b. Brooklyn, N.Y.; A.B.. St. Francis Coll., Brooklyn. Marine ins and shipping business; mem. N.Y. Assembly, 1896-98, Senate, 1899-1918; mem. 66th to 78th Congresses (1919-45), 4th N.Y. Dist. Democrat. Home: 215 Congress St., Brooklyn, N.Y. Died Feb. 29, 1944.

CULLER, Arthur Jerome, clergyman, educator; b. near Canton, O., Mar. 14, 1883; s. John and Amanda (Kurtz) C.; A.B., Juniata Coll., Huntingdon, Pa., student U. of Pa., 1908-09, U. of Leipzig, summer 1910; B.D., Union Theol. Sem., 1911; Ph.D., Columbia, 1912; m. Mary S. Stover, Sept. 28, 1911; children—Robert Dale (dec.), George D., Arthur D. Ordained ministry Disciples of Christ, 1911; pastor Geiger Memorial Ch., Phila., 1911-14; coll. preacher and dean Div. Sch., McPherson (Kan.) Coll., 1914-21; chautauqua lecturer, 1920, 22; dean and professor N.T., Hiram College, 1921-29; pastor Heights Christian Church, Cleveland, 1930-45. Pastor Emeritus, 1945. American Red Cross organizer, Southwestern Division, 1917-18; Liberty Loan speaker, 1917-18; American Red Cross service in Palestine and Turkey, 1919-20, and organized Near East Relief in Central Turkey; chmn. Social Welfare and Health, Cleveland Office Civilian Defense, since 1942. President National Conference of Christians and Jews since 1933. Mem. American Psychol. Assn., A.A.A.S., American Assn. Univ. Profs., Soc. Bibl. Lit. and Exegesis, English-Speaking Union. Republican. Clubs: Rotary, City. Author: Interference and Adaptability—Experimental Study of their Relations, 1912; The Bethany Bible Teacher, 1924. Co-author: Influence of Caffein on Mental and Motor Efficiency, 1912; Creative Religious Literature—A New Literary Study of the Bible, 1929. Corr. of Associated Press, Russia and Germany, 1935, Oxford Conf., 1937, Mexico, 1938. Address: 16815 Holbrook Rd., Cleveland, O. Died Nov. 27, 1946.

CULVER, Frank Pugh, clergyman; b. Lawrenceville, Ala., July 31, 1863; s. Maj. Isaac Franklin and Nancy (McSwean) C.; M.A., Southern U., Greensboro, Ala., 1888; D.D., Southwestern U., 1912; m. Ella Taylor (died Aug. 28, 1896); children—Frank Pugh, Elizabeth; m. 2d, Mary Lee White, Apr. 23, 1901; children—Anna, Nancy. Ordained M.E. Ch., S. ministry, 1888; pastor, Oxford, Ala., 1888-91, Anniston, 1892-96, Tuscaloosa, 1897-1902, Huntsville, 1902-05, Eleventh Av. Ch., Birmingham, 1906-08; presiding elder Birmingham Dist., 1909-11; pres. Polytechnic Coll., Ft. Worth, Tex., 1911-15; pastor Austin Av. Ch., Waco, Tex., 1915-18, 1st. Ch., Ft. Worth, 1918-21; presiding elder Ft. Worth Dist., 1921-25 and since 1929, Waco Dist., 1925-26; pastor of First Ch., Corsicana, 1926-29. Presiding elder Ft. Worth District, 1930-34. Pres. bd. trustees Texas Wesleyan Coll.; trustee Texas Woman's Coll., Fort Worth, Tex. Mem. General Conference 11 times; del. Ecumenical Meth. Conf., Toronto, 1911, Atlanta, Ga., 1931; mem. Unification Commn. M.E. Ch. and M.E. Ch., S., 1922-25; mem. Uniting Conf., 1939; mem. General Conf., Meth. Ch., 1940. Mem. Kappa Alpha. Democrat. Mason (32°). Home: 2119 Park Pl., Fort Worth, Tex. Died June 26, 1949.

CULVER, Harry H(azel), banker, realtor; b. Milford, Neb.; s. Jacob H. and Ada I. (Davidson) C.; ed. Doane Coll., Crete, Neb., and U. of Neb.; LL.D., Loyola U., Los Angeles, Calif., 1930; m. Lillian Roberts, June 11, 1916; 1 dau., Patricia. Founder and builder of Culver City, Calif., 1914, University City Calif., 1927. Pres. Harry H. Culver & Co., Culver City Co., Arizona Development Co. (Phoenix, Ariz.), Pacific Military Acad.; formerly dir. Security-1st National Bank of Los Angeles. Served as sergt. maj., cav., U.S. Vols., Spanish-American War; lt. col., U.S. Army Specialists Res.; now asst. real estate officer, war Dept. Engrs., Pacific Div. Ex-pres. National Assn. Real Estate Boards, Calif. Real Estate Assn., Los Angeles Real Estate Bd.; chmn. finance com. Los Angeles Chamber of Commerce; executive vice-pres. Royce-Linnard Hotels; mgr. Fairmont Hotel, San Francisco. Mem. bd. regents Loyola U., Los Angeles. Republican. Conglist. Mason (32°. Shriner). Clubs: California, California Country, Los Angeles Country. Address: 1705 E. Central Av., Balboa, Calif. Died Aug. 17, 1946; buried at Inglewood, Calif.

CUMMING, Hugh S., surgeon; b. Virginia, 1869; M.D., U. of Va., 1893, Univ. Coll. of Medicine, Richmond, 1894; Sc.D., U. of Pa.; LL.D., Yale Univ.; m. Lucy Booth, Oct. 28, 1896; children—Lucy Booth (dec.), Hugh S., Diana. Apptd. asst. surgeon, U.S. P.H.S., May 25, 1894; passed asst. surgeon, May 16, 1899; surgeon, Mar. 15, 1911. Pub. Health Service expert on duty with the Navy during war, 1917-19; nom. surg. gen. U.S.P.H.S., Jan. 27, 1920; retired as surgeon general, Feb. 1, 1936. Director Pan-American San. Bureau, 1920-47; v.p. health sect. League of Nations; representative of U.S. on Cannes Conf.; Am. mem. and president, Office International d'Hygiene Publique; pres. Allied Med. Mission to Poland; mem. A.M.A., Med. Soc. of Va., Am. Pub. Health Assn., Chi Phi, Eli Banana, Phi Beta Kappa, Alpha Omega Alpha, Delta Omega, Sigma Xi; hon. fellow Am. Coll. Surgeons, Am. Coll. Physicians, Am. Coll. Dentists; fellow Nat. Acad. Medicine of Mexico, and of Peru; hon. life mem., Royal Soc. of Med., London, Assn. Mil. Surgeons of Mexico, Canadian Pub. Health Assn. Comdr. Legion of Honor (France); comdr. with Star, Polonia Restituta (Poland); decorated by govts. of Peru, Ecuador, Chile, Dominican Republica, Mexico, Cuba, Columbia, Haiti, Guatamala Paraguay, Venzuela. Episcopalian. Clubs: Cosmos, Chevy Chase, Nat. Press (Washington). Author: Various works and pamphlets on pub. health. Home: 2219 California St. Office: Pan American Sanitary Bureau, Washington, D.C. Died Dec. 20, 1948.

CUMMINS, Alexander Griswold, clergyman, editor; b. Smyrna, Del., Apr. 8, 1869; s. Alexander Griswold and Louisa (Hayes) C.; A.B., Swarthmore Coll., 1889, Litt.D., 1909; student Gen. Theol. Sem., 1889-93; A.M., Columbia, 1893; studied and traveled abroad, 1894-96; D.D., Washington Coll., Md., 1921; LL.D., Gettysburg Coll., 1926; m. Evelyn Atwater, Sept. 8, 1915. Deacon, 1892, priest, 1894, P.E. Ch.; rector Christ Ch., Poughkeepsie, N.Y., since 1901. Founder and editor The Chronicle (monthly mag. of P.E. Ch.); sec. Protestant Episcopal Soc. for Promotion of Evangelical Knowledge; pres. St. Barnabas Hosp. Fund; state charities visitor Hudson River State Hosp.; mem. bd. of trustees Evangelical Edn. Soc.; Dutchess County Health Assn.; pres. Poughkeepsie Community House and Rescue Mission Foundation; chmn. Archdeaconry of Dutchess, Diocese of N.Y.; dir. Mid-Hudson Grenfell Assn.; formerly mem. standing com. and chmn. social service commn., Diocese of N.Y.; deputy for Diocese of N.Y. Provincial Synod N.Y. and N.J., 1918; mem. exec. com., sec.-treas. Protestant Episcopal Ch. League; sec.-treas., The Clergyman's Mutual Ins. League. Sec. and part owner Enterprise Pub. Co. 1914-18; editor, Evening Enterprise, Poughkeepsie, 1917-18. Dir. Farmers and Mfrs. Nat. Bank, 1919-21. Mem. Churchman's Assn., Ministers Assn. of Poughkeepsie, The Club, Rectory Club, The Pilgrims Soc., S.C.W., S.R., Phi Kappa Psi, Phi Beta Kappa. Republican. Clubs: Union League, Hunters Frat., Columbia U. (New York); Graduate (New Haven, Conn.); National, Connaught, Dartmouth House (London, Eng.); Clove Valley Rod and Gun (pres. 1909-1934); Amrita (Poughkeepsie); Organizer and dir. Three Brooks Associates Gun Club. Formerly prominent in athletic and field sports; sportsman; literary critic. Exchange preacher Great Britain and U.S., 1933, 34, 35, 36, 37, 38. Address: The Woodside, Poughkeepsie, N.Y. Died Sept. 22, 1946; buried in Poughkeepsie Rural Cemetery.

CUNNINGHAM, William Burgess, clergyman; b. Troy, Obion County, Tenn., Jan. 15, 1883; s. William Monroe and Mary Tennessee (Brown) C.; A.B., Bethel Coll., McKenzie, Tenn., 1910 (pres. of class), D.D. from the same coll., 1932; m. Una Owen, Oct. 25, 1911; 1 dau., Mary Margaret. Ordained ministry of the Cumberland Presbyn. Ch., 1907; pastor rural chs. and at Humboldt, Hickman and Rutherford, Tenn., until 1916, Union City since 1916; sec. and treas. Bd. of Edn. Cumberland Presbyn. Ch.; permanent engrossing clk., Gen. Assembly Cumberland Presbyn. Ch.; elected moderator Gen. Assembly, 1933; declined presidency Bethel Coll., 1932. Democrat. Mason. Home: Union City, Tenn.* Deceased.

CUNLIFFE, John William (kŭn'lĭf), author, educator; b. Bolton, Lancashire, Eng., Jan. 20, 1865; s. Thomas and Mary Anne (Kershaw) C.; B.A., U. of London, 1884, M.A. (in classics), 1886, M.A. (modern langs.), 1888, D.Lit., 1892; Shakespeare scholar, Owens Coll. (now U. of Manchester), 1885-86, Berkeley fellow, 1891-92; Litt.D., Columbia U., 1929; m. Jane Erskine, 1897. Lecturer in English, 1899-1905, asso. prof., 1906-07, McGill U., Montreal, Can.; lecturer at Columbia, 1907; prof. English and chmn. dept., U. of Wis., 1907-12; prof. English and asso. dir. Sch. of Journalism, Columbia Univ., 1912-20, dir., 1920-23, dir. emeritus since 1931. First v.p. Modern Lang. Assn. of America, 1910. Dir. London Br. Am. Univ. Union in Europe, 1918-19; trustee and sec. of bd., same, 1919-25. Author: The Influence of Seneca on Elizabethan Tragedy, 1893; A Canadian Soldier, 1917; English Literature During the Last Half Century, 1919; (in collaboration with P. de Bacourt) French Literature During the Last Half Century, 1923; Modern English Playwrights, 1927; Pictured Story of English Literature, 1933; English Literature in the Twentieth Century, 1933; Leaders of the Victorian Revolution, 1934; England in Picture, Song and Story, 1936. Editor: Gascoigne's Supposes and Jocasta, 1906; Gascoigne's Complete Works, 1907-10; Browning's Shorter Poems, 1909; Shakespeare's As You Like It, 1910; Century Readings in English Literature, 1910, 5th edit., 1940; Midsummer Night's Dream, 1911; Thackeray's English Humorists, 1911; Early English Classical Tragedies, 1912; Shakespeare's Principal Plays, 1914, 3d edit., 1935; Writing of Today (with G. R. Lomer), 1915, 4th edit., 1925; Poems of the Great War, 1916; Century Readings in the Old Testament, 1923; Century Readings in the New Testament, 1923; Century Readings in European Literature (Medieval and Modern), 1925; Century Readings in the English Novel, 1930; Century Readings in Victorian Prose, 1935. Contbr. to philol. jours. and to Cambridge History of English Literature. Joint Editor, revised edit. of Warner Library, 1917-18. Chmn. editorial bd., Columbia U. Course in Literature, 1928-29.* Died Mar. 18, 1946.

CUNLIFFE-OWEN, Sir Hugo, pres. and dir. British-Am. Tobacco Co., Ltd; Chmn. bd. and dir. Cunliffe-Owen Aircraft, Ltd.; vice chmn. Tobacco Securities Trust, Ltd.; dir. Midland Bank, Eagle Star Insurance Co. Home: Sunningdale Park, Ascot, England. Office: British-American Tobacco Co., Ltd., Westminster House, 7 Millbank, London S.W. 1, England. Died Dec. 14, 1947.

CUNNINGHAM, Benjamin B., judge; b. Rochester, N.Y., Apr. 1, 1874; s. Michael and Mary (Hanly) C.; ed. pub. and high schs., Rochester; studied law in office of W.B. Crittenden, Rochester; m. Eleanore MacKearin, 1911. Admitted to N.Y. bar, 1895, and began practice at Rochester; asst. to corp. counsel, Rochester, 1898-1916; corp. counsel, 1916-19 (resigned); justice Supreme Court of N.Y., 7th Dist., Jan. 1, 1920), for term of 14 yrs., ending Dec. 31, 1934. Republican. K.C. Club: Genesee Valley. Home: 1330 Park Av., Rochester, N.Y. Died Jan 2, 1946.

CUNNINGHAM, Bert, biology; b. McLean County, Ill., June 3, 1883; s. Parker Dresser and Susie (Hammond) C.; B.S., Ill. Wesleyan U., 1908, M.S., 1909; A.M., Trinity Coll. (now Duke U.), 1916; Ph. D., U. of Wis., 1920; m. Jean Knapton, Oct. 1, 1907. Prof. science, Mo. Wesleyan Coll., 1909-11; Durham (N.C.) High Sch., 1911-16; instr. biology, Trinity Coll., 1917-20; prof. biology, Duke U., since 1920. Fellow A.A.A.S.; mem. Am. Soc. Zoölogists, Am. Mus. Natural History, N.C. Acad. Science (ex-pres., sec.), Sigma Xi, Phi Sigma, Kappa Delta Pi, Phi Gamma Delta. Methodist. Author: Axial Duplicity in Serpents (monograph), 1937. Home: 1200 Markham Av., Durham, N.C. Died Sep. 27, 1943.

CUNNINGHAM, Charles Henry, govt. career service; b. Dubois, Neb., May 7, 1885; s. Charles Richard and Louise (Crump) C.; B.L., U. of Calif., 1909, M.L., 1910, Ph.D., 1915, traveling fellow in Spain and S.A., 1915-17; m. Goldie C. Shellenberger, July 28, 1908; children—Helen Louise, Frances Ione, Mary Goldie; m. 2d, Henrietta Wright, 1936; 1 son, Charles Henry, Jr. Teacher, P.I., 1910-13; instr., later asst. prof. Latin Am. history, U. of Tex., 1917-20; spl. work for U.S. Govt. in Mexico, rank of vice consul (on leave from U. of Tex.), 1918-19; U.S. trade commr., Mexico City, Mexico, May-Nov. 1920; commercial attaché, U.S. Dept. Commerce, Spain, 1920-23, Portugal, 1921-23, Cuba, 1923-24, Spain and Portugal, 1924-27; prof. foreign trade, New York U., 1927-29; commercial attaché, U.S. Dept. Commerce, Peru and Ecuador, 1929-31, Mexico City, 1931-33; research asso. in polit. science and economics, U. of Calif., since 1933; apptd. dep. adminstr. NRA at Washington, D.C., was in charge Los Angeles office with jurisdiction over S. Calif., N.M. and Ariz.; apptd. field rep. Social Security Bd., Southern Calif. area, June 1936, and mgr. Los Angeles office since Nov. 1936; representative of Division of Exports, Board of Economic Warfare, Mexico City, since 1942; special research work, U.S. Tariff Commission and a New York investment bank, 1927-29. Member Phi Beta Kappa, Spanish Academy History. Mason (32°, Shriner). Author: The Audiencia in the Spanish Colonies, 1919. Contbr. commerce reports, U.S. Dept. Commerce, also econ. and hist. articles to mags. Home: 21736 Roscoe Blvd., Canoga Park, Calif. Office: Federal Bldg., Los Angeles, Calif. Deceased.

CUNNINGHAM, Donnell LaFayette, lawyer; b. Gaylesville, Ala., Apr. 21, 1866; s. Ebenezer and Martha (Clayton) C.; ed. high sch., Gaylesville: studied law in office of Hon. John L. Burnett, of Gadsden, Ala.; m. Mrs. Louisa (Cornelius) Leavenworth, Mar. 10, 1904. Admitted to Ala. bar, 1887; practiced in Ala. until 1893; removed to Colo. and entered mining and stock brokerage business, at Cripple Creek; lost entire property by fire, 1896; went to Flagstaff, Ariz.; and began as common laborer; reëntered law practice at Williams, Ariz., 1899; city atty., Williams, 1900; removed to Tombstone, 1902; dist. atty., Cochise County, 1903-04; del. Ariz. Constl. Conv., 1910; asso. justice Supreme Court of Ariz., 1911-20 (chief justice, 1919, 20); resumed practice at Willcox, Ariz.; formerly with legal dept. Industrial Commn. of Ariz. Democrat. Home: Willcox, Ariz. Deceased.

CUPPY, William Jacob (Will Cuppy) (kŭp'pĭ), writer; b. Auburn, Ind., Aug. 23, 1884; s. Thomas Jefferson and Mary Frances (Stahl) C.; Ph.B., U. of Chicago, 1907, A.M., 1914. Served as 2d lt., U.S. Army, World War. Mem. Phi Gamma Delta. Democrat. Presbyterian. Author: How to Be a Hermit, 1929; How to Tell Your Friends from the Apes, 1931; How to Become Extinct, 1941; The Great Bustard, 1944; Murder Without Tears, 1946; The Decline and Fall of Everybody, 1948. Writes a column in Weekly Book Review, N.Y. Herald Tribune. Home: 130 W. 11th St., New York, N.Y. Died Sep. 19, 1949.

CURETON, Calvin Maples, judge; b. nr. Walnut Springs, Tex., Sept. 1, 1874; s. William E. and Mary (Odle) C.; student U. of Va.; m. Nora Morris, Apr. 28, 1901. Began practice at Meridian, Bosque Co., Tex., 1899; mem. Tex. Ho. of Rep. 2 terms, 1909-12 inclusive; 1st asst. atty. gen. of Tex., 1913-18; atty. gen. of Texas, 2 terms, 1919-23, resigned; chief justice Supreme Court of Tex., since 1921. Served as pvt. Co. A, 3d Tex. Vol. Inf., Spanish Am. War, 1898. Democrat. Mem. Am. Bar Assn. K. of P. Editor: Banking Laws of Texas (with W. M. Harris), 1916. Home: 1300 Blanco St., Austin, Tex. Died Apr. 8, 1940.

CURLEY, Michael Joseph, archbishop; b. Golden Island, Athlone, Ireland, Oct. 12, 1879; s. Michael and Maria (Ward) C.; A.B., Royal U. of Ireland, 1900; B.D., Propaganda Theol. U., Rome, Italy, 1901, S.T.L., 1903. Ordained R.C. priest, 1904; missionary in Florida, 1904-14; apptd. bishop of St. Augustine by Pope Pius X, Apr. 2, 1914; consecrated June 30, 1914; apptd. archbishop of Baltimore to succeed Cardinal Gibbons, Aug. 1, 1921; installed in Baltimore, Nov. 30, 1921. Address: 408 N. Charles St., Baltimore, Md.* Died May 16, 1947.

CURME, George Oliver (kûrm), univ. prof.; b. Richmond, Ind., Jan. 14, 1860; s. Arthur A. and Elizabeth Jane (Nicholas) C.; student De Pauw U., irregularly, 1876-81, A.M., 1885; A.B., U. of Mich., 1882; student U. of Berlin, 1890; D.Litt., De Pauw, 1908; Ph.D., Heidelberg U., 1926; LL.D., U. of Southern Calif., 1935; Litt.D., Northwestern, 1937; m. Caroline C. Smith, July 14, 1881; children—Herta, Gertrude, George Oliver, Henry. Instr. German and French, Jennings Sem., Aurora, Ill., 1882-84; prof. modern langs., U. of Wash., 1884-86; instr. German and French, 1886-87, prof. German lang. and lit., 1887-96, Cornell Coll., Ia.; prof. Germanic philology, Northwestern U., 1896-1933; lecturer in German in U. of Southern Calif., 1934-39; retired. Mem. Linguistic Soc. America, Modern Lang. Assn. of America, Nat. Inst. of Social Sciences, Phi Beta Kappa. Author or Editor: Selected Poems from Premières et Nouvelles Méditations of Lamartine, 1888; Lessing's Nathan der Weise, 1898; A Grammar of the German Language, 1905, revised edit., 1922; Grillparzer's Libussa, 1913; A First German Grammar, 1913; College English Grammar, 1925; English Syntax, 1931; Parts of Speech and Accidence, 1935; Principles and Practice of English Grammar, 1946. Contbr. to Am. and German philol. jours. Address: 11 Murchison Place, White Plains, N.Y. Died Apr. 29, 1948.

CURRAN, Charles Courtney (kûr'rän), artist; b. Hartford, Ky., Feb. 13, 1861; s. Ulysses Thompson and Elizabeth (Thompson) C.; studied at Cincinnati Sch. Design, Nat. Acad. Design, and Art Students' League, New York, and Académie Julian, Paris; m. Grace Winthrop Wickham, of Norwalk, O., June 12, 1888. Hon. mention, Paris Salon, 1890; Clarke prize and 2d and 3d Hallgarten prizes, Nat. Acad. Design; $500 Carnegie prize, Soc. Am. Artists; $200 1st Corcoran prize, Washington; 1st Altman prize, Nat. Acad. Design, 1920; medals at Chicago and Cotton States Internat. expns.; silver medal, Buffalo Expn., 1901, St. Louis Expn., 1904; Shaw Fund prize, Soc. Am. Artists, 1906; A.N.A., 1888, N.A., 1904; corr. sec. N.A.D.; mem. Am. Water Color Soc., N.Y. Water Color Club, N.Y. Art Commn. Assn.; trustee Am. Fine Arts Soc. Clubs: Lotos (life), Fencers (life), Nat. Arts (life), Salmagundi. Address: 39 W. 67th St., New York, N.Y. Died Nov. 9, 1942.

CURRELL, William Spenser, educator; b. Charleston, S.C., May 13, 1858; s. William and Agnes (Wilkie) C.; A.B., B.P., Washington and Lee, 1878, A.M., 1879, Ph.D., 1882 (LL.D., U. of Ala. and Davidson Coll., 1914, and U. of Florida, 1916); m. Sarah Scott Carrington, June 28, 1888; children—Susan McDowell, Sarah Carrington, Agnes Wilkie (dec.), Mary Spenser, Lilly Preston (Mrs. F. M. Simrill), Elise Hay, Helen Nolting (Mrs. W. H. Burruss), Isabel Wilkie. Prof. English, Hampden-Sidney Coll., Va., 1882-86, Davidson Coll., N.C., 1886-95; prof. English and modern langs., 1895-99, prof. English, 1899-1914, Washington and Lee U., Lexington, Va.; pres., U., of S.C., 1914-22, dean of Grad. Sch., 1922-29, prof. of English, 1929-35; now prof. emeritus. Home: 810 Sumter St., Columbia, S.C. Died July 17, 1943.

CURRICK, Max Cohen, rabbi; b. Boston, Mass., Sept. 1, 1877; s. Fishel and Hannah (Ganut) C.; A.B., U. of Cincinnati, 1898; rabbi, Hebrew Union Coll., Cincinnati, 1898; D D. (hon.), 1939; m. Florence L. Baker, Jan. 27, 1910. Rabbi United Hebrew Congregation, Fort Smith, Ark., 1898-1901, Congregation Anshe Hesed, Erie, Pa., since 1901, editor Erie Dispatch (daily and Sunday), 1912-16; columnist Erie Daily Times, Erie Dispatch-Herald, Erie Observer, Chairman, regional panel War Labor Board. President Central Conference of Am. Rabbis, 1937-39, v.p. same, 1935-37, chmn. Com. on Internat. Peace, 1927-35. Chmn., Liberal Judaism, a monthly mag. Vice-pres. Community Chest of Erie County since 1918, Erie Pub. Library, 1923-37, pres. since 1937. Mem. bd. govs. Hebrew Union Coll., 1932-39, Union of Am. Hebrew congregations, 1937-39; board of governors B'Nai B'rith Home for Children, Fairview, Pa., since 1912, pres. since 1939; hon. mem. Erie Chapter, Am. Red Cross; chmn. The Playhouse, 1916-27 (mem. bd. to 1936); mem. bd. Erie Boys' Club, Anti-Tuberculosis Soc., The Child-Parent Bur. Hon. past pres. Dist. Grand Lodge, I.O.B B. No. 3, 1941. Mason. Author: (monographs) Jewish Apologetics, 1911; The Synagogue and the Philanthropies, 1916; The History of Congregation Anshe Hesed (Erie, Pa), 1929; and many others. Home: 523 W. 9th St. Office: 930 Liberty St., Erie, Pa. Died May 23, 1947.

CURRIE, Thomas White; b. Durango, Falls County, Tex., Jan. 23, 1879; s. David Mitchell and Ira Ione (White) C.; B.A., Austin Coll., Sherman, Tex., 1907, D.D., 1915; B.D., Austin Presbyn. Theol. Sem., 1911; M.A., U. of Tex., 1911; LL.D., Daniel Baker Coll., Brownwood, Tex., 1937; m. Jeannette E. Roe, Aug. 26, 1913; children—Thomas White, David Mitchell, Stuart Dickson, Elizabeth Jeannette. Formerly clk., bookkeeper, salesman; gen. sec. U. of Tex. Y.M.C.A., 1911-20; asso. prof. English Bible, 1911-20, pres. and prof. ch. history and English Bible since 1920, Austin Presbyn. Theol. Sem.; also pastor of the Highland Park Presbyterian Church of Dallas, Texas, 1932-37. Sec. Y.M.C.A. war work dept., 1917-18, also active in Liberty Loan Red Cross and European relief drives. Teacher Bible, summer camps, Kan., Colo., Mo., Tex., N.C., La and S.C., Neb. and Va. Moderator of Gen. Assembly of Presbyn. Ch. in U.S., May 1930-May 1931; mem. exec. com. Schs. and Colls., Synod of Tex., Presbyn. Ch. in U.S. Rep. Presbyn. Ch. U.S., to Universal Christian Conf. on Life and Work, Stockholm, Sweden, 1925, also to Pan-Presbyn. Conf., Cardiff, Wales, 1925; sec. Tex. Ednl. Endowment ($1,-350,000), Presbyn. Ch.; del. of Presbyn. Ch. to World Conf. on Faith and Order, Edinburgh, Scotland, 1937; chmn. Com. on Coöperation and Union for the Presbyn. Ch. in U.S. since 1938. Mason. Mem. Alpha Tau Omega. Clubs: University, Rotary. Author: Studies in the Psalms; also author of extension courses in English Bible, given through U. of Tex. Home: 2621 Speedway. Office: 100 W. 27th St., Austin, Tex. Died Apr. 22, 1943.

CURRIER, Richard Dudley (kûr'rĭ-ēr), lawyer, educator; b. Bridgeport, Conn., Aug. 25, 1877; s. Levi Wheeler and Sarah Elizabeth (Ayer) C.; B.A., Yale, 1900; student Boston U. Law Sch., 1900-01; LL.B., New York Law Sch., 1902; LL.D., U. of Newark, 1939; m. Adèle Josephine Ames, Oct. 20, 1909; children—Elizabeth Adèle (Mrs. Thomas Jefferson Morris), Ruth Prentice (Mrs. Forrest P. Gates, Jr.), Richard Dustin, Eleanor Ames (dec.). Began practice in New York City, 1902; founder, 1908, and president New Jersey Law Sch., Newark, New Jersey, 1908-34; founder, 1930, and pres. Dana Coll., Newark, 1930-34, treas., 1934-36; organizer Seth Boyden Sch. of Business, 1930; founder with Dr. T. Lawrence Davis of Stoneleigh Coll., Rye, N.H., pres. since 1934; pres. Dorec Press, Inc. Mem. Am. Bar Assn., N.Y. State Bar Assn., Am. Soc. Internat. Law, Internat. Law Assn., Acad. Polit. Science. Republican. Unitarian. Clubs: Dorset (Vt.) Field; Bankers (New York). Author: Cases on Torts (with Oscar M. Bate), 1914; Negotiable Instruments, 1922. Editor: Commercial Law, 1922. Home: 95 S. Mountain Av., Montclair, N.J. Died June 2, 1947.

CURRIER, Thomas Franklin, retired; b. Roxbury, Mass., Feb. 26, 1873; s. Thomas Florian and Lucinda Franklin (Reed) C.; grad. Boston Latin Sch., 1890; A.B., Harvard, 1894; m. Florence May Wyman, Oct. 14, 1908; children—Margaret, Jean (dec.). Asst. in Boston Athenæum Library, 1894; asst. Harvard Coll. Library, 1894-1913; asst. librarian, Harvard U., 1913-37, asso. librarian, 1937-40; hon. curator of New Eng. literature and consultant in Am. literary bibliography in Harvard Univ. Library since 1941; hon. curator of the Whittier Collection, Haverhill (Mass.) Public Library. Mem. American Antiquarian Soc., Mass. Historical Soc., A.L.A., Am. Library Inst., Bibliographical Soc. America, Friends Hist. Assn., Phi Beta Kappa. Republican. Conglist. Mason. Club: Appalachian Mountain. Compiler of the Catalogue of the Molière Collection in Harvard College Library (with Ernest Lewis Gay), 1906; Catalogue of Graduates of the Public Latin School in Boston, 1918; Selective Cataloging, 1923; A Bibliography of John Greenleaf Whittier, 1937; Elizabeth Lloyd and the Whittiers, 1939; collaborator in Catalogue Rules compiled by committees of the Am. Library Assn. and the British Library Assn., 1908, 2d edit., 1941. Home: 19 West St., Belmont, Mass. Died Sep. 14, 1946.

CURRY, Charles Madison, editor; b. Whiteland, Ind., May 16, 1869; s. Oliver P. and Catherine (Brown) C.; A B., Franklin (Ind.) Coll., 1891, A.M., 1895; studied U. of Mich., U. of Chicago and Oxford U., Eng.; m. Mabel Dunlap, Sept. 8, 1892; children—Margaret, Harriet, Charlotte. With Ind. State Normal Sch. from 1892, as asst. prof. lit., 1892-93, actg. head of dept., 1893-94, prof. lit., 1894-1925; ednl. editor for Rand, McNally & Co., Chicago, 1926-28; special editor for Am. Book Co., New York, since 1928. On leave as chmn. Ind. Edn. Survey Commn., 1921-22; supervisor teacher training for Ind., 1922-23. Editor: Literary Readings (introduction to study of literature), 1903; (with M. Adelaide Holton) Holton-Curry Readers (8 books), 1914; (with L. P. Powell) The World and Democracy, 1919; (with E. E. Clippinger) Children's Literature, 1921; (with M. B. Huber and H. B. Bruner) The Poetry Book (9 vols.) and Children's Interests in Poetry; (with T. H. Briggs and L. W. Payne) Literature for the Junior High School. Address: 88 Lexington Av., New York, N.Y. Died Mar. 14, 1944.

CURRY, George, ex-governor; b. Bayou Sara, La., Apr. 3, 1862; s. George and Clara C.; ed. country schs. Worked on ranches, 1875-85; dep. county treas., 1888, county clk., 1888-90, assessor, 1890-92, sheriff, 1892-94, Lincoln County, N.M.; mem. N.M. Territorial Senate 1894-96 (pres. 1895-96); clk. U.S. Dist. Ct., 1895; 1st lt. and capt. 1st U.S. Vol. Cav. ("Rough Riders"), Spanish-Am. War, 1898; sheriff Otero County, N.M., Mar.-Aug. 1899; lt. 11th Vol. Cav., 1899, and comd. regtl. scouts in P.I.; capt. Troop K, 11th Cav., 1900-01; 1st civ. gov. Province of Ambos Camarine, P.I., Apr.-Aug 1901; chief of police of Manila and organized 1st civ. police force under Am. Govt., Aug. 1902; mgr. Camarines Mercantile Co., 1902-03; gov. Province of Isabella, P.I., 1904-05; gov. of Samar, 1905-07; gov. of N.M., 1907-11; mem. 72d Congress (1911-13), State of N.M.; mem. Internat. Boundary Commn., U.S. and Mexico, until 1928; chmn. New Mexico Draft bd., N.M. rationing bd. during World War II; now state historian for N.M. Republican. K.P. Elk. Home: Kingston, N.M. Died Nov. 24, 1948; buried National Cemetery, Santa Fe, N.M.

CURRY, John Steuart, artist; b. Dunavant, Kan., Nov. 14, 1897; s. Smith and Margaret (Steuart) C.; student Art Inst. Chicago, 1916-18, Geneva Coll., Beaver Falls, Pa., 1919-20, Russian Acad., Paris, 1926-27, Art Students League, New York, 1927; m. Clara H. Derrick, Jan. 23, 1923 (died July 10, 1932); m. 2d, Kathleen Muriel Gould, June 2, 1934. Rep. by paintings in permanent collections of Metropolitan Museum, Whitney Museum of Am. Art, Addison Gallery, Phillips Andover Acad., U. of Neb.; frescos in Bedford Jr. High Sch., Westport, Conn.; decorations for Dept. of Justice and Dept. of Interior bldgs., Washington; murals in Kansas State Capitol, Topeka, Kan., Biochemistry Bldg., U. of Wis., Law Library, U. of Wis., First National Bank, Madison, Wis. Art instr. Art Students League (New York); artist in residence, Coll. of Agriculture, U. of Wis., since 1936. Awarded 2d prize, Carnegie Internat. Exhbn., 1933. Served as pvt., U.S. Army, World War I. Ref. Presbyn. Home: R.F.D. 3, Madison, Wis. Died Aug. 29, 1946.

CURTIS, Carlton Clarence, botanist; b. Syracuse, N.Y., Aug. 26, 1864; s. Harlow and Martha (Shumway) C.; A.B., Syracuse U., 1891, A.M., Ph.D., 1893; A.M., Columbia, 1892; student universities of Cambridge, 1899, Leipzig, 1900; married. Principal, Fayette Union Sch., N.Y., 1892-94; instr. natural science, Brooklyn Poly. Inst., 1894-96; instr. botany, Columbia, since 1899. Mem. Am. Soc. Naturalists, Bot. Soc. Am. and other bot. socs., Phi Beta Kappa. Contbr. to bot. jours. Author: Text-Book of General Botany, 1897; Nature and Development of Plants, 1922; Guide to the Trees, 1927. Address: Columbia University, New York. Died Apr. 10, 1945.

CURTIS, Charles Minot, judge; b. Newark, Del., Aug. 19, 1859; s. Frederick Augustus and Harriet L. (Hurd) C.; A.B., Delaware Coll., 1877; LL.B., Harvard, 1881; m. Phœbe George Bradford, Mar. 31, 1886; children—Frederick A., Stephen. Admitted to bar, 1883; practiced at Wilmington, Del.; city solicitor Wilmington, 1891-93; chancellor, and presiding judge Supreme Court of Del., 1909-21. V.p. Delaware Trust Co.; judge Juvenile Court, 1926-39. Republican. Mgr. Del. Industrial Sch. for Girls, Babies' Hosp.; trustee Del. Coll.; trustee and chancellor of the P.E. Diocese of Del. Home: Granby, Mass.* Died Apr. 15, 1945.

CURTIS, Charles Pelham, lawyer, trustee; b. Winchester, Mass., Sept. 7, 1860; s. Charles Pelham and Caroline Gardiner (Cary) C.; desc William Curtis, of England, who settled in Roxbury, Mass., 1632; A.B. Harvard University, 1883; married Ellen Amory Anderson, July 30, 1890; children—Charles Pelham, Jr., Richard Cary, Ellen Sears Minot. Admitted to Mass. bar, 1886, and since practiced at Boston; v.p. Provident Instn. for Savings; dir. Dwight Mfg. Co., New Eng. Trust Co., Boston Ins. Co.; formerly pres. Lowell Bleachery and Collateral Loan Co.; formerly v.p. Mass. Hosp. Life Ins. Co. and dir. Boston & Roxbury Mills Corp. Mem. Met. Dist. Commn. on Greater Boston, 1894; mem. Boston Bd. of Police, 1895-1905; mem. Finance Commn. of City of Boston, 1909-13; pres. bd. of incorporators, Peter Bent Brigham Hosp., 1915-36; former dir. Boston Lying-in Hosp.; former mem. bd. mgrs. and chmn. admission com., Farm and Trades Sch.; formerly pres. and chmn. standing com. Humane Soc. of Mass.; mem. bd. mgrs. Mass. Eye and Ear Infirmary. Served as ensign and lt., U.S.N.R., World War I; in Office of Comdr. U. S. Naval Aviation Forces, Paris; aide on staff comdr. and liaison officer to British; aide to comdr. of Naval Air Station, Ireland. Mem. Nat. Audubon Soc., Mass. Soc. Mayflower Descendants, Mil. Order World War, Mil. Order Foreign Wars, East African Professional Hunters Assn. (hon.); fellow Royal Geog. Soc. and Zoöl. Soc. (London). Clubs: Somerset, Tavern, Harvard (Boston); Country (Brookline); Harvard Varsity; Essex Country; Eastern Yacht (commodore 1929-30); Corinthian Yacht; Boston Yacht. Home: 244 Beacon St. Office: Ames Bldg., Boston, Mass. Died Apr. 26, 1948.

CURTIS, Eugene Newton, prof. history; b. White Plains, N.Y., June 23, 1880; s. Newton Freeman and Gertrude I. (Preudhomme) C.; grad. Phillips Acad., Andover, Mass., 1897; B.A., Yale, 1901; B.D., Episcopal Theol. Sch., Cambridge, Mass., 1904; M A., Harvard, 1904; studied U. of Paris, 1912-14, U. of Munich, 1914; Ph.D., Columbia, 1917; m. Blanche O'Neill; 1 son, Franklin O'Neill. Instr. in history, U. of Wis., 1915-17; asst. prof. history, Goucher Coll., Baltimore, Md., 1917-19, asso. prof., 1919-20, prof. since 1920, also acting dean, 1919-21. Mem. Am. Hist. Assn., Md. History Teachers' Assn. Republican. Episcopalian. Author: The French Assembly of 1848 and American Constitutional Doctrines, 1918; Saint-Just, Colleague of Robespierre, 1935; also hist. articles in Am. and European mags. Home: 4323 Wickford Rd., Baltimore, Md. Died Apr. 20, 1944.

CURTIS, Florence Rising, librarian, educator; b. Ogdensburg, N.Y.; d. Gen. Newton Martin and Emeline (Clark) Curtis; Wells Coll., Aurora, N.Y., 1891-94; diploma N.Y. State Library Sch., Albany, 1896, B L.S., 1911; A.B., U. of Ill., 1911; M.A., U. of Minn., 1917. Asst., Osterhout Library, Wilkes-Barre, Pa., 1894-97; librarian and sec. State Normal Sch.,

Potsdam, N.Y., 1900-06; librarian Atheneum Library, Saratoga Springs, N.Y., 1906-08; successively instr., asso., and asst. prof. U. of Ill. Library Sch., 1908-20; teacher govt. schs., Kaifeng, China, and Manila, P.I., 1920-22; asst. dir. Drexel Inst. Library Sch., 1922-25; dir. Hampton Inst. Library Sch., 1925-39. Mem. A.L.A. Unitarian. Author: (brochures), The Collection of Social Survey Material, 1915; The Libraries of the American State and National Institutions for Delinquents, Dependents and Defectives, 1918. Home: 417 Elizabeth St., Ogdensburg, N.Y. Died Oct. 6, 1944.

CURTIS, Otis Freeman, plant physiology; b. of Am. parents, Sendai, Japan, Feb. 12, 1888; s. William Willis and Lydia Virginia (Cone) C.; A.B., Oberlin, 1911; Ph.D., Cornell U., 1916; m. Lucy Marguerite Weeks, Aug. 27, 1913; children—Otis Freeman, William Edgar, Margaret Ann. Tutor Oberlin Acad., 1911-12; with Cornell U. since 1913, instr., later asst. prof. botany until 1922, prof. botany, plant physiologist, Expt. Sta., since 1922; visiting prof., U. of Leeds, Eng., 1926-27, Ohio State U., 1930-31. Mem. A.A.A.S., Bot. Soc. America, American Assn. Naturalists, Am. Soc. for Hort. Science, Am. Society Plant Physiologists (v.p. 1936-37, pres. 1937-38), Phi Kappa Phi, Gamma Alpha, Sigma Xi. Unitarian. Author: Translocation of Solutes in Plants; Introduction to Plant Physiology, 1949. Contributed findings of research along lines of translocation of foods in green plants, vegetative propagation and water and temperature relations of plants. Home: Forest Home, Ithaca, N.Y. Died July 4, 1949.

CURTISS, Charles Franklin, agriculturist; b. Nora, Ill., Dec. 12, 1863; s. Franklin and Margaret (Schmitz) C.; B.Agr., Ia. Agrl. Coll., 1887, M.Agr., 1894; D.Sc., Mich. Agrl. Coll., 1907; m. Olive Wilson, Feb. 15, 1893. Managed farm, 1887-90; asst. dir., 1890-97, dir., 1897-32, Ia. Expt. Sta., and sr. dean of agr., now dean emeritus. A founder, dir., mem. exec. com. Internat. Live Stock Expn. Assn.; mem. Am. Soc. Promotion Agrl. Science. Club: Saddle and Sirloin (Chicago). Home: Ames, Ia. Died July 30, 1947.

CURTISS, Julian Wheeler; b. Fairfield, Conn., Aug. 29, 1858; s. Henry Tomlinson and Mary Eliza (Henderson) C.; A.B., Yale, 1879, hon. A.M., 1926; m. Mary Case, Oct. 12, 1880; children—Jean Beardslee (Mrs. Lee Wallis Gibbons), Mary Louise (Mrs. Herbert Hoyt Pease), Henry Tomlinson (dec.), Margaret Burr (dec.). Sec. A. G. Spalding & Bros., 1885-98, v.p. 1898-1920, pres., 1920-33, chmn. bd., 1933-38. Chmn. Greenwich War Bur., World War. One of 2 neutral arbitrators between N.Y.C. R.R. and Shop Craft employees. Pres. Y.M.C.A., Greenwich, 1916-24. Mem. U.S. Chamber Commerce, Conn. Chamber Commerce, Grad. Assn., Delta Kappa Epsilon, Scroll and Key. Republican. Clubs: Yale (pres. 1904-06), Special Car, Greenwich Country (pres. 1924-33), Yale Golf, Round Hill Golf. Grad. coach of Yale crew, 1902-11; referee Intercollegiate Assn. Poughkeepsie Regatta, 1918-40, and Yale-Harvard race, 1933; retired 1940. Home: Oak Farm, Greenwich, Conn. Office: 19 Beekman St., New York, N.Y. Died Feb. 17, 1944.

CUSHING, Oscar K., lawyer; b. 1865. Partner Cushing & Cushing, San Francisco. Mem. Am. Bar. Assn., State Bar of Calif., Bar Assn. of San Francisco. Home: 37 7th Av. Office: 1 Montgomery St., San Francisco, Calif. Died Oct. 6, 1948.

CUSHMAN, Joseph Augustine, biologist; b. Bridgewater, Mass., Jan. 31, 1881; s. Darius and Jane Frances (Fuller) C.; student Bridgewater (Mass.) Normal School 4 yrs.; S.B., Harvard U., 1903; Ph.D. from same, 1909, hon. Sc.D., 1937; m. Alice Edna Wilson, Oct. 7, 1903 (died Jan. 25, 1912); children—Robert Wilson, Alice Eleanor, Ruth Allerton; m. 2d, Frieda G. Billings, Sept. 3, 1913. Museum dir. Boston Soc. Natural History, 1913-23; dir. Cushman Laboratory for Foraminiferal Research since 1923. Lecturer in micropalæontology, Harvard, 1926-40; research asso. in micropaleontology, Harvard, since 1940. Consulting geologist U.S. Geol. Survey; mem. Carnegie Instn. Expdn. to Jamaica, 1912. Chairman com. on micropaleontology National Research Council since 1930. Fellow Am. Acad. of Arts and Sciences; mem. Geol. Soc. America (v.p. 1938), Washington Acad. Sciences, Paleontol. Soc. (pres. 1937), Am. Geog. Soc., Boston Soc. Natural History (trustee), N.E. Bot. Club, Am. Assn. Petroleum Geologists, A.A.A.S., Soc. Econ. Paleontology and Mineralogy (pres. 1930-31), Calif. Acad. Sciences, Sigma Xi; hon. fellow Royal Microscopical Society of London. Recipient of Hayden Memorial gold medal, 1945. Unitarian. Mason. Author: Monograph of Foraminifera of North Pacific Ocean (Smithsonian Instn.), Parts I-VI, 1910-17; Foraminifera of Atlantic Ocean, Parts I-VIII, 1918-31; also various papers on fossil and living Foraminifera in publs. U.S. Geol. Survey, U.S. Nat. Museum, Carnegie Instn., Washington, and publs. of Cushman Lab. Editor Jour. of Paleontology, 1927-30. Home: Brook Rd., Sharon, Mass. Died Apr. 16, 1949.

CUSTER, Omer N(ixon), banker; b. Fayette County, Pa., Dec. 25, 1873; s. Hernon Kyle and Dorcas Anne (Nixon) C.; ed. pub. schs., Fayette County; m. Olive Frances Temple, Dec. 24, 1894; children—Mrs. Ethel Mae Pritchard, Howard Temple (dec.). Pres. 1st Galesburg Nat. Bank & Trust Co. Purington Paving Brick Co., pub. Galesburg Register Mail; pres. Intra-State Telephone Co., Beatrice Creamery Co., Abingdon Sanitary Mfg. Co., Gazette Pub. Co., pubs. Hawkeye Gazette (Burlington, Ia.). Co. treas., Knox County, Ill., 1906; postmaster of Galesburg, 1908-13; mem. Ill. State Industrial Commn., 1917-21; state treas., Ill., 1925-27, 1929-30; chmn. State Tax Commn., 1930-31. Trustee Lombard College, Galesburg. Republican. Presbyterian. Mason. Club: Rotary (Galesburg). Home: 81 E. Grove St., Galesburg, Ill. Office: 154 E. Simmons St., Galesburg, Ill. Died Oct. 17, 1942.

CUSTIS, John Trevor, editor; b. Philadelphia, Pa., Dec. 17, 1875; s. Rev. John William and Henrietta Elizabeth (Sheldrake) C.; student Central High Sch., Phila., 1890-93; m. Mary C. Farrell, Nov. 3, 1900. With the Philadelphia Inquirer since 1894, reporter until 1899, city editor, 1899-1908, mng. editor, 1908-33, editor since 1933; v.p. and dir. Phila. Inquirer Co. Member of the Colonial Society of Pennsylvania. Republican. Episcopalian. Club: Union League. Author: The Public Schools of Philadelphia, 1897. Home: 7620 Lincoln Dr., Chestnut Hill. Office: Inquirer Bldg., Philadelphia. Died Dec. 3, 1944; buried in St. Luke's Churchyard, Germantown, Pa.

CUTHELL, Chester Welde (kŭth-ĕl'), lawyer; b. N.Y. City, Jan. 10, 1884; s. James M. and Louise (Welde) C.; A.B., Columbia, 1905, LL.B., 1907; m. Dorothy Banta, May 21, 1913; children—Robert, Mary, David, Priscilla. In law office Ward, Hayden & Satterlee, New York, several yrs.; mem. Cuthell, Appleby, Osterhout & Mills, New York; gen. counsel U.S. Shipping Bd. Emergency Fleet Corp., Mar. 1918-Jan. 1919; spl. rep. of sec. of war, Jan.-Oct. 1919, and effected collection of War Dept.'s claims against Eng., France and Italy; organized many aviation cos.; spl. counsel N.Y. State Transit Commn. in unification of all New York City subway and elevated railroads, 1937-41. D.S.M.; Chevalier Legion of Honor (French); Commendatore Order of the Crown of Italy. Mem. Assn. Bar City of New York, Am. Bar Assn., Phi Gamma Delta Fraternity. Lutheran. Clubs: Downtown Assn., University, Columbia Univ., Wee Burn, Congressional. Home: 1160 Park Av., New York. Office: American Security Bldg., Washington, D.C., and 630 Fifth Av., New York, N.Y. Died Dec. 11, 1942.

CUTLER, Elliott Carr, prof. surgery; b. Bangor, Me., July 30, 1888; s. George Chalmers and Mary Franklin (Wilson) C.; A.B., Harvard, 1909, M.D., 1913; hon. doctorate U. of Strasbourg, 1938; D.Sc., U. of Vermont, 1941, University of Rochester, 1946; m. Caroline Parker, May 24, 1919; children—Elliott Carr, Thomas Pollard, David, Marjorie Parker (dec.), Tarrant. Surgical house officer, Peter Bent Brigham Hosp., 1913-15; resident surgeon, Harvard Unit, Am. Ambulance Hosp., Paris, 1915; resident surgeon, Mass. Gen. Hosp., 1915-16; alumni asst. in surgery, Harvard, 1915-16; voluntary asst., Rockefeller Inst., N.Y. City, 1916-17; resident surgeon, Peter Bent Brigham Hospital, 1919-21, associate in surgery, 1921-24; instructor in surgery, Harvard, 1921-24; professor of surgery, Western Reserve Univ., School of Medicine, 1924-32; dir. of Surgical Service, Lakeside Hosp., Cleveland, 1924-32; consulting surgeon, New England Peabody Home for Crippled Children, since 1932, Children's Hosp., Boston, since 1945; Moseley Prof. of surgery, Harvard, since 1932; surgeon in chief, Peter Bent Brigham Hosp., since 1932; chief consultant to professional services division, Vet. Adminstrn., 1945; civilian consultant to Sec. of War since May, 1946; acting asst. med. dir. Vets. Adminstrn., since 1947. Trustee, Dexter Sch., 1938-43 (chmn. med. com., 1938-43), Noble and Greenough School, Boston Sch. Occupational Therapy, Mass. State Infirmary; mem. exec. com., Hugh Cabot Memorial Fund; mem. Mass. Med. Benevolent Soc., trustee, 1934-37; sponsor Walter Cannon Memorial Fund, 1946. Served as lt. Med. Res..ve Corps, 1916-17; capt., M.O.R.C., 1917-18, major, 1918-24, lt. col., 1924-42, col., 1942-45, brig. gen., A.U.S., 1945, retired April, 1946; chief surgical consultant, E.T.O., U.S. Army, 1942-45; chief, professional services div., E.T.O., U.S. Army, 1945. Awarded Distinguished Service Medal with Battle Clasps for Champagne-Marne, Aise-Marne, St. Mihiel, (Meuse-Argonne Defensive Sector), Victory Medal World War I; Campaign Medal, E.T.O., World War II, Legion of Merit, Croix de Guerre with Palm, Order of British Empire; Oak Leaf Clusters & D.S.M., World War II. Fellow, Am. Coll. Surgeons, Boston Med. Library, Internat. Society of Surgery (chmn. Am. Com., 1929-47, del., chmn., U.S. Exec. Com., 1932). Mem. A.A.A.S., Am. Assn. Advancement of Sci., Am. Geog. Soc., Mass. Foundation, Am. Acad. Surgery, Am. Assn. for Thoracic Surgery, Am. Bd. of Surgery, Founders Group, 1937, Am. Bur. for Med. Aid to China, Inc., Am. Soc. for Clinical Investigation (emeritus, 1931), Am. Heart Assn., Inc., A.M.A., Am. Soc. for Exptl. Pathology, Am. Surgical Assn. (pres. 1947), Am.-Soviet Medical Soc. (regional v.p. 1945-47; American Committee for the Protection of Medical Research, (chmn., 1926-42), Assn. Mil. Surgeons of the U.S.; Boston Surgical Soc.; Boylston Med. Soc. of Harvard U., L'Europe Medicale (hon. scientific mem., patronage com.), Friends of Med. Progress; Federation of Am. Socs. for Exptl. Biology (chmn. of com. for defense of Biological Research), Gerontological Soc., Inc., Harvard Med. Alumni Assn., Mass. Med. Soc.; Med. Exchange Club; New England Heart Assn.; New England Surgical Soc.; Norfolk Med. Soc., Omaha Med. Soc., Soc. for Exptl. Biology and Medicine, Soc. of Clinical Surgery, (senior mem. 1943, pres., 1941-46); Soc. of Univ. Surgeons, (hon. mem. 1938); Suffolk Dist. Med. Soc., Soc. U.S. Med. Consultants of World War II (pres. 1946). Mem. Town of Brookline Unemployment Com., U.N. (official, Mass. Com.), Mass. Foundation, exec. com., Mass. com. on Public Safety, (dir. Med. Div.), Mass. Com. for retaining wild life, Parker River Wild Life Refuge. Mem. Alpha Omega Alpha, Sigma Xi, American Legion Inc. (Also corresponding member of many foreign medical societies.). Unitarian. Clubs: Harvard, Somerset, Thursday Evening, Friday Evening, (all Boston), Aesculapian, Asso. Harvard Clubs (pres. 1936), Porcellian, Hasty Pudding (all affiliated Harvard U.), Harvard (New York), Mayfield Country (Cleveland), Country (Brookline), N. American Yacht Racing Union, Vineyard Haven Yacht Club (Commodore, 1938-42; 1946), Bonaventure Assos., Rotary (distinguished service award, 1946); Henry Jacob Bigelow medal from Boston Surg. Soc., 1947. Editor: America Clinica (adv. bd.), American Heart Journal, (adv. bd.), Macmillan Co. Surgical Monograph Series, (editor), Journal of Clinical Investigation (editorial com.), Surgery (adv. council), Am. Jour. of Surgery, (asso. editor), Brit. Jour. Surgery, (editorial bd. and exec. com.), Washington Inst. of Medicine, (editorial and consulting bd. in surgery). Author: Atlas of Surgical Operations (with R. Zollinger), 1939. Home: 61 Heath St., Brookline, Mass. Office: Peter Bent Brigham Hospital, 721 Huntington Av., Boston 15, Mass. Died Aug. 16, 1947

CUTLER, Frederick Morse, educator; b. Elizabeth, N.J., Apr. 23, 1874; s. Edward Morse and Josephine Adelaide (Macfarlane) C.; A.B., Columbia, 1895; B.D., cum laude, Union Theol. Sem., 1898; fellow Clark U., 1920-21, Ph.D., 1922; m. Lillian Maria Metcalf, Nov. 25, 1903. Gen. sec. Y.M.C.A. of Columbia U., 1895-97; pastor Presbyn. Ch., Wallington, N.J., 1897-98; home missionary (Congl.), Armour, S.D., 1898-1901; pastor Ashland, Mass., 1901-03, Edgartown, 1903-08, Hudson, 1908-12, Wenham, 1912-17; exec. sec. Worcester Fedn. of Chs., 1920-21; prof. history, U. of Porto Rico, 1922-25; asst. prin., State Teachers Coll., Worcester, 1925-26; in charge of anthropology and sociology, Mass. State Coll., since 1926. Chaplain 55th Arty., C.A.C., U.S. Army, with A.E.F., 1917-19; in battles at Aisne-Marne, Champagne, Oise-Aisne and Meuse-Argonne; lt. col. U.S. Army (Res.). Charter mem. S.A.R., S.D., 1899; Grand Rep., K.P., South Dakota, 1901; del. to Congl. Nat. Council, 1907; mem. council Boy Scouts America, 1911-36; chaplain Ancient and Hon. Arty. Co., Boston, 1916; dept. chaplain for Mass., Am. Legion, 1919; chaplain Mass. Commandery, Mil. Order Foreign Wars, 1921; dept. pres. for P.R., Reserve Officers' Assn. of U.S., 1925; councillor for Mass., Order of Founders and Patriots, 1925-29, historian Amherst Hist. Soc. since 1939. Mem. Am. Congl. Assn., 7th Regt. Vets. (N.Y. City), Soc. Clan MacFarlane (London), Sigma Phi Epsilon and Pi Gamma Mu fraternities. Club: City (sec.). Author: The Old First Massachusetts Coast Artillery in War and Peace, 1917; The 55th Artillery in the A.E.F., 1920; History of Military Conscription (monograph), 1922; Sociological Laws, 1924, 29, 32 and 37; contbr. to periodicals. Home: 43 Butterfield Terrace, Amherst, Mass. Died Dec. 26, 1944.

CUTTER, Irving Samuel, physician; b. Keene, N.H., Dec. 5, 1875; s. Charles H. and Frances (Prescott) C.; B.Sc., U. of Neb., 1898, M.D., 1910, D.Sc., 1925; LL.D., Jefferson Medical College, 1931; Sc.D., Northwestern University, 1941; m. Mary L. Stearns, July 26, 1909; 1 son, Richard Stearns. Instructor high school, Humboldt, Nebraska, 1896; principal Beatrice High School, 1898-1900; gen. agt. Ginn & Co., 1900-06; practicing physician and instr. physiol. chemistry, U. of Neb., 1910-13; prof. biochemistry and dir. of lab., 1913-15, dean, 1915-25, Coll. of Medicine, U. of Neb.; asso. prof. medicine and dean Northwestern U. Med. Sch., 1925-41, dean and professor of medicine emeritus since Sept. 1941; med. dir. Passavant Memorial Hospital since 1928. Editor Neb. State Med. Jour., 1916-18; mem. editorial bd. Annals of Med. History. Health editor The Chicago Tribune since 1934. Capt. Med. Corps U.S. Army, 1918-19; lt. col. med. sect. O.R.C., 1920-29. Fellow A.A.A.S., A.M.A.; mem. Am. Chem. Soc., S.A.R., Alpha Omega Alpha, Sigma Xi, Phi Rho Sigma (pres. 1927-34), Chi Phi. Clubs: University, Glen View. Author: (with F. E. Clements) Laboratory Manual of High School Botany, 1899; also wrote The School of Medicine, 1930; History of Physical Therapy, 1932; History of Obstetrics and Gynecology, 1933; and numerous other monographs on med. and ednl. topics. Home: 1307 Ashland Av., Wilmette, Ill. Office: 303 E. Superior St., Chicago, Ill. Died Feb. 2, 1945.

CUTTING, Elisabeth Brown, editor; b. Brooklyn, N.Y.; d. Churchill Hunter and Mary (Dutton) Cutting; A.B., Vassar; A.M., Columbia. Editorial staff Harper's Bazar, 1907-10; asso. editor North Am. Review, 1910-21, mng. editor, 1921-27. Mem. bd. mgrs. Am. Bible Soc. since 1925. Mem. Am. Hist. Assn., N.Y. State Hist. Assn., Vassar Alumnæ Assn. (pres. 1916-18), Am. Soc. of French Legion of Honor (dir. 1934-37). Officier de l'Instruction Publique and Chevalier Légion d'Honneur (France). Club: Cosmopolitan. Author: Jefferson Davis, Political Soldier, 1930. Address: 955 Lexington Av., N.Y. City. Died, Aug. 13, 1946.

CYR, Paul Narcisse, ex-gov.; b. Jeanerette, La., Sept. 9, 1878; s. Joseph and Emilie Julie (Hoffer)

Cyr; grad. Atlanta Dental Coll., 1900; m. Mary McGowen, Feb. 6, 1907; children—Louie, Marjorie, Emily, Charles. Began practice of dentistry at Jeanerette, 1900; was pres. Dental Examining Bd., La.; identified with banking business since 1907; dir. First Nat. Bank, Jeanerette, also dir. Consolidated Grocery Co.; elected lt. gov. of La., 1928; succeeded Huey P. Long as gov. for term expiring May 1932. Democrat. Presbyterian. K.P., Woodman, Elk. Home: Jeanerette, La. Died Aug. 24, 1946.

ÇZERWONKY, Richard Rudolph (chĕr-vŏn′kĭ), violin virtuoso; b. Birnbaum, Provinz Posen, Germany, May 23, 1886; s. Gustav and Marie (Gartheis) C.; studied with Floian Zajic, Andreas Moser and Joseph Joachim, in Berlin; at Klindworth-Scharwenka Conservatory, 3 yrs., Royal High Sch. of Music, 4 yrs.; m. Hildegard Maurer, June 28, 1910. Début, Berlin, with Philharmonic Orch., 1906; played in Germany, Sweden, Holland, France, Russia, etc.; asst. concertmaster, Boston Symphony Orchestra, 1907-08; concertm., asst. condr. and soloist Minneapolis Symph. Orchestra, 1909-18; head of violin dept. Bush Conservatory of Music, Chicago, Ill., 1918-32; founder and dir. Bush Conservatory Symphony Orchestra; v.p. Chicago Conservatory, 1932-35; founder Women's Symphony Orchestra of Chicago; condr. Chicago Philharmonic Orchestra, 1925-45, condr. Kenosha Symphony Orchestra. Guest conductor, violin soloist, Berlin Symphony Orchestra, 25th Artists' Jubilee, 1931. Head of the violin and orchestral department at De Paul University School of Music, Chicago, since 1935. Has appeared as soloist in leading musical centers of U.S. Became naturalized citizen of U.S., 1915. Mem. Am. Soc. Composers, Artists and Pubs.; nat. hon. mem. of Phi Mu Gamma; hon. mem. Phi Mu Alpha Sinfonia. Lutheran. Mason (32°, Shriner). Has composed extensively for violin, piano, voice, orchestra, etc. Home: 2622 N. Lakeview Av. Studio: 64 E. Lake St., Chicago. Died Apr. 16, 1949.

D

DABNEY, Charles William (dăb′nē), univ. pres.; b. Hampden-Sydney, Va., June 19, 1855; s. Robert L. D. (Stonewall Jackson's chief of staff) and Lavinia (Morrison) D.; A.B., Hampden-Sydney Coll., 1873; Univ. of Va., 1874-77; Ph.D., Göttingen, 1880; LL D., Davidson, 1889, Washington & Lee Univ., 1900, Yale U., 1901, Johns Hopkins U., 1902, U. of Cincinnati, 1937; m. Mary Brent, Aug. 24, 1881. Prof. chemistry, Emory and Henry Coll., 1877-78; studied Berlin and Göttingen, 1878-80; prof. chemistry, University of N.C., and state chemist, 1880-81; director North Carolina Agricultural Experimental Sta., 1880-87; prof. agr. chemistry and dir. Tenn. Expt. Sta., 1887-90; pres. U. of Tenn., 1887-1904; pres. U. of Cincinnati, 1904-20; retired, 1920; state chemist of N.C., 1880-87; asst. sec. Dept. of Agr., 1893-97. Chief dept. of govt. and states exhibits, New Orleans Expn., 1883-84; chmn. bd. mgrs. of govt. exhibits, Atlanta Expn., 1895, Tenn. Centennial Expn., 1897; mem. Jury Awards, Paris Expn., 1900. Fellow A.A.A.S. Mem. Inst. Publique Instruction, Chevalier French Legion d'Honneur, N.E.A., Wash. Acad. of Science, etc. Clubs: Cosmos (Washington); Authors' (London). Author: Universal Education in the South; also other books on hist., scientific and ednl. subjects. Home: 2719 Digby Av., Clifton, Cincinnati, O. Died June 15, 1945.

DABNEY, Richard Heath, univ. prof.; b. Memphis, Tenn., Mar. 29, 1860; s. Virginius (author of Don Miff) and Ellen Maria (Heath) D.; M.A., U. of Va., 1881; student University of Munich, Berlin and Heidelberg, 1882-85; Ph.D., Heidelberg, 1885; m. Mary A. Bentley, June 19, 1888 (died May 18, 1889); 1 dau., Mary Bentley (dec.); m. 2d, Lily H. Davis, Nov. 28, 1899; children—Virginius, Lucy Davis (dec.), Alice Saunders. Taught in N.Y. Latin Sch., 1881-82; prof. history, Ind. U., 1886-89; adj. prof., 1889-96, asso. prof. history, 1896-97, prof. history and economics, 1897-1906, prof. history, 1897-1938, dean dept. grad. studies, 1905-23, U. of Va. Retired, 1938. Author: The Causes of the French Revolution, 1888; John Randolph, a Character Sketch, 1898; also numerous hist. and miscellaneous revs. and articles. Address: University, Va. Died May 16, 1947.

DAFOE, John Wesley (dā′fō), editor, author; b. Combermere, Ont., Mar. 8, 1866; s. C. W. and Mary (Elcome) D.; ed. high school, Arnprior, Ont.; hon. LL.D., U. of Manitoba, Queen's U. (Kingston), U. of Alberta, U. of N.D.; m. Alice Parmelee, June 17, 1890; 4 daughters, 3 sons. Began as school teacher in Ont.; reporter Montreal Star and corr., 1883-85; editor Evening Journal, Ottawa, 1885-86; mem. staff Winnipeg Free Press, 1886-92; editor in chief Daily Herald, Montreal, 1892-95; mem. staff Montreal Star and editor Family Herald and Weekly Star, 1895-1901; editor in chief Winnipeg Free Press since 1901; chancellor, U. of Manitoba, since 1934. Delegate to Commercial Congress of the Empire, 1906, Imperial Press Conf., London, 1909, 30, Melbourne, Australia, 1925; representative of Department of Public Information, Canadian delegation to Peace Conference, 1919; chairman Institute Pacific Relations, 1936-38, president Canadian Inst. Internat. Affairs, 1936-38; mem. Royal Commn. on Dominion-Provincial Relations, 1937-40. Fellow Royal Soc. of Can. Mem. Manitoba Club, Winnipeg. Author: Over the Canadian Battlefields, 1919; Laurier, a Study of Canadian Politics, 1922; Clifford Sifton in Relation to His Times, 1931; Canada, an American Nation, 1934. Editor: Canada Fights; An American Democracy at War, 1941. Contbr. to Great Britain and the Dominion (Harris Foundation lecturer, U. of Chicago), 1925. Lecturer under Beer Foundation, Columbia U. Home: 1325 Wellington Crescent, Winnipeg, Manitoba. Died Jan. 9, 1944.

DABNEY, Samuel Gordon, physician; b. nr. Charlottesville, Va., Aug. 6, 1860; s. William S. and Susan Fitzhugh (Gordon) D.; M.D., U. of Va., 1882, U. of Louisville, 1883; studied in Zurich and Vienna; m. Louisa Higgins Allen, Dec. 21, 1887; children—Mary Allen (Mrs. George Ezra Woodruff), William Cecil. Practiced at Louisville since 1885; prof. diseases of ear, nose and throat and clin. prof. diseases of the eye, U. of Louisville, Med. Dept.; mem. staff Louisville City Hosp., Norton Memorial Infirmary. Fellow Am. Coll. Surgeons; mem. A.M.A., Ky. State Med. Assn., Am. Acad. Ophthalmology and Oto-Laryngology. Episcopalian. Club: Pendennis. Home: 1329 S. Third Av. Office: 870 Starks Bldg., Louisville. Died Dec. 14, 1935.

DAGGETT, Leonard Mayhew, lawyer; b. New Haven, Conn., Nov. 23, 1863; s. David Lewis and Margaret Donaldson (Gibbons) D.; A.B., Yale U., 1884, LL.B., 1887; m. Eleanor E. Cutler, Feb. 17, 1906. Admitted to Conn. bar, 1887; asso. with Henry C. White, 1887-1913; mem. law firm Bristol & White, 1913-34, Daggett & Hooker, since 1934; instr. on wills, Yale Law Sch., 1894-1910; judge advocate gen. on staff of Gov. Coffin, 1896-97; corp. counsel, City of New Haven, 1901-08. Chmn. Dist. Draft Exemption Bd., 2d Conn. Dist., World War I. Mem. Am. Bar Assn., Am. Law Inst., New Haven Colony Hist. Soc. (dir.). Republican. Conglist. Home: 60 Wall St. Office: 205 Church St., New Haven, Conn. Died March 3, 1949.

DAHLERUP, Ioost Baron (däl′ĕr-ŭp), author; b. Copenhagen, Denmark, Aug. 7, 1874; s. Baron Hans Ioost Vilhelm and Ursula Sophie (Holbech) D.; ed. St. Andreas Coll., Denmark; m. in Cape Town, S. Africa, Alma Bech-Bróndum, Feb. 12, 1898; children—Ida-Gro, Ioost Hans Birch. Came to America in 1893. Author: Hvad Ingen Ser (What Nobody Sees), 1905; For Vind og Vove (For Wind and Weather), 1908; Mit Livs Begivenheder (The Events of My Life), 4 vols., dealing with life of grandfather, Admiral Baron Hans Birch Dahlerup, 1908-12; Danske Foregangsmænd i Amerika (Progressive Danish Emigrants in America), 1911; Vi Udvandrere (We Emigrants), 1924. Translator (into Danish): The Making of an American (by Jacob A. Riss), 1912. Knight Order of Dannebrog (Denmark). Address: "Osborne," 205 W. 57th St., New York, N.Y. Died Aug. 7, 1944.

DAHLGREN, Ulric, biologist; b. Brooklyn, N.Y., Dec. 27, 1870; s. Charles Bunker and Augusta (Smith) D.; student State Model Sch., Trenton, N.J., 1883-85; grad. Mt. Pleasant Mil. Acad., Ossining, N.Y., 1890; A.B., Princeton, 1894, M.S., 1896; m. Emillie Elizabeth Kuprion, Sept. 3, 1896. Instr., 1896, prof. biology, 1911-39, prof. emeritus since 1939, Princeton U. Asst. dir. Marine Biol. Lab., Woods Hole, Mass., 1899; trustee Harpswell (Me.) Biol. Lab., 1912-16; dir. Mount Desert Island Biol. Lab., Bar Harbor, 1921, pres. of Corp. since 1937. Pres. Princeton (N.J.) Bd. of Health. Fellow A.A.A.S., Phila. Acad. Sciences; mem. Am. Soc. Zoölogists, Am. Soc. Naturalists, Am. Philos. Soc., N.J. Soc. of the Cincinnati, N.J. Soc. S.R., Loyal Legion, Sons Colonial Wars. Clubs: Princeton (Phila.), Nassau (Primate President), 1942-45. Author: Principles of Animal Histology (with W. A. Kepner), 1908. Wrote series on Production of Light by Organisms (Jour. of Franklin Inst.), 1915; also zoöl. memoirs in German and Am. jours., mostly on production of light and electricity by animals. Home: 7 Evelyn Pl., Princeton, N.J. Died May 30, 1946.

DAINS, Frank Burnett, chemist; b. Gouverneur, N.Y., Jan. 15, 1869; s. Rev. George G. and Celestia Stone (Burnett) D.; Ph.B., Wesleyan U., Conn., 1890 M.S., 1891, D.Sc., Wesleyan U., 1940; Ph.D., U. of Chicago, 1898; Freiburg and Berlin, 1901-02; m. Alice, d. Rev. W. H. Haight, Sept. 24, 1898. Asst. in chemistry, Wesleyan U., 1891-93; asst. prof., U. of Kan., 1893-94; fellow U. of Chicago, 1894-95; asst. prof. chemistry, Northwestern U. Schs. of Medicine and Pharmacy, 1895-1901; prof. chemistry, Washburn Coll., 1902-11; prof. chemistry, U. of Kan., since 1911, emeritus professor since Feb. 1942, acting dean Graduate School, 1926-27. Original investigator in chemistry and contributor of numerous papers on chem. subjects in Am. and fgn. jours. Mem. Sigma Xi, Phi Beta Kappa, Kan. Acad. Science, Am. Chem. Soc., History of Science Soc., Psi Upsilon; fellow A.A.A.S. Club: University (Lawrence). Home: 1224 Louisiana St., Lawrence, Kan. Died Jan. 5, 1948.

DAINES, Lyman Luther (dānz), univ. dean; b. Hyde Park, Utah, Mar. 15, 1883; s. Robert and Jemima (Seamons) D.; A.B., Brigham Young Coll., 1908; M.A., U. of Utah, 1910; Ph.D., U. of Calif., 1912; M.D., Rush Medical Coll., 1931; m. Agnes Purdie, June 4, 1908; children—Norma, Lyman G., William P., Donald R. Instr. in biology, Brigham Young Coll., 1912-15; prof. of bacteriology and pathology, U. of Utah, since 1915, dean Coll. of Medicine, since 1932; pathologist Latter Day Saints Hosp. (Salt Lake City) since 1918. Capt. Med. R.C., 1923-28. Trustee Utah Sch. for Deaf and Blind. Mem. Utah and Salt Lake County med. socs., Utah Acad. of Science, Arts and Letters, Am. Assn. of Univ. Profs., Am. Pub. Health Assn., Sigma Xi, Phi Kappa Phi, Phi Sigma, Phi Beta Pi, etc. Democrat. Mem. Ch. of Latter Day Saints. Club: Timpanagos. Author: Comunity Health and Hygiene (with Dr. A. L. Beely), 1931. Home: 1366 Butler Av., Salt Lake City, Utah.* Died 1941.

DAKE, Charles, physician; b. Pittsburgh, July 13, 1860; s. Jabez P. (M.D.) and Elizabeth (Church) D.; prep. edn. high sch., Nashville, Tenn.; student Southwestern Bapt. Univ., Jackson, Tenn., 1 yr.; M.D., U. of Tenn., 1881; m. Emily J. Hurley, July 29, 1900. Practiced in Hot Springs, Ark., since 1881, except short time in Louisville, Ky.; specializes in chronic diseases. Mem. Am. Inst. Homoeopathy, Southern Homoe. Med. Assn., Southern Med. Assn., A.M.A. Home: Hot Springs, Ark. Died Sept. 11, 1937.

DALLIN, Cyrus Edwin, sculptor; b. Springville, Utah, Nov. 22, 1861; s. Thomas and Jane (Hamer) D.; ed. Springville, Utah; art studies at École des Beaux Arts, Paris, 1889; Julian Acad., Paris; studied under Henri Michel Chapu, Jean Dampt, Paris; hon. M.A., Tufts Coll., 1923; hon. Dr. of Art, Boston U., 1937; m. Vittoria Colonna Murray, June 16, 1891. Received gold medal, Am. Art Assn., New York, 1888; hon. mention Paris Salon, 1890; first-class medal and diploma, Chicago Expn., 1893; silver medals, Mass. Charitable Mechanics' Assn., Boston, 1895, Paris Expn., 1900, Buffalo Expn., 1901; gold medal, St. Louis Expn., 1904; first prize competition for soldiers' and sailors' monument, Syracuse, N.Y., 1906; silver medal, Johnstown Expn., gold medal, Salon, 1909; gold medal, Panama P.I. Exposition, 1915. Instr. in sculpture, Mass. School of Art, Boston. Principal works: Signal of Peace, Lincoln Park, Chicago, 1894; Sir Isaac Newton, Congressional Library, Washington; Pioneer Monument, Salt Lake City; Angel, Temple, same; Don Quixote; Apollo and Hyacinthus; Medicine Man, Fairmount Park, Phila.; equestrian statue, The Cavalryman, Hanover, Pa.; soldiers' monument, Syracuse; Appeal to the Great Spirit, Mus. Fine Arts, Boston; Indian Hunter, Arlington, Mass.; The Scout, Kansas City; Statue of Massasoit, Plymouth, Mass., 1921; Alma Mater, Mary Inst., St. Louis; Signing the Compact, Provincetown, Mass.; "The Spirit of Life," Brookline, Mass., 1928; statue of Anne Hutchinson, State House, Boston. Mem. Mass. State Art Commn. Fellow Am. Acad. Arts and Sciences; mem. Nat. Inst. Arts and Letters, Royal Soc. Arts, London, Nat. Sculpture Soc., Archtl. League, New York, Boston Soc. Architects. N.A., 1931. Clubs: St. Botolph, Boston Art. Address: 69 Oakland Av., Arlington Heights, Boston, Mass. Died Nov. 14, 1944.

DALTON, James L., army officer; b. New Britain, Conn., Jan. 20, 1910; s. Charles and Gladys D.; B.S., U.S. Mil. Acad., 1933; m. Kaye Starbird, Oct. 16, 1937; children—Catherine Starbird, Elizabeth Hodgman. Commd. 2d lt., U.S. Army, 1933, and advanced through the grades to brig. gen., 1945; stationed at Schofield Barracks, Hawaii, at time Japanese attack, 1941; served in Guadacanal, New Georgia and Solomon Islands campaigns; landed Lingayen Gulf, P.I., Jan. 1945, fought up to Balete Pass; killed by sniper fire, May 1945. Decorated Silver Star with oak leaf cluster, Bronze Star, Combat Infantryman's Badge, Purple Heart. Died May 1945.*

DALTON, Test, dramatist; b. Chicago, Ill., Sept. 13, 1875; s. Nathan Ford and Mary (Test) D.; Racine Coll. Grammar Sch., 1887-92; A.B., Butler College, 1896; Harvard, 1897; married; 1 dau., Mezzie Test. Corr. in London, 2 yrs.; asso. editor Black Cat, London. Dramatic dir. Camp Logan, Tex., and Camp Merritt, N.J., 1918-19. Mem. American Legion, Veterans of Foreign Wars, Sigma Chi Fraternity. Club: National Liberal (London, England). Author: The Rôle of the Unconquered, 1902; (plays) Navarre, 1913; Letorière, 1914; The Eleventh Hour, 1915; "System" Marmaduke, 1915; Three Fourths, 1916; It Begins at Home, 1916; Not According to Hoyle, 1917; Little Theatre Plays (one-act), 1917; Uncle John, 1920; The Mantle of Lincoln, 1921; The Scarlet Night, 1922; Adam's Apple, 1923; For Brides Only, 1923; The Blue Orchid, 1925; Among Those Present, 1926; Red Light—Green Light, 1928; T.N.T., 1930; The Richest Man on Earth (novel), 1931; The Golden City, 1936; High Tide (a novel), 1940. Address: care Samuel French, 25 W. 45th St., New York, N.Y. Died Dec. 10, 1945.

DALY, J. J., pres. Regal Shoe Co. Address: 401 South Av., Whitman, Mass. Died June 23, 1948; buried in St. Francis Xavier Cemetery, Centerville, Mass.

DALY, Thomas Augustine, writer; b. Phila., May 28, 1871; s. John Anthony and Anne Victoria (Duckett) D.; ed. pub. schs., Villanova Coll., Pa., Fordham U. to close of sophomore yr., 1889; hon. M.A., Fordham U., 1901, Litt.D., same, 1910; LL.D., Notre Dame U., 1917; LL.D., Boston Coll., 1921; m. Nannie Barrett, June 24, 1896; children—Leonard Barrett, John Anthony, Thomas Augustine, Ann Elizabeth, Stephen Barrett, Brenda Rutledge (dec.), Frederic Rutledge, Frances Joan. Clerk, 1889-91, reporter and editorial writer, 1891-98, Phila. Record; gen. mgr. Catholic Standard and Times, Phila., 1898-1915; asso. editor Evening Ledger, Phila., 1915-18; asso. editor Philadelphia Record, 1918-29; columnist, Philadelphia

Evening Bulletin, since 1929. Lecturer since 1905. Author: Canzoni, 1906; Carmina, 1909; Madrigali, 1912; Little Polly's Pomes, 1913; Songs of Wedlock, 1916; McAroni Ballads, 1919; Herself and the Houseful (prose), 1924; A Little Book of American Humorous Verse (anthology), 1926; The House of Dooner (with Christopher Morley, prose); McAroni Medleys, 1931; Selected Poems of T. A. Daly, 1936; Late Lark Singing, 1946. Compiler: The Wissahickon, 1922. Home: 4937 Rubicam Rd., Germantown, Pa. Office: Bulletin Bldg., Philadelphia, Pa. Died Oct. 4, 1948.

DALY, William Barry, mining engr.; b. Smartsville, Yuba County, Calif., Jan. 4, 1873; s. Lawrence and Ann (Barry) D.; grad. high sch., Smartsville, 1889; m. Mary E. Nevin, June 28, 1905; 1 son, Eugene William. Teacher, pub. grade schs., Brady, Calif., 1890-91; admitted to Calif. bar, 1894, and practiced at San Francisco until 1899; successively foreman, supt., efficiency engr., gen. supt. mines, asst. gen. mgr. mines, Anaconda Copper Mining Co., until 1924, gen. mgr. mines, 1924-40; cons. mining engr. since Jan. 1, 1940. Mem. Am. Inst. Mining and Metall. Engrs., Am. Mining Congress. Democrat. Mem. Knights of Columbus. Clubs: Silver Bow, Country. Home: 808 W. Galena St. Office: Hennessey Bldg., Butee, Mont. Deceased.

DAMON, Alexander M(artin) (dā'mŏn), Salvation Army officer; b. Lowell, Mass., July 28, 1874; s. Alexander M. and Laura E. (Stiles) D.; ed. pub. schs. of Lowell and Boston, Mass.; D.D., Oskaloosa (Ia.) Coll., 1917, Bob Jones Coll., Ky., 1934; L.H.D., Am. Internat. Coll., Mass., 1937; m. Annie Barrow, Dec. 19, 1895; 1 dau., Gladys Mina (Mrs. Lyell M. Rader). Began as Salvation Army officer, 1890; advanced through all ranks from lt. to commr. After Corps and Headquarters appointments commanded Atlantic Coast Province, 1906; field sec. U.S. 17 years; chief sec. Central Territory, 1924-30; territorial comdr. 15 Southern States, 1930-35; comdr. Eastern Territory, 1935-42, retired Feb. 1, 1942. Club: Rotary (New York). Home: 85 Stockton Av., Ocean Grove, N.J.* Died Nov. 26, 1947.

DANA, Harvey Eugene, clergyman, educator; b. nr. Vicksburg, Miss., June 21, 1888; s. Charles Martin and Eva Grace (Smith) D.; Ph.B., Mississippi Coll., Clinton, Miss., 1911, A.B., 1919; Th.D., Southwestern Bapt. Theol. Sem., Ft. Worth, Tex., 1920; studied U. of Chicago, U. of Dubuque; hon. LL.D., Ottawa (Kansas) U., 1939; m. Tommy Elizabeth Pettit, July 13, 1909; children—Eugenia Elizabeth and Elsie Marie. Ordained Baptist ministry, 1908; pastor Port Gibson, Miss. and Utica, Miss., Allen Av. Ch., Ft. Worth, Tex., Alvord, Tex., until 1919; prof. N.T. interpretation, Southwestern Bapt. Theol. Sem., 1919-38; pres., Kansas City (Kan.) Bapt. Theol. Sem. (now Central Bapt. Theol. Sem.) since 1938. Pastor First Ch., Ardmore, Okla., 1931-35. Mem. Soc. Bibl. Lit. and Exegesis, Am. Research Soc. Mason, Woodman. Author: Manual for the Study of the Greek Testament, 1923; Authenticity of the Holy Scriptures, 1923; Introduction to the Critical Interpretation of the New Testament, 1924; New Testament Criticism, 1924; New Testament Message, 1925; Christ's Ecclesia, 1926; New Testament World, 1926; Manual Grammar of the Greek Testament, 1927; Searching the Scriptures, 1936; The Epistles and Apocalypse of John, 1937; Jewish Christianity, 1937; the Ephesian Tradition, 1940; The Heavenly Guest, 1943. Address: Central Baptist Theological Seminary, Kansas City, Kan. Died May 17, 1945.

DANDY, Walter E(dward), surgeon; b. Sedalia, Mo., Apr. 6, 1886; s. John and Rachel D.; A.B., U. of Mo., 1907, LL.D., 1928; M.D., Johns Hopkins, 1910, A.M., 1911; m. Sadie Martin, Oct. 1, 1924; children—Walter E., Mary Ellen, Kathleen Louise, Margaret Martin. Began practice, Baltimore; now prof. neurol. surgery, in charge surgery of nervous system, Johns Hopkins. Mem. Am. Surg. Assn., Am. Neurol. Assn., Southern Surgical Assn., Phi Beta Kappa, Sigma Xi. Author of a textbook on neurological surgery and several books on various lesions of the brain. Contr. numerous articles to surgical and neurological journals. Introduced new operative procedures for tumors and aneurysms of the brain, for hydrocepholus, neuralgias and other disturbances of cranial nerves; introduced ventriculography, ventricular estimation and cerebral pneumography, for diagnosis and localizing of tumors of the brain and intracranial lesions; discovered ruptured intervertebral disks which cause low backaches and sciaticas, and introduced surgical procedure for their cure. Home: 3904 Juniper Rd., Baltimore 18. Office: Johns Hopkins Hosp., Baltimore 5, Md. Died Apr. 19, 1946.

DANE, Ernest Blaney, banker; b. Brookline, Mass., Oct. 17, 1868; s. Edward S. and Emma C. D.; A.B., Harvard, 1892; m. Helen Folsom Pratt, Oct. 8, 1903. Now pres. Brookline Trust Co., Earnshaw Knitting Co.; dir. Tampa Elec. Co., Merchants Nat. Bank, Northern Tex. Electric Co., John Hancock Mut. Life Ins. Co. Pres., treas. and trustee Boston Symphony Orchestra; trustee N.E. Conservatory of Music, Provident Instrn. for Savings. Home: 360 Heath St., Chestnut Hill, Mass. Office: 6 Beacon St., Boston, Mass. Died Apr. 5, 1942.

DANEY, Eugene, lawyer; b. Bordeaux, France, Oct. 11, 1862; s. Michel and Marguerite (Dutruch) D.; brought to U.S. at age of 3; LL.B., U. of Calif., 1885; m. 2d, Alma Cherry Dietzsch, Nov. 27, 1912; children—Eugene, Florence E. (Mrs. R. J. Stork), Constance (Mrs. J. H. Dunn). Admitted to Calif. bar, 1885, and began practice at San Francisco; dir. and atty. for First Nat. Trust and Savings Bank, Southern Title and Trust Co. (San Diego). Permanent mem. Legal Advisory Bd. San Diego County and mem. exec. com. Am. Red Cross, World War. Trustee and sometime pres. San Diego County Law Library. Mem. Am. Bar Assn., Calif. Bar Assn. (pres. 1915-16); mem. bd. govs. State Bar Calif. (1927-34), San Diego Bar Assn. (1st pres., serving 7 terms), Lawyer's Inst. of San Diego (1st pres.). Republican. Mason (32°, Shriner), Elk. Club: Cuyamaca. Home: 208 W. Juniper St. Office: 1st National Bldg., San Diego, Calif.* Died Dec. 4, 1946.

DANGAIX, William Joseph (dăn'gā), capitalist; b. Phila., Pa., Sept. 16, 1864; s. Joseph and Mary (Lasserre) D.; student Sorbonne, Paris, and Inst. d'Études françaises de Touraine, Tours, France; studied Spanish 1 yr. in Spain; unmarried. Began at 18 as dept. clerk Superior Court, Brunswick, Ga.; in ins. and real estate business at Birmingham, Ala., many yrs.; gen. agt. for Southern States of Agrl. Ins. Co. of Watertown, N.Y., 10 yrs.; organizer and first pres. Birmingham Savings Bank, merged with Am. Trust & Savings Bank, of which was a dir. for many yrs.; bank merged into Am.-Traders Nat. Bank which was merged into First Nat. Bank of Birmingham; retired from active business, 1908, and has since spent most of time abroad, principally at Paris, but maintains legal citizenship at Birmingham. Under apptmt. as spl. asst. of Dept. of State, served, 1918-19, as foreign agt. of War Trade Bd., at Berne, Switzerland, and at Paris. Democrat. Catholic. Wrote booklets, How Latin America Affects Our Daily Life, 1917; How We Affect Latin America's Daily Life, 1919. Has traveled widely in Europe, Asia, Australasia, Africa and North, Central and South America. American Address: Care First National Bank, Birmingham, Ala. Foreign Address: Care Guaranty Trust Co., 4 Place de la Concorde, Paris, France. Died 1943.

DANIEL, J(ohn) Frank(lin), zoölogist; b. O'Fallon, Mo., July 31, 1873; s. Dr. John Franklin and Martha Short (Henry) D.; Southern Ill. Normal U., 1901; with dept. of edn., P.I., 1901-05; S.B., U. of Chicago, 1906; Adam T. Bruce fellow from Johns Hopkins, Pasteur Inst., Lille, France, 1908-09; Ph.D., Johns Hopkins, 1909; m. Menetta White Brooks, Feb. 16, 1909. Instr. zoölogy, U. of Mich., 1910-11; instr. zoölogy, 1911-12, asst. prof., 1912-17, asso. prof., 1917-19, prof. zoölogy since 1919, U. of Calif. U.S. del. to 12th Internat. Congress of Zoölogy, Lisbon, 1935. Decorated Chevalier of Legion of Honor (France), 1936. Fellow A.A.A.S., Am. Acad. of Arts and Sciences; mem. Am. Zoöl. Soc., Western Soc. of Naturalists, Soc. Exptl. Biology and Medicine, Calif. Acad. Sciences, Am. Genetic Assn., Société Zoölogique de France, Assn. des Anatomistes. Author: Animal Life of Malaysia, 1905; The Elasmobranch Fishes, 1922; also papers on breeding of mice for scientific purposes, experimental studies on alcohol, morphogenesis, etc. Chmn. U. of Calif. Publs. in Zoölogy; collaborator Internat. Jour. of Cytology (Japan). Home: 615 Woodmont Av., Berkeley, Calif. Died Nov. 2, 1942.

DANIELLS, Arthur Grosvenor, clergyman; b. West Union, Fayette Co., Ia., Sept. 28, 1858; s. Thomas Grosvenor and Mary Jane (McQuillen) D.; ed. Battle Creek (Mich.) Coll.; m. Mary Ellen Hoyt, Nov. 30, 1876. Ordained ministry Seventh Day Adventist Ch., 1882; sent as missionary to South Seas, 1886; pres. New Zealand Conf., 1889-91. Australian Conf., 1892-96, Australian Union, 1897-1900. World's Gen. Conf. Seventh Day Adventists, 1901-22, sec. same, 1922-26; sec. Ministerial Assn. Seventh Day Adventists; pres. bd. Coll. of Med. Evangelists, Los Angeles. Has preached in nearly every country in the world. Author: The World War, 1916; A World in Perplexity, 1917; Christ Our Righteousness, 1926. Address: College of Medical Evangelists, Los Angeles. Died 1935.

DANIELS, Francis Potter, college prof.; b. Ionia, Mich., Aug. 1, 1869; s. Newton Russell and Rosina Frances (Potter) D.; A.B., U. of Mich., 1895; teaching fellow, U. of Mo., 1896-97, A.M., 1897, Ph.D., 1905; Hopkins scholar, Harvard, 1897-98; m. Louise Grimmer, June 21, 1899. Ordained Unitarian ministry, Oct. 8, 1898; pastor Sturgis, Mich., 1898-99, Manistee, Mich., 1900-01; acting dir. foreign langs., Manual Training High Sch., Kansas City, 1906; prof. Romance langs., U. of Colo., summer session, 1906, Cornell Coll., Ia., 1906-09, Wabash Coll., Crawfordsville, Ind., 1909-16, Columbia U., New York, Summer 1916; asst. prof. modern langs., U. of Mo. Sch. of Mines and Metallurgy, Rolla, 1916-20; asst. prof., 1920-21, asso. prof. Romance langs., 1921-22, asso. prof. Spanish and head depts. of Spanish and Italian, 1922-23, U. of Ariz.; prof. French and acting head Latin dept., Ga. State Coll. for Women, 1923-28, prof. Latin and chmn. sch. of foreign langs., 1928-32, prof. Latin since 1932, emeritus since 1935; assistant curator, U.S. National Herbarium, summer 1911. Was first fellow on Kahn Foundation for Foreign Travel of American Teachers, 1911-12; deviser of National Doctors' Academy, also of the Doctors' Academy of U. of Ariz. and pres., 1922-23; pres. Doctors' Acad. of Ga. State Coll. for Women, 1928-29, and 1932-41. Fellow A.A.A.S.; mem. Modern Lang. Assn. America, Phonétique Internationale, Acad. Polit. Science, Am. Assn. Teachers of Spanish, Eugenics Soc. of U.S.A., History of Science Soc., Eugene Field Soc., Classical Assn. of Mid-West and South, Phi Beta Kappa, Pi Gamma Mu, Sigma Pi Rho; asso. mem. Am. Museum of Natural History. Democrat. Baptist. Kiwanian (lt. gov. of 5th Div. of Ga., 1935-36). Author: Flora of Columbia, Mo., 1907; Flora of Boulder, Colo., 1911; French Scientific Reader, 1917; The Golden Trove (verse), 1934; also poems in many anthologies. Home: Milledgeville, Ga. Deceased.

DANIELS, Josephus, ex-ambassador, ex-sec. Navy; b. Washington, N.C., May 18, 1862; s. Josephus and Mary (Cleves) D.; ed. Wilson (N.C.) Collegiate Inst., law, U. of N.C.; Litt.D., Washington and Lee U.; LL.D., University of North Carolina, Wesleyan University and other universities and colleges; m. Addie W., d. Maj. W. H. Bagley, May 2, 1888; children—Josephus, Worth Bagley, Jonathan Worth, Frank A. Became editor of Wilson (North Carolina) Advance at age of 18; admitted to the bar, 1885; but did not practice; state printer for North Carolina, 1887-93; chief clerk Dept. of Interior, 1893-95; became editor Raleigh (N.C.) State Chronicle, 1885; consolidated the State Chronicle and the North Carolinian with the News and Observer, 1894, and since editor News and Observer; secretary of the navy in cabinet of President Wilson, March 5, 1913-March 6, 1921; Am. ambassador to Mexico, 1933-42. Member of Democratic National Com. from N.C., 1896-1916; dir. publicity Bryan and Wilson campaigns. Trustee and mem. exec. com. U. of N.C.; trustee Wilson Foundation, Jefferson Memorial Commn.; mem. Woodrow Wilson and Franklin D. Roosevelt Foundations. Author: The Navy and the Nation (addresses), 1919; Our Navy at War, 1922; Life of Worth Bagley, 1898; Life of Woodrow Wilson, 1924; Tar Heel Editor, 1939. Editor: In Politics, 1940; The Wilson Era (Peace 1913-17), 1944; The Wilson Era (War 1917-23), 1945; Shirt Sleeve Diplomat, 1947. Methodist (mem. gen. Conf.). Home: Raleigh, N.C. Died Jan. 15, 1948.

DANIELS, Milton J., ex-congressman; b. Cobleskill, N.Y., Apr. 18, 1838; s. Hon. John V. and Hester Ann (Wheeler) D.; ed. Middlebury (N.Y.) Acad.; m. Jennie E. Booth, May 27, 1869. Enlisted 9th Minn. Inf., Apr., 1861; 2d lt., Aug. 28, 1862; 1st lt., Apr. 24, 1864; capt., May 20, 1864; bvtd. maj. vols., Dec. 9, 1865, hon. mustered out, Dec. 13, 1865. Engaged in banking in Minn., 1868; mem. Minn. Legislature, 1882-9; mem. 58th Congress, (1903-5), 8th Calif. Dist.; Republican. Mem. G. A. R., Loyal Legion. Address: Riverside, Calif. Died Dec. 1, 1914.

DANIELS, Winthrop More, prof. transportation; b. Dayton, O., Sept. 30, 1867; s. E.A.D.; A.B., Princeton, 1888, M.A., 1890; studied 1 yr. U. of Leipzig; hon. M.A., Yale, 1923; m. Joan Robertson, Oct. 12, 1898; 1 son Robertson Balfour. Prof. polit. economy, Princeton, 1892-1911; mem. Bd. Pub. Utility Commrs. of N.J., 1911-14; mem. Interstate Commerce Commn., 1914-23 (chmn. 1918-19), resigned, 1923; prof. of transportation, Yale, 1923-40, now emeritus. Trustee of N.Y., N.H.&H. R.R. Co., 1935-37, retired. Club: Graduate (New Haven). Author: Revision and Continuation of Alexander Johnston's History of the United States, 1897; Elements of Public Finance, 1899; Continuation of Alexander Johnston's History of American Politics, 1902; American Railroads—Four Phases of Their History, 1932; The Price of Transportation Service, 1932. Contbr. to Atlantic and other mags. Home: Saybrook Point, Conn. Died Jan. 2, 1944.

DANSINGBERG, Paul, state librarian. Office: State Library, St. Paul, Minn. Died July 30, 1946.

D'ARCY, William Cheever, advertising counselor; founder and pres. D'Arcy Advertising Co. (offices in St. Louis, New York, Cleveland, Atlanta, Toronto and Mexico City), 1906-45; dir. Coca-Cola Co., dir. Mississippi Valley Trust Co., Presstite Engring. Co., Coca-Cola Bottling Co. of St. Louis, Laclede Gas Light Co. Past pres., past exec. dir. Jefferson Memorial Expansion Assn. Clubs: St. Louis Country, Bogey Golf, Noonday (St. Louis); Seigniory of Canada. Home: 6 Hortense Place, St. Louis, Mo. Died July 21, 1948.

DARDEN, Thomas Francis, ry. official; b. Hamilton, N.C., July 11, 1870; s. Thomas Edward and Mary Anne (Boyle) D.; student common schs. and Hamilton Acad., 1878-85; m. Bessie Coles Davis, Oct. 20, 1896; children—Mary Nixon, Thomas Francis, Robert Davis. Clerk and telegraph operator A.C.L. R.R., 1888-91; agt. and chief clk. gen. office Wilmington, New Bern & Norfolk R.R., 1891-97; cashier and mgr. New York Dock Co., and Terminal Ry., Brooklyn, 1897-1903; chief clk. and asst. auditor Old Dominion Steamship Co., 1903-09; examiner and asst. chief examiner Bur. of Accounts, Interstate Commerce Commn., Washington, 1909-13; special accountant A.C.L. R.R., Wilmington, N.C., 1913-14, asst. to pres., 1914-18, asst. to federal mgr., 1918-20, asst. to exec. v.p., 1920-23, v.p. since 1923; also officer or dir. various subsidiary cos. Mem. bd. mgrs. James Walker Memorial Hosp. Episcopalian. Clubs: Cape Fear, Cape Fear Country, Carolina Yacht. Home: 410 S. Front St. Office: Atlantic Coast Line R.R., Wilmington, N.C. Died Feb. 25, 1943

DARGUE, Herbert Arthur (därg), army officer; b. Brooklyn, N.Y., Nov. 17, 1886; s. Arthur Percy and Madeline (Newins) D.; B.S., U.S. Mil. Acad., 1911; grad. Air Corps Engring. Sch., 1920, Command and Gen. Staff Sch., 1924, Army War Coll., 1929, Navy War Coll., 1930; m. Marie Virginia Salmon, Nov. 17, 1915; 1 son, Donald Salmon. Commd. 2d lt. C.A.C., U.S. Army, 1911, and advanced through the grades to maj. gen. U.S. Army, 1941; formerly command of

Observers School, Air Corp, Post Field, Okla., comdg. gen. 19th Wing, 1938; comdg. 1st Air Force, Mitchell Field, New York since 1941. Decorated Distinguished Flying Cross, 1927. Mem. Daedalian, Early Bird. Presbyterian. Mason (Shriner). Club: Army and Navy (Arlington, Va.). Home: 3215 Rowland Place N.W. Address: War Dept., Washington, D.C. Died Dec. 8, 1942.

DARLING, Charles Hial, lawyer; b. Woodstock, Vt., May 9, 1859; s. Jason L. and Ellen L. (Paul) D.; A.B., Tufts, 1884, LL.D., 1903; m. Agnes Christmas Norton, Nov. 6, 1889 (died Jan. 27, 1941); children—Margaret Norton (Mrs. John Randall Roberts) (dec.), Alice Godfrey (Mrs. Hamilton Armstrong), Elizabeth Paul (Mrs. Donald Armstrong). Admitted to bar, 1886; municipal judge, 15 yrs.; pres. village of Bennington, 1895; mem. Gen. Assembly, Vt., 1896-97; asst. sec. of the navy, 1901-05; collector of customs, dist. of Vt., 1905-14; now pres. Am. Fidelity Co. Trustee Tufts Coll. State dir. Am. Red Cross Christmas membership drive, 1917, and for 3d Liberty Loan. Mem. Vt. Bar Assn. (pres. 1900), Zeta Psi (nat. pres. 1904), S.A.R. (pres. Vt. Soc.). Mason (33°), Grand Master of Masons of Vt., 1914-16. Address: 184 S. Winooski Av., Burlington, Vt. Died Oct. 31, 1944.

DARLINGTON, Thomas, physician; b. Brooklyn, Sept. 24, 1858; s. Thomas and Hannah Anne (Goodliffe) D.; C.E., and Ph.B., New York Univ.; Litt.D. from Juniata (Pa.) Coll., 1924; M.D., Coll. Physicians and Surgeons (Columbia), 1880; m. Josephine A. Sargeant, June 9, 1886 (died 1890); children—Clinton Pelham, Dorothea. Practiced Newark, N.J., 1880-82, New York, 1882-88, Bisbee, Ariz., 1888-90, New York, since 1891. Commr. and pres. New York Bd. of Health, 1904-10; mem. New York State Workmen's Compensation Commn., 1914-15; cons. physician N.Y. Foundling Hosp. Formerly lecturer indsl. hygiene, Stevens Inst. Tech., and Fordham U. Sanitary engr. N.Y. City Dept. of Health until January 1, 1934. Trustee, 1st v.p. Met. Savings Bank (New York); dir. Morris Plan Bank. Chmn. Mayor's Com. on Sanitation and Harbor Pollution, 1927-28. Trustee N.Y. City Mission Society, also trustee of Grant Monument Association. Maj. Med. Corps, U.S. Army, 1917-18. Asst. to pres. Am. Iron and Steel Institute. Fellow A.A.A.S., N.Y. Acad. of Science; mem. Soc. Med. Jurisprudence, A.M.A., Am. Institute, Am. Climatol. and Clin. Assn., Am. Assn. for Promoting Hygiene and Pub. Baths (v.p.), Nat. Inst. of Social Science (v.p.), Harvey Soc., Internat. Sunshine Soc. (care of blind children), Med. Soc. of County of N.Y., N.Y. Acad. Medicine, Greater N.Y. Med. Assn. (v.p.), Physicians Mut. Aid Assn., Sachem Tammany Soc. (Grand Sachem), Thomas Hunter Assn. (pres. 1923-24, 1929-37), Alumni N.Y. Univ., N.Y. Chamber of Commerce (hon. physician), N.Y. Soc. Mil. and Naval Officers World War. Huguenot Soc., St. Nicholas Soc., Soc. Colonial Wars, S.R., Alpha Mu Pi Omega; hon. mem. Kings County Med. Soc. Deacon 1st Presbyterian Ch., trustee Archdeaconry of New York, 1905-11. Club: Iroquois (New York). One of 14 exec. members Congress of Physicians and Surgeons, 1907-39. Writer on med. and climatol. subjects and sanitation. Home: R.D. No. 1, Monticello, N. Y. Died Aug. 23, 1945; buried in Woodlawn Cemetery, New York.

DARMS, John Martin George (därms), (originally D'Arms), ch. official; b. Philadelphia, Pa., July 24, 1873; s. Lorenz and Ursula von (Anliueser) D.; A.B., Mission House Coll., Plymouth, Wis., 1892; D.D., 1912; grad. Theol. Sem. of same instn., 1895; postgrad. study Columbia U. and Teachers Coll., 1923; m. Charlotte von Tacky, May 2, 1900; 1 son, Edward Francis. Ordained ministry Ref. Ch. in U.S., 1895; organized ch. in Buffalo, N.Y., with 4 members and continued as pastor 16 yrs. (now nearly 1,000 members); pastor Emanuel Ch., Rochester, 8 yrs., Salem Ch., Allentown, Pa., 1914-23 ($300,000 ch. erected); pres. Mission House Coll. and Sem., also prof. comparative religion and religious edn., 1923-30; asst. exec. sec. of exec. com. Reformed Ch. in U.S. since 1930; exec. sec. Reformed Churchman's League, 1938; exec. sec. Churchman's Brotherhood since 1937; pastor Zion Evangelical and Reformed Church, Buffalo, N.Y., since 1941. Formerly v.p. United Stewardship Council of North America and Canada; member Board of Foreign Missions of Reformed Church, Council Fedn. Churches in U.S.A., Alliance of Presbyn. and Reformed Churches, National Service Commn. Trustee Huping Coll., Hunan, China, Central China College, Wuchang. Active at war work at Camp Meade (Cape May, N.J.) and Camp Allentown, Pa. Republican. Rotarian. Author: On the Threshold of the Christian Ministry, 1912; Manual of Christian Stewardship, 1915; With Christ Through Lent, 1927; Men of the Church (handbook for Churchman's Brotherhood), 1940. Wrote adult lessons for 10½ yrs.; also editor of Christian Forum (monthly) and asso. editor The Churchmen's Brotherhood and Men's Dept. of Outlook of Missions. Home: 6 Seneca Parkside, Buffalo, N.Y. Deceased.

DARRACH, William (där'rä), surgeon; b. Germantown, Phila., Pa., Mar. 12, 1876; s. William and Edith Romeyn (Aertsen) D.; grad. The Hill Sch., 1893; A.B., Yale, 1897, hon. A.M., 1920; A.M., M.D., Columbia, 1901 (1st Harsen prize), D.Sc., 1929; LL.D., St. Andrews U., 1928; D.Sc., Jefferson, 1930; m. Florence Borden, May 22, 1907; children—Edith, William, Effie Brooks (dec.), Judith (dec.). Interne, 1901-03, asso. attending surgeon, 1913-16, Presbyn. Hosp.; demonstrator anatomy, 1903-09, instr. surgery, 1903-16, prof. of clinical surgery since 1916, and dean of the med. faculty, 1919-30, dean emeritus since 1930, Coll. Phys. and Surg. (Columbia); attending surgeon Vanderbilt Clinic, 1903-06; 2d asst. attending surgeon, 1906-08, 1st asst., 1908-10, jr. surgeon, 1910-13, Roosevelt Hosp.; dir. 1st surg. div., Bellevue Hosp., 1916-19; attending surgeon, Presbyn. Hosp., to 1946, now cons. surg.; cons. surg. Neurol. Inst., N.Y. Orthopedic Dispensary and Hosp., Greenwich, Beekman St., Babies', Sloane, Willard Parker, Morristown Memorial, N. Westchester hosps., Neuro-Psychiatric Inst. of Hartford (Conn.) Retreat. Captain Med., May 10, 1917, later major and lt. col. N.A., col. M.C., U.S. Army; sailed for France, May 14, 1917; comdg. officer, Base Hospital 2, U.S.A. (No. 1 General Hospital, B.E.F.), February 20-July 30, 1918; consultant surgeon 42d Division, A.E.F., later asst. consultant 1st Corps then 1st Army, then sr. consultant 3d Army; participated in Passchendael Campaign, B.E.F., and Château-Thierry, St. Mihiel, Meuse-Argonne campaigns, A.E.F.; hon. discharged, Apr. 12, 1918; col. M.C., U.S. Civilian cons. to Surg. Gen., and Vets. Adminstrn. Trustee, Fay Sch. Fellow Am. Coll. Surgeons (mem. bd. govs.), Chicago Surg. Soc. (hon.), Am. Assn. Surgery of Trauma (hon.); mem. Am. Acad. Orthopedic Surg.; mem. A.M.A., Assn. Am. Anatomists, Am. Surg. Assn. (pres. 1944), N.Y. Surg. Soc., Soc. Clin. Surgery (pres. 1929-31), N.Y. State Med. Soc., N.Y. County Med. Soc., Société de Chirurgiens de Paris, N.Y. Acad. of Medicine, Société Internationale de Chirurgie, Nat. Research Council (sub-com. on orthopedics), A.A.A.S., Am. Philos. Soc., Soc. Colonial Wars, Psi Upsilon, Phi Beta Kappa, Sigma Xi, Alpha Omega Alpha, etc. Republican. Episcopalian. Clubs: Century, Manursing Island. Contbr. articles on surgery, anatomy and med. edn. Home: Greenwich, Conn. Office: 180 Fort Washington Av., New York, N.Y. Died May 24, 1948.

DARROW, George Potter, congressman; b. Waterford, Conn., Feb. 4, 1859; s. Edmund and Elizabeth (Potter) D.; A.B., Alfred U., 1880, LL.D., 1922; m. Sarah Johnson, Feb. 8, 1887 (died Sept. 18, 1888); m. 2d, Elizabeth Shore, Sept. 16, 1897. Mem. bd. mgrs. Mut. Fire Ins. Co., Germantown, Phila.; pres. 22d sectional Sch. Bd., Phila., 3 yrs.; mem. Common Council, Phila., 1910-15; mem. 64th to 74th Congresses (1915-37), 6th and 7th Pa. Dists., 76th Congress (1939-41), 7th Pa. Dist. Republican. Baptist. Club: Union League. Home: 5625 Germantown Av., Philadelphia. Died June 7, 1943.

DARST, Thomas Campbell, retired; b. Pulaski, Va., Nov. 10, 1875; s. Thomas Welsh and Margaret (Glendy) D.; student Roanoke Coll., Salem, Va., 1899; grad. Theol. Sem. in Va., 1902; D.D., same, 1914, U. of the South, 1915, Roanoke Coll., 1918, U. of N.C., 1927, Duke U., 1935; m. Florence N. Wise, Nov. 5, 1902 (died, 1914); children—George Wise, Thomas C., Meade C.; m. 2d, Fannie Lauriston Hardin, Apr. 26, 1916; 1 daughter, Margaret G. Deacon. Priest, 1903, P.E. Ch.; asst. Fairmount, W.Va., 1902-03; rector Meade and John's parishes, Va., 1903-05, St. Mark's Ch., Richmond, 1905-09, St. Paul's Ch., Newport News, 1910-14, St. James Ch., Richmond, 1914-15; consecrated bishop of E. Carolina, Jan. 6, 1915. Former pres. Province of Sewanee. Trustee U. of the South, St. Mary's and St. Augustine schs. (Raleigh, N.C.), Theol. Sem. of Va. Dir. of Bishops' Crusade, 1926-27; retired since May 1, 1945. Mem. Pi Kappa Alpha. Democrat. Mason. Home: Box 84 A, R. 3, Wilmington, N.C. Died Sept. 1, 1948.

DARTON, Nelson Horatio (där'tŭn), geologist; b. Brooklyn, N.Y., Dec. 17, 1865; s. William and Caroline M. (Thayer) D.; hon. D.Sc., U. of Ariz., 1922; m. Alice Weldon Wasserbach, 1903. Chemist in N.Y., 1880-86; geologist, U.S. Geol. Survey, 1886-1910 and 1913-36 (ret.); geologist, Bur. Mines, 1910-13. Inventor of a sugar process; researches in tannic acid and water analysis, etc. Lectured at various colleges. Fellow Geol. Soc. America (ex-v.p.), A.A.A.S.; mem. Washington Acad. Sciences (former vice-pres.), Geol. Soc. Washington (former pres.), Soc. Econ. Geologists, Mining and Metall. Soc., Am. Inst. Mining and Metall. Engrs., Soc. Linn de Lyons, Inst. Français, Pi Gamma Mu, Soc. Géol. de France, Assn. Am. Geographers, Internat. Geol. Congress, Soc. Fine Arts, Wyo. Valley Geol. Soc., Am. Geophysical Union, Archæol. Soc., Federal Bd. of Surveys and Maps, English-Speaking Union, Italy-America Soc., Alliance Française (v.p.), Spanish Atheneum (ex-pres.), Instituto de las Españas; hon. mem. Am. Assn. of Petroleum Geologists; mem. sub-com. Nat. Council. Awarded Daly gold medal by Am. Geog. Soc., 1930, and Penrose gold medal by Geol. Soc. of Am., 1940; Legion of Honor, Am. Inst. Mining and Metall. Engrs., 1944. Wrote: The Story of the Grand Canyon; Geologic Guide to Santa Fe R.R.; Geologic Guide to Southern Pacific R.R.; Geology of Great Plains, Black Hills, Bighorn Mts., Owl Creek Mts.; Geology Dist. Columbia region; Geologic maps Great Plains, Grand Canyon, S.D., Neb., Ariz., N.M., Lower Calif. and Tex.; many folios U.S. Geol. Survey, etc. Contributor on geol. subjects; geol. maps and reports on many districts, topog. maps states of Ariz., N. M., Tex., Nebr., N.D., S.D.; many articles in Ency. Americana and other publications. Explored ruins of the temple of Cuicuilco, Mexico, for Nat. Geog. Soc. and oil geology of Lower Calif., Santo Domingo, Eastern Cuba and Central Venezuela. Clubs: Cosmos, Inquirendo. Home: 6969 Brookeville Rd., Chevy Chase, Md. Office: U.S. Geological Survey Washington, D.C. Died Feb. 28, 1948.

DAU, William Herman Theodore (dow), educator; b. Lauenburg, Pomerania, Germany, Feb. 8, 1864; s. Herman and Augusta (Blaschke) D.; came to U.S., 1881; A.B., Concordia Coll., Fort Wayne, Ind., 1885; grad. Concordia Sem., St. Louis, Mo., 1886; D.D., Sem. of Adelaide, Australia, 1923; D.D., Concordia Sem., 1930; Litt.D., Valparaiso U., 1939; m. Marie Louise Becker, Aug. 14, 1888 (died 1928); children—Marie Concordia (Mrs. P. F. Miller), Walther Martin, Emma Magadelene (Mrs. M. Bertram), Anna Pauline (Mrs. E. P. Merkel), William Herman, Gertrude Margaret (Mrs. W. Peters), Erna Martine (Mrs. W. Schreyers); m. 2d, Mrs. Elizabeth K. Friedrichs, Apr. 28, 1932. Ordained Luth. ministry, 1886; pastor Trinity Ch., Memphis, Tenn., 1886-92; pres. Concordia Coll., Conover, N.C., 1892-99; pastor St. Paul Ch., Hammond, Ind., 1899-1905; prof. theology, Concordia Sem., 1905-26; pres. Valparaiso (Ind.) U., 1926-29, now pres. emeritus. Mem. Am. Soc. Church History Pi Gamma Mu, Gesellschaft der Freunde der Deutschen Bücherei, Gesellschaft der Freunde der Wartburg. Author: Luther Examined and Reëxamined, 1917; The Leipzig Debate of 1518, 1918; The Great Renunciation, 1919; At the Tribunal of Cæsar, 1921; He Loved Me and Gave Himself for Me, 1921; Utterances of Jesus, 1938. Co-author: Walther and the Church, 1938. Translator: Starcke's Prayerbook, 1921; Walther's Law and Gospel, 1929; The Planting of the Christian Church in Europe, 1943. Wrote numerous essays and tracts. Formerly editor Lutheran Witness and Homiletic Magazine; served as co-editor of Triglot Concordia, and mng. editor Theological Monthly. Home: 40 Brookside Av., Berkeley, Calif. Died Apr. 21, 1944.

DAUGETTE, Clarence William (dawg'gĕt), educator; b. Belle's Landing, Ala., Oct. 14, 1873; s. Thomas William and Clara Jeanette (Rankin) D.; B.Sc., Ala. Poly. Inst., Auburn, 1893, M.Sc., 1894; work at U. of Chicago, summers, 1901, '02; LL.D., from U. of Ala., 1916; m. Annie Rowan Forney, Dec. 22, 1897; children—Kathleen Forney, Palmer, Clarence William, Forney Rutledge, Rankin Middleton. Began teaching at Repton, Ala., 1889; pres. State Teachers Coll., Jacksonville, Ala., since Oct, 1899. Pres. 1st Nat. Bank, Ex-pres. Ala. Edn. Assn. Democrat. Episcopalian. Mason. Past Grand Master I.O.O.F. Home: Jacksonville, Ala. Died Aug. 9, 1942; buried at Jacksonville.

DAULTON, Agnes (Warner) McClelland, author; b. New Philadelphia, O., Apr. 29, 1867; d. Lewis Robert and Lucy (Warner) McClelland; student Oberlin Coll.; m. George Daulton, Dec. 9, 1900. Author: Wings and Stings, 1903; Autobiography of a Butterfly, 1905; Dusk Flyers; Fritzi, 1908; From Sioux to Susan, 1909; The Gentle Interference of Bab, 1912; The Capers of Benjy and Barbie, 1913; The Marooning of Peggy, 1915; Uncle Davie's Children, 1919; Froken Robinson, 1924; Green Gate, 1926. Contbr. serials and stories to St. Nicholas, Outlook, etc. Lecturer on literature and childhood. Home: Woodstock, N.Y. Died June 5, 1944.

DAVENPORT, Charles Benedict, biologist; b. Stamford, Conn., June 1, 1866; s. Amzi B. and Jane Joralemon (Dimon) D.; B.S., Poly. Inst., Brooklyn, 1886; A.B., Harvard, 1889, A.M., Ph.D., 1892; m. Gertrude Crotty, June 23, 1894; children—Mrs. Millia Davenport Harkavy, Mrs. James A. deTomasi, Charles Benedict (dec.). Engr. survey of Duluth, S. Shore & Atlantic Ry., 1886-87; asst. zoölogy, 1888-90, instr., 1891-99, Harvard; asst. prof. zoölogy and embryology, 1899-1901, asso. prof. and curator Zoöl. Mus., 1901-04, U. of Chicago; dir. dept. of genetics, Carnegie Instn., comprising Sta. for Experimental Evolution, 1904-34, and Eugenics Record Office, 1910-34, Cold Spring Harbor, N.Y.; dir. Biol. Lab., Brooklyn Inst. Arts and Sciences, 1898-1923. Maj. Sanitary Corps, U.S. Army, in charge of anthropology, 1918-19. Asso. editor Jour. Experimental Zoölogy since 1898, Jour. of Physical Anthropology since 1918, Genetics since 1916, and others. Fellow Am. Acad. Arts and Sciences, A.A.A.S. (vice-pres. 1900-01, 1925-26), New York Zoöl. Soc.; mem. Nat. Acad. Sciences, Am. Philos. Soc., Am. Soc. Zoölogists (pres. 1902-03, 29-30), Am. Genetic Assn., Am. Soc. Naturalists (sec. 1899-1903, v.p. 1906), Soc. Exptl. Biology and Medicine, Eugenics Research Assn. (hon. pres. 1937), N.Y. Acad. Medicine (asso.), Galton Soc. (pres. 1918-30), Nat. Inst. of Social Sciences (gold medal, 1923), L.I. Biol. Assn. (sec.), Internat. Fedn. of Eugenic Organizations (pres. 1927-32), Anthropologische Gesellschaft in Wien, Kaiserlich Deutsche Akad. Naturforscher (Halle), Berliner Gesellschaft für Anthropologie, Ethnologie und Urgeschichte (corr. mem.), Acad. Royale de Belgique; foreign corr. Zoöl. Soc., London; pres. Third Internat. Eugenics Congress, New York City, 1932. Author: Graduate Courses, 1893; Experimental Morphology Part 1, 1897, Part 2, 1899; Statistical Methods in Biological Variation (4th edit.), 1936; Introduction to Zoölogy (with G. C. Davenport), 1900; Elements of Zoölogy, 1911; Inheritance in Poultry, 1906; Inheritance of Characteristics of Fowl, 1909; Eugenics, 1910; Heredity in Relation to Eugenics, 1911; Heredity of Skin Color in Negro-White Crosses, 1913; The Feebly-inhibited—Nomadism and Temperament, 1915; Naval Officers—Their Development and Heredity (with M. Scudder), 1919; Physical Examination of First Million Draft Recruits, 1919; Defects Found in Drafted Men, 1920; Army Anthropology, 1921 (the last 3 with Major A. G. Love); Body Build and Its Inheritance, 1923; Race-Crossing in Jamaica (with M. Steggerda), 1929; Genetical Factor in Endemic Goiter, 1932; How We Came by Our Bodies, 1936. Contbr. to biol. jours. Home: Cold Spring Harbor, L.I., N.Y. Died Feb. 18, 1944.

DAVENPORT, Walter Rice, clergyman; b. Williamstown, Vermont, Apr. 10, 1885; s. Rice and Susan D.; ed. Montpelier Seminary and Boston U.; D.D. from Norwich U.; m. Flora L. Thomson, Apr. 10, 1884; m. 2d, Mrs. Emma L. Putnam, Aug. 20, 1913; m. 3d, Mrs. Edith L. Hamilton, April 26, 1925. Joined Vermont (Methodist) Annual Conf., 1880; pastor Waterbury, Vt., 1888-93, Barre, Vt., 1893-98; presiding elder Montpelier District, 1898-1900; pastor Orleans, Vt., 1905-09, Bellows Falls, 1910-12, Springfield, 1913-20; supt. St. Albans Dist., 1919-26. Sec. Vt. Conf. Hist. Soc., 1887-1935, Vt. Conf. Bd. Ch. Extension, 1889-97, 1902-06; mem. Vt. Conf. Bd. Exam., 1892-98 and 1909-18, sec. bd., 1892-93, chmn. bd., 1913-19; sec. Vt. Conf., 1895-99 and 1911, Vt. Conf. Sustentation Fund Soc., 1909-19; sec. Bd. of Conf. Claimants, 1917-20. Pres. Municipal League, Barre, 1894-95; mem. bd. of health, Barre, 1896-97; pres. Bd. of Trade, Orleans, 1909, Hosp. Aid Soc., Springfield, 1913-16; field sec. Vt. State Anti-Saloon League, 1905-06; state supt. S.S. temperance work, 1908-11; state supt. Adult Bible Class Work, 1922-26. Editor and pub. People's Monthly, 1881-82; asst. editor Vt. Christian Messenger, 1882-84; editor Barre Daily Telegram, 1904, Vt. Issue, 1905-11, Springfield Reporter, 1915-16. Supt. schs., Waterbury, 1889-90; mem. Washington County Bd. of Edn., 1891-92, sec., 1892; trustee Montpelier Sem., 1889-90 and since 1920, sec. bd., 1889-1901; prin. Montpelier Sem., 1901-03. Mem. Gen. Conf. M.E. Ch., Des Moines, Ia., 1920; pres. N.E. Dist. Supts.' Assn., 1923; treas. Vt. Ann. Conf., 1927-29; pres. Vt. Ann. Conf. Hist. Soc. since 1929. Chaplain Vt. legislature, 1929-30; pres. Retired Preachers Assn., 1931—. Author: The Biography of Thomas Davenport, inventor, 1929; also booklet, Hymns for Annual Conferences; History of Methodism in Barre, Vt.; History of Methodism in Williamstown, Vt.; History of Newbury (Vt.) Seminary; History of Montpelier Seminary; Random Recollections of a Long Life. Contbr. verse. Address: 67 E. State St., Montpelier, Vt. Died Oct. 12, 1942.

DAVEY, Martin L., ex-gov.; b. at Kent, Ohio, July 25, 1884; s. John Davey (father of tree surgery) and Bertha (Reeves) D.; student Oberlin Coll., 1904-07; m. Berenice M. Chrisman, Aug. 31, 1907; children—Evangeline, Martin L. Pres. and treas. The Davey Tree Expert Co., Inc., pres. Davey Compressor Co., Davey Investment Co. Mayor of Kent, 1914-18 (resigned); elected to 65th Congress Nov. 1918 to fill unexpired term, and elected at same time to 66th Congress (1919-21), reëlected to 68th to 70th Congresses (1923-29), 14th Ohio Dist.; Dem. candidate for gov. of Ohio, 1928; elected governor, 1934, reelected, 1936. Mem. Chamber of Commerce of United States, Kent Chamber Commerce, Ohio Soc. of New York. Mem. Church of Christ (Disciples). Mason (K.T., Shriner), Odd Fellow, K.P., Elk, Moose, Eagle; mem. Grange, Grotto. Clubs: Akron City, Masonic, Cleveland City, Twin Lakes Golf, Kent Rotary; National Press (Washington). Home: 453 W. Main St., Kent, O. Died Mar. 31, 1946.

DAVIDSON, David J., govt. official; b. Pinos Altos, N.M., Oct. 10, 1899; s. Arnard Russel and Mina Isabel (Scott) D.; A.B., Occidental Coll., 1923; m. Betty Ward Rose, Sept. 10, 1928. Farm supt., Calif. Farming Co., 1926-31; has operated own farm since 1931; in field service br., U.S. Dept. of Agriculture, Agrl. Adjustment Adminstrn., head field officer, prin. field officer, exec. field officer, administrative officer, chmn., state com., state (Calif.) dir., since 1935, dir., Washington, D.C., br., since 1946. Served with U.S. Army, 1918-19. Mem. Phi Beta Kappa. Conglist. Club: Commercial, San Francisco. Home: 6680 32d Place, N.W. Office: U.S. Dept. of Agriculture, Washington, D.C. Died May 28, 1948.

DAVIDSON, James Edward, shipbuilder, banker; b. Buffalo, N.Y., Dec. 7, 1865; s. James and Ellen M. (Rogers) D.; A.B., Hillsdale (Mich.) Coll., 1887, LL.D., 1925; m. June Lolette Cobb, Feb. 12, 1890 (died 1918); children—James Lorenzo (deceased), Lt. Comdr. Edward Cobb; married 2d, Helen Forrest Knox, July 28, 1919; children—Helen Forrest (Mrs. G. B. Paull, Jr.), Laura Isabelle (Mrs. R. P. Beattie II), Shirley Knox (Mrs. Horton R. Prudden), Ashley. Chmn. bd. Hillsdale County Nat. Bank, Bay Trust Co.; pres. Peoples Comml. and Savings Bank, Davidson Building Co., Bay Trust Co.; v.p. Robert Gage Coal Co. (Bay City); president Inter-Ocean Steamship Co., Continental S.S. Co., Duluth Steamship Company, (Duluth, Minn.), Globe Steamship Corporation (Indianapolis, Ind.), United Steamship Company, Triton S.S. Co., Sumatra S.S. Co., Consolidated S.S. Co. (Wilmington, Del.); v.p., treas., dir. Am. Ship Building Co. (Cleveland); dir. Pere Marquette Ry. Co., Bay City Building Co., Tanner Investment Co., Great Lakes Towing Co., Industrial-Brown-Hoist Corp. (Bay City). Chmn. Local Draft Bd. No. 1, Bay City, World War. Mem. Soc. Naval Architects and Marine Engrs., Phi Delta Theta, Epsilon Delta Alpha. Mem. Rep. State Central Com., Mich., since 1902; mem. Rep. Nat. Com. 1923-40; chmn. Bay County Rep. Com., 1920-34 and 1936-38, mem. since 1896; del. Rep. Nat. Conv., Chicago, 1920. Mem. St. Lawrence Waterway Commn., appointment President Coolidge, 1924; mem. advisory bd. Detroit Loan Agency, R.F.C.; dir. Detroit Br., Federal Reserve Bank of Chicago, Jan. 1936-Dec. 1942. Chairman board trustees, Hillsdale Coll., 1925-32; chmn. board of trustees Y.W.C.A., Bay City; mem. exec. council Am. Bankers Association, 1935-38; president Michigan Bankers Association, 1934-35; executive council Michigan Bankers Assn. for life. Episcopalian. Mason (33°); Past Grand Comdr. K.T. of Mich.; Past Potentate, Shrine; Past Comdr. Bay City Comdry. 26; bd. control Mich. Masonic Home: Elk. Clubs: Saginaw Country, Detroit Athletic, University (Detroit); Kitchi Gammi (Duluth); Saturn (Buffalo); Union, Mid-Day, Terminal (Cleveland); Metropolitan, India House, Lambs (New York). Home: 1710 Center Av. Office: Foot of Randolph St., Bay City, Mich. Died July 25, 1947.

DAVIDSON, Royal Page, educator; b. Somerville, N.J.; s. Harlan Page and Adelaide S. (Ford) D.; grad. Northwestern Mil. Acad., 1889; studied Mass. Agrl. Coll.; U. of Wis.; m. Clara M. Colwell, July 4, 1892. Comdt., 1891-1911, supt. since 1912, Northwestern Mil. & Naval Acad., Lake Geneva, Wis. Col. Res., U.S. Army. Conglist. Mem. S.A.R., Delta Upsilon (Wis. Chapter); pres. North Central Academic Assn., 1914; sec.-treas. Assn. of Mil. Colls. and Schs. of U.S., 1919-21, pres. 1925. Inventor first military automobile in U.S., 1889; later designed field hospital, radio and other military equipment. Contributor to numerous publications on military and pedagogical subjects. Clubs: Union League, University oif Wisconsin, Army and Navy (Chicago); Big Foot and Lake Geneva (Wis.) Country. Home: Avon Park, Fla. Address: Northwestern Military and Naval Academy, Lake Geneva, Wis. Died Jan. 16, 1943; buried on grounds of Northwestern Military and Naval Academy, Lake Geneva.

DAVIES, William Preston (dā'vēz), newspaper editor; b. nr. Brantford, Ont., Can., Oct. 29, 1862, of Am. parents; s. John Matthews and Mary Ann Elizabeth (Gill) D.; ed. country sch.; LL.D., Wesley College, Grand Forks, N.D., 1929; m. Rachel Spence, of Ethel, Ont., Aug. 19, 1885 (died Aug. 25, 1939); children—Russell Gladstone, Mabel Spence. Clerk, farmer, carpenter and schoolteacher until 1896; with Grand Forks Herald since 1897, editor since 1898; pres. Grand Forks Bldg. & Loan Assn. Park commr., Grand Forks, 1905-14 (pres. bd. 1908-14). Mem. N.D. Press Assn. Republican. Methodist. Odd Fellow. Clubs: Kiwanis, Fortnightly, Franklin, Civic and Commerce Assn. Home: 922 Walnut St. Address: Grand Forks Herald, Grand Forks, N.D. Died May 19, 1944.

DAVIN, John Wysor (dăv'ĭn), pres. N.Y.,C.&St.L. R.R.; b. Montgomery, W.Va., Mar. 10, 1892; s. John and Mary Elizabeth (Montgomery) D.; student W.Va. Univ., Prep. Branch, 1908-10; widower; children—Virginia (Mrs. Andrew Douds, Jr.), Margaret Ann (Mrs. Jack Jackson), Patricia Ruth. Check clerk, C.&O. Ry. Co., 1910-14, car distbr., 1914-16, chmn. allotment commn., 1920-23, asst. supt. transportation, 1923-31, asst. gen. supt. transportation, 1931-33, asst. to the pres., 1933-39, v.p., 1939-42; pres., New York, Chicago & St. Louis R.R. Co. since Dec. 16, 1942; dir. Peoria & Pekin Union Ry. Co., Cleveland Union Terminals. Clubs: Recess, Cloud (New York); Duquesne (Pittsburgh); Union, Country, Pepper Pike and Shaker Heights (Cleveland, O.); Guyan (Huntington, W.Va.); Kanawha (Charleston, W.Va.). Home: 18001 Shaker Blvd., Shaker Heights. Address: 2910 Terminal Tower, Cleveland, O Died Jan. 7, 1949.

DAVIS, Alfred Cookman, pres. Marlin-Rockwell Corp.; b. Meyersdale, Pa., Aug. 26, 1875; s. Rev. Samuel Wesley and Catherine (Stone) D.; E.E., U. of Pittsburgh, 1897; m. Ethel Falconer, June 20, 1906 (died Oct. 1916); children—Catherine, Samuel McMillen, Richard Hallock; m. 2d, Ruth Ford, Oct. 11, 1930. Motive power dept., Pa. R.R., Ft. Wayne, Ind., successively as machinist apprentice, motive power inspector, elec. engr., master mechanic, 1897-1910; v.p. and gen. mgr. Am. Mfg. Co., Falconer, N.Y., 1910-16; with Marlin-Rockwell Corp., mfrs. ball bearings, Jamestown, N.Y., since 1916, cons. engr., 1916-18, works mgr. 1918, v.p., 1918-37, pres. and gen. mgr. since 1937; chmn. bd. Art Metal Constrn. Co.; exec. dir. Jamestown Mutual Ins. Co.; chmn. First Nat. Bank; dir. Erie R.R. since 1941. Chmn. Bd. Public Utilities, Jamestown, since 1936. Mem. Mfrs. Assn. (dir.). Republican. Clubs: University (N.Y. City and Jamestown, N.Y.). Home: R.F.D. 1, Ashville, N.Y. Office: Marlin-Rockwell Corp., Jamestown, N.Y. Died May 17, 1946.

DAVIS, Arthur William, lawyer; b. Maynard, Fayette County, Ia., Nov. 16, 1873; s. William E. and Helen Josephine (Wells) D.; B.Sc., Upper Ia. Univ., Fayette, 1893; student U. of Ia., 1900-01; m. Florence A. Carpenter, Dec. 24, 1900; children—Florence Rachel, John Benjamin (dec.), Arthur William. Prin. at various Ia. schs., 1893-98; supt. schs., Pocahontas County, 1898-1900; admitted to Ia. bar, 1900, and practiced at Fonda until 1905, when removed to Spokane, Wash.; v.p. Bremen Investment Co. Vice chmn. State Progressive Campaign Com., 1912-14, Rep. Campaign Com., 1918-20; mem. Rep. State Central Com., 1918-20; mem. Bd. of Edn., Spokane, 1908 12, State Law Bd., 1916-19; state rep. Nat. Uniform Laws Commn., 1919-24; regent State Coll. of Wash. since 1921 (now pres.). Mem. Chamber of Commerce (Spokane), Sigma Nu, Phi Delta Phi. Mason (33°, Shriner); Past Grand Master, Wash. Clubs: Spokane City, Rotary. Home: Spokane Estates. Office: Ziegler Bldg., Spokane, Wash. Died June 29, 1945.

DAVIS, Bert Byron, educator; b. Lenawee Jct., Mich., Apr. 24, 1880; s. Maxon and Laura (Hibbard) D.; B.A., U. of Calif., 1919, M.A., 1920; m. Rosella Amelia Snyder, Sept. 14, 1904. Teacher pub. schs., Kalamazoo County, Mich., 1898-1904; identified with Seventh Day Adventist schs. since 1904; successively prin. at Fresno, Calif.; critic teacher Pacific Union Coll.; prin. at Edendale Sch., Los Angeles; critic teacher and normal dir. San Fernando Acad.; normal dir. Walla Walla Coll., later at Union Coll., College View, Neb.; ednl. supt. Seventh Day Adventist schs. for Mich., 1926-31; dean of edn., Philippine Union Coll., Manila, since 1932 (mem. exec. bd.).* Died Feb. 11, 1944.

DAVIS, Charles B., judge; b. Hannibal, Mo., Mar. 9, 1877; s. William A. and Mary F. (Mills) D.; grad. high sch., Hannibal, 1897; A.B., U. of Mo., 1902, LL.B., 1905; m. Elizabeth L. Jackson, Dec. 25, 1915; children—Helen M., Mary L., Elizabeth L., Dorothy J. Admitted to Mo. bar, 1905, and began practice at St. Louis; asst. circuit atty., 1909-12; asso. city counselor, St. Louis, 1914-15; judge Circuit Court of Mo., 1916-24; judge U.S. Dist. Court, Eastern Dist. of Mo., by apptmt. of President Coolidge, since Jan. 31, 1924. Mem. Am., Mo. State and St. Louis bar assns., Phi Delta Phi, Phi Beta Kappa. Republican. Mem. Christian (Disciples) Ch. Mason. Home: Webster Groves, Mo. Address: U.S. Dist. Court, St. Louis, Mo. Died Mar. 3, 1943.

DAVIS, Dwight Filley, ex-gov. gen. P.I.; b. St. Louis, July 5, 1879; s. John Tilden and Maria (Filley) D.; A.B., Harvard U., 1900; LL.B., Washington U., 1903; m. Helen Brooks, Nov. 15, 1905 (died Oct. 10, 1932); children—Dwight F., Alice Brooks (Mrs. Roger Makins), Cynthia (Mrs. William McC. Martin), Helen Brooks (Mrs. Allen Hermes); m. 2d, Pauline Sabin, May 8, 1936. President of Davis Estate. Mem. Pub. Baths Commn., 1903-06; Public Library Bd., 1904-07; bd. control, Mus. Fine Arts, 1904-07 and 1911-12; Public Recreation Commn., 1906-07; mem. St. Louis Ho. of Dels., 1907-09; Bd. Freeholders, 1909-11; City Plan Commn., 1911-14; park commr., 1911-14. Capt., 5th Mo. Inf., May 18, 1917; maj., Nov. 1917; lt. col., Oct. 1918; col., O.R.C., 1923. Director general Army Specialist Corps, 1942. Mem. executive committee Nat. Municipal League, 1908-12, Playground and Recreation Assn. America, 1910-14; dir. Civic League, 1904-07; v.p. St. Louis Playgrounds Assn., 1905-08; dir. Tenement House Assn., 1907-09, Soc. Prevention Tuberculosis, 1909-12; mem. Bd. of Overseers, Harvard, 1915-21, 1926-32; dir. War Finance Corp., 1921-23; asst. sec. of war, 1923-25, sec., 1925-29; governor gen. of the Philippine Islands, 1929-32. Mem. bd. dirs. Lehman Corporation, 1941-42. Chmn. bd. trustees Brookings Instn. since 1939. Awarded D.S.C., Mar. 1923, "for extraordinary heroism" in operations at Bauiny and Chaudron Farm, France, Sept. 29-30, 1917; also awarded Legion of Honor (France), 1932. Republican. Baptist. Member Alpha Delta Phi, Phi Delta Theta, Phi Delta Phi, Comdr. St. Louis Post No. 4, Am. Legion, 1919. Clubs: Noonday Club (St. Louis, Mo.); Chevy Chase, Metropolitan, Burning Tree, Alibi (Washington, D.C.); University (New York). Home: Meridian Plantation, Tallahassee, Fla., and Washington, D.C. Died Nov. 28, 1945; buried in Arlington National Cemetery.

DAVIS, Ewin Lamar, member Federal Trade Commission; b. Bedford County, Tenn., Feb. 5, 1876; s. McLin H. and Christina Lee (Shoffner) D.; ed. Webb Sch. and Vanderbilt U.; LL.B., Columbian (now George Washington) University, 1899; recipient (1945) from George Washington U. of its Alumni Achievement Award (for notable achievement in law); m. Carolyn Windsor, Dec. 28, 1898; children—John Windsor, Margaret (Mrs. George K. Taylor), Ewin Lamar II (Mrs. George W. Williams), Latham Shoffner, Carolyn Windsor (Mrs. Lloyd W. Parrish). Began practice at Tullahoma, 1899; Dem. presdl. elector, 1904; judge 7th Jud. Circuit of Tenn., 1910-18; chmn. Dist. Exemption Bd. Middle Dist. of Tenn., 1917-18; mem. 66th to 72d Congresses (1919-33), 5th Tenn. Dist.; chmn. Com. on Merchant Marine, Radio, and Fisheries, 72d Congress; mem. Fed. Trade Commn., term 1933-39; reappointed term ending Sept. 25, 1946; reappointed term ending September 25, 1953; chairman Federal Trade Commission, 1935, 1940, and 1945; mem. Nat. Emergency Council, 1935; mem. Temp. Nat. Econ. Com., 1938-40. Mem. Am. Nat. Com. of 3d World Power Conf. Mem. of bar, all courts of Tenn., D.C., and U.S. Supreme Court. Mem. Am., D.C., Federal and George Washington bar assns., Alpha Tau Omega (mem. Golden Circle), Phi Delta Phi. Missionary Baptist. Mason (32°). U.S. Treasury Award and Medal for patriotic service in War Finance, 1941-45. Home: Tullahoma, Tenn. Address: 2150 Wyoming Av., Washington. Died Oct. 23, 1949; buried Oakwood Cemetery, Tullahoma, Tenn.

DAVIS, Fay, actress; b. in U. S.; became public reader; went to England, 1895; made debut on dramatic stage at Criterion Theatre, London, Nov. 5, 1895; has played Princess Flavia in Prisoner of Zenda, Rosalind in As You Like It, Hero in Much Ado About Nothing, Elsie in A Man of Forty, Queen Flavia in Rupert of Hentzau, Gypsy Floyd in A Debt of Honor, Georgina in The Wisdom of the Wise, Olive Laurence in The Awakening, Iris 1901, and other leading roles in St. James Theatre Co. Address: Garrick Theatre, W. C., London, England. Died Feb. 26, 1945.

DAVIS, James John, senator; b. Tredegar, South Wales, Oct. 27, 1873; s. David James and Esther Ford (Nicholls) D.; LL.D., Bucknell, Pa. Mil. Acad., U. of Pittsburgh, Drake U., St. Bonaventure's Sem.; m.

Jean Rodenbaugh, Nov. 26, 1914; children—James, Jane, Jean, Joan, Jewell. Came to U.S. with parents, 1881; began as puddler's asst. in iron works at Sharon, Pa., later in Pittsburgh, at 11; was a puddler at 16; moved to Elwood, Ind., 1893, and worked in steel and tin plate mills; city clk. Elwood, 1898-1902; recorder Madison County, Ind., 1903-07; dir. gen. Loyal Order of Moose since 1906 (membership increased from 247 to over 600,000); sec. of labor, by apptmt. of President Harding, Mar. 5, 1921, and continued under Presidents Coolidge and Hoover until Dec. 9, 1930; elected U.S. senator from Pa. to fill vacancy, for term expiring 1933, reëlected for terms 1933-1939, 1939-45. Founder Mooseheart Home and Sch.; chmn. Mooseheart govs., also Home for Old Folks, Moosehaven, Florida. Mem. Almagamated Assn. Iron, Steel and Tin Workers of America. Mem. Veterans of Foreign Wars, Spanish Am. War Veterans. Mason, Odd Fellow, K.P., Elk., etc. Clubs: Press, Chevy Chase (Washington, D.C.). Home: Pittsburgh, Pa. Died Nov 22, 1947

DAVIS, Jackson, educator; b. Cumberland County, Va., Sept. 25, 1882; s. William Anderson and Sally Wyatt (Guy) D.; A.B., Coll. William and Mary, 1902, LL.D., 1931; A.M., Columbia, 1908; LL.D., U. of Richmond, 1930; m. Corinne Mansfield, May 9, 1911 (died 1941); children—Helen Mansfield (Mrs. John P. Lynch, Jr.), Ruth Elizabeth (Mrs. Charles R. Langhorne). Prin. public sch., Williamsburg, Va., 1902-03; asst. sec. Y.M.C.A., Roanoke, Va., 1903-04; prin. pub. sch., Marion, Va., 1904-05; supt. schs., Henrico County, Va., 1905-09; mem. State Bd. Examiners and Inspectors, Va. State Bd. of Edn., 1909-10; state agt. for Negro rural schs., Va. State Dept. Edn., 1910-15; gen. field agt. Gen. Edn. Bd., N.Y. City, 1915-29, asst. dir., 1929-33, asso. dir. since 1933; Carnegie visitor to Africa, 1935; sec. Internat. Edn. Bd., 1923-38. Mem. Commn. on Interracial Coöperation; mem. Advisory Com. on Edn. in Liberia; pres. bd. trustees Booker Washington Inst., Liberia; mem. bd. visitors Coll. of William and Mary, 1913-20; trustee Phelps-Stokes Fund since 1939, v.p. since 1940. Mem. Va. Acad. Science, Va. Hist. Soc., New York Colonization Soc. (pres.), S.A.R., Phi Beta Kappa, Theta Delta Chi, Phi Delta Kappa. Democrat. Methodist Clubs: Town Hall, Century (New York). Contbr. to ednl. jours. Home: Cartersville, Va. Office: General Education Board, 49 W. 49th St., New York 20, N.Y. Died Apr. 15, 1947; buried in Hollywood Cemetery, Richmond, Va.

DAVIS, Joe L., judge; b. Atlanta, Ark., Dec. 20, 1869; s. James Evan and Mary Rebecca (Morgan) D.; ed. Atlanta (Ark.) Acad.; m. Ella Arnold, Jan. 16, 1901; children—Ruth Spears (Mrs. J. H. White), Joe Lamar, Mary M. (Mrs. W. A. G. Woodward), Lottie Arnold. V.p. Magnolia Cotton Mill Co.; sec. Columbia Cotton Oil Co.; dir. Camden (Ark.) Milling Co.; elected mem. Ark. Ho. of Rep., 1932; practicing law; county and probate judge, Columbia County, Ark., since 1937. Pres. Columbia County Bd. of Edn. Mem. Ark. State Bd. Charities, 1907-09, Constl. Conv., Ark, 1917-18; supervisor census, 7th Ark. dist, 1920. Democrat. Methodist. Mason. Club: Ben Venue. Home: 420 E. Main St. Office: 130 S. Jefferson St., Magnolia, Ark. Died July 25, 1941.

DAVIS, John Marcus, transportation; b. Anderson County, Tex., Nov. 5, 1871; s. Henry Clay and Mary Elizabeth (Rogers) D.; ed. pub. and pvt. schs. and Houston (Tex.) Business Coll.; m. Janet Heslip Shearer, Oct. 14, 1908; children—Mary Mildred, Bernice Elizabeth. Successively clk., stenographer and chief clk., supts. and gen. mgrs. offices, S.P., Santa Fe and G.N. rys., until 1896; asst. supt. Northern S.S. Co., Buffalo, N.Y., 1896-98; asst. supt., later supt., G.N. Ry., 1898-1900; supt., Erie R R., 1900-03; supt. and asst. gen. supt. G.N. Ry., 1903-06; gen. supt. U.P. and S.P. systems, Salt Lake City, Utah, later at San Francisco, Calif., 1906-14; gen. mgr. and v.p. in charge maintenance and operation B.&O. R.R., 1914-18, mgr. New York terminals same and S.I. Rapid Transit R.R., also mem. U.S. R.R. Administration Gen. Mgrs. Com., 1918-19; pres. Manning, Maxwell, & Moore, Inc., 1920-25; pres. D.L.&W. R.R. Co., 1925-41, chmn. bd. since 1941. Mem. advisory bd. N.Y. Ordnance Dist., U.S. War Dept. Dir. Cancer Research Fund and Moses Taylor Hosp. Mem. advisory bd. Sch. of Business (Columbia). Mem. New York Travelers Aid Society, Metropolitan Mus. of Art, Municipal Art Society, Soc. of the Genesee, Steuben County Society, Pilgrims of the United States. Clubs: Metropolitan, Recess, Railroad, Blind Brook Country, Sleepy Hollow Country (New York); Bohemian (San Francisco). Home: 1035 5th Av. Office: 140 Cedar St., New York, N.Y. Died Mar. 21, 1944.

DAVIS, John Staige, plastic surgeon; b. Norfolk, Va., Jan. 15, 1872; s. William Blackford and Mary Jane (Kentie) Howland; Ph.B., Yale U., 1895, A.M., 1925; M.D., Johns Hopkins, 1899; m. Kathleen Gordon Bowdoin, Oct. 26, 1907; children—Kathleen Staige (Mrs. Charles E. Scharlett, Jr.), William Bowdoin (capt. Med. Corps, U.S. Army), Howland Staige (lt. comdr. Naval Aviation). Surgeon, Baltimore, Md., since 1899; asso. prof. surgery, Johns Hopkins U. since 1923; visiting plastic surgeon, Johns Hopkins Hosp., Union Memorial Hosp., Hosp. for Women of Md., Children's Hosp. Sch. Served as capt., M.C., U.S. Army, 1917-19. Fellow Am. Coll. Surgeons; mem. Am. Surg. Assn. (vice pres. 1939), Am. Bd. of Surgery, Southern Surg. Assn. (pres. 1940), Am. Assn. for Surgery of Trauma, Interurban Surg. Soc., Surg. Research Soc., Am. Assn. Plastic Surgeons (pres. 1945). Chmn. Am. Board of Plastic Surgery. Democrat. Episcopalian. Clubs: Maryland, Yale (New York). Home: 215 Wendover Rd., Baltimore 18. Office: 701 Cathedral St., Baltimore 1, Md. Died Dec. 23, 1946.

DAVIS, Jonathan McMillan, ex-governor; b. Franklin Twp., Bourbon County, Kan., Apr. 26, 1871; s. Jonathan McMillan and Eve (Holeman) D.; student U. of Kan., 1888-91, U. of Neb., 1892-93; m. Mollie Purdom, Sept. 26, 1894 (died July 13, 1926); m. 2d, Mary E. (Winston) Raymond, Dec. 16, 1931. Farmer; mem. Dem. County Committee, Bourbon County, Kan., 1893-1900; chmn. Dem. Congressional Com., 2d Dist., Kan., 1898; alternate at large, Dem. Nat. Com., 1900; mem. Kan. Ho. of Rep. 4 terms until 1913, Senate, 1913-17; Dem. candidate for gov., 1920; gov. of Kan., Jan. 1923-25. Endorsed by Kan. Democrats for President, 1924, and received votes on 55 ballots, also in balloting for Vice President, at Dem. Nat. Conv., 1924; Dem. candidate for gov., 1926, for U.S. Senate, 1930; candidate for Dem. nomination for gov., 1936; independent candidate for gov., 1938. Methodist. Mason, Odd Fellow, K.P., Eagle, Moose, Elk. Club: Kiwanis (Ft. Scott, Kan.). Home: Bronson, Bourbon County, Kan. Died June 27, 1943.

DAVIS, Norman H.; b. Bedford County, Tenn., Aug. 9, 1878; s. Maclin H. and Christina Lee (Shofner) D.; Vanderbilt U., 1897-98, Stanford, 1899-1900; D.C.L., U. of the South, 1921; LL.D., Columbia, 1933, Harvard, 1935, Princeton U., 1937, N.Y. U., 1939; m. Mackie Paschall, Oct. 1898. Began business career in Cuba, 1902, became interested in banking, sugar and other enterprises; organized, 1905, The Trust Co. of Cuba, and was pres. until 1917; adviser to sec. of treasury in connection with fgn. loans, 1917; spl. U.S. del. to Spain and rep. of treasury in London and Paris, 1918; apptd. finance commr. of U.S. to Europe, 1919; Am. mem. Armistice Commn.; mem. Supreme Econ. Council (chmn. finance sect.); financial adviser to President Wilson and Am. Commn. to Negotiate Peace; mem. Reparations and Financial commns.; asst. secretary of United States Treasury, Nov. 1919-June 1920; served as undersec. of state, June 15, 1920-Mar. 7, 1921; chmn. commn. of League of Nations to determine status of territory of Memel, 1924. Mem. Am. Delegation to Internat. Econ. Conf., Geneva, May 1927; mem. League of Nations Financial Com.; apptd. mem. organizing com. for Internat. Monetary and Econ. Conf., 1932; del. from U.S. to Disarmament Conf., Geneva, Switzerland, 1932, and chmn. of Am. delegation, 1933; apptd. head of Am. delegation to London Naval Conf., Dec. 1935; chmn. Am. Delegation to Internat. Sugar Conf., 1937; U.S. del. to Nine Power Conf. at Brussels, Nov. 1937; chmn. Am. Red Cross, Washington, D.C.; chmn. bd. of govs. League of Red Cross Societies (composed of 61 nations). Member board of trust Vanderbilt University; trustee Bank of New York & Trust Company; director Pan American Airways. Democrat. Episcopalian. Clubs: Metropolitan, Burning Tree (Washington); Century, The Links (New York). Home: 804 Prince St., Alexandria, Va. Office: American Red Cross, Washington, D.C. Died July 1, 1944.

DAVIS, Paul A., 3d, architect; b. Philadelphia, Pa., June 18, 1872; s. Paul A. and Henrietta Scull (Duy) D.; grad. William Penn Charter Sch., Phila., 1890; B.S., U. of Pa., 1894; diploma, Ecole des Beaux Arts, Paris, 1900; m. Frances Ward Smillie, Mar. 18, 1903; children—Elizabeth Smillie (Mrs. Edwin Frayne Nimmo), Paul A., 4th, David Richard. Began practice at Philadelphia, 1909. Principal works: Univ. of W.Va. Buildings; High Sch. and Jr. High Sch., Camden, N.J.; Am. Bank & Trust Co., Holmesburg Trust Co., 9th Bank & Trust Co. and Presbyn. Ministers' Fund Life Ins. bldgs., Phila.; Overbrook Presbyn. Ch.; Chaltenham High Sch., Elkins Park, Pa., etc. Fellow Am. Inst. Architects (dir. 1926-29; pres. Phila. chapter); mem. Société des Beaux Arts, Société des Architectes Diplômes, Acad. Fine Arts, Pa. Clubs: Union League, Egypt Mills Club. Home: Forgedale Rd., Barton, Berks County, Pa. Office: 1717 Sansom St., Philadelphia, Pa. Died Nov. 24, 1948; buried at Colestown, N.J.

DAVIS, Robert Courtney, army officer; b. Lancaster, Pa., Oct. 12, 1876; s. Thomas J. and Lydia (Leaman Audenreid) D.; grad. U.S. Military Academy, 1898; Sc.D., Washington and Jefferson College, 1941; m. Ruby Caroline Hale, Nov. 12, 1902. Commissioned 2d lt. 17th Inf., Apr. 26, 1898; promoted through grades to major gen., Sept. 1, 1922; brig. gen. N.A., June 26, 1918; col. U.S. Army, July 1, 1920; brig. gen., July 3, 1920; commission expired Mar. 4, 1921; maj. gen., the adj. gen., 1922, reappointed, 1926; retired July 1, 1927. Participated in campaign against Santiago de Cuba, 1898, taking part in battles of El Caney and San Juan; Philippine Insurrection, 1899-1901; with Rio Grande Expedition, later in numerous engagements with Filipino insurgents; instructor Department of Tactics, U.S. Military Academy, 1901-05; with Army of Cuban Pacification, 1906-09; with Mass. Nat. Guard, summers 1907-09; a.d.c. to Major Gen Barry, 1909-11; adj. U.S. Mil. Acad., 1911-12; inspector and instr. Philippine Scouts, 1914-16; duty office of the adj. gen., U.S. Army, 1917; arrived in France, July 28, 1917; asst. to adj. gen., A.E.F., July 28-Nov. 26, 1917; acting adj. gen., A.E.F., Nov. 27, 1917-Jan. 22, 1918; asst. to adj. gen. A.E.F., Jan. 23,-Apr. 30, 1918; apptd. adj. gen., A.E.F., May 1, 1918; returned to U.S., Sept. 8, 1919; designated by Sec. of War to take charge of Dept.'s part in administrn of World War Adjusted Compensation Act, upon its passage, May 19, 1924. Exec. dir. N.Y. chapter, Am. Red Cross since 1932; pres. Assn. of Grads. U.S. Mil. Acad., 1936-38. Chmn. Commercial Radio Internat. Com. since 1942. Awarded D.S.M. (U.S.); Silver Star, with Oak Leaf Cluster (U.S); companion of the Bath (Great Britain); Comdr. Legion of Honor (France); Comdr. Order of the Crown (Italy); Comdr. Order of the Crown (Belgium); Grand Officer, Order of Prince Danilo (Montenegro); Order of La Solidaridad, 2d Class (Panama). Clubs: Knollwood Country (White Plains, N.Y.); Army and Navy, Chevy Chase (Washington, D.C.). Home: 277 Park Av. Office: 315 Lexington Av., New York, N.Y. Died Sep. 2, 1944.

DAVIS, Robert Hobart, editor, dramatist; b. Brownsville, Neb., Mar. 23, 1869; s. Rev. George Ransome and Silvia (Nichols) D.; ed. pub. sch., Carson City, Nev.; m. Madge Lee Hutchinson, Sept. 20, 1899. Compositor on Carson Appeal in youth; reporter on San Francisco Examiner, Call, Chronicle; founder and editor Chic, fortnightly, San Francisco, 1894; with New York Journal and American, 1895-1903, New York Sunday World, 1903; mng. editor New York Sunday News, 1904; joined editorial staff Frank A. Munsey Co.; asso. editor Munsey's Mag.; started and was 1st mng. editor of All-Story Mag., Scrap Book, Railroad Man's Mag., Woman, The Ocean, The Live Wire, The Cavalier. Member executive board New York Sun, also world corr. of same. Honorary pres. Stevenson Society. Clubs: Lotos, Players, Overseas Press, the Century Assn. Author: (plays) The Family; The Welcher; Efficiency and Laughter (with Perley Poore Sheehan); and books: We Are French (with Perley Poore Sheehan); Ruby Robert—Alias Bob Fitzsimmons; Over My Left Shoulder; Bob Davis Recalls; Bob Davis Again—In Many Moods; Bob Davis Abroad; On Home Soil with Bob Davis; Bob Davis Hither—and Yon; Islands Far and Near; Bob Davis at Large; Let's Go with Bob Davis; The Caliph of Bagdad—Life of O. Henry (with Arthur B. Maurice); Tree Toad; Autobiography of a Small Boy; The More I Admire Dogs—True Tales of Man's Best Friend; People, People Everywhere (published in England as Footprints of a Wanderer), Canada Cavalcade; Oriental Odyssey; Hawaii, U.S.A. As amateur photographer has made more than 3,000 portraits of prominent people and published "Man Makes His Own Mask," a collection of portraits, with biographical notes, of 130 notable subjects. For interview with Mussolini, Rome, Sept. 13, 1926, was made hon. life mem. staff Associated Press. Writer for last 17 yrs. "Bob Davis Reveals" column, New York Sun. Office: 280 Broadway, New York, N.Y. Died Oct. 11, 1942.

DAVIS, Roblin Henry, banker; b. Rawlins, Wyo., Apr. 29, 1885; s. John Charles and Ella Mary (Castiday) D.; A.B., Princeton, 1907; m. Margaret Evans, Apr. 29, 1915; children— Roblin Henry, Margaret, David Gray, William Evans. Began as wholesale druggist, 1907; pres. and mgr. Davis Brothers Drug Co., Denver, Colo., 1907-32; chmn. bd. since 1933; pres. Denver Nat. Bank since 1933; pres. Bolten & Davis Livestock Co. Served as lt., U.S. Naval Reserve, 1916-19. Pres. Denver Chamber of Commerce, 1923. Alumni trustee, Princeton U. since 1937. Episcopalian. Clubs: Mile High, Athletic, Country, Denver, University. Home: P.O. Box 60. Office: Denver Nat. Bank, Denver, Colo. Died Oct. 1945.

DAVIS, Royall Oscar Eugene, chemist; b. at Newberry, S.C., July 11, 1880; s. of William Alexander and Sarah Isabelle (Payne) D.; Ph.B., U. of N.C., 1901, Ph.D., 1903; student University of Leipzig, 1904; m. Birdie Pritchard, July 26, 1905. Instr. chemistry, U. of N.C., 1903-09, asso. prof., 1909; soil physicist, 1910-27, U.S. Department of Agr., Washington; in charge soil water investigations, same, 1912-13, in charge soil physics investigations, 1915-26; sr. chemist fertilizer and fixed nitrogen investigations, 1927-29, in charge nitrogenous fertilizer materials, fertilizer investigations, 1930-42; asst. head soil, fertilizer investigations, 1942-45; asst. Div. Soils, Fertilizer and Investigation since 1944. Mem. Am. Chem. Soc., A.A.A.S., Soc. Agronomy, Internat. Soc. Soil Science. Democrat. Methodist. Mason. Club: Cosmos. Contbr. numerous articles on soils, nitrogen, fertilizers and related subjects; asst. editor Chemical Abstracts. Home: 7130 Alaska Av. N.W., Washington. Died Oct. 30, 1949; buried at Chapel Hill, N.C.

DAVIS, Tenney Lombard, chemist; b. Somerville, Mass., Jan. 7, 1890; s. Thomas Lombard and Martha W. (Tenney) D.; student, Dartmouth Coll., 1907-08; B.S., Mass. Inst. Tech., 1913; M.S., Harvard, 1914, Ph.D., 1917; U. Calif., 1916-17; m. Dorothy Theresa Münch, Aug. 28, 1923. Austin teaching fellow, Harvard, 1913-16; instr. organic chem., Mass. Inst. Tech., 1919-20, asst. prof., 1920-26, asso. prof., 1926-38, prof., 1938-42, prof. emeritus since 1942; summer lecturer, Western Reserve Univ., 1931, 1938; sect. chairman National Defense Research Committee, June 1940-April 1941; director of scientific research and development, National Fireworks, Incorporated since 1942; trustee South Scituate Savings Bank. First lieutenant Ordnance Department, U.S. Army, 1917-19. Mem. Am. Chem. Soc. (chmn. history chem. div., 1932-39), History of Science Soc. (v.p. 1941), A.A.A.S., Am. Acad. Arts and Sciences (corr. sec. 1930-37, rec. sec. 1937-38), corresponding mem. Royal Soc. Bohemia (Prague, Czechoslovakia), Newcomen Soc. Editor-in-chief Chymia. Associate editor, Journal of Chemical Education, Isis, Tech. Review. Author: The Chemistry of Powder and Explosives. Contributor various articles on chemical subjects, history of chemistry, Chinese alchemy. Home: Central St., Norwell, Mass. Died Jan. 25, 1949.

DAVIS, Thomas Bealle, chmn. bd. Island Creek Coal Co.; officer or dir. other cos. Home: 477 Park Av. Office: 20 Exchange Pl., New York, N.Y. Died July 3, 1948.

DAVIS, Warren Bartlett, osteopath; b. Fort Atkinson, Wis., Jan. 27, 1869; s. John Henry and Esther (Hopkins) D.; D.O., Northern Coll. Osteopathy, Minneapolis, Minn., 1899; m. Nettie J. Adams, Aug. 16, 1893; children—Earl Adams, Paul Herbert. In practice as osteopathic physician and surgeon at Milwaukee, Wis., 1899-1920, Long Beach, Calif., since 1920; pres. Calif. Bd. of Osteopathic Examiners, 1933, '37, '41. Mem. Am. Osteopathic Assn. (pres. 1930), Calif. Osteopathic Assn. (pres. 1925); pres. Wis. Osteopathic Assn., 1908. Baptist. Mason. Clubs: Rotary, Long Beach Masonic (pres. 1928), Virginia Country. Home: 769 Cherry Av. Office: First Nat. Bank Bldg., Long Beach, Calif. Died Sept. 15, 1944; buried in Inglewood Park Cemetery, Inglewood, Calif.

DAVIS, Westmoreland, ex-gov.; b. of Am. parents, at sea, Aug. 21, 1859; s. Thomas Gordon and Annie Lewis (Morriss) D.; grad. Va. Mil. Inst., 1877; student U. of Va., 1883; LL.B., Columbia, 1885; LL.D., Washington and Lee U., 1921, Coll. of William and Mary, Williamsburg, Va., 1921; certificate of merit, Va. Poly. Institute, 1929; m. Margaret Inman. Admitted to N.Y. bar, 1885, and practiced at N.Y. City; began farming in Loudoun County, Va., 1901; elected gov. of Va. for term Feb. 1, 1918-Feb. 1, 1922; pres. and pub. Southern Planter. Mem. bd. of visitors Virginia Poly. Institute. Democrat. Episcopalian. Pres. Va. State Farmers' Inst., 1908-15; pres. Va. State Fair Assn. Mem. Phi Beta Kappa, Omicron Delta Kappa. Home: Morven Park, Leesburg, Va. Died in Johns Hopkins Hospital, Baltimore, Md., Sept. 2, 1942.

DAVIS, William Rees, coll. dean; b. Oshkosh, Wis., Aug. 12, 1877; s. Rees and Anne (Hughes) D.; A.B., Ripon Coll., 1901; student University of Chicago, 1902-12; A.M., Harvard, 1910; m. Edith Blackman, Merrell, Aug. 22, 1907; children—Margaret, Merrell, Elizabeth. Instr. Sch. of Edn., U. of Chicago, 1903-12; head of English dept., Whitman Coll., since 1912, dean since 1917, dean Division of Arts and Letters since 1935; prof. English, U. of Wash., summers 1921, 22; Wash. State Coll., summer 1923. Moderator Wash. Congl. Conf., 1930, 1931. Mem. Modern Lang. Assn. America, American Assn. of University Profs., Nat. Council Teachers of English, Archaeol. Inst. America, Delta Sigma Rho, Phi Delta Theta, Phi Beta Kappa, etc. Republican. Conglist. Kiwanian. Home: 116 Stanton St., Walla Walla, Wash. Died Mar. 13, 1947.

DAVIS, William Thornwall, ophthalmologist; b. Little Rock, Arkansas; son William Thornwall and Terese (Akin) D.; student Ky. Military Institute, 1890-92; M.D., George Washington, 1901; grad. U.S. Army Med. Sch., 1902-03, Univ. of Vienna, 1906, 12, Royal Ophthalmic Hosp., London, 1906; m. Reneé Tolson, 1912; children — William Joseph Graham, Roger Has Brouck, René Sheldon, Akin Thornwall. Interne Garfield Memorial Hosp., Washington, D.C., 1901-02; 1st lt., later capt. Med. Corps, U.S. Army, 1902-13 (under Gen. Leonard Wood, Moro campaigns, 1904-05; surgeon under Gen. Frank McCoy, Datto Ali Campaign, 1905); maj. Med. Corps, U.S. Army, World War; prof. ophthalmology, U.S. Army Med. Sch., 1917-18; prof. same, George Washington, since 1920; sr. surgeon Episcopal Eye and Ear Hosp.; cons. ophthalmologist at Garfield, Columbia, Gallinger, Casualty hosps.; ophthalmologist in chief George Washington U. Hosp.; consultant in ophthalmology to the surg. gen. U.S. Army, Feb. 1943. Mem. advisory bd. Selective Service Draft, 1941. Mem. bd. dirs. Washington Loan & Trust Co. Official Orden Nacional de Merito Carlos J. Finley (Cuba). Fellow American College Surgeon; mem. A.M.A., Southern Med. Assn., Am. Acad. Ophthalmology and Otolaryngology, Med. Soc. of D.C., S.A.R.; Mil. Order of Foreign Wars of U.S., Soc. of the Cincinnati of State of Va., The Filson Club of Ky., Pan-Am. Med. Assn., Acad. of Medicine (Washington, D.C.), Mil. Order Carabao, Spanish Am. War Veterans, Am. Legion (A.P. Gardner Post), Phi Sigma Kappa, Sigma Xi. Episcopalian. Mason. Rotarian. Clubs: Army and Navy, Metropolitan (Washington); Chevy Chase (Maryland). Contributed papers read before Am. Acad. Ophthalmology, Ophthal. Sect. A.M.A., etc. Office: 927 Farragut Sq., Washington, D.C. Died June 16, 1944.

DAVIS, Wirt, banker; b. Liberty, Tex., Nov. 20, 1873; s. George W. and Camilla (Hardin) D.; grad. Lawrenceville (N.J.) Sch., 1893; A.B., Yale, 1897; m. Kate G. Wilson, Sept. 18, 1918; children—Camilla G., Wirt, Patricia. Admitted to Tex. bar, 1898; mem. George W. Davis & Son, 1897-98; pres. Tex. Farm Mortgage Co., 1906-34; pres. Republic Trust and Savings Bank, Dallas, 1924-23; pres. Davis-Johnson Lumber Co. since 1925; vice chmn. Republic Nat. Bank & Trust Co., Dallas, 1925-34; chmn. bd. Republic Nat. Bank, Dallas, since 1934; dir. Liberty State Bank, Oak Cliff State Bank; director, Employers Casualty Company, Dallas. Pres. bd. trustees Tex. Country Day Sch. for Boys. Mem. Delta Kappa Epsilon. Democrat. Episcopalian. Clubs: Yale (N.Y. City); Critic, Dallas Country (Dallas). Home: 4512 Lakeside Drive. Office: Republic National Bank, Dallas, Tex. Died Aug. 5, 1945.

DAVISON, Charles Stewart, lawyer; b. N.Y. City, April 14, 1855; s. Edward Francis and Charlotte Sewell (White) D.; 8th in descent from Daniel D., Mass. Bay Colony, 1651; Harvard, 1871-72; B.A., Cambridge U., Eng., 1876, M.A., 1914; student Inner Temple, London, Eng., 2 yrs.; LL.B., Columbia, 1877; hon. fellow Magdalene Coll., Cambridge, Eng., 1928; unmarried. Practiced in N.Y. City, since 1877; specialist in constl. and comml. law. Mem. Assn. Bar City of N.Y. (ex-chmn. exec. com.), N.Y. Law Inst., Nat. Assn. Constl. Govt., Am. Defense Soc. (hon. chmn.), Am. Coalition Patriotic Socs. (bd. govs.), Nat. Lafayette Day Com. (hon. sec.), Immigration Restriction League, Civil Service Reform Assn., Civil Legion, Dutch Belted Cattle Assn., Hampshire Swine Assn., Nat. Parks Com., etc.; hon. chmn. Good Government Clubs of New York; mem. exec. com. League of Rep. Clubs; formerly chmn. Citizens Com. of Welcome; formerly sec. and chmn. Sailing Com. of Isle of Purbeck Yacht Club (Eng.) and sec. and chmn. Sailing Com. of Corinthian Yacht Club of N.Y. Chevalier Legion of Honor (France), 1920. Unitarian. Clubs: Century, Down Town, Harvard, Boone and Crockett (formerly v.p.), United University (London, Eng.), Pitt, A.D.C. (Cambridge, Eng.), Author brochures: Letters to Hiram Freeborn; Treason; Freedom of the Seas (book); Selling the Bear's Hide (book); Dealers in Money; Reprisal in War; Maritime Neutral and Belligerent Rights; etc., also short stories. Author and Editor: The Alien in Our Midst (book); The Founders of the Republic on Immigration (book). Contbr. on constl. topics. Devised "The Mystery Ships" for British and French navies, 1915. Collaborator with Madison Grant on The Passing of the Great Race (book) and Conquest of a Continent (book). Home: Columbia University Club. Office: 64 Wall St., New York, N.Y. Died Nov. 23, 1942.

DAVISON, Donald Angus, army officer; b. San Carlos, Ariz., Oct. 26, 1892; s. Lorenzo Paul and Carolyn (Shannon) D.; student, Colgate Univ., 1910-11, B.S., U.S. Military Acad., 1915; m. Marjorie Risk, Dec. 28, 1920; children—Carolyn Maclean (Mrs. Hugh McCormick Hayden), Wilhemina Shannon, Margaret Angeline. Commd. 2d lt., 1915, and advanced through grades to brig. gen., 1942; Corps of Engrs., 1917-42; awarded Legion of Merit, 1943. Chief engr., Northwest African Air Force, 1943. Christian Scientist. Clubs: Army-Navy, Country (Washington, D.C.). Home: 3804 Fulton St. N.W., Washington, D.C. Died May 5, 1944.

DAVISON, George Stewart, civil engr.; b. Pittsburgh, Pa., Sept. 21, 1856; s. Edward and Isabel (Kennedy) D.; C.E., Rensselaer Poly. Inst., 1878; D.Sc., U. of Pittsburgh, 1926; Dr. Engring., Rensselaer, 1926; m. Clara Elizabeth Lape, May 19, 1881; 1 son, Allen Stewart. Began with engring. dept. Pa. Lines West, 1878; with U.S. Engring Corps, 1879; with engring. dept. A.T.&S.F. Ry. and Pa. Lines West, 1880-82; chief engr. Pittsburgh, Chartiers & Youghiogheny R.R., 1882, gen. supt., 1883-90; mem. Wilkins & Davison, 1890-1900; gen. mgr. Monongahela and Pittsburgh and Birmingham Ry. Lines, Pittsburgh, 1900-02; president Pa. Water Co. since 1902; asst. to pres. subsidiary cos. of Gulf Oil Corp., 1905-11. In 1911 became pres. Gulf Refining Co. and other subsidiaries of Gulf Oil Corp., resigned, 1929; v.p. Green Bag Cement Company of West Va.; chairman of the board Pittsburgh Coke & Iron Company, Pittsburgh & Ohio Valley R.R., Green Bag Cement Company of Pa., Allegheny River Limestone Co.; dir. Bellefield Co., Schenley Hotel Co.; pres. bd. mgrs. Homewood Cemetery; trustee Rensselaer Poly. Inst.; pres. and dir. West Penn Hosp., Pittsburgh; mem. Bd. of Industrial Preparedness, 1916, Com. of Public Safety of Pa., oil sub-com. Nat. Council of Defense and Nat. Petroleum War Service Commn., World War. Mem. Am. Soc. C.E. (past-pres.), Am. Inst. Consulting Engrs. Soc. of Western Pa. (past-pres.), Delta Phi. Republican. Presbyterian. Clubs: Pittsburgh, Athletic, Duquesne (Pittsburgh). Home: Pittsburgh Athletic Assn. Office: Oliver Bldg., Pittsburgh, Pa. Died Oct. 3, 1942.

DAVISON, John A., clergyman; b. Woodville, Ga., July 15, 1888; s. Thomas Cobb and Sarah (Armstrong) D.; A.B., U. of Ga., 1908; student Harvard Law Sch., 1909; M.Th., Southern Bapt. Theol. Sem., 1912, D.Th., 1913; D.D., Mercer U., Macon, Ga., 1933; m. Anne Victoria Greene, June 28, 1919; children—Sarah Quinn, Anne, Margaret. Ordained to ministry of Bapt. Church, 1910; pastor, 1st Bapt. churches, Camden, S.C., 1913-17, Selma, Ala., 1917-22, Columbus, Ga., 1922-27, Clarksville, Tenn., 1927-37; pastor First Bapt. Church, Selma, Ala., since 1937; commencement speaker at various colls.; speaker on religious programs. Has served as mem. Bapt. state exec. bds. of S.C., Ala., Ga., Tenn.; bds. of trustees Southern Bapt. Theol. Sem., Judson Coll., Shorter Coll., Tenn. Coll. for Women, Relief and Annuity Board and Home Mission Board, Hospital Board Southern Baptist Convention. Served as 1st lt. (chaplain) U.S. Army, World War I. Member Phi Beta Kappa, Sigma Nu, Am. Legion. Independent Democrat. Mason. Club. Kiwanis. Home: 724 Alabama Av. Office: First Baptist Church, Selma, Ala. Died May 6, 1947.

DAWE (George) Grosvenor, researcher, writer, lecturer; b. at Hersham (Surrey), England, July 15, 1863; s. John Ward and Sarah (Grosvenor) D.; student ungraded sch., 1872-78; Wilbraham (Mass.) Acad., 1884-86; came to U.S., 1883, naturalized, 1894; m. Angeline Baldwin, July 14, 1886 (now dec.); children—John Grosvenor, George Lyman, Charles Gridley; m. 2d, Cynthia Ann Shaen, Jan. 1, 1900; children—Robert Shaen, Allen Shaen. Circulation man Funk-Wagnalls, 1888-92; with Review of Reviews, 1892-98; Butterick Pub. Co., 1898-1907; sec. Society of Am. Authors, 1898-1903; mng. dir. Southern Commercial Congress, 1908-12; editor Nation's Business, 1912-14; orgn., research and development work, 1914-17; Y.M.C.A. work with A.E.F., France, 1918-20; Washington rep., research since 1908; organized early boys' clubs in Melrose, N.Y., and N.Y. City; comml. body reorgn., Southern U.S., 1907-12, throughout the U.S., 1912-18; with various British commissions, 1942-45. Unitarian. Publisher: Philosophy of the State (with Rev. Charles A. Hart), 1940; biography of Melvil Dewey, 1932; also author several bulls. on Florida and other subjects and numerous articles; conducted column, "Rambling Thoughts by Nemo," 1895-1900; "Date Briefs as a Gateway to Knowledge." Address: 272 Plainfield Av., Floral Park, N.Y. Died Sept. 13, 1948.

DAWSON, Allan, foreign service officer; b. Washington, D.C., Feb. 16, 1903; s. Thomas Cleland and Luisa Guerra (Duval) D.; B.S., U. S. Mil. Acad., 1924; m. Jane Dodge Myers, Jan. 3, 1947; 1 son, Thomas Cleland III. Newspaper reporter in Washington and New York, 1919-20; foreign service officer since 1925; vice consul, Rio Janeiro, Brazil, 1925-26, Bahai, Brazil, 1926-27; 3d secretary of Legation, Panama, 1927; 3d secretary of embassy, Mexico, Mexico, 1927-30; assigned to Dept. of State, 1930-31; 3d sec. of legation, Bogota, Colombia, 1931-32, 2d sec., 1932-34; 2d sec. legation, Managua, Nicaragua, 1934-35; assigned to Dept. of State, 1935; asst. and acting U.S. delegate, Chaco Peace Conf., Buenos Aires, Argentina, 1935-36; 2d sec. of embassy, Rio de Janeiro, Brazil, 1936-37; consul, Hamburg, Germany, 1937-39; 2d sec. of legation, La Paz, Bolivia, 1939-41, 1st sec. 1941-42; 1st sec. of embassy, Rio de Janeiro, Brazil, 1942; assigned to Dept. of State 1942-44, acting asst. chief Div. Am. Republics, Dept. of State, 1941, 1943-44; counselor of Embassy, Havana, Cuba, 1944, Caracas, Venezuela, 1945-47; chief div. Brazilian Affairs, Dept. of State, since 1947; chargé d'affaires ad interim, Colombia, Nicaragua, Bolivia, Cuba and Venezuela; detailed to 6th Pan-Am. Conf., Havana, Cuba, 1928, Pan-Am. Arbitration and Conciliation Conf., Washington, D.C., 1928-29; United Nations Conf. on Internat. Orgn., San Francisco, 1945; 4th gen. assembly of Pan-Am. Inst. of Geog. and Hist., Caracas, Venezuela, 1946. Address: Dept. of State, Washington. Died Oct. 15, 1949; buried in Arlington National Cemetery.

DAWSON, Edgar, educator; b. at Scottsville, Va., Dec. 22, 1872; s. George W. and Sarah S. (May) D.; A.B., Davidson Coll., N.C., 1895; M.A., U. of Va., 1899; Ph.D., U. of Leipzig, 1902; m. Anna King McKemy, Aug. 31, 1897 (died 1933). Prof. of history and polit. sci., Delaware Coll., 1902-06; asst. prof. history and polit. science, Princeton, 1906-09; prof. same, Hunter Coll., New York, Sept., 1909-39; retired 1939. Visiting prof., U. of Calif., 1920 and summer 1917, Columbia, 1918, Calif., 1919, Ore., 1920, Colo., 1921, 22. Sec. Assn. of History Teachers Middle States and Md., 1913-18, pres., 1912-13; sec. Nat. Council Social Studies, 1921-28; pres., 1930. Mem. Am. Hist. Assn., Nat. Civil Service Reform League, Am. Polit. Science Assn., Phi Beta Kappa. Presbyterian. Democrat. Club: City. Author: The Public Archives of Delaware, 1908; Practical History of the World (in part), 1908; The Teaching of Government (with others), 1916; Organized Self-Government, 1920; Preparation of Teachers of Social Studies in Civic Education, 1923; Outlines of Responsible Government (in part), 1923; The History Inquiry, 1924; Teaching the Social Studies, 1927; Classroom Teacher (in part), 1927; also articles and revs. on ednl. subjects. Editor City History Series, 1930-31; Civil Service in Modern Government, 1937. Actively interested in promoting civil service reform and world organization for peace. Address: 55 E. 76th St., New York, N.Y. Died Apr. 30, 1946.

DAWSON, Edward, clergyman; b. Walden, N.Y., Oct. 10, 1871; s. Joseph Thomas and Sarah Catharine (McKinney) D.; A.B., Rutgers, 1898, M.A., 1901, D.D., 1924; studied New Brunswick Theol. Sem., 1898-01; D.D., Central Coll., Ia., 1924; m. Sadie Estelle Voorhees, Apr. 30, 1902; 1 dau., Edna Voorhees. Ordained ministry Protestant Ref. Ch., 1901; pastor Ref. Ch., Union City, N.J., 1901-12; organized First Ref. Ch., Union City, N.J., 1903; pastor Old First Protestant Ref. Ch., of Acquackanonk, Passaic, N.J., 1912-41, pastor emeritus, 1941-1947; president of General Synod, Reformed Church in America, 1932-34; vice pres. Board of Fgn. Missions, 1932-35, pres. 1935-46. Member Ministerial Assn., Passaic, N.J. (pres.), Chi Psi, Alpha Rho. Clubs: Clerical, Alpha Sigma (New York); Rotary (Passaic, N.J.). Home: 32 North Spring Garden Av., Nutley, N.J. Died Oct. 25, 1947; buried at Walden, N.Y.

DAWSON, Miles Menander, actuary, lawyer; b. Viroqua, Wis., May 13, 1863; s. John and Martha (Ady) D.; ed. pub. schs. and Ky. (now Transylvania) U., to close of junior year; LL.B., New York U.; LL.D., Transylvania; m. Grace Luenette Burnette. Genl. practice as cons. actuary; actuary of Armstrong investigating com., N.Y., 1905-06, of Royal Commn. on Life Insurance of Can., 1906, of Wisconsin Legislative committee, 1906; adviser War Risk Bur., 1917, 21, also N.Y. gov. and commn. re workmen's compensation, 1914; spl. counsel U.S. in tax litigation, 1915, 17; spl. atty. exmr. U.S. Shipping Bd. Emergency Fleet Corp., 1918-19; counsel and actuary commn. to investigate N.Y. State ins. fund, 1919. Mem. Assn. Bar City of N.Y., Am. Bar Assn., Poetry Soc. America (treas.); hon. mem. Swiss So-

ciety of Actuaries; fellow Am. Soc. Actuaries, Inst. of Actuaries, Am. Inst. Actuaries, Casualty Actuarial Assn., Fraternal Actuarial Association. Clubs: Authors' (London); Arts and Letters (Toronto); City, Authors, Delta Upsilon. Author: Elements of Life Insurance, 1892, 1902, 11; The Effect of Free Surrender and Loan Privileges in Life Insurance, 1894; Assessment Life Insurance, 1895; Principles of Insurance Legislation, 1896; Practical Lessons in Actuarial Science, 1897, 1905; The Function of Insurance in Modern Society, 1898; Various Derived Tables, American Experience, 1900, 05, 15; Things Agents Should Know, 1900; Development of Insurance Mathematics, 1901; Poems of the New Time, 1902; The Business of Life Insurance, 1905; Comparative Reserve Tables, 1907, 15; Workingmen's Insurance in Europe (with Dr. L. K. Frankel), 1910; Survivorship Annuity Tables, 1910, 15; Ethics of Confucius, 1915; Ethics of Socrates, 1924; Ethical Religion of Zoroaster, 1931; Wisdom of Confucius, 1931. Translator: Elsie, a novel (from Norwegian of Alexander Kjelland), 1892; Brand, a poetical tragedy by Henrik Ibsen, 1916. Office: 500 Fifth Av., New York, N.Y.
Died Mar. 27, 1942.

DAWSON, William Warren, prof. law; b. Wooster, O., Mar. 2, 1892; s. Rev. William Chambers and Mary Elizabeth (Nail) D.; A.B., Ohio Wesleyan U., 1914; LL.B., Western Reserve U, 1921; student Harvard U. Law Sch., Jan.-June 1927; hon. LL.D., Washington & Jefferson Univ., 1942; married Marguerite Sague Shafer, Sept. 3, 1929. Admitted to Ohio bar, 1920; practiced with Stanley & Horwitz, Cleveland, 1920-23, Dawson & Meyer, 1923-27; instr. law, Western Reserve U., 1927-30, asso. prof., 1930-33, prof. since 1933 (on leave since 1942); pub. rep. Regional Labor Bd., 1935-42. Mayor Brecksville, O., 1931-36. Enlisted 166th Inf., 42d Div., U.S. Army, 1917, commd. 2d lt., July 1918, 1st lt., Jan. 1919; hon. disch., July 1919; commd. maj. Inf., A.U.S., Oct. 1942; asst. exec. Tank Destroyer Sch., Camp Hood, Texas; promoted lt. col., June 1943; enrolled, Sch. of Mil. Govt., Charlottesville, Va., Sept. 1, 1943; dir. Training Division, European Civil Affairs Div., Aug. 1944; promoted to col., Mar. 1945; dir. office Military Govt. Wuerttemberg-Baden, Germany, July 1945; director regional government, Coordinating Office, August 1946. Awarded Bronze Star, Jan. 1946, Legion of Merit, 1947; Croix de Guerre with palm, Chevalier de la Legion d'Honneur (France). Mem. Cuyahoga County Charter Commission, 1935. Mem. American Ohio and Cleveland bar assns., Phi Beta Kappa, Beta Theta Pi (pres. 1940-46), Phi Delta Phi, Omicron Delta Kappa. Republican. Methodist. Clubs: University, Philosophical (Cleveland). Author: Ohio Appellate Review, 1935; Dawson & Andrews Ohio Forms, 1928. Editor: Am. Bar Assn. Inst. on Federal Rules, 1938. Address: Windover, Brecksville, O. Died Feb. 10, 1947; buried in Arlington National Cemetery

DAY, Charles Manley, newspaper pub.; b. Sidney, Ia., Nov. 4, 1863; s. James Gamble and Minerva (Manley) D.; A.B., Tabor (Ia.) Coll., 1886; m. Annie Louise Davenport, Dec. 18, 1888; children—Herbert James, M.D., Dorothy Davenport (Mrs. Holton Davenport). Began in newspaper business, Sioux Falls, S.D., 1886; editor Daily Argus-Leader and pres. Angus-Leader Co. since 1905. Mem. S D. State Bd. Charities and Corrections, 1917-25; member of Mount Rushmore National Commn. Del. to Rep. Nat. Conv., 1932, 36, 40. Republican. Mason (Shriner), Elk. Clubs: Rotary, Minnehaha Country (Sioux Falls); Athletic Club (Los Angeles). Home: 631 W. 10th St. Office: 109-111 N. Main Av., Sioux Falls, S.D. Died Sep. 7, 1945.

DAY, Edward Marvin, lawyer; b. Colchester, Conn., Aug. 20, 1872; s. Erastus S. and Catherine (Olmsted) D.; B.A., Yale, 1894; LL.B., 1896; unmarried. Admitted to Conn. bar, 1896, and since practiced at Hartford; mem. Conn. Ho. of Rep., 1897-99; exec sec. State of Conn., 1899-1901, 1905-07; chmn. Employees' Liability Commn., 1907. Dir. Aetna Life Ins. Co., Aetna Casualty & Surety Co., Automobile Ins. Co. of Hartford, Phoenix Ins. Co., Hartford Courant Co., Hartford-Conn. Trust Co., J. B. Williams Co., North and Judd Mfg. Co., New Britain Machine Co. Mem. Delta Kappa Epsilon. Republican. Conglist. Clubs: Hartford, Twentieth Century. Home: 236 Girard Av. Office: 750 Main St., Hartford, Conn. Died May 2, 1947.

DAY, Ewing Wilber, physician; b. Deerfield, O., Nov. 1, 1862; s. Edgar M. and Frances (Reed) D.; A.B., Allegheny Coll., Meadville, Pa., 1884, A.M., 1886; M.D., Georgetown U., 1889; m. Annie A. Mosier, July 23, 1890; children—Edgar Mortimer (dec.), Ewing W., Kenneth Mosier, Percival Eaton, Mrs. Elizabeth Autrey (dec.). Practiced in Pittsburgh, Pa., 1899-1928 (retired); emeritus prof. otology of the U. of Pittsburgh; member of the Collegium Oto-Rhino-Laryngolicum. Mem. A.M.A., Pa. State Med. Soc., Am. Laryngol., Rhinol. and Otol. Soc. (pres.), Am. Otol. Soc. (pres.), Allegheny County Med. Soc. (pres.), Pittsburgh Acad. Medicine (pres.), S.A.R., Patriots and Founders of America. Episcopalian. Lt. col. Med. R.C., 1917. Club: University. Home: 616 Commercial St., Provincetown, Mass. Office: 121 University Pl., Pittsburgh, Pa. Died Nov. 24, 1942.

DAY, Francis, painter; b. Le Roy N.Y., Aug. 12, 1863; s. James and Jennie (McKane) D.; student Art Students' League, New York, and at École des Beaux Arts, Paris, under Herbert Merson and Colin; m. Mary Evelyn Smith, July 3, 1887. Has been represented in numerous exhbns.; took 3d Hallgarten prize, Nat. Acad. Design, 1895, for picture "Patience." A.N.A. Episcopalian. Republican. Home: Lanesboro, Mass. Deceased.

DAY, G. Z., pres. Northern Insurance Co. of New York. Address: 83 Malden Lane, New York, N.Y. Deceased.

DAY, Joseph Paul, real estate; b. New York, N.Y., Sept. 22, 1873, s. John W. and Catherine A. (Hayes) D.; educated public schools; m. Pauline M. Pope, June 1, 1898 (died July 1932); children—Joseph P., Bernard Pope, Charles Pope, Pauline Pope, Laura Pope (deceased), Fairfield Pope; m. 2d, Mrs. Agnes Y. Cole, May 31, 1942. Entered real estate and insurance business at 21; negotiated, 1898, what is said to be the largest accident policy ever written, covering insurance against accidents resulting from change of motive power on 3d Av. surface ry.; sold at auction, 1910, the 3d Av. R.R. which brought $26,000,000, etc.; active in negotiating many large purchases of real estate at pvt. sale; sold for U.S. Shipping Bd. Emergency Fleet Corp. 6 war villages, involving over $6,000,000; also more than $100,000,000 real estate in United States and Canada, in 1922; sold at Auction over $1,500,000 real estate holdings of closed nat. banks, 1937. Pres. Real Estate Auctioneers' Assn., N.Y.; pres. Castle Hill Estates, Inc., Joseph P. Day, Inc.; dir. R. H. Macy & Company, National Horse Show Association, Westchester Fire Insurance Co., Metropolitan Life Insurance Co., Union Carbide & Carbon Co., Phoenix Indemnity Co., Imperial Assurance Co. Hon. chmn. Interstate Sanitation Commn. Was one of organizers Am. Relief Com. in London, Eng., at outbreak of European War, to bring Americans back to U.S. Mem. Real Estate Bd. of New York (pres. 2 terms, honorary governor), Chamber of Commerce of N.Y., Geneal. Society. Clubs: Metropolitan, New York Yacht, Friendly Sons of St. Patrick, Lake Placid. Home: 34 Gramercy Park, N.Y. City; (country) Short Hills, New Jersey. Office: 405 Lexington Avenue, New York, New York. Died Apr. 10, 1944.

DAY, Ralph E., pres. Bridgeport Brass Co.; b. Peckville, Pa., 1885; ed. Lehigh Univ.; m. Ernestine Brown, Dec. 14, 1938; children—Ellen E., David K. Pres. and gen. mgr. Bridgeport Brass Co., 1930-42; pres. Bridgeport Engravers Supply Co.; dir. City Savings Bank, First Nat. Bank & Trust Co., Gray Mfg. Co., Silex Co.; Lava Cap Gold Mining Corp. Dir. Bridgeport Hosp. Mem. Chamber of Commerce, Bridgeport. Mason (Shriner). Home: High Oakes, Maitland, Fla. Office: 774 E. Main St., Bridgeport, Conn. Died May 2, 1946; buried at Wilkes-Barre, Pa.

DAY, Stephen A., ex-congressman; b. Canton, O. July 13, 1882; s. Justice William Rufus and Mary Elizabeth (Schaefer) D.; ed. Univ. Sch., Cleveland, O., and Asheville (N.C.) Sch.; A.B., U. of Mich., 1905; m. Mary Thayer (deceased); children—Mary Elizabeth, Helen, Stephanie, Stephen A., Jr.; m. 2d, Shirley Spoerer. Served as private secretary to Chief Justice Melville W. Fuller, of the Supreme Court of the U.S., 1905-07; admitted to Ohio bar, 1907, and practiced in Cleveland; with Pam, Hurd & Day, Chicago, 1908-12; practiced alone since 1920; mem. of the 77th and 78th Congresses (1941-45), Ill. at large. Devotes special attention to federal court matters and corp. organization and reorganization. Revised and annotated "Appellate Jurisdiction and Procedure in all Courts of the United States," 1917. Author: The Constitutionalist, 1936; We Must Save the Republic, 1941. Home: 2144 Forestview Rd., Evanston, Ill. Died Jan. 5, 1950.

DAY, William Horace, clergyman; b. Bloomingdale, Ill., Nov. 26, 1866; s. Warren Finney (D.D.) and Rachel (Beith) D.; A.B., Amherst, 1889, A.M., 1892; student Yale Div. Sch.; B.D., Chicago Theol. Sem., 1892; U. of Chicago traveling fellow, Oxford, Eng., 1894-95, Berlin, Ger., 1895-96, grad. student, 1896-98; D.D., Amherst, 1906; m. Julia Huntington Lyman, Oct. 11, 1897. Ordained Congl. ministry, 1892; asst. pastor New England Ch., Chicago, 1892-94, First Ch., Aurora, Ill., 1896-1900, First Ch., Los Angeles, 1900-17 (asso. with father until latters death, 1913, one of the few cases where father and son occupied same pulpit); pastor United Congl. Ch., Bridgeport, Conn., 1917-37, active emeritus since 1937. Moderator Nat. Council Congl. Chs. of U.S., 1917-19; pres. Am. Missionary Assn., 1923-27, Congl. Home Bds., 1927 Congl. del. to Stockholm Conf. on Life and Work, 1925; del. to Lausanne Conf. on Faith and Order, 1927, Oxford Conf. on Life and Work, 1937, Edinburgh Conf. on Faith and Order, 1937. Elected chmn. exec. com. Internat. Congl. Council. Pres. Fairfield County, Amherst Club. Mem. Delta Kappa Epsilon. Clubs: University, Rotary; Yale (New York); Chicago Literary. Home: 464 Park Pl., Bridgeport, Conn. Died March 16, 1942.

DAYTON, Arthur Spencer, lawyer; b. Philippi, W. Va., May 6, 1887; s. Alston Gordon and Lummie (Sinsel) D.; A.B., W.Va. U., Morgantown, W.Va., 1907, LL.B., 1908; M.A., Yale, 1909; m. Ruth Woods, June 14, 1916. Admitted to W.Va. bar, 1908; practiced at Philippi, W.Va., 1909-23; practiced at Charleston, West Virginia, since 1923; mem. firm Blue, Dayton & Campbell, Charleston, 1926-45 (firm became Dayton, Campbell and Love, 1945). Approved for 1st lt., Army Service Corps, U.S. Army, during World War. Mem. Kanawha County Pub. Library Bd., Charleston. Mem. Am. Bar Assn., W.Va. State Bar Assn., City of Charleston Bar Assn., Phi Beta Kappa, Delta Tau Delta, Phi Alpha Delta. Republican. Presbyterian. Clubs: Edgewood Country (Charleston, W. Va.); Yale (N.Y. City); Duquesne, University (Pittsburgh, Pa.). Author various legal articles. Home: 19 Bradford St. Office: Security Bldg., Charleston, W.Va. Died May 21, 1948; buried in Sunset Memorial Park, Charleston, W.Va.

DEADERICK, William Heiskell (dĕd'rĭk), physician; b. Knoxville, Feb. 7, 1876; Thomas Oakley and Josephine (Heiskell) D.; Southwestern Presbyn. U., 1891-95; U. of Louisville Med. Dept., 1895-97; M.D., Vanderbilt U., Tenn., 1898; m. Ava Van Leer Lusby, Jan. 8, 1921; children—Elizabeth, Margaret, William H. Practiced at Clarksville, Tenn., 1898-99, at Marianna, Ark., 1899-12, Hot Springs, Ark., since 1912. Mem. med. advisory bd. Hot Springs Clinic, U.S. Pub. Health Service; mem. advisory com. div of venereal diseases, U S. Pub. Health Service. Editor Am. Jour. of Syphilis, 1920-30. Ex-pres. Ark. Child Welfare Assn.; fellow. mem. bd. govs. Am. Coll. Physicians; hon. mem. Nat. Malaria Com., Am. Congress on Internal Medicine. Author: A Practical Study of Malaria, 1909. Joint Author: The Endemic Diseases of the Southern States (with L. O. Thompson), 1915. Home: Hot Springs, Ark. Deceased.

DEAKYNE, Herbert (dē-kīn'), army officer; b. Deakyneville, Del., Dec 29, 1867; s. Napoleon B. and Mary A. (David) D.; student Delaware Coll. (now U. of Del.), 1884-85; grad. U.S. Mil. Acad., 1890; Engr. Sch. of Application, 1893; Army War Coll., 1917; m. Sadie M. Nickerson, June 15, 1899; children—Ramona (Mrs. John B. Hughes), Rosalind (Mrs. George W. Waldron). Commd. additional 2d lt. engrs., June 12, 1890; promoted through grades to lt. col., Feb. 27, 1914; col. Nat. Army, July 6, 1917; brig. gen. (temp.), Oct. 1, 1918-May 31, 1919; col. engrs., Feb. 6, 1920; brig. gen., June 27, 1926; retired, Dec. 31, 1931. River and harbor improvements, California, 1893-96; fortification works, Calif., 1896-1900; mem. Calif. Debris Commn., 1897-1901; in charge fortification works and river and harbor improvements in Fla., 1901-03; at Fort Leavenworth, Kan., 1903-05; in Philippines, 1905-07; chief engr. officer Philippines Div., Aug.-Nov. 1907; mem. Bd. Engrs. for Rivers and Harbors, 1909-12; at Phila., Pa., in charge of fortification works and river and harbor improvements, 1908-12; at Kansas City, Mo., in charge of river and harbor improvements, 1912-16; duty office of Chief of Engrs., Washington, D.C., 1916; at Army War Coll., 1916-17. Organized 19th Engrs. (Ry.) at Phila., May-Aug. 1917; sailed for France via Halifax and Eng., Aug. 9, 1917; arrived in France Aug. 30, 1917; comd. 19th Engrs. at St. Nazaire, Sept. 1917-Jan. 1918; comd. 11th Engrs. (Ry.) on British Front and with A.E.F., Jan.-May, 1918; at G.H.Q., A E.F., as dir. of Light Rys. and Roads, May-July 1918; chief engr. Paris Group, Aug.-Sept. 1918; chief engr., 2d Army, Sept. 1918-Apr. 1919; at New Orleans, La., in charge of fortification works and river and harbor improvements, May 1919-Sept. 1920; mem. Miss. River Commn., Mar.-Sept. 1920; at San Francisco, Calif., as div. engr. Pacific Div., and in charge fortification works and river and harbor improvements, Sept. 1920-Jan. 1925; mem. California Debris Commn., 1920-25; as division engineer Northeast division and in charge river and harbor improvements, Feb. 1925-June 1926; asst. chief of engrs., June 1926-June 1930; acting chief of engrs., Aug. 8-Sept. 30, 1929. Mem. Board of Engineers for Rivers and Harbors, Feb, 6, 1925-Dec. 31, 1931; mem. Permanent Internat. Commn. of Internat. Assn. of Navigation Congresses; pres. Soc. Am. Mil. Engineers, 1932; cons. engr. to Chamber of Commerce, Eureka, Calif., Mar.-May, 1934, to Trinity River Canal Assn., Fort Worth, Tex., Jan.-May 1937. Clubs: Army and Navy, Army, Navy, and Marine Corps Country (Washington, D.C.). Home: San Francisco, Calif. Address: 2248 Washington St., San Francisco 15, Calif. Died May 28, 1945.

DEAL, Joseph T., ex-congressman; b. in Va., Nov. 19, 1860; s. John J. and Virginia Elizabeth D.; C.E., Va. Mil. Inst., 1882; m. Juliette D. Spartley, Oct. 28, 1885; children—Thurman, Roy C., Joseph D. Lumber mfr. since 1883; moved to Norfolk, Va., 1891; acquired large lumber holdings in S.C., 1900, later became owner large land areas on James River, Va. Chmn. Improvement Bd., Norfolk City, 1905-10; del. Dem. Natl. Conv., 1908; mem. Va. Ho. of Dels., 1910-12; Dem. candidate for Congress, 1912; mem. Va. Senate, 1919; mem. 67th to 70th Congresses (1921-29), 2d Va. Dist.; candidate at primary election for gov., 1933. Mem. S.A.R. Democrat. Episcopalian. Mason (K.T., Shriner). Home: 7457 N. Shore Rd., Norfolk, Va. Died March 7, 1942.

DEALEY, George Bannerman, publisher; b. Manchester, Eng., Sept. 18, 1859; s. George and Mary Ann (Nellins) D.; ed. primary schs., Liverpool, Eng., and primary and night schs., Galveston, Tex.; came to U.S., 1870; LL.D., Southern Meth. U., 1921, Austin Coll., 1924, U. of Mo., 1925; m. Olivia Allen, Apr. 9, 1884; children—Annie, Fannie, Walter Allen (dec.), Edward Musgrove, Mary. Began with Galveston News, Oct. 12, 1874, as office boy; promoted through various grades and was business mgr. and mgr. Dallas News, 1885-1906; v.p. and gen. mgr. A. H. Belo & Co., pubs. Galveston News, Dallas News and other newspapers, 1906-20; pres. and gen. mgr. same, 1920-26; purchased controlling interest and reorganized A. H. Belo & Co., July 1926; pres. A. H. Belo Corp., 1926-40; chmn. bd. A. H. Belo Corp., pubs. Dallas Morning News and Texas Almanac and State Industrial Guide; part owners of Radio Station WFAA and KGKO; pres. G. B. Dealey Land

Co., West Commerce Realty Co. Pres. Family Service, Dallas; dir. Children's Hosp. of Texas; Dallas; chmn. exec. com. Richmond Freeman Mem. Clinic; hon. v.p. Nat. Housing Assn., 1920-21; mem. bd. govs. Am. City Planning Inst., 1920-21; v.p. Nat. Municipal League, 1923-24; mem. advisory council Am. Planning and Civic Assn.; 1st v.p. Southwestern Polit. Science Assn., 1920-29; 2d v.p. Asso. Press, 1923-24; dir. Greater Texas and Pan-Am. Expn., 1937; hon. mem. Sigma Delta Chi (nat. hon. pres. 1940-41); elected hon. mem. Phi Beta Kappa, 1943; Phi Beta Kappa Associates, 1944; hon. mem. Jas. B. Bonham chapter Daughters of Republic of Tex., Thos. J. Rusk chapter Sons Republic of Texas; received Order of the Knights of San Jacinto at annual meeting of Sons of Republic of Texas, April 18, 1944; mem. Philos. Soc. of Tex. (pres. 1939), Texas State Hist. Assn. (life mem.), Tex. Geog. Soc., Dallas Hist. Soc. (pres.), Eng.-Speaking Un., Dallas Advt. League (hon. life), Press Congress of the World, Tex. Press Assn., Tex. Forestry Assn.; hon. mem. Dallas Post No. 156, Vets. Foreign Wars; hon. life member Internat. Printing Pressmen and Assistants Union; life member Dallas Y.M.C.A.; director Dallas Scottish Rite Temple Assn.; chmn. bd. trustees Westminster Presbyterian Church; member national committee of Commn. on Interracial Coöperation; sponsor Dallas Foundation, organized in 1930. Mem. Navy League of U.S.; life mem. Texas Congress of Mothers and Parent-Teachers Assn.; hon. mem. Dallas Big Brothers, Salesmanship Club, Pan American Round Table. Called dean of Am. journalists having been with one newspaper concern since 1874. Independent Democrat. Presbyterian. Scottish Rite Mason (33°, K.T., Shriner); mem. Red Cross of Constantine. Clubs: Critic, Athletic, Country (hon. mem.), Knife and Fork, Salesmanship of Dallas (hon.); Nat. Press (Washington). Home: 3704 Alice Circle (Highland Park), Dallas. Office: The News, Dallas, Tex. Died Feb. 26, 1946.

DEAN, Arthur Davis, educator; b. Cambridge, Mass., Sept. 15, 1872; s. Daniel H. and Lizzie (Reed) D.; grad. Rindge Tech. Sch., Cambridge, 1891; B.S., Mass. Inst. Tech., 1895; Sc.D., Alfred U., 1913; m. Amy Joanna Chattle, Dec. 24, 1896; m. 2d, Rose Elizabeth Sherman, September 8, 1941. Asst. prin., Tech. High Sch., Springfield, Mass., 1899-1905; supervising evening schs. of Y.M.C.A. in Mass. and R.I., 1906-07; chief div. vocational schs., N.Y. State Edn. Dept., Sept. 1908-17; prof. of vocational edn., Teachers Coll. (Columbia), 1917-23. Investigated possibilities of industrial and agrl. edn. in P.R. for insular govt.; editor of investigation of conditions in shoe industry, bull. 8, Nat. Soc. Promotion Industrial Edn., 1908; asst. in investigation apprenticeship systems, for bull. U.S. Dept. Interior, 1907; dir. survey of N.Y. Prison Survey Com., 1919; asso. editor, Industrial Edn. Mag. Maj. U.S. Army, in reconstruction work in army hospitals, 1918-19. Filled U.S. Civilian Defense assignment to Connecticut State Forestry Service, 1942-43. President Eastern Art and Manual Training Teachers' Assn., 1911, etc. Club: Nat. Arts (New York). Author: The Worker and the State, 1910; Our Schools in War Time—and After, 1917; Just Between Ourselves, 1923; also newspaper syndicate feature "Your Boy and Your Girl" and "Let's Talk it Over," since 1924. Address: National Arts Club, 15 Gramercy Park, New York, N.Y. Died Nov. 19, 1949.

DEAN, Edwin Blanchard, clergyman, educator; b. of American parents, Satara, India, July 21, 1866; s. Rev. Samuel Chase and Augusta Elizabeth (Abbott) D.; B.A., Doane Coll., Crete, Neb., 1888, D.D., 1917; B.A., Amherst, 1889 M.A., 1904; B.D. Chicago Theol. Sem., 1893; m. Georgia DeCou, July 8, 1896; children—Berta DeCou, Carol Chase (Mrs. Glenn R. Oertli). Ordained Congl. ministry, 1893; pastor First Ch., Wilmette, Ill., 1893-99, First Ch., Clinton, Ia., 1899-1905 First Ch., Northfield, Minn. 1905-20; asst. to pres. and chmn. bd. of deans, Carleton Coll., Northfield, 1920-25; pres. Doane Coll., Jan. 1925-Aug. 1936, pres. emeritus since 1936. Introduced Boy Scouting to Minnesota, 1910. Member War Personnel Board, Nat. War Work Council Y.M.C.A., New York, 1918; mem. same and hdqrs. chaplain Y.M.C.A., Paris, 1919; chmn. com. in charge steamship Haverford, arriving in Phila., Aug. 1, 1919. Moderator Minn. Congl. Conf., 1916; mem. com. on interchurch relations, Nat. Council Congl. Chs., 1929-37, mem. com. on ministry, 1931-41, mem. com. on broadcasting, 1931-33; dir. Neb. Congl. Conf., 1926-32; pres. Assn. of Colls. of Congl. Affiliation, 1928-29; trustee Doane Coll., 1925-39, trustee emeritus since 1939; dir. Doane Corp. since 1929 chmn. Neb. State Com. of Selection for the Rhodes Scholarships 1935 to World War II. Fellow Am. Geog. Soc. Clubs: Knife and Fork, Lincoln Pioneers Golf. Home: 1112 C St., Lincoln 2, Neb. Died Nov. 8, 1948; buried Riverside Cemetery, Crete Neb.

DEAN, Lee Wallace, otolaryngologist; b. Muscatine, Ia., Mar. 28, 1873; s. Henry Munson and Emma (Johnson) D.; B.S., State U. of Ia., 1894, M.S., 1896, M.D., 1896; studied in Vienna, 1896-97; m. Ella May Bailey, Dec. 29, 1904; 1 son, Lee Wallace. Prof. and head of otolaryngology and oral surgery, State U. of Ia. until July 1, 1927; also dean Coll. of Medicine, same univ., 1912-27; prof. otolaryngology, Washington U. Sch. of Medicine, since 1927; mem. staff Barnes, St. Louis Children's and Jewish hosps.; otolaryngologist in chief McMillan Eye, Ear, Nose & Throat Hospital and Oscar Johnson Research Inst., St. Louis (emeritus 1943). Served as lieut. col. Med. O.R.C., comdg. offr. Gen. Hosp. No. 54, World War. Mem. Am. Bd. Otolaryngology; editor Annals of Otology, Rhinology and Laryngology. Fellow Am. Coll. Surg.; mem. Am. Laryngol. Assn. (past pres.), Am. Laryngol., Rhinol. and Otol. Soc. (past pres.), Am. Otol. Soc. (past pres.), Am. Peroral Endoscopists, Mo. State Med. Soc., Am. Acad. of Ophthalmology and Otolaryngology (pres), La Société de Laryngologie des Hopitaux de Paris. Home: Kirkwood, Mo. Recipient of de Roaldes prize award, 1937. Address: Washington University Medical School, St. Louis, Mo. Died Feb. 9, 1944.

DEAN, Willis Johnson, cons. engr.; b. Owensboro, Ky.; s. John Allen and Mary (Hale) D.; B.C.E., Univ. of Kentucky, 1908; m. Margaret Elizabeth Gage. Engaged in design and supervision of constrn. of comml. bldgs. and indsl. plants. Representative buildings and plants: Spalding Bldg., Multnomah Hotel, Portland, Ore.; Bryson Apt. Hotel, Los Angeles; Watts Office Bldg., San Diego; Robbins & Myers Co., Plant, Springfield, O.; Army Supply Base, Brooklyn, N.Y.; Goodyear Tire & Rubber Co. plants, Akron, O., and Los Angeles, Calif.; Hamilton Club, Edgewater Beach Hotel, Union League Club, Daily News Bldg., Cook County Nurses Home, Chicago, etc. Capt. constrn. div. U.S. Army, during the World War. Kappa Alpha (Southern). Baptist. Mason (32°, Shriner). Home: Hotel Sovereign. Office: 400 W. Madison St., Chicago, Ill. Died Oct. 5, 1944.

DEAN, Willis Leonard, educator; b. Waverly, Pa., Feb. 5, 1857; s. Nelson and Clarissa (Searle) D.; grad. Wyoming Sem., 1873; hon. A.M. Dickinson Coll., 1890; m. Mary Goodwin, June 20, 1878 (died July 14, 1933); children—Searle Goodwin (dec.), Marjorie (Mrs. George W. Carey). Began as teacher, Lowell's Commercial Coll., Binghamton, N.Y., 1873; teacher, Wyoming Sem., Kingston, Pa., 1875-1882; prin. Dean Sch. of Business, Wyoming Sem. since 1882. Republican. Methodist. Home: Kingston, Pa. Died Dec. 20, 1942.

DEAR, Joseph Albert, judge, pub.; b. Jersey City, N.J., Nov. 28, 1871; s. Joseph Albert and Katharine Augusta (Barbour) D.; grad. Hasbrouck Inst., Jersey City, 1889; A.B., Princeton, 1893; m. Julia Allene Reid, Oct. 21, 1897 (dec.); children—Joseph Albert, Bertha Allene (dec.), Helen. Began as reporter Jersey Journal, Jersey City, N.J., 1893, editor and pub. since 1908; pres Evening Journal Assn.; apptd. judge N.J. Court of Errors and Appeals, 3 terms, 1926-44. Trustee and treas. Jersey City Free Pub. Library. Mem. Princeton U. Grad. Council, Princeton Alumni Assn. of Paterson, Passaic and Ridgewood (New Jersey). Republican. Presbyterian. Clubs: Arcola Country, Ridgewood Country; Princeton (New York). Home: 325 Heights Rd., Ridgewood, N.J. Address: Jersey Journal, Journal Sq., Jersey City, N.J. Died July 17, 1947.

DEARBORN, Richard Harold, dean engring.; b. Salem, Ore., Nov. 2, 1874; s. Richard H. and Helen Azubah (Flint) D.; A.B., Willamette U., 1895; E.E., Cornell U., 1900; m. Julia Isabelle Braun, June 23, 1903; children—Katherine (Mrs. Henry Frulan DeBoest), Isabelle (Mrs. L. B. Forbes). Electrical engineer Portland General Electric Company, 1900; inaugurated course in electrical engineering, U. of Ore., Sept. 1901, successively instr., asst. prof. and prof., 1901-14; part time appraisal engr. Ore. State Tax Commn., 1908-10; half-time elec. engr. Ore. Pub. Utilities Commn., 1912-14; prof. elect. engring. and head of department, Oregon State College, 1914-33 (consolidation of all engineering instruction at Oregon State College); became dean of engring., 1933, now dean emeritus. Dir. Engineering, Science, and Management War Training for Oregon. Member administrative council Ore. State Coll. Fellow Am. Inst. Elec. Engrs.; mem. Soc. for Promotion Engring. Edn., Northwest Electric Light & Power Assn., Corvallis Chamber of Commerce, Delta Upsilon, Tau Beta Pi, Sigma Tau, Pi Tau Sigma, Eta Kappa Nu. Republican. Episcopalian. Club: Corvallis Country. Writer of tech. articles. Home: 6212 S.E. 28th Av., Portland 2, Ore. Died Mar. 21, 1946.

DEARMONT, Washington Strother, educator; b. Clark County, nr. Berryville, Va., Sept. 22, 1859; s. Peter and Mary Eliza Ferguson (Bell) D.; A.B., Pd.B., Univ. of Mo., 1885, A.M., 1890; Litt.D., Westminster Coll., Fulton, Mo., 1907; m. Julia Lee McKee, May 29, 1890. Supt. pub. schs., Mound City, Mo., 1888-93, Kirkwood, 1893-99; pres., Southeast Mo. State Teachers Coll., Cape Girardeau, since June 1899. County commr. schs., Holt County, 1891-93. Mem. N. E. A., Nat. Soc. Study of Edn., Nat. Council Normal Sch. Presidents (pres. 1914), Mo. State Teachers Assn. (pres. 1901), Nat. Peace Soc., Mo. Peace Soc., Mo. Y. M. C. A. (exec. com.); chmn. County Council of Defense, 1917-18, County Food Adminstrn., 1917-18. Democrat. Presbyterian. Contbr. to ednl. jours. Home: Cape Girardeau, Mo. July 17, 1944.

DEAVER, Bascom S., judge; b. Union County, Ga., Nov. 26, 1882; s. Reuben Miles and Nancy Jane (Chastain) D.; A.B., Mercer U., 1907, LL.B., 1910; m. Emily Cook, Oct. 6, 1917; children—Jeannette, Bascom S. Admitted to Ga. bar, 1910, and began practice at Macon; asst. U.S. atty. Southern Dist. of Ga., 1922-26; U.S. atty. Middle Dist. of Ga., 1926-28; U.S. dist. judge, same dist. since Mar. 24, 1928. Republican. Baptist. Mason, Odd Fellow. Office: Federal Bldg., Macon, Ga. Died Oct. 13, 1944; buried at Copperhill, Tenn.

DeBARDELEBEN, Charles Fairchild (dē-bär'dĕl-ē-bĕn), pres. Ala. Fuel & Iron Co.; b. Prattville, Ala., July 4, 1876; s. Henry Fairchild and Ellen (Pratt) DeB.; student Ala., Polytechnic Inst., 1890-9?; m. Margaret Prince, Apr. 15, 1896; children—Charles Fairchild, Thomás Prince, Walter Percy. With engring. corps, Tenn. Coal, Iron & R.R. Co., 1893; mine foreman Bessemer Coal, Iron & Land Co., 1896-98, supt., 1904-05; operating ore mine, 1898-1901; supt. Little Cahaba Coal Co., 1901-04; became gen. mgr. Ala. Fuel & Iron Co., 1905, pres. since 1921; chmn. bd. Chas. C. Steward Machine Co. Pres. Birmingham Chamber of Commerce, 1917. Mem. Kappa Alpha. Episcopalian. Mason. Clubs: Southern, Mountain Brook Country. Home: 2460 Milner Heights. Office: Webb Crawford Bldg., Birmingham, Ala.* Died 1941.

DE BECK, William, cartoonist; b. Chicago, Ill., Apr. 16, 1890; s. Louis and Jessie Lee (Morgan) D.; ed. Chicago Acad. Fine Arts; married. Began by contributing to Chicago Daily News, 1908; polit. cartoonist Pittsburgh Gazette Times and Chronicle Telegraph, 1912-16; comic artist, Chicago Herald, 1916-17; with William Randolph Hearst pubs. since 1918. Created series, "Married Life"; also creator "Barney Google," 1918, "Spark Plug" and "Bunky," 1922, "Snuffy Smith," 1934, "Feather Merchants," 1938; U.S. Army "Yard Bird," 1940. Mem. Illustrators' Soc., Authors' League America. Presbyterian. Clubs: Dutch Treat, Coffee House, Artists and Writers Golf, North Hemstead Golf (Long Island); Lakewood Golf (Fla.). Address: 235 E. 45th St., New York, N.Y.; also 321 Brightwaters Blvd. St. Petersburg, Fla. Died Nov. 11, 1942.

DeBERRY, William Nelson, clergyman; b. Nashville, Tenn., Aug. 29, 1870; s. Caswell and Charlotte (Mayfield) D.; B.S., Fisk U., Nashville, 1896; B.D., Oberlin Theol. Sem., 1899; D.D., Lincoln U., Pa., 1914; m. Amanda McKissack, Sept. 6, 1899; children—Charlotte Pearl (Mrs. Henry George Tracy), Anna Mae (Mrs. Arthur H. Johnson); m. 2d, Louise Scott, October 9, 1943. Ordained ministry Congregational Church, 1899; pastor St. John's Church, Springfield, Mass., 1899-1931. Second Assistant moderator Nat. Council Congregational Chs., 1919. Trustee Fisk University executive secretary Dunbar Community League, 1914-17. Apptd. by mayor, mem. Springfield Bd. of Pub. Welfare, 1935; apptd. by Gov. Saltonstall mem. of Governor's Committee on Religious and Interracial Understanding in 1913. Dir. New England Camping Assn. Member Massachusetts Home Missionary Society (trustee), Alpha Phi Alpha. Republican. Lecturer on race problems; received first award from Harmon Foundation of New York for distinguished service in religion among Negroes of the United States, 1927; awarded William Pynchon medal by city of Springfield "for distinguished public service," 1928. Represented Gov. Ely of Mass. at 50th anniversary of founding of Tuskegee Normal and Industrial Inst., 1931. Home: 31 Westminster St.; Springfield Cemetery.

DE BLOIS, Austen Kennedy (dē-blwä') educator; b. Wolfville, N.S., Dec. 17, 1866; s. Dr. Stephen W. and Mary S. (Fitch) D.; Horton Acad., 1881; in Europe, 1885; grad. Acadia Coll., N.S., 1886, A.M., Brown, 1888, Ph.D., 1889, D.D., 1914; student Newton (Mass.) Theol. Inst., 1889; U. of Berlin, 1890; U. of Leipzig, Germany, 1891; LL.D., Franklin Coll., 1897; D.D., Acadia Univ., 1925; citation of honor, Brown U., 1938; m. Erminie A. Day, June 25, 1890; children—Stephen George, Cedric (dec.), Mary Ailsa, Charles Austen, Laurier St. John, Erminie Stanhope. V. prin. Union Baptist Sem., St. Martins, N.B., 1892, prin., 1892-94; pres. Shurtleff Coll., Alton, Ill., 1894-99; traveled in Europe and Africa, 1900-01; pastor First Bapt. Ch., Elgin, 1899-1902, First Bapt. Ch., Chicago, 1902-11; First Bapt. Ch., Boston, 1911-26; editor The Watchman-Examiner, New York, 1926-28; president Eastern Baptist Theol. Seminary, 1926-36; pres. emeritus since 1936. Lecturer psychology of religion, Newton Theology Instn., 1913-17, philosophy of religion, 1914-15; annual course on Pastoral Experience, Colgate, 1915. Trustee Shurtleff Coll., West China Union U., Div. Sch. U. of Chicago, Newton Theol. Instn., Gordon Coll.; pres. N E. Acadia Alumni Assn.; pres. Chicago Bapt. Orphanage, 1900-11, Home for Missionaries' Children, Morgan Park, Ill., 1909-11; mem. bd. of mgrs. Am. Bapt. Fgn. Mission Soc.; mem. laymen's commn. to the Orient, making around the world tour of Christian missions, 1907; mem. exec. com. and chmn. ednl. work Ill. State Y.M.C.A., 1898-1910; commr. Relation of Y.M.C.A. to Churches, 1911-18; mem. adminstrn. com. of Northern Bapt., Conv., 1922-30; pres. Bapt. Council of Greater Boston, 1915-16; Northern Bapt. Edn. Soc. since 1917. Pres. Evang. Alliance of Greater Boston, 1918; chaplain Canadian Club, 1917-23; v.p. Am. Brit. Federation, 1917; mem. Brit. Recruiting Mission of N.E., 1917-18; mem. bd. mgrs. Am. Bapt. Home Mission Soc. since 1922; chmn. Nation-wide Home Mission Centenary Campaign, 1930-32; mem. Am. Commn. of Ten; mem. continuation com. World Conf. on Faith and Order. Mem. Delta Upsilon, Phi Beta Kappa. Mason. Clubs: Classical, Canadian, Penn Athletic; City, Brit. Schools and Univs. (N.Y.); Royal Automobile (London). Author: Bible Study in American Colleges, 1899; The Pioneer School, 1900; Imperialism and Democracy, 1901; History of the First Baptist Church in Boston, 1665-1915, 1916; Life of John Mason Peck, Prophet of the Prairies, 1917; The Message of Wisdom; Studies in the Book of Proverbs, 1920; Some Probelms on the Modern Minister, 1928; John Bunyan, the Man, 1928; Fighters for Freedom, 1929; Evangelism in the New

Age, 1933; The Church of Today—and Tomorrow, 1934; The Making of Ministers, 1936; Christian Religious Education: Principles and Practice, 1939. Translator and editor: Borelius Grundriss der Jetzigen Lage in der Deutschen Philosophie. Editor: The Evangelical Faith, 1931. Editor of The Christian Rev. since 1931. Am. del. to many internat. confs.; in U.S. 9, Oxford, Eng. 3, Edinburgh 2, Tokyo and Shanghai. Home: 2902 Morris Road, Ardmore, Pa. Died Aug. 10, 1945.

DEBUCHI, Katsuji, ambassador; b. Morioka, Japan, July 25, 1878; s. Katsumasa and Jiu D.; grad. Tokyo Commercial Coll., 1902; m. Hama Kikuchi, Sept. 23, 1906; children—Masaru, Takako. Eleve-consul, Seoul, Korea, 1903-07; 3d sec. of embassy, Berlin, Germany, 1907-14; 1st sec. of legation, Peking, China, 1914-18; 1st sec. of embassy, Washington, D.C., Mar.-Nov. 1918, counselor, 1918-20; charge d'ffaires, Berlin, 1920; mem. Disarmament Com., Washington, 1921; dir. Asiatic Bur., Dept. Foreign Affairs, 1923-24, vice minister for foreign affairs, 1924-28; A.E. and P., Washington, Oct. 17, 1928-Feb. 13, 1934. Decorated 1st class, Order of Sacred Treasure. Address: 103 Ayamamachi, Tamagawa Oyamamchi, Setagaya, Tokyo, Japan. Died Sept. 16, 1947.

de CARTIER de MARCHIENNE, Baron Emile, diplomat; b. Brussels, Belgium, Nov. 30, 1871; ed. in Belgium; LL.D., Princeton, 1917, Villa Nova, 1918, Brown, 1921, Columbia, 1922, Rochester, 1923. Hon. capt. 106th Regt. N.Y. Nat. Guard, 1923; m. Marie Dow, 1919. A.E. and P. from Belgium to U.S. since Aug. 1919. Catholic. Address: 1780 Massachusetts Av. N.W., Washington. Died May 10, 1946.

DeCASSERES, Benjamin (dê-kăs-ĕr-ĕs), author; b. Phila., Pa.; s. David and Charlotte (Davis) DeC.; collateral descendant of Benedict de Spinoza; educated public schools to 13; m. Bio Terrill, Oct. 12, 1919. Proofreader Philadelphia Press, 1892-99, New York Sun, 1899-1903, New York Herald, 1903-19, except when serving as co-founder and editorial writer, El Diario, City of Mexico, 1906-07; book reviewer New York Sun, Times, Bookman, etc., 1912-23; spl. Sunday writer New York Times, 1919-24; contbr. to Philistine, Cosmopolitan, Metropolitan, Life, Judge, American Mercury, Smart Set, American Spectator, New York World, Herald Tribune, The Thinker, The Mercure de France, Theatre Mag., Vanity Fair, etc.; dramatic critic Arts and Decorations, 1922-33, also Screenland and Motion Picture Herald; mem. editorial staff Famous Players-Lasky Corp., 1919-23, Universal Pictures Corp., 1924-25; now "March of Events" columnist, and chief edit. writer on the N.Y. Daily Mirror and book reviewer for the N.Y. Journal and Am. and asso. Hearst newspapers. Author: The Shadow-Eater (poems), 1915; Chameleon—Being the Book of My Selves, 1922; Mirrors of New York, 1925; James Gibbons Huneker, 1925; Forty Immortals (essays), 1925; Anathema! (prose-poem), 1928; The Superman in America, 1929; Mencken and Shaw, 1930; The Love Letters of a Living Poet, 1931; Spinoza, 1932; The Muse of Lies, 1936; Don Marquis (a parable and a tribute), 1938; The Works of Benjamin DeCasseres (3 vols.), 1939. Also compiled and wrote foreword of Germans, Jews and France, by Nietzsche, 1935. Writings translated and introduced into France by Remy de Gourmont. Author of 12 written partly unpublished books. Home: 593 Riverside Dr., New York, N.Y. Died Dec. 6, 1945.

DECELL, John Lloyd (dê-sĕl'), clergyman; b. Brookhaven, Miss., Aug. 12, 1887; s. William A. and Mary (Smith) D.; student Union Coll., Barbourville, Ky., 1906-09; D.D., Millsaps Coll., Jackson, Miss., 1929; LL.D., Union Coll., 1938, Athens Coll., 1938; m. Bertha Whitley, Aug. 16, 1910; children—Frances Elizabeth, William James. Licensed to preach M.E. Church, South, 1906; admitted Miss. Annual Conf., 1910; successively pastor at Osyka, Mt. Olive, Waynesboro, McComb—all Miss., 1910-19, St. Paul's Ch., Fresno, Calif., 1919-20, Central Ch., Meridian, Miss., 1921-24, Galloway Memorial Ch., Jackson, Miss., 1932-38; elected bishop M.E. Ch., S., 1938; bishop Methodist Ch., May 1939; presiding elder Jackson (Miss.) Dist., 1925-28, Brookhaven (Miss.) Dist., 1929-31. Del. to Gen. Conf., 1926, 30, 34, 38, mem. Edn. Commn., 1926-30, sec. Interdenominational Relations Commn., 1930-34; sec. Gen. Conf. Commn. Church Union with M.E. and M.P. chs., term 1934-38; mem. Gen. Bd. Christian Edn.; dir. Greater Millsaps Coll. Movement, 1937-38. Mem. Kappa Alpha, Internat. Soc. of Theta Phi, Omicron Delta Kappa. Democrat. Mason. Kiwanian. Home: 757 Belhaven, Jackson, Miss. Died Jan. 10, 1945.

DE CISNEROS, Eleonora, opera singer; b. New York City; d. John C. and Eleonor (Small) Broadfoot; ed. St. Agnes Sem., Brooklyn; studied grand opera singing with Madame Murio Celli; m. Count Francois G. de Cisneros, Nov. 16, 1900. Debut Met. Opera House, New York, season 1899-1900; first Am. singer to appear in leading role at Met. Opera House without previous experience or foreign training; has sung at Rome, Milan, Madrid, Lisbon, Vienna, St. Petersburg, Berlin, Covent Garden, London, Rio Janeiro, Mexico City, etc., also in Australia with Melba, and in extensive concert tours. Mem. Chicago Opera Assn., 1910-16. Sold $30,000,000 Liberty Bonds during World War (said to have been the highest record of any individual worker); decorated by Am. Red Cross for war work. Guest appearances, 1921, New York, spl. operatic roles. Mem. Wagnerian Opera Co. (in America), 1923-24, singing Brunhilde in "Walkure," Ortrud in "Lohengrin," etc. Address: Georgian Hotel, W. 35th St., New York. Died Feb. 3, 1934.

De COU, Edgar Ezekiel (dê-kōō), mathematics; b. Thamesville, Ont., July 13, 1868; s. Ezekiel Cleveland and Margaret Ann (Ingalls) D.; grad. State Normal Sch., Madison, S.D., 1890; B.S., U. of Wis., 1894; M.S., U. of Chicago, 1897; grad. study, 1899-1900; grad. study Yale, 1900-01; m. Elizabeth Freeman Fox, Sept. 2, 1922; children—Margaret Ann (Mrs. James Robert McGill), Elizabeth Catherine, Edgar John. Instructor State Normal School, Madison, S.D., 1890-92; prin. high school, Evansville, Wis., 1894-96; professor mathematics, Bethel Coll., Russellville, Ky., 1897-99, 1901-02, acting pres., 1902; dean U. of Ore. Acad., 1902-04; prof. mathematics, 1902-39, prof. emeritus, 1939 (teaching part time, 1939-44); founder and dir. Oregon High School part time); founder and dir. Oregon High School Debating League, 1907-10. Mem. Am. Math. Soc., Math. Assn. America, Am. Assn. Univ. Profs., Pi Mu Epsilon. State rep. for Ore. Nat. Council of Teachers of Mathematics. Republican. Conglist. Author: Socialized Mathematics for Freshmen, 1937. Contbr. math. and ednl. jours. Home: 929 Hilyard St., Eugene, Ore. Died Oct. 15, 1947.

DEEGAN, William Joseph, telegraph official; b. New York, N.Y., July 29, 1885; s. John and Jane (Segrave) D.; ed. New York Evening High Sch. and New York U. Sch. of Commerce Accounts and Finance; m. Anna Foster, Apr. 24, 1916; children—William Foster (Capt. U.S.M.C.R.), Frank Vincent (Lt. U.S.N.R.). Messenger Commercial Cable Co., 1898-1900, clerk, 1900-18, sec., 1918-22, vice pres., 1922; v.p. Postal Telegraph land line wire system, 1922; later president until merger with Western Union in 1943; vice pres. and dir. Mackay Radio & Telegraph Company from its formation in 1927 to 1940, when radio and cable companies divorced from Postal Telegraph land wire system; v.p. Western Union Telegraph Co.; chmn. exec. com. Commercial Pacific Cable Co.; member Industry Advisory committee Board of War Communications (U.S.). Chairman Public utilities committee of Archbishop's Committee of the Laity, Catholic Charities of New York City. Mem. Morse Telegraph Club of America, China Soc., Am.-Irish Hist. Soc., Friendly Sons of St. Patrick of City of N.Y. (pres.). Catholic. Mem. K.C. (past dist. dep.). Clubs: Manhattan, Broad Street, Economic, Century (N.Y. City); Longshore Country (Westport, Conn.); Wheatley Hills Golf (East Williston, N.Y.). Home: 975 Park Av., New York, N.Y. Died Jan. 6, 1947.

de FOREST, Alfred Victor, pres. Magnaflux Corp.; b. New York City, Apr. 7, 1888; s. Lockwood and Meta (Kemble) de F.; S.B., Mass. Inst. Tech., 1911; m. Izette Taber, Aug. 22, 1912; children—Taber, Judith B. Draftsman, New London Ship & Engine Co., 1912-13; instr. Princeton, 1913-15; asst. research engr., Remington Arms Co., 1915-18; research engr., Am. Chain Co., 1918-30, consultant on strength and fatigue of metals and methods of inspection, since 1928; pres. Magnaflux Corp. since 1930; asso. prof., Mass. Inst. Tech., 1934-37, prof. since 1937; partner, Ruge-de Forest. Awarded Dudley medal, Am. Soc. Testing Materials, 1928, Longstreth medal, Franklin Inst., 1936, Sylvanus Albert Reed award, Inst. Aeronautical Sciences, 1938, Modern Pioneers award, 1941. Member American Society for Metals, American Society Testing Materials, Am. Inst. Mining and Metall. Engrs., Newcomen Soc., Century Assn., Am. Acad. Arts and Sciences; fellow Inst. Aeronautical Sciences. Home: Marlboro, N.H. Office: Mass. Inst. Tech., Cambridge, Mass. Died April 5, 1945; buried at Sky Farm, Marlboro, N. H.

de FOREST, Charles Mills (dê-fŏr'ĕst), social economist; b. Waterloo, Ia., July 9, 1878; s. Rev. Henry Swift and Anna Margaret (Robbins) de F.; prep. edn. Talladega (Ala.) Coll., Mt. Hermon (Mass.) Sch. and New Haven High Sch.; A.B., Yale, 1901, M.A., 1902, law study, 1902-04; m. Mary Eugenia Benjamin, Sept. 3, 1908 (died Jan. 18 1928); children—Walter Robbins, Jean Marie; m. 2d, Mrs. Bess (Cole) Fuller, Sept. 30, 1939. In business with brother, Lee de Forest (radio inventor), 1904-13; sales mgr. for Am. Red Cross Christmas seals, Westchester County, N.Y., 1913, N.Y. State, 1914, U.S., 1915-18; field sec. N.Y. State Charities Aid Assn., 1914-15; field sec. Nat. Tuberculosis Assn., 1915-19; founder, 1916, exec. until 1924, Modern Health Crusade; founder, 1924, dir. until 1926, Knighthood of Youth (movement of Nat. Child Welfare Assn.); founder and exec. v.p. Am. Provident Soc., since 1928; founder Provident Legion of America (under the Provident Soc.), and Clinic in Money Management. Mem. Am. Econ. Assn., Phi Beta Kappa. Ind. Republican. Dutch Reformed. Club: Yale. Author: Hygiene for Success, 1924; How Old Am I Financially?, 1930. Home: 135 W. 16th St. Office: 130 W. 42d St., New York 18. Died Apr. 12, 1947; buried in Mount Hope Cemetery, Westchester County, N.Y.

de FOREST, Henry Pelouze, obstetrician, surgeon; b. Fulton, N.Y., Dec. 29, 1864; s. John Teller and Emeline (Stephens) D.; Ph.B., Cornell, 1884, grad. course, 1886-87, M.S. (with distinction), 1887; med. student Columbian U., 1887-88; M.D., Coll. Phys. and Surg. (Columbia), 1890; m. Anna Catherine Gilmour (A.B., Smith, 1889), Dec. 6, 1891. Began practice Brooklyn, 1890; in M.E. Hosp., Brooklyn, 1890-91, Vienna U. and Hosp., 1891-92, U. of Freiburg, 1892, Sloane Maternity Hosp., New York, 1892-93, U. of Paris and hospitals, 1897, Dublin and Edinburgh hospitals, 1902, Dresden and Berlin hospitals, 1907; police depts. of Christiana, Stockholm, Helsingfors, St. Petersburg, Moscow and Copenhagen, studying methods of personal identification, 1912. Inventor Dactyloscope, 1912; est. first finger print file in U.S., 1902. Sanitary inspector Department of Health, New York City, 1894-1902; medical examining departments, fire and police, N.Y. City, 1902-03; police surg., New York, 1902-12; chief med. exam. municipal civil service commn., 1912-19; pres. med. bd., Teachers' Retirement System, City of N.Y., 1917-28. Lecturer on obstetrics, L.I. Coll. Hosp., 1893-1903; asso. prof. obstetrics, New York Post-Grad. Med. Sch., 1903-21. Capt., asst. surgeon 13th Inf. Nat. Guard, N.Y., 1893-98; acting asst. surg. 3d Div. Hosp. 7th Corps, Spanish-Am. War, 1898-99; maj. and surg. 13th C.A., Nat. Guard, N.Y., 1899-1912; maj. M.C. (retired). Mem. N.Y. Acad. Medicine, Brooklyn Pathol. Soc. (pres. 1900-02), U.S. Soc. Mil. Surgeons, Brooklyn Gynecol. Soc. (pathologist 1898-1902), N.Y. State Med. Soc.; sec. Am. Soc. Sanitary and Moral Prophylaxis, 1911-15; pres. Cornell Assn. Class Secs., 1912-14; pres. Internat. Soc. of Personal Identification, 1920-35; grand historian Alpha Mu Pi Omega, 1919-25; librarian Cornell Club of N.Y. since 1924; charter mem. University Club of Brooklyn, Asso. Physicians of Long Island; hon. member Assn. of Alumni of the College of Physicians and Surgeons. Contributor and member editorial staff Medico-Surgical Bulletin, 1897-99, Brooklyn Medical Jour., 1890-1903, Annals of Surgery since 1890, The Post Graduate, 1904-21; Diseases of the Blood and Ductless Glands in Butler's "Internal Medicine," 1902. Wrote (at personal request of Clara Barton) Textbook for First Aid Classes of the Am. Red Cross, 1903. Author: One Thousand Miles Afoot, 1895; Class Secretaries and Their Duties, 1913; Infectious Abortion of Cattle—As a Complication of Pregnancy in Women, 1917; The Evolution of Dactyloscopy in the United States, with an Historical Note on the First Fingerprint Bureau in the United States and a Bibliography of Personal Identification, 1931; Peanut Worms and Pellagra—Is the Indian Meal Moth, Plodia interpunctella, the Cause of Pellagra?, 1933; also about 100 miscellaneous articles on med. subjects. Life sec. Class of 1884 (Cornell), Class of 1890 (Columbia); rep. of Coll. of Physicians and Surgeons in Columbia Fed., 1930-39; medalist Columbia U., 1933. Inventor binaural stethoscope, Vienna, 1892. Home: 419 E. 57th St. Address: The Harbor, 667 Madison Av., New York, N.Y. Died June 13, 1948; buried in Mount Adnah Cemetery, Fulton, N.Y.

de FREYRE y Santander, Manuel (dā-frā'ē-rā' ē sän'tän-där'), diplomat; b. Washington, D.C., Nov. 29, 1872; s. Manuel and Clementina (Santander y Ponton) de F.; studied civ. engring., U. of Pisa and U. of Lausanne; m. Dolores Na Honer, Jan. 17, 1919 (dec.); children—Francisco, Margarita. Attaché of Peruvian Legation, Bern, Switzerland, 1902-03; 2d sec. of legation, Bogota, Colombia, 1903-07; 1st sec. of legation, Washington, D.C., 1907-17; minister plenipotentiary, Washington, 1917-19, Tokyo and Peking (now Peiping), 1919-22; minister to Bogota, 1922, Buenos Aires, 1923; del. to Plebiscitary Commn., Arica, 1924; minister to London, 1925-30; ambassador to Washington since 1930. Address: Peruvian Embassy, Washington, D.C. Died Apr. 1, 1944.

DE GARMO, William Burton, physician; b. West Troy, Wis., Apr. 24, 1849; s. John and Emeline (Coleman) D.; med. student U. of Mich., 1870-71; M.D., Univ. Med. Coll., New York U., 1875; m. Elizabeth Emory Milligan, Feb. 20, 1873 (died 1910); m. 2d, Alice K. Hormby, June 17, 1914. Prof. special and clin. surgery, N.Y. Post-Grad. Med. Sch. and Hosp., 1888-1918, cons. surgeon since 1948. Capt. Med. Res. Corps U.S.A., 1917. Fellow Am. Coll. Surgeons, N.Y. Acad. Medicine, Am. Geog. Soc.; hon. mem. Va. State Med. Soc.; mem. N.Y. State Hist. Soc. Author: Abdominal Hernia—Its Diagnosis and Treatment, 1907. Contbr. to med. jours. Home: Coral Gables, Fla. Died Jan. 3, 1936.

de GERSDORFF, Carl August (dê-gĕrs'dôrf), lawyer; b. Salem, Mass., July 10, 1865; s. Ernst Bruno and Caroline (Choate) de G.; grad. Boston Latin Sch., 1883; A.B., Harvard, 1887; student Harvard Law Sch., 1887-89; m. Helen Suzette Crowninshield, Sept. 28, 1895; children—Josephine (Mrs. Frederick J. Bradlee, Jr), Alma (Mrs. David Percy Morgan), Caspar Crowninshield. Admitted to N.Y. bar, 1890, and practiced in N.Y. City; now mem. Cravath de Gersdorff, Swaine & Wood; dir. Chemical Bank & Trust Co. Mem. Assn. of Bar City of N.Y., N.Y. State Bar Assn. Republican. Clubs: Knickerbocker, Union, University, Century, Harvard (N.Y. City); Harvard (Boston). Home: 635 Park Av. Office: 15 Broad St., New York, N.Y. Died Jan. 21, 1944.

De HAAN, John, Jr. (dê-hän), clergyman; b. Hollaway, Raisin County, Mich., July 15, 1891; s. John, Sr., and Trientje (Cramer) De H.; student Calvin Coll., Grand Rapids, Mich., 1913-18, Calvin Sem., 1918-21; m. Pauline Wagner, June 18, 1913. Ordained to ministry of Christian Reformed Church, 1921; pastor, Lamont (Mich.) Ch., 1921-25, Ninth Street Ch., Holland, Mich., 1925-29; Broadway Av. Ch., Grand Rapids, Mich., since 1929; stated clerk Christian Reformed Ch., hdqrs at Grand Rapids, since 1942. Home: 825 N. Ottilia, S.E., Grand Rapids 4, Mich. Died Oct. 28, 1945.

De HAVEN, David William (dē-hā'vĕn), judge; b. Oxford, Miss., Oct. 26, 1872; s. David and Mary Thomas (Dobyns) DeH.; ed. Kemper Mil. Sch., 1888-92; studied law under Judge Bedford M. Estes, Memphis, Tenn.; m. Anna H. Hays, Sept. 12, 1895. Admitted to Tenn. bar, Oct. 1893, and began practice in Memphis; apptd. judge of Chancery Court, Memphis, 1925, and re-elected for terms, 1926-42 (resigned 1935); apptd. asso. justice Supreme Court of Tenn., Jan. 1935, and elected without opposition for terms, 1936-42 and 1942-50. Life dir. Memphis Y.M.C.A. Mem. Tenn. and Am. bar assns. Democrat. Episcopalian (vestryman). Club: Idlewild (Memphis). Home: 1784 Linden Av., Memphis. Office: Supreme Court Bldg., Nashville, Tenn. Died June 4, 1942.

DeHAVEN, John B., chmn. bd. and pres. Allied Mills, Inc., Chicago, Ill. Home: 599 Woodlawn Av., Glencoe, Ill. Office: Board of Trade Bldg., Chicago, Ill.* Deceased.

DELABARRE, Edmund Burke (dĕl'á-bär), psychologist; b. Dover, Me., Sept. 25, 1863; s. Edward and Maria (Hassell) D.; student Brown U., 1882-83; A.B., Amherst, 1886; A.M. Harvard, 1889; Ph.D., U. of Freiburg, 1891; m. Dorothea Esther Cotton, Mar. 14, 1907; children—Maria Elizabeth, Edmund Burke, Barbara Melville, Dorcas Hope. Asso. prof. psychololgy, 1891-96, prof., 1896-1932, Brown U., now prof. emeritus. Dir. Psychol. Lab., Harvard, during absence of Prof. Münsterberg, 1896-97. Fellow A.A.A.S., Am. Acad. of Arts and Sciences; member Am. Psychol. Assn., R.I. Hist. Soc., Old Colony Hist. Soc., Phi Beta Kappa, Sigma Xi; corr. mem. Geog. Soc. Phila., Geog. Society, Lisbon, Archæol. Soc. of Portugal. Officer of Mil. Order St. James of the Sword (Portugal). Author: Ueber Bewegungsempfindungen, 1891; Report of Brown-Harvard Expedition to Nachvak, Labrador, in 1900, 1902; Dighton Rock History, 1916, 17, 19; Inscribed Rocks of Narragansett Bay, 1919-23; Dighton Rock—A Study of the Written Rocks of New England, 1928. Contbr. to psychol., archæol., hist. publs. Mem. Colonial Soc. of Mass. Address: 9 Arlington Av., Providence, R.I. Died Mar. 16, 1945.

DeLACOUR, Reginald Beardsley, adj. gen., Conn.; b. Wichita, Kan., Nov. 8, 1886; s. Joseph Walter and Margaret Starr (Beardsley) D.; grad. Stratford High Sch., 1904; Comd. and Gen. Staff Sch., Leavenworth, Kan., spl. class 1926, Army War Coll., Washington, D.C., spl. G-1 class, 1927. Enlisted 1st Ill., Cav., Ill. Nat. Guard, Nov. 8, 1915; disch. sergt., Dec. 1916; commd. 1st lt., inf. Plattsburg Training Camp, Aug. 1917; 1st lt. machine gun co., 165th Inf., 42d Div. (Rainbow), A.E.F., disch. capt. May 9, 1919. Mem. Officers Reserve Corps., capt. inf. advancing to col., inf., commd. brig. gen., A.G.D., Conn. Nat. Guard, Sept. 19, 1939; commd. adj. gen., rank of major gen., Apr. 1947. Mem. Conn. Gen. Assembly, 1925-27. Vice chmn. State Aeronautics commn. Conn.; chief of staff, Governors Staff, Conn., 1947. Awarded Distinguished Service Cross, Silver Star, Purple Heart, Conspicuous Service Cross, (N.Y.). Mem. Sons of American Revolution, Huguenot Society of North Carolina, Society of Colonial Wars, Army-Navy Legion of Valor. Republican. Mason (K.T., 32°, Shriner), Sojourners, Elk. Clubs: Wings, Army-Navy, Washington, D.C., Hartford Golf, Hartford (Hartford, Conn.). Home: Prayer Spring Farm, Oronoque, P.O., Stratford, Conn. Office: State Armory, 3360 Broad St., Hartford, Conn. Died Mar. 21, 1948.

DELAFIELD, E. M. (pseudonym; real name, Edmée Elizabeth Monica Dashwood), author; daughter Count Henry de la Pasture of Llandogo; m. Arthur Paul Dashwood, 1919; 1 dau. Author: Way Things Are, 1928; First Love, 1929; Consequences, 1929; Zella See Herself, 1930; Women Are Like That, 1930; Turn Back the Leaves, 1930; House Party, 1931; Diary of a Provincial Lady, 1931; Good Man's Love, 1932; Provincial Lady in London, 1933; General Impressions, 1933; Gay Life, 1933; Provincial Lady in America, 1934; Provincial Lady at Home and Abroad, 1935; Faster! Faster!, 1936; Nothing is Safe, 1937; Ladies and Gentleman in Victorian Fiction, 1937; I Visit the Soviets, 1937; As Others Hear Us, 1937; Love Has no Resurrection, 1939; Provincial Lady in Wartime, 1940; No One Now Will Know, 1941; Late and Soon, 1943. Address: Croyle, Cullompton, Devon, England. Died Dec. 2, 1943.

DELAFIELD, Lewis Livingston, lawyer; b. New York, N.Y., Jan 30, 1863; s. Lewis L. and Emily (Prime) D.; ed. private schs. in Switzerland, St. Paul's School, Concord, N.H., Columbia Coll., Harvard Law School; LL.B., Columbia, 1884; m. Charlotte Hoffman Wyeth, Apr. 25, 1885; Children—Lewis L., Jr., Charlotte (Mrs. Robert McCurdy Marsh); Emily (Mrs. Edmund W. Peaslee). Admitted to N.Y. bar, 1884; later to Federal courts and U.S. Supreme Court; practiced in New York since 1884; mem. of Com. of Seventy of 1894; sec. Rapid Transit Commn., 1894-99; nominated for justice N.Y. Supreme Court by bar of 1st Judicial Dist. (Judiciary Nominators Movement), 1906; mem. Dist. Bd. City of New York, having jurisdiction of appeals in all draft matters, 191.-18, mem. com. on character and fitness of Appellate Div. N.Y. Supreme Court, 1st Dept., 1923-27 (chmn. 1926-27); mem. Charter Revision Commn., New York, apptd. by Gov. Miller; spl. U.S. atty. Southern Dist. N.Y. for war purposes, 1917-18; senior mem. Hawkins, Delafield & Longfellow until 1934, now retired; dir. Farmers' Loan and Trust Co. (now City Bank Farmers Trust Co.). Mem. Assn. of Bar of City of New York (past v.p. and chmn. exec. and judiciary coms.), N.Y. State Bar Assn. (past v.p. and chmn. exec. com.), Harvard Law Sch. Assn. of New York (past pres.); hon. mem. Marine Soc. of New York; former mem. Am. Law Institute. Trustee N.Y. Hist. Society. Episcopalian. Clubs: Union, Century Assn. (New York). Home: 630 Park Av. Office: 67 Wall St., New York, N.Y. Died Sep. 27, 1944.

DELAFIELD, M(aturin) Livingston, broker; b. N.Y. City, March 17, 1901; s. Edward Coleman and Margaretta Stockton (Beasley) D.; ed. Browning Sch., Hotchkiss Sch.; A.B., Princeton U., 1923; m. Mary Peirce Lyon, Oct. 25, 1924; children—Mary L., Maturin Livingston. Associate J. Henry Schroeder & Co., London, Eng., 1923-26, Kuhn, Loeb & Co., N.Y. City, 1926-27, Dominick & Dominick, N.Y. City, 1927-37; partner in stock exchange firm Delafield & Delafield, N.Y. City, since 1937. Chmn. bd. and mem. exec. com. Kansas City Southern Ry. Co. since 1943; vice-pres. and dir. Delafield Allied Corp. Asst. sec. and dir. Delafield Family Assn. Trustee N.Y. Dispensary. Mem. Assn. Stock Exchange Firms (gov. and chmn. investment advisory com., treas. and vice chmn. exec. com.); mem. Down Town Assn., S.R., Soc. Descendants Signers Declaration Independence, Pilgrim Soc., Soc. St. Nicholas. Republican. Episcopalian. Clubs: Union (gov.), Rockaway Hunt (governor), Lawrence Beach. Home: Hewlett, Long Island, N.Y. Office: 14 Wall St., New York 5, N.Y. Died Aug. 15, 1945.

DE LAND, Clyde Osmer (dē-lănd'), artist; b. Union City, Pa., Dec. 27, 1872; s. Theodore D. and Nancy F. (Howard) D.; U. of Rochester, 1891-92; grad. Drexel Inst., Phila., 1898; studied Pyle Sch. of Illustration, Phila.; unmarried. Teacher of music and concert pianist, 1889-94; art editor Sotheran's Mag., Phila., 1896; artist and illustrator since 1897. Mem. Alpha Zeta, Delta Upsilon, Hist. Soc. of Pa. (Phila.). Has furnished many important illustrations to leading weeklies and mags., especially on subjects of Am. history. Paintings: "First Am. Flag" (property of the City of Somerville, Mass; "Balboa—Discoverer of the Pacific"; "Inauguration of Washington"; "First Shot of 1812"; in the U.S. Nat. Museum—"The First Steamboat," "The First Automobile," "The First Street Railway"; in Carpenters' Hall, Phila.—(painting) "The First Continental Congress." Books illustrated: The Count's Snuff-Box (Rivers), 1898; Cinderella (Crockett), 1901; Barnaby Lee (John Bennett), 1902; A Forest Hearth (Major), 1903; Mr. Kris Kringle (Weir Mitchell), 1904; Captain Blood (Sabatini), 1923; Nicholas Rowntree (Kauffman), 1924; The Carolinian (Sabatini), 1925. Lecturer (with stereopticon) on "Drama of American History." Deacon in Baptist Church, Phila. Home and Studio: 19 N. 50th St., Philadelphia, Pa. Died Mar. 27, 1947.

DELAND, Margaretta Wade, author; b. (Campbell) Allegheny, Pa., Feb. 23, 1857; ed. at pvt. schs.; m. Lorin F. Deland, 1880. Mem. Nat. Institute of Arts and Letters. Author: John Ward, Preacher; The Old Garden and Other Verses; Philip and His Wife; Florida Days; Sidney; The Story of a Child; The Wisdom of Fools; Mr. Tommy Dove and Other Stories; Old Chester Tales; Dr. Lavendar's People; The Common Way, 1904; The Awakening of Helena Richie, 1906; An Encore, 1907; The Iron Woman, 1911; The Voice, 1912; Partners, 1913; The Hands of Esau, 1914; Around Old Chester, 1915; The Rising Tide, 1916; The Vehement Flame, 1922; New Friends in Old Chester, 1924; The Kays, 1926; Captain Archer's Daughter, 1932; If This Be I (As I Suppose It Be), 1935; Old Chester Days, 1935; Golden Yesterdays, 1941. Home: Kennebunkport, Maine; and Hotel Sheraton, Boston, Mass. Died Jan. 13, 1945.

DELANEY, John J. (dē-lā'nē), congressman; b. Brooklyn, N.Y., Aug. 21, 1878; s. Charles J. and Jane (Brazier) D.; student Manhattan Coll., 1896-97; LL.B., Brooklyn Law Sch., 1914; m. Lotti S. Brochert, Feb. 24, 1925; children—Joanne Cornelia, John Steven. Engaged in business in New York; formerly dep. commr. of pub. markets, New York; mem. 65th, 72d to 80th Congresses (1917-19 and 1931-49) 7th N.Y. Dist. Mem. St. Patrick's Soc. Democrat. Catholic. K.C., Elk. Clubs: Seneca, Cathedral. Home: 25 Clark St., Brooklyn, N.Y. Died Nov. 18, 1948.

DELANO, Edith Barnard, author; b. Washington; d. William Theodore and Emma J. (Thomas) Barnard; m. James Delano, 1908. Author: Zebedee V, 1912; The Land of Content, 1913; The Colonel's Experiment, 1913; Rags, 1915; The White Pearl, 1916; June, 1916; To-morrow Morning, 1917; Two Alike, 1918; The Way of All Earth, 1925. Home; Deerfield, Mass. Died Sept. 8, 1946.

DELANO, Lyman, ry. official; b. Newburgh, N.Y., Jan. 16, 1883; s. Warren and Jennie (Walters) D.; A.B., Harvard, 1906; m. Leila Burnett, June 1908; children—Warren, Leila, Frederic A., Margaret, Jane W. With Stone and Webster, Boston, 1906-10; with Atlantic Coast Line R.R. Co. since 1910 (chmn. bd.); also chmn. bd. The Atlantic Coast Line Co., Charleston & Western Carolina Ry. Co., L.&N. R.R. Co.; chmn. exec. bd. Clinchfield R.R. Co.; v.p. Atlanta, Birmingham & Coast R.R. Co., Atlantic Land & Improvement Co., Wilmington Ry. Bridge Co.; dir. Charleston Union Station Company, Fort Myers Southern Railroad Company, Moore Haven & Clewiston Railway Company, Savannah Union Station Company, Fruit Growers Express Co., Richmond Terminal Ry. Co., Jacksonville Terminal Co., P. & O. Steamship Co., Columbia, Newberry & Laurens R.R. Co., Ry. Express Agcy., Inc., C., I.&L. Ry. Co., East Carolina Ry., Holston Land Co., Pan American Airways Corp., Richmond, Fredericksburg & Potomac R.R. Co., Richmond-Washington Co., New Boston Land Co., South Carolina Pacific Ry. Co., Tampa Southern R.R. Co., Winston-Salem Southbound Ry. Co., Atlanta & West Point R.R. Co., Western Ry. of Alabama, Safe Deposit & Trust Co. of Baltimore, Fed. mgr. for U.S. Railroad Adminstrn. of A.C.L. R.R. and other railways during war period. Clubs: Union, Harvard, Recess, Union League, River (New York); Metropolitan, University (Washington, D.C.). Home: Barrytown, N.Y. Office: 570 Lexington Av., New York; also 71 Broadway, New York. Died July 23, 1944; buried at Rhinebeck, N.Y.

DELANY, Joseph Francis (dē-lā'nĭ), clergyman; b. N.Y. City, Jan. 9, 1866; s. John and Julia (O'Neil) D.; A.B., St. Francis Xavier Coll., New York, 1883, A.M., 1884; S.T.D., Am. Coll., Rome, 1889. Ordained priest R.C. Ch., 1889; prof. philosophy, St. Joseph's Sem., Troy, N.Y., 1892-96; asst. rector Holy Name Ch., New York, 1896-1904; rector St. Malachy's Ch., 1906-17, Ch. of the Incarnation since 1917. Home: 1290 St. Nicholas Av., New York, N.Y.* Died Mar. 9, 1943.

DELAVAN, D(avid) Bryson (dĕl'á-văn), physician; b. N.Y. City, May 1, 1850; s. Edward Close and Margaretta (Bryson) D.; A.B., Yale, 1872; M.D., Coll. Physicians and Surgeons (Columbia), 1875; m. Marion Rumsey, June 14, 1899 (dec.); 1 dau., Elma R. (Mrs. Wm. Randolph Moore). Consultant St. Luke's and Memorial hosps., and Hosp. for Ruptured and Crippled, New York, Stony Wold Sanitarium, St. Luke's Home (pres. med. bd.), Soc. Alumnæ N.Y. Hosp. School of Nursing. Pres. Russell Sage Inst. Pathology. Hon. fellow Am. Laryngol. Assn. (pres. 1893, 1918) Am. Coll Surgeons, A.M.A., N.Y. Acad. Medicine, Congress Am. Physicians and Surgeons; hon. fellow Phila. Laryngol. Soc., Asso. Physicians of L.I., N.Y. Odontol. Soc.; hon. pres. Continental Anglo-Am. Med. Soc.; mem. Am. Soc. Control of Cancer, Harvey Soc., New York Clinical Soc., N.Y. Laryngol. Soc. (pres.; hon. mem.), Am. Museum of Health (hon. life mem.), Soc. Alumni City Hosp., Society Alumni Presbyterian Hospital, Am. Scenic and Historic Preservation Soc. (hon. pres.), Grenfell Assn. America (ex-pres.), Scroll and Key, Delta Kappa Epsilon (Yale), etc. Clubs: Century, University, Yale. Home: 30 E. 60th St., New York, N.Y. Died May 23, 1942.

De LEE, Joseph Bolivar, (dē-lē'), obstetrician; b. Cold Springs, N.Y., Oct. 28, 1869; s. Morris and Dora (Tobias) D.; ed. 1 yr. at Coll. City of New York; M.D., Chicago Med. Coll. (now Northwestern U. Med. Sch.), 1891; interne Cook County Hosp., 1891-92; studied in univs. of Vienna and Berlin, 1893-94, Paris, 1894; hon. A.M., Northwestern, 1906; unmarried. Demonstrator anatomy, Chicago Med. Coll., 1892-93; lecturer in physiology, Dental Sch., 1892-93; became demonstrator obstetrics, Northwestern U. Med. Sch., 1894; lecturer on obstetrics same, 1895; took chair of obstetrics, 1896, and given title prof. obstetrics, 1897; now prof. emeritus obstetrics and gynecology, U. of Chicago. Founded, 1895, Chicago Lying-in Hosp. and Dispensary, opened hosp. in connection with same, 1899, now consultant in obstetrics Chicago Lying-In Hosp. and Dispensary; founder, 1932, and cons. obstetrician Chicago Maternity Center. Hon. fellow Edinburgh Obstet. Soc.; fellow Am. Gynecol. Soc. (v.p., 1929), Am. Coll. Surgeons; mem. A.M.A., Chicago Med. Soc. (councillor 1902), Ill. State Med. Soc. (sec. 1899), Chicago Gynecol. Soc. (pres. 1908), Miss. Valley Med. Assn., Chicago Hist. Soc. Author: Obstetrics for Nurses, 1904, 12th edit., 1941, Notes on Obstetrics, 1904; Yearbook of Obstetrics, 1904-41, The Principles and Practice of Obstetrics, 1913, 7th edit., 1938. Home: 5028 Ellis Av. Office: 5841 Maryland Av., Chicago, Ill. Died Apr. 2, 1942.

DELL, Francis William, clergyman; b. Charlbury, Eng., June 18, 1877; s. Francis and Sarah (Lamb) D.; prep. edn., Friends Acad., Saffron Walden, Eng.; student Leeds U., Yorkshire, Eng., 1894-96; B.D., Hartford (Conn.) Theol. Sem., 1917; D.D., Whittier (Calif.) Coll., 1929; m. M. E. Adaline Johnson, Dec. 27, 1905 (died Oct. 8, 1931); children—Sarah Catherine, Francis Johnston, Loreen Elaine, Olive Eleanor, Margaret (dec.), Norma Nina, John William; m. 2d, Rebecca H. Collins, Nov. 8, 1932. Came to U.S., 1908, naturalized, 1915. Teacher, Friends Acad., Waterford, Ireland, 1898-1902; mission worker, Leeds, Eng., 1902-04; pastor Friends Ch., Ont., Can., 1904-08, Central City, Neb., 1908-10; supt. Neb. Yearly Meeting, 1910-14; pastor 1st Presbyn. Ch., Thompsonville, Conn., 1917-19, 1st Friends Ch., Whittier, 1919-24, 1st Friends Ch., Long Beach, Calif., 1924-26; Supt. Calif. Yearly Meeting, 1927-36; pastor College Av. Friends Ch., Oskaloosa, Ia., 1936-37; lecturer and evangelist 1937-39; pastor 1st Friends Ch., Huntington Park, Calif., 1939-44, now retired. Conducted religious services in Ireland, May-Nov., 1938. Author of "What It Means to be a Christian" and "Personality, What It Is and How to Realize It," courses in Bible study illustrated by lantern slides and films, "Making America Safe for Boys and Girls" (religious motion picture), "Fishers of Men," "Broken Vessels." Editor 6 Studies in Alcohol Edn.; also Great Hymns of the Church (illustrated), 1940; Hymn Series for Youth (illustrated), 1943; Seven Illustrated Studies in the Ten Commandments, 1945. Contbr. to Am. Friend, Pacific Friend. Home 109 Grande Vista Place, Whittier, Calif. Died May 25, 1945.

DEL MAR, Eugene, author, lecturer; b. New York, N.Y., Sept. 6, 1864; s. Alexander and Emily Del M.; LL.B., U. of Calif., 1883; m. Lulu Curtis, Nov. 24, 1917. Admitted to Calif. bar, 1885, and began practice at San Francisco; admitted to the New York bar, 1889; later mem. of New York Stock Exchange and partner with brother in banking business, London, Eng.; asso. editor magazine "Freedom," Sea Breeze, Fla., 1901, "Mind" New York, 1904; editor "Common Sense," Denver, 1903; various branches comml. business until 1922; has lectured widely on metaphysical subjects. Formerly mem. Am. Acad. Polit. and Social Science, A.A.A.S., Science League of America, etc. Author: Spiritual and Material Attraction, 1901; The Divinity of Desire, 1906; Living Ideals, 1907; Fulfillment, 1908; The Conquest of Disease, 1922; Man the Master, 1925. Founder Mental Science Temple (New York), 1899, New Thought Federation (New York), 1904, League for the Larger Life, 1916. Trustee Univ. of Life Science, Fla., 1924. Address: 450 S. Benton Way, Los Angeles, Calif. Died Nov. 27, 1941.

DE LONG, Ira Mitchell, prof. mathematics; b. Monroe, Jasper County, Ia., Jan. 7, 1855; s. William and Susan Adaline (Tool) D.; B.A., first honors, Simpson Coll., Indianola, Ia., 1878, M.A., 1881; LL.D., U. of Denver, 1914; m. Elizabeth A. Wright, Aug. 28, 1879; children—Edith E., Ruth; m. 2d, E. Vivian Sloan, April 3, 1929. Prof. mathematics, Central Bapt. Coll., Pella, Ia., 1878-86; prof. Latin and principal Preparatory Sch., Ia. Wesleyan Coll., Mt. Pleasant, 1886-88; prof. mathematics, U. of Colo., 1888-1925, now prof. emeritus. Organizer, mgr. Boulder Bldg. & Loan Assn. since 1890; an organizer, and dir. Merc. Bank & Trust Co., 1904-11, dir., 1918-37, pres. 1924-37. Organizer, and ex-pres. Colo. Chautauqua Assn. Del. Prog. Nat. Conv., 1912, 16; mem. Prog. Nat. Com., 1914-16; del. and pres. Boulder City Charter Conv., Aug.-Sept. 1917. Del. Gen. Conf. M.E. Ch., 1900; Colo. M.E. del. London Ecumenical Conf., 1921. Life mem. Am. Math. Soc., A.A.A.S.; mem. Math. Assn. of America, Colo. Math. Soc. (pres.), Colo. Ednl. Council (ex-pres.), Sigma Xi (charter mem.), Delta Tau Delta. Mason (32°, Scottish Rite) Home: 201 Faculty Club House, Boulder, Colo.* Died Sep. 2, 1942.

de los RIOS, Fernando (dĕ-lôs-rē'ôs), univ. prof. and diplomat; b. Ronda (Malaga), Spain, Dec. 8, 1879; s. José and Fernanda Urruti de los R.; LL.D., University of Madrid; student Sorbonne, Paris, London School for Economics and Polit. Science, London University, and German Universitys of Jena, Berlin, Marburg; m. Gloria Giner, July 1, 1912; 1 daughter, Laura de los Rios (Mrs. F. Garcia Lorca). Chair of polit. law and science, U. of Granada, 1911-30; chair of grad. studies in polit. science, U. of Madrid, 1930-38, rector, 1938; president of the Ateneo, of Madrid, 1934; A.E. and M.P. to U.S., 1936-39; prof. of polit. sci., Grad. Faculty of New School for Social Research, New York, 1939-47, retired and apptd. prof. emeritus grad. faculty, New Sch., 1948. Minister of justice in Cabinet of newly established Spanish Republic, 1931; minister of education, 1932-33; minister of fgn. affairs, 1933 Came to U.S. in 1919 as tech. adviser to Spanish dels. to Internat. Labor Conf.; Spanish envoy to Internat. Congress of Philosophy, presenting 2 treatises, 1926. Lectured at the U. of Mexico, 1926, Morelia (Mexico), 1927. U. of Havana, 1927, 1940, Columbia, 1928, U. of Puerto Rico, 1928, 1941, King Coll. of London U., Oxford and Cambridge, 1934, Sorbonne, 1935; lectured at Univs. of Panama, Bogota, Quito, Cuzco, La Paz, Potosi, Sucre and Santiago de Chile, 1941. U. of Montevideo, 1942, University of Caracas, 1944. Hon. prof. univs. of Quito, Cuzco and Santiago de Chile; Doctor honoris cause, univs. of La Paz, Sucre (Bolivia), Caracas, Middlebury (U.S.); prof. extraordinary (Mexico); professor U. of Rio Pedras, Puerto Rico, summer, 1943; mem. Congress of Professors of Spanish Universities, Havana, 1943. Member Internat. Inst. Public Law, Acad. Polit. Science, Am. Polit. Science Assn. Hon. mem. Wilson Club (N.Y. City); pres. juridical sect., Pan European Conference, 1943. Author of many books and pamphlets on philosophy, history, politics, Ibero-American instns., social sciences, in Spanish, French and English. Address: 448 Riverside Dr., New York, N.Y. Died May 31, 1949. Buried Kensico Cemetery, West Chester Co., N.Y.

DELWICHE, Edmond Joseph (dĕl'wich), prof. agronomy; b. Orbais, Belgium, Mar. 25, 1874; s. Désiré Joseph and Marie Joseph (Dethy) D.; brought to U.S., 1879; Dixon (Ill.) Coll.; Interstate Sch. of Correspondence (Northwestern U.); B.S.A., U. of Wis., 1906, M.S., 1909; m. Alice Josephine Collin, 1899; children—Mary A. (Mrs. W. E. Hansen), Anthony J., Edmond D., Joseph J., Francis R., Richard O., Eugene A., Constant C. Teacher country schs. until 1903; with U. of Wis. since 1904, successively as field asst. Expt. Sta., supt. branch stations, asst. prof. agronomy, 1910-12, asso. prof., 1913-19, prof. agronomy, 1920-45 (emeritus since 1945), also supt. branch experiment stations. Fellow of the A.A.A.S.; mem. Am. Society Agronomy, Am. Genetics Assn., Wis., Acad. Art Letters and Sciences, Alpha Zeta Fraternity. K.C. Originator two varieties of corn, also varieties of wheat, disease resistant peas, oats, soybeans. Author numerous expt. sta. publications. Home: R.F.D. 2, Green Bay. Office: Green Bay, Wis. Died Jan. 19, 1950.

DEMERS, Albert Fox (dē-mĕrz'), editor; b. Troy, N.Y., June 28, 1863; s. George Washington and Margaret (Forrest) D.; ed. pub. schs., business coll., Troy Academy; student at Rensselaer Poly. Inst., 1882-85; m. Abigail Ellsworth Boughton, Sept. 11, 1893; children—Madeleine Lorilla (Mrs. James J. McCarthy, Jr.), Agnes Ellsworth (Mrs. Floyd D. Wander), Margaret Alberta (Mrs. John S. Woodhouse). Reporter Albany Evening Jour., 1885, sketch artist same, 1886-87; studied under Gillam, cartoonist "The Judge," 1886; reporter Troy Press, 1887-90; legislative corr. United Press, 1890-91; news editor Albany Press-Knickerbocker, 1891-92; reporter and news editor Troy Times, 1892-99; mng. editor Albany Press-Knickerbocker-Express, 1899-1906; asso. editor Troy Record since 1906. Baptist. Author: Like and Unlike (novel), 1888; A Master Passion, 1888. A Colonial MacGregor, 1893; The Finest Lass, 1897; History of the Class of 1886, Rensselaer Polytechnic Institute, 1930; also short stories, poems and essays. Mem. New York advistory council Yenching Univ., Peiping, China. Home: 206 Spring Av. Address: The Troy Record, Troy, N.Y. Died Jan. 23, 1943.

DEMING, Edwin Willard, artist; b. Ashland, O., Aug. 26, 1860; s. Howard and Celestia Velutia (Willard) D.; ed. pub. and pvt. sch.; student Art Students' League under Boulanger and Le Favre, Paris; m. Therese Osterheld, Oct. 22, 1892; children—Alden O., Kathryn O., Henrietta Hall, John O., Hall Mather and Edwin Willard (twins). Painter of Indian and animal subjects (folk-lore, domestic, hunting and war); sculptor; mural decorator. Received silver medal at Phila.; hon. mention, Buffalo Expn., 1901; hon. mention, Turin, Italy, 1902; bronze medal, St. Louis Expn., 1904; won competition for 2 mural paintings, Municipal Art Soc., 1906; bronze medal, Panama P.I. Expn., 1915, "Landfall of Jean Nicholet" selected by Wisconsin and reproduced as federal three cent stamp to commemorate Wisconsin Tercentennial. Permanently represented in Black Hawk Museum, Wis. Hist. Soc., Madison, Met. Museum of Art, Am. Museum Natural History, Nat. Museum, Brooklyn Museum of Arts and Sciences, Herron Art Institute of Indianapolis, Milwaukee Museum, National Museum, Washington, D.C., Museum of the American Indian, Montclair (N.J.) Art Museum. Captain, U.S. Army; senior officer camouflage dept. of Inf. Sch. of Arms, Camp Benning, Ga. Mem. Soc. Mural Painters (life), Soc. Washington Artists, Ethnol. and Anthrop. Soc., Soc. of Am. Mil. Engrs., Soc. of N.Y. Artists, Soc. Indian Wars, S.A.R., Ohio Soc. in New York, Bison Soc., Oregon Trail Memorial Soc., D.C. Soc. of North Dakota. Clubs: Cosmos, Arts (Washington, D.C.); Campfire of America (life), Explorers (life), Army and Navy, Mil. Engineers', Nat. Arts (N.Y.); Adventurers (life), Yorktown Country of Va. (life). Illustrator: Lone Star Rises—History of Texas; Indian Life series (written by wife); Cosel, on the Trail with Geronimo. Exploration work among Motalone Indians, Colombia, S.A., 1921. Home: West Redding, Conn. Studio: 15 Gramercy Park, New York, N.Y. Died Oct. 15, 1942.

DEMING, Therese O. (Mrs. Edwin Willard Deming), author; b. in Bavaria, of American parents; d. Gen. Henry and Kathryn Brehm (Eickemeyer) Osterheld; grad. Halsted Sem., Yonkers, N.Y., 1890; m. Edwin Willard Deming, Oct. 22, 1892; children—Alden, Kathryn, Henrietta, John, Hall and Willard (twins). Has traveled widely among Indian tribes and adopted by Blackfoot and Pueblo Indians. Episcopalian. Author (illustrated by husband): Indian Child Life, 1899; Indian Pictures, 1899; Red Folk and Wild Folk, 1902; American Animal Life, 1916; E. W. Deming, His Work, 1925; Many Snows Ago, 1929; Little Eagle, 1931; Indians in Winter Camp, 1931; Red People of the Wooded Country, 1932; Pueblo Indian Children, 1935; Cosel, on the Trail with Geronimo, 1938; Indians of the Wigwam, 1939. Mem. Soc. of Women Geographers. Has given talks on Indians to sch. groups and on radio, specializing on Indian Child Life for children groups. Home: West Redding, Conn. Studio: 15 Gramercy Park, New York, N.Y. Died July 14, 1945; buried in Umpawog Hill Cemetery, Redding, Conn.

DEMING, William Chapin, editor, publisher; b. Mt. Olivet, Ky., Dec. 6, 1869; s. Osmer S. and Leona (Rigg) D.; A.B., Allegheny Coll., Pa., 1890, A.M., 1893, LL.D., 1924. Editor and mgr. Warren (O.) Tribune, 1894-1901; moved to Cheyenne, Wyo., 1901; editor and pub. Wyo. State Tribune-Leader, and Wyo. Stockman-Farmer, sold interests and retired, 1937; v.p. Tribune Co. of Warren, Ohio; pres. Deming Realty Co., Cheyenne. Mem. Wyo. Ho. of Reps., 1903-05; mem. and sec. Wyo. Commn., St. Louis Expn., 1904, Lewis and Clark Expn., Portland, Ore., 1905; receiver pub. moneys, U.S. Land Office, Cheyenne, 1907-13; pres. bd. of trustees, U. of Wyo., 1921-23; pres. U.S. Civil Service Commn., 1923-30. Mem. Lake Mohonk Conf. Internat. Arbitration, 1912-14. Mem. S.A.R., Phi Beta Kappa (hon.). Mason (32°). Wrote: Roosevelt in the Bunk House; How a Letter of a Country Lawyer Became International Law; The Press in Relation to World Peace; Application of the Merit System in U.S. Civil Service; Presidents I Have Known. Address: 820 E. 17th St., Cheyenne, Wyo. Died Apr. 9, 1949.

DEMPSEY, Elam Franklin, clergyman, editor, writer; b. Atlanta, Ga., July 6, 1878; s. Thomas Jackson and Narcissa America (Smith) D.; A.B., Emory Coll. (now Univ.), 1899; B.D., Vanderbilt, 1906; D.D., Southern U., 1915; m. Georgia Page Hunnicutt, Nov. 7, 1906. Began on trial as jr. preacher M.E. Ch., S., at City Mission, Atlanta, 1899; pastor Trinity Ch., Atlanta, 1909-10. 1st Ch., Milledgeville, 1910-14; dean theol. dept. Emory Coll., later prof. Bibl. lit., Emory U., 1914-19; pastor 1st Ch., Athens, Ga., 1919-20, 1st Ch., Rome, 1920-21; sec.treas. Christian Edn. Movement, 1921-26; presiding elder Oxford Dist., Ga., 1926-30; editor and business mgr. The Wesleyan Christian Advocate, 1930-32; pastor First Ch., Madison, Ga., 1932-34, Toccoa, Ga., 1934-38; on sabbatical leave completing some literary work, 1938-39; secretary Historical Society since 1939. Mem. International Anti-Saloon League Conf., Washington, D.C., Jan. 1924; del. Study Confs. on the Churches and World Peace, Columbus, O., and Chicago; mem. Commn. on Internat. Justice and Good Will, Federal Chs. of Christ in America, Apr. 1929. Mem. Eugene Field Soc., St. Louis. Mem. Gen. Confs. M.E. Ch., S., Atlanta, 1918, Hot Springs, Ark., 1922; called session of Gen. Conf., Chattanooga, July 1924; alternate del. Gen. Conf., Memphis, May 1926. Pres. legal conf. of N. Georgia Conf.; v.p. Widows' and Orphans' Aid Soc. and sec. of edn. same, 1921-30; chmn. headquarters com., Ga. Anti-Saloon League; curator N. Ga. Conf. Hist. Soc. Trustee Emory Univ., 1922-30, Reinhardt Coll., LaGrange Coll., The R. B. Holmes' Industrial Inst. (for negroes), Atlanta. Editor: The Wit and Wisdom of Warren Akin Candler, 1919. Wrote: Sermons to Live By (daily newspaper feature); Life With Christ in God (translated and pub. in Korean tongue); Life of Bishop J. E. Dickey; Life of Bishop Atticus G. Haygood; Souvenir of First General Conference of the Methodist Church. Contbr. prose and verse to ch. periodicals, newspapers and revs. Home: 34 Rockyford Road, N.E., Atlanta, Ga. Office: Glenn Memorial Church, Emory University, Ga. Deceased.

DEMPSEY, S(tephen) Wallace, ex-congressman; b. Hartland, N.Y., May 8, 1862; s. John and Anne (Bell) D.; DeVeaux Coll., Niagara Falls, N.Y., 1880; m. Laura Hoag, June 26, 1889. Admitted to N.Y. bar, 1886; asst. U.S. atty., 1899-1907; spl. asst. to atty. gen. U.S., 1907-12, in prosecutions in western New York of the Standard Oil Co., and the N.Y.C. R.R. Co., and Pa. R.R. on charges of giving and accepting concessions on freight rates; mem. 64th to 71st Congresses (1915-31), 40th N.Y. Dist.; was chmn. Rivers and Harbors Com. of the House; in practice of law at Washington since 1931. Republican. Episcopalian. Clubs: Army and Navy, Chevy Chase (Washington, D.C.); Nat. Republican (New York). Address: Investment Bldg., Washington, D.C. Died Mar. 1, 1949.

DEMPWOLF, Reinhardt, architect; b. Vlotho on the Weser River, Westphalia, Germany; s. Carl and Wilhelmine (Becker) D.; came to U.S., naturalized, 1872; student, York County Acad. and Collegiate Inst., 1880, Acad. of Fine Arts, Phila., Pa., 1880-84, Ecole des Beaux Arts, Paris, France, 1884-87; m. Nellie Schaszberger June 1, 1897; 1 son, John Armour. Wood and stone carver, 1888; v.p. York Chem. Works, 1935. Gold Medal of Pa. State Sunday Sch. (services as teacher for 50 years). Fellow A.I.A.; mem. Hist. Soc. of York County (sec.). Address: R.D. No. 3, York, Pa. Died Feb. 22, 1945.

DENBIGH, John Halliday, educator; b. Leeds, Eng., June 17, 1868; s. John and Mary (Halliday) D.; B.A., Oxford, 1891, M.A., 1895; hon. M.A., Columbia, 1909, Princeton, 1915; L.H.D., Union Coll., 1919; LL.D., U. of Rochester, 1919; unmarried. Came to U.S., 1895, naturalized citizen, 1901. Teacher, Trinity Sch., New York, 1895-97; head of mathematics dept., Morris High Sch., 1897-1904, prin., 1904-18; prin. Packer Collegiate Inst., Brooklyn, 1918-38. Mem. Headmasters' Assn., New York Acad. Pub. Ed. Episcopalian. Clubs: Century (New York), British Schools and Universities Club. Home: 540 Argye Rd., Brooklyn, N.Y. Died July 24, 1943.

DENISON, Arthur Carter, lawyer; b. Grand Rapids, Nov. 10, 1861; s. Julius Coe and Cornelia (Carter) D.; LL.B., U. of Mich., 1883 (LL.D., same, 1916); m. Susie L. Goodrich, 1886 (died 1896); children—John Walter, Donald Goodrich, Arthur Curtis (dec.); m. 2d, Julia B. Barlow, 1898; 1 dau., Ruth Barlow. Admitted to bar, 1883; practiced at Grand Rapids; U.S. district judge, Western Dist. of Mich., Feb. 2, 1910-11; U.S. circuit judge, 6th Circuit, 1911-32; presiding judge, U.S. Court of Appeals, Cincinnati, 1925-32, resigned and reentered law practice; with Baker, Hostetler and Patterson, Cleveland, since 1932; mem. President's Aircraft Bd., Sept.-Nov. 1925. Republican. Pres. Grand Rapids Bar Assn., 1903, Mich. State Bar Assn., 1906-07. Pres. Bd. of Edn., Grand Rapids, 1904-05. Clubs, Peninsular, Kent Country (Grand Rapids); Cosmos (Washington). Home: Moreland Court. Office: Union Commerce Bldg., Cleveland, O. Died May 27, 1942.

DENNETT, Fred, ex-commr. General Land Office; b. Valparaiso, Chile, S.A., June 17, 1863; s. Rev. Dr. Richard and Eleanor (Garforth) D.; ed. Great Malvern Coll., Eng.; came to U.S., 1885; LL.B., Columbian (now George Washington) U., 1895, LL.M., 1896; J.D., Catholic U. of America, 1903; m. Elizabeth E. Comerford, Nov. 23, 1892; children—Dorothy Dixon (Mrs. Patten Wise Slemp), Richard Rodney. Editor and propr. Milton (N.D.) Globe, 1887-92, part owner, 1892-1903; mem. N.D. Ho. of Rep. 1891; sec. U.S. Senate Com. on Public Lands, 1898-1905; in charge agency force, pub. lands, Washington state, 1905-07; asst. commr., 1907-08, commr., Mar. 4, 1908-June 16, 1913, Gen. Land Office; practicing law, Washington since 1913. Del. Brazilian Centennial Expn., 1922 Mem. Archaeol. Inst. America, Phi Delta Phi. Republican. Mason.

Contbr. articles to Washington Law Reporter, National Magazine, Peace Forum. Home: Milton, N.D. Address: The Cairo, Washington. Died Sept. 28, 1928.

DENNETT, Tyler, author; b. Spencer, Wis., June 13, 1883; s. Rev. Wilbur Eugene and Roxie (Tyler) D.; student Bates Coll., Lewiston, Me., 1900-01; A.B., Williams, 1904; Ph.D., Johns Hopkins; LL.D., Wesleyan, 1934, Harvard, 1934, Amherst, 1934, Columbia, 1935, Beloit, 1935; L.H.D., Williams Coll., 1934; Litt.D., Princeton U., 1934; LL.D., Lafayette Coll., 1936, Clark Univ., 1937; m. Maybelle Raymond, Mar. 15, 1911; children—George Raymond, Tyler Eugene, Audrey, Laurence. Lecturer in Am. history, Johns Hopkins, 1923-24, Columbia, 1927-28; chief Div. of Publs. and editor Dept. of State, 1924-29, hist. adviser, 1929-31; prof. internat. relations, Princeton, 1931-34; pres. Williams Coll., 1934-37. Carnegie visitor to Australia and New Zealand, 1938-39. Fellow Am. Acad. Arts and Sciences; mem. Am. Hist. Assn., Soc. of Internat. Law. Republican. Conglist. Clubs: Century (New York); Cosmos (Washington, D.C.). Author: The Democratic Movement in Asia, 1918; Americans in Eastern Asia, 1923; Roosevelt and the Russo-Japanese War, 1924; Biography of John Hay (Pulitzer prize), 1933; Lincoln and the Civil War—Hay Diaries, 1939; also articles in scientific and popular periodicals. Home: Hague, N.Y. Died Dec. 29, 1949.

DENNEY, Oswald Evans, officer U.S. Pub. Health Service; b. Smyrna, Del., July 21, 1885; s. Robert and Henrietta (Holding) D.; M.D., U. of Pa., 1913; D.T.M., U. of Philippines, 1915; m. Bertha Oliva Harris, Oct. 27, 1920; children—Robert Harris, Philip Holding, Oswald Evans, Mary Elizabeth Anne. Resident physician at Philippine General Hospital, 1913-14, San Lazaro Hospital, Manila, 1914-15; resident physician and later chief, Culion Leper Colony, P.I., 1915-19; exec. officer 4th dist. U.S. Pub. Health Service, 1919-20; med. officer in charge Nat. Leprosarium, Carville, La., 1921-35; chief quarantine officer Panama Canal Zone, 1936-39; traveling rep. Pan-Am. Sanitary Bureau, 1940; med. officer in charge U.S. Marine Hosp. and chief quarantine officer, Galveston, Texas, since 1940. Fellow Am. Coll. Physicians; mem. A.M.A., Am. Soc. Tropical Medicine, Assn. Mil. Surgeons of U.S., Internat. Leprosy Assn., Am. Legion, Phi Chi, Sigma Xi. Democrat. Presbyterian. Clubs: Marine Hospital Golf (Carville). Author numerous papers on tropical medicine, particularly on Asiatic cholera and leprosy. Home: Smyrna, Del. Address: U.S. Marine Hospital, Galveston, Texas. Died Feb. 19, 1944.

DENNIS, Charles Henry, editor; b. Decatur, Ill., Feb. 8, 1860; s. Andrew and Matilda Lavina (Baker) D.; B.L., U. of Ill., 1881, M.A., 1905; LittD., Northwestern U., 1934; m. Rachel Shelby Wilson, 1884 (died 1891); m. 2d, Jeannelle Caldwell Wilson, 1894 (died 1933); children—Ruth Elizabeth (Mrs. John C. Langtry), William Andrew, Herbert Wilson (dec.), Mildred Blackburn (Mrs. Julian P. Anderson). Began career in newspaper work in Chicago, 1881; reporter, dramatic critic, editorial writer, city editor The Chicago Daily News, 1882-91; managing editor Chicago Record, 1892-1901; chief editorial writer and mgr. foreign news service, Chicago Daily News, 1901-07, asso. editor, 1907-12, mng. editor, 1912-25, editor, 1925-34, editor emeritus, 1934. Clubs: Union League, City (Chicago); University (Evanston). Evanston Golf. Author: Eugene Field's Creative Years, 1924; Victor Lawson, 1935. Home: 1225 Michigan Av., Evanston, Ill. Office: Daily News, Chicago. Died Sept. 25, 1943.

DENNIS, Ralph (Brownell), educator; b. Tama, Ia., Sept. 21, 1876; s. Jabez and Alice (Reynolds) D.; B.L., Northwestern U., 1901, M.A., 1914; L.H.D., Wabash, 1931; m. Myrta McKean, 1904 (died 1937); m. 2d, Dorothy Critchfield, 1940. Teacher, Northwestern U., 1901-09; dir. and dean School of Speech, Northwestern U., since 1913. Address: Northwestern University, Evanston, Ill. Died Aug. 23, 1942.

DENNY, Collins, bishop; b. Winchester, Va., May 28, 1854; s. William R. and Margaret A. (Collins) D.; A.B., Princeton, 1876, A.M., 1879; LL.B., U. of Va., 1877; student U. of Va., 1889-91; D.D., Emory and Henry, Washington and Lee U.; LL.D., Emory and Henry, Va., and Emory (Ga.) U., 1910; m. Lucy C. Chapman, July 5, 1881; children—Margaret Collins (wife of Rev. J. W. Dixon), Elizabeth Chapman (Mrs. E. E. Vann), William Ritenour (dec.), Edith Allan (wife of Rev. R. M. White), Lucy Chase (wife of Prof. P. W. Slosson), Collins. Practiced law, Baltimore, 1877-79; entered M.E. Ch., S., ministry, Baltimore Conf., 1880, visited Asiatic missions of M.E. Ch., S., by episcopal appointment, 1886-87; chaplain U. of Va., 1889-91; prof. mental and moral philosophy, Vanderbilt U., 1891-1910; elected bishop, M.E., Ch., S., May 1910; retired from active work in ministry, May 1934. Offered bishopric in Meth. Ch. but declined. Sec. Coll. of Bishops M.E. Ch., S., 1910-27; acting sec. Gen. Conf., 1894; chmn. book com., 1898-1910; del. Gen. Conf., 1894, 98, 1902, 06, 10; fraternal del. M.E. Ch., S., to M.E. Ch., Baltimore, 1908. Mem. Va. State Council of Defense, 1917; mem. Va. War History Commn. Contbr. Library of Southern Literature, and frequent contbr. to The Methodist Review Quarterly and periodicals of the Meth. church. Mem. Phi Beta Kappa, Phi Kappa Psi, Phi Delta Phi. Author: Analysis of Davis's Elements of Deductive Logic and of His Elements of Psychology, 1916; A Manual of the Discipline of the M.E. Ch., S., 17th Edit., 1920, 18th edit., 1924, 19th edit., 1930. Home: 1619 Park Av., Richmond, Va. Died May 12, 1943.

DENNY, Harold Norman, newspaperman; b. Des Moines, Ia., Mar. 11, 1889; s. Charles Oscar and Lily (Wisner) D.; student Drake U., 1907-11, granted A.B. degree nunc pro tunc, 1939; m. Jean Bullitt Lowry, June 5, 1936. Employed in reportorial and editorial capacities on Des Moines (Ia.) Register, St. Paul Pioneer Press, Minneapolis (Minn.) Tribune, N.Y. Tribune, Chicago Tribune (Paris Edition) and other newspapers, 1913-22; with New York Times since 1922, assigned to crossing of Sahara and exploration of Hoggar with Franco-Am. Archæol. Mission, 1925, Moroccan War, 1926, Am. tour of Queen Marie of Roumania, 1926, Lindbergh's Central Am. flight, 1928, Nicaraguan crisis, 1927-28, Forbes Commn. to Haiti, 1930, Cuban crisis, 1930-31, Pennsylvania coal strike, 1933, Italo-Ethiopian War, 1935, Moscow corr., 1934-39, covered Moscow treason trials and Soviet purge, 1936-38; German investiture of Czecho-Slovakia, 1939. Served as enlisted man, inf., U.S. Army, World War I; wounded in Argonne. War corr. with Brit. Army, 1939-41, in Flanders and Middle East, and with Finnish Army, 1939-40; captured by Marshal Rommel's tanks in Lybia, Nov. 23, 1941; exchanged and returned to U.S. after 6 months imprisonment by Gestapo in Berlin and Italian Army in Italy. Mem. Phi Beta Kappa. Author: Dollars for Bullets, 1929; Behind Both Lines, 1942. Address: 229 W. 43d St., New York, N.Y. Died July 3, 1945.

DENSLOW, Herbert McKenzie, clergyman; b. Lynn, Mass., Aug. 20, 1852; s. Dwight Bennett and Loise Atkinson (Staple) D.; B.A., Yale, 1873; (hon. M.A., Kenyon Coll., O., 1896; D.D., Gen. Theol. Sem., 1907); m. Anna Mary Olmsted, June 28, 1877; children—Dwight Norton, Rebekah, Theodore North, Helen Elizabeth. Deacon, 1878, priest, 1879, P.E. Ch.; rector Grace Ch., New Haven, Conn., 1878-82, Trinity Ch., Rutland, Vt., 1882-85, Trinity Ch., Seneca Falls, N.Y., 1885-93; rector and chaplain Kenyon Coll. and instr. in liturgics, 1893-96; rector Grace Ch., Muncie, Ind., 1896-1901, St. John's Ch., Lafayette, Ind., 1901-02; prof. pastoral theology, Gen. Theol. Sem., Aug. 1, 1902-27. Deputy to Gen. Conv. P.E. Ch., Indianapolis, 1901. Mem. Torrey Bot. Club (pres. 1928-29), Conn. Bot. Soc., Alpha Delta Phi, Phi Beta Kappa. Home: 36 Wethersfield Av., Hartford, Conn. 1944.

DENSMORE, John Hopkins, composer; b. Somerville, Mass., Aug. 7, 1880; s. Charles Dana and Ellen Josephine (Brennen) D.; direct desc. of Myles Standish of the Mayflower and of Capt. Samuel Brocklebank of England; A.B., Harvard, 1904 (honors in music; elected chorister of the class); post-grad. work same Univ., in music, composition, orchestration, etc.; Harvard Law School, 1904-05; unmarried. Began writing music while at college. Mem. First Corps Cadets, Boston, 1905-08. Mem. Delta Kappa Epsilon, Inst. of 1770, Signet Club, Spee Club, Hasty Pudding Club (Harvard), Harvard Musical Assn., Musical Manuscript Club of Boston, Brookline Civic Soc. (music com.), Soc. Mayflower Descendants, Soc. Colonial Wars, Harvard Law Sch. Assn., Vet. Assn. 1st Corps Cadets, 101st Engrs., Mil. Hist. Soc. of Mass., Am. Soc. Composers, Authors and Publishers. Club: Harvard of Boston. Composer and condr. operettas for Hasty Pudding Club, 1904, First Corps Cadets, 1905; also numerous choral works. Compositions include many songs, cantata, pieces for piano, band and orchestra, etc. Recent songs composed: The Lamb; Memory; I Must Down to the Seas Again; Roadways; Elf and Fairy; A Spring Fancy; The Voice and the Flute; Nocturne; The South Winds Are Blowing; Good Tidings of Great Joy; The Nightingale; Daffodil Comes Home Today; I Know Where a Garden Grows; Love Song; All to Myself; My Garden; If God Left Only You; The Searchlight; Laughing Song; Just for To-day; God Made a Heart of Gold; April, April, Laugh Thy Girlish Laughter; Starry-Night; Cigarette Tango; Sea-Fever; In Love; Longing, Dear, for You; A Baby's Epitaph; The Unfurling of the Flag; cantata for chorus and orchestra, Hail, Ceres, Hail!; piano solo or orchestra, Butterfly, Gardenia, Veritas March; also compositions "Only A Rose," "Just A Pal Like You," "The Nicest Kind of Smile," "My Only Song," "A Spring Fancy" (operetta), "A Forest Fantasy," for piano and orchestra, "A Newport Novelty" (operetta). Named as a representative writer of Am. music by Nat. Federation of Music Clubs. Address: Westhampton Beach, L.I., N.Y. Died Sep. 21, 1943.

DENTON, James Clarence, lawyer; b. Newport, Tenn., Mar. 18, 1882; s. James Jefferson and Elizabeth (Loyd) D.; student Emory and Henry Coll., Emory, Va.; B.S., U. of Tenn., 1903; LL.B., 1904; m. Clara M. Murchison, July 1, 1912; 1 son, James C. Admitted to bar, Indian Ty., 1904, and began practice at Nowata; gen. practice, Muskogee, Okla., 1912-20, gen. counsel Mid-Continent Petroleum Corp., Tulsa, Okla., since 1920, v.p. since 1925; dir. Nat. Bank of Tulsa, Atlas Life Ins. Co. Mayor of Nowata, 1907-08; asst. U.S. atty., Eastern Dist., Okla., 1909-12. Served as lt., later capt. Okla. Nat. Guard, 1918-21. Mem. bd. trustees U. of Tulsa. Mem. Am. Bar Assn. (v.p. from Okla., 1924; gen. council, 1925-27), Mid-Continent Oil and Gas Assn. (pres.), Alpha Tau Omega, Phi Kappa Phi and Theta Lambda Phi fraternities. Republican; delegate at large from Oklahoma to Republican National Convention, Kansas City, 1928. Methodist. Mason, Elk. Clubs: Tulsa, University, Tulsa Town and Country. Home: 15 W. 22nd St. Office: Cosden Bldg., Tulsa, Okla. Died June 4, 1942.

DEPUTY, Manfred Wolfe, coll. pres.; b. Vernon, Ind., Oct. 27, 1868; s. James A. and Martha Ann (Wolfe) D.; B.S., Southern Ind., Normal Sch. Mitchell, 1892; A.B., Ind. U., 1904, A.M., 1905; grad. study Columbia, summer 1911; m. Carrie Gault, Aug. 14, 1895; 1 dau., Mary Lois (Mrs. F. Vernon Lamson). Teacher, country schs., 1887-89; prin. high sch., Hayden, Ind., 1892-94, Paris, Ind., 1895-97; county supt. schs., Jennings Co., Ind., 1897-1903; supt. city schs., Columbia City, Ind., 1905-09; supervisor model sch., Eastern Ill. State Normal Sch., 1909-11; dir. elementary sch. and teacher of pedagogy, State Normal Sch., Mankato, Minn., 1911-16; prin. City Normal Sch., Kansas City, Mo., 1916-19; organizer, 1919, since pres. State Teachers Coll., Bemidji, Minn. Mem. N.E.A., Minn. Edn. Assn. (exec. com.; 1st pres. Northern Div.), Bemidji Civic and Commerce Assn. Republican. Methodist. Mason. Club: Philomathean. Home: 1121 Bemidji Av., Bemidji, Minn. Died March 12, 1947.

DERBY, Stephen Hasket, maritime law; b. Boston, Mass., Dec. 25, 1877; s. Hasket and Sarah (Mason) D.; A.B., Harvard, 1899; LL.B. cum laude, 1902; m. Nora Purcell Leary, Apr. 25, 1911 (died Sept. 10, 1935); married 2d, Sylvia M. Webster, June 14, 1945. Admitted to bar of Territory of Hawaii, 1902, and began practice at Honolulu; police judge, Honolulu, 1906-1907; in practice of maritime law, San Francisco, California, since 1907; member firm, Derby, Sharp, Quinby and Tweedt, since 1926; writer and lecturer on maritime law. Member Derby, Sharp, Quinby & Tweedt since 1926. Mem. Draft Bd., San Francisco, World War. Democrat Catholic. Clubs: Commercial, Commonwealth, Harvard, Olympic, Lakeside Country (San Francisco); University (Hawaii). Home: 320 San Leandro Way, San Francisco 16 Died April 2, 1947.

DE RESZKE, Jean, operatic singer; b. Varsovie, Poland, Jan. 14, 1850; studied under Ciaffei, Cotogni and Sbriglia. m. Countess Maria de Goulaine. Debut as baritone singer in Favorita, Venice, Jan., 1874; tenor debut, Madrid, 1879; has appeared in leading roles in grand opera in Europe and U. S. Mem. Victorian Order (4th class), England. Address: Metropolitan Opera House, New York. Died Apr. 3, 1925.

DERN, Alfred L., business exec.; b. Hooper, Neb., Oct. 10, 1885; s. Philip and Hermin (Klingbeil) D.; ed. pub. schs. of Hooper, Neb.; m. Alma C. Aldrich, Aug. 26, 1914; children—John Philip, James Richard. Began career as life ins. Agent, 1906-07; with Miles Menander Dawson, Cons. Actuary, New York, 1907-12; actuary and asst. sec., Pioneer Life Ins. Co., Fargo, N.D., 1912-17; supt. of agents, Lincoln Nat. Life Ins. Co., Fort Wayne, Ind., 1917-33, vice pres. since 1933, mem. bd. dirs. since 1923. Mem. Fort Wayne Chamber of Commerce (mem. bd. dirs.), Fort Wayne Y.M.C.A. (past v.p., mem. bd. dirs.), Anthony Wayne Area Boy Scouts of Am. (past v.p.), Taxpayers Research Assn. (v.p. and mem. bd.), Life Ins. Agency Management Assn. (bd. dirs.), Life Ins. Sales Research Bur. (past chmn. bd. dirs.), Am. Life Conv. (past chmn. agency sect.), Photographic Soc. of Am. Republican. Conglist. Mason (Scottish Rite, Shriner, Jester). Club: Fort Wayne Country. Home: 451 Arcadia Court, Fort Wayne 6. Office: Fort Wayne 2, Indiana. Died May 29, 1947; buried Lindenwood Cemetery. Fort Wayne, Ind.

DE ROUEN, Rene L., congressman; b. nr. Ville Platte, La., Jan. 7, 1874; s. Fabius and Alma (De Baillon) De R.; A.B., Holy Cross Coll., New Orleans, 1892; m. Christina Currie, 1896; children—Mrs. L. V. Dupuis, Mrs. Albert Tate, Louis R., Alvin F. Identified with merchandising, banking and farming; pres. Evangeline Bank & Trust Co.; v.p. First Nat. Bank (both of Ville Platte); mem. La. Constl. Conv., 1921; mem. 70th to 76th Congresses (1927-41), 7th La. Dist. Democrat. Roman Catholic. Home: Ville Platte, La. Died March 27, 1942.

de ROUSSY de SALES, Raoul (Jean Jacques Francois) (dĕ-rōōs'sī dĕ-säls), journalist; b. Paris, Mar. 5, 1896; s. Jean Emmanuel and Rose Lilly (Rheims) de R.; ed. Lycee Janson deSailly, 1904-12, Gresham Sch., Norfolk, Eng., 1912-13; m. Reine Marie Melanie Tracy, Feb. 5, 1925; 1 son, Aymon Bertrand Francois Jacques Raoul. Came to U.S., 1932. Clerk, Compagnie d'Exportations de l'Afrique Occidentale Francaise, exporting firm, France, 1913-14; served as liaison officer (1st lt.) Am. Red Cross, 1918; asst. dir. Rockefeller Foundation, in tuberculosis prevention in France, 1918-21; asst. dir. League of Red Cross Socs., Paris, 1922-31; U.S. corr. for Paris-Soir and Paris-Midi, 1934; diplomatic corr. in U.S. for Havas News Agency, 1937; lecturer in U.S. on European situation; U.S. corr. newspaper France (pub. in London). Decorated Chevalier Legion of Honor (France). Pres. Assn. of Foreign Press Correspondents, 1937-39. Roman Catholic. Editor: Mein Kampf, 1939; My New Order (Hitler's speeches), 1941. Contributor to You Americans (book), 1939; contbr. to Atlantic Monthly, Revue de Paris, l'Europe Nouvelle. Home: 12 E. 82d St., New York, N.Y. Died Dec. 3, 1942.

DERRICK, Sidney Jacob, prof. history; b. Little Mountain, S.C., Nov. 10, 1867; s. Jacob and Martha Catherine (Kesler) D.; A.B., Newberry (S.C.) Coll., 1892, A.M., 1897; studied Cornell U. and Columbia; LL.D., Lenoir Coll., Hickory, N.C., 1921; m. Mary V. Hiller, Dec. 21, 1898. Teacher, White Rock Sch., 1892-94; supt. schs., Lexington, S.C., 1894-96; prin. prep. dept. Newberry Coll., 1896-1905, asst. prof. history and psychology, 1905-11, prof. history and economics, 1911-18, pres., 1918-30, prof. history since 1930, dean of faculty, 1939. Mem. Bd. of Education, Newberry, 1900-16; mem. State Board of Education, S.C., 1916-20 and since 1924; chmn. local Exemption Bd., 1917-18. Del. Dem. State Convention, 1914, 20. Mem. exec. com. Interracial Conf.; mem. exec. com. Luth. Synod of S.C. Democrat. Clubs: Rotary, Country. Home: Newberry, S.C. Died June 13, 1948.

DERRY, George Hermann, educator; born Portland, Me., May 27, 1878; s. Adolphus and Katherine (Doran) D.; ed. Holy Cross College, Worcester, Mass., 1895-96; St. John's Juniorate, S.J., Frederick, Md., 1896-99; grad. summa cum laude, Schs. of Social Science and Philosophy, Stonyhurst Coll., Eng., 1902; post-grad. student Johns Hopkins, 1902-04; Ph.D., Holy Cross Coll., 1908; S.T.B., Catholic U., Paris, 1910; LL.D., Marquette, 1927; Litt.D., Xavier U., Cincinnati, 1940; m. Agnes Lurana Mann, July 22, 1913; children—Jeanne, Geo. Hermann, Marie. Prof. Latin, Greek and comparative lit., St. Francis Xavier's Coll., N.Y. City, 1904-06, Holy Cross Coll., 1906-08; asst. prof. polit. science, U. of Kan., 1917-19; acting head dept. of economics, Bryn Mawr Coll., 1919-20; head dept. of economics, Union U., Schenectady, N.Y., 1920-25; lecturer on sociology, Catholic Summer Sch. of America, Cliff Haven, N.Y., since 1920; prof. and head dept. of sociology, Marquette U., 1925-27; pres. Marygrove Coll., Detroit, 1927-37; nat. dir. social edn., Knights of Columbus, 1937-39; pres. St. Joseph's Coll., Portland, 1941-47; dir. social edn. Supreme Council, Knights of Columbus since 1947. Decorated Knight Comdr. St. Gregory the Great by Pope Pius XI, 1932. Member Mediæval Academy of America, American Catholic History Assn., Nat. Catholic Industrial Conf., Nat. Cath. Charities Conf., Am. Cath. Philos. Assn., K.C. Hist. Commn., Phi Kappa. Asso. editor K.C. Hist. Series; contbr. to Catholic Ency., etc. Has lectured in seven langs. in U.S., Can., Gt. Britain and France. Internat. dir. of social edn., K.C., 1946-48. Home: Mendon, Mass. Address: 45 Wall St., New Haven, Conn. Died Jan. 17, 1949.

de SAINT EXUPERY, Antoine (dĕ-săɴ-tĕks-ōō-pă-rĕ', ăn-twăn), author, aviator; b. Lyon, France, June 29, 1900; s. Jean and Marie (de Fonscolombe) de Saint-Exupery; m. Consuelo Suncin, Apr. 1931. Began as airplane pilot, 1921; participated in creation of airlines in France, Africa, S. America; served in World War II; returned to French Army Air Force, reported missing, Aug. 1944. Decorated Croix de Guerre; Officer Legion of Honor (France). Author: Night Flight, 1939; Wind, Sand and Stars, 1940; Flight to Arras, 1942. Home: 2 Beekman St., New York, N.Y. Deceased.

DESMOND, Daniel Francis, bishop; b. Haverhill, Mass., Apr. 4, 1884; s. Daniel C. and Catherine (Lynch) D.; A.B., Holy Cross Coll., Worcester, 1906; LL.D., Duquesne U., 1935. Ordained Roman Catholic priest, 1911; asst. priest Beachmont, Mass., 1911-12, Medford, 1913-16, Somerville, 1917-32; consecrated bishop of Alexandria, La., Jan. 5, 1933; installed Feb. 15, 1934. First lt. (chaplain) U.S. Army, 1918-19. Dir. Somerville Cath. Charities, 1926-32. Address: 1805 Jackson Av., Alexandria, La. Died Sep. 11, 1945.

Des PORTES, Fay Allen (dā-pōrt'), diplomat; b. Winnsboro, S.C., June 16, 1890; s. Ulysee G. and Sarah (Wolfe) D.; student Clemson (S.C.) Coll., and N.C. State Coll.; m. Elsie Lyles, Sept. 14, 1914; children—Bernard Baruch, Fay Allen. Mem. S.C. Ho. of Representatives 1926-28, Senate, 1928-36, resigned to accept appmt. as E.E. and M.P. to Bolivia, 1933-36; E.E. and M.P. to Guatemala, 1936-43; A.E. and P. to Costa Rica since March 28, 1943; represented S.C. at gov.'s confs., 1931-32; del. Dem. Nat. Conv., 1932, nat. platform and resolutions committeeman of S.C., one of committeemen selected to present Dem. Platform to Conv.; dir. Assn. Against Nat. Prohibition. Chmn. of U.S. del. of Regional Radio Conv. for Central America, Panama and the Canal Zone, 1938. Democrat. Episcopalian (former mem. exec. council and financial com. Diocese of S.C.). Home: Winnsboro, S.C. Address: U.S. Embassy, San Jose, Costa Rica. Died Sep. 1944.

de STEIGUER, Louis Rodolph (dĕ-stī'gĕr), admiral U.S. Navy, retired; b. Athens, Ohio, Mar. 18, 1867; s. Judge R. and Mary (Carpenter) de S.; student Ohio University, Athens, hon. LL.D.; graduate United States Naval Academy, 1889; m. Katharine Constable. Commd. ensign, 1891; promoted through grades to rear admiral, Dec. 31, 1921. Served on Montgomery, Spanish-Am. War, 1898; Nashville Philippine insurrection, 1900, O.N.I. Washington; U.S. Ill., 1901-04; supervisor New York Harbor; ordnance officer, Ill. and exec. officer U.S. Conn. in cruise around the world, 1907-09; in charge 5th lighthouse dist., Baltimore, 1909-11; comdg. U.S. Panther, 1911-13; capt. yard and acting comdt., Norfolk, Va.; comdg. U.S. Kearsage and receiving ship (Maine) Navy Yard, New York; Naval War. Coll., 1916-17; chief of staff, 3d naval dist., comdg. U.S. Arkansas British Grand Fleet, U.S. fleet comdt. Navy Yard, Portsmouth, N.H., 1920; hydrographer, Washington, D.C., 1921; comdr. U.S. Train, 1922; comdt. Navy Yard, Boston; comdg. 4th div. battle fleet; vice adm., comdr. battleship divs.; adm. comdr.-in-chief Battle Fleet, 1927; comdt. 3d Naval Dist. and Navy Yard, New York, until retired, Apr. 1, 1931. Clubs: Army-Navy Country, Army and Navy (Washington, D.C.); New York Yacht (New York) Address: 1302 18th St. N.W., Washington, D.C. Died April 19, 1947.

DETT, R(obert) Nathaniel, composer; b. Drummondsville, Ont., Can., Oct. 11, 1882; s. Robert Tue and Charlotte (Johnson) D.; student Oliver Willis Halsted Conservatory of Music, Lockport, N.Y., 1901-03; Mus. B., Oberlin Conservatory of Music, Oberlin, Ohio, 1908; studied Columbia, U. of Pa., Am. Conservatory of Music (Chicago), Harvard Univ.; Mus.D., Howard Univ., 1924; Mus.D., Oberlin, 1926; Mus.M., Eastman Sch. of Music, U. of Rochester, 1931; m. Helen Elise Smith, pianist, Dec. 27, 1916. Church and social pianist, Niagara Falls, N.Y., 1898-1903; dir. of music, Lane Coll. (colored), Jackson, Tenn., 1908-11, Lincoln Inst. (colored), Jefferson City, Mo., 1911-13, Hampton (Va.) Inst., from 1913; dir. of School of Music of same since 1926; dir. Hampton Choral Union; condr. Hampton Inst., Choir (80 voices) on tours in U.S., Canada and 7 countries of Europe; dir. Am. Choir, Sta. WHAM, 1930-31; dir. Negro Community Chorus, 1933-34; became dir. music, Bennett Coll., Greensboro, N.C., since 1937. Mem. N.E.A., Nat. Assn. Teachers of Colored Schs., Nat. Assn. of Negro Musicians (chmn. advisory bd., 1919; pres., 1924-26). Republican. Presbyterian. Mason, K. of P. First American to utilize Negro folk tune for classic development. Composer: Album of a Heart (verse), 1911; The Magnolia Suite (piano); In the Bottoms (suite for piano); Listen to the Lambs, The Chariot Jubilee (motets); America the Beautiful (chorus); Enchantment Suite (for piano); Cinnamon Grove Suite; Tropic Winter Suite; The Chariot Jubilee (for 8 part mixed chorus and orchestra); The Ordering of Moses (oratorio for 4 part mixed chorus and orchestra); also anthems, songs, etc. Bowdoin prize, Harvard, 1920, for essay, "The Emancipation of Negro Music"; Francis Boott prize, Harvard, 1920, for Molet on a Negro Motive, "Don't Be Weary, Traveler"; Harmon first award for creative achievement in music, 1927. Author and editor of Religious Folk Songs of the Negro as Sung at Hampton Institute; pub. The Dett Collection of Negro Spirituals (4 books), 1937. Organized Musical Art Soc. of Hampton Inst. (800 members), 1919. Address: 1087 Plymouth av. S., Rochester, N.Y.* Died Oct. 3, 1943.

DEVENDORF, James Franklin, philanthropist; b. Lowell, Mich., Apr. 6, 1856; s. Thomas Jefferson and Grace (Condon) D.; ed. pub. schs.; m. Lillie A. Potter; children—Edwina, Mrs. Myrtle Gibbs, Mrs. Lillian Hohfeld, Mrs. Marian Angus. Topographical engr.; pres. Carmel Development Co.; known as community organizer and patron of art, literature and music. Founder of Artists' and Writers' Colony at Carmel-by-the-Sea, and of Carmel Highlands; promoter of Carmel Forest Theatre, for prize contests and for prodn. of original drama; also promoter Carmel Arts and Crafts Soc. and allied organizations. Republican. Methodist. Home: Oakland, Calif. Died Oct. 9, 1934.

DEVINE, Edward Thomas (dĕ-vīn'), author, lecturer; b. Union, Hardin County, Ia., May 6, 1867; s. John and Laura (Hall) D.; A.B., Cornell Coll., Ia., 1887, A.M., 1890; LL.D., 1904; Ph.D., U. of Pa., 1893, fellow, 1891-95; U. of Halle, 1890-91; m. Hattie Evelyn Scovel, Aug. 15, 1889; children—Thomas, Ruth (Mrs. F. B. Hunt). Principal of schools in Albion, Ia., 1886-87, Marshalltown, Ia., 1887-88, Mt. Vernon, Ia., 1889-90; staff lecturer economics for American Society Extension of University Teaching, 1891-96, secretary 1894-96; general secretary Charity Organization Soc., New York, 1896-1912. Editor of the Survey (formerly Charities and the Commons), 1897-1912; prof. social economy, Columbia, 1905-19; dir. New York Sch. of Philanthropy, 1904-07, 1912-17; sec. Charity Orgn. Soc., New York, 1912-17; asso. editor of the Survey, 1912-21; chief bur. of refugees and relief under Am. Red Cross Commn. to France, 1917-18; mem. U.S. Coal Commn., 1922-23; prof. social economy and dean Grad. Sch. American U., Washington, D.C., 1926-28; dir. Bellevue-Yorkville Health Demonstration, N.Y. City, 1929-30. Pres. Nat. Conf. of Charities and Correction, 1906; special representative Am. Red Cross, in charge of relief at San Francisco, 1906; pres. sect. of hygienic, social, indsl. and econ. aspects of tuberculosis, Internat. Congress on Tuberculosis, Washington, 1908; advisory com. Internat. Prison Congress, 1910; chmn. com. on industrial relations, 1912; spl. rep. Am. Red Cross, in charge of storm and flood relief in Dayton, O., 1913; spl. agt. Am. Embassy, Petrograd, 1916. Vice chmn. New York Com. of 1000, 1931; exec. dir. Emergency Work Bur., Nassau County, N.Y., 1931-33; exec. dir. Emergency Relief Bureau, Nassau County, 1933-35. Mem. Am. Econ. Assn., British Economical Assn.; dept. research and education and department of race relations of Federal Council Churches of Christ in America, chairman committee on revision of social ideals of the churches, 1930-32. Author: Economics, 1898; The Practice of Charity, 1901, new edit., 1904; The Principles of Relief, 1904; Efficiency and Relief, 1906; Misery and Its Causes, 1909; Report on the Desirability of Establishing an Employment Bureau in the City of New York, 1909; Social Forces, 1909; The Spirit of Social Work, 1911; The Family and Social Work, 1912; The Normal Life, 1915, revised edition, 1917; Disabled Soldiers and Sailors, 1919; Social Work, 1921; Coal—Economic Problems of the Mining, Marketing, and Consumption of Anthracite and Soft Coal in the United States, 1925; Progressive Social Action, 1933; When Social Work Was Young, 1939. Home: 642 N Elmwood Av., Oak Park, Ill. Died Feb. 27, 1948.

De VINE, James Herbert, lawyer and corp. exec.; b. Ia., May 2, 1880; s. Michael and Margaret (Herbert) De V.; B.S., Valparaiso Coll., 1898; LL.B., Ind. Law Sch., Valparaiso, Ind., 1900; LL.B., U. of Mich., 1904; m. Dolly Maloney, Nov. 27, 1907; children—Dolly Louise (Mrs. James C. Donnell, II), James Maloney. Admitted to bar, 1905; city atty., Ogden, Utah, 1906-10; gen. counsel, Bamberger Elec. R.R., 1910-25, Utah-Idaho Central R.R. Co., 1915-39; one time head firm De Vine, Howell & Stine, Ogden; pres. Am. Packing and Provision Co. since 1936, Western Gateway Storage Co. since 1936; exec. v.p. Park City Consol. Mines Co., 1928-43; gen. counsel Utah Sperry Flour Co. (General Mills) 1917-41; Utah Globe Grain and Milling Co. (Pillsbury Flour Mills Co.), 1920-41; Utah counsel Mountain Fuel Sup. Co. since 1929; Utah counsel Am. Can Co. since 1914. Pres. Ogden C. of C., 1926-28. Republican. Elk. Clubs: Weber, Elks, Country (Ogden); Alta (Salt Lake City, Utah). Home: 2843 Fillmore Av. Office: 625 Eccles Bldg., Ogden, Utah. Died Dec. 7, 1943.

DE VOE, John M., pres. U.S. Tobacco Co. Home: 133 Otter Rock Dr., Greenwich, Conn. Office: 630 5th Av., New York, N.Y.* Died Jan. 20, 1946.

DeVORE, Harry S. (dĕ-vôr'), coll. pres.; b. Johnstown, Pa., July 27, 1891; s. Samuel and Dora (Lape) D.; A.B., Southern Methodist University, 1918, B.D., 1920; D.D. Southwestern Univ. 1932; student at Chicago Theol. Sem., summers 1928-32; LL.D., McMurry Coll., Abilene, Tex., 1944; m. Ann Elizabeth George, November 2, 1920; children—John Woodrow, James Kilgore, Mary Elizabeth. Minister, Meth. Ch., Oklahoma City, 1920, Elk City, Okla., 1920-23, Miami, Okla., 1923-25, Sapulpa, Okla., 1925-27, Grace Ch., Oklahoma City, 1927-31, Ardmore, Okla., 1931-35, Texarkana, Ark., 1935-38, Dallas Dist., 1938-42; pres. Central Coll., Fayette, Mo., since 1942; clerical member at large, Comm. on World Service and Finance, Meth. Ch., since 1940. Curator of Central College. Mem. National Academy of Political Science, Pi Gamma Mu, Tau Kappa Alpha, Pi Kappa Alpha, Theta Phi. Mason (Scottish Rite). Club: Rotary (Fayette). Home: 502 Linn St. Office: Central Coll., Fayette, Mo. Died Oct. 14, 1947.

DEVRIES, Herman, vocal teacher; b. New York City, Dec. 25, 1858; s. David and Rosa (Van Os) D.; ed. Paris Lycee Condorcet; m. Hattie Van Buren, Oct. 14, 1904; children—Rene, Mercedes. Singer 20 yrs. in Paris Grand Opera, Opera Comique, Metropolitan Opera Co. (2 yrs.), Covent Garden, Brussels, etc.; est. Herman Devries Studios, Chicago, 1900; music critic Chicago American. Decorated by French Govt. as Chevalier Legion d'Honneur, Officier Nicham Iftikar, Officier d'Academie, Officier de l'Instruction Publique. Compositions include: Le Meilleur Moment des Amours; Bonjour Suzon; Souvenir de l'Orient; Si J'etais Dieu; several pieces for piano and orchestra, etc. Home: Congress Hotel, Chicago. Died Aug. 24, 1949.

DEWART, William Thompson, publisher; b. Fenelon Falls, Ont., Can., Jan. 29, 1875; s. William and Jessie (Graham) D.; student U. of Rochester, class of 1896; Doctor of Letters, Union College, Schenectady, N.Y., 1937; m. Mary Louise, d. of Commodore and Mrs. Thomas H. Wheeler, Apr. 21, 1908; children—William Thompson, Thomas Wheeler, Mary (Mrs. Frederick Brockway Gleason, Jr.). Came to U.S., 1881. Pres. New York Sun, Inc., Frank A. Munsey Co., Mohican Co., Mohican Stores, Inc., Mohican Hotel Co., Merlis Real Estate Co., Inc.; chmn. bd. Munsey Trust Co., Washington, D.C. Chevalier Legion of Honor (France), 1928; Officer Legion of Honor (France), 1933; Commander of the Order of The White Rose of Finland, 1934; v.p. Am. Soc. of French Legion of Honor. Fellow Metropolitan Museum of Art (life). Republican. Episcopalian. Clubs: Pilgrims, Union League, Union, Advertising; Empire State (New York City); Round Hill (Greenwich, Conn.), Home: 660 Park Av., New York, N.Y., and "Willmary Manor, North St., Greenwich, Conn.; (summer) "Keewaydin," Alexandria Bay, New York. Office: 280 Broadway, New York, N.Y. Died Jan. 27, 1944.

DEWEY, Davis Rich, economist; b. Burlington, Vt., Apr. 7, 1858; s. Archibald S. and Lucina A. (Rich) D.; brother of John D. (q.v.); A.B., U. of Vt., 1879; Ph.D., Johns Hopkins, 1886; LL.D., U. of Vt., 1910; m. Mary C. Hopkins, June 29, 1886; children—Bradley, Dorothy (Mrs. A. Barr Comstock). Prin. Hyde Park High Sch., Chicago, 1881-83; asst. prof. economics and statistics, 1886-92, prof., 1893-1933, prof. emeritus since 1933, Mass. Institute Tech. Chmn. Mass. Bd. to Investigate Subject of Unemployed, 1893, and mem. Commn. to Investigate Public Charitable and Reformatory Interests of Mass., 1897; mem. com. on relations between employer and employe, 1904; spl. expert agt. on wages, 12th U.S. Census, 1902. Mem. Am. Statis. Assn. (sec. 1886-1906), Am. Econ. Assn. (pres. 1909), etc. Trustee Mass. Agrl. Coll., 1909-39. Mng. editor Am. Economic Review, 1911-40. Author: Syllabus on Political History since 1815, 1887; Financial History of the United States, 1902; Employees and Wages—Special Report, 12th Census, 1903; National Problems, 1907; Banking and Credit (with M. J. Shugrue), 1922. Editor: Discussions in Economics and Statistics, by Francis A. Walker, 1899. Dir. economic sect. of information and edn. service under the

Dept. of Labor, Washington, 1919. Fellow Am. Acad. Arts and Sciences; mem. Internat. Statis. Inst. Mem. emergency boards in disputes of r.r. employees where strikes were threatened, 1928-33; mem. 3 boards of arbitration set up by U.S. Board of Mediation, 1931-33. Home: 985 Memorial Drive, Cambridge, Mass. Died Dec. 13, 1942.

DEWEY, Lyster Hoxie, botanist; b. Cambridge, Mich., Mar. 14, 1865; s. Francis Asbury and Harriet (Smith) D.; B.S., Mich. Agrl. Coll., 1888; m. Etta Conkling, Aug. 22, 1889; children—Grace Marguerite, Mary Genevieve (dec.). Instr. botany, Mich. Agrl. Coll., 1888-90; asst. botanist, 1890-1902, botanist in charge of fiber investigations since 1902, U.S. Agrl. Dept. Conducted investigations on grasses and troublesome weeds; U.S. rep. to Internat. Fiber Congress, Soerabaia, Java, 1911. Fellow A.A.A.S.; mem. Washington Acad. of Sciences, Bot. Soc. Washington, Biol. Soc. Washington. Democrat. Presbyterian. Home: 4512 9th St., Washington. Died Nov. 1944.

DeWOLF, Richard Crosby, lawyer; b. Des Moines, Ia., July 13, 1875; s. Israel H. and Eliza (Crosby) DeW.; student Mass. Inst. Tech., 1896-98; LL.B., George Washington U., 1913; unmarried. Became govt. employe, 1898; clerk, U.S. Navy Yard, Portsmouth, N.H., 1898-1900, Manila, P.I., 1901-02; entered copyright office, 1907; engaged in practice of law, 1918-23; counsellor to Lithuanian Exec. Com. (later Lithuanian Legation), Washington, D.C., 1921-22; with copyright office since 1923, asst. register of copyrights, 1930-37 and 1942-43, acting register, 1944, spl. consultant, Feb.-May, 1945; ret. Served with U.S.M.C. in Spanish-American War. Club: Cosmos (Washington). Author: An Outline of Copyright Law, 1925. Decorated Order of Gediminas (Lithuania). Home: 23 Second St. N.E., Washington, D.C. Deceased.

DEXTER, Clarence Sawyer, mfr.; b. Chicago, Ill., June 4, 1883; s. George W. and Laura A. (Sawyer) D.; student Chicago Manual Training Sch., 1897-99; Armour Scientific Acad., 1900-01; m. Emma H. Foote, June 16, 1908; children—Frances Juanita (Mrs. Platt Dockery), Dorothy Muriel (Mrs. George T. Aitken). Manufacturer furniture since 1907; pres. and mem. bd. dirs. Imperial Furniture Co.; past pres. and dir. Furniture Mutual Ins. Co.; v.p. Furniture Mfrs. Warehouse Co.; mem. bd. dirs., and exec. com. Mich. Trust Co., Old Kent Bank. Dir. Grand Rapids Industries, Inc.; dir. Grand Trunk Western R.R. Company; past pres., dir. Grand Rapids Exposition Assn.; member bldg. com. Grand Rapids Civic Auditorium; dir. Furniture Manufacturers Association (past president); former member Library Commission of Grand Rapids; by invitation mem. Rice Foundtion Society. Republican. Episcopalian. Mason (32°, Shriner). Clubs: Peninsular, Kent Country. Home: 460 Fountain St. Office: 1642 Broadway N.W., Grand Rapids, Mich. Died Apr. 4, 1947; buried Grand Rapids Graceland Mausoleum.

DEXTER, Walter Friar, educator; b. Chicago, Ill., Nov. 21, 1886; s. Harry and Margaret (Bell) D.; A.B., Penn Coll., 1916; A.M., Columbia, 1919; Ed.M., and Ed.D., Harvard, 1921; m. Ethel Lenore Smith, Aug. 25, 1910; 1 son, Walter Franklin. Head Department of Education, Earlham Coll, Richmond, Ind., 1921-23; lecturer University of Virginia, summer 1923; pres. Whittier Coll., 1923-34; exec. sec. to gov. of Calif., 1935-37; supt. of pub. instrn. of State of Calif. and dir. of edn. since 1937. Mem. Phi Delta Kappa, Phi Beta Kappa. Republican. Quaker. Club: Lions (internat. pres. 1938-39). Address: Library-Courts Bldg., Sacramento, Calif. Died Oct. 1945.

DEXTER, William, lawyer, trustee; b. Beverley, Mass., July 15, 1897; A.B., Harvard, 1919, LL.B., 1922. Partner Choate, Hall & Stuart; mem. exec. com. and trustee Amoskeag Co., Boston & Maine R.R.; trustee and dir. many banks, trusts, transportation cos. and mfg. cos. of New England. Home: 67 Marlborough St. Office: 30 State St., Boston, Mass. Died Feb. 8, 1943.

DIAMANTOPOULOS, Cimon P. (thyā-măn-tŏ'pōō-lōs), E.E. and M.P. from Greece. Address: 2221 Massachusetts Av., Washington, D.C.* Died Dec. 6, 1946.

DICK, Charles, senator; b. Akron, Ohio, Nov. 3, 1858; s. Gottlieb and Magdalena D.; publ sch. edn.; m. Carrie R. Peterson, June 30, 1881. Admitted to bar, 1893, and since in practice at Akron. Served in Ohio N.G., since 1876; maj.-gen., since 1899; in active service 8th Ohio Vols. during Spanish-Am. War. Auditor Summit County, O., 1880-93; chmn. Rep. Co. Com., 1887-91; chmn. Rep. State Exec. Com., 1892-4, and 1899-1907; sec. at Chicago headquarters, Rep. Nat. Com., 1896; sec. Rep. Nat. Com., 1897-1900; del. Rep. Nat. convs., 1892, 96, del.-at-large, 1900, 04; mem. 55th to 58th Congresses, 1898-1904 (author of present Militia Bill); elected U.S. senator Mar. 2, 1904, for short and long terms to succeed late senator M. A. Hanna; term expired, 1911. Address: Akron, O. Died March 13, 1945.

DICK, George Alexander, dean; b. Cheapside, Ont., Can., Nov. 29, 1877; s. John and Jennie (Young) D.; came to U.S., 1880, parents U.S. citizens; prep. edn. Port Allegany pub. schs.; V.M.D., U. of Pa. Sch. of Vet. Medicine, 1904; B.S. in Animal Husbandry, Ia. State Coll., Ames, Ia., 1919; m. Cornelia Eugenie Colony, Sept. 5, 1905; 1 son, John Mandeville, Veterinarian, Kane, Pa., 1904-16; with Sch. of Vet. Medicine, U. of Pa., since 1917, dean, 1931-46; resigned June 1946; dir. operations, Sch. Animal Pathology, since 1937. Mem. Am. Vet. Med. Assn., U.S. Live Stock Sanitary Assn. Home: 234 Sagamore Rd., Upper Darby, Pa. Address: 39th and Woodland Av., Philadelphia, Pa. Died Oct. 15, 1948.

DICK, Paul Stephens, banker; b. La Grande, Ore., July 1, 1877; s. Franklin Taylor and Marquis Eleanor (Lewis) D.; student pub. schs. of La Grande and Portland, Ore.; LL.B., U. of Ore., 1902; m. Emma B. Timms, Aug. 27, 1903; children—Harvey Franklin, Philip Van, Robert Lewis. Successively bank messenger, clk., receiving teller Ainsworth Nat. Bank, Portland, 1895-1902; then paying teller, credit mgr., asst. cashier, cashier, v.p. U.S. Nat. Bank, Portland, pres. since 1931, dir. since 1923; pres. and dir. Central National Bank, 1929-31. Chmn. advisory bd. Nat. Credit Corp., 1931-32; chmn. advisory com. local agency R.F.C. since 1932; past pres. Portland Clearing House; former mem. adv. council of Federal Res. System; mem. Commerce and Marine Commn. Mem. Am. Bankers Assn., Phi Delta Phi. Republican. Baptist. Mason. Clubs: Arlington, Waverly (Portland). Home: 1914 N.E. 22d Av. Office: U.S. National Bank, Portland, Ore. Died May 9, 1945.

DICKERMAN, William Carter, locomotive builder; b. Bethlehem, Pa., Dec. 12, 1874; s. Charles Heber and Joy Ivy (Carter) D.; M.E., Lehigh U., 1896, D.Eng., 1938; m. Alice Carter, June 19, 1905; children—William Carter, Joy Ivy, Honour Redington, Cornelia Redington. Began with Milton Car Works, Milton, Pa., 1897, and on formation of Am. Car and Foundry Co., 1899, was made asst. mgr. Milton dist.; continued with same co. as sales agt., 1900-05, v.p. 1905-29, in charge of operations, 1919-29, in charge war div. of co. during World War; pres. Am. Locomotive Co. since 1929, now chmn. board of directors; dir. First Milton National Bank, Milton Mfg. Co.; chairman Montreal Locomotive Works, Ltd. (exec. com.); dir., mem. exec. com. Gen. Steel Castings Corp., Am. Car & Foundry Co., Am. Car & Foundry Export Co., Am. Car & Foundry Investment Corp.; dir., Flannery Bolt Co., Shippers Car Line Corp., Carter Carbureter Co., Superheater Co., Gen. Electric Co., Internat. Gen. Electric Co., Inc. Private, batt. adj. and 1st lt. Pa. N.G., 1897-1901. Trustee Lehigh U.; pres. and mem. Guild of Brackett Lecturers (Princeton U.); mem. U.S. and New York chambers of commerce. Member Am. Soc. Mech. Engrs., Am. Inst. Mining & Metall. Engrs., Am. Acad. Polit. and Social Science, N.Y. Society Colonial Wars, N.Y. Soc. S.R., Newcomen Soc. of England, Royal Soc. of Arts (London), Delta Phi. Clubs: Railroad, Manursing Island, Union, Pennsylvania Society, The Recess, University, Metropolitan; University (Phila.); Devon Yacht, Maidstone (East Hampton, N.Y.). Home: 955 Fifth Av., New York; also "Dune Dee," East Hampton, N.Y. Office: 30 Church St., New York, N.Y. Died Apr. 25, 1946.

DICKEY, Herbert Spencer, physician, explorer; b. Highland Falls, N.Y., Feb. 24, 1876; s. Charles Henry and Marie (Brosseau) D.; prep. edn., Phillips Exeter Acad., Exeter, N.H.; student New York U. Med. Sch., 1895-98; M.D., Boston, 1899; m. Elizabeth Staley, Oct. 6, 1925 (divorced 1933). Served as surgeon for the Tolima Mining Company, Colombia, S.A., 1900-06; resident physician, Peruvian Amazon Co., 1907-08, Antunes Rubber Estates, Remate de Males, Brazil, 1908-10, again with Peruvian Amazon Co., 1911-12, La Romana Sugar Estates, Dominican Republic, 1914-16; chief surgeon, Guayaquil & Quito R.R., 1923-25. Served as officer, rank of capt., Mil. Intelligence Div., U.S. Army, Southern Dept., 1918-19; maj., Mil. Intelligence Div. Res. Associate in South American research, Southwest Museum, Los Angeles. Decorated Order Al Merito by Ecuador, "for important services to the Country," 1937. Mem. American Ethnological Society. Presbyterian. Clubs: Explorers, Ends of the Earth (N.Y.); Adventurers (Los Angeles). Author: The Misadventures of a Tropical Medico (with Daniel Hawthorne), 1929; My Jungle Book, 1932. Contributor to the New York Times. Believed to be 1st white man to descend Caqueta River from Colombia to its mouth. Principal explorations: 5 times on foot over Ecuadorian Andes, exploring affluents of Amazon; explored River Tomo, affluent to Orinoco; located source of Orinoco, July 14, 1931; organized and led first "Dude" expdn. over the Andes and down the Amazon, 1932; accompanied Sir Roger Casement on his trip to Amazon, 1911; discovered and removed from Ecuador nearly 500 archæol. specimens for Southwest Mus., 1936; originated process for extracting quinine from low-grade cinchona bark in Ecuador, 1941. Address: Explorers Club, 10 West 72d St., New York, N.Y.; and Huigra, Ecuador. Died Oct. 28, 1948.

DICKEY, James Allen, rural economics and sociology; b. Burlington, North Carolina, Apr. 18, 1892; s. James Andrew and Permelia Cecelia D.; A.B., Elon (N.C.) Coll., 1912; A.M., U. of N.C., 1922; Ph.D., Cornell U., 1931; m. Naomi Cecelia Joyner, Oct. 19, 1913; children—Allen Joyner, Virginia Katharine. Instr. Univ. of N.C., 1920-21; research asst. Cornell U., 1922-24; prof. rural economics and sociology, U. of Ark., 1924-31; sr. economist, Federal Farm Bd., June 1931-32; with U.S. Dept. of Agr., 1932-36; dir. Assn. of Sugar Producers of Puerto Rico since 1936; editor Bulletin of Public Service. Mem. Ark. State Indusl. Commn. Made survey of industrial resources of Ark.; survey of summer camping in the South for Playground and Recreation Assn. America; econ and social survey of 500 dairy farms in Schoharie County, N.Y. for Cornell U., in cooperation with U.S. Dept. Agr.; survey of agr. in Porto Rico, 1929, as mem. Brookings Inst. of Economics staff. Mem. Ark. Real Estate Assn., Alpha Kappa Delta, Sigma Xi. Democrat. Mem. Christian (O'Kelley) Ch. Wrote (U. of Ark. bulletins): Farm Organization and Management; Three Years' Study of Farm Management and Income in a Typical Upland Section of Arkansas. Home: 3201 N. Wakefield St., Arlington, Va. Office: 732 Shoreham Bldg., Washington, D.C. Died Nov. 20, 1943.

DICKEY, Samuel, theologian; b. Oxford, Pa., Nov. 27, 1872; s. Rev. Samuel and Jennie (Rutherford) D.; A.B., Princeton, 1894, A.M., 1897; grad. Princeton Theol. Sem., 1897; student univs. of Berlin, Marburg, Erlangen, 1897-99, Athens, 1901, Jena, 1904; m. Louise Parke Atherton, Feb. 26, 1908. Ordained Presbyn. ministry, 1899; prof. classical and Hellenistic Greek, Lincoln U., Pa., 1899-1903; adj. prof., 1903-05, prof. N.T. literature and exegesis, 1905-23, McCormick Theol. Sem., Chicago. Author: The Constructive Revolution of Jesus, 1923. Contbr. to theol. reviews, Standard Bible Dictionary, The Outline of Christianity, etc. Home: Runnymede Orchards, Oxford, Pa. Died June 27, 1944.

DICKIE, Alexander Jack, editor; b. San Francisco, Calif., Sept. 30, 1876; s. George William and Anna (Jack) D.; A.B. in Mech. and Elec. Engring. U. of Calif., 1898; m. Clara Gertrude Paulin, Apr. 3, 1901; children—Arthur William, Gordon Alexander. Engaged in marine elec. engring., Union Iron Works, San Francisco, Calif., 1898-1904; in fruit growing, real estate and farm management, San Jose, Calif., 1904-18; editor Pacific Marine Review, San Francisco, Calif., 1918-47, cons. editor since 1947. Fellow Am. Soc. M.E. (mgr. nat. council; chmn. San Francisco sect.); mem. examining com. for engring. curriculae, Engineering Council Professional Development. Elder of Presbyterian Ch. U.S.A. Club: Engineers (San Francisco). Home: 1036 Mariposa Av., Berkeley, Calif. Office: 500 Sansome St., San Francisco, Calif. Died Aug. 17, 1948.

DICKINSON, Hobart Cutler, physicist; b. Bangor, Me., Oct. 11, 1875; s. George Lyman and Emma T. (Cutler) D.; A.B., Williams Coll., 1900, A.M., 1902; studied Clark U., 1902-03, Ph.D., 1910; m. Elizabeth Wells, 1903 (died 1921); children—David (dec.), Bradley Wells (adopted); m. 2d, Mabel V. Kitson, 1923; 1 dau., Anne Katherine. Became connected with Bur. of Standards, Washington, 1903, asst. physicist, 1906-10, asso., 1910-16; physicist, 1916-21; research mgr. Soc. Automotive Engrs., 1921-23; chief Div. of Heat and Power, Bur. of Standards, 1923-45. Fellow A.A.A.S., Am. Physical Soc.; mem. Am. Soc. Testing Materials, Am. Soc. Refrigerating Engrs., Washington Acad. Sciences, Washington Philos. Soc. Conglist. Clubs: Cosmos (Washington, D.C.); Williams (New York). Home: 4629 30th St. N.W., Washington. Died Nov. 27, 1949; buried Washington.

DICKINSON, Luren Dudley, ex-governor; b. Niagara County, N.Y., Apr. 15, 1859; s. Dani and Hannah (Leavens) D.; ed. district sch. and Charlotte (Mich.) High Sch.; m. Zora Della Cooley, Oct. 16, 1888; 1 adopted dau. (niece), Rilla Ethel (Mrs. Laverne Patterson; now dec.). Taught rural schs., winters, for 19 yrs.; formerly prin. Potterville (Mich.) High Sch.; farmer, fruit grower, stock raising many years; served as assessor of sch. dist., 11 yrs., also town clerk, supervisor and supt. of schools. Mem. State Ho. of Reps., 1897-98, 1905-06, 1907-08; State Senate, 1909-10; lt. gov. of Mich., 1915-21, 1927-33 and 1939; became governor of Michigan, March 17, 1939, at the death of Gov. Frank D. Fitzgerald remaining in office to Jan. 1941, when term expired. Mem. County Rep. Com. 24 yrs. Mem. Charlotte Grange; trustee Eaton Meth. Ch.; del. 8 times to Gen. Conf. M.E. Ch. and served as mem. of inter-church commn. of Meth. churches; also del. Uniting conf. of Meth. churches; v.p. Men's Work Commn. of M.E. Ch.; pres. Laymen's Assn. M.E. Ch.; state chmn. Near East Relief. Hon. LL.D., conferred by Huntington Coll., 1940. Republican. Home: R.F.D., Charlotte, Mich. Died Apr. 22, 1943.

DICKINSON (Clinton) Roy, editor, writer; b. Newark, N.J., Mar. 14, 1888; s. Philemon Olin and Anna Elizabeth (Van Riper) D.; grad. Newark Acad., 1905; Litt.D., Princeton, 1909; m. Marjorie S. Bostick, Feb. 15, 1916; children—Philemon, Katharine (Mrs. James L. Macwithey), Clinton Roy, Jr. With Cosmopolitan Mag., 1910-15, Puck, 1915-16, New York Times, 1916, Frank Presbrey Co., advt. agts., 1916-17; asso. editor Printers' Ink and Printers' Ink Monthly, 1919-33; pres. Printers' Ink Pub Co., 1933-42; resigned to enter Army of the U.S. with rank of colonel, 1942. First lt. and later capt. and major, office of chief of staff, U.S. Army, World War; lt. col. O.R.C. Mem. President Harding's Unemployment Conf. (with Samuel Gompers signed minority report against cut in wages). Dir. Council for Democracy. Mem. National Publishers Assn. (dir.), Asso. Business Papers, Inc. (dir.). Methodist. Clubs: Princeton, Dutch Treat, Advertising, Players, Essex County Country, National Press. Contbr. short stories to Harper's, Scribner's, Ladies' Home Journal, Am. Legion Monthly, Elks Magazine, Liberty, etc., articles to Printers' Ink, etc.; included in O'Brien's Best Short Stories of the Year, 1918, 26 and 28. Author: Wages and Wealth, 1931; The Cowards Never Started, 1933;

The Ultimate Frog, 1939. Office: 21st and C St. N.W., Washington, D.C.* Deceased.

DICKINSON, Roscoe Gilkey, univ. prof.; b. Brewer, Me., June 10, 1894; s. George Edward Mott and Georgie Estelle (Gilkey) D.; B.S., Mass. Inst. Tech., 1915; Ph.D., Calif. Inst. Tech., 1920; m. Madeline Grace Haak, Apr. 7, 1917; children—Robert Winchester, Dorothy. Asst. in theoretical chemistry, Mass. Inst. Tech., 1915-16, asst., 1916-17, research associate in chemistry, Calif. Inst. Tech., 1917-26, nat. research fellow, 1920-23, Internat. Edn. Bd. fellow (Europe), 1924-25, asst. prof. physical chemistry, 1926-28, asso. prog., 1928-38, prof. since 1938, acting dean of Grad. Sch., 1942-45. Engaged in war research, Office of Sci. Research and Development, since 1941. Mem. Am. Chem. Soc., Sigma Xi. Home: 530 Bonita Av., Pasadena 8. Office: California Inst. of Technology, E. California St., Pasadena 4, Calif. Died July 13, 1945.

DIEFENBACH, Elmer G., business exec.; b. Ebenezer, N.Y., Aug. 4, 1893; s. Michael and Anna Mary (Schneckenburger) D.; B.C.S., New York Univ., 1917; m. Mary Elizabeth Demarest, Dec. 17, 1928; children—Robert Elmer, Richard Peter, John Michael, Mary Anne. In bond Dept., Guaranty Trust Co., New York, N.Y., 1917-19; Bonbright & Co., New York, 1919-22; vice pres. and pres., G. E. Barrett & Co., New York, 1923-32; vice pres. Blair & Co., 1934-39; chmn. exec. com. and dir. Am. Securities Corp. since 1946, Certain-teed Products Corp. since 1944; chmn. bd. dirs. Marion-Power Shovel Co. since 1946; pres. and dir. Electric Ferries, Inc. since 1933. Dir. Freeport Sulphur Co., Panhandle Eastern Pipe Line Co. Served in U.S. Army, World War I. Mem. Nat. Planning Assn. (mem. bus. com.), New York State Chamber of Commerce, Pan-Am. Soc. Republican. Clubs: The Recess, Canadian (New York); Manursing Island, Apawamis. Home: Purchase Lane, Rye, N.Y. Office: 25 Broad St., New York 4, N.Y. Died Feb. 27, 1949; buried Gate of Heaven Cemetery, Valhalla, N.Y.

DIEHL, Charles Sanford, journalist; b. Flintstone, Md., Aug. 8, 1854; s. Carl F. and Amanda F. D.; ed. pub. schs., Ottawa, Ill.; m. Ellen Watson Chandler, Sept. 9, 1879 (died May 21, 1937); children—Chandler (dec.), Grace Chandler (Mrs. S. F. Shaw). Published "Our Boys," 1871-73; on staff Chicago Times, 1873-83; day mgr. Associated Press service, Chicago office, 1883, supt. Pacific coast division, San Francisco, 1887-93, assistant general manager at New York and Chicago, 1893-1911; owner and publisher San Antonio (Tex.) Light (with Harrison L. Beach), 1911-24. Reported Sioux Indian campaign of 1876, 1877, and winter campaign against Sioux, 1881; prepared plans to report Spanish-American War for Associated Press, 1898, taking personal charge staff war corrs. in field during war. Organized 1st Regt. Ill. N.G., 1874 (now 131st Inf., 33d Div., U.S. Army), filling all grades from 2nd lt. to lt.-col. Author: The Staff Correspondent, 1931. Club: San Antonio Country. Home: 301 Terrell Rd., San Antonio, Tex. Died Aug. 19, 1946.

DIEHL, Jacob, clergyman and educator; b. at Greencastle, Pa., Feb. 20, 1884; s. John Luther and Martha Ellen (Kuhn) D.; A.B., Gettysburg (Pa.) College, 1903; hon. LL.D., 1930; student at Gettysburg Theol. Seminary, 1907, Leipzig U., 1908-09 and 1914; D.D., Carthage (Ill.) Coll., 1920; m. Sara Matilda Klapp, Apr. 22, 1914; children—Dorothea Prieson, Sara Matilda, William Adolph, Marian Louise. Ordained ministry Luth. Ch., 1910; pastor St. John's Luth. Ch., Lock Haven, Pa., 1909-15, Trinity Luth. Ch., Carthage, Ill., 1915-22; prof. religious edn., Carthage Coll., 1920-22; pastor Trinity Luth. Ch., Selinsgrove, Pa., 1924-29; acting pres., Susquehanna U., 1927-28; pres. Carthage Coll., 1929-33. Dir. Luth. Mutual Life Ins. Co.; spl. rep. Board of Pensions, United Luth. Ch. Served as chaplain, 1st lt., U.S. Army, Camp Custer, Battle Creek, Mich., Feb. 1918-Jan. 1919. Mem. A.A.A.S., Alpha Tau Omega, Pi Gamma Mu, Phi Beta Kappa. Republican. Mason. Home: Lock Haven, Pa. Died May 19, 1946.

DIETZMAN, Richard Priest, ex-judge; b. Louisville, Ky., Aug. 13, 1883; s. Albert S. and Nellie Priest (Chamberlin) D.; A.B., Harvard, 1905, LL.B., 1907; m. Esther Elisabeth Sesmer, Nov. 13, 1935; children—Elisabeth Priest, Anne Chamberlin. Admitted to Kentucky bar, 1907; began practice at Louisville; mayor's counsel, City of Louisville, 1922-23; first assistant city attorney, Louisville, 1923-24, city attorney, July-Nov. 1924; asso. judge Court of Appeals of Ky. (Supreme Court), term beginning 1924, reëlected 1927; chief justice of Ky., 1931-35, now practicing law also prof. Jefferson Sch. of Law; dir. Federal Home Loan Bank of Cincinnati, Kentucky Home Mutual Life Ins. Co. Mem. Sewerage Commn. City of Louisville. Trustee King's Daughters Home for Incurables, Louisville. Republican. Episcopalian. Mason, Elk. Mem. Am., Ky. State and Louisville bar assns., Am. Legion. Clubs: University, Filson (Louisville). Home: 2223 Millvale Road. Office: Kentucky Home Life Bldg., Louisville, Ky. Died Dec. 22, 1943.

DIFFENDERFER, George M. (dĭf'ĕn-dĕr-fĕr), clergyman; b. East Petersburg, Lancaster County, Pa., Jan. 5, 1869; s. Emanuel G. and Frances L. (Knier) D.; A.B., Gettysburg (Pa.) Coll., 1893, A.M., 1896, D.D., 1911; grad. Luth. Theol. Sem., Gettysburg, 1896; attended lectures in philosophy, U. of Berlin, 1910; m. Laura A. Diehl, June 30, 1896; children—Isabel Romayne (Mrs. John Russell Yates), George M. Ordained Luth. ministry, 1896; pastor St. Paul's Ch., Newport, Pa., 1896-1900, First Ch., Carlisle, 1900-14 (built ch., $130,000, and hosp., $125,000), Luther Place Memorial Ch., Washington, D.C., 1919-1930. Lecturer on Comparative Religions, Dickinson Coll., 1910-11, Washington Sch. of Religious Edn., 1922-24, on Evolution of North American Indian, Oberammergau, God's Garden of Wonders. Chaplain U.S. Industrial Indian Sch., Carlisle, 1900-10; exec. sec. ministerial relief, Luth. Ch., 1914-17; mem. Pa. Relief Bd.; chaplain at Newport News, Va., 1917-18; maj., chaplain O.R.C., U.S. Army. Pres. Washington Fed. of Chs., 1922-23; trustee Tressler Orphanage (v.p. since 1924); trustee Standard Woman's Coll. since 1923; mem. Com. on Army and Navy Chaplains, Washington Com. of Federal Council Churchs of Christ; trustee United Christian Endeavor Soc. Grand Chaplain Pa. A.F. and A.M., 1924-25; K.P. Republican. Editor of Army Chaplain, 1934-36. Home: 2 N. Hanover St., Carlisle, Pa.* Died May 16, 1943.

DIGGES, Dudley, actor; b. Dublin, Ireland, June 9, 1880; s. James Dudley and Catherine (Forsythe) D.; student Christian Bros. Sch., Dublin, 1886-90; student St. Mary's Coll., Dublin, 1890-93; m. Mary T. Quinn, Aug. 27, 1907. Came to U.S., 1904, naturalized, 1933. Co-founder of The Irish Nat. Theatre, 1902, appeared in 1st prodn. of Yeat's, Cathleen-ni-Houliham and AE's Deirdre, 1902; engaged for Irish Theatre, World's Fair, St. Louis, Mo., 1904; with Charles Frohman prodns., New York, 1907-11; with George Arliss as stage mgr., 1911-18; played Jimmy Caesar in St. John Ervine's John Ferguson, 1st New York Theatre Guild success, 1919; played leading characters with Guild 1919-29; dir. several Shaw plays including Heartbreak House, New York; starred in, On Borrowed Time, 1938, The Masque of Kings, 1937, The Searching Wind, 1944, Listen Professor, 1943; has played Harry Hope in Eugene O'Neill's The Iceman Cometh, New York 1946-47. Recipient gold medal award of Am.-Irish Hist. Soc., New York, for leadership in Irish and Am. drama, 1939. Club: The Players. Home: One West 64th St., New York, N.Y. Died Oct. 24, 1947.

DILLER, Theodore, physician; b. Lancaster, Pa., Aug. 25, 1863; s. of George J. and Mary (Kreider) D.; M.D., U. of Pa., 1886; m. Rebecca Chambers Craig, Sept. 8, 1899 (died 1908); children—Theodore Craig, George E., Winifred (Mrs. A. C. Mann). Practiced at Lancaster and Danville, Pa., 1886-90, Pittsburg since 1890. Republican. Episcopalian. Mem. A.M.A., Am. Neurol. Assn., Pittsburgh Neurol. Soc., Pittsburgh Acad. Medicine. Clubs: Duquesne, University. Author: Franklin's Contribution to Medicine, 1911; Washington in Western Pennsylvania, 1916; Pioneer Medicine in Western Pennsylvania, 1927. Home: 6861 Penn Av., Pittsburgh, Pa. Died Oct. 6, 1943.

DILLON, Charles, editor; b. Brooklyn, N.Y., Jan. 9, 1869; s. Joseph and Eliza (Halligan) D.; ed. pub. schs., night schs.; m. Florence Voris Pierson, Dec. 30, 1901; children—John Knox, Ralph Paul, Millicent Meredith. With Kansas City Star 10 yrs.; mng. editor for Senator Capper, at Topeka, Kan., 6 yrs.; asst. to chmn. Western Ry. Presidents' Com. on Public Relations, Chicago, 5 yrs., also same position on Eastern Presidents' Com., New York; pres. Publication Corp., Chicago, and mng. editor Railway Review, 1926; v.p. and mng. editor of Transportation (monthly mag.), Los Angeles, 1927-31; pres. Publications, Inc., San Bernardino, Calif., 1933-35; columnist Beverly Hills Citizen and Rogers allied publs., Beverly Hills, Calif., 1937. With Exclusive Features, syndicate, 1938; mem. faculty U. of Southern Calif., Sch. of Journalism, 1939. Decorated by King Albert of Belgium, 1920, for war service; mem. Belgian League of Honor. Founded chair of industrial journalism in Kansas State College, Manhattan, Kans., 1910. Mem. Sigma Delta Chi. Republican. Presbyterian. Mason (32°). Club: Authors' (Hollywood). Author: Journalism for High Schools, 1919, enlarged edit., 1931; Dillon's Desk Book, 1919; Speaking of Presidents; also many articles and stories in Saturday Evening Post, American Magazine, World's Work, Collier's etc. Address: 16 Josephine St., Sausalito, Calif. Died Aug. 16, 1942.

DILLON, Edmond Bothwell, judge; b. Ironton, O., Feb. 9, 1869; s. Rev. John W. and Mary Catharine (Cox) D.; student Ohio Wesleyan U., 1885-9, M.A., 1906; m. Marian Daisy Whitney, May 8, 1895. Admitted to Ohio bar, 1891, and practiced in Columbus; judge Ct. of Common Pleas, Franklin County, since 1903; prof. of law, Ohio State U., since 1904. Mem. Ohio State Bd. Law Examiners, 1897-03; mem. Columbus Civil Service Commn., 1899-03; nominated for gov. of Ohio by Rep. State Conv., 1912 (declined). Mem. Phi. Kappa Psi. Methodist. Mason, Elk, K.P. Clubs: Athletic, Arlington Country. Home: 83 Wilson Av. Address: Court House, Columbus, O. Died Nov. 11, 1919.

DILLON, Fannie (Charles), pianist, composer; b. Denver, Colo., Mar. 16, 1881; d. Henry Clay and Florence Hood Dillon; moved with family to Long Beach, Calif., 1890; studied composition with Heinrich Urban, Hugo Kaun and Rubin Goldmark, piano with Leopold Godowsky, Berlin, Germany, 1900-06. Teacher, pianist and composer, Los Angeles, 1906-10; teacher at Pomona Coll., 1910-13, in Los Angeles high schs., 1918-1941; on invitation of Beethoven Soc. of N.Y., gave concert of her compositions, New York, Feb. 9, 1918; selected as California's first representative woman composer and sent to MacDowell Colony, Peterboro, N.H., June-Sept. 1921, and in 1923, 1933, 1942, 1944 Composer of piano, vocal, orchestral and chamber music compositions; composer of music for outdoor dramas, "Nevertheless—Old Glory," "The Desert Calls," "Tahquitz." Founder of Woodland Theater at Fawnskin, Big Bear Lake, 1921, gen. mgr. of successful seasons, 1926-29. Mem. League of Western Writers. Clubs: Southern Calif. Women's Press (hon. mem.), Big Bear Lake Women's, Schubert, Pasadena Fine Arts, Matinee Musical. Home: Robins Wold, Fawnskin, Calif.; also 429 Sturtevant Drive, Sierra Madre, Calif. Died Feb. 21, 1947; buried in Forest Lawn Memorial Park, Glendale, Calif.

DILLON, John Jordan, coll. pres.; b. Derby, Conn., Sept. 2, 1898; s. David Joseph and Mary Jane (Houlihan) D.; A.B., Providence (R.I.) Coll., 1924; A.M., Catholic U. of America, 1929; S. T. Lr., Coll. of Immaculate Conception, Washington, D.C., 1930; Ph.D., Internat. Pontifical U., "Angelicum," Rome, Italy, 1932; LL.D., Brown U., 1941, R.I. State Coll., 1942; Professor philosophy, Providence College, 1932-36, asst. dean, 1932-36, pres. since 1936; superior Dominican Fathers since 1936; treas. Providence Coll. Corp. Served in U.S.N., 1918-19. Mem. Am. Legion, Thomistic Inst., Delta Epsilon Sigma. Roman Catholic. K.C. Home: 55 Chapel St., Derby, Conn. Died Dec. 1, 1944.

DILLON, John Richard; b. Highland Falls, N.Y., Feb. 16, 1890; graduate New York U., class of 1912; m. Marie Treanor; children—Marjorie Palmer (Mrs. Conrad H. Pinches), John R. Partner, Hayden, Stone & Co., 1929-44; dir. Lone Star Cement Corp., Am. Agrl. Chem. Co., Continental-Diamond Fibre Co., Carey, Baxter & Kennedy, Inc.; dir. and mem. exec. com. Twentieth Century-Fox Film Corp.; dir. and mem. finance com. Raybestos-Manhattan, Inc., National Theatres Corp.; dir. Skouras Theatres Corp., Haveg Corp.; chmn. bd. Unexcelled Chem. Corp. Home: 322 Corlies Av., Pelham 65, N.Y. Office: 25 Broad St., New York 4, N.Y. Died Sept. 20, 1948.

DILLON, Thomas J., newspaper editor; b. Baldwin, Wis., May 20, 1878; s. Patrick C. and Mary (Maloney) D.; ed. St. Boniface (Manitoba, Can.) Coll. and U. of Notre Dame; m. Clarissa Church, June 28, 1906; 1 son, Thomas Church. Began, 1897; reporter successively at Minneapolis and St. Paul, Minn., Helena and Butte, Mont., Salt Lake City, Utah, Santa Fe, N.M., El Paso, Tex., Kansas City, Mo., then with Tacoma Ledger, later editor Everett Herald and spl. writer Seattle Star; founder, 1906, and was first editor Portland News; successively, 1910-20, editorial writer and mng. editor Seattle Post-Intelligencer; editor of Minneapolis Morning and Evening Tribune, 1920-40; editor-in-chief Minneapolis Morning Tribune, 1940-45, editorial writer and columnist 1945-46; retired 1946. Clubs: Seattle Press (life mem.), San Francisco Press (life). Home: 6107 Ascot Drive, Piedmont Pines, Oakland 11, Calif. Died Jan. 27, 1949.

DIMAN, John Hugh (dī'măn), clergyman, educator; b. Brookline, Mass., May 24, 1863; s. Rev. J. Lewis and Emily Gardner (Stimson) D.; A.B., Brown U., 1885, hon. A.M., 1903; B.D., Episcopal Theol. Sch., Cambridge, Mass., 1888; A.M., Harvard U., 1896; student St. Charles House Oxford, England, 1918-19, Ecclesiastical Academy, Rome, 1919-20. Ordained deacon Episcopal Ch., 1898; with St. Columbia's Chapel, Middletown, R.I., 1888-92; teacher University Grammar Sch., Providence, R.I., 1892-95; founder and headmaster St. George's School, Middletown, R.I., 1896-1917; founder of the Diman Vocational School, Fall River, Massachusetts, 1912; entered Roman Catholic Church, 1917; captain Am. Red Cross in Europe, 1918; ordained priest, 1921, curate, Our Lady of Lourdes, N.Y. City, 1922-23; joined Benedictine Order, 1923; changed name of John Byron Diman (legal name) to John Hugh Diman; mem. Community of St. Anselm's Priory, Washington, D.C., 1924-26; headmaster Priory Sch., Portsmouth, R.I., 1926-42 (except Sept. 1932-June 1934); prior, Portsmouth Priory, Nov. 1929-Aug. 1940. Pres. Harvard Teachers Assn., 1908-10. Address: Portsmouth Priory, Portsmouth, R.I. Died March 17, 1949.

DINAND, Joseph Nicholas, clergyman; b. Boston, Mass., Dec. 3, 1869; s. John Patrick and Julia Elizabeth (Looney) D.; ed. Jesuit Novitiate, Frederick, Md.; studied philosophy and theology, Woodstock Coll. Ordained R.C. priest, 1903; prof. classics and mathematics, Coll. of St. Francis Xavier, New York, N.Y., 5 yrs.; headmaster, Coll. of St. George, Kingston, Jamaica, 3 yrs.; asst. superior novitiate of St. Andrew-on-Hudson, Poughkeepsie, N.Y., 3 yrs.; later pres. College of the Holy Cross; became vicar apostolic and R.C. bishop in Jamaica; now bishop at Boston, Mass. Address: Boston. Died July 29, 1943.

DINEHART, Alan (dīn'härt), actor, producer, writer; b. St. Paul, Minn., Oct. 3, 1890; s. Mason Alan and Elizabeth (Green) D.; grad. high sch., Butte, Mont.; student U. of Mont.; m. Louise Dyer; 1 son, Alan; m. 2d, Mozelle Britton, June 28, 1933; 1 son, Mason Alan 3rd. First appearance on stage in "Woman of the West," Chicago, 1912; part of Michael in "The Gypsy Trail" at Chicago, 1918; appeared in plays in N.Y. City and elsewhere to 1931; appeared in "The Alley Cat," of which he was co-author, in 1934; collaborated on "In Love with Love," "Applesauce" and others; staged "The Patsy," "The Merry-Go-Round" and others, 1925-29; in motion pictures since 1931, his later pictures being "The Pay-

Off," "Thanks a Million, "It Had to Happen," "Big Town Girl," "Ali Baba Goes to Town," "Dangerously Yours," "This is My Affair," "Step Lively Jeeves," "Fifty Roads to Town," "Midnight Taxi," "Peach Edition," "Love on a Budget," "Up the River," "Fast and Loose," "Rebecca of Sunnybrook Farm," "Second Fiddle," "Elsa Maxwell's Hotel for Women," "Two Bright Boys," "Strictly Dishonorable," "Girl Trouble," "Mr. Smug," "Blondie Buys a Horse," "Sweet Rosie O'Grady," "The Heat's On," and "Ten Percent Woman," appeared in play, "Separate Rooms" (co-author, director and co-producer same), Plymouth Theatre, N.Y. City. Author: (with Joseph Carole) "Thanks for My Wife"; (with Joseph Carole) "Salutary Lodge." Radio entertainer. Chmn. of entertainment Nat. Defense Week for Pacific Coast. Full legal name: Mason Alan Dinehart II. Home: 3061 Lake Hollywood Dr., Hollywood, Calif.; (ranch) 6400 Hawarden Dr., Riverside, Calif. Address: 8776 Sunset Blvd., Beverly Hills, Calif. Died July 17, 1944.

DINNEEN, Fitz-George (dĭn-nēn'), clergyman; b. Chateaugay, N.Y., July 10, 1866; s. Michael J. and Katherine (Fitzgerald) D.; grad. St. Mary's (Kan.) Coll., 1889; student St. Louis U., 1895-98. Mem. Soc. of Jesus (Jesuits). Teacher Creighton U., 1898-1902, Loyola U., Chicago, 1906-19; pastor St. John's Collegiate Ch., Omaha, 1919-22; pastor, St. Mary's, Kan., 1922-24; in charge St. Ignatius Ch., Chicago, since 1924. Trustee Loyola U. Dir. Legion of Decency (dealing with the motion picture problem, clean and unfit pictures, etc.), Chicago Archdiocese. Home: 6559 Glenwood Av., Chicago, Ill. Died Sep. 13, 1944.

DINSMORE, Carlos Millson, church official; b. nr. St. Mary's, Ont., Can., Jan. 28, 1875; s. Andrew and Mary B. (Millson) D.; brought to U.S., 1881; A.B., Kalamazoo (Mich.) Coll., 1900; B.D., U. of Chicago, 1907; D.D., Franklin (Ind.) Coll., 1920; m. Bertha Irwin Buschman, Aug. 26, 1903; children—Dorothy Irwin (Mrs. N. P. Bloom), Margaret Millson (Mrs. H. A. Lynes), William James, Bertha Elizabeth Tedder. Ordained to the Baptist ministry, 1902; pastor at Ocoya and Harvey, Ill., until 1907, Anderson, Ind., 1907-14, Evansville, 1914-15; gen. supt. Ind. Bapt. Conv., 1915-31; sec. Am. Bapt. Home Mission Soc., 1931-Sept. 1941; pastor First Bapt. Ch., South Haven, Mich., since Oct. 1941. Republican. Home: Beechwood Hills, Covert, Mich. Died Apr. 5, 1948.

DINWIDDIE, Courtenay, sociologist; b. Alexandria, Va., Oct. 9, 1882; s. William and Emily Albertine (Bledsoe) D.; grad. Greenwood (Va.) Sch. for Boys, 1898; A.B., Southwestern U., 1901; grad. work U. of Va., 1901-03; m. Susan Anderson Ellis, May 8, 1907; children—Courtenay Lee (dec.), Hope (dec.), Jean (Mrs. John Jay Weldon), Donal. Mgr. Greenwood (Va.) Fruit Farm, 1903-04; sec. to pres. bd. of Bellevue and Allied Hospitals, New York, 1905-06; exec. sec., N.Y. City Visiting Com. of State Charities Aid Assn., 1906-10; sec. Duluth Asso. Charities and supt. City Bd. of Pub. Welfare, 1910-13; supt. Cincinnati Anti-Tuberculosis League, 1913-18; organizer Public Health Federation, active in Cincinnati Social Unit Experiment, 1917-20; instructor community organization Johns Hopkins U., 1921-22; exec. sec. Nat. Child Health Council, 1920-23; dir. Am. Child Health Assn., 1923-25; dir. of Child Health Program, Commonwealth Fund, 1922-30; consultant U.S. Children's Bureau, consultant in child hygiene N.Y. City Health Dept., 1930-31; gen. sec. Nat. Child Labor Com. since 1930. Awarded Mack gold medal for Bible Study, Southwestern U., 1900. Mem. advisory com. Ednl. Policies Commn., N.E.A.; mem. com. on research and prevention Internat. Soc. for Crippled Children, Inc. Mem. Am. Acad. Polit. and Social Science, Nat. Soc. for the Study of Edn., Soc. for the Exptl. Study of Edn.; fellow Am. Pub. Health Assn. Presbyterian. Author: Community Responsibility, 1921; Child Health and the Community, 1931. Contbr. Ency. of the Social Sciences. Home: Brookside Av., Irvington, N.Y. Office: 419 4th Av., New York, N.Y. Died Sep. 16, 1943.

DISMUKES, Douglas Eugene (dĭs-mūks), rear admiral (retired); b. Macon, Miss., Oct. 1, 1869; s. George and Agnes Salina (Harrison) D.; grad. U.S. Naval Academy, 1890; married Maude A. Hench, September 16, 1897; children—Ann Ellen (deceased), Judith Lee, Douglas Eugene. Advanced through grades to captain, United States Navy, 1918; promoted by special act of Congress to rear admiral upon retirement from active service, 1925, in recognition of bring U.S.S. Mt. Vernon into port after being torpedoed 200 miles off coast of France. Served in Spanish-Am. War; comd. U.S.S. Petrel, Haiti Revolution, 1911; capt. eastern terminal port, Panama Canal Zone, 1913-14; comdr. U.S. Naval Training Sta., Newport, R.I., 1919-21; comdr. U.S.S. Nevada, special mission to Rio de Janeiro Internat. Expn., 1922; comdt. Navy Yard, Portsmouth, N.H., 1923-25; recalled to active duty, Jan. 1942; comdg. Me. Maritime Acad., Castine, Me. Awarded D.S.M.; citation for "exceptionally meritorious services" (U.S.); decorated Officer Legion of Honor (France). Home: 32 Livermore St., Portsmouth, N.H. Died Dec. 2, 1949.

DISTLER, Carl Martin, lawyer; b. Baltimore, Mar. 24, 1886; s. John C. and Elizabeth E. (Felber) D.; A.B., Johns Hopkins, 1907; LL.B., U. of Maryland, 1909; unmarried. Admitted to Md. bar, 1909, in general practice of law, Baltimore, Md., since 1909; vice pres. and dir. Riggs, Distler and Co., Inc. Mem. jail board City of Baltimore since 1943; mem. draft advisory bd., 1917, and since 1941. Pres. and dir bd. social missions United Lutheran Ch. of America, dir. leadership training school corp. of parish and ch. Sch. Bd. Pres., trustee Ch. Mission Soc. of Evangelical Luth. Ch., Baltimore City and Vicinity, Inc., 1913-28 and since 1943; del. to Nat. Conf. on Ch. and Econ. Life of Fed. Council of Churches, 1947; mem. Investment Commn., United Lutheran Chs. of Am., since 1946; mem. exec. com., Laymen's Movement for Stewardship, U.L.C.A. Mem. Am., Md., and Baltimore bar assns. Home: 2905 N. Calvert St. (18). Office: American Bldg., Baltimore and South Sts., Baltimore 2, Md. Died March 22, 1947.

DITMARS, Raymond Lee, curator; b. Newark, N.J., June 20, 1876; grad. Barnard Mil. Acad., 1891; Litt.D. degree. Asst. curator entomology, Am. Museum Natural History, 5 yrs.; court reporter on New York Times, 1898-99; entered N.Y. Zoöl. Park as curator of reptiles, July 1899 and in charge department mammals since 1910. Fellow N.Y. Zoölogical Society, American Institute; correspondent member, Zoöl. Soc., London. Author: The Reptile Book, 1907; Reptiles of the World, 1909; Snakes of the World, 1931; Strange Animals I Have Known, 1931; Thrills of a Naturalist's Quest, 1932; Forest of Adventure, 1933; Confessions of a Scientist, 1934; The Book of Zoögraphy, 1934; The Book of Prehistoric Animals, 1935; The Book of Living Reptiles, 1936; The Making of a Scientist, 1937; The Book of Insect Oddities, 1938; The Fight to Live. Contbr. on entomology and herpetology. Erected a studio at Scarsdale, N.Y., 1913, for the production of ednl. motion pictures. Home: 885 Post Road, Scarsdale, N.Y. Address: Zoölogical Park, New York, N.Y. Died May 12, 1942.

DITTER, J. William, congressman; b. Philadelphia, Pa., Sept. 5, 1888; s. George and Elizabeth (Weissgerber) D.; LL.B., Temple U. Law Sch., 1913, LL.D., Ursinus Coll., 1940; m. Mabel Sylvester Bearné, Sept. 2, 1913; children—Mabel Bearné, John William. Prof. history and commerce, Phila. High, 1913-25; sr. mem. law firm Ditter and Ditter; mem. 73d to 78th Congresses (1933-45), 17th Pa. Dist. Chmn. Nat. Rep. Congressional Com. Mem, Pa. and Montgomery bar assns. Republican. Protestant. Mason, Moose; Club: Rotary. Home: Tennis Av. Office: Old Nat. Bank Bldg., Ambler, Pa. Died Nov. 21, 1943.

DITTMAR, George Walter; b. Derinda Centre, Ill., Apr. 1, 1872; s. Albert and Anna M. (Praeger) D.; student normal dept. Philomath (Ore.) Coll., 1892-93; D.D.S., Northwestern U., Dental Sch., Chicago, 1898; m. Agnes C. Dooling, Sept. 7, 1904; children—Agnes Charlotte, Katherine Louise, George Walter. Practiced in Chicago since 1898; mem. faculty Coll. of Dentistry (formerly Ill. Sch. of Dentistry), U. of Ill., since 1898, prof. prosthetic dentistry since 1910. Mem. Med. Advisory Bd., Chicago, World War. Ex-pres. Am. Dental Assn., Ill. State, Chicago Dental and Chicago Odontological socs.; mem. Am. Dental Assn., Odontographic Soc. Chicago, Delta Sigma Delta (past supreme grand master), Omicron Kappa Upsilon; fellow Am. Coll. Dentists. Republican. Rotarian. Club: Lake Shore Athletic. Lecturer. Home: 1423 Fargo Av. Office: 30 N. Michigan Av., Chicago. Died May 18, 1949; buried Saint Michael Cemetery, Galena, Ill.

DITTO, Rollo C., army officer; born Pa., Sept. 27, 1886; grad. Command and Gen. Staff Sch., 1923, Army War Coll., 1927. Served as private, corpl. and sergt., C.A.C., U.S. Army, Mar. 1907-Nov. 1909; commd. 2d lt., Inf., Nov. 1909; transferred to Chem. Warfare Service as major, 1921, and advanced through the grades to brig. gen., Sept. 1941; served as major, Inf., World War I; on Gen. Staff Corps, 1929-31. Awarded Silver Star with oak leaf cluster, Purple Heart. Address: Huntsville Arsenal, Huntsville, Ala.* Died Jan. 7, 1947.

DIX, William Frederick, life ins.; b. Newark, N.J., Nov. 18, 1867; s. John Edwin and Mary Fisher (Joy) D.; student Princeton, 1889; m. Mary Alice Tennille, June 2, 1900; children—Tennille Dix, Alison Joy, Norman B. World tour, 1890-92; literary editor The Churchman, 1894; editor The Home Journal, New York, name changed to Town and Country, 1900-06; sec. Mut. Life Ins. Co. of New York, May, 1906-33. Trustee Adelphi Coll., Brooklyn, 1913; chmn. bd. trustees Carnegie Fund. Mem. Soc. Colonia Wars (gov. 1910-12; dep. gov. gen. 1913; N.J. Soc.), Soc. Founders and Patriots (gov. N.J. Soc., 1918-21; sec. gen. of Gen. Ct., 1920-22); formerly chmn. Bd. Internat. Hospitality of N.Y., chmn. exec. com. Nat. Security League; treas. and trustee Carteret Acad. (Orange). Capt. E. Orange Rifles; col. 1st Regt., New York Police Reserve. Consul gen. of Montenegro in New York, 1918-21, in charge of Legation, 1920-21. Decorated by King Nicholas with Grand Cross of the Order of Danilo I, in recognition of services for Montenegro. Clubs: Authors (former treas.), Princeton (New York); Westhampton Country (L.I.), Orange Lawn Tennis, Rock Spring Country. Author: The Face in the Girandole; The Lost Princess; Daphne of the Forest; (in collaboration) Man and the Two Worlds. Home: South Orange, N.J.; and Westhampton Beach, L.I., N.Y. Deceased.

DIXEY, Henry E., actor; b. Boston, Jan. 6, 1859. Became mem. stock co. of Howard Athenaeum, 1868; afterward in various cos.; 1st great success was in Adonis; since then in many plays as comedian in England as well as U.S. Home: Wassaic, N.Y. Died Feb. 25, 1943.

DIXON, Frank Haigh, educator; b. Winona, Minn., Oct. 8, 1869; s. Alfred C. and Caroline A.D.; Ph.B., U. of Mich., 1892, Ph.D., 1895; m. Alice L. Tucker, Apr. 17, 1900; children—William Tucker, Caroline Moorhouse, Roger Coit. Asst. polit. economy, 1892-95, instr. history, 1896-97; asst. prof. polit. economy, 1897-98, U. of Mich.; asst. prof. economics, 1898-1903, prof. 1903-19, Dartmouth Coll.; prof. economics, Princeton Univ., 1919-38, prof. emeritus since 1938. Sec. Amos Tuck Sch. of Adminstrn. and Finance, Darthmouth, 1900-04; expert for Interstate Commerce Commn., 1907-08, Nat. Waterways Commn., 1909; chief statistician, Bur. of Ry. Economics, 1910-18; spl. expert U.S. Shipping Bd., 1918. Mem. exec. com. N.H. Com. on Pub. Safety, 1917-18. Mem. Am. Econ. Assn. (vice-pres. 1927), Am. Assn. University Profs. Club: Princeton (New York). Author: State Railroad Control, 1896; A. Traffic History of the Mississippi, 1909; (joint author) War Adminstrn. of Railways in U.S. and Great Britain, 1918; Railroads and Government, Their Relations in the United States, 1922. Joint Author: Stabilization of Business, 1923; Facing the Facts, 1932. Contbr. to mags. Home: 123 Patton Av., Princeton, N.J. Died Jan. 27, 1944.

DIXON, Maynard, painter; b. Fresno, Calif., Jan. 24, 1875; s. Harry St. John and Constance (Maynard) D.; limited edn. pub. sch.; self-ed. in art; m. Lillian West Tobey, May 7, 1905; 1 dau., Constance Maynard; m. 2d, Dorothea Lange, Mar. 21, 1920; children—Daniel Rhodes, John Goodnews; m. 3d, Edith Hamlin, Sept. 7, 1937. Began in newspaper work, San Francisco; made illustrations for numerous vols. of western fiction and for leading mags.; began professional painting, 1920; represented in Emmanuel Walter and A.M. Bender collections (San Francisco), San Francisco Mus. of Art, M. H. de Young Mus. (San Francisco), Mills Coll., Pasadena Art Mus., Phoenix (Ariz.) Municipal Collection, Brooklyn (N.Y.) Mus., Brigham Young U., U. of Ida.; murals in Calif. State Library, San Francisco Water Dept., Mark Hopkins Hotel (San Francisco), Arizona Biltmore (Phoenix), Oakland (Calif.) Tech. High Sch.; The Kit Carson Cafe, 1936; Post Office, Martinez, Calif., 1938; 2 walls Dept. of Interior Bldg., Washington, D.C., 1939; Post Office, Canoga Park, Calif., 1942; also numerous residential and commercial murals. Illustrator: Oregon Trail (for Limited Editions Club, New York), 1942-1944; commd. to paint Desert Southwest for 75th (Jubilee) edition Encyclopædia Britannica and Collection of Contemporary Am. Painting. Paintings and mural work, principally interpreting life and country of the West. Mem. Foundation of Western Art (Los Angeles), San Francisco Art Assn., Southwest Soc. Club: California Art (Los Angeles). Address: 2255 E. Prince Rd., Tucson, Ariz. Died Nov. 13, 1946.

DIXON, Thomas, novelist, playwright; b. Shelby, N.C., Jan. 11, 1864; s. Rev. Thomas and Amanda Elizabeth (McAfee) D.; A.M., Wake Forest Coll., N.C., 1883; LL.B., Greensboro (N.C.) Law Sch., 1886; admitted to bar all courts, N.C. and U.S. Dist. and Supreme cts., 1886; scholarship, history and politics, Johns Hopkins, 1883-84; m. Harriet Bussey, Mar. 3, 1886; children—Jordan (dec.), Charlotte Louise, Thomas; m. Madelyn Donovan, Raleigh, N.C., Mar. 20, 1939. Mem. N.C. legislature, 1885-86; resigned to enter Bapt. ministry, Oct., 1886; pastor Raleigh, N.C., 1887, Boston, Mass., 1888-89, New York, N.Y., 1889-99; popular lyceum lecturer, 1889-1903; clerk U.S. Dist. Ct., Eastern Dist., N.C., 1938-43. Democrat. Author: Leopard's Spots, 1902; The One Woman, 1903; The Clansman, 1905; The Life Worth Living, 1905; The Traitor, 1907; Comrades, 1909; The Root of Evil, 1911; The Sins of the Father, 1912; The Southerner, 1913; The Victim, 1914; Foolish Virgin, 1915; The Birth of a Nation (photoplay), 1915; Fall of a Nation, 1916; The Way of a Man, 1918; A Man of the People, 1920; The Man in Gray, 1921; The Black Hood, 1924; The Love Complex, 1925; The Sun Virgin, 1929; Companions, 1931; The Inside Story of the Harding Tragedy (with Harry M. Daugherty), 1932; A Dreamer in Portugal, 1934; The Flaming Sword, 1939. Home: Raleigh, N.C.* Died Apr. 3, 1946.

DOANE, Ralph Harrington, architect; b. Middle Musquoduobitt, N.S., Can., Oct. 2, 1886; s. Howard Payne and Sarah H. (Simson) D.; brought by parents to U.S., 1889; grad. Mt. Hermon (Mass.) Boys Sch., 1908; grad. Mass. Inst. Tech., 1912; m. Katharine Dorr, June 10, 1920; 1 dau., Josephine Swift. Cons. architect to Philippine Islands, 1916-18; in practice at Boston since 1918; instr. in archtl. design, Mass. Inst. Tech., 1919; schoolhouse commr., City of Boston, 1920-21. Prin. works: Capitol Bldg., Manila, P.I.; Motor Mart, Boston (awarded Harleston Parker gold medal as "most beautiful piece of architecture within limits of City of Boston or Metropolitan Parks Districts," 1927); Rindge Tech. School, Cambridge, Mass. Served as 1st lt. Engr. Corps, U.S. Army, World War. Mem. Am. Inst. Architects, Boston Soc. Architects, Chi. Phi. Republican. Episcopalian. Home: 2 Whitelawn Av., Milton, Mass. Office: 7 Water St., Boston, Mass. Died Nov. 6, 1941.

DOBBINS, Donald Claude, lawyer; b. in Champaign County, Ill., Mar. 29, 1878; s. Foster and Margaret (Beard) D.; student U. of Ill., 1895-96, Dixon (Ill.) Business Coll., 1899-1900, George Washington U., 1903-06; m. Nellie Irene Vernam, Dec. 25, 1901 (died Mar. 20, 1919); children—Elinor Elizabeth (dec.), Donald Vernam; m. 2d, Mrs. Grace R. Maxwell, May 7, 1921; step-daughter, Mrs. Margaret Maxwell Clone. Teacher, 1896-99; stenographer and correspondent, 1900-06; post office inspr., 1906-09; in practice of law since 1909; sr. mem. Dobbins, Dobbins & Thomas. Del. Dem. Nat. Conv., 1936. Mem. 73d and 74th Congresses (1933-37). Presidential elector, 1940. Mem. Am., Ill. State and Champaign County bar assns., Acad. Polit. Science, Ill. Hist. Soc., Phi Delta Phi (hon.), Order of Coif (hon.). Democrat. Presbyterian. Clubs: Rotary, Champaign Country. Home: 110 N. Prospect Av. Office: 30 Main St., Champaign, Ill. Died Feb. 14, 1943.

DOBBS, John Francis, clergyman, educator; b. Liberty Corner, N.J., July 2, 1870; s. Francis and Anna (Crampton) D.; B.A., Lafayette Coll., Pa., 1897; M.A., 1900; studied Columbia, 1898; grad. Union Theol. Sem., 1900; D.D., Lafayette, 1913; m. Caroline Conseylea, June 6, 1899. Ordained Prebyn. ministry, 1900; pastor, Mott Haven Ref. Ch., New York, 1898-1908, 1st Ref. Ch., Syracuse, 1908-15, First Congl. Ch. Malden, Mass., 1915-25; pres. Pacific U., Forest Grove, Ore., since May 4, 1925. Clubs: Rotary (Forest Grove); University, Progressive Business Men's (Portland, Ore.). Author: The Call of the Nation, 1907; The Modern Man and the Church, 1911. Home: Forest Grove, Ore. Died Sept. 20, 1949.

DOBIE, Charles Caldwell, author; b. San Francisco, Calif., Mar. 15, 1881; s. William and Mary Ida (Slocomb) D.; grammar sch. edn.; unmarried. In fire and marine ins. business until 1916; first short story appeared in San Francisco Argonaut, 1910. Mem. Authors' League Am., Calif. Soc., S.A.R. Clubs: Bohemian (San Francisco); P.E.N. (New York); Authors (London). Author: (novels) Blood Red Dawn, 1920; Broken to the Plow; Less Than Kin, 1926; Portrait of a Courtezan, 1934; (plays) Ilya of Murom; Ramati; The Hidden Pool; Charity; Doubling in Brass; The Cracked Teapot; Retribution; Believe It or Not; Three Times a Day; also The Arrested Moment (short stories), 1927; San Francisco—A Pageant, 1933; San Francisco Tales (short stories), 1935; San Francisco's Chinatown, 1936; San Francisco Adventure (short stories), 1937. Contbr. to mags. Home: 840 Green St., San Francisco. Died Jan. 11, 1943.

DOBYNS, Fletcher (dŏb'ĭns), lawyer, author; b. nr. Columbus, O., 1872; s. William Alexander and Anne M. (Kidwell) D.; A.B., Harvard, 1898; Northwestern U., Law Sch., 1899-1901; m. Winifred Ursula Starr, Oct. 21, 1909. Admitted Ill. bar, 1901, began practice at Chicago. Asst. state's atty., Cook County, 1903-06; spl. asst. U.S. dist. atty. Northern Dist. of Ill., 1907-09; spl. asst. atty. gen. of U.S., 1911; candidate for atty. gen. of Ill. on Progressive Ticket, 1912; spl. counsel for U.S. Shipping Bd. and spl. asst. to atty. gen. of U.S., 1921-22. Mem. Am. Bar Assn. Author: Cases on Criminal Law and Procedure; Justice Holmes and the Fourteenth Amendment; The Underworld of American Politics; The Amazing Story of Repeal—An Exposé of the Power of Propaganda. Home: 870 Chula Vista Av., Pasadena. Office: Title Guarantee Bldg., Los Angeles, Calif. Died Dec. 13, 1942.

DOCKWEILER, Isidore Bernard (dŏk'wī-lėr), lawyer; b. Los Angeles, Calif., Dec. 28, 1867; s. Henry and Margaretha (Sugg) D.; A.B., St. Vincent's (now Loyola) Coll., 1887, A.M., 1889, LL.D., 1911; m. Gertrude Reeve, June 30, 1891; children—Thomas Aloysius Joseph, Henry Isidore, Mrs. Mary Gertrude D. Young, John Francis (deceased), Mrs. Rosario Margaret D. Crahan, George Augustine, Edward Vincent, Mrs. Ruth Ysidora D. Brady, Robert Reeve (deceased), Frederick Charles, Louis Bernard. Began business career as bookkeeper, 1883-85; surveyor, 1887-88; studied law with Anderson, Fitzgerald & Anderson, Los Angeles, Calif.; admitted to Calif. bar, Oct. 14, 1889, later to Federal Courts in Calif., U.S. Supreme Court and bars of Ariz. and Nev.; senior mem. Dockweiler & Dockweiler, Los Angeles; dir. Calif. Rendering Co., Ltd., Copra Oil & Meal Co., Forthmann Estate Co., Lincoln Savings & Loan Assn., Los Angeles Public Market Co., Los Angeles Soap Co., Los Angeles Union Terminal Co., Monterey Park Land Corporation, Mullen Estate Co., National Title Insurance Co., Pacific Electric Ry. Co., Security-First Nat. Bank of Los Angeles, Wilson Land Co., White King Soap Co. Dem. candidate for lt. gov. of Calif., 1902; del. Dem. Nat. Convs., Denver, 1908, Philadelphia, 1936, Chicago, 1940; mem. Dem. Nat. Com., 1916-32. Trustee St. Vincent's Coll., 1890-1911; dir. Los Angeles Pub. Library, 1897-99, 1901-11 (ex-pres.); trustee State Normal School, San Diego, 1898-1919; mem. Bd. U.S. Indian Commrs., by appointment Pres. Wilson, 1913-29; mem. Calif. State Park Commn.; chmn. Housing Authority of Los Angeles County. Created Knight St. Gregory by Pope Pius XI, 1924. Mem. Am., Calif., and Los Angeles County bar assns., Native Sons Golden West, Elks, K.C., Young Men's Inst., St. Anthony's Benevolent Soc. Catholic. Democrat. Clubs: California Newman; National Democratic (New York); Jefferson Islands. Home: 366 S. June St. 5. Office: Van Nuys Bldg., Los Angeles 14, Calif.* Died Feb. 6, 1947.

DOCKWEILER, John Francis, ex-congressman; b. Los Angeles, Calif., Sept. 19, 1895; s. Isidore Bernard and Gertrude (Reeve) D.; A.B., Loyola Coll., Los Angeles, 1918; J.D., U. of Southern Calif., 1921; student Harvard Law Sch., 1921-22; m. Angelia Irene McManus, Apr. 13, 1925. In practice of law, Los Angeles, since 1922; mem. 73d to 75th Congresses (1933-39), 16th Calif. Dist. Mem. Calif. Dem. State Central Com. since 1922. Dist. atty. Los Angeles County (Calif.), since Dec. 2, 1940. Mem. Am., Calif. State and Los Angeles County bar assns. Mem. Delta Chi. Democrat. Catholic. Home: 935 S. Dunsmuir Av. Office: Hall of Justice Bldg., Los Angeles, Calif. Died Jan. 31, 1943.

DODD, Anna Bowman, author; b. (Blake) Brooklyn, N.Y.; m. Edward Williams Dodd, 1883. Began early to write for newspapers and mags., especially Harper's. Author: Cathedral Days; The Republic of the Future; In and Out of Normandy Inns; Glorinda (a novel); On the Norfolk Broads; Struthers; Falaise. Address: 15 Rue La Perouse, Paris, France. Died Jan. 30, 1929.

DODDS, George William, newspaper editor; b. Yarm, Yorkshire, Eng., Aug. 5, 1864; s. John and Kate (Ruddock) D.; ed. pub. schs.; m. Kate Emma Lynes, May 17, 1888; 1 dau., Kate (Mrs. Laurence A. Spear). Came to U.S., 1888, naturalized, 1893. Began as reporter Northern Echo, Darlington, Eng., 1884; reporter and asst. city editor St. Paul Globe, 1888-91; asst. city editor Minneapolis Tribune, 1891-93; city editor St. Paul Dispatch, 1893-1905; mng. editor, 1905-09; mng. editor Spokesman-Review, Spokane, Wash., 1909-43, editor emeritus since 1943. Pres. Spokane River Parkway Assn., 1927-40; mem. Spokane Civilian Defense Council, 1942-44. Republican. Episcopalian. Elk. Clubs: Spokane City, University. Address: Box 132, Kaloma, Wash. Died 1947.

DODDS, Samuel, clergyman, educator; b. Prospect, Pa., Feb. 28, 1858; s. Ebenezer and Sarah Jane (Gill) D.; B.S., Grove City (Pa.) Coll., 1881, Ph.D., 1898; Ph.D., Pittsburgh Theol. Sem., 1889; D.D., Westminster (Pa.) Coll., 1902; m. Alice A. Dunn, July 8, 1885; children—Harold Willis, Joseph Leroy, John Wendell. Ordained ministry U.P. Ch., 1889; prof. Biblical doctrine, Wooster Coll., since 1918. Republican. Author: Progressive Studies in The Bible, 1901; Friendship's Meaning, 1919. Home: 646 College Av., Wooster, O. Died Dec. 26, 1947.

DODGE, Raymond, prof. psychology; b. Woburn, Mass., Feb. 20, 1871; s. George S. and Anna (Pickering) D.; A.B., Williams, 1893, D.Sc., 1918; Ph.D., U. of Halle, 1896; D.Sc., Wesleyan U., 1931; m. Henrietta C. Cutler, Aug. 18, 1897. Asst. librarian, Williams Coll., 1893-94; asst. to Prof. Benno Erdmann, U. of Halle, 1896-97; prof. philosophy, Ursinus Coll., 1897-98; instr. in psychology, 1898-99, asso. prof., 1899-1902, prof., 1902-24, Wesleyan U.; prof. Inst. of Psychology, Yale, 1924-29, prof. psychology, Inst. Human Relations, Yale, 1929-36, prof. emeritus since 1936. Asso. editor Psychological Bulletin, 1904-10, Psychol. Review, 1910-15, Psychobiology, 1917-20, Journal Exptl. Psychology since 1916, Jour. Comparative Psychology since 1921. Exptl. psychologist of nutrition lab., Carnegie Instn., 1913-14; nonresident lecturer in psychology, Columbia, 1916-17; E. K. Adams research fellow same, 1916-18. Mem. psychology com. of Nat. Research Council; chmn. div. anthropology and psychology, same, 1922-23; dir. Psychol. Corp. 1920-23. Mem. com. on classification of personnel in army, and com. on fatigue of Council Nat. Defense; cons. psychologist, Chem. Warfare Service, Bur. of Mines, June 10, 1918; lt. comdr. U.S. N.R.F., Oct. 10, 1918. Chmn. Program Com. of IX Internat. Congress of Psychology, 1929; mem. Am. Psychol. Assn. (pres. 1916-17), Am. Philos. Assn., Am. Acad. Arts and Sciences, Nat. Acad. Sciences. Republican. Conglist. Author: Die Motorischen Wortvorstellungen, 1896; Psychologische Untersuchengen über das Lesen, 1898; Experimental Study of Visual Fixation, 1907; Psychological Effects of Alcohol (with F. G. Benedict), 1915; Elementary Conditions of Human Variability, 1927; Sensorimotor Consequences of Passive Oscillation (with R. C. Travis), 1928; Autobiography—A History of Psychology in Autobiography (Vol. 1), 1930; Conditions and Consequences of Human Variability, 1931; The Craving for Superiority (with Dr. Eugen Kahn), 1931; also numerous scientific articles. Home: Tryon, N.C. Died Apr. 8, 1942.

DODSHON, Joseph Henry (dŏd'shŏn), clergyman; b. Spennymoor County, Durham, Eng., pr. 19, 1868; s. Joseph and Mary (Wilkinson) D.; ed. Durham Coll.; Mus. Dr., London Coll. of Music, 1890, Calif. Coll. of Music, 1920; m. Carsonette Porter, Apr. 24, 1913; m. 2d, Mrs. Elsé Constance Lamb, Dec. 22, 1945. Came to U.S., 1895, naturalized citizen, 1900. Deacon, 1898, priest, 1900, P.E. Ch.; missionary in Wyo., 1898-1903 (built chs. at Douglas and Lusk); traveled abroad, 1903-04, 1906-07; archdeacon of Western Mich., 1905-06; in charge English Cathedral, Gibraltar, 1907; archdeacon of Southern Ohio since 1907; rector St. Simeons Ch., N.Y. City, 1931-44, rector emeritus. Vice president New York Morning Telegraph, Russell Securities Corporation. Chaplain Camp Sherman, Ohio, several months, World War; four-minute speaker; national speaker Society for Promoting Internat. Goodwill among Nations. In England, 1945-47; in charge various parishes, North Wales and England. Mem. Sons of St. George, Ohio State Automobile Assn. (v.p.), Ohio Soc. of New York (chaplain), Church Temperance Soc. (pres.), Sons of St. George, Pioneer and Hist. Soc., Academy Political Science. Republican. Mason, Elk. Clubs: Motor (pres. 7 yrs.), Exchange (Zanesville); Columbus (Columbus); Union League, Dramatic, National Travel (New York); Rotary, Larchmont Yacht, Horseshoe Yacht (Larchmont, N.Y.), Stuyvesant Yacht (rear commodore and fleet chaplain), City Island, N.Y. Mem. Bronx Council Boy Scouts of New York. Author: God's Word and Man's; One Line Wisdom; Hints on Visiting the Sick; (booklet) The Truth about Prohibition; also (brochures) Aids to Family Prayers, What Is Faith?, The League of Nations, Can We Believe in the Virgin Birth?, etc. Address: 551 Minneford Av. City Island, New York, N.Y. Died July 22, 1948.

DOERING, Edmund Janes, physician; b. New York, Nov. 7, 1854; s. Rev. Dr. C. H. and Nancy (McLaughlin) D.; M.D., Northwestern U., 1874; studied univs. of Berlin and Vienna, 1875 (M. Sc., Northwestern U., 1916); m. Julia Whiting, May 24, 1877 (died Oct. 1939); 1 son, Edmund Janes. Practiced in Chicago since 1881; cons. physician, Chicago Lying-In and Michael Reese hosps. Editor Chicago Med. Recorder, 1891. First lt. U.S.A. Med. Res. Corps, 1911; capt., later major, 1917; lt. col. M.C., U.S.A., 1918; col. M.R.C., Sept. 1922; apptd. sr. surgeon U.S. P.H.S., Oct. 1919. Late surgeon U. S. Marine Hosp. Service; pres. U.S. Examining Bd., Med. R.C., 1918; apptd. dist. med. officer for Ill., Mich. and Wis., of Federal Bd. for Vocational Edn., 1919; chief cons. U.S. Vet. Bur. of Chicago. Fellow Am. Coll. Surgeons; mem. A.M.A., Ill. Med. Soc., Chicago Med. Soc. (pres. 1886-87), Chicago Gynecol. Soc. (ex-pres.), Medico-Legal Soc. (pres.), Inst. Medicine of Chicago (gov.). Sr. v. comdr. Hyde Park Post Am. Legion; pres. Ill. Div. Med. R.C., U.S.A.; gov. Nat. Reserve Officers' Assn., 1922-23 (hon. pres. Med. Chapter); gov. Mil. Order World War (elected comdr. Chicago Chapter 1930). Clubs: Chicago Athletic, University, South Shore Country, Physicians, Executives, Chicago Medical (Chicago); Army and Navy (Washington and Chicago). Mem. adv. council The Living Age. Mem. Bd. Pub. Health Advisors in Dept. of Pub. Health, State of Ill., 1936. Home: 215 E. Chestnut St., Chicago. Died March 1, 1943.

DOERSAM, Charles, Henry (dâr'săm), teacher, musician, concert organist; b. Scranton, Pa., Sept. 29, 1878; s. Philip and Elizabeth (Schlager) D.; ed. Scranton High Sch.; studied piano under August Spanuth (N.Y. City) and Karl Beving (Leipzig), organ under Samuel P. Warren (N.Y. City) and Wallace Goodrich (Boston), theory under Cantor Gustav Schreck (Leipzig), counterpoint and composition under Geo. W. Chadwick; received highest honors New Eng. Conservatory of Music, 1909 (made mem. faculty); m. Mary Davenport, June 20, 1916; children—Philip Davenport, Charles Henry. Mem. faculty and head organ dept., Columbia U., since 1920, in charge chapel choir, summer sessions, since 1933; with theatre orchestra, conducting Gilbert & Sullivan operas, 1901-03; condr. Scranton Symphony Orchestra, 3 yrs.; accompanist for nationally known artists; director and organist First and Second Presbyn. Chs., Scranton, First M.E. Ch., Wilkes-Barre, also chs. in Carbondale, Pa., Wellesley, Dorchester and Boston, Mass., Rye, N.Y., Park Av. Synagogue and Rutgers Presbyn. Ch., N.Y. City. Has given many organ recitals throughout U.S. Warden Am. Guild Organists, 1932-39, dean Northeastern Pa. Chapter, sec. New England Chapter. Fellow Am. Guild Organists. Mem. Pi Kappa Lambda. Presbyterian. Clubs: Sinfonia (Boston); Men's Faculty (Columbia U.); St. Wilfrid (N.Y. City). Composer church anthems, songs and chamber music. Home: 7 Buckingham Road, Palisade, N.J. Died July 14, 1942.

DOGAN, Matthew Winfred, pres. emeritus, Wiley Coll.; b. Pontotoc, Miss., Dec. 21, 1863; s. William and Jennie (Martin) D.; A.B., Rust Coll., 1886, A.M., 1897, D.D., New Orleans Univ., Ph.D., 1906, m. Fannie Faulkner, June 1888; children—Lucile (Mrs. Lucile Dogan Teycer), Clara (Mrs. Clara Dogan Feaman; dec.), Ruth (Mrs. Ruth Dogan Shelton), Blanche (Mrs. Blanche Dogan Hughes), Mathew Winfred. Prof. mathematics, Central Tenn. Coll. (Later Walden Coll.), 1890; became pres. Wiley Coll., 1896, pres. emeritus since 1942. Bd. of Edn. Meth. Ch., Tex. Conf. Meth. Ch., Central Jurisdiction (treas.), Resettlement Adminstrn. of Tex., Tex. Inter-racial Comm. (charter mem.), State of Tex. Y.M.C.A. Council. Mem. Tex. Assn. of Negro Colleges, Tex. State Colored Teachers Assn., Gamma Mu, Phi Beta Sigma. Author: Progress of the Negro. Home: 603 S. Carter St., Marshall, Tex. Died June 17, 1947.

DOLAN, Arthur W., judge; b. Boston, Mass., Sept. 22, 1876; s. John and Delia (Murphy) D.; A.B., Boston Coll., 1897, LL.D., 1922; LL.B., Harvard Univ. Law Sch., 1900; m. Christine M. Barr, Sept. 29, 1903; children—Arthur Barr, John Barr, Helen Barr, William Barr, Mary Christine. Admitted to Mass. bar, 1900; practiced law until 1907; register of Probate Court, Suffolk County, 1907-22; became judge same, 1922; now asso. justice Supreme Court of State of Mass. Mem. Common Council, Boston, 1900-05, pres. 1902-05; sec. to mayor of Boston, 1906-07; mem. Judicial Council of Mass., 1902-06. Mem. Mass. and Boston bar assn., Am. Judicature Soc., Am. Bar Assn. Democrat. Catholic. Home: 1514 Beacon St., Brookline, Mass. Died Sep. 28, 1949.

DOLAN, George W., business exec.; b. Cleveland, O., Jan. 11, 1902; s. Denis J. and Sarah G. (Smith) D.; Western Reserve Univ., 1921-25; m. Adele T. Corcoran, Oct. 16, 1933; 1 son, George E. Pres. and dir. The Mathieson Alkali Works, Inc., N.Y. City, since 1943; pres. Southern Carbonic Co., N.Y. City, since 1943, Bray Chem. Co. (Chicago), since 1942;

mem. adv. bd. Marine Midland Trust Co., since 1946. Served as pvt. 1st class U.S. Army, World War I; served as asst. chief Chem. Warfare Service, U.S. Army Procurement Dist. No. 1, World War II. Roman Catholic. Clubs: Athletic, Uptown, The Niblicks, Winged Foot Golf (New York); Columbia Country (Md.); Niagara (Niagara Falls). Home: 22 Larchmont Av., Larchmont, N.Y. Office: 60 E. 42d St., New York 17, N.Y. Died July 24, 1948.

DOLE, Helen James Bennett, translator; b. Worcester, Mass.; d. William Montgomery and Frances (Fletcher) Bennett; ed. pvt. schs., Worcester; made spl. study of music; m. Nathan Haskell Dole, June 28, 1882; children—Robert Montgomery, Arthur Alexander, Margaret Aliona (Mrs. M. D. McCall), Harold Sanford. Translator: Rudolph Baumbach's Tales, 1888; Victor Hugo's Ninety-Three, 1888; Theuriet's Abbé Daniel, 1894; Paul Marguéritte's Avril, 1895; Pierre Loti's Iceland Fisherman, 1896; Theuriet's Rustic Life in France, 1896; Champfleury's Faience Violin, 1896; Rostand's Cyrano de Bergerac, 1899; Spyri's Heidi, 1899 and 1940; Klemens Brentano's Gockel, Hinkel and Gackeleia, 1914; Spyri's Moni the Goat Boy, 1914; Spyri's The Rose Child, 1916; What Sami Sings with the Birds, 1917; Little Miss Grasshopper, 1918; Little Curly-Head, the Pet Lamb, 1919; Spyri's Toni, the Little Wood-Carver, 1920; Spyri's Tiss, a Little Alpine Waif, 1920; Spyri's Trini, the Little Strawberry Girl, 1921; Spyri's The Children's New Year's Carol, 1921; Spyri's Jo, the Little Machinist, 1922; Spyri's A Little Alpine Musician, 1923; Spyri's Arthur and Squirrel, 1925; Ulrich's Johanna Spyri's Childhood, 1925; Spyri's Cornelli, 1927; Spyri's Castle Wonderful; revised centennial edit. of Spyri's Heidi, 1927; Spyri's Eveli and Beni, 1928; Spyri's Stories of Swiss Children, 1928; Spyri's Boys and Girls of the Alps, 1929; Spyri's In the Swiss Mountains, 1929; Spyri's Renz and Margritli, 1931; Spyri's Eric and Sally, 1932. Home: "The Moorings," Ogunquit, Me.; and 525 W. 238th St., Riverdale-on-Hudson, New York, N.Y. Died June 9, 1944.

DOLL, William DeBerge, lawyer; b. Milwaukee, Wis., Nov. 17, 1897; s. George Edward and Magdalene (DeBerge) D.; A.B., Lawrence Coll., Appleton, Wis., 1920; student U. of Wis., 1920-21, U. of Wash., 1921-22; m. Bernice O. Buehler, Dec. 21, 1921; children—Robert William (dec.), William Irving. Instr. of speech, U. of Wash., 1921-22, U. of Wis., 1922-27; admitted to Wash. bar, 1922; mem. firm Field & Doll, Milwaukee, 1927-40, Doll & Kinzer, Milwaukee, since 1941. Served in S.A.T.C., 1918; major, Judge Adv. General's Dept., Res. Corps, 1936-42. Trustee Lawrence Coll., 1939-45. Del. to Nat. Rep. Conv., 1940, alternate, 1944; dir. Speakers Bureau, Wisconsin Council of Defense, 1941-43; founder and pres., Milwaukee Speakers Forum. Mem. American Bar Association (chmn. section on bar activities, 1943-44, chmn. spl. commn. public relations, 1944-45; chmn. of "Let's Face the Issue" broadcasts, 1944-45), Wis. State Bar Assn. (pres. 1940-41), Milwaukee Bar Assn. (president 1937-38), American Judicature Soc., American Legion, Beta Theta Pi, Phi Alpha Delta frats. Republican. Conglist. Mason (K.T., 32°, Shriner). Club: Tripoli Country (Milwaukee). Author: The Art of Public Speaking, 1924; You Can Make a Speech, 1941; Real Estate Brokers, 1945. Home: Milwaukee, Wis. Died Oct. 8, 1945.

DONAHEY, James Harrison (dŏn'á-hā), cartoonist; b. Westchester, Tuscarawas County, Ohio, Apr. 8, 1875; s. John C. and Catherine (Chaney) D.; ed. pub. schs., and Cleveland School of Art; m. Josephine Rhodes, 1941. Began as cartoonist, 1897; cartoonist, Cleveland Plain Dealer, since 1899. Life mem. Cleveland Mus. Art; hon. mem. Hermit Club. Methodist. Books: Sketches in Egypt; Sketches in Yucatan; Sketches in Ohio Western Reserve; Sketches in Alaska; Romance of the Great Lakes. Home: Aurora, O. Died June 1, 1949.

DONAHEY, Vic, ex-senator; b. Cadwallader, Tuscarawas County, O., July 7, 1873; s. John C. and Catherine (Chaney) D.; common sch. ed.; m. Mary Edith Harvey, Jan. 5, 1897; 10 children living. Learned printer's trade; clk. of Goshen Twp., Tuscarawas County, 1898-1903; county auditor, 1905-09; mem. Bd. of Edn., New Philadelphia, O., 1909-11; mem. 4th Ohio Constl. Conv., 1912; state auditor, Ohio, 1912-20; Dem. candidate for gov. of Ohio, 1920 (defeated); elected gov., 1922; reëlected, 1924 and 1926; U.S. senator, 1935-41; pres. Donahey Clay Products Co., Motorists Mutual Ins. Co., dir. Ohio Nat. Bank. Home: Huntsville, O. Address: 471 E. Broad St., Columbus, O. Died Apr. 8, 1946.

DONDORE, Dorothy Anne, educator; b. Iowa City, Ia., Feb. 7, 1894; d. Francis Hamilton and Josephine Elesa (Haas) D.; grad. high sch., Iowa City, 1911; A.B., State U. of Ia., 1916, A.M., 1917; Ph.D., Columbia, 1926; unmarried. Asst. librarian Iowa City Pub. Library, 1912-17; teacher of English, Scarborough (N.Y.) Sch., 1918-19; asst. in English, State U. of Ia., 1913-17, instr. in English, 1917-18, 1920-22; asst. prof. English, Elmira (N.Y.) Coll., 1924-25, asso. prof. 1925-27, prof. since 1927; mem. editorial staff Ency. Britannica, 1927-1929. Mem. Modern Lang. Assn. America, Am. Hist. Assn., Miss. Valley Hist. Assn., Am. Assn. Univ. Women, Phi Beta Kappa, Pi Lambda Theta, Mortar Board. Author: The Prairie and the Making of Middle America, 1927. Contbr. to Dictionary of Am. Biography, Encyclopedia Britannica, Am. Speech, Miss. Valley Hist. Review, etc. Home: 214 N. Capitol St., Iowa City, Ia. Address: Elmira Coll., Elmira, N.Y. Died 1946.

DONHAM, Harold Gregory, exec. vice-pres. United Shoe Machinery Corp.; b. Portland, Me., July 28, 1875; s. Grenville M. and Sarah A. (Gregory) D.; LL.B., Harvard Law Sch., 1899; m. Elizabeth A. Schneller, June 27, 1906; children—Clarissa Gregory (Mrs. Lovett Morse), Elizabeth Howe (Mrs. Osborne Goodrich). Admitted to Mass. bar, 1899; with United Shoe Machinery Corp., Boston, Mass., since 1902, dir. and vice-pres., 1917, exec. v.p., 1939; treas. and dir. Ansonia O. & C. Co.; dir. Ansonia Nat. Bank; v.p. and dir. United Shoe Machinery Co. of Canada, etc. Clubs: Algonquin, Union, Beacon Society (Boston, Mass.); Country (Brookline, Mass.); Graduates (New Haven, Conn.); Chevy Chase (Washington, D.C.). Home: Salem End Rd., Framingham Centre, Mass. Office: 140 Federal St., Boston, Mass.* Died Apr. 13, 1946.

DONNELLY, Lucy Martin, prof. English; b. Ithaca, N.Y., Sept. 18, 1870; d. Henry D. and Abby (Martin) D.; A.B., Bryn Mawr (Pa.) Coll., 1893; studied univs. of Oxford and Leipzig, 1893-4, Sorbonne and College de France, 1894-5. Instr. in English, Bryn Mawr Coll., 1895, prof. since 1909. Mem. Modern Lang. Assn. Am., Am. Assn. Univ. Profs., Assn. Collegiate Alumnae. Unitarian. Clubs: Cosmopolitan, Bryn Mawr (New York); College (Phila.). Home: Bryn Mawr, Pa. Died Aug. 3, 1948.

DONNELLY, Samuel Bratton, printer; b. Concord, Pa., Nov. 7, 1866; s. James M. and Hannah M. (Bratton) D.; ed. high schools, Lewistown, Pa., State Normal Sch., Shippensburg, Pa. Teacher country schs., Franklin Co., Pa., 1883-86; began learning printing trade, 1886; pres. New York Typographical Union No. 6, 1895-98; Internat. Typographical Union, Indianapolis, 1898-1900; sec. Nat. Civic Federation, 1901-02, Joint Arbitration Bd. of New York Bldg. Trades Employers Assn., 1903-08; commr. New York Bd. Edn., 1901-08; public printer, Dec. 1, 1908-June 25, 1913; now sec. Bldg. Trades Employers' Assn., New York. Clubs: Republican (New York); Invincible (Brooklyn), South Shore Yacht. Home: 25 Brooklyn Av., Brooklyn. Address: 34 W. 33d St., New York. Died Jan. 26, 1946.

DONOVAN, Edward Francis (dŏn'ō-văn), editor, writer, lexicographer; b. Kingston, Ont., Can.; s. Peter and Catharine (Kelly) D.; came to U.S. as a child; LL.B., John B. Stetson U., DeLand, Fla.; m. Elizabeth Snowdon, Nov. 16, 1904. Admitted to Fla. bar, 1916, to practice in U.S. courts, 1916; mem. editorial staff, Standard Bible Dictionary, 1908-09; editor Unabridged New Standard Dictionary, 1909-14; wrote and revised legal articles for Ency. Americana, 1917-18, 1926-27; editor Practical Standard Dictionary, 1920-23; style editor and head of transcription and proofreading depts. in the New York editorial offices of the Ency. Britannica (14th edit.), Nov., 1927-Aug., 1929; editor and orthoepist Weedon's Modern Encyclopedia, 1930-31; editor Funk & Wagnalls' New Standard Encyclopedia, Sept.-Nov. 1931; revised legal articles Nelson's Encyclopedia, 1934; asso. editor Unabridged Standard Dictionary, 1937 and 1938 edits., Practical Standard Dictionary, 1938 and 1939 edits. Mem. Phi Alpha Delta. Home: 1288 Longfellow Av., West Englewood, N.J. Died Jan. 25, 1943.

DONOVAN, Jerome Francis, lawyer, former congressman; b. New Haven, Conn., Feb. 1, 1872; s. Jeremiah C. and Ellen (Collins) D.; LL.B., Yale, 1894; m. Mary E. Fahy, Oct. 12, 1898; children—Jerome Francis, Jr. (capt. U.S. Navy), Mrs. Mary Bodkin, Mrs. Elinor Tower, Paul, Robert. Admitted to Conn. bar, 1894; practiced at New Haven; removed to N.Y. City, 1910; mem. Connecticut House of Representatives, 1901-03; auditor, later sec. New Haven Civil Service Commn., 1904-09; elected to 65th Congress (1917-19), 21st N.Y. Dist., Mar. 5, 1918, for an unexpired term; reelected to 66th Congress (1919-21), same dist.; mem. Special Com. Investigating World War Expenditures; dep. atty. gen. in charge New York City office, 1922-23, for atty. gen. state of N.Y. Capt. Conn. Nat. Guard, 1897-1907. Democrat. Catholic. Club: Yale. Home: Stony Creek, Conn. Died Nov. 2, 1949.

DONOVAN, Richard, army officer; born at Paducah, Kentucky, Dec. 2, 1885; B.S., U.S. Military Acad., 1908; M.S., Mass. Inst. Tech., 1921; grad. Army War Coll., 1931, Command and Gen. Staff Sch., 1926, Coast Arty. Sch. (advanced course), 1925. Commd. 2d lt., Coast Arty. Corps, 1908; promoted through grades to maj. gen., Apr. 1941; retired with rank of maj. gen., 1947. Home: Melrose Hotel, Dallas, Tex. Died Feb. 7, 1949.

DONWORTH, George, lawyer; b. Machias, Me., Nov. 26, 1861; s. Patrick Enright and Mary Eliza (Baker) D.; A.B., Georgetown U., 1881; LL.D., from same; m. Emma Tenney, Aug. 22, 1889 (died 1936); children—Charles Tenney, Robert Baker, Mary (Mrs. John S. McFarland). Admitted to Me. bar, 1883; practicing at Ft. Fairfield; removed to Seattle, 1888; elected mem. commission to frame a new charter for Seattle, 1890; corp. counsel, Seattle, 1892-94; mem. Seattle Sch. Bd., 1907-09; apptd. U.S. dist. judge, Western Dist. of Wash., May 1909; resigned 1912, and resumed practice; mem. firm Donworth, Donworth & Smith. Apptd. by U.S. Supreme Court, 1935, mem. Adv. Com. of 14 to prepare gen. rules of practice and procedure in federal courts. Dir. Seattle Trust & Savings Bank. Pres. Wash. State Bar Assn., 1899; pres. Wash. Soc. S.R., 1910. Civilian aide to the adjutant gen. U.S. Army, 1918-22, to sec. of war for State of Wash., 1923. Mem. of Bd. of Regents U. of Wash., 1923-25. Trustee of Seattle Chamber of Commerce. Mem. American Bar Assn., Washington State Bar Assn., American Academy Social and Polit. Science, Am. Soc. Internat. Law, Am. Br. Internat. Law Assn., Am. Law Inst. (mem. Council), Society Colonial Wars, Sons of Italy in America (hon.). Received decoration of Knight Order of the Crown of Italy, 1923, and Commendatore of same, 1925. Republican. Catholic. Clubs: Rainier, Monday, University (Seattle); University (New York). Address: Hoge Bldg., Seattle, Wash. Died Sept. 6, 1947.

DONWORTH, Grace, author; b. Machias, Me.; d. Patrick Enright and Mary Eliza (Baker) Donworth; ed. pvt. sch., Boston; unmarried. Mem. D.A.R., Boston Authors' Club. Honorary mem. International Mark Twain Society, Women's Republican Club of Mass. Author: Letters of Jennie Allen to Her Friend, Miss Musgrove, 1908; Down Home with Jennie Allen, 1910; contbr. to mags. Home: Machias, Me. Died Nov. 25, 1945.

DOOLAN, John Calvin (dōō'lăn), lawyer; b. Shelby County, Ky., June 15, 1868; s. Thomas Jefferson and Rowena E. (Weakley) D.; ed. pvt. sch. conducted by father; B.L., U. of Va., 1890; m. Katherine Clark, Apr. 29, 1905. Gen. and corporate practice, Louisville, Ky., since 1890; mem. Doolan, Helm, Stites & Wood. District attorney for Kentucky of I.C. R.R. Co. and of C.I.&L. Ry. Co. (Monon). Mem. American Law Inst., Am. Bar Assn., Ky. State Bar Assn. (pres. 1925-26), Louisville Bar Assn. (pres. 1917); asso. mem. Association Bar City of N.Y. and various historical societies. Democrat. Baptist. Clubs: Pendennis, Louisville Country. Author magazine articles, addresses and papers. Home: Dunmanway, Upper River Rd. Office: Ky. Home Life Bldg., Louisville, Ky. Died Oct. 25, 1947.

DOOLAN, Leonard Weakley, clergyman; b. Finchville, Shelby County, Ky., May 13, 1872; s. Thomas Jefferson and Rowena Elizabeth (Weakley) D.; grad. Shelby Acad., Shelbyville, Ky., 1888; A.B., Central U. of Ky., 1895; student Rochester Theol. Sem.; Th.D., Southern Bapt. Theol. Sem., Louisville, Ky., 1901; m. Elizabeth Todd Hodges, Oct. 23, 1901; children—Elizabeth Hodges, Leonard W., Rowena Lewis. Instr. Chemistry, Central U. of Ky., 1893-94, in Greek, 1894-95; pres. Hardin Collegiate Inst., Elizabethtown, Ky., 1895-97; ordained ministry Southern Bapt. Ch., 1897; pastor Madison, Ind., later Henderson, Ky., until 1904; prof. Hebrew and practical theology, Baylor U., 1904-07; pastor Louisville and Bowling Green, Ky., Columbus, O., and Hopkinsville, Ky., until 1924, Danville, Ky., 1924-35, Lyndon Bapt. Ch., Louisville, Ky., 1935-41. Mem. Sigma Nu Fraternity. Author: The Scarlet Thread, 1933. Lesson writer Southern Bapt. Sunday School Board, 1925-26; contbr. to Internat. Standard Bible Ency., 1915. Home: R.F.D. 6, Box 350, Louisville, Ky. Died Jan. 13, 1943.

DOOLEY, William Henry (dōō'lē), educator, author; b. Boston, Mass., Feb. 26, 1880; s. James Edward and Mary Elizabeth (McCarty) D.; S.B. Harvard, 1905; A.M., Columbia, 1918; Ph.D., Fordham, 1925; m. Ellen V. Kenney, 1909. Science teacher, high sch., Fitchburg, Mass., 1905-06, Lawrence, Mass., 1906-08; organizer, and prin. Lawrence Day Industrial Sch., 1909, Lowell Day Industrial Sch., 1911, Fall River Tech. High Sch., 1913-16; in charge of apprentice sch. Brooklyn Navy Yard, 1917-19; prin. N.Y. Textile High Sch. since 1919. Mem. Friendly Sons of St. Patrick. Clubs: Catholic, New York Athletic. Editor: The Wiley Pre-service Series of textbooks and handbooks for teachers in pre-induction and war training courses in Textile High School; Fundamentals of Electricity, Fundamentals of Shop Work, Fundamentals of Machines, Fundamentals of Radio and Fundamentals of Auto Mechanics, 1942. Author: Textiles, 1910, 25; Boot and Shoe Manufacturing, 1912; Education of the Ne'er Do Well, 1914; Vocational Mathematics for Boys, 1915; Vocational Mathematics for Girls, 1917; Principles and Methods of Industrial Education, 1918; Applied Science for Metal Workers, 1919; Applied Science for Wood-Workers, 1919; Drill Book on Vocational Mathematics, 1926; Clothing and Style, 1927; Economics of Textiles and Clothing, 1934; Attractive Clothing (with Frances H. Consalus), 1937; Distinctive Clothing, 1939; History of Costume, 1939. Buying and Selling (with Louis Tanz), 1943. Home: Hotel Leville, Madison Av. and 29th St., New York, N.Y. Died Dec. 7, 1944.

DORAN, James M., chemist; b. Grand Forks, N.D., August 17, 1885; s. Frank and Edwinna (Brainerd) D.; B.S. in Chemistry, U. of Minn., 1907; post-grad. study, George Washington U., 1912-13; m. Roxana Brook, Aug. 22, 1908; children—James Edward, Frances. Chemist Internal Revenue Bur., U.S. Treasury, since 1907, head of chem. and tech. div. since 1920; commr. of prohibition, 1927-30; commr. of industrial alcohol 1930-33; supervisor Assn. of Distilled Spirits Industry (code authority), Dec. 1933-May 1935; tech. dir. Distilled Spirits Inst. since Dec. 1933. Mem. Am. Chem. Soc., Sigma Xi. Republican. Protestant. Club: Cosmos. Contbr. on industrial alcohol to scientific periodicals. Home: 1231 31st St. N.W., Washington. Died Sept. 8, 1941.

DORCHESTER, Daniel, clergyman; b. Dudley, Mass., Apr. 28, 1851; s. Rev. Dr. Daniel and Mary Payson (Davis) D.; A.B., Wesleyan U., Conn., 1874,

A.M., 1880, D.D., 1900; U. of Berlin, Germany, 1887-88; Ph.D., Boston U., 1891; m. Cleora Clark, July 1, 1875. Entered M.E. ministry, 1876; pastor Springfield, Vt., 1876-78, Hopkinton, Mass., 1878-81, Boston, 1881-82, Newton, Mass., 1882-83; prof. English lit., Boston U., 1883-95; pastor Christ Ch., Pittsburgh, Pa., 1895-1900, Lindell Av. Ch., St. Louis, 1900-03, Christ Ch., Pittsburgh, 1903-10, St. Mark's Ch., Brooklyn, 1910-16. Mem. Gen. Conf. 1908, and received 201 votes for bishop. Lecturer, Boston U., since 1916; pastor, Westbury, N.Y., 1920-25. Mem. Authors Club (London), Phi Beta Kappa, Psi Upsilon. Contbr. articles on lit. subjects to Shakespeare Soc., London, Browning Soc., Boston, Poet Lore, Meth. Review, etc. Author: Sovereign People, 1914; Bolshevism and Social Revolt, 1919. Home: Lexington, Mass. Died Jan. 10, 1944.

DOREMUS, Frank Ellsworth, ex-congressman; b. Venango Co., Pa., Aug. 31, 1865; s. Sylvester and Sarah (Peake) D.; ed. pub. schs., Portland, Mich., and Detroit Coll. of Law; m. Elizabeth Hatley, June 26, 1890. Established Portland Review, 1885, editor until 1899. Postmaster, Portland, 1895-99; in law practice at Detroit, 1899-1924. Mem. Mich. Ho. of Rep., 1890-92; asst. corp. counsel, Detroit, 1903-07; city comptroller, 1907-10; mem. 62d to 66th Congresses (1911-21), 1st Mich. Dist.; mayor of Detroit, 1923-24. Democrat. Home: 257 E. Philadelphia St., Detroit. Died Sept. 1, 1947.

DOREY, Halstead (dō-rā), army officer; b. St. Louis, Mo., Feb. 7, 1874; s. William A. and Georgiana (Banks) D.; grad. Shattuck Sch., Fairbault, Minn., grad. U.S. Mil. Acad., 1897; m. Theodora Cheney, Sept. 20, 1905; children—Georgiana (wife Col. M. F. Grant, U.S. Army), Ednah Cheney. Additional 2d lt., June 1897; promoted through grades to maj. gen. Nov. 1, 1933; retired, 1936. In Santiago Campaign, Spanish-Am. War, 1898; Philippine Insurrection, 1899-1901; various fights with Moros, 1903-05; Vera Cruz Expdn., 1908; comdr. 4th Inf. (emergency col.), in France, May-Oct. 1918; participated in battles, Aisne, Aisne-Marne, Champaigne-Marne, St. Mihiel, Meuse-Argonne. Decorated D.S.C. and D.S.M. (U.S.); Officer Legion of Honor and Croix de Guerre (French); Purple Heart and Silver Star (U.S., each 3 oak leaf clusters). Episcopalian. Clubs: Army and Navy (Washington, and Manila); University (New York). Address: Salsipuedes, Boerne, Tex. Died June 19, 1946; buried at West Point, N.Y.

DORLAND, Ralph E., Sr., business exec.; b. Elyria, O., Aug. 22, 1879; s. Charles Johnson and Ida Belle (McNabb) D.; Ph.G., Purdue, 1901; m. Edith E. Green, June 17, 1902; children—Grant A., Wayne E., Jack A., Ralph E. Began career as proprietor, Dorland Drug Co., Williamsfield, Ill., 1901-07; proprietor, Dorland Pharmacy Co., Springfield, Ill., 1912-16; mgr. pharmaceutical dept., Dow Chemical Co., Midland, Mich.; New York mgr., Dow Chemical Co. since 1919. Pres. Ill. Pharm. Assn., 1913; pres. Am. Chem. Salesmen, 1923-25. Chmn. drug chemical sect., New York Bd. of Trade, 1940; pres. N.Y. Bd. of Trade, 1946. Republican. Presbyterian. Clubs: Chemists of New York (vice pres. 1941-42), Rockefeller Luncheon. Home: 115 Central Park West, New York. Office: 30 Rockefeller Plaza, New York 20, N.Y. Died May 14, 1948.

DORR, George Bucknam, scientist, student; b. Jamaica Plain, Mass., Dec. 29, 1853; s. Charles Hazen and Mary Gray (Ward) D.; A.B., Harvard, 1874, post-grad. work, 1888-91, hon. M.A., 1923; hon. M.Sc., U. of Me., 1924; unmarried. Studied and traveled in Europe and Near East; has devoted much time to plant life, pub. reservations and landscape gardening; founder, and supt. under U.S. Govt., of Acadia National Park, on coast of Me. Fellow Harvard Travellers Club; mem. N.E. Bot. Soc.; treas. The Wild Gardens of Acadia. Home: (legal) Bar Harbor, Me. Died Aug. 5, 1944.

DORR, Rheta Childe, author; b. Omaha, Neb.; d. Edward P. (M.D.) and Lucie M. Childe; student U. of Neb. 2 yrs.; married; 1 son, Julian C. Editor Woman's dept., New York Evening Post, 1902-06; staff writer, Hampton's and other mags. since 1907; war corr. for New York Evening Mail, and syndicate of 21 newspapers, 1917-18; fgn. corr. with hdqrs. at Prague, 1921-23. Author: What Eight Million Women Want, 1910; Inside the Russian Revolution, 1917; A Soldier's Mother in France, 1918; A Woman of Fifty (autobiography), 1924; Susan B. Anthony, 1928; Drink—Coercion or Control?, 1929. Contbr. to Columbia Ency., 1934-35. Address: Town Hall Club, New York. Died Aug. 8, 1948.

DORRANCE, Arthur Calbraith (dŏr'răns), manufacturer; b. Bristol, Pennsylvania, June 21, 1893; s. John and Eleanor Gillingham (Thompson) D.; prep. edn., Episcopal Acad., Philadelphia; B.S., Mass. Inst. Tech., 1914; m. Elsie Allan Ross, Feb. 7, 1918; children—Arthur Calbraith, David Ross. Asso. with canning industry since 1914; asst. gen. mgr. Campbell Soup Co., 1923-28, gen. mgr. since 1928, pres. since 1930; pres. The Franco-Am. Food Co. since 1921; dir. Federal Reserve Bank, Philadelphia, 1928-31, Phila. National Bank, 1932-35; mem. of bd. mgrs. Girard Trust Co.; dir. Guaranty Trust Co. of N.Y., Bell Telephone Co. of Pa., Pa. R.R. Co.; trustee Penn Mut. Life Ins. Co. Served as 1st lt., later capt. arty., U.S. Army, World War; maj. Reserve Corps. Term mem. corp. Massachusetts Institute Tech., 1935-40. Mem. Am. Legion, Sigma Alpha Epsilon. Republican. Episcopalian. Clubs: Technology, Rittenhouse, Racquet, (Phila.) Merion Cricket; Gulph Mills Golf; Fishers Island (N.Y.); Chicago. Home: "Leahurst," Ardmore, Pa. Office: Campbell Soup Co., Camden, N.J. Died Sep. 21, 1946.

DORRANCE, George Morris, surgeon; b. Bristol, Bucks County, Pa., Apr. 24, 1877; s. John and Eleanor Gillingham (Thompson) D.; prep. edn., Peekskill Mil. Acad., Ossining, N.Y.; M.D., U. of Pa., 1900; m. Emily Fox, Nov. 10, 1921; children—George Morris, Emily Fox. Practiced at Phila. since 1900; prof. surgery Women's Med. Coll. of Pa., 1923-24; prof. maxillo-facial surgery, Thomas Evans Inst., U. of Pa.; surgeon in chief Am. Oncologic Hosp.; surgeon to Doctors Hosp., Philadelphia; surgeon, Cooper Hospital, Camden, N.J.; consultant oral surgeon State and Montgomery Hospitals, Norristown, Pa.; chmn. bd. Campbell Soup Co. Served overseas as maj. Med. Reserve Corps, U.S. Army. Fellow Am. Coll. Surgeons, Coll. Physicians of Phila.; mem. A.M.A., Pa. State Med. Soc., Phila. County Med. Soc., Pathol. Soc., Phila. Acad. Surgery. Republican. Episcopalian. Clubs: Raquet, Medical, Physicians, Motor, Phila. Country. Home: 2218 Delancey St. Office: 2101 Spruce St., Philadelphia, Pa.* Died Nov. 21, 1949.

DORSEY, Clayton Chauncey, lawyer; b. Sandusky, O., Mar. 21, 1871; s. Stephen W. and Helen M. (Wack) D.; A.B., Yale, 1890; m. Marguerite Montgomery, June 22, 1897. Admitted to Colo. bar, 1893; with Teller & Orahood, 1892-99; practiced alone, 1899-1900; mem. Teller & Dorsey, 1900-05, Dorsey & Hodges, 1905-11, Hughes & Dorsey, 1911-45, now retired. Republican. Episcopalian. Mem. Am., Colo. State and Denver bar assns. Clubs: Denver, University, Denver Country (Denver). Home: 330 Gilpin St. Office: International Trust Bldg., Denver, Colo. Died Sept. 22, 1948.

DORSEY, Frank J. G., ex-congressman; b. Phila., Pa., April 26, 1891; s. John Henry and Ellen Catherine (Maher) D.; B.S., U. of Pa., 1917; m. Cecelia Mae Alphonsene Ward, Apr. 14, 1920; 1 daughter, Cecelia Marie. Assistant in finance Wharton Evening School (Univ. of Pennsylvania), 1916-17; with Henry Disston & Sons, Inc., saw, steel file manufacturers, 1919-34; member 74th and 75th Congresses (1935-39), 5th Pa. Dist.; director Northeast Nat. Bank, Fidelity Fed. Savings & Loan Assn. Enlisted as pvt. in U.S. Army, June 1917; hon. disch. as lt., April 1919. Mem. Mil. Order of World Wars, Am. Legion, Sigma Nu, Beta Gamma Sigma. Democrat. Mem. Knights of Columbus. Clubs: Frankford, Torresdale Country. Home: Primrose Rd., Torresdale, Philadelphia, Pa. Died July 13, 1949.

DORSEY, Hugh Manson, judge; b. at Fayetteville, Ga., July 10, 1871; s. Rufus Thomas and Sarah Matilda (Bennett) D.; A.B., U. of Ga., 1893; student law dept. U. of Va., 1893-94 (non-grad.); m. Adair Wilkinson, June 29, 1911; children—Hugh Manson, James Wilkinson. Associated in practice of law at Atlanta, Ga., under title of Dorsey, Brewster, Howell & Heyman, 1894-1916; apptd. solicitor-general of Atlanta Judicial Circuit, elected for term ending 1916; gov. of Ga. 2 terms, 1917-19, 1919-21; defeated for U.S. senate, 1920, by Thomas E. Watson; resumed law practice; apptd. judge City Court of Atlanta, Sept. 1926, and elected to same office Nov. following, and served until 1935; judge Superior Ct. Atlanta Judicial Circuit, 1935-48. Democrat. Methodist. Mem. Kappa Alpha. Clubs: Piedmont Driving, Atlanta Athletic. Home: 141 Bolling Rd. Address: Court House, Atlanta, Ga. Died June 11, 1948.

DOSS, Roscoe James (dŏs), railroad exec.; b. nr. Canton, Ga., Mar. 30, 1884; s. Lemuel J. and Luray Virginia (Low) D.; student Etowah Mil. Inst., Canton, Ga., 1896-98; m. Lucy Humphreys, June 30, 1914. Clerk, later telegraph operator, Atlanta, Knoxville & Northern Ry. (now Louisville & Nashville R.R.), 1900-04; overcharge claim investigator, office of freight claim agent, Southern Ry., Washington, D.C., 1904-05; local agent, Atlanta, Knoxville & Northern Ry. (L&N), 1906-08, rate clerk, general freight office, L. & N. R.R., Knoxville, Tenn. and Louisville, Ky., 1908-13; chief rate clerk and chief clerk, gen. freight office, Atlantic Coast Line R.R., Savannah, Ga., 1913-16, asst. to gen. freight agent, Wilmington, N.C., 1916 to period of Federal control; during Fed. control attached to staff Southern rate com. U.S. Railroad Adminstrn.; asst. gen. freight agent, Atlantic Coast Line R.R., Wilmington, N.C., 1920-26; gen. freight agent, 1926-30, asst. freight traffic mgr., 1930-35, freight traffic mgr., 1935-40, gen. freight traffic mgr., 1940-41, gen. traffic mgr., 1941-42, v.p. traffic since May, 1942; vice pres. Charleston and Western Carolina Ry.; traffic mgr., Columbia, Newberry & Laurens R.R., Rockingham R.R.; dir. and traffic manager, East Carolina Railway. Member Association Interstate Commerce Commission Practitioners. Elk. Clubs: Cape Fear, Cape Fear Country, Carolina Yacht, Surf (Wilmington, N.C.); Traffic (New York). Home: 707 Market St. Office: Atlantic Coast Line Railroad Bldg. "D," Wilmington, N.C. Died June 26, 1949.

DOSTER, James Jarvis (dŏs'tẽr), univ. dean; b. Ariosto, Dale County, Ala., Dec. 20, 1873; s. Simeon J. and Sarah (Tucker) D.; Ph.B., State Teachers Coll., Troy, Ala., 1902; B.S., Teachers Coll., Columbia Univ., 1906, A.M., 1909; LL.D., Univ. of Alabama, 1917; m. Mabel Cowart, Aug. 11, 1909; 1 son, James Doster. Prin. high sch., Troy, 1900-02; prof. secondary edn., 1907-11, apptd. prof. philosophy and education, dean Coll. of Edn. and dir. of summer session since 1911, acting dean of university, 1918-19, U. of Ala. Asso. of Internat. Inst., Teachers Coll., Columbia, for study of secondary edn. in Argentine Republic, Chile, Uruguay and Brazil, 1925-26. Sec.-treas. Assn. of Ala. Colls., 1910-23; pres. Assn. of Ala. Colleges, 1923-1924. State ins. county high schs. of Ala., 1908-11; mem. Univ. Race Commn., Ala. State Text-Book Commn., Ala. Bd. for Vocational Edn. Democrat. Methodist. Rotarian, K.P. Mem. Am. Assn. Univ. Profs., Soc. Coll. Teachers Edn., N.E.A. (legislative com.), Ala. Ednl. Assn., Alabama Alpha, Phi Beta Kappa (sec. 1915-23), Delta Chi, Omicron Delta Kappa. Home: University, Ala. Died Oct. 21, 1942.

DOTEN, Carroll Warren (dō'tĕn), statistician; b. Panton, Vt., Jan. 27, 1871; s. Elisha Morton and Ida Lucretia (Hatch) D.; Ph.B., U. of Vt., 1895, A.M., 1899; A.M., Harvard U., 1902; m. Carrie Kingsland Mitchell, Sept. 6, 1899 (died July 9, 1933); children—Robert Kingsland, Dana Morton; m. 2d, Mary Helen Wyman, May 2, 1936. Instructor, 1895-1903, sec. and register, 1896-1903, U. of Vt.; instr., 1903-05, asst. prof. economics, 1905-14, asso. prof., 1914-18, prof. of economics, 1918-36, emeritus since Feb. 1, 1936, Mass. Inst. of Tech. Head of research work, Boston School for Social Workers, 1907-09; expert spl. agt. U.S. Bur. of Census, 1909; chief investigator, Mass. Commn. on Compensation for Industrial Accidents, 1910-12; pres. Cambridge (Mass.) Asso. Charities, 1914-17; pres. Cambridge Park Commission, 1921-1928 and 1934-1939; member Mass. Bureau Immigration, 1917-19. Head of industrial service section of U.S. Shipping Board Emergency Fleet Corp., 1918; in charge statis. audit, U.S. Central Bur. of Planning and Statistics, 1919; mem. advisory com. U.S. Census, 1919-24; cons. specialist Bur. Agrl. Economics, U.S. Dept. of Agr., 1922-27; cons. economist Nat. Retail Dry Goods Assn. since 1929; cons. specialist to secretary of interior, 1933-34; collaborator, consumers' counsel, Agricultural Adjustment Adminstrn. since 1934. Trustee U. of Vt., 1925-30 and since 1936. Pres. Am. Statis. Assn., 1920-21; member American Economics Association, Massachusetts Reform Club (president), N.E.R.R. Club (pres. 1921-22), Phi Beta Kappa, Phi Delta Theta. Republican. Conglist. Clubs: Cosmos (Washington); City (Boston); Cambridge. Home: Basin Farm, Brandon, Vt. Office: 222 Charles River Rd., Cambridge, Mass. Died June 14, 1942.

DOUBLEDAY, Nelson, chairman board, Doubleday & Co., Inc.; pres. Nelson Doubleday, Inc., Garden City Pub. Co., Inc., Windward House, Inc., The Blakiston Co., Childrens Literary Guild, Inc., Country Life Press Corp. Home: Oyster Bay, N.Y. Office: 500 Franklin St., Garden City, N.Y. Died Jan. 11, 1949.

DOUBLEDAY, Russell, author; b. Brooklyn, May 26, 1872; s. William Edwards and Ellen M. (Dickinson) D.; ed. in pvt. schs.; m. Janet MacDonald, Oct. 10, 1901. Served in naval militia during Spanish-Am. War, 1898. Advertising mgr., 1909-12, formerly v.p., sec., dir. and in charge editorial dept. Doubleday, Page & Company (now Doubleday & Co.); now retired. Author: A Gunner Aboard the Yankee, 1898; Cattle Ranch to College, 1899; A Year in a Yawl, 1901; Stories of Inventors, 1904; Photography Is Fun, 1938; Long Island, 1939; Tree Neighbors, 1940. Clubs: Century Assn., Piping Rock. Home: Glen Cove, N.Y. Died June 14, 1949.

DOUDNA, Edgar George (dou'dnȧ), educator; b. Viola, Wis., Sept. 21, 1877; s. William F. and Mary (Brewer) D.; grad. State Normal Sch., Platteville, Wis., 1900; Ph.B., University of Wisconsin, 1916; hon. M.A., Lawrence College, Appleton, Wis., 1926; L.H.D., from Milton College, 1942; married Carrie Parnell, Dec. 22, 1903; children—William Lester, Dorothy (dec.). Prin. high sch., Sextonville, Wis., 1900-03; teacher of English, high schs., Dodgeville, 1903-07; prin. high school, Watertown, 1907-08; supt. schs., Richland Center, 1908-16; head of English dept. State Teachers Coll., Eau Claire, 1916-18; supt. schs., Wisconsin Rapids, 1918-23; sec. Wis. Teachers Assn. and editor Wis. Jour. of Edn., 1923-28; sec. Bd. of Regents of Normal Schs. of Wis. and dir. teacher training since 1928. Mem. Nat. End. Assn.; chmn. board of trustee, Wisconsin Ednl. Assn. (president, 1939), Wisconsin Historical Society, Phi Delta Kappa. Democrat. Conglist. Mason (32°). Rotarian (dist. gov. 13th Dist., 1935-36). Author: Our Wisconsin (sch. history of Wis.), 1918; Our Government (Wis. edition), 1940; also articles on Wis. in cyclos., newspapers, etc. Lecturer on ednl. subjects. Home: 2017 Monroe St., Madison 5. Office: Capitol, Masison 2, Wis. Died April 16, 1948.

DOUGHERTY, Edward E., architect. Fellow Am. Inst. Architects since 1918. Address: Dougherty & Clemmons, Clarkston Hotel, Nashville, Tenn.* Deceased.

DOUGHERTY, Paul, artist; b. Brooklyn, N.Y., Sept. 6, 1877; s. J. Hampden and Alice (Hill) D.; B.S., Brooklyn Poly. Inst., 1896; LL.B., New York Law Sch., 1898; traveled and studied art alone, 5 yrs. at Paris, London, Florence, Venice, Munich; m. Anna Bertha Lund, Aug. 12, 1902 (died July 19, 1903); 1 dau., Anne Elizabeth; m. 2d, Marthe Wisner, Jan. 12, 1907; m. 3d, Marian Averell Clark, June 17, 1916; m. 4th, Paula Gates, Aug. 10, 1928. Exhibited Paris Salon, 1901, Nat. Acad. Design, Soc. Am. Artists, Pa. Acad. Fine Arts, Carnegie Inst., Pittsburgh, Venice, 1909, Berlin, 1910, Rome, 1911. Awarded

Osborn prize, 1905, silver medal Carnegie Internat. exhbn., 1912; Inness gold medal, 1913; Carnegie prize and 1st Altman prize, Nat. Acad. Design, 1913; gold medal, Panama-Pacific Expn., San Francisco, Calif., 1915; Palmer Memorial prize Nat. Acad. Design, 1941. Represented in permanent collections of Metropolitan Museum, N.Y. City; Luxembourg, Paris; Nat. Gallery, Corcoran Gallery and Phillips Memorial Gallery, Washington, D.C.; Carnegie Inst., Pittsburgh, Pa.; Art Inst. Chicago; Toledo (O.) Art Gallery; Hackley Art Inst., Muskegon, Mich.; Portland (Ore.) Museum, Fort Worth (Tex.) Museum; Albright Gallery, Buffalo, N.Y.; Memorial Gallery, Rochester, N.Y.; Art Museum, St. Louis, Mo.; Phillips Andover Gallery, Andover, Mass.; Nat. Gallery, Ottawa, Can. A.N.A., 1906, N.A., 1907; Wm. Rockhill Nelson Museum, Kansas City; mem. Nat. Inst. Arts and Letters, Soc. Am. Artists. Clubs: Century, National Arts (life), (N.Y.); Bohemian (hon.) (San Francisco). Address: R.F.D. 1, Carmel, Calif. Died Jan. 9, 1947.

DOUGHTY, Howard Waters, prof. chemistry; b. Baltimore, Md., Aug. 13, 1871; s. Thomas Paramour and Margaret Mustard (Waters) D.; student Johns Hopkins, 1890-93, 1900-04, Ph.D., 1904; M.A., Amherst Coll., 1916; Bachelor of Engring. extra ordinem, Johns Hopkins, 1927; m. Anna Elizabeth Bates, Nov. 29, 1905 (died Jan. 22, 1913); children—Mary Elizabeth (dec.), Odbert Bates, Howard Waters; m. 2d, Rebecca Thompson Pue, Dec. 22, 1920. Research asst., Carnegie Foundn, 1904-05; instr. chemistry, U. of Mo., 1905-06, U. of Wis., 1906-07; mem. faculty, Amherst since 1907, prof. chemistry 1913 since. Fellow A.A.A.S.; mem. Am. Chem. Soc., Phi Gamma Delta, Phi Beta Kappa, Sigma Xi, Phi Lambda Upsilon. Presbyterian. Home: Amherst, Mass. Died Jan. 25, 1949.

DOUGLAS, Alice May, author; b. Bath, Me., June 28, 1865; d. Joshua Lufkin and Helen Lauraman (Harvey) Douglas. Ex-state supt. peace and arbitration, Me. W.C.T.U.; ex-sec. Young People's Work of Woman's Home Missionary Soc. M.E. Ch., Me. Conf.; exec. Me. Branch Am. Sch. Peace League; Me. corr. Lake Mohonk Conf. on Internat. Arbitration; geneal. investigator for Eugenics Sect. Carnegie Instn., Cold Spring Harbor, N.Y.; ex-dir. Me. Conf. Deaconess Home, Portland. Formerly wrote S.S. lessons primary dept. Sunday School Journal; was editor of Pacific Banner, and The Acorn. First state primary S.S. sec. (for Me.) in U.S.; ex-4th v.p. Me. State Epworth League; ex-dist. sec. Woman's Foreign Missionary Soc., and conf. sec. of Woman's Home Missionary Soc. of M.E. Ch.; del. to Boston Peace Congress; founder of Peace Makers' Bands; ex-sec. of Lay Electoral Conf. of Me. Conf. of M.E. Ch.; ex-sec. Sagadahoc Historical Soc. Organizer of Bands of Mercy for Am. Humane Edn. Soc. Mem. New England Woman's Press Assn., Me. Woman's Suffrage Assn., Internat. Magna Carta Day Assn. (v.p. for Maine), Bath W.C.T.U. (pres.). Author: Phlox (verse); May Flowers (verse); Gems Without Polish, 1889; The Pine and the Palm (verse); Olive Leaves (songs); Peace Bells (songs). Serials: Quaker John in the Civil War; Self-exiled from Russia; How the Little Cousins Formed a Museum; The Peace Makers; A Friend Indeed; Jewel Gatherers. Home: Bath, Me. Died Jan. 6, 1943.

DOUGLAS, Archibald, lawyer; b. Tarrytown, N.Y., May 5, 1872; s. Henry Livingston D.; student Sch. of Mines (Columbia), 1890-92, literary course, 1892-93; LL.B., Columbia, 1896; m. Edith M. Douglas, of Spuyten Duyvil, N.Y., Oct. 8, 1901; children—Archibald, John Waldo, Mrs. Martin Fenton. Admitted N.Y. bar, 1896, and since practiced in N.Y. City; mem. firm Douglas, Armitage & McCann (now Douglas, Armitage & Holloway), since 1907; admitted to practice before U.S. Supreme Court, 1924; specializes in mining and corporate law; chairman board Solar-Sturges Mfg. Co. of Chicago; dir. G. R. Kinney Co. Trustee Columbia U. (twice elected alumni trustee; now life trustee), Bard College; chairman board Memorial Hospital for Treatment of Cancer. Chairman Committee for Republican Reorganization of Bronx County 1941. Mem. American, N.Y. State bar assns., Bar Assn. City of New York, Am. Inst. Mining and Metall. Engrs. (gen. counsel), Mining & Metall. Soc. America, Psi Upsilon (pres. 1932-37). Republican. Episcopalian. Clubs: Columbia University (a founder), Century, Down Town, University, Pilgrims, St. Andrew's Golf, Adirondack League, Anglers. Contbr. chapter on mining law in Peele's Engineering Handbook. Home: Spuyten Duyvil, N.Y. Office: 30 Rockefeller Plaza, New York, N.Y. Died Dec. 14, 1943.

DOUGLAS, Bruce Hutchinson, pub. health adminstrn.; b. Des Moines, Ia., Aug. 26, 1892; s. John Henry, Jr., and Mabel (Hutchinson) D.; A.B., Whittier (Calif.) Coll., 1915; M.D., Rush Medical Coll., U. of Chicago, 1921; m. Lorena Kelsey, Aug. 29, 1917; 1 dau., Mabel (Mrs. Eldon Hamm); m. 2d, Anita Kelsey, Feb. 3, 1926. Interne, Harper, Children's and Herman Kiefer hosps., Detroit, Mich., 1920-21; resident physician, Herman Kiefer Hosp., Detroit, Mich., 1921-22; asst. med. dir. Wm. H. Maybury Sanatorium, Northville, Mich., 1922-23, med. dir., 1923-24, supt., 1924-33; tuberculosis controller Detroit Dept. of Health, 1933-40; acting supt. Herman Kiefer Hosp., 1940-41; commr. of health Detroit, Mich., since 1941. Lecturer on tuberculosis, U. of Mich. Med. Sch., 1923-24; lecturer on tuberculosis U. of Mich. Postgrad. Medicine Dept. since 1930; prof. preventive medicine and pub. health, Wayne U., 1935-41, prof. and head dept. since 1941; special lecturer on tuberculosis U. of Mich. Sch. of Pub. Health since 1941. Commd. surgeon U.S.P.H.S., Reserve Corps, 1942. Mem. com. on tuberculosis Nat. Research Council, 1940-46. President Mississippi Valley Tuberculosis Conference, 1940-41. Fellow Am. Medical Association, American College Physicians, Am. Pub. Health Assn.; mem. Nat. Tuberculosis Assn. (pres. 1941-42). Am. Trudeau Soc. (formerly Am. Sanatorium Assn.), Mich. Trudeau Soc., Internat. Union Against Tuberculosis, Mich. State and Wayne County med. socs., Mich. Acad. Science, Arts and Letters, A.A.A.S. Mem. editorial bd. Am. Rev. of Tuberculosis. Author of chapter on tuberculosis, Top's Handbook of Communicable Diseases, 1941. Contbr. articles on tuberculosis to sci. jours. Home: 18066 Warrington Drive, Detroit 21. Office: 3919 John R St., Detroit 1, Mich. Died Aug. 11, 1949.

DOUGLAS, Charles Winfred, clergyman; b. Oswego, N.Y., Feb. 15, 1867; s. Virgil Chittenden and Caroline (Church) D.; Mus.B., Syracuse U., 1891; student St. Andrew's Div. Sch., Syracuse, 1893; studied ch. music in Eng., France and Germany, 1903-04; Mus.D., Nashotah House, Wis., 1916; m. Mary Josepha Williams, M.D., 1896; 1 son, Frederic Huntington. Deacon, 1893, priest, 1899, P.E. Ch.; asst. organist St. Paul's Cathedral, Syracuse, 1889-91; organist Ch. of Zion and St. Timothy, New York, 1892-93; curate Ch. of the Redeemer, New York, 1893-94; minor canon St. John's Cathedral, Denver, Colo., 1894-97; canon St. Paul's Cathedral, Fond du Lac, Wis., 1907-34; canon St. John's Cathedral, Denver, 1934; asso. editor New Hymnal, P.E. Ch.; editorial work, lecturing and teaching; lecturer Union Theol. Sem., N.Y. City, 1928, 34; Hale lecturer, Seabury Northwestern Seminary, 1935; mem. advisory bd. and lecturer, St. Dunstan's Coll. Sacred Music; v.p. The Evergreen Conference. Trustee Nashotah House, Hoosac Sch., Schola Cantorum, New York. Fellow Am. Ecclesiol. Soc. (chmn. dept. of music), Plainsong Soc. (pres.); mem. Delta Kappa Epsilon, Theta Nu Epsilon. Clubs: Explorers', Delta Kappa Epsilon (New York); Bohemians. Editor or Compiler: Ordinary and Canon of the Mass, 1913; The Canticles at Evensong, 1915; The Order of Matins, 1916; The Psalms of David, 1917; The St. Dunstan Psalter, Parts 1 and 2; The Ceremonial Noted, 1923; (with Kurt Schindler) A Cappella Choruses from the Russian Liturgy; (with same) Twelve Old Spanish Motets; Songs of the Church, 1921; (with Wallace Goodrich) The Choral Service, 1927; The American Psalter, 1929; The American Missal, 1931; The American Plainsong Psalter, 1931; The Monastic Diurnal, 1932; The Midnight Mass, 1933; The St. Dunstan Kyrial, 1933; The Praise of God—Church Music in History and Practice, 1936; A Missionary Service Book, 1937. Home: 2588 Dexter St., Denver, Colo.* Died Jan. 18, 1944.

DOUGLAS, Fred James, surgeon, ex-congressman; b. Clinton, Mass., Sept. 14, 1869; s. Andrew and Adelaide (Brennan) D.; M.D., Dartmouth Med. Sch., Hanover, N.H., 1895; m. Catherine McGrath, Dec. 1, 1897; children—James Glass, Katherine Jean (Mrs. Mason F. Sexton), Fred John. Interne Faxton Hosp., Utica, N.Y., 1895-97, mem. surgical staff since 1923; cons. surgeon Utica State Hospital; member 75th-79th Congresses (1937-47), 33d N.Y. Dist. Mem. bd. Edn., Utica, 1910-20, mayor, 1922-23; commr. for lit. gov. of N.Y., 1934. Fellow Am. Coll. Surgeons; mem. A.M.A., N.Y. State Med. Assn., Oneida County Med. Assn., Utica Acad. of Medicine, Alpha Kappa Kappa. Republican. Mason, Elk. Clubs: Ft. Schuyler (Utica); Nat. Republican. Home: 285 Genesee St., Utica, N.Y.* Died Jan. 1, 1949.

DOUGLAS, George William, editor; b. Liberty, Sullivan County, N.Y., Apr. 8, 1863; s. Rev. Samuel J. and Annie Suthers (Jackson) D.; A.B., Colgate U., 1888, A.M., 1891, Litt.D., 1915; m. Gertrude Douglas Greenwood, Dec. 4, 1895; children—Mrs. John M. Compton, Gertrude Wellesley. Asso. with brothers in pub. amateur paper in Springfield Center, N.Y., 1872-76; reporter Brooklyn Citizen, 1888-91; law reporter Brooklyn Daily Eagle, 1891; Albany legislative corps, same, 1892, asso. editor and editorial writer on Eagle, 1892-1902; asso. editor Youth's Companion, 1902-14; asso. editor Phila. Public Ledger, 1914-15; asso. editor Evening Public Ledger, 1915-34, lit. editor, 1917-24. Mem. Phi Beta Kappa. Delta Upsilon; mem. Pa. Hist. Soc. Alumni trustee Colgate U.; 1896-1937. Author: The Many-Sided Roosevelt; The American Book of Days; also various short stories and spl. articles on pub. topics. Contbr. to Ency. Britannica and Britannica Book of the Year. Office: Evening Public Ledger, Philadelphia, Pa. Died Feb. 17, 1945.

DOUGLAS, James Stuart, miner, banker; b. Megantic Twp., Quebec, Can., June 19, 1868; s. James and Naomi (Douglas) D.; ed. pub. schs.; m. Josephine Leah Williams, Nov. 11, 1891; children—Lewis W., James. Assayer for Copper Queen mine, Ariz., 1891-92; time-keeper and assayer Senator mine of the Commercial Mining Co., Prescott, Ariz., 1892-94, assayer, bookkeeper and supt, 1892-94, supt. Big Bug Smelter, 1896-99; supt. Piacho mine, Sonora, Mexico, 1900; supt. Moctezuma Copper Co., 1901-09; became pres. Bank of Douglas, 1909; pres. United Verde Extension Mining Co.; vice pres. and gen. mgr. Cananea Cons. Copper Co., 1913-14. Decorated Chevalier Legion d'Honneur (France). Democrat. Episcopalian. Club: Cercle Interallie (Paris). Home: Douglas, Ariz. Died Jan. 2, 1949.

DOUGLAS, Thaddeus, judge; b. Clinton, Iowa, May 2, 1872; s. William R. and Lurana (Duncan) H.; A.B., Grant U., Athens, Tenn., 1891; LL.B., Cumberland U., 1892; LL.D., Chattanooga U., 1923; LL.D., Cumberland Univ., 1940; m. Effie May Sawyer, Oct. 22, 1896; children—Louise, Elizabeth. Began practice at Clinton, 1892; city atty., 1892-93; county atty. Anderson County, 1894-96; capt. 6th U.S. Vol. Inf., Spanish Am. War, 1898; alderman and mayor of Clinton; mem. Tenn. Senate, 1911; asst. atty. general 2d Circuit of Tenn., 1911-13; judge Criminal and Law Court, 1913-18; judge Circuit Court, 19th Circuit of Tenn., 1918-23; U.S. dist. judge, East and Middle dists. of Tenn., 1923-28; U.S. circuit judge, Sixth Circuit, since June 12, 1928, Presiding judge since 1938, chief judge since 1948. Mem. Beta Theta Pi, Phi Delta Phi. Republican. Methodist. Club: University (Cincinnati). Home: Clinton, Iowa. Address: Federal Bldg., Nashville, Tenn. Died Aug. 11, 1949.

DOUGLAS, Walter, mining engr.; b. Quebec, P.Q., Can., Dec. 19, 1870; s. James and Naomi (Douglas) D.; ed. Upper Can. Coll., Morrin Coll., Royal Mil. Coll., all of Can.; Sch. of Mines (Columbia); m. Edith Margaret Bell, Sept. 10, 1902; children—Elizabeth Margaret, Katherine Stuart, Naomi Margaret, Walter, Robert Bell. Engr. Commercial Mining Co. of Prescott, Ariz., 1890-92; metallurgist, Consol. Kansas City Smelting & Refining Co., 1892-94; chemist Copper Queen Consol. Mining Co., 1894-95; Detroit Copper Mining Co., 1896-99; supt. 1899-1902, gen. mgr. since 1902, Copper Queen Consol. Mining Co.; gen. mgr. Phelps Dodge & Co. since 1910; ex-pres. Phelps Dodge Corp., now dir.; officer numerous allied corps.; formerly chmn. bd. in active charge of property Southern Pacific R.R. Co. of Mexico; dir. Southern Pacific Co., etc. Mem. Am. Mining Congress (ex-pres.), Am. Inst. Mining Engrs., Mining and Metall. Soc. of America, St. Andrew's Soc., etc. Clubs: Century, Grolier, Down Town, St. Andrew's Golf. Home: "Glenalla," Chauncey, N.Y. Office: 233 Broadway, New York, N.Y. Died Oct. 3, 1946.

DOUGLAS, William Harris, ex-congressman; b. New York, Dec. 5, 1853; s. Alfred and Rebecca A. (Harris) D.; ed. New York City and boarding schs., Ft. Washington and Ossining, N.Y., and one yr. at Coll. City of New York; m. Juliette H. Thorne, Apr. 11, 1889. Pres. Arkell & Douglas, Inc., shipping and commn., New York. Mem. 57th and 58th Congresses (1901-05), 14th (now 15th) N.Y. Dist. Mem. C. of C., Produce Exchange (pres., 1906-07), Maritime Exchange, Merchants' Exchange, S.R., Soc. Colonial Wars, Soc. Cincinnati. Clubs: Union League, Republican. Home: 317 W. 76th St. Office: 22 Exchange Pl., New York. Died Jan. 27, 1944.

DOUGLASS, Matthew Hale, librarian emeritus; b. Osage, Ia., Sept. 16, 1874; s. Rev. Truman Orville and Maria (Greene) D.; A.B., Grinnell Coll., 1895, A.M., 1898; m. Minnie Griswold, June 25, 1905 (died Apr. 5, 1943). Librarian Grinnell Coll., 1899-1908; librarian, U. of Ore., 1908-42, librarian emeritus since 1942. Mem. Ia. Library Assn. (pres. 1906), Pacific Northwest Library Assn. (treas. 1910-14, sec. 1921-22, pres. 1924-26), Phi Beta Kappa (pres. U. of Ore. chapter 1934-35). Club: Rotary (Eugene, Ore.). Home: 2293 Birch Lane, Eugene, Ore.* Died Oct. 3, 1945.

DOW, Alex (dou), chmn. exec. com. Detroit Edison Co.; b. Scotland, 1862; hon. Master Engring., U. of Mich., 1911; hon. D.Engring., U. of Mich., 1924; D.Sc., U. of Detroit, 1936; Dr. of Arts, Wayne U., 1938; m. Vivienne Kinnersley, 1889. Came to U.S., 1882, naturalized, 1895. Elec. engr. City of Detroit, 1893-96; water commr., Detroit, 1916-21, reapptd., 1925-32; pres. Detroit Edison Co., 1932-40, now chmn. exec. com. Mem. Am. Soc. C.E., Am. Soc. M.E., Am. Inst. E.E., Inst. Elec. Engrs., Inst. Mech. Engrs. (Great Britain), etc. Republican. Episcopalian. Clubs: Detroit, etc. Home: Barton Hills, Ann Arbor, Mich. Office: 2000 2d Av., Detroit, Mich. Died Mar. 22, 1942.

DOW, Edward Albert, Am. consul gen.; b. Ft. Dodge, Ia., Apr. 20, 1879; s. Charles Noble and Nora Gertrude D.; A.B., Ambrose Coll., Davenport, 1897; studied langs. and sciences, St. Paul, Minn., 2 yrs.; m. Rose C. Rush; children—Edward Albert, Rose Mary. Real estate and ins. business, 1900-15; apptd. consul at St. Stephen, N.B., Can., Nov. 1915; at Ft. William and Port Arthur, Can., 1917, Ciudad Juarez, Mexico, 1917-20, Algiers, Algeria, 1920-24, Rotterdam, Netherlands, 1924-28, Frankfort-on-Main, Germany, 1928-30; consul gen., St. John's, Newfoundland, 1930-33, at Santiago, 1933-39, Leipzig, Germany, 1939—. Catholic. Clubs: Union, Rotary, Automobile. Home: Omaha, Neb. Address: State Dept., Washington, D.C.* Died July 31, 1945.

DOW, Willard Henry, corp. official; b. Midland, Mich., Jan. 4, 1897; s. Herbert Henry and Grace Anna (Ball) D.; Bachelor of Science, University of Mich., 1919, D.E., from same university, 1941; D.Sc., Mich. Coll. of Mining and Tech., 1939; D. Eng., Illinois Inst. of Tech., 1944; m. Martha L. Pratt, Sept. 3, 1921; children—Helen Dow Whiting, Herbert Henry II. Began as chem. engr. Dow Chem. Co., 1919, dir. since 1922, asst. gen. mgr., 1926-30, pres. and gen. mgr. since 1930, chmn. board since 1941; pres. Ethyl-Dow Chem Co., 1933-46; Midland Ammonia Co., 1937-45, Dow of Can., Ltd., 1942-46, Io-Dow Chem. Co., 1936-39, Dowell Inc., 1932-39, Cliffs Dow Chem. Co., 1935-39; dir. Dowell, Inc., Dow Magnesium Corp., Dow Corning Corp., Midland Ammonia Co., Dow Chem. of Can., Ltd., Saran Yarns Co., Ethyl-Dow Chem. Co. (1933-46), Cliffs Dow

Chem. Co. (1935-42). Mem. Chem. Corps Adv. Bd., chmn. adv. com. Munitions Bd., 1940-49; adviser to Resources Div. Office Quartermaster Gen., 1942-49. Mem. bd. control Mich. Coll. of Mining and Tech., 1946-49; Corp. of Mass. Inst. Tech., 1942-46. Mem. Am. Chem. Soc. (dir. 1945-49), Am. Inst. Chem. Engrs., Am. Inst. of Chemists, Soc. Chem. Industry, A.A.A.S., N.E. Historic Geneaol. Soc., Engring. Soc. of Midland, Newcomen Soc., Tau Beta Pi, Theta Delta Chi, Alpha Sigma. Chandler Medalist, Columbia, 1943; recipient; Gold Medal of Am. Inst. Chemists, 1944; Chem. Industry Medal of Am. sect. of Soc. of Chem. Industry, 1946; Medal for Advancement of Research by Am. Soc. for Metals, 1948. Chosen one of America's 50 foremost bus. leaders by Forbes Mag., 1948. Presbyterian. Mason (33°, Shriner). Clubs: Chemists, Rockefeller Center (New York); Detroit, Midland Country; Bohemian (San Francisco); York (Toronto); Crystal Downs Country (Frankfort, Mich.). Home: 923 W. Park Drive. Office: Dow Chemical Co., Midland, Mich. Died Mar. 31, 1949.

DOWLING, John Joseph, lawyer; b. New York, N.Y., Dec. 1, 1903; s. John Joseph and Eva (Morris) D.; student Fordham Coll., 1925-26; LL.B., Fordham Law Sch., 1929; m. Anne Chisholm, June 30, 1936; children—John Lawrence, Peter Chisholm, Roderick Anthony, Brian Richard, Robert Morris, II. Admitted to N.Y. bar, 1932, and asso. with Compton & Delaney, New York, 1929-31, Laughlin, Gerard, Bowers & Halpin, New York, 1931-34; asst. U.S. atty., Southern Dist. of N.Y., 1934-39; dir. Catholic Lawyers Guild; trial counsel Securities and Exchange Commn., New York, Mar. 1, 1939-Mar. 30, 1940; counsel to trustees in reorganization of Asso. Gas & Electric Corp., 1940-42; partner Krisel, Lessall & Dowling. Served 7th Regt., N.Y. Nat. Guard. Mem. Bar Assn., City of New York, Am. Bar Assn., Gamma Eta Gamma. Democrat. Roman Catholic. Clubs: N.Y. Athletic, New Rochelle Shore, National Democratic, Scarsdale Golf. Home: 3 Hamilton Rd., Scarsdale, N.Y. Office: 1450 Broadway, New York. Died May 4, 1949.

DOWNES, William Augustus, surgeon; b. Crockett, Tex., Dec. 2, 1872; s. James E. and Elizabeth (Brown) D.; M.D., Coll. Phys. and Surg., Columbia, 1895; m. Lucile K. Griffin, Sept. 1927; children—Helen C., Elizabeth K. (Mrs. John Atkins Payne), Margaret (Mrs. Leonard Courtlandt Linkroum, Jr.). Practiced in New York City since 1900; prof. clin. surgery, Coll. Phys. and Surg., Columbia Univ., since 1913; attending surgeon St. Luke's and Babies' hosps.; cons. surgeon Memorial, Manhattan State hosps.; Hosp. for Ruptured and Crippled, New York Nursery, since practiced at Boston; mem. Mass. Ho. of Rep. 4 terms between 1899-1913; mem. Mass. Constl. Conv., 1917-18; mem. 69th to 72d Congresses (1925-33), 10th Mass. Dist., and 73d Congress (1933-35), 11th Mass. Dist. Democrat. Home: 51 Landseer St., West Roxbury, Mass. Died May 10, 1948.

DOWNEY, Francis Xavier, clergyman, educator; b. New Haven, Conn., Aug. 12, 1887; s. Michael Joseph and Mary A. (McMahon) D.; student Holy Cross Coll.; grad. Novitiate of St. Andrew, Poughkeepsie, N.Y., 1910; B.A., Woodstock Coll., Md., 1913, M.A., 1918. Joined Soc. of Jesus (Jesuits) 1906; ordained priest, R.C. Ch., 1921; prin. Regis High Sch., New York, 1922-23; dean and sec. trustee, Holy Cross Coll., 1924-29. Founder Pro Parvulis (Boys' and Girls') Book Club; editorial sec. Spiritual Book Assos. Mem. N.E.A., N.E. Classical Assn. (v.p.), Nat. Council Teachers of English. K.C. Author: Greek Grammar (with F. M. Connell); Taking Down the Crib; contbr. fiction and essays. Dir. presentation of Euripides' Hecuba, at Sesquicentennial, Phila., 1926. Lecturer and occasional preacher as mem. Jesuit mission band; spiritual dir. of retreats to religious orgns. Editor Jesuit Seminary News. Home: 300 Newbury St., Boston, Mass. Address: Empire State Bldg., New York, N.Y. Died Apr. 14, 1942.

DOWNING, Elliot Rowland, zoölogist, educator; b. Boston, Mass., Nov. 21, 1868; s. Orrien Elliot and Mary Jane (Rowland) D.; B.S., Albion (Mich.) Coll., 1889; M.S., 1894; Ph.D., U. of Chicago, 1901; Columbia, 1907-08; U. of Würzburg, Naples Aquarium, 1908; m. Grace Emma Manning, June 24, 1902; children—George Elliot, Mary Elizabeth, Lucia Grace. Instr. science, Ft. Payne (Ala.) Acad., 1890-91, Beloit (Wis.) Coll. Acad., 1891-96; supt. Brooklyn Training Sch. for Boys, 1896-98; sec. Brooklyn Children's Aid Soc., 1898-99; fellow in zoölogy, U. of Chicago, 1899-1901; instr. embryology, summer sessions same, 1900, 1901; prof. biology, Northern State Normal Sch., Marquette, Mich., 1901-11; asst. prof. natural science, 1911-13, asso. prof., 1913-34, emeritus asso. prof. since 1934; asst. dean School of Edn., 1913-16, Univ. of Chicago. Editor Nature Study Review, 1911-17. Pres. Mich. State Non-Game Bird Commn., 1907-11. Fellow A.A.A.S.; mem. Am. Eugenics Assn., Wis. Acad. Science, Am. Nature Study Soc., Nat. Assn. Research in Science Teaching (pres. 1930-32), Sigma Xi, Alpha Tau Omega. Republican. Conglist. Club: Quadrangle. Author: Elementary Eugenics; A Naturalist in the Great Lakes Region; Our Living World; Our Physical World; Teaching Science in the Schools; Science in the Service of Health; Introduction to the Teaching of Science; Living Things and You. Home: Williams Bay, Wis. Died Sep. 10, 1944.

DOWNING, Harold Kemp, banker; b. Troy, N.Y., Sept. 21, 1875; s. Edward Halley and Anna (Cantrell) D.; ed. high sch., Troy; m. Jane Riggs Luckerhoff, June 1, 1899; 1 dau., Eleanor. Clk. Nat. State Bank, Troy, 1893-98; receiving teller Mfrs. Nat. Bank, 1898-1901; asst. sec. and treas. The Troy Trust Co., 1901-07, treas., 1907-13, sec. and treas., 1913-18, v.p. and sec., 1918-20, president, 1920-41, chmn. bd., Jan. 15-Nov. 1, 1941; treas., mng. dir. and dir. Rensselaer Improvement Co. Mem. N.G.N.Y., 1890-98. Treas. Rensselaer County Red Cross. Mem. Am. Bankers Assn., N.Y. State Bankers Assn., Rensselaer County Bankers Assn. (chmn.), Trust Companies Assn. of N.Y. (exec. com.), Atlantic States Shippers Advisory Board, Troy Chamber of Commerce (ex-pres.). Republican. Episcopalian. Mason. Clubs: Troy, Rotary, Masonic, Troy Country. Home: The Caldwell. Office: 33 3d St., Troy, N.Y. Deceased.

DOWNING, Paul M., elec. engr.; b. Newark, Mo., Nov. 27, 1873; s. Thomas B. and Margaret (Sanford) D.; A.B., Stanford, 1895; m. Frances Stevenson, July 20, 1897. With Tacoma (Wash.) Light & Power Co., 1895-96, Market St. Ry. Co., San Francisco, 1896-97, Blue Lakes Water Co., 1898-99; Standard Consol. Mining Co., 1899-1901; mgr. Colusa Gas & Electric Co., 1901-02; div. supt. Bay Counties Power Co., 1902-03; various positions with Calif. Gas and Electric Corp. and Pacific Gas and Electric Co.; 1st v.p. and general manager Pacific Gas and Electric Co., 1929-43, executive vice-president since August 1943, Vice-president Edison Electric Institute; mem. Am. Inst. Elec. Engrs., Pacific Coast Elec. Assn., Pacific Coast Gas Assn. Republican. Mason (K.T., Shriner). Clubs: Engineers', Olympic, Commonwealth, Sutter, Commercial, Pacific Union, Lakeside Country, Menlo Country, San Francisco Golf. Home: 1980 Washington St. Office: 245 Market St., San Francisco, Calif. Died Dec. 11, 1944.

DOWNING, Robert L., actor; b. Washington, 1857; m. Eugenie Blair, actress. Entered profession, 1877, at Baltimore, and later supported Mary Anderson, Edwin Booth, John McCullough, John E. Owens, Joseph Jefferson and others. Since 1889 has starred unler his own management as Virginius, Spartacus in The Gladiator, Othello, Ingomar and other heroic roles. Died Oct. 1, 1944.

DRACHMAN, Bernard (drăk'măn), rabbi; b. New York, June 27, 1861; s. Benjamin D.; A.B., Columbia, 1882; grad. U. of Breslau Jewish Theol. Sem., Breslau; Ph.D. multa cum laude, Heidelberg, 1884; rabbi, Breslau, 1885; spl. studies Jewish theology, Semitic langs. and philosophy; m. Sarah, d. Jonas Weil, philanthropist, of New York, Feb. 15, 1888 (died Feb. 11, 1925); m. 2d, Hadassah Levine (educator and social worker), July 12, 1927. One of few Am.-born rabbis to give warm and consistent adherence to the orthodox faith of Judaism; prof. Bibl. exegesis and Hebrew philosophy, 1887-1902, and dean, 1889-1902, Jewish Theol. Sem. of New York; prof. Bible and Rabbinical Codes, Jewish Theol. Sem. of America until 1908; now lecturer Hebrew lang. and lit., Yeshiva Coll., N.Y. Rabbi Congregation Zichron Ephraim, New York, since 1889, also of Congregation Ohab Zedek, May 1909-Oct. 1922. Pres. Jewish Sabbath Alliance of America; hon. pres. Union of Orthodox Jewish Congregations of America; dir. Synagogue Council of America; mem. Hebrew Language Com. of Vaad Ha-Lashon of Palestine. Author: Die Stellung and Bedeutung des Jehuda Hajjug in der Geschichte der Hebräischen Grammatik, 1885; From the Heart of Israel, 1905; Looking at America, 1935. Translator: The Nineteen Letters of Ben Uziel, from the German of Samson Raphael Hirsch, New York, 1899; The Second Book of Samuel, from the original Hebrew. Edited and published Dibré Ha-Riboth, a mediæval Hebrew manuscript, 1908. Author of many essays and monographs on Jewish scientific and theol. subjects. Formerly editor Sabbath Jour. and Jewish Forum. Awarded Columbia U. medal for excellence, June 1941. Address: 245 E. 72d St., New York. Died March 12, 1945; buried in Mount Zion Cemetery, L.I., N.Y.

DRAIN, James Andrew, past nat. comdr. Am. Legion; b. Warren County, Ill., Sept. 30, 1870; s. Andrew Hazlett and Virginia (Wornem) D.; ed. high sch. and Western Normal Coll., Shenandoah, Ia.; m. Ethel Mary Marsland, June 24, 1891. Mem. Supreme Court of U.S., Dist. of Columbia, Wash. State and Am. bar assns.; owner, pub. and editor Arms and the Man, New York and Washington. Brig. gen. and adj. gen. Nat. Guard of Washington; chmn. exec. com. Nat. Guard Assn. of U.S.; chmn. Nat. Militia Bd., etc. World War, Apr. 20, 1917-June 9, 1919; original ordnance officer 1st Div., A.E.F., France, June 1917; D.S.M. (U.S.); Legion of Honor (French); Cross of Italy. Nat. comdr. Am. Legion, 1924-25. Lawyer Spokane, Wash., and Washington, D.C. Staff Social Security Board; asst. to Federal Security Administrator. Clubs: University, National Press, Washington Golf and Country. Author: Stories of Some Shoots, 1912; various articles. Home: Stoneleigh Court, Washington, D.C. Died May 30, 1943.

DRAKE, J(ohn) Walter, automobile mfr.; b. Sturgis, Mich., Sept. 27, 1875; s. Alfred G. and Anna Maria (Patrick) D.; LL.B., Detroit Coll. of Law, 1896; m. Martha Myler, Sept. 27, 1900; children—Rosalie (Mrs. Robert Wendell Hodge), John Alfred, Ruth Barbara (Mrs. Robert Charles Lake), Elizabeth Myler (Mrs. Robert Thompson Garrison). Practiced law at Detroit, Mich., 1896-1908; pres. Hupp Motor Car Co., 1908, chmn. bd., 1923; now pres. Hupp Motor Car Corp.; asst. sec. of commerce of U.S., 1923-27. Mem. Detroit Bd. of Commerce, Soc. Automotive Engrs., Detroit Bar Assn. Served on U.S.S. Yosemite, Spanish-Am. War. Republican. Episcopalian. Clubs: Detroit, Detroit Boat, Country Club of Detroit, Detroit Automobile. Home: Lake Angelus, Pontiac, Mich. Office: Hupp Motor Car Corp., Detroit, Mich. Died Nov. 27, 1941.

DRAKE, Joseph Horace, Sr., prof. law; b. Lebanon, O., May 16, 1860; s. Isaac Lincoln and Sarah (Evans) D.; A.B., U. of Mich., 1885, Ph.D., 1900, LL.B., 1902; univs. of Jena and Munich, 1890-92, U. of Greifswald, 1899; m. Maude Elizabeth Merritt, June 20, 1894 (died Sept. 29, 1920); children—Joseph Horace, Charles Merritt, Robert Lincoln, Elizabeth Maude. Prin. high sch., Battle Creek, Mich., 1885-88; asst. prof. Latin, 1890-1900, jr. prof. Latin and Roman law, 1900-02, prof. Roman law, 1902-07, prof. law, 1907-30, now emeritus, U. of Mich. Mem. Mich. Bar Assn., Phi Beta Kappa, Delta Upsilon, Phi Delta Phi. Republican. Clubs: Scientific, Research. Author: The Principales of the Early Roman Empire, 1904. Translator: Menæchmi of Plautus; Stammler's Fundamental Tendencies in Modern Jurisprudence; Wolff's Jus Gentium. Annotated The Fables of Phædrus, and revised Jones' Beginning Latin Book, and Jones' Latin Prose. Contbr. articles to class and law journals on Contract, Partnership, Damages, etc. Home: 903 Lincoln Av., Ann Arbor, Mich. Died Aug. 4, 1947.

DRAKE, Noah Fields, geologist; b. Summers, Washington County, Ark., Jan. 30, 1864; s. Wesley and Martha (Kellam) D.; C.E., U. of Ark., 1888; A.B., 1894, A.M., 1895, Ph.D., 1897, Stanford U.; m. Mary Elenor Shockley, July 30, 1904 (died Dec. 25, 1926); m. 2d, Lota West Fairchild, Dec. 23, 1932. Geologic work, Ark. Geol. Survey, 1887, Texas Geol. Survey, 1889-93, U.S. Geol. Survey, 1897; prof. geology and mining, 1898-1900 and 1905-11, Pei Yang U., Tientsin, China; asso. prof. economic geology, Leland Stanford Jr. U., 1911-12; prof. geology and mining, U. of Ark., 1912-20; cons. geologist since 1920. Engr. Pub. Works Dept., Tientsin, China, 1900-01; cons. geologist Am. China Development Co., 1902-04; chmn. bd. Tientsin Land & Investment Co., Ltd., 1904-11; v.p. Am. Machinery & Export Co., Tientsin, 1910. Fellow Geol. Soc. America; mem. Am. Inst. Mining Engrs., Seismol. Soc. America, Royal Asiatic Soc. (N. China branch), China Philos. Soc. Home: Fayetteville, Ark. Died May 4, 1945.

DRANE, Herbert Jackson; b. Franklin, Ky., June 20, 1863; s. Ossian A. and Josephine F. (Dickey) D.; ed. pub. schs. and by home study; honorary LL.D., Florida Southern Coll., Lakeland, Fla., 1929; m. Mary Wright, Dec. 31, 1885; children—Ossian Wright (1st lt. in World War; died as result of service), Mabel (Mrs. W. S. Moore), Josephine (Mrs. James W. Passmore). Went to Fla., 1883, as a r.r. builder and was a founder of Lakeland; engaged in fire ins., real estate business and orange growing. Served as mayor of Lakeland and county commr., Polk County, Fla.; mem. Fla. Ho. of Rep., 1903, Senate, 1913-17 (pres. 2 yrs.); mem. 65th to 72d Congresses (1917-33), 1st Fla. Dist.; mem. Federal Power Commn., 1933-37; pres. H. J. Drane & Son, Inc., ins. and real estate (founded 1884), Lakeland Building and Investment Co. Hon. mem. Army and Navy Club of Tampa, Spanish-Am. War Vets. (Gen. Leonard Wood Post of St. Petersburg, Fla.), Sigma Nu Phi (Joseph H. Choate Chapter, Washington, D.C., 1921). Democrat. Episcopalian. Mason (32°), Elk, Woodman. Drane Field, U.S. Army air base at Lakeland, named in his honor. Home: "Hillcrest." Office: Drane Bldg., 311 E. Main St., Lakeland, Fla. Died Aug. 12, 1947.

DRAPER, Benjamin Helm Bristow, textile machinery mfr.; b. N.Y. City, Feb. 28, 1885; s. Eben Sumner and Nannie (Bristow) D.; prep. edn., St. Mark's Sch., Southboro, Mass., and Phillips-Exeter Acad.; Harvard, 1903-06; m. Queena Sanford, Mar. 17, 1907; children—Benjamin Helm Bristow, Eben, Robert Caulfield. Pres. Draper Corp., mfrs. textile machinery; dir. First Nat. Bank of Boston, United Shoe Machinery Corp., Calhoun Mills. Served as pvt., Field Artillery, U.S. Army, World War. Mem. Am. Legion. Republican. Unitarian. Clubs: Somerset, Harvard, Tennis and Racquet, Brookline Country (Boston); River (New York); The Bath, Indian Creek Country (Miami Beach, Fla.). Home: Hopedale, Mass. Died June 4, 1944.

DRAPER, Edward Bailey, timberlands, mfr., lawyer; b. Canton, Mass., Mar. 27, 1876; s. Thomas Bailey and Sarah D. T. (Sumner) D.; A.B., Harvard, 1899, LL.B., 1902; married. Treas., gen. mgr. Katahdin Pulp & Paper Co., 1910-14; pres. Lincoln (Me.) Trust Co., 1912-14. Treasurer Puerto Rican plantation and processing cos., 1942-45. Mem. Mass. Ho. of Rep., 1907, 08. Trustee U. of Me., 1922-28; pres. Canton Taxpayers' Assn. for 2 years; dir. of Mass. Fed. of Taxpayers' Assns. since 1936; dir. Mass. Forest and Park Assn.; member New Eng. Forestry Foundation. Republican. Unitarian. Mason. Home: 150 Chapman St., Canton, Mass. Died Feb. 3, 1947.

DRAYTON, Samuel, chmn. bd. Hudson County Nat. Bank; b. Jersey City, N.J., 1863. Elk. Address: Hudson County National Bank, 75 Montgomery St., Jersey city 2, N.J. Died Jan. 16, 1949.

DREISER, Theodore (drī'sēr), author, journalist; b. Terre Haute, Ind., Aug. 27, 1871; s. John Paul and Sarah (Schanab) D.; ed. pub. schs. of Warsaw, Ind., and Indiana U. Began newspaper work, Chicago Globe, June 15, 1891; dramatic editor and traveling corr. St. Louis Globe-Democrat, 1892-93;

traveling corr. St. Louis Republic, 1893-94; editor Every Month, 1895-96; subsequently special work for Harper's, McClure's, Century, Cosmopolitan and Munsey's; editor of Smith's Magazine, 1905-06; mng. editor Broadway Magazine, 1906-07; editor-in-chief of the Butterick Publs. (Delineator, Designer, New Idea, English Delineator), 1907-10. Organized Nat. Child Rescue Campaign, 1907. Asso. editor: American Spectator until Jan. 1934. Author: Sister Carrie (novel), 1900; Jennie Gerhardt, 1911; The Financier, 1912; A Traveller at Forty, 1913; The Titan, 1914; The Genius, 1915; Plays of the Natural and the Supernatural, 1916; A Hoosier Holiday, 1916; Free and Other Stories, 1918; Twelve Men, 1919; The Hand of the Potter (tragedy), 1919; Hey Ruba-Dub-Dub—a Book of Essays and Philosophy, 1920; Newspaper Days (a Book About Myself), 1922; The Color of a Great City, 1923; An American Tragedy, 1925; Moods (verse), 1926; Chains (lesser novels and stories), 1927; Dreiser Looks at Russia, 1928; A Gallery of Women, 1929; My City, 1929; Epitaph, 1930; Dawn, 1931; Tragic America, 1932; Thoreau. 1939; America Is Worth Saving, 1941. Home: 1015 N. King's Rd., Hollywood, Calif. Address: care P. Putnam's Sons. 2 W. 45th St., New York, N.Y. Died Dec. 28, 1945.

DREWRY, Patrick Henry, congressman; b. Petersburg, Va., May 24, 1875; s. Dr. E. A. and Alta L. (Booth) D.; B.A., Randolph-Macon Coll., Ashland, Va.; LL.D., Randolph-Macon Coll., 1946; studied law at U. of Va.; m. Mary E. Metcalf, Apr. 18, 1906; children—Patrick Henry, John Metcalf, William Emmett. Admitted to Va. bar, 1901, and began practice at Petersburg; mem. bd. dirs. Petersburg Savings and Am. Trust Co., Petersburg. Served as chmn. state auditing com., chmn. Economy and Efficiency Commn. of Va. and chmn. State Advisory Bd.; mem. Va. Senate, 1912-20; elected without opposition as mem. 66th Congress, Apr. 27, 1920, to fill unexpired term of Walter A. Watson, and to 67th to 72d Congresses (1921-33), 4th Va. District; reëlected 73d and 74th Congresses (1933-37), Va. at large, and 75th to 80th Congresses (1937-49), 4th Virginia District. Chmn. Dem. Nat. Congressional Com.; del. at large to Dem. Nat. Conv. in 1916, and del. from Va. to all succeeding national convs. and Va. state convs. since 1912 (chmn. resolutions com. 1924). Methodist. Mem. Am. Hist. Assn., Va. Hist. Soc., Sons Confed. Vets., Sigma Chi, Phi Beta Kappa, Omicron Delta Kappa; ex-pres. Alumni Assn. Randolph-Macon Coll.; mem. bd. visitors U.S. Naval Coll., 1925, 30. Clubs: Petersburg, Country. Author: Story of a Church; also monographs, and mag. articles on hist. subjects. Home: 200 S. Sycamore St., Petersburg, Va. Died Dec. 21, 1947.

DREXEL, George W. Childs; b. Long Branch, N.J., July 1868; s. Anthony Joseph D., banker and philanthropist; ed. pvt. schs. and by tutors; m. Mary S. Irick, Nov. 18, 1891. Succeeded George W. Childs as editor and pub. the Public Ledger; sold paper and retired, 1903. Home: "Wootton," Bryn Mawr, Pa. Office: 350 Drexel Bldg., Philadelphia, Pa. Died Sep. 9, 1944.

DREYER, Jorgan Christian, sculptor; b. Tromsö, Norway, Dec. 26, 1878; s. Hans Peter and Regina Margareta (Michelsen) D.; ed. Latin Sch., Tromsö, and Royal Sch. of Art and Industries, Oslo; m. Lorena Ellene McWilliams, Nov. 15, 1918. Mem. Architectural League (Kansas City, Mo.); hon. mem. Am. Inst. Architects. Sculptures include portraits, medals, fountains architectural designs, etc.; among them: figure, Dawn, Phillips Hotel, Kansas City; Autumn, St. Louis Art Mus.; Lionesses, Kansas City Life Ins. Co. Bldg.; Sphinxes, Scottish Rite Temple, Kansas City; portrait bust John P. Greene, pres. William Jewell Coll., Liberty, Mo., and of Jerome Uhl, painter, Washington, D.C.; Bishop Lillis' Jubilee medal; the De Molay medal for heroism; Grotesques, Philtower Bldg., Tulsa, Okla.; Dean Marvin Memorial, Univ. of Kan.; and many others; instr. sculpture Fine Arts Inst., Kansas City, Mo., 1907-09; Private School, Studio Bldg., Kansas City, Mo., 1910-14. Home-Studio: 3721 Michigan Av., Kansas City, Mo. Died Nov. 17, 1948.

DREYSTADT, Nicholas, automotive exec.; b. Germany, Sept. 30, 1889; s. John and Margaret (Henne) D.; ed. in college at Saarbrucken, Germany; m. Georgia Humphrey, Sept. 5, 1928; children—Margaret Mary, John Nicholas. With General Motors Corp., Detroit, Mich., since 1916, beginning in service dept. of Chicago branch and advancing through positions of responsibility, became gen. parts and service mgr. Cadillac factory, 1926, became works mgr. Cadillac Motor Car Div., 1932, gen. mgr. since 1934, also vice pres. Gen. Motors Corp. since 1942, mem. Gen. Motors adminstrn. com. since 1945, gen. mgr. Chevrolet Motor Div. since June 4, 1946; dir. Goebel Brewing Co. Mem. Detroit Bd. of Commerce; dir. Detroit Economic Club. Clubs: Recess, Detroit Athletic (mem. bd. dirs.), Orchard Lake Country (Detroit), Bloomfield Hills Country. Home: 4895 W. Maple Rd., Birmingham, Mich. Office: 3044 W. Grand Blvd., Detroit 2. Died Sept. 3, 1948.

DRIGGS, Edmund Hope, congressman, fire ins. surveyor; b. Brooklyn, N.Y., May 2, 1865; ed. Adelphi Coll.; married. Mem. Congress since 1897-1901. Democrat. Home: 672 Ocean Av. Office: 13 Broadway, Brooklyn, N.Y. Died Oct. 1946.

DRIGGS, Laurence La Tourette, author, lawyer, aviation specialist; b. Saginaw, Mich., Dec. 1, 1876; s. LeRoy Channing and Mary (La Tourette) D.; ed. U. of Mich.; LL.B., New York Law Sch., 1900; m. Mary Ogden, June 29, 1904; children—Ogden, Laurence L. Practiced law in N.Y. City. Rep. nominee for Congress, 11th N.Y. Dist., 1908; dep. atty. gen. of N.Y. State, 1909-10; apptd. mem. Market Commn. of N.Y., 1913; operated cattle ranch in Tex. Panhandle, 1913-16; mem Rep. County Com., 1908-20. Mem. Troop C, N.G.N.Y., 1902-05; mem. Veteran's Corps Artillery since 1906; learned to fly, 1913; invited by British Govt. to visit battle front in France, 1914-16, as aviation specialist; attached to Royal Air Force headquarters, 1918; examined German aviation fields after Armistice. Formed Am. Flying Club at the front, 1918, composed of Am. aviators who had flown over lines, and elected first pres. of the club, at New York, 1919, reëlected, 1920; organized New York-Toronto aeroplane races, 1919, aviators' armistice dinner, aviators' annual ball. Commd. maj. N.Y.G. Air Service, 1921; organized 102 Observation Squadron, N.Y.G., as comdg. officer; commd. lt. col. by governor and attached to staff, 1921. Lecturer on aviation throughout U.S. since 1919; engaged in commercial air transport in N.Y. and N.E. since 1927; pres. Prudential Airways; v.p. Colonial Air Transport, Colonial Western Airways, Canadian Colonial Airways. Special rep. of sec. of agr. in lending govt. funds to form credit corps, in drought area, 1931. Mem. Early Birds. Club: Cosmos (Washington). Author: Arnold Adair, 1917; Heroes of Aviation, 1918, 26; Fighting the Flying Circus (with Eddie Rickenbacker), 1919; Golden Book of Aviation, 1920; Arnold Adair with the English Aces, 1921; Secret Air Service, 1930; The Secret Squadron, 1931; Flight, 1933. Home: Broadwater, Oxford, Md. Died May 26, 1945.

DRISCOLL, Clara; b. St. Mary's, Tex., Apr. 2, 1881; d. Robert and Julia (Fox) Driscoll; ed. pvt. schs., Tex., New York and France. Honored by the organization of the Daughters of the Republic of Texas by title of "Custodian of the Alamo" on account of her successful efforts to save the historic site to the state. V. chmn. exec. bd. Texas Centennial Expn.; dir.-gen. Austin Pan-Am. Round Table; pres. Daughter of the Republic of Texas since 1925. Pres. and owner Corpus Christi Bank & Trust Co.; sole owner and mgr. of the ranches, petroleum fields, farms and other properties of the R. Driscoll Estate. Democratic nat. committeewoman for Texas since 1928. Dir. Women's War Bonds and Stamps Sales for Tex. Clubs: Violet Crown Garden (pres.); Texas of N.Y. City (hon. life pres.). Author: The Girl of La Gloria, 1905; In the Shadow of the Alamo, 1906. Wrote "Mexicana," a comic opera, 1906. LL.D., Baylor U., 1943. Awarded Distinguished Citizenship Medal by Veterans of Foreign Wars; scholarship dedicated to U. of Tex. by Daughters of Rep. of Tex., named the "Clara Driscoll Scholarship for Research in Texas History," 1943. Acted as sponsor to launching of U.S.S. Corpus Christi, Wilmington, Calif., Aug. 17, 1943. Home: Corpus Christi, Tex. Died July 17, 1945.

DRUCKER, Arthur Eilert, educator, metall. engr.; b. San Francisco, Calif., Aug. 25, 1877; s. Eilert and Emma Florence (Cootey) D.; grad. Calif. Sch. Mech. Arts, 1897; B.S., Univ. of California, 1902; LL.D., Washington State College, 1944; married Minnie Barstow, Feb. 14, 1912. Assayer and mill foreman, Minas del Tajo, Sinaloa, Mexico, 1902-04; mill foreman, Roosevelt M. & M. Co., Calif., 1904-05; cyanide foreman and research metallurgist. Oriental Con. Mining Co., Korea, 1905-08; metall. exams. in Japan, Philippines, Malay States, Australia, U.S., etc., 1908-10; chief metallurgist and constn. engr. Oriental Con. Mining Co., Korea, 1910-13; technical mgr. Concession Miniere Française, North Korea, 1913-14; cons. metall. engr., London, 1914-15; engaged in metall. exams. and constn. of plants for Pellew-Harvey & Co., in Colombia, S.A., 1915-16; cons. engr., New York, 1916-20; prof. metall. engring., Wis. State Sch. of Mines, 1920-21; asst. prof. mining engring., U. of Ill., 1921-26; dean Sch. of Mines and Geology, Washington State College, 1926-45; dir. Mining Expt. Sta., State Electrometall. Research Labs., 1937-45; dean emeritus since 1945. Tech. adviser Wash. State Planning Council. Mem. Northwest Mining Assn., Asso. Engrs. Spokane, Central Washington Mining Assn., Eastern Oregon Mining Assn. (hon. life), Newcomen Soc of England (hon.), Northwest Sci. Assn., Pullman Chamber Commerce, S.A.R., Sigma Xi, Tau Beta Pi, Sigma Tau, Epsilon Chi, Sigma Gamma Epsilon, Delta Mu Epsilon, Phi Eta, Acacia. Mason (32°, Shriner). Clubs: Kiwanis, Wranglers, Cosmopolitan; Seoul (Korea). Contbr. of many articles to mining jours. Home: Hotel Washington, Pullman, Wash. Died Feb. 7, 1949

DRUMHELLER, Roscoe Maxson, business exec.; b. Walla Walla, Wash., Feb. 19, 1882; s. Jesse and Martha Alvira (Maxson) D.; student Whitman Acad., 1896-98, Willamette U., 1898-99; m. Hazel Jaycox, Sept. 21, 1904 (dec.); children—James, Martha (Mrs. John Wiley), Mary (Mrs. Robert L. Mattison), Jean; m. 2d, Helen Payne, Aug. 29, 1933. President Drumheller & Ennis, Inc., real estate and insurance, 1908-14; collector of customs, State of Washington, 1915-21; chairman Drumheller, Ehrlichman Company, investment bankers, since 1921; chmn. bd. United Pacific Ins. Co. since 1932; chmn. bd. United Nat. Corp.; pres. Pacific Northwest Oriental Line, Inc., 1939-41; dir. Equity Fund, Inc., Shareholders Corp., Northern Life Ins. Co., United Pacific Realty & Investment Corp. Engaged in farming and stock breeding in Eastern Wash. since 1904. Mem. Wash. State Council of Defense, 1939-40. Chmn. Pacific Northwest Group of Investment Bankers Assn. America 1928-29; chmn. Wash. State Recovery Bd., 1933-34; mem. Dem. Nat. Com., 1932-36. Mason: Clubs: Tacoma, Tacoma Country (Tacoma); Rainier (Seattle). Home: R. 1, Box 789. Office: Med. Arts Bldg., Tacoma, Wash. Died Aug. 27, 1943.

DRURY, Walter Maynard, mining engr.; b. Chicago, Ill., Feb. 8, 1880; s. Myron M. and Ida (Osborn) D.; B.S., Mass. Inst. Tech., 1903; m. Mary Kane, 1915; children—Maynard Kane, Innes. Gen. mgr. mining dept. Am. Smelting & Refining Co. of New York since 1912; dir. Cia Minera Asarco, Cia Minera Nacional, Cia Minera Loteria, Cia Minera Magistral, Cia Metalurgica Mexicana, Potosi & Rio Verde R.R., Montezuma Lead Co., Sombrerette Mining Co., Descubridora Mining Co., Cia Minera Tepic, Cia Minera La Ventura, Brandreth Mfg. Co., Intercontinental Rubber Co., Towne Securities Co. Mem. Am. Inst. Mining and Metall. Engrs. Clubs: Bankers, Tuxedo, Sleepy Hollow Country (New York). Address: care American Smelting & Refining Co., 120 Broadway, New York, N.Y. Died July 16, 1946.

DUANE, William J., univ. pres.; b. N.Y. City; A.B., St. Francis Xavier Coll., 1887. Entered Soc. of Jesus (Jesuits), 1887; prof., Boston Coll., 1893-98; pres. Fordham U. since 1924. Address: Fordham University, New York.

DUCKER, Edward Augustus, judge; b. Visalia, Calif., Feb. 26, 1870; s. Benjamin Franklin and Augusta (Woodward) D.; ed. pub. schs.; m. Dollie B. Guthrie, Mar. 30, 1903; children—Helen Claire (dec.), Edward Augustus, Robert Varian, Marian. Admitted to Nev. bar, 1902, and began practice at Winnemucca; dist. atty., Humboldt County, Nev., 1905-10; judge Dist. Court, 6th Jud. Dist., Nev., 1911-18; justice Supreme Court of Nev. since 1918, chief justice 1923, 24, 29, 30, 35, 36, 41, 42 (dean of Supreme Court of Nevada). Nevada delegate to World War Conv., Phila., 1918. Chmn. of hon. bd. of visitors U. of Nev., 1923, 24, 29, 30, 35, 36, 41, 42; personal representative of Governor to Western States Parole and Probation Conference, Portland, 1936. Mem. State Bar of Nevada, American Bar Association. Democrat. Mason (K.T., Knight of Constantine; Grand Master of Masons of Nevada, 1925; Grand High Priest R.A.M. of Nevada, 1927-28; Grand Commander K.T. of Nevada 1941), Eagle, O.E.S. Home: Carson City, Nev. Address: Supreme Court and Library Bldg., Carson City, Nev. Died Aug. 14, 1946.

DUDLEY, Bide, humorist, dramatic critic; b. Minneapolis, Minn., Sept. 8, 1877; s. James Todd and Ida (Bronson) D.; ed. pub. schs.; m. Taney Keplinger, Sept. 21, 1916; children—Doris, Bronson. Began with St. Joseph (Mo.) News, 1903; successively with Kansas City Journal, Kansas City Star, Denver Post, Denver Times, New York Morning Telegraph; with New York Evening World and New York World-Telegram since 1914. Episcopalian. Club: Friars. Author: Bolivar Brown, 1921. Co-Author: Odds and Ends of 1917; The Little Whopper; Sue, Dear; The Matinee Girl; Bye, Bye, Bonnie; Come Along (all musical comedies); Oh, Henry (comedy); Borrowed Love (drama). Home: Lambs Club, 130 W. 44th St. Office: 1476 Broadway, New York, N.Y. Died Jan. 4, 1944.

DUDLEY, Frank Alonzo, hotel exec., lawyer; b. Wilson, N.Y., Jan. 30, 1864; s. John Alexander and Henrietta Marie (Wright) D.; ed. State Normal Sch., Whitewater, Wis.; m. Etta Brown, Dec. 17, 1890. Admitted to N.Y. bar, 1887, and began practice at Niagara Falls; mem. firm Dudley, Gray, Phelps & Gray; organizer and pres. North Coast R.R. of State of Wash.; organizer, 1910, since pres. United Hotels Co.; also pres. or v.p. 24 subsidiary hotel cos.; 1st v.p. Am. Hotels Corp. Pres. Niagara Falls Hist. Soc. Mem. N.Y. Assembly (chmn. com. of taxation), 1896-98. Mem. N.Y. State Bar Assn., Am. Hotel Association (past pres.), Sovereign Colonial Society of Royal Descent, Society of Colonial Wars, Society Am. Revolution. Republican. Presbyterian. Clubs: Lawyers, Niagara Falls Country (organizer); Bankers (New York). Home: "Amigari," Lewiston Heights. Office: United Office Bldg., Niagara Falls, N.Y. Died Sep. 21, 1945.

DUDLEY, Samuel Madison, lawyer, church sec.; b. Mobile, Ala., Aug. 2, 1873; s. Calvin and Maria E. Dudley; grad. Broad St. Acad., Mobile, Ala., 1892; student accounting, U. of Chicago, 1900-02; LL.B., Howard U., m. Leonea B. Barbour, Apr. 30, 1924. Teacher of math., Broad St. Acad., Mobile, Ala., 1892-1900; practiced law, Washington, D.C., statistician of Religious Bodies, Bur. of Census, 1909-28.; became exec. sec. Tercentenary movement, a campaign for evangelism and edn., 1919; elected del. to Nat. Laymen's Conf. of the Interchurch world movement for studying Protestant Chs. of the world, 1920; church extension and home mission sec., A.M.E., Zion, 1924-32, gen. sec., 1938-47 Mem. bd. mgrs. Y.M.C.A., Washington, D.C.; pres. Bethel Literary Soc.; mem. Washington Bar Assn.; officer of the Universal Development and Loan Co., Inc. for better housing conditions. Honored with cup for 40 yrs. of leadership as civic worker, counselor and Christian layman. Club: Musolit. Editor and compiler: The Year Book of the A.M.E. Zion Church, Editions 1942-43-44. Republican. Address: 3536 13th St. N.W., Washington, D.C. Died, Jan. 6, 1947.

DUERR, Alvan Emile (dü'ër); b. Cleveland, Dec. 20, 1872; s. Rev. John William Casimir and Emily (Princehorn) D.; student Kenyon Mil. Acad., Gambier, O., 1886-89, Kenyon Coll., 1889-91, hon. M.A.,

1932; B.A., Williams Coll., Williamstown, Mass., 1893; hon. LL.D., Lawrence College, 1941; m. Virginia Allen, June 18, 1895; children—Winslow Alvan (dec.), William Allen. Master Holbrook Sch., Ossining, N.Y., 1893, Phillips Exeter (N.H.) Acad., 1894, William Penn Charter Sch. (Phila.), 1895; headmaster Poly. Prep. Sch., Brooklyn, 1906-12; headmaster and dir. Storm King Sch., Cornwall, N.Y., 1912-27; personnel dir. Chatham Phoenix Nat. Bank & Trust Co., N.Y. City, 1927-30; dir. public relations, Mfrs. Trust Co., N.Y. City, since 1930; also dir. various corps. Received distinguished Service medal for service to youth through the Am. College fraternity, 1940. Mem. Nat. Interfraternity Conf. (chmn. 1930-32); mem. various coms. on coöperation between colls. and fraternities; leader of movement to weave fraternities more closely into ednl. fabric of schs.; mem. Schoolmasters Assn. of New York (pres. 1905-06), Headmasters Assn., Cum Laude Soc., Nat. Council at Nat. Econ. League, Com. on Vocation Training of N.Y. City Y.M.C.A., United Neighborhood Guild, Wallmen, Delta Tau Delta (nat. pres. 1925-27); pres., bd. trustees National Interfraternity Foundation; chmn. America's Tomorrow—College Discussions. Republican. Episcopalian. Club: Williams. Author: Essentials of German Grammar, 1906; People, Business and You, 1945. Editor of Annual Survey of Scholarship of College Fraternities since 1927. Contbr. on ednl. subjects. Editor Baird's Manual; asso. editor, Banta's Greek Exchange. Home: 242 E. 19th St., 3. Office: 55 Broad St., New York 15. Died Nov. 18, 1947.

DUFF, Edward Aloysius, clergyman; b. Philadelphia, Pa., Jan. 5, 1885; s. Patrick James and Mary Eleanore (Bergen) D.; student St. Charles Coll., Md., 1901-03, St. Charles Seminary, Overbrook, Pa., 1904-06; A.B., St. Mary's Seminary, Baltimore, also A.M. and S.T.B. Ordained priesthood Catholic Ch., 1911; sec. to bishop, Cathedral St. John the Baptist, Charleston, S.C., 1911-13; chaplain Charleston Navy Yard, 1911-13; appt. chaplain U.S. Navy 1915 and has served on ships at sea, Navy Headquarters, London, Graves Registration Unit, Paris, Navy Yards at Philadelphia, New York, U.S. Marine Base, Paris Island, Bureau of Navigation; commd. Capt., U.S. Navy; appt. chief of Chaplain Corps; retired Sept. 1, 1938. Served on staff of Admiral Sims, comdr. U.S. Naval forces in European Waters, World War. Decorated Chevalier of the Crown of Italy. Accompanied body of Unknown Soldier from France to U.S. Clubs: Army and Navy, Army and Navy Country. Lecturer. Home: 3200 16th St. N.W., Washington, D.C. Died Feb. 11, 1943.

DUFFIELD, Pitts, publisher; b. Detroit, Jan. 22, 1869; s. Henry Martyn and Frances (Pitts) D.; A.B., Harvard, 1892; m. Isabel McKenna, Jan. 6, 1904; 1 dau., Carolyn Pitts. Editor New York Tribune, New York Globe, 1894; instr., Harvard, 1896-97; lit. editor Charles Scribner's Sons, New York, 1898-1902; sec. Fox, Duffield & Co., 1903-05; pres. Duffield & Co., pubs., 1905-18. Mem. Delta Kappa Epsilon, Hasty Pudding Club, O.K. Soc. Clubs: Players, Harvard, University (New York). Author: Blind Man's Bluff, play, prod. 1918; The Fan (adapted), 1921. Home: 168 E. 61st St., New York. Died Aug. 12, 1938.

DUFFY, John A.; bishop Roman Catholic Ch. Address: Buffalo, N.Y. Died Sep. 27, 1944.

DUFFY, Richard, editor; b. New York, Nov. 26, 1873; s. John Giblon and Annie (O'Brien) D.; ed. St. Mary's Coll., Northeast, Pa.; m. Louise Chauvet, 1895. Editor Ainslee's Magazine, 1898-1904; mng. editor Watson's Magazine, 1904-06; editorial staff F. A. Munsey Co., 1906-09. Author: An Adventure in Exile (novel), 1908; The Night of the Wedding (play); The Leeches (novel). Contbr. stories and essays to mags. Address: 260 W. 78th St., New York. Died March 5, 1949.

DUGGAN, Laurence (dŭg'gȧn); b. New York, N.Y., May 28, 1905; s. Stephen Pierce and Sarah (Elsesser) D.; grad. Phillips Exeter Acad., Exeter, N.H., 1923; A.B., Harvard, 1927; m. Helen Bushong Boyd, Sept. 17, 1932; children: Stephanie, Laurence, Robert, Christopher. Stockroom clk. and salesman Harper & Bros., 1927-29; with Inst. of Internat. Edn., 1929-30; with U.S. Dept. of State, Washington, D.C., 1930-44, chief division of American Republics, 1935-44; asst. diplomatic adviser, U.N.R.R.A., 1944-45; Latin-Am. cons., 1945-46; pres. Inst. Internat. Edn. since 1946. Adviser U.S. delegation to 8th Internat. Conf. of Am. States, Lima, Peru, 1938; apptd. adviser on political relations, Oct. 1940; adviser to meeting of treas. reps. of the Am. Republics, Guatemala City, Nov. 1939; adviser to sec. of state, second meeting of foreign ministers of the Am. Republics, Havana, Cuba, 1940. Dir. Foreign Policy Assn., Am. Civil Liberties Assn., East and West Assn. Home: 46 Walworth Av., Scarsdale, N.Y. Address: 2 W 45th St., New York, N.Y. Died Dec. 20, 1948.

DUGGAR, John Frederick, agriculturist; b. Faunsdale, Ala., Aug. 24, 1868; s. Dr. Reuben Henry and Margaret Louisa (Minge) D.; brother of Benjamin Minge D.; ed. Southern U., Greensboro, Ala.; B.S., Miss. Agrl. and Mech. Coll., 1887, M.S., 1888; student Columbian (now George Washington) U., Cornell U., and U. of Colo.; m. Frances Ambrose Camp, June 17, 1891; children—John Frederick, Frances Camp, Mrs. Margaret McCormick, Ambrose Camp, Llewellyn Goode, Dorothy. Asst. prof. agr., Tex. Agrl. and Mech. Coll., Bryan, Tex., 1887-89; editor Southern Live Stock Journal, Starkville, Miss., 1890; asst. dir. Expt. Sta., Clemson Coll., S.C., 1890-92; editor dept. field crops, Expt. Sta. Record, U.S. Dept. Agr., 1893-95; prof. agr., Alabama Poly. Inst., 1896-1921; also dir. Alabama Expt. Sta., 1903-21, and dir. Ala. Extension Service, 1911-20; research prof. farm management and special investigations, Ala. Poly. Inst., 1922-31. research prof. since 1931. Lecturer in agronomy, U. of Calif., 1922-24. Mem. Phi Kappa Phi. Recipient (1939) medal for distinguished service, from Assn. Southern Agrl. Workers. Author: Agriculture for Southern Schools; Southern Field Crops; Southern Forage Crops; also numerous articles and pamphlets. Home: Auburn, Ala. Died Dec. 25, 1945.

DUKE, William Waddell, physician; b. Lexington, Mo., Oct. 18, 1882; s. Henry Buford and Susie (Waddell) D.; Ph.B., Yale, 1904; M.D., Johns Hopkins, 1908; grad. study, Mass. Gen. Hosp., Boston, 1909-10, U. of Vienna, 1910-12, U. of Berlin, m. Frances Thomas, May 18, 1920; children—Henry Basil, Frances Suzanne. Practicing physician in Kansas City, Mo., since 1912, limiting practice to internal medicine; prof. exptl. medicine U. of Kan. Sch. of Medicine, Rosedale, 1914-18; visiting physician Christian Ch. Hosp., Kansas City, 1918-24. Mem. Council of Nat. Defense and capt. in Am. Red Cross, World War; lt. col. O.R.C. since World War. Fellow A.M.A.; mem. Am. Coll. Physicians. Awarded silver medal, 1924. by A.M.A. for research in allergy; annual gold medal, 1941, by the Midwest Forum of Allergy for "distinguished and outstanding contributions in the field of allergy." Episcopalian. Mason (K.T., Shriner). Clubs: Kansas City, University, Kansas City Country. Author: Oralsepsis in Relationship to Systemic Disease, 1918; Allergy, Asthma, Hay Fever, Urticaria and Allied Manifestations of Reaction, 1925; also chapters in Practitioners' Library of Medicine and Surgery, Cyclo. of Medicine, Modern Home Med. Adviser. Contbr. tech. articles. Discoverer in field of allergy and physical allergy, oral sepsis, transfusion and anemia, palm color test, bleeding time, relation between platelets and hemorrhagic disease; co-discoverer physiology of heart beat in relationship to the potassium and calcium content of the blood; also made pollen surveys. Home: 1220 W. 62nd St. Office: Professional Bldg., Kansas City, Mo. Died Apr. 10, 1946.

DUKES, Charles Alfred, physician, surgeon; b. Numa, Ia., Apr. 23, 1872; s. Harrison C. and Isabella Jane (Shaw) D.; studied Drake U., 1892-93; M.D., Cooper Med. Sch., San Francisco, 1895; m. Mable Saxe, May 17, 1897; children—Dorothy (Mrs. Stanley Dimm), Helen (Mrs. Reimer R. Lahann). Staff Merritt Hosp., Oakland, Calif., 1912-34; chief West Surgical Service, Highland and Fairmont Hosp., since 1926; chmn. cancer clinic, Highland Hosp., since 1930; vis. surgeon Vet. Adminstrn. Facilities, Livermore, Calif., since 1932; dir. First Nat. Bank, Oakland. Col., Med. Corps, Calif. N.G., retired. Fellow Am. Coll. Surgeons (v.p.); mem. Calif. Med. Assn. (chmn. Cancer Commn., Pub. Relation Com.), Alameda County Med. Assn., Acad. of Medicine, Alpha Kappa Kappa. Republican. Methodist. Mason, Elk. Clubs: Commonwealth (San Francisco); Athenian-Nile, Claremont Country, Kiwanis (Oakland). Home: 211 The Uplands, Berkeley, Calif. Office: 426 17th St., Oakland, Calif. Died March 13, 1942.

DULANY, Henry Rozier, Jr., lawyer; b. Washington, D.C., Oct. 11, 1889; s. Henry Rozier and Anne Willing (Carter) D.; student Woodbury Forest Sch., Orange, Va., 1905-06; A.B., U. of Va., 1910, B.L., 1912; m. Kate Allen Weems, Dec. 4, 1915; children—Juliet Carter, Benjamin Weems, Anne Willing. Admitted to District of Columbia bar, 1912; counsel to Comptroller of Currency and asst. counsel Fed. Reserve Bd., 1914-17; engaged in pvt. practice since 1917; president A. S. Pratt & Sons, Inc.; chmn. bd. Griffith-Consumers Co., dir. Nat. Savings & Trust Co., Frederick County Products Co., Potomac Electric Power Co. Mem. Delta Kappa Epsilon, Phi Delta Phi, Phi Beta Kappa. Episcopalian. Mason. Club: Chevy Chase Country. Home: 2445 California St. Office: 815 15th St., Washington, D.C. Died Nov. 2, 1948.

DULANY, William Henry, lumber; b. at Salisbury, Mo., June 16, 1874; s. Thomas Gates and Mary Thomas (Dulany) D.; grad. Mo. Mil. Acad., Mexico, Mo., 1892; student U. of Va., 1892-93, U. of Mo., 1893-96; unmarried. Began in lumber business, Hannibal, Mo., 1896; pres. R. J. Hurley Lumber Co.; vice-pres. St. Louis Lumber Co.; dir. Eclipse Lumber Co.; dir. La. Long Leaf Lumber Co., Hannibal Nat. Bank, Mound City Trust Co. Capt., Mo. Home Guards, World War I. Trustee Culver-Stockton Coll., Canton, Mo., William Woods Coll., Fulton, Mo., Christian Coll., Columbia, Mo., Nat. Benevolent Assn. Disciples of Christ. Mem. Sons of Am. Revolution, Beta Theta Pi. Mem. Christian (Disciples) Ch. Clubs: Bellerive Country, Glen Echo Country, Hannibal Country. Home: 265 Union Blvd. Office: 1234 S. Kingshighway, St. Louis, Mo. Died Mar. 9, 1948.

DULLES, Joseph Heatly, librarian; b. Phila., May 27, 1853; s. Rev. John Welsh and Harriet Lathrop (Winslow) D.; A.B., Princeton, 1873, A.M., 1876; grad. Princeton Theol. Sem., 1877; unmarried. Ordained Presbyn. ministry, 1877; stated supply Jenkintown and Edge Hill, Pa., 1877. First Ch., Nebraska City, Neb., 1877-78; pastor Second Ch., Belvidere, N.J., 1881-83; travel and study in Europe, 1883-85; librarian Princeton Theol. Sem., 1886-1031. Mem. Phi Beta Kappa. Editor Semicentennial Anniversary of Prof. William Henry Green; compiler General Catalogue of Princeton Theol. Sem., 1894; wrote historical sketch of Princeton Theological Seminary, Bibliography of James McCosh, Bibliography of William Henr yGreen. Compiler Biographical Catalogue of Princeton Theol. Sem., 1909. Home: Princeton, N.J. Died March 8, 1937.

DU MEZ, Andrew Grover (dŭ-mā'), pharmaceutical chemist; b. Horicon, Wis., Apr. 26, 1885; s. Andrew Alexander and Anna (Meister) Du M.; Ph.G., U. of Wis., 1904, B.S., 1907, M.S., 1910, Ph.D., 1917; m. Mary Elizabeth Fields, June 9, 1912. Instr. in pharm. chemistry, U. of Wis., 1905-10; prof. chemistry, Pacific U., Forest Grove, Ore., 1910-11; asst. prof. chemistry, Okla. Agrl. and Mech. Coll., 1911-12; dir. Sch. of Pharmacy, U. of the Philippines, 1912-16; Hollister fellow, U. of Wis., 1916-17; asso. pharmacologist, Hygenic Lab., U.S. Public Health Service, Washington, D.C., 1917-26; dean of Sch. of Pharmacy, U. of Md., since 1926. Pharmacy consultant to the surgeon general, U.S. Army. Sec. spl. com. Treasury Dept. to investigate traffic in narcotics in United States, 1918-19; vice chairman Revision Com. of Pharmacopœia of U.S., for term 1930-40; chairman sub.-com. on nomenclature since 1920; U. S. Govt. del. to Second Conf. on Unification of Standards for Potent Remedies, Brussels, 1925; sec. Am. Council on Pharmaceutical Edn. since 1932. Fellow A.A.A.S.; member American Association Colleges of Pharmacy (pres. 1929), Am. Chem. Soc., Am. Pharm. Assn. (pres. 1939-40, awarded Remington Medal, 1948), Am. Pub. Health Assn., Wis. Acad. Science, Arts and Letters, Sigma Xi, Phi Delta Chi. Congregationalist. Mason. Joint Author: Quantitative Pharmaceutical Chemistry (with Glenn L. Jenkins), 1931. Advisory editor, joint author, American Pharmacy. Editor: Digest of Comments on the Pharmacopœia of the U.S. and the National Formulary, 1916-22; Yearbook of Am. Pharm. Assn., 1921-34, Pharm. Abstracts, 1935-41. Science editor Jour. Am. Pharm. Assn., 1938-41. Contbr. to Philippine Jour. Science, Jour. Am. Med. Assn., Jour. Am. Pharm. Assn., Am. Jour. Pharmacy, etc. Home: Stony Run Lane and 40th St., Baltimore 10. Office: 32 S. Greene St., Baltimore 1, Md. Died Sept. 26, 1948.

DUMMEIER, Edwin F. (dŭ'mīr), prof. economics; b. Metropolis, Ill., Apr. 4, 1887; s. Louis F. and Amelia (Hausman) D.; A.B., La. State U., 1918; A. M., U. of Colo., 1921; Ph.D., U. of Chicago, 1926; m. Binna Mason, June 19, 1944. Teacher, high sch. principal and school supt. in Louisiana, 1905-18; instructor economics, State Coll. of Washington, 1921-23; asst. prof., 1923-25; research asst. in agrl. marketing, U. of Chicago, 1925-26; prof. economics and expt. sta. economist, State Coll. of Wash., since 1926. Mem. Wash. State War Food Adminstrn. Wage Bd. Member Am., Am. Farm, Pacific Coast Economics Assn., Western Farm Economics Assn. (pres. 1937-38), Am. Acad. Polit. Science, The Grange, Phi Kappa Phi, Alpha Kappa Psi, Delta Sigma Rho, Tau Kappa Epsilon. Co-Author: (with R. B. Heflebower) Economics with Applications to Agriculture (textbook), 1934, revised edit., 1940. Contbr. agrl. station bulls. and articles to professional jours. Home: Pullman, Wash. Died June 17, 1946.

DU MOULIN, Frank, bishop; B.A., Trinity Coll., Toronto, 1894, M.A., 1894, D.D., 1916; LL.D., St. Francis Xavier U., Can., 1905; D.D., Kenyon Coll., 1914; m. Ethel King, 1902; children—Françoise, Rockwell, Emily; m. 2d, Cora Stiles, 1929. Ordained to ministry P.E. Ch., deacon, 1894, priest, 1895; asst. Holy Trinity Ch., Toronto, 1895-96. Trinity Ch., Chicago, 1896-97; rector Emanuel Ch., Cleveland, 1897-99, St. Peter's Ch., Chicago, 1899-1907; dean Trinity Cathedral, Cleveland, 1907; elected bishop coadjutor of Ohio, 1914, resigned 1924; rector Ch. of the Saviour, Phila., 1925-31; rector St. John's Ch. of Lattingtown, Locust Valley, L.I., N.Y., 1931-43; retired from active ministry, Jan. 1, 1943. Home: 6641 Lincoln Dr., Philadelphia 19, Pa. Died July 9, 1947; buried in Phila.

DUNBAR, James Whitson, ex-congressman; b. New Albany, Ind., Oct. 17, 1860; s. John and Margaret (Whitson) D.; grad. New Albany High Sch., 1878. Began with New Albany Gas Co., New Albany, Ind., as a street gas lamp lighter, 1872; became v.p. United Gas & Electric Co., New Albany and Jeffersonville, Ind., and New Albany Water Co. (resigned from both cos., 1918). Sec. Am. Gas Inst. 1906-08, Western Gas Assn., 1894-1906; pres. Indiana Gas Assn., 1908-10. Rep. presdl. elector, 1917; mem. 66th, 67th, 71st Congresses (1919-23, 1929-31), 3d Ind. Dist. Del. to Rep. Nat. Conv., Chicago, 1932. M.W. Grand Master of Ind. Masonic Grand Lodge, 1902-03. Home: New Albany, Ind. Died May 18, 1943.

DUNCAN, Luther Noble, educator; b. on farm near Russellville, Alabama, October 14, 1875; s. Thomas A. and Margaret S. (Hargett) D.; B.S., Ala. Poly. Inst., 1900, M.S., 1907, LL.D., 1933; grad. study Univ. of Tenn. and U. of Ill.; m. Annie Elizabeth Smith, Feb. 26, 1902; children—Mary Elizabeth, Margaret Susan, Robert Smith. Teacher of agr., high schs. and dir. expt. farms of same, Ala, 1900-05; supervisor agromony research, Ala. Expt. Sta. and instr. in agr., Ala. Poly. Inst., 1905-09; organizer and supervisor boys' and girls' 4-H club work, and extension work in home economics, Ala., 1909-20; dir. extension service, Ala. Poly. Inst., 1920-37, sec. to administrative com., 1932-35; pres. since Feb.

1935. Awarded distinguished service agr. medal, Am. Farm Bur. Fed., 1929. Mem. Assn. Land Grant Colls. and Univs., Ala. Farm. Bur. Fed. (advisory mem. executive committee), Gamma Sigma Delta, Phi Kappa Phi, Kappa Sigma. Democrat. Methodist. Kiwanian, K.P. Co-author farm life readers. Contbr. to numerous scientific agrl. publs. Home: Auburn, Ala. Died July 26, 1947.

DUNCAN, Oscar Dibble, lawyer; b. Ala.; s. John W. and Mary (Moragne) D.; student U. Ala., 1891-93; grad. U.S. Naval Acad., 1897; law student Columbia, 1906; LL.B., New York Law Sch., 1908; m. Jean Ray Waterman, Nov. 19, 1902; children—John W., Jean (Mrs. Howard W. Soule, Jr.). Commd. ensign, U.S. Navy, 1897, retiring with rank of lt. (s.g.), 1905; served in U.S.S. Maine and U.S.S. New York, 1897; mem. staff of Adm. Sampson, 1898; in U.S.S. Texas, 1899, U.S.S. Culgoa and U.S.S. Frolic in Philippines; comd. U.S.S. gunboat Panay during Samar and Philippine insurrections; on shore duty and in dept. of discipline and dept. of astronomy and navigation, U.S. Naval Acad., and in charge exptl. torpedo work, U.S. Torpedo Sta., Newport, R.I.; became associated with Robinson, Biddle & Benedict, N.Y. City, 1907; mem. firm Goulder, Day, White, Gary & Duncan, Cleveland, O., 1910-13, Van Iderstine, Duncan & Barker, N.Y. City, 1913-16; sr. partner Duncan & Mount since 1916; counsel to Am. Bureau of Shipping, 28 yrs.; acted as atty. in establishing Am. Trust of Excess Ins. Co., Ltd., Am. Trust of Brit. Marine Ins. Cos., and Am. Trust of Lloyds, London; represented Underwriters at Lloyds, London, many years; general counsel in the U.S. for Lloyd's London. Elected hon. mem. of Lloyd's, London (Eng.), 1946. With U.S. Navy during World War I; in Judge Adv. Gen.'s Office, Washington, D.C., with Bd. of Inspection and Survey, and counsel for Inland Waterways; also with Railroad Adminstrn. Decorated West Indian Campaign Medal with 7 bars (Spanish-Am. War). Mem. Am. and N.Y. State bar assns., Am. Bureau of Shipping, Bar Assn. City of N.Y., Brit. Empire Chamber of Commerce (New York) and Columbia Law Sch. Alumni, Maritime Law Assn., Commerce and Industry Assn. of N.Y., Montclair (N.J.) Art Assn., Montclair Horse Show, Inc., N.Y. Law Inst., N.Y. Southern Soc., U.S. Naval Acad. Alumni Assn. U.S. Naval Acad. Assn. (New York), Navy Athletic Assn. U.S. Naval Inst., Soc. Naval Architects and Marine Engrs., St. George's Soc., Ins. Fedn. of N.Y., Fedn. of Ins. Counsel, Internat. Assn. Ins. Counsel, Sigma Nu. Presbyterian. Clubs: American (London); Army and Navy (Washington); India House; Montclair (N.J.) Golf, Montclair Riding; Seigniory (Can.); Skytop. Home: 150 South Mountain Av., Montclair, N.J. Office: 27 William St., New York 5, N.Y. Died June 12, 1947.

DUNCAN, William Cary, writer; b. North Brookfield, Mass., Feb. 6, 1874; s. Timothy Mason and Harriet Indiana (Eaton) D.; A.B., Amherst, 1897; m. Louise Van Cleaf, Dec. 18, 1901; 1 son, William Cary. Teacher of English and pub. speaking Poly. Prep. Sch., Brooklyn, N.Y., 1897-1917; engaged as writer musical comedy since 1911. Mem. Society Am. Dramatists, American Society Composers, Authors and Publishers, Chi Phi Fraternity. Republican. Presbyterian. Author: The Amazing Madam Jumel (biography), 1935; Golden Hoofs (serial in The Sportsman; also appeared in form of motion picture and was published as book); Dog Training Made Easy, 1940; also author or co-author of musical comedies; Katy Did; The Love Wager; The Purple Road; When Love Is Young; His Little Widows; A Regular Girl; Sunshine; The Royal Vagabond; Fiddlers Three; The Rose Girl; The Blue Kitten; Molly Darling; Mary Jane McKane; In Dutch; Princess April; Talk About Girls; Yes, Yes, Yvette; Sunny Days; Great Day; Lady Luck (London). With Famous Players-Lasky Corp., Hollywood, Calif., 1929. Clubs: Am. Kennel (dir.), Irish Setter Club of America (ex-pres.). Editor of Am. Kennel Gazette; also of dog dept., Outdoor Life; contbr. to mags. Address: North Brookfield, Mass. Died Nov. 21, 1945.

DUNCAN, William McKinley, lawyer; b. Pittsburgh, May 19, 1873; s. Andrew Jackson and Sarah (McKinley) D.; ed. Pittsburgh and Rayen high schs.; Cornell U.; m. Viola Deetrick, Oct. 18, 1899; children—William McKinley, John Allison, Andrew Jackson, III. Practiced, Cleveland, since 1894; mem. Squire, Sanders & Dempsey. Apptd. gen. atty. Wheeling & Lake Erie R.R. Co., 1905, and continued after appointment of receiver, June 1, 1908; receiver same road, June 20, 1912-16, and pres. reorganized co., Wheeling & Lake Erie Ry. Co., Jan. 1, 1917-22, chmn. bd. since July 1, 1922. Atty. for conf.-com. of mgrs. of eastern rys. in engineers' wage arbitration, Manhattan Beach, summer, 1912. Mem. McKinley Memorial Board. Republican. Presbyterian. Clubs: Union, Mayfield, Mid-Day. Home: S.O.M. Center Rd., Solon, O. Office: Union Commerce Bldg., Cleveland, O. Died, Sept. 6, 1945.

DUNCAN, W(alter) Wofford T(ucker), clergyman; b. Moncton, N.B., Can.; s. Robert and Maria C. (Higgs) D.; B.D., Drew U., 1896; D.D., Syracuse U., 1923; LL.D., Lincoln Memorial U., 1928; m. Clara Bishop, Sept. 23, 1896; children—Wayland Pierce, Mildred Bishop. Came to U.S., 1887, naturalized citizen, 1898. Ordained ministry M.E. Ch., 1900; pastor St. John's M.E. Ch., New Rochelle, N.Y., 1907-14, Janes Memorial Ch., Brooklyn, 1914-20, Emory M.E. Ch., Pittsburgh, Pa., 1920-31, Lakewood Meth. Ch., Cleveland, O., 1931-42; Florida representative of Foreign Division Methodist Bd. of Missions, Orlando, Fla., 1943; pastor Meth. Ch., Columbia Station, Ohio, since 1943. Formerly trustee Saint Luke's Hosp., Cleveland, O., Anti-Saloon League, Nat. Reform Assn., Ohio Northern Univ., Cleveland Church Fed. Mem. Gen. Conf. M.E. Ch., 1920; pres. Cleveland Ministerial Assn., 1941-42. Mason (32°, K.T., Shriner). Club: Lions. Author: Our Protestant Heritage, 1922; The Preacher and Politics, 1930; Inflexible in Faith, 1942. Lecturer. Home: Columbia Station, O. Died Aug. 2, 1945.

DUNGAN, Paul Baxter (dŭn'găn), naval officer; b. Hastings, Neb., July 21, 1877; s. William Witherspoon and Isabella (Woods) D.; grad. U.S. Naval Acad., 1899; m. Mabel Miller, June 3, 1903; 1 dau., Catharine. Commd. ensign U.S. Navy, Feb. 1901; promoted through grades to rear admiral, Nov. 13, 1933; assigned to engring. duty, Aug. 1917; participated in Spanish-Am. War, Battle of Santiago, Philippine Insurrection, Boxer Campaign in China and World War. Mem. Soc. Naval Engrs., Naval Inst. Congregationalist. Home: Hastings, Neb. Died Nov. 27, 1941.

DUNHAM, Frederic G(ibbons), lawyer; b. Buffalo, N.Y., Mar. 22, 1878; s. John C. and Abby Louise (Gibbons) D.; A.B., Cornell U., 1902; LL.B., A.M., Columbia, 1905; m. Caroline L. Allen, Apr. 10, 1909; children—Anna Louise, Elizabeth (Mrs. William M. Aurelius). Admitted to N.Y. bar, 1904; law clk., 1904; mem. Finegan & Dunham, 1905-09; chief Liquidation Bur., N.Y. State Ins. Dept., 1909-16; atty. Assn. of Life Ins. Pres., 1916-27; asst. gen. counsel Metropolitan Life Ins. Co., 1927-36; gen. counsel since 1936. Served as capt. and admiralty claims officer U.S. Army, with A.E.F., 1918-19; maj. Judge Advocate Gen. Dept. (Res.), 1920-35. Mem. Am. Bar Assn., Assn. of Bar of City of N.Y., N.Y. County Lawyers Assn. Home: 450 Beverly Rd., Ridgewood, N.J. Office: 1 Madison Av., New York, N.Y. Died Dec. 24, 1943.

DUNHAM, Henry Kennon, physician; b. Fairview, O., Mar. 3, 1872; s. Dr. William Henry and Mary (McPherson) D.; student U. of Cincinnati, 1888 to 1891; Miami Med. Coll., 1891-94; M.D. Univ. of Cincinnati Dept. of Medicine, 1894; post-grad. work Johns Hopkins Hosp. and research work there to demonstrate specific Roentgen markings characteristic of pulmonary tuberculosis; Great Ormond St. Hosp. and St. George's Hosp., London; m. Amelia Hickenlooper, Mar. 14, 1905; children—Harry, Amelia. Assistant in medicine, Miami Medical Coll., 1896-99; prof. electro-therapeutics, U. of Cincinnati Med. Dept., 1904-40; dir. tuberculosis clinic, 1914-40; head of dept. of tuberculosis, and asso. prof. of medicine, Medical Coll., U. of Cincinnati, and dir. tuberculosis service of Cincinnati Gen. Hosp. until 1940. Special war work without rank or pay, 1917-18; capt., M.C., U.S. Army, May 1918; maj., Apr. 1919. Ex-pres. Cincinnati Anti-Tuberculosis League. Mem. A.M.A., Am. Roentgen Ray Soc., Cincinnati Acad. Medicine, Am. Coll. Chest Phys., Am. Coll. Tuberculosis Phys., Am. Clinical and Climatological Soc., Nat. Tuberculosis Assn., Ohio State Med. Soc., Ohio Pub. Health Assn., Beta Theta Pi, Nu Sigma Nu. Presbyterian. Clubs: Country, Golf, University, Queen City. Author: Stereo-Roentgenography-Pulmonary Tuberculosis, 1915; also many tech. articles. Home: 3011 Vernon Pl. Office: Union Central Bldg., Cincinnati, O. Died Apr. 27, 1944.

DUNHAM, Sturges Sigler, patent lawyer; b. Toledo, O., Nov. 28, 1874; s. Edmund Sehon and Anna Hull (Sigler) D.; B.A., Ohio Wesleyan U., 1897; LL.B., Nat. Law Sch., Washington, D.C.; m. Stella Warren Secrest, Jan. 30, 1906; 1 son, Robert Secrest. Examiner U.S. Patent Office, 1898-1901; admitted to bar, 1901, and began practice at N.Y. City; with Kerr, Page & Cooper, 1902-08, Kerr, Page, Cooper & Hayward, 1908-20; mem. Cooper, Kerr & Dunham 1920-41. Served as non-commd. officer Ohio Vol. Inf., Spanish-Am. War. Mem. Ohio Soc. of N.Y., N.Y. Hist. Soc., Kipling Soc. (London), A.A.A.S., Am. Museum of Nat. History (N.Y.), Met. Museum of Art (New York), Soc. Colonial Wars, S.R., Phi Beta Kappa, Sigma Alpha Epsilon. Ind. Democrat. Methodist. Clubs: Bankers of America (New York). Homes: 200 W. 86th St., New York, N.Y.; and Over Rock Lane, Westport, Conn. Office: 233 Broadway, New York, N.Y. Died Sep. 11, 1944.

DUNIWAY, Clyde Augustus, educator; b. at Albany, Ore., Nov. 2, 1866; s. Benjamin Charles and Abigail (Scott) D.; A.B., Cornell, 1892; A.M., Harvard, 1894; Ph.D., 1897; LL.D., U. of Colo., 1914, U. of Denver, 1914, Colorado Coll., Colorado Springs, Colo., 1923; m. Caroline M. Cushing, June 11, 1901 (died Dec. 15, 1926); children—John (dec.), Benjamin, David. Instr. history, Harvard and Radcliffe, 1896-97; asst. prof. history, 1897-99, asso. prof., 1899-1908, prof., 1908, Leland Stanford Jr. U.; pres. U. of Mont., 1908-12, U. of Wyo., 1912-17; pres. Colo. Coll., 1917-24; prof. history, Carleton Coll., 1924-37; Carnegie vis. prof., Australia and Japan, 1930-31. Acting prof. U. of Calif., summer 1926, Stanford, summer 1929. Dir. Brit. Div. Am. Univ. Union, 1923-24. Mem. Am. Hist. Assn., Soc. Am. Archivists, Nat. Econ. League, Nat. Peace Conf., Minn., Wash., and Ore. State hist. socs., N.E.A., Am. Fgn. Policy Assn., Nat. Assn. State Universities, Commonwealth Club of California, Palo Alto Peace Council, Phi Beta Kappa, Elector, Hall of Fame since 1900. Author: Handbook of Graduate Courses, 1895-96-97; Freedom of the Press in Massachusetts, 1906; Daniel Webster (in Am. Secretaries of State), 1927. Contbr. Am. Hist. Rev., Proc. Am. Hist. Assn., Am. Jour. Internat. Law, Miss. Valley Hist. Rev., Proc. N.E.A., Encyclopedia Britannica, Dictionary of Am. Biography. Home: Stanford University, Calif. Died Dec. 24, 1944.

DUNKEL, J(oel) Ambrose (dŭnk''l), clergyman; b. Circleville, O., Apr. 20, 1871; s. Samuel and Susanah (Berger) D.; A.B., Heidelberg U., Tiffin, O., 1894 (winner all oratorical contests); M.A., Princeton, 1907; Ph.D., Oskaloosa (Ia.) Coll., 1911; D.D., Alma (Mich.) Coll., 1914; m. Lulu Dell Baker, June 29, 1898; children—Wilbur Dwight, Harold Baker. Ordained ministry Presbyn. Ch., 1897; pastor successively at Jonesboro, Gas City and Elwood, Ind., and Saginaw, Mich., until 1918, then Tabernacle Ch., Indianapolis (builder of $1,000,000 ch.); now minister First Presbyn. Ch., Napoleon, O. Has served as moderator synods of Mich. and Ind.; mem. Nat. Council Presbyn. Ch. (exec. com., 1923); del. Pan Presbyn. Council, Boston, 1929. Mem. bd. dirs. Princeton Theol. Sem. Mem. Indianapolis Ministers' Assn., S.A.R., Soc. War of 1812, Hist. Soc. of Ind. Republican. Mason (33°, K.T.), Odd Fellow, K.P. Club: Kiwanis. Home: 304 W. Main St., Napoleon, O. Died Oct. 16, 1944.

DUNLAP, Charles Kephart, ry. official; b. Greenfield, O., Apr. 8, 1863; s. Dr. Milton and Frances L. D.; ed. pub. schs.; m. Martha Simpson, Feb. 10, 1891. Began as clk, material dept., Mexican Internat. R.R., 1887, cashier, Torreon, Mex., agt., Sabinos, rate clk, traffic dept, commercial agt. at Monterey, and Mexico City, gen. freight and pass. agt., to 1901; gen. freight agt., Galveston, Harrisburg & San Antonio Ry., Houston & Tex. Central R.R., and Houston, E. & W. Tx. Ry., 1901-06; became traffic mgr., same rds. and Tex. & New Orleans and Houston & Shreveport rys., 1906; pres. Southern Pacific Lines in Tex. and La., 1918-20, traffic mgr., 1920-27. Home: 125 E. 84th St., New York. Died Feb. 4, 1940.

DUNLAP, Knight, psychologist; b. Diamond Spring, California, November 21, 1875; s. Elon and Sarah Calista (Knight) D.; Ph.B., U. of Calif., 1899, M.L., 1900; A.M., Harvard, 1902, Ph.D., 1903; L.H.D., Gallaudet Coll., Washington, D.C., 1931; m. Mary Durand, May 3, 1906; children—Anna Cecelia, Mary Knight, Sarah Calista. Le Conte fellow, Univ. of Calif., 1900-01; James Walker fellow, Harvard, 1901-02; asst. and instr. psychology, U. of Calif., 1902-06; instr., asso. and asso. prof. psychology, 1906-16, prof. exptl. psychology, 1916-36, Johns Hopkins U.; prof. psychology, U. of Calif., at Los Angeles, 1936-47; professor emeritus since 1947. Major Sanitary Corps, in charge of psychological section of Medical Research Laboratory, Air Service, to August 30, 1918. Chmn. div. of anthropology and psychology, Nat. Research Council, 1927-29. Democrat. Fellow A.A.A.S.; mem. Am. Psychol. Assn., Am. Philos. Assn., Phi Beta Kappa, Sigma Xi, Omicron Delta Kappa, Pi Gamma Mu. Club: National Press. Author: A System of Psychology, 1912; An Outline of Psychobiology, 1914; Personal Beauty and Racial Betterment, 1920; Mysticism, Freudianism and Scientific Psychology, 1920; Elements of Scientific Psychology, 1922; Social Psychology, 1925; Old and New Viewpoints in Psychology, 1925; Habits, Their Making and Unmaking, 1932; The Dramatic Personality of Jesus (with R. S. Gill), 1933; Civilized Life, 1935; Elements of Psychology, 1936; Personal Adjustment, 1946; Religion, Its Functions in Human Life, 1946. Address: R. 3, Arcadia, S.C. Died Aug. 14, 1949.

DUNLAP, Renick William, agrl. scientist; b. Kingston, O., Oct. 21, 1872; s. Nelson J. and Elizabeth J. (Bell) D.; B.Sc., Ohio State U., 1895; Dr. Agriculture, Rhode Island State Coll., 1929; m. Maxine C. Cummins, June 9, 1897; children—Nelson Henderson (deceased in 1942), Mary Maxine. Farmer; president Columbus Wire Fence Company. Member Ohio Senate, 76th General Assembly; dairy and food commissioner of Ohio, 1907-11; secretary of agriculture, Ohio, 7 mos., 1915; asst. sec. of agr. by appointment of President Coolidge, April 1, 1925, reapptd. by President Hoover, Mar. 1929 (resigned Mar. 1933), apptd. mem. Com. on Recent Economic Changes by Sec. of Commerce Hoover, Mar. 1928; chmn. Am. delegation to World's Dairy Congress, London, 1928. Advocate of enforcement of pure food laws; author of the commercial feed stuff law of Ohio. Mem. Ohio Farm Bur., The Grange, Alpha Zeta, Kappa Sigma. Mem. Com. on Agr. Kiwanis Internat. Republican. Presbyn. Mason (Shriner). Clubs: Torch, Kiwanis. Named one of 48 leading alumni of O. State U., 1929; presented with testimonial by Am. Soc. Annual Production and other orgns., 1931, and portrait hung in Saddle and Sirloin Club, Chicago. Home: Kingston, Ohio. Died Mar. 2, 1945.

DUNMORE, Walter Thomas, dean law sch.; b. Cleveland, July 15, 1877; s. Thomas and Elizabeth (Wright) D.; A.B., Oberlin, 1900, A.M., 1905; LL.B., Western Reserve U., 1904; LL.D., Oberlin, 1925; m. Mabel Curtis Dunmore, Nov. 10, 1904 (died 1921); children—Marjorie Dunmore Oliver, Helen Dunmore Ayres; m. 2d, Mrs. R. J. Firestone, June 29, 1939. Instr. law of property, 1905-07, prof. law of property, evidence, and conflict of laws since 1907, also dean Law Sch., Western Reserve U. Pres. Cleveland Legal Aid Soc. since 1923. Republican. Methodist. Mem. Order of Coif, Theta Lambda Phi. Author: Ship Subsidies, 1907; also articles on "Decedents' Estates" and "Executors and Administrators," in Cyclo. of Procedure. Home: 15900 South Park Blvd., Shaker Heights, O. Died Jan. 23, 1945.

DUNN, Edward Gregory, lawyer; b. Nora Springs, Ia., Aug. 18, 1879; s. Michael and Anna (Ryan) D.; grad. Nora Springs Sem., 1895; student U. of Ia., 1902-03; m. Laura Helen Delker, June 26, 1912; children—Edward Michael, Dorothy Ann, George Delker. Rural school teacher, Ia., 1896-1901; operated Farmers' Elevator Co., Burchinal, Ia., 1904-05; organizer of co-operative elevators, Farmers' Grain Dealers Assn. of Ia., 1905-12, also with Chicago Grain Commn.; admitted to Ia. bar, 1913; mem. firm Dunn & Danforth; became U.S. dist. atty. Northern Dist. of Ia.; now asst. atty. gen. state of Ia. Dem. candidate for gov. of Ia., 1912. Former pres. Ia. Cooperative Grain Co. Democrat. Roman Catholic. K. of C. (state dept. 1911-13). Home: 211 5th St., N.E. Office: 114 Third St. N.E., Mason City, Ia. Died June 19, 1948.

DUNN, Fannie Wyche, prof. edn.; b. Petersburg, Va., Jan. 17, 1879; d. Thomas Robert and Mary Steele (Schoolfield) Dunn; student Peabody Coll., Nashville, Tenn., 1895-97; B.S., Teachers Coll., Columbia, 1915; A.M., 1917, Ph.D., 1920; unmarried. Teacher in pub. and private schs., 1897-1903; supervisor State Normal Sch., Farmville, Va., 1903-10, rural supervisor and dir. high sch. training, 1910-13, dir. rural edn., 1914-16; with Teachers Coll., Columbia, since 1918, professor education, assigned to rural edn. 1921-44, prof. emeritus, 1944. Mem. Kappa Delta Pi, Delta Kappa Gamma. Democrat. Author: Interest Factors in Primary Reading Material, 1921; Primer and First Reader, Everyday Classics (with F. T. Baker and A. H. Thorndike), 1922; Four Years in a Country School (with M. A. Everett), 1926; Primary Readers, Mother Nature Series (with Eleanor Troxell), 1928; Religion in the Highlands (with Elizabeth Hooker), 1933. Editor: Organization of Curriculum for One-Teacher Schools, 1934; Materials of Instruction, 1935; Motion Pictures in Education (with Etta Schneider, Edgar Dale, Chas. F. Hoban, Jr.), 1937; Guidance in Rural Schools, 1942. Editor of Rural Education, 1921-26. Contbr. to ednl. mags., Ency. of Research, Ency. Americana and yearbooks. Home: Sharon, Conn., R.D. 2. Died Jan. 17, 1946.

DUNN, John Randall, Christian Sci. practitioner; b. in Massillon, Ohio; s. James Randall and Caroline Rebecca (Brown) D.; educated in grammar and high schs., Massillon; C.S.B., Mass. Metaphysical Coll., Boston, 1919; m. Katherine Cornelia Wasson, San Francisco. In U.S. Govt. Service, Chinese Bur., San Francisco, 1899-1907; entered Christian Science practice, St. Louis, Mo., 1907; apptd. to Bd. of Lectureship of First Ch. of Christ, Scientist, in Boston, July 1, 1916; first reader of The Mother Church (Christian Science), Boston, 1920-23, apptd. pres., 1942-43. Republican. Mason. Club: Hyannisport (Mass.) Golf. Editor in chief: Christian Science Journal, Sentinel and Herald, 1943. Home: Centerville, Cape Cod, Mass.; and Longwood Towers, Brookline, Mass. Died Dec. 22, 1948.

DUNN, Matthew A., congressman; b. Braddock, Pa., Aug. 15, 1886; ed. pub. schs., Pittsburgh and Meyersdale, Pa., and schs. for blind, Pittsburgh and Phila., after loss of sight at age of 20. Agt. Birmingham Fire Ins. Co., since 1920; mem. Pa. Ho. of Rep., 1926-32; mem. 73d and 76th Congresses (1933-41), 34th Pa. Dist. Home: Mount Oliver, Pa. Died Feb. 13, 1940.

DUNN, Richard J., insurance official; b. Ottawa, Ill., June 16, 1894; s. Richard and Margaret (O'Neill) D.; LL.B., Notre Dame Univ., 1918; m. Margaret Jennett, Sept. 16, 1922; children—Richard, William, Margaret, Kathleen, John, Robert, Edwin Rydell, Rydell James; m. 2d, Clara Rydell Fellinger, July 1, 1941. Admitted Ill. and Mass. bars; trial lawyer office of John A. Bloomington, Chicago, 1919-21; atty. Lumberman's Mutual Casualty Co., 1921-28; transferred to Boston and New England counsel since 1928; second vice pres. Lumberman's Mutual Casualty Co., Am. Motorists Ins. Co.; dir. public relations for Kemper Group; dir. Fed. Mut. Liability Ins. Co., Fed. Mut. Fire Ins. Co., Associated Mutuals, Inc., Index Bur., Inc.; prof. of insurance, Boston Coll. Law Sch. Mem. Am. Law Inst. Served as 2d lt. inf., U.S. Army, World War I. Author articles on ins. laws. Home: 1111 Sheridan Road, Wilmette, Ill. Office: 4750 Sheridan Road, Chicago, Ill. Died February 2, 1947; buried in St. Joseph's Cemetery, W. Roxbury, Mass.

DUNN, Robert A., banker; b. Sulphur Springs, Ark., Mar. 18, 1862; s. Milas Robinson and Elizabeth (Ingram) H.; ed. pvt. schs.; LL.D., Davidson (N.C.) Coll.; m. Haselline Norwood, Sept. 1896 (died 1899); m. 2d, Adele Brenizer, June 1902. Pres. Burwell & Dunn Co., wholesale mfg. druggists, Charlotte, N.C.; pres. Commercial Nat. Bank, Charlotte, 1906-11 and from 1918, now chmn. of bd. Former pres. bd. trustees Davidson Coll.; moderator General Assembly Presbyn. Ch. in U.S., 1931. Mem. Omicron Delta Kappa. Home: 511 N. Tryon St. Office: Commercial Nat. Bank, Charlotte, N.C. Died Feb. 21, 1945.

DUNNE, James Edward, ex-mayor; b. Providence, R.I., Oct. 3, 1882; s. James and Mary Ellen (Reed) D.; ed. pub. schs.; m. Genevieve Rita Rawdon, Sept. 18, 1908; children—James Edward, Robert Rawdon, Ellen Reed, Richard Barry, John (dec.), Stephen (dec.). Owner and mgr. retail grocery stores, 1902-16; in chem. and oil business with Daniel Minogue, Phila., 1916; prop. Strand Chem. Co. since 1919. Mem. Common Council, Providence, 1915-21, Bd. of Aldermen, 1923-27; chmn. Dem. State Central Com., 1922-25; became mayor of Providence, 1927, now retired. Roman Catholic. Home: 18 Flora St., Providence. Died Feb. 28. 1942.

DUNNING, N. Max, architect; b. Kenosha, Wis., Aug. 4, 1873; s. Frank B. and Frances A. (Baker) D.; student U. of Wis., 1891-94. Practiced at Chicago since 1894, specializing in schools, clubs, hotels, industrial work; won 1st traveling scholarship of Chicago Archtl. Club, 1900; traveled in France, Italy, England and Germany; mem. Bd. of Park and Bldg. Advisers of Ill., by appointment Gov. Lowden, 1917-19; mem. requirements div. U.S. Housing Corp. during World War and chmn. adjustment com. after Armistice; mem. President's Conf. on Home Bldg. and Home Ownership; mem. President Hoover's Emergency Com. on Unemployment; archtl. adviser R.F.C., 1933; asst. dir. housing Public Works Adminstrn., 1934; special asst. Public Works Branch, Procurement Div., Treasury Dept., 1935; architect asst. to commr. of Public Bldgs. Adminstrn., Federal Works Agency, 1939. One of organizers Architectural League America and sec. of its 1st conv. at Cleveland, 1903 (pres. 1904); fellow A.I.A. and past pres. Ill. Chapter same; dir. Am. Inst. Architects 3 yrs. (1st v.p. 1924; chmn. structural service com.); chmn. ways and means com. Central Housing Com.; mem. and past dir. Ill. Soc. of Architects; mem. Chicago Assn. Commerce. Clubs: Architects (life), Univ. of Wis., Lake Shore (Chicago); (hon. mem.) Producers Council Club (Washington). Home: Roger Smith Hotel, Washington, D.C. Deceased.

DUNSMORE, John Ward, artist; b. nr. Oxford, O., Feb. 29, 1856; s. Joseph Pollock and Margaret Annette (Ward) D.; ed. U. of Cincinnati; studied art with Thomas Couture, Paris; married. Dir. Detroit Mus. of Art, 1888-90, Detroit Sch. of Arts, 1890-94. Specializes in hist. subjects. Exhibited in U.S., Eng. and France. Rep. in Nat. Acad. Design, New York Hist. Soc. and Salmagundi Club, New York; Cincinnati Mus. Art and Ohio Mechanics Inst., Cincinnati; Lasell Sem., Auburndale, Mass.; entire room in Wagnall's Memorial Library, Lithopolis, O.; 30 hist. paintings of Am. Revolution in gallery of S. R. at Frances Tavern and 11 in offices of Title Guarantee & Trust Co., New York. Medal for "Macbeth," Boston, 1881; Evans prize, for "The Music Room," Salmagundi Club, 1914. A.N.A.; pres. Cincinnati Art Club, 1898-1901; mem. Am. Water Color Soc. (pres.), Am. Fine Arts Soc. (pres.), Am. Artists Professional League, New York Water Color Club, N.Y. State Hist. Assn., Cincinnati Art Club (hon.), Salmagundi Club (v.p. 1924-25), S.R., etc. Cannoneer Vet. Corps Artillery, N.Y., and did field service on Aqueduct, 1917; mem. 9th C.A.C., 1918; maj. with regular army in charge Red Cross activities, U.S. Gen. Hosp. No. 5, and U.S. Gen. Hosp. No. 41 until end of 1920. Home: Hoboken, N.J. Studio: 96 Fifth Av., New York, N.Y. Died Sep. 30, 1945.

DU PONT, A. Felix (dū-pŏnt'), vice pres. E. I. duPont de Nemours & Co.; b. Wilmington, Del., Apr. 14, 1879; s. Francis G. and Elise (Simons) duP.; student U. of Pa.; m. Mary Richard Chicester, Apr. 9, 1902; m. 2d, Ann Burton DeArmond, Sept. 3, 1937. Vice pres. and dir. E. I. duPont de Nemours & Co. since 1916. Trustee U. of Pa. Address: Wilmington, Del. Died June 29, 1948.

DU PRÉ, Arthur Mason (dū-prē'), educator; b. Abbeville, S.C., Nov. 22, 1869; s. Julius Franklin Carne and Mary Power (Huckabee) Du P.; A.B., Wofford College, 1895, A.M., 1896; studied, summers at Vanderbilt, Chicago, Cornell, Wis., and Columbia univs.; LL.D., Furman Univ., 1933; m. Caroline Elizabeth Chambers, June 1905; children—Arthur Mason, Mrs. Caroline Elizabeth Wells. Teacher, later head master, Wofford Coll. Fitting Sch., 1895-1912; prof. Latin and mathematics, Wofford Coll., since 1912, dean 1920-25, 1926-40, acting pres., 1920-21, now dean emeritus and prof. mathematics. Dean Spartanburg Hosp., 1913-18. Mem. S.C. State Teachers' Assn. (pres. 1922-23). Prominent in Prohibition movement in S.C. Mem. Phi Beta Kappa, Kappa Alpha. Democrat. Methodist. Mason. Home: Spartanburg, S.C. Died Oct. 28, 1949.

DURAND, Sir Henry Mortimer, British ambassador; b. England, 1850; s. Sir Henry Durand, and Anne (McCaskill) D.; ed. Blackheath Sch. and Eton House, Tonbridge, Eng.; called to bar at Lincoln's Inn, London, 1872; m. Ella Sandys, 1875. Entered Bengal Civil Service, 1873; polit. sec. to Sir Frederick (now Earl) Roberts during Kabul campaign, 1879; Foreign Sec. in India, 1884-94; conducted Mission to Ameer of Afghanistan, 1893; minister to Teheran, 1894-1900, ambassador and consul-gen. at Madrid, 1900-03; ambassador at Washington since 1903. Edited Sir Henry Durand's History of the First Afghan War, 1879. Author: Life of Sir Henry Durand, 1883; Helen Trevelyan, 1891. Clubs: Athenaeum, St. James (London). Address: British Embassy, Washington. Died June 8, 1924.

DURANT, William Crapo, mfr.; b. Boston, Mass., Dec. 8, 1861; s. William Clark and Rebecca Folger (Crapo) D.; g.s. Hon. H. H. Crapo, governor of Mich., 1864-68; ed. public schs., Flint, Mich.; m. Catherine Lederer, May 28, 1918. Founder Durant-Dort Carriage Co., Flint, 1886, and developed business reaching 150,000 carriages a yr.; organized the Buick Motor Car Co., 1905, the General Motors Co., 1908; purchased the Cadillac, Oakland, Oldsmobile and Northway motor cos., 1908-09; secured controlling interest in Gen. Motors Co., 1915, and in same yr. organized the Chevrolet Motor Co., an $80,000,000 corp., with plants in 11 prin. cities of U.S.; held controlling interest in Gen. Motors Co. and Chevrolet Motor Co. until Nov. 1920; organized Durant Motors, Inc., Jan. 1921; pres. Crown Point Products, Inc., Pomeroy-Day Land Co.; v.p. C.V.S. Mfg. Co.; dir. Huntman Stabilizer Corp. Republican. Presbyterian. Clubs: Detroit, Detroit Athletic, Flint Country, Calumet, Lotos (New York). Home: 45 Gramercy. Office: 230 Park Av., New York, N.Y. Died Mar. 18, 1947.

DURANTE, Oscar (dū-rän'tē), editor, publisher; b. Naples, Italy; s. Louis and Teresa (Cannavale) D.; ed. Istituto e Collegio Liebler, Naples; m. Jean Andrews, Oct. 30, 1899; 1 dau., Marion (Mrs. Frank Schneberger). Came to Chicago, 1885, naturalized. At age of 16 established L'Italia (The Italian News); cable corr. Chicago Daily Tribune, Rome, 1899-1900. Apptd. U.S. consul at Catania, Italy, by President William McKinley, Jan. 22, 1898; mem. Am. Commn. for establishment of U.S. Postal Service in Porto Rico, 1898; official interpreter U.S. Army, asst. postmaster, San Juan, Porto Rico, 1899; spl. rep. Sec. of Labor, at Chicago, 1923; apptd. mem. Bd. of Edn., Chicago, 1927, elected v.p., 1931. Mem. Ill. Commn. for Relief of Earthquake Sufferers, Messina, Italy, 1909. Decorated Order of Crown of Italy, 1918, Officer Knight, 1930, Comdr., 1934. Republican. Catholic. Translator: (from the Italian) De Amici's Heart of a Boy, 1904. Compiler: Vest Pocket Italian-English and English-Italian Dictionary; English Language Grammar for Italian-Speaking People; Italian Language Grammar for English-Speaking People. Home: 7426 Paxton Av., Chicago, Ill. Died Feb. 22, 1945.

DURFEE, William Pitt, coll. dean; b. Livonia, Mich., Feb. 5, 1855; s. R. S. and Mary (Wightman) D.; A.B., U. of Mich., 1876; Ph.D., Johns Hopkins U., 1883; LL.D., Hobart Coll., 1922; m. Charlotte E. Racao, Apr. 3, 1888; children—Walter Hetherington, Elizabeth Racao; m. 2d, Katharine S. Butts, June 29, 1898; 1 dau., Mary Katharine Perry. Teacher, Berkeley (Calif.) Gymnasium, 1877-81, prof. mathematics, 1884-1929, prof. of mathematics emeritus since 1929, dean, 1888-1925, acting pres., 1897, 1901-03, 1912-13, 1917-19, Hobart Coll., dean meritus since 1926. Fellow A.A.A.S.; mem. Am. Math. Soc., Math. Assn. of Am. Episcopalian. Republican. Author: Elements of Trigonometry, 1901. Home: Geneva, N.Y. Died Dec. 17, 1941.

DURHAM, Charles Love, educator; b. Shelby, N.C., Jan. 2, 1872; s. David Noah and Esther Ruth (Coleman) D.; M.A., Furman U., 1891; Ph.D., Cornell U., 1899; univs. of Leipzig and Munich, 1905-06; Litt.D., Furman U., 1922; m. Jean Liddell Glendinning, Mar. 4, 1903; children—Charles Glendinning (dec.), Helen Coleman (Mrs. Erwin John McGuire), Archibald Glendinning, David Hughes, Forrest, George. Instructor at Furman U., 1891-96; fellow in Latin and Greek, 1896-97, instr. in Latin, 1897-1901, asst. prof., 1901-09, prof. since 1909 (first incumbent of the John Wendell Anderson Professorship), emeritus 1940, Cornell U. Apptd. vice consul at Geneva, Switzerland, 1918; Dem. candidate for Congress, 1920 and 1924, from 37th N.Y. Dist. Presbyterian. Mem. Chi Psi and holder of its Distinguished Service Award, Kentucky Colonel. Author: Subjunctive Substantive Clauses in Plautus (Cornell Studies in Classical Philology, Vol. 13), 1901; The Amphitruo of Plautus, 1904. Home: 101 West Upland Rd., Cayuga Heights, Ithaca, N.Y. Died Apr. 15, 1949.

DURHAM, Robert Lee (dûr'ŭm), college president; b. Shelby, N.C., May 4, 1870; s. Plato and Catherine Leonora (Tracy) D.; descendant of Lt. Thomas Tracy, Norwich, Conn. (1610-85); preparatory education, Kings Mountain (N.C.) High Sch. and Horner Mil. Sch.; B.Sc., Trinity Coll. (now Duke U.), 1891; studied law at Trinity Coll. and Dick's Law Sch.; m. Mary Willie Craton, Dec. 27, 1893; children—Robert Lee (dec.), Margaret (Mrs. H. Russell Robey), Joshua Forman (dec.), Ben Dixon (dec.). Began practice of law, Rutherfordton, N.C., 1893; teacher Davenport Coll., Lenoir, N.C., 1909-10, Centenary Coll., Cleveland, Tenn., 1910-11; dean Martha Washington Coll., Abingdon, Va., 1911-19; pres. Southern Seminary, Buena Vista, Virginia, 1919-44. Mem. North Carolina State Dem. Com. 1894-98; mem. platform com. Dem. State Conv., 1906. Served as capt. Co. G, 2d N.C. Inf., Spanish-Am. War, 1898. Trustee Trinity Coll., 1895-1912. Mem. Phi Beta Kappa, Omicron Delta Kappa, Alpha Tau Omega. Mem. Methodist Ch. (mem. Gen. Conf., 1918, 36). Mason, K.P., Red Man. Club: Rotary of Buena Vista (ex-pres.). Author: Call of the South, 1908; A Simple Construction for the Approximate Trisection of an Angle, 1944; Since I Was Born (autobiography), 1948; also verse and various college songs. Known as football and baseball player. Home: Buena Vista, Va. Died Jan. 1, 1948.

DUSCHAK, Lionel Herman (dōō'shăk), univ. prof., cons. engineer; b. Buffalo, N.Y., Sept. 25, 1882; s. Adolf and Agnes Hannah (Day) D.; A.B., U. of Mich., 1904; M.A., Ph.D., Princeton, 1908; m. Frances Eschenburg, Oct. 13, 1909. Instr. in chemistry, Princeton, 1907-09; research engr. Corning (N.Y.) Glass Works, 1909-13; chem. engr. U.S. Bur. Mines, in charge Expt. Sta., Berkeley, Calif., 1915-21; cons. practice since 1921; prof. metallurgy, U. of Calif., since 1938. Mem. Am. Chem. Soc., Am. Inst. Mining and Metall. Engrs., Pacific Assn. of Cons. Engrs., A.A.A.S., Phi Gamma Delta, Theta Tau, Sigma Xi, Tau Beta Pi. Republican. Unitarian. Clubs: Engineers (San Francisco); Commonwealth Club of Calif., Faculty. Home: 86 Tamalpais Rd., Berkeley 8, Calif. Office: Hobart Bldg., San Francisco, Calif. Died Nov. 27, 1948; buried at Santa Barbara, Calif.

DU SHANE, Donald (dū-shān), educator; b. at South Bend, Indiana, June 5, 1885; s. James and Emma (Anderson) Du S.; B.S., Hanover (Ind.) Coll., 1906, M.A., 1913; M.S., U. of Wisconsin, 1916; LL.D., from Wabash Coll., 1939; LL.D., from Butler University, 1941; m. Harriette McLelland, June 29, 1907; children—Donald McLelland, Graham Phillips, James William. Teacher pub. schs., 1906-10; prin. Shelbyville (Ill.) High Sch., 1910; supt. schs., Madison, Ind., 1911-16, Clinton, 1916-18, Columbus, 1918-41; exec. sec. National Commn. for Defense of Democracy Through Education, Washington, D.C., since 1941; prof. sch. adminstrn. Butler U., 1924-25. Trustee Ind. State Teachers' Retirement Fund (1921-33), Hanover Coll. Pres. bd. Southern Ind. Tuberculosis Hosp., 1938-41. Mem. Ind. Soc. Mental Hygiene (past pres.), Ind. Conf. on Social Work (pres. 1926), Ind. Tuberculosis Assn. (pres. 1937), Ind. State Teachers' Assn. (pres. 1921), N.E.A. (chmn. com. on Tenure 1934-40; pres. 1940-41), Phi Delta Theta. Presbyterian. Mason. Wrote and secured passage through Ind. legislature of tenure and other laws promoting interest of pupils and teachers; author articles and pamphlets on Teacher Tenure and other edul. subjects. Dir. investigations, N.Y. and Chicago pub. schools. Club: Rotary (Columbus). Address: Washington, D.C. Died March 11, 1947.

DUTTON, Emily Helen (dŭt'tŭn), coll. dean; b. Shirley, Mass., Sept. 29, 1869; d. Rev. Albert Ira and Helen Abby (Reed) Dutton; A.B., Mt. Holyoke Coll., 1891; A.M., Radcliffe Coll., 1896; student U. of Berlin, winter 1901, U. of Munich, summer 1902; Ph.D., U. of Chicago, 1913; unmarried. Teacher secondary sch., Park City, Utah, 1888-89; teacher Latin and Greek Mankato (Minn.) High Sch., 1891-95; teacher Latin and Ancient History, Girls' High Sch., Brooklyn, 1896-97; instr. Latin, Vassar Coll., 1897-1906; prof. Latin and Greek, Tenn. Coll., Murfreesboro, 1909-23, dean, 1922-23; dean and prof. Greek and Latin, Sweet Briar Coll., 1923-40, dean emeritus since 1940; fellow in Latin, U. of Chicago, 1906-09. Received Algernon Sydney Sullivan award, Sweet Briar Coll., 1939. Dir. Auxiliary Fund of Am. Classical Sch., Athens, 1938-41; chmn. Southern Conf. Academic Deans, 1937-38. Mem. Archæol. Inst. America, Am. Philol. Assn., Classical Assn. of Middle West and South (1st v.p. 1922-23), Classical Assn. of Great Britain, Nat. Assn. Deans of Women, Am. Assn. Univ. Profs., Am. Assn. Univ. Women (nat. com. on standards of colls., 1921-33, chmn., 1925-33), Am. Assn. for the United Nations, Americans United for World Orgn., Foreign Policy Association, English-Speaking Union, Phi Beta Kappa. Conglist. Club: Women's University (New York). Author: Studies in Greek Prepositional Phrases, 1916; Reflections on Rereading Vergil, 1916; also papers, articles and reports on classical subjects, etc. Address: Sweet Briar Coll., Sweet Briar, Va. Died June 18, 1947.

DUTTON, George Elliott, coll. dean; b. Seaford, Del., Dec. 16, 1881; s. James E. and Mary R. (Elliott) D.; A.B., Del. Coll. (now one of the two colleges of U. of Del.) 1904; grad. student Johns Hopkins U., 1905-08; A.M., Harvard U., 1911; m. Elsie Smith, Apr. 6, 1912; 1 son, George Elliott. Instr. English, U. of Mo., 1908-10; instr. English, U. of Del., Newark, Del., 1911-13, asst. prof., 1913-17, asso. prof., 1917-18, prof. English since 1918, dean and registrar Del. Coll. since 1923. Mem. Assn. Deans of Land Grant Colls., Nat. Assn. Deans and Advisers, Nat. Assn. Coll. Registrars, Sons of Del. of Phila. Ind. Democrat. Presbyterian. Co-author (with W. O. Sypherd): Outline of Survey Course in English Literature; Specimens of English Compositions; English Composition for College Freshmen. Contbr. to sch. journals. Home: 183 W. Main St., Newark, Del.* Died Feb. 29, 1944.

DUVEL, Joseph William Tell (dū-vĕl'), crop technologist; b. Wapakoneta, O., Nov. 16, 1873; s. August and Amanda (Myers) D.; B.Sc., Ohio State U., 1897; D.S., U. of Mich., 1902; m. Elva Smith, May 11, 1904; children—Maxine, William August. Asst. botanist, Ohio Agrl. Expt. Sta., 1898-99; with Bur. Plant Industry, U.S. Dept. of Agr., Washington, 1902-18, crop technologist, in charge of grain standardization investigations, 1910-18; with U.S. Grain Corp., New York, 1918-20; grain mcht., Winnipeg, Can., 1920-21; U.S. grain exchange supervisor, Chicago, 1922-25; chief, Commodity Exchange Adminstrn., Washington, D.C., 1925-42; retired March 1, 1942. Fellow A.A.A.S.; mem. Washington Botanical Soc., Potomac Grange, Washington Biologists' Field Club, Kappa Sigma, Pi Gamma Mu; hon. life mem. of Royal Agrl. Soc. of New South Wales, Australia. Club: Cosmos. Home: 1225 Decatur St., N.W. Office: U.S. Dept. Agr., Washington, D.C.* Died Jan. 8, 1946.

DWIGHT, Arthur Smith, mining and metall. engr.; b. Taunton, Mass., Mar. 18, 1864; s. Benjamin Pierce and Elizabeth Fiske (Dwight) S.; assumed maternal surname on coming of age—authorized by Kings' County (N.Y.) Court, Dec. 15, 1886; grad. Poly. Inst., Brooklyn, 1882; E.M., Sch. of Mines (Columbia), 1885, hon. M.Sc., 1914, hon. D.Sc., 1929; m. Jane Earl Reed, June 4, 1895 (died Feb. 1929); m. 2d, Mrs. Anne Howard Chapin. Mining and metallurgical work, 1885-1906, in charge smelting operations at Pueblo and Leadville (Colo.), El Paso (Tex.), Argentine (Kan.), San Luis Potosi and Cananea (Mexico); cons. practice, and directing business of Dwight & Lloyd cos., New York, since 1906; pres. Dwight & Lloyd Sintering Co.; pres. Dwight & Lloyd Metall. Co. Commd. major engrs., U.S.R., Jan. 23, 1917; assisted organizing 1st Reserve Engrs., later 11th Engrs., the first A.E.F. unit in action in France (Cambrai); served in Somme sector, Cambrai offensive, Lys defensive, N. Picardy sector, Meuse-Argonne offensive; in France 22 mos., on British front 9 mos., comdg. 1st Batt., 11th Engrs.; later on spl. duty as metall. consultant French companies; engr. salvage officer A.E.F.; now colonel engrs., U.S.R. (inactive); vice chmn. mineral advisory com. Army and Navy Munitions Board. Alumni trustee Columbia U., 1915-21. Mem. American Institute Mining and Metallurgical Engineers (life, ex-pres.; Douglas medallist), Mining and Metallurgical Society America, Society American Mil. Engrs. (ex-pres. N.Y. Post), Mass. Society of Mayflower Descendants, Mil. Order of the World War, Am. Legion, Great Neck Post, American Vets. Assn., Institution Mining and Metallurgy of London (hon.), Mass. Soc. of the Cincinnati, Sigma Xi, Tau Beta Pi; hon. mem. Soc. Engineers of Louvain Univ., Belgium. Citation by Gen. Pershing; Order of Purple Heart (U.S.); Companion D.S.O. (British); Chevalier Légion d'Honneur (French). Republican. Episcopalian (hon. Warden All Saints Church, Great Neck). Clubs: University, Engineers', Mining, Columbia Univ., North Hempstead Country, Hobe Sound Yacht (vice commodore), Jupiter Island; Army and Navy (Washington); Union Interalliée (Paris). Co-inventor with R. L. Lloyd of Dwight and Lloyd system of ore treatment. Home: West Shore Rd., Great Neck, L.I., N.Y., Pine Hill Road, New Fairfield, Conn. and "Beau Rivage," Hobe Sound, Fla. Office: 19 Rector St., New York, N.Y. Died Apr. 1, 1946.

DWIRE, Henry Rudolph, editor; b. Winston-Salem, N.C., Oct. 8, 1882; s. Henry Xenophon and Mary (Hanes) D.; A.B., Trinity Coll. (now Duke U.), 1902, A.M., 1903; LL.D., Davidson College, North Carolina, 1943; assistant in English, Trinity College, 1903; instr., Fishburne Mil. Sch., Waynesboro, Va., 1903-04; editor Winston-Salem Sentinel, 1904-26, co-pub., 1918-26; dir. pub. relations and alumni affairs, Duke U., since 1929; elected vice-pres. Duke U., 1941; also editor South Atlantic Quarterly, Duke U. Alumni Register. Chmn. Winston-Salem Sch. Commn., 1923-30; sec. bd. dirs. N.C. State Hosp. for Insane, 1929-33; founder Winston-Salem Fine Arts Foundation. Mem. N.C. State Board of Edn. Mem. bd. of lay activities Western N.C. Conf. M.E. Ch., S., 1925-29. Trustee Duke U. Mem. N.C. Art Soc. (dir. 1931) Am. Red Cross (chmn. Winston-Salem Chapter, 1927-29), Alpha Tau Omega, Phi Beta Kappa, Omicron Delta Kappa. Awarded Winston-Salem trophy for distinguished community service, 1928. Democrat. Methodist. Clubs: Rotary (dist. gov. Rotary Internat., 1929-30), Cosmos (Winston-Salem); Hope Valley Country. Home: Durham, N.C. Died July 17, 1944.

DWYRE, Dudley G. (dwīr), business exec.; b. London, Eng., Jan. 30, 1880; s. Charles Golding and Bessie (Fox) D.; grad. Colo. State Agr. Coll., 1901; student George Washington U., 1917-18; m. Emma Blanch Nicholson, Aug. 28, 1902; children—Dorothy Cora (Mrs. Eyre Branch), Jack Golding. Came to U.S., 1884; citizen by father's naturalization. With U.S. Indian Service, 1902-03; Philippine Service, 1904; chief clerk and asst. supt. U.S. Indian Agency, 1904-08; clerk U.S. Indian Warehouse, 1909-17; chief of sec., Bureau of Indian Affairs, 1917-18; Dept. of State, 1918-19; apptd. U.S. consul, 1919, and served successively at Maracaibo (Venezuela), Fort William and Port Arthur (Canada), Guadalajara and Mexico City (Mexico); London; then consul gen. at London, Panama, Montevideo (Uruguay) and Costa Rica; 1st sec. of Legation at Montevideo, San Jose (Costa Rica) and Guatemala City; also charge d'affaires at Montevideo, Guatemala City and San Jose; counselor of embassy, Montevideo, 1942; retired from Service with rank of counselor of embassy and consul general; now pres. Negociacion Sur Peruana, S.A., hdqrs. in Arequipa, Peru. Mason. Home: 222 Ximeno Av., Long Beach 3, Calif. Address: Casilla 382, Arequipa, Peru. Died March 1, 1948.

DYE, Clair Albert, pharmacy; b. Zeno, O., June 23, 1869; s. Elza A. and Emma O'Neil (Garrett) D.; Ph.G., Ohio State U., 1891, grad. study, 1895-97; Ph.D., U. of Berne, Switzerland, 1901; m. Oleta Sinclair, June 30, 1902; m. 2d, Flora Alice Elder, June 19, 1930. Asst. in chemistry and pharmacy, Ohio State U., 1890-94, asst. in pharmacy, 1894-98, asst. prof. pharmacy, 1898-1906, asso. prof., 1906-09, prof. since 1909, also acting dean of Coll. of Pharmacy, 1915-21, dean, 1921-39, dean emeritus since 1939. Mem. revision com. U.S. Pharmacopoeia. Pres. Am. Assn. Colleges of Pharmacy, 1921-22, chmn. sect. edn. and legislation, 1919-20. Mem. Am. Pharm. Assn., Ohio State Pharm. Assn., Sigma Xi, Phi Delta Chi. Republican. Club: Faculty. Contbr. papers and reports to drug jours., pharm. assns., etc. Home: 2201 Starr Rd., Columbus, O. Died Oct. 10, 1949.

DYER, H(ezekiah) Anthony, artist; b. Providence, R.I., Oct. 28, 1872; s. Elisha and Nancy Anthony (Viall) D.; prep. edn. St. Paul's Sch., Concord, N.H.; B.S., Brown U., 1894, hon. A.M., 1919; studied in France, Holland, Italy and Germany; m. Charlotte Osgood Tilden, Oct. 16, 1900; 1 dau., Nancy A. Exec. sec. to father, gov. of R.I., 1897-1900, and col. and a.-d.-c. on staff of gov. during same period. Landscape painter; works on permanent exhbn. in Corcoran Gallery, Washington, D.C., R.I. Sch. of Design; Providence Art Club; New Bedford (Mass.) Library; Fall River (Mass.) Library, etc. Univ. extension lecturer Brown U.; docent lecturer and mem. advisory com. Rhode Island Sch. of Design. Mem. Archtl. Commn., Diocese of R.I. Ex-pres. R.I. Rep. Club. Mem. Providence Art Club (ex-pres.), Providence Water Color Club (ex-pres.), Newport Art Assn. (mem. council), Boston Water Color Soc., R.I. Society Colonial Wars (gov. 1929-31), R.I. Hist. Soc. (ex-pres.), Phi Beta Kappa (hon.), Sigma Chapter Psi Upsilon (pres. local club). Republican. Episcopalian (mem. Standing Com. of Diocese); warden St. Stephens' Ch.; mem. Diocesan Council, del. Gen. Conv. Lectures on art and travel. Dir. Community Council of R.I. Council of Defense; dir. R.I. Speakers' Bur. ("Four-Minute Men"); dir. of speaking for R.I. Food Adminstrn.; mem. State War Memorial Com., Roosevelt Memorial Com.; Monument Com. Lincoln Memorial Commn. of R.I.; mem. of Providence Tercentennial Commn.; Am. del. and speaker, Anglican Catholic Congress, London, 1930. Comdr. Order of the Crown of Italy, by King, 1926; Chevalier Order S.S. Maurizio and Lazzaro, by same, 1931; awarded silver medal and diploma by French Govt. for children's relief work; hon. diploma Italian Touring Club. Address: 170 Blackstone Blvd., Providence, R.I.*Died Aug. 24, 1943.

DYER, Joseph Henry, ry. official; b. Colfax, Calif., Mar. 13, 1872; s. John and Katherine (Robinson) D.; educated in public schools; m. Kate McGrail, Oct. 8, 1898; children—Joseph H., Lorene, Helen. With Southern Pacific Co. since 1888, beginning as section laborer, advanced to freight conductor, 1894, traveling conductor, 1900, gen. yardmaster, Sacramento, 1902, trainmaster, 1905, supt. Shasta div., 1908-11, Tucson div., 1911-14, Sacramento div., 1914-16, asst. gen. mgr., 1916-18, gen. mgr. operating dept. Southern Pacific System, at San Francisco, 1918-29, now v.p. in charge operations; pres. Ogden Union Ry. and Depot Co.; dir. Southern Pacific Golden Gate Co., Sunset Ry. Co., Northwestern Pacific R.R. Co., Southern Pacific Golden Gate Ferries, Ltd., Southern Pacific R.R. Co. of Mexico. Republican. Clubs: Bohemian, Family (San Francisco); Sutter (Sacramento). Home: Hotel Mark Hopkins. Office: 65 Market St., San Francisco, Calif. Died June 14, 1947.

DYER, Walter Alden, author; b. Roslindale, Mass., Oct. 10, 1878; s. Ebenezer Porter and Martha Augusta (Fearing) D.; A.B., Amherst, 1900; m. Ethelind Thorp Childs (died March 1904); m. 2d, Muriel Worthington Childs, June 1, 1907. On staff of Springfield (Mass.) Union, 1900-01, Criterion, New York, 1901; editor Wall Paper News, New York, 1901-05; on staff, 1905-06, mng. editor, 1906-14, Country Life in America. Mem. Amherst Hist. Soc. (pres. 1924-26), Phi Kappa Psi, Phi Kappa Phi. Author: The Lure of the Antique, 1910; The Richer Life, 1911; Pierrot, Dog of Belgium, 1915; Early American Craftsmen, 1915; Gulliver the Great, and Other Dog Stories, 1916; Humble Annals of a Back Yard, 1916; Creators of Decorative Styles, 1917; Five Babbitts at Bonnyacres, 1917; The Dogs of Boytown, 1918; Handbook of Furniture Styles, 1918; Ben, the Battle Horse, 1919; With the Help of God and a Few Marines (with Brig. Gen. A. W. Catlin), 1919; Sons of Liberty, 1920; Many Dogs There Be, 1924; All Around Robin Hood's Barn, 1926; The Breakwater, 1927; Country Cousins, 1927; The Rocking-Chair—an American Institution (with Esther Stevens Fraser), 1928; Chronicles of a Countryman, 1928; Sprigs of Hemlock —A Tale of the Shays Rebellion, 1931. Editor Amherst Graduates' Quarterly and dir. Amherst Coll. Press (news bur. and publicity). Home: "Rock Walls Farm," Amherst, Mass. Died June 20, 1943; buried in Wildwood Cemetery, Amherst.

E

EAGLETON, Wells Phillips, surgeon; b. Brooklyn, N.Y., Sept. 18, 1865; s. Thomas Aston Proud and Mary Emma (Phillips) E.; Polytechnic Inst., Brooklyn; M.D., Coll. Phys. and Surg. (Columbia), 1888; D.Sc. (hon.), Univ. of Newark, 1942; D.Sc. (hon.), Rutgers Univ., 1943; m. Florence Pershine Riggs, May 24, 1913; med. director board trustees Newark Eye and Ear Infirmary; chief division of head surgery, Newark City Hosp.; cons. cranial surgeon St. Barnabas, St. Michael's, Memorial, Presbyn., and Beth Israel hosps. (Newark), Mountain Side Hosp. (Montclair), Muhlenberg Hosp. (Plainfield), All Souls Hosp. (Morristown, N.J.), Irvington General Hospital, Orange Memorial Hospital, Elizabeth General Hosp., West Hudson Hosp. of Kearny (all N.J.); cons. ophthalmologist and otologist Women's and Children's Hosp., Newark, Hosp. & Home for Crippled Children, Newark, Morristown (N.J.) Memorial Hosp.; mem. cons. staff of Essex County Hospital, Overbrook, N.J., div cranial surgery, Essex County Isolation Hosp., Soho; former director Federal Trust Co. Vol. U.S. Army, April 10, 1917; served as chief of surgery of the head Base Hosp., Camp Dix, until after signing of Armistice; col. Officers' Reserve Corps, M.D. President Newark Council of Social Agencies; trustee Welfare Fedn. of Newark, Newark Museum. Recipient first Edward J. Ill award, 1930, Award of Merit Medical Soc. of N.J., hon. membership, 1939; Diplome de Membre, Associe du College International de Chirurgiens, 1940; gold medal, by Kings County Medical Society, 1938. Member of the board of governors, American College of surgeons, A.M.A.

(house of delegates), N.J. State Med. Soc. (pres. 1923-24 and chmn. welfare com.), Am. Otol. Soc. (pres. 1921), N.Y. Otol. Soc. (pres. 1929), Am. Acad. Ophthalmology and Otolaryngology (pres. 1934-35), Nat. Med. Acad. Rio de Janeiro (hon.); hon. mem. Kansas City Ophthalmology, Otology, Rhinology and Laryngology Soc., Washington (D.C.) Med. and Surg. Soc., Sociedad Otorinoloargingologica (Madrilena, Spain); trustee Am. Coll. of Surgeons; former N.J. rep. on the Med. Adv. Bd. of the Veterans' Bur.; formerly mem. N.J. Com. for the Blind. Clubs: Essex, Essex County Country. Author: Brain Abscess—Its Surgical Pathology and Operative Treatment, 1922; Cavernous Sinus, 1925; Thromboses (both translater into French), 1925; also numerous published speeches and monographs. Home: 212 Elwood Av. Office: 15 Lombardy St., Newark 2, N.J. Died Sept. 11, 1946; buried in Mount Pleasant Cemetery, Newark, N.J.

EAMES, Charles Holmes; b. Andover, Mass., Nov. 17, 1875; s. Lemuel Holmes and Helen Maria (Eames) E.; B.S. in E.E., Mass. Inst. Tech., 1897; m. Mary Wood Richardson, Nov. 18, 1901. Supt. Light, Heat & Power Corp., Lowell, Mass., 1898-99; elec. engr. with Stone & Webster, 1899-1904; instr. in physics and math.; sec. Lowell Textile Sch., 1904-07, prin., 1907-08, pres., 1918-45; retired; v.p., Central Savings Bank. Moderator Town of Billerica since 1912. Trustee of Rogers Hall (Lowell). Mem. Am. Inst. of Elec. Engrs., A.A.A.S., Nat. Assn. Cotton Mfrs. Republican. Unitarian. Mason. Home: Blanchard Av., Billerica, Mass. Died Jan. 29, 1948.

EARL, Charles, lawyer; b. Cambrige, Mass., Apr. 21, 1869; s. Charles and Katharine (Sullivan) E.; LL.B., Georgetown, U., 1895, LL.M., 1896; m. Kathleen Rogers; children—Charles Rogers, Richard Philip. Admitted to bar, 1896; practiced D.C. and Md., 1896-1903; spl. atty. Bur. of Corps., Dept. Commerce and Labor, 1903-06; spl. atty. Dept. Justice, June 18-Sept. 1, 1906; solicitor Dept. Commerce and Labor, Sept. 1, 1906-Mar. 31, 1913; v.p. and gen. counsel Am. Smelting & Refining Co., N.Y. Trustee John Simon Guggenheim Memorial Foundation; mem. Am. Bar Assn., Am. Assn. Internat. Law, Am. Geog. Soc. Home: Great Neck, N.Y.; (summer) Westhampton Beach, L.I., N.Y. Office: 120 Broadway, New York, N.Y. Died July 26, 1943.

EARL, Robert, surgeon; b. Lansing, Ia., Aug. 27, 1872; s. Peter O. and Hannah (Anderson) E.; M.D., U. of Minn., 1896; m. Clara Swanstrom, June 1, 1900; children—May Earl Slocum, John Robert. Surgeon Midway Hospital and Mound Park Hospital. Diplomate American Board of Surgery; fellow Am. Coll. Surgeons; mem. Western Surg. Assn., A.M.A., Minn. State Med. Assn., Ramsey County Med. Soc., Minn. Acad. Medicine, St. Paul Surgical Soc. Mason. Clubs: Athletic, St. Paul Automobile. Home: 1645 Summit Av. Office Lowry Bldg., St. Paul, Minn. Died Aug. 11, 1948.

EARLY, Gilbert Garfield, railroad exec.; b. Pittsburgh, Pa., July 25, 1881; s. James and Anna Elizabeth (Kerr) E.; m. Mellie Guthridge, Nov. 18, 1903; children—Wilda, Gilbert G., Jr., Oren, Robert. Entered railway service with Erie R.R. as clerk, 1900; chief rate clerk, Wabash lines, east of Toledo, O., 1907; general freight passenger agent, Pittsburgh & W.Va. R.R. at Pittsburgh, 1917, assistant general freight agent, same, 1918; reopened an off-line of Wabash Ry. at Phila., 1920; asst. gen. freight agent, Wabash Ry. at St. Louis, 1921, gen. freight agent, 1924, asst. freight traffic manager, 1927, freight traffic manager, 1931; apptd. chief traffic officer for receivers of Wabash Ry. and Ann Arbor R.R., and v.p. traffic Manistique & Lake Superior R.R., Sept. 1, 1936; apptd. v.p. traffic Corporate Orgns., Wabash Ry. and Ann Arbor R.R., and v.p. traffic Lake Erie & Ft. Wayne R.R. Co., Sept. 29, 1936. Presbyterian. Mason (Shriner). Clubs: Noonday, Traffic, Wabash, Glen Echo Country (St. Louis, Mo.); Union League, Traffic, Chicago Towers (Chicago). Home: 7485 Washington St., University City, Mo. Office: 1455 Railway Exchange Bldg., St. Louis, Mo. Died Mar. 8, 1943.

EARLY, John Jacob, supt. of schools; b. South Bend, Ind., Jan. 15, 1878; s. Isaac and Mary Elizabeth (Irvin) E.; A.B., Indiana University, 1901; A.M., Columbia University, 1927; m. Mary Whitmer, August 20, 1902; 1 daughter, Ruth Evelyn (Mrs. J. W. Sampson). Country school teacher, 1895-98; teacher physics and chemistry, Warsaw (Ind.) High Sch., 1901-03, prin. high sch., 1903-05; supt. schs., 1905-08; supt. schs. Sheridan, Wyo., 1908-1945; supt. emeritus since Aug. 1, 1945. Mem. State Bd. Ednl. Examiners, State Bd. Edn. (pres.), Y.M.C.A. Bd., Boy Scouts Council; trustee Perkins Foundation. Mem. Nat. and Wyo. edn. assns., Phi Delta Kappa, Phi Gamma Delta. Republican. Presbyterian. Mason (Shriner). Club: Rotary. Home: 326 Coffeen Av., Sheridan, Wyo. Died Nov. 25, 1945.

EASLEY, Claudius Miller (ēz'lē), army officer; b. Thorp Spring, Tex., July 11, 1891; s. Alexander Campbell and Claudia (Miller) E.; B.S., Tex. A. and M. Coll., 1916; student Army Service Schs., 1927-30; grad. Army War Coll., 1940; m. Inez Wickline, Oct. 13, 1917; 1 son, Claudius Miller. Commd. 2d lt., U.S. Army, Aug. 7, 1917, and advanced through the grades to brig. gen. Awarded Distinguished Marksman medal. Mason. Home: Lake Waco, Waco, Tex. Address: 3601 Connecticut Av. N.W., Washington. Died June 19, 1945; buried in 96th Inf. Div. Cemetery, Okinawa.

EASTMAN, Joseph Bartlett, pub. official; b. Katonah, N.Y., June 26, 1882; s. Rev. John Huse and Lucy (King) E.; B.A., Amherst Coll., 1904, hon. LL.D., 1926; LL.D., Syracuse U. and Temple U., 1934; LL.D., Oberlin College, 1938, Dartmouth College, 1941, U. of Michigan, 1942. Holder of Amherst fellowship at South End House (social settlement), Boston, 1905; sec. Public Franchise League, Boston, 1906-13; counsel for employes of various st. ry. cos. in wage arbitration cases, 1913-14; mem. Mass. Pub. Service Commn., 1915-19; mem. Interstate Commerce Commn. for many years from 1919; federal coördinator of transportation, June 1933-June 1936; dir. Office of Defense Tranportation since Dec. 1941. Trustee of Amherst Coll. Mem. Psi Upsilon, Phi Beta Kappa. Clubs: Boston City; Cosmos (Washington, D.C.); Chevy Chase Club. Home: 2266 Cathedral Av. N.W., Washington, D.C. Died Mar. 15, 1944.

EASTMAN, Joseph Rilus, surgeon; b. Indianapolis, Ind., Apr. 18, 1871; s. Joseph and Mary Katherine (Barker) E.; B.Sc., Wabash Coll., Ind., 1891 (A.M., 1904); M.D., magna cum laude, U. of Berlin, 1897; spl. work, Princeton Univ., 1 yr.; LL.D. from Wabash Coll., 1926; m. Frieda Grumpelt, Feb. 1, 1910 (dec.); 1 son, Joseph Rilus; m. 2d, Neva Bonham, 1926. Surgeon, Indianapolis City Hospital since 1900; prof. surgery, Indiana U. School of Medicine since 1909. Major, M.C. U.S. Army; mem. Gen. Med. Bd. of Council Nat. Defense; dir. American Hosp., Vienna, Austria, 1916. Received Austrian Imperial decoration of the Red Cross, officers class, 1917. Letter of appreciation sent by Austrian govt. to American govt. Fellow Am. Coll. Surgeons (founder and ex-gov.); mem. Am. Surg. Assn., Western Surg. Assn. (pres. 1913-14), A.M.A. (diploma of honor awarded for pathology exhibit), Ind. State Med. Assn. (pres. 1919), Indianapolis Med. Assn. (pres. 1925), Société Internationale de Chirurgie, Sigma Chi, Phi Rho Sigma, Sigma Xi. Republican. Episcopalian. Mason. Clubs: University, Indianapolis Literary. Contbr. many articles to Am. and fgn. med. publs. Original worker in surg. pathology; has devised surg. procedures and instruments. Home: 970 N. Meridian St., Indianapolis, Ind. Died Nov. 29, 1942.

EASTMAN, Lucius Root, food products; b. Framingham, Mass., July 29, 1874; s. Lucius Root and Rebecca Porter (Crane) E.; B.A., Amherst, 1895; LL.B., Boston U., 1898; m. Eva L. Hills, June 14, 1905; children—Margaret Hills (Mrs. Paul C. French), John Hills (dec.), Lucius Root. Pres. The Hills Bros. Co., 1906-38, chmn. bd. since 1938. Pres. Am. Arbitration Assn., 1926-38, chmn. bd. since 1938; Am. rep. econ. com., League of Nations, 1928-33; mem. exec. com. Am. sect. Internat. Chamber Commerce; mem. bd. Merchants Assn. of New York since 1920 (pres. 1924-28); pub. dir. Federal Home Loan of New York. Pres. Congl. Bd. of Ministerial Relief, 1923-27; pres. Alumni Assn. of Amherst Coll., 1929-31; trustee Amherst Coll. since 1931, Hartford Foundation since 1939; trustee Museum of Science and Industry (New York). Mem. Beta Theta Pi Fraternity. Clubs: Amherst, Bankers, Century. Home: "Axonwold," Scarsdale, N.Y. Office: 110 Washington St., New York, N.Y. Died Mar. 14, 1943.

EATON, Barney Edward, pub. utility exec.; b. Taylorsville, Miss., Dec. 5, 1878; s. James Samuel and Olivia (Sharbrough) E.; A.B., Millsaps Coll., Jackson, Miss., 1901, LL.B., 1903, LL.D., 1922; m. Helen Grey Simpson, Aug. 5, 1905; children—Margaret Simpson (Mrs. Robert A. Murphy), Barney Edward, James Samuel, William Douglas. Admitted to bar of State of Miss., 1903, and began practice of law at Hattiesburg; dist. attorney 13th Mississippi dist., 1906-09; atty. Gulf & Ship Island R.R., 1909-11, gen. counsel, 1911-24; pres. Miss. Power Co. since 1924; v.p. Gulfport & Miss. Coast Traction Co. Mem. Am. and Miss. State bar assns. Democrat. Methodist. Mason (Shriner). Home: 2106 E. Beach. Office: G. & S. Bldg., Gulfport, Miss. Died July 18, 1944.

EATON, Edward Dwight, educator; b. Lancaster, Wis., Jan. 12, 1851; s. Rev. Dr. Samuel W. and Catharine E. (Demarest) E.; A.B., Beloit Coll., 1872, A.M., 1875; B.D., Yale, 1875; univs. of Leipzig and Heidelberg, 1875-76; D.D., Northwestern, 1887, Yale, 1900; LL.D., U. of Wis., 1887, Marietta College, 1910; L.H.D., Beloit (Wis.) College, 1936; m. Martha E., d. Honorable J. Allen Barber, Aug. 23, 1875; children—Ethelwyn (Mrs. Charles F. Read), Allen Barber, Katrina Elizabeth (Mrs. Henry W. Hincks), Mildred Lois (Mrs. Howard B. Lewis), Mattie Carolyn (dec.), Aldyth Lillian Frances (Mrs. Donald M. Jack). Ordained to ministry of Congl. Church, 1876; pastor Newton, Iowa, 1876-79; pastor First Congl. Ch., Oak Park, Ill., 1879-86; pres. Beloit Coll., 1886-1905, 1907-17, pres. emeritus since 1917, and pres. ad interim, 1923; pastor North Church, St. Johnsbury, Vt., 1905-07; pastor Cleveland Park Ch., Washington, 1918-20; sec. ad interim Nat. Congl. Council, 1920-21. One of del. of 3 sent, 1898, to inspect missions of A.B.C.F.M. in China; spent 1901-02 abroad, in study at Berlin and in travel; mem. com. of 19 to reorganize Congl. benevolent socs., 1910-13; Southworth lecturer, Andover (Mass.) Theol. Sem., 1904; Pond lecturer, Bangor Theol. Sem., 1906; Porter lecturer, Beloit Coll., 1918. V.p. A.B.C.F.M., 1910-17, mem. Prudential Com., 1917-23, chmn. 1922-23; pres. bd. trustees Internat. Coll., Smyrna, Asia Minor, 1921-32; trustee Anatolia Coll. (Salonica, Greece), American Coll. (Sofia, Bulgaria); dir. Congl. Edn. Soc., Boston, 1917-25; pres. Isles of Shoals Congl. Conf., 1924-26. Mem. sect. of coöperating orgns. of U.S. Food Administration, Washington, 1917. Member Phi Beta Kappa. Clubs: Theta Sigma (Washington); Winthrop (Boston). Author: Historical Sketches of Beloit College, 1928, 35; Two Wisconsin Pioneers, 1933; Thronging Echoes, 1938; Along Life's Pathway, 1941. Editor: The Hymnal of Praise, 1913, 24; The Student Hymnary, 1937; The New Hymnal of Praise, 1941. Writer of over 20 articles in Dictionary of American Biography. Home: Fairfield, Conn. Address: 147 Algonquin Road, Bridgeport, Conn. Died June 19, 1942.

EATON, George Francis, zoölogist and archeologist; b. New Haven, Conn., May 30, 1872; s. Daniel Cady and Caroline (Ketcham) E.; B.A., Yale, 1894, Ph.D., 1898; m. Julia Henrietta Hammer, Oct. 24, 1899. Curator of osteology, 1899-1920, asso. curator vertebrate paleontology, 1904-10, asso. paleontologist, 1919-20, Yale. Sec. Conn. Acad. Arts and Sciences, 1905-46, editor publs., 1916-46; now retired. Mem. A.A.A.S., Am. Soc. Naturalists. Home: 85 Laurel Rd., New Haven, Conn. Died Nov. 6, 1949.

EATON, John Wallace, univ. prof.; b. Lancaster, Eng., July 7, 1886; s. Alexander John and Edith Helen (Batten) E.; student Dublin Trinity Coll., 1904-09, Sorbonne (Paris), 1909-10, Marburg U. (Germany), 1913, Munich (Germany), 1914; M.A., LL.B., Litt.D., Dublin U.; m. Jane Bigelow, Aug. 4, 1933; 2 sons, John Wallace, Michael Bigelow. Assistant lecturer in German and French, University of Bristol, England, 1910-12; lecturer in French, Queen's Univ., Kingston, Ont., 1912-13; prof. of German, U. of Saskatchewan, Can., 1913-29; prof. of German, U. of Mich., since 1929. Served with 28th Batn., C.E.F., and Brit. Intelligence Corps, 1916-19. Mem. Modern Lang. Assn. America, Scandinavian Am. Assn., Mich. Acad. Clubs: Authors (London); University, Rotary (Ann Arbor). Author: German Influence in Danish Literature, 1929. Contbr. to professional jours. Address: University Hall, Ann Arbor, Mich. Died Dec. 26, 1948.

EATON, William Robb, ex-congressman; b. Pugwash, N.S., Can., Dec. 17, 1877; s. Cyrus Black and Margaret (Whidden) E.; brought by parents to U.S., 1878; LL.B., U. of Denver, 1909; m. Leila Carter, Sept. 16, 1909. In banking business, 1889-99, mercantile business, 1900-09; admitted to Colo. bar, 1909; dep. dist. atty., Denver, 1909-13; mem. Colo. Senate, 1914-18, 1922-26; mem. 71st and 72d Congresses (1929-33), 1st Colo. Dist. Mem. Am., Colo. State and Denver bar assns., Internat. Law Assn., Internat. Assn. of Ins. Counsel, Nat. Assn. for Constl. Govt., State Hist. Soc. of Colo., Sons and Daughters of the Pilgrims, Kappa Sigma (alumni sec. 7 yrs.). Republican. Baptist. Mason (32°, K.C.C.H., K.T., Shriner), K.P. Clubs: University, City, Lincoln, Denver Athletic, Denver Country, Motor Club of Colorado. Sponsor of Industrial Commn. of Colo., 1915. Home: 1430 Vine St. Office: 1st Nat. Bank Bldg., Denver, Colo. Died Dec. 16, 1943.

EBERHARDT, Frederick L., machinery mfr.; b. Newark, N.J., Feb. 27, 1868; s. Ulrich and Emeline Taylor (Hudson) E.; ed. grammar and pvt. schools, Newark, and Newark Tech. Sch.; m. Martha Lou Boals, Oct. 16, 1895; children—Ruth Boals, Frederick Gordon, Eleanor Hudson. Began as gen. machine apprentice, 1881; with Gould & Eberhardt, Inc., mfrs. of machine tools, shaping machines, automatic gear cutting machines, Newark, N.J., since 1901, pres. since 1927; advisory dir. Fidelity Union Trust Co. Pres. bd. trustees Newark Tech. Sch. and Newark Coll. of Engring. Republican. Methodist. Mason (K.T., Shriner). Home: 629 Prospect St., Maplewood, N.J. Office: 433 Fabyan Pl., Irvington 11, N.J. Died July 18, 1946.

EBERHART, Nelle Richmond, writer; b. Detroit; d. John Thomas and Cora Amelia (Newton) McCurdy; m. Oscar Eberhart, Aug. 22, 1894; 1 dau., Constance. Teacher in country schs., Neb., until 1895; settled in Pittsburgh, 1900. Mem. Kansas City Musical Club (honorary), American Society Composers, Authors and Pubs., Illinois Women's Press Assn. (life), Ill. Fedn. Music Clubs, League Am. Pen Women (hon.), Society Midland Authors, Theosophical Soc. Began collaboration with Charles Wakefield Cadman, 1902; joint librettist with Francis La Flesche in Indian opera, "Daoma," 1909 (revised and called "Ramala"); wrote libretto of opera, "The Garden of Mystery," 1914, produced at Carnegie Hall, N.Y. City, 1925; also cycles, Four American Indian Songs (Cadman), Sayonara, Three Songs to Odysseus, From Wigwam to Tepee, Idyls of the South Sea, First Love, Birds of Flame, etc., and over 200 songs; cantata "Spring Rapture," music by Harvey B. Gaul; best known lyrics, "From the Land of the Sky-blue Water," and "At Dawning." Wrote opera, "The Robin Woman" (Shanewis), music by Cadman, 1917, prod. at Met. Opera House, New York, seasons of 1917-18 and 1918-19; also opera, "A Witch of Salem," music by Cadman, 1920, prod. by Chicago Civic Opera Co., 1926-27, 1927-28; opera "Hypatia," music by Mana-Zucca, 1924-25; wrote "Father of Waters," "The King and the Star," "The House of Joy," "The House of Cortelyou" (cantatas); 2 operatic quartet cycles, "Full Moon," and "White Enchantment," music by Cadman, 1929; wrote with Cadman, the first radio opera—"The Willow Tree," prod. by NBC, Oct. 4, 1932. Unitarian. Clubs: Woman's Univ. (hon.); Cameo Salon. Gives operalogues and lectures on music subjects illustrated by her daughter. Home: 420 E. Armour Blvd., Kansas City, Mo. Died Nov. 5, 1944.

EBERLE, Abastenia St. Leger (ĕb'ēr-lē), sculptor; b. Webster City, Ia., Apr. 6, 1878; d. Harry A. (M.D.) and Clara Vaughan (McGinn) Eberle; studied Art Students' League, New York, under C. Y. Harvey, Kenyon Cox and George Grey Barnard; unmarried. Has exhibited in leading cities America and Europe. Represented in Met. Museum, Whitney Museum of American Art (both N.Y. City); Worcester (Mass.) Art Mus.; Newark (N.J.) Mus.; Art Institute of Chicago; Peabody Institute, Baltimore; Carnegie Institute, Pittsburgh; Detroit Museum; Brookgreen Gardens Museum, S.C., etc. Bronze medal, St. Louis Expn., 1904; H. F. Barnett prize N.A.D., New York, 1910; bronze medal, Panama P.I Expn., 1915; Lindsay Morris Sterling award, Allied Artists America. Mem. Nat. Sculpture Soc., A.N.A., 1921. Home: 2211 Broadway, New York, N.Y.; and Southport, Conn. Died Feb. 27, 1942.

EBERSOLE, J(ohn) Franklin, prof. finance; b. North Tonawanda, N.Y., July 16, 1884; s. Levi D. and Annie Elizabeth (Brown) E.; Ph.B., U. of Chicago, 1907 (with honors in polit. economy); A.M., Harvard, 1909; m. Blanche Brenneman, Aug. 27, 1908; children—Katherine Elizabeth (dec.), Dorothy Franche (Mrs. Charles J. Gould, Jr.), Betty Turner (Mrs. Walter F. Ames, Jr.), John Franklin, Jr. (dec.), Laurence Donald. Instructor in history, Goshen (Ind.) College, 1907-08; asst. instr. pub. finance, U. of Chicago, 1909-10; prof. economics, Marquette U., 1910-11; asst. prof. economics, 1911-17, professorial lecturer banking, 1918-27, U. of Minn.; vis. prof. U. of Chicago, summer, 1914; mng. dir., State Deposit Bank, Minneapolis, Minn., 1917-20; asst. federal reserve agt., Federal Reserve Bank of Minneapolis, 1920-27; economic adviser U.S. Treasury, 1927-30; prof. finance, Harvard, 1930-41; Edmund Cogswell Converse prof. banking and finance, Harvard, since 1941; visiting lecturer law Sch. Yale, 1934, 1936 and 1938; vis. prof. and lecturer Stanford U., summers, 1937, 38, 40; lecturer, Pacific Northwest Banking Sch., summers, 1938, 39, 41; consulting economist to Central Bank of Mass., for Coöperative Banks, 1932-37, State Street Trust Co. since 1936; member board directors Banco National de Nicaragua, 1937. Member exec. com. Economists' National Com. on Monetary Policy, 1933-37 (resigned); mem. Code Authority for savings, building and loan assns., 1934-35. Fellow Am. Acad. Arts and Sciences; mem. Alpha Kappa Psi. Baptist. Mason. Author: Bank Management—A Case Book, 1931. Home: 104 Fletcher Rd., Belmont, Mass. Died June 24, 1945.

EBY, Kerr, artist; b. of Canadian parents at Tokyo, Japan, Oct. 19, 1889; s. Rev. Charles Samuel and Ellen (Keppel) E.; came to U.S., 1907; ed. Art Student's League, N.Y. City, and Pratt Inst., Brooklyn, N.Y.; m. Frances Sheldon, Apr. 26, 1920 (died 1932); m. 2d, Phyllis Brevoort Barretto, June 5, 1935. Etcher. Served as sergt. engrs., U.S. Army, 2 yrs., World War; artist war correspondent with Marines in Southern Pacific, 1943, 44. A.N.A., 1930, N.A., 1934; mem. Soc. American Etchers, Chicago, Soc. Etchers, Phila. Soc. Etchers, Cleveland Soc. Etchers, Inst. of Arts and Letters, Century Club of N.Y. City, Rep. by volume in Am. Etchers Series, 1930; Book of war pictures entitled "War," pub. by Yale University Press, 1936. Home: Westport, Conn. Died Nov. 18, 1946.

ECKARDT, Lisgar Russell, coll. prof.; b. Unionville, Ont., Can., Oct. 22, 1876; s. Joseph and Joanna (Thompson) E.; came to U.S., 1902, naturalized Am. citizen; A.B., Toronto U., 1902; S.T.B., Boston U., 1907, A.M., 1907, Ph.D., 1911; student U. of Berlin, 1908-09; m. Ethel Wilson, Oct. 22, 1907; children—Frances Dyer (Mrs. Rockwell Carter Smith), Mona Jean (Mrs. Walter E. Darnell), Lisgar Bowne, Wilbert Joseph. Supply asst., dept. of philosophy, Syracuse (N.Y.) U., 1910-11; head dept. philosophy of religion, Iliff Sch. of Theology, Denver, Colo., 1911-13; head dept. of philosophy, DePauw U., Greencastle, Ind., 1913-45; prof. emeritus, 1945-46; visiting prof. philos., West Maryland Coll., 1945-46. Prince of Wales Gold Medalist (Toronto U.), Jacob Sleeper fellow (Boston U.). Mem. Am. Philos. Assn. Home: Greencastle, Ind. Died July 12, 1946.

ECKEL, Edwin Clarence (ĕk'ĕl), engr., geologist; b. New York, Mar. 6, 1875; s. August and Helena S. K. (Butt) E.; B.S., New York U., 1895, C.E., 1896; m. Julia Egerton Dibblee, July 9, 1902; children—Edwin Butt, Julia Dibblee, Richard Egerton. Asst. geologist of N.Y., 1900-02; asst. geologist, 1902-05, U.S. Geol. Survey, and geologist in charge sect. of iron ores and structural materials, 1906-07; spl. commr. in charge cement exhibits, Jamestown Expn., 1907; cons. engr. and geologist since 1907; pres. Dominion Cement Co., 1910-12. Expert on southern and eastern iron ores for U.S. Steel Corp. during the Stanley investigation and dissolution suit, 1911-13; iron ore investigations in Europe, 1928-30; cement mill valuations for U.S. Treasury Dept., 1931-32; chief geologist Tenn. Valley Authority since 1933. Commd. capt., Engr. R.C., Jan. 23, 1917; maj. engrs., U.S. Army, Apr. 1919; service in France, July 1917-July 1919. Fellow Geol. Soc. America; mem. Soc. of Econ. Geologists, Am. Inst. Mining Engrs., Delta Kappa Epsilon; life mem. Am. Soc. C.E. Author: Cements, Limes and Plasters, 1905; Portland Cement Industry from the Financial Standpoint, 1908; Building Stones and Clays, 1911; Iron Ores, 1914; Coal, Iron and War, 1920; Le Ciment Portland, 1927; Report on Economic Sanctions, 1931. Wrote Ency. Britannica article on Iron Ore Resources of World; Engineering Geology of Tennessee Valley, 1939. Home: 1503 Decatur St. N.W., Washington, D.C. Died Nov. 22, 1941.

ECKFELDT, Howard, mining engr.; Conshohocken, Pa., Oct. 17, 1873; s. Jacob B. and Jeanette R. (Latch) E.; B.S., Lehigh U., 1895; E.M., 1896; m. Catalina Trousselle, Oct. 3, 1898; children—Jacob Trousselle, Emily Catherine, Jeannette Matilde. Mining engr. for Mazapil Copper Co., Concepcion del Oro, 1896-1900; instr. in mining engring., Lehigh U., 1900-02, prof. since 1902, now head of dept. In charge survey of F. C. de Zacatecas Oriente, June-Sept. 1907. Absent on leave from Lehigh U., Aug. 1910-Sept. 1911, on engring. work in Mexico. Mem. Am. Inst. Mining and Metall. Engrs., Soc. Promotion Engring. Edn., Sigma Xi. Presbyterian. Home: Bethlehem, Pa. Died March 4, 1948.

ECKHARD, George Frederick, coll. dean; b. Waverly, Ia., Nov. 21, 1878; s. George and Katherine E.; M.Di., Ia. State Teachers Coll., 1900; B.S., U. of Ia., 1905, C.E., 1910; m. Henrietta Plock, Sept. 1, 1908; 1 dau., Elizabeth. With Cuba Eastern R.R. Co., 1905-06; U.S. mineral surveyor for N.M., 1908-09; prof. of civil engring., N.M. Sch. of Mines, 1907-09, James Milliken U., 1909-12; asso. prof. Pa. State College, 1912-15; prof. structural engring, U. of Vt., 1915-32, dean College of Engring. since 1932. Member American Society of Civil Engineers, Vermont Soc. of Engrs. (past pres.); mem. Vt. State Board of Registration for Professional Engrs., Soc. for Promotion of Engring. Edn., Sigma Xi. Republican. Congregationalist. Home: 178 Summit St., Burlington, Vt. Died Dec. 28, 1945.

ECKSTEIN, Nathan, wholesale grocer; b. Bavaria, Jan. 10, 1873; s. Lazarus and Johanna (Haas) E.; ed. Sch. of Commerce, Munich, Bavaria; came to U.S., 1888; m. Mina Alice Schwabacher, Oct. 30, 1902; children—Joanna, Babette (Mrs. Edwin Joseph). Began in wholesale grocery business in N.Y. City, 1888; moved to Seattle, Wash., 1898; with Schwabacher Bros. & Co., wholesale grocers, Seattle, since 1898, pres. since 1916; chmn. bd. Schwabacher Hardware Co., dir. Peoples Nat. Bank of Wash. Asst. sec. of war, Seattle, Winter Plattsburg, 1924-26; civilian aid to sec. War, Wash. Citizens Mil. Training Camps, 1927-29. Mem. Sch. Bd., Seattle, 1914-20, pres. 2 yrs.; chmn. Tax Investigation Com., Wash., 1921-22; mem. Freeholders Charter Commn. to revise charter of Seattle, 1925; mem. Wash. Commn. Century of Progress Expn.; pres. Seattle Community Fund, 1925; pres. Wash. State Conf. Social Work, 1935; v.p. Am. White Cross Assn. on Drug Addictions; mem. bd. dirs. Nat. Farm School, Seattle Symphony Orchestra, Seattle Art Museum, Seattle Chamber of Commerce; v. chmn. Wash. State Planning Council since 1933. Designated Seattle's most useful citizen, 1926. Jewish religion. Mason (Shriner), Elk. Clubs: Rainier, Arctic, Glendale Golf and Country. Home: 1000 14th Av. N. Office: 300 Occidental Av.; Seattle. Died Oct. 21, 1945.

ECKSTORM, Fannie Hardy, author; b. Brewer, Me., June 18, 1865; d. Manly and Emma F. (Wheeler) Hardy; grad. Smith Coll., Mass., 1888; hon. M.A., U. of Maine, 1929; m. Rev. Jacob A. Eckstorm, Oct. 24, 1893; children—Katharine Hardy (dec.), Paul Frederick (dec.). Hon. mem. Me. Hist. Soc.; cofounder Folk-Song Soc. of Northeast. Author: The Bird Book, 1901; The Woodpeckers, 1901; The Penobscot Man, 1904; David Libbey (True American Types Series), 1907; The Minstrelsy of Maine—Folk Songs and Ballads of the Maine Woods and Coast (with Mary W. Smyth), 1927; British Ballads from Maine (with Phillips Barry and Mary W. Smyth), 1929; Handicrafts of the Modern Indians of Maine (bull. III, Lafayette Nat. Park Mus.), 1932; Indian Brother (with H. V. Coryell), 1934; The Scalp Hunters (with H. V. Coryell), 1936; Indian Place-names of Penobscot Valley and the Maine Coast, 1941; Old John Neptune and Other Maine Indian Shamans, 1945. Has written on birds, the Maine woods, game laws, Indians, folk songs, local history, etc. Home: Brewer, Me. Died Dec. 31, 1946.

EDDY, David Brewer, denominational sec.; b. Leavenworth, Kan., June 20, 1877; s. George Alfred and Margaret L. (Norton) E.; B.A., Yale, 1898, M.A., 1901; D.D., Wesleyan U., Conn., 1921; m. Josephine Russell, Apr. 25, 1906; children—George A., Frances, C. Russell, David B., Priscilla. Ordained Congl. ministry, 1904; pastor Trinity Ch., E. Orange, N.J., 1906-09; Am. Bd. Commrs. for Foreign Missions since 1909; retired Jan. 1, 1945. Republican. Took rôle of David Livingstone in "Pageant of Light and Darkness," Missionary Expositions, "World in Boston," 1911, and "World in Chicago," 1913. Y.M.C.A. service in France and with British Ministry of Information, 1918. Six months Japan and China, 1922, inter-racial problems in Hawaii, 1924; made a 7 months' journey around the world, 1934-35, in Europe, studying present-day problems, 1937. Clubs: Boston City, Yale. Pres. Eddy Family Assn. of America. Author: What Next in Turkey, 1913. Home: Newtonville, Mass. Office: 114 Beacon St., Boston, Mass. Died June 1, 1946.

EDDY, Henry Stephens, artist; b. Rahway, N.J., Dec. 31, 1878; s. Charles and Edith Harriet (Stephens) E.; student Art Students League, New York; pupil of Volk, Cox, Twachtman, Alphonse Mucha, George Elmer Browne; m. Catherine Day Cleveland, Apr. 17, 1901; 1 dau., Catherine Edith (Mrs. Norman LaCour Olsen). Represented in collections of Milwaukee (Wis.) Art Inst., Reid Memorial Library, Passaic, N.J., Arnot Art Gallery, Elmira, N.Y., Lotus Club, N.Y. City, etc. Awarded hon. mention N.J. State annual exhbn. (1932), Art Museum, Montclair, N.J.; first and popular prizes annual mem. exhbn. (1939), Plainfield Art Assn., Plainfield, N.J. Mem. Artists Fellowship, Artists Fund Soc., Guild Am. Painters, Allied Artists of America, Westfield (N.J.) Art Assn., Am. Assn. Museums, Plainfield Art Assn. Clubs: Salmagundi, Lotos (life mem.), Nantucket Yacht (life mem.). Home: Springfield Rd., Westfield, New Jersey. Died Aug. 9, 1944.

EDELSTEIN, M. Michael (ĕd'ĕl-stīn), congressman; b. Meseritz, Poland, Feb. 5, 1888; s. Jacob and Rose Mandelbaum E.; LL.B., Brooklyn Law Sch., 1909; unmarried. Admitted to N.Y. State bar, 1910; admitted to practice in U.S. dist. courts for southern and eastern dists. of N.Y., 1911, U.S. Circuit Court for the Second Dist., 1911, U.S. Supreme Court, 1923; in practice in N.Y. City since 1910; elected to the 76th Congress by a special election to fill unexpired term of Dr. William I. Sirovich, 1940; re-elected, Nov. 1940, to the 77th Congress (1941-43). Active in local politics as mem. Democratic party. Mem. N.Y. County Lawyers Assn., N.Y. Law Inst., N.Y. County Criminal Bar Assn. Democrat. Jewish religion. Home: 170 Second Av. Office: 111 Broadway, New York, N.Y. Died June 4, 1941.

EDGAR, Randolph, writer; b. Minneapolis, Aug. 31, 1884; s. William Crowell and Anne Page Randolph (Robinson) E., grad. Flexner Sch., Louisville, Ky., 1904; Harvard 1904-7; unmarried. Traveled and wrote for papers, 1907-08; mng. editor and dramatic critic, The Bellman, Minneapolis, since 1908. Mem. Theta Delta Chi. Clubs: Harvard (New York); Minneapolis, Lafayette (Minneapolis). Author: Frank Norris, An Appreciation, 1906. Contbr. to mags. Home: 66 Groveland Terrace. Office: 118 S. 6th St., Minneapolis. Died July 10, 1931.

EDGERTON, Alice Craig, writer, lawyer; b. Caldwell, Wis., July 25, 1874; d. Asa H. and Rebecca Craig; grad. Carroll Coll., Waukesha, Wis., 1893; LL.B., Chicago-Kent Coll. of Law, 1910; LL.M., 1911; m. Charles H. Edgerton, July 30, 1896 (died July 30, 1905). Admitted to Ill. bar, 1910, Wis. bar, 1926; practiced in Chicago until 1923, Mukwonago, Wis., since 1926. Justice of the peace, Mukwonago. Received award from Wis. Fedn. Women's Clubs for professional achievement and public service, 1941. Sole shipper of the famous Craig Honey Melon, originated by Asa H. Craig, father. Founder and hon. pres. Kappa Beta Pi (first international legal sorority in the world). A founder of Women's Bar Assn. of Ill. Member Am., Wis. State and Waukesha Co. bar assns., Order of Bookfellows, Waukesha Women's Club. Democrat. Congregationalist. Mem. Order of Eastern Star. Author: Queen Nature's Fairy Helpers, 1921; Thirty Complete Debates (with Asa H. Craig), 1926; A Speech for Every Occasion (original speeches), 1931; Juvenile Selections and Dialogues (original), 1931; More Speeches and Stories for Every Occasion, 1936; History Kappa Beta Pi Legal Sorority, 1937, revised, 1941. Contributor to: A Bookfellow Anthology, 1929; Complete George Washington Programs, 1931; How to Organize and Conduct a Meeting, 1938; other books, newspapers and mags. Home: Mukwonago, Wis. Died Jan. 7, 1946.

EDGETT, Edwin Francis (ĕd'jĕt), journalist, author; b. Boston, Mass., Jan. 12, 1867; s. Reuben and Eveline (Pray) E.; A.B., Harvard, 1894; m. Evelyn Torrey, 1896. Harvard corr. New York Times, 1894; dramatic editor, 1894-99, lit. editor, 1901-38, Boston Transcript; asst. editor The King, London, 1899-1900; on publicity and literary staffs of David Belasco, John Craig, Henry Jewett and James K. Hackett, 1901-30. Author: Plays of the Present (with J. B. Clapp), 1901; Players of the Present (with same), 1901; Life of Edward L. Davenport, 1901; Slings and Arrows, 1922; I Speak for Myself: an Editor in His World, 1940. Contbr. of 70 articles to Dictionary of American Biography, 1928-36; commentator on books and authors over Nat. Broadcasting and Columbia Broadcasting systems, 1927-37. Home: 135 Pleasant St., Arlington, Mass. Died Mar. 12, 1946.

EDMONDS, Franklin Spencer, lawyer; b. Phila., Mar. 28, 1874; s. Henry R. and Catharine Ann (Huntzinger) E.; A.B., Central High Sch., Phila., 1891, A.M., 1896; Ph.B., U. of Pa., 1893, LL.B., 1903; Andrew D. White fellow, Cornell, 1894-95; LL.D., Juniata Coll., 1929, Ursinus Coll., 1932; m. Elise Julia, d. Hon. Abraham M. and Julia L. Beitler, Dec. 6, 1909. Asst. sec. Am. Soc. for Extension of University Teaching, 1893-94; instr. history, 1895-97, asst. prof. polit. science, 1897-1902, prof. polit. science, 1902-04, hon. lecturer in polit. science since 1904, Central High Sch., Phila.; prof. law, Swarthmore (Pa.) Coll., 1904-10; in practice of law, Phila., since 1904; mem. Edmonds, Obermayer & Rebmann. Solicitor for Pa. Museum of Art. Editor The Teacher, 1898-1901. Candidate for Select Council on City Party ticket, 1905; receiver of taxes, 1907; chmn. City Com. of City Party, 1905; mem. Lincoln Party State Com., 1905, 06; chmn. 2 City Party county convs. Mem. Bd. Pub. Edn., Phila., 1906-11; chmn. citizens' campaign com. of Washington party (Progressive), 1912; mem. Pa. Ho. of Reps., 1921, 23 and 25; chmn. Pa. Tax Commn., 1924-27; pres. Nat. Tax Assn., 1932-33; mem. State Senate from Montgomery Co. since 1938; re-elected, 1942. Rep. Pres. Ednl. Club of Phila., 1900-03, Phila. Teachers' Assn., 1903-05; mem. Am. Econ. Assn., Am. Hist. Assn., Am. Polit. Sci. Assn., Am. Acad. Polit. and Social Sci., Am. Bar Assn., Hist. Soc. of Pa., American Statistical Assn., Beta Theta Pi, Phi Delta Phi. Clubs: Union League, Franklin Inn, Lawyers, Schoolmen's and Church clubs. Author: Century's Progress in Education (pamphlet), 1899; History of Central High School of Philadelphia, 1838-1902, 1902; Life of Ulysses S. Grant (Am. Crisis Biographies); Reciprocity in State Inheritance Taxation (pamphlet). Organizer, and head of Savoie leave area, France, 1918; head of soldiers' leave dept. and of legal dept., Y.M.C.A., A.E.F., 1918-19. Home: Whitemarsh, Montgomery County, Pa. Office: 111 S. 15th St., Philadelphia, Pa. Died Oct. 29, 1945.

EDMONDS, Harry Marcus Weston, physicist; b. Oshkosh, June 25, 1862; s. Marcus A. and Mary E. (Weston) E.; A.B., U. of Calif., 1882; M.D., Hahnemann Med. Coll., Phila., 1893; postgrad work; univs. of Gottingen, Bonn and Leipzig; m. Mary D. Bigelow, June 8, 1889; children—Marc Weston, Dorothy, Katherine. With U.S. Coast and Geol. Survey, 1889-1909; magnetician, Dept. Terrestrial Magnetism, Carnegie Instn., 1909-30, retired. Comdr. yacht Carnegie, 1917-18; in charge Huancayo Magnetic Obs., Peru, 1919-21; co-operated with New Zealand in the operation of Apia Observatory, Samoa, 1921-22. Address: Carnegie Institution, Washington. Died Apr. 4, 1945.

EDMONDSON, Clarence Edmund, educator; b. at Ellettsville, Ind., Apr. 9, 1883; s. John Ewing and Nancy Florence (Buzzaird) E.; A.B., Ind. U., 1906, A.M., 1912, Ph.D., 1914; student Med. Sch., Ind. U., 1909-11; m. Edna Elder Hatfield, July 31, 1913. Teacher of biology, Crawfordsville (Ind.) High Sch., 1906-09; instr. in physiology, Ind. U. Sch. of Medicine, 1912-16, asst. prof., 1916-19; asso. prof. of hygiene, Ind. U., 1919-25, prof. of hygiene since 1925, dean of men since 1919, emeritus since July 1, 1944. Fellow A.A.A.S.; mem. Ind. Acad. Science, Nat. Assn. Deans of Men (pres. 1932), Mayflower Soc., Phi Beta Kappa, Sigma Xi, Nu Sigma Nu, Delta Tau Delta. Mason (32°). Home: 1915 Mill Rd., South Pasadena, Calif. Died Dec. 14, 1946; buried in Forest Lawn Memorial Park, Glendale, Calif.

EDMUNDS, Albert Joseph, librarian; b. Tottenham, Middlesex, Eng., Nov. 21, 1857; s. Thomas and Rebecca (Hallat) E.; ed. Friends' Sch., Croydon, and Flounders Inst., Ackworth; matriculated U. of London, 1877; pvt. student of N.T., James Rendel Harris, 1890-95; hon. A.M., U. of Pa., 1907, fellow, 1914; unmarried. Sec. to T. W. Backhouse, astronomer, 1879-83; emigrated to U.S., 1885; asst. librarian, Haverford Coll., 1887-89; classifier Phila. Library, 1889-90; cataloguer Hist. Soc. of Pa., 1891-1936. Prepared Catalogue Sunderland (Eng.) Library, 1881-84. Author: English and American Poems, 1888; Songs of Asia Sung in America, 1896; Marvelous Birth of the Buddhas, 1899; Hymns of the Faith (Dhammapada), 1902; Buddhist and Christian Gospels, 1902, 3d edit., Tokyo, 1905, 4th edit., Phila., 1908-09, with postscripts, 1912, 14, 21, 26, 28, 35, 37, 38; Italian transl., Palermo, 1913; Buddhist Bibliography, 1903; Buddhist Texts in John, 1906, 2d edit., 1911; Fairmount Park and Other Poems, 1906; A Dialogue Between Two Saviors, 5th edit., 1931; Lucy Edmunds (1859-1935) in The Two Worlds, 1935; Leaves from the Gospel of Mark, 1936. Contbr. to jours. on subjects of comparative religion. Home: 213 Ryers Av., Cheltenham, Pa. Died Dec. 17, 1941.

EDMUNDS, Charles Keyser, coll. pres.; b. Baltimore, Sept. 21, 1876; s. James Richard and Anna Smith (Keyser) E.; A.B., Johns Hopkins, 1897, prize essayist, 1895, Univ. scholar, 1897-98, Ph.D., 1903; m. Sarah Katharine Poorbaugh, June 30, 1909; children—Elizabeth P., Richard (dec.). Acting prof. physics, U. of Utah, 1898-99; magnetic observer, United States Coast and Geodetic Survey, 1899-1900; fellow in physics, Johns Hopkins University, 1902-03; prof. physics and elec. engring., 1903, v.p., 1907-08, pres., 1907-24, Am. dir., 1926-28, Lingnan University, Canton, China; provost Johns Hopkins, 1924-27; president Pomona College, 1928-41, emeritus since 1941. Magnetic observer for Carnegie Institution of Washington, in China, 1906-17. Member American Physical Society, Phi Beta Kappa, Phi Gamma Delta. Club: University (Los Angeles). Author of papers on Modern Education in China, etc. Address: Pomona College, Claremont, Calif. Died Jan. 8, 1949.

EDMUNDS, Sterling Edwin, lawyer, publicist; b. St. Louis, Mo., June 5, 1880; s. Sterling Edwin and Mollie (Garnhart) E.; prep. edn., pub. schs., Louisville, Ky.; student Benton Coll. of Law, St. Louis, 1901-03, U. of Va., 1927; LL.D., St. Louis U., 1917; m. Eugenia Howard, May 26, 1906; 1 dau., Eugenie (Mrs. Alexander B. Carver). Reporter St. Louis Post Dispatch, 1897-98; city editor St. Louis Chronicle, 1899-1901, mng. editor, 1901-03, editor in chief, 1903-04; admitted to Mo. bar, 1906; spl. asst. U.S. Dept. State, 1918. Lecturer on internat. law, St. Louis U. Law Sch., 1909-26. Organizer and dir. Nat. Com. for the Protection of Child, Family, Sch. and Ch. Vice-pres. U.S. Golf Assn., 1919-20. Member American Bar Association, St. Louis Bar Association, American Society International Law, American Judicature Society. Democrat. Presbyterian. Clubs: Noonday, Saint Louis Country (Saint Louis). Author: International Law Applied to the Treaty of Peace, 1919; The Lawless Law of Nations, 1925; The Federal Octopus, 1932, 1933; The Roosevelt Coup D'Etat of 1933-40. Contbr. to various law and other periodicals. Home: 28 Westmoreland Pl. Office: 1218 Olive St., St. Louis. Died July 12, 1944.

EDSALL, David Linn (ĕd'săl), physician; b. Hamburg, N.J., July 6, 1869; s. Richard E. and Emma E. (Linn) E.; A.B., Princeton, 1890; M.D., Univ. of Pa., 1893; Sc.D. from Princeton U., 1913, Harvard U., 1928; m. Margaret Harding Tileston, 1899 (died 1912); children—John Tileston, Richard Linn, Geoffrey; m. 2d, Elizabeth Pendleton Kennedy, June 1915; m. 3d, Louisa C. Richardson, 1931. Prof. therapeutics and pharmacology, 1907-10, medicine, 1910-11, U. of Pa.; prof. preentive medicine, Washington U., 1911-12; Jackson prof. clin. medicine, 1912-23, dean, 1918-35, Harvard Med. Sch.; also dean Harvard Sch. of Pub. Health, 1921-35; dean of the faculty of medicine, Harvard Med. Sch. and dean of the Harvard Sch. of Public Health, emeritus, since 1935; chief of med. service, Mass. Gen. Hosp., 1912-23. Fellow Am. Acad. Arts and Sciences; mem. Assn. Am. Physicians, Am. Philos. Soc. Club: Harvard. Contbr. to med jours. Home: Tryon, N.C. Died Aug. 12, 1945.

EDWARD, Harvey, army officer; b. New York, Oct. 1, 1893; grad. Q.M.C. Sch., 1928, Army Indsl. Coll., 1931, Command and Gen. Staff Sch., 1934, Chem. Warfare Sch., field officers course, 1938, Army War Coll., 1938. Commd. 2d lt., U.S. Army, 1917, and advanced through the grades to brig. gen., 1945. Address: care The Adjutant General's Office, War Department, Washington 25. Deceased.

EDWARDS, (F.) Boyd, clergyman, educator; b. Lisle, N.Y., May 5, 1876; s. Mortimer Burr and Harriett Louise (Boyd) E.; grad. Phillips Acad., Andover, Mass., 1896; B.A., Williams Coll., 1900, D.D., 1920; Union Theol. Sem., 1902-04; S.T.D., Univ. of Pa., 1925; LL.D., Franklin and Marshall Coll., 1931; m. Frances McCarroll (A.B., Smith Coll., 1903), May 24, 1904. Ordained Congl. ministry, 1904; asst. pastor Tompkins Av. Ch., Brooklyn, 1904; asso. pastor South Ch., Brooklyn, 1905-10; pastor same, 1908-10; pastor Hillside Ch., Orange, N.J., 1910-22; headmaster and trustee The Hill Sch., Pottstown, Pa., 1922-28; headmaster Mercersburg Acad., 1928-41; trustee Mt. Holyoke Coll., 1920-37, Williams Coll., 1923-28. Chairman National Preparatory School Committee of National Y.M.C.A., 1915-35. Member Nat. Headmasters' Assn., Assn. Schs., Colls. and Sems. of Ref. Ch. in U.S. (v.p.), Phila. Headmasters' Assn., Zeta Psi. Clubs: Century, Zeta Psi (New York). Author: Have Faith in Youth; Boys Will Be Men. Editor: Mr. Rolfe of the Hill; Prayers in the Hill School Chapel; Religion in the Preparatory Schools; The Chapel Hymnal (co-editor). Home: Arlington, Vt. Died Nov. 10, 1944.

EDWARDS, Edward B., artist; b. Columbia, Lancaster County, Pa., Feb. 8, 1873; s. Edward B. and Mary Elizabeth (Kistler) E.; ed. pub. schs.; Art Students' League, New York; Académie Colarossi, Acad. Vitti, Acad. Castellucho—all in Paris; m. Amelia F. England, Sept. 27, 1893; children—Edward Norman, Albert K., Llewellyn, Lucien (dec.), Madeleine. Designer and illustrator of books, magazine pages and advertisements; formerly dir. Am. Inst. Graphic Arts; instr. dynamic symmetry and design, Master Inst. of Roerich Mus., N.Y. City. Hon. mem. New York Soc. of Craftsmen; mem. The Stowaways, Artists' Guild, Architectural League, New York, Met. Mus. Republican. Protestant. Clubs: Salmagundi, Marshall Chess (mem. bd. of govs. Designer of decorations of Life of Count Hoym (Grolier Club), 1899; designer and illustrator, A Book of Shakespeare's Songs, 1903; illustrator and designer of handbooks for Met. Mus. of Art; The Lord's Prayer (illuminated page), Ladies' Home Jour.; The Great Chalice of Antioch, 1923; decorator of The Altoviti Aphrodite (pvtly. printed for John D. Rockefeller), 1920. Author Dynamarhythmic Design, 1932. Awarded gold medal of honor for distinguished contribution to Am. art, Am. Artists Professional League, 1943. Died Feb. 16, 1948.

EDWARDS, George Herbert, ex-mayor; b. St. Louis, Mo., May 25, 1860; s. Richard and Betsey Josslyn (Samson) E.; student Ill. State Normal U.; m. Isabella Dix, Nov. 20, 1889; children—Alice Louise (dec.), George Herbert (dec.), Lucile Belle (Mrs. S. E. Cutler), Richard Dix, Betsey Josephine (Mrs. Hubert O. Sheidley), Gertrude Martha (Mrs. Eldon W. Michaels), Grace Eleanor (Mrs. L. J. Marshall, Jr.). Traveling salesman for various jewelry concerns, 1879-89; settled in Kansas City, Mo., 1889, as sec. S. D. Mills Jewelry Co.; title changed to Edwards & Sloane Jewelry Co., 1892, now Edwards-Ludwig-Fuller Jewelry Co., of which is pres.; pres. Mercantile Bank, 1912-1915 until consol. with Commerce Trust Co., of which is dir. Mem. Upper House of Common Council 2 terms, 1906-14; mayor of Kansas City, term 1916-18; apptd. mem. commn. to build new water works for Kansas City, 1921. Republican. Club: Chamber of Commerce. Home: 5223 Mission Woods Terrace, Kansas City, Kan. Office: 1115 Walnut St., Kansas City, Mo. Died Dec. 28, 1941.

EDWARDS, George Wharton, portrait and mural painter; b. Fair Haven, Conn.; s. of William and Margaret Edwards; acad. education at Antwerp and Paris; pupil of Eugene Féyén, Paris; m. Anne Johns, d. Gen. John C. Cox, of Quincy, Ill., Mar., 1886. Dir. art dept., Collier's, 1898-1903; mgr. art dept. Am. Bank Note Co., 1904-12. Bronze and silver medals, Boston, 1884, 90; hon. mention for black and white drawing; bronze medal and silver medal for paintings, Buffalo Expn., 1901; silver medal and diploma for paintings, S. C. Expn., 1902; mural decoration "Henrik Hudson," U.S. Mil. Acad. Asso. National Academician, 1930; mem. Allied Artists America, Am. Water Color Soc., Nat. Arts Club, N.Y. Water Color Club, Authors Club. Author: Thumbnail Sketches, 1886; P'tit Matinic, Monotones, 1887; The Rivalries of Long and Short Codiac, 1888; Break o' Day, and Other Stories, 1889; A Reading Journey in the Hollowland, 1908; Holland of Today, 1909; Brittany and the Bretons, 1910; Some Old Flemish Towns, 1911; Marken and Its People, 1912; The Forest of Arden, 1914; Vanished Towers and Chimes of Flanders, 1916; Vanished Halls and Cathedrals of France, 1917; Alsace-Lorraine, 1918; Holland of Today, 1919; Belgium Old and New, 1920; London, 1921; Paris, 1924; Spain, 1925; Rome, 1928; Constantinople, 1929-30. Illustrator: Oliver Wendell Holmes' Last Leaf, 1885; Austin Dobson's Sun Dial, 1892; Spenser's Epithalamium, 1895; Old English Love Songs, 1896; Old English Ballads, 1897; The Jackdaw of Rheims, 1919. Was awarded the medal of the Order of King Albert of Belgium (Reconnaissance Belge), conferred by the King, 1920; gold palms of l'Académie Française for art, and made Officer of Public Instruction, France, 1921; Chevalier Legion of Honor (France), 1925; Chevalier Order Crown (Belgium), 1927; Chevalier Order of Isabella the Catholic (Spain), 1927; Chevalier Royal Order of the Crown of Italy, 1929; Belgian League of Honor, 1936. Mem. Am. Inst. Arts and Letters. Clubs: Nat. Arts (life), Salmagundi, Authors. Home: 145 Milbank Av., Greenwich, Conn. Died Jan. 18,1950.

EDWARDS, Ira, geologist; b. Hulberton, N.Y., Apr. 22, 1893; s. Frank S. and Alice M. (Sherman) E.; B.S., U. of Rochester, 1913, M.S., 1914; Ph.D., George Washington U., 1930; m. Nora E. Dicke, July 17, 1917. Began as lab. asst., U. of Rochester, 1910; expert in paleontology, N.Y. State Museum, Albany, 1914-16; asst. Milwaukee Pub. Museum, 1916-19, asst. curator geology, 1919-20; adjunct prof. geology, U. of Tex., 1920-21; curator of geology, Milwaukee Pub. Museum, 1922-39, dir. since 1940; geologist Wis. Natural History and Geol. Survey, 1924-30, asst. editor Museum publs., 1925-39, editor since 1940; instr. U. of Wis. Extension Div., 1935-39. Fellow Paleontol. Soc., Geol. Soc. America; mem. A.A.A.S., Wis. Acad. Sciences, Arts and Letters, Am. Museums Assn., Wis. Archeol. Soc., British Museums Assn., Theta Chi, Sigma Gamma Epsilon, Sigma Xi. Conglist. Club: Rotary (Milwaukee). Contbr. to Milwaukee Pub. Museum Yearbook. Home: 2651 N. 60th St. Address: Milwaukee Public Museum, Milwaukee, Wis. Died Oct. 31, 1943.

EDWARDS, John Homer, former asst. sec. dept. interior, lawyer; b. Mitchell, Ind., Sept. 10, 1869; s. William Henry and Cornelia A. (McCoy) E.; A.B., Indiana U., 1891; LL.B., Northwestern U., 1894; unmarried. Mem. Ind. Ho. of Rep., 3 terms, 1903-07; solicitor U.S. Post Office Dept., 1921-23; solicitor U.S. Interior Dept., 1923-25, asst. sec. Mar. 2, 1925-Mar. 4, 1933. Served as chmn. 4th Ind. Dist. Bd., Vincennes, Ind., World War I. Mem. Sigma Chi. Republican. Home: Mitchell, Ind. Address: La Salle Apts., Washington, D.C. Died Aug. 18, 1945.

EDWARDS, John Rogers, clergyman; b. Cornwall, Eng., Aug. 16, 1871; s. Philip Corin and Amelia (Rogers) E.; came to U.S., 1881; student Shepherd Coll. State Normal Sch., Shepherdstown, W.Va.; A.B., Dickinson Coll., Carlisle, Pa., 1896, D.D., 1917; m. Ellen Brown Rumsey, 1900; children—Philip Corin, Ruth Rumsey. Deacon M.E. Ch., 1896; elder, 1901; pastor Highland, Baltimore, Md., 1896-1900, Towson, 1900-05. Catonsville, 1905-10. Walbrook, Baltimore, 1910-17; dist. supt., Washington Dist., 1917-24; corr. sec. Bd. of Foreign Missions M.E. Ch., 1924-36; dist. supt., Jacksonville, Illinois, 1936-37; pastor Union M.E. Church, Washington, D.C., 1937-41; district supt. Wash. W. Dist., 1941-44; asso. pastor Foundry Church, Washington, D.C., 1944-45. Mem. board trustees Dickinson College. Missionary travels, 1926, North Africa and Europe, 1929-30, China and Japan. Mem. Ecumenical Conf. of Methodism, 1931; mem. Western Div. Ad Interim Com. of Ecumenical Methodism; treas. Baltimore Conf. of M.E. Ch., 1909-12; mem. Bd. of Examiners, 1904-17; mem. Com. on Chaplains in World War; mem. and recording sec. Bd. of Prohibition, 1918-24; mem. Bd. of Foreign Missions and Exec. Com., 1920-24; mem. Com. of Conservation and Advance, 1920-24; mem. Gen. Conf. of M.E. Ch., 1920, 24, 28, 32, 36; mem. Uniting Conf. of Methodism, 1939. Mem. Phi Kappa Sigma. Mason, Odd Fellow. Home: 1634 Hobart St. N.W., Washington, D.C. Died Feb. 18, 1945.

EDWARDS, Loren McClain, clergyman; b. Rising Sun, Ind., Nov. 14, 1877; s. Rev. Charles C. and Belle (McClain) E.; A.B., Moore's Hill (Ind.) Coll., 1899, A.M., 1902; B.D., Drew Theol. Sem., 1905; studied Columbia, United Free Ch. Coll., Glasgow, Scotland; D.D., DePauw, 1913; m. Florence Mary; d. Rev. James A. Sargent, of Seymour, Ind., Sept. 14, 1905; 1 son, Rev. Justin S. Ordained M.E. ministry, 1899; pastor Milroy, 1899-1900, Anderson, 1901, Noblesville, 1905, Westfield, 1906, Simpson Church, Ft. Wayne, 1906, 07, Portland, 1908-11, Mishawaka, 1912-16 (all of Indiana), Grace Church, Baltimore, Md., 1917-19; Trinity Church, Denver, Colo., 1920-32, Grace Church, St. Louis, 1932-37, First Church, Colorado Springs, 1937-41, Newton, Ia., since 1941. Republican. Mason (32°). Clubs: Rotary, Country. Author: Every Church Its Own Evangelist, 1917; The Spectrum of Religion, 1918; Light of Christmas and Other Poems, 1923; What Is Left of the Apostles' Creed, 1927; also many articles in newspapers and religious jours. Frequent speaker at clubs, convs., etc.; mem. Gen. Conf. Commn. of World Service and Finance of the Meth. Church; mem. Gen. Confs., Meth. Ch., 1928, 32, 36, 40. Home: 209 N. 2d Av. E., Newton, Ia. Died July 20, 1945.

EDWARDS, Vere Buckingham, shipbuilding; b. Glenburn, Pa., Jan. 17, 1890; s. James E. and Jennie (Buckingham) E.; C.E., Lehigh U., 1912; m. Edith Hitchcock, Nov. 15, 1915; children—Virginia, Marion, Ruth, Alan, Carol. With Dravo Corp., since 1912, beginning as junior civil engr., dir. since 1922, pres. since 1934; dir. Nat. Council Am. Shipbuilders, Union Barge Line Corp. Republican. Presbyterian. Clubs: Duquesne (Pittsburgh); Montour Heights Country. Home: R.D. 1, Coraopolis, Pa. Office: Neville Island Station, Pittsburgh. Died May 8, 1946.

EFROYMSON, Gustave A. (ĕ'frŭm-sŭn), hosiery, mfr.; b. Evansville, Ind., Jan. 21, 1870; s. Jacob and Minnie (Paul) E.; m. Mamie W. Wallenstein, Apr. 14, 1896; children—Clarence W., Robert A. Pres. Real Silk Hosiery Mills, Inc., Occidental Realty Co.; dir. Indiana Nat. Bank, Union Trust Co. Pres. William E. English Foundation; dir. Union of Am. Hebrew Congregation, Jewish Fedn. of Indianapolis, Indianapolis Foundation. Jewish religion. Clubs: Columbia, Highland Golf and Country, Broadmoor Country. Home: Marott Hotel. Office: 611 N. Park Av., Indianapolis, Ind. Died Nov. 3, 1946.

EGAN, Hannah M., teacher; b. New York City, Nov. 25, 1891; d. John Joseph and Catherine (O'Leary) Egan; A.B., Hunter Coll., 1911; A.M., Columbia, 1913; Ph.D., Fordham U., 1922; m. Leo Francis Kengla, Sr., July 8, 1946. On staff Hunter Coll., 1911-14 and 1915-46, in office of dean of students, 1928-46, prof. and dean 1934-46, retired since Aug. 1946. Mem. Nat. Assn. Deans of Women, N.Y. chapter, Administrative Women in Edn., Newman Club, Phi Beta Kappa. Home: 1311 Kowalski Av., Santa Barbara, Calif. Died Sep. 12, 1949.

EGAN, Joseph L., business exec.; b. New York, N.Y., Aug. 9, 1886; s. Joseph Martin Francis (M.D.) and Sarah Josephine (Phillips) E.; student St. Francis Xavier Prep. School, 1899-1903, Coll. of St. Francis Xavier, 1903-04, Columbia U., 1904-07; LL.B., N.Y. Law Sch., 1909; m. Irene Gerken, Nov. 23, 1915; children—Irene Marie (Mrs. Lawrence J. O'Brien), Joseph L. (dec.), Ronald Gerken. Pvt. practice of law, N.Y. City, 1911-12; atty. Western Union Telegraph Co., N.Y. City, 1912-25, dir. of contracts, 1925-39, vice pres., 1939-45, pres. and dir. since 1945; chmn. bd. and dir. Am. Dist. Telegraph Co.; pres. and dir. Gold & Stock Telegraph Co., Internat. Ocean Telegraph Co., Washington and New Orleans Telegraph Co.; and numerous other subsidiaries of Western Union Telegraph Co.; dir. Am. Dist. Telegraph Co. (N.J.), Am. Express Co., The Teleregister Corp., The Chase Nat. Bank of The City of N.Y. Mem. Friendly Sons of St. Patrick, Assn. of Alumni of Columbia Coll., Theta Delta Chi. Clubs. Arkwright, Economic, N.Y. Athletic, Railroad (N.Y.); Metropolitan (Washington); Mercier, Montclair Golf, Monmouth Beach (N.J.); Deal (N.J.) Golf and Country (dir.). Address: care Western Union Telegraph Co., 60 Hudson St., New York. Died Dec. 6, 1948.

EGBERT, James Chidester, educator, author; b. New York, May 3, 1859; s. Rev. James C. and Louisa (Drew) E.; A. B., Columbia, 1881, A.M., 1882, Ph.D., 1884, Litt.D., 1929; LL.D., Rutgers University, 1926; m. Emma G. Pennington, 1884 (now dec.); children—James C. Pennington (dec.), Harry Drew (dec.), George Pennington, Lester Darling; m. 2d, Mrs. Agnes Pennington Lester, 1936. Held prize fellowship, 1882-85, asst. in Greek, 1885-87, tutor Latin, 1888-91, instr., 1891-95; adj. prof., 1895-1900, prof. Roman archæology and epigraphy, 1900-06, prof. Latin, 1906-42, dir. Sch. of Bus., 1916-31, dean of sch., 1931-32, Columbia. Dir. summer session, Columbia, 1902-19; dir. Univ. Extension, 1910-42, emeritus since 1942. Del. Rep. Nat. Conv., Cleveland, O., 1936. Pres. Long Island Coll. Hosp., 1917-30; pres. L.I. Coll. Medicine, 1930-31. Prof. Latin, Am. Sch. Classical Studies, Rome, 1903-04; mem. exec. com. Am. Acad. in Rome (1st v.p.); mem. Jersey City Bd. Edn., 1898-1903. Republican. Mem. Archæol. Inst. America (pres. 1917-21), Am. Philol. Assn., Phi Beta Kappa, New York (pres. 1904-05). Author: Macmillan's Shorter Latin Course, 1892; Cicero, deSenectute, 1895; Introduction to the Study of Latin Inscriptions, 1895; Livy, Book XXI and selections, 1913; also wrote The Equestrian Cursus Honorum, in Classical Studies in Honor of Henry Drisler, 1894; also several articles in Harper's Dictionary of Classical Antiquity, and New Internat. Ency. Gen. editor Macmillan's Series of Latin Classics. Home: 924 West End Av., New York, N.Y. Died July 17, 1948.

EGGIMANN, Edward Daniel, business exec.; b. Fort Wayne, Ind., Feb. 9, 1877; s. Conrad and Lydia (Fry) E.; student pub. schs. of Fort Wayne, Ind.; m. Mildred Evelyn Russell, Oct. 15, 1898 (died Aug. 4, 1939); children—Paul Harold, Naomi Ruth; m. 2d, Ruth Rowena McDaniel, Nov. 4, 1940. Began as clerk with S. F. Bowser & Co. (now Bowser, Inc.) manufacturers of meters, pumps, tanks and liquid control systems, Fort Wayne, Ind., 1898-1908, mgr. collection dept., 1908-18 office mgr., 1918-20, asst. sec. and treas., 1918-25, sec., 1925-27, sec. and treas. 1927-37, exec. v.p. and treas., 1937-45, chmn. bd. since 1945; chmn. bd. dirs. Johnson Fare Box Co., Chicago, Ill., since 1932; v.p., dir. Fostoria Screw Co. since 1941; exec. v.p. and dir. S. F. Bowser Co. Ltd. (Toronto) since 1936; v.p. and dir. Eagle Lock Co., Terryville, Conn., since 1943. Admitted to Ind. bar, 1929. Dir. Y.M.C.A. (Fort Wayne), Fort Wayne Meth. Hospital. Democrat. Baptist (trustee First Ch., Fort Wayne). Mason. Home: 302 N. Cornell Circle, Fort Wayne 6. Office: 1302 E. Creighton Av., Fort Wayne 2, Ind. Died Jan. 9, 1948; buried Lindenwood Cemetery, Fort Wayne, Ind.

EGNER, Arthur Frederick (ĕg'nẽr), lawyer; b. Newark, N.J., Sept. 20, 1882; s. Henry William and Emily Susan (Nasher) E.; A.B., Columbia, 1903, A.M., 1905; LL.B., N.Y. Law Sch., 1905; m. Adele Badgley Gifford, June 21, 1923; children—Mary Gifford, Emily Nasher. Admitted to N.J. bar, 1905; mem. McCarter, English & Egner since 1912; v.p. and dir. Kresge Dept. Stores, Inc., Del., since 1936; chmn. bd. and counsel N.J. Realty Title Ins. Co. since 1937, N.J. Realty Co. since 1937; counsel and dir. Art Metal Works, Inc., N.J. Worsted Mills; dir. Armstrong Rubber Co., Eagle Fire Ins. Co. Employee, Gen. Staff, U.S. Army, 1918. Mem. City Planning Commn., Newark, N.J., 1912-14. Pres. Newark Mus. Assn. since 1932, Hosp. and Home for Crippled Children since 1930; v.p. of trustees Newark U. since 1936. Mem. Essex County Bar Assn. (pres. 1924-25). Received award of Advertising Club of Newark, 1938. Democrat. Lutheran. Clubs: Grolier (New York); Essex (Newark); Carmel (N.Y.) Country. Home: 406 Centre St., South Orange, N.J. Office: 13 Commerce St., Newark, N.J. Died June 7, 1943.

EHNES, Morris Wellington (ĕn'ĕs), clergyman; b. Dashwood, Ont., Can., Mar. 3, 1873; s. August G. and Sarah (Haist) E.; came to U.S., 1891; A.B., Ohio Wesleyan U., Delaware, O., 1898; spl. work, Columbia, 1907-08; D.D., Ohio Wesleyan U., 1923; m. Belle Gates, Aug. 22, 1898; children—Margaret Gates (Mrs. Wm. R. Canner), Bayard Freeman, Elizabeth Ruth (Mrs. Frederick G. Welsh), Robert Morris (deceased), Helen Belle (Mrs. Henry E. Grammerstorf). Began as missionary to Rhodesia, 1898-1901; gen. secretary College Y.M.C.A., Delaware, O., 1902-04; asst. gen. sec. Student Volunteer Movement for Fgn. Missions, 1904-05; editorial sec. Missionary Edn. Movement and editor missionary text books, 1905-16; exec. sec. Ohio Wesleyan U., 1916-19; asst. treas. Methodist Centenary movement, 1919-20, treas. Com. on Conservation and Advance of M.E. Ch., 1920-24; treas. Bd. of Foreign Missions M.E. Ch. 1924-40; treas., Div. of Foreign Missions Meth. Ch., 1940-43; treas. Board of Missions and Church Extension Meth. Ch., 1940-43; treas. Meth. Com. for Overseas Relief, 1940-43; treas. Institution for the Chinese Blind, Shanghai, China; mem. Associated Boards for Christian Colleges in China; pres. Nanking Realty Corp., New York; mem. bd. trustees Santiago Coll., Santiago, Chile, Ward Coll., Buenos Aires, Argentina; member Committee on Permanent Funds and Investments of the Woman's Division of Christian Services of the Board of Missions and Church Extension of the Methodist Church; treas. Wendel Foundation, New York, 1934-43. Mem. Phi Beta Kappa, Phi Gamma Delta. Republican. Mason. Home: 196 Park Av., Leonia, N.J. Office: 156 Fifth Av., New York, N.Y. Died July 3, 1945.

EHRINGHAUS, John Christoph Blucher (ē'ring-hous), ex-gov.; b. Elizabeth City, N.C., Feb. 5, 1882; s. Erskine and Carrie Colville (Mathews) E.; grad. Atlantic Collegiate Inst., 1898; A.B., U. of N.C., 1901, LL.B., 1903; m. Matilda Bradford Haughton, Jan. 4, 1912; children—John C. B., Haughton, Matilda. Admitted to N.C. bar, 1903, and practiced at Elizabeth City; became mem. Ehringhaus & Hall. Mem. N.C. Ho. of Rep., 1905-08; solicitor, 1st Jud. Dist., N.C., 1910-22; gov. of N.C., term 1933-37; now practicing law at Raleigh, N.C.; dir. Equitable Life Assurance Society of the U.S. Mem. N.C. Judicial Conference; mem. Pasquotank County and N.C. State Dem. exec. coms. Mem. Am. and N.C. State bar assns., N.C. Hist. Soc., Phi Beta Kappa, Delta Kappa Epsilon, Theta Nu Epsilon. Episcopalian. Mason (Shriner), Odd Fellow, Elk. Co-author of bill establishing E. Carolina Teachers Training Sch. and present system of rural high schools.‡ Died July 29, 1949.

EICHER, Edward Clayton (ĭk'ẽr), b. Noble, Ia., Dec. 16, 1878; s. Benjamin and Lydia (Sommer) E.; student Washington (Ia.) Acad., 1894-97, Morgan Park (Ill.) Acad., 1898-99; Ph.B., U. of Chicago, 1904; law student, 1903-05; m. Hazel Mount, Aug. 19, 1908; 1 dau., Elizabeth (foster child). Admitted to Ia. bar, 1906; asst. registrar U. of Chicago, 1907-09; asst. atty. Ia. dist., C.,B.&Q. R.R. Co., 1909-18; in practice at Washington, Ia., 1918-33; member Securities and Exchange Commission, 1938-42, chmn., 1941-42; now chief justice U.S. Dist. Ct. for District of Columbia. Member 73d to 75th Congresses (1933-39), 1st Iowa District. Member Temporary Nat. Econ. Com., 1938. Mem. bars Ia., Ill. State and U.S. Supreme Court, Alpha Delta Phi, Phi Delta Phi. Democrat. Mennonite. Home: 12 Wilton Rd., Alexandria, Va. Address: U.S. Court House, Washington, D.C. Died Nov. 30, 1944.

EICHHEIM, Henry, musician; b. Chicago, Jan. 3, 1870; s. Meinhard and Augusta (Pellage) E.; grad. (1st prize in violin) Chicago Musical Coll.; m. Ethel Roe, April 17, 1917 (died June 15, 1931). First violin, Boston Symphony Orchestra, 1890-1912; mem. Thomas Orchestra, N.Y. City, 1899-1900; condr. Winchester (Mass.) Orchestra, 1913-17. Has conducted own works with Boston, Chicago, Cleveland, San Francisco, Los Angeles orchestras; made chamber music concert tours of U.S. and England; lecturer on oriental music. Mem. Pro Musica, Japan Soc. Boston, Japan Soc. New York. Composer: Oriental Impressions (small orchestra, piano); Malay Mosaic; The Rivals (Chinese ballet); Burma; Java (symphonic poem); Sonata (violin); etc. Made 4 trips to Orient for musical research. Home: 99 Mesa Rd., Santa Barbara, Calif. Died Aug. 22, 1942.

EILSHEMIUS, Louis Michel (īl-shē'mĭ-ŭs), artist; b. Laurel Manor, N.J., Feb. 4, 1864; s. Henry Gottfried and Cecile Eugenie (Robert) E.; student Cornell U., 1882-84, Acad., N.Y. City, 1883-86, Julian Acad., Paris, 1886-89; unmarried. Rep. in Phillips Memorial Gallery, Washington, D.C., Metropolitan Mus. of Art, Mus. of Modern Art, Whitney Mus. of Art, N.Y. City; Detroit Inst. of Art; Cleveland Mus.; Luxembourg Mus., Paris; Museum of Fine Arts, Boston. Author, painter, composer. Home: 118 E. 57th St., New York, N.Y.* Died Dec. 29, 1941.

EINSTEIN, Lewis, diplomat; b. New York, Mar. 15, 1877; s. David L. and Caroline E.; A.B., Columbia, 1898, A.M., 1899; m. Helene Ralli, 1904. Third sec. Am. Embassy, Paris, 1903-05, at London, 1905-06; sec. U.S. delegation, Moroccan Conf., 1906; 2d sec. Am. Legation, Constantinople, Mar. 1-June 28, 1906; 2d sec. Am. Embassy, Constantinople, June 28, 1906, 1st sec. of embassy and chargé d'affaires, Nov. 13, 1908; apptd. sec. Am. Legation at Peking, China, Dec. 1909; E.E. and M.P. to Costa Rica, July 1911-June 1913; special agent of the State Dept. at Constantinople, Jan.-Sept. 1915; Am. diplomatic rep. to Bulgaria, in charge British interests, Oct. 1915-June 1916 (received thanks of King of England); E.E. and M.P. to Czechoslovakia, Oct. 1921-Feb. 1930. Comdr. Legion of Honor (France); Grand Officer S.S. Maurice and Lazarus (Italy); Grand Cross Order of the White Lion (Czechoslovakia); presentation plate from British Govt.; Medal of Excellence from Columbia Univ., 1934. Mem. Sons of the Revolution, Phi Beta Kappa, The Athenaeum (London, Eng.). Author: Luigi Pulci and the Morgante Maggiore, 1902; The Italian Renaissance in England, 1902; The Relation of Literature to History, 1903; Napoleon III and American Diplomacy at the Outbreak of the Civil War, 1905; American Foreign Policy by a Diplomatist, 1909; Inside Constantinople, 1917; Prophecy of the War, with introduction by Theodore Roosevelt; Tudor Ideals, 1921; Roosevelt, His Mind in Action, 1930; Divided Loyalties—Americans in England During the War of Independence, 1933; Verses, 1938; The Winged Victory, 1941; Historical Change, 1946; also contbr. of Lewis Cass and American Diplomacy under President Buchanan (in Lives of Secretaries of State), 1927; articles in American, English, French, Italian jours. on diplomatic history and art subjects. Editor: The Humanists Library (reprints and original contbns. relating to the Renaissance); Leonardo da Vinci—Fragments, 1907. Address: care Central Hanover Trust Co., New York, N.Y. Died 1949.

EKBLAW, Walter Elmer (ĕk'blaw), geographer; b. Rantoul, Ill., Mar. 10, 1882; s. Andrew and Ingrid (Johnson) E.; prep. edn., Austin Prep. Coll., Effingham, Ill., and Central Y.M.C.A. Night Sch., Chicago; A.B., U. of Ill., 1910, A.M., 1912; hon. fellow Clark Univ., 1924-26, Ph.D., 1926; Sc.D. (hon.) Upsala College, 1947; married Augusta May Krieger, February 28, 1918; children—Walter Elmer, Neil William, Elsa May; m. 2d, Ellen L. Lindblad, Jan. 23, 1933. Geologist and botanist, Crocker Land Arctic Expdn., 1913-17; research fellow, U. of Ill., 1917-20; also research asso. Am. Museum Natural History, 1917-22; consultant geologist, 1922-24; editor Economic Geography since 1924; prof. geography, Clark U., since 1926. Decoration: Order of the North Star (Sweden). Member Assn. American Geographers, Am. Assn. of Professional Geographers (vice pres.), Mass. Archeol. Soc. (pres.), A.A.A.S., Am. Anthrop. Soc., Soils Science Society of America, Am. Ornithol. Union, Swedish Colonial Society, Sigma Xi, Gamma Alpha, Theta Nu Epsilon, Acacia. Republican. Episcopalian. Mason. Clubs: Explorers (N.Y.); Cosmos (Washington); Kiwanis (Champaign, Ill.). Contbr. to Annals of Assn. Am. Geographers. Explored large areas of Grant Land and Ellesmere Land. Home: The Homelands, N. Grafton, Mass. Office: Clark University, Worcester, Mass. Died June 5, 1949.

ELDER, Paul, publisher, bookseller; b. Harrisburg, Pa., Jan. 1, 1872; s. Scott and Mary A. (Eyster) E.; ed. Lowell High Sch.; m. Emma Moore, May, 1896; children—Pauline, Scott, Paul. Apprenticed to William Doxey, bookseller; started business under name of D. Paul Elder, 1898; co-partnership Paul Elder and Morgan Shepard, 1900; head of Paul Elder and Co., Inc., 1903. Republican. Unitarian. Mason. Clubs: Commonwealth, Rotary. Author: Mosaic Essays, 1906; California the Beautiful, 1911; Old Spanish Missions of California, 1913. Home: 701 Post St. Office: 239 Post St., San Francisco, Calif. Died Jan. 24, 1948.

ELDRIDGE, Francis Howard, lawyer; b. Americus, Ga., January 31, 1896; s. Archibald Ronaldson and Minnie (Kelly) E.; A.B., Georgetown U., 1914; LL.B., Northwestern U., 1917; unmarried. Admitted to Ill. bar, 1917, and began practice at Chicago; asso. with law firm Rosenthal, Hamill & Wormser, 1917-26, mem. firm, 1926-37; mem. successor firms Rosenthal, Hamill, Eldridge & King, 1937-42, Rosenthal, Eldridge, King & Robin since Mar. 1942. Served as ensign, U.S. Naval Res. Force, World War I. Mem. Am. Bar Assn., Ill. State Bar Assn. (mem. bd. govs. 1940-43), Chicago Bar Assn. (mem. bd. mgrs. 1940-42), Chicago Law Inst., Law Club, Art Inst. Chicago,

Chicago Hist. Soc. Catholic. Clubs: University, Chicago, Tavern, Chicago Literary (pres. 1943-44), Knollwood, Caxton. Occasional contbr. to legal periodicals. Home: 503 Barry Av. Office: 105 W. Monroe St., Chicago, Ill. Died Aug. 21, 1944.

ELIOT, Christopher Rhodes, clergyman; b. St. Louis, Mo., Jan. 20, 1856; s. William Greenleaf and Abby (Adams Cranch) E.; grad. Smith Acad., 1872; A.B., Washington U., 1876, A.M., 1881, LL.D., 1925; S.T.B., Harvard, 1881; m. Mary Jackson May, Sept. 7, 1888 (died 1926); children—Frederick May, Martha May, Abigail Adams. Minister First Parish Unitarian Ch., Dorchester, Mass., 1882-93; asso. minister Bulfinch Pl. Unitarian Ch., Boston, Mass., 1894-96, minister, 1896-1927, minister emeritus since 1927; minister at large, Benevolent Fraternity of Churches, Boston, 1927-30. Pres. Lend a Hand Soc., Unitarian Historical Society (emeritus); vice-president Boston Federation of Churches; director Unitarian Temperance Soc.; dir. Children's Mission to Children; moderator Mass. Conv. Congl. Ministers, 1935-36. Club: Twentieth Century. Home: 21 Francis Av., Cambridge, Mass. Died June 21, 1945.

ELKINS, William McIntire, investment banking; b. Phil., Pa., Sept. 3, 1882; s. George W. and Stella (McIntire) E.; grad. St. Marks Sch., 1901; student Harvard, 1901-05; m. Elizabeth Wolcott Tuckerman, June 10, 1905 (died 1941); children—William L. (deceased), Elizabeth W., Bayard T. (deceased); m. 2d, Lisa Cushing Norris. Began in investment banking business at Philadelphia, 1906; member of firm Elkins, Morris & Company since 1911; vice-president Land Title Building Corporation; director Land Title Bank & Trust Co., Penn Mutual Life Ins. Co. Member New York Stock Exchange. Lieut. U.S. N.R.F., 1917-19. Vice-pres. Pa. Museum and Sch. of Indsl. Art; trustee St. Mark's Sch.; trustee The Church Foundation; dir. Phila. Free Library; mem. Am. Antiquarian Soc., Worcester, Mass. Republican. Episcopalian. Clubs: Philadelphia, Pine Valley, Sunny Brook, Farmers'. Home: Chestnut Hill, Pa. Office: Land Title Bldg., Philadelphia, Pa.* Died June 5, 1947.

ELKUS, Abram I., lawyer; b. New York, Aug. 6, 1867; s. Isaac and Julia E.; ed. pub. schs. and Coll. City of New York; LL.B., Columbia, 1888; D.C.L., St. Lawrence U., 1913; LL.D., Middlebury, 1918; Syracuse, 1918; m. Gertrude R. Hess, Apr. 15, 1896; children—James Hess, Ethel J., Katharine. In practice at New York; apptd. ambassador E. and P. to Turkey, July 1916, for 3 yrs.; apptd. judge Ct. of Appeals of N.Y., Nov. 1919; appointed commr. of League of Nations to decide the Aaland Islands dispute, 1920. Was spl. U.S. attorney to prosecute fraudulent bankrupts, 1908; counsel for Mchts.' Assn., etc. Trustee and hon. pres. Baron de Hirsch Fund; pres. Hebrew Tech. Sch. for Girls; counsel N.Y. State Factory Investigating Commn.; regent U. State of New York, 1911-19; chmn. Reconstruction Commn., N.Y. State, 1918-19. Decorations: Grand Officer Legion of Honor (France); Grand Cross of the British Empire; l'Ordre de la Rose Blanche (Finland). Mem. Am., N.Y. State bar assns., N.Y. County Lawyers Assn. (dir.), Assn. Bar City of New York. Clubs: Manhattan, City, Lotos, Lawyers', Metropolis, Harmonie, Bankers, Rumson Country, National Democratic (New York); Fort Orange (Albany); Cosmos (Washington); Union Interalliée (Paris, France). Author: Secret Liens and Reputed Ownership, 1910. Home: 420 Park Av.; also Red Bank, N.J. Office: 40 Wall St., New York, N.Y. Died Oct. 15, 1947.

ELLENWOOD, Frank Oakes, univ. prof.; b. Little Hocking, O., Nov. 10, 1878; s. Douglas Harlow and Cynthia Clough (Oakes) E.; A.B. in Mech. Engring., Stanford, 1904, M.E., 1922; m. Cecelia Freeman Atherton, June 30, 1909; children—Ruth Cecelia (Mrs. Prince McGuyre), Hazel Adaline (Mrs. Warner S. Hammond), Cecelia Atherton (dec.). Asst. to erection foreman, steam power plants, C. C. Moore & Co., San Francisco, Calif., 1904-05; asst. to master mechanic, Tonopah (Nev.) R.R. Co., 1905-06; asst. engr. Am. Smelting and Refining Co., South San Francisco, Calif., 1907-08; instr. mech. engring., Stanford, 1908-11; asst. prof. heat-power engring., Cornell U., 1911-15, prof., 1915-40, head of dept. heat-power engring. since 1940, John Edson Sweet prof. engring. since 1941. Served as head of engine dept. U.S. Army Sch. of Mil. Aeronautics, Cornell U., 1917-19. Mem. Am. Soc. M.E. (chmn. com. on thermodynamic terminology, 1936; mem. com. on symbols for heat and thermodynamics 1927-44), Am. Soc. Refrigerating Engrs., Soc. Promotion Engring. Edn., Sigma Xi, Tau Beta Pi, Phi Kappa Phi, Atmos, Triangle. Mem. First Unitarian Ch., Ithaca, N.Y. Clubs: Research Cornell U., Ithaca Country (Ithaca, N.Y.). Author: Steam Charts, 1914. Co-author: Heat-Power Engineering, Vol. I, 1926, Vol. II, 1932, Vol. III, 1933; Vapor Charts, 1939; Thermodynamic Charts, 1944. Home: 111 Harvard Place, Ithaca, N.Y. Died Sept. 7, 1947.

ELLENWOOD, Fred Alden, sheep and wool; b. Marietta, O., Apr. 10, 1876; s. Douglas H. and Cynthia (Oakes) E.; ed. normal schs., Lebanon, O., and Valparaiso, Ind.; m. Minnie Hickman, Jan. 6, 1904. Teacher pub. schs., Ohio, 1894-95; removed to Calif., 1896, and went to work in sheep camp; associated with T. H. Ramsay and Corinne S. Ramsay, 1912, in purchase of ranch of 25,000 acres; led in fight of wool growers for reform in wool tariff and secured change in tariff act in Congress so that wool duties were assessed on scoured content instead of the grease basis; pres. Northern Calif. Wool Warehouse Co., 1920-30 and its successor, the Calif. Wool Marketing Assn.; owner and mgr. Ellenwood & Ramsay Sheep Co., Ellenwood & Co.; dir. Red Bluff Branch Bank of America. Pres. Calif. Wool Growers Assn., 1918-22, Nat. Wool Growers Assn., 1934-36. Republican. Mason (K.T., Shriner). Elk. Home: Red Bluff, Calif. Died Dec. 13, 1946.

ELLER, Adolphus Hill, lawyer, banker; b. Wilkes County, N.C., Apr. 9, 1861; s. James and Mary Ann (Carlton) E.; prep. edn., Moravian Falls (N.C.) Acad., 1879-81; A.B., U. of N.C., 1885; Folks Law Sch., Cilly, N.C., 1885-86; m. Laura Winifred Newland, Nov. 19, 1896; children—Mary (dec.), John DeWalden, Adolphus Hill. Admitted to N.C. bar, 1886, and began practice at Winston-Salem; mem. Eller & Starbuck, 1888-94; sec. and treas. N.C.R.R. Company, 1905-13; vice-pres. and chmn. of trust dept. coms. Wachovia (N.C.) Bank & Trust Co.; organizer, 1908, since pres. Standard Bldg. & Loan Assn. Mem. N.C. State Senate, 1905-07; chmn. State Dem. Exec. Com., 1908-12; chmn. Winston-Salem Commn. of Pub. Sch., 1927-33. Trustee U. of N.C., 1905-33, N.C. Bapt. Hosps. (a founder), Winston-Salem Teachers Coll. for Negroes. Mem. Sigma Alpha Epsilon. Baptist. Mason. Clubs: Twin City, Forsyth Country; Cosmos. Home: 129 Cascade Av. Office: Main and 3d Sts., Winston-Salem, N.C. Died Dec. 7, 1941.

ELLETT, Edward Coleman (ĕl'lĕt), physician; b. Memphis, Tenn., Dec. 18, 1869; s. Henry Thomas and Katherine (Coleman) E.; Southwestern Presbyn. U., Clarksville, Tenn., 1884-86; B.A., U. of the South, Sewanee, Tenn., 1888; M.D., U. of Pennsylvania, 1891; LL.D., Southwestern University, 1942; hon. D.Sc., University of the South, 1943; married Nina Polk Martin, Nov. 12, 1896. Practiced medicine at Phila., 1891-93, Memphis Tenn., since 1893; prof. diseases of eye, U. of Tenn., 1906-22. Lt. col. M.C., U.S. Army, in active service, 1917. Fellow Am. Coll. Surgeons; mem. Memphis and Shelby County med. socs., West Tenn. Med. and Surg. Assn., Tenn. State Med. Soc., A.M.A., Am. Acad. of Ophthalmology and Otolaryngology, Am. Ophthalmol. Soc., Kappa Sigma, Phi Alpha Sigma. Clubs: Memphis Country; Memphis University. Home: 1545 Central Av. Office: Exchange Bldg., Memphis, Tenn. Died June 8, 1947.

ELLETT, Walter Beal, prof. agrl. chemistry; b. Radford, Va., Nov. 11, 1874; s. Robert Thadius and Sue Virginia (French) E.; B.S., Va. Agrl. and Mech. Coll. (now Va. Poly. Inst.), 1894, M.S., 1896; M.A., Ph.D., U. of Göttingen, 1904; m. Anna B. Burton, Aug. 12, 1926. Chemist Va. Agrl. Expt. Sta. since 1906 and prof. agrl. chemistry, Va. Poly. Inst. since 1916. Home: Blacksburg, Va. Died May 12, 1943.

ELLICK, Alfred George, lawyer; b. Fremont, Neb., Aug. 29, 1878; s. Francis Ignatius and Josephine (Lauth) E.; LL.B., U. of Mich. Law Sch., 1900; m. Frances Purvis, Dec. 16, 1903; children—Josephine (Mrs. Edward B. Crofoot), Robert Purvis, Alfred George. In practice at Omaha, Neb., since 1900; coach Haskell Indians football team, 1900, 01, Creighton U. football team, 1902; asst. city atty., Omaha, 1904-05; dep. county atty., Douglas County, Neb., 1906-12; asst. gen. atty. Union Pacific R.R., 1912-18; partner law firm Ellick, Fitzgerald & Smith, Omaha, Neb. Pres. Neb. State Bar Assn., 1921; pres. Neb. Grain Improvement Assn. since 1938. Served as capt. Neb. Home Guards, 1917-18. Mem. Am. Bar Assn., Neb. State Bar Assn., Omaha Bar Assn., Omaha C. of C. Jeffersonian Democrat. Clubs: Omaha, Omaha Country, Omaha Athletic, Rotary. Home: 105 S. 53d St. Office: 810 Insurance Bldg., Omaha, Neb. Died June 21, 1942.

ELLINWOOD, Everett E., lawyer; b. Rock Creek, Ashtabula County, O., July 22, 1862; s. John P. and Cornelia (Sperry) E.; ed. Knox Coll., 1881-83; LL.B., U. of Mich., 1890; LL.D., U. of Ariz., 1941; m. Minnie L. Walkley, Nov. 17, 1886 (dec.); children—Mrs. Cornelia Morris, Ralph Everett (dec.); m. 2d, Hazel J. Nesbit, May 10, 1933. Admitted to Ill. bar, 1889; went to Ariz., where has since practiced; mem. Ellinwood & Ross; gen. atty. Phelps Dodge Corp. interests in Ariz. U.S. dist. atty., Ariz., 1893-98; Commr. for Promotion of Uniform Laws in U.S., 1897-1911; del. Dem. Nat. Conv., 1892; chmn. Dem. Territorial Com., 1900-02, and 1904-06; mem. Ariz. Constl. Conv., 1910, but did not sign constitution because of provision relating to recall of judiciary; chancellor U. of Ariz., 1923-27, regent, 1932-41, pres. bd. regents, 1937-41; ex-pres. Phoenix Nat. Bank, Phoenix Savings Bank and Trust Co. Mem. Am. Bar Assn. (gen. council, 1897-1907, 1911-14; v.p. for Ariz., 1910-11, 1915); del. Universal Congress Lawyers and Jurists, St. Louis, 1904. Conglist. Home: N. Central Av. Office: Title & Trust Bldg., Phoenix, Ariz. Died Aug. 8, 1943.

ELLIOTT, Daniel Stanley, coll. prof., physicist; b. Baltimore, Md., Aug. 3, 1885; s. George Herbert and Minnie (Prinz) E.; A.B., Johns Hopkins U., 1911, A.M., 1913, Ph.D., 1914, fellow, 1913-14; m. Nora A. Nilson, June 11, 1917. Instr. physics, Ga. Inst. Tech., 1914-15, asst. prof., 1915-16, asso. prof., 1916-17, acting prof., 1918-19; W. R. Irby prof. of physics and head dept., Tulane U., New Orleans, La., since 1920. Served as v.p. acad. bd. and head depts. radio and airplanes, Ga. Tech. Sch. of Mil. Aeronautics, U.S. Army, 1917-18; at O.T.C., Plattsburg, N.Y., 1918. Fellow Am. Phys. Soc., A.A.A.S.; mem. Am. Assn. Physics Teachers (mem. exec. com. 1938-39), Soc. for Promotion of Engring. Edn. (council mem., 1937-39); Southeastern Sect. of Am. Phys. Soc. (chmn. 1936), New Orleans Acad. of Sciences (treas. 1933), La. Sect. of Am. Assn. Physics Teachers (chmn. 1940), La. Engring Soc., Gamma Alpha, Phi Kappa Phi, Omicron Delta Kappa, Kappa Delta Phi. Democrat. Methodist. Contributor articles to technical journals, etc. Home: 7922 Freret Street, New Orleans, La. Died Dec. 1, 1944.

ELLIOTT, Edward, banker; b. Murfreesboro, Tenn., Aug. 3, 1874; s. William Yandell and Margaret Graham (Johnston) E.; A.B., Princeton, 1897, A.M., 1900; studied univs. Berlin and Heidelberg, 1900-02; Ph.D., Heidelberg, 1902; m. Margaret Randolph Axson, Sept. 8, 1910. Teacher, Bolton, Tenn., 1897-98; instr. in Latin, 1898-1900, in jurisprudence, 1902-05, preceptor in dept. of history, politics and economics, 1905-09, prof. politics, 1909-15, dean of the college, 1909-12, Princeton U.; lecturer internat. law, 1913-16, prof., 1916-20, U. of Calif. Admitted to San Francisco bar, 1913; dir. Fed. Res. Bank of San Francisco, 1917-20; vice-pres. Security-First Nat. Bank, Los Angeles, Calif, 1921-47. Mem. Am. Bankers Assn. (member com. on bank taxation, 1928-47), Association of Reserve City Bankers (director 1935-37, commission on banking law and practice 1934-38; member committee on public relations, 1937-39; trustee Banking Research Fund, 1937-45; president 1939-40); California Bankers Association (member com. on legislation and taxation, chmn. 1928-35, chmn. com. on research, 1936-39). Author: Die Staatslehre John C. Calhoun's 1903; The Biographical Story of the Constitution, 1910; American Government and Majority Rule, 1915; also monographs Selected Documents in International Law, State Bank Membership in the Federal Reserve System. Writer of numerous articles. Home: Princeton, N.J. Died Dec. 12, 1947.

ELLIOTT, George Blow, ry. pres.; b. Norfolk, Va., Mar. 22, 1873; s. Warren G. and Margaret (Blow) E.; C.E., Va. Mil. Inst., 1892; B.L., Harvard, 1896; m. Mabel E. Green, Apr. 19, 1899; children—Mabel (dec.), Margaret B. (Mrs. George G. Carey), Esther (Mrs. Thorne Sparkman). Began with law dept. Atlantic Coast Line R.R., 1896, chaiman executive committee to 1945, retired since October, 1945. Democrat. Episcopalian. Clubs: Cape Fear. Home: 207 S. 3d St., Wilmington, N.C. Died Feb. 18, 1948.

ELLIOTT, Harriet Wiesman, dean of women; b. Carbondale, Ill., July 10, 1884; d. Allan Curtis and Elizabeth Ann (White) Elliott; prep. edn., Park Coll., Parkville, Mo.; A.B., Hanover (Ind.) Coll., 1910, LL.D., 1941; A.M., Columbia U. 1913. Teacher history and political science, Women's Coll., U. of N.C., since 1913, prof. since 1921 and dean of women since 1935; chief Consumer Div., Office of Price Adminstrn. Member administrative board, N.C. Legislative Council; mem. Women's Nat. Council of Defense during World War, 1918-19; mem. White House Conf. on Children, 1928; mem. Advisory Commn. N.C. Emergency Relief Adminstrn., 1933-35; mem. com. White House Conf. on Children in a Democracy, 1940; mem. Washington Conf. on Unemployment among Young Women of America, 1940; pres. N.C. Social Service Conf., 1939-40; mem. Gov. Hoey's N.C. com. of Conf. of Southern Govs., 1940; apptd. by President consumer mem. of Advisory Commn. to the Council of Nat. Defense, May 1940; apptd. by Secretary Morgenthau head of Women's Div., War Savings Staff, U.S. Treasury, June 1942. Adviser, representing U.S. State Department, London Educational Conference, 1945; member Committee of the South (branch of National Planning Council. Del. large from N.C. to Dem. Nat. Conv., 1932, 36; dir. edn. program for Women's Div. of Nat. Dem. Com., 1935; alternate mem. platform com. of Dem. party from N.C., 1936. Chmn. nat. legislative com. Am Assn. Univ. Women, 1937-43. Mem. Am. Polit. Science Assn., Nat. Assn. Deans of Women, N.C. Fedn. of Women's Clubs. Alpha Delta Phi. Presbyterian. Address: 316 McIver St., Greensboro, N.C. Died Aug. 6, 1947.

ELLIOTT, Huger, educator; b. Sewanee, Tenn., Oct. 5, 1877; s. John Barnwell and Lucy (Huger) E.; B.S., Sch. of Architecture (Columbia), 1900; École des Beaux Arts, Paris, 1903-05; m. Elizabeth Shippen Green, June 3, 1911. Instr. Sch. of Architecture, U. of Pa., 1899-1901, 1905-07, Harvard, 1907-08; dir. R.I. Sch. of Design, 1908-12; supervisor of ednl. work, Museum of Fine Arts, Boston, and dir. dept. of design, Mus. Sch., 1912-20; prin. of the Pa. Museum Sch. of Industrial Art, Phila., 1920-25; dir. ednl. work, Met. Museum of Art, 1925-41. Awarded Medal of Excellence, Columbia U., 1941. Member Alpha Tau Omega, Sigma Xi. Democrat. Episcopalian. Author: Memorial Art, 1923; The Significance of the Fine Arts (part author), 1923; Fashions in Art, 1937, An Alliterative Alphabet for Adult Abecedarians, 1947. Home: Cresheim Rd. and Emlen St., Philadelphia 19, Pa. Died Nov. 13, 1948.

ELLIOTT, J. M., pres. and gen. mgr., Jacksonville Times Union. Address: Jacksonville, Fla. Died Apr. 15, 1948.

ELLIOTT, Jackson S., newspaperman, writer of biographies; b. La Salle County, Ill., Mar. 9, 1876; s. John B. and Minerva D. (Johnston) E.; self ed.; m. Isabel R. Joyce, Aug. 18, 1909 (died 1934); children—Jackson S., Joyce; m. 2d, Frances Savage, sculptress, 1940. Began with Sioux City (Ia.) Journal, 1894, and continued in various cities of Ia. for 8 yrs.; reporter Washington Times, 1902-03; with Associated Press, 1903-38 (honorarily retired); assigned to all major polit. convs. and directed Associated Press reportorial staffs, 1904-1924; manager Congress staff, Asso. Press, 1909-11, chief of staff of Washington office, 1911-12, and supt. eastern div., New York, 1912-15; resumed direction of Washington bureau, June 1915, and also in charge of Southern div. until Mar. 1918, when became chief of the news dept. at New York; in direct charge Associated Press News Service during World War; became gen. supt., Oct. 1920, and asst. gen. mgr., Apr. 1921. Congregationalist. Home: 967 E. 18th St., Brooklyn, N.Y. and Palm Springs, Calif. Died Mar. 10, 1942.

ELLIOTT, John Lovejoy, teacher; b. Princeton, Ill., Dec. 2, 1868; s. Isaac Hughes and Elizabeth (Denham) E.; L.B., Cornell U., 1892; Ph.D., U. of Halle, 1894; unmarried. Has been engaged in ednl. and social work since 1894; instr. in ethics, Ethical Culture School, New York, since 1894; organizer, 1895, and since headworker, Hudson Guild (a neighborhood centre). Member board governors Ethical Culture School; president National Federal Settlements, 1919-23, United Neighborhood Houses of New York, 1926, 27; chairman trustees Sch. for Printers' Apprentices; senior leader of New York Society for Ethical Culture and rector Ethical Culture Schools. Clubs: City, Town Hall. Home: 470 W. 24th St. Office: 2 W. 64th St., New York, N.Y. Died Apr. 12, 1942.

ELLIOTT, Lewis Grimes, pres. La Salle Extension Univ.; b. Platte County, Mo., Nov. 28, 1872; s. Alexander K. and Mollie (Grimes) E.; ed. pub. schs., Liberty, Mo.; m. Martha Keller, Oct. 20, 1897; children—Theodore Keeton, Virginia Lee (Mrs. Pope Lancaster), Alexander Keller. Employed in banking and publishing business until 1904; treas. DeBower-Elliott Co. publishers, Chicago, 1904-11; pres. Elliott-Madison Co., subscription books, 1911-16; organizer and pres. Lakeland (Fla.) Highlands Coop. Assn., 1913-18; co-founder La Salle Extension Univ., 1908, treas. 1916-37, pres. since 1937; pres. Stenotype Co., dir. Central Nat. Bank in Chicago; pres. Nat. Home Study Council (Washington, D.C.). Mem. exec. com. and recording sec. Ill. State Assn. of Y.M.C.A., 1912-24; pres. Bd. of Edn., La Grange, 1917-21. Democrat. Presbyterian. Clubs: La Grange Country (pres. 1914-15), La Grange, Civic, Union League (Chicago); The Chicago Federated Advertising Club, Ill. Seniors Golf Assn. Home: 101 S. Spring Av., La Grange, Ill. Office: 4101 S. Michigan Av., Chicago 5. Ill. Died Oct. 22, 1946.

ELLIOTT, Maud Howe, author; b. Boston, Nov. 9, 1854; d. of Dr. Samuel Gridley and Julia (Ward) Howe; pvt. edn. in America and Europe; m. John Elliott, Feb. 7, 1887. Has lectured, Chicago, Boston, Newport; v.p. Newport County Woman's Republican Club; sec. Art Assn. of Newport. Author: A Newport Aquarelle; The San Rosario Ranch; Atalanta in the South; Mammon; Phyllida; Laura Bridgman (with Florence M. Hall), 1903; Roma Beata, 1904; Two in Italy, 1905; Sun and Shadow in Spain, 1908; Sicily in Shadow and in Sun, 1910; The Eleventh Hour in the Life of Julia Ward Howe, 1911; Life and Letters of Julia Ward Howe (with Laura E. Richards), 1915; Three Generations, 1923; Lord Byron's Helmet, 1927; John Elliott, The Story of An Artist, 1930; My Cousin, F. Marion Crawford, 1934; Uncle Sam Ward and His Circle, 1938; Recollections of the Civil War, 1943; This Was My Newport, 1944; What I Saw and Heard in Panama, 1947. In 1917, awarded, with Laura E. Richards, the Joseph Pulitze rize, Columbia University, for The Life of Julia Ward Howe. Decorated Golden Cross of the Redeemer (Greek); Queen Mary's Needlework Guild (British). Mem. exec. com. N.E. Italian War Relief Fund; mem. R.I. Food Conservation Com., 1917; mem. Miantonomi Memorial Park Commn.; hon. pres. Soc. of the Four Arts (Palm Beach, Fla.). Clubs: Chilton (Boston), Cosmopolitan. Citation from U.S. Treasury Dept. in recognition of service as chmn. Newport Book and Author Rally, 7th War Loan, 1945. Home: Lilliput, Lovers Lane, Newport, R.I. Died March 19, 1948.

ELLIOTT, Richard Nash, asst. comptroller gen.; b. Fayette County, Ind., Apr. 25, 1873; ed. pub. schs.; studied law in offices of Connor & McIntosh, Connersville, Ind.; m. Lizzie A. Ostheimer, Jan. 20, 1898. Admitted to Ind. bar, 1896, and since practiced at Connersville. Mem. Ind. Ho. of Rep., 2 terms, 1905-09; elected to 65th Congress, 6th Ind. Dist., June 26, 1917, for unexpired term of Daniel W. Comstock; reëlected 66th to 71st Congresses (1919-31); asst. comptroller gen. of U.S., 1931-36, now acting comptroller gen. Republican. Home: Connersville, Ind.; and 110 Maryland Av. N.E., Washington, D.C. Address: 5th and F Sts., Washington, D.C.* Died Mar. 21, 1948.

ELLIOTT, Robert Irving, educator; b. Worth, Cook County, Ill., Apr. 18, 1883; s. John and Marion Elizabeth (Tobey) E.; grad. Wayne (Neb.) Normal Coll., 1901; A.B., U. of Neb., 1914; M.A., Columbia University, 1928; m. Annie L. Babcock, Nov. 27, 1913; 1 son, Robert Irving. Teacher rural sch., Neb., 1901-03; supt. schs., Pilger, Neb., 1903-05; county supt. schs., Wayne County, Nebraska, 1905-06; supt. schs., Chadron, 1908-09, Broken Bow, 1909-12; dep. state supt. instruction, Neb., 1912-15; head dept. of mathematics, Neb. Teachers' Coll., Kearney, Neb.; 1915-16; pres. Neb. State Teachers Coll., Chadron, 1916-40, emeritus since Apr. 1, 1940. Consultant Ednl. Policies Commn. Mem. N.E.A., Neb. State Teachers' Assn., Delta Sigma Rho, Phi Alpha Tau, Phi Gamma Delta, Kappa Delta Pi, Acacia. Republican. Conglist. Mason (32°). Rotarian. Home: 511 Main St., Chadron, Neb. Died Sep. 26, 1944.

ELLIOTT, Thompson Coit, investment banking; b. Barkhamstead, Conn., Sept. 10, 1862; s. John Euclid and Mary Ann (Thompson) E.; A.B., Amherst Coll., 1885, Litt.D., 1930; hon. A.M., U. of Ore., 1919; m. Anna Baker, Sept. 18, 1890; children—Mary Elizabeth, Romie Josephine, Dorothy Amelia, Dorsey John, Thompson Baker, Anna-Louise, Barbara Coit (Mrs. David L. Davies). Title examiner Central Loan and Land Co., Emporia, Kan., 1885-86; land examiner and cashier Washington Loan and Trust Co., Walla Walla, 1886-98; mng. mem. Elliott & Co., Walla Walla, investment securities since 1900. Treas. Whitman Coll., 1895-1900; dir. Walla Walla Pub. Library, 1895-1925, pres., 1925-40. Fellow Royal Hist. Soc.; hon. mem. British Columbia Hist. Soc.; mem. Wash. State Hist. Soc. (dir.), Ore. Hist. Soc. (dir.), Am. Hist. Assn., New England Soc. of City of N.Y., Beta Theta Pi, Phi Beta Kappa (hon.). Republican. Conglist. Clubs: University (Portland, Ore., and Seattle, Wash.). Author of many brochures on the history of Pacific Northwest; contbr. to hist. jours. Home: 314 E. Poplar St. Office: 17 N. 2d Av., Walla Walla, Wash. Died May 5, 1943.

ELLIOTT, William, lawyer; b. Beaufort, S.C., Mar. 30, 1872; s. William and Sallie (Stuart) E.; prep. edn., Episcopal High Sch., Alexandria, Va.; U. of Va., 1893; m. Leila G. Sams, Nov. 15, 1900; children—William, Leila E. (Mrs. Albert L. Wardlaw), Margaret S. (Mrs. John A. Manning). Admitted to S.C. bar, 1893, and began practice at Beaufort; moved to Columbia, S.C., 1900; mem. Elliott, McLain, Wardlaw & Elliott; dir. Union-Buffalo Mills Co., Santee Mills, Nuckasee Mfg. Co., Union Mfg. & Power Co., Buffalo-Union Carolina R.R., Citizens and Southern Nat. Bank of S.C.; former receiver Peoples State Bank of S.C.; pres. The State Co. and pub. The State (newspaper). Lt. j.g., U.S. Navy, Spanish-Am. War; state food adminstr., S.C., World War. Code Commr. S.C., 1903-11; former mem. S.C. State Port Commn.; mem. Nat. Council Boy Scouts of America for many years. Mem. S.C. Bar Assn., Delta Psi. Democrat. Episcopalian. Mason. Club: Kosmos. Editor of Acts of Gen. Assembly of South Carolina, 1903-10. Home: 1819 Pendleton St. Office: Liberty Life Bldg., Columbia, S.C. Died Apr. 7, 1943.

ELLIS, A(lexander) Caswell, univ. prof.; b. Franklin County, N.C., May 4, 1871; s. Dr. Orren Littleberry and Mary Louisa (McKnight) E.; A.B., U. of N.C., 1894; Harvard, summer of 1894; Ph.D., Clark U., 1897; U. of Berlin, 1905; m. Mary Heard, July 30, 1901. Adj. prof. pedagogy, 1897-1903, asso. prof. science and art of edn., 1903-08, prof. philosophy of edn., 1908-26, dir. dept. of extension, 1911-13, 1914-16, U. of Tex.; dir. of Cleveland Coll. of Western Reserve University, 1926-41, director emeritus since 1941; consultant on adult edn., U. of Tex., since 1942. Member board visitors United States Naval Academy, 1903-04. Fellow A.A.A.S., Texas Acad. Science; pres. Assn. Deans and Directors Univ. Evening Colleges, 1940, 1941; mem. Southern Edn. Assn. (council), Soc. Scientific Study of Edn., N.E.A., Am. Assn. Coll. Teachers of Edn., So. Soc. for Philosophy and Psychology, American Assn. Adult Education (council, and exec. com.), Am. Council on Education, Kappa Alpha, Phi Beta Kappa. Democrat. Author of monographs and mag. articles concerning investigations in child psychology, ednl. adminstrn., and adult edn. Joint Author: Fundamentals of Farming and Farm Life (with E. J. Kyle), 1912. Home: 904 A West 22½, Austin, Tex. Died Oct. 9, 1948.

ELLIS, Anderson Nelson, author, physician; b. Ellis Landing, Adams County, O., Dec. 19, 1840; s. Washington and Aris (Parker) E.; B.S., Miami U., 1864, hon. A.M., 1886); M.D., Berkshire Med. Coll., Pittsfield, Mass., 1867; M.D., Ohio Med. Coll., 1868; post-grad. work Vienna, London and Heidelberg, m. Laura Caroline Murphy, Dec. 30, 1891; 1 son, William Nelson. Clin. asst., London Central Throat and Ear Hosp., 1880; asst. phys., Longview Insane Asylum, Cincinnati, O., 1881; prof. larnygology, Cincinnati Coll. Phys. and Surg., 1882-90. Served as 2d lt. and capt. U.S.V., 1862-63; med. officer, U.S.A., in Kan., N.M., and Colo., 1871-75; maj. and surgeon, 1st Regt. Ohio N.G., 1888-89; examiner of pensions since 1899, Mem. Soc. Army of the Cumberland, G.A.R. (med. dir., rank of col., Dept. of Ky.). Republican. Presbyterian. Author: Land of the Aztec, 1874; Life of Maj. General William Nelson, 1886; Rambles Through Italy, 1887; Influence of the Trade Winds on the Health of the World, 1888. Home: Maysville, Ky. Died Jan. 25, 1927.

ELLIS, Challen Blackburn, lawyer; b. Covington, Ky., Nov. 20, 1876; s. Alexander Campbell and Kate (Blackburn) E.; A.B., U. of Cincinnati, 1898; LL.B., Harvard, 1900; unmarried. Admitted to Ohio bar, 1900, and began practice at Cincinnati; moved to Washington, D.C., 1912; mem. Ellis, Houghton & Ellis. Mem. Beta Theta Pi. Republican. Mem. Christian (Disciples) Ch. Clubs: Metropolitan, University. Co-author and editor: Ellis' Ohio Municipal Code, 1908. Co-author: Fed. Securities Act Manual, 1933. Home: 1026 16th St. N.W. Office: Southern Bldg., Washington, D.C. Died Jan. 31, 1948.

ELLIS, Charles Alton, educator; born Parkman, Me., June 23, 1876; s. David B. and Eliza Wharff (Lombard) E.; A.B., Wesleyan U., 1900; C.E., U. of Ill., 1922; m. Elsie Louise Ney, Sept. 29, 1913. Draftsman, checker, squad foreman, Am. Bridge Co., 1902-08; asst. prof. civil engring., U. of Mich., 1908-12; designing engr., Dominion Bridge Co., 1912-14; asst. prof. civil engring., U. of Ill., 1914-15, prof. structural engring., 1915-21; v.p. Strauss Engring. Corp., 1921-32; cons. engr., private practice, 1932-34; prof. and head of div. (structural engring., Purdue U., 1934-46; prof. emeritus since 1946; lecturer in Civil engring., Northwestern Tech. Inst., since 1946; designer (with P. L. Pratley), Montreal Harbor Bridge; designing engineer, Golden Gate Suspension Span. Member Am. Soc. C.E. (life), Am. Ry. Engr. Assn., Am. Concrete Inst., Soc. Promotion Engring. Edn., Sigma Xi, Tau Beta Pi, Chi Epsilon, Delta Kappa Epsilon, Triangle. Contbr. articles on engring. to jours. Home: 638 Garrett Place, Evanston, Ill. Died Aug. 22, 1949.

ELLIS, Edgar Clarence, ex-congressman; b. Vermontville, Mich., Oct. 2, 1854; s. Elmer Eugene and Jane Maria (Halstead) E.; A.B., Carleton Coll., 1881; m. Emily Hatch Roy, July 20, 1882 (died Oct. 31, 1931); children—Joseph Roy, Ralph Edgar, Frank Hale; m. 2d, Katherine M. Morgan, Nov. 5, 1936. Admitted to bar, 1885; moved to Kansas City, Mo., 1888; now mem. Gossett, Ellis, Dietrich & Tyler. Mem. 59th and 60th (1905-09), 67th 1921-23), 69th (1925-27), and 71st (1929-31), Congresses, 5th Mo. Dist. Republican. Conglist. Home: (winter) 737 2d Av. N., St. Petersburg, Fla. Office: Dwight Bldg., Kansas City, Mo. Died Mar. 15, 1947.

ELLIS, Griffith Ogden, publisher; b. Urbana, O., Nov. 19, 1869; s. Griffith and Jane Hoge (Woods) E.; ed. Urbana U., 1888-90; Columbian U., Washington, D.C., 1890-91; LL.B., U. of Mich., 1893; m. Ellen Winifred Scripps, Apr. 21, 1897. In govt. service at Washington, 1890-91; became connected with the Sprague Pub. Co., Detroit, 1891, pres. 1908-39; pres. William A. Scripps Co.; editor American Boy, pub. by Sprague Pub. Co., 1908-40. Participated in orgn. of Boy Scouts of America, 1910; serving on National Council since 1910; awarded Silver Buffalo, 1931; vice president, Bank of Detroit, 1921-30; dir. Guardian-Detroit Bank, 1930-33. Pres. Detroit Street Ry. Commn., 1920-30, which municipalized Detroit's System. Trustee Detroit Mus. of Art, Cranbrook Sch. for Boys (Bloomfield Hills, Mich., 1924-45). Mem. Detroit Bd. of Commerce, Fine Arts Soc., Beta Theta Pi. Republican. Episcopalian. Mason (32°). Clubs: Detroit, Detroit Boat, Country, Old Club. Home: 2535 Iroquois Av., Detroit 14, Mich. Died Feb. 4, 1948.

ELLIS, (Harold) Milton, prof. English; b. Belfast, Me., Aug. 2, 1885; s. Gilbert Randall and Ida Melissa (Rowe) E.; B.A., U. of Maine, 1907, M.A., 1908; A.M., Harvard University, 1909, Ph.D., 1913; married Carrie Voadicia White, August 5, 1914; children—Gilbert Milton, Ernest Randall, George Hathaway; married 2d, Leola B. Chaplin, June 6, 1942. Instructor English, Muhlenberg College, 1909-11, U. of Tex., 1913-17; prof. English, Trinity Coll., N.C., 1917-19, U. of N.C., summer 1919, U. of Chicago, summer 1928, U. of Mich., summer 1930, Harvard, summer 1932, Duke, summer 1940; head dept. of English, U. of Maine, since 1919, also dir. summer session, 1925-30. Mem. Modern Lang. Assn. America (chmn. Am. Lit. sect. 1942), Am. Assn. Univ. Profs., College English Assn. (dir. since 1942), Colonial Soc. of Massachusetts, Maine Historical Society (standing com.), Phi Eta Kappa, Phi Beta Kappa, Phi Kappa Phi (president University of Maine Chapter). Democrat. Unitarian. Author: Joseph Dennie and His Circle, 1915; "Philenia"—The Life and Works of Sarah Wentworth Morton (with Emily Pendleton), 1931; The College Book of American Literature (with Louise Pound and G. W. Spohn), 1939. Editor: The Power of Sympathy (Facsimile Text Soc. 1937); The Lay Preacher Essays of Joseph Dennie, Scholars' facsimiles and Reprints, 1943. Mem. editorial bd. N.E. Quarterly since 1932, mng. editor, 1938-1944. Contbr. to geneal. and scholarly publs. Home: Orono, Me. Died May 18, 1947.

ELLIS, Samuel Meryl, newspaper man; b. Cerro Gordo, Ill., June 19, 1889; s. Joshua Green and Rose (Brown) E.; grad. Northwestern Mil. Acad., Highland Park, Ill., 1910; m. Helen Cole, Oct. 6, 1912; 1 dau., Barbara Miriam. Began as reporter Decatur (Ill.) Herald, 1910; held reportorial, desk or exec. positions on Ill. State Journal and Ill. State Register (Springfield), Quincy (Ill.) Whig, Cedar Rapids (Ia.) Republican, Mobile (Ala.) Register, Jacksonville (Fla.) Journal, Tallahassee (Fla.) Democrat, Pensacola (Fla.) News and Journal. Contbr. to mags. Editor of Florida Highways magazine since 1940. Democrat. Methodist. Elk. Address: Winter Garden, Fla. Died Apr. 27, 1944.

ELLIS, Wade H., lawyer; b. Covington, Ky., Dec. 31, 1866; s. A. C. and Kate (Blackburn) E.; ed. Hughes High Sch. and Chickering Inst., Cincinnati; LL.B., Washington and Lee U., 1889; LL.D., Miami U., 1904, Washington and Lee, 1909; Litt.D., Lincoln Memorial U., 1923; m. Dessie Corwin Chase, Oct. 3, 1894. Admitted to bar, 1890; editor Cincinnati Tribune and later of Commercial Tribune, 1895-97; asst. corp. counsel, Cincinnati, 1897-1903; atty. gen. Ohio, 1904-08; asst. to atty. gen. of U.S., Nov. 6, 1908-Feb. 1910; now practicing law in Washington, D.C. Mem. Archeol. Soc. of Washington (pres.), Phi Beta Kappa (pres.), S.A.R. (pres.). Clubs: Metropolitan, University, Chevy Chase, Racquet, Congressional Country, City (Washington); Queen City (Cincinnati); Lawyers, Union League, Grolier (New

York). Author: Ellis' Annotated Ohio Municipal Code; lectures on law of pvt. corp., etc. Home: 1440 Massachusetts Av. N.W., Washington, D.C.; (country) "Rippon Lodge," Woodbridge, Prince William County, Va. Office: Southern Bldg., Washington, D.C. Died July 4, 1948.

ELLIS, Willard Drake, banker; b. Ogden, Utah, Apr. 8, 1887; s. John Gregory and Rose Amelia (Drake) E.; ed. pub. schs. and high sch., Ogden, Utah; m. Louise Woodbury, Sept. 6, 1923; children—Willard Eldan, Rosemary, Frank Woods, Gordon Woodbury, Ann Louise. With John Scowcroft & Sons Co., Ogden, Utah, 1902-06; sec. New Zealand Mission, 1906-09; with Pingree Nat. Bank, 1909-17; with Federal Land Bank of Berkeley, Calif., since 1917, pres. and chmn. bd., 1920-34 and since 1943; with Federal Intermediate Credit Bank of Berkeley since 1923, pres. and chmn. bd. since 1923; chmn. bd. Berkeley Bank of Cooperatives, Production Credit Corp. (Berkeley). Gen. agent Farm Credit Adminstrn. Democrat. Clubs: Claremont Country (Oakland); Commonwealth (San Francisco). Home: 825 Contra Costa Av., Berkeley 7. Office: Center and Milvia Sts., Berkeley 4, Calif. Died Aug. 1, 1947.

ELLIS, William Hull, judge; b. Pensacola, Fla., Sept. 17, 1867; s. Charles H. and Julia F. (Wilson) E.; LL.D., John B. Stetson U., Deland, Fla., 1937; m. M. Ramelle Nicholson, June 1894 (died Dec. 25, 1902); m. 2d, Ena H. Taylor, Apr. 1906. Admitted to bar, 1889; mem. Ellis & Love, 1897-1901; Dem. presdl. elector, 1900; state auditor of Fla., 1903; apptd. atty. gen. of Fla., Feb. 1904, and elected for term 1905-09; mem. Ellis & Watson, 1910; gen. counsel Trustees Internal Improvement Fund of Fla., 1911-15; justice Supreme Court of Fla., term 1915-21; renominated without opposition, 1920, 27 and 33, and reelected; retired Nov. 1, 1938. Mem. State Bar Assn. (pres. 1919), U. of Fla. Endowment Corp. (bd. govs., 1935), Phi Alpha Delta (hon. mem.), Pi Gamma Mu. Episcopalian. Mason; K. of P. (mem. Supreme Tribunal, 1906-13). Home: Tallahassee, Fla. Died Apr. 14, 1948.

ELLIS, William John; b. Muncy, Pa., Nov. 18, 1892; s. Rev. John R. and Annie (Thomas) E.; A.B., Hobart Coll., 1914, M.A., 1914, LL.D., 1929; grad. study, Columbia, 1914-17; Ph.D., Rutgers, 1928; m. Marie Law, June 27, 1917; children—Janet Lee, Mary Ellen, John. Teacher, Morse Sch., Englewood, N.J., 1914-17; asst. in classification work, Dept. Instns. and Agencies, N.J., 1919-21, dir. div. of classification and edn., 1921, commr. of dept. since 1926; sec. N.J. Social Security Commn. and of N.J. Crime Commn.; mem. N.J. Police Radio. Served as lieut. Sanitary Corps, U.S. Army, 1917-19. Member President's White House Conf. (chmn. com. on physically and mentally handicapped), 1928-29; mem. N.J. State Rehabilitation Commn.; United States delegate Am. Prison Congress, Prague, 1929; N.J. del. to First Internat. Conf. on Mental Hygiene; mem. advisory council N.J. tSate Emergency Relief Adminstrn.; mem. Advisory Com. on Prisons, Probation and Parole (of which Dr. Hastings H. Hart was chmn.), apptd. by the Wickersham Com. on Law Enforcement and Observance; mem. N.J. Juvenile Delinquency Commn.; past pres. N.J. Hosp. Assn., N.J. Conf. of Social Work; mem. N.J. Commn. on Inter-state Coöperation; chmn. Interstate Commn. on Social Security of State Govts.; mem. bd. The Osborne Assn.; chmn. Nat. Com. to Survey Juvenile Instns.; pres. N.J. Tuberculosis League; chmn. com. on preparation for parole, Nat. Parole Conf. called by President Roosevelt and Atty. Gen. Frank Murphy, April 1939; mem. N.J. Unemployment Relief Commn., 1939; rep. of N.J. White House Conf. on Children, 1939; mem. exec. com. Nat. Com. on Mental Hygiene; mem. N.J. Defense Council (chmn. Com. Health, Welfare and Recreation); chmn. Community War Services Div., State Defense Adminstrn.; mem. N.J. Postwar Economic Planning Commission. Trustee Hobart College. Trustee (life) Rutgers University (life), Vineland Training School. Honorary fellow Am. Coll. Hosp. Adminstrs.; fellow Am. Assn. on Mental Deficiency; mem. American Public Welfare Assn. (past pres.), Am. Prison Congress (past pres.), Nat. Conf. for Social Work, Am. Legion, Phi Beta Kappa. Presbyterian. Kiwanian. Author of many articles and reports on crime, pub. welfare, institutional management. Home: Station A, Trenton. Office: State Office Bldg., Trenton, N.J. Died Mar. 11, 1945.

ELLISTON, George (Miss), author; b. Mt. Sterling, Ky.; d. Joseph Lillard and Ida (Givens) Elliston; ed. high sch., Covington, Ky., and under pvt. tutors; m. Augustus T. Coleman, Jan. 2, 1907 (died 1935). Staff writer with the Cincinnati Times-Star; editor Gypsy Poetry Mag., 1925-39. Mem. League of Am. Pen Women, Ohio Newspaper Women's Assn., Cincinnati MacDowell Soc., Daughters of Am. Revolution; hon. mem. New England Women and Woman's Art Club. Author: Every Day Poems, 1921; Changing Moods, 1922; Through Many Windows, 1924; Bright World, 1927; Cinderella Cargoes, 1929; also spl. articles in magazines and newspapers, and many song-texts; syndicates daily poem series under title of "Every Day Poems," with Associated Newspapers. Won, with Ilse Huebner, Oesterreichische Music Pad Reichaverband Award, Vienna. Home: "Catalpa Cabin," Morrow, Ohio; also 340 W. 4th St., Cincinnati, O. Address: The Times-Star, Cincinnati, Ohio. Deceased.

ELLWOOD, Charles Abram, sociologist; b. nr. Ogdensburg, N.Y., Jan. 20, 1873; s. Gibson and Maria (Walrath) E.; Ph.B., Cornell U., 1896; student U. of Chicago, 1896-97, U. of Berlin, 1897-98, U. of London, 1915; fellow in sociology, U. of Chicago, 1898-99; Ph.D., from same, 1899; LL.D., Bethany Coll., 1922; m. Ida M. Breckenridge, June 30, 1897; 1 son, Walter Breckenridge. Sec. Charity Organization Soc., Lincoln, Neb., 1899-1900; lecturer and later instr. in sociology, U. of Neb., 1899-1900; prof. sociology, U. of Mo., 1900-30; prof. of sociology, Duke University, 1930-44. Visiting prof. of sociology, summer terms, Columbia, 1913, U. of Chicago, 1916, 20, U. of Colo., 1911, 15, 17, 21, 22, 24, U. of Southern Calif., 1923, 26, Nat. Summer Sch., Logan, Utah, 1925, Colorado Agrl. Coll., 1927, U. of Wis., 1928, Harvard, 1934, Northwestern, 1936, U. of Calif. at Los Angeles, 1939. Lecturer Yale Div. Sch., 1922. Cole lecturer, Vanderbilt, 1929. Chmn. social psychology, Internat. Congress Arts and Sciences, St. Louis, 1904; pres. Mo. Conf. Charities, 1904. Fellow A.A.A.S.; mem. American Sociological Soc. (pres. 1924); corr. mem. Deutsche Gesellschaft für Soziologie; hon. mem. Masaryk Sociological Society (Czechoslovakia), Société de Sociologie de Genève; nat. pres. Pi Gamma Mu, 1931-37; pres. Internat. Congress Sociology, Brussels, 1935; pres. Internat. Inst. Sociology, 1935-36. Scottish Rite Mason (32°). Club: University. Author: Public Relief and Private Charity in England, 1904; Sociology and Modern Social Problems, 1910, revised edit. titled, Sociology: Principles and Problems, 1943 (Chinese translation, 1923); Sociology in Its Psychological Aspects, 1912 (French transl. 1914); The Social Problem, 1915, 1919 (Japanese translation 1917, Chinese translation 1923, German translation 1925); An Introduction to Social Psychology, 1917 (Japanese transl. 1922, Chinese transl., 1923); The Reconstruction of Religion—A Sociological View, 1922 (German transl., 1924, Japanese transl., 1926); Christianity and Social Science, 1923 (Japanese transl., 1926); The Psychology of Human Society, 1925 (German transl., 1927); Cultural Evolution: A Study of Social Origins and Development, 1927; Man's Social Destiny in the Light of Science, 1929; Methods in Sociology—A Critical Study, 1933; A History of Social Philosophy, 1938 (Spanish translation, 1939); The World's Need of Christ, 1940. Contbr. of more than 100 articles to Ency. Americana, Am. Jour. Sociology, and other scientific periodicals. Address: 129 Pinecrest Rd., Durham, N.C. Died Sep. 25,1946.

ELMQUIST, Axel Louis (ĕlm'kwĭst), coll. prof.; b. Parker's Prairie, Minn., Feb. 3, 1884; s. Peter John and Ida Charlotta (Johansson) E.; grad. Acad. of Northwestern U., Evanston, Ill., 1901; A.B., Northwestern U., 1904, A.M., 1905; studied univs. of Leipzig, Germany, Upsala, Sweden, and Copenhagen, Denmark; m. Minna Louise Harter, June 15, 1907 (dec.); 1 son, Karl Erik. Instr. Greek and Latin, Northwestern U., 1906-08, instr. Scandinavian langs., 1909-11, asst. prof. Scandinavian langs., 1911-15, asst. prof. Germanic langs., 1915-20; instr. Germanic langs., U. of Nebraska, 1936-39, asst. prof. Germanic languages since 1940. Lecturer general phonetics, Garrett Bibl. Inst. and other instrns. Asso. editor Scandinavian Studies and Notes, 1915-19, 1938-46. Mem. Soc. Advancement Scandinavian Study, Augustana Inst. of Swedish Culture, Phi Beta Kappa. Republican. Author: An Elementary Swedish Grammar, 1914; Swedish Phonology, 1915. Editor: Selma Lagerlöf's En Herrgårdssägen, 1910; Helena Nyblom's Det Ringer, 1910; Selections from Selma Lagerlöf's Nils Holgersson, 1912; Runeberg's Fänrik Ståls sägner, 1915, rev. edit., 1936; Swedish Reader, 1917. Gen. editor Bonnier's College Series of Swedish Textbooks (Albert Bonniers förlag, Stockholm). Contbr. to philol. jours. America and Europe. Co-editor: Scandinavian Studies. Address: University of Nebraska, Lincoln 8, Neb. Died Oct. 13, 1949.

ELLSLER, Effie (Mrs. Frank Weston), actress; b. Phila., 1858; m. Frank Weston. Appeared at Madison Sq. Theatre, New York, then to Union Sq. Co.; was original Hazel Kirke in play of that name, and of many other stage heroines; has played leading parts in her own co. since 1886. Died Oct. 8, 1942.

ELSBERG, Charles Albert, retired; b. N.Y. City, Aug. 24, 1871; s. Albert and Rebecca (Moses) E.; A.B., Coll. City of New York, 1890; M.D., Coll. of Physicians and Surgeons (Columbia), 1893. Practiced at N.Y. City since 1893; prof. emeritus neurol. surgery, Coll. Physicians and Sur.; surgeon-in-chief emeritus N.Y. Neurol. Institute; cons. surgeon Mt. Sinai Hospital. Fellow Am. Coll. Surgeons; mem. A.A.A.S., N.Y. County Med. Soc., Acad. Medicine, N.Y. Surg. Soc., Soc. Neurol. Surgeons, Am. Neurol. Assn., New York Neurol. Soc., Assn. for Research in Nervous and Mental Diseases, New York Pathol. Soc. Home: Long Ridge Road, Stamford, Conn. Died March 18, 1948.

ELSON, Alfred Walter, art pub.; b. Boston, Mass., 1859; s. Julius and Rosalie (Schnell) E.; ed. English and Roxbury high schs.; m. Maud Spooner, Dec. 16, 1886. Began in art printing business, 1888; pres. and treas. Elson Co., Inc., pubs. of pictures for schoolroom decoration, also ednl. art books. Home: 527 Concord Av. Office: Locust St., Belmont, Mass.* Died 1944.

ELTING, Arthur Wells, surgeon; b. S. Cairo, N.Y., Oct. 6, 1872; s. Francis and Margaret M. (Snyder) E.; A.B., Yale, 1894; M.D., Johns Hopkins, 1898; on staff, Johns Hopkins Hosp., 1898-99; (LL.D., St. Lawrence Univ., 1916); m. Mary B. Lord, Sept. 5, 1900; m. 2d, Harriet Corning Rawle, October 24, 1917. Practiced, Albany, N.Y., since 1900. Became prof. of surgery, Albany Medical Coll., May 1911. Lt. col. Med. Corps, U.S. Army, active service in France, 1918. Fellow American Surgical Association (president); chmn. of Am. Board of Surgery; mem. A.M.A., Clin. Surg. Soc., Interurban Surg. Soc., Albany County and N.Y. State med. socs., Eclat Soc., Phi Beta Kappa. Republican. Home: 119 Washington Av., Albany, N.Y. Died Jan. 2, 1948.

ELTON, John Prince, mfr.; b. Waterbury, Conn., June 30, 1865; s. James Samuel and Charlotte Augusta (Steele) E.; B.S., Trinity Coll., Conn., 1888; m. Deborah Steele, July 9, 1902; children—Deborah R., Charlotte. Entered mfg. business, 1888; pres. Dime Savings Bank, Waterbury, later chmn. bd., and now dir. Waterbury Savings Bank into which it is merged; pres. Blake & Johnson Co.; v.p. Colonial Trust Co.; dir. Landers, Frary & Clark (New Britain, Conn.), Scovill Mfg. Co. (Waterbury, Conn.), and various other companies. Mayor of Waterbury, 1904-06. Mem. War Industries Board, Washington, 1917-18. Pres. Park Bd., Waterbury, Conn. Pres. board of trustees Westover Sch. (Middlebury, Conn.); trust and chmn. board Trinity Coll. (Hartford, Conn.), Hotchkiss School. Member Delta Psi. Republican. Episcopalian (sr. warden St. John's Parish). Clubs: Waterbury (Conn.); University, St. Anthony, New York Yacht (New York); Graduate (New Haven). Home: Waterbury, Conn. Died March 8, 1948.

ELVINS, Politte, lawyer, ex-congressman; b. at French Village, Mo., Mar. 16, 1878; s. Jesse Mahagan and Zelma (Politte) E.; A.B., Carleton College, 1897; LL.B., Univ. of Mo., 1899, U. of Sorbonne, Paris, 1924; m. Florence Kells, Nov. 25, 1901; 1 son, Kells Elvins. Has been in practice of law since 1899. Mem. 61st Congress (1909-11), 13th Mo. Dist.; ex-chmn. Rep. State Com. of Mo.; mem. and chmn. com. on rules and order of business, Mo. Constl. Conv., 1922-23; mem. Mo. legislature, 1929-30. Grower of citrus fruit in Texas. Life mem. Sigma Alpha Epsilon. Home: Price Rd., St. Louis County; and Jackson Road, Pharr, Tex. Died Jan. 14, 1943.

ELY, Richard Theodore, economist; b. Ripley, N.Y., Apr. 13, 1854; s. Ezra Sterling and Harriet G. E.; A.B., Columbia, 1876, A.M., 1879; Ph.D., U. of Heidelberg, 1879; LL.D., Hobart Coll., 1892, U. of Wis., 1923, Columbia, 1929; fellow in Letters, Columbia U., 1876-79; student univs. of Halle, Heidelberg, Geneva and at Royal Statis. Bur., Berlin, 1877-80; m. Anna Morris Anderson, June 25, 1884 (died Mar. 13, 1923); children—Richard S., Josephine Anderson (dec.), John T. A., Mrs. Anna Ely Morehouse; m. 2d, Margaret Hahn, 1931; children—William Brewster, Mary Charlotte. Professor polit. economy, Johns Hopkins U., 1881-92; head of dept. polit. economy, U. of Wis., 1892-1925, hon. prof. economics since 1925; prof. economics, Northwestern U., 1925-33; pres. Inst. for Econ. Research and School of Land Economics, hon. asso. in economics, Columbia U., since 1937. Mem. Baltimore Tax Commn., 1885-86, Maryland Tax Commn., 1886-88. Mem. President's Conf. on Home Building and Home Ownership, 1931-32. Lecturer on political economy, U. of London, 1913. One of founders, sec., 1885-92, pres., 1899-1901, Am. Econ. Assn.; 1st pres. Am. Assn. for Labor Legislation, 1907-08; founder, dir. and pres. Inst. for Economic Research, Inc. (formerly Inst. for Research in Land Economics and Pub. Utilities). Mem. Internat. Statis. Institute. Clubs: Pilgrims, Town Hall. Author: French and German Socialism in Modern Times, 1883; Taxation in American States and Cities, 1888; Introduction to Political Economy, 1889; Outlines of Economics (with Prof. Ralph H. Hess); 6th edition, 1937; Monopolies and Trusts, 1900; Studies in the Evolution of Industrial Society, 1903; Property and Contract in their Relation to the Distribution of Wealth, 2 vols., 1914; Elementary Economics (with Prof. G. R. Wicker), 1904, 17, new edition in collaboration with Dr. S. J. Brandenburg, 1923; Foundations of National Prosperity (in collaboration), 1917; Elements of Land Economics (with E. W. Morehouse), 1926; Hard Times—The Way in and the Way Out, 1931; The Great Change (with Dr. Frank Bohn), 1935; Ground Under Out Feet, 1938; Land Economics (with George S. Wehrwein), 1940; also articles in various periodicals; editor, Macmillan's Citizen's Library of Economics, Politics and Socialogy, Macmillan's Social Science Text Book Series, Macmillan's Land Economics Series. Founder and editor of Journal of Land and Public Utility Economics. Home: R.F.D. 2, Old Lyme, Conn. Died Oct. 4, 1943.

ELY, Robert Erskine, educator; b. Binghamton, N.Y., Sept. 13, 1861; s. Richard and Sarah (Roseboom) E.; A.B., Amherst Coll., 1885; grad. Union Theol. Sem., New York, 1888; m. Rudolphine Scheffer, June 7, 1905; children—Robert S., Mia R., Rudolph S., Wilhelmina R. Pres. Prospect Union, Cambridge, 1891-1901; dir. League for Polit. Edn., New York, 1901-37, now dir. emeritus. Dir. Economic Club, New York. Clubs: Town Hall (New York); 20th Century (Boston). Home: 35 Overton Road, Scarsdale, N.Y. Office: Town Hall, 123 W. 43d St., New York. Died July 13, 1948.

EMERSON, Jay N(oble), merchant; b. Bloomdale, O., Nov. 24, 1879; s. Rufus A. and Ellen B. (Shirk) E.; ed. pub. schs. of Bloomdale, O.; m. Amelia M. Gerding, June 20, 1901; children Frances Willard, Robert R. Mercantile experience in father's store, Bloomdale, O., 1895 to 1905; part owner of the Burgan-Emerson store, Pullman, Wash., 1906-12; operator chain of ten general stores in northern Ida. and eastern Wash. since 1912; pres. Pullman Savings and

Loan Assn. since 1927; pres. Post War Employment Commn. since 1946. State chmn. Rep. State Central Com. since 1925. Dir. Wash. State Retailers Assn. Mem. Meth. Episcopal Ch. (trustee). Club: Kiwanis (gov. Pacific Northwest dist.; pres. Kiwanis Internat. 1947). Home: 1209 Maple. Office: Main St., Pullman, Wash. Died June 12, 1947.

EMERSON, Merton Leslie, engineer; b. Brockton, Mass., Aug. 11, 1882; s. Edwin Leslie and Lora Gertrude (Kingman) E.; student Thayer Acad., Braintree, Mass., 1900; S.B., Mass. Inst. Technology, 1904; m. Frances Elizabeth Dike, Oct. 25, 1906; children—Elizabeth Kingman (dec.), Merton Leslie (dec.), Mary Leslie (wife of Major Thos. B. Mechling, U.S.A.). Engineer with U.S. Geological Survey, 1903-04; engr. Boston Pneumatic Transit Co., 1904-06; mng. dir. The Housing Corp., 1920-21; operating mgr. Am. Pneumatic Service Co., 1906-16, v.p., 1916-27, pres., 1927-29; treas. The Lamson Co., 1916-18, pres., 1927-29; pres. Boston Pneumatic Transit Co., New York Pneumatic Service Co., Chicago Pneumatic Service Co., St. Louis Pneumatic Tube Co.; cons. engr. with Scovell Wellington & Co. and Unifed Engrs. & Constructors; dir. Arkwright Mut. Fire Ins. Co., Braintree Nat. Bank. Mem. Tech. Board of Rev., U.S. Fed. Adminstrn. Pub. Works; New England dir. NRA, 1935; consultant Nat. Resources Com., asst. dir. U.S. Drainage Basin Studies; tech. adviser Social Security Bd. Served as major, U.S. Army, chief of adminstrn., gas defense div., Chem. Warfare Service, 1918-19; Army Specialist Corps, 1942. Trustee Wentworth Inst., Boston, Thayer Acad., Thayerlands Sch.; term mem. Mass. Inst. Tech. Corp. Mem. Am. Soc. C.E., Am. Soc. Mil. Engrs., Am. Inst. Cons. Engrs., Soc. Advancement of Management, Am. Soc. Public Adminstrn., Am. Legion, Mil. Order World War, Tech. Alumni Council, Tau Beta Pi, Soc. Mayflower Descendants, Republican, Unitarian, Mason. Clubs: Engineers, Technology (New York); University (Boston); Cosmos, Army and Navy Country (Washington). Home: Braintree, Mass.; 218 S. Royal St., Alexandria, Va. Office: 75 Federal St., Boston, Mass. Died Feb. 1945.

EMERSON, Rollins Adams, geneticist; b. Pillar Point, Jefferson County, N.Y., May 5, 1873; s. Charles D. and Mary C. (Adams) E.; moved to Neb., 1880; B.Sc., U. of Neb., 1897, LL.D., 1917; Sc.D., Harvard, 1913; m. Harriet Hardin, May 23, 1898; children—Mrs. Thera Kahler, Sterling Howard, Eugene Hardin, Mrs. Myra Ryan. Horticulturist, office of expt. stas., U.S. Dept. Agr., Washington, D.C., 1897-98; asst. prof. and prof. horticulture, U. of Neb., 1899-1914; prof. plant breeding, Cornell U., 1914-42, and dean grad. school, 1925-30. Mem. A.A.A.S., Am. Soc. Naturalists, Am. Assn. Univ. Profs., Nat. Acad. Sciences, Am. Genetic Assn. Home: 501 Dryden Rd., Ithaca, N.Y. Died Dec. 8, 1947.

EMERY, Ambrose R., army officer; born Ind., July 26, 1883; B.S. in Elec. Engring., Ga. Sch. Tech., 1904; grad. Inf. Sch., Advanced Course, 1925, Command and Gen. Staff Sch., 1926, Army War Coll., 1932. Commd. 2d lt., Inf., U.S. Army, Apr. 1905, and advanced through the grades to brig. gen., Oct. 1941; retired Feb. 1944. Address: War Dept., Washington 25, D.C.*Died Nov. 28, 1945.

EMMERT, John Harley, chmn. The Pacific Lumber Co.; b. Hedgesville, W.Va., Aug. 31, 1858; s. John and Louise (Burkhart) E.; student pub. schs. of Washington County, Md., and Fort Scott, Kan.; m. Cynthia Finney, Dec. 6, 1883 (dec. 1932); children—Helen, Doris, Barbara (dec. 1927). Various positions railroad companies 1874-99; asst. to pres. Santa Fe, Prescott & Phoenix Ry., Prescott, Ariz., 1899-1905; auditor later trustee Murphy Family Trust, Detroit, Mich., 1905-35; pres. and dir. Murphy Ranch Co., Whittier, Calif., since 1929; v.p. and dir. Simon J. Murphy Co., Detroit, Mich., since 1915; v.p. and dir. Penobscot Iron Ore Co., Detroit, since 1933; chmn. The Pacific Lumber Co., San Francisco, Calif., since 1930. Republican. Clubs: Pacific Union (San Francisco); California (Los Angeles); Detroit, Boat (Detroit, Mich.). Home: 2619 Wilshire Boulevard, Los Angeles, California. Office: 100 Bush St., San Francisco, Calif. Died Nov. 19, 1943.

EMMETT, Daniel Decatur, minstrel and song writer; b. Mt. Vernon, O., 1815; ed. public schools Mt. Vernon, O. As a boy learned printer's trade; abandoned it to join the regular army; became mem. of Oscar Brown's Circus Co., 1835; in 1842 with Frank Brown, William Whitlock and Richard Phelam formed what was the 1st negro minstrel co.; 1st appearance at the old Chatham Theatre, New York, known as the Virginia Minstrels, and went from New York to Boston, and later to England; returned to U. S. in 1844; with Dan Bryant, 472 Broadway, New York, 1858-65, while mem. of Bryants Co., 1859, he wrote the famous song of "Dixie"; became independent mgr., 1865, returned to Mt. Vernon, O., 1878. Author: numerous songs, including Old Dan Tucker, Boatman's Dance, The Road to Richmond, and many old-time favorites. Address: Mount Vernon, O. Died June 29, 1904.

EMMONS, George Thorton, lt. U.S. navy; b. Md.; grad. U.S. Naval Acad., Oct. 15, 1874, ensign, July 17, 1875, master, Oct. 15, 1881, lt. (j.g.), March 3, 1883; lt., Nov. 1, 1887; on duty at World's Columbian Expn., 1892-93. Mem. Nat. Geog. Soc. Address: Navy Dept., Washington. Died June 11, 1945.

EMMONS, Grover Carlton, clergyman; b. Walnut Hill, Fla., Feb. 13, 1886; s. John Davidson and Martha Jane (Huggins) E.; student Ala. Poly. Inst., Auburn, 1903-05; A.B., U. of New Mexico, 1909; grad. student, Vanderbilt U., Nashville, Tenn., 1909-12; D.D., Asbury Coll., Wilmore, Ky., 1929; m. Helen Keith Boulware, Dec. 11, 1920; children—Mary Helen, Carlton Boulware, David Rucker. Entered ministry of M.E. Ch., South, 1912; pastor, Salem, Ark., 1912-13, San Marcial, N.M., 1913-14, Gallup, N.M., 1914-17; war work evangelist and sec. to Bishop Walter R. Lambuth, 1917-18; Y.M.C.A. sec. with A.E.F., France, 1918-19; sec. to Bishop Lambuth in Orient, 1919-20; pastor Santa Rosa, Calif., 1920-25, San Diego, Calif., 1925-27, Long Beach, Calif., 1927-28, Fresno, Calif., 1928-30; presiding elder Los Angeles Dist., 1930-34; sec. of home missions and hosps., Bd. Missions, M.E. Ch., South, 1934-40; sec. Pacific Annual Conf., M.E. Ch., South, 1928-39; sec. Southern Calif.-Ariz. Annual Conf., Methodist Church, 1939; editor, founder The Upper Room (religious quarterly) and coordinate exec. sec. of the Gen. Commission on Evangelism of the Methodist Church. Pres. bd. mngrs. Textile Industrial Institute, Spartanburg, South Carolina, 1935-41; mem. bd. of trustees Paine Coll., Augusta, Ga. Mem. bd. of trustees Miles Memorial Coll., Birmingham, 1935-43; mem. Glide Foundation, San Francisco; exec. sec. Week of Dedication, Meth. Ch., 1943-44; mem. Joint Commn. on Meth. Union, 1934-39; mem. Gen. Conf. M.E. Ch., South, 1930, 34, 38; mem. Meth. Uniting Conf., Kansas City, Apr. 1939; mem. 1st Gen. Conf. The Meth. Ch., Atlantic City, 1940. Mem. Pi Kappa Alpha. Mason (K.T., 32°, Shriner). Contbr. articles to jours. Home: Enquirer Av. Office: Medical Arts Bldg., Nashville, Tenn. Died Apr. 14, 1944.

EMMONS, William Harvey, geologist; b. Mexico, Mo., Feb. 1, 1876; s. St. Clair Peyton and Elizabeth Harvey (Ford) E.; A.B., Central Coll., Fayette, Mo., 1897; Ph.D., U. of Chicago, 1904; m. Virginia Cloyd, Sept. 6, 1910; children—Elizabeth, William Cloyd. Geologic aid, 1904-06, asst. geologist, 1906-10, geologist, 1910-15, U.S. Geol. Survey; lecturer on ore deposits, 1907, on petrology, 1908, asst. prof. petrology and econ. geology, 1908-09, asso. prof. econ. geology, 1909-12, U. of Chicago; prof. and head of dept. geology and mineralogy, University of Minnesota since 1911, professor emeritus since 1944; also director Minnesota Geol. Survey. Asso. editor Jour. of Geology. Mem. Am. Commn. to China, 1920, to study coal and iron for S. Manchurian Ry. Mem. Geol. Soc. America (v.p. 1923), Geol. Soc. Washington, Am. Inst. Mining Engrs., Soc. Econ. Geology (pres. 1928); mem. (hon.) American Assn. Petroleum Engrs., Geological Societies of France and of Belgium, Sigma Xi, Sigma Nu, Gamma Alpha. Methodist. Author: Ore Deposits of Maine, 1910; Ore Deposits of Bull Frog, Nev., 1910; Ore Deposits of Elko, Lander and Eureka Counties, Nev., 1910; Ore Deposits of Phillipsburg, Mont. (with F. C. Calkins), 1913; Enrichment of Ore Deposits, 1917; Ore Deposits of Ducktown, Tenn., 1926—(all pub. by U.S. Geol. Survey); also several text books on ore deposits and on petroleum. Home: 1225 7th St. S.E., Minneapolis. Died Nov. 5, 1948.

EMRICH, Jeannette Wallace (Mrs. Richard Stanley Merrill Emrich) (ĕm′rĭk), writer, lecturer; b. Saxonville, Mass., July 15, 1878; d. William Bruce and Maria Ann (Fitzgerald) Wallace; grad. kindergarten course Pratt Inst., Brooklyn, 1900; studied Hartford Theol. Sem. and Hartford Sch. Religious Edn., 1904-05. Boston U., 1915-16; m. Rev. Richard Stanley Merrill Emrich, July 5, 1904 (died 1919); children—Philip Melvin (dec.), Dr. Duncan Black Macdonald, Rev. Richard Stanley Merrill, Wallace Chandler (dec.). Missionary under A.B.C.F.M., Mardin, Turkey, 1905-19; spl. lecturer on Y.W.C.A., 1918; organized relief work, Constantinople, Turkey, among 6,000 children, 1921-22; asso. sec. Commn. of Internat. Justice and Good Will of Federal Council of Chs. of Christ of America, 1926-31; in community service dept. Motion Picture Producers and Distributors of America; mem. faculty Extension Div., Hunter Coll. Clubs: Chautauqua Woman's, Framingham Woman's (hon.), Constantinople American. Home: 454 Riverside Drive. Office: 28 W. 44th St., New York, N.Y. Died May, 1946.

ENDELMAN, Julio, college prof., dean; b. Lima, Peru, Jan. 9, 1879; s. Seferino and Antonia (de Fabra) E.; student Scientific Inst., Lima, Peru, and U. of Paris (France); D.D.S., U. of Pa., 1900; M.S., Loyola U., Los Angeles, 1920; D.D.Sc., U. of Southern Calif., 1929; unmarried. Lecturer in materia medica, U. of Pa., 1901-08; practice of dentistry, 1908-14; prof. pathol. and therapeutics U. of Southern Calif. since 1914, dean Coll. of Dentistry since 1944. Fellow Am. Coll. Dentists, New York Acad. Dentistry; hon. mem. Calif. State Dental Assn., Nat. Dental Soc. of Chile; mem. Am. Dental Assn., Southern Calif. (pres. 1923), State Dental Assn., Hollywood Acad Medicine, Wilshire Acad. Dentistry, Sigma Xi, Phi Kappa Phi, Delta Sigma Delta, Omicron Kappa Upsilon. Home: 901 S. Kingsley Drive, Los Angeles. Died Nov. 10, 1948.

ENGEL, Carl, musician, writer; b. Paris, France, July 21, 1883; s. Joseph C. and Gertrude (Seeger) E.; was educated in univs. of Strasbourg and Munich; studied musical composition with Ludwig Thuille, Munich; hon. Mus.Doc., Oberlin, 1934; m.* Abigail Josephine Carey, July 29, 1916; 1 dau., Lisette. Came to U.S., 1905, naturalized citizen. Editor and musical adviser, Boston Music Co., 1909-21; chief of music div., Library of Congress, 1922-34; pres. G. Schirmer, Incorporated, music publishers, 1929-32 and since 1934. Hon. consultant in musicology, Library of Congress, since 1934. Editor Musical Quarterly since 1929. First chmn. com. on musicology, Am. Council Learned Socs.; pres. Am. Musicol. Soc., 1937-38; fellow Am. Acad. Arts and Sciences; mem. Musical Assn., London; hon. mem. Harvard Musical Assn.; corr. mem. Société Française de Musicologie; U.S. del. to Beethoven Centenary, Vienna, 1927. Chevalier Legion of Honor (France), 1937. Clubs: Cosmos (Washington, D.C.); Century Assn. (New York). Address: 3 E. 43d St., New York, N.Y. Died May 6, 1944.

ENGEL, Edward J., ry. official; b. Havana, O., July 28, 1874; s. Ephraim Hunter and Maria Almina (Myers) E.; ed. pub. schs. and business coll.; m. Nellie Edwards Grover, July 1, 1902 (died 1905); 1 son, Edward Kenneth (dec.); m. 2d, Louisa Carpenter DeCew, Apr. 3, 1912. With A.T.&S.F. Ry. since Mar. 23, 1899 as stenographer, chief clk., asst. to pres., 1910-18, v.p., 1918-35, exec. vice-pres., 1935-39, pres. and chmn. exec. com., since Mar. 28, 1939, retired Aug. 1, 1944; mem. bd. dirs. also dir. Trustee Museum of Science and Industry, Chicago. Mason. Clubs: Chicago, Chicago Athletic, Chicago Traffic, Western Railway; non-resident member, California Club (Los Angeles). Home: Huntington Hotel, Pasadena, Calif. Died March 30, 1947.

ENGELHARDT, Fred (ĕng-ĕl-härt), university president; b. Naugatuck, Conn., Apr. 15, 1885; s. Georg John and Helena (Deubel) E.; preparatory edn., Phillips Acad., Andover, Mass., and Haverford (Pa.) Sch.; Ph.B., Yale, 1908, grad. study, 1908-09; A.M., Columbia, 1915, Ph.D., 1924; grad. study, Harvard, summers 1909-10, U. of Pa., 1916-17; LL.D., U. of Me., 1940; m. Marion E. Haskell, Aug. 29, 1929. Asst. instr., Yale, 1908-09; teacher and prin. pub. schs., N.Y., and pvt. schs., Pa. and Ill., until 1919; insp., elementary edn., N.Y. State Dept. Edn., 1919; dir. Bur. of Adminstrn., Pa. State Dept. Edn., 1919-22; asst. dean, in charge Coll. Liberal Arts, U. of Pittsburgh, 1922-24; prof. ednl. administration, Coll. of Edn., U. of Minn., 1924-37; pres. U. of N.H. since 1937. Visiting prof. (summers), Peabody Coll., 1929, Univ. of Winnipeg, 1932, Stanford Univ., 1933, Duke U., 1934, Northwestern and Yale, 1935. Maj. Heavy Arty., U.S. Army, 1917-19. Mem. bd. trustees Austin-Cate Acad., Brewster Acad., Northern New England Sch. of Religious Edn. Chmn. State Planning and Development Commn. Mem. N.E.A., Nat. Soc. Study of Edn., Nat. Acad. of Polit. Science, Pa. State Teachers Assn., N.H. Hist. Soc., New England Council, Newcomen Society, Am. Legion, Scabbard and Blade, Grange, Phi Delta Kappa, Kappa Delta Pi, Alpha Sigma Pi. Mason. Clubs: Rotary (Dover); University (Boston). Author: Forecasting School Population, 1924; Public School Organization and Administration, 1931; Syllabus for Public School Organization and Administration, 1930. Co-author: Gunnery for Heavy Artillery, 1915; Public School Accounting Procedure, 1927; First Course in Algebra, 1927; Public School Business Administration (with N. L. Engelhardt), 1927; Second Course in Algebra, 1929; School Plant Programs (with N. L. Engelhardt), 1930; Mathematics for Junior High Schools (3 vols.), 1931; Minnesota Public Schools, 1934; Survey of Public Schools Business Administration (with N. L. Engelhardt), 1936; The Story of Fulling Mill Brook, 1937; Secondary Education Principles and Practices (with A. V. Overn), 1937. Editor: Appleton-Century Administration Series. School surveys: Robinsdale, Minnesota, 1925; Aurora, Minnesota, 1926; Superior, Wis., 1926; Austin, Minn., 1927; Albert Lea, Minn., 1927; Ortonville, Minn., 1928; specialist in administration, Nat. Secondary Survey Commn., 1930-32; on staff Chicago Pub. Sch. Survey, 1932; mem. advisory com. Nat. Finance Survey, 1931-33; mem. Commn. for Study of N.H. Resources, 1937. Contbr. to ednl. publs. Home: Durham, N.H. Died Feb. 3, 1944.

ENGLEBRIGHT, Harry Lane (ĕng′gĕl-brīt), congressman; b. Nevada City, Calif., Jan. 2, 1884; s. Hon. William F. and Kittie F. (Holland) E.; student U. of Calif.; m. Marie Grace Jackson, Dec. 14, 1912; 1 son, Harry Jackson. Identified with mining enterprises in Calif. since 1906; mineral insp. for Gen. Land Office, San Francisco, 1911-14, also engr. State Conservation Commn. of Calif.; elected to 69th Congress at spl. election Aug. 31, 1926, and reelected 70th to 77th Congresses (1927-43), 2d Calif. Dist. Mem. Am. Mining Congress, Native Sons of Golden West. Republican. Episcopalian. Elk, Eagle, Red Man (Past Great Sachem of Calif.). Home: Nevada City, Calif. Died May 13, 1943.

ENGLEMAN, James Ozro, educator; b. Jeffersonville, Ind., Sept. 13, 1873; s. Jefferson and Sarah H. Emeline (Byrne) E.; grad. Ind. State Normal Sch., Terre Haute, 1901; A.B., Ind. U., 1905; A.M., U. of Chicago, 1918; LL.D., James Millikin U., 1923; Ph.D., Ohio State U., 1932; m. Anna Ulen, June 25, 1897; children—James Kemp (dec.), Lois Eleanor, Buryl Frederick, Edward Ulen, Helen, Clarence Clarke, John Philip. Began teaching in rural sch. at 19; prin. high schs., Ind., 8 yrs.; prin. Borden (Ind.) Inst., 1905-06; supt. schs. Loogootee, 1906-07; prin. training dept. Ind. State Teachers Coll., Terre Haute, 1907-09; state institute condr., head dept. of edn. and v.p. State Normal Sch., La Crosse, Wis., 1909-13; supt. schs., Decatur, Ill., 1913-21, Joliet, 1921-22; dir. div. of field service N.E.A., 1922-24; supt. schs., Terre Haute, 1924-27; pres. Kent. (O.) State Univ., 1928-38, emeritus prof. of ednl. administration since 1938, prof. sch. administration, summers, Ohio State U., U. of

Chicago; ednl. lecturer. Mem. N.E.A. (life) and Dept. of Superintendence, Horace Mann League America, Ohio Ednl. Assn., Ohio Coll. Assn., Phi Delta Kappa, Pi Gamma Mu. Republican. Conglist. Mason. Club: Rotary (pres.). Author: Moral Education in School and Home, 1918; (with Lawrence McTurnan) Guide Books to Literature (3 vols.), 1924-26. Contbr. ednl. jours. Home: Kent, Ohio. Died Sep. 15, 1943.

ENGLISH, Charles Henry, lawyer; b. Erie, Pa., Oct. 30, 1883; s. Michael Martin and Maria (Sheridan) E.; LL.B., Georgetown U., 1905, LL.M., 1906, LL.D., 1935; m. Mary O'Brien, June 16, 1910 (died Oct. 8, 1928); children—Richard O'Brien, John William, Mary Patricia; m. 2d, Aline Walker Warfel, Nov. 23, 1929. Admitted to Pa. bar, 1907, and since practiced in Erie; mem. firm English, Quinn, Leemhuis & Tayntor; dir. Erie Coach Co., General Telephone Corporation, Union Bank of Erie, Griffin Manufacturing Company; city solicitor of Erie, 1912-16; member Pa. Commission on Constl. Amendment and Revision, 1919; mem. Tax Law Revision Commn., 1922; chmn. com. on municipalities in Constl. Conv., 1920; apptd. by Supreme Court of Pa. on com. of 5 on Revision of Rules of Practice, 1922; mem. State Bd. of Law Examiners since 1925, chmn. since 1930. Mem. Erie Chamber of Commerce (pres. 1919); 1st pres. Erie Community Chest, 1918; trustee and treas. St. Vincent's Hosp. Decorated Knight Commander, Order of Saint Gregory. Mem. Am. Bar Assn., Pa. Bar Assn. (pres. 1937), Am. Law Inst., Am. Judicature Soc., Delta Chi. Republican. Roman Catholic. K.C. Clubs: Erie, Kahkwa (Erie). Contbr. legal articles to jours. Home: 2050 South Shore Dr. Office: Erie Trust Bldg., Erie, Pa. Died Feb. 18, 1944.

ENGLISH, George Letchworth, mineralogist; b. Phila., Pa., June 14, 1864; s. John A. and Amanda (Evans) E.; grad. Friends' Central Sch., Phila., 1881; m. Louise T. Baltz, June 17, 1890 (died Mar. 10, 1920); children—Mrs. Gwendolen Burleson, Henry Rowland, Kathrine Louise (dec.); m. 2d, Jane Parsons Hanna, Mar. 29, 1923. Collected minerals in Europe, North and South America, Africa and Australia; head firm George L. English & Co., Phila. and New York, dealers in scientific minerals, 1886-1904; monazite expert, and in charge of mining monazite in N. and S. Carolina for Nat. Light & Thorium Co., 1903-13; mgr. dept. of mineralogy and petrography, Ward's Natural Science Establishment, Rochester, N.Y., 1913-21; cons. mineralogist for the same (later The Frank A Ward Foundation of Natural Science of the University of Rochester), 1921-34. Has lectured on mineralogy for N.Y. City Board of Edn., also before various socs. Fellow and life mem. Rochester Acad. Science (pres. 1919-21); mem. Phila. Acad. Natural Sciences, Brooklyn Inst. Arts and Sciences (life), New York Mineral Club, Mineral. Soc. America (v.p. 1927), etc. Author: Getting Acquainted with Minerals; Descriptive List of the New Minerals, 1892-1938; A Catalogue of Minerals, and articles on mineralogy in Ency. Americana, etc. Home: 50 Brighton St., Rochester, N.Y. Died Jan. 2, 1944.

ENGLISH, Merle Neville, clergyman; b. Jacksonville, Ill., 1878; s. Daniel Wilbur and Winnie Farmer (Minear) E.; A.B., Ill. Wesleyan U., Bloomington, 1898, D.D., 1911; student Garrett Bibl. Inst., 1900-01; m. Margaret McMurray, 1899 (died 1924); children—Helen Virginia (Mrs. John A. Hoadley), Margaret Ruth (Mrs. Donald E. Stier); m. 2d, Sarah R. Shufelt, 1926. Ordained ministry M.E. Ch., 1898; pastor successively in Westfield, Owaneco, Macon, Jacksonville, Bloomington, Danville, Ill.; dist. supt. Decatur Dist. and pastor First M.E. Ch., Oak Park, Ill., 1920-28; sec. Bd. of Edn. M.E. Ch., in charge of religious edn., 1928-38; nat. dir. field activities Church Com. for China Relief, 1938-39. Pastor First Meth. Ch., Woodstock, Ill., 1940. Mem. exec. com. Internat. Council of Religious Edn. Trustee Ill. Wesleyan U., Chicago Training Sch.; mem. Gen. Conf. M.E. Ch., 1920-28; mem. Nat. Council Boy Scouts of America and numerous denom. and interdenom. bds. Home: 205 W. South St., Woodstock, Ill.* Died Feb. 1945.

ENGLISH, Robert Henry (ing'lish), rear adm., U.S. Navy; b. Warrenton, Ga., Jan. 16, 1888; s. William Columbus and Mary Cornelia (Fitzpatrick) E.; student Ga. Sch. of Tech., 1904-06; B.S., U.S. Naval Acad., 1911; m. Eloise Shuford Walker, April 19, 1919; children—Eloise Walker, Robert Henry, Eleanor Cornelia. Commd. ensign U.S. Navy, 1911, and advanced through the grades to rear adm., 1942; in command of Pacific Submarine Force, 1943. Decorated Navy Cross, World War I Campaign, Mexican Campaign; D.S.M. (posthumously). Club: Army and Navy Country (Washington, D.C.). Home: 4445 Lowell St., Washington, D.C. Killed in airplane crash, Jan. 21, 1943.

ENNIS, H. Robert; b. County Down, Ireland, Nov. 1, 1870; s. Thomas and Annie (Menown) E.; ed. nat. schs., Ireland; m. M. Kate Patterson, Oct. 29, 1896; children—Alice Louise, Catharine Elizabeth. Came to America, 1887; pres. H. R. Ennis Real Estate & Investment Co. Rep. presdl. elector 5th Congressional District of Missouri, 1912. Directed Kansas City Provident Association (president 1910-11, life member), Research Hosp. (pres. bd. 1921); mem. Board Public Welfare, Kansas City (president 1917-18); president board directors Real Estate Bd. of Kansas City, 1920-21. Mem. personal staff of Gov. Hadley of Mo., 1912, with rank of col., also of Gov. Hyde of Mo., 1921, rank of col. Mem. Chamber of Commerce of Kansas City (v.p. 1913-14), Nat. Assn. Real Estate Bds. (dir. 1922-23, pres. 1924). Presbyterian. Club: Croatan Country of Va. (life). Engaged actively for a number of yrs. in prosecution of persons illegally selling habit-forming drugs. Home: 402 E. 43d St. Office: 400 Victor Bldg., Kansas City, Mo. Died Mar. 19, 1946.

ENNIS, William Duane, engineer; b. in Bergen County, N.J., Jan. 6, 1877; s. William C. and Kate E. (Burroughs) E.; M.E., Stevens Inst. Tech., 1897, Dr. Engring., 1934; married Margaret Schuyler, December 28, 1898. Mechanical engineer in various companies, including Am. Linseed Co., 1897-1905; engr. Am. Locomotive Co., 1905-07; served as prof. mech. engring., Poly. Inst. of Brooklyn, Columbia U., U.S. Naval Acad. Consultant in mech. engring. and industrial management. Commd. maj. U.S.R. and on active duty, Ordnance Dept., Washington, and Watervliet Arsenal, N.Y., 1917-18. Vice pres., Technical Advisory Corp., N.Y., 1920-29. Alexander Crombie Humphreys prof., economics of engring., Stevens Inst. Tech., 1929-44; now professor emeritus. Fellow A.A.A.S., Royal Econ. Soc.; Am. Soc. M.E. (treas. 1935-44); mem. American Economic Assn., Tau Beta Pi. Author: Linseed Oil, 1909; Applied Thermodynamics, 1910; Vapors for Heat Engines, 1912; Flying Machines Today, 1911; Works Management, 1911; Thermodynamics Abridged, 1920; Business Fundamentals for Engineering Students, 1941. Home: Wyckoff, N.J. Died Oct. 14, 1947.

ENO, William Phelps, highway traffic engr.; b. N.Y. City, June 3, 1858; s. Amos Richards and Lucy Jane (Phelps) E.; B.A., Yale, 1882, M.A., 1923; m. Alice Rathbone, Apr. 4, 1883 (died Dec. 21, 1911); m. 2d, Alberta Averill Paz, Apr. 18, 1934. Studied highway traffic regulation in Europe many yrs.; actively identified with the cause in U.S. since 1899; incorporated the Eno Found. for Highway Traffic Regulation, 1921; organized and directed Home Defense League of D.C. (an auxiliary police force); now mem. adv. bd. on Highway Research of Nat. Research Council. Served as chmn. div. of transportation of War Industries Bd. and as chmn. adv. bd. highway transport com of Council of Nat. Defense. Chevalier Legion of Honor (France), 1925, promoted to officer, 1935. Hon. mem. Inst. of Traffic Engrs., Traffic Squad Benevolent Assn. of Police Dept., N.Y. City; hon. pres. Nat. Pedestrian Assn., Nat. Highway Traffic Assn.; hon. mem. Chember Syndicale des Cochers et Chauffeurs de Voitures de Place de la Seine (Paris). Clubs: Yale, University, New York Yacht (New York); Cosmos, Metropolitan (Washington, D.C.); Union Interalliee, American (Paris). Author: Street Traffic Regulation, 1909; Le Probleme de la Circulation, 1912; The Science of Highway Traffic Regulation, 1920; Fundamentals of Highway Traffic Regulation, 1926; Simplification of Highway Traffic, 1929. Home: Washington, D.C.; and Saugatuck, Conn. Died Dec. 3, 1945.

ENT, Uzal Girard, army officer; b. Northumberland, Pa., Mar. 3, 1900; s. Oscar Wellington and Elizabeth (Girard) E.; ed. Susquehanna U. (Selinsgrove, Pa.), 1917-18; B.S., U.S. Mil. Acad., 1924; m. Eleanor Marwitz, Nov. 24, 1929; 1 son, Girard Wellington. Promoted through grades from pvt., aviation sect. Signal Corps, 1918, to maj. gen., 1944; mil. attaché, Am. Embassy, Lima, Peru, 1939-42; chief of staff, U.S. Army Forces in Middle East, 1942; comdg. maj. gen. 9th Bomber Command since Mar. 1943. Decorated D.S.C., D.S.M. (with oak leaf cluster), D.F.C. (with oak leaf cluster), Air Medal (with oak leaf cluster), Legion of Merit, Presidential Unit Citation, Peruvian Flying Cross 1st class, Peruvian Order of Ayacucho, Comdr. Bolivian Condor of the Andes, Comdr. Order of the British Empire. Mason. Home: Northumberland, Pa. Died Mar. 5, 1948.

ENSLEN, Eugene F. (ĕnz'lĕn), banker; b. Wetumpka, Ala., Feb. 11, 1858; s. Christian F. and Elizabeth (Flynn) E.; grad. Eastman Business Coll., Poughkeepsie, N.Y., 1877; m. Della W. Evans, 1878 (dec.); children—Mrs. Julia V. Kidd, Eugene F., Gladys E. (Mrs. John M. Lutz). In mercantile business until 1885; cashier, 1885-1909, pres., 1909-15, Jefferson County Savings Bank, Birmingham, Ala. Trustee, Howard Coll., Birmingham. 1st lt. arty., Ala. N.G., 1876-80. Mem. Bd. of Aldermen, Birmingham, 1885-89. Democrat. Baptist. Clubs: Country, University, Newspaper. Home: 2200 22d Av. S. Office: Comer Bldg., Birmingham, Ala. Died July 30, 1941.

ENWALL, Hasse Octavius, clergyman, educator; b. Tuna (Kalmarlän), Sweden, June 9, 1873; s. Jacob August and Clara (Rosenquist) E.; grad. Naval Sch., Sweden, 1891; student U. of Calif., 1898; Ph.B., Northwestern U., 1902; S.T.B., Boston U. Sch. of Theology, 1905; Ph.D., Boston U., 1915; student U. of Chicago, Grad. Sch., 1915-18; m. Rose Berthema Christianson, Sept. 26, 1902; 1 son, Hayford Octavius. Came to U.S., 1891, naturalized citizen, 1896. Ordained M.E. ministry, 1904; pastor Plainville, Mass., 1904, Mt. Auburn, Cincinnati, O., 1905-09, Trinity Ch., Chicago, 1909-11, First Ch., Aurora, Ill., 1911-13, First Ch., West Lafayette, Ind., 1917-20; prof. philosophy U. of Fla., 1921-45, prof. emeritus since 1945. Mem. Southern Philos. Assn., Delta Tau Delta, Delta Sigma Rho, Phi Kappa Phi. Home: 326 S. Roper Av., Gainesville, Fla. Died Dec. 20, 1947.

EPSTEIN, Abraham (ĕp'stīn), exec. sec. Am. Assn. for Social Security; b. Russia, Apr. 20, 1892; s. Leon and Bessie (Levovitz) E.; B.S., U. of Pittsburgh, 1917, grad. work, 1917-18; grad. work Columbia, 1929-31; m. Henriette Castex, Feb. 24, 1925; 1 son, Pierre Leon. Came to U.S., 1910, naturalized, 1917. Research dir. Pa. Commns. on Old Age Pensions, 1918-21, and 1923-27; exec. sec. Am. Assn. for Old Age Security (now Am. Assn. for Social Security, Inc.) since 1927. Am. rep. Social Insurance Com., Internat. Labor Office, 1934-37; instr. Brooklyn Coll. and N.Y. Univ. Cons. economist Social Security Bd. Mem. City Affairs Committee (New York). Author: Negro Migrant in Pittsburgh, 1918; Facing Old Age, 1922; Problem of Old Age Pensions in Industry, 1926; The Challenge of the Aged, 1928; Insecurity—A Challenge to America, 1933. Contbr. to mags. Editor of Social Security (official publ. of Am. Assn. for Social Security). Home: 389 Bleecker St. Office: 22 E. 17th St., New York, N.Y. Died May 5, 1942.

EPSTEIN, Jacob, sculptor; b. of Russian-Polish parents, N.Y. City, 1880; student of art at Ecole des Beaux Arts and Julian Acad.; m. Margaret Gilmour Dunlop. Executed 18 figures for the bldg. of the British Med. Assn., 1908; designed tomb of Oscar Wilde, Père Lachaise Cemetery, Paris, 1912; memorial to W. H. Hudson, Hyde Park, London, 1925; carved two groups, "Day" and "Night," 1928, for Underground New Bldg., Westminster, London S.W.; 5 works in Nat. Gallery of Modern British Art; portraits, Admiral Lord Fisher, Joseph Conrad, Duchess of Hamilton, Lady Gregory, Prof. John Dewey (Columbia Univ.), Winston Churchill; also "Adam," a 3-ton statue in pink alabaster, exhibited in N.Y. City, 1940, and "Genesis." Author: Let There Be Sculpture, 1940, autobiographical. Address: 18 Hyde Park Gate, London, Eng. Died Dec. 27, 1945.

EPSTEIN, Louis M., rabbi; b. Onixt, Lithuania, Oct. 19, 1887; s. Ezriel and Rebecca (Mehler) E.; came to U.S., 1904; naturalized, 1907; B.S., Columbia U., 1911, A.M., 1915; A.M., Harvard, 1921; Rabbi, Jewish Theol. Sem. 1913, D.H.L., 1921, D.D., 1937; m. Minnie Hannah Winer, Aug. 5, 1914. Rabbi at Dallas, Tex., 1913-15, Toledo, O., 1915-18; instr. in philosophy, Toledo U., 1915-18; rabbi Roxbury, Mass., 1918-25, Brookline, Mass., 1925-47, emeritus since 1947. Dir. Rabbinical Assembly of America (pres. 1918-22), dir. Jewish Theol. Sem. of America; hon. mem. Rabbinical Assn. of Greater Boston; Fellow Am. Acad. Jewish Research, Jewish Academy Arts and Science. Author: The Jewish Marriage Contract, 1927; A Solution to the Agunah Problem (Hebrew), 1940; Marriage Laws in the Bible and the Talmud, 1942; Sex Laws and Customs in Judaism, 1948. Home: 302 W. 77th St., N.Y. City. Died 1949.

ERB, Donald Milton, univ. pres.; b. Brooklyn, N.Y., Aug. 3, 1900; s. John Lawrence and Ethel Bernice (Heydinger) E.; B.S., U. of Ill., 1922, M.S., 1925; A.M., Harvard, 1927, Ph.D., 1930; m. Roxane Catherine Stuart, Mar. 24, 1923; children—Barbara Stuart, Elizabeth Jean. Asst. in economics, U. of Ill., 1923-25; asst. prof. of economics, U. of Ore., 1927-30, prof., 1930-33; prof. of economics, Stanford U., 1933-38; pres. and prof. of economics, U. of Ore., since 1938. Adminstr. E. C. Brown Trust for social hygiene education. Dir. Northwest Regional Council. Mem. Am. Econ. Assn., Pacific Coast Economic Assn., Am. Newcomen Soc., Phi Gamma Delta. Republican. Club: University (Portland, Ore.). Home: 2315 McMorran Drive, Eugene, Ore. Died Dec. 23, 1943.

ERB, John Warren, prof. of music; b. Massillon, O.; s. John Samuel and Ida (Steele) E.; ed. Massillon High School; studied piano with Xavier Scharwenka, theory with Hugo Leichtentritt, choral conducting with Siegfried Orchestras, also studied with Felix Weingartner and others; hon. Mus.D., Washington and Jefferson College, 1934, Cincinnati Conservatory of Music, 1940; unmarried. Director instrumental music, New York University, since 1920; dir. music dept., Lafayette Coll., Easton, Pa., since 1928; now condr. Symphonic Soc. of New York U., Musical Arts Chorus, N.Y. City, and Musical Arts Chorus, Easton, Pa. Has appeared as condr. of Nat. Chorus for Federated Music Clubs, Baltimore Conv., 1939; mass chorus of 1200 at N.Y. World's Fair, 1939; orchestra and chorus in Pilgrim's Progress (festival), N.Y. City, 1940; Maine State Festival Chorus, 1940, Pilgrim's Progress with Portland (Me.) Symphony and chorus of 500, 1941. Elected, 1941 and re-elected 1943, nat. choral chmn. Nat. Federated Music Clubs and commd. to organize and conduct nat. chorus at conv. in 1943; conducted a chorus of 400 in Victory Concert at Biennial Convention, N.Y. City, 1943. Conducted North American Venezuelan Friendship Concert, Apr. 8, 1945, N.Y. City, under patronage of His Excellency Dr. Diogenes Escalante, Ambassador of Venezuela (concert was performance by orchestra, Musical Arts Chorus of Easton and soloists, of Dr. Stillman Kelley's musical miracle play "Pilgrim's Progress" and Venezuelan compositions by Gayetano Carreno, Jose Angel Lamas, Juan Manuel Olivares, Juan B. Plaza, Manuel M. Rodriquez and Vincente Emilio Sojo), program was repeated Apr., 1945, at Colton Memorial Chapel, Lafayette Coll., Easton, Pa. Compositions: A Greek Christmas (for string orchestra); Thou Wilt Keep Him in Perfect Peace (mixed choral); also various choral works. Mem. Nat. Fedn. Music Clubs (nat. chmn. Chamber Music and Orchestra, 1939-40), Assn., Am. Condrs. and Composers, Phi Mu Alpha-Sinfonia. Republican. Mason. Christian Scientist. Home: 20 W. 10th St., New York, N.Y. Office: New York Univ., New York, N.Y.; Lafayette College, Easton, Pa. Died July 1, 1948.

ERICHSEN, Hugo, physician; b. Detroit, June 22, 1860; s. Claus Detlef and Elise (Ruslaub) E.; ed. German Am. Sem., Detroit, and Realschule, Kiel, Germany; M.D., Detroit Med. Coll., 1882, Univ. of Vt., 1882; licentiate, Royal Coll. Phys. and Surg., Kingston, Ont., 1883; Litt.D. from College of City of Detroit, 1932; m. Emma Amelia Eggeman, June 1, 1886; children—Elsa Victoria, Agnes Editha. Prof. diseases of brain and nervous system, Sch. of Medicine, Chaddock Coll., Quincy, Ill., 1883-85; asst. editor Detroit Clinic, 1883; asso. editor Western Med. Reporter, 1883-84; city physician, Detroit, 1888-90. Dir. med. service Burroughs Adding Machine Company, Detroit, Mich., 1919-26; again engaged in writing since 1926. Founder Mich. Cremation Assn., 1886, Detroit Crematorium, 1887, and Cremation Assn. of America, 1913; hon. mem. nine foreign cremation socs.; pres. Cremation Assn. Am., 1913-16, Mich. Cremation Assn. since 1936; hon. mem. Detroit Florists' Club and Wayne County Med. Assn. Editor Photographic Dept. American Boy, 1903-13. Author: Medical Rhymes, 1884; The Cremation of the Dead, 1887; The Methods of Authors, 1894; Herbstlese (German poems), 1912; Roses and Ashes, 1917. Contbr. to med. jours. and to many mags. Home: 415 Harmon Av., Birmingham, Mich. Died Oct. 10, 1944.

ERICKSON, John E., ex-senator; b. Stoughton, Wis., Mar. 14, 1863; s. E. and Olene Alma E.; A.B., Washburn Coll., 1890; m. Grace Vance, 1898; children—Vance B., Ellen D., John C. Admitted to Kan. bar, 1891; moved to Mont., 1894; county atty., Teton County, 3 terms, 1897-1903; dist. judge 11th Jud. Dist. of Mont., 1904-15; practiced at Kalispell, Mont., 1916-25; del. Dem. Nat. Conv., San Francisco, 1920; chmn. Dem. State Central Com., Mont., 1920-24; gov. of Mont., 2 terms, 1925-33; apptd. U.S. senator, Mar. 14, 1933, to fill vacancy caused by death of Hon. T. J. Walsh, serving until Nov. 6, 1934. Lutheran. Home: Helena, Mont. Died May 25, 1946.

ERIKSSON, Herman, ambassador of Sweden to United States. Address: Swedish Embassy, Washington, D.C. Died Feb. 18, 1949.

ERNST, Alwin Charles, audits; b. Cleveland, O.; ed. Cleveland High Sch.; LL.D., Wooster Coll., 1931, Kenyon Coll., 1940; m. Charlotta Elizabeth Fawcett, 1903; children—Ruth (Mrs. H. S. L. Reno, Jr., dec.), Frances (Mrs. Peter Hallaran), Harriett (Mrs. Tinkham Veale, II), Allayne (Mrs. Douglas Wick), Joan. Organized firm of Ernst & Ernst, public accountants, auditors and systematizers, 1903 (this firm now operates 46 offices in U.S. and 1 in Toronto, Canada); chairman Liquidating Com. of Union Properties, Inc. Mem. Cleveland Museum of Art, Cleveland Museum of Natural History (life mem.), Early Settlers Assn. of Western Reserve (life mem.), Cleveland C. of C. (pres. 2 terms), Musical Arts Assn. (Cleveland Symphony Orchestra), Northern Ohio Metropolitan Opera Assn. (mem. exec. com.), organizer and mem. Greater Cleveland Defense Savings Com.; mem. Cuyahoga County Civilian Defense Com.; trustee and mem. corp. Case Sch. of Applied Science; chmn. bd. Gates Mills Park Commn.; mem. and trustee Gates Mills Improvement Soc.; trustee and mem. exec. bd. Boy Scouts of Am. (Cleveland Council); mem. Cleveland Council Inter-Am. Affairs; trustee Conn. (New London) Coll. for Women, Kenyon Coll.; trustee mem. Corp. Cleveland Clin. Foundation; mem. Council Navy League U.S., Newcomen Soc. of London (Am. br.) Gates Mills Hist. Soc. (pres.). Member board trustees, Lake Erie College (Painesville, Ohio). Received Cleveland Gold Medal of Honor, 1939. Clubs: The Union, Chagrin Valley Hunt, Pepper Pike Country, Mayfield Country, Mid-Day (Cleveland); Recess, Cloud (New York). Author of special articles on bus. and financial matters for various institutions and organizations. Home: (winter) 2540 Fairmount Blvd., Cleveland Heights, Ohio; (summer) "Fair Elm," Gates Mills, O. Office: 1356 Union Commerce Bldg., Cleveland, O. Died May 13, 1948; buried Knollwood Mausoleum, Knollwood Cemetery, Cleveland.

ERNST, Clayton Holt, publisher, editor; b. Franconia, N.H., Dec. 29, 1886; s. Frederick William and Harriet Emeline (Holt) E.; A.B., Harvard Univ., 1910; m. Dorothy Haynes Puffer, Sept. 20, 1924; children—Eleanor Holt, Dorothy Wynkoop. Asst. editor The Youth's Companion, 1911-19; editor and part owner The Open Road for Boys since 1919; pres. The Open Road Pub. Co. since 1928, Outdoor Publs., Inc., 1939-42, Child Life, Inc., since 1941. Mem. Mag. and Periodical Industry Adv. Com. War Prodn. Bd. since 1942. Director, New England Town Planning Assn. Unitarian. Clubs: Harvard, Boston Authors, Laurel Brook Club. Author: First Aid for Boys (with Norman B. Cole, M.D.), 1917; Blind Trails, 1919; The Mark of the Knife, 1920; What Shall I Be?, 1924; The Secret of Coffin Cove, 1926. Editor: (with Prof. Trentwell White) Opportunity Ahead!, 1929. Trustee, Dow Academy, Franconia, N.H. Home: 38 Chestnut St., Wellesley Hills, Mass. Office: 729 Boylston St., Boston. Died Oct. 15, 1945; buried in Woodlawn Cemetery, Wellesley Hills, Mass.

ERNST, Edward Cranch, U.S. Pub. Health Service; b. Chicago, Ill., Sept. 4, 1886; s. Edward F. and Bertha (Cranch) E.; student U. of Munich, Germany, 1903-04; M.D., Columbia, 1911; unmarried; adopted 2 boys, Edward C., William C. Commd. asst. surgeon, U.S. Pub. Health Service, 1916, passed asst. surgeon, 1921, surgeon, 1923, sr. surgeon, 1936; on coast guard Arctic cruise, 1917; quarantine officer, Manila, P.I., 1918; dir. San Lazaro Hosp., 1919, P.I. Health Service, 1920; assigned to Office Industrial Hygiene, Washington, D.C., 1922; med. dir. U.S. Employees Compensation Commn., 1922-34; asst. dir. Pan-Am. Sanitary Bur. since 1937. Fellow A.M.A.; member American Public Health Association, American Hospital Association, Royal Tropical Med. Soc., Far Eastern Tropical Medicine Assn., Assn. Industrial Hygiene, Assn. Mil. Surgeons. Clubs: Cosmos, Columbia Country (Washington, D.C.). Contbr. articles on industrial medicine and med. economics to jours. Home: 3212 Wisconsin Av. Office: Pan-American Union, Washington, D.C. Died Nov. 6, 1944.

ERRETT, Edwin Reeder (ĕr′rĕt), religious editor; b. Carnegie, Pa., Jan. 7, 1891; s. William Russell and Jane (McCallen) E.; ed. Western U. of Pa., 1907-08, Bethany (W.Va) Coll., 1903-11 (A.B.), Divinity Sch. and Grad Sch., Yale, 1911-12; D.D., Butler, 1929; Phillips U., 1939; Litt.D., Cincinnati Bible Sem., 1930. Bethany Coll., 1939; m. Clara K. Luskey. Aug. 27, 1917 (died July 12, 1923); m. 2d, Bessie Taylor Eldredge, June 11, 1925. Office editor Christian Standard, 1912-18; commentator and lesson writer of Sunday school materials, Standard Pub. Co., Cincinnati, 1918-25, editor in chief of Sunday school publs., 1925-29; editor in chief Christian Standard since 1929; minister Ch. of Christ, Felicity, O., 1921-39. Mem. continuation com. World Council of Churches; del. World Conf. on Faith and Order, Edinburgh, 1937. Dir. Butler U.; trustee Christian Foundation, Indianapolis. Mem. Sigma Nu. Democrat. Mem. Disciples of Christ. Ch. Contbr. to religious jours. Home: R.F.D. 6, Box 84, Cincinnati, O. Office: 640 W. 8th St., Cincinnati, O. Died Jan. 29, 1944.

ERTEGUN, Mehmet Munir (âr-tă-gün′), ambassador; b. Istanbul, Turkey, 1883; s. Mehmet Cemil and Hamida M.; student U. of Istanbul; m. Hayrünnisa Rüstem, 1917; children—Nesuhi, Ahmet, Selma. Began as asst. legal adviser to Ministry of Fgn. Affairs, 1909, then head legal adviser; jurist at Lausanne Conf., 1922-23; minister to Switzerland, 1925-30; ambassador to France, 1930-32, to England, 1932-34, to U.S. since 1934. Decorated Independence medal (Turkey). Address: Turkish Embassy, Washington, D.C. Died Nov. 11, 1944.

ERVIN, Charles Edwin, ry. official; b. Turner, Kan., July 26, 1880; s. William Wallace and Susan Mildred (Martin) E.; ed. grade and high schs., Kansas City, Kan.; m. Lucey Glenn Ivie, Nov. 18, 1903; children—Marion Ivie (Mrs. Charles M. Monroe, Jr.), Dorris Glenn (Mrs. M. J. Epley), Sara Perry (Mrs. William F. Nesbit), Charles Edwin, Jr. Messenger A.,T.&S.F. Ry., Kansas City, Mo., 1896-97, yard clerk, 1897-98, asst. chief yard clerk, 1898-1900; clerk 1897-98, asst. chief yard clerk, 1898-1900; clerk Southern Ry., Sheffield, Ala., 1900-01, machinists' helper, 1901-02, chief clerk to roadmaster, 1902-06, track supervisor, 1906-11, asst. engr., 1911-12, roadmaster Atlanta Div., 1912-17, supt. Atlanta Div., 1917-20; gen. supt. M.&O. R.R., St. Louis, 1920-25, gen. mgr., 1925-32, chief operating officer, 1932-33; appt. receiver M.&O. R.R., St. Louis, 1933; now v.p. Gulf, Mobile & Ohio R.R. Co. Baptist. Club: Alba (Mobile, Ala.). Home: 2067 Springhill Av. Office: 104 St. Francis St., Mobile, Ala. Died Dec. 16, 1946.

ERVIN, Joe W. (ĕr′vĭn), congressman; b. Morganton, N.C., Mar. 3, 1901; s. Samuel James and Laura (Powe) E.; A.B., U. of North Carolina, 1921; m. Susan Graham. Admitted to North Carolina bar, 1923, and since engaged in practice of Law, Charlotte, N.C.; mem. 79th Congress (1945-47), 10th N.C. Dist. Democrat. Mem. Myers Park Presbyterian Ch., Charlotte, N.C. Mason. Home: 168 Cherokee Road, Charlotte, N.C. Office: House Office Bldg., Washington, D.C. Died Dec. 25, 1945.

ESENWEIN, Joseph Berg (ĕs′ĕn-wīn), editor; b. Phila., Pa., May 15, 1867; s. Dr. Augustus and Katherine (Angelo), E.; B.S., Albright Coll., 1884; student Millersville (Pa.) Teachers Coll., 1886; A.M., Lafayette Coll., 1894; Ph.D., Richmond Coll., 1896; Litt.D., Univ. of Omaha, 1896; Master Humanics, Springfield Coll., 1937; m. Caroline Deats Miller, Mar. 21, 1889. Pres. Albright Collegiate Inst., 1895-96; ednl. dir. Y.M.C.A., Washington Heights, New York City, 1897; lit. work and foreign travel, 1898-99; prof. English lang. and lit., Pa. Mil. Coll., Chester, 1899-1903; mgr. Booklovers' Magazine, 1903-05; editor and mgr. Lippincott's Mag., Phila., 1905-14, and lit. adviser to J. B. Lippincott Co., 1908-14; editor The Writer's Monthly, Springfield, Mass., since 1915, Nature League News, Worcester, Mass., 1936-38. Head of lit. faculty, Home Correspondence Sch., 1910-41; instructor in public speaking Springfield Coll., 1920-37; lecturer on educational, ethical and popular topics. Fellow Royal Society Arts; mem. Society of Arts and Letters, etc. Presbyterian. Republican. Mason. Kiwanian. Author: Songs for Reapers, 1895; Modern Agnosticism, 1896; Feathers for Shafts, 1897; How to Attract and Hold an Audience, 1901; Writing the Short-Story, 1909; Lessons in the Short-Story, 1910; Short-Story Masterpieces, 1912; Studying the Short Story, 1912; The Art of Versification (with Mary E. Roberts), 1913; Writing the Photoplay (with Arthur Leeds), 1913; The Art of Story Writing (with Mary D. Chambers), 1914; The Art of Public Speaking (with Dale Carnegie), 1915; Writing for the Magazines, 1916; Children's Stories and How to Tell Them (with Marietta Stockard), 1917; Writing Good English, 1925. Contributed over 100 critical summaries to Charles Dudley Warner's Library of the World's Best Literature; has published many songs and hymns, words and music. Compiled and edited 6 vols. of juvenile fiction, 1937. Home: Longmeadow, Mass. Office: Myrick Bldg., Springfield, Mass. Died Nov. 7, 1946; buried in Mount Lebanon Cemetery, Lebanon, Pa.

ESHNER, Augustus Adolph (ĕsh′nĕr), physician; b. Memphis, Tenn., Nov. 17, 1862; s. James and Jane E.; A.B., Central High Sch., Phila., 1879, A.M., 1884; M.D., Jefferson Med. Coll., 1888; m. Julia Friedberger, 1904; children—Mrs. Annette E. Dalsimer, Mrs. Juliet E. Nathanson. Resident physician Philadelphia Hosp., 1888-89; registrar neurology dept. same, 1891-96; chief clin. asst. outpatient med. dept., Jefferson Med. Coll. Hosp., 1892; prof. clin. medicine, Phila. Polyclinic, 1895-1918; phys. Phila. Hosp., 1896-1914; asst. phys. Orthopædic Hosp. and Infirmary for Nervous Diseases, 1900-17; visiting physician Hosp. for Diseases of the Lungs, 1901-02; cons. physician Mercy Hosp. since 1910. Asst. editor Medical News, 1891-95, Phila. Med. Journal, 1898-99; asso. editor Pa. Medical Journal, 1904-22. Commd. 1st lt. Med. R.C., 1917. Fellow Coll. Physicians of Phila., A.A.A.S.; mem. Phila. Co. Med. Soc. (chmn. dirs. 1904-05), Pa. State Med. Soc., A.M.A., Pathol. Soc. Phila., Northern Med. Assn., Science League America, Franklin Ist. Pa., Pa. Museum and Sch. Industrial Art, Pa. Acad. Fine Arts, Hist. Soc. Pa., Phila. Zoöl. Soc., Acad. Natural Sciences of Phila., Valley Forge Hist. Society, Assn. Alumni Central High Sch. of Phila., Fairmount Park Art Assn., Jewish Publ. Soc. America. Author: Essentials of Med. Diagnosis (with Dr. Solomon Solis-Cohen), 1892, 2d edit., 1900; Hand-Book of Fevers, 1895. Asst. editor: American Text-book of Applied Therapeutics, 1896. Transl. and edited: Atlas and Methods of Clinical Investigation (Dr. Christfried Jakob), 1898; Elements of Clinical Bacteriology (Dr. Ernest Levy and Dr. Felix Klemperer), 1900; A Text-book of the Practice of Medicine (Dr. Hermann Eichhorst), 1900. Collaborator on Annual of the Universal Med. Sciences, 1890-95; Sajous' Annual and Cyclo. of Practical Medicine, 1899; Cyclo. of Practical Medicine and Surgery, 1900; System of Physiologic Therapeutics, 1902-03; Reference Handbook of the Medical Sciences, 1903; A Textbook of Human Physiology (L. Landois), 1904. Has written many med. monographs and articles in med. jours., etc. Editor: Trans. Phila. County Med. Soc., 1896, 97; Phila. General Hospital Reports, Vol. IX, 1913. Address: 1019 Spruce St., Philadelphia 7, Pa. Died Dec. 20, 1949.

ESSARY, Jesse Frederick (ĕs′să-rē), newspaper man; b. Washburn, Tenn., Aug. 22, 1881; s. John Thurman and Maetta (Hill) E.; student Emory and Henry Coll., 1900-01, LL.D., 1933; LL.D. from George Washington U., 1935; m. Helen Forman Kerchner, Sept. 28, 1910. Sec. to commr. of agr., Tenn., 1898; clk. N.&W. and S.A.L. rys., 1901-03; reporter Pub. Ledger and Norfolk (Va.) Landmark, 1903-08; financial editor, Baltimore Star, 1908-09; Washington corr. Baltimore News, New Orleans Item and Boston Journal, 1910-12, Baltimore Sun since 1912; London corr. Baltimore Sun, 1926; pres. National Press Building Corp. since 1931. Sec. Chamber of Commerce, Norfolk, Va., 1907, and awarded medal and diploma by Jamestown Expn.; sec. Shipping League of Baltimore, 1909; sec. Maryland Commn. to Seattle Exposition, 1909. Member Sigma Delta Chi and Pi Delta Epsilon. Baptist. Mason. Clubs: National Press (pres. 1928), Gridiron (president 1925), Cosmos (Washington, D.C.); Maryland (Baltimore); Authors' (London). Author: Maryland in National Politics; Life of Isidor Rayner; Your War Taxes; Covering Washington; Reverse English; Ships (with B. N. Baker); Washington Sketch Book (with Helen Essary); Crisis (with Lord Kilanin). Editor: Spirit of the Courts. Contbr. to mags. Lecturer. Winner of Pugsley journalistic award, 1932. Home: 3121 Newark St. Office: National Press Bldg., Washington, D.C. Died Mar. 11, 1942.

ESTBERG, Edward Robert, banker; b. Waukesha, Wis., Nov. 25, 1862; s. Claes A. and Sophia (Schlitz) E.; ed. pub. schs.; m. Sara Brown, Nov. 8, 1893; children—Lola Sophia (Mrs. William Floyd Clarkson), John Edward, Margaret (dec.), Edward Frame, Charles Byron. Began as messenger Waukesha Nat. Bank, 1880, successively bookkeeper, teller, asst. cashier until 1906, cashier, 1906-15, v.p., 1915-19, pres., 1919-38, chmn. of bd. since Jan. 11, 1938; dir. and mem. exec. com. Fed. Reserve Bank of Chicago; dir., treas. Waukesha Motor Co., Hein-Werner Motor Parts Corp., Co. chmn. Liberty Loan drives, Waukesha County, World War. Mayor of Waukesha, 1914-19; pres. Bd. of Edn., Waukesha, 1921-36. Mem. Am. Bankers Assn. (mem. exec. council 3 yrs.), Wis. Bankers Assn. (mem. exec. council 3 yrs.). Republican. Episcopalian. Mason (32°). Home: 229 Wisconsin Av. Office: Waukesha Nat. Bank, Waukesha, Wis. Died Mar. 3, 1944.

ESTIGARRIBIA, Jose Felix (ĕs-tē-găr-rē′bē-ā), President of Paraguay; b. Caraguatay, 1888; s. Mateo Estigarribia and Casilda Insaurralde de Estigarribia; ed. Colegio Nacional de Asunción; École Supérieure de Guerre, Paris; m. Julia Miranda Sueto de Estigarribia; 1 dau., Graciela. Director Mil. School, Asunción, 1923-24; chief of gen. staff, 1928-29; inspector gen. of army, 1931; commander-in-chief of Paraguayan Army; minister plenipotentiary to U.S., 1938-39; pres. of delegation to Peace Conf., Buenos Aires, 1938; elected pres. of Paraguay, 1939; officially proclaimed himself dictator, 1940. Mem. Union Club (Asunción).

Latin Am. Club (Paris). Address: Presidential Palace, Asunción, Paraguay. Died Sep. 7, 1940.

ESTILL, Harry Fishburne, educator; b. Lexington, Va., Aug. 12, 1861; s. Charles Patrick and Katherine (Fishburne) E.; Austin (Tex.) Coll., 1875-77; grad. Sam Houston Normal Inst., 1880; Litt.D., Austin Coll., 1907; m. Loulie Sexton, Aug. 3, 1892; children—Frank Sexton, Katherine Fishburne, Mary Sexton, Harry Fishburne, Ruth. Teacher pub. schs., Grimes County, Tex., 1880-81; prin. High Sch., Navasota, Tex., 1881-82; instr. State Sch. of Methods, Austin, Tex., 1888; conductor summer normal institutes, Orange, Jewett, Sulphur Springs and Huntsville, Tex., 1890-1908; prof. Latin and history, Sam Houston State Teachers Coll., 1882-1908, pres., 1908-37, pres. emeritus and prof. history since 1937. Fellow Tex. Hist. Soc.; mem. N.E.A. (vice pres. teachers coll. sec., 1934-35), Texas State Teachers' Assn. (pres. 1902), Southern Ednl. Assn., Pi Gamma Mu. Democrat. Presbyn. Mason (K.T., Shriner). Rotarian. Author: History of Our Country (with others), 1893; Beginner's History of the United States, 1900, 29. Home: Huntsville, Tex. Died Feb. 12, 1942.

ESTY, Edward Tuckerman, lawyer; b. Amherst, Mass., Aug. 30, 1875; s. William Cole and Martha Ann (Cushing) E.; A.B., Amherst College, 1897; LL.B. Harvard U., 1901; LL.D., Amherst Coll., 1937; m. Grace Heward, Mar. 1, 1919; 1 dau., Martha Cushing. Instr. mathematics, Amherst Coll., 1897-98; admitted to Mass. bar, 1901; with Hammond & Field, Northampton, Mass., 1901-02; practiced law in Worcester since 1902; mem. Vaughan, Esty, Clark & Crotty, Worcester. Mem. Worcester Common Council, 1906-11 (pres. 1910-11); spl. justice Central Dist. Court of Worcester, 1904-10; asst. dist. atty. for Middle Dist., Mass., 1911-16, dist. atty., 1917-22. Dir. Home for Aged Men (treas. 1907-37); trustee Worcester Pub. Library, 1911-16, Worcester County Instn. for Savings, Amherst Coll., Memorial Hosp. Mem. Am. Law Inst., Am., Mass., and Worcester County bar assns., Am. Antiquarian Soc., Worcester Fire Soc., St. Wulstan Soc., Psi Upsilon, Phi Beta Kappa. Republican. Episcopalian. Mason. Clubs: Worcester, Tatnuck Country. Home: 85 Elm St. Office: 332 Main St., Worcester, Mass. Died July 4, 1942.

ETTER, William Kirby, ry. official; b. Shippensburg, Pa., Jan. 16, 1874; s. Josiah and Mary (Bowen) E.; ed. pub. schs. and McPherson (Kan.) College; m. Locky Fort, Dec. 10, 1902; children—William Kirby, Lewis Fort; m. 2d, Mrs. Julia Miller Brown, Aug. 14, 1934. Began as axeman and chainman with the A.,T.&S.F. Ry., 1891; held various subordinate positions, later exec. offices, v.p. since 1932; also v.p. subsidiary lines. Mason. Clubs: Chicago, Lake Shore Athletic (Chicago); California (Los Angeles); Riverside (Ill.) Golf. Home: 850 Lake Shore Dr. Office: 80 E. Jackson Blvd., Chicago, Ill. Died Aug. 16, 1943.

ETTINGER, George Taylor (ĕt'ing-ẽr), college dean; b. Allentown, Pa., Nov. 8, 1860; s. Amos and Susan (Laudenschläger) E.; A.B., Muhlenberg Coll., 1880, A.M., 1883, Litt.D., 1920, LL.D., 1937; Ph.D., New York U., 1891; m. Emma C. Aschbach, Aug. 17, 1899; 1 son, Amos Aschbach. Teacher Muhlenberg Coll. since 1880; now dean emeritus and prof. Latin emeritus. Was lit. editor Allentown Morning Call; teacher and dean Pa. Chautauqua, 9 yrs.; mem. bd. sch. dirs., Allentown, 15 yrs. (ex-sec., ex-pres.); mem. bd. prison inspectors Lehigh County, Pa., 12 years (ex-sec.); first president Allentown Library Assn., 1912-43, now president emeritus; ex-president trustees' section Pennsylvania State Library Association; member A.L.A. many years; many years alumni editor Muhlenberg Weekly. Ex-pres. Lehigh Valley Classical League, 1924-25. Often del. conf., to ministerium of Pa. and to Gen. Council Lutheran Ch. N. America; dir. Luth Theol. Sem., Phila., 1924-33. Mem. Lehigh County Hist. Society (ex-pres.), Am. Philol. Assn., Pa. German Soc. (ex-pres.), Nat. Inst. Social Sciences, Am. Assn. Univ. Profs., Phi Beta Kappa, Phi Gamma Delta, Omicron Delta Kappa, Eta Sigma Phi; ex-pres. Alumni Assn. Muhlenberg Coll. Clubs: Contemporary, Schoolmen's, Lions, Rotary (Allentown). Republican. Lutheran. Home: 1114 Hamilton St., Allentown, Pa. Died Apr. 20, 1949.

ETTINGER, William L., supt. schs.; b. N.Y. City, Dec. 29, 1862; s. Louis L. and Mary E. E.; A.B., Manhattan Coll., 1881 (LL.D., 1918); M.D., Univ. Med. Coll., 1891; m. Emma R. McCarthy, Dec. 26, 1894; children—William L., Albert M., Thomas C. Teacher in De LaSalle Acad., 1881; later teacher and prin. pub. schs., Manhattan; elected dist. supt., 1909, asso. supt., 1913, supt. schools, New York City, 1918, supt. emeritus, 1926. Originated duplicate sch. system in congested dists., 1903, later modified for upper grades; organized pre-vocational training, 1914, also developed continuation classes, cooperative classes and vocational schs. Ex-pres. N.Y. City Teachers' Assn.; ex-pres. Principals' Assn. of Greater New York; mem. Assn. Principals and Teachers of N.Y. City, etc. Democrat. Roman Catholic. Clubs: Staten Island, White Beeches Country, N.Y. Athletic. Home: 3671 Broadway, New York. Died Dec. 25, 1945.

EUBANK, Earle Edward (ū'băngk), sociologist; b. Columbia, Mo., Mar. 20, 1887; s. Peyton Adams and Laura Boardman (Houchens) E.; A.B., William Jewell College, 1908, A.M., 1913; fellow in sociology and Ph.D., cum laude, U. of Chicago, 1916; m. Eva Maude Stephens, 1910 (died 1923); children—Evelyn Laile, Edward Earle (dec.), Laurel Elsabeth, Lois Lilian; m. 2d, Jessie Logan Burrall, 1928. Supervisor of schs., Philippines, 1908-12; prof. sociology, George Williams College, 1914-21, also dean, 1918-21; prof. sociology and head of dept., U. of Cincinnati, since 1921, also founder and dir. Sch. of Social Work, 1923-31; prof. sociology, summers, U. of Chicago, 1927, U. of Southern Calif., 1928, Colo. State College, 1932, 33, Univ. of Denver, 1935, Univ. of Colo., 1937. Member American Seminar to Europe, 1921, 1934. Acting dir. Bur. of Social Surveys, Chicago, 1916. Dir. of training, Central Mil. Dept., Nat. War Work Council, Y.M.C.A., World War. Mem. Y.M.C.A. Nat. Constitutional Conv., 1924. Mem. White House Conf. on Child Welfare, 1931. Delegate Bapt. World Congress, Berlin, 1934. Mem. Am. Sociol. Soc., Am. Assn. Univ. Profs., Ohio Valley Sociol. Soc. (pres. 1926-27), Alpha Kappa Delta, Phi Eta, Beta Epsilon; associate Internat. Institut de Sociologie; hon. mem. Masaryk Sociol. Soc. (Czechoslovakia). Baptist. Clubs: Faculty, Torch (pres. 1939-40). Author: A Study of Family Desertion, 1916; (with C. L. Clark) Lockstep and Corridor, 1927; The Concepts of Sociology, 1931; (with others) Introduction to Western Civilization, 1933; (with others) Social Problems and Social Processes, 1933; (with others) Fields and Methods of Sociology, 1934; (with others) Contemporary Social Theory, 1940. Asso. editor: Dictionary of Sociology. Advisory editor Am. Jour. Sociology, Sociology and Social Research. Contbr. to sociol. and religious jours.; speaker in same field. Home: Vernon Manor, Cincinnati, O.; and Under the Bent Twig, Sharpes, Fla. Died Dec. 17, 1945.

EVALD, Emmy (ē-väld'); b. Geneva, Ill., Sept. 18, 1857; d. Rev. Erland (D.D.) and Eva (Charlotta) Carlson; ed. pub. schs., girls' coll., Kalmar Sweden, and Rockford Coll.; M. A., Augustana Coll., L.H.D., Upsala College; m. Carl A. Evald (D.D.), May 1883 (now dec.); children—Anna Fedelia (wife of Rev. C. E. Hofsten, D.D.), Lillian Charlotta (Mrs. A. R. Carlson). Engaged in missionary and religious organization work since 1886; founder, and dept. editor of Mission Tidings since 1906; sent by Women's Missionary Soc. on inspection tour of mission stations in India, China and Holy Land, 1926-27; founder of homes for women—Mission Home and Immanuel Woman's Home, Chicago (pres. of both), Home for Women (N.Y. City) and a home in Vancouver, Canada. Organizer, 1892, of the Woman's Missionary Soc. N.A. of Lutheran Augustana Ch., which built 75 buildings in different parts of the world; pres. Lutheran Woman's Congress, Chicago Expn., 1893; organizer of Nat. Lutheran Woman's League; pres. Fredrika Bremer Association; mng. dir. Luth. Home for Women Assn., 1930; mem. Nat. Com. of the Am. Swedish Hist. Foundation (Phila.), Swedish Am. Tercentenary Assn., American Sons and Daughters of Sweden (v.p.), Internat. Suffrage Assn. Decorated Knight Order of Vasa, by the King of Sweden, 1922. Section in new library at Rockford College, Rockford, Ill., given in Dr. Emmy Evald's honor, 1940. Was college mate of Jane Addams and classmate of judge and lawyer Catharine Waugh McCullough. Author: Dr. Carl Evald's Life, 1909; 9 Calendars of Woman's Missionary Society for Years 1910-27; Tenth Anniversary Lutheran Home for Women. Home: 318 E. 82d St., New York, N.Y. Died Dec. 10, 1946.

EVANS, Anthony Harrison, clergyman; b. Bryncellyn, Wales, Jan. 1, 1862; s. Robert Trogwy and Mary (Blackwell) E.; B.A., Hamilton Coll., Clinton, N.Y., 1882, A.M., 1885, D.D., 1895; graduate Union Theol. Seminary, 1888; LL.D., Tusculum Coll., Greeneville, Tenn., 1930; m. Ethel Kelsey, July 31, 1890 (died Dec. 2, 1920). Instr. Poly. Inst. of Brooklyn, 1882-85, Hamilton Coll., 1888-89; ordained Presbyn. ministry, 1889; pastor First Ch., Lockport, N.Y., 1889-95; West Ch., New York, 1895-1911; copastor West Park Ch., New York, 1911-18, pastor same since 1918. Moderator N.Y. Presbytery, 1903-04, 1915-16, Synod of New York, 1906; trustee N.Y. Presbytery (pres. bd.), N.Y. Synod (pres. bd. 1914-31); dir. N.Y. City Mission Soc.; trustee Hamilton Coll. (1927-31), Union Theol. Sem.; mem. com. evangelism Federal Council Chs. Mem. Clerical Conf. of New York, Hamilton Coll. Alumni Assn. (pres. 1907-08), St. David's Soc. (pres. 1908-10), Nat. Inst. Social Sciences, Chi Alpha, Sigma Chi, Theta, Delta Kappa Epsilon, Phi Beta Kappa. Club: Century. Author: Each Returning Day, 1904. Home: 225 W. 86th St., New York, N.Y. Died Aug. 29, 1942.

EVANS, Arthur Thompson, botanist; b. Wellington, Ill., May 22, 1888; s. Robert M. and Anna Caldwell (Johnstone) E.; A.B., U. of Ill., 1912; studied U. of Mich., summers, 1913, 14; M.A., U. of Colo., 1915; Ph.D., U. of Chicago, 1918; m. Anna Mathilde Hansen, Aug. 22, 1914; children—Margaret Louise, Arthur T., Lewis Hansen, Dorothy Ann. Grad. asst. in botany, U. of Colo., 1914-15, instr., 1915-17; fellow in botany, U. of Chicago, 1917-18; in charge cereal disease investigations, U.S. Dept. of Agr., in Great Plains Region, World War, 1918, corn investigations, 1919; dean of coll. and prof. botany, Huron (S.D.) Col., 1919-20; asso. prof. agronomy, 1920-23, head of dept. and prof. botany and plant pathology, 1923-28, S.D. State Coll.; now prof. botany, Miami University. Fellow A.A.A.S., Ohio Academy of Science; member Botanical Society America, Phi Sigma (biological), Sigma Xi, Delta Pi. Republican. Presbyterian. Mason (K.T., Shriner). Author: (textbook) First Course in Botany (with R. J. Pool); Laboratory Manual for First Course in Botany. Contbr. on original research in morphology and cytology, also coll. bulls, etc. Home: Oxford, O. Died Oct. 5, 1943.

EVANS, Curtis Alban, surgeon; b. Wales, Wis., Apr. 20, 1879; s. Rowland Hill and Sarah (Alban) E.; student Ripon Acad. and Coll., 1894; A.B., U. of Mich., 1902, M.D., 1904; m. Nellie S. Schwartzburg, June 24, 1908; children—Robert Curtis, John Alban, Edward Sifton, Nancy Jane. Instr. anatomy, 1904-08, prof., 1908-12, Wis. Coll. Phys. and Surg.; asso. prof. surgery, Marquette U., 1912-25; chief of staff, Milwaukee Hosp., 1928-1941; cons. surgeon Johnson Emergency Hosp.; surg. staff Columbia Hosp.; Cons. Surgeon Milwaukee Children's Hosp. Commd. lt. M.R.C., U.S. Army, May 27, 1916; maj., Aug. 23, 1917; lt. col., Aug. 20, 1918; dir. and chief surg. service U.S. Army Base Hosp. 22, A.E.F., 1917-Mar. 15, 1919; U.S. Army citation, 1919; col. Med. O.R.C. Mem. of Founders Group Am. Board of Surgery. Fellow Am. Coll. Surgeons (mem. bd. govs. since 1925), A.M.A.; mem. Milwaukee Surg. Soc. (pres. 1922), Milwaukee Acad. Medicine (pres. 1922), Phi Rho Sigma, Pi Gamma Mu. Awarded Order of Purple Heart, 1932. Conglist. Club: University. Home: 2914 E. Newberry Blvd. Office: 324 E. Wisconsin Av., Milwaukee, Wis. Died May 3, 1947.

EVANS, Daniel, clergyman; b. S. Wales, Aug. 22, 1866; s. Michael and Hannah (Thomas) E.; came to Am. with parents, 1869; attended 1 yr. Wyoming Sem., Kingston, Pa., 3 yrs. at Bangor Theol. Sem.; A.B., Bowdoin Coll., 1890, D.D., 1906; student advanced course, Andover Theol. Sem., 1 year; m. Addie Seavey Ames, June 17, 1891. Ordained Congl. ministry, 1891; pastor, E. Weymouth, Mass., 1891-99, North Av. Ch., Cambridge, Mass., 1899-1909; prof. Christian theology, Andover Theol. Sem., Cambridge, 1909-31, Andover Newton Theol. Sch. since 1931. Trustee Bowdoin Coll., Webber Foundn. Clubs: Fortnightly, Winthrop, Ministers'. Home: 42 Hillside Terrace, Belmont, Mass. Died Apr. 24, 1943.

EVANS, Edward Steptoe, manufacturer; b. Thaxtons, Va., May 24, 1879; s. Thomas Davis and Mary Elizabeth (Murrell) E.; law student Columbian (now George Washington) Univ., Washington, D.C., 2½ yrs.; spl. course in library science; m. Virginia Epes McCormick, Apr. 5, 1905; children—Edward Steptoe, Robert Beverly. In Library of Congress, 1900-04; asst. state librarian, Va., 1904-07; founder, 1915, pres. and treas. Evans Products Co., Inc., mfrs. loading material and devices for loading automobiles loading material and devices for loading freight cars, airplanes and trucks, road and rail locomotives and vehicles and other equipment for railroads, battery separators, heating and ventilating units for motor vehicles and airplanes, molded plywood, airplane engine mounts, etc.; president and treasurer Saven Corporation, investments; farmer, breeder of registered Guernseys. Served as captain in Q.M.C., U.S. Army, 1918-19 inclusive; lieutenant colonel specialist reserve attached to U.S. Air Corps. Fellow American Geographical Society; member Society Automotive Engrs. Episcopalian. Mason (32°, K.T., Shriner). Clubs: Explorers (New York); Detroit, Detroit Athletic, Detroit Boat, Country, Players, Adventurers (Chicago); Commonwealth (Richmond, Va.). Held record for circumnavigating the globe in 28 days, 14 hours and 36 minutes, 1926; mgr. Detroit Arctic Expdn., 1925, 26. Founder and 1st pres. Nat. Glider Assn. Donor annual silver trophy U.S. nat. glider champion and bronze trophy U.S. Army Air Corps grand glider champion presented to U.S. War Department, 1941. Author: Encyclopædic Guide to Richmond, Va., 1907; History of Seals of Virginia (monograph), 1908. Compiler: Calendar of Virginia Transcripts, 1906. Contbr. to numerous mags. on freight transport. Pioneer in aircraft mfr. and air transportation. Home: 1005 Three Mile Drive, Grosse Pointe, Mich. Office: 15310 Fullerton St., Detroit, Mich. Died Sep. 6, 1945.

EVANS, Elwyn, pres. Wilmington Trust Co.; b. Racine, Wis., Jan. 20, 1895; s. Thomas and Ellen (Rogers) E.; B.A., Beloit Coll., Beloit, Wis., 1916; ed. Harvard, 1919-20; B.A., M.A., B.C.L., Oxford (Eng.) U., 1922; m. Mary Railey Boyd, June 2, 1926; children—Elwyn, Katherine Lloyd, Tilghman Boyd. Admitted to Wis. bar, 1923, Del. bar, 1928; engaged in practice of law, 1923-28; asst. trust officer First Wis. Trust Co., Milwaukee, 1928; v.p. Wilmington (Del.) Trust Co., 1928-33, exec. v.p., 1933-42, pres. since 1942; dir. and member finance com., E. I. du Pont De Nemours & Co.; pres. Coca-Cola Internat. Corp.; dir. Milwaukee Journal, Del. Power & Light Co., Continental Am. Life Ins. Co., Coca-Cola Bottling Plants, Inc., Nat. Vulcanized Fibre Co., Phila., Baltimore & Washington R.R. Co. Republican. Conglist. Clubs: Wilmington, Wilmington Country, Vicmead Hunt (Wilmington, Del.); Milwaukee Country, University (Milwaukee, Wis.). Home: Greenville, Del. Office: Wilmington Trust Co., 10th & Market Sts., Wilmington, Del. Died Sep. 27, 1948.

EVANS, Evan Alfred, judge; b. Spring Green, Wis., Mar. 19, 1876; s. Evan W. and Mary Ellen (Jones) E.; B.L., U. of Wis., 1897, LL.B., 1899, LL.D. 1933; LL.D., Lake Forest Coll., 1944, Northwestern U., 1946; m. Mary Rountree, Sept. 16, 1902 (died Sept. 12, 1921); children—Evan A., Orrin B., George A.; m. 2d, Mrs. Ferne Ryan Allen, June 1926 (died Apr. 5, 1940). Practiced law at Baraboo, Wis., 1900-16; judge U.S. Circuit Court of Appeals since May 17, 1916. Unitarian. Clubs: University, Union League. Home: 104 7th Av., Baraboo, Wis.

Address: 1212 Lake Shore Drive, Chicago, Ill. Died July 7, 1948.

EVANS, Frank Edgar, officer U.S.M.C.; b. Franklin, Pa., Nov. 19, 1876; s. Frederick and Frances (Williams) E.; student Princeton 3 yrs. (non-grad.); grad. Naval War Coll., 1925, Army War Coll., 1926; m. Esther Caldwell Townsend, Oct. 16, 1909 (divorced); m. 2d, Alleen Fisk Lambert, June 19, 1937. Began service as enlisted man, 1st Wis. Regt., Spanish-Am. War; commd. 2d lt. U.S.M.C., Jan. 26, 1900; 1st lt., Feb. 19, 1902; capt., July 26, 1905; maj., May 25, 1917; lt. col., July 1, 1918; col., June 24, 1924; retired with rank of brig. gen., 1940. Served in Philippines, Panama, Porto Rico and at Culebra; on relief expdn. to West Indies following eruption of Mt. Pelee, Apr. 1902; on Isthmus of Panama, 1904; with 4th Brigade, 2d Div., A.E.F., in France, Nov. 1, 1917-Oct. 1, 1918; regtl. adj. 6th Marines, at Belleau Wood; on staff American High Commissioner to Haiti, 1922-24; on staff Naval War Coll., 1926-27; comdt. Garde d'Haiti, with rank of maj. gen., Apr. 1927-Apr. 1930. Member Am. Assn. Internat. Rifleman; adjutant Am. Palma Rifle Team, 1907, Am. Olympic Rifle Team, 1908; capt. U.S.M.C. Rifle Team, 1905-07. Mem. Comite de Patronage Les Amis de la Legion Etrangere. Awarded Navy Cross for services with 6th Regt. Marines in France; officer Legion of Honor, and hon. private, 1st Class, 2d Regt., Foreign Legion (France). Republican. Clubs: Chevy Chase (Chevy Chase, Md.), Tiger Inn (Princeton), Princeton (New York); Bohemian (San Francisco); Racquet (Philadelphia). Author: Marvel Book of American Ships (with O. P. Jackson), 1916; Daddy Pat of the Marines, 1919; New Book of American Ships (with O. P. Jackson), 1927. Contbr. of fiction to mags. Died November 25, 1941.

EVANS, Frederick Noble, landscape architect; b. Youngstown, O., July 26, 1881; s. Daniel Henry and Sarah Jane (Livingston) E.; A.B., Harvard; Technische Hochschule, Charlottenberg, Germany, 1905-06; M.L.A., Harvard Grad. Sch. Applied Science, 1910; m. Belle Spencer Sanford, 1912; children—Sarah June (wife of Comdr. Franklin G. Hess, U.S. Navy), and Janet Sanford (wife of Lt. Alan White, U.S. N.R.). Mem. Evans & Punchard, Cleveland, O., 1910-14; winter practice Calif., 1913-14; instr. landscape gardening, 1913-15, asst. professor, 1915-20, U. of Ill.; city landscape architect, Sacramento, Calif., since 1920. President Western Shade Tree Conference, 1937-38. Fellow Am. Inst. Park Executives, Am. Soc. Landscape Architects (pres. Pacific Coast chapter, 1934); mem. Sacramento Garden Club (permanent vice-pres.), Sigma Alpha Epsilon; hon. mem. Calif. Garden Clubs, Inc.; mem. Am. Planning and Civic Assn. Republican. Episcopalian. Mason. Author: Town Improvement, 1919. Lecturer on garden design. Home: 1341 40th St., Sacramento, Calif. Died Nov. 30, 1946.

EVANS, George Edward; b. Freeport, O., Feb. 1, 1876; s. Philip Spiker and Marganna (Beebe) E.; student Phillips Exeter Acad., 1900; LL.B., Univ. of Pittsburgh, 1914; m. Daisy Lillian Best, June 20, 1900; children—Elinore Rose, Mildred Josephine, Samuel Beamer. Engaged in bldg. constrn. and retail lumber bus., 1905-39. Mem. bd. dirs. of Retail Lumber Dealers Assn. of Pa., 1918-24; pres. Retail Lumber Dealers Assn., 1920, mem. council, City of Pittsburgh, since 1935. Chmn. com. on pub. works, city council, Pittsburgh, Carnegie Free Library, Allegheny, Housing Authority, Pittsburgh, Pa. State Bd. of Housing; pioneered in development of pub. housing in Pittsburgh and Pa.; served on com. to promote better housing and town planning. Mem. bd. of trustees Carnegie Free Library of Pittsburgh, Carnegie Inst. of Tech., Carnegie Museum, Buhl Planetarium and Inst. of Popular Science, Bldg. Owners and Mgrs. Assn., Pa. Housing and Town Planning Commn., Irene Kaufman Settlement, Urban Law Institute. President National Association of Housing Officials, 1941, Henry George Foundation. Member Allegheny County Bar, Pittsburgh Real Estate Board, Chamber of Commerce, Sons of American Revolution, Sons of Union Vets. of the Civil War. Democrat. Mason (32°, Shriner). Club: Highland Country. Author pamphlets on home bldg. Home: 197 Watson Blvd. Office: 510 City-County Bldg., Pittsburgh, Died June 8, 1945.

EVANS, Henry Ridgely, author; b. Baltimore, Nov. 7, 1861; s. Henry Cotheal and Mary Elizabeth (Garrettson) E.; ed. Georgetown Coll., D.C., and Columbian Coll. (now George Washington U.); LL.B., U. of Md., 1884, Litt.D., 1914; m. Florence Kirkpatrick, Dec. 31, 1891. Student psychical research and Masonic antiquities. Mem. Society of Colonial Wars. Author: Historical Introduction and Bibliography to Hopkins' Magic, Illusions and Scientific Diversions, 1901; The Spirit World Unmasked, 1902; The Napoleon Myth, 1905; The Old and the New Magic, 1909; The House of the Sphinx, 1907; History of the York and Scottish Rites of Freemasonry, 1924; Adventures in Magic, 1927; History of Conjuring and Magic, 1928; Cagliostro and his Egyptian Rite of Freemasonry, 1930; Cagliostro, Sorcerer of the Eighteenth Century, 1931, rev. edit., 1941; A Master of Modern Magic—Life and Adventures of Robert Houdin, 1932; Old Georgetown on the Potomac, 1933; Founders of the Colonial Families of Ridgely, Dorsey, and Greenberry, of Maryland, 1935; Progenitors of the Howards of Maryland, 1938; Edgar Allan Poe and Baron von Kempelen's Chess-Playing Automaton, 1939; Some Rare Old Books on Conjuring and Magic, 1943. Compiled list of writings of William Torrey Harris, 1907. Episcopalian. Scottish Rite Mason (33°). Address: Wyman Park Apts., 40th St. and Beech Av., Baltimore, Md. Died Mar. 29, 1949.

EVANS, John Gary, ex-governor; b. Cokesbury, S.C., Oct. 15, 1863; s. Nathan George and Ann Victoria (Gary) E.; ed. Union Coll., Schenectady, N.Y., class of 1883, to close jr. yr.; read law under Judge W. T. Gary, of Augusta, Ga.; m. Emily Mansfield Plume, Dec. 17, 1897; 1 dau., Emily Victoria (Mrs. Dag Knutson). Admitted to S.C. bar, 1886; elected to S.C. Ho. of Rep. 1888, 1890, Senate, 1892, gov. of S.C., 1894-97; pres. S.C. Constl. Conv., 1895. Maj. and insp.-gen. 1st Div, 7th Army Corps, Spanish-Am. War, 1898; transferred to staff of Major-Gen. William Ludlow, Havana, Cuba; assisted in organizing civic govt. for Havana after war. Del.-at-large from S.C. to Dem. Nat. Conv., 1896, del., 1900, del.-at-large, 1912, 16; chmn. State Dem. Exec. Com., 1912-16; chmn. City Democracy; mem. Dem. Nat. Com. for S.C., 1918-30; mem. S.C. Ho. of Rep. Mem. S.C. Hist. Soc., Delta Phi. Episcopalian. Home: Spartanburg, S.C. Died June 27, 1942.

EVANS, John Morris, clergyman; b. Aberdare, Wales, July 12, 1877; s. Thomas S. and Esther Morris E.; brought to U.S., 1880; student Bucknell U., Lewisburg, Pa., 1896-9. Oxford U., Eng., 1901-3; m. Lettie Louise Lewis, Sept. 10, 1906. Ordained Bapt. ministry, 1903; pastor Memorial Ch., Builth Wells, Breconshire, Wales, 1903-5, King's St. Ch., Abertillery, Monmouthshire, Wales, 1905-10, Bapt. Ch., Lowville, N.Y., 1912-16, 1st Unitarian Ch., Dayton, O., 1916-19, All Souls' Ch., Chicago, since Oct. 1, 1919; also head resident Abraham Lincoln Centre. Mason. Author: Conflict in Christian Belief, 1908. Home: 4031 Ellis Av., Chicago. Died Nov. 21, 1948.

EVANS, John William, artist-engraver; b. at Brooklyn, Mar. 27, 1855; s. Felix and Sarah (Pitt) E.; pupil of P. R. B. Pierson; m. Hannah M. Armstrong, Jan. 9, 1878. Exhibited Chicago Expn., 1893, Paris Expn., 1900, also in London, Berlin, Vienna, Munich and New York; bronze medal, Buffalo Expn., 1901, St. Louis Expn., 1904; silver medal, Panama P.I. Expn., 1915. Home: 822 Elm Av., Ridgefield, N.J. Died Mar. 10, 1943.

EVANS, Joseph Spragg, prof. medicine; b. West Chester, Pa., Mar. 6, 1875; s. Joseph S. and Ruth Ann (Peirce) E.; B.A., Haverford Coll., 1895; M.D., Sch. of Medicine, U. of Pa., 1899; m. Mary E. Eagan, Apr. 9, 1907 (died Dec. 18, 1924); 1 dau., Clara Mary. Practiced Phila., 1899-1909; instr. clin. medicine, U. of Pa., and asso. Wm. Pepper Lab. Clin. Medicine, 1902-09; prof. clin. medicine, University of Wisconsin, 1910-24, prof. of medicine, 1924-45, prof. emeritus since Sept. 1945. Fellow Am. Coll. Physicians; mem. A.M.A., College Physicians (Philadelphia), Alpha Tau Omega, Phi Alpha Sigma, Sigma Xi, Alpha Omega Alpha, Mil. Order Loyal Legion. Clubs: University (Phila., and Milwaukee). Mem. Wis. State Council of Defense, 1917. Address: 1300 University Av., Madison 6, Wis. Died Feb. 3, 1948.

EVANS, Newton (Gurdon), pathologist; b. Hamilton, Mo., June 1, 1874; s. William and Emma Beulah (Newton) E.; student Battle Creek (Mich.) Coll., Am. Med. Missionary Coll., Chicago; B.S. Union College, Lincoln, Neb., 1895; M.D., Cornell Univ. Med. Sch., New York, 1900; m. Cora Mildred Deming, Aug. 27, 1901 (died 1942); children—Emma Elizabeth (Mrs. Howard A. Ball), William Dustin. In general practice until 1914, prof. pathology, Med. Dept. U. of Tenn., 1908-11; prof. pathology, College Medical Evangelists, Loma Linda and Los Angeles, California, since 1914, president, 1914-27, dean, 1928-31, and since 1943; vice-pres., 1931-36; pathologist Los Angeles County Gen. Hosp. since 1928, Lt. col. Med. Res. (now retired), comdg. officer U.S. Gen. Hosp. 47, 1926-32 and 1935-37. Chmn. bd. Alumni Research Foundation, Coll. Med. Evangelists. Fellow A.M.A., Am. Coll. Physicians, A.A.A.S.; mem. Am. Soc. Clin. Pathologists, Los Angeles Acad. Medicine, Los Angeles Pathological Soc. (pres. 1929), Los Angeles Cancer Soc. (pres. 1936), Am. Assn. Pathologists and Bacteriologists, Med. Assn. State of Calif. Republican. Seventh Day Adventist. Contributor results of research to various med. jours. Home: 2000 Milan Av., South Pasadena. Address: 312 N. Boyle Av., Los Angeles, Calif. Died Dec. 19, 1945.

EVANS, William Augustus, hygienist; b. Marion, Ala., Aug. 5, 1865; s. William Augustus and Julia Josephine (Wyatt) E.; B.S., Agrl. College of Miss., 1883, M.S., 1898; M.D., Tulane Univ. of La., 1885, med. dept. U. of Ill., 1899; LL.D., Tulane, 1910; D.P.H., Univ. of Mich., 1911; LL.D., Univ. of Miss., 1921; m. Ida May Wildberger, Nov. 20, 1907 (died Jan. 13, 1926). In practice of medicine since 1885; demonstrator pathology, 1891-95, prof., 1895-1908, Coll. of Medicine of U. of Ill.; commr. of health of Chicago, 1907-11; prof. san. science, Northwestern U. Med. Sch., 1908-28, now emeritus. Home: Aberdeen, Miss. Died Nov. 8, 1948.

EVERARD, Lewis Charles (ĕv'ẽr-ärd), editor; b. Corsicana, Tex., Nov. 7, 1884; s. Richard and Carrie L. (Cantine) E; B A., Yale, 1908, M.A., 1910, post-grad. work, 1910; Phi Beta Kappa fellow from Yale at Sorbonne and Coll. de France, 1908-09; m. Juanita Maginnis Norman, Sept. 16, 1908; children—Nathaniel (dec.), William Phelps, Howard (dec.), Marion (dec.), Frank Norman. Began as stenographer Wells Fargo & Co., New Orleans, 1900; sec. to William Lyon Phelps, professor, Yale, 1904-08, also to Alfred K. Merritt, registrar of Yale; instr. English, Yale, 1910-15; asst. editor U.S. Forest Service, 1915-18, chief of its publs., 1918-20; chief editor U.S. Dept. Agr., 1920-21; economist and statistician War Finance Corp., 1921-23; v.p. Med. Standard Book Co., Baltimore, 1923-25; editor, chief of ednl. cooperation and asst. chief div. of information, U.S. Forest Service, 1925-29; editor Am. Assn. Museums, including Museum News (semi-monthly), since 1929. Mem. Phi Beta Kappa, Beta Theta Pi. Republican. Spiritualist. Author: (brochure) Arbor Day—Its History and Observance (U.S. Dept. Agr.), 1926; Zoölogical Parks, Aquariums and Botanical Gardens (Am. Assn. Museums), 1932; also (songs for Arbor Day) On Forest Land, Made of Wood. Editor: Year Book, U.S. Dept. Agr., 1920; Handbook of American Museums, 1932. Contbr. article on Museums and Exhibitions to new Ency. of Social Sciences, 1933; article on Museums in Dictionary of the Arts, 1942; yearly article on museums in the Yearbook of the World Book Ency. Home: 3820 Tenth St. N.W. Address: Smithsonian Institution, Washington, D.C. Died 1943.

EVERETT, Sidney Johnston, lawyer; b. Weakley County, Tenn., July 5, 1862; s. Elbert Green and Maleita (Busey) E.; B.S., Bethel Coll., McKenzie, Tenn., 1885; LL.B., Cumberland U., 1888; m. Annie McCallum, Oct. 22, 1890; children—Roxie May (Mrs. Albert Ezzell), Grace, Eleanor (Mrs. B. C. Arnold), Maleita (Mrs. Wynn Smith), Virginia (Mrs. Byron Alexander). Mem. Tenn. House of Rep., 1886-88; practiced at Jackson, Tenn., 1891-1905; mem. Dem. Exec. Com., Tenn., 1900-04; apptd. judge 16th Circuit, Mar. 25, 1905, elected for unexpired term, 1906-10, and reëlected for term, 1910-18; resumed practice at Jackson, Sept. 1, 1918. Mem. Jackson and Madison County bar associations (pres. both), Tennessee Bar Association. Elected delegate to General Assembly of Presbyterian Church, 1941. Mem. Sigma Alpha Epsilon. Presbyterian. K.P. Home: 365 Highland Av. Office: Elks Bldg., Jackson, Tenn. Deceased

EVERETT, Willis Mead, lawyer; b. Randolph, N.Y., Nov. 18, 1863; s. Timothy Amos Cowles and Lydia (Van Rensselaer) E.; A.B., Allegheny Coll., Meadville, Pa., 1885; LL.D., Presbyterian Coll., Clinton, S.C., 1939; m. Mary Catherine Gillette, Aug. 18, 1887; children Charles Gillette (dec.), Edward Van Rensselaer (deceased), Mary Louise (deceased), Willis Mead. Professor mathematics and German, Chamberlain Inst. and Female Coll., Randolph, N.Y., 1885-86; admitted to O. bar, 1887, practiced in Cincinnati, 1887; admitted to Ill. bar, 1887, practiced Chicago, 1888; admitted to Ga. bar, 1888, and since practiced in Atlanta; mem. with son, Everett & Everett. Pres. exec. com. Home Missions of Presbyn. Ch. in U.S.; moderator Gen. Assembly Presbyn. Ch. in U.S., 1938-39; chmn. stewardship and finance com. Presbyn. Ch. U.S., 1938-39. Trustee Clark U., Atlanta, Gammon Theol. Sem., Atlanta. Mem. Atlanta Bar Assn., Phi Kappa Psi. Mason. Home: Ponce de Leon Apts. Office: 402 Connally Bldg., Atlanta, Ga. Died Oct. 12, 1943.

EVERITT, Charles Raymond, book publisher; b. New York, N.Y., Dec. 31, 1901; s. Charles Percy and Elizabeth (Thompson) E.; grad. Hotchkiss Sch., 1919; A. B., Yale, 1923; student Oxford U., England, 1923-24; m. Helen Goetzmann, Sept. 4, 1924; children—Rae Alexander, Jeanne, Charles Bell, Samuel Agar. With Harcourt, Brace and Co., New York City, 1924-29; mgr. Curtis Brown, Ltd., New York, 1930-35; with Little, Brown and Co., Boston, since 1936, exec. vice pres., Chief of publ. div., European Theatre of Operations, Office of War Information, London, since 1945. An editor of "Free America." Mem. Psi Upsilon. Clubs: St. Botolph (Boston); Dutch Treat (New York). Translator: (with Helen Everitt) Egyptian Day, 1927. Home: Miles River Farm, Ipswich, Mass. Office: 34 Beacon St., Boston, Mass. Died May 23, 1947.

EVVARD, John Marcus (ĕv-värd'), consultant animal nutrition and prodn., author; b. Saunemin, Ill., Nov. 6, 1884; s. John B. and Mary (Leitel) E.; B.S., U. of Ill., 1907; M.S. in Agr., U. of Mo., 1909; Ph.D., U. of Ariz., 1927; m. Mattie Casey Cooper, Aug. 10, 1911; children—Mary Margaret Batman, John Cooper, Martha Jane Shemer. Asst. city editor Pontiac Daily Sentinel, 1904; asst. to dean and dir. Mo. Agrl. Coll. and Mo. Agrl. Expt. Sta., 1907-10; asst. chief, animal husbandry, Ia. Agrl. Expt. Sta., 1910-14; charge animal husbandry sect. and chief in swine prodn., 1911-30, chief in beef cattle and sheep production, 1919-30, Ia. Agrl. Expt. Sta.; asso. prof. animal husbandry, 1916-18, prof., 1918-30, Ia. State Coll. Agr. and Mechanic Arts, chief in nutrition, 1914-19; special assistant in the Office of Secretary of Agriculture, 1922-23; staff of Am. Inst. of Agriculture, 1922-23; v.p. McMillen Co., Allied Mills, Ft. Wayne, Ind., 1930-33; research consultant Soya Products, Inc., Chicago, since 1932; advisory to exec. staff Allied Mills, Inc., since 1933; pres. Universal Supply, Inc., Phoenix, 1933-36; professor and head of dept. of agriculture, Ariz. State Coll., Tempe, (part time), 1935-37. Contbg. editor Chester White Journal, 1920-30, corr. editor Farm and Fireside, 1924-30. Chmn. swine commn. U.S. Food Administration, 1917-18; mem. U.S. Livestock Industrial Com., 1917; member Farmers' Livestock Marketing Com. of 15. Fellow A.A.A.S., Ia. Acad. Science; mem. Am. Soc. Animal Production (ex-pres.), Alpha Zeta, Sigma Xi, Phi Lambda Upsilon, Phi Kappa Phi, Gamma Sigma Delta, Sigma Delta Chi, Lambda Gamma Delta. Advanced Unitarian. Author over 700 bulls., papers, etc., covering investigations principally in field of animal feeding and nutrition. Home: "Casita Querida," 317 W. Cypress, Phoenix, Ariz. Died July 30, 1948.

EWART, Frank Carman, college prof.; b. Marietta, O., Sept. 4, 1871; s. Thomas West and Jerusha Sage (Gear) E.; grad. Granville (O.) Acad., 1888; A.B., Denison U. 1892, A.M., 1894, L.H.D., 1919; student univs. of Chicago, 1892-93, Heidelberg, Germany, 1895-96, Grenoble, France, summer 1912, U. of Havana, Cuba, 1914-15; m. Nettie Luella McVeigh, Aug. 22, 1894; children—Brainerd Gilliam (dec.), Beatrice Marie (Mrs. Roy N. Anderson), Donald McVeigh (deceased). Instr. in Latin, Granville (O.) Acad., 1893-95; acting asst. prof. of modern langs., Denison U.; Granville, 1896-97; instr. in French, Kalamazoo Col., Mich., 1897-99; asso. prof. modern languages, Colgate U., 1899-1904, prof. Romanic langs., 1904-39, prof. emeritus since 1939. Fellow Inst. of Am. Genealogy. Mem. Modern Lang. Assn. Am., Am. Assn. Teachers of Spanish, Am. Assn. Teachers of French, Am. Assn. Teachers of Italian, Am. Assn. Univ. Pros., Phi Beta Kappa, Kappa Delta Rho. Baptist. Mason. Club: Torch (Utica, N.Y.). Author: Cuba y las costumbres cubanas, 1919. Annotated Rostand's L'Aiglon. Home: Hamilton, N.Y. Died Sept. 28, 1942.

EWING, James, pathologist; b. Pittsburgh, Dec. 25, 1866; s. Thomas and Julia R. (Hufnagel) E.; A.B., Amherst, 1888, A.M., 1891; Sc.D., 1923; M.D., Coll. Phys. and Surg. (Columbia), 1891; Sc.D., U. of Pittsburgh, 1911, Amherst, 1923, U. of Rochester, 1932, Union U., 1938; LL.D., Kenyon, 1931, Western Reserve, 1931; m. Catherine C. Halsted, June 19, 1900; 1 son, James Halsted. Tutor histology, 1893-97. Clark fellow, 1896-99, instr. clin. pathology, 1897-98, Coll. Physicians and Surgeons; prof. pathology, Cornell, 1899-1932, prof. of oncology since 1932. Charles Mickle fellow, Toronto, 1935; John Scott medalist, Phila., 1937; hon. mem. Phila. Pathol. Soc., Acad. Med., Brazil, Swedish Roentgen. Soc., Acad. Med. Budapest; mem. Nat. Acad. Sciences, Assn. Am. Physicians, Am. Roentgen Ray Soc., Am. Med. Museums Soc., Am. Assn. Pathologists and Bacteriologists, Soc. Exptl. Biology and Medicine, Harvey Soc., Am. Assn. for Cancer Research, N.Y. Acad. Med., N.Y. Pathol. Soc. Decorated Officer Order Southern Cross, Brazil; Officer Order of Leopold, Belgium. Republican. Presbyterian. Clubs: Century, University, Amherst. Author: Clinical Pathology of Blood, 1900-03; articles on Identity, The Signs of Death, and Sudden Death, in Text-Book of Legal Medicine and Toxicology, 1903; on Blood, etc., in Text-Book of Legal Medicine, 1910; Neoplastic Diseases, 1919-27, 40. Home: 415 Central Park W. Office: 444 E. 68th St., New York, N.Y. Died May 16, 1943.

EWING, Samuel Edgar, church official; b. Sandoval, Ill., May 12, 1865; s. Robert and Minerva Jane (Martin) E.; A.B., William Jewell Coll., 1893; Th.M., Southern Bapt. Theol. Sem., Louisville, Ky., 1896; D.D., Ewing (Ill.) Coll., 1915; m. Mattie James McCourt, 1896 (died 1923); 1 son, Samuel E.; m. 2d, Eunice E. Ringer, 1926. Ordained Bapt. ministry, 1893; pastor successively First Ch., Kansas City, Kan., Logan Street Ch., Louisville, Ky., Holden, Mo., and Euclid Ch., St. Louis, until 1910; supt. St. Louis Bapt. Mission Bd. and Sec. St. Louis Bapt. Assn., 1910-40. Recording and statis. sec. Mo. Bapt. Gen. Assn.; trustee and sec. Mo. Bapt. Hosp. since 1915; trustee Southern Bapt. Theol. Sem., Southern Bapt. Hosp., New Orleans. Republican. Mason. Author: (booklet) St. Louis, A Mission Field, 1912. Address: 5939 DeGiverville Av., St. Louis, Mo. Died Sep. 11, 1941.

EWING, Thomas, lawyer; b. Leavenworth, Kan., May 21, 1862; s. Gen. Thomas and Ellen Ewing (Cox) E.; student U. of Wooster, Ohio, 1879-81; A.B., Columbia, 1885, A.M., 1886, law sch., 1887-88, tutor Sch. of Mines, 1885-88; LL.B., Georgetown U., 1890, LL.D., 1914; m. Anna Phillips, d. William F. Cochran, Oct. 24, 1894; children—Alexandra (Mrs. Thomas A. Stone), Thomas (died Feb. 8, 1933), William Francis Cochran, Sherman, Gifford Cochran, Ellen Cox (Mrs. Thomas A. Stone, she died June 18, 1931), Bayard. Asst. examiner U.S. Patent Office, 1888-90; practiced in N.Y., 1891-1913, making splty. of patent law; commr. patents, U.S., 1913-17, resigned and resumed practice, N.Y. City, Aug. 1917; lecturer on patent law, Georgetown U. Law Sch., 1914-32. Has solicited some well-known patents, notably fundamental patent of Frank J. Sprague on multiple unit system of elec. train operation, fundamental patent of David T. Kenney on vacuum cleaning, and Prof. M. I. Pupin's patents on long distance telephony. Dem. candidate for mayor of Yonkers, 1897-99; mem. Yonkers sch. bd., 1897-1903, police bd., 1905-07; pres. Yonkers Tuberculosis Hosp. Commn., 1910-13. Chmn. Munitions Patent Bd., U.S. War and Navy depts., 1918-20. Pres. Am. group Internat. Assn., for Protection of Industrial Property, 1933-35; del. of U.S. to Internat. Conf., London, 1935. Member Ohio Society of New York (pres. 1927-29), Sigma Chi, Phi Beta Kappa. Clubs: University, Century (New York, N.Y.); Metropolitan (Washington, D.C.). Author: Jonathan, a Tragedy, 1902; also poems in anthologies and some metrical transls. of Horace, in Poet Lore. Home: Yonkers, N.Y. Office: 405 Lexington Av., New York, N.Y. Died Dec. 7, 1942.

EXNER, Max Joseph, public health; b. Austria, Mar. 31, 1871; s. Franz and Marie (Zöllner) E.; came to U.S., 1882; M.P.E., Y.M.C.A. Coll., Springfield, Mass., 1892; B.S., Carleton Coll., Northfield, Minn., 1898; M.D., Univ. Med. Coll., Kansas City, Mo., 1906; m. Elizabeth Wells, May 26, 1899; children—Donald W., Max V., Willard B., Robert M. Physical dir. Carleton Coll., 1892-98, Y.M.C.A., Troy, N.Y., 1898-99, Y.M.C.A., Kansas City, Mo., 1899-1908, Y.M.C.A., China, 1908-11; dir. sex edn., Internat. Com. Y.M.C.A., since 1911. In charge social hygiene edn. for U.S. Army, during World War, coöperating with War Dept. Commn. on Training Camp Activities. A pioneer in sex edn.; started 3 lines of work in China—nat. physical training, training sch. for native physical directors, ednl. propaganda in hygiene and sanitation. Dir. endl. dept. Am. Social Hygiene Assn., 1920-36, now consultant; epidemiologist Dept. of Health, Newark, N.J., 1936-38, dir. of venereal division since 1938. Author: The Rational Sex Life for Men, 1914; The Sexual Side of Marriage, 1932; also many pamphlets. Home: 357 Lake St. Address: Dept. of Health, Newark, N.J. Died Oct. 8, 1943.

EXTON, William Gustav, pathologist, urologist; b. Savannah, Ga., Feb. 25, 1876; s. Gustav and Rosalie (Unger) E.; M.D., Coll. Physicians and Surgeons (Columbia), 1896; house physician, Mount Sinai Hosp., N.Y. City, 1896-99; post grad. and research work, Pathol. Inst., Vienna, also in London and Paris, 1906-07; m. Florence Phillips, Sept. 20, 1905; children—William, Manning Mason, John Marshall. Practiced, N.Y. City, 1901-06; spl. practice and research in urology-metabolism, 1907-16; dir. laboratories Prudential Ins. Co., Newark, N.J., since 1914, planned and directed longevity service since 1917. Mem. A.M.A., Med. Soc. State of N.Y., New York County Med. Soc., Am. Pub. Health Assn., Am. Urol. Assn., Am. Soc. Clinical Pathologists (pres.), Assn. Life Ins. Med Dirs., Optical Society of America, Am. Assn. Advancement of Science, Am. Chem. Soc. Inventor of gastroscope, 1906; urological table, 1907; immiscible balance, 1915; protein tests, 1918; turbidimeter, 1918; euscope, 1920; spectroscopic method of colorimetry, 1921; scopometer, 1924; junior scopometer, 1927; quantitative microscopy, 1928; photoelectric scopometer, 1929; a new test for sugar tolerance, 1930; new methods for identifying the various sugars that occur in urine, 1932; new method for measuring the number, diameters, volume and hemoglobin content of red blood cells, 1933; the one-hour-two-dose dextrose tolerance test, 1934; incidence of sugars and reducing substances other than glucose in 1000 consecutive cases, 1934; instrument and method for measuring size of sub-microscopic particles photoelectrically by transmitted light and Tyndall beam, 1934; fibrinogen as an index of disease and its clinical determination by photoelectric scopometry, 1935; partition of blood fats, 1936; one hour renal condition test, 1937; colorimetric determination of oxygen in blood, 1938; determination of blood water and its distribution between cells and plasma, 1940; inventor of Photo-panometer: a photoelectric photometer and spectrophometer having scale readings linear with concentration, 1940; clinical significance and measurement of acidosis and alkalosis by colorimetry of carbon dioxide in blood. Author: The Prudential Urinalysis System, 1934. Contbr. on preclinical medicine, longevity, clinical pathology, etc. Awards Ward Burdick memorial medal, Am. Soc. Clin. Pathologist; N.Y. State and N.J. State Med. socs and others. Home: Flofields, Millbrook, N.Y.; also 240 Central Park S., New York, N.Y. Office: Prudential Ins. Bldg., Newark, N.J. Died Mar. 12, 1943.

EYRE, Wilson, architect; b. Florence, Italy, Oct. 30, 1858; s. Wilson and Louisa (Lear) E.; ed. in Italy until 1869, Newport, R.I., 1869-72, Lenoxville, Can., 1872-74; and 1875, Woburn to prepare for inst.; M. I. T., 1876; unmarried. With James P. Sims, architect, 1876-81; since then in independent practice. Has built many bldgs. in Phila. and New York, also several bldgs. for Newcomb Memorial Coll., New Orleans; the Detroit Club, Detroit, etc. A.N.A., 1910; mem. A.I.A., Am. Social Science Assn. Address: 1003 Spruce St., Philadelphia, Pa. Died Oct. 23, 1944.

F

FABER, Lothar W., pres. Eberhard Faber Pencil Co.; b. N.Y. City, Sept. 27, 1861; s. Eberhard and Jenny (Haag) F.; prep. edn., Trinity Sch., New Brighton, S.I.; Ph.B., Columbia, 1882; m. Anna Prieth, June 17, 1885 (dec.); children—Theodora (Mrs. J. Whitney Baker, dec.), Margaret (wife of lt. col. Brock Putnam), Eberhard Lothar. Began with Eberhard Faber Pencil Co., 1885, pres. since 1898; v.p. Eberhard Faber Rubber Co., Newark, 1910-29. Mem. Chem. Soc. America, Beta Theta Pi. Clubs: Richmond County Country, Wykagyl Country. Home: 335 Riverside Drive, New York, N.Y. Office: 37 Greenpoint Av., Brooklyn, N.Y. Died May 12, 1943.

FABER, Eberhard (fä'bĕr), manufacturer; b. New York, Mar. 14, 1859; s. Eberhard and Jenny (Haag) F.; educated Columbia School of Mines; m. Abby B. Adams, Dec. 22, 1886 (died May 25, 1898); m. 2d, Roberta A. Heim, Apr. 20, 1904. Entered office of his father (the well-known lead-pencil mfr.), and in 1879 took charge of the business; later his brother, Lothar W., became asso. with him in the plants at Brooklyn, N.Y., and Newark, N.J., the former being incorporated as the Eberhard Faber Pencil Co., and latter as Eberhard Faber Rubber Co. Home: 820 5th Av. Office: 200 5th Av., New York. Died May 16, 1946; buried in Moravian Cemetery, Staten Island.

FAGET, Guy Henry, U.S. Pub. Health Service; b. New Orleans, La., June 15, 1891; s. Francois and Alice (Beegg) F.; M.D., Tulane U., 1914; m. Isabelle Le Blanc, Feb. 8, 1917; children—Frank Alfred, Max Allen, Elsie Alice, Guy Edmund. Interne Marine Hosp., New Orleans, 1914-16; physician Brit. Colonial Service, British Honduras, 1916-22; aptd. asst. surgeon U.S.P.H.S., 1922, surgeon, 1934; U.S. Marine Hosp., Mobile, 1922-23, Marine Hosp., San Francisco, 1923-24, Seattle, 1924-26, Fort Stanton, 1926-30, New Orleans, 1930-33, Norfolk, 1933-37, U.S. Marine Hospital, San Francisco, Calif., 1937-40; med. officer in charge, Nat. Leprosarium, Carville, La., since July, 1940; senior surgeon, U.S. Public Health Service, 1942; medical director, U.S. Pub. Health Service, Cons. adv. bd. Leonard Wood Memorial; elected chmn. Pan Am. Conf. on Leprosy, Sect. on Therapeutics, Rio de Janeiro. Awarded Liber Medal in sci. exhibit of Centennial meeting, A.M.A., for exhibit in chemotherapy in leprosy, 1947. Pioneered new sulfone treatment of leprosy. Fellow Am. Col. Physicians, Am. Med. Assn.; mem. Internat. Leprosy Assn., Associated Mil. Surgeons, Am. Pub. Health Assn., Am. Physicians Lit. Guild, Alpha Omega Alpha. Roman Catholic. Contbr. several papers to Med. Jours. Address: U.S. Marine Hospital, Carville, La. Died July 17, 1947.

FAIRBANK, Alfred, life insurance officer; b. De Soto, Mo., Aug. 3, 1887; s. William Cooper and Mary Emma (McConnell) F.; LL.B., Benton Coll. of Law, St. Louis, 1909; m. Abby Jane Downing, Oct. 14, 1915; children—Charlotte Lucille (Mrs. Fred H. Mason), Dorothy May (Mrs. Robert E. Newton). Teacher in pub. schs., Cleveland and St. Louis, 1905-11; admitted to Mo. bar, 1909; asst. supt. St. Louis Industrial Sch., 1911-13; exec. agent Bd. of Children's Guardians, City of St. Louis, 1913-17; dir. civilian relief S.W. Div. Am. Red Cross, 1917-18; mgr. of div., 1918-20; investment banking, St. Louis, Mo., 1920-30; v.p. and trust officer Boatmen's Nat. Bank, St. Louis, 1930-38; pres. Central States Life Ins. Co., St. Louis, since 1938; dir. Barnard Stationery Co., Nat. Oats Co. Mem. and pres. University City, Mo., Sch. Bd., 1926-30; gen. chmn. St. Louis Community Fund Campaign, 1927; sec. St. Louis Chapter Am. Red Cross and dir. disaster relief com.; pres. bd. dirs. Barnard Free Skin and Cancer Hosp.; v.p. St. Louis Mercantile Library Assn.; dir. St. Louis and Mo Chambers of Commerce; dir. United Charities formerly mem. exec. com., trust div., Am. Bankers Assn. Mem. St. Louis and Mo. bar assns., Delta Theta Phi. Republican. Conglist. (Mem. Prudential Com. Bd. of Commrs. of Foreign Missions.) Mason. Club: Noonday. Home: 6612 Waterman Av. Office: 3663 Lindell Blvd., St. Louis, Mo. Died March 6, 1945.

FAIRBANKS, Arthur, educator; b. Hanover, N.H., Nov. 13, 1864; s. Henry and Annie S. (Noyes) F.; A.B., Dartmouth, 1886, Litt.D., 1909; student Union Theol. Sem., 1887-88, Yale Div. Sch., 1888-89; Berlin and Freiburg, 1889-90; Ph.D., Freiburg, 1890; m. Elizabeth L. Moody, May 2, 1889. Instr. Greek, Dartmouth Coll., 1886-87 and 1890-91, asst. prof. German and instr. logic, 1891-92; lecturer social science and philosophy of religion, Yale, 1892-94, instr. comparative religion, 1894-99; acting assistant prof. ancient philosophy, Cornell, 1899-1900; prof. Greek lit. and archæology, U. of Ia., 1900-06; prof. Greek and Greek archæology, U. of Mich., 1906-07; dir. Boston Museum Fine Arts, 1907-25; prof. fine arts, Dartmouth Coll., 1928-33. Fellow Am. Sch. Classical Studies, Athens, 1898-99; editor The Classical Journal, 1905-07. Mem. Am. Philol. Assn., Archæol. Inst. America, Deutsches Archæol. Institut, Phi Beta Kappa; fellow Am. Acad. Arts and Sciences. Author: Introduction to Sociology, 1896-1901; First Philosophers of Greece, 1898; A Study of the Greek Pæan, 1900; The Mythology of Greece and Rome, 1907; Athenian White Lekythoi, U. of Mich. Studies VI-VII, 1907, 1914; Handbook of Greek Religion, 1910; Greek Gods and Heroes, 1915; Catalogue of Greek and Etruscan Vases in the Boston Museum of Fine Arts, Vol. I, 1928; Greek Art—The Basis of Modern European Art, 1933. Translator: Riehl's Introduction to the Theory of Science and Metaphysics, 1894; Philostratus' Imagines, 1931. Contbr. to philol. pubs. Home: Hanover, N.H. Died Jan. 13, 1944.

FAIRBANKS, John Leo, artist and sculptor; b. Payson, Utah, Apr. 30, 1880; s. John B. and Lillie Anetta (Huish) F.; student U. of Chicago, 1906-07, New York U., 1909-10, Columbia, 1912-13; studied Julien Academie and Academie Colorossi Paris; m. Pauline White, Dec. 25, 1916. Painter and sculptor since 1912; mural sculptural decorations, Temple at Laie (Hawaii), Salt Lake Temple, Mesa Temple, Ariz. State Coll. Library; stained glass windows, Hall of Religion (Century of Progress Exposition, Chicago); murals, Officers Club, Adair, Oregon; professor art, Ore. State Coll., since 1923; supervisor of art, Salt Lake City Schools, 1905-23. Sec. Salt Lake City Planning Commn.; pres. Utah Art Inst.; mem. Kappa Kappa Alpha, Alpha Delta Sigma, Professional Artists League, Am. Fed. of Arts, Soc. Ore. Artists, New York Architectural League, Pacific Arts Assn. (treas.). Club: Triad (Corvallis, Ore.). Home: 316 N. 32d St., Corvallis, Ore. Died Oct. 3, 1946; buried in Mt. Olivet Cemetery, Salt Lake City.

FAIRBANKS, Richard, publisher; b. Indianapolis, Ind., Oct. 8, 1883; s. Charles Warren and Cornelia (Cole) F.; student Phillips Acad., Andover, Mass., 1900-01; A.B., Yale U., 1905; LL.B., Ind. Law Sch., 1909; m. Louise Hibben, 1911 (died 1912); 1

son, Richard; m. 2d, Robertine Buchanan, Nov. 14, 1918; 1 son, Michael Buchanan. Admitted to Ind. bar, 1909; practiced law at Indianapolis, 1909-17; pres. Am. Trust & Savings Bank, Springfield, O., 1919; v.p. Indianapolis News, 1920-40, pres. and pub. since 1940; pres. Indianapolis Switch & Frog Co., 1938-40. Served as capt., Inf., with A.E.F., 1917-18. Mem. Delta Kappa Epsilon. Republican. Methodist. Mason (Shriner), Odd Fellow. Clubs: Columbia, Woodstock, Dramatic (Indianapolis). Home: 4171 Washington Blvd. Office: Indianapolis News, Indianapolis, Ind.* Died July 26, 1944.

FAIRBURN, William Armstrong, pres. Diamond Match Co.; b. Bath, Me., Oct. 12, 1876. Apprentice Bath Iron Works, 1890-94; student in naval architecture and engring., U. of Glasgow, Scotland, 1896-97; designed vessels for James J. Hill and Edward H. Harriman; with Diamond Match Co. since 1909, became gen. supt., 1910, pres. since 1915. Home: Center Lovell, Me.; Ojai Valley, Calif.; Morristown, N.J. Office: 30 Church St., New York, N.Y.* Died Oct. 1, 1947.

FAIRCHILD, Benjamin Lewis, former congressman; b. Monroe County, N.Y., Jan. 5, 1863; s. Benjamin and Calista (Scheaffer) F.; lived in Washington, D.C., in childhood; LL.B., Columbian (now George Washington) U., 1883, LL.M., 1885; m. Anna E. Crumbie, Feb. 28, 1893 (died Nov. 24, 1902); 1 son, Franklin Crumbie (dec.); m. 2d, Elinor Gardiner Parsons, Apr. 21, 1922; children—Elinor, Mabelle. Draughtsman, Patent Office, at 14; clerk, Treasury Dept., 1879-85; practicing law since 1885. Mem. 54th Congress (1895-97), 16th N.Y. Dist., 65th Congress (1917-19), 67th to 69th Congresses (1921-27), 24th N.Y. Dist. Mem. Am., N.Y. State and Westchester County bar assns., Med. Jurisprudence Soc. Club: Union League. Home: Pelham, N.Y. Office: 280 Madison Av., New York. Died Oct. 25, 1946.

FAIRLIE, John Archibald (fâr'lĭ), univ. prof.; b. Glasgow, Scotland, Oct. 30, 1872; s. James Mitchell and Margaret Simpson (Miller) F.; A.B., Harvard, 1895, A.M., 1896; Ph.D., Columbia, 1898; unmarried. Sec. to com. on canals of N.Y., 1899-1900; asst. prof., 1900-06, jr. prof., 1906-09, U. of Mich.; spl. agt. Bur. of Corps., 1908, 09; asso. prof. polit. science, U. of Ill., 1909-11, prof., 1911-41, head of dept., 1938-41; chmn. senate library com., 1938-41; mem. grad. faculty, 1939-41; emeritus, 1941; visiting prof., Ohio State University, 1942, 1943. Mem. Mich. Constl. Conv., 1907-08. Dir. Ill. Efficiency and Economy Com., 1914-15; War Dept. (chief of section), 1918-19. Mng. editor Am. Political Science Review, 1916-25. Mem. Am. Polit. Science Assn. (pres. 1929), Nat. Municipal League, Phi Beta Kappa Fraternity. Clubs: Harvard (New York City); Cosmos (Washington, D.C.); University (Chicago and Urbana). Author: Centralization of Administration in N.Y. State, 1898; Municipal Administration, 1901; National Administration of U.S., 1905; Local Government in Counties, Towns and Villages, 1906; Essays in Municipal Administration, 1908; Taxation and Revenue System of Illinois, 1910; Town and County Government in Illinois, 1913; Revenue and Finance Administration (Ill.), 1915; British War Administration, 1919; Administrative Procedure in Great Britain, 1927; County Government and Administration (with C. M. Kneier), 1930; Biography of J. W. Garner, 1943; also various bulls., Ill. Constl. Conv., 1919-20. Contbr. to encys. and tech. jours. Mem. bd. editors Ill. Studies in Social Sciences, 1912-41. Home: 1203 W. Illinois St., Urbana, Ill. Died Jan. 23, 1947; buried at Jacksonville, Fla.

FAIRFIELD, Arthur Philip, naval officer; b. Saco, Me., Oct. 29, 1877; s. Rufus Albert and Frances Mary (Patten) F.; student Thornton Acad., Saco, Me., 1892-1895; Bowdoin Coll., Brunswick, Me., 1895-97, hon. A.M., 1924; B.S., U.S. Naval Acad., 1901; m. Nancy Douglas Duval, June 14, 1906. Began as naval cadet, 1897; served as such in U.S.S. Columbia during Spanish-Am. War; advanced through the grades to rear adm., 1934; during World War comdr. U.S.S. McDougal and U.S.S. Gregory, later on staff Adm. Sims, Queenstown, Ireland; mem. Gen. Bd., Navy Dept., Washington, D.C., 1937-39; later comdr. Battleship Div. 3, U.S.S. Idaho, flagship; retired with rank of vice admiral November 1, 1941; in active service after retirement until Dec. 1946. Decorated Spanish-Am. War campaign badge, Victory medal, Navy Cross, Victory medal World War II (U.S.); Order of Crown of Leopold (Belgium), Order of St. Olaf (Norwegian); hon. comdr. Order Brit. Empire. Mem. Naval Inst., Delta Kappa Epsilon. Unitarian. Clubs: N.Y. Yacht, Ends of the Earth (N.Y. City); Army and Navy (Washington, D.C.); Wardroom (Boston). Home: 2400 16th St., N.W. Address: U.S. Maritime Commission, Commerce Bldg., Washington. Died Dec. 1946.

FAIRWEATHER, Jack Hall Alliger Lee, judge; b. Rothesay, N.B., Jan. 9, 1878; s. Arthur Clarence and Annie Rebecca (Lee) F.; student Bishops Coll. Sch., Lennoxville, Quebec, 1889-90, Rothesay (N.B.) Collegiate Sch., 1890-94; B.A., U. of New Brunswick, Fredericton, 1898, LL.D., 1936; LL.B., Harvard Law Sch., 1902; D.C.L., U. of King's Coll., Halifax, 1939; m. Agnes Clifton Tabor, Aug. 29, 1906; children—Barbara Lee (wife of Dr. F. Ralph Connell), Hamlin Lee (wife of Capt. Kingsley Hume); m. 2d, Agnes Charlotte MacKeen, May 11, 1922; children—Robert Gordon Lee, Jack Lee, Richard Lee (dec.), David Stewart Lee. Called to New Brunswick bar, 1901; judge, Supreme Court, New Brunswick, Kings Bench Div., since 1935. Mem. Canadian Inst. of Internat. Affairs. Mem. senate U. of New Brunswick; gov. King's Coll., Halifax; gov. Rothesay Collegiate Sch. Mem. New Brunswick Legislature, as rep. King's County, 1930-35. Served with Canadian Artillery, overseas, World War I. Awarded Military Cross, 1917. Clubs: Union, Cliff (Saint John, N.B.). Mem. Ch. of England. Home: Rothesay, Kings County. Address: Provincial Bldg., Saint John, N.B., Can. Died Jan. 19, 1948.

FALK, Maurice; b. Pittsburgh, Pa., Dec. 15, 1866; s. Charles and Sarah (Sanders) F.; ed. pub. schs., Pittsburgh; m. Laura Klinordlinger, 1888 (died Dec. 21, 1928); m. 2d, Mrs. Selma K. Wertheimer, Sept. 25, 1930. In clothing business until 1893; organizer, 1893, with brother, Leon Falk, of Duquesne Reduction Co.; dir. Nat. Steel Corp., Edgewater Steel Co., Blaw-Knox Co., Farmers Deposit Nat. Bank, Farmers Deposit Savings Bank, Farmers Deposit Trust Co., Reliance Life Ins. Co. Dir. Fed. Jewish Philanthropies, Montefiore Hosp., Pittsburgh Y.M.H.A., Pittsburgh Y.W.H.A. Republican. Jewish religion. Clubs: Concordia (dir.), Hundred, Westmoreland Country. With brother, Leon Falk, donor of Falk Clinic to U. of Pittsburgh, designed to treat 750 daily free patients; established The Maurice and Laura Falk Foundation ($10,000,000 foundation for religious, charitable and ednl. purposes). Home: Hotel Schenley. Office: Farmers Bank Bldg., Pittsburgh, Pa. Died Mar. 18, 1946.

FALK, Myron Samuel, cons. engr.; b. New York, N.Y., Sept. 13, 1878; s. Arnold and Fannie (Wallach) F.; C.E., Columbia, 1899, Ph.D., 1903; M.E., Stevens Inst. Tech., 1900; m. Milly Einstein, June 3, 1903 (died Nov. 9, 1915); children—Eleanor Arnold (Mrs. Joseph B. Lenzner), Myron Samuel, Mildred (Mrs. Edgar P. Loew). Successively tutor, instr., lecturer in civil engring., Columbia, 1900-10; mem. N.Y. Bay Pollution Commn., 1903-05; cons. engr. N.Y. State Water Supply Commn., 1905-08; chief engr. Godwin Constrn. Co., New York, 1905-30, H.H. Oddie, Inc., 1909-28; chmn. bd. dirs. Wonham, Bates & Goode Trading Corp., 1920-23; v.p. Am. Bemberg Corp., 1925-27. Served as major, later lt. col., Ordnance Dept., U.S. Army, 1918-19. Chmn. bd. trustees Lavanburg Found.; trustee Mount Sinai Hosp. Mem. Am. Soc. Civil Engrs., Am. Soc. Testing Materials. Clubs: Engineers, Columbia University, Harmonie (New York); Century Country (White Plains, N.Y.); Tamarack Country (Port Chester, N.Y.). Author: Cements, Mortars and Concretes, 1904; Graphic Method by Influence Lines for Bridge and Roof Computation (with Wm. H. Burr), 1908; Design and Construction of Metallic Bridges (with Wm. H. Burr), 1908. Address: King St., Greenwich, Conn. Died Nov. 26, 1945.

FALL, Albert Bacon, ex-senator, ex-sec. of the Interior; b. Frankfort, Kentucky, Nov. 26, 1861; s. William R. and Edmonia (Taylor) F.; ed. country schools, principally self-taught; m. Emma Garland Morgan, May 7, 1883. Taught sch. and read law 1879-81; practiced law 1889-1904; worked on farm, cattle ranch, and as a miner; became interested in mines, lumber, lands, and railroads; now engaged in farming, stock raising and mining. Served as mem. N.M. legislature, asso. justice Supreme Ct. of N.M., twice as atty-gen. N.M. Terr. and as mem. Constl. Conv.; elected by legislature, to U.S. Senate, Mar. 27, 1912, and drew term expiring Mar. 4, 1913; reelected June 1912, and credentials not being signed by gov. was again elected Jan. 23, 913, for term, 1913-19; reelected, term 1919-25, resigned 1921; sec. of the interior in cabinet of President Harding, Mar. 4, 1921, resigned, Mar. 4, 1923. Republican. Capt. Co. H, 1st Territorial Vol. Inf., 1898-99. Clubs: Toltec (El Paso, Tex.); Foreign Club (Chihuahua, Mex.). Home: Three Rivers, N.M. Died Nov. 30, 1944.

FALVEY, Timothy J. (fawl'vē), pres. Mass. Bonding and Ins. Co.; b. Lebanon, Conn., Jan. 17, 1868; s. John and Ellen (Neal) F.; ed. high sch., Norwich, Conn.; m. Mary E. Cosgrove, Oct. 26, 1892; children—Wallace J., Donald. Organizer, 1907, and since pres. Mass. Bonding and Ins. Co. Home: White Court, Little's Point, Swampscott, Mass. Office: 10 Post Office Square, Boston, Mass. Died Dec. 2, 1947.

FANT, Lester Glenn (fănt), lawyer; b. Holly Springs, Miss., Oct. 29, 1875; s. Selden and Nannie Bell (Williams) F.; prep. edn., Webb Sch., Bell Buckle, Tenn.; A.B., Vanderbilt, 1897, LL.B., 1899; m. Cordelia Leach, June 29, 1904; 1 son, Lester Glenn. Admitted to Miss. bar, 1899, and practiced since at Holly Springs; U.S. dist. atty., Northern Miss. Dist., 1912-14 and 1933-37; asst. U.S. attorney, 1924-29; U.S. dist. atty., ad interim, 1929-33, same dist.; dir. Standard Life Ins. Co. Trustee Webb Sch. Mem. Delta Kappa Epsilon. Democrat. Methodist. Mason (K.T.). Home: Holly Springs, Miss.* Died Dec. 6, 1946.

FARIS, John Thomson (fâ'rĭs), editor, clergyman; b. Cape Girardeau, Mo., Jan. 23, 1871; s. William Wallace (D.D.) and Isabella Hardy (Thomson) F.; student Lake Forest (Ill.) Coll., 1 year; A.B., Princeton, 1895 (Phi Beta Kappa); grad. McCormick Theol. Seminary, Chicago, 1898; D.D., Jamestown College, 1913; Litt.D., Blackburn Coll., 1932; married Clara Lee Carter, Feb. 2, 1898 (died Dec. 28, 1934); children—Bethann Beall (Mrs. Noble Van Ness), Clara Lee Carter (Mrs. Condit D. Brown), Phoebe (Mrs. Gerald MacGilvray). Local editor, business mgr. The Talk, Anna, Ill., 1890; business mgr. The Occident, San Francisco, 1891-92; foreman composing room The North and West, Minneapolis, 1892; ordained Presbyn. ministry, 1898; served as supply, Blissfield, Michigan, 1897; pastor Mount Carmel, Illinois, 1898-1903, Markham Memorial Ch., St. Louis, 1903-07; mng. editor Sunday Sch. Times, Phila., 1907-08; asso. editor Presbyn. Bd. Publn. and Sabbath Sch. Work, Phila., 1908-14, editor, 1914-23; dir. editorial div. Bd. of Christian Edn. of the Presbyn. Ch. in U.S.A., 1923-37; travel free-lance writing and lecturing in schools and colls. since 1937. Apptd. div. of coöperating orgns. of U.S. Food Adminstrn., for vol. service in organizing religious press publicity, 1917. Stated clerk, Cairo Presbytery, 1901-03, moderator, 1902; pres. S.S. Council of Evangelical Denominations, 1920; mem. Internat. Uniform Lessons Com., 1917-35; mem. World's S.S. Com., 1918-37; mem. program com. World's S.S. Conv., Tokio, 1920, Glasgow, 1924. Mem. John Milton Foundation, 1928-35. Mem. bd. of corporators Presbyn. Ministers Fund, Phila. Republican. Author: The Sunday School and the Pastor, 1906; Pleasant Sunday Afternoons for the Children, 1907; Winning Their Way, 1909; Romance of the English Bible, 1911; Making Good, 1911; Winning the Oregon Country, 1911; Life of J. R. Miller, 1912; Men Who Made Good, 1912; The Alaskan Pathfinder, 1913; The Book of God's Providence, 1913; Seeking Success, 1913; The Book of Answered Prayer, 1914; The Book of Faith in God, 1915; Reapers of His Harvest, 1915; The Mother Heart, 1916; The Christian According to Paul, 1916; How It Was Done in Harmony, 1916; The Book of Personal Work, 1916; Real Stories from Our History, 1916; Old Roads Out of Philadelphia, 1917; Makers of Our History, 1917; The Book of Joy, 1917; The Romance of Old Philadelphia, 1918; Historic Shrines of America, 1918; The Virgin Islands (with Theodoor de Booy), 1918; The Victory Life (awarded prize in George Wood competition), 1918; Seeing Pennsylvania, 1919; The Book of Courage, 1920; On the Trail of the Pioneers, 1920; Seeing the Far West, 1920; Seeing the Sunny South, 1921; Seeing the Eastern States, 1922; Men Who Conquered, 1922; Seeing the Middle West, 1923; Where Our History Was Made, Book One, 1923, Book Two, 1924; Seeing Canada, 1924; The Romance of Forgotten Towns, 1924; The Book of Every Day Heroism, 1924; Real Stories of the Geography Makers, 1925; When America Was Young, 1925; The Romance of the Boundaries, 1926; Old Churches and Meeting Houses In and Around Philadelphia, 1926; The Romance of the Rivers, 1927; Nolichucky Jack, 1927; Old Trails and Roads in Penn's Land, 1927; The Romance of Forgotten Men, 1928; The Paradise of the Pacific, 1929; Roaming the Rockies, 1930; Roaming American Highways, 1931; Seeing South America, 1931; Roaming the Eastern Mountains, 1932; The New Winning Their Way, 1932; Old Gardens In and Around Philadelphia, 1932; Roaming American Playgrounds, 1934; Against Head Winds, 1935; also wrote chapters in The Skill of Living, 1921, and chapters in the revised edition of Hill Towns of Italy, 1930. Editor: The Sunday School at Work, 1913; The Glory of the Commonplace, 1913; Intimate Letters on Personal Problems, 1914; The Sunday School and World Progress, 1921; The Sunday School and the Healing of the Nations, 1924; Thy Kingdom Come, 1928. Home: Jonwood, Golf Club Lane, Nashville 5, Tenn. Died Apr. 13, 1949.

FARISH, Frederick Garesché (fâr'ĭsh), mining engr.; b. St. Louis, Sept. 14, 1866; s. Edward Tilghman and Elizabeth (Garesché) F.; ed. St. Mary's Coll., Montreal, Can., 1880-86; St. Louis (Mo.) U., 1887-88; m. Alice Harwood, Oct. 1, 1898; 1 son, Edw. T. Asst. supt. Old Dominion Mining Co., Ouray, Colo., 1892-93; supt. Silver Age Mining Co., Idaho Springs, Colo., 1893-95; assayer and chemist, Grand Central Mining Co., Ltd., Torres, Sonora, Mex., 1896-99; mgr. Japan-Flora Mining Co., Telluride, Colo., 1900-01; cons. and exam. engr., 1902-11; supt. Humboldt mine, Sneffels, Colo., 1912-13; mgr. Lluvia de Oro Gold Mining Co., Chihuahua, Mex., 1915-16; mgr. Mineral Hill Consol. Copper Co., Ariz., 1917-18; gen. mgr. Metals Exploration Co., 1919-23; gen. supt. Silvermane Mines Co., Lake City, Colo., 1924-25; gen. mgr. Rico Mining & Reduction Co. since 1926. Cons. practice N.Y. City since 1927; cons. engr. to Campbell Mining Co., Inc., N.Y. City, 1934-40; retired. Mem. Am. Inst. Mining and Metall. Engrs. Catholic. Home: "The Pines," R.F.D. 2, Bel Air, Md. Died Aug. 14, 1946; buried in Calvary Cemetery, St. Louis.

FARISH, Hunter Dickinson, historian, dir. of research; b. Montgomery, Ala., Sept. 12, 1897; s. James Hunter and Sallie (Dickinson) F.; B.S., Princeton, 1922; A.M., Harvard, 1926, Ph.D., 1936. Asst. prin. Choudrant Agrl. High Sch., 1923-24; asst. prof. Westminster Coll., 1926-30; instr., tutor in history, Harvard and Radcliffe Coll., 1936-37; dir. dept. of research and record, Colonial Williamsburg, Inc., since 1937; visiting prof. colonial history, Coll. of William and Mary, 1939; gen. editor Williamsburg Restoration Historical Studies since 1939; mem. editorial bd. William and Mary Quarterly since 1943. Mem. Am. Antiquarian Soc., Soc. of Cincinnati in the State of Va. Methodist. Clubs: Cloister Inn (Princeton); Commonwealth (Richmond). Editor: The Present State of Virginia and the College, 1940; Journal and Letters of Philip Vickers Fithian, 1943. Author: The Circuit Rider Dismounts, 1938. Address: Williamsburg, Va. Now deceased.

FARISH, William Stamps, pres. Standard Oil Co. (N.J.); b. Mayersville, Miss., Feb. 23, 1881; s. Wm. Stamps and Katherine Maude (Power) F.; grad. St. Thomas Hall, Holly Springs, Miss., 1897; LL.B., U. of Miss., 1900; m. Libbie Randon Rice, June 1, 1911;

children—William Stamps, Martha Botts. Admitted to Miss. bar, 1900, and practiced 3 mos. at Clarksdale; moved to Beaumont, Tex., 1900, Houston, 1905; with Texas Oilfield, Ltd., 1900-01; one of organizers Brown-Farish Oil Co., 1902; engaged in contract drilling, 1905-17; one of organizers Humble Oil Co., 1917, v.p., 1917-22, pres. 1922-33; chmn. board Standard Oil Co. (N.J.), 1933-37, pres. since 1937. Mem. Nat. Petroleum War Service Com., World War; mem. Federal Oil Conservation Board and Com. of 9, 1927. Pres. Gulf Coast Producers Assn., 1915, Tex.-La. Oil and Gas Assn., 1917; mem. Am. Petroleum Inst. (one of founders; pres. 1926), Delta Tau Delta. Episcopalian. Clubs: Houston, Houston Country (Houston); River, Links, Turf and Field. Home: 10 Remington Lane, Houston, Tex. Office: Humble Bldg., Houston, Tex.; and 30 Rockefeller Plaza; New York, N.Y. Died Nov. 29, 1942.

FARLEY, Frank Edgar, college prof.; b. Manchester, N.H., Apr. 25, 1868; s. George W. and Lucina C. (Baker) F.; A.B., Harvard, 1893, A.M., 1894, Ph.D., 1897; m. Mrs. Amy Elwell Crane, Aug. 5, 1903. Asst. in English, Harvard, 1893-95, Radcliffe Coll., 1894-97; inst. English, Haverford Coll., 1897-98; instr., asso. prof. and prof. English, Syracuse U.; 1898-1903; asso. prof. and prof. English, Simmons Coll., Boston, 1903-18; prof. English lit., Wesleyan U., 1918-36, prof. emeritus since 1936. Vis. lecturer, Harvard U., 1925. Fellow Am. Acad. Arts and Sci. Editor: Milton's Paradise Lost, Books I and II, 1898. Author: Scandinavian Influences in the English Romantic Movement, 1903; (with G. L. Kittredge) An Advanced English Grammar, 1913; A Concise English Grammar (with G. L. Kittredge), 1918. Home: Middletown, Conn. Died March 25, 1943.

FARLEY, James I., ex-congressman; b. near Hamilton, Ind., Feb. 24, 1871; s. Franklin and Nancy Jane (McCurdy) F.; ed. Tri-State Coll., Angola, Ind., and Simpson Coll., Indianola, Ia.; m. Charlotte Gramling, Apr. 15, 1893; children—Frank G., Frances P. (Mrs. James D. Spurrier), Paul E., Thain L. Maxine. Began teaching in pub. schs. 1889; salesman Studebaker Corp., 1906-08; salesman, later sales mgr. Auburn Automobile Co., 1908, then vice pres. and pres. until 1926, retired. Del. to Dem. Nat. Conv., 1928. Mem. 73d to 75th Congresses (1933-39), 4th Ind. Dist. Methodist. Mason, K.P., Moose. Club: Auburn Country. Home: Auburn, Ind. Died June 16, 1948.

FARMER, Alfred Gibson, ophthalmologist, b. Elizabethtown, Ky., June 4, 1877; s. Benjamin Dew and Elizabeth (Giles) F.; M.D., Ky. U., 1904; grad. work N.Y. Post Grad. Med. Sch., 1915-16, Ohio U., Athens, 1916; m. Minnie L. Cuckler, Jan. 20, 1910; 1 dau., Margaret Louise. Began practice of medicine, 1904; in med. service Panama Canal, U.S. Govt., 1905-15; phys. Gorgas Hosp., dist. phys. Gatun and Cristobal, chief of med. service Colon Hosp.; med. officer Army and Navy Gen. Hosp., Hot Springs, Ark., 1916-17; since 1919 in Dayton, O., practice limited to eye, ear, nose and throat; cons. ophthalmologist Miami Valley Hospital, Dayton, since 1919; ex-chief of staff Miami Valley Hospital; medical examiner, Civil Aeronautics Adminstrn. Served as med. officer and post surgeon (maj.) aviation service, U.S. Army, Wilbur Wright Aviation Field, Dayton, 1916-19; lt. col. U.S. Army-Med. Res. since 1919. Licentiate of Am. Bd. of Ophthalmology; fellow Am. Coll. Surgeons, A.M.A., Am. Acad. Ophthalmology and Otolaryngology; mem. Aero Med. Assn., Montgomery County Med. Soc. (pres. 1935), Phi Chi. Methodist. Mason. Contbr. professional articles. Home: 707 Superior Av. Office: Fidelity Medical Bldg., 209 S. Main St., Dayton, O., Died April 2, 1945; buried at Athens, O.

FARNHAM, Sally James, sculptor; b. Ogdensburg, N.Y.; d. Col. Edward C. and Sarah Welles (Perkins) James; ed. pub. schs.; m. Paulding Farnham. Prin. works: Statue of Gen. Bolivar (won in competition), presented to City of N.Y. by Venezuelan Govt.; frieze of discoverers (Pan-Am. Union, Washington); Soldiers and Sailors monument, Ogdensburg, N.Y.; Soldiers and Sailors monument, Holy Sepulchre and Mt. Hope cemeteries, Rochester, N.Y.; Soldiers and Sailors monument, Bloomfield, N.J.; World War memorial, Fultonville, N.Y.; fountain, Baltimore, Md.; monument to Gen. Chaffee, Nat. Cemetery, Arlington, Va.; memorial to Vernon Castle, Woodlawn, N.Y.; monument, Junipero Serra, San Fernando Mission, Calif.; portraits of President Harding, Herbert Hoover, Theodore Roosevelt, Marshal Foch, Senator W. A. Clark, portraits Gen. Sucre, gift of Colombia, and Hippolito Unanue, gift of Peru, at Pan-Am. Union, Washington, D.C.; Will Rogers on his pony; cowboy group "Pay Day"; portraits Gen. Sucre and Hidalgo, Rio de Janeiro, Brazil; etc. Decorated Order of Bolivar (Venezuela). Studio: 1 W. 67th St., New York, N.Y.* Died Apr. 28, 1943.

FARQUHAR, S(ilas) Edgar, editor; b. near Evansville, Ind., Oct. 1887; s. Daniel Webster and Louella (Kight) F.; B.S., Earlham Coll., 1909; M.S., Univ. of Ill., 1913; M.P.J., Ill. Press Assn., 1931; married Myrtle Bell Smith, 1919; children—Donald Edgar, Doris Ann. Asst. in chemistry, Purdue U., 1910-11, univ. of Ill., 1911-12; salesman, sales mgr. Chicago and N.Y. City, 1913-23; editor The Midland Press, Chicago, 1923-30; editor Quarrie Corp., Chicago, 1931-40; editor The Grolier Soc., Inc., N.Y. City, since 1940. Mem. Sigma Xi. Mem. Soc. of Friends. Editor: The New Human Interest Library, 6 vols., 1928; World Book Encyclopedia, 19 vols., 1933-40; World Book Encyclopedia Annual, 1932-40; Childcraft, 20 vols., 1934-39; The Progress of Science (annual), 1941-42; Grolier Encyclopedia, 11 vols., since 1944. Home: 210 Knapp Terrace, Leonia, N.J. Office: 2 W. 45th St., New York 19, N.Y. Died Mar. 31, 1948.

FARNSWORTH, Charles Hubert, prof. music; b. of Am. parents, Cesarea, Turkey, Nov. 29, 1859; s. Wilson Amos and Caroline E. (Palmer) F.; ed. Robert Coll., Constantinople; studied music with pvt. teachers U.S. and Europe; m. Charlotte Joy Allen, 1890. Teacher of music, Worcester, Mass., 8 yrs.; head music dept. U. of Colo., 12 yrs.; head dept. of music and speech, Teachers Coll., (Columbia), 1901-26; now prof. emeritus. Pres. The Hanoum Camps, Inc. Trustee Thetford (Vt.) Acad. Mem. Music Teachers' Nat. Assn. (pres. 1912-15). Conglist. Author: Education Through Music, 1909; How to Study Music, 1920; The Why and How of Music Study, 1927; Short Studies in Musical Psychology, 1929. Compiler: Songs for Schools, 1907; Folk Songs (Farnsworth and Sharp), 1916; Songs for Grammar Grades, 1916; Tonal Phrase Book (Farnsworth and Kraft), 1920. Editor: The World's Music, 1927; Singing Youth, 1935. Adv. editor: Our Songs, 1939. Collaborator: NBC Music Appreciation Hour Notebooks since 1931. Home: Thetford, Vt. Died May 22, 1947.

FARRAH, Albert John (fär'á), dean law school; b. Adrian, Mich., July 15, 1863; s. Thomas and Catherine (Chase) F.; student U. of Mich., 1884-85, LL.B., 1896: A.M., Cornell Coll., Mt. Vernon, Ia., 1906; LL.D., U. of Ala., 1924; D.C.L., U. of Fla., 1935; m. Eva A. Wilson, Aug. 28, 1888; 1 dau., Elvira Katherine. Supt. schs., Michigamme, Mich., 1889-94; admitted to Mich. bar, 1896, and practiced at Ann Arbor and Battle Creek 3 yrs.; instr., law dept. U. of Mich., 1897-1900; dean and prof. law, John B. Stetson U. Coll. of Law, DeLand, Fla., 1900-09; same, in U. of Fla. Coll. of Law, 1909-12; same, University of Alabama School of Law since 1913. Chmn. Ala. Bd. of Law Examiners. Mem. Am. and Ala. State bar assns., Phi Beta Kappa, Omicron Delta Kappa, Phi Delta Phi. Democrat. Presbyterian. Mason. Home: University, Ala. Died June 29, 1944.

FARRAND, Max, library director; b. Newark, N.J., Mar. 29, 1869; s. Samuel A. and Louise (Wilson) F.; A.B., Princeton, 1892, A.M., 1893, Ph.D., 1896; grad. study history, Princeton, Leipzig, Heidelberg, 1892-96; hon. A.M., Wesleyan, 1900, Yale, 1908; L.H.D., Wesleyan U., Middletown, Conn., 1928; LL.D., Occidental Coll. and Pomona Coll., 1928, U. of Southern California, 1930, Univ. of Mich., 1931, Univ. of California, 1937; Litt.D., Princeton Univ., 1942; m. Beatrix Jones, Dec. 17, 1913. Instr., asso. prof. and prof. history, Wesleyan U., 1896-1901; prof. and head dept. history, Stanford, 1901-08; acting prof. Am. history, Cornell U., 1905-06; prof. history, Yale, 1908-25; gen. dir., 1919-21, adviser in ednl. research, 1921-25, dir. div. edn., 1925-27, Commonwealth Fund; dir. Henry E. Huntington Library and Art Gallery, 1927-41, research associate since 1941. Fellow New York Genealogical and Biographical Society American Academy Arts and Sciences; trustee American Academy in Rome since 1940; mem. Am. Antiq. Soc., Am. Philos. Soc., Am. Hist. Assn. (pres. 1940); corr. mem. Mass. Historical Soc., Colonial Soc. of Mass; asso. N.Y. Hist. Soc. Clubs: Century; Sunset, Zamorano (Los Angeles); Valley Club of Montecito (Santa Barbara). Author: Legislation of Congress for Government of Organized Territories of United States (1789-1895), 1896; Translation of Jellinek's Declaration of Rights of Man and of Citizens, 1901; Framing of Constitution, 1913; Development of U.S., 1918; Fathers of the Constitution, 1921. Editor: Records of Fed. Convention of 1787, 3 volumes, 1911, 4th vol., 1937; M. V. H. Dwight's A Journey to Ohio in 1810, 1913. Contbr. to American Historical Review and other hist. periodicals. Home: Reef Point, Bar Harbor, Me. Died June 17, 1945.

FARRAND, Wilson, head master, emeritus; b. Newark, N.J., Sept. 22, 1862; s. Samuel Ashbel and Louise (Wilson) F.; grad. Newark Acad., 1878; A.B., Princeton, 1886, A.M., 1889; hon. A.M., Columbia, 1907; L.H.D., Hamilton Coll., 1918; Litt.D., Princeton Univ. 1935; L.H.D., Rutgers U., 1936; LL.D., U. of Newark, 1940; m. Margaret Washburne Walker, Nov. 23, 1889; children—Margaret L. Katharine (dec.), Dorothy W. Asst. editor Scribner's Magazine, 1886-87; master, Newark (N.J.) Acad., 1887-89, asso. head master, 1889-1901, head master, 1901-35, emeritus since 1935. Mem. College Entrance Examination Bd. since 1900. Mem. Schoolmasters' Assn. of New York (pres., 1895-96), Middle States Assn. Colls. and Prep. Schs. (pres. 1902), Head Masters Assn. of U.S. (pres., 1911), New Eng. Soc. of Orange (pres., 1906-08); pres. Princeton Alumni Fed. of N.J., 1909-11. Alumni trustee Princeton U., 1909-19, life trustee and clerk bd. since 1919; mem. Commn. on Higher Institutions, Middle States Assn. Presbyn. Clubs: University, Century, Princeton (New York); Nassau (Princeton). Editor: Carlyle's "Essay on Burns," 1896; Tennyson's "Princess," 1898. Has written many papers and delivered many addresses on ednl. topics, especially coll. entrance requirements and relation of sch. and coll. Address: Princeton, N.J. Died Nov. 4, 1942.

FARRAR, Roy Montgomery, banker, lumberman; b. St. Louis, Mo., Dec. 16, 1870; s. John H. and Sarah (Rose) F.; ed. pub. schs., St. Louis; m. Emily Taylor, 1897 (died 1902); 1 dau., Ellen Taylor (Mrs. Dallas H. Moore); m. 2d, Margaret Campbell, Apr. 30, 1906; children—Margaret (Mrs. Wm. A. Cline), Ruth (Mrs. Clifton Iverson). Began with Houston Lumber Co., 1887; organizer, 1902, vice-pres. until 1914, South Texas Lumber Co.; organizer, 1912, since pres. Farrar Lumber Co.; pres. Nat. Bank of Commerce, Houston, 1915-21; dir. Houston Br. Fed. Res. Bank of Dallas, 1919-35; pres. Union Nat. Bank of Houston since 1924; director Houston Compress Co., Mo. Pacific Lines. Member Houston Port Commission, 1913-25. Mem. Houston Chamber Commerce (ex-pres.). Democrat. Methodist. Clubs: Houston, Houston Country. Home: 511 Lovett Blvd. Address: Union Nat. Bank, Houston, Tex. Died Aug. 17, 1943.

FARRELL, Benjamin Peter (făr'ĕl), orthopedic surgeon; M.D., Long Island Coll. Hosp., 1906; prof. orthopedics, Columbia; chief of staff, House of the Holy Comforter; surgeon-in-chief New York Orthopedic Dispensary and Hosp.; asst. consultant in orthopedics, Presbyterian Hosp.; consultant in orthopedics, Englewood (N.J.) Hosp. Fellow Am. Coll. Surgeons; mem. A.M.A. Office: 654 Madison Av., New York, N.Y. Died Dec. 27, 1947.

FARRELL, James A(ugustine); b. New Haven, Conn., Feb. 15, 1863; s. John Guy and Catherine (Whalen) F.; LL.D., Georgetown U. and St. Bonaventure Coll.; Eng.D., Stevens Inst. of Technology; m. Catherine McDermott, June 11, 1889; children—John Joseph, Mary Theresa (Mrs. Joseph B. Murray), Catherine (Mrs. Luke D. Stapleton, Jr.), James Augustine, Rosamond (Mrs. Richard J. Buck). Began work in steel wire mill, New Haven, at 16; laborer in mills of Pittsburgh Wire Co., 1888, later supt. and mgr.; organized wire co. at Braddock, Pa., which became part of Am. Steel & Wire Co., of which was gen. mgr. of exports until 1903; pres. U.S. Steel Products Export Co., 1903-11; pres. U.S. Steel Corp., 1911-32, then dir., now retired. Decorated Comdr. Order of Crown of Italy; Knight of St. Gregory the Great; Knight Order of Malta. Hon v.p. Iron and Steel Inst. of Great Britain; mem. Am. Iron and Steel Inst. (awarded 1st Gary memorial medal), Nat. Foreign Trade Council (chmn.). Catholic. Clubs: Metropolitan, India House (pres.). Home: 1060 5th Av., New York; (summer) South Norwalk, Conn. Office: 26 Beaver St., New York, N.Y. Died Mar. 28, 1943.

FARRELL, William Elliston, mfr.; b. Nashville, Tenn., Feb. 7, 1870; s. Norman and Josephine (Elliston) F.; prep. edn., Webb's Sch., Culleoka, Tenn.; E.M., Vanderbilt U., 1891; m. Emily W. Cottrell, June 5, 1900; children—Joseph Cottrell, William Elliston, Emily Cottrell. Began as chemist North Branch Steel Co., Danville, Pa., 1891, later master mechanic; successively gen. mgr. Phila. Roll & Machinery Co., Birdsboro Steel Foundry & Machine Co., and v.p. Treadwell Engring. Co., Easton, Pa.; pres. Easton Car & Constrn. Co., mfrs. industrial cars, since 1914. Mem. Phi Delta Theta. Republican. Presbyterian. Clubs: Pomfret, Northampton Country (Easton); University (Phila.). Home: Easton, Pa. Office: 50 Church St., New York. Died Aug. 22, 1949.

FARWELL, John Villiers, merchant; b. Chicago, Ill., Oct. 16, 1858; s. John Villiers and Emeret (Cooley) F.; A.B., Yale, 1879; m. Ellen S. Drummond, May 20, 1884 (died Aug. 6, 1912); 1 dau., Katharine Drummond; m. 2d, Harriet (Flower) Smith, Apr. 3, 1919 (died Dec. 26, 1938). Chmn. bd. of dirs. J. V. Farwell Co., dry goods, until business was purchased by Carson Pirie Scott & Co., 1925; dir. Harris Safe Deposit Co. Pres. 1st State Pawners' Soc.; pres. trustees Y.M.C.A.; mem. corp. Yale U., 1911-31. Was pres. Y.M.C.A., Chicago, when new La Salle St. bldg. was erected; dir. Chicago World's Fair, 1893; chmn. com. which secured passage of new revenue law of 1897; pres. Nat. Citizens' League for Promotion of Sound Banking System, 1911-14; mem. advisory com. Municipal Voters' League; mem. exec. com. Chicago Plan Commn. since organization. Republican. Clubs: Yale (New York); Commercial, Chicago, University. Onwentsia, Old Elm. Home: 229 Lake Shore Drive, Chicago, Ill.; and Lake Forest, Ill. Office: 208 S. La Salle St., Chicago, Ill. Died June 17, 1944.

FASSETT, Helen Mary Revere; b. Lancaster, Mass., Aug. 26, 1875; d. Frank Exavier and Adelaide Adela (Pratt) Fassett; A.B., Radcliffe Coll., 1897; A.M., Sorbonne, Paris, France, 1901; student École des Beaux Arts, Paris, 1905. Mem. Soc. Arts and Crafts (Boston), Société des Amis de l'Art (Paris, France), Decorative Art Soc. (London), Royal Art Soc. of Belgium, etc. Apptd., 1917, by King and Queen of Belgium as representative in America of the lace workers of Belgium. Mem. Société de Amiches de Arts of Florence, Italy, 1918; del.-at-large to Woman's Internat. Alliance; mem. Select Council of Liberal League America; mem. at large Pi Gamma Mu. Contbr. to mags. Now engaged in translations of modern French and Italian authors with sister, Lillian J. Fassett. Home: 411 Cherry St., Grand Rapids, Mich. Died Dec. 25, 1947.

FAST, Gustave, cons. engr.; b. Sweden, May 18, 1884; s. Johan P. and Maria Charlotta (Swenson) F.; ed. Chalmers Tech. Coll., Goteborg, Sweden, 1900-04, City and Guild Tech. Coll., London, Eng., 1904-06; m. Ganna Kjaergaard-Nielsen, Aug. 23, 1929; 1 son, Jon Gustave Viking. Came to U.S., 1910, naturalized, 1924. Mech. engr. Gwynne's, Ltd., London, Eng., 1906-07, Atlas Iron Works, Birmingham, Eng., 1908-09, Swedish State Ry., 1909-10, Worthington Pump & Machinery Co., Harrison, N.J., 1910-12, Crown Cork & Seal Co., Baltimore, 1912-15, Poole Engine & Machine Co., Baltimore, 1915-25, Bartlett Hayward Co., Baltimore, since 1919, pres.

Gustave Fast Engring. Co., Annapolis, since 1931; pres. The Fast Bearing Co., Annapolis, since 1936; cons. engr. Koppers Co., Baltimore, since 1919. Fellow Am. Soc. M.E. Awarded John Price Wetherill medal by Franklin Inst. for "discovery and invention in the physical sciences," 1929; "Modern Pioneer" plaque, by Am. Assn. Mfrs., 1939. Club: Cosmos (Washington, D.C.). Home: Salisbury, Md. Office: Gustave Fast Engineering Co., Annapolis, Md. Died May 9, 1946; buried at Goteborg, Sweden.

FAUCETTE, William Dollison (faw-set), civil engr.; b. Halifax, N.C., June 27, 1881; s. Charles William and Florence Relinda (Dickens) F.; B.E., N.C. State Coll., Raleigh, N.C., 1901, C.E., 1910, D. Sc., 1929; m. Belle Edwards Nash, Nov. 11, 1908; children—Ellen Nash (Mrs. W. E. Black, Jr.), Florence Wilcox (Mrs. J. L. Weller, Jr.), Belle Dollison. Began with Seaboard Air Line Ry., 1901, and served as asst. engr., in Savannah office and adjacent region until 1906; in chief engineer's office, 1906-10, chief clk. to pres., 1910-12; chief engr., all Seaboard Air Line Railway System 1913-44; executive rep. of receivers, Seaboard Airline Railway System, 1944-46, executive, representative of receivers and chairman of committee, for Research and Planning, Seaboard Air Line Railroad Co. since 1946. Del. for Va., at Southern Forestry Congress, 1923-26; official del. for Ga., to Southern Appalachian Power Conf., Chattanooga, Tenn., 1927; on council American Inst. Weights and Measures; chmn. Joint Comm. on Metric System, Assn. Am. R.R. (mem. spl. com. on grade crossing elimination; railroad com. to study post-war transportation); chmn. zone 3, Assn. Am. R.A. com. on Waterway Projects. For many yrs. mem. exec. com. U. of N.C. (former trustee). Mem. Norfolk (Va.) City Council com. on higher edn. Mem. bd. dirs. Central Y.M.C.A., Travelers Aid Society, Norfolk. Mem. Am. Ry. Engring. Assn. (past pres.); mem. spl. com. on uniform gen. control forms and cooperative relations with univs., waterways and harbors, Am. Soc. C.E. (ex-pres. Va.), N.C. Soc. Engrs., Phi Kappa Phi, Tau Beta Pi. Democrat. Episcopalian (vestryman St. Andrews Church, Norfolk). Mason. Clubs: Engrs. of Hampton Roads; Norfolk German (past pres.), Norfolk Yacht and Country, Virginia (Norfolk, Va.). Home: 1024 Graydon Av. Office: 756 Seaboard Air Line Railroad, General Office Bldg., Norfolk, Va. Died May 19, 1947.

FAULEY, Wilber Finley (Wilber Fawley, pen name), author, journalist; b. Fultonham, Muskingum County, O., Oct. 15, 1872; s. Calvin Buckingham and Mary Eleanor (Finley) F.; grad. Fultonham (O.) Acad., 1890; studied music in Phila. under pvt. instr.; unmarried. Spent 1 yr. abroad, earning way by writing, and later contributed lit. and hist. articles to the Bookman, Harper's Bazaar, etc.; with N.Y. Evening Journal, 1900-05, N.Y. American, 1905-06, Globe, 1906-07, Herald (Brooklyn Sunday sect.), 1907-09; with N.Y. Times since 1909, social editor, 1910-24, gen. staff since 1924. Directed and produced children's plays at Waldorf-Astoria Hotel, New York, 1909, also in home of late John Jacob Astor; owns and operates a ranch in Terry County, Tex. Mem. Authors League America, Inc., S.R. Republican. Presbyn. Author: Seeing Europe on Sixty Dollars, 1912; Jenny Be Good, 1919; Queenie, 1921; Fires of Fate, 1922; Princess Charming, 1927; Virginity—Story of the Middle West, 1931; Misalliance, 1934; Shuddering Castle, 1936; Burnt Earth (published play), 1936; also wrote melodrama, "After Midnight" and a novel version of the play, 1904; "King of Diamonds" (melodrama), 1906; "Within Four Walls" (play), 1914. Home: 15 E. 48th St., New York; also 836 Lexington Av., Zanesville, O. Address: New York Times, 229 W. 43d St., New York, N.Y. Died Dec. 21, 1942.

FAULKNER, Leon Charles, sociologist; b. Owego, N.Y., Nov. 22, 1884; s. John Charles and Estella (Harrison) F.; ed. Owego Free Acad.; m. M. Vivian Ballou, Dec. 24, 1906; 1 dau., Vivienne Ballou. Drill master and disciplinarian Berkshire Industrial Farm, Canaan, N.Y., 1904-08; supt. Fairview Home for Friendless Children, Watervliet, 1908-11; business mgr. George Jr. Republic, Freeville, N.Y., 1911-14; supt. Md. Training Sch. for Boys, Loch Raven, 1914-24; director The Children's Village (private training sch. for study, education and development of unadjusted children), Dobbs Ferry, N.Y., since 1924. Official del. from N.Y. to Internat. Penitentiary Congress, London, 1925, Prague, 1930. Dir. Am. Prison Assn. (pres. 1931-32); mem. Internat. Boys' Work Council, Nat. Conf. Juvenile Agencies, Nat. Assn. of Training Schs., Conf. of Supts. of Training Sch. and Reformatories, Am. Assn. Social Workers, Nat. Conf. of Social Work, Nat. Crime Prevention Inst., Reserve Officers Assn. (pres. West County 1933-34; v.p. state dept. 1934-35, 1939-40), Vets. of Foreign Wars, Advertising Fedn. of America, Advertising Club of N.Y., Nat. Aeronautic Assn. of U.S. Army, hon. mem. Grand Jurors Assn. of Baltimore. Served in U.S. Army in Philippines, Spanish-Am. War; formerly lt. col., Adj. Gen.'s Dept., U.S. Reserve. Republican. Episcopalian (mem. Church Club of N.Y.). Mason (K.T.), Elk. Club: Rotary (New York) (pres. 1932-33, gov. 29th dist. Rotary Internat., 1933-34). Address: 3 Mather St., Binghamton, N.Y. Died Oct. 27, 1945.

FAULKS, Theodosia (Mrs. Frederic J. Faulks), author; b. Newark, N.J., 1874; d. Silas Wright and Annie (Bedell) Pickering; ed. pvt. schs. at Newark; m. Joseph Garrison, Mar. 2, 1898; m. 2d, Frederic J. Faulks, 1911. Mem. Authors' League, Poetry Soc. Author: The Joy o' Life and Other Poems, 1909; Earth Cry and Other Poems, 1910; The Dreamers, 1917. Contbr. of verse and stories to mags. Home: Short Hills, N.J. Died Oct. 9, 1944.

FAUSTMANN, Edmund C., pres. Royal Typewriter Co. Home: Darien, Conn Office: 2 Park Av., New York, N.Y.* Died Aug. 29, 1946.

FAUVER, Edgar, prof. physical edn.; b. North Eaton, O., May 7, 1875; s. Alfred and Elizabeth M. (King) F.; A.B., Oberlin, 1899; studied Harvard, summer 1903, Columbia, summers 1904, '06; M.D., Coll. Phys. and Surg. (Columbia), 1909; m. Alice Chipman MacDaniels, Sept. 9, 1908. Dir. physical training, Centre U., Ky., 1899-1900; tutor in Greek and asst. in gymnastics, Oberlin, 1900-03; instr. in gymnastics, 1903-07, Columbia, lecturer in physical training, 1907-09, asst. prof. physical edn., 1909-11; prof. physical edn. and coll. phys., Wesleyan U., since 1911. Pres. Middlesex Hosp. since 1929. Mem. Am. Phys. Edn. Assn., Am. Student Health Assn. (pres N.E. div. 1933-34), Soc. Dirs. Phys. Edn. in Colls. (pres. 1922), Assn. N.E. Colls. on Athletics (sec. 1919-20). Republican. Conglist. Home: Middletown, Conn. Died April 1946.

FAVILLE, William Baker, architect; b. San Andreas, Calif., Nov. 13, 1866; s. Charles and Emma Louise (Baker) F.; ed. high sch., Buffalo, N.Y., student architecture, Mass. Inst. Tech., 1894-95; instr. architecture, Mass. Inst. Tech., for short period; m. Ada Cockbaine, Sept. 20, 1901 (died Sept. 1929). Archtl. training with R. A. Waite and Green & Wicks (Buffalo); with McKim, Mead & White, 1895-98; partner Bliss & Faville, San Francisco, 1898-1925; practiced alone since 1925. Archtl. works: Bank of California; American Trust; St. Francis Hotel; State Building, Civic Center; Masonic Temple; Children's Hospital; Presbyn. Orphanage; Gary Theatre; Liverpool, London & Globe Ins. Co.; Eastman Kodak; Moore Office Bldg.; Oakland Public Library; James Flood residence. One of three original mems. Archtl. Commn. Panama-Pacific Internat. Expn.; fellow Am. Inst. Architects (mem. Northern Calif. chapter), dir. 8 yrs., pres., 1922-24; mem. State Assn. Calif. Architects, San Francisco Architectural Club, San Francisco Symphony Assn., English Speaking Union, Marin County Musical Chest. Clubs: Pacific Union; Bohemian, Commonwealth. Affiliated with Mechanics Inst. Home: 35 Central Av., Sausalito, Calif. Office: Crocker First National Bank Bldg., San Francisco. Died Dec. 15, 1947.

FAWCETT, Howard S(amuel) (faw'sĕt), plant pathologist; b. Salem, O., Apr. 12, 1877; s. Thomas F. and Sidney Ann (Bonsall) F.; B.S., Ia. State Coll., 1905; M.S., U. of Fla., 1908; Ph.D., Johns Hopkins, 1918; m. T. Helen Tostenson, Sept. 15, 1909; 1 dau., Rosamond Annette. Asst. prof. botany and horticulture, U. of Fla., 1905-06; plant pathologist Fla. Agrl. Expt. Sta., 1906-11, Calif. Commn. of Horticulture, 1911-13; asso. prof. plant pathology, U. of Calif., 1913-18, prof. since 1918; collaborator for U.S. Dept. Agr. for study of citrus and date diseases, N. Africa and Mediterranean lands, 1929-30. Fellow A.A. A.S.; mem. Bot. Soc. America, Phytopathol. Soc. (pres. 1930), Am. Soc. Naturalists, Western Soc. Naturalists, Phi Beta Kappa, Sigma Xi. Mem. Soc. Friends—Quakers (went to Russia to aid their relief work 1922). Author: Citrus Diseases and Their Control (used by the citrus industry as authority), 1926; revised, 1936; also many scientific papers and bulletins. Home: 3594 Larchwood Pl. Address: Citrus Experiment Station, Riverside, Calif. Died Dec. 12, 1948.

FAY, Charles Norman, author; b. Burlington, Vt., Aug. 13, 1848; s. Rev. Charles (D.D.) and Charlotte Emily (Hopkins) F.; A.B., Harvard, 1869; m. Lillian Hale, Aug. 26, 1922. Began with 1st Nat. Bank, Marquette, Mich., 1869, advancing to cashier; moved to Chicago, 1877; gen. mgr. Bell Telephone Co. of Ill., 1879, later v.p. and gen. mgr. Chicago Telephone Co.; pres. Chicago Gas Trust Co. (now Peoples Gas Co.), 1887-89; pres. Chicago Arc Light and Power Co., 1888-93, Remington-Sholes Co., mfrs. typewriters, Chicago, 1896-1909. Indsl. editor N.Y. Commercial, 1922-23. Organizer, v.p. and active exec. Orchestral Assn., supporting Theodore Thomas Orchestra, 1889-1910; trustee hosps., etc.; retired 1911, and settled at Cambridge, Mass., 1915. Mem. Boston C. of C., Phi Beta Kappa. Republican. Episcopalian. Clubs: Harvard (Boston); University (Chicago); Boat (Cambridge). Author: Big Business and Government, 1912; Labor in Politics, 1920; Where Do the Union Men Get Off? 1921; Too Much Government—Too Much Taxation, 1923; Business in Politics, 1925; Social Justice, 1926; Rugged Individualism, 1929. Home: 983 Memorial Drive, Cambridge, Mass. Died Apr. 7, 1944.

FAY, Frederic Harold, civil engr.; b. Marlboro, Mass., July 5, 1872; s. John Sawyer and Elizabeth (Ingalls) F.; S.B., Mass. Inst. Tech., 1893; M.S., 1894; m. Clara May Potter, Apr. 21, 1897; children—Allen Potter (dec.), Beatrice, Mildred E., Dorothy C., Eleanor P., Elizabeth. Transitman, with city engr., Marlboro, Mass., summer, 1892; draftsman Boston Bridge Works, summer, 1894; city engr.'s office, Boston, as draftsman and asst. engr. in charge design and constrn. of city's bridges, 1895-1911; engr. in charge bridge and ferry div. Pub. Works Dept., Boston, 1911-14 (resigned), also commr. for Boston on Boston and Cambridge Bridge Commn.; mem. Fay, Spofford & Thorndike, cons. engrs., since June 1914. Served as cons. engr. for railroads, Federal, State and provincial authorities, municipalities, etc., in U.S. and abroad, and as engr. to War Dept. on design and supervision of Boston army base, 1918-19, and Newfoundland and other northern army bases since 1940, also jointly with other firms, engr. to Navy Dept. on design of dry docks and Navy Yard improvements since 1940; former chmn. Boston City Planning Bd. and vice chmn. Met. Planning Div. of Mass.; chmn. Boston Bd. Zoning Adjustment; mem. Mass. State Planning Board, N.E. Regional Planning Commn. and Nat. Conf. of City Planning (dir. 1931-34); alumni mem. Corp. Mass. Inst. Tech. 1914-19; trustee Northeastern Univ., Dorchester Savings Bank. Fellow Am. Acad. Arts and Sciences, A.A.A. S.; mem. Am. Inst. Cons. Engrs. (pres. 1927), Am. Soc. C.E., Engring. Inst. of Canada, Boston Soc. C.E. (pres. 1913-14), Engineers Soc. Western Mass., N.E. Water Works Assn., Am. Concrete Inst., Internat. Assn. Navigation Congresses, Mass. Highway Assn., Mass. Charitable Mechanics' Assn., Boston Chamber Commerce (ex-v.p. and chmn. com. on municipal and met. affairs), Alumni Assn. Mass. Inst. Tech. (pres. 1913). Life mem. and dir. Am. Unitarian Assn.; v.p. Unitarian Laymen's League. Clubs: Union, Engineers, Boston City, Wollaston Golf (Boston); Engineers, Technology (New York). Compiler of "The Population and Finances of Boston," 1901. Home: 227 Savin Hill Av., Dorchester. Office: 11 Beacon St., Boston, Mass. Died June 5, 1944.

FAY, James H., congressman; b. New York, N.Y., Apr. 29, 1899; ed. public schools and De La Salle Inst.; LL.B., Brooklyn Law Sch., 1929. Dep. and acting commr. of hospitals, N.Y. City, 1929-34; chief field dep., 3d N.Y. Dist., Internal Revenue, 1935-38; mem. 76th and 78th Congresses (1939-41, 1943-45), 16th N.Y. Dist. Democrat. Served with 165th Inf., U.S. Army, World War I; wounded in action. Home: New York. N.Y.* Died Sep. 10, 1948.

FAY, Oliver James, surgeon; b. Postville, Ia., July 2, 1874; s. James M. and Elizabeth (Shriner) F.; B.S., Ia. State Coll., 1898; M.D., Coll. Physicians and Surgeons (U. of Ill.), 1902; m. Helen Knapp, Mar. 17, 1904; children—Helen L. (Mrs. William O. Purdy), Betty (Mrs. Ansel T. Blake). Interne, Augustana Hosp., Chicago, Ill., 1902-03; in practice surgery, Des Moines, Ia., since 1904. Med. adviser to Ia. State Industrial Service since its inception, 1913. Fellow Am. Coll. Surgeons, A.M.A.; mem. Western Surg. Assn., Ia. State Med. Soc. (pres. 1924), Am. Assn. Railroad Surgeons, Am. Assn. Industrial Physicians and Surgeons. Home: 1435 Casady Dr. Office: Bankers Trust Bldg., Des Moines, Ia. Died June 1, 1945.

FEAD, Louis H., judge; b. Lexington, Mich., May 2, 1877; s. John Lawrence and Augusta (Walthers) F.; grad. prep. dept., Olivet (Mich.) Coll., 1899, LL.D., 1928; LL.B., U. of Michigan, 1900, hon. LL.D., 1934; m. Marion McPherson, Sept. 19, 1919; children—Marion Augusta, William Alexander, Nancy Louise, Louis McPherson. Admitted to Mich. bar, 1900, practicing at Newberry; v.p. Newberry State Bank since 1908; mem. F. P. Bohn & Co. Pros. atty. Luce County, Mich., 1901-13; circuit judge, 11th Jud. Circuit, Mich., 1913-28; asso. justice Supreme Court, Mich., 1928-Dec. 31, 1937. Served as capt. Am. Red Cross, overseas, World War. Republican. Episcopalian. Mason (Grand Master Mich., 1917-18). Clubs: Rotary, Kiwanis, Lions, Newberry Golf. Home: Newberry, Mich. Office: 3456 Penobscot Bldg., Detroit, Mich. Died Feb. 4, 1943.

FEARON, Henry Dana, banker; b. Pratts Hollow, N.Y., Jan. 18, 1864; s. Robert and Juliette M. J. (Dana) F.; grad. Cazenovia (N.Y.) Sem., 1882; A.B., Syracuse U., 1886, A.M., 1889; m. Mary Fuller, Jan. 8, 1890; children—Spencer Fuller, Gladys Dana, Carroll Dana, Robert Henry, Charles Fuller, Henry Dana. With Cochran & Fearon, drygoods, Oneida, N.Y., 1886-91; spl. agt. Northwestern Mut. Life Ins. Co., 1891-1914; cashier Oneida Valley Nat. Bank, 1914-27, pres. since 1927; pres. Thousand Island Park Assn., Sylvan Spring Water Co. Pres. Asso. N.Y. State Sch. Bds., Bd. of Edn. Oneida. Del. to Gen. Conf. M.E. Ch., 1900. Mem. N.Y. State Bankers Assn. (treas 1920-21), Phi Beta Kappa, Delta Kappa Epsilon. Republican. Methodist. Rotarian. Home: 506 Main St. Office: 160 Main St., Oneida, N.Y. Died Dec. 12, 1941.

FEATHERS, William C., banker; b. Nassau, N.Y., Mar. 24, 1870; s. John and Orcelia F. (Ives) F.; ed. Lansingburg (N.Y.) Acad. and Troy (N.Y.) Bus. Coll.; m. Alice Eddy Potter, Jan. 26, 1892; 1 son, Leonard Clark. Clk. and bookkeeper, Gilbert Car Mfg. Co., Troy, 1887-93; with Manufacturers Nat. Bank, Troy, since 1893, pres., 1925-34, chmn. of bd., 1934-36, chmn. exec. com. since 1936. Republican. Baptist. Clubs: Troy, Lake Placid. Office: Manufacturers Nat. Bank, Troy, N.Y. Died Aug. 14, 1944.

FECHET, James Edmond (fe-shay), army officer; b. Ft. Ringgold, Tex., Aug. 21, 1877; s. Edmond Gustav and Rachel Morrow (Forsythe) F.; A.B., U. of Neb., 1899; grad. Inf. and Cav. Sch., 1904; hon. Dr. Aeronautical Sch., Pa. Mil. Coll., 1929; m. Catharine Luhn, Apr. 10, 1907; children—Catharine, Mary. Enlisted as non-commd. officer cav., U.S. Army, 1898; commd. lt., July 25, 1900; promoted through grades to brig. gen. A.S., Apr. 26, 1925. Identified with A.S. since 1917; comdg. officer Kelly Field, San Antonio, Tex., 1918-20; chief of Training and War Plans Div., Office Chief of A.S., 1920-24; comdg. officer U.S. Training Fields and 3d Attack

Group, Kelly Field, 1924-25; asst. chief of Air Service, 1925-27; apptd. chief of Air Corps, with rank of maj. gen., Dec. 14, 1927; retired Dec. 1931. Recalled to active duty Mar. 15, 1942; re-retired, Dec. 31, 1946. Decorations: D.S.M., Legion of Merit, African Medal, Pearl Harbor Medal. President Air Corps Promotion Board, Air Corps Decoration Board, Air Corps Procurement Board, Air Corps Naming Bd. Mem. Sigma Chi. Clubs: Army and Navy, Army and Navy Country (Washington, D.C.). Address: Air Corps., War Dept., Washington, D.C. Died Feb. 10, 1948; buried in Arlington National Cemetery.

FEGAN, Joseph Charles, marine corps officer; b. Dallas, Tex., Nov. 6, 1886; grad. Field Officers Course, Marine Corps Schs., Naval War Coll., 1936; married; 1 son, Joseph Charles (officer Marine Corps). Apptd. 2d lt., U.S. Marine Corps, 1909, advancing through the grades to maj. gen., 1942; served in Panama, Cuba, Philippines, Santo Domingo and Haiti; on active sea duty in U.S.S. Florida, 1911-13, U.S.S. Cincinnati, 1917; served as comdr. Dept. of the North, Garde D'Haiti, hdqrs. Cap Haitien, 1929-32; comd. 4th Marines, Shanghai, China, 1938-39, 2d Marines, 2d Marine Div., Fleet Marine Force, Marine Corps Base, San Diego, Calif., 1940-41; became comdt. Camp Joseph H. Pendleton, Oceanside, Calif., 1942; comdg. gen. Marine Corps Dept. of the Pacific, hdqrs. San Francisco, Calif., since May 1944. Decorated Distinguished Service Medal, Medaille Militaire (comdr. and officer), Order of Honor and Merit (Haiti), Gold Medal (Dominican Republic), Expeditionary Ribbon, Victory Medal with Asiatic Clasp, China Service and Am. Defense medals (U.S.). Home: 2020 S. Pacific Av., Oceanside, Calif. Died May 26, 1949.

FEGTLY, Samuel Marks (fĕk'lē), dean emeritus; b. West Unity, O., Aug. 30, 1867; s. Jacob and Sarah (Wolph) F.; student Simpson Coll., Indianola, Ia.; Ph.B., Northwestern U., 1897, LL.B., 1900; m. Mary A. Archer, June 30, 1903; 1 dau., Mrs. Margaret Fegtly Nichols. Practiced law, Chicago, 1900-15; joined faculty of U. of Ariz., 1915, head prof. of law, 1916-19, dir. Sch. of Law, 1919-25, dean College of Law, 1925-38, retired. Mem. Am., Ariz. State and Pima County bar assns., Am. Acad. Polit. and Social Science, Am. Assn. Legal Authors, Am. Judicature Soc., Phi Beta Kappa, Delta Rho Sigma, Phi Kappa Phi, Pi Gamma Mu, Order of Coif. Republican. Conglist. Mason. Home: 621 N. Tyndall Av., Tucson, Ariz. Died Aug. 11, 1947; buried University Plot, Evergreen Cemetery, Tuscon.

FELDMAN, Herman, prof. industrial relations; b. N.Y. City, Mar. 20, 1894; s. Joseph and Rebecca (Kramer) F.; grad. Townsend Harris Hall, N.Y. City, 1911; A.B., Coll. City New York, 1915; student Bur. Municipal Research, N.Y. City, 1915-16; A.M., Columbia, 1917, Ph.D., 1925; unmarried. Mem. editorial board American City Magazine, 1915-17; organizer War, Navy depts. commns. on training camp activities, 1917-19; mem. staff Legislative Drafting Service, Columbia Univ., 1919-20; mem. staff Bur. of Personnel Administration, N.Y. City, 1920-21; mem. research staff President Harding's Unemployment Conf., Oct.-Dec. 1921; prof. industrial relations, St. John's Coll., Brooklyn, spring term 1922; asst. prof. industrial relations, Amos Tuck Sch. of Bus. Adminstrn., Dartmouth Coll., 1923-29, prof., 1929-40, and since 1942; lecturer, Columbia, spring 1926; dean Sch. Business and Civic Adminstrn., College of City of New York, 1940-42; research consultant to various companies and associations since 1926. Investigator in industrial relations, Social Science Research Council, N.Y. City, Jan.-July 1928; econ. adviser, U.S. Personnel Classification Bd., Washington, D.C., July 1928-Feb. 1930; research asso., Nat. Commn. on Law Observance and Enforcement, Washington, Oct., 1930-May 1931. Chmn. N.H. Commn. on Unemployment Res., 1933-34. Pub. mem. Nat. Apparel Com., Wage-Hour Act, arbitrator labor disputes since 1935; chmn. paper mfg. adv. bd. of New England Regional War Labor Bd., 1944; sec. com. on employee orgns. in Civil Service, Nat. Civil Service League, 1944-46. Member American Economic Association, Am. Management Assn., Soc. for the Advancement of Management, National Civil Service League, American Association University Professors, Phi Beta Kappa, Beta Gamma Sigma. Club: Town Hall. Author: The Regularization of Employment, 1925; Prohibition—Its Economic and Industrial Aspects, 1927; Research in the Field of Industrial Relations, 1928; Racial Factors in American Industry, 1931; A Personnel Program for the Federal Service, 1931; Problems in Labor Relations, 1937; Stabilizing Jobs and Wages, 1940. Editor of volume on Labor Relations and the War, of Annals Am. Acad. Polit. and Social Science, Nov. 1942; Volume on Labor Relations and the Public, Nov. 1946; Readings on Industrial Relations and Personnel Management, 1947. Contbr. to Am. Polit. Science Review, Nat. Municipal Rev., Personnel, The Annals, Advanced Management, Ency. Social Sciences, N.Y. Times Sunday Mag., etc. Address: P.O. Box 147, Hanover, N.H. Died Oct. 16, 1947.

FELGAR, James Huston, mechanical engr.; b. Stuart, Ia., July 27, 1874; s. David and Margaret (Huston) F.; A.B., U. of Kan., 1901; B.S., Armour Institute Technology (now Illinois Institute of Technology), Chicago, 1905, M.E., 1911, honorary Dr. Engring. 1929; m. Etta Judd, 1906. Instr. mech. engring., Okla. Agrl. and Mech. Coll., 6 mos., 1906; instr. mech. engring., coll. of engring., U. of Okla., 1906-08, prof., 1908-37, dean coll. of engring., 1909-37, dean emeritus and prof engring. since 1937. Mem. Am. Soc. M.E., Okla. Soc. Engrs. (ex-pres.), Okla. Society Professional Engrs., Soc. Promotion Engring. Edn., Phi Beta Kappa, Tau Beta Pi, Sigma Tau, Beta Theta Pi, Lions Internat. (ex-pres.). Presbyterian. Home: 749 De Barr Av., Norman, Okla. Died July 19, 1946.

FELL, Thomas, college pres.; b. Liverpool, Eng., July 15, 1850; s. Thomas and Hannah (Corry) F.; ed. at King's Coll., London, and London U., 1874; LL.D., Hampden-Sydney Coll., 1889; Ph.D. St. John's Coll., Md., 1889; D.C.L., U. of the South, 1907; LL.D., U. of Pittsburgh, 1912, William and Mary, 1921; Litt.D., U. of Md., 1923; m. Isabella Louisa Hunter, Apr. 1881 (died Dec. 25, 1934); children—Thomas T. (dec.) Francis C.D. (dec), Edgar T., John Corry (dec.). Prof. of ancient and modern languages, New Windsor Coll., Md., 1884-86; pres. St. John's Coll., 1886-1923, now emeritus; vice-chancellor, U. of Md., 1907, provost, 1913-20. Mem. Phi Sigma Kappa. Mem. standing com. Diocese of Md. Clubs: University (Washington, D.C., Baltimore, Annapolis, Md.); Press, Churchman of Md. Home: "Sherborne," Markham, Va. Died Apr. 13, 1942.

FELLOWS, William Kinne, architect; b. Winona Minn., Sept. 3, 1870; s. J. B. and Antoinette (Kinne) F.; grad. Sch. of Mines and Architecture (Columbia), 1894; m. Elizabeth Steele, May 19, 1898. Began practice as architect in 1894; instr. in architecture, Art Inst. Chicago, 1894-96; Columbia scholarship in architecture at Am. Acad. in Rome, 1896-97; mem. Nimmons & Fellows, Chicago, 1898-11. Perkins, Fellows & Hamilton, 1911-27, Hamilton, Fellows & Wilkinson, 1927-29, Hamilton, Fellows & Nedved, 1929, ret. 1936. Mem. Bd. of Ed., Chicago, 1923-25. Fellow American Institute Architects, American Academy of Rome; member Art Institute, Chicago, Field Museum, Chicago Hist. Soc. Republican. Mem. Kenwood Evang. Church. Clubs: University, Cliff Dwellers, South Shore Country, Flossmoor Country. Home: 4530 Lake Park Av., Chicago, Ill. Died Aug. 8, 1948; buried in Oakwoods Cemetery.

FELT, Ephraim Porter, entomologist; b. Salem, Mass., Jan. 7, 1868; s. Charles Wilson and Martha Seeth (Ropes) F.; grad. Mass. Agrl. Coll., 1891; appointed specialist in entomolgy by Gypsy Moth Commn., Mass., S.D., Cornell, 1894; m. Helen Maria Otterson, June 24, 1896; children—Margaret, Ernest Porter, Helen, Elizabeth. Taught natural sciences, Clinton Liberal Inst., Ft. Plain, 1893-95; asst. to state entomologist, 1895; acting state entomologist, 1898, state entomologist of N.Y., 1898-1928; dir. and chief entomologist Bartlett Tree Research Labs. since 1928. Published extended work on park and woodland insects, a manual of tree and shrub insects, key to American insect galls, our shade trees, plant galls and gall makers, pruning trees and shrubs, shelter trees in war and peace, 25 official reports, a number of bulletins and many articles in agricultural, horticultural and scientific jours. Hon. editor Jour. of Econ. Entomology. Collaborator U.S. Bur. of Entomology, New York State Museum. Emeritus life mem. A.A.A.S.; fellow Entomol. Soc. of America; mem. Am. Assn. Econ. Entomologists (pres. 1902), Conn. Tree Protective Assn. (pres.), Entomol. Soc. Washington, N.Y. Entomol. Soc., Sigma Xi; hon. mem. Entomol. Soc. Ontario. Chief Entomologist, Gypsy Moth Bur., N.Y. State Conservation Commn., 1923-24. Co-author: (with W. H. Rankin) Insects and Diseases of Ornamental Trees and Shrubs. Address: Stamford, Conn. Died Dec. 14, 1943.

FENLON, John F., univ. pres.; b. Chicago, Ill., June 23, 1873; s. Thomas and Mary (O'Keeffe) F.; student St. Ignatius Coll., Chicago, 1891; A.B., St. Mary's Sem., Baltimore, 1895, A.M., 1896; D.D., Angelico U., Rome, Italy, 1900; grad. study Johns Hopkins, 1894-96, Sapienza U., Rome, 1898-1900; LL.D., Loyola Coll., Baltimore, Md., 1938. Ordained priest R.C. Ch., 1896; curate Holy Name Cathedral, Chicago, 1896-98; prof. Holy Scriptures, St. Joseph Sem., Yonkers, N.Y., 1901-04, St. Mary's Sem., Baltimore, 1904-19; pres. St. Austin's Coll., Washington, D.C., 1904-11; pres. Divinity Coll., Cath. U. of America, Washington, 1911-24; pres. Sulpicia Sem., Washington, 1924-25; pres. St. Mary's Sem. and Univ., Baltimore, since 1925; provincial of Sulpicians in U.S. since 1925. Secretary to Cardinal Gibbons at the orgn. of Nat. Cath. War Council, 1917, Nat. Cath. Welfare Conf., 1919. Contbr. to the Catholic World, Ecclesiastical Review, etc. Address: St. Mary's Seminary, Roland Park, Baltimore. Died July 31, 1943; buried at St. Charles College, Catonsville, Md.

FENNEMAN, Nevin M., geologist; b. Lima, O., Dec. 26, 1865; s. William Henry and Rebecca (Oldfather) F.; A.B., Heidelberg Coll., Tiffin, O., 1883; Ph.D., U. of Chicago, 1901; LL.D., Cincinnati, 1940; m. Sarah Alice Glisan, Dec. 26, 1893 (died 1920). Prof. physical sciences, Colo. State Normal Sch. (now Colo. State Coll. of Edn.), 1892-1900; prof. geology, U. of Colo., 1902-03, U. of Wis., 1903-07, U. of Cincinnati, 1907-37, emeritus prof. since 1937; asst. geologist, 1901-19, asso. geologist, 1919, geologist, 1924, U.S. Geol. Survey; geologist, Wis. Geol. and Natural History Survey, 1900-02, Ill. State Geol. Survey, 1906-08, Ohio Geol. Survey, 1914-16. Awarded gold medal, Geog. Soc. Chicago, 1938. Fellow A.A.A.S. (v.p., chmn. sec. E., 1923), Geol. Soc. America (pres. 1935); mem. Assn. Am. Geographers (pres. 1918), Am. Soc. Naturalists, Sigma Xi, Phi Beta Kappa (hon.). Mem. Nat. Research Council, 1917-24, 1932-35, chmn. div. of geology and geography, 1922-23. In charge science work on Africa for inquiry preparatory to Paris Peace Conf. Presbyterian. Clubs: Literary of Cincinnati (pres. 1924-25); Cosmos (Washington, D.C.). Author: Physiographic Divisions of the United States; Physiography of Western United States; Physiography of Eastern United States; also numerous government bulls. and scientific papers. Home: 348 Shiloh St. Address: Univ. of Cincinnati, Cincinnati, O. Died July 4, 1945.

FENNER, Edward Blaine, naval officer; b. Rochester, N.Y., Aug. 2, 1876; s. Edward Bela and Margaret Virginia (Taylor) F.; student U. of Rochester 2 yrs.; grad. U.S. Naval Acad., 1899; m. Louise Arnold, Sept. 7, 1904. Commd. ensign U.S. Navy, Jan. 28, 1901; promoted through grades to rear adm., Nov. 1, 1930. Served in Spanish-Am. War (Battle of Santiago), Philippine Insurrection, Boxer Campaign N. China, establishment of Republic of Panama, Mexican Campaign; comd. U.S.S. Denver, World War; chief of staff, U.S. Asiatic Fleet, 1923-25; comd. U.S.S. Mississippi, 1928-30; apptd. comd. 16th Naval Dist. and stas. Cavite and Olongapo, Aug. 1930; comdg. Cruiser Div. 2, 1932-33, Cruisers of Battle Force, 1933-34; comdg. 6th, 7th and 8th Naval Dists., May 1934-Mar. 1936; comdr. Battle Div. One, April-June 1936; comdr. Cruisers Scouting Force, 1936-37; comdt. 13th Naval Dist. and Puget Sound Navy Yard, July 1937-Aug. 1940; retired Sept. 1940. Mem. Psi Upsilon. Club: Army and Navy (Washington, D.C.). Home: 6230 Wilson Av., Seattle, Wash. Died Feb. 13, 1943.

FENNER, Erasmus Darwin, orthopedist; b. New Orleans, La., Dec. 21, 1868; s. Charles Erasmus and Caroline (Payne) F.; A.B., Tulane, 1888; student med. dept. U. of Va., 1888-89; M.D., Tulane Med. Coll., 1892; m. Sadie Cameron McDonald, Apr. 28, 1920. Practiced at New Orleans since 1892; emeritus prof. orthopedics and surgical diseases of children, Tulane Med. College; chief in orthopedics and fractures, Independent Unit, Charity Hospital; consultant in orthopedics, Mercy Hospital-Soniat Memorial. Captain Medical Reserve Corps, U.S. Army, June 15, 1917; assigned to duty with Base Hospital 24, Aug. 31, 1917; liaison officer 12th Region, June 1918-Jan. 1919; major Medical Corps, Nov. 9, 1918; hon. disch. Apr. 24, 1919. Decorated Officer d'Académie by French Govt. Fellow Am. Coll. Surgeons; mem. A.M.A., Southern Med. Assn., La. State and Orleans Parish med. socs., Clin. Orthopedic Soc., Am. Acad. of Orthopedic Surgeons, Sigma Chi. Democrat. Episcopalian. Club: Boston. Home: 6323 St. Charles Av., New Orleans. Died June 7, 1944; buried in Metairie Cemetery, New Orleans.

FENNING, Frederick Alexander, lawyer; b. Washington, D.C., Oct. 23, 1874; s. James Alexander and Mary (Anderson) F.; LL.B., Nat. U. Law Sch., 1900, LL.M., 1901; m. Blanche Alisan Hine, Oct. 18, 1899; children—Katharine Hine (Mrs. Walter L. Wright, Jr.), James Frederick. Resigned as asst. chief clerk, U.S. Disbursing Pension Agency, 1902; in law practice Washington since 1902; dir., mem. trust com., Nat. Savings and Trust Co. Active duty as capt. and maj. Q.M.C., June 28, 1917-Mar. 15, 1919, in charge of officers allotments branch; col. R.C. Dir. Washington Bd. Trade, 1917-20; v.p. Am. Bar Assn., 1910-11, mem. gen. council, 1911-13, 1915-17; mem. Bd. of Med. Supervisors, D.C., 1915-25; mem. Board of Commissioners, D.C., 1925-1926; general counsel med. soc. D.C., 1924-38, advisory counsel since 1938, also honorary mem. of same society; hon. mem. Med. Soc. of St. Elizabeth's Hosp., D.C. Mem. bd. of trustees Am. Univ., 1921-27. Pres. The Anson Mills Foundation; pres. Washington Law Reporter Co. Mem. Bar Assn. D.C., S.A.R., Kiwanis (honorary), Republican. Presbyn. Clubs: Chevy Chase, Army and Navy. Wrote chapter on "Legal Measures in Their Remedial Bearings," in work White and Jelliffe on Treatment of Nervous and Mental Diseases, 1913; contbr. papers on legal aspect of insanity and medical jurisprudence to law and medical publs. Home: The Kennedy-Warren, Washington, D.C.; (summer) "Grayledge," Brooklin, Me. Office: 1029 National Press Bldg., Washington, D.C. Died Sep. 17, 1944.

FENWICK, Edward Taylor, patent lawyer; b. Washington, D.C., Apr. 18, 1869; s. Robert Washington and Annie Elizabeth (Munson) F.; direct descendant of Cuthbert Fenwick, who settled in southern Maryland, 1632; student Corcoran Scientific Sch., Washington, 1887-88; LL.B. and Master Patent Laws, George Washington U., 1891; m. Clara Louise Gulager, Sept. 3, 1895; children—Louise (Mrs. John R. Browning), Edward Gulager, Charles Rogers, Mary Virginia (Mrs. Donald K. Addie), Robert Munson (dec.), Lawrence Mason, Ellen (Mrs. John L. Demarest), Katherine Elizabeth. Admitted to D.C. bar, 1890; practiced patent and trade-mark law in Washington since 1887; offices also in N.Y. City; sr. partner Mason, Fenwick & Lawrence, patent and trade mark lawyers. Mem. Am. Bar Assn., Bar of Ct. of Appeals of D.C., Washington Bd. of Trade S.S. supt. since 1901; licensed as lay preacher, 1912; moderator Potomac Bapt. Assn. of Va., 1918-19; often del. to Gen. Bapt. Assn. of Va. and Southern Bapt. Conv. Democrat. Mason (K.T.). Rotarian, Knight of the Round Table. Contbr. to legal and religious articles. Home: E. Falls Church, Va. Office: Woodward Bldg., Washington, D.C. Died Oct. 10, 1942.

FERBERT, Adolph Henry, steamship exec.; b. Cleveland, O., Apr. 26, 1883; s. John Calhoun and Caroline (Striebinger) F.; student Cleveland pub. schs., 1889-1901; m. Ruby Bertha Winzer, Feb. 17, 1919; children—Edward Albert, Frederick Winzer. Stenographer Pittsburgh Steamship Co., Cleveland, O., 1904-06, in furnace order dept., 1906-12, dispatcher, 1912-22, traffic mgr., 1922-24, v.p., 1924-40, pres. since 1940, dir. since 1930; dir. Pittsburgh Supply Co. Mem. Cleveland Chamber of Commerce. Clubs: Westwood Country, Union of Cleveland, Mid-Day, Rotary (Cleveland). Home: 1080 Erie Cliff Drive, Lakewood, O. Office: Rockefeller Bldg., Cleveland, O Died May 23, 1948.

FERGUSON, James Edward, governor, b. Bell County, Tex., Aug. 31, 1871; s. James Edward and Fannie (Fitzpatrick) F.; ed. dist. sch.; m. Miriam Wallace, Dec. 31, 1899. Spent 2 yrs. on Pacific Coast and in Rocky Mountains as laborer, teamster, miner, etc.; foreman of bridge-building crews on various rys. in Tex.; engaged in farming in Bell County and now extensive land owner; admitted to Tex. bar, 1897; practiced in Belton, later in Temple, Tex.; an organizer of Temple State Bank, 1907; candidate for gov. of Tex., on a business man's platform, 1914; nominated at primaries and elected gov. for term, 1915, 1916; Democrat. Mason, Woodman, K. of P., Odd Fellow, Elk. Home: Temple, Tex. Address: Austin, Tex. Died Sept. 21, 1944.

FERGUSON, John Calvin, Adviser to the Executive Yuan of the National Government of China; b. Ontario, Can., Mar. 1, 1866; s. Rev. John and Catherine Matilda (Pomeroy) F.; A.B., Boston University, 1886, Ph.D., 1902; LL.D., 1939; also LL.D., U. of Southern California, 1939; m. Mary E. Wilson, Aug. 4, 1887 (died Oct. 6, 1938); children—Luther Mitchel (dec.), Helen Matilda (Mrs. John C. Beaumont), Alice Mary (dec.), Florence Wilson (Mrs. Raymond Mackay), Charles John, Mary Esther, Robert Mason, Duncan Pomeroy, Peter Blair (dec.). Pres. Nanking U., 1888-97, Nanyang Coll., Shanghai, 1897-1902; sec. Chinese Ministry of Commerce, 1902; chief sec. Imperial Chinese Ry. Administration, 1903-07; foreign adviser to viceroys of Nanking, 1898-1911, and of Wuchang, 1900-10; fgn. sec. Ministry of Posts and Communications, Peking, 1911; resigned to devote himself to lit. and art studies; returned to official life and became counselor of dept. of state of China, 1915-17; adviser to the Pres. of Republic of China, 1917-28. Chmn. Central China Famine Relief Com., 1910-11, raising nearly one million dollars; v.p. Red Cross Soc. of China, 1911, and counselor same, 1912-22; mem. Chinese Commn. to revise treaties with U.S. and Japan, 1902-03; sent on spl. missions for Chinese Govt. to U.S., 1901, 4, 7, 16, 17, 18, 19, also to 9th Internat. Conv. of Red Cross Socs., Washington, 1912; mem. Conf. on Limitation of Armament, 1921; pres. Sin Wan Pao, Shanghai (Chinese daily newspaper), 1899-1929; adviser of Executive Yuan of Nat. Govt., Nanking. Propr. Shanghai Times (daily), 1907-11. Held 2d class button of Chinese Govt.; Order of Double Dragon, 2d grade, 3d class, under former dynasty; Chevalier de la Légion d'Honneur (France); Order of Sacred Treasure (Japan); Order of St. Anna (Russia); 1st class Chia-ho Order of the Chinese Republic; 2d class of Wen-hu Order; Order of Merit of the Red Cross Soc. of China, same of Japan; received by pub. mandate thanks of Chinese govt. for gift of art collection to U. of Nanking, 1935; 1st class Order of Brilliant Jade (Nat. Govt. China). Hon. sec. North China br. of Royal Asiatic Soc., 1902-11, pres. 1911-12, hon. mem., 1919, editor jour., 1902-11. Editor China Journal of Science and Art, 1923-30. Trustee Boston U., since 1918; hon. fellow (1923), and fellow in perpetuity (1913), Met. Mus., New York; hon. adviser Govt. Mus. and Old Palace Mus., Peking; hon. mem. Phi Beta Kappa. Clubs: Century (New York); Peking, Shanghai, American (Shanghai). Author: Outlines of Chinese Art; Chinese Mythology; Chinese Paintings; Survey of Chinese Art; Catalogue of Recorded Paintings (in Chinese); Porcelains of Successive Dynasties; Catalogue of Recorded Bronze. Home: Newton, Mass. Address: Peking, China.* 1945.

FERREE, Clarence Errol (fĕr-rē'), psychologist; b. Sidney, O., Mar. 11, 1877; s. Jeremiah Dixon and Arvesta (Line) F.; B.S. and A.M., Ohio Wesleyan U., 1900, M.S., 1901; Sage fellow in psychology, Cornell U., 1902-03, Ph.D., 1909; D.Sc. Ohio Wesleyan U., 1939; m. Gertrude Rand, Sept. 28, 1918. Assistant in psychology, Cornell U., 1903-05, 1906-07; instr. in physics and psychology, U. of Ariz., 1905-06; lecturer in exptl. psychology, 1907-09, asso., 1909-12, asso. prof., 1912-17, prof., 1917-28, dir. Psychol. Lab., 1912-28, Bryn Mawr Coll.; dir. Research Lab. Physiol. Optics, and resident lecturer in ophthalmology, 1928-32, prof. physiol. optics and dir. Research Lab. Physiol. Optics, 1932-36, Wilmer Ophthal. Inst., Johns Hopkins Med. Sch.; dir. Research Lab. Physiol. Optics, Baltimore, since 1936. Fellow A.A. A.S.; mem. Am. Psychol. Assn., Illuminating Engring. Soc., Optical Soc. Amer., Franklin Inst., Phi Gamma Delta, Sigma Xi, P.B.K. (hon.). Apptd. mem. Engr. Reserve Corps Com., May 1917. Inventor (with G. Rand) various lighting appliances, apparatus for measuring speed of accommodation and convergence of the eye, apparatus for testing visual acuity and the light and color sense, perimeter, pupilometer, central-vision scotometer and other optical and ophthalmic instruments. Author: Radiometric Apparatus for Use in Psychological and Physiological Optics, 1917; Studies in Physiological Optics, 2 volumes (with G. Rand), 1934; The Light Sense, Chapter XV, Modern Trends in Ophthalmology, London, 1940. Editor and author: Studies in Psychology, 3 volumes, 1916, 1922, 1925. Contbr. more than 275 articles in scientific, technical and ophthal. jours. on lighting in its relation to the eye, hygiene of the eye, methods and apparatus for refracting the eye, etc. Contbr. (with same) of apparatus and research, air service of army and lookout and signal service of navy. Contbr. Fourth Internat. Congress Sch. Hygiene, 1913, Internat. Congress of Ophthalmology, 1922, English-speaking Congress of Ophthalmology, London, 1926, Joint Discussion on Vision, The Physical and Optical Societies, London, 1932. Member committee of 4 on standards of field taking in study of eye diseases, Internat. Congress of Opthalmology, 1922, Nat. Research Council's Com. on Industrial Lighting, 1924, Inter Soc. Com. on Color, 1931. Granted several patents on illuminating devices and optical instruments. Home: 2609 Poplar Drive, Baltimore. Address: Research Laboratory of Physiological Optics, Baltimore, Md. Died July 26, 1942.

FERRIER, William Warren, editor, historian; b. Metz, Ind., July 18, 1855; s. William and Olive (Thompson) F.; A.B., Otterbein Coll., Westerville, O., 1878, A.M., 1879, D.D., 1904; student Lane Theol. Sem., Cincinnati, O., 1887-88; m. Adessa J. Jarvis, Feb. 23, 1881; 1 son, William Warren; m. 2d, Rosa M. Buel, Feb. 10, 1910. Editor and co-propr. Steuben Republican, Angola, Ind., 1880-86, Daily Times, Muncie, Ind., 1887; ordained to ministry Conglist Ch., 1889; pastor Port Townsend, Wash., 1889-90, University Ch., Seattle, Wash., 1891-92, Mayflower Ch., Pacific Grove, Calif., 1894-96. Editor The Pacific, organ of Pacific Coast Congl. chs., 1897-1920; writer of Calif. hist. articles in Daily Gazette, Berkeley, Calif., 1921-33; author Calif. histories since 1927. Author: Pioneer Church Beginnings and Educational Movements in California, 1927; Origin and Development of the University of Calif., 1930; Berkeley, California—The Story of the Development of a Hamlet into a City of Culture and Commerce, 1933; Ninety Years of Education in California, 1846-1936, 1937; Henry Durant, First President of the University of California, 1941; Congregationalism's Place in California History, 1943; also several booklets on hist. subjects. Contbr. to periodicals. Home: 2716 Hillegass Av., Berkeley, Calif. Died Aug. 20, 1945.

FERRIS, David Lincoln, bishop; b. Peekskill, N.Y., Dec. 31, 1864; s. James Augustus and Catherine Sophia (Clark) F.; prep. edn. Peekskill Mil. Acad. and Cuyaga Lake (N.Y.) Mil. Acad.; B.A., Hobart Coll., Geneva, N.Y., 1888, M.A., 1891, D.D., 1920; grad. Berkeley Div. Sch., Middletown, Conn., 1893, D.D., 1921; L.H.D., St. Stephen's, 1921; m. Mary Eversley Stuart, Oct. 24, 1893; 1 son, Eversley Stuart. Deacon, 1893, priest, 1894, P.E. Ch.; rector St. Matthew's Ch., Horseheads, N.Y., and St. John's Ch., Big Flats, N.Y., 1893-96; sr. curate St. John's Ch., Stamford, Conn., 1896-1900; asso. rector Calvary Ch., Pittsburgh, Pa., 1900-12; rector Christ Ch., Rochester, N.Y., 1912-20; bishop suffragan, Diocese W. New York, 1920-24, bishop coadjutor, 1924-1929, bishop, 1929-32 (until its division); bishop Episcopal Diocese of Rochester, New York, 1932-38, resigned, 1938. Secretary of the Standing Committee, Diocese of Pittsburgh, 1905-12; dep. to Gen. Conv. P.E. Ch., 1916-1919; v.p. trustees P.E. Ch. Home, Rochester; trustee Gen. Theol. Sem., Berkeley Div. Sch. Mem. Phi Beta Kappa, Theta Delta Chi. Republican. Mason (33°, K.T.). Clubs: University, Genesee Valley, Chamber of Commerce. Home: 325 Park Av., Rochester, N.Y. Died June 9, 1947.

FESSENDEN, Russell Green, banker; b. Boston, Mass., Oct. 21, 1869; s. Sewall Henry and Louisa Green (Bursley) F.; A.B., Harvard, 1890; m. Mrs. J. L. Snelling, Mar. 10, 1910. Mem. Edward H. Eldredge & Co. until 1907; pres. and chmn. bd. Am. Trust Co., 1907-27, chmn. bd., 1927-30; now with Old Colony Trust Co. (director, and chairman of the real estate committee); president, trustee, Boston Five Cents Savings Bank; director Scott & Williams, Inc. Pres. and mem. bd. mgrs. Mass. Eye and Ear Infirmary; mem. bd. mgrs. Boston Provident Assn. Member Delta Kappa Epsilon. Clubs: Harvard (Boston); Country (Concord). Home: Concord, Mass. Office: One Federal St., Boston, Mass. Died Feb. 11, 1945.

FETTER, Frank Albert, univ. prof.; b. Peru, Ind., Mar. 8, 1863; s. Henry G. and Ellen (Cole) F.; A.B., Ind. U., 1891; Ph.M., Cornell, 1892; post-grad. studies, Sorbonne, Ecole de Droit, Paris, 1892-93, Halle, 1893-94, Ph.D., 1894; LL.D., Colgate, 1909, Occidental, 1930, Ind. U., 1934, Princeton, 1945; m. Martha Whitson, July 16, 1896; children—Frank Whitson, Ellen Cole, Theodore Henry. Bookseller, Peru, Ind., 1883-90; winner Interstate Oratorical Contest, Des Moines, Ia., 1891; instr. polit. economy, Cornell, 1894-95; prof. Ind. U., 1895-98, Leland Stanford Jr. U., 1898-1900; prof. polit. economy and finance, Cornell U., 1901-10; economics and distribution, 1910-11; prof. polit. economy, Princeton, 1911-31; prof. emeritus since 1931; chmn. dept. of economics and social instns., 1911-22; visiting prof. Harvard, 1906-07, Columbia, 1912-13, The Claremont Colleges, 1928-29, U. of Ill., 1934-36; lecturer at various times at Johns Hopkins, U. of Chicago, Northwestern U. Commr. N.Y. State Bd. Charities, 1910-11; gen. mgr. Nat. War Camp Community Service, 1918-19; mem. bd. mgrs. N.J. State Home for Boys, 1918-28; pres. N.J. Conf. for Social Welfare, 1919; vice pres. Princeton Bd. of Edn., 1923-28; economic adviser to the Asso. States opposing Pittsburgh-Plus, 1923; special expert on the basing-point practice, for the Fed. Trade Commn., 1938-39. Sec.-treas. Am. Economic Assn., 1901-06, pres. 1912. Mem. Am. Philos. Soc., Am. Acad. Arts and Sciences, Beta Gamma Sigma, Phi Kappa Psi, Phi Beta Kappa, Delta Sigma Rho. Clubs: Cosmos. Author: Versuch einer Bevolkerungslehre, 1894; The Principles of Economics, 1904; Economic Principles, 1915; Modern Economic Problems, 1916, 22; The Masquerade of Monopoly, 1931; also many articles, monographs, etc., on econ. subjects. Home: 168 Prospect Av., Princeton, N.J. Died March 21, 1949.

FICKE, Arthur Davison (fĭk'ĕ), author; b. Davenport, Iowa, Nov. 10, 1883; s. Charles August and Frances (Davison) F.; A.B., Harvard, 1904; student Coll. of Law, State U. of Ia.; m. Evelyn Bethune Blunt, Oct. 1, 1907; 1 son, Stanhope Blunt; m. 2d, Gladys Brown, Dec. 8, 1923. Taught English, State U. of Ia., 1906-07. Author (poems): From the Isles, 1907; The Happy Princess, 1907; The Earth Passion, 1908; The Breaking of Bonds, 1910; Twelve Japanese Painters, 1913; Mr. Faust, 1913; Sonnets of a Portrait Painter, 1914; The Man on the Hilltop, 1915; Chats on Japanese Prints, 1915; An April Elegy, 1917; Spectra (with Witter Bynner), 1916; Sonnets of a Portrait Painter, 1922; Out of Silence, 1924; Selected Poems, 1926; Mountain Against Mountain, 1929; The Secret and Other Poems, 1936; Tumultuous Shore, 1942; Mrs. Morton of Mexico (novel), 1939. Home: Hardhack, Hillsdale, N.Y. Died Nov. 30, 1945; buried Hardhack, Hillsdale.

FIELD, Harry Hubert, organizer Nat. Opinion Research Center; b. Harrogate, Eng., Oct. 29, 1897 s. Harry and May Elizabeth (Thomas) F.; student private schools and Shrewsbury School, England; m. Helen Knowlton, 1931 (deceased, December 4, 1944). Asst. secretary Houston Publishing Company, 1921-23; Am. business rep. Asso. Newspapers Ltd., London, Eng., 1923-25; asso. with Blackman Co., later Young & Rubicam, Inc.; v.p. and dir. Hawley Advt. Co., 1929-39; organized with Dr. George Gallup, British Inst. of Pub. Opinion, 1936; pres. People's Research Corp., 1939-41; initiated and organized Nat. Opinion Research Center (non-profit, non-commercial orgn. to measure public opinion; has grant from Marshall Field Foundation, Inc., and U. of Denver). Served in British Army, 1914-18, capt., 1917; instr., A.E.F., 1918. Mentioned in Sir Douglas Haig dispatch, Apr. 1918. Hon. mem. Nat. Guard (N.Y.) Regt., 1920-29. Episcopalian. Clubs: Naval Military (New York); Royal Automobile (London); Denver Country, Cactus (Denver). Author: After Mother India, 1929; contbr. general and scientific mags., various newspapers. Home: 128 Gilpin St. Office: Nat. Opinion Research Center, U. of Denver, Denver 10, Colo. Died Sep. 4, 1946.

FIELD, Henry, seedsman; b. Shenandoah, Ia., Dec. 6, 1871; s. Solomon Elijah and Celestia Josephine (Eastman) F.; student, scientific course, Western Normal Coll., Shenandoah, 1890-91; m. Edna L. Thompson, May 8, 1900; children—Frank, Faith, Hope, Philip, Josephine, Jessie, Mary, Ruth, Georgia, John Henry, Letty. Seed growing and seed selling, 1894-1907; organized and incorporated, 1907, Henry Field Seed Co., of which he is pres.; pres. Henry Field Co., KFNF, Inc. County surveyor Page County about 1892. Methodist. Editor Field's Seed Sense; contbr. hort. and agrl. articles to various publs. Candidate of Rep. party for U.S. senator, 1932. Home: 403 Sycamore St., Shenandoah, Ia.

Died Oct. 17, 1949.

FIELD, Rachel (Mrs. Arthur S. Pederson), writer; b. New York, N.Y., Sept. 19, 1894; d. Matthew D. (M.D.) and Lucy (Atwater) Field; ed. pub. schs.; spl. student Radcliffe, 1914-18; m. Arthur S. Pederson, June 1935. Awarded John Newberry medal for most distinguished contribution to lit. for children, 1929. Author: The Pointed People, 1924; Six Plays, 1924; Taxis and Toadstools, 1926; Eliza and the Elves, 1926; The Magic Pawnshop, 1927; The Cross-Stitch Heart and Other One-Act Plays, 1927; Little Dog, Toby, 1928; Hitty, Her First Hundred Years, 1929; Points East, 1930; Calico Bush, 1931; Hepatica Hawks, 1932; God's Pocket (biography), 1934; Branches Green (verse), 1934; Time Out of Mind (novel), 1935; Fear Is the Thorn, 1936; To See Ourselves (with Arthur Pederson), 1937; All This and Heaven Too, 1938; Ava Maria, 1940. Editor: The White Cat and Other French Fairy Tales, 1928; American Folk and Fairy Tales, 1929. Address: care Macmillan Co., 60 Fifth Av., New York, N.Y. Died Mar. 15, 1942.

FIELD, Robert Michael, lawyer, corp. official; s. Robert Michael and Frances (Ward) F.; A.B. and LL.B., grad. study Oxford U., Eng., and Sorbonne, Paris; m. Mary Louise Gardner; children—Robert Michael III, Christopher Burnet, Deidre Damaris. Admitted to practice, New York bar and before the bar of the United States Supreme Court; contributing editor New York Evening Post; chmn. board directors, Indusco. Served as pvt., later lt., inf., 28 months, 13 mos. with A.E.F. in France, 1917-19. Asst. U.S. atty. gen., asst. chmn. Business Advisory Council, spl. advisor N.R.A. Del. to Brussels congress of La Fédération des Anciens Combattants; chmn. Nat. Advisory Council; dir. and mem. exec. com. United China Relief. Mem. Am. Asiatic Assn. (dir. and vice-pres.), Pan American Soc. (dir.), Nat. Foreign Trade Council, Am. Brazilian Assn., Internat. Chamber of Commerce, Chamber of Commerce of State of N.Y., Argentine C. of C., Export Managers Club, Acad. Polit. Science, Am. Bar Assn., Council on Foreign Relations, Am. Legion, Phi Beta Kappa, Delta Sigma Rho, Sigma Upsilon. Clubs: Riverdale Tennis, St. Andrews Golf, Riverdale Yacht, India House. Author: From Tilden to Wilson; Epochs in American Banking. Contributor articles to various magazines. Home: Field Lane, Riverdale-on-Hudson, New York, N.Y. Died Nov. 1, 1949.

FIELDS, Annie Adams, author; b. Boston, June 6, 1834; d. Dr. Zabdiel Boylston and Sarah May (Holland) Adams; m. James Thomas Fields, 1854 (died 1881). Author: A Shelf of Old Books; Memoirs of James T. Fields; How to Help the Poor; Whittier, Notes of His Life and Friendship; Authors and Friends; Under the Olive; The Singing Shepherd, and Other Poems; Nathaniel Hawthorne, 1899; Orpheus, 1900. Address: 148 Charles St., Boston. Died Jan. 1915.

FIELDS, W. C. (Dukenfield), stage, motion picture, radio comedian; b. Philadelphia, Pa., Jan. 29, 1880. In vaudeville for several years. Appeared in musical productions on Broadway, including the Ziegfield Follies and Earl Carroll's Vanities. Motion pictures: So's Your Old Man, It's the Old Army Game, The Potters, Six of a Kind, One in a Million, It's a Gift, David Copperfield, Mississippi, The Man on the Flying Trapeze, Poppy, The Big Broadcast of 1938, The Bank Dick, Never Give a Sucker an Even Break, My Little Chickadee, etc. On the Chase and Sanborn Radio Hour, 1937. Address: Hollywood, Calif. Died Dec. 25, 1946; buried in Forest Lawn Memorial Park, Glendale, Calif.

FIFE, Joseph Paull; A.B., Stanford U., 1896; LL.B., Harvard, 1900. In practice of law at Pittsburgh; mem. firm Douglass, Fife & Young. Office: Frick Bldg., Pittsburgh, Died Mar. 10, 1947.

FIFER, Orien Wesley, clergyman; b. Mendon, Ill., May 4, 1868; s. John and Ruth Amelia (Megrue) F.; B. Litt., U of Neb., 1889, A.M., 1895; student Garrett Bibl. Inst., 1890-91; D.D., Neb. Wesleyan U., 1912; D.D., DePauw, 1933; LL.D., University of Nebraska, 1939; married Georgia Taylor, September 2, 1891 (died February 28, 1945); children—Warren Taylor, Paul Megrue, Ruth Mary (Mrs. Herschel E. Davis), Orien Wesley. Entered ministry M. E. Ch., 1891; pastor Emmanuel Ch., Lincoln, 1891-94; Wahoo, 1895, Geneva, 1896-98, York, 1898-1904, Grace Ch. Des Moines, Ia., 1904-13, Warren Memorial Ch., Denver, Colo., 1913-17, Central Av. Ch., Indianapolis, Indiana, 1917-27; supt., Indianapolis dist., 1927-32; editor Christian Advocate, Cincinnati, 1932-40; columnist, Christian Advocate, Chicago, 1941-43. Chaplain Neb. Nat. Guard, 1903-04; camp pastor and Y.M.C.A. asst., Camp Gordon, Atlanta, Ga., 1918. Mem. Bd. Foreign Missions M.E. Ch., 1924-40. Del. to Gen. Conf. M. E. Ch., 1912, 24, 28, 32, 36 (chmn. episcopacy com. 1928, 1932 and 1936); del. to Uniting Conf., 1939 (chmn. com. on ministry, including episcopacy and judicial administration); del. Ecumenical Conf., Atlanta, 1931; del. Gen. Conf. and Jurisdictional Conf., 1940 (chmn of com. on ministry, including episcopacy); exec. sec. Methodist Emergency Commn., Jan.-Mar. 1941; pastor emeritus Central Av. Ch., Oct., 1941-1945; acting supt. Indianapolis Methodist Hosp., Mar.-June, 1946; acting supt. Ft. Wayne Methodist Hosp. since 1946. Mason (33°). Clubs: Indianapolis Literary, Rotary. Home: 3515 Winthrop Av., Indianapolis, Ind. Died Sept. 18, 1947.

FIKE, Pierre Hicks, newspaper editor; b. Tylersville, Laurens County, S.C., May 24, 1873; s. Claudius Lucien and Mary (Goodwin) F.; prep. edn. Laurens (S.C.) Male Acad.; student Wofford Coll., Spartanburg, S.C., 1894-95; m. Lula Justice, Dec. 24, 1910; children—Pierre Hicks, Claudius Lemuel, William Russell, Louise. City editor Spartanburg Herald, 1896-1904; sec. to Congressman J. T. Johnson, 1904-12; postmaster, Spartanburg, 1913-21; editor Spartanburg Journal since 1923. Mem. Pi Kappa Alpha. Methodist. Mason. Home: 189 Hampton Drive. Office: Herald-Journal Bldg., Spartanburg, S.C. Died May 12, 1943.

FILBERT, William J., steel mfr.; b. Palatine, Ill., ed. pub. schs., Palatine. In purchasing dept., later accounting div. C.& N.-W. Ry.; asst. auditor Federal Steel Co., 1898-1901; with U.S. Steel Co., 1901-36, asst. controller, 1901-02, controller, 1902-33, chmn. finance com., 1933-36, retired Jan. 1, 1936. First sec. Am. Iron & Steel Inst., and awarded Gary Medal by same, 1931, for outstanding service to steel industry. Rated an authority on accountancy. Home: 898 Park Av. Office: 71 Broadway, New York. Died Feb. 4, 1944.

FILLMORE, Parker, author; b. Cincinnati, Sept. 21, 1878; s. William Aden and Adelaide Martha Susan (Molloy) F.; B.A., U. of Cincinnati, 1901; m. Louise Dutton; 1 dau., Rose. Gov. teacher in P.I., 1901-04; mem. firm W. H. Fillmore & Co., bankers, Cincinnati, 1904-18. Author: The Hickory Limb, 1910; The Young Idea, 1911; The Rosie World, 1914; A Little Question in Ladies' Rights, 1916; Czechoslovak Fairy Tales, 1919; The Shoemaker's Apron, 1920; The Laughing Prince, 1921; Mighty Mikko, 1922; The Wizard of the North, 1923; Yesterday Morning, 1931; The Stuffed Parrot, 1931. Home: 434 E. 87th St., New York. Died June 5, 1944.

FILSINGER, Ernst B., foreign trade expert; b. St. Louis, June 10, 1880; s. Henry J. and Kate (Ernst) F.; ed. pub. schs., St. Louis; m. Sara Teasdale, Dec. 19, 1914. Fgn. sales mgr. Lawrence & Co., textiles, New York and Boston. Author: Exporting to Latin America, 1916; Commercial Travelers' Guide to Latin America, 1920. Contrb. to tech. jours.; occasional lecturer at Harvard Grad., Sch. of Business Administration. Clubs: Export Managers (pres.), Wool Club, Arkwright, The Players. Home: 146 Central Park West. Office: 24 Thomas St., New York. Died May 24, 1937.

FINAN, Joseph B. (fī'năn), editor, pub.; b. Cumberland, Md., June 10, 1869; s. James and Anne (McDonough) F.; ed. Carroll Hall Acad., Cumberland; m. Clara Helen Doerner, June 12, 1895; children—Rev. Gerald J., Anna Irene, Mary Josephine. Editor and gen. mgr. Cumberland Times since 1918; pres. Times & Alleganian Co. Democrat. Catholic. Rotarian. Home: 527 Washington St. Office: 7 S. Mechanic St., Cumberland, Md. Died Aug. 2, 1943.

FINCH, Thomas Austin, pres. Thomasville Chair Co.; b. Randolph County, N.C., Apr. 7, 1890; s. Thomas Jefferson and Hannah (Brown) F.; A.B., Trinity Coll. (now Duke U.), 1909; m. Daisy Ernestine Lambeth, Nov. 6, 1919; 1 son, Thomas Austin. With Thomasville Chair Co. since 1909, sec.-treas., 1914-29, pres. since 1929; v.p. HighPoint,Thomasville&Denton R.R.; pres. First Nat. Bank (Thomasville); mem. bd. govs. Am. Furniture Mart; dir. Southern Furniture Bldg. Corp., Home Bldg. and Loan Assn. Mayor of Thomasville, N.C., 1922-24; mem. N.C. Transportation Council, 1926-28, N.C. Employment Council, 1930, Industrial Adv. Board, NRA, 1933, Business Advisory Council, U.S. Dept. of Commerce since 1933. Mem. Furniture Club of America. Democrat. Methodist. Mason. Rotarian. Address: Thomasville, N.C. Died Jan. 11. 1943.

FINFROCK, Clarence Millard, prof. law; b. New Paris, O., Feb. 9, 1881; s. Charles Milton and Mary Angeline (Cable) F.; A.B., Ohio Wesleyan U., 1902, M.A., 1907; LL.B., Western Reserve University, 1907; LL.D., Ohio Wesleyan University, 1946; married Zoe Ellen Hoskinson, June 23, 1909; children—Charles Millard, Mary Ellen (Mrs. Wright Morris), Principal high school, Tippecanoe City, Ohio, 1902-05; professor of law, Western Reserve University since 1907; secretary of faculty, 1910-45, associate medical jurisprudence Medical School, 1914-45; lecturer on dental jurisprudence Dental School, 1918-45, dean School of Law, since 1945; lecturer on negotiable paper and trust business, American Institute Banking, 1914-45. Chairman Selective Service Board 41, Cuyahoga, O., since 1941; pub. member Regional War Labor Board, 5th Area, 1943-46. Trustee Cuyahoga County Conservation Council; v.p. League of Ohio Sportsmen, 1939. Chmn. bd. in charge intercollegiate athletics, Western Reserve U., 1930-36. Treas. Cleveland Chapter Com. to Defend America by Aiding the Allies. President League of Ohio Law Schools, 1940-41. Mem. Am. Ohio State and Cleveland bar assns., Order of the Coif, Am. Ornithol. Union, Wilson Ornithol. Club, Lake Erie Wild Flower and Conservation Club, Phi Beta Kappa, Phi Delta Phi. Democrat. Presbyterian. Mason. Clubs: Cleveland Bird, Inc. (trustee), Professional, Western Reserve University Faculty, University. Home: 3186 Oak Rd., Cleveland Heights 18, O. Died March 7, 1948.

FINGERHOOD, Boris, hospital administrator and consultant; born in Russia, April 19, 1887; s. Schmaryohu and Israelevitch F.; preparatory education, Gymnasium, Warsaw, and Real Schule, Dvinsk, Russia; student New York U., 1916-19; m. Sylvia Golden. Supt. Israel-Zion Hosp., Brooklyn, 1920-44, emeritus since 1944; hosp. editor Medical Review of Reviews. Mem. Am. Hosp. Assn., Kings County Med. Assn., N.Y. State Hosp. Assn. (pres. 1932-33), Hosp. Council of Brooklyn (pres. 1930-31); charter fellow Am. Coll. Hosp. Adminstrs.; mem. com. on training hosp. adminstrs. and com. on nomenclature in uniform staff orgn. of Am. Hosp. Assn. Has written A Minimum Standard for Dispensaries and Hospital Service and the Physician. Contbr. to Modern Hospital, Hospital Management, etc. Home: Miami Beach, Fla.; also 333 W. 86th St., New York, N.Y. Died Apr. 21, 1946.

FINK, Emil C., chmn. bd. and pres. Mack Trucks, Inc.; officer or dir. other cos. Address: 48th Av. and 34th St., Long Island City, N.Y. Died Jan. 1, 1942.

FINKEL, Benjamin Franklin (surname formerly Finckel), coll. prof.; b. near E. Ringgold, Fairfield County, O., July 5, 1865; s. John Philip and Louise Frederica (Stickle) F.; B.S., Ohio Northern U., 1888, M.S., 1891; studied U. of Chicago, 1895-96, and 5 summers; spl. fellow in mathematics, 1903-04, Harrison fellow, 1905-06, U. of Pa., A.M., 1904, Ph.D., 1906; LL.D., Drury Coll., 1923; m. Hannah Cokely, July 17, 1890 (died Jan. 29, 1938); children—Calvin Randell (dec.), Mrs. Lucile Whitney, Mrs. Louise Lockwood; married 2d, Mary Frances Ford, August 24, 1944. Teacher in rural schs., O., 1884-89; instr. in mathematics, Fostoria (O.) Acad., 1889; prin. Gibson Male and Female Acad., Tenn., 1889-90; supt. schs., N. Lewisburg, O., 1890-91, West Middleburg, O., 1891-92; instr. mathematics and astronomy, Kidder (Mo.) Inst., 1892-95; prof. mathematics and physics; Drury Coll., Springfield, Mo., 1895-1937, prof. emeritus of mathematics and physics since 1937; dir. summer sessions, Drury Coll., 1915-18; instr. in mathematics, summer sessions, U. of Colo., 1913-18; instr. physics, U.S. Army classes, U. of Mo., 1944. Fellow A.A.A.S.; mem. Am. Math. Soc., London Math. Soc., Circolo Matematico di Palermo, Sigma Xi (U. of Pa. chapter), Mo. Soc. Mathematics and Science (sec.), Math. Assn. of America (council; v.p. 1920-21), Am. Assn. Univ. Profs., Mo. Acad. Science (chmn. Mathematics Sect. 1934, 35). Republican. Conglist. Club: University (pres. 1932). Author: Mathematical Solution Book, 1892; A History of American Mathematical Journals, 1940. Founder, and editor Am. Math. Monthly (now official jour. Math. Assn. America), 1894-1913, now dept. editor. Lecturer on scientific subjects. Home: 1227 N. Clay Av., Springfield, Mo. Died Feb. 5, 1947.

FINLAYSON, Frank Graham, lawyer; b. of naturalized Am. parents, Bendigo, Australia, Mar. 24, 1864; s. James Ross and Elizabeth (Goodsir) F.; LL.B., Hastings Coll. of Law (U. of Calif.), 1885; m. Agnes Thayer, July 10, 1895 (died Oct. 4, 1936); 1 dau., Beatrice (Mrs. Charles S. Forve); m. 2d, Grace Reiniger, April 22, 1939. Brought to America, 1867. Admitted to Calif. bar, 1885; practiced in San Francisco until 1886, since at Los Angeles; mem. Calif. Assembly,1893-94; asst. U.S. dist. atty., Southern Dist. of Calif., 1895-97; judge Superior Court, Los Angeles County, 1911-19; presiding justice Dist. Court of Appeals, Div. 2, 2d Appellate Dist., 1919-26; apptd. justice Supreme Court of Calif. to fill unexpired term, Oct. to Dec. 1926; sr. partner Finlayson, Bennett & Morrow since 1926. Mem. Calif. State Bar Assn. (mem. bd. govs.), Am. Bar Assn., Los Angeles Bar Assn. Republican. Mason (33°). Clubs: California, University, Sunset. Author: Street Laws of California, 1893. Home: 500 S. Gramercy Pl. Office: Van Nuys Bldg., Los Angeles, Calif. Died Feb. 9, 1947.

FINLEY, Ernest Latimer, editor, pub. and farmer; b. Corvallis, Ore., Sept. 15, 1875; s. William Asa and Sarah E. (Latimer) F.; ed: pub. schs.; m. Ruth Woolsey, 1912; children—Ruth, Robert Woolsey. Owner and editor Morning Press Democrat, Santa Rosa, Calif., since 1897; owner Evening Republican since 1924, also Weekly Coast Defender; owner radio station KSRO. Postmaster of Santa Rosa, 1936-39. Pres. bd. trustees Santa Rosa Pub. Library 2 terms. Pres. North Bay Counties Development Assn. 3 terms, Santa Rosa Chamber Commerce 2 terms; president Symphony Orchestra Assn., 1 term; pres. Redwood Empire Pubs. Assn. Democrat. Episcopalian. Elk. Home: 1020 McDonald Av. Office: The Press Democrat, Santa Rosa, Calif. Died Oct. 24, 1942.

FINLEY, John Huston, editor, educator, author; b. Grand Ridge, Ill., Oct. 19, 1863; s. James Gibson and Lydia Margaret (McCombs) F.; A.B., Knox Coll., 1887, A.M., 1890; Johns Hopkins, 1887-89; LL.D., Park Coll., 1895, Knox Coll., 1899, U. of Wis., 1904, Princeton, 1905, Tulane, 1906, Williams, 1908, Dartmouth, 1909, Hobart, 1913, Columbia, 1914, Brown U., 1915, U. of State of N.Y., 1921, U. of Mich., 1925, Miami U., 1927, Hamilton Coll., 1927, U. of Toronto, 1927, McGill, 1932, Colby, 1932, Middlebury, 1933, Marietta Coll., 1935, U. of Calif., 1936, Johns Hopkins, 1938; L.H.D., Colgate, 1914, New York Univ., 1915, Univ. of Vt., 1925, Yeshiva, 1933, Trinity, 1933, St. Lawrence U., 1935; J.U.D., Univ. of Pa., 1927; Litt.D., Lafayette, 1930, U. of Rochester, 1931, Butler, 1932; m. Martha Ford Boyden, June 29, 1892; children—Ellen Boyden, Margaret Boyden (dec.), Robert Lawrence, John Huston. Sec. State Charities Aid Assn., N.Y., and editor Charities Rev., 1889-92. Pres. Knox Coll., 1892-99; editor Harper's Weekly, 1899; prof. politics, Princeton, 1900-03; pres. Coll. City of New York, 1903-13; commr. of edn., State of N.Y., and pres. U. of the State of New York, 1913-21; asso. editor New York Times, 1921-37, editor-in-chief, 1937-38, editor emeritus since 1938. Dir. Hall of Fame, New York U., since 1938. Harvard exchange lecturer on the Hyde Foundn., at The Sorbonne, Paris, 1910-11; lecturer on the Weil Foundn., U. of N.C., 1922, on Page-Barbour Foundn., Univ. of Va., 1924, on Watson Foundn., Univ. of Edinburgh, 1929, on the Evangeline Wilbour Blashfield Foundn., Am. Acad. of Arts and Letters, 1930, on Earl Foundn., Pacific Sch. of Religion, 1931; Phi Beta Kappa orator, Harvard, 1925; Laureate Chapter Kappa Delta Pi, 1935. Mem. bd. of arbitration in eastern ry. controversy, 1913-14; chmn. N.Y. State Commn. for Blind, 1913; pres. N.Y. Assn. for Blind; mem. New York State Constl. Conv. Commn., 1914-15; dir. New York Life Ins. Co., 1910-22; trustee, majority stock of Equitable Life Ins. Co., 1919-25; trustee Sage Foundn., Knox Coll., Berea Coll.; also trustee of N.Y. Public Library; special rep. of Regents of U. State of N.Y. on ednl. mission to France, 1917; mem. Am. Army Edn. Com. in France, 1918; head of Am. Red Cross in Palestine and Near East, 1918-19. Decorated Order Rising Sun (Japanese); Officer Legion of Honor (French); Comdr. Order of Crown of Italy; Knight of the Holy Sepulchre; Comdr. Order of St. Sava (Serbian); Comdr. Polonia Restituta (Polish); Comdr. Order of White Rose (Finnish), Order of St. Olaf (Norwegian); Knight of Dannebrog (Danish); Knight of Gediminas (Lithuanian); Cmdr. Order of the Savior (Greek); Comdr. Order of the White Lion (Czechoslovakia); Comdr. Order of the Royal North Star (Sweden); Book on French in America crowned by Academie Francaise and awarded gold medal Geographic Soc., Paris. Mem. Nat. Inst. Arts and Letters (ex-v.p.); mem. Am. Acad. Arts and Letters, 1927; pres. Am. Social Science Assn., 1910-11; pres. Nat. Dante Com., 1921; pres. Nat. Child Welfare Assn.; v.p. Nat. Recreation Assn.; chmn. Com. on Internat. Justice and Goodwill, Fed. Council Chs. of Christ in Am., 1921-25; mem. Nat. Council of Boy Scouts; hon. v.p. Boy Scouts of Scotland; vice chmn. Near East Relief; v.p. Nat. Inst. Social Sciences, N.Y. State Hist. Assn., Internat. Auxiliary Lang. Assn.; pres. New York Adult Edn. Council, Grover Cleveland Birthplace Assn.; hon. life mem. Met. Mus. Art; hon. pres. Am. Geog. Soc.; senator Phi Beta Kappa; chmn. Phi Beta Kappa Foundn.; hon. mem. N.Y. Hist. Soc., Soc. of Cincinnati of State of New York. Clubs: Century, Players (N.Y.). Author: Taxation in American States and Cities (with Richard T. Ely), 1889; The American Executive and Executive Methods (with John F. Sanderson), 1908; The French in the Heart of America, 1914; French Schools in War Time, 1917; A Pilgrim in Palestine, 1918; The Debt Eternal, 1923; The

Mystery of the Mind's Desire, 1936. Editor Nelson's Ency. Contbr. to revs., etc. Home: 1 Lexington Av. Address: New York Times, New York. Died March 7, 1940.

FINLEY, Solomon Henderson, civil engr.; b. Lincoln County, Mo., Oct. 10, 1863; s. Andrew Ramsey and Caroline (Gibson) F.; A.B., Monmouth (Ill.) College, 1886, A.M., 1889; m. Ida Hedges, Jan. 8, 1891; children—Gailene (Mrs. Donald Mynard Swarthout), Malcolm Hedges, Knox Henderson, Wendell William, Rhodes Andrew. Began practice as civ. engr., Santa Ana, Calif., 1886; city engr. (installed original municipal water system), 1891-97; planned and built Modjeska Dam for Madam Modjeska, 1900; planned and built agrl. drainage systems for 5 dists., Orange County, Calif., 1889-1905; as chief engr. built Santa Ana Newport R.R., 1891-99; mem. bd. trustees, Santa Ana, 1900-02, mayor, 1902-04; chief engr. Orange County Highway Commn., 1915-16; supervisor of Orange County, 1916-28; an organizer, 1928, since sec., and dir. from Santa Ana, The Met. Water Dist. of Southern Calif. Mem. Nat. Guard of Calif., 1890-1908; capt. 7th Calif. Vols., Spanish-Am. War; col. 7th Regt. Nat. Guard of Calif., 1904-08; assigned for duty with Red Cross in France, 1918, war closed before reaching front. Apptd. by Gov. Young as mem. Calif. com. to adjust Colorado River water claims with Ariz. and Nev. Mem. S.R., Spanish War Vets. Democrat. Presbyterian. Club: Rotary. Home: 1633 E. 4th St., Santa Ana, Calif. Died Dec. 4, 1944.

FINNEY, Benjamin Ficklin; b. Society Hill, S.C., Mar. 26, 1870; s. William Wood and Constance (Williams) F.; student U. of the South, 1885-86, D.C.L., 1938; B.S., Va. Poly. Inst., Blacksburg, Va., 1888; spl. course, U. of Va., 1890; LL.D., Hobart Coll., 1924; m. Elizabeth Bridgers, Jan. 3, 1899 (died 1902); 1 son, Benjamin Ficklin. Asso. chemist Va. Expt. Sta., 1888-90; chemist Va. State Dept. Agr., 1890-91; analyst and chem. engr., Savannah, Ga., 1892-1908; sec., 1908-21, vice chancellor Brotherhood of St. Andrew, U. of the South, 1922-38, pres., 1932-38, vice chancellor emeritus since 1938, regent since 1913. Mem. Va. branch Soc. of the Cincinnati, Alpha Tau Omega, Phi Beta Kappa, Omicron Delta Kappa, Pi Gamma Mu. Dep. to Gen. Conv. P.E. Ch., 1919, 28, 31, 34, 37. Democrat. Mason (32°). Home: Sewanee, Tenn. Died Oct. 21, 1943; buried at St. Luke's Church, Powhatan County, Va.

FINNEY, John Miller Turpin, surgeon; b. June 20, 1863; s. Ebenezer D. and Annie L. (Parker) F.; A.B., Princeton, 1884; M.D., Harvard, 1889, LL.D., 1937; LL.D., Tulane U., New Orleans, 1935; m. Mary E. Gross, Apr. 20, 1892; children—John Miller Train, Eben Dickey, George Gross, Mary Elizabeth. In practice at Baltimore since 1889; prof. surgery emeritus, Johns Hopkins. Fellow Am. Surg. Assn. (ex-pres.), Am. Coll. Surgeons (ex-pres.), Southern Surg. and Gynecol. Assn. Brig. gen., Med. R.C. U.S. Army; chief consultant in surgery A.E.F. Decorated D.S.M. (U.S.); Comdr. de l'Ordre de la Couronne (Belgian); Officier de la Légion d'Honeur (French). Club: Maryland. Home: 200 Goodwood Gardens, Roland Park. Office: 2947 St. Paul St., Baltimore, Md. Died May 30, 1942.

FINNEY, William Parker; b. near Natchez, Miss., September 9, 1861; s. Ebenezer Dickey and Annie Louise (Parker) F.; A.B., Princeton, 1883, A.M., 1886; grad. Princeton Theol. Sem., 1886; D.D., Cumberland (Tenn.) U., 1910; m. Pamela Richardson, Oct. 5, 1887 (died 1889); m. 2d, Katherine Richardson, Oct. 5, 1897 (died 1907); m. 3d, Eleanor Hoopes, June 11, 1910. Ordained Presbyn. ministry, 1886; pastor Cream Ridge and New Egypt, N.J., 1886-92, Moorestown, N.J., 1892-1910; prof. English, Lincoln U., Chester Co., Pa., 1910-26; gen. sec. Presbyn. Hist. Soc., Phila., 1926-33. Mem. Soc. of Cincinnati of Pa. (pres.), Order of Founders and Patriots of America. Home: Wood-Norton Apt., 6347 Wayne Av., Philadelphia. Died Aug. 11, 1944.

FISCHER, George August, music pub.; b. Dayton, O., Sept. 13, 1870; s. Joseph and Eleanor (Heineman) F.; m. Frances Stickler, Nov. 21, 1895; children—Antoinette (Mrs. Herbert Gardner), Joseph, Eugene, Victor. Pres. J. Fischer & Bro. music pubs., N.Y. Ctiy, since 1903; mem. bd. dirs. Am. Soc. Authors, Compasers and Pubs., N.Y. City; treas. St. Gregory Soc. of America. Home: 1 Midland Gardens, Bronxville, N.Y. Office: 119 W. 40th St., New York, N.Y. Died Aug. 21, 1941

FISCHER, Leo J.; chmn. bd. Thompson-Starrett Co. Address: 444 Mackson Av., New York, N.Y.* Died June 22, 1948.

FISCHER, Louis, M.D.; b. Kaschau, Austria-Hungary, Nov. 21, 1864; s. Ignetz and Louisa F.; came to New York in childhood; student Coll. City of N.Y. 2 yrs.; grad. Coll. of Pharamacy, 1882; M.D., Univ. Med. Coll. (New York U.), 1884; also studied in Berlin; m. Clara Robert, Mar. 20, 1895; children—Alfred E., Robert M. Specialist in diseases of children; visiting phys. Riverside Hosp., Willard Parker Hosp.; formerly lecturer on diseases of children, N.Y. Post-Grad. Hosp. and phys.-in-chief babies' wards, Suydenham Hosp. Mem. A.M.A. (sec. sect. diseases of children, 1900), Acad. of Medicine, New York, N.Y. County Med. Soc., Harlem Med. Soc. Author: Infant Feeding in Health and Disease, 1901; The Health Care of the Baby, 1906; Diseases of Infancy and Childhood, 1907; Health Care of the Growing Child, 1915. Contbr. on diphtheria, infantile diseases and feeding to various mags. Address: 73 E. 90th St., New York, N.Y. Died Apr. 9, 1945.

FISH, Bert, fgn. service; b. Bedford, Ind., Oct. 8, 1875; s. George Washington and Sarah Minty (Lee) F.; LL.B., John B. Stetson U., 1902, LL.D., 1935; unmarried. Admitted to Florida bar, 1902, in practice at DeLand; retired, Dec. 31, 1926; judge Criminal Court, Volusia County, 8 yrs.; E.E. and M.P. to Egypt since 1933, to Saudi, Arabia, since Aug. 1939, to Portugal since Mar. 1941. Chmn. delegation to the Capitulations Confs., Montreux, Switzerland, April-May, 1937. Mem. Sigma Nu, Phi Alpha Delta. Democrat. Mason (32°). Engaged in citrus industry. Home: DeLand, Fla. Address: Am. Legation, Lisbon, Portugal. Died July 21, 1943.

FISH, Irving Andrews, lawyer, b. Racine, Wis., Aug. 25, 1881; son of John T. and Eliza (Sampson) F.; student U. of Wis., 1899-1904; m. Margaret Carswell Richards, Apr. 25, 1908; 1 son, James Fish. Admitted to Wis. bar, 1903, and began practice at Madison; asso. with law firm Burr W. Jones, (Madison); mem. Fish & Storms (Racine, Wis.), Quarles, Spence & Quarles (Milwaukee); now mem. Fish, Marshutz & Hoffman (Milwaukee). Served as 2d lt., capt. and major, Wis. Nat. Guard, 1903-16; major Infantry and Signal corps and lt. col. Cavalry and Field Arty., U.S. Army, 1916-19; col. O.R.C., 1919-27; brig. gen., later major gen., Wis. Nat. Guard, 1927-40; major gen. U.S. Army, since Oct. 1940. Awarded Mexican Border, World War medals, Legion of Merit. Member Am., Wis. and Milwaukee Co. bar assns., Wis. Hist. Soc., Psi Upsilon, Phi Delta Phi. Episcopalian. Clubs: Milwaukee, Milwaukee Country. Home: 9185 N. Range Line Rd., Milwaukee 9. Office: Wells Bldg., Milwaukee, Wis. Died Apr. 22, 1948.

FISHER, Albert Kenrick, biologist; b. Sing Sing (now Ossining), N.Y., Mar. 21, 1856; s. Hiram and Susan E. (Townsend) F.; ed. Holbrook's Mil. High Sch., Sing Sing; M.D., Coll. Phys. and Surg. (Columbia U.), 1879; m. Alwilda Merritt; children—Harry Townsend (dec.), Walter Kenrick, Mrs. Ethel Merriam White (dec.), and Mrs. Alberta Merritt Marble (twins). Was with Death Valley Expdn., 1891, sent out by Dept. Agr., made biol. survey of portions of Calif., Nev., Ariz. and Utah; also made biol. survey in various other western states, 1892-98; member Harriman (Alaska) Expdn., 1899; member Pinchot South Sea Expdn., 1929. In charge econ. investigations U.S. Biol. Survey; collaborator U.S. Nat. Museum. One of founders of the Am. Ornithologists' Union (pres.); hon. mem. Am. Game Protective Assn.; corr. mem. Linnaean Soc. N.Y., Nuttall Ornithol. Club; hon. mem. Cooper Ornithol. Club, Delaware Valley Ornithol. Club; Internat. Assn. Game and Fish Commissioners; member Biological Society of Washington, Washington Biological Field Club; associate Boone and Crockett Club; president Baird Ornithol. Club. Club: Cosmos. Author: Hawks and Owls of the United States, 1893; Ornithology of the Death Valley Expedition of 1891, 1893; also 160 shorter papers. Address: Cosmos Club, Washington 5, D.C. Died June 12, 1948.

FISHER, Charles Asbury, dir., extension service, Univ. of Mich.; b. Huntington, Ind., July 3, 1885; s. Isaac Emory and Elizabeth Jane (Heiney) F.; A.B., DePauw U., 1910, M.A., Columbia, 1918, Ph.D., U. of Mich., 1930; m. Anna Moore, Dec. 25, 1910 (now deceased); children—Charles Eugene, Joseph Vincent, Paul Moore; m. 2d, Elsa Wilhelmina Apfel, Dec. 20, 1919; children—William Edward (dec.), John Apfel. Country sch. teacher, 1905-06; high sch. teacher, Lafayette, Ind., 1910-11; prin., Huntington, Ind., 1911-12, Warsaw High Sch., 1912-14, Benton Harbor High Sch., 1914-19, Kalamazoo High Sch., 1919-26; asst. dir. extension service, U. of Mich., 1926-37, dir. since 1937, instr. sociology, 1927-28. Member State Com. on Juvenile Delinquency, 1943, Nat. Jurisdictional Conf. of Meth. Ch., 1944; vice-pres. Mich. Congress of Parents and Teachers, 1938-40; mem. Nat. Univ. Extension Assn. (v.p. 1942-43, pres. 1944-45; chmn. com. on war effort and information, 1943-44; N.U.E.A. member Joint Com. for The Study of Adult Edn., Policies, Principles and Practices. Mem.N.E.A., Am. Sociological Soc., National Univ. Extension Assn., Am. Assn. for Adult Edn., Delta Kappa Epsilon, Phi Delta Kappa, Sigma Delta Chi. Mason. Methodist. Clubs: Economic (Detroit); University, Ann Arbor Golf and Outing (Ann Arbor). Home: 532 S. Fifth Av., Ann Arbor, Mich. Died Mar. 30, 1948.

FISHER, (George) Clyde, curator; b. near Sidney, O., May 22, 1878; s. Harrison Jay and Amanda (Rhinehart) F.; student Ohio Northern U.; A.B., Miami Univ., 1905, LL.D., 1926; Ph.D. in Botany, Johns Hopkins, 1913; m. Bessie Wiley, Aug. 29, 1905; children—Ruth Anna, Beth Elinor, Katherine Wiley; m. 2d, Te Ata, of the Chickasaw Nation, Sept. 28, 1933. Teacher in the public schools of Ohio 6 years; teacher of astronomy, botany and zoology, high sch., Troy, Ohio, 1905-07; prin. Palmer Coll. Academy, De Funiak Springs, Fla., 1907-1909; acting pres. Palmer College 1909-1910; in charge courses in ornithology, 3 summers, U. of Fla., 1 summer, U. of Tenn., courses in nature study, Cornell U., summer 1931; mem. scientific staff Am. Museum Natural History since 1913, now hon. curator a tronomy and of Hayden Planetarium. Conductor photog. expdn. to Bermudas, 1924. Arctic Lapland expdn. 1924: visited astron. museums and observatories of Europe 1925, to gather material for proposed Hall of Astronomy at Am. Museum; mem. of Harvard-Mass. Inst. Tech. Eclipse Expdn. to Siberia, 1936; leader of Am. Museum Eclipse Expdn. to Peru, 1937; mem. Am. Museum expdn. to volcano Paricutin in Mexico 1943 and 1944. Group of islands off coast of N. Labrador named in his honor, 1944. Made Hon. Chief, Blood Tribe of Blackfoot Confederacy, 1946. Fellow Royal Astron. Soc., A.A.A.S., N.Y. Acad. Sc ences, New York Zool. Soc.; mem. Am. Ornithol. Union (asso.), Am. Astron. Soc., Am. Assn. Variable Star Observers, Amateur Astron. Assn. (past pres.), Soc. for Research on Meteorities, Torrey Bot. Club, New York Bot. Garden, N.Y. Bird and Tree Club (pres.), Am. Nature Study Soc.; mem. Lima (Peru) Geog. Soc. (hon.). Phi Beta Kappa, Tau Kappa Alpha. Rep. Club: Explorers (pres.). Lecturer on astron. travel, natural history. Author: Nature's Secrets (Present edition called Nature Encyclopedia), 1921; Exploring the Heavens, 1937; Astronomy (co-author), 1940; The Story of the Moon, 1943 (trans. into Spanish, 1944; printed for the U.S. Armed Forces, 1945); The Life of Audubon, 1949. Home: 41 W. 72d St. Address: American Museum of Natural History, 79th St. and Central Park W., New York. Died Jan. 7, 1949.

FISHER, Edwin, banker; b. 1883. Chairman Barclays Bank, Ltd., since 1936. Address: 54 Lombard St., London, E.C. 3, England. Died Jan. 1947.

FISHER, Irving, polit. economist; b. Saugerties, N.Y., Feb. 27, 1867; s. Rev. George Whitefield and Ella (Wescott) F.; A.B., Yale, 1888, Ph.D., 1891; LL.D., Rollins Coll., 1932, University of Athens and U. of Lausanné, 1937; studied Berlin and Paris, 1893-94; m. Margaret, d. Rowland Hazard, June 24, 1893 (dec.); children—Margaret (dec.), Caroline (Mrs. Carol Fisher Baumann), Irving Norton. Tutor math., 1890-93, asst. prof., 1893-95, asst. prof. polit. economy, 1895-98, professor political economy, 1898-1935, now prof. emeritus, Yale Recuperating health in Colorado, California, 1898-1901. One of editors Yale Review, 1896-1910; Hitchcock lecturer, University of California, 1917; lecturer University of London School of Economics and Polit. Science, 1921, Geneva School of Internat. Studies, 1927. Gave lectures on income tax reform, U. of Southern Calif., Feb.-Apr. 1941. President for U.S. of Third Internat. Commn. on Eugenics; mem. Theodore Roosevelt's Nat. Conservation Commn.; chmn. Hygiene Reference Bd. of Life Extension Inst. since 1914; chmn. sub-com. on Alcohol of Council Nat. Defense, 1917-18; pres. Citizens' Com. on War-Time Prohibition, 1917; pres. Com. of 60 on Nat. Prohibition, 1917; chmn. bd. scientific dirs. Eugenics Record Office, 1917; dir. of Cowles Com. for Econ. Research. Vice pres., dir. Gotham Hosp., Gotham Med. Center. Chmn. bd. and dir. Check Master Plan, Inc., Gyrobalance Corp., Automatic Signal Corp.; dir. and mem. exec. com. Remington Rand Inc.; dir. Buffalo Elec. Furnace Corp., Sonotone Corp., Latimer Lab., Life Extension Inst. President American Assn. Labor Legislation, 1915-17, Nat. Institute Social Sciences, 1917, Am. Econ. Assn., 1918, Eugenics Research Assn., 1920, Pro-League Independents, 1920, Econometric Soc. 1931-33, Am. Statis. Assn., 1932; founder and 1st pres. Am. Eugenics Soc., 1923-26; founder Vitality Records office, 1937; founder Stable Money Assn.; fellow Royal Statis. Soc., A.A.A.S. (chmn. com. of 100 to promote pub. health and to advocate establishing a nat. dept. of health); rec. sec. New Haven County Anti-Tuberculosis Assn., 1904-14; mem. editorial bd. of Econometrics; mem. Phi Beta Kappa, Sigma Chi. Royal Econ. Society, Conn. Acad. Arts and Sciences, Am. Acad. Polit. and Social Science, Am. Statis. Assn., Am. Ethnographical Soc., N.E. Free Trade League, Internat. Free Trade League, Nat. Assn. Study and Prevention Tuberculosis, Am. Assn. for Study and Prevention Infant Mortality, Nat. Consumers League, League of Nations Assn., Am. Philos. Soc., Reale Accademia dei Lincei (Rome), Institut Internat. Statisque, Norwegian Acad. of Sci. and Letters, Instituto Lombardo (Milan, Italy), Com. for the Nation. Conglist. Club: Cobden (hon.), Civic, Yale, Reform (New York); Faculty Graduate (New Haven). Published weekly index number of wholesale prices in business jours. since 1923, founded Index Number Institute. Author: Mathematical Investigations in the Theory of Value and Prices, 1892, transl. into French, 1917, into Japanese, 1925; Elements of Geometry (with Prof. A. W. Phillips), 1896 (transl. into Japanese, 1900); Bibliography of Mathematical Economics in (and asst. in translating and editing) Cournot's Mathematical Theory of Wealth, 1897; A Brief Introduction to the Infinitesimal Calculus, 1897 (transl. into German, 1904, Italian, 1909); The Nature of Capital and Income, 1906, transl. into French, 1911, Japanese, 1913, Spanish, 1921, Italian, 1922; The Rate of Interest, 1907, transl. into Japanese, 1912; National Vitality, 1909; The Purchasing Power of Money, 1911, transl. into Japanese, 1911, transl. into German, 1916, and transl. into Russian, 1926; Elementary Principles of Economics, 1910; Why is the Dollar Shrinking?, 1914; How to Live (with Dr. E. L. Fisk, in collaboration with 93 members of hygiene reference board of Life Extension Institute, 1915, translated into Japanese, 1917, Spanish, 1918, Chinese, 1919, Norwegian 1929, 20th rev. ed., with Dr. Haven Emerson, 1938, 21st edition appeared, 1945. Stabilizing the Dollar, 1920; The Making of Index Numbers, 1922, trans. into Russian; League or War?, 1923; America's Interest in World Peace, 1924; Prohibition at Its Worst, 1926; The Money Illusion, 1928 (transl. into German, French, Dutch, Polish, Italian, Greek); Prohibition Still at Its Worst (with H. B. Brougham) 1928; The Theory of Interest, 1930 (trans. into German); The Noble Experiment (with H. B. Brougham), 1930; The Stock Market Crash, 1930; Booms and Depressions, 1932; Inflation, 1933; Stamp Scrip, 1933; After Reflation, What?, 1933; Stable Money, a History of the Movement, 1934; 100% Money, 1935, revised edit., 1936; Constructive Income Taxation, 1942; World Maps and Globes (with O. M. Miller), 1944; also numerous articles, monographs, etc. Home: 113 Park Av., Hamden, Conn., Post Office Box 1825, New Haven, Conn. Died Apr. 29, 1947; buried in Evergreen Cemetery, New Haven.

FISHER, Mahlon Leonard, author; b. Williamsport, Pa., July 20, 1874; s. John Stires and Mary Elizabeth (Jamison) F.; ed. high sch. and pvtly. Studied architecture in various offices, and in practice many yrs. Founder, 1917, and editor The Sonnet; asso. editor The Golden Galleon, Kansas City, Mo., since 1924. Mem. Poetry Soc. America, Friends of the Harvard Library, Pa. Assn. of Architects, Humane Soc. of New York (asso.). Author: Sonnets—A First Series, 1917; Lyrics Between the Years, 1928; (verse) River's Gift, 1928; also wrote the words for "White Silence," arranged for a four-part chorus of women's voices by Nicola A. Montani, and sung by choruses of 200 persons, in Philadelphia and elsewhere; wrote sonnet "November," given a musical setting for solo purposes by Pearl Adams; wrote, To a Humming Bird in a Garden, arranged for string quartet. Contbr. of verse to mags. Represented in various anthologies. Address: P.O. Box 173, Williamsport, Pa. Died Sept. 25, 1947.

FISHER, Martin Luther, univ. dean; b. near Murray, Ind., Oct. 24, 1871; s. Samuel and Margaret Jane (Crawford) F.; student Central Normal Coll., Danville, 1890-91; B.S. in agr., Purdue, 1903; M.S., U. of Wis., 1911; m. Mary Ella Fishbaugh, May 26, 1894; children—Beatrice Louise (dec.), Frances Elizabeth (dec.), Barbara Catherine (Mrs. Edgar D. Harder). Began as teacher of pub. schs., 1890; with Purdue U. since graduation 1903, beginning as instr. in agr., became prof. and asst. dean of agr., 1920, dean of men since 1926. Mem. Ind. Acad. Science, Ind. State Audubon Soc., N.E.A., Sigma Pi, Sigma Xi, Kappa Delta Pi. Ind. Republican. Methodist. Clubs: Kiwanis (Lafayette, Ind.); University (Purdue). Author: Agriculture for Common Schools (with F. A. Cotton), 1909; also many agrl. expt. station bulletins. Home: 325 Vine St., West Lafayette, Ind.*
Died Dec. 1, 1942.

FISHER, Ralph Talcott, banker, v.p. Am. Trust Co.; b. Oakland, Calif., Sept. 26, 1877; s. Galen Merriam and Susan (Talcott) F.; A.B., University of California, 1901, A.M., 1903, LL.D., 1942; m. Margaret Reid Merriam, June 26, 1919; children—Ralph Talcott, Galen Reid, Margaret Merriam (Mrs. Albert W. Stone). With Asso. Oil Co., San Francisco, 1903-18; mem., later asst. dir., Federal Board for Vocational Edn., at San Francisco, N.Y. City and Washington, D.C., 1918-21; dir. Calif. State Dept. Instns., 1921-22; v.p. Am. Trust Co., San Francisco, 1922-24, Oakland since 1924. Pres. Civil Service Bd., Oakland, 1915-18, Bd. of Port Commrs., 1928-39; mem. California State Commission on Pensions, 1927-28. Chmn. Governor's Old Age Pension Com., 1943. Mem. State Board of Education since 1943. Pres. California War Chest, Inc., since 1943. Director Alameda County Tuberculosis and Health Assn., Oakland; director Oakland Community Chest, pres., 1940-42; director National War Fund, 1945-46; member of State Council on Educational Planning and Coordination, 1940-41. Mem. Nat. Assn. of Credit Men (dir. 1933-35, nat. v.p. 1935-36), Pacific School of Religion (Berkeley), U. of Calif. Alumni Council (Berkeley), Internat. House (Berkeley); mem. bd. govs. Alameda County Community Foundation; pres. U. of Calif. Alumni Assn. and mem. bd. regents U. of Calif., 1936-38. Mem. Beta Theta Pi. Presented honor shield by Oakland Real Estate Bd. as most distinguished in community service, 1928. Republican. Mason. Clubs: Kiwanis (ex-pres.), Athenian-Nile, Athens Athletic. Home: 3247 Kempton Av. Office: American Trust Co., Oakland 4, Calif. Died Aug. 7, 1948.

FISHER, William Arms, editor; b. San Francisco, Apr. 27, 1861; s. Luther Paine and Katharine (Arms) F.; ed. pub. schs.; studied harmony and organ under John P. Morgan, Oakland, Cal.; counterpoint, canon and fugue under Horatio W. Parker, New York; composition under Anton Dvořák, New York; singing under William Shakespeare, London; m. Emma Roderick Hinckle, Feb. 14, 1922. Editor and pub. mgr. for Oliver Ditson Co., Jan. 1, 1897-Dec. 31, 1937, also v.p. of the company. His published compositions include numerous anthems and part songs, over 75 separate songs, a volume of 60 Irish songs, and a volume of negro spirituals. Editor of The Musicians Library, The Music Students Library, The Music Students Piano Course and A Course of Study in Music Understanding. Past pres. Music Teachers Nat. Assn., Music Publishers Assn. of U.S.; mem. Am. Soc., Composers, Authors and Publishers. Author: Notes on Music in Old Boston; Ye Olde New England Psalm-Tunes; The Music That Washington Knew; One Hundred and Fifty Years of Music Publishing in the United States (1783-1933); Music Festivals in the U.S. Home: 200 St. Paul St., Brookline, Mass. Died Dec. 18, 1948.

FISKE, Bradley Allen, naval officer; b. Lyons, N.Y., June 13, 1854; s. Rev. William Allen and Susan (Bradley) F.; grad. U.S. Naval Acad. (2d in class), 1874; m. Josephine, d. Joseph Wesley Harper, 1882; 1 dau., Caroline Harper. Ensign, July 17, 1875; promoted through grades to rear-adm., Aug. 3, 1911; retired June 13, 1916. Served on various duties and stations; was on "Yorktown," under Commander Robley D. Evans, in Valparaiso, during critical times following the "Baltimore" incident; on board Admiral Benham's flagship, "San Francisco," in Rio, in 1894, when the U.S. fleet cleared for action, and enforced neutral rights; navigator of "Petrel" at battle of Manila; reported by capt. of "Petrel" for "eminent and conspicuous conduct in battle," and by Admiral Dewey for "heroic conduct" at battle of Manila; navigator of monitor "Monadnock" during 4 mos. following outbreak of the Filipino insurrection; took part in bombardments of Parañaque and Malabon; as exec. officer of "Yorktown" took part in bombardment of San Fernando, Aug. 1899; comd. the Minneapolis, the Arkansas and the Tennessee; comd. 5th, 3d and 1st divs. Atlantic Fleet, 1912; aid for operations, Navy Dept., 1913, till May 1915, when resigned. Mem. 1st Electrical Conf., Phila., 1884; mem. naval wireless telegraph bd., 1904-05; mem. Gen. Bd. of Navy, also Joint Bd. Army and Navy, 1910-11 and 1913-15. Invented boat detaching apparatus, system of elec. communication for interiors of warships, stadimeter, an electric range finger, an electric ammunition hoist, a range indicator, a battle-order telegraph, an elec. engine telegraph, a helm-indicator, a speed and direction indicator, a system of turning turrets of war ships by electricity, the naval telescope mount, the naval telescope sight, gun director system, wireless control of moving vessels, the torpedo-plane, system for detecting submarines, prism system of target practice, electro-magnetic system for exploding torpedoes under ships, and also the reading machine. The naval telescope sight has been adoptel by all the navies of the world, and is the main cause of the recent great improvement in the accuracy of naval gunnery; the torpedoplane has been adopted by all the leading navies. Awarded Elliott Cresson gold medal by Franklin Institute, 1893; gold medal for prize essay by U.S. Naval Institute, 1905; gold medal by Aero Club of America for invention of torpedoplane, 1919. Pres. U.S. Naval Inst., 1911-23. Club: Army and Navy of New York (hon. pres.). Author: Electricity in Theory and Practice, 1884; 10 edits.; War Times in Manila; The Navy as a Fighting Machine, 1917, 2d edit., 1918; From Midshipman to Rear Admiral, 1919; The Art of Fighting, 1920; Invention, 1921; also numerous articles on elec. and naval subjects. Home: Waldorf Astoria, New York, N.Y.
Died Apr. 7, 1942.

FISKE, George Walter, educator, author; b. Holliston, Mass., June 3, 1872; s. George Batchelder and Ada M. (Perry) F.; A.B., Amherst, 1895, A.M., 1898, D.D., 1925; B.D., Hartford Theol. Sem., 1898; Ph.D., Boston U., 1919; m. Alice M. Stewart, Aug. 1, 1898; 1 dau., Margaret S. (Mrs. Margaret F. Hilliard). Ordained Congl. ministry, 1898; pastor, Huntington, Mass., 1898-1900, S. Hadley Falls, Mass., 1900-03, High St. Ch., Auburn, Me., 1903-07; prof. practical theology and religious education, 1907-37, emeritus since 1937, junior dean, 1908-21, acting dean, 1928, Graduate Sch. of Theology of Oberlin College; study and lecturing in the Near East, 1933; exchange prof. Am. U. of Beirut, Syria, Near East School of Theology, 1937-38. Mem. Commn. on Worship and Com. on Marriage and the Family, both of Federal Council of Churches of Christ in America. Member Am. Sociol. Soc., Am. Country Life Assn., Religious Edn. Assn., Am. Assn. of Univ. Profs., A.A.A.S., Phi Beta Kappa (pres. Oberlin College chapter, 1937). Theta Phi, Phi Delta Theta, Pi Gamma Mu. Republican. Author: Boy Life and Self Government, 1910; The Challenge of the Country, 1912; Finding the Comrade God, 1918; Community Forces for Religious Education, Middle Adolescence, 1921; Community Forces for Religious Education, Early Adolescence, 1922; Jesus' Ideals of Living, 1922; Purpose in Teaching Religion, 1927; The Changing Family, 1928; The Christian Family, 1929; The Recovery of Worship, 1931; In a College Chapel, 1932; A Study of Jesus' Own Religion, 1932; Studies in Spiritual Energy, 1933; Problems of Christian Family Life Today, 1934. Co-Author: Education and Religion, 1929; The Lesson Round Table, 1930; Studies in Religious Education, 1931; The Quest for God Through Worship, 1935; The Quest for God Through Understanding, 1937; Creative Personalities, Vol. III, Founders of Christian Movements, 1941. Contributor mags. Home: 151 State St., Framingham Center, Mass.; (winter) Orlando, Fla. Died Oct. 10, 1945; buried Lake Grove Cemetery, Holliston, Mass.

FISKE, Harrison Grey, theatrical mgr., play director, journalist; b. Harrison, N.Y., July 30, 1861; s. Lyman and Jennie M. F.; student New York U., 2 yrs.; m. Minnie Maddern Davey, Mar. 19, 1890 (died 1932). Was editor and dramatic critic of newspapers and contbr. to various publications. Served as mgr. of Mrs. Fiske, Otis Skinner, Bertha Kalich, George Arliss, Lydia Lopokova and other stars; lessee Manhattan Theatre, New York, 1901-06; dir. Kismet, A Doll's House, Hedda Gabler, Rosmersholm, Pillars of Society, Ghosts, The Merry Wives of Windsor, Much Ado About Nothing, The Rivals, Tess of the D'Urbervilles, Becky Sharp, Magda, Mary of Magdala, Leah Kleschna, The New York Idea, Salvation Nell, Hannele, Mrs. Bumpstead-Leigh, Lady Patricia, Erstwhile Susan, Mis' Nelly of N'Orleans, Wake Up, Jonathan, Mary, Mary, Quite Contrary, Ladies of the Jury, Marta of the Lowlands, Monna Vanna, The Kreutzer Sonata, Sapho and Phaon, The Devil. Septimus, The Green Cockatoo, A Light from St. Agnes, Where Ignorance Is Bliss, The Fear Market, A Night at an Inn, Sonya, In the Shadow of the Glen, We Moderns, and 50 others. Author: Hester Crewe; The Privateer (with others); The District Attorney; The Dice of the Gods; Helena's Boys; (adaptations) Marie Deloche; Divorcons; Cesarine; Frou Frou; Therese Raquin. Democrat. Club: Lotos. Address: 162 W. 13th St., New York. Died Sept. 2, 1942.

FISKE, Thomas Scott, univ. prof.; b. New York, May 12, 1865; s. Thomas Scott and Clara (Pittman) F.; A.B., Columbia, 1885, A.M., 1886, Ph.D., 1888; m. Natalie Page, Feb. 1, 1913 (died Jan. 23, 1920); 1 dau., Natalie Page. Fellow asst. in mathematics, Columbia, 1885-88, tutor, 1888-91, instr., 1891-94, adj. prof., 1894-97, prof., 1897-1935, emeritus, 1935; acting dean, Barnard Coll., 1899; sec. Coll. Entrance Exam. Bd., 1902-36; examiner mathematics, N.Y. State Edn. Dept., 1909-11. Fellow A.A.A.S.; mem. Am. Math. Soc. (founder; 1st sec., 1888-95; editor Bull., 1891-99; editor Transactions, 1899-1905; pres. 1902-04), Math. Assn. Am., London Math. Soc., Assn. Teachers Mathematics of Middle States and Md. (pres. 1905-06). Wrote Theory of Functions of Complex Variable, 1906; author of math. and ednl. papers and articles in Am. and foreign periodicals. Home: 6 Platt St., Poughkeepsie, N.Y. Address: Columbia University, New York. Died Jan. 10, 1944.

FISKEN, John Barclay, electrical engr.; b. Helensburgh, Dumbartonshire, Scotland, Nov. 2, 1861; s. Archibald and Sarah A. (Kerr) F.; grad. Coll. of Science and Arts, Glasgow, Scotland, 1886 (1st class honor diploma); m. Helen Kyle Binnie, of Barassie, Ayrshire, Scotland, June 4, 1889 (died June 30, 1901); children—Mary Carolyn (Mrs. Louis Kapek), Ruth Kerr (Mrs. Thomas Large), James Binnie; m. 2d, Eva Jane Weymouth, Sept. 3, 1907. With office of Anchor Line Steamship Co., Glasgow, Scotland, 4 yrs.; came to U.S., 1886; with Washington Water Power Co. and its predecessors since 1887, except 1 yr., chief engr. same, 1918-20, and consulting engr. from 1920 until date of retirement, December 31, 1942. Fellow Am. Inst. Elec. Engrs. (v.p. 1919-20); mem. Associated Engineers of Spokane. Republican. Conglist. Clubs: Tesemini Outing, Spokane Country, Spokane City and University, Seniors North West Golf Assn., Rotary (Spokane). Home: W. 28 28th Av., Spokane 9, Wash. Died June 6, 1946; buried in Fairmount Memorial Park, Spokane.

FITCH, Albert Parker, educator; b. Boston, Mar. 6, 1877; s. Henry Hubbard and Elizabeth Anne Frances (Smith) F.; A.B., Harvard, 1900; B.D., Union Theol. Sem., 1903; D.D., Amherst, 1909, Williams Coll., 1914; m. Flora May Draper, June 4, 1903. Ordained Congl. ministry, Apr. 9, 1903; pastor First Ch., Flushing, L.I., 1903-05, Mt. Vernon Ch., Boston, 1905-09; pres. Andover Theol. Sem., Cambridge, 1909-17; prof. history of religion, Amherst Coll., 1917-23, Carleton Coll., 1924-27; minister Park Avenue Presbyn. Ch., 1928-33, now emeritus. Beecher lecturer at Yale, 1919-20. Mem. Delta Upsilon; hon mem. Harvard Chapter Phi Beta Kappa, 1911. Author: The College Course and the Preparation for Life, 1914; Religion and the Undergraduate (monograph); Can the Church Survive in the Changing Order?, 1920; Preaching and Paganism, 1920; None So Blind, 1924. Home: Windsor, Vt. Died May 22, 1944.

FITCH, Edward, prof. Greek; b. Walton, N.Y., May 27, 1864; s. George William and Harriet (Sinclair) F.; A.B., Hamilton College, 1886, hon. L.H.D., 1934; Ph.D., University of Goettingen, 1896; married Annie Louise MacKinnon, July 3, 1901 (died September 12, 1940). Professor Greek, Park College, 1886-89; asst. professor Greek, 1889-99, asso prof., 1899-1902, prof., 1902-34, emeritus since 1934, Hamilton Coll., also acting dean, 1922-23 and dean, 1926-32. Mem. Am. Philol. Assn., Am. Dialect Soc., Archæol. Inst. America, Phi Beta Kappa; mem. managing com. Am. Sch. Classical Studies in Athens, annual prof., 1932-33; examiner in Greek, N.Y. State Dept. Edn., 1927-31. Republican. Presbyterian. Author: De Argonautarum Reditu, 1896; also articles in professional jours. Compiler: The Class of 1886 of Hamilton College, 1916, the same, 1916-36; Necrology of Hamilton College, yearly, 1917-22. Historian and an editor, Journal of the John More Association, since 1910. Editor-in-chief Hamilton Alumni Review, 1935-38. Home: Walton, N.Y. Died Apr. 15, 1946; buried in Hamilton College Cemetery.

FITCH, William Edward, physician, author; b. Burlington, N.C., May 29, 1867; s. William James and Mary Elizabeth (King) F.; M.D., Coll. Physicians and Surg., Baltimore, Md., 1891; m. Minnie Crump, Oct. 5, 1892; children—Lucille, Elizabeth, William Edward. Specialist in diseases of metabolism, med. hydrology and dietotherapy; lecturer on principles of surgery, Fordham U. Sch. Medicine, 1907-09; attending physician Vanderbilt Clinic; attending gynecologist outpatient dept. Presbyn. Hosp.; asst. in surg. clinic, St. Luke's Hospital; med. dir. and cons. med. hydrologist at French Lick (Ind.) Springs, 1931; cons. med. hydrologist Crazy Hotel and Spa Mineral Wells, Tex. Served as editor Gaillard's Southern Medicine, 1900-09; editor Pediatrics, 1908-17; co-editor and pub. Am. Jour. Electrotherapeutics and Radiology, 1918-19. Served as acting asst. surg. U.S.P.H. and M.H. Service. Spanish-Am. War, 1898; commd. 1st lt. Med. R.C., U.S. Army, July 3, 1912; capt., July 16, 1917; maj., Sept. 25, 1917; comdg. officer hosp. at Ft. Terry, N.Y., 18 mos., later at Ft. Totten and Ft. Schuyler, N.Y., and chief nutrition and dir.

mess, Base Hosp., Camp Jackson, S.C.; later adviser to camp surgeon's office; hon. disch., Dec. 3, 1918. Mem. Hudson-Fulton Celebration Commn. Pres. Alamance Battle Ground Commn. Mem. med. soc. states of Va., Ind., Am. Med. Editors' and Authors' Assn., Med. Assn. Greater N.Y., Nat. Soc. Advancement Gastroenterology, Am. Soc. Balneology, Internat. Soc. Med. Hydrology (London), N.Y. Soc. Founders and Patriots Am. (council, gen. court), Soc. Cincinnati, Soc. Fgn. Wars, Soc. Am. Wars, Soc. Vets. World War, Southern Soc. (New York). Democrat. Episcopalian. Clubs: Lotos (New York); Burlington Country. Author: Fitch's Medical Pocket Formulary, 1914, now in 7th edit.; Dietotherapy (3 vols.), 1918, now in 3d edit.; Mineral Waters of the U.S. and Greater American Spas, 1926; Diseases of Metabolism; The Battle of Alamance; also various writings on early history of N. Carolina. Address: 3707 Segovia St., Coral Gables, Fla. Died Sept. 12, 1949; buried Burlington, N.C.

FITTERER, J(ohn) C(onrad), engr. and mathematician; b. at Clyde, Ohio, Dec. 15, 1871; s. Jeremiah S. and Rosena E. (Mook) F.; B.Sc., Ohio State U., 1898; B.S. in C.E., U. of Colo., 1904, C.E., 1912; m. Lucy E. Kamp, Dec. 27, 1899. In charge dept. Am. Clay Machinery Co., Bucyrus, O., 1898-1903; with U.S. Reclamation Service, various projects, until 1908; prof. civ. and irrigation engring., U. of Wyo., 1908-28, also irrigation engr. Agrl. Expt. Sta., and acting dean Coll. Engring., 1922-24; prof. math., head dept. Colo. Sch. Mines, Golden; cons. practice, Mem. Am. Soc. C.E., Am. Math. Soc., Math. Assn. America, Soc. for Promotion Engring. Edn., A.A. A.S., N.E.A., Tau Beta Pi, Phi Kappa Phi. Republican. Presbyterian. Wrote: Reclamation by Drainage, 1911; co-author of Meteorology for Twenty Years, 1913. Home: 1620 Maple St., Golden, Colo. Died Mar. 1947; buried Crown Hill Park, Denver.

FITZGERALD, David Edward, lawyer; b. New Haven, Conn., Sept. 21, 1874; s. Edward and Ann (Conway) F.; LL.B., Yale, 1895, M.L., 1896; m. Alice Clark, Nov. 14, 1900; children—David Edward, John Clark. Admitted to Conn. state bar, 1895; mem. FitzGerald & Walsh, 1897-1920, FitzGerald & Haddon, 1920-32, FitzGerald Foote & FitzGerald since 1932; pres. and treas. New Haven News Pub. Co., Commercial Realty Finance Co. Mayor of New Haven, 1918-26. Chmn. Dem. State Central Com.; 1914-22; del. at large every Dem. Nat. Conv., 1912-40, vice-chmn. and mem. of the Dem. Nat. Com. Chevalier Order of Crown of Italy. Portrait in Hall of Fame, Sterling Memorial, New Haven, as one of 30 Immortals of Yale. Mem. Am., Conn. and New Haven County bar assns., Am. Branch of Internat. Law Assn.; hon. mem. G.A.R. (Adm. Foote Post), Vets. of Foreign Wars, Spanish War Vets.; judge advocate Second Co. of Gov.'s Footguard of Conn. Catholic. K.C., Elk, Eagle, Moose, Hibernian, Forester. Clubs: Quinnipiack, Union League (New Haven); Hartford Club; Catholic (New York); Racebrook Country, Woodbridge Country. Home: 149 Fountain St., New Haven; (country) Geraldine Manor, Woodbridge, Conn. Office: 185 Church St., New Haven, Conn. Died Nov. 17, 1942.

FITZGERALD, James J., ins. exec.; b. Saginaw, Mich., Jan. 26, 1878; s. Edmond and Ann (Reynolds) F.; ed. pub. and parochial schs. and business coll.; m. Helen O. Wilson, Apr. 19, 1904 (died 1917); children—John Sheridan (dec.), Lawrence A., Francis E., Dorothy A. (Mrs. Donald E. Schick), Louis (dec.); m. 2d, Emma L. Hardegen, June 2, 1919. Stenographer with Saginaw Valley Fire & Marine Ins. Co., 1893-99; with Mich. Mfrs. Mut. Fire Ins. Co., 1899-1902; insp. Grain Dealers Nat. Mut. Fire Ins. Co., 1902-07, zone mgr., 1907-14, asso. Western mgr., 1914-18; asst. sec., later sec., 1918-35, pres. since 1935; dir. Improved Risk Mutuals, New York; pres. Hoosier Adjustment Bureau, Indianapolis, Mut.-Co. Assn. (Chicago); sec.-treas. Grain Dealers Mut. Agency, Inc.; dir. Mut. Fire Prevention Bur., Cath. Charities Bur. Mem. Nat. Assn. Automotive Mut. Insurance Companies, National Association of Mutual Insurance Companies. Mem. Indianapolis Chamber of Commerce. Democrat. Catholic. K. of C. Clubs: Indianapolis Athletic, Illinois Athletic, Meridian Hills Country. Editor of Mutual Forum (mag.). Home: 4832 Graceland Av. Office: 1740 N. Meridian St., Indianapolis, Ind. Died July 1, 1942.

FITZ-GERALD, John Driscoll, II, univ. prof.; b. Newark, N.J., May 2, 1873; s. Aaron Ogden and Harriet Minerva (Haines) F.-G.; A.B., Columbia, 1895, scholar and fellow Romance langs., 1895-96, 1897-98, Ph.D., 1906; Litt.D. from Syracuse U., 1920; student Romance philology, 1896-97, and 1900-02, U. of Leipzig, Berlin, Paris, and Madrid; Élève titulaire, 1897, Élève diplômé, 1902, de l'École Pratique des Hautes Études (Sect. des Sciences Historiques et Philologiques), U. of Paris; Diploma Honor, Academia Mexicana; m. Leora Almita Hartpence, May 16, 1900; children—Nesta, Gerald Hartpance, Linda. Asst. in Romance langs. and lits., 1898-1902, tutor, 1902-07, instr., 1907-09, Columbia; asst. prof. Romance langs. and lits., 1909-15, prof. of Spanish, 1915-25, prof. Romance philology, 1925-29, U. of Ill.; prof. Romance philology and head of dept. Spanish, University of Arizona, 1929-43; prof. Romance Philology since 1943. Visiting prof. U. of Madrid, Spain, 1922-23; visiting prof. Nat. U. of Mexico, 1936, univs. of Puerto Rico, Santo Domingo and Habana, 1941. Good Will Lecturer in Mexico City (Acad. Mexicana, Biblioteca Benjamin Franklin and Colegio Americano), 1944. Awarded Columbia University medal for excellence, 1931; Knight Comdr., with plaque, Royal Order of Isabella the Catholic. Mem. Modern Lang. Assn. America, Hispanic Soc. America, S.R. (apptd. sec. Ariz. Soc., 1942; awarded Veteran Member medal, 1943), Phi Beta Kappa Fraternity (pres. Arizona Alpha 1940-41); elected founding mem. Phi Beta Kappa Assos., 1942; corr. mem. Reales Academias Española de la Lengua, de la Historia de Madrid, de Buenas Letras de Barcelona, de Ciencias, Bellas Letras y Nobles Artes de Córdoba, Sevillana de Buenas Letras, Gallega, de Bellas Artes y Ciencias Históricas de Toledo, Hispano-Americana de Ciencias y Artes de Cadiz, and Academias de Bellas Artes de Valladolid, de Bellas Artes de San Luis de Zaragoza, Nacional de Artes y Letras de Cuba, Dominicana de la Historia, and Colombiana, and hon. mem. Academia Chilena; Ateneo Puerto Riqueño and Ateneo Dominicano. Steward of the Central Methodist Church, Newark, N.J., since 1913, First Methodist Ch. Tucson, Ariz. since 1932; chmn. bd. mgrs. Wesley Foundation, Tucson, since 1933. Delegate to South America for Am. Assn. for Internat. Conciliation, 1914. Asst. sec. 2d Pan-Am. Scientific Congress, 1915-16. Pres. Am. Assn. Teachers Spanish, 1921-23; pres. Nat. Fed. Modern Lang. Teachers, 1924-26; pres. Modern Lang. Teachers of Central West and South, 1929-30. Del. of Nat. Fedn. Modern Lang. Teachers to congresses of Féd. Internat. des Profs. de Langues Vivantes (Bruxelles), and World Fed. of Edn. Assns. (Oxford), 1935; del. of Nat. Edn. Assn. to VII World Conf. of World Fed. of Edn. Assns. (Tokyo), 1937; del. Nat. Fedn. Modern Lang. Teachers and N.E.A. to VIII World Conf. of World Fed. Edn. Assns., Rio de Janeiro, 1939; del. Acad. Chilena and Acad. Dominicana de la Historia, to 8th Pan-Am. Scientific Congress (Washington), 1940; del. Inter-American Bibliog. and Library Association (Washington), 1941; national honorary pres. of Span. (national honor fraternity), Sigma Delta Pi. Associate editor of Romanic Rev.; Cons. editor of Hispania; member Internat. advisory editorial bd. of Inter-America; editor of Hispanic Series; editor dept. of Hispanic subjects to New Internat. Encyclopedia. Editor: La Vida de Santo Domingo de Silos, par Gonzalo de Berceo, 1904; Lope de Vega—Novelas a la Señora Marcia Leonarda (with Leora A. F.-G.), 1913. Author: Versification of the Cuaderna Via as found in Berceo's Vida de Santo Domingo de Silos, 1905; Rambles in Spain, 1910; Apuntes Sobre Literatura Americana, 1924; Relaciones Hispano-Americanas, 1925; Historia de la Universidad de Arizona, 1942. Translator (with Thacher Howland Guild); A New Drama, by Manuel Tamayo y Baus, 1915. Home: 708 W. Nevada, Urbana, Ill. Address: Tucson, Ariz. Died June 8, 1946.

FITZGERALD, Michael Edward, supt. schools; b. Rockland, Mass., Nov. 22, 1863; s. John Cushing and Mary Collins (Donovan) F.; grad. State Normal Sch., Bridgewater, Mass., 1886; A.B., Boston Coll., 1913, LL.D., 1927, also M.A. and Ph.Lic.; m. Mary Elizabeth Brassill, Aug. 24, 1892; children—Pierce Edward Brassill (dec.), Gerald Cushing, Robert Brassill, Walter Adams, John Cushing, Pierce Joseph, Edward Norton Drum, Leon Carew. Admitted to Mass. bar, 1900; teacher and ednl. exec. since 1886; supt. schs., Cambridge, Mass., since 1912. Resigned on Jan. 15, 1945, in the 33d year of his service. Catholic. K.C., Elk. Clubs: Cambridge, Rotary, Kappa Beta Phi (Bridgewater). Home: South Weymouth, Mass. Died Apr. 4, 1945; buried at Rockland, Mass.

FITZ GERALD, Susan Walker (Mrs. R. Y. Fitz Gerald); b. Cambridge, Mass., May 9, 1871; d. John Grimes and Rebecca White (Pickering) Walker; A.B., Bryn Mawr Coll., 1893; m. Richard Y. Fitz Gerald, Aug. 3, 1901; children—Anne, Rebecca Pickering, Susan, Richard Leigh. Sec. to the dean, Bryn Mawr Coll., 1893-94, sec. to pres., 1894-95; head of Fiske Hall, Barnard Coll. (Columbia), 1898-1901; head worker West Side Branch, New York U. Settlement (later Richmond Hill House), 1901-04; mem. New York Child Labor Com., 1902-04 (the 1st child labor com. in Am.); truant officer, New York, 1903-04; sec. Boston Equal Suffrage Assn., 1907-10, School Voters' League, 1910-18. Trustee Women's Ednl. and Indsl. Union, 1908-11; sec. Mass. Woman Suffrage Assn., 1911-Oct. 1912; rec. sec. Nat. Am. Woman Suffrage Assn., 1911-15; sec. Mass. Polit. Equality Union, Dec. 1912-16. Mem. exec. com. Women's Trade Union League, 1913-20; chmn. Mass. League for Progressive Democracy, 1916-18; alt. del.-at-large from Mass. to Dem. Nat. Conv., San Francisco, 1920, del.-at-large, same, New York, 1924; mem. Mass. Legislature, 1923-24; mem. State Special Commn. on Necessaries of Life, 1926-30. Club: Bryn Mawr (Boston). Home: 19 Dunster Rd., Jamaica Plain, Mass. Died Jan. 20, 1943

FITZGERALD, Thomas Edward, lawyer, newspaper pub.; b. Elroy, Wis., May 10, 1879; s. Michael C. and Catherine (Lambert) F.; student John B. Stetson U., Deland, Fla., 1904, 05; m. Edna L. Vandewater, Aug. 10, 1900; children—Franklin Edward, Raymond Vandewater, Frederic Charles. Admitted to Fla. bar, 1905, and practiced at Daytona, 1905-37; pub. The Observer and The Recorder. Lt. col. and aide on staff Gov. John W. Martin, 1925-29. Democrat. Mason (32°, Shriner), Elk. Author: Present Great Religions of the World; Volusia County—Past and Present. Home: Daytona Beach, Fla. Died July 25, 1944.

FITZGERALD, Walter James, clergyman, educator; b. Peola, Garfield County, Wash., Nov. 17, 1883; s. Patrick Sarsfield and Johanna Frances (Kirk) F.; normal course, Los Gatos, Calif., 1906; B.A., Gonzaga U., 1910; M.A., 1912; studied theology, Immaculate Conception Coll., Montreal, Can., 1915-19, ascetic theology, Los Gatos, 1920-21. Joined Soc. of Jesus (Jesuits), 1902; ordained priest R.C. Ch., 1918; prof. ancient classics, Seattle (Wash.) Coll., 1906-09, prof. classics, English, history, Gonzaga U., 1912-15, 1919-20, pres. Corp. Gonzaga U., 1921-27; pres. Jesuit Sem., Manresa Hall, Port Townsend, Wash., 1927-29; pres. Seattle Coll., 1929-30; vice provincial Rocky Mountain Region of Soc. of Jesus (Jesuits), 1931; provincial superior of Jesuit Province of Ore., 1932-38; consecrated coadjutor bishop of Alaska, Feb. 24, 1939; vicar-apostolic of Alaska since May 20, 1945. Address: Bishop's Residence, Juneau, Alaska. Died July 19, 1947; buried in Mount St. Michael's Cemetery, Spokane.

FITZGERALD, William Joseph, lawyer; b. Brooklyn, N.Y., Nov. 19, 1877; s. Daniel H. and Margaret J. (Kelly) F.: student St. Thomas' Coll. (now U. of Scranton), 1892-94, Holy Cross Coll., 1894-96; A.B., Georgetown U., 1898; m. Clare P. McGrath, Nov. 9, 1916. Prin. pub. sch., Scranton, Pa., 1898-1902; admitted to Lackawanna County (Pa.) bar, 1902; and since in practice at Scranton; partner Fitzgerald & Kelly, Scranton. Mem. American Bar Association, Pa. Bar Assn. (president, 1932-33), Lackawanna Bar Assn. (pres., 1928-32). Catholic. Club: Scranton Country (Clarks Summit, Pa.). Author articles on legal subjects. Home: 1617 Madison Av., Dunmore, Pa. Office: 600 Scranton Life Bldg., Scranton, Pa. Died May 6, 1947.

FITZSIMMONS, Cortland, author; b. Richmond Hill, L.I., N.Y., June 19, 1893; s. Simon Michael and Martha Emma (Gritman) F.; student Miner's Business Acad., Brooklyn, 1912-13, New York U., 1916-17, Coll. City of N.Y., 1923-24; m. Menie Muriel Simpson, Apr. 30, 1927. Clerk, later export mgr. for McKesson & Robbins, N.Y. City, 1916-18; owner of bookshop, 1918-19; salesman Baker & Taylor, pubs., N.Y. City, 1920-24, for Am. News Co., N.Y. City, 1924-29; sales mgr. Viking Press, Incorporated, N.Y. City, 1929-34; screen writer and novelist since 1934. Author: Better Bridge, 1928; Bainbridge Murder, 1929; Manville Murders, 1930; 70,000 Witnesses, 1931; No Witness, 1932; Red Rhapsody, 1933; Death on the Diamond, 1934; Crimson Ice, 1935; Whispering Window, 1936; Moving Finger, 1937; Sudden Silence, 1938; Mystery at Hidden Harbor, 1938; The Girl in the Cage, 1939; One Man's Poison, 1940; The Evil Men Do, 1941; This Is Murder, 1941; Death Rings a Bell, 1942; Tied for Murder, 1943; If You Can Read You Can Cook (with Muriel S. Fitzsimmons), 1946. Contbr. fiction to mags. Home: 10526 National Blvd., Los Angeles 34. Died July 25, 1949.

FITZ SIMONS, Ellen French; b. New York, N.Y., June 15, 1881; d. Francis Ormond and Ellen (Tuck) French; ed. private tutors in England, France and Germany; m. Alfred Gwynne Vanderbilt, 1901; 1 son, William H. (gov. of R.I., 1938-40); m. 2d, Paul FitzSimons, lt. comdr., U.S. Navy, 1919. Rhode Island member Republican National Committee, 1930-44; mem. Republican National Executive Com. 1936-44; elected eastern vice chmn. Rep. Nat. Com., 1940-44. Organized Newport County (R.I.) Chapter Am. Red Cross, 1916, and vice chmn., 1916-19; awarded Victory medal of Soc. of Social Sciences for war work, 1919; pres. Newport County Women's Republican Club, 1926-37. Home: "Harbourview," Newport, R.I. Died Feb. 26, 1948; buried at St. Mary's Church, Portsmouth, R.I.

FLAGG, Ernest, architect; b. Brooklyn, Feb. 6, 1857; s. Rev. Jared B. and Louisa (Hart) F.; m. Margaret Elizabeth Bonnell, 1899. Practicing architecture at New York since 1891; architect of St. Luke's Hosp., New York, Corcoran Gallery of Art, Washington, U.S. Naval Acad., Annapolis, Md., Singer Bldg., New York, and many other pub. bldgs. and pvt. residences. Author; The Parthenon Naos; Small Houses—Their Economic Design and Construction, 1922; Genealogical Notes on the Founding of New England, 1927. Office: 111 E. 40th St., New York, N.Y. Died Apr. 10, 1947.

FLANAGAN, Edward Joseph, dir. Father Flanagan's Boys' Home; b. Roscommon, Ireland, July 13, 1886; s. John and Honora (Larkin) F.; came to U.S., 1904, naturalized 1919; A.B., Mt. St. Mary's Coll., Emmitsburg, Md., 1906, A.M., 1908, LL.D., 1938; student St. Joseph's Sem., Dunwoodie, N.Y., 1906-07, Gregorian Univ., Rome, Italy, 1907-08, Jesuit Univ., Innsbruck, Austria, 1909-12; LL.D., St. Benedict's Coll., Atchison, Kan., 1939; LL.D., Creighton University, Omaha, Nebraska, 1941. Ordained priest Roman Cath. Ch., Innsbruck, 1912; asst. pastor St. Patrick's Parish, O'Neill, Neb., 1912-13; asst. pastor St. Patrick's Parish, Omaha, 1913-16; started Workingmen's Hotel, Omaha, 1914; founded Home for Homeless Boys, Omaha, 1917, later moved 10 miles west of Omaha and est. Boys Town, serves as sec.-treas. and dir. Was pres. Omaha Welfare Bd. for 10 years; mem. children's com. Nat. Conf. Catholic Charities. Elected Omaha's First Citizen by Post No. 1, Am. Legion, Omaha, 1930; received Humanitarian award, Variety Clubs of America, 1938. Made domestic prelate with title of Right Rev. Monsignor, 1937. At request of U.S. govt. made study of youth problems, Korea and Japan, 1947, Austria, Ger. and Italy, 1948. Appd. member Atty. Gen. Tom Clark's adv. panel to study juvenile delinquency. Mem. K. of C. Club: Omaha Athletic. Contbr. articles on child welfare to periodicals. Life and purposes of Father Flanagan's Boys' Town portrayed by motion picture "Boys Town," 1938; second picture of similar nature,

"Men of Boys Town," 1941. Address: Boys Town, Neb. Died May 15, 1948; buried in Dowd Memorial Chapel, Boys Town.

FLANNERY, John Rogers, mfr.; b. Pittsburgh, Pa., Nov. 3, 1879; s. James Joseph and Harriet (Rogers) F.; A.B., Mt. St. Mary's Coll., Emmitsburg, Md., 1899, A.M., 1902, LL.D., 1916; LL.B., U. of Pittsburgh, 1902; m. Adelaide Naomi Friday, Oct. 24, 1907; children—John Rogers, Adelaide Elizabeth, Hilda Adelaide. Admitted to Pa. bar, 1902; investigating rubber and mineral concessions, Nicaragua, 1903; began in bolt manufacturing, 1904, vanadium metals manufacturing, 1909; president Flannery Bolt Company, American Vanadium Company, Collier Land Company. In 1914 was sent by Herbert Hoover into Belgium to assist in organizing Belgian Relief Commission operations and was first American to return from war torn Belgium to United States; active throughout country in securing funds and was decorated by Belgium. Director of service and supplies, American National Red Cross in Washington, May-October 1917; assistant to chairman U.S. Shipping Board, dir. housing, October 1917-May 1918; dir. ry. equipment and supplies, War Industries Bd., May-Nov. 1918; lt. col. ordnance, U.S. Army, 1918. Pres. Mercy Hosp.; trustee Duquesne U., De Paul Inst., St. Barnabas Free Home, St. Paul's Orphan Asylum. Republican. Catholic. Club: Pittsburgh Athletic Assn. Home: 1544 Beechwood Blvd. Office: Flannery Bldg., Pittsburgh, Pa. Died Dec. 26, 1947.

FLEISCHER, Charles (flīsh'ĕr), publicist; b. Breslau, Germany, Dec. 23, 1871; s. Nathan Oskar and Frederica (Silberstein) F.; who emigrated to America in 1880; A.B., Coll. City of New York, 1888; Litt.B., U. of Cincinnati, 1893; rabbi Hebrew Union Coll., Cincinnati, 1893; m. Mabel R. Leslie, lawyer, Sept. 30, 1919. Rabbi Temple Israel, Boston, 1894, until 1911; organized, 1911, and since leader of the Sunday Commons, Boston. Lecturer; contbr. to mags. and newspapers. Editor of "Democracy"; editor N.Y. American editorial page since 1922. Radio "commentator" over Columbia Broadcasting System. Free lance lecturer, writer, journalist. Home: 129 E. 17th St., New York, N.Y. Died July 2, 1942.

FLEISHER, Benjamin Wilfrid (flīsh'ĕr), editor; b. Phila., Pa., Jan. 6, 1870; s. late Simon B. and Cecilia (Hoffheimer) F.; Ph.B., U. of Pa., 1889; m. Marie Blanche Blum, Mar. 26, 1896; children—Wilfrid, Mrs. William Stix Wasserman, Mrs. S. Walter Washington. Pub. and editor, The Japan Advertiser, daily newspaper, Tokyo, Japan, 1908-Oct. 15, 1940, when paper was sold under duress to the Japan Times, daily owned by the Foreign Office of the Japanese government; returned to the U.S. and retired from business; was publisher and editor The Trans-Pacific (weekly review of far eastern affairs and developments), and pres. The Trans-Pacific Advertising and Service Bureau. A founder, and gen. manager The China Press, Shanghai, China, 1911-13. Founder and first v.p. American-Japan Soc., Tokyo. Corr. in Japan and for Far East at various times for leading newspapers and news agencies. Contbr. to periodicals on Far Eastern subjects. Home: 2022 Columbia Road, N.W., Washington. Died Apr. 29, 1946; buried in Forest Lawn Memorial Park, Glendale, Calif.

FLEISHER, Samuel S., retired mfr., philanthropist; b. Phila., Pa., 1872; s. Simon B. and Cecilia (Hoffheimer) F.; student Wharton Sch. of Finance (U. of Pa.), class of 1892. Was v.p. S. B. & B. W. Fleisher, Inc., mfrs. worsted yarn. Dir. Jewish Foster Home and Orphan Asylum, 1903-15, now hon. dir.; trustee Baron de Hirsch Fund of America, 1903-32; chmn. Baron de Hirsch Fund Agrl. Sch., 1908-20, Woodbine Community Center, 1926-32; mem. Nat. Conf. on Care of Dependent Children, 1909; v.p. Juvenile Protective Assn., 1909-13; mem. exec. com. Phila. Vice Commn., 1913; dir. Court Aid Soc., 1913-18; v.p. Ellis Coll. for Fatherless Girls, 1919-32; hon. v.p. Phila. Art Alliance, Nat. Plant, Fruit and Flower Guild; mem. Pa. Council for Edn., 1925-33; v.p. Phila. Playgrounds Assn.; dir. S.E. Pa. Chapter Am. Red Cross, Jewish Welfare Soc., Phila., Emergency Aid Soc. Pa., Nat. Economic League, also advisory com. Pa. League of Women Voters, and hon. com. Scholastic Awards of Pa. (art div.); hon. pres. Asso. Amateur Art Clubs of America, Phila.; founded Phila. Sch. Art League; mem. Phila. Commn. for Beautification of Metropolitan Area, 1925-32; chmn. bd. trustees Pa. State Home for Training in Speech of Deaf Children, 1932-33. Mem. Phila. Advisory Com. of Housing for the Federal Emergency Adminstrn. of Pub. Works since 1934; mem. bd. trustees Neighborhood Centre and of Reform Congregation of Keneseth Israel; sponsor Foreign Policy Assn., 1926-33; one of the founders and charter members Phila. Sch. Occupational Therapy; dir. Sesqui-Centennial Expn., 1926; chmn. Mayor's Com. on Child Welfare and Recreation, 1929; mem. Regional Planning Com., 1928-32; mem. Phila. Zoning Com., 1929-32, Greater Pa. Council, 1931-33, Com. for Employment Artists under Pub. Works Art Project, 1933-34; mem. advisory bd. Housing Com. of Phila. Assn. of Settlements; mem. bd. dirs. Nat. Com. on Enrichment Adult Life, 1931-34; sponsor Nat. Theater Movement; mem. Nat. Recreation Congress; elected trustee Phila. Award, 1935; mem. advisory com. Acad. of Nat. Sciences; apptd. Mayor Wilson as mem. Phila. Recreation Commn., 1936; apptd. commr. of Fairmount Park, 1936; chmn. Recreation Com. Fairmount Park Commn.; mem. gen. advisory council Nat. Assn. for Art Edn., 1936; apptd. by Gov. Earle mem. Pa. Constitution Commemoration Com., 1937; mem. bd. dirs. Crime Prevention Assn. since 1936; official Norfolk Museum of Arts and Sciences since 1934. Honorary mem. Am. Inst. Architects; hon. Knight Am. Order Round Table; mem. Am. Fed. of Arts, Art Alliance, Art Teachers Assn., Hist. Soc. Pa., Fairmount Park Art Assn., Pa. Acad. Fine Arts, Regional Planning Fedn. of Phila., Y.M. Hebrew Assn., Y.W. Hebrew Assn., Gen. Alumni Soc. Received 1923, the Phila. Award (gold medal and $10,000) conferred each year upon the citizen "advancing the best and largest interest of Philadelphia." Founder and sole supporter of Graphic Sketch Club (free, non-sectarian art school, 2,200 students). Mem. Phila. Zoning Commn. Mason. Clubs: T-Square (hon.), Business Men's Art Club of Phila. (a founder and dir.), Men's Temple, Penn Club, Art Alliance. Home: 2220 Green St. Office: 1616 Walnut St., Philadelphia, Pa.
Died Jan. 20, 1944.

FLEMING, Bryant, landscape architect; b. Buffalo, July 19, 1877; s. Emmet and Mary (Harris) F.; spent yr. 1896 and summer, 1898, under Dir. Cowell, Buffalo Botanic Garden, compiling herbarium and gen. study; B.S. Agr., Cornell, 1901; Coll. of Architecture, Cornell, 1 yr.; unmarried. In employ Warren H. Manning, landscape architect, Boston, 1901-04; traveled and studied abroad summers 1903, 1908, 1914; landscape architect at Buffalo, since 1904. Prof. in charge Dept. Landscape Architecture, Cornell, 1904-15, advisory prof. since 1915; mem. plan commn. and landscape adviser to Cornell Univ.; also landscape adviser to Am. Scenic and Historic Preservation Society at Letchworth Park, N.Y. Among his principal works are preservation and restoration of Watkins Glen, N.Y.; plans for the insular fair, and restorations and additions to the city of San Juan, P.R.; Chilmark Farm, estate V. Everitt Macy, Scarborough, N.Y.; estate and gardens for Andrew Carnegie, Lenox, Mass.; W. E. Scripps estate, of Orion, Mich.; residence and estate of W. C. Winter, Lake Forest, Ill., of Leslie Cheek, Nashville, Tenn., of Roy King, and R. M. Carrier, Memphis, Stephen Clarke, Cooperstown, N.Y., Louis Lee Haggin, Lexington, Ky., Keeneland Racing Assn., Lexington, Ky., etc.; designer and adviser, Town of Grand Mere, Quebec; landscape designer plans for U. of Toronto. Mem. Am. Acad. in Rome, Jury of Landscape Architecture; trustee Foundation for Architecture and Landscape Architecture. Lake Forest, Ill. Registered architect N.Y. State. Pres. Wyoming County Pioneers Assn.; fellow Am. Soc. Landscape Architects; mem. A.I.A.; mem. com. on Nat. Capitol, com. on city and regional planning, Architectural League of New York, Buffalo Guild Allied Arts; Delta Phi, Scalp and Blade. Republican. Episcopalian. Clubs: University (Buffalo); Stafford (N.Y.) Country. Home: Tower Hill. Office and Studio: The Academy, Wyoming, N.Y. Died Sep. 19, 1946.

FLEMING, Francis Philip, lawyer; b. Jacksonville, Fla., Jan. 23, 1874; s. Francis Philip and Floride Lydia (Pearson) F.; ed. Sem. West of Suwanee, Tallahassee, Fla.; hon. A.B., U. of Fla., 1915; m. Julia Eleanor Spades, Dec. 31, 1902; children—Hester Ann (Mrs. Herbert E. Williams), Floride Lydia (Mrs. Kenneth M. Keefe), Julia Eleanor (Mrs. Dana Brown), Elizabeth Legere (Mrs. Frederick C. Hixon). Admitted to Fla. bar, 1894, and began practice at Jacksonville; mem. firm Fleming & Fleming, 1895-1926; Fleming, Hamilton, Diver & Lichliter, 1926-37, Fleming, Hamilton & Diver, 1937, Fleming, Hamilton, Diver & Jones, 1938, now Fleming, Jones, Scott & Botts; dir. and gen. counsel Barnett Nat. Bank of Jacksonville, Florida Pub. Co. Chancellor St. John's Parish. Dir. Jacksonville Humane Soc.; chmn. Duval County Defense Council. Mem. Am., Fla. State and Jacksonville bar assns., Am. Law Inst., Am. Judicature Soc. Democrat. Episcopalian. Clubs: Bankers (New York); Seminole, Florida Yacht (Jacksonville); Everglades (Palm Beach). Home: 1550 Riverside Av. Office: Barnett Nat. Bank Bldg., Jacksonville, Fla. Died June 27, 1948.

FLEMING, Harvey Brown, street railway exec.; b. Newburgh, N.Y., Jan. 14, 1873; s. Henry Fleming and Jane (Hill) F.; ed. Newburgh Acad.; B.S., Washington Univ. (St. Louis, Mo.), 1896, C.E., 1904; m. M. Elsie Carruthers; children—Harvey Carruthers, Richard Hill, Elsie C. (Mrs. Joseph W. Cummings). Asso. with T. M. Marvel Co., shipbuilders, Newburgh, N.Y., 1889-92; asst. engr., St. Louis Water Works Dept., St. Louis, Mo., 1896-98; engr., Nat. St. Ry. Lines, St. Louis, Mo., 1898-99; became engr. in charge tracks, bldgs. and electrical work, Chicago City Ry. Co., 1899, chief engr., 1905, dir., 1912, vice president, 1912-30, pres., chmn. bd. dirs., chmn. exec. com., 1930-45, receiver, Nov. 1933-Feb. 1941; mem. Bd. Supervising Engrs., Chicago Traction, representing Chicago City Ry. Co., 1907-45, Southern Street Ry. Co., 1909-45, Calumet & S. Chicago Ry. Co., 1914-45; became dir. Calumet & S. Chicago Ry. Co., Southern Street Ry. Co., 1915, vice president, 1921, pres., chmn. bd. dirs., 1930-45, receiver, Nov. 1933-Feb. 1941; became vice president Chicago & Western Ry. Co., 1921, dir., 1930, chmn. bd. dirs., Sept. 22, 1930-45; became dir. Hammond, Whiting & E. Chicago Ry. Co., 1922, pres., chmn. bd. dirs., 1930-45; mem. governing Com., Chicago City and Connecting Rys. Collateral Trust, 1930-45; chief engr., Chicago Surface Lines, 1914-45; mem. bd. operation, Sept. 1930-Feb. 1941, mem. exec. com., bd. operation, Sept. 1930-Feb. 1941. Life mem. Am. Soc. Civil Engineers and Western Soc. Engrs. Member American Transit Association. Mason (K.T., Shriner). Clubs: Chicago Athletic Association, Mid-Day. Presbyterian. Republican. Home: Prairie View, Ill. Died Oct. 3, 1947.

FLEMING, Matthew Corry, lawyer; b. Xenia, O., June 24, 1864; s. Ebenezer Caldwell and Rachel (Corry) F.; B.A., Princeton, 1886, M.A., 1889; LL.B., Cincinnati Law Sch., 1889; m. Angeline Wilson, Oct. 11, 1893; children—Wilson Fleming (dec.), Matthew C., William W. Began practice at Cincinnati, 1889; moved to New York; asst. corp. counsel, N.Y. City, 1902-04; asst. counsel N.Y. Gas Investigating Com., 1905, New York Ins. Com., 1905, 06; now mem. Osborn, Fleming & Whittlesey; dir. and gen. counsel Phelps Dodge Corp.; gen. counsel St. Joseph Lead Co. Formerly mem. Squadron A, N.Y. Nat. Guard. Trustee Princeton U., 1912-42, now trustee emeritus (chmn. finance com., 1927-42); trustee and sec. Presbyn. Hosp. Mem. Am. and N.Y. State bar assns., Bar Assn. City of New York, S.R., Phi Beta Kappa. Republican. Clubs: Century; University, Princeton, Down Town, Colony, Piping Rock, Holland Lodge. Home: 1060 Fifth Av. Office: 20 Exchange Pl., New York, N.Y. Died Feb. 20, 1946.

FLEMING, Victor, motion picture dir.; b. Pasadena, Calif.; s. William Richard Lonzo and Elisabeth Evelyn (Hartman) F.; m. Lucile Rosson, 1933; children—Victoria Susan, Sally Elisabeth. Began in automobile business; later racing driver in Vanderbilt Cup Races; became camera man Am. Film Co., Santa Barbara, 1912; camera man with Douglas Fairbanks many years, starting to direct him, 1919. Directed "The Virginian," "Treasure Island," "Captains Courageous," "Test Pilot," "Wizard of Oz," "Gone with the Wind," and many others; producer-dir. on film, Joan of Arc. Served as 1st lt., Photographic Sect. Signal Corps, World War I, 1917; made ednl. pictures for Army; developed speed cameras for analytical photography. Member President Wilson's staff during European Peace Conf. Home: 1050 Moraga Drive, Bel Air, Los Angeles 24, Calif. Address: Roach Studio, Culver City, Calif. Died Jan. 6, 1949.

FLETCHER, Emerson Armor, urologist; b. Detroit, Mich., 1860; student U. of Mich.; M.D., U. of Pa., 1892; grad. study Johns Hopkins; unmarried. Licensed to practice medicine, 1900; genito-urinary surgeon Milwaukee Hosp. Fellow Am. Coll. Surgeons, A.M.A.; mem. Am. Urol. Assn. Republican. Home: 2804 Newbury Blvd. Office: 208 E. Wisconsin Av., Milwaukee, Wis. Died Dec. 6, 1946.

FLETCHER, Jefferson Butler, prof. emeritus; b. Chicago, Nov. 13, 1865; s. Isaac Dudley and Mary Elizabeth (Pickering) F.; A.B., Harvard, 1887, A.M., 1880; Litt.D., Bowdoin Coll., Brunswick, Me., 1932; m. Agnes Peabody Herrick, May 29, 1893. Instr. English, 1890-1902; asst. prof. comparative lit., 1902-04, Harvard; prof. comparative lit., Columbia, 1904-39, now professor emeritus. First lieutenant A.E.F., 1917-18. Mem. Nat. Inst. Arts and Letters. Club: Century. Author: The Religion of Beauty in Woman, 1911; The Overture and Other Poems, 1911; Dante, 1916; Symbolism of the Divine Comedy, 1921. Translator: Divine Comedy, 1931; Literature of the Italian now professor emeritus. Served as first lieutenant American Field Service, A.E.F., 1917-18. Awarded Distinguished Service Cross, Croix de Guerre. Member National Institute Arts and Letters. Club: Renaissance, 1934. Home: York Village, Me. Died Aug. 17, 1946.

FLETCHER, John Madison, psychologist; b. nr. Murfreesboro, Tenn., June 27, 1873; s. Burrell Dickinson and Elizabeth Ann (Alexander) F.; grad. Webb Sch., Bell Buckle, Tenn., 1896; B.A., Vanderbilt, 1901; M.A., U. of Colo., 1904; student Stanford, 1907-10; Ph.D., Clark U., 1912; m. Annie Cooper, Dec. 25, 1907; 1 dau., Olive May. Teacher, Webb Sch., 1901-02; prin. Univ. Training Sch., Granberry, Tex., 1902-03, Vanderbilt Training Sch., Elkton, Ky., 1904-05; asst. in edn., U. of Colo., 1905-06; asst. in philosophy, Stanford, 1909-10; fellow Clark U., 1910-11, lecturer, 1911-12; asst. prof. exptl. and clin. psychology, Tulane Univ., 1912-13, prof. and head of dept., 1913, acting dean grad. dept., 1919-20, dean grad. dept., 1920-24, also dir. Collender Lab. of Psychology and Edn., absent on leave, 1923-24; prof. psychology, 1928-38, prof. emeritus, 1938; prof. psychology, Vanderbilt U. and lecturer in Vanderbilt Med. Sch., 1926-28. Fellow A.A.A.S., A.A.A.P., New Orleans Acad. (pres. 1916-17); mem. Am. Psychol. Assn., Southern Assn. Psychology and Philosophy (pres., 1920-21), Phi Beta Kappa, Sigma Xi. Democrat. Methodist. Author: The Problem of Stuttering, 1928; Psychology in Education, 1934. Home: 1220 Henry Clay Av., New Orleans. Died Dec. 12, 1944.

FLETCHER, William Meade, corp. commr., author; b. Sperryville, Va., Oct. 21, 1870; s. James William and Catherine (Meade) F.; LL.B., U. of Va., 1891; m. Florence Lea, Feb. 18, 1896 (died Apr. 19, 1911); 1 son, William Meade; m. 2d, Martha Ball Buckner, Sept. 30, 1914; children—Anne Buckner, James William. Admitted to bar 1891; practiced in Mont., 1891-94, at Chicago, 1895-1904, Phila. and Chicago, 1905-12, Va., since 1912. Prof. law John Marshall Law Sch., Chicago, 1899-1901, Northwestern U., 1901-04; spl. judge Dist. Court, Cascade County, Mont., 1893; judge of Court of Juvenile and Domestic Relations, Rappahannock County, Va., 1925-26; mem. Commn. to Suggest Amendments to Constn. of Va., by apptmt. of Gov. H. F. Byrd, 1926; mem. since 1928 and now chmn. State Corp. Commn. of Va. Del. Dem. Nat. Conv., 1932. Mem. Am., Ill. State, Chicago and Va. bar assns., Phi Kappa Psi. Democrat. Episcopalian. Author: Taxation of Franchises, 1900; Treatise on Equity Pleading and Practice, 1902; Corporation Forms and Precedents, 1913;

Treatise on the Incorporation and Management of Corporations in Illinois, 1910; Equity Pleading and Practice Forms, 1912; Cyclopedia of the Law of Private Corporations, 10 vols., 1917-1920; Supplement to Corporation Forms and Precedents, 1923; Corporation Forms and Precedents (2d edit.), 1928. Home: Sperryville, Va. Office: State Office Bldg., Richmond, Va. Died Dec. 19, 1943.

FLEXNER, Bernard, lawyer; b. Louisville, Ky., Feb. 24, 1865; s. Morris and Esther (Abraham) F.; pub. schs. of Louisville; LL.B., U. of Louisville, 1898; law dept. U. of Va.; unmarried. Admitted to Ky. bar, 1898, Ill. bar, 1911, N.Y. bar, 1919; in law practice since 1898; moved to Chicago, 1911, to N.Y. City. 1919. Chmn. Juvenile Court Bd.. Jefferson County (Louisville), Ky., 1906-11; chmn. com. apptd. by atty. gen. U.S. to study the need for legislation affecting children in the D.C., 1914; mem. Ky. Bd. Tuberculosis Commrs., 1913. Mem. Am. Red Cross Commn. to Roumania, July 1917. Counsel Zionist delegation to the Peace Conf., Paris, 1918-19; organizer Palestine Economic Corp., 1925, pres. to 1931 and since chmn. bd.; founder Mary Flexner lectureship on humanities at Bryn Mawr Coll., 1928, Abraham Flexner lectureship on med. science at Vanderbilt U., 1929. Mem. at large U. of Louisville. Mem. Assn. of Bar of City of N.Y., Council on Foreign Relations. Promoted and assumed responsibility for publication and free distribution to libraries throughout world of complete record of trial of Sacco and Vanzetti (6 vols.), 1928. Club: Cosmos (Washington). Joint Author: Juvenile Courts and Probation (with R. N. Baldwin), 1914; The Legal Aspect of the Juvenile Court (with Reuben Oppenheimer), 1922. Home: 1000 Park Av. Office: 570 Lexington Av., New York, N.Y. Died May 3, 1945.

FLEXNER, Simon, physician; b. Louisville, Ky., Mar. 25, 1863; s. Morris and Esther (Abraham) F., ed. Louisville pub. schs.; M.D., U. of Louisville, 1889; post-grad. student Johns Hopkins, univs. of Strassburg, Berlin, Prague and Pasteur Inst.; D.Sc., Harvard, 1906, Yale, 1910, Princeton, 1913, U. of Pa., 1929, Nat. U. of Ireland, 1936, U. of Louisville, 1937; LL.D., U. of Md., 1907, Washington U., Brown, Johns Hopkins—all 1915, Cambridge U. (England), 1920, Western Reserve, 1929; Doctor, Univ. of Strassburg, 1923, Univ. of Louvain (Belgium), 1927, Univ. Libre, Brussels, 1930; M.A., Oxford U.; Fellow, Balliol Coll., Oxford, U., 1937; m. Helen Whitall Thomas, 1903; children—William Welch, James Carey Thomas. Asso. prof. pathology, 1895-98, prof. pathol. anatomy, 1898-99, Johns Hopkins; prof. pathology, U. of Pa., 1899-1903; dir. Ayer Clin. Lab., 1901-03; pathologist, Univ. Hosp., Phila. Hosp., 1900-03; dir. laboratories Rockefeller Inst., Med. Research, 1903-35, dir. Inst., 1920-35, emeritus since 1935; Eastman prof., Oxford U., 1937-38. Col., O.R.C., United States Army. Trustee Carnegie Instn. Washington, 1910-14., Rockefeller Foundation, 1913-28, Johns Hopkins University, 1937-42. Chairman Public Health Council of New York. Chevalier Legion of Honor, France, 1914, Officer, 1919, Commander, 1923; Order of the Sacred Treasure, Japan, 1915. Fellow American Academy Arts and Sciences (Boston). Academy Medicine, A.A.A.S.; member National Acad. Sciences, Assn, Am. Physicians, Am. Philos. Soc., Am. Assn. Pathologists and Bacteriologists, A.M.A., Harvey Soc.; corr. mem. Medico-Chirurgical Soc. of Bologna, Reale Istituto Lombardo di Scienza e Lettere, Milan, Soc. Path. Exotique (Paris), Academy of Medicine (Paris), Academy of Sciences, Inst. of France (Paris, foreign associate), Gesellschaft d. Aerzte in Wien, Wiener Gesellschaft für Mikrobiologie, Berliner Medical Gesellschaft, Academy Medicine Caracas, Society Med. Chirg. del. Guyas, Guyaquil, Ecuador; hon. mem. Inst. for Exptl. Therapy, Frankfurt am M., Deutsche Akademie Naturforscher, Halle, Swedish Medical Society, Société Med. des Hôpitaux, Paris, Société de Biologie, Paris; fgn. mem. Royal Soc. (London); hon. fellow Royal Society of Medicine (London); fgn. mem. Royal Soc. Trop. Med. and Hygiene, Brit. Med. Assn., Soc. belge de Med. Trop., Soc. belge de Biol., Royal Acad. Medicine, Brussels, Soc. Royale des Sciences Med. et Nat., Brussels, Bataafsch Genootschap d. Proefonder-vindelijke Wijsbegeerte, Rotterdam, Copenhagen Medical Soc., Royal Danish Scientific Soc., Soc. Argentina de Biol. (Buenos Aires), Microbiol. Soc., Leningrad. Author of many papers and monographs relating to bacterial and pathol. subjects, including: The Pathology of Toxalbumin Intoxication; biochemical constitution of snake venoms, experimental pancreatitis and fat necrosis; epidemic cerebrospinal meningitis, and its serum treatment; poliomyelitis, its cause, mode of transmission and prevention; epidemic encephalitis; experimental epidemiology, etc. Author: (with James Thomas Flexner) Biography of William Henry Welch, 1941. Home: 530 E. 86th St., New York. Died May 2, 1946.

FLICK, Alexander Clarence, historian; b. Galion, O., Aug. 16, 1869; s. Enos H. and Elizabeth Jane (Johnson) F.; A.B., Otterbein U., Westerville, O., 1894, A.M., 1897, Litt.D., 1904; Ph.D., Columbia, 1901; LL.D., Alfred (N.Y.) Univ., 1928; L.H.D., Syracuse (N.Y.) Univ., 1935; m. Laura T. Page, June 10, 1899; children—Dorothy Jean, John Williston, Alexander C., Hugh M. Univ. fellow in history, Columbia, 1895-96; prof. European history, Syracuse U., 1899-1923, head dept. of history and polit. sci., 1916-23; State historian and dir. of archives and history State of N.Y., 1923-1939 (retired). Traveled and studied in Europe, 1902-11; lecturer on hist. subjects, U. S. and Europe, and through Far East, 1912-13. Mem. Am. Hist. Assn., Am. Acad. Polit. and Social Science. Organizer Univ. Travel-Study Club. Author: Loyalism in New York, 1901; History of New York (with J. J. Anderson), 1902; History in Rhymes and Jingles, 1902; Rise of the Mediaeval Church, 1909; Recent World History, 1926; The American Revolution in New York, 1926; The Decline of the Mediaeval Church, 1929; the Sullivan-Clinton Campaign, 1929; History of the State of New York, 1933-37; Modern World History Since 1775, 1935; Samuel J. Tilden, 1939. Contbr. of hist. articles to various publs. Home: 127 Manning Blvd., Albany, N.Y. Died July 30, 1942.

FLICKINGER, Roy Caston (flĭk'ĭng-ẽr), univ. prof.; b. Seneca, Ill., Dec. 17, 1876; s. George Harnish and Nina Theresa (Parker) F.; A.B., Northwestern U., 1899, A.M., 1901; Ph.D., U. of Chicago, 1904; studied at U. of Berlin, summer, 1905, leave of absence for travel and study, 1923-24; m. Lillian Hortense Cook, Aug. 25, 1904; m. 2d, Minnie A. Keyes, Dec. 21, 1932. Instr. Greek, Evanston (Ill.) Acad., 1899-1901; prof. Greek and Latin, Epworth U., Oklahoma City, 1904-05; instr. Greek and Latin, 1905-08, asst. prof. Greek, 1908-10, asso. prof., 1910-16, prof. Greek and Latin, 1916-25, sec. of faculty, 1908-19, dean Coll. Liberal Arts, 1919-23, Northwestern U.; head-prof. Latin and Greek, since 1925, ann. research lecturer, 1925-26, State U. of Ia. On staff Am. Sch. Classical Studies, Athens, summer, 1933. Mem. Am. Philol. Assn. (exec. com., 1921-23 and 1930-40; sec.-treas., 1932-35), Classical Assn. of Middle West and South (pres. 1932-33), Archeological Inst. America (pres. Chicago Society of same, 1921-25; pres. Iowa Soc. since 1925), Humanist Soc. (pres. 1927-28), Am. Assn. Univ. Profs. (chmn. com. on promotion of teachers, 1923-26; chmn. com. on required courses in edn., 1929-31; pres. U. of Iowa chapter, 1928-29), Assn. of Coll. Honor Socs. (exec. com. since 1941), Archeol. Soc. Athens (hon.), Horatian Soc. (London), Classical Assn. (London), Assn. Budé (Paris), Phi Beta Kappa (pres. U. of Ia. chapter 1937-38, del. to triennial councils 1922, 37, 40; chmn. North Central Dist. and mem. nat. nominating com. since 1937; senator, 1940-46); mem. Eta Sigma Phi (chmn. bd. trustees, 1940). Pres. Chicago Classical Club, 1918-20; mem. exec. com. Am. Classical League, 1919-34; mem. Advisory Com. for Investigation of Classical Teaching, financed by Gen. Edn. Bd.; mem. classical jury, Am. Acad. in Rome, 1929-33, chmn. advisory council, 1933; initiated and designed Eta Sigma Phi medal for honor students in Latin, 1929; chmn. Com. for Horace Bimillenary; del. to Rep. State Conv., 1936, 38, 40; chmn. Rep. Central Com. of Iowa City, 1937-41; Iowa City chairman for Greek War Relief, 1940. Clubs: University (Evanston); University (Chicago); Triangle, Research. Author: Plutarch and the Greek Theater, 1904; The Greek Theater and Its Drama, 1918, 4th edit., 1936; Horace's First Bimillennium, 1936. Editor: Carmina Latina, 1919, 4th edit., 1929; Songs for the Latin Club, 1924. Asso. editor Philol. Quarterly; business mgr. Classical Jour., 1927-33, editor in chief, 1928-33, asso. ed. since 1933; editor Iowa Studies in Classical Philology since 1934. Contbr. to philol. jours. Home: 301 N. Capitol St., Iowa City, Ia. Died July 6, 1942; buried at Morris, Ill.

FLINN, Richard Orme, clergyman; b. Milledgeville, Ga., Aug. 8, 1870; s. Rev. William (D.D.) and Mary (Orme) F.; student Southwestern Presbyn. U., Clarksville, Tenn., 1886-90; grad. Columbia (S.C.) Theol. Sem., 1894; D.D., Presbyterian Coll. of S.C., June 1911; m. Anna Emery, Mar. 8, 1898; children—Emery, Mary Orme (dec.), Richard Orme, Elizabeth F., William Adams. Ordained Presbyn. ministry, 1894; pastor Kirkwood, Ga., 1894-98; stated supply 1st Ch., Atlanta, Jan., 1899, until resignation July, 1939; councillor and helper in various fields, now pastor emeritus North Av. Presbyn. Ch.; State Supply Roswell Public Resources, Georgia, 1941-46. Delegate to Pan Presbyn. Council, Glasgow, Scotland, 1896, Cardiff, Wales, 1925; ex-mem. exec. commn. on evangelism of the Federal Council of Chs. of Christ in America; 1st sec. systematic beneficence com., Presbyn. Ch., 1911-14; was mem. campaign com. and home mission com. Mem. Com. on Coöperation and Union, Gen. Assembly of Presbyn. Ch. U.S.; mem. Ch. Coöperation Com., Atlanta; former chmn. Work Com. Synod of Ga., commn. on evangelism of Ch. Council of Atlanta; dir. North Av. Presbyn. Synodical Sch., Rabun-Gap-Nacoochee School (chmn. executive com.), Agnes Scott Coll., Ga. Former chmn. war time Food Conservation Com. Synod of Ga.; mem. com. Presbyn. Ch. U.S. care of soldiers in camps; spl. speaker with "flying squadron" of Y.M.C.A.; overseas in France and Germany, 1919-20. Counsellor for 4th Corps Area Reforestation Camps, 1933. Democrat. Mason. Mem. Pi Kappa Alpha, Sons of Confederate Vets. Home: 1020 Springdale Rd., N.E., Druid Hills, Atlanta, Ga. Died Mar. 25, 1948.

FLIPPER, Joseph Simeon, bishop; b. Atlanta, Ga., Feb. 22, 1859; student Atlanta U., 1869-76; ordained to ministry African M.E. Ch., 1880; bishop since May 20, 1908. Address: 488 Houston St., Atlanta, Ga.* Died Oct. 10, 1944.

FLOOD, Henry, Jr., cons. engr.; b. Elmira, N.Y., Feb. 9, 1887; s. Henry and Ella Louise (Seeley) F.; grad. Elmira Acad., 1904; grad. Wertz Sch., Annapolis, Md., 1905; M.E., Cornell U., 1909; m. Iona Grace Sandford, Apr. 6, 1912; 1 dau., Iona Sandford. Chief engr. Central Hudson Gas & Electric Co., 1909-17; mech. engr. Am. Smelting & Refining Co., 1917-19; associated in practice with Dr. John Price Jackson, New York, 1920; engineers secretary U.S. Superpower Survey, 1920-21; president and director M. & F. Management Corp.. Murray and Flood, Inc.; chmn. and dir. Lanova Corp.; pres. Flood & Watson, cons. engs. Fellow Am. Inst. E.E.; mem. Am. Soc. M.E., Phi Gamma Delta; asso. mem. Soc. Automotive Engrs. Episcopalian. Club: Engineers. Home: 36 Riverside Av., Red Bank, N.J. Died June 17, 1948; buried in Fairview Cemetery, Red Bank.

FLORE, Edward (flôr'ē), gen. pres., Internat. Labor Union; b. Buffalo, N.Y., Dec. 5, 1877; s. George and Catherine (Hassenfratz) F.; m. Mary Katherine Schneider, Sept. 27, 1911. County supervisor, 1908-20. Elk, Eagle. Home: 426 Woodbridge Av. Office: 422 Sidway Bldg., Buffalo, N.Y. Died Sep. 27, 1945.

FLOWER, Henry Corwin, banker; b. Mt. Vernon, Ind., Aug. 15, 1860; s. Richard and Rebecca (McArthur) F.; A.B., U. of Mich., 1885; m. Lida Carr, Dec. 18, 1895; children—Henry Corwin, Ruth (Mrs. Robert R. Lester), Elizabeth Fordham. Practiced law, Kansas City, Mo., 1885-99; organized Fidelity Trust Co., 1899, pres. until consolidation with Nat. City Bank, June 1, 1919, under name of Fidelity Nat. Bank & Trust Co., chmn. of bd.; also chmn. bd. Fidelity Savings Trust Co. Mem. Capital Issues Com., Washington, during the war. Democrat. Clubs: Country, Athletic, University. Office: Fidelity National Bank & Trust Co., Kansas City, Mo. Died June 20, 1938.

FLOWERS, Alan Estis, engineer; b. St. Louis, Mo., Oct. 4, 1876; s. William Pitts and Mary Emma (Cummins) F.; M.E., Cornell U., 1902, M.M.E., 1914, Ph.D., 1915; m. Ida Vandergrift Burns, June 29, 1907; children—George Schluederberg, Nancy Holmes, Priscilla (dec.). Engr. apprentice with Westinghouse Electric & Mfg. Co., 1902-04; instr. and asso. prof. elec. engring., U. of Mo., 1904-12; with Gen. Electric Co., 1912-13; prof. elec. engring., Ohio State U., 1913-18; appraisal engr., Columbus Electric Power & Light Co., 1917-18; capt. Signal Corps, U.S. Army, on duty in radio development sect., Washington, D.C., Mar. 31, 1918-Mar. 8, 1919; test engr. engring. dept., Nat. Aniline & Chem. Co., New York, 1919-20; research engr. in charge of Research Engring. Sect., 1921-22; mgr. and cons. engr. Chem. Machinery Construction Co., 1922-23; engr., in charge development, De Laval Separator Co., 1923-43, research engr. since 1943; dir. Flakice Corp. since 1943. Mem. Am. Inst. Elec. Engrs., Am. Soc. Mech. Engrs. (mem. spl. research com. on lubrication), Am. Soc. for Testing Materials (chmn. sub-com. on sampling and gaging), Am. Phys. Soc., Am. Soc. Metals, Am. Assn. Univ. Profs., Phi Mu Alpha, Lambda Phi Rho, Sigma Xi, Tau Beta Pi. Conglist. Developed apparatus for measuring cylinder friction and lubrication in steam engines, also invented a viscosimeter; developed processes for oil reclamation, improvements in centrifugal separators and ultra high speed test tube centrifuge. Contbr. on tech. topics.; chapter on "Centrifuges" in Chemical Engineers' Handbook. Home: 148 College Av., Poughkeepsie, N.Y. Died Dec. 4, 1945.

FLYNN, Benedict Devine, insurance exec.; b. Hartford, Conn., July 6, 1880; s. Daniel and Elizabeth (Devine) F.; ed. Trinity Coll., hon. M.A., 1913; m. Genevieve Brady, July 3, 1917. With The Travelers Ins. Co., Hartford, Conn., since 1902, as asst. actuary, 1907, actuary casualty dept., 1911, asst. sec., 1913, sec., 1922, sec. and actuary, 1930, v.p. and actuary since 1930. Fellow Actuarial Soc. of America, Am. Inst. of Actuaries, and Casualty Actuarial Soc. (past pres.); mem. Inst. Actuaries of Great Britain. Home: 160 Kenyon St. Office: 700 Main St., Hartford, Conn. Died Aug. 22, 1944.

FLYNN, Joseph Crane, educator; b. Cincinnati, O., Mar. 3, 1876; s. John Walter and Isabella Mary (Crane) F.; ed. St. Xavier Acad. and Coll., 1892-98, St. Louis U. Normal, 1898-1902, St. Louis U. Sch. of Philosophy, 1902-05, St. Louis Sch. of Divinity, 1910-14; unmarried. Teacher, St. Louis U. High Sch., 1905-10, St. Ignatius High Sch., Chicago, Ill., 1915-19; chmn. dept. English, St. Xavier Coll., 1919-23; dean Coll. Arts and Sciences, Marquette U., 1923-25; dean Coll. Arts and Sciences, and dir. summer sessions, Creighton U., 1925-31; dean of Arts and Sciences, U. of Detroit, since 1931. Dir. Catholic Women's Study Club, Cincinnati, O., 1919-22, Laymen's Retreats, Cleveland, O., 1934-38, Men of Milford Jesuit Retreat League (for laymen) since 1938. Republican. Catholic. Club: Professional Men's. Address: Retreat House, Milford, O. Died June 8, 1948.

FLYNN, P. J., ry. official; b. Granville, N.Y., Mar. 12, 1856; ed. pub. schs. Section work, Phila. & Reading Ry., 1870; telegraph operator, agt. and clk., various rds. until 1880; sta. agt. A.T.&S.F.Ry., Trinidad, Colo., 1880-83, gen. agt., successively, Salt Lake City, Cincinnati and Denver, Colo., until 1887, gen. agt. and asst. supt. in charge Denver terminals, 1887-89; gen. western freight and passenger agt. Mo.P.Ry., Denver, 1889-90; gen. freight and passenger agt. Rio Grande-Midland Route, Denver, 1890-91; commr. Colo.-Utah Traffic Assn., 1891-99, also chmn. Colo. Passenger Assn., 1892-99; gen. freight agt., 1899-1903, freight traffic mgr., 1903-11, v.p. in charge of traffic, 1911, now sec. and treas. D.L.&W.R.R. Office: 90 west St., New York. Died Oct. 12, 1936.

FOCKE, Theodore Moses (fōk), mathematician; b. near Massillon, O., Jan. 3, 1871; s. Theodore H. and Katherine M. (Brown) F.; B.S. in C.E., Case Sch. of Applied Science, Cleveland, O., 1892; Ph.D., U. of Göttingen, Germany, 1898; Sc.D. (hon.), Case Sch. of Applied Science, 1944; m. Anne L. Bosworth,

Aug. 7, 1901 (died 1907); children—Helen Metcalf, Theodore Brown, Alfred Bosworth. Instr. mathematics, Case Sch. Applied Science, 1892-93; tutor in physics and chemistry, Oberlin Coll., 1893-96; instr. mathematics and civ. engring., 1898-1902; asst. prof. mathematics, 1902-08, Kerr prof. and head of dept. mathematics, 1908-44, dean of the faculty, 1918-44, dean emeritus Case Inst. Tech., since 1944. Fellow A.A.A.S., mem. Am. Math. Soc., Math. Assn. America, Am. Society for Engring., Sigma Xi, Phi Kappa Psi, Tau Beta Pi. Republican. Episcopalian Home: 2517 Wellington Rd., Cleveland Heights 18, O. Died Mar. 2, 1949.

FOGDALL, Sorenus P. (fōg'dawl), educator, clergyman; b. nr. Kolding, Denmark, Sept. 2, 1879; s. Peter Iversen and Karen Madison (Schmidt) F.; studied Dano-Norwegian Bapt. Theol. Sem., identified with U. of Chicago, diploma from U. of Chicago, 1906; Ph.B., Des Moines Coll., 1910; M.A., U. of Chicago, 1915; Ph.D., State U. of Ia., 1921; m. Louise Swansen, Aug. 31, 1910; children—Vergil Swansen, Gordon Swansen. Instr., Sac City Inst., 1910-12; prof. history, Des Moines Coll., 1912-18; prof. history and govt., Des Moines U. (union of Des Moines and Highland Park Colls.), 1918-29; became prof. history and govt., Penn. Coll., Oskaloosa, Iowa, 1929, Ottawa (Kan.) University, 1931; pastor First Baptist Church of Clarks Grove, Minnesota, 1937-44, retired from active pastorate. President Danish Baptist General Conference of America, and chairman board of trustees, 1937-39, mem. board of trustees since 1939. Mem. State Com. (Ia.) on High Sch. Curriculum, 1929. Instr., Automobile Corps, Des Moines, World War. Mem. Am. Hist. Assn., Ia. State Teachers' Assn., Miss. Valley Hist. Assn. Republican. Baptist (ordained Bapt. ministry, 1906). Mason (32°). Author: Teaching of Civics and Training for Citizenship (monograph), 1918; Danish-American Diplomacy, 1922; An Outline of American Government, 1926; History of Des Moines University (chapter in History of Baptists in Iowa), 1933; also hist. articles and numerous articles based on archeol. research; Am. corr. Kolding Folkeblad since 1928 (temporarily suspended during war). Asso. editor The Baptist Record, Pella, Ia. Contbr. to Dictionary of Am. History. Lecturer on America's Relation to Europe, World Peace, etc. Archaeol. research in Cimbrian mounds, Jutland, 1921. Address: 2837 Kingman Blvd., Des Moines 11, Ia Died June 13, 1947.

FOGEL, Edwin Miller (fō'gĕl), educator; b. Fogelsville, Pa., May 29, 1874; s. Rev. Dr. Edwin J. and Jennie E. (Miller) F.; A.B., Ursinus Coll., Collegeville, Pa., 1894; student Johns Hopkins, 1894-96; Ph.D., U. of Pa., 1907; unmarried. Editor German-American Annals, 1914-17; business mgr. Americana Germanica Press since 1914; asst. prof. German, U. of Pennsylvania, 1925-28. V.p. and dir., Fogelsville Nat. Bank, 1926-38. Formerly chmn. Office Price Adminstrn. Rationing Bd. 39-2. Mem. Anthrop. Soc. of Phila. (pres.), German-Am. Hist. Soc. (ex-sec.), Acacia. Mem. bd. of directors of Ursinus Coll., 1930; mem. exec. com., Lehigh County Hist. Soc., since 1923, treas. since 1939; one of organizers Pa. German Folk-Lore Soc., dir. and treas. since 1935. Clubs: Lenape (treas.), Livingston. Author: Beliefs and Superstitions of Pennsylvania Germans, 1914; Proverbs of the Pennsylvania Germans, 1929; The Pennsylvania Germans in Peace and War, 1933; also wrote History of St. John's Reformed Church. Contbr. to New History of the Lehigh Valley, 1941; also to German American Annals, Jour. English and Germanic Philology, Handwörterbuch des Deutschen Volkstums im Auslande (Leipzig), vols. V and VI of Pa. German Folklore Soc., etc. Home: Fogelsville, Pa. Died Dec. 16, 1949.

FOKINE, Michel (fō-kēn), ballet master; b. Petrograd, Russia, Apr. 26, 1880; s. Michel and Ekaterin (Kind) F.; student Imperial Theatrical Sch., Russia, 1889-98; m. Vera Antonova, Mar. 5, 1905; 1 child, Vitale. First visit to U.S., 1919, naturalized citizen, 1932. Dancer Imperial Theater, Petrograd, 1898-1918; teacher of classical ballet, Imperial Ballet Sch., Petrograd, 1902-12; ballet master Imperial Theater, Petrograd, 1909-18, and Diaghileff Ballet Russe, 1909-14; ballet master Royal Opera, Stockholm, 1910, La Scala, Milan, 1911, Grand Opera, Paris, 1921, Royal Opera, Copenhagen, 1925, Nat. Theater, Riga, 1929, Teatro Colon, Buenos Aires, 1931, Rene Blum Ballet de Monte Carlo, 1936, Ballet Russe, 1937, Education Ballet, 1939, Ballet Theatre, 1940; head of ballet studio since 1920, and of the Michel Fokine and Vera Fokina Am. Ballet since 1925, making tours with Vera Fokina over Russia, 1915-17, Scandinavia, 1918, United States, Germany, Scandinavia, France, 1919-25. Creator of 77 ballets including Les Sylphides, Cleopatra, Carnival, Fire Bird, Petrouchka, Le Coq d'Or, Scheherazade, Don Juan. etc. Address: 170 Shonnard Terrace, Yonkers, N.Y. Died Aug. 22, 1942.

FOLEY, Arthur Lee, physicist; b. Hancock County, Ind., Feb. 22, 1867; s. Mansfield Calvin and Clara Alice (Myers) F.; student Central Normal Coll., Danville, 1882-84 (Litt.D., 1941), Hayward Coll., Fairfield, Ill., 1886-87; A.B., Ind. U., 1890, A.M., 1891; University of Chicago, 1894; Ph.D., Cornell, 1897; European univs., 1908; m. Lorettie Hayworth, Apr. 15, 1885; children—Ernest Lee, Mrs. Eupha May Tugman. Teacher pub. sch., Vivalia, Ind., 1884-85; prin. pub. sch., Cleveland, Ind., 1885-86, Johnsonville, Ill., 1887-88; instr. physics, Ind. U., 1890-91, asso. prof., 1891-97, prof. and head of dept. of physics, 1897-1938, emeritus prof. since 1938, Waterman research prof., 1917-25, also chmn. Bur. of Science Service, 1926-35. Dir. of physics research, Affiliated Coll. of Ind., 1917-25; chmn. research com. Ind. State Council of Defense, 1915-18; dir. U.S. Radio Sch., Ind. U., 1918. Mem. Nat. Research Council. Republican. Methodist. Fellow A.A.A.S., Ind. Acad. Science (pres. 1909); chmn. research com. since 1924), Am. Phys. Soc., Accustical Soc. America; mem. Am. Assn. Physics Teachers, Sigma Xi (pres. 1892), Phi Beta Kappa (pres. 1914). Acoustical engineer, inventor, investigator, author of 90 scientific papers and 4 editions of a physics text. Home: Bloomington, Ind. Died Feb. 13, 1945.

FOLEY, James A., judge; b. N.Y. City, 1882; s. James and Anna (Moran) F.; A.B., Coll. of the City of N.Y., 1901; LL.B., N.Y. Law Sch., 1903; LL.D., Fordham, 1928, Columbia, 1934, N.Y.U., 1945; m. Mabel Graham, 1919. Admitted to N.Y. bar, 1903, and began practice in N.Y. City; mem. N.Y. Assembly, 1907-12, Senate, 1912-19 (Dem. leader of Senate, 1919); while in legislature actively promoted Workmen's Compensation Law, direct primary, welfare legislation and pub. service laws; del. N.Y. Constl. Conv., 1915, 38; judge Surrogate's Court (Probate Court), New York County, since 1920; trial judge of Amos F. Eno will contest, Ella Wendel and Ida Wood will contest; elected leader of Tammany Hall, 1924, but declined. Chmn. N.Y. State Commn. to Investigate Defects in Laws of Estates, 1927-33. Mem. N.Y. State Commn. to Revise Civil Practice, 1918-19; mem. N.Y. State Pan-Pacific Expn. Commn., 1915, Mem. N.Y. State World's Fair Commn., 1939-40. Knight Commander Equestrian Order of Holy Sepulchre, 1931, Papal Knight of Malta, 1941. Member American Bar Association, Bar Association City of New York; pres. Asso. Alumni Coll. of the City of N.Y., 1923; mem. Soc. of Friendly Sons of St. Patrick of New York (pres. 1931-34), Phi Beta Kappa. Clubs: Manhattan (pres. 1933-37), Nat. Democratic, Nat. Golf Links of America. Author of several articles and addresses on the law of wills, estates, inheritance and procedure of Probate Courts. Home: 243 E. 17th St. Address: Hall of Records, New York, N.Y. Died Feb. 11, 1946.

FOLGER, Alonzo Dillard (fōl'gĕr), congressman; b. Dobson, N.C., 1888; s. Thomas W. and Ada D. Folger; A.B., U. of N.C., 1912, LL.B., 1914; m. Gertrude Reece, Oct. 13, 1919; children—Alonzo Dillard, Jack. Admitted to N.C. bar, 1914, and began practice at Mt. Airy; mem. firm Folger and Folger since 1914; judge Superior Court of N.C., 1936-37; mem. 76th to 80th Congresses (1939-49), 5th N.C. Dist. Dem. nat. committeeman from N.C. since 1936; mem. Dem. Nat. Exec. Com. and dir. of finance for N.C.; campaign mgr. for Lt. Gov. A. H. Graham; candidate for gov. N.C., June 1936. Trustee Greater U. of N.C. since 1934. Mem. N.C. Bar Assn. Home: Mt. Airy, N C. Deceased.

FOLLAND, William Henry (fōl'land), lawyer; b. Salt Lake City, Utah, Dec. 5, 1877; s. Eli A. and Rachel A. (Lewis) F.; ed. Latter Day Saints Coll., 1897-98; U. of Utah, 1909; m. Grace Freeze, Nov. 6, 1903; children—Harold Freeze, Donald Freeze, Edward Freeze. Formerly official court reporter, 3d Dist. Court, Utah; admitted to Utah bar, 1910, and practiced at Salt Lake City as mem. Evans, Evans & Folland; asst. city atty., Salt Lake City, 1913-17, city atty., 1917-28; became asso. justice Supreme Court of Utah, 1929, chief justice, 1937-38; now practicing law Salt Lake City. Mem. Am. Bar Assn. Chmn. Am. Red Cross, Salt Lake County, 1926-30; dir. Community Chest; mem. Conf. of Commrs. of Uniform State Laws, 1915-28. Mem. Am. Law Inst., Univ. of Utah Law Alumni, Sigma Chi. Phi Alpha Delta. Republican. Mormon. Home: 1471 Michigan Av. Office: Utah Oil Bldg., Salt Lake City, Utah. Died June 4, 1941.

FOLSOM, Alfred Iverson (fōl'sŭm), physician and surgeon; b. McGregor, Tex., May 9, 1883; s. Dr. Alfred Iverson and Mary Frances (Powell) F.; A.B., Southwestern U., Georgetown, Tex., 1904; M.D., Southwestern Med. Coll., Dallas, Tex., 1908; m. Ann Rebecca Hodge, Sept. 29, 1909 (died Jan. 12, 1938); children—Frances Davidella (Mrs. George Crofford), Ann Rebecca (Mrs. Joseph O. Neuhoff), Alfred Iverson; m. 2d, Mrs. Erma (Hewitt) Matthews, Mar. 26, 1939. Practiced as physician, Alba, Tex., 1908-09; asst. to Drs. R. W. Baird and E. J. Reeves, Dallas, Tex., 1909-12; did post grad. work, Mayo Brothers, Rochester, Minn., 1912; specializing in urology, Dallas, Tex., since 1912; asso. prof. urology, Baylor U. Med. Coll., Dallas, Tex., 1921-23, prof., 1923-43; prof. urology Southwestern Med. Coll., since 1943; chief of urol. dept., Parkland Hosp., Dallas, since 1923. Hon. prof. urology U. of Guadalajara, Guadalajara, Jalisco, Mexico. Mem. Tex. Surg. Soc. (pres. 1937), Dallas County Med. Assn., Tex. State and Am. med. assns., Dallas Southern Clin. Soc., South Central (past pres.) and Am. (pres.-elect 1945) urol. assns., Kappa Alpha. Club: Dallas Country. Author numerous articles in med. jours. Home: 8211 Inwood Road 9. Office: Medical Arts Bldg., Dallas, Tex. Died Oct. 3, 1946.

FOLWELL, William Hazelton, textile mfr.; b. Phila., Pa., Dec. 5, 1876; s. William H. and Mary R. (Pearsol) F.; student University of Pennsylvania, 1895, Ecole Nationale des Arts Industrielles, Roubaix, France, 1896, Bradford Technical College, England, 1897-98; m. Miriam E. Neff, March 30, 1904; children—Miriam, Elizabeth. Began as apprentice in textile mill; vice-president Folwell Brothers & Company, 1900-30, pres. since 1930. Pres. Mfrs. Assn. Casualty Ins. Co., Pa. Mfrs. Assn. Fire Ins. Co.; dir. Fidelity Mutual Ins. Co., Girard Life Ins. Co. Dir. Industrial Trust Co. Spl. Dep. Alien Property Custodian, World War. Republican. Theosophist. Club: Union League (Philadelphia). Home: The Kenilworth Apartments, Germantown, Phila., Pa. Office: 250 W. Cambria St., Philadelphia, Pa. Died Nov. 12, 1945.

FONDE, George H(eustis) (fŏn-dā'), physician; b. Mobile, Ala., May 12, 1873; s. Charles H. and Lydia (Wragg) F.; M.D., Univ. of Alabama, 1897; post-graduate study Chicago Polyclinic, 1899; married Mary Crawford, Jan. 10, 1902; children—Comdr. Georg. Heustis, U.S.N.R., Major Edgar C. (M.C., U.S.A., killed in action, Germany, Apr. 1, 1945), Robert Maiben (dec.), Capt. William Gorgas, Mary C. Intern, Mobile City Hospital, 1897-98; general practice, Mobile since 1899; in charge yellow fever camp, Mobile, 1898; acting asst. surgeon, 1st lt., Med. Corps, U.S. Army, detached, spl. yellow fever service, Spanish-Am. War. Mem. A.M.A., Ala. State Med. Soc., Mobile County Med. Soc.; charter mem. League of Nations Assn. Democrat. Episcopalian. Home: 151 Chatham St., Mobile 20. Office: Annex 1st National Bank Bldg., Mobile 13, Ala.

Died Sep. 3, 1947.

FOOTE, Harry Ward, chemist; b. Guilford, Conn., Mar. 21, 1875; s. Christopher Spencer and Hannah Jane (Hubbard) F.; Ph.B., Yale, 1895, Ph.D., 1898; studied in Leipsic and Munich, 1899-1900; m. Martha Babcock Jenkins, June 22, 1904; children—William Jenkins, Mary, Margaret Spencer. Instr. in chemistry, Sheffield Scientific Sch., Yale, 1898-1904, asst. prof., 1904-12, prof. physical chemistry since 1912. Fellow Royal Geog. Soc., mem. Conn. Acad. Science, Am. Chem. Soc. Episcopalian. Address: 209 Livingston St., New Haven, Conn. Died Jan. 14, 1942.

FOOTE, John Taintor, author, playwright; b. Leadville, Colo., Mar. 29, 1881; s. George Ward and Margaret Gilson (Moore) F.; ed. Kenyon Mil. Acad., Gambier, O.; m. Jessie Florence Todhunter, Aug. 3, 1920; children—John Taintor, Timothy. Author: Blister Jones, 1913; The Look of Eagles, 1916; Dumbbell of Brookfield, 1917; The Lucky Seven, 1918; The Song of the Dragon, 1923; Toby's Bow (comedy), prod. New York, 1919; (with John Golden) Flying Colors (comedy), 1920; The Song of the Dragon (play); A Wedding Gift, 1925; Pocono Shot, 1925; The Number One Boy, 1926; Trub's Diary, 1928; Fatal Gesture, 1933; Tight Britches (tragedy—with H. Hayes), 1934; Full Personality, 1935; Change of Idols, 1935; Daughter of Delilah, 1936; Julie the Great, drama, prod., 1936; Jing (limited edition), 1936; Hell Cat, 1936; Broadway Angler, 1937; Sporting Days, 1937. Mem. Soc. of the Cincinnati in the State of Va. Clubs: Honga River Gun, Brooklyn Fly Fishers; Newport Harbor Yacht; Los Angeles Yacht. Home: Beaverkill, N.Y.* Died Jan. 29, 1950.

FOOTE, Nathaniel, jurist, b. Morrisville, N.Y., Nov. 15, 1849; s. Nathaniel and Olivia M. (Knox) F.; A.B., Hamilton Coll., 1870, A.M., LL.D., 1907; LL.D., Rochester U. and Hobart Coll.; m. Charlotte A. Campbell, Jan. 10, 1872; children—Nathaniel Frederick, Franc Estelle (Mrs. Charles N. Perrin), Louise Knox (Mrs. John C. Jessup), Charlotte Campbell (Mrs. Jerome B. Chase), Olive Jeannette (Mrs. Edmund H. Barry). Practiced law at Morrisville, N.Y., 1871-73, at Rochester, N.Y., 1873-1905; apptd., 1905, and elected Nov. 1905, justice Supreme Court of N.Y., for term 1906-20; asso. justice Appellate Div., 4th Dept., Jan. 1, 1912-Dec. 1919; retired upon reaching constl. age of 70 yrs. Official referee since Jan. 6, 1920. Republican. Del. N.Y. Constl. Conv., 1894. Mem. Am. Judicature Soc., Am. Bar Assn., N.Y. State Bar Assn., Rochester Bar Assn. (1st pres., 1892-94), Delta Kappa Epsilon. Episcopalian. Clubs: Genesee Valley, Rochester Country. Home: 112 Brunswick St. Office: 800 Powers Bldg., Rochester, N.Y. Died Jan. 26, 1944.

FOOTNER, Hulbert, author; b. Hamilton, Can., Apr. 2, 1879; s. Harold John and Frances Christine (Mills) F.; ed. evening high sch., New York; m. 1916, Gladys, d. Dr. W. H. Marsh; children—Mary Ann, Phoebe, Jane, Geoffrey. In newspaper work, New York, 1905, Calgary, Alberta, Can., 1906. Author: Two on the Trail, 1911; New Rivers of the North, 1912; Jack Chanty, 1913; The Sealed Valley, 1914; The Fur Bringers, 1917; The Huntress, 1917; The Fugitive Sleuth; Thieves' Wit, 1918; The Substitute Millionaire, 1919; The Owl Taxi, 1921; Country Love, 1922; The Deaves Affair, 1922; Ramshackle House, 1923; Officer!, 1924; The Wild Bird, 1925; The Under-Dogs, 1925; Antennae, 1926; Queen of Clubs, 1927; Cap'n Sue, 1928; The Doctor Who Held Hands, 1929; The Mystery of the Folded Paper, 1930; Easy to Kill, 1931; Dead Man's Hat, 1932; The Ring of Eyes, 1933; Dangerous Cargo, 1934; Scarred Jungle, 1935; The Murder of a Bad Man, 1936; Dark Ships, 1937; New York—City of Cities, 1937; More Than Bread, 1938; Charles' Gift, 1939; Sailor of Fortune: the Life and Adventures of Commodore Joshua Barney, 1940; Maryland Main and the Eastern Shore, 1942; The House with the Blue Door, 1942; The Death of a Saboteur, 1943; Rivers on the Eastern Shore, 1944; also Shirley Kaye, comedy, prod. Hudson Theatre, New York, Dec. 25, 1916. Contbr. stories to mags. Home: Charles' Gift, Lusby, Md. Died Nov. 25, 1944.

FORAKER, Forest Almos, prof. of mathematics; b. Sharon, O., Dec. 26, 1881; B.S. Ohio Northern Univ., 1904, M.S., 1905; Sc.D. U. of Pittsburgh, 1942; student U. of Chicago, 1907; Columbia, 1911. Taught sci. and math. Fairmount (Ind.) Acad., 1904-08; math. Bradley Polytechnic Inst., 1908-12; U. of Pittsburgh since 1912. Mem. Am. Math. Soc., Am. Math. Assn., Am. Assn. for Advancement of Scis., Am. Assn. Univ. Profs., Sigma Xi. Home: 1313 Macon Av. Office: Univ. of Pittsburgh, Pittsburgh. Died June 30, 1949.

FORBES, Allyn Bailey, librarian, editor; born Taunton, Mass., Nov. 2, 1897; s. Harrie Wilson and Bertha (Wilbur) F.; A.B., Amherst Coll., 1919; A.M., Harvard, 1927; m. Lois Whitney Perry, June 15, 1938. Instr. in history, Deerfield Acad., 1920-25, Harvard, 1928-31; editor Colonial Soc. of Mass. since 1931; librarian Mass. Hist. Soc., 1934-40, dir. since 1940. Fellow Am. Acad. Arts and Sciences; mem. Mass. Hist. Soc., Colonial Soc. of Mass., Am. Antiquarian Soc. Episcopalian. Clubs: Harvard, Odd Volumes (Boston). Home: 11 Fayerweather St., Cambridge, Mass. Office: 1154 Boylston St., Boston, Mass. Died Jan. 21, 1947.

FORCE, Juliana, fine arts; b. Doylestown, Bucks County, Pa.; ed. private schools and abroad; m. Dr. Willard Burdette Force (dec.). Dir. Whitney Museum of American Art since its inception in 1931; chmn. of Am. Art Research Council, organized in Apr. 1942. Vice pres., trustee Am. Fedn. of Arts. Mem. Am. Assn. Mus., Museums Council N.Y. City, Architectural League of N.Y., Nat. Audubon Soc., Art Advisory Com. of Girl Scouts Inc., The Municipal Art Soc., Am. Defense Soc., N.Y. Zool. Soc. Clubs: Cosmopolitan, Women's City of N.Y. Home: 825 Fifth Av. Office: 10 W. 8th St., New York 11, N.Y. Died Aug. 28, 1948.

FORD, Alexander Hume; b. Florence, S.C., Apr. 3, 1868; s. Frederick Winthrop and Mary Mazyc (Hume) F.; father a rice planter and owner of a thousand slaves at outbreak of Civil War; ed. high sch. and acad. Began as reporter Charleston News and Courier, 1885, later with New York and Chicago dailies and editor monthly mags.; made 1st tour of world, 1899, and settled in Honolulu, 1907; pub. Mid-Pacific Mag.; retired; dir. gen. Pan Pacific Union. Clubs: Cosmos (Washington); Japan Soc., China Soc., Pan Am. Soc. (New York); Outrigger Canoe (Honolulu); America Japan (Tokyo); Pan Pacific (Shanghai); Millions (Sydney); New Zealand (Wellington). Home: Honolulu, T.H. Died Oct. 14, 1945.

FORD, Edsel Bryant, automobile mfr.; b. Detroit, Mich., Nov. 6, 1893; s. Henry and Clara J. (Bryant) F.; ed. Detroit Univ. Sch. (coll. prep.); m. Eleanor Clay, Nov. 1, 1916; children—Henry II, Benson, Josephine Clay, William Clay. Identified with father in mfr. of automobiles from beginning of active career; later pres. and treas. Ford Motor Co. Pres. Arts Commn. of Detroit Inst. of Arts. Clubs: Detroit, Country, Grosse Pointe, Grosse Pointe Hunt; New York Yacht. Home: 1100 Lake Shore Rd., Grosse Pointe Shores, Mich. Office: Ford Motor Co., Dearborn, Mich. Died May 26, 1943; buried in Woodlawn Cemetery, Detroit.

FORD, Ford Madox, writer. Author: New York Is Not America, 1927; New York Essays, 1927; Some Do Not, 1928; Man Could Stand Up, 1928; Little Less Than Gods, 1928; Last Post, 1928; No Enemy, A Tale of Reconstruction, 1929; Mirror to France, 1929; English Novel, From the Earliest Days to the Death of Joseph Conrad, 1929; When the Wicked Man, 1931; Ladies Whose Bright Eyes, 1931; Return to Yesterday, 1932; Rash Act, 1933; It Was the Nightingale, 1933; Henry for Hugh, 1934; Provence, From Minstrels to Machine, 1935; Vive Le Roy, 1936; Collected Poems, 1936; Portraits from Life, 1937; Great Trade Route, 1937; March of Literature, From Confucius' Day to Our Own, 1938. Address: Paris, France.* Died June 27, 1939.

FORD, Henry, automobile manufacturer; b. Dearborn Township, Wayne County, Mich., July 30, 1863; s. William and Mary (Litogot) F.; ed. in dist. sch., Dearborn, Mich., D.Eng., U. of Mich., 1926; LL.D., Colgate U., 1935; m. Clara J. Bryant, Apr. 11, 1888; 1 son, Edsel Bryant. Learned machinist's trade; in Detroit since 1887; was chief engr. Edison Illuminating Co.; organizer, 1903, pres. many yrs. Ford Motor Co. (largest mfr. of automobiles in the world, employing over 100,000 persons). Announced, 1914, plan of profit-sharing involving distribution of ten to thirty millions of dollars annually to employees. Mem. Soc. Automotive Engrs., Detroit Board of Commerce. Clubs: Detroit, Detroit Athletic, Country, Detroit Boat, Automobile of America. Chartered ship, and at own expense conducted party to Europe, leaving New York, Dec. 4, 1915, with object of organizing a conf. of peace advocates to influence belligerent govts. to end the war; returned home after reaching Christiania, Norway, but members of the party proceeded to Stockholm, Sweden, and Copenhagen, Denmark, and through Germany to The Hague. Built Henry Ford Hosp. at cost of $7,500,000. Apptd. by Pres. Wilson mem. Wage Umpire Bd., July 13, 1918; Dem. candidate for U.S. Senate against Truman H. Newberry, 1918. Author: My Life and Work, 1925; Today and Tomorrow, 1926; Moving Forward, 1931. Home: Dearborn, Mich.* Died Apr. 7, 1947.

FORD, Henry Clinton, educator; b. Charlotte County, Va., Dec. 12, 1867; s. Luther Rice and Pernette (Smith) F.; student Va. Poly. Inst., Blacksburg, 1884-85; B.S., Va. Mil. Inst., Lexington, 1889; Ph.D., U. of Va., 1899; m. Agnes Palmer, Jan. 10, 1900 (died Sept. 9, 1902); children—Thomas Lewis (dec.), Mary Lewis; m. 2d, Elizabeth Walker, July 12, 1905; children—Virginia Easton, Henry Clinton, Medora Beall. Instr. in French, English and tactics, Va. Mil. Inst., 1889-90; comdt. cadets and instr., Wentworth Mil. Acad., Lexington, Mo., 1890-93; asst. prof. modern langs. and tactics, Va. Mil. Inst., 1895-96; master St. Albans' Sch., Radford, Va., 1896-98; adj. prof. Latin, English and history, Va. Mil. Inst., 1892-1902, comdt. of cadets, 1901-03, prof. Latin, English and history, 1902-10, prof. history since 1919. Mem. Va. State Bd. of Edn., 1911-23, 1927-30; mem. Town Council, Lexington, 1913-19. Col. and chief of engrs., staff of Gov. James Hoge Tyler, 1898-1902. Del. to Dem. Congressional Conv., Va., 1890; Dem. Gubernatorial Conv., 1897; Dem. State Conv., 1916; Dem. Nat. Conv., 1916. Mem. Va. Social Science Assn., Assn. Am. Univ. Profs., Phi Beta Kappa, Kappa Alpha, Pi Gamma Mu, Raven, Tilka (U. of Va.). Episcopalian. Contbr. to Library of Southern Lit. Home: Lexington, Va. Died Sept. 1, 1936.

FORD, James, sociologist, author; b. Clinton, Mass., Oct. 1, 1884; s. Andrew Elmer and Ellen Louise (Burdett) F.; A.B., Harvard, 1905, A.M., 1906; grad. work Coll. Libre des Sciences Sociales, France, 1906-07, U. of Berlin, 1907; Ph.D., Harvard, 1909; m. Marian Willard Tyler, Sept. 4, 1909; children—Margaret (Mrs. Edward Lownes Francis), Caroline (Mrs. Edward Mason Read III), James Andrew; m. 2d, Katherine Morrow, Feb. 21, 1936; 1 daughter, Margaret Morrow. Inst. in social ethics, Harvard U., 1909-13; asst. prof., 1913-21; asso. prof. since 1921. Dir. Internat. Housing Assn. Pres. and trustee Prospect Union Ednl. Exchange. Mgr. Homes Registration and Information Div., U.S. Housing Corp., 1918-19; asso. dir. President's Conf. on Home Bldg. and Home Ownership, 1930-33; mem. exec. com. of the com. on hygiene of housing Am. Pub. Health Assn. (chairman sub. committee on standards of occupancy); consultant to U.S. Defense Housing Co-ordinator, 1940-42; consultant Nat. Housing Agency since 1942. Fellow A.A.A.S. (sec. sect. K., social and econ. sciences), Am. Acad. of Arts and Sciences. Editor: Social Problems and Social Policy, 1923; Report of President's Conf. on Home Bldg. and Ownership (with John M. Gries), 1932-33. Author: Slums and Housing (with Katherine Morrow and George N. Thompson), 1936; The Abolition of Poverty (with Katherine Morrow Ford), 1937; Social Deviation, 1939; the Modern House in America (with Katherine Morrow Ford), 1940; Design of Modern Interiors (with Katherine Morrow Ford), 1942. Home: Woods End Rd., Lincoln, Mass. Office: Harvard University, Cambridge, Mass. Died May 11, 1944.

FORD, James Buchanan, ry. official; b. Raleigh, N.C., July 18, 1879; s. Rufus Jones and Arkans S. (Mullin) F.; student N.C., Coll. Agr. Mechanical Arts, Raleigh, North Carolina, 1896-98; m. Lurline Walsh, Apr. 18, 1917; children—James Buchanan, Richard Alexander. Began as corr. clk., div. freight office, Raleigh, N.C., Southern Ry. Co., 1898; held various positions with same company and was made chief clk. and office asst., to freight traffic mgr., at Louisville, Ky., 1906; apptd. chief clk. to v.p. same co. and Queen & Crescent Route, Cincinnati, 1910; asst. gen. freight agt., at Cincinnati, 1912, and gen. freight agt. Southern Ry. System, 1917; chmn. Com. of Freight Traffic Control, Ohio River Gateways, under U.S.R.R. Administration, World War; freight traffic mgr. Erie R.R. Co., at Chicago, 1920-25; and at New York, Jan.-Aug. 1925; v.p. C.&E.I. Ry. since Aug. 1, 1925. Baptist. Clubs: Traffic (Detroit); Traffic (New York); Traffic, Union League (Chicago); Transportation Club of Louisville (hon.). Home: 5460 Cornell Av. Office: McCormick Bldg., 332 S. Michigan Av., Chicago, Ill.* Died Apr. 22, 1947.

FORD, John Battice, corp. official; b. New Albany, Ind., Oct. 25, 1866; s. Edward and Mittie (Penn) F.; ed. Western U. of Pa., Pittsburgh and Harvard U.; special course in law sch., 1888; m. Helen Sloane, 1895; children—John B., Jr., Frederick Sloane. Began career as treas. Pittsburgh Plate Glass Co.; moved to Detroit and founded Mich. Alkali Co., 1893; now pres. same; also pres. Huron Portland Cement Co., Huron Transportation Co.; dir. Parke, Davis & Co., Libby-Owens-Ford Glass Co., etc. Trustee and donor of Ford Memorial Chapel, Allegheny Coll. Home: 91 Touraine Rd., Grosse Pointe Farms. Office: 1622 Ford Bldg., Detroit. Died Oct. 8, 1941.

FORD, Shirley Samuel, banker; b. Sun River, Mont., Mar. 9, 1887; s. Robert Simpson and Sue (McClanahan) F.; student St. Paul's Sch., Concord, N.H., 1899-1904; A.B., Harvard, 1909; m. Elizabeth Floweree Wallace, Aug. 25, 1915; 1 dau., Shirley Gertrude (Mrs. Robert Faegre). Began as bank clerk, 1909; v.p. Great Falls (Mont.) Nat. Bank, 1913-30; v.p. U.S. Nat. Bank of Omaha, Neb., 1930-34; v.p. Northwest Bancorporation, Minneapolis, 1934-39, dir. since 1939; pres. Northwestern Nat. Bank of Minneapolis since 1939; trustee Equitable Life Ins. Co. of Ia. Trustee Minneapolis Foundation; dir. General Mills, Inc., Minn. & Ontario Paper Co., Fed. Reserve Bank of Minneapolis. Dir. Assn. of Reserve City Bankers. Democrat. Episcopalian. Clubs: Minneapolis, Woodhill, Minikahda. Home: Route 3, Wayzata, Minn. Office: Northwestern Nat. Bank, Minneapolis. Died June 25, 1945; buried at Sun River, Mont.

FORDYCE, Samuel Wesley, lawyer; b. Hot Springs, Ark., Aug. 11, 1877; s. Samuel Wesley and Susan Elizabeth (Chadick) F.; A.B., Harvard, 1898; LL.B., St. Louis Law Sch. (Washington Univ.), 1901; LL.D., Missouri Valley College, 1923; m. Harriet Frost, Dec. 18, 1900. Practiced in St. Louis since 1901; mem. Fordyce & Polk, 1903-05, Fordyce, Holliday & White, 1908-31, Fordyce, White, Mayne & Williams, 1932-37, Fordyce, White, Mayne, Williams & Hartman since Jan. 1, 1937; counsel War Finance Corp., May 23, 1918-March 1, 1919; director American Zinc, Lead & Smelting Company, St. Louis Union Trust Co., Coca-Cola Bottling Co., Houston Oil Co., Met. Life Ins. Co., Lambert Pharmacal Co., Municipal Theatres Assn., Ex-chmn. Dem. State Com. of Mo. Mem. American, Mo. State and St. Louis bar assns., Bar Assn City of New York. Clubs: Racquet, Log Cabin (St. Louis); The Links (New York). Home: Berkeley, St. Louis County, Mo. Office: 506 Olive St., St. Louis, Mo. Died Jan. 9, 1948.

FORREST, Nathan Bedford, army officer; b. Memphis, Tenn., Apr. 7, 1905; s. Nathan Bedford and Mattie Patterson (Patton) F.; student Ga. Tech., 1923-24; A.B., U.S. Mil. Acad., 1928; m. Frances Bassler, Nov. 22, 1930. Commd. 2d lt., U.S. Army, 1928, and advanced through the grades to brig. gen., Nov., 1942; became chief of staff, Second Air Force. Reported missing in action while on plane bombing Kiel, Germany, June 1943. Home: 115 W. 9th St., Spokane, Wash. Died June 4, 1944.

FORRESTAL, James, sec. of defense; b. Beacon, N.Y., Feb. 15, 1892; s. James and Mary A. (Toohey) F.; student Dartmouth Coll., 1911-12, Princeton U., 1912-15; LL.D. (hon.), Princeton, 1944, Williams Coll., 1946; m. Josephine Ogden, Oct. 12, 1926; children—Michael, Peter. With New Jersey Zinc Co., Tobacco Products Corp., N.Y. City, 1915-16; with Dillon, Read & Co., 1916-40, pres., 1937-40; administrv. asst. to President of U.S., June-Aug. 1940; under secretary of navy, 1944-47; sec. of defense, Sept. 17, 1947-Mar. 28, 1949. Served as lt., U.S. Naval Reserve Force, 1917-19. Democrat. Home: 3508 Prospect Av. N.W. Office: The Pentagon, Washington. Died May 22, 1949; buried in Arlington National Cemetery, Washington.

FORRESTER, Graham, editor; b. White Plains, Ga., May 4, 1870; s. Redmond Vincent and Martha (Holtzclaw) F.; ed. at home and pvt. schs.; m. Leonede Tharpe, Dec. 24, 1890 (died May 11, 1926); children—Tharpe, Redmond Vincent, Richard, Julia (Mrs. John Ryle Lawson), Christine. Admitted to Ga. bar, 1893; practiced at Buena Vista; solicitor gen., Stewart County Court, 1895-99, 1902-07; ordained ministry Bapt. Ch., 1907; pastor in Ga. and S.C. until 1924; asso. editor Tampa Daily Times, 1924-33. Alternate Dem. presdl. elector, Ga., 1904; served as mem. Ga. State Dem. Exec. Com. and Dem. Congl. Com., 3d Ga. Dist. Mem. Mission Bd. Ga. Bapt. Conv. 5 terms; v.p. Ga. Bapt. Conv. 3 terms; moderator Western Assn., Baptists, 2 terms; mem. exec. com. Valdosta (clk.), Columbus, Western, Reheboth (chmn.) and Broad River (chmn.) assns. Trustee Ga. State Tuberculosis Sanitarium; dir. Tampa Municipal Hosp., 1928-31. Home: 2406 Prospect Rd., Tampa 6, Fla. Died Aug. 19, 1948.

FORSTALL, Armand William, coll. prof.; b. Chaumont, France, July 5, 1859; s. Eugene Forstall and Armande (Carette) F.; ed. Jesuit College, Dole-Jura, France, 1870-72, Amiens, Somme, 1872-78; B.A., U. of Douai (North), 1877; student St. Stanislaus Coll., Paris, 1878-79, Tronchiennes (Belgium) Sem., 1880-82, Jesuit Sem., Louvain, 1882-85; A.M., Woodstock (Maryland) College, 1894; student Angers Seminary, Angers (Maine et Loire), France, 1894-95; D.Sc., U. of Denver, 1935. Came to U.S., 1885. Ordained to ministry R.C. Ch., 1892; instr. mathematics, Coll. of Sacred Heart, Morrison, Colo., 1885-86, instr. in physics, chemistry, mathematics, Las Vegas (N.M.) Coll., 1886-88, Regis Coll., Denver, 1888-90, and 1898-99; instr. physics, Georgetown U., 1895-96 and 1900-02, Holy Cross Coll., Worcester, Mass., 1899-1900; prof. of chemistry, Woodstock Coll., Md., 1902-04; prof. of mathematics, physics, chemistry, Regis Coll., 1904-25, prof. of physics and chemistry, 1904-23, prof. of physics and engring. drawing, 1904-31, prof. engring. drawing, 1923-32, also head of dept., 1923-32, prof. of analytic chemistry since 1932, and dir. Seismic Station, 1909-34. Mem. Seismol. Soc. of America, Jesuit Seismol. Assn., Soc. for Research on Meteorites. Has written many reports on mining resources of Colo., especially uranium, molybdenum and tungsten; also publs. of Observatory—U.S. Weather Review to 1921, U.S. Geodetic Survey Publications, 1922-26; publs. of St. Louis Univ. on Geophysics, etc. Address: Regis College, Denver. Died Apr. 21, 1948; buried in Regis College Cemetery, Denver.

FORSTER, Frank Joseph, architect; b. New York, N.Y., Dec. 12, 1886; s. William and Margaret (Black) F.; ed. Cooper Union, New York, 1903-08, archtl. study in Europe, 1908, Art Students League, New York, 1912; m. Mary Viola Tackleson, May 4, 1925. Archtl. draftsman, 1908-09; in partnership with Edward King, 1910; practice in own name since 1911; a winner in competition for design of N.Y. City Slum Clearance projects; apptd. architect for Harlem Houses project. Served with 7th Regt., New York Militia, 1917; private, Officers Training Sch., Va., 1918. Awarded Archtl. League medal for domestic architecture, 1927, 1929; Archtl. League honorable mention, 1928; Better Homes in America medal, 1933. Fellow A.I.A.; mem. Archtl. League of New York. Author: Country Houses, The Work of Frank J. Forster, 1931. Contbr. articles to archtl. jours. Home: Killingworth, Deep River, Conn. Died Mar. 4, 1948.

FORT, Rufus Elijah, surgeon; b. Fort Station, Robertson Co., Tenn., Mar. 19, 1872; s. Col. Edmund Augustus and Julia (Garth) F.; academic dept. U. of the South, 1887-89; M.D., Vanderbilt, 1894; hon. D.Sc., U. of South, 1936; m. Louise Clark, Oct. 12, 1909; children—Rufus E., Dudley Clark, Garth Edmund, Cornelia Clark, Louise Clark. Supt. and chief surgeon Nashville Hosp., 1897-1903; chief surgeon Tenn. Central R.R., 1902-16, Fort's Pvt. Hosp., 1904-20; visiting surgeon, chmn. exec. com. Nashville Protestant Hosp.; visiting gynecologist and abdominal surgeon, Nashville Gen. Hosp.; v.p. and med. dir. Nat. Life and Accident Ins. Co. Trustee Cumberland U. Fellow Am. Coll. Surgeons (bd. govs.); mem. A.M.A., Davidson County Med. Soc., Southern Surg. and Gynecol. Assn., Assn. Am. Med. Dirs., Sigma Nu. Democrat. Clubs: Hermitage (pres.), Belle Meade Country. Home: Riverside Blvd. Office: 303 7th Av. N., Nashville, Tenn. Died 1940.

FOSTER, Alexis Caldwell, banker; b. Nashville, Tenn., July 25, 1867; s. Turner Saunders and Harriet (Erwin) F.; ed. Montgomery Bell Acad., Nashville, Tenn.; m. Alice Eddy Fisher, Oct. 28, 1898; children—Lucius Fisher, Turner S. (dec.), Katharine Louise Baroness Walram von Schoeler), Cynthia Bethell (Mrs. Paul Wolf). Settled in Denver, Colo., 1890; bookkeeper, later receiver, Denver Hardware & Mfg. Co.; became credit man Daniels & Fisher Stores Co. 1898, later dir.; made cashier, 1904, of Daniels Bank, nucleus for U.S. Nat. Bank, of which was cashier, later v.p.; in bond business as mem. Sweet, Causey, Foster & Co., 1912-20; elected, 1920, pres. Bankers Trust Co., consolidated, 1923, with U.S. Nat. Bank; now partner Calvin Bullock, N.Y. City. Republican. Club: Knollwood Country. Home: 8 Brooklands, Bronxville. Office: 1 Wall St., New York. Died Apr. 30, 1945; buried at Denver.

FOSTER, Charles Kendall, dir. Am. Radiator & Standard Sanitary Corp.; b. Detroit, Mich., Oct. 19, 1867; s. Fred S. and Adelaide V. (Grose) F.; ed. high sch., Detroit, and St. Johnsbury (Vt.) Acad.; m. Janet May Brien, Apr. 26, 1905. Began with Am. Radiator Co. (now Am. Radiator and Standard Sanitary Corp.) at its formation, 1892, successively asst. sec., mgr. sales, v.p. in charge sales and v.p. and treas., exec. v.p., now dir.; dir. 1st Nat. Bank, Chicago, American Steel Foundries. Vice-chairman priorities com., War Industries Bd., Washington, 1918. Clubs: Chicago, Commercial, Casino, Old Elm, Shoreacres. Home: 1260 Astor St., Chicago, Died July 28, 1945.

FOSTER, Edna (Abigail), author; b. Sullivan Harbor, Me.; d. Charles W. (architect) and Sarah J. (Dyer) Foster; grad. Lowell (Mass.) High Sch.; pupil Berlitz Sch. of Languages; unmarried. Contbr. to jours. and mags., since 1893; asst. editor, The Household, 1895-1900, editor, 1900; apptd. asso. editor Youth's Companion, 1900; contbr. to Presbyterian Bd. of Christian Edn. (Phila.), 1923; advt. copy writer since 1927; became editorial writer for Nat. Magazine, 1928. Author: Hortense, a Difficult Child, 1902; Cordelia's Pathway Out, 1905; Barbara's Bridge, 1917. Editor: Something-To-Do Boys, 1916; Something-To-Do Girls, 1916. Home: 19 Chester St., Allston, Mass. Died July 11, 1945.

FOSTER, George Sanford, surgeon; b. at Barrington, N.H., Apr. 20, 1882; s. George Sanford and Etta Frances (Moulton) F.; student Harvard Summer Sch. of Physical Edn., 1900, Harvard Summer Sch. of Obstetrics, 1905; M.D., cum laude, Tufts Coll. Med. Sch., 1906 (pres. of class); post grad. study in Europe; m. Elizabeth Russell Danforth, Dec. 27, 1905; children—Clayton Reginald, Virginia Frances, George Sanford, Jr., Russell Danforth. Athletic dir. various high schs. and Y.M.C.A.'s for several years; interne Children's Hosp., Boston, Boston City Hosp., Sacred Heart Hosp., Manchester, N.H., 1905-07; began practice at Manchester, Feb. 1, 1907; surgeon and pathologist to Notre Dame Hosp., Manchester, N.H., 1907-25; surgeon Lucy Hastings Hosp., Manchester, 1925-38; cons. surgeon Peterboro (N.H.) Hosp. Trustee Manchester Boys' Club (pres. 12 yrs.). Founded clin. lab. and training school for nurses, Notre Dame Hosp., Manchester; founded Lucy Hastings Hosp., also training schools for nurses and technicians and cancer research lab. at same, Manchester. Served as capt. Med. Corps, U.S. Army, during World War I. Now serving as lt. comdr., Med. Corps, U.S.N.R. Fellow Internat. Coll. Surgeons (Geneva). Mem. N.H. Surg. Club, Manchester Med. Soc. (past pres.), Hillsboro County Med. Soc., N.H. Med. Soc., Am. Med. Assn., Am. Assn. for Study of Neoplastic Diseases (founder Northern New England Assn.), Am. Med. Editors and Authors Assn., Wild Life Soc., Am. Forestry Assn., Nat. Assn. Audubon Socs., Mass. Audubon Soc., Northern New England Bird Banding Assn. (treas.), Fed. Boys' Clubs of Am. (exec. com. New Eng. div.), Clin. Congress Surgeons of N. America (rep. from N.H., 1908-11; sen. from N.H., 1911-14), Manchester Hist. Assn., N.H. Hist. Soc., N.H. S.A.R., Manchester Inst. Arts and Sciences, Phi Chi (ex-pres. Delta Chapter), Mil. Order of the World War, Mil. Order of Foreign Wars, Assn. Mil. Surgeons of U.S., Am. Legion, Res. Officers Assn. of U.S. Army, Eugene Field Soc. (hon.). Mason. Odd Fellow. Clubs: Manchester Country, Y.M.C.A. (Manchester); University (Boston); Army and Navy (Washington). Author: Post Operative Treatment; Qualifications of a Model Nurse; Health Day by Day; Health; Art of Living; Birds and Bird Clubs; They Know Not; Why I Believe in God and Immortality; Trapping the Common Cold; Our Youth (Helping Them to Help Themselves); also numerous monographs, brochures and articles on med. subjects, etc. Home: Manchester, N.H. Died Aug. 13, 1945.

FOSTER, Henry Hubbard, lawyer, educator; b. Buffalo, N.Y., Dec. 3, 1876; s. Hubbard A. (M.D.) and Florence A. (Jenkins) F.; A.B., Cornell U., 1899; LL.B., Harvard, 1908; m. Emma B. Adams, Dec. 29, 1910; children—Henry H., Margaret Adams, Virginia Beatrice. Admitted to Ill. bar, 1908, and practiced at Peoria until 1910; prof. law, U. of Okla., 1910-20; prof. law, U. of Neb., since 1920, dean of Coll. Law since 1926. Mem. Am. and Neb. State bar assns., Sigma Xi, Phi Delta Phi, Alpha Tau Omega. Conglist. Mason. Contbr. articles on real property law to law periodicals. Annotator for Nebraska, Restatement of Trust Law; editor Nebraska Law Review. Home: 1821 Pershing Rd. S., Lincoln, Neb. Died Feb. 1947.

FOSTER, Herbert Hamilton, prof. education; b. Huron, N.Y., Feb. 13, 1875; s. Owen and Emeline (Hibbard) F.; Ph.B., Cornell U., 1900, post-grad. work, 1904-06; post-grad. work U. of Jena, 1906-07, Ph.D., 1907; Teachers Coll. (Columbia), 1914-15; m. Florence Robinson, Jan. 2, 1912. Pub. sch. teacher and adminstr., 1892-96; supt. schs., Smethport, Pa., 1900-04; prof. edn. Ottawa (Kan.) U., 1907-15; same, U. of Ariz., also head of dept., 1915-20; prof. edn., U. of Colo., various summers; dir. Summer Sch., U. of Ariz., 1918-20; head of dept. of edn., U. of Vt., 1920-21; prof. secondary edn., Summer Sch., U. of Pa., 1922-26, and 1932-40, U. of Ill., 1927, 29, 30, U. of Tenn., 1931; head of dept. of education, Beloit College, since 1923. Mem. N.E.A., National Soc. Coll. Teachers of Edn., Am. Assn. Univ. Profs., Nat. Assn. Secondary Sch. Principals, Rock River Schoolmasters Club (pres.), Phi Delta Kappa, Pi Gamma Mu. Republican. Episcopalian. Rotarian. Author: Principles of Teaching in Secondary Education, 1921; High School Administration, 1928; High School Supervision, 1939. Home: 1408 Emerson St., Beloit, Wis. Died Dec. 1, 1942.

FOSTER, John Shaw, clergyman; b. Mobile, Ala., Nov. 17, 1870; s. William Story and Margaret (Shaw) F.; prep. edn., Barton Acad., Mobile; A.M., Southwestern Presbyn. U., Clarksville, Tenn., 1891, B.D., 1894; D.D., Hampden-Sidney (Va.) Coll., 1906; m. Bessie Goss, June 20, 1894; children—Bessie (Mrs. W. L. Harsh), Juliet E. (Mrs. Geo. W. Speer), Margaret H. (Mrs. Starke B. Sullivan). John S. Ordained ministry Presbyn. Ch. in U.S., 1894; pastor successively Senatobia, Miss., Franklin, Tenn., Tabb Street Ch., Petersburg, Va., First Ch., Birmingham, Ala., and First Ch., Anderson, S.C., until 1921, First Ch., Winston-Salem, N.C., 1921-36; prof. homiletics and practical theology, Columbia Theol. Sem., Decatur, Ga., since Jan., 1936 (on leave of absence from Decatur for 1936). Mem. Bd. of Edn., Petersburg, Va., 5 yrs. Trustee Southwestern Presbyn. U., 7 yrs., Barlum Springs Orphanage, 4 yrs.; mem. exec. com., Home Missions, Presbyn. Ch. in U.S., 27 yrs., Gen. Assembly's Work Com. of 44; chmn. Gen. Assembly's Systematic Beneficence Com.; moderator Synod of N.C., 1929-30; chmn. Home Mission Com., Synod of N.C., 1927-33. Mem. Pi Kappa Alpha. Democrat. Mason (K.T.). Club: Civitan. Address: Columbia Theological Seminary, Decatur, Ga. Died May 26, 1943.

FOSTER, Julian Barringer, foreign service officer; b. Colorado Springs, Colo., July 29, 1897; s. Edwin Hardy and Margaret Massey (Chumm) F.; student U. of Ala., 1917; B.F.S., Georgtown Univ. Sch. of Foreign Service, Washington, D.C., 1923; grad. work in economics, Columbia U., 1923-24; N.Y. Univ., 1924-25; m. Henrietta Winning Leckie, Feb. 23, 1929; children—Juliette, Margaret Irene, Beverley Leckie. Began as journalist, 1917; France-Civilian official with U.S. Quartermaster Depot, 1920-21; spl. agt., Bureau of Foreign and Domestic Commerce, N.Y., 1923-24; asst. trade commr. for the Dept. of Commerce, Sydney, Australia, 1925, Melbourne, 1925; trade commr., Wellington, New Zealand, 1927-33; trade commr., Singapore, Straits Settlements, 1933-37; commercial attaché, Am. Legation, Copenhagen, Denmark, 1937-42; assigned as liaison officer for Dept. of State with War Shipping Adminstrn. and Maritime Commn., 1942-43; delegate for State Dept. at Internat. Chamber of Commerce Convention, Copenhagen, 1939; tech. advisor of State Dept. at Internat. Refugee Congress, Bermuda, 1943. Mem. Lambda Chi Alpha, Delta Sigma Pi. Clubs: Wellesley, Wellington, New Zealand; Athenum, Melbourne, Australia. Home: University of Ala., Tuscaloosa, Ala. Address: Dept. of State. Washington, Died June 17, 1944.

FOSTER, Marcellus Elliott, newspaper pub.; b. Pembroke, Ky., Nov. 29, 1870; s. Marcellus Aurelius and Mariella (Fitzhugh) F.; grad. Sam Houston Normal Inst., 1890; student U. of Tex., 1 year; married; children—(by 1st marriage) Howard Fitzhugh (dec.); (by 2d marriage) Zadie Lee, Madora. Established the Houston Chronicle, 1901, sold controlling interest in 1926; now editor emeritus Houston Press. Dir. City Bank & Trust Co. Democrat. Episcopalian. Mem. Kappa Sigma. Clubs: Elks, Houston, Knife and Fork, Country (Houston). Address: 5367 Institute Lane, Houston, Tex. Died Apr. 1, 1942.

FOSTER, Reginald, lawyer; b. Worcester, Mass., Jan. 2, 1863; s. Hon. Dwight and Henrietta Perkins (Baldwin) F.; A.B., Yale, 1884; LL.B., Boston U., 1886; m. Harriette Story Lawrence, Mar. 8, 1893. Admitted to Mass. bar, 1887, and began practice at Boston; vice-president and counsel N.E. Mut. Life Ins. Co.; dir. Boston & Me. R.R., Continental Mills, Old Colony Trust Co.; trustee Pemberton Bldg. Trust, Provident Instn. for Savings. Home: Manchester, Mass., and 48 The Fenway, Boston. Office: 501 Boylston St., Boston, Mass. Died Dec. 21, 1944.

FOSTER, Richard Clarke, univ. pres.; b. Demopolis, Ala., July 12, 1895; s. John Manly and Kathleen Mary (Clarke) F.; A.B., U. of Ala., 1914, LL.D., 1936; LL.B., Harvard, 1917; D.C.L., U. of the South, 1937; m. Lida Scarborough, Feb. 27, 1923 (died Sept. 1936); 1 dau., Lida Scarborough. Admitted to the bar, 1919; mem. Foster, Verner & Rice, 1920, Foster, Rice & Foster, 1923-37; pres. U. of Ala. since Jan. 1, 1937; dir. Merchants Bank & Trust Co. of Tuscaloosa. Served as lt. and capt. F.A., U.S. Army, 1917-18. Mem. State Dem. Exec. Com., 1924-36; mem. Tuscaloosa County Dem. Exec. Com., 1932-36. Trustee Ala. Insane Hosps. Mem. Am. and Ala. State bar assns., Am. Legion, Phi Beta Kappa, Alpha Tau Omega, Omicron Delta Kappa, Phi Delta Phi. Democrat. Episcopalian. Mason, Odd Fellow, K.P. Clubs: Rotary, Tuscaloosa Country. Died November 19, 1941.

FOSTER, Robert Frederick, authority on card games; b. Edinburgh, Scotland, May 31, 1853; s. Alexander Frederick and Mary E. (Macbrair) F.; m. Mary E. Johnson, 1900. Architect and civil engr. until 1893, became writer on games of cards; card editor New York Sun, since 1895, with New York Tribune and Vanity Fair, 1919; inventor of Foster's whist markers and self-playing whist and bridge cards; originator of the "eleven rule" at bridge. Mem. Soc. Am. Magicians. Clubs: Savage, Nat. Liberal (London), Knickerbocker Whist; Wheatley Hills Golf; Los Angeles Athletic; Deauville Beach; Cavendish. Author: The Coming Faith (philosophy); Not Guilty (fiction); Cab. No. 44 (fiction); also many books on cards and many mag. stories. Author of the Pelman-Foster system of mind training. Address: 135 William St., New York. Died Dec. 25, 1945.

FOSTER, Rufus Edward, judge; b. Mathews County, Va., May 22, 1871; s. Gustavus and Catherine (Moore) F.; student Soule Coll., 1885-88; LL.B., Tulane Univ. Law School, 1895 (hon. LL.D., 1935); m. Blanche Ahrons, Sept. 7, 1899; children—Alice Catherine, Blanche Marian. Second lt. 2d La. Vol. Inf., Spanish-Am. War, May 2, 1898-Apr., 1899; adj.-gen. staff of Brig.-Gen. W. W. Gordon, 2d Brigade, 1st Div., 7th Army Corps. Asst. U.S. atty., Eastern Dist., La., 1905-08, U.S. atty., 1908, 1909; apptd. U.S. dist. judge, Eastern Dist. of La., Feb. 2, 1909; U.S. circuit judge, 5th circuit, Jan. 2, 1925. Prof. law, Tulane U., since 1912; dean Coll. of Law, Tulane U., 1920-27 (emeritus); reëmployment dir. for La., under NRA. V.p. Am. Olympic Com.; dir. Am. Athletic Union of U.S. Mem. La. Bar Assn., Am. Bar Assn., Am. Law Inst., S.A.R., Phi Delta Phi, Order of Coif. Comdr. in chief United Spanish War Veterans, 1940-41. Republican. Episcopalian. Clubs: Boston, New Orleans Country (both of New Orleans). Home: 21 Richmond Pl. Address: Post Office Bldg., New Orleans Died Aug. 23, 1941; buried in Metairie Cemetery, New Orleans.

FOSTER, Sheppard Walter, dentist; b. on farm nr. Troy, Ala.; s. John Lewis and Martha A. (Rountree) F.; D.D.S., Dept. Dentistry, Vanderbilt, 1887; m. Sophie Lee Jackson, Nov. 11, 1891. Began practice of dentistry, 1887; dean of Southern Dental Coll., 1896-1917; pres. Atlanta-Southern Dental Coll., 1917-45; now. pres. emeritus Atlanta-Southern (now School Dentistry, Emory University. Fellow Am. Coll. Dentists, Ga. State Dental Soc. (pres. 1925-26); mem. Dental Edn. Council of Am., 1914-32, mem. Am. Dental Assn. (ex-pres.; trustee 1923-32), Psi Omega, Omicron Kappa Upsilon. Democrat. Methodist. Mason (Shriner). Rotarian. Home: 407 2d St. No., St. Petersburg, Fla. Office: 106 Forrest Av. N.E., Atlanta, Ga. Died Aug. 16, 1947.

FOSTER, Warren William, corp. exec.; b. Riverhead, N.Y., July 26, 1859; s. Nat W. and Fanny (Miller) F.; A.B., Dartmouth, 1881, A.M., 1883; LL.B., Columbia, 1883; unmarried. Judge Court of Gen. Sessions, New York, 1899-1914; retired pres. River Rouge Corp.; dir. and mem. exec. com. Cities Service Corp., Empire Gas & Oil Co., Fashion Farm Corp., Dominion Copper Co., Cities Fuel & Power Co.; mem. exec. com. Am. Light & Traction Co.; dir. Southern Light & Traction Co., Am. Distilling Co.; chmn. bd. of dirs. Am. Commercial Alcohol Co. Mem. Psi Upsilon. Home: 17 Arch St., Norwalk, Conn. Died Aug. 8, 1943.

FOSTER, William Garnett, editor; b. Dancyville, Tenn., Nov. 11, 1884; s. Thomas Jefferson and Annie (Shivers) F.; B.A., Southwestern Bapt. U. (now Union U.), 1905; m. Queenie Rowles, July 19, 1911 (died 1924); 1 son, Rev. William Garnett; m. 2d, Quintene Brown, May 12, 1930; children—George Lane, James Quentin. Reporter Jackson (Tenn.) Whig, June-Sept. 1905, became editor Sept. 1905; reporter Chattanooga News, 1906-08, Louisville (Ky.) Herald, 1908; part owner Jackson Whig, 1908-09; polit. writer Chattanooga Times, 1909, sports editor, 1910-25, news editor, 1926-31, mng. editor, 1932-35; editor Chattanooga News-Free Press since 1935. Dir. Boy Scouts of America, Am. Red Cross. Democrat. Methodist (mem. bd. stewards 15 yrs.; teacher men's bible class). Clubs: Chattanooga Executives, Kiwanis (past dist. gov.), Automobile. Home: Route 6. Office: Chattanooga News-Free Press, Chattanooga, Tenn.* Died Sep. 26, 1946.

FOSTER, William Heber Thompson, packer; b. Brooklyn, N.Y., July 20, 1873; s. Thomas Dove and Lizzie M. (Thompson) F.; student at Parsons Coll., Fairfield, Ia., and Pa. Mil. Coll., Chester, Pa.; hon. LL.D. from Huron (S.D.) College, 1935; m. Jeannette Pattison, June 22, 1909 (died 1919); children—Ann Elizabeth, Thomas, D., John Pattison; m. 2d, Isabelle Crawford, Apr. 7, 1921 (died Oct. 1946); married 3d, Bessie M. McElroy, January 10, 1948. Entered packing business of John Morrell & Co., Ottumwa, Ia., 1893; trans. to Sioux Falls, S.D., 1913, became v.p. and gen. mgr. of co., now dir. Pres. Sioux Falls Y.M.C.A.; mem. Internat. Com., Y.M.C.A.; mem. Sioux Falls Chamber Commerce (pres. 1915). Trustee Huron (S.D.) Coll. Republican. Presbyterian. Past pres. Rotary Club of Sioux Falls. Actively interested in civic and philanthropic enterprises. Home: Penmarch Place, Sioux Falls, S.D. Died July 7, 1949.

FOUILHOUX, Jacques Andre (fōō-yōō'), architect; b. Paris, France, Sept. 27, 1879; s. Jean Baptiste and Leonie Gasparine (d'Etcheverry) F.; B.A., B.S., Ph.B., Sorbonne, Paris, 1898; C.E., M.E., École Centrale des Arts et Manufactures, Paris, 1901; m. Jean Butler Clark, July 8, 1908; 1 dau., Anita Clark (Mrs. Isaac Hayne Houston). Came to U.S., 1904, naturalized, 1913. With Baltimore Ferro Concrete Co., 1904-07; mem. Whitehouse & Fouilhoux, architects, Portland, Ore., 1908-17; architect, office of Albert Kann, Detroit, 1919; asso. with Raymond M. Hood, architect, New York, 1920-34; mem. Hood & Fouilhoux, 1927-34; mem. W. K. Harrison & J. A. Fouilhoux, 1935-41; mem. Harrison, Fouilhoux & Abramovitz since 1941. Works: News Building, New York City (asso. with Raymond M. Hood and John Mead Howells); McGraw-Hill Bldg., New York City (asso. with Raymond Hood); addition to Am. Radiator Bldg., N.Y. City; one of 3 firms of architects of Rockefeller Center, New York; Theme Bldg., New York World's Fair (asso. with Wallace K. Harrison); now engaged in defense work, Naval Base, Canal Zone. Treasurer and trustee Beaux Art Institute of Design; chmn. advisory council Art Schools of Cooper Union; visiting critic Schools of Architecture, Columbia University; trustee French Benevolent Society; vice-pres. French Hospital; member. bd. mgrs. Lincoln Hall; mem. board trustees St. Vincent de Paul Institute; pres. New York Building Congress. Served as capt. and maj. F.A., U.S. Army, 1917-19; in battles of St. Mihiel and Meuse-Argonne. Decorated Chevalier de la Legion d' Honneur, 1939. Member Am. Inst. Architects, Architl. League of N.Y., Am. Soc. Civil Engrs. Democrat. Roman Catholic. Clubs: Baltusrol Golf (Short Hills, N.J.); University, Century, Catholic Assn., Rockefeller Center Luncheon (New York). Home: 930 Fifth Av. Office: 45 Rockefeller Plaza, New York. Died June 20, 1945; buried at Baltimore.

FOUNTAIN, Claude Russell, prof. physics; b. Ashland, Ore., Nov. 2, 1879; s. James Davis and Grace (Russell) F.; A.B., U. of Ore., 1901; univ. scholar in mathematics, Columbia, 1901-02, Ph.D. in physics, 1908; m. Lucy E. Landru, June 16, 1914; children—Betty Grace Edwards, Margaret Louise Pinkston. Asst. in physics, Columbia, 1902-05, also assistant in Columbia Summer School of Practical Astronomy and Geodesy; associate professor physics, University of Idaho, 1905-06; instructor physics, Williams Coll., 1906-09; asst. prof. physics, Kenyon Coll., Gambier, O., 1909-13; adj. prof. physics, U. of Ga., 1913-18; prof. physics and astronomy, Mercer U., 1918-26; prof. mathematics and physics, 1926-27, prof. teaching of physics, 1927-40, George Peabody Coll. for Teachers; also prof. physics, same instn., summers 1915-19, 1923-26; prof. of Aeronautics (teaching all courses at Ground Sch. of the Civil Aeronautics Authority), Southwestern Coll., Memphis, summer, 1940; prof. applied science and mathematics Hume-Fogg Technical High Sch., 1940-41; vis. prof. physics, Amherst Coll., 1941-42; vis. prof. of physics, Mass. Inst. of Technology, 1942-43; senior physicist U. S. Signal Corps, ground signal service, Camp Evans, Belmar, N.J., 1943-46; research physicist Naval Research Lab. since 1946. Assistant district ednl. dir. Dist. 5, S.A.T.C., 1918. Fellow A.A.A.S.; mem. Am. Physical Society, Am. Meteorol Society, Am. Assn. Physics Teachers, Tenn. Acad. of Sciences (pres. 1936), Kappa Delta Pi. Club: Freolac. Democrat. Conglist. Author: Laboratory Manual of Practical Physics, 1925. Inventor of simplified types of laboratory apparatus and devices in automechanics, heat and radio. Developed a lab. course in which the student is led to discover the fundamental laws instead of trying to verify them. Home: 4708 Nichols Av. S.W., Washington 20. Office: Naval Research Laboratory, 4th St. near Chesapeake S.W., Washington, D.C. Died Nov. 28, 1947.

FOUNTAIN, Richard Tillman, lawyer; b. Edgecombe County, N.C., Feb. 15, 1885; s. Almon Leonidas and Sarah Louisa (Eagles) F.; law study, U. of N.C., 1905-07; m. Susan Rankin, Oct. 3, 1918; children—Susan Rankin Fountain Thurston, Anne Sloan Fountain Dill, Margaret Eagles Fountain Paylor, Richard Tillman. Practiced at Rocky Mount, N.C. since 1907; judge Municipal Court of Rocky Mount, 1911-18; mem. N.C. Ho. of Rep. 5 terms, 1919-29 (speaker of House, 1927-29); lt. gov. of N.C. for term 1929-32. Director City Industrial Bank, 11 yrs.; director New Home Building & Loan Association. Member of School Board, Rocky Mount, 1917-35 (chmn. 7 yrs.); trustee U. of N.C.; chmn. bd. Eastern Carolina Training Sch. for Boys, and author of bill establishing same; chmn. State Bd. of Equalization; mem. Great Smoky Mountain Nat. Park Commn. Candidate for gov., Dem. primary, 1932, received 173,000 votes; candidate for U.S. Senate, 1936, received 188,000 votes. Mem. N.C. Bar Assn. (v.p. 1932). Democrat. Presbyn. K.P. Club: Civitan. Home: Rocky Mount, N.C. Died Feb. 21, 1945.

FOURNIER, Alexis Jean (fōōr-nyā), landscape painter; b. St. Paul, Minn., July 4, 1865; s. Isaie and Annie M. F.; ed. Minneapolis Sch. Fine Arts under Douglas Volk; Julian Acad., Paris, under J. P. Laurens, Benjamin Constant, Henri Harpignies; m. Emma M. Fricke, 1887 (died 1921); children—Grace Dulin, Paul; m. 2d, Mrs. L. Clarence Ball (died Jan. 1937); m. 3d, Coral T. Lawrence, Oct. 1, 1944. Exhibited Paris Salon; rep. in Print Dept. of Congl. Library, Washington, District of Columbia; Minneapolis Art Institute; Minneapolis Library Gallery and Woman's Club; St. Paul Art Institute; Detroit Art Institute; Muskegon Art Institute; Kenwood Club, Chicago; Public Library, East Aurora, New York; et cetera. Prize for outstanding landscape at the Hoosier Salon, Chicago, 1934; prize for outstanding painting, Brown County (Ind.) Art Assn., 1940; medals from Minn. Agrl. Soc., St. Paul Pub. Library, Minneapolis Club. Painted 20 pictures of the haunts and homes of the Barbizon Masters. Founder Minneapolis Art League; mem. Soc. Western Artists, Am. Art Assn., Paris, Buffalo Society of Artists (honorary member). Clubs: Nat. Arts Club (New York), Cliff Dwellers (Chicago); Indiana Club of South Bend (hon.), Art Klan (Toledo), Rotary Internat. Author: The Homes of the Men of 1830; Among the Cliff Dwellings in San Juan Country, 1893. Address: 54 Walnut St., East Aurora, N.Y. Died Jan. 20, 1948.

FOUST, Julius Isaac (foust), educator; b. Graham, N.C., Nov. 23, 1865; s. Thomas C. and Mary E. (Robbins) F.; Ph.B., U. of N.C., 1890, LL.D., 1910; m. Sallie Price, Nov. 22, 1892 (dec.); m. 2d, Clora McNeill, Aug. 25, 1932. Prin. schs., Goldsboro, N.C., 1890-91; supt. schs., Wilson, N.C., 1891-94, Goldsboro, 1894-1902; prof. pedagogy, 1902-07, pres. 1907-34, emeritus since 1934, N.C. Coll. for Women, now Woman's Coll. of Univ. of N.C. Mem. bd. trustees A. & T. Coll. (for Negroes), chmn. many years, mem. com. supervisors of state normal schs. (for Negroes); mem. 1st textbook commn. of N.C.; conducted teachers' insts. in various counties of North Carolina. President North Carolina Association City Sch. Supts., 1902, N.C. Teachers' Assembly, 1904, N.C. Assn. of Colls., 1912. Author: Geography of North Carolina; also article on N.C. for ency. Coauthor: A Spelling Book. Presbyterian. Address: Greensboro, N.C. Died Feb. 15, 1946.

FOUT, Henry H., bishop; b. Maysville, W.Va., Oct. 18, 1861; s. Henry and Susan Catharine (Powell) F.; grad. Shenandoah Collegiate Inst., Dayton, Va., 1885; grad. Bonebrake Theol. Sem., Dayton, O., 1890; m. Adah C. Pierson, Dec. 11, 1900; 1 dau., Lois Virginia. Began preaching at Edinburg, Va., 1885; ordained U.B. ministry, 1890; pastor Oak St. Ch., Dayton, O., 1891-99; conf. supt., 1899-1901; editor S.S. periodicals, U.B. Ch., 1901-13; became bishop U.B. Ch., May 4, 1913; now retired. Home: 800 Middle Drive, Woodruff Pl., Indianapolis. Died Dec. 4, 1947.

FOWLE, Frank Fuller, consulting electric engineer; b. San Francisco, Calif., Nov. 29, 1877; s. Edward Osborne and Helen (Fuller) F.; S.B. in E.E., Mass. Institute of Technology, 1899; m. Alice Edna, d. William H. and Ida Thomas Cowper, October 17, 1905 (died March 17, 1944); children—Frank Fuller, William Cowper. With Am. Telephone & Telegraph Co., N.Y. City engineering department, 1892-1903, special agent, ry. dept., 1903-06, mgr. Chicago operating district (long lines dept.), 1906-08; cons. engr., Chicago, 1908-12; asso. editor in joint charge of Electrical World, 1912-13; cons. engr., 1913-14; receiver Central Union Telephone Co., an associated co. of Bell System operating in Ohio, Ind. and Ill., 1914-19; mem. Fowle & Cravath, cons. engrs., Chicago, 1919-20; head of Frank F. Fowle & Co., cons. elec. and mech. engrs. since 1920; practice covers electric power and telephone utilities and allied industries; cons. engr. Nat. Elec. Light Assn., 1920-32; expert in numerous court and commn. cases. Editor-in-chief Standard Handbook for Electrical Engineers, 1913-38; dir. Ill. Engring. Council since 1938, pres. 1943-44; mem. Am. Inst. E.E. (mgr. 1919-23), Western Soc. Engrs. (pres. 1935-36), Washington Award Commn., 1938-41 (chmn. 1940-41), Illuminating Engring. Soc., Am. Soc. for Testing Materials, Assn. Am. R.R.s, Am. Soc for Metals, Winnetka (Ill.) Zoning Commn. and Bd. of Zoning Appeals, Newcomen Soc., Indiana Soc. Professional Engrs., Ry. and Locomotive Hist. Soc., N.E. Historic Geneal. Soc., Art Inst. Chicago (life), Ill. State Hist. Soc. (life), Wis. State Hist. Society (life). Member Winnetka Conglist Church. Clubs: University, Engineers (Chicago); Engineers (New York). Author: Transmission Line Crossings, 1909; numerous professional papers. Home: 233 Ridge Av., Winnetka, Ill. Office: 35 E. Wacker Drive, Chicago. Died Jan. 21, 1946; buried at Hancock, N.H.

FOWLER, Carl Hitchcock, lawyer; b. Evanston, Ill., Aug. 24, 1873; s. Rev. Charles Henry (bishop of M.E. Ch.) and Myra A. (Hitchcock) F.; student U. of Calif., 1891-92; B.A., U. of Minn., 1895, B.S., 1896; M.A., Columbia, 1897, LL.B., 1899; m. Henrietta R. Brown; 1 son, Carl Henry. Admitted to N.Y. bar, 1898; asso. in practice with Carter, Hughes (Charles Evans) & Dwight, 1898-1905. Pres. Meth. Social Union, New York, 1909-12; pres. trustees Drew Sem. (Carmel, N.Y.), 1910-18; pres. trustees Christ M.E. Ch., 1916-37; sec. trustees, John St. M.E. Ch.; mem. Gen. Bd. of Edn. M.E. Ch., 1916-24; del. to four Gen. Confs. of M.E. Ch.; del. to Uniting Conf. of Meth. Ch., 1939; pres. Laymen Assn. N.Y. Conf., 1920-22; trustee The Broadway Temple of New York, N.Y. State Inst. for Applied Agriculture on L.I., N.Y. City Soc. of M.E. Ch. Mem. Am., N.Y. State, County and City bar assns., New York Alumni Assn. of U. of Minn. (pres.), Psi Upsilon, Phi Delta Phi, etc. Republican. Clubs: Nat, Republican, Economic, Clergy, Mountain Golf. Author: Life of Luke Hitchcock, 1906. Editor: Patrioite Oration of Bishop C. H. Fowler, 1910. Home: 338 W. 72d St., New York; (summer) Twilight Park, N.Y. Office: 100 E. 42d St., New York, N.Y. Died Mar 30, 1942.

FOWLER, Charles Evan, civil engr.; b. Bartlett, Washington County, O., Feb. 10, 1867; s. Chalkley T. and Phebe W. (Hobson) F.; Ohio State U.; Master C.E.; m. Lucille H. Doyle, Dec. 4, 1890; children—Harold D., Louise H., Margaret E., Robert C. In practice as civ. engr. since 1886; bridge engr. Hocking Valley (O.) Ry., 1887; designing engr. Berlin (Conn.) Iron Bridge Co., 1889; engr. Bear Valley (Calif.) Irrigation Co., 1891; chief engr. Youngstown (O.) Bridge Co., 1891-98; built Knoxville (Tenn.) cantilever and Youngstown arch, also bridges for 60 American rys.; consulting engr., New York, 1898-1900, erection Williamsburg suspension 1,600 ft. span, numerous other bridges and bldgs. U.S. and Can.; pres. and chief engr. constrn. cos., 1900-13; built White Pass (Alaska) arch and navy coaling plant; asso. on Manila (P.I.) harbor; filling Seattle tide flats and dredging contracts 20 million yards; asso. in planning Seattle park system and Seattle port improvements; foundations 42 story bldg. and 600 ft. brick chimney; plans for three 2,000 ft. spans, three 2,400 ft. sus. spans, San Francisco-Oakland Bay bridge, 1915, and 4,850 foot suspension; cons. engr. N.Y. City, 1917-41; rebuilt Niagara Ry. arch, 1919, receiving Rowland prize Am. Society Civil Engrs.; plans for Detroit, 1,850 ft. suspension bridge, 1920-21, for 1,650 ft. arch bridge, Sydney, Australia, foundations 34 story bldg., Detroit; 24 mile causeway over Lake Pontchartrain at New Orleans, Narrows Bridge, N.Y. City, 4,550 ft. suspension, Mackinac Cantilever Bridge and Causeway, 25 miles, Soo Internat. Bridge, 2,000 ft. suspension; cons. engr. other long span bridge projects, plans 1,500 ft. high bldg., N.Y.; 2,500 ft. television tower, N.Y.; harbor work including 50 mile ship canal and 24 mile ry. and hy. bridge and causeway, U.S., Mexico and Cuba; 250-ft. piers, Tacoma-Lincoln bridge, and others; consulting engineer in defense work, 1941-43. Past president bd. park commrs. Madrona Heights Improvement Club; trustee Seattle Chamber Commerce, 10 yrs., Seattle Expn., 1909. Mem. Inst. Am. C.E., Engring. Inst. of Can., Pacific Northwest Soc. Engrs. (past pres.), Soc. of Terminal Engrs. Author: Cofferdam Process for Piers, 1898; Ordinary Foundations, 1904; General Specifications for Steel Roofs and Buildings, 1894; Engineering Studies (12 parts), 1899; Contracts and Specifications, 1907; Law and Business of Engineering and Contracting, 1909; Sub-Aqueous Foundations, 1913; Seaport Studies, 1913; San Francisco-Oakland Bridge, 1915; Engineering and Building Foundations, 1919; World Ports and Harbor Data, 1921; The Ideals of Engineering Architecture, 1929; The Mississippi Flood Problem, 1929; Fowler Family, 1937; Engineering Epics. Owner of large Napoleon collection. Contbr. to engring. jours. Home: Everett Av. N., Seattle, Wash. Office: 92 Liberty St., New York, N.Y. Died 1944.

FOWLER, Chester Almeron, judge; b. Rubicon, Wis., Dec. 24, 1862; s. Franklin Dwight and Maria Antoinette (Cole) F.; grad. Whitewater (Wis.) Normal Sch., 1884; B.L., U. of Wis., 1887; m. Carrie J. Smith Mar. 30, 1892; children—Dwight Smith, Mary Lucile (Mrs. Verne Knox Boynton). In practice of law at Omaha, Neb., 1889-94, Portage, Wis., 1894-1905, judge Circuit Court, 18th Wis. Jud. Circuit, 1905-29; justice Supreme Court of Wis. since 1929, present term ends 1952. Mem. Wis. State Bar Assn. Democrat. Club: Madison (Wis.). Home: 1933 Regent St., Madison, Wis. Died Apr. 8, 1948.

FOWLER, Elbert Hazelton, banker; b. Watford, Ont., Can., Dec. 31, 1883; s. Henry John and Elizabeth Ellen (Hazelton) F.; came with parents to U.S. 1892; student U. of Mich., 1901 to 1910; m. Fanny Livingston Ptolemy, 1909; children—Hugh Stratton, Ruth Elizabeth, Marian Louise, Janet Helena. Admitted to Mich. bar, 1910, and practiced at Detroit until 1921; chmn. bd. Commonwealth-Commercial State Bank, Detroit Investment Co.; treas. Mich. Home & Realty Co.; dir. Peoples State Bank of Pontiac. Methodist. Mason (32°, Shriner). Clubs: Lochaven, Wayne County Republican (treas.), Bankers, Union League of Mich., Williams Lake Country (pres.). Home: 2031 Chicago Blvd. Office: Guaranty Trust Bldg., Detroit. Died May 22, 1930.

FOWLER, Frederick Hall, civil engr.; b. Fort Custer, Mont., Mar. 30, 1879; s. J. L. and Marion (Hall) F.; A.B., Stanford, 1905; m. Elsie Branner, Dec. 20, 1909. Engr. in charge constrn. Calif. sect. Laguna dam, Colo. River, 1905-06; engr. on surveys for proposed American River water supply for San Francisco, 1906-07; instr. in civ. engring., Stanford, 1907-08; in Europe and Egypt, 1908-09; engr. on topographic surveys, Mich., 1909; same on sewer constrn., Calif., 1910; hydro-electric engr. and dist. engr. U.S. Forest Service, San Francisco, 1910-22; engring. rep. in Calif. and Nev. of Federal Power Commn., 1920-22, and cons. civ. engr., San Francisco, since

1922. Adviser for U.S. Fuel Administration, Calif., 1917-18; capt. and topographic officer 211th Engrs., U.S. Army, Camp Meade, Md., 1918. Has made valuations for oil corporations to amount of 75 millions; reported to American Petroleum Institute on power requirements of 7 western states. Mem. cons. bd. San Gabriel River Flood Control, 1927, financial com. Sewage Disposal Research Com., northern Calif.; mem. Calif. Forest Research Adv. Com.; mem. Governor's Commn. to Investigate Causes Leading to Failure of St. Francis Dam, 1928; mem. State Com. on Water Resources Investigation of Southern Calif., 1929-30; mem. Tech. Board of Review, Federal Emergency Adminstrn. of Public Works, 1933-35, with spl. cons. assignment by Public Works Adminstrn. on Fort Peck, Grand Coulee and Bonneville dams, Casper-Alcova Project, and on Platte Valley Pub. Power and Irrigation, and Loup River Pub. Power dists.; mem. President's Bd. of Review, Atlantic-Gulf (Fla.) Ship Canal, 1934; mem. San Luis Valley Drain Com. (Rio Grande Basin) 1935; cons. engr. Federal Emergency Adminstrn. of Pub. Works, 1935-36; consultant to Corps of Engrs., U.S. Army, on dams on Yuba, Bear and Am. rivers, Calif., and on power on the Yuba, 1934; consultant to Flood Protection Planning Com. Greater Kansas City, 1935-41; dir. Nat. Drainage Basin Study; Nat. Resources Com., 1936, and water consultant thereafter; consultant Dept. of Water and Power, City of Los Angeles, 1938-41; chief civil engring. group, Construction Div., Office of the Q.M. General, 1941; chief consulting civil engr., Office of Chief of Engrs., Power Procurement officer, War Dept., 1943; valuations for Federal Works Agency, Puerto Rico, July-Dec. 1943; resumed private practice, San Francisco, Feb. 1944; consultant Dept. of Water and Power, City of Los Angeles, and State of California, Colorado River and Mexican Treaty matters, 1944-45. Mem. Am. Society C.E. (dir. 1928-30; pres. San Francisco Section, 1930; nat. pres. 1941), Society American Military Engineers (dir. 1941, pres. 1943-44), Seismological Society of America, American Ornithologists Union, Cooper Ornithological Club, Calif. Acad. of Sciences, Newcomen Society, Stanford Alumni Association (ex-pres.), Delta Upsilon. Clubs: Engineers (San Francisco); Cosmos, Army and Navy (Washington). Author: Hydro-electric Power Systems of California, 1923, also of various papers on power development, flood control, dam design, Colo. River, etc., and on ornithol. subjects. Home: 360 Forest Av., Palo Alto, Calif. Office: 1300 Crocker First Nat. Bank Bldg., San Francisco 4, Calif. Died Nov. 7, 1945.

FOWLER, Henry Thatcher, univ. prof.; b. Fishkill, N.Y., Mar. 4, 1867; s. Hon. Milton A. and Catharine Putnam (Sykes) F.; B.A., Yale, 1890, Div. Sch., 1892-94, Ph.D., 1896; m. Harriet Mansur Nesmith, July 1897 (died Feb. 1932). Teacher in Norwich (Conn.) Acad., 1891-92; gen. sec. Yale U. Y.M.C.A., 1892-94; asst. in bibl. lit., Yale, 1895-96; asst. prof. philosophy, 1896-97, prof., 1897-1901, Knox Coll., Ill.; prof. bibl. lit. and history, Brown U., 1901-34, now emeritus. Mem. publ. com. editing Journal of Bibl. Lit., 1916-21. Fellow Am. Acad. Arts and Sciences; mem. Soc. Bibl. Lit. and Exegesis, Soc. of the Cincinnati, Am. Oriental Soc. 1944, Palestine Oriental Soc. (Jerusalem), Nat. Assn. Biblical Instrs., Phi Beta Kappa, Alpha Delta Phi frats., S.A.R. Member chapter and corporation of the Cathedral of St. John, Providence, Rhode Island, 1930-42. Member Town Council, Gloucester, R.I., 1935-37. Author: The Books of the Bible, with Relation to Their Place in History (with Dr. M. C. Hazard), 1903; The Prophets as Statesmen and Preachers, 1904; Outlines for Study of Biblical History and Literature (with Dr. F. K. Sanders), 1906; Studies in the Wisdom Literature of the Old Testament, 1907; History of the Literature of Ancient Israel, 1912; The Origin and Growth of the Hebrew Religion, 1916; Great Leaders of Hebrew History, 1920; The History and Literature of the New Testament, 1925; General Knox and His Home in Maine, 1931; also many articles in professional journals and general reviews. Clubs: Faculty (Providence); Gloucester (R.I.) Country; Authors' (London). Home: "Wyndcliff," Harmony, R.I. Died Jan. 23, 1948.

FOWLER, Leonard Burke, lawyer; b. Visalia, Calif., Oct. 20, 1877; s. Thomas and Mary E. (Farley) F.; student classical dept. St. Joseph Coll., San Jose, Calif. (later consolidated with Santa Clara U.), 1894-97; m. Ellen Claire Lucey, Aug. 25, 1925. Began practice at San Jose, 1899; removed to Carson City, Nev., 1908; 1st asst. atty. gen. of Nev., 1908-11; atty. gen. of Nev., 1919-23; resumed pvt. practice Jan. 1923. Author various publications. Home: Reno, Nev. Died June 13, 1942.

FOWLER, Raymond Foster, army officer; b. Alexandria, Neb., Oct. 14, 1884; s. Charles Addison and Abbie V. (Church) F.; student U. of Neb., 1904-06; B.S., U.S. Mil. Acad., 1910; grad. Engr. Sch., 1912; honor grad., Command and Gen. Staff Sch., 1925; grad. Army War Coll., 1935; m. Katharine Van Dorn Wagner, Nov. 24, 1924; children—Helen Frederica (Mrs. Bradford G. Woolley), Gordon (lt. comdr. U.S. Navy). Commd. 2d lt., Corps of Engineers, U.S. Army, June 15, 1910, and advanced through the grades to brig. gen.; served as sect. engr. on constrn. in base sects., A.E.F., and ry. constrn., B.E.F., 1917-18; asst. brigade comdr., 1st Tank Brigade, 1918; chief of supply div., Office of Chief of Engrs., since 1941; div. engrs., South Atlantic Div.; engr. staff 4th Service Command; retired Dec. 1945; exec. Ga. State Ports Authority. Mem. Soc. Am. Mil. Engrs. Clubs: Army and Navy (Washington); Engineers (Phila.); Capital City, Atlanta Athletic. Home: 999 Mt. Paran Rd. N.W., Atlanta, Ga. Died Jan. 19, 1949.

FOX, A(braham) Manuel, economist; b. Phila., May 14, 1889; s. Louis Dembitz and Anne (Berner) F.; C.E., Cornell, 1911 (N.Y. State and Pulitzer scholarships, 1907); A.M., New York U., 1924; m. Dorothy Convissor, Sept. 7, 1911; children—Myra Crandall, Melvin James. Fellow in transportation and instr., U. of Mich., 1911-14; with cost dept., Dodge Bros. Motor Co., Detroit, 1915; investigator, Detroit Street Ry. and telephone cases, 1916; examiner, Mich. State Tax Commn., also efficiency expert, Empire Art Metal Co., College Point, N.Y., 1917; asst. to valuation counsel, N.Y.C. R.R., 1918-21; lecturer dept. of economics and Sch. of Business and Civ. Administration, Coll. City of N.Y., 1920-24; economist, U.S. Tariff Commn., Washington, D.C., 1923-24, chief of economics div., 1924-37, chmn. advisory bd. and mem. planning and reviewing com., 1924-35; lecturer, Knights of Columbus Evening Sch., Washington, 1923-26; asso. prof. economics, Catholic U. of America, Washington, 1924-29; dir. research, U.S. Tariff Commn., Washington, 1934-37, and chmn., planning and reviewing com., 1935-37; mem. U.S. Tariff Commn., 1937-41; v. chmn., Com. for Reciprocity Information, 1938-41; Chairman, Am. Advisory Econ. Mission to Venezuela, 1939; American member of American-Chinese Stabilization Fund Board since 1941. Mem. Am. Econ. Assn., Am. Statis. Soc., Beta Sigma Rho, Pi Gamma Mu. Mason. Clubs: Cornell, Cosmos. Home: 3002 P St. N.W. Office: Old Land Office Bldg., Washington, D.C. Died June 21, 1942.

FOX, Daniel Frederick, clergyman; b. Huntingberg, Ind., Sept. 25, 1862; s. John and Mary (Bott) F.; A.B., Northwestern Coll., Naperville, Ill., 1886, D.D., 1898; grad. Union Bibl. Inst., Naperville, 1888; post-grad. work in univs. of Germany; D.D., Pomona Coll., 1925; m. Anna M. Schneider, May 29, 1890; children—Donald Frederick, Ethel Emma. Ordained Congl. ministry, 1887; pastor California Av. Ch., Chicago, 1891-1909, First Ch., Pasadena, Calif., 1909-30. Republican. Mason (32°). Club: Twilight (Pasadena). Lyceum lecturer on hist. and lit. topics; has lectured in every state in the Union and through Great Britain. Address: 993 N. Madison Av., Pasadena, Calif. Died Jan. 21, 1939.

FOX, Dixon Ryan, college pres.; b. Potsdam, N.Y., Dec. 7, 1887; s. James Sylvester and Julia Anna (Dixon) F.; Potsdam Normal Sch., 1903-07; A.B., Columbia, 1911; A.M., 1912, Ph.D., 1917; L.H.D., Union Coll., 1931, Syracuse U., 1934; Litt.D., Columbia, 1935, Keuka Coll., 1937; Pd.D., N.Y. State Coll. for Teachers, 1936; LL.D., Bates Coll., 1934, U. of Rochester, 1935, Knox, Williams, and Franklin and Marshall colls., 1937, Dickinson Coll., 1938; D.C.L., Alfred University, 1936; m. Marian Stickney, d. Prof. H. L. Osgood, June 7, 1915; children—Herbert Osgood, Harold Dixon. With Columbia U. as lecturer on history, 1912-13, instr., 1913-19, asst. prof., 1919-22, asso. prof., 1922-27, prof., 1927-34; pres. Union Coll. and chancellor Union U. since 1934; visiting prof., Yale, 1929-30. Research asso. Carnegie Instn., 1918-20. Editorial staff Yale U. hist. motion pictures since 1923 Trustee Carnegie Foundation for Advancement of Teaching; trustee New York State Historical Association, joint editor its quarterly mag. and 1st v.p., 1927-29, pres. since 1929; 1st v.p. Westchester County (N.Y.) Hist. Assn., 1922-34, acting pres., 1930; pres. Conf. of Am. Local Hist. Socs., 1929-30; dir. Am. U. Union, London, 1927-28, lecturing in 18 British univs. and colls.; mem. Am. Council of Learned Socs. (mem. com. on fellowships 1931-36, chmn., 1934-36); pres. Assn. Colls. and Univs. of N.Y., 1939, Am. Council on Edn. (mem. exec. council since 1942); mem. Coll. Council, U. of State of N.Y., since 1939; chmn. N.Y. State Fed. Art Project, 1940; chmn. adv. bd., N.Y. State War Council (citizen unity sect.), since 1941. Chmn. Schenectady County World's Fair Com., 1939-40; pres. Schenectady Philharmonic Orchestra Soc. since 1941; v.p. Mohawk Drama Festival since 1935; chmn. Empire State Town Meeting of the Air (weekly, over WGY) since 1937. Member Antique Collectors' League America (pres. since 1935), Am. Philos. Soc., English-Speaking Union, Am. Hist. Assn. (exec. com. 1930-35), Am. Antiquarian Soc., N.Y. and Mass. hist. socs., Alpha Chi Rho (sec. 1913-19; national councillor 1919-22; pres. 1929-32), Phi Beta Kappa, Phi Alpha Theta, Delta Sigma Rho; hon. mem. N.J. Hist. Soc., Vt. Hist. Soc., Rotary International. Presbyterian. Clubs: Andiron (N.Y.); Torch, Fortnightly, Executive (Schenectady); Scarsdale Town (pres. 1929-30). Author: Decline of Aristocracy in the Politics of New York, 1919; An Historical Atlas of the United States, 1920; An Outline of Early American History, 1922; Herbert L. Osgood, an American Scholar, 1923; Caleb Heathcote, Gentleman Colonist, 1926; Ideas in Motion, 1935; Yankees and Yorkers, 1940. Co-author: Aspects of Social History, 1931; The Completion of Independence (with J. A. Krout), 1943. Editor: Westchester Court Minutes (1657-1696), 1924; (with A. M. Schlesinger) A History of American Life (12 vols.), 1927; J. F. Cooper's New York, 1930; A Quarter Century of Learning, 1931; Sources of Culture in the Middle West, 1934; N.Y. State History Assn. Series since 1932; Crofts' Am. History Series since 1932. Editor Columbia University Quarterly, 1930-34; Cavalcade of America, 1935-38; asso. editor Pageant of America, 1926-29, History of the State of New York (10 vols.), 1933; contbr. forewords to numerous books. Received Schenectady Advg. Club annual award as "having done most for good name of Schenectady," 1940. Address: Union College, Schenectady, N.Y. Died Jan. 30, 1945.

FOX, Early Lee, coll. prof.; b. Warren County, Va., Feb. 9, 1890; s. Lafayette and Katherine V. (Stoneburner) F.; student Randolph-Macon Acad., Front Royal, Va., 1901-06; A.B., Randolph-Macon Coll., 1909; M.A., Johns Hopkins U., 1914, Ph.D., 1917; m. Dec. 18, 1920. Teacher Randolph-Macon Acad., 1909-12; prin. Accomac (Va.) High Sch., 1914-15; prof. history and govt., W.Va. Wesleyan Coll., 1917-18, Randolph-Macon College since 1918; instr. summer sessions, U. of Va., U. of N.C., U. of Richmond, Duke U., Johns Hopkins U. Mem. advisory com. Nat. Broadcasting Co.; mem. state advisory com. Columbia Broadcasting System. Former mem. bd. dirs. Va. Industrial Schs. for Colored Children; former chmn. consultative bd. Va. Youth Serving Agencies; former sec. Va. Welfare Council; mem. Va. Com. Nat. Foundation of Infantile Paralysis; chmn. Education Com., Va. War Fund, Va. Edni. Policies Commn., Nat. Panel of Arbitrators; mem. Va. Cancer Foundation; former member nat. bd. mgrs., Nat. Congress of Parents and Teachers; sec. Va. Council of Churches, chmn. its dept. of social education and action; State chairman Russian War Relief Committee; mem. bd. mgrs. Trinity Institutional Ch., Richmond; former mem. state advisory com. Farm Security Adminstrn.; former vice chmn. Va. State Conf. of Church Social Work. Mem. Am. Acad. Polit. and Social Science, Am. Polit. Science Assn., Am. Hist. Assn., Va. Social Science Assn. (ex-pres.), Cooperative Edn. Assn. (pres.), Southern Assn. Colls. and Secondary Schs. (curriculum com.), Phi Beta Kappa, Tau Kappa Alpha, Sigma Upsilon, Omicron Delta Kappa. Dem. Club: Torch (sec.). Author: American Colonization Society, 1817-1840. Contbr. 5 articles to Dictionary of Am. Biography and book reviews to Jour. of Southern History and Christendom. Address: Randolph-Macon Coll., Ashland, Va. Died 1946.

FOX, Emma Augusta (Mrs. Charles Edgar Fox), parliamentarian; born in Binghamton, New York, March 29, 1847; d. of Allen Goff and Caroline (Scott) Stowell; ed. pub. and pvt. schls.; Dr. of Humanics, Hillsdale (Michigan) College, 1937; Litt.D. from Wayne University, 1942; m. Charles Edgar Fox, November 8, 1876; children—Maurice Winslow, Howard Stowell. Was teacher in North Division High Sch., Chicago, at time of marriage; has since resided in Detroit; devoted many yrs. to scientific study of parliamentary law and has served as official parliamentarian at convs. of many nat. and state orgns. Was recording sec. and 2d v.p. Gen. Fed. of Women's Clubs; treas. and pres. bd. trustees Women's Hosp., Detroit; pres. Michigan Fed. of Women's Clubs; mem. Bd. of Edn., Detroit, 2 yrs.; mem. exec. com. Nat. Council of Women of the U.S., 1925-27; hon. v.p. Gen. Federation of Women's Clubs since 1920. Mem. Nat. Woman's Party. Conglist. Mem. D.A.R., Soc. Mayflower Descendants, League of Women Voters, Kenmore Assn., Stowell Family Assn. Clubs: Detroit Parliamentary Law Club (a founder, 1899, and now pres.), Twentieth Century (a founder and ex-pres.), Women's City, Detroit Garden. Author: Your Rights as a Member, 1941; Parliamentary Usage, 1902, 4th edit., 1943. Home: 5832 2d Blvd., Detroit, Mich. Died Feb. 8, 1945.

FOX, Felix, pianist; b. Breslau, Germany, May 25, 1876; s. Baruch and Bertha F.; brought to U.S. in infancy; studied piano and composition with Reinecke and Jadassohn, in Leipzig, also with I. Philipp in Paris, 2 yrs.; m. Mary Vincent Pratt, 1910; children—Richard B., Francis E. Appeared in concerts abroad and made concert tour in United States, 1897; settled in Boston, 1898; active in concert work; soloist with important symphony orchestras in U.S.; head of Felix Fox Sch. of Pianoforte Playing, Boston, 1908-35; dir. music dept., Miss Porter's Sch., Farmington, Conn. Decorated Chevalier Legion of Honor (French). Composer pianoforte pieces and songs; editor many musical works. Composer: The King Fishers (an operetta, with George Mitchell), 1932 (produced Repertory Theater, Boston, 1934); The Baker of Bunsdorf (an operetta, with George Mitchell), 1933; The White Knight (operetta for puppets with George Mitchell), 1939. Home: 403 Marlborough St., Boston, Mass. Died Mar. 24, 1947.

FOX, Herbert, pathologist; b. Atlantic City, N.J., June 3, 1880; s. Samuel Tucker and Hannah Ray (Freas) F.; A.B., Central High Sch., Phila., 1897; M.D., Med. Dept., U. of Pa., 1901; studied U. of Vienna; m. Louise Carr Gaskill, Nov. 9, 1904 (died Nov. 16, 1933); children—Margaret, John Freas (dec.), Samuel Tucker; m. 2d, Mary Harlan Rhoads, Dec. 3, 1938. Volunteer asso. in William Pepper Clin. Lab. 1903-06; pathologist to Rush Hosp., since 1904; pathologist to Phila. Zoöl. Soc., since 1906; chief of Labs., Pa. Dept. of Health, 1906-11; dir. William Pepper Lab. of Clinical Medicine, Hosp. U. of Pa., since 1911; pathologist to the Children's Hosp., 1915-26; prof. comparative pathology, U. of Pa., since 1927. Mem. Coll. of Physicians, Am. Philos. Society, Acad. of Natural Sciences, County Med. Soc., Pathol. Society (all of Phila.), A.M.A., Am. Assn. Pathologists and Bacteriologists; fellow A.A.A.S. Served as chief cantonment lab., Camp Zachary Taylor, Ky., 1917-19; maj. M.C. U.S. Army. Republican. Author: Elementary Bacteriology and Protozoölogy, 1912, 5th edit., 1931; Text Book of Pathology (with Alfred Stengel), 8th edit., 1927; Disease in Captive Wild Mammals and Birds, 1923. Home: Hamilton Court, 39th and Chestnut Sts., Philadelphia, Pa. Died Feb. 27, 1942.

FOX, Herbert Henry Heywood, bishop; b. Montclair, N.J., Mar. 11, 1871; s. James and Ann (Wood) F.; prep. edn. Newark (N.J.) Tech. Sch.; St. Andrew's Div. Sch., Syracuse, N.Y.; B.A., Hobart, 1897, S.T.D., 1921; grad. Gen. Theol. Sem., 1900, S.T.D., 1924; m. Alma Walther, Sept. 3, 1902. Deacon and priest P.E. Ch., 1900; missionary in charge Slaterville Spgs., Speedsville and Dryden, N.Y., 1900-01; vicar All Saints Chapel, Lockport, N.Y., 1901-05; rector All Saints Ch., Pontiac, Mich., 1905-14, St. John's Ch., Detroit, 1914-20; consecrated suffragan bishop of Mont., Nov. 10, 1920; elected co-adjutor bishop, May 1925; bishop, July 20, 1934; retired, Nov. 10, 1939. Mason (32°, K.T.). Author: The Church in Oakland County (Mich.), 1912. Home: 244 Lewis Av., Billings, Mont. Died Nov. 24, 1943.

FOX, Jesse William, cotton grower; b. Slate Springs, Miss., Aug. 11, 1867; s. Hally and Angeline (Cooke) F.; B.S., Miss. Agrl. and Mech. Coll., 1889, M.S., 1891; post-grad. study, U. of Va., 1890, U. of Chicago, 1891-93; m. Lucy Gay, Dec. 16, 1897; children—Mary Francis (Mrs. John Lyttleton Lyon), Judith Virginia, Jesse William. Dir. cotton expt. sta., Stoneville, Miss., 1906-10; dir. Federal Expt. Sta., A. and M. Coll., 1910-12; gen. mgr. Delta & Pine Land Co. (40,000 acres), Scott, Miss., since 1912; maintains a widely-known experiment station for cotton breeding. Trustee U. of Miss., and Miss. Agrl. and Mech. Coll. Democrat. Baptist. Recognized as an authority on scientific growing of cotton. Delivered address before Internat. Cotton Conf., Brussels, Belgium, 1910. Home: Scott, Miss.*Died Oct. 4, 1944.

FOX, Philip, astronomer; b. Manhattan, Kan., Mar. 7, 1878; s. Simeon M. and Esther (Butler) F.; B.S., Kan. State Agrl. Coll., 1897, M.S., 1901; B.S., Dartmouth Coll., 1902; Univ. of Berlin, 1905-06; grad. Army Gen. Staff Coll., Langres, France, 1918; LL.D., Drake Univ., 1929; D.Sc., Kans. State, 1931; m. Ethel L. Snow, Aug. 28, 1905; children—Stephen Snow, Bertrand, Gertrude, Robert Temple. Commandant and teacher of math., St. John's Mil. Sch., Salina, Kan., 1899-1901; asst. in physics, Dartmouth, 1902-03; Carnegie research asst., Yerkes Obs., U. of Chicago, 1903-05; instr. astro-physics, Univ. of Chicago, 1907-09; prof. astronomy and dir. Dearborn Obs., Northwestern Univ., 1909-29; dir. of Adler Planetarium and Astron. Museum, Chicago, 1929-37; dir. Museum of Science and Industry, Chicago, 1937-40. In active duty as col. Inf. since Mar. 21, 1941. Fellow American Academy Arts & Sciences, A.A.A.S., Royal Astron. Soc.; mem. Am. Astron. Soc. (v.p.), Société Astronomique de France, Astronomische Gesellschaft, Alpha Delta Phi, Phi Beta Kappa, Phi Kappa Phi, Sigma Xi. Mason. Served as 2d lt. 20th Kan. Inf., U.S. Vols., in P.I., 1898-99; maj. inf., May 1, 1917-Sept. 23, 1919; in France, asst. chief of staff, 7th Div.; col. inf., R.C. Officier de l'ordre du Sauveur (Greece); Chevalier Legion d'Honneur. Author: Annals of the Dearborn Observatory (vols. I, II and III), also scientific brochures and contbns. to astron. jours., principally on double stars, stellar parallax and solar physics. Home: 816 Milburn St., Evanston, Ill. Died July 21, 1944.

FOX, William Joseph, librarian; b. Phila., Nov. 21, 1872; s. Benjamin F. and Elizabeth (Quirk) F.; ed. pub. schs., Phila.; m. Margaret Muldoon, Apr. 27, 1897; 1 son, Edward Nolan; m. 2d, Louise P. Hellyer, June 22, 1904. Asst. librarian Acad. Nat. Sciences of Phila., 1888-1933, librarian since 1933-44, librarian emeritus since 1944. Editor publs., 1921-38. Original investigator in entomology. Mem. Acad. Natural Sciences, Phila. Zoöl. Society. Address: 1611 Diamond St., Philadelphia. Died Aug. 24, 1947.

FOY, Robert Cherry, army officer; b. Eufaula, Ala., Aug. 20, 1876; s. William Humphrey and Mary Louise (Wilson) F.; B.S., Ala. Poly. Inst., 1894; grad. U.S. Mil. Acad., 1899, Mounted Service Sch., Ft. Riley, Kan., 1915; distinguished grad. Army Sch. of the Line, Ft. Leavenworth, Kan., 1916; grad. Gen. Staff Sch., 1922, Army War Coll., 1923; m. Helene Hummel, Aug. 7, 1923. Commd. 2d lt. U.S. Army, Feb. 15, 1899; promoted through grades to brig. gen., Mar. 1, 1935. Served in Cuba, 1899-1900, in Philippines, 1902-03, Texas, 1903-04; asst. q.m., West Point, N.Y., 1904-08; again in Philippines, 1908-11; on Mexican border with 3d Cav., 1911-14 and 1916-17; in Hawaii with 1st F.A., 1917; organized 332d F.A., Camp Grant, Ill., and comd. the regt. in France, Sept.-Dec. 1918; returned to U.S., Aug. 1919. Comd. 15th F.A. at Fort Sam Houston, Tex., 1920; with 17th F.A., Ft. Bragg, N.C., 1921; mil. attaché, Bucharest, Roumania and Constantinople, Turkey, 1923-26; comd. 4th F.A. at Ft. McIntosh, Tex., 1926-28; served on War Dept. Gen. Staff, Washington, D.C., 1928-32; comdg. officer sch. troops, F.A. Sch., Ft. Sill, Okla., 1932-35; comdr. 2d F.A. Brig., Ft. Sam Houston, Tex., March 1, 1935-March 1937; comdr. 11th F.A. Brigade, Schofield Barracks, Hawaii, 1937-39; retired Dec. 31, 1939. Awarded Polish Commanders' Cross, Order of Polonia Restituta; Czechoslovakia Nat. Order of White Lion. Mem. Sigma Nu. Methodist. Clubs: Army and Navy, Chevy Chase Country (Washington, D.C.). Address: Boerne, Tex. Died Feb. 6, 1944.

FRAME, Nat T(erry), U.S. Dept. of Agriculture; b. Depauville, Jefferson County, N.Y., Feb. 25, 1877; s. S. W. (M.D.) and Harriet (Terry) F.; A.B., Colgate, 1899, D.Sc., 1928; m. Grace Roomer; children—Luke W., Robert N., Silas W. Formerly public sch. teacher and prin.; engaged as orchardist and farmer in W.Va.; county agrl. agt., Louisville, Ky., 1912-13; dir. agrl. extension W.Va. U., 1919-33; ednl. supervisor Civilian Conservation Corps, Fort Hayes, Columbus, Ohio, 1934-37; dir. Oglebay Inst., Wheeling, W.Va., 1937-39; social science analyst, Leader Area III, Div. of Farm Population and Rural Welfare, Bureau of Agrl. Economics, Milwaukee, Wis., since 1939. Originator West Virginia Community Score Cards; organized "4-H" clubs for country boys and girls; chairman West Virginia Beautification Conference, 1925-27; sec. Am. Country Life Assn., 1920-28; vice chmn. and sec. W.Va. Conservation Commn., 1925-29; pres. Nat. Coöp. Extension Workers Assn., 1930-31; v.p. and pres. Am. Country Life Assn., 1933-34. Hon. Col. staff of Gov. Hatfield. Pres. Sons of the Am. Revolution in W.Va., 1939. Mem. Phi Kappa Psi. Republican. Kiwanian; chmn. agrl. com. Kiwanis Internat., 1925-26; gov. W.Va. Kiwanis Dist., 1928. Wrote bulls., Focusing on the Country Community; Helping the Country Community Lift Itself by Its Own Bootstraps; Whither Rural Youth (1940-42); also numerous pamphlets and articles on rural life. Home: Milwaukee, Wis.

Died Mar. 22, 1948.

FRANCIS, William Howard, lawyer; b. Denton, Tex., Mar. 12, 1885; s. William Byrne and Mattie Elizabeth (Melugin) F.; LL.B., U. of Tex., 1907; m. Frances Blair Lysaght, Dec. 6, 1911; children—Frances Margaret, William Howard, Edward Lysaght, James Byrne. Admitted to Tex. bar, 1907, and began practice at Fort Worth; with Thompson & Barwise, 1907-12; moved to Dallas, 1918; asst. gen. atty. Magnolia Petroleum Co., 1912-20, gen. atty. and v.p., 1920-39; retired. Mem. Am., Tex. State and Dallas bar assns., Beta Theta Pi. Democrat. Methodist. Mason (Shriner). Clubs: Dallas Country, Brookhollow Country. Home: 4201 Armstrong Parkway. Address: P.O. Box 900, Dallas 1, Tex. Died Apr. 3, 1946; buried in Grove Hill Memorial Park, Dallas.

FRANK, Alfred, mining engr.; b. Cincinnati, O., Jan. 27, 1879; s. Charles and Amalia (Binger) F.; student U. of Cincinnati, 1895-96; C.E., Cornell U., 1898; unmarried. Mine engr. and surveyor, Butte, Mont., 1900-02; mine foreman, 1903; chief engr., mines of F. Aug. Heinze, 1904-07; supt., Davis-Daly Copper Co., 1907-09; gen. mgr. Ohio Copper Co., Salt Lake City, Utah, 1910-14; cons. engr., Stewart Mining Co., 1910-15; mgr. mining properties since 1915; pres. and gen. mgr. Nat. Parks Airways, 1928-37; v.p. Keystone Mining Co.; pres. The Exploration Syndicate; dir. Western Air Lines, Inc., 1937-42. Mem. Am. Inst. Mining Engrs. Clubs: Alta, Commercial, Country (Salt Lake City); Silver Bow, Country (Butte). Home: Walker's Lane, Halloday. Office: Continental Bank Bldg., Salt Lake City, Utah.

Deceased.

FRANKLIN, Leo M., rabbi; b. Cambridge City, Ind., Mar. 5, 1870; s. Michael H. and Rachel (Levy) F.; LL.B., U. of Cincinnati, 1892 (Phi Beta Kappa); Rabbi, Hebrew Union Coll., Cincinnati, 1892; LL.D., U. of Detroit, 1923; D.D., Hebrew Union Coll., 1939; LL.D., Wayne Univ.; m. Hattie M. Oberfelder, July 15, 1896; children—Ruth Lucile (Mrs. Raymond H. Einstein, dec.), Leo I., Margaret Helen Fleishaker. Rabbi, Temple Israel, Omaha, 1892-99, Temple Beth El, Detroit, Michigan, 1899-41, rabbi emeritus since 1941. Pres. Detroit Public Library, 1928-34, 1939; chairman of book com. since 1929; trustee Detroit Symphony Orchestra since 1924; trustee Detroit Historical Soc. since 1940, Citizens' Housing and Planning Commn. since 1939; dir. World Union of Progressive Judaism, 1926. Chairman of Tract Commission of Union American Hebrew Congregations and Central Conference of Amer. Rabbis. Mem. Central Conf. Am. Rabbis (ex-pres.), Hebrew Union Coll. Alumni Assn. (ex-pres.). Wrote: Christ and Christianity from the Standpoint of the Modern Jew; Practical Problems of the Ministry; The Rabbi—The Man and His Message, 1938; Light at the Eventide, 1939; The Way to Understanding Between Christian and Jew, 1939. First person to receive citation from Round Table of Catholics, Jews and Protestants for "Distinguished Living." Clubs: Economics, Wranglers, Great Lakes, Franklin Hills Country, Torch. Mem. Eugene Field Soc., hon. mem. Internat. Mark Twain Soc. Home: 26 Edison Av. Study: Temple Beth El, Woodward and Gladstone, Detroit 2, Mich. Died Aug. 8, 1948.

FRANKS, John B., army officer; b. Kansas, Mar. 10, 1890; B.S. in Civil Engring., U. of Michigan, 1917; M.S., Mass. Inst. Tech., 1925; grad. Army Indsl. Coll., 1936, Q.M. Sch., 1937. Commd. 2d lt., F.A., U.S. Army, 1918, promoted 1st lt., 1918; commd. 1st lt., Q.M.C., 1920, and advanced through the grades to brig. gen., 1945. Decorated Legion of Merit, Oak Leaf Cluster; Bronze Star; Croix de Guerre with Palm. Home: 2700 Connecticut Av., Washington, D.C. Died Nov. 13, 1946; buried in Arlington National Cemetery.

FRASER, Cecil Eaton, educator; born at Champaign, Ill., October 7, 1895; s. of Wilber John and Alice May (Eaton) F.; student U. of Ill., 1914-15, Harvard, 1915-17, B.S. (war degree as of 1918), M.B.A., 1921; M. Clara Foster; children—Diana, Constance. Field agt., Harvard Business Sch., 1921-22, research supervisor, 1922-26, also instr. in finance, 1923-26, asst. prof. finance, 1926-29, asso. prof., 1929-31; treas. and dir. Incorporated Investors, 1930-36; pres. and dir. Boston Fund, Inc. and Boston Management and Research Corp., 1936-39; returned to Harvard Business School, mem. of staff on industrial mobilization, 1940-47, asso. prof. since 1941 and assistant dean, 1942-47. Pres. and dir. The Buckingham School, 1934-47. Served as 2d lt., later 1st lt. F.A., U.S. Army, A.E.F., Aug. 1917-May 1919; 1st lt. F.A. Res., 1919, capt., 1924, major, 1930-34; instr. Army Air Force since 1942; dir. Army Air Force War Adjustment Commission, 1945. Mem. Harvard Bus. Schl. Alumni Assn. (pres. 1928-29, mem. exec. council 1922-28, 1929-38). Pres. Cambridge Republican Council, 1934, 35; del. Mass. Republican Pre-Primary Convention, 1934; Mass. del. to Rep. Nat. Conv., 1936; mem. Cambridge Sinking Fund. Commn., 1935-45; corporator Cambridge Savings Bank, 1934-47, trustee, 1939-47; trustee Avon Home; dir. East End Union; mem. Commn. on Inter-Governmental Relationship, 1942-46. Conglist. Clubs: Harvard (Boston); Harvard (New York); Faculty (Cambridge). Author: Finance (vol. X) of Manuals of Business Management, 1927; Problems in Finance, 1927 (also repub. in 3 vols., Investments, Banking, Corporation Finance, 1928), revised edit. 1930; Analyzing Our Industries (with Georges F. Doriot), 1932. Editor: The Case Method of Instruction, 1931; Industry Goes to War (with Stanley F. Teele), 1942. Home: 20 Gray Gardens W., Cambridge, Mass. Office: Morgan Hall, Harvard Business School, Soldiers Field, Boston. Died Feb. 23, 1947; buried at Fairhaven, Mass.

FRASER, Leon, banker; b. Boston, Mass., Nov. 27, 1889; s. John and Mary (Lovat) F.; adopted by Ronald E. and Susan (Dayton) Bonar; B.A., Columbia Univ., 1910, M.A., 1911, Litt.B., 1913, Ph.D., 1915; LL.D., Colgate Univ., 1935; m. Margaret M. Maury, 1922 (dec.). Reporter N.Y. World, 1913; admitted to N.Y. bar, 1914; lecturer on political science and instr. public law, Columbia, 1914-17. Private United States Army, 1917; major judge advocate; 1st assistant judge advocate, Service of Supply, A.E.F. Decorated D.S.M. (U.S.); Grand Officer Legion Honor (France), Grand Officier Order Leopold (Belgium); Officer Order of Saints Maurizo e Lazzaro (Italy); Officer d'Académie (France); Comdr. Order of St. Sava (Jugoslavia). Asso. counsel and asst. dir. Bur. of War Risk Insurance, 1920; exec. officer and acting dir. U.S. Vets.' Bur., 1921; practiced internat. law with Coudert Bros, Paris, 1922-24; legal adviser to Am. delegation, London Prime Ministers Conf., 1924; gen. counsel Dawes Plan and Paris rep. of agent general reparation payments, 1924-27, New York corr. Ropes, Gray, Boyden & Perkins, of Boston, 1927-30; attended Paris Conf. of Financial Experts which drafted Young Plan, 1929; mem. prep. com. of experts, London Monetary and Econ. Conf., 1933 (del.); v.p., dir. Bank for Internat. Settlements, 1930-33, pres. and chmn. bd., 1933-35; v.p. First National Bank of City of New York, 1935-37, pres., 1937; dir. Gen. Electric Co., International General Electric Company, First Nat. Bank of N.Y., N.Y. Central R.R. Co., U.S. Steel Corporation, Federal Reserve Bank of New York; trustee Mutual Life Ins. Co. of New York; chmn. N.Y. Clearing House Com., 1944. Trustee Union Coll., Trinity Sch. (New York), Academy Political Science, American Historical Assn., Am. Red Cross Endowment Fund (nat. chmn. 1944 War Fund); treasurer American Academy in Rome. Member Pilgrims, Council on Foreign Relations, Delta Sigma Rho, Phi Kappa Psi. Clubs: Knickerbocker, Faculty, Century; University, The Creek, Broad Street, Columbia Univ. (N.Y.). Home: North Granville, N.Y. Address: 1060 5th Av.; and 2 Wall St., New York, N.Y. Died Apr. 8, 1945.

FRASER, Wilber John, dairy husbandman; b. Lockport, Ill., July 1, 1869; s. John Alexander and Mary Ann (Van Horn) F.; B.S., U. of Ill., 1893, M.S., 1902; studied dairy conditions in Europe 6 mos. at 2 different times; m. Alice May Eaton, Sept. 12, 1894. Asst. agriculturist, Ill. Agrl. Expt. Sta., 1895-96; instr. in dairy husbandry, 1896-1901; prof. since 1901, U. of Ill.; chief in dairy farming, Ill. Agrl. Expt. Sta., since 1897. Studied agrl. economics, Harvard, Sept. 1915-Feb. 1917. Mem. Am. Soc. Animal Production, Am. Econ. Assn., Am. Farm Econ. Assn., Am. Dairy Science Assn., Sigma Xi. Presbyterian. Author: Dairy Farming, 1930; Profitable Farming and Life Management, 1937; Dairy Profit, 1940; also numerous bulls. and circulars of the Ill. Agrl. Expt. Sta., and many articles in Hoard's Dairyman. Home: Urbana, Ill.

Died Apr. 16, 1945.

FRAZER, John G., lawyer; b. Mansfield, Pa., July 19, 1880; s. Robert S. and Loretta (Gilfillan) F.; A.B., Princeton, 1901; LL.B., U. of Pittsburgh, 1904; m. Katharine Reed, Apr. 24, 1911; children—Katharine (Mrs. George D. Lockhart), John G. Admitted to Pennsylvania bar, 1904; mem. Reed, Smith, Shaw and McClay; dir. Am. Fruit Growers, Inc., Farmers Deposit Nat. Bank, Reliance Life Ins. Co., Duquesne Light Co., Pa. Water Co., Bessemer & Lake Erie Railroad Co., Union R.R. Co., Consol. Ice Co. Trustee Carnegie Inst., Carnegie Inst. of Tech., U. of Pittsburgh; dir. Western Pa. Hosp.; mem. Carnegie Hero Fund Commn. Mem. Am., Pa. and Allegheny County bar assns. Republican. Presbyterian. Clubs: Princeton (New York) City; Duquesne, University, Pittsburgh, Harvard-Yale-Princeton, Pittsburgh Golf, Fox Chapel Golf (Pittsburgh). Home: 720 Amberson Av. Office: Union Trust Bldg., Pittsburgh, Pa.

Died Apr. 17, 1942.

FRAZER, Joseph Christie Whitney, prof. chemistry; b. Lexington, Ky., Oct. 30, 1875; s. Joseph George and Mary Jane (Filson) F.; B.S., Ky. State U., 1897, M.S., 1898; Ph.D., Johns Hopkins, 1901; Sc.D., Kenyon Coll., 1926; m. Grace Carvill, Sept.

16, 1903; children—Joseph Hugh, Grace Carvill, Jean Cameron (dec.), Jeanne Henry. Asst. and asso. in chemistry, Johns Hopkins, 1901-07; chemist, U.S. Bur. of Mines, 1907-11; prof. chemistry since 1911, chmn. dept. of chemistry, 1916-36, B.N. Baker, prof. since 1921, Johns Hopkins. Foreign mem. Soc. of Arts and Sciences, Utrecht; mem. Kappa Alpha, Phi Beta Kappa, Tau Beta Pi (hon.). Democrat. Presbyterian. Research work on osmotic pressure and vapor tension of solutions, catalysis and the chem. behavior of surfaces. Address: 3937 Cloverhill Rd., Baltimore, Md. Died July 28, 1944.

FRAZER, Leslie, first asst. commr. of patents, U.S. Patent Office; b. Beaver, Utah, Jan. 16, 1889; s. David I. and Mary (Woolfenden) F.; student U. of Utah, 1915; LL.B., Georgetown U., 1918; m. Eleanor Florence Anderson (died Mar. 23, 1932), December 21, 1922; 1 son—Robert Anderson; m. 2d, Anna Rush Poindexter, June 28, 1937. Asst. county attorney, Salt Lake County, 1920-22; private practice, Salt Lake City, 1922-34; asst. commr. of patents, U.S. Patent Office, 1934-41, first asst. commr. of patents since 1941. Mem. Am. Patent Law Assn. (hon.), Phi Delta Theta. Democrat. Home: 4000 Cathedral Av., Washington. Died Sept. 16, 1947.

FRAZIER, Kenneth, artist; b. Paris, France, 1867; s. Benjamin West and Alice (Clark) F.; B.A., Lehigh U., 1887; art studies at Julian Académie, pupil of Lefèbvre and Constant; m. Julia Fish Rogers, 1894; children—Veronica (Mrs. Cecil D. Murray), Susan (Mrs. Donald MacInnes), Harriette (Mrs. M. W. Openhovski). Professionally engaged as artist since 1889. A.N.A. Club: Century. Home: Garrison, N.Y. Died Aug. 31, 1949; buried in St. Philips in the Highlands Cemetery, Garrison, N.Y.

FRAZIER, Lynn Joseph, ex-senator; b. Steele County, Minn., Dec. 21, 1874; s. Thomas and Lois B. (Nile) F.; B.A., U. of N.D., 1901; m. Lottie J. Stafford, Nov. 26, 1903 (died Jan. 14, 1935); children—(twins) Unie Mae (Mrs. Emerson C. Church) and Versie Fae (Mrs. Stanley H. Gaines), Vernon, Willis, Lucille; m. 2d, Mrs. Cathrine W. Paulson, Sept. 7, 1937. Has been engaged in farming since boyhood; endorsed for governor by Nonpartisan League, 1916, and elected on the Rep. ticket; reelected, 1918, 1920; elected to U.S. Senate, 1922, and reelected, 1928, 1934. Progressive Republican. Home: Hoople, N.D. Died Jan. 11, 1947.

FREAR, Walter Francis, ex-governor, banker; b. Grass Valley, Calif., Oct. 29, 1863; s. Walter and Fannie (Foster) F.; grad. Oahu Coll., Honolulu, 1881; A.B., Yale, 1885, LL.B., 1890, Jewell prize for best examination at graduation; LL.D., Yale, 1910, University of Hawaii, 1937; m. Mary Emma Dillingham (A.B., Wellesley, author verse, music, stories, etc., Litt.D., Univ. of Hawaii, 1943), Aug. 1, 1893; children—Virginia, Margaret. Taught Greek, mathematics, polit. economy, Oahu Coll., 1886-88; 2d judge, 1st circuit, Kingdom of Hawaii, Jan. 1, 1893; 2d asso. justice Supreme Ct., Provisional Govt., Hawaii, Mar. 7, 1893; 1st asso. justice Supreme Ct., Republic of Hawaii, Jan. 6, 1896; mem. Hawaiian commn. to recommend to Congress legislation concerning Hawaii, Aug. 1898; chief justice, 1900-07; chmn. Hawaiian Code Commn., 1903-05; gov. of H.T., 1907-13. Now v.p. Bishop Trust Co. Chmn. Hawaiian delegation to Rep. Nat. Conv., 1912; mem. Code Revision Commn., 1923; vice chmn. Hawaiian Crime Commn., 1930; mem. Commn. on the Illegal Practice of Law, 1931. Mem. Hawaiian Hist. Soc. (ex-pres.), Honolulu Social Science Assn., Royal Geog. Soc. Australasia. Contbr. on legal and hist. subjects. Home: 1434 Punahou St. Office: Bishop Trust Co., Ltd., Honolulu, Hawaii. Died Jan. 22, 1948.

FREDRICK, John E., steel mfr.; b. Randolph County, Ind., Oct. 27, 1865; s, John Phillip and Rebecca (McFarland) F.; student Heidelberg Coll., Tiffin, O., 1887-89; M.D., Ohio Med. Coll., 1892; m. Bessie Kitselman, July 21, 1896; children—Waneta, Ruth Louise, John, Betty. In practice of medicine at Ridgeville, Ind., 1892-96; organized Kokomo Fence Machine Co., 1896; organized Kokomo Nail & Wire Co., 1899; organized, 1901, Kokomo Steel & Wire Co., merged with others as Continental Steel Corp., of which is chmn. bd.; chmn. board Union Bank & Trust Co.; pres. of First Federal Loan & Savings Bank. One of organizers and 1st pres. Ind. Mfrs. and Shippers Assn., 1908; mem. Workmen's Compensation Commn., 1912; co-author of present Ind. workmen's compensation law. Pres. Ind. State Chamber of Commerce 18 years. Mem. Sch. Bd., Kokomo, 1915; chmn. Howard County Thrift Stamp orgn., later chmn. for 9th Congl. Dist.; mem. Bd. of Safety, Kokomo, 1918. Mem. Kokomo Chamber Commerce (pres. 3 yrs.). Democrat. Conglist. Mason, Elk. Clubs: Rotary, Indianapolis Athletic. Home: 516 W. Walnut St. Office: Continental Steel Corp., Kokomo, Ind. Died Mar. 3, 1943.

FREDERICKS, John Donnan, ex-congressman; b. Burgettstown, Pa., Sept. 10, 1869; s. James T. and Mary (Patterson) F.; hon. LL.D., Washington and Jefferson, 1937; m. Agnes M. Blakeley, 1896; children—Mrs. Doris Toney, John D., Mrs. Deborah F. Fort, James B. Admitted to Calif. bar, 1895, and since practiced in Los Angeles; deputy dist. atty., Los Angeles County, 1899-1903, dist. atty. 3 terms, 1903-15; now chmn. bd. dirs. Pacific Clay Products, Inc.; dir. Associated Telephone Co.; pres. Rio Horedo Water Co. Served with 7th Regt. Calif. Vols., Spanish-Am. War. Pres. Los Angeles Chamber of Commerce, 1922. Mem. 68th and 69th Congresses (1923-27), 10th Calif. Dist. Republican. Presbyterian. Mason (K.T., Shriner). Club: California. Home: 10778 Chalon Rd., Bel Air. Office: Pacific Southwest Bldg., Los Angeles, Calif. Died Aug. 26, 1945.

FREEDLANDER, Joseph Henry, architect; b. New York, N.Y.; grad. Mass. Inst. Tech.; grad. École des Beaux Arts, Paris; architecte diplômé par le Gouvernement Français; m. Gladys Mate Cullen, Aug. 31, 1937. Architect of following bldgs.: Importers and Traders' Nat. Bank Bldg., New York; New Harlem Hosp.; Nat. Home for Disabled Vol. Soldiers, Tenn.; Perry Memorial, Put-in-Bay, O.; Portland (Ore.) Auditorium; Library for Andrew Carnegie; Fifth Av. Traffic Towers, New York; Municipal Bldg., White Plains, N.Y.; Museum of the City of New York; Saratoga Spa; Bronx County Court House; Bronx County Jail; Supreme Court, Appellate Division, First Department; also architect of various city and country residences, also various commercial buildings; memorial for Lieutenant General Nelson A. Miles; various other memorials. Past president Fine Arts Federation of New York; past pres. Am. Group Société des Architectes Diplômés par le Gouvernement Français. Chevalier Legion of Honor, France. Academician, Nat. Acad. of Design; fellow A.I.A. (mem. N.Y. chapter); mem. Archtl. League, Nat. Sculpture Soc., Beaux-Arts Institute of Design, Soc. of the Legion of Honor. Club: The Players. Home: 245 E. 72d St. Office: 101 Park Av., New York, N.Y. Died Nov. 23, 1943.

FREEMAN, Edmond Wroe, editor, publisher; b. Hawesville, Ky., Feb. 9, 1866; s. Amos and Sarah (Wroe) F.; ed. pub. schs.; m. Blanch Newman, 1893; children—Gordon Newman, Edmond Wroe. Editor and pub. Pine Bluff Commercial since 1897. Trustee Ark. Haygood Indsl. School; mem. bd. Davis Hosp. Mem. S.A.R. Democrat. Baptist. Clubs: Civitan (ex-pres.), Airport. Each year donates silver loving cup to the citizen selected by popular vote as having performed the most outstanding service for the community during the previous year; awards annually cash prize to outstanding member in Journalistic Class of Pine Bluff High School. Home: 1220 Main St. Office: 106 W. Barraque St., Pine Bluff, Ark. Died Jan. 28, 1945.

FREEMAN, Francis Breakey, ry. official; b. Dublin, Ireland, Apr. 2, 1867; s. William and Anne (Breakey) F.; ed. Rathmines Sch. and Royal Coll. of Science, Ireland; come to U.S., 1892; m. Mary Louisa Brewer, Nov. 1893; children—Ellen Breakey (dec.), William Morten Breakey. Mech. apprentice, later constrn. engr. and sub. agt. various rys. in Ireland; asst. engr. Kingsley & Brewer, civil engrs., New York, 1892-94; with S. Orange & Maplewood St. Rys., 1894; asst. engr. bridge dept. Erie R.R., 1894-1900; chief draftsman, later asst. engr., N.Y.C. & H.R. R.R., 1900-02; supt. constrn. Catawba Power Co., S.C., 1902-03; with H. DeB. Parsons, civil engr., New York, 1903; asst. engr. joint facilities and agreements, N.Y.C. & H.R., R.R., 1903-05, continuing with same rd. as designing engr., 1905-07, and engr. of constrn., 1907-09; chief engr. B. & A. R.R., at Boston, 1909-27; chief engr. N.Y.C. R.R.Co. (Buffalo and East). Mem. A.R. Engrs. Assn. Republican. Clubs: St. Andrew's Golf (New Brunswick); Siwanoy Country. Home: 145 E. 52d St. Address: 466 Lexington Av., New York. Died June 14, 1934.

FREEMAN, Harrison Barber, lawyer, corp. official; b. Hartford, Conn., Aug. 22, 1869; s. Harrison Belknap and Frances Hall (Bill) F.; A.B., Yale, 1892, LL.B., Yale Law Sch., 1894; m. Alma Newell Crowell, Sept. 9, 1901 (died Aug. 22, 1910); children—Harrison Crowell, Horace Hoyt; m. 2d, Marguerite Gibson, June 26, 1919. Admitted to Conn. bar, 1894; pros. atty. City of Hartford, 1895-1906; one of organizers Conn. Investment Management Corp., 1931, and pres. since 1932; also pres. Enfield Constrn. Co., Hartford Belknap Co.; treas. Home & Gardens Co. Mem. Conn. Legislature, 1899-1903; mem. Aviation Commn. of Hartford, 1920-24; trustee Conn. Coll. for Women since 1924, chmn. of bd. since 1931. Pres. Almada Lodge-Times Farm Corp. (summer camp for poor children). Dir. Div. of War Rallies, Speaker Bur., and chmn. Com. Law Enforcement, Conn. State Council of Defense, World War. Mem. Delta Kappa Epsilon, Elihu Club (Yale). Republican. Conglist. Clubs: Hartford, 20th Century, Yale (New York); Graduate (New Haven); Pacific (Nantucket, Mass.). Home: 176 N. Beacon St., Hartford, Conn.; (summer) 117 Main St., Nantucket, Mass. Office: 50 State St., Hartford, Conn. Died Apr. 9, 1942.

FREEMAN, James Edward, bishop; b. New York, N.Y., July 24, 1866; ed. pub. schs., and 15 yrs. in legal and accounting depts. L.I. and N.Y.C. &H.R. rys.; theol. course under Bishop Henry C. Potter and diocesan chaplains; D.D., Seabury Div. Sch., 1913; LL.D., Kenyon College, 1925, Brown U., 1926, Dickinson College, 1931; S.T.D., Bowdoin Coll., 1932; D.C.L., George Washington U., 1933; LL.D., U. of California, 1937; m. Ella Vigelius, April 19, 1890. Deacon, 1894, priest, 1895, P.E. Church; asst. St. John's Ch., Yonkers, N.Y., 1894-95; rector St. Andrew's Memorial Ch., Yonkers, 1894-1910, St. Mark's Ch., Minneapolis, 1910-21, Epiphany Ch., Washington, D.C., 1921; consecrated bishop of Washington, 1923. Lyman Beecher lecturer, Yale, 1928. Chaplain, rank of maj., O.R.C. Founder of Hollywood Inn (workingmen's club), Yonkers; also developed similar clubs in Minneapolis. Elected bishop coadjutor of Western Texas, 1911 (declined). Clubs: Cosmos, Chevy Chase (Washington, D.C.); Yale (New York); Elks, Traffic, Dunwoody Country (Yonkers, N.Y.). Author: If Not the Saloon—What?, 1902; The Man and the Master, 1905; Themes in Verse, 1904; The Ambassador, 1928; also Everyday Religion, Little Sermons. Home: Bishop's House, Washington, D.C. Died June 6, 1943.

FREEMAN, John Dolliver, theologian; b. Milton, Nova Scotia, Aug. 12, 1864; s. James Willard and Augusta Clara (Smith) F.; prep. edn., Liverpool Acad., N.S., 1876-82; grad. McMaster U., 1890, D.D., 1914; hon. M.A., Acadia U., 1896; m. Clara Bell Dakin, Sept. 6, 1884; children—Frank Foster, John Starr (dec.), Ralph Evans, William Dakin (killed in action), Joyce M'Leod (Mrs. Ebenezer Bushnell). Came to U.S., 1927. Teacher public schools, Nova Scotia, 1882-86; ordained ministry Baptist Ch., 1890; pastor Guelph, Ont., 1890-94, Brunswick St. Baptist Church, Fredericton, N.B., 1894-1900, Germain St. Baptist Church, St. John, N.B., 1900-02, Bloor St. Bapt. Ch., Toronto, 1902-07, Belvoir St. Bapt. Ch., Leicester, Eng., 1907-22, Hinton Bapt. Ch., Chesham, Eng., 1922-25, First Bapt. Ch., Winnipeg, Man., Can., 1926-27; prof. philosophy, N.T. interpretation and homiletics, Mercer U. Sch. of Christianity, 1927-39 (retired); now engaged in preaching and editorial writing. Mem. Alpha Chi Omega, Blue Key. Author: Life on the Uplans, 1907; Concerning the Christ, 1910; The Edge of the Age, 1916; Fan of Belseys, 1920; This My Son, 1921; Punch and Holy Water, 1923; God's Infidel, 1925; Kennedy's Second Best, 1926; also to religious publs. Home: Massee Apts., Macon, Ga. Died Feb. 17, 1943.

FREEMAN, R(ichard) Austin, author; b. Eng., 1862; student private schs. and Middlesex Hosp. Med. Coll.; m. Annie Elizabeth Edwards, 1887; 2 sons. Began in Middlesex Hosp., 1880, became house physician, 1886; became asst. colonial surgeon, Gold Coast Colony, 1887; med. officer, surveyor and naturalist to the expdn. to Ashanti and Bontuku, 1889; served as Anglo-German boundary commr., 1890, invalided, 1891; became acting surgeon in charge of throat and ear dept., Middlesex Hosp., 1892; acting dep. med. officer, Holloway Prison, 1901; acting asst. med. officer of Port of London, 1904; served in Royal Army Med. Corps, Territorial Forces, and comd. field ambulances, 1916-17; retired, 1922; has been writing since 1898. Mem. Royal Coll. of Surgeons; licentiate and freeman of Soc. of Apothecaries of London; elected to the Livery, 1929. Author: Travels and Life in Ashanti and Jaman, 1898; The Golden Pool, 1905; The Red Thumb Mark, 1907; John Thorndyke's Cases, 1909; The Eye of Osiris, 1911; The Mystery of 31 New Inn, 1912; The Singing Bone, 1912; The Unwilling Adventurer, 1913; A Silent Witness, 1914; The Exploits of Danby Croker, 1916; The Great Portrait Mystery, 1918; A Savant's Vendetta, 1920; Social Decay and Regeneration, 1921; Helen Vardon's Confession, 1922; The Cat's Eye, 1923; Dr. Thorndyke's Case Book, 1923; The Mystery of Angelina Frood, 1924; The Puzzle Lock, 1925; The Shadow of the Wolf, 1925; The D'Arblay Mystery, 1926; The Magic Casket, 1927; The Surprising Experiences of Mr. Shuttlebury Cobb, 1927; A Certain Dr. Thorndyke, 1927; Flighty Phyllis, 1928; As a Thief in the Night, 1928; Mr. Pottermack's Oversight, 1930; Pontifex, Son and Thorndyke, 1931; When Rogues Fall Out, 1932; Dr. Thorndyke Intervenes, 1933; For the Defence: Dr. Thorndyke, 1934; Stoneware Monkey, 1940; Mr. Polton Explains, 1941; Dr. Thorndyke's Crime File, 1941. Address: Rosemount, 94 Windmill St., Gravesend, Kent, Eng. Died Sep. 30, 1943.

FREEMAN, Richard Patrick, ex-congressman; b. New London, Conn., Apr. 24, 1869; s. Richard Patrick and Mary Belle (Maganis) F.; A.B., Harvard, 1891; LL.B., Yale, 1894; m. Mrs. Fredricca Baile Hunt, Nov. 24, 1915. Admitted to Conn. bar, 1894, and since practiced in New London. Mem. 64th to 72d Congresses (1915-33), 2d Conn. District. Republican. Maj. and judge advocate, Conn. N.G., 1901-08; regtl. sergt. maj., 3d Conn. Vols., during Spanish-Am. War. Conglist. Mason. Home: 72 Mott Av., New London, Conn. Died July 8, 1944.

FREEMAN, Rowland Godfrey, pediatrist; b. New York, N.Y., June 11, 1859; s. Alfred and Amelia (Taylor) F.; A.B., Columbia, 1883; M.D., Coll. Physicians and Surgeons (Columbia), 1886; interne Bellevue Hosp., 1886-87; post-grad. work, Berlin, Vienna and Paris, 1887-88; m. Henrietta Taylor, Mar. 20, 1887 (dec.). Prof. emeritus, Univ. and Bellevue Hosp. Med. Coll.; cons. pediatrist Foundling Hosp., N.Y., Nursery and Child's Hosp., Roosevelt Hosp., Seaside Hosp. of St. John's Guild, Somerset Hosp., St. Agnes Hosp. for Crippled and Atypical Children, Holy Name Hosp. Mem. Assn. Am. Physicians, Am. Pediatric Soc., A.M.A., N.Y. Acad. Medicine. Club: Century. Home: 103 E. 75th St., New York, N.Y. Died Nov. 14, 1945.

FREER, Eleanor Everest; b. Phila., Pa.; d. Cornelius and Ellen Amelia (Clark) Everest; musical edn. under parents, and Mathilde Marchesi and Benjamin Godard, Paris, and Bernhard Ziehn, Chicago; awarded hon. degree of Dr. of Music; m. Archibald E. Freer, Apr. 25, 1891. Began publishing, 1902; advocate of vocal music in English, in English-speaking countries, as a necessary step towards progress of nat. musical art. Hon. pres. The Melodists, Chicago Chapter League of Am. Penwomen; hon. chmn. of music, Ill. Acad. of Fine Arts; hon. life mem. Soc. for Promotion of Am. Music; hon. mem. Nat. Fed. of Music Clubs, Musicians Club of Women (Chicago), Chicago Artists Assn., Chicago Women's Musical Club, Chicago Colony of N.E. Women, Lake View Musical Soc., Swedish-Am. Art Assn. Decorated by French and Belgian govts. for war work, 1914-20; awarded David Bispham medal, Century of Progress medal, 1933-34;

founder Am. Opera Soc. of Chicago, 1921. Episcopalian. Home: 179 Lake Shore Drive, Chicago, Ill. Died Dec. 13, 1942.

FRELINGHUYSEN, Joseph Sherman (frē'lĭng-hī-zĕn), ex-senator; b. Raritan, N.J., Mar. 12, 1869; hon. A.M., Rutgers Coll.; m. Emily Brewster. Chmn. bd. J. S. Frelinghuysen Corp.; pres. Raritan Valley Farms, Inc.; dir. Stuyvesant Ins. Co. Chmn. Somerset County Rep. Exec. Com., 1902-05; mem. Rep. State Com.; candidate for N.J. Senate, 1902; elected to Senate terms 1905-08, 1908-11; pres. of Senate, 1909 and 1910, and acting gov. of N.J. ad interim; mem. U.S. Senate, 1917-23. Club: University (New York). Served as lieutenant Spanish-American War. President State Board of Edn. New Jersey several yrs.; pres. State Bd. of Agr. of N.J. Trustee Rutgers Coll. Home: "Brookwoods," Far Hills, N.J. Office: J. S. Frelinghuysen Corp., 20 Vesey St., New York. Died Feb. 8, 1948.

FRENCH, Allen, author; b. Boston, Nov. 28, 1870; s. John James and Frances Maria (Stratton) F.; S.B., Mass. Inst. Tech., 1892; studied U. of Berlin, 1892-93; A.B., Harvard, 1894; m. Ellen R. Dorrance, Apr. 14, 1898 (died Apr. 28, 1918); children—Maude Dorrance, Frances Stratton, Ellen; m. 2d, Aletta A. Lillibridge, June 17, 1922. Instr. in English, Harvard, 1908-13, 1919-20. Author: The Junior Cup, 1901; The Colonials, 1902; Sir Marrok, 1902; The Barrier, 1904; The Story of Rolf and the Viking's Bow, 1904; Heroes of Iceland, 1905; The Reform of Shaun, 1905; Pelham and His Friend Tim, 1906; The Story of Grettir the Strong, 1908; How to Grow Vegetables, 1911; The Siege of Boston, 1911; The Runaway, 1914; The Beginner's Garden Book, 1914; Old Concord, 1915; The Hiding Places, 1917; At Plattsburg, 1917; The Golden Eagle, 1917; The Day of Concord and Lexington, 1925; A British Fusilier in Revolutionary Boston, 1926; The Taking of Ticonderoga, 1775, 1928; General Gage's Informers, 1932; The First Year of the American Revolution, 1934; The Drama of Concord, 1935; The Red Keep, 1938; The Lost Baron, 1940; Historic Concord, 1942. Home: Concord, Mass. Died Oct. 6, 1946.

FRENCH, Amos Tuck, banker; b. Boston, July 20, 1863; s. Francis Ormond and Ellen (Tuck) F.; A.B., Harvard, 1885; m. Pauline Le Roy, Dec. 2, 1885. Mem. New York Stock Exchange, 1887-91; treas., Manhattan Trust Co., 1888, sec., 1891, v.-p. and dir., 1893-1908; retired. Dir. Northern Securities Co., C.B. & Q. Ry. Co., N.P. Ry. Co., Lying In Hosp. Republican. Clubs: Knickerbocker (treas. and gov.), Union, Harvard, Metropolitan, Grolier, New York Yacht, Coney Island Jockey, Tuxedo (gov.), Turf and Field, Down Town (New York); Newport Reading Room, Newport Casino (Newport, R.I.); gov. Breeders Club of N.H. Residences: Tuxedo Park, N.Y., and Chester, N.H. Office: 20 Wall St., New York. Died Nov. 15, 1941.

FRENCH, Herbert Greer, v.p. Procter & Gamble Co.; b. Covington, Ky., Jan. 17, 1872; s. Jeremiah Henry and Katharine (Smith) F.; grad. Woodward High Sch., Cincinnati, O., 1891; student U. of Cincinnati, 1891-93; unmarried. Began with The Procter & Gamble Co., soap mfrs., 1893, treas., 1903-19, dir. since 1903, v.p. since 1919. Dir. Cincinnati, New Orleans & Texas Pacific Ry. Co. Gen. chmn. Cincinnati Community Chest Campaign, 1931. Dir. U. of Cincinnati; trustee Cincinnati Art Mus.; pres. Cincinnati Inst. Fine Arts; trustee Cincinnati Symphony Orchestra. Republican. Episcopalian. Clubs: Literary, Commercial, University, Cincinnati, Queen City, Cincinnati Country. Home: Reachmont Farm, Pleasant Ridge, Cincinnati. Office: Gwynne Bldg., Cincinnati, O. Died June 25, 1942.

FRENCH, Ralph Lines, mfr. brass, bronze and nickel silver; b. Thomaston, Conn., Oct. 17, 1861; s. Asabel N. and Huldah (Churchill) F.; ed. Thomaston Acad.; m. Aurelia McBurney, Apr. 21, 1888; children—Clifford Ralph (dec.), Walter Leroy, Hazel Aurelia. Began in casting dept. of Plume & Atwood Mfg. Co., 1887, pres. since 1918; dir. Waterbury Nat. Bank. Mem. Conn. Ho. of Rep., 1921, Senate, 1923. Republican. Conglist. Club: Waterbury. Home: Thomaston, Conn. Died Apr. 2, 1945.

FRENCH, Thomas Ewing, univ. prof.; b. Mansfield, O., Nov. 7, 1871; s. Daniel Houston (D.D.) and Janette Helen (Methven) F.; M.E., Ohio State U., 1895; D.Sc., Monmouth Coll., 1921; m. Ida J. Richards, June 28, 1898 (died Apr. 14, 1903); 1 dau., Janet. Draftsman and chief draftsman, Smith-Vaile Co., Dayton, O., 1888-91; instr. drawing, Y.M.C.A., Dayton, 1889-91; asst. in drawing, 1892-98, asst. prof., 1898-1901, asso. prof. architecture and drawing, 1901-06, prof. engrng. drawing since 1906, Ohio State U. Mem. Edw. H. French & Co., cons. chem. engrs. Fellow A.A.A.S.; mem. Am. Society of Mech. Engrs., Society for Promotion Engrng. Edn., Newcomen Society of England, Sigma Xi, Phi Beta Kappa, Tau Beta Pi, Tau Sigma Delta, Epsilon Pi Tau, Phi Gamma Delta. Republican. United Presbyterian. Clubs: Engineers', Kit-Kat, Rotary. Author: A Manual of Engineering Drawing, 1911, 6th edit., 1941; The Essentials of Lettering (with Robert Meiklejohn), 1912; Agricultural Drawing and the Design of Farm Structures (with F. W. Ives), 1915; Mechanical Drawing for High Schools (with C. L. Svensen), 1919, 4th edit., 1940; Lessons in Lettering (with W. D. Turnbull), 1921; Engineering Drawing Sheets (with H. M. McCully) 1937, 1941. Home: 1994 Suffolk Road, Columbus, O. Died Nov. 2, 1944.

FRENCH, Will(iam) J(ohn), industrial counselor; b. Auckland, New Zealand, Aug. 13, 1871; s. Robert and Marian (Hunter) F.; ed. pub. schools in New Zealand; m. Eva Mildred Dean, Sept. 12, 1899 (died 1903); m. 2d, Margaret Loretta Powers, Dec. 1, 1905 (died, 1933); m. 3d, Grace Amy Blake, Feb. 28, 1935 (died, 1946); m. 4th, Rose Gragert, Jan. 27, 1947. Came to U.S., 1892, naturalized, 1898. Learned printing trade in New Zealand and began as printer in Calif., 1892; active in trade union movement and pres. San Francisco Labor Council, 1904-05; sec. and treas. San Francisco Typographical Union No. 21, 1907-09, pres., 1904-05; pres. San Francisco Allied Printing Trades Council, 1904-05; editor Pacific Union Printer, 1898-99; editor Labor Clarion, 1909-11; mem. Calif. Industrial Accident Commn., 1911-33, chmn. 6 years, served under 5 govs.; organized industrial safety movement in Calif.; surveyed social and labor legislation of Australia and New Zealand, 1925; dir. State Dept. Industrial Relations and chmn. Indsl. Accident Commn., Calif., 1928-32; part time lecturer in economics, U. of Calif., 1927-32; mem. Federal commn. to investigate labor situation in Imperial County, Calif., 1934; NRA compliance officer for Calif. and labor mem. 9th Regional Compliance Council for 8 Western States, 1934-35; dir. state Works Progress Adminstrn. Div. of Labor Management, and state dir. Div. of Employment, 1935-36; apptd. by President Roosevelt on President's Emergency R.R. Bd. to adjust railway labor controversies, 1934, 1936. Life mem. Commonwealth Club of Calif. (ex-mem. bd. govs.); member California Constitutional Commission, 1930; member State Unemployment Commission, 1930-32. Mem. San Francisco Red Cross and Liberty Loan Coms. during World War I. Member American Soc. Safety Engineers. Republican. Presbyterian. Odd Fellow. Contributor numerous articles on labor and social problems to periodicals; also speaker and lecturer. Selected for list of arbitrators in several indsl. agreements in Calif. Home: 1416 Cabrillo Av., Burlingame, Calif. Died March 24, 1947.

FRENZEL, John Peter, Jr., banker; b. Indianapolis, Ind., Mar. 9, 1881; s. Otto Nicholas and Caroline (Goepper) F.; A.B., Cornell U., 1903; m. Anne Jillson, Nov. 1, 1919. Began as bank messenger, 1897, advancing to cashier and v.p., pres. since 1927, Merchants Nat. Bank, Indianapolis; pres. Western Savings & Loan Assn. since 1925; v.p. and dir. Ind. Trust Co. since 1925; dir. Continental Steel Corp. Pres. Indianapolis Clearing House. Chairman of board Mchts. Nat. Bank 1945; vice chairman board Ind. Trust Co. Home: R.R. 2, Carmel, Ind. Office: 11 S. Meridian St., Indianapolis, Ind. Died Dec. 7, 1949.

FRETZ, Franklin Kline, clergyman, educator; b. Line Lexington, Pa., Apr. 6, 1876; s. Henry Landis and Wilhelmina (Kline) F.; A.B., Muhlenberg Coll., Allentown, Pa., 1897, D.D., 1921; grad. Luth. Theol. Sem., Mt. Airy, Phila., 1900, A.M., same yr.; Ph.D., U. of Pa., 1911; m. Cora Weikel, Nov. 7, 1900; 1 dau., Barbara Catherine. Ordained Luth. ministry, 1900; pastor St. John's Ch., Easton, Pa., since 1912; organized psychol. clinic, Temple U., Phila., 1911; prof. research dept. of theology, Temple U., since 1909; prof. sociology, Temple U., Sch. of Theology, 1910-40. Chaplain City of Easton, by apptmt. of mayor, 1916-20. Dir. Phila. Sem. Ministerium of Pa.; v.p. bd. of dirs. of the Luth. Seminary at Phila.; v.p. bd. of edn. of the United Lutheran Church; v.p. bd. of trustees Eastern Public Library; chmn. Theol. Commn. of the United Luth. Ch. in America. Mem. Pa. German Soc. (pres.), Northampton County Geneal. and Hist. Soc. (pres.). Republican. Kiwanian. Author: The Furnished Room Problem in Philadelphia, 1911; The Family, 1924. Home: 330 Ferry St., Easton, Pa. Died June 25, 1941.

FREUDENBERGER, Clay Briscoe (froi'dĕn-bĕrg-ĕr), anatomist; b. Centertown, Mo., Apr. 30, 1904; s. Henry Clay (M.D.) and Daisy Myrtle (Briscoe) F.; A.B., Colo. Coll., 1925; A.M., U. of Colo., 1926; Ph.D., U. of Minn., 1931; M.D., Rush Med. Coll. (U. of Chicago), 1938; m. Olive Eckhardt, Dec. 18, 1926; children—Jimmie David, Robert Louis. Instr. biology, Colorado Coll., 1926-28; teaching fellow in anatomy, U. of Minn., 1928-29, instr. anatomy, 1929-31; asso. prof. anatomy, U. of Utah, 1931-32, prof. and head of dept. since 1932, acting dean, Sch. of Medicine, 1939-40 and 1941-42, asso. dean 1942-44. Fellow A.A.A.S., American Medical Assn.; mem. Am. Assn. of Anatomists; Soc. Exptl. Biology and Medicine, Utah State Med. Soc., Salt Lake County Med. Soc., Acacia, Phi Beta Pi, Phi Beta Kappa, Phi Kappa Phi, Alpha Omega Alpha, Sigma Xi. Baptist. Mason. Club: Aztec (Salt Lake City). Contbr. to Anatomical Record, Am. Jour. Anatomy, Endocrinology, Jour. of Nutrition, Jour. of A.M.A., etc. Home: 441 Douglas St., Salt Lake City. Died May 28, 1946, buried at Colorado Springs, Colo.

FREW, William, pres. bd. trustees Carnegie Inst.; b. Pittsburgh, Pa., Nov. 24, 1881; s. William Nimick and Emily Wick (Berry) F.; ed. St. Paul's Sch.; A.B., Yale, 1903, LL.B., U. of Pittsburgh, 1906; LL.D., Washington and Jefferson Coll., 1944; m. Margaretta Park, 1909; children—Emily Berry (Mrs. Henry Oliver, Jr.), Margaretta Park (Mrs. Theodore H. Conderman). Admitted to Allegheny County bar, 1906; assistant district attorney, 1907-10; practiced law, 1910-17; connected with Union Trust Company, 1919-22; member firm Hill, Wright & Frew, 1922-32, merged with Moore, Leonard & Lynch, 1932, partner, 1932-43; president of the boards of trustees, Carnegie Inst., Carnegie Library; chmn. bd. trustees Carnegie Inst. Tech., Pittsburgh, Pa.; trustee Carnegie Corp., N.Y. City since 1943. Served as capt. air corps, U.S. Army, 1917-19. Member Scroll and Key. Episcopalian. Clubs: Pittsburgh, Pittsburgh Golf, Duquesne, Fox Chapel Golf, Century Assn. (N.Y.). Home: 1060 Morewood Av. Office: Carnegie Institute, Pittsburgh, Pa. Died Jan. 31, 1948.

FREY, Calvin Alexander, express transportation; b. Sidney, O., July 27, 1887; s. Frederick F. and Sarah (Condell) F.; grad. Ottawa (O.) High Sch., 1904; m. Bess J. Cowic, Dec. 19, 1908; clerk U.S. Express Co. at Ottawa, O., Toledo, O., and Jackson, Mich., 1904-07; with Pacific Express Co. and Wells Fargo & Co., Little Rock, Newport, Pine Bluff, Ark., San Antonio, Corpus Christi, Houston, Tex., 1907-17; asst. traffic mgr. Wells Fargo & Co., N.Y. City, 1917-18; asst. mgr. mail and express traffic, U.S. R.R. Adminstrn., Washington, D.C., 1919-20; asst. traffic mgr., asst. to v.p. Am. Ry. Express and Ry. Express Agency, 1920-36, v.p. since 1936; v.p. Railway Express Motor Transport, Inc., Railway Express Agency of Calif., Railway Express Agency of Va.; mem. exec. com. and dir. Expressmen's Mut. Life Ins. Co. Mem. N.Y. State Chamber of Commerce. Club: Traffic (New York). Home: 16 Park Av., New York 17. Office: Railway Express Agency, Inc., 230 Park Av., New York 16, N.Y. Died Jan. 1, 1947.

FREYVOGEL, C(harles) Ernest Cecil (frä'vō-jĕl), banker; b. Bombay, British India, Feb. 5, 1888; s. Ernest Edward and Nona Gregory (Wright) F.; student Swiss schs. and pvt. comml. sch. (Lausanne), 1895-1905; m. Irma Jacqueline Cas, Oct. 21, 1935. Came to U.S., 1933; naturalized 1942. Probationer with Ehinger & Co., bankers, Basle, Switzerland, 1905-08; sub-mgr., Comptoir Nat. d'Escompte de Paris (Bombay and Calcutta), 1908-14; sub-mgr. Westminster Bank, Paris, 1918-20; mgr. Bankers Trust Co., Paris, 1920-26, v.p. Bankers Trust Co., New York, since 1926. Dir. French Chamber of Commerce, Alliance Francaise. Decorated Knight French Legion of Honor. Clubs: Cercle Union Interallie (Paris); India House (New York). Home: Sunset Hill, Redding, Conn. Office: 16 Wall St., New York, N.Y. Died Jan. 24, 1950.

FRICK, William Jacob, surgeon; b. Montgomery City, Mo.; s. William E. and Elenor J. (Fulkerson) F.; student William Jewell Coll., Liberty, Mo.; M.D., Kansas City Med. Coll., 1888; m. Katherine J. Menet, Apr. 28, 1904. Practiced in Kansas City, since 1895; surgeon Research Hosp., Kansas City Gen. Hosp. Maj. Med. R.C., 1917. Fellow Am. Coll. Surgeons; mem. A.M.A., Mo. State Med. Assn., Kansas City Med. Soc., Western Surg. Assn., Nu Sigma Nu. Democrat. Baptist. Clubs: University, Blue Hills Country. Home: Oak Grove, Mo. Office: Professional Bldg., Kansas City, Mo. Died Apr. 1, 1942.

FRICKS, Lunsford Dickson, sanitarian; b. Walker County, Ga., July 18, 1873; s. Asa T. and Virginia A. (Park) F.; A.B., U. of Ga., 1894, D.P.H., 1926; M.D., Chattanooga Med. Coll. (Grant U.), 1897; m. Grace Beene, July 22, 1907 (died 1939); children—Lunsford Dickson (died March 3, 1944), Patton Cotnam, Hugh Doran (died Nov. 23, 1943, Tarawa); m. 2d, Ethel M. Collishaw, 1942. Apptd. asst. surgeon U.S. P.H.S., 1898; dir. yellow fever control operations, Key West and Miami, Fla., 1899; asst. dir. Hygienic Lab., Washington, D.C., 1900; passed asst. surgeon, 1903; surgeon, 1912, sr. surgeon, 1929, med. dir., 1930; dir. Rocky Mountain spotted fever investigation, 1912-17; dir. malarial field investigation, 1919-27; sec. Nat. Malaria Co., 1919-27; med. dir. Dist. VI, headquarters, Seattle, Wash., 1927-35; chief quarantine officer Hawaiian Islands, 1935-37, Seattle, Wash., 1937-38; retired, Feb. 1, 1938. Sanitary officer in Cuba, Spanish-Am. War, 1898; organizer and dir. extra cantonment sanitation, Camp Zachary Taylor, World War, 1917-19; U.S. del health sect. League of Nations, 1925. Health Officer, Helena, Lewis and Clark counties, Mont., 1942-43. Mem. A.M.A., Am. Pub. Health Assn., Assn. Mil. Surgeons, Nat. Malaria Com., Southern Med. Assn., Vets. Spanish-Am. War, Am. Legion, Med. Vets. World War, Sigma Nu. Democrat. Unitarian. Club: University (Washington, D.C.) Author of various govt. bulls. and articles on pub. health. Home: 5310 Roosevelt Way, Seattle 5, Wash. Died July 9, 1947.

FRIDAY, David, economist; b. Coloma, Mich., Sept. 30, 1876; s. Jacob and Elizabeth (Butzbach) F.; student Benton Harbor (Mich.) Coll., 1893-95; A.B., U. of Mich., 1908; m. Florence Knowlton Middaugh, Jan. 2, 1930. Instructor in economics, 1908-12, prof., 1912-16, sec. courses in commerce, 1913-16, U. of Mich.; prof. economics, 1916-19, head of dept., 1917-19, New York U.; prof. polit. economy, U. of Mich., 1919-21; pres. Mich. Agrl. Coll., 1921-23; prof. of political economy, New Sch. for Social Research, N.Y. City, 1923-25; research and cons. economist since 1925. Statistician for Mich. Commn. of Inquiry into Taxation, 1911; valuation expert Mich. R.R. Commn., 1915; statis. adviser to U.S. Treas., 1918, to U.S. Telephone and Telegraph Adminstrn., 1919. Director Overseas Securities Co. Member American Economic Association, Nat. Tax Assn., Am. Statis. Assn., Mich. State Tax Assn. (dir., ex-pres.), Am. Acad. Polit. and Social Science, Royal Econ. Soc., Phi Beta Kappa; dir. Nat. Bur. Econ. Research (pres. 1938, 39; chmn. bd. 1940, 41). Clubs: Banker's of America (New York); Bass River Yacht. Author: Problems in Accounting, 1915; Readings in Economics, 1916; Profits, Wages and Prices, 1920. Address: 4525 Garfield St., Washington, D.C.;

(summer) South Yarmouth, Mass. Died Mar. 16, 1945; buried in Rock Creek Cemetery, Washington.

FRIEDENWALD, Herbert, author; b. Baltimore, Sept. 20, 1870; s. Moses and Jane (Ahlborn) F., A.B., Johns Hopkins, 1890; Ph.D., U. of Pa., 1894; m. Rose Diebold Davenport, 1927. Chief div. MSS., Library Congress, 1897-1900; editor Am. Jewish Year Book, 1907-13. Sec. Am. Jewish Com., 1907-13; founder Am. Jewish Hist. Society, and of Am. Hist. Review, 1895; mem. Am. Hist. Assn. Founded with wife, 1936, the Friedenwald Foundation for Promotion of Higher Learning, Baltimore, Md. Clubs: Franklin Inn (Phila.), Cosmos (Washington, D.C.). Author: The Continental Congress; The Journal and Papers of the Continental Congress; Material for the History of the Jews in the British West Indies, 1897; Some Newspaper Advertisements of the 18th Century, 1897; Historical Manuscripts in the Library of Congress, 1898; A Calendar of Washington MSS. in the Library of Congress, 1901; The Declaration of Independence, 1904; Preparedness, a play, 1915; (in collaboration) The Embrace (play), 1919; The Showdown (play), 1921. Editor: Termination of Treaty of 1832 between U.S. and Russia, 1911 (Govt. Printing Office). Address: Wardman, Park Hotel, Washington, D.C. Died Apr. 28, 1944.

FRIEDLANDER, Israel (frēd'lănd-ēr), building and loan official; b. Waco, Tex., July 22, 1888; s. Adolph and Mina (Frank) F.; student Toby's Business Coll., 1904; L.L.B., Houston Law Sch., 1928; m. Reva Davidson, Sept. 18, 1913. Began as stenographer, 1904; pres. Gibraltar Savings & Bldg. Assn. (Houston); past pres. U.S. Bldg. & Loan League (Chicago); elected chmn. advisory council Federal Home Loan Bank Bd., Washington, D.C.; former chmn. bd. Federal Home Loan Bank, Little Rock, Ark.; dir. City Nat. Bank of Houston. Mem. exec. com. Am. Jewish Com. (N.Y.). Trustee and sec. Pauline Sterne Wolff Memorial Home; trustee and ex-pres. Temple Beth Israel; v.p. Jewish Community Council, Jewish Welfare Bd.; dir. Houston Community Chest and Council of Social Agencies. Mem. Tex. and Am. bar assns. Hebrew religion. Clubs: Houston, Westwood Country; International Building (London). Home: 2623 Riverside Drive. Office: 1201 Capitol Av., Houston, Tex.* Died Nov. 27, 1944.

FRIEDMAN, William Sterne, rabbi; b. Chicago, Oct. 24, 1868; s. Nathan and Bertha (Sternberg) F.; B.A., U. of Cincinnati, 1889; grad. Hebrew Union Coll., as rabbi, 1889; LL.D., U. of Colo., 1906; m. Juliet Freyhan, Apr. 29, 1903; children—J. Freyhan, Pauline A. Rabbi of Temple Emanuel, Denver, 1889-1939, rabbi emeritus since 1939. Founder of National Jewish Hospital for Consumptives, 1890 (first free tubercular sanatorium in America, non-sectarian), chairman board managers since 1911 and president since 1929; William S. Friedman Building, named in appreciation of 25 yrs. of service and as founder of the instn.; v.p. Charity Organization Soc. of Denver, 1890-1901; mem. bd. Denver Library Commrs. since 1906 (v.p. 1910); mem. State Bd. Charities and Corrections, Colo., 1901-23 (pres. 1904-10); v.p. Colo. State Conf. of Charities and Corrections, 1905-07, Hosp. Saturday and Sunday Assn. since 1905, Big Brothers; mem. Colo. State Bd. of Peace Commrs.; exec. com. Colo. Red Cross; mem. advisory council of Bd. of Charities and Corrections of gov. of Colo., 1923; mem. bd. dirs. Colo. Soc. for Mental Hygiene. Temporary residence: Hotel Del Coronado, Coronado, Calif. Died Apr. 25, 1944.

FRIES, Adelaide Lisetta (frēz), archivist, genealogist; b. Salem, N.C., Nov. 12, 1871; d. John William and Agnes Sophia (de Schweinitz) Fries; grad. Salem Acad. and Coll., 1888, A.B., 1890, A.M., 1916; research abroad, 1899, 1909; Litt.D., Moravian Coll., 1932; Dr. Letters, Wake Forest Coll., U. of N.C., 1945. Archivist of Southern Province, Moravian Ch. Mem. Moravian Hist. Soc., Wachovia Hist. Soc., N.C. Lit. and Hist. Assn. (pres. 1922-23), N.C. Folk Lore Soc., Nat. Geneal. Soc., N.E. Geneal. Soc., Inst. Am. Genealogy, N.C. Fed. Women's Clubs (pres. 1913-15). Author: History of Forsyth County, N.C., 1898; The Moravians in Georgia, 1735-1740, 1905; Records of the Moravians in N. Carolina (7 vols.), 1922, 25, 26, 30, 40, 43, 47. The Moravian Ch. Yesterday and Today (with J. Kenneth Pfohl), 1926; Moravian Customs—Our Inheritance, 1936; Some Moravian Heroes, 1936; The Road to Salem, 1944 (awarded Mayflower Cup, 1944). Editor: A Brief History of the Moravian Church (also part author), 1909. Home: 224 S. Cherry St., Winston-Salem 3. Office: 4 East Bank St., Winston-Salem, N.C. Died Nov. 29, 1949.

FRIESELL, H. Edmund (frē-zĕl'), dental educator; b. Pittsburgh, Pa., Nov. 10, 1873; s. Jacob and Margaret J. (McClaren) F.; D.D.S., Pa. College Dental Surgery, 1895; B.S., U. of Pittsburgh, 1911; LL.D., Marquette Univ., 1919; D.Sc., U. of Pittsburgh, 1930; m. Esther J. Hutchison, Aug. 1898; children—Dorothy Marion, Charles Edmund, Aimee Elizabeth. Prof. operative dentistry, and dean Sch. Dentistry, U. of Pittsburgh, since Oct. 1903; prof. operative dentistry and dental pathology, Western Reserve University, Cleveland, 1906-17. Assistant editor The Journal of Dental Research. Mem. Nat. Board of Dental Examiners, Commn. on Survey of the Dental Curriculum; ex-pres. Nat. Assn. Dental Faculties, Dental Council of Pa., Am. Inst. Dental Teachers, Pa. State Dental Soc.; hon. mem. Northern Ohio, Ohio State and R.I. State dental socs.; pres. Nat. Dental Assn., 1920-21; pres. Am. Assn. of Dental Schs.; 1st v.p. Seventh Internat. Dental Congress; pres. Omicron Kappa Upsilon; fellow Am. Coll. of Dentists (pres.), Am. Acad. Dental Surgeons; advisory fellow Mellon Inst. Industrial Research; mem. Ill. State, Chicago, Pittsburgh, and Lake Erie dental socs., Odontol. Soc. Western Pa., American Medical Association, International Association of Dental Research, Fed. Dentaire Internationale, Psi Omega (past supreme grand master), Delta Tau Delta, Omicron Delta Kappa, Scabbard & Blade. Mason (32°). Republican. United Presbyterian. Clubs: University; Chemists (New York). Extensive contbr. on dental subjects; also writer on history; pub. speaker. Home: Murrysville, Pa. Died Oct. 27, 1946.

FRISBIE, Robert Dean (frĭz'bē), author, South Sea trader; b. Cleveland, O., Apr. 16, 1896; s. Arthur G. and Florence (Johnston) F.; student Manor Sch., Stamford, Conn., 1909-10; Raja Yoga Acad., San Diego, Calif., 1911-12; m. Ngatokourua Kaitapuaa, Jan. 2, 1928 (died 1939); children—Charles Mataa, Florence Nga, William Hopkins, Elaine M., Ngatakoruaimatauea. Began as newspaper reporter, 1917; editor United States Army publisher, The Saber, 1917-19; reporter Fresno (California) Morning Republican, 1919-20; trader, navigator and author of South Sea stories since 1920; employed as trader for A. B. Donald, N.Z. Ltd., 1923-28; writer and ind. trader since 1928. Served as musician with 8th U.S. Cav. Band, 1916-19. Author: Book of Puka-Puka, 1929; A Kanaka Voyage (serial), 1930; My Tahiti, 1937; Mr. Moonlight's Island, 1939; The Island of Desire, 1944; Amaru, 1945. Contbr. to Atlantic Monthly, Harpers, Forum and other mags. Home: Danger Island, Rarotonga, Cook Islands. Address: Care of Harold Ober, 40 E. 49th St., New York, N.Y. Deceased.

FRISON, Theodore Henry (frī-sŭn), entomologist; b. Champaign, Ill., Jan. 17, 1895; s. Joseph and Helen (O'Neal) F.; B.A., U. of Ill., 1918, M.A., 1920, Ph.D., 1923; m. Ruby Gertrud Dukes, Aug. 22, 1919; children—Theodore Henry, Jr., Patricia Ann. Began as asst. Wis. state entomologist, 1920; asst. entomologist U.S. Bur. Entomology, 1921-22; asst. in dept. of entomology, U. of Ill., 1922-23; systematic entomologist Ill. State Natural History Survey, 1923-30, also acting chief of same, 1930-31, chief of Ill. State Natural History Survey since July 1, 1931. Dir. Central States Forest Exptl. Sta., Central States Forestry Congress. Entered U.S. Army, Apr. 1918; commd. 2d lt., Aug. 1918; resigned, Dec. 1918. Fellow A.A.A.S., Entomol. Soc. America (v.p. 1936); member American Association Economic Entomologists (1st vice president 1945). Ecol. Society Am. (rep. on Nat. Research Council, 1937), Ill. Audubon Soc. (dir. 1942), Limnological Soc. America, Soc. Wildlife Specialists, Am. Wildlife Inst., Am. Soc. Naturalists, Wilderness Soc., Ill. State Florists Assn., Conservation Council of Ill., Ill. Hort. Soc., Ill. State Nurserymen's Assn. (hon.), Ill. State Acad. Science (2d vice-president 1929-30; 1st vice-president 1939-41; president 1941-42), Izaak Walton League of America, Alpha Sigma Phi and Sigma Xi fraternities. Methodist. Club: Urbana Golf and Country. Author: Fall and Winter Stoneflies, or Plecoptera, of Illinois, 1929; The Plant Lice, or Aphiidae, of Illinois (with Frederick Hottes), 1931; The Stoneflies, or Plecoptera, of Illinois, 1935; and over eighty other scientific articles. Compiler: List of Insect Types in the Collections of Illinois State Natural History Survey and University of Illinois, 1927. Editor of Journal of Economic Entomology, 1936-40; mem. editorial board of Ecology, 1938-40. Mem. Thomas Say Foundation Bd., 1942-44. Home: 1005 S. Douglas St. Address: Natural Resources Bldg., Urbana, Ill. Died Dec. 9, 1945.

FROLICH, Finn Haakon, sculptor; b. Norway, Aug. 13, 1868; s. Ernest and Sara S. Victoria (Jacobsen) F.; ed. in Norway; also student Art Students League, N.Y.; pupil of D. O. French and St. Gaudens; studied under Ernest Barrias at Ecole des Beaux Arts, Paris; m. Ragnhild Sjoholm, 1898; m. 2d, Helen Manson, 1910; m. 3d, Kala Coronada Guilford, 1914; children—Virginia, Guilford. Came to U.S., 1885, naturalized, 1899. Dir. of sculpture Alaska-Yukon-Pacific Expn., 1909-11; official sculptor Pan-Am. Expn., 1913; instr. Art and Crafts Sch., U. of Calif., 1917-18; founded Plastic Arts Dept., Fairfax High Sch., Hollywood, 1926; condr. of Frolich Sch. of Sculpture, Hollywood, since 1928. Works: portrait and monument of Paul Kruger at Johannesburg, South Africa; monuments of Edward Grieg, James J. Hill, Jack London; portraits of Luther Burbank, Senator Shortridge; bust of Amundsen; monument in Forest Lawn Park, Glendale, Calif. Awarded silver medal, San Francisco Fair; silver medal, Paris, 1900. Studio: 5152 La Vista Court, Hollywood, Calif. Died Sept. 5, 1947.

FROST, Albert D., ophthalmologist; b. Pittsburgh, Pa., May 20, 1889; s. Albert Ellis and Mary Addie (Dalbey) F.; B.S., U. of Pittsburgh, 1912, M.D., 1919; m. Isabel McCloskey, Sept. 9, 1922; children—Dorothy Jane, Albert Ellis, James Dalbey; m. 2d, Martha White Craig, Mar. 8, 1940. Private practice of medicine, specializing in ophthalmology in Pittsburgh, 1923, Columbus, O., 1924; prof. of ophthalmology, Ohio State Univ., since 1930. Mem. Am. Ophthalmological Soc., Internat. Coll. of Surgeons, Sigma Chi, Phi Rho Sigma, Alpha Omega Alpha. Mason (32°, Scottish Rite, Shriner). Clubs: University, Faculty, City, Kiwanis, Columbus, Scioto Country. Home: 2375 Tremont Rd. Office: 150 E. Broad St., Columbus, O. Died Nov. 15, 1945; buried at Greenlawn, Columbus.

FROST, Edward J., merchant; b. Waupaca, Wis., Feb. 9, 1873; s. David and Adelia (Owen) Frost; ed. Bellevue (Mich.) High Sch.; m. Gertrude C. Mead, of St. Johns, Mich., June 30, 1897; children—Owen Carlisle, Edith Anne, Mary Elizabeth. Employed in general store, 1888; cashier Bellevue Bank, Mich., 1891-1901; asst. credit mgr., purch. agt., Western Electric Co., Chicago, 1901-02, mgr. Pittsburgh, Pa., 1902-03, New York office, 1904-06; pres. and dir. William Filene's Sons Co., Boston, treas., dir. Federated Dept. Stores, Inc., Federated Service, Inc., New York City; dir. R.H. White Co., Bloomingdale Brothers, Inc., Federal Reserve Bank (Boston), Liberty Mut. Ins. Co.; trustee Copenhagen Real Estate Trust, F. N. Day Estate. Treas. Asso. Merchandising Corp., Retail Research Assn.; dir. Boston Municipal Research Bur., Boston C. of C. Trustee Andover-Newton Theol. Sch., Northeastern Univ., Simmons Coll., Huntington Sch., Lasell Jr. Coll., Newton Hosp., Newton Y.M.C.A.; dir. Newton Community Chest. Home: Hillcrest, Auburndale, Mass. Office: 426 Washington St., Boston, Mass. Died June 6, 1944.

FROST, Harry Talfourd, city planner, architect; b. Hanley, Eng., Feb. 3, 1887; brought to U.S., 1892; s. Samuel and Annie Maria (Hughes) F.; student Ohio State U., 1903-06; B.S., George Washington U., 1910; m. Charlette Quinn Wright, Apr. 4, 1940. Began in office U.S. supervising architect, Washington, 1910; became asso. with Edward H. Bennett, 1912; mem. Bennett, Parsons & Frost, 1922-37, Bennett & Frost since 1937. Prepared city development plans for Phoenix, Pasadena, St. Paul, Ft. Wayne, Palm Beach, Davenport, Quezon City (P.I.) and others; designer of Camp Las Casas, P.R., Camp Grant, U.S. Botanic Garden Conservatory, Federal Trade Commn. Bldg. (Washington), William Wrigley, Jr. Memorial (Santa Catalina Island, Calif.), City Park (New Orleans), etc.; tec. adviser Chicago Bd. of Zoning Appeals, 1923-24; city planning and architectural adviser to Commonwealth of P.I., 1940-41, on the new Capital City, resort cities of Tagaytay and Dansalan, Nat. Expn., U. of Philippines and Capitol Bldg. Mem. Am. Inst. Architects, Sigma Chi. Clubs: Army and Navy of Manila, Tavern, Arts. Home: 105 E. Delaware Place. Office: 80 E. Jackson Blvd., Chicago, Ill. Died Dec. 28, 1943.

FROST, Stanley, author; b. Oberlin, O., Oct. 26, 1881; s. William Goodell and Louise (Raney) F.; B.S., Berea (Ky.) Coll., 1902; m. Katherine May Fairchild, June 1, 1904; m. 2d, Alta N. Morse, Oct. 17, 1925 (died Jan. 5, 1928); m. 3d, Marion Yingling, Sept. 21, 1935. Began as reporter New York Tribune, -1902; with Berea Citizen, 1907-10, Detroit News, 1910-14; New York Tribune, 1915-20, Author: Germany's New War Against America, 1919; Labor and Revolt, 1920; Challenge of the Klan, 1924. Contbr. to The Outlook, Collier's, Review of Reviews, Forum, World's Work, etc. Home: 120 N. 2d St., Richmond, Va. Died June 14, 1942.

FROST, Thomas Gold, lawyer; b. Galesburg, Ill., Feb. 17, 1866; s. Thomas Gold and Elizabeth (Bancroft) F.; student Northwestern U., 1880-81; A.B., Knox Coll., Galesburg, 1886, A.M., 1888, LL.D., 1905; Seligman prize fellow, Columbia, 1887-88, LL. B., 1888, Ph.D., 1890; m. Mary A. Kennedy, Oct. 26, 1893; children—Mrs. Barbara Gold Shively, Dorothy Dean. Admitted to Minnesota bar, 1888, and practiced at Minneapolis until 1899, at New York since 1899. As counsel for Jewel Palmer Macdonald before Canadian Ministry secured commutation of sentence for first Am. woman sentenced to be hanged in Can., 1928. Organized, with Luther H. Gulick, the Camp Fire Girls of America, 1912. Republican. Presbyterian. Author: French Constitution of 1793, 1890; Incorporation and Organization of Corporations, 1904; Law of Guaranty Insurance, 1908; Man of Destiny (novel), 1909; New York Corporations, 1910; Federal Corporation Tax, 1911; Federal Income Tax, 1913. Asso. editor Medico-Legal Journal, 1888-1910. Home: 125 Prospect Av., Mount Vernon, N.Y.; also (summer) Lake Winnepesaukee, N.H. Office: 291 Broadway, New York, N.Y. Died Feb. 13, 1948.

FROTHINGHAM, Jessie Peabody, author; b. Boston; d. Arthur Lincoln and Jessie (Peabody) Frothingham; ed. abroad; unmarried. Lived for some yrs. in Italy, later in Baltimore and Princeton, N.J. Writer of stories and articles for magazines and newspapers. Translator: (from French) Journal of Maurice de Guerin, 1891; Obermann (by Senancour), with intro., 1901. Author: Sea-Fighters from Drake to Farragut, 1902; Sea Wolves of Seven Shores, 1904; Running the Gantlet, 1906; Success in Gardening, 1913. Address: Princeton, N.J. Died Jan. 17, 1949.

FRY, John Hemming, artist; b. Greene County, Ind., July 7, 1860; s. Jacob and Mahala (Morris) F.; student St. Louis Sch. of Fine Arts, 1880-84, Julian's (Paris), under Boulanger, Lefebvre and Cormond, 1884-87; m. Georgia Timken, 1891 (died 1921). Teacher of art, St. Louis Sch. of Fine Arts, 1887-92; served on jury of painting, Chicago Expn., 1893. Painter of numerous works, chiefly themes from classic poets and legends. Collection of reproductions published, 1927. Color reproductions of his paintings, with text by Lilian Whiting, published under title of Greek Myths and Other Symbols, 1927; L'Evangile de la Laldeur (in French, 1928); The Revolt Against Beauty, 1934, in French, 1935. Decorated Chevalier Legion of Honor, 1928, Officier, 1932; Commander of the Crown of Italy, 1933. Painting Ode to Sappho awarded hon. mention at Paris Salon, 1931. Elected corr. mem. Sect. of Fine Arts, Inst. of France, 1933. Clubs: Union League, Press (New York); Greenwich Country, Indian Harbor Yacht. Contbr articles dealing with art. Home: Stanwich Rd., Coscob, Conn.* Died Feb. 24, 1946.

FRY, Lawford H., mech. engr.; b. Richmond, P.Q., Can., June 16, 1873; s. Howard and Eliza Tyrell (Lawford) E.; brought to U.S., 1873, naturalized, 1929; ed. Bedford (Eng.) Grammar Sch.; City and Guilds Tech. Inst., London; U. of Goettingen and Hannoversche Technische Hochschule (Germany); m. Marjorie Stockton Canan, Sept. 9, 1905 (died Sept. 1932); children—Frances Elizabeth, Lucy Howard, Humphrey Lawford, Christopher Arthur, Alison Marjorie (Mrs. Nelson Orr Wieman); m. 2d, Mildred Lucinda Kolb, Dec. 2, 1935. Engr., Baldwin Locomotive Works, 1897-1913; metall. engr., Standard Steel Works, 1913-30; railway engr., Edgewater Steel Co., 1930-43; dir. of research The Locomotive Inst., New York, N.Y., since 1943. Mem. Inst. Civil Engrs., Inst. Mech. Engrs. (Bernard Hall prize 1927), Inst. Locomotive Engrs., Am. Soc. M.E. (Warner Reed Medal 1938), Am. Soc. Testing Materials, Newcomen Soc. of England; affiliated mem. mech. div., A.A.R. Author: A Study of the Locomotive Boiler, 1924; Contbr. papers and articles to tech. socs. and jours. Home: 15 Wales Place, Mt. Vernon, N.Y. Office: 60 E. 42d St., New York 17, N.Y. Died July 10, 1948.

FRYE, John H., banker; b. Monroe County, Ala., Dec. 23, 1871; s. John H. and Amanda (Parker) F.; U. of Ala., 1890; m. Helen Mushat, 1906; children—John H., Helen Mushat (dec.), Roland Mushat. Began with First Nat. Bank, Anniston, Ala., 1888; organizer, 1903, and for 24 yrs. pres. Traders Nat. Bank, Birmingham; mng. dir. Birmingham br., Fed. Reserve Bank of Atlanta, 1932-36; retired, 1936. Mason. Presbyterian. Home: Roebuck Springs, Birmingham, Ala. Died Aug. 1, 1943.

FUERBRINGER, Ludwig Ernest (für'bring-ẽr), theologian; b. Frankenmuth, Mich., Mar. 29, 1864; s. Ottomar and Agnes E. (Buenger) F.; grad. Concordia Coll., Ft. Wayne, Ind., 1882; grad. Concordia Theol. Sem., St. Louis, 1885; D.D., Concordia Coll., Adelaide, Australia; Litt.D., Valparaiso (Ind.) Univ.; m. Anna Zucker, Nov. 5, 1896; children—Agnes Maria, Clara Charlotte, Alfred Ottomar, Irmgard Theodora, Ottomar Ernest. Ordained ministry Evang. Luth. Ch., 1885; pastor Frankenmuth, Mich., 1885-93; prof. Bibl. introduction, exegesis and liturgics, Concordia Theol. Seminary since 1893; pres., 1931-43. Pres. Evang. Luth. Synodical Conf, N.A., 1927-44. Member Missouri Hist. Soc., State Hist. Soc. of Mo. Editor: Populaere Symbolik (by Guenther), 1898, and 1913; Briefe von C. F. W. Walther, Vol. 1, 1915, Vol. 2, 1916; Men and Missions (10 vols.), 1924-33; The Book of Job. 1927; Die Evangelischen Perikopen des Kirchenjahres, 1932; Persons and Events, 1947; The External Why, 1947. Co-editor of Concordia Cyclopedia, 1927. Gen. editor: The Thomasius Gospel Selections, 1937; Eighty Eventful Years, 1944. Editor: Der Lutheraner, 1896-1912, and since 1917. Home: 6253 Southwood Av., St. Louis. Died May 6, 1947; buried Concordia Cemetery, St. Louis.

FULBRIGHT, James F., judge; b. in Millerville, Cape Girardeau County, Mo., Jan. 24, 1877; B.S.D., State Teachers Coll., Cape Girardeau, Mo., 1900; m. Maude Estelle Barfield, Oct. 8, 1905; children—James W., Carleton B. Admitted to Missouri bar, 1903, to bar of Supreme Court of U.S., 1925; appointed prosecuting attorney for Ripley County, Mo., 1906, and elected to same office, 1906, 08, 10; mem. Mo. Ho. of Rep., 3 terms (speaker pro tem. of House, 2 terms); mayor of Doniphan, 1919-23; mem. 68th, 70th and 72d Congresses (1923-25, 1927-29, 1931-33), 14th Mo. Dist.; judge Springfield Court of Appeals since 1936, now presiding judge. Democrat. Methodist. Mason, Odd Fellow. Home: Doniphan, Mo. Office: Woodruff Bldg., Springfield, Mo. Died Apr. 5, 1948.

FULLER, Oliver Clyde, banker; b. Clarkesville, Ga., Sept. 13, 1860; s. Henry A. and Caroline M. (Wyly) F.; ed. pub. and pvt. schs., Atlanta, and U. of Ga., class 1880; m. Kate FitzHugh Caswell, May 25, 1881; children—Mrs. H. L. Willoughby, Jr., Mrs. Elizabeth Coffin, Mrs. George B. Miller, Mrs. William Bradford Stryker, Clyde H., Robert S. Clk. and later partner wholesale mercantile business, with father, as H. A. Fuller & Son; mem. Jones & Fuller (bonds), 1886-89; located in Milwaukee, 1891; est. firm of Oliver C. Fuller & Co., bonds, 1893; organized, 1903, pres. Wis. Trust Co.; later chmn. bd. First Wis. Nat. Bank (consol. of First Nat. and Wis. Nat. Banks of Milwaukee), First Wis. Trust Co., First Wisconsin Co.; retired, 1926. Mem. Am. Bankers' Assn. (pres. Trust Co. Sect., 1910-11), Wis. Sec. S.A.R., Soc. Colonial Wars. Republican. Episcopalian. Clubs: Milwaukee, Town, Country, University, Athletic (Milwaukee). Home: Laurel Park, Hendersonville, N.C. Died Aug. 17, 1942.

FULLER, Paul, Jr., lawyer; b. South Orange, N.J.; s. Paul and Léonie (Coudert) F.; student St. Francis Xavier Coll., Columbia Coll., 1897-99 (nongrad.); LL.B., New York Law Sch., 1901; spl. course, U. of Va., 1901; m. Marie A. de Florez, Jan. 25, 1905; 5 children. Began practice at N.Y. City, 1902; partner Coudert Bros.; U.S. commr. to Hayti, 1915; consul gen. S.A.S., Prince de Monaco, since 1920; dir. Bur. War Trade Intelligence, July 1917-Dec. 1918; acting dir. Bur. Enemy Trade, 1917-19; mem. Censorship Bd., 1917-18; formerly chmn. Foreign Trade Com. of New York Merchants' Assn., and legal adviser to French Govt. Dir. The Budd Co., Coty, Inc., Coty Internat., Savannah & Atlanta R.R. Mem. N.Y. State Bar Assn. Bar Assn. City of N.Y., Soc. Internat. Law, Delta Psi. Officier Legion d'Honneur, France; Officier Order St. Charles. Democrat. Roman Catholic. Clubs: Union, Century Assn., Down Town, Rockaway Hunting, St. Anthony (New York); Cercle de l'Union, The Travellers (Paris). Home: Hewlett, L.I. Office: 2 Rector St., New York. Died May 12, 1947.

FULMER, Hampton Pitts, congressman; b. nr. Springfield, S.C., June 23, 1875; s. James Riley and Marthenia (Evans) F.; ed. high sch. and business coll.; m. Willa E. Lybrand, Oct. 20, 1901; children—Margie Louise (Mrs. C. G. Smith), Ruby Maxine (Mrs. J. B. Sloan), Willa Juanita (Mrs. W. T. Reed). Farmer. Mem. S.C. Ho. of Rep., 1917-20; mem. 67th to 78th Congresses (1921-45), 2d S.C. District (chmn. agr. com.); author of U.S. Standard Cotton Grading Act. and Agrl. Adjustment Act. Democrat. Baptist. Mason, Woodman. Home: Orangeburg, S.C. Died Oct. 19, 1944.

FUNK, Eugene Duncan, farmer, seedsman; b. Shirley, Ill., Sept. 3, 1867; s. LaFayette and Elizabeth (Paullin) F.; student Wyman's Inst., Upper Alton, Ill., 1883-84, Phillips Acad., Andover, Mass., 1885-88, Yale, 1888-90; studied agr. in Europe, 1890; hon. recognition in Agrl., U. of Wis., 1920; m. Mary Anderson, July 19, 1894; children—Gladys (Mrs. Curtis Rehtmeyer), LaFayette, Elizabeth (Mrs. Robert McCormick), Eugene Duncan, Paul Allen, Theadore, Ruth (Mrs. Waldo Roth), Mary Alice (Mrs. Lester Ahroon). Began plant breeding (primarily corn), 1892; established Funk Bros. Seed Co. at Bloomington, Ill., 1901, and since pres.; v.p. Funk's Grove Grain Co. Served as mem. advisory bd. Food Adminstrn., World War. Chmn. McLean County Corn Loan Com.; mem. advisory bd. Ill. Coll. Agr.; dir. Bloomington Assn. Commerce. Mem. Nat. Corn Assn. (pres.), Ill. Farmers' Club (pres.), Ill. Live Stock Assn. (treas.), Am. Seed Trade Assn. (pres.), Ill. Council of Defense, Ill. Products Commn. (chmn.), etc. Republican. Mason (32°). Clubs: Bloomington, Rotary (charter mem.) Apptd. mem. Champion Farmers of America, 1940. Home: Shirley, Ill. Address: Bloomington, Ill. Died Nov. 28, 1944.

FUNKHOUSER, William Delbert, zoölogist; b. Rockport, Ind., Mar. 13, 1881; s. Hugh Clark and Laura Josephine (Mobley) F.; A.B., Wabash Coll., Crawfordsville, Ind., 1905, ScD., 1929; M.A., Cornell U., 1912, Ph.D., 1916, honor fellow, 1916-17; m. Josephine H. Kinney, June 29, 1910. Instr. biology, high sch., Brazil, Ind., 1905-07; high sch., Greencastle, Ind., 1907; headmaster, high sch., Ithaca, N.Y., 1908-14; prin. Cascadilla Sch., July 1, 1915-Aug. 15, 1918; head dept. zoölogy and entomology since 1918, prof. of anthropology and dean of Grad. Sch. since 1925, U. of Ky. Fellow A.A.A.S., Entomol. Soc. Am. (pres. 1940); mem. New York and Brooklyn entomol. socs., Ky. Acad. Sciences, Ky. Ednl. Assn., Wilson Orinthol. Club, Am. Zoöl. Soc., Am. Anthrop. Soc., Kappa Sigma (past dist. grand master Ky. and Tenn.), Phi Beta Kappa, Sigma Xi (pres. Ky. Chapter, 1923-24); pres. Ky. Research Club, 1922-23, pres. Rotary Club (Lexington), 1925-26; pres. Ky. Archæol. Soc., 1933; sec. of Southeastern Athletic Conf. since 1934; president Conference of Deans of Southern Graduate Schools, 1944-45 (secretary 1935-40); mem. com. on instns. of higher edn. 1941-43; mem. com. on grad. instrn., Southern Univ. Conf., 1940-44. Mem. exec. com. Oak Ridge Inst. Mem. Filson Club, Bradford Soc., Ky. Hist. Soc. Republican. Conglist. Rotarian. Author: Biology of Membracidæ of Cayuga Lake, 1917; Outlines of Zoölogy, 1919; Wild Life in Kentucky, 1923; Birds of Kentucky, 1925; Catalogue of Membracidæ, 1927; Kentucky Prehistory, 1931; Autobiobraphy of an Old Man, 1940; Ethnology Behind the War, 1943; Portraits of Kentuckians, 1943; Dead Men Tell Tales, 1944; The Days That Are Gone, 1945; also about 300 articles in entomol. jours. Home: 468 W. Second St. Lexington, Ky. Died June 9, 1948.

FUQUA, Stephen Ogden (fū-kā'), army officer; b. Baton Rouge, La., Dec. 25, 1874; s. James Overton and Jeannette M. (Foules) F.; student Tulane U., 1888-89, U. of La., 1889-92, U.S. Mil. Acad., 1892-93; distinguished grad. Inf.-Cav. Sch., 1907; grad. Army Staff Coll., 1908, A.E.F. Staff Coll., Langres, France, 1918; refresher course, Inf. Sch., 1924; m. Pauline Stafford, Apr. 25, 1906; children—Jeannette Stafford, Stephen Ogden. Commd. capt., Inf., U.S. Vols., July 8, 1898; 2d lt., U.S. Inf., Feb. 2, 1901; advanced through grades to col., (temporary) Oct. 30, 1918, (permanent) Jan. 14, 1928; became chief of inf., rank of maj. gen., Mar. 28, 1929; formerly mil. attaché Am. Embassy, Madrid, Spain; now military Affairs editor, Newsweek, New York. Awarded D.S.M. Mem. Sigma Nu. Mason. Address: War Dept., Washington, D.C. Died May 11, 1943.

FURMAN, Franklin De Ronde, educator; b. Ridgely, Md., Aug. 30, 1870; s. John Lewis and Adelia Catherine (De Ronde) F.; grad. Hasbrouck Inst., Jersey City, 1888; M E. Stevens Inst. Tech., Hoboken, N J., 1893; m. Minnie Adelaide Thompson, Nov. 3, 1894 (died Dec. 30, 1936); m. 2d, Alice Martha Nazarian, Sept. 24, 1942. Successively instr., asst. prof. and prof. mechanism and machine design, Stevens Inst. of Tech., 1893-1941, dean of coll., 1928-41, prof. emeritus and dean emeritus since 1941. Conducted course for Steam Engring. Sch., U.S. Navy, during World War. Trustee Stevens-Hoboken Acad. since 1929, and vice-pres. since 1939. Mem. Am. Soc. Mech. Engrs., Newcomen Society, Society Promotion Engring. Edn.; fellow A.A.A.S.; chmn. Nat. Com. on Standardization of Drawings and Drafting Room Practice. Editor: Stevens Institute Indicator, 1897-1902. Author: Valves and Valve Gears for Steam Engines, 1903, Steam Turbines added, 1911; History of the Stevens Family of Engineers; History of Stevens Institute of Technology; Biographies of Alumni of Stevens Institute, 1905; Career of Graduates in Mechanical Engineering, 1908; Cams for Automatic Machinery, 1911; Questions and Problems in Machine Design, 1912; Valves and Valve Gears for Gas, Gasoline and Oil Engines, 1915; Questions in Engineering Drawing, 1919; Cams, Elementary and Advanced, 1921; Planetary Gearing, 1924; Mechanism, 1929; also ednl. notes on mech. subjects and tech. articles to engring. mags. Home: 36 Reid Av., Passaic, N.J. Died Nov. 21, 1943.

FURNALD, Henry Natsch, religious education; b. S. Manchester, Conn.; s. Henry Natsch and Louisa (Bodmer) F.; A B., Brown U., 1902; grad. Union Theol. Sem., 1905, grad. student, same, 1912-13; D.D., College of Idaho, Caldwell, Idaho, 1941; m. Ethel Helena Budington, Dec. 2, 1914; 1 son, Henry Natsch. Ordained Presbyn. ministry, 1905; pastor First Ch., Liberty, N.Y., 1905-09; world travel, 1909-12; dir. religious edn., First Ch., Greenwich, Conn., 1914-17, St. Nicholas Av. Ch., New York, 1917-27, Presbytery of New York, 1929-40; field rep. Presbyn. Bd. of Christian Edn., 1929-40. Director Greater N.Y. Federation of Chs.; secretary bd. trustees N.Y. State Council of Chs.; mem. bd. mgrs. Seamen's House of Y.M.C.A., N.Y. City, Y.M.C.A. sec. Camp Merritt Base Hosp., 1918. Mem. Phi Delta Theta. Clubs: Nat. Republican, Clergy, Quill, Brown Univ. of N.Y. Home: Riverdale, New York, N.Y. Died Mar. 20, 1945.

FUSSELL, Joseph Hall (fū-zĕl'); b. Nottingham, Eng., 1863; s. Joseph and Susannah (Hall) F.; ed. University Coll., Nottingham; D.Theos., Theosophical University, 1929; unmarried. Came to U.S., 1890; teacher, pvt. sch., Savannah, Ga., 1890-91; pvt. tutor, N.J. and N.Y. City, 1891-92; pvt. sec. to William Q. Judge (co-founder of Theos. Soc.), New York, 1893-96, and to Katherine Tingley, 1896-1929; sec.-gen. The Theosophical Society; trustee, Theosophical University; asso. editor, Theosophical Forum. Mason (32°). Wrote: Theosophy and Occultism; More Light—A Study of Theosophy and Freemasonry; also various brochures. Home: Internat. Theosophical Hdqrs., Point Loma, Calif. Died May 7, 1942.

G

GAARDE, Fred William (gär'dē), physician; b. Minden, Neb., June 20, 1887; s. John Frederick and Anna Dorothy (Klith) G.; B.S., U. of Chicago, 1909; M.D., Rush Medical Coll., 1912; in practice of internal medicine, Chicago, 1913-14; instr. medicine, Rush Med. Coll., 1913-20; m. Hazel Holhman, May 20, 1915. Asso. in med., Mayo Clinic, Sept. 1920; asso. prof. med., Mayo Foundation, Univ. of Minn.; head diagnostic section in med., Mayo Clinic. Major, Med. Corps, U.S. Army; with A.E.F., World War I. Mem. Chicago Inst. Medicine, Am. Medical Assn., Central Clin. Research Club, Minn. Soc. of Internal Medicine, Am. Coll. Physicians, Sigma Xi. Author: chapter in Nelson's Loose-leaf System of Medicine, and in Blumer's Bedside Diagnosis. Contbr. about 25 articles to med. jours. Address: 102 2d Av. S.W., Rochester, Minn. Died Feb. 10, 1948.

GADSDEN, Philip Henry (gădz'dĕn), pub. utility exec.; b. Charleston, S.C., Oct. 4, 1867; s. Christopher Schulz and Florida I. (Morrall) G.; student Porter Mil. Acad., Charleston, 1880-84; A.B., U. of S.C., 1888, LL.D., 1918; m. Sallie Pelzer Inglesby, Apr. 19, 1895 (died July 22, 1900); children—Philip Henry, Lavinia Inglesby (Mrs. Douglas M. Dimond); m. 2d Estelle Blanche White, June 17, 1910; children—Henry White, Margaret Eleanor, Charles Christopher. Admitted to S.C. bar, 1890, and practiced at Charleston, mem. firm Mordecai & Gadsden, 1890-1907; v.p. Charleston Consol. Ry. & Lighting Co., 1900-03, pres., 1903-26; v.p. Charleston Light & Water Co., 1907-17; v.p. United Gas Improvement Co. since 1919; dir. Fidelity Mut. Life Ins. Co. Mem. S.C. Ho. of Rep., 1893-98; mem. Federal Electric Rys. Commn., 1919. Chmn. war bd. Am. Electric Ry. Assn. and chmn. Nat. Com. on Pub. Utility Conditions, World War; chief Phila. Dist. Ordnance Office, War Dept. Pres. Southern Gas Assn., 1922, and Eastern States Gas Conf., 1923. Mem. bd. trustees Edison Electric Inst.; chmn. com. Utility Executives; mem. Am. Gas Assn., Am. Electric Ry. Assn. (pres. 1921), Am. Acad. Polit. and Social Science, U.S. Chamber Commerce (dir. 1921-29), Pa. State Chamber Commerce (dir.), Phila. Chamber Commerce (pres. 1926-35), Army Ordnance Assn. (pres. Phila. post), Kappa Alpha. Democrat. Episcopalian. Mason (Shriner), K.P. Clubs: Engineers, Midday, Rittenhouse, Philadelphia Country (Philadelphia); Congressional Country, Metropolitan (Washington); City Midday (New York). Home: 6420 Drexel Rd. Office: 1401 Arch St., Philadelphia, Pa.* Died Feb. 27, 1945.

GAEBELEIN, Arno Clemens (gā'bĕ-lin), clergyman, editor, author; b. Germany, Aug. 27, 1861; s. Hugo and Fannie (Weidhaas) G.; ed. gymnasium and pvt studies; D.D., Wheaton Coll., 1922; m. Emma F Grimm, Apr. 9, 1885; (died November 21, 1938) children—Paul W., Aino W., Frank E. Came to U.S.

of Am., 1879. Ordained to the ministry of the M.E. Church, 1885; held various pastorates in Baltimore, Md., N.Y. City and Hoboken, N.J., 1894-97; supt. Hope of Israel Mission in connection with N.Y. City Mission, 1894-99. Editor of Our Hope (Bible study mag.), since 1894; Spl. lecturer Evang. Theol. Coll., Dallas, Tex. since 1925. V.p. Stony Brook (L.I., N.Y.) Sch. for Boys. Pres. Am.-European Fellowship; mem. Mediæval Acad. America, N.Y. Hist. Soc., Pi Gamma Mu Fraternity; hon. mem. Eugene Field Literary Society. Republican. Author: Harmony of the Prophetic Word, 1905; Studies in Zachariah, 1906; Commentary on Matthew (2 vols.), 1908; The Work of Christ, 1909; The Prophet Daniel, 1909; The Lord of Glory, 1911; The Book of Revelation, 1916; Studies in Prophecy, 1917; The Jewish Question, 1917; The Annotated Bible (9 vols.), 1912-20; The Angels of God; The Holy Spirit; The Healing Question; Exposition of the Gospel of John; also Commentaries on The Acts of the Apostles, Ezekiel, Joel, Ephesians; Prayer in the Light of the Bible, 1925; Christianity or Religion?, 1927; Half a Century, an Autobiography, 1930; Meat in Due Season, 1932; The Conflict of The Ages, 1933; World Prospects, 1934; Among the Red Autocrats, translated from the German, 1935; Hopeless—Yet There Is Hope, 1935; Listen—God Speaks!, 1936; As It Was—So Shall It Be, 1937; The Hope of the Ages, 1938; The Prophet St. Paul; Moses, His First and Second Coming; What will become of Europe?, 1941; The Mystery of Unanswered Prayer; Gabriel and Michael the Archangel, 1945. Lecturer on biblical subjects in principal cities of U.S. and Canada, and in seminaries and Bible insts. Home: 229 E. Sidney Av., Mount Vernon, N.Y. Office: 456 4th Av., New York. Died Dec. 25, 1945.

GAERTNER, William, instrument maker; b. Merseburg, Germany, Oct. 24, 1864; s. Karl and Louise (Pippel) G.; ed. pub. sch. and Tech. Sch. for Instrument Makers, Berlin; m. Belva Eleanora Boosinger, June 14, 1917. Apprentice in instrument shop, Halle, at 16; worked for various firms in Germany, later in London, and Vienna; came to U.S., 1889, naturalized citizen, 1896; instrument maker for Coast and Geodetic Survey, 1890-93; with Smithsonian Instn., 1893-96; opened shop in Chicago, Ill., 1896, later William Gaertner & Co. and since 1924, Gaertner Scientific Corp., of which is pres. and treas.; mfr. of the "interferometer," for Prof. Albert A. Michelson; the photographic zenith tube, for the Internat. Geodetic Assn., to determine variations of latitude, etc.; has practically solved the problem of eliminating error in accurate precision screws. Awarded Howard N. Potts gold medal, "for notable achievements as a designer and maker of scientific instruments," by the Franklin Inst., 1924. Mem. Am. Astron. Soc., Army Ordnance Assn., Chicago. Assn. Commerce. Lutheran. Club: Press. Active in developing new instruments and improving old designs for U.S. Air Corps. Home: 115 Garrison St., Wilmette, Ill. Office: 1201 Wrightwood Av., Chicago, Ill.* Died Dec. 3, 1948.

GAFFEY, Hugh J., army officer; b. Hartford, Conn., Nov. 18, 1895; s. Peter John and Anne Elizabeth (Conley) G.; grad. Worcester (Mass.) Acad., 1916; student U. of Pa., 1916-17; grad. F.A. Sch., 1923, Command and Gen. Staff Sch., 1936; m. Eleanor Schmitt, Jan. 5, 1922; 1 dau., Eleanor Anne. Commd. 2d lt., F.A., Aug. 15, 1917, and advanced through the grades to maj. gen., Apr. 28, 1943; chief of staff 3d Army, for Lt. Gen. George Patton; comdr. 2d Armored Div., landings in Africa, Sicily; now comdr. 4th Armored Div. sent to rescue of Bastogne. Decorated Silver Star citation, D.S.M., Legion of Merit. Mem. Delta Kappa Epsilon. Home: 3207 Clearview Av., Austin, Tex. Died June 17, 1946; buried in Fort Knox (Ky.) National Cemetery.

GAFFNEY, John J(erome), naval officer; b. Charleston, S.C., Mar. 5, 1891; s. Patrick John and Ellen Frances (O'Conner) G.; A.B., Coll. of Charleston, 1912; student St. Lawrence U. (Brooklyn Law Sch.), 1925-26; m. Wahneta Walsh, Jan. 16, 1915; children—John Jerome, Mary Yetive (Mrs. Edward W. Bridewell), Gloria Louise (Mrs. Francis Van Dyke Andrews), Lurline Loretta (Mrs. Charles R. Eisenbach). Entered supply corps, U.S. Navy, 1912; promoted through grades to rear adm., 1943; served in Chinese waters, 1913-16; built and managed naval clothing factory, Charleston, S.C., 1917; sec. Virgin Islands, 1920-23; bought navy fuel, 1937-39; staff comdr. Aircraft Battle Force, 1939-41; headed supply work ashore, Pearl Harbor, 1941-45; comdr. Naval Supply Depot, Oakland, Calif. since Aug., 1945. Awarded Silver Star, spl. commendation letter, Sec. of Navy, Legion of Merit. Home: 11 Mill St., Charleston, S.C. Address: U.S. Naval Supply Depot, Oakland 4, Calif. Died Nov. 21, 1947.

GAFFNEY, T(homas) St. John, consul gen.; b. Limerick, Ireland, 1864; s. Thomas Gaffney; ed. Clongowes Wood Coll. (Ireland), Royal U. of Ireland; m. Fannie Smith Humphreys. Strong supporter of all movements in behalf of Irish Nationality; actively identified with Rep. party; sec. McKinley League, State of N.Y., campaign of 1896; consul-gen. at Dresden, Saxony, 1905-13, at Munich, Bavaria, 1913. Decorated Cross Legion d'Honneur, France, 1902; officer Order of King Leopold, Belgium, 1905. Frequent contbr. to mags. and journals on nat. and internat. subjects. Mem. Am.-Irish Hist. Soc., Gaelic Soc., K.C. Clubs: Republican (New York); Royal Saxon Automobile; Touring Club of France; German Touring (Munich); Royal Saxon Aeronautic. Home: New York. Address: American Consulate General, Munich, Bavaria. Died Jan. 13, 1944.

GAG, Wanda (gŏg), artist, author; b. New Ulm, Minn., Mar. 11, 1893; d. Anton and Lissi (Biebl) Gág; studied St. Paul Art School, 1913-14, Minneapolis Art School, 1915-17, Art Students League, N.Y., 1917-18; married Earle Marshall Humphreys. Permanently represented at Metropolitan Museum of Art, N.Y. Pub. Library, Newark Museum, Art. Inst. Chicago, Library of Congress, Addison Gallery Am. Art, Phillips Acad. (Andover, Mass.), Mus. Fine Art (Cleveland O.), Acad. Fine Arts (Honolulu), Los Angeles Art Assn., Wisconsin Art Inst., Evander Childs High Sch. (N.Y. City), Vassar Coll., San Francisco Mus. Art, Phila. Mus. Art, Wadsworth Athenaeum, British Mus., So. Kensington Mus., Bibliotheque Nationale (Paris) Kupferstich Kabinett (Berlin), Whitney Mus., Am. Art. Boston Mus. Fine Arts, Mus. Fine Arts (Houston); exhibited in Am. Printmakers show, 1927-36. Awarded 1st prize Phila. Lithograph Show, 1930; Purchase prize for lithograph, Artists for Victory show, Met. Mus. New York, 1942; purchase prize for lithograph, Library Congress (Washington), 1944. Translator and illustrator; Tales from Grimm, 1936; Snow White and the Seven Dwarfs, 1938; Three Gay Tales from Grimm, 1943. Author and illustrator: Millions of Cats, 1928; Snippy and Snappy, 1931; The Funny Thing, 1929; The A.B.C. Bunny, 1933; Gone is Gone, 1935; Growing Pains, 1940; Nothing at All, 1941. Died June 27, 1946.

GAGE, Brownell, educator; b. Astoria, L.I., N.Y., Apr. 14, 1874; s. Charles Tyler and Sarah Anne (Perrin) G.; student Coll. City of N.Y., 1889-92; B.A., Yale, 1898, M.A., 1911, Ph.D., 1924; B.D., Union Theol. Sem., 1911; m. Helen Robertson Howe (M.D., D.P.H.), Jan. 12, 1904 (died Jan. 6, 1937); children—Katharine Perrin, Robertson (dec.), Emily Thornton, Eleanor Williams (Mrs. Dean F. Betts); m. 2d, Delight Walkly Hall, May 27, 1938. A founder, 1904, of Colls. of Yale, Changsha, China, serving as dean, later provost and chmn. governing board until 1923, now trustee; headmaster Suffield Acad., 1924-39, headmaster emeritus since July 1, 1939; pastor, Bolton Congregational Church since 1940; trustee Suffield Acad. since Feb. 1939, also exec. sec. of bd. Served with Y.M.C.A. in France 1 yr., World War. Mem. Appalachian Mountain Club, Phi Beta Kappa. Republican. Conglist. Home: Bolton, Conn. Died Feb. 3, 1945.

GAGE, Simon Henry, biologist; b. Otsego County, N.Y., May 20, 1851; s. Henry V. and Lucy (Grover) G.; B.S., Cornell U., 1877; studied in Europe, 1889; m. Susanna Phelps, Dec. 15, 1881 (died Oct. 5, 1915); 1 son, Henry Phelps; m. 2d, Clara C. Starrett, Apr. 14, 1933. Instructor, 1878-81, asst. prof., 1881-89, asso. prof. physiology, 1889-93, asso. prof. anatomy, histology and embryology, 1893-95, prof., 1895-96, prof. histology and embryology, 1896-1908, Cornell; apptd. prof. histology and embryology, emeritus, June 1908, after 25 yrs'. service to undertake spl. investigations, on an allowance from Carnegie Foundation for the Advancement of Teaching; resumed teaching, 1918-19, to take place of instrs. who entered military service. Co-editor Am. Jour. Anatomy, 1901-21; pres. Comstock Publishing Co., Inc., 1932-44. Chmn. section embryology, Internat. Congress Arts and Sciences, St. Louis, 1904; fellow A.A.A.S. (v.p., 1885, 1892, 1899); mem. Assn. Am. Anatomists, Am. Soc. Naturalists, Am. Micros. Soc., Am. Soc. Zoölogists, Am. Soc. of Amateur Microscopists (pres. 1939), Royal Soc. of Arts, London. Mem. advisory bd. Wistar Inst. Anatomy since 1905; trustee Cornell U., 1921-22. Author: The Microscope and Microscopic Methods, 17th Edit., 1941; History of Microscopy in America, 1943 (in manuscript); Anatomical Technology (with Prof. Burt G. Wilder); Optic Projection with the Magic Lantern, the Reflecting Lantern, the Projection Microscope, and the Moving Picture Machine (with Henry Phelps Gage, Ph.D.), 1913-14; also numerous papers on biol. subjects; collaborator or contbr. to Foster's Encyclopaedie Medical Dictionary, Wood's Reference Handbook of the Medical Sciences, Johnson's Cyclopedia. Editor and contbr. Record of the Class of 1877, Cornell U., 1923; librarian Van Cleef Memorial Library, Cornell U., 1921-40; life sec. Class of 1877, Cornell. Home: Interlaken, N.Y. Office: Stimson Hall, Ithaca, N.Y. Died Oct. 20, 1944; buried at Worcester, Otsego County, N.Y.

GAGER C(harles) Stuart, botanist; b. Norwich, N.Y., Dec. 23, 1872; s. Charles Carroll and Leora Josephine (Darke) G.; A.B., Syracuse U., 1895; Pd.B. and Pd.M., N.Y. State Normal Coll., Albany, 1897; Harvard summer, 1898; Ph.D., Cornell U., 1902; D.Sc., Syracuse, 1920; Pd.D., N.Y. State Coll. for Teachers, 1921; m. Bertha Woodward Bagg, June 25, 1902; children—Benjamin Stuart (dec.), Ruth Prudence (Mrs. Kenneth G. Bucklin). Laboratory asst., Syracuse U., 1894-95; vice-principal, Ives Sem., Antwerp, N.Y., 1895-96; prof. biol. sciences and physiography, N.Y. State Normal Coll., 1897-1905; dir. labs., N.Y. Bot. Garden, 1906-08; prof. botany, U. of Mo., 1908-10; dir. Brooklyn Botanic Garden since 1910. Asst. in botany, 1901-02, instr., 1904, Summer Sch., Cornell; lab. asst., N.Y. Bot. Garden, 1904-05; acting prof. botany, Rutgers Coll., 1905; teacher botany, Morris High School, New York, 1905; prof. botany, summer session, New York U., 1905-06. Editor Brooklyn Botanic Garden Record since 1912; bus. mgr. Am. Jour. Botany, 1914-35, Ecology since 1920, Genetics since 1922. Mem. com. on plant quarantines and their adminstrn. of Merchants Assn. of N.Y. City since 1922, chmn. since 1933; mem. com. on bot. exhibits, A Century of Progress, Chicago, 1933; v.p. Hortus, Inc. (hort. section, N.Y. World's Fair, 1939, 40); mem. various commns. Nat. Research Council; chmn. sub-com. on edn. and public relations, U.S. Botanic Garden; mem. and dir. Corp. of Bermuda Biological Station for Research; member board directors N.J. Federation of Shade Tree Commissions; trustee Adelphi College, 1932-40. Honorary life mem. Pa. Hort. Soc.; fellow A.A.A.S. (v.p. and chmn. of Sect. G, 1917), N.Y. Acad. Sciences, Brooklyn Inst. Arts and Sciences; mem. Bot. Soc. America (pres. 1936), Soc. Exptl. Biology and Medicine, Torrey Bot. Club (sec. 1905-08; v.p. 1911, 1917-31), Am. Soc. of Biol. Chemists, Am. Soc. Naturalists, Nat. Inst. Social Sciences (vice pres. 1928-31 and since 1935; pres. 1932-35), Sch. Garden Assn. America (hon.), Horticultural Soc. of N.Y. (vice chmn. board since 1937), Internat. Flower Show Commn. since 1932; N.J. Federation of Shade Tree Commissions since 1934; Svenska Linné Sällskapet, Société Linnéene de Lyon, Royal New Zealand Inst. of Horitculture, Phi Beta Kappa, Sigma Xi, Delta Upsilon, Gamma Sigma Delta. Clubs: Century, N.Y. Bird and Tree Club (dir.), Twentieth Century of Brooklyn (pres. 1933-35). Author: Errors in Science Teaching, 1901; Effects of the Rays of Radium on Plants, 1908; Fundamentals of Botany, 1916; Laboratory Guide for General Botany, 1916; Heredity and Evolution in Plants, 1920; The Relation between Science and Theology, 1925; General Botany with Special Reference to Its Economic Aspects, 1926; The Plant World, 1931; also numerous papers in scientific and ednl. jours. Abstractor Biol. Abstracts, 1926-31; bot. editor and contbr. Nat. Cyclo., 1932. Contbr. Ency. Brittanica, Standard Cyclo. Horticulture, Cyclo. Edn. Translator: (from the German of de Vries) Intracellular Pangenesis, 1910. Home: 29 Linden Blvd., Brooklyn, N.Y. Died Aug. 9, 1943.

GAIGE, Crosby, theatrical producer; b. Nelson, N.Y., July 26, 1882; s. George Edward and Jane (DeMaine) G.; ed. Cazenovia (N.Y.) Sem., 1896-99, Columbia, 1899-1903; married Hilda Wilson, Mar. 12, 1908 (divorced 1928); 1 son, Jeremy; married 2d, Cecelia Bauer, January 3, 1945. Began as play-broker, 1903; joined Selwyn & Co., 1905; started producing business with "Within the Law," 1912; independent producer since 1926; prod. Silence, The Butter and Egg Man, The Enemy, Beware of Widows, The Shannons of Broadway, Night Stick, Little Accident, House Beautiful, I Loved You Wednesday, (with Jed Harris) Broadway, and Coquette starring Helen Hayes, Accent on Youth. Mem. Bibliog. Soc. of London, de l'Union des Sommeliers de Paris, Latin Soc. of America. Republican. Episcopalian. Author: New York World's Fair Cook Book; Crosby Gaige's Cocktail Guide and Ladies' Companion, 1941; The Standard Cocktail Guide, 1944; Crosby Gaige's Macaroni Manual, 1947; Footlights and Highlights (autobiography), 1948. Compiled official World's Fair food guide book, Food at the Fair. Editor: Prunier's Fish Cookery Book (Am. edit.); Andre Simon's French Cook Book, 1948; Footlights and Highlights, 1948. Contbr. to periodicals; wrote weekly column on food for United Feature Syndicate; food and wine editor of Country Life Magazine; broadcasts column on food for United Feature Syndicate; food and wine editor of Country Life Magazine; broadcasts on subjects of food and cooking; specialist on spices and seasoning; advisor on flavor to Am. Spice Trade Assn.; consultant on food generally with special reference to dehydration and dehydrated foods. Home: Watch Hill Farm, Peekskill, N.Y. Office: 630 5th Av., New York, N.Y. Died Mar. 8. 1949.

GAINER, Joseph Henry, lawyer; b. Providence, R.I., Jan. 18, 1878; s. John and Margaret (Keogh) G.; A.B., Holy Cross Coll., Worcester, Mass., 1899, LL.D., 1919; LL.B., Catholic U. of America, 1902; A.M., Brown U., 1924; m. Christina McPherson, 1915; children—Christine, Margaret, Joseph. Practiced law in Providence since 1902; became mem. Gainer, Carr & Mulhearn 1903, O'Shaunessy, Gainer and Carr, 1911, Gainer and Carr, 1922, Curran, Hart, Gainer and Carr, 1927; now mem. Hart, Gainer and Carr; mem. Providence Sch. Com. 2 yrs.; mem. Common Council 2 yrs., Bd. of Aldermen 3 yrs.; mayor City of Providence, R.I., 1913-27. Trustee Citizens Savings Bank; dir. The Morris Plan Co. of R.I. Trustee St. Joseph's Hosp., St. Vincent de Paul Infant Asylum; mem. R.I. State Council of Defense; State chmn. U.S.O.; mem. exec. com. Am. Red Cross. Mem. Am. and R.I. bar assns., Gen. Alumni Assn. of Holy Cross Coll. (ex-pres.), Phi Beta Kappa, Phi Kappa. Catholic. Democrat. Clubs: University, Catholic, Columbus. Home: 55 Grotto Av. Office: Hospital Trust Bldg., Providence, R.I.* Died Dec. 15, 1945.

GAINES, Charles Kelsey (gānz), univ. prof.; b. Royalton, Niagara County, N.Y., Oct. 21, 1854; s. Rev. Absalom Graves and Emma Clara (Hurd) G.; B.A., St. Lawrence U., Canton, N.Y., 1876, M.A., 1879, LL.D., 1917; Ph.D., Lombard U., 1892; m. Campbellina Pendelton Woods, July 2, 1878; 1 son, Clarence Hurd. Prof. Greek, St. Lawrence U., 1876-95, and since 1900. Engaged in newspaper work, New York, 1895-1900. Mem. Phi Beta Kappa, Beta Theta Pi, Am. Phiol. Assn., Authors' League of America. Author: Gorgo, a Romance of Old Athens, 1903; revised and enlarged edit. of Cushing's Manual, 1911; revised "Sixty Years of St. Lawrence," 1916; Echoes of Many Moods (verse), 1926; also articles and poems in mags. Home: 20 Pine St., Canton, N.Y. Died Jan. 2, 1944.

GAINES, Edward Franklin, prof. genetics in agronomy; b. Avalon, Mo., Jan. 12, 1886; s. Charles Samuel and Mattie (Millay) G.; grad. State Normal Sch., Cheney, Wash., 1907; B.S., State Coll. of Wash., 1911, M.S., 1913; Sc.D., Harvard, 1921; m. Xerpha McCulloch, June 6, 1912; children—Edward McCulloch, Xerpha Mae, John Charles, Irene (dec.), Grant Robert. Instr. in agronomy, State Coll. of Wash., 1911-17, asst. prof. farm crops, 1917-21, asso. prof., 1921-30, prof. genetics in agronomy since 1930; cerealist, Washington Expt. Station, since 1917. Fellow A.A.A.S., Am. Soc. Agronomy; mem. Am. Phytopathol. Soc., Am. Bot. Soc., Northwest Scientific Assn. (pres. 1939), Alpha Gamma Rho, Alpha Zeta, Phi Kappa Phi, Phi Beta Kappa, Sigma Xi. Contbr. agrl. publs. Home: Pullman, Wash. Died Aug. 17, 1944.

GALBRAITH, Nettie May, educator; b. Walla Walla, Wash., June 17, 1880; d. James William and Margaret Ellen Breckenridge (Kerr) Galbraith; grad. Central Wash. Coll. of Edn., Ellensburg; A.B., Whitman Coll., 1905; A.M., Wash. State Coll., 1916; grad. study U. of Calif., Columbia, U. of Ore.; scholastic course, Europe, 1925; unmarried. Teacher public schs., Walla Walla, 1900-05; prin. Green Park Sch., Walla Walla, 1905-10; prin. St. Paul's Sch. for Girls, Walla Walla, since 1910, also instr. in history. Mem. N.E.A., Administrative Women in Edn. (nat. council), Am. Assn. Univ. Women (past president; past 1st vice-president), English-Speaking Union (hon.), Archæol. Inst. America (regent Walla Walla br.), Chamber of Commerce, Whitman Guild (program chairman), Kappa Kappa Gamma (past province v.p.), Phi Beta Kappa, Pi Gamma Mu, Pi Lambda Theta. Episcopalian. Clubs: Kiwanis, Walla Walla Symphony (dir. and v.p.), Walla Walla Art (pres.), Park and Civic Arts (pres.), Presidents' Council (pres.). Lecturer on ednl. subjects, state and national. Awarded Episcopal Cross for Service, Dist. of Spokane. Address: St. Paul's School, Walla Walla, Wash. Died Jan. 21, 1943.

GALE, Edward Chenery, lawyer; b. Minneapolis, Minn., Aug. 21, 1862; s. Samuel Chester and Susan (Damon) G.; U. of Minn., 2 yrs.; A.B., Yale, 1884; Harvard Law Sch., 1886-87, A.M., 1887; m. Sarah Belle Pillsbury, June 28, 1892; children—Edward Pillsbury (dec.), Richard Pillsbury. Practiced at Minneapolis since 1888; mem. Snyder, Gale & Richards. Pres. Pub. Library Bd., 1915-41; pres. Hennepin County Sanatorium Commn. in charge pub. tuberculosis hosp.; mem. exec. council Minn. State Hist. Society (pres. 1936-38). Decorated Officer Order Leopold II (Belgium), 1930. Mem. bd. of dirs. Minneapolis Orchestral Assn (v.p.), Minneapolis Soc. Fine Arts, Minneapolis Bar Assn. (pres. 1919-20), Psi Upsilon, Phi Beta Kappa, Scroll and Key. Republican. Clubs: Minneapolis, Skylight, Minikahda, LaFayette, Woodhill Country. Home: 2115 Stevens Av. Office: Rand Tower, Minneapolis, Minn.* Died Sep. 12, 1943.

GALE, Henry Gordon, physicist; b. Aurora, Ill., Sept. 12, 1874; s. Eli Holbrook and Adelaide (Parker) G.; A.B., U. of Chicago, 1896, grad. student, 1896-97, fellow in physics, 1897-99, Ph.D., 1899; m. Agnes Spofford Cook, Jan. 5, 1901; 1 dau., Beatrice Gordon. Asst. in physics, 1899-1900, asso., 1900-02, instr., 1902-07, asst. prof., 1907-11, asso. prof. physics, 1911-16, prof., 1916-40, dean in Junior Colls., 1908-40, dean of science in the Colls., 1912-40, dean of Ogden Grad. Sch. Science, 1922, chmn. dept. of physics, 1925, dean div. of phys. sciences, 1931, emeritus, Univ. of Chicago. Physicist, Solar Observatory, Mt. Wilson, Calif., 1906; research associate of Carnegie Inst. at Mt. Wilson, 1909, 10, 11; editor Astrophys. Jour. since 1912. Capt. of Inf., N.A., 1917; maj. Sig. Corps, Jan. 1918, lt. col., Mar. 1919; in charge spl. service div., Tours, France, 1918-19. Cited by comdr.-in-chief A.E.F. for "especially meritorious and conspicuous service"; Chevalier Legion of Honor, France. Mem. bd. John Crerar Library. Fellow A.A.A.S. (v.p. 1934), Am. Physical Soc. (v.p. 1927-29; pres. 1929-31), Am. Optical Society; mem. Delta Kappa Epsilon, Sigma Xi and Gamma Alpha fraternities. Clubs: Quadrangle, Wayfarers, University, Lake Zurich (Ill.) Golf. Republican. Author: (with R. A. Millikan) A First Course in Physics, 1906; A Laboratory Course in Physics, 1906; Practical Physics, 1920; Elements of Physics, 1926; (with R. A. Millikan and C. W. Edwards) A First Course in College Physics, 1928. Vice chmn. div. of phys. sciences, Nat. Research Council, 1920-21, chmn., 1921-22. Home: 5646 Kimbark Av., Chicago, Ill. Died Nov. 16, 1942.

GALE, Philip Bartlett, chmn. bd. Standard Screw Company; b. Peoria, Illinois; s. Edward and Ellen (Maxwell) G.; ed. Lewis Institute, Chicago; m. Bernadine Dodd, 1898. With Standard Screw Co., Hartford, Conn., since beginning career, chairman of board since 1930; director Smyth Mfg. Co., The Collins Co., Hartford National Bank & Trust Co., Hartford Fire Insurance Co., Hartford Steam Boiler & Inspection Co., Hartford Accident & Indemnity Co., Terry Steam Turbine Co., Chicago Screw Co., Western Automatic Machine Screw Co.; v.p. Conn. Humane Soc. Trustee, Society for Savings, Hartford Y.M.C.A. Dir. Hartford Hospital, Conn. Children's Aid Soc., Hartford Community, Hartford, Conn. Died July 25, 1945.

GALLAGHER, William J., congressman; b. Minneapolis, Minn., May 13, 1875; s. Patrick J. and Louisa (Knaeble) G.; grad. North Side High Sch., Minneapolis, 1894; m. Mabel Pierson, June 6, 1936; children—Mary (Mrs. Russell Thomson), Lois (Mrs. Theodore Newman). Worked as railroad checker and as city laborer; became editorial writer The National Single Taxer, Minneapolis, 1895; mem. 79th Congress (1945-47), 3d Minn. Dist. Democrat. Home: 2206 James Av. N., Minneapolis 11. Minn. Died Aug. 13, 1946.

GALLAND, Joseph Stanislaus (găl'lănd), Romance langs.; b. Biddeford, Me., Sept. 20, 1883; s. Joseph and Léa (Labonté) G.; A.B., U. of Me., 1906, B.S., 1907; M.A., U. of Wis., 1909, Ph.D., 1914; m. Margaret Michels, Dec. 28, 1909; 1 dau., Margaret Léa (Mrs. Burton A. Milligan). Has been a teacher of the Romance languages in various capacities at Kemper Mil. Sch., U. of Wis., Grove City (Pa.) Coll., Syracuse U., U. of Mich., Indiana U., until 1925, prof. Romance langs. since 1925, head of dept., 1925-34, Northwestern U.; visiting prof. U. of Southern California, summer 1930. 2d and 1st lt. Intelligence Dept., U.S. Army, World War, specializing in codes and ciphers; with English and French armies on Arras and Amiens fronts, spring of 1918; with Am. Army in St. Mihiel, Argonne, Woevre and Moselle movements, and Army of Occupation with 4th Corps, at Cochem-am-Moselle, Germany. Mem. Modern Lang. Assn. America, Am. Assn. Univ. Profs., Nat. Fedn. of Modern Lang. Teachers, Société des Amis de la Bibliothèque Nationale, Am. Cryptogram Assn., Am. Legion, Vets of Foreign Wars, Les Camarades de Combat (vice-pres. 1936), U.S. Naval Institute (associate member), American Society French Legion of Honor, Alpha Tau Omega Fraternity. Decorated Chevalier Legion of Honor (France), 1932. Democrat. Club: University. Author: French Composition, 1922; Spanish Grammar Review (with Brenes-Mesén), 1923; Spanish Composition (with same), 1924; Elementary Spanish Reader (with same), 1925; Progressive French Reader (with A. E. Du Gord), 1929; Nineteenth Century French Prose (with Roger Cros), 1930; Nineteenth Century French Verse (with same), 1931; Progressive French Grammar (with Ethel Vaughan), 1932, revised edit., 1941; A Study of the structural elements of the French language, 1941; An Historical and Analytical Bibliography of the Literature of Cryptology, 1945. Editor: Balzac's Le Colonel Chabert, 1929; Ten Favorite French Stories, 1935. Home: 1609 Ridge Av., Evanston, Ill. Died Nov. 28, 1947.

GALLUP, Clarence Mason (găl-lŭp'), clergyman; b. Norwich, Conn., Oct. 2, 1874; s. Loren Aborn and Elizabeth Hooker (Kinney) G.; grad. Norwich Free Acad., 1891; A.B., Brown Univ., 1896; B.D., Divinity School U. of Chicago, 1900; D.D., Brown Univ., 1915; m. Mary Alice Hovey, June 28, 1899; 1 son, Frederick Sherer. Ordained ministry Bapt. Ch., 1900; pastor Second Ch., Southington, Conn., 1900-01; asst. pastor Emmanuel Ch., Albany, N.Y., 1901-03; pastor First Ch., New Bedford, Mass., 1904-11, Central Ch., Providence, R.I., 1911-31. Recording sec. Ministers and Missionaries Benefit Board, 1927-44; rec. sec. Northern Bapt. Conv., 1928-46. Mem. N.E. Baptist Hist. Soc., S.A.R., Phi Beta Kappa, Pi Gamma Mu, Phi Delta Theta. Mem. New York Q. Clubs: Quill, Republican (White Plains, N.Y.). Wrote: (dramas) Conscience—Freedom; The High Calling; From Tarsus to Rome; Lazarus; The Singing Shepherd; The Angel of the Church; Abraham Lincoln; The Double Gift; Haystack Harvest; The Song of a Nation's Soul; Out of the Rock; Roger Williams Passes By; A Hero of Conscience; (dissertation) The Political Menace of Atheism. Contbr. essays, poems, etc. Home: 83 Waller Av., White Plains, N.Y. Died July 16, 1947.

GAMMELL, William, capitalist; b. Providence, R.I., May 20, 1857; s. William and Elizabeth Amory (Ives) G.; A.B., Brown U., 1878; m. Bessie Gardner Bowen, Feb. 20, 1884; children—William, Arthur Amory, Robert Hale Ives. Engaged as mfr. and in investments since 1880; mem. Brown & Ives; pres. Beverly Land Co. Trustee Brown U. since 1915. Mem. Psi Upsilon. Clubs: University, Hope, Agawam, Squantum (Providence); University, Garden City (New York). Home: 170 Hope St. Office: 50 S. Main St., Providence, R.I. Died Nov. 12, 1943.

GAMMON, Robert William, clergyman; b. California, Missouri, July 15, 1867; s. Noah and Adaline (Buchanan) G.; A.B., Earlham Coll., Ind., 1895; B.D., Chicago Theol. Sem., 1899; D.D., Tabor, 1912, Chicago Theol. Sem., 1920; m. May E. Thomas, Aug. 27, 1891; 1 dau., Mrs. Marie Elizabeth Quinn. Ordained Congl. ministry, 1898; pastor Whitewater Friends' Meeting, Richmond, Indiana, Congregational Church, Big Rock, Illinois, Pilgrim Church, Pueblo, Colorado, First Church, Decatur, Illinois, until 1911; edn. sec. for the interior, Congregational Educational Soc., 1911-25, asso. sec., 1925-36; spl. rep., Congl. Edn. Soc. since 1936. Western corr. Congregationalist and its successor The Advance, 1914-42. Exec. sec. Midwest Pastoral Relations Com. since 1938. Founder, Tower Hill Camp, Sawyer, Michigan. Republican. Mason (K.T.). Home: 531 Clinton Av., Oak Park, Ill. Office: 19 S. La Salle St., Chicago, Ill. Died Feb. 27, 1948.

GANDHI, Mohandas (Karamchand), Mahatma (gän-dē), Indian nationalist and religious leader; b. Oct. 2, 1869; mem. Vaisya or merchant caste; ed. Samaldas Coll., Kathiawai, India; m. Kasturbai, 1882, at age of thirteen. Practiced law in Rajkot since 1891. Induced All-India Cong. Com. at Poona meeting to offer co-operation in war effort in event British agreed to set up immediate provisional govt.; arrested and sentenced to 1 yr. imprisonment, Dec., 1940. During Boer War helped Brit. by forming Indian Ambulance Corps of which became asst. supt., for which service received Boer War Medal (this returned together with gold Kaiser-i-Hind Medal to Brit. Viceroy, 1928). Led Indians in nursing European victims of the Black Plague, Johannesburg, Africa, brought about formation of another Indian Ambulance Corps during Zulu rebellion and made possible compromise with Gen. Smuts, over tax imposed on Indians coming out of indenture, 1908. Jailed three times for leading civil disobedience campaigns. Formed Satyagrapha League, 1919, after appearing for first time as leader in Indian Nat. Cong. at spl. session at which Montagu-Chelmsford proposals and Rowlatt bills were denounced; resigned both as pres. and mem. of Congress, Oct. 1934 (however has continued to use influence with both British and leaders of new Indian govt. and continues as leading power). Opposed to modern science and inventions, violence and bloodshed, industrialism; believes in individual reform. Address: Segaon near Wardha, India. Died Jan. 30, 1948.

GANNETT, William Howard, publisher; b. Augusta, Me., Feb. 10, 1854; s. Joseph Farley and Mary E. (Patterson) G.; ed. Augusta pub. schs.; m. Sarah N. Hill, Oct. 20, 1878; children—Grace B. (dec. wife of Dr. D. B. Cragin), Guy Patterson, Florence Lillian (wife of Francis H. Farnum, U.S. Army). Clerk in Augusta stores until 1888; established Comfort Magazine, 1888. Mem. Me. Legislature, 1903-05. Mem. Nat. Aeronautic Assn. (former gov. for Me.). Republican. Mason (K.T.), Odd Fellow. Clubs: Centenarian of East Aurora, N.Y. (life); Abnaki (Augusta). Has travelled extensively in U.S. and Europe by air. Club: 100,000 Mile Club, United Air Lines; commodore, Am. Air Lines. Home: 114 Western Av., Augusta, Me. Died July 30, 1948.

GANNON, Sinclair, naval officer; b. Columbia, Tex. Mar. 19, 1877; s. William Andrew and Nancy Clementine (Robinson) G.; grad. U.S. Naval Acad., 190 Naval War Coll., Newport, 1921; m. Dell Triplet Sept. 25, 1902; children—Nancy Stuart (wife Comdr Hilyer Fulford Gearing), Mary Sinclair (Mrs. Ott Lang), commd. ensign July 1, 1902; promoted throug grades to rear adm., July 1, 1933; with landing part from U.S.S. Machias, Colon, Colombia, 1901-02; participated Abyssinian Expdn. in U.S.S. Machias, 1903-04; with Atlantic Fleet world cruise in U.S.S. Glacier, Kearsarge and Connecticut, 1907-09; flag sec. t comdr. in chief U.S. Asiatic Fleet in U.S.S. Saratoga, Cincinnati and Rainbow, 1911-12, and comdg. officer U.S.S. Elcano on Yangtze River, 1912-14, during overthrow of Manchu Dynasty; comdg. officer U.S.S. Saranac participated in laying North Sea mine barrage, 1918; comdg. officer U.S.S. San Francisco and comdr. Mine Detachment, 1919-20; mem. War Plans Div., Office of Naval Operations, Joint Army and Navy Planning Com. and Joint Bd., 1921-23; asst. chief of staff to commander in chief U.S. Fleet in U.S.S. Seattle, 1923-25; commandant of midshipmen U.S. Naval Academy., 1925-28; commanding officer U.S.S. New York, 1928-29; chief of staff to comdr. U.S. Scouting Fleet, in U.S.S. Wyoming, 1929-30; comdg. officer U.S. Naval Training Sta., San Diego, Calif., 1930-33; comdr. Aleutian Islands Survey Expdn., 1934, and comdr. Minecraft, Battle Force, in U.S.S. Oglala, 1934-35; comdr. Destroyers Scouting Force, in U.S.S. Raleigh, Dobbin, Whitney and Aylwin, 1935-36; comdt. 11th Naval Dist. and San Diego Naval Operating Base, 1936-39; sr. mem. Pacific Coast sect. U.S. Navy Bd. of Inspection and Survey, 1939-41; retired Apr. 1941. Awarded D.S.M., Victory medal, Expeditionary medal, Spanish War medal. Clubs: Army and Navy (Washington); Army and Navy (Manila); N.Y. Yacht (New York, N.Y.). Address: 14 Thompson St., Annapolis, Md. Died Oct. 21, 1948.

GANTT, Ernest Sneed, judge; b. Centralia, Mo., Jan. 11, 1867; s. Patrick Henry and Martha Jane (Fish) G.; student U. of Mo., 1885-87; m. Helena Pettingill, Mar. 30, 1918; children—Ernest Sneed, Grace. Admitted to Mo. bar, 1892, and began practice at Mexico, Mo.; city atty., Mexico, 1894-98; pros. atty., Audrain County, Mo., 1909-13; judge Circuit Court, Audrain County, 1916-27; judge Supreme Court, Mo., since 1927, present term expires 1947. Democrat. Home: 1114 Moreau Drive, Jefferson City, Mo. Died Mar. 4, 1947.

GARBER, Milton C(line), ex-congressman; b. Humboldt, Calif., Nov. 30, 1867; s. Martin and Lucy A. (Rife) G.; student Upper Iowa Univ., 1887-90, A.M. (hon.), 1906; law dept. State U. of Ia., 1891-93; m. Lucy M. Bradley, 1900; children—Ruth, Martin, Martha, Milton, Lucy Ann. Settled in Okla. upon opening of Cherokee strip; began practice at Guthrie, 1893; in company with father and brother, founded town of Garber, and with brother opened up Garber oil field; probate judge, Garfield County, Okla. Ty., 1902-06; asso. justice Supreme Court of Okla., 5th Jud. Dist., 1906-08; elected judge 20th Jud. Dist. of Okla., 1908; resigned to resume practice; mayor of Enid, 1919-21; mem. 68th to 72d Congresses (1923-33), 8th Okla. Dist.; pres. Enid Pub. Co., publishing Enid Morning News and Enid Daily Eagle. Republican. Mem. Christian (Disciples) Ch. Eagles. Home: Enid, Oklahoma. Died Sept. 12, 1948.

GARCELON, William Frye (gär-sē-lŏn'), lawyer; b. Lewiston, Me., Oct. 24, 1868; s. William F. and Lucy A. (Tatterson) G.; A.B., Bates Coll., Lewiston, 1890; LL.B., Harvard, 1895; m. Grace F. Merrill, Sept. 13, 1899; children—Merrill, Grace. Admitted to Mass. bar, 1895, and began practice at Boston; dir. Boston Garden Arena Corp.; grad. treas. Harvard Athletic Assn., 1908-13; treas. Am. Tool & Machine Co.; dir. Am. News Co., Armstrong Co.;

trustee Boston Five Cents Savings Bank. Mem. Mass. Ho. of Rep., 1907-09; mem. bd. of fellows Bates Coll. Mem. Bar Assn. City of Boston. Republican. Mason. Home: 300 Franklin, Newton, Mass. Office: 199 Washington St., Boston, Mass.*Died May 1, 1949.

GARDINER, Curtiss C., pres. Hartford Steam Boiler Inspection and Ins. Co.; b. St. Louis, Mo., May 19, 1874; s. Curtiss Crane and Mary Parmelee (Thurston) G.; student Shady Side Acad., Pittsburgh, Pa.; m. Alice Dana Knox, June 4, 1926. With Hartford Steam Boiler Inspection and Ins. Co., St. Louis, Mo., 1894-1901, v.p. 1927, exec. v.p., 1941, pres., 1942-47, chmn. bd., since 1947. Dir. Hartford Nat. Bank & Trust Co., Boiler Inspection and Ins. Co. of Canada. Trustee Soc. for Savings, Hartford. Member Conn. Historical Soc., Military Order of the Loyal Legion. Club: Hartford and Hartford Golf. Home: 238 N. Whitney St. Office: 56 Prospect St., Hartford, Conn. Died Feb. 23, 1948.

GARDNER, Charles Spurgeon, professor homiletics; b. Gibson County, Tenn., Feb. 28, 1859; s. Stephen Eddy and Eveline Ellen (Wood) G.; student Union U., Jackson, Tenn., 1877-81, Richmond (Va.) Coll., 1881-82; student Southern Baptist Theological Seminary, Louisville, Ky., 1882-83; m. Ariadne Turner, of Brownsville, Tenn., Apr. 17, 1884 (died 1914); m. 2d, Mary Carter Anderson, of Richmond, Virginia, September 1, 1920. Ordained Baptist ministry, 1883; pastor Trenton, Tenn., 1884-85, Brownsville, 1885-86, Edgefield Ch., Nashville, 1886-94, 1st Ch., Greenville, S.C., 1894-1901, Grace St. Ch., Richmond, 1901-07; became prof. homiletics and sociology, Southern Bapt. Theol. Sem., 1907, now emeritus. Mem. Am. Acad. Polit. and Social Science, Am. Sociol. Society, Kappa Alpha. Addressed Baptist World's Congress in London, 1905; preached ann. sermon before Southern Bapt. Conv., 1911; delivered address before World's Social Progress Congress, San Francisco, 1915. Author: The Ethics of Jesus and Social Progress, 1914; Psychology and Preaching, 1918. Club: Authors (London) Home: Gresham Court Apts., Richmond, Va. Died Apr. 1, 1948.

GARDNER, Frank, ex-congressman; b. Scott County, Ind., May 8, 1872; s. William and Eliza J. (Ray) Gardner; grad. Borden Inst., Clark Co., Ind., 1896; LL.B., Ind. U., 1900; m. Bertha A. Warner, Oct. 15, 1908; 1 dau., Frances Aldine. County auditor Scott County, 1903-11; county atty., 6 yrs.; chmn. Dem. County Com., Scott County, 10 yrs.; mem. 68th to 70th Congresses (1923-29), 3d Ind. Dist. Democrat. Presbyterian. Home: Scottsburg, Ind. Died Feb. 1, 1937.

GARDNER, Helen, educator; b. Manchester, N.H.; d. Charles Fredrick and Martha W. (Cunningham) G.; B.A., U. of Chicago, 1901, M.A., 1918. Instr. and asst. prin. Brooks Classical Sch., Chicago, 1901-10; mem. staff Sch. of Art Inst. Chicago since 1920, prof. history of art and chmn. dept. since 1933; lecturer U. of Calif. at Los Angeles, 1927 U. of Chicago, 1928. Mem. Am. Assn. Univ. Women, Am. Soc. Aesthetics, Midland Authors, Phi Beta Kappa. Author: Art Through the Ages, 1926, 3d edit., 1946; Understanding the Arts, 1932. Home: 5749 Dorchester Av., Chicago 37, Ill. Died June 6, 1946.

GARDNER, Herman, pres. Phoenix Hosiery Co. Adress: 320 E. Buffalo St., Milwaukee, Wis. Died Sept. 13, 1947.

GARDNER, Hugh Miller, coll. prof.; b. Goshen, Ind., Aug. 6, 1893; s. Benjamin Franklin and Barbara (Miller) G.; B.S. in Agr., Purdue U., 1916; M.S., Cornell U., 1922; student U. of Southern Calif., summers 1932-33; m. Vina Robertson, May 28, 1926; children—Hugh Robert, Helen Louise. Instr. biology and agr. high schs., Frankfort, Ind., 1916-17; instr. agr. high sch., Oxford, Ind., 1919-21; instr. agrl. edn. and economics, N.M. College of Agriculture and Mechanic Arts, 1922-23; state supervisor of agrl. edn. for N.M., 1923-28; vice dean Sch. of Agr. and prof. of agrl. edn., N.M., College of Agriculture and Mechanic Arts, 1928-29, dean, prof. agrl. edn., director summer sessions, 1929-45, acting president, 1935-36; acting dean of students, 1944-45; pres. Las Cruces Chamber Commerce, 1943-45. Served as chief pharmacist's mate, U.S. Navy, 1917-19. Member N.M. Ednl. Assn., N.M. Schoolmasters Club (pres. 1932-33), Alpha Zeta, Pi Gamma Mu, Alpha Tau Alpha, Acacia. Presbyterian. Mason. Club: Lions (pres. 1932-34). Home: 1001 N. Armijo St., Las Cruces, N.M. Address: State College, N.M. Died, May 1947.

GARDNER, J(ohn) Howland, naval architect; b. Newport, R.I., Feb. 28, 1871; s. Stephen Ayrault and Mary (Sherman) G.; B.S., Mass. Inst. Tech., 1894; m. Helen M. Douglas, Dec. 26, 1900; children—John Howland, Helen Douglas (Mrs. George W. Elkins). Vice-pres. New England Steamship Co., 1913-28, pres., 1928-31; cons. engr. and mem. bd. dirs. Keerfoot Engring Co.; dir. New England Steamship Co., Hartford-New York Transportation Co. Mem. Bd. of Survey and Cons. Engrs., World War; commr. to Peruvian govt. for purchase of German vessels seized by Peru, 1918; co-founder (at request of U.S. Shipping Bd.) U.S. Bur. of Survey, 1920; was for over twenty years chmn. joint equipment com. of President's Conf. Com. and of Bur. of Valuation of Interstate Commerce Commn. Past pres. and hon. mem. Soc. Naval Architects and Marine Engrs. (mem. of exec. com. and member of com. on applications); trustee Webb Inst. Naval Architecture (20 yrs.); Republican. Conglist. Clubs: Engineers (past pres., and mem. admission com.), India House (New York). Home: Old Lyme, Conn. Died July 7, 1944.

GARDNER, John Henry, army officer; b. Meadowdale, N.Y., Oct. 10, 1893; s. John Henry and Fanny Brooks (Ostrander) G.; B.S., Union Coll., 1913; M.S. in E.E., 1915; M.S., Yale, 1924; m. Mercedee Latham Crum, Oct. 15, 1921; children—Frances Patricia, John Underhill. With Gen. Electric Co., 1913-17; commd. 2d lt. F.A., 1917 and advanced through the grades to brig. gen., 1943; with F.A., A.E.F. and Army of Occupation, 1918-21; transferred to Signal Corps in 1923 and served in various research and development activities since 1927; comdg. gen., Signal Corps Aircraft Signal Service, Wright Field, Dayton, O., 1943; asst. chief, Procurement and Distribution Service, Office Chief Signal Officer, Washington, D.C., since August 1943. Mem. Am. Inst. E.E., Chi Psi. Home: 1719 37th St. N.W., Washington. Died Oct. 11, 1944; buried in Arlington National Cemetery

GARDNER, Karl Dana, merchant; b. Warren, R.I., Jan. 23, 1892; s. Dana Leonard and Katherine Esther (Macomber) G.; A.B., Brown U., 1913; m. Laura Borden Batt, Sept. 23, 1916. Connected with W. T. Grant Co., nat. chain stores, since 1913; asst. mgr., store mgr., later dist. mgr., 1924-28; dir. of sales promotion, 1928-30; dir. of merchandising, 1930-35; v.p. and gen. mgr., 1935-37; pres. and gen. mgr., 1937-40; chmn. exec. com., May 1940-Mar. 1942. Lt. col., Army United States, dir. procurement, Army Exchange Service, Jan. 1942-July 1942, col. since July 1942. Trustee Brown University. Mem. Beta Theta Pi. Mem. Reformed Ch. Clubs: Brown (New York); Siwanoy Country. Home: 43 Greenfield Av., Bronxville, N.Y. Died Feb. 25, 1944.

GARDNER, Leroy Upson, physician; b. New Britain, Conn., Dec. 9, 1888; s. Irving Isaac and Inez Baldwin (Upson) G.; B.A., Yale, 1912, M.D., 1914; graduate study Boston City Hospital and Harvard Medical School, 1914-17; honorary M.S., Yale, 1940; m. Carabelle McKenzie, June 22, 1915; children—Margaret, Dorothy. Instructor in pathology, Harvard Medical School, 1916-17; asst. prof. pathology, Yale Sch. of Medicine, 1917-18; pathologist Trudeau Foundation, Saranac Lake, N.Y., 1919-27, director of same since 1936; director Saranac Lab. for Study of Tuberculosis since 1927. Lecturer in medicine, U. of Rochester. Served as lt. Med. Corps, U.S. Army, 1917. Trustee Village of Saranac Lake, 1932-33; mem. water bd., same, 1929-30; mem. Village Planning Commn.; trustee of Trudeau Sanatorium; dir. Trudeau Foundation since 1938. Mem. Corr. Com. on Silicosis, Internat. labor Office, 1930. Fellow A.A.A.S.; mem. Am. Assn. Pathologists and Bacteriologists, Nat. Tuberculosis Assn. (bd. dirs.), A.M.A. (Council Industrial Health), Beta Theta Pi, Nu Sigma Nu. Republican. Presbyterian. Author: Tuberculosis—Bacteriology, Pathology and Laboratory Diagnosis (with S. A. Petroff), 1927. Contbr. to med. publs. on silicosis and related disease due to dust. Home: 36 Old Military Rd., Saranac Lake, N.Y. Died Oct. 24, 1946.

GARDNER, Oliver Max, ex-governor; b. Shelby, N.C., Mar. 22, 1882; s. Oliver Perry (M.D.) and Margaret (Blanton) G.; B.S., N.C. State Coll. Agr. and Engring., 1903; student law, Univ. of N.C., 1905-07, LL.D., 1931; m. Fay Lamar Webb, Nov. 6, 1907; children—Margaret, James W., Ralph, Max, Jr. Practiced at Shelby since 1907, also pres. Cleveland Cloth Mills, Shelby; director Sperry Corp., 1942; chmn. adv. bd. Office of War Mobilization and Reconversion, 1944; chairman Democratic Exec. Com., Cleveland County, N.C., 1907-08; state organizer Dem. clubs, 1908; mem. Dem. State Exec. Com., 1910-14; mem. State Senate 2 terms, 1911 and 1915 (pres. pro-tem, 1915); lt. gov. of N.C., 1916-21; candidate for nomination for gov. of N.C., 1920; del. at large and chmn. state delegation, Dem. Nat. Conv., New York, 1924, Chicago, 1932; gov. of N.C., term 1929-33. Teamster 2d Ill. Regt., Spanish-Am. War, 1898; capt. Co. G, 1st N.C. Inf., 1907-14. Trustee Univ. of N.C., Julius Rosenwald Fund, 1943. Mem. Am. and N.C. bar assns., Sigma Nu. Odd Fellow, Elk. Baptist. Home: Shelby, North Carolina. Address: Woodward Bldg., Washington 5, D.C. Died Feb. 6, 1947.

GARDNER, Walter Pennett, banker; b. Jersey City, N.J., May 27, 1869; s. Edward Charles and Content Wilkinson (Scobey) C.; LL.D., Lafayette Coll., 1933; m. Rebecca C. Horstmann, Oct. 7, 1896; 1 son, Arthur. In banking business since 1888; with N.J. Title Guarantee & Trust Co., 1912-39, dir., 1912-39, pres., 1935-39; judge N.J. Court of Errors and Appeals, 1915-25. Trustee Central R.R. of N.J. in reorganization since 1940. N.J. Commr. Panama-Pacific Expn., 1913-15; chmn. Jersey City Liberty Loan Com. World War. Decorated Chevalier Legion of Honor (France), 1934. Mem. Am. Friends of Lafayette, New York and New Jersey hist. sccs. Home: 131 Kensington Av., Jersey City 4, N.J. Died Nov. 12, 1949.

GARFIELD, Harry Augustus, educator; b. Hiram, Portage County, O., Oct. 11, 1863; s. James Abram (20th President of the U.S.) and Lucretia (Rudolph) G.; A.B., Williams Coll., 1885; student Columbia Univ. Law Sch., 1886-87; also Oxford Univ., England; LL.D., Princeton, and Dartmouth, 1908, Amherst, Wesleyan, 1909, William and Mary, 1921, Harvard Univ., 1928, Toronto Univ., 1933; Williams Coll., 1934; L.H.D., Whitman Coll., 1919; m. Belle Hartford Mason, June 14, 1888; children—James, Mason, Lucretia (Mrs. John Preston Comer), Stanton. Teacher of Latin and Roman history, St. Paul's Sch., Concord, New Hampshire, 1885-86; practiced law as mem. firm Garfield, Garfield & Howe, Cleveland, 1883-1903; prof. contracts, Western Reserve Univ. Law Sch., 1891-97; prof. politics, Princeton Univ., 1903-08; pres. Williams Coll., 1908-34; pres. emeritus since 1934. Chmn. Inst. of Politics since 1920; chmn. Price Com. of U.S. Food Adminstrn. Apptd. U.S. fuel adminstr. by Pres. Wilson, Aug. 1917. Pres. Cleveland Chamber of Commerce, 1898-99; an organizer, 1896, and later pres. Municipal Assn., Cleveland. Mem. Am. Hist. Assn., Am. Econ. Assn., Am. Polit. Science Assn.; (pres. 1923), Am. Soc. Internat. Law, Am. Bar Assn., Nat. Municipal League, Nat. Inst. Social Sciences, League of Nations Non-Partisan Assn., Am. Acad. Polit. and Social Science; council on foreign relations World Peace Foundation (trustee). Mem. U.S. Constl. Sesquicentennial Commission; Washington Nat. Monument Soc. Pres. Outdoor Cleanliness Assn. of D.C., Inc. Home: (summer) Williamstown, Duxbury, Mass. (winter) 2435 Kalorama Road N.W., Washington, D.C. Died Dec. 12, 1942.

GARLAND, Robert, mfr.; b. North Ireland, Sept. 27, 1862; s. Robert and Eliza Jane (Atwell) G.; ed. pub. schs.; came to U.S., 1876; m. Alice Noble Bailey, Apr. 12, 1888; children—Robert (dec.), Alice Gertrude (Mrs. Roy H. McKnight). Began as clk., Oliver Iron & Steel Co., Pittsburgh, 1876, gen. sales mgr., 1886-90; began as mfr., 1890; pres. Garland Mfg. Co., mfrs. electric conduits, Pittsburgh, since 1898. Mem. advisory bd. American Hardware Mfrs. Assn. Chairman War Resources Com., Western Pa. and W.Va., World War I. Mem. City Council, Pittsburgh, 1911-40; trustee Grove City (Pa.) Coll.; mem. Hist. Soc. Western Pa. (pres.). Republican. Episcopalian. Mason (K.T., Shriner). Club: Pittsburgh Athletic. Author: History of the Scotch Irish in Western Pennsylvania; Ten Years of Daylight Saving, from the Pittsburgh Standpoint. Home: 1428 Inverness Av. Office: 4338 Bigelow Blvd., Pittsburgh, Pa. Died Apr. 19, 1949.

GARLAND, William May; b. Westport, Me., Mar. 31, 1866; s. Jonathan May and Rebecca (Jewett) G.; ed. high sch., Waterville, Me.; m. S. Blanche Hinman, Oct. 12, 1898; children—William Marshall, John Jewett. With Ill. Trust & Savings Bank, Chicago, till 1890; moved to Los Angeles, Calif.; auditor Pacific Cable Co., 1890-94; in real estate business since 1894; head of W. M. Garland & Co. Pres. Calif. State Chamber Commerce, 1929-30; hon. pres. Calif. Real Estate Assn. Pres. Automobile Club of Southern Calif., 1906. Mem. Nat. Association of Real Estate Bds. (twice pres.), Los Angeles Realty Bd. (3 times pres.). Dollar a year man, Washington, World War. Col. on staff of Gov. Gillette, 1906-10; ex-mem. Los Angeles Bd. of Edn., Pub. Library Bd.; mem. Rep. Nat. Convs., 1900, 24, 28, 36, 40. Mem. Internat. Olympic Com. that went to Rome, 1923, and secured celebration of the X Olympiad at Los Angeles, for 1932; pres. Organizing Com. X Olympiad, Los Angeles, 1932; pres. Los Angeles Art Assn., 1934-39. Decorated Order of Leopold (Belgium); Officer Order of the White Lion (Czechoslovakia); Legion d'Honneur (France); Cross of Honor, Red Cross—First Class (Germany); Officer Order of Crown (Italy); Comdr. Order of Orange-Nassau (Netherlands); Officer, Royal Order of the Polar Star (Sweden); Comdrs. Cross Order of Polonia Restituta (Poland). Mem. Sons of Revolution. Republican. Episcopalian. Clubs: California (pres. 1908), Los Angeles Athletic (pres. 19 years), Los Angeles Country, Jonathan, Crags Country (president 10 years), Bolsa Chica Gun (president 6 years); Bohemian (San Francisco); Cypress Point Country (Pebble Beach, Calif.); Union Interalliée (Paris). Received award presented by Los Angeles Realty Bd., Los Angeles Chamber of Commerce, Los Angeles Clearing House Assn., Merchants and Mfrs. Assn. as most useful citizen for year 1923. Home: 815 W. Adams Blvd., Los Angeles 7. Office: 117 West Ninth St., Los Angeles 15, Calif. Died Sep. 26, 1948.

GARLINGTON, Creswell, army officer; b. Rock Island, Ill., June 23, 1887; s. Ernest Albert and Anna Bowers (Buford) G.; ed. St. Paul's Sch., Concord, N.H., 1902-06; B.S., U.S. Mil. Acad., 1910; grad. Engr. Sch., 1912, Ecole Superieure de Guerre, Paris, 1923; distinguished grad. Command and Gen. Staff Sch., 1925; grad. Army War Coll., 1928; m. Alexandrine Fitch, Feb. 5, 1921; children—Creswell, Henry Fitch, Sally. Command. 2d lt., Corps of Engrs., U.S. Army, 1910, and advanced through the grades to temp. brig. gen.; temp. col., Corps of Engrs., 1918; comdg. gen., Engr. Replacement Training Center, Ft. Leonard Wood, Mo., since Jan. 20, 1943. Decorated D.S.C.; Purple Heart; Officer, Order of the Crown (Belgium); Legion of Merit (posthumous). Mem. Soc. of Am. Mil. Engrs. Clubs: Chevy Chase (Md.); Army and Navy Country (Arlington, Va.). Address: Hotel General Oglethorpe, Savannah, Ga. Died Mar. 11, 1945; buried in Arlington National Cemetery.

GARNSEY, Elmer Ellsworth (gärn'sē), artist; b. Holmdel, N.J., Jan. 24, 1862; s. John C. and Louisa J. (Fenton) G.; pupil of the Cooper Inst., Art Students' League, George W. Maynard, and Francis Lathrop, New York; m. Laurada Davis, Oct. 6, 1886. Awarded bronze medal as one of the designers of the Chicago Expn., 1893; hon. mention and silver medal, Paris Expn., 1900. Decorations in: Library of Congress; Boston Pub. Library; R.I. State House; Carnegie Inst., Pittsburgh; U.S. Nat. Pavilion, Paris Expn., 1900; New York Stock Exchange; Prudential Life Ins. Bldg., Newark, N.J.; University and Union Clubs, Columbia Univ.; residence of Andrew Carnegie, New York; U.S. Capitol; Ryerson Library, Chicago; Minn., Ia. and Wis. capitols; Yale U.; St. Louis Pub Library; U.S. Custom House, New York; Art Museum, St. Louis. Mem. Nat. Soc. Mural Painters, Architectural League, New York; hon. mem. A.I.A.; charter mem. Am. Acad. in Rome. Club: Century. Address: care Fifth Av. Bank, New York, N.Y. Died Oct. 26, 1946.

GARRAN, Frank W., coll. prof.; b. Boston, Mass., June 17, 1894; s. George F. and Priscilla (Stevens) G.; B.S., Norwich U., 1917, M.S., Mass. Inst. of Tech., 1924; A.M., Dartmouth Coll., 1933; m. Harriet E. Whitney, 1917; children—Frank W., Priscilla E., Philip W., Edward F. Headmaster Atkinson Acad., 1919-20; instr. and asst. prof. civil engring., Norwich U., 1920-24; asst. prof., U. of Ariz., 1924-26; prof. engring., Coll. of Charleston, 1926-29; asst. prof. civil engring., Thayer Sch. of Civil Engring., Dartmouth, 1929-33, prof. and dean since 1933. Served as 1st lt. of engrs., U.S. Army, 1917-19. Trustee Norwich U. Mem. Am. Soc. C.E., Soc. for Promotion Engring. Edn., Theta Chi. Episcopalian. Home: Hanover, N.H. Died Sept. 18, 1945.

GARRECHT, Francis Arthur (gär'rĕkt), judge; b. Walla Walla, Wash., Sept. 11, 1870; s. Daniel and Caroline T. (Hess) G.; grad. St. Patrick's Academy, Walla Walla, Wash., June 21, 1888; LL.D., Gonzaga U., Spokane, Wash., 1914; LL.D., U. of San Francisco, 1933; Doctor of Civil Law, Whitman College, June 1945; m. Frances T. Lyons, November 23, 1898; children—Francis Arthur (colonel U.S. Army), Ann L., Caroline T., Grace A. Admitted to Wash. bar, 1894, Wash. Supreme Court, 1900, Ore. Supreme Court, 1909, U.S. Supreme Court, 1913; practiced in Walla Walla, 1895-1913; dep. clk. Superior Court, Walla Walla County, 1890-94; mem. Wash. Ho. of Rep., 1911-13; U.S. atty., Eastern Dist. of Wash., 1914-21; lecturer on waters, Gonzaga U., 1911-24; mem. Garrecht & Twohy, 1922-32; legal adviser Gov. Clarence D. Martin, Legislative session, 1933; apptd. judge U.S. Circuit Court of Appeals, May 4, 1933. Dir. Walla Walla Pub. Library, 1910-13. Mem. Am. Bar Assn., Wash. State Bar Assn., Phi Delta Phi. Del. Dem. Nat. Conv., 1932. Supreme rep. Catholic Knights of America, 1893; grand pres. Young Men's Inst., 1897, and supreme rep., 1898; mem. Knights of Columbus, Elks. Elected a chief of Yakima Indian Nation at general council of affiliated tribes Jan. 1921, in recognition of efforts resulting in vindication of treaty rights to ancient fisheries; awarded De Smet medal, May 30, 1935, by Gonzaga Univ. "for outstanding service to church and state." Clubs: Pacific Union, Commonwealth (San Francisco). Home: Spokane, Wash. Address: P.O. Bldg., San Francisco, Calif. Died. Aug. 11, 1948.

GARRELS, Arthur (gär'ĕls), b. St. Louis, Jan. 3, 1873; s. William and Antonie (Wiebe) G.; ed. Smith Acad., St. Louis, Mo.; m. Elinor McEwen Norfleet, Nov. 10, 1923. Employed in banking and mfg. business, 1890-98; connected with theatrical and amusement enterprises in U.S. and Far East, 1898-1903; in bond and stock brokerage business, 1903-08; apptd. consul to Zanzibar, June 22, 1908; consul at Catania, 1910-12, Alexandria, Egypt, Aug. 1912-Dec. 1919; consul gen. at large, dist. Near East and Africa, 1919-22, dist. Mexico and West Indies, 1922-24; consul gen., Athens, Greece, 1924-26, Melbourne, Australia, 1926-30, Tokyo, Japan, 1930-38; retired Jan. 31, 1938. Fellow Am. Geog. Soc. Unitarian. Clubs: Tokyo, American (Tokyo); British (New York). Address: 24 E. 82d St., New York, N.Y. Died June 29, 1943.

GARRETT, Alfred Cope, religious edn. and church unity; b. Germantown, Philadelphia, Pa., Nov. 3, 1867; s. Philip C. and Elizabeth Waln (Cope) G.; ed., Germantown Friends Sch., Philadelphia; pvt. sch., Lausanne, Switzerland, 1878; Argyle Coll. (boys' sch.) London, Eng., 1878-79; A.B., Haverford Coll., Pa., 1883-87; M.A., Ph.D., Harvard, 1889-92; m. Eleanor Evans, June 18, 1896; children—Eleanor Wistar (Mrs. Paul H. Sangree), Thomas Cresson and Philip Cresson (twins), Alfred Cope, Jr. (dec.). Instr. of English, Harvard, 1892-1900; lecturer on Biblical lit. and New Testament Greek, Haverford Coll., 4 yrs.; chmn. com. on teacher training of church schools, Phila.; rep. Soc. of Friends of U.S. at World Conf. on Ch. Unity, Lausanne, Switzerland, 1927, at Conf. in Edinburgh, Scotland, 1937 (mem. of continuation coms. of these confs. in various European countries, 1927-39). Author: The Man from Heaven (life of Christ) 1939, One Mystic (an autobiography), 1945; and other publs. Home: 5301 Old York Rd., Logan, Philadelphia 41, Pa. Died Sep. 28, 1946.

GARRETT, John Work, foreign service; b. Baltimore, May 19, 1872; s. T(homas) Harrison and Alice Dickinson (Whitridge) G.; B.S., Princeton 1895, LL.D., 1922; LL.D., St. John's Coll., Annapolis, 1934; m. Alice Warder, Dec. 24, 1908. Partner in banking firm of Robert Garrett & Sons, Baltimore, 1896-1934 (firm founded by great-grandfather). Sec. Am. Legation at the Hague, 1901-03, to the Netherlands and Luxemburg, 1903-05; 2d sec. Am. Embassy at Berlin, 1905-08; 1st sec. Am. Embassy at Rome, 1908-11; E.E. and M.P. to Venezuela, Dec. 15, 1910-Nov. 1911, to Argentina, 1911-14; spl. agent Dept. of State to assist Am. Ambassador, Paris, Aug. 6, 1914-Aug. 23, 1917; in charge of German and Austro-Hungarian civilian prisoners of war, etc., 1914-17; rep. at Bordeaux of the Am. Embassy at Paris, Sept. 3-Dec. 9, 1914; E.E. and M.P. to The Netherlands and Luxemburg, Aug. 23, 1917-Aug. 1919; A.E. and P. to Italy, 1929-33. Was delegate to fifth and seventh National Irrigation Congresses, 1896, 98; sec. Am.-Russian sealing arbitration, The Hague, 1902; sec. Arbitral Tribunal in Venezuela preferential treatment case, The Hague, 1903-04; del. Hosp. Ship Conf., The Hague, 1904, and signed the Hosp. Ship Convention, Dec. 21, 1904. At request of the French Government inspected camps of French prisoners in Germany, 1916; chmn. spl. diplomatic mission to negotiate treaty regarding prisoners of war with Germany; jointly negotiated and signed such treaty at Berne, Nov. 11, 1918; sec. gen. Conf. on Limitation of Armaments, Washington, 1921-22. Mem. Am. Soc. Internat. Law, Archæol. Inst. America, English Speak. Union, Am. Forestry Assn., Council on Foreign Relations, Am. Geog. Soc., Am. Numismatic Soc., Am. Acad. Polit. and Social Science. Delegate at large from Md. to Republican National Conv., Chicago, 1920, Cleveland, 1924. Clubs: Metropolitan (Washington); Century, Princeton, Grolier, N.Y. Yacht (New York); Maryland, Elkridge Kennels, Merchants', Bachelors' Cotillon (Baltimore). Home: "Evergreen," 4545 N. Charles St., Baltimore, Md. Died June 26, 1942.

GARRETT, Rufus Napoleon, banker; b. nr. Arkadelphia, Ark., Dec. 24, 1858; s. Mancil and Mathilda Caroline (Street) G.; ed. Okolona (Ark.) Acad. and Little Rock Commercial Coll., grad. 1882; m. Uarda Rosamond, 1910; children—Uarda Rosamond, Rufus Napoleon. Began in gen. store, Okolona, and bought out the business, 1886; an organizer, 1892, South Arkansas Lumber Co., of which was sec. and treas., company building Ark. Southern R.R. Co.; sold to C.,R.I.&P. R.R. Co., in 1904; an organizer, 1903, pres. 14 yrs., now chmn. bd. First Nat. Bank, of El Dorado; v.p. El Dorado Foundry & Machine Co.; partner Cargile & Garrett Ranch, San Angelo, Tex.; stockholder various corps. Trustee Ouachita Coll., Arkadelphia, Ark. Democrat. Baptist. Mason (32°). Clubs: Rotary, El Dorado Golf and Country. Home: El Dorado, Ark.; (summer) Garrett Lodge, Epworth Heights, Ludington, Mich. Died April 8, 1942; buried at Eldorado, Ark.

GARRICK, James P., coll. pres.; b. Weston, S.C., Aug. 7, 1875; s. Grover and Frankie (Weston) G.; student Benedict Coll., Columbia, S.C., 1892-98; A.B., Morris Coll., Sumter, S.C., 1908, B.D., 1909, D.D., 1912; m. Mittie G. Watson, Dec. 26, 1900; children—Paralee E. (Mrs. H. D. Dupree), Gardenia E., Mittie Irma Rosemelle. Began as teacher, 1898; ordained to ministry of Baptist Ch., 1904; pastor Ebenezer Ch., 1904-16, New Bethel Ch. since 1916, St. John Ch., 1918-25, Mt. Zion Ch. since 1922, Enon Ch. since 1935; pres. Morris Coll. since 1939. Republican. Mason, K.P. Home: Morris College, Sumter, S.C.* Deceased.

GARRISON, Sidney Clarence, college pres.; b. Lincolnton, N.C., Oct. 17, 1887; s. Rufus J. and Susie Elizabeth (Mooney) G.; A.B., Wake Forest (N.C.) Coll., 1911; A.M., 1913; A.M., George Peabody Coll. for Teachers, 1916; Ph.D., 1919; m. Sara Elizabeth McCurry, Oct. 16, 1918; children—Sidney Clarence, Lucy Fuqua, Wm. Louis, Frank McMurry, Rufus James. County supt. schools, Lincoln County, N.C., 1912-14; supt. of schs., Crouse, N.C., 1911-12; prof. psychology, 1919-33, dean Grad. School, 1933-36, pres. since 1937, George Peabody College for Teachers. Captain U.S. Army, 1918-19. Trustee Meharry Med. Coll.; mem. State Bd. of Education. Fellow A.A.A.S.; member Am. Psychol. Assn., Am. Ednl. Research Assn., Southern Soc. for Psychology and Philosophy, Phi Delta Kappa, Kappa Delta Pi. Democrat. Baptist. Co-Author: Things to Do in the Teaching of Reading, 1928; (with Karl C. Garrison) Psychology of Elementary Education, 1929; Psychology of Secondary Education, 1934. Home: Peabody Campus, Nashville, Tenn. Died Jan. 18, 1945.

GARTH, Schuyler Edward, bishop; b. Saffordville, Kan., September 1, 1898; s. Christian and Lura Mabel (Ream) G.; B.A., Baker Univ., 1922, D.D., 1933; B.D., Garrett Biblical Inst., 1924, D.D., 1935; D.D., Ohio Wesleyan Univ., 1941; m. Lola Mabel Stroud, June 20, 1922; children—Lynn Doré, Lura Belle, Doris LaVerne. Ordained ministry M.E. Ch., 1920; pastor Welda, Kan., 1920-22, Henning, Ill., 1922-24; asso. pastor White Temple, Miami, Fla., 1924-26; supt. Miami Dist. and dir. religious edn., St. John's River Conf., Fla., 1926-30; pastor First Av. Church, St. Petersburg, Fla., 1930-33, Christ Church, Pittsburgh, Pa., 1933-36, Trinity Church, Youngstown, O., 1936-44; consecrated bishop, Methodist Church, Minneapolis, Minn., July 2, 1944, assigned to Wisconsin Area; assigned with wife by Meth. Ch., to make survey of Chinese mission field. Y.M.C.A. sec., Emporia, Kan., 1916-17; with Army Y.M.C.A., 1917-18; enlisted S.A.T.C., 1918. Trustee Mt. Zion (Ga.) Sem. Mem. Bd. Foreign Missions M.E. Ch.; del. to Ecumenical Meth. Conf., Atlanta, Ga., 1931, M.E. Gen. Conf., Columbus, O., 1936, Meth. Ch. Gen. Conf., Atlantic City, 1940. Meth. Ch. North Central Jurisdictional Conf., Chicago, 1941. Republican. Mason. Rotarian. Home: Madison, Wis. Killed in airplane crash near Hankow, China, Jan. 28, 1947; buried in International Cemetery, Hankow, China.

GARTON, Will Melville, naval officer; b. Des Moines, Ia., Oct. 31. 1875; s. William Thomas and Minerva (Allum) G.; student Des Moines Coll., 1890-93; M.D., State U. of Ia., 1896; post grad. work Naval Med. Coll., 1906, Naval War Coll., 1922-23; hon. LL.D., Sioux Falls (S.D.) University; m. Beatrice Farquhar, 1900 (died 1923); children—Norman Farquhar (U.S. Navy), Will Melville; m. 2d, Katharine Ballou, Oct. 15, 1927. Commd. ensign Med. Corps, U.S. Navy, 1898; advanced through grades to rear adm., 1930; retired, Nov. 1, 1939. Awarded campaign medals for Spanish-Am. War, Mexican Service, World War, Haitian and Dominican campaigns. Fellow Am. Coll. Surgeons; mem. A.M.A., Phi Delta Theta. Mason (32°, Shriner). Clubs: Metropolitan, Army and Navy, Army and Navy Country (Washington, D.C.); New York Yacht, New York Athletic, Lambs (N.Y. City). Died June 7, 1946.

GARVIN, Margaret Root, author; born N. Y. City; d. Henry Mitchell and Margaret Rockwell (Root) Garvin; great, great uncle, Roger Sherman, signer of Declaration of Independence; ed. "The Oaks," Lakewood, N.J. Mem. Poetry Soc. of America. Episcopalian. Clubs: Leisure Hour, Civic. Mem. League of Am. Pen Women, Order of Bookfellows; mem. Utica Chapter Red Cross; corr. sec. Oneida Hist. Soc.; a founder Acad. Am. Poets; mem. Berkeley Poetry Society, New York Library Association (mem. Citizens' Committee); active member Oneida County Tuberculosis Assn., mem. Nat. Cathedral Association. Author: A Walled Garden and Other Poems, 1913; Peacocks in the Sun, 1925. Contbr. poems to Harper's, Century, The Carillon, The Independent, Boston Transcript, Voices, etc.; one poem included in the "Lyric Year" collection of 100 poems, selected from 10,000 poems, and other of her poems in various collections. Home: 1500 Oneida St., Utica 3, N.Y. Died Dec. 4, 1949.

GARY, Hunter Larrabee, business executive; b. Macon, Mo., May 27, 1884; s. Theodore and Helen (Larrabee) G.; ed. high sch. and mil. acad., Macon, and business course; m. Lamora Sauvinet, June 28, 1905; children—Mary Lamora (Mrs. Edward T. Harrison), Theodore S.; m. 2d, Lazzetta Barth, Dec. 1936. Partner Theodore Gary & Partners (N.Y.); pres., dir. Nemo Corp., Adaven Corp., Nat. Service, Inc., Nevada Trust Co., Natser Corp. (all of Reno, Nev.), Island Real Estate Corp. (Wis.), Gary-Loomis Co. (Kansas City, Mo.), Walnuts Residence Co. (Kansas City, Mo.); chmn. bd. Asso. Telephone & Telegraph Co., Wilmington, Del.; v.p. Anglo-Canadian Telephone Co. (Montreal), Compania Dominican de Telefonos (Dominican Republic); chairman Theodore Gary & Co. (Kansas City, Missouri), York Investment Co., Allied Syn. Inc., General and Telephone Investments, Inc. (Wilmington, Del.); dir. Linwood Investment Co., Whitewater Power and Mining Co.; chairman board Philippine Long Distance Telephone Co., Telephone Investment Corp.; v.p., dir. Compania Telefonica Central (Bogota, Colombia), Continental Telephone Co.; v.p., dir. Theodore Gary and Co. (London, Eng.), Mo. Telephone Co.; dir. Telephone Bond and Share Co., Missouri-Kansas-Texas Railroad Co.; also officer and dir. many other corps. Episcopalian. Mason (K.T.), K.P., Elk, Maccabee. Clubs: Kansas City Country, Kansas City, Mission Hills Country (Kansas City); Chicago, Attic, Union League (Chicago); Recess, Metropolitan, Bankers (New York). Home: 17 S. Virginia St., Reno, Nev. Office: 313 First National Bank Bldg., Reno, Nev.; and Telephone Bldg., Kansas City, Mo.; and 1100 King St., Wilmington, Del. Died Nov. 30, 1946.

GASS, Sherlock Bronson, prof. English; b. Mansfield, O., Oct. 17, 1878; s. Florien Preston and Harriet Elizabeth (Bronson) G.; Ph.B., U. of Chicago, 1904; m. Alice Virginia Dougan, June 7, 1926; children—Geoffrey Alan, Alison Estabrook. Instr. in English, Univ. High Sch., U. of Chicago, 1905-06; with U. of Neb. since 1906, prof. English since 1917. Mem. Phi Beta Kappa. Episcopalian. Author: English Composition, 1910; A Lover of the Chair, 1919; Criers of the Shops, 1925; A Tap on the Shoulder, 1929; Family Crisis, 1940. Home: 2121 Euclid Av., Lincoln, Neb. Died Aug. 31, 1945.

GAST, Robert Shaeffer, lawyer; b. Pueblo, Colo., Sept. 27, 1879; s. Charles Edwin and Elizabeth Shelly (Shaeffer) G.; B.A., Yale, 1902; LL.B., Columbia Law Sch., 1905; m. Corinne Neville Busey, May 16, 1908; children—Elizabeth Busey (Mrs. Lewis Jerroldton Powers), Charles Edwin, Robert S. Practiced in Pueblo with father until latter's death, 1908; member Adams (Alva B.) & Gast, 1908-Dec. 1, 1941, when Senator Alva B. Adams died; chmn. bd. First Nat. Bank, Florence, Colo.; dir. Pueblo Savings & Trust Co., Ideal Cement Co. Civilian aide to the adj. gen. Mem. Am. Bar Assn. (gen. council 1926-27, 1931), Colo. Bar Assn. (pres. 1923-24), Pueblo Bar Assn., Assn. Bar City of N.Y., Newcomen Society of England. Trustee Fountain Valley School of Colo. Republican. Episcopalian. Clubs: Pueblo Golf (Pueblo); University, Denver, Mile High, Cactus, Denver Press (Denver); Cheyenne Mountain Country (Colo. Springs, Colo.); Yale, Lawyers (New York). Home: 1801 Greenwood St. Office: Thatcher Bldg., Pueblo, Colo. Died Apr. 4, 1948.

GASTON, Charles Robert (găs'tŭn), teacher; b. Detroit, Sept. 6, 1874; s. Charles Henry and Mary Beatrice (Warren) G.; A.B., Cornell, 1896, Ph.D., 1904; m. Edith Gertrude Fales, Sept. 28, 1907; children—Edith Gertrude (Mrs. Kelso V. Young), Robert Stephen (deceased). Teacher of English, Cornell University, Ithaca, N.Y., 1896-1900; head of dept. of

English, Richmond Hill High Sch., New York, 1900-25; 1st asst. in English and chmn. of English department, Theodore Roosevelt High Sch., N.Y. City, 1926-45; evening session, Columbia U., 1910-18, Coll. of City of N.Y., 1919-23; asst. prof. English, Bay View U. Summer Sch., 1920-22; Middlebury Coll. Summer Sch., 1924, Syracuse U. Summer Sch., 1928; lecturer, Bay View Assembly, 1921. Mem. Am. Dialect Soc., N.Y. City Assn. Teachers of English (sec.-treas. 1905-13, pres. 1915-17), N.Y. State Assn. Teachers of English (sec. 1914-15, pres. 1915-16), Nat. Council Teachers English (pres. 1922-23); chmn. English question com. of the Univ. of State of N.Y., 1916-20; lecturer Columbia Scholastic Press Assn., 1935-43; mem. Phi Beta Kappa. Editor: Hawthorne's Twice Told Tales, 1901; Shakespeare's As You Like It, 1902; Irving's Life of Goldsmith, 1903; Washington's Farewell Address and Webster's First Bunker Hill Oration, 1906; Ruskin's Sesame and Lilies, 1909; Selections from American Poetry, 1909 (revised and enlarged, 1913); Stevenson's Treasure Island, 1911; Shakespeare's The Merchant of Venice, 1913; Forum Papers—Second Series, 1925; Modern Lives (with Gertrude F. Gaston), 1927. Co-author: English in Daily Life. Club: Faculty of Columbia U. Home: Great Oak Lane, Pleasantville, N.Y. Died Nov. 28, 1945.

GATES, C(larence) Ray, educator, author; b. Baker, Kan., Dec. 23, 1885; s. James Lyman and Annie Vio (Racey) G.; B. Ed., State Teachers Coll., Peru, Neb., 1911; A.B., U. of Neb., 1916; A.M., Columbia, 1920, Ed.D., 1938; m. Maude Beatrice Nixon, Sept. 1, 1909; children—Esther Nixon (Mrs. Paul B. Newell), Clarence Ray. Supt. schs., Pilger, Neb., 1906-07; prin. high sch., Oakland, 1907-08, Nebraska City, 1908-11, Blair, 1911-16; supt. schs. West Point, Neb., 1916-18, Columbus, Neb., 1918-22, Grand Island since 1922. Mem. Men's Work Commn., M.E. Ch., 1927-35; mem. Gen. Conf. M.E. Ch., 1932; mem. Book Com. M.E. Ch., 1932-40; trustee Neb. Wesleyan U., 1931-35. Mem. Commn. on Problems of Sch. Administration, Dept. of Superintendence, N.E.A. (1934 Yearbook), 1932-34; mem. Neb. Ednl. Planning Commn., 1933-39, chmn., 1938-39; chmn. study committee, Neb. Educational Survey, 1939. Mem. Nat. Soc. for Study of Edn., Am. Assn. School Adminstrs. (mem. adv. commn. since 1939), Neb. State Teachers' Assn. (pres. 1931), Neb. Schoolmasters' Club (pres. 1925-26), Phi Delta Kappa. Republican. Methodist. Mason; Grand Orator, Grand Lodge of Neb., 1933. Clubs: Rotary (pres. 1927); Riverside Country. Author: The Management of Smaller Schools, 1923, A Leisure Emphasis in Education, 1937. Contbr. to ednl. periodicals. Home: 1810 W. Charles St. Office: 504 N. Elm St., Grand Island, Neb. Died Sep. 21, 1944.

GATES, Caleb Frank, college pres.; b. Chicago, Oct. 18, 1857; s. Caleb Foote and Mary Eliza (Hutchins) G.; A.B., Beloit (Wis.) Coll., 1877; grad. Chicago Theol. Sem., 1881; D.D., Knox Coll., 1897; LL.D., Edinburgh U., 1899; same degree from Beloit College, 1927; m. Mary Ellen Moore, May 31, 1883; children—Edward Caleb (Dec.), Herbert Frank, Moore, Elizabeth Davidson (dec.), Caleb Frank. Ordained Congl. ministry, 1881; missionary A.B.C.F.M., Mardin, Turkey in Asia, 1881-94; pres. Euphrates Coll., Harpoot, Turkey, 1894-1902; pres. Robert Coll., Constantinople, 1903-32. Chmn. Near East Relief Commn. in Constantinople, 1917-19. Mem. Nat. Inst. of Social Science, Acad. of Polit. Science. Decorated Knight Comdr. George I (Greece), Knight Comdr. Alexander (Bulgaria), III and II. Author: A Christian Business Man, 1893; Not to Me Only (a half century in Turkey); also (article) "Caliphate in The Modern Moslem World." Address: 1640 E. 3d Av., Denver, Colo. Died Apr. 9, 1946.

GATES, Herbert Wright, clergyman, educator; b. Geneva, Ill., Oct. 30, 1868; s. Caleb Foote and Mary Eliza (Hutchins) G.; brother late Caleb Frank G.; A.B., Amherst, 1890, A.M., 1904; B.D., Chicago Theol. Sem., 1904, D.D., 1919; post-grad. univs. of Leipzig, Halle, and Chicago; m. Harriet J. Kirk, of Wilmette, Ill., June 16, 1898; children—Edward Stuart (dec.), Catharine Everald Margaret Wright, Esther Kirk. Librarian and instr. religious pedagogy, Chicago Theol. Sem., 1896-1904; dir. religious work, Central Dept., Chicago Y.M.C.A., 1904-08; general sec. Coll. Y.M.C.A., Northwestern U., 1908-10; supt. Brick Church Inst., Rochester, N.Y., 1910-20; sec. Missionary Edn. Dept., 1920, gen. sec., 1925-38, Christian Edn. Div.—Bd. of Home Missions of Congl. and Christian Chs. Exec. sec. Adv. Commission Chicago Public Library, 1909; board managers Missionary Education Movement, 1938; field sec. Boston Seaman's Friend Society since 1940. Member Ration Board, Newton, Mass., 1942-45. Member Religious Education Association, Alpha Delta Phi. Author of various books on religious edn. Lesson writer with Pilgrim Press, Boston, Mass., since 1943. Home: 38 Kenwood Av., Newton Center 59, Mass. Died Feb. 8, 1948.

GATES, Thomas Sovereign, univ. chmn.; b. Germantown, Phila., Pa., Mar. 21, 1873; s. Jabez and Isabel (Sovereign) G.; Ph.B., U. of Pa., 1893, LL.B., 1896, hon. LL.D., 1931, Ph.D., 1946; hon. LL.D., Villanova Coll., 1923, Allegheny Coll., 1928, Haverford College, Dickinson College, Lafayette College and Lehigh University, 1931, New York University, 1932, U. of Pittsburgh, 1933, Temple Univ., 1933, Harvard University, 1936, Jefferson Med. College, 1940, Princeton University, 1940, Swarthmore College, 1942; m. Emma Barton Brewster Waller, July 18, 1929. Admitted to Pennsylvania bar, 1896; asst. in law office of John G. Johnson, of Phila., 1895-1906; trust officer The Pa. Co. for Insurances on Lives and Granting Annuities, 1906-10, v.p. and trust officer, 1910-12, v.p., 1912; pres. Phila. Trust Co., 1912-18; partner Drexel & Co., 1918-30, J. P. Morgan & Co., 1921-30; pres. U. of Pa., 1930-44, chmn. since 1944; pres. and dir. Beaver Coal Corp.; dir. Pa. R.R. Co. (chmn. road com.), Phila., Baltimore & Washington R.R. Co., Pittsburgh, Fort Wayne & Chicago Ry. Co., Pittsburgh, Cincinnati, Chicago & St. Louis R.R. Co., Manor Real Estate & Trust Co., Fidelity-Philadelphia Trust Co.; trustee Penn Mutual Life Ins. Co., Church Life Ins. Corp., Nat. Health and Welfare Retirement Assn., Inc.; mgr. Phila. Saving Fund Soc. (finance com.). Dir. Phila. Orchestra Assn. (chmn., Metropolitan Opera Assn., Community Chest for Phila. (adv. com.), Pa. Acad. Fine Arts, Church Soc. for College Work; pres. Union Library Catalogue of Phila.; v.p. Phila. Council of Churches. Trustee University of Pennsylvania, Thomas W. Evans Dental Museum and Institute Society, Moore School of Elec. Engring. (chmn.), Acad. of Natural Sciences of Phila., Divinity Sch. of the P.E. Church in Phila., Nat. Tuberculosis Assn., Pension Fund of P.E. Ch., Internat. Cancer Research Foundation, Phila. Commercial Museum, Exhibition and Convention Halls, The Morris Arboretum, The University Museum (Phila.), Philadelphia Museum of Art, Leamy Home; councillor Hist. Soc. of Pa.; mem. exec. com. Red Cross War Fund, 1945; member Am. Philos. Soc. (president), American Academy Political and Social Science, Washington Cathedral Council, Nat. Industrial Conf., Board, Inc., Nat. Safety Council (advisory com.), National Institute of Social Sciences, Newcomen Society, Wistar Assn., Phi Beta Kappa, Phi Kappa Sigma. Episcopalian. Clubs: Rittenhouse, Philadelphia, University (Phila. and New York), Art Alliance, Colonial Soc. of Pa., Contemporary, Legal Lenape, Mask and Wig, Midday, Penn Athletic, Print, Racquet, Seaview Golf, Sunnybrook Golf, U. of Pa. in N.Y. City, Union League, Wianno (Mass.). Mem. Nat. Commn. UNESCO. Home: Rex and Seminole Avs. Office: Packard Bldg., Philadelphia 2, Pa. Died Apr. 8, 1948.

GAUL, Harvey B., organist, composer; b. N.Y. City, 1881; s. James Harvey and Louise (Bartlett) G.; studied with George F. Lejeune (New York), Alfred R. Gaul (Birmingham, Eng.), Dr. Armes (Durham, Eng.). Schola Cantorium and Paris Conservatory with Guilmant, Widor, Decaux and D'Indy; with Mons. Rella of Sistine Chapel Choir and Mons. Rienzi of St. Peter's (Rome); hon. Dr. Mus., U. of Pittsburgh, 1933; m. Harriette Avery, a writer, June 13, 1908; children—James Harvey and Ione Avery (Mrs. Hudson D. Walker). Associate organist, Saint John's Chapel, N.Y. City, 1899; organist Emmanuel Church, Cleveland, 1901-09, Calvary Church, Pittsburgh, since 1910. Formerly mem. faculty, U. of Pittsburgh, Carnegie Inst. Tech., Washington and Jefferson Univ.; condr. Singers Club, Cleveland, O., 1924-26. Pittsburgh Apollo Male Chorus, 1925-30, Pittsburgh Chamber of Commerce Chorus, 1925-29; condr. of Y.M.& W.H.A. Choral Soc., 1925-42; condr. Civic String Orchestra since 1936; mem. faculty Fillion Studio of Music since 1931; music critic Pittsburgh Post-Gazette, 1914-34, editor of music, art, drama and book dept., 1929-34; feature editor Mus. Forecast since 1934; dir. Savoyard Opera Company since 1939. Mem. American Guild Organists, Musicians' Club. Episcopalian. Composer of over 400 published works, including cantatas, anthems, part-songs, solos, organ and orchestral works; awarded first prize, "Water Lillies," Tuesday Mus. Club, Pittsburgh; "Madrigal," Chicago Madrigal Clubs; "Ode to Vulcan," Pittsburgh Male Chorus; "Euridice," Federated Clubs: "Cry of Micah," Art Society of Pittsburgh, 1939; Mendelssohn Club prize, Phila.; Strawbridge & Clothier's prize, Phila; first prize for woodwinds ensemble "John Brashear Sings in the Night," by Pittsburgh Art Soc., 1936. Celebration of Harvey Gaul Day by proclamation of Mayor Scully of Pittsburgh, Mar. 28, 1941; concert of Gaul's Works and Harvey Gaul scholarship established by State Fedn. of Music Clubs, as tribute for civic work. Lecturer on mus. subjects. Choir House of Calvary Episcopal Ch., Pittsburgh, dedicated to him, June 1946. Home: 12 Dunmoyle Pl., Pittsburgh. Died Dec. 1, 1945; ashes placed in wall of Choir House, Calvary Episcopal Ch., Pittsburgh.

GAUSE, Fred C. (gaws), lawyer; b. Wayne County, Ind., Aug. 29, 1879; s. Thomas and Christena (Boone) G.; student Ind. U., 1898; law student, 1898-1900; m. Mollie Cummins, May 10, 1904; 1 dau., Katherine. Admitted to Ind. bar, 1900 and began practice at Newcastle; county atty., Henry County, Ind., 1902-12; judge, Circuit Court, Henry County, 1914-23 (resigned); judge, Supreme Court, Ind., 1923-25 (resigned); practicing law as successor to firm Pickens, Gause & Pickens of Indianapolis. President Indiana State Bar Assn., 1936; pres. Indianapolis Bar Assn., 1941. Mem. Beta Theta Pi. Republican. Methodist. Clubs: Columbia, Indianapolis Country. Home: 3545 Watson Rd. Office: Consolidated Bldg., Indianapolis, Ind. Died Feb. 15, 1944.

GAY, Charles Richard, broker; b. Brooklyn, N.Y., Sept. 14, 1875; s. Charles Abram and Anna Mitchell (Campbell) G.; student pub. schs., Brooklyn, 1881-89; Polytechnic Inst. of Brooklyn, 1889-94; honorary Sc.D., Dickinson College, 1937; m. Jennie Campbell Bowdish, Oct. 26, 1898; 1 son, William Campbell. Clerk Faulkner, Page & Co., 1894-96, Associated Mfrs. Ins. Co., 1896-98; partner Barber & Ziegler, wholesale coal, 1898-1901; asst. sec. Long Island Loan & Trust Co., 1901-11; mem. N.Y. Stock Exchange since 1911, gov., 1923-35, pres. 1935-38; partner Gude, Winmill & Co.; trustee Dime Savings Bank, Packer Collegiate Inst. of Brooklyn, N.Y. Trustee Drew U. (Madison, N.J.), Dickinson Coll., Carlisle, Pa., M.E. Hosp. (Brooklyn), Brooklyn Assn. for Improving Condition of the Poor. Republican. Methodist. Mason. Clubs: The Lunch; Stock Exchange Luncheon. Home: 440 E. 19th St., Brooklyn, and Huntington, L.I., N.Y. Office: 1 Wall St., New York, N.Y. Died Mar. 23, 1946.

GAY, Edwin Francis, economist; b. Detroit, Mich., Oct. 27, 1867; s. Aaron F. and Mary L. (Loud) G.; A.B., U. of Mich., 1890; Ph.D., U. of Berlin, 1902; LL.D., Harvard, 1918, U. of Mich., 1920, Northwestern, 1927, Tulane, 1935, Occidental, 1940; Litt.D., Manchester U., England, 1933; m. Louise Fitz Randolph, 1892; children—Edward Randolph, Margaret Randolph. Instructor, 1902-03; assistant prof., 1903-06, prof. economics, 1906-19, dean Grad. Sch. of Business Adminstrn., 1908-19, prof. economic history, 1924-36, Harvard; mem. research staff Huntington Library, San Marino, Calif., since 1936, chairman since 1941. Dir. Council on Foreign Relations, N.Y. City. Pres. New York Evening Post, 1920-23. Mem. Commercial Economy Bd. Council Nat. Defense, 1917-18; dir. div. planning and statistics, U.S. Shipping Bd., Feb. 1918-Mar. 1919; mem. War Trade Bd., Feb. 1918-June 1919; chmn. div. planning and statistics, War Industries Bd., June 1918-Jan. 1919; dir. Central Bur. of Planning and Statistics, June 1918-July 1919. Mem. A.A.A.S. (Boston), Am. Econ. Assn., Am. Statis. Assn., Am. Hist. Assn., Royal Econ. Soc. (Eng.); fellow Am. Philos. Soc. (Phila). Club: Century (New York). Home: 1650 Orlando Road, San Marino 5, California. Died Feb. 8, 1946.

GAYLORD, Franklin Augustus, retired Y.M.C.A. official; b. Glenwood near Yonkers, N.Y., May 1, 1856; s. Gen. Augustus and Martha (Champlin) G.; A.B., Yale, 1876; grad. Union Theol. Sem., 1881; studied at College de France, Paris, 1883; m. Mary Louise Robinson, Sept. 10, 1891. Gen. sec. Y.M.C.A., Paris, France, 1887-93; ordained Presbyn. ministry, Oct. 1, 1894; transferred to Manhattan Congl. Assn., 1895; pastor Trinity Congl. Ch., New York, 1895-99; gen. sec. Russian Y.M.C.A., St. Petersburg, 1899-1911; dir. Russian Soc. for Moral and Physical Development of Young Men, 1911-18. Sec. Am. Hosp. for wounded Russian soldiers, 1916; sec. Internat. Com. Y.M.C.A., 1918-19; trustee Jas. Stokes Soc. for forwarding work of Y.M.C.A., 1920; rep. at Odessa, Russia, of Internat. Com. Y.M.C.A., 1919-20, also at Constantinople and in Egypt; lectured in U.S.; again in Europe, at Berlin, Warsaw, Belgrade, Sophia, Constantinople; returned to New York, Nov. 1921; was sent to Washington to invite delegates to Conf. on Disarmament to lecture in U.S. Chevalier Order St. Anne, Russia, 1902; presented to Czar, 1907, 1911; Chevalier, Order St. Stanislaus, 1916, Chevalier Russian Red Cross, 1920. Mem. Congl. Assn. Ministers of New York City since 1895; mem. The Hymn Soc. of Am., Delta Kappa Epsilon, Phi Beta Kappa. Clubs: Yale, Town Hall, Clergy (New York); Graduate (New Haven); Authors' (London). Author: The Builders of the Atoll and other poems. Translator into English verse of various Russian poems. Home: 47 Englewood Av., W. Englewood, N.J. Died Aug. 14, 1943.

GEBELEIN, George Christian (gā'bĕl-lin), silversmith; b. Wuestenselbitz, Oberfranken, Bavaria, Nov. 6 1878; s. Nicholas and Margaretha (Solger) G.; brought to U.S. by parents, 1879; ed. public schools, Cambridge, Mass.; m. Eva Mary Pelren, Mar. 31, 1901; children—Margaretha Pelren (Mrs. Shirley M. Leighton, Jr.), Ernest George, John Herbert, Esther Marie (Mrs. Richard Swain), Arthur David, Eleanor Eva (Mrs. Gardiner G. Greene), George Christian. Silversmith apprentice, pupil of Adolph Krass, with Goodnow & Jenks, Boston silversmiths, 1893-97; journeyman silversmith with Tiffany & Co. and Wm. B. Durgin Co., 1898-1903; individual silversmith in Handicraft Group, Boston, 1903-09; established own studio, Boston, and conducting same since 1909; also instr. to scholarship students from schs. of fine arts; consultant and authority on antique metalcraft. Works include silver services for U.S.S. Lexington, U.S. Mil. Acad. Chapel, William and Mary Coll. Chapel, Phillips Andover Acad. Chapel, Washington (D.C.) Cathedral, ecclesiastical pieces in numerous churches, Percy D. Haughton Memorial Cup, Alexander Agassiz Cup (Harvard), Halcyon and Shattuck Trophy (St. Paul's Sch., Concord, N.H.); a silver tankard, a tribute to James Grafton Rogers, first master of Timothy Dwight Coll., Yale; also miscellaneous special trophies, presentations to distinguished individuals; domestic silver in private ownership of prominent families; restoration of Old Mace for Williamsburg, Va.; represented in exhbns. at Portland (Ore.), Museum of Fine Arts, 1908, Addison Gallery of American Arts (Andover, Mass.) 1932, Metropolitan Museum (N.Y.), 1937. The Currier Gallery of Art (Manchester, N.H.), 1937, Brooklyn Museum, 1937-38, N.E. Handicrafts Exhibition, Worcester Art Museum, 1943, Boston Soc. of Arts and Crafts Traveling Exhibits, Ella Parsons Collection, Phila. Memorial Museum. Awarded Master Craftsman's medal by Boston Soc. of Arts and Crafts, 1919; received Art Inst. Chicago award, group exhibit, 1905; medalist Panama Pacific Expn., 1915; Mass. Tercentenary Exhbn., 1930. Home: 4 Cliff Rd., Wellesley Hills, Mass. Office: 79 Chestnut St., Boston, Mass. Died Jan 25, 1945.

GEDDES, James, Jr. (gĕd'dĕs), univ. prof.; b. Boston, July 29, 1858; s. James G. and Laure (Sazy) G.; A.B., Harvard, 1880, A.M., 1889, Ph.D., 1894; m. Mathilde Hugèl, June 27, 1894. Clk. U.S. Consulate, Trieste, 1880-82; pvt. sec. Theodore Lyman, Washington, 1883-85; master Groton (Mass.) Sch., 1885-86; clk. president's office, U.P. Ry. Co., 1887; instr. Romance langs., Boston U., 1887-90, asst. prof., 1890-92, prof., 1892-1937, now emeritus. In charge Italian and Spanish depts., Oswego (N.Y.) Summer Sch. of Langs., 1888-89, French dept., Martha's Vineyard (Mass.) Summer Sch., 1894. Mem. Modern Lang. Assn. of America (council 8 yrs.), Am. Dialect Soc., Assn. Phonétique Internationale; com. courses of instrn., Harvard, 1900-13; mem. com. research humanities, Harvard, 1926-37; pres. Circolo-Italiano di Boston, 1906-37, hon. pres. 1938; pres. Am. Assn. Teachers of Italian, 1926-27; v.p. Alliance Française, Boston-Cambridge, 1911-36; founder Boston Chapter Am. Assn. Teachers of French, 1928, and Boston Chapter Am. Assn. Teachers of German, 1929; treas. Italian Benevolent Aid Soc., Boston, 1906-12; hon. v.p. Soc. Historique Franco-Americaine, N.E. League Am. Teachers of Spanish; mem. council of the Simplified Spelling Board; fellow Am. Acad. Arts and Sciences; pres. Boston U. group Am. Assn. Univ. Profs., 1920-24. Decorated Cavaliere Order of Crown (Italy), 1909, Ufficiale, 1932, Commendatore, 1937, Sòci dóu Felibrige, 1938, Chevalier Légion d'honneur, 1940. Editor French, Spanish and Italian texts, with introduction, notes and vocabulary; Calderon's El mágico prodigioso, 1929. Author: Canadian French, the Language and Literature, 1902; (with A. Rivard) Bibliographie du Parler français au Canada, 1906; Study of an Acadian French Dialect, 1908; also French prose transl. of Müller text of old French poem, La Chanson de Roland, 1906; French Pronunciation, 1913. Contbr. to mags. on Romance langs. and especially on Acadian and Canadian-French dialects; contbr. of articles on Italian and Spanish subjects to Ency. Americana. Home: 39 Fairmount St., Brookline, Mass. Died Sept. 30, 1948.

GEDDES, John Joseph, banking exec.; b. Chicago, Sept. 3, 1880; s. Adam and Ellen (O'Connell) G.; student pub. schs., Chicago Bus. Coll.; m. Anna E. Enright, June 10, 1908; children—Anna Marion, John Joseph, Isabel, Frank M., William H. Vice pres. Continental Ill. Nat. Bank & Trust Co., Chicago, since 1929. Clubs: Bankers, South Shore Country, Union League (Chicago). Home: 7321 South Shore Dr. Office: 231 S. LaSalle St., Chicago. Died Jan. 29, 1950.

GEER, William Clarke, corp. official; b. Orange, N.J., Sept. 29, 1859; s. George Spencer and Martha Clarke (Hamilton) G.; ed. high sch., Troy, N.Y.; m. Kate Everingham, Sept. 1882; 1 dau., Olive Edson (Mrs. Norman Kley); m. 2d, Blanche G. Van Every. Began as clk., Geer & Co., Troy, N.Y., 1876; pres. Gilbert Geer, Jr., & Co., 1888-1931; pres. Albia Box & Paper Co., Geer Hydro Electric Co., Faith Knitting Co., Troy Cemetery Assn.; v.p. Internat. Pulp Co., U.S. Talc Co., Oswegatchie Light & Power Co., Troy Parkway Villa Site Co., La Fargeville Electric Light Co. (N.Y. City), Rossie Electric and Mfg. Co. (N.Y. City); dir. Mfrs. Nat. Bank, Troy Waste Mfg. Co., Rensselaer Improvement Co. Dir. Samaritan Hosp., Troy Orphan Asylum; mem. bd. govs. Marshall's Infirmary; trustee, Troy Y.W.C.A. Baptist. Clubs: Troy, Troy Country; Everglades (Palm Beach); Yacht, Juniper Island (Hobe Sound). Home: Springwood, Troy, N.Y.; also (winter) Agua Vista, Hobe Sound, Fla.* Died Mar. 1943.

GEIGER, Roy Stanley, marine officer; b. Middleburg, Fla., Jan. 25, 1885; s. Marion Francis and Josephine (Prevatt) G.; student Fla. State Normal Sch., 1900-04; LL.B., John B. Stetson U., 1907; LL.D., 1940; distinguished grad., Commd. and Gen. Staff Sch., 1925; grad. Army War Coll., 1929, Naval War Coll., 1940, student advanced course, 1941; completed naval aviation course, Pensacola, Fla., 1916; m. Eunice Renshaw Thompson, July 18, 1917; children—Joyce Renshaw (wife of Lt. Col. Robert J. Johnson, U.S.M.C.), Maj. Roy Stanley, Jr. Commd. 2d lt., U.S. M.C. and promoted through grades to lt. gen., 1945; comd. Squadron A, 1st Marine Aviation Force, France, World War I; apptd. head Marine Corps Aviation, Washington, D.C., 1931; asst. naval attaché for air, London, England, 1941; directed operations of all Allied aviation activities on Guadalcanal, 1942 (1st Allied offensive, World War II); assumed command 1st Marine Amphibious Corps, 1943, seized Bougainville; comdr. 3d Marine Amphibious Corps which seized Guam, 1944, Palaus, 1944, participated in invasion and capitulation of Okinawa, 1945; comdr. U.S. 10th Army, Okinawa upon death of Lt. Gen Simon B. Buckner; U.S. Marine rep. at formal surrender of Japan, Tokyo Bay, 1945; comdr. Fleet Marine Force, Pacific, 1945; sr. Marine rep. Bikini, during Atomic tests Able and Baker, 1946. Returned to U.S., duty Marine Corps Hdqrs., Washington, D.C., Nov., 1946. Awarded Navy Cross, Gold Star in Lieu of 2d Navy Cross, Navy Distinguished Service Medal, Distinguished Flying Cross, 2 Gold Stars in lieu of 2d and 3d D.S.M.'s, Air Medal, Presidential Unit Citation with 2 stars, 1st Nicaraguan with stars, Victory Medal, Haitian Campaign, 2d Nicaraguan, American Defense Medal, Pacific Area Medal with 1 silver star, Nicaraguan Medal of Distinction, Dominican Medal of Merit with 2 Silver Stars. Member American Legion. Clubs: Army and Navy, Army-Navy Country (Washington, D.C.). Home Rosemont, Pensacola, Fla. Died January 23, 1947; buried in Arlington National Cemetery.

GEISSLER, Arthur H., diplomatic service; b. Oct. 30, 1877; ed. pub. schs. and under tutors; studied comparative jurisprudence and diplomacy at Columbian (now George Washington) U., 1903-04; made several study trips to Europe and Latin America; LL.D., Lincoln Memorial U., Cumberland Gap, Tenn., 1929; m. Julia Henderson Adams, May 2, 1905 (died Mar. 1, 1925). Instr. modern langs., 1895; admitted to bar, 1896; pres. bank in Okla., 1902-09; pres. ins. co. in Oklahoma City, Okla., 1904-23; E.E. and M.P. to Guatemala, 1922-29, to Siam since Dec. 1929. Chmn. Rep. County Com., Oklahoma County, 1910-14; chmn. Rep. State Com., 1912-18; pres. Nat. Assn. Rep. State Chairmen, 1918; del. at large Rep. Nat. Conv., 1916. Mem. Am. Soc. Internat. Law, Academie Diplomatique Internationale. Mason (Shriner). Home: Oklahoma City, Okla. Address: care Dept. of State, Washington. Died Feb. 18, 1945.

GEIST, Samuel Herbert, physician; b. New York, N.Y., July 1, 1885; s. Ralph Roger and Frances (Davis) G.; A.B., Coll. of City of New York, 1904; M.D., Coll. of Physicians and Surgeons, Columbia, 1908; grad. study, U. of Freiburg, 1911-12; m. Juliet Beecher, July 1, 1933; 1 dau., Joyce B. Interne Mt. Sinai Hosp., New York, 1908-10; mem. attending staff since 1913; gynecologist since 1936; clin. prof. of gynecology, Coll. of Physicians and Surgeons, Columbia, since 1936. Served as capt. Med. Corps, U.S. Army, 1917-19; with A.E.F., 14 months. Mem. Am. Gynecol. Soc., N.Y. Obstet. Soc., Harvey Soc., N.Y. Acad. Medicine, N.Y. Pathol. Soc. Club: Sunnydale Country (Scarsdale, N.Y.). Contbr. to textbooks on surgery and gynecology; also articles to med. jours. Home: 969 Park Av. Office: 100 E. 74th St., New York, N.Y.* Died Dec. 14, 1943.

GENNET, Charles Westcott, Jr. (jĕn-ĕt), vice-pres. Sperry Rail Service; b. Binghamton, N.Y., Aug. 1, 1876; s. Charles Wescott, Sr., and Julia (Park) G.; M.E., Cornell U., 1898; m. Margaret Hughes, June 10, 1907; 1 son, Charles Wescott III (dec.). Specialized in inspection and testing ry. material, notably rails; with Baldwin Locomotive Works, Phila., 1898-99, Southern Ry., 1899-1907; in charge inspection and testing steel rails Robert W. Hunt Co., engrs., Chicago, Ill., 1908-28; v.p. Sperry Rail Service, Chicago, testing rails in track, since 1928. Awarded Chanute Medal by Western Soc. of Engrs., 1941. Mem. Am. Soc. C.E., Am. Ry. Engring. Assn., Western Soc. Engrs., Chi Psi. Episcopalian. Mason (32°, Shriner). Clubs: University, South Shore Country. Contbr. articles to tech. publs. Home: 1648 E. 50th St. Office: 80 E. Jackson Blvd., Chicago, Ill. Died Oct. 26, 1943.

GENTHE, Arnold (gĕn'tē), photographer, author; b. Berlin, Germany, Jan. 8, 1869; s. Hermann and Louise (Zober) G.; ed. Wilhelm Gymnasium, Hamburg, until 1888; studied classical philology, archeology and philosophy, U. of Jena and U. of Berlin, Ph.D., Jena, 1894; studied at the Sorbonne, Paris, 1894-95; unmarried. Came to U.S., 1895, naturalized citizen, 1918. Became interested in photography as a hobby, and has devoted himself to it professionally since 1898; studio in San Francisco, California, until 1911, and since in New York City. Club: Dutch Treat (of New York City). Author: Deutsches Slang, 1892; De Lucani Codice Erlangensi, 1894; Acht Briefe Hegel's and Goethe, 1895; Rebellion in Photography, 1900; Old Chinatown (text by Will Irwin), 1913; The Book of the Dance, 1916; Impressions of Old New Orleans, 1926; Isadora Duncan—24 Studies, 1929; As I Remember (autobiography), 1936; Highlights and Shadows, 1937. Illustrated The Yellow Jacket (by George C. Hazelton and Benrimo), The Sanctuary (by Percy Mackaye). Compiler: Four Hundred Japanese Color Prints. Contbr. illustrated articles in mags. Home: 212 E. 48th St. Studio: 41 E. 49th St., New York, N.Y. Died Aug. 8, 1942.

GENTRY, North Todd, lawyer; b. Coluumbia, Mo., Mar. 2, 1866; s. Thomas Benton and Mary E. (Todd) G.; B.A.S., U. of Mo., 1884, Surveyor and A.B., 1886, LL.B., 1888; m. Ulie Denny, Oct. 8, 1896; children—Mary T. (Mrs. H. K. Hannah, Jr.), Nadine (Mrs. H. M. Lovan). Began law practice at Columbia, 1888; served as atty. for banks, ins. cos. and various rys.; atty. for plaintiff in case of Howell vs. Hines, dir. gen. of rys., wherein the Supreme Court of U.S. held that a written contract for shipment of live stock would not release the ry. co. from damages on account of breach of a prior oral contract; active in legal reforms. City atty., Columbia, 1889; asst. atty. gen. of Mo., 1905-08; mem. Mo. Statute Revision Commn., 1909; atty. gen. Mo., 1925-28; judge Mo. Supreme Ct., 1928; judge 34th Judicial Circuit, 1932; conciliation commr. and referee in bankruptcy, 1934-40; practicing law. Chmn. Council of Defense, and County Food Administrn., 1917-18. Mem. Columbia br. Am. Red Cross; trustee Boone County Pub. Hosp. President Board of Education, Columbia; pres. Columbia Chamber of Commerce, 1911-13. Mem. Am. Bar Assn., Mo. Bar Assn. (v.p.), Boone County Bar Assn. (pres. 1913-16), Boone Co. Hist. Soc. (pres. 1933), Phi Beta Kappa, Phi Delta Phi. Republican. Presbyterian; moderator Synod of Mo. Mason, K.P. Clubs: Kiwanis, Columbia Country; Jefferson City Country. Author: Missouri Laws Made Plain, 1905, Bench and Bar of Boone County, Mo., 1915; articles on Mo. history. Home: Columbia, Mo.* Died Sep. 18, 1944.

GEORGE, Charles P., army officer; b. Aug. 10, 1886; grad. Mounted Service Sch., 1915, Command and Gen. Staff Sch., 1925, Army War Coll., 1927. Commd. 2d lt., Jan. 1, 1908; promoted through grades to brig. gen., Apr. 1941, major gen., 1942; served as lt. col., later col., Field Arty., World War I; served with 4th Army; retired Oct. 1946. Died Dec. 30, 1946; buried in National Cemetery, Fort Sam Houston, Tex.

GEORGE, William, banker; b. Aurora, Ill., Sept. 23, 1861; s. Alonzo and Lydia Rosetta (May) G.; student State U. of Ia., 1881-83; LL.B., Union Coll. of Law (U. of Chicago and Northwestern U.), 1885; m. Alice Maude Lounsbury, Oct. 11, 1887; children—Mrs. Alice May Morrill, Elizabeth M. Admitted to Ill. bar, 1885, and practiced about 3 years with U.S. Senator Albert J. Hopkins and with his partners, N. J. Aldrich and F. H. Thatcher; later alone and as mem. firm Aldrich, Winslow & George; largely engaged in commercial and business affairs; v.p. Old Second Nat. Bank, 1891-95, pres. (succeeding father) since 1895; owner of George Stock Farms and breeder of pure bred stock; also pres. Aurora Cotton Mills, Bankers Mutual Fidelity & Casualty Co., Chicago; v.p. for Ill. Nat. Surety Co. Republican. Baptist. President Ill. Bankers Assn., 1903-04; v.p. for Ill., Am. Bankers' Assn. (exec. council, 1905-08, 1909-12, 1929-32); ex-pres. Illinois Cattle Breeders' Assn.; v.p. Am. Genetic Assn; ex-pres. Am. Hereford Cattle Breeders' Assn.; mem. advisory bd. Nat. Soil Fertility League; pres. Kane County (Ill.) Bankers' Assn.; dir. Kane County Farm Improvement Assn. Mem. Phi Delta Theta, Phi Delta Phi. Mem. Aurora Patriots' Com., World War; chmn. Kane County Y.M.C.A. War Work; chmn. Kane County United War Work; mem. Kane County Council of Defense; treas. Jewish Relief for Kane County; sole trustee Henderson Estate, Old People's Home; mem. Aurora Centennial Bd., Aurora Red Cross Bd. Clubs: Union League, Hamilton, Saddle and Sirloin (Chicago); Union League, Rotary, Country (Aurora). Home: 461 Downer Pl. Office: Old Second Nat. Bank, Aurora, Ill. Died Jan. 21, 1943.

GERARD, Felix Roy, r.r. exec.; pres. and dir. Lehigh Valley R.R. Co., New York, N.Y., and numerous subsidiaries. Address: care Lehigh Valley R.R., 143 Liberty St., N.Y. City. Deceased.

GERHARDT, August Edward (gĕr'härt), surgeon; b. Fayette County, Ill., Oct. 1, 1882; s. Julius and Caroline (Berg) G.; student Concordia Coll., Springfield, Ill., 1897-1900, Ill. Sch. Pharmacy, Chicago, 1903-05; M.D., Northwestern U., Chicago, 1909; m. Elizabeth Walsh, July 17, 1912. Practiced in Wenatchee, Wash., since 1915; chief of staff Deaconess Hosp., 5 yrs.; asst. div. surgeon G.N. Ry.; dir. Columbia Valley Bank. Served as maj. M.C., World War; lt. col. Med. O.R.C. Fellow Am. Coll. Surgeons, A.M.A.; mem. Wash. State Med. Soc. (trustee), Pacific Coast Surg. Assn., Puget Sound Surg. Soc., Seattle Surg. Soc., Spokane Surg. Soc. Republican. Clubs: Rainier, University (Seattle). Home: R.R. 3, Wenatchee. Office: 32 S. Wenatchee Av., Wenatchee, Wash. Died May 3, 1942.

GERIG, William, civil engr.; b. Columbia, Boone County, Mo., Mar. 25, 1866; s. Francis Joseph and Caroline (Degen) G.; B.S., U. of Missouri, 1885, C.E., 1886, hon. LL.D., 1938; m. Fannie Crow, Jan. 21, 1890; children—Frank Austin, Mildred. Asst. engr. St. Louis & San Francisco R.R., 1886-89; U.S. asst. engr. Miss. River Commn., 1889-90; asst. engineer Chicago Drainage Canal, 1890-1900; chief engr. Southwest Ark.& I.Ty. Ry., 1890-91; U.S. asst. engr. Miss. River Commn., 1891-1905; div. engr. Panama Canal, 1905-08; pvt. practice, 1908-09; v.p., treas., chief engr. and gen. mgr. Pacific & Eastern Ry., cons. engr. Spokane, Portland & Seattle Ry. and St. Paul Union Depot, and consulting highway engr. Jackson County, Ore., 1909-15; cons. engr. N.Y. Barge Canal, etc., 1916; engr. Alaskan Engring. Commn., 1917; engr. and engr. in charge Anchorage div., Alaska R.R., 1918; asst. chief engr., Alaskan Engring. Commn., 1919-23; U.S. asst. engr., 1923, asso. engr., 1926, later sr. engr., head engr. Office of Chief Engrs. U.S. Army, 1923-38; retired Apr. 1, 1938. Mem. bd. engrs. Saluda Dam and cons. engr. Fort Peck Dam on Mo. River; cons. engr. Muskingum River Dams, Tygert Dam, Conchos Dam, etc. Mem. Am. Soc. C.E., Soc. Am. Mil. Engrs., Phi Beta Kappa, Tau Beta Pi. Presbyn. Mason. Contbr. to periodicals. Home: 9th and Pine St., Arkadelphia, Ark. Died Apr. 3, 1944.

GERKEN, Rudolph A. (gĕr'kĕn), archbishop; b. Dyersville, Ia., Mar. 7, 1887; s. Wm. and Elizabeth (Sudmeier) G.; ed. Pio Nono Coll., Milwaukee, Wis., and St. Joseph's Coll., Rensselaer, Ind. Teacher, pub. schs., Tex., 1910-12; instr., Dallas (Tex.) U., 1912-13; instr. in langs., Kenrick Sem., St. Louis, Mo., 1913-17; ordained priest, R.C. Ch., 1917; pastor Sacred Heart Parish, Abilene, Tex., 1917-19, St. Rita's Ch., Ranger, Tex., 1919-27; bishop, diocese of Amarillo (Tex.), 1927-33; installed as archbishop of Santa Fe, Aug. 23, 1933. Home: 219 Cathedral Pl., Santa Fe, N.M. Died Mar. 2, 1943.

GERLACH, Charles L. (gĕr'läk), congressman; b. Bethlehem, Pa., Sept. 14, 1895; s. Charles L. and Amanda (Rodenbach) G.; ed. pub. schs. of Bethlehem, Pa.; m. Florence I. Hillegase, Nov. 16, 1916. Treas. Allentown Supply Co.; mem. 76th, 77th and 78th Congresses (1939-45), 9th Pa. Dist. Republican. Mem. Travelers Protective Assn. Mem. Moravian Ch. Mason (32°, Shriner), Moose, Owl, Eagle. Clubs: Lehigh Valley Shrine, American Business (Allentown). Home: 2233 Liberty St. Office: 123 Hamilton St., Allentown, Pa.* Died May 1947.

GERMAN, John S., clergyman; b. Baltimore, Md., Aug. 26, 1879; s. William Henry and Sarah Rebecca (Slade) G.; B.A., Johns Hopkins University, Baltimore, Md., 1908; D.D., Morgan State College, Baltimore; D.D., Dickinson College, 1947; married to Cora May German, June 4, 1913; 1 dau., Cora Elizabeth. Joined Baltimore Conf. of Meth. Churches, 1908; served 3 pastorates; then pastor, Broadway Meth. Ch., Baltimore, since 1917; organizer and supt., Baltimore Goodwill Industries, since 1919; chmn., dept. of cities of Meth. Ch.; v.p., Nat. Assn. Goodwill Industries; trustee, Goucher Coll. Clubs: Internat. Torch (pres. Baltimore, 1944), Baltimore Exchange (chaplain since 1942). Home: 2408 Erdman Av., Baltimore 13. Office: 1713 E. Pratt St., Baltimore 31, Md. Died Oct. 17, 1947; buried London Park, Baltimore.

GERMANE, Charles E. (jẽr-măn′), educator; b. Riverdale, Mich., Dec. 9, 1885; s. Cassius and Mary Ann (Melia) G.; B.A., Tri-State Coll., Angola, Ind., 1910; M.A., State U. of Ia., 1918, Ph.D., 1920; m. Edith Gayton, July 21, 1915; children—Gayton Elwood, Edith Marie. Fellow State U. of Ia., 1918-19; dean Coll. of Education, Des Moines Univ., 1920-25; prof. edn., U. of Mo., since 1925. Mem. Nat. Soc. for Study of Edn., Phi Delta Kappa. Republican. Baptist. K.P. Author: (with wife) Silent Reading, 1922; Character Education, 1929; Character Training, 1929; Guidance and Counseling for Elementary Grades, 1938; Guidance and Counseling for Secondary Schools, 1941; The Value of Summarizing as Compared with Re-reading, 1941; Personnel Work in High Sch., 1941. Home: Columbia, Mo. Died Apr. 21, 1942.

GERNERD, Fred B(enjamin) (gẽr′nẽrd), ex-congressman; b. Spring Creek Lehigh Co., Pa., Nov. 22, 1879; s. C. W. B. and Ellen V. (Schmoyer) G.; A.B., Franklin and Marshall Coll., 1901; A.M., Columbia, 1903, LL.B., 1904; m. May G. M. Klein, Feb. 18, 1915; children—David Klein, Margaret Ellen. Admitted to bar, N.Y. City, 1904; began practice at Buffalo, N.Y., 1904; admitted to practice, Allentown, Pa., 1905; dist. atty. Lehigh County, Pa., 1908-12; mem. Rep. State Com., Pa., 1912-20; mem. 67th Congress (1921-23), 13th Pa. Dist. Del. Rep. Nat. Com., Kansas City, Mo., 1928. Chmn. and del. Pa. Bar Assn. to Inter-Am. Bar Conf., Havana, Cuba, 1941; del. Inter-American Bar Conf., Mexico City, 1944; del. Inter-Amer. Bar Conf., Santiago, Chile, 1945. Trustee Franklin and Marshall Coll., Cedar Crest Coll.; pres. Allentown Hosp. Assn.; organizer and first pres. Allentown Council Boy Scouts of America (now hon. pres.); founder and first pres. John Hay Rep. Assn. of Allentown (now hon. pres.). Hon. mem. Am. Huguenot Soc.; v.p. Valley Forge chapter S.A.R. Mem. Am. Bar Assn. (mem. house of dels. 1940-42), Pa. Bar Assn. (pres., 1941-42, mem. bd. govs.), Lehigh County Bar Assn., Sigma Chi. Republican. Mem. Reformed Ch. Home: 1519 Hamilton St., Allentown, Pa. Died Aug. 7, 1948.

GEROULD, Katharine Fullerton, writer; b. Brockton, Mass., Feb. 6, 1879; d. Bradford Morton (D.D.) and Julia M. (Ball) Fullerton; A.B., Radcliffe Coll., 1900, A.M., 1901; m. Gordon Hall Gerould, June 9, 1910; children—Christopher, Sylvia. Reader in English, Bryn Mawr Coll., 1901-10, on leave of absence in England and France, 1908-09. Author: Vain Oblations, 1914; The Great Tradition, 1915; Hawaii, Scenes and Impressions, 1916; A Change of Air, 1917; Modes and Morals (essays), 1919; Lost Valley, 1922; Valiant Dust, 1922; Conquistador, 1923; The Aristocratic West, 1925; The Light That Never Was, 1931; Ringside Seats, 1937. Winner of prize for best story in the Century's competition for coll. grads., 1900; contbr. stories, essays and verse to mags. Home: Princeton, N.J. Died July 27, 1944.

GERRY, Martin Hughes, Jr. (gẽr′ĭ), electrical engr.; b. Boston, Mass., October 16, 1868; s. Martin Hughes and Mary (Kernan) G.; grad. University of Minnesota, mechanical and electrical engineer, 1890; M.M.E., Cornell University, 1894; m. Altha Child, September 1900. In employ Sprague Elec. Ry. Co., and Thomson-Houston Co., and later with Gen. Elec. Co.; later at work on construction Met. Elevated Ry. of Chicago, and its supt. of motive power until 1898, when went to Mont. to take charge of engring. and construction for Helena Water & Elec. Power Co. (Missouri River Power Co.) in building dams and power plants for transmission of power to Helena, 18 miles, Butte, 65 miles, and Anaconda, 100 miles, upon completion of which he became its chief engr. and gen. mgr.; also consulting engr. Mont. Power Co., operating lighting plants in all large Mont. towns and power plants at Great Falls and Thompson Falls, 250,000 h.p.; also constructed elec. pumping plants for irrigation at Helena and other points in Mont. During World War served as Federal Fuel Administrator for Mont. Chief engr. and agent, St. Anthony Falls Water Power Co. and Minneapolis Mill Co. until 1924; Am. rep. Benguet Consolidated Mining Co., Manila, P.I.; now consulting engr. Address: 1107 Hobart Bldg., San Francisco, Calif. Died Dec. 30, 1941.

GERSON, Felix Napoleon, editor and author; b. Philadelphia, Oct. 18, 1862; s. Aaron and Eva (Goldsmith) G.; ed. Central High Sch., Philadelphia; studied civil engring.; m. Emily Goldsmith, 1892 (died 1917); children—Mrs. Cecelia G. Reinheimer, Dorothy G.; m. 2d, Emma Brylawski, 1936. Departmental chief clerk Reading Ry. Co., 1880-90; corr. for various papers; managing editor Chicago Israelite, 1890-91; manager, 1891-1908, mng. editor since 1908, pres. since 1919, Jewish Exponent. Staff writer for Philadelphia Public Ledger, 1895-1916; contbr. prose and verse to various publs. Mem. publ. com., Jewish Publ. Soc. America. Clubs: Franklin Inn, Philmont, Judæans, Pharisees. Author: Some Verses (collection of his poems). Translations of hist. and dramatic works: The Jews of Regensburg and Augsburg, 1939; The Ship of Hope, 1941; Rembrandt, the Bible and the Jews, 1945. Home: The Sprucemont, 16th and Spruce Sts., Philadelphia, Pa. Died Dec. 13, 1945.

GERSTENBERG, Charles William, publisher; b. Brooklyn, N.Y., May 25, 1882; s. Charles H. T. and Harriet (Hall) G.; Ph.B., New York U., 1904, LL.B., 1905; J.D., 1916; m. 2d, Mary E. Perry, Sept. 10, 1925; 1 dau., Mary Perry. Practiced law in N.Y. City, 1906-12; apptd. sec. Sch. of Commerce, Accounts and Finance, New York U., 1912, asso. prof. finance, 1915-17, prof., 1917-24; prof. constl. law, St. Lawrence U., since 1920. Mem. Pan-Am. Financial Conf., 1919. Chmn. bd., Prentice Hall, Inc.; trustee and mem. exec. com. West Side Savings Bank. Treas. Village of Oldfield, 1934-45. Sec. of Interfraternity Conf., 1928-29, chmn., 1929-30. Trustee George Washington University; president, Emma S. Clarke Memorial Library; pres. National Tax Association, 1940; mem. com. on taxation and pub. revenue of Commerce and Industry of New York; advisory com. on taxation, Am. Legislators' Assn.; mem. Joint Com. Nat. Tax Assn. and Am. Bar Assn. on Coordination of Federal, State and Local Taxation. Mem. American Economic Association, Delta Chi, Phi Beta Kappa, Beta Gamma Sigma, Theta Sigma Lambda. Episcopalian (vestryman Trinity Church. Author: Commercial Law (with T. W. Hughes), 1909; Materials of Corporation Finance, 1913; Organization and Control, 1916; Law of Bankruptcy, 1917; Principles of Business, 1918; Financial Organization and Management, 1924; Constitutional Law, 1926; American Constitutional Law, 1937. Address: Setauket, L.I., N.Y.; and 18 W. 9th St., New York. Died Sept. 15, 1948; buried in Caroline Churchyard, Setauket, L.I., N.Y.

GESSNER, Hermann Bertram, surgeon; b. New Orleans, La., Feb. 19, 1872; s. George and Josephine (Nicks) G.; A.B., Tulane U., 1889, A.M., 1891, M.D., 1895; studied Johns Hopkins Med. Sch., 1905, West London Hosp. Med. Sch., 1907; m. Jessie Hayes Gessner, Feb. 27, 1900; children—Leonard Edward, Josephine Hayes, Barbara Jessie, Edward Heim. Acting asst. surgeon, U.S. P.H.S., 1897, 1905; same, U.S. Army, Spanish-Am. War, 1898; practiced in New Orleans since 1895; prof. clin. surgery emeritus, Tulane Univ. First lieut. Med. R.C., U.S. Army, 1909-17; Mexican border duty, 1916. Chmn. Conf. Com. of Charity Hosp., New Orleans, 1913-16. Mem. A.M.A., Louisiana State Medical Society (president 1930-31), Orleans Parish Med. Soc. (pres. 1902), Southern Surg. Assn., Phi Delta Theta, Phi Beta Kappa, Alpha Kappa Kappa. Democrat. Unitarian. Club: Round Table. Author: Laboratory Exercises in Operative Surgery, 1910. Home: 119 Audubon Blvd., New Orleans, La. Died Aug. 8, 1944.

GEST, Morris, theatrical producer; b. Wilna, Russia, Jan. 17, 1881; s. Leon and Louise G.; came to U.S., 1893; ed. pub. schs. Boston; m. Reina Victoria Belasco, June 1, 1911. Began in theatrical business at Boston, 1893; mem. firm F. Ray Comstock and Morris Gest, 1905-28; firm prod. more than 50 plays; notable successes: Experience, 1914; The Wanderer, 1917; Chu Chin Chow, 1918; Aphrodite, 1919; Mecca, 1920. Lessee Manhattan Opera House, 1911-20; personal lessee and dir. Century Theatre, New York, 1917-20; first impresario to bring original Russian ballet to Am., first to introduce Michel Fokine, famous Russian ballet master, to Am.; first to introduce to Am., with extraordinary success, Balieff's Chauve-Souris, 1922, and the Moscow Art Theatre, in a repertory of 13 plays during the seasons 1923-25; reintroduced Eleanora Duse to Am. stage in repertory of 5 plays, 1923-24; brought Max Reinhardt to New York to stage "The Miracle," 1924; brought the Moscow Art Theatre Musical Studio of Vladimir Nemirovitch-Dantchenko to America for the first time, 1925; produced "Wonderbar," with Al Jolson, 1931. Signed contract with United Artists, 1926, to produce one motion picture annually for 6 yrs., beginning with Belasco's "The Darling of the Gods" operating independently as Morris Gest, Inc., since 1928. Jewish religion. Home: 71 E. 52d St. Address: 16 W 39th St., New York. Died May 16, 1942.

GETHOEFER, Louis Henry (gĕth-o′fẽr), chmn. bd. Peoples-Pittsburgh Trust Co.; b. Sept. 20, 1866; s. George and Emelie (Rudolf) G.; ed. pub. schs. Employed by Bank of Buffalo (N.Y.), 1890-93, City Bank of Buffalo, 1893-1901, Marine Bank of Buffalo, 1901-03, v.p., 1903; cashier Columbia Bank of Buffalo, 1903-13; v.p. Bankers Trust Co. of Buffalo, 1913-16; pres. and dir. Pittsburgh Trust Co., 1916-29; v.p. and dir. Peoples-Pittsburgh Trust Co., 1929-31, pres. and dir., 1931-40, chmn. bd. Peoples-Pittsburgh Trust Co. since 1940; pres. and dir. Nufer Cedar Co.; dir. Mercantile Bridge Co. Pres. and dir. Passavant Hosp. of Pittsburgh. Mason (32°, K.T., Scottish Rite). Clubs: Duquesne, Pittsburgh Athletic Assn., Oakmont Country. Home: Schenley Apts. Office: Fourth Av. and Wood St., Pittsburgh, Pa. Died July 27, 1946.

GETMAN, Frederick Hutton, chemist; b. Oswego, N.Y., Feb. 9, 1877; s. Charles Henry and Alice (Peake) G.; ed. Rensselaer Poly. Inst., Troy, N.Y., and Lehigh U.; grad. chem. dept., U. of Va., 1896; Ph.D., Johns Hopkins, 1903; m. Ellen M. Holbrook, Nov. 26, 1906. Instr. chemistry and physics, Stamford High Sch., 1897-1901; fellow physical chemistry, 1902-03, fellow by courtesy, 1903-04, Carnegie research asst. in phys. chemistry, 1903-04, Johns Hopkins; lecturer in phys. chemistry, Coll. City of New York, 1904-05; instr. in phys. science, Stamford High Sch., 1905-1906; lecturer physics, Columbia, 1907-08; asso. prof. chemistry, Bryn Mawr (Pa.) Coll., 1909-15; dir. Hillside Laboratory, Stamford, Conn.; dir. Stamford Trust Co.; pres. The Getman & Judd Co. Dir. and v.p. Ferguson Library; v.p. Stamford Hosp. Fellow A.A.A.S., Am. Inst. of Chemists; mem. Am. Chem. Soc., Am. Electrochem. Soc., History of Sciences Soc., London Chem. Soc., Nederlandsche Chemische Vereeniging, Phi Beta Kappa. Club: Chemists (New York). Presbyterian. Republican. Author: Blow-pipe Analysis, 1899; Laboratory Exercises in Physical Chemistry, 1904; Introduction to Physical Science, 1909; Outlines of Theoretical Chemistry, 1913; Electrochemical Equivalents (with Dr. Carl Hering); Life of Ira Remsen; also scientific papers on various problems in phys. chemistry and chem. biography. Died Dec. 2, 1941.

GHENT, William James (jĕnt), author; b. Frankfort, Ind., Apr. 29, 1866; s. Ira Keith and Mary Elizabeth (Palmer) G.; ed. pub. grammar and high schs.; m. Amy Louise Morrison, July 17, 1909. Worked as a compositor and proofreader in various cities and sub-editor of various trade papers in New York. Aid to Samuel M. Jones, of Toledo, as lit. mgr. of mayoralty and gubernatorial campaigns of 1899. Regular contbr. to The Independent, New York, 1900-13; occasional contbr. to various publs.; editor American Fabian, 1897-98. One of the founders Social Reform Club, New York, 1894. Sec. Rand Sch. of Social Science from its founding, 1906-09; pres. Rand Sch., 1909-11; sec. to Victor L. Berger, 1911-12; editor California Outlook, 1915-17; regular contbr. The Weekly Review (New York), 1919-20; on staff Dictionary of Am. Biography, 1927. Mem. Authors' League America, Am. Hist. Assn.; hon. mem. Order of Indian Wars; mem. exec. com. Am. Alliance for Labor and Democracy, 1917-19. Clubs: X, Authors. Author: Our Benevolent Feudalism, 1902; Mass and Class, 1904; Socialism and Success, 1910; The Reds Bring Reaction, 1923; The Road to Oregon, 1929; The Early Far West, 1931; (with LeRoy R. Hafen) Broken Hand, The Life Story of Thomas Fitzpatrick, 1931. Editor: Appeal Socialist Classics (12 vols.), 1916. Home: 1809 Belmont Rd., Washington, D.C. Died July 10, 1942.

GIANNINI, Amadeo Peter (jä-nē′nē), banker; b. San Jose, Calif., May 6, 1870; s. Luigi and Virginia (Demartini) G.; ed. pub. sch. and bus. coll.; m. Clorinda Agnes, d. Joseph Cuneo, Sept. 14, 1892; children—L.M., V.D. (dec.), Claire E. Began at 12 yrs. of age with L. Scatena & Co., wholesale commn. mchts., San Francisco, and at 19 was admitted to firm; became mgr. Estate of Joseph Cuneo, and dir. Columbus Savings & Loan Soc.; founder 1904, Bank of Italy (now Bank of America Nat. Trust & Savings Assn.) founder, chairman; chmn. bd. Transamerica Corp.; hon. chmn. Banca d'America e d'Italia; dir. Nat. City Bk. and dir. City Bk. Farmers Trust Co., New York; director First National Bank of Portland, Oregon. director Fireman's Fund Insurance Co., and Fireman's Fund Imdemnity Co., San Francisco. Member board regents University of Calif.; dir. San Francisco Chamber Commerce 3 terms; mem. Native Sons of Golden West. Catholic. Clubs: Olympic, Bohemian, Commonwealth, San Francisco Commercial, Union League, San Francisco Golf (San Francisco); Country, Athletic, California (Los Angeles); Burlingame (Calif.) Country; Broad Street, New York Athletic (New York); Congressional Country (Washington, D.C.); Union Interallée (Paris). Home: "Seven Oaks," San Mateo. Office: 300 Montgomery St., San Francisco. Died June 3, 1949; buried in Holy Cross Cemetery, San Francisco.

GIANNINI, Attilio H., banker; b. Calif., 1874; s. Louis Giannini; A.B., U. of Calif., 1894, M.D., 1896; m. Leontine Denker; 1 son, Bernard. Began practice at San Francisco, 1896; moved to New York; became chmn. bd. Bank of Am. and vice pres. Transamerica Corp.; formerly chmn. gen. exec. com., Bank of Am. N.T.&S.A.; formerly chmn. bd. and pres. United Artists Corp. Served as surgeon in Spanish-Am. War. Mem. A.M.A., Med. Soc. State of Calif. Catholic. Clubs: Lambs, Bankers, Westchester-Biltmore, New York Athletic; Bohemian, Olympic Family, San Francisco Golf and Country. Home: 161 S. Mapleton Dr., Holmby Hills, Los Angeles, Calif. Office: 8278 Sunset Boul., Los Angeles. Deceased.

GIBBINS, Henry, army officer; b. Knoxville, Tenn., May 20, 1877; s. William E. and Ellen M. (Henry) G.; ed. Holbrook Coll., Knoxville, 1894-95; grad. Mounted Service Sch. (U.S. Army), 1910, Army Sch. of the Line, 1916; m. Grace McGonigle, Jan. 19, 1907; children—Margaret, Henry, Jr. Enlisted in Tenn. N.G., 1896; 1st lt. 3d Tenn. Inf., May 1898-Jan. 1899; 2d and 1st lt., 31st U. S. Vol. Inf., 1899-1901; commd. 2d lt. cav., regular army, Feb. 2, 1901; promoted through grades to col., Aug. 31, 1929; asst. to q.m. gen., with rank of brig. gen., Feb. 6, 1935-Apr. 1, 1936; apptd. q.m. gen., with rank of maj. gen., Apr. 1, 1936; retired Apr. 1, 1940. Participated in Spanish-Am. War, Philippine Insurrection, Cuban Occupation and World War. Awarded Mexican border and Victory medals. Home: 2139 Wyoming Av. Office: 923 15th St., Washington, D.C. Deceased.

GIBBONEY, Stuart Gatewood, lawyer; b. Wytheville, Va., Nov. 1, 1877; s. David Kyle and Frances G. (Crockett) G.; ed. Wytheville Mil. Acad., University Sch., Richmond, Va.; LL.B., U. of Va., 1903; m. Constance F. Whitehead, Nov. 30, 1907; 1 dau., Constance (Mrs. Frederick Randolph Bailey). Entered practice of law in N.Y. City, 1903; practiced in London, England and Paris, France, 1904; returned to N.Y. and became mem. Barber, Watson & Gibboney; then mem. Gibboney & Harris; retired April 1943; chairman board of directors and director The Angostura-Wuppermann Corporation. Served in United States Army, Spanish American War in Cuba and the U.S. and later on staff General Adna R. Chaffee, Pekin, China, during Boxer outbreak, 1900; asso. with Senator W. G. McAdoo and Wm. F. McCombs, Wilson pre-convention campaign, 1911-12; sec. Nat. Wilson and Marshall League Campaign, 1912; organized Thomas Jefferson Memorial Foundation, 1923, which maintains Monticello as a national shrine, pres. and dir. since its orgn.; elected chmn. Sesquicentennial of Am. Independence and Thomas Jefferson Centennial Commn., created by Act of Congress, 1926; apptd. member Jefferson Memorial Commn., 1934, elected chmn., 1939; apptd. mem. Thomas Jefferson Bi-centennial commission by President Roosevelt, 1940. Sec. "The Virginians," Soc. in New York, 1907-10; sec. New York Southern Soc., 1908-12. Mem. Am. Bar Assn., N.Y. State Bar Assn., N.Y. County Lawyers Assn., Federal Bar Assn. of N.Y., N.J. and Conn., Phi Delta Phi. Clubs: Sons of the Revolution of New York; Lawyers; National Democratic; Farmington Country (Va.); "The Virginians." Democrat. Episcopalian. Home: "Monticello," Charlottesville, Va. Died Apr. 24, 1944.

GIBBS, George, author, illustrator; b. New Orleans, Mar. 8, 1870; s. Benjamin Franklin and Elizabeth Beatrice (Kellogg) G.; U.S. Naval Acad., 1886-88; studied art, Corcoran Sch. of Art and Art Students' League, Washington; m. Maud Stovell Harrison, Apr. 24, 1901; children—George Fort, Theodore Harrison, Sarah Stovell. Progressive. Episcopalian. Clubs: Art, Franklin Inn, Pegasus. Author and Illustrator: Pike and Cutlass, 1900; In Search of Mademoiselle, 1901; The Love of Monsieur, 1905; The Medusa Emerald, 1907; Tony's Wife, 1909; The Bolted Door, 1911; The Forbidden Way, 1911; The Maker of Opportunities, 1912; The Silent Battle, 1913; Madcap, 1913; The Flaming Sword, 1914; The Yellow Dove, 1915; Paradise Garden, 1916; The Secret Witness, 1917; The Golden Bough, 1918; The Black Stone, 1919; The Splendid Outcast, 1920; The Vagrant Duke, 1921; Youth Triumphant, 1921; The House of Mohun, 1922; Fires of Ambition, 1923; Sack Cloth and Scarlet, 1924; Mad Marriage, 1925; How to Stay Married, 1925; The Up Grade, 1927; The Joyous Conspirator, 1927; The Castle Rock Mystery, 1927; The Shores of Romance, 1928; The Isle of Illusion, 1929; The Fire Within, 1930; Old Philadelphia, 1931; Foul Weather, 1932; Honor Among Women, 1933; The Yellow Diamond, 1934; Out of the Dark, 1935; The Vanishing Idol, 1936; Hunted, 1937; The Road to Bagdad 1938; The Silver Death, 1940; The Sleeper Wakes, 1941; also American Sea Fights (a portfolio of colored drawings), 1903. Address: Rosemont, Pa. Died Oct. 10, 1942.

GIBBS, George Couper, lawyer; b. Jacksonville, Fla., Oct. 28, 1879; s. George Williams and Margaret (Watkins) G.; LL.B., Washington and Lee, 1903; m. Lenora B. Warnock, Oct. 14, 1908; children—Margaret (Mrs. William Worthington), William Warnock, Kingsley (dec.), Harriet Crossman. Admitted to Fla. bar, 1903; law asst., A. W. Cockrell & Son, 1903-07; in practice at Jacksonville, 1907-12; additional judge Circuit Court, Duval County, 1912-13; judge Circuit Court, 4th Fla. Circuit, 1913-35; law practice, Jacksonville, 1935-38; atty. gen. of Fla., 1938-41; resumed law practice at Jacksonville, 1941; chief atty., Fla., Office Price Administrn., 1942-43, counsel to director, 1943; resumed private practice, Feb. 1943. Served with Fla. Nat. Guard, 1896-99; corpl. U.S. Vol. Inf., 1898. Chmn. Vice Commn., Jacksonville, 1905-06. Mem. exec. com. Interracial Commn., Fla.; chmn. advisory bd., Brewster Hosp. Fellow Am. Geog. Soc.; mem. Am. Bar Assn., Fla. State Bar Assn. (ex-sec.), Jacksonville Bar Assn. (ex-sec.); Acad. of Political Science, Spanish War Vets.; Phi Kappa Psi; hon. mem. Phi Delta Phi. Democrat. Presbyterian. Clubs: Civitan, Seminole; Florida Yacht. Home: 2717 Riverside Av. Office: Florida Bank Bldg., Jacksonville, Fla. Died Sep. 17, 1946.

GIBBS, George Sabin, army officer, industrialist; born in Harlan, Iowa, December 14, 1875; son of George Sabin and Della (Baughn) Gibbs; B.S., State Univ. of Iowa., 1897, M.S., 1901; grad. Army Signal School, 1912; also grad. of Army War College, 1920; m. Ruth Annis Hobby, Oct. 9, 1899; children—Jessie Louise (Mrs. George K. Perkins), Robert Henry (capt. U.S. Navy), George Wareham (lt. col. U.S. Army), David Parker (lt. col. U.S. Army). Private and q.m. sergt. Co. C, 51st Ia. Inf., and 1st class sergt. Signal Corps U.S.V., May 30, 1898-Jan. 30, 1899; commd. 2d lt. signal officer vols., Jan. 13, 1899; promoted through grades to col., May 9, 1921; col. and brig. gen. (temp.), World War. Served in the Philippines in Spanish-Am. War and Philippine Insurrection, 1898-1900; built north central sect. of the Alaska telegraph system, 1901-03. Chief signal officer, Army of Cuban Pacification, 1907-09; chief signal officer Hawaiian Dept., 1913-15, and of the El Paso Dist., 1917; assistant chief signal officer A.E.F. in France, 1917-19, with the rank of brig. general; General Staff, 1920-21; in charge of laying of new Alaska cable, 1924; chief signal officer of Army, with rank of maj. gen. for 4 years from Jan. 9, 1928; retired from active service, June 30, 1931, to become v.p. Internat. Telephone and Telegraph Corp.; became pres. Postal Telegraph-Cable Co., Oct. 15, 1931, apptd. a trustee in reorganization of the co., 1936, director, 1940; director and vice chairman Federal Telephone and Radio Corporation since 1943. Recommended "for especially gallant and meritorious conduct" in the Battle of Manila, Aug. 13, 1898. Decorated D.S.M.; Officer Legion of Honor (France); Companion of the Order of St. Michael and St. George (Great Britain); Commandeur, Ordre de la Couronne (Belgium); Commendatore dell'Ordine della Corona d'Italia (Italy). Mem. Nat. Inst. Social Sciences, Sigma Nu, Sigma Xi. Mason (K.T.). Clubs: Army and Navy, Army, Navy Country (Washington, D.C.). Home: Lime Rock, Conn. Office: 67 Broad St., New York, N.Y. Died Jan. 9, 1947.

GIBBS, Lincoln Robinson, coll. prof.; b. Wiscasset, Me., Dec. 9, 1868; s. Lincoln Watts and Sarah Eliza (Baker) G.; grad. Me. Wesleyan Sem., Kents Hill, 1888; A.B., Wesleyan U., Conn., 1892, A.M., 1893; A.M., Harvard, 1897; Northwestern U., Evanston, Ill., 1907-08; m. Kate Peters, Aug. 17, 1905; children—Robert Edmund, Katherine. Instr. English, Lehigh U., S. Bethlehem, Pa., 1894-95, Boston U., 1896; prof. English, Mt. Union Coll., Alliance, O., 1899-1901, Territorial Normal Sch., Edmond, Okla., 1901-03, Wells Coll., Aurora, N.Y., 1903-04, Mt. Union Coll., 1904-09, U. of Pittsburgh, 1909-22, Antioch Coll., Yellow Springs, O., 1922-26, U. of Miami, 1926-28, Antioch Coll. since 1928. Mem. Am. Assn. Univ. Profs., Phi Beta Kappa, Psi Upsilon. Methodist. Editor; Coleridge's Ancient Mariner (sch. edit.), 1898; Selections from Coleridge (sch. edit.); Selections from Robert Browning. Home: Yellow Springs, O. Died Dec. 14, 1943.

GIBSON, Ben J., ex-atty. gen. of Ia.; b. Corning, Ia., Nov. 13, 1881; s. William and Virginia G.; U. of Neb., 1902-06, A.B. and LL.B.; m. Anna Rolston, Sept. 5, 1905; children—Wayne, Wendell, Ben. Began practice at Corning, 1906; co. atty. Adams County, 1908-12; mem. Ia. Senate, 1916-18 (resigned); atty. gen. of Ia., 1921-27. Mem. Iowa Nat. Guard, 1901-17; lt. col., 1923-38, then col. U.S.R., Ia. Nat. Guard, now retired; Mexican border service; capt. and operations officer 72d Inf., U.S. Army, World War. Mem. Am. and Ia. State bar assns. Republican. Presbyterian. Mason (32° Shriner), Odd Fellow, K. of P., etc. Clubs: Des Moines, Acacia, Wakonda, Alumni Club (U. of Neb.). Home: 405 37th St. Office: 1204 Equitable Bldg., Des Moines, Ia. Died July 8, 1949.

GIBSON, Charles Dana, illustrator; b. Roxbury, Mass., Sept. 14, 1867; s. Charles DeWolf and Josephine Elizabeth G.; ed. at Flushing, L.I., also Art Students' League, New York, 1884-85; m. Irene Langhorne, Nov. 7, 1895. Has done much illustrating in principal mags.; also illustrated numerous books. Mem. Am. Acad. Arts and Letters. Author: Sketches in London; People of Dickens; Drawings, 1894; Pictures of People, 1896; Sketches and Cartoons, 1898; The Education of Mr. Pipp, 1899; Sketches in Egypt, 1899; The Americans, 1900; A Widow and Her Friends, 1901; Social Ladder, 1902. National Academician, 1932. Address: 127 E. 73d St., New York, N.Y.* Died Dec. 23, 1944.

GIBSON, Charles Langdon, surgeon; b. Boston, Mass., May 5, 1864; s. Charles Langdon and Margarette Carter (Smith) G.; A.B., Harvard, 1886, M.D., 1889; unmarried. Prof. emeritus surgery, Cornell Med. Coll.; cons. surgeon, N.Y. Hosp., St. Luke's Memorial, State Hosp. for Deformed and Crippled Children, and Southside (Babylon) hospitals. Commanding major Medical Corps, U.S. Army; director Base Hospital 9, A.E.F., in France, 1917-18. Commander of Crown (Belgian). Fellow American Surg. Assn.; mem. Soc. Clin. Surgery, Am. Assn. Genito-Urinary Surgeons, Internat. Surg. Assn., Practioners' Soc., N.Y. Clin. Soc., N.Y. Surg. Soc., Soc. Colonial Wars, S.R., Mil. Order Foreign Wars; asso. mem. Academie de Chirurgie, Paris; corr. mem. Academie de Medecine, Paris. Club: University. Address: 1 W. 54th St., New York, N.Y. Died Nov. 24, 1944.

GIBSON, James Lambert, mathematician; b. Kamas, Utah, Mar. 10, 1873; s. William and Mary Adelia (Lambert) G.; B.S., U. of Utah, 1895; A.M., Columbia, 1898; Ph.D., Vienna, 1923; studied Cambridge U., Eng., 1902-03, Bonn., Germany, 1922, Vienna, 1922-23, Paris, 1923, Göttingen, 1931; m. Sarah Pope, Feb. 11, 1904; children—Marl D., Rhea, James L., Vera, Keath P., Earle. Prof. mathematics, University of Utah, 1904-41, dean School of Arts and Sciences, 1915-41, now emeritus. Pres. Utah Conservation and Research Foundation since 1937. Fellow A.A.A.S., Utah Acad. of Sciences, Arts and Letters; mem. Am. Math. Soc., Math. Assn. America, Phi Kappa Phi, Sigma Xi. Home: 1337 Harrison Av. Salt Lake City 3, Utah.* Died Feb. 10, 1945.

GIBSON, Robert Murray, judge; b. Duncansville, Pa., Aug. 20, 1869; s. William James (D.D.) and Elizabeth (Murray) G.; student Pa. State Coll.; A.B., Washington and Jefferson Coll., 1889; m. Lorena G. Core, Oct. 4, 1897; U.S. dist. judge Western Dist. of Pa. since July 29, 1922. Republican. Presbyn. Mason. Home: 6101 Stanton Av. Address: Federal Bldg., Pittsburgh, Pa.* Died Dec. 19, 1949.

GIDDINGS, Howard Andrus, ins. exec., author; b. Hartford, Conn., Oct. 2, 1868; s. Edwin Alden and Susan M. (Keep) G.; ed. high sch.; m. Florence Chase Starkweather, Apr. 7, 1892; children—Helen, Florence, Elizabeth, Bradford, Chase, Marion, Constance, Marston Todd. With Conn. Mut. Life Ins. Co., Hartford, 1887-1901; with Travelers Ins. Co. since 1901, now vice-pres. Maj. brig. staff Conn. Nat. Guard, 1893-1902; capt. Vol. Signal Corps, Spanish-Am. War; acting chief signal officer 7th A.C. Mem. Conn. State Council of Defense, World War; mem. Am. Liberty Loan Mission to Europe, 1918. Mem. Soc. Mayflower Descendants, The Pilgrims, Mil. Order Foreign Wars of U.S. (formerly vice comdr. gen.), Naval and Mil. Order Spanish War; fellow Royal Geog. Soc. (London). Republican. Clubs: Hartford; Explorers (New York). Author: Hand Book of Military Signaling, 1896; New Handbook of Military Signaling, 1917; Exploits of the Signal Corps in the War with Spain. Contbr. on outdoor and insurance subjects. Home: 182 Fern St. Office: 700 Main St., Hartford, Conn. Died Mar. 10, 1949.

GIDEON, Dave, pres. Huntington Pub. Co.; pub. Huntington Herald-Dispatch. Address: Huntington, W.Va.* Died Jan. 5, 1950.

GIE, Stefanus Francois Naudé, M.P. and E.E. from Union of South Africa; b. Worcester, South Africa, July 13, 1884; s. C.J.C. and M. (Naudé) G.; ed. Victoria Coll., U. of Stellenbosch, U. of Amsterdam, U. of Berlin; holds degree Dr. Phil.; m. Johanna Jordaan, Dec. 1911; 2 sons. Prof. history and prin., U. of Stellenbosch, 1918-26; sec. for edn., Union of South Africa, 1926-34; M.P. and E.E. from Union of South Africa to Germany, 1934-39, to Sweden, 1934-44, to U.S. since Mar. 1944. Address: South African Legation, Washington, D.C. Died Mar. 1945.

GIESY, John Ulrich (gē'sē), physician, author: b. Chillicothe, O., Aug. 6, 1877; s. William Sommers and Anna Kate Hutton (Heckerman) G.; M.D., Starling Med. Coll., Columbus, O., 1898; m. Juliet Galena Conwell, Dec. 8, 1904. Practiced at Salt Lake City, Utah, since 1898; asst. city physician, 1899. Capt. Med. Corps, U.S. Army, May 28-Dec. 23, 1918, retired lt. col. Med. R.C. Prime mover in securing officers' training camp at Ft. Douglas, Utah, 1916; gen. sec. Citizens' Mil. Training Camp Assn., Salt Lake City, 1916. Mem. Pub. Safety Com., Salt Lake City, 1917. Section leader, medical section, American Legion Alerte (auxiliary police unit) Salt Lake Post No. 2, 1943. Examiner U.S. Recruiting and Induction Station on civilian status, Salt Lake City, 1942-43. Fellow American Medical Association; mem. Am. Congress Physiotherapy, Utah State and Salt Lake Co. med. socs., Authors League of America, Am. Legion, Am. Forestry Assn., Reserve Officers Assn. U.S. (past pres. Salt Lake chapter), Utah State R.O.A. (v.p.), S.A.R.; life mem. U.S. Inf. Assn. Republican. Protestant. Author: All For His Country, 1914; The Other Woman (with O.R. Cohen), 1917; Mimi, 1918. Contbr. fiction and detective stories to mags. also science articles to med. jours.. Home: 207 Maryland Apts. Office: Medical Arts Bldg., Salt Lake City, Utah. Died Sept. 8, 1947.

GIFFORD, Charles L., congressman; b. Cotuit, Mass., Mar. 15, 1871; s. William C. and Mary A. (Baker) G.; common sch. edn.; m. Fannie H. Handy, Sept. 6, 1892; 1 dau., Mrs. Florence Claussen. Formerly teacher high schs. in Conn. and Cotuit; in real estate business since 1900. Mem. Gen. Court, Mass., 1912-13, Senate, 1914-19; elected mem. 67th Congress (1921-23) to fill vacancy; mem. 68th to 72d Congresses (1923-33), 15th Mass. Dist. and 73d to 80th Congresses (1939-49), 9th Mass. Dist. Republican. Conglist. Mason. Odd Fellow. Home: Cotuit, Barnstable, Mass. Died Aug. 23, 1947.

GIFFORD, John Clayton, forester; b. May's Landing, N.J., Feb. 8, 1870; s. Daniel and Emily (Frazier) G.; B.S., Swarthmore Coll., 1890; special student U. of Mich., Johns Hopkins; studied forestry in Germany; D.Oec. (Doctor of Economics), U. of Munich, 1899; m. 2d, Martha Wilson, Jan. 1, 1923. Instr. econ. botany, Swarthmore, 1890-94; forester N.J. Geol. Survey, 1895-96; asst. prof. forestry, N.Y. State Coll. Forestry (Cornell), 1900-03; spl. agt. Bur. of Forestry, U.S. Dept. of Agriculture, 1905; prof. tropical forestry, U. of Miami, Fla. Engaged in tropical forestry and horticulture. Founder of "The Forester," now "American Forests and Forest Life," official organ Am. Forestry Assn. Mem. Swarthmore Meeting Society of Friends. Fellow A.A.A.S.; sr. mem. Soc. Am. Foresters. Author: Practical Forestry, 1901; The Everglades of Florida, 1911; Billy Bowlegs and the Seminole War, 1925; Living by the Land, 1945; also U.S. Bulls. on the Luquillo Forest Reserve, Porto Rico, The Subsistence Homestead, The Rehabilitation of the Floridan Keys, The Reclamation of the Everglades with Trees; Bulletin 77 Fla. Keys State Dept. of Agr., Tallahassee, Fla. Address: 2937 S.W. 27th Av., Miami, Fla. Died June 25, 1949. Buried Elliot's Key, Dade Co., Fla.

GIFFORD, Sanford Robinson, ophthalmologist; b. Omaha, Neb., Jan. 8, 1892; s. Harold and Mary (Millard) G.; A.B., Cornell U., 1913; M.A. and M.D., U. of Nebr., 1918; m. Alice Carter, July 11, 1917; children—Sanford R., Carter. Bacteriologist, rank of 1st lt. U.S. Army Base Hosp., in France, 1918-19; in practice with father, Omaha, 1919-29; instr. in ophthalmology, U. of Neb. Med. Sch., 1919-24, asst. prof. ophthalmology, 1924-29; prof. ophthalmology, Northwestern U. Med. Sch., also ophthalmologist to allied hosps. since 1929; attending ophthalmologist Cook County Hosp. since 1932. Mem. Am. Ophthal.

Soc., Am. Acad. Ophthalmology and Oto-Rhino.-Laryngology, Chicago Inst. Medicine, Phi Rho Sigma, Alpha Omega Alpha and Sigma Xi fraternities. Clubs: Tavern, University, Saddle and Cycle, Bohemian (San Francisco, Calif.). Author: Handbook of Ophthalmic Therapeutics, 3d edit., 1942; Textbook of Ophthalmology, 2d edit., 1941. Asso. editor Archives of Ophthalmology since 1928. Contbr. to Am. Jour. Ophthalmology, 1919-28. Corr. editor Klinische Monatsblätter für Augenheilkunde, 1928-40. Author of articles on bacteriology of the eyes, especially diseases due to fungi and higher bacteria. With Dr. J. M. Patton reported probable etiological agent of hitherto unknown disease, agricultural conjunctivitis. Home: 1430 Lake Shore Drive. Office: 720 N. Michigan Av., Chicago, Ill. Died Feb. 25, 1944.

GILBERT, George Blodgett, clergyman; b. Randolph, Vt., Jan. 23, 1872; s. Henry Charles and Martha Pamelia (Blodgett) G.; A.B., Trinity Coll., Hartford, Conn., 1896; grad. Berkeley Divinity Sch., Middletown, Conn., 1898, Hartford Sch. Religious Pedagogy, 1910; m. Mary Jane Shelley, Feb. 4, 1903; children—Shelley Tingle, George Blodgett, Henry Closson, Mary Virginia, Charles Nathaniel. Ordained to ministry of Episcopal Ch. as deacon, 1898, priest, 1899; rector Christ Ch., Middletown, Conn., 1899-1909; missionary Middlesex County, Conn., since 1909; archdeacon of Middlesex County, 1937-40; minister in charge of Emmanuel Ch., Killingworth, Conn., since 1910, Epiphany Ch., Durham, Conn., 1924-41, St. James Ch., Ponset, Conn., 1938-41. Mem. Common Council, City of Middletown; mem. town school bd., 1922-42; pres. Middlesex County Regional Assn. of School Boards, 1941; mem. Conn. Legislature, 1927-29; chaplain State Senate, 1937-39. Selected as typical country parson of U.S. by Christian Herald and Harper Bros. Pub. Co., 1939. Mem. Phi Beta Kappa. Democrat. Author: Forty Years a Country Preacher (autobiography), 1940. Contbr. of column, "Pastoral Parson and His Country Folks" to Rural New Yorker; also contbr. to religious jours. Home: Millbrook Road, Middletown, Conn. Died Feb. 20, 1948.

GILBERT, Joseph Walter, newspaper man; b. Green County, Wis., May 20, 1875; s. Franklin H. and Clara (Tait) G.; grad. high sch., Chetek, Wis., 1890; m. Rose Poindexter, Oct. 4, 1904; children—Miles Poindexter, Jo Janette. Licensed as pharmacist, S.D., 1897, and practiced in Deadwood; reporter Fargo (N.D.) Call, 1899, Anaconda (Mont.) Standard, 1900-03; Sunday editor Standard, 1903-04; reporter Butte Intermountain, 1905-06; news editor Missoulian, Missoula, Mont., 1906; with Seattle Post-Intelligencer, 1907-21, as reporter, city editor, Washington corr., polit. editor, editorial writer, and mng. editor; editorial writer, later polit. editor, Seattle Times, since 1922. Republican. Clubs: Washington State Press, Elks. Home: 1920 38th Av. N., Seattle, Wash. Died July 10, 1944.

GILBERT, Osceola Pinckney, editor; b. Rockford, Ala., Sept. 22, 1875; s. John Fleming and Susann (Thomas) G.; student Mercer U., Macon, Ga., 1895-97, D.D., 1930; U. of Ga., 1899-1900; Crozer Sem., Chester, Pa., 1901-02; m. Talula Zuleme Jordan, Dec. 7, 1904; children—Wright Courtland, John Jordan, William Andrew (dec.), Osceola Pinckney, Benjamin Pierce, James Brown. Ordained ministry Bapt. Ch., 1895; pastor Second Bapt. Ch., Augusta, Ga., 1900-05, 1908-16, First Bapt. Ch., Americus, Ga., 1905-08, First Bapt. Ch., Brunswick, Ga., 1916-30; moderator Hephzibah Bapt. Assn. 1915-16; mem. exec. com. Georgia Baptist Conv., 1919-29; editorial writer Brunswick Banner, 1917-19; book editor The Christian Index, 1922, editor and mgr. of publ., 1930-47. Mem. adv. bd. to pres. Mercer Univ. Trustee Bapt. Bible Inst., New Orleans. Office: Baptist Bldg., 291 Peachtree St., Atlanta, Ga. Died April 6, 1947.

GILBERT, Samuel T., corp. exec.; b. Kalamazoo, Aug. 29, 1881; s. Julius and Hannah (Goldwin) G.; ed. pub. schs.; m. Sylvia Goodman, June 3, 1907; 1 son, Julius. Pres. The Deisel-Wemmer-Gilbert Corp., Lillies Cigar Co. (Kalamazoo, Mich.), Consol. Cigar Co. (N.Y. City), Webster Cigar Co. (Detroit, Mich.), Otto Eisenlohr & Bros. (Philadelphia, Pa.). Clubs: Columbia Yacht (N.Y. City); Franklin Hills Country, Great Lakes (Detroit). Home: 31 Arden Park. Office: 2180 E. Milwaukee Av., Detroit, Mich.* Died Mar. 3, 1947.

GILBERT, William Edward, banking; b. Springfield, Mass., Aug. 28, 1870; s. George Stebbins and Ella (Parkhurst) G.; student Springfield pub. schs.; m. Jessie Morgan Dewey, Oct. 10, 1894; children—George Dewey, Morgan Parkhurst. In employ Third Nat. Bank, 1888-93; teller City Nat. Bank, 1893-99, cashier, 1899-1906; v.p. and treas. Union Trust Co., 1906-16, chmn. bd. dirs. since Dec. 1940; trustee Hampden Savings Bank; dir. The Torrington Co., Bowles Lunch, Inc. Trustee Springfield Hosp. Republican. Unitarian. Mason. Clubs: Canadian (New York); Colony (Springfield). Home: 172 Long Hill St. Office: Union Trust Co., Springfield 2, Mass. Died Dec. 25, 1948.

GILCHRIST, Harry Lorenzo (gĭl'krĭst), army officer; b. Waterloo, Ia., Jan. 16, 1870; s. Lorenzo D. and Margaret Jane (Ohl) G.; M.D., Western Res. U., 1896; honor grad. and medalist, Army Med. Sch., 1903; m. Mayme L. Morgan, June 30, 1909. Contract surgeon, U.S. Army, 1898-1900; asst. surgeon, U.S. Army, 1900-05, capt., Med. Corps, Oct. 3, 1905, maj., Jan. 1, 1909, lt. col., May 15, 1917, col., Oct. 1, 1920, maj. gen., Mar. 28, 1929. Health officer, Manila, P.I., 1900-01; experimented with X-ray in treatment of leprosy, 1903-04; commanded 1st U.S. expdn. to Europe in World War, Lakeside Hospital Unit No. 4; comdr. British General Hosp. No. 9, Rouen, France, May-Dec. 1917; med. director Chemical Warfare Service, A.E.F., Dec. 1917-Dec. 1918, comdr. American Typhus Expdn. to Poland, 1919; chief of med. research div., Washington, D.C., and Edgewood Arsenal, Chem. Warfare Service, 1921-29; chief of Chem. Warfare Service, March 28, 1929-May 16, 1933; retired Jan. 16, 1934; editor of The Military Surgeon, 1934-Sept. 1940. Awarded D.S.M., Purple Heart (U.S.); General Service Medal (Gt. Britain); Officer Legion of Honor, Médaille d'Honneur Epidemies (France); Cross of the Valiant, Comdr. Order of Polonia Restituta (Poland); Order of Star of Abdon Calderón (Ecuador); Spanish-Am. War decoration (Cuba); campaign medals for Spanish War, Philippines, Cuba, Mexican Border, World War; cited in spl. orders by Sir Douglas Haig; cited by Gen. Pershing for "especially meritorious service with Chem. Warfare Service." Fellow Am. Coll. Surgeons; mem. Assn. Mil. Surgns. (pres. 1933-34; sec. since 1934); hon. prof. Polish Army Med. Sch.; hon. mem. Mexican Assn. Mil. Surgeons. Clubs: Army and Navy (Washington); Army, Navy and Marine Corps (Arlington, Va.). Home: 2219 California St., Washington, D.C. Died Dec. 26, 1943.

GILL, Charles Clifford, author, naval officer; b. Junction City, Kan., Aug. 24, 1885; s. Clifford Belcher (lt. U.S. Navy) and Sarah Stoddard (Frothingham) G.; grad. St. John's Mil. Acad., Manlius, N.Y.; grad. U.S. Naval Acad., 1906; grad. Naval War Coll., 1920; m. Helen, d. Rear Admiral W. L. Howard, U.S. Navy, Apr. 25, 1911; children—Anne Alden, Charles Howard; m. 2d, Golda Chase Munroe; m. 3d, Marie Meuffels. Passed as midshipman, 1903; was promoted through the grades to captain, September 1, 1932; commander U.S.S. Vestal, 1932; was senior member United States Naval Mission to Brazil; commanded U.S.S. Astoria, 1937-38; was professor of naval science and tactics, and commanding officer Naval Training Unit, Yale Univ. Author: Naval Power in the War 1918; The War on the Sea (vol. IV Harper's Pictorial Library of the World War), 1920—. Edited Part I—Naval Strategy and Major Naval Operations; What Happened at Jutland, 1921. Lectures delivered at Army and Navy War Colleges in Brazil and pub. in Portuguese, 1927, Escape of the Goeben and Breslau, Army and Navy Coöperation in the Civil War, Strategic and Tactical Analysis North Sea Battles, 1936. Died Jan. 9, 1948.

GILL, Corrington, economist; b. Grand Rapids, Mich., Jan. 17, 1898; s. William E. and Florence Nightingale (Calhoun) G.; student Detroit Univ. Sch., 1915-17; A.B., U. of Wis., 1923; m. Julia Turnbull, Apr. 21, 1922. Business mgr. and corr. Washington (D.C.) Press Service, 1923-27; independent research and consulting work in economics and business, Washington, 1927-30; economist and statistician Federal Employment Stabilization Bd., 1931-33; dir. research statistics and finance, Federal Emergency Relief Administration, 1933, and asst. administrator F.E.R.A. since 1934; asst. adminstr. Federal Civic Works Adminstrn., 1933-34; asst. adminstr. Works Progress Adminstrn., 1935-39; asst. commr. Work Projects Administration, 1939-41; deputy dir. in charge of operations Office of Civilian Defense, Washington, D.C., 1941; consultant to War Department, since May 1942; dir. C.C.P.A., 1943-44; deputy dir. gen. UNRRA, March, 1945. Served in U.S. Navy, destroyer service on French Coast, 1917-19. Mem. Central Statistics Bd., Am. Statistics Association, Am. Econ. Assn., Am. Acad. Polit. Science, Am. Soc. for Pub. Adminstrn., Beta Theta Pi. Club: Cosmos. Author: Wasted Manpower: The Challenge of Unemployment. Contbr. economic articles. Home: 2630 Adams Mill Rd., S.W. Office: 1211 Dupont Circle Bldg., Washington. Died July 12, 1946; buried in Arlington National Cemetery.

GILL, Joe Henry, electric engr.; b. Kerrville, Tex., Sept. 25, 1886; s. Wm. Francis and Miriam (Fort) G.; E.E., U. of Tex., 1910; m. Mabel Jenkins, Oct. 2, 1918; 1 son, Wm. Haywood. With Gen. Electric Co., Schenectady, N.Y., 1910-12; with Tex. Power & Light Co., Dallas, 1912-17, advancing to gen. supervision design and constrn. of elec. distribution and transmission systems; with Dallas Power & Light Co., 1919-25, beginning as salesman and advancing to asst. gen. mgr. design, construction and operation of co.'s plants and systems; with Fla. Power & Light Co., Miami, 1925-35, pres. and gen. mgr., 1929-33; pres. Electric Power & Light Corp. since 1935. Served as pvt., later 2d and 1st lt. C.A.C., U.S. Army, 1917-20. Asso. mem. Am. Inst. E.E.; mem. Kappa Sigma. Democrat. Presbyterian. Club: Round Hill (Greenwich). Home: 5108 Gaston Av., Dallas, Tex. Office: 2 Rector St., New York, N.Y. Died June 16, 1944.

GILLANDERS, John Gordon, judge; born Highgate, Ontario, Aug. 26, 1895; s. Angus and Helen (Learmonth) G.; ed. Ridgetown Coll. Inst., Faculty of Education, Toronto, Ontario, 1913, Osgoode Hall, 1921; m. Kathleen M. White, London, Ontario, Sept. 17, 1927; children—Ellen Jean, John Ross. Called to the bar of Ontario, 1921; created King's Counsel, 1934; practised as partner, Ivey, Elliott & Gillanders, London, 1922-34, Ivey & Gillanders from 1934-38; justice in appeal, Supreme Court of Ontario since 1938. Served in World War I, capt., R.A.F. Awarded D.F.C. Chmn., Ontario Cancer Commn., 1938. Club: London Hunt and Country (London, Eng.). Home: 24 Chestnut Park. Office: Osgoode Hall, Toronto, Ontario, Canada. Died May 15, 1946.

GILLESPIE, Dean Milton, business exec., U.S. congressman; b. Salina, Kan., May 3, 1884; s. David Morton and Isabel (Black) G.; student Salina Normal University, 1903 04; married to Lillie May Baldwin, January 29, 1908; children—Jeanne (Mrs. Walter W. Land), Ruth (Mrs. Edward Lehman): Proprietor, Dean Gillespie Sign Co., 1907-08; sales manager, Mead Auto Cycle Co., 1909-10; dist. mgr., White Motor Co., 1913-25; mgr. western dist., 1925-34; pres., Dean Gillespie and Co., since 1937. Pres., Power Equipment Co., Motoroyal Oil Co.; v.p., treas., Bluhill Foods, Inc. Mem. 78th and 79th Congresses (1944-47). Mem. U.S. Chamber of Commerce, Denver Chamber of Commerce, Soc. of Automotive Engrs., Soc. of Mil. Engrs., Soc. for Research of Meteorites. Republican. Mason (K.T., S.R.). Clubs: Denver, Rotary (treasurer), Wigwam, Denver Athletic, Denver Rifle. Owner one of largest pvt. collections of meteorites in world. Home: 632 Humboldt St. Office: 601 E. 18th Av., Denver. Died Feb. 2, 1949.

GILLESPIE, William, mathematician; b. Hamilton, Ont., Can., Nov. 1879; s. George Hamilton and Elizabeth Agnes G.; B.A., Toronto U., 1893; Ph.D., U. of Chicago, 1900; unmarried. Teacher of mathematics, Princeton U., since 1897, prof., 1905-39, emeritus prof., 1939. Presbyterian. Address: 160 Springdale Rd., Princeton, N.J. Died Sept. 13, 1947.

GILLETT, Arthur Dudley Samuel (jĭl-lĕt'), educator; b. Ogden, Ia., Aug. 6, 1881; s. John Dudley and Lucina Adelphia (Clark) G.; grad. Superior State Normal School Wis., 1897; B.L., U. of Wis., 1902, M.A., 1907; LL.D., Northland Coll., 1931; m. Lulu Pickering, Aug. 13, 1907; children—Elizabeth (Mrs. John H. Nason), Genevieve (Mrs. William H. Bennetts). Teacher in rural and elementary schools, high school; later teacher economics and sociology, Superior State Normal School (now State Teachers College), 1903-20, pres., 1925-31; supt. schs., Eveleth, Minn., since 1934. Finance commr., Superior, 1920-25; mem. bd. of Edn. and Library Bd., 1920-25; mem. Midwest Commission on Post-War Planning; mem. St. Louis County (Minnesota) Safety Council; pres. Nat. St. Lawrence Seaway Assn. since 1933. Mem. board of visitors, University of Wisconsin since 1937, president since 1945. Mem. Nat. Edn. Assn., Minn. Ednl. Assn., Assn. of Dirs. of Teacher Training, Nat Soc. for Study of Edn., John Dewey Soc., Am. Assn. of Sch. Adminstrn., Progressive Edn. Assn., Phi Kappa Sigma, Sigma Delta Phi, Pi Gamma Mu; pres. Lake Superior Edn. Assn., 1918. Conglist. Mason; Grand Chancellor K. of P., 1922; lt. gov. Kiwanis Internat., 1929-31. Clubs: Kiwanis, Owl and Serpent, Riley. Author: George Anderson of Wisconsin (textbook in civics); The Marvelous Mesaba; A Community School on the Mesaba Range; The Mesaba Will Win the War; War Activities of the Eveleth Schools; A Mesaba Range Community Re-examines Itself. Home: 804 Jones St., Eveleth, Minn. Died Dec. 11, 1946.

GILLETTE, Leon N. (jĭl-lĕt'), architect. Fellow Am. Inst. Architects since 1934. Address: Walker & Gillette, Fuller Bldg., 57th and Madison Av., New York, N.Y.* Died May 3, 1945.

GILLIES, Andrew (gĭl'ēz), clergyman; b. Glasgow, Scotland, Aug. 3, 1870; s. Peter and Agnes (Clark) G.; was brought to America, 1870; grad. Genesee Wesleyan Sem., Lima, N.Y., 1891; A.B., cum laude, Wesleyan U., Conn., 1895, D.D., 1911; m. Martha Elizabeth Smith, Sept. 25, 1895; children—Faith (Mrs. John Compton Leffler), Brooks (dec.). Ordained M.E. ministry, 1895; pastor, White River Junction, Vt., 1895-97, Montpelier, Vt., 1897-99, State St. Ch., Troy, N.Y., 1899-1903, St. Andrew's Ch., New York, 1903-07, Hennepin Av. Ch., Minneapolis, 1907-16, pastor Third Presbyn. Ch., Rochester, 1925-37, now emeritus, Chaplain Vt. State Senate, 1898. Mem. Phi Nu Theta (Wesleyan), Phi Beta Kappa. Author: The Minister as a Man, 1913; The Individualistic Gospel, 1919. Contbr. to religious periodicals. Home: 134 Nunda Blvd., Rochester, N.Y. Died Apr. 4, 1942.

GILLIES, James Lewis, clergyman; b. Glasgow, Mo., May 2, 1871; s. Rev. Dr. John and Fannie (Bartholow) G.; grad. high sch., St. Joseph, Mo., 1887; A.B., Missouri Wesleyan College, 1891, D.D., 1908; D.D., from University of Southern California, 1941; m. Zorah Margaret, d. Rev. Dr. John H. Poland, 1895 (she died June 5, 1941); children—Ruth Virginia (Mrs. Wm. H. Warnes), Frances Olive (Mrs. Eugene D. Barton), Zorah Margaret (dec.), Kathleen (Mrs. W. A. Applegate), Marion Louise (Mrs. P. B. Howell); m. 2d, Mary F. Judd, August 24, 1942. Y.M.C.A. secretary in St. Joseph, and Chicago, 1891-94; ordained M.E. ministry, 1896; pastor Mo. Conf., 1894-1900, Odebolt, Ia., 1904-07; dist. supt. Sheldon (Ia.) dist., 1907-13; sec. Morningside Coll., Sioux City, Ia., 1913-15; pastor, Clear Lake, Ia., 1915-17, Trinity Ch., Des Moines, 1917-21, First Ch., Riverside, Calif., 1921-28; dist. supt. San Diego Dist., 1928-29, Los Angeles Dist., 1929-34; pastor First Ch., Monrovia, Calif., 1935-38, Holliston Av. Ch., Pasadena, 1938-41, Santa Barbara Avenue Ch., Los Angeles, 1941-43; chaplain, Pacific Home, Los Angeles, since 1943. Executive secretary Los Angeles Missionary and Ch. Extension Soc. M.E. Ch., 1931-34. Del. Gen. Conf. M.E. Ch., 1912, Meth. Ecumenical Conf., Atlanta, 1931; ex-pres. State Ch. Federation;

trustee Pacific Palisades Assn., Spanish-Am. Institute, Pacific Home (pres. bd.), University Religious Conf. of Univ. of Calif. at Los Angeles (ex-pres.). Republican. Mason (32°). Clubs: Present Day, "Twenty"; University Club of Los Angeles. Former editor of The Methodist and contbr. to Church Advocate. Home: 725 Lorraine Blvd., Los Angeles 5, Calif.
Died Aug. 1, 1946.

GILLIES, John A. (gĭl'lēz), ry. exec.; b. Winnipeg, Manitoba, Aug. 15, 1889; ed. public schools, Manitoba, Puerto Rico, Colo.; m. Tollee Pierson; children—John A., Alice Jean. With A.,T.&S.F. Ry. and its subsidiaries since 1906; inspector and surveyor, 1906-12; draftsman, 1912-15; engr. Southern Dist., 1915-17; Northern Dist., 1917-18; trainmaster Western Dist., 1918-23, asst. supt., 1923-28; supt. Slaton Div., 1928-32, Colo. Div., 1932-37; asst. gen. mgr. Northern Dist., Western lines, 1937-38, Eastern Div., Eastern lines, 1938-39; gen. mgr. Western lines and v.p. and gen. mgr. Panhandle & Santa Fe Ry. since 1939. Home: 1908 Harrison St. Office: 900 Polk St., Amarillo, Tex.* Died Feb. 1942.

GILLMORE, Frank, actor, union exec.; b. New York, N.Y., May 14, 1867; s. Parker and Emily (Thorne) G.; ed. Chiswick Collegiate Sch., London, Eng.; m. Laura MacGillivray, July 30, 1896; children—Margalo (Mrs. Robert Ross), Ruth Emily (Mrs. Max Sonino). Began as actor, 1879; played in provinces of Eng. 3 yrs., on London stage 5 yrs., with Charles Frohman in U.S. 2½ yrs., with Forbes-Robertson, Beerbohm Tree and John Hare in Eng., in New Theater, N.Y. City, 1 yr.; leading man with Minnie Maddern Fiske, Henrietta Crosman, Mary Mannering, Bertha Kalich, Elsie Ferguson, Mme. Nazimova; exec. sec. Actors Equity Assn. (affiliate of Am. Fed. of Labor), 1918-29, pres. 1929-37; also pres. Chorus Equity Assn. to 1937; now internat. pres. Asso. Actors and Artists of America. Awarded gold medal of Am. Arbitration Assn. Democrat. Episcopalian. Mason. Clubs: Players, Lambs. Home: 191-24 Palmero Av., Hollis, L.I., N.Y. Office: 45 W. 47th St., New York, N.Y. Died Mar. 29, 1943.

GILLMORE, William E., army officer; b. Lorain, O., Nov. 29, 1876; s. Q. A. and Mary J. (Fitzgerald) G.; student U.S. Mil. Acad., 1896-99.; m. Florence Edgerton Nelson, Dec. 14, 1901; children—Martha Huntington (wife of Frederick W. Huntington, U.S.A.), William N. Commd. 2d lt. U.S.A. Feb 2, 1901; promoted through grades to lt. col., July 1, 1920; served in Air Corps, 1917-31; now retired. Successively chief of Personel Div., chief of Planning Div., exec. officer A.C., pres. Control Bd., comdg. officer Kelly Field (San Antonio, Tex.), air officer 9th Corps Area (San Francisco), and chief of Supply Div.; apptd. asst. chief A.C., July 17, 1926, rank of brig. gen., term of 4 yrs. Col. Air Service, U.S.A., Aug. 24, 1918-June 30, 1920. Mem. Nat. Aeronautic Assn., Soc. Automotive Engrs. Republican. Conglist. Clubs: Army and Navy, Columbia Country; Engineers, Dayton City, Dayton Country. Address: War Dept., Washington. Died Nov. 7, 1948.

GILMAN, Luthene Clairmont, lawyer, ry. pres.; b. Levant, Me., Jan. 28, 1857; s. Henry and Mary (Twombley) G.; grad., Me. Central Inst., Pittsfield, 1879; LL.B., Columbia Sch. of Law, New York, 1883; m. Eva A. Stinson, Aug. 24, 1887. Admitted to Wash. bar, 1884, and practiced at Seattle, firm Lewis & Gilman, 1884-92, Stratton, Lewis & Gilman, 1892-97, Preston, Carr & Gilman, 1897-1903; city atty., Seattle, 1887-88; mem. Wash. Ho. of Rep., 1893; became Western counsel for G. N. Ry., 1903; removed to St. Paul, Minn., 1909, as asst. to pres. G. N. Ry.; removed to Portland, Ore., 1913; pres. Spokane, Portland & Seattle Ry. Co., and affiliated lines, Jan. 1, 1914-June 30, 1918; dist. dir. Puget Sound Dist. (Wash. and Ore.), at Seattle, U.S. R.R. Administration, June 20, 1918-March 1, 1920; pres. Spokane, Portland & Seattle Ry. Co., and affiliated lines, Mar. 1-Nov. 15, 1920; v.p. G.N. Ry. Co., Seattle, 1920-37, retired, Jan. 28, 1937. Mem. Am. Bar Assn. Democrat. Clubs: Rainier, University, Transportation, Monday (Seattle). Office: 1101 Second Av., Seattle. Died Sept. 7, 1942.

GILMAN, Mary Rebecca Foster, author; b. Worcester, Mass., 1859; d. Dwight and Henriette P. B. Foster; m. Bradley Gilman, 1886. Mem. Mass. Soc. Colonial Dames of America. Author: The Life of Ste. Theresa (in Famous Women series), 1888. Compiled, with intro., The Pilgrim's Scrip, a collection of the wit and wisdom of George Meredith, 1888. Editor: Philip G. Hamerton's Posthumous Quest for Happiness, 1898; Mrs. Fawcett's Life of Queen Victoria, 1901. Translator: 'Les Dames du Palais'' (''Love Versus Law''), from French of Colette Yver, 1911. Contbr. to mags. and newspapers. Address: Hotel Brunswick, Boston. Died May 5, 1943.

GILMAN, W. Stewart, real estate; b. Sioux City, Ia., Jan. 20, 1877; s. Daniel T. and Mary (Stewart) G.; grad. Phillips Exeter Acad., Exeter, N.H., 1895; B.A., Yale, 1899; m. Marjorie King, June 6, 1900; children—Mrs. Harry Flory, Daniel T., Henry K. (deceased). Has engaged in real estate and banking business since 1899; president Sloan (Ia.) State Bank, American State Bank (Newcastle). Member Board of Education, Sioux City, 1910-19; mayor of Sioux City under commn. form of govt., 1924-28. Chmn. Greater Sioux City Com.; chmn. Interim Com. for Reduction of Govt. Expenditure, State of Ia.; mem. Appraisal Board of Sioux City Real Estate Assn., 1910-35; apptd. mem. bd. of Pub. Docks, Sioux City, term 1939-42; mem. Miss. Valley Assn., Mo. River Navigation Assn., Nat. Rivers and Harbors Congress, Phi Beta Kappa, Beta Theta Pi. Republican. Episcopalian. Mason (32°), Elk. Clubs: Sioux City Boat; University (Chicago); University (Winter Park, Fla.); Rotary (Orlando, Fla.); life mem. Sioux City Boat Club. Author of articles on tax reduction, waterway improvements, etc.; editor of column entitled "Driftwood" (devoted to waterway improvement) in Sioux City Jour. Home: (winter) 511 Osceola Av., Winter Park, Fla. Office: Insurance Exchange Bldg., Sioux City, Ia. Died Sep. 4, 1945.

GILMORE, Albert Field, editor; b. Turner, Me.; s. Sidney M. and Elvira (Alden) G.; A.B., Bates Coll., 1892, A.M., 1895; Litt.D., 1924; C.S.B., 1922; m. Katie May Fish (dec.); m. 2d, Mrs. Davye M. Haefele, May 1933. Was prin. high sch., Kennebunk, supt. schs., Turner and prin. Litchfield Acad. (all of Me.); with Am. Book Co., 1897-1917. First reader, First Ch. of Christ, Scientist, Brooklyn, N.Y., 1914-17; Christian Science Com. on Publ., N.Y., 1917-22; pres. of The Mother Church, 1922-23; editor Christian Science weekly and monthly mags., 1922-29; mem. Board of Lectureship, Christian Science Ch., 1930-32; trustee Christian Science Pub. Soc., since 1932; mem. Monitor Editorial Bd., 1932-35. Teacher of Christian Science. Mem. Me. Ho. of Rep., 1901-02. Mem. board of fellows, Bates Coll. Mem. Am. Ornithol. Union, Phi Beta Kappa. Republican. Mason. Club: University. Author: Birds Through the Year, 1909; Birds of Field, Forest and Park, 1918; East and West of Jordan, 1929; Fellowship—The Story of a Man and a Business, 1929; Yes 'Tis Round (story of a world journey), 1933; The Bible—Beacon Light of History, 1935; Links in Christianity's Chain, 1938, Who Was This Nazarene, 1940. Lecturer and writer on nature. Home: (summer) 34 Hosmer St., Hudson, Mass.; (winter) 90 The Fenway, Boston, Mass.
Died June 8, 1943.

GILMORE, Charles Whitney, vertebrate paleontologist; b. Pavilion, N.Y., Mar. 11, 1874; s. John Edward and Caroline M. (Whitney) G., B.S., U. of Wyo., 1901; m. Laure Coutant, Oct. 22, 1902; children—Eloise Elizabeth (dec.), Dorothy Caroline (dec.), Helen Rosalie Collector dept., vertebrate paleontology, Carnegie Mus., 1901-04; with U.S. Nat. Museum since 1904, as preparator dept. vertebrate paleontology until 1908, custodian, 1908-11, asst. curator, 1911-18, asso. curator, 1918-23, curator since 1923. Specialized in extinct reptiles. Served as sergt. Spanish-American War. Mem. Paleontol. Soc. (pres. 1938), Biol. Soc. Washington, Geol. Soc. Washington, Geol. Soc. of America, Paleontol. Soc. Washington (pres. 1935), Soc. Vertebrate Paleontol. (pres. 1943). Presbyterian. Club: Explorers. Home: 451 Park Rd. N.W., Washington, D.C. Died Sept. 27, 1945.

GILMORE, John Washington, univ prof.; b. White County, Ark., May 9, 1872; s. Thomas Griffin and Emma Frances (Landrum) G.; B.Sc. in agr., Cornell U., 1898, M.S.A., 1905; m. Elizabeth May Vetter-Hitchcock, Aug. 23, 1900; children—John Landrum, Raymond Maurice, Harold Vetter. Established Agrl. Coll., Wuchang, China, 1898-1900; Agriculture Normal Sch., Honolulu, H.T., 1900-01; organizer agrl. schs. in P.I., 1901-02; from asst. to asst. prof. agr., Cornell U., 1902-07; prof. agr., Pa. State Coll., 1907-08; pres. Coll. of Hawaii, Aug. 1908-Sept. 1, 1913; prof. agronomy, Univ. of Calif., since 1913. Agrl. expert and counsellor to Chile, 1921, to Dominican Republic, summer, 1925, to Mexico, summers 1931, 32; advisor to Ministry of Agr., Chile, Feb.-Aug, 1936. Fellow A.A.A.S.; mem. Am. Genetic Assn., Sigma Xi, Alpha Zeta. Mem. Jury of Awards, Panama P.I. Expn., 1915. Exchange prof., at Santiago, Chile, 1921; hon. prof. with diploma, Univ. of Chile, 1936. Address: College of Agriculture, Davis. Calif. Died June 25, 1942.

GILMORE, Robert, physician, surgeon; b. Belfast, Ireland, June 4, 1856; s. James and Jean (McCroberts) G.; student Belfast-Royal Acad., Queen's U., Ireland (now Royal Irish U.); hosps., Belfast, Dublin and Edinburgh; grad. Royal Coll. Physicians, Edinburgh, 1879, Royal Coll. Surgeons, 1879, Queen's U., Ireland, 1880; m. Gretta Campbell Burrows, Oct. 25, 1884. Came to U.S., 1887, since practiced, Omaha, Neb.; physician in chief Wise Memorial Hosp. Office: Arthur Bldg., Omaha, Neb. Died July 31, 1937.

GILMOUR, Ray Bergantz, osteopathist; b. Blackfoot, Ida., Feb. 27, 1888; s. George H. and Ella (Ray) G.; D.O., Am. Sch. Osteopathy, Kirksville, Mo., 1908, grad. work, 1909-10; hon. D.O., Kansas City Coll. Osteopathy and Surgery, 1929; m. Goldie Boon, May 5, 1911. Began practice at Kirksville, 1908; settled in Sioux City, 1910. Served in Ia. N.G., 1914-17; mem. Ia. State Bd. of Osteopathy, 1921-26. Vice-pres. Professional Ins. Corp.; trustee A. T. Still Research Inst., Am. Osteopathic Foundation. Mem. Am. Osteopathic Assn. (pres. 1926-27; chmn. exec. com. and bur. professional edn., 1927-30), Ia. Osteopathic Assn. (pres. 1928-29), Central States Osteopathic Assn. (pres. 1926-27), Northwest Iowa Osteopathic Assn. (pres. 5 years), Am Assn. Osteopathic Oto-laryngologists, Sioux City Chamber Commerce, Theta Psi (nat. pres. 1924-25, 27-28). Independent. Unitarian. Mason (32°, Shriner), Elk. Clubs; Rotary (pres. 1930-31), Auto, Boat, Rod and Reel, Sioux City Golf. Home: 2208 Kennedy Drive. Office: Security Bldg., Sioux City, Ia. Died Mar. 5, 1947.

GIMBEL, Jacob, humanitarian; b. Vincennes, Ind., Apr. 17, 1876; s. Seleman and Mary (Hyman) G.; Vincennes U. to sr. yr., 1892; Rauscher's Inst., Stuttgart, Germany, 1892-93; LaChatalaine, Geneva, Switzerland, 1893-94; hon. M.A., Indiana U., 1933; unmarried. Organizer of the "dollar savings bank plan" among poor boys of Vincennes. Financed the Gimbel Expdn. to S. America, 1910, headed by Dr. Max M. Ellis, of U. of Colo., to explore rivers of British Guiana, and especially to study the life habits of the Gymnotids; resulted in the discovery of numerous rare forms, among them Porotergus Gimbeli. Mem. Pi Gamma Mu. Has assisted many young men to secure high edn.; donor of medals on mental attitude. Address: care Bank of America, 7th and Olive Sts., Los Angeles, Calif. Died Jan. 28, 1943.

GIMMESTAD, Lars Monson (gĭm'mē-städ), clergyman; b. Nordford, Norway, Jan. 20, 1868; s. Mons Mathiason and Anne (Vasenden) G.; came with parents to U.S., 1879; A.B., Luther Coll., Decorah, Ia., 1891; C.T., Luther Theol. Sem., Robbinsdale, Minn., 1894; m. Amalie Bergine Anderson, July 22, 1896 (died Mar. 23, 1922); children—Marie Helen (Mrs. J. Norton Wells, Jr.), Agnes Olava (Mrs. A. Dewey Arnold), Herman, Laura Mathilde (Mrs. Walter L. Peppers), Bernard Oscar, Victor Edward. Ordained ministry Norwegian Luth. Ch. of America, 1894; pastor Eau Claire, Wis., 1894-95, Columbia County, Wis., 1895-1901; pres. Gale Coll., Galesville, Wis., 1901-18; pastor Orfordville, Wis., 1918-38; now retired. Pres. Council of Federated Norwegian Socs. America, 1928-31; former v.p. eastern dist. Norwegian Luth. Ch. America. Del. to Millennial Celebration, Iceland, 1930. Home: Clinton, Wis.
Died Sep. 13, 1943.

GIRDNER, John Harvey, physician, surgeon; b. Cedar Creek, Greene Co., Tenn., Mar. 8, 1856; s. William and Mary Ann (Link) G.; A.B., Tusculum Coll., Tenn., 1876; M.D., Univ. Med. Coll., New York U., 1879; m. Adela Pratt of Opelousas, La., Sept. 23, 1886. Interne, Bellevue Hosp., 1879-80; lecturer on surgery, New York Post-Grad. Med. Sch. and Hosp. (mem. corp.). Was 1st to graft skin successfully from dead body onto the living; inventor of telephonic bullet probe, 1887, and phymosis forceps. Fellow New York Acad. Medicine. Democrat. Author: "New-yorkitis," 1901; also contbr. many essays on med. and other subjects. Home: 47 W. 71st St., New York. Died Nov. 25, 1933.

GIRL, Christian, retired mfr.; b. nr. Elkhart, Ind., Dec. 31, 1874; s. Joseph and Catherine G.; ed. country sch.; m. Hittie Agnes Schottler, Sept. 15, 1909. Mail carrier, Cleveland, O., 8 yrs.; founded Perfection Spring Co., mfr. automobile springs, 1906, absorbed by Standard Part Co., 1916, pres. until dissolution; purchased Kalamazoo Spring & Axle Co., 1920; later organized C. G. Spring & Bumper Co., merged, 1929, with Houdaille-Hershey Corp., Chicago; retired 1929. Served as dir. Truck Prodn., World War I. Awarded D.S.M. (U.S.). Mem. Soc. Automotive Engr., Ohio Soc. of N.Y. City. Club: Detroit Athletic Home: Grand River Rd, Madison, O. Died June 10, 1946.

GLASGOW, Ellen (Anderson Gholson), author; b. Richmond, Va., Apr. 22, 1874; d. Francis Thomas and Anne Jane (Gholson) Glasgow; private edn.; Litt.D., U. of N.C., 1930; LL.D., U. of Richmond and Duke U., 1938, Coll. of William and Mary, 1939. Awarded, 1940, by the Am. Academy of Arts and Letters, the quinquennial Howells medal for "eminence in creative literature as shown in the novel"; received Saturday Review of Literature's special award for distinguished service to American literature, 1940; awarded Southern Authors prize, 1941, the Pulitzer prize for novel, 1941. Author: The Descendant, 1897; Phases of an Inferior Planet, 1898; The Voice of the People, 1900; The Freeman and Other Poems, 1902; The Battle-ground, 1902; The Deliverance, 1904; The Wheel of Life, 1906; Ancient Law, 1908; The Romance of a Plain Man, 1909; The Miller of Old Church, 1911; Virginia, 1913; Life and Gabriella, 1916; The Builders, 1919; One Man in His Time, 1922; The Shadowy Third, 1923; Barren Ground, 1925; The Romantic Comedians, 1926; They Stooped to Folly, 1929; The Sheltered Life, 1932; Vein of Iron, 1935; In This Our Life, 1941; A Certain Measure: An Interpretation of Prose Fiction, 1943. Mem. Am. Acad. Art and Letters, Nat. Inst. Arts and Letters, Soc. of Authors, Playwrights and Composers (British), Phi Beta Kappa (hon.), P.E.N., Modern Lang. Assn., Colonial Dames of America, Richmond Soc. Prevention of Cruelty to Animals (pres. since 1924). Clubs: Woman's Country (Richmond); Cosmopolitan (New York). Home: Richmond, Va.
Died Nov. 21, 1945.

GLASGOW. Hugh, entomologist; b. Tennessee, Ill., Nov. 17. 1884; s. Douglass and Margaret Matilda (Walker) G.; A.B., U. of Ill., 1908; Ph.D., 1913; m. Beulah P. Ennis, Dec. 28, 1935. Asst. entomologist, U. of Ill., 1912-13, instr. entomology, 1913-14; asst. in research, N.Y. Agrl. Experiment Station (Cornell University), Geneva, N.Y., 1914-20, asso. in research, 1920-26, chief in research, 1926-38, professor of entomology and chief division of entomology since 1938. Member A.A.A.S., American Association of Econ. Entomologists, Entomological Soc. of America, Sigma Xi. Author: Experiment Sta. Bulls. on Applied Entomology and articles in Jour. of Econ. Entomology. Home: 665 Castle St. Office: 630 W. North St., Geneva, N.Y. Died July 16, 1948.

GLASGOW, William Hargadine, retired; b. St. Louis, Mo., Nov. 9, 1880; s. Edward James and Julia (Hargadine) G.: A.B., Harvard, 1903; m. Yvonne Elizabeth Merrill, Aug. 11, 1923; children—William Hargadine, Walter Merrill. With Hargadine-McKittrick Dry Goods Company, St. Louis, 1903-14; entered employ of the Federal Reserve Bank of St. Louis, 1914, in charge of Memphis office same company, 1916-17, asst. cashier at St. Louis, 1918-21; asst. to dirs. War Finance Corp., Washington, 1921-22; mng. dir. Memphis Br. Federal Res. Bank of St. Louis, 1926-45; now retired. Democrat. Unitarian. Clubs: Noonday, Racquet, Country (St. Louis); Memphis, Fifty, Country (Memphis). Home: 7 Morningside Park, Memphis, Tenn. Died June 21, 1947.

GLASPELL, Susan (glăs′pĕl), author; b. Davenport, Ia., July 1, 1882; d. Elmer S. and Alice (Keating) Glaspell; Ph.B., Drake Univ., Ia.; post-grad. Univ. of Chicago; m. George Cram Cook, Apr. 14, 1913 (died 1923). Was State House and Legislative reporter, The News and The Capital, Des Moines. Contbr. of stories to mags., etc. Identified with the Little Theatre movement through the Provincetown Players. Author: The Glory of the Conquered, 1909; The Visioning, 1911; Lifted Masks, 1912; Fidelity, 1915; Trifles, 1917; (with George Cram Cook) Suppressed Desires, 1917; Plays (including Bernice and other plays), 1920; Inheritors (play), 1921; Verge (play), 1922; The Road to the Temple, 1926; The Comic Artist (in collaboration with Norman Matson), 1927; Brook Evans, 1928; Fugitive's Return, 1929; Alison's House (awarded Pulitzer prize for plays), 1930; Ambrose Holt and Family, 1931; The Morning Is Near Us, 1940; Norma Ashe, 1942; Judd Rankin's Daughter, 1945. Home: Provincetown, Mass. Died July 27, 1948.

GLASS, Carter, U.S. senator; b. Lynchburg, Va., Jan. 4, 1858; s. Robert Henry and Augusta (Christian) G.; ed. pub. and pvt. schools, Lynchburg; LL.D., Lafayette Coll., U. of N.C., Washington and Lee U., Wesleyan U. (Conn.), Tufts, William and Mary (Va.), Yale, Princeton, Columbia, Dartmouth, Hamilton College, University of New York; LL.D., Lynchburg College, 1941; married Aurelia Caldwell; children—Powell, Carter, Mary Archer, Augusta Christian; m. 2d, Mrs. Mary Scott Meade, June 22, 1940. Owner Daily News (morning), and Daily Advance (afternoon), Lynchburg. Mem. Va. Senate, 1899-1903; mem. State Constitutional Conv., 1901; mem. 57th to 65th Congresses, inclusive (1902-19), 6th Va. Dist.; as chmn. Com. on Banking and Currency, was patron and floor mgr. of Federal Reserve Bank Act in House of Representatives; chmn. of Joint Congressional Com. reporting Federal Farm Land Bank Act; resigned from Congress, 1918; sec. of treasury in Cabinet of President Wilson, Dec. 1918-Feb. 1920; resigned to accept U.S. senatorship, by appmt. of gov. of Va., elected 1924 and re-elected 1930, 36, 42; pres. pro tem. of Senate since 1941; chmn. Appropriations Com., member Foreign Relations Com. Mem. board visitors, U. of Va., 8 years. Mem. Nat. Dem. Com., 1916-28; chmn. Com. on Resolutions of Nat. Dem. Conv., 1920, and drafted platform; mem. com. on Resolutions, Dem. Nat. Conv., 1932, and assisted in drafting platform; declined secretaryship of U.S. Treasury in Roosevelt cabinet. Mem. Phi Beta Kappa (William and Mary Coll.). Democrat. Methodist. Home: Lynchburgh, Va. Died May 28, 1946; buried in Spring Hill Cemetery, Lynchburg.

GLASS, Powell, journalist; b. Lynchburg, Va., Oct. 9, 1886; s. Carter and Aurelia McDearmon (Caldwell) G.; A.B., Washington and Lee U., 1907; m. Anne Elizabeth Cleghorn, Oct. 21, 1915; 1 son, Powell. Reporter, The News and The Daily Advance, Lynchburg, Va., 1907-10, state editor, 1910-12, mng. editor, 1912-30, asso. pub. since 1930, gen. mgr., The News and The Daily Advance, since 1943. Served as maj., U.S. Army, 1917-19; comd. 1st Batt., 317th Inf. in France; on staff of Am. Commn. to negotiate peace. Dir. Glamorgan Pipe & Foundry Co. Mem. Va. Press Assn. (pres. 1944-45), Lynchburg Chamber of Commerce (dir.), Phi Beta Kappa, Kappa Sigma, Delta Sigma Chi, Omicron Delta Kappa. Club: Sphex (Lynchburg, Va.); Commonwealth (Richmond, Va.). Home: 210 Lee Dr. Office: The News, Lynchburg, Va. Died July 8, 1945.

GLASSCOCK, Carl Burgess, writer; b. Ferndale, Calif., May 4, 1884; s. Aldea (M.D.) and Sarah McNeely (DeLany) G.; student U. of Calif., 1902-05; m. Marion Tannahill, Mar. 2, 1917. Reporter San Francisco Examiner, 1905; founder, 1906, editor, 1906-07, Death Valley Chuck-Walla; newspaperman with Cleveland Plain Dealer, Montreal Star, United Press, New York Telegram, Santa Barbara News, Chicago Examiner, 1908-20; editorial writer Chicago Tribune, 1920-24; production mgr. Liberty Mag., 1925-27. Pvt. U.S. Army, 1918. Author: Bandits and the Southern Pacific, 1929; The Big Bonanza, 1931; Gold in Them Hills, 1932; Lucky Baldwin, 1933; The Treasure of Drowning River, 1933; A Golden Highway, 1934; The War of the Copper Kings, 1935; The Gasoline Age, 1937; Then Came Oil, 1938; Here's Death Valley, 1940. Contbr. short stories to mags. Home: Laguna Beach, Calif. Died Nov. 13, 1942.

GLASSON, William Henry (glăs′ŭn), educator, economist; b. Troy, N.Y., July 26, 1874; s. John and Agnes Allen (Pleming) G.; Ph. B., Cornell U., 1896; Ph.D., Columbia U., 1900; LL.D., Duke Univ., 1939; m. Mary Beeler Park, July 12, 1905; children—Mrs. Lucy Glasson Wheeler, Mrs. Mary Glasson Brinn, Mrs. Marjorie Glasson Ross, John. Fellow in political economy and finance, Cornell, 1896-97; Harrison fellow economics, U. of Pa., 1897-98; fellow in adminstrn., Columbia, 1898-99; head dept. of history and of civics, George School (Soc. of Friends), nr. Newtown, Pa., 1899-1902; prof. polit. economy and social science, Duke U. (formerly Trinity Coll.), N.C., 1902-40, emeritus since September 1, 1940; director South Atlantic Publishing Co., 1940-45; prof. economics, summer session, Cornell U., 1907; acting prof. economics and politics, Cornell U., 1910-11; prof. economics, U. of Va., summer quarter, 1928; dean Grad. School Arts and Sciences, Duke U., 1926-38. Mem. Phi Beta Kappa (sec. South Atlantic dist. 1925-37), Kappa Delta Pi, Am. Econ. Assn. (mem. exec. com. 1916-18), Dean's Conf. Southern Graduate Schools, 1927-37 (pres. 1929), Quill and Dagger (Cornell). Specialty—writing on the pension system of the United States; contbr. poetry to magazines and newspapers; feature writer, Cornell Countryman, 1945. Joint editor South Atlantic Quarterly, 1905-19, mng. editor, 1909-19; advisory editor Nat. Municipal Rev., 1912-22. Mem. City Charter Com., Durham, 1921, Bd. Edn., Durham, 1919-23; mem. N.C. State Commn. Unemployment Ins., 1934-35. Author: History of Military Pension Legislation in the United States, 1900; Federal Military Pensions in the United States, 1918. Contbr. to South in the Building of the Nation, 1910; Cyclopædia of American Government, 1913. Collaborator in division of economics and history, Carnegie Endowment for Internat. Peace, 1913-18. Home: 710 Buchanan Rd., Durham, N.C. Died Nov. 11, 1946; buried in Lakewood Cemetery, Durham.

GLEASON, Clarence Willard, teacher, author; b. Holden, Mass., Aug. 11, 1866; s. Charles Willard and Jane Grey (Story) G.; A.B., Harvard, 1888, A.M., 1889, M.A. (hon.), Trinity Coll., 1934; m. Ellen Frances Morrison, July 1, 1890; children—Harold Willard, Elisabeth Story (dec.). Taught in Roxbury Latin Sch., 1889-1905, and since 1912, acting headmaster, 1932-33; teacher Volkman Sch., Boston, 1905-12; taught at Columbia Summer School, 1929, 31. Pres. Classical Assn. of N.E., 1923-24 (sec. Eastern Mass. Sect.). Mem. Am. Philol. Assn., Phi Beta Kappa. Clubs: Friday Evening, Harvard, Cleveland Democrat. Asso. editor Classical Journal. Author: Gate to the Anabasis, 1894; The First Greek Book, 1895; Xenophon's Cyropaedia, 1897; Gate to Virgil, 1898; A Term of Ovid, 1899; Story of Cyrus, 1900; Greek Primer, 1903; Greek Prose Composition, 1905; A Latin Primer, 1926. Home: 460 Huntington Av., Boston. Died Nov. 3, 1942.

GLENN, Garrard, prof. law; b. Atlanta, Aug. 17, 1878; s. John Thomas and Helen Augusta (Garrard) G.; A.B., U. of Ga., 1899 (Phi Beta Kappa); LL.B., Columbia U. Law Sch., 1903; m. Rosa Aubrey Wood, Sept. 9, 1909; children—Garrard W., John Forsyth Cobb. Admitted to N.Y. bar, 1902, and practiced at N.Y. City until 1929; was asso. prof., Columbia; now prof. law, U. of Va. Mem. War Dept. Special Board on Tax Amortization Cases, 1941; Tax Amortization Board, 1942. Mem. American Bar Association, Association Bar City of New York, Va. Bar. Assn., Am. Law Institute, Soc. Colonial Wars, Sigma Alpha Epsilon (Ga. Beta Chapter), Phi Delta Phi. Catholic. Clubs: University (New York); Farmington Country (Albemarle County, Va.); Colonnade (Univ. of Va.). Author: Creditors' Rights, 1915; The Army and the Law, 1918; Fraudulent Conveyances, 1931; Glenn on Liquidation, 1935; Glenn on Fraudulent Conveyances and Preferences (2d edit., revised and enlarged), 1940; Cases on Creditors' Rights, 1940; Glenn on Mortgages, 1943. Joint author: Secret Liens, 1910. Contbr. articles on legal and other subjects. Argument as counsel for defense in prosecution of publ. of Cabell's "Jurgen" was included in "Jurgen and the Law," pub. 1923. Former mem. council Am. Law Inst., former adviser in Institute's restatement of law of security; former advisory member National Bankruptcy Conf.; mem. Faculty Com. of Virginia Quarterly Review. Recipient of Raven Award (U. of Va.), 1941. Home: "Spring Hill," Ivy Depot, Va. Address: Law School, University, Va.

Died Jan. 25, 1949.

GLENN, Thomas Kearney, banker; b. Vernon, Miss., Jan. 21, 1868; s. Wilbur Fisk and Florella (Harper) G.; ed. common schs.; m. Agnes Raoul, Apr. 21, 1904 (died Nov. 3, 1914); children—Wadley R., Wilbur F.; m. 2d, Elizabeth E. Woodhouse, Sept. 10, 1927. With Maddox-Rucker Banking Co., Atlanta, 1887-91, Atlanta Consolidated Street Ry. Co., 1891-1902; v.p. Ga. Ry. & Electric Co., 1902-08; pres. Atlantic Steel Co., 1908-21, chmn. bd. since 1921; elected pres. Trust Co. of Ga., 1921, consolidated with Lowry Nat. Bank, 1923; pres. Atlanta and Lowry Nat. Bank and Trust Company, of Georgia, 1923-29; chmn. bd. First Nat. Bank of Atlanta and pres. Trust Co. of Ga., 1929-33; pres. Trust Co. of Ga., 1933-37, chmn. of bd. since 1937; chmn. of bd. Trust Co. of Ga. Associates; dir. Atlantic Steel Co., The Coca-Cola Co., Continental Gin Co., Atlantic Co. Chmn. board of trustees Grady Hospital, Atlanta, Ga.; trustee Emory Univ., L.H. Beck Foundation, Crawford W. Long Memorial Hosp. (Atlanta), Reinhardt Coll. (Waleska, Ga.), Rabun Gap-Nacoochee Sch. (Rabun Gap, Ga.). Methodist. Mason (32°). Clubs: Capital City, Atlanta Athletic, Druid Hills Golf, Piedmont Driving, Rotary (Atlanta); Bankers, New York Southern Society (New York). Home: Glenridge Hall, Dunwoody, Ga. Office: Trust Company of Georgia, Atlanta, Ga.

Died Oct. 11, 1946.

GLENNON, John Joseph, archbishop; b. Kinnegad, County Meath, Ireland, June 14, 1862; prepared at St. Mary's Coll., Mullingar; grad. All Hallows Coll., Dublin, 1883; ordained R.C. priest, 1884. Asst. pastor St. Patrick's Ch., Kansas City, 1884-87; pastor cathedral there, under Bishop Hogan, 1887-92; vicar-gen. of diocese, 1892-94; adminstr. of diocese, 1894-95; apptd. coadjutor bishop of Kansas City, with right of succession, and consecrated titular bishop of Pinara, June 29, 1896; became coadjutor archbishop of St. Louis, Apr. 27, 1903, and archbishop, Oct. 13, 1903. Erected New Cathedral of St. Louis, 1913; Kenrick Sem., 1915; St. Louis Prep. Sem., 1930. Address: 4510 Lindell Blvd., St. Louis, Mo.*
Died Mar. 9, 1946.

GLINTENKAMP, H(endrik), artist; b. Augusta, N.J., Sept. 10, 1887; s. Hendrik and Sophie (Dietz) G.; ed. by pvt. tutors; student Nat. Acad. of Design, 1903-06; studied under Robert Henri, 1906-08; m. Helena Ruth Gibbs, 1916; m. 2d, Eleanor Wilson Parker, 1922; 1 dau., Brünnhilde; m. 3d, Fann Rosenthal, 1930; 1 son, Hendrik. Artist, painter, sculptor, wood engraver, etcher, illustrator and teacher since 1908; instr. Hoboken (N.J.) Art Club, 1912-17; cartoonist on staff Hudson Dispatch, 1912; instr. in drawing and mem. bd. of control Am. Artists Sch., New York. On editorial board, Art Front, 1935. Mem. exec. bd. and chmn. nat. exhbn. cdm. of Am. Artists Congress, 1938, 39, nat. exec. sec., 1940-41, vice-chmn., 1941. Mem. N.Y. City council for Nat. Art Week, 1940; mem. N.Y. Jury for Nat. Art Week, 1941. Represented by wood block, Victoria and Albert Mus. (London); Birobijan, U.S.S.R.; wood block and bookplates in print collection and also reproductions in circulating picture collection, N.Y. Pub. Library; wood cuts, Newark Pub. Library, Metropolitan Museum of Art (N.Y. City), Museum of Modern Art; Cleveland (O.) Museum; Baltimore Museum and private collections; also represented in exhbns. at Pa. Acad. of Fine Arts, Am. Water Color Soc., New York Water Color Club, Salon of Am. Artists, Whitney Studio Club, Phila. Print Club, McDowell Club (New York), Peoples Art Guild, Am. Salon of Humorists, British Soc. of Painters (London), Syracuse (N.Y.) Mus., N.J. State Museum, N.C. State Art Assn., New York U. and many others. Represented in 50 prints of the year, Inst. of Graphic Arts. Mem. council and asst. sec., Artists Conf. of The Americas, 1939; member Independent Citizens Committee of Arts, Sciences and Professions; member executive board of the American Commiittee fror Spanish Freedom. Honorable mention 3d Exhbn. of Illustration, Print Club of Phila., 1939. Organized and pres. Gamut Arts Club (embracing all the arts), 1941. Mem. American Artists Congress, Artists Union, Teachers Union, Gamut Arts Club (N.Y. City), Artists for Victory, Inc., Artists' League of America (1942). Author: A Wanderer in Woodcuts, 1932; also illustrator of books and mags. Home: Sparta, N.J. Studio: 19 E. 16th St., New York 3, N.Y. Died Mar. 19, 1946.

GLOVER, Arthur James (glŭv′ẽr), editor; b. Zumbro Falls, Minn., Apr. 3, 1873; s. James Bradley and Olive (Whaley) G.; ed. Minn. Sch. Agr., St. Paul and U. of Minn.; m. Maymie S. Scofield, Dec. 25, 1899; children—Robert Bradley, Arthur James, Wilbur Hillman, Myra Lucile. Insp. Dairy and Food Commn. of Minn., 1899-1901; asst. prof. dairy husbandry, Ill. Coll. Agr., Urbana, 1901-04; editor Hoard's Dairyman since 1904. Former mem. Sch. Bd., Fort Atkinson, Wis.; mem. bd. of regents Univ. of Wis., 1937-43 (pres. 1939-43). Pres. Am. Dairy Fedn.; sec. Wisconsin Dairymen's Assn., 1909-15; pres. Holstein-Friesian Assn. of America, 1934-37. Republican. Mason. Home: Ft. Atkinson, Wis. Died May 8, 1949.

GLOVER, Robert Hall, clergyman; b. Leeds, Quebec, Can., Oct. 17, 1871; s. Thomas and Jennie (Hall) G.; ed. Collegiate Inst. and U. of Toronto; grad. New York Missionary Training Coll., 1893; M.D., Univ. Med. Coll. (New York U.), 1894; m. Caroline Robbins Prentice, Nov. 20, 1902; children—Bernard Prentice (dec.), Florence Jennie, Marjorie Evelyn, Robert Prentice. Missionary in China under Christian and Missionary Alliance, 1894-1913; ordained to Christian ministry, 1896; founded Bible Training Sch., Wuchow, 1900, and Blackstone Bible Inst., Wuchang, 1905; deputational sec. Christian and Missionary Alliance, 1911-13; foreign sec. same, 1913-21; dir. Missionary Course, Moody Bible Inst., Chicago, 1921-26; asst. home dir. China Inland Mission, 1926-29, home dir., 1930-43, now home dir. emeritus. Visited Christian missions in many parts of world. Fellow Royal Geog. Soc. Author: Ebenezer—A Record of Divine Deliverances in China, 1905; The Progress of World-Wide Missions, 1924; also many magazine articles on travel and missions. Home: 237 W. School Lane, Germantown, Philadelphia, Pa. Died Mar. 23, 1947; buried in Ardsley Burial Park, Ardsley, Pa.

GODBEY, Allen Howard (gŏd′bē), educator; b. Cooper County, Mo., Nov. 21, 1864; s. Rev. William Clinton and Caroline Malvina (Smith) G.; A.M., Morrisville (Mo.) Coll., 1883; fellow in Semitics, U. of Chicago, 1902-05; Ph.D., 1905; m. Emma Lizbeth Moreland, June 16, 1892 (now dec.); 1 dau., Elizabeth Beulah (Mrs. Glenn W. Johnson). Prof. mathematics and natural science, Morrisville Coll., 1883-86; asst. editor Southwestern Methodist, 1887-89; in literary and pastoral work, Kansas City, 1890-94; prof. Latin and Eng. lit., St. Charles (Mo.) Coll., 1894-95; licensed minister M.E. Ch., S., 1891, deacon, 1895, elder, 1897; pastor Russellville, Mo., 1895-98,

Corder, Mo., 1898-99; prin. acad. dept., Central Coll., 1899-1902; fellow in Semitics, U. of Chicago, and corr. editor Ark. Methodist, 1902-05; prof. Latin and Greek, Morrisville Coll., 1905-06, pres. 1906-09; pastor Bellefontaine Ch., St. Louis, Mo., 1909-13, Immanuel Ch., 1913-14, Bridgeton and Stephan Memorial Ch., 1914-17, Beech Grove, Ky., 1917-19, Carrsville, Ky., 1919-26; prof. Old Testament, Duke U., 1926-32, emeritus professor of Old Testament since 1932; engaged, since 1932, in new researches in archeological backgrounds of Old Testament and in recovering lost documents of Methodism in Missouri; other pursuits are natural history and paleontology. Food administrator, McLean County, Ky., 1917-19. Secretary, since 1915, of commission to recover Methodist beginnings west of the Mississippi River. Mem. com. on law and philosophy, World Conf. on Narcotic Edn. Mem. Am. Oriental Soc., Soc. Oriental Research, Archæological Inst. of America, Society for Am. Archæology, Palestinian Oriental Soc., New Orient Society, Society of Biblical Literature, Pi Gamma Mu. Mason. Author: Light in Darkness (with J. E. Godbey), 1888; Stanley in Africa, 1890; Great Disasters, 1890; Code of Hammurabi (with R. F. Harper), 1904; Notes on Some Officials of the Sargonid Period, 1905; The Lost Tribes, A Myth, 1930; The Psychology of Narcotism Among American Indians, 1931; New Light on the Old Testament, 3d edit., 1936; Pre-Mosaic Hebrew Religion, 1935. Contbr. to Methodist Quarterly Rev., Monist, Am. Jour. Semitic Langs. and Lit., etc. Address: 408 Milton Av., Durham, N.C. Died May 8, 1948.

GODBEY, Earle (god'bē), newspaper editor; b. Cleveland County, N.C.; s. James M. and Sarah (Hogue) G.; m. Margaret Albright, Aug. 25, 1930. Asso. editor Asheville Gazette-News, 1906-14; asso. editor Greensboro Daily News, 1914-18, sec. and editor, 1918-34; v.p. and editor-in-chief Greensboro News Co., pubs. of Greensboro Daily News and the Greensboro Record since 1934. Address: Daily News, Greensboro, N.C. Died Oct. 22, 1941.

GODCHARLES, Frederic Antes, librarian, historian; b. Northumberland, Pa., June 3, 1872; s. Charles Aiken and Elizabeth (Burkenbine) G.; E.E., Lafayette Coll., Easton, Pa., 1893; Litt.D. from Susquehanna Univ., 1928; m. Mary Walls Barber, June 15, 1904. Elec. engr., city hall, Phila., Pa., 1893-95; pres. F. A. Godcharles Co., Milton Nail Works, 1895-1914; editor and pub. The Miltonian and Milton Morning Bulletin, 1910-26; dir. Pa. State Library and Museum, 1927-31. Mem. Pa. N.G., 1893-98; served with same, Spanish-Am. War, mem. staff Brig. Gen. J.P.S. Gobin; regimental insp. of rifle practice, rank of capt., 1900-10; capt. ordnance, on staff Maj. Gen. Leonard Wood, World War I. Mem. Pa. Gen Assembly, 1900; Pa. Senate, 1904, 08; dep. sec. Commonwealth of Pa., 1915-23. Mem. A.L.A., Pa. Federation Hist. Socs. (past pres.), Pa. Hist. Soc., Northumberland County Hist. Soc. (pres.), Pa. Hist. Assn. (dir.), Eastern States Archeol. Fedn. (ex-pres.), Pa. Soc. Archæology (past pres., editor), Pa. Folk-Lore Soc. (v.p.), Huguenot Soc., Pa. German Soc. (dir.), Mil. Order Foreign Wars, Sons of Union Vets. of Civil War (past state comdr.), S.A.R., Am. Legion, Newcomen Soc. of Great Britain, Phi Kappa Psi. Republican. Presbyn. Mason (33°). Clubs: Manufacturers, Rotary (ex-pres.), Acacia (Williamsport); Union League (Phila.); Explorers (New York); Tilghman Island (Md.). Author: Freemasonry in Northumberland and Snyder Counties, 1911; Daily Stories of Pennsylvania, 1924 and 1927; Pennsylvanians Past and Present, 1926; also Daily Stories of New York. Editor Ency. of Pennsylvania Biographies; Pennsylvania, Political, Governmental, Military and Civil; Chronicles of Central Pennsylvania, also writer of syndicate hist. articles. Expert marksman. Home: Milton, Pa. Died Dec. 30, 1944.

GODDARD, Edwin C., prof. law; b. Winnebago, Ill., Aug. 20, 1865; s. James W. Goddard and Mary (Blodgett) G.; Ph.B., U. of Mich., 1889, LL.B., 1899; m. Lillian Rosewarne, July 7, 1892. Instr. mathematics, Saginaw (Mich.) High School, 1889-91, prin., 1891-95; instr. mathematics, U. of Mich., 1895-1900, prof. law, 1900-35, prof. emeritus of law since 1935, sec. faculty, 1901-17. Mem. Am. and Mich. State bar assns., Am. Law Inst., Phi Beta Kappa, Phi Delta Phi, Order of the Coif. Republican. Conglist. Clubs: University, Michigan Union. Author: Plane and Spherical Trigonometry (with E. A. Lyman), 1899; Outlines of the Law of Bailments and Carriers, 1904; Cases on Bailments and Carriers, 1904; Cases on Agency, 1914; Cases on Principal and Agent and Master and Servant, 1925; Cases on Bailments and Public Utilities, 1928. Collaborator: Principal and Agent (in cyclo.), 1909. Home: 1212 Hill St., Ann Arbor, Mich. Died Aug. 14, 1942.

GODDARD, John Calvin, clergyman; b. New York, Sept. 18, 1852; s. James Edward and Catherine Fredericka (Jennings) G.; A.B., Yale, 1873; B.D., Chicago Theol. Sem., 1881; S.T.D., Pa. Coll., Gettysburg, 1915; m. Harriet Warren Allen, Aug. 2, 1883 (died Feb. 2, 1923); children—Catherine (Mrs. Howard L. Aller), Miriam (Mrs. Charles H. Davis), Rose (Mrs. William M. Clark), Charles Allen, John Calvin, Louisa Page (Mrs. J. B. Stamp), Ruth Salisbury (Mrs. L. C. Morton), Priscilla Alden (Mrs. E. L. Allen, Jr.); m. 2d, Kathryn C. Belden, Nov. 26, 1932. Sec. Yale, 1873. Pastor Congl. Church, Salisbury, Conn., 1884-1920, now emeritus. Feature writer Hartford Times, 1922-33 and Courant since 1933. Lecturer. Sec. Bd. Edn., Salisbury, 1889-93; moderator Gen. Assn. of Conn., 1895; pres. Salisbury Choir, Trustee Hotchkiss School. Mem. S.A.R., Conn. Hist. Soc., Alpha Delta Phi, Litchfield County University Club; pres. Scoville Memorial Library; chaplain Soc. Colonial Wars of Conn. Republican. Author: The 150th Anniversary of the Congregational Church in Salisbury, Connecticut, 1895; A Leave of Absence, and Other Leaves, 2d edit., 1901; Protestant Church History of Connecticut, 1925, Salisbury. Feature writer for Conn. newspapers. Perpetual toastmaster of Yale '73 annual banquets; frequently called upon to speak on "These United States." Home: Salisbury, Conn. Died March 17, 1945.

GODDARD, Robert Hale Ives, mfr.; b. Providence, R.I., Feb. 12, 1880; s. Robert Hale Ives and Rebekah B. (Groesbeck) G.; A.B., Yale, 1902; m. Margaret Hazard, July 15, 1908; 1 son, Robert Hale Ives. With Lonsdale Co., mfrs. cotton goods, Providence, since 1903, now partner; ex-pres. Providence Nat. Bank; pres. Lonsdale Co.; dir. R.I. Hospital Trust Co., Providence Washington Ins. Co. Mem. common council, Providence, 1912-24. Trustee Butler Hosp. Home: 66 Power St. Office: 50 S. Main St., Providence, R.I.* Died Aug. 10, 1945.

GODDARD, Robert Hutchings, physicist; b. Worcester, Mass., Oct. 5, 1882; s. Nahum Danford and Fannie Louise (Hoyt) G.; B.Sc., Worcester Poly. Inst., 1908; A.M., Clark U., 1910, Ph.D., 1911, Sc.D., 1945; m. Esther Christine Kisk, June 21, 1924. Instr., Worcester Poly. Inst., 1909-11, Princeton, 1912-13; instr. and fellow, physics, 1914-15, assistant prof., 1915-19, prof., 1919-43, Clark Univ., also dir. Physical Laboratories; leave of absence, 1930-32 and 1934-42, engaged in rocket research, under Daniel and Florence Guggenheim Foundation grants; director of research, Bureau of Aeronautics, Navy Department, 1942-45; consulting engineer, Curtiss-Wright Corporation, 1943-45. Served as dir. research, U.S. Signal Corps, Worcester Poly. Inst. and Mt. Wilson Observatory, Calif., World War, 1918. Fellow A.A.A.S.; mem. Am. Physical Soc., Am. Meteorological Soc., Institute Aeronautical Sciences, National Aeronautic Assn., Geophysical Union, Sigma Xi, Sigma Alpha Epsilon. Made extensive researches upon rocket method for reaching extreme altitudes. Home: Mescalero Ranch, Roswell, N.M.; also 1 Talawanda Drive, Worcester, Mass. Died Aug. 10, 1945.

GODFREY, Stuart C. (gŏd'frē), army officer; b. Milford, Mass., Jan. 1, 1886; s. Charles Boker and Cora Anna (Chapin) G.; ed. Phillips Exeter Acad., 1902-04; student Mass. Inst. of Tech., 1904-05; B.S., U.S. Mil. Acad., 1909; honor grad. Command and Gen. Staff Sch., 1926; grad. Army War Coll., 1933; m. Dorothy Severeance Rich, Sept. 2, 1915; children—Dorothy Hope (Mrs. Christopher McGrath), Charles Stuart, Pearce. Commd. 2d lt., Engr. Corps, U.S. Army, June 15, 1909, and advanced through the grades to brig. gen., Mar. 1942, Air Forces. Decorated Legion of Merit, Air Medal (1944); D.S.M. of Soc. Am. Mil. Engrs.; French Order of Palms. Awarded Silver Beaver, Boy Scouts of America. Mem. Am. Soc. C. E., Soc. of Am. Mil. Engrs. Bd. of Visitors, Civil Engring. and Mil. Science, Mass. Inst. of Tech. Club: Army and Navy (Washington). Home: 3619 O St. N.W., Washington, D.C. Died Oct. 19, 1945.

GOFF, Thomas Theodore (gawf), textbook author; b. near Eldorado Springs, Mo., Mar. 28, 1882; s. James Nelson and Missouri Adaline (Burch) G.; B.S., Okla. Agrl. and Mech. Coll., 1900; Master of Accounts, Gem City Business Col., Quincy, Ill., 1904; grad. study U. of Tex., summer 1927, U. of Wis., summers 1929, 30, 31; m. Myrta Louise Hixon, Sept. 3, 1905; 1 dau., Cleo Myrtilla. Teacher of mathematics, Gem City Bus. Coll., 1904-16; prof. mathematics and supervisor of arithmetic, State Teachers Coll., Whitewater, Wis., since 1916. Mem. Home Guards, Whitewater, 1918. Mem. Nat. Council Mathematics Teachers, Nat. Commercial Teachers' Fedn., N.E.A., Wis. Edn. Assn., Inst. of Am. Genealogy, Phi Delta Kappa. Democrat. Baptist. Mason (32°, K.T.); mem. O.E.S. Clubs: Walworth County Consistory (pres. 1931), Kiwanis (pres. 1933), Whitewater Country. Author: Self-Proving Business Arithmetic, Part I, 1924, Part I revised and Part II, 1928; Exercise Book for Business Arithmetic, 1928. Co.-Author (with John Guy Fowlkes): Modern Life Arithmetics, 8 book series, 1928, 6 book series, 1929; Practice Tests in Arithmetic, 1928; (with Fowlkes, Kingsbury and Wallace) Work Book in Algebra, 1928; (with Fowlkes, Taylor and Wright) Practical Arithmetic Work Books, 1929; (with Fowlkes and Lynch) My Number Book, 1931. Home: 1007 Main St., Whitewater, Wis.* Died Sep. 23, 1945.

GOLDBLATT, Nathan, dept. store mcht.; b. Staszow, Poland, March 24, 1895; s. Simon and Hannah G.; brought to U.S., 1904; ed. pub. schs., Chicago; m. Frances Abrams, June 22, 1924; children—Mavis, Renee, Lionel, Cherie Joy. Asso. at age 19 with brother Morris on combined capital of $2,000 in establishment of a small dry goods store, Chicago; opened a second store in Chicago, 1928, others in 1929, 30, 31, and in 1936 acquired Loop store formerly operated as The Davis Co., Chicago; also owner stores in Hammond and Gary, Ind., and Joliet, Ill.; sec. and treas. Goldblatt Bros., Inc. Mem. bd. dirs. Orthodox Jewish Home for the Aged, Hias Society. Mason. Home: Wilmette, Ill. Office: 333 S. State St.. Chicago, Ill. Died Nov. 3, 1944.

GOLDER, Benjamin M., ex-congressman; b. Vineland, N.J., Dec. 23, 1891; LL.B., U. of Pa., 1913. Admitted to Pa. bar, 1913, and began practice at Phila.; mem. 69th to 72d Congresses (1925-33), 4th Pa. Dist. Served as ensign Naval Aviation Service, World War I. Republican. Home: 2011 N. 33d St. Office: 1622 Chestnut St., Philadelphia. Died Dec. 1946.

GOLDMAN, Edward Alphonse, naturalist; b. Mt. Carroll, Ill., July 7, 1873; s. Jacob Henry and Laura Carrie (Nicodemus) G.; ed. pub. schs. and under pvt. tutors; m. Emma May Chase, June 23, 1902; children—Nelson Edward, Orville Merriam, Luther Chase. With U.S. Biol. Survey since 1892; much of time, 1892-1906, in biol. investigations in Mexico; in biol. survey of Panama, 1911-12, of Ariz., 1913-17; in charge div. of biological investigations, 1919-25; in charge div. of game and bird reservations, 1925-28; senior biologist since 1928. Fellow A.A.A.S.; mem. Am. Ornithologists' Union, Am. Soc. Mammalogists, Washington Acad. of Science, Biol. Soc. of Washington (pres. 1927-29), Am. Forestry Assn., Cooper Ornith. Club of Calif., Washington Biologists' Field Club. Commd. major, Sanitary Corps N.A., 1918, and with A.E.F. in France; maj. Sanitary Officers' Res. Corps, 1921-37, now retired. Clubs: Cosmos (Washington), Explorers (New York). Author: Revision of Wood Rats of Genus Neotoma, 1910; Revision of Spiny Pocket Mice (Heteromys and Liomys), 1911; Plant Records of an Expedition to Lower California, 1916; Rice Rats of North America (Oryzomys), 1918; Mammals of Panama, 1920; The Wolves of North America (with Stanley P. Young); also numerous shorter papers, mainly on mammals and birds and conservation of wild life. Home: 2702 17th St. N.E. Office: U.S. National Museum, Washington, D.C. Deceased.

GOLDSBOROUGH, Phillips Lee, dir. Federal Deposit Insurance Corp.; b. Cambridge, Md., Aug. 6, 1865; s. M. Worthington and Nettie M. (Jones) G.; educated in private and public schools of Maryland; studied law in office of Daniel M. Henry, Jr., and admitted to Maryland bar, 1886; LL.D., University of Pa., University of Md., Washington College, and St. John's College; m. Mary Ellen Showell, 1893 (dec.); children—Phillips Lee, Brice W., II. Practiced, Dorchester County; elected state's attorney, 1891, and reëlected, 1895; comptroller of Md., 1898-1900; apptd. collector internal revenue, District of Md., by President McKinley, and twice reapptd. by Presidents Roosevelt and Taft; gov. of Md., term Jan. 1912-Jan. 1916; mem. U.S. Senate, term 1929-35. Mem. bd. dirs. Federal Deposit Insurance Corp. since Apr. 29, 1935. Republican. Episcopalian. Home: Tudor Arms Apts., University Parkway, Baltimore, Md. Office: National Press Bldg., Washington 4. Died Oct. 22, 1946; buried in Christ Churchyard, Cambridge, Md.

GOLDTHWAIT, James Walter, prof. geology; b. Lynn, Mass., Mar. 22, 1880; s. James Wesley and Olive Jane (Parker) G.; A.B., Harvard, 1902, A.M., 1903, Ph.D., 1906; D.Sc. (hon.) Univ. of New Hampshire, 1945; married Edith Dunnels Richards, June 25, 1906; children—Richard Parker, Lawrence. Asst. prof. geology, Northwestern U., 1904-08; asst. prof. geology, 1908-11, prof. geology since 1911, Dartmouth. Engaged during summers in geologic field work for state surveys of Wis. and Ill., for U.S. Geol. Survey and for Geol. Survey of Can. Served as capt. U.S. Army, Apr. 8-Dec. 31, 1918, in charge of map room, Office Chief of Staff, Washington. Geologist, N.H. State Highway Dept. since 1917. Fellow Geol. Soc. America, Am. Acad. Arts and Sciences; mem. Phi Beta Kappa, Sigma Xi, Gamma Alpha fraternities. Conglist. Author: Abandoned Shorelines of Eastern Wisconsin (Wis. Geol. Survey), 1906; Physiography of Nova Scotia (Geol. Survey of Can.), 1925; Geology of New Hampshire (N.H. Acad. Science Handbook No. 1), 1925; also numerous reports and papers, dealing with extinct shorelines, earth movements, river floods, glacial and physiographic studies in N.E. and Can. Home: Hanover, N.H. Died Dec. 31, 1947.

GOLDTHWAITE, Anne, artist; b. Montgomery, Ala.; d. Richard and Lucy (Armistead) Goldthwaite; ed. Acad. of Design (New York), Acad. Moderne (Paris, France). Painter and etcher; work on permanent exbn. at Met. Museum and Public Library, New York; Congressional Library, Washington, D.C.; Art Institute Chicago; Museum of Rue Spontini, Paris; N.Y. Metropolitan Museum; N.Y. Museum of Modern Art; also museums of Brooklyn, Baltimore, Phila., Boston, Whitney Mus. (New York), Montgomery (Ala.), and others. Home: 112 E. 10th St., New York, N.Y. Died Jan. 29, 1944.

GOLDTHWAITE, Nellie Esther, coll. prof.; b. Jamestown, N.Y.; d. Lucian and Octavia (Churchill) Goldthwaite; student Wellesley, 1884-86; B.S., U. of Mich., 1894; fellow chemistry, U. of Chicago, 1894-97, Ph.D., 1904. Teacher, Jamestown (N.Y.) High Sch., 1886-89, Chicago pub. schs., 1889-91; head chemistry dept. Mt. Holyoke Coll., 1897-1905; research work, Rockefeller Inst., 1906-08; asso., U. of Ill., 1908-11, asst. prof. household science, 1911-15; dean of women and head of Home Economics Dept., N.H. Coll., 1915-16; traveled and studied in Orient, 1916-19; asso. prof. home economics, in charge of research, Colo. Coll. of Agr., 1919-25. Mem. A.A.A.S., Am. Chem. Soc., Am. Home Economics Assn., Am. Assn. Univ. Women, N.E.A., Sigma Xi, Omicron Nu, Phi Beta Kappa, Kappa Mu Sigma. Conglist. Contbr. to scientific mags. Home: South Hadley, Mass. Died Nov. 25, 1946.

GOLDWATER, Sigismund Schultz, hospital administrator; b. New York, Feb. 7, 1873; s. Henry and

Mary (Tyroler) G.; student Columbia, 1894-95; M.D., Univ. and Bellevue Hosp. Med. Coll. (N.Y. U.), 1901; D.Sc. Marquette, 1925; Dr. Pub. Health, New York University, 1939; m. Clara Aub, Feb. 8, 1904; children—Janet Teres, Robert John, Mary Margaret. Supt. Mt. Sinai Hosp., 1903-16, dir. 1917-29; commr. of health, New York City, Jan. 1914-15; commr. of Dept. of Hosps., City of N.Y., 1934-40; pres. Asso. Hosp. Service, New York, since 1940. Municipal expert in hosp. constrn. and administration, New York, 1908; advisory expert to many hosps. Mem. Am. Hosp. Assn. (pres. 1908), N.Y. Acad. Medicine (v.p. 1913), Nat. Inst. Social Sciences (v.p. 1918-21); hon. mem. Brit. Hosp. Assn.; pres. Am. Conf. on Hosp. Service, 1924-26; v.p. research council, Dept. of Hospitals, N.Y. City, since 1941. Med. Counselor U.S. Vet. Bur., 1924; cons. expert, U.S. pub. Health Service; cons. expert Inst. of Exptl. Medicine, Leningrad, Russia, 1933; consultant Murry & Leonie Guggenheim Foundation; consultant, Pan-American Sanitary Bureau. Trustee United Hosp. Fund (N.Y.), Huntington (L.I.) Hosp. Mem. Soc. for Ethical Culture. Home: 320 Central Park W., New York, N.Y.; and Bay Av., Huntington, L.I., N.Y. Died Oct. 22, 1942.

GOMBERG, Moses, chemist; b. Elizabetgrad, Russia, Feb. 8, 1866; s. George and Marie Ethel (Resnikoff) G.; ed. Elizabetgrad Gymnasium, 1878-84; B.S., U. of Mich., 1890, M.S., 1892, Sc.D., 1894; studied at U. of Munich, 1896-97, U. of Heidelberg, 1897; hon. Sc.D., U. of Chicago, 1929, Poly. Inst., Brooklyn, 1932; LL.D., U. of Mich., 1937; unmarried. Instr. chemistry, 1893-99; asst. prof. organic chemistry, 1899-1902, jr. prof., 1902-04, prof., 1904-36; also chmn. dept. of chemistry, 1927-36, Univ. of Mich., prof. emeritus since 1936. Consulting chemist, Bureau of Mines, 1917-18; maj. Ord. Department, North America, July 1918. Contbr. to various chemical jours. Awarded Nichols medal, Am. Chem. Soc., 1914, Willard Gibbs medal, 1925, Chandler medal, 1927; fellow A.A.A.S. (vice-pres. and chmn. sect. C, 1935); mem. Nat. Acad. Sciences, Am. Philos. Soc., Am. Chem. Society (pres. 1931); hon. mem. Netherlands Chem. Soc., Am. Inst. of Chemists. Home: 712 Onondaga St., Ann Arbor, Mich. Died Feb. 12, 1947.

GOMPERT, William Henry (gŏm'pẽrt), architect; b. N.Y. City, June 10, 1875; s. Christian and Catherine G.; studied Pratt Inst., Brooklyn, 1892; art study, Adelphi Acad., Brooklyn, and Brooklyn Inst. Arts and Sciences; unmarried. Began practice at N.Y. City, 1906; architect and supt. sch. bldgs., Bd. of Edn., N.Y. City, 1923-28. Architect of Pullman Bldg., Cuyler Bldg., Burrell Bldg. and Embassy Hotel, Theodore Roosevelt High Sch., N.Y. Teachers Training Coll., DeWitt Clinton High Sch. (all of N.Y. City) and 170 high and grade sch. bldgs. and many residences, banks, churches, amusement structures; architect Empire City Race Track; asso. architect U.S. Marine Hosp., Stapleton, S.I.; Lincoln Baths, Saratoga Springs; consulting architect N.Y. County Court House; architect of first health center of N.Y. City. Mem. Am. Inst. Architects (mem. N.Y. chapter; past pres. Brooklyn chapter), Architectural League New York, Beaux Arts Inst. of Design; mem. bd. of Municipal Art Soc., Am. Artists Professional League, Henry Bacon Memorial Foundation, Architects Emergency Com. Episcopalian. Mason. Architect for buildings in New York and vicinity aggregating upward of $200,000,000. Office: 330 E. 43d St., New York 17, N.Y. Died May 19, 1946.

GOOD, Irby J., college pres.; b. Nappanee, Ind., Mar. 16, 1885; s. Isaiah R. and Anna (Rohrer) G.; Otterbein Coll., Westerville, O., 1904-05; A.B., Ind. Central Coll., 1908, A.M., 1911, LL.D., 1923; m. Mabel Rivir, Sept. 2, 1908; children—Julia Marie, Lowell Herbert, Ida Mae. Prin. Acad. of Indiana Central Coll., 1909-13; business mgr., 1914-15, pres. since Sept. 9, 1915, Indiana Central Coll. Republican. Mem. U.B. Ch. Home: 4202 Otterbein Av., Indianapolis, Ind. Died Feb. 25, 1945.

GOODE, Clement Tyson (good), prof. English; b. Mooresboro, N.C.; s. Rev. James Millard and Sarah Amy (Walker) G.; A.B., Wake Forest (N.C.) Coll., 1905, A.M., Harvard, 1911; Ph.D., Cornell, 1920; m. Bessie Mae Trimble, Sept. 2, 1916; children—Sara Trimble, Clement Tyson. Principal high school and superintendent schools, Oxford, N.C., 1905-08; head dept. of English, city schs., Durham, N.C., 1908-10; instr. in English, 1911-12, asso. prof., 1912-14, U. of Ark.; prof. English, Sweet Briar (Va.) Coll., 1915-22; instr. in English, Cornell, 1919-20; prof. English, Mercer U., 1922-24; Bostwick prof. English, Univ. of Richmond, 1924-41. Mem. Modern Lang. Assn. America, Am. Assn. Univ. Profs., Modern Humanities Research Association, Pi Gamma Mu, Omicron Delta Kappa, Phi Beta Kappa. Democrat. Baptist. Author: Byron as Critic, 1923; An Atlas of English Literature (with E. F. Shannon), 1925; Heath Readings in the Literature of England (with T. P. Cross), 1927; A Literary Map of the British Isles, 1941; Composition and Rhetoric (with T. P. Cross and R. A. Law), 1932. Compiler of selected short stories, 1932. Contbr. to critical periodicals. Home: Lonoke, Ark. Died Nov. 8, 1943.

GOODELL, Reginald Rusden, coll. prof.; b. Portland, Me.; s. Charles Raymond and Susan Watson (Anderson) G.; A.B., Bowdoin Coll., 1893, A.M., 1895; post-grad. studies Johns Hopkins, and the Sorbonne, Paris; unmarried. Instr., U. of Me., 1898-99; instr. Romance langs., Mass. Inst. Tech., 1901-02; head of dept. of Romance langs., Simmons Coll., Boston, since 1904; professor emeritus since 1938. Pres. Warren Memorial Foundation and trustee of several schools and colleges. Home: Anderson Farm, S. Windham (Portland, R.F.D. 3), Me. Died Jan. 23, 1945.

GOODLAND, Walter Samuel, gov. of Wis.; born Sharon, Wis., Dec. 22, 1862; s. John and Caroline Melissa (Clark) G.; grad. high sch., Appleton, Wis.; student Lawrence Coll., Appleton; m. Christena Lewis, Apr. 26, 1883 (died Nov. 24, 1896); children—Mary Caroline, John James, Rudyard Lewis, Doris Martha (Mrs. Earl Roethke); m. 2d, Annie Lewis, Feb. 17, 1898 (died Dec. 3, 1930); 1 dau., Clarice (Mrs. George Kimpel); m. 3d, Mrs. M. A. Risney (nee Roache), Jan. 7, 1933. Admitted to Wis. bar, 1885 and began practice at Wakefield, Mich.; founder, 1887, Wakefield Bulletin; founder, 1889, pub. to 1896, Ironwood (Mich.) Times; editor, part owner, Beloit (Wis.) Daily News, 1899-1900; became pub. and editor Racine Times, 1900, consol. with Racine Daily Call as Racine-Times-Call, 1915; pres. and treas. Call Pub. Co. Postmaster of Ironwood, 1895-98; mayor of Racine, 1911-15; del. Rep. Nat. Conv., 1912, 28; pres. Racine City Water Commn. 12 years; mem. Wis. State Senate, 1926-30, reëlected term, 1930-34; lt. gov. of Wis., 1938-41, reëlected, 1940-42; became gov. of Wis., Jan. 3, 1943, upon death of governor-elect for term, 1943-45; elected Gov. of Wisconsin for term, 1945-47; reelected gov. Nov. 5, 1946, for term 1947-49. Episcopalian. Mason. Home: 1632 Wisconsin St., Racine, Wis. Died March 12, 1947; buried Graceland Cemetery, Racine.

GOODMAN, Charles, surgeon; b. Hungary, June 14, 1871; s. Albert and Frances (Richman) G.; brought to U.S., 1874; M.D., Western Reserve U., 1892; post-grad. work, Berlin, Goettingen and Halle; m. 2d, Adele Frederica Prauger, July 11, 1923; 1 dau., Jane Helen. On staff Lying-in Hosp., N.Y. City and City Hosp., Blackwell's Island, 1892; mem. resident staff, surg. div., Mt. Sinai Hosp., 1893-96, chief of surg. dept., 1896-1916; attending surgeon Sydenham Hosp. 3 yrs., Montefiore Hosp. 15 yrs., Beth Israel Hosp. 20 yrs.; clin. prof. surgery, N.Y. Univ. and Bellevue Hosp. Med. Coll. since 1914; cons. surgeon Rockaway Beach Hosp., Beth Israel Hosp.; surgeon Park West Hosp.; asso. surgeon, Polyclinic Hospital. Member of Nobel Prize nominating committee in medicine, 1936. Successively capt. U.S. Med. Reserve Corps, comdg. officer of reinforcement of Presbyn. Hosp. (Gen. Hosp. No. 1, A.E.F.), major, head of operating team, Paschendale offensive, dir. Field Hosp. Sect., 42d Div., 1917-19; lt. col. Med. Res., U.S. Army. Cons. vascular surgeon to U.S. Veterans Facilities, II Corps Area, U.S. Veterans Hosp., No. 81. Fellow Am. Coll. Surgeons; mem. A.M.A., Acad. Medicine, Internat. Surg. Soc., N. Y. State and N.Y. Co. med. socs., Metropolitan, Harlem and Riverside med. socs., Harvey Soc., Eastern Med. Soc. (ex-pres.), Assn. Alumni of Mt. Sinai Hosp. (ex-sec.), Physicians' Mut. Aid Assn., Am. Legion, Mil. Order World War, Reserve Officers' Assn., Assn. Mil. Surgeons, Am. Public Health, Internat. Med. Club (v.p.), Union Médicale Latine. Republican. Clubs: Army and Navy, Central Park Riding, Lakeville Golf and Country. Author of 64 reprints of med. articles pub. in various scientific journals on file at N.Y. Acad. of Medicine. Home: 125 E. 72d St., New York 21. Address: 745 5th Av., New York 22, N.Y. Died May 23, 1945.

GOODMAN, John Forest, army officer; b. Texas, Aug. 22, 1891; B.S., U.S. Mil. Acad., 1916; grad. Inf. Sch., field officers course, 1922, Command and Gen. Staff Sch., 1931, Chem. Warfare Sch., field officers course, 1940, Army War Coll., 1940. Commd. 2d lt., U.S. Army, 1916, and advanced through the grades to brig. gen., 1945. Decorated Silver Star, Purple Heart, Legion of Merit, Croix de Guerre. Address: care The Adjutant General's Office, War Department, Washington 25, D.C. Died Mar. 6, 1947.

GOODRICH, Donald Reuben, army officer; b Marshall, Mich., Oct. 17, 1894; grad. Army Indsl. Coll., 1931, Air Corps Tactical Sch., 1938. Commd. 2d lt., Air Service, U.S. Army, 1920, and advanced through the grades to brig. gen., 1944; served as flight adjutant and supply officer, 2d Observation Squadron, Camp Nichols, Rizal, P.I., 1927-29; asst. chief, personnel div., training group, Office Chief of Air Corps, also liaison officer Adj. Gen.'s Office, 1938-40; exec. officer, military personnel div. Office Chief of Air Corps, 1940-42; comdg. officer, 3d Air Service Area Command, Atlanta, Ga., 1942-43; became chief of staff, Eighth Air Force Service Command, European Theater of Operations, Mar. 1943, assuming command of an air depot area, European Theater of Operations, Aug. 1943. Address: care The Adjutant General's Office, War Department, Washington 25, D.C.* Died July 12, 1945.

GOODRICH, Lowell Pierce, city supt. schs.; b. Ripon, Wis., June 16, 1891; s. Rudolph Ormsby and Ella Elizabeth (Stewart) G.; A.B., Ripon Coll., 1913; A.M., U. of Wis., 1923; student Columbia, 1927, Harvard, 1937; m. Jane Blodwyn Jones, Aug. 24, 1915; 1 son, William Pierce. Science teacher, Wausau (Wis.) High Sch., 1913; supt. of schs., Phillips, Wis., 1915-18, Ripon, Wis., 1918-23, Fond du Lac, 1923-40; asst. supt. of schs., Milwaukee, 1940-43, superintendent since 1943; visiting instructor Northwestern Univ., summer 1945; Univ. of Wisconsin, summer 1946. Chairman Wisconsin Council on Edn., 1932-38. Mem. N.E.A., Am. Assn. Sch. Administrs., Wis. City Supts. Assn. (pres., 1923-24), Newcomen, Am. Interprofessional Inst., Phi Delta Kappa. Mason. Clubs: City, Rotary (Milwaukee). Home: 2311 E. North Av. Address: 1111 N. Tenth St. Milwaukee, Wis. Died Mar. 29, 1949.

GOODSELL, Charles True, college prof.; b. Medina, N.Y., Mar. 2, 1886; s. William Edward and Josephine (Chase) G.; A.B., U. of Rochester (N.Y.), 1909; D.B., Colgate-Rochester Divinity School, 1912; A.M., Univ. of Chicago, 1924; LL.D., Kalamazoo Coll., 1936; m. Frances Elizabeth Comee, Sept. 10, 1920; children—Betty Jo, Barbara Jean, Charles True. Ordained Bapt. ministry, 1912; pastor Emmanuel Ch., Sparks, Nev., 1912-18, Central Ch., Olympia, Wash., 1918-21, First Ch., Mendota, Ill., 1921-24, First Ch., Lafayette, Ind., 1924-28; head of history dept., Kalamazoo (Mich.) Coll., since 1928, v.p., 1933-35, acting president, 1935-36. Served with Y.M.C.A., A.E.F., 1917-18. Mem. Theta Chi, Delta Theta Chi. Mason, Odd Fellow, K.P. Club: Outlook. Author: (with W. F. Dunbar) A Centennial History of Kalamazoo College, 1933. Home: 1316 W. Lovell St., Kalamazoo, Mich. Died Nov. 25, 1941.

GOODSPEED, Charles Barnett; b. Cleveland, O., Feb. 8, 1885; s. Wilbur F. and Harriett (Howe) G.; M.E., Cornell U., 1908; m. Elizabeth Fuller. Dir. Buckeye Steel Castings Co., City Nat. Bank & Trust Co. Served as capt. 32d, 29th, 42d Division, A.E.F., World War I. President bd. managers Presbyterian Hospital. Trustee U. of Chicago, Art. Inst. Chicago, Chicago Symphony Orchestra Assn., Fourth Presbyn. Ch., Ill. Children's Home and Aid Soc.; citizen fellow Inst. Med. of Chicago. Republican. Home: 2430 Lake View Av., Chicago, Ill. Died Feb. 23, 1947; buried at Columbus, O.

GOODSPEED, Charles Ten Broeke, lawyer; b. Quincy, Ill., May 19, 1869; s. Thomas Wakefield and Mary Ellen (Ten Broeke) G.; A.B., Denison U., 1890; LL.B., Chicago Coll. of Law (Lake Forest U.), 1893; grad. student U. of Chicago, 1892-93; unmarried. Admitted to Ill. bar, 1893, and since practiced in Chicago; atty. for Prairie State Bank 8 yrs. until its merger, 1912; mem. firm Goodspeed, Bates & Amundson. Mem. Commn. on protection of residence dists., by apptmt. of Mayor Harrison; pres. South Park Improvement Assn., 1904-28, 1930-35; ex-pres. Neighborhood Improvement League of Chicago. Served as mem. Legal Advisory Bd., Division No. 15, Chicago, Selective Service, 1917-18. Trustee Divinity Sch., U. of Chicago, chmn. to 1941; trustee George Williams Coll. Mem. Am., Ill. State and Chicago bar assns., Chicago Law Institute (pres. 1916), Chicago Historical Society, Illinois Historical Soc.; mem. Y.M.C.A. (mem. National Council of U.S., 1925; Ill. State Com. to 1925; mem. and recording sec. bd. mgrs., Chicago, since 1911). Baptist (mem. Law Com. Northern Bapt. Conv., 1937-38; v.p. Chicago Baptist Social Union, 1924, 29; mem. bd. dirs. Chicago Bapt. Assn.). Chmn. church council Hyde Park Bapt. Ch., Chicago, 1937-38; chmn. finance com. 30 years. Republican. Club: Quadrangle. Author: Thomas Wakefield Goodspeed (a biography), 1932; Loring Wilbur Messer (biog. sketch), 1934. Home: 828 Simpson St., Evanston, Ill. Office: 189 W. Madison St., Chicago, Ill. Died Nov. 18, 1949.

GOODWIN, Cardinal (Leonidas), coll. prof.; b. Pine Bluff, Ark., May 1, 1880; s. Iverson S. and Sally (Pierce) G.; B.A., Brown U., 1905, M.A., 1910; Ph.D., U. of Calif., 1916; m. Mildred Louise Smith, Mar. 25, 1907; children—Cardinal Wayne, Margaret Louise. Prin. high sch., Essex, Mass., 1906-07; Lyndon Inst., Lyndonville, Vt., 1907-10; teaching fellow in history, U. of Calif., 1910-11; teacher history, high sch., Alameda, Calif., 1911-13; head of history dept. Stockton (Calif.) High Sch., 1913-14, Fremont High Sch., Oakland, Calif., 1914-18, and vice prin., 1917-18; prof. Am. history, Mills Coll., Calif., since 1918; prof. Am. history at Stanford U. fall quarter, 1927, and Sch. of Citizenship, Syracuse U. (leave of absence from Mills Coll.), 1928-29; taught in summer schs. U. of Kan., U. of Ia., U. of Ore. (Eugene and at Portland), U. of Calif. (Berkeley and Los Angeles), U. of Colo. and U. of Texas. Mem. American Historical Assn., Mississippi Valley Historical Assn., Phi Beta Kappa, Pi Gamma Mu. Mason. Author: The Establishment of State Government in California, 1914; A Larger View of the Yellowstone Expedition, 1918; The Trans-Mississippi West from 1803 to 1853—a Brief History of Its Acquisition and Settlement, 1922; A Syllabus of United States History, 1927; John Charles Fremont—An Explanation of His Career, 1930. Editor: New Spain and the Anglo-American West, Vol. 2, 1932. Contbr. to Dictionary of Am. Biography. Writer various articles in mags., relating to hist. topics. Address: Mills College, Oakland, Calif. Died June 23, 1944.

GOODWIN, Frederick C., lawyer; b. New Hartford, Conn., 1877; grad. U. of Rochester (N.Y.), 1898. Admitted to N.Y. bar, 1900, and practiced in Rochester; sr. partner Goodwin, Nixon, Hargrave, Middleton & Devans; chmn. Rochester Telephone Corp.; dir. Lincoln Alliance Bank & Trust Co., Rochester Gas & Electric Corp., Stromberg-Carlson Telephone Mfg. Co., Bausch & Lomb Optical Co., Pfaudler Co., Curtice Bros. Co., Vogt Mfg. Corp. Home: 860 Rock Beach Road. Office: 31 Exchange St., Rochester, N.Y. Died Dec. 3, 1942.

GOODWIN, John Edward, librarian; b. East Middleton, Dane County, Wis., Oct. 1, 1876; s. Henry and

Mary (Hope) G.; B.L., U. of Wis., 1901; B.L.S., N.Y. State Library Sch., 1905; m. Jeannette Boynton Storms, Sept. 20, 1904 (died Nov. 18, 1944; m. 2d, Fanny Alice Coldren, Feb. 28, 1946. Asst. in Free Pub. Library and Legislative Reference Bur., Madison, Wis., 1901-03; asst. librarian Stanford, 1905-12; librarian U. of Tex., 1912-23, U. of Calif. at Los Angeles, 1923-44, librarian emeritus since 1944. Mem. Am. Calif. and Tex. library assns. Democrat. Methodist. Home: 1539 Calmar Court, Los Angeles 24, Calif. Died Nov. 18, 1948.

GOODYKOONTZ, Wells, ex-congressman; b. Newbern, Pulaski County, Va., June 3, 1872; s. William M. and Lucinda K. (Woolwine) G.; ed. Oxford (Va.) Acad.; studied law under Judge Z. T. Dobyns, of Floyd C.H., Va., and at Washington and Lee U.; m. Irene Hooper, Dec. 22, 1898. Practiced at Williamson, W.Va., since 1894; mem. Goodykoontz, Slaven & Kopp; mem. W. Virginia Ho. of Del., 1911-12, Senate, 1914-18 (Rep. floor leader, 1915-16, pres. of Senate, 1917-18); the only one of the presidents of W.Va. Senate concerning whose rulings no appeal was ever taken; mem. 66th to 67th Congresses (1919-23), 5th W.Va. Dist. Pres. Nat. Bank of Commerce, Williamson. Mem. Am. Bar Assn., W.Va. Bar Assn. (pres. 1917-18); chmn. com. of lawyers that directed W.Va. bar in assisting registrants in connection with draft and in aiding soldiers, sailors and their families. Apptd. 1926, by President Coolidge, commr. from W.Va. to Sesquicentennial, Phila.; also apptd., same yr., by gov. of W.Va., mem. State Tax Commn. Mason. Home: Williamson, W.Va. Died Mar. 2, 1944.

GORDON, Charles; b. at Indianapolis, Ind., May 5, 1890; s. Samuel and Anna (Finsten) G.; B.S., Univ. of Ill., 1912; m. Rinda Morgan, Nov. 29, 1912; children—Sylvia Lucile, Charles Byron. Engr. of equipment, Chicago Surface Lines, 1912-23; Western editor Electric Ry. Jour., 1923-26, editor, 1926-29; mng. dir. Am. Electric Ry. Assn. (now Am. Transit Assn.) since 1929; sec., dir. Transit Research Corp. since 1926. Served as engineering officer 276th Aero Squadron, U.S. Army, during World War. Protestant. Clubs: Uptown, Engineers (New York). Leader in modernization of local transportation. Office: 292 Madison Av., New York, N.Y. Died May 3, 1945.

GORDON, Douglas, editor; b. Richmond, Va., July 27, 1876; s. James Roy and Evelyn (Croxton) G.; grad. McGuire's Univ. Sch., Richmond, 1894; LL.B., U. of Va., 1898; m. Mabel Walker, Apr. 27, 1916. Practiced law at Richmond as mem. Cannon and Gordon; dramatic and music critic, Richmond Times-Dispatch, 1909, later book reviewer and editorial writer; editor Norfolk (Va.) Ledger-Dispatch, 1917-23, and since 1928; asso. editor, later editor Richmond Times-Dispatch, 1923-28. Mem. Bd. Police Commrs., Richmond, 8 yrs.; sec. Va. State Fair Assn., 7 yrs. Mem. bd. dirs. Norfolk Newspapers, Inc.; mem. Phi Beta Kappa (hon.), Delta Psi. Democrat. Episcopalian. Address: Norfolk Ledger-Dispatch, Norfolk, Va. Died May 3, 1944.

GORDON, Frank Malcolm, banker; b. Birmingham, Eng., Nov. 22, 1876; s. Hugh Benjamin and Clara (Walsh) G.; brought to U.S. at age of 3 yrs.; ed. public schools and business college, Chicago; married Sarah Marie Corboy, 1910; children—Isabel Marie (Mrs. Edmond M. Sullivan), Marion R. (Mrs. Harmar D. Ker), Evelyn R. (Mrs. William E. Comstock). Became identified with First National Bank, Chicago, 1892; transferred to First Trust and Savings Bank upon its organization in 1903; asst. mgr. bond dept. same, 1909-11, mgr. 1912-16, v.p., 1916; became v.p. First Nat. Bank of Chicago, 1925, also v.p. First Trust Joint Stock Land Bank, First-Chicago Corp., National Safe Deposit Co.; dir. Minnesota & Ontario Paper Co., Horlicks Malted Milk Corp., M. J. Corboy Co.; chmn. bd. College Inn Food Products Co. Treas. U. of Ill. Mem. Investment Bankers Assn. (pres. 1932-33). Republican. Roman Catholic. Clubs: Chicago Athletic Assn., Bankers; Chicago Golf (Wheaton). Home: 1300 N. State St. Office: First Nat. Bank, Chicago, Ill. Died Nov. 28, 1946.

GORDON, Jacques, violinist; b. Odessa, Russia, grad. Imperial Conservatory of Music, Odessa, Russia, 1913, Imperial Gymnasium, Odessa, 1913; student Inst. Musical Art, N.Y. City, 1914-17; m. Ruth Janeway, June 11, 1922; children—Richard Seymour, Nicholas. Concertized in Europe, 1913-14; mem. Berkshire String Quartet, N.Y. City, 1917-20; concertmaster, Chicago Symphony Orchestra, 1921-30; head of violin dept., Am. Conservatory of Music, Chicago, 1921-30; founder Gordon String Quartet, 1921; condr. of Hartford (Conn.) Symphony Orchestra Jan. 1, 1936-39; head of violin department, Eastman School of Music, University of Rochester, 1942. Director Federated Settlement Music Schools of Chicago. Founder 1930, and since director Gordon Musical Association. Member Phi Mu Alpha. Awarded Gold Medal by Czar of Russia, 1913; Coolidge medal by Library of Congress, 1938. Clubs: Cliff Dwellers, Tavern, Arts (Chicago); Bohemians, Beethoven Assn. (New York). Composer of much violin music. Home: Falls Village, Conn. Died Sept. 15, 1948; buried in Old Country Graveyard, Music Mountain, Falls Village.

GORDON, Leon, artist; b. Borisov, Minsk, Russia, May 25, 1889; s. Issaac Borisovitch and Sonia (Slutskov) G.; ed. under pvt. tutors, Russia and U.S.; studied Art Inst. Chicago, Nat. Acad. Design, N.Y. City, Kunst Academie, Vienna, and Julian Acad., Paris; m. Ella Loeb, May 10, 1913 (died Dec. 5, 1918); 1 dau., Louise; m. 2d, Natalie Hutchinson McCloskey, July 14, 1921; children—Gerome, Sonia. Came to U.S., 1904, naturalized citizen. 1913. Illustrator, portrait painter. Mem. Soc. of Illustrators. Authors' League America, Artists and Writers. Clubs: Salmagundi, Dutch Treat. Home: 11 Rue Schoelcher, Paris, France. Died Dec. 31, 1943.

GORDON, Neil Elbridge, chemist; b. Spafford, N.Y., Oct. 7, 1886; s. William James and Ella C. (Mason) G.; Ph.B., Syracuse U., 1911, M.A., 1912, Pd.B., 1921; Ph.D., Johns Hopkins, 1917; m. Hazel A. Mothersell, June 29, 1915; children—Neil Elbridge, Fortuna Lucille. Asst. prof. chemistry, Goucher Coll., Baltimore, Md., 1917-19; prof. phys. chemistry, U. of Md., 1919-21, dir. chem. dept., 1921-28; state chemist of Md., 1921-28; Francis P. Garvan prof. chemical edn., Johns Hopkins U., 1928-36; head chemistry dept., Central Coll., Fayette, Mo., 1936-42; chmn. chemistry dept., Wayne University since Sept. 1942; dir. Nat. Fellowships, Johns Hopkins, 1930-36. Organizer and editor Jour. of Chem. Edn., 1924-33. Dir. Hooker Scientific Library, 1936-46; dir. Friends of the Kresge-Hooker Scientific Library, since 1946. Organizer and editor, Record of Chemical Progress, since 1939. Fellow A.A.A.S. (organizer and director Gibson Island Research Conferences, 1938-46; mem. Am. Chem. Soc., Mo. Acad. Science, Faraday Soc., Royal Soc. Arts and Sciences, Sigma Xi, Alpha Chi Sigma. Methodist. Author: Project Study of Chemistry, 1925; Introductory College Chemistry, 1926, 2d edit., 1941; Introductory Chemistry, 1927, revised 1940; College Chemistry, 1928; Record Book for Introductory Chemistry, 1928. Contbr. numerous articles in scientific jours. Home: The Wardell Sheraton Hotel, Detroit 2. Died May 20, 1949.

GORDON, Peyton, judge; b. Washington, D.C., Apr. 30, 1870; s. Malcolm Burkhead and Sarah (Thompson) G.; LL.B., Columbian U., 1890, LL.M., 1891; LL.D., National U., Washington, D.C., 1931; m. Evelyn Briley, June 4, 1902; 1 dau., Mrs. H. Wells March (pen name Evelyn Peyton). Appointed assistant United States attorney for D.C.; 1901; pardon atty., 1904-07; spl. asst. to Attys. Gen. Bonaparte and Wickersham, 1907-13, in charge land fraud cases in Western States and sent to Japan on customs cases, 1912; U.S. dist. atty., Washington, D.C., by apptmt. of President Harding, Aug. 11, 1921; reapptd. by President Coolidge in 1926, term of 4 yrs.; apptd. associate justice of Supreme Court of District of Columbia by President Coolidge, April 3, 1928; retired February 4, 1941. Major, Judge Advocate Gen.'s Corps, 18 mos., World War, 6 mos. at G.H.Q., Chaumont, France. Mem. Bar Assn. of D.C. (pres. 1923-24), Am. Law Inst. (incorporator), Alumni Assn. Columbian-George Washington Law Sch. (ex-pres.), Am. Legion, Phi Beta Gamma. Republican. Methodist. Club: Chevy Chase. Home: 2139 Wyoming Av. N.W., Washington. Died Sept. 17, 1946; buried in Arlington National Cemetery.

GORDON, Robert Loudon, corp. exec.; b. New York, N.Y., Apr. 16, 1874; s. Robert and Mary (Loudon) G.; M.E., Cornell U., 1895; m. Helen Ferguson, Apr. 17, 1900; children—Helen Barrie (Mrs. John P. Kniffin), Mary Loudon (Mrs. R. Arthur Spaugh, Jr.), Isabel Ferguson (Mrs. Dempster McIntosh). With Baldwin Locomotive Works, 1895-97; mech. engr. Fox Pressed Steel Equipment Co., 1897-99, Pressed Steel Car Co., 1899-1902; salesman Standard Steel Car Co., 1902-05, asst. to pres., 1905-17, v.p. and dir., 1917-30; v.p. and dir. Standard Steel Car Corp., 1930-35; v.p. and dir. Pullman-Standard Car Mfg. Co. since 1935; v.p. and dir. Pullman-Standard Car Export Corp.; dir. The Foundation Co., Trans-Lux Corp. Mem. Phi Gamma Delta. Presbyterian (trustee Fourth Presbyn. Ch., New York). Clubs: Metropolitan, Engineers, Cloud, New York Railroad, Cornell, Phi Gamma Delta (New York); Siwanoy Country (Bronxville, N.Y.). Home: 3 Brooklands, Bronxville, N.Y. Office: 52 Vanderbilt Av., New York, N.Y. Died Feb. 12, 1946.

GORDON, William, lawyer; b. Oak Harbor, O., Dec. 15, 1862; s. Washington and Margaret (Rymers) G.; LL.B., U. of Mich., 1893; m. Elizabeth M. Gernhard, Sept. 12, 1893. Began practice, Oak Harbor, 1893; pres. Gordon Lumber, Basket & Mfg. Co. Mem. county bd. sch. examiners, Ottawa Co., 1890-96; dep. county treas., under father, 1887-91; pros. atty., Ottawa Co., 1894-1900; del. Dem. Nat. Conv., 1896; mem. Dem. State Central Com., 1903, 04; mem. 63d to 65th Congresses (1913-19), 20th Ohio Dist. Trustee Andrews Inst. for Girls, Willoughby, O. Mason (K.T., Shriner). Club: City. Home: 6904 Franklin Av. Office: Guarantee Title Bldg., Cleveland. Died Jan. 16, 1942.

GORDON, William Knox, oil exec.; b. Spotsylvania Co., Va., 1862. Chmn. of bd. and dir., Texas Pacific Coal & Oil Co., Fort Worth; mem. exec. com. and dir., Southwestern Life Ins. Co., Dallas, Texas. Home: 2624 Edgewood, Fort Worth. Office: Texas Pacific Coal & Oil Company, Fort Worth, Texas.* Died Mar. 13, 1949.

GORE, Howard Mason, ex-governor; b. at Clarksburg, W.Va., Oct. 12, 1887; s. Solomon D. and Marietta Payne (Rogers) G.; B.A., W.Va. U., 1900; m. Roxilene Corder Bailey, Sept. 30, 1906 (died 1907). Largely engaged in agriculture and live stock raising, also in hotel, banking and mercantile business; mem. State Bd. of Edn., W.Va., 1920-25; asst. sec. agr., Washington, D.C., 1923-24; sec. of agr., Nov. 1924-Mar. 1925; gov. of W.Va., term 1925-29; commr. agr. W.Va., 1931-33; W.Va. adminstr. Farm to Market Roads Adminstrn.; mem. (chmn. since Jan. 1944) W.Va. Pub. Service Commn.; mem. State Council of Defense. Served as asst. food administrator, W. Va., and mem. Council of Defense, World War. Pres. of West Virginia Livestock Assn., 1912-16; pres. of W.Va. Hereford Breeders Assn., 1918-21; was mem. of Com. of Fifteen of Am. Farm Bureau Fedn.; mem. first bd. dirs. Nat. Producers Livestock Coop. Assn.; life mem. Internat. Livestock Expn.; a founder and patron of boys' and girls' organization work; pres. W.Va. Farm Bureau Coop. Assn.; dir. Producers Coop. Live Stock Assn.; chmn. Drouth Relief Com. of W.Va. Mem. Phi Sigma Kappa, Phi Beta Kappa. Rep. Baptist. Mason, Odd Fellow, Elk, Moose, K.P. Club: Cosmos (Wash.). Home: Clarksburg, W.Va. Died June 20, 1947.

GORE, John Kinsey, actuary; b. Newark, N.J., Feb. 3, 1864; s. George W. and Mary L. (Kinsey) G.; A.B., Columbia U., 1883, A.M., 1886; received the Univ. medal from Columbia, 1932; m. Jeannette Littell, Feb. 16, 1898. Teacher and prin. Woodbridge Sch., New York, 1884-92; clerk actuarial dept., 1892-94; mathematician, 1894-95, assistant actuary, 1895-97, became actuary, March 1897, director, 1907, v.p., 1912, now retired, Prudential Ins. Co. of Am.; dir. Nat. State Bank of Newark. Inventor of a system of tabulating machines. Fellow Actuarial Soc. America (pres. 1908-10); mem. N.E. Soc. of Orange (pres. 1912-13). Mem. Newark Bd. of Edn., 1895-96. Republican. Clubs: Phi Gamma Delta, Columbia U. (New York). Writer scientific papers pub. in trans. of Actuarial Soc. of America, Internat. Congress of Actuaries, and "A World War Against Disease," pub. by Assn. Life Ins. Presidents, 1927. Home: 69 High St., Orange, N.J. Died June 22, 1943.

GORE, Thomas Pryor; b. Webster County, Miss., Dec. 10, 1870; s. Thomas Madison and Carrie Elizabeth (Wingo) G.; at age of 8 lost left eye by being accidentally struck with a stick by a playmate and at 11 lost right eye by an arrow from a cross bow; grad. normal sch., Walthall, Miss., 1890; B.L., Cumberland U., 1892, LL.D., 1921; admitted to bar, 1892; m. Nina Kay, Dec. 27, 1900. Taught sch., 1890-91; nominated for state legislature, 1891, but withdrew on account of minority as to age; began practice in Miss., 1892; removed to Texas, 1896; delegate Populist Nat. Conv., St. Louis, 1896; nominated for Congress by People's party, 6th Dist., Texas, 1898 (defeated); joined Dem. party, 1899, and campaigned in S.D., 1900 and in Ill., Ohio, N.Y. and Ind., 1904; removed to Okla., 1901; mem. Territorial Council, 1903-05; U.S. Senator from the admission of Oklahoma as a state, 1907-March 4, 1921, reëlected for term 1931-37. Delegate-at-large Dem. National Conv. 1912, 1928 and 1936, mem. exec. com. Dem. Nat. Com., 1912-16; in charge bureau of organization for Dem. Nat. Com., 1912. Mem. U.S. Rural Credits Commn., 1913; mem. Joint Com. on Short Time Rural Credits, 1921-22. K.P., Moose, Elk, Woodman. Home: Oklahoma City, Okla. Office: 525 Union Trust Bldg., Washington, D.C. Died Mar. 1, 1949.

GORMAN, James Edward, ry. official; b. Chicago, Ill., Dec. 3, 1863. With C.B.&Q. R.R., 1877-81; then C.R.I.&P. R.R., until 1884; Chicago Lumber Co., 1884-85; C.&N.W. Ry., 1885-87; Chicago,SantaFe& Cal. Ry., 1887-89; I.C. R.R., 1889-90; Chicago,Santa Fe&Cal. Ry., 1890-93; traffic mgr. Joy Morton & Co., 1893-95; with A.T.&S.F. R.R., as chief clk. to traffic mgr., Mar.-Sept. 1895; asst. gen. frt. agt., same rd., at Chicago, 1895-99; gen. frt. agt., 1899-1904, asst. frt. traffic mgr., 1904-05, frt. traffic mgr., 1905-09; 1st v.p. in charge of frt. traffic, C.R.I.&P. R.R., 1909-15, chief exec. officer under receivership, 1915-17, pres. 1917-18, federal mgr. 1918-20, pres. Mar. 1, 1920-Dec. 1, 1933, since trustee and president, Chicago, RockIsland&Pacific Ry. Office: La Salle Station, Chicago, Ill. Died Mar. 23, 1943.

GORRELL, Edgar Staley (gôr'rĕl), industrial engr.; b. Baltimore, Md., Feb. 3, 1891; s. Charles Edgar and Pamelia Stevenson (Smith) G.; ed. Baltimore City Coll., 1904-07; B.S., U.S. Mil. Acad., 1912; M.Sc., Mass. Inst. Tech., 1917; D.Sc., Norwich Univ., Northfield, Vt., 1937; m. Ruth Maurice, Dec. 10, 1921; children—Mary (dec.), Edgar Staley; m. 2d, Mary Frances O'Dowd Weidman, Feb. 22, 1945. Served in inf., 1912-14; trans. to Aviation Sect. Signal Corps (now Army Air Corps), 1914; joined 1st Aero Squadron, as lt., San Antonio, Tex., Jan. 1916; participated in Punitive Expdn., Mexico, under General Pershing; detailed to Mass. Inst. Tech., then at hdqrs., Washington, D.C.; promoted to capt., 1917; sent to Europe by Pres. Wilson, as mem. Bolling Mission; to visit Allies to determine what aerial material should be produced in United States and what purchased in Europe; served as chief engr. officer of Air Service, A.E.F.; promoted to colonel October 28, 1918; later assistant chief of staff, Air Service; representative of U.S. at more than 200 internat. confs.; participated in campaigns on all five fronts during war; chief of staff of Air Service, A.E.F., with rank of col.; resigned from army, Mar. 1920. With the Nordyke & Marmon Co., 1920-25, vice-pres., 1923-25; with Stutz Motor Car Co., 1925-39, dir., v.p. and gen. mgr., 1925-29, dir. and pres., 1929-35, also chmn. board; pres., dir. and chmn. of bd. Edgar S. Gorrell Investment Co. since 1935; pres. and dir. Air Cargo, Inc., since 1940; apptd. mem. Army Air Service Investigating Com., Mar. 1934; now mem. Transportation Advisory Group, U.S. Army. Mem. bd. of trustees Norwich U. since 1935; pres. Air Transport Assn. of America since 1936; mem. visitors com. Mass. Inst.

of Tech. since 1936; mem. com. of nat. sponsors Air Youth of America, 1940; mem. Aeronautical Advisory Council, 1940. Mem. Soc. Automotive Engineers, Nat. Aeronautic Assn.; mem. Inst. of Aeronautical Science, Am. Meteorological Soc. Awards: medal, Mexican Punitive Expdn., 1916; Victory medal, 1918; Distinguished Service medal (U.S.); British D.S.O.; Legion of Honor (French). Presbyterian. Clubs: Country (Indianapolis); Racquet and Tennis, Wings (New York); The Attic (Chicago); Winter Lake (Lake Forest); Conquistadores del Cielo, New Mexico. Author of Study in Aerofoils, 1917. Member editorial board Journal of Air Law and Commerce, Northwestern U., Jan. 1939. Home: 777 N. Washington Rd., Lake Forest, Ill. Office: 1515 Massachusetts Av. N.W., Washington. Died Mar. 5, 1945; ashes scattered by Army Air Corps over West Point.

GORSKI, Martin, congressman; b. Poland, Oct. 30, 1886; came to U.S., 1889; ed. grammar, high sch. and business coll., Chicago; LL.B., Chicago Law Sch., 1917. Admitted to Ill. bar, 1917; asst. states atty., 1918-20; master in chancery, Superior Court, Cook County, Ill., 1929-42. Mem. 78th Congress (1943-45), 4th Ill. Dist. Democrat. Mem. Chicago Bar Assn. Home: Chicago, Ill.* Died Dec. 4, 1949.

GORTNER, Ross Aiken (gôrt'nẽr), biol. chemist; b. nr. O'Neill, Holt County, Neb., Mar. 20, 1885; s. Rev. Joseph Ross and Louisa E. (Waters) G.; B.S., Neb. Wesleyan U., 1907; M.A., U. of Toronto, 1908; univ. fellow in chemistry, Ph.D., Columbia University, 1909; hon. Sc.D., Lawrence Coll., 1932; m. Catherine V. Willis, Aug. 4, 1909 (died 1930); children—Elora Catherine, Ross Aiken, Willis Alway, Alice Louise; m. 2d, Rachel Rude, Jan. 12, 1931. Research asst. in agrl. chemistry, U. of Neb., 1906-07; asst. in chemistry, Faculty of Arts, U. of Toronto, 1907-08; resident investigator in biol. chemistry, Sta. for Exptl. Evolution of the Carnegie Instn. of Washington, Cold Spring Harbor, N.Y., Sept. 1, 1909-Aug. 1, 1914; asso. prof. soil chemistry, 1914-16, asso. prof. agr. biochemistry, 1916-17, Coll. of Agr. of U. of Minn.; prof. agrl. biochemistry and chief of div. of agrl. biochemistry, Coll. of Agr. of U. of Minn. and Minn. Agrl. Expt. Sta., since Aug. 1, 1917. Consultant Chem. Warfare Service, U.S. Army, since 1926. Asso. editor Jour. Am. Chem. Soc., Jour. Physical Chemistry, 1929-30 and 1934-35; asst. editor of Chemical Abstracts (zoölogy). Mem. Nat. Research Council (div. chemistry and chem. technology, 1930-33; div. biol. agr., 1930-33; mem. exec. com. 1931-32); chmn. U.S. com. of Internat. Com. on Biochem. Nomenclature of Union of Pure and Applied Chemistry, 1930-37. Wis. Alumni Foundation lecturer, 1930; George Fisher Baker non-resident lecturer Cornell U., 1935-36 (1st sem.). Priestly lecturer, Pa. State Coll., 1934. Mem. jury Willard Gibbs medal award, Am. Chem. Soc., 1933-39; mem. jury Borden medal award, Am. Chem. Soc. since 1939. Fellow A.A.A.S.; mem. Am. Chem. Society (councillor 1918-25, 1929-39; v. chmn. and sec., 1919; chmn. biol. div., 1920; sec. colloid div., 1929; chmn. 1931), Nat. Acad. of Sciences, Am. Soc. Biol. Chemists, Soc. Exptl. Biology and Medicine, Am. Society Naturalists (pres. 1932), Sigma Xi (exec. com. 1936-40), Phi Lambda Upsilon (nat. pres. 1921-26; hon. mem. 1939), Gamma Sigma Delta, Gamma Alpha, Phi Kappa Phi; hon. mem. Des Moines Acad. Medicine, Eugene Field Society (hon.), Alpha Zeta, Alpha Chi Sigma. Author: Outlines of Biochemistry, 1929, 2d edit., 1938; J. Arthur Harris, Botanist and Biometrician (with others), 1936; Selected Topics in Colloid Chemistry, 1937; also extensive contbr. on topics pertaining to biol. chemistry. Home: 1460 Raymond Av., St. Paul, Minn. Died Sep. 30, 1942.

GOSLINE, William A., Jr. (gŏs'lĭn); b. Toledo, O., Oct. 25, 1873; s. William A. and Mary Elizabeth (Card) G.; prep. edn., Phillips Acad., Andover, Mass.; student Harvard, 1892-93; m. Margaret M. Taylor, Oct. 30, 1902; children—Margaret (Mrs. C. Lockhart McKelvy), William A. III. Partner W. A. Gosline & Co., coal mchts., since 1902; dir. Toledo Trust Co., Gendron Realty Co. Pres. Toledo Chamber of Commerce, 1915; mem. bd. Social Service Fedn. since 1915; dir. Community Chest, Toledo, since 1918 (1st pres.); trustee Toledo Chapter Red Cross since 1918; trustee Toledo Art Museum (pres. since 1933). Served on Liberty Loan campaigns, World War I, and as dir. local Am. Soc. of Fatherless Children of France; mem. Ohio Inst., Northwestern Hist. Soc., etc. Republican. Episcopalian. Club: Toledo. Home: Perrysburg, O. Address: Toledo Museum of Art, Toledo, O. Died Feb. 21, 1947.

GOSNEY, Ezra Seymour (gŏz'nē); b. Kenton County, Ky., Nov. 6, 1855; s. Daniel B. and Eloiza (Griffing) G.; left home at 17; worked way through coll. and law sch.; B.S., Richmond (Mo.) Coll., 1877; LL.B., St. Louis Law Sch. (a dept. of Washington U.), 1880; m. Tyrene Noyes, 1886 (died 1887); m. 2d, May Hawkey, 1893 (died 1923); children—Gladys (Mrs. Joe G. Crick), Mrs. Lois G. Castle; m. 3d, Sarah H. Dearborn, 1924. Asst. gen. atty. K.C., St. Joseph & Council Bluffs R.R., St. Joseph, 1881-87; at Flagstaff, Ariz., 1888, and engaged in law practice, banking, stock growing, etc. Organizer, 1898, and pres. for 10 yrs. Ariz. Wool Growers' Assn.; v.p. and dir. Commercial Discount Co. of Los Angeles; mem. adv. bd. Pasadena Branch, Security-First Nat. Bank of Los Angeles. Founder and pres. Human Betterment Foundation; founder and trustee Polytechnic Elementary Sch., Pasadena. Active in Boy Scouts' work and community playground and recreation service. Mem. Am. Eugenics Soc., Am. Social Hygiene Soc., Eugenic Research Assn., Am. Assn. on Mental Deficiency, Am. Genetics Assn., Eugenics Soc. (London), Internat. Conf. of Social Work. Republican. Club: Twilight. Author: Sterilization for Human Betterment (with Paul Popenoe), 1929. Home: 1051 Woodbury Rd. Office: Security Bldg., Pasadena, Calif. Died Sep. 5, 1942.

GOSS, John Henry, pres. and gen. mgr. Scovill Mfg. Co.; b. Waterbury, Conn., 1872; s. Chauncey and Caroline (Ketcham) G.; grad. Yale U., 1894. Pres., gen. mgr. Scovill Mfg. Co.; v.p. Nazareth (Pa.) Cement Co.; dir. Citizens and Mfrs. Nat. Bank, Waterbury, Conn.; dir. Mfrs. Mutual Fire Ins. Co., New Britain Machine Co.; dir. Waterbury Savings Bank (Conn.). Mem. Mfrs. Assn. of Conn. (v.p.). Home: 70 Hillside Av. Office: 99 Mill St., Waterbury, Conn. Died Oct. 16, 1944.

GOSSETT, Alfred Newton (gŏs'sĕt), lawyer; b. Sharpsburg, Ky., Nov. 13, 1861; s. Jacob Dunham and Joan Frances (Ratliff) G.; B.A., Woodland Coll., Independence, Mo., 1880; LL.B., Washington U., St. Louis, 1883; m. Daisy Vera Galbaugh, Nov. 23, 1887 (died Mar. 2, 1892); 1 dau., Gale Galbaugh (Mrs. Roy Kaiser Dietrich). Admitted to Mo. bar, 1883, and since practiced in Kansas City; sr. partner Gossett, Ellis, Dietrich & Tyler; sec. Kansas City bd. election commrs., 1911-14; mem. 53d Gen. Assembly, Mo.; mem. Mo. constl. conv., 1922-23; mem. at large City Council, Kansas City, 1926-39. Mem. Am. and Mo. State bar assns., Kansas City Bar Assn. (past pres.). Democrat. Protestant. Mason (K.T.). Home: 2626 E. 28th St. Office: Dwight Bldg., Kansas City, Mo.* Died 1943.

GOSSLER, Philip Green, corp. officer; b. Columbia, Pa., Aug. 6, 1870; s. Philip and Emily (Washabaugh) G.; B.S., Pa. State Coll., 1890, E.E., 1892; post-grad. course, Columbia, 1893. With Chester (Pa.) Foundry & Machine Co., and Edison Gen. Electric Co., 1890-91; asst. engr. United Elec. Light & Power Co., New York, 1891-95; supt. and engr. Royal Elec. Co., Montreal, Can., 1895-1901; gen. supt. and engr. Montreal Light, Heat & Power Co., 1901-04; v.p. J. G. White & Co., and various other cos., 1904-09; chmn. bd. Columbia Gas & Electric Co., 1909-22, pres. and chmn. bd., 1922-26; pres., Columbia Gas & Electric Corp., 1926-36, chmn. bd. since 1936, also dir. various subsidiary companies. Dir. Guaranty Trust Co. of N.Y. Mem. Am. Inst. Elec. Engrs., N.Y. Elec. Soc. (ex-v.p.), Edison Pioneers (ex-v.p.), Am. Gas Assn., Assn. Edison Illuminating Cos., Edison Elec. Inst. (trustee), Phi Kappa Sigma, Pennsylvania Soc. Republican. Presbyterian. Clubs: Metropolitan (gov.), University, Recess (gov.); Piping Rock; Porcupine (gov.), Emerald Beach (Nassau, Bahamas); Royal Nassau Sailing; Cincinnati (O.). Home: 14 E. 65th St. Office: 61 Broadway, New York, N.Y.* Died May 11, 1945.

GOTT, Edgar N(athaniel), airplane mfr.; b. Detroit, Mich., May 2, 1887; s. Edward Alonzo and Stephanie (Ortmann) G.; prep. edn., Detroit Univ. Sch., 1900-05; B.S. in Chem. Engring., U. of Mich., 1909; m. Arline Elizabeth Biggs, June 2, 1914 (died Feb. 18, 1939); children—John Edgar, Stephanie E.; m. 2d, Gertrude Agnes Koenig, May 2, 1940. Resident engr., Chicago, Ill., and Tacoma, Wash., Griffin Wheel Co., 1909-15; v.p. Boeing Airplane Co., Seattle, Wash., 1915-22, pres., 1922-25; v.p. Fokker Aircraft Corp., 1925-26; pres. Keystone Aircraft Corp., 1926-32; v.p. Consolidated Aircraft Corp., San Diego, 1935-43; asst. to pres. Consolidated Vultee Aircraft Corp. since 1943. Vice-pres. and dir. Mfrs. Aircraft Assn. since 1937; dir. Aeronautical Chamber of Commerce of America since 1939; dir. San Diego Chamber of Commerce since 1935. Chmn. San Diego War Transportation Commn. since 1942, San Diego War Housing Commn. since 1942. Mem. Chi Psi. Episcopalian. Clubs: Army and Navy (Washington, D.C.); San Diego, Cuyamaca, San Diego Yacht. Home: San Diego, Calif. Died July 17, 1947.

GOUDY, Frank Burris (gou'dē), jurist; b. Ouray, Colo., Feb. 16, 1881; s. Frank Curtis and Ida Joella (Gephart) G.; student Colo. Sch. of Mines, 1900-01; A.B., Stanford U., 1905; A.M., Columbia, 1908; student Denver U. Law Sch., 1913-15; m. Blanche Estelle Johnson, Oct. 10, 1910; children—Marian Elizabeth, Robert Curtis. Mining engr., 1906-24; admitted to Colo. bar, 1915; justice of Supreme Court of Colo. since Sept. 1, 1942. Dir. Carnegie Pub. Library, Monte Vista, Colo. Mem. Colo. Denver, and San Luis Valley bar assns., Sigma Alpha Epsilon, Phi Delta Phi, Legal. Mason (Colo. Consistory, Scottish Rite). Eastern Star. Clubs: University, Rotary (Denver, Colo.); Commercial (Monte Vista, Colo.). Home: Monte Vista, Colo. Residence: 825 St. Paul St., Denver, Colo. Business Address: State Capitol, Denver, Colo. Died Oct. 14, 1944.

GOUDY, Frederic William (gou'dē), designer, printer; b. Bloomington, Ill., Mar. 8, 1865; s. John Fleming and Amanda M. (Truesdell) G.; grad. high sch., Shelbyville, Ill., 1883; H.L.D., Syracuse University, 1939; Litt.D., Mills College, 1941; LL.D., University of California, 1942; made 8 trips for study to England, Belgium, Holland and France; married Bertha M. Sprinks, June 2, 1897 (died 1935); 1 son, Frederic T. Began as accountant; engaged as designer since 1898; proprietor Village Press; president Village Press and Letter Foundry (destroyed by fire 1939); art advisor Lanston Monotype Company. Has designed over 100 type faces; bronze medal for book printing, St. Louis Exposition, 1904; Gold medal American Institute Graphic Arts; gold medal, A.I.A., Friedsam gold medal, Architectural League of N.Y.; medal of honor Sch. of Journalism, Syracuse U., 1936; medal of honor, Ulster-Irish Soc. of N.Y., 1937. Del. to Expn. of Industrial and Modern Art (Paris), 1925. Republican. Presbyterian. Clubs: Grolier, Typophiles, Stowaways (New York). Author: The Alphabet, 1918; Elements of Lettering, 1921; Capitals from the Trajan Column, 1936; Typologia, 1940. Contbr. on typography, also lecturer schs., clubs, etc. Home: Marlborough-on-Hudson, N.Y. Died May 11, 1947.

GOUGH, Emile Jefferson (gŏf), newspaperman; b San Francisco, Calif., Apr. 22, 1889; s. Thomas Jefferson and Rebecca (Patterson) G.; ed. Poly. High Sch., San Francisco; m. Nellie Marie Sweeney, Aug. 20, 1912 (died June 23, 1923); 1 son, Dr. Emile Jefferson; m. 2d, Mary Elizabeth Brennan, March 27, 1943. Reporter, sporting editor San Francisco Post and The Globe; joined The Call staff, 1913, asst. city editor until Apr. 1916, city editor; mng. editor of The Call, 1917-27; vice-pres. Hearst Radio, Inc., to Dec. 20, 1937; with Sesac, Inc., 1938-46 (both N.Y. City). Home: 2201 Sacramento St., San Francisco 15. Died Oct. 14, 1947.

GOULD, Arthur Robinson, ex-senator; b. East Corinth, Me., Mar. 16, 1857; s. Robinson and Elizabeth (Huse) G.; ed. pub. schs. and East Corinth Academy; m. Mary Donovan; 4 children. Formerly engaged in lumber business at Presque Isle; built power plant for Maine & New Brunswick Co., also an electric railroad from Presque Isle to Caribou; pres. Aroostook Valley R.R. Co. Mem. Me. Senate, 1921-22; elected mem. U.S. Senate Nov. 1926, for unexpired term ending Mar. 3, 1931, of Hon. Bert M. Fernald. Republican. Mason. Rotarian. Home: Presque Isle, Me. Died July 24, 1946

GOULD, Charles Newton, geologist; b. Lower Salem, O., July 22, 1868; s. Simon G. and Arvilla A. G.; grad. Southwestern Coll., Winfield, Kan., 1899; special studies geology and paleobotany; A.M., U. of Neb., 1900, Ph.D., 1906, hon. D.Sc., 1928; hon. LL.D., Oklahoma City Univ., 1933; m. Nina Leola Swan, Sept. 24, 1903; children— Lois Hazel, Donald Boyd. Prof. of geology U. of Okla., 1900-11; resident hydrographer U.S. Geol. Survey, 1902-06; dir. Okla. Geol. Survey, 1908-11; consulting geologist, engaged chiefly in petroleum investigations, 1911-24; director Okla. Geol. Survey, 1924-32, with rank of dean in Univ. of Oklahoma. Chmn. of Am. Com. on Revision of Rules of Stratigraphic Nomenclature, 1929-33. Member Am. Inst. Mining and Metall. Engrs., Geol. Soc. America, Am. Assn. State Geologists, Paleontol. Soc. America, A.A.A.S., Internat. Geol. Congress, Inst. Petroleum Technologist, Sigma Xi, Phi Beta Kappa, Sigma Gamma Epsilon, Phi Sigma, Pi Gamma Mu. Okla. Acad. Science (twice pres.), Am. Assn. Petroleum Geologists, Royal Soc. Arts, Okla. Bd. of Geographic Names; past vice pres. American Mining Congress; member American Geophysical Union; Oklahoma Hall of Fame. Methodist. Clubs: University, Rotary, Men's Dinner. Author: Geology and Water Resources of Oklahoma, 1905; Geography of Oklahoma, 1909; Petroleum and Natural Gas in Oklahoma, 1912; Index to the Stratigraphy of Oklahoma, 1926; Travels Through Oklahoma, 1928; Humanizing Geology, 1928; Oklahoma Place Names, 1933; Covered Wagon, Geologist, 1947; also numerous bulletins and articles. Director structural materials survey Oklahoma State, Federal Emergency Relief Administration, 1934; state director mineral survey, Oklahoma Geology Survey, Works Progress Adminstrn., 1935; hon. member Am. Assn. of Petroleum geologists, 1944; regional geologist Nat. Park Service, 1936-40; Am. Geographical Union, 1947. Home: 420 Chautauqua St., Norman, Okla. Died Aug. 13, 1949; buried in I.O.O.F. Cemetery, Norman.

GOULD, Frank Miller, ry. official; b. New York, N.Y., Feb. 6, 1899; s. Edwin and Sarah (Cantine) G.; student Browning Sch., N.Y. City, 1912-16, Yale to 1920; m. Florence Amelia Bacon, Nov. 16, 1924 (divorced May 1944); children—Marianne Alice, Edwin Jay; m. 2d, Helen Roosen Canan, June 7, 1944. Assistant secretary St. Louis Southwestern Railway Company, 1920-24, vice president since 1924. Trustee (chairman board) Edwin Gould Foundation for Children. Mem. Yale R.O.T.C., 1917; lt. U.S. Army, 1918; lieutenant 212th Artillery, New York National Guard, 1921-22. Commissioned captain, Army Air Corps, March 21, 1942. Mem. United Hunt Racing Assn., Virginia Gold Cup Assn. Clubs: New York Yacht, Racquet and Tennis, Turf and Field, University (New York); Jekyll Island (Ga.); Seminole Golf (Palm Beach); Sewanhaka-Corinthian Yacht (L.I.). Home: Oyster Bay, L.I., N.Y. Office: 165 Broadway New York. Died Jan. 13, 1945; buried in Woodlawn, New York.

GOULD, Harris Perley, horticulturist; b. North Bridgton, Me., Sept. 6, 1871; s. Charles Henry and Bethia Spring (Wadsworth) G.; B.S., U. of Maine, 1893; M.S. in Agr., Coll. of Agr., Cornell U., 1897; m. Alice Hewes Peabody, Apr. 24, 1905; children—Lawrence P., Stanley W. (dec.). Asst. in horticulture, Me. Expt. Sta., 1892-96; asst. in Cornell U. Expt. Sta., 1897-98; state nursery insp., N.Y., 1898; asst. entomologist and asst. horticulturist, Md. Agrl. Coll. Expt. Sta. and Md. State Hort. Dept., 1899-1900, and acting state entomologist, Jan.-June, 1901; asst. pomologist and pomologist, U.S. Dept. of Agr., 1901-28, sr. pomologist, 1928-38, prin. horticulturist in charge Div. Fruit and Vegetable Crops and Diseases, Bur. Plant Industry, U.S. Dept. of Agr., 1938-1941, retired as Collaborator, 1941. Conglist. Fellow A.A.A.S.; mem. Am. Pomol. Society, Am. Soc. Hort. Science, Bot. Soc. of Wash., Phi Kappa Phi, Beta Theta Pi. Author many circulars, bulls. and pub. addresses on pomol. subjects. Author: Peach-Growing (in Rural Science Series), 1918. Home: 3909 13th St. N.W. Office: Bureau of Plant Industry, Station, Beltsville, Md. Died Oct. 31, 1946.

GOULD, Harry; b. at East Machias, Me., June 18, 1869; son of Simeon H. and Sophia N. (Hanscom) G.; educated Washington Acad. East Machias; m. Carrie A. Chedell, Oct. 28, 1891; children—Helen (Mrs. Fenn Bailey Newell), Virginia (Mrs. Kenneth L. Peck). Began as office boy, 1883; with R. I. News Co., 1883-98, New York Herald, 1898-1905, Am. News Co. since 1905, pres. since 1927 and treas. since 1929, chmn. bd. and treas. since 1939; also treas. and dir. Union News Co., dealers and distributors of newspapers and mags. and operators of restaurants on eastern rys. and ry. terminals; retired, Mar. 12, 1941. Republican. Protestant. Club: Union League. Home: 54 Church Lane, Scarsdale, N.Y. Died July 17, 1945.

GOULD, Kingdon, capitalist; b. New York, Aug. 15, 1887; s. George Jay and Edith M. (Kingdon) G.; ed. Lakewood (N.J.) Sch. and pvt. instrn.; E.M., Columbia, 1909; m. Annunziata Lucci, July 2, 1917; children—Silvia Annunziata Maria, Edith Kingdon, Kingdon. Entered U.S.A., Sept. 1917; sent to France, May 11, 1918; commd. 1st lt. Corps of Interpreters, Apr. 15, 1918; assigned to 79th Div. and served as divisional observation officer to signing of armistice; discharged, Apr. 25, 1919. Home: 160 E. 72d St. Office: 39 Broadway, New York. Died Nov. 7, 1945.

GOURLEY, Joseph Harvey (gōr'lē), horticulturist; b. Homer City, Pa., July 1, 1883; s. John and Elizabeth Anna (Harvey) G.; B.S., Ohio State U., 1908, also M.S., 1915; Ph.D. from U. of Chicago, 1931; m. Lucy M. Kinney, June 7, 1911; children—Margaret Cruickshank, Elizabeth. Asst. horticulturist Ohio Agrl. Expt. Sta., 1908-10; asst. prof. horticulture, Ohio State U., 1910-12; prof. horticulture, N.H. Coll., and horticulturist, N.H. Agrl. Expt. Sta., 1912-20 (v. dir. 1920); prof. horticulture W.Va. U. and horticulturist W.Va. Agrl. Expt. Sta., 1920-21; horticulturist, Ohio Agrl. Expt. Sta., since 1921; chmn. dept. of horticulture, Ohio State U., since 1929. Fellow A.A.A.S. (v.p. sect. O), Ohio Acad. Science; hon. mem. Ohio Nursery Assn., Columbus Hort. Soc.; mem. Am. Soc. Hort. Science (president 1923), Ohio State Hort. Soc. (pres. 1940-41), Alpha Zeta, Sigma Xi, Alpha Tau Omega, Gamma Alpha, Pi Alpha Xi, Phi Upsilon Phi. Republican. Presbyterian. Mason. Grange. Clubs: Wooster Country, Century. Author: Text-Book of Pomology, 1922; Orchard Management, 1924; Modern Fruit Production (with F. S. Howlett), 1941. Cons. editor Am. Fruit Grower Mag. Home: Wooster, O. Died Oct. 7, 1946.

GRACE, William Russell, corp. official; b. New York, Apr. 11, 1878; s. William Russell and Lillius (Gilchrist) G.; student Columbia; m. Elise W. Ladew, Apr. 1914. First v.p. Ingersoll-Rand Co.; v.p. Belgrave Realty Co., Inc.; v.p. A. S. Cameron Steam Pump Works, Gilchrist Realty Corp.; dir. Canadian Ingersoll-Rand Co., Ltd., W. R. Grace & Co. Catholic. Home: Old Westbury, N.Y. Office: 11 Broadway, New York, N.Y. Died Mar. 31, 1943.

GRACE, Frank W.; v.p. and gen. mgr. M.K.&T. Ry.; b. Denison, Tex., 1880. Home: 7003 Lakewood Blvd. Office: Missouri, Kansas & Texas Ry., Dallas, Tex.* Deceased.

GRACEY, William Adolphe, newspaperman; b. Nynee Tal, India (parents Am. missionaries), Aug. 4, 1866; s. John T. (D.D.) and Annie (Ryder) G.; student U. of Rochester (N.Y.), 1884-88; m. Luella Warfield, Sept. 5, 1889 (died Jan. 4, 1941); children—Katharine (Mrs. William F. Merrill), Howard Warfield (dec.), Lawrence Williams, Lewis Adolphe, Robert Stuart. Mem. staff Rochester Democrat and Chronicle, 1889-98; editor and one of pubs. Geneva (N.Y.) Daily Times since 1898. Park commr. City of Geneva, 1916-40. Member American Newspaper Publishers Assn., N.Y. Publishers Assn., N.Y. Associated Dailies (pres. 1914), N.Y. State Soc. Newspaper Editors, Am. Soc. Newspaper Editors, Geneva Hist. Soc. (pres. since 1942), Psi Upsilon. Presbyn. (moderator Geneva Presbytery, 1941-42). Rotarian. Home: 71 Hamilton St., Geneva, N.Y. Died Oct. 16, 1944.

GRAF, Robert Joseph (grăf), investment banking; b. Washington, D.C., Nov. 13, 1882; s. Frederick John and Amalia (Boyland) G.; ed. common and prep. schs.; m. Helen Harriet Martin, Feb. 6, 1907 (died July 8, 1937); children—Robert J., Barbara Helen (Mrs. Charles Stickney Connell); m. 2d, Mrs. Margaret Brown Johnson, June 25, 1941. Began with H. M. Byllesby and Co. as sec. and asst. treas. upon its incorporation in 1903, elected v.p., 1914, and 1st v.p., 1924, elected pres. 1936; pres. and dir. Byllesby Corp. Mem. Am. Inst. E.E., Western Soc. Engrs., Art Inst. of Chicago, Chicago Hist. Soc., Field Museum. Clubs: Chicago, Union League, Attic, Tavern (Chicago); Recess (New York). Home: Route 1, St. Mary's Road, Libertyville, Ill. Office: 135 S. La Salle St., Chicago 3, Ill. Died Jan. 2, 1949.

GRAHAM, Alexander William (grā'ăm), civil engr., postmaster; b. Mineola, Mo., Aug. 6, 1884; s. William A. and Epsey Ann (McGhee) G.; student William Jewell Coll., 1902-04; B.S., U. of Mo., 1908; m. Edna Grace Ramsey, Aug. 4, 1912; 1 son, William Alexander. Gen. engring. work, 1908-17; state highway engr. of Mo., 1917-22; dealer in heavy constrn. machinery, 1922-27; pres. Graham-Hobson Tractor Co., 1927-33; postmaster at Kansas City, Mo., since 1933; served as asst. resident engr. on constrn. of Armour Swift Burlington Bridge, Kansas City; Miss. River bridges near Keithsburg, Ill.; Yellowstone River bridge near Fairview, Mont. Pres. Nat. Assn. of Postmasters, 1936-37. Mem. Kansas City Safety Council (dir.), Better Business Bur. (dir.), Chamber of Commerce. Democrat. Clubs: Automobile of Mo., Indian Hills Country. Home: 11 East Winthrop Rd. Office: U.S. Post Office, Kansas City, Mo. Died Jan. 30, 1949.

GRAHAM, Ben George, supt. schools; b. East Moravia, Pa., May 18, 1880; s. Benjamin and Caroline (Palmer) G.; A.B., Westminster Coll., Pa., 1904, A.M., 1908, Sc.D., 1924; M.A., U. of Pittsburgh, 1925, LL.D., from same, 1932; LL.D., Juniata Coll., 1934; LL.D., from Harvard University, 1941; married Zelma Burroughs, June 7, 1908; children—Ben G., Burns, Betty, Harriet Inez, John Muir, David, Paul, Ella Ruth. Teacher, Lawrence County, Pa., 1900-03, high sch., McKeesport, Pa., 1903-07; prin. high sch., Greensburg, Pa., 1907-09; teacher of chemistry, Central High Sch., Pittsburgh, 1909-16; prin. Latimer Jr. High Sch., Pittsburgh, 1916-19; supt. schs., New Castle, Pa., 1919-26; asso. supt. schs., Pittsburgh, 1926-27, first asso. supt., 1927-30. supt. since 1930. Mem. N.E.A., Am. Assn. of Sch. Adminstrs. (pres. 1939-40), Pa. State Edn. Assn. (pres. 1935), Phi Delta Kappa, Omicron Delta Kappa. Republican. United Presbyterian. Mason. Clubs: University, Rotary (Pittsburgh); Alcoma Country. Contbr. to ednl. periodicals. Home: 5614 Woodmont St. Office: 341 Bellefield Av., Pittsburgh, Pa. Died Mar. 20, 1942.

GRAHAM, Frank Dunstone, economist; b. of Am. parents, Halifax, N.S., Jan. 1, 1890; s. George and Jessie (Woodill) G.; B.A., Dalhousie U., 1913; LL.B., 1915; A.M., Harvard, 1917, Ph.D., 1920; m. Mary Louise Power, Sept. 14, 1920; children—Frank Dunstan, Hugh, John. Instr. in economics, Rutgers College, 1917-20; assistant professor economics, Dartmouth College, 1920-21; with Princeton University since 1921, asst. prof. economics, until 1925, asso. prof., 1925-30, prof. since 1930. Sec. Am. Commn. Financial Advisers to Poland, 1926; economic adviser to Business Men's Commn. on Agr., 1927; Guggenheim fellow, Germany, 1927-28; economic adviser, Federal Farm Bd., 1930-31; prof. of internat. economics, Institut Universitaire de Hautes Etudes Internationales, Geneva, Switzerland, 1931-33; mem. of the Commission on Cuban Affairs, 1934; Oberlaender Trust fellow, 1936, Knight Order of Polonia Restituta. Mem. Am. Econ. Assn., Am. Assn. Univ. Profs. Mem. of Unitarian Ch. Author: Exchange, Prices and Production in Hyper-Inflation, Germany (1920-23), 1930; The Abolition of Unemployment, 1932; Protective Tariffs, 1934; Golden Avalanche (with C. R. Whittlesey), 1939; Social Goals and Economic Institutions, 1942; (with Abba P. Lerner and others) Planning and Paying for Full Employment, 1946; also writer on agriculture, money, finance and internat. trade. Home: 214 Western Way, Princeton, N.J. Died Sep. 24, 1949.

GRAHAM, Horace French, governor; b. N.Y. City, Feb. 7, 1862; s. Samuel H. and Lucy F. (Swett) G.; prep. edn. Craftsbury (Vt.) Acad.; LL.B. cum laude, Columbia Law Sch., 1888 (also course in polit. sci.); unmarried. Practiced at Craftsbury; state's atty., Orleans County, Vt., 1898-1902; mem. Vt. Ho. of Rep., 1892 and 1900; Rep. presdl. elector, 1900; auditor of accounts for Vt., 1902-17; gov. of Vt., 1917-19. Home: Craftsbury, Vt. Address: Montpelier, Vermont. Died Nov. 23, 1941.

GRAHAM, James M., congressman; b. Ireland, Apr. 14, 1852; s. Hugh and Sarah (McMahon) G.; came to America, 1868; ed. Northern Normal U., Valparaiso, Ind.; m. Kate Wallace, Aug. 15, 1876. Admitted to bar, 1885, and since in practice at Springfield, Ill.; asso. in practice with Gen. John M. Palmer and Hon. William E. Shutt, as Palmer, Shutt & Graham; since death of Gen. Palmer and Senator Shutt, mem. firm of Graham & Graham. Mem. Ill. Ho. of Rep., 1885; state's atty., Sangamon Co., 1892-6; mem. 61st to 63d Congresses (1909-15), 21st Ill. Dist.; Democrat. Roman Catholic. Home: 413 S. 7th St. Office: 216 S. 5th St., Springfield, Ill. Died Oct. 23, 1945

GRAHAM, Walter James, prof. English; b. Waldoboro, Me., Apr. 17, 1885, s. Rev. James and Emily (Cox) G.; A.B., Bates Coll., Lewiston, Me., 1911; A.M., Columbia, 1912, fellow, 1914-15, Ph.D., 1918; m. Mary Elizabeth Whiteford, Mar. 31, 1931; 1 dau., Jane Graham. Instr. English, Western Res. U., 1912-14, 1916-18, asst. prof. English, 1918-24, asso. prof., 1924-27; acting head of English dept., Adelbert Coll., same U., 1927-28; prof. English, U. of Ill., since 1928, head of dept., 1928-35; prof. of English, summers, U. of Tex., 1936, U. of Southern Calif., 1937. Mem. Modern Lang. Assn. America, Modern Humanities Research Assn., Am. Assn. Univ. Profs., Phi Beta Kappa, Sigma Delta Chi. Clubs: University, Urbana Golf and Country; Authors (London). Author: Notes for Young Writers, 1918; The Beginnings of English Literary Periodicals, 1926; English Literary Periodicals, 1930. Editor: The Double Falsehood (attributed to Shakespeare), 1921; Henry Esmond, 1926; The Tatler, Spectator and Their Followers, 1928; Poetry of Tennyson, 1930; Modern Reader's Browning, 1934; The Letters of Joseph Addison, 1941. Editor: Journal of English and Germanic Philology since 1942. Contbr. to Modern Philology, Philol. Quarterly, Modern Lang. Notes, etc. Home: 1208 W. California St., Urbana, Illinois. Died Sep. 21, 1944.

GRAMMER, Carl Eckhardt, clergyman; b. Smyrna, Del., Nov. 11, 1858; s. Julius Eckhardt (D.D.) and Elizabeth Anne (Sparrow) G.; A.B., Johns Hopkins University, 1880; grad. P.E. Theol. Sem. in Va., 1884; S.T.D., Trinity Coll., Conn., 1895; m. Mary W. Page, July 3, 1889; children—Mrs. Elizabeth Torrey, Mary Page, Mrs. Dorothy Croyder. Deacon, 1884, priest, 1885, P.E. Ch.; rector Hancock, Md., 1884-87, Ch. of the Epiphany, Walnut Hills, Cincinnati, O., 1887; prof. ch. history, P.E. Theol. Sem. in Va., 1887-98; rector Christ Ch., Norfolk, Va., 1898-1905, St. Stephen's Ch., Phila., Pa., 1905-36, rector emeritus, 1937; deputy to Gen. Conv. P.E. Ch., 1895, 1901, 04, 07, 10, editor P.E. Review (now defunct), 1890-98; pres. Inter Church Fedn. of Philadelphia, 1918-20, president Evang. Ednl. Society; emeritus pres. Bd. of Sweet Briar Coll., Va. Member Phi Beta Kappa, Beta Theta Pi. Mason. Clubs: Old Guard (Summit, N.J.). Author of Bohlen lectures for 1928, entitled Things That Remain, etc., and of numerous pamphlets on religious and humanitarian topics, also mag. articles and a history of St. Stephen's Club. Contbg. editor Chronicle. Home: 6 Valley View Av., Summit, N.J. Died Mar. 17, 1944.

GRANT, Arthur Rogers, surgeon; b. Binghamton, N.Y., Nov. 21, 1871; s. Bradley M. and Cornelia (Rogers) G.; student Columbia, 1895-96; M.D., Univ. and Bellevue Hosp. Med. Coll. (New York U.), 1897; m. Lillian M. Clark, Sept. 1, 1897; 1 dau., Mrs. Priscilla Morehouse; m. 2d, Grace Allen, 1930. Practiced in Utica, N.Y., since 1897; surgeon in chief, Utica Homœ. Hosp., since 1906; gynecologist, Utica General Hospital, since 1906. Commissioned major Med. R.C., 1917, and assigned to Metropolitan Base Hosp. Unit No. 48, in France, Jan. 1918. Fellow Am. Coll. Surgeons; mem. Am. Inst. Homœopathy, N.Y., Homœopathy, N.Y., Homœ. Soc., etc. Republican. Presbyterian. Mason. Author of numerous papers read before med. socs. Clubs: Ft. Schuyler, Yahnundasis Golf. Home: 321 Genesee St., Utica, N.Y. Died Nov. 6, 1945.

GRANT, Elihu, college prof.; b. Stevensville, Bradford County, Pa., July 12, 1873; s. William Thomas and Amanda Lewis (Bird) G.; des. Matthew and Priscilla Gray Grant of Boston (1630), Windsor (1635); A.B., Boston U., 1898, A.M., 1900, Ph.D., 1906, S.T.B., 1907; m. Almy Chase, June 6, 1899; 1 dau., Rachel (Mrs. John L. Powell). Engaged in business in Boston, Mass., 1889-94; student pastor, Wilmington, Mass., 1894-98, Revere, 1898-1901; ordained M.E. ministry, 1900; supt. American Friends' schs., Ram Allah Jerusalem, 1901-04; pastor E. Saugus, Mass., 1904-07; asso. prof., later prof., Bibl. lit., Smith Coll., 1907-17; prof. Bibl. lit., Haverford (Pa.) Coll., 1917-38, now emeritus, dir. Grad. School, 1923-27; associated with Tell en Nasbeh Archæol. expdn., Palestine, 1927; dir. Am. excavations, Ain Shems, Palestine, 1928-33. Pres. Am. Friends of the Arabs; chmn. Palestine Relief Commn. Mem. Am. Oriental Soc., Soc. Biblical Lit. and Exegesis (pres. 1935), Phi Beta Kappa, Theta Delta Chi. Republican. Mem. Soc. of Friends. Club: Oriental (Phila.). Author: The Peasantry of Palestine, The Life, Manners and Customs of the Village, 1907; The Orient in Bible Times, 1920; The People of Palestine, 1921; Beth Shemesh Progress of the Haverford Archæological Expedition, 1929; Ain Shems Excavations, I, II, 1931, 32; Rumeileh, 1934; Ain Shems IV (with G. E. Wright), 1938, V, 1939; Sunlight—A Tribute, 1935; Palestine Today, 1938; Palestine, Our Holy Land, 1940. Co-Author: The Bible as Literature, 1914. Editor and contbr. Haverford Symposium on Archæology and the Bible, 1938. Home: Stamford, Conn. Died Nov. 2, 1942; buried at Haverford, Pa.

GRANT, Heber J.; b. Salt Lake City, Utah, Nov. 22, 1856; s. Jedediah M. and Rachel R. (Ivins) G.; ed. pvt. schs. and Deseret U. (now U. of Utah); m. Lucy Stringham, Nov. 1, 1877; m. 2d, Augusta Winters, May 26, 1884; m. 3d, Emily Wells, May 27, 1884. Ins. business on own account and as pres. Heber J. Grant & Co. since 1876, organized Utah Home Fire Ins. Co., pres. same; pres. Zion's Coöperative Mercantile Instn., Utah-Ida. Sugar Co., Zion's Savings Bank & Trust Co., Utah State Nat. Bank, Beneficial Life Ins. Co., Consol. Wagon & Machine Co.; dir. U.P. Ry. Co. Formerly mem. City Council of Salt Lake City and upper house of Utah territorial legislature. Mem. Latter Day Saints; elected mem. Council of Twelve, 1882, pres. 1916; filled ch. missions in Japan, 1901-03; presided over European mission, 1904-06; elected to First Presidency, Nov. 23, 1918; served long as pres. Prohibition and Betterment League. Home: 201 Eighth Av. Office: 47 E. South Temple St., Salt Lake City, Utah. Died May 14, 1945.

GRANT, James Benton, lawyer; b. Denver, Colo., May 6, 1888; s. James Benton and Mary Matteson (Goodell) G.; Phillips Andover Acad., 1905; B.A., Yale, 1909; LL.B., Harvard, 1912; m. Mary Urquhart Brooke, Apr. 18, 1914 (dec.); children—Mary Urquhart, James Benton; m. 2d, Carolan Alton Hayward, July 16, 1943. Admitted to N.Y. and Colo. bars, 1913; law clerk Masten and Nichols, N.Y. City, 1912-13; asso. with Wm. V. Hodges, Denver, 1913-

15; partner law firm Lewis & Grant, Denver, since 1915; chmn. bd. Potash Co. of America since 1935, also of the Denver National Bank since 1945; vice pres. and general counsel American Crystal Sugar Co. since 1932; dir. Denver Dry Goods Co., Colo. Milling & Elevator Co. Dir. Boettcher Foundation, Bonfils Foundation. Served as capt., Air Service, 1918, Field Arty. Res. Corps, 1919-24. Mem. Am., Colo., Denver and N.Y. County bar assns. Episcopalian. Clubs: Denver, Country, Mile High, Cherry Hills (Denver); Yale (New York); Graduate (New Haven). Home: 3909 S. University Blvd. Office: First Nat. Bank Bldg., Denver, Colo. Died May 21, 1947.

GRANT, John Prescott, surgeon; b. New Glasgow, N.S., Can., Oct. 31, 1872; s. Donald Cameron and Mary (Fraser) G.; M.D., McGill U., Montreal, 1895; Kings Coll. Hosp., London, 2 years, 1899, 1900; house surg. Royal United Hosp., Bath, Eng., 1901; m. Edith G. Quirk, 1901. Came to U.S., 1902, naturalized, 1917. Chief of surg. clinic Cornell Med. Coll., 1907-12; instr. in operative and clin. surgery, Cornell U. Med. Coll., 1906-12; adj. prof. surgery, New York Polyclinic Med. Sch., and Hosp., 1912-14, clin. prof. surgery, 1914-17, prof. surgery, 1917-38, emeritus since 1938, pres. of faculty, 1924-26; dir. Dept. of Surgery, 2 yrs., cons. surgeon, 1938; surgeon to Polyclinic Hosp.; cons. surgeon N.Y. City Hosp., Midtown Hosp. (New York); dir. surgery Long Beach (N.Y.) Hosp.; cons. surg. Peoples Hosp. and Bronx Maternity Hosp. (New York). Fellow N.Y. Acad. Medicine, Nat. Soc. Advancement of Gastroenterology, Am. Coll. Surgeons; mem. Royal Coll. Surgeons, A.M.A., Gastro-enterol. Soc. of New York, Alpha Mu Pi Omega. Republican. Presbyn. Clubs: Lotus (New York); Yacht (Wayne, Me.). Author of surg. sect. in Dr. Samuel Weiss' textbook, Diseases of the Stomach, Liver and Pancreas, 1935. Home: "Sunnycroft," Wayne, Me.; (winter) 2901 Columbus Blvd., Coral Gables, Fla. Office: 27 W. 55th St., New York. Died May 27, 1946; buried in Woodlawn Cemetery, Coral Gables, Fla.

GRANT, Joseph Donohoe, merchant; b. San Francisco, Calif., Mar. 28, 1858; s. Adam and Emma F. (Gummer) G.; U. of Calif., 1876-79; m. Edith M. Macleay, June 23, 1897. President of the Grant Company; dir. Bank of California, North Am. Investment Corp., Norwalk Oil Co. V.p. Save-the-Redwoods League; life trustee Stanford U., Calif. Acad. Sciences. Mem. Society of Calif. Pioneers. Republican. Clubs: Pacific Union, Bohemian, Burlingame Country, Olympic (San Francisco); Union (New York); St. James (London, Eng.). Home: 2200 Broadway. Office: 114 Sansome St., San Francisco, Calif. Died Feb. 9, 1942.

GRANT, Robert John, mining engr.; b. Pictou County, N.S., Nov. 12, 1862; s. Peter J. and Christy Ellen G.; ed. pub. schs., N.S.; Boston Evening High Sch.; m. Leslie Hayden, June 14, 1894. Mining, Colo. and Ariz., 1889-1902, in Mexico, 1903, Australia, 1904-05; mine engr. and mgr. since 1906; supt. U.S. Mint, Denver, 1921-23; dir. of Mint, Washington, D.C., 1923-33; adviser Central Mint, Shanghai, China, since 1933. Executive mgr. U.S. Food Administration for Colo., 1917-19. Republican. Presbyterian. Mem. Am. Inst. Mining and Metall. Engrs. Clubs: Denver Country; American, Columbia Country (Shanghai). Address: 832 Equitable Bldg., Denver, Colo. Died Nov. 24, 1949.

GRANVILLE, William Anthony, insurance exec.; b. White Rock, Minn., Dec. 16, 1863; s. T. Pearson and Hannah (Olson) G.; Gustavus Adolphus Coll.; Ph.B., Sheffield Sci. (Yale), 1893; Ph.D., Yale, 1897; LL.D., Lafayette Coll., 1911, Muhlenberg Coll., 1921; m. Ida Irvin, July 11, 1888; children—Irene (Mrs. S. F. Lehman), Rachel, Leone (dec.). Instr. mathematics, Yale, 1895-1909; pres. Gettysburg (Pa.) Coll., 1910-23; pres. of Am. Fedn. of Luth. Brotherhoods, 1925-29; vice-pres. Washington Nat. Insurance Co. Has designed various devices for use of math. students. Mem. Am. Math. Soc., A.A.A.S., Sigma Xi, Delta Phi, Am. Soc. Swedish Engrs., Insurance Economics Soc. America; fellow Casualty Actuarial Soc. America. Author: Differential and Integral Calculus, 1905; Plane Trigonometry, 1909; Spherical Trigonometry, 1909; Logarithmic Tables, 1909; Elementary Analysis (with P. F. Smith), 1910; The Fourth Dimension and the Bible, 1922; also several accident and health ins. manuals. Home: 513 Aldine Av., Chicago Office: 610 Church St., Evanston, Ill. Died Feb. 4, 1943; buried in Evergreen Cemetery, New Haven, Conn.

GRASSELLI, Thomas Saxton (gräs'sĕl-lī), mfr.; b. Cleveland, O., Nov. 14, 1874; s. Caesar A. and Johanna (Ireland) G.; ed. Mt. Saint Mary's Coll., Emmitsburg, Md.; m. Emilie Smith, May 29, 1899; children—Caesar A., II, Thomas Fries, Harry Williams. Engaged in chem. mfg. since 1893; pres. The Grasselli Chemical Co., 1916-36, when co. became div. of E. I. du Pont de Nemours & Co., v.p. and dir. latter co.; retired as mem. exec. com. Nov. 1939. Captain 1st Ohio Vol. Cav., Spanish-Am. War, 1898, later capt. q.m. dept. Mem. Ohio Soc. of New York, Cleveland Chamber Commerce. Republican. Catholic. Clubs: Union, Chagrin Valley Hunt, Kirtland Country (Cleveland); Wilmington (Del.) Club; Chemists (New York). Home: 2775 S. Park Blvd., Shaker Heights, Cleveland, O. Died Aug. 22, 1942.

GRASSHAM, Charles C., lawyer, corp. exec.; b Salem, Ky., Mar. 20, 1871; s. Montgomery and Martha Elizabeth (Mahan) G.; ed. McCully and Kemp Sch., Madisonville, Ky., and Nat. Normal U., Lebanon, O.; m. Corrie Bush, Aug. 19, 1896; children—Roscoe Bush (dec.), Pauline Bush. Teacher, pub. schs., 1886-91; admitted to Ky. bar, 1891, later to practice in U.S. dist. cts. of Ky. and Ind. in U.S. Circuit Court of Appeals (6th Circuit), and before Supreme Court of U.S., 1915; began practice at Smithland, Ky., gen. counsel Ayer & Lord Tie Co., mfrs. and preservers of wood, ry. ties and bridge timbers, now The Wood Preserving Corp., and Koppers Co., since 1894, gen. mgr., 1916-20; commd. spl. judge, by gov. of Ky., and chief justice of Ky. Court of Appeals; first appellate dist. judge of Special Court of Appeals of Kentucky to try judges' pension case, 1940; vice president and general manager Mineral Ridge Fluorspar Company, Salem, Ky., producer of Fluorspar. Dem. presdl. elector, 1st Ky. Dist., 1904. Active in Woodrow Wilson campaign for pres. of U.S., 1912; served as mem. Dem. Finance Com. of McCracken County, Ky.; mem. advisory board representing local draft board No. 109, of McCracken County, Ky.; mem. Nat. Reemployment Com. for McCracken County. Was aide de camp, rank of col., staff of Gov. J. C. W. Beckham. Del. from Ky. to Conservation Congress, St. Paul, Minn., to Rivers and Harbors Congress, Washington, D.C. Mem. Am. Bar Assn., Ky. State Bar Assn. (v.p.), Am. Law Inst., Am. Judicature Soc. Presbyterian. Clubs: Paducah (Ky.) Country; Forest Hills Country (Paducah). Home: 105 Fountain Av. Office: Citizens Savings Bank Bldg., Paducah, Ky. Died May 25, 1945.

GRATKE, Charles (Edward) (grăt'kē), newspaperman; b. Astoria, Ore., Aug. 11, 1901; s. John Edward and Fredda (Reinhart) G.; student, U. of Ore., 1919-21; m. Elisabeth James Whitehouse, Aug. 28, 1922. Editorial staff Astoria (Ore.) Evening Budget, Oregon City Enterprise, Portland Oregonian, Detroit News, 1920-26; with Christian Science Monitor since 1927, New York staff, 1927-29, asst. to exec. editor, 1929-32, Berlin corr., 1932-33, European editorial mgr., London, 1933-34, gen. news editor, 1934-37, foreign editor since 1937. Mem. Sigma Delta Chi. Mason. Clubs: Nat. Press (Washington, D.C.), University (Boston). Home: 456 Beacon St. Office: 1 Norway St., Boston 15, Mass. Died July 15, 1949.

GRAUPNER, Adolphus Earhart (grōp'nēr), lawyer; b. Clinton, Ia., Feb. 3, 1875; s. Louis Carl and Mazilpha Josephine (Earhart) G.; prep. edn., Boys' High Sch., San Francisco; LL.B., U. of Calif., 1897; m. Elise Wenzelburger, Apr. 22, 1903; children—Adolphus Earhart, Eleanor Louise. Admitted to Calif. bar, 1897, and began practice at San Francisco; asst. city atty., San Francisco, 1908-13; judge Superior Court, Calif., 1913-15; pvt. practice, 1916-17; gen. counsel Calif. Industrial Accident Commn., 1919-23; mem. U.S. Bd. of Tax Appeals, Washington, D.C., 1924-26; member faculty of Hastings College of Law, Univ. of Calif., 1931-40. Member firm of Graupner, Janin & Haven, San Francisco, Calif. Served in U.S. Army, May 8, 1917-May 5, 1919; capt. 364th Inf., 91st Div.; wounded in action at battle of Meuse-Argonne, and cited for courage and efficient leadership in face of enemy. Awarded Order of the Silver Star for Valor and Order of the Purple Heart. Mem. Am., Calif. and San Francisco bar assn., Phi Alpha Delta, Am. Legion. Republican. Unitarian. Mason. Home: 209 Walnut St. Office: 1104 Mills Tower, San Francisco, Calif. Died Sept. 19, 1947.

GRAVATT, William Loyall (grá-văt'), bishop; b. Port Royal, Va., Dec. 15, 1858; s. Dr. John James and Mary Eliza (Smith) G.; ed. Blacksburg Mil. Coll.; grad. Va. Theol. Sem., 1884; D.D., Washington and Lee U., 1904, U. of the South, 1907; m. Sidney S. Peyton, Oct. 13, 1887; children—Thomas Peyton (dec.), William Loyall, Anne Cary, Mary Elizabeth. Deacon, 1884, priest, 1885, P.E. Ch.; asst. rector St. Paul's, Richmond, Va., 1885-87; rector St. Peter's Norfolk, Va., 1887-93, Zion Ch., Charles Town, W.Va., 1893-99; elected, July 26, 1899, consecrated, Nov. 10, 1899, coadjutor bishop of W.Va., and bishop of W.Va., 1916. Home: 1583 Virginia St., Charleston, W.Va. Died Feb. 14, 1942.

GRAVE, Caswell, biologist; b. Monrovia, Ind., Jan. 24, 1870; s. Thomas C. and Anna (Hubbard) G.; B.S., Earlham Coll., Richmond, Ind., 1895; awarded LL.D. from same college, 1928; scholar and fellow and Adam T. Bruce fellow, Johns Hopkins Univ., 1898-1901, Ph.D., 1899; m. Josephine Grave, Sept. 24, 1896; 1 son, Thomas Brooks. Temporary asst., U.S. Fish Commn., 1899-1900; asst. in zoölogy, 1901-02, asso., 1902-06, asso. prof., Johns Hopkins; Rebstock prof. zoölogy and head dept., Washington U., 1919-40, emeritus prof. of zoölogy since 1940. Dir. U.S. Fisheries Lab., Beaufort, N.C., 1902-06; shellfish commr., Md., 1906-12; instr. in charge course in invertebrate zoölogy, Marine Biol. Lab., Woods Hole, Mass., 1912-19. Capt. Chem. Warfare Service, U.S. Army, 1918-19. Fellow A.A.A.S. (ex-v.p. sect. F); mem. Am. Soc. Zoologists (sec.-treas. 1913-18; v.p. 1920; pres. 1928), Am. Soc. Naturalists, Phi Beta Kappa, Sigma Xi. Trustee Marine Biol. Lab., 1936-40, emeritus trustee since 1940; mem. Bd. Nat. Research Fellowship in the Biol. Sciences, 1935-38. Club: University (Winter Pk.). Author scientific papers. Home: Winter Park, Fla. Died Jan. 8, 1944.

GRAVES, Bibb, ex-gov.; b. Hope Hull, Ala., Apr. 1, 1873; s. David and Martha (Bibb) G.; B.C.E., U. of Ala., 1893; LL.B., Yale, 1896; m. Dixie Bibb, Oct. 10, 1900. Admitted to Ala. bar, 1897, and began practice at Montgomery. Mem. Ala. Ho. of Rep., 1898-99, 1900-01; city atty., Montgomery, 1901-02; chmn. Ala. State Dem. Exec. Com., 1914-18; gov. of Ala., terms 1927-31, and 1935-39. Capt. Ala. Nat. Guard, 1897-98; maj., 1898-1905; adj. gen. Ala., 1907-11; lt. col. 1st Ala. Cav., 1916, col., 1917; served as col. 117th F.A., U.S. Army, 1917-19. Trustee Bob Jones Coll. Address. Montgomery, Ala. Died Mar. 14, 1942.

GRAVES, Charles, clergyman; b. Earith, Huntingdonshire, Eng., Sept. 23, 1868; s. Henry and Elizabeth (Wilkins) G.; ed. pub. schs., Eng., and Meadville (Pa.) Theol. Sch.; m. Annie Louise Fish, 1895; children—Robert Collyer, Elizabeth Porter. Ordained Unitarian ministry, 1894; pastor Anamosa, Ia., 1893-95, Humboldt, Ia., 1895-98, Littleton, N.H., 1898-1901, Barneveld, N.Y., 1901-07, Passaic, N.J., 1907-11, Albany, N.Y., 1911-18, 1st Unitarian Congl. Ch., Hartford, Conn., 1918-41, now minister emeritus. Chaplain N.Y. Ho. of Assembly, 1917-18; mem. Sch. Board, Passaic, N.J., 1910-11; on editorial staff Knickerbocker Press, Albany, N.Y., 1912-14; v.p. Am. Unitarian Assn., 1933-36. Club: City (Hartford). Author: A Century of Village Unitarianism, 1904. Contbr. articles "Unitarianism," "Civilization," "Future Life," etc., to Ency. Americana; also contbr. to Dictionary of Am. Biography. Apptd. by Centenary Com. of Am. Unitarian Assn. of Boston, to write a history of the origin and development of the Am. Unitarian Assn. Apptd. pub. service counselor to radio stations WDRC and W65H. Home: 194 Garden St., Wethersfield, Conn. Died May 11, 1948.

GRAVES, George Keene, merchant; b. Lexington, Ky., Nov. 7, 1865; s. George W. and Mary J. (Keene) G.; ed. Ky. State Agrl. and Mech. Coll., 1879-83; m. Kate Lewis Clark, Nov. 30, 1899; children—George Keene, Joseph C., Katherine Lewis. A founder, now v.p. Graves, Cox & Co.; a founder Indian Refining Co., Fayette Home Telephone Co., Ky. Joint Stock Land Bank (dir.); v.p. Security Trust Co.; dir. Ky. Union Land Co., Lexington Cemetery Co. Dep. food adminstr. Fayette County, World War; formerly mem. Bd. of Edn., Lexington; ex-pres. Good Samaritan Hosp. Mem. Soc. Colonial Wars, Kentucky Soc. of S.R., Huguenot Soc. S. C., S.C.V. Democrat. Episcopalian. Clubs: Rotary (hon.), Lexington Country. Home: 248 S. Ashland Av. Office: 122 W. Main St., Lexington, Ky. Died Mar. 18, 1943.

GRAVES, Jay P.; b. Plymouth, Ill., June 27, 1859; s. John J. and Orilla L. (Berry) G.; ed. Carthage (Ill.) Coll.; hon. LL.D., Whitworth Coll., Spokane, 1940; m. Amanda Cox, 1879; 1 son, Clyde M.; m. 2d, Alice Hardin Towne, July 6, 1921. Settled at Spokane, Wash., 1887; actively engaged for many years in copper mining and smelting and railroad building. Pres. Columbia Mines Corp., Spokane-Idaho Mining Co. Trustee Whitworth Coll. Republican. Presbyterian. Clubs: Spokane City, University. Address: The Huntington, Pasadena, Calif. Died April 27, 1948.

GRAVES, Lulu Grace, cons. dietitian; b. Fairbury, Neb.; d. Warren Jacob and Elizabeth (Babcock) Graves; student Neb. State Normal Sch., 1894-96, U. of Chicago, 1906-09; unmarried. Teacher, primary grades, Fairbury and Plymouth, Neb., 1896-1906; asso. prof. home economics, Ia. State Coll., 1909-10; head dietitian, Michael Reese Hosp., Chicago, 1911-14, Lakeside Hosp., Cleveland, 1914-18; prof. home economics, Cornell U., 1918-21; head dietitian, Mt. Sinai Hosp., N.Y. City, 1921-24; cons. dietitian, N.Y. City, 1924-39. Advisory editor Practical Home Economics. Member American Dietetic Association (organizer, president 3 years; now honorary president), Am. Hospital Assn. (chmn. dietetics section 4 yrs.), Am. Home Econ. Assn., N.Y. Dietetic Assn., N.Y. Home Economics Assn., Calif. Home Economics Assn., Calif. Dietetic Assn. Presbyterian. Co-Author: Dictionary of Food and Nutrition, 1938. Author: Modern Dietetics, 1917; Foods in Health and Disease, 1932. Contributor to Careers for Women, 1928, 1934; consultant in nutrition, kitchen plans and equipment. Home: 2605 Haste St., Berkeley, Calif. Died July 31, 1949; buried, Fairbury, Neb.

GRAVES, Mark, tax commr.; b. Willing N.Y., Dec. 29, 1877; s. Marlin and Susan E. (Beaver) G.; student Buffalo Law Sch., 1900-01; LL.D., Syracuse U., 1933; LL.D., Union Coll., 1937; m. Clara Belle Gale, Oct. 7, 1903; children—Mildred, Evelyn, Eleanore. Began as teacher; admitted to N.Y. bar, 1901; in practice, 1901-07; with N.Y. State Govt. since 1907, serving successively as examiner of municipal accounts in bureau of comptroller's office, dir. same, counsel to comptroller, dir. income tax bureau, research dir. bd. of estimate and control, tax commr., budget dir. and since 1933 as commr. of taxation and finance and pres. tax commn. Dir. Albany City and County Savings Bank; mem. Council of State Govts. (former v.p., mem. planning bd.), Interstate Commn. on Conflicting Taxation, Nat. Tax Assn. (ex-pres.); mem. State Planning Council; advisory mem. Joint Legislative Com. on Interstate Cooperation. Dir. Albany Y.M.C.A., Albany Symphony Orchestra. Mem. N.Y. State Bar Assn. Democrat. Methodist. Mason, Knight of Pythias. Clubs: University, Rotary (ex-pres.), Ft. Orange, Albany Country (trustee); Houvenkopf Country (Suffern). Contbr. articles on pub. finance to mags. Home: 152 S. Allen St. Office: State Office Bldg., Albany, N.Y. Died June 1, 1942.

GRAVES, William Lucius, prof. English; b. Davenport, Ia., Apr. 4, 1872; s. Lucius Velorus and Adaline

(Bowman) G.; A.B., Ohio State U., 1893, A.M., 1897; m. Anise Colburn, Mar. 1, 1941. Instr. in high sch., Coshocton, O., 1894-95; fellow and asst. in English lang. and rhetoric, Ohio State U., 1916, asst. prof. rhetoric, 1896-1904, asst. prof. English, 1904-08, associate professor, 1908-12, professor, 1912; now professor emeritus. Member Modern Language Association, American Association Univ. Profs., National Council Teachers of English, English-Speaking Union, Beta Theta Pi, Phi Beta Kappa, Alpha Sigma Chi. Republican. Methodist. Clubs: University, Kit-Kat (Columbus); Faculty (Ohio State U.). Editor and compiler: Prose Specimens (with E. L. Beck, C. S. Duncan), 1913; Prose Models (with E. L. Beck), 1928; Models of Description and Narration (with E. L. Beck), 1928. Contbr. verse to periodicals; contbr. weekly column, "The Idler's Chronicle and Comment," to Ohio State Univ. Lantern since 1900. Home: 380 Alden Av., Columbus, O.* Died Sep. 7, 1943.

GRAY, Baron De Kalb, clergyman; b. Waynesboro, Miss., June 18, 1855; s. Maj. John L. and Caroline (Salter) G.; A.M., Miss. Coll., Clinton, 1878; grad. Southern Bapt. Theol. Sem., Louisville, 1883; D.D., Miss. Coll., 1890; LL.D., 1904; LL.D., Baylor U., 1920; m. Alma Ratliff, Dec. 9, 1884; children—Carol, Mary Ratliff, Baron De Kalb. Licensed, Bapt. ministry, 1873, ordained, 1878; pastor Mound Bluff, New Hope, Miss., 1878-79, Midway, Ky., 1879-80, Buffalo Lick, Ky., 1881-82, East Ch., Louisville, 1882-84, Clinton, Miss., 1884-87, Hazelhurst, Miss., 1888-93, First Ch., Birmingham, Ala., 1893-1901; pres. Georgetown (Ky) Coll., 1901-03; corr. sec. Home Mission Bd., Southern Baptist Conv., 1903-28; retired as exec. sec. emeritus. Trustee Miss. Coll. 7 yrs.; mem. 1893-1901, pres. 1898-1901, bd. trustees Howard Coll., East Lake, Ala.; chmn. com. on Cecil Rhodes Scholarships for Ky., 1902-03. Home: 614 N. Main St., College Park, Ga. Died Nov. 25, 1946.

GRAY, Campbell, bishop; b. Bolivar, Tenn., Jan. 6, 1879; s. William Crane (D.D.) and Fannie Campbell (Bowers) G.; father 1st bishop of Southern Fla.; B.A., U. of the South, Sewanee, Tenn., 1901, M.A., 1902; student in theology, same univ., 1901-02, D.D., 1926; grad. Gen. Theol. Sem., 1904, S.T.D., 1926; D.D., Nashotah, 1925; m. Virginia Neil Morgan, Nov. 1, 1905; children—William Crane, Virginia Marshall, Francis Campbell, Mary Morgan, Joseph Alberti. Deacon, 1904, priest, 1905, P.E. Ch.; missionary in Fla., 1904-14; vicar St. Augustine's Ch., Rhinelander, Wis., 1914-22; rector St. Paul's Church, Peoria, Ill., 1922-25; exam. chaplain Diocese of Quincy, Ill., 1922-25; elected bishop coadjutor of Diocese of Northern Ind., Jan. 21, 1925, but on account of death of Bishop John Hazen White did not become coadjutor; consecrated bishop of Diocese of Northern Ind., May 1, 1925. Selected St. Paul's Ch., Mishawaka, Ind., as pro-cathedral (temp.). Mem. Gen. Conv., P.E. Ch., 1910-43; trustee U. of the South, 1911-13; mem. Cathedral Chapter of Southern Fla., 1911-14; mem. Diocesan Bd. of Missions, 1914-15, Standing Com., 1915-22, Diocesan Bd. of Religious Edn., 1916-22, Provincial Synod, 1918-42; pres. board trustees Howe Mil. Sch.; trustee Nashotah (Wis.) House; president Synod of Prov. of Mid-west since 1926; the Am. mem. Doctrinal Commn. of Anglican and Orthodox Chs. as authorized by Lambeth Conf., 1930. Democrat. Home: 710 Lincoln Way E., Mishawaka, Ind. Died May 16, 1944.

GRAY, Chester Earl; b. Columbus Junction, Ia., May 16, 1881; s. James Edward and Margaret Jane (Dawdy) G.; B.S., Ia. State Coll., 1901, M.S., 1924; m. Rachel L. Mosier, Apr. 25, 1905; children—Catherine Jane, Annabel. Asst. in agrl. chemistry, Ia. State Coll., 1901-02; chemist Continental Creamery Co., Topeka, Kan., 1902-03, Beatrice (Neb.) Creamery Co., 1904-05; chemist in charge Research Lab., Dairy Div. Bur. of Animal Industry U.S. Dept. Agr., 1905-08; asst. gen. mgr. Central Creamery Co. (now Golden State Co., Ltd.), Eureka, Calif., 1908-15; gen. mgr. Calif. Central Creameries (now Golden State Co., Ltd.), San Francisco, 1915, pres., 1915-33; chmn. bd. Golden State Co., Ltd., 1931-37, now dir. Mem. Calif. State Board of Agr., 1929-40; mem. com. advisory to dir. Giannini Foundation of Agrl. Economics, University of California; dir. Am. Dry Milk Institute (chairman board), California Dairy Council, Pacific Slope Dairy Show. Inventor and patentee processes and apparatus for desiccating and for mfg. of products from milk and cream. Republican. Mem. Am. Chem. Soc., Am. Dairy Science Assn., A.A.A.S. Clubs: Commonwealth, Commerical (San Francisco); Athens Athletic (Oakland); Univ. of Calif. Club (Berkeley). Author of bulls. pub. by Dept. of Agr., Dry Milk Inst., to encourage outstanding contbns. and meritorious achievements in dry milk production, distribution and research established the C. E. Gray Award in his honor, Apr. 1943. Home: 6263 Chabot Rd., Oakland, Calif. Office: 425 Battery St., San Francisco, Calif. Died Sep. 19, 1944.

GRAY, Clifton Daggett, coll. pres.; b. Somerville, Mass., July 27, 1874; s. Jefferson Jenness and Alida Mazella (Daggett) G.; A.B., Harvard, 1897, A.M., 1898; B.D., Newton Theol. Instn., 1899; S.T.B., U. of Chicago, 1900, Ph.D., 1901; LL.D., U. of Me., 1922; L.H.D., Colgate, 1940; D.D., Bates Coll., 1947; research work in British Museum, London, Eng., 1900; m. Neva B. Ham, June 26, 1900 (died Sept. 12, 1946); children—Malcolm Jefferson, Paul Judson (dec.), Clifton Daggett. Ordained to ministry Baptist Church, 1899; pastor First Bapt. Church, Port Huron, Mich., 1901-05, Stoughton St. Ch., Boston, 1905-12; editor of The Standard, Chicago, Oct. 1912-Dec. 1919, and pres. and treas. Goodman & Dickerson Co., pubs. same; mng. editor of The Baptist, official weekly of Northern Bapt. Conv., Jan.-Apr. 1920; pres. Bates Coll. (Me.), May 1, 1920-Sept. 1, 1944, president emeritus since Sept. 1, 1944. Hon. sec. Bapt. World Alliance. Mem. Phi Beta Kappa, Phi Kappa Phi. Chevalier Legion of Honor (French). Republican. Trustee Newton Theol. Instn.; mem. many denom. bds. Club: University (Claremont, Calif.). Author: The Shamash Religious Texts, Youth on the March. Home: Ocean Park, Me. (summer), Claremont, Calif. (winter). Died Feb. 21, 1948; buried in Woodlawn Cemetery, Everett, Mass.

GRAY, Edward Winthrop, writer, pub., b. Jersey City, N.J., Aug. 18, 1870; s. Edward and Elizabeth (Beggs) G.; ed. pub. schs.; m. Altha R. Hay, 1898; children—Altha R., Julia B. (dec.), Elizabeth. Reporter New York Herald, 1894, New York World, 1894-96; owner and pub. Summit (N.J.) Herald, 1897-98; city editor and mng. editor, Newark Daily Advertiser, 1898-1902; pres. and gen. mgr. Newark Daily Advertiser Pub. Co., 1902-04; sec. to Gov. Edward C. Stokes, 1904-07; organizer, 1909, Commercial Casualty Ins. Co. of Newark. Mem. 64th and 65th Congresses (1915-19), 8th N.J. Dist.; candidate for Republican nomination for U.S. Senate on anti-prohibition platform, 1918-28. Appointed by Gov. Murphy comm. to investigate tenement house conditions, 1902; mem. Bd. Tenement House Supervision of N.J. 8 yrs.; see Rep. State Com. of N.J., 1908-13. Club: Newark Athletic (1st pres. and 1st hon. mem.). Home: 141 Wakeman Avenue. Office: 16 Park Place, Newark, N.J. Died June 10, 1942.

GRAY, George Herbert, consultant in architecture and city planning; b. Redwood City, Calif., Apr. 5, 1874; s. Rev. Edward Powers and Maria Louisa (Clark) G.; A.B., Johns Hopkins, 1895; study of architecture atelier Masquery (New York) with York & Sawyer (New York), atelier Laloux, Ecole des Beaux Arts (Paris), Delano & Aldrich (New York), 1896-1907; m. Mary Belknap, June 16, 1909. Engaged in practice of architecture as George H. Gray, Louisville, Ky., 1906-07; mem. firm Gray & Hawes, 1909-12, Gray & Wischmeyer, 1912-17; practiced as George H. Gray, New Haven, Conn., 1919-23, Gray & Lawrence, 1923-25; as George Herbert Gray, architect and city planner since 1925. Organized dept. of architecture, U. of Louisville, 1912, lecturer on history and theory of architecture, 1916-17; town planning consultant and architect to Berea Coll., 1914-23; head dept. of city planning, Columbia, 1920-23; lecturer on city planning, Dartmouth Coll., 1925-26. Pres. Prospect Homes, Inc. Major, U.S. Engrs. (inactive); comdg. officer 516th Engrs., 1918-19; comdg. officer A.E.F. Art Training Center, Bellevieu, Seine et Oise, France, 1919. Mem. Conn. Archtl. Examining Bd., 1933-40. Chmn. zoning commn. of New Haven, 1921-23; dir. Conn. State Planning Bd., 1934; planning consultant Nat. Research Planning Bd., 1934; city planning consultant to Housing Authority of New Haven, 1939-42; mem. engring. adv. com. Comm. State Defense Council, 1941-44. Fellow A.I.A. (life mem.; pres. Conn. chapter 1929-30; dir. N.E. region, 1931-34); mem. Soc. Planning Officials (charter), Am. Inst. of Planning, Internat. Fedn. Housing and Town Planning, Graduates Club Assn. of New Haven, Cream Hill Lake Assn. (West Cornwall). Mason (32°), Kiwanian. Author of treatise "Housing and Citizenship," a Study of Low-cost Housing (published June 1946). Contbr. numerous articles relating to planning and architecture to various publs. Home: 6 Prospect Ct., New Haven, Conn. Died Oct. 19, 1945; buried in Cave Hill Cemetery, Louisville.

GRAY, Jessie, educator; b. London, Eng., June 2, 1876; d. Alfred and Sarah Jane (Percy) Gray; came to U.S., 1881; grad. Phila. Normal Sch., 1896; student U. of Pa., 1922-24, Temple U., 1925-26, Columbia, 1928; hon. A.M., U. of Pa., 1935; unmarried. Teacher elementary sch., Phila., 1896-1914; training teacher Thaddeus Stevens practice dept., Phila., Normal Sch., since 1914. Mem. N.E.A., state dir., 1925, v.p., 1930-31, pres. 1933-34, 1st v.p., 1934-35, mem. legislative com., 1921-36, mem. tenure com., 1929-32; del. to World Fed. of Edn. at Edinburgh, 1925, Toronto, 1927, Dublin, 1933; mem. Pa. State Edn. Assn., pres. 1925-26, mem. legislative com., 1921-38, mem. welfare com., 1929-38, chmn. com. on management of teachers home; mem. Phila. Teachers Assn., pres. 1928-31, 34-35; mem. Women's Legislative Council of Pa., v.p., 1927-35, sec. 1935-44, v.p. 1945; mem. Women's Sesquicentennial com., chmn. First Brick House, High St., 1926; mem. Mayor Wilson's Constl. Celebration Com., 1938; mem. Gov. Earle's Com. to Supervise Civil Service Exam., 1937; sec. Women's Auxiliary Frankford Hosp. Mem. League of Women Voters (chairman education committee, 1935-38), Philadelphia Normal School Alumni (president 1927-31), Business and Professional Women's Club (chairman education committee 1937-38): recording sec., Phila. Diabetic Soc., 1944-45. Mem. Delta Kappa Gamma (pres. Alpha Chapter of Pa., 1938-43; chmn. nat. com. on retirement, 1938-42); mem. N.E.A. (life mem.), Pa. State Teachers Assn., Phila. Teachers Assn. Methodist. Clubs: Temple University Women's; Am. Rocky Mt. Alpine; Frankford Country (capt. hockey team). Contbr. articles to jours. Home: 1210 Filmore St., Philadelphia 24. Died May 29, 1948.

GRAY, John Henry, economist; b. Charleston, Ill., Mar. 11, 1859; s. James Cowan and Mary A. (Mitchell) G.; ed. full course and diploma, Ill. State Normal U.; A.B., Harvard, 1887; Ph.D., U. of Halle, 1892; studied also at Paris, Vienna and Berlin; m. Helen Rockwell Bliss, June 14, 1894 (died 1922); children—James Bliss (dec.), Evelyn (Mrs. George E. Talmage, Jr., dec.). Instr. polit. economy, Harvard, 1887-89; prof. polit. and social science, Northwestern U., 1892-1907; prof. economics, U. of Minn., 1907-20, Carlton Coll., 1920-25; chief analyst and examiner, Interstate Commerce Commn. Bur. of Valuation, 1917-19, examiner valuation, 1925-28; prof. and head dept. of economics, Grad. Sch. of Am. Univ., 1928-32. Prof. economics, Univ. of Calif., summer 1914. Chmn. World's Congress Auxiliary on Polit. Science, Chicago, 1893; chmn. municipal com. Civic Fedn. of Chicago, 1894-96; expert U.S. Dept. Labor, 1902-03, to investigate restrictions of output in Great Britain; represented U.S. Commr. of Labor at Internat. Coöperative Congress, Manchester, Eng., 1902; represented U.S. at Internat. Congress on Ins. of Laboring Men, Düsseldorf, Germany, 1902, and at Internat. Congress of Commerce and Industry, Ostend, Belgium, 1902; mem. Nat. Civic Federation Commn. on Municipal Ownership, 1905, and expert to commn. for Am. investigation; mem. exec. council dept. Nat. Civic Federation to investigate regulation of pub. service corps., 1911-14; sec. of the dept. and dir. of investigation. Published Commission Regulation, a compilation and analysis of all Am. statutes relating to regulation of public service corps. (1284 pp.), 1913; Urban Mortgages in U.S. since 1920 (with G. W. Terborgh), 1929; Regulation and Valuation of Public Utilities (with Jack Levin), 1933; also more than 100 articles in scientific journals; mem. Minnesota Efficiency and Economy Commission, 1914-15. Lt. col. U.S. Army and mem. bd. appraisers for all property commandeered for the army. Asso. editor Economic Bulletin, 1908-10, Journal of Accountancy, 1908-15. Specialist in pub. utilities and railroads. Pres. Am. Econ. Assn., 1913-14. Treas. People's Lobby since 1935. Has traveled most of the time since 1928 in Asia, Europe, Africa, the West Indies, South and Central America and the U.S. Clubs: Cosmos (Washington); University (hon. mem.; Evanston). Address: 1323 Jackson St. N.E., Washington, D.C. Died Apr. 4, 1946.

GREACEN, Edmund (grē'ā-sĕn), artist; b. N.Y. City, 1877; s. Thomas Edmund and Isabella (Wiggins) G.; A.B., New York U., 1897; studied Art Students League and Chase Sch. of Art, New York; m. Ethol Booth, 1904; children—Edmund, Nannette. Exhibited portraits and landscapes at Paris Salon, Nat. Acad., Pa. Acad. Fine Arts, Corcoran Gallery, etc.; represented in Butler Art Museum, Youngstown, O., Newark, N.J., Art Museum, etc. Organizer and pres. Grand Central Sch. of Art, New York. Awarded Salmagundi Shaw Prize, 1922; Nat. Arts Club prize and medal, 1923, 35. Served as pvt., 7th regt., N.G.N.Y.; Y.M.C.A. sec. in France, World War I; Nat. Academician; charter mem. Painters and Sculptors Gallery Assn. (New York); mem. Am. Water Color Soc. Clubs: Salmagundi, Zeta Psi, Nat. Arts (v.p.), Lotos. Address: 12 Gracie Sq., New York, N.Y. Died Oct. 4, 1949.

GREEN, Addison Loomis, lawyer; b. Westfield, Mass., Oct. 23, 1862; s. Thomas Jefferson and Alvira Eunice (Loomis) G.; A.B., Wesleyan U., 1885, (D.C.L.); m. Maud Ingersoll Bennett, 1890 (died 1901); children—Addison Bennett, Donald Ross, Mrs. David D. Milne, David Loomis; m. 2d, Gertrude Metcalf, 1911; children—Clarissa (Mrs. Fritz Hopf), Gertrude (Mrs. William C. Hammond, Jr.), Marshall. Admitted to Mass. bar, 1887, began practice at Holyoke. Mem. of the Judicature Commn. appointed, 1919, to investigate the judicature of the Commonwealth; chmn. Judicial Council of Mass., 1927-29. Member board trustees Wesleyan University; chairman board Am. School Prehistoric Research. Mem. Mass. Bar Assn. (pres. 1922), Psi Upsilon, Phi Beta Kappa. Republican. Episcopalian. Mason. Club: Union (Boston). Home: "Meadowview," Holyoke, Mass. Died June 24, 1942.

GREEN, Bert, cartoonist, author; b. Sutton, Surrey, Eng., Jan. 28, 1885; s. Francis William and Gertrude Eleanor (Scarman) G.; brought to U.S., 1887; ed. pub. schs. and privately tutored; student art schools, Pratt Inst. and Chase Art School; m. Catherine Porter, Mar. 25, 1908 (died Feb. 1, 1943); 1 son, Robert Barrington; m. 2d, Evelyn Virginia Betts, Jan. 8, 1944. Around the world before the mast, 1900-04; q.m., S.S. Arizonian, Am.-Hawaiian Line, 1904; successively lathe hand, E. W. Bliss Co., Brooklyn, N.Y., asst. electrician, Old Times Bldg., N.Y. City, with art depts. New York Herald, New York World, New York Sunday American, New York Journal, Atlanta Georgian, 1905-13; art mgr., Chicago Examiner, 1914-15; animated cartoonist, Hearst-Pathe, later Pathe News, 1915-23; in business for self, creator of industrial animated cartoons, 1923-26; creator of comic strip "Kids," Chicago Tribune, 1928; asso. with George Palmer Putnam, Inc., N.Y. City, 1926-30, with Hal Roach and Metro-Goldwyn-Mayer, Culver City, Calif., 1927; creator of U.S. Navy cartoons for the Vocafilm Corp., since 1943; creator of newspaper cartoon, Wise Guys, 1947. Authors agent, Myron Selznick, New York. Episcopalian. Club: Lotos (N.Y.). Author 230 humorous articles for Liberty Mag. and others, including: Love Letters of an Interior Decorator (1927-31); Diana's Diary (1932); Love Letters of a Prizefighter and a Hollywood Extra (1935); Free Air from a Taxi Pilot (1937-38); The Gold Rushers (1939); Susie, 1940; Bread Line, 1941. Diesel engr. auxiliary schooner on anti-submarine patrol Atlantic Theatre of Operations, U.S. Coast Guard Reserve, since 1942.

Home: 13 E. 34th St., New York, N.Y. Died Oct. 5, 1948.

GREEN, Fitzhugh, naval officer, author; b. St. Joseph, Mo., Aug. 16, 1888; s. Charles Edward and Isabelle Fitzhugh (Perryman) G.; grad. U.S. Naval Acad., 1909; M.Sc., George Washington U., 1913; grad. Naval War Coll., 1924; m. Natalie Wheeler Elliot, Nov. 27, 1916; children—Fitzhugh, Elisabeth Farnum, Richard Elliot; m. 2d, Margery Durant, Nov. 15, 1933. Commd. ensign, June 19, 1911; promoted through grades to comdr., Mar. 1927. Served 2 yrs. with Atlantic Fleet; duty Bur. of Ordnance, 1912-13; sent as engr. and physicist, 1913, to Arctic regions, with Donald B. MacMillan, in S.S. Erik, in search of Crocker Land and to explore unknown areas of Polar Sea, returning, 1916. Aide and flag lt. to Adm. Rogers in World War, in European waters; apptd. officer in charge proving and testing all ordnance material for the Navy, Mar. 1919, at Naval Proving Grounds, Indian Head, Md.; detailed as gunnery officer U.S.S. Texas, June 1921; was aide to pres. of Naval War Coll.; shifted to Naval Reserve, May 31, 1927; recommissioned in U.S. Navy, duty at Bureau of Ordnance, Navy Department, Washington, D.C., 1940, rank of lt. comdr.; transferred to staff of vice adm. Ghormley, comdg. South Pacific Area, May 1942; took part in preparation and execution of Guadalcanal Campaign. Commissioned Commander, U.S.N.R., July 19, 1942. Served on Staff of Comdr. South Pacific Area World War II. Became temporary technical film director for Richard Barthelmess, 1925; managing editor George Matthew Adams Newspaper Service, 1925-26; assistant to president Putnam Publishing Co., 1927. Fellow Am. Geog. Soc. Mem. Phi Lambda Epsilon, Phi Sigma Kappa. Democrat. Episcopalian. Clubs: Explorers', Army and Navy (New York and Washington); Racquet (Phila.); N.Y. Yacht, Knickerbocker, Dutch Treat (New York); Appawamis. Author: Arctic Duty, 1917; Clear the Decks, 1918; Won for the Fleet, 1921; The Mystery of Erik, 1923; ZR Wins, 1924; Midshipmen All, 1925; Fought for Annapolis, 1925; Our Naval Heritage, 1925; History of American Navy; Life of Robert E. Peary, 1926; I'll Never Move Again, 1926; Uncle Sam's Sailors, 1926; Hold 'em Navy, 1926; Anchor's Aweigh, 1927; Famous Sea Fights (with H. H. Frost), 1927; Bob Bartlett, Master Mariner, 1929; Martin Johnson, Lion Hunter, 1928; Dick Byrd, Air Explorer, 1928; The Film Finds its Tongue, 1929. Co-author with Chas. A. Lindbergh of "We," 1927; also collaborator with Rear Adm. Richard E. Byrd, Martin Johnson, etc. Address: Lambert Road, New Canaan, Conn. Died Dec. 2, 1947.

GREEN, George Rex, univ. prof.; b. Glen Hope, Pa., June 29, 1884; s. Abraham Keagy and Emma Jane (Rex) G.; student Dickinson Coll., 1904-05; A.B., U. of Mich., 1907-11; M.S., Pa. State Coll., 1915; student Cornell U., 1924, U. of Pa., 1927-29; m. Edith Newton, Apr. 16, 1913; children—George Rex, Betty Irene. Pub. sch. teacher, 1903-04; asst. state forester of Ohio, 1911-12; asst. prof. of forestry, Pa. State Coll., 1912-15, asso. prof. of dendrology and wood tech., 1915-21, professor of dendrology and nature study, 1921-24, prof. of nature edn., head of dept. and dir. of nature camp since 1924; chief wood inspector U.S. Naval Aircraft Factory, Phila., 1918-20. Fellow A.A.A.S.; mem. N.E.A. (life), Pa. State Edn. Assn. (life), Am. Assn. Univ. Profs., Am. Assn. Coll. Teachers, Am. Nature Study Soc. (past pres.), Nat. Council Supervisors Elementary Science, Nat. Assn. for Research in Science Teaching, Soc. Am. Foresters, Am. Ornithol. Union, Am. Nature Assn., Nat. Geog. Soc., Pa. Acad. Science, Nat. Soc. Coll. Teachers of Edn., Am. Science Teachers Assn., Acacia, Sigma Alpha Epsilon, Pi Gamma Mu, Xi Sigma Pi, Kappa Delta Pi, Phi Delta Kappa. Republican. Mason. Club: Rotary. Author: Survey of Nature, 1926; Trees of North America, Vol. I, The Conifers, 1933, Vol. II, The Broadleaves, 1934. Home: 215 Woodland Drive, State College, Pa. Died Oct. 31, 1947.

GREEN, Grafton, judge; b. Lebanon, Tenn., Aug. 25, 1872; s. Nathan, Jr. and Betty (McClain) G.; A.B., Cumberland U., Lebanon, 1891, LL.B., 1893; m. Pauline Dinges, Dec. 10, 1898. Practiced law at Nashville, Tenn., 1893-1910; justice Supreme Court of Tenn., terms, 1910-18, 1918-26, chief justice, terms, 1926-34, 1934-42, 1942-50. Democrat. Home: Lebanon, Tenn. Died Jan. 26, 1947.

GREEN, H. T. S., banker; b. Hong Kong, China, July 30, 1864; s. Thomas and Jane (Stewart) G.; ed. pvtly.; m. Winifred Rudge, Nov. 14, 1901. Began in London, Eng., with Hong Kong & Shanghai Banking Corp., later with San Francisco (Calif.) br., and with accounting dept. New York br., 1892-98; asst. mgr. London, Paris and Am. Bank, San Francisco, 1902-06. With Internat. Banking Corpn., mgr. Japan branch, 1906-08, China br., 1909-10, mgr. New York, 1910, became pres. and gen. mgr., 1912; became v.p. Nat. City Bank of N.Y., 1925; retired, 1931. Home: 520 E. 86th St. Office: 55 Wall St., New York. Died Apr. 29, 1942.

GREEN, Horace, author, publisher; b. N.Y. City, Oct. 13, 1885; s. George Walton and Harriet Brodhead (Atwater) G.; grad. Groton (Mass.) Sch., 1904; A.B., Harvard, 1908; student Harvard Law Sch.; m. Eleanor Rodman Townsend, June 4, 1915; children—Barbara, Alison, Georgina Walton, Eleanor Sheldon. On staff of the New York Evening Post, 1911-14; went to Europe as corr. for New York Evening Post at outbreak of World War; taken prisoner at the front, sent to interior of Germany; released and made his way back into Antwerp; present at bombardment and capture of city; returned to U.S., Jan. 1915; corr. for Post in France and the Balkans, 1915-16; editor U.S. Air Service Magazine, and treas. Air Service Pub. Co., Washington, D.C., 1919-21; asso. editor Leslie's Weekly, 1921-22; polit. editor The Forum, short periods; with Duffield & Co. (later Duffield & Green), pubs., 1923-34, pres., 1925-34. Commd. 1st lt. U.S. Air Service, Aug. 1917; capt. Aug. 1918; licensed pilot; maj. O.R.C. Clubs: Harvard, Century Assn. (New York City); Nat. Press, Overseas Writers (Washington, D.C.). Author: The Log of a Non-Combatant, 1915; The Life of Calvin Coolidge, 1924; General Grant's Last Stand (biography), 1936; Triumph (play), 1938. Edited The Contemporary Statesman Series. Home: Cow Lane, King's Point, Great Neck, L.I., N.Y. Died Nov. 14, 1943.

GREEN, John, ophthalmologist; b. Templeton, Mass., Aug. 2, 1873; s. John and Harriet Louisa (Jones) G.; A.B., Harvard, 1894; M.D., Washington U., 1898; m. Lucretia Hall Sturgeon, Oct. 29, 1902; children—Helen C. (Mrs. Leonard Lee Bacon), Harmon, John, Nathaniel Pope, Lucretia H. (Mrs. William C. Lindsley), Elizabeth. Engaged in practice as physician since 1899; specializing in ophthalmology since 1902; dir. St. Louis (Mo.) Mutual Life Ins. Co. Mem. bd. of edn., University City, Mo., 1910-20, mem. bd. of health, 1921-26. Sec. Joint Med. Council, an organization to change plan of adminstrn. and control of pub. hosp., in St. Louis, 1906-10. Pres. Am. Ophthalmological Soc., 1944; sec. Am. Bd. of Ophthalmology, 1933-43, chmn. 1944; chmn. sect. on ophthalmology A.M.A., 1936; vice-pres. Am. Acad. Ophthalmology and Otolaryngology, 1917-18; vice-pres. St. Louis Med. Soc., 1927; sec., later pres., Soc. of City Hosp. Alumni, 1904. Home: 243 Westgate Av., University City 5, Mo. Office: 3720 Washington Av., St. Louis 8. Died Apr. 7, 1949.

GREEN, John Edgar, Jr., lawyer; b. Selma, Ala., Apr. 19, 1880; s. John Edgar and Susan Morgan (Bridges) G.; A.B., Southwestern U., Georgetown, Tex., 1901; LL.B., U. of Tex., 1909; m. Anne Gentry Skinner, Apr. 29, 1914. Reporter on Houston (Tex.) Chronicle, 1901-03; reporter 1904-05, city editor, 1906-07, Houston Post; admitted to Tex. bar, 1908, and practiced in Houston; asst. criminal dist. atty., Galveston and Harris counties, Tex., 1910-12; U.S. atty., Southern Dist. of Tex., 1914-19; asst. gen. atty., Gulf Refining Co., Gulf Production Co., and Gulf Pipe Line Co., of Houston, Tex., 1919-28; general atty. Gulf Oil Corp. and its subsidiaries since 1929. Mem. Tex. Bar Assn., Harris County Bar Assn., Phi Delta Theta, Phi Delta Phi. Democrat. Clubs: Houston, Tejas, River Oaks, Houston Country. Home: 2970 Lazy Lane. Office: Gulf Bldg., Houston, Tex. Died Nov. 8, 1947.

GREEN, Marcellus, lawyer; b. Jackson, Miss., Aug. 12, 1851; s. Joshua and Elizabeth (Jarvis) G.; ed. Soule's Commercial Coll., 1868, U. of Va., 1872; m. Lucy Edelin Garner, Apr. 24, 1879; children—Garner Wynn, Lulah Edelin (Mrs. G. W. F. Rembert), Gertrude Elizabeth (Mrs. O. M. Turner), Elise Langdon (Mrs. Edwin L. Herring), Marcellus (dec.), Lewis Jarvis (dec.), Ada (Mrs. Alfred Harden Coon, dec.). Admitted to bar Supreme Court of Miss., 1874, Supreme Court of U.S., 1886; sec. to Gov. J. M. Stone, 1876; v.p. Jackson Fertilizer Co. Commr. from Miss. to Centennial of promulgation of Constitution at Phila., 1889; pres. commn. to build Colored Insane Annex to Insane Asylum, Jackson, Miss., 1890; pres. commn. to rebuild Hosp. for Insane, Jackson, after fire, 1892; trustee State Hosp. for Insane, 1884-94, State Blind Asylum, 1882-84. Mem. Standing Com. Diocese of Miss.; sr. warden St. Andrew's P.E. Church, Jackson; del. Diocese of Miss. to Gen. Conv. P.E. Ch., New Orleans, La., 1925; mem. Com. Revision Federal Equity Rules from 5th U.S. Circuit. Fellow Royal Soc. Arts (London); mem. Miss. Bar Assn., Am. Bar Assn. (v.p. for Miss.), Nat. Econ. League, etc. Trustee Jackson Pub. Schs. (pres. 1893-96). Mem. Ala., Fla., Ga., Miss., La., Southern Editors Assn., Biol. Univ. of Va. Alumni, Virginian Patriarch. Portrait installed by Law Dept. on U. of Miss. Contbr. Biographical Ency. Club: Rotary (hon. mem.). Address: 633 North State St., Jackson, Miss. Died June 3, 1949.

GREEN, Robert Gladding, prof. bacteriology; b. Wadena, Minn., Jan. 11, 1895; s. George Henry and Ella Augusta (Banta) G.; student Valparaiso (Ind.) U., 1914-16; A.B., U. of Minn., 1919, A.M., 1920, M.B., 1921, M.D., 1922; m. Beryl Bertha Sparks, Apr. 7, 1917 (died Apr. 23, 1941). Asst. in bacteriology, U. of Minn., 1918, instr., 1921, asst. prof., 1922-25, asso. prof., 1925-29, became prof. 1929, head dept. of bacteriology, Univ. of Minn. 1946-47. Served in Med. R.C., 1917, Students' Army Training Corps, 1918-19, World War I. Capt. and Med. Officer, Civil Air Patrol, Wing No. 71, Air Corps, Minnesota State Guard, 1942-43. Fellow N.Y. Zoöl. Soc.; mem. A.A.A.S., Soc. Am. Bacteriologists, Am. Assn. Pathologists and Bacteriologists, A.M.A., Society for Exptl. Biology and Medicine, Am. Soc. Mammalogists, Am. Assn. of Immunologists, American Legion, Sigma Xi, Alpha Omega Alpha. Republican. Episcopalian. Mason. Club: Minneapolis Athletic. Author of many scientific publs. and contbr. numerous tech. articles. Home: 3948 1st Av. S. Office: 223 Millard Hall, Dept. of Bacteriology, University of Minnesota, Minneapolis. Died Sept. 6, 1947.

GREEN, Roy Monroe, coll. pres.; b. Carrollton, Mo., Mar. 12, 1889; s. Calvin and Sophia Ann (Tripp) G.; B.S., University of Mo., 1914; M.S., Kan. State College, 1923, D.Sc., 1941; grad. student U. of Chicago, 1929-30; m. Mary Ethel Miller, May 4, 1915; children—Roy Raymond, Dorothy Mae, Mary Frances, Russell Lee. Science assistant United States Department of Agriculture, 1914; instructor in farm management, U. of Mo., 1915-16; asst. prof., 1915-20; asso. prof. in agr. econ., Kan. State Coll., 1920-25, prof., 1925-33; v.p. Prodn. Credit Corp., Wichita, Kan., 1934-35; chief div. agr. finance, Dept. of Agr., 1936-38; exec. officer Federal Crop Ins. Corp., Dept. of Agr., 1938; gen. agent, Farm Credit Adminstrn., Wichita, Kan., 1938-39; dep. gov. of Land Bank Commr., Farm Credit Adminstrn., 1939-40; pres. Colo. Agricultural and Mechanical Coll. since 1940. Served in Instrs. Unit, U. of Mo., 1917-18. Mem. Am. Farm Econ. Assn., Phi Kappa Phi, Alpha Zeta, Gamma Sigma Delta (nat. pres., 1935-39). Independent. Clubs: Kiwanis, Country (Manhattan, Kan.); Rotary (Wichita, Kan.; Fort Collins, Colo.). Author: of expt. sta. bulls. for U. of Mo. Agr. Coll. and Kan. State Coll. Contbr. articles on agr. to jours. Address: Colorado Agricultural and Mechanical College, Ft. Collins, Colo. Died Jan. 22, 1948.

GREEN, Warren Everett, ex-gov.; b. Jackson County, Wis., Mar. 10, 1870; s. Chester and Mary Jane (Crawley) G.; ed. pub. and high schs., Castlewood and Watertown, S.D.; m. Elizabeth Jane Parliament, Jan. 17, 1899; children—Maxwell Eldon, George Chester, Mildred Grace, Edson Richard. Engaged in farming and stock raising nr. Hazel, S.D., since 1895. Mem. S.D. State Senate, 1907, 23, 25; mem. State Bd. Charities and Corrections, 1913-19; gov. of S.D., term 1931-33; head of S.D. del. to Nat. Republican Conv., Cleveland, 1936. Republican. Methodist. Mason. Kiwanian. Home: Hazel, S.D. Died Apr. 27, 1945.

GREEN, William Marvin, supt. schs.; b. Roanoke, Tex., Mar. 21, 1884; s. William Pinkney and Jane Elizabeth (Wolff) G.; student N. Tex. State Teachers Coll., Denton, 1901-04, Tex. Christian U., Ft. Worth, 1913-14, U. of Colo., 1917; A.B., State Teachers Coll., Greeley, Colo., 1923; A.M., Columbia, 1930; LL.D., Tex. Christian U., 1939; m. Lucy Melton, Sept. 21, 1904. Teacher pub. sch. Amarillo, 1904-08; with pub. schs., Ft. Worth, since 1908, asst. supt., 1922-31, supt. since 1931. Mem. Phi Delta Kappa, Kappa Delta Phi. Democrat. Methodist. Mason. Clubs: Rotary, Fort Worth, Torch. Home: 2934 Fifth Av. Office: 409 E. Weatherford St., Ft. Worth, Tex.* Died Oct. 5, 1946.

GREEN, William Mercer, bishop; b. Greenville, Miss., July 12, 1876; s. Rev. Duncan Cameron and Belle (Bott) G.; B.A., U. of the South, 1896, M.A., 1898, B.D., 1899, D.D., 1919; m. Pauline Leila Priestley, Nov. 16, 1904. Deacon, 1899, priest, 1900, P.E. Ch.; minister in charge St. Colomb's, Jackson, St. Luke's, Ridgeland, and St. John's, Fla.; rector Grace Ch., Canton, Miss., 1900-02; asst. rector St. John's Church, Knoxville, Tenn., 1902-04; rector St. Paul's Church, Meridian, Miss., 1904-09; dean All Saints Coll., Vicksburg, 1909-11; rector St. Andrew's Ch., Jackson, Miss., 1911-19; consecrated bishop coadjutor of Miss., May 29, 1919; bishop of Miss. by succession, Nov. 2, 1938; Hale Memorial preacher, Seabury Western Theol. Sem., Oct. 20, 1936. Trustee U. of the South, All Saints Coll., DuBose Memorial Ch. Training Sch., Instns. of Higher Learning of State of Miss. Democrat. Mason, K. of P. Mem. Kappa Sigma. Home: Battle Hill, Jackson, Miss. Died Nov. 12, 1942.

GREEN, William Raymond, judge, economist; b. Colchester, Conn., Nov. 9, 1856; s. Timothy Franklin and Sarah Maria (Raymond) G.; A.B., Oberlin, 1879, LL.D., 1927; m. Luella Washington Brown, June 1887; children—William Raymond, Mrs. Margaret Thorp Campbell. Admitted to Ill. bar, 1882; practiced, Dow City, Ia., 1882-84, Audubon, from 1884. Judge Dist. Ct., 15th Dist. Ia., 1894-1911, resigned; elected to 62d Cong., 9th Ia. Dist., June 5, 1911, to fill unexpired term (1911-13) of Walter I. Smith, resigned; reëlected 63d to 70th Congresses (1913-29); chmn. Ways and Means Com., 68th to 70th Congresses; also chmn. Joint Com. of House and Senate on Internal Revenue, 1926-28; resigned from Congress to become judge Court of Claims of U.S., 1928. Republican. Wrote: The Theory and Practice of Modern Taxation; Tariff Facts and Fallacies; articles on pub. and govt. matters in Saturday Evening Post, etc. Mem. Acad. Polit. Science. Club: Cosmos (Washington, D.C.). Address: Court of Claims, Washington. Died July 11, 1947; buried in Rock Creek Cemetery, Washington.

GREENBAUM, Sigmund Samuel, dermatologist; b. Philadelphia, Pa., Mar. 17, 1890; s. Joseph and Sarah (Klein) G.; B.S., Central High Sch., Phila., 1909; M.D., Jefferson Med. Coll., 1913; certificate from U. of Paris, faculty of medicine Hosp. St. Louis Clinic of Skin Diseases and Syphilis, 1919; married Rae Refowich, Nov. 30, 1922; children—Charles, Edwin, Carol (dec.), Janet. Practiced Phila. since 1913; professor clinic dermatology and syphilology, University of Pennsylvania; graduate School of Medicine since 1935; attending dermatologist, Philadelphia General Hospital since 1922; dermatologist Graduate Hosp. University of Pennsylvania, Rush Hosp., Phila. Psychiatric Hosp., Med. Adv. Bd. 1 of Pa. Selective Service; lecturer on skin and social diseases, Phila. Occupational Sch. of Therapy; cons. dermatologist,

Bamberger Home and Betty Bacharach Home, Atlantic City, N.J., Eagleville Sanitarium, Camden (N.J.) General Hospital; fellow in research, Inst. of Cutaneous Medicine; director Bankers Securities Corporation. Trustee National Farm School. Diplomate Am. Bd. Dermatology and Syphilology. Fellow Am. Acad. Dermatology and Syphilology. Served as capt. Med. Corps, U.S. Army. Mem. A.M.A., West Phila. Med. Assn., Med. Club of Phila., A.A.A.S., Northern Med. Assn. of Phila., Phila. Dermatol. Soc., Phila. Defense Council (venereal disease sub-com.), Med. Soc. State of Pa., Phila. County Med. Soc. (chmn. com. on cutaneous and social diseases), Am. Coll. of Physicians, Phila. Coll. of Physicians, Am. Legion, Phi Delta Epsilon. Author: (with H. Prinz) diseases of the Mouth, 1935; Dermatology in General Practice, 1947. Contbr. to med. jours. Home: 320 S. 18th St., Philadelphia. Died Oct. 3, 1949; buried Roosevelt Cemetery, Philadelphia.

GREENE, Charles Jerome, clergyman, educator; b. Barnwell County, S.C., July 23, 1867; s. William Holland and Florence Virginia (Heath) G.; A.B., Arkadelphia (Ark.) Meth. Coll., 1894; Vanderbilt U., 1899-1901, B.D., 1917; D.D., Hendrix Coll., 1919; m. Euella Pettus, June 29, 1892 (died July 7, 1919); children—Verna Jerome (dec.), Ruby Caroline (dec.), Charles Jerome; m. 2d, Irma Frances Funk, Dec. 1, 1920; 1 dau., Irma Katherine. Ordained ministry M.E. Ch., S., 1895; pastor, Washington, Ark., 1895-97, Mena, Ark., 1898-99, Fordyce, Ark., 1902-03; head dept. of English, Hendrix Coll., Conway, Ark., 1904-25, acting pres., 1920-21, v.p. and head of dept. of religion, 1925-41, retired 1941, now v.p. and prof. emeritus. Formerly sec. Little Rock Annual Conf. and editor of its annual; mem. Nat. Assn. Bible Instrs., Soc. Biblical Study and Research. Mem. Gen. Conf. of M.E. Ch., S., 1918. Democrat. Mason, Woodman, Kiwanian. Home: Conway, Ark. Died July 1, 1944.

GREENE, Evarts Boutell, univ. prof.; b. Kobe, Japan, July 8, 1870; s. Daniel Crosby and Mary Jane (Forbes) G.; student Northwestern U., 1885-88; A.B., Harvard, 1890, A.M., 1891, Ph.D., 1893; LL.D., U. of Ill., U. of Rochester, 1931; Litt.D., Dartmouth Coll., 1931; L.H.D., Lehigh Univ., 1931; unmarried. Asst. in history, Harvard, 1890-93. Harris traveling fellow, Harvard U. (Berlin U.), 1893-94; asst. prof., 1894-95, asso. prof., 1895-97, prof. history, 1897-1923, dean Coll. Lit. and Arts, 1906-13, U. of Ill.; prof. Am. history since 1923, De Witt Clinton prof., 1926-39, prof. emeritus since 1939, Columbia Univ.; lecturer on Early American History on the Stokes Foundation, N.Y. Univ., 1940; chmn. Institute of Japanese Studies (Columbia), 1936-39; president trustees Illinois State Hist. Library, 1910-23; mem. Ill. State Centennial Commn., 1913-19. Sec. council Am. Hist. Assn., 1913-19 (mem. council 1908-11; v.p. 1927-29; pres. 1930); mem. Am. Council of Learned Socs., 1933-36; mem. Am. Philos. Soc., Am. Antiquarian Soc.; corr. mem. Chicago Hist. Soc., Minn. Hist. Soc., Colonial Soc. of Mass.; hon. mem. German-Am. Hist. Soc. of Ill.; fellow, American Academy Arts and Sciences. Chmn. Nat. Bd. for Hist. Service (coöperating with Com. on Pub. Information and other Govt. depts.), 1917-18; mem. bd. of editors American Historical Review, 1923-27; mem. editorial bd. Journal of Econ. and Business History, 1931-32; member editorial bd. Review of Religion since 1941. Clubs: Century (New York); Rotary (Croton-on-Hudson, N.Y.). Author: The Provincial Governor in English Colonies of North America, 1898; Government of Illinois, 1904; Provincial America, 1905; American Interest in Popular Government Abroad (War Information Series), 1917; Lieber and Schurz (War Information Series), 1918; Foundations of American Nationality, 1922, rev. edit., 1935; A New Englander in Japan (Daniel Crosby Greene), 1927; Guide to Sources for Early American History in New York City (with R. B. Morris), 1929; American Population before the First Federal Census (with V. D. Harrington), 1932; Religion and the State in America, 1941; The Revolutionary Generation, 1763-1790, 1943. Contributor to historical and educational periodicals. Editor: Governor's Letter Books, 1818-34 (with C. W. Alvord); Governor's Letter Books, 1840-53 (with C. M. Thompson). Chmn. editorial com. Am. Legal Records, 1930-34. Home: Mount Airy, Croton-on-Hudson, N.Y. Address: Box 285 Croton-on-Hudson, N.Y. Died June 27, 1947.

GREENE, Herbert Eveleth, univ. prof.; b. Newton, Mass., Aug. 27, 1858; s. William Lyman and Sarah (Eveleth) G.; A.B., Harvard, 1881, A.M., 1884, A.M. and Ph.D., 1888; studied in Germany (U. of Leipzig) and in France, 1881-82; m. Harriet Savage Chase, July 15, 1886; children—William Chase, Harold Chase, Theodore Chase. Prof. English, Wells Coll., 1891-93; collegiate prof. English, Johns Hopkins, 1893-1925, prof. emiritus of English lit. since 1925. Treas. Modern Lang. Assn., Am., 1896-1901, v.p., 1906; pres. Johns Hopkins Chapter Phi Beta Kappa, 1921-22; pres. Johns Hopkins Philol. Assn., 1923-24; pres. Harvard Club of Md., 1903. Club: Harvard of Boston. Editor of Shakespearean texts, including The Tempest in the Tudor Shakespeare and King Richard the Second in the Arden Shakespeare. Has written many criticisms, literary, musical, dramatic. Home: 33 Somerset Rd., West Newton, Mass. Died Sept. 3, 1942.

GREENE, Katherine Glass (Mrs. Harry Rayner Greene), educator; b. Frederick County, Va., Nov. 24, 1865; d. William Wood and Nancy Rebecca (Campbell) Glass; g.g.g.d. Col. James Wood, Va., abt. 1759, who was founder of Winchester; grad. Fairfax Hall, Winchester; studied summers, Harvard, Columbia, Johns Hopkins, U. of Va. and abroad; m. Harry Raynor Greene, Dec. 20, 1921. Founder, 1905, and pres. Ft. Loudoun Sem., coll., prep. and vocational sch. for girls; now retired. Founder and 1st regent Ft. Loudoun Chapter D.A.R.; founder and 1st pres. Lawrence Augustine Washington Soc. Children of Revolution; mem. Colonial Dames of America in State of Va., D.C. Branch of League of Am. Penwomen, D.A.R. (state librarian 1928-31, and state chaplain, 1931-34), U.D.C., United States Daughters of 1812, Pi Gamma Mu. Democrat. Presbyterian. Clubs: Century, Civic, Music, Garden. Author: Winchester and Its Beginnings (1743-1814), 1926; Stony Mead, 1929; Sketch of Winchester, Va., for University of Virginia Record Extension Series, 1930; The Evolution of the Conception of God, 1934; (in collaboration) Gen. and Gov. James Wood and the Society of the Cincinnati in Virginia, 1945. Asso. editor of True Stories of Winchester, 1931. Address: Fort Loudoun Apts., Winchester, Va. Died May 11, 1948.

GREENE, Roger Sherman; b. Westborough, Massachusetts, May 29, 1881; s. Daniel Crosby and Mary Jane (Forbes) G.; A.B., Harvard, 1901, A.M., 1902; m. Kate Brown, May 8, 1920; children—Edward Forbes, Katharine Curtis. Vice and deputy consul-gen. at Rio de Janeiro, Brazil, 1903-04; vice consul at Nagasaki, Japan, 1904-05; vice and deputy consul at Kobe, 1905; commercial agent and later consul at Vladivostok, Siberia, 1905-07; consul at Dalny, Manchuria, 1907-09, at Harbin, China, 1909-11; consul-gen. at Hankow, China, 1911-14; resident dir. in China of China Med. Bd. of Rockefeller Foundation, 1914-21, dir., 1921-25, gen. dir., 1925-27; v.p. in Far East of Rockefeller Foundation, 1927-29; dir. China Med. Bd., Inc., 1929-35, World Citizens Assn., Chicago, 1939; acting dir. Peiping Union Med. Coll., 1927-35; chmn. Am. Com. for Non-Participation in Japanese Aggression, 1938-41; asso. dir., Com. to Defend America by Aiding the Allies, 1940-41; consultant, Div. of Cultural Relations, Dept. of State, 1942-44. Fellow American Academy of Arts & Sciences; mem. Am. Soc. Internat. Law, Council on Fgn. Relations, American Oriental Soc., Chinese Med. Assn. (hon.), Chinese Physiol. Soc.; trustee and vice chmn. China Foundation for Promotion of Education and Culture, Harvard-Yenching Inst., Bancraft School, Worcester. Home: 548 Lincoln St., Worcester, Mass. Died Mar. 27, 1947.

GREENMAN, Walter Folger, clergyman; b. Nantucket, Mass., Jan. 21, 1865; s. George Washington and Sarah Wood (Folger) G.; A.B., Harvard, 1885, A.M., 1888; B.D., Harvard Div., 1888; m. Mabel Josephine Henshaw, Dec. 26, 1888; 1 son, Raymond Henshaw. Ordained Unitarian ministry, 1890; pastor Winona, Minn., 1888-91, Fitchburg, Mass., 1891-1900, Watertown, Mass., 1900-08, Milwaukee, Wis., 1908-19, Greenfield, Mass., 1920-25, Augusta, Me., 1926-31; retired. Gen. sec. Gen. Conf. Unitarian and other Christian Chs., 1903-10; pres. Wis. State Conf. Charities and Corrections, 1911-12; chmn. advisory com. dirs. Milwaukee Assn. Chs., 1910-19, Milwaukee Juvenile Protective Assn., 1913-19; pres. Milwaukee Central Council of Social Agencies, 1913-15; hon. vice-pres. Mass. Anti-Tuberculosis League. Chmn. dept. pub. welfare Milwaukee County Council of Nat. Defense, 1917-19; mem. council Gen. Unitarian Conf., 1919-23. Mem. A.A.A.S., Am. Pub. Health Assn. Author: Sociological Charts for Milwaukee, 1914. Home: 320 Otis St., West Newton, Mass. Died July 25, 1945.

GREENOUGH, William (grēn'ō), lawyer; b. Quincy, Mass., July 15, 1874; s. William and Alice Mary (Patterson) G.; student King's Sch., Stamford, Conn.; St. Paul's Sch., Concord, N.H., 1890-92; A.B., Harvard, 1896, LL.B., 1899; m. Charlotte Warren, Dec. 27, 1907; 1 dau., Beatrice (Mrs. John A. Warple). Admitted to bar, 1899; practiced in office Strong & Cadwalader, New York, N.Y., 1899-1904; atty N.Y., N.H., & H. R.R., 1904-08; partner Patterson, Eagle, Greenough & Day since 1908; formerly trustee and sr. vice pres. Union Square Savings Bank. Mem. New York Community Trust (pioneer in its creation, 1920; vice chmn. distribution com.; counsel), Charity Organization Soc. (former mem. exec. com.). Mem. Am. and N.Y. State bar assns., Bar Assn. City of New York. Republican. Episcopalian. Clubs: New York Yacht (former fleet capt.). Knickerbocker, Racquet and Tennis, Clambake, Reading Room, (Newport); Home: 860 Park Av., New York 21. Office: 120 Broadway, New York 5, N.Y. Died Feb. 1, 1949.

GREENSLADE, John Wills, naval officer; b. Bellevue, O., Jan. 11, 1880; grad. U.S. Naval Acad., 1899, Naval War Coll., 1926; children—John Francis (Capt. U.S. Navy), Robert Wills (Lt. U.S.N.R.). Service: Cuban and Puerto Rican campaigns, Spanish-American War, 1898; Philippines, 1899-1902; head dept. ordnance and gunnery, Naval Acad., 1917; comd. U.S.S. Housatonic, Northern Mine Barrage, North Sea, 1918; inspector of ordnance, Naval Powder Factory and Proving Ground, 1920-23; comdr. Mine Squadron 1, U.S. Fleet, 1923-25; head operations dept., Naval War Coll., 1926-28; comd. U.S.S. Pennsylvania, 1928-29; chief of staff, Battleship Divs., U.S. Fleet, 1929-30; mem. Gen. Bd., 1931-32, 1934-36, 1939-41; comdr. Submarine Force, U.S. Fleet, 1932-34; vice admiral, comdr. battleships, U.S. Fleet, 1938-39; sr. mem. President's Bd. to select sites for Atlantic bases in Brit. possessions, 1940; comdt. 12th Naval Dist., 1941; comdr. Western Sea Frontier, 1942-Feb. 1944; retired; coordinator of naval logistics, Pacific Coast, 1944; resources coordinator, Western Sea Frontier, 1945. Awards (service) D.S.M., 1918, 1944; (campaign) Spanish-Am., Philippines, Cuban and Mexican Interventions, World Wars I and II; (foreign) Mexican Nat. Order of Aztec Eagle, Merito Naval; Chilean Orden del Merito; Panamanian Order of Vasco Nunez de Balboa. Address: 226 Greenwood Heights, Bellevue, O. Died Jan. 6, 1950.

GREENWOOD, Allen, surgeon; b. Chelsea, Mass., Mar. 1, 1866; s. William Allen and Caroline (Carleton) G.; M.D., Harvard, 1889; house officer, Boston City Hosp., 1888-90; m. Bertha Underhill, June 23, 1892 (dec.); m. 2d, Hope Whipple, Mar. 8, 1917 (dec.); children—Allen, Carolyn; m. 3d, Marion Tucker, Aug. 16, 1924; 1 dau., Grace Tucker. Instructor Waltham Training Sch., 1890-1901; bacteriologist, Waltham Bd. of Health, 1894-98; asst. instructor in ophthalmology, Harvard Med. Sch., 1904-05; ophthalmic surgeon to the Boston City Hosp., 1901-18, since consulting ophthalmologist; visiting surgeon, 1895-1900, visiting ophthalmic and aural surgeon since 1900, Waltham Hospital; now cons. ophthalmic surgeon, Mass. Eye and Ear Infirmary, Beth Israel Hosp. (Boston); Union Hosp. (Framingham), Milford Hosp., lecturer in ophthalmology, Harvard Graduate Sch. of Medicine; prof. emeritus ophthalmology, Tufts Med. Sch. Apptd. acting asst. surgeon U.S. Army, Aug. 22, 1898, and assigned to 19th U.S. Inf., Ponce, P.R.; hon. disch., Oct. 19, 1898; hon. lt. col. Royal Army Med. Corps, with B.E.F. in France, summer 1916; mem. sub-com. on ophthalmology Gen. Med. Bd. of Council Nat. Defense, Apr. 26, 1917; commd. maj. Med. R.C., 1917, and on duty surgeon gen.'s office, Washington; lt. col. Med. Corps, sr. consultant in ophthalmology for A.E.F., 1918; col. Med. R.C. U.S. Army, 1919. Mem. A.M.A. (chmn. ophthal. sect.), Mass. Med. Soc., Am. Ophthalmology Society (president), American Academy Ophthalmology and Oto-Laryngology (president 1918), New England Ophthalmology Society (president 1913), Waltham Med. Club, Waltham Edn. Soc. (pres. 1904-05), etc. Club: Harvard. Home: 84 Commonwealth Av. Office: 82 Commonwealth Av., Boston, Mass. Died Oct. 24, 1942.

GREENWOOD, Thomas Benton, lawyer; b. Louisburg, N.C., July 2, 1872; s. Thomas Benton and Lucy H. (Gee) G.; student U. of Tex., 1888-90; LL.D., Austin Coll., 1924; m. Mary Ezell, Aug. 12, 1908. Admitted to Tex. bar, 1893, practiced in Palestine to 1918. Author "I.&G.N. Bill," enacted by Tex. Legislature, 1910, which prevents purchase of franchises and properties of a railroad corp. from acquiring old charter or right to new one unless provision is made for payment of liabilities incurred in operation of railroad during preceding two years; leading counsel for City of Palestine, 1911-18, in preventing same rd. from removing its gen. offices and shops from Palestine; asso. justice Supreme Court of Tex., 1918-35; practicing law at Austin with Greenwood, Moody & Robertson since 1935. Regent U. of Texas, 1907-11. Member Travis County Bar Association, Texas State Bar Association. Democrat. Elder Presbyn. Ch. Home: 2528 Harris Blvd., Austin, Tex. Died Mar. 26, 1946.

GREER, Frank U., army officer; b. Washington, D.C., Sept. 24, 1895; s. William Alexander and Cecelia (Throckmorton) G.; student Catholic Univ., 1915-18; LL.B., George Washington Univ., 1926; grad. Inf. Sch., 1921, Chem. Warfare Sch., 1934, Command and Gen. Staff Sch., 1934, Army War Coll., 1938; hon. M. Mil. Science, R.I. State Coll., 1941; m. May Imogene Mann, December 26, 1917; children—Mary Imogene (Mrs. P. J. McCaskey), Charles Francis, Thomas Upton, Frank Upton, Rebecca Ellan. Commd. 1st lt., 1917 and advanced through the grades to brig. gen., 1943. Awarded Purple Heart, Silver Star (Africa, 1943), oak leaf cluster to both Purple Heart and Silver Star (France, 1944), Bronze Star (France, 1944); Legion of Honor, Croix de Guerre with Palm (French). Mem. Alpha Tau Gamma, Odd Fellow, K.C. Home: 859 Second Av., Gainesville, Fla. Died May 17, 1949.

GREER, Herbert Chester, steel mfr.; b. Sharon, Pa., Aug. 11, 1877; s. Charles and Mary (Park) G.; grad. Kiskiminetas Springs Sch., Saltsburg, Pa., 1895; B.S., Mass. Inst. Tech., 1899; m. Agnes J. Reeves, June 3, 1908; 1 dau., Jane. Began as steel mill employee with Sharon Steel Co., 1899; successively with Tenn. Coal, Iron & Steel Co., La Belle Iron Works, Preston County (W.Va.) Coke Co., Reeves Mfg. Co., Greer Steel Co. of Dover, O.; pres. Reeves Steel and Mfg. Co., Greer Steel Co., Preston County Coke Co., Preston County Light & Power Co., Greer Limestone Co., and W.Va. Newspaper Co.; owner of five newspapers in W.Va. Republican. Methodist. Mason. Clubs: Morgantown Golf and Country; Gibson Island Yacht (Md.); Duquesne, Long Vue Country (Pittsburgh); Union (Dover); Everglades, Bath and Tennis, Sail Fish, Soc. Four Arts (Palm Beach, Fla.). Homes: Morgantown, W.Va.; Dover, O.; Palm Beach, Fla. Died Aug. 5, 1948.

GREER, Samuel Miller, banker; b. Brooklyn, N.Y., Jan. 25, 1875; s. Samuel M. and Margaret Agnes (Huey) G.; ed. pub. schs., N.Y. City; m. Helen Penta, Feb. 11, 1902 (died May 27, 1946). With Bell telephone system, 1890, various positions with New York Telephone Co.; head of development work, Chesapeake & Potomac Telephone Co., Baltimore, Md., 1913-18; v.p. Bankers Trust Co., New York, 1918-24. Dir. dept.

of development Am. Red Cross, in charge membership and production work, July 1917-June 1918, asst. gen. mgr. since June 1918; v.p. Chesapeake & Potomac Telephone Co. and associated cos., 1924-27; associated with Jeremiah Milbank, New York, since 1927. Dir. Commercial Solvents Corp., Am. Steel Foundries, Combined Metals Reduction Co., Milchester Realty Corp. Trustee Inst. for Crippled and Disabled. Republican. Clubs: Union League, Wall Street of New York. Home: 1016 5th Av. Office: 44 Wall St., New York, N.Y. Died Sept. 19, 1948.

GREGG, James Edgar, clergyman, educator; b. Hartford, Conn., Nov. 24, 1875; s. James Bartlett and Mary (Needham) G.; A.B., Harvard, 1897, A.M., 1901; B.D., Yale, 1903, D.D., 1918; D.D., Williams, 1923; LL.D., Wilberforce, 1924; m. Pauline Pumpelly, Mar. 16, 1903 (died May 27, 1911); children—Elise Pumpelly (wife of Dr. Emir Allen Gaw), James Bartlett; m. 2d, Mary Livingston Hinsdale, June 10, 1914; children—Theodore Hinsdale, Gerald Hinsdale (dec.). Ordained to ministry Congl. Church, 1903; pastor Pilgrim Memorial Church, Pittsfield, Mass., 1903-09, Kirk Street Church, Lowell, Mass., 1909-12, and First Church of Christ, Pittsfield, Mass., 1912-18; prin. Hampton (Va.) Normal and Agrl. Inst. (colored), 1918-29; pastor First Ch., Waterbury, Conn., 1929-41; acting pastor Congl. Ch., Adams, Mass., 1942, and Williamstown, Mass., 1942-45. Trustee Penn Sch., S.C., Southern Edn. Foundation. Mem. Phi Beta Kappa, Delta Upsilon. Club: Century (New York). Home: East Lenox Road, Pittsfield, Mass. Died Feb. 23, 1946.

GREGG, John Robert, educator, author, pub.; b. Rockcorry, Ireland, June 17, 1867; s. George and Margaret (Johnston) G.; pub. sch. edn.; hon. S.C.D., Boston Univ., 1930, Litt.D., Rider College, Trenton, New Jersey, 1942; m. Maida Wasson, July 3, 1899 (died June 28, 1928); m. 2d, Janet Fraser, d. David Kinley, ex-pres. U. of Ill., Oct. 23, 1930; children—Kate Kinley, John Robert. Inventor of Gregg Shorthand and author of many text books on shorthand and comml. edn.; editor The Gregg Writer (monthly mag.) since 1900, Am. Shorthand Teacher (now Business Edn. World) since 1920; pres. Gregg Coll., Inc., Chicago, Gregg Pub. Co., New York, Chicago, Boston, San Francisco, Dallas, Toronto; chairman bd. dirs. The Gregg Pub. Co., Ltd., London, Gregg Schs., Ltd., London (22 schs.). Chmn. Liberty Loan Com., Long Beach, L.I., 1917-18. Fellow Nat. Acad. of Design; mem. Metropolitan Museum of Art, National Commercial Teachers Federation (hon. life), National Shorthand Reporters' Association (charter mem.). N.Y. State Shorthand Reporters' Assn. (hon. life mem.); vice-pres. Internat. Shorthand Congress, Paris, 1931. Democrat. Episcopalian. Clubs: Illinois Athletic (Chicago); Nat. Arts (pres.), Players, Advtg. (New York). Author: Gregg Shorthand Manual (over eighteen million copies sold), 1888; Progressive Exercises in Gregg Shorthand, 1890; The Gregg Shorthand Dictionary, 1901; The Gregg Phrase Book, 1901; Gregg Speed Practice, 1907; The Gregg Reporter, 1909; Gregg Speed Studies, 1917; Reporting Shortcuts, 1921; Basic Principles of Shorthand, 1923; Secretarial Studies (with R. P. SoRelle), 1924; The Q's and A's of Shorthand Theory, 1924; Gregg Speed Bldg., 1932; Applied Secretarial Practice, 1941; The Private Secretary, 1943. Del. to Internat. Congress on Comml. Edn., Amsterdam, 1929 (chmn. Am. delegation and v.p. of Congress), London, 1932. Awarded medal for "distinguished services to commercial education," Eastern Commercial Teachers Assn., 1931; presented with scroll signed by over 1000 Spanish-speaking people, Latin-Am. Goodwill Luncheon, New York, 1931; Ulster-Irish Soc. medal for "notable service to the nation," 1936; award of New York Acad. of Pub. Edn. for "distinguished service to public education," 1938. Awarded King George Medal, for services to the cause of freedom, 1947. Home: The Ovals, Cannondale, Conn. Office: 270 Madison Av., New York, N.Y. Died Feb. 23, 1948; buried at New Canaan, Conn.

GREGG, William C.; b. Pittsburgh, Pa., July 17, 1862.; s. Cephas (educator) and Mary (Newton) G.; student U. of Neb., 1880-82; m. Mary A. Damarin, Sept. 18, 1889; children—Louis D., Otis T., W. Burr, Mrs. Rachel de Clairmont, Mrs. Mary Young. Inventor of ry. applianced; founder and pres. Gregg Co., Ltd. An authority on nat. parks, forests and reclamation; vice chmn. Southern Appalachian Nat. Park Commn., 1924. In Y.M.C.A. service in France, 1918; visited (by request) Am. and British fronts and reported to hdqrs. on uses of light rys. Fellow Nat. Acad. of Design; mem. Nat. Parks Assn., Council of Nat. Parks, Forests and Wild Life, Audubon Soc., Am. Civic Assn., etc. Republican. Clubs: Arts, Cosmos (Washington, D.C.); Nat. Arts (New York). Author: Three Months in France in 1918. Contbr. to mags. on travel and polit. economy. Collector of old masters and antiques. Home: 330 Prospect Av., Hackensack, N.J. Died Jan. 22, 1946.

GREGORY, Clifford V., editor; b. Mason City, Ia., Oct. 20, 1883; s. Elmer O. and Millie E. (McFarlin) G.; ed. Iowa State Coll., 1906-10; m. Edna L. Springer, June 27, 1910; children—Gwendolyn Ruth, Merrill Clifford, Howard Verne, Barbara, David Walter, Shirley Ann. Prof. Iowa Agrl. Coll., 1910-11; editor Prairie Farmer, Chicago and v.p. Prairie Farmer Pub. Co., 1911-37; v.p. Agricultural Broadcasting Co. (WLS), 1928-37; asso. pub. Wallace's Farmer and Iowa Homestead, also Wis. Agriculturist and Farmer since 1937; dir. Federal Reserve Bk. of Chicago. Trustee Farm Foundation; v.p. Des Moines Flying Service. Methodist. Mason. Clubs: Union League, National Press. Died November 18, 1941.

GREGORY, Jackson, author; b. Salinas, Calif., Mar. 12, 1882; s. Durell Stokes and Amelia (Hartnell) G.; B.L., U. of Calif., 1906; m. Lotus McGlashan, Dec. 20, 1910; children Jackson, Roderick. Formerly prin. high schools in Calif.; newspaper reporter in larger cities of U.S. and Can. Mem. Authors' League America. Democrat. Catholic. Author: Under Handicap, 1914; The Outlaw, 1916; The Short Cut, 1916; Wolf Breed, 1917; The Joyous Trouble Maker, 1918; Six Feet Four, 1918; Judith of Blue Lake Ranch, 1919; The Bells of San Juan, 1919; Ladyfingers, 1920; Man to Man, 1920; Desert Valley, 1921; The Everlasting Whisper, 1922; Timber-Wolf, 1923; The Maid of the Mountain, 1925; The Desert Thoroughbred, 1926; Captain Cavalier, 1927; Redwood and Gold, 1928; Sentinel of the Desert, 1929; Mystery at Spanish Hacienda, 1929; The Trail to Paradise, 1930; The Silver Star, 1931; The House of the Opal, 1932; Splendid Outlaw, 1932; A Case for Mr. Paul Savoy, 1933; The Shadow on the Mesa, 1933; Ru, the Conqueror, 1933; Red Rivals, 1933; Riders Across the Border; Second Case of Mr. Paul Savoy, 1933; High Courage, 1934; Emerald Murder Trap, 1934; Island of Allure, 1934; Valley of Adventure, 1935; Lords of the Coast, 1935; White Water Valley, 1935; Into the Sunset, 1936; Mountain Men, 1936; Third Case of Mr. Paul Savoy, 1936; Sudden Bill Dorn, 1937; Powder Smoke on Wandering River, 1938; Dark Valley, 1937; The Secret of Secret Valley, 1939; Girl at the Crossroads, 1940; The Far Call, 1940; Guardians of the Trail, 1940; Ace in the Hole, 1941. Home: Auburn, Calif., and Altadena, Calif. Died June 12, 1943.

GREGORY, Laurence Wilcoxson, teacher; b. Norwalk, Conn., May 10, 1887; s. Giles Abijah and Mary Esther (Wilcoxson) G.; grad. Hopkins Grammar Sch., New Haven, Conn., 1905; A.B., Yale, 1909; m. Luella Burton Coley, Sept. 15, 1919; children—Roger Coley, John Burton. Apprentice in bus. enterprises, 1909-11; instr. Kiskiminetas Springs Sch., Saltsburg, Pa., 1911-13, Hotchkiss Sch., Lakeville, Conn., 1913-17; instr., Milford Sch., 1917-33, headmaster since 1920. Republican. Episcopalian. Mason. Club: Yale (New York). Home: Milford, Conn. Died July 29, 1946.

GREGORY, William Benjamin, engineer; b. Penn Yan, N.Y., Mar. 13, 1871; s. Ezra Eugene and Mary Elizabeth (Bush) G.; grad. Penn Yan Acad., 1890; M.E., Cornell, 1894, post-grad. work, 1907-08, master mech. engring., 1908; m. Selina Elizabeth Bres, June 21, 1898; children—Elizabeth (Mrs. Henry S. Ferris, now deceased), William Bres, Angela. Instructor drawing, Tulane University, 1894-97, asst. prof. exptl. engring., 1897-1902, asso. prof., 1902-05, prof. 1905-38, prof. emeritus experimental engineering and hydraulics since 1938. Irrigation engr., U.S. Dept. Agriculture; summer vacations devoted largely to the latter work and to drainage work (specialty rice irrigation) since 1902; cons. engineer Mississippi River Commn., in tests of hydraulic dredges, 1903; cons. engr. to U.S. Army Engineers in hydraulic tests, Bonnet Carré Spillway, 1928-29. Pres. New Orleans Acad. Sciences, 1914. Awarded Warner medal by Am. Soc. M.E., 1940 for distinguished work in hydraulic engineering. Major engrs., U.S.R.; service with A.E.F. in France, Oct. 1917-Jan. 1919; col. (inactive), U.S. Engrs. Res. Corps. Decorated Order of Purple Heart and awarded citation.. Mem. Engring. Com., "Safe River," New Orleans. Mem. adv. com. Nat. Hydraulic Lab. Fellow Am. Soc. M.E. (council 1916-19; v.p. 1920-21); mem. Am. Soc. C.E. (life), La. Engring. Soc. (pres. 1910; hon. life mem.), New Orleans Acad. Sciences (past pres., hon. mem.); Am. Soc. for Testing Materials, Sigma Xi (pres. Tulane chapter), Tau Beta Pi; formerly mem. Soc. des Ingenieurs Civils de France. Unitarian. Club: Round Table (hon. 1942). Contbr. to trans. engring. socs. and bulls. on engring. Inventor Tulane Pitot Tube used to measure flow of water. Home: 630 Pine St., New Orleans. Died Jan. 29, 1945; buried in Cypress Grove Cemetery, New Orleans.

GREINER, John E. (grīn'ẽr), consulting engr.; b. Wilmington, Del., Feb. 24, 1859; s. John and Annie (Steck) G.; B.S., Delaware Coll., 1880, later C.E., Sc.D.; Dr. Engring., Johns Hopkins U., 1937; m. Lily F. Burchell, Dec. 16, 1886; children—Lillian Burchell, Gladys Houston. Practiced, Baltimore, since 1908; has served as cons. engr. B.&O. R.R., Erie R.R., Norfolk&Southern R.R., State of Pa., State of Md., etc.; designed and built nine bridges across the Ohio River and many others east of the Mississippi River; also railroad ocean terminals, dams and highways; now mem. J. E. Greiner Co., consulting engrs. Mem. Am. Ry. Commn. to Russia, 5 months, 1917. Chmn. Port Development Commn., authorized to expend $50,000,000 in improving the port of Baltimore. Mem. Am. Inst. Consulting Engrs., Am. Soc. Testing Materials, Am. Ry. Engring. Assn. (chmn. com. which adopted specifications for iron and steel structures); hon. mem. Am. Soc. C.E. Clubs: University, Elkridge Fox Hunting. Home: Ruxton, Md. Office: 1201 St. Paul St., Baltimore, Md. Died Nov. 15, 1942.

GREIS, Henry Nauert (grīs), bus. exec.; born Buffalo, N.Y., July 5, 1880; s. Jacob N. and Amelia (Nauert) G.; m. Bertha de Lace Westcott, Oct. 1 1907; 1 dau., Elizabeth (wife of Lt. J. Donald McBirney). Clerk, Marine Trust Co., Buffalo, N.Y., 1904; pres. Burke-Greis Oil Corp. since 1910; pres. Atlantic Petroleum, 1917, Lago Petroleum Corp. of Venezuela, 1924; trustee Deep Rock Oil Corp., Tulsa, Okla., 1933-41, pres. since 1941; dir. Mid-Continent Petroleum Corp., Okla. Natural Gas Corp., First Nat. Bank and Trust Co. of Tulsa. Dir. Tulsa Chamber of Commerce, Mid-Continent Oil and Gas Assn., Am. Petroleum Inst. Mem. U.S. Chamber of Commerce. Mason (33°), Elk. Clubs: Tulsa, Southern Hills Country (Tulsa, Okla.). Home: 1550 E. 29th St. Office: Mid-Continent Bldg., Tulsa, Okla. Died July 17, 1947

GREUSEL, John Hubert (grī'zĕl), journalist; b. Detroit, Mich., Mar. 20, 1866; s. Joseph and Sophia (Stumm) G.; of New England stock, through Warren, Wyant and Lockwood (1630), and officers in Colonial and Revolutionary wars. B.Litt., U. of Mich., 1888; post-grad. work same, 1888-90; m. Stella Tolsma, Mar. 27, 1892. Special writer New York World, New York Herald, Detroit Free Press, Detroit News, San Francisco Chronicle, Los Angeles Times, Asso. Sunday Mag., McClure's Syndicate, etc.; was mem. famous "all-star" staff, New York Recorder, under John W. Keller and Julius Chambers, 1892-95. Has interviewed and written character studies of more than 500 Am. leaders in all walks of life; wrote interview for New York World with Walt Whitman in his home, a few nights before the poet's death; 14-column illustrated story of Grover Cleveland's boyhood; wrote Story of the Monroe Doctrine (obtained by researches in Nat. archives at Washington), 1892, which was widely quoted; wrote notable brochure on Champ Clark, 1912, Edison, 1913; character-study of Bismarck, Blood and Iron, 1915; satire on conventional lies of society, The Rogue's March, 1916; etc. Lectured before class in journalism, U. of Mich., 1910. Wrote propaganda for U.S. during World War I and World War II; also tabloid editorial feature, Time and Tide, 1928-32; wrote character sketches of world-celebrities of Western Europe, 1923-33. For some years past has studied main instl. development during various hist. periods, with spl. reference to condition of the Masses (Rise of the Common Man); author of numerous manuscripts on hist. subjects and social analysis. Address: 6061 Hollywood Blvd., Hollywood, Calif. Died May 2, 1946.

GRICE, Warren, judge; b. Perry, Ga., Dec. 6, 1875; s. Washington Leonidas and Martha Virginia (Warren) G.; student Mercer U., Macon, Ga., 1892-94; m. Clara Elberta Rumph, June 18, 1901; children—Ruth, Warren (dec.), Samuel Rumph, Benning Moore, Elia. Admitted to Ga. bar, 1894, and practiced in Hawkinsville; mem. Ga. Ho. of Rep., 1900-04; atty.-gen. of Ga., 1914-15; prof. law of real property, Atlanta Law Sch., 1914-15; lecturer same, Law Sch., Mercer U., 1916-23; asso. justice Supreme Court of Ga. since 1937. Mem. Commn. to Revise Constitution of Ga., 1943-44; trustee and mem. exec. com. Mercer U. Served as 1st lt. and capt. 2d Inf., Nat. Guard of Ga., 1896-1903. Pres. Macon Circuit Bar Assn., 1927; mem. Am. Bar Assn., Ga. Bar Assn. (pres. 1926-27), Macon Bar Assn. (pres. 1926); Kappa Alpha. Democrat. Baptist. Clubs: Atlanta-Burns, Atlanta Athletic, Capitol City. Author: Law of Administrators, Executors and Guardians, 1923; Georgia Bench and Bar—A History of the Development of Georgia's Judicial System, 1931. Home: Della Manta Apts. Address: State Capitol, Atlanta, Ga. Died May 27, 1945.

GRIFFIN, James Aloysius, bishop; b. Chicago, Ill., Feb. 27, 1883; s. Thomas J. and Catherine (Woulfe) G.; St. Ignatius Coll., Chicago; Ph.D., and D.D., Propaganda U., Rome. Ordained priest Roman Cath. Ch., 1909; asst. St. James Ch., 1910-15, St. Brendan's Ch., 1915-17, both of Chicago; pastor Assumption Ch., Coal City, Ill., 1917-21; pastor downtown ch. of St. Mary's, Joliet, Ill., 1921-24; bishop of Springfield Diocese since Feb. 28, 1924. Has conducted two successful fund raising campaigns, netting over million dollars each, one for Cathedral building group, other for post-war expansion program. Dedicated Cathedral in Springfield, Oct. 14, 1928; patriotic note especially emphasized in style of architecture. Lectures on patriotic subjects; author of articles on Church and State. Inaugurated social welfare program in Diocese; sponsored CYO movement; active in representing church interests in legislature. Successfully conducted million dollar drive for Catholic postwar needs in Springfield diocese, 1944; first to inaugurate physical ednl. techniques in Catholic schools on a diocesan-wide basis, 1945; speaker at labor convs., jubilee occasions, etc. Mem. Ancient Order Hibernians; state chaplain K.C. Address: 524 E. Lawrence Av., Springfield, Ill. Died Aug. 5, 1948; buried in Cathedral Crypt, Springfield.

GRIFFIN, Martin Luther, cons. chem. engr.; b. Northampton, Mass., May 21, 1859; s. John and Naomi (Estabrook) G.; A.B., Amherst, 1883, A.M., 1886; m. Ada Riggs, Mar. 28, 1894; children—Archer Estabrook, Carroll Riggs. Expert in pulp and paper-making processes and raw materials therefor, also in textile finishing of cotton, silk and woolen fabrics, combustion of fuels, destructive distillation, deportment of gases, processes of evaporation and drying, the electrolytic cell for the production of caustic soda and chlorine and the application of their products to industry, the treatment of water and trades wastes in industry. Mem. various chem. socs. and author of tech. papers. Home: 4 Prospect Pl., Taunton, Mass. Died Aug. 28, 1942.

GRIFFIN, William Aloysius; R.C. bishop of Trenton, N.J., since July 1940. Address: Trenton, N.J. Died Jan. 1, 1950.

GRIFFIN, William Richard, bishop; b. Chicago, Ill., Sept. 1, 1883; s. Patriel and Margaret (Bourke) G.; student St. Ignatius Coll., Chicago, 1897-99; A.B., De Paul U., Chicago, 1903; studied for priesthood of R.C. Ch., Kenrick Sem., Webster Groves, Mo., 1903-07. Ordained priest, 1907; asst. pastor in Chicago chs. until 1923; pastor Mary Queen of Heaven Ch., Cicero, Ill., 1923-30, St. Andrew's Ch., Chicago, 1930-35; diocesan consultor, 1932-35; apptd. auxiliary bishop, La Crosse, Wis., 1935. Invested with title of Very Rev. Monsignor, 1926; domestic prelate with title of Right Rev., 1930. Address: 11th and Market Sts., La Crosse, Wis. Died Mar. 18, 1944.

GRIFFITH, David (Lewelyn) Wark, motion pictures; b. La Grange, Ky., 1880; s. late Brig. Gen. Jacob Wark G. (C.S.A.); ed. pub. schs.; m. Linda Avidson, 1905 (divorced); m. 2d, Evelyn Marjorie Baldwin, Mar. 2, 1936. Actor for 2 yrs.; identified with motion picture business since 1908, first as actor, then as dir. for Biograph Film Co. Independent producer; principal productions include The Birth of a Nation, Intolerance, Hearts of the World, Way Down East, Broken Blossoms, Orphans of the Storm, and America. Address: Players' Club, 16 Gramercy Park, New York, N.Y.* Died July 23, 1948.

GRIFFITH, John L., athletics; b. Mt. Carroll, Ill.; s. Hugh Jordan and Lucy Luella (Cummings) G.; grad. Warren (Ill.) Acad., 1898; B.A., Beloit (Wis.) Coll., 1902; m. Alice Kelley, Aug. 17, 1904; 1 son, John L., Jr. Director of athletics Yankton (S.D.) Coll., 1902-05, Morningside Coll., Sioux City, Ia., 1905-08, Drake U., Des Moines, Ia., 1908-18; commr. of athletics, Intercollegiate Conf. ("Big Ten") since 1922; editor and pub. Athletic Journal, tech. mag. for coaches and athletic dirs. Athletic dir. U.S. Army, at Camp Dodge, Ia., Aug. 1917-Aug. 1918; commd. capt. and had charge of organized recreation at the camp, of 30,000 men; sent to Camp Gordon, Aug. 1918, to assist in est. a sch. of physical training and bayonets, and in Sept. 1918, to Camp Pike to take charge of physical and bayonet sch. there; aptd. exec. officer, Washington, D.C., Jan. 1919, of Athletic Div. of Commn. on Training Camp Activities; promoted maj. June 1919. Mem. Nat. Collegiate Athletic Assn. (pres.), Am. Olympic Com., Paul Reveres (gov.). Baptist. Clubs: Rotary (pres. 1934-35), Executives (dir.). Home: 717 Walden Rd., Winnetka, Ill. Office: Hotel Sherman, N. Clark and W. Randolph Sts., Chicago, Ill.* Died Dec. 7, 1944.

GRIFFITHS, Frederick J., business exec.; b. Buffalo, N.Y., Oct. 13, 1879; s. Joseph and Elizabeth (Stucky) G.; m. Grace Gould, June 30, 1902; m. 2d, Julia Elizabeth Flynn, Feb. 22, 1927; 1 dau., Barbara Ann. Started in retail drug bus., Buffalo, N.Y., 1895; pres. Pa. Drug Co., New York, N.Y., 1927-46, chmn. bd. since 1946; pres. Whelan Stores Corp., New York, N.Y., 1928. Mem. bd. trustees Columbia Univ. Coll. of Pharmacy of City of New York. Dir. Am. Foundation for Pharmaceutical Edn., New York, N.Y. Mem. Nat. Assn. Chain Drug Stores, New York, N.Y. (sec.-treas. 1933-47). Republican. Presbyterian. Clubs: Advertising, Sales Executives. Home: 421 Fieldpoint Rd., Greenwich, Conn. Office: 4 Park Av., New York 16, N.Y. Died Feb. 5, 1949.

GRIGGS, Herbert Lebau, banker; b. Newton, Mass., 1855; grad. English High Sch., Boston; m. Emily Thompson, 1889. Began with Kidder, Peabody & Co., Boston, 1869; removed to New York, 1877; pres. Bank of New York, 1901, now trustee; trustee in U.S. of Sun Ins. Co., of London, Eng., also Atlantic Mut. Ins. Co. of New York. Episcopalian. Club: Metropolitan. Home: 375 Park Av., New York. Died Sept. 19, 1944.

GRIMES, Waldo Ernest, agrl. economist; b. Lee's Summit, Mo., Oct. 5, 1891; s. Arch Theodore and Anna (Hess) G.; B.S. in Agr., Kansas State Coll., 1913; studied Cornell U., 1914-15; Ph.D., U. of Wis., 1923; m. Ethel Roseberry, Sept. 15, 1914; children—Sarah Anna, Rosethel, Waldo Eugene, James Theodore. With Kansas State Coll. since 1913, respectively supt. of agronomy, exptl. farm of Agrl. Expt. Sta. 1 yr., asst. prof. farm management, 1915-18, asso. prof. agrl. economics, 1918-21, prof. in charge dept. since 1921, head dept. economics and sociology since 1936; acting dir. Kan. Agrl. Expt. Sta., 1934; visiting prof. of economics, U. of Chicago, spring quarter, 1939. Trustee Wesley Foundation Kan. State Coll. Mem. Am. Econ. Assn., Am. Farm Econ. Assn. (pres. 1935), Kansas State College Alumni Assn. (dir.), A.A.A.S., Phi Kappa Phi, Sigma Xi, Alpha Zeta, Gamma Sigma Delta (past nat. pres.), Pi Kappa Delta, Pi Kappa Alpha. Republican. Methodist. Author: (with others) Making the Most of Agriculture, 1927; Modern Agriculture (with E. L. Holton), 1931. Home: 203 N. Delaware St., Manhattan, Kan. Died May 23, 1947.

GRIMMER, Ward Chipman Hazen, judge, Appeal and Chancery Courts, N.B.; b. Saint Stephen, N.B., Oct. 31, 1858; s. Geo. Skeffington and Mary Allan (Hazen) G.; B.A., M.A., U. of New Brunswick, Fredericton, 1877-79, LL.D., 1914; m. Bessie Emily Gove, Nov. 24, 1884 (dec.); children—Don Skeffington, Lois Hazen (dec.). Called to N.B. bar, Oct. 1880; practiced in St. Stephen; apptd. King's counsel, 1903; mem. Legislative Assembly, 1903-14; surveyor general, 1908-11; atty. gen., Nov. 1911-Jan. 1914; mayor, St. Stephen, 1888; judge, Appeal and Chancery Courts, N.B., since Jan. 10, 1914; judge of Divorce Court, 1932-39. Chmn. Royal Commn. for Lumber Industry, N.B., 1927, Royal Commn Old Age Pensions, 1929, Workmen's Compensations Bd., 1931, N.B. Forestry Commn., 1934. Mem. Knights of Pythias. Mem. Conservative Party. Mem. Anglican Ch. Club: Cliff (Saint John, N.B.). Home: 216 Germain St. Address: 55 Canterbury St., St. John, N.B., Can. Died Oct. 1945.

GRINNELL, Russell (grĭ-nĕl'), corp. exec.; b. Providence, R.I., Aug. 3, 1875; s. Frederick and Mary Brayton (Page) G.; B.S., Brown U., 1897; m. Rose Lamb Gifford, Oct. 24, 1900 (died Jan. 6, 1943); children—Russell, Rose; married second, Maud E. Waters, August 7, 1945. With Grinnell Corp., Providence, R.I., since 1898, pres. since 1925, dir. since 1906; dir. Automatic Fire Alarm Co., Firemen's Mutual Ins. Co., Gorham Mfg. Co., Metals and Controls Corp. State senator, Rhode Island, 1924-28. Clubs: Hope, Squantum Association, Turks Head (Providence). Home: Locust Valley Farm, Exeter, R.I. Office: 260 W. Exchange St., Providence, R.I. Died July 2, 1948.

GRISWOLD, Benjamin Howell, Jr. (grĭz'wōld), lawyer, banker; b. Hagerstown, Md., Aug. 1, 1874; s. Benjamin Howell and Carrie G. (Robertson) G.; A.B., Johns Hopkins, 1894; LL.B., U. of Md., 1897; m. Bessie M., d. Alexander and Bessie (Montague) Brown, Dec. 7, 1904; children—Capt. Alexander Brown, Carolyn Howell (Mrs. J. McKenney W. Egerton), Lt. Benjamin Howell, Betty Tailer (Mrs. L. McLane Fisher). Admitted to Md. bar, 1897; became senior mem. Griswold, Thom & Jenkins, 1900; mem. Alex. Brown & Sons, bankers, since 1904, sr. mem. since 1924; judge advocate general of Maryland, 1916-20. President Board of Trade, Baltimore, 1915-21. President Alliance of Charitable and Social Agencies of Baltimore, 1916-21; mem. Maryland Council Defense; chmn. Md. Ednl. Survey Commn., 1915-16. Trustee Johns Hopkins since 1911; pres. bd. trustees Walters Art Gallery since 1933; chmn. code com. Investment Bankers under NRA, 1934-35, Investment Bankers Conf., Inc., 1936-39, Nat. Assn. Securities Dealers, Inc., 1939-42; Md. chmn. Com. for Economic Development. Mem. Newcomen Soc. of England. Author of pamphlets and articles on economics, educational subjects and public affairs. Clubs: Maryland, Johns Hopkins, Alpha Delta Phi. Home: Roland Park, Md. Address: Alex. Brown & Sons, Baltimore and Calvert Sts., Baltimore, Md. Died July 27, 1946.

GROAT, Benjamin Feland (grōt), cons. engr., patent atty.; b. Hannibal, Mo., Oct. 18, 1867; of Colonial and Revolutionary ancestry; s. Peter Benjamin and Ann Garnett (Ritter) G.; B.Sc. in Engring., U. of Minn., 1901, LL.B., 1908, LL.M., 1910; m. Harriet Grace Mitchell, June 25, 1906; 1 dau., Lucy Mitchell (Mrs. George Ashmun Morton). Identified with railroad service, various branches, for a number of yrs.; instr. physics, 1895, prof. in charge mechanics and mathematics, U. of Minn. Sch. of Mines, 1898-1910, admitted to bar, 1908; hydro-electric engr. Aluminum Co. of America, 1910-20; cons. practice since 1910; made alloy lead pipe coupling with adjusted expansion properties; developed precise turbine tests, measuring water chemically, 1914; planned and directed dredging and power improvements of Grasse River, N.Y., 1914; inventor-patentee method of automatic ice diversion; originated plan and wrote application for permit to install ice diversion, St. Lawrence River, which was granted by Internat. Joint Commn.; advocate of Nat. Hydraulic Laboratory (citing its value in planning means to stop erosion of soils); advocate of a "standard-of-living-wage-price-dollar"; etc. Awarded silver medal, Engrs.' Soc. Western Pa., 1915; Norman medal, Am. Soc. Civil Engrs., 1917. Former fellow A.A.A.S.; mem. Am. Soc. Civil Engrs., Soc. for Promotion Engring. Edn., Am. Math. Soc., Sigma Xi; former mem. Am. Soc. Mech. Engrs.' Soc. Western Pa.; asso. Am. Inst. Elec. Engrs. Protestant. Author of scientific papers relating to force of New Richmond tornado; summation of differences; inversions and determinants; back-water slopes; chemihydrometry; ice diversion; rod float theory and tables; dimensional theory; similarity and models (founding a proposed new branch of accurate engring. design); gas flow with frictional and received (rejected) heat; rules of quadrature, Generalized Maxwell's Viscosity Theory, disclosing an error not previously recognized. Address: Emlen Arms, Philadelphia 19. Died June 16, 1949; buried in Princeton Cemetery, Princeton, N.J.

GROAT, William Avery, physician; b. Canastota, N.Y., Nov. 9, 1876; s. William Robert and Elizabeth Morgan (Avery) G.; B.S., Syracuse U., 1897, M.D., 1900; m. Nellie Nichols Bacon, Oct. 2, 1901; children—William Avery, Robert Andrews, Elsie (Wade). In practice Syracuse, N.Y., since 1901; mem. faculty, Coll. of Medicine, Syracuse U., since 1902, prof. clin. pathology since 1911; sr. attending physician and dir. Hazard Lab., Memorial Hosp.; sr. attending physician diseases of metabolism and dir. Jacobson Memorial Lab., St. Joseph Hosp.; consultant University, City and Psychopathic hosps. and Syracuse Free Dispensary. Chmn. advisory com. on pub. health, City of Syracuse. Served as capt., later maj., M.C., U.S. Army, World War; lt. col. Med. O.R.C. Mem. Am. Pharmacopœia Convs., 1910, 20, 30, 40 (com. on constl. revision, 1940). Trustee Syracuse Univ. Fellow American College Physicians, A.A.A.S. Diplomate and member exec. committee American Board Internal Medicine, A.M.A. (delegate), N.Y. State Medical Society (chmn. bd. trustees, ex-president and member house of delegates; ex-chairman committee on scientific work; ex-president 5th district branch), American Assn. Immunologists, Am. Assn. Clin. Pathologists, Am. Assn. for Study of Goitre, Am. Assn. for Diseases of Internal Secretions, Delta Kappa Epsilon, Nu Sigma Nu, Sigma Xi, Alpha Omega Alpha, Phi Kappa Phi, Phi Kappa Alpha. Republican. Episcopalian. Clubs: Faculty, Onondaga Golf and Country, Thousand Island Park Golf; Holland Society of N.Y. (ex-v.p.). Contbr. articles and reports of researches, particularly diseases of the blood and metabolism, to med. publs. Cons. editor N.Y. State Med. Jour. Home: 1352 Teall Av., Syracuse; (summer) Cedar Island, Fishers Landing, N.Y. Died Sept. 9, 1945.

GROESBECK, Clarence Edward, public utilities; b. Frankfort, Ill., July 24, 1876; s. Edward C. and Rose G.; U. of Mich., 1894-97, B.S., 1898, D.Eng., 1931; m. Alice Hughes Ball, Jan. 3, 1900. With Electric Bond & Share Co., New York, since 1914, now director; chmn. bd., member executive com. Am. Gas and Elec. Co.; mem. exec. com. Assn. of Edison Illumination Companies. Mem. Alpha Delta Phi. Republican. Conglist. Clubs: University, Bankers, Recess, Alpha Delta Phi, The Creek, Piping Rock. Address: 325 Dunsmore Dr., La Jolla, Calif. Died Aug. 21, 1948.

GROGAN, James J., ry. exec.; b. Chicago, Ill., Dec. 26, 1884; s. James H. and Mary (Gorman) G.; student DeLaSalle Inst.; LL.B., Loyola Univ.; widower; children—James E., Mary P. (Mrs. E. T. Clemmons). Entire career with A.T. & S.F. Ry., Chicago; clerk, chief clerk; service Chicago Western Dist. Freight Traffic Com., 1919-20, fgn. frt. agt., gen. frt. agt., asst. frt. traffic mgr., frt. traffic mgr., gen. frt. traffic mgr., asst. vice pres. traffic, now vice pres.; served as asst. mgr. Inland Traffic, U.S. Food Adminstrn., Washington, D.C., Aug. 1917-Feb. 1919. Mem. Ill. bar., Chicago Athletic Assn. Clubs: Traffic (New York and Chicago); Bohemian (San Francisco). Home: 5000 East End Av., Chicago 15. Office: 80 E. Jackson Blvd., Chicago 4, Ill. Died Dec. 20, 1949.

GRONER, Frank Shelby, church official; b. Collin County, Tex., Jan. 3, 1877; s. William Christopher and Cleopatra Clementine (Dunnegan) G.; ed. under father until 14; M.S., North Texas Baptist Coll., 1896; student law, U. of Tex., 1 yr.; D.D., Baylor Univ., 1915; LL.D., Howard Coll., 1937; m. Laura Virginia Wyatt, June 30, 1903; children—Willie Lee, Edward Russell (dec.), Frank Shelby, Laura Virginia, Riley (dec.), Pat Neff. Teacher pub. schs., 1896-99; county atty., Jack County, Tex., 1900-04, also atty. R.I. Ry. 3 yrs.; pastor Stamford, Tex., and Columbus Street Ch., Waco, until 1918; gen. sec. exec. bd. Bapt. Gen. Conv. of Tex., 1918-28; pres. Coll. of Marshall, Tex., 1928-42, now pres. emeritus; chmn. Southern Bapt. Hosp. Commn. since 1916; led in building Hillcrest Memorial Hosp., Waco, and in movement to build Southern Bapt. Hosp., New Orleans. Democrat. Mason (32°; Shriner); mem. K.P., Woodmen of the World. Author: The Witness of Great Minds to Christian Verities; The Bible—The Book; Christian Education; Heaven and Our Sainted Loved Ones. Home: Marshall, Tex. Died Nov. 8, 1943.

GROSE, Clyde Leclare, educator; b. Deweyville, O., Apr. 8, 1889; s. Peter John and Harriet E. (Bolton) G.; A.B., Findlay Coll., 1910; A.M., Harvard, 1914, Ph.D., 1918; m. Carolyn Trowbridge, June 28, 1921; children—Trowbridge, Virginia, Peter. Teacher, high sch., Spencer, Ia., 1910-12; asst. in history, Harvard, 1914-16; mem. faculty Northwestern U. since 1916, director summer sessions, 1922-30, chairman of department of history since 1941; Harvard traveling fellow, 1919-20; recipient of research grants by Am. Council Learned Socs., 1926-28, by Social Science Research Council, 1928-31, 1937-38. 2d lt. 19th Arty. Brigade, U.S. Army, World War. Mem. Am. Hist. Assn., Royal Hist. Soc. Baptist. Club: University (Evanston). Author: A Select Bibliography of British History, 1660-1760, 1939. Contbr. on hist. subjects to jours. Home: 1600 Lincoln St., Evanston, Ill. Died May 6, 1942.

GROSS, Fred Louis, lawyer; b. Brooklyn, N.Y., Aug. 27, 1878; s. Louis F. and Christiana (Waldenmayer) G.; ed. Brooklyn Prep. Sch. and New York Law Sch.; m. Caroline Kelland, Apr. 16, 1906; children—Kelland Frederick, Edward Valentine. Admitted to N.Y. bar, 1900; mem. law firm Gross & Keck, Brooklyn, N.Y., since 1927; dir. Long Island Safe Deposit Co. Mem. Am., N.Y. State (pres. 1940), Brooklyn (pres. 1930-34) and Nassau County bar assns., Brooklyn-Manhattan Trial Lawyers Assn. Clubs: Union League (Brooklyn); Huntington (L.I.), Crescent. Author: The Law of Real Estate Brokers, 1910, rev. edit., 1917; What Is The Verdict?, 1944. Home: 436 Washington Av., Brooklyn 5. Office: 16 Court St., Brooklyn 2, N.Y. Died Jan. 16, 1947.

GROSS, Mervin E., army officer; b. Bowyer, S.C., Feb. 16, 1900; s. Rufus Barnwell and Carrie Sutton (Kane) G.; B.S., U.S. Mil. Acad., 1922; grad. Air Service Bombardment Sch., 1924, Air Corps Engring. Sch., 1933, Tactical Sch., 1938; rated command pilot, combat observer, aircraft observer. Commd. 2d lt., Air Service, U.S. Army, and advanced through the grades to brig. gen., 1943. Instr. mathematics U.S. Mil. Acad., 1928-32; engaged in aeronautical engring. and procurement Army Air Force Materiel Command, 1933-Dec. 1944; chief of requirements div. Hdqrs. Army Air Forces, determining all type requirements for aircraft, aircraft accessories, organization and organizational equipment for A.A.F.,

Mar. 1942-Dec. 1944; acting chief of staff U.S. Forces, China Theater, Jan. 1945; comdt. Air Inst. of Technology, Wright Field, Dayton, O., April 1946. Decorated Distinguished Service Medal. Address: 1511 - 44th St. N.W., Washington 25, D.C. Died Oct. 18, 1046; buried at Holly Hill, S.C.

GROSS, William J(ennings), newspaper editor; b. Williamstown, Ky., Jan. 5, 1897; s. Luther Martin and Laura Lee (Lemon) G.; grad. Elwood (Ind.) High Sch., 1913; student Ind. U., 1914-16; m. (Jule) Evangeline Rogers, Nov. 28, 1916; children—F. Mark, Margaret Evangeline. Chemist Fajardo (P.R.) Sugar Co., 1916-17; Ill. Steel Co., Gary, Ind., 1917, Sherwin-Williams Co., Chicago, 1917-18; chief chemist Marmon Automobile Co., Indianapolis, Ind., 1918; research and investigation New York, France, Italy, Germany, Rumania, 1918-20; reporter and branch city editor South Bend (Ind.) Tribune, 1921-23; editorial writer Fort Wayne (Ind.) News-Sentinel, 1923-37; editorial editor, 1937-45. Chmn. sub-com. on foreign policy for 3d Region, Rep. Nat. Com. on Program, 1938-40. Mem. Com. on Food for the Small Democracies, 1940-45. Ind. del.-at-large, Rep. Nat. Convention, 1944; del. memorial address, 150th anniversary of foundation of Ft. Wayne, 1944; mem. advis. com. on State educational methods, 1944. Founder and 1st pres., Old Fort Players (Fort Wayne Civic Theater), 1931-32, mem. of bd., 1931-34. Mem. Am. Soc. Newspaper Editors, Am. Acad. Polit. and Soc. Sci., Fort Wayne Chamber of Commerce, Allen County-Fort Wayne Hist. Soc., Allen Co. Rep. Club, Sigma Delta Chi. Catholic. Mason (32°). Clubs: Quest, Fortnightly. Wrote report on Foreign Policy for 3d Region Rep. Nat. Com. on Program; also numerous pamphlets on polit. and econ. subjects. Home: 2108 Kensington Blvd. Office: News-Sentinel, Fort Wayne, Ind. Died Feb. 5, 1945.

GROSSMAN, Moses Henry (grōs'măn), lawyer; b. N.Y. City, Feb. 18, 1873; s. Henry and Catherine (Jasnigi) G.; LL.B., New York U. Law Sch., 1894; LL.D., Nat. U., 1927, Lincoln Memorial U., 1930; m. Lillian Viola Berliner, June 28, 1900; children—Ethel B. (Mrs. Francis Fels Rosenbaum), William H. B. Admitted to N.Y. bar, 1894, and practiced since at N.Y. City; asst. dist. atty., 1894; city magistrate, 1918; sr. mem. House, Grossman, Vorhaus & Hemley; also admitted to bars of Calif., D.C., Fla., Mass., Mich., Hawaii. Founder, 1922, Arbitration Soc. of America, consolidated later with Am. Arbitration Assn., of which is now hon. pres. and dir.; an organizer, 1923, and now v.p. and dir. Thomas Jefferson Memorial Foundation; pres. Alumni Assn. of N.Y. Univ. Law Sch., 1936-37; dir. Am. Judicature Society and Lexington Avenue Civic Association; hon. life mem. Internat. Printing Pressmen and Assistants' Union of North America. Mem. Am. and N.Y. State bar assns., N.Y. County Lawyers Assn. (dir.), Am. Law Inst., Am. Branch Internat. Law Assn., Am. Soc. Internat. Law, Soc. Med. Jurisprudence, Federal Bar Assn. of N.Y., N.J. and Conn., N.Y. Law Inst., Am. Acad. of Polit. and Social Science, Nat. Puzzles League, Fifth Av. Assn. of New York, Foreign Policy Assn., Acad. Polit. Science City New York, Nat. Amateur Press Assn., Merchants Assn. of N.Y., Eastern Puzzlers League, Alumni Assn. of New York Univ., George White Alumni Assn. Jewish religion. Mason (Shriner, Mecca Temple, Past Master and Right Worshipful), Elk, K. of P. Clubs: Lawyers Club, Economic Club, City Club, National Democratic, Newspaper, City, New York Press, Advertising, The Fossils, Inwood Country. Donor of rare collection of English legal documents of 13th century to New York U. Law Sch. Home: 111 E. 56th St. Office: 521 5th Av., New York, N.Y.
Died June 6, 1942.

GROSVENOR, Graham Bethune (grōs'vĕn-ôr); b. Dubuque, Ia., July 22, 1884; s. George B. and Jesse (Lyon) G.; ed. pub. schs.; m. Mary Alice Ritchie, Feb. 28, 1910. Began with Otis Elevator Co., Chicago, Ill., 1902, gen. sales engr., N.Y. City, 1908-09, v.p. Otis Elevator Co. of Tex., 1911-15, western mgr., San Francisco, Calif., 1915-18, v.p. Otis Elevator Co., 1918-24; cons. engr. for N.Y. City banking interests, 1924-27; pres. Fairchild Airplane Mfg. Corp. and v.p. Fairchild Aviation Corp., 1928; pres. The Aviation Corp., 1929-30, dir. Pan-Am. Airways, Inc. Republican. Protestant. Home: Old Westbury, N.Y. Office: 135 E. 42d St., New York, N.Y.
Died Oct. 28, 1943.

GROSVENOR, William Mason (grō'vĕ-nŏr), cons. chem. engr.; b. St. Louis, Mo., Oct. 5, 1873; s. Col. William and Ellen (Sage) G.; father was econ. editor N.Y. Tribune and Dun's Weekly Rev.; prep. edn. Roots Acad., Greenwich, Conn.; B.S., Polytechnic Inst., Brooklyn, 1893; Johns Hopkins Univ., Baltimore; Ph.D., U. of Pa., 1898; m. Marie Dexter, Apr. 9, 1901; children—Mary Dexter (Mrs. Ralph O. Ellsworth), William Mason. Served as industrial investigator for New York Tribune, 1895; was chemist Mathieson Alkali Works, 1896; Millview Mining Co., 1898; engr. and asst. treas. Ampere Electrochem Co., 1899; asst. supt. Gen. Chem. Co., 1900-02; asst. mgr. investigating dept. same, 1903-04; supt. Contact Process Co., Buffalo, N.Y., 1905; engr., treas. George F. Westcott Co., 1906; engr., sec. Dryer Engring. Co., 1907; cons. practice and chem. expert since 1907. Mem. Textile Com., Council of Nat. Defense, World War. Mem. Am. Chem. Soc., Soc. Chem. Industry (chmn. 1915), Am. Inst. Chem. Engrs. (charter mem.), Electrochem Soc., Am. Institute of Chemists, Professional Engrs. Assn., A.A.A.S., Soc. de Chimie et Industrie. Presbyterian. Clubs: Chemists' of New York (charter mem.), Lawrence Beach, Lido. Contbr. to professional jours. First to introduce high speed moving picture and projection to analysis of rapid motion in industrial work; etc. Holder of numerous U.S. patents. Home: R.F.D. No. 1, New Canaan, Conn. Office: Chemists' Bldg., 50 E. 41st St., New York, N.Y.* Died May 30, 1944.

GROUT, Abel Joel, teacher; b. Newfane, Vt., Mar. 24, 1867; s. Joel and Martha J. G.; Ph.B., U. of Vt., 1890, Ph.D., Columbia, 1898; m. Grace E. Preston, July 21, 1893. Specialist in study of mosses; was 1st asst., N.H. State Normal Sch.; teacher botany, Boys' High Sch., Brooklyn, 1899-1908; 1st asst. teacher biology, Curtis High Sch., S.I., N.Y., since Nov., 1908. Editor Bryologist, 1911-12. Fellow A.A.A.S. Author: Mosses with a Hand-Lens; Mosses with a Hand-Lens and Microscope; also monographs on several genera. Address: New Dorp, Richmond County, N.Y. Died March 27, 1947.

GROVES, Charles Stuart, newspaperman, b. Montreal, Can., Dec. 29, 1867; s. Charles and Jeannette (McGillivary) G.; brought to U.S. in infancy; ed. pub. schs. of Mass.; m. Emily Cross Blossom, Dec. 25, 1893; children—Louise, John, Churchill B. Reporter and polit. writer, Boston Globe, 1890-1907; sec. to gov. of Mass., 1907; exec. sec. Rep. State Com. of Mass., 1908-13; Washington corr. Boston Globe since 1914. Episcopalian. Clubs: Gridiron (pres. 1930), Nat. Press. Author: Henry Cabot Lodge—The Statesman. Home: 1742 Q St. Office: Evening Star Bldg., Washington, D.C. Died Nov. 15, 1948; buried at Hingham, Mass.

GROVES, Ernest Rutherford, prof. sociology; b. Framingham, Mass., May 6, 1877; s. Henry Hunt and Hannah (Seward) G.; A.B., summa cum laude, Dartmouth College, 1903; B.D., Yale Divinity School, 1901; Litt.D., Florida Southern College, 1943; m. Dorothy, daughter of Chief Justice Charles Doe, of Rollinsford, N.H., Oct. 1906 (died 1916); children—Catherine, Ernestine Dorothy; m. 2d, Gladys Hoagland, Feb. 1919; children—Ruth Elva, Lois Mary. Instr. in Eng. and philosophy, U. of New Hampshire, 1903-04, asso. prof. of Eng., 1904-06, prof., 1908-10, sec. faculty, 1903-13, prof. psychology, 1910-15, prof. sociology, 1910-20, dean arts and sci. div., 1915-20; asso. prof. social science, Boston U., 1920-22, professor social science, lecturer on educational sociology, 1922-27; professor sociology, Univ. of N.C. since 1927. Lecturer on the family, Duke Univ., 1935-42. First pres. N.C. Mental Hygiene Soc., 1936-38; chmn. Com. on the Family, Federal Council of Churches of Christ in America, 1938-41; pres. Nat. Conf. Family Relations, 1941; pres. Am. Assn. of Marriage Counselors, 1945; est. at U. of N.C., annual Groves Conf. on Conservation of Marriage and the Family (oldest nat. con. for marriage educators and marriage counselors). Member American Sociological Society, Authors' Guild, Associe Institut Internationale de Sociologie, The Am. Orthopsychiatric Assn. (fellow) and Am. Assn. for Advancement of Sci. (fellow), Southern Sociol. Soc., Phi Beta Kappa. Independent Democrat. Congregationalist. Author: Personality and Social Adjustment, 1923; Social Problems and Education, 1925; (with wife) Wholesome Childhood, 1924; Drifting Home, 1926; Social Problems of the Family, 1926; (with wife) Wholesome Marriage, 1927; Introduction to Sociology, 1928; The Marriage Crisis, 1928; American Marriage and Family Relations (with W. F. Ogburn), 1928; Parents and Children, 1929; Wholesome Parenthood (both with wife), 1929; Introduction to Mental Hygiene (with Dr. Phyllis Blanchard), 1930; Sex in Marriage (with wife), 1931; The Family and Its Relationships (with others), 1932; Sex in Childhood (with wife), 1933; The American Family, 1934; Readings in the Family (with L. M. Brooks), 1934; Understanding Yourself, 1935; Readings in Mental Hygiene (with Phyllis Blanchard), 1936; Preparation for Marriage, 1936; The American Woman, 1937; Our Changing Social Order, 1938; The Family and its Social Functions, 1940; Marriage, 1933, 2d edit., 1941; Christianity and the Family, 1942; Sex Fulfillment in Marriage (co-author), 1942; Conserving Marriage and the Family, 1944; Dynamic Mental Hygiene (1946); The Contemporary American Family (co-author with wife), 1947; also brochures, pamphlets and articles. Editor Longmans, Green Sociology Series, 1926-46; asso. ed. Social Forces, Education; corr. editor Parents Magazine. Started first credit course in preparation for family life at Boston Univ., 1924, and later at summer session of Teachers Coll. (Columbia); developed at Univ. of N.C. first univ. credit course in preparation for marriage. Home: Chapel Hill, N.C. Died Aug. 28, 1946; buried in Sleepy Hollow Cemetery, Concord, Mass.

GROZIER, Richard, newspaperman; b. Brooklyn, New York, January 12, 1887; s. Edwin Atkins and Alice G. (Goodell) G.; grad. Phillips Exeter Acad., Exeter, N.H., 1905; A.B., Harvard, 1909; m. Margaret E. Murphy, Oct. 28, 1929 (now dec.); m. 2d, Helen V. Doherty, Jan. 18, 1935. Editor and pub. Boston Post since 1924. Address: 259 Washington St., Boston, Mass. Died June 19, 1946.

GRUBBS, Samuel Bates, pub. health service; b. Indianapolis, Ind., Feb. 11, 1871; s. Daniel Webster and Matilda (Miller) G.; prep. edn., Boys Classical Sch., Indianapolis, and Abbott Sch., Farmington, Me.; grad. Hogsetts Acad., Harrodsburg, Ky., 1888; A.B., U. of Mich., 1893; M.D., Coll. Physicians and Surgeons, Columbia, 1896; grad. study, Paris, 1900-01, Vienna, 1908; m. Mary Evelyn Noble, June 17, 1903; 1 son, Daniel Dean. In United States Public Health Service since 1897, specializing in yellow fever, bubonic plague, typhus fever and meningitis prevention, advanced through ranks to med. dir. retired, Sept. 1, 1933; service in Europe, Mexico, South America, P.I. and Orient; was chief quarantine officer, Porto Rico, 1908-12; visiting physician, Presbyn. Hosp., San Juan, Porto Rico, 1910-12; chief of extra cantonment sanitary area, Newport News, Va., 1917-18, and sanitary inspector U.S. Army, post of embarkation, N.Y.; served in France; chief quarantine officer, Panama Canal, 1919-20; health officer, Port of New York, 1921-25; chief of foreign quarantine div., 1925-27; dir. Great Lakes dist., 1928; adviser to Los Angeles Health Dept., 1929; chief guarantine officer, Hawaiian Islands, 1929-33. Sanitary insp. on board transport Sedgwich, Spanish-Am. War. Am. del. orgn. office Internat. d'Hygiene Publique. Mem. A.M.A., A.A.A.S., Nu Sigma Nu, Delta Upsilon. Republican. Clubs: University (Washington); Delta Upsilon (New York); Columbia, Indianapolis Literary (Indianapolis). Contbr. to Pub. Health Reports. Originator of vacuum cyanide method of disinfecting clothing, ratproofing of ships and cheopis index for bubonic plague. Home: Carmel, Ind. Address: U.S. Public Health Service, Washington, D.C.
Died Sep. 19, 1942.

GRUBER, L. Franklin, clergyman, educator; b. near Reading, Pa.; s. Franklin H. and Matilda (Himmelberger) G.; student Neff Coll. Elocution and Oratory, 1898-1900; grad. Pa. State Teachers Coll., 1892; A.B., Muhlenberg Coll., Pa., 1898, A.M., 1901; grad. Mt. Airy Luth. Theol. Sem., 1901; D.D., Muhlenberg, 1918; LL.D., Thiel, 1921; m. Amelia Louise Hoehn, Oct. 7, 1902; 1 son, Luther (dec.). Ordained Luth. ministry, 1901; prof. mathematics and English, Wagner Coll., Rochester, N.Y., 1901-02; pastor, Ch. of Holy Communion, Utica, N.Y., 1902-08, St. Mark's Ch., Minneapolis, Minn., 1908-14, Ch. of Reformation, St. Paul, 1914-27; pres. and prof. systematic theology, Chicago Luth. Theol. Sem. since 1927. Lecturer, Chicago Div. Sch., 1920-21, Northwestern Theol. Sem., 1921-22, Theol. Sem., Gettysburg, Pa., 1922; spl. lecturer on apologetics, Western Theol. Sem., 1922-26; lecturer Christian Evidences, Chicago Theol. Sem. since 1925; lecturer Chautauqua and other summer assemblies since 1921. Statis. sec. Synod of Northwest, 1914-27; sec.-treas. Gen. Council Com. on Religious Work in Am. Univs. and Colls., 1911-18; mem. Bd. of Edn. United Luth. Ch. in America, 1918-28; mem. Spl. Commn. on Theol. Edn., 1924-30, Spl. Commn. on Relationship between Science and Religion, 1926-28, Commission of Adjudication since 1936. Mem. A.A.A.S., Ill. Acad. Science, Am. Interprofessional Inst., Soc. of Biblical Research, Soc. of Biblical Literature and Exegesis, Am. Theol. Society, Philos. Soc. of Great Britain, History of Science Society, Astron. Soc. of the Pacific, Eugene Field Soc., American Society Church History, Pi Gamma Mu. Author: The Version of 1611, 1913; The Truth About Tyndale's New Testament, 1917; Documentary Sketch of the Reformation (from original documents), 1917; The Wittenberg Originals of the Luther Bible, 1918; Creation ex Nihilo, 1918 (issued, 1921, under title, Whence Came the Universe?); The Theory of a Finite and Developing Deity Examined, 1918; The Creative Days, 1919; Is the Doctrine of an Infinite and Unchangeable Deity Tenable? 1921; The Freedom of the Will, 1923; The Einstein Theory—Relativity and Gravitation, 1923; What After Death? 1925; The First New Testament and Luther, 1928. Contbr. "Nicholas von Amsdorf," in Leaders of the Lutheran Reformation, 1917; "The September Testament (1522)," "Luther the Prince of Translators," "The Bible in English," in The Translated Bible, 1934. Asso. editor Bibliotheca Sacra, 1920-34; contbg. editor The Bible Champion, 1920-23, World Book Ency. and its Annual. Died Dec. 5, 1941.

GRUEN, Frederick G(ustavus) (groo'en), horologist, watch mfr.; b. Delaware, O., Apr. 15, 1872; s. Dietrich and Pauline (Wittlinger) G.; student Ohio State U.; grad. Horological Inst., Glashutte, Dresden, Germany; m. Mathilda Louise Fischer, Apr. 5, 1906; children—Paul (dec.), Margaret Suzanne (wife of Dr. J. J. Longacre IV). A founder, pres. and chmn. bd. and horol. adviser Gruen Watch Co., Cincinnati; former dir. Western Bank, Cincinnati, dir. Ohio Nat. Life Ins. Co. Founder of modern watchmakers' guild idea. Hon. life mem. Horological Inst. of Am. (Washington, D.C.); hon. mem. Rice Leaders of World Assn., Alpina Uhrmacher Genossenschaft (Berlin). Chamber Music Soc., Cincinnati Fine Arts Inst., Cincinnati Mus. Assn. Mason (32°). Clubs: Queen City, Cincinnati. Inventor VeriThin and Curvex watches. Home: 3460 Oxford Terrace, Cincinnati, O. Died Sept. 15, 1945; buried in Spring Grove Cemetery, Cincinnati.

GRUMBINE, Harvey Carson, educator; b. Fredericksburg, Pa., May 1, 1869; s. Ezra (M.D.) and Annie (Beaver) G.; A.B., valedictorian, Albright College, Pa., 1888; Lafayette College, 1889; Ph.B., Wesleyan U., Conn., 1892; student Germanic and Romance philology, U. of Munich, 1897-1900, Ph.D., 1900; studied Bibliothèque Nationale, Paris, and British Museum, London; m. at Paris, C. Estelle Uhler, 1897. Asso. editor Lebanon (Pa.) Daily Report, 1892-94; on staff Philadelphia Record, 1894-95; prof. English and civics, Central State Normal Sch., Lock Haven, Pa., 1895-97; instr. English and German, Pa. State Coll., 1900-01; asst. prof. English, Washington U., St. Louis, 1901-02; prof. English lang. and lit., Coll. of Wooster, 1902-16; hon fellow, 1916-18, lecturer, 1918-19, Clark U.; prof. English, 1919-25, W.Va. Univ. Author: Vol. XIV of Literarhistorische Forschungen (Berlin), 1900; The Misfortunes of Arthur, 1900; Love, Faith and Endeavor, 1909; Stories from Browning, 1914; Humanity or Hate—Which?, 1917; The Chase, 1928; The Web, 1929; also monograph Reflections of an Immature Introspectionist, 1917. Contbr. of verse and articles to Outlook, Putnam's, Scribner's, Unpartizan Review, etc. Alternate del. at large from Ohio to Nat. Progressive Conv., 1912. Mem. Am. Assn. of Univ. Profs., A.A.A.S., Chi Psi, Phi Kappa Phi, Pi Gamma Mu. Address: Lebanon, Pa. Died Dec. 24, 1941.

GRUNN, Homer, pianist, composer; b. West Salem, Wis., May 5, 1880; s. John Ludwig and Sarah Catherine (Eublee) G.; studied music under Emil Liebling, Chicago, Ernest Jedliczka, Berlin; m. Nell Celeste Denhart, Dec. 28, 1905; children—Catherine Lydia, Nell Celeste, Sylvia Isabell. Début at Kimball Hall., Chicago, 1900; teacher of piano, Chicago Musical Coll., 1903-07; moved to Los Angeles, Calif., 1910; soloist with Los Angeles Symphony Orchestra and People's Orchestra, 1913-15; assisting artist with Zollner Quartet, 1921-24; a founder, Brahmns Quintet, 1910, and continued with it 8 seasons; soloist with Los Angeles Chamber Music Soc. Fellow MacDowell Colony, Peterboro, N.H. Mem. Am. Soc. Composers, Authors and Publishers, Calif. Soc. Composers (pres. 1937-38), First Am. (Indian) Assn. of N.M. Democrat. Clubs: Musicians (pres. 1924), MacDowell of Los Angeles (life); Uplifters (Santa Monica) Composer: Desert Suite; Zuni Indian Suite; symphonic poem, "Shadow World," for orchestra; also 5 operas, 2 ballets and many songs and piano pieces. Home: 911 Westchester Pl., Los Angeles, Calif.* Died June 6, 1944.

GRYLLS, Humphry John Maxwell (grĭlz), architect; b. England, Mar. 8, 1865; s. Humphry Millett and Henrietta Elizabeth (Fox) G.; ed. in England; came to America, 1881; m. Mary Field, Oct. 4, 1893; children—Humphry Millet Kercheval, Richard Gerveys Field, Maxwell Miles, John Robert Jefferson. In employ of W. E. Brown, architect, Detroit, 1883-85; became connected with William Scott & Co., 1885, and mem. of firm, 1889, when the title became John Scott & Co.; v.p. and treas. Smith, Hinchman & Grylls. Episcopalian. Fellow A.I.A.; mem. Detroit Chapter A.I.A., Arts and Crafts Soc., Mich. Soc. of Architects. Mem. Detroit Bd. of Commerce. Clubs: Detroit, Witenagemote, Detroit Automobile, Country (Detroit). Home: 1038 Parker Av. Office: 800 Marquette Bldg., Detroit, Mich.* Died June 21, 1942.

GUCK, Homer, newspaper pub.; b. L'Anse, Mich., June 11, 1878; s. Herman and Emma (Beehler) G.; grad. high sch., Calumet, Mich.; student U. of Chicago; m. Beatrice Clendenon Ferguson, Jan. 24, 1908. Began as reporter Chicago Journal, 1900; reporter Houghton (Mich.) Mining Gazette, 1902, mng. editor, 1902-04, v.p. and editor, 1904-20; asst. pres. Detroit Life Ins. Gas., 1920-24; dir. pub. relations, Union Trust Co., Detroit, 1924, v.p., 1925-27; asst. business mgr. New York Evening Journal, 1927; gen. mgr. San Francisco Examiner, 1928; pub. Chicago Herald and Examiner, 1929-36, Detroit Times, 1937. Served as pvt. 34th Mich. Inf., Spanish-Am. War. Mem. bd. dirs. Century of Progress, 1933. Mem. Phi Gamma Delta. Clubs: Chicago. Home: Eagle Harbor, Mich. Died June 15, 1949; buried Calumet, Mich.

GUDAKUNST, Donald Welsh (good'â-koonst), med. dir.; b. Paulding, O., Aug. 18, 1894; s. William Edward and Fannie May (Welsh) G.; B.S., U. of Mich., 1917, M.D., 1919; Dr. P.H., Wayne U., 1937; m. Jen Fray, June 20, 1921; 1 dau., Betty Sue; m. 2d, Bernice Drahner, Sept. 16, 1932. Industrial physician Solway Process Co., Detroit, Mich., 1920; county health officer, Roswell, N.M., 1921-23; dir. sch. health service, Detroit Dept. of Health, 1924-37; prof. pub. health and preventive medicine, Wayne Univ., 1937-41; dep. health commr. Detroit Dept. of Health, 1932-37; state health commr., Mich. State Dept. of Health, 1938-39; sr. surgeon (R.), U.S. P.H.S., 1939; med. dir., Nat. Foundation for Infantile Paralysis since Jan. 1, 1940. Fellow Am. Pub. Health Assn., N.Y. Acad. of Medicine, A.M.A.; mem. Alpha Kappa Kappa, Delta Omega. Contbr. to med. jours. Home: North Av., Westport, Conn. Address: 120 Broadway, New York, N.Y. Died Jan. 20, 1946.

GUEDALLA, Philip (gwĕ-däl'â), Brit. author; b. London, Eng., Mar. 12, 1889; Rugby Sch., Balliol Coll.; Oxford (B.A., 1912, M.A., 1916, pres. Oxford Union Soc., 1911); m. Nellie Maude Reitlinger, July 14, 1919. Admitted to the bar, 1913; retired from practice, 1923; in War Office as legal adviser of Contracts Dept.; organized Flax Control Bd., 1917-20; Liberal candidate from various sections, 1922-31; hon. dir. Ibero-American Inst. of Great Britain; chmn. Ibero-American and Film Coms., Brit. Council; mem. Cinematograph Films Council, Bd. of Trade; head of Latin-Am. sect. of Ministry of Information, 1940. Jewish religion. Author: Ignes Fatui, a Book of Parodies, 1911; Metri Gratia, Verse and Prose, 1911; The Partition of Europe, 1715-1815, 1914; Supers and Supermen, 1920; The Industrial Future, 1921; The Second Empire, 1922; Masters and Men, 1923; A Gallery, 1924; A Council of Industry, 1925; Napoleon and Palestine (Davis lecture), 1925; Independence Day, 1926; Palmerston, 1926; Conquistador, 1927; Gladstone and Palmerston, 1928; Bonnet and Shawl, 1928; The Missing Muse, 1929; The Duke, 1931; Argentine Tango, 1932; The Queen and Mr. Gladstone, 1933; The Hundred Days, 1934; The Hundred Years, 1936; 1936: The Hundredth Year, 1940; Mr. Churchill, 1941; The Two Marshals, 1943. Home: 15 Hyde Park St., London W 2, England; and The Laundry, Easton Park, Dunmow, Essex, England. Died Dec. 16, 1944.

GUERIN, Jules (gĕr'ĭn), artist; b. St. Louis, Mo., 1866; s. Richmond L. and Louise (Davis) G.; pupil of Benjamin Constant and Jean Paul Laurens; Litt.D., Dartmouth Coll., Hanover, N.H.; m. Mary Mulford. Awarded Yerkes Medal; silver medal, St. Louis Expn., 1904; gold medal, Panama P.I. Expn., 1915. Dir. color and decoration, Panama P.I. Expn. Painted decorations for Lincoln Memorial Building, Washington; Pa. Sta., New York City; decorations in Federal Reserve Bank, San Francisco, Ill. Merchants Bank (Chicago), Union Trust Bank (Cleveland), Civic Opera (Chicago), Cleveland Terminal Bldg., Merchandise Mart, Chicago, State Capitol, Baton Rouge, La. N.A.; mem. Architectural League, N.Y., Nat. Inst. of Arts and Letters, Am. Water Color Society, American Institute of Architects, Soc. of Am. Illustrators, Beaux Arts Society (New York). Clubs: Tavern (Chicago); Amateur Comedy, New York Water Color, Century, Coffee House, Players (New York). Address: 24 Gramercy Park, New York, N.Y. Died June 13, 1946.

GUERRY, Alexander (gĕr'rĭ), univ. pres.; b. Lincolnton, N.C., Oct. 17, 1890; s. William Alexander and Anne (McBee) G.; grad. Sewanee Mil. Acad., 1906; B.A., U. of the South, 1910, D.C.L., 1929; LL.B., Chattanooga Coll. of Law, 1913; m. Charlotte Holmes Patten, Dec. 17, 1914; children—Alexander, John Patten. Commd. 1st lt. U.S. Army, Sept. 12, 1918; served with 320th Machine Gun Batt., 82d Div., A.E.F.; participated in St. Mihiel and the Argonne campaigns; hon. discharged, May 11, 1919; headmaster Baylor Sch., Chattanooga, 1919-29; pres. U. of Chattanooga, 1929-38; vice chancellor (pres.) U. of the South since 1938. Pres. Tenn. Coll. Assn., 1931-33; mem. bd. dirs., Assn. Am. Colleges since 1947; mem. exec. com. Southern Assn. of Colleges and Secondary Schools, 1940; pres. Southern Univ. Conf., 1946; mem. Tenn. Civil Service Commn. since 1940. Mem. Am. Legion (comdr. Chattanooga Post 1922-23), Phi Beta Kappa. Independent. Episcopalian. Rotarian. Address: University of the South, Sewanee, Tenn. Died Oct. 19, 1948.

GUERRY, Le Grand, surgeon; b. Florence, S.C., Feb. 3, 1873; s. Le Grand Felder and Julia (Evans) G.; student U. of the South, 1890-93, D.C.L., 1924; M.D., U. of Ga. Med. Sch., 1895; LL.D., U. of S.C., 1928; D.Sc., U. of Ga., 1931; m. Anne Elizabeth Hawkins, June 5, 1899; children—Le Grand, Emily, Annie Elizabeth (Mrs. Walter Newton), Virginia Felder (Mrs. John Conn). Demonstrator of anatomy in the U. of Georgia Medical Department, 1897-99; practiced at Columbia since 1899; surgeon Columbia Hospital. Fellow Am. Coll. Surgeons; mem. A.M.A., S.C. Med. Assn. (ex-pres.), Am. Surg. Assn. (1st v.p.), Southern Surg. Assn. (pres. 1924), Tri-State Med. Assn. (ex-pres.), Columbia Med. Soc. (ex-pres.), Phi Beta Kappa. Democrat. Episcopalian. Home: 1831 Pendleton St. Office: 1417 Hampton Av., Columbia, S.C.* Died Aug. 14, 1947.

GUESS, Harry Adelbert, mining engr.; b. Hartington, Ont., Can., Nov. 21, 1875; s. Charles Wellington and Augusta (Shorey) G.; M.A., Queen's Univ., Kingston, 1895, LL.D., 1926; m. Eva Young, Winnipeg, Can., June 19, 1901 (died Mar. 13, 1935); 1 son, Shorey Cameron; m. 2d, Vista Brabham, Mar. 18, 1936 (died Dec. 24, 1940); 1 son, Harry Adelbert Jr. Came to United States, 1901, naturalized citizen, 1923. Has been connected with the American Smelting & Refining Co. since 1901, as manager various mines, in charge metal mining explorations and operations, v.p. since 1917, in charge of mining operations and explorations; chmn. Big Bell Mines, Ltd. (Western Australia); pres. Neptune Gold Mining Co., Buchans Mining Co., Ltd., Premier Gold Mining Co., Ltd. (Can.), Montezuma Lead Co. and Cia Metalurgica Mexicana, Silbak Premier Mines, Ltd. (Can.), Toburn Gold Mines Co. (Can.); v.p. Northern Peru Mining & Smelting Co., Federal Mining & Smelting Co., N.Y. and Honduras Rosario Mining Co.; dir. Compania Minera Asarco (Mexico), Revere Copper & Brass Co., Inc., Towne Mines, Inc., Gen. Cable Corp. Mem. Am. Inst. Mining & Metall. Engrs., Mining and Metall. Soc. America. Republican. Presbyterian. Clubs: University, Bankers. Home: 8 Markwood Rd., Forest Hills, L.I., N.Y. Office: 120 Broadway, New York, N.Y. Died Apr. 11, 1946.

GUGGENHEIM, Solomon R., mining; b. Phila., Feb. 2, 1861; s. Meyer and Barbara (Myers) G.; ed. pub. and pvt. schs., Phila., and St. Gall and Zürich, Switzerland. Mem. Guggenheim Bros.; dir. Braden Copper Co., Nev. Northern Ry. Co., Kennecott Copper Corp., Pacific Tin Consol. Corp. Pres. Solomon R. Guggenheim Foundation. Mem. Am. Inst. Mining and Metall. Engrs. Home: Trillora Court, Port Washington, N.Y. Office: 120 Broadway, New York, N.Y.* Died Nov. 3, 1949.

GUILD, Courtenay (gild), editor, pub.; b. Boston, Mass., Dec. 6, 1863; s. Curtis and Sarah Crocker (Cobb) G.; A.B., Harvard, 1886; hon. Dr. Fine Arts, Boston U., 1940; unmarried. Formerly connected with banking business; sec. to mayor of Boston, 1895; city tax collector of Boston, 1900-02, associated with brother (the late Gov. Curtis Guild), 1907, under title of Curtis Guild & Co., pubs. The Commercial Bulletin (founded by father, 1859), of which is owner, also with bro. organized the Anchor Linotype Printing Co., of which is pres. and treas.; Trustee, Military Historical Society, Trustee; Oliver Ditson Fund. Honorary Pres. Mass. Anti Saloon League. Director, General Theological Library v.p. Franklin Savings Bank dir. The Exolon Co. Mem. 1st Corps Cadets, 1891-1900; mem. Rep. City Com. 54 yrs.; mem. Boston Finance Com., 1918-32, etc. Pres. Closed Shop Employing Printers of Greater Boston; trustee Boston Univ. Vice-president Bunker Hill Monument Assn., Bostonian Soc. (pres.), Industrial Aid Soc. (v.p.), Harvard Musical Assn. (pres.), Handel and Haydn Soc. (pres.), Veteran Journalists Assn. (pres.). Unitarian. Clubs: Union, Union Boat, Harvard, Round Table, Shakespeare, Apollo (pres. since 1904); Harvard (New York). Author of "Thirty Years More," history of Handel and Haydn Soc., 1903-1933. Home: 26 Mt. Vernon St. Office: 144 High St., Boston, Mass. Died Apr. 24, 1946.

GUILD, George A. (gĭld), banker; b. Galesburg, Ill., Sept. 28, 1863; s. Rufus B. and Susan (Bergen) G.; student Knox Coll., Galesburg, Ill., 1879-81; m. Gertrude Irish, Nov. 10, 1886; children—Mildred (wife of Dr. Walter H. Weidling), Herbert H. Began as store clk., 1881; with bank, Sabetha, Kan., 1883-1908; pres. Capitol Nat. Bank, Topeka, 1908-10; v.p. Central Nat. Bank, 1910-32, chmn. bd. since 1932; v.p. Central Trust Co., Kansas Bankers Surety Co.; dir. Capitol Federal Savings & Loan Assn. Trustee Washburn Co., Topeka. Republican. Conglist. Mason (32°). Club: Topeka Country. Home: 2220 W. Euclid. Office: Central National Bank, Topeka, Kan.* Died Aug. 14, 1944.

GUILD, Lewis Thurber (gĭld), clergyman; b. nr. Des Moines, Ia., May 5, 1864; s. Rev. J. Ellis and Sarah (Ramsey) G.; Ph.B., Ill. Wesleyan U., 1898, Ph.D., 1901; D.D., Neb. Wesleyan Univ., 1903; m. Ruth Thomas, June 21, 1884; children—Ellis Darwin, Ruth Edna, Bartlett Paine, Lewis Thurber. Learned printers' trade; supt. schs., Holdrege, Neb., 1884-86; editor Holdrege Republican; entered M.E. ministry, 1888; in Bulgaria, 1893-94, as supt. Publs. M.E. Ch. in Eastern Europe; pastor Crete, Neb., 1891-93, again 1895-96, Grace Ch., Lincoln, Neb., 1897-1899, Grace Ch., Des Moines, 1900-04. Wesley Ch., Minneapolis, Minn., 1905-07, First Ch., San Diego, Calif., 1907-11, St. Paul's Ch., Toledo, Ohio, 1911-13; Chautauqua lecturer, Redpath Bureau, 1906-07; editor and manager of Daily Courier-News, Fargo, N.D., 1913-17, Daily Outlook, Santa Monica, Calif., 1917-18; pastor Wilshire Ch., Los Angeles, 1918-19, First Ch., Long Beach, 1919-22; del. Ecumenical Conf., London, Eng., 1921; area sec., San Francisco Area, M.E. Church, 1922-23; supt. Los Angeles Dist., M.E. Ch., 1923-29; sec. Los Angeles Missionary and Ch. Extension Soc. M.E. Ch., 1927-29; preacher in England under Internat. Com. on Pulpit Exchanges, 1930; lecturer Auditorium Bible Class, First M.E. Ch., Los Angeles, 1932-39. Mem. Southern Calif.-Ariz. Methodist Conf. Republican. Mason. President Los Angeles Celtic Club, 1920. Author: The Romance of Religion, 1924; The Cosmic Ray in Literature, 1929. Contbr. to religious periodicals. Traveled abroad, 5 times, visiting mission fields, Palestine and Egypt twice, around the world, 1929-30. Home: 149 S. Kingsley Dr., Los Angeles, Calif. Died Dec. 21, 1944.

GUILD, Roy Bergen (gĭld), clergyman; b. Galva, Ill., Dec. 1, 1871; s. Rufus Barnard and Susan Fidelia (Bergen) G.; student Washburn Coll., Topeka, Kan., 1891-92; A.B., Knox Coll., 1894, A.M., 1897, D.D., 1911; grad. Chicago Theol. Sem., 1897; m. Winifred A. Everhard, June 21, 1898; children—William Everhard, Roland Bergen, George Scoville. Ordained Congl. ministry, 1897; pastor Woodstock, Ill., 1897-1900, Leavitt St. Ch., Chicago, 1900-06; sec. Ill. Home Missionary Soc., 1906-08; N.E. sec. Congl. Ch. Building Soc., Boston, 1908-10; exec. sec. Men and Religion Forward Movement, 1911-12; pastor Central Ch., Topeka, Kan., 1912-15. Chmn. Kan. State Commn. on Pub. Health, 1913-15; exec. sec. Commn. on Councils of Churches of Federal Council Chs. of Christ in America, 1915-25; pastor Trinitarian Congl. Ch., New Bedford, Mass., 1925-29; asso. gen. sec. Federal Council of Chs. of Christ in America since 1929; sec. Com. on Religious Work in Canal Zone; exec. of Gen. Com. on Army and Navy Chaplains, Washington, D.C.; sec. emeritus Federal Council of Chs., 1937. Fla. exec. sec. Save the Children Fedn., since 1939. Mem. Florida Conf. of Congl. Christian Churches, Beta Theta Pi, Phi Beta Kappa, Quill. Republican. Decorated La Croix de Chevalier de l'Ordre de la Couronne (Belgium), 1919. Editor: Manual of Interchurch Work; Community Programs for Cooperating Churches, 1933. Author: Practicing Christian Unity, 1919. Home: 333 Vitoria Av., Winter Park, Fla. Office: 297 4th Av., New York, N.Y. Died Jan. 13, 1945.

GUILD, William Huntoon (gĭld), railroad exec.; b. Omaha, Neb., Oct. 25, 1883; s. John and Laura (Reed) G.; ed. grade and high schs., Omaha; m. Ethel Lawrie, Oct. 7, 1909; children—William H., Harriet L. (Mrs. George M. Seymour). Began as office boy, 1899, successively clk., sec. and chief clk., asst. to gen. mgr., gen. supt., gen. mgr., vice-pres. Union Pacific R.R. since 1940. Republican. Presbyterian.

Mason (Shriner). Home: 119 S. Orange Dr., Los Angeles, Calif. Died July 29, 1948.

GUILDAY, Peter (gĭl'dā), clergyman, educator; b. Chester, Pa., Mar. 25, 1884; s. Peter Wilfrid and Ellen (Keenan) G.; Overbrook Sem., Phila., 1902-07; U. of Louvain, Belgium, 1907-14, Docteur en Sciences Historiques, 1914; LL.D., U. of Notre Dame; 1925; L.H.D., Marquette U., 1928: J.U.D., Georgetown U., 1930. Instr. in history, Catholic U. of America, 1914-19, asso. prof. history, 1919-23, prof. Am. ch. history since 1923. Asst. dir. S.A.T.C. for Middle States, 1917-18. Founder Catholic Hist. Assn., 1919; fellow Royal Hist. Soc., 1918. Made domestic prelate by Pius XI, title Right Rev. Monsignor, 1935. Decorated Chevalier de l'Ordre de Léopold II (Belgium). Republican. Author: English Colleges and Convents in the Low Countries, 1914; The Three Hours' Agony of Our Lord Jesus Christ, 1917; Life and Times of John Carroll, 1922; National Pastorals of the American Hierarchy, 1923; The Church in Virginia (monographs), 1924; Graduate Studies (brochure), 1924; Life of John Gilmary Shea (monograph), 1926; Life and Times of John England, 1927; History of the Councils of Baltimore, 1932. Editor: Church Historians, 1926; The Catholic Church in Contemporary Europe, 1932. Editor Catholic Hist. Review (founder); formerly asso. editor Speculum. Address: Catholic University of America, Washington, D.C. Died July 31, 1947.

GUITERMAN, Arthur (gĭt'ẽr-măn), author; b. of Am. parentage, Vienna, Austria, Nov. 20, 1871; s. Alexander and Louisa (Wolf) Guiterman; B.A., Coll. City of New York, 1891; Litt.D., Rollins College, 1940; m. Vilda Lindo, 1909. In editorial work on Woman's Home Companion, Literary Digest and other mags., 1891-1906. Author: Betel Nuts, 1907; Guest Book, 1908; Rubaiyat, including The Literal Omar, 1909; Orestes (with André Tridon), 1909; The Laughing Muse, 1915; The Mirthful Lyre, 1918; Ballads of Old New York, 1920; Chips of Jade, 1920; A Ballad Maker's Pack, 1921; The Light Guitar, 1923; A Poet's Proverbs, 1924; I Sing the Pioneer, 1926; Wildwood Fables, 1927; Song and Laughter, 1929; (play) The School for Husbands (with Lawrence Langner, adapted from Molière), 1933; Death and General Putnam and 101 Other Poems, 1935; Gaily the Troubadour, 1936; Lyric Laughter, 1939; libretto of opera "A Man Without a Country" (score by Walter Damrosch), produced by the Met. Opera Co., 1937-38. Was lecturer on magazine and newspaper verse in the New York U. Sch. of Journalism, 1912-15. Contributor of "Rhymed Reviews," to Life, and of ballad and lyric verse to various mags. Pres. Poetry Soc. of America, 1925-27, Authors' League Fellowship, 1925-27. Mem. Authors' League of America. Address: 187 E. 64th St., New York, N.Y.; and Hillhouse, Arlington, Vt. Died Jan. 11, 1943.

GULICK, Sidney Lewis, missionary; b. Ebon, Marshall Islands, Apr. 10, 1860; s. Luther Halsey and Louisa (Lewis) G.; A.B., Dartmouth, 1883, A.M., 1886; D.D., 1903; grad. Union Theol. Sem., 1886; D.D., Yale, 1914, Oberlin, 1914; m. Cara May Fisher, Sept. 14, 1887; children—Susan Fisher, Luther Halsey, Leeds, Ethel, Sidney Lewis. Ordained Congl. ministry, Dec. 1886; stated supply Willoughby Av. Mission, Brooklyn, 1886-87; missionary A.B.C.F.M. in Japan, 1887-1913; prof. theology, Doshisha, Kyoto, 1906-13; lecturer Imperial U., Kyoto, 1907-13; sec. dept. of internat. justice and good will Federal Council Chs. of Christ in America, 1914-34; sec. Am. Branch of World Alliance for Promotion of Internat. Friendship through the Churches, 1916-19; sec. Nat. Committee for Constructive Immigration Legislation, 1919-34; sec. Nat. Com. on Am. Japanese Relations, 1921-1934; sec. Com. on World Friendship Among Children, 1926-34. Retired. Author: The Growth of the Kingdom of God, 1896; Evolution of the Japanese, Social and Psychic, 1903; The White Peril in the Far East, 1905; A Sketch of the History of German Theology (in Japanese), 1909; Evolution (cosmic, terrestrial and biological, also in Japanese), 1910; Evolution of the Human Race (in Japanese), 1913; The American-Japanese Problem, 1914; General Cyclopedia, with Classification of Human Knowledge (in Japanese), 1914; The Fight for Peace, 1915; Working Women of Japan, 1915; America and the Orient, 1916; Anti-Japanese War-Scare Stories, 1917; American Democracy and Asiatic Citizenship, 1918; The Korean Situation, 1919; The Korean Situation No. 2, 1920; Problems of the Pacific and the Far East, 1921; Should Congress Enact Special Laws Affecting Japanese?, 1922; The Christian Crusade for a Warless World, 1922; The Winning of the Far East, 1923; Making the Peace Pact Effective, 1929; Dolls of Friendship, 1929; Churches and the World Disarmament Conference, 1931; Toward Understanding Japan, 1935; Mixing the Races in Hawaii, 1937. Home: 2451 E. Manoa Rd., Honolulu, T.H. Died Dec. 20, 1945.

GULLION, Allen Wyant (gŭl'yŭn), major general, United States Army; b. Carrollton, Kentucky, Dec. 14, 1880; s. Edmund A. and Atha (Hanks) G.; A.B., Centre Coll., Ky., 1901; B.S., U.S. Mil. Acad., 1905; LL.B., U. of Ky., 1914; grad. Gen. Service Sch., Leavenworth, Kan., 1928, Army War Coll., Washington, D.C., 1931; grad. Naval War College, Newport, R.I., 1932; General Staff Corps Eligible List; hon. LL.D., University of Hawaii, 1935, Centre College, 1939, University of Kentucky, 1942; m. Ruth Mathews, September 9, 1905 (deceased); children—Ruth, Edmund, Atha, Margaret (dec.), Phillip, Allen. Commd. 2d lt. U.S. Army, June 13, 1905; promoted through grades to lt. col., Aug. 31, 1929; col., 2d Ky. Inf., Mexican Border, 1916; lt. col. (temp.) World War. Prof. mil. science and tactics, U. of Ky., 1912-14. Chief of Mobilization Div., Office of Provost Marshal Gen., Nat. Selective Service, Washington, D.C., 1917; judge advocate Third Corps, A.E.F., 1918; legal adviser to Gen. R. L. Bullard, Governors Island, N.Y., 1919-24; chief of Mil. Affairs Div., Office Judge Advocate Gen., Washington, 1928-30; sr. War Dept. rep. at Geneva, 1929, participating with representatives of 47 nations in formulation of code for prisoners of war, and in revision of Geneva Convention of 1906; senior judge adv. Hawaiian Dept., 1932-33; sole U.S. del. to Congress of Juridical Experts, Luxembourg, 1938, addressing the conf. on the "present state of international law regarding protection of civilians against the new war technics"; senior War Dept. rep. and del. of Am. and Federal bar assns. at first convention of Inter-American Bar Assn., Havana, 1941. Deputy administrator, NRA, Territory of Hawaii, 1933-35; chief of mil. affairs div., Office of Judge Advocate Gen., Washington, D.C., 1935, asst. judge advocate gen., 1936, acting judge advocate gen., 1937, judge advocate general (major general), 1937; provost marshal general (major general), July 31, 1941-Apr. 28, 1944; overseas (France) 1944; retired as major general, December 1944. Honorary president Kentucky Soc., Washington. Awarded D.S.M. (U.S.); Oak Leaf cluster to D.S.M., 1944; Legion of Merit (1944); Estralla d'Abdon Calderon (Ecuador). Clubs: Army and Navy (Washington, D.C.); Army and Navy Country (Arlington, Va.). Home: 2737 Devonshire Pl. N.W., Washington, D.C. Died June 19, 1946.

GUNN, Selskar Michael; b. London, Eng., May 25, 1883; s. Michael and Barbara Elizabeth (Johnston) G.; student Kensington Park Coll., London, 1896-1900; came to America, 1900; S.B., Mass. Inst. Tech., 1905; C.P.H., Harvard Technology School of Public Health, 1917; m. Carroll McComas, July 1933. Bacteriologist, Boston Biochem. Lab., 1905-06; 1st asst. bacteriologist, State Bd. of Health, Ia., 1906-08; lecturer on hygiene, U. of Ia., 1906-08; health officer, Orange, N.J., 1908-10; instr. sanitary biology, 1910, asst. prof. sanitary biology and pub. health, 1911-14, asso. prof., 1914-19, Mass. Inst. Tech. Asst. prof. biology, Simmons Coll., 1912-14. Sec. Am. Pub. Health Assn., 1912-18. Mng. editor, 1912-14, editor, 1914-18, Am. Jour. Pub. Health. Mem. State Bd. Labor and Industries of Mass., 1913-14; dir. div. hygiene, State Health Dept. of Mass., 1915-16; asso. dir. of Commn. for the Prevention of Tuberculosis in France, 1917-20; advisor ministry of health, Czechoslovakia, 1920-22; dir. Paris office Internat. Health Board of Rockefeller Foundation, 1922-27; vice-pres. Rockefeller Foundation since 1927. Capt., Am. Red Cross, 1918-19. Legion of Honor (France), 1919, Officier, 1925, Comdr., 1938; Comdr. Chevalier Order Polonia Restituta (Poland), 1923; Grand Officier Order Saint Sava (Jugoslovakia), 1925; Officer Order White Lion (Czechoslovakia), 1924; "Meritul Sanitar" (Rumania), 1926; Comdr. Royal Order of St. Olav (Norway), 1926; Comdr. Order of Dannebrog (Denmark), 1927. Was sanitary expert of the Bureau of Economy and Efficiency, Milwaukee, 1911; asst. sec.-gen. 15th Internat. Congress on Hygiene and Demography, Washington, 1912. Sec. health com. Office of Foreign Relief, State Dept. since 1943. Mem. A.A.A.S., Am. Pub. Health Assn., Nu Sigma Nu, Cercle Interalliée (Paris); corr. mem. Royal Budapest Med. Soc., 1924. Club: Cosmos (Washington). Author of various papers on sanitary subjects. Address: Rockefeller Foundation, 49 W. 49th St., New York, N.Y. Died Aug. 2, 1944.

GUNNISON, Royal Arch, war correspondent, broadcaster, author; b. Juneau, Alaska, Feb. 7, 1909; s. Royal Arch and Helena (Cobb) G.; grad. George Washington U., Washington, D.C.; studied for U.S. Foreign Service; student The Principia, St. Louis, Mo.; Univ. of Washington, Seattle, Wash.; grad. student internat. politics and economics, U. of Geneva; m. Marjorie Hathaway, 1935. Began as fgn. corr. Associated Press, Europe, assigned to cover League of Nations, 1934; later staff corr. Christian Science Monitor, working fgn. news desk (Boston), writing front page column The World's Day, also conducting daily newscast; assigned by Monitor to West Coast News Bureau, covering Australia, New Zealand, Hawaii, Alaska, 11 western states; joined staff North Am. Newspaper Alliance, 1940, sent Alaska first Clipper flight, June, 1940, to New Zealand and Australia first Pan Am. Clipper flight, Aug. 1940; remained on assignment in East Asia, Australia, Netherlands East Indies, Singapore, Malaya, free and occupied China and Philippine Islands; broadcast from Australia for M.B.S., 1941, later from Chunking, China. Became Collier's corr., in Far East prior war with Japan; caught last Clipper from Hongkong to Manila, arriving just before Philippines attacked, Dec. 7, 1941; covered Philippines campaign for M.B.S., Collier's, North Am. Newspaper Alliance. Captured by Japanese Army in Manila, Jan. 2, 1942, repatriated to U.S. aboard M.S. Gripsholm, December 1943; correspondent for M.B.S. and Collier's covering Philippine liberation campaign, 1944-45. Now M.B.S. news analyst. Received 1942 National Headliner's Journalism award for radio reporting under combat conditions; United Nations Association, award for "unceasing effort and contribution to cause of internat. cooperation," Jan. 1944; citation from Alaska for remaining in Manila to report the invasion. Mem. Sigma Chi. Author: So Sorry—No Peace, 1944. Was in Vienna when Premier Dolfuss was assassinated; in Berlin just after first blood purge, Nazi Party. Address: care Mutual Broadcasting System, New York, N.Y. Died Sep. 25, 1946.

GUNTHER, Ernest Ludolph, naval officer; b. Louisville, Ky., Sept. 7, 1887; s. Marius Harrison and Fanny Lee (Aroni) G.; B.S., U.S. Naval Acad., 1909; m. Helen St. Goar, May 20, 1922; children—Ernest Harrison, Charles Frederick. Commd. ensign U.S. Navy, 1909, advancing through the grades to rear adm., 1942; comd. U.S.S. Jarvis (destroyer) in European waters, World War I; naval attaché to Chile, 1931-34; comd. Naval Air Station and Naval Air Center, San Diego, Calif., 1942-43; comdr. aircraft, South Pacific Force, 1943-45; comdr. Air Force Pacific Fleet Subordinate Comd. Forward Areas, Feb. 1945-May 1946; comdr. Fleet Air, Quonset Pt. since 1946. Decorated Navy Cross, Legion of Merit (U.S.), Orden del Merito (Chile), Presidential Medal of Merit (Nicaragua), British Order of the Bath. Clubs: New York (N.Y.) Yacht; Philadelphia (Pa.) Racquet; Army and Navy (Washington, D.C.). Home: 9241 Peabody Av., Memphis. Died Mar. 27, 1948.

GURD, Fraser Baillie, surgeon; b. Montreal, Quebec, Can., Jan. 7, 1883; s. David Fraser and Mary (Baillie) G.; B.A., McGill U., 1904, M.D., C.M., 1906; m. Jessie Gibson Newman, Jan. 4, 1910; children—Fraser Newman (M.D.), Katharine Mary (Currie), Frank Ross Newman. Instr., lecturer in pathology, Tulane U.; pathologist Touro Infirmary, New Orleans, 1909-11; lecturer in immunology, McGill U., 1911-20, consecutively demonstrator, lecturer, asst. prof., asso. prof., prof. of surgery, since 1911; asst. in surgery, Montreal Gen. Hosp., consecutively asso. surgeon, attending surgeon, chief of surgical service, surgeon-in-chief, since 1911; surgeon-in-chief Grace Dart Home Hosp. (for pulmonary tuberculosis), since 1932. Served as capt., Royal Army Med. Corps, 1915-18, officer commanding dept. exptl. surgery, Alder Hey Hosp., Liverpool; surgery specialist, 22 casualty Clearing Stations; maj. Royal Canadian Army Med. Corps, officer comdg. St. Annes Mil. Hosp., 1918-21. Fellow Canadian Med. Assn., Am. Assn. of Pathologists and Bacteriologists, Am. Assn. for Tropical Medicine, A.M.A., Am. Coll. of Surgeons (2d vice pres., 1938-39), Am. Assn. for Thoracic Surgeons (vice pres., 1939, pres., 1940-41), Am. Surgical Assn. Royal Coll. Surgeons of Can.; mem. Canadian Assn. Clin. Surgeons (pres., 1938-40), Am. Assn. for Surgery of Trauma (founders group; vice pres., 1938-39, pres., 1939-40), Am. Bd. of Surgery (founders group), Surg. Research Soc., Central Surg. Soc. (founders group), McGill regional Com. of Surgery (chmn.), Nat. Research Council of Can., Nat. Research Council (mem. subcom. on surgery, 1942-46), Phi Rho Sigma, Delta Upsilon, Sigma Xi. Mem. Conservative party. Mem. United Ch. of Canada. Clubs: Mount Royal, University, Faculty (McGill U.), Royal Montreal Golf, Rotary, Canadian (Montreal). Home: 3180 The Boulevard, Westmount 6, Quebec, Can. Office: 1538 Sherbrooke St. W., Montreal 25, Quebec, Can. Died Feb. 22, 1948; buried Mount Royal Cemetery, Montreal.

GUTHRIE, Ernest Graham, clergyman; b. Dunedin, New Zealand, Dec. 21, 1879; s. Henry and Isabella Allen (Graham) G.; B.A., U. of New Zealand, 1900, M.A. (1st class honors in philosophy), 1901; studied Presbyn. Theol. Hall, New Zealand, 2 yrs.; B.D., Yale, 1904, fellow, 1905; D.D., Chicago Theol. Sem., 1927, Carleton Coll., 1927; D.D., Olivet (Mich.) Coll., 1928; LL.D., 1933; unmarried. Ordained Presbyn. ministry, 1906; asso. pastor Third Ch., Rochester, N.Y., 1906-07; temporarily in ministry for a yr. in New Zealand; minister 1st Ch. (Congl.), Burlington, Vt., 1908-14, Union Ch., Boston, Mass., 1914-26; gen. dir. Chicago Congl. Union since 1926. Gen. officer Am. Field Service, with French Army, 1917. Trustee Chicago Church Federation, Olivet (Mich.) Coll.; mem. Chicago City Mgr. Com., Christian Unity Com.; chmn. College-Church Movement; chmn. Ill. Com. for Assistance to War Victims; mem. Nat. Fight for Freedom Com., Union for Democratic Action, Nat. Commn. on Inter-Church Relations. Home: 152 E. Superior St. Office: 19 S. La Salle St., Chicago, Ill. Died Jan. 20, 1944.

GUTHRIE, William Norman, clergyman; b. at Dundee, Scotland, Mar. 4, 1868; s. of William Eugene and Frances Sylva (d'Arusmont) G.; B.Litt., U. of the South, 1889, A.M., 1891, D.D., 1915; m. Anna Norton Stuart, Jan. 4, 1893. Asst. prof. modern langs., U. of the South, 1889-90; prof. modern langs., Kenyon Coll., 1892-93; ordained P.E. ministry, 1893; missionary in charge, Christ Ch., Kennedy Heights, 1893-94; asst. Ch. of the Advent, Cincinnati, 1894-96; lecturer comparative lit., U. of Cincinnati, 1898-1900; rector Ch. of Resurrection, Fern Bank, O., 1899-1903, Christ Ch., Alameda, Calif., 1903-08; prof. gen. lit. and dir. Univ. Extension Dept., U. of the South, 1908-11; rector St. Marks in the Bouwerie, New York, 1911-37, now rector emeritus of St. Marks in the Bouwerie. Author: Love Conquereth, 1890; Modern Poet Prophets, Essays Critical and Interpretative, 1897, 1899; To Kindle the Yule Log, 1899; Songs of American Destiny, 1900; The Old Hemlock, 1901; The Christ of the Ages in Words of Holy Writ, 1903; Orpheus Today; St. Francis of the Trees and Other Verse, 1907; The Vital Study of Literature, 1911; Beyond Disillusion; A Dramatic Study of Modern Marriage, 1915; Uncle Sam and Old World Conquerors, 1915; The Gospel of Osiris, 1916; Leaves of the Greater Bible, 1917. Editor Forensic Quarterly, 1909-10, Dramatic Quarterly, 1910-11, Leaves of the Greater Bible, 1916; The Religion of Old Glory, 1919; From

Ragnarock to the Immediate Presence of God, 1922; The Birth and Progress of the Human Soul, 1923; Offices of Mystical Religion, 1927; Twenty-four Evangelical Offices, 1930; Seven Oracles from the Cross, 1935; The Lord's Prayer (a series of mystery dramas in 7 short dramatic episodes), 1940. Club: National Arts. Address: 242 Sound View Av., Stamford, Conn. Died Dec. 9, 1944; buried at Alexandria, Va.

GUYER, Ulysses Samuel, congressman; b. Pawpaw, Lee County, Ill.; s. Rev. Joseph and Sarah (Lewis), G.; ed. Lane U., Lecomton, Kan., Southwestern College of Commerce, Wichita; grad. Leander Clark Coll. (now merged with Coe Coll., Cedar Rapids, Ia.), 1894; School of Law, Univ. of Kan., 1895-97; LL.B., Kansas City School of Law, 1902; LL.D., Coe Coll., Cedar Rapids, Ia.; m. Della Alforetta Daugherty, Jan. 15, 1919. Prin. St. John (Kan.) high sch., 1897-1901; admitted to Kansas bar, 1902, and practiced at Kansas City, Kan. since 1902. Judge City Court of Kansas City, 1907-09; resigned to become mayor of Kansas City, Kan., term 1909-10; mem. 68th Congress (1923-25) to fill unexpired term of E. C. Little (dec.), also 70th to 77th Congresses (1927-43), 2d Dist. Kan. (ranking Republican on Com. on the Judiciary). Mem. Am. Bar Assn. Republican. Conglist. Mason, Odd Fellow. Home: The Cedars, Fort-to-Fort Highway. Office: Occidental Life Bldg., Kansas City, Kan. Died June 5, 1943.

GWATHMEY, James Tayloe, physician; b. Norfolk, Va., Sept. 10, 1863; s. William Watts and Margaret (Tayloe) G.; ed. Norfolk Male Acad., Va. Mil. Inst.; M.D., Vanderbilt U. Med. Dept., 1899; m. Margaret L. Riddle, Dec. 1890. Practiced in N.Y. City, since 1902; anesthetist New York Skin and Cancer Hosp., People's Hosp., Mem. A.M.A., Am. Assn. Anaesthetists, N.Y. Acad. Med., N.Y. Anes. Soc., Kappa Alpha, Southeast. Episcopalian. Club: New York Athletic. Author: Anaesthesia, 1914. Read paper "An Attempt to Abolish Inhalation Anaesthesia" (by mixing ether and oil and placing in lower bowel), before Internat. Med. Congress, London, Eng., 1913; contbr. results of original research in anaesthetics. Introduced (with Capt. Howard T. Karsner) method of giving ether and oil by mouth for painful dressings; with Asa B. Davis, instituted "Obstetrical Analgesia" at Lying-in Hosp., New York, 1923. Home: New York Athletic Club, 180 Central Park S. Office: 133 E. 58th St., New York. Died Feb. 1944.

GWYNNE, Charles Thomas (gwin), chamber of commerce executive; b. New York, N.Y., July 12, 1874; s. Charles and Sarah Price (Jones) G.; ed. pub. and high schs., N.Y. City, and East Orange, N.J.; LL.D., Alfred U., 1929; m. Lilian Eade, Sept. 20, 1900 (died 1931); children—Dorothy Eade (Mrs. Wm. M. Wilson), Charles Allan, John Thomas; m. 2d, Katherine L. McCarter, July 12, 1935. With Edison Phonograph Works, Orange, 1889; with U.S. Express Co. and Pratt & Whitney, N.Y. City, 1890-94; with Chamber Commerce of State of N.Y. since 1894, sec., 1915-22, v.p. and sec., 1922-24, exec. v.p. since 1924. Director National Rivers and Harbors Congress. Mem. N.Y. Nat. Guard, 1898-1907; lt. col. Officers Res. Corps, U.S. Army. Sec., treas. and mem. board trustees N.Y. Museum of Science and Industry. Mem. Nat. Assn. Commercial Orgn. Secretaries, Am. Arbitration Assn. (vice chmn.) bd. dirs. N.Y. State Hist. Society, N.E. Society Oranges (ex-pres.), St. David's Soc., N.Y. State Secs' Conf. (ex-pres.), N.Y. City Secs' Conf. (ex-pres.), N.Y. Soc. Mil. and Naval Officers of World War, Reserve Officers' Assn. of U.S. Army, N.Y. Mil. Intelligence Reserve Soc. (ex-pres.), Edison Pioneers, Pilgrims. Conglist. Mason. Clubs: Men's Faculty of Columbia U. (New York); Rip Van Winkle Golf and Country (Palenville, N.Y.). Home: Saugerties, New York. Office: 65 Liberty St., New York, N.Y. Died Jan. 31, 1945.

H

HACK, Roy Kenneth, prof. classics; b. Ballston, Spa, N.Y., July 3, 1884; s. Rollin Therman and Miriam Matilda (Forbes) H.; A.B., Williams, 1905; Rhodes scholar Oxford U., Eng., 1905-08, B.Litt., 1908; m. Apphia Thwing, Dec. 22, 1913; 1 dau., Apphia. Instr. in classics, Williams Coll., 1908-12; instr. in classics, Harvard, 1912-18, asst. prof., 1918-23; prof. classics, Grad. Sch., U. of Cincinnati, since 1923. Mem. Am. Acad. Arts and Sciences, Phi Beta Kappa. Conglist. Clubs: University, Literary. Author: God in Greek Philosophy, 1931. Home: 619 Evanswood Pl., Cincinnati, O. Died Aug. 25, 1944.

HACKNEY, Thomas, ex-congressman; born Giles County, Tenn., December 11, 1861; s. Edward Jones and Frances Josephine (Langham) H.; ed. Southern Ill. Normal U., Carbondale, and Mo. State U.; m. Addie K. Newell, May 8, 1888. Admitted to bar, 1886; mem. law firm Thomas & Hackney, since 1886. Mem. Mo. Legislature, 1901-02; mem. 60th Congress (1907-09), 15th Mo. Dist.; defeated for 61st Congress. Democrat. Mem. Christian Ch. Address: Carthage, Mo. Died Dec. 24, 1946.

HADLEY, Carleton Sturtevant, lawyer, railroad official; b. Lowell, Mass., Dec. 24, 1902; s. Everett A. and Lilla M. (Sturtevant) H.; A.B., Wash. U., 1925, LL.B., 1928; m. Elizabeth Jane Rucker, April 11, 1931; children—Anne Carleton, Jane Everett. Admitted Mo. state bar, 1928, and practiced with firm Carter, Jones & Turney, St. Louis, Mo., 1928-33; asst. atty. St. Louis Southwestern R.R., 1929-33, asst. gen. atty., 1933-36, asst. gen. solicitor, and asst. gen. counsel for trustee, 1936; gen. counsel Terminal R.R. Assn., St. Louis, Mo., 1939-41, v.p. and gen. counsel, 1941-42, exec. officer, dir. and counsel numerous subsidiaries, 1939-42; gen. counsel Wabash R.R. since 1942. Gen. counsel Ann Arbor R.R., N.J., Ind. & Ill. R.R., Toledo Central Sta. Ry., Manistique & Lake Superior R.R., Menominee & St. Paul Ry., Ann Arbor Boat Co., Wabash Radio Corp.; gen. counsel and dir. Detroit & Western Ry., Frankfort Realty Co.; gen. counsel, dir. and mem. exec. com. Lake Erie & Ft. Wayne R.R., Wabash Motor Transit Co.; dir. Des Moines Union Ry., Am. Refrigerator Transit Co. Mem. Am., Mo., St. Louis bar assns., Am. Judicature Soc., Mo. Hist. Soc., Wash. U. Law Alumni Assn. (past pres.), Phi Beta Kappa, Phi Delta Theta, Phi Delta Phi. Republican. Conglist. Clubs: Noonday, Racquet (St. Louise). Home: 4 N. Kingshighway. Office: 1667 Railway Exchange Bldg., St. Louis, Mo. Died Feb. 16, 1945.

HADLEY, Lindley Hoag, ex-congressman; b. nr. Sylvania, Parke Co., Ind., June 19, 1861; s. Jonathan and Martha (McCoy) H.; student Ill. Wesleyan U., Bloomington, 1880-82; m. Lavalette Cross, June 1, 1887; children—Mrs. Virginia Trafton, Gordon (dec.), Mrs. Helen Gander. Admitted to Ind. bar, 1889; removed to Whatcom (now Bellingham), Wash., 1890, and practiced law there from 1890 until election to Congress; mem. 64th to 72d Congresses (1915-33), 2d Wash. Dist. Republican. Mem. Am., Wash. State and Whatcom County bar assns. Mason (K.T.). Home: (legal) Bellingham, Wash.; and Hotel Roosevelt, Washington. Died Nov. 1, 1948.

HAECKER, Theophilus Levi, dairy husbandry; b. Liverpool (now Valley City), O., May 4, 1846; s. Henry and Barbara (Drohman) H.; ed. pub. schs., and U. of Wis., 1867-68; m. Marie Brown, Mar. 1879; children—Harry C., Archibald Louis, Mrs. Elfleda H. Lansing, Mrs. Mary Haecker Palmer, Mrs. Barbara H. Bartlett; m. 2d, Fanny Main, Oct 22, 1888. Est. Ackley (Ia.) Independent; removed to Wis., 1874; exec. clk. to gov. of Wis., 15 yrs., also engaged in dairy farming; dir. Minn. Dairy Sch. and prof. dairy husbandry, U. of Minn., May 1893-1918, now emeritus. Enlisted Co. A, 37th Wis. Vol. Inf., Mar. 11, 1864; in Grant's campaign before Richmond and Petersburg; participated in Grand Review, Washington; hon. discharged, July 27, 1865. Awarded testimonial for distinguished services in animal nutrition research, by U. of Wis 1923, by U. of Minn., 1925. Home: 2134 Knapp St. Address: University Farm, St. Paul. Died 1938.

HAENSEL, Fitzhugh William, impresario; b. Richmond, Va., Jan. 11, 1879; s. Guy Henry and Marian (Dielman) H.; student Coll. City of New York, 1894-96; spl. course, Columbia; m. Florence A. Owen, July 11, 1905. Formerly engaged in newspaper work in N.Y. City specializing in musical reviews and criticism; founder, 1905, pres. and gen. manager of Haensel & Jones; dir. and vice. pres. Columbia Concerts Corp.; pres. Community Concerts Corp. Mem. 7th Regt., Nat. Guard N.Y., 7 yrs.; lt. M.I. and Corps of Interpreters, A.E.F., World War. Presbyterian. Mason (32°, K.T., Shriner). Clubs: Metropolitan, Lotos, Southern Society. Home: Venice, Fla. Address: 113 W. 57th St., New York, N.Y. Died May 3, 1944.

HAENSEL, Paul (hĕn'zĕl), economist; b. Moscow, Feb. 8, 1878; s. Peter M. and Bertha F. (Grevsmuehl) H.; grad. Classical Gymnasium, Moscow, 1896; B.Commerce (gold medal), Acad. of Commerce, Moscow, 1898; grad. Univ. of Moscow, 1902, Masters degree, 1907, LL.D., 1910; doctor œconomiæ publicæ honoris causa, Munich Univ., 1926; m. Nina von Tugenhold, May 8, 1904; children—Andrew, Vladimir, Konstantin. Came to U.S., 1930. Prof. Univ. of Moscow, 1903-28; prof. Institute of Economics, Moscow, 1908-28 dean, 1909-16; prof. Tauric Univ., 1918-20; lecturer London School of Economics, 1928, Univ. of Chicago, 1929; prof. Univ. of Graz, Austria, 1929-30; prof. pub. finance, Northwestern Univ., 1930-43, emeritus; prof. Mary Washington Coll., Virginia 1943-48; mem. board dirs. Imperial Bank of Russia and various governmental coms. during Tsarist regime; pres. finance section Inst. of Econ. Research and consultant in Commissariat of Finance, Soviet Russia, 1921-28. Mem. American Economic Assn., Royal Econ. Soc., Internat. Inst. Public Finance. Author: Inheritance Tax (in Russian and German), 1907; Bibliography of Public Finance (in Russian), 1908; Recent Tendencies in Local Taxation (in Russian), 1909; Die Finanz- und Steuerverfassung d. U.S.S.R., 1928; The Economic Policy of Soviet Russia (German and Spanish trans.), 1930; American Tax Problems, 1935; Public Finance of U.S.S.R., 1939; Illinois Tax Reform, 1941; War Taxation, 1941-45; Economic Reconstruction of Europe, 1943; Soviet Finances, 1946; Financing World War II, 1946. Over 200 articles in various langs. Extensive tours in Europe, lecturing, 1937, 39. Home: 706 W. North St., Hinsdale, Ill. Died Feb. 28, 1949.

HAFF, Delbert James, lawyer; b. Oakland County, Mich., Feb. 19, 1859; s. Ethan Clark and Sarah M. (Bush) H.; A.B., U. of Mich., 1884, LL.B., 1886 (hon. M.A., 1909); m. Grace Isabel Barse, Jan. 28, 1891; children—Carroll Barse, Madeline (Mrs. Richard H. Field), Gertrude (Mrs. Matthew R. Liddon Blood-Smyth). Admitted to Mich. bar, 1885; asst. to Judge Thomas M. Cooley, of Ann Arbor, Mich., 1885-86; practiced alone, Kansas City, Mo., 1886-89; mem. firm Haff & Valkenburgh (Arba S.), 1889-96; practiced alone, 1896-1900; associated with William C. Michaels, 1900-11; then mem. Haff, Meservey German & Michaels, later Haff, Meservey, Michaels, Blackmar & Newkirk. Pres. Bd. Park Commrs., Kansas City, 1910-12; formulated and successfully upheld the law under which was created the park and boulevard system of Kansas City; mem. Bd. of Freeholders that framed charter of Kansas City, Mo., 1905, also elected, 1908, mem. bd. which framed city charter. Republican. Life member Am. Unitarian Assn.; member American Bar Assn., Missouri Bar Assn., Kansas City Bar Assn., Am. Soc. Internat. Law, Am. Acad. Polit. and Social Science, Soc. Colonial Wars (Mo. chapt.), S.R. (Kansas City chapt.), Holland Soc. of New York, Mexican Acad. Jurisprudence and Legislation, Phi Beta Kappa. Mason (32°). Clubs: University, Kansas City, Country Club of Kansas City. Home: 416 E. 36th Street. Office: Commerce Bldg., Kansas City, Mo. Died Aug. 10, 1943.

HAGA, Oliver Owen (hä'gȧ), lawyer; b. Luverne, Minn., Nov. 19, 1872; s. O. O. and Julia (Emerick) H.; A.B., Northern Ind. U., Valparaiso, 1894, A.M., 1899; m. Jennie E. Bartlett, Aug. 28, 1900 (died 1939); children—Eleanor Louise (Mrs. J. F. Harris), Margaret Virginia (Mrs. Hubbell Carpenter). Prin. Boise High Sch., 3 yrs.; began practice in Boise, 1901; mem. Richards & Haga, since 1901; specializes in law of corp., mining, and water rights; dir. financial, industrial, mining and other corps.; pres. Boise Community Hotel Co. Idaho commr. uniform state laws. Pres. board trustees Boise Public Schools, 1908-24, State Industrial Sch., 1911-12, Boise Junior Coll. since 1934; ex-pres. Boise Chamber Commerce; dir. commercial economy for Ida., during the World War. Apptd. by President Coolidge mem. Sesquicentennial Commn., 1926. Chmn. Board of Appeal, Selective Service Act. Mem. Am. and Idaho State bar assns. Republican. Conglist. Gov. of Kiwanis Clubs for Utah-Ida. Dist., 1922. Home: Hotel Boise. Office: 517 Idaho Bldg. Boise, Ida. Died Mar. 10, 1943.

HAGER, Clint Wood, lawyer; b. Bristol, Tenn., June 19, 1890; s. John Jackson and Maude Livingston (Caldwell) H.; ed. King Coll., Bristol, 1908-12, Harvard Law Sch., 1913-16; m. Mary Agnes Kelley, Feb. 4, 1918. Admitted to Tenn. bar, 1916, and practiced at Kingsport until 1918; practiced at Atlanta, Ga., 1919-21; became U.S. dist. atty., 1921; now in practice of law. Republican. Presbyn. Mason, Elk. Home: 112 Peachtree Hills Av. Office: Atlanta National Bldg., Atlanta, Ga.* Died May 5, 1945.

HAGER, Luther George, cartoonist; b. Terre Haute, Ind., Mar. 19, 1885; s. John Ross and Anna (Hyde) H.; ed. pub. and high schs. and 1 yr. at U. of Wash., Seattle; studied 7 months at Art Students' League, New York; m. Beatrice Holbrook Dearborn, Jan. 1, 1910; children—Carol Louise, Beatrice Minnie (dec.). Cartoonist for Seattle Post-Intelligencer, Jan. 1905-Sept. 1910, July 1911-Sept. 1913; contbg. cartoonist to Christian Science Monitor since 1926. Also illustrator. Mem. Beta Theta Pi. Home: 5221 15th Av., N.E. Office: Smith Tower, Seattle, Wash. Died Jan. 1945.

HAGERTY, James Edward, educator; b. La Porte County, Ind.; s. John and Jane E. (Crilly) H.; grad. Northern Ind. Normal Sch., Valparaiso, 1888; A.B., Ind. U., 1892; grad. student, economics and sociology, U. of Chicago, 1896-97; hon. fellow economics, U. of Wis., 1897-98; univs. of Berlin and Halle, 1898-99; fellow sociology, 1899-1900; sr. fellow, 1900-01, U. of Pa., Ph.D., 1900; m. Lucile Joyce, Oct. 26, 1907; children—James Edward, Eliza Joyce, Lawrence Vincent, Lucile. Teacher mathematics, La Porte (Ind.) High Sch., 1892-96; asst. prof., 1901-03, acting head of dept., 1903-04, prof. economics and sociology and head of dept., 1904-22, prof. of sociology and chmn. dept., 1922-32, organized Coll. of Commerce and Journalism, 1916, dean, 1916-26, dir. Sch. of Social Adminstrn., 1927-32, prof. social adminstrn., 1932-40, prof. emeritus since 1940, Ohio State U. Taught 1st marketing course in Am. univs., 1905. Head div. on marketing Federal Food Adminstrn. for O., 1918, and deputy food administrator for Ohio, June 1918-Jan. 1919. Pres. Ohio State Conf. Charities and Corrections, 1908, Nat. Assn. of Collegiate Schools of Business Edn., 1924; mem. State Bd. Charities of Ohio, 1919-21; mem. exec. com. on social action of Nat. Welfare Council; pres. Nat. Catholic Conf. on Industrial Problems, 1928-37. Mem. Am. Econ. Assn., Am. Sociol. Soc., Phi Beta Kappa, Beta Gamma Sigma. Author: Mercantile Credit; The Training of Social Workers; Twentieth Century Crime—18th Century Methods of Control; Early Financial History of Indiana; The Prevention of Delinquency. Home: 94 15th Av., Columbus, O. Died Nov. 10, 1946.

HAGOOD, Johnson (hăg'wood), army officer; b. Orangeburg, S.C., June 16, 1873; s. Lee H.; nephew of Brig. Gen. Johnson Hagood, Confederate Army, and governor of South Carolina; student Univ. of S.C., 1888-91, LL.D., 1921; grad. U.S. Mil. Acad., 1896; m. Jean Gordon Small, Dec. 14, 1899; children—Jean Gordon (wife of Adm. J. L. Holloway, U.S.N.), Johnson (U.S. Army), Francesca (wife of A. B. Packard, U.S. Army). Commd. add. 2d lt. 2d Artillery, June 12, 1896; promoted through grades to brig. gen. N.A., Apr. 12, 1918; brig. gen. U.S. Army, July 3, 1920 (recess apptmt. exp. Mar. 4, 1921), reapptd. Apr. 27, 1921; maj. gen. Aug. 2, 1925. Garrison duty in R.I., Conn. and S.C., 1896-1901; instr. dept. of philosophy, U.S. Mil. Acad., 1901-04; asst. to chief of arty., Washington, D.C., 1905-07; mem. Gen. Staff Corps, 1908; a.d.c. Maj. Gen. J. F. Bell, 1908-10; asst. to Maj. Gen. Leonard Wood, re-detail to Gen. Staff Corps until 1912; comdr. Ft. Flagler, Wash., 1912-13; in Philippines, 1913-15; various commands, coast defense, 1915-17, detailed as commander of 7th regt. 1st Expeditionary Brigade, Coast Arty. Corps, July 16, 1917. Arrived in France, Sept. 11, 1917; duty in battlefield nr. Soissons, Sept.-Oct.; organized and in comd. advance sect. Line of Communications, A.E.F., Oct. 24; in comd. Neufchâteau, Nov. 1-Dec. 1; chief of staff, Line of Communications, Dec. 2; Gen. Staff, A.E.F., Jan. 10, 1918; pres. of bd. that reorganized A.E.F. staff and created S.O.S.; chief of staff S.O.S., until Armistice; rep. Am. Army in replying to address of Marshal Joffre, Paris, May 12, 1918; in battle sectors along Am., French, and British fronts, June-July 1918; Meuse-Argonne offensive, Oct. 1918; designated by comdr. in chief to be maj. gen. N.A., Oct. 20, 1918, but apptmt. failed on account of Armistice; apptd. comdr. 30th C.A. Brigade, Nov 10, trans. to 66th F.A. Brigade, Nov. 24; crossed Rhine River Dec. 31, 1918, and estab. hdqrs. at Hohr, Germany; comd. army arty. of 3d Army and corps arty. of 3d Corps until Apr. 10, 1919; sailed for U.S., May 16, 1919; assigned to comd. 30th Brigade (Ry.), C.A.C., and Camp Eustis, Va., Nov. 24, 1919; comd. South Atlantic Coast Arty. Dist., Nov. 1920-Sept. 1921; apptd. comdr. Camp Stotsenburg, P.I., Feb. 1, 1922, 2d Coast Arty. Dist., Ft. Totten, N.Y., Aug. 1924, 4th Corps Area, Oct. 5, 1925-Mar. 1927; comdg. Philippine Div., Apr. 25, 1927-June 22, 1929; comdg. 7th Corps Area Aug. 26, 1929-Oct. 2, 1933, 4th Army, Aug. 9, 1932-Oct. 2, 1933, 3d Army and 8th Corps Area, 1933-36, 2d Army and 5th Corps Area, May 1, 1936; retired, May 31, 1936. Decorated with Distinguished Service Medal, Jan. 9, 1919; Comdr. Legion of Honor (French), 1919; Comdr. Order of Crown of Italy; Grand Officer Order of the Sacred Treasure (Japanese). Member United Confederate Vets., Soc. of the Cincinnati, Am. Legion. Episcopalian. Rotarian (hon.). Clubs: Army and Navy (Washington, D.C.); Army and Navy of Manila (past pres.), Charleston. Devised Hagood tripod mount, mortar deflection board, and other apparatus connected with sea-coast defense. Author: The Services of Supply—A Memoir of the Great War, 1927; We Can Defend America, 1937; Soldiers Handbook; Meet Your Grandfather, 1946; General Wood as I Knew Him, Closing the Gap in National Defense, I Had a Talk with the President (Saturday Evening Post) and other articles in leading mags. and newspapers. Home: Charleston, S.C.; also San Antonio, Tex. Died Dec. 22, 1948.

HAGUE, Maurice Stewart, artist; b. Richmond, O., May 13, 1862; s. James Russel and Susan (Stewart) H.; ed. pub. schs., Columbus; studied medicine 3 yrs., but abandoned it for art; self-educated in art; m. Edith M. McGrew, Feb. 4, 1922. Followed portrait painting and modeling until 1895, then took up landscape painting. Represented in pvt. collections in New York, Baltimore, Buffalo, Pittsburgh, Cleveland, Rochester and Columbus (O.) Gallery of Fine Arts; exhibited at Boston, St. Louis, Minneapolis, Buffalo, Cleveland and Columbus. Chmn. Ohio Bd. Motion Picture Censors, 1917-20. Charter mem. Orpheus Club (noted male chorus); basso in Scottish Rite Quartette, 1888-1903. Republican. Quaker. Mem. Am. Federation of Arts, Soc. of Independent Artists, Chicago No-Jury Soc. Artists, Am. Artists Professional League, Ohio Archaeol. and Hist. Soc., Soc. for Sanity in Art. Mason (32°). Club: Kit Kat (pres. 1924-25). Home: 1470 Fair Av., Columbus, O. Died Feb. 3, 1943.

HAHN, Frederick E., violinist; b. N.Y. City, Mar. 23, 1869; s. Henry and Clara (Mayer) H.; ed. Eastburn Acad., Phila., Pa.; studied violin under father; grad. Leipzig Conservatory of Music, 1890 (1st prize for violin); hon. degree of Doctor of Music from Zeckwer-hahn Phila. Music Academy, 1940, also from the Curtis Institute of Music, 1941; unmarried. Toured U.S., 1890-91; 1st violinist Boston Symphony Orchestra, 1892; head of string quartet 25 yrs.; founder Hahn Conservatory of Music, Phila., 1902; pres. and dir. Zeckwer-Hahn Phila. Musical Acad. since 1917. Author: Practical Violin Study, 1930. Composer of violin works, songs and orchestra pieces, also editor violin pieces and études. Home: Bellerich Apt. Studio: 1617 Spruce St., Philadelphia, Pa. Died Nov. 25, 1942.

HAID, Paul L., insurance pres.; b. New Castle, Pa., Sept. 25, 1887; s. Augustine and Winifred (McGraw) H.; ed. Belmont Abbey Coll., Belmont, N.C.; m. Anna M. Beach, May 21, 1913; 1 son, Paul L. Entered ins. business in office of Justus Mulert, Pittsburgh, Pa., 1904; with Edwards, George & Co., Pittsburgh, 1908-10; spl. agt. Girard Fire & Marine Ins. Co., 1910-14, Phila. Underwriters, 1912-14; spl. agt., Western Pa., of Fidelity-Phenix Ins. Co., 1914-18, exec. spl. agt. N.Y. City, 1918-19; asst. sec., "America Fore" cos., 1919-20, asst. to pres., 1920-21, sec., 1921; first v.p., Continental Ins. Co., 1921-24; pres. Fidelity-Phenix Ins. Co., 1924, pres. "America Fore" companies, Continental Ins. Co., Fidelity-Phenix Ins. Co., Am. Eagle Ins. Co., First Am. Ins. Co., since 1924, and since 1929, pres. Niagara Fire Ins. Co., Md. Ins. Co., Fidelity & Casualty Ins. Co. of New York; v.p. Fire Cos. Bldg. Corp., Am. Eagle Investing Co.; resigned from foregoing cos., 1932, to become pres. Insurance Executives Assn. and Fire Cos'. Adjustment Bur. Republican. Catholic. Clubs: Drug and Chemical, Down Town, Down Town Athletic, New York Yacht (New York); Racquet (Chicago); Westchester Country (Rye, N.Y.). Home: 37 Washington Sq. W. Office: 116 John St., New York, N.Y. Died Aug. 31, 1942.

HAIGHT, Raymond LeRoy, lawyer; b. San Jose, Calif., July 18, 1897; s. George Washington and Icadora Maude (Gillette) H.; A.B., U. of Southern Calif., 1919, J.D., 1921; m. Heloise Marie Davis, Apr. 15, 1920; children—Raymond LeRoy, Fulton Wilbur, Heloise Maureen. Admitted to Calif. bar, 1921, and since practiced in Los Angeles; with Newlin & Ashburn, 1920-27; sr. partner Haight, Trippet & Syvertson since 1927; city atty. Venice, Calif., 1925; commr. of playgrounds, Los Angeles, 1930, of corps., State of Calif., 1931; mem. commn. of Police of City of Los Angeles; gubernatorial nominee of Progressive and Commonwealth parties, 1934; Progressive party, 1938; chmn. State Central Com., Progressive Party of Calif., 1937-38; gen. chmn. Gov. Warren Gubernatorial Com., 1942; elected Republican Nat. Committeeman, Calif., 1944-48. In U.S. Army Air Service, 1917-18. Mem. bd. dirs. Wilshire Y.M.C.A. (Los Angeles). Mem. Am. and Los Angeles Bar Assns., State Bar of Calif., Los Angeles County Bar Assn. (trustee), Delta Sigma Rho, Phi Alpha Delta, Kappa Alpha. Methodist. Clubs: California, Los Angeles Athletic, Hollywood Athletic, Editor Southern Calif. Alumni Review, 1923-32. Home: 351 N. Fuller Av. Office: 458 S. Spring St., Los Angeles. Died Sept. 2, 1947.

HAINES, Charles Grove, univ. prof.; b. Lineboro, Md., Sept. 20, 1879; s. Henry Wertz and Ceranda (Grove) H.; A.B., Ursinus College, Pa.; Columbia University, 1903-06, A.M., 1904, Ph.D., 1909; LL.D., from Ursinus College, 1941; m. Bertha Harner Moser, Nov. 27, 1906. Prof. history and polit. science, Ursinus Coll., 1906-10; prof. polit. science and dean philos. group, Whitman Coll., 1910-14; exec. sec. League of the Pacific Northwest Municipalities, 1912-14; prof. govt., 1914-22, prof. law, 1922-25, chmn. Dept. of Govt., 1916-17 and 1918-22, U. of Tex.; in charge Bur. of Govt. Research, same univ., 1918-22, and organized there the 1st chapter Pi Sigma Alpha; asso. prof. polit. science, U. of Chicago, for yr. 1917-18; prof. polit. science, U. of Calif. at Los Angeles, since 1925; also research lecturer, 1926-27; visiting prof. dept. of govt. and research in Law Sch., Harvard, 1936-37; commr. Dept. of Water and Power, City of Los Angeles, 1939; public panel member, National War Labor Bd., 1943-44. Trustee John Randolph Haynes and Dora Haynes Foundation, 1938-46. Fellow Am. Acad. Arts and Scis.; dir. Los Angeles Inst. of Public Affairs—A Center of the Am. Acad. of Polit. and Social Science, 1925-27; mem. Am. Polit. Science Assn. (pres. 1939), Am. Acad. Polit. and Social Science (vice-pres. 1931-37), Southwest Polit. and Social Science Assn. (a founder and mng. editor of Quarterly, 1920-22), Pacific Southwest Acad (pres. 1928-29 and 1933-35), Phi Beta Kappa, Pi Sigma Alpha. Author: The Conflict Over Judicial Powers in the United States to 1870, 1909; The American Doctrine of Judicial Supremacy, 1914, revised edition, 1932; The Movement for the Reorganization of State Administration (University of Texas Bulletin), 1920; Principles and Problems of Government (with Bertha Moser Haines), 1921, 3d edition, 1934; The Revival of Natural Law Concepts, 1930; The Role of the Supreme Court in American Government and Politics, 1789-1835, 1944. Editor: The Teaching of Government (rept. to Am. Polit. Science Assn.), 1916. Contbr. papers on constl. law and legal philosophy. Home: 487 Myrtle St., Laguna Beach, Calif. Address: 405 Hilgard Av., Los Angeles, Calif. Died Dec. 27, 1948.

HAINES, Elwood Lindsay, bishop; b. Phila., Pa., March 12, 1893; s. John Batten and Jennie (Lindsay) H.; A.B., U. of Pa., 1916; S.T.B., Phila. Divinity Sch., 1920; D.D., 1945; D.D., Parsons Coll., 1944, Seabury-Western Theological Sem., 1944; m. Cornelia McCoy Smith, Oct. 7, 1933; children—Evelyn Viola, Juliet Lindsay. Ordained to the ministry of the Protestant Episcopal Ch., York, Pa., 1920; missionary, Liberia, 1920-24; rector Trinity Ch., Bethlehem, Pa., 1924-28; exec. sec. diocese N.C., 1928-31; rector Christ Ch., Glendale, O., 1931-37; dean Christ Ch. Cathedral, Louisville, Ky., 1937-44; 5th bishop of Iowa, Davenport, Ia., since May 1944. Served as corp. 6th Regt. 84th Co., U.S. M.C., April 1918-Sept. 1919; with Army Occupation, Nov. 1918-Aug. 1919. Dep. to Gen. Conv. Episcopal Ch., 1940-43; mem. Nat. Council Episcopal Ch., 1943-44; various types of service in ministry, 1920-44. Mem. Alpha Sigma Phi. Author: Poems of the African Trail, 1928; A Children's Service Book, 1931. Home: Cathedral Close, 1103 Main St. Office: 1102 Brady St., Davenport, Ia. Died Oct. 29, 1949.

HAINES, Harry L., ex-congressman; b. Red Lion, Pa., Feb. 1, 1880; s. Benjamin Ambrose and Rebecca (Wallick) H.; ed. Pa. State Normal Sch., Lock Haven; m. Cora Ness, May 22, 1898; children—Henry Luther, Mary Rebecka (Mrs. Stuart S. Stabley), Charlotte Ruth, George Woodrow, Martha Jeanette Mfr. cigars since 1906; chief exec. Red Lion Boro 3 terms, 1921-33; mem. 72d to 75th Congresses (1931-39), 22d Pa. Dist.; now acting state treas. of Pa. Democrat. Mem. United Brethren Ch. Mason. Odd Fellow, Red Man. Club: Lions. Home: Red Lion, Pa. Office: State Treasury, Harrisburg, Pa. Died March 30, 1947.

HALDEMAN, Bruce; b. Knoxville, Tenn., Nov. 5, 1862; s. Walter Newman and Elizabeth (Metcalfe) H.; ed. U. of Va.; m. Annie Ford Milton, Jan. 20, 1892; children—Florence (Mrs. Charles Baird Price), Elizabeth (Mrs. Isaac Hilliard), Walter N., Annie Bruce. Advanced from reporter to mng. editor Louisville Courier Journal and Louisville Times, 1885-95; also agt. Associated Press; pres. Louisville Courier Journal Co. and Louisville Times Co., 1902-18; retired from newspaper business. Pres. Am. Newspaper Publishers' Assn., 1910-11; chmn. Ky. bd. dirs. Assn. Against Prohibition Amendment. Democrat. Presbyterian. Clubs: Pendennis, Country (Louisville). Home: Glenview, Ky. Died Nov. 29, 1948.

HALE, Annie Riley, author; b. on plantation in eastern Tenn., May 1, 1859; d. John D. and Ailsie (Kyle) Riley; grad. Stonewall Jackson Inst., Abingdon, Va., 1876; m. J. R. Hale, Sept. 17, 1885. Author: Rooseveltian Fact and Fable, 1908. Writer of numerous mag. and newspaper articles; lecturer on negro problem. Address: 1113 P St., Washington. Died Dec. 26, 1944.

HALE, Ellen Day, artist; b. Worcester, Mass., Feb. 11, 1855; d. Edward Everett and Emily Baldwin (Perkins) H.; pvt. edn.; studied art in U.S. and Paris; unmarried. Worked in London and Paris, later settling in Boston, then in Washington. Ch. subjects, portraits, landscapes and genre paintings. Home: 1673 Columbia Rd., Washington. Died Feb. 11, 1940.

HALE, Harry Clay, army officer; b. at Knoxville, Ill., July 10, 1861; s. T. J. and Sarah (Pierce) H.; grad. U.S. Mil. Acad., 1883, LL.D., Knox Coll., 1924; m. Elizabeth C. Smith, Dec. 2, 1886. Commd. 2d lt., June 13, 1883, and promote dthrough grades to col., Mar. 26, 1915; trans. to China in command of 15th Inf., Nov. 30, 1915; brig. gen. R.A., 1917; maj. gen. N.A., Aug. 5, 1917. At Ft. Sully, S.D., in charge Sioux Indian prisoners of war, Jan.-June 1891; a.d.c. to Brig. Gen. Wesley Merritt, at St. Paul, Chicago, and Governor's Island, N.Y., 1893-99; adj. gen. and actg. aide to Maj. Gen. Wesley Merritt during Manila campaign, 1898; batt. comdr. 44th U.S. Vols., Philippine Insurrection, 1899-1902; comd. Bilibid Prison, Manila, 1902; acting batt. comdr. 20th U.S. Inf., Luzon Campaign, 1902; duty Gen. Staff, 1903-06; again in Philippines, 1906-09; adj. gen. Dept. of the Lakes, 1909-10, Dept. of Mo. 1910-11; apptd. comdr. Camp Zachary Taylor, Louisville, Ky., Sept. 1917; comdr. 84th Div. A.E.F., in France, 1918; after armistice comdr. Combat Div. 26; comdg. 2d Brigade A.F. in Germany, Dec. 17, 1920-Feb. 3, 1922, promoted maj. gen., Nov. 2, 1921; comd. 1st Div., U.S. Army, Camp Dix, N.J., Feb.-Dec. 1922; comd. 6th Corps Area Chicago, 1922-25; retired, July 10, 1925. Awarded D.S.M., 1920. Home: 1275 Rockville Pike, Rockville, Md. Died Mar. 20, 1946.

HALE, Marshal, merchant; b. Schoolcraft, Mich., Feb. 14, 1866; s. Marshal and Prudence T. (Dyckman) H.; B.S., U. of Pacific, 1886; m. Mae Miller, Jan. 19, 1898. Began dry goods bus., Sacramento, 1886; moved to San Francisco, 1894; chmn. exec. com. and dir. Hale Bros. Stores, Inc.; ex-pres. Liberty Bank; v.p. and dir. Hale Real Estate Co.; pres. and dir. Residential Development Co.; vice pres., treas. and dir. Panama Realty Co.; dir. Bank of America Nat. Trust & Savings Assn.; past pres. Down Town Assn. Pres. Hahnemann Medical College and Hahnemann Hospital; playground commr., San Francisco, 6 yrs.; pres. State Bd. Harbor Commrs., Calif., 1911. Chmn. San Francisco Chapter Am. Red Cross; mgr. Pacific Div. Am. Red Cross, 1917, 18; in France for Am. Red Cross as mgr. S. Intermediate Zone, hdqrs. Lyons, 1918, rank of maj. Pres. San Francisco Retail Dry Goods Assn., 1914, Calif. Retail Dry Goods Assn., 1915; dir. Merchants' Assn. of San Francisco, 5 yrs. Mason. Clubs: Bohemian, Commonwealth. Home: Fairmont Hotel. Address: Hale Bros. Stores, Inc., San Francisco, Calif. Died Nov. 3, 1945.

HALE, Morris Smith, college dean and registrar; b. Albany, Ga., Sept. 7, 1895; s. Frank Simmons and Mary Anna (Morgan) H.; student Emory U., 1914-17; B.S., Peabody Coll., Nashville, Tenn., 1928, A.M., 1931; m. Alice Lois Sellers, Aug. 20, 1919; children—Morris Smith, Robert Frank, James Morgan. Teacher pub. schs., Lee County, Ga., 1915-16; prin. high sch., Morven, Ga., 1916-17, city supt., 1918-20; supt. schs., Gore, Ga., 1920-24; pres. Sparks (Ga.) Jr. Coll., 1924-26; supt. schs., Arlington, Ga., 1926-31; supervisor, Tampa pub. schs., 1931-32, city supt., 1932-34; dean and bus. mgr., U. of Tampa, 1934-40. acting pres., 1936-37; dean and registrar, Orlando Jr. Coll., since 1941. Commd. 2d lt., U.S. Army, serving in World War, 1917. Mem. bd. dirs. Tampa Urban League; sec. Fla. High Sch. Music Festival Assn. Mem. Court of Honor, Tampa Boy Council, Boy Scouts of America. Mem. N.E.A. (mem. com. on internat. relations), Fla. Edn. Assn., Am. Legion, Fla. Assn. Colls. and Univs. (pres., 1946-47. dir.), Am. Assn. Collegiate Registrars. Presidents' Round Table of Tampa, Pi Kappa Phi, Phi Delta Kappa, Kappa Delta Pi. Democrat. Methodist. Mason. Club: Optimist of Tampa (ex-pres., bd. dirs.). Home: 1207 Hillcrest, Orlando, Fla. Died Dec. 16, 1948.

HALE, Richard Walden, lawyer; b. Milton, Mass., June 30, 1871; s. George Silsbee and Ellen (Sever) H.; desc. ancestors who arrived in Mass. before 1650; student Mass. Inst. Tech., 1887-88; A.B., Harvard Coll., 1892; LL.B., Harvard Univ. Law Sch., 1895; m. Mary Newbold Patterson, May 14, 1903; 1 son, Richard Walden, Jr. Admitted to Mass. bar, 1895; mem. Hale Fiske, 1895-97; alone 1897-99; mem.

Hale & Grinnell, 1899-1914, Hale, Grinnell & Swaim, 1914-18, Hale & Dorr since 1918; treas. Old South Meeting House; v.p. Ford Hall Forum. Mem. Mass. Ho. of Reps., 1910; has held various town offices, Dover, Mass. Sec. and treas. for U.S. of Selden Soc. (English). Republican. Conglist. Clubs: Union (Boston); Century (New York). Author: The Dreyfus Story (book). Editor Letters of Warwick Greene (book); also articles in various mags. Home: Dover (P.O. Needham), Mass. Office: 60 State St., Boston, Mass. Died Mar. 5, 1943.

HALE, William Browne, lawyer; b. Chicago, Ill., Dec. 7, 1875; s. William E. and Mary (Scranton) H.; B.A., Yale, 1898; LL.B., Northwestern U. Law Sch., 1901; A.M., Harvard, 1902; m. Eunice D. Follansbee, June 27, 1912; children—George Ellery, William B., Jr. (dec.), Mary S., Eunice, John E. Admitted to Ill. bar, 1901, and since in practice at Chicago; mem. Wilson & McIlvaine; lecturer on corp. law, Northwestern Law School, 1919-20. Mem. Illinois State Board of Law Examiners, 1921, 1922, 1923. Member Am. Bar Assn. (Ho. of Del., 1941-42), Am. Law Inst. (council), Ill. State Bar Assn., Chicago Bar Assn., Council on Foreign Relations, Chicago Council on Foreign Relations. Clubs: University, Indian Hill (Chicago). Author: Private Corporations in Illinois, 1916. Home: 900 Mt. Pleasant St., Winnetka, Ill. Office: 120 W. Adams St., Chicago, Ill. Died Jan. 18, 1944.

HALE, Wyatt Walker, educator; b. Gadsden, Ala., June 30, 1901; s. William Walker and Julia Mariah (Williamson) H.; B.S., Birmingham-Southern Coll., 1923, A.M., 1926; student Johns Hopkins Univ., 1924-25; Teachers Coll., Columbia Univ., summer 1927, Univ. of Minn., summer 1930, U. of Chicago, summer 1939; Ed.D., Stanford University, 1932; m. Madelyn Thomas, April 8, 1937. Shoe and ins. salesman, 1917-20; with Birmingham-Southern Coll. since 1923 serving successively as sec. to pres., registrar, alumni sec., dir. of extension, registrar and asst. to pres., registrar and prof. edn., registrar and acting dean, and since 1934 as dean and registrar; acting examiner, University of Minnesota, summer 1930. Holder of $1,000 fellowship of American Assn. of Collegiate Registrars, 1929-30, of $2,500 fellowship of Phi Delta Kappa, 1930-31. Mem. Am. Assn. of Collegiate Registrars, Omicron Delta Kappa, Phi Delta Kappa, Kappa Phi Kappa, Theta Chi Delta, Tau Kappa Alpha, Phi Beta Kappa; pres. Association of Alabama Colleges, 1941-42. Democrat. Methodist. Club: Ensley Rotary (ex-pres. and dir.). Address: Birmingham-Southern Coll., Birmingham, Ala. Died Apr. 10, 1943.

HALL, Arthur Jackson, educator; b. Richardsville, Va., Oct. 5, 1874; s. Alexander Charles and Mary Appleton (Childs) H.; B.A., Richmond (Va.) Coll., 1898, M.A., 1899; B.D., Crozer Theol. Sem., 1903, Th.M., 1905; Ph.D., U. of Chicago, 1911; m. Fonce B. Smith. Ordained ministry Bapt. Ch., 1896; pastor First Ch., Pottsville, Pa., 1903-08; pres. Coker Coll., Hartsville, S.C., 1911-14; with Baylor U. since 1915, prof. psychology, philosophy and education, also head of dept., 1915-20, prof. psychology and philosophy, also head of dept. psychology and philosophy, 1921-35, prof. philosophy and head of dept. since 1935, head of both philosophy and psychology depts. since 1945. Author: Religious Education in the Public Schools of the State and City of New York. Home: Waco, Tex. Deceased.

HALL, Arthur Fletcher, chmn. Lincoln Nat. Life Ins. Co.; b. Baxter Springs, Kan., May 11, 1872; s. Truman Walter and Harriet (Beeler) H.; ed. pub. schs., Indianapolis, Ind.; m. Una Fletcher, June 1897 (died Feb. 1920); children—Arthur Fletcher, William Baldwin Fletcher, Aileen; m. 2d, Ann O'Rourke, Oct. 1920. Began as printer's devil, Indianapolis Journal, 1889, advertising mgr., 1900-02, asst. bus. mgr., 1902-04; field supt. Equitable Life Assurance Soc., 1904-05; organizer, 1905, since officer Lincoln Nat. Life Ins. Co.; pres. Greater Ft. Wayne Development Corp.; dir. Wabash Valley Improvement Assn. Gen. chmn. 4th Liberty Loan campaign, Allen County, Y.M.C.A. war fund drive; head of Am. Protective League, Fort Wayne dist., World War. Mem. Ind. Lincoln Union (exec. com.); chmn. Indiana Lincoln Memorial Highway Commn.; mem. advisory com. Industrial Research Division, State Planning Board of Indiana. Republican. Episcopalian. Mason (Shriner), Elk. Club: Fort Wayne Country. Home: 2530 Beechwood Circle. Office: Lincoln Life Bldg., Fort Wayne, Ind. Died Nov. 9, 1942.

HALL, Fitzgerald, ry. pres.; b. Nashville, Tenn., Dec. 6, 1889; s. Allen Garland and Lillie (Gunn) H.; B.A., Vanderbilt Univ., 1911, LL.B., 1913; m. Marcelle Ball Lake of Memphis, Tenn.; children—Elizabeth Gardner, Mary Fitzgerald. Began practice at Nashville, 1913; asst. U.S. atty. Middle Dist. of Tenn., 1914-15; asst. gen. counsel N.,C.&St.L. Ry., May 1915-Jan. 1918; counsel for U.S.R.R. Administration, operating Tenn. Central, N.,C.&St.L. and Birmingham & N.W. rys. Jan. 1918-Mar. 1920; gen. counsel N.,C.&St.L. Ry., 1920-26, v.p. and gen. counsel, 1926-34, pres. since Nov. 30, 1934; dir. Federal Reserve Bank of Atlanta, Fruit Growers Express Co. Dir. C. of C. of U.S. Mem. board of trust, Vanderbilt Univ. Mem. Am. and Tenn. bar assns., Phi Beta Kappa, Sigma Upsilon, Phi Delta Theta. Democrat. Clubs: Round Table, Coffee House (Nashville); Bellemeade Golf and Country. Home: Wellington Arms Apt. Office: 930 Broadway, Nashville, Tenn. Died Feb. 7, 1946.

HALL, George Elisha, lawyer; b. May 10, 1870; s. Elisha and Mary (Hayden) H.; grad. high sch., New Haven; LL.B., Yale, 1894; D.P.E., Arnold Coll., New Haven, 1929; m. Harriet F. Blakeslee, Dec. 4, 1908; children—William Blakeslee, George Elisha. Practiced in New Haven since 1894; served as alderman, city atty., judge of City Court, and chmn. Zoning Bd. of Appeals, New Haven; mem. Conn. State Senate, 1925-29, also Tuberculosis Commn. of Conn. Secretary, dir. New Haven Trap Rock Co., Branford Steam R.R. Co., Wilcox Crittenden & Co. Formerly pres. and trustee Arnold Coll. for Hygiene and Physical Education. Enlisted as private Conn. Nat. Guard, 1896, and advanced through grades to brig. gen.; served on Mexican border; lt. col. U.S. Army, 1917-19; col. U.S. Inf. Res., May 1, 1926; regtl. comdt. 417th Inf., 1926-34, retired 1934; inactive reserve, 1934-41. Mem. Am. Bar Assn., Conn. State and County of New Haven bar assns., Internat. Law Assn., Am. Judicature Soc., Acad. of Polit. Science, Am. Museum of Natural History, New Haven Colony Hist. Soc., Edgewood Civic Assn., English-Speaking Union, National Travel Club, American National Red Cross, American Legion, Military Order World War (past comdr.), Yankee Division Vets. Assn., Reserve Officers Assn. of U.S. Republican. Universalist. Mason (32°). Odd Fellow, Woodman. Clubs: Graduate (New Haven); Waterbury (Conn.). Home: 1 West Park Av. Office: 718 Second Nat. Bank Bldg., New Haven, Conn. Died Feb. 4, 1944.

HALL, Henry Noble, newspaperman, lecturer; b. Penge, nr. Croydon, Eng., Dec. 11, 1872; s. Henry Nissen and Lillian (Porter) H.; ed. King's Sch., Canterbury, Victoria Coll., Jersey, and La Sorbonne, Paris; m. Suzanne Arot, June 24, 1893 (died 1919); m. 2d, Jean Oertel, Oct. 27, 1920. Worked on French newspapers and travelled extensively throughout Europe, 1890-1900; visited West Indies; owner-editor The Pioneer and the Trinidad Mag., 1901-05, Phila. North American, 1905-07, New Orleans Item, 1907; conducted investigation into telephone conditions in New Orleans for New Orleans Bd. of Trade, 1907; staff corr., New York World, 1908-17, war corr., 1914-15, lent to Dem. Nat. Com. for President Wilson's campaigns, 1912, 16; apptd. by Mayor Mitchell as asst. sec. of Com. to Honor and Welcome British and French War Missions, 1917; acting corr. London Times in Washington and war corr. with A.E.F., also covered Peace Conf. and all meetings of Supreme Council, 1917-22; hon. sec. Anglo-Am. Press Assn. in Paris; pub. relations officer Internat. Chamber of Commerce, 1925-30; dir. Office Britannique in Paris and from its inception, rep. of British Council in charge British propaganda in France, 1930-39; 1st sec. (temp.) British Embassy in Paris in charge of Information, 1939-40; asso. with Lord Bessborough in French Welfare Work in London, 1940-41; Am. corr. of News of the World, 1941-46. Decorated Comdr. Order of the British Empire, Officer of the Legion of Honor, Officier de L'Instruction Publique, Knight of Order of Leopold (Belgium). Clubs: National Press (Washington; Lotos, Dutch Treat (New York), Overseas Press of America (sec.), Silurians, Adventurers, Am. Platform Guild; Anglo-American Press Assn. (Paris). Author: History of the IVth (Ivy Div.) in the World War (with Col. Bach), 1919; Why Palestine?, 1946; How I Was Cured of Cancer by Radioactivity, 1947. Translator: Andre Tardieu's "Truth About the Treaty," "France and America," Voltaire's "Candide"; Odic's "Stepchildren of France." Dekobra's "Paradise in Montparnasse." Home: 150 E. 49th St., New York, N.Y. Died Mar. 26, 1949.

HALL, Howard Judson, prof. English; b. Lansingburgh, N.Y., Feb. 6, 1869; s. Rev. Joshua Beers and Eugenia (Campbell) H.; B.S., Mich. State Coll., 1890; A.B., Leland Stanford Jr. U., 1896; A.M., Harvard, 1900; m. Kalene Louise Timlan, 1894; 1 dau., Elizabeth Pierson. Successively instr., acting prof., librarian and prof. English, U. of Ariz., 1891-1904; asst. and prof. English, Stanford, 1905-35, now emeritus. Instr. Army Ednl. Corps, A.E.F., in France, Jan.-July 1919. Presbyn. Mem. Modern Lang. Assn. America; corr. mem. Colonial Soc. of Mass. Author: Three Centuries of American Poetry and Prose (with Alphonso Gerald Newcomer and Alice E. Andrews), 1917, 2d edit., 1929; Types of Poetry, 1927, 2d edit., 1931; Twelve Centuries of English Poetry and Prose (with Alphonso Gerald Newcomer and Alice E. Andrews), 2d edit., 1929. Compilations: Selections from the Poetry of William Wordsworth, 1924; Benjamin Tompson's Collected Poems, 1924. Edited Nathaniel Morton's New Englands Memorial, 1937. Home: Los Altos, Calif. Died Dec. 14, 1942.

HALL, James King, physician; b. Iredell County, N.C., Sept. 28, 1875; s. Eugenius Alexander and Amanda McCullough (Howard) H.; A.B., U. of N.C., 1901, LL.D., 1935; M.D., Jefferson Med. College, Phila., 1904; m. Laura Witherspoon Ervin, Feb. 29, 1912; children—James King, Dorman Thompson, Samuel Ervin. Intern Phila. Poly. and Coll. for Graduates in Medicine, 1904-05; asst. physician State Hosp., Morganton, N.C., 1905-11; pres. Westbrook Sanatorium, Richmond, since 1911; mem. Nat. Com. for Mental Hygiene. Pres. Am. Psychiatric Assn., 1941-42; pres. Nat. Assn. of Private Psychiatric Hosps., 1940-41; mem. A.M.A., Va. State Med. Soc., N.C. State Med. Soc., Richmond Acad. Medicine, Tri-State Med. Assn., Am. Psychiatric Assn., Southern Psychiatric Association (pres.), A.A.A.S., Va. Acad. of Science, Am. Assn. on Mental Deficiency, Am. Prison Assn., N.C. Hist. Soc., Phi Beta Kappa. Club: Commonwealth. Asso. editor Southern Medicine and Surgery, Diseases of the Nervous System. Home: 3011 Seminary Av. Office: Westbrook Sanatorium, Richmond, Va. Died Sept. 10, 1948; buried in Forest Hill Cemetery, Morganton, N.C.

HALL, John Ellsworth, lawyer; b. Griffin, Ga., Feb. 15, 1876; s. John Iredell and Elizabeth (McMichael) H.; A.B., Emory Coll., Oxford, Ga., 1896; LL.B., U. of Georgia, 1900; m. May Louise Kennedy, Oct. 17, 1901; children—Elizabeth Lynde, John Iredell, Louise Kennedy, Ellsworth, Francis Kennedy, Benjamin Campbell, May Kennedy. Admitted to bar, 1900; asso. with father's firm, 1900-06; mem. Hall & Hall (father and son), 1907 until death of father, 1912; mem. Hall & Grice, now Hall & Bloch; has specialized in railway litigation, as gen. or division counsel various Ga. rys. Trustee Macon Free Sch., Alexander Free Sch.; mem. Bibb County Bd. of Edn. and Orphanage. Mem. Kappa Alpha, Phi Beta Kappa, Sphinx (U. of Ga.). Democrat. Episcopalian. Home: 231 High St. Office: 615 Georgia Casualty Bldg., Macon, Ga. Died Dec. 13, 1945.

HALL, Lemuel C., newspaper pub.; b. Harwich, Mass., Dec. 13, 1874; s. Gershom and Sophie Louise (Parker) H.; ed. high sch., Harwich; m. Lettice M. G. Foster, Dec. 25, 1896 (died 1911); children—Clarence J., Lillian L. (Mrs. Ralph B. Cudworth). Editor and pub. Wareham (Mass.) Courier since 1904; clk. and dir. Courier-Independent Pub. Co., Cape Cod Cranberry Growers Assn. Mem. Mass. Ho. of Rep., 1927-28. Pres. Mass. Press Assn., 1921, N.E. Press Assn., 1928, Nat. Editorial Assn., 1929-30. Republican. Conglist. Mason, Red Man. Clubs: Rotary, Community Associates. Home: 65 High St. Office: 173 Main St., Wareham, Mass. Died Oct. 18, 1946.

HALL, Louis Phillips, prof. operative dentistry; b. Toledo, O., June 1, 1860; s. Israel and Olivia (Bigelow) H.; student lit. dept. U. of Mich., 1879-80; grad. in dentistry, same univ., 1889; m. Elizabeth Campbell Douglas, Feb. 14, 1885; children—Douglas, Louis Phillips, Richard Nelville (killed in France), Elizabeth Olivia (Mrs. J. R. Hayden). Asst. to prof. clin. and operative dentistry, U. of Mich., 1889, advanced through various positions to prof. operative and clin. dentistry, 1903, prof. operative dentistry since 1922. Chmn. local br. Am. Red Cross, 1917-21. Mem. Am., Mich. State and 1st Dist. dental socs., Delta Sigma Delta. Republican. Episcopalian. Clubs: Rotary (pres. 1923), Barton Hills, Ann Arbor Golf, Ann Arbor br. Detroit Auto. Home: Ann Arbor, Mich. Died Dec. 19, 1944.

HALL, Matthew Alexander, lawyer; b. Scarboro, Ont., Can., July 31, 1862; s. Thomas Hewitson and Janet (Burns) H.; student Toronto Collegiate Inst., 1878-1880; teacher's certificate, County of York, 1880; taught Glenville and Kettleby schs., 1881-82; LL.B., U. of Wis., 1888; m. I. May Wurtele, Sept. 2, 1890; children—Percy Wurtele, Charles Alexander (dec.), Donald James, Robert Andrew. Came to U.S., 1885, naturalized, 1892. Admitted to Neb. bar, 1888, and began practice at Omaha; formerly mem. Hall, Young & Williams; then practicing alone; apptd. U.S. commr. for Dist. of Neb., 1938. Member Neb. Senate, 1903-04. British vice-consul at Omaha, 1898-1931. Mem. Am. Bar Assn., Neb. State Bar Assn., Omaha Bar Assn. (pres.), Commercial Law League of America, Phi Delta Theta. Republican. Presbyterian. Mason (Shriner). Home: 3871 Dewey Av. Office: Post Office Bldg., Omaha, Neb. Died June 17, 1942.

HALL, Oliver Leigh, editor, librarian; b. Rockland, Me., May 6, 1870; s. Oliver Gray and Sarah Frances (White) H.; student Coburn Classical Inst., Waterville, Me., 1887-89, Colby Coll., 1890-92; A.M., Colby Coll., 1914, U. of Me., 1927; m. Marie Agnes Bunker, June 3, 1896; children—Oliver Gray, Miriam Adelaide, Leonora Edith (Mrs. Herschel L. Good). Editor of Waterville (Me.) Sentinel, 1892-94; city editor of Rockland (Me.) Daily Star, 1895-97, editor, 1897-1900; city editor Bangor (Me.) Evening Commercial, 1905-11, editor, 1911-37 and since 1942; exec. sec. to Governor of Maine, 1937-38; state librarian, Me., 1938-41. Served as sr. lt. U.S.N.R., 1927-34. Member Bangor City Council, 1908-09, Bangor Bd. of Aldermen, 1910-11; chmn. Republican Com. of Hampden, 1928-38. Director of Port of Portland Authority, 1937-42. Editor Colby Alumnus (mag.), 1936-41. Trustee Hampden Acad. (pres. of bd.), Coburn Classical Inst., Good Samaritan Home. Past pres. of Me. Daily Newspaper Pubs. Assn., past pres. of Maine S.A.R.; mem. Reserve Officers Assn. of Bangor, Patrons of Husbandry (Hampden), Society of Mayflower Descendants, Zeta Psi. Republican. Mason. Clubs: Masonic, Hampden Community Assn. Author: The Man from East Corinth, biography of Arthur R. Gould, former U.S. Senator from Me., 1941. Home: Hampden, Me. Died Nov. 17, 1946.

HALL, William Shafer, mathematician; b. Chester, Pa., June 27, 1861; s. Stephen Cloud and Mercie Emma (Baker) H.; C.E., Lafayette Coll., 1884 (Phi Beta Kappa Fraternity), M.E., 1885, M.S., 1887, LL.D. from the same college, 1934; Sc.D., Gettysburg Coll., 1922 (Tau Beta Pi); m. Rachel Estelle Kline, Aug. 11, 1891; children—Rachel Elizabeth, Margaret (dec.), Mary Estelle, William Arthur (dec.), Eleanor Bassett. Tutor in Eng. and graphics, 1884-88, adj. prof. mining engring. and graphics, 1890-98, prof., 1898-1912, prof. tech. mathematics, 1912-14, prof. mathematics and head dept., 1914-34, emeritus professor of mathematics since 1938, Lafayette College, also secretary of faculty. Fellow A.A.A.S.; mem. Math. Assn. of America, Am. Assn. Univ. Profs., Math. Assn. Middle States and Md., Pa. Soc. S.R. Republican. Presbyterian. Elder. Mason (Past Eminent Comdr. K.T.). Author: Mensuration, 1893; Descriptive Geometry, 1904; Differential and Integral Calculus, 1897; Mine Surveying, 1911. Address: 310 March St., Easton, Pa. Died Dec. 17, 1948.

HALLAERT, Charles (hä-lärt'), consul general of Belgium; b. Belgium, April 1, 1894; s. Charles and Marie (De Simpel) H.; student Univ. of Louvain, 1912-14, 1918-20; m. Marie-Thérèse Leclercq, May 9, 1926; 1 dau., Anne-Marie. Vice consul of Belgium in New York in 1921; chargé d'affaires of Belgium in Guatemala, 1925-26; vice consul, New York, 1926-34, consul general, 1940. Served in Belgian Army, World War I. Decorated Ordre de Leopold, Ordre de la Couronne; Ordre de Leopold II; Croix de Guerre; Croix de Feu; Médaille de la Victoire; Médaille Commémorative. Clubs: Rockefeller Centre, Manhattan, Hackensack Golf, New York Athletic (N.Y. City); Columbia Golf (Washington, D.C.). Home: 232 Knox Av., Grantwood, N.J. Office: Belgian Consulate General, 630 Fifth Av., New York 20. Died Jan. 2, 1948; buried in Madonna Cemetery, Fort Lee, N.J.

HALLAM, Oscar, lawyer; b. Town of Linden, Wis., Oct. 19, 1865; s. Joseph and Mary (Wood) H.; A.B., U. of Wis., 1887, LL.B., 1889; m. Edith L. Lott, July 27, 1892. Began practice at St. Paul, 1889; dist. judge, 2d Jud. Dist. of Minn., 1905-13; asso. justice Sup. Ct., Minn., Jan. 1913-23; candidate at primary election for U.S. Senate, 1924. Dean St. Paul Coll. of Law. Conglist. Mem. Am., Minn. State, and Ramsey County bar assns. Home: 2230 Fairmount Av. Office: Endicott Bldg., St. Paul, Minn. Died Sep. 23, 1945.

HALLETT, George Hervey, mathematician; b. Manchester, Me., Dec. 30, 1870; s. James Hervey and Sarah Louise (Hawkes) H.; student Lehigh U., 1889-90; A.B., U. of Pa., 1893, A.M., 1894, Ph.D., 1896; m. Gertrude Amy Hawkes, Feb. 21, 1894; children—George H., Henry M., Mrs. Rebecca Richie, Margaret E. (Mrs. Margaret Pittman), Winslow N. Instructor in mathematics, 1894-1904, asst. prof., 1904-09; prof. 1909-33, Thomas A. Scott prof. of mathematics, 1933-41, emeritus since Jan. 1, 1942, University of Pa. Mem. Assn. Teachers of Math. Middle States and Md., Pa. State Ednl. Assn. (ednl. council 1910-16), Am. Math. Soc., Pi Mu Epsilon, Sigma Xi, Phi Beta Kappa. Club: Meridian (Philadelphia). Author: (with Robert F. Anderson) Elementary Algebra, 1917. Home: West Chester, Pa. Died Aug. 12, 1947.

HALLOCK, Frank Hudson, prof. Old Testament; b. N.Y. City, Aug. 15, 1877; s. Joseph Treadwell and Emma (Moore) H.; student Columbia; student Gen. Theol. Sem., 1905, S.T.D., 1919; S.T.B., Seabury Div. Sch., Faribault, Minn., 1913; LL.D., Nashotah House, 1940; m. Anne Walbridge Brown, Dec. 9, 1901; children—Elisabeth Walbridge (Mrs. Albert Daniel Klein), Richard Treadwell, Donald Hathaway. Deacon and priest P.E. Ch., 1906; pastor successively Marquette, Mich., Newark, N.J. and Schenectady, N.Y., until 1919; prof. dogmatic theology, Western Theol. Sem., Chicago, 1919-20; prof. O.T. and Semitic langs., Seabury Div. Sch., 1920-29, later Western Theological Seminary, now Nashotah (Wisconsin) House. Fellow Society Oriental Research, American Oriental Society, Society Biblical Literature. Republican. Author: Moral Theology (with F. J. Hall), 1924; The Gifts of the Holy Ghost, 1935; The Tell el-Amarna Tablets (with S. A. B. Mercer), 1939; also many articles, revs., etc.; editor rev. edit. Hall's Theological Outlines, 1933. Address: Nashotah House, Nashotah, Wis. Died Dec. 13, 1944.

HALSTEAD, Albert, consul gen.; b. Cincinnati, Sept. 19, 1867; s. Murat and Mary (Banks) H.; A.B., Princeton U., 1889; m. Aline Wilcox, Dec. 8, 1896; children—Albert Halstead, Aline Halstead Amon, Margaret Halstead Mason. Col. and a.-d.-c. on staff of William McKinley, gov. Ohio, 4 yrs. Washington corr. Cincinnati Commercial Gazette, 1891-96; editor Springfield (Mass.) Union, 1896-99; Washington corr. Brooklyn Standard Union, Phila. Evening Telegraph, etc., 1900-06. Consul at Birmingham, Eng., 1906-Feb. 1915; consul gen. at Vienna 1915-17; consul gen. at Stockholm, Sweden, Jan. 1918-May 1919; commercial adviser Am. Legation, Stockholm, June 1918-May 1919; consul gen. class 2, July 1918; U.S. commr. in Austria, at Vienna, 1919-20; consul gen., Montreal, P.Q., 1920-28; foreign service officer, class 1, July 1, 1924, consul gen., London, Eng., Oct. 1, 1928-Sept. 30, 1932, retired; now engaged in writing and in political study. Address: Bank of N.Y. and 5th Avenue Bank, N.Y. City 19. Died May 20, 1949.

HALSTEAD, Alexander Seaman, naval officer; b. Phila., Pa., Dec. 17, 1861; s. David and Janet (Gunn) H.; A.B., Central High Sch., Phila., 1879; grad. U.S. Naval Acad., 1883; grad. Naval War Coll., Newport, R.I., 1917; unmarried. Promoted asst. engr., July 1, 1885; passed asst. engr., Sept. 11, 1895; transferred to line as lt., Mar. 3, 1899; lt. comdr., Jan. 1, 1904; commander, July 1, 1908; capt., July 1, 1911; rear admiral (tem.), July 1, 1918; rear admiral (permanent), July 1, 1919. Served on Raleigh, Spanish-American War, participating in the Battle of Manila Bay, May 1, 1898, also capture of Corregidor Island, Manila Bay, capture of Grand Island, Subig Bay, and assault on Manila, Aug. 1898; on Chicago, 1904-06; insp. ordnance, San Francisco, Calif., 1906-09; comd. Vicksburg, 1909-10, Pensacola, 1910-11, comd. West Virginia, flagship 2d Div. Pacific Fleet, 1911-12; comd. California, flagship of Pacific Fleet, 1912-13, participating in operations of U.S. forces in connection with revolution in Nicaragua; supervisor New York Harbor, 1915; comdr. Utah, 1915-16, Naval War Coll., Newport, R.I., 1916-17; apptd. sr. mem. Bd. of Appraisal for Mcht. and Pvt. Vessels, N.Y. City, Apr. 2, 1917. Comdr. dist. of Brest, France, Oct. 1918-Jan. 1919; comdr. U.S. naval forces in France, hdqrs., Brest, Jan. 30, 1919; cooperated with U.S. Army in returning troops to U.S.; demobilized and returned to U.S. naval personnel and materiel of naval units ashore and afloat; duty completed, returned to U.S., Oct. 1919; comdt. Navy Yard, Portsmouth, N.H., Dec.-Oct. 1920; comdt. 12th Naval Dist., San Francisco, Oct. 1920 to June 1923; retired Nov. 13, 1923. Holder Dewey medal, and Spanish-Am. War and Nicaragua campaign badges; awarded D.S.M. by War Dept. and Navy Cross by Navy Dept. Comdr. Legion of Honor (French). Presbyn. Home: Pacific Union Club, San Francisco 6, Calif. Died Aug. 19, 1949.

HAM, William Felton, public utilities; b. Lewiston, Me., Mar. 15, 1870; s. John Stockbridge Patten and Abigail Lincoln (Stetson) H.; student Bates Coll., Lewiston, 1891; m. Suzanne Mulford, Oct. 10, 1899. Entered pub. utility business, 1895; chmn. bd. Potomac Electric Power Co. Mem. Soc. Mayflower Descendants, S.R. Clubs: Metropolitan, Chevy Chase; Blue Ridge Rod and Gun (Virginia); Alfalfa, Old Guard Soc. (Palm Beach, Fla.). Home: 2621 Woodley Pl., Washington, D.C.; (summer) Turner, Me. Office: 10th and E Sts. N.W., Washington, D.C. Died May 1949.

HAMBRECHT, George Philip (hăm'brĕkt), state dir. vocational and adult edn.; b. Milwaukee, Wis., Feb. 1, 1871; s. William and Mary (Cleary) H.; student U. of Wis., 1892-95; Ph.B., U. of Chicago, 1903; LL.B., Yale, 1904; hon. Sc.D. from The Stout Inst., 1932; traveled and studied in Europe, 1922; m. Mrs. Kate Magee (Barrows) Brace, Aug. 4, 1896 (died Oct. 12, 1939); 1 dau., Elizabeth (Mrs. Peter W. Krier). Supt. of schs., Wisconsin Rapids, Wis., 1899-1902; admitted to bar, 1903; city atty. Wisconsin Rapids, 1903-15; mem. Wis. Ho. of Rep. 1909-15; mem. Industrial Commn. of Wis., 1915-21 (chmn. 1917-21); state dir. vocational and adult edn., Wis., since July 1, 1921; mem. law firm Hambrecht & Calkins, Wisconsin Rapids. Chmn. State War Labor Bd., 1917-18, also state dir. of labor, state dir. U.S. Pub. Service Reserve, and four minute man, same period. Mem. Bd. of Visitors, U. of Wis., since 1910 (pres. 1922-23); pres. Assn. Govt. Labor Officials, 1919-20; dir. Nat. Safety Council, 1918-21; mem. Wis. Council Edn. since 1939; apptd. by Federal Government Wis. rep. for vocational training of defense workers, 1940; State dir. vocational training for war production workers since 1941, apptd. by U.S. Office of Edn.; hon. life mem. American Vocational Assn. (pres. 1935-36); mem. Nat. Econ. League, Nat. Safety Code Com. of Bur. of Standards, Nat. Assn. State Dirs. Vocational Edn. (pres. 1930), Am. and Wis. bar assns., Madison Civic Music Assn. (pres. 1928-37), Theta Delta Chi, Delta Chi, Book and Gavel (Yale), Phi Alpha Delta. Republican. Mason (32°, Shriner, Jester); Potentate of Zor Temple, 1935; dir. of Jesters 126, 1936-37. Elk. Clubs: Wisconsin, Rotary (pres. 1927-28), Madison (Madison); Milwaukee City, Calumet (Milwaukee). Author: Abraham Lincoln—His Spirit Lives, 1926; Lincoln Literature, 1937; Abraham Lincoln in Wisconsin, 1941; also many monographs, among which are Problem of Education, Learn While You Earn, Out of School Youth Problem, and Hobbies—the Use of Leisure Time. Contbr. to mags. on industrial and economic problems. Lecturer and collector of Lincolniana, and owner of over 3,000 volumes and pamphlets on Lincoln; elected mem. The Abraham Lincoln Assn., Springfield, Ill.; v.p. Lincoln Scholarship Fund (New York) since 1929; hon. mem. Southern Calif. Abraham Lincoln Assn.; charter mem. and pres. of Lincoln Fellowship of Wisconsin. Apptd., by U.S. sec. of labor, mem. Nat. Advisory Council for U.S. Employment Service; chmn. Local NRA Compliance Bd., 1933-34. Apptd. hon. Texas Ranger by Gov. Allred, 1936. Mem. Wis. Council of Defense, 1940-42. Home: 515 E. Gorham St. Address: State Office Bldg., Madison, Wis. Died Dec. 23, 1943.

HAMILL, Samuel McClintock, pediatrician; b. Oak Hall, Pa., Nov. 3, 1864; s. Robert and Margaret E. (Lyon) H.; student Princeton, 1886; M.D., U. of Pa., 1888; hon. D.Sc., U. of Pa., 1940; m. Lila Clarke Kennedy, Apr. 17, 1895; children—Kennedy, Samuel McClintock, Hugh Maxwell. Practiced in Phila. since 1890; demonstrator physical diagnosis, 1892-94, instr. medicine, 1894-1901, U. of Pa.; prof. diseases of children, Phila. Polyclinic and Coll. for Graduates in Medicine, 1901-19; prof. same, Post-Graduate Dept. of Medicine, U. of Pa., 1919-20; cons. pediatrician, Presbyn. Hosp.; formerly visiting pediatrician to St. Christopher's Hosp. for Children and Phila. Polyclinic; chmn. sect. I, med. service, and chmn. follow-up com. of sect. I, White House Conf. on Child Health and Protection. Mem. bd. mgrs. Babies' Hospital of Phila. Mem. exec. com. of Pa. mental hygiene com. of Public Charities Assn. Mem. Am. Med. Assn. (chmn. sect. on diseases of children, 1911), Am. Academy Pediatrics (pres. 1932), Am. Pediatric Soc. (pres. 1913-14), Med. Soc. State of Pa. (1st chmn. sect. on pediatrics), Phila. Pediatric Soc. (pres. 1901-02), Phila. Pathol. and Neurol. socs., Coll. of Physicians of Phila. Chmn. Pa. Emergency Child Health Com., 1933-39; mem. Gen. Med. Bd. and chmn. Nat. Child Welfare Com. of Council Nat. Defense; dir. child welfare for State of Pa., 1917-18; del. Cannes Med. Conf. of Red Cross Socs., 1919; pres. dirs. of Phila. Child Health Soc., 1919-42; mem. Am. Assn. Study and Prevention Infant Mortality (pres. 1915-16), Am. Child Health Assn. (pres. 1931-35); former mem. trustees Lawrenceville Sch. Republican. Presbyterian. Home: 1822 Spruce St., Philadelphia. Died May 3, 1948.

HAMILTON, Arthur Stephen, neurologist and psychiatrist; b. Wyoming, Ia., November 28, 1872; s. Arthur A. and Ada O. (Fisher) Hamilton; B.S., Univ. of Ia., 1894; M.D., Univ. of Pa., 1897; m. Susanna P. Boyle, Dec. 25, 1903; 1 son, David Arthur. Asst. physician, Independence (Ia.) State Hosp., 1897-1904; instr. neuropathology, U. of Minn., 1904-12, clin. instr. and asst. prof. nervous and mental diseases, 1905-12, asso. prof., 1912-16, prof. since 1916, also chief div. since 1912; neurologist to Univ., St. Mary's, Swedish, Fairview, Abbott, New Asbury, St. Andrews and Northwestern hosps.; dir. neurol. service U.S. Vets.' Hosp. No. 68. Capt. M.C., U.S.A., 1918; maj. 1919. Mem. Am. Neurol. Soc., Chicago Neurol. Soc., Minn. Neurol. Soc. (ex-pres.), Central Neuropsychiatric Assn. (ex-pres.), Am. Psychiatric Soc., Am. Med. Psychol. Assn., A.M.A. (ex-chmn. sect. nervous and mental diseases), Minn. State Med. Soc., Minn. Acad. Medicine (ex-pres.), Hennepin County Med. Soc. (ex-pres.), Phi Delta Theta, Nu Sigma Nu, Sigma Psi. Republican. Episcopalian. Clubs: Minneapolis, Campus, Minneapolis Golf. Home: 1432 Minnehaha Parkway W. Office: Medical Arts Bldg., Minneapolis. Died June 2, 1940.

HAMILTON, Clayton (Meeker), author, lecturer, editor; b. Brooklyn, N.Y., Nov. 14, 1881; s. George Alexander and Susie Amelia (Corey) H.; B.A., Poly. Inst. of Brooklyn, 1900; M.A., Columbia, 1901; awarded University Medal, Columbia, 1932; hon. fellow for drama, Union Coll., since 1936; m. Gladys Coates, May 24, 1913; children—Donald, Gordon. Tutor in English, Columbia and Barnard colls., 1901-04; extension lecturer, Columbia, 1903-23; lecturer, Classical Sch. for Girls, 1900-20, New York Dept. of Edn., 1903-06, Gardner Sch., 1904-20, Finch Sch., 1906-08, Miss Spence's Sch., 1908-20, Jacobi School, 1918-19, Chautauqua Summer Assembly, 1911, Brooklyn Inst. Arts and Sciences, 1913-19, Dartmouth Coll., summer session, 1916, 17, Utah. Agr. Coll., 1927, Pa. State Coll., 1927, Bread Loaf Summer Conf., 1931, 32, 33, Leland Powers Foundation, Boston, 1934-35, Mohawk Drama Festival, 1935, 36, 38, 39. Dir. edn. Palmer Photoplay Corp., 1922-25; pres. Palmer Inst. of Authorship, 1925-29. Dramatic critic and asso. editor Forum, 1907-09; dramatic editor, The Bookman, 1910-18, Everybody's Mag., 1911-13, Vogue, 1912-20; asso. in theatrical prodn. with George C. Tyler, Mrs. Fiske, William Gillette, Norman Bel Geddes, Walter Hampden, Playwrights' Company, Sam H. Harris, Vinton Freedley, since 1924; lecture tours of U.S., 1924-26 and 1932-33. Administrative assistant, U.S.O. Camp Shows, Inc., 1940; radio commentator WOR-Mutual, 1945. Mem. National Institute Arts and Letters, Phi Kappa Psi. Clubs: Players, P.E.N. (N.Y.); Writers (Hollywood). Author: (plays) The Love That Blinds (with Grace Isabel Colbron), for Mary Shaw, 1906; The Stranger at the Inn, for Tyrone Power, 1913; The Big Idea (with A. E. Thomas), for Cohan and Harris, 1914; Thirty Days (with A. E. Thomas), for A. H. Woods, 1916; The Better Understanding (with A. E. Thomas), for Henry Miller, 1917; Friend Indeed (with B. H. Voigt), prod. 1926; (books) Materials and Methods of Fiction, 1908; The Theory of the Theatre, 1910; Studies in Stagecraft, 1914; On the Trail of Stevenson, 1915; Problems of the Playwright, 1917; The Big Idea, 1917; A Manual of the Art of Fiction, 1918; Seen on the Stage, 1920; Thirty Days, 1923; The Better Understanding, 1924; Conversations on Contemporary Drama (lecture series), 1924; Wanderings, 1925; Friend Indeed, 1926; So You're Writing a Play!, 1935; The Theory of the Theatre, Consolidated Edition, 1939; The Art of Fiction, 1939. Contbr. of Hawaiian Chapter in These United States, 1924. Editor: Robert Louis Stevenson's Treasure Island, 1910; Kenyon's Kindling, 1914; Mackaye's A Thousand Years Ago, 1914; H. A. Jones' Mary Goes First, 1914; Clark's Three Modern Plays from the French, 1914; Pinero's R. L. Stevenson as a Dramatist, 1914; The Social Plays of A. W. Pinero (4 vols.), 1917-22; Calvert's Problems of the Actor, 1918; Yvette Guilbert's How to Sing a Song, 1918; Hooker's Translation of Cyrano de Bergerac, 1923; Representative Plays, by H. A. Jones (4 vols.), 1925; Goodrich's Caponsacchi, 1927; Hugo's Notre Dame de Paris, 1928; Stevenson's Mediaeval Tales, 1929; Goodrich's Richelieu, 1929; Hooker's translation of Ruy Blas, 1930. Contbr. to Ency. Americana, New Internat. Year Book, Nelson's Ency., and many mags. Asso. editor Goldwyn Studios, 1920-22. Address: The Players, 16 Gramercy Park, New York 3, N.Y. Died Sep. 17, 1946.

HAMILTON, E(dward) Wilbur Dean, portrait painter; b. Summerfield, O., Feb. 17, 1863; s. Rev. W. C. P. and Henrietta M. (Dean) H.; studied in Mass. State Sch. of Art (Boston), Julian Acad., and École des Beaux Arts (Paris); pupil of Jules Eli Delaunay; m. Mrs. Lilian Derby Holmes, July 24, 1894; 1 son, Dean Derby. Formerly head, now mem. Fine Arts Dept., Mass. State Sch. of Art. Hon.

mention Municipal Art Soc.; medal, Atlanta, 1895; Phila. Court House prize competition, 1894; Jordan prize, Boston, 1894; gold medal, San Francisco Expn., 1915; gold medal, Internat. Expn., San Francisco, 1939. Portraits of Justice McKenna of Supreme Court of U.S.; President W. F. Warren, Boston U.; Francis L. Higginson, Boston; Mrs. Travis Cochran, Phila.; Mrs. Hilborne Roosevelt, N.Y. City; also portrait of late President Harding for Am. Univ., Washington, D.C.; portrait of Bishop Francis Asbury for First Wesleyan Ch., Bristol, Eng.; portrait of Bishop John W. Hamilton for Boston U.; decorated John Wesley Memorial Room, Lincoln College, Oxford; decorated altar of Ch. of All Nations; now working on transcript "The Religions in America" for same ch.; group of three portraits for Battelle Memorial, late John G. Battelle, wife and son; portraits for McLean Hospital, Waverly, of late Dr. Frank Cowles, late Dr. George T. Tuttle and replica to be placed in Dartmouth College, late Dr. Arthur Jelley; group portrait of Mrs. Davenport Brown and daughter, Boston; portraits of Dr. Elwood Worcester, of the Emmanuel Movement; late Charles C. Glover, pres. of Cochran Art Gallery for American U.; Miss Eleanor Ames, now Mrs. Alexander North Easton; Miss Natalie Gourley, now Mrs. Frank Appleton, Boston; Robert Vose, Jr., Boston; Mrs. Wilbur Dean Hamilton, Kingston; late Mrs. George Stoddard. Home: Landing Rd., Kingston, Mass. Died Jan. 23, 1943.

HAMILTON, Elwood, judge; b. Benson, Ky., Feb. 22, 1883; s. Allen and Sophia (Stigers) H.; student University of Kentucky, 1902-03; LL.B., University of Louisville, 1904; m. Maude Pence, Dec. 28, 1904 (died Feb. 9, 1945); children—Hazel Pence (Mrs. Charles Gatz), Helen Prentice (Mrs. Harry Earl Gatz), Allen Scott, Elizabeth Elwood (Mrs. Charles Conrad Meyer, Jr.). Admitted to Kentucky bar, 1905; practiced at Frankfort, 1905-22, partner Scott & Hamilton, 1908-17, Hamilton & Polagrove, 1917-22; settled in Louisville, 1922; mem. Beckham, Hamilton & Beckham, 1922-29, Woodward, Hamilton & Hobson since 1929; mem. Gen. Assembly of Ky., 1912-14; collector internal revenue for Ky., 1917-22; U.S. dist. judge, Western Dist. of Ky., 1935-38; judge U.S. Circuit Ct. of Appeals, 6th Circuit, since Apr. 1, 1938. Mem. Am., Ky. State and Louisille bar assns. Democrat. Mem. Christian (Disciples) Ch. Club: Pendennis. Home: 2735 Field Av. Address: Federal Bldg., Louisville, Ky. Deceased.

HAMILTON, George E., lawyer; b. Charles County, Md., Mar. 5, 1855; s. John and Mary Emily H.; A.B., Georgetown University, D.C., 1872, LL.B., 1874, A.M., 1882, LL.D., 1889, and J.U.D. from same univ., 1922; m. Louise F. Merrick, 1891. Began law practice, 1876, associated with Merrick & Morris; on the death of Richard T. Merrick, 1885, became mem. Morris & Hamilton; now sr. mem. Hamilton & Hamilton; gen. counsel Washington Terminal Co., counsel B.&O. and other ry. corps.; v.p., gen. counsel and trust officer of Union Trust Co., Washington; gen. counsel Capital Transit Company. Lecturer on legal ethics and dean emeritus, Law School of Georgetown University; regent Georgetown University; pres. and trustee Corcoran Gallery of Art. Clubs: Cosmos, Chevy Chase. Home: Stone Ridge, Bethesda, Md. Office: Union Trust Bldg., Washington, D.C. Died May 24, 1946.

HAMILTON, George Henry, banker; b. Wellington, Ill., Apr. 4, 1875; s. John Lawrence and Ann Eliza (Leemon) H.; B.S., Olivet Coll., 1894; grad. work Harvard, 1894-96; student Northwestern U. Law Sch., 1898-1901; m. Anna C. Russell, Sept. 18, 1907; children—George Russell, Elizabeth Ann. Admitted to Ill. bar, 1901; entered banking business in Watseka, Ill., 1903; removed to Wichita, Kan., and purchased State Savings Bank, Wichita, 1912; merged with Fourth Nat. Bank, 1922; v.p., later pres. of same, 1924-32; gov. of Federal Reserve Bank of Kansas City, Mo., 1932-37, pres. 1937-41; v.p. Fourth Nat. Bank, Wichita, Kan., since 1941. Apptd. chief renegotiator Midwestern Procurement Dist., Army Air Forces, Dec. 9, 1942. Regent of Wichita Municipal U., 1927-32. Served in Ill. State legislature, 1906-12; city commr. city of Wichita, 1921-22, mayor of Wichita, 1922. Mem. Phi Delta Phi. Republican. Mason. Clubs: Wichita, Kansas City, Wichita Country, Mission Hills Country. Home: 348 N. Roosevelt. Office: Fourth National Bank, Wichita, Kan. Died Jan. 18, 1948.

HAMILTON, Gilbert Van Tassel, physician; b. Frazeyburg, O., Jan. 15, 1877; s. Joseph Gilbert and Margaret (Van Tassel) H.; A.B., Ohio Wesleyan U., 1896; M.D., Jefferson Med. Coll., 1901; student Harvard U. Grad. Sch., 1905-06 and 1907-08; m. Mary Sisson, June 27, 1906; 1 son, Dr. Joseph Gilbert. Interne, Jewish Hosp., Phila., 1901-02; asst., 1st asst. physician, State Hosp. for Insane, Warren, Pa., 1902-05; resident med. officer, McLean Hosp., Waverley, Mass., 1905-07; clinical psychiatry and privately endowed research in comparative psychology, 1908-17; psychiatric clinical survey, Newark, O., 1921-22; dir. Div. of Psychobiological Research of Bur. of Social Hygiene, N.Y. City, 1924-28; clinical psychiatry, Santa Barbara, since 1928; dir. Santa Barbara Socialization Inst., 1939-41; mem. visiting staff, Cottage Hosp., Dir. West Coast Apartments Co. Diplomate Am. Bd. Neurology and Psychiatry. Mem. A.M.A., Am. Psychiatric Assn., Am. Psychol Assn., Phi Kappa Psi. Author: Introduction to Objective Psychopathology, 1925; A Research in Marriage, 1929; What Is Wrong with Marriage (with Kenneth Macgowan), 1929; The Adversary in Tomika, 1930. Home: 824 Moreno Rd. Address: Edgerly Court, Santa Barbara, Calif. Died Dec. 1943.

HAMMAN, Louis, physician; b. at Baltimore, Dec. 21, 1877; s. John A. and Agatha (Haseneyer) H.; Calvert Hall Coll., Baltimore, 1893; A.B., Rock Hill Coll., Ellicott City, Md., 1895; studied Johns Hopkins, 1896; M.D., Johns Hopkins, 1901; m. Mary Brereton Sharretts, Oct. 10, 1906; children—Mary Sharretts, Ellen Power, Louis; m. 2d, Marian Campbell Bond, February 6, 1943. Interne, 1901-02, resident physician, 1902-03, New York Hosp.; began practice at Baltimore, Mar. 1903; asst. in medicine, 1903-06, instr., 1906-08, asso., 1908-15, asso. prof. clin. medicine, 1915-32, asso. prof. medicine since 1932, Johns Hopkins U.; asst. visiting physician, Johns Hopkins Hosp., 1908-28, visiting physician since 1928. Mem. Assn. Am. Physicians, A.M.A., A.A.A.S., Phi Beta Kappa; corr. sec. Internat. Anti-Tuberculosis Assn. Catholic. Club: Elkridge. Contbr. on med. subjects. Home: 8 W. Read St. Office: 9 E. Chase St., Baltimore, Md. Died Apr. 28, 1946.

HAMMER, Trygve, sculptor; b. Arendal, Norway, Sept. 6, 1878; s. Christopher Natvig and Caroline (Dreyer) H.; student Royal Arts Trade Sch., Oslo, Norway, 1895-98, Art Students League, Nat. Acad. of Design and Beaux-Arts School of Sculpture, 1906-13; m. Emma Tronboll, June 15, 1905; children—Agnes Gudrun (Mrs. John J. Clutz), Olaf Trygveson. Came to U.S., 1903, naturalized, 1913. Interior designer and decorator, 1903-16, sculptor and designer since 1916, with Fed. Telephone and Radio Corp., E. Newark, N.J. Works: Theodore Roosevelt Memorial, Tenafly, N.J.; War Memorial Window, Crescent Athletic Club, Brooklyn; Benson Memorial, Zion Norwegian Ch., Brooklyn; heroic size busts of Roald Amundsen and Henrik Ibsen; Humphries bronze memorial, Stevens Inst., Hoboken, N.J.; Scofield Memorial, Am. Scandinavian Foundation, New York; Trophy Room, Princeton University; Norse grill room, Hotel Waldorf-Astoria; collaborator on sculpture for the John Philip Sousa Memorial, Washington, D.C.; Bishop Otto Fabricius Memorial Tablet in bronze for Greenland. Work reptd. in Brooklyn Museum, Newark Museum, Brookgreen Gardens open-air sculpture collection of Mr. and Mrs. Huntington, S.C. Painted decorations in the Waldorf Savarin, New York; murals in the Hotel Ambassador, Washington, D.C. Home: 67 Jane St., New York, N.Y. Died June 28, 1947.

HAMMOND, Alonzo John, civil engr.; b. Thorntown, Ind., Apr. 23, 1839; s. John W. and Mary Ann (Padgett) H.; B.S., Rose Poly. Inst., 1889; M.S., 1894, C.E., 1898, Dr. Engring., 1933; grad. study, Mass. Inst. Tech., 1891; m. Flora Troll, May 23, 1893; children—Alonzo John, Mary A. (Mrs. George E. Davies). City engr. Frankfort, Ind., 1888-98; asst. engr. Terre Haute & Ind. R.R., 1898-1901; city engr. South Bend, Ind., 1901-09; cons. engr., Chicago, since 1910; chief engr. Bur. Public Efficiency, Chicago, 1911; engr. of bridges and harbors, Chicago, 1912-13; asst. chief engr. Chicago Union Station Co. (in charge engring. design and constrn. $75,000,000 station), 1914-22; asso. with James O. Heyworth, 1922-25, constructing hydroelectric plants and bridges; with Mellon-Stuart Co., 1926-27, rep. of company in negotiations for $130,000,000 internal improvement program for Cuba; since 1927 in cons. engring. practice (City of Chicago on river straightening, viaducts and bridges; Des Moines and Sioux City, Ia., union stations; vehicular tunnel under Delaware River; high level bridge Pittsburgh and report on Minneapolis and St. Louis R.R.). Mem. Building Code Com., Chicago; gen. chmn. Construction League of U.S., 1933-34; pres. Am. Engring. Council, 1940-41; mem. bd. mgrs. Rose Poly. Inst., mem. advisory com. Army and Navy Munitions Bd. on engring. and construction; consulting engr. construction div. of War Dept. on all field operations; now member construction contract board of construction division, War Department, Washington. Vice-president Am. Inst. Consulting Engrs., 1943. Member American Society of Civil Engineers (pres. 1933; elected hon. mem. Jan. 1943), Western Soc. Engrs., Am. Ry. Engring. Assn., Am. Inst. Cons. Engrs. Republican. Presbyterian. Mason (Shriner). Clubs: Chicago Engineers, Shawnee Country. Home: Hotel Claridge, 820 Conn. Av. N.W., Washington, D.C. Office: 120 S. La Salle St., Chicago, Ill. Died Dec. 2, 1944.

HAMMOND, Graeme Monroe, neurologist; born Phila., Feb. 1, 1858; s. William A. and Helen (Nisbet) H.; Sch. of Mines (Columbia), 1874-77; M.D., Univ. Med. Coll. (New York U.), 1881; LL.B., New York Law Sch., 1900; m. Louise Elsworth, Apr. 27, 1881. Interne, N.Y. Post-Grad. Med. Sch. and Hosp., 1881, since been identified with that instn., now prof. nervous diseases; frequently called as expert in insanity cases. Served maj. Med. R.C., Apr. 1917-Feb. 1919. Mem. Am. Neurol. Assn. (sec. and treas. 25 yrs., pres. 1911-12), Am. Psychiatric Assn., A.M.A., New York Psychiatric Soc., New York Neurol. Soc. Home: 145 E. 52d St. Office: 140 E. 54th St., New York. Died Oct. 30, 1944.

HAMMOND, John Henry, lawyer; b. Louisville, Ky., Oct. 3, 1871; s. late Gen. John Henry and Sophia Vernon (Wolfe) H.; Ph.B.; Sheffield Scientific Sch. (Yale), 1892; LL.B., Columbia, 1895; admitted to bar, 1895; m. Emily V. Sloane, Apr. 5, 1899; children—Mrs. Emily Franklin, Mrs. Adele Olyphant, Mrs. Alice Goodman, Mrs. Rachel Speiden, John Henry. Deputy attorney general of New York State, 1899-1901, in charge of election cases; brought charges against Asa B. Gardiner, dist. atty. N.Y. County, resulting in his removal by Gov. Roosevelt. Mem. exec. com. Rep. County Com., 29th Assembly Dist., 1907-08. Formerly mem. Cadwalader, Wickersham & Taft, later Brown Brothers, Harriman & Co., bankers; now mem. Door, Hammond, Hand & Dawson, N.Y. City; formerly chmn. Bangor & Aroostook Railroad Co.; dir. All America Cables, W. & J. Sloane, Sloane-Blabon Corporation, Greenwich Savings Bank; trustee National Industrial Conference Board. Director Bureau of Enemy Trade of War Trade Board. Trustee New York Public Library (1911-19), Community Service Society. Mem. American Bar Association, Assn. Bar City of New York. Clubs: Union, Yale, St. Anthony, Republican, Down Town, Yeaman's Hall, Blind Brook. Author: Hammond on Taxation of Business Corporations in New York State, 1901. Home: 778 Park Av., N.Y. Office: 61 Broadway, New York, N.Y. Died June 28, 1949.

HAMMOND, William Churchill, organist; b. Rockville, Conn., Nov. 25, 1860; s. Joseph C. and Kate (Burr) H.; studied music in Hartford and New York with N. H. Allen and S. P. Warren; m. Fanny Bliss Reed, June, 1898. Organist Congl. Ch., Rockville, Conn., and Pearl St. Ch., Hartford; organist Second Congl. Ch., Holyoke, since 1885; instr. of organ at Smith Coll., 1890-1900; prof. of music, Mt. Holyoke Coll., S. Hadley, Mass., since 1900. Address: Holyoke, Mass. Died Apr. 16, 1949.

HAMPSON, Alfred Aubert, lawyer; b. Washington, D.C., Oct. 9, 1882; s. Thomas Evans and Martha Rogers (Hale) H.; A.B., Stanford Univ., 1907; m. Ethel M. Stevenson, June 25, 1917; children—Patricia, Alfred A.; m. 2d, Cyetta McClaskey, July 25, 1925. Admitted Ore. bar, 1906, and since in practice at Portland; partner Hampson, Koerner, Young and Swett; became gen. atty. Southern Pacific Co., Ore. lines, 1930. Dir., Northern Pacific Terminal Co., Ore., Calif. & Eastern Ry. Co. Mem. Am., Ore. and Multnomah bar assns. Mem. Sigma Nu, Phi Delta Phi. Clubs: Arlington (pres. 1936), Waverley Country, University (Portland). Home: 01411 S.W. Radcliffe Rd. Office: Pacific Bldg., Portland, Ore. Died Apr. 9, 1946.

HAMPTON, Ireland, lawyer; b. Boyd County, Ky., Apr. 6, 1871; s. John Warring and Louisa Virginia (Ireland) H.; ed. by pvt. tutors, 2 yrs. Ky. Wesleyan U., Winchester (formerly Millersburg), Ky., and pvt. study of law; m. Marian Reger (dec.); children—John Howard, Ireland; m. 2d, Hally Bradley. Admitted to Tex. bar, 1894, and practiced in Fort Worth; specializes in laws relating to conservation of water resources; author of or consultant for practically all major legislation of Texas, enacted since 1922, relating to the conservation of water and other natural resources; consultant for cities and districts on water control problems; adviser com. on water resources, Tex. Planning Bd. Mem. Tex. Bar Assn. Home: 4501 E. Lancaster. Office: Capps Bldg., Fort Worth, Texas. Died July 23, 1943.

HANCH, Charles Connard (hănsh), automotive, bus. counsel; b. Maywood, Ind., Nov. 19, 1867; s. George B. N. and Emma W. (Eaglesfield) Hanch; student Butler University, 1887-88; m. Dorothy Martin Davis (died 1945); 1 dau. Hazel M. Deputy treas. City of Indianapolis, 1888-89; general accountant, Bank of Commerce, Indianapolis, 1890-91; sec. and treas. C. L. Storrs Lumber Co., Evansville, Ind., 1892-93; mgr. Helena (Mont.) Pub. Sampling Works, 1894-95; credit mgr. and treas. Nordyke and Marmon Co., Indianapolis, 1896-1914; treas. Studebaker Corp., South Bend, Ind., 1915-18; chief of automotive products sect. of War Industries Bd., June 20, 1918, to end of war; trade commr. Bur. Foreign and Domestic Commerce, U.S. Dept. Commerce, Feb.-May 1919; gen. factory mgr. Maxwell Motor Co., Detroit, 1919-20; exec. v.p. Lexington Motor Co., Connersville, Ind., 1921-22; consulting expert various automobile mfrs. since 1923; gen. mgr. Nat. Assn. of Finance Companies, 1925-34. Prominent in Indianapolis Mfrs. Assns. for 19 yrs., and 1st pres. Chamber of Commerce, Indianapolis; was v.p. Automobile Bd. of Trade and Nat. Automobile Chamber Commerce, New York. Initiated movement that led to pooling of patents in Nat. Automobile Chamber of Commerce. Led fight of automobile industry for repeal of excise taxes; former dir. Automobile Mutual Ins. Co., R.I. (charter policy holder). Inventor automotive devices. Author of numerous financial and tech. articles. Contributor to jours. Protestant. Scottish Rite Mason (Shriner). Clubs: Columbia (Indianapolis); Indiana Society of Chicago, Adventurers (Chicago); Society of Automotive Engineers of New York. Home: 1400 Lake Shore Drive. Office: 185 N. Wabash Av., Chicago 1. Died Oct. 12, 1946.

HANCOCK, Clarence Eugene, ex-congressman; b. Syracuse, N.Y., Feb. 13, 1885; s. Theodore E. and Martha B. (Connelly) H.; A.B., Wesleyan U., Middletown, Conn., 1906; LL.B., New York Law Sch., 1908; m. Emily W. Shonk, Oct. 5, 1912; 1 son, John Shonk. Admitted to N.Y. bar, 1908, and began practice with Hancock, Hogan & Hancock, Syracuse; mem. same firm, 1911-16; mem. Hancock, Dorr, Ryan & Shove since 1919. With N.Y. Cav., Mexican border, 1916; capt. machine gun batn. U.S. Army, World War. Corp. counsel, Syracuse, 1926-27; mem. 70th to 79th Congresses (1927-47), 36th N.Y. Dist. Mem. N.Y. State, Onondaga County bar assns., Phi Beta Kappa, Phi Delta Phi, Alpha Delta Phi. Republican. Presbyterian. Clubs: Century, Cazenovia Country (Syracuse); Nat. Republican (New York). Home: 1650 James St. Office: Hills Bldg., Syracuse, N.Y. Died Jan. 3, 1948.

HANCOCK, Thomas Hightower, surgeon; b. Ellerslie, nr. Charlottesville, Va., Jan. 9, 1869; s. Richard Johnson and Thomasia Overton (Harris) H.; M.D., Coll. Phys. and Surg. (Columbia), 1891; m. Marie Louise Price, Sept. 26, 1894; children—Elizabeth Erskine, Richard Harris, Emma Louise, John Overton. Interne, Polyclinic Hosp., New York, 1891-92, practiced at Atlanta, Ga., since 1893; founder, 1907, pres. and chief surgeon, Atlanta Hosp.; gen. surgeon Ga. Power Co.; surgeon Southern Ry.; consulting surgeon S.A.L. Ry. Mem. Am., Southern, Ga. State and Fulton County med. assns., Southern States Assn. Ry. Surgeons (ex-pres.), Assn. of Surgeons of Southern Ry. Co. (charter mem. and ex-pres.), Phi Chi, etc. Democrat. Episcopalian. Mason. Odd Fellow, K.P. Home: 300 Crumley St. S.W. Office: 320 Crew St. S.W., Atlanta, Ga.* Deceased.

HAND, William Flowers, chemist; b. Shubuta, Miss., Dec. 1, 1873; s. Albert Powe and Florence May (Flowers) H.; B.S., Mississippi State Coll., 1893, M.S., 1895; Ph.D., Columbia, 1903. Asst. in chemistry, Miss. State Coll., 1893, prof. chemistry since 1899, v.p. since 1935, also dean Science Sch., 1916-46; state chemist, Miss., 1899-1946 (now emeritus). Pres. Assn. Feed Control Officials of U.S., 1922. Mem. Am. Chem. Soc., Assn. Official Agrl. Chemists of North America (pres. 1921), Sigma Alpha Epsilon. Democrat. Address: State College, Mass. Died Sept. 25, 1948.

HANDFORTH, Thomas, artist; b. Tacoma, Wash., Sept. 16, 1897; s. Thomas Jefferson and Ruby Edwardine (Shera) H.; student U. of Wash.; art edn., Nat. Acad. Design and Art Students' League, N.Y. City, Ecole des Beaux Arts and Académie Colarossi, Paris, Charles Hawthorne Sch., Provincetown, Mass.; unmarried. Etcher, lithographer, illustrator, portraitist. Represented in Metropolitan Museum Art, N.Y. City; New York Public Library; Bibliothèque Nationale, Paris; Honolulu (H.T.) Acad. Arts; Pa. Museum, Phila.; Fogg Art Museum, Cambridge, Mass.; Omaha Art Mus.; Baltimore (Md.) Museum of Art; Library of Congress; Boston (Mass.) Museum of Fine Arts; Carnegie Inst., Pittsburgh, Pa.; also represented in Fine Prints of the Year, 1926-37; Fifty Prints of the Year, 1926-29. Awarded Emil Fuchs prize, Brooklyn Soc. Etchers, 1927; Charles M. Lea prize, Phila. Soc. Etchers, 1929; Guggenheim fellowship for study in Far East, 1931; purchase prizes, Northwest Soc. of Printmakers, 1934, Chicago Soc. for Etchers, 1937, Boston Soc. of Ind. Artists, 1937, Calif. Soc. of Etchers, 1941; Caldecott medal for "Mei Li," 1939. Illustrator of "Mei Li" by Thomas Handforth, 1938. Served as sergt. Med. Dept., U.S. Army, 1918-19. Pvt., U.S. Army Air Corps, 1942-43. Member Society American Etchers, Chicago Soc. Etchers, Zeta Psi. Illustrator of "Sidonie," by Pierre Coalfleet, 1921; Toutou in Bondage, by Elizabeth Coatsworth, 1929; Tranquilina's Paradise, by Susan Smith, 1930; Secret of the Porcelain Fish, by Margery Evernden, 1946. Author and illustrator: Faraway Meadow, 1939; Sleeping Arrow, 1941. Contbr. to Forum, Asia and to Foreign Policy Assn. publs. Address: 604 Lindsey Rd., Wilmington 280, Del. Died Oct. 19, 1948.

HANDY, Anson Burgess, educator; b. Bourne, Mass., May 15, 1883; s. Henry Thomas and Lydia Perkins (Ellis) H.; grad. Bridgewater Normal Sch. (now Teachers Coll.), 1904; A.B., Harvard Coll., 1908, M.Edn., 1930; m. Clara Grace Jones, June 14, 1910; children—Henry King, Dr. Allan Ward, Carol Sayres. Instr. East Greenwich (R.I.) Acad., 1904-06; teacher Medford (Mass.) High Sch., 1908-09, Winn Sch. for Boys, Asheville, N.C., 1909-10; prin. York (Me.) High Sch., 1910-12, Barre (Mass.) High Sch., 1912-15, Putnam (Conn.) High Sch., 1915-18; supt. schs. and prin. Stafford High Sch., 1918-22; supt. schs., Thompsonville, Conn., 1922-26, Plymouth, Mass., 1926-41; pres. Hyannis State Teachers Coll., May 1, 1941-Sept. 1, 1944; Dean Hyannis Technical School, Sept. 1, 1944. Mem. N.E.A., American Assn. Sch. Administrators, Mass. State Teachers Assn., Mass. Superintendents Assn., N.E. Superintendents Assn., Cape Cod Chamber of Commerce (Hyannis). Mason. Club: Rotary (Hyannis). Address: 17 Harbor Bluff Road, Hyannis. Died Mar. 24, 1946.

HANES, Frederic Moir, physician; b. Winston-Salem, N.C., Sept. 18, 1883; s. John Wesley and Anna (Hodgin) H.; A.B., Univ. of N.C., 1903; A.M., Harvard, 1904; M.D., Johns Hopkins, 1908; m. Elizabeth Peck, Dec. 16, 1913. Interne Johns Hopkins Hosp., 1908-09; asso. prof. of pathology, Columbia, and pathologist, Presbyn. Hosp., New York, 1909-12; asso. Rockefeller Inst., 1912-13; asso. prof. of medicine, Washington U. Med. Dept., 1913-14; asst. in neurology Queen Square Hosp., London, 1914; prof. of therapeutics, Med. Coll. of Va., 1914-16; internist, Winston-Salem, N.C., 1918-31; physician Duke Hosp., 1931, prof. of medicine since 1933. Served as lt. col., Med. Corps, U.S. Army, Comdg. Base Hosp. 65, A.E.F., 1917-19. Fellow Am. Coll. Physicians; mem. Assn. Am. Physicians, A.M.A., Clin. and Climatol. Assn., N.C. State Med. Soc., Sigma Alpha Epsilon, Nu Sigma Nu, Phi Beta Kappa, Alpha Omega Alpha. Contbr. to med. jours. Home: Campus Road, Durham, N.C. Died Mar. 25, 1946.

HANEY, Bert Emory, judge; b. LaFayette, Ore., Apr. 10, 1879; s. John Haney and Mary (Harris) H.; student Willamette U., 1896-99; LL.B., U. of Ore., 1903; LL.D., Linfield Coll., 1937; m. Jessie Holmes, November 21, 1906; 1 son, John Robert (deceased). Began practice at Portland, Oregon, 1903; deputy district attorney 4th Judicial District, Oregon, 1904-08; mem. firm Joseph, Haney & Littlefield, 1908-28; chmn. Dem. State Com., Ore., 1910-15; U.S. atty. Dist. of Ore., by apptmt. of President Wilson, 1918-20; chmn. State Bd. Pardons and Paroles (Ore.), 1922-23; mem. U.S. Shipping Bd., June 1, 1923-Mar. 1, 1926 (resigned); judge U.S. Circuit Court of Appeals, 9th Circuit, by apptmt. of President Franklin D. Roosevelt, since Aug. 20, 1935. Chmn. State Advisory Board, Pub. Works Administration and Home Owners Loan Corp.; chmn. Port of Portland. Pres. Ore. League of Nations Assn.; trustee Ore. Hist. Soc. Mem. Am. and Ore. State bar assns., Sons and Daughters of Ore. Pioneers (pres.), Phi Delta Phi. Democrat. Presbyn. Clubs: University (Portland); Waverly Country. Home: 2308 N.E. Alameda Drive, Portland, Ore. Office: U.S. Court House, Portland, Ore.; and 332 Post Office Bldg., San Francisco, Calif. Died Sep. 18, 1943.

HANEY, Dick, lawyer; b. Lansing, Ia., Nov. 10, 1852; s. John and Fanny (Toll) H.; ed. Ia. Wesleyan U. and State U. of Ia.; LL.B., State U. of Ia., 1874; m. Roxie W. Doe, Jan. 22, 1876 (died 1907); children—John D., Harriet H.; m. 2d, Florence May Tredway, Sept. 14, 1909; children—Elinor, Mary Patricia. Practiced law at Lansing, Ia., 1875-85; removed to S.D.; elected circuit judge, Oct. 1889; re-elected Nov. 1893; judge Supreme Court of S.D., Feb. 1, 1896-Jan. 7, 1913; chief reviser S.D. Code Commn., July 1, 1917-July 1919; elected state senator, 1924; municipal judge Huron, 1925-33. Home: Huron, S.Dak. Died May 3, 1948.

HANGER, William A., lawyer; b. Tarrant County, Texas; s. Robert N. and Hannah E. (Swan) H.; ed. Trinity U., Tehuacana, Tex., 1886-89; grad. Cumberland U., Lebanon, Tenn., 1890; hon. LL.D., Cumberland U., 1933, Trinity Univ., Waxahachie, Tex., 1935; m. Mattie Scruggs, Aug. 23, 1893; children—Robert K., Ruth (dec.). Admitted to Texas bar, 1890, and since in practice at Fort Worth; mem. Cantey, Hanger, McMahon, McKnight & Johnson since 1905; mem. State senate of Texas, 1899-1907. Democrat. Presbyterian. Club: Fort Worth. Home: 2308 Winton Terrace West. Office: Sinclair Bldg., Fort Worth, Tex.* Died June 8, 1944.

HANK, Oscar Charles, vice-pres. U.S. Tobacco Co.; b. Paducah, Ky., 1877; s. Peter and Pauline (Haefner) H.; m. Inez Trent, Oct. 2, 1916; children—Oscar Charles, Jr., Virginia. Asso. with U.S. Tobacco Co. and predecessors, 43 yrs, mgr. leaf dept., later v.p. and dir.; ret. 1945. Presbyterian. Home: 2830 Broadway. Address: Box 116, Paducah, Ky. Died June 8, 1946; buried in Oak Grove Cemetery, Paducah.

HANKS, Marshall Bernard, publisher; b. Dallas, Tex., Sept. 10, 1884; s. Robert Taylor and Mattie Bernard (Jones) H.; B.A., Simmons Coll., 1904; Baylor U., 1906; m. Eva May Hollis, Nov. 16, 1906; 1 dau., Patty (Mrs. A. B. Shelton). With Abilene Reporter-News since 1900, beginning as delivery boy, pres. and pub. since 1926; mem. Harte & Hanks, pubs. of Abilene Reporter-News, San Angelo Evening Standard, San Angelo Morning Times, Corpus Christi Times, Corpus Christi Caller, Paris Morning News, Big Spring Herald, Marshall News Messenger and Denison Herald. Democrat. Baptist. Home: 898 Sayles Blvd. Office: Box 20 Abilene, Tex. Died Dec. 12, 1948.

HANNA, Edward J., archbishop; b. Rochester, N. Y., July 21, 1860; s. Edward and Anne (Clarke) H.; ed. Rochester Free Acad., Propaganda (Rome, Italy), U. of Cambridge, Eng.; U. of Munich; D.D., Rome, 1886. Ordained priest R.C. Ch., 1885; teacher Propaganda, 1886-87; prof. theology, St. Bernard's Sem., Rochester, 1893-Dec. 1912. Apptd. by Pope Pius X auxiliary bishop of San Francisco, Oct. 22, 1912, and consecrated bishop of Tetopolis, Dec. 4, 1912; apptd. archbishop of San Francisco, June 1, 1915; resigned Mar. 4, 1935. Home: Rome, Italy. Died July 10, 1944.

HANNA, Frank Willard, water supply engr.; b. Geneseo, Ill., Sept. 16, 1867; s. James Steel and Harriet Louise (Hunt) H.; B.S., Highland Park Coll., Des Moines, Ia., 1893, M.S., 1898, C.E., 1902; m. Frances Grace Gore, Aug. 28, 1901; 1 son, John Alden. Dean of civ. engring. dept., Highland Park Coll., 1895-1902; hydrographer U.S. Geol. Survey, 1903-05; tech. engr. U.S. Reclamation Service, Washington, D.C., 1906-08, project engr., Boise, Ida., 1909-12, tech. engr., Washington, 1913, supervising engr., Phoenix, Ariz., 1914-15, cons. engr., Ankney, Ia., 1915-17, 1919-21, engr., Soldier Settlement investigations, northern div., 1918-19; gen. mgr. Canada Land & Irrigation Co., Medicine Hat, 1921-23; hydraulic and designing engr., East Bay Municipal Utility Dist., Oakland, Calif., 1924-28, chief engr. and gen. mgr., 1929-34; cons. engr. since 1934. Mem. Am. Soc. C.E. Republican. Methodist. Clubs: Lions, Oakland Engineers' Lunch. Author: Logical Methods in Arithmetic, 1900; Tables for Reinforced Concrete, 1913; Measurement of Irrigation Water, 1913; Agriculture by Irrigation, 1913; The Agricultural Value of Peat Soils, 1919; The Design of Dams (with R. C. Kennedy), 1931. Contbr. to Engring. News Record, Western Constrn. News. Inventor of an angle multisector, irrigation water meter, automatic stop and relief valves. Home: Webster City, Ia. Died Jan. 26, 1944.

HANNA, Howard Melville, chmn. bd. M. A. Hanna Co.; b. Cleveland, O., Dec. 14, 1877; s. H. Melville and Kate (Smith) H.; prep. edn., University Sch., Cleveland; student Sheffield Scientific Sch., 1900; m. Jean Claire Hanna, Jan. 15, 1907; children—Mrs. Fanny Bolton, Howard M. (dec.), Mrs. Jean Palmer, Mrs. Kate Bicknell, Mrs. Constance McIntosh. One of incorporators, 1922, pres. until 1929, M. A. Hanna Co., chmn. bd. since 1929; dir. Nat. Biscuit Co., Nat. Steel Corp., Howe Sound Co. Home: 11505 Lake Shore Blvd. Office: 1300 Leader Bldg., Cleveland, O.* Died Mar. 17, 1945.

HANNA, Hugh Sisson, economist; b. Baltimore, June 2, 1879; s. Hugh Bell and Letitia (Lindsay) H.; A.B., Johns Hopkins, 1899, Ph.D., 1907; m. Helen Lamson Mabry. With U.S. Bur. Labor Statistics, Washington, 1908-18; chief examiner Nat. War Labor Bd., 1918-19; chief research and editorial div., and editor Monthly Labor Rev., U.S. Bur. Labor Statistics, 1926-1944. Mem. Anthracite Fact Finding Commn. of Nat. Labor Bd., 1933; official observer U.S. govt. at Internat. Labor Conf., Geneva, 1934; tech. adviser to U.S. govt. delegation to Internat. Labor Conf., Geneva, 1935. Mem. Beta Theta Pi. Clubs: Cosmos, Unitarian. Various reports and articles on labor conditions in United States and foreign countries. Home: 2522 Wilson Blvd., Arlington, Va. Died Jan. 9, 1948.

HANNA, John Hunter, civil engr.; b. Henderson, Ky., Dec. 9, 1871; s. William M. (M.D.) and Mary Virginia (Matthews) H.; C.E., Princeton, 1892; m. Jane Edwards Soaper, Nov. 18, 1896; children—Nancy P., William M., John H., Robert C., Francis H., Jane E. Ry. constrn. in Ky., 1892-94; with Washington & Georgetown R.R. Co., 1894, and continued with its successor, the Capital Traction Co., chief engr., 1908-16, v.p., 1916-26, pres. since 1926; pres. Capital Transit Co., a new corp. organized to take over all st. ry. and bus lines in D.C., 1933-37, chairman board since 1937; director Capital Transit Company. Member American Society Civil Engring., Am. Transit Assn. (ex-pres.), Washington Soc. Engrs., Washington Bd. of Trade, Columbia Hist. Soc. Presbyn. Clubs: Cosmos, Columbia Country (Washington); Blue Ridge Rod and Gun (Harpers Ferry, W.Va.). Home: 3009 Q St. N.W. Office: 36th and M St. N.W., Washington, D.C. Died June 28, 1947.

HANNA, Louis Benjamin, ex-gov.; b. New Brighton, Pa., Aug. 9, 1861; s. Jason R. and Margaret A. (Lewis) H.; ed. public schools; LL.D.; m. Lottie L. Thatcher, Nov. 1884 (died Jan. 2, 1933); children—Margaret E. (dec.), Jean E., Dorothy L., Robert L. Moved to N.D., 1881; pres. First Nat. Bank, of Page, N.D. Mem. N.D. Ho. Rep., 1895-97, Senate, 1897-1901, 1905-09; mem. 61st and 62d Congresses (1909-13), N.D. at large; gov. for terms 1913-15, 1915-17. Chmn. N.D. Rep. State Central Com., 1902-08. Served with Am. Red Cross in France, 1918. Decorated Grand Cross of St. Olav, 1st rank (Norway), 1915; Officer Legion of Honor (France), 1926. Trustee Fargo Coll.; apptd. by President Hoover, mem. Mount Rushmore Nat. Memorial Commn. Pres. N.D. State Elks Assn. since 1930. Conglist. Mason (33°). Club: Minneapolis (Minneapolis). Home: Fargo, N.D. Died Apr. 23, 1948.

HANNA, Richard Henry, lawyer; b. Kankakee, Ill., July 31, 1878; s. Isaac Bird and Belle (Hall) H.; grad. Northwestern U. Acad., 1898; LL.B., U. of Colo. Sch. of Law, 1903; m. Clara Zimmer, Feb. 8, 1905; 1 son, Richard John. Mem. Hanna & Wilson, 1909-12 and 1922-37, Hanna, Wilson & Brophy since 1937-43; justice Supreme Ct. of N.M., 1912-19 (chief justice, 1917); special asst. to the U.S. atty. gen. since 1936. Dem. candidate for gov., 1920; Dem. candidate at spl. election for U.S. senator, 1921; mem. Dem. Nat. Com. for N.M., 1928-32. Sec. Territorial Law Library Bd., 1904-11; ex-sec. Territorial Bar Assn.; mem. Alpha Tau Omega. Mason (33°, Scottish Rite). Home: 601 North Thirteenth St., Albuquerque, N.M. Died Aug. 17, 1946.

HANNAH, Harvey Horatio, lawyer; b. Louisville, Aug. 30, 1868; s. John H. and Lillie L. (Gerding) H.; ed. mil. coll.; LL.B., Univ. of Tenn., 1891; unmarried. Began practice at Oliver Springs, Tenn., 1891; pvt. sec. to Gov. Robert L. Taylor; Dem. presdl. elector, 1896; U.S. commr.; state railroad commr. since Jan. 1, 1907. Served as capt. Tenn. N.G.; lt. col. 4th Tenn. Vols., Spanish-Am. War; adj. gen. Tenn., 1903-07. Presbyterian. Mem. Sigma Nu. Residence: Oliver Springs, Tenn. Address: Nashville, Tenn. Died Nov. 8, 1936.

HANNEGAN, Robert E., former postmaster gen. U.S.; b. St. Louis, Mo., June 30, 1903; s. John Patrick and Anna (Holden) H.; LL.B., St. Louis U., 1925; m. Irma Protzmann, Nov. 14, 1929; children—Patricia, Robert Emmet, William, Sally. Practiced law, St. Louis, 1925-41; apptd. collector of internal revenue, Eastern Dist. of Mo., St. Louis, 1942; apptd. commr. of internal revenue, Washington, D.C., 1943; postmaster general, U.S., July 1945-Nov. 1947; chmn. Democratic City Com., St. Louis, 1933-42; became chmn. Democratic National Com., Jan. 22, 1944. Dir. Am. League Baseball Co., St. Louis; v.p., then pres., 1947-49, Jefferson Club (St. Louis). Mem. Mo. Supreme Court Com. on Civil Procedure; chmn. Fed. Div. St. Louis War Chest Drive, 1942-43; v.p. Lawyers Assn. of St. Louis since Apr. 1944. Made Knight of Saint Gregory, Grand Order of the Holy Cross, by His Holiness Pope Pius XII, July 1946. Mem. Am., Mo. bar assns., Sigma Nu Phi. Clubs: University, Missouri Athletic, Glen Echo Country (St. Louis); Burning

Tree (Bethesda, Md.); Westchester Country, Metropolitan (New York). Home: 5745 Lindell Blvd. Office: 3623 Dodier St., St. Louis. Died Oct. 6, 1949.

HANSEN, A. B., pres., gen. mgr., Northern Paper Mills; b. Racine, Wis., June 7, 1896; s. John Peter and Emma (Olsen) H.; B.S., Thiel Coll., Greenville, Pa., 1918; student U. of Wis., 1920-21; m. Helen Delbridge, Jan. 12, 1924; children—James, Barbara Ann. Chief chemist, Marinette & Menominee Paper Co., Marinette, Wis., 1922-29, purchasing agt. and safety dir., 1928-29, mill mgr., 1929-35; exec. v.p. and gen. mgr., Northern Paper Mills, 1935-41, pres. and gen. mgr., since 1941. Pres. Northern Paper Mills Ltd., Can., since 1936; pres. Patten Logging Company, Amasa, Michigan, North Shore Timber Co., president Cloverland Supply Co., Crystal Falls, Mich., Falls Paper & Power Co., Ocohto Falls, Wis. Organized and served as exec. sec. of Brown County Council of Defense; resigned to be Dep. Director (dollar a yr.) for Pulpwood, War Production Bd., Washington, D.C. Served as ensign U.S. Navy, World War I. Mem. Tech. Assn. Pulp & Paper Industry. Director State Chamber of Commerce, Rotary, Delta Sigma Phi, Phi Alpha Delta; hon. mem. Am. Paper & Pulp Mills Supts. Mason. Lutheran. Home: 905 S. Monroe Av., Green Bay, Wis. Office: Northern Paper Mills, Green Bay, Wis. Died July 4, 1948.

HANSEN, Paul, engineer; b. Arlington, Va., Aug. 9, 1879; s. John and Pauline (Meyenberg) H.; grad. in sanitary engring., Mass. Inst. Tech., 1903; m. Alison May Scott, Oct. 3, 1905; children—Elizabeth Scott (Mrs. Henry Pope, Jr.), Dr. Paul Scott. Mem. U.S. Geol. Survey party, Ind., summer, 1901; in engring. dept. Mass. State Bd. of Health, summer, 1902, June 1903-May 1904); on water supply and sewerage improvements, Columbus, O., May-Dec. 1904; chief engr. Pittsburgh (Pa.) Filter Mfg. Co., Jan.-Oct. 1905; 1st asst. and later chief engr. Ohio State Board of Health, 1906-10; state sanitary engr. of Ky., Aug. 1910-Oct. 1911; chief engr. Ill. State Waterway Survey, 1911-15, Ill. State Bd. of Health, 1915-17 and 1919-20; member Greeley & Hansen, Chicago, since May 1920. Engaged in design and constrn. of numerous water supply and drainage works, including projects for New York, Boston, Washington, Chicago, Buffalo, etc. Spent 19 mos., 1917-19, with A.E.F. in France as staff officer with Gen. Pershing. Mem. Am. Soc. C.E., Western Soc. Engrs., Am. Soc. Municipal Improvements, Boston Soc. C.E., Am. Pub. Health Assn., Am. Water Works Assn., N.E. Water Works Assn., Sigma Xi, Theta Xi. Author of numerous engring. and tech. reports and papers. Home: 223 E. Delaware Place. Office: 6 N. Michigan Av., Chicago, Ill. Died Feb. 1944.

HANSON, Frank Blair, zoologist; b. Bloomington, Ill., July 15, 1886; s. Warren John and Lozetta (Adreon) H.; A.B., George Washington U., 1913; A.M., U. of Ill., 1916; Ph.D., Am. U., 1919; m. Harriet R. Cavender, June 21, 1910; children—Betty Blair, Phyllis Claire, Frank Blair (dec.) Instr. zoology, Washington U., 1916-18, asst. prof., 1918-20, asso. prof., 1919-24. Prof., 1924-33; fellowship administrator for Natural Sciences of Rockefeller Foundation in Europe, 1930-32, asst. dir. in New York City, 1933-35, asso. dir., 1935. Received traveling fellowship, Am. U., 1915-16. Fellow A.A.A.S., Mem. Am. Soc. Naturalists, Am. Soc. Zoologists, Am. Assn. Anatomists, Genetics Soc. of Am., Phi Beta Kappa, Sigma Xi. Contbr. articles to professional jours. Home: 8 McKinley St., Bronxville 8, N.Y. Office: 49 W. 49th St., New York 20, N.Y. Died July 21, 1945.

HANSON, James Christian Meinich, librarian; b. Nordre Aurdal, Valdres, Norway, March 13, 1864; s. Gunnerius and Eleanore H.; A.B., Luther Coll., Iowa, 1882, LL.D., 1931; student Concordia Theol. Sem., St. Louis, 1882-84; teacher in Chicago, 1884-88; post-grad. work, Cornell U., in history, economics, Romance languages (Andrew D. White, fellow in history), 1888-90; m. Sarah Nelson, 1892; children—Karl B., Mrs. Valborg Enerson, Mrs. Eleanore B. Rustman, Thorfin A., Harald B. Cataloguer and classifier, Newberry Library, Chicago, 1890-93; chief catalogue dept., U. of Wis., 1893-97; investigator for Venezuelan Commission, 1896-97; chief catalogue div., Library of Congress, 1897-Nov. 1910; asso. dir. of Libraries, U. of Chicago, 1910-27, acting dir., 1927-28; prof. library science Graduate Library School same univ., 1928-34, emeritus. On mission to Rome, 1928, to reorganize Vatican library system. Knight and Comdr. of St. Olaf (Norway). Mem. A.L.A., Kappa Sigma. Author: A Comparative Study of Cataloging Rules Based on the Anglo-American Code of 1908, 1939. Editor and compiler Anglo-American Catalogue Rules, 1908. Home: Sister Bay, Wis. Died Nov. 8, 1943.

HANSON, Richard Burpee, former leader of opposition House Leader Conservative Party, Commons, Canada; b. Bocabec, N.B., March 20, 1879; s. Richard B. and Hannah P. (Mann) H.; B.A., Mount Allison U., Sackville, N.B., 1899, hon. D.C.L., 1942; LL.B., Dalhousie Law Sch., Halifax, 1901; hon. LL.D., U. of New Brunswick, 1935; hon. D.C.L. Mt. Allison U., Sackville, N.B., 1942; m. Jean B. Neill, Aug. 15, 1906; 1 dau., Mary Hope (Mrs. George C. Thompson). Barrister, 1902; King's counsel, 1917; gen. counsel and chief solicitor for Fraser Cos. and subsidiaries, 1917-34; consulting counsel to Hanson, Dougherty & West, Fredericton, N.B.; dir. Fraser Cos., Ltd., Restigonche Co., Ltd., New Brunswick Telephone Co., Ltd., New Brunswick & Can. R.R. Co. City solicitor, Fredericton, 1920-25; elected to House of Commons of Can., 1921, 25, 26, 30, defeated, 1935, re-elected, 1940; chmn. standing com. on govt. railways and shipping, 1933; chmn. com. on banking and commerce, 1934 (Bank of Can. Act). Sworn to Privy Council of Can. and apptd. minister of trade and commerce, Nov. 1934, resigned Oct. 1935, on defeat of Bennett adminstrn. Leader of Conservative Party and of the Opposition, House of Commons of Can., May 1940-Jan. 1943; retired from public life, June 1945. Mem. board regents, Mount Allison University. Member Canadian Bar Assn., Empire Parliamentary Assn. Mason. Mem. United Ch. of Can. Progressive-Conservative. Club: Rideau (Ottawa); City (Fredericton, N.B.). Home: 270 Church St. Office: 61 Carleton St., Fredericton, N.B., Can. Died July 14, 1948; buried in Forest Hill Cemetery, Fredericton, N.B.

HANSON, Thomas Grafton, army officer; b. San Rafael, Calif., May 1, 1865; s. Thomas Hawkins and Carlotta (Milewater) H.; grad. U.S. Mil. Acad., 1887, Inf. and Cav. Sch., 1891; m. Pauline De Forest, Sept. 13, 1893; children—Thomas Grafton, Elizabeth D. (Mrs. B. R. Alexander). Commd. 2d lt., 19th Inf., June 12, 1887; 1st lt., June 7, 1894; capt., Mar. 2, 1899; maj. 8th Inf., Mar. 24, 1910; maj. Q.-M. Corps, May 11, 1915; lt. col. inf., June 12, 1916; col., May 15, 1917; brig. gen. N.A., Aug. 5, 1917. Served in Spanish-Am. War, 1898, Philippine Insurrection, 1899-1901; asst. prof. modern langs., U.S. Mil. Acad., 1901-05; sr. instrn. modern langs., Army Sch. of the Line, and Army Staff Coll., Ft. Leavenworth, Kan., 1910-12; assigned to comd. 178th Inf. Brigade, 89th Div., Camp Funston, Kan., Aug. 1917; comd. 178th Brig., 89th Div., in Am. capture of St. Mihiel salient, operations beginning Sept. 12, 1918, and in final Am. assault, Nov. 1-Nov. 9, 1918, Meuse-Argonne. Retired at own request, Jan. 4, 1919. Home: Union League Club, San Francisco. Died May 23, 1945.

HANSON, Victor Henry, newspaper pub.; b. Barnesville, Pike County, Ga., Jan. 16, 1876; s. Henry Clay and Anna (Bloodworth) H.; ed. pub. schs., Macon, Ga., and Gordon Inst., Atlanta; D.Litt., U. of Ala., 1922; LL.D., Howard Coll., Birmingham, Ala., 1923; D.H.L., Birmingham Southern Coll., 1925; Litt.D., Oglethorpe U., 1930; m. Weenona White, Dec. 27, 1897 (died Jan. 17, 1933); m. 2d, Mrs. Ruth Lawson Smith, May 14, 1936. Advertising mgr. Montgomery Advertiser, 1896-1909; with Birmingham News since 1909, became pres., 1910, chmn. of bd. since Jan. 1936; purchased Birmingham Ledger, 1920, Birmingham Age-Herald, 1927, The Huntsville (Ala.) Times, 1932. Purchased radio sta. WSGN, Birmingham, Ala., 1936. Member executive and finance committee and dir. First National Bank of Birmingham; dir. Protective Life Ins. Company (exec. and finance coms.), Birmingham Fire Ins. Co. Trustee and mem. exec. and finance coms. Ala. Poly. Inst., Auburn; dir. Birmingham Community Chest since 1924; dir. Jefferson County Tuberculosis Assn., Birmingham Boys' Club, Birmingham Children's Hosp. (trustee). Mem. Am. Newspaper Pubs. Assn., Southern Newspaper Pubs. Assn. (ex-pres., dir.). Mem. Omricon Delta Kappa, Pi Gamma Mu, Alpha Tau Omega, Sigma Delta Chi; elected hon. mem. Phi Beta Kappa at Birmingham-Southern Coll., Mar. 1941. Del. Dem. Nat. Conv., 1924. Presbyterian. Chief donor girls' dormitory (Weenona Hanson Hall), Huntingdon Coll., Montgomery, also of girls' dormitory (Weenona Hanson Hall), Alabama Coll., Montevallo, Ala. Clubs: Rotary, Birmingham Country, Mountain Brook Club. Home: 2641 Crest Road, Milner Heights (Birmingham). Office: The Birmingham News, Birmingham, Ala. Died March 7, 1945; buried Elmwood Cemetery Birmingham, Ala.

HANUS, Paul Henry, university prof.; b. Hermsdorf u.d. Kynast, Silesia, Prussia, Mar. 14, 1855; s. Gustaf and Ida (Aust) H.; came to U.S., 1859; B.S., U. of Mich., 1878; LL.D., U. of Colo., 1906, U. of Mich., 1925; m. Charlotte Hoskins, Aug 10, 1881; 1 dau., Winifred (Mrs. Edward Clark Whiting). In drug business, Denver, 1 yr.; teacher since 1878, except for 1 yr.; prof. pedagogy, Colo. State Normal Sch., Greeley, 1890-91; asst. prof. history and art of teaching, Harvard, 1891-1901; prof., 1901-21, prof. emeritus since 1921. Chmn. Mass. State Commn. on Indsl. Edn., 1906-09; mem. Mass. State Board of Edn., 1909-19; chmn. exec. bd., Boston Vocation Bur., 1909-17. In charge ednl. aspects of an inquiry undertaken by a com. on sch. inquiry of Bd. of Estimate and Apportionment of New York City, June 1, 1911-July 1, 1912; survey of Hampton Inst. (Va.) for Gen. Edn. Bd., 1917. Dir. sch. surveys in various cities since 1912; counselor on coll. problems; prin. founder Grad. Sch. of Edn., Harvard, 1920. Pres. Colo. Teachers Assn., 1889; trustee Wellesley Coll., 1916-36, Internat. Coll., Izmir, Turkey, 1930-35. Pres. Nat. Soc. Coll. Teachers of Edn., 1909-10. Mem. editorial bd. School Review, Chicago, 1906-15; collaborator, Ednl. Adminstrn. and Supervision, Baltimore, 1915-17; lecturer Sch. of Edn., U. of Chicago, 1st term summer quarter, 1914, also summer sessions a number of state univs. Fellow A.A.A.S. (v.p. 1914); mem. Nat. Soc. for Study of Edn. (hon.), Am. Ednl. Research Assn. (hon.), Delta Tau Delta, Phi Beta Kappa, Phi Delta Kappa, Kappa Delta Pi. Pres. Mass. Schoolmasters Club, 1903-04. Club: Faculty. Author: Elements of Determinants, 1886; Geometry in the Grammar School, 1894; Educational Aims and Educational Values, 1899; A Modern School, 1905; Beginnings in Industrial Education and Other Educational Discussions, 1908; School Efficiency, 1913; School Administration and School Reports, 1920; Opportunity and Accomplishment in Secondary Education, 1926; Adventuring in Education, 1937. Editor: School Efficiency Series. Contbr. to ednl. journals and other periodicals. Home: 3 Channing Circle, Cambridge, Mass. Died Dec. 14, 1941.

HANWAY, J. E., editor, pub.; b. Greensburg, Ind., June 25, 1866; s. Israel Gilpin and Martha (Lowe) H.; ed. country and pub. schs.; m. Effie Em Grice, Sept. 18, 1889; children—Earl Edwin, Isabel Martha (Mrs. Clifford L. Fitzgerald). Circulation traveler Kansas City Star, Kansas City World, Kansas City Times and Topeka Journal, 1893-04; pub. Horton (Kan.) Commercial, Richfield (Utah) Reaper, Sterling (Colo.) Advocate and 10 other small papers, 1904-40; pub. Casper Tribune-Herald since 1914; pres. Casper Tribune-Herald, Wyoming Weekly Review. Author: Memoirs, 1942. Republican. Christian Scientist. Elk. Home: 704 S. Park St. Office: Tribune-Herald Bldg., Casper, Wyoming.* Died Jan. 27, 1946.

HAPGOOD, Hutchins, author; b. Chicago, May 21, 1869; s. Charles H. and Fanny Louise (Powers) H.; A.B., Harvard, 1892, A.M., 1897; m. Neith Boyce, June 1899; children—Boyce (dec.), Charles Hutchins, Miriam, Beatrix. Teacher, Harvard and Chicago U. (English composition); studied 2 yrs. at German univs. Contbr. to magazines, weeklies and reviews. Dramatic critic Chicago Evening Post, 1904; editorial writer on Evening Post, Press, and Globe, New York. Author: Paul Jones, 1901; The Spirit of the Ghetto, 1902; The Autobiography of a Thief, 1903; The Spirit of Labor, 1907; An Anarchist Woman, 1909; Types from City Streets, 1910; Enemies (with Neith Boyce), 1916; The Story of a Lover, 1919; Victorian in the Modern World, 1939. Address: Route 3, Winchester, N.H. Died Nov. 19, 1944.

HARBORD, James Guthrie, army officer, hon. chmn. Radio Corp. of America; b. Bloomington, Ill., Mar. 21, 1866; s. George W. and Effie Critton (Gault) H.; B.S., Kan. State Agrl. Coll., Manhattan, Kan., 1886, M.S., 1895; grad. Inf. and Cav. Sch., 1895, Army War College, 1917; LL.D., Trinity College, 1924, Colgate, 1926, Marietta College, 1927, Yale, 1928; Washington and Jefferson College, 1938; m. Emma Yeatman Ovenshine, Jan. 21, 1899 (died May 29, 1937); m. 2d, Mrs. Anne Lee Brown, Dec. 31, 1938. Pvt., corpl. and sergt. and q.-m. sergt. 4th Inf., 1889-91; commd. 2d lt. 5th Cav., July 31, 1891; maj. 2d Vol. Cav., May 24, 1898; hon. mustered out vols., Oct. 24, 1898; 1st lt. 10th U.S. Cav., July 1, 1898; capt. 11th Cav., Feb. 2, 1901; assigned to 1st Cav., Jan. 1, 1914; maj. Dec. 10, 1914; lt. col. Gen. Staff, May 15, 1917; brig. gen. N.A., Aug. 5, 1917; maj. gen. N.A., June 26, 1918; brig. gen. U.S. Army, Nov. 30, 1918; maj. gen. U.S. Army, Sept. 8, 1919. Served as asst. chief Philippine Constabulary with rank of col., Aug. 18, 1903-Jan. 1, 1914; chief of staff, A.E.F., in France, May 15, 1917-May 6, 1918; comd. Marine Brigade nr. Château Thierry, June-July 1918; comd. 2d Div. in Soissons offensive, July 18, 19, 1918; comd. Service of Supply, July 29, 1918-May 26, 1919; re-apptd. chief of staff, A.E.F., May 25, 1919; dep. chief of staff, U.S. Army, July 1, 1921-Dec. 29, 1922; retired lieutenant general, U.S. Army July 9, 1942; pres. Radio Corp. of America, Jan. 1, 1923-30, chmn. bd., 1930-47; honorary chairman and director since July 1947; chairman board RCA Communications, Inc.; director and member exec. com. A.T.&S.F. Ry.; mem. exec. com. N.Y. Life Ins. Co., Employers Liability Assurance Corp., Ltd. (London); dir. Bankers Trust Co., Nat. Broadcasting Co., New York Life Insurance Company. Chief of American Mil. Mission to Armenia, 1919. Hon. chmn. Am. Red Cross, N.Y. Chapter. Awarded D.S.M. of both Army and Navy; Comdr. Legion of Honor, Croix de Guerre, two palms (French); Knight Comdr. St. Michael and St. George (British); Grand Officer Order of the Crown (Belgian); Comdr. St. Maurice and St. Lazarus (Italian); Order of Prince Danilo (Montenegrin); Order of La Solidaridad (Panamanian); Grand Officer Order Polonia Restituta (Polish); gold medal of 2d Div. Mason (32°, Knights Templar). Clubs: Army and Navy (Washington, D.C.); Knickerbocker, Nat. Republican, Century (New York); Army and Navy (Manila); Apawamis (Port Chester, N.Y.). Home: Dogwood Lane, Rye, N.Y. Office: 30 Rockefeller Plaza, New York, N.Y. Died Aug. 20, 1947; buried in Arlington National Cemetery.

HARDESTY, Irving, anatomist; b. Beaufort, N.C., Oct. 8, 1866; s. Washington Irving and Katherine (Harrell) H.; A.B., Wake Forest College, N.C., 1892; Ph.D., Univ. of Chicago, 1899; D.Sc., Wake Forest Coll., 1918; m. Anne Myatt Kinnard, Dec. 21, 1904; children—Mary (Mrs. William Larkin Duren, Jr.), Katharine (Mrs. Chester McArthur Destler), Irving. Prin. Wakefield Acad., 1892-03; asst. in biology, U. of Mo., 1895-96; asso. in anatomy (neurology), U. of Chicago, 1899-1900; instr. and asst. prof. anatomy, 1901-06, asso. prof., 1906-09, U. of Calif.; prof. anatomy and head of dept., Tulane U., 1909-34, prof. emeritus since 1934. Mem. Assn. Am. Aanatomists, A.A.A.S., Society of Exptl. Biology and Medicine, Sigma Xi, Nu Sigma Nu. Democrat. Baptist. Author: Neurological Technique, 1902; The Nervous System (Part III of Morris's Human Aanatomy), 1907, 14, 21, 33; A Laboratory Guide for Histology, 1908. Contbr. to jours. involving research of nervous system, including organ of hearing. Home: 1301 Pine St., New Orleans. Died Nov. 7, 1944; buried in Metairie Cemetery, New Orleans.

HARDIN, John Ralph, lawyer and pres. Mutual Benefit Life Insurance Co.; b. Sussex County, N.J., Apr. 24, 1860; s. Charles and Abbie M. (Hunt) H.; A.B., Princeton, 1880, A.M., 1883; LL.D., New Jersey Law Sch. (now U. of Newark); m. Jennie J. Roe, Feb. 1, 1894 (died Mar. 29, 1939); children—Charles R., Elizabeth A. (Mrs. Wright D. Goss, Jr.), John R. Admitted to N.J. bar as atty., 1884, as counsellor, 1887; practiced Newark, N.J., since 1884; mem. firm of Pitney, Hardin & Ward; pres. Mutual Benefit Life Ins. Co. since Jan. 1924, dir.; dir. Nat. Newark and Essex Banking Co., Am. Ins. Co., Howard Savings Instn., United N.J. Railroad & Canal Co., N.J. Bell Telephone Co., Newark Museum Assn.; atty. bd. of health, Newark, 1887-90; alderman, Newark, 1890-91; mem. N.J. Ho. of Reps., 1891-92; mem. N.J. Constl. Conv. to suggest jud. changes, 1905; mgr. N.J. Epileptic Village, 1900-03; mem. Essex County Park Commn. since 1903; mem. Newark Sinking Fund Commn. since 1904; mem. from N.J. of Nat. Conf. on Uniform Law, 1902-28. Trustee (life) Princeton U.; mem. bd. trustees Inst. for Advanced Study, Louis Bamberger and Mrs. Felix Fuld Foundation, Newark Eye & Ear Infirmary, Babies' Hosp. of Newark; pres. Marcus L. Ward Home for Aged and Respectable Bachelors and Widowers. Awarded gold medal, N.J. Bar Assn., 1940, for service to the bar. Mem. Am., N.J., and Essex County bar assns. Democrat. Episcopalian. Mason. Clubs: Essex (dir., Newark); Essex County Country (West Orange) Baltusrol Golf (Short Hills, N.J.); Somerset Hills Country (Far Hills, N.J.); Princeton, University (New York). Home: 40 Mt. Prospect Pl. Office: 744 Broad St., and 300 Broadway, Newark, N.J. Died Dec. 7, 1945.

HARDING, Arthur McCracken, univ. pres.; b. Pine Bluff, Ark., Sept. 3, 1884; s. Charles Taylor and Florence May (Brewster) H.; A.B., U. of Ark., 1904; A.M., U. of Chicago, 1913, Ph.D., 1916; m. Edna Earle Nance, Aug. 9, 1905; children—Arthur Leonidas, Mary Frances. Instr. mathematics, U. of Ark., 1905-07, adj. prof., 1907-10, asso. prof., 1910-16, prof., 1916-41, dir. gen. extension service, 1919-41, pres. univ., July 1, 1941-47. Mem. Math. Assn. America, Am. Math. Soc., Am. Astron. Soc., Am. Assn. for Advancement of Science, Phi Beta Kappa, Sigma Xi, Sigma Nu. Democrat. Episcopalian. Author: (with John S. Turner) Plane Trigonometry, 1915; (with George W. Mullins) Analytic Geometry, 1924; College Algebra (with same), 1927; Plane Trigonometry (with same), 1928; Astronomy, 1935. Contbr. to scientific jours. of America and Europe. Home: Fayetteville, Ark. Died Dec. 24, 1947.

HARDING, C(harles) Francis, electrical engr.; b. Fitchburg, Mass., Sept. 11, 1881; s. Charles Theodore and Ellen (Lane); B.S. in E.E., Worcester Polytechnic Inst., 1902, E.E., 1910, hon. Dr. Engring., 1931; post-grad. work, Dartmouth Coll. and Cornell U.; m. Mabelle C. Brooks, July 14, 1903. With testing dept. Gen. Electric Co., Schenectady, N.Y., 1902; elec. engr. Worcester & Southbridge St. Ry Co., Worcester, 1903-04, D.&W. Fuse Co., Providence, R.I., 1904-05; asst. prof. elec. engring., Cornell U., 1905-06; elec. engr. Stone & Webster Engring. Corp., Boston, 1906-08; head prof. elec. engring. and dir. Elec. Lab., Purdue U., 1908—; also consulting engr. Fellow Am. Inst. E.E. (v.p. 1937-38); mem. Soc. Promotion Engring. Edn. (v.p. 1931), Am. Assn. Univ. Profs., Sigma Xi, Tau Beta Pi, Eta Kappa Nu, Alpha Tau Omega, etc. Presbyn. Clubs: Rotary (past pres.), Country. Author: Electric Railway Engineering, 1911; Business Administration for Engineers; Legal and Ethical Phases of Engineering, 1936; also over 50 articles in tech. jours. Home: 503 University St., West Lafayette, Ind. Died Apr. 13, 1942.

HARDING, Nelson, cartoonist; b. N.Y. City, Oct. 31, 1879; s. Charles N. and Flora (McGregor) H.; ed. Greenwich (Conn.) Acad.; art edn., Art Students' League, N.Y. City, Chase Sch., New York Sch. of Art; studied under Robert Henri; m. Anna Seamon, Mar. 8, 1911; children—Peggy Rives, Jean McGregor. Cartoonist Brooklyn (N.Y.) Eagle, 1908-29, New York Journal since 1929. Served as pvt. inf., U.S. Vols., Spanish-Am. War; at San Juan Hill and siege of Santiago; mem. N.G.N.Y., 1898-1908, 1st lt., 1917-18. Mem. 71st Regt. Vets'. Assn. Awarded Pulitzer prize for best cartoon published in any Am. newspaper in immediately preceding yrs., 1927, 28. Episcopalian. Address: Care New York Journal, New York, N.Y.* Died Dec. 30, 1944.

HARDING, John Thomas, lawyer; b. St. Louis, Mo., Nov. 15, 1866; s. Joseph Nathan Monroe and Emily Dyer (Badger) H.; ed. S.W. Normal Sch., 1882-83, U. of Mo., 1884-87; m. Mary Joel Atkinson, Nov. 4, 1892 (died 1914); children—Patti Atkinson (Mrs. Taylor S. Abernathy), Douglas; m. 2d, Lucia Byrne, July 12, 1916. Admitted to Mo. bar, 1890, practiced in Nevada, Mo., 1890-99, in Kansas City since 1899; partner Harding, Murphy & Tucker; city counselor Nevada, Mo., 1896-98, of Kansas City, 1909; pres. John M. Byrne Lumber Co.; dir. Traders Gate City Nat. Bank. Trustee Kansas City Conservatory of Music, Kansas City Philharmonic Orchestra, Kansas City Art Inst. and Sch., Liberty Memorial Assn.; advisory trustee U. of Mo., Kansas City U.; mem. Kansas City Chamber Commerce; chmn. Mo. State Social Security Com. Mem. Am., Mo. State and Kansas City bar assns., Mayflower Soc., Beta Theta Pi. Christian Scientist. Mason (33°, Shriner, past potentate). Home: 3715 Belleview Av. Office: Scarritt Bldg., Kansas City, Mo. Died Aug. 18, 1946.

HARDINGE, Hal Williams, cons. engr.; b. San Antonio, Tex., Sept. 30, 1855; s. George and Sarah A. L. (Bumstead) H.; E.M., Colo. Sch. of Mines, 1883; m. Bertha Wilson, Nov. 12, 1889; children—Mrs. Arlene H. Greening, Harlowe. Mgr. mines and smelters in West many yrs.; now chmn. bd. Hardinge Co., Steacy-Schmidt Mfg. Co., Ruggles-Coles Engring Co. With Bur. of Mines, Washington, during World War, as "dollar-a-year man." Awarded John Scott medal, 1915, Franklin Inst., Phila., for inventions; also Longstreth medal, 1927; awarded James Douglas gold medal, 1938, for metall. inventions. Mem. Am. Inst. Mining and Metall. Engrs., Mining and Metall. Soc. of America, Tau Beta Pi. Republican. Mason (K.T., Shriner). Clubs: Engineers', Nat. Arts, Mining, Engineers Country. Home: 75 Greenway S., Forest Hill, L.I., N.Y. Office: 122 E. 42d St., New York, N.Y. Died Sep. 15, 1943.

HARDT, Frank McCulley, business executive; born Frederick, Maryland, July 14, 1879; s. William McCulley and Mary Ida (Keller) H.; B.S., U. of Pa., 1901; hon. LL.D., Hahnemann Med. Coll. and Hosp.; m. Helen C. Liscom, Feb. 6, 1905; children—William McCulley II, Frances (wife of Thomas Francis Furlong, Jr., M.D.). Asst. cashier Nat. Bank of Northern Liberties, 1904-14; cashier and dep. gov. Federal Reserve Bank of Phila., 1914-18; v.p. Phila. Trust Co., 1918-26, merged into Fidelity-Phila. Trust Co. and v.p., 1926-46; pres. Business Liquidation Corp.; dir. Phila. Life Ins. Co., Pocono Hotels Corp., Bellevue-Stratford Co.; gen. partner Montgomery Scott & Co. Mem. Community Fund of Phila. and Vicinity; director Philadelphia Chamber of Commerce; dir. Dunwoody Home. Mem. Am. Acad. Polit. and Social Science, Pa. Soc. S.R., U.S. Golf Assn. (mem.), Golf Assn. of Phila., Phi Delta Theta. Republican. Presbyterian (trustee and treas. Overbrook Church). Clubs: Union League, Midday (treas.), Bank Officers' (treas.), Merion Cricket, Phila. Country (treas.). Home: York Lynne Manor, Overbrook, Pa. Office: 123 S. Broad St., Philadelphia 9. Died Jan. 30, 1949; buried in West Laurel Hill Cemetery, Bala-Cynwood, Pa.

HARDWICK, Thomas William, ex-governor; born Thomasville, Ga., Dec. 9, 1872; s. Robert William and Zemula Schley (Matthews) H.; A.B., Mercer U., Ga., 1892; B.L., Lumpkin Law Sch. (U. of Ga.), 1893; m. Maude Elizabeth Perkins, Apr. 25, 1894 (died 1937). Admitted to bar, 1893, practicing at Sandersville, Ga.; pros. atty., Washington County, 1895-97; mem. Ga. Ho. of Rep., 1898-1901; mem. 58th to 63d Congresses (1903-15), 10th Ga. Dist. Democrat. Elected U.S. senator, 1914, for unexpired term (1914-19) of Senator Bacon, dec.; gov. of Ga., term June 1921-June 1923; spl. asst. to atty. gen. of U.S. and mem. adv. council. War Transactions Sect. of Dept. of Justice of U.S., July 1, 1924. Home: Sandersville, Ga. Died Jan. 31, 1944.

HARDY, Charles Oscar, economist; b. Island City, Mo., May 2, 1884; s. Charles Webster and Martha Louisa (Spilman) H.; A.B., Ottawa (Kan.) University, 1904, LL.D., 1935; Ph.D., U. of Chicago, 1916; married Myra May Moore, 1909; children—Margaret Ruth (Mrs. Pitman B. Potter), Frederick Leland. Teacher of mathematics, Hiawatha (Kansas) Academy, 1904-06; clerk, government service, 1906-08; prof. history and economics, Ottawa U., 1910-18, dean of coll., 1916-18; lecturer, Sch. Commerce and Administration, U. of Chicago, 1918-19, asst. prof. finance, 1919-22; prof. finance, State U. of Ia., 1922-24; mem. research staff, Inst. Economics, Brookings Institution, Washington, D.C., 1924-43; economic adviser, Office of Alien Property Custodian, 1942-43; vice president, Federal Reserve Bank of Kansas City 1943-46; Economist, Chicago Association of Commerce, 1946-47; staff dir. Congressional Joint Com. on the Econ. Report, since Apr. 1947. Mem. Am. Econ. Assn., American Statistical Association, Royal Economic Society, Phi Beta Kappa, Pi Kappa Delta, and Alpha Kappa Psi fraternities. Baptist. Editor: Readings in Risk and Risk Bearing, 1924. Author: Risk and Risk Bearing, 1923; (with R. N. Owens) Interest Rates and Stock Speculation, 1925; Tax Exempt Securities and the Surtax, 1926; (with G. V. Cox) Forecasting Business Conditions, 1927; Credit Policies of the Federal Reserve System, 1932; (with H. G. Moulton and others) The American Transportation Problem, 1933; The Housing Program of the City of Vienna, 1934; Is There Enough Gold?, 1936; Odd-lot Trading on the New York Stock Exchange, 1939; War Time Control of Prices, 1940. Del. to Internat. Conf. sponsored by Carnegie Endowment for Internat. Peace, Chatham House, London, 1935. Home: Avenel, Silver Springs, Md. Office: U.S. Capitol, Senate P.O., Washington 24, D.C. Died Nov. 30, 1948.

HARDY, George Fiske, cons. engr.; b. Poquonock, Hartford County, Conn., Feb. 12, 1865; s. George F. and Jane (Smyth) H.; B.S., Dartmouth, 1888; hon. Sc.D. from same college, 1926; m. Johnetta Beall, Jan. 29, 1896 (died Nov. 3, 1925); children—George Fiske, John Alexander. Engr. in employ of D. H. & A. B. Tower, of Holyoke, Mass., specialists in pulp and paper mills, 1888-93; jr. mem. of firm under name of A. B. Tower & Co., 1893-96; resigned 1896, to build a mill for the Hudson River Pulp & Paper Co., Corinth, N.Y.; built mill for making news paper for the Laurentide Paper Co., Grand Mere, P.Q., 1897; was apptd. chief engr. Internat. Paper Co. (controlling prin. news paper mills of the country after they were combined), 1898, but resigned, 1901, to acquire Tower business, which had been moved to New York; now sr. partner George F. Hardy & Son; has built numerous paper and pulp mills and power plants since 1901, including 275,000 horsepower hydroelectric plant, Abitibi Canyon, Ont., 1930-32; since 1932 engaged in kraft pulp and paper development in Southern states (Savannah, Georgia, and St. Marys, Georgia, Fernandina, Florida, Port St. Joe, Florida, Bogalusa, La., Monroe, La.); first mill to make newsprint from Southern pine at Lufkin, Tex., later added Sulphate Pulp Mill: now engaged in work on kraft mill, Atenquique, Mex.; doubling newsprint capacity, Lufkin; liner board mill, Macon, Ga.; also work on improvements in pulp and paper industry; dir. St. Croix Paper Co. (Woodland, Maine). N.Y. dist. manager, div. of supply Emergency Fleet Corp., 1918. Republican. Episcopalian. Mem. Am. Soc. C.E., Am. Soc. M.E., Engring. Inst. of Can.; F.R.S.A. (Great Britain). Clubs: Union League, University (New York). Home: Cryders Point, Whitestone Landing, L.I., N.Y. Office: 441 Lexington Av., N.Y. City 17. Died Oct. 2, 1947.

HARDY, Guy U., ex-congressman; b. Abingdon, Ill., Apr. 4, 1872; s. U. W. and Virginia (Moorehead) H.; student Albion Normal U., 1888-90, Transylvania U., Lexington, Ky., 1892-94; m. Jessie Mack, Aug. 2, 1899; children—Max, Marion, Donald, Lyman. Began in newspaper bus. at Canon City, 1894; owner and pub. Canon City Daily Record, Canon City Weekly Record. Postmaster, Canon City, 1900-04; mem. 66th to 72d Congresses (1919-33), 3d Colo. Dist. Republican. Pres. N.E.A., 1918-19. Mem. Christian (Disciples) Ch. K. of P., Elk, Moose. Home: Canon City, Colo. Died Jan. 26, 1947.

HARDY, Marjorie, educator; b. Adrian, Mich., Mar. 10, 1888; d. Clinton Dewey and Nida Marion (Pennock) Hardy; Ph.B., U. of Chicago, 1921; M.A., Columbia, 1930. Teacher in pub. schools, Chisholm, Minn., 1911-13; teacher state sch., Owatonna, Minn., 1914-17; teacher in laboratory sch., U. of Chicago, 1918-29; prin. lower sch., Germantown Friends Sch., Philadelphia, Pa., 1930-45. Dean's Scholar, Teachers Coll. Columbia U., summer 1930. Mem. Assn. for Childhood Edn. (pres. 1941-43), Nat. Edn. Assn., Soc. Progressive Edn., Am. Assn. Univ. Women, Kappa Delta Pi, Delta Phi Epsilon, Pi Lambda Theta. Author: Child's Own Way," series of school readers with teachers' manuals, wordbooks, etc., 1926 to 1929, with later revisions. Home: 221 Winona Av., Philadelphia. Died June 20, 1948.

HARE, Clifford LeRoy, educator; b. Lee County, Ala., Mar. 19, 1869; s. Joseph S. and Susan (Bullard) H.; B.S., Ala. Poly. Inst., 1891, M.S., 1892; M.A., U. of Mich., 1903; m. Dabney Bondurant, Sept. 15, 1903; children—Emily Morrison (Mrs. Phillip H. Hardie), Catherine Lee Bullard (Mrs. Paul Mayo), Dabney Bondurant (Mrs. William C. Sugg), Susan Mizelle (Mrs. C. H. McGehee), Joseph Lee. Assistant in chemistry, Alabama Polytechnic Institute, 1891-1903, assistant professor, 1903-15, asso. prof., 1915-20, prof., 1920-32, dean Sch. of Chemistry since 1932, faculty chmn. of athletics since 1918; state chemist since 1930. Dir. Bank of Auburn. Mem. Southern Conference (athletic) Assn. (member exec. com. 1918-22, pres. 1932), Assn. Official Agrl. Chemists (mem. exec. com. 1937), Phi Delta Theta, Gamma Sigma Epsilon, Phi Lambda Upsilon, Phi Kappa Phi. Democrat. Methodist. Mason. Club: Rotary. Home: Auburn, Ala. Died Oct. 27, 1948.

HARE, James H., war corr.; b. London, Eng., Oct. 3, 1856; s. George and Margaret (Ball) H.; student St. John Coll., London, 1870-71; m. Ellen Crapper, Aug. 2, 1879; children—George James, Margaret Ellen, Dorothy, Ruth Kate. Came to U.S., 1889; photographer and corr., revolution in Cuba, 1898, Spanish-Am. War, 1898, Russo-Japanese War for Collier's Weekly, 1904-05; also of revolutions in Haiti, Venezuela and Panama, Madero revolution in Mexico, 1911, Balkan War, 1912, landing of U.S. Marines in Vera Cruz, Apr. 1914, for Collier's Weekly; in France, Belgium, Salonica and Italy, for Leslie's Weekly, at various times during World War I. A pioneer in aerial photography. Republican. Episcopalian. Home: 3111 Farragut Rd., Brooklyn, N.Y. Died June 24, 1946.

HARGEST, William M(ilton), judge; b. Winchester, Va., Aug. 5, 1868; s. Thomas Sewell and Virginia (Diffenderfer) H.; graduate Harrisburg Acad., 1886; grad. study, 1886-88; LL.D., Lebanon Valley Coll., 1922, Lafayette Coll., 1923; m. Kingsley Le-Galliene, Oct. 17, 1895 (now deceased); children—Thomas Sewell II (dec.), William Milton. Began practice of law at Harrisburg, 1891; dept. atty. Gen. State of Pa., 1909-20; pres. judge Common Pleas Court, 12th Pa. Dist., since 1920. Pres. Nat. Conf. of Commrs. on Uniform State Laws, 1930-33. Mem. bd. dirs. Harrisburg Y.M.C.A., Harrisburg Hosp. Mem. Am. Bar Assn., Pa. Bar Assn. (ex-pres.). Republican. Presbyn. Mason, Elk; mem. Royal Arcanum. Home: 3314 N. 2d St., Harrisburg, Pa. Died Feb. 16, 1948.

HARLAN, Byron Berry, lawyer; b. Greenville, O., Oct. 22, 1886; s. Benjamin B. and Margaret H. (Bond) H.; A.B., U. of Mich., 1909, LL.B., 1911; m. Sada Shaw, June 16, 1914; children—Richard S., Bruce S., Eleanor L. (Mrs. Frederick E. Batrus, Jr.). Admitted to Ohio bar, 1911; practiced law in Dayton, O., 1911-31; mem. 72d to 75th Congresses (1931-39) 3d Ohio Dist.; U.S. dist. atty. for Southern Dist. Ohio, 1944-46; judge Tax Court of U.S. since March 1946. Pres. Ohio Fedn. Humane Soc., 1927-44; hon.

vice pres. Am. Humane Assn. Mem. Ohio State Bar Assn., American Bar Assn. Democrat. Mason. Office: Reibold Bldg., Dayton, O. Died Nov. 11, 1949

HARLAN, Henry David, lawyer; b. Churchville, Md., Oct. 23, 1858; s. David H. (med. dir. U.S. Navy) and Margaret Rebecca (Herbert) H.; A.B., St. John's Coll., Md., 1878; A.M., 1884, LL.D., 1894; LL.B., U. of Md., 1881; LL.D., St. Lawrence U., 1935; m. Helen Altemus, Dec. 19, 1889; children—Helen (Mrs. R. Marsden Smith), Henry Altemus, Mary Leita (wife of Dr. John R. Paul), David. Admitted to bar, 1881; asso. prof. and later prof. elementary law and domestic relations, 1883-1900, prof. constl. law, 1900-13, prof. domestic relations, 1900-24, and treas. of law faculty, 1883-1910, dean, 1910-32, dean emeritus since 1932, U. of Md.; chief judge Supreme Bench of Baltimore, Oct. 23, 1888-Jan. 1, 1914; counsel Fidelity Trust Co., Baltimore, since Jan. 1, 1914. Democrat. Mem. Standing Com. P.E. Church, Diocese of Md., 1912-1941. Pres. trustees Johns Hopkins Hosp., 1903-1941. Trustee Johns Hopkins U. since 1904. Home: 4909 Falls Road. Office: Fidelity Trust Co., Baltimore, Md. Died Sep. 7, 1943.

HARMAN, Arthur Fort, coll. pres.; b. Lexington, S.C., Aug. 10, 1875; s. Marion DeKalb and Ellen Scotto (Rawl) H.; grad. Peabody Coll. for Teachers, 1896; spl. student same and U. of Nashville, 1 yr.; B.S., Teachers Coll. (Columbia), 1928, grad. study, summers, 1928, 29; LL.D., U. of Ala., 1924; m. Anna Rebecca Fuller, Dec. 24, 1900; children—John Fuller, Arthur Fort, Marion DeKalb. Teacher of English and Latin and asst. prin. Brewton (Ala.) Collegiate Inst., 1898-1901; prin. high sch., Centerville, Ala., 1901-02; supt. city schs., New Decatur, Ala., 1902-04, 1906-08, Florence, 1904-06; Selma, 1908-20; supt. edn., Montgomery County, Ala., 1920-28; dir. Div. Ednl. Administration, Ala. State Dept. Edn., Jan. 1928-Oct. 1929; state supt. edn., Ala., Oct. 1, 1929-Jan. 15, 1935; pres. Alabama Coll.-State College for Women, 1935-47, president emeritus since Sept. 1, 1947. Member National Conference on the Financing of Edn., Columbia U., 1933; ex-officio mem. State Bd. of Edn., 1929-35; ex-officio trustee Ala. Coll., Ala. Poly. Inst., U. of Ala., 1929-35. Mem. advisory com. Local Sch. Units Project, U.S. Office of Edn., 1936, 37. Mem. Am. Assn. of School Administrators of N.E.A. (mem. 1933 Yearbook Commn), N.E.A. (v.p. 1933-34; life mem.; pres. dept. rural edn., 1926; mem. com. on Instns. of higher learning 1936 and 1937), Ala. Edn. Assn. (life mem.; pres. 1911; mem. exec. com. 1908 and 1909; chmn. of exec. com. 1910; mem. com. on legislation several years including 1945-46, 1946-47; pres. dept. city superintendence, 1907), Nat. Congress Parents and Teachers (5th v.p.); dir. dept. of edn., 1934-37), Phi Delta Kappa, Kappa Delta Pi; honorary member of the Future Farmers of Alabama. Democrat. Presbyterian. Mason. Pres. Selma (Ala.) Rotary Club, 1918-19, Montgomery (Ala), 1924-25. Author of numerous articles, addresses and reports, chiefly on ednl. topics. Address: 512 S. Hull St., Montgomery Ala. Died Oct. 12, 1948.

HARMON, Millard Fillmore, army officer; b. Fort Mason, San Francisco, Calif., Jan. 19, 1888; s. Millard Fillmore and Madelin (Kendig) H.; B.S., U.S. Military Acad., 1912; grad. Signal Corps Aviation Sch., 1916, Command and Gen. Staff Sch., 1923, Army War Coll., 1925; m. Alberta Clark, Mar. 7, 1917; children—Helen Clark, Millard Fillmore, III. Commd. 2d lt., Inf., U.S. Army, advanced through ranks to maj. gen., Air Corps, July 1941, lieut. general, February 1943; served 9th, 24th and 28th Regts. Inf., U.S. and Philippines, 1912-15; aviation sect. Signal Corps, since 1915; airplane pilot, Perishing expdn. to Mexico, 1916-17, World War, Aviation Hdqrs. A.E.F. and French Group de Combat No. 13, 1917-18; comdr. successively, 1st Provisional Wing, France Field, Panama, Canal Zone; March Field, Calif.; Barksdale Field, La.; 20th Pursuit Group; Luke Field, Hawaii; 5th Bombardment Group, Hamilton Field, Calif.; 10th Pursuit Wing; 4th Interceptor Command; instr. Command and Gen. Staff Sch., 1930-32; asst. comdt., Air Corps Tactical Sch., 1938-40; mil. observer in England and air adviser Harriman Mission to Great Britain, Feb. to Mar., 1941; maj. gen. comdg. 2d Air Force, July 1941-Jan. 1942; chief of Air Force, 1942-43; apptd. comdr. all army forces on Guadalcanal and S. Pacific islands, Feb. 1943. Awarded Service medal Mexican Punitive Expdn., Victory medal (2 clasps), Croix-de-Guerre (Star). Became jr. military aviator, military aviator, airplane pilot, command pilot, combat and tech. observer, French military pilot (badge No. 4446). Pilot Certificate Aero Club of America, 1916. Episcopalian. Address: War Dept., Washington, D.C. Died Mar. 3, 1945.

HARMS, John Henry, clergyman; b. Savannah, Ga., Jan. 27, 1876; s. C. H. and Elizabeth (Bruker) H.; A.B., Newberry (S.C.) Coll., 1893, A.M., 1902; grad. Luth. Theol. Sem., Gettysburg, Pa., 1897; D.D., Erskine Coll., Due West, S.C., 1910; m. Sarah Bowers Wheeler, Apr. 20, 1898; children—Kathryn Wheeler (Mrs. W. C. Beasley), Elizabeth Wheeler (Mrs. John E. Slaughter, Jr.). Ordained Lutheran ministry, 1897; pastor Trinity Ch., Chambersburg, Pa., 1897-1900, St. Paul's Ch., Newport, Pa., 1900-01, Bethlehem Ch., Harrisburg, 1902-08; pres. Newberry (S.C.) Coll., Oct. 1908-June 1918; pastor Ch. Holy Communion, Phila., since 1918. Mem. editorial staff Augsburg Teacher since 1909. Pres. Fedn. of Chs., Phila.; pres. bd. dirs. Grace Coll., Luth. Bd. of Publ. Frequently del. to gen. ch. convs. Home: 2111 Sansom St., Philadelphia, Pa. Died Aug. 22, 1946.

HARNED, Virginia, actress; b. Boston; m. E. H. Sothern, Dec. 3, 1896 (marriage dissolved, 1910). Joined George Clark's Co. at 16 and appeared as Lady Despar in "The Corsican Brothers"; metropolitan début at 14th St. Theatre, Mar. 31, 1890, in "A Long Lane, or Green Meadows"; soon after was engaged as leading woman for E. H. Sothern under Daniel Frohman's management; subsequently played leading rôles in A. M. Palmer's Stock Co. Created the title rôle in "Trilby" (Paul Potter's dramatization), Park Theatre, Boston, Mar. 11, 1895; starred in that play one season. Died Apr. 29, 1946.

HARPER, George McLean, univ. prof.; b. Shippensburg, Pa., Dec. 31, 1863; s. William Wylie and Nancy J. (McLean) H.; A.B., Princeton, 1884, A.M., Ph.D., 1891; m. Belle Dunton Westcott, May 9, 1895; children—Isabel Westcott (Mrs. R. F. Blount) George McLean. Employed on New York Tribune, 1884; studied abroad, 1885-87; employed Scribner's Mag., 1887-89; instr., Princeton U., 1889-91, asst. prof., 1891-94, prof. Romance langs., 1894-1900, English lit., 1900-26, Woodrow Wilson prof. of lit., 1926-32, emeritus and spl. lecturer English lit., 1932. Dir. C.R.B. Ednl. Foundation; del. Am. Commn. for Relief in Belgium, 1915. Officer Order Crown of Belgium, 1919. Mem. Nat. Inst. Arts and Letters. Author: Masters of French Literature, 1901; Life of Charles Augustin Sante-Beuve, 1909; William Wordsworth, His Life, Works and Influence, 1916; John Morley and Other Essays, 1920; Wordsworth's French Daughter, 1921; Dreams and Memories, 1922; Spirit of Delight, 1928; Literary Appreciations, 1937. Joint-translator: Rein's Japan, Vol. II, 1888. Edited edits. of several French texts and addresses of President Wilson, 1918; Wordsworth, in the Modern Student's Library, 1923; introduction and notes to the Standard Oxford Edition of the Poetical Works of Wordsworth, 1933. Contbr. to the Coleridge Memorial Volume, 1934. Lecturer on Anglo-American Union, 1939-43. Home: 36 Mercer St., Princeton, N.J. Died July 14, 1947.

HARPER, Harry F., business executive; vice pres. and dir. Capital Trust Co., Duplex Truck Co., Michigan Surety Co., Am. State Savings Bank, Michigan Steel Tube Products Co.; dir. Motor Wheel Corp. Home: 1408 Cambridge Rd. Office: 701 E. Saginaw St., Lansing 10, Mich. Died Aug. 8, 1949.

HARPER, Henry Winston, chemist, educator; b. Boonville, Mo., Sept., 20, 1859; s. James W. and Virginia (Crenshaw) H.; ed. Mound City Coll.; Ph.G., Phila. Coll. Pharmacy, 1881; M.D., U. of Va., 1892; spl. study with Dr. J. W. Mallet, U. of Va., summer 1894, and in Europe, summer 1897; LL.D., Baylor U., Waco, Tex., 1914; m. Susan Randolph West, July 9, 1895; children—Henry Winston, Virginia Randolph. Mfg. chemist and perfumer, Ft. Worth, Tex., 1881-84; chemist and metallurgist to mining cos. in Mex., 1884-86; chemist, Ft. Worth, Tex., 1887-90; asst. resident phys., Rockbridge Alum Springs, Va., 1892; adj. prof. chemistry in charge of Sch. of Chemistry, and dir. Chem. Lab., 1894-97, asso. prof., 1897-1903, prof. since 1903, chmn. grad. council, 1900-13, and dean Graduate Sch., 1913-36, U. of Tex., dean emeritus of Grad. Sch. since 1936. Chemist to U. of Tex. Mineral Survey, 1901-06. Has investigated and reported upon mining and reduction properties, U.S. and Mexico. Honorary chmn. 95th meeting Am. Chemical Society, Dallas, Tex., 1938. Fellow Chem. Soc. London, A.A.A.S. (emeritus life mem.), A.M.A., Tex. Acad. Sciences (pres. 1900-01), Am. Inst. of Chemists; mem. Am. Chem. Soc., 5th, 7th and 8th Internat. Congress Applied Chemistry, Soc. Chem. Industry (London, Eng.), Texas State Med. Assn., Southern Med. Assn., Philos. Soc. of Tex.; charter mem. Am. Assn. Univ. Profs.; mem. Beta Theta Pi, Phi Beta Kappa, Alpha Mu Pi Omega, Phi Lambda Upsilon, Pi Gamma Mu, Alpha Epsilon Delta; asso. mem. Am. Museum Natural History (New York), S.A.R. Member committee to draft ednl. plan for S.A.T.C., 1918; field aide to Texas dirs., Com. on Industrial Preparedness, Naval Consulting Bd., Southern Div., 1917-18, etc. Clubs: University, Town and Gown, University Science. Has written many articles on chem. and med. subjects in tech. jours. and proc. of learned socs. Home: 2216 Rio Grande St., Austin, Tex. Died Aug. 28, 1943.

HARPER, Paul Vincent, lawyer; b. New Haven, Conn., Jan. 5, 1889; s. William Rainey and Ella (Paul) H.; B.A., U. of Chicago, 1908, J. D., 1913; student U. of Born (Germany), 1908; student Harvard, 1912; m. Isabel Vincent, Aug. 31, 1914; children—Paul Vincent, Jane Vincent. Admitted to Illinois bar, 1913, and since in practice of law; member law firm Sidley, Austin, Burgess and Harper. Served as capt. F. A., U.S. Army, 1917. Baptist. Home: R.F. D. 1, Libertyville, Ill. Office: 11 S. La Salle St., Chicago, Ill.* Died Sep. 16, 1949.

HARPER, Robert Almer, botanist; b. Le Claire, Ia., Jan. 21, 1862; s. Rev. Almer and Eunice (Thomson) H.; A.B., Oberlin, 1886, A.M., 1891; Ph.D., U. of Bonn, 1896; m. Alice Jean McQueen, June 25, 1899; m. 2d, Helen Sherman, Jan. 2, 1918; 1 son, Robert Sherman. Prof. Greek and Latin, Gates Coll., 1886-88; instr. in acad., 1889-91, prof. botany and geology, 1891-98, Lake Forest U.; prof. botany, U. of Wis., 1898-1911, Columbia U., 1911-30, now emeritus. Mem. Nat. Acad. Sciences. Am. Acad. Arts and Sciences, Am. Philos. Soc., Bot. Soc. America, A.A. A.S. Home: Route 5, Bedford, Va. Died May 12, 1946.

HARPER, Samuel Northrup, coll. prof.; b. Morgan Park, Ill., Apr. 9, 1882; s. William R. (ex-pres. U. of Chicago) and Ella (Paul) H.; A.B., U. of Chicago, 1902; grad. l'Ecole des langues Orientales Vivantes, Paris, 1905; studied Columbia; unmarried. Asso. in Russian; U. of Chicago, 1905-09; lecturer in Russian institutional history, U. of Liverpool, Eng., 1911-13; asst. prof. Russian lang. and instns., U. of Chicago, 1915, now prof. Clubs: University, Quadrangle; Cosmos (Washington, D.C.). Author: Russian Reader (with Boyer and Speransky); Civic Training in Soviet Russia; Making Bolsheviks; The Government of the Soviet Union. Home: 5728 Woodlawn Av. Address: University of Chicago, Chicago, Ill. Died Jan. 18, 1943.

HARPER, Theodore Acland, author; b. Christchurch, New Zealand, Dec. 17, 1871; s. Leonard and Joanna Dorothea (Acland-Troyte) H.; student New Zealand U. Sch. of Mines, 1895-97; m. Winifred Mary Hunter-Brown, Nov. 8, 1908 (died July 5, 1933). Sailed before the mast 6 mos., 1897; was engaged in mining engring. in Arizona, 1897-1900; in gold rush, Cape Nome, Alaska, 1900-01; general manager mining concession, Eastern Siberia, 1902-10; also traveled in Manchuria, Mongolia, Japan, Central America, etc., reporting on mines; mgr. mines, Juneau, Alaska, 1910-11; resigned mining connection and bought fruit ranch in Ore. Elected mem. Inst. Mining and Metallurgy, London, 1906; mem. Ore. Writers' League, 1924. Mason. Author: The Mushroom Boy, 1924; Singing Feathers, 1925; Siberian Gold, 1927; The Janitor's Cat, 1927; Kubrik the Outlaw, 1928; Forgotten Gods, 1929; His Excellency and Peter, 1930; Windy Island, 1931 (last 6 titles with wife); Red Sky, 1935; Allison's Girl, 1936; Seventeen Chimneys, 1938. Home: 3055 N. W. Vaughn St., Portland, Ore. Died May 6, 1942.

HARPER, William Allen, univ. prof.; b. Berkley, Va., Apr. 27, 1880; s. Joseph and Mary Melissa (McCloud) H.; grad. Berkley Mil. Acad., 1895; A.B., Elon Coll., N.C., 1899; Yale U., 1903-05, M.A., 1904; Litt.D., Defiance (O.) Coll., 1912; LL.D., Union Christian Coll., Ind., 1912; m. Estelle Walker (Ph.B.), Oct. 19, 1899. Latin teacher, Franklin Mil. Acad., 1899-1900; prin. Kenly Acad., N.C., 1900-03; prof. Latin, 1905-11, pres. Elon Coll., 1911-31; visiting prof. religious edn., Div. Sch., U. of Chicago, summer 1931; prof. religious edn., Vanderbilt Univ. Sch. of Religion, since Jan. 1932; visiting prof. of religious edn., Northwestern U., summer, 1935, Chautauqua, N.Y., summer, 1937, Boston U., summers, 1938, 39. Special rep. of Am. Bd. Commrs. for Foreign Missions, in Moslem lands, Sept.-Dec. 1931. General secretary Board of Christian Edn. of Christian Ch. since 1922; chmn. com. on religious edn., Council of Ch. Bds. of Edn.; pres. Coll. Conf., Congl.-Christian Colls.; mem. Foundation for Edn.; pres. N.C. and Va. Christian Conf., 1905-16; chmn. N.C. S.S. Assn., 1913-19; pres. N.C. Coll. Conf., 1928; v.p. Council of Ch. Bds. of Edn., 1929; mem. bd. trustees Elon Coll. since 1931; mem. strategy com. Gen. Council Congl. and Christian Chs., 1934-36; mem. continuation com. World Conf. on Faith and Order. Mem. Southern Ednl. Assn., Classical Assn. Middle States and South, N.C. Teachers' Assembly (v.p.), N.C. Folk-Lore Soc., N.E.A. (life), Religious Edn. Assn., Pi Gamma Mu. Democrat. Rotarian. Author: Preparing the Teacher, Vol. I, 1909, Vol. II, 1910; The Making of Men, 1915; The New Layman for the New Time, 1917; The New Church for the New Time, 1918; Reconstructing the Church, 1920; The Church in the Present Crisis, 1921; An Integrated Program of Religious Education, 1926; Youth and Truth, 1927; Character Building in Colleges, 1928; A New Technique for Teaching Religion (pamphlet), 1933; Personal Religious Beliefs, 1937; The Minister of Education, 1939; also many articles and addresses in religious and educational publications. Editor in chief The Journal of Christian Education; asso. editor Christian Quarterly; an advisor of "Character," the publication of Character Associates, Inc. Home: Black Mountain, N.C. Died May 11, 1942.

HARRE, T. Everett, author; b. Marietta, Pa., Dec. 17, 1884; unmarried. On staff Phila. Press, 1905-07; spl. writer Phila. N. American, 1907-09; associate editor Hampton's, 1909-11, for which went North to meet Robert E. Peary on his return from his 8th Arctic expedition and with the collaboration of Elsa Barker secured the serial rights to story of trip to the North Pole; was first person after a 4 months' search, to get into touch, Oct. 1910, with Dr. Frederick A. Cook, the explorer, after his long disappearance, finding him in London, and securing the first exclusive statement for publication. Literary and dramatic critic Phila. Evening Ledger, 1914. Spl. contbr. Am. Weekly of New York American, 1915-16; publicity dir. League for Nat. Unity and Nat. Civic Federation, 1917-20; mng. editor Nat. Civic Fed. Rev., 1919-21; spl. contbr. to Red Book Mag., also articles and stories in Cosmopolitan, Ladies' Home Jour., Liberty, The Dance, Good Housekeeping, etc. Author: The Eternal Maiden, 1913; Behold the Woman!, 1916 (re-published 1925, 1937); One Hour—and Forever, 1925; The Heavenly Sinner, 1935; You Can Not Miss That Inn, 1939; The Little Poor Man of Graymoor, 1947; Heroes of Peace, 1947. Compiler: Beware After Dark, 1929; The Treasury of Love—Supreme Stories of Romance, Passion and Tragedy, 1945; Treasures of the Kingdom, 1947; Ways to the Kingdom, 1948. Collaborated with Very Rev. Paul James Francis, Father General of Franciscan

Soc. of the Atonement: Theresa Neumann—the Mystic Maid, 1939. Home: 257 West Market St., Marietta, Lancaster Co., Pa. Deceased.

HARRELL, Alfred, publisher; b. Merced County, Calif., Nov. 10, 1863; s. Alfred and Louise Alpha (Ward) H.; ed. pub. and high schs., Merced and Alameda counties, Calif.; m. Virginia McKamy, July 10, 1886; 1 dau., Bernice (Mrs. William F. Chipman). Teacher and county supt. schs., Calif., 1882-99; pub. and owner Bakersfield Californian since 1897. Mem. Native Sons of the Golden West. Democrat. Elk. Clubs: Bohemian (San Francisco); Stockdale Country (Bakersfield). Home: 1161 Oleander Av. Office: 1701 I St., Bakersfield, Calif. Died Dec. 14, 1946.

HARRER, Gustave Adolphus, prof. Latin; b. Brooklyn, N.Y, May 14, 1886; s. Gustave Adolphus and Letitia (Morrison) H.; A.B., Princeton, 1910, Ph.D., 1913; m. Florence M. Wagner, July 8, 1914; children—Gustave Adolphus, Joseph Wagner, Marcella Caroline, Letitia Mary. Instr. in classics, Princeton, 1913-15; with Univ. of N.C. since 1915, instr. in Latin until 1918, asst. prof., 1918-21, asso. prof., 1921-24, prof., 1924-34, Kenan prof. Latin, since 1934, head dept. of Latin since 1936, head dept. of classics since 1938; chmn. Div. of Humanities since 1940; in Italy, on leave, Kenan Foundation, 1922, 23. Mem. exec. com. Classical Assn. Middle West and South, 1928-32, 1934-38, pres., 1933-34; mem. Am. Philological Association, American Association University Professors, Phi Beta Kappa Fraternity. Democrat. Presbyterian. Author: Studies in the History of the Roman Province of Syria, 1915; also (with George Howe) Roman Literature in Translation, 1924; Greek Literature in Translation, 1924; A Handbook of Classical Mythology, 1929. Contbr. to classical jours. in field of Latin inscriptions, Roman history, chronology and institutions. Home: Laurel Hill Rd., Chapel Hill, N.C. Died Nov. 26, 1943.

HARRIMAN, Charles Conant, clergyman; b. Somerville, Mass., June 2, 1876; s. Charles Franklin and Mary White (Conant) H.; grad. Boston Latin Sch., 1893; B.A., Harvard, 1897; B.D., Cambridge Episcopal Theol. Sch., 1905; m. Edith Lee Wells, Nov. 25, 1908 (died 1911); children—Florence Conant, Mary Wells; m. 2d, Mary Hilliard Phillips, Jan. 18, 1916; 1 dau., Julia (dec.). Deacon and priest P.E. Ch., 1905; curate St. George's Ch., New York, 1905-07; rector St. Ann's Ch., Morrisania, Bronx, New York, 1907-12, Saint Peter's Church, Albany, New York, 1912-39, rector emeritus, 1939, archdeacon of Albany, 1926-27. Pres. Standing Com. Diocese of Albany, 1930-36, trustee, 1915-39; trustee William Croswell Doane Fund, 1920-37, Albany Diocese Foundation, 1922-39; chairman Diocesan Com. on Pension Fund, 1926-37. Clubs: Torch (pres. 1933), Eau Gallie Yacht Club. Home: Highland Av., Eau Gallie, Fla. Died July 28, 1946.

HARRIMAN, Joseph Wright, banker; b. Belleville, N.J., Jan. 31, 1867; s. John Neilson and Elizabeth Grainger (Hancox) H.; grad. Charlier's French Inst., New York, 1883; m. Augusta Barney, Nov. 21, 1892; children—Miriam, Alan. Began as clk. U.S. Nat. Bank, New York, 1883, advancing to asst. cashier; asst. cashier, Merchants Nat. Bank, 1894, cashier, 1896, v.p., 1902; mem. firm Harriman & Co., bankers, 1902-24 (est. 1871); founder, 1912, pres. many yrs., Harriman Nat. Bank (name changed to Harriman Nat. Bank & Trust Co.); has also been officer or dir. various other corps. Mem. B. Co., 7th Regt., N.G.N.Y., 1887-92. Episcopalian. Died Jan. 23, 1949.

HARRINGTON, John Lyle, cons. engr.; b. Lawrence, Kan., Dec. 7, 1868; s. Robert Charles and Angeline Virginia (Henry) H.; A.B., B.S., C.E., U. of Kan., 1895; B.S., McGill U., Montreal, 1906, M.S., 1908; Dr. Engring., Case Sch. of Applied Science, 1930; m. Daisy June Orton, June 21, 1899; 1 son, Thomas Orton. With J. A. L. Waddell, Kansas City, 1895-96; with Elmira Bridge Co., 1896, Pencoyd Iron Works, Phila., 1896-97, Keystone Bridge Works, 1897-98, designing Monongahela R.R. bridge and other heavy structures for Pittsburgh, Bessemer & L.E. R.R.; asst. supt. structural dept. Cambria Steel Co., Johnstown, Pa., Jan.-Sept. 1898; asst. chief engr. and asst. supt. Bucyrus Co., Milwaukee, Sept. 1898-Mar. 1899; asst. to chief engr. Northwestern Elevated R.R. Co., Chicago, Mar.-Dec. 1899; designing engr. Berlin Iron Bridge Co., E. Berlin, Conn., 1899-1900; asst. engr. bldgs. and bridges, B.&O. R.R., 1900-01; with C.W. Hunt Co., New York, in charge engring., estimating and contracting, 1901-05; chief engr. and mgr. Locomotive & Machine Co., Montreal, Ltd., 1905-06; mem. firm Waddell & Harrington, cons. engrs., Kansas City, Mo., 1907-14, Harrington, Howard & Ash, 1914-28, Harrington & Cortelyou since 1928. Designed 6 bridges over Chesapeake and Del. Canal; 18 bridges over Welland Canal; bridge over San Francisco Bay; bridge over Mobile River; bridge over Ohio R. at Paducah, Ky., over Missouri R. nr. St. Louis, Mo., at Kansas City, Mo., at Blair, Neb., and at Rulo, Neb., over Mississippi River at Cape Girardeau and Louisiana, Mo., Alton, Ill., Vicksburg, Miss., and railway and highway at Baton Rouge, La.; railroad and highway bridge over Piscataqua River between New Hampshire and Maine; bridges over St. John's River at Jacksonville, Fla., and over Atchafalaya River at Simmesport, La., over Don River, Rostoff, Russia, Yalu River, Manchuria, docks at Beaumont, Tex., and water supply, Brownwood, Tex., etc. Mem. Engineers Advisory Board and chief engr., R.F.C. Has taken out many patents on movable bridges. Trustee Robert College, Turkey. Mem. Am. Soc. C.E., Am. Soc. M.E. (v.p. 1920-22, pres. 1923), Am. Railway Engring. Assn., The Newcomen Soc., Am. Soc. Testing Materials, Instn. Civ. Engrs. (Eng.), Engring. Inst. Can., A.A.A.S., Sigma Nu, Sigma Xi, Tau Beta Pi (pres. 1917), Theta Tau; mem. Am. Engring. Council, 1926-32. Presbyterian. Clubs: University, Engineers' (ex-pres.), Mission Hills Country (Kansas City); Cosmos (Washington, D.C.). Home: 4909 Belinder Terrace, Kansas City, Kan. Office: 1004 Baltimore Av., Kansas City, Mo. Died May 20, 1942.

HARRINGTON, John Thomas, physician; b. Buena Vista, Miss., Jan. 7, 1858; s. John Thomas and Margaret (Belk) H.; ed. St. Louis Medical Coll., 1879, Louisville Medical Coll., 1886, Polyclinic Medical Coll., 1895 (M.D.); m. Genoa Cole, June 5, 1884; children—Genoa (Mrs. A. D. Brinkerhoff) and Jessie (Mrs. P. S. Durham). Began practicing medicine in 1879 and still in active practice; pres. Board of Health, El Paso, Tex.; dir. epileptic colony, Abilene, Tex.; city physician, Waco, Tex.; supervisor of Texas penitentiaries; one of the founders and first sec.-treas. of board of trustees Hardin Simmons Univ., Abilene, Tex.; pres. board of trustees Baylor Univ., Waco, Tex.; on medical staff at Providence and Hillcrest Memorial hosps., Waco, Tex. Mem. A.M.A.; Texas Med. Assn. Democrat. Baptist. Office: Amicable Bldg., Waco, Tex. Died Apr. 29, 1947.

HARRINGTON, Philip, chmn. Chicago Transit Authority; b. Worcester, Mass., Jan. 28, 1886; s. Michael and Ellen (Ryan) H.; B S., Armour Inst. Tech., 1906; LL.D., Kent Coll. of Law, 1915; Doctor Engring., 1944; children—Marjorie, Ann, Michael. Admitted to Illinois bar, 1916. Connected with Sanitary District of Chicago, Ill., 1906-35, beginning as rodman, chief engr. 1933-35; directed design and construction tunnels, bridges, pumping stations and sewage disposal works costing over $100,000,000; special traction engr., City of Chicago, 1935-38; author study and report of Comprehensive Transportation Plan for City of Chicago, Nov. 22, 1937; apptd. commr. of subways, City of Chicago, Nov. 3, 1938; designed and constructed first transportation subway, City of Chicago ($60,000,000); author comprehensive superhighway plan for City of Chicago, Oct. 30, 1939; apptd. commr. subways and superhighways, City of Chicago, Jan. 1, 1940; chmn. Chicago Transit Authority since 1945. Mem. Chicago Plan Commn. Chief Civilian Defense Communications and administrator of Defense Transportation for Chicago Metropolitan Area during World War II. Mem. Am. Soc of Civil Engrs., Western Soc. Engrs. Clubs: Chicago Athletic Assn., Exmoor Country. Life mem. Art. Inst. of Chicago. Co-inventor system of flash-drying and incineration of sewage sludge and other waste materials. Alumni award of merit Ill. Inst. Tech., 1942. Home: 219 South Av., Glencoe, Ill. Office: 20 N. Wacker Dr., Chicago 6, Ill. Died Feb. 11, 1949.

HARRINGTON, Samuel Milby, Marine Corps officer; born, Md., Nov. 13, 1882; commd. 2d lt., Marine Corps, 1909, and advanced through the grades to brig. gen., Mar. 1941; pres. Naval Examining Bd. Address: U.S. Marine Corps Headquarters, Washington, D.C.* Died Mar. 31, 1948.

HARRINGTON, Vincent Francis, congressman; b. Sioux City, Ia., May 16, 1903; s. Thomas Francis and Maria (O'Leary) H.; student Trinity Coll., Sioux City, Ia., 1917-21; A.B., U. of Notre Dame, 1925; m. Catherine O'Connor; children—Catherine Tim, Patricia Ann. Instr. history, economics, and athletic dir., U. of Portland (Ore.), 1925-26; v.p., gen. mgr., Continental Mortgage Co., Sioux City, since 1927; mem. Iowa State Senate, 1933-37; mem. 75th to 77th Congresses (1937-43), 9th Ia. Dist. (resigned). Entered Army Air Force (U.S.) as major, May 1943, assigned I Troop Carrier Command, Hdqrs., Stout Field, Indianapolis (asst. A-3). Democrat. Catholic, K.C., Elk, Eagle. Clubs: Country (Sioux City), Monogram (U. of Notre Dame). Home: Warrior Hotel, Sioux City, Ia. Address: 320 E. Maple Rd., Indianapolis, Ind. Died Nov. 29, 1943.

HARRIS, Albert Mason, univ. prof.; b. Old Mystic, Conn., Jan. 13, 1868; s. William Clifford and Elizabeth (Comer) H.; grad. Emerson Coll. of Oratory, Boston, 1893, grad. student, 1894, hon. B.L.I., 1931; A.B., Cornell Coll., Ia., 1901, A.M., 1902; m. Florence Blackwell, Dec. 31, 1902; children—Lucy Elizabeth, Katherine Louise. Mem. staff Hartford (Conn.) Times, 1887-91; instr. Harrington's Sch., Waterbury, Conn., 1895; asst. in oratory, Oberlin, 1895-96; instr. in oratory, 1896-98, dir. Sch. of Oratory, 1898-1902, Cornell Coll.; asso. prof. pub. speaking and debate, 1902-23, prof., 1923-41, Vanderbilt U., retired, 1941. Has served as professor of public speaking in summer schools of Cornell College, University of Texas, University of California, University of Southern Calif. Mem. N.E.A., Nat. Speech Arts Assn., Southern Assn. Teachers of Speech; ex-pres. Southern Intercollegiate Oratorical Assn., Tenn. Oratorical League. Mem. Phi Beta Kappa Fraternity. Methodist. Compiler: Selected Orations, 1924; Old Testament Readings for Schools, 1925. Editor: Citizenship Readers. Platform lecturer and reader. Home: 2700 Woodlawn Drive, Nashville, Tenn. Died Aug. 6, 1945.

HARRIS, Alfred F., chmn. bd. Harris-Seybold-Potter Co.; b. Covington, Ky., Apr. 17, 1860; s. James and Hannah (Carpenter) H.; ed. pub. schs., Niles, O.; m. Minnie L. Stull, May 22, 1890; 1 son, Alfred Stull. Began as apprentice jeweler, 1885; opened store in New Philadelphia, with brother Charles G., as Harris Brothers, jewelers, 1885; moved business to Niles, O., 1889; experimented with printing presses and developed a press with automatic feed for printing envelopes, later developing offset litho graphic press; discovered and developed the method of paper feeding to printing presses now in general use; with brother was organizer of Harris Automatic Press Co., 1894, firm later became Harris-Seybold-Potter Co., Cleveland and Dayton, chmn. bd. since June 24, 1929. Republican. Methodist. Home: Surrey and Derbyshire Roads, Cleveland Heights, O. Office: 4510 E. 71st St., Cleveland, O. Died June 26, 1943.

HARRIS, Alfred S., business exec.; b. Warren, Ohio, 1891. Pres. and dir. Harris-Seybold Co. Mason. Home: 2375 Woodmere Drive. Office: 4510 E. 71st St., Cleveland, Ohio. Died Aug. 22, 1947.

HARRIS, Basil; b. Pullman, Ill., Oct. 31, 1889; s. William Rees and Florence (Lewis) H.; prep. edn., Lawrenceville (N.J.) Sch., 1905-08; Litt.B., Princeton, 1912; hon. LL.D., Georgetown U., 1939; m. Mary Ursula Dempsey, Oct. 19, 1914; children—Basil, Richard Lewis. With MacAndrews & Forbes Co., commn. house, Camden, N.J., 1912-19; with Norton Lilly & Co. of New York, shipping, 1919-23; partner Roosevelt Steamship Co., 1923-39; v.p. Internat. Mercantile Marine Co., 1930-39; sr. v.p. U.S. Lines, 1931-39, exec. v.p., 1941-42, pres. since Mar. 1942; asst. to U.S. sec. of treasury and commr. of customs, Sept. 1939-July 15, 1940; special partner, Phelps Fenn & Co.; pres. and dir. Internat. Mercantile Marine Co., Roosevelt Steamship Co., Inc.; trustee, Emigrants Industrial Savings Bank, Atlantic Mutual Ins. Co., Am. Bur. Shipping, Northern Ins. Co., Chmn. bd., St. Vincent's Hosp. Decorated Knight of Malta. Roman Catholic. Clubs: India House (New York); National (Southampton); Apawamis (Rye, N.Y.). Home: Dogwood Lane, Rye, N.Y. Address: 1 Broadway, New York, N.Y. Died June 18, 1948.

HARRIS, Beverly Dabney; pres. Second Nat. Bank of Houston. Address: Houston, Tex. Died Jan. 25, 1948.

HARRIS, Charles, retired univ. prof.; b. Albion, Ill., Nov. 19, 1859; s. George and Catharine (Smith) H.; A.B., Ind. U., 1879, LL.D., 1929; Ph.D., U. of Leipzig, 1883; m. Mary McCalla, Dec. 24, 1884; 1 son, John McCalla. Teacher in acad., Vincennes, Ind., 1883-86; prof. French and German, Southern Ill. State Normal Sch., 1886-88; prof. German, Oberlin, 1888-93, Western Reserve U., 1893-1930 (emeritus). Mem. Modern Lang. Assn. America, Phi Beta Kappa, Phi Kappa Psi. Episcopalian. Author: German Composition, 1890; German Lessons, 1892; German Reader, 1895; German Grammar, 1914. Editor: Wichert's An der Majorsecke, 1895; Goethe's Poems, 1899; Lessing's Hamburgische Dramaturgie (abridged edit.), 1901. Home: Cleveland Heights, Ohio. Died Sept. 1943.

HARRIS, Charles Joseph, capitalist; b. Putnam, Conn., Sept. 11, 1853; s. William and Zilpah (Torrey) H.; ed. Yale, class of 1874, and St. Louis Law Sch. Has been largely interested in development of Western N.C. and especially identified with mining of kaolin in the U.S. President Harris Co., Jackson County Bank (Sylva, N.C.), Harris Granite Quarries (Salisbury, N.C.); pres. Asheville Daily Times Co., 1920; retired, 1941. Del.-at-large Rep. Nat. Conv., Chicago, 1908; Rep. candidate for gov. of N.C., 1904, mem. U.S. Industrial Commn., 1898-1902. Pres. Yale Alumni Assn. of N.C. Clubs: Metropolitan (Washington); University (New York); Asheville (Asheville, N.C.). Home: Dillsboro, N.C. Died Feb. 14, 1944.

HARRIS, Edwin Ewell, physician; b. Thurman, Ia., Jan. 2, 1867; s. Jared Junius and Mary Elizabeth (Ewell) H.; B.S., Tabor (Ia.) Coll., 1891; M.D., Howard U., Washington, 1894; studied U. of Vienna, U. of Chicago, Johns Hopkins, Mayo Clinic, Rochester, Minn.; further study in U.S. and Europe, 1922-25; m. Louise Allen Fairfield, 1895 (died 1919); children—Frederic F. (dec.), Mrs. Eleanor Curtis. Practiced at Tabor until 1908, at Grinnell since 1909; specialized in neuro-psychiatry; chmn. staff Community Hosp., 1921-22; bus. mgr. and treas. Grinnell Clinic. Mem. M.C., U.S.A., 1918; mem. Exemption and Adv. Bds., Poweshiek County, Ia., World War. Mem. Ia. State Med. Soc., Mo. Valley Med. Soc., Poweshiek Med. Soc. (sec.), Am. Legion. Republican. Conglist. Mason (32°, Shriner), Elk. Home: Grinnell, Iowa. Died Nov. 12, 1938.

HARRIS, George Simmons, cotton mfr.; b. Cedartown, Polk County, Ga., Jan. 16, 1881; s. James Coffee and Ellen (Simmons) H.; ed. U.S. Naval Acad., Ga. Sch. of Technology and Lowell (Mass.) Textile Sch.; m. Minnie Teague, May 10, 1904; children—Gertrude Ellen, Margaret Simmons. Began as supt. Sycamore (Ala.) Cotton Mills, 1902; supt. Gate City (Atlanta) Cotton Mills, 1905-07, Lanett (Ala.) Cotton Mills, 1907-20; also agt. Lanett (Ala.) Bleachery and Dye Works, 1916-20; pres. Exposition Cotton Mills, Atlanta, Ga., 1920-30; dir. 6th Dist. Federal Res. Bank, 1928-33; mem. Ga. State Bd. Vocational Edn., 1929-32; pres. Cascade Mills, Lowe Mfg. Co., Hunter Securities Co., treas. Shelbyville Mills, 1930-32; exec. v.p. Springs Cotton Mills of South Carolina, 1932-40; now pres. and treas. Dan River Mills, Inc. (formerly Riverside and Dan River Cotton Mills), Danville, Va.; dir. Cotton Clothing Relief, converting govt. owned cotton, Am. Red Cross

Hdqrs., Washington, D.C., 1932-33. Mem. Am. Cotton Mfg. Assn. (pres. 1927-28), Ga. Cotton Mfg. Assn. (pres. 1924-26). Chmn. bd. Cotton Textile Inst., 1948-49. Democrat. Presbyterian. Club: Country. Home: Danville, Va. Died Feb. 16, 1950.

HARRIS, Frederic Robert, retired rear adm.; b. N.Y. City, Apr. 10, 1875; s. Siegmund and Rose (Leeberg) H.; M.E., Stevens Inst. Tech., Hoboken, 1896, hon. E.D., 1921; m. 2d, Dena Sperry, Mar. 4, 1931 (died July 21, 1945). Engineering practice, 1896-1903; commissioned lieutenant (j.g.) Navy Corps, civil engineers, January 3, 1903; promoted through grades to chief Bur. Yards and Docks of Navy, temp. rear adm., 1916; permanent rear adm., Aug. 1916; retired Feb. 1927. In charge navy war construction, shore program in the U.S. and abroad, 1915-17; general manager Emergency Fleet Corp., U.S. Shipping Bd., in charge war emergency merchant marine constrn.; rep. Emergency Fleet Corp., U.S. Shipping Bd.; cons. and mng. engr., specializing in harbor and river work, bridges, etc.; pres. Frederic R. Harris, Inc.; consulting engr. U.S. Navy, 1939-45; designed water-front facilities, floating drydocks (including largest in world); cons. engr. Brit. admiralty. Mem. Am. Soc. Civil Engrs., Soc. Naval Architects and Marine Engrs., Naval Inst., Soc. Am. Mil. Engrs., N.Y. State Soc. Professional Engrs. and Land Surveyors, N.J. Soc., Am. Legion. Clubs: Army and Navy, University (Washington, D.C.); Union League (hon.), Collectors (New York); City Midday; Nat. Sojourners; Royal Philatelic (London). Asso. editor Am. Civ. Engrs.' Handbook, River and Harbor Works. Home: 420 Park Av. Address: 27 William St., New York. Died July 22, 1949; buried in Arlington National Cemetery.

HARRIS, James A., business exec.; b. Henry, Ill., July 26, 1870; s. George H. and Emma H. (Rowe) H.; ed. common schs. and business coll.; unmarried. Began in mercantile bus., Wagoner, Okla., 1893, also real estate and farming; mem. Harris Bros., Harris Bros. & Brann, and Harris Bros. & Strawn (oil producers), Wagoner, Okla.; pres. Harris-Strawn Oil Co. Chmn. Creek Nation Com. of Ind. Ty.; mem. Okla. Constl. Conv., 1907; del.-at-large Rep. Nat. Conv., 1908; chmn. Rep. State Com., Okla., 1910-12, 1920-21; mem. Rep. Nat. Com., 1912-16, 1920-24; mem. Com. of 21 on Amendments to Okla. Constn., 1931. Methodist. Mason. Address: Wright Bldg., Tulsa, Okla. Died Apr. 16, 1947.

HARRIS, Lee A., chmn. bd. Am. Automobile Ins. Co.; b. St. Louis, Mo., July 17, 1880; ed. St. Louis U.; m. Elsie McLain, Oct. 8, 1910. Public accountant, 1905-11; comptroller Southern Surety Co., 1911-17; chief auditor U.S. Shipping Bd., 1917-20. With Am. Automobile Ins. Co. since 1920, comptroller, 1920-25, then pres. and treas., now chmn. bd.; dir. Jefferson Hotel Co., McLain Orthopedic Sanitarium (St. Louis), Farm and Home Savings & Loan Assn. (Nevada, Mo.). Clubs: Bellerive Country, Noonday, Racquet, Mo. Athletic (St. Louis). Home: 6 Beverly Pl. Office: Pierce Bldg., St. Louis, Mo.
Died May 30, 1944.

HARRIS, Morris Bedford, lawyer; b. Albion, Ill., Sept. 10, 1866; s. Lucius and Constance Katherine (Thompson) H.; ed. U. of Ind. and Wittenberg Coll., Springfield, O.; m. Jessie Hayward Boggs, Feb. 21, 1889; children—Marjorie Hayward (Mrs. August F. Muenter), Ronald Biddle. Began practice at Fresno, Calif., 1895; sr. mem. firm Harris, Willey & Harris; attorney for various coöperative corps. and irrigation dists.; dir. Rowell, Chandler Co. Roosevelt presdl. elector, 1904-12; mem. State Bd. of Edn., 1915-16; mem. Calif. Senate, 1918-22, reëlected for term 1922-26; chmn. Rep. State Conv., 1918; asso. state dir. Four Minute Men, World War; pres. trustees Calif. State Normal Sch., Fresno, 1910-19; mem. Calif. Highway Commn., 1927-31; pres. Calif. R.R. Commn. during 1936. Mem. Mayflower Society, Sons of American Revolution, Phi Kappa Psi Fraternity. Clubs: Commercial, Commonwealth (San Francisco). Leader of "dry" forces in Calif. legislature, 1919-21, and author of the Harris Law for enforcement of 18th Amendment to the Constitution of U.S., which was defeated by referendum; led successful fight for enactment of Wright enforcement act, 1921. Home: 711 Ashlan Av. Office: 6 W. Patterson Bldg., Fresno, Calif. Died Aug. 23, 1941.

HARRIS, Paul Percy, originator Rotary Club movement; b. Racine, Wis., Apr. 19, 1868; s. George H. and Cornelia (Bryan) H.; Ph.B., U. of Vt., 1889, LL.D., 1933; LL.B., State U. of Ia., 1891; m. Jean Thomson, July 2, 1910. In practice at Chicago since 1896; mem. Harris, Reinhardt & Bebb. Founder, 1905, Rotary Club movement of the world; president emeritus Rotary Internat. Mem. Am. Bar Assn., Illinois State Bar Assn., Chicago Bar Assn. Awarded Silver Buffalo Token by Boy Scouts of America, 1934; Order of the Southern Cross (Brazil); Order of Merit (Chile); Order of the Sun (Peru and Ecuador), 1936; Officer Legion of Honor (France), 1937. Republican. Home: 10856 Longwood Drive. Office: Rotary International, 35 E. Wacker Dr., Chicago, Ill. Died Jan. 27, 1947.

HARRIS, Robert Le Roy, bishop; b. Cleveland, O., Feb. 12, 1874; s. E. Clark and Susan (Shaw) H.; A.B., Kenyon Coll., Gambier, O., 1896, M.A., 1911, D.D., 1918; grad. Bexley Hall (theol. dept., Kenyon), 1899; m. Katheryn Brandon, Aug. 25, 1897 (died 1903); children—Mrs. Katheryn Brandon, Baird, Robert Brandon; m. 2d, Mrs. Annie Reynolds Macomber, Jan. 2, 1911; children—Charles Reynolds Macomber (foster son), Rosalind Susanne; m. 3d, Mrs. Mary Parsons Sowers, Jan. 18, 1930. Ordained deacon, 1899, and priest, 1900, Episcopal Church; rector Calvary Church, Toledo, Ohio, 1899-1901, St. Paul's Ch., Newport, Ky., 1901-04; Grace Ch., Cincinnati, O., 1904-06, St. Mark's Ch., Cheyenne, Wyo., 1906-09, St. Mark's Ch., Toledo, 1909-18; elected bishop of Marquette, Nov. 6, 1917, consecrated Feb. 7, 1918, now retired. Formerly bishop in charge Episcopal Chs. in Europe. Trustee Kenyon Coll., pres. Nat. Ch. League. Mem. Delta Tau Delta (Distinguished Service Chapter). S.A.R. Progressive Republican. Mason (33°). Clubs: Exchange, Country, Marquette. Author: The Invisible Temple; The Challenge; etc., also lecturer. Home: 3807 Hawk St., San Diego 3, Calif. Ranch: Hacienda De La Luz, Dulzura, Calif. Died Feb. 7, 1948; buried Cheyenne, Wyo.

HARRIS, Thomas Jefferson, otolaryngologist; b. Claremont, N.H., July 26, 1865; s. Thomas J. and Myra (Beaumont) H.; desc. of Walter Harris, Dorchester, Mass., 1632; and Elder Wm. Brewster of the Mayflower; A.B., Dartmouth, 1886, A.M., 1889; M.D., U. of Pa., 1889; grad. work, U. of Berlin, 1890-91; m. Lena Breed, Oct. 21, 1896; 1 dau., Elizabeth (Mrs. Francis Lowell Barton). Practiced in N.Y. City since 1891; formerly prof. diseases of nose and throat, New York Post-Grad. Med. Sch., and jr. surgeon (throat), Manhattan Eye, Ear and Throat Hosp.; cons. otolaryngologist New York Post-Grad. Hosp. Lt. col., Med. Corps, U.S. Army, 1918-19, in charge dept. otolaryngology, Gen. Hosp. No. 14, Ft. Oglethorpe, Ga., and dir. sch. of laryngology, Camp Greenleaf, Ga. Pres. Jennie Clarkson Home for Children, 1922-1940; former sec. N.Y. City Bapt. Mission Society since 1914; former dir. Baptist Fresh Air Home Soc., Westchester Hist. Society. Fellow Am. Coll. Surgeons; mem. A.M.A., Med. Soc. State of N.Y., Am. Laryngol., Rhinol. and Otol. Soc. (sec. 1906-16, pres. 1916-17), Am. Laryngol. Assn., Am. Otol. Soc. (pres. 1925-26), N.Y. Laryngol. Soc. (sec. 1928-32, pres. 1932), N.Y. Physicians Mut. Aid Assn. (pres. 1930), Theta Delta Chi; mem. permanent com. Internat. Oto-Laryngol. Congress; hon. dir. Am. Bd. Oto-Laryngology. Baptist. Club: Quill (pres. 1907-08). Formerly historian of Town of Scarsdale. Home: Hopatcong, N.J. Address: care Irving Trust Co., 100 E. 42d St., New York, N.Y. Died Mar. 14, 1943.

HARRIS, William, Jr., theatrical mgr.; b. Boston, Mass., July 22, 1884; s. William and Rachel (Freefield) H.; prep. edn., Berkeley Sch., N.Y. City; spl. student, Columbia, 4 yrs. (no degree); m. Sibyl Klein, Apr. 23, 1907; m. 2d, Oello Houston, May 17, 1929. Theatrical business, New York, since 1912. Producer: "The Yellow Jacket"; "Twin Beds"; "Abraham Lincoln"; "Mary Stuart"; "Robert E. Lee"; "The Outsider"; "Outward Bound"; "In Love with Love"; "Madame Pierre"; "The Criminal Code"; "The Greeks Had a Word for It," etc. Club: Lambs. Address: 130 W. 44th St., New York, N.Y.
Died Sep. 2, 1946.

HARRISON, Harvey Thomas, lawyer; b. Lockesburg, Ark., Jan. 6, 1884; s. William Ringgold and Alice Virginia (Grady) H.; A.B., Hendrix Coll., 1906, LL.D., 1940; m. Ellen Evans McCaughey, Dec. 14, 1911; 1 son, John McCaughey. Admitted to Ark. bar, 1911; practiced at Fordyce, Ark., 1911-15, Little Rock since Mar. 1915; partner Buzbee, Harrison & Wright since Ja. 1916. Mem. Am. Bar Assn., Bar Assn. of Ark. (pres. 1939-40), Little Rock Bar Assn. Democrat. Methodist. Clubs: XV, Country (Little Rock). Home: 1915 Battery St. Office: 1025 Pyramid Bldg., Little Rock, Ark. Died Sep. 29, 1942.

HARRISON, James Jabez, pub. official; b. Hot Springs, Ark., June 26, 1891; s. Rev. William R. and Alice Virginia (Grady) H.; A.B., Hendrix Coll., 1914; m. Julia Turner, Apr. 28, 1920; children—Virginia, Julia. In life ins. business, 1922-41; v.p. Home Life Ins. Co., 1922-30; state mgr. Union Central Life Ins. Co., 1931-41. State director of Nat. Emergency Council and Office of Government Reports, 1934-43; chmn. Ark. State Planning Bd.; vice-chmn. State Defense Council; mem. exec. com. Am. Soc. Planning Officials; dir. of Ark. State Y.M.C.A.; chmn. bd. trustees Hendrix Coll.; dir. Ark. chapter Nat. Foundation for Infantile Paralysis. Commd. capt. inf., U.S. Army, 1917; maj., 1918. Comdr. Ark. Dept. Am. Legion, 1919 (one of founders; mem. rehabilitation ins. advisory com.); pres. Little Rock Chamber of Commerce, 1930. Democrat. Methodist. Home: 209 Ridgeway. Office: Donaghey Bldg., Little Rock, Ark. Died May 1, 1943.

HARRISON, John B., jurist; b. Anderson County, Ky., Apr. 10, 1861; m. Etta Wallach, Apr. 20, 1891. Admitted to Tex. bar, 1888, and began practice in Wheeler County; later moved to Oklahoma City; then asso. justice Supreme Court of Okla.; now retired. Home: 133 N.E. 14th St., Oklahoma City, Okla. Died Apr. 12, 1947.

HARRISON, Mary Scott Lord (Mrs. Benjamin Harrison); b. Honesdale, Pa., Apr. 30, 1858; d. Russell Farnham Lord (chief engr. and gen. mgr. Del. & Hudson Canal Co.) and Elizabeth (Scott) Lord; ed. by private tutors, and at Mrs. Moffat's Sch., Princeton, N.J., and Elmira Coll.; m. Walter Erskine, s. Samuel E. Dimmick, atty. gen. Pa., 1881 (the former died Jan. 1882); m. 2d, Apr. 6, 1896, Benjamin Harrison (President of the United States, 1889-93, who died Mar. 13, 1901); 1 dau., Elizabeth (Mrs. James Blaine Walker, Jr.). Club: Cosmopolitan (New York). Home: 29 E. 64th St., New York, N.Y. Died Jan. 5, 1948.

HARRISON, Milton (Whately); b. Brooklyn, N.Y., Feb. 12, 1889; s. William Henry and Martha Ella (Jackson) H.; grad. St. Lawrence U., Brooklyn Law School; New York U. School of Accounts, Commerce and Finance; grad. Am. Institute Banking; m. Irene H. Seiberling, Dec. 25, 1923; children—Sally Anne, Gertrude Faith, Robert Frank. Teacher commercial and banking law, 1912-15; sec. savings bank section Am. Bankers Assn., 1914-19; asst. ednl. dir., Am. Inst. Banking, 1915-19; dir. in charge banks and schools in war savings orgns., Washington, D.C., 1917-18; exec. mgr. Savings Banks Assn., State of N.Y., 1919-20; pres. Natamsa Pub. Co., National Ry. Service Corp.; dir. Franklin Nat. Bank, 1922-24; dir. Coal & Iron Nat. Bank, Seiberling Rubber Co.; trustee and member of executive committee Bowery Savings Bank; chmn. bd. Midland Continental Railroad. Pres. of the Security Owners Assn., Inc., 1924-1935; consultant and mem. governing bd. Railroad Security Owners Assn., Inc., 1935-39; hon. v.p. Nat. Assn. of Mutual Savings Banks; mng. dir. Save-to-Travel Assn., 1924-28; president, Thrift Economics Consultants, Inc. Mem. Com. on International Trade and Improvement, 1921-24; publisher and editor Savings Bank Journal; chmn. debenture com. Equitable Office Building Corp., New York, 1940-41; treas. and mem. exec. com. Citizens Emergency Com. on Non-defense Expenditures, 1941-43; chmn. Housing Authority, City of Yonkers, N.Y., 1943-45; mem. bd. trustees and asst. treas. Am. Inst. of City of N.Y.; economic consultant, 1939-46; dir. Research in Public Points of View; dir. Citizens Nat. Com.; mem. Chamber Commerce State of N.Y. (com. public service in Metropolitan Dist. 1924-27), National Assn. State Chambers of Commerce (mem. com. on Federal finance), American Economic Assn., Nat. Tax Assn., Nat. Publishers' Assn., Am. Inst. Polit. Science, Soc. Colonial Wars, Huguenot Soc., St. Nicholas Soc., Soc. of Am. Wars, Phi Delta Phi; hon. mem. Vt. Bankers Assn., N.Y. Chapter Am. Inst. Banking. Clubs: Union League; Metropolitan (Washington, D.C.); Coreleigh. Home: 56 Highland Circle, Bronxville, N.Y. Office: 100 Stevens Av., Mt. Vernon, N.Y.; 110 E. 42nd St., New York 17, N.Y. Died Aug. 8, 1949.

HARRISON, Thomas Perrin, prof. English; born Abbeville, S.C., Oct. 11, 1864; s. Francis Eugene and Mary Eunice (Perrin) H.; Abbeville Acad.; B.S., The Citadel, 1886, LL.D., 1929; Ph.D., Johns Hopkins, 1891; m. Adelia Lake Leftwich, Jan. 9, 1894; children—James Leftwich, Thomas Perrin, Florence Leftwich, Lewis Wardlaw. Instr. English, The Citadel, 1886-88; asso. prof. English, Clemson Coll., S.C., 1891-96; prof. English, Davidson (N.C.) Coll., 1896-1909; prof. English, N.C. State Coll., since 1909, dean, 1910-35. Y.M.C.A. ednl. sec., A.E.F., in France, July 1918-Apr. 1919; with Army Edn. Corps, A.E.F., France, Apr.-July 1919. Mem. Nat. Council Teachers of English, N.C. State Teachers' Assembly, Kappa Alpha (Southern). Democrat. Presbyterian. Mason. Home: 1800 Park Drive, Raleigh, N.C. Died Nov. 1, 1949.

HARRISON, William Benjamin, business exec.; b. Louisville, Ky., July 28, 1889; s. William and Virginia L. (Trezevant) H.; B.L., U. of Va., 1910; m. Margaret W. Allis, June 4, 1912; children—William H., Winston P., Penelope A. Dixon, Margaret T. Reynolds, Dorothy F. Seelbach. Adjuster, Travelers Ins. Co., Louisville, Ky., 1910-12; asst. mgr. Am. Surety Co. of New York, 1912-17; sec., treas. Foundry Products Co., 1919-22; pres. Ky. Refrigerating Co., 1922-30; pres. Louisville Indsl. Foundation since 1934; chmn. Mengel Co.; dir. B. F. Avery & Sons Co., Puritan Cordage Mills, Wheatley Foods, Inc., Porcelain Metals Corp., Morton Packing Co., Castlewood Mfg. Co. Dir. Louisville Bd. of Trade. Mayor of Louisville, 1927-33. Served as capt. F.A., U.S. Army, 1917-19. Mem. Louisville Area Development Assn., Zeta Psi. Republican. Presbyterian. Clubs: Pendennis, Louisville Country. Home: 1460 St. James Ct. Office: Columbia Bldg., Louisville, Ky. Died July 13, 1948.

HARROLD, Charles Cotten, surgeon; b. Americus, Ga., Dec. 9, 1878; s. Uriah Bullock and Mary Elizabeth (Fogle) H.; grad. high sch., Americus, 1895; B.S., U. of Ga., 1898; A.M., Columbia, 1902, M.D., 1902; m. Helen Sophia Shaw, Oct. 23, 1906; children—Helen Shaw (Mrs. Sinclair Alfred Frederick), Mary Fogle (Mrs. John Emory Seals), Charles Cotton. Began practice, Macon, 1904; limited to surgery since 1911; pres. Middle Ga. Hosp. since 1925; dir. Citizens & Southern Nat. Bank since 1929; v.p. Macon Federal Savings & Loan Assn. since 1930. Served in Ga. Nat. Guard, 1904-16; maj. U.S.M.C. 1916-19, World War. Fellow Am. Coll. Surgeons A.A.A.S.; mem. A.M.A., Am. Soc. for Control of Cancer, Soc. for Ga. Archæology (pres.), Phi Beta Kappa, Phi Delta Theta. Democrat. Episcopalian. Mason. Clubs: Kiwanis, Idle Hour Country. Contbr. surg. articles. Home: 550 Orange St. Office: 700 Spring St., Macon, Ga. Died Oct. 11, 1948.

HARROP, George Argale, Jr., med. research; b. Peru, Ill., Nov. 5, 1890; s. George Argale and Mary Belle (Cole) H.; U. of Wis., 1908-10; A.B., Harvard, 1912; M.D., Johns Hopkins Univ., 1916; research, U. of Copenhagen, 1920-21; m. Esther Caldwell, Mar. 16, 1924; children—George Argale III, William Caldwell, David Cole, Esther. Intern and asst. resident phys. Johns Hopkins Hosp., 1916-21; resident phys. and instr. in medicine, Columbia U., 1921-23; asso. prof. medicine, Peking U. Med. Coll., China, 1923-24; asso. prof. medicine, Johns Hopkins, 1925-33 in charge chem. lab. and work in diseases of metabolism and endocrinology; dir. of research Squibb Inst. for Med. Research, New Brunswick, N.J., since 1938; v.p., dir. of research, E. R. Squibb and Sons, N.Y., since 1943. Fellow Am. Scandinavian Foundation; mem. A.M.A., Assn. Am. Physicians, Am. Coll. Physicians, Am. Soc. for Clin. Investigation, Am. Soc. Biol. Chemists, Soc. for Exptl. Biology and Medicine, Société Biologique (Paris), Cosmopolitan Clinical Clubs, New York Academy of Medicine, American Clinical and Climatol. Association, Phi Beta Kappa, Alpha Omega Alpha, Phi Kappa Psi, Nu Sigma Nu, Sigma Xi. Clubs: Harvard University (New York); Nassau (Princeton); Maryland (Baltimore). Author: Management of Diabetes, 1925; Diet in Disease, 1930; also numerous articles on metabolism, diabetes, the use of diet in therapy, etc. Home: 33 Cleveland Lane, Princeton, N.J. Died Aug. 4, 1945.

HARRY, Joseph Edward, univ. prof.; b. Harford County, Md., Oct. 1, 1863; s. David and Maria Jane H.; grad. State Normal Sch. of Md., 1880; A.B., Johns Hopkins, 1886, Ph.D., 1889; post-grad. study in Germany, 1887; m. Cora Day, 1890. Prof. Greek and German, Georgetown Coll., Ky., 1889-1900; prof. Greek, U. of Cincinnati, 1900-16, dean Coll. of Liberal Arts, 1904-06, acting-pres., 1904, dean Grad. Sch., 1906-16; writer in New York, and in service of U.S. Govt., 1916-19; lecturer at Sorbonne, Paris, 1919-22; traveler, writer, and master of languages in various institutions, 1922-26; asso. prof. classics, St. Stephen's Coll. (now Bard Coll.), Columbia U., 1926-28, Hoffman prof. Greek lang. and lit., 1928-39, now prof. emeritus in residence. Mem. bd. of trustees Am. Iona Soc. since 1925. Mem. Am. Philol. Assn., Am. Oriental Soc., Archaeol. Inst. America, Internat. Congress Archaeologists; sec. Greek sect. Congress of Arts and Sciences, St. Louis Expn., 1904. Republican. Mem. Soc. of Friends. Editor: The Hippolytus of Euripides, 1900; Prometheus Bound of Aeschylus, 1905. Author: The Greek Tragic Poets; also many articles on Greek Philology in tech. periodicals and encys. Translation: Antigone of Sophocles; Dog and Dogs; Greek Tragedy, Vol. I, Aeschylus and Sophocles, 1933; Vol. II, Euripides; and other books, and articles in the Golden Book and other mags. Home: Annandale-on-Hudson, N.Y. Died Aug. 12, 1949.

HARSHA, William McIntire, surgeon; b. Harshaville, O., June 15, 1855; s. William B. and Rachel (McIntire) H.; B.S. and A.B., Nat. Normal U., Lebanon, O.; studied medicine at U. of Mich.; 1st yr., Cincinnati, 2d yr.; M.D., Chicago Med. Coll. 1883; m. Adelia S. Hutchinson, June 1, 1880; children—William Thomas, Edward Houston. Practiced at Cerro Gordo and Decatur, Ill., until 1890, then at Chicago; emeritus prof. surgery, College of Medicine, U. of Ill., Chicago; surgeon to St. Luke's Hosp. Fellow Am. Coll. Surgeons (a founder); mem. Am. Med. Assn., Chicago Surg. Society (pres. 1916-17), Inst. of Medicine, Chicago (emeritus). Republican. Club: University. Extensive contbr. to med. jours. Address: 5121 Kimbark Av., Chicago, Ill. Died Feb. 26, 1943.

HART, Albert Bushnell, univ. prof.; b. Clarksville, Pa., July 1, 1854; s. Dr. Albert Gailord and Mary Crosby (Hornell) H.; A.B., Harvard, 1880; Ph.D., Freiburg, Baden, 1883; LL.D., Richmond, 1902, Tufts, 1905, Western Reserve, 1907; Litt.D., Geneva, Switzerland, 1909; m. Mary Hurd Putnam, July 11, 1889. Instr. Am. history, 1883-86, history, 1886-87, asst. prof. history, 1887-97, prof. history, 1897-1910, prof. govt., 1910-26, prof. emeritus since 1926, Harvard U. Mem. Mass. Constl. Conv., and chmn. Com. on Amendment and Codification, 1917-19; mem. and historian of U.S. Commn. for Celebration of 200th Anniversary of Birth of George Washington, 1926-32; chmn. and mem. Mass. George Washington Commn., 1932. Joint editor Harvard Graduates' Mag., 1894-1902, Am. Hist. Rev., 1895-1909. Pres. Am. Hist. Assn., 1909, Am. Polit. Science Assn., 1912; mem. council Mass. Hist. Soc., 1908; mem. Pa. and Minn. hist. socs. Trustee Howard U., 1930-37; mem. bd. govs. Mooseheart, Ill. Author: Formation of the Union, 1892, new edit., 1925; Guide to the Study of American History (with Edward Channing), 1897; same, with Edward Channing and F. J. Turner, 1912; Salmon Portland Chase, 1899; Foundations of American Foreign Policy, 1901; Actual Govt., 1903, 08, 18; Essentials of American History, 1905; Slavery and Abolition, 1906; National Ideals Historically Traced, 1907; Manual of American History, Diplomacy and Government, 1908; Southern South, 1911; Obvious Orient, 1911; Monroe Doctrine, 1915; New American History, 1917; School History of the U.S., 1917; Wall Maps of American History, 1918, 2d edit., 1926; Handbook of the War (with A. C. Lovejoy), 1917; America at War, 1917; Causes of the War (Harper's Pict. Lib.), 1920; We and Our History, 1923; Wall Maps of American Government, 1927. Editor: Epochs of American History (4 vols.), 1891-1926; American History Told by Contemporaries (5 vols.), 1898-1929; American Citizen Series (7 vols.), since 1899; Source Book of American History, 1899, enlarged edit., 1924; Source Readers in American History (5 vols.), 1901-27; The American Nation (28 vols.), 1903-18; American Patriots and Statesmen (5 vols.), 1916; Am. Year Book, 1911-20, 1926-32; Commonwealth History of Massachusetts (5 vols.), 1927-29; George Washington Pamphlets, 1930-32. Joint editor: American History Leaflets, 1895-1913; Cyclopædia of American Governments (3 vols.), 1914. Editor of Roosevelt Ency., since 1927; chmn. bd. Current History Associates, Current History, 1923-31. Author, joint author or editor of about 100 volumes. Home: 8 Plympton St., Cambridge, Mass. Address: 46 Widener Library, Cambridge, Mass. Died June 16, 1943.

HART, Boies Chittenden, banker; b. Adrian, Mich., Jan. 27, 1885; s. Herman V. C. and Clara (Boies) H.; prep edn., Trinity Hall, Washington, Pa., 1899-1903; U. of Mich., 1903-04; m. Ruth Higby Hart, Dec. 30, 1909; 1 son, Boies Chittenden; m. 2d, Eloise Grayston. Gen. mgr. Big Horn Irrigation Co., Basin, Wyo., 1905-12; mem. Wyo. Ho. of Rep., 1911-12; pres. Pioneer Trust & Savings Bank, Basin, 1912-16; with Nat. City Bank of New York since 1917, at Moscow, 1917-18, Sao Paulo, Brazil, 1918-20, Pernambuco, 1920-21, again at Sao Paulo, 1921-24; mgr. Brazilian branches, 1924-27; v.p. in charge South Am. Dist., 1927-31, v.p. in charge of Far Eastern Dist., 1931-43, v.p. and mgr. Overseas Div. since Jan. 1943. Mem. Psi. Upsilon. Republican. Episcopalian. Mason (32°). Clubs: Jockey (Buenos Aires); Jockey (Rio de Janeiro); Automobile (Sao Paulo); American (Shanghai and Tokyo); Metropolitan, Washington Union League; India House (New York). Address: 55 Wall St., New York. Died June 15, 1946; buried in Oakwood Cemetery, Adrian, Mich.

HART, Frances Noyes, author; b. Silver Spring, Md., Aug. 10, 1890; d. Frank Brett and Janet Thurston (Newbold) Noyes; ed. pvt. schs., Farmington, and Florence, Italy, and the Sorbonne and Collège de France, Paris, extension courses, Columbia U.; m. Edward Henry Hart, Jan. 6, 1921; children—Janet Mary, Ann. Served as a translator with Naval Intelligence Bur. 6 mos., 1917-18; Y.M.C.A. canteen worker in France, 1918-19. Mem. Authors' League America. Clubs: Colony, National Woman's Country. Author: Mark, 1913; My A.E.F., 1920; Contact, 1923; The Bellamy Trial, 1927; Hide in the Dark, 1929; Pigs in Clover, 1931; The Crooked Lane, 1934; also short stories in mags. Address: The Colony Club, Park Av. and 63d St., New York. Died Oct. 25, 1943.

HART, Howard Stanley, mfr.; b. New Britain, Conn., July 9, 1867; s. William Henry and Martha (Peck) H.; student pub. schs. New Britain, Conn.; m. Bessie Stanley, March 26, 1891 (dec. 1935), children—Alice (Mrs. Stanley Robbins Eddy), William Henry, Stanley; m. 2d, Helen Cromwell Howland, May 2, 1936. Est. Hart & Cooley Mfg. Co., Chicago, Ill., pres. 1891-1900; est. Hart & Cooley Co., Inc., registers and grilles, New Britain, Conn., pres., 1901-12, chmn. since 1912; est. Fafnir Bearing Co., New Britain, pres. 1911-20, chmn. bd., 1920-30, chmn. exec. com. since 1911; est. Hart & Cooley Mfg. Co. of Holland, Mich., dir. since 1928; dir. Tuttle & Bailey Co., Goss and Deleeu Mach. Co. Trustee Martha's Vineyard (Mass.) Hosp. Mem. Am. Soc. M.E., Nat. Econ. League. Republican. Conglist. Clubs: New Britain Shuttlemeadow (New Britain, Conn.); Edgartown (Mass.) Yacht; Vineyard Haven Yacht (Martha's Vineyard, Mass.) Home: Vineyard Haven, Mass. Office: Hart & Cooley Co., Inc., New Britain, Conn. Died Mar. 8, 1944.

HART, John William, banker; b. Ogden, Utah, Nov. 14, 1866; s. John L. and Martha (Barton) H.; ed. pub. and high schs. to 1884; m. Elizabeth J. Hogge, Dec. 2, 1885; children—John W., Elizabeth E., Clarence, Charles O., Vera (dec.), George L., Martha (dec.), Sarah Z., Veda L., David F., Cecil E., Joseph I., Ivy Katheryn. Began as sheep raiser, 1886, later entered cattle business; located on farm in Snake River Valley, Ida., 1896; v.p. C. A. Smith Mercantile Co.; pres. First Nat. Bank, Jefferson State Bank, Menau, Ida.; pres. Snake River Valley Dairy Products Co.; dir. Farmers & Merchants Bank, Idaho Falls; dir., gen. supt., Wood Live Stock Co. Chmn. Water Com. Dist. No. 36, covering whole of Snake River Valley. Mem. Ida. Ho. of Rep., 1898-99, State Senate, 4 terms, 1905-10, 1913-14 (pres. pro tem. and Rep. leader last 2 terms); acting gov. of Ida. 30 days, Jan. 1910; mem. Rep. Nat. Com., 1912-24; mem. State Rep. Com., Utah. Trustee Acad. of Idaho (sec. bd.), 1902-12; pres. bd. trustees Ricks Coll.; trustee Idaho Falls Latter Day Saints Hosp.; mem. auditing com. Ch. of Jesus Christ of Latter Day Saints; pres. Rigby Stake. Home: Rigby, Ida. Died April 5, 1936.

HART, Joseph Kinmont, educator; b. nr. Columbia City, Ind., Feb. 16, 1876; s. David N. and Lucy (Kinmont) H.; A.B., Franklin (Ind.) Coll., 1900; Ph.D., U. of Chicago, 1909; m. 2d, Frances Stuyvesant Uhrig, 1929. Prof. philosophy and psychology, Baker U., Kan., 1909-10; asst. prof. edn., U. of Wash., 1910-15; prof. edn., Reed Coll., Portland, Ore., 1916-19; editor dept. of edn., The Survey, 1920-26; prof. of edn., U. of Wis., 1927-30, same and head of dept., Vanderbilt, 1930-1934; prof. edn. Teachers College, Columbia Univ., 1934-40. Author: Critical Study of Current Theories of Moral Education, 1910; Democracy in Education, 1918; Community Organization, 1920; The Discovery of Intelligence, 1924; Social Life and Institutions, 1924; Light from the North, 1927; Adult Education, 1927; Prophet of a Nameless God, 1927; Inside Experience, 1927; A Social Interpretation of Education, 1929; Creative Moments in Education, 1931; Education for an Age of Power, 1935; An Introduction to the Social Studies, 1937; Mind in Transition, 1938. Address: 44 Worth Av., Hudson, N.Y. Died March 10, 1949.

HART, Sophie Chantal, college prof.; b. Boston, Aug. 20, 1868; d. Eugene and Anne Hart; A.B., Radcliffe Coll., Cambridge, Mass., 1892; A.M., U. of Mich., 1898; unmarried. Tutor in English, Wellesley Coll., 1892, instr., 1893-97, asso. prof. English and head of dept., 1897-1906, prof. rhetoric and English composition and head of dept., 1906-37, prof. emeritus since 1937. Conglist. Clubs: Twentieth Century, Authors. Editor: Gareth and Lynette, Launcelot and Elaine and The Passing of Arthur, 1903; Nicholas Rowe, 1907, Carlyle's Essay on Burns and Songs of Burns, 1912; The Coming of Arthur, 1915; The Holy Grail, 1915. Home: Wellesley, Mass. Died Dec. 8, 1948.

HART, William S., motion pictures; b. Newburgh, N.Y., Dec. 6, 1872; ed. in Minn. and Dak.; married; 1 son, William S. Début as actor at age of 19 with Daniel E. Bandmann; leading man with Modjeska, Madame Rhea and Julia Arthur; played rôle of Messala in "Ben Hur" in New York 2 yrs.; starred as Cash Hawkins in "The Squaw Man," also in "The Virginian"; appeared in "The Barrier," "The Trail of the Lonesome Pine," etc. Began in motion pictures, 1914, with New York Motion Picture Corp.; made first 5-reel picture, "The Bargain"; produced, 1917-24, at his own studio and released through Famous Players Lasky—later Paramount—27 William S. Hart pictures that grossed approximately half a million dollars each. Has appeared in "The Passing of Two-Gun Hicks"; "The Aryan"; "The Disciple"; "The Patriot"; "The Apostle of Vengeance"; "The Narrow Trail"; "Wagon Tracks"; "The Toll Gate"; "The Cradle of Courage"; "The Testing Block"; "O'Malley of the Mounted"; "Travelin' On"; "Tumbleweeds," 1926. Author: A Lighter of Flames, 1923; My Life East and West (autobiography), 1929; Hoofbeats, 1933; The Law on Horseback and Other Stories, 1935; And All Points West, 1940. Home: Horseshoe Ranch, Newhall, Calif. Died June 23, 1946.

HARTER, George Abram, former univ. pres.; b. Leitersburg, Md., Nov. 7, 1853; s. Peter Koontz and Mary (Poe) H.; A.B., St. John's Coll., Md., 1878, A.M., 1880, Ph.D., 1892; LL.D., U. of Del., 1925; m. Ellen Studdiford Graff, 1882; 1 dau., Elinor Theodora (Mrs. R. W. Kumler). Asst. prof. mathematics and Latin, St. John's Coll., 1878-80; prin. Leitersburg grammar sch., 1880-81; prin. of acad., Hagerstown, Md., 1881-85; prof. mathematics and modern langs., U. of Del., 1885-88, mathematics and physics since 1888, pres., 1896-1914. Mem. A.A.A.S., Am. Math. Soc., Am. Math. Assn., Soc. for Promotion Engring. Edn., Am. Statis. Assn. Home: Newark, Del. Died July 23, 1943.

HARTER, J. Francis, ex-congressman; b. Perry, N.Y., Sept. 1, 1897; s. Eugene L. and Elizabeth (Battin) H.; LL.B., U. of Buffalo, 1919; m. Ruth Wiesseman, 1922 (died June 25, 1930); children—Charles Eugene, Geraldine Ruth; m. 2d, Lillian Unholz, July 28, 1932; 1 son, Russell Gordon. Admitted to N.Y. bar, 1920, since practiced in Buffalo, N.Y.; mem. 76th Congress (1939-41), 41st N.Y. Dist. Served at C.O.T.C., Camp Lee, Va., World War. Mem. Am. Legion, Delta Chi. Republican. Baptist. Mason, Moose, Eagle. Home: 120 Ruskin Rd., Eggertsville, N.Y. Office: Prudential Bldg., Buffalo, N.Y. Died Dec. 20, 1947.

HARTIGAN, Charles Conway, naval officer; b. Middletown, N.Y., Sept. 13, 1882; s. William C. and Minnie (Conway) H.; B.S., U.S. Naval Acad., 1906; m. Margaret Thompson, May 5, 1910; children—Margaret Alden (Mrs. James A. B. Barton), Charles Conway (lt., U.S. Navy). Commd. ensign, U.S. Navy, 1906, and advanced through the grades to rear admiral, 1941; retired July 1941; served in Mexican campaign, 1913; comd. U.S.S. Cassin (destroyer), June 1918-Mar. 1919; mem. U.S. Naval mission to Brazil, 1919-21, 1925-27; comd. Destroyer Div. 25 (U.S.S. Isherwood, flagship), 1927-29; U.S. naval attaché, Peking, China, 1929-32; comd. U.S.S. Relief, 1932-34; Office Chief of Naval Operations, 1934-36; Naval War Coll., Newport, 1936-37; comd. U.S.S. Oklahoma, 1937-39; Office Chief of Naval Operations, 1939-41. Awarded Medal of Honor, 1913; Mexican campaign, World War, Dominican campaign and Yangtse campaign medals. Clubs: Chevy Chase; Army and Navy; New York Yacht. Home: Edgewater, Ann Arundel County, Md. Died Feb. 25, 1944.

HARTLEY, James Joseph, bishop; b. June 6, 1858; ed. Mt. St. Mary's Coll. and Holy Angel's Sem., Niagara, N.Y. Consecrated bishop of Columbus, O., Feb. 25, 1904. Roman Catholic. Home: 198 E. Broad St., Columbus, O.* Died 1944.

HARTMAN, Edwin Mitman, educator; b. near Applebachville, Bucks County, Pa., Oct. 6, 1869; s. William Fulmer and Susan (Mitman) H.; student State Normal Sch., Kutztown, Pa., 1890-91; A.B., Franklin and Marshall College, 1895, A.M., 1898 (Pd.D., same college, 1921); grad. Theol. Seminary of Reformed Church in U.S., 1900; post-grad. study, U. of Pa.; m. Helen Russell Stahr (A.B., Wellesley, 1894), d. of John S. Stahr, June 5, 1905; children—Frances Andrews (Mrs. Louis S. May), William Fulmer, Charles Stahr. Teacher pub. schs., Bucks County, Pa., 1886-90; prin. Franklin and Marshall Acad. 1897-1943; asst. to pres. Franklin & Marshall Coll. since 1943, directing financial campaign, 1903-07; sec. dept. field work and dir. financial campaign of Forward Movement, Ref. Ch. in U.S., 1919-25; chmn. Civil Service Commn. for Lancaster Dept. of Police, 1926-30; chmn. Lancaster City Shade Tree Commn., 1929-42; pres. Head Masters' Club of Phila. Dist., 1928; vice-chmn. Alliance of Reformed Chs. holding Presbyn. System (Western Sect.), 1939-40. Mem. Pa.

German Soc., Phi Beta Kappa, Phi Sigma Kappa. Democrat. Home: Lancaster, Pa. Died June 20, 1947.

HARTMAN, John Peter, lawyer; b. nr. Harveysburg, Ind., July 3, 1857; s. John P. and Mary Anne (Sines) H.; student U. of Neb., 1876-80, hon. LL.M., 1908, LL.D., 1930; m. Caroline E. Dryden, Sept. 16, 1883; children—Dwight D., Harold H., Robert N. Admitted to Neb. bar, 1882, and began practice at Kearney; moved to Tacoma, Washington, 1891, to Seattle, 1896; largely retired from practice of law, January 1, 1943, but continues as special partner with sons, Dwight and Harold, Fred W. Catlett, David H. Jarvis and Gail M. Williams, under firm name Catlett, Hartman, Jarvis & Williams; was in charge of first railroad built into Butte, Montana; a promoter and builder of the Brackett Wagon Road over White Pass, Alaska, also of White Pass & Yukon Railway, the Northwestern Steamship Co.; secured terminals and franchises at Seattle and Tacoma for Harriman Lines, 1906-09; one of 14 organizers of the Wash. Good Roads Assn., of which was pres., now life mem.; dir. many corps. and promoter of farm orgns.; author of act creating Mt. Rainier Nat. Park. Mem. Rep. Nat. Conv. that nominated Benjamin Harrison for President, and often delegate to Republican Party conventions. One of citizens active in promotion and completion of Grand Coulee Dam and Columbia Basin Reclamation; now also engaged in war work. Member of Loyal Legion, American and Washington State bars. Republican. Presbyterian. Clubs: Rainier, Arctic, Press. Wrote important parts of "Building a State," printed by Washington State Hist. Society, 1940. Privately pub. and distributed many addresses of which most prominent are "Creation of Mt. Rainier National Park" and "Epic of American Transportation," also has prepared about 100 volts. of briefs before appellate courts. Active in general development in Wash. Mem. Grange (7°). Home: Bellevue, Wash. Office: Hoge Bldg., Seattle, Wash. Died Oct. 29, 1945.

HARTMAN, Leon Wilson, univ. pres.; b. Downsville, N.Y., June 18, 1876; s. Henry and Sarah Eleanor (Wilson) H.; B.S., Cornell Univ., 1898, A.M., same, 1899; Ph.D., Univ. of Pa., 1903; Univ. of Göttingen, 1903-04; m. Edith Dabele Kast, July 31, 1907; children—Margaret Eleanor, Sara Louise (dec.), Paul Leon, Charles Frederick, David Kast. Asst. in physics, Cornell U., 1900-01; prof. physics, Kan. Agrl. Coll., 1901-02; Fraser fellow in physics, U. of Pa., 1902-03, Tyndale fellow, 1903-04; instr. physics, Cornell, U., 1904-05; asst. prof. physics, 1905-06, asso. prof., 1906-09, U. of Utah; prof. physics, U. of Nevada since 1909, acting pres., 1938, pres. since 1939. With Utah Power and Light Co., summer, 1906, U. of Utah, summers, 1907, 08, 09, U. of Calif., summers, 1924, 25; investigator Nela Research Lab. of Gen. Electric Co., Cleveland, O., summer, 1916; with Pacific Telephone and Telegraph Co., summer, 1927, Leeds & Northrup Co., Phila., summers, 1928, 29, Bureau of Standards, Washington, D.C., autumn 1929 and summer 1930. Mem. A.A.A.S., Am. Phys. Soc., Utah Acad. Science, Illuminating Engring. Soc., Am. Assn. Univ. Profs., Sigma Xi, Phi Kappa Phi. Author: Laboratory Manual of Experiments in Physics, 1906; An Introduction to Electrical Measurements, 1930; Measurement of Coefficient of Self-Inductance in Terms of Resistance and Time (joint author), 1940. Contbr. to various scientific journals, articles on raditaion, pyrometry, acetylene, Nernst lamp, spectro-photometry, visibility, etc. Home: Reno, Nev. Died Aug. 27, 1943.

HARTMANN, Jacob Wittmer, college prof.; b. Brooklyn, N.Y., Oct. 23, 1881; s. Jacob, Jr., and Mary (Wittmer) H.; B.S., Coll. City of N.Y., 1901; student Columbia, 1901-06, Ph.D., 1912; m. Marie Schwartje, June 18, 1908. Tutor in German, Coll. City of N.Y., 1901-06; prof. English lang. and lit., Imperial Higher Commercial Sch., Kobe, Japan, 1906-07; instr. German, Coll. City of N.Y., 1908-15, asst. prof. German language and lit., 1915-19; prof. German, St. John's Coll., 1925-27; prof. Germanic langs., L.I. Univ. since 1927. Mem. Modern Lang. Assn. Am., Soc. Advancement Scandinavian Study, Am. Scandinavian Soc., Brooklyn C. of C. Author: Göngu-Hrolfssaga—a Study in Old Norse Philology, 1912. Translator: Hellas, Travels in Greece (Georg Brandes), 1926; Mrs. Socrates (by Fritz Mauthner), 1926; The Mantle of Caesar (by F. Gundolf), 1928; Days in the Sun (by M. A. Nexö), 1929; also translations of brochures and articles from the German, Swedish, Danish, Norwegian, Russian and mod. Icelandic langs. Home: 194 Park Pl., Brooklyn, N.Y. Died Jan. 13, 1934.

HARTNEY, Harold Evans, tech. adviser in aviation; b. Packenham, Ont., Can., Apr. 19, 1888; s. James Harvey and Annie Evans (Cuthbert) H.; B.A., U. of Toronto, 1911; grad. U. of Saskatchewan, 1912; student Law Soc. of Saskatchewan, 1911-14; married to Irene McGeary, November 11, 1914; children—Mrs. Frederick Yeager, Mrs. Robert Gensel, Harold Evans (killed in action May 13, 1944), James Cuthbert. Came to United States, 1917, naturalized, 1923. Began with Royal Flying Corps, Canada; comdg. 1st Pursuit Group, U.S. Army Air Service, with A.E.F., 1917-19; chief of training, Washington, D.C., 1919-21; discharged with rank of lt. col. (Reserve); organizing sec. and 1st gen. mgr. Nat. Aeronautic Assn., 1921-23; tech. adviser to several aeronautic corps; tech. adviser to U.S. Senate Com. on Air Safety, 1935-38; tech. adviser Civil Aeronautics Adminstrn., 1938-41; active duty Ferrying Command Air Corps (lt. col.); mgr. Washington Bureau, Ziff-Davis Publications, 1941-42; has been active in efforts to make air power recognized in war and industry. Decorated Distinguished Service Cross, Silver Star, Purple Heart (U.S.); Legion of Honor, Croix de Guerre (France); Silver Medal for Valor (Italy); Service Decoration (Brit.); Victory medals U.S. and Great Brit. Mem. Early Birds, Quiet Birdmen, Inst. Aeronautical Sciences, Am. Legion (past comdr. Aviators Post), Nat. Aeronautic Assn. Episcopalian. Author: Up and At 'Em, 1940; Complete Flying Manual, 1940; Aircraft Spotters' Guide, 1942; What the Citizen Should Know about the Air Force, 1942. Home: 3130 16th St., N.W., Washington, D.C. Died Oct. 5, 1945.

HARTRIDGE, Emelyn Battersby, educator; b. Savannah, Ga., July 17, 1871; d. Alfred Lamar and Julia Smythe (Wayne) Hartridge; A.B., Vassar, 1892; L.H.D., Smith Coll., Northampton, Mass., 1928. Founder The Hartridge Sch., Savannah, Ga., 1892; prin. The Hartridge Sch., Plainfield, N.J., since 1903, and pres. since incorporation, 1908, trustee and principal, 1933-40. One of organizers Plainfield Chapter of American Red Cross, 1914; organizer Plainfield Jr. Red Cross, 1917; treas. Plainfield Belgian Relief Soc., 1914-19; chmn. Plainfield Com. of Vassar Salary Endowment Fund, 1922-25; mem. standing com. Vassar Students' Aid, 1924-29; representative at large, Vassar Alumnæ Council (chmn. 1928-30); pres. Asso. Alumnæ of Vassar Coll., 1930-33; treas. N.J. Vassar 75th Anniversary Com., 1939-40; vice-chmn. of exec. com. Cooperative Bur. for Women Teachers, 1928-31; exec. mem. Ginling 25th Anniversary Com., 1940-41; rep. of girls' schs. U.S. Com., 1940, Internat. Education Council since 1941. Mem. Head Mistresses Assn. of the East (pres. 1924-28; chmn. pub. issues com. 1936-38; hon. mem.), Internat. Student Hospitality Assn. (mem. advisory com.), Am. Assn. Univ. Women, Parents League of New York, Poetry Soc. of Ga. Episcopalian. Clubs: College, Monday Afternoon of Plainfield (pres. 1924-27; hon. mem.). Address: Oakwood, Plainfield, N.J. Died Sep. 24, 1942.

HARTT, Rollin Lynde, writer; b. Ithaca, N.Y., Nov. 20, 1869; s. Prof. Charles Frederick (of Cornell U.) and Lucy Cornelia (Lynde) H.; A.B., Williams Coll., 1892; grad. Andover Theol. Sem., 1896; m. Jessie Clark Knight, Dec. 25, 1901 (died Apr. 18, 1917); children—John Francis (adopted), Charles Frederick; m. 2d, Helen Harrington, June 1, 1921. Ordained Congl. ministry, 1896; pastor, Helena, Mont., 1896-97, Leverett, Mass., 1897-98. Traveled extensively in America, 1899-1900, gathering magazine material; staff Boston Transcript until 1917, Chicago Tribune, 1917-18, Lit. Digest, 1919; publicity work for Meth. Centenary, 1920; traveling reporter for World's Work, 1923-24. Author: The People at Play; Ruth of the Dolphin; Understanding the French; Confessions of a Clergyman (anon.); The Man Himself (The Nazarene), 1923; The Clerk of the Day (Transcript semi-weekly column); As I Was Saying (daily in N.Y. Tribune); and many mag. articles. Home: New York. Died June 17, 1946.

HARTWICH, Herman, painter; b. New York, July 8, 1853; s. George G. and Dorothea (de Luce) H.; ed. schs. and acad., Jersey City, N.J.; received first instrn. in drawing and painting from father; studied in Royal Acad., Munich, 1877; pupil Profs. Diez and Loefftz; unmarried. Specialized in painting figures, landscapes, portraits, animals, etc.; has painted many subjects in Upper Bavaria in the Tyrol, etc.; in U.S., painting portraits, 1893-96; in Munich since 1896. Gold medals in Munich and Berlin; medals in Madrid, London; hon. mention and 2d gold medal, Paris Salon; hors Concours, Paris Salon, 1902; silver medal, St. Louis Expn., 1904; 1st class gold medal, Munich and Salzburg. Pictures in mus. in Leipzig and Cleveland, O., and in collections of Prince Regent of Bavaria, Grand Duchess of Modena, Gallery Forbes, London, Royal Gallery, Stuttgart, and Pinakothek, Munich. Address: Landwehr St., 46, Munich, Bavaria. Died March 8, 1926.

HARVEY, Alexander, editor, author; b. Brussels, Belgium, Dec. 25, 1868; s. Alexander and Bridget Maria (Canavan) H.; came to America with parents at 2 yrs. of age; pub. sch. edn.; m. Eva Augusta Schubert, 1895 (died 1946). Reporter, Phila. Press, 1892, N.Y. Evening Telegram, 1893; editor Irving Bacheller's Newspaper Syndicate, 1893-95, Twentieth Century, 1895-98; sec. to diplomatic agt. and counsel-gen. of U.S. in Egypt, 1898-99; asst. Sunday editor of New York Herald, 1900; foreign editor Literary Digest, 1901-05; asso. editor Current Opinion, 1905-22; asso. editor Am. Monthly, 1922-29. Author: The Toe and other stories, 1913; William Dean Howells, 1917; Shelley's Elopement, 1919; Essays on Sophocles, 1922; Essays on Euripides, 1923; Oedipus, 1923; Essays on Jesus, 1924; Friends of Jesus, 1925; Iphigenia, 1925; The Bacchantes, 1926; Love Life of Hellenic Heroines, 1927. Home: 314 Washington Av., Dumont, N.J. Died Nov. 20, 1949.

HARVEY, Andrew Magee, physician and surgeon; b. Galesburg, Ill., Jan. 14, 1868; s. William Nathaniel and Lovina (Brewer) H.; B.S., Knox Coll., 1889, M.S., 1892; M.D., Coll. of Physicians and Surgeons, 1893; D.Sc. (hon.), Knox Coll., 1939; m. Edith Dorset Earle, June 1, 1898; children—Andrew Magee, Lovina Brewer (Mrs. Lawrence A. Williams), John Earle. Interne, St. Elizabeth Hosp., Chicago, 1893-95; attending surgeon, West Side Free Dispensary, Frances Willard Hosp., Garfield Park Sanitarium, Chicago; asst. health offr., Long Beach Calif., since 1942; med. dir. and chief surgeon Crane Co. (retired); capt. No. 6 Calif. State Guard (retired). President of Grace Hospital, 1905-10, second section preventive medicine and public health, A.M.A., chief med. officer, Republican nat. convention, 1932. Dir. Nat. Safety Council; bd. dirs. The Edward Sanitarium, 1920-39; bd. edn., LaGrange, Ill. Fellow American College Surgeons, A.M.A.; honorary fellow (co-founder) Am. Assn. Indsl. Physicians and Surgeons, Tuberculosis Assn. Mem. Chicago Public Policy Com., Ill. State Med. Soc., Chicago Council for Indsl. Safety (first pres.), Alumni Assn. Coll. of Physicians and Surgeons (pres.), Alumni Assn. Knox Coll., (pres.) Chicago Med. Soc., Calif. State, Los Angeles County Med. Assns., Instructor for Traumatic Surgery, West Suburban Council Boy Scouts of Am. Health officer, Village LaGrange Park. Phi Gamma Delta, Nu Sigma Nu. Mason. Pioneered in systematically protecting eyes of indsl. workers, reducing eye injuries by placing safety glasses on those exposed to eye accidents. Home: 21 Redondo Av. Office: 218 E. 1st St., Long Beach, Calif. Died July 18, 1949; buried in Rose Hill Cemetery, Chicago.

HARVEY, George U.; pres. Borough of Queens. Address: Board of Estimates, New York, N.Y.* Died Apr. 6, 1946.

HARVEY, Harold Brown, engr. and mfr. nonferrous forgings; b. Parkman, Me., June 20, 1884; s. Daniel Genthner and Ida Gertrude (Brown) H.; grad. high sch., Wakefield, Mass., 1902; Mass. Inst. Tech., 1905; lecturer courses Northwestern U. Sch. of Commerce; m. Alwilda Fritsch, May 20, 1911. Elec. engr. with Becker Bros., Chicago, and chief engr. Am. Maintenance Co., 1906; factory mgr. Henry Newgard & Co., elec. constrn. and mfg., 1910-15; founder 1915, and pres. until 1920, Marquette Electric Switchboard Co.; pres. Harvey Electric Co. (now Chicago Forging & Mfg. Co.), brass forgings, 1919-21; founder, 1923, and since pres., The Harvey Metal Corp., aluminum, brass and copper forgings for automotive, aircraft, railroad, and gen. industries; pres. Burr Oak Coal Co.; Fed. reorganization mgr. Interstate coal properties, 1941-46; mgr. Marquette Indsl. Bldgs. Inventor magnetic metal separator and early high voltage equipment; pioneer in aluminum and brass forging industry; originator of drop forgings of brass and various processes in the forging of nonferrous metals. Developed ins. plan maintaining elec. machinery. Pres., 1919-20, Rotary Club of Chicago, which originated and sponsored first Boys' Week in Chicago, also originated scholarship for city boys in agrl. course, U. of Ill. Charter mem. Nat. Assn. Brass Forging Industries, and dir., 1932-33; sec. Aluminum Forging Council, 1933. Under N.R.A., successively sec. code com. and chmn. Nat. Code Authority Brass Forging Industry; chmn. code com. and nat. chmn. Aluminum Forging Div.; dir. Aluminum Code Authority, Inc. Since N.R.A. chmn. com. to reorganize nationally the brass forging industry forming the Brass Forging Assn. of which was first pres.; also mem. com. to organize assn. for aluminum industry and first chmn. of the Aluminum Forging Div.; western vice pres. and dir. Assn. Mfrs. in Aluminum Industry, 1935. Mem. Aluminum Assn. (western v.p., dir. and mem. various coms.), Aluminum Forging Div. (chmn.) Brass Forging Assn. (pres. since 1936), Nat. Assn. of Mfrs. (com. on Nat. Defense), Army Ordnance (mem. nat. endowment com.), U.S. C. of C., Ill. Mfrs. Assn., Ill. C. of C., Soc. Automotive Engrs. (com. on nat. defense), Am. Soc. of Metals, Am. Soc. Mech. Engrs.; trustee mem. corp. Mass. Inst. Tech. (various coms.), Chicago Assn. of Commerce, Soc. for Oriental Research. Mason (32°, Shriner). Clubs: Rotary (past pres.), Technology (M.I.T. Alumni, past pres.), Chicago Motor; New York Athletic. Author of Rotary's Message to Garcia, Renaissance of the Bronze Age, and several statistical treatises on non-ferrous forgings. Home: 320 23d St., Santa Monica, Calif. Died Dec. 3, 1949; buried Forest Lawn Cemetery, Glendale, Calif.

HARVEY, Paul, lecturer, publicist; b. Chicago, Ill., Dec. 31, 1878; s. Turlington Walker and Belle Sheridan (Badger) H.; grad. Acad. of Marietta (O.) Coll., 1896; studied at Marietta Coll., Harvard, and U. of Chicago; student Art Inst., Chicago, Sch. of Fine Arts, Boston; m. Lillian Fancher Howe, July 7, 1934. Began in business, 1902, sec., later v.p. and pres. Acme Gas Co., Chicago; pres. Industrial Gas Co., New York, 1904-07; mgr. sales dept. Lee, Higginson Company, Chicago, 1907-10; partner Unit Air Conditioning Company; artist, Santa Barbara, California, 1910-17; became connected with Christian Science Pub. Soc., Boston, 1917; mem. bd. of trustees Christian Science Pub. Soc., pubs. of Christian Science Monitor, 1921-22 (resigned); pub. Internat. Interpreter (weekly), New York, 1922, also editor same, 1923; lecturer on internat. subjects. Mem. Internat. Chamber Commerce, Inst. of Politics, Williamstown, Mass. Clubs: Harvard (New York and Boston); Overseas Press, Shanghai Tiffin (New York). Lecturer on international relations. Home: 2921 211th St., Bayside, L.I., N.Y. Office: 37 W. 39th St., New York 18, N.Y. Died Jan. 8, 1948.

HARVEY, Rodney Beecher, prof. plant physiology; b. Monroeville, Ind., May 26, 1890; s. Aaron Lawrence and Mary Vandervort (Hester) H.; Ph.C., Purdue U., 1912, D.Sc. causa honoris, 1939; B.S., U. of Mich., 1915; Ph.D., U. of Chicago, 1918; student Cambridge (Eng.) U., 1927-28, U. of Bonn, Germany, summer 1928; m. Helen M. Whittier, June 17, 1916; children—Hale M. Whittier (dec.), Rodney Bryce, Rhoda Beatrice, Helen Elizabeth, Eleanor

Whittier. Asst. botanist Eli Lilly Co., 1912-13; asst. pharmacognosist U.S. Bur. Chemistry, 1915; asso. pharmacognosist U.S. Bur. Plant Industry, 1918, plant physiologist, 1918-20; asst. prof. botany, U. of Minn., 1920-21, asso. prof. plant pathology and botany, 1921-31; prof. plant physiology, agrl. botany and horticulture since 1931; dir. Fla. Citrus Expt. Sta., 1936-37; dir. division of industrial microbiology, General Mills Research Laboratory, 1942-43. John Simon Guggenheim fellow, 1927-28. Fellow A.A.A.S.; mem. Bot. Soc. America, Am. Chem. Soc., Am. Soc. Plant Physiologists (pres. 1936-37), Minnesota Academy of Science (v.p. 1938-39, pres. 1942-43), Am. Phytopathol. Soc., Ecol. Soc. of America, Bot. Soc. of Czechoslovakia (corr. mem.), Phi Lambda Upsilon, Sigma Xi, Gamma Sigma Delta, Alpha Zeta, Gamma Alpha. Mason. Author: Plant Physiological Chemistry, 1930; A Textbook of Plant Physiology (with A. E. Murneek). 1930; An Annotated Bibliography of Low Temperature Relations of Plants, 1935; Plant Physiology (with A. E. Murneek), 1938. Discoverer of ethylene process of ripening fruits and holder of patents on fruit ripening and coloration. Home: R.F.D. 2, Box 116, Stillwater, Minn. Address: University Farm, St. Paul, Minn. Died Nov. 4, 1945.

HARVEY, Rowland Hill, prof. history; b. Battle Creek, Ia., Mar. 24, 1889; s. Frank and Jessie Anderson (Preston) H.; B.A., U. of Southern Calif., 1918, M.A., 1920; Ph.D., Stanford U., 1923; m. Claire M. Edwards, July 28, 1914; 1 dau., Elizabeth Claire. Social worker, Chicago, 1910-12; Redpath Chautauqua lecturer, 1912; social worker, Los Angeles, 1912-15; Boy Scout exec., Prescott, Ariz., 1918-19; instr. history, Porterville (Calif.) High Sch., 1919-21; university fellow Stanford University, 1922-23; instructor history, State U. of Ia., 1923-24; instr. history, U. of Calif. at Los Angeles, 1924-25, asst. prof., 1925-30, asso. prof. since 1930. Mem. Kappa Alpha, Phi Beta Kappa. Democrat. Presbyterian. Author: Samuel Gompers—Champion of the Toiling Masses, 1935; "John L. Lewis," in Famous Americans, 1941; also mag. articles and reviews. Home: 369 Homewood Road, Los Angeles, Calif. Died Mar. 10, 1943.

HARVIE, John Bruce, surgeon; b. Ottawa, Ont., Can., 1857; s. Peter and Mary (Reid) H.; M.D., C.M., McGill U., 1881; m. Helena Dickson, 1884 (died May 2, 1924); children—Mildred (Mrs. Barry C. Ritchie), Helen. Practiced at Troy since 1881; surgeon St. Joseph's Maternity Hosp., Samaritan Hosp.; consulting surgeon, Leonard Hosp. Fellow Am. Coll. Surgeons; mem. A.M.A., Med. Soc. State of N.Y. Clubs: Troy, Troy Country, Troy Riding. Home: 41 2d St., Troy, N.Y.; (country) Petersburg, N.Y.* Died 1941.

HARVIE, Peter Lyons, surgeon; b. Binghamton, N.Y., Aug. 13, 1885; s. Peter and Lulu Olmstead (Lyons) H.; A.B., Harvard, 1908, M.D., 1911; grad. student Post Grad. Hosp., 1914, Univ. of Nancy, France, 1919; m. Ruth Hyde, Sept. 29, 1926; children—Harriet Virginia, Ruth Hyde, Diana Lyons, Peter. Interne Boston City Hosp., 1911-13; Boston Lying-In-Hosp., 1913; staff Samaritan Hosp., Troy, New York, 1914-43, retired; instructor Albany Med. Coll., 1915-36; attending surgeon James A. Eddy Memorial Foundation, 1932-43; consulting surgeon Putnam Mem. Hosp., Bennington, Vermont, 1937-43. Served as lt. Medical Corps, U.S. Army, Mexican Border, 1916; capt., Tex., 1917; capt. of Ambulance Co., No. 5, 3d Div., A.E.F., 1918-19; gassed in action; received citation. Fellow Am. Coll. Surgeons; mem. Founders Group Am. Bd. Surgery; mem. A.M.A., N.Y. State and Rensselaer County med. socs., Sons of the Revolution, Am. Legion, Disabled Am. Vets., Mil. Order Purple Heart, Harvard Assn. Eastern N.Y. Awarded Purple Heart, Silver Star. Episcopalian (vestryman). Club: Troy Country. Home: Glen Finert Farm, R.D. 3, Troy, N.Y. Died Feb. 4, 1944.

HASBROUCK, Gilbert D. B., lawyer; b. Esopus, Ulster County, N.Y., Feb. 19, 1860; s. Josiah and Ellen J. (Blauvelt) H.; A.B., Rutgers Coll., 1880, A.M., 1883, LL.D., 1920; attended Columbia Law Sch., 1881-82; m. Julia M. Munn, Jan. 13, 1886 (died May 18, 1926). Began practice at Kingston, N.Y., 1882. Mem. New York Assembly, 1884-85; corp. counsel, Kingston, 1887-94; 2d dep. atty. gen., 1894, 1st dep. atty. gen., 1895-99; asso. judge, Jan. 1, 1902, to Dec. 1, 1903, presiding judge to Dec. 16, 1904, Court of Claims; justice Supreme Court of N.Y., by appmt. Gov. Odell, 1904-05; again justice Supreme Court of N.Y., for term expiring 1926; reëlected for term expiring 1930; in Appellate Div., 3d Dept., 1922-23 and 1928-31; dir. of State of New York National Bank. Represented Gov. Morton in the case of People ex rel. Broderick vs. Morton, Woodruff & Fish, and Gov. Odell in re Guden, to uphold the constitutionality of political executive acts when challenged by judiciary. Official referee, N.Y., since 1931. V.p. Federation of Bar Assns., 3d Judicial Dist., 1932, pres., 1934; chmn. emergency relief, Kingston, 1931; trustee Kingston City Library, 1932, now pres.; v.p. Home for the Aged, 1935, now pres. Pres. State Hist. Assn., 1921-23; trustee Rutgers Coll., 1913-18; chmn. sesquicentennial celebration of orgn. of state govt. at Kingston, 1927; mem. Tercentenary Com. to Celebrate Founding of Reformed Ch. in New Netherland, 1928; pres. New Paltz Normal Sch. Bd., Wiltwyck Cemetery Assn., Ulster County Hist. Assn., Mid-Hudson Grenfell Assn.; v.p. Huguenot Soc. of America for New Paltz; mem. Dutchess County, Greene County, Constitution Island, Temple Hill, Woodstock Historical and Holland socs., Zeta Psi; city historian, Kingston, mem. Bd. of Edn., 1937-38. Chmn. Ulster County Home Defense Com., Ulster County Chapt., A.R.C., during war, vice-chmn. after war, now chmn. Clubs: University (New York); Fort Orange (Albany); Twaalskill and Kingston (Kingston). Home: Kingston, N.Y. Died June 5, 1942.

HASELTINE, Burton, oculist, aurist; b. Richland Center, Wis., Sept. 27, 1874; s. Hascal and Martha (Pierce) H.; Allegheny Coll., Pa., 1889-91; Cleveland (O.) U. of Medicine, 1894-95; M.D., Hahnemann Med. Coll., Chicago, 1896; m. Marie Leitch, Aug. 25, 1906. Former prof. diseases of throat and nose; Hahnemann Med. Coll.; cons. eye, ear and throat surgeon, Cook County and Ill. Masonic hosps.; attending ear and throat surgeon, Henrotin and Am. hosps. Office: Peoples Gas Bldg., Chicago, Ill. Died 1941.

HASKELL, Mellen Woodman, univ. prof.; b. Salem, Mass., Mar. 17, 1863; s. Rev. Augustus Mellen and Catherine (Woodman) H.; A.B., Harvard, 1883, A.M., 1885; Ph.D., Göttingen, 1889; m. at Cambridge, Mass., Mary P. Brown, June 5, 1902 (died Jan. 15, 1928); m. 2d, Isabel W. Brown, Dec. 29, 1928. Instr. mathematics, Univ. of Mich., 1889-90; asst. prof., 1890-94, asso. prof., 1894-1906, prof. of mathematics, 1906-33, prof. emeritus since 1933; dean of Social Sciences, 1899-1900, dean Coll. of Letters, 1900-01, U. of Calif. Vis. prof. Columbia Univ., 1916, Univ. of Chicago, summer 1920. Mem. Am. Math. Soc., Deutsche Mathematikervereinigung, Circolo Matematico di Palermo. Clubs: University, Harvard (pres. 1912, 13); Chit Chat (San Francisco); Berkeley, Faculty (Berkeley). Contbr. to math. jours. Home: 2019 Durant Av., Berkeley, Calif. Died Jan. 15, 1948.

HASKIN, Frederic J., newspaper corr.; b. Shelbina, Mo., Dec. 13, 1872; s. Ephrahn G. and Rosetta (Jennings) H.; common school edn.; m. Olive G. Nagel, May 20, 1905; children—Nagel, Frederic J. While pub. The Torchlight at Shelbina, Mo., 1894, became writer for Globe Democrat, St. Louis; gradually added other papers, and is now regular contbr. of spl. articles to over 100 papers; owner of the largest free information bureau in existence. Has traveled in principal countries of the world. Club: Nat. Press (Washington). Author: The American Government, 1911, 23; The Immigrant, An Asset and a Liability, 1913; The Panama Canal, 1913; Uncle Sam at Work (motion pictures), 1915; Answers to Questions, 1926; 5000 New Answers to Questions, 1933; 10,000 Answers to Questions, 1937; The American Government Today, 1935; The Quiz and Answer Book, 1938; The America Quiz and Answer Book, 1941; The American Government, 1941. Home: The Kennedy-Warren. Office: 316 I St. N.E., Washington, D.C. Died Apr. 24, 1944.

HASKINS, Charles Nelson, mathematician; b. New Bedford, Mass., May 7, 1874; s. Herbert Kinsley and Sarah Kinsley (Nelson) H.; B.S., Mass. Inst. Tech., 1897; M.S., Harvard Univ., 1899, M.A., 1900, Ph.D., 1901; hon. Sc.D. from Dartmouth College, 1928; m. Edith Delano Dexter, Sept. 4, 1909. Asst. in physics, 1897-98, instr. mathematics, 1902-03, Mass. Inst. Tech.; instr. mathematics, Yale, 1903-04, Cornell, 1904-06; asst. prof. mathematics, U. of Ill., 1906-09; asst. prof. mathematics, 1909-16, prof. since 1916, Dartmouth. Fellow A.A.A.S.; mem. Am. Math. Soc. Republican. Club: Harvard (Boston). Contbr. Trans. Am. Math. Soc., Annals of Mathematics and bulletins of U.S. Govt. Home: Hanover Rd., Lebanon, N.H. Died Nov. 13, 1942.

HASTINGS, George Everett, prof. English; b. Fredericktown, Pa., Oct. 27, 1878; s. Francis Luellen and Matilda Ann (Fulmer) H.; graduate Southwestern State Normal School (now State Teachers College), California, Pa., 1899; student Washington and Jefferson Coll., 1899-1902; A.B., Princeton, 1904, A.M., 1912; A.M., Harvard, 1917, Ph.D., 1918; m. Mary Frances Rudolph, Aug. 15, 1922. With traffic dept., Bell Telephone Co., Pittsburgh, Pa., 1904-09; miner and prospector, Utah, 1909; instr. in English, U. of Utah, 1909-10; same, Shattuck Sch., Faribault, Minn., 1910-16, 1918-19; asst. prof. English, U. of Ark., 1919-21, asso. prof., 1921-27, prof. since 1927; visiting member summer school faculty, U. of Utah, 1923, Univ. of Texas, 1927, 29, 30, 35, 36. Mem. Modern Language Assn. of America, Am. Assn. Univ. Profs., Beta Theta Pi, Phi Beta Kappa. Author: The Life and Works of Francis Hopkinson, 1926. Contbr. Americana, Am. Hist. Rev., Pa. Mag. of History and Biography, South Atlantic Quarterly, Dictionary of Am. Biography, Am. Literature, etc. Joint editor of Brownie, a Tale Written in Youth by George Gissing, 1931. Home: 210 W. Maple St., Fayetteville, Ark. Died Nov. 8, 1942.

HASTINGS, John Russel, editor; b. San Francisco, Calif., Oct. 25, 1878; s. Howard Franklin and Emma (Cunningham) H.; m. Katharine Bagg. Mem. staff of San Francisco Chronicle, San Francisco Examiner, New York Press and Evening Telegram; later night editor New York Daily News; then writer for N.Y. Globe; asst. city editor New York Times, mng. editor New York Journal, 1906-26; supervising editor Hearst Service since 1926. Club: Players. Home: 230 E. 50th St. Office: Hearst Magazine Bldg., New York, N.Y. Died Apr. 2, 1942.

HASTINGS, Paul Pardee, ry. official; b. Farmington, Kan., Oct. 22, 1872; s. Zachariah Simpson and Rosetta (Butler) H.; ed. public schools and Nat. Business Coll., Kansas City, Mo.; m. Charlotte Reed, Nov. 20, 1901; children—Ross Reed, Marylyn (Mrs. J. E. Bardwell). Began with A., T. & S.F. Ry., Aug. 1891; freight clerk Santa Fe, Prescott & Phoenix Ry., Prescott, Ariz., 1895-98; traffic mgr. United Verde Copper Co., Jerome, Ariz., 1898-1900; auditor and gen. freight and passenger agent United Verde & Pacific Ry., Jerome, 1900-02; with mining interests in Ariz. and Mexico, 1902-03; auditor Santa Fe, Prescott & Phoenix Ry., Prescott, 1903-07, gen. freight and passenger agent, 1907-12; asst. gen. freight agent A., T.&S.F. Ry., San Francisco, 1912-18; asst. dir. of traffic in charge freight rate dept., U.S.R.R. Adminstrn., Washington, D.C., 1918-20; mem. standing rate com., Trans-Continental Freight Bureau, Chicago, 1921-22; general freight agent A.,T.&S.F. Ry., San Francisco, 1922-36, asst. freight traffic mgr., 1936-37, freight traffic mgr., Chicago, 1937-38, v.p. in charge of traffic, Chicago, since Mar. 1, 1938. Clubs: Chicago Athletic, Traffic (Chicago); Associated Traffic Clubs of America. Home: 200 E. Chestnut St. Office: 80 E. Jackson St., Chicago, Ill.* Died Sep. 16, 1947.

HASTINGS, Samuel Miles, dir. Internat. Business Machines Corp.; b. Rimersburg, Pa., Aug. 14, 1860; s. Eli and Rachel Whitehall (Kerr) H.; ed. pub. schs., Gardner, Ill.; m. Jeannette Rankin, Sept. 16, 1881 (died 1922); 1 son, Rolland Thomas Rankin; m. 2d, Nettie A. Moore, 1925. In retail dry goods business, Braidwood, 1879-84, Streator, 1884-89; removed to Chicago, 1889; engaged in mfr. and sale of computing scales since 1893; pres. Dayton Scale Co. until 1927, merged with Internat. Business Machine Corp., former chmn. finance com., now dir. Mayor of Highland Park, 1915-28. Mem. S.A.R. Republican. Presbyterian. Mason (K.T.). Clubs: Chicago Athletic, Old Elm, Exmoor. Home: 812 Waverly Rd., Highland Park, Ill. Office: 233 W. Madison St., Chicago, Ill. Died Oct. 23, 1943.

HATCH, Harry C., business exec.; b. Ameliasburg, Ont., Can., Apr. 12, 1884; s. William and L. (Allison) Hatch; ed. public and high schools; m. Elizabeth Carr, 1909. In hotel business with father, 1911. Began in liquor business as owner of store, Whitby, 1911-13, and part owner with brother at Toronto, 1913-16; in mail order liquor bus., Montreal, 1916-21; asst. to pres. Canadian Industrial Alcohol Co., Ltd., 1921. Reorganized Gooderham & Worts, Ltd., 1923; elected pres.; pres. Hiram Walker's, Ltd., 1927; Hiram Walker-Gooderham & Worts, Ltd., 1928, became chmn. bd., 1928; pres. and chmn. bd. since 1938; vice pres. Canada Malting Co. Dir. T. G. Bright & Co., Ltd. Dir. Canada Steamship Lines, Ltd., Canadian Indsl. Alcohol, Ltd. Clubs: Royal Canadian Yacht; Royal St. Lawrence Yacht, Engineers (Montreal); Albany, Granite, Rosedale Golf, Ontario Jockey. Home: 38 Roxborough Dr. Office: 2 Trinity St., Toronto, Ont., Can. Died May 8, 1946.

HATCHER, Eldridge Burwell, clergyman, educator; b. Fork Union, Va., Oct. 16, 1865; s. William Eldridge and Virginia (Snead) H.; M.A., Richmond (Va.) Coll., 1886; studied Johns Hopkins; Th.M., Southern Bapt. Theol. Sem., Louisville, Ky., 1892; D.D., William Jewell Coll., 1903; m. Anna Granville Denson, Mar. 28, 1899; children—William Eldridge, Anna Granville. Ordained ministry Bapt. Ch., 1893; pastor First Ch., Norfolk, Va., 10 yrs.; supt. state missions, Md., 11 yrs.; pastor Christiansburg, Va., 3 yrs.; editor The Baptist World and The Western Recorder, 1918-20; pastor Lowrey Memorial Ch., Blue Mountain, Miss., 1920-23; head dept. of Christianity, Blue Mountain Coll., 1923-36; now head of dept. of Bible, Harcum Junior Coll., also lecturer in Bible. Democrat. Author: The Bible and the Monuments, 1893; The Young Professor, 1901; Dorothy Page, 1912; Life of William E. Hatcher, 1915; Woodrow Carlyle, 1927. Home: Bryn Mawr, Pa. Died July 21, 1943.

HATCHER (Orie) Latham, b. Petersburg, Va., Dec. 10, 1868; d. William Eldridge and Oranie Virginia (Snead) Hatcher; A.B., Vassar, 1888; Ph.D., U. of Chicago, 1903. Joined faculty of Bryn Mawr, 1904; head of dept. comparative lit., 1910-15, asso. prof. English, 1912-15. Founder, 1914, and pres. Southern Woman's Ednl. Alliance (now Alliance for Guidance of Rural Youth) since 1914; chmn. rural section, 1928-38, trustee, 1933-37, National Vocational Guidance Assn.; co-founder and mem. exec. bd. Richmond School of Social Work and Pub. Health since 1917; mem. vocational guidance com. Nat. Adv. Council Radio in Edn., 1932; mem. exec. bd. Nat. Council of Women, 1932-35; mem. Nat. Occupational Conf., 1933-39; consultant Youth Conf., Dept. of Interior, 1934; mem. bd. or reps. Council of Guidance and Personnel Assn. since 1935; mem. White House Conf. on Children in a Democracy, 1940-41; mem. White House Conf. on Rural Education, 1944. On Va. Roll of Honor, 1940. Chmn. Inst. Rural Youth Guidance, Washington, D.C., 1941-44; chmn. monthly Luncheon Forum, Washington Youth Serving Agencies, since 1942; tech. director Pine Mountain Guidance Institute, Harlan County, Ky., 1936-42. Clubs: Virginia Writers (founder); American Association University Women; Dixie Club of New York (hon.); Vassar Club of Virginia (ex-president). Author: John Fletcher, 1904; A Book for Shakespeare's Plays and Pageants, 1915; Occupations for Women, 1927; Guiding Rural Boys and Girls, 1930; Child Development and Guidance in Rural Schools (with Ruth Strang), 1943 (chosen for microfilming for use in China). Co-author: A Mountain School (also editor), 1930; Rural Girls in the City for Work (also editor), 1930; Experimentation in Simple Guidance Programs for Rural Schools, 1931. Editor: Guidance at Work in Schools of Craven County, N.C., 1930; Handicaps of Elementary School Girls in Especially Underprivileged Rural Communities, 1931. Wrote Rural Guidance Programs in report White House Conf. Com.

on Vocational Guidance and Child Labor, 1930. Contbr. bulletins and mag. articles, first on Elizabethan Age, later on youth guidance. Former mem. advisory editorial bd. Vocational Guidance Mag., and advisory council Vassar Alumnae Quarterly. Office: Gresham Court, Richmond 20, Va. Died Apr. 1, 1946.

HATCHER, Robert Anthony, pharmacologist; born New Madrid, Mo., Feb. 6, 1868; s. Richard H. and Harriet Hinton (Marr) H.; Ph.G., Phila. Coll. Pharmacy, 1889, Pharm.M., 1929; M.D., Tulane, 1898; D.Sc. in Pharmacy, Columbia, 1929; m. Mary Q. Burton, Dec. 28, 1904; 1 son, Robert Lee. Prof. materia medica, Cleveland Sch. Pharmacy, 1899-1904; demonstrator pharmacology, Western Reserve Medical Coll., 1901-03; instr. pharmacology, Cornell U. Med. Sch., 1904-06; asst. prof. pharmacology and materia medica, 1906-08, prof., 1908-35, prof. emeritus pharmacology, since 1935. Mem. A.M.A. (mem. council on pharmacy and chemistry), Am. Physiol. Soc., Am. Soc. Biol. Chemists, Am. Soc. Pharmacology and Exptl. Therapeutics, Am. Pharm. Assn., Harvey Soc., N.Y. Acad. Medicine. Republican. Author: (with Torald Sollmann) Textbook of Materia Medica, 1904; (with M. I. Wilbert) Pharmacology of Useful Drugs, 1915. Editor: Useful Drugs, 1934. Contbr. to med. and scientific jours. Home: Flushing, L.I. Office: 1300 York Av., New York. Died Apr. 1, 1944.

HATCHER, William Bass, coll. president; b. Ripley, Miss., Dec. 12, 1888; s. Thomas W. and Ida M. (Hobgood) H.; A.B., La. State U., 1916, A.M., 1923, Ph.D., 1937; student Yale, 1930-31; m. Mary Amelia Devall, Oct. 14, 1934; 1 dau., Joan Amelia. Prin. Baker (La.) High Sch., 1914-16; supt. Baton Rouge pub. schs., 1916-35; state dir. N.Y.A., 1935-36; asso. prof. Am. history, La. State U., 1936-41, prof. since 1941, dean John McNeese Jr. Coll., 1941, asso. dean, Coll. of Arts and Sciences, in charge freshman div., 1941-42, dean of the junior div., 1942-44, pres. La. State U. since 1944; armed services rep., 1942-43; academic coordinator army specialized training program, 1943-44. Served as officer cand., U.S. Army, 1918. Mem. Am. Hist. Assn., Miss. Valley Hist. Assn., Southern Hist. Assn., La. Hist. Assn., Assn. Am. U. Profs., Phi Theta Kappa, Phi Kappa Phi, Kappa Phi Kappa. Democrat. Episcopalian. Mason. Club: Rotary. Author: Edward Livingston, Jeffersonian Republican and Jacksonian Democrat, 1940. Contbr. articles to La. Hist. Quarterly, Dictionary of Am. History. Home: President's House. Office: Louisiana State U., Baton Rouge, La. Died Apr. 3, 1947.

HATFIELD, Charles Sherrod, judge; b. West Millgrove, O., June 29, 1882; s. Nathan Sherrod (M.D.) and Aura (Foster) H.; A.B., Hanover (Ind.) Coll.; studied Ind. U.; LL.B., Ohio State U.; LL.D., National U., Washington; married; children—Margaret Taylor, Dos Taylor, Norma Sherrod. Admitted to Ohio bar, 1907; was pros. atty. Wood County O.; apptd. judge U.S. Court of Customs and Patent Appeals, Washington, D.C., Mar. 4. 1923. Address: 4335 Cathedral Av. N.W. Office: Internal Revenue Bldg., Washington.* Died Feb. 9, 1950.

HATFIELD, Henry Rand, educator; b. Chicago, Ill., Nov. 27, 1866; s. Rev. Robert M. and Elizabeth Ann (Taft) H.; A.B., Northwestern, 1892, LL.D., 1923; Ph.D., U. of Chicago, 1897; LL.D., U. of California, 1940; m. Ethel A. Glover, June 15, 1898; children—John Glover, Robert Miller (dec.), Elizabeth (Mrs. C. A. Glover). In bond business 1886-90; instr. polit. economy, Washington Univ., 1894-98; instr. 1898-1902, asst. prof. and dean Coll. of Commerce and Administration, 1902-04, U. of Chicago; asso. prof. accounting, 1904-09, prof. 1909-37, prof. emeritus since 1937; dean Coll. Commerce, 1909-20, 1927-28, dean of faculties, 1916, 1917-18, 1920-23, U. of Calif.; Dickinson lecturer, Harvard Sch. of Bus. Adminstrn., 1942. Pres. Berkeley Commn. of Charities, 1914-18; dir. div. planning and statistics, War Industries Bd., 1918; expert with Adv. Tax Bd., 1919; mem. Berkeley War Appeals Bd., 1942. Mem. Am. Accounting Assn. (pres. 1918), Am. Econ. Assn. (v.p. 1918), Beta Theta Pi, Phi Beta Kappa (senator, 1923-28). Methodist. Clubs: Berkeley, Faculty (Berkeley); Commercial (San Francisco). Author: Modern Accounting, 1908; Accounting, 1927; A Statement of Accounting Principles (with T. H. Sanders and U. Moore), 1938; Accounting Principles and Practices (with T. H. Sanders and N. L. Burton), 1940; Surplus and Dividends, 1942. Contbr. to American and foreign accounting periodicals. Home: 2605 Le Conte Av., Berkeley, Calif. Died Dec. 25, 1945.

HATFIELD, James Taft, Germanist; b. Brooklyn, N.Y., June 15, 1862; s. Rev. Robert M. and Elizabeth Ann (Taft) H.; A.B., Northwestern U., 1883, A.M., 1886, Litt.D., 1937; studied Japan, China, India, 1883-84; Ph.D., Johns Hopkins U., 1890, Berlin, Tübingen, Oxford, 1896-97; m. Maude Hollingsworth Wilson, Mar. 13, 1890 (died 1906); children—Wilson (dec.), Margaret, Theodore; m. 2d, Ann Estelle Caraway, Apr. 7, 1910 (died 1940); children—Henry, Elizabeth, Ann, Blanche. Prof. classical langs., Rust U., Miss., 1884-85; fellow Johns Hopkins, 1887-90; prof. German lang. and lit., Northwestern U., 1890-1934. Served in Spanish-American War on United States cruiser Yale, from June-Aug. 1898. Awarded Poe Medal, University of Virginia, 1909. Special Berlin corr. Chicago Daily News, 1919. Guest of Govt. of Anhalt, Müller Centenary, 1927. Lectured at 10 chief German universities, 1936. Hon. corr. mem. Deutsche Akademie; mem. Modern Language Assn. America (pres. 1934), Soc. Midland Authors, MacDowell Soc., Beta Theta Pi, Phi Beta Kappa. Unitarian. Clubs: Germania, University (hon.), Cliff Dwellers, Chicago Classical (ex-pres.). Author (or editor): Elements of Sanskrit Grammar, Lucknow, 1884; A Study of Juvencus, Bonn, 1890; Freytag's Rittmeister von Alt-Rosen, 1894; Goethe's Hermann und Dorothea, 1899; German Lyrics and Ballads, 1900; Diary and Correspondence of Wilhelm Müller (with P. S. Allen), 1903; From Broom to Heather, 1903; Goethe's Egmont, 1904; Gedichte von Wilhelm Müller (complete critical edit.), Berlin, 1906; Ernst's Überwunden, 1908; Early Romantic School, 1913; Shorter German Poems, 1915; Rathenau's Addresses, 1928; New Light on Longfellow, 1933; German Culture in the U.S., 1936. Frequent contbr. to philol. and lit. jours. in U.S., Germany and Eng. Home: 1704 Hinman Av., Evanston, Ill. Died Oct. 3, 1945.

HATHAWAY, Harle Wallace; b. Norwalk, O., Oct. 24, 1866; s. Israel Wister (D.D.) and Lucy Brownell (Fay) H.; A.B., Princeton, 1890 (class poet, commencement orator); A.M., 1894; grad. Princeton Theol. Sem., 1894; m. Eva Pauline Bellows, Apr. 2, 1895; children—Mildred Marie (Mrs. Leslie S. Betts), John Wallace. Ordained Presbyn. ministry, 1894; pastor Madison Av. Ch., Elizabeth, N.J., 1894-1903; mercantile business several yrs.; minister Eastminster Chapel, Germantown, Phila., 1907-10; pastor Covenant Ch., Germantown, 1911-25; became exec. secretary Presbytery of Philadelphia North, 1925, established six new Presbyterian churches in the bounds of Presbytery, honorably retired, October 1, 1938. Member Com. of 100, Phila.; mem. Reconstructed Fourth Assn.; organizer and pres. East Germantown Improvement Assn. Republican. Clubs: Union League, City. Writer of comments on Internat. Lessons in Union Quarterly for 10 years. Home: Emlen Arms. Germantown, Philadelphia 19, Pa. Died Nov. 22, 1945.

HATTON, Augustus (Raymond) Rutan, educator; b. Vevay, Ind., Sept. 27, 1873; s. Augustus and Mary Lavinia (Howard) H.; Ph.B., Franklin Coll., 1898; Ph.D., U. of Chicago, 1907; LL.D., Franklin Coll., Franklin, Ind., 1920; m. Nancy Mathews, Nov. 11, 1903 (died 1931); 1 dau., Martha Mathews; m. 2d, Esther Rutan, Nov. 25, 1936. Instr. in history and polit. science, 1898-99, prof., 1900-01, Franklin Coll.; fellow in polit. science, 1901-03, fellow and asst., 1903-07, asso. prof. in extension div., 1907, U. of Chicago; asso. prof. polit. science on Marcus A. Hanna Foundation (1st incumbent), Western Reserve U., 1907-10, prof., 1910-27; prof. and chmn. polit. science, Northwestern University, 1927-40, prof. emeritus since 1940; visiting professor of government, University of Texas, 1942-43; visiting professor and advisor to the Chancellor, Univ. of Puerto Rico, 1943-44. Lecturer on municipal government, Harvard, 1911; lecturer on civic problems and cons. specialist on city charters and state constns.; mem. of and draftsman for Cleveland Charter Commn., 1913; author charter of Cleveland, in effect Jan. 1, 1923, providing for a mgr. and council elected by proportional representation; mem. Cleveland City Council, 1923-27. Charter consultant for Nat. Municipal League, 1920-25; pres. Proportional Representation League since 1929; hon. mem. Internat. City Managers' Assn. Mem. Sigma Alpha Epsilon. Club: City (Cleveland). Editor: Digest of City Charters, 1906; Public Budgets, 1915; also articles on municipal govt. Home: Lazy H Ranch, Dripping Springs, Tex. Died Nov. 12. 1946.

HATHAWAY, King, cons. engr.; b. San Francisco, Calif., Apr. 9, 1878; s. John Dudley and Susan (King) H.; ed. pub. schs. of San Francisco, Calif.; m. Ethel Cramer, in Paris, France, Aug. 12, 1929; children—Pierre, Taylor, Joan. With Midvale Steel Works, Phila., 1896-1901; supt. Payne Engine Co., 1902-04; supt., v.p., mgr. Tabor Mfg. Co., 1904-16; asso. with Dr. F. W. Taylor, 1904-15; lecturer on scientific management, Harvard Grad. Sch. of Business Adminstrn., 1912-17, Wharton Sch., U. of Pa., 1921-22; cons. engr. in foundry operation Industrial Assn. of San Francisco, 1923-26; gen. mgr. Schlage Lock Co., 1927-28; cons. work in Japan and Europe, 1929; cons. engr. Manning, Maxwell & Moore and gen. mgr. Consol. Ashcroft Hancock Co., 1930-32; consultant in orgn. and management, 1906-17, 1919-22, and since 1932; also cons. prof. of scientific management, Stanford U., since 1937. Served as capt. and lt. col. Ordnance Dept., U.S. Army, with A.E.F., 1917-18. Decorated Officier de l'Ordre de l'Etoile Noir. Mem. Masaryk Acad. of Work (Prague), Soc. for Advancement of Management, Am. Soc. Mech. Engrs. Republican. Episcopalian. Contbr. articles to professional societies and jours. Home: 200 Lowell Av., Palo Alto, Calif. Died June 12, 1944.

HAUCK, Louise Platt, author; b. Argentine, Kan., Aug. 15, 1883; d. Emory Melzar and Elizabeth Landon (Prescott) Platt; ed. high sch., St. Joseph, Mo.; m. Leslie Franklin Hauck, May 21, 1907; children—Elizabeth Prescott, Jean Louise, Leslie Franklin. Began writing for newspapers and magazines in 1915; has specialized in treating of quaint features of Missouri history, legend and romance. Mem. Authors' League of America, Soc. Midland Authors, also of Pen and Brush Club. Republican. Author: Missouri Yesterdays, 1920; The Mystery of Tumult Rock, 1920; Joyce, 1927; High Jinks Ranch, 1927; The Youngest Rider, 1927; May Dust, 1929; The Gold Trail, 1929; Marise, 1929; Partners, 1929; Rosaleen, 1930; At Midnight, 1930; Cherry Pit, 1930; Anne Marries Again, 1930; Lucky Shot, 1931; Sylvia, 1931; Wild Grape, 1931; Blazing Tumbleweed (nom de plume, Peter Ash), 1931; Untarnished (nom de plume, Peter Ash), 1931; The Green Light (nom de plume, Louise Landon), 1931; Mystery Mansion (nom de plume, Lane Archer), 1931; Prince of the Moon, 1931; The Wifehood of Jessica, 1932; Two Together, 1932; The Story of Nancy Meadows, 1933; The Strange Death of a Doctor (nom de plume, Louise Landon), 1933; The Pink House, 1933; His Own Rooftree (nom de plume, Peter Ash), 1933; Life, Love, and Jeanette, 1933; Bill Had an Umbrella, 1934; Friday's Child, 1934; Family Matters, 1934; Rainbow Glory, 1935; The Crystal Tree, 1935; If with All Your Hearts, 1935; Blackberry Winter (nom de plume, Peter Ash), 1934; A Little Aversion (nom de plume, Louise Landon), 1934; In Lilac Time (nom de plume, Jean Randall), 1934; The Little Doctor, Truce with Life, Whippoorwill House, 1936; Bridesmaid (nom de plume, Jean Randall), 1936; Without Charm, Please; One Is Beloved; Marriage for Rosamond, 1937; After a Man's Heart (nom de plume, Jean Randall), 1937; The Shortest Street (nom de plume, Jean Randall), 1938; Climax (nom de plume, Peter Ash); Chan Osborne's Wife; Juliet Inc.; Dear Deborah; Priscilla Won't (nom de plume, Jean Randall); Just Like a Girl (nom de plume, Jean Randall); Beloved Buff; Lance Falls in Love; Peppertree Inn (nom de plume Jean Randall), 1941; Soft as Silk (nom de plume Jean Randall), 1942; Gardenias for Sue, 1942; The Little Secretary, 1942; A Woman Will or Won't, 1942; Careless Rapture (nom de plume Jean Randall), 1943; Evergreen House, 1943; Cary Fordyce, 1943; Traveler's End (under pseudonym, Jean Randall), 1943; No Sweeter Woman, 1943. Home: 2211 Francis St., St. Joseph, Mo. Died Dec. 10, 1943.

HAUCK, Minnie (Mme. von Wartegg), prima donna; b. New Orleans, 1853; m. Chevalier Hesse von Wartegg. Sang in concert before going to Europe to study; operatic début in Vienna, as Violetta in La Traviata; 1st appeared in London as Amina in La Sonnambula; later returned to U.S., appeared in many leading roles; best known in title rôle of Carmen. Died Feb. 6, 1929.

HAUPTMANN, Gerhart (houpt'män), dramatist; b. Obersalzbrunn, Silesia, Germany, Nov. 16, 1862; s. Robert and Marie Strahler) H.; student Acad. of Arts, Breslau, and U. of Jena, Germany; hon. dr. Oxford U., 1902, Leipzig U., 1909, U. of Prague, 1921, Columbia U., 1932; m. Marie Thienemann, 1885; 3 children; m. 2d, Magarete Marschalk, 1904; 1 son. Began as sculptor, 1884; gave up sculpture for writing, 1885. Awarded Nobel Prize for Literature, 1912; became senator of German Acad., Munich, 1932; holds numerous other honors and awards. Author: Vor Sonnenaufgang, 1889; Das Friedensfest, 1890; Einsame Menschen, 1891; Die Weber, 1892; College Crampton, 1892; Der Biberpelz, 1893; Hanneles Himmelfahrt, 1894; Florian Geyer, 1896; Die versunkene Glocke, 1897; Fuhrmann Henschel, 1899; Helios, 1899; Schluck und Jau, 1900; Michael Kramer, 1900; Der rote Hahn, 1901; Der arme Heinrich, 1902; Rose Bernd, 1903; Elga, 1905; Und Pippa tanzt, 1906; Das Hirtenlied, 1906; Die Jungfern vom Bischofsberg, 1907; Kaiser Karls Geisel, 1908; Griselda, 1909; Die Ratten, 1911; Gabriel Schillings flucht, 1912; Festspiel in deutschen Reimen, 1913; Der Bogen des Odysseus, 1913; Die Winterballade, 1917; Der Weisze Heiland, Indipohdi, 1920; Peter Brauer, 1921; Veland, 1924; Dorothea Angermann, 1925; Spuk, 1929; Vor Sonnenuntergang, 1932; Die goldene Harfe, 1933; Hamlet in Wittenberg, 1935. Epics: Promethidenlos, 1885; Der Apostel, Bahnwärter Thiel, 1892; Griechischer Frühling, 1908; Der Narr in Christo Emanuel Quint, 1910; Atlantis, 1912; Lohengrin, Parcival (for children), 1913; Der Ketzer von Soana, 1918; Anna, 1921; Fasching, Phantom, 1922; Ausblicke, 1922; Die Insel der Groszen Mutter, 1923; Die Blaue Blume, Till Eulenspiegel, 1927; Wanda, 1928; Buch der Leidenschaft, 1929; Spitzhacke, Drei Reden, 1930; Hochzeit auf Buchenhorst, 1931; Um Volk und Geist, 1932; Das Meerwunder, 1934; Im Wirbel der Berüfung, 1935; Das Abenteuer Meiner Jugent, 1937. Lyrics: Bas Bunte Buch, 1888; Sonette, 1920; Gesammelte Werke: deutsch: Ges. W. in 12 Bdn., 1922; engl: The Dramatic Works, 9 vol., New York, 1913-29; Ulrich von Lichtenstein, Komödie, 1939. Address: Der Wiesenstein, Agnetendorf im Riesengebirge, Germany.* Died June 8, 1946.

HAUSER, Conrad Augustine, church official; b. Frederick, Md., May 17, 1872; s. John Conrad and Mary (Rommel) H.; A.B., Johns Hopkins, 1894; grad. Theol. Sem. Ref. Ch. in U.S., Lancaster, Pa., 1897; studied U. of Berlin, 1900-01; A.M., U. of Pa., 1921, Ph.D., 1922; m. Sophia M. Hartig, Oct. 24, 1901; 1 son, Paul Martin Conrad. Ordained ministry Ref. Ch. in U.S., 1897; pastor successively Salem Ch., Frostburg, Md., St. Mark's Ch., Cumberland, and Emanuel Ch., Rochester, N.Y., until 1911; apptd. ednl. supt. for Publ. and Sunday Sch. Bd., Ref. Ch., Sept. 1911, editor, 1923, ednl. sec. and editor religious publs. same bd., 1925-39; dir. field promotion, Bd. of C.E. of Evang. and Reformed Ch. Mem. Com. on Edn. Pa. Council of C.E., and Phila. Council of C.E.; mem. Internat. Council of Religious Edn., Phi Delta Kappa. Author: A Course of Supplemental Lessons on the Sunday School, 1910; Outline Studies on the Old Testament, 1912; Outline Studies on the Church, 1915; Latent Religious Resources in Public School Education, 1924; Teaching Religion in the Public Schools, 1942. Home: 43 Windsor Avenue, Highland Park, (Upper Darby, P.O.), Pa. Office: 1505 Race St., Philadelphia, Pa. Died Mar. 13, 1943.

HAVENS, Valentine Britton, lawyer; b. Brooklyn, N.Y., July 11, 1889; s. Edwin Taylor and Edith (Murphy) H.; A.B., Rutgers, 1912; Rhodes scholar, Oxford U., Eng., 1913-16, B.A. in Jurisprudence, 1916; m. Nellie Laycock, Sept. 3, 1919 (divorced); children—Patricia Valerie, Leston Laycock; m. 2d, Louise R. Mygatt, August 1935 (div.); m. 3d, Katherine S. Mapp, July 1943 (div.). Practiced N.Y.

City since 1916; partner Holmes, Lynn, Paul & Havens, 1922-26, Holmes, Paul & Havens, 1926-30, Olcott, Holmes, Glass, Paul & Havens, 1930-32, now Olcott, Havens, Wandless and Stitt; lecturer in law, Brooklyn Law Sch., 1922-41; identified with much important litigation in state and federal courts; dir. Radio Frequency Labs., Inc., Aircraft Radio Corp., Tech-Art Plastics Co.; dir. Greenville Finishing Co., Glasgo Finishing Co. Served as lt. j.g. U.S.N.R.F., 1917-19. Member Phi Beta Kappa, Delta Upsilon. Club: Maidstone (East Hampton, L.I.). Home: One Fifth Av., New York 3. Office: 70 Pine St., New York 5. Died July 21, 1948.

HAWES, Charles Henry, anthropologist; b. New Southgate, Middlesex, Eng., Sept. 30, 1867; s. Frederic and Mary Ann (Nesbit) H.; A.B., Trinity Coll., Cambridge U., 1899, A.M., 1902; m. Harriet Boyd, Mar. 3, 1906; children—Alexander Boyd, Mary Nesbit. In mercantile business, 1882-95; social and ednl. work, London, Eng., 1899-1900; travel and research in the Orient and Crete, 1900-06, making anthropol. survey of Sakhalin and Crete; mem. faculty U. of Wis., 1907-09, Dartmouth, 1910-17; war service in England, 1917-19; asst. dir. Mus. of Fine Arts, Boston, 1919-24, asso. dir., 1924-1934. Rep. British Assn. Advancement of Science, in Crete, 1905, 09. Episcopalian. Author: In the Uttermost East, 1903; Crete, the Forerunner of Greece (with H. B. Hawes), 1909. Wrote monographs for use of British Peace Delegation, Paris, 1919. Home: 2 Belfield Road, Belle Haven, Alexandria, Va. Died Dec. 13, 1943.

HAWES, Harry Bartow, ex-senator; b. Covington, Ky., Nov. 15, 1869; s. Smith Nicholas and Susan Elizabeth (Simrall) H.; LL.B., St. Louis Law Sch. (Washington U.), 1896; m. Eppes Osborne Robinson, Nov. 15, 1899; children—Mrs. Peyton Hawes Dunn, Eppes Bartow (Mrs. William Fahnestock, Jr.). Began practice of law, St. Louis, 1896; represented the Republic of Hawaii during annexation to the U.S., 1898; mem. Mo. Ho. of Rep., 1916-17; pres. Bd. Police Commrs., St. Louis, 4 yrs.; mem. 67th to 69th Congresses (1921-27), 11th Mo. Dist.; mem. U.S. Senate, 1927-33, resigned, Feb. 3, 1933; was candidate for gov.; now in practice of law at Washington and St. Louis. Major U.S. Army, and apptd. to mil. intelligence bur.; mil. attaché, Madrid, World War. Democrat. Episcopalian. Mem. Am., Mo., D.C. and St. Louis bar assns., Am. Soc. Internat. Law, Am. Geog. Soc., Am. Econ. Assn., Mo. Hist. Soc., Soc. of St. Louis Authors, Am. Soc. Polit. and Social Science, Chamber of Commerce, Izaak Walton League, Am. Game Assn., Audubon Soc., Am. Forestry Assn., Nat. Rifle Assn., Reserve Officers Assn., S.A.R., Sons Confederate Vets., Am. Legion, Mil. Order World War. Clubs: St. Louis, Racquet, Noonday, Miss. Valley Kennel (pres. many yrs.), Mo. Athletic (St. Louis); Chevy Chase, Metropolitan, National Press (Washington); Lotos (New York); pres. Jefferson Islands Club (Sherwood, Md.); Camp Fire of America, Corinthian Yacht. A leader in behalf of good roads; author of the State Highway Law of Mo., known as the "Hawes Law"; ex-pres. Federated Roads Council of St. Louis and Mo. Good Roads Federation which directed campaign for $60,000,000 road bond issue; an organizer Lakes to Gulf Deep Waterways Assn.; joint author of Hawes-Cutting bill giving Philippines independence; counsel for Philippine Commonwealth. Author: My Friend the Black Bass, 1930; Philippine Uncertainty—An American Problem, 1932; Fish and Game, Now or Never, 1935; also of brochures on "The Dog," and "Conservation." Counselor for great game orgns. of America; apptd. mem. representing U.S. Senate, on Migratory Bird Conservation Commn. Home: 4822 Quebec St. N.W. Office: Transportation Bldg., Washington, D.C. Died Aug. 1, 1947.

HAWES, Richard S., banker; b. Covington, Ky., Dec. 15, 1873; s. Smith N. and Susan Elizabeth (Simrall) H.; ed. pub. schs.; m. Mary T. Kemp, June 30, 1897 (dec.); children—Richard S., Mary Bartow, Robert N., Susan Elizabeth; m. 2d, Mrs. Oliver C. Smith, Apr. 5, 1924. Began in retail jewelry store, Kansas City, 1889, later in employ Miss. River Commn., and in railroad business, Cincinnati; became connected with Chemical Nat. Bank, St. Louis, 1893, and in 1897 with its successor, the Third Nat. Bank, of which was elected v.p., 1911; Third Nat. Bank consolidated, July 1919, with new First Nat. Bank, of which is sr. v.p. Mem. Am. Bankers Assn. (1st v.p. 1918-19, pres., 1919-20), Mo. Bankers Assn. (ex-pres.), Assn. Reserve City Bankers (ex-pres.), St. Louis Chamber of Commerce (ex-pres.). Served as gen. chmn. bankers' com. of Liberty Loan, as chmn. Home Guard Com., chmn. Free Bridge Campaign, chmn. "Buy in St. Louis" League; state treas. United War Work Campaign. Pres. St. Louis Clearing House Assn.; mem. exec. com. Jefferson Nat. Expansion Memorial Assn. Democrat. Episcopalian. Clubs: Bellerive, Noonday, Racquet, Industrial. Home: 4943 Maryland Av., St. Louis, Mo. Died March 23, 1949.

HAWKES, Herbert Edwin, educator; b. Templeton, Mass., Dec. 6, 1872; s. Gen. George P. and Abigail Elizabeth (Sparhawk) H.; A.B., Yale, 1896, Ph.D., 1900, M.A., same, 1920; L.H.D., Hobart Coll., 1928; LL.D., Wabash Coll., 1928, U. of Rochester, 1929, Columbia, U., 1929, Bethany College, 1941; student University of Göttingen, 1901-02; m. Nettie M. Coit, July 8, 1896 (died Oct. 10, 1932); m. 2d, Anna L. Rose, Feb. 17, 1934. Instr. mathematics, 1898, asst. prof., 1903-10, Yale; prof. mathematics, Columbia, since July 1910, acting dean of Columbia Coll., 1917-18, and dean since July 1918. Chmn. bd. Ednl. Records Bur.; pres. Assn. Colls. and Univs. of State of N.Y., 1934-35; chmn. Am. Council on Edn., 1938-39 and mem. exec. com., 1939-42; chmn. Com. on Measurement and Guidance of Am. Council on Edn.; pres. Nat. Council on Religion in Higher Edn., 1930-34; mem. Nat. Com. for Mental Hygiene, Com. on Edn. of Nat. Research Council; pres. Middle States Assn. of Colls. and Secondary Schs., 1927-28, mem. Am. Math. Soc. Mem. bd. trustees Williston Academy. Mem. bd. trustees Hood College. Clubs: Columbia, University, Century. Author: Advanced Algebra, 1905; Higher Algebra, 1913; College, What's the Use?, 1927. Co-author: First Course Algebra, 1910; Second Course Algebra, 1911; Complete School Algebra, 1912; Plane Geometry, 1920; Solid Geometry, 1921; New Plane Geometry, 1929; First Year Algebra, 1934; Second Year Algebra, 1935. Contbr. to Am. and German math. publs. Address: 415 W. 117th St., New York, N.Y. Died May 4, 1943.

HAWKESWORTH, Alan Spencer, clergyman; b. New Orleans, Aug. 10, 1867; s. William Colomb and Gertrude (Victor) H.; taken to England at 4 yrs. of age; ed. Ch. Missionary Coll., London; unmarried. Went to San Antonio, Tex., 1891; ordained deacon P.E. Ch., 1892; went to Buenos Aires, S.A.; ordained priest, 1894; English chaplain, Sao Paulo and Santos, Brazil, 1893-97; rector, Georgetown, St. Vincent, British W.I., 1897, Sheridanville, Pittsburgh, 1905-17. Mathematician in Bur. of Ordnance, Navy Dept., 1917-23. Has traveled extensively in nearly all countries of world; passed through 4 revolutions in S.A., and saw heavy fighting in W.I. (Spanish Main) and China Seas. Fellow A.A.A.S.; perpetual fellow Circolo Matematico di Palermo, 1923; life fellow Royal Society of Arts (England); mem. of Philosophical Society of Washington, Washington Soc. Engrs.; mem. 4th Internat. Math. Congress, Rome, 1908. Mason. Author: Identity of Hebrew and Aryan Roots, 1896; De Incarnatione Verbi Dei, 1897; also various brochures on theol. subjects. Lecturer on philosophy. Has discovered and published nearly 100 new theorems in geometrical conics. Address: 1216 Madison St. N.W., Washington, D.C. Died Oct. 31, 1942.

HAWKINS, Horace Norman, lawyer; b. in Dickson County, Tenn., Feb. 19, 1867; s. Ashton W. and Sarah Ann (May) H.; LL.B., Vanderbilt, 1893; m. Frances Rubin, May 14, 1896 (died Feb. 27, 1913); children—Mary O'Neil, Margaret Marsh, Frances Rubin, Horace Norman, Agnes Luten. Practiced at Huntingdon, Tenn., 1888-92; moved to Denver, Colo., 1893; in office of Hon. T. M. Patterson (later U.S. Senator), 1893-95; mem. Patterson, Richardson & Hawkins, 1895-1903, Richardson & Hawkins, 1903 until death of Mr. Richardson, 1911; practiced in association with son, Horace N., since 1925; lecturer Westminster Law Sch. since 1928, pres. since 1940; special representative 1941, acting as hearing officer for Dept. of Justice regarding pleas for exemption from military service on grounds of conscientious scruples. Mem. Colo. Bar Examining Bd., 1902-05, Civil Service Bd., 1911-13; mem. Colo. State Council Defense during World War, also mem. exec. com. Denver Liberty Loan League; mem. City Council, Denver, 1918, 19. Mem. advisory bd., U. of Colo.; chmn. bd. trustees Westminster Law School, 1941. Mem. Am. and Colo. bar assns., Denver Bar Assn. (pres. 1908), Phi Delta Theta. Del. to Dem. Nat. Conv., San Francisco, 1920, and mem. com. on resolutions and platform. Club: Denver. Home: Lakewood, Colo. Office: Ernest and Cranmer Bldg., Denver, Colo. Died May 24, 1947.

HAWKINS, Morris Seymour, ry. official; b. Norfolk, Va., Jan. 21, 1882; s. Edward A. and Ella (Morris) H.; ed. pub. schs.; m. Genevieve Elizabeth Parker, Nov. 14, 1907; 1 dau., Genevieve Hawkins Knoll. Clk. Southern Ry. Co., 1899-1909, agt. at Norfolk, Va., 1909-10; sec. Norfolk Southern R.R. Co., 1910-12, sec. and asst. to pres., 1912-18, and 1920-32; asst. to Fed. mgr. Norfolk Southern R.R. and Va. Ry., 1918-19; Fed. mgr. Norfolk Southern R.R., Kingston Carolina R.R., Carolina R.R., 1919-20; asst. to pres. and sec. Kingston Carolina R.R., Carolina R.R., 1920-32; asst. to receivers of Norfolk Southern R.R., 1932-33; co-receiver Norfolk Southern R.R., 1933-42, when receivership ended, now pres. and dir. Norfolk Southern Railway Co.; pres., dir. Norfolk & Portsmouth Belt Line R.R. Co., Norfolk Southern Bus Corp., Princess Anne Power Co.; dir. Seaboard Citizens Nat. Bank. Clubs: Virginia, Norfolk Yacht and Country (Norfolk); Princess Anne Country. Home: North Shore Point. Office: Norfolk Terminal Railway Co. Bldg., Norfolk, Va. Died Mar. 14, 1946.

HAY, Charles Martin, lawyer; b. Brunot, Wayne County, Mo., Nov. 10, 1879; s. William Henry and Lucy (Pease) H.; A.B., Central Coll., Fayette, Mo., 1901 (prizes in scholarship and oratory), LL.D., 1926; LL.B., Washington U., 1904 (class orator); m. Rosella Lanius, Sept. 8, 1904; children—Frances, Mrs. Lucille Thoele, James Lanius. Practiced at Greenville, Mo., 1904, Fulton, 1905-13; in St. Louis since 1913; mem. Hay & Flanagan, general law practice, since 1925. Mem. Mo. Ho. of Rep., 1913-14; del.-at-large Dem. Nat. Conv., 1924; chmn. Dem. State Conv., 1924, 28; Dem. nominee for U.S. Senate, 1928; counselor City of St. Louis, Apr. 1932-Dec. 1935; apptd. vice chmn. Railroad Pension Commn., Dec. 1935; spl. assistant to U.S. Atty. Gen. engaged to defend Railroad Retirement Act, 1936; counsel for Ry. Labor Execs. Assn. in R.R. retirement and R.R. unemployment insurance legislation, and in trial in 1938 R.R. Wage case before President's Emergency Bd.; counsel for Operating Brotherhoods in railroad wage case, 1941; part time mem. 7th region War Labor Bd., 1942-43; gen. council, War Manpower Commn. since 1943; chmn. St. Louis Bd. of Election Commrs., 1939-41. Trustee Central Coll. Mem. Am. Bar Assn. (Mo. del. to House of Dels.), Mo. State and St. Louis bar assns., S.A.R., Phi Delta Phi. Methodist; lay mem. Gen. Conf. M.E. Ch., S., 1926. Mason. Club: Mo. Athletic. Home: 9 Windermere Pl. Office: 506 Olive St., St. Louis, Mo. Died Jan. 16, 1945.

HAY, Logan, lawyer; b. Springfield, Ill., Feb. 13, 1871; s. Milton and Mary (Logan) H.; prep. edn., Lawrenceville (N.J.) Sch.; B.A., Yale U., 1893; LL.B., Harvard University, 1897; LL.D., Illinois College, 1929; m. Lucy Langdon Bowen, November 9, 1899; children—Mary Douglass (Mrs. Donald S. Funk), Alice Houghton (Mrs. Albert C. Schlipf). Admitted to Ill. bar, 1897, and practiced since at Springfield; mem. Brown, Hay & Stephens since 1921. Mem. City Council, Springfield, 1903-06; mem. Ill. State Senate, 1907-15. Vice-pres. Associated Welfare Agencies of Springfield, Abraham Lincoln Council of Boy Scouts (president 1920-23). Mem. Am. Bar Assn., Ill. State Bar Assn. (pres. 1920-21), Am. Law Inst., Assn. Bar of New York. Abraham Lincoln Assn. (pres. since 1924). Republican. Clubs: Sangamo, Illini Country (Springfield); University (Chicago); Century (New York). Home: 1220 S. Grand Av. W. Office: First Nat. Bank Bldg., Springfield, Ill. Died June 2, 1942.

HAY, Samuel Ross, bishop; b. Decatur County, Tenn., Oct. 15, 1865; s. William and Martha Jane (England) H.; ed. Southwestern U., Tex.; D.D., Southwestern; LL.D., Centenary Coll., La., Southern Coll., Lakeland, Fla.; m. Della Binford, June 11, 1889 (died Jan. 1899); children—Horace, Sam R.; m. 2d, Margaret Gulick, Aug. 21, 1900; 1 dau., Margaret (Mrs. Clay J. Berry). Licensed to preach, 1886; ordained deacon, 1889; elder, 1893; junior preacher 1st Ch. Paris, Tex., 1887; pastor Lamar Av. Ch., Paris, 1888, Oak Cliff, Dallas, 1889-90, Abilene, 1891-92, Trinidad, Colo., 1892-93, Belton, Tex., 1893-95, Vernon, Tex., 1895-97, Mexia, Tex., 1897-98, Corsicana, Tex., 1898-99, Shearn Ch., Houston, 1900-04; presiding elder Houston Dist., 1905-06; pastor Centenary Ch., St. Louis, 1906-07, Beaumont, Tex., 1907-08; presiding elder Ft. Worth (Tex.) Dist., 1908-10; pastor St. Paul's Ch., Houston, 1910-14, 1st Ch., Dallas, 1914-17; presiding elder Dallas Dist., 1917-19; pastor Amarillo, Tex., 1919, 1st Ch., Houston, 1919-22; elected bishop, May 16, 1922, and appointed bishop in charge of work in China, 1922-23; bishop in charge Ark. and La., 1924-25, in charge east half of Tex. and Pacific coast, 1926-30, in charge west half Tex. and N.M., 1930-34, then in charge Ala. and Fla.; now retired. Mem. Joint Hymnal Commn. to prepare Methodist Hymnal, 1930-34; mem. Gen. Conf. of Methodist Ch., S., 1906, 10, 14, 18, 22. Was mem. Lausanne World War Conf. on Faith and Order; mem. Ecumenical Conf. of Methodism, Toronto, 1911; mem. Ecumenical Conf., Atlanta, Ga., 1931; pres. Bd. of Missions of Methodist Ch., S., 1932-34; mem. Bd. of Ch. Extension, 1910-34. Sent to Mexico, 1930, to set up the autonomous Methodist Ch. of Mexico. Democrat. Address: 4004 Mt. Vernon St., Houston, Tex.* Died Feb. 19, 1944.

HAY, William Henry, army officer; b. Fla., July 16, 1860; grad. U.S. Mil. Acad., 1886, Inf. and Cav. Sch., 1891, Army War Coll., 1913; married; children—Thomas Robson, William Wren, Edward Northup, Richard Carman. Second lt. 3d Cav., July 1, 1886; 1st lt. 10th Cav., July 21, 1893; capt. a.q.m. vols., Nov. 26, 1898; hon. discharged volunteers, March 15, 1901; capt., U.S.A., Feb. 2, 1901; advanced through grades to the rank of col., July 1, 1916; brig. gen. N.A., Oct. 31, 1917; maj. gen. N.A., Oct. 1, 1918; brig. gen. regular army, Apr. 11, 1922; maj. gen., Nov. 5, 1923; retired, Nov. 6, 1923. Apptd. comdr. 15th Cav., Manila, P.I., 1916; comdr. 184th Brig., 92d Div., Nov. 5, 1917-Oct. 24, 1918; comdg. 28th Div., Oct. 25, 1918-Apr. 17, 1919; demoted grade of col. regular U.S. Army, Mar. 15, 1920; insp. gen., July 1920; Gen. Staff and chief of staff, Am. Forces in Germany, May 9, 1921-Apr. 25, 1922; comdr. 1st Cav. Brig., 1st Cav. Div., Aug. 18-Nov. 17, 1922. Campgians: St. Die sector, Vosgres, Pont-à-Mousson sector, Thiancourt sector, Meuse-Argonne offensive, offensive of 2d Army. Awarded D.S.M. (U.S.); Croix de Guerre with two palms, and Comdr. Legion of Honor (French); Comdr. Black Star; Comdr. Order of Leopold (Belgian). Address: War Dept., Washington. Died Dec. 17, 1946.

HAY, William Perry, biologist; b. Eureka, Ill., Dec. 8, 1872; s. Oliver Perry and Mary Emily (Howsmon) H.; B.S., Butler U., Ind., 1890, M.S., 1891; m. Annie Aletha McKnew, Dec. 19, 1902. Teacher zoölogy, Central High Sch., Washington, 1892-98, biology, 1898-99; head dept. biology, Washington high schs., 1899-01; asst. prof. zoölogy, Columbian, 1898-99; prof. biology and geology, Howard U., 1901-07; head dept. biology and chemistry, Washington high schs., since Sept., 1907. Lecturer on zoölogy, Georgetown U., 1898; engaged in investigations for U.S. Bur. of Fisheries, 1900-15. Contbr. to various publs. on zoöl. subjects. Fellow A.A.A.S.; mem. Biol. Soc. Washington (pres. 1916-17), Washington Acad. Sciences, Nat. Fisheries Soc., Washington Biologists' Field Club (pres. 1901-04, 1915-16). Home: Kensington, Md. Died Jan. 26, 1947.

HAYDEN, Joel Babcock, clergyman; b. Reading, Pa., Feb. 12, 1888; s. Harry Johnson and Jessie

Evelyn (Hinds) H.; prep. edn., Oberlin (O.) Acad.; A.B., Oberlin Coll., 1909; B.D., Union Theol. Sem., 1912; D.D., Western Reserve, 1928; m. Hazel Bernice Petty, June 15, 1912; children—Mrs. Jean Guarnaccia, Joel Babcock. Ordained Presbyterian ministry, 1912; immigration fellow, Bd. National Missions, Presbyterian Ch. U.S.A., in Russia and Poland, 1912-13; pastor St. Paul's Presbyn. Ch., Baltimore, Md., 1914-17, Woodland Av. Presbyn. Ch., Cleveland, O., 1917-23, Fairmount Presbyn. Ch., Cleveland, 1923-31; dir. Woodland Center, 1923-26; headmaster Western Reserve Acad., Hudson, Ohio, 1931-47, emeritus since Aug. 1947. Trustee Oberlin College American Farm Sch. (Salonica, Greece), Brush Foundation; mem. Headmasters Assn., Nat. Prep. Sch. Com. Y.M.C.A., Citizens Library Com. of Ohio; v.p. New England Soc. (Cleveland); mem. bd. dirs. Am. Relief for Czechoslovakia, Inc. Mem. Adult Edn. Assn., Cleveland (pres. 1926-27). Mem. Bd. Nat. Missions, Presbyn. Ch., U.S.A., 1913-30; mem. Boys Work Com., Internat. Y.M.C.A., 1935-37. Mem. A.A.A.S., Phi Beta Kappa (Oberlin, 1909). Clubs: University, City, Alathians. Contbr. to Whither Christianity, 1929; also to Adult Edn. (mag.). Home: Hudson, Ohio. Died Jan. 10, 1950.

HAYDEN, Joseph Ralston, prof. polit. science; b. Quincy, Ill., Sept. 24, 1887; s. Philip Cady and Mary Neely (Ralston) H.; B.S., Knox Coll., Galesburg, Ill., 1910, LL.D., 1928; M.A., U. of Mich., 1911, Ph.D., 1915; m. Elizabeth Olivia Hall, Aug. 25, 1917; children—Mrs. Elizabeth Douglas Pearson, Mary Ralston, Ralston. Reporter Constitution-Democrat, Keokuk, Ia., 1905-06; asst. in Am. history, U. of Mich., 1910-12, mem. faculty of polit. science since 1912, prof. of polit. science since 1924, chmn. dept. since 1937, James Orrin Murfin prof., 1941; was on leave absence as vice gov. and sec. of pub. instrn. P.I., 1933-35; exchange prof., U. of Philippines, 1922-23; visiting prof., same, 1930-31; Ernest A. Hamill visiting prof., U. of Chicago, summer quarter, 1940; member board of analysts Office of Strategic Services, 1941; civil affairs advisor in Philippines, 1945. Director East Indies Institute of America since 1942. Chairman Commission on Reform and Modernization of Government, State of Mich., 1938-39. Dir. round table on Philippine Islands, Inst. of Politics, Williamstown, 1927; spl. corr. in Far East, Christian Science Monitor, 1922-23, 1926, 1930-31; mem. bd. Current History Associates. Current History, 1925-30; civilian adviser, cons. on Philippine civil affairs for War Dept. on staff of Gen. MacArthur, 1943-45. Lt. Mich. Naval Militia, sr. officer univ. divs., 1917; lt. U.S.N.R.F., active service, Apr. 1917-Feb. 1919. Mem. Am. Polit. Science Assn. (sec.-treas. 1925-29; 3d v.p. 1931), Am. Council of Inst. Pacific Relations (trustee, 1940), Detroit Com., Council on Foreign Relations. Phi Beta Kappa, Phi Kappa Phi, Phi Gamma Delta. Awarded silver star citation by secretary of Navy. Episcopalian. Author: The Senate and Treaties, 1789-1817, 1920; The Philippines: a Study in National Development, 1941; The Philippines, Past and Present (with Dean C. Worcester), 1930. Contbr. articles on govt. and politics. Home: 1530 Hill St., Ann Arbor, Mich. Died May 19, 1945.

HAYES, Arthur Badley, lawyer; b. in Warren County, Ia., Nov. 8, 1859; s. Rev. James and Elizabeth K. (Middleton) H.; student Northwestern Normal Sch. for short time, 2 terms at Lake Language Sch. and Ohio Wesleyan U.; studied law in offices at Fostoria and Tiffin, O., 3 yrs.; m. Ida E. Walker, Mar. 23, 1893; 1 son, Arthur Badley. Taught sch. for 3 yrs. at Fostoria; engaged in newspaper work for 10 yrs.; mng. editor and editorial writer, Nebraska State Journal, Lincoln, 1885-89; went to Utah, 1890; engaged in newspaper work at Ogden, then in mining and later in practice of law since 1892; state's dist. atty., 2d Jud. Dist., Utah, 1901-03; solicitor of internal revenue, Dept. of Justice, 1903-08; practicing in Washington since 1908, making a specialty of interstate commerce law. Apptd. judge of U.S. Dist. Court, Dist. of Alaska, by Pres. Roosevelt, 1902, but declined. Actively engaged in politics since 1883. Republican. Mason (33°, S.J.U.S.A.); gen. sec. Scottish Rite bodies in Washington. Home: 3041 Sedgewick St. N.W. Office: 2800 16th St., N.W., Washington, D.C. Died Sep. 26, 1942.

HAYES, Hammond Vinton, engr.; b. Madison, Wis., Aug. 28, 1860; s. William Allen and Elisabeth (Vinton) H.; A.B., Harvard, 1883, A.M., Ph.D., 1885; Mass. Inst. Tech., 1884-85; unmarried. Entered employ Am. Bell Telephone Co., 1885, in charge of lab. and later was made elec. engr., asst. chief engr. and chief engr., Am. Telephone & Telegraph Co., 1902-07; consulting engr., 1907-24; pres. Submarine Signal Corp., 1925-30. Fellow Am. Inst. E.E., Am. Acad. Arts and Sciences; mem. A.A.A.S. Republican. Episcopalian. Clubs: Union (Boston); University (New York). Author: Public Utilities—Their Cost New and Depreciation; Public Utilities—Their Fair Present Value and Return. Assisted in development of telephony and infra-red signaling. Home: 48 Beacon St. Office: 253 Summer St., Boston, Mass. Died Mar. 22, 1947.

HAYES, James Edward, retired business executive; b. Brooklyn, N.Y., Oct. 28, 1872; s. James Edward and Anna (Lincoln) H.; student Brooklyn Poly. Inst., 1885-91; C.E., Princeton, 1895, E.E., 1897; unmarried. Retired since Sept. 30, 1946. Mem. Am. Mining Congress, Am. Inst. Mining and Metall. Engrs., Am. Inst. E.E., Princeton Engring Soc., Pa. Soc. Republican. Clubs: University, Princeton, Down Town Assn., New York Yacht (New York); Blue Ridge Country; Wallkill Golf; University Cottage. Home: 299 Park Av., N.Y. City. Died Aug. 6, 1948.

HAYES, Jay Orley, newspaper pub.; b. Waterloo, Wis., Oct. 2, 1857; s. Anson Everis and Mary (Folsom) H.; LL.B., U. of Wis., 1880; m. Clara Isabel Lyon, June 16, 1885; children—Mildred Mary (Mrs. Almon E. Roth), Lyetta Adelia, Elystus Lyon, Miriam Folsom (Mrs. Edgar C. Kester), Jay Orlo. Admitted to Wis. bar, 1880, and began practice at Madison; moved to Santa Clara County, Calif., 1887, and since engaged in mining, fruit raising; pub. (with brother) San Jose Daily Mercury Herald since 1901; pres. Mercury Herald Co., Sierra Buttes Canal & Water Co.; sec.-treas. Hayes-Chenoweth Co. Mem. Rep. State Central Com. of Calif., 1902-35; del. at large to Rep. Nat. Conv., 1916; del. to Rep. Nat. Conv., 1928; Rep. candidate for gov. of Calif., 1918. Former mem. Bd. of Regents, U. of Calif. Mem. Wis. State Hist. Soc., San Jose C. of C. Mem. True Life Ch. Mason, Odd Fellow. Clubs: Commercial, Country. Home: Eden Vale, San Jose. Office: Mercury Herald Bldg., San Jose, Calif. Died Aug. 31, 1948.

HAYES, John William, labor leader; b. Phila., Dec. 26, 1854; s. Edward and Mary (Galbreath) H.; entirely self taught; m. Nellie A. Carlen, July 1882. With Pa. R.R. Co. as brakeman in early life; lost right arm, May 28, 1878, on N.Y. div. Pa. R.R. Learned telegraphy; worked at it until strike of 1883; mem. gen. exec. bd., 1884-88, sec.-treas., 1888-1902, gen. master workman since Nov. 1902, Knights of Labor; was editor Journal of the Knights of Labor, and National Labor Digest. Pres. North Chesapeake Beach Land and Improvement Co. Home: North Beach, Md. Died Nov. 24, 1942.

HAYES, Max S., newspaper editor; b. Havana, Huron County, O., May 25, 1866; s. Joseph and Elizabeth (Borer) H.; moved with parents to Fremont, O., 1876, to Cleveland, 1883; common sch. edn.; m. Dora Schneider, Dec. 11, 1900; 1 dau., Maxine Elizabeth. Learned printer's trade; aided in establishing the Cleveland Citizen, Feb. 1891, and has edited it since 1892. Paper was Populist until 1896, since then trade union organ of the Cleveland Federation of Labor. Was nominated for v.p. U.S. at Nat. Conv. Socialist Labor Party at Rochester, N.Y., Feb. 2, 1900, but resigned from ticket 2 months later when that party united with Social Dem. Party; candidate for Congress, 21st Ohio Dist., 1900, for sec. of state Ohio (Socialist party), 1902. Held many positions of trust in trade unions and the Socialist orgns.; elected by Nat. Conv. Am. Federation of Labor, Nov. 1902, fraternal del. to Brit. Trade Union Congress, Leicester, Eng., Sept. 1903; chmn. exec. com. Nat. Labor Party, 1919; candidate for vice-pres. Farmer-Labor Party ticket, 1920. Apptd. to Met. Housing Authority for slum elimination, 1933, to State Adjustment Bd. NRA, 1934. Home: 2829 Coventry Rd. Office: E. 12th St. and Chester Av., Cleveland, O. Died Oct. 11, 1945.

HAYES, Philip, army officer; b. Portage, Wis., June 16, 1887; B.S., U.S. Mil. Acad., 1909; grad. F.A. Sch., 1923; distinguished grad. Command and Gen. Staff Sch., 1924; grad. Army War Coll., 1930. Commd. 2d lt., Inf., 1909, transferred to F.A., 1915, and advanced through the grades to major gen., Jan. 17, 1944; instr., U.S. Mil. Acad., 1912-17; with 2d F.A., Camp Stotsenburg, P.I., 1917-18, F.A., Camp Grant, Jan.-July 1918; with War Plans Div., War Dept. Gen. Staff, Washington, D.C., 1918-19; exec. for athletics, U.S. Mil. Acad., 1919-22; instr., F.A. Sch., Ft. Sill, 1924-27; exec. of F.A. Sch., 1927-29; instr., Command and Gen. Staff Sch., Ft. Leavenworth, Kas., 1930-35; comdr., 19th F.A., Fort Benjamin Harrison, Ind., 1935-37; asst. chief of staff, G-3 (Operations and Training), Hawaiian Dept., Ft. Shafer, Hawaii, 1937-39, chief of staff, 1939-41; prof. mil. science and tactics, Harvard U., Dec. 1941-Mar. 1942; chief of staff, hdqrs. 1st Corps Area (1st Service Command), Boston, Mar. 1942-May 1943; exec. for Deputy chief of staff for Service Commands, May-Aug. 1943; acting deputy chief of staff for service commands to Nov. 30, 1943; commanding general, Third Service Command, Army Service Forces, since December 1, 1943. Retired as major general U.S. Army May 31, 1946. President, Tower Realty Co. since 1946. Home: 10 St. Martins Rd., Baltimore 18. Office: American Bldg., Baltimore 2, Md. Died Nov. 25, 1949.

HAYES, Watson McMillan, missionary; b. near Greenfield, Mercer County, Pa., Nov. 23, 1857; s. David and Margaret Jane (Watson) H.; A.B., Westminster Coll., Pa., 1879; grad. Western Theol. Sem., Pittsburgh, 1882; D.D., Westminster, 1900; LL.D., Washington and Jefferson and Westminster, 1913; m. Margaret Ellen Young, July 5, 1882; children—John D., Agnes Irene (dec.), Ernest M. Ordained Presbyn. ministry, 1882; prof., 1893-95, pres., 1896-1901, Tengchow Coll., China; founder and pres. Provincial U. of Shantung, 1901-03; prof. Union Theol. Sem., Tsinan, Shantung, China, 1904-19; pres. North China Theol. Sem., 1919-37, pres. emeritus since 1937. Founder North China Women's Bible Sem., 1924. Translator in Chinese and author of 31 scientific theol. and math. text-books; editor and pub. Shantung Times (first newspaper published in Shantung). Drew up system of edn. approved by Empress of China as system for the Empire, embodying in same provision that Sunday shall be a holiday in all govt. schs. and colls. With D. McGillivray, gen. editor New Critical and Expository Commentary N.T. (Chinese); mem. revision com. Chinese edit. Internat. Standard Biblical Ency. Address: Tenghsien, Sung, China (via Shanghai). Died Aug. 2, 1944.

HAYNES, George Henry, college prof.; b. Sturbridge, Mass., Mar. 20, 1866; s. Henry Dunton and Eliza Marshall (Carter) H.; A.B., Amherst, 1887, L.H.D., 1933; Ph.D., Johns Hopkins, 1893; Sc.D., Worcester Polytechnic Institute, 1944; m. Annie Bliss Chapman, Nov. 4, 1903. Instr., 1887-90, prof. economics and government, 1893-1937, prof. emeritus since 1938, Worcester Polytechnic Inst.; Schouler lecturer Johns Hopkins, 1929. Sec. Worcester Associated Charities, 1894-1920, pres., 1920-23; mem. Worcester Welfare Investigating Commn., 1929. Mem. Am. Antiq. Soc., The Bohemians, Phi Beta Kappa, Sigma Xi, Delta Kappa Epsilon. Mng. ed., Jour. of Worcester Poly. Inst., 1905-22. Author: Representation and Suffrage in Massachusetts (1620-1691), 1894; Representation in State Legislatures, 1900; The Election of Senators, 1906; Charles Sumner, 1909; The Life of Charles G. Washburn, 1931; The Senate of the United States: Its History and Practice, 1938. Contbr. many articles on representation, suffrage, initiative, referendum, and the U.S. Senate, also sketches in Dictionary of Am. Biography. Address: 7 Otsego Rd., Worcester, Mass. Died Oct. 30, 1947.

HAYNES, Irving Samuel, physician; b. Saranac, N.Y., Aug. 29, 1861; s. Samuel and Phebe (Ayre) H.; Ph.B., Wesleyan, 1885; M.D., University Med. Coll. (New York U.), 1887; (Sc.D., Wesleyan U., 1915); m. Charlotte E. Scribner, Mar. 19, 1890 (died Dec. 7, 1897); m. 2d, Laura C. Marsh, July 5, 1899 (died July 26, 1935); children—Harriett Marsh, Dorothy Helen, Irving Samuel (dec.). Interne Bellevue Hosp., 1887-88; visiting surgeon Harlem Hosp., 1895-1922, cons. surgeon since 1922; visiting surgeon New York Park Hosp., 1909-17; cons. surgeon Reconstruction Hosp., Glens Falls Hosp.; supt. Physicians Hospital (Plattsburg), 1931-1943; prof. practical anatomy, Univ. Med. Coll., 1888-98; prof. applied anatomy, 1898-1917, prof. clin. surg., 1911, now emeritus, Cornell U. Med. Coll. Fellow Am. Coll. Surgeons; mem. A.M.A., Clinton County Med. Soc., N.Y. Surg. Soc., D.K.E., S.A.R.; hon. Phi Beta Kappa (Wesleyan, 1914). Pres. trustees Park Av. M.E. Ch., 1900-28; mem. bd. govs. Lake Champlain Assn., 1909-28; mem. bd. dirs. Physicians Hosp. since 1944. Author: Practical Guide for Beginners to the Dissection of the Human Body, 1893; Manual of Anatomy, 1896. Contbr. to various med. jours. Home: Plattsburg, N.Y. Died Oct. 9, 1946.

HAYS, Charles Thomas, judge; b. New London, Mo., May 9, 1869; m. Sarah Margaret Brashears, May 25, 1897; children—Agnes (Mrs. J. C. Ferguson), Margaret Ann (Mrs. R. E. Hibbard), George Campbell, Charles Thomas, Jr. (deceased). Has been city atty. Town of New London, also mayor; removed to Hannibal, Mo., 1907; mayor City of Hannibal, 1911-12; became judge of 10th Judicial Circuit, 1919; elected asso. judge of the Mo. Supreme Court, 1932, elected chief justice, 1937, retired from bench, Dec. 31, 1942. Mem. Beta Theta Pi. Mem. Christian Ch. Mason. Home: R.F.D. 1, New London, Mo. Died Feb. 6, 1949.

HAYWARD, Nathan, corp. official; b. Boston, Mass., Aug. 27, 1872; s. James Warren and Sarah Bancroft (Howard) H.; student Roxbury Latin Sch., 1885-91; A.B., Harvard, 1895; S.B., Mass. Inst. of Tech., 1897; m. Anna Howell Lloyd, April 30, 1907; children—Anna Howell, Nathan, Sarah Howard, Malcolm Lloyd, Esther Lloyd. Instr. in Mass. Inst. of Tech., 1897-98; with Bell Telephone Co. of Pa., as engr., later cons. engr., 1898-1922; pres. Am. Dredging Co. since 1917; Am. Shipyard Co. since 1919; director Bell Telephone Company of Pennsylvania, Philadelphia and Reading Coal and Iron Co., Philadelphia Saving Fund Society, Philadelphia Belt Line R.R. Co., Fidelity-Phila. Trust Co. Served asso. chief on War Industries Bd., World War. Pres. Franklin Inst., 1928-37; mem. bd. of overseers of Harvard U.; mem. advisory com. Pa. Hosp.; dir. Philadelphia Maritime Exchange. Member American Philosophical Soc., New England Soc. of Pa., Am. Inst. of Elect. Engrs., Newcomen Soc. (Eng.), Telephone Pioneers of America, Hist. Soc. of Pa., Acad. of Natural Sciences of Phila., Fairmount Park Art Assn., Nat. Assn. of River and Harbor Contractors, Dredge Owners Protective Orgn. Republican. Unitarian. Clubs: Harvard, Rittenhouse, Engineers (Philadelphia); Harvard (Boston); Harvard (New York); Jean Ribaut (Florida); Manchester Yacht (Mass.). Home: Brook Rd., Wayne, Pa. Office: 12 S. 12th St., Philadelphia, Pa. Died June 21, 1944.

HAYWARD, William, lawyer; b. Nebraska City, Neb., Apr. 29, 1877; s. Monroe Leland and Jane (Pelton) H.; studied Munich, Germany, 1896-97; LL.B., U. of Neb., 1897; mem. varsity football and baseball teams (manager), and pres. Class of 1897; married; 1 son, Leland; m. 2d, Mrs. Mae C. Plant, June 21, 1919. Began practice at Nebraska City, 1897; captain 2d Nebraska Inf. in Spanish-Am. War; col. 2d Inf., Neb. N.G., 1898-1901; pvt. sec. M. L. Hayward, U.S. senator from Neb., 1899; county judge Otoe County, Neb., 1901-02; chmn. Rep. State Central Com., 1907-09; sec. Rep. Nat. Com., 1908-12. Traveled around world, 1910-11. Mem. law firm Wing & Russell, New York, May 1, 1911-12; asst. dist. atty., 1913-14; counsel to the gov. (Whitman), 1915, and to N.Y. legislative com. to investigate pub. service commns.; pub. service commr. 1st Dist. N.Y., term 1915-20, resigned Jan. 1, 1918. Recruited, organized and trained 15th Inf. N.G.N.Y. (colored), later the 369th U.S. Inf.; regt. was with 1st contingent A.E.F. in France, 1917; brigaded with 4th French Army under Gen. Gouraud to end of war; under fire 191 days (longer than any other Am.

regt.); participated in battles of 1918, and in Sept.-Oct. offensives as picked shock unit; regt. awarded citation for gallantry and colors decorated with Croix de Guerre; after armistice led French armies to the Rhine, being 1st Allied unit into Germany; 1st combat unit to return to U.S. Personally awarded D.S.M. and extra citation (U.S.); awarded Croix de Guerre and Officier Légion d'Honneur (French). U.S. atty. Southern Dist. of N.Y., 1921-25. Chmn. Rep. State Conv., 1920; del. Rep. Nat. Conv., 1924. Traveled and hunted big game in East and Central Africa, 1926-27; made Arctic expdn. to Franz Josef Land, 1929; captured live polar bears for New York Zoo. Mem. Assn. Bar City of New York, S.R., Spanish War Vets., Am. Legion, Phi Delta Theta, Phi Delta Phi. Clubs: Union League, Circumnavigators (New York); Everglades, Seminole (Palm Beach, Fla.); Sand Point (N.Y.) Golf. Home: 1051 5th Av. Office: 1 E. 42d St., New York, N.Y. Died Oct. 13, 1944.

HAZARD, Caroline, ex-college pres.; b. Peace Dale, R.I., June 10, 1856; d. Rowland and Margaret Anna (Rood) Hazard; ed. by governess and tutors, and at Miss Mary A. Shaw's Sch., Providence; pvt. study abroad; hon. A.M., U. of Mich., 1899; Litt.D., Brown Univ., 1899, Mills Coll., 1931; LL.D., Tufts College, 1905, Wellesley College, 1925, Rhode Island State College, 1942. President Wellesley College, 1899-1910. Life member R.I. Hist. Society; mem. Am. Acad. Polit. and Social Science, Am. Hist. Assn., Am. Polit. Science Assn., Am. Social Science Assn., Archæol. Inst. America, N.E. Hist.-Geneal. Soc., Religious Edn. Assn.; corporate mem. A.B.C.F.M., Colonial Dames of R.I., Narragansett Chapter D.A.R. Elector Hall of Fame. Chmn. for S. Kingston (R.I.) Census, under Woman's Council Nat. Defense, 1916; chmn. Woman's Council Nat. Defense, July-Dec. 1916; 1st Liberty Loan, 1916; War Savings Campaign, 1917; United War Work Campaign, 1918; pres. South County Hosp. Assn., 1919-29. President Gilbert Stuart Memorial, Incorporated; hon. pres. South County Hosp.; hon. pres. Santa Barbara (California) Museum of Natural History. Author: Life of J. L. Diman, 1886; Thomas Hazard, Son of Robert, 1893; Narragansett Ballads, 1894; The Narragansett Friends' Meeting, 1899; Some Ideals in the Education of Women, 1900; A Scallop Shell of Quiet, 1908; A Brief Pilgrimage in the Holy Land, 1909; The College Year, 1910; The Yosemite and Other Verse, 1917; Anchors of Tradition, 1924; From College Gates, 1925; Songs in the Sun, 1927; The Homing (verse), 1929; Shards and Scarabs (verse), 1931; Threads from the Distaff, 1934; The Golden State (verse), 1939; Introduction to an Academic Courtship, 1940; also essays, revs., verses, etc., in mags. Editor: Works of R. G. Hazard (4 vols.), 1889; South County Studies (by Esther Bernon Carpenter), 1924; John Saffin His Book, 1664-1707, 1928; Nailer Tom's Diary, 1778-1840, 1930. Home: Peace Dale, R.I. Died Mar. 19, 1945.

HAZELTINE, Mary Emogene, librarian, bibliographer; b. in Jamestown, New York, May 5, 1868; d. of Abner and Olivia (Brown) Hazeltine; B.S., Wellesley (Mass.) Coll., 1891. Librarian of James Prendergast Free Library, Jamestown, N.Y., 1893-1906; prin. Library Sch. and asso. prof. bibliography, U. of Wis., 1906-38. Mem. A.L.A., N.Y. Library Assn. (pres. 1902), Wis. Library Assn., Am. Assn. Univ. Women, Y.W.C.A., D.A.R., Phi Beta. Republican. CongList. Clubs: College, Fortnightly, Mozart. Author: Anniversaries and Holidays, 1928, revised edit, 1944; One Hundred Years of Wisconsin Authorship, 1836-1937—A Contribution to a Bibliography of Books by Wisconsin Authors, 1937. Contbr. to Wis. Library Bull., professional jours. and Encyclopaedia Britannica. Home: 109 Price St., Jamestown, N.Y. Died June 16, 1949; buried Lakeview Cemetery, Jamestown, N.Y.

HAZEN, Charles Downer, educator; b. Barnet, Vt., Mar. 17, 1868; s. Lucius Downer and Orinda (Kimball) H.; A.B., Dartmouth, 1889; Johns Hopkins, 1889-90; univs. of Göttingen, Berlin, and Paris, 1890-92; Ph.D., Johns Hopkins, 1893; L.H.D., Hobart, 1911, Rollins Coll., 1933; Litt.D., Dartmouth, 1914; LL.D., Smith Coll., 1937; m. Sara Sefton Duryea, June 26, 1901. Prof. history, Smith Coll., 1894-1914, Columbia, 1916-38; prof. emeritus, Columbia, since 1938. Lecturer, Columbia, 1910-11, Johns Hopkins, 1915-17; prof. at U. of Strasbourg, France, 1920-21. Mem. Am. Acad. Arts and Letters, Am. Acad. Arts and Sciences, Am. Philos. Soc., Royal Hist. Soc., Am. Geog. Soc., Am. Hist. Assn., Am. Polit. Science Assn., Am. Acad. Polit. and Social Science, Am. Soc. Internat. Law, N.Y. Hist. Soc., France-America Soc., Mass. Hist. Soc., New England Soc. of New York, Société d'Historie Moderne (Paris, France), Institut International d'Histoire de la Révolution Française, Phi Beta Kappa, Delta Kappa Epsilon; hon. mem. Vt. Hist. Soc. Chevalier Légion d'Honneur (France). Clubs: Century, University (N.Y. City); Union Interalliée (Paris). Author: Contemporary American Opinion of the French Revolution, 1897; Old Northampton, 1904; Europe since 1815, 1910 (enlarged edit., 2 vols., 1923); Modern European History, 1917, 37; The French Revolution and Napoleon, 1917; Alsace-Lorraine under German Rule, 1917; The Government of Germany, 1917; Fifty Years of Europe, 1919; Modern Europe, 1920; French Revolution (2 vols.), 1932. Co-author: Historical Sources in Schools, 1902; Three Peace Congresses of the Nineteenth Century, 1917. Editor: Historical Essays (by Lord Macaulay), 1921; The Kaiser vs. Bismarck, 1921; The Letters of William Roscoe Thayer 1926. Translator: Adoption and Amendment of Constitutions (by Charles Borgeaud, U. of Geneva), 1895. Home: 42 E. 75th St., New York, N.Y. Died Sept. 18, 1941.

HAZEN, William Livingston, educator; b. Elizabeth, N.J., May 4, 1861; s. Aaron Coursen and Sarah (Young) H.; A.B., Columbia, 1883, LL.B., 1885; LL.D., Manhattan Coll., N.Y. City, 1933; m. Olive Starr, Oct. 23, 1889; children—Starr (dec.), Eleanor (dec.), Elizabeth Starr (Mrs. Burritt Alden Cushman, Jr.). Began as teacher, 1883; founder Barnard Sch. for Boys, N.Y. City, 1886, and since headmaster; founder Barnard Sch. for Girls, 1896, and since headmaster; founder Camp Iroquois for Boys, Mallett's Bay, Vt., 1899, and since pres.; founder Camp Barnard for Girls, Mallett's Bay, 1902, and since dir. Served as capt. Co. B, 71st Regt. Inf. N.Y. Vols., Spanish-Am. War, 1898; participated in Santiago campaign. Pres. mem. Schoolmasters Assn. of New York and Vicinity; mem. Country Day Sch. Assn. of U.S., Vets. of Seventh Regt. of N.Y., United Spanish War Vets. (Dept. of New York.), Soc. of Army of Santiago de Cuba, Phi Gamma Delta (pres. 1889), Phi Delta Phi, Phi Beta Kappa. Awarded Columbia U. Medal for Service, 1933, medal for conspicuous Columbia alumni service, 1938. Republican. Baptist. Clubs: Columbia Univ., Phi Gamma Delta. Home: 440 Riverside Drive. Office: Barnard School for Boys, W. 244th St., New York. Died Apr. 13, 1944; buried, Newton, N.J.

HAZLETT, Robert, banker; b. Wheeling, W.Va., Dec. 24, 1863; s. Robert W. (M.D.) and Mary Elizabeth (Hobbs) H.; prep. edn., Linsly Inst., Wheeling; C.E., Ohio State U., 1887; m. Anne Cummins, Mar. 18, 1909; children—Robert C., James C., Catharine H. Civ. engr., Washington, D.C., 1891-93, N.Y. City, 1893-95, Wheeling, 1895-1914; was county engr., Ohio County, W.Va.; now chmn. bd. Wheeling Dollar Savings & Trust Co.; pres. Wheeling & Belmont Bridge Co., Greenwood Cemetery, Investment Building Co.; sec. and treas. Wheeling Bridge Co.; dir. Wheeling Steel Corp. Formerly mem. City Council, and also postmaster of Wheeling, 1911-14, W.Va. Ho. of Dels. and W.Va. State Senate; was vice-pres. for W.Va., Nat. Rivers and Harbors Congress. Treas. Linsly Inst. (trustee). Mem. Sigma Chi; asso. mem. Am. Soc. C.E., W.Va. Soc. C.E. Republican. Presbyterian. Elk. Club: Fort Henry. Home: Echo Point. Office: Dollar Savings & Trust Company, Wheeling, W. Virginia. Died June 9, 1944.

HEADLAND, Isaac Taylor, missionary; b. Freedom, Pa., Aug. 16, 1859; s. Jacob and Eliza (Smith) H.; A.B., Mt. Union Coll., Alliance, O., 1884, A.M., 1888, Ph.D., 1900; S.T.B., Boston U., 1890; D.D., Mt. Union, 1911; Litt.D., Coe Coll., 1914; m. Anor Arelia Eckert, 1886 (died 1890); m. 2d, Mariam Sinclair, M.D., 1894; children—Marion, Courtenay. Ordained to the Methodist Episcopal ministry, 1890; sailed as missionary to Peking, 1890; prof. science, Peking U., 1890-1907; apptd. pres. Foochow Anglo-Chinese Coll., 1901; teacher comparative religions, and philosophy, Mt. Union College, 1914-37, now emeritus. Offered presidency Beaver Coll., Pa., 1917. Hazlett lecturer and Stinson prof. Missions, Wesley Coll., North Dak., 1919-20. In charge Chinese art exhibit, Methodist Centenary, Columbus, O., 1919. Member Peking Oriental Soc., British Royal Asiatic Society, Authors Club, London, Authors' League Am., Phi Beta Kappa, Pi Gamma Mu. Author: Chinese Mother Goose Rhymes, 1900; Chinese Boy and Girl, 1901; Chinese Heroes, 1902; Our Little Chinese Cousin, 1903; Tourists' Guide to Peking, 1905; Court Life in China, 1909; Some By-Products of Missions, 1912; China's New Day, 1912; Young China Hunters, 1912; Home Life in China, 1914; Chinese Rhymes for Children, 1933; Tao Picture Puzzles, 1933. Wrote articles on China for Monroe's Ency. of Education; contbr. to Am. mags. on Chinese subjects; lecturer on Chinese life, art, lang., lit., history, etc., has made a large collection of Chinese paintings, now in Boston Mus. Chautauqua lecturer. Home: Alliance, O. Died Aug. 2, 1942.

HEADLEE, Thomas J., entomologist; b. at Headlee, Ind., Feb. 13, 1877; s. Josephus and Ruann (Mattix) H.; grad. State Normal Sch., Terre Haute, Ind., 1900; A.B., Ind. U., 1903, A.M., 1904; Ph.D., Cornell U., 1906; m. Blanche Ives, Oct. 11, 1903; children—Mary Ruanna, Josephine (dec.), Miriam Esther, Ruth Margaret. Asst. entomologist, 1906-07, asso., July-Sept. 1907, State Agrl. Expt. Sta., N.H.; head dept. of entomology and zoölogy, State Agrl. Coll. and Expt. Sta., Kan., 1907-12; prof. entomology, Rutgers U., and entomologist N.J. Expt. Sta., and state entomologist, Oct. 1912-Dec. 31, 1943, emeritus professor of entomology since Jan. 1, 1944. Fellow A.A.A.S. (council, 1920-24); mem. Am. Assn. Econ. Entomologists (pres. 1929), Entomol. Soc. America (charter mem.), Sigma Xi, Phi Beta Kappa. Author: The Mosquitoes of New Jersey and Their Control, 1945; of repts., bulls. and articles in tech. jours. Home: Dayton, N.J. Office: New Brunswick, N.J. Died June 14, 1946; buried in Masonic Cemetery, Delphi, Ind.

HEALE, Charles J., publisher; b. Brooklyn, N.Y., May 20, 1900; s. Charles and Eugenie (Andrews) H.; ed. pub. schs., N.Y. City; m. Martha L. Windeler, May 31, 1922. Office boy, advt. dept., Iron Age, 1916; Hardware Age, 1917, advt., asso. editor, 1919, Cleveland editor, 1923, v.p. and editor, 1934, pres., gen. mgr. since 1946. V.p. and dir. Chilton Co., Inc., pubs. Mem. Hardware Boosters, Nutmeggers, Keystoners, Nat. Conf. of Bus. Paper Editors (chmn., exec. com.). Republican. Episcopalian. Mason. Club: Engineers. Home: Massapequa, Long Island, N.Y. Office: 100 E. 42d St., New York, N.Y. Died Dec. 1, 1949; buried Amityville, L.I., N.Y.

HEALEY, Arthur Daniel, judge; born Somerville, Mass., Dec. 29, 1889; son of Dennis and Mary (Ireland) H.; student Dartmouth, 1909-10; LL.B., Boston U., 1913; m. Tresla Fisher, Jan. 27, 1923; Children—Robert Fisher, Arthur Daniel, Elaine Teresa, Ruth, Mary. Began practice of law at Boston, 1914; mem. firm Healey & Healey. Served as pvt., advancing to 2d lt. Q.M.C., U.S. Army, World War. Chmn. Somerville Dem. City Com. Mem. 73d to 77th Congresses (1933-43), 8th Mass. Dist.; resigned from Congress to accept appointment to U.S. Dist. Ct., Mass., Aug. 3, 1942. Mem. Am. Legion, Sigma Alpha Epsilon. Catholic. Knight of Columbus, Elk. Home: 156 Sycamore St., Somerville, Mass. Office: Post Office Bldg., Boston. Died Sept. 16, 1948.

HEALY, Fred Albert, vice-pres. Curtis Pub. Co.; b. Bristol, Ill., July 7, 1889; s. Arthur N. and Jennie E. (Palmer) H.; B.S., U. of Ill., 1915; m. Alice Riley, Mar. 3, 1917; children—Doris (Mrs. William P. Schuber), Margaret (Mrs. Donald S. Martin), Frances (Mrs. Robert A. Eagle). Salesman, Osgood Lens Co., 1915-17; advtg. solicitor Curtis Pub. Co. 1917-21; mgr. Chicago office Country Gentleman, 1922-25, Detroit, 1925-28, New York, 1928; advtg. director Curtis Pub. Co., Phila., since 1928, v.p., dir. since 1930. Mem. Delta Tau Delta. Republican. Baptist. Clubs: Racquet, Poor Richard, Mid-Day, Down Town (Phila.); Merion Cricket and Golf (Haverford); University (Chicago); Pine Valley Golf (Clementon, N.J.). Home: 250 S. 18th St. Office: Curtis Publishing Co., Philadelphia 5. Died Oct. 11, 1947.

HEALY, Robert E., mem. Securities Exchange Commn.; b. Bennington, Vt., Mar. 25, 1883; s. John M. and Sarah J. (Corbet) H.; ed. Bennington High Sch.; studied law in office of O. M. Barber; m. Sarah S. Houlihan, Sept. 3, 1907. Admitted to Vt. bar, 1904, and practiced with preceptor until latter was apptd. judge U.S. Court of Customs Appeals, 1910; asso. justice Supreme Court of Vt., Dec. 1, 1914-Feb. 1, 1915 (resigned); chief counsel Federal Trade Commn., 1928-34; mem. Securities Exchange Commn. since 1934. Republican. Catholic. Elk. Home: Pastorius Court Apts., Germantown, Phila. Office: Securities and Exchange Commn., 18th and Locust Sts., Philadelphia, Pa.* Died Nov. 16, 1946.

HEALY, Thomas Henry, prof. internat. law; b. Washington, D.C., Aug. 26, 1894; s. John Paul and Katherine Virginia (Worthington) H.; A.B., magna cum laude, Georgetown U., 1914, A.M., cum laude, 1915, LL.B., 1917, Ph.D., 1925; grad. study, Acad. Internat. Law, The Hague, Holland, 1925, 29; m. Elizabeth Josephine Maurin, June 10, 1919; 1 son, Michel Henry. Admitted to D.C. bar, 1917, Supreme Court of U.S., 1927; sec. exec. faculty, Georgetown U., Foreign Service Sch., since 1920, prof. internat. law and foreign relations, dean since 1935; prof. internat. law, Acad. Internat. Law, The Hague, 1925-29, Am. Sect. L'Institut de Droit Internationale, 1929; lectured Naval and Army war colls., U.S. Naval Acad., Army Industrial Coll. and various universities. Served in France as 1st lieut. regtl. and camp adj. heavy arty., U.S. Army, World War. Del. of U.S. Govt. to Internat. Congress Commercial Edn., Amsterdam, 1929. Mem. Am. Soc. Internat. Law, Am. Assn. Teachers of Internat. Law, Internat. Law Assn., Am. Peace Society, American Academy Political and Social Science, Am. Econ. Assn., Am. Acad. Polit. Science, Assn. Acad. Internat. Law (The Hague), L'Institut Français de Washington, Am. Legion (former nat. chmn. for nat. defense), Delta Chi; corr. mem. Belgian Acad. Comparative Law; hon. mem. Astra Soc. (Rumania). Decorated Officer and Comdr. Order of Crown (Rumania); Knight Royal Order Isabella the Catholic (Spain); Comdr. Order of Leopold II (Belgium); Comdr. Order of Cespedes (Cuba); Comdr. of Order of St. Sava (Jugoslavia), 1932; Comdr. Order of Crown (Italy); Chevalier Legion of Honor (France); Comdr. Order of White Lion (Czechoslovakia); Comdr. Order of Merit (Chile); Comdr. Order of Boyaca (Colombia). Club: Cosmos (Washington). Author: L'Ordre Public dans le Droit Internationale Privé, 1926; La Condition Juridique de L'Etranger aux Etats Unis, 1929; National Defense and Peace, 1936; Why Meddle in the Orient? (co-author), 1938. Home: 3934 Legation St., Washington. Died July 5, 1943; buried in Arlington National Cemetery.

HEATH, Hugh Austin, clergyman; b. Jackson, Minn., Sept. 1, 1867; s. Charles H. and Eliza (Kenyon) H.; A.B., Des Moines (Ia.) Coll., 1893, D.D., 1896; B.D., Rochester Theol. Sem., 1896; m. Flora Northrop Robinson, May 21, 1896. Ordained Bapt. ministry, 1892; pastor Genesee St. Ch., Rochester, N.Y., 1895-96, Waverly, Ia., 1896-98, Keokuk, 1898-1901, Wakefield, Mass., 1901-13; gen. sec. Mass. Bapt. Missionary Soc. (Mass. Bapt. Conv.), 1913-19; exec. sec. convs. and confs. of Gen. Bd. of Promotion of Northern Bapt. Conv., 1919-22; gen. sec. Mass. Bapt. Conv., 1922-40; retired. Home: 195 Morton St., Newton Center, Mass. Died Mar. 10, 1942.

HEATH, S. Burton, writer; b. Lynn, Mass., Dec. 20, 1898; s. Horace Burton and Ida Victoria (Morine) H.; Ph.B., Univ. of Vermont, 1926; m. Emily J. Dodge, June 30, 1923; children—Nancy Emily, Burton Dodge. Began as apprentice printer Bradford (Vt.) Opinion, 1913; editor Groton (Vt.) Times, 1917-21, owner, 1920-21; asst. campaign mgr. for U.S. Senator P. H. Dale, 1926; reporter Associated Press, 1926-28; reporter N.Y. Telegram, 1928-30; sec. St. Lawrence Power Development Commn., 1930-31; reporter New York World-Telegram 1932-40; editor and columnist, McClure Newspaper Syndicate, 1941; writer, Newspaper Enterprise Association since 1942; publicity consultant in several political campaigns; manager two political campaigns. Member executive com. Citizens Union of City of N.Y. Served in 102d Inf., 26th Div., U.S. Army, A.E.F., World War. Former state officer 40 and 8. Mem. Phi Beta Kappa, Sigma Alpha Epsilon, Tau Kappa Alpha, Boulder (sr. hon. soc., U. of Vt.), Nat. Press Club, Am. Legion. Independent Republican. Methodist. Awarded 1939 Pulitzer prize for reporting exposé resulting in resignation and conviction of Judge Manton, Second Court of Appeals. Author: Yankee Reporter, 1940, and mag. articles. Home: 49 Brookside Road, Darien, Conn. Office: 461 Eighth Av., New York. Killed in air crash, while returning from news-gathering trip to Indonesia, at Bombay, India, July 12, 1949; buried in Arlington National Cemetery.

HEAVEY, John William, army officer; b. Vandalia, Ill., Feb. 19, 1867; s. Patrick and Susan (Mahan) H.; grad. U.S. Mil. Acad., 1891, Command and Staff Sch., 1912, Army War Coll., 1913, Inf. Sch., 1923; m. Julia Baggette, Apr. 19, 1894; m. 2d, Katherine Theresa Sullivan, Jan. 19, 1915; children—William Francis, Thomas Jackson, Wade Hampton. Commd. 2d lt. inf., U.S. Army, June 12, 1891, and advanced through grades to col., Aug. 15, 1917; retired with rank of brig. gen., Feb. 28, 1931. Mem. Mil. Order Carabao. Republican. Catholic. Clubs: Army and Navy (Washington); Union League, Penn Athletic (Philadelphia); Army and Navy (Manila). Died Nov. 18, 1941.

HEBARD, Arthur Foster, industrial management; b. Brooklyn, N.Y., Oct. 18, 1878; s. George Whiting and Mary Francis (Foster) H.; grad. Worcester (Mass.) Acad., 1896; A.B., Williams, 1900; m. Marjorie Dexter Stone, June 7, 1904; children—Bertha (Mrs. Stanton G. Litchfield), George Whiting, Arthur Foster (dec.). With Remington Arms Co., advancing to gen. sales mgr., 1900-17; vice pres. and treas. Savage Arms Corp., 1919-21; vice pres. and gen. mgr. Noiseless Typewriter Co., 1921-24; vice pres. Gorham Mfg. Co. and The Gorham Co., 1924-26; in indsl. management bus. since 1926; dir. Scarsdale (N.Y.) Nat. Bank, Scarsdale Improvement Co.; pres., dir. Dardelet Threadlock Corp. Mem. bd. govs. White Plains Hosp. Served as capt., Ordnance Dept., U.S.A., 1918-19; maj., later lt. col., Ordnance R.C. Mem. Am. Legion (past comdr. Post 52, Scarsdale), Zeta Psi. Republican. Presbyterian (trustee Hitchcock Memorial Ch.). Clubs: Lawyers (New York); Scarsdale Town (past pres.); Army and Navy (Washington). Home: 6 Rectory Lane, Scarsdale, N.Y. Office: 55 Liberty St., New York. Died Jan. 9, 1946.

HECHT, Selig, prof. biophysics; b. Glogow, Austria, Feb. 8, 1892; s. Mandel and Mary (Mresse) H.; brought to U.S., 1898; B.S., Coll. of City of N.Y., 1913; Ph.D., Harvard, 1917; m. Cecilia Huebschman, June 3, 1917; 1 dau., Maressa. Research asst. U.S. Bureau Fisheries, 1912-13; asst. pharmacologist Bureau of Chemistry, 1913-14; Austin teaching fellow, Harvard, 1915-17; asst. prof. physiology, Creighton Med. Coll., Omaha, 1917-21; nat. and internat. research fellow at Liverpool, Harvard, Naples, Cambridge (Eng.), 1921-26; prof. biophysics, Columbia University, since 1926; lectureships at Cornell, 1929, Harvard, 1930, Harvey Society, 1937; lecturer, New Sch. for Social Research, since 1935; national lecturer, Sigma Xi, 1944; research in chemistry and physics of the processes involved in vision and light reception since 1917. Official investigator, Nat. Defense Research Com., and with Office of Scientific Research and Development (Office of Emergency Management); mem. sub-committee on visual problems, Nat. Research Council; mem. com. Army-Navy Office of Scientific Research and Development Vision Com. Mem., Army-Navy Nat. Research Council Vision Com. Awarded Frederic Ives medal, Optical Soc., 1941; Townsend Harris Medal, Associate Alumni City Coll. of N.Y., 1942. Fellow A.A.A.S.; mem. Am. Soc. Naturalists, Am. Society Zoölogists, Am. Physiol. Society, Optical Society of America, Harvey Society, Phi Beta Kappa, Sigma Xi (v.p. 1940-41, pres. 1941-42, Kappa Chapter), National Academy of Sciences. Editor of Columbia Biological Series, Monographs on Experimental Biology, Biological Bulletin. Asso. editor Journal Optical Society of America. Author: The Retinal Processes Concerned with Visual Acuity and Color Vision, 1931; La Base Chimique et Structurale de la Vision, 1938; Explaining The Atom, 1947. Contbr. artcles to scentfic jours. Home: 35 Claremont Av., New York 27. Died Sept. 18, 1947.

HECKMAN, James Robert, merchant, banker; b. Nova Scotia, Oct. 17, 1866; s. Cecil M. and Elizabeth H.; came to U.S. with parents, 1874; ed. pub. schs.; m. Marie C. Capp, 1894. Pres. J. R. Heckman & Co., Miners & Merchants Bank (both Ketchikan). Republican. Mason (32°, K.T., Shriner); mem. Odd Fellows, Knights of Pythias, Eagles, Moose, Redmen, Pioneers of Alaska. Club: Arctic (Seattle, Wash.). Home: Ketchikan, Alaska.* Died Aug. 21, 1939.

HECKSCHER, August, capitalist; b. Hamburg, Germany, Aug. 1848; s. John Gustav Maurice and Antoinette (Brautigam) H.; ed. high sch.; m. Anna Atkins, Oct. 13, 1881; children—G. Maurice, Antoinette (Viscountess Esher). With importing house of E. Nolting & Co., Hamburg, 3 yrs.; came to U.S., 1868, engaged in coal bus. until 1884; an organizer of Lehigh Zinc & Iron Co., 1881, later consolidated with others into the New Jersey Zinc Co., gen. mgr. until 1904, later dir.; pres. Anahama Realty Corp.; dir. Union Bag and Paper Corp., Empire Trust Co., Crucible Steel Co., etc. Chmn. Heckscher Foundn. for Children. Home: Pent House, 52 Vanderbilt Av. Office: 52 Vanderbilt Av., New York. Died Apr. 26, 1941.

HEDERMAN, T. M., editor, Daily Clarion-Ledger, Jackson, Miss.* Died Feb. 25, 1948.

HEDGE, William Russell, insurance; b. Plymouth, Mass., 1876; s. William and Catharine (Russell) H.; B.S., Mass. Inst. Tech., 1896; m. Alice Paine Nowell; children—Susan, Lucia Russell, Alice Nowell. Pres. Boston Insurance Co., Old Colony Ins. Co. Mem. advisory bd. Bur. War Risk Ins. (marine and seamen's div.), World War; also served as mem. ins. com. U.S. Shipping Bd. Pres. Pilgrim Soc. Clubs: Exchange, Union, Odd Volumes (Boston); The Country Club of Brookline (Brookline, Mass.); Plymouth Country (Mass.); Down Town Assn. (New York); Pilgrim Yacht (Plymouth, Mass.). Office: 87 Kilby St., Boston, Mass. Died Apr. 18, 1943.

HEDGES, Samuel Hamilton, civil engr.; b. Ira, N.Y., Apr. 18, 1866; s. David Talmadge and Jane (Hamilton) H.; M.S. in C.E., Ia. State Coll. Agr. and Mechanic Arts, 1886; m. Jessie Jackson, June 29, 1892. Began as rodman with Cedar Rapids & Manchester R.R., 1887; asst. city engr. Cedar Rapids, 1887-88; contracting engr. Clinton Bridge & Iron Works, 1888-92; partner John Ward & Co., bridge builders, 1892-93; northwestern agt. Chicago Bridge & Iron Works, at St. Paul, Minn., 1893-99; contracting and designing engr., same, at Chicago, 1899-1905; pres. Puget Sound Bridge & Dredging Co., 1905-28. Mem. Seattle Chamber of Commerce (pres. 1920; trustee, 1921-24). Mem. Am. Soc. C.E. (dir. 1913-16), Western Soc. Engrs., Engineers' Club of Seattle, Sigma Nu. Mason (32°, K.T., Shriner). Clubs: Rainier, Broadmoor Golf. Home: 702 14th Av. N. Office: 2929 16th St. S.W., Seattle, Wash.* Deceased.

HEDRICK, Charles Baker, theologian; b. Palatka, Fla., Jan. 31, 1877; s. Andrew Jackson and Ella Augusta (Baker) H.; B.A., Trinity Coll., Conn., 1899, D.D., 1929; grad. Gen. Theol. Sem., New York, 1906, B.D., 1921; D.D., Berkeley Div. Sch., Middletown (now New Haven), Conn., 1922; studied Oxford U., Eng., 1910; m. Hedwig von Bötticher, Aug. 8, 1912; children—Ella von Bötticher, Walter (dec.), Margaretha, Doris Ingeborg. Master, St. Luke's Sch., Wayne, Pa., 1900-03; deacon, 1907, priest, 1908, P.E. Ch.; rector St. Mark's Ch., Starke, Fla., 1908-09; instr. in N.T., 1911, prof. lit. and interpretation N.T., 1912-41, acting dean since 1941, Berkeley Divinity School. Member Society Biblical Literature and Exegesis, American Theological Society, National Assn. Bibl. Instrs., Alpha Delta Phi, Phi Beta Kappa. Address: 599 Whitney Av., New Haven, Conn. Died Jan. 12, 1943.

HEDRICK, Earle Raymond, college prof.; b. Union City, Ind., Sept. 27, 1876; s. Simon and Amy Isabella (Vail) H.; A.B., U. of Mich., 1896, hon. D.Sc., 1936; A.M., Harvard, 1898; Ph.D., U. of Göttingen, 1901; École Normale Supérieure, Paris, 1901; LL.D., U. of Mo., 1939; m. Helen Breeden Seidensticker, Oct. 21, 1901; children—Edith Vail, Helen Breeden, Dorothy Janet, Earle R., Amy Isabella, Rachel Esther (dec.), Clyde Lewis, Frank Jerome, Marjorie Bertha (dec.), Elisabeth Busch, Marjorie Janet (adopted daughter). Instr. mathematics, Sheffield Scientific Sch. (Yale), 1901-03; prof. mathematics, U. of Mo., 1903-24; prof. mathematics, U. of Calif. at Los Angeles, since 1924, provost since 1937 and v.p. U. of Calif. Dir. mathematics, Army Ednl. Corps, A.E.F., Jan.-June 1919. Editor in chief Bull. of Am. Math. Soc., 1921-37. Mem. Am. Math. Soc. (v.p. 1916; pres. 1929-30), Math. Assn. of America (pres. 1916), Nat. Research Council (div. of physical sciences, 1921-24 and 1929-32), Société Mathématique de France, Circolo Matematico di Palermo, Am. Soc. Mech. Engrs., Am. Inst. E.E., A.A.A.S. (v.p.; chmn. Sect. A 1931; sec. Sect. A 1933-40), Soc. for Promotion of Engring. Edn., Am. Assn. Univ. Profs., Deutsche Mathematiker Vereinigung, Phi Beta Kappa, Sigma Xi. Decorated Officier d'Academie (France), 1932. Clubs: University (Los Angeles); Faculty (Berkeley); Bohemian (San Francisco). Author: A Course in Mathematical Analysis (Goursat and Hedrick), 1904; An Algebra for Secondary Schools, 1908; Applications of the Calculus to Mechanics (with O. D. Kellogg), 1909; also articles in math. and educational jours. Editor for the Macmillan Company, of A Series of Mathematical Texts, and of the Engineering Science Series. Address: Univ. of Calif. at Los Angeles, Los Angeles. Died Feb. 3, 1943; buried in Forest Lawn Memorial Park, Glendale, Calif.

HEELAN, Edmond, bishop; b. Elton, County Limerick, Ireland, Feb. 5, 1868; s. John D. and Anne (Quish) H.; studied in private schs.; grad. in philosophy and theology, All Hallows Coll., Dublin, 1890. Ordained priest at Dublin, Ireland, 1890; came to U.S., 1890, naturalized citizen, 1895. Asst. pastor St. Raphael's Cathedral, Dubuque, Ia., 1890-93, rector, 1893-97; pastor Sacred Heart Ch., Ft. Dodge, Ia., 1897-1919; apptd. auxiliary bishop of Sioux City, Dec. 21, 1918; consecrated bishop, Apr. 8, 1919; rector Epiphany Cathedral, Sioux City, 1919-20; apptd. bishop of Sioux City, Mar. 8, 1920; apptd. asst. at the Pontifical Throne and Count of the Apostolic Palace, Oct. 10, 1941. Home: 2221 Nebraska St., Sioux City, Ia. Died Sept. 20, 1948.

HEES, William Rathbun, corp. official; b. Oswego, N.Y., June 18, 1867; s. George H. and Antoinette (Rathbun) H.; student Hamilton Acad., 1882-83; Packard Commercial Sch., New York, 1884-85; m. Cora Jane Reed, Sept. 16, 1891; children—Marion Lockman (Mrs. William Merle Sebring), William Rathbun. In window shade and shade cloth business since 1885, at Oswego, N.Y., 1885-87, Toronto, 1887-95, Detroit, 1895-1903, New York since 1903; v.p. Columbia Shade Cloth Co., 1905-18; pres. Columbia Mills, Inc., 1918-32, chmn. bd. since 1932; dir. bd. Northern N.Y. Power Corp.; chmn. and treas. Geo. H. Hees Son & Co., Ltd., Toronto, Ont. Clubs: Union League (New York); Long Island Country; Seigniory (Can.). Home: 860 Park Av. Address: 225 5th Av., New York. Died Dec. 31, 1947.

HEGGEN, Thomas Orlo, author; b. Fort Dodge, Ia., Dec. 23, 1919; s. Thomas O. and Mina (Paulson) H.; A.B., U. of Minn., 1941; unmarried. Member editorial staff Reader's Digest. Author: Mister Roberts, 1946. Home: 4621 Beard Av. S., Minneapolis. N.Y. Office: 8 E. 62d St., N.Y. City. Died May 1949.

HEGNER, Robert William, zoölogist; b. Decorah, Ia., Feb. 15, 1880; s. Charles G. and Wilhelmina (Busch) H.; B.Sc., U. of Chicago, 1903, M.S., 1904; Ph.D., University of Wisconsin, 1908; hon. ScD., Mt. Union College, 1939; m. Jane Zabriskie, Sept. 12, 1906; children—Janette La Tourette Zabriskie, Mary Elizabeth (dec.), Isabel McKinney (dec.). Instr. and asst. prof. zoölogy, U. of Mich., 1908-18; asso. prof. protozoölogy, Sch. of Hygiene and Pub. Health, Johns Hopkins, 1918-20; prof. and head of dept. med. zoölogy, same univ., since 1922; visiting prof. of parasitology, Sch. of Hygiene and Pub. Health, U. of the Philippines, 1929-30, London Sch. of Tropical Medicine, 1926. Mem. scientific expedition to Mexico, 1903; del. to Royal Inst. Pub. Health, Brussels, Belgium, 1920; in chg. expdn. for study of tropical medicine, Porto Rico and Venezuela, 1921; del. to Internat. Congress on Health Problems in Tropical America, Jamaica, 1924; mem. Scientific Board of Gorgas Memorial Institute. Fellow A.A.A.S., Royal Inst. Pub. Health (London), Royal Soc. Tropical Medicine; mem. American Soc. Zoölogists, Am. Soc. Parasitologists, Am. Soc. Naturalists, Sigma Xi, Phi Beta Kappa, Delta Omega, Alpha Pi Lambda; corr. mem. Belgium Soc. of Tropical Medicine. Unitarian. Author: Introduction to Zoölogy, 1910; College Zoölogy, 1912; Germ Cell Cycle in Animals, 1914; Practical Zoölogy, 1914; Diagnosis of Protozoa and Worms Parasitic in Man (with Dr. W. W. Cort), 1921; Outlines of Medical Zoölogy (with Dr. Cort and Dr. F. M. Root), 1923; Human Protozoölogy (with Dr. W. H. Taliaferro), 1924; Host-Parasitic Relations between Man and His Intestinal Protozoa, 1927; Animal Parasitology (with Dr. F. M. Root and D. L. Augustine), 1929; Problems and Methods of Research in Protozoölogy (with Dr. Justin Andrews), 1930; Invertebrate Zoölogy, 1933; Parade of the Animal Kingdom, 1935; Big Fleas Have Little Fleas, 1938. Editor of Century Biol. series; contbg. editor Quarterly Rev. of Biology; mem. editorial board, Jour. of Morphology, Am. Jour. of Hygiene, Jour. of Parasitology; hon. editor Revista di Malariologia. Contbr. to mags. Home: 218 Hawthorne Rd., Baltimore, Md. Died Mar. 11, 1942.

HEIDINGER, James Vandaveer, congressman; b. Mt. Erie, Ill., July 17, 1882; s. W. B. and Elizabeth (Vandaveer) H.; ed. Northern Ill. Normal Sch., Northern Ill. Coll. of Law (Dixon), Valparaiso (Ind.) U.; m. Bessie Summers, Jan. 10, 1911; 1 son, James Summers. Admitted to Ill. bar, 1908, and since practiced law at Fairfield; county judge Wayne County, 3 terms, 1914-26; asst. atty. gen. of Ill., 1927-33; mem. 77th and 78th Congresses (1941-45), 24th Ill. Dist.; dir. Fairfield Nat. Bank, 1918-38, actively engaged in farming. Mem. Wayne County Bar Assn. (pres.). Republican. Methodist. Mason, Shriner. Home: Fairfield, Ill. Died Mar. 22, 1945.

HEIKES, Victor Conrad, statistician; b. Dayton, O., May 21, 1867; s. William Fletcher and Lettie (Conard) H.; grad. as assayer and chemist, Colo. State Sch. of Mines, 1889; m. Anna Sellier, Oct. 25, 1899; 1 son, George Conrad. Railroad surveys, Wyo., 1886; chemist, spl. mining investigation for Rio Grande Western Ry., 1890; chemist, La Gran Fundicion Nacional Mexicana, Monterey, Mex., 1891; asst. and chief, Colo. mining dept., Chicago Expn., 1892-93; curator economic geology, Field Columbian Museum, Chicago, 1894; supt. of mill, Sunshine Gold Mining Co., Utah, 1895-96; chemist, Mingo Smelter, Utah, 1896; mem. firm Watts & Heikes, assayers and chemists, Boulder, Colo., 1897-99; spl. agt., asst. and acting dir. mines and metallurgy, U.S. Commn. to Paris Expn., 1899-1900; field asst. Div. of Mineral Resources, U.S. Geol. Survey, 1901; chief clk., 1902, asst. chief, 1903-04, Dept. Mines and Metallurgy, St. Louis Expn.; statistician in charge Salt Lake Region branch U.S. Geol. Survey, 1904-25; engr. in charge Salt Lake sect. mineral resources and statistics, including Ariz., Ida., Mont., Nev., Utah and Wash., 1925-27; in charge mine production statistics of Calif. and Ore., San Francisco office of U.S. Bur. of Mines, 1928-33 (retired). Mem. Am. Inst. Mining and Metall. Engrs. Author (with G. F. Loughlin) of treatises on arsenic, bismuth, selenium, tellurium; also on platinum and allied metals. Mason. Home: Carmel, Calif. Died June 29, 1948; buried Piedmont Cemetery, Oakland, Calif.

HEIL, Julius Peter, ex-gov.; b. Dusemond, Germany, 1876; s. Franz and Barbara (Krebs) H.; ed. rural sh.; m. Elizabeth Conrad, June 4, 1900; 1 son, Joseph F. Began with Winton Gen. Store at age of 12; later drill press operator Internat. Harvester Co., Milwaukee, pr.; apprentice blacksmith and machine shops, 7 yrs.; became expert welder and traveled throughout country completing welding contracts, built street ry., Buenos Aires, Argentine. Founded The Heil Co., 1901, served as president until 1946; now active in business as chmn. of board. Governor of Wisconsin, 1938-43. Was head of Nat. Recovery Adminstrn. for State of Wis. Republican. Mason (Potentate 1927; sec.-treas. Tripoli Temple since 1921; chmn. finance com. and mem. bldg. com., 1927-28), Elk, Moose. Clubs: Wisconsin, Milwaukee Athletic. Mem. publ. com. Shrine Mag. Address: 3014 W. Montana, Milwaukee, Wis. Died Nov. 30, 1949.

HEILMAN, William Clifford (hīl'man), composer; b. Williamsport, Pa., Sept. 27, 1877; s. Abraham H. and Catherine Updegraff (Clapp) H.; student Mercersburg Acad., 1895-96; A.B., Harvard, 1900, hon. A.M., 1925. Instr. music, Harvard U., 1905-10, asst. prof., 1910-20, lecturer, 1920-30; composer of music for pianoforte, voices, chamber instruments and orchestra. Mem. Am. Acad. Arts and Sciences. Lutheran. Club: Harvard (Boston). Home: 992 Memorial Drive, Cambridge, Mass. Died Dec. 20, 1946.

HEIN, Carl, musical dir.; b. Rendsburg, Germany, Feb. 2, 1864; s. Fritz and Alwine (Schorr) H.; studied at Hamburg Conservatory Music; m. Marta Krüger, Jan. 1890 (died 1925); children—Illo, Yrsa, Castor, Pollux, Uarda. Came to U.S., 1890. Mem. Philharmonic Soc., Hamburg, Germany, 1885-90; mus. dir. German singing socs., etc., since 1890; dir. Franz Schubert Männerchor, 1890-1928, Mozart Verein, 1894-1928, Harmonie, 1891-1926, Concordia, 1894-1922, Einigheit, 1894-1927; now pres. New York Coll. Music. Mem. internat. jury of awards in music, San Francisco Expn., 1915, Sesquicentennial Expn., Philadelphia, 1926. Pres. United German Choral Dirs. America. Author: Thirty-one Daily Exercises for the Voice, 1915; Tone Production in 20 Lessons, 1918. Home: Woodcliff Lake, N.J. Office: 114-116 E. 85th St., New York, N.Y. Died Feb. 27, 1945.

HEINDEL, Mrs. Augusta Foss (Mrs. Max Heindel); b. nr. Mansfield, O., Jan. 27, 1865; d. William and Anna Mary (Wright) Foss; ed. pub. schs.; m. Max Heindel, author, Aug. 10, 1910 (died 1919). Engaged many yrs. in humanitarian work; cofounder, 1911, Rosicrucian Fellowship, Mount Ecclesia, Oceanside, Calif. Past mem. Oceanside Planning Commn., 1928. Author: The Message of the Stars (with husband), 1918; also Evolution, Earthbound, Astro Diagnosis. Editor Rosicrucian (mag.) and publisher of Rosicrucian Cosmo Conception, by Max Heindel, and various other works by him. Lecturer and writer on Christian mysticism. Mem. Federated Womans Club, Oceanside Woman's, Business and Professional Woman's clubs (hon.), Eugene Field Soc., Desert Club. Vice pres. and life mem. Oceanside Humane Society. Home: Oceanside, Calif. Died May 9, 1949.

HEINER, Gordon Graham, army officer; b. Washington, D.C., Nov. 2, 1869; s. Robert Graham and Helen Gordon (Slemaker) H.; B.A., U. of W.Va., 1889; grad. U.S. Mil. Acad., 1893; hon. grad. Arty. Sch., Fort Monroe, Va., 1910; m. Elizabeth Cloyd Kent, Nov. 12, 1895; children—Gordon G., Mary Grant, Robert Graham, Elizabeth Kent. Commd. 2d lt. 2d Arty., June 12, 1893; transferred to 4th Arty., Nov. 29, 1893; 1st lt., Mar. 2, 1899; capt. Arty. Corps, July 1, 1901; maj. Coast Arty. Corps, Jan. 24, 1910; lt. col., July 1, 1916; brig. gen. N.A., Aug. 5, 1917; col. C.A., Mar. 21, 1919; appt. comdr. Coast Defenses, Honolulu, T.H., Feb. 12, 1921; comd. Coast Defenses, Honolulu, 1921-23; exec. officer 2d Coast Arty. Dist., 1923-26; chief of staff, Field Arty. Group Organized Res., 3d Corps Area, hdqrs. Harrisburg, Pa., Apr. 6, 1926-Aug. 1928; comd. 30th C.A. Brig. and Fort Eustis, Va., Sept. 1928-May 1929; retired, Sept. 10, 1929. (For details as to career see Vol. XI, 1920-21.) Home: 313 Suffolk Road, Guilford, Baltimore, Md. Died Dec. 23, 1943.

HEINGARTNER, Robert Wayne, American foreign service officer, retired; b. Canton, Ohio, February 20, 1881; son of Alexander and Kate C. (Bachert) H.; educated in public schools of Ohio, tutors in Europe 4 years; m. Lily Kraus, January 6, 1920 (died Nov. 21, 1934); children—Gladys Ruth, Alexander. Apptd. consular agt. at Carini, Italy, 1904; deputy consul, Trieste, 1904-06, vice and deputy consul, 1906-07; vice and dep. consul gen., Vienna, 1907-15, vice-consul, 1915-17; assigned to Spanish Embassy, Vienna, 1917-18, to Am. Legation, Berne, Switzerland, 1918-20; apptd. consul class 6, 1920, and detailed to Vienna, Kovno, 1926-28, Frankfort-on-the-Main, 1928-39, Regina, 1939-42; apptd. class 4, Oct. 1, 1935; sec. in diplomatic service, Aug. 17, 1937; retired from Am. foreign service, Oct. 1, 1942. Address: 143 Forest St., Oberlin, O.* Died Feb. 18, 1945.

HEINRICHS, Jacob, missionary; b. Allenstein, Germany, Mar. 2, 1860; s. Jacob and Wilhelmine (Dobrizinski) H.; came to U.S., 1881; student U. of Rochester, 1885-86, D.D., 1914; grad. Rochester Theol. Sem., 1889; S.T.D., Northern Baptist Theol. Sem., 1933; m. Lydia V. Fleischmann, Aug. 6, 1889; children—Edgar J. (dec.), Waldo H., Doris L. (dec.), Margaret M., Conrad L. Ordained Bapt. ministry, 1889; sent as missionary to India, 1889; evangelistic work, 1889-95; pres. Bapt. Mission Theol. Sem., Ramapatnam, S. India, 1895-1917. Sent on special mission to Persia, 1907, to Russia, 1909, to Alsace, 1920. Author: Introduction to the Bible, 1898; Ecclesiology, 1898; Commentary on Romans, 1903; New Testament History, 1915; Commentary on Revelation, 1916—all in Telugu lang. Dean and prof. systematic theology, Northern Bapt. Theol. Sem., Chicago, 1918-33, retired as dean emeritus. Home: 44A South St., Middlebury, Vt. Died Aug. 30, 1947.

HEINTZ, Philip Benjamin, casket mfr.; b. Boston, Mass., May 29, 1861; s. John and Marie H.; ed. pub. schs.; m. Frances Viola LeCain, May 29, 1882 (dec.); 1 dau., Phyllis Wainwright (Mrs. John Timothy McGillicuddy); m. 2d, Laura Sheldon Graham, July 12, 1939. Began with Bay State Casket Co., Boston, 1879; organizer, 1884, Boston Casket Co., merged with Nat. Casket Co., 1890, mgr. Boston Br., 1890-1918, gen. mgr., 1918-21, pres. since 1921; pres. Hornthal & Co. (Chicago), Necrosan Co. (E. Cambridge, Mass.), Nat. Casket Co. of Dallas, Internat. Casket Hardware Co. (Thompsonville, Conn.), Clark Mfg. Co. (Providence), Gleason Board Co. (Rochester). Republican. Universalist. Mason (32°). Clubs: Algonquin, Boston Athletic, Hyannisport Golf. Home: 195 St. Paul St., Brookline, Mass. Office: 60 Massachusetts Av., Boston, Mass.* Died July 28, 1943.

HEINTZLEMAN, Percival Stewart, consular service; b. Fayetteville, Pa., July 24, 1880; A.B., Pa. Coll., Gettysburg, 1901; A.B., U. of Pa., 1902. Apptd. student interpreter in China, Oct. 25, 1902; vice and dep. consul gen., Canton, 1904-06, Dalny, 1907; asst. to 3d asst. sec. in Far Eastern Affairs, Washington, D.C., 1907-08; asst. in Div. of Far Eastern Affairs, Mar.-Aug. 1908; vice consul gen., Shanghai, 1908-09, in charge consulate gen. at Shanghai, July-Sept. 1909; again with Div. Far Eastern Affairs, 1909-10; 2d sec. of Legation, Peking, 1910-11; asst. chief Far Eastern Affairs, 1911-14; consul gen. at Mukden, 1914-16, at Canton, 1916-18, at Tientsin, 1918-19, Hankow, 1919-25, Winnipeg, Can., since 1925. Republican. Lutheran. Address: American Consulate, Winnipeg, Manitoba, Can. Died Oct. 22, 1942.

HEISE, Fred H. (hī'sē), med. dir.; b. Baltimore, Md., Nov. 18, 1883; s. John Henry and Katherine (Ernst) H.; M.D., U. of Maryland, 1907; m. Ethel Roberts, Oct. 8, 1914. Asst. resident physician, Trudeau (N.Y.) Sanatorium, 1909-11, Md. State Sanatorium, 1911-12; resident physician, Trudeau Sanatorium, 1912-29, med. dir. since 1929, chmn. med. bd., 1932-37 and since 1944; lecturer Trudeau Sch. of Tuberculosis; part-time lecturer in tuberculosis U. of Rochester (N.Y.). Mem. Nat. Tuberculosis Assn. (pres.), Am. Trudeau Soc. (mem. council), Am. Trudeau Soc. Eastern Section, Am. Clin. and Climatol. Assn. (emeritus), A.M.A. Trustee Potts Memorial Inst. Dir. Saranac Lake Study and Craft Guild. Mason, Elk. Author: The Lungs (with Lawrason Brown), 1931. Editor: Nelson's Abstracts (Tuberculosis) with Lawrason Brown), 1929, 30, 31; 1000 Questions and Answers on T.B., 1935, 2d edit., 1941. Contbr. numerous articles to sci. periodicals. Address: Trudeau Sanatorium, Trudeau, N.Y. Died June 8, 1946.

HEKMA, Jacob (hĕk'mȧ), public utilities; b. Leens, Groningen, Netherlands, Apr. 29, 1879; s. Nicholas and Jacoba (Albertsma) H.; ed. pub. schs.; m. Bessie Barry, 1902; children—Nicholas Barry, Frank Jacob. Started with Michigan Trust Co. in 1896 and resigned as auditor in 1905; with Hodenpyl, Walbridge & Co., New York, mem. of firm in 1911; asst. sec. and sec. and treas. Consumers Power Co., 1910-20, vice pres. and director since 1920; director Ohio Edison Co., since 1938; v.p. and dir. The Commonwealth and Southern Corp., N.Y. City, since 1929. Mem. The Netherland-America Foundation. Clubs: Bras Coupe Hunting & Fishing (Quebec); Huguenot Yacht, Lawyers, Round Hill, Blind Brook. Home: North St., Greenwich, Conn. Office: 20 Pine St., New York, N.Y. Died 1949.

HELFENSTEIN, Edward Trail, bishop; b. St. Louis, Mo., Apr. 7, 1865; s. Cyrus G. and Annie E. (Trail) H.; prep. edn., Frederick Acad. and Episcopal High Sch. of Va.; student Johns Hopkins, Va. Theol. Sem., D.D., 1916; m. Grace Fenton Nelson, Apr. 8, 1890; 1 dau., Grace Nelson (dec.). Deacon, 1889, priest, 1890, P.E. Ch. rector Christ Ch., Rock Spring, Md., 1889-90, St. Mark's Parish, Frederick and Washington counties, 1890-1900, St. John's and St. Peter's Chs., Howard County, 1900-20; archdeacon of Md., 1920-26; consecrated coadjutor bishop of Md., Dec. 28, 1926, bishop since Oct. 3, 1929. Dep. to Gen. Conv. Protestant Episcopal Ch., 4 times. Retired Nov. 1st, 1943. Home: 5318 Tilbury Way, Baltimore, Md. Died Dec. 22, 1947.

HELLENTHAL, John Albertus, lawyer; b. Allegan County, Mich., Sept. 17, 1874; s. Albertus and Riemka (Sluiter) H.; grad. Hope Coll., Holland, Mich., 1891; student U. of Mich., 1896-97; m. Bertha Emily Linsley, Feb. 12, 1900. Admitted to bar, 1897; practiced in Utah and Wyo. until 1900; moved to Juneau, Alaska, 1900; counsel Alaska Treadwell Gold Mining Co. and allied corps., including Alaska Juneau Gold Mining Co., since 1910. Author: The Alaskan Melodrama, 1936. Home: Juneau, Alaska. Died May 25, 1945.

HELLINGER, Mark, writer and motion picture producer; born at New York, N.Y., March 21, 1903; son of Paul and Millie H.; student at Townsend Harris Hall High School, New York City, 1916-19; m. Gladys Glad, July 11, 1929. Began in advertising business, 1921; writer New York Daily News and Chicago Tribune Syndicate, 1923-30; daily columnist for New York Daily Mirror and King Features Syndicate, 1930-38. Writer of Sunday page for "March of Events" sect., Hearst Newspapers. Author: Moon Over Broadway, 1931; The Ten Million, 1934; also wrote last Ziegfeld Follies that was produced, and the play Hot-Cha; writer motion picture plays: Broadway Bill, The Roaring Twenties. Producer of films A Torrid Zone, Brother Orchid, High Sierra, They Drive by Night, Manpower, Rise and Shine, Moon Tide, Thank Your Lucky Stars, The Doughgirls, The Two Mrs. Carrolls, The Killers, Swell Guy, Brute Force. On leave from picture activities, served as war corr. in South Pacific and India for Hearst newspapers, 1944; pres. Mark Hellinger Productions, Inc. Producer films: The Killers, Swell Guy, Brute Force, The Naked City. Home: Hollywood, Calif. Office: Mark Hellinger Productions, Inc., Universal City, Calif. Died Dec. 21, 1947.

HELLER, Joseph Milton, M.D., surgeon; retired; b. Staunton, Va., Jan. 29, 1872; s. Jonas and Pauline (Frank) H.; prep. edn., Emerson Inst., Washington, D.C.; M.D., Georgetown U., 1896; post-grad. study, New York Polyclinic Sch. and Hosp.; m. Renee V. Manning, Mar. 31, 1923. Demonstrator of anatomy, Georgetown Med. Sch., 1896-98; in pvt. practice, Washington, 1903-17; mem. dispensary staff, Emergency and Garfield hosps., Washington, 1896-98; prof. tropical medicine, George Washington U. Med. Sch., 1904-10. First volunteer accepted for Spanish-Am. War; apptd. asst. surg. U.S. Army, Apr. 18, 1898; served as surg. 3d Cav., P.I., 1899; detailed regtl. surgeon 5th Cav., 1901; commd. major and surgeon by President McKinley; in charge water supply, Manila, during cholera epidemic, 1902 (commended by William Howard Taft, then gov. gen. of Philippines; post surgeon Governor's Island, N.Y.; commd. maj. M.R.C., U.S. Army, May 11, 1917; served as div. sanitary inspector and acting chief surgeon, 90th Div., later comdg. officer Base Hosp., Ft. Riley, Kan., Gen. Hosp. No. 23, Hot Springs, N.C., and No. 22, Phila, Pa.; lt. col. Med. Corps, U.S. Army, 1918-22; col. Med. R.C. Participated in Gen. Lawton's advance in Northern Luzon and was surgeon of Maj. Batchelor's "Lost Battalion." Recommended for Congl. Medal of Honor, 1915. Fellow A.M.A., Am. Coll. Physicians; mem. Med. Soc. D.C., Assn. Mil. Surgeons U.S. Army, Internat. Med. Club, Assn. Oldest Inhabitants (D.C.), Mil. Order Foreign Wars (surgeon 1917-23), Naval and Mil. Order of Spanish-Am. War, Mil. Order of the Carabao (nat. comdr. 1929; nat. sec. since 1910), Mil. Order World War (surgeon gen. since 1938, Assn. War Surgeons, Am. Legion, United Spanish War Veterans. Received citation and silver star, War Dept., for attending wounded under fire, Battle of Naguilan, Northern Luzon, Feb. 7, 1899. Mason. Clubs: Army and Navy, Nat. Sojourners, Nat. Press, Alfalfa, Congressional Country, Army Navy Country. Address: 1028 Connecticut Av. N.W., Washington, D.C. Died Oct. 11, 1943.

HELLMAN, Milo, orthodontist; b. Jassy, Roumania, Mar. 26, 1872; s. Wolf and Fanny (Hellman) H.; came to U.S., 1888, naturalized, 1893; prep. edn., New York Prep. Sch.; D.D.S., University of Pennsylvania, 1905; hon. Sc.D., 1933; graduate student Angle School of Orthodontia, N.Y. City, 1908; hon. Sc.D., Witwatersrand Univ., Johannesburg, South Africa, 1938; m. Helen Michelson, Nov. 30, 1905; children—Doris, Edith (Mrs. John L. Bull Jr.), Marion (Mrs. William T. Sandalls). Practiced dentistry, N.Y. City, 1905-08; in practice of orthodontia 1908-42, consultant since 1942; lecturer in orthodontia, Univ. of Pa. School of Dentistry, 1924-26, Harvard Dental Sch., 1927-28; prof. comparative dental anatomy, New York U. Coll. of Dentistry, 1927-28, prof. of orthodontia, 1928-29; prof. of dentistry, Sch. Dental and Oral Surgery, Columbia U., since 1932; research associate in phys. anthropology, Am. Museum of Natural History since 1917. Mem. com. on growth and development, White House Conf. on Child Health and Protection, 1930. Participated in Internat. Symposium on Early Man, Phila., 1937, Symposium on Development of Occlusion at Bicentennial Celebration U. of Pa., 1940, Orthodontic Conf., U. of Southern Calif., 1940; hon. pres. 1st Internat. Orthodontic Congress, N.Y. City, 1926, 2d, London, 1931; mem. exec. group of coms. for standardization of anthrop. techniques, Internat. Congress Anthropologists and Ethnologists, 1937-38; mem. S. African Expdn. of Am. Mus. of Nat. History, 1938; consultant Bur. of Med. Information, N.Y. Acad. of Medicine. Received hon. citation by Assoc. Founds. in Lab. of Anatomy, Western Reserve Univ., Cleveland, O., 1937; Albert H. Ketcham Memorial award, 1939. Fellow N.Y. Acad. Science (v.p. 1932, 33), A.A.A.S., Am. Coll. of Dentists, N.Y. Acad. Dentistry, Odontological Soc. Union of S. Africa; asso. fellow N.Y. Acad. Med.; mem. Am. Dental Assn. (life), N.Y. State Dental Soc. (Scientific research com.), 1st Dist. Dental Soc., Internat. Assn. Dental Research (pres. N.Y. Sect. 1933), Soc. for Research in Child Development (mem. field com. on physical environment and nutrition), Am. Association Physical Anthropologists (life), American Assoc. Mammalogists, Am. Ethnol. Soc., N.Y. Soc. of Orthodontists, Am. Assn. Orthodontists (exec. and research coms.; v.p. 1941), Eastern Assn. Grads of Angle Sch. of Orthodontia (president 1911), American Association of Dental Editors, Delta Sigma Delta, Sigma Xi, Omicron Kappa Upsilon; hon. mem. Southern Soc. of Orthodontists, Mexican Orthodontic Soc.; charter mem. Soc. of Vertebrate Paleontology. Author: The

Dentition of Dryopithecus and the Origin of Man (with W. K. Gregory), 1926; Fossil Anthropoids of the Yale-Cambridge Expedition of 1935 (with others), 1938. Mem. editorial board Archives of Clinical and Oral Pathology. Editor American Orthodontist, 1910-12. Contributor of chapter "The Evidences of the Dentition on the Origin of Man" in Early Man, 1937; chapter "The Face in Its Developmental Career" in The Human Face, 1935; chapter "The Factors Influencing Occlusion" in Development of Occlusion, 1941; chapter "White House Conf. on Child Health and Protection, Part II," 1931. Contributor over 70 articles to scientific and dental journals. Home: 49 Merrall Road, Far Rockaway, N.Y. Died May 11, 1947.

HELLMUND, Rudolph Emil, electrical engr.; b. Gotha, Germany, Feb. 2, 1879; s. Louis and Katharina (Wenzel) H.; grad. realschule, Gotha, 1895; studied Tech. Coll., Ilmenau, and U. of Charlottenburg, 1896-99 and 1902-03; m. Hetty Borgmann, May 24, 1913. Came to U.S., 1903, naturalized citizen, 1920. Asst. to William Stanley, Great Barrington, Mass., 1904-05; designing engr. Western Electric Co., Chicago, 1905-07; with Westinghouse Electric & Mfg. Co. since 1907; apptd. chief engr., 1933, responsible for adequacy of company's engring. and design work, covering all branches of the orgn., also chmn. ednl. com., etc. Inventor elec. devices covered by more than 250 U.S. and foreign patents. Fellow Am. Inst. of E.E. (bd. dirs.; chmn. standards com.); mem. standards council, Am. Standards Assn. Lutheran. Mason (K.T., Shriner). Awarded Benjamin Lamme medal, Am. Institute Electrical Engineers, 1929. Club: Pittsburgh Athletic. Writer of numerous papers and articles in American and European publications. Home: Swissvale, Pa. Died May 16, 1942.

HELM, Harry Sherman, flour milling; b. Byron, Ill., Dec. 17, 1867; s. Clinton and Hannah S. (Poyneer) H.; Beloit (Wis.) Coll., 1886-87; U. of Ill., 1887-88; m. Miss Bowler, Nov. 18, 1911; children—Jane, Virginia, Harriet. In flour milling business since 1888; chmn. bd. Russell Miller Milling Company; dir. Millers Nat. Insurance Co. Republican. Clubs: Minneapolis, Minikanda, Minneapolis Athletic, Automobile. Home: 2400 Blaisdell Av. Office: Security Bldg., Minneapolis, Minn. Died May 6, 1947.

HELMICK, Eli Alva, army officer; b. in Ind., Sept. 27, 1863; s. Hiram T. and Matilda Ann Helmick; graduate U.S. Military Academy, 1888; grad. Army Sch. of the Line, 1909; Army War Coll., 1910; LL.D., Kan. State Agrl. Coll.; m. Elizabeth Allen Clarke, Nov. 20, 1889; children—Charles Gardiner, Florence (Mrs. John Macaulay), George Randall. Apptd. add. 2d lt. 11th Inf., June 11, 1888; promoted through grades to brig. gen. Mar. 5, 1921. Duty in Idaho during Cœur d'Alene riots, Sept.-Nov. 1892; at Chicago Expn., 1893; duty Hillsdale (Mich.) Coll., 1894-96; participated in expdn. to Santiago de Cuba, 1898; comd. Ft. Reno, Okla., 1898-99; provost marshal and insp. rural guard of Cuba, 1900-01; comd. Puerto Princessa, P.I., 1901-02; comd. prov. batln. against Moros, in Mindanao, 1902; recruiting, Springfield, Mass., 1903-06; comd. Fort Liscum, Alaska, 1906-07; on Mexican border, 1910-11; insp. gen., 1911-14; comdg. bn. 27th Inf., 1914-15; comdg. troops, Donna, Tex., on Mexican patrol, 1915-16; duty Insp. Gen.'s Dept., as lt. col., col. and brig. gen. (temp.), Sept. 9, 1916-Aug. 8, 1918; maj. gen. (temp.), Aug. 26, 1918-Sept. 30, 1919, comdg. 8th Div., Sept.-Nov., 1918, comdg. Base Sect. 5, Service of Supplies, at Brest, France, Nov. 23, 1918-Aug. 24, 1919; detailed to General Staff and chief of staff, Central Dept., Aug. 22, 1919-May 10, 1921; apptd. insp. gen. of the Army, rank of maj. gen., Nov. 7, 1921, reapptd. insp. gen. Nov. 7, 1925; retired Sept. 27, 1927. Awarded D.S.M. Home: 2746 Ferdinand Av., Honolulu, T.H. Died Jan. 13, 1945; buried in Arlington National Cemetery.

HELVERING, Guy Tresillian, judge; b. Felicity, O., Jan. 10, 1878; s. William J. and Samantha Jane (Jones) H.; U. of Kan., 1899-1900; U. of Mich., 1903-06, LL.B., 1906 (pres. class); m. Tinnie Ludoweine Koester, Mar. 16, 1910. Began practice Marysville, Kan., 1906; mem. Helvering & Helvering, 1909—; Corpl. Co. M, 22d Kan. Vol. Inf. Spanish-Am. War; pros. atty., Marshall County, Kan., 2 terms, 1907-11; defeated for Congress, 1910; mem. 63d to 65th Congresses (1913-19), 5th Kan. Dist.; mem. Ways and Means Com. in 64th and 65th Congresses; chmn. Dem. State Com. of Kan., 1930-34; formerly dir. of highways, State of Kan.; now chmn. bd. Planters State Bank, Salina, Kan.; commr. internal revenue, 1933-43; apptd. U.S. district judge for Kansas, 1943. Democrat. Address: Federal Bldg., Topeka, Kan. Died July 4, 1946.

HEMENWAY, Charles Reed, chmn. board Hawaiian Trust Co., Ltd.; b. Manchester, Vt., June 12, 1875; s. Lewis Hunt and Maria (Reed) H.; ed. Burr and Burton Sem., Manchester, Vt., 1888-93; A.B., Yale University, 1897; LL.D., University of Hawaii, 1944; m. Jane Munson Colburn, July 25, 1901. Became teacher Punahou Sch., Hawaii, 1899; in practice of law, 1901-07 and 1910-15; atty. gen. of Hawaii, 1907-10; asso. with Alexander & Baldwin, Ltd., 1915-38, v.p. and asst. gen. mgr., 1918-38; pres. Hawaiian Trust Co., 1937; chmn. bd., 1945; dir. Am. Factors, Ltd., Hawaiian Commercial & Sugar Co., Ltd., Maui Agrl. Co., Ltd., McBryde Sugar Co., Bank of Hawaii, Inter-Island Steam Navigation Co., Hawaiian Electric Co., Hawaii Consol. R.R. Co. Regent U. of Hawaii, 1910-40, chmn. bd., 1920-40; past pres. and dir. Queen's Hosp.; hon. pres. Honolulu Community Chest. Past pres. Bar Assn. of Hawaii, Honolulu Chamber of Commerce. Clubs: Pacific, University (pres. 1914); Waialae Country. Address: Hawaiian Trust Co., Ltd., Honolulu, T.H. Died Oct. 15, 1947.

HEMENWAY, Herbert Daniel, lecturer, author; b. Barre, Mass., Jan. 2, 1873; s. Chauncey Columbus and Sarah (Parker) H.; B.Sc., Mass. Agrl. Coll., 1895; B.Sc., Boston U., 1895, post-grad. work, 1898; m. Myrtle L. Hawley, Nov. 25, 1903; children—Clyde Herbert, Truth Mary, Charles Daniel. Dir. Sch. of Horticulture, Hartford, Conn., 1900-06; gen. sec. People's Inst., Northampton, Mass., 1906-13; pres. Northampton Playground Assn., 1910-13; staff lecturer on civic improvement, Nat. Soc. for Broader Edn., Carlisle, Pa., 1913-15; community inst. lecturer State of Ind.; in charge boys' and girls' work Worcester County (Mass.) Farm Bur., 1915-16; expert, engaged in landscape community development work and food production gardens, since 1916; supt. grounds and their development, U.S. Vets.' Hosp. 89, Rutland, Mass. Expert in charge of war gardens, City of Cambridge, Mass., 1917; ednl. and publicity agt. for Nat. War Garden Commn., 1918-19; State Bd. of Agr. canning demonstrator. Mem. City Council, Northampton, 1911-13. Mem. Mass. Hort. Soc., Civil Legion (exec. com. from State of Mass.), County Civil Legion. Author: How to Make School Gardens, 1903; Hints and Helps for Young Gardeners, 1906; How to Make Home and City Beautiful, 1911; also 11 nature leaflets. Better homes lecturer extension dept. Art Inst., Chicago. Author of correspondence courses. Home: Holden, Mass. Died Feb. 15, 1943.

HEMINGTON, Francis, organist, choral condr.; b. London, Eng., Aug. 22, 1866; s. James Alexis and Emily (Allen) H.; asso. Royal Coll. Organists, London, 1885; Mus.D., N.Y. Conservatory of Music, 1910; m. Sarah Jane Horn, Mar. 2, 1892. Came to America, 1893; organist and choirmaster, Grace Episcopal Ch., Oak Park, Ill., 1893-94; St. Paul's Universalist Ch., Chicago, 1894-98; Ch. of the Epiphany, Chicago, 1898-1922; Zion Temple (Jewish), Chicago, 1910-20; Pilgrim Congl. Ch., Oak Park, since 1922; founder, 1894, since dir. Oak Park Sch. of Music; dir. Pilgrim Choral Soc. since 1923. Conglist. Mason. Pres. Ill. Council Nat. Assn. of Organists, 1917-23. Home: 614 N. Ridgeland Av., Oak Park, Ill. Died Dec. 31, 1942.

HEMINGWAY, Harold Edgar, banker; b. Aylmer, Ont., Can., Aug. 22, 1887; s. Silas and Thirza (Marchant) H.; A.B., U. of Toronto, 1909; m. Isabel Whittam, 1911 (died 1927); children—Robert, Richard; m. 2d, Marie Christiansen, Aug. 6, 1923. Came to U.S., 1915, naturalized, 1920. Bond salesman and realty operator, Can., 1909-15; cashier First Nat. Bank (Bryant, S.D.), 1915-16, Mason Valley Bank (Nev.), 1917-19, Bingham State Bank (Utah), 1919-22; pres. Burley (Ida.) Nat. Bank, 1922-34; pres. Commercial Security Bank (Ogden, Utah), since 1929, Ida. Bank & Trust Co., Pocatello, since 1934, Nev. Bank of Commerce, Elko, Nev., 1939-42; pres. Mutual Creamery Co., Salt Lake City, since 1943; dir. Ogden Union Stock Yards. Dir. Salt Lake City br., Federal Reserve Bank, 1930-35. Republican. Club: Alta (Salt Lake City); Weber (Ogden); Ogden Golf and Country. Home: Hotel Ben Lomond. Office: Commercial Security Bank, Ogden, Utah.* Deceased.

HEMMETER, Henry Bernard, college pres.; b. Baltimore, Md., Dec. 24, 1869; s. Christopher and Caroline (Weismueller) H.; student Baltimore City Coll., 1883-86; grad. Concordia Sem., St. Louis, Mo., 1892, D.D., 1939; M.A., Concordia Coll., Conover, N.C., 1917; D.D., Lenoir-Rhyne Coll., Hickory, N.C., 1920; married Anna Helen Heitmueller, April 4, 1893; children—Bernard H., Anna (Mrs. Albert Schneider), Carolyn J. (Mrs. George Tiedemann), Henrietta (Mrs. Edwin Engerer), Pauline, Henry, Marie (Mrs. William Nehrenz). Pastor Our Savior Lutheran Church, Baltimore, 1892-95, St. Andrew's Luth. Ch., Pittsburgh, Pa., 1895-1902; prof. English and Latin, Concordia Coll., Conover, 1902-05; also editor Lutheran Witness, 1902-05; pastor Trinity Luth Ch., Pittsburgh, 1905-08, Bethlehem Luth. Ch., St. Louis, Mo., 1908-14; pres. Concordia Coll., Conover, 1914-18; pastor St. Matthew's Luth. Ch., Rochester, N.Y., 1918-28; pres. Concordia Coll., Conover, N.C., 1928-36; pres. Concordia Theol. Sem., Springfield, Ill., 1936-45; now emeritus. President Southeastern Mission Bd.; v.p. Eastern Dist., 1921-28, chmn. publ. bd. of English Synod, 1896-1902 and 1905-08, Lutheran Ch. Editor of Church Record. Mem. Am. Acad. Polit. and Social Science, Foreign Policy Soc., Concordia Hist. Soc. (v.p.), Genesee Soc., Metropolitan Museum, Pi Gamma Mu. Author: Family Prayers, 1931; Modernism in Religion, 1931. Editor: Life of Walther, 1900; Sunday School Hymnal, 1901. Home: 2907 Woodland Av., Baltimore 15. Died July 2, 1948.

HENDERSON, Charles William, mining engr.; b. Valley City, N.D., Sept. 10, 1885; s. David and Jane Louise (Morton) H.; A.B., in geology and mining, Stanford Univ., Calif., 1910; D.Sc., Colo. Sch. of Mines, 1930; unmarried. Statistical and geological work, San Francisco, 1907-08, in charge, Denver, 1908-25, U.S. Geol. Survey; in charge Denver office economic br. U.S. Bur. of Mines, 1925-35; supervising engr. of field offices, mineral production and economics div., U.S. Bur. of Mines, 1935—, acting asst. to dir., bureau, Feb. 5-Apr. 18, 1940. Cons. engr. U.S. Geol. Survey on Colo. Coöp. Geol. Survey since 1925. Chmn. Colo. sect. 16th Internat. Geol. Congress, 1932-33; v.p. Colo. Engring. Council, 1932-34. Advisor on copper, lead and zinc codes, NRA, 1933-34; mem. sub-com. on vanadium, mineral advisory com., Army and Navy Munitions Board, 1939-40. Fellow Am. Assn. for Advancement of Science; mem. Am. Assn. Petroleum Geologists, Am. Inst. Mining and Metall. Engrs. (ex-sec. and chmn. Colo. sect.), Mining and Metall. Soc. of America, Colo. Scientific Soc. (pres. 1931-43), Teknik Club (Denver), Sigma Xi, Phi Gamma Delta, Sigma Gamma Epsilon. Clubs: University (Denver, Washington, D.C.), Phi Gamma Delta (New York). Author: History of Mining in Colorado (U.S. Geological Survey); Gold and Silver Am. Year Book, 1928-36; History and Influence of Mining in the Western United States, Lindgren vol. (A.I.M.M.E.), 1933. Author of ann. reports on mineral resources (U.S. Geol. Survey and Bur. of Mines), 1908-43; also articles in mining jours. and U. of Ore. Bull. Home: University Club. Office: Custom House Bldg., Denver, Colo. Died Jan. 26, 1945.

HENDERSON, Robert, actuary; b. Russell, Ont., Can., May 24, 1871; s. Walter and Janet (Eadie) H.; ed. Collegiate Inst.; B.A., Toronto, 1891, D.Sc., 1930; m. Anna Magee, July, 1896. Fellow in mathematics, U. of Toronto, 1891-92; with Canadian Govt. Ins. Dept., 1892-97; came to U.S., 1897, naturalized, 1920. With Equitable Life Assurance Soc. of U.S., 1897-1936, actuary, 1911-36, 2d v.p., 1920-29, v.p., 1929-36, ret., 1936. Fellow Actuarial Soc. Am. (pres. 1922-23), Inst. of Actuaries Great Britain; mem. Am. Philos. Soc., Am. Math. Soc., Math. Assn. America, Am. Statis. Assn. Republican. Presbyterian. Club: University. Author: Examinations, 1906; Mortality Laws and Statistics, 1915; Graduation of Mortality and Other Tables, 1919. Home: Crown Point, N.Y. Died Feb. 16, 1942.

HENDERSON, W(alter) B(rooks) Drayton, prof. English; b. Brown's Town, Jamaica, B.W.I., Aug. 4, 1887; s. Rev. George Edward and Katharine Alice (Clark) H.; came to U.S., 1901; Ph.B., Brown U., 1910; Ph.D., Princeton, 1915; unmarried. Lit. editor Macmillan Co., 1915-17, 1919-20; instr. in English, Yale, 1920; asst. prof. English, Dartmouth, 1925-28, prof. since 1928. Served as 2d lt. Royal Horse and Royal F.A., 1918. Author: Swinburne and Landor, 1918; The New Argonautica (epic poem), 1928. Home: Hanover, N.H. Died July 10, 1939.

HENDERSON, William D., university prof.; b. Ingersoll, Can., Nov. 27, 1866; s. Robert and Sarah Ann (Crawford) H.; A.B., U. of Mich., 1903, A.M., 1904, Ph.D., 1906; m. Mary Bartron, Sept. 1, 1894; children—Margaret (dec.); Robert Bartron. Instr. physics, 1903-05, asst. prof., 1906-09, asso. prof., 1909-19, dir. extension div., 1916-36, U. of Mich., now emeritus. Chmn. standardization com. Nat. Univ. Extension Assn. (pres. 1919-20); mem. Phi Beta Kappa, Sigma Xi, Economic Club of Detroit (mem. bd. of dirs.). Democrat. Presbyterian. Author: One Hundred Twenty Laboratory Exercises in Physics, 1915; Problems in Physics, 1916; Physics in Everyday Life, 1921; Guide to the Study of Physics. Home: Ann Arbor, Mich. Died May 26, 1944.

HENDERSON, William Price, lawyer, educator; b. Delaware, O., Aug. 24, 1867; s. Isaiah R. and Frances Anna (Price) H.; A.B., Ohio Wesleyan U., 1888; LL.D., Taylor U., Upland, Ind., 1922; m. Olive R. Sagebiel, Feb. 25, 1890; children— Berkeley, Woodruff, Mrs. Dorcas Mary Shaffer. Admitted to Ohio bar, 1889, and began practice at Kenton; judge Court of Common Pleas, 10th Jud. Dist. of Ohio, 1909-21; resumed practice at Kenton, 1921; mem. firm Henderson & Kaylor; dean of Warren G. Harding Coll. of Law, Ohio Northern U., Ada, O., since 1921. Mem. Phi Kappa Psi (Ohio Wesleyan), Delta Theta Phi (Ohio Northern). Democrat. Methodist. Elk. Home: 642 N. Main St., Kenton, O. Died Feb. 20, 1943.

HENDERSON, William Penhallow, artist and architect; b. Medford, Mass., 1877; s. William Oliver and Sallie Augusta (LeGalle) H.; ed. Mass. Normal Art Sch., Boston Museum Fine Arts; m. Alice Corbin, 1905; 1 dau., Alice Oliver (Mrs. Edgar L. Rossin). Represented in Art Inst., Chicago, Denver Art Assn., and in private collections. Work includes mural decorations, portraits and landscapes, pastels and lithographs. Work as architect includes Sena Plaza Office Bldg., Museum of Navajo Ceremonial Art and prt. residences in Santa Fe. With Camouflage Dept. U.S. Navy, Southern Pacific Dist., stationed at San Francisco, World War. Studio: Santa Fe, N.M. Died Oct. 15, 1943.

HENDERSON, William Williams, college prof.; b. Clarkston, Utah, May 23, 1879; s. James and Mary (Williams) H.; A.B., Brigham Young Coll., 1903; post-grad. work, U. of Chicago, 1904; A.M., Cornell, 1905; Ph.D., U. of Calif., 1924; m. Survina Wheeler, June 26, 1901. Prof. zoölogy, Brigham Young Coll., 1905-10; pres. Weber Normal Coll., Ogden, Utah, 1910-14; state entomologist, Utah, 1917-20; prof. and head of dept. zoölogy and entomology, Utah Agrl. Coll., 1917-21 and since 1926; entomologist, Utah Expt. Sta., 1917-20, 1926—, Utah Crop and Pest Commn., 1917-21; pres. Brigham Young Coll., 1921-26. Mem. Sigma Xi, Gamma Sigma Delta, Phi Kappa Phi. Democrat. Mem. Ch. of Latter Day Saints (Mormon). Contbr. numerous articles, mostly on agrl. edn. Home: Logan, Utah. Died Oct. 13, 1944.

HENDERSON, Yandell, physiologist; b. Louisville, Ky., Apr. 23, 1873; s. Isham and Sally Nielson

(Yandell) H.; B.A., Yale, 1895, Ph.D., 1898; univs. of Marburg, 1899, and Munich, 1900; m. Mary Gardner Colby, Apr. 2, 1903; children—Malcolm Colby, Sylvia Yandell (Mrs. G. McL. Harper, Jr.). Instr. physiology, 1900-03, asst. prof., 1903-11, prof., 1911-21, prof. applied physiology, 1921-38, prof. emeritus since 1938, Yale. Conn. physiologist, U.S. Bur. of Mines, 1913-25. Mem. Naval Militia, C.N.G., 1897-99; ensign U.S. Navy, during Spanish-American War; served on U.S.S. Yale in Cuban waters and on 1st expdn. to P.R. Chief of physiol. sect. U.S. war gas investigation, 1917-18; chmn. Med. Research Bd., Aviation Sect., Signal Corps, U.S. Army, 1917-18. Mem. Charter Revision Commn., New Haven, Conn. V.-chmn. Conn. delegation to 1st Prog. Nat. Conv., 1912; Prog. candidate for Congress, 3d Conn. Dist. Mem. A.M.A., Am. Physiol. Soc. Am. Pharm. Soc., Nat. Soc. Anæsthetists, Physiol. Soc. (Gt. Britain), A.A.A.S., Nat. Acad. Sciences, Am. Philos. Soc.; hon. mem. Am. Climatol. Assn., Assn. Physicians of Vienna, Austria, Coal Mining Inst. America. Clubs: Graduate (New Haven); Yale (New York). Honorary M.D., Conn. State Med. Soc., 1942. Home: 440 Prospect St., New Haven, Conn. Died Feb. 18, 1944.

HENDRICK, Burton Jesse, writer; b. New Haven, Conn., Dec. 8, 1870; s. Charles B. and Mary Elizabeth (Johnston) H.; B.A., Yale, 1895, M.A., 1897; Litt.D., Allegheny Coll., 1924; LL.D., Duke U., 1928; m. Bertha Jane Ives, Dec. 29, 1896; children—Ives, Hobart Johnston. Editor New Haven Morning News, 1896-98; on staff New York Evening Post, 1899-1905; staff McClure's Magazine, 1905-13; associated editor of World's Work, 1913-27. Member National Institute Arts and Letters (secretary 1926-32), Psi Upsilon, Chi Delta Theta. Clubs: University, Century, Dutch Treat, Coffee House, Yale (New York City); Graduates Club of New Haven, Connecticut. Author: The Story of Life Insurance; The Age of Big Business (in Yale Chronicles of America); Life and Letters of Walter H. Page, American Ambassador to Great Britain, 1913-18 (awarded Pulitzer prize for this work as the best Am. biography of 1922; (privately published posthumous work) Louise Whitfield Carnegie. also edited Vol. III, containing letters of Walter H. Page to Woodrow Wilson; The Jews in America, 1923; The Training of an American (awarded Pulitzer prize as best American biography of year), 1928; Life of Andrew Carnegie; The Lees of Virginia; Bulwark of the Republic, a Biography of the Constitution, 1937 (Book of the Month Club selection, June 1937); Statesmen of the Lost Cause, 1939 (Literary Guild Selection, Nov. 1939; Lincoln's War Cabinet, 1946. Co-author: (with Adm. William Sowden Sims) The Victory at Sea (awarded Pulitzer prize of $2,000, as best book on history of U.S. pub. in 1920); (with Marie Doughty Gorgas) William Crawford Gorgas, His Life and Work, Editor of Miscellaneous Writings of Andrew Carnegie. Mem. Pulitzer Prize jury in history, 1930-38, in biography since 1940. Address: 1 W. 54th St., New York, N.Y. Died Mar. 23, 1949; buried New Haven, Conn.

HENDRICK, John Thilman, mfr., broker; b. Clarksville, Tenn., Nov. 12, 1876; s. David Stewart and Pattie (Warfield) H.; Vanderbilt U., 1892-94; LL.B., George Washington U., 1897; m. Elizabeth Graff, Mar. 2, 1918. Began as agt. Manhattan Life Ins. Co., 1895, and became gen. mgr. Central Eastern div.; entered real estate and stock brokerage business about 1915; now spl. partner W. B. Hibbs & Co., members New York Stock Exchange; chmn. bd. Lanston Monotype Machine Co. Pres. Bd. of Commrs. of D.C. during latter part of President Wilson's administration. Mem. Chi Phi, Phi Delta Phi. Democrat. Presbyn. Mason, K.P. Clubs: Racquet (Washington); Columbia Country (Chevy Chase, Md.); Blue Ridge Rod and Gun (Harpers Ferry, W.Va.). Home: 2443 Kalorama Road. Office: Hibbs Bldg., Washington, D.C.* Died Mar. 26, 1944.

HENDRICKS, Thomas Armstrong, supt. schs.; b. Pulaski County, Ky., Mar. 20, 1871; s. Samuel Bailey and Orlean (Adams) H.; B.S., Centre Coll., Ky., 1897, M.A., 1905, LL.D., 1935; studied summers, U. of Tenn. and U. of Ky.; M.A., Teachers Coll. (Columbia), 1922; m. Katherine Cox, 1901; children—Thomas A., Katheryne Neil, Samuel Francis, Joseph Clay; m. 2d, Mrs. Doris B. Piatt, Mar. 5, 1939. Superintendent schs. Junction City, 1899-1905, Versailles, 1905-08, Cynthiana, 1908-13, Paris, 1913-18; pres. Hamilton Coll., Lexington, Ky., 1918-19; supervisor country schs., Winchester, Ky., 1919-21; supt. schs., Winchester, 1922-23, Berea since 1923; dean and prof. education, Berea Coll. Mem. Phi Delta Kappa. Democrat. Mem. Disciples of Christ. Mason (K.T.). Home: Berea, Ky. Deceased.

HENDRIX, William Samuel, prof. romance langs.; b. Ragland, Ala., May 27, 1887; s. William D. and Indiana Cornelia (Martin) H.; A.B., Howard Coll., Ala., 1907, A.M., 1909; A.M., Cornell U., 1910; studied U. of Caen and at Madrid; Ph.D., U. of Chicago, 1922; m. Bertha Estella Bourdette, June 25, 1913; children—Edith Bourdette, William Edwin. Asistant in romance languages, University of Illinois, 1910-13; instructor romance languages, University of Tex., 1913-16, adj. prof., 1916-20; prof. romance langs., Ohio State U., since 1920, chmn. of dept. since 1926. Mem. Modern Lang. Assn. America, Am. Assn. Teachers of Spanish (pres. 1926), Am. Assn. Teachers of French, Nat. Federation Modern Language Teachers, Acacia; corr. mem. Hispanic Soc. America, Caballero de la Real Orden de Isabel la Católica. Baptist. Author: Elementary Spanish, 1923; Some Native Comic Types of the Early Spanish Drama, 1924; Elementary Spanish Reader, 1933; Cultural Spanish Reader, 1936; Cultural Shortwave Broadcasts from Spanish America, 1938; Beginning French (with W. E. Meiden), 1940; Beginning Spanish, 1943. Editor: Breton de los Herreros, Marcela, 1922; Caballeros y escuderos, 1928; Fernán Caballero's La Familia de Alvareda, 1928; Palacio Valdés' La Novela de un Novelista, 1931; Bécquer's Short Stories and Poems, 1936. Managing editor of Modern Lang. Jour. since 1947. Contbr. to philol. jours. Home: 423 W. 9th Av., Columbus, O. Died March 22, 1948; buried at Sylacauga, Ala.

HENING, Benjamin Cabell, clergyman; b. Powhatan County, Va., Sept. 15, 1863; s. William Henry (M.D.) and Pocahontas Bolling (Megginson) H.; alumnus Richmond (Va.) Coll.; grad. Crozer Theol. Sem., 1891; D.D., U. of Richmond; m. Peachey Fleet Bagby, June 1, 1892; children—Wave Randolph (dec.), Clarice Shackford. Ordained ministry Bapt. Ch., 1891; successively pastor Bruington, Va., Richmond, Va., Bristol, Va., Knoxville, Tenn., Elizabeth City, N.C., Miami, Fla., until 1908; sec. Bapt. Edn. Commn. of Va. 10 yrs., 1908-18; asso. gen. dir. Bapt. $75,000,000 campaign, 1919; supt. Home Missions Southern Bapt. Conv. (resigned). Led movement to establish West Hampton Coll. at Richmond, Va., and to move Richmond Coll. Trustee Southern Bapt. Theol. Sem., Southwestern Bapt. Theol. Sem., Va. Intermont Coll. Democrat. Home: 532 San Esteban Av., Coral Gables, Fla. Died Aug. 11, 1949; buried in Riverview Cemetery, Richmond, Va.

HENNRICH, Kilian Joseph, director gen. Cath. Boys Brigade of U.S.; b. Leeuwarden, Holland, Nov. 9, 1880; s. James and Helen (Meurer) H.; student secondary schs., Holland and Germany, 1892-1900; A.B., St. Lawrence Coll., Mt. Calvary, Wis., 1904, A.M., 1910; student St. Francis Capuchin Sem., Milwaukee, Wis., 1904-11. Came to U.S., 1900, naturalized, 1909. Ordained priest R.C. Ch., 1911; chief commr. Cath. Boys Brigade of U.S., 1916-23, dir. gen. since 1923, moderator nat. ednl. com. same since 1929; pres. Cath. Boys Brigade Corp. since 1929; spl. lecturer, U. of Notre Dame, 1925. Mem. editorial com. Catholic School Journal; chmn. Honor Ct. "Star Pro Juventute." Mem. White House Conf. on Edn. and Training of Youth, 1922, Conf. on Outdoor Recreation, 1924, Conf. on Child Health and Protection, 1930, Nat. Third Order Conv. (local chmn., New York, 1926), Motion Picture Research Council, Welfare Council (New York); del. Internat. Congress on Child Welfare, Geneva, 1925, Cath. Youth Internat. Congress, Rome, 1925; Youth chmn. San Francisco, 1931. Mem. Franciscan Capuchin Order, Cath. Writers Guild, St. Lawrence Coll. Alumni Assn. Decorated Knight Comdr. Order of the Holy Sepulchre, Jerusalem, 1937. Author: Boy Guidance, 1925; Boy Leader's Primer, 1930; Christ, 2 vols., 1940; Youth Guidance, 1941; The Better Life, 1942 (an international tertiary book selection). Forming A Christian Mentality, 1945; Watchful Elders, (enlarged edit.). Editor Boys Brigade Guide, 1930-35; editorial com. of Cath. Sch. Jour. since 1932 and Franciscan Studies since 1941. Contbr. transl., pamphlets and articles on ednl. subjects. Home: 213 Stanton St., New York 2, N.Y. Died Nov. 23, 1946.

HENRICI, Arthur Trautwein (hĕn-rē'sē), bacteriologist; b. Economy, Pa., Mar. 31, 1889; s. Jacob Frederick and Viola (Irons) H.; M.D., U. of Pittsburgh, 1911; m. Blanche Ressler, Aug. 7, 1913; children—Carl Ressler, Ruth Elizabeth, Hazel Jean. Pathologist St. Francis Hosp., Pittsburgh, 1912-13; instr. in pathology and bacteriology, U. of Minn., 1913-16, asst. prof. bacteriology, 1916-20, asso. prof., 1920-25, prof. since 1925; Walker-Ames Prof., U. of Wash., 1941. Served as capt. Med. Corps, U.S. Army, 1917-19. Mem. Soc. Am. Bacteriologists (pres. 1939), Soc. Exptl. Biology and Medicine, Limnological Soc. of America, Mycological Soc. of Am., Sigma Xi, Gamma Alpha, Alpha Omega Alpha. Author: Morphologic Variation and the Rate of Growth of Bacteria, 1928; Molds, Yeasts and Actinomycetes, 1930; The Biology of Bacteria, 1934, 2d edit., 1939. Contbr. to bacteriological jours. Home: 130 Arthur Av. S.E., Minneapolis, Minn. Died Apr. 23, 1943.

HENRIQUEZ-UREÑA, Pedro (ĕn-rē'kĕs), Dominican writer and educator; b. Santo Domingo, 1884; s. Dr. Francisco Henríquez y Caravajal, and Salomé Ureña de Henríquez; ed. Professional Institute of Santo Domingo (degree of bachelor of science and letters, 1901); U. of Mexico, lawyer, 1914; U. of Minn., M.A., 1917, Ph.D., 1918; m. Isabel Lombardo Toledano; children—Natalia and Sofía. Chief official of secretariat, U. of Mexico, 1910-14; prof. of Spanish and Spanish-Am. lit., Nat. Preparatory School, Mexico City, 1912-13; joint editor of Las Novedades, N.Y., 1915-16; prof. Spanish and Spanish lit., U. of Minn., 1916-19, 1920-21; associate editor of the Revista de Filología Española of Center of Historical Studies of Madrid, 1919-20; Dominican del. to Internat. Students' Congress of Mexico City, 1921; dir.-founder Summer School, U. of Mexico, 1923; prof. of Spanish language and lit., Colegio of National University of La Plata since 1924; prof. of Latin-Am. Lit. in School of Philosophy and Letters, U. of Buenos Aires since 1935. Mem. Sociedad de Conferencias of Mexico; Ateneo de Mexico; Asociacion de las Artes de la Plata; Academia Argentina de Letras. Author: Horas de estudio, 1919; La versificación irregular en la poesía castellana, 1920; Seis ensayos en busca de nuestra expresión, 1928; Literary currents in Hispanic America, 1945. Address: Ayacucho 890, Buenos Aires, Argentina. Died 1947.

HENRY, Frederick Augustus, judge; b. Bainbridge, Geauga County, O., June 16, 1867; s. Charles Eugene and Sophia Marcia (Williams) H.; A.B., Hiram Coll., Ohio, 1888; A.M., LL.B., U. of Mich., 1891; m. Louise Adams, E. Smithfield, Pennslyvannia, Jan. 25, 1893; children—Marcia L. (Mrs. H. C. Rosenberger) Charles A., Charlotte S., Rhoda (Mrs. V. E. Messner), and Polly M. In law practice at Cleveland, 1891-1905; judge Circuit Court, Ohio, 1905-12; resigned Jan. 2, 1912, and resumed law practice, Cleveland; conservator Chagrin Falls Banking Co., 1933-34, counsel and secretary of liquidating committee, 1934-45; dir. Van Sweringen Co., Shaker Co., New Amsterdam Co., Williamson Co. (all Cleveland, Ohio). Professor of law, Western Reserve University, 1894-1911. Trustee Hiram Coll. since 1899 (pres. bd. 1908-38), Cleveland Y.M.C.A. since 1908 (pres. 1936-39); pres. Gen. Conv. of Disciples of Christ, 1913, Cleveland Federated Chs., 1914, Business Men's Commn. of Men and Millions Movement, 1915-19; dir. Municipal Research Bur. of Cleveland, 1915-20; v.p. Federal Regional Road Advisory Com. of Cleveland. Mem. Cleveland Chamber Commerce (v.p. 1912-14), N.E. Hist. Geneal. Soc., Western Reserve, Bradford County (Pa.) Hiram, (O) and Geauga County (O.) hist. socs., Philos. Club of Cleveland (pres. 1915-16), Loyal Legion (jr. vice-comdr. O. Commandery 1934-35), Sons of Vets., Phi Delta Phi. Republican. Author: Henry Family Record (genealogy), 1905; Capt. Henry of Geauga, 1942. Home: Geauga Lake, O. Office: Williamson Bldg., Cleveland, O. Died Jan. 15, 1949.

HENRY, George Frederick, prof. chemistry; b. Ainsworth, Ia., Nov. 20, 1870; s. William and Margaret (Frederick) H.; student Albion (Mich.) Coll., 1895-96; B.S., Wash. State Coll., 1903; M.S., Northwestern U., 1915; studied U. of Chicago, 1915; m. Julia M. Reeve, Oct. 31, 1903 (died 1914); children Dorothy Eleanor, George Frederick; m. 2d, Louise McIntosh, June 5, 1927. Teacher rural schs. until 1900; teacher high sch., Lewiston, Wash., 1903-06; head dept. science, Lucknow (India) Christian Coll., 1906-14, v. prin., 1912-14; prof. chemistry and physics, Mt. Union Coll., 1915-16, Fargo (N.D.) Coll., 1916-21, asst. dean, 1919-21; prof. chemistry, Coll. of Puget Sound, 1921-38, prof. emeritus since 1938, dean, 1922-26. Fellow of A.A.A.S., Am. Inst. of Chemists; mem. Am. Chem. Soc., Pi Kappa Delta, Phi Kappa Phi, Phi Beta Kappa. Republican. Methodist. Author: Laboratory Manual of General Chemistry, 1911. Home: 1011 11th St., N.W., Puyallup, Wash. Died May 9, 1945.

HENRY, Hugh Carter, physician; b. New Kent County, Va., Oct. 31, 1875; s. Hugh and Mildred Carter (Selden) H.; M.D., Med. Coll. of Va., 1896; m. Annie Smith, Dec. 3, 1898; children—Van Meter Allen (Mrs. Raymond Barker), Hugh Carter; m. 2d, Bessie McGehee, Nov. 14, 1911. Private practice of medicine, Charlotte County, Va., 1898-1906, 1908-11; asso. Dr. Barringer's Sanitarium, U. of Va., 1906-07; asst. physician Central State Hosp., Va., 1911-24, supt., 1924-38; dir. State Hosps. of Va., 1938-42; commr. of mental hygiene and hospitals since 1942. Mem. A.M.A., Va. Neuropsychiatric Society (pres. 1939), Am. Psychiatric Assn., Southern Psychiatric Assn., Tri-State Med. Assn. Democrat. Presbyterian. Home: 5405 Matoaka Av. Office: 309 N. 12th St., Richmond, Va. Died Oct. 14, 1945.

HENRY, Philip Walter, consulting engr.; b. Scranton, Pa., Mar. 24, 1864; s. Eugene Thomas and Emma Elizabeth (Walter) H.; C.E., Rensselaer Poly. Inst., 1887; m. Clover Cox, Jan. 22, 1906; children Clover Eugenia. With Barber Asphalt Paving Co., 1887-1902, becoming v.p. and gen. mgr.; v.p. Medina Quarry Co., 1902-04; v.p. A. L. Barber Asphalt Co., and Pan Am. Co. of Del., 1904-09; pres. S. American Contsrn. Co., 1907-09; pres. Central R.R. Co., of Haiti, 1909-17; v.p. Am. Internat. Corp., 1916-23, Siems-Carey Ry. & Canal Co., 1921-23. Mem. Tech. Bd. Review, Public Works Adminstrn., 1933-35. V.p. Rensselaer Poly. Inst. Has been identified with engring. and contsrn. work in Mex., Haiti, Venezuela, Peru, Boliva, Argentine, Spain and China. Dir. N.Y. City Mission Soc. Mem. Am. Soc. Civil Engrs., American Institute Consulting Engrs. (past president; secretary since 1924), American Inst. Mining Engrs., Am. Geog. Soc. (councillor), Pan-Am. Soc., (hon.) Assn. Chinese and Am. Engrs. Republican. Presbyn. Clubs: University, Engineers', Century (New York). Author of various articles and papers. Home: Scarborough, N.Y. Office: 75 West St., New York. Died Nov. 7, 1947.

HENRY, Robert K., congressman; b. Jefferson, Wis., Feb. 9, 1890; s. Will Sayre and Jessie (Harris) H.; ed. Jefferson (Wis.) High Sch., and U. of Wisconsin; m. Claire Stevens, Dec. 13, 1911. Clerk, Jefferson County Bank, 1913-18, asst. cashier, 1918-28, cashier and dir. since 1928; served as state treas., Wis., 1933-36; mem. Wis. state banking commn., 1940-44; served as city clerk, Jefferson, 1914-24; mem. 79th Congress (1945-47), 2d Wis. Dist. Mason (32°), Odd Fellow. Club: Madison (Wis.). Home: Jefferson, Wis. Office: House Office Bldg., Washington, D.C. Died Nov. 20, 1946.

HENRY, Thomas P., pres. Am. Automobile Assn.; b. Brookhaven, Miss., Dec. 28, 1877; s. Robert Hiram and Ida (Johnson) H.; ed. pub. schs. and Milsaps Coll.; m. Beatrice Morris, of Parkersburg, W.Va., Mar. 23, 1905; children—Thomas P., Beatrice, Eleanor, Anne. Worked on newspapers in Miss. and New Orleans, later with Chicago Tribune, N.Y. Times, N.Y. Commercial, Detroit Free Press; founded Thos.

P. Henry Co., Detroit, 1906; pres, Am. Automobile Assn. since 1923. Consumer adviser petroleum code, NRA; consultant on transportation, Office for Emergency Management, 1941-42; v.p. Assn. Internat. des Automobile Clubs Reconnus (governing com.), Internat. Assn. of Execs. Mason, Rotarian. Clubs: Detroit Club, Detroit Golf, Detroit Athletic, Miami Beach Surf. Contbr. articles on motoring to mags. Home: 19515 Cumberland Way. Office: 41 Burroughs Av., Detroit, Mich. Died Sep. 7, 1945.

HENSCHEL, George, musician, singer, composer; b. Breslau, Silesia, Feb. 18, 1850; s. Moritz and Henriette H.; ed. in Breslau; mus. edn., Leipzig and Berlin; came to U.S., 1880; m. Lillian Bailey, Mar. 9, 1881 (died 1901); m. 2d, Amy Louis, 1907. Lived in Boston, 1881-84; then in London, made numerous visits to U.S. First conductor Boston Symphony Orchestra until 1884; est. and was conductor, London Symphony Orchestra 11 yrs.; first conductor Scottish Symphony Orchestra. Retired as singer, 1901; prof. singing, Inst. of Musical Art, New York, since 1905. Compositions: Serbisches Liederspiel; Te Deum; Stabat Mater; Requiem; Nubia (opera), and other vocal works; many songs, duets, quartettes, etc. Music to Hamlet and other instrumental works. Address: Allt-na-criche, Aviemore, Scotland. Died Sept. 10, 1934.

HENSHAW, Samuel, zoölogist; hon. A.M., Harvard, 1903. Dir. Mus. Comparative Zoölogy, Harvard, 1911-27. Fellow Am. Acad. Arts and Sciences; mem. Am. Soc. Naturalists, Am. Soc. Zoölogists. Address: 28 Fayerweather St., Cambridge, Mass. Died Feb. 5, 1941.

HENSLEY, Walter Lewis, ex-congressman; b. Jefferson County, Mo., Sept. 3, 1871; s. Thomas J. and Emily E. H.; ed. pub. schs., U. of Mo.; married; children—Robert Thornton, Emily Elyzbeth, Walter Lewis, John Clark. Admitted to bar, 1894, and practiced in St. Francois County; pros. atty., St. Francois County, 1898-1902; mem. 62d to 65th Congresses (1911-19), 13th Mo. Dist.; U.S. atty. for Eastern Dist. of Mo., 1919-20; resigned to engage in private practice; member firm Hensley, Krause & Hensley. Democrat. Home: 419 Polo Drive, Clayton, Mo. Office: Boatmen's Bank Bldg., St. Louis, Mo. Died July 18, 1946.

HERING, Frank Earl, editor; b. Northumberland County, Pa., Apr. 30, 1874; s. Solomon and Mary Elizabeth (Neuer) H.; student U. of Chicago, 1892-95, 1897, Bucknell U., 1895-96; Ph.D., U. of Notre Dame, 1898, LL.B., 1902; m. Claribel Ormsby Orton, Jan. 20, 1910. Teacher of English and history, U. of Notre Dame, 1898-1904; nat. pres. Fraternal Order Eagles, 1909-10, 1911-12, now nat. chmn. Eagles' Old Age Pension Commn.; sec. Eagles' Nat. Stabilization of Employment Commn.; mng. editor and advertising mgr. The Eagle Mag. since 1912. Vice-pres., sec. and mng. organizer Ind. State War Savings Stamp Com., 1917-18. Trustee U. of Notre Dame. Mem. Alumni Assn. U. of Notre Dame (nat. pres. 1930-31), Phi Gamma Delta; hon. mem. Vets. of Foreign Wars. Mason, Elk. Clubs: Rotary (ex-pres.), University (ex-pres.), South Bend Knife and Fork (ex-pres.). Author: At the Edge of Day (verse), 1909. Public speaker. Active in promoting mothers' pension laws, old age pension laws. Decorated by Am. War Mothers, named by Mont. legislature and credited in Congress as the first nationwide sponsor of Mothers' Day. Bronze tablet erected in his honor at English Opera House, Indianapolis, Ind., commemorating first Mothers' Day address, Feb. 7, 1904. Home: 919 E. Jefferson Blvd. Office: Lafayette Bldg., South Bend, Ind. Died July 11, 1943.

HERING, Henry, sculptor; b. N.Y. City, Feb. 15, 1874; s. Michael and Magdalene (Compter) H.; Art Students' League, New York, 1894-98; École des Beaux Arts and Colorossi Acad., Paris, France, 1900-01; pupil of Augustus St. Gaudens, 1900-07; m. Elsie Ward, June 1910. Principal works: (portrait busts) Augustus St. Gaudens; Bishop Ethelbert Talbott; Stephen H. Olin and his father for Middletown Coll. Library; Roger Platt, N.Y. City; John Freeman, N.H.; Edward C. Simmons, St. Louis, Mo.; F. J. V. Skiff, Field Museum, Chicago; Ernest R. Graham, Chicago; Dr. Richard H. Hoffmann; Russ Whytll; (portrait reliefs) Mr. Sam Scribner; Peirce Anderson; Stephen H. Olin, Rhinebeck, New York; Mrs. Tracy Dows and son, Rhinebeck, New York; Miss Irom, Portland Library, Oregon; Charles Albert Coffin, N.Y.; Evarts Tracy, N.Y.; Dr. Andrew McCosh, Presbyterian Hospital, New York City; William Cullen Bryant, Williams College; (medals) John Mulholland; Apartment House for N.Y. Chapter A.I.A.; Official Seal P.P. Internat. Expn. Calif.; Searsdale Golf Club championship medal; (memorial reliefs) Robert Collyer, Ch. of Messiah, N.Y. City, Huntington Wolcott Jackson, Crerar Library, Chicago, and Princeton University; Mcl. Craig, Metropolitan Life Insurance, New York City; General Fitzgerald, 71st Armory, New York City; Henry Bacon, St. George's Church, N.Y. City; Josiah Kirby Lilly, Indianapolis; pediment and symbolic figures, Eli Lilly Research Laboratories, Indianapolis; (architectural sculpture) Field Museum Natural History, Chicago; Industrial Arts Bldg., Chicago; Union Station, Chicago; two groups South Pylons "Defense of Fort Dearborn and Regeneration of Chicago," Rush Street Bridge, Chicago; Civic Opera House pediment, Chicago; (Federal Reserve Banks) Dallas, Tex., Kansas City, Mo., Chicago, Ill., Cleveland, O., Pittsburgh, Pa., Clarksburg, W.Va.; four bronze panels, Religion, Science, Law, Knowledge, for Obelisk, Indianapolis, Ind.; pediment Severance Hall, Cleveland, O., Med. Arts Bldg., Cleveland, O.; eight heroic bridge pylon figures for Cleveland, O.; Spandrils for Museum, Yale U.; (portrait statues) of Pere Marquette, Gary, Ind.; Seated Abraham Lincoln, Woodrow Wilson, Indianapolis, Ind.; (war memorials) Civil War Memorial, Yale Univ.; Ind. State War Memorial with heroic bronze figure of Pro Patria, Indianapolis; war memorial, Ridgewood, N.J.; (memorial tablet) Myron T. Herrick, Paris, France; trophy for Am. Legion Champion Color Guard; also many fountains. Nat. Academician, 1937. Served with 40th Engrs., U.S. Army, 1918. Mem. Nat. Sculpture Soc., Archtl. League of N.Y., Fine Arts Federation of N.Y.; served on Art Commn. of N.Y. City, 1937-41; N.Y. City Art Commn. Assos. (pres. 1944-45), Am. Legion. Clubs: Players (New York); Scarsdale (N.Y.) Golf. Studio: 10 W. 33d St., New York. Died Jan. 15, 1949.

HERING, Hollis Webster, librarian; b. Brooklyn, N.Y.; d. Daniel Webster and Mary Hollis (Webster) Hering; A.B., Vassar Coll., 1908 (Phi Beta Kappa); B.L.S., Pratt Inst. of Library Science, Brooklyn, 1910; M.A., New York U., 1919. Asst. in reference dept., Union, Theol. Sem., New York, 1910-14, also acting head dept. various times; librarian Missionary Research Library, New York, 1914-48; ret. 1948; chmn. book selection com., A.L.A. Religious Books Sect., 1936, 37; chmn. A.L.A. Religious Books Sect., 1940, 41. Mem. A.L.A., Special Libraries Assn., New York Library Club. Presbyn. Contbr. to Library Jour., Foreign Missions Year Book, Moslem World, New China Rev., Internat. Rev. of Missions, Special Libraries. Compiler: Recommended Titles on Missions and Related Subjects, 1924; Christian Missions in World Perspective, 1931; A World-Wide Christian Outlook—a selected bibliography, 1935. Home: 2208 Andrews Av., N.Y. City. Died April 30, 1949.

HERLIHY, Charles Michael, educator; b. Cambridge, Mass., Oct. 1, 1891; s. John William and Mary Ann (Murphy) H.; A.B., Boston Coll., 1912, A.M., 1914, LL.D., 1934; grad. Boston Normal Sch., 1914; m. Emma Cutter, Sept. 19, 1918; children—Charles Cutter, John Joseph, Mary Isabel. Served as teacher, pub. schs., Cambridge, 1912-16, asst. supt. schs., 1916-20; asst. supervisor of Americanization, Mass. State Dept. Edn., 1920-22, supervisor, 1922-27; pres. State Teachers Coll., Fitchburg, Mass., since 1927. Served as 2d lt., Sanitary Corps, U.S. Army, 1918-19. Pres. Nat. Dept. Adult Edn., 1922-24; mem. Americanism com. Am. Legion, 1924-27; mem. advisory bd. Div. Immigration and Americanization, 1926-39; sec. bd. trustees Fitchburg Pub. Library since 1935; mem. exec. com. Fitchburg Art Center since 1929; mem. N.E. Teacher Training Assn. (pres.), N.E. Sch. Supts. Assn., N.E.A., Mass. Schoolmasters Club, Mass. School Supts. Assn., Mass. Teachers College Assn., Fitchburg Council of Social Agencies, October Conference for Exchange of Educational Opinion. Democrat. K.C. Rotarian (past pres.). Co-author: First Steps in Americanization, 1918. Writer of federal and state bulls. on adult edn. Contbr. ednl. articles to School and Society, School Board Journal and Journal of the N.E.A. Home: 112 Pearl St., Fitchburg, Mass. Died Jan. 27, 1945.

HERMAN, Abraham, business exec.; b. Niejin, Russia, Mar. 25, 1878; s. Elias and Temma (Dullberg) H.; came to U.S., 1891, naturalized, 1899; Ph.G., Brooklyn Coll. of Pharmacy, 1902; m. Sylvia Lewis, Dec. 25, 1906 (died Jan. 30, 1931); 1 dau., Renée (dec.); m. 2d, Marie Silberman, July 21, 1932. In business as pharmacist, 1902-05; mem. Crown Pad Co., 1905-12; sec.-treas. William Herman Co., Inc., 1912-28; dir. and chmn. bd. Nat. Container Corp., Long Island City, N.Y., since 1928; dir. and mem. exec. com. Pennsylvania Exchange Bank. Trustee Lebanon Hosp. Associates. Pres. Hebrew Sheltering and Immigrant Aid Soc. since 1926. Asso. mem. New Sch. Social Research. Mem. N.Y. County Grand Jury Assn., Grand Street Boys Assn. Mason. Mem. B'nai B'rith. Home: 302 W. 12th St., New York 14, N.Y. Office: 30-01 Review Av., Long Island City 1, N.Y. Died Mar. 25, 1947.

HERMAN, Raphael, mfr.; b. nr. Königsburg, Germany, Dec. 15, 1865; s. Sampson J. and Celia (Lumenfels) H.; ed. in Germany; hon. degree Fellowship of Educational Inst. of Scotland, Edinburgh, July 21, 1925; LL.D., U. of Southern Calif., 1927; unmarried. Came to America, 1890; engaged in business in N.Y. State; one of the officials of the Pan-Am. Expn., Buffalo, 1901; pub. Acetylene Journal, 1895-1903; pres. Nat. Acetylene Assn., 1900-02; pres. and treas. Diamond Power Specialty Co., mfrs. of steam specialists, Detroit, since 1905; pres., treas. Power Efficiency Corp., Calorizing Corp. of American. An organizer and trustee, until 1912, of Detroit Tuberculosis Sanitarium; a founder and life mem. Detroit Mus. of Art; founder and trustee Los Angeles U. of Internat. Relations; mem. Detroit Board of Commerce, Am. Mus. Natural History (New York); mem. bd. trustees World Federation of Ednl. Assns; advisory mem. Council on Internat. Relations; nat. v.p. League of Nations Assn.; mem. Council of Foreign Relations; mem. Com. on Cultural Relations with Latin America; mem. advisory bd. Inst. Internat. Relations, China Inst. in America. Trustee U. of Southern Calif.; trustee Abraham Lincoln Home for Boys, Los Angeles. Donor of $25,000 competitive peace prize, won by Dr. David Starr Jordan, of Stanford Univ. Mem. Am. Acad. Polit. and Social Science, Am. Soc. Internat. Law; colleague Florence Nightingale Inst. of Honorables. Unitarian. Mason (32°). Clubs: Detroit, Detroit Country, Detroit Athletic, Players (Detroit); Union League (Chicago); National Arts (New York). Home: Reno, Nev. Died Apr. 7, 1946.

HERMAN, Theodore Frederick, theologian; b. Göttingen, Germany, Mar. 22, 1872; s. Henry and Caroline (Gardner) H.; Gymnasium, Göttingen; came to America, 1887; B.A., Calvin Coll., Cleveland, 1892; Theol. Sem. Ref. Ch., Lancaster, Pa., 1892-95; U. of Berlin, 1895-97; D.D., Franklin and Marshall Coll., 1910; LL.D., Catawba Coll., 1940; m. Emma Lane Garrigan, July 19, 1899; children—Dorothea Elizabeth, Theodore Frederick, John Eldredge. Ordained Ref. Ch. ministry, 1897; asst. pastor Grace Ch., Cleveland, 1897-98; pastor, Salem Ch., Lafayette, Ind., 1898-1903, Allentown, Pa., 1903-09; prof. systematic theology, Theol. Sem. Ref. Ch., Lancaster, September 1909-47, pres., 1939-47; prof. ethics Coll. for Women, Allentown, Pa., 1904-10. S.S. editor Messenger of Evang. and Reformed Church; editor Reformed Church Review. Mem. Am. Theol. Soc., Phi Kappa Sigma. Clubs: Contemporary (Allentown); Cliosophic (Lancaster). Address: 914 New Holand Av., Lancaster, Pa. Died Apr. 30, 1948.

HEROD, William Pirtle, lawyer; b. Columbus, Ind., July 27, 1864; s. William Wirt and Susan Coons (Rogers) Herod; B.A., Yale, 1886; m. Mary Beaty Applegate, June 5, 1890 (died 1923); children—Bergen, Mary Beaty (Mrs. Nelson M. Graves), William Rogers. Admitted to Indiana bar, 1887, to bar of U.S. Supreme Court, 1905; mem. Herod & Herod, 1887-1904; now gen. counsel Grain Dealers Nat. Mutual Fire Ins. Co. U.S. commr. Dist. of Ind., 4 yrs.; mem. faculty and prof. med. jurisprudence, Central Coll. Phys. and Surg., Indianapolis, 4 yrs.; has served as spl. judge Superior Court, Marion Co., Ind. Trustee Boys Prep. Sch., Indianapolis; dir. James Whitcomb Riley Memorial Assn. Receiver Central Ind. Ry. Co., Lexington Motor Co. Mem. Indianapolis Bar Assn., Ind. State Bar Assn., Indianapolis Art Assn., Delta Kappa Epsilon, Vol. at War Coll., Washington, winter 1917, 1918, Mil. Intelligence Sect. Gen. Staff; mem. exec. com. War Camp Community Service; br. chmn. Mil. Training Camps Assn.; civilian aide to adj. gen. U.S.A., etc. Republican. Clubs: University, Woodstock, Indianapolis Athletic, Dramatic (Indianapolis); University (Chicago); Yale (New York); Country (Connersville, Ind.). Home: Indianapolis Athletic Club, 350 N. Meridian St. Office: Guaranty Bldg., Indianapolis. Died Feb. 1931.

HERRICK, Christine Terhune, author; b. Newark, N.J.; d. Rev. Edward Payson and Mary Virginia Terhune ("Marion Harland"); ed. by governess, pvt. schs. and teachers in Rome, Italy, and Geneva, Switzerland; m. James Frederick Herrick, Apr. 23, 1884 (died 1893). Writer on domestic topics. Mgr. with Florence E. Bate of the Chamber Recital Co., 1908-12. Author: Liberal Living Upon Narrow Means (a cook-book), 1890, Chafing-dish Supper, 1895; Cradle and Nursery, 1889; First Aid to Young Housekeeper, 1900; Housekeeping Made Easy, 1888; Little Dinner, 1893; What to Eat, 1891; The National Cook-Book (with Marion Harland), 1897; Cottage Kitchen (with same), 1895; In City Tents, 1902; The Expert Maid Servant, 1904; Sunday Night Suppers, 1907; Like Mother Used to Make, 1912; The Helping Hand Cook-Book (with Marion Harland), 1912; My Boy and I, 1913; The ABC of Housekeeping, 1915; The Letters of the Duke of Wellington to Miss J., 1894. Revised "Common Sense in the Household" (by Marion Harland), for gas and elec. cookery, under name of "The New Common Sense." Home: Hotel Chastleton, Washington. Died Dec. 2, 1944.

HERRICK, Frederick Cowles, M.D., surgeon; b. Cleveland, O., Oct. 31, 1872; s. Henry Justus and Mary (Brooks) H.; A.B., Amherst Coll., 1894; M.D., Western Reserve U., 1897; grad. study U. of Göttingen, Germany, 1898-1900, London Gen. Hosp., 1905-06; m. Annie Bayard Crowell, July 22, 1908; children — Henry Crowell, Frederick Cowles, Bayard Brooks, Anne Frances. Demonstrator of surgery, Western Reserve University, 1905-07, instructor in surgery, 1908-11, assistant clinical prof. in surgery, 1920-29, became associate clinical professor in surgery, 1933; now retired; visiting surgeon Cleveland City Hospital; visiting surgeon and visiting urologic surgeon, Charity Hosp., also chief surg. teaching staff; cons. surgeon St. John's Hosp. Served as captain U.S. Army, 1917-18, major 1918-19, lt. col., 1919, A.E.F.; chief surgeon Base Hosp. 83, France; col. Med. Res., 1929. Fellow Am. Coll. Surgeons (bd. govs.); mem. A.M.A., Am. Urol. Assn. (pres. Ohio sect.), Cleveland Acad. Medicine, Am. Board of Surgery, Am. Board of Urology, Cleveland Chamber Commerce, Delta Tau Delta. Republican. Presbyn. Clubs: University, Union, Cleveland; Mayfield Country. Contbr. surg. articles to Annals of Surgery, Surgery, Gynecology and Obstetrics, Experimental Medicine, etc. Home: 2211 Harcourt Drive, Cleveland, O. Died Apr. 5, 1943.

HERRICK, Robert Frederick, lawyer; b. Medford, Mass., Aug. 8, 1866; s. Frederick Chamberlin and Josephine (Flanagan) H.; LL.B., Boston U., 1886; A.B., Harvard, 1890; m. Alice Taft, Sept. 20, 1892; m. 2d, Margaret Perkins Rice, Oct. 3, 1922. Mem. law firm Herrick, Smith, Donald & Farley, Boston; pres. The Mfrs.' Co.; treas., dir. A. J. Tower Co., F. S. Webster Co.; chmn. bd. Pacific Mills, Scott & Williams, Inc., American Felt Co.; First National Bank, United Fruit Co., Daniel Green Co., U.S. Smelting, Refining & Mining Co., Calumet & Hecla Cons. Copper Co., Revere Sugar Refinery, United Shoe Machinery Corp., Boston Edison Co., Wyman Gordon

Co., Saco-Lowell Shops, etc.; trustee, mem. bd. of investment, Boston Five Cents Savings Bank; trustee Post Office Sq. Bldg. Trust (Boston). Ex-overseer Harvard; ex-chmn. Harvard Graduate Rowing Com. Clubs: Harvard (Boston and New York); University, Union, Home Market, Eastern Yacht, Somerset (Boston); Miramichi Fish and Game (Canada); Leander Club (Eng.). Home: 25 Commonwealth Av. Office: 1 Federal St., Boston, Mass. Died Oct. 13, 1942.

HERRING, Clyde LaVerne, ex-senator; b. Jackson, Mich., May 3, 1879; s. James Gwynn and Stella Mae (Addison) H.; ed. pub. schs.; m. Emma Pearl Spinney, Feb. 7, 1901; children—LaVerne Barlow, Lawrence Winthrop, Clyde Edsel. Rancher, Colo., 1902-06; moved to Massena, Ia., 1906; farmer, 1906-08; in automobile business, Atlantic, Ia., 1908-10; moved to Des Moines, Ia., 1910; pres. Herring Motor Co., Herring-Wissler Co. Dem. nominee for gov. of Ia., 1920; Dem. nominee for U.S. Senate, 1922; mem. Dem. Nat. Com., Ia.; elected gov. of Ia. for term 1933-35, reëlected term 1935-37; mem. U.S. Senate for term 1937-43. Mem. bd. curators State Hist. Soc. of Ia.; dir. Greater Des Moines Com. Conglist. Clubs: Des Moines, Wakonda Country (Des Moines); Detroit (Mich.) Athletic. Home: 180 37th St., Des Moines, Ia. Died Sept. 15, 1945.

HERRIOTT, Frank Irving, univ. prof.; b. nr. New Liberty, Scott County, Ia., Oct. 19, 1868; s. John (lt.-gov. Iowa, 1902-07) and Nellie F. (Moss) H.; A.B., Ia. (now Grinnell) Coll., 1890, A.M., 1893; Ph.D., Johns Hopkins, 1893; m. Mary Haines, 1896; children—Maxwell Haines, Frances Helen, Roberta Haines, Roger Moss, Charles Burton. Instr. in polit. economy, Woman's Coll., Baltimore, Md., 1892-93; editor University Extension Magazine, Phila., 1893-94; prof. polit. science, Ia. Coll., 1895-96; deputy treas., State of Ia., 1897-1901; prof. social science, Drake U., 1903-37, prof. of political science since 1937. Dir. Des Moines Morris Plan Bank, 1914-21. Statistician to Bd. of Control of State Instns. of Ia., 1903-16. Trustee Ia. Coll., 1899-1904. Treas. Ia. Soc. for Study and Prevention of Tuberculosis, 1905-08; pres. Ia. State Conf. of Charities and Corrections, 1905-09; del. of Commercial Club of Des Moines to Nat. Conf. on Trusts, 1907; mem. exec. com. Associated Charities, Des Moines, 1897-1911; pres. Ia. Children's Home Soc., 1909-11, and since 1912; dir. Bur. Municipal Research, Des Moines, since 1920, v.p., since 1922; investigated initiative, referendum and recall in Pacific Coast states, 1918, for Mass. Mfrs.' Assn. Mem. Nat. Inst. Social Sciences, 1914, Nat. Economic League, 1921, Am. Soc. Internat. Law, Am. Econ. Assn. (1892-1908), Phi Beta Kappa (a founder Beta Chapter, Grinnell, and charter mem. Gamma Chap., Drake, pres. since 1923); hon. mem. German-Am. Hist. Soc. of Ill., Concord Soc. Mem. Com. on Uniform Accounting, League of Ia. Municipalities, 1905-06, and author of law providing for publication of municipal accounts, uniform system of accounts, reports and audit in cities and towns of Ia., enacted by Gen. Assembly of Ia., 1906, and now in operation. Del. to Nat. Conf. for Social Work, 1929, Interracial Commn. of Des Moines, 1936-38; mem. of com. on health, Iowa State Planning Board, 1937-39. Republican. Clubs: Cosmopolitan, Frontier, Prairie, University (ex-pres. of all these clubs), Economic Club. Writer on hist., econ. and polit. subjects. Home: 1206 W. 21st St., Des Moines, Ia. Died Sept. 14, 1941.

HERRMANN, Richard, mfr.; b. Chemnitz, Saxony, Mar. 10, 1849; s. John G. and Therese (Bachman) H.; ed. Chemnitz, Wheeling, W.Va., Pittsburgh, Pa.; m. Lena Jungk, Feb. 22, 1878. Farmed 5 yrs. nr. Centralia, Ill.; employe of I.C.R.R., section hand to civ. engr.; sec., pres., treas. Dubuque Cabinet Makers' Assn., furniture mfrs., 1877-1909; now head R. Herrmann & Sons, furniture, etc. Known as student of geology, paleontology, archaeology and ethnology; founder the Herrmann Mus. of Natural History, Dubuque, Ia.; one of promoters and builders of monument to Julien Dubuque, founder of city; treas. Dubuque Monument Assn. Has a large private collection of geol. specimens; sec. in charge Iowa Inst. of Arts and Sciences. Mason (32°); sec. Masonic Hall Assn. 21 yrs. Author: Life and Adventures of Julien Dubuque; Geology—a Plea for Higher Education; Curriculum Vitae, Memoirs of Life; Collection of Choice German Songs; Mound Builders of the Mississippi Valley; also papers on geol. and other scientific subjects, etc. Home: 2419 Central Av. Office: 545 Main St., Dubuque, Ia. Died Apr. 29, 1941.

HERRON, Charles, clergyman; b. Pittsburgh, Jan. 29, 1863; s. Samuel Davidson, Jr. and Mary Jane (Pomeroy) H.; A.B., Western U. of Pa., Pittsburgh, 1883, A.M., 1886; grad. Western Theol. Sem., Allegheny, Pa., 1887; New Coll. (Theology) Free Ch. of Scotland, 1893-94; D.D., Miami U., 1901, U. of Pittsburgh, 1912; m. Mary Thompson Herron, Dec. 1, 1887. Ordained Presbyn. ministry, 1887; pastor Curwensville, Pa., 1887-93; supply 1st Ch., Wooster, O., 1894-95; pastor Troy, O., 1895-1903, Crowley, La., 1903-04; prof. ecclesiastical history and missions, Presbyn. Theol. Sem., Omaha, Neb., 1904-35, prof. emeritus, since 1935. Republican. Traveled extensively in Europe, studying Church history and lecturing. Home: 2024 Emmet St., Omaha, Neb. Died Apr. 16, 1942.

HERRON, James Hervey, cons. engr.; b. Girard, Pa., Jan. 4, 1875; s. James Hervey and S. Josephine (Fuller) H.; student U. of Mich., 1897-99, B.S. in Mech. Engring., 1909; student Grad. Sch., U. of Mich., 1916-17, 1920-21; Dr. of Engring. (hon.) 1943, Case Sch. of App. Sci.; m. Cora E. Lewis, June 19, 1900. Apprentice, Stearns Mfg. Co., Erie, Pa., 1889-95; asst. and chief engr. Erie City Iron Works, 1895-97; draftsman and asst. engr. Cambria Steel Co., Johnstown, Pa., 1899-1902; v.p. and chief engr., Bury Compressor Co., Erie, Pa., 1902-05; mgr. Motch and Merryweather Machinery Co., Detroit, 1905-07; chief engr. and works mgr. Detroit Steel Products Co., 1907-09; pres. The James H. Herron Co., cons. engrs., Cleveland, O., since 1909; dir. Forest Glen Estate, Youngstown, O. Pres. Bd. of Edn., Cleveland Heights, 1914-20. Life mem. Cleveland Engring. Soc. (pres. 1917-18, hon. mem. 1940); fellow Am. Soc. M.E. (mgr. 1922-25; v.p. 1934-36; pres. 1936-37), A.A.A.S., Am. Inst. Elec. Engrs.; mem. Am. Soc. Civil Engrs. (pres. Cleveland sect. 1935), Am. Inst. Mining and Metall. Engrs., American Chemical Society, Am. Soc. for Testing Materials, Brit. Iron and Steel Inst., Am. Concrete Inst., Tau Beta Pi. Christian Scientist. Mason. Club: Mid-Day (Cleveland). Asso. editor and contbr. chapter on "Iron and Steel" to Hool and Johnston, Handbook of Building Construction; Hool and Kinne, Bldg. Constrn. Home: 17612 Winslow Rd., Shaker Heights 20, O. Died March 29, 1948.

HERSEY, Henry Blanchard, meteorologist and balloonist; b. Williamstown, Vt., July 28, 1861; s. Joel and Recta Wheelock (Blanchard) H.; B.S., Norwich U., Vt., 1885, M.S., 1906; course at U.S. Signal Service Tech. Sch., Va.; m. Mrs. Laura A. Saunier, Mar. 13, 1926 (died 1940). Service of U.S. Weather Bur., 1885-1932. Maj. 1st U.S. Vol. Cav. ("Roosevelt's Rough Riders"), Spanish-Am. War; exec. officer Wellman Chicago Record-Herald Polar Expdn., 1906-07; experienced meteorologist and balloonist, being a licensed aeronautic pilot of the Aero Club of France, and of the Aero Club of America. Assisted Lt. Frank P. Lahm, U.S. Army, in the internat. balloon race at Paris, 1906, helping to win the James Gordon Bennett cup; sailed the balloon "United States" in the internat. race at St. Louis, 1907, crossing lakes Michigan, St. Clair and Erie, and landing in Canada. Apptd. maj., Aviation Sect., Signal Corps, May 1917, and placed in command U.S. Army Balloon Sch., Ft. Omaha, Neb.; rated as jr. mil. aeronaut, July 24, 1917; promoted lt. col. Signal Corps, U.S. Army, Sept. 27, 1917; served with balloon div., Air Service, in France, Oct. 1918-Mar. 1919. Fellow Royal Meteorol. Soc., London; mem. Southern Calif. Acad. Sciences, A.A.A.S., etc. Elected permanent hon. comdr. Los Angeles Bd. No. 4, Am. Balloon Corps Vets. Mason (32°). Club: Cosmos (Washington). Contbr. on aeronautical subjects to Century Mag. Home: 135 East Laurel Av., Sierra Madre, Calif. Died Sept. 24, 1948.

HERSEY, Ira Greenlief, ex-congressman; b. Hodgdon, Me., Mar. 31, 1858; s. Samuel B. and Elizabeth (White) H.; ed. Ricker Classical Inst., Houlton; m. Annie Dillen, Jan. 6, 1884. Began practice of law in Houlton, 1880; candidate of Prohibition Party for gov., 1886; mem. Me. Ho. of Rep., 1909-10, Senate, 1913-16 (pres. 1915-16); mem. 65th to 70th Congresses (1917-29), 4th Me. Dist.; in practice of law, Washington, since 1929. Republican. Methodist. Mason, Odd Fellow, Elk. Club: Meduxnekeag (Houlton). Home: 517 Cedar St., Takoma Park, Washington. Died March 6, 1943.

HERSHEY, J(ohn) Willard, chemist; b. Gettysburg, Pa., Feb. 6, 1876; s. Abraham and Hosie (Eyster) H.; B.S., Gettysburg Coll., 1907, M.S., 1910; student Harvard, 1907-08, Johns Hopkins, 1910-11; Ph.D., U. of Chicago, 1924; m. Effie Bowman, Aug. 24, 1910; 1 son, Ardys Willard. Taught 5 yrs. in Pa. pub. schs.; prof. chemistry, Bridgewater (Va.) Coll., 1908-10, Defiance (O.) Coll., 1911-18, McPherson (Kan.) Coll. since 1918. Fellow A.A.A.S., Internat. Coll. of Anesthetists (life); mem. Am. Chem. Soc. (councilor 1930-32; pres. Wichita sect. 1937-39), Am. Inst. Chemists, Kan. Acad. Science (pres. 1933-34), Physical Science Teachers Soc. (pres. 1933-37), Sigma Xi, Phi Beta Kappa. Democrat. Mem. Ch. of Brethren. Rotarian. Author: A Laboratory Guide to Study of Qualitative Analysis, 1927; (with L. A. Enberg) Laboratory Manual for General Chemistry, 1933; The Book of Diamonds, 1940; also research papers on synthetic diamonds and components of the atmosphere and synthetic gases in relation to animal life. Home: McPherson, Kan. Died Sept. 27, 1943.

HERSHEY, Milton Snavely, mfr.; b. Derry Twp., Dauphin County, Pa., Sept. 13, 1857; s. Henry H. and Fannie (Snavely) H.; ed. pub. schs.; m. Catharine Sweeney, 1898 (died 1915). Began mfr. of chocolate at Lancaster, Pa., 1893; now chmn. bd. Hershey Chocolate Corp., Hershey, Pa.; pres. Hershey Trust Co. Founder, 1905, chmn. bd. mgrs. Hershey Industrial Sch. for orphan boys; donated, 1918, fortune, estimated at $60,000,000, as a trust for the maintenance of the school. Republican. Home: Hershey, Pa. Died Oct. 13, 1945; buried in Hershey Cemetery, Hershey, Pa.

HERT, Mrs. Alvin T. (Sally Aley); b. Bedford, Ind.; d. Calvin Reuter and Susan Louisa Aley; m. Alvin T. Hert, Nov. 20, 1893 (died June 7, 1921). Chmn. bd. Am. Creosoting Co., and active in connection with various large business enterprises with which her husband was identified, including Hurstbourne Farms, Jefferson County, Ky. Vice chmn. Rep. Nat. Com., 1924-36 (resigned); state chairman for Republican women in Ky., 1923-35; mem. Rep. Nat. Com. for Ky., 1924-35. Episcopalian. Clubs: Pendennis, Country (Louisville); Women's Nat. Republican (New York); Everglades, Bath & Tennis (Palm Beach). Home: 1800 South Ocean Blvd., Palm Beach, Fla. Office: 401 W. Main St., Louisville, Ky. Died June 8, 1948.

HERTZ, Alfred, musician; b. Frankfort-on-the-Main, Germany, July 15, 1872; s. Leo and Sara (Koenigswerther) H.; ed. Frankfort Gymnasium; musical edn. at Raff Conservatorium, Frankfort; married. Conductor at Hoftheater, Altenburg, Saxony, 1892-95; Stadttheater, Barmen-Elberfeld, 1895-99; spring, 1899, concerts in London, Stadttheater, Breslau, 1899-1902; German opera at Met. Opera House, New York, 1902-15; dir. San Francisco Symphony Orchestra, 1915-30. Dir. royal opera, Covent Garden, London, spring and fall 1910; directed 1st performance of "Parsifal" outside of Bayreuth, Dec. 24, 1903, Met. Opera House, New York, and first and only performance of Richard Strauss' "Salome" in New York, Jan. 22, 1907; directed 1st performance of "Königskinder," Dec. 28, 1910; original productions of such Am. operas as Mona, by Horatio Parker; Cyrano de Bergerac, by Damrosch; Fairyland, by Parker; directed San Francisco Spring Music Festivals, 1924-25; inaugurated and directed summer series of symphony concerts in the Hollywood Bowl, Los Angeles, 1922-34; dir. Standard Symphony Hour over the radio, 1932-39; regional director Federal Music Project, 1937-1939. Decorated with an order for Art and Science, of Saxony; Order of Merit for Art, of Rumania; hon. citizen of San Francisco. Home: 770 Camino del Mar, San Francisco, Calif. Died Apr. 17, 1942.

HERTZLER, Arthur Emanuel, surgeon; b. West Point, Ia., July 26, 1870; s. Daniel and Hannah M. (Krehbiel) H.; B.S., Southwestern Coll., Winfield, Kan., 1897; M.D., Northwestern U., 1894; grad. work, Berlin, 1899-1901; Ph.D., Ill. Wesleyan U., 1902; LL.D., Washburn Coll.; LL.D., Southwestern Coll., 1939; Sc.D., Boston U., 1939; m. Myrtle Arnold, May 1, 1894; children—Agnes H., Helen L., Margaret L.; married 2d, Irene A. Koeneke, M.D., June 8, 1945; Teacher of pathology, 1902-07, surgeon and gynecologist, 1907-09, Univ. Med. Coll., Kansas City, Mo.; prof. surgery, U. of Kan., since 1909; founder, 1902, and pres. Agnes Hertzler Memorial Hosp. Has conducted researches in diseases of peritoneum since 1894, and has made important discoveries as to local anæsthesia and as to the diseases of the thyroid gland. Mem. A.M.A., Western Surg. Assn., Am. Micros. Soc. (pres. 1911), Assn. Am. Anatomists, Am. Acad. Medicine, etc. Mason. Clubs: City, Kansas City. Author: Treatise on Tumors, 1912; Surgical Operations Under Local Anæsthesia, 1913; Principles of Abdominal Surgery, 1918; Diseases of the Peritoneum, 1919; Case Histories in Surgery, 1919; Diseases of the Thyroid Gland, 1922; Treatise on Minor Surgery (with V. E. Chesky), 1925 Pathology of the Surgical Diseases of Bone, 1930; Pathology of Genitourinary Diseases, 1930; Pathology of the Diseases of the Skin, 1931; Pathology of the Female Generative Organs, 1931; Surgical Pathology of the Diseases of the Mammary Gland; Surgical Pathology of the Diseases of the Peritoneum; Surgery of General Practice (with Chesky), 1934; Surgical Pathology of the Gastro Intestinal Tract, 1936; Surgical Pathology of the Thyroid Gland, 1936; Surgical Pathology of Diseases of the Neck, 1937; The Horse and Buggy Doctor, 1938; Surgical Pathology of Diseases of the Mouth and Jaws, 1938; The Doctor and His Patient, 1940; Study of the Diseases of the Thyroid Gland, 1941. Grounds of an Old Surgeon's Faith, 1944; Ventures in Science of a Country Surgeon, 1944; Always the Child, 1944. Home: Halstead, Kan. Died Sept. 12, 1946.

HESSLER, John Charles, college pres.; b. Syracuse, N.Y., Nov. 27, 1869; s. Jacob R. and Mary (Shane) H.; A.B., U. of Chicago, 1896, Ph.D., 1899; m. Maud C. Hutchins, 1891; children—Margaret Constance, Herbert Eugene. Teacher Chicago high schs., 1890-99; instr. chemistry, U. of Chicago, 1899-1907; prof. chemistry, 1907-20, dean, 1917-20, acting pres., 1919, James Millikin U.; asst. dir. Mellon Inst. Industrial Research, Pittsburgh, 1920-21; prof. chemistry, Knox Coll., 1921-34; pres. James Millikin U. since 1934. Fellow A.A.A.S.; mem. Am. Chem. Soc., Ill. State Acad. Science (ex-pres.), N.E.A., Ill. Assn. Chemistry Teachers (ex-president), Phi Beta Kappa, Sigma Xi, Phi Lambda Upsilon. Republican. Presbyterian. Author: (with Albert L. Smith) Essentials of Chemistry, 1902; First Year of Science, 1915; Junior Science, 1919; First Year of Chemistry, 1931; Workbook Manual of Chemistry, 1932 (with Henry C. Shoudy), Understanding Our Environment, 1939; also research and education articles. Home: 1313 W. Main St., Decatur, Ill. Died July 29, 1944.

HESS, Herbert William, univ. prof.; b. St. Louis, Mo., March 10, 1880; s. William Henry and Agnes Christina (Tuche) H.; A.B, Northwestern U., 1904; Ph.D., U. of Pa., 1914; unmarried. Teacher, Ft. Scott (Kan.) High Sch., 1904-05; St. Louis (Mo.) High Sch., 1905-09; promotive work and one of founders, City Coll. Law and Commerce, St. Louis, 1908-09; advertising and sales expert, 1914; instr. Wharton Sch., U. of Pa., 1909-14, head of merchandising dept., 1909-33, prof. since 1916. Mem. Am. Acad. of Polit. and Social Science, Am. Econ. Assn., Phila. Art. Alliance, Am. Teachers of Advertising and Marketing, Beta Gamma Sigma, Sigma Kappa Phi. Clubs: Manufacturers and Bankers, Sales Manager's, Poor Richard (Phila.); Wranglers (Northwestern U.). Republican. Author: Productive Advertising, 1915; Creative Salesmanship, 1923; Advertising Its Economics, Philosophy and Technique, 1930. Lecturer; advisory editor of The Plan, pub. by Middle Atlantic Lumberman's Assn., 1935-36. Home: Alden

Park Manor, Germantown, Philadelphia. Died Feb. 20, 1949.

HESSBERG, Irving Kapp, bus. exec.; b. New York, N.Y., Oct. 20, 1894; s. Magnus M. and Fanny (Kapp) H.; ed. public schools, Townsend Harris Hall and City Coll. of N.Y.; m. Peggy Finkelstein, June 25, 1924; 1 dau., Fern E. Began as clerk, Julius Kayser & Co., 1911; employed in stock dept., Wimelbacher & Rice; with Van Raalte Co., Inc., since 1917, pres. since 1933, dir. since 1928. Served with U.S. Army during World War I. Dir. and past chmn. bd. Nat. Assn. of Hosiery Mfrs.; dir. Full Fashioned Hosiery Assn. Clubs: Empire State (gov.); Metropolis Country (White Plains). Home: 451 West End Av. (24). Office: 417 Fifth Av. N.Y. City. Died Oct. 4, 1948.

HETZEL, Ralph Dorn, college pres.; b. Merrill, Wis., Dec. 31, 1882; s. Henry Clayton and Sadie (Dorn) H.; A.B., U. of Wis., 1906, LL.B., 1908; studied U. of Calif., summer 1909; LL.D., Dartmouth Coll., 1918, U. of Me., 1924, Bucknell U., 1927; Litt.D., Lafayette Coll., 1928; LL.D., U. of Pa., 1934, University of New Hampshire, 1937, University of Pittsburgh, 1943; m. Estelle Helene Heineman, Aug. 4, 1911; children—Ralph Dorn, Helene Estelle (Mrs. B. K. Johnstone), Roger Harry, Harriett Elizabeth (Mrs. J. A. Williams), Philip Edgar. Instr. English, 1908-09, asst. prof., 1909-11, prof. English and polit. science, 1911-13, dir. extension service, 1913-17. Ore. State Coll.: pres. N.H. Coll. Agr. and Mechanic Arts, 1917-23; pres. U. of N.H., 1923-26; pres. Pa. State Coll. since Jan. 1927. Admitted to Wisconsin bar, 1908, Oregon bar, 1910. President Association of College Presidents of Pennsylvania, 1933. Member Committee for Consideration of Inter-Governmental Debts, 1933. Member advisory committee, Army Specialized Training Division. Mem. Assn. Land-grant Colls. and Univs. (exec. com. 1924-32, 1935-37; pres. 1947), Nat. Assn. State Univs. (pres. 1934; chmn. com. on mil. affairs since Dec. 1943); Am. Council Edn. (mem. exec. com. 1941-44); area chmn. Pa. War Fund; adv. com. on edn., State Council of Defense, Pennsylvania Chamber of Commerce (director 1927-43), Phi Beta Kappa, Delta Upsilon, Phi Delta Phi, Gamma Sigma Delta, Phi Kappa Phi, Kappa Phi Kappa, Pi Delta Epsilon, Phi Sigma Iota, Phi Eta Sigma. Republican. Conglist. Mason. Home: State College, Pa. Died Oct. 3, 1947.

HETZLER, Theodore, banker; b. N.Y. City, June 13, 1875; s. Bernhard H.; ed. pub. schs. of N.Y. City; m. Mary Regis Smith, July 6, 1914. With Fifth Av. Bank, N.Y. City, since 1890, pres., 1916-40, chmn. bd. since 1940; trustee Franklin Savings Bank. Served in U.S. Vols., Spanish-Am. War, 1898, participating in the principal battles in Cuba. Mem. Nat. Sculpture Soc., Artists' Aid Soc., Met. Mus., Museum of Natural History, Soc. Santiago de Cuba. Republican. Lutheran. Clubs: Century Assn., Union League. Office: 530 Fifth Av., New York, N.Y. Died Aug. 12, 1945.

HEWETT, Edgar Lee, univ. prof.; b. Warren County, Ill., Nov. 23, 1865; s. H. H. and Tabitha (Stice) H.; student Tarkio (Mo.) Coll.; M.Pd., Teachers Coll., Greeley, Colo., 1898; D.Sc., U. of Geneva, Switzerland, 1908; LL.D., U. of Ariz., 1917; L.H.D., U. of N.M., 1934; D.Sc., Knox Coll., 1939; m. Cora E. Whitford, Sept. 16, 1891 (died 1905); m. 2d, Donizetta A. Wood, Dec. 30, 1911. Teacher rural schools, Mo., 1884-86; prof. lit. and history, Tarkio Coll., 1886-87; supt. schs., Fairfax, Mo., and Florence, Colo., 1889-92; supt. training dept. State Normal School, Greeley, Colo., 1894-98; pres. N.M. Normal U., 1898-1903; student U. of Geneva, Switzerland, and research work in Italy, Greece, Palestine, Egypt and Mexico, 1903-08; dir. Am. research for Archeol. Inst. of America, since 1906; dir. Sch. of Am. Archeology (now School Am. Research) since 1907, pres., exec. bd. since 1930, dir. Mus. of N.M., Santa Fe, since 1909; dir. exhibits in science and art, Panama-Calif. Expn., San Diego, 1911-16; dir. San Diego Mus., 1917-29; prof. anthropology, State Teachers' Coll., San Diego, 1922-27; prof. of archeology and anthropology, State U. of N.M., 1927-40, also in University of Southern California since 1932, now emeritus; special lecturer American School of Oriental Research, Jerusalem, and Bagdad, and with Yale-Babylonian Expedition in Palestine, Syria, Arabia and Mesopotamia, 1923; explorations in Morocco, Algeria, Tunisia and Sahara Desert, 1926, Asia Minor and Mediterranean Islands, 1930. Directed excavation of ancient Maya City of Quirigua, Guatemala, and numerous excavations among the ancient cliff dwellings and pueblos of Colorado, Utah, Ariz. and N.M., also anthropol. expdns. there and in Calif.; dir. field classes, Mexico, Guatemala, Peru, Bolivia and Ecuador; made known and named the cliff-dwelling region of Pajarito Plateau, N.M.; prepared federal laws (passed 1906) for preservation of Am. antiquities and at. monuments and state laws, N.M. (passed 1931), for conservation scientific resources; made archeol. survey on which Mesa Verde Nat. Park was established. 1906. Fellow A.A.A.S. (pres. Southwestern div., 1920); life mem. Archeol. Inst. of America (v.p. since 1930). Chmn. state hist. service and dir. state child welfare service, N.M. State Council Defense, 1917-19. Vice-pres. Am. Federation of Arts since 1919, Himalayan Research Inst. since 1928. Mason (32°). Author: Ancient Life in the American Southwest; Ancient Life in Mexico and Central America; Ancient Andean Life; Quirigua Papers; Les Communautés Anciennes dans le Désert Américain; Chaco Canyon and Its Monuments; Indians of the Rio Grande Valley (with Adolph Bandelier); Pajarito Plateau and Its Ancient People; The Pueblo Indian World (with Bertha Dutton); New Mexico Landmarks (with Wayne Mauzy); Mission Monuments of New Mexico (with Reginald Fisher); From Cave Dwelling to Mount Olympus; Man and Culture; Man and the State; Camp Fire and Trail; also numerous papers on Am. archeology, anthropology, sociology, and edn. Home: Santa Fe, N.M. Died Dec. 31, 1946.

HEWITT, A., business exec. Pres. and dir. Leslie Salt Co.; dir. Schilling Estate Co., Calif. Rock Salt Co., Redwood City Harbor Co. Address: 310 Sansome St., San Francisco, Calif. Died Jan. 19, 1947.

HEWITT, Herbert Edmund, architect; b. Bloomington, Ill., July 20, 1871; s. Charles Edmund and Helen (Thompson) H.; student U. of Ill., 1889-91, Mass. Inst. Tech., 1892-94, U. of Chicago, 1895; B.S., Mass. Inst. Tech., 1911; m. Helen Richmond Carter, Oct. 10, 1906; children—Maj. Carter Edmund, Gillette Hewitt (Mrs. Robert C. Barker). Engaged in practice alone in Peoria, Ill., 1897-1907; then mem. firm Hewitt & Emerson, 1907-27, Hewitt, Emerson & Gregg since 1927. Designer (with partners) of Peoria Life Bldg., Commercial Nat. Bank Bldg., Consistory Cathedral, Shrine Temple, Barker Memorial, Proctor Recreation Center, State Reformatory for Women (Dwight, Ill.), etc. Fellow A.I.A. (dir.); mem. Ill. Architects' Examining Commn., Art Inst. of Peoria (ex-pres.), Ill. Soc. of Architects, Delta Upsilon. Republican. Presbyn. Elk. Clubs: Creve Coeur, Orpheus (ex-pres.), Country Club of Peoria. Home: 204 Callender Av. Office: Alliance Life Bldg., Peoria, Ill.* Died Oct. 24, 1944.

HEYE, Carl T. (hī), consulting director, Guardian Life Insurance Co. of America; b. Quakenbruck, Germany, May 13, 1871; grad. Real Gymnasium, Quakenbruck, 1889; grad. New York U. Law Sch., 1905. With Guardian Life Ins. Co. of America since 1889, as sec., 1902-15, v.p. and sec., 1915-21, pres., 1921-40, chmn. bd., 1940-45, now consulting dir. Trustee Lenox Hill Hospital, New York City. Home: 34 Ridgeview Av., White Plains, N.Y. Office: 50 Union Square, New York, N.Y. Died June 22, 1946.

HEYMANN, Hans, economist; b. Koenigsberg, Prussia, June 27, 1885; s. Johann Richard and Johanna (Sommerfeld) H.; student Royal Friedrichs Coll., Koenigsberg; studied philosophy, polit. economy and law, U. of Berlin; Ph.D., Albertina U., Koenigsberg; m. Ella Jeannette Catz, Sept. 8, 1913; children—Ilse, Inge-Maria, Hans, Eva. Became naturalized citizen of U.S., Feb. 15, 1943. Formerly exec. and chmn. of life insurance companies and mortgage banks, Berlin; founded Assn. for Currency and Finance Reform, Berlin, 1920, and was chmn. During the Weimar Republic was economic adviser on credit and currency to the German Foreign Office, 1921-32; worked for Franco-German understanding, Paris, 1930-32; research, Berlin and London, 1932-36; came to U.S., 1936, and introduced property life insurance; granted charter for company to sell property life insurance in N.Y. and Ill., 1937; research prof. of economics, Rutgers U., 1939-43; prof. of Economics, Sampson Coll., Sampson, N.Y., 1946-48; vis. lecturer in economics, U. of Ill., 1948-49; lectures on private and social ins., long-term credit, mortgage banking, econ. geography and significance of atomic energy. Mem. Am. Assn. of Univ. Teachers of Ins., Am. Econ. Assn. Unitarian. Decorated Austrian War Cross. Author: Property Life Insurance, 1939; Plan for Permanent Peace, 1941; We Can Do Business with Russia, 1945; also several books published in Germany. Contbr. about 200 economic articles to Am. publs. Address: University of Illinois, Urbana, Ill. Died Oct. 1, 1949.

HEYWARD, Duncan Clinch, ex-governor; b. Richland County, S.C., June 24, 1864; ed. Cheltenham Acad., Pa., and Washington and Lee U. Extensive rice planter; ex-pres. Standard Warehouse Co., Columbia Savings Bank & Trust Co. Gov. of S.C. two terms, 1903-07; apptd. collector of internal revenue, Dist. of S.C., 1913; later spl. agt. group div., Protective Life Ins. Co., now retired. Democrat. Home: 3910 Kilbourne Rd., Columbia, S.C. Died Jan. 23, 1943.

HIBBARD, Addison, coll. dean; b. Racine, Wis., Aug. 29, 1887; s. Daniel Osmer and Ida (Brightman) H.; B.A., U. of Wis., 1909, M.A., 1919; m. Ruth Barr, June 20, 1918; children—John Barr, Ruth Margaret, Jean Scott, Sarah Brightman. Prof. English, Imperial Coll. of Commerce, Nagasaki, Japan, 1909-14; instr. in English, U. of Wis., 1916-17; asst. prof. English, Miami U., Oxford, O., 1917-18; asst. prof. English, U. of N.C., 1918-21, asso. prof., 1921-26, prof. English and dean Coll. of Liberal Arts, 1926-30; dean of Coll. Liberal Arts, Northwestern U., since 1930. Mem. U.S. Navy, 1918. Mem. Phi Beta Kappa, Sigma Delta Chi, Sigma Nu. Independent. Author: (with W. F. Thrall) A Handbook to Literature. Editor: The Lyric South, 1929; The Book of Poe, 1930; Stories of the South, 1931; Writers of the Western World, 1942. Newspaper corr. while in Orient; contbr. to mags. Home: 1416 Hinman Av. Address: Coll. Liberal Arts, Northwestern Univ., Evanston, Ill. Died May 17, 1945.

HIBBARD, Angus Smith, elec. engr.; b. Milwaukee, Feb. 7, 1860; s. William B. and Adaline H.; ed. Milwaukee Acad. and Racine Coll.; D.Sc., Carleton Coll., Northfield, Minn., 1939; m. Lucile Ray, Dec. 4, 1884; 1 dau., Janet (Mrs. Janet H. Henneberry). Began bus. experience in railroading; later sec. to gen. supt. Northwestern Telegraph Co.; studied telephony; supt. Wis. Telephone Co., 1881-86; first gen. supt. Am. Telephone & Telegraph Co., 1886-93, inaugurating their long-distance lines; gen. mgr. Chicago Telephone Co., 1893-1911, later also 2d v.p.; adviser to exec. dept. Am. Telephone & Telegraph Co., New York, 1911-16; now cons. engr. Invented and patented many improved devices for use with telephone. Designer of the "Blue Bell" sign of the telephone, used throughout the world. Editor emeritus The Diocese Magazine, since 1937. Mem. Am. Inst. Elec. Engrs., Wis. Soc. of Chicago (pres. 1911), Chicago Assn. of Commerce (hon.). Republican. Episcopalian. Clubs: Union League, University, Industrial, Glen View (hon.). Composer of song, The U.S.A. Forever, music for song, Hail Chicago, etc. Capt. Am. Red Cross, with A.E.F. in France, June-Dec. 1918. Chmn. Camp Roosevelt Assn., 1919-23. Home: 2440 Lake View Av. Office: 212 W. Washington St., Chicago. Died Oct. 21, 1945.

HIBBS, Henry C., architect; b. Camden, N.J., Jan. 26, 1882; s. Jonathan K. and Anna Waples (Kirkpatrick) H.; B.S., U. of Pa., 1904; M.F.A., Southwestern, Memphis, Tenn., 1932; m. Agnes Robertson Bryan, Sept. 28, 1909; children—Elizabeth Burton, Isabel Robertson, Harriet Twinning, Agnes Allison. Began as draftsman, 1904; began practice as architect, Nashville, Tenn., 1916. Architect various bldgs. of Southwestern (Coll.), Peabody Coll., Ward Belmont School, Hendrix Coll., Vanderbilt Univ., Fisk Univ., Univ. of Tulsa, Davidson Coll., Scarritt Coll., Southern Grad. Sch.; psychiatry bldgs. of Western State Hosp. at Bolivar, Tenn., Obstetric and Pediatric Bldg. for Vanderbilt Med. Sch. and Hosp. at Nashville, Tenn., Mary Baldwin Coll., Staunton, Va., and Univ. of South Carolina; also American Trust Building, Nashville, Kennedy Gen. Hosp., Memphis, Tenn.; Joint Univ. Library of Peabody Coll., Scarrett Coll., Vanderbilt U. Fellow A.I.A. Awarded gold medal for ecclesiastical and gold medal for ednl. architecture, Southern Exhibit, Memphis, 1929. Presbyterian. Mason (32°). Club: Coffee House. Home: 1804 18th Av. S. Office: Nashville Trust Bldg., Nashville, Tenn. Died March 3, 1949; buried Mount Olivet Cemetery, Nashville, Tenn.

HICKEY, Andrew J., ex-congressman; b. Albion, N.Y., Aug. 27, 1872; ed. high sch.; studied law 3 yrs.; unmarried. Admitted to N.Y. bar; later removed to LaPorte, Ind.; mem. firm Hickey & Dilworth; sec. 1st Dist. Exemption Bd., Ind.; mem. 66th to 71st Congresses (1919-31), 13th Ind. Dist.; v.p. LaPorte Foundry & Furnace Co. Republican. Mem. Ind. State and LaPorte County bar assns. Home: Rumely Hotel. Office: First Nat. Bank Bldg., LaPorte, Ind. Died Aug. 20, 1942.

HICKMAN, Emily, coll. prof.; b. Buffalo, N.Y., July 12, 1880; d. Arthur Washington and Alice (Gregory) H.; A.B., Cornell U., 1901, Ph.D., 1911; student Yale, 1909-10; unmarried. Prof. of history, Wells Coll., Aurora, N.Y., 1911-27, New Jersey Coll. for Women, New Brunswick, N.J., since 1927. Lecturer summer sessions Cornell U., Rutgers U., U. of Colo.; also made 2 lecture tours across the U.S. Chmn. commn. on world community Nat. Peace Conf.; chmn. Com. on Participation of Women in Postwar Planning; chmn. pub. affairs com. Nat. Bd. of Y.W.C.A.; chmn. ednl. com., Commn. to Study Orgn. of Peace; chmn. ednl. com. Woman's Action Com. Pres. United Nations Assn. of N.J. Mem. Am. Assn. Univ. Profs., Am. Hist. Assn., Phi Beta Kappa. Mem. of Institute of Intensive Study of Contemporary Russian Civilization, Cornell U., 1944; mem. public liaison staff, Am. delegation, United Nations Conf., 1945. Contbr. articles to Dictionary of Am. Biography, New England Quar.; book reviews and editorials to Woman's Press, Democratic Digest. Home: 27 Seaman St., New Brunswick, N.J. Died June 12, 1947.

HICKOK, Paul Robinson, clergyman; b. Nebraska City, Neb., Apr. 6, 1877; s. Rev. Francis M. (D.D.) and Mary Matilda (Robinson) H.; grad. prep. dept. Hastings (Neb.) Coll.; student Hanover (Ind.) Coll., D.D., 1920; B.A., Coll. of Wooster, O., 1897; grad. Auburn Theol. Sem., 1900; m. Mary, d. Rev. John Calvin Elliott, Sept. 6, 1900. Ordained Presbyn. ministry, 1900; asst. pastor "Old Stone" (First) Ch., Cleveland, O., 1900-02; pastor First Ch., Delaware, O., 1902-09; Metropolitan Ch., Washington, 1909-17; 2d Ch., Troy, N.Y., 1917-28; pastor Forest Hill Ch., Newark, N.J., 1928-43, pastor emeritus since September 1, 1943. Chaplain Fifth Infantry, Ohio N.G., 1900-09; dir. religious work Nat. War Work Council of Y.M.C.A. in group of camps of Washington Dist., 1918. Mem. Presbyn. Bd. of Ch. Erection since 1912; trustee Coll. of Wooster, 1915-22; dir. Auburn Theol. Sem. Nat. Chaplain Alpha Tau Omega since 1900 (nat. pres. 1908-10). Mem. Pi Gamma Mu, Theta Phi. Republican. Mason (32°, K.T.); past grand chaplain, Ohio, 1008-10, and in D.C., 1912-17; grand sovereign Knights of Red Cross of Constantine, 1938-39. Rotarian. Dir. of "Told by Paul Hickok" sect. in Alpha Tau Omega "Palm" since 1928. Asso. editor of hymnal, "Christian Worship and Praise." Contbr. to mags. Home: 1117 Chenango St., Binghamton, N.Y. Died Jan. 21, 1945.

HICKOK, Ralph Kiddoo, clergyman, educator; b. Humboldt, Neb., Jan. 14, 1880; s. Rev. Francis Marion (D.D.) and Mary Matilda (Robinson) H.; B.A., Coll. of Wooster, 1899, D.D., 1923; M.A., Princeton, 1904; B.D., Princeton Theol. Sem., 1904; studied New York U., 1913-14, Cornell U., 1920-22, Columbia summer 1921; LL.D., Miami U., 1934; Litt.D., Waynesburg (Pa.) Coll., 1939; m. Grace Anderson Oct. 26, 1904; children—Thomas Anderson, Frances

Anderson (Mrs. Winthrop P. Moore), Mary Anderson (Mrs. Nixon L. Ballard). Prof. of mathematics. Hastings (Neb.) Coll., 1899-1901; was ordained to Presbyterian ministry, 1904; asst. pastor Univ. Place Ch. (now First Presbyn. Ch.), New York, 1904-07; pastor First Ch., East Aurora, 1907-12; dir. religious edn., First Ch., Brooklyn, N.Y., 1912-14; professor Biblical literature and history, Wells College, Aurora, N.Y., 1914-31; became pres. Western College, Oxford, Ohio, 1931, resigned, 1942. Served as Y.M.C.A. religious work dir., Camp Humphreys, Va., and over Washington Dist., May 1918-Aug. 1919, World War. Mem. Soc. Bibl. Lit. and Exegesis, Nat. Assn. Bibl. Instrs. (sec. 1923-28; pres. 1929), Alpha Tau Omega, Phi Beta Kappa, Pi Gamma Mu, Theta Pi. Mason. Home: Aurora-on-Cayuga, N.Y. Died Apr. 24, 1947.

HICKS, Clarence John; b. Omro, Wis., Mar. 7, 1863; s. Reuben P. and Sophia B. (Kimball) H.; A.B., U. of Wis., 1884, LL.B., 1888; hon. A.M., Princeton, 1933; LL.D., U. of Mich., 1937; m. Mary B. Riddell, July 22, 1890 (died 1913); m. 2d, Esther Collins Chappell, June 23, 1917. In Y.M.C.A. work, 1888-1915; as head of railroad dept., investigated condition of Russian railroad employes for Russian govt.; asso. gen. sec. Internat. Com. Y.M.C.A., 1901-11, making 13 trips to Europe on Y.M.C.A. business, also supervising Y.M.C.A. club work in Canal Zone; with exec. dept. (welfare work) of Internat. Harvester Co., 1911-15, hdqrs. at Chicago; exec. asst. to pres. of Colo. Fuel and Iron Co., 1915-17, to pres. of Standard Oil Co. (N.J.), 1917-33; chmn. exec. com. Industrial Relations Counselors, Inc., since July 1933. Occasional lecturer on industrial relations, Princeton, Harvard, Yale and several other universities. Mem. President's Conf. on Unemployment, 1921. Author: My Life in Industrial Relations, 1941. Home: Pelham Manor, N.Y. Office: RKO Bldg., Rockefeller Center, New York. Died Dec. 21, 1944; buried at Omro, Wis.

HIEBERT, Joelle C. (hē'bērt), physician; b. Hillsboro, Kan., Sept. 24, 1892; s. Rev. John K. and Sarah (Eitzen) H.; A.B., Tabor Coll., 1917; M.D., Boston U., 1923; m. Susie Pauls, Sept. 5, 1920; children—Joelle Cornelius, Clement Arthur, Gordon Lee, Ruth Evelyn, Dorothy, Victor Allen (dec.). House officer, Mass. Memorial Hosp., 1923-24; resident physician and supt., Med. Mission Dispensary, Boston, 1924-31; clin. instr. obstetrics, Boston U., 1924-31; instr. preventive medicine and first aid, Gordon Coll. Sch. of Theology and Missions, Boston, 1929-31; supt. Central Maine Gen. Hosp., Lewiston, since 1931. Pres. Lewiston Parent-Teacher Assn., 1943; trustee Oak Grove Sch., Vassalboro, Me.; dir. Boy Scouts of America, Lewiston-Auburn Dist. Treas. Women's Field Army, Me. br.; dir. Androscoggin County Tuberculosis Assn.; mem. adv. council Me. State Dept. of Health and Welfare; mem. adv. com. Pine Tree Soc. for Crippled Children. Mem. Am. Coll. of Hosp. Adminstrs., Am. Hosp. Assn. (chmn. sect. on bus. management and personnel 1943), A.M.A., Am. Protestant Hosp. Assn., N.E. Hosp. Assembly (pres. 1941-42), Me. Hosp. Assn. (pres. 1937-38, v.p. 1943-44), Mass. Med. Soc., Me. Med. Assn., Am. Soc. Control of Cancer, Phi Chi. Clubs: Boston Hosp. Supts., Rotary (Lewiston, Me.). Contbr. to hosp. and med. jours. On editorial bd. Me. Med. Journal. Home: 240 College St. Office: Central Maine Gen. Hosp., 300 Main St., Lewiston, Me. Died June 8, 1944.

HIERONYMUS, Robert Enoch (hī-ēr-ŏn'ĭ-mŭs), educator; b. nr. Atlanta, Ill., Dec. 8, 1862; s. B.R.H.; grad. Ill. State Normal U., 1886; A.B., Eureka Coll., 1889, A.M., 1890, LL.D., 1914; at U. of Mich., 1887-88; m. Minnie S. Frantz, June 26, 1890 (died Oct. 27, 1898); children—Faith Helene, Frantz Mountjoy, Rex Eugene; m. 2d, Lois Campbell, Aug. 30, 1900; children—Grace (dec.), Robert Crawford. Taught in Carrollton (Ill.) High Sch., 1886-87; prof. dept. of English lang. and lit., 1890-97, v.p., 1895-97, Eureka Coll.; teacher English and history, State Normal Sch., Los Angeles, Calif., 1897-98; supt. univ. extension work in Southern Calif., 1898-99; professor dept. English, 1899-1900, pres., 1900-09, Eureka (Ill.) Coll.; mem. Ednl. Commn. State of Ill., 1907-09, sec., 1910-13; community adviser, U. of Ill., since 1914, now emeritus. Pres. Federation of Ill. Colls., 1906-08, Ill. Schoolmasters' Club, 1907-08, Ill. Chautauqua Alliance, 1911-13, Ill. Conf. on Pub. Welfare, 1926-27; chmn. Community Com. of Ill. Ch. Council, 1935. Address: 1605 S. Orchard St., Urbana, Ill. Died Dec. 18, 1941.

HIGBIE, Edgar Creighton, educator; b. Berlin, Wis., July 31, 1875; s. Columbus Jerome and Ann Electa (Wilson) H.; student U. of Minn. Sch. of Agr.; Carleton Coll., U. of Chicago; A.B., U. of Minn., 1907, A.M., 1909; Ph.D., Columbia, 1921; m. Nellie May Leslie, June 15, 1904; children—Howard Ernest, Leslie Wilson. Director West Central Minn. Sch. of Agr., 1910-17; pres. Eastern S.D. State Teachers Coll., 1920-31, J. Ormond Wilson Teachers College, Washington, D.C., 1931-41. Visiting instr., summer sessions, Boston U. and George Peabody Coll. for Teachers since 1924. Mem. N.E.A., Federal Schoolmen's Club, Phi Delta Kappa. Republican. Conglist. Mason. Home: 4624 N. Chelsea Lane, Bethesda, Md. Died Nov. 24, 1944.

HIGGINS, Aldus Chapin, mfr. abrasives and machinery; b. Worcester, Mass., Dec. 7, 1872; s. Milton Prince and Katharine Elizabeth (Chapin) H.; desc. of Richard Higgins, from Eng. to Plymouth, Mass. Colony, 1633, also Mayflower ancestry through Elder William Brewster; B.S., Worcester Poly. Inst., 1893, D.Eng., 1931; LL.M., Nat. Univ. Law Sch., Washington, D.C., 1896; m. Edgenie G. Brosius, 1898 (died 1911); children—Elizabeth B. (Mrs. Ernest Angell), Milton Prince; m. 2d, Mary Sprague Green, Jan. 16, 1914. Asst. examiner, U.S. Patent Office, Washington, D.C., 1893-96; practiced law at Worcester, 1890-1900; gen. counsel, later mgr. abrasive plants, Norton Co. (of which father was pres.), 1901-13, sec. and gen. counsel, 1913-19, treas., 1919-33, pres. and gen. mgr., 1933-40; chmn. bd. dirs., 1941; chmn. bd. Riley Stoker Corp.; chmn. bd. Indian Hill Co., Norton Company of Canada, Ltd.; dir. Boston & Maine Railroad, Worcester County Trust Co., Merchants & Farmers Mutual Fire Insurance Company; director Liberty Mutual Insurance Company. Invented electric furnace in which abrasive "Alundum" is made, and awarded John Scott medal by Franklin Inst. for this invention, 1913. Active in war work, World War. Trustee Worcester Poly. Inst., Worcester Memorial Hosp., Worcester Foundation for Exptl. Biology; pres. Worcester Art Mus.; v.p. Worcester Children's Friend Soc.; mem. Com. on China Relief; mem. nat. advisory bd. Met. Jr. Achievement, Inc. Mem. Am. Soc. M.E., Worcester County Bar Assn., Am. Antiquarian Soc. (mem. council), Foreign Policy Assn., Worcester C. of C., Newcomen Soc., Bohemians, Worcester Fire Society, Worcester Poly. Inst. Alumni Assn., Worcester Hist. Soc., Worcester Natural History Soc., Worcester County Republican Club, Mass. Soc. Mayflower Descendants. Republican. Unitarian. Clubs: Worcester, University, Economic, Players, Odin, Tatnuck Country (Worcester); Union (Boston), Odd Volumes (Boston); American (Paris). Home: 1 John Wing Rd. Address: Norton Co., Worcester, Mass. Died Sep. 11, 1948.

HIGGINS, Archibald Thomas, judge; b. Algiers, La.; s. Thomas Patrick and Lillian (Cartel) H.; LL.B., Tulane U. Law Sch., 1916; LL.M., Loyola U., 1924; m. Emelda Niklaus, Apr. 4, 1923; children—Archibald Thomas, Robert Allen. Admitted to La. bar, 1916, and became mem. firm Terriberry, Rice & Young; city atty. Town of Gretna, 1916-18; mem. La. House of Reps., 1920-24; asst. dist. atty., 24th Judicial Dist., 1927-29; judge Court of Appeals, Orleans Parish, 1929-34; asso. justice of La. Supreme Court since 1934; instr. in civic code, Loyola U., 1927-31. Mem. Am., La. State and New Orleans bar assns. Methodist. Mason (Grand Master of the Grand Lodge of La.), K.T., Shriner. Club: Young Men's Business. Home: Gretna, La. Address: 420 Civil Court Bldg., New Orleans, La.* Deceased.

HIGGINS, Joseph, lawyer; b. Coldwater, Tenn., May 13, 1872; s. George Washington and Susan (Carrigan) H.; student Oak Hill Acad., at Bellville, Tenn., 1884-88; m Mary Hill, Jan. 13, 1893; children—Jimmie Margaret (Mrs. Charles F. Bagley), Joseph. Admitted to Tenn. bar, 1893; in practice, Fayetteville, Tenn., 1893-1902; city Atty., Fayetteville, 1900-02; judge circuit ct., 7th Dist., 1902-10, Tenn. Ct. of Appeals, 1910-18; in practice, Nashville, since 1918; dir. and atty. Bankers Securities Trust Co. Mem. Am. Bar Assn., Tenn. Bar Assn. (ex-pres.), Nashville Bar Assn., Nashville Chamber of Commerce. Democrat. Presbyn. Mason (Shriner). Clubs: Shakespeare (pres.), Froelac, Civitan. Author: Administration of Estates in Tennessee, 1943. Wrote: Legal and Social Essays, 1908; Civil Procedure (with Arthur Conover, Jr.). Compiler of Reports of Tenn. Court of Appeals, 8 vols. (covering decisions 1910-18). Contbr. to law jours. Home: 1705 Acklen Av. Office: Fayetteville, Tenn. Died Oct. 1, 1946.

HIGGINS, Victor, artist; b. Shelbyville, Ind., June 28, 1884; s. John Tilson and Rose (Dolan) H.; ed. Art Inst. of Chicago, Chicago Acad. Fine Arts, Académie de la Grande Chaumeire, Paris, France, and under H. von Hyeck, Munich; 1 dau., Joan. Exhibited in American galleries and by invitation in Paris and Venice. Represented in permanent collections: Mus. Fine Arts (Boston), Art Inst. of Chicago, Pa. Acad. Fine Arts, Dallas Art Mus., Corcoran Gallery of Art Washington), Butler Art Institute (Youngstown, O.), Chicago City and Terre Haute (Ind.) collections, Rockford (Ill.) Club Art Guild, Municipal Art League (Chicago). Awarded gold medal, Pallette and Chisel Club, Chicago, 1914; Chicago Municipal Art League prize, 1915; Martin B. Cahn and Edward B. Butler prizes, Art Inst. of Chicago, 1916; 2d Logan medal of same, 1917, 1st Logan medal ($500), 1918; 1st Altman prize ($1,000) for figure, Nat. Acad. Design, 1918; 1st Altman prize for landscape, 1927; John C. Schaffer prize, Chicago, 1918. A.N.A., 1921, Nat. Academician, 1936. Trustee Harwood Foundation, Taos, N.M. Mem. Taos Heptagon. Home: Taos, N.M. Died Aug. 23, 1949.

HIGHT, Clarence Albert (hīt), lawyer; b. Scarboro, Me., Jan. 26, 1868; s. Horatio and Clara E. (Milliken) H.; A.B., Harvard, 1889; LL.B., 1892; m. Emily L. Coyle, Nov. 9, 1892. Admitted to Me. bar, 1892, and began practice at Portland; also practiced at Boston, Mass., since 1899; mem. firm Coolidge & Hight, 1901-23; chmn. of bd. U.S. Smelting, Refining & Mining Co.; pres. Niagara Mining Co., Richmond-Eureka Mining Co., U.S. Smelting, Refining and Mining Exploration Co. Compania de Real del Monte y Pachuca; v.p. and dir. Island Creek Coal Co.; dir. U.S. Lead Refinery, Inc. Mem. Am. Bar Assn., Bar Assn. City of Boston, Cumberland (Me.) Bar Association. Republican. Clubs: Harvard, Union (Boston); Cumberland (Portland); Harvard (New York). Home: 122 Carlton St., Brookline, Mass. Office: 75 Federal St., Boston, Mass. Died June 30, 1945.

HIGHTOWER, William Harrison, cotton goods mfr.; b. Thomaston, Ga., Nov. 25, 1887; s. Robert Edgar and Mattie Lou (Harrison) H.; B.S. in Tech. Engring., Ga. Tech., 1909; m. Annie Turner, June 14, 1911; children—William Harrison, George Harrison, Martha (Mrs. Harry J. Davis). Started as office clerk Thomaston (Ga.) Cotton Mills, 1909, made asst. treas., 1914, v.p., 1919, pres. since 1924; dir. Central of Ga. Ry. Co. Mem. Sigma Nu. Methodist. Home: 409 N. Church St. Office: Thomaston Cotton Mills, Thomaston, Ga.* Died Feb. 9, 1947.

HIGLEY, Brodie Gilman, lawyer; b. Hartford, N.Y., Sept. 6, 1872; s. Julius Henry (capt. N.Y. Vols., Civil War) and Lydia Maria (Duel) H.; desc. of Capt. John Higley of Conn., and of Day, Duel, Stark and Denio (Denoyen, French), and Whitney, New England families; A.B., Stanford U., 1899; m. Eleanor Luceria Weatherhead, June 12, 1901. Admitted to N.Y. State bar, 1896, U.S. Supreme Court, 1918; practiced law, Hudson Falls, N.Y., 1900-18; N.Y. City since 1918; now asso. with Baar, Bennett & Fullen, N.Y. City; from 1901-22 was pres., vice-pres., treas. and/or general counsel independent telephone companies, electric, gas and water corps., paper, pulp and wall paper corps., shipbuilding and steamship corps.; chmn. exec. com. and dir. Adirondack Trust Co., and dir. Dunkirk Trust Co.; pres. Hudson Falls Nat. Bank; dir. Nat. Container Corp. Mem. Stanford U. Nat. Board, 1923-27. Mem. N.Y. Dem. County Com., New York State Bar Assn. Mem. Soc. of Colonial Wars, Sons of the Revolution. Mason (K.T., 32°, Shriner). Democrat. Home: 242 E. 19th St. Office: 29 Broadway, New York, N.Y. Died June 3, 1946.

HIGLEY, Adelbert Pankey, clergyman; b. Rutland, Meigs County, O., Jan. 2, 1872; s. Milo Harvey and Mary P. (Pankey) H.; A.B., Coll. of Wooster, 1898; graduate McCormick Theological Seminary, 1901; D.D., Wooster, 1915, Ill. Coll., 1918; LL.D., Tusculum Coll., Greenville, Tenn.; m. Elizabeth Parker, Sept. 8, 1904; children—John Parker, Mary Graham. Ordained Presbyn. ministry, 1901; pastor Knox Ch., Cincinnati, 1901-04, 1st Ch., Sandusky, O., 1904-06, 2d Ch., Springfield, Ill., 1906-11, 1st Ch., Troy, 1911-14, Calvary Ch., Cleveland, O., since 1914. Trustee Coll. of Wooster, Pikeville (Ky.) Coll.; mem. bd. dirs. McCormick Theol. Sem. Moderator of Synod of Ohio, 1931, of Cleveland Presbytery, 1921-24 (3 terms); chaplain Ill. State Senate, 2 terms. Mem. Cleveland Chamber of Commerce, Associated Charities of Cleveland (life). Mem. S.A.R., N.E. Soc., Abraham Lincoln Assn. (Springfield, Ill.), Phi Beta Kappa. Republican. Mason. Home: 2681 Scarborough Rd., Cleveland Heights, O. Died Feb. 17, 1944.

HILDEBRAND, Daniel Munroe (hĭl'dē-brănd), cattleman; b. Morganton, N.C., Feb. 22, 1880; s. Miles Pinkney and Delia E. (Smith) H.; student U. of Neb., 1910-19; m. Victoria A. Hedden, Mar. 6, 1905; children—Helen B. (Mrs. Vernon Hershberger), Paul Hedden, Victor Dan. Clk. in drug store, later clothing store, later C.,B.&Q. Ry. Co., 1892-1909; with F. D. Wead, Omaha, Neb., 1909-10; engaged in farm rentals, ranching and the raising of livestock since 1910; pres. Protective Fire Ins. Co.; v.p. Midwest Life Ins. Co. Pres. U.S. Live Stock Assn.; mem. exec. bd. Neb. Feeders and Breeders Assn.; mem. Nat. Live Stock and Meat Bd., Chamber of Commerce; dir. Neb. Turkey Federation. Named as one of two men from Neb. to serve on the policy com. of the Rep. Party, 1937. Republican. Methodist. Mason. Home: Seward, Neb. Died Dec. 5, 1942.

HILDEBRAND, Ira Polk, prof. Law Sch. U. of Tex.; b. Lagrange, Tex., Dec. 19, 1876; s. William Jackson and Narcissa (Whittenberg) H.; A.B., Tex. Christian U., Ft. Worth, 1897; A.B., and LL.B., U. of Tex., 1899, LL.M., 1900; LL.B., Harvard, 1902; m. Mabel Shiner, June 3, 1909; children—Ira Polk, Frances Mabel. Admitted to Tex. bar, 1899; began practice in partnership with Judge T. D. Cobbs, San Antonio, 1902; prof. law, U. of Tex., since 1907, dean of Law Sch. since 1924. Mem. Am. and Tex. State bar assns., Am. Law Inst., Assn. Am. Law Schs., Kappa Sigma. Democrat. Mem. Christian (Disciples) Ch. Mason (32°, Shriner). Author: (with Prof. E. H. Warren) Select Cases and Other Authorities on the Law of Private Corporations, 1912; Hildebrand Texas Corporations, 4 vols., 1942. Contributor on legal subjects. Home: 2431 Wooldridge Drive, Austin, Tex. Died Nov. 11, 1944.

HILDRETH, Melvin Andrew, lawyer; b. Watertown, N.Y., Oct. 27, 1859; s. Curtis L. and Sarah Ann (Luther) H.; ed. Whitestown (N.Y.) Sem.; m. Luella Davis, Feb. 13, 1889. Began practice at Watertown, 1883; removed to Fargo, N.D., 1888; spl. asst. atty. gen., N.D., 1892; city atty., Fargo, 1892-94, 1902-04; asst. U.S. atty., N.D., 1913-14, U.S. atty., 1914-24; now atty. in Cass County for Home Owners Loan Corp. Enlisted in Nat. Guard N.D., Oct. 1890; mem. 1st N.D. Vols., Spanish-American War; service as colonel, Philippine Insurrection, 1898-99; detailed as judge advocate by Maj. Gen. Otis; mem. commn. under treaty, 1899, to settle mil. affairs with Spanish Govt. in Philippines; brig. gen. N.D. N.G., 1908. Awarded Congressional Medal of Honor for active service. Life mem. Am. and N.D. State bar assns. Democrat. Presbyterian. Mason (K.T., Shriner). Home: 300 8th St. S. Office: 11 Broadway, Fargo, N.D. Died Jan. 13, 1944.

HILL, Albert Ross; b. in Nova Scotia, Can., Oct. 4, 1869; s. Daniel and Esther (Davison) H.; A.B., Dalhousie U., 1892; Ph.D., Cornell, 1895; univs. of

Heidelberg, Berlin and Strassburg, 1893-94; Clark U., Worcester, Mass., summer 1896; LL.D., U. of S.C., 1905, Westminster, 1909, Washington U., 1915, Lafayette, 1915, U. of Colo., 1916, U. of Mich., 1916, U. of Calif., 1918, U. of Ark., 1919, U. of Mo., 1933; m. Agnes S. Baxter, Aug. 20, 1896 (died Mar. 17, 1917); children—Jessie Methven, Esther Davison; m. 2d, Mrs. Vassie James Ward, Sept. 6, 1919. Taught in schs. of N.S., 1885-87; prof. psychology and edn., State Teachers College, Oshkosh, 1895-97; asso. prof. philosophy, 1897-98, prof. philosophy and dir. psychol. labs., 1898-1903, U. of Neb.; prof. ednl. psychology and dean Teachers Coll., U. of Mo., 1903-07; prof. philosophy of edn., dir. Sch. of Edn. and dean Coll. Arts and Sciences, Cornell, 1907-08; pres. U. of Mo., 1908-22; dir. Foreign Operations, Am. Red. Cross, 1921-23; gen. mgr. Ward Investment Co., Kansas City, Mo., since Mar. 1923. Fellow A.A. A.S.; mem. Western Philos. Assn. (sec. 1900-04, pres. 1904-05), Am. Philos. Assn., N.E.A., Phi Beta Kappa, Phi Mu Alpha, Sigma Xi, Phi Delta Kappa. Mem. Bd. U.S. Naval Acad., 1917-21; trustee Carnegie Foundn. Clubs: University (Kansas City); Cosmos (Washington, D.C.). Author: The Epistemological Function of the "Thing in Itself" in Kant's Philosophy (monograph); also numerous ednl. articles in jours. and procs. of ednl. socs. Home: 52d and Summit Sts. Office: Pioneer Trust Bldg., Kansas City, Mo. Died May 6, 1943.

HILL, Arthur Dehon, lawyer; b. Paris, France, June 25, 1869; s. Adams Sherman and Caroline Inches (Dehon) H.; spl. student, Harvard, 1888-90, LL.B., 1894; m. Henriette Post McLean, June 20, 1895. Practiced at Boston, since 1894; dist. atty., County of Suffolk, 1908-09; mem. firm Hill, Barlow, Goodale & Wiswall; mem. corp. Provident Instn. for Savings. Prof. law, Harvard, resigned in 1916; corp. counsel City of Boston, 1919-23. Commd. maj., Judge Advocate's Dept., U.S. Army, Dec. 27, 1917; lt. col., Apr. 23, 1919; hon. discharged July 7, 1919. Served in France, Jan. 1918-June 1919. Mem. Am. Bar Assn., N.Y. Bar Assn., Mass. Bar Assn., Assn. Bar City of Boston, Am. Legion. Mason, Elk. Clubs: Somerset, Union, Tavern, Union Boat; Harvard (Boston). Home: 61 Mount Vernon St., (summer) Portsmouth, N.H. Office: 53 State St., Boston, Mass. Died Nov. 29, 1947.

HILL, E(rnest) Rowland, consulting engr.; b. Pompton, N.J., Jan. 29, 1872; s. Benj. Rowland, Jr., and Hetty M. (Van Duyne) H.; prep. edn., Pratt Inst., Brooklyn, N.Y.; M.E. and E.E., Cornell U., 1893; m. Grace G. Crider, June 1, 1904; 1 dau., Jean S. (Mrs. E. C. Johnson). Gen. shop training, Westinghouse Electric & Mfg. Co., 1893-95; special engr. same co., 1895-1901; engr. in chief British Westinghouse Electric & Mfg. Co., London, in charge of all elec., steam, mech. and gen. engring. work of the co., design and constrn. stations, lines, etc., in Gt. Britain, 1901-06; asst. to chief engr. of electric traction in electrification of New York Terminal and tunnels of Pa. R.R. and extension of electrification L.I. R.R., 1906-12; partner Gibbs and Hill, cons. engrs., 1912-24; now pres. Gibbs & Hill, Inc., engaged in gen. consulting engring. practice, designing construction, including electrification work on Pa. R.R., New York-Washington-Harrisburg electrification, Norfolk & Western Railway and Virginian Railway electrification; changes and additions in Cos Cob Power House and other electric power equipment of N.Y., N.H.&H. R.R.; electrification of N.Y. Connecting R.R., I.C. R.R. (Chicago, Ill.), Broad St. Subway, Philadelphia, Pa.; engaged in consulting, designing, construction, general practice, power plants, Army and Navy bases, industrial plants, etc. Dir. Ampere Bank & Trust Co.; mem. bd. Orange Memorial Hosp. Mem. and past pres., Am. Inst. Cons. Engrs. Fellow Am. Inst. Electrical Engrs.; mem. Am. Soc. C.E., Am. Soc. M.E., Inst C.E. (London), S.A.R. Presbyterian. Clubs: Cornell, Bankers, Rock Spring Country. Home: 111 S. Munn Av., East Orange, N.J. Office: Pennsylvania Station, 7th Av. and 32d St., New York, N.Y. Died Aug. 25, 1948.

HILL, George Alfred, Jr., pres. Houston Oil Co. of Tex.; b. Corsicana, Tex., Jan. 12, 1892; s. George Alfred and Julia (McHugh) H.; student U. of Tex., 1907-11; m. Mary Van Den Berge, June 24, 1916; children—Joanne (Mrs. Pieter Cramerus), George Alfred, Raymond Monroe. Admitted to Tex. bar, 1911; assistant general attorney, I.G.N. Railroad, 1911-17; partner Kennerly, Williams, Lee & Hill, 1917-32; vice president and general counsel Houston Pipe Line Company, 1925-32, pres. since 1932; vice president and gen. counsel Houston Oil Co. of Texas, 1930-32, pres. since 1932; v.p. Houston Natural Gas Corp., 1928-32. Capt., Troop C, 7th Tex. Cav., during World War. Dir. gen., Houston Community Chest, 1933; dir. gen., Endowment Fund Campaign (1934) Mus. of Fine Arts, Houston, and pres. and trustee of mus., 1935-38; vice-pres. for production, Am. Petroleum Inst., 1934-46; vice-pres. San Jacinto Centennial Assn., Oil World Expn.; pres. San Jacinto Museum of History (1938-47), pres. The Philos. Society of Tex.; chmn. City of Houston Water Dept. Bd.; chmn. U. of Tex. Development Bd.; mem. Business Advisory Council of Dept. of Commerce; adv. to Am. Delegation, London, 1945, in re. Anglo-American Oil Treaty. Director of Federal Reserve Bank of Dallas. Chmn. exec. com. S. Tex. C. of C. Dir. Houston Chamber of Commerce. Mem. Petroleum Industry War Council. Mem., chmn. Agenda Com., Nat. Petroleum Council; Chmn. Facilities Security Com. of Petroleum Administrator for War. Received Distinguished Service Award, 1946, Tex. Mid-Continent Oil and Gas Assn. Director Am. Petroleum Inst., Independent Pet. Assn., Mid-Continent Oil and Gas Assn.; mem. Tex. Petroleum Council, Am. Inst. Min. assns., Tex. State Hist. Soc. (vice pres. and fellow), Texas Folk-Lore Society, Yanaguana Society, Sociedad Bibliographia de Mexico, Kappa Alpha, Phi Delta Phi. First Knight of the Order of San Jacinto of the Sons of the Republic of Texas. Democrat. Episcopalian. Clubs: Houston Country, Bayou, River Oaks, Tex., Corinthian Yacht, Tejas, University (Austin). Home: 1604 Kirby Drive. Office: Petroleum Bldg., Houston, Tex. Died Nov. 2, 1949.

HILL, George Washington, pres. American Tobacco Co.; b. Phila., Pa., Oct. 22, 1884; s. Percival S. and Cassie Rowland (Milnes) H.; A.B., Williams Coll.; m. Mary Barnes, July 8, 1935. With American Tobacco Co. since 1904, succeeding father as pres. 1925; also officer or dir. of various other companies. Officer Legion of Honor (France). Clubs: Metropolitan, Williams (New York); Westchester Country. Office: President, American Tobacco Co., 111 5th Av., New York, N.Y. Died Sep. 13, 1946.

HILL, Grace Livingston, author; b. Wellsville, N.Y., April 16, 1865; d. Rev. Charles Montgomery and Marcia (Macdonald) Livingston; educated at public school and high school; m. Rev. Thomas G. F. Hill, Dec. 8, 1892 (died 1899); children—Margaret Livingston (Mrs. Wendell H. Walker), Ruth Glover (Mrs. Gordon Munce). Presbyterian. Author: A Chautauqua Idyl, 1887; A Little Servant, 1890; The Parkerstown Delegate, 1892; Katharine's Yesterday, 1896; In the Way, 1897; Lone Point, 1898; A Daily Rate, 1899; An Unwilling Guest, 1901; The Angel of His Presence, 1902; According to the Pattern, 1903; The Story of a Whim, 1902; Because of Stephen, 1903; The Girl from Montana, 1907; Marcia Schuyler, 1908; Phoebe Dean, 1909; Dawn of the Morning, 1910; The Mystery of Mary, 1911; Aunt Crete's Emancipation, 1911; Lo, Michael, 1913; The Best Man, 1914; The Man of the Desert, 1914; Miranda, 1915; The Obsession of Victoria Gracen, 1915; The Finding of Jasper Holt, 1916; A Voice in the Wilderness, 1916; The Witness, 1917, The Red Signal, 1918; The Enchanted Barn, 1918; The War Romance of the Salvation Army, 1919; The Search, 1919; Cloudy Jewel, 1920; Exit Betty, 1920; The Tryst, 1921; The City of Fire, 1922; The Big Blue Soldier, 1923; Tomorrow About This Time, 1923; Recreations, 1924; Not Under the Law, 1925; Ariel Custer, 1925; A New Name, 1926; Coming Through the Rye, 1926; Job's Niece, 1927; The White Flower, 1927; Crimson Roses, 1928; Blue Ruin, 1928; Duskin, 1929; The Prodigal Girl, 1929; Ladybird, 1930; The Gold Shoe, 1930; Silver Wings, 1931; The Chance of a Lifetime, 1931; Kerry, 1931; Happiness Hill, 1932; The Challengers, 1932; The Patch of Blue, 1932; The Ransom, 1933; Matched Pearls, 1933; The Beloved Stranger, 1933; Rainbow Cottage, 1934; Amorelle, 1934; The Christmas Bride, 1934; Beauty For Ashes, 1935; White Orchids, 1935; The Strange Proposal, 1935; April Gold, 1936; Mystery Flowers, 1936; The Substitute Guest, 1936; Sunrise, 1937; Daphne Deane, 1937; Brentwood, 1937; Marigold, 1938; Homing, 1938; Maris, 1938; The Seventh Hour, 1939; Patricia, 1939; Stranger Within the Gates, 1939; Head of the House, 1940; Rose Galbraith, 1940; Partners, 1940; By Way of the Silverthorns, 1941; In Tune With Wedding Bells, 1941; Astra, 1941; Crimson Mountain, 1942; The Girl of the Woods, 1942; The Street of the City, 1942; Spice Box, 1943; The Sound of the Trumpet, 1943; Through These Fires, 1943; More Than Conqueror, 1944; Time of the Singing of Birds, 1944; All Through the Night, 1945; A Girl To Come Home To, 1945; also (under nom de plume of Marcia Macdonald), The Honor Girl, 1927; Found Treasure, 1928; Out of the Storm, 1929; The White Lady, 1930. Home: 215 Cornell Av., Swarthmore, Pa. Died Feb. 23, 1947.

HILL, Herbert Wynford, prof. English; b. Stanstead, Quebec, Can., Apr. 14, 1875; s. Herbert Curtis and Julia (Morrill) H.; B.L., U. of Calif., 1900; Ph.M., U. of Chicago, 1904, fellow, 1906-07, Ph.D., 1911; m. Nina Burtis, June 22, 1911. Instr. in English, Utah State Agrl. Coll., 1900-03; instr. in English, U. of Tex., 1904-06; prof. English and head of dept., U. of Nev., 1907-27; prof. English, U. of Southern Calif., since 1927, also univ. editor since 1928. Mem. Modern Lang. Assn. America, Philol. Assn. Pacific Coast, Phi Kappa Phi, Psi Upsilon. Republican. Methodist. Mason. Club: Faculty. Author: Sidney's Arcadia and the Elizabethan Drama, 1909; La Calprenède and the Restoration Drama, 1911; The Semicentennial Celebration of the Founding of the University of Southern California, 1930; Twenty-Fifth Anniversary of the Inauguration of Graduate Studies at the University of Southern California, 1935. Home: 3806½ W. Adams Blvd., Los Angeles, Calif. Died Feb. 16, 1943.

HILL, Horace Greeley, chain store mcht.; b. Sparta, Tenn., Sept. 21, 1873; s. George M. and Hulda (Rogers) H.; ed. Montgomery Bell Acad., Nashville, Tenn., and Draughons Bus. Coll.; m. Mamie Wilson, Nov. 24, 1897; children—Elizabeth (Mrs. W. E. Penick), Horace Greeley, Frances (Mrs. Wentworth Caldwell). Began in grocery business at Nashville, 1895; organizer, 1907, pres. since 1907, H.G. Hill Co.; chmn. bd. Nashville Trust Co. Dir. George Peabody Coll. for Teachers. Past pres. Nashville Chamber Commerce. Presbyn. Mason (32°). Club: Belle Meade Country. Home: 5-Mile Harding Rd. Office: 500 2d Av. N., Nashville, Tenn. Died Oct. 17, 1942.

HILL, Julien Harrison, banker; b. Richmond, Va., Sept. 15, 1877; s. William Maury and Frances Cadwallader (Harrison) H.; prep. edn., pub. sch. and McCabe's Sch., Richmond; student U. of Va.; m. Lucy Kearny, Apr. 22, 1903. Chmn. State-Planters Bank & Trust Co., Richmond; dir. Va. Fire & Marine Ins. Co., Chesapeake Corp., Albemarle-Chesapeake Corp., Universal Motor Co., Chesapeake & Potomac Telephone Co. of Va. Mem. Va. State Chamber of Commerce (dir.); dir. Police Benevolent Assn., Va. State Fair Assn., Chesapeake-Camp Corp.; mem. bd. visitors Med. Coll. of Va. Mem. bd. mgrs. University of Va. Alumni Assn.; trustee Church Schs. of Va.; mem. local bd. St. Christopher's Sch., advisory bd. Pan-American Sch. Mem. Beta Theta Pi, Lambda Pi, Eli. Democrat. Episcopalian. Clubs: Commonwealth, Richmond German, Country, Virginia Boat; Colonnade (U. of Va.). Home: 1810 Monument Av. Office: 900 E. Main St., Richmond, Va. Died Dec. 1, 1943.

HILL, Louis Warren, retired ry. official; b. St. Paul, May 19, 1872; s. James Jerome and Mary Theresa (Mehegan) H.; Ph.B., Yale, 1893; m. Maud Van Cortlandt Taylor, June 5, 1901. Has held various positions on Great Northern and rys. of which his father was pres. and succeeded him as pres. of G.N. Ry. systems, Apr. 1, 1907, chmn. bd. dirs., 1912-29, now dir.; trustee G.N. Iron Ore Properties. Clubs: Minnesota, University, St. Paul Athletic, Somerset Country. Home: 260 Summit Av., St. Paul 2. Office: Great Northern Ry. Bldg., St. Paul 1, Minn. Died Apr. 27, 1948.

HILL, Max, radio commentator, former foreign corr.; b. Colorado Springs, Colo., Apr. 23, 1904; s. Roscoe C. and Edith (Ritterskampf) H.; A.B., U. of Colorado, 1927; married June White, 1928 (deceased); 1 dau., June; married 2d, Phoebe Ray Adams, 1946. City editor, Denver Post, 1932; with Associated Press, 1934-43, as Washington feature and photo editor, 1935-37, chief of N.Y. Bureau, 1937-40, chief of Tokio, Japan, bureau, 1940-41, special assignments, 1942-43. Arrested in Japan at outbreak of war, 1941; imprisoned in Sugamo prison, Tokio, 6 mos.; sentenced to 18 mos. for sending stories "detrimental to Japan's diplomacy," May 1942; permitted under exchange agreement to return to U.S. on Asama Maru and Gripsholm, June 1942; arrived in New York, August 1942. Representative of NBC in North Africa, Italy, Turkey and Greece, 1943-45; commentator on Sheaffer World Parade, 1945-46. Mem. Phi Gamma Delta. Clubs: American, Tokio (Tokio); Press (Denver); Advertising (N.Y.); Lambs (N.Y.); Overseas Press. Author: Exchange Ship, 1942. Contbr. of articles to periodicals. Commentator for Nat. Broadcasting Co.; lecturer. Address: 1259 N. Dearborn, Chicago 10. Died Oct. 18, 1949; buried at Denver, Colo.

HILL, Patty Smith, kindergartner; b. Louisville, Ky.; d. William Wallace and Martha J. (Smith) Hill; grad. Louisville Collegiate Inst., 1887, Louisville Kindergarten Training Sch., 1889; unmarried. Dir. Model Kindergarten, Louisville, 1889-93; prin. Louisville Kindergarten Training Sch. and supervisor pub. sch. kindergartens, 1893-1905; instr. kindergarten edn., 1905-10, dir. Kindergarten Dept. and asst. prof. kindergarten edn., 1910, associate professor kindergarten education and director dept. of lower primary edn., since 1918, Teachers Coll. (Columbia). Lecturer kindergarten edn. N.Y. U., Summer Sch. of South. and elsewhere. Pres. Internat. Kindergarten Union, 1908-09; v.p. Child Conf. for Research and Welfare; mem. Com. of 19, Presbyterian. Joint-Author: Kindergarten; Song Stories for the Kindergarten. Contbr. ednl. mags. Home: 620 W. 116th St., New York. Died May 25, 1946.

HILL, Robert Carmer, chmn. bd. Pittsburgh Consolidation Coal Co.; b. Phila., Pa., July 12, 1869; s. William and Harriet (Chapin) H.; grad. Episcopal Acad., Phila., 1885; A.B., U. of Pa., 1889; m. Anna Gilman, June 2, 1894. Vice-pres. Madeira Hill & Co., 1894-1928, also pres. and v.p. various affiliated cos. until 1928; served as chmn. bd. Consolidation Coal Co., receiver and trustee, 1932-35; chmn. bd. Pittsburgh Consolidation Coal Co. (formed by merger Consolidation Coal Co. and Pittsburgh Coal Co.) 1945-46; honorary chairman board Pittsburgh Consolidation Coal Company since 1946; director Empire-Hanna Coal Co. Ltd., Avonmore Coal Co.; trustee Bank of New York; dir. Eagle Fire Co., of New York, Norwich Union Indemnity Co., Equitable Life Assurance Society of the United States, North Western-Hanna Fuel Co., Parish Safe Deposit Co. Mem. Co. K, 7th Regiment, N.G.N.Y., 1893-99. Dir. New York Post-Grad. Hosp.; trustee U. of Pa. Mem. Zoöl. Soc. N.Y., Pa. Soc., Soc. Colonial Wars, S.R., Associated Engrs. Corps 7th Regt., Delta Phi, St. Nicholas Soc., Yeamans Hall. Republican. Episcopalian (vestryman). Clubs: University, Union, Univ. of Pa., Church, Boone and Crockett, Rockland County Country (New York); Rittenhouse, St. Elmo (Phila.). Home: 101 E. 72d St., New York; (summer) Palisades, Rockland County, N.Y. Office: 30 Rockefeller Plaza, New York, N.Y. Died Feb. 28, 1947.

HILL, William Bancroft, college prof.; b. Colebrook, N.H., Feb. 17, 1857; s. Rev. Joseph Bancroft and Harriet (Brown) H.; A.B., Harvard, 1879; Columbia Law Sch., 1880-81, Baltimore Law Sch., 1881-82; Union Theol. Sem., 1883-86; D.D., Rutgers U., 1905; Litt.D., Hope Coll., 1924; LL.D., Central Coll., 1938; m. Elise Weyerhaeuser, Dec. 29, 1892. Practiced law at Baltimore, 1882-83; prof. philosophy, Park Coll., Mo., 1883; pastor, Ref. (Dutch) Ch.,

Athens, N.Y., 1886-90, Poughkeepsie, N.Y., 1890-1902; lecturer on Bible, 1899-1902, prof. Bibl. lit., 1902-21, Vassar Coll.; prof. emeritus, 1922. Visited mission fields Japan, China, India, 1915-16; pres. Gen. Synod Ref. Ch. in America, 1925-26; pres. Bd. Foreign Missions, 1933-35. Trustee and chmn. Am. U., Cairo (Egypt), Fukien Christian U. (China), Am. Indian Inst. Mem. Phi Beta Kappa (Harvard), Nat. Inst. of Social Sciences, Am. Oriental Soc., Audubon Soc., Victoria Inst., Archeol. Inst. America, Japan Soc., China Soc., Egypt Exploration Fund, Soc. Bibl. Lit. and Exegesis, Egypt Research Account, etc. Club: Harvard (New York). Author: Present Problems in New Testament Study, 1903; Guide to the Lives of Christ, 1905; Introduction to the Life of Christ, 1911; Life of Christ, 1917; Graves Lectures on Missions, 1920; Apostolic Age, 1922; Mountain Peaks in the Life of Our Lord, 1925; The Resurrection of Jesus Christ, 1930; Chimham and His Khan, 1934. Home: 112 Raymond Av., Poughkeepsie, N.Y. Died Jan. 23, 1945; buried at Rock Island, Ill.

HILLES, Charles Dewey (hil'lēs), former chairman Republican National Committee; b. Belmont County, O., June 23, 1867; s. Samuel and Elisabeth (Lee), H.; grad. Barnesville (O.) High Sch., 1885; student acad., Oxford, Md., 1885-87; m. Dollie Bell Whiley, 1896; children—Elisabeth Lee (wife of Lt. Col. Geo. S. Reynolds), Lt. Col. Frederick W., Charles Dewey. Financial officer and supt. Boys' Industrial Sch., of Ohio, at Lancaster, 1890-1902, mng. dir. Children's Village, Dobbs Ferry, N.Y., 1902-09; asst. sec. U.S. Treasury, Apr. 20, 1909-Apr. 4, 1911; sec. to the Pres. (Taft), Apr. 4, 1911-Mar. 4, 1913; chmn. Rep. Nat. Com., 1912-16, mem. same to 1938. In charge Eastern Hdqrs., Rep. Nat. Campaign, 1924. Resident mgr., N.Y. State of Employers' Liability Assurance Corp., 1913, also vice chairman, executive com.; resident mgr. for N.Y. State of Employers' Fire Insurance Co., Am. Employers' Liability Ins. Co.; dir. Otis Elevator Co., Am. Smelting & Refining Co., Otis Fenson Elevator Co., New York Life Ins. Co., Bankers Trust Co., Waygood-Otis Company, Anglo-Chilean Nitrate Company, General Cable Corporation; member U.S. Treasury War Bond Com. and chmn. for Long Island. Trustee John Simon Guggenheim Foundation, Children's Village. Treas. Protestant Council, N.Y. Mem. N.Y. State C. of C., Merchants' Assn. of N.Y., Surety & Casualty Club, Loyal Legion, Ohio Soc. of New York (ex-pres.). Dir. Fedn. Protestant Welfare Agencies. Trustee Madison Av. Presbyterian Ch. Clubs: Union League, Metropolitan, Century, Quill, Pilgrims, Lawyers, Manhattan, Downtown, The Links, National Golf Links, Long Island Country, Mountain Lake (Florida), National Republican (former pres.). Home: 888 Park Av. Address: 120 Williams St., New York, N.Y. Died Aug. 27, 1949.

HILLMAN, Sidney, labor leader; b. Zagare, Lithuania, Mar. 23, 1887; s. Schmuel and Judith (Paikin) Gilman; came to United States at age of 20; received Rabbinical education; m. Bessie Abramowitz, 1916; children—Philoine (Mrs. Milton Fried), Selma (Mrs. Irving Lerner). Department under United Garment Workers, at Hart Schaffner & Marx, Chicago, 1911-14; chief clk. under Brandeis' protocol in Cloakmaker's Union, New York, Feb.-Oct. 1914; pres. Amalgamated Clothing Workers of America since 1915; chmn. bd. Amalgamated Bank of New York; dir. Amalgamated Trust & Savings Bank, Chicago. Led strike, Hart Schaffner & Marx, which resulted in collective agreement with that firm, 1910; strike in New York which achieved 48-hour week, 1916, the 44-hour week, 1919; organized Rochester market, 1918; organized Chicago market, 1919; visited Russia, 1921, and made agreement for transmission of Am. dollars; made agreement with Arthur Nash Co., Cincinnati, 1925; organized Phila. market, 1929; built coöperative houses in New York; established Unemployment Insurance Fund, Rochester, Chicago, and New York; mem. of Labor Advisory Board, NRA, 1933, Nat. Industrial Recovery Bd., 1935; mem. advisory bd. Nat. Youth Adminstrn., 1935; reached first nat. collective bargaining agreement in men's clothing industry in 1937; mem. textile and apparel industry coms. Fair Labor Standards Bd., 1938; v.p. Congress of Industrial Organizations; chmn. Textile Workers Organization Com., 1937-39; chmn. exec. council, Textile Workers' Union of America, since May 1939; apptd. labor mem. Nat. Defense Advisory Commn., 1940; became asso. dir.-gen. O.P.M. and dir. labor div. of same, 1941; apptd. to Supply Priorities and Allocation Bd., Sept. 1941, dir. labor div., W.P.B., 1942. Mem. Acad. Polit. and Social Science. Home: 237 E. 20th St., New York, N.Y. Office: Social Security Bldg., Washington. D.C., also 15 Union Sq., New York, N.Y. Died July 10, 1946.

HILLYER, Homer Winthrop, chemist; b. Waupun, Wis., Jan. 26, 1859; s. Edwin and Angeline C. (Coe) H.; B.S., U. of Wis., 1882; Ph.D., Johns Hopkins, 1885; m. Hariet A. Robbins, July 12, 1887. Asst. instr. and asst. prof. organic chemistry, U. of Wis., 1885-1905; with research dept. Gen. Chem. Co., 1907-17. Nat. Aniline & Chem. Co., 1917-25. Conglist. Author: Laboratory Manual of General Chemistry. Inventor fungicide known as atomic sulfur. Home: Farmington, Conn. Died Jan. 3, 1949.

HILTON, Clifford L., lawyer, judge; b. Kenyon, Minn., Dec. 8, 1866; s. Addison and Harriet E. (Bullis) H.; LL.B., U. of Wis., 1888; m. Frances C. Moll., Sept. 23, 1891. Began practice at Fergus Falls, Minn., 1888; city atty., 1897-99; county atty. Otter Tail County, 1899-1909; asst. atty. gen. of Minn., 1909-17; dep. atty. gen., 1917-18; atty. gen. of Minn., Mar. 8, 1918-28; apptd. asso. justice Supreme Court of Minn., Jan. 1, 1928, and elected to same office, Nov. 1928, for term of 6 yrs., beginning January 7, 1929; reelected, Nov. 1934, and Nov. 1940. Mem. Assn. Attys. Gen. (ex-pres.), Internat. Assn. Attys. Gen. (ex-pres.), Am. Bar Assn., S.A.R. Republican. Presbyn. Mason (K.T., 33°, Shriner), K. of P., Woodman, Elk. Home: Fergus Falls, Minn. Address: Supreme Court, Capitol, St. Paul, Minn.* Deceased.

HILTON, David Clark, surgeon; b. Saline County, Neb., Apr. 22, 1877; s. John Bulin Whitehead and Mary Elizabeth (Redgate) H.; A.B., U. of Neb., 1900, A.M., 1901; M.D., Rush Med. Coll., Chicago, 1903; m. Sarah Luella O'Toole, Aug. 23, 1900; children—Blossom Virginia (Mrs. Harold Stanley Gish), Ruth Acacia (Mrs. Woodward Burgert), Hiram David (M.D.). Practice Lincoln, Neb., since 1903; head of science depts., Cotner U., 1904-05; demonstrator in anatomy, U. of Neb., 1903-05; attending surgeon St. Elizabeth's Hosp. since 1905; attending surgeon Bryan Memorial Hosp. since 1926; consultant-surgeon U.S. Vets. Bur. Hosp. since 1930. Served as captain Med. Corps, U.S. Army, World War; col. comdg. 110th Med. Regt., Neb. N.G. 1925-40; div. surgeon, 35th Div., N.G., 1927-40; brig. gen. of the line, Neb. N.G., since Sept. 1940 (unassigned). U.S. del. to 5th Internat. Congress of Mil. Medicine and Pharmacy, Warsaw, Poland, 1927, VIth, London, Eng., 1929. Awarded cross of the Army Med. Sch. (Poland), 1927. Fellow A.A.A.S., Am. Coll. Surgeons; mem. A.M.A., S.A.R., Soc. Colonial Wars, Lancaster County Medical Soc., Inter-Professional Men's Inst., Neb. Ornithol. Union, The Audubon Soc., Neb. Geneal. Soc., Lincoln Chamber of Commerce, Acacia, Sigma Xi. Republican. Anglican. Mason (33°, K.T., R.C. of Constantine). Author of various papers on med., mil. and ornithol. subjects. Home: 2500 Woodscrest Blvd. Office: Continental Bldg., Lincoln, Neb. Died Dec. 12, 1945.

HILTON, Henry Hoyt, publisher; b. Cambridge, Mass., Apr. 17, 1868; s. Lucius W. and Louisa B. (Leighton) H.; A.B., Dartmouth, 1890, A.M., 1894; LL.D., Northwestern U., 1928, Colby Coll., 1930, Dartmouth Coll., 1938; m. Charlotte T. Sibley, 1897; children—Katharine L., Charlotte W., Thorndike (dec.), Henry Hoyt, Ruth S. (dec.), Edward L. With Ginn & Co., Boston, 1890, member of firm and one of Chicago managers, 1894, chmn., subsequently pres. then chmn. of corporation. Retired 1946. Chief of settlement div. S.A.T.C., World War; mem. Tax Simplification Bd., by appmt. of President Harding. Treas. Chicago Theological Seminary; trustee Colby Coll., Dartmouth Coll. 2 terms, Constantinople Woman's Coll., 1 term. Congregationalist. Mason. Clubs: Union League, University (Chicago). Home: 5644 Kimbark Av., Chicago 37; (summer) R.D., Lowell, Mass. Office: 2301 Prairie Av., Chicago 16 Died Apr. 10, 1948.

HIMES, Norman Edwin, sociologist, med. historian; b. Jersey City, N.J., Aug. 4, 1899; s. Edward and Sarah Teresa (Bush) H.; B.S., Harvard, 1923, M. A., 1924, Ph.D., 1932; m. Vera Carola Hokanson, June 14, 1924 (deceased); m. 2d, Marian King Bailey, Jan. 9, 1947. Robert Treat Paine fellow in social ethics, Harvard, 1923-25; instr. economics and sociology, Cornell (Ia.) Coll., 1925-26; traveling fellow, Social Sci. Research Council, 1926-27; instr. economics, Simmons Coll. and Simmons Sch. Social Work, 1928-30; asst. editor, sociology sec., Social Science Abstracts, 1929; asso. prof. economics and sociology, Clark U., 1930-31; asst. prof. sociology, Colgate U., 1932-38, prof. 1938-42; major, office Surgeon General, U.S. Army, Washington, D.C., 1943-44; chief, Wages, Hours and Comn. Facility, W. M. C., Washington, D.C., 1944-45; prof. sociology Biarritz (France) American U., 1945-46; chief Office of Special Education, Office Mil. Govt. for Germany, U.S. Zone, Berlin, 1946-48, Information Control Div. Office Mil. Govt., Bremen, Germany, U.S. Zone, 1948-49. Editor, Marriage Hygiene (Bombay), 1934-37; Am. corr. Eugenics Rev. (London), 1935-38; editor Sociology series for Longmans, Green, 1940-45; research in birth control and its history since 1925; research on marriage since 1932; consultant in med. hist. to Nat. Com. on Maternal Health, N.Y. City, 1932-36. Mem. Am. Sociol. Soc. (past chmn. div. population and social biology; exec. com. 1941-44), Eastern Sociol. Soc. (mem. founding group; mem. exec. com. 1941-44), Population Assn. of America (past dir. bd.), Am. Assn. U. Profs. (past pres. Colgate U. chapter), Eugenics Soc. (London), Nat. Conf. on Family Relations (dir. bd.), Nat. Advis. Com., Consumers Union, Delta Sigma Rho, Tau Kappa Alpha. Mem. Soc. for Ethical Culture. Author: Truth About Birth Control, 1931; A Guide to Birth Control Literature, 1931; Medical History of Contraception, 1936; Practical Birth Control Methods, 1938 (Portugese transl., Métodos Pratico de Impedir a Conçepcão, 1931); Your Marriage, 1940, 1941 (Portugese transl., Nossa Vida Conjugal, 1943), Happy Marriage, 1941. Coauthor: Men, Groups and the Community, 1940. Editor: Illustrations and Proofs of the Principle of Population, 1930; Economics, Sociology and the Modern World; Essays in Honor of T. N. Carver, 1935; C. K. Knowlton, Fruits of Philosophy, 1937. Contbr. to Ency. of Social Sciences, Dict. Am. Biog., Ency. Sexualis, and to sociol. econ. and med. jours. Address: 4429 38th St. N., Arlington, Va. Died June 6, 1949; buried in Arlington Nat. Cemetery.

HINCKLEY, Edwin Smith, educator; b. Cave Creek Fort, Utah, July 21, 1868; s. Ira Nathaniel and Adelaide Cameron (Noble) H.; B.S., U. of Mich., 1895; B.S., Brigham Young U., Provo, Utah, 1903; m. Addie Henry, Sept. 3, 1891. Prof. geology and geography, Brigham Young U., 1895-15; supt. State Industrial Sch., Ogden, Utah, since Jan. 21, 1915. Fellow A.A.A.S., Nat. Soc. for Broader Edn. Democrat. Mem. Ch. of Jesus Christ of Latter Day Saints (Mormon). Address: State Industrial School, Ogden, Utah. Deceased.

HINDLEY, Howard Lister (hind'lē), editor; b. Frome, Ont., Can., July 23, 1870; s. John Ingham and Hannah (Lister) H.; desc. of the Hindleys and Listers, pioneers in Eramosa, Ont.; student McGill U., 1 yr.; m. Mary Ella Caldwell, June 1893; children—Mary Vivien, Miriam Joyce, Lister Caldwell. Began as railroad telegraph operator, 1886; train dispatcher, Central Vt. and Rutland ry. cos., 1888-99; editor Vergennes Enterprise, 1899-1901, Ludlow Tribune, 1901-05, Rutland Herald since 1905, except 18 mos. on Montpelier Journal and 4 yrs. in the West. Directed 1st political bur. of publicity in Vt., Percival W. Clement's 1906 campaign for governor. Republican. Conglist. Mason. Author: The Gentleman from Hayville, 1908. Address: The Herald, Rutland, Vt. Died May 10, 1943.

HINDS, Frederick Wesley, dean of dental coll.; b. Hubbard, Minn., Mar. 5, 1888; s. Edward Roswell and Mary Ann (Wilkins) H.; student St. Cloud Normal Sch., 1908; D.D.S., U. of Minn., 1915; m. Sara Marie Holm, Jan. 15, 1916; children—Edward Copas, Charlotte. Practice of dentistry, St. James, Minn., 1915-16, Park Rapids, Minn., 1916-26, Dallas, Tex. (part time), since 1929; with Baylor U., Dallas, since 1926, as instr. in Coll. of Dentistry, 1926, supt., 1927, dean since 1927. Mayor of Park Rapids, 1923-25. Fellow Am. Coll. Dentists, A.A.A.S.; mem. exec. com. Am. Assn. of Dental Schs.; mem. Am. Dental Assn., Tex. State Dental Assn.; Dallas County Dental Assn., Xi Psi Phi, Omicron Kappa Upsilon. Episcopalian. Mason (York Rite, Shriner). Clubs: Rotary, Lakewood Country, Dallas Athletic. Contbr. to dental jours. Lectured and presented clinics, U.S. and Can., since 1919. Home: 6300 Tremont St., Dallas, Tex. Died June 4, 1943.

HINKE, William John (hin'kē), prof. Semitic langs.; b. Giershofen, Rhine Province, Germany, Mar. 24, 1871; s. William Henry Christian and Maria Louisa (Haag) H.; Gymnasium, Elberfeld, Germany, 1880-87; A.B., Calvin Coll., Cleveland, 1890, A.M., 1893; Ursinus Sch. of Theology, Pa., 1892-94; Princeton Theol. Sem., 1894-95; Grad. Sch. of U. of Pa., 1900-06; Ph.D., 1906; D.D., Heidelberg U., 1906; m. Bertha Agnes Berleman, Nov. 23, 1898. Came to U.S., 1887, naturalized citizen, 1897. Prof. Latin and Greek, Calvin Coll., 1890-92; instr. German, Ursinus Coll., Pa., 1892-94; instr. Hebrew, 1895-97, prof. Hebrew lang. and lit., 1897-1907, Ursinus Sch. of Theology; asst. prof. in O.T. dept., 1907-09, prof. Semitic langs. and religions, 1909-39, now emeritus, Auburn (N.Y.) Theol. Sem.; annual prof. Am. Sch. of Archaeology at Jerusalem, 1921-22; librarian, Auburn Theological Seminary, 1923-39. Member Society of Biblical Literature and Exegesis, Presbyterian Hist. Soc., Pa. German Soc., Cayuga County Hist. Soc. Republican. Author: Bibliography of Reformed Church in United States, 1901; A New Boundary Stone of Nebuchadnezzar I, from Nippur, 1907; Selected Babylonian Kudurru Inscriptions, 1911; Life and Letters of the Rev. John Philip Boehm, 1916; History of Goshenhoppen Reformed Charge (1727-1833), 1920; History of the Tohickon Union Church (1745-1854), 1925. Editor and translator of Minutes and Letters of the Coetus of Pennsylvania, 1747-1792, Phila., 1903; General Biog. Cat. of Auburn Theol. Sem. (1818-1918), 1918; The Latin Works of Huldreich Zwingli (Vol. II), 1922; Pennsylvania German Pioneers (3 vols.), 1934. Contbr. many hist. articles to mags. and ch. revs. Home: Auburn, N.Y. Died Jan. 1, 1947.

HINKLE, Thomas Clark, author; b. Laclede, Ill., June 12, 1876; s. William R. and Sarilda Catherine H.; grad. high sch., Junction City, Kan., 1898; M.D., U. of Kan., 1904; m. Roxana E. Stevens, Dec. 1908; children—Thomas Clark, Rolland Theodore. Republican. Conglist. Author: (juveniles) Snowy Tail; Tiny Cottontail; Doctor Rabbit and Ki-Yi Coyote; Doctor Rabbit and Tom Wild Cat; Doctor Rabbit and Old Bill Horned Owl; Doctor Rabbit and Slinky Black Wolf; Doctor Rabbit and Brushtail Fox; Doctor Rabbit and Grumpy Bear; How to Eat (adult), 1921; Waddy Rabbit, 1922; Jolly White Tail, 1922; A Coyote of the Republican Valley; Split-Ear—A Battling Coyote, 1925; Tawny, A Dog of the Old West; Trueboy, The Story of a Great Dog; Bugle, A Dog of the Rockies; Black Storm, A Horse of the Kansas Hills; Tornado Boy, A Horse of the West; Shag, The Story of a Dog; Bing, the Story of a Tramp Dog; Silver, the Story of a Wild Horse; Hurricane Pinto, the Story of an Outlaw Horse; King, the Story of a Sheep Dog; Crazy Dog Curly, The Story of a Mongrel Dog; Barry, The Story of a Wolf Dog; Cinchfoot, The Story of a Range Horse; Buckskin, The Story of a Western Horse; Dusty, The Story of a Wild Dog; Old Nick and Bob: Two Dogs of the West; Mustang, a Horse of the Old West; Shep, a Collie of the Old West; Tomahawk, The Story of a Fighting Horse; Jube, The Story of a Trapper's Dog; Blaze Face, the story of a horse; Wolf; Blackjack; Vic. Home: Onaga, Kan. Died May 13, 1949; buried Wamega, Kan.

HINSDALE, Guy, M.D.; b. Brooklyn, N.Y., Oct. 26, 1858; s. Theodore and Grace (Webster) H.; 7th in descent from Robert Hinsdale who came from

Eng. and was a propr. of Dedham, Mass., 1637, and was slain by Indians in massacre at Deerfield, 1675; A.B., Amherst, 1878, A.M., 1881; M.D., U. of Pa., 1881; m. Mary P. Graham, Mar. 11, 1890; 1 dau., Jean Graham. Assisted late Dr. S. Weir Mitchell and Dr. William Osler in hosp. and pvt. practice several yrs.; asso. prof. climatology, Medico-Chirurgical Coll., Phila., 1905-17; prof. climatology, Univ. of Pa., 1917-19; practiced at Hot Springs, Va., 1904-29; med. dir. White Sulphur Springs, Inc., 1929-42, when U.S. Army purchased The Greenbrier for a gen. hosp. An instr. in medicine and med. diagnosis of student med. officers, U.S. Navy, Phila., 1917. Mem. Am. Acad. Medicine (v.p. 1906-07), Coll. Physicians Phila., Am. Climatol. and Clin. Assn. (sec. 1894-1918, pres. 1919), Am. Neurol. Assn., A.M.A., Pa. Soc. Prevention Tuberculosis (pres. 1900-02), Am. Meteorological Soc., Am. Assn. History of Medicine; fellow Royal Soc. Medicine, London; mem. Comite d'Honneur de Congrès Internat. du Tourisme, du Thermalisme et du Climatisme, Paris, 1937; hon life mem. West Va. Med. Soc. Clubs: Medical Club of Phila. (hon.); Colonnade, Farmington Country (Charlottesville). Author Am. Med. Argonauts, Pupils of Pierre Charles Alexander Louis, 1830-40, 1898. Writer of essays, articles, etc. Contbr. to Bull. of Am. Meteorol. Soc. and med. jours. Address: 1401 Rugby Rd., Charlottesville, Va. Died April 27. 1948.

HINSDALE, Wilbert B., physician; b. Wadsworth, O., May 25, 1851; s. Albert and Clarinda (Eyles) H.; B.S., Hiram (O.) Coll., 1875, M.S., 1878; M.D., Cleveland Homoe. Med. Coll., 1887; hon. A.M., Hiram Coll., 1897; hon. A.M., U. of Mich., 1934; m. Estella Stone, Nov. 25, 1875 (dec.); 1 son, Albert Euclid (dec.). Prof. internal. and clin. medicine, homoe. dept. U. of Mich., since 1895; dean homoe. med. dept. same, 1895-1922, also med. dir. of coll. hosp.; retired as prof. emeritus, 1922; custodian Mich. archaeology, Univ. Museums, 1922-29; asso. in charge of div. of the Great Lakes, Mus. of Anthropology, U. of Mich. since 1929. Pres. Mich. Acad. of Science, Arts and Letters, 1931. Mem. Am. Assn. Archaeologists, etc. Author: Primitive Man in Michigan; The Indians of Washtenaw County; The First People of Michigan; Archaeological Atlas of Michigan; Distribution of the Aboriginal Population of Michigan; Perforated Indian Crania in Michigan (with E. F. Greenman), 1936. Home: Ann Arbor, Mich. Died July 25, 1944.

HINSHAW, William Wade, singer, conductor, operatic producer; b. near Union, Hardin County, Ia., Nov. 3, 1867; s. Thomas Doane and Anna Harriett (Lundy) H.; grad. Friends Acad., New Providence, Ia., 1886; B.S. in C.E., Valparaiso U., 1888, Mus.B., 1890, LL.B., 1897, hon. Mus.D., 1926; studied singing in U.S. and Germany; hon. Ph.D., Bethany Coll., Lindsborg, Kan., 1901; m. Anna Tannahill Williams, Sept. 28, 1893 (died Nov. 1905); children—John Carl Williams, William Wade, Thomas Doane, Anne Marie Wing; m. 2d, Mabel Clyde, June 3, 1911. Leader of boys' band at age of 15; teacher and choir leader, Chicago, 1890-99; dean of music department, Valparaiso U., 1895-99; debut with Castle Square Opera Co., as Mephisto in "Faust," St. Louis, 1899; pres. Chicago Conservatory of Music, 1903-07, Hinshaw Conservatory of Music, Chicago, 1907-09; concert tours, U.S. and Can., 1908-10; leading Am. baritone with Metropolitan Opera Co., New York, 1910-13; sang "Wotan" and "Wandrer" in Niebelungen Ring Festival, Graz, Austria, summer 1912; same roles 15 times in Niebelungen Ring Festival, Berlin, Germany, summer 1914; concertized in U.S. and Can., 1913-18; created role of "Gloom" in Parker's prize opera Mona, Metropolitan Opera, 1912; created role of "King" in Parker's prize opera "Fairyland," Los Angeles, Calif., 1915; opera producer, New York, as pres. Soc. Am. Singers, 1918-20; opera producer with own company, giving Mozart operas in English, U.S., Can. and Cuba (800 performances), 1920-26; gave 1st Cuban Mozart Festival, Havana, Dec. 1925; gave 1st Am. Mozart Festival, Cincinnati, O., May 1926. Mem. New England Hist. Geneal. Soc., N.Y. Geneal. Biog. Soc., Va. Hist. Soc., Pa. Geneal. Soc. Phila., Friends Hist. Soc., Inst. Am. Genealogy (fellow), S.A.R. Republican. Mem. Soc. of Friends. Mason (32°, K.T., Shriner), K.P., Elk. Clubs: Apawamis (Rye, N.Y.); Tedesco Country (Boston); Chevy Chase, Columbia Country (Washington, D.C.); U.S. Seniors' Golf Assn.; Augusta (Ga.) National Golf. Retired from musical activities, June 1926, and engaged (as a hobby) in assembling, compiling and publishing an Encyclopedia of Am. Quaker Genealogy (Vol. I, containing all Quaker genealogical records, 1678-1890, in N.C., S.C., Ga. and Tenn., pub. Dec. 1936; Vol. II, containing all Quaker genealogical records, 1676-1937, of Salem and Burlington Mo. Mtgs., N.J. and of Philadelphia and Falls Mo. Mtgs., Pa., pub. Mar. 1938; Vol. III, containing all Quaker genealogical records, 1657-1937, of all Mtgs. in N.Y. City and L.I., pub. April 1940; Vols. IV and V containing records of the 46 oldest mo. mtgs. in Ohio, 1 mtg. in Mich., 4 in Western Pa., 1946; Vol. VI containing the records of mtgs. in Va., on press; records of other mtgs. to follow. Home: Mayflower Hotel, Washington 6. Died Nov. 27, 1947.

HIPSHER, Edward Ellsworth, musician, editor; b. Caledonia, O., Mar. 28, 1871; s. Francis Marion and Elizabeth (Dickin) H.; grad. dept. of music, Valparaiso (Ind.) U., 1890, grad. study gold medalist, 1893; student Royal Acad. Music, London, 1894-95, 99; pupil of Carpi, Florence, Italy, 1914; Associate Royal Academy of Music, London, 1916; hon. Mus. Doc., Temple U., 1933; unmarried. Musical dir. Humeston (Ia.) Normal Coll., 1890-91, Mendota (Ill.) Coll., 1893-94, Holbrook Normal Coll., Fountain City, Tenn., 1898-1901, Marion (O.) Conservatory of Music, 1901-05, Southern Normal Inst., Douglas, Ga., 1905-07; dir. vocal dept. Centenary Coll., Cleveland, Tenn., 1909-10; musical dir. Marion Conservatory of Music and Claridon Twp. Schs., also condr. Marion Choral Soc., 1910-13; musical dir. Morris Harvey Coll., Barboursville, W.Va., 1913-20; asso. editor The Etude, 1920-40. Dir. Phila. Operatic Soc., and Italo-American Philharmonic Orchestra. Mem. Phila. Music Teachers' Assn. (pres.), China Inst. of America, English-Speaking Union, Phila. Art Alliance, Phila. Soc. for Preservation of Landmarks (life), Ohio Soc. of Phila. (exec. com.), Dickens Fellowship (exec. council), Arts and Sciences Soc. of Pa. (v.p. for music); founder-pres. The Mozart Soc. of Phila. Metropolitan Opera Guild, Italo-American Orchestra (mem. bd. dirs.), Italian Symphony Orchestra, Marion Branch of Dickens Fellowship (founder-pres.). Author: Choir Book for Women's Voices, 1912; American Opera and Its Composers, 1927; Choral Art Repertoire, 1933. Translator of libretto of Bizet's Pearl Fishers, 1928. Composer of songs, piano pieces and ch. music; contbr. to mags. Home: 218 N. State St., Marion, O. Died March 7. 1948.

HIRONS, Frederic C(harles), architect; born Birmingham, Eng., Mar. 28, 1882; s. Charles Frederic and Esther (Rushton) H.; came with parents to U.S., 1892; grad. Boston Tech., 1903; student École des Beaux Arts, Paris, 1904-09; Rotch scholar, 1904; Paris prize fellow, 1906; M.S. (hon.) Catholic U. of Am.; m. Edna Bushnell Post, Aug. 24, 1910; children—Cornelia Post, Priscilla Bushnell (Mrs. D. C. Watson), Frederic Charles. Began practice as architect at N.Y. City, 1909. Principal works: George Rogers Clark Memorial, Ind.; Worcester (Mass.) War Memorial Auditorium; Rockland County Court House, New York City, N.Y.; Beaux-Arts Inst. of Design Bldg., New York; Davidson Co. Courthouse, Nashville. A.N.A., 1931; mem. Am. Inst. Architects, Beaux Arts Inst. Design, Cercle Interallie, Beaux Art Soc. of Architects (pres. 1937-39). Decorated Legion of Honor (France), 1926. Clubs: Yale, Century. Home: 40 E. 49th St., New York. Died Jan. 23, 1942.

HIRSCH, Isaac E., editor, pub.; b. Carver County, Minn., May 11, 1859; s. Max and Helene (Einstein) H.; pioneer settlers of Minn.; ed. pub. schs. and grad. Old Central High Sch. of Pittsburgh, Pa., 1873; m. Margaret Bradley, 1885 (died May 2, 1935); 1 dau., Annette (wife of Dr. J. W. Frey, of Pittsburgh). Began as office boy foreign steamship and banking firm of Max Schamberg & Co., Pittsburgh, 1873, mgr., 1880, propr., 1887, and sold out to First Nat. Bank, Pittsburgh, 1900; part owner Pittsburgh Volksblatt, 1885, consolidating with Freiheits Freund, 1901; then v.p. Neeb-Hirsch Pub. Co. until dissolution, 1929. Mem. Acad. Science and Art (councilor, 1899-1921; pres. 1922), Art Soc. (dir. 1907-20). Mem. German-Am. Tech. Soc., Western Pa. Hist. Soc., Humane Soc. of Western Pa., Assn. of Masonic Vets. of Western Pa. Clubs: Civic, Press, German (pres. 1917-19). Author: Tante Lotte beim Freitag Nachmittag Kaffeeklatsch, 1887; poems set to music by various composers. Home: 214 Bellefield Av., Pittsburgh, Pa. Died Mar. 2, 1942.

HIRSCHHORN, Fred, cigar mfr.; b. N.Y. City, Dec. 22, 1870; s. Louis and Severine (Lippmann) H.; ed. grade sch., New York; m. Hannah Scharps, Sept. 9, 1912; children—Rose, Hannah, Fred. Chmn. bd. Gen. Cigar Co. Republican. Jewish religion. Club: Harmonie. Home: 417 Park Av. Office: 119 W. 40th St., New York. Died Apr. 30, 1946.

HIRSCHFELDER, Arthur Douglass, prof. pharmacology; b. San Francisco, Calif., Sept. 29, 1879; s. Joseph Oakland and Clara (Honigsberg) H.; B.S., U. of Calif., 1897; student Pasteur Inst., Paris, 1898-99, U. of Heidelberg, 1899; M.D., Johns Hopkins, 1903; m. May R. Straus, June 26, 1905; children—Rosalie Claire (Mrs. Gosta C. Akerlof), Joseph Oakland. Resident house officer Johns Hopkins Hosp., Baltimore, 1903-04; asst. in medicine, Cooper Med. Coll., San Francisco, 1904-05; successively vol. asst., instr., asso. in medicine Johns Hopkins, 1905-13; prof. pharmacology, U. of Minn., since 1913. Served as pharmacologist, War Dept., 1918. Fellow A.A. A.S.; mem. A.M.A. (chmn. sect. on pharmacology 1917-18), Am. Soc. Clin. Investigation, Soc. Exptl. Biology and Medicine, Am. Soc. Pharmacology and Exptl. Therapeutics, Am. Physiol. Soc., Am. Soc. Biol. Chemistry, Am. Chem. Soc., Minn. Acad. Science, Sigma Xi, Gamma Alpha. Club: Campus (Minneapolis, Minn.). Author: Diseases of the Heart and Aorta, 1910; An Investigation of the Louse Problem (with Wm. Moore), 1918. Contbr. professional jours. Home: 2364 Lake of the Isle Blvd., Minneapolis, Minn. Died Oct. 11, 1942.

HISCOCK, Frank Harris (hĭs'kŏk), judge; b. Tully, N.Y., Apr. 16, 1856; s. L. Harris and Lucy (Bridgman) H.; A.B., Cornell Univ., 1875; LL.D., Syracuse Univ., 1914, Columbia University, 1917, Williams College, 1924; University of State of New York, 1926; m. Elizabeth Barnes, October 22, 1879; children—Rebecca Cornelia (deceased), Helen Lucy, George Barnes, Luther Harris. Admitted to bar, 1877, and engaged in practice at Syracuse, N.Y. Elected justice Supreme Court of N.Y., 5th Dist., 1896; asso. justice 4th Appellate Div., 1901-05; judge Court of Appeals, 1906, chief judge, 1916-Dec. 31, 1926; sr. mem. Hiscock, Williams & Cowie and Hiscock, Cowie, Bruce and Lee, 1926-35; official referee N.Y. Court of Appeals; dir. various corps. Chmn. bd. trustees Cornell U., 1917-39, chmn. emeritus since 1939; ex-pres. N.Y. State Bar Assn.; member Cornell Law Assn.; mem. Syracuse Chamber Commerce. Republican. Formerly v.p. Laymen's League Unitarian Church. Clubs: Century, University of Syracuse, Citizens, Cornell (New York and Syracuse). Home: Syracuse, N.Y. Died July 2, 1946.

HITCHCOCK, Curtice, publisher; b. Pittsford, Vt., Mar. 4, 1892; s. Ernest and Caroline Ann (Curtice) H.; A.B., U. of Vt., 1913; m. Margaret Unwin, July 21, 1920; children—Joan, John Raymond. Registrar, Lake Forest (Ill.) Acad., 1913-15; reporter, later mem. Washington Bur. of N.Y. Times, 1915-17; Council of Nat. Defense, Washington, D.C., 1917; 2d lt. U.S. Army, 1918; travel in Europe, 1919; mem. U. of Chicago faculty, 1920-23; asst. to pres., later v.p., The Macmillan Co., N.Y. City, 1924-31; v.p. The Century Co., N.Y. City, 1932-33; pres. and dir. Reynal & Hitchcock, Inc., since 1934. Represented Am. publishers and Office of War Information on spl. mission to England, Nov.-Dec. 1942. Mem. Phi Beta Kappa, Delta Psi. Clubs: Century (N.Y. City); Cosmos (Washington); Eight Mile River (Lyme, Conn.). Author: The Worker in Modern Economic Society (with Paul H. Douglas, W. E. Atkins), 1923. Home: 36 Gramercy Park, New York, N.Y.; (summer) Lyme, Conn. Office: 8 W. 40th St., New York 18, N.Y. Died May 3, 1946.

HITCHCOCK, Embury Asbury, engineer, educator; b. Henrietta, N.Y., June 26, 1866; s. Julius Charles and Finett Rosett (Potter) H.; student Syracuse U., 1885; M.E., Cornell U., 1890; m. Hattie Isabel Mortimore, July 7, 1896 (died 1933); children—Isabelle, Mortimore, Harriett; m. 2d, Florence Estelle Mortimore, Apr. 27, 1940. Designer Corliss Steam Engine Co., Providence, R.I., 1890-93; mem. faculty, Ohio State U., 1893-1912; engr. with E. W. Clark Co. Management Corp., 1912-19; v.p. Bailey Meter Co., Cleveland, O., 1919-20; dean Coll. of Engring., Ohio State U., 1920-36, dean emeritus since 1936. Represented Appalachian Power Co. at First World Power Conf., London, 1924. Member American Society Engineering Education (v.p. 1929-30), National Soc. Professional Engrs., Sigma Xi, Tau Beta Pi, Scabbard and Blade, Triangle. Chmn. engring. section Association Land-Grant Colleges, 1925-26; vice-president Columbus Chamber Commerce, 1926-27; hon. judge Fisher Body Craftsmen's Guild, 1930-37. mem. nat. council Boy Scouts America, 1937-45. Republican. Methodist. Author: My First Fifty Years in Engineering. Conducted first complete heat balance tests of locomotives on road. Home: 348 W. Eighth Av., Columbus, O. Died April 29, 1948; buried in Amaranth Abbey, Columbus, O.

HITCHCOCK, Lucius Wolcott, artist; b. West Williamsfield, O., Dec. 2, 1868; s. Elizur and Lucretia (Kellogg) H.; pupil Art Students' League, New York, Jules Lefebvre, Benjamin Constant, Jean Paul Laurens and the Colarossi Acad., Paris; m. Sarah McNeil, Feb. 1895; children—James M., Ethan Wolcott. Bronze medal, Paris Expn., 1900, Buffalo Expn., 1901; silver medal, St. Louis Expn., 1904. Home: Southport, Me. Died June 18, 1942.

HITCHENS, Arthur Parker, health commissioner; b. Delmar, Delaware, Sept. 14, 1877; s. William Smith and Fannie (Parker) H.; Prep. Sch., Temple Coll., Phila.; M.D., Medico-Chirurg. Coll., Phila., 1898; studied U. of Pa., St. Mary's Hosp. (London), Woods Hole, Mass.; grad. Army Med. Sch., 1923; also grad. course preventive medicine; m. Ethel Mary Bennett, June 20, 1906. Dir. biol. labs., Glenolden, Pa., 1900-18; commd. maj. M.C., U.S. Army, 1920, lt. col. 1937; spl. lecturer on infection and immunity, Sch. for Grads., Dept. of Agr., 1922; advisory prof. bacteriology, Am. Univ., Washington; inrst. Army Med. Sch.; tech. adviser to gov. gen. P.I. in pub. health matters, 1925-29; professorial lecturer on epidemiology, Sch. Hygiene and Pub. Health, U. of Philippines, 1928-29; in charge Corps Area Lab., Fort Sheridan, Ill., 1929-33; instr. in bacteriology and chief dept. bacteriology, Army Medical Sch. Washington, 1935-38; asst. prof. military science and tactics, U. of Pa., 1938, prof. of public health and preventive medicine, 1939-44; commissioner of health, Wilmington, Del., since 1944; staff mem. Wilmington General Hospital, since 1945; dir. State of Pa. Bur. of Labs., 1948-49. Mem. Phila. City Bd. of Health, 1940-43. Editor Abstracts of Bacteriology; chmn. editorial bd., sect. on microbiology, Biol. Abstracts, 1937-45; member exec. com. Union of Am. Biol. Societies, Fellow A.M.A., Phila. Coll. Physicians, Am. Public Health Assn. (chmn. laboratory sect. 1923-24; chairman coordinating com. on standard methods, lab. sect., 1931-46); mem. Soc. Am. Bacteriol. (sec. 1912-22, v.p. 1923, pres. 1924; pres. Washington local 1936-37), Am. Assn. Immunologists, North Shore Science Club (founded 1931, pres.). Episcopalian. Mason. Clubs: Union League (Phila.); Cosmos (Washington); Army and Navy, Manila; Polo (Manila, P.I.); Laboratory (founder 1944), Torch, Rotary, Masonic (Wilmington). Address: 906 S. 48th St., Phila. 43. Died Dec. 10, 1949.

HITE, Lewis Field (hī'tē), clergyman, educator; b. "Belle Vue," near Middletown, Va., Aug. 1, 1852; s. Hugh Holmes and Ann Randolph (Meade) H.; U. of Va., 1873-76, 1878-79, 1881-82; Harvard, 1893-1902, 1903-04, M.A., 1901; New Ch. Theol. Sch., Cambridge, Mass., 1890-92; U. of Heidelberg, Germany, 1910-11; attended lectures at U. of Paris and Coll. de France, 1911; m. Abbe Bailey James, July 19, 1893; children—Harriet James, Hugh Maury.

Teacher Urbana U., 1884-90; with New Ch. Theol. Sch. since 1893, prof. philosophy since 1893. Mng. editor New Ch. Review, 1916-34. Minister Ch. of the New Jerusalem; pres. Swedenborg Scientific Assn., 1917-35. Mem. A.A.A.S., Am. Philos. Assn., S.R. Democrat. Club: New Church (Boston). Author: Swedenborg's Historical Position, 1928; Ultimate Reality, 1937; Urbana University and Higher Education, 1939. Home: 42 Arlington St., Cambridge, Mass. Died Apr. 26, 1945.

HOBART, Henry Metcalf, engr.; b. Boston, Mass., Nov. 29, 1868; s. Arthur William and Martha Lambard (Nichols) H.; B.S. in E.E., Mass. Inst. Tech., 1889; m. Edith Walpole, Aug. 26, 1909. With Thomson-Houston Electric Co., and its successor, the Gen. Electric Co., 1889-94, British Thomson-Houston Co., London, 1894-99; cons. engr., Union Elektricitäts Gesellschaft, Berlin, 1900-03; independent cons. practice, London, Eng., 1903-11; cons. engr. Gen. Electric Co. of America, 1911-40; consulting engineer since 1940. Fellow Am. Inst. Elec. Engrs.; mem. Inst. Civil, Mech. and Elec. Engrs. (England), Am. Soc. M.E. Author: Electric Motors, 1904, 2d edit., 1910, 3d edit., 1923; Continuous Current Dynamo Design, 1906; Heavy Electrical Engineering, 1908; Electricity, 1909; Electric Trains, 1910; Design of Static Transformers, 1911; Electric Propulsion of Ships, 1911; Design of Polyphase Generators and Motors, 1913; also other books with collaborators. Editor: Dictionary of Electrical Engineering, 1910. Office: 10 Balltown Rd., Schenectady, N.Y.*Died Oct. 11, 1946.

HOBBS, James Randolph, clergyman; b. Hinds County, Miss.; s. Rev. James Augustus and Elizabeth Caroline (Wyatt) H.; Ph.B., Miss. Coll., 1903; D.D., Union U., Jackson, Tenn., and Carson and Newman Coll., Jefferson City, Tenn., 1916; LL.D., Georgetown (Ky.) Coll. and U. of Ala., 1926; m. Elizabeth Brown Drake, June 14, 1905 (now dec.); children—James Randolph, Sara Elizabeth (Mrs. Derwood A. Norris). Ordained ministry Southern Bapt. Ch., 1901; pastor successively Mt. Sterling, Owensboro, Ky., Shelbyville, Tenn., Jonesboro, Ark., until 1918; pastor First Bapt. Ch., Birmingham, Ala., 1919-38; pastor emeritus since 1938. Mem. exec. com. that planned and instituted $75,000,000 Bapt. Campaign; v.p. Southern Bapt. Conv., 1921-22, 1935-36; increased membership of First Ch., Birmingham, from 500 to 2,900 and built S.S. bldg. at cost of $275,000. Preached conv. sermon, Southern Bapt. Conv., Washington, 1920, Chattanooga, 1928. Pres. Ala. Bapt. State Conv., 1926-27, chmn. Bapt. State Exec. Bd., Ala., 1929-32; pres. Ala. Anti-Saloon League, 1931-32; pres. Anti-Saloon League of America, 1937-39. Mason (32°, Shriner). Author: The Pastor's Manual, 1924. Toured Europe, Asia and Africa, 1923, contbg. articles to Birmingham News. Frequent speaker before univs. and colls. Office: Education Bldg., Birmingham, Ala. Died April 23, 1942.

HOBLITZELLE, Harrison (hŏb-lĭt-zĕl'), chmn. Gen. Steel Castings Corp.; b. St. Louis, Mo., Oct. 17, 1896; s. George Knapp and Laura Trimble (Harrison) H.; student Smith Acad., St. Louis, 1908-13; A.B., Cornell U., 1917; m. Mary D. Jones, Jan. 14, 1920; children—George Knapp, Harrison. Clk., Commonwealth Steel Co., 1917, asst. purchasing agt., 1919, mgr. of purchases, 1922, v.p. and mgr. of purchases, 1926, v.p. and mgr. sales, 1929; v.p. and gen. mgr. Commonwealth Div. of Gen. Steel Castings Corp., 1929-31, exec. v.p., 1931, pres., Sept. 1931-June 1945, chairman board since June 1945, also dir.; mem. bd. mgrs. Western Saving Fund Soc.; mem. bd. govs. Ry. Business Assn.; mem. Pa. advisory bd. Am. Mutual Liability Ins. Co.; mem. state bd. Pa. Economy League. Dir. Bryn Mawr (Pa.) Hosp. Mem. Am. Iron and Steel Inst., Newcomen Soc. (Eng.), Mo. Hist. Soc., Kappa Alpha. Ind. Democrat. Episcopalian. Clubs: Racquet, Gulph Mills Golf, Pohoqualine Fishing (Phila.); St. Louis Country. Home: Conestoga Rd., Ithan, Pa. Office: General Steel Castings Corp., Eddystone, Pa. Died Dec. 5, 1949.

HOCH, Homer (hōk), judge; b. Marion, Kan., July 4, 1879; s. Edward Wallis and Sarah Louisa (Dickerson) H.; A.B., Baker U., 1902, LL.D., 1937; law student George Washington U., 1903-05; LL.B., Washburn Coll., Topeka, Kan., 1909; m. Edna Wharton, June 7, 1905 (died 1935); children—Wharton, Jean; m. 2d, Ruth Beatie, 1938. Chief of Apptmt. Div., Post Office Dept., Washington, D.C., and confidential clk. to purchasing agt., 1903-05; sec. to gov. of Kan., 1907-08; practicing atty.; mem. 66th to 72d Congresses (1919-33), 4th Kan. Dist.; mem. State Corp. Commn. of Kan., 1933-39; judge Kan. Supreme Court since Jan. 1939. Republican. Methodist. Mem. Delta Tau Delta. Mason. Legal Address: Marion, Kan. Home: 3120 Westover Rd. Address: State Capitol, Topeka, Kan. Died Jan. 30, 1949.

HOCKER, Lon O., lawyer; b. Harrisonville, Mo., Nov. 21, 1873; s. James E. and Katherine S. (Railey) H.; ed. high sch.; studied law in office of uncle, Col. Robt. T. Railey; m. Mary Norris Berry, June 15, 1904; children—Edward Berry, Lon O., Marion Blackwell. Admitted to Mo. bar, 1894; now mem. Jones, Hocker, Gladney & Grand, St. Louis; former teacher night classes of St. Louis U. Law Sch.; was mem. St. Louis Draft Appeals Bd., World War; served as spl. atty. gen. of U.S. in Miss. River Barge litigation; pres. Bd. of Police Commrs. of St. Louis by apptmt. of Gov. Caulfield. Mem. Am. and Mo. State bar assns., St. Louis Bar Assn. (pres. 1927-28), St. Louis Chamber Commerce, Mercantile Library Assn., Phi Delta Phi (hon.). Republican. Clubs: Noonday, Glen Echo, Normandie. Home: 39 Portland Pl. Office: 407 N. 8th St., St. Louis, Mo. Died July, 1948.

HODGE, Edward Blanchard, surgeon; b. Burlington, N.J., Aug. 21, 1875; s. Edward Blanchard and Alice C. (Van Rensselaer) H.; A.B., Princeton, 1896; M.D., U. of Pa., 1899; m. M. C. Gretchen Greene, Feb. 10, 1904; children—Edward Blanchard, Mary Stewart (wife of C. Alexander Hatfield, M.D.). Asst. surgeon, Childrens Hosp., Phila., 1902-07, surgeon, 1907-25; asst. surgeon, Pennsylvania Hosp., Phila., 1903-20, asso. surgeon since 1920; asst. surgeon, Presbyterian Hosp., Phila., 1903-10, surgeon, 1910-41, cons. surgeon since 1941; surgeon, Germantown Hosp., 1925-41, cons. surgeon since 1941; chief surgeon, Chester County Hosp., West Chester, Pa., 1927-44, cons. surgeon since 1944. Served as capt., Med. Corps, U.S. Army, World War I; with Base Hosp. 10, overseas, 1917-19; disch. with rank of lt. col. Charter trustee Princeton U.; trustee Princeton Theol. Sem. Mem. bd. mgrs. Children's Hosp. (Philadelphia), Children's Seashore House (Atlantic City, N.J.). Mem. bd. dirs., bd. of Christian education, Presbyterian Ch. of U.S.A. Mem. Am. Surg. Assn., A.M.A., Am. Bd Surgery (founders group), Phila. Acad. Surgery, Coll. of Physicians of Phila. (vice pres.). Club: Princeton (Philadelphia). Home and office: 2019 Spruce St., Philadelphia 3, Pa. Died June 19, 1945.

HODGES, Campbell Blackshear (hŏj'ĕz), army officer, univ. pres.; b. Bossier Parish, La., Mar. 27, 1881; s. Campbell Bryan and Luella Virginia (Sockwell) H.; prep. edn. Mount Lebanon (La.) College, and Louisiana Polytechnic Institute, Ruston; grad. U.S. Mil. Acad., 1903; A.M., La. State U., 1918; LL.D., Laval U., 1941, La. Coll., Pineville, 1943; unmarried. Commd. 2d lt. inf., U.S. Army, June 11, 1903; advanced through grades to maj. gen., 1940. Lieut. col. 1st La. Inf., N.G., 1916-17; col. (temp.), 1918-20. Served in Philippines, 1903-05, 1908-09, with A.E.F., France, 1918-19, Am. forces in Germany, 1921. Prof. mil. science and tactics, La. State U., 1911-12; detailed for duty on Gen. Staff, Militia Bur., Bur. Insular Affairs; mil. attaché to Spain and Portugal, 1923-26; comdt. of cadets, West Point, 1926-29; mil. aide to President of U.S., Mar. 1929-June 1933; with 14th Inf., Canal Zone, 1933-36; chief of staff 4th Corps Area, Atlanta, Ga., Aug.-Dec. 1936; in command 14th Brigade and Fort Snelling, Minn., 1936-39; comdg. 5th Div., Oct. 1939-May 1940; 5th Corps Area, May-Oct. 1940; 5th Army Corps, 1940-41; retired from active military service, June 30, 1941; pres. La. State U. since July 1, 1941. Awarded D.S.M. (U.S.). Address: University Station, Baton Rouge, La. Died Nov. 23, 1944; buried at West Point, N.Y.

HODGDON, Anderson Dana, foreign service officer; b. Baltimore, Md., May 8, 1890; s. Dr. Alexander Lewis and Lillian Dana (Coolbaugh) H.; student Charlotte Hall Mil. Sch., 1902-08; A.B., Washington and Lee Univ., 1911; LL.B., U. of Md., 1914; grad. work, Johns Hopkins, 1912-14; m. Virginia May Lehrs, July 17, 1935; children (by former marriage), Anderson Dana, Jr., Alpheus Hyatt, Samuel Carter (deceased). Admitted to Md. bar, 1913; with trust company, 1913-14; law practice, 1914-17, 1919-23; with U.S. Foreign Service since 1923; appointed vice consul of career, June 21, 1923; vice consul, Prague, 1923, Stuttgart, June 1924; foreign service officer unclassified, 1924-27; vice consul, Windsor, June 1927; consul, Windsor, Aug. 1927; Dept. of State, Mar. 1928; asst. chief Visa Office, Feb. 1929, chief, July 1930; detailed to attend consular conferences at London, Stuttgart and Warsaw in connection with enforcement of laws and regulations relating to issuance of visas, 1930; chief Visa Div., Jan. 1931; sec. in Diplomatic Service and consul Jan. 15, 1934; foreign service officer at Moscow, Feb. 7, 1934, consul, Moscow, Feb. 1934, Riga, Oct. 1934; consul, Berlin, June 1936, and 2d sec., Berlin, May 1939; consul, Naples, December 6, 1940, Rome, February 1941; secretary, Rome, April 1941; relieved of duties as consul July 1941 and continued as sec. of Embassy; class 4, June 1942; assigned to Dept. of State, June 19, 1942, following the exchange of Diplomats in May 1942, between U.S. and Italy; asst. to the liaison officer, Dept. of State with War and Navy Depts., Mar. 1943; also duty with Joint Intelligence Staff, Sept. 1943; chief liaison office, Dept. of State with War and Navy Depts., June 1, 1944; first sec. Am. embassy, London and consul gen. for duty S.H.A.E.F., Aug. 1944; mem. staff polit. advisor, U.S. Group, Control Council for Germany, June 18, 1945, hdqrs., Berlin, later office polit. affairs, Office Mil. Govt., U.S.-Berlin, in charge consular affairs; consul general (temp.), Hamburg, Feb. 1946, Stuttgart, March 1946. Mem. bd. trustees Charlotte Hall Mil. Sch. (founded 1774). Served with Md. Naval Militia, 1914-17, Nat. Naval Vols., 1917, U.S. Naval Res. Force, 1918-19, lt. comdr. (at sea World War I, 1917-19). Vice comdr. Dept. of Md., Am. Legion, 1920-22. Mem. Am. Foreign Service Assn., Am. Bar Assn., Md. Hist. Soc., Phi Gamma Delta, Phi Beta Kappa, Am. Legion, Mil. Order of the World Wars. Clubs: Maryland, Bachelors (Baltimore): Army and Navy, Chevy Chase (Washington, D.C.). Home: "Brambly," Maddox P.O., St. Mary's County, Md.; 2905 32d St. N.W., Washington 8, D.C. Address: Dept. of State, Washington, D.C. Died July 12, 1948.

HODGES, George Hartshorn, ex-governor; b. Orion, Wis., Feb. 6, 1866; s. William W. and Lydia Ann (Hartshorn) H.; moved with parents to Kan., 1869; ed. pub. schs., Olathe, Kan.; m. Ora May Murray, Mar. 1899; children—Georgia Ferree, Murray Hartshorn. Began as lumber yard salesman and bookkeeper, Olathe, 1886; traveling salesman 2 yrs., and studied commercial law; now sr. mem. Hodges Bros., owning 12 lumber yds. and 12 hardware stores, also owners of Johnson County (Kan.) Democrat; pres. Olathe Building and Loan Co.; dir. of numerous banks; mem. Kan. Senate 2 terms, 1904-12; author of Hodges hard surface road law, and the pioneer of the benefit plan of road building; gov. of Kan., 1913-15. As gov. inaugurated movement to collect food and supplies for the Belgians, the state of Kan. and its citizens, donating 50,000 barrels of flour, meal and other food supplies, which were delivered to the Belgians within 90 days after the call was issued; civilian on staff of Maj. Gen. Wood, World War I. Decorated by King Albert with the Golden Cross, Officer of the Crown. Advocated constl. amendment abolishing the two branches of the state legislature and substituting a single body of 12 men to pass and repeal laws for the state; an authority on commission form of govt. Formerly adj. 1st Regt., Kan. N.G.; served as maj. Am. Red Cross, at Ft. Funston and Ft. Riley, World War. Lecturer and writer. Mem. Christian (Disciples) Ch. Mason (33°). Home: Olathe, Kan. Died Oct. 7, 1947.

HODGES, LeRoy, economist; b. Tarboro, N.C., July 12, 1888; s. Eli Blucher and Rosa Hammond (Warrington) H.; Washington and Lee U., 1906-10, D.C.Sc., 1929; m. Almeria Orr Hill, Jan. 18, 1911; children—LeRoy, Rosa Batte, Almeria Hill (dec.). Lieut. col., Ord. Dept., Nat. Guard U.S. (Va.). Mem. Pi Kappa Alpha, Omicron Delta Kappa, Phi Beta Kappa (Washington and Lee). Decorated Officer Order White Lion (Czechoslovakia); Officer, Order of the Crown (Italy); Distinguished Service Medal, The Va. Musketeers (U.S.). Democrat. Episcopalian. Clubs: Commonwealth, Country Club of Virginia (Richmond); Petersburg (Virginia) Country; Farmington Country (Charlottesville); Nat. Press (Washington). Author: Agricultural Credit Systems Abroad, 1913; Petersburg, Virginia—Economic and Municipal, 1917; Post-War Ordnance, 1923; also "Ordnance Notes," The Va. Guardsman, 1931-39; and numerous pamphlets and articles. Editor: The South's Physical Recovery, 1911; Agricultural Coöperation and Rural Credit in Europe, 1913. Home: 3505 Seminary Av., Richmond, Va. Died Dec. 18, 1944.

HODGES, Walter Edward, railway official; b. Fall River, Mass., July 23, 1860; s. Wm. and Harriot L. (Horton) H.; grad. Rogers High Sch., Newport, R.I., 1879; m. Caroline E. Taylor, Jan. 21, 1885; children—Robt. Taylor, Elizabeth (dec.). Began as clk. gen. supt's office, C.,B.&Q.R.R., 1881, chief clerk to trainmaster, Chicago, 1883-86, clerk, general freight agent, 1886-88, asst. to general mgr., 1888-89; traffic mgr., Fraser & Chalmers, Chicago, 1889-95; pvt. sec. to pres. A.,T.&S.F. Ry., 1896-97, gen. purchasing agt., 1897-1909, v.p. A.,T.&S.F. Ry. System since 1909, in charge dept. of purchases and stores, timber and fuel properties, 1909-18, in charge certain properties in Calif. since 1918. Republican. Unitarian. Clubs: Chicago Athletic; Santa Barbara, Montecito Country, La Cumbre Golf (Santa Barbara). Home: 2112 Santa Barbara St., Santa Barbara, Calif. Office: Korckhoff Bldg., Los Angeles. Died June 16, 1942.

HODGES, William Thomas, coll. dean; b. Chatham, Va., Nov. 19, 1881; s. Isham Thomas and Marianne (Motley) H.; A.B., Coll. of William and Mary, 1902; A.M., Columbia, 1916; Ed.D., Harvard, 1925; m. Euphemia Lee Walton, 1910 (died 1924); children—William Walton, John, Julia Lee; m. 2d, Annie Marion Powell, 1927. Teacher and prin. high schs., Va. and N.C., 1903-09; supt. schs., Arlington County, Va., 1909-16; Va. State supervisor rural schs., 1916-20; prof. edn., Coll. of William and Mary, 1920-28, dir. of extension, 1921-24 and 1928-32, dean of men, 1928-32; prof. of philosophy and psychology and dean of Norfolk Div., same coll., 1933-42; now retired. Exec. officer Hampton Roads Regional Defense Council, 1941-42. Mem. American Assn. Univ. Profs., Phi Beta Kappa, Theta Delta Chi, Phi Delta Kappa. Democrat. Episcopalian. Wrote bulletin, Important Features in Rural School Development, 1914. Home: Stuart Hall, Staunton, Va. Died Apr. 23, 1947; buried in Cedar Hill Cemetery, Williamsburg, Va.

HODGKINSON, Francis, mech. engr., inventor; b. London, Eng., June 16, 1867; s. Francis Otter and Margaret H.; ed. Royal Naval Sch., New Cross, London; night courses, Durham U.; m. Edith Marion Kate Piercy, June 1, 1897; children—Francis Piercy, George Arthur, William Sampson. Apprentice Clayton & Shuttleworth, agrl. engrs., 1882-85; with C. A. Parsons Co., advancing to supt. field work, 1885-90; engr. Chilean Navy, 1890-92, later identified with telephone and elec. light engring. in Peru; with C. A. Parsons & Co., 1894-96; with Westinghouse Electric & Mfg. Co. since 1896, cons. mech. engr. of its South Phila. and East Pittsburgh works on retirement in 1936; appointed hon. prof. mech. engring., Columbia U. Widely known as designer and builder of steam turbines. Awarded Elliott Cresson gold medal, Franklin Inst., 1925; Holley gold medal, Am. Soc. Mech. Engrs., 1938; awarded 101 patents, principally in field of steam turbines. Mem. Am. Soc. Mech. Engrs., Am. Inst. E.E., Engrs. Soc. of Western Pa., Inst. of Mech. Engrs. of Great Britain. Clubs: Engineers' (New York). Contbr. many articles on tech. subjects. Home: 138 E. 36th St., New York, N.Y.* Died Nov. 4, 1949.

HODGSON, Albert James (hŏd'sŭn), surgeon; b. Waukesha, Wis., Nov. 9, 1858; s. John and Hannah (Seller) H.; student Carroll Coll., Waukesha, 1872-77; M.D., Rush Medical Coll., Chicago, 1886 Sc.D., Carroll Coll., 1916; m. 2d, Flora Christensen, Nov. 3, 1925. In gen. practice in Waukesha, 1886-92; specialized in treatment of diabetes and Bright's disease since 1892 (recognized as an authority on the subjects); founder Still Rock Hosp. for treatment of diabetes mellitus and Bright's disease, 1909, Still Rock Spa, 1912, inc. as Waukesha Spa Co., of which is ex-pres. Mem. Am., Wis. State and Waukesha County med. socs. Republican. Has read various papers on treatment of kidney diseases before A.M.A. and Can. Med. Assn. Home: Jupiter, Fla.
Died Oct. 5, 1943.

HODOUS, Lewis (hō'dŭs), educator; b. Bohemia, Dec. 31, 1872; s. John and Mary (Barres) H.; brought to U.S., 1882; A.B., Western Reserve U., 1897, D.D., 1919; B.D., Hartford Theol. Sem., 1900; studied U. of Halle, 1900, U. of Leyden, 1909; m. Anna Jelinek, Oct. 7, 1901. Ordained Congl. ministry, 1901; missionary, A.B.C.F.M., Foochow, China, 1901-17; pres. Foochow Theol. Sem., 1902-12; assisted in organizing Foochow Union Theol. Sch., 1911, pres. 1914-17; head of Chinese Dept. Kennedy Sch. of Missions, Hartford Sem. Foundation, 1917-45; lecturer, Union Theol. Sem., 1922; Columbia Univ., 1923-1928; translator for govt., World War I and II; prof. emeritus in Chinese culture since 1945; prof. history and philosophy of religion, Hartford Theological Seminary, 1928-41. Member bd. trustees Fukien Christian U., Foochow, China. Mem. N. China br. Royal Asiatic Soc. (life), Phi Beta Kappa. Author: Buddhism and Buddhists in China, 1924; Folkways in China, 1929; Editor of Careers for Students of Chinese Language and Civilization, 1933; Co-author (with W. E. Soothill) A Dictionary of Chinese Buddhist Terms, 1937. Home: Mount Hermon, Mass. Died Aug. 9, 1949.

HODSON, William, commr. pub. welfare; b. Minneapolis, Minn., Apr. 25, 1891; s. William and Anna (Redding) H.; A.B., U. of Minn., 1913; LL.B., Harvard, 1916; m. Gertrude Prindle, May 4, 1918; children—Judith, William, Jeremy. Admitted to Minn. bar, 1916; chief counsel Legal Aid Bur., Minneapolis, 1916; exec. sec. Child Welfare Com. State of Minn., 1917; dir. Children's Bur. of Minn., State Bd. of Control, 1918; dir. div. child welfare legislation, Russell Sage Foundation, 1922, dir. dept. social legislation, 1924; exec. dir. Welfare Council of N.Y. City, 1925; commr. of pub. welfare City of N.Y. since 1934. Former chairman and executive director N.Y. City Emergency Relief Bureau; former mem. N.Y. State Temp. Emergency Relief Adminstrn. President American Public Welfare Association, 1940-41; member Am. Assn. of Social Workers (ex-president), Nat. Conf. of Social Work (ex-pres.), Phi Beta Kappa, Beta Theta Pi. Episcopalian. Clubs: Harvard, City and Church (New York). Home: 246th St. and Palisade Av., Riverdale. Address: 902 Broadway, New York, N.Y. Died Jan. 14, 1943.

HOEHLING, Adolph August (hā'lĭng), judge; b. Phila., Pa., Nov. 3, 1868; s. Rear Adm. Adolph August (U.S. Navy) and Annie (Tilghman) H.; student Rensselaer Poly. Inst. and Lehigh U.; LL.B., Columbian (now George Washington) U., 1889, LL.M., 1890; m. Louise G. Carrington, June 9, 1906; children—Louise Carrington, Adolph August. Admitted to D.C. bar, 1890, and practiced at Washington; mem. firm Hoehling, Peele & Ogilby, 1913-21; asso. justice Supreme Court of D.C., 1921-27; resigned to resume pvt. practice; mem. firm Hoehling & Ogilby; v.p., Nat. Metropolitan Bank, Washington. Mem. Bar Assn. D.C. (pres. 1916), Lawyers' Club (pres. 1902-04), Psi Upsilon, Phi Delta Phi.* Republican. Episcopalian. Home: 5 Newlands St., Chevy Chase, Md. Office: 613 15th St. N.W., Washington. Died Feb. 17, 1941; buried in Arlington National Cemetery.

HOEY, James J., gen. ins.; b. N.Y. City, Dec. 15, 1877; s. John F. and Catherine (Mullen) H.; ed. pub. schs., N.Y. City; unmarried. In ins. business, N.Y City, since 1904; v.p. Continental Fire Ins. Co. Fidelity Phenix Fire Ins. Co. and Am. Eagle Fire Ins. Co., 1915-22; mem. firm Hoey & Ellison, gen. insurance agts., since 1922 (now Hoey, Ellison & Frost, Inc.); pres. Hoey & Ellison Life Agency, Inc., 99 William St. Corp.; dir. Am. Eagle Fire Insurance Co., City of New York Insurance Co. Member N.Y. State Assembly, 1907-11; dep. state supt. ins., N.Y., 1911-15; collector of internal revenue, 2d Dist. N.Y.; chmn. bd. dirs. N.Y. Bd. of Fire Underwriters. Catholic. Clubs: Catholic, Manhattan, New York Athletic, Chamber of Commerce, Merchants Association. Home: 135 Central Park W. Office: 99 William St., New York, N.Y. Died Nov. 10, 1941.

HOFFENSTEIN, Samuel (Goodman), writer; b. Lithuania, Oct. 8, 1890; s. Josiah Mayer and Taube Gita (Kahn) H.; Ph.B., Lafayette Coll., Easton, Pa., 1911; m. Edith M. Morgan, May 11, 1927. Reporter New York Sun, 1912, spl. writer, 1913, dramatic critic, 1914-15; press agt. for Al Woods, Theatrical producer, 1916-27; columnist, "The Dome," New York Tribune, 1923-25; now, writing for the screen. Author: Life Sings a Song, 1916; Poems in Praise of Practically Nothing, 1928; Year In, You're Out, 1930. Home: Los Angeles, Calif., and New York, N.Y. Address: care Leland Heyward, Inc., 654 Madison Av., New York, N.Y.; and 9460 Wilshire Blvd., Beverly Hills, Calif. Died Oct. 1947.

HOFFMAN, Arthur G(ilman), industrialist; v.p. Great Atlantic & Pacific Tea Co.; v.p. Second Nat. Bank of Orange, N.J.; dir. Chase Nat. Bank of New York. Home: 93 Ridge St., Orange. N.J. Office: 420 Lexington Av., New York, N.Y. Died Feb. 16, 1947.

HOFFMAN, Carl, editor; b. San Jose, Calif., Sept. 29, 1882; s. Carl and Regula (Baumgartner) H.; student U. of Calif., 1903-06; unmarried. Reporter San Francisco Bulletin, 1901; co-founder, 1906, Berkeley Independent (sold to E. W. Scripps, 1908); telegraph editor San Francisco Bulletin, 1908-10, city editor, 1910-18; asst. editor San Francisco Call, 1918-22; editor Oakland Post Enquirer, 1922-40, pub., 1938-39; chief editoriol writer, Oakland Tribune since 1942. Mem. Calif. Hist. Soc., Delta Upsilon. Republican. Methodist. Clubs: Athenian-Nile (Oakland); Commonwealth of California. Home: 56 Lake View Av., Piedmont, Calif. Died Nov. 14, 1946.

HOFFMAN, Frederick Ludwig, statistician; b. Varel, N. Germany, May 2, 1865; s. Augustus Franciscus and Antoinette (von Laar) H.; common school and private education in Germany; LL.D., Tulane U., 1911; m. Ella G. Hay; children—Ella, Frances, Armstrong, Virginia, Gilbert Hay, Barbara, Victoria. Cons. statistician of Prudential Ins. Co. of America, 1894-1934; cons. statistician Biochemical Research Foundation of Franklin Institute, Phila., to 1938; retired. Ex-pres. Am. Statis. Assn.; fellow A.A.A.S., Royal Statis. Soc., Royal Anthropol. Inst.; hon. corr. mem. Actuarial Soc. Switzerland; asso. fellow A.M.A.; asso. mem. Am. Acad. Medicine; hon. mem. Nat. Inst. Homœopathy, German Cancer Research Soc.; charter mem. Nat. Tuberculosis Assn.; dir. Am. Public Health Assn., Am. Society Control of Cancer; mem. Nat. Safety Council, Safety Inst. of America, Am. League to Abolish Capital Punishment (v.p.); hon. pres. Nat. Malaria Soc., 1944; dir. Nat. Foundation for Care of Advanced Cancer Patients, 1944. Awarded Clement Cleveland medal by Am. Soc. for Control of Cancer, 1943. Dir. Health Survey of the Printing Trades; dir. San Francisco Cancer Survey; mem. London Cancer Conf., 1928. Author of numerous brochures, books, etc., some of which are The Race Traits and Tendencies of the American Negro, 1896; History of the Prudential Ins. Co. of America, 1900; Insurance Science and Economics, 1911; Facts and Fallacies of Compulsory Health Insurance, 1917; Annual Record of Homicide and Suicide (Spectator, N.Y.), 1910-23; Cancer and Civilization, Belgian Nat. Cancer Congress, 1923; also in 1926, Cancer in Canada; Cancer in Native Races; The Homicide Problem; Windstorm and Tornado Insurance; and in 1927, Cancer and Overnutrition; Industrial Insurance; fourth to seventh reports on San Francisco Cancer Survey, 1928-31; Suicide Problem, 1928; Earthquake, Hazards and Insurance, 1928; Problems of Longevity, 1929; also repts. and papers; Malaria in Mississippi and Adjacent States, 1931; 9th and final San Francisco Cancer Rept., 1934; Final Results of the San Francisco Cancer Survey, 1932; Malaria in India and Ceylon, 1933; Cancer in British Malaya and the Philippine Islands, 1933; Cancer in Spain, 1933; Cancer in Iceland, Cancer and Diet, 1937; Deaths from Lead Poisoning, 1943 and Earlier Years. Was v.p. Congress of Royal Inst. of Pub. Health, Ghent, Belgium; mem. 8th Internat. Actuarial Congress, London; mem. 1st Internat. Civil Aeronautics Congress, Washington, D.C., 1928; speaker on cancer before Pan Pacific Surg. Conf., Honolulu, H.T. Home: 1978 Sunset Blvd., San Diego, Calif.
Died Feb. 24, 1946.

HOFFMAN, Horace Addison, university dean; born nr. Auburn, Ind., July 30, 1855; A.B., Ind. U., 1881; A.M., Harvard, 1884; studied in Europe, 1890; m. Anna Bowman, June 13, 1888. Instr. Greek and Latin, 1881-83, prof. Greek, since 1885, dean dept. Liberal Arts, 1894-1908, dean coll. Liberal Arts since 1908, Ind. U. Wrote (with David Starr Jordan): A Catalogue of the Fishes of Greece, with notes on the names now in use and those employed by classical authors, Proc. Acad. Natural Sciences, Phila., Aug. 1892. Author: Everyday Greek, 1919. Address: Bloomington, Ind. Deceased.

HOGAN, Aloysius Gonzaga Joseph (hō'găn), univ. dean; b. Philadelphia, Pa., Aug. 5, 1891; s. John and Anna Mary (Good) H.; prep. edn., Gesu Parochial Sch. and St. Joseph's Prep. Sch., Philadelphia; A.B., St. Joseph's Coll., Philadelphia, 1908; studied Jesuit House of Classical Studies, Poughkeepsie, N.Y., 1908-12, Woodstock (Md.) Coll., 1912-15, 1920-24, A.M., 1915; S.T.D., Gregorian U., Rome, 1924; Ph.D., Cambridge U., England, 1927. Joined Soc. of Jesus (Jesuits), 1908; ordained priest R.C. Ch., 1923; teacher of classics, Boston Coll., 1915-20; dean of house of Classical Studies, Poughkeepsie, N.Y., 1927-30; dean of Jesuit House of Classical Studies, Wernersville, Pa., 1930; pres. Fordham U., 1930-36; dean Grad. Sch. Georgetown U. since June 1936. Mem. N.E.A., Assn. Am. Colls., Am. Classical League, The Classical Assn., Mediæval Acad. America, Middle States Assn., Nat. Cath. Ednl. Assn. Clubs: Fordham University; Cambridge (Eng.) Union. Research in mediæval mystery plays; writer on ednl. and lit. subjects. Address: Georgetown U., Washington, D.C.
Died Dec. 19, 1943.

HOGAN, Dana, oil producer; b. Minneapolis, Minn., June 28, 1891; s. James M. and Mary (Mangan) H.; A.B., U. of Wis., 1912; m. Ida G. Hollister, June 26, 1935. Oilwell worker, geol. engr., supt. and asst. purchasing agent for various subsidiaries of Calif. Petroleum Corp., 1912-17; filled positions as geologist, scout, land agent, mgr. lands and exploration, and vice pres. of various companies controlled by E. L. Doheny, 1919-32; formed Hogan Petroleum Co., 1933, and since has served as pres. Served with U.S. Navy, 1917-19; deck and engr. officer at sea, 1917-18; aviation officer and aviator, 1918-19. Pres. San Joaquin Valley Oil Producers Assn.; dir. Am. Petroleum Inst., Independent Petroleum Assn. America. Mem. Am. Assn. Petroleum Geologists, Am. Inst. M.E., Sigma Chi. Clubs: California, University, Los Angeles Country, Bel-Air (Los Angeles); Pacific-Union (San Francisco); Cypress Point (Pebble Beach, Calif). Home: 239 Muirfield Rd., Los Angeles 4. Office: 714 W. Olympic Blvd., Los Angeles 15, Calif. Died Dec. 14, 1945.

HOGAN, Frank J., lawyer; b. Brooklyn, N.Y. Jan. 12, 1877; s. Maurice and Mary E. (McSweeney) H.; ed. pub. schs.; LL.B., Georgetown U., 1902; hon. LL.D., Georgetown U., 1925, Litt.D., 1939; hon. D.C.L., U. Southern Calif., 1939; hon. LL.D., Manhattan Coll., 1939; hon. LL.D., Laval U., Quebec, Can., 1939; m. Mary Cecil Adair, Feb. 14, 1899; 1 dau., Dorothy (Mrs. John W. Guider). Sec. to chief quartermaster, U.S. Army, Cuba, 1898-99; to quartermaster general, Washington, D.C., 1899-1903; to chief of staff of The Army, 1904; began practice of law at Washington, D.C., 1902. Lecturer on law of wills, evidence and partnership, Sch. of Law, Georgetown U., 1912-19. Mem. Prog. Nat. Com., 1912-16; del. Rep. Nat. Conv., 1916, 20. Pres. D.C. Bar Assn., 1932-33, Washington Lawyers Club, 1930-31; pres. Am. Bar Assn., 1938-39, mem. exec. com. and bd. of govs., 1933-36, mem. house of delegates, 1937-39; pres. Georgetown Alumni Assn., 1925-39; v.p. Shakespeare Assn. of America. Catholic. Clubs: Metropolitan, Nat. Press, Blue Ridge Rod and Gun (Washington); California, Zamorama (Los Angeles); Bohemian (San Francisco); Grolier (New York). Book collector. Home: 2320 Massachusetts Av. N.W. Office: Colorado Bldg., Washington, D.C. Died May 15, 1944.

HOGATE, Kenneth Craven (hō'găt), pres. The Wall Street Jour.; b. Danville, Ind., July 27, 1897; s. Julian DePew and Etta (Craven) H.; A.B., DePauw University, 1918; LL.D., Atlanta (Georgia) Law School, 1939; L.H.D., DePauw University, 1942; m. Anna Ruth Shields, August 5, 1918; children—Sarah Shields (Mrs. Theodore Spaulding Bacon, Jr.), Barbara Ann (Mrs. Allan Wheeler Ferrin), Anne Shields. Reporter Cleveland and Detroit newspapers, 1917-21; became manager Detroit office Wall Street Jour., 1921; mng. editor Wall Street Jour., 1923, v.p., 1926, v.p. and gen. mgr., 1928, pres. since 1933; pres. The Financial Press Cos. of America, Dow, Jones & Co., Barron's Pub. Co., Phila. News Bureau. Trustee DePauw U. (Greencastle, Ind.). Mem. com. on orgn. N.Y. Stock Exchange, 1937. Mem. Scarsdale Village Board, 1938-41, mayor, 1941-43. Mem. Am. Soc. of Newspaper Editors, Chamber of Commerce State of N.Y., Sigma Delta Chi (ex-pres.), Phi Beta Kappa, Sigma Chi. Republican. Methodist. Clubs: Columbia (Indianapolis); National Press (Washington); Bankers, Downtown Athletic, Bond (New York). Home: Glen Arden Farm, Pawling, N.Y. Office: 44 Broad St., New York. Died Feb. 11, 1947; buried in churchyard of St. James-the-Less, Scarsdale, N.Y.

HOHLFELD, Alexander Rudolf, univ. prof.; b. Dresden, Germany, Dec. 29, 1865; s. Karl Gottlieb and Helene (Libbert) H.; ed. Annen Real-Gymnasium, Dresden; Ph.D., Univ. of Leipzig, Ger., 1888; Litt.D., Middlebury (Vt.) College, 1937; teacher in Eng. 1888; student at Paris, 1889; m. Helen Voss, June 24, 1890; children—Ralph Alfred (dec.), Helen Minnie, Karl Voss (dec.), Rudolph L. (dec.). Instr. French, Vanderbilt U., 1889-90, adj. prof. Romance langs., 1890-92, prof. Germanic langs., 1892-1901, dean Acad. Dept., 1900-01; prof. German, U. of Wis., 1901-36, emeritus since 1936. Mem. Modern Lang. Assn. Am. (chmn. central div., 1904, pres. 1913), Am. Assn. Teachers of German (pres. 1933), Goethe-Gesellschaft in Weimar, Goethe-Verein in Vienna; hon. senator Deutsche Akademie (München, Germany). Author: Die altenglischen Misterienspiele, 1888. Editor of two stories by Marie von Ebner-Eschenbach, 1898. Editor-in-chief of Deutsches Liederbuch für amerikanische Studenten, 1906; editor Neues deutsches Liederbuch, 1931, and of The Goethe Centenary at the University of Wisconsin, 1932. Co-author: Wortindex zu Goethe's Faust, 1940. Contbr. to Am. and German periodicals. Home: 1911 Vilas Av., Madison, Wis. Deceased.

HOKE, Kremer J., educator; b. Emmitsburg, Md. Nov. 19, 1878; s. Jacob and Mary Elizabeth (Keilholtz) H.; B.A., Mt. St. Mary's Coll., Emmitsburg, 1904; M.A., Columbia U., 1911, Ph.D., 1915; D.C.L., Mount St. Mary's Coll., 1938; m. Annie Lee Bland, June 19, 1911; children—George Bland, Robert Lee. Elementary sch. prin. Richmond, Va., 1907-10; asst. supt. schools, Richmond, 1910-16; supt. schs., Duluth, Minn., 1910-20; dean of coll. and School of Edn., dir. summer session, Coll. of William and Mary, 1920-38; dean summer semester and dept. of edn., since 1938. Member Moseley Education Commn. to England, 1908; chairman Committee on Work Conferences. Commission on Curricular Problems Schs., 1936-43; mem. adv. com. on teaching in school and college, State Bd. of Edn., 1936-40; mem. adv. com. Va. State Chamber of Commerce since 1942. Mem. Nat. Soc. Coll. Teachers, Nat. Ednl. Research Assn., N.E.A., Va. State Teachers' Assn., Soc. of Friends of Lafayette, Phi Delta Kappa, Phi Beta Kappa. Democrat. Episcopalian. Mason. Author: Placement of Children in the Elementary Grades (U.S. bull.), 1915; (with Guy M. Wilson) How to Measure, 1920, 27. Home: Williamsburg, Va.
Died Feb. 6, 1944.

HOKE, Michael, orthopædic surgeon; b. Lincolnton, N.C., June 28, 1874; s. Robert Frederick and Lydia (Van Wyck) H.; M.D., U. of Va., 1895; B.Engring., U. of N.C., 1893, LL.D., 1931; m. Laurie Hendree Harrison, Apr. 20, 1904; children—Laura Hendree, Lydia Van Wyck. Practiced at Atlanta since 1897; cons. Scottish Rite Hosp. for Crippled Children; orthopædic surgeon, Piedmont Hosp. Mem. A.M.A., Med. Assn. of Ga., Am. Orthopædic Assn. Democrat. Protestant. Address: Beaufort, S.C. Died Sep. 24, 1944.

HOKE, Robert Frederick, soldier, ry. official; b. Lincolnton, N.C., May 27, 1837; s. Michael and Frances (Burton) H. Maj., 1st N.C. inf., early in 1861; later maj., lt.-col., and col., 33d N.C. inf.; col., 21st N.C.; apptd. brig.-gen., C.S.A., Jan. 17, 1863; maj-gen., Apr. 20, 1864. His brigade served in Army of Northern Va., in Gen. Early's Div.; comd. div. at battle of Cold Harbor; comdr. dist. of N.C., 1865; surrendered with Johnston at Durham Sta., N.C., Apr. 26, 1865. Engaged in business in N.C., and became pres. Seaboard Air Line system. Address: Raleigh, N.C. Died July 3, 1912.

HOLABIRD, John Augur (hŏl'ā-bûrd), architect; b. Evanston, Ill., May 4, 1886; s. William and Maria (Augur) H.; grad. Hill Sch., Pottstown, Pa., 1903, U.S. Mil. Acad., 1907, Engrs. Sch., Washington Bks., 1909, École des Beaux Arts, Paris, 1913; m. Dorothy Hackett, May 12, 1917; children—John Augur, Christopher. Mem. firm Holabird & Root; firm designed Palmolive, Daily News and Board of Trade bldgs., Chicago, Ill., also Ramsey County Court House, St. Paul, Minnesota, Lafayette Building, Statler Hotel, Washington, D.C. Commd. 2d lt. Engrs., U.S. Army, 1907; capt. Ill. Nat. Guard, 1914-17; maj., later lt. col. F.A., U.S. Army, Aug. 1918-Mar. 1919. Awarded D.S.M. Trustee Art Institute, John Crerar Library, Newberry Library, Morton Arboretum. Fellow Am. Inst. Architects. Republican. Episcopalian. Mason (32°). Clubs: University, Commercial, Chicago Saddle and Cycle, Glen View Golf, Tavern. Home: 2236 Lincoln Park W. Office: 333 N. Michigan Av., Chicago, Ill. Died May 4, 1945.

HOLADAY, William P., congressman; b. Ridgefarm, Ill., Dec. 14, 1882; s. George M. and Martha (Smith) H.; Penn. Coll., Oskaloosa, Ia.; student U. of Mo., 1902-03, U. of Ill., 1903-05; m. Blanche Gorman, Sept. 12, 1906; children—Helen, William. Began practice at Danville, Ill., 1905; now mem. Hall & Holaday; asst. state's atty. Vermilion County, Ill., 1905-07; mem. Ill. Ho. of Rep., 1909-23; mem. 68th to 72d Congresses (1923-33), 18th Ill. Dist. Republican. Mem. Soc. of Friends. Home: Georgetown, Ill. Died Jan. 29, 1946.

HOLCOMB, Lynn Howe, newspaperman and editor; b. Youngstown, O., Feb. 25, 1903; s. Dello Adonius and Maude (Bostwick) H.; A.B., Ohio State U., 1927; m. Cathryn Wentsler, June 29, 1935; children—Barbara, Barry. Reporter and desk man, Youngstown (O.) Telegram, and Oklahoma City (Okla.) News, 1927-30; with Akron (O.) Beacon Journal since 1930, managing editor since Mar. 1945. Member executive committee Summit County (Ohio) United Community Chest, Ohio, Welfare Council, Aviation Indsl. and Nat. Affairs Coms. of Akron C. of C., Army Advisory Com., Naval Res. Advisory Council; trustee Summit County Tuberculosis Assn.; member board of directors Akron Safety Council. Mem. bd. trustees Cancer Control Commission, American Society Newspaper Editors, Associated Press Managing Editors Assn., Chi Phi. Elk. Clubs: Akron City, Fairlawn Country (Akron, O.). Home: 2131 Stabler Rd. Office: Akron Beacon Journal, Akron 8, O. Died Nov. 12, 1948.

HOLDEN, Charles Revell, lawyer, banker; b. Chicago, Ill., Jan. 9, 1871; s. William Hiram and Sarah J. (Revell) H.; desc. of one of original proprs. of Groton, Mass., from Sussex, Eng., 1630; A.B. Yale, 1892; student Northwestern U. Law Sch.; m. Mertie Towne, Dec. 1893; m. 2d, Cora Eaton, Aug. 12, 1901; 1 son, William H. T. Student with law firm of Moran, Kraus & Mayer; admitted to bar, 1893; began as clk. Moran, Kraus & Mayer, admitted as jr. partner, 1899; withdrew, 1900, with Adolf Kraus, to form firm of Kraus & Holden, which changed, 1901, on admission of Samuel Alschuler, to Kraus, Alschuler & Holden; entered Union Trust Co., 1914, as v.p. and counsel; later v.p. First Nat. Bank until 1936; now engaged in scientific research in Calif. Mem. Ill. State and Chicago bar assns. Trustee U. of Chicago (hon.). Ex-pres. Chicago Crime Commission; mem. sr. council Chicago Assn. Com. Republican. Home: 2039 Midlothian Dr., Altadena, Calif. Deceased.

HOLDEN, Edwin Chapin, mining engr.; b. New York, Nov. 8, 1872; s. Albert James and Henrietta V. (Chambers) H.; B.S., Coll. City of New York, 1893; E.M., Sch. of Mines (Columbia), 1896; m. Grace E. Morgenroth, Sept. 19, 1908; children—Florence, Edwin C. Mining engr., supt. and mgr. various properties in British Columbia and U.S., 1897-1903; cons. mining engr., New York, 1903-08, with work in U.S., Can., Mex. and W.I.; prof. mining and metallurgy, U. of Wis., 1908-16; gen. mgr. Davison Sulphur & Phosphate Co., 1916-19; cons. engr., Davison Chem. Co. and Silica Gel Corp., 1919-32; developing mines in British Columbia, 1930-34, and in Colo. since 1934. Mem. Am. Inst. Mining and Metall. Engrs., Mining and Metall. Soc. America, Phi Gamma Delta, Sigma Xi. Unitarian. Co-author Mining Handbook. Home: 202 E. Chase St., Baltimore, Md. Deceased.

HOLDEN, Frederick Clark, obstetrician, gynecologist; b. Tremont, Me., Nov. 4, 1868; s. Simeon A. and Hannah A. (Verrill) H.; M.D., New York U., 1892, D.P.H., 1941; m. Rachel Maud Wilson, Nov. 17, 1897; 1 son—W. Wilson. Intern St. Mary's Hosp., Brooklyn, N.Y., 1892-93; asst. attending surgeon, same, 1895-98; asst. obstetrician and gynecologist, Williamsburg Hosp., 1902-06; same, Methodist Hosp., 1906-08; attdg. obstetrician, same hosp., 1908-14; asst. attdg. obstetrician and gynecologist, L.I. Hosp., 1908-14; chief obstetrician and gynecologist, Greenpoint Hosp., 1914-19; asst. prof. gynecology and obstetrics, L.I. Coll. Hosp., 1914-19; dir. dept. gynecology, Bellevue Hosp., 1919-34; prof. obstetrics and gynecology N.Y. Univ. Med. Coll., 1919-32, now prof. emeritus; dir. of gynecology Jersey City Medical Centre since 1940; attending obstetrician and gynecologist, French Hospital; consulting gynecologist, Harlem Hosp., Broad St. Hosp. (N.Y. City); consulting obstetrician, Bellevue Hosp., Methodist Hosp. (Brooklyn), Margaret Hague Memorial Hosp. (Jersey City). Fellow Am. Coll. Surgeons; mem. Am. Gynecol. Soc. (past pres.), A.M.A., Am. Soc. for Control of Cancer, N.Y. Acad. Medicine, N.Y. Obstet. Soc. (past pres.), Brooklyn Gynecol. Soc., Am. Bd. Obstetrics and Gynecology (diplomate); Corr. mem. King's County Med. Sch. (past pres.). Mem. S.R., Phi Gamma Delta, Alpha Kappa Kappa, Alpha Omega Alpha. Presbyterian. Clubs: Oakland Golf, University. Home: 116 E. 53d St. Office: 59 E. 54th St., New York, N.Y. Died Aug. 27, 1944.

HOLDEN, Gerry Rounds, surgeon; b. Concord, N.H., Sept. 12, 1874; s. Benjamin F. and Sarah E. (Rounds) H.; B.A., Yale, 1897; M.D., Johns Hopkins, 1901; spl. student, Berlin, 1901; m. Anne Ridgway Milliken, Nov 8, 1905; children—Katharine, Gerry R. House surgeon, Roosevelt Hosp., New York, 1903; resident gynecologist, Johns Hopkins Hosp., Baltimore, 1905; attending gynecologist to St. Luke's Hosp., Jacksonville, Fla., since 1906, to Duval County Hosp. since 1922; cons. surgeon, Flagler Hosp., St. Augustine, Fla., since 1935. Specialist in gynecology. Presbyterian. Fellow Am. Coll. Surgeons; member A.M.A., Fla. State Med. Assn. (past pres.), Duval County Med. Soc., Southern Med. Assn., Southeastern Surg. Congress (past pres.), Southern Surg. Assn., South Atlantic Assn. of Obstetricians and Gynecologists. Contbr. to med. jours. Home: 1525 Goodwin St. Office: 1022 Park St., Jacksonville, Fla. Died July 21, 1945.

HOLDEN, James Austin, state historian; born Glens Falls, N.Y., Sept. 17, 1861; s. Austin Wells and Elizabeth (Buell) H.; A.B., Williams, 1885; m. Mary Belle Everest, June 12, 1889. State historian of N.Y. State, since May 22, 1911. Trustee Glens Falls, 1893-94; commr. Bd. of Pub. Safety, 1908-15; mem. Bd. of Edn. Town of Queensbury, 13 yrs., pres. 7 yrs.; treas. Glens Falls Home for Aged Women. Democrat. Episcopalian. One of founders, treas., trustee N.Y. State Hist. Assn.; corr. mem. N.Y. Geneal. and Biog. Soc., etc. Mason (32°, K.T.). Elk. Club: University (Albany). Author various monographs on hist. subjects. Home: 382 Morris St. Office: Dept. of Edn., Albany, N.Y. Died 1918.

HOLDEN, Louis Edward, educator; b. Rome, N.Y. April 30, 1863; s. William Rufus and Ann Eliza (Davis) H.; A.B., Beloit Coll., 1888, A.M., 1891; grad. Princeton Theol. Sem., 1891; D.D., Beloit, 1899; LL.D., Lake Forest, 1900, Washington and Jefferson College, 1902, The College of Wooster (Ohio), 1937; m. Harriet Eliza Simmons, Sept. 29, 1890 (died Jan. 29, 1917); m. 2d, Mary L. Murray, Apr. 20, 1918; children—Anne Elizabeth, Louis Edward. Ordained Presbyn ministry, 1891; prof. oratory, Beloit Coll., 1891-99; pres. College of Wooster, Ohio, 1899-1915; asso. sec. Gen. Bd. of Edn., Presbyn. Ch., U.S.A., 1917-20; pres. James Millikin U., Decatur, Ill., 1920-23; v.p. Beloit Coll., 1923-33, resigned. Mem. Phi Beta Kappa. Home: 346 E. Bowman St., Wooster, Ohio. Died Apr. 12, 1943.

HOLDEN, Roy Jay, geologist; b. Sheboygan Falls, Wis., Oct. 21, 1870; s. Harvey J. and Sarah Diana (Danforth) H.; prep. edn., high sch., Sheboygan Falls and Wayland Acad.; B.S., U. of Wis., 1900, Ph.D., 1915; m. Elizabeth Virginia Evans, June 29, 1915; children—Sarah Virginia, Elizabeth Flora, Roy Jay. Teacher country schs., 1892-95, high sch., Sheboygan Falls, 1895-97; science teacher high sch., Beloit, Wis., 1900-02; with Va. Poly. Inst. since 1905, successively asso. in geology and mineralogy, asso. prof. and prof. geology; also consulting commercial geologist. Determined geological structure of the Valley Coal Field of Va., adding 100 sq. miles to the previously known coal-bearing territory; located the first gas well in Virginia. Fellow A.A.A.S., Geological Society America; member American Inst Mining and Metall. Engrs., Am. Assn. of Petroleum Geologists, Soc. of Economic Geologists, Va. Acad. of Science, Phi Kappa Phi, Sigma Xi. Baptist. Author of various articles and reports on geological resources in Wis., Va., etc. Home: Blacksburg, Va.* Died Dec. 16, 1945.

HOLGATE, Thomas Franklin (hōl'gāt), univ. prof.; b. Hastings County, Ont., Apr. 8, 1859; s. Thomas and Eleanor (Wright) H.; A.B., Victoria College, Toronto, 1884, A.M., 1889; fellow Clark University, 1890-93, Ph.D., 1893; LL.D., University of Ill., 1905, Queen's University, 1910, Northwestern University, 1937; married Julia Caroline Sharp, Aug. 12, 1885 (died 1887); m. Georgina Angela Burdette, July 23, 1890 (died 1934); children—Eleanor (Mrs. Owen Lattimore), Robert Burdette, Barbara, Frances Burdette. Prof mathematics, Northwestern U., 1893-1934, retired 1934; dean of coll., 1902-19, acting pres., 1904-06 and 1916-19; visiting prof. U. of Nanking, China, 1921-22. Sec. Internat. Congress of Mathematicians, Rome, 1908. Mem. Chicago Pub. Library Commn., 1909; pres. North Central Assn. Colls. and Secondary Schs., 1917-18; mem. Bd. Edn. for Negroes, M.E. Ch., 1920-24; mem. Bd. of Edn., 1924-44, treas., 1934-38; pres. Chicago Ch. Fed., 1923 25. Mem. Gen. Conf. M.E. Ch., 5 times, 1920-36. Fellow A.A.A.S.; mem. Am. Math. Soc. Clubs: University (Chicago and Evanston). Author: Elementary Geometry, 1901; Projective Pure Geometry, 1930. Translator: Reye's Geometry of Position, 1898. Home: 617 Library Pl., Evanston, Ill. Died April 11, 1945.

HOLLAMAN, Rich William, maps; b. Brooklyn, N.Y., Mar. 11, 1885; s. Rich George and Mary (Matheson) H.; student Yale; m. Janet Buchanan, June 3, 1915; children—Joan, Richard Buchanan, Mary Lou. Admitted to bar; in practice law with Murray, Hollaman & Lockwood, N.Y. City; pres. and treas. Sanborn Map Co., N.Y. City. Republican. Clubs: Lawyers, Yale (N.Y. City); Apawamis, Manursing Beach (Rye, N.Y.). Home: 565 Park Av. Office: 10 Cedar St., New York, N.Y.* Died Mar. 1947.

HOLLAND, Rush LaMotte, lawyer; b. Union County, O., Nov. 18, 1867; s. Gabriel H. and Ruthana L. (Reynolds) H.; student Madison Acad., Mt. Perry, O., and Ohio Wesleyan U., Delaware, O., 1884-88; m. Mrs. Mary L. Fox (née Davis), Aug. 20, 1910. Editor Zanesville (O.) Times Recorder, 1889-93; admitted to Ohio bar, 1895, Colo. bar, 1900, bar United States Supreme Court, 1913; bar of Supreme Court of D.C., 1925; practiced at Zanesville, O., 1895-1900, Colorado Springs, Colo., 1900-21; asst. atty. gen. of U.S. 1921-25; now in practice of law alone. Chmn. Republican State Com. of Colo., 1918-22. Episcopalian. Mem. Am. Bar Assn., Bar Assn. of D.C., Sigma Chi; hon. life mem. Internat. Assn. Chiefs of Police. Mason (32°, Shriner), Past Grand Exalted Ruler B.P.O.E. Clubs: El Paso, Broadmoor (Colorado Springs, Colo.); Washington Gun, Congressional Country, Nat. Press (Washington, D.C.). Home: The Shoreham. Office: Metropolitan Bank Bldg., Washington, D.C. Died Jan. 16, 1944.

HOLLAND, Thomas Leroy, army officer; born Ind., Aug. 10, 1879; LL.B., St. Lawrence U., 1906, LL.M., 1907. Commd. capt. Q.M. Sect., O.R.C., Apr. 1917; called to active duty, May 1917, and advanced to lt. col., 1940; retired June 1942; recalled to active duty July 1942; made brig. gen., Mar. 1943. Address: Quartermaster Corps, Atlanta, Ga. Died Aug 19, 1944.

HOLLIDAY, Robert Cortes, author; b. Indianapolis, Ind., July 18, 1880; s. Wilbur F. and Minerva J. (Kendrick) H.; student Art Students' League, New York, 1899-1902, U. of Kan., 1903-04; m. Estelle Alice Hickman, July 12, 1913 (divorced). Illustrator for mags., 1904-05; book-seller, Charles Scribner's Sons, 1906-11; librarian New York Pub. Library, 1912; reference librarian, New York Sch. of Philanthropy, 1913; asst. lit. editor, New York Tribune, 1913-14; reporter and editor The Fishing Gazette, New York, 1915; with editorial dept. Doubleday, Page & Co., 1916, George H. Doran Co., 1917; asso. editor The Bookman, 1918, editor, 1919-20, contbg. editor, 1921-23; lit. adviser Henry Holt & Co., 1921-23; staff writer for Leslie's Weekly, 1921; feature writer McNaught Syndicate, 1921; publicity work with John Price Jones, 1923; lit. critic for Life, 1923; account exec. Barton, Durstine & Osborn, 1923-24; journalism and advertising, 1925; instr. in writing for publication since 1926. Mem. Sigma Alpha Epsilon. Clubs: Players, Authors. Author: Booth Tarkington, 1918; The Walking-Stick Papers, 1918; Joyce Kilmer, A Memoir, 1918; Peeps at People, 1919; Broome Street Straws, 1919; Men and Books and Cities, 1920; Turns About Town, 1921; A Chat About Samuel Merwin, 1921; In the Neighborhood of Murray Hill, 1922; The Business of Writing (with Alexander Van Rensselaer), 1923; Literary Lanes and Other Byways, 1925; Our Little Brother Writes a Play, 1928; Unmentionables—From Figleaves to Scanties, 1933; An Asylum for the Elite: A History of Gramercy Park; The Player's Book, 1938. Contbr. to ednl. jours. and other publs.; lit. executor of Joyce Kilmer; occasional lecturer. Address: 16 Gramercy Park, New York 3, N.Y. Died Jan. 1947.

HOLLERITH, Herman, inventor; E.M., Columbia, 1879, Ph.D., 1890. Inventor electric tabulating machines used by the U.S. and foreign govts. in the tabulation of census returns. Office: 1054 31st St., Washington. Deceased.

HOLLINGTON, Richard Deming, clergyman; b. Toledo, O., May 21, 1870; s. Ambrose and Sophronia Elizabeth (Deming) H.; A.B., Ohio Wesleyan U., 1892, A.M., 1894, Ph.D., 1896, D.D., 1917; S.T.B., Boston U., 1895; studied U. of Jena, 1896-97; m. Maud Francis Thomas, June 16, 1896; children—Mary Maud (Mrs. Marston Burnham), Ethel Annette (Mrs. George Murch). Ordained to ministry of M.E. Ch., 1895; pastor First Ch., Fostoria, O., 1898-1901, Kenton, 1901-05, St. Paul's Ch., Toledo, O., 1905-11, First Ch., San Diego, Calif., 1911-17, Mathewson St. Ch., Providence, R.I., 1917-27; became professor church administration and preaching Garrett Bibl. Institute, Evanston, Ill., 1927, now prof. emeritus. Honorary life chaplain 121st Regiment, O.V.I.; chaplain British Empire Club. Mem. S.A.R., Loyal Legion, Phi Delta Theta. Republican. Mason (32°). Clubs: Rotary, Kildeer Golb Club. Lecturer on the history of art, and on religious psychology; chaplain and lecturer on tours of the world, 1908, 13. Author: Psychology for Pastors, 1927; Psychology Serving Religion, 1938; Technique of Preaching, 1942. Home: 3720 Wellborn St., San Diego, Calif. Died Aug. 7, 1944.

HOLLIS, Henry French, ex-senator; b. West Concord, N.H., Aug. 30, 1869; s. Abijah and Harriette V. M. (French) H.; A.B. magna cum laude, Harvard, 1892; law student Harvard and under Hon. William L. Foster and Hon. Harry G. Sargent; admitted to bar, 1893; m. Grace Bruerton Fisher, June 14, 1893; children—Henry French, Mrs. Anne Richardson Harris; m. 2d, Anne White Hobbs, Mar. 21, 1922. Dem. candidate for Congress, 1900, for gov., 1902 and 1904; formerly mem. Dem. State Central Com.; U.S. senator, 1913-19. Regent Smithsonian Instn., 1914-19. Apptd. mem. U.S. Liquidation Commn., War Dept., for Europe, Feb. 1919. Officer Legion of Honor (France); awarded Polish and Serbian decorations for war service. Unitarian. Clubs: Metropolitan, Chevy Chase (Washington, D.C.); Cercle Interallié (Paris). Address: 39 Av. George V, Paris, France. Died July 7, 1949.

HOLLMANN, Harry Triebner (hŏl'mȧn), physician; b. Phila., Pa., Dec. 13, 1878; s. Harry and Mary (Thomas) H.; M.D., Medico-Chirurg. Coll., Phila., 1898; m. Amelia Thomas Duncalfe, Apr. 17, 1900; m. 2d, Bonita Clarke, July 12, 1929; children—Bonita L., Pamela Jane, Harry Triebner. Instr. in pathology, Medico-Chirurg. Coll., 1903-05; physician to Dept. of Charities, Phila., 1903-06; asst. eye, ear, nose and throat surgeon, Phila. Gen. Hosp., 1905-06; with U.S. Public Health Service, 1907-18. On duty at Leprosy Investigation Sta., Honolulu, 1907-18; med. supt. Kalihi Hosp.; supt. Queen's Hosp., 1918, 19. Chmn. Territorial Radio Commn. (Hawaii). First lt. Med. Corps, Hawaiian Nat. Guard. Mem. Ky. State Med. Soc., Hawaiian Territorial Med. Soc., W. E. Hughes Med. Soc. Baptist. Mason, Odd Fellow. Club: Commercial. Author of various bulls. setting forth original research on leprosy; specialist in diseases of the skin. Home: 2154 Atherton Road. Office: 1124 Miller St., Honolulu, T.H. Died Dec. 13, 1942.

HOLLZER, Harry Aaron (hŏl'zẽr), judge; b. N.Y. City, Nov. 4, 1880; s. Joseph and Anne (Gray) H.; B.L., U. of Calif., 1902, LL.B., 1903; m. Louise Green, May 5, 1907; children—Alma (Mrs. O. N. Srere), Herbert. Admitted to Calif. bar, 1902, began practice at San Francisco, 1903; apptd. judge Superior Ct. of Calif., May 1924; elected to same office, Nov. 1924, to fill unexpired term, and elected to full term, Nov. 1926; judge U.S. Dist. Court, Calif., since 1931. Apptd. mem. Judicial Council of Calif. for 2-yr. term, 1926-28, reapptd., 1928, 30 (dir. survey and research); chmn. Nat. Conf. of Jud. Councils, 1929-31; trustee Univ. Religious Conf., Los Angeles, Mem. advisory bd. Selective Draft Bd., Los Angeles, 1917-18. Mem. exec. bd. Los Angeles Area United Service Orgns.; chmn. Los Angeles County Army and Navy Com. of Jewish Welfare Board. Mem. Am. Bar Assn. Republican. Hebrew religion. Mason (Shriner), Elk. Clubs: Los Angeles Athletic, Santa Monica Swimming. Home: 450 N. Rossmore Av. Address: Federal Bldg., Los Angeles, Calif. Died, Jan. 1946.

HOLMES, Donald Safford, lawyer; b. Fergus Falls, Minn., Sept. 20, 1888; s. Willis Jerome and Ida Corinne (Safford) H.; student U. of Minn., 1907-09; LL.B., U. of Wis. Law Sch., 1912; m. Ruth Neimeyer, Oct. 7, 1916; children—Katharine, Mary Louise. Admitted to Wis. and Minn. bars, 1912; clerk with Baldwin & Baldwin, Duluth, 1912-16, partner since 1916 (firm now Holmes, Mayall, Reavill & Neimeyer). Served as 1st lt., Inf., U.S. Army, 1917-18. Col., 2d Inf., Minn. State Guard, 1941-47. President Duluth (Minn.) Community Fund, 1939-40. Mem. Minn. (pres. 1941-42), Am. bar assns., Duluth C. of C. (pres. 1930-31), Sigma Chi, Phi Delta Phi. Republican. Episcopalian. Home: 4040 Minnesota Av. Office: 900 Alworth Bldg., Duluth, Minn. Died Feb. 20, 1949.

HOLMES, Frederick Lionel, writer; b. Waukau, Winnebago County, Wis., May 9, 1883; s. Michael and Jane Ann (Bridle) H.; A.B., University of Wisconsin, 1906; Litt.D., Marquette University, 1942; m. Helen D. Pollack, Apr. 14, 1915 (died July 19, 1939). Polit. reporter, Wis. State Journal, Madison, 1906-09; mgr. La Follette's Weekly, Madison, 1909-13; mng. editor La Follette's Magazine, 1917-29. Mem. Wis. Ho. of Rep., 1913-15 (chmn. pub. utility com.); spl. newspaper corr.; mgr. Holmes News Service; dir. Quality Printers; dir. and chmn. bd. dirs. Madison Bank and Trust Co.; admitted to Wis. bar, 1927. Chmn. commn. to appraise 10,565 acres of land for Badger Ordnance Co., 1942. Vice-pres. Lincoln Fellowship of Wis. Mem. Wis. State Hist. Soc. (curator since 1935), Wis. State Bar Assn.; nat. publicity dir. La Follette-Wheeler presdl. campaign, 1924. Mem. Sigma Delta Chi. Roman Catholic. Mem. Knights of Columbus, Madison Literary Club. Author: Regulation of Railroads and Public Utilities in Wisconsin, 1915; Wisconsin's War Record, 1919; Abraham Lincoln Traveled This Way, 1930; George Washington Traveled This Way, 1935; Alluring Wisconsin, 1937; Badger Saints and Sinners, 1939; The Voice of Trappist Silence, 1941; Old World Wisconsin, 1944; Wisconsin, Stability, Progress and Beauty (editor), 1945. Editor Wisconsin Blue Book (official state publ.), 1923, 1925-27. Home: 2106 Hollister Av. Office: 1 W. Main St., Madison, Wis. Died July 27, 1946.

HOLMES, Gerald Anderson, architect; b. Phila., Pa., Feb. 20, 1887; s. Gerald and Margaret Wellwood (Anderson) H.; A.B., B.S., U. of Pa., 1908; m. Mary Elizabeth Hunt. Archtl. draftsman, Day & Klander, Phila., 1908-10, McKim, Mead & White, New York, 1910-23; mem. Thompson, Holmes & Converse, 1923-38; designer bldgs. for City College, Hunter College, Bellevue Psychopathic Hospital, New York City; designer, Bureau of Constrn., Board of Edn., New York, 1938-42, asst. supt. of sch. bldgs. since 1942. Fellow A.I.A.; mem. Archtl. League of New York, Century Assn., New York. Home: 126 E. 19th St., New York, N.Y. Address: 49 Flatbush Av., Ext., Brooklyn, N.Y. Died April 19, 1948.

HOLMES, Guy Earl, composer, musician; b. Baraboo, Wis., Feb. 14, 1873; s. Lucian O. and Vira (Johnson) H.; ed. pub. schs.; studied theory and harmony with G. Mitchell and Capt. W. F. Heath, cornet with Vandercook and Rigdon, saxophone with Lattimer, flute with Weldon; m. Lotus F. Spring, May 8, 1915. Formerly flute soloist with Weldon's Band, dir. Ben Hur Band, dir. and arranger Vogel's Minstrels, teacher harmony and instrumentation, Prior's Conservatory, Danville, Ill.; mem. faculty Vandercook Sch. of Music. Composer: The Prospector (official march of St. Louis Expn.); March Courageous (dedicated to United Nations, World War II); over 200 mil. marches and overtures for band and orchestra; many songs and characteristic pieces; numerous pieces for saxophone. Mem. Am. Fedn. Musicians, Am. Soc. Composers, Authors and Pubs. Republican. Methodist. Mason. Address: 2322 Farragut Av., Chicago, Ill. Died Feb. 10, 1945; interment Baraboo, Wis.

HOLMES, Major Edward, coll. dean; b. La Grange, Ky., Jan. 8, 1882; s. Jesse Munroe and Laura N. (Maddox) H.; A.B., Ind. U., 1908; M.S., Cornell U., 1910, Ph.D., 1920; m. Florence Juanita Garr, Apr. 27, 1922. Teacher and high sch. prin., Kempton, Ind., 1901-06; development engr. Nat. Carbon Co., 1910-19; mgr. chemistry dept. and acting gen. mgr., Nat. Lime Assn., 1919-22; development engr. U.S. Gypsum Co., 1922-23, Dolomite, Inc., 1923-26; prof. and head dept. ceramic engring. and dir. Mo. Clay Testing and Research Lab., U. of Mo., 1926-32; dean State College of Ceramics, Alfred U., since 1932. Sec. and treas. N.Y. Ceramic Industries Assn.; fellow Am. Ceramic Soc. (v.p. 1942-43); mem. Am. Soc. for Testing Materials, Sigma Xi, Alpha Chi Sigma, Klan Alpine, Keramos. Mason. Club: Rotary (pres. Wellsville Club 1936-37). Contbr. manuals and scientific articles. Invented and improved electric dry cells, quick setting lime plaster and stable dolomite clinker and refractories of various kinds. Home: Alfred, N.Y. Died May 2, 1946; buried at LaGrange, Ky.

HOLMES, Morris Grant, architect; b. LaPorte, Ind., Apr. 27, 1862; s. Isaac Newton and Susan B. (Miller) H.; ed. high sch., LaPorte; m. Maud Josephine Harvey, Dec. 31, 1887; 1 dau., Kathryn Langley. Consulting architect. Designer American Board Mission Sch. and Hosp., Fenchow, China; Skinner Memorial Chapel and coll. group of Carleton Coll., Northfield, Minn.; McKinley Foundation, U. of Ill.; numerous school and college buildings, churches, hospitals, public libraries. Mem. Am. Inst. Architects. Home: 136 155th St., Harvey, Ill. Died Aug. 13, 1945.

HOLMES, Jesse Herman, college prof.; b. W. Liberty, Ia., Jan. 5, 1864; s. Jesse and Sara Morgan (Paxson) H.; B.S., U. of Neb., 1884, grad. student and librarian, 1884-85; grad. student, 1885-86 and 1888-90, Ph.D., 1890, Johns Hopkins; student Harvard Summer Sch., 1894, spl. student Oxford U., 1899-1900; m. Rebecca Sinclair Webb, June 16, 1892; children—Elizabeth Webb (dec.), J. Herman, Robt. S. Teacher Friends' Select Sch., Washington, 1886-88, 1890-93; collector bot. specimens for U.S. Herbarium, Dept. of Agr. in Potomac Valley, N.J., pine barrens and Rocky Mountains, 1888-90; teacher George Sch., Bucks Co., Pa., 1893-99; prof. history of religion and philosophy, Swarthmore Coll., 1900-34; emeritus prof. philosophy, since 1934. Socialist candidate for gov. of Pa., 1932, 38; Pa. state chmn. of Socialist party, 1935-39. Active worker, Society of Friends, especially in S.S. work. Lecturer and platform supt., Chautauqua Assn. of Pa., 1912-23. Pres. Nat. Fedn. Religious Liberals, 1915-27. Commr. for Am. Friends relief work in Europe, 1920. Mem. Phi Beta Kappa. Author of several courses of lessons on Old and New Testament, ch. history, etc., for Friends' Sunday schools. Home: 700 Manchester Av., Moylan, Pa. Died May 27, 1942.

HOLMES, Phillips, actor; b. Grand Rapids, Mich., July 22, 1909; s. Taylor and Edna (Phillips) H.; prep. edn., Harvard Mil. Sch., Los Angeles, and tutoring sch., Tunbridge Wells, Eng.; studied Cambridge U. and Princeton; unmarried. Began in small role in screen play, "Varsity," at Princeton; played with father in "The Great Necker," then signed to appear in Paramount pictures; has played leading rôles in "The Devil's Holiday," "Her Man," "The Criminal Code," "Stolen Heaven," "An American Tragedy," "Broken Lullaby," "Two Kinds of Women," etc. Clubs: Triangle (Princeton); Footlights (Cambridge, Eng.). Address: Metro-Goldwyn-Mayer Studios, Culver City, Calif. Died Aug. 12, 1942.

HOLMES, William Henry, educator, curator; born Augusta, Me., Sept. 13, 1874; s. William Henry and Emma Augusta (Penney) H.; A.B., Colby Coll., 1897; Ph.D., Clark U., 1910; spl. courses in edn., New York U. and Teachers Coll. (Columbia); m. Louise Macdonald, July 19, 1898; 1 son, Lt. Richard M. Prin. Israel Putnam Grammar Sch., Putnam, Conn., 1897-98, Putnam High Sch., 1898-99; supt. schs., Grafton and Upton, Mass., 1899-1903, Westerly, R.I., 1903-13, Mt. Vernon, New York, 1913-40; restorer, curator "Victoria Mansion" Museum, Portland, Me., 1941, best standing example of early Victorian Art and Architecture in Northeastern U.S. Lecturer on sch. adminstrn., Dartmouth Coll., summer 1913, Pa. State Coll., summer, 1924, Bates Coll., summers, 1926, 27; lecturer on school publicity, Pa. State Coll., 1927; surveyor N.Y. City Sch. Survey, 1925. Asst. in charge of personnel and chmn. com. on extension lectures under Army Ednl. Commn., A.E.F., Paris, Nov. 1918-Apr. 1919; gen. field supervisor Army Ednl. Corps U.S. Army, Beaune, France, Apr.-July 1919. Life member N.E.A. (N.Y. state dir. 1926-29; v.p. 1930-31), Nat. Parent Teacher Assn., National Association of School Administrators; member American Institute Instruction (vice-pres.), World Federation of Ednl. Associations, Delta Upsilon. Republican. Author: School Organization and the Individual Child, 1912; Key to Number, 1929. Co-author: Key to Reading, 1928; Along the Way (school poems), 1938. Wrote nat. sch. songs, "We'll Carry On" and "Stand By the Schools." Editor of Educational Work (mag.), 1906. Contbr. to ednl. jours. Home: The Eastland, Portland, Me. Died Jan. 6, 1948; buried Augusta, Me.

HOLT, Andrew, judge; b. East Union, Minn., May 20, 1855; s. John and Catharine (Swanson) H.; ed. St. Ansgar's Acad. (now Gustavus Adolphus Coll.), St. Peter, Minn.; LL.B., U. of Minn., 1880; m. Hilda C. Turnquist, Oct. 1, 1885; children—Agnes Evelyn, John Elmer. Admitted to Minn. bar, 1881; later mem. Ueland, Shores & Holt, and Ueland & Holt; judge Municipal Court, Minneapolis, 1894-1904; judge Dist. Court, 1904-11; now asso. justice Supreme Court of Minn., 1912-42, now retired. Republican. Lutheran. Home: 324 Prospect Av., Minneapolis, Minn. Died Feb. 11, 1948.

HOLT, Frank O., educator; b. Janesville, Wis., Oct. 2, 1883; s. John and Augusta (Brunk) H.; Ph.B., U. of Wis., 1907, Ph.M., 1921; student U. of Chicago, 1923; Dr. pedagogy, Milton Coll., 1933; m. Grace M. Rood, Sept. 1, 1909; children—Gweneth May (Mrs. George W. Field, Jr.), Fred Rood, Frank, Jr. Supt. Schs. Sun Prairie, Wis., 1907-11, Edgerton, 1911-20, Janesville, 1920-27; registrar and dir. Bur. of Guidance, U. of Wis., 1927-35, dean U. Extension Div. since 1935. Director Public Service U. of Wis., 1943. Mem. Madison Bd. of Education; dir, Madison-Wis. Foundation; dir.-treas. Wis. Conf. of Social Work. Mem. Wis. Alumni Assn. (dir.-treas.), Wis. Edn. Assn. (past pres.); State Council Edn., Nat. Assn. Collegiate Registrars (past pres.), Wis. Vocational Guidance Assn. (past pres.), Nat. Univ. Extension Div. Assn. Chmn. State Radio Council, chmn. State Educational Advisory Committee, Phi Delta Kappa. Conglist. Mason, K.P. Club: University (Madison). Home: 1929 Regent St., Madison, Wis. Died April 1, 1948.

HOLT, Henry Winston, jurist; b. Isle of Wight County, Va., Sept. 14, 1864; s. Micajah Quincy and Virginia Henry (Winston) H.; C.E., Va. Mil. Inst., 1886; B.L., Washington and Lee Univ., 1888, LL.D., 1929; Phi Beta Kappa; m. Mary Caperton Braxton, June 6, 1894 (died 1935); children—Henry Winston, Virginia Henry, Eliza Braxton (died 1942), Esta Carter, Mary Caperton, Margaret Pegram. Practiced Wichita, Kan., 1888-91; moved Staunton, Va., 1891; judge Corp. Court, Buena Vista, Va., 1893-96 (resigned); judge Corp. Court for City of Staunton, 1900-12; judge 18th Jud. Dist. of Va., 1912-24; apptd. mem. Special Court of Appeals, 1924, reapptd., 1926; justice Supreme Court of Appeals of Va., 1928-46; chief justice since 1946. Democrat. Episcopalian. Mem. Sigma Chi. Club: Commonwealth (Richmond, Va.). Home: Staunton, Va. Died Oct. 4, 1947.

HOLT, Winifred (Mrs. Rufus Graves Mather), sculptor, writer and philanthropist; b. New York City; d. Henry and Mary Florence (West) H.; educated various private schools, ending with Brearley Sch., New York; studied anatomy, drawing and sculpture in Florence, Italy; received criticism and instruction from various famous artists in America and Europe; m. Rufus Graves Mather, Nov. 16, 1922. Exhibited at Nat. Sculpture Soc., Architectural League, etc., New York, Florence, Italy, Berlin, Germany, and England (examples of these are bronzes in the Metropolitan Opera House, New York, and Dept. of the Interior, Washington. Principal works and commissions have been portraits, busts, bas-reliefs. Founder and hon. sec. N.Y. Assn. for the Blind; through her efforts the following brs. of the assn. were opened: The Emma L. Hardy Memorial Home at Cornwall-on-Hudson, N.Y. (1912), and the Bourne Workshop for the Blind in N.Y. City (1913), and new headquarters of the assn., better known as "The Lighthouse" (last by President Taft); founder Ticket Bur. for the Blind in America and Europe, and Com.

for Men Blinded in Battle; del. to Internat. Conv. of Workers for the Blind, Manchester, Eng., 1908 and 1914 (bearing autograph letter of the President); witness on care of the blind and Prevention of Blindness for the Departmental Com. of the House of Commons, 1914; organized Phare de Bordeaux (1st lighthouse for the blind on the Continent), 1915, organized the Phare de France, opened by Pres. of France and Am. ambassador, 1916; pres. Comite Franco-Amercain pour les Aveugles de la Guerre, etc. Fall of 1916 and Spring of 1917, lectured in leading cities of U.S. and Can. on work for blinded soldiers; opened in France, 5th, 6th and 7th Lighthouses for the Blind, 1917, and the 8th Rome (under presidency of Benito Mussolini), 1919. Went to Poland in 1921 as the guest of the Polish Govt. for relief of Polish blind, founding 9th Lighthouse in Warsaw. With husband made trip around the World twice stimulating interest in prevention of blindness; through their efforts Lighthouses have been opened in many of the leading cities of the World. Awarded Legion of Honor, France, and various medals, including gold medal of Nat. Inst. Social Sciences, and the French Gold Medal of Foreign Affairs, also Italian and Belgian medals, etc. Life mem. Italy-America Soc.; mem. National Institute Social Sciences, Metropolitan Museum, English-Speaking Union. Clubs: Colony (New York City); Sulgrave (Washington, D.C.); Sesamee, American Woman's (London, England). Author: A Short Life of Henry Fawcett, the Blind Postmaster General of England, for Children Everywhere, 1911; The Beacon for the Blind, 1914; The Light Which Cannot Fail, 1922; also numerous papers on the blind. Founder of first Braille magazine for blind children, the Searchlight, which is printed at Lighthouse Number One, the New York Association for the Blind and sent all over the World. With her husband lectures and writes on modern treatment and prevention of blindness; together made tour to the North Cape and lectured in Sweden, Norway and Denmark, being honored by the presence of the King in Norway and members of the Royal Family in Denmark, subsequently the King and Queen of Bulgaria were present at lecture given in the capital; lectured on prevention of blindness, 1935, before members of governments of Ireland, Greece, Turkey, Bulgaria, Jugoslavia and Austria, also before royalty and at universities, resulting in fresh efforts in behalf of the blind; founder, with husband, of "Lighthouse" coms. in many parts of the world; in 1936 with husband lectured in Japan on prevention of blindness and justice for the blind and present at inauguration of first "Lighthouse" for blind in Osaka which was result of their visit in 1929; in China lectured and started a nat. "Lighthouse" movement under the presidency of Madame Chiang Kai-shek and Lighthouse No. 10. Lectured in Florida, 1939-40. Spl. Corr. in France for N.Y. Times, 1916-18. Address: 111 E. 59th St., New York, N.Y.

Died June 14, 1945.

HOLTON, Holland, educator; b. Dobson, N.C., May 13, 1888; s. Samuel Melanchthon and Aura Barrett (Chaffin) H.; A.B., Trinity Coll. (now Duke U.), 1907; student Trinity Coll. Law Sch., 1910-11, 14-15; U. of Chicago, summers 1915, 16, 17, J.D., 1927, grad. study, 1926-27; m. Lela D. Young, Dec. 24, 1911; children—Winfred Quinton (dec.), Samuel M., Holland Young. Prin. high sch., East Durham, 1907-09; head of history dept., Durham High Sch., 1909-10; prin. high sch., West Durham, 1911-14, 1915-19; instr. in public speaking, Trinity Coll., 1912-19; asst. supt. schs., Durham County, 1915-19, supt., 1919-21; prof. history of edn. and legal phases of sch. adminstrn., and head of dept., Trinity Coll. and Duke U., since 1921; dir. summer sch., same, since 1920. Sec. North Carolina State Commission on High School Textbooks, 1919-23; secretary Durham County and City Bd. of Health, 1922-26; mem. Commn. on Secondary Schs. of Assn. Colls. and Secondary Schs. of Southern States since 1927; elected, 1933, to N.C. Constitutional Conv. Against Repeal of 18th Amendment of Federal Constitution. Pres. N.C. Coll. Conf., 1937-38; mem. Selective Service System since 1940. Mem. N.C. Edn. Assn., Tau Kappa Alpha, Phi Beta Kappa, Kappa Delta Pi, Phi Delta Kappa. Republican. Methodist. Mason. Kiwanian. Editor of Southern Assn. Quarterly since 1937. Home: 809 Watts St., Durham, N.C. Died Aug. 20, 1947.

HOLZHEIMER, William Andrew (hōlts'hīmẽr), lawyer; b. Saginaw, E.S., Mich., Sept. 29, 1870; s. Christopher F. and Mary Louise (Cornell) H.; ed. pub. schs., Saginaw; LL.B., U. of Mich., 1898; m. Georgina McCall Nesbit, June 17, 1900; 1 dau., Mary Catherine (wife of Lt. Samuel Gregory, U.S. Navy). Admitted to bar, 1898; practiced at Eureka, Utah, 1898-1901, Pocatello, Ida., 1901-05, Seattle, Wash., 1905-15, Juneau, Alaska, 1915-16; asst. U.S. atty., Ketchikan, Alaska, Jan. 1-Nov. 1, 1917; apptd. U.S. dist. judge, 2d div., Alaska, 1917; now U.S. dist. atty., 1st Alaska Div. Was chmn. Sch. Bd., Eureka, Utah; asst. county atty., Juab County, Utah, 1899-1900; chmn. Dem. county and city coms., Eureka, Utah, and Pocatello, Ida.; 1st city chmn. under direct primary law, Seattle, Wash.; was Dem. candidate for Ida. legislature, 1904, for atty. gen. of Wash., 1908. Mem. Am. Bar Assn., Ketchikan Bar Assn. (ex-pres.), Arctic Brotherhood. Episcopalian (chancellor Alaskan Diocese). Mason, Elk, K.P., Eagle, etc. Del. Dem. Nat. Conv., 1936. Home: Ketchikan, Alaska. Address: Juneau, Alaska. Deceased.

HOMER, Louise Dilworth Beatty, singer; b. Pittsburgh, Pa.; d. Rev. Wm. Trimble and Sarah Colwell (Fulton) Beatty; studied Phila., Boston and 2 yrs. in Paris, France; M.A., Tufts College, 1925, Smith College, 1932; Mus. Doc., Russell Sage College, 1932, Middlebury College, 1934; Litt.D., Miami U., Oxford, Ohio, 1933; m. Sidney Homer, Jan. 9, 1895; children—Louise (Mrs. Ernest V Stires), Sidney, Katharine (Mrs. Douglas Fryer), Anne Marie (Mrs. Robert Warner), Hester Makepeace (Mrs. Robert E. Henry, Jr.), Helen Joy (Mrs. William M. Doerflinger). Made début as opera singer, Vichy, France, 1898; engaged for following season, Covent Garden, London, and appeared as Amneris in Aida, May, 1899; with Royal Opera, Brussels, 8 mos.; New York début with Met. Opera Co., 1900; has sung nineteen successive seasons at Met. Opera House; with Chicago Civic Opera Co. since 1920, San Francisco and Los Angeles Opera cos., 1926; Metropolitan Opera Co., 1927, and in recital throughout the country. Address: Homeland, Bolton, N.Y. Died May 6, 1947.

HOOBLER, B(ert) Raymond (hō'blẽr), pediatrist; b. Standish, Mich., May 5, 1872; s. Saml. R. and Mary Roselia (Worth) H.; B.S., Wabash Coll., Ind., 1901, M.A., 1903; M.D., Cornell U., 1905; studied in Europe, 1914; m. Madge Sibley, Oct. 15, 1906; m. 2d, Icie G. Macy, June 11, 1938. Practiced at N.Y. City, 1905-14, also teaching in Cornell U. Med. Coll.; prof. diseases of children, Wayne U., 1914-37, emeritus since 1937; cons. Children's Hosp. of Mich. Mem. A.M.A., Am. Pediatric Soc., Phi Beta Kappa, Sigma Xi, Phi Gamma Delta, Nu Sigma Nu. Republican. Presbyterian. Mason (K.T.). Author of numerous papers on nutrition of children. Home: 805 Three Mile Drive, Grosse Pointe, Mich. Died June 11, 1943.

HOOD, Frazer, psychologist; b. Tupelo, Miss., June 2, 1875; s. Charles Buren and Martha Leontine (Wiley) Hood; B.A., Southwestern Presbyn. Univ., Clarksville, Tenn., 1896; Johns Hopkins, 1898-99; M.A., Yale, 1900, Ph.D., 1902; Litt.D., Presbyn. Coll. of S.C., 1923; studied in France and Eng., 1925-26; m. Kalista Wagner, Apr. 15, 1903; 1 dau., Kalista Wagner. Fellow in psychology, Yale, 1901-02; prof. ethics and English lit., Hanover (Ind.) Coll., 1902-03; actg. prof. psychology, U. of Okla., 1903-04; prof. psychology, West Tenn. State Normal Sch., also head dept. of edn., 1913-18; 1st lt., Sanitary Corps, U.S. Army, Mar. 19, 1918; asst. chief ednl. service and head of div. psychology and statistics, Gen. Hosp. 36, Dec. 12, 1918-Aug. 1, 1919; dir. psychol. lab. and instr. psychology, Northwestern U., Sept. 1, 1919-20; asst. state high school insp. for N.C.; prof. psychology, Davidson Coll., since 1920; prof. ednl. psychology, Univ. of N.C., summers, 1923-25; prof. psychology, Ohio State U., summers, 1930, 33. Past pres. bd. trustees Edgar Tufts Memorial Assn., Banners Elk, N.C.; past pres. North Carolina Coll. Conf.; pres. Presbyn. Ednl. Assn. of the South, 1942-43. On labor panel Am. Arbitration Assn. since Mar. 5, 1943. Chmn. psychology sect., N.C. Acad. of Science; mem. Am. Statis. Assn., Ill. Acad. Sciences, N.C. Acad. Sci., Am. Psychol. Assn., Southern Society of Philosophy and Psychology, Phi Beta Kappa, Kappa Alpha, Sigma Upsilon, Scabbard and Blade. Democrat. Presbyterian. Mason, Odd Fellow. Author: A Manual of Psychology Every Parent Ought to Know, 1917; The Steps in the Sale (booklet), 1923; Everyman's Insurance, 1925; College Trustees—Their Selection, Duties and Responsibilities. Appointed lecturer on Smythe Foundation, Columbia Theol. Seminary, Atlanta, Ga., 1934. Home: Davidson, N.C.

Died June 19, 1944.

HOOD, Frederic Clark, rubber goods mfr.; b. Chelsea, Mass., Mar. 11, 1865; s. George Henry and Frances Henrietta (Janvrin) H.; A.B., Harvard, 1886; m. Myra Tucker, Nov. 24, 1891; 1 son, Donald Tucker. Began with Boston Rubber Co., 1886, mfrs. rubber clothing, rubber boots, shoes and moulded goods, and became supt. and asst. treas.; founder, 1896, gen. mgr. and treas., Hood Rubber Co., until 1916, pres., 1916-29. Served on Nat. War Labor Bd., 1918; pres. Associated Industries of Mass., 1917-18, now mem. exec. com.; pres. Rubber Assn. of Am., 1911-13; treas. Nat. Ind. Conf. Bd., 1917-18. Clubs: Harvard, University, (Boston); Country (Brookline); Kittansett (Marion, Mass.). Republican. Episcopalian. Home: 6 Arlington St. Address: 6 Arlington St., Boston. Died Dec. 24, 1942.

HOOKER, (William) Brian, author; b. at New York, Nov. 2, 1880; s. William Augustus and Elisabeth (Work) H.; A.B., Yale, 1902, A.M., 1904; (M.A., honoris causa, Yale, 1912); m. Doris Redfield Cooper, Aug. 18, 1911; children—Belinda, Elisabeth, Pamela. Asst. in English, Columbia, 1903-05; instr. rhetoric, Yale, 1905-09; lecturer extension teaching at Columbia, 1915-18. Mem. Nat. Inst. Arts and Letters, Am. Soc. Composers, Authors and Pubs., Dramatists Guild of Authors League of America, Gamma Delta Psi, Zeta Psi, Chi Delta Theta. Club: The Players (New York City). Author: The Right Man, 1908; The Professor's Mystery (with Wells Hastings), 1911; Mona (opera), 1911 (awarded prize in Met. Opera Co. competition; music by Horatio Parker); Fairyland (opera), 1915 (awarded prize in Am. Opera Assn. competition; music by same); Morven and the Grail, 1915 (music by same); Poems, 1915; commemorative poem, "A.D. 1919" (music by Horatio Parker). Author or collaborator: June Love, 1920; Marjolaine, 1921; Our Nell, 1922; Fashion, 1923; Engaged, 1925; The Vagabond King, 1925; White Eagle, 1927; Falstaff, 1928; Through the Years, 1932; The O'Flynn, 1934. Translator: Cyrano de Bergerac, 1923, Ruy Blas, 1933. Lit. editor New York Sun, 1917. Home: Old Lynne, Conn.

Died Dec. 28, 1946.

HOOKER, Donald Russell, physiologist; b. New Haven, Conn., Sept. 7, 1876; s. Frank Henry and Grace (Russell) H.; B.A., Yale, 1899, M.S., 1901; M.D., Johns Hopkins, 1905; student U. of Berlin, 1906; m. Edith Houghton, June 14, 1905; children—Donald Houghton, Russell Houghton, Edith Houghton, Elizabeth Houghton, Beatrice Houghton. Asst. instr. and asso. in physiology, 1906-10, asso. prof. 1910-20, Johns Hopkins Med. Sch.; lecturer on physical hygiene, Johns Hopkins U. Mng. editor Am. Journal Physiology, since 1914; also mng. editor Physiological Revs. Mem. Am. Physiol. Soc. Home: 1016 St. George's Rd. Office: 19 W. Chase St., Baltimore, Md. Died Aug. 1, 1946.

HOOKER, Harry Mix, business exec.; b. Rochester, N.Y., July 18, 1872; s. Horace B. and Susan P. (Huntington) H.; A.B., U. of Rochester; m. L. May Kirkpatrick, May 7, 1917; step-children—Nathalie M., John Ashmead Rodgers. With Hooker Electrochem. Co. since 1913 as supt. of constrn., exec. development dept., sales mgr., 1918-35, v.p. sales, 1936-38, pres. 1938-45, chmn. bd. since June 1945. Mem. Alpha Delta Phi. Clubs: Niagara Falls Country, Niagara (Niagara Falls, N.Y.). Home: Lewiston Heights, Niagara Falls, N.Y. Died April 9, 1949.

HOOVER, Charles Lewis, consul gen.; b. Oskaloosa, Ia., Jan. 11, 1872; s. Samuel A. and Miriam J. (Beardsley) H.; ed. U. of Mo., Cotner U., U. of Chicago, and by pvt. tutors; m. Helen E. Lowrie, Oct. 1, 1901; children—Lois, Wilford Samuel. Supt. schools, Edgemont, S.D., 1895-98; div. supt. schs., P.I., 1902-09; consul at Madrid, Spain, June 29, 1909-Aug. 21, 1912; at Carlsbad, Austria, Aug. 22, 1912-July 17, 1914; at Prague, Austria, July 18, 1914-Aug. 1916, Sao Paulo, Brazil, 1916-20 (resigned); reapptd. as consul to Free City of Danzig July 1921, Batavia, Java, July 19, 1922; consul gen. at Batavia May-Oct. 1927, at Amsterdam, Jan. 1928-July 1934, at Hong Kong since Aug. 1934. Rep. Dept. State at Nat. Fgn. Trade Council meeting, Cincinnati, O., 1918, Internat. Chamber Com. meeting, Amsterdam, July, 1929. Silver medal, St. Louis Exposition, 1904, for scientific exhibit of collection of econ. plants of P.I. Mem. Am. Geog. Soc. Presbyn. Author of brochures: The Wild Tribes of Mindanao; Flora of Mindanao; The Dialects of the Philippines; The Constitution of Aragon. Home: New York, N.Y. Address: "On Lee," Mt. Davis Rd., Hong Kong. Died May 30, 1949.

HOOVER, C(harles) R(uglas), chemist; b. Oskaloosa, Ia., Sept. 30, 1885; s. Hiram Alonzo and Edith Adaline (Crane) H.; Ph.B., Penn Coll., Oskaloosa, Ia., 1906; B.S., Haverford, 1907, M.A., 1908; Ph.D., Harvard, 1915; m. Anna Mary Johnson, Sept. 7, 1912; children—Albert Charles, John Crane. Prof. chemistry, Penn Coll., 1909-10; Austin fellow in chemistry, 1910-12, Carnegie research fellow in chemistry, 1912-13, Harvard; asso. prof. chemistry, Syracuse U., 1913-15; asso. prof. chemistry, 1915-18, prof. since 1918, v.p., 1926-27, Wesleyan U., Conn. Gas chemist research div. C.W.S., U.S. Army, 1918; cons. chemist same, 1917-19; cons. chemist, State Water Commn. and State Commn. Fisheries and Game, Conn., since 1928. Consultant Nat. Defense Research Com. Mem. Conn. State Board of Registration for Engineers; mem. State Flood Control and Water Policy Commn. Mem. of committees of Nat. Research Council and Assn. Harvard Chemists; fellow Am. Inst. Chemists, A.A.A.S.; mem. Am. Chem. Soc. (councillor, also pres. Conn. Valley sect.). Conn. Soc. Civil Engrs., New England Sewage Works Assn., Soc. Chem. Industry, Am. Public Health Assn., N.E.A., Sigma Xi, Phi Beta Kappa, Alpha Chi Sigma. Conglist. Rotarian. Inventor of gas absorbent and gas detector. Author: Laboratory Construction and Equipment; contbr. on chem. topics. Home: 10 Wesleyan Pl., Middletown, Conn. Died June 8, 1942.

HOOVER, Lou Henry (Mrs. Herbert Hoover); b. Waterloo, Ia.; d. Charles D. and Florence (Weed) Henry; A.B., Stanford, 1898; awarded honorary degrees by Worcester, Elmira, Whittier and other colleges; m. Herbert Hoover (31st President of U.S.), February 10, 1899; children—Herbert, Allan Henry. Mem., officer and hon. officer many ednl. and philanthropic orgns. Translator: (with Herbert Hoover) de Re Metallica from Latin of Georg Agricola, 1556 1912. Home: Stanford University, Calif.

Died Jan. 7, 1944.

HOOVER, Samuel Earle; b. Phila., Pa., July 12, 1879; s. Frederick Lyman and Caroline (Seltzer) H.; student Peirce Sch. Business Adminstrn., 1896-97; m. Jennie Lachot, Oct. 1, 1902. Began as clk. F. L. Hoover & Sons Co., Phila., building constrn., 1897, becoming pres., 1933. Ruling elder Carmel Presbyn. Ch., Edge Hill, Pa., since 1902; former vice moderator Presbyn Ch. in U.S.A.; former pres. Presbyn Social Union, Philadelphia Elders Association, Abingdon (Pa.) Y.M.C.A.; former mem. bd. dirs. Phila Y.M.C.A.; dir. Am. Sunday Sch. Union, Tennent Coll. mem. exec. com., Federal Council of Chs. of Christ in America; candidate for Congress on the Dry Ticket (Republican), 1932. Republican. Clubs: Transportation (New York), Art Manufactures and City (Philadelphia). Home: Cathcart Home, Presbyterian Hospital, Devon, Pa. Died June 6, 1945.

HOOVER, William D., banker; b. Washington, D.C., Oct. 6, 1864; s. Adam M. and Harriet (Sims) H.; grad. high school and Emerson Inst., Washington, D.C., LL.B., Georgetown U., 1888; LL.M., 1889; m. Louise M. Reeve, Jan. 5, 1897 (dec.); children—

Mrs. Eleanor S. Landstreet, Reeve. Admitted to the D.C. bar, 1889; officer Real Estate Title Ins. Co., 1897-1902; trust officer Nat. Savings & Trust Co., 1902-09, pres. 1909-34, chmn. bd. since 1934; dir. and mem. exec. com. Real Estate Title Ins. Co.; dir. Norfolk & Washington Steamboat Co., Terminal Refrigerating and Warehousing Corp. Mem. Bd. of Edn., D.C., 1907-12. Republican. Episcopalian. Mason. Clubs: University, Lawyers' Chevy Chase. Home: 1028 Connecticut Av. N.W. Office: National Savings and Trust Co., Washington, D.C. Died Sep. 24, 1943.

HOPE, Walter Ewing, lawyer; b. Bristol, Pa., Sept. 15, 1879; s. Peter Ewing and Isabella Hunter (Baker) H.; A.B., Princeton University, 1901; LL.B., New York Law School, 1903; married Florence Hazen Talcott-Rogers, April 14, 1909; children—Marian Talcott (Mrs. Robert McNeal Smith), Helen Talcott (Mrs. David E. Austen). Admitted to New York bar, 1903; with Masten & Nichols since 1901, member firm since 1909 (now Milbank, Tweed, Hope, Hadley & McCloy); dir. Office Realty Corp., Metropolitan Life Insurance Co. President Institute for Crippled and Disabled; trustee Watch Hill Chapel Society, Princeton Univ. (chmn. exec. com.), Presbyn. Hosp., N.Y. City; trustee and mem. exec. com. United Hosp. Fund; chmn. United Hosp. Fund Campaign, 1939. Apptd. by Pres. Hoover asst. sec. U.S. Treasury, Oct. 1929. Member New York State Banking Board since 1945. Dir. State Organizations in charge of 48 state fuel orgns., U.S. Fuel Administration, 1917; chmn. spl. commn. to investigate fuel conditions in Eng., France, Italy, reporting to Peace Conf., 1918; Eastern vice treas. Rep. Nat. Com., 1928; chmn. United Rep. Finance Com., 1944; chairman National Republican Finance Com., 1946. Mem. Am. Bar Assn., N.Y. State Bar Assn., Assn. Bar City of New York, New York County Lawyers Assn., Acad. Polit. Sci., Metropolitan Museum, S.R., St. Andrews Soc., Phi Beta Kappa (ex-pres. Alumni in N.Y.), Phi Delta Phi. Republican. Presbyn.; trustee Madison Av. Ch. Clubs: University (pres. 1934-39), Princeton (pres. 1924-27), Century, Down Town, Piping Rock, Links (New York), Princeton of New York, Metropolitan (Washington), Nassau (Princeton). Home: 43 E. 70th St. Office: 15 Broad St., New York, N.Y. Died Aug. 16, 1948.

HOPF, Harry Arthur, management engr.; b. London, Eng., Apr. 3, 1882; s. Charles and Franziska (Grote) H.; came to U.S., 1898; naturalized, 1903; prep. edn. in Germany, 1892-98; B.C.S., New York U., 1906, M.C.S., 1914, M.B.A., 1922; post-grad. student, Columbia, 1927-28; hon. M.S., Bryant Coll., Providence, R.I., 1937; Dr. Engring., Rensselaer Polytechnic Institute, 1942; m. Flora Paine, 1908; children—Elliott Arthur, Gordon Allen; m. 2d, Rita Hilborn, 1926. Underwriting and organization work Germania (now Guardian) Life Ins. Co., New York, 1902-14; organization and office planning Phoenix Mutual Life Ins. Co., Hartford, Conn., 1914-17, E. I. duPont de Nemours & Co., Wilmington, Del., 1917-18; professional practice as management engr., New York, 1918-19; orgn. counsel Federal Reserve Bank of New York, 1919-22; management engr. as H. A. Hopf & Co. since 1922; pres. Hopf Inst. of Management, Ossining, N.Y.; adviser to President Taft's Commn. on Economy and Efficiency, 1909; lecturer in office management, New York U., 1919-25, Columbia, 1931-33, adjunct prof. management Grad. Sch. Bus. Adminstrn., New York U., 1947-49. Mem. engrs. adv. com. Div. of Contract Distribution, Office of Production Management, 1941. Licensed professional engineer, N.Y.; chmn. bd. trustees Bard Coll., Annandale-on-Hudson, 1948-49. Del. 1st Internat. Management Congress, Prague, 1925, 5th Congress, Amsterdam, 1932, 6th Congress, London (chairman U.S. del.), 1935, 7th Congress, New York (chmn. organizing com.), 1938. Fellow Inst. of Industrial Administration (London). Mem. Acoustical Soc. America, A.A.A.S., Am. Management Assn. (v.p. 1929), Am. Marketing Soc., Am. Soc. Mech. Engrs., N.Y. State Soc. Professional Engrs., Am. Soc. for Pub. Adminstrn., Am. Statis. Assn., Assn. of Cons. Management Engrs. (charter mem.; pres. 1933-35; dir. 1935-36), Inst. of Management of Am. Management Assn. (charter fellow, pres. 1929), Econometric Soc., Nat. Bureau Economic Research, Nat. Office Management Assn. (hon. fellow; president 1932-34; director 1934-36), Personnel Research Federation. Special Libraries Association, Comité Nat. de l'Organisation Française (Paris), Comité Nat. Belge d'Organisation Scientifique (Brussels), Internat. Com. Sci. Management (dep. pres., 1935-38, hon. mem. council, 1938-49), Internat. Indsl. Relations Inst. (The Hague), Masaryk Acad. Work (Praha), Nat. Management Council of the U.S.A. (founder; chmn. 1932-35). Soc. for Advancement of Management (advisory council, v.p. and mem. operating council 1937-39); fellow Royal Econ. Soc., Royal Soc. of Arts (both London); mem. Alumni Assn. of Sch. of Commerce of New York U. (pres. 1929-31), New York U. Alumni Fed. (dir. 1930-33), Beta Gamma Sigma, Alpha Kappa Psi (grand pres. 1909-10). Recipient: New York U. Alumni medal for meritorious service, 1932; gold medal by Internat. Com. of Scientific Management, 1938; Taylor Key award for distinguished services in management Soc. Advancement Management, 1947; Knight Royal Order of North Star by direction of King Gustaf VI of Sweden, 1947. Lutheran. Mason (K.T., Shriner). Clubs: Engineers, Columbia University, Lawyers' (New York). Author of numerous articles and brochures on management and organization; contributing editor, The Spectator. Home: Windrose Farm, Ossining. Office: Hopf Institute Bldg., Ossining, N. Y. Died June 3, 1949; buried Washington Cemetery, Brooklyn.

HOPKINS, Edwin Mortimer, univ. prof.; b. Kent, Putnam County, N.Y., Sept. 16, 1862; s. William Ambrose and Hannah Elizabeth (Sunderlin) H.; student N.Y. State Normal Coll., 1880-81; A.B., Princeton, 1888, math. fellow, 1889, A.M., 1890, Ph. D., 1894; study U. of Oxford (on leave), 1901-02; m. Madeleine May Mundy, of Metuchen, N.J., June 17, 1900. Teacher N.Y. pub. schools, 1878-84; tutor, Princeton U., 1888-89; asst. prof. and asso. prof. English, U. of Kan., 1889-93, prof. since 1893, dept. head, 1902-09, acting dir. dept. of journalism, 1903-05, retired 1937. Mem. Phi Beta Kappa, Modern Language Association, Nat. Edn. Assn., Coll. English Assn.; American Dialect Society; Kiwanis Club; charter mem. Am. Assn. Univ. Profs., Nat. Council Teachers of English (pres. 1916, dir. 1911-38), Kan. Soc. Mayflower Descendants (gov. 1917-20), American College Quill Club, Kan. Educator's Club Kan. Assn. Teachers of English; sometime mem. Simplified Spelling Board, American Guild Organists, Institute of American Genealogy. Associate editor English Journal, 1911-26; special collaborator U.S. Bureau Edn., 1913-21. Author: Handbook on the Teaching of English, 1904, The Labor and Cost of English Teaching, 1913, 16th edit., 1923. Contbr. professional and literary articles to periodicals. Home: 1234 Mississippi St., Lawrence, Kan.; (summer) Woodland Park, Colo. Died June 13, 1946; buried in Presbyterian Cemetery, Metuchen, N.J.

HOPKINS, Harry L., government official; b. Sioux City, Ia., Aug. 17, 1890; S. David and Anna (Picket) H.; grad. Grinnell (Ia.) Coll., LL.D., 1935; m. Ethel Gross, 1913; children—David, Stephen, Robert; m. 2d, Barbara Duncan, 1929 (died 1937); 1 dau., Diana; m. 3d, Mrs. Louise Macy, July 30, 1942. Began as supervisor Assn. for Improving Conditions of Poor, N.Y. City; executive sec. Bd. Child Welfare, 1915-17; dir. mgr. New Orleans for Am. Red Cross, 1917-22; then asst. dir. Assn. for Improvement Condition of the Poor; then dir. New York Tuberculosis and Health Assn.; apptd. exec. dir. N.Y. State Temporary Emergency Relief Administration, 1931, chmn., 1932; apptd. federal administrator of emergency relief, 1933. Works Progress Adminstr., 1935-38; apptd. Sec. of Commerce, 1938, resigned Aug. 1940; apptd. head Lease-Lend Program, 1941. Apptd. adviser and asst. to President Roosevelt 1941; resigned, 1945; apptd. impartial chmn., Woman's Cloak and Suit Industry, New York, July 1945; chmn. munitions assignments board; mem. central com. the Am. Nat. Red Cross; trustee, Franklin D. Roosevelt Library. Awarded D.S.M. by President Truman, Sept. 1945. Home: 1046 Fifth Av., New York 28. Office: 450 7th Av., New York 1, N.Y. Died Jan. 29, 1946.

HOPKINS, John Henry, clergyman; b. Burlington, Vt., Sept. 17, 1861; s. Rev. Theodore Austin and Alice Leavenworth (Doolittle) H.; A.B., U. of Vt., 1883, also D.D.; grad. Gen. Theol. Sem., 1890, S.T.B., 1893; S.T.D., Western Theol. Sem.; m. Marie Moulton Graves, June 10, 1890 (died 1933). Organist St. Paul's Ch., Burlington, 1878-83; fire ins. agt., Oakland, Calif., 1884-87, also organist First Presbyn. Ch., Oakland; organist Chapel of the Good Shepherd, Gen. Theol. Sem., New York, 1888-90, and of Calvary Episcopal Ch., New York, 1889-90; deacon, 1890, priest, 1891, P.E. Ch.; asst. Calvary Chapel, New York, 1890-91; asst. St. James' Ch., Chicago, 1891-93; rector Trinity Ch., Atchison, Kan., 1893-95, Christ Ch., St. Joseph, Mo., 1895-99, Ch. of the Epiphany, Chicago, 1899-1909; sec. 5th Missionary Dept., 1909-10; rector Ch. Redeemer, Chicago, Dec. 1, 1910-29 (now rector emeritus). Mem. Episcopal Hymnal Revision Commn., 1936. Chaplain 4th Regt., Mo. Nat. Guard, 1897-99. Mem. Phi Beta Kappa Fraternity. Mason (32°). Clubs: Church Club (Chicago); University (Winter Park, Fla.). Autnor: Life of Marie Moulton Graves Hopkins, 1934; The Great Forty Years of the Diocese of Chicago, 1936; Practical Confirmation Instructions, 1941. Contbr. Am. Church Monthly, The Living Church, etc. Editor Bible Lessons in St. Andrew's Cross, 1891-92. Composer of Communion Service in B flat. Republican. Home: Grand Isle, Vt. Died Nov. 1, 1945.

HOPKINS, Nevil Monroe, engineer, educator; b. Portland, Me., Sept. 15, 1873; s. Francis Nevil and Frances Anna (Monroe) H.; B.S., Columbian (now George Washington) U.; 1899, M.S., 1900, Ph.D., 1902; grad. student, Harvard, 1901; m. Katherine Guy, Jan. 5, 1897; children—Anne Dorsey (Mrs. James W. Allison), Frances Monroe (Mrs. Horace W. Peaslee); m. 2d, Raymonde Briggs, June 22, 1932. Instr. chemistry, Columbian Univ., 1899-1902; asst. prof. chemistry since 1902, George Washington U.; professional engr. lecturer, Coll. of Engring., New York U., since 1934; mem. faculty Institute for Industrial Progress; mem. Munroe, Hall & Hopkins, cons. engrs. Electrician, Gen. Electric Co., Schenectady, N.Y.; editorial rep. Electrical World and Engineer, N.Y.; trustee and in charge div. elec. engring., Inst. of Industrial Research; v.p. and elec. engr. Electric Tachometer Co. Elec. engr. Navy Dept. in charge power plant design and constrn. at all navy yards and stas., 1905-08; expert engr. U.S. Office of Public Roads, Washington, D.C., since 1909. Inventor of electric and mech. devices, instruments for high temperature measurements, etc.; awarded John Scott medal, Franklin Inst., 1900. Temporary asst. Am. Embassy, Paris, during outbreak European war; vol. to French Red Cross and with French army in retreat from Mons to Paris. Lectured in Am. theatres on European war for benefit of Belgian destitute; chmn. Belgian Scholarship Com., for bringing to America worthy Belgian professors and scholars and providing funds for their support with free use of Am. univs. Lecturer on the navy and national defense, auspices of Navy League U.S. Tech. adviser, design sect. of gun div. Bur. of Ordnance, since 1917; maj. of ordnance, U.S. Army, 1917. Consulting engr. Rys. Electric Equipment Co., Philadelphia; cons. engr. Aircraft Fireproofing Corp., New York, also of Union Carbide and Carbon Co., New York, and in charge dept. of mech. research, Union Carbide and Carbon Research Labs., Long Island; dir. research Burnot Fireproofing Products; pres. New-Mix Products, Inc., Internat. Tube Co. Inventor and developer "Televotes," "Radiovotes"; also submersible battle cruiser and long range naval and antiaircraft guns, high explosive antiaircraft shells and battleship wrecking bombs; new blast meter and system for U.S. Army for measuring force of high explosives in the field; new electro chronograph for ballistic measurements; inventor Synchronous Electric Registration and Voting System, and Home Registration Voting Stations therefor, making possible mass voting by radio and newspaper announcement; automatic radio-electric survey system showing the number of radio receiving sets tuned in to any particular broadcasting station wave length, at any time; inactivators for destroying criminal time bombs and infernal machines; designer of torpedo and magnetic-mine protection equipment for freighters at sea; also super rocket guns and rocket missiles. President National Electric Ballots, Inc. Consultant in high explosives in regard to bomb-proofs and shelters for animals to American Society for Prevention of Cruelty to animals. Recipient of George Washington U. Alumni Award for notable achievement in science and conspicuous service, June 1942. Fellow A.A.A.S., American Institute Mech. Engrs., mem. Am. Chem. Soc., Am. Electrochem. Soc., Am. Soc. Testing Materials, Am. Soc. M.E., Am. Inst. Chem. Engrs., Soc. Am. Mil. Engineers, Army Ordnance Assn., Inst. of Social Sciences, Military Order of World War, Master Marines' Assn. (Gloucester, Mass.), Loyal Legion, United States Power Squadron, S.R., Society Colonial Wars (lt. gov. and gov.). Clubs: Metropolitan, Cosmos, Chevy Chase, Adventurers, Corinthian Yacht (Washington, D.C.); MacDowell, National Arts (v.p.), New York Yacht (New York). Author: Model Engines and Boats, 1898; Twentieth Century Magic, 1904; Experimental Electro-Chemistry, 1905; The Strange Cases of Mason Brant, 1916; The Racoon Lake Mystery; Over the Threshold of War; The Outlook for Research and Invention; The Inventor and His Workshop; The Horrors in the Grew Mystery; also over 100 articles in scientific and engring. jours., and short stories in mags. Home: 12 Washington Square N., New York. Died Mar. 26, 1945; buried in Rock Creek Cemetery, Washington.

HOPKINS, Richard J., judge; b. Jefferson City, Mo., Apr. 4, 1873; s. William Robert and Elizabeth (Murphy) H.; U. of Kan., 1893-96; LL.B., Northwestern U., 1901; m. May Cathcart, Sept. 16, 1909 (died Nov. 18, 1918); children—Isabelle, Richard Cathcart, Daniel Roberts; m. 2d, Lida Hafford, Jan. 22, 1935. Began practice of law, Chicago, 1901; practiced with father at Garden City, 1906 until father's death, 1913; mem. Kan. Ho. of Rep., 1909 (speaker pro tem. of House); lt. gov. of Kansas, 1911, 12; city atty., Garden City, 1913-18; atty. gen. of Kan., 1919-23; asso. justice Supreme Court of Kan., term 1923-29; apptd. by President Hoover judge U.S. Dist. Court, Kan., Dec. 19, 1929. Mem. Am. and Kan. State bar assns., Sigma Nu. Republican. Methodist Mason (32°, K.T., Shriner), Rotarian. Home: Mission Hills, Kan.; also 1501 W. 59th St., Kansas City, Mo. Office: Federal Bldg., Kansas City, Kan. Died Aug. 28, 1943.

HOPLEY, Russell James, public utilities; born in Blue Island, Ill., Apr. 28, 1895; son of John Barnes and Mary Elizabeth (Russell) Hopley; educated in public schools and business college of Fort Madison, Ia.; married Helen Joyce Kreymborg, February 6, 1931; children—Russell J., Jr., John K. Collector Northwestern Bell Telephone Co. (formerly Iowa Telephone Co.), Fort Madison, Ia., 1915-17, manager offices McGregor and Waterloo, Ia., 1919-22, gen. staff Omaha, Neb., 1922-23, mgr. Des Moines, 1923-25, dist. mgr. Des Moines, 1925-29, commercial operations-supervisor, Omaha, 1929-37, gen. mgr. states of Neb. and S.D., 1937, v.p. of operations, dir. and mem. exec. com. 1937-42, pres. since 1942; pres., dir. and mem. exec. com. The Tri-State Telephone and Telegraph Co.; vice pres., dir. and mem. exec. com. Dakota Central Telephone Co., Omaha, 1937-42; dir. Neb. Savings & Loan Assn. and United States Nat. Bank, Omaha; mem. proxy com. Northwest-Bancorporation, Minneapolis. During World War I (1917-19), served with Field-Signal Battalion, A.E.F. (Haute-Alsace, Meuse-Argonne), during World War II (1941-45), served as civilian adv. army air service. Trustee United Seamans Service; vice chmn. United War and Community Fund. Member Omaha C. of C. (chmn. finance com. 1943-44; post war planning bd., municipal tax com.); international vice president Int'l dir. Conopos Clubs, 1926-29; trustee U. of Neb. Foundation; trustee Children's Memorial Hosp.; vice president and trustee World War II Memorial Park Association; Salvation Army Advisory Bd.; gen. chairman Mayors City-wide Planning Commission. Mem. Newcomen Soc. of Eng., Telephone Pioneers of Am. Am. Legion, Neb. Table Tennis Assn. (hon. vice pres.). Republican. Presbyterian. Mason (32°, Shriner,

Jesters), Clubs; Country, Omaha, Athletic, Engineers (Omaha); University (Lincoln); Minneapolis (Minneapolis, Minn.); Minnesota (St. Paul); Des Moines (Des Moines, Ia.). Home: 725 N. 57th St., Omaha 3. Office: 118 S. 19th St., Omaha 2, Neb. Died Nov. 23, 1949.

HOPPIN, William Warner, lawyer; b. N.Y. City, Dec. 13, 1878; s. William W. and Katharine (Beekman) H.; A.B., Yale, 1901; m. Mary Gallatin, Mar. 31, 1902. Began practice at N.Y. City, 1906; of counsel to alien property custodian; asst. U.S. atty. gen. in charge of customs cases, June 16, 1921-Nov. 15, 1925; resigned to resume pvt. practice; apptd. city magistrate, Apr. 1940. Mem. Mayor Mitchel's Com. of Defense, World War; govt. appeal agt. in first draft; enlisted in U.S. Army for service in Field Arty.; former capt. O.R.C. City Magistrate of City of N.Y. Mem. bd. mgrs. Ruptured and Crippled Hosp., secretary New York Assn. for the Blind. Director Florence Crittenton League. Member Field Artillery Reserve Assn. (dir.), First Av. Assn. (dir.), St. Nicholas Soc. Republican. Clubs: Union, Yale, Nat. Republican. Home: 53 E. 66th St., New York, N.Y. Died May 27, 1948.

HORMEL, George Albert (hôr'mĕl), chmn. bd., Geo. A. Hormel & Co.; b. Dec. 4, 1860, Buffalo, N.Y.; s. John G. and Susana (Decker) H.; m. Lillian B. Gleason, Feb. 24, 1892; 1 son, Jay C. Began as helper on surfacing machine Mitchell & Roland Lumber Co., Toledo, O., 1873; helper on wood tenon machine Wabash Ry. shops, Toledo, 1874-76; cashier packing house market, Chicago, 1876-77; employed by Gale & Decker, pork packers, Chicago, 1878-79; traveling buyer for J. N. Du Bois, Kansas City, 1880, for Oberne Hosick & Co., Chicago, 1881-87; partner Frederich & Hormel, retail meats, Austin, Minn., 1887-91; organized, 1892, Geo. A. Hormel & Co., chmn. bd. since 1928. Clubs: Union League (Chicago); Los Angeles Country, Bel-Air Bay. Address: 630 Nimes Rd., Bel-Air, Los Angeles, Calif. Died June 5, 1946.

HORN, Henry John, ry. official; b. St. Paul, Minn., 1864; s. Henry J. and Francenia (Banning) H.; B.S. in C.E., Mass. Inst. Tech., 1888; m. Josephine M. Robinson, Feb. 15, 1898; children—Henry J., Francenia (Mrs. Ralph Shattuck Stevens). Asst. engr. Chicago, St. Paul & Kansas City Ry., 1888-89; entered service of Northern Pacific Ry. as draftsman, engrng. dept., 1889, and continued as chief draftsman, middle dist., 1890-91, resident engr., 1891-1893, supervisor bridges, Minn. div., 1893-97, supt. Mont. div., 1897-1902, asst. gen. supt. middle dist., 1902-03, gen. mgr. coal dept. Northwestern Improvement Co. (an auxiliary corp.), 1903-04, gen. mgr. N.P. Ry., 1904-07; in comml. bus., 1907-10; asst. gen. mgr., C.,B.&Q. Ry., May-Dec. 1910; asst. to pres., N.Y., N.H. & H.R.R., Dec. 1, 1910-Jan. 1, 1911; v.p., 1911-13; v.p. in charge of operation, 1912-13; railroad analysis since 1913. Dep. commr. Am. Red Cross, 1917-18; Am. Commn. to Russia, also for a time vice chmn. Am. Ry. Commn. to Russia. Pres. Alumni Assn. Mass. Inst. Tech., 1915, and for 5 yrs. term mem. of that corp. Home: 1791 Beacon St., Brookline, Mass. Died Dec. 29, 1940.

HORNADY, John Randolph, author, editor; b. Ringgold, Ga., May 15, 1872; s. John Randolph and Janie Lawton (Mulkey) H.; m. Maude Morel Simmons, Nov. 28, 1896; children—Jack Randolph, Cecil Carr, Ernestine. Asso. editor, mng. editor Birmingham, Ala., News, 1908-15; editor Rome, Ga., News Tribune, since 1930. Chmn. Coosa-Ala. Rivers Improvement Assn.; vice pres. City Commn. of Birmingham, Ala., 1915-21. Mem. Ala. Com. Newcomen Soc. of Eng. Mason (32°). Clubs: Rome Country, Rotary. Author: (books) Soldiers of Progress, 1930; Book of Birmingham, 1921; History of Atlanta, 1922; Editorials of J. R. H., 1914; contbr. mags. including McClure's, Metropolitan, Leslie's; author, lecturer on commn. form of govt. Address: General Forrest Hotel, Rome, Ga. Died Mar. 1, 1948.

HORNBEAK, Samuel Lee, univ. pres.; b. Bosqueville, Tex., Jan. 13. 1865; s. Samuel M. and Harriet Jane (Rice) H.; A.B., Trinity U., Tex., 1885, A.M., 1886; U. of Chicago, 1894-95; Ph.D., Cumberland U., Tenn., 1895; LL.D., 1908; post grad. U. of Wis., summer 1918, Columbia, 2d sem. 1920-21, U. of Chicago, summer 1926; LL.D., Baylor U. and Trinity U., 1920; m. Mattie A. Gee, May 27, 1891; children—Harriet Lee, Louise Sloan, Katherine Gee. Teacher pub. schs., Tex., 1885-91; prof. chemistry and physics, Trinity U., 1891-1907, chmn. of faculty, 1899-1901, dean, 1901-07; supt. State Sch. for Blind, Austin, Tex., 1907-08; pres. Trinity U., Waxahachie, Tex., Sept. 1908-20, trustee Trinity U., 1907-08, dir. million dollar endowment campaign, 1919-21, pres. emeritus and prof. social sciences since 1921, chmn. administrative council, 1933-34; retired, 1942. Chairman of Waxahachie Public Forum. Chmn. bd. trustees Sims Library; mem. Texas Society for Crippled Children. Mem. American Economic Assn., National Education Assn., Southwestern Polit. and Social Science Assn., Nat. Conf. Social Work, Am. Social Hygiene Assn., Am. Sociol. Soc., Inter-racial Commn. of Tex., Nat. Council of Nat. Econ. League. Democrat. Presbyterian (elder). Author: The History of Trinity University. Home: Waxahachi Tex. Died June 15, 1949.

HORNBLOW, Arthur, editor, author and dramatist; b. Manchester, Eng.; s. William and Sarah Jane (Rodgers) H.; studied lit. and art, Paris; corr. English and Am. jours. from Paris; came to U.S., 1889; m. Natalie Lambert, May 26, 1892 (died 1912); m. 2d, Nora Marie Geoghegan, 1914. On staff Kansas City Globe, 1889, later on Dramatic Mirror; asst. play reader for A. M. Palmer, 1892-94; asst. fgn. editor and fgn. editor, 1894-96, on staff Paris edit., 1896-97, asst. cable editor at London, 1897-99, New York Herald; on staff New York Times, 1899; editor The Theatre Magazine, 1901-26; dean John Murray Anderson-Robert Milton Sch. of The Theatre, 1927-29. Club: Authors' (London). Author: (books) The Lion and the Mouse, novelized from Charles Klein's play, 1906; The End of the Game, 1907; The Profligate; By Right of Conquest, 1909; The Third Degree (with Charles Klein); John Marsh's Millions (with Charles Klein); The Gamblers (with Charles Klein); The Easiest Way (with Eugene Walter); Bought and Paid For (with George Broadhurst); Kindling (with Charles Kenyon); The Talker (with Marion Fairfax); The Mask; The Argyle Case (with Harriet Ford and Harvey J. O'Higgins in coöperation with William J. Burns); The Money Makers (with Charles Klein); The Price (with George Broadhurst); Training for the Stage, 1916; A History of the Theatre in America, 1919. Translations: The Demi-Virgins, 1896, and Letters of Women, 1897 (both by Marcel Prévost); Triumph of Death, 1897. The Intruder, 1898 (both by Gabriele d'Annunzio); Private Life of the Sultan (Dorys), 1901. Plays: Musotte, 3 acts (adaptation Guy de Maupassant), 1894; Twilight (collaborator), 1896; Strolling Players (adaptation), 1906; The System of Dr. Tarr (collaborator). Home: 9 The Drive, Golders Green, London, England. Address: care Fifth Av. Bank, 44th St. and 5th Av., New York, N.Y. Died May 6, 1941.

HORNE, Charles Francis, author, editor, teacher; b. Jersey City, N.J., Jan. 12, 1870; s. George E. and Margaret A. (Cooper) H.; B.S., Coll. City of New York, 1889, M.S., 1897; Ph.D., New York U., 1905; m. Sarah Durham, Feb. 14, 1896; children—Winifred Durham, Enid Warren, Charles F. Instr. English, Coll. City of New York, 1897, asst. prof., 1906-15, prof., 1915-40, also head of dept. of English, 1935-40. Lecturer in various univ. extension movements, on lit. and hist. topics. Mem. Modern Lang. Assn. America, Phi Beta Kappa, Phi Gamma Delta. Club: City College. Author: The Birth of the Novel, 1897; The Story of Germany and Austria, 1901; The Story of France, 1902; The Story of Our Country, 1903; Outline Narrative of the Great Events of History, 1905; The Story of Turkey, 1906; The Technique of the Novel, 1908; History of New York State, 1915; The World and Its People, 1924; The Story of Our American People, 1926; Europe the Mother of America, 1930; Young America, 1931. Editor: Great Men and Famous Women (8 vols.), 1894-96; Story of the Greatest Nations, 10 vols. (with Edward Sylvester Ellis), 1901-06; Great Events by Famous Historians (20 vols.), 1904-05; History of the College of the City of New York, 1907; The Meaning of Modern Life, 1907; The Bible and Its Story (10 vols.), 1908-10; Life and Works of Jules Verne, 1911; The World's Famous Events (10 vols.), 1914; Sacred Books and Early Literature of the East (14 vols.), 1917; Universal Library of Autobiography, 1918; Great Events of the Great War (7 vols.), 1921; Source Records of the Post-War Period (4 vols.), 1931; World Epochs (12 vols.), 1936. Mem. U.S. Army Ednl. Corps with A.E.F. in France; editor and author of the Am. history textbooks of the Am. Legion. Home: "Landfall." Annapolis. Md. Died Sep. 14, 1942.

HORNE, Edmund Campion, univ. pres.; b. Meadville, Pa., Mar. 12, 1898; s. Martin Charles and Johanna (Murphy) H.; ed. St. Charles Coll., Baltimore, 1916-19, John Carroll U., Cleveland, O., 1919-20, St. Louis U., 1920-24; A.B., Gonzaga U., Spokane, Wash., 1926, A.M., 1927; grad. student Cath. U., Washington, D.C., 1934-37. Mem. Soc. of Jesus since 1920; ordained priest R.C. Ch., 1927. Instr. St. Ignatius High Sch., Cleveland, 1927-30; instr. in English, Creighton U., 1933-34; pres. John Carroll U. since 1937. Mem. Am. Assn. Sch. Adminstrs., Ohio Coll. Assn. (v.p. 1939), Ohio College Assn. (pres. 1940), Alpha Sigma Nu. Mem. K.C. Contbr. to Thought (Jesuit publ.). Address: John Carroll University, Cleveland, O. Died May 25, 1948.

HORNE, Herman Harrell, univ. prof.; b. Clayton, N.C., Nov. 22, 1874; s. Hardee and Ida Caroline (Harrell) H.; A.B., A.M., U. of N.C., 1895; A.M., Harvard U., 1897, Ph.D., 1899; studied U. of Berlin, 1906-07; LL.D., Wake Forest (N.C.) Coll., 1924, Muhlenberg Coll., 1927, U. of N.C., 1934; New York U., 1943; m. Alice Elizabeth Herbert Worthington, Aug. 20, 1901 (died Apr. 4, 1934); children—Julia Carolyn, Betsy Worthington, William Henry, Ida Battle; m. 2d, Mrs. Mary D. W. Williamson, Apr. 9, 1944. Instructor, modern languages, Univ. of N.C., 1894-96; instr. philosophy, Dartmouth Coll., 1899-1900, asst. prof. philosophy and pedagogy, 1900-05, prof. philosophy, 1905-09; prof. history of edn. and history of philosophy, New York University, 1909-42, emeritus since September 1, 1942. Lecturer in Harvard Summer School of Theology, 1903, in Martha's Vineyard Summer Institute, 1902-04, University of N.C. Summer Sch., 1903, Columbia U. Summer Session, 1905, Harvard Summer Sch., 1907, U. of Calif., Summer Session, 1909, N.Y.U., summers 1911-13 and since 1922, Summer Sch. of the South, Knoxville, Tenn., 1914, Auburn Summer Schs., 1915-17, Southern Coll. of Y.M.C.A., summers, 1920, 21; Norton lecturer Southern Bapt. Theol. Sem., 1923; Carew lecturer, Hartford Theol. Foundation, 1935; James Sprunt lecturer, Union Theol. Sem., 1937; McDowell lecturer, Ohio Wesleyan University, 1943. Mem. Religious Edn. Assn., Am. Philos. Assn., Am. Acad. Polit. and Social Science, N.C. Hist. Soc., Soc. Coll. Teachers Edn., Phi Beta Kappa, Phi Delta Kappa; fellow A.A.A.S., Soc. for Advancement of Edn. Presbyterian. Clubs: Authors (New York), Scholia. Author: The Philosophy of Education, 1904, 27; The Psychological Principles of Education, 1906; Idealism in Education, 1910; Free Will and Human Responsibility, 1912; Leadership of Bible Study Groups, 1912; Story-Telling, Questioning, and Studying, 1916; The Teacher as Artist, 1917; Jesus—Our Standard, 1918; Modern Problems as Jesus Saw Them, 1918; Jesus—The Master Teacher, 1920; Christ in Man-Making, 1925; Jesus as a Philosopher, 1927; This New Education, 1931; The Essentials of Leadership, 1931; John Dewey's Philosophy (pamphlet), 1931; The Democratic Philosophy of Education, 1932; Syllabus in The Philosophy of Education, 1934; Quintilian on Edn. (with Catherine Ruth Smith), 1936; The Philosophy of Christian Education, 1937; Introduction to Modern Education (with others), 1937; Tomorrow in the Making (with others), 1939. Editor: Simple Southern Songs, 1916; Songs of Sentiment (by Ida Caroline Horne), 1917; Romantic Rambles, 1925. Contbr. to Monroe's Cyclo. of Education and Nelson's Ency. of Sunday Schools, and to 41st Yearbook of Nat. Soc. for Study of Edn. Home: 341 Summit Av., Leonia, N.J. Died Aug. 16, 1946.

HORNER, J(ames) Richey, M.D.; b. Tarentum, Pa., June 7, 1861; s. Rev. Joseph and Caroline (McCracken) H.; grad. Pittsburgh Central High Sch.; M.D., Homœ. Hosp. Coll., Cleveland, 1883; M.D., New York Homœ. Med. Coll., 1884; M.D., Western Reserve U., 1907; hon. A.M., Allegheny Coll., Pa., 1885; m. Belle Benton, June 12, 1900; children—William Wattles, James Richey. Resident surgeon Ward's Island (N.Y.) Homœopathic Hosp., 1884; phys., 1885, and later staff obstetrician, Homœ. Hosp., Pittsburgh; gen. practice, Pittsburgh and Allegheny until 1896; abroad 7 months, 1896; asst. to Hughlings Jackson, neurologist, Queen's Square Hosp., London; spl. study diseases of nervous system; asst. phys., staff of State Homœ. Hosp. for the Insane, Middletown, N.Y., 1897; now in exclusive practice in mental and nervous diseases; was registrar and prof. neurology and electro-therapeutics, was prof. psychiatry and insanity, Cleveland-Pulte Med. Coll.; neurologist, Huron Street Hosp. Mem. Am. Inst. Homœopathy, Cleveland Acad. of Medicine, Ohio State Med. Soc., A.M.A. Member Cleveland Chamber of Commerce. Republican. Methodist. Club: Big Ten University. Home: 12924 Forest Hill Av., East Cleveland 12. Office: 663 Rose Bldg., Cleveland 15, O. Died Mar. 20, 1947.

HORNER, Leonard Sherman, elec. engr.; b. Marshall, Va., Mar. 26, 1875; s. Frederick (U.S. Navy) and Maria Elizabeth H.; prep. edn. Bethel Mil. Acad., Warrenton, Va.; E.E., Lehigh U., 1898; m. Julia Stuyvesant Barry, Nov. 8, 1902; children—H. Mansfield, Helen N. Began with engr. constrn. dept., Am. Telephone & Telegraph Co., New York, 1898; with Crocker-Wheeler Co. as sales engr. and mgr. for Conn., 1900-08; v.p. Acme Wire Co., 1908-26, now dir.; pres. Niles-Bement-Pond Co., 1926-30; v.p. and dir. The Bullard Co. Chmn. com. on census of mfrs., Dept. Commerce, 1931-32, chmn. Nat. Research Council Com., 1929-30, in preparation of aircraft prodn. study and report, which study covered factors affecting increased output and reduced cost of prodn. and embodied recommendations in methods, etc.; dep. adminstr. National Recovery Administration, 1933-34; now active in estate management and supervision of investments; also active on indsl. surveys and as indsl. advisor to mfrs. With troop A, New York Cavalry, in Puerto Rico, Spanish-Am. War, 1898; with Air Service at Washington, D.C., World War, 1917-18, as chief of staff, Bureau Aircraft Production, rank of maj.; promoted to lt. col. Mem. U.S. Chamber Commerce (dir. 1929, 30), Chamber Commerce of New Haven (v.p.; dir.). Mem. Nat. Industrial Conf. Bd., Nat. Assn. Mfrs., New England Council, Va. Hist. Soc., New Haven Hist. Soc., Sigma Chi, Am. Legion. Republican. Episcopalian. Clubs: Graduate, New Haven Country (New Haven); Army and Navy (Washington, D.C.). Home: 870 Prospect St., New Haven, Conn. Died Aug. 1, 1943.

HORNIBROOK, William Harrison (hôr'nĭ-brŏok); b. Cherokee, Ia., July 6, 1884; s. Dr. Edward and Rosina H.; Shattuck Sch., Faribault, Minn., 1900-02; grad. prep. dept., Drake U., 1902-03; student U. of Mich., Dept. of Law, 1903-04; LL.B., Nat. U., 1905; m. Miss Yolande Wilson, Nov. 23, 1906; children—John Wilson (M.D.), Frances Virginia. Purchased Condon (Ore.) Globe, 1906; moved to Twin Falls, Ida., 1908; established Twin Falls Chronicle, 1908; purchased Albany (Ore.) Daily Democrat, 1912, Vancouver (Wash.) Daily Columbian, 1919. Mem. Ida. Senate, 1910-12; mem. and sec. Dem. State Central Com., Ore., 1913-15; E.E. and M.P. to Siam, 1915-17; resigned and resumed charge of newspaper; elected Ore. mem. Dem. Nat. Com., 1918; resigned Apr. 1919; settled at Boise, Ida., 1921; pres. Security Abstract & Title Co.; elected chmn. Dem. State Central Com. of Ida., Aug. 1, 1922; resigned and purchased The Evening Recorder, Porterville, Calif.; moved to Provo, Utah, Oct. 1924, and purchased the Provo Evening Herald; purchased the Salt Lake Times, Dec. 1926, and Salt Lake Mining and Legal News, Jan. 1929; E.E. and M.P. to Iran (Persia), 1933-36, to Afghanistan, 1935-36 (resigned), to Costa Rica, 1937-41 (resigned). Episcopalian. Purchased Pacific Grove Tribune (Calif.), Nov. 15, 1943. Address: 188 Laurel Av., Pacific Grove, Calif. Died Mar. 20, 1946.

HORSBURGH, Robert Homer, business exec.; b. Sarnia, Ont., Can., Apr. 4, 1883; s. William and Elizabeth (Courtney) H.; m. Flora Larimer, Oct. 15, 1908; children—Delbert Larimer, Elizabeth Alice (Mrs. Charles Vernay Molesworth), Janet Courtney (Mrs. Alexander Fullerton Phillips), Robert Homer. Naturalized Am. citizen since 1904. Comptroller, The Sherwin-Williams Co., to 1917; then became sec.-treas., The Glidden Co., Cleveland, O., exec. vice pres., now vice chmn. of bd. Mem. Selective Service Bd. No. 43, Lakewood, O. Trustee and treas. Hiram House, Cleveland. Clubs: Union, Mid-Day (Cleveland); Clifton (Lakewood). Home: 15410 Edgewater Drive, Lakewood 7, O. Office: Union Commerce Bldg., Cleveland 14, O. Died Feb. 11, 1949.

HORSFALL, R(obert) Bruce (hôrs'fal), artist-naturalist; b. Clinton, Ia., Oct. 21, 1868; s. John Tomlin and Anne (Battersby) H.; ed. pub. schs.; studied Cincinnati Art Acad., 1886-89; awarded European scholarship and studied at Art Acad., Munich, and at Paris, France, 1889-93; m. Carra Elisabeth Huntting, May 27, 1906; 1 son, R. Bruce. First exhibited at Chicago, Ill., in 1886; also at Chicago Expn., 1893, and at Midwinter Expn., San Francisco, 1893-94; scientific illustrations for Am. Museum Natural History, New York, 1898-99, for Princeton Patagonian Report, 1904-14; illustrator for Century and St. Nicholas, 1899-1921; illustrated Land Mammals of the Western Hemisphere, 1912-13; also many natural history books. Permanently represented by backgrounds for Habitat Groups, Am. Museum Natural History, Peabody Museum (Yale), Kent Scientific Museum (Grand Rapids, Mich.), State Museum (Springfield, Ill.), Zoöl. Museum (U. of Minn.); life size paintings of Great Auk, Calif. condor, Pallas cormorant in Adminstrn. Bldg., New York Zoöl. Park; Great Auk, Dinosaur, in U.S. Nat. Museum; by portraits of Dr. William John Sinclair and Alexander H. Phillips in Guyot Hall, Princeton University. Asst. biologist, Oregon Fish and Game Commn., 1914-16. Mem. Am. Ornithologists' Union, Cooper Ornithological Club, Northwest Bird and Mammal Soc., Am. Soc. Mammalogists, Am. Museum Natural History. Address: Route No. 2, Fairport, N.Y. Died Mar. 24, 1948.

HORSKY, Edward (hôr'skĭ), lawyer; b. Helena, Mont., June 12, 1873; s. John and Louise (Seykora) H.; A.B., Central High Sch., Phila., 1890, A.M., 1896; studied medicine but changed to law; LL.B., U. of Mich., 1895; m. Grace A. Johnston, Jan. 18, 1934. Was admitted to practice Michigan bar, 1895, Mont. bar same yr., U.S. Circuit Court, 1897, U.S. Circuit Court of Appeals, at San Francisco, 1899, U.S. Supreme Court, 1904; practiced in Helena since 1895; city atty., 1898-1904, 1908-11, 1915-18; mayor of Helena, 1911; ex-chmn. Rep. City Com., Helena. Mem. Sons and Daughters of Mont. Pioneers (ex-pres.; v.p. 1938-40). Scottish Rite Mason (32°), Shriner. Protestant. Mem. Mont. Bar Assn. "Four-Minute Man." Grad. Field Arty., Central Officers T.S., 53d Battery, Camp Taylor, Ky., 1918. Mem. American Legion. Home: 320 North Benton Av. Office: Horsky Bldg., Helena, Mont. Died Jan. 28, 1948.

HORSLEY, John Shelton (hôrs'lĕ), surgeon; b. Lovingston, Va., Nov. 24, 1870; s. John and Rose Evelyn (Shelton) H.; student acad. dept. U. of Va., 1888-90, M.D., 1892; post-graduate courses, New York; LL.D., U. of Richmond; D.Sc., Medical Coll. of Va.; m. Eliza Braxton, Feb. 14, 1899; children—John Shelton (dec.), Elizabeth Braxton (dec.), Caperton Braxton, Guy Winston, Mary Caperton, Braxton, Frederick, Alice Cabell. Began practice in Nelson County, Va.; moved to Staunton, 1894; asst. to Dr. John A. Wyeth, of New York, 1896; editor New York Polyclinic Med. Jour., 1897-98; at El Paso, Tex., 1898-1903; propr. and surgeon in chief St. Luke's Hosp., El Paso, 1899-1903; prof. principles of surgery, Med. Coll. of Va., Richmond, 1903-12; surgeon in charge St. Elizabeth's Hospital. Certified by American Board of Surgery. Fellow American Surg. Assn., Southern Surg. Assn., Am. Med. Assn., hon. mem. Soc. of Alumni of Bellevue Hosp.; mem. Internat. Soc. of Surgery; Richmond Acad. Medicine (former president), Phi Beta Kappa, Alpha Omega Alpha, Sigma Xi; honorary member N.M. Medical Soc., St. Louis Med. Soc.; ex-pres. Med. Soc. of Va.; ex-pres. Southern Med. Assn.; ex-pres. Va. Acad. of Science. Democrat. Unitarian. Clubs: Commonwealth, Country of Va.; Colonnade. Author: Surgery of Blood Vessels; Operative Surgery; Surgery of Stomach and Small Intestines; Research and Medical Progress; Surgery of Stomach and Duodenum. Associate editor of Lewis Practice of Surgery. Contbr. to medical press on surgical subjects. Home: Westmoreland Pl. Office: 617 W. Grace St., Richmond, Va. Died Apr. 7, 1946.

HORST, John Joseph, univ. dean; b. Duesseldorf, Germany, July 29, 1880; s. Johann and Margareta (Euler) H.; student Canisius Coll., Exaeten, Holland, 1900-01, Campion Coll., Prairie du Chien, Wis., 1901-04; A.M., St. Louis U., 1913; Ph.D., Gregorian Univ., Rome, Italy, 1931. Came to U.S., 1901, naturalized 1911. Mem. Society of Jesus. Instr. in mathematics and history St. John's High Sch., Toledo, O., 1904-09; ordained priest Roman Cath. Ch., 1912; prof. philosophy and biology, U. of Detroit, 1914-31, dean, Coll. of Arts and Sciences, 1925-31; prof. philosophy, St. Louis U., 1931, dean of Sch. of Philosophy and Science, 1932-44; mem. faculty, Creighton U., Omaha, 1944-45. Trustee U. of Detroit, 1925-31, St. Louis U. since 1937. Mem. Jesuit Ednl. Assn., Jesuit Philos. Assn. of the Miss. Valley. Home: 221 N. Grand Blvd., St. Louis, Mo. Died July 8, 1945.

HORTON, Elmer Grant, M.D., educator; b. Horton Hill, Erie County, N.Y., May 22, 1868; s. Lorenzo Lincoln and Phila Ann (Chase) H.; B.S., Cornell U., 1892; fellow U. of Pa., 1895-96; M.D., Ohio Med. U., Columbus, 1906; grad. study, Harvard, 1912-14; m. Belle Fisher, Sept. 4, 1894; children—Vivian Fisher, Mildred Mae (Mrs. Harry R. Ansel). Teacher dist. schs., 1885-88, Cornell U. Summer Sch., 1892; instr. in sciences, Detroit School for Boys, 1892-93; prof. hygiene and physical culture, Wabash Coll., 1893-95; instr. in hygiene, U. of Pa., 1896-98; bacteriologist and chemist in charge Ohio State Bd. of Health labs., 1898-1907; health commr., Columbus, O., 1907-09; practice in pediatrics since 1912; pediatrist and asst. chief of staff Children's Hosp.; head of pediatric dept. University Hosp.; in charge Isolation Hosp.; lecturer on communicable diseases, Grant Hosp. Prof. hygiene, Ohio Med. U., 1902-07, prof. pediatrics 1912-14; prof. pediatrics, Starling Ohio Med. Coll., 1907-12; asst. prof. pediatrics, Ohio State U., 1914-24, prof., 1924-37, clin. prof. of pediatrics, 1937-39, emeritus prof. of pediatrics since 1939. Recalled 1940 to active duty as professor and in charge of Isolation Hospital. Member Franklin County Board of Health, 1928-33. Member A.M.A., American Academy of Pediatrics, Ohio State Medical Assn., Columbus Acad. Medicine (pres. 1935; hon. life mem. since 1941), Alpha Mu Pi Omega, Nu Sigma Nu. Republican. Methodist. Clubs: University Faculty, Lions (past pres., zone-chmn., Ohio, 1938-39; deputy dist. gov., 1939-40, dist. gov., 1940-41; internat. counselor, 1941), Columbus Automobile. Contbr. to med. publs. Home: 285 E. Lane Av. Office: 350 E. State St., Columbus, O. Died May 30, 1949.

HORTON, Frank Ogilvie, mem. Rep. Nat. Com.; b. Muscatine, Ia., Oct. 18, 1882; s. Col. Charles Cummings and Isabel (Ogilvie) H.; grad. Morgan Park Mil. Acad., Chicago, Ill., 1899, U. of Chicago, 1903; m. Henriette Stuart, 1937; children—William Scovel, John Ogilvie, Ovid Butler. Engaged in livestock ranching many years. Mem. 76th Congress (1939-41), Wyoming at large; mem. Rep. Nat. Com. since 1937. Home: Saddlestring, Wyo. Died Aug. 17, 1948.

HORTON, George, author; b. Fairville, New York, Oct. 11, 1859; s. Peter Davis and Mary Sophia (Aiken) H.; A.B., U. of Mich., 1878; Litt.D., George Washington U., 1903; m. Catherine Sacapoulo (former pres. Mixed Tribunal of Egypt), of Athens, Greece, Feb. 4, 1909; 1 dau., Nancy Phyllis. Consul at Athens, Greece, 1893-98; lit. editor Chicago Times-Herald, 1899-1901; editor lit. supplement, Chicago American, 1901-03; consul, 1905-06, consul-gen., 1906-10, at Athens, Greece; consul at Saloniki, Turkey, 1910-11; consul-gen. at Smyrna, Turkey, 1911-17, and again assigned there May 1919; at Saloniki, 1917-19, at Budapest, Hungary, 1923-Oct. 1924 (retired). Was in charge of the interests of Great Britain, France, Italy, Russia, Serbia, Montenegro, and Rumania, in Asia Minor from the outbreak of World War I until Apr. 6, 1917, distributing relief among needy civilians and prisoners of war; on rupture of relations with Turkey transferred to Saloniki. Received thanks of British and French Govts. for services during war; decorated Knight Order of Gregory the Great (Papal) for protection afforded Christian populations in Turkey; Comdr. Order of the Savior (Greek); del. Am. High Commn. to Turkey, 1920-21; received vote of thanks from Am. missionaries for efforts at Smyrna in behalf of Christian population. Hon. mem. Athens "Parnassos," 1908. Has lectured extensively in U.S. for Am. Archaeol. Soc. Mem. Phi Beta Kappa. Episcopalian. Clubs: Cosmos, Nat. Press (Washington). Author: Songs of the Lowly, 1891; In Unknown Seas, 1895; Aphroessa, 1897; A Fair Brigand, 1898; Like Another Helen, 1901; Modern Athens, 1901; The Tempting of Father Anthony, 1901; The Long Straight Road, 1902; In Argolis, 1902; The Monk's Treasure, 1905; The Edge of Hazard, 1906; Miss Schuyler's Alias, 1913; The Blight of Asia, 1926; Recollections Grave and Gay, 1927; The Home of Nymphs and Vampires, 1929; Poems of an Exile, 1931. Address: care Cosmos Club, Washington. Died Jan. 5, 1942.

HORTON, George Terry, civil engr., mfr.; b. Waupun, Wis., 1873; s. Horace E. and Emma (Babcock) H.; C.E., Rensselaer Poly. Inst., 1893; m. Hazel Heath, Nov. 27, 1907; 1 dau., Florence (Mrs. Arnold Gillatt). Became identified with the Chicago Bridge & Iron Works, 1893, pres. and mgr. since 1912. Chairman Chicago Plan Commission; life trustee Rensselaer Poly. Inst. Lt. comdr. U.S.N.R., retired. Mem. Am. Soc. C.E., Western Soc. Engrs., Chicago Hist. Soc., Am. Welding Soc. (pres.), Am. Soc. for Testing Materials, Soc. Naval Architects and Marine Engrs., Chicago Engrs., New Eng. Historic Geneal. Soc., Art Inst. of Chicago, Am. Petroleum Inst., Am. Water Works Assn., Delta Kappa Epsilon. Clubs: Engineers', University, South Shore Country, Commercial Club, Aero Club of Illinois (Chicago). Home: 4940 Woodlawn Av. Office: 1305 W. 105th St., Chicago, Ill. Died Mar. 19, 1945.

HORTON, Lydiard Heneage, cons. psychologist; b. London, Eng., 1879; s. Samuel Dana H. of Ohio and Blanche (Lydiard) H.; ed. prep. schs., Switzerland, France, Eng., U.S.; A.B., Williams Coll., 1901; A.M., Columbia, 1911, Ph.D., 1922; grad. study Harvard and U. of Pa. Med. Schs.; also research with Prof. Wm. James. Aide to guardian, Dr. F. W. Holls, 1897-1903, in promotion of internat. arbitration, first Hague Court, and Internat. Congress of Art and Sciences; industrial research in mech. dept., C.& A. R.R., 1901-08; on house staff, Boston Psychopathic Hosp., 1912-14; collaborator with Dr. Morton Prince in Journal Abnormal Psychology, 1912-21; founder, 1920, since dir. Cartesian Research Soc.; editor bulletin same, Biopsychology; asso. Evans Memorial Clinic, 1928-36; representative on Boston Noise Commn., 1931-32; lecturer on biopsychology, Boston University School of Medicine since 1929. Member American psychopathol. Association (vice-pres. 1937-38), A.A.A.S., Assn. Research Human Heredity, Am. Assn. for Applied Psychology, Mass. Medico-Legal Society, Chi Psi. Clubs: Williams (New York); University (Boston). Author: The Dream Problem and the Mechanism of Thought, 2 vols., 1925, 26; contbr. to Problems of Personality, 1925. Articles disputing validity of psychoanalytic techniques; devised precision method for analysis of dreams and war neuroses; mental hygiene promotional article "Everything Improved but the Mind." Address: 175 Dartmouth St., Boston, Mass. Died Jan. 19, 1945.

HORTON, Robert Elmer, hydraulic engr.; b. Parma, Mich., May 18, 1875; s. Van Rensselaer W. and Rowena Spencer (Rafter) H.; B.Sc., Albion Coll., 1897, Sc.D., 1932; m. Ella H. Young, June 19, 1901. Asst. on U.S. Deep Waterways Survey, 1898-99; dist. engr. U.S. Geol. Survey, 1900-06; engr. in charge Bur. Hydraulics, N.Y. State Barge Canal, 1906-11; cons. practice since 1911; hydraulic expert Dept. Pub. Works and Atty. Gen.'s Dept., State of N.Y., 1911-25; engr. in charge Del. River Case before Supreme Court of U.S., for State of N.J., 1922-30; cons. engr. Bd. of Water Supply, Albany, N.Y., 1924-32; cons. engr. The Power Authority, State of N.Y., 1932-33; mem. advisory council of Federal Board Surveys and Maps, 1918-39, and Engring. Board of Review, Sanitary Dist. of Chicago, 1925-27; engineer consultant, Nat. Resources Com., 1934-37; cons. U.S. Soil Conservation Service, 1939-41; consultant Tenn. Valley Authority, 1942-44, City of Rochester, N.Y., 1942-43; dir. Horton Hydrologic Lab. Member Am. Society C.E., Am. Water Works Assn., N.E. Water Works Assn., Am. Geophys. Union, Sigma Nu, Inst. C.E. (London), Instn. of Water Engrs. (England); fellow Am. Meteorol. Soc. (pres. 1939), Royal Meteorol. Soc., Am. Geog. Soc. Republican. Author: Weir Experiments, Coefficients and Formulas, 1905; Turbine Water Wheel Tests and Power Tables, 1906; Water Wheels, 1907; Determination of Stream Flow during the Frozen Season (with H. K. Barrows), 1907; Hydrography of N.Y. State (N.Y. State Annuals) 1900-11; Hydrology of the Gt. Lakes (with C.E. Grunsky), 1926; Rainfall Runoff and Evaporation (with L. K. Sherman), 1933; Surface Runoff Phenomena, 1935; Apples from Eden (stories), 1938; also numerous scientific papers. Inventor water level gauge; joint for wood stave pipe. Home: Voorheesville, N.Y. Died Apr. 22, 1945.

HORTON, Wilkins P., Dem. nat. committeeman; b. Corning, Kan., Sept. 1, 1889; s. Thomas B. and Mary Ellen (Wilkins) H.; student Draughn's Business Coll., Raleigh, N.C., 1910-11, U. of North Carolina, 1912-14; m. Cassandra C. Mendenhall, June 12, 1918. 1 son, Harry P. Admitted to N.C. bar, 1915; atty. for Chatham County, N.C., since 1922; pres. North Carolina R.R., fiscal year, 1943-44; state senator, 1918, 26, 30, 35; lt. gov. North Carolina, 1936-40; chmn. Dem. Exec. Com., Chatham City, N.C., since 1922. Dem. nat. committeeman for N.C., 1944-47; resigned; elected chmn. State Dem. Exec. Com. of N.C., May 1947; practiced law since 1915; mem. law firm Horton & Bell, since June 1946. Chmn. N.C. State Sch. Com., 1937-41; chmn. Judicial Dist. Commn. of N.C., 1941-44. Mem. N.C. State Bar, Inc., Am., N.C. bar assns., Sigma Chi. Mason (Shriner); Grand Lodge of N.C., since Apr. 1947. Home: Hillsboro St., Pittsboro, N.C.* Died Feb. 1, 1950.

HOSFORD, Harry Lindley, artist; b. Terre Haute, Ind., Aug. 19, 1877; s. Charles Eugene and Lida (Showalter) H.; ed. pub. schs.; art edn., Nat. Acad. Design, N.Y. City, and New York Sch. of Art; studied under William M. Chase, Frank V. DuMond, Francis Jones, F. Louis Mora; m. Gertrude Lillian Gile, June 7, 1905; children—Dorothy, Gertrude, Jane, Harry Lindley. Has specialized on etchings. Represented in Library of Congress, Smithsonian Instn., New York Pub. Library, Minneapolis Art Inst., Bibliothèque Internationale, Paris, collection of Crown Prince of Sweden. Awarded 2d prize in prints, Minneapolis Art Inst., 1931, 1st prize, prints, same inst., 1934. Sec. State Dept. Health, Pa., 1911-17. Mem. Chicago Soc. of Etchers, Lyme Art Assn. Republican. Unitarian. Clubs: Century (N.Y.), Nat. Press (Washington, D.C.). Home: Lyme, Conn. Died Sept. 5, 1945.

HOSKINS, James Preston, corp. official; b. Lexington, Miss., Dec. 2, 1864; s. E. and Louisa (Pinkston) H.; ed. Miss. Agrl. and Mech. Coll.; m. Jean Dobbins, Apr. 30, 1914. Record clk., later chief clk. and cashier, Queen & Crescent R.R., 1882-87; bookkeeper, later asst. cashier, Chattanooga (Tenn.) Nat. Bank, 1887-99, cashier, 1899-1905; cashier 1st Nat. Bank, Chattanooga, 1905-25, pres., 1925-33; formerly pres. Chattanooga Gas Co.; dir., sec., treas. Signal Mountain Portland Cement Co.; also dir. many cos. Democrat. Presbyterian. Clubs: Mountain City, Fairyland Golf and Country. Home: Lookout Mountain, Tenn. Died Aug. 2, 1948.

HOSMER, Charles Bridgham (hŏz'mẽr), foreign service officer; b. Hudson, Mass., July 15, 1889; s. Frederick Prescott and Velona (Bridgham) H.; LL.B., U. of Me., 1911; grad. Nat. U., Havana, Cuba, 1921-

22; LL.M., George Washington U., 1929; m. Faye Hood Durham, Mar. 15, 1931; children—Charles Bridgham, Stephen Durham. Admitted to Me. bar, 1911; practiced in Lewiston, 1911-18; sec. to congressman, 1917-19; vice consul, Havana, 1919-22, Santo Domingo, 1922-23; consul Santo Domingo, 1923-25, Sherbrooke, Canada, 1925-26; assigned to Dept. of State, 1926-30; lecturer consular practice, Georgetown U., 1927-30; consul, Naples, Italy, 1930-36; chief Office of Fiscal and Budget Affairs, Dept. of State, 1937-40; diplomatic sec. and consul gen. detailed as foreign service inspector. 1940. Address: Dept. of State, Washington, D.C. Died Nov. 16, 1942.

HOSTETLER, Theodore Allen, patent lawyer; b. McLean County, Ill., May 8, 1864; s. John and Henrietta (Nafziger) H.; B.S. and A.B., Valparaiso (Ind.) U., 1892; LL.B., Chicago Law Sch., 1898; m. May Minier, Oct. 28, 1898; children—George Minier, Imogen. Began as teacher, 1882; asst. examiner U.S. Patent Office, Washington, D.C., 1902-15, prin. examiner, 1915-17, law examiner, 1917-22, became solicitor, 1922; now in practice as patent lawyer; instr. patent law, Nat. U., Washington, 1927-28. Sr. patent lawyer for Alien Property Custodian, 1942-45. Mem. Federal Bar Assn. of D.C. Mem. Christian (Disciples) Ch. Home: 1711 Surrey Lane N.W. Office: Nat. Press Bldg., Washington. Died Nov. 5, 1948.

HOTCHKISS, H(enry) Stuart; b. New Haven, Conn., Oct. 1, 1878; s. Henry L. and Jane (Trowbridge) Hotchkiss; Ph.B., Yale University, 1900; m. Elizabeth Wyndham Washington, Oct. 9, 1907; children—Henry, Mary Bolling Washington, Stuart Trowbridge, Joseph Washington. With L. Candee & Co., a subsidiary of U.S. Rubber Co., 1901-30, advancing to vice-pres. of latter; pres. Cambridge Rubber Co., 1937-40, now chmn. bd.; devoted much time to development of rubber plantations in Sumatra and the Malay Peninsula; chmn. bd. General Rubber Co. and subsidiaries until 1930; pres. U.S. Rubber Plantations, Inc., and subsidiaries until 1930; chmn. bd. General Latex & Chemical Corp.; director Union & New Haven Trust Co.; member board of management U.S. Govt. Synthetic Rubber Plant, Baytown, Texas. Representative in Europe of trustee in bankruptcy of International Match Corporation, 1932-33; industrial advisor to Swedish liquidators of Kreuger & Toll, 1934-35. Member Connecticut Naval Reserve, 1899-1901; apptd. chmn. Com. on Rubber, Council of Nat. Defense, Apr. 1917; commd. capt. S.C., Oct. 25, 1917; maj., Jan. 28, 1918; lt. col. Air Service, Oct. 8, 1918; served as asst. chief insp. equipment div. and as sr. asst. mil. attaché, Am. Embassy, London; with A.E.F. in France, and as chief of raw material production, Air Service, Washington, D.C. Trustee Bermuda Biol. Sta. for Research; asso. fellow of Silliman College, Yale. Mem. Am. Council, Inst. of Pacific Relations, Am. Geog. Soc. (v.p.; chmn. council), Mayflower Soc., Soc. Colonial Wars, Conn. Soc. (ex-gov.), Delta Psi; fellow Royal Geog. Soc., London. Conglist. Mason (32°). Clubs: Century Assn., Yale, St. Anthony (New York); Graduate, New Haven Lawn (New Haven, Conn.). Home: "Wyndham," East River, Conn. Office: 205 Church St., New Haven, Conn.; and 748 Main St., Cambridge, Mass. Died Sept. 16, 1947.

HOUGH, Henry Hughes, naval officer; b. St. Pierre, Miquelon (island nr. Newfoundland), Jan. 8, 1871; s. Charles Thacher and Sarah (Hughes) H.; grad. U.S. Naval Acad., 1891; m. Flaurence Oliphant Ward, Apr. 16, 1901. Ensign, July 1, 1893; promoted through grades to rear adm. Sept. 16, 1924. Served on Morris, Spanish-Am. War, 1898, Cleveland, 1903-06; duty Office of Naval Intelligence, Navy Dept., 1907-08; ordnance officer Idaho, 1908-09; navigator same, 1909; exec. officer Virginia, 1909-10; with Office Naval Intelligence, Navy Dept., 1910; naval attaché, Paris, France, and St. Petersburg, Russia, 1911-14; comd. Wilmington, 1914-15; assigned to duty U.S. Naval Acad., 1915; dist. comdr. Brest, France, 1918; commr. Prisoner of War Conf., Berne, Switzerland, 1918; comdg. U.S.S. Utah, 1919-21; comdg. receiving ship New York, 1921-22; governor Virgin Islands of the U.S., 1922-23; dir. Naval Intelligence, 1923-25; comdr. Yangtse (China) Patrol Force, 1925-27; mem. General Board, 1928-30; comdt. 15th Naval Dist. and Naval Operating Base, Canal Zone, 1930-31; Commander Base Force, U.S. Fleet, 1931-33; Commandant 1st Naval Dist. and Navy Yard, Boston, Mass., 1933-35; retired, Feb. 1, 1935. Decorated Officer of the Legion of Honor (French). Episcopalian. Clubs: Army and Navy, Chevy Chase (Washington); New York Yacht (New York). Address: Navy Dept., Washington, D.C. Died Sep. 9, 1943.

HOUGH, Samuel Strickler, church official; b. West Moreland County, Pa., Oct. 4, 1864; s. David W. and Polly (Reynolds) H.; student Shenandoah Normal Sch., Middletown, Va., and Nat. Normal U., Lebanon, O.; B.S., Glasgow (Ky.) Normal Coll., 1887; grad. Bonebrake Theol. Sem., Dayton, O., 1892; D.D., Otterbein Coll., 1905; m. Mrs. Mary R. Albert, July 16, 1914. Teacher, pub. schs., Pa., 1883-86, and prin. East Brady (Pa.) Schs., 1887-89; ordained ministry U.B. Ch., 1892; pastor Madison Circuit, Allegheny Conf., 1892-94; Madison Sta., 1894-95, 2d Ch., Altoona, Pa., 1895-1905; gen. sec. Foreign Mission Soc., U.B. Ch., 1905-19; exec. sec. bd. of adminstrn., U.B. Ch., 1919-37, gen. sec. emeritus since 1937. Mem. exec. com. Federal Council Chs. of Christ in America, also a member of United Stewardship Council America since 1913. Del. Ecumenical Missionary Conf., New York, 1900; World's S.S. Conv., Jerusalem, 1904; World's Missionary Conf., Edinburgh, 1910. Writer of books: Our Church Abroad; Our Foreign Missionary Enterprise (with J. S. Mills and W. R. Funk); China and the Islands (with G. M. Mathews); Partners in the Conquering Cause (with H. F. Shupe); (booklets) Continuing the Fellowship; Life Complete through Stewardship; Church Commission on Growth and Service; Christian Newcomer, His Life, Journal and Achievements. Home: 809 Manhattan Av., Dayton, O. Died July 15, 1944.

HOUGHTON, Will H., pres. Moody Bible Inst ed. in Boston and Providence, R.I.; D.D., Wheaton Coll.; m. Elizabeth Andrews; children—Adelaide Maude, Everett Arthur, Firman Andrews. Formerly pastor Bapt. Tabernacle, Atlanta, Ga.; pastor Calvary Bapt. Ch., N.Y. City, 1930-34; pres. Moody Bible Inst. since Nov. 1934; also editor of Moody Monthly. Author: The Living Christ; Let's Go Back to the Bible, 1939; Back to the Bible, 1940. Address: 153 Institute Pl., Chicago, Ill. Died June 14, 1947.

HOUSE, Homer Doliver, botanist; b. Oneida, N.Y., July 21, 1878; s. Doliver E. and Alice J. (Petrie) H. B.S., Syracuse U., 1902; M.S., Columbia, 1903, Ph.D. 1905; m. Erma N. H. Hotaling, Dec. 21, 1908. Prof botany and bacteriology, Clemson Coll., S.C., 1906-07; asso. dir. and lecturer botany and dendrology, Biltmore (N.C.) Forest Sch., 1908-13; asst state botanist, N.Y., 1913-14, state botanist since 1914. Mem. Torrey Bot. Club, Am. Bot. Soc., Am. Mycolo. Soc., Am. Fern Soc. Author: North American Species of Ipomoea. 1908; Wild Flowers of New York, 1923; Annotated List of Ferns and Flowering Plants of New York State, 1924; Wild Flowers, 1935; also ann. repts. of State Botanist of N.Y. State since 1915. Contbr. bot. articles. Home: Loudonville, N.Y. Address: N.Y. State Museum, Albany, N.Y. Died Dec. 21, 1949.

HOUSER, Frederick Wilhelm (hou'zẽr), judge; b. Jones County, Ia., Apr. 15, 1871; s. Justus Christian and Martha (Rodman) H.; ed. Lenox Coll., Hopkinton, Ia., Woodbury, and Los Angeles Business Coll., Los Angeles, and U. of Southern Calif. (LL.B., 1899); m. Sara L. Wilde, Jan. 1, 1903; children—Frederick Francis, Rodman Wilde. Admitted to Calif. bar, 1897, and began practice in Los Angeles, judge Superior Court, Los Angeles County, 1907-23; justice Court of Appeal, 1923-35, presiding justice, 1935-37; became asso. justice Supreme Court of Calif., 1937. Mem. State Legislature, 1903-07. Mem. Order of Coif. Republican. Mason (K.T., 32°, Shriner). Home: Granada Hotel, San Francisco, Calif. Died Oct. 12, 1942.

HOUSER, Shaler Charles, civil engr.; b. Lincolnton, N.C., June 7, 1879; s. Thomas Lawson and Elizabeth (James) H.; B.S., U. of Ala., 1898, C.E., 1899; hon. D.Sc., 1938; m. Mary George Cruikshank, June 11, 1911 (died Mar. 8, 1918); 1 son, Shaler Charles; m. 2d, Anna Taylor Donoho, July 16, 1927 (died May 26, 1928); m. 3d, Martha Warren Parham, Aug. 5, 1930; 1 dau., Martha Parham. Began as asst. engr., City of Mobile, Ala., 1899; gen. contractor, Anniston, Ala., 1900-01; designing engr. Stewart Coal Washer and engr. Mobile & Ohio R.R. and coal mines, Ala., 1901-04; engr. in charge Marx & Windsor, Cuba, on railroad location, irrigation and constrn. work, 1904-11; chief engr. Guantanamo & Western R.R., 1912; prof. engring., supervising engr. and treas., U. of Ala., since 1912. Mem. Am. Soc. C. E., Am. Soc. for Engring. Edn., Phi Beta Kappa, Omicron Delta Kappa, Alpha Tau Omega. Clubs: Rotary, Country of Tuscaloosa. Democrat. Presbyterian. Home: 154 The Highlands, Tuscaloosa, Ala. Died Jan. 11, 1948.

HOUSTON, George Harrison (hous'tŭn), industrial consultant; b. Covington, Ky., Jan. 4, 1883; s. Charles R. and Elizabeth (Mapes) H.; ed. Cincinnati Tech. Inst.; m. Mary Stuart Hoge, Apr. 29, 1909. Began with Houston, Stanwood & Gamble Co., Cincinnati, O.; asso. with Root and Vandervoort Engring. Co., Moline, Ill., 1910-15; became partner, Jamieson and Houston, cons. industrial engrs., N.Y. City, 1915; firm succeeded by George W. Goethals & Co., in which was partner, retiring from latter in 1922; pres. Wright-Martin Aircraft Corp. 1917-19, Wright Aeronautical Corp., 1919-22, Marlin Rockwell Corp., 1920-22; with others organized General Sugar Co., 1922, to engage in reorganizing group of West Indian sugar properties; completed this work, and resumed gen. cons. work, 1927; pres. Baldwin Locomotive Works, 1929-38; mem. Houston & Jolles (name later changed to Geo. W. Houston & Co.), consultants on indsl. management, financing and reorgn.; dir. Causejero Delegado and Financiera Técnica de Mexico, S.A. Mem. Soc. Automotive Engrs., Am. Soc. Mech. Engrs. Clubs: Metropolitan, Knickerbocker, City Midday, Broad Street (New York); Rittenhouse (Phila.); Round Hill (Greenwich, Conn.); Metropolitan (Washington); Chicago (Chicago); Bankers (Mexico City). Address: care Financiera Técnica de Mexico, S.A., Venustiano Carranza 944, Mexico, D.F. Died July 10, 1949; buried at Louisville, Ky.

HOUSTON, Robert Griffith, ex-congressman; born Milton, Del., Oct. 13, 1867; s. David H. (M.D.) and Comfort Tunnell (Hitchens) H.; ed. pub. schs. and under tutelage; read law in office of Judge Houston, 1885-88; m. Margaret White, Dec. 20, 1888; children—John Wallace, Mary Comfort (Mrs. J. Thomas Robinson), Elizabeth Wiltbank. Admitted to Del. bar, 1888, and began practice at Georgetown; owner and editor Sussex Republican since 1893; recommended by members of bar for asso. judge Supreme Court of Del., 1910, 22; asst. atty. gen., Del., 1921-24; atty. and chief, bur. of law, alien property custodian, Washington, 1923-25; mem. 69th to 72d Congresses (1925-33). Mem. Bd. Bar Examiners, Del.; vice chmn. State Com. for Feeble Minded; former trustee or sec. Sch. Bd., Georgetown; pres. State S.S. Assn. 3 yrs.; etc. Mem. Del. State Bar Assn. Republican. Presbyterian. Mason. Co-editor Vols. VII, VIII, IX, Houston's Delaware Law Reports. One of three authors of Del. Sch. Law, 1921. Home: Georgetown, Del. Died Jan. 29, 1946.

HOVEY, George Rice, educator; b. Newton Centre, Mass., Jan. 17, 1860; s. Alvah and Augusta M. (Rice) H.; A.B., Brown U., 1882, A.M., 1885; grad. Newton Theol. Instn., 1885, post-grad. work, 1885-86; D.D., Temple U., Phila., 1901, Brown, 1902; m. Clara K. Brewer, Sept. 15, 1890; children—Alvah Brewer (dec.), Ruth. Instr. Yale Summer Sch. of Hebrew, 1887; prof. Hebrew, 1887-97, N.T. Greek, 1890-97, Richmond (Va.) Theol. Sem.; pres. Wayland Sem. and Coll., Washington, D.C., 1897-99; prof. theology and philosophy, 1899-1919, pres., 1905-19, Va. Union U. (colored), Richmond, Va.; dir. Summer Normal Sch., Richmond, 1911-18; sec. for edn. Am. Bapt. Home Mission Soc., 1919-30; dir. Nat. Ministers' Inst., 1930-1935. Republican. Author: Hebrew Word Book, 1902; Alvah Hovey—His Life and Letters, 1927; The Bible—Its Origin and Interpretation, 1930; Christian Ethics for Daily Life, 1932; Bible Study—A Natural Method Illustrated, 1935. Home: Upper Montclair, N.J. Died Jan. 28, 1943.

HOVEY, Otis Ellis, civil engr.; b. E. Hardwick, Vt., Apr. 9, 1864; s. Jabez Wadsworth and Hannah Catherine (Montgomery) H.; B.S., Dartmouth Coll., 1885; C.E., Thayer School of Civil Engring., Dartmouth, 1889; D.Eng., Dartmouth Coll., 1927; D.Sc., Clarkson Coll., 1933; m. Martha W. Owen, Sept. 15, 1891; children—Otis Wadsworth, Mrs. Ellen Catherine Davis. Engr. Hoosac Tunnel and Wilmington R.R., Vt., 1885-86; draughtsman Edge Moor Iron Co., Wilmington, Del., 1887; asst. engr. for D.H.&A.B. Tower, Holyoke, Mass., in charge of Dam at Chicopee, Mass., and various improvements in paper mills, 1888; instr. civ. engring., Washington U., St. Louis, 1889-90; asst. engr. with George S. Morison, engaged on bridge designs, in Miss. valley and other engring. work, 1890-96; engr. Union Bridge Co., New York, and Athens, Pa., 1896-1900; in engring. dept. since 1900; asst. chief engr., 1907-31, cons. engr., 1931-34, Am. Bridge Co.; private practice since 1934. Dir. The Engring. Foundation since 1937. Mem. bd. overseers Thayer Sch. of Civ. Engring. (Dartmouth), Mem. Am. Soc. C.E. (hon.), Am. Soc. Mech. Engrs., Am. Soc. Testing Materials, Am. Ry. Engring. Assn., Am. Welding Soc., Am. Inst. of Consulting Engrs., Beta Theta Pi, Phi Beta Kappa. Republican. Presbyterian. Club: Engineers. Author: Movable Bridges (2 vols.), 1926, 27; Steel Dams, 1935. Home: 425 Riverside Drive. Office: 11 W. 42d St., New York, N.Y. Died Apr. 15, 1941.

HOVGAARD, William (hov'gärd), naval architect; b. Aarhus, Denmark, Nov. 28, 1857; s. Ole Anton and Louise Charlotte (Munch) H.; grad. Naval Acad., Denmark, 1879; grad. Royal Naval Coll., Greenwich, Eng., 1886; hon. D.Eng., Copenhagen (Denmark) Poly. Inst., 1929; hon. D.Eng., Stevens Inst. Technology, 1934; m. Marie Ludolphine Elisabeth Nielsen, Sept. 19, 1896; children—Ole Mogens, Annette. Served as sub-lt., lt., and comdr. Royal Danish Navy; mem. Danish expdn. to St. Croix, W.I., to observe transit of Venus, winter, 1882-83; studied naval construction Royal Naval Coll., Greenwich, Eng., 1883-86; on naval tech. and administrative duties, dockyard and sea-service, Denmark, to 1895; gen. mgr. shipyard, Burmeister and Wain, Copenhagen, 1895-97; naval service, 1897-1901; prof. naval construction, Mass. Inst. Tech., 1901-33, prof. emeritus and honorary lecturer, 1933-34; resigned from Danish Navy, 1905. On scientific tech. duty, Bur. Constrn. and Repair, Navy Dept., May 1917-Sept. 1918; cons. naval architect for same, 1919-26; mem. sub-com. on airships ZR-1 and RS-1, under the Nat. Adv. Com. for Aeronautics, 1922-25; tech. adviser to Court of Inquiry, Shenandoah disaster, 1925, mem. Special Com. on Airship Design and Construction, 1935; consulting naval architect for Bur. of Yards and Docks, Navy Dept., 1935-38; mem. Advisory Bd. on Battleship Plans, 1937-38. Naturalized as American citizen, 1919. Trustee Am. Scandinavian Foundation, New York. Mem. Instn. Naval Architects (Eng.), Am. Soc. Naval Architects and Marine Engrs., U.S. Naval Inst., Am. Assn. of Univ. Profs., Mass. Hist. Soc.; fellow American Geographical Soc., Inst. Aeronautical Sciences; mem. American Acad. Arts and Sciences, A.A.A.S., Nat. Acad. Sciences; hon. mem. Am. Soc. Danish Engineers, Danish Luncheon Club, Tau Beta Pi. Decorated Commander of Order of Dannebrog (Denmark), etc. Awarded gold medal by Brit. Instn. Naval Architects, for paper on Submarine Boats, 1917, hon. member of same, 1944. Awarded David W. Taylor Medal by Soc. of Naval Architects and Marine Engrs., 1913. Lutheran. Author: Submarine Boats (London), 1887; The Voyages of the Norsemen to America, 1914; Structural Design of Warships (London), 1915, 2d edition, 1940 (U.S. Naval Institute); Modern History of Warships, 1920; General Design of Warships, 1920; The United World, 1944; also brochures and papers on technical and mil. subjects. Home: Hotel Margaret, 97 Columbia Heights, Brooklyn 2, N.Y. Died Jan. 5, 1950.

HOW, Louis, author; b. St. Louis, Mo.; s. James Flintham and Eliza Ann (Eads) H.; A.B., Harvard

1895; unmarried. Pvt. in Spanish-Am. War. Author: Penitentes of San Rafael (novel), 1900; James B. Eads, 1900; Lyrics and Sonnets, 1911; The Youth Replies:, 1912; Barricades, 1914; A Hidden Well, 1917; Nursery Rhymes of New York City, 1919, with additions, 1931; Ruin and Gold, 1924; Narcissus, 1928; The Other Don Juan, 1932; The Years Relent, 1936; Regional Rhymes of New York City (all verse). Translator: Montaigne's Essay on Friendship and 29 Sonnets by Etienne de La Boetie, 1915; Lazarillo de Tormes, 1917; Caesar or Nothing (by Pio Baroja), 1919; Dante, Inferno, 1934; Dante, Purgatorio, 1938; Dante, Paradiso, 1940; An Evening with Ninon, 1941. Home: 167 W. 12th St., N.Y. City. Died Oct. 3, 1947.

HOWARD, Alfred Taylor, bishop; b. Schoolcraft, Mich., Mar. 12, 1868; s. Cornelius and Harriet L. (Guilford) H.; A.B., Otterbein U., Westerville, O., 1894, A.M., 1898; post-grad. work, U. of Chicago, D.D., Otterbein, 1905; m. May D. Stevenson, June 14, 1894; children—John Gordon, Donald Stevenson, Florence Cronise. Ordained ministry U.B. Ch., 1894; sent as missionary to Africa; prin. Clark Training Sch., Sierra Leone, 1894-98; supt. Japan Mission of U.B. Ch., 1898-1912; supt. U.B. missions in Orient (Japan, China and P.I.), 1912-13; gen. supt. (bishop), foreign dist. of U.B. Ch. (Sierra Leone, Porto Rico, Japan, China and P.I.), 1913-21; pres. Bonebrake Theol. Sem., Dayton, Ohio, 1921-29 and 1933-38, prof. missions and sociology, 1921-42, retired 1942. Home: 821 Five Oaks Av., Dayton 6, O. Died Nov. 12, 1948.

HOWARD, Charles Danforth, chemist and sanitarian; b. Westford, Mass., July 31, 1873; s. Calvin L. and Mary Jane (Hale) H.; B.S., Worcester Poly. Inst., 1893; m. Ada Yates, Aug. 5, 1901; children—John Adams, Charlotte Danforth. Pvt. asst. to Dr. Wolcott Gibbs, at his lab., Newport, R.I., 1893-94, to Prof. L. P. Kinnicutt, Worcester Poly. Inst., 1894-95; asst. chemist, N.H. Expt. Sta., Durham, 1895-98; asst. and asso. chemist, W.Va. U. Expt. Sta., 1898-1905; chemist and sanitarian, N.H. Bd. of Health, since 1905, dir. div. of chemistry and sanitation since 1920. State water coordinator; chmn. N.H. Commn. on Stream Classification. Mem. federal Com. on Definitions and Standards for Foods, 1918-42. Fellow Am. Pub. Health Assn.; mem. Am. Chem. Soc., Am. Water Works Assn., N.E. Water Works Assn., N.E. Assn. Dairy Food and Drug Officials (ex-pres.), N.H. Acad. Science (pres. 1942), Sigma Xi; hon. mem. N.H. Med. Soc., N.H. Pharm Assn. Conglist. Author of numerous articles in bulls. and scientific jours.; various sanitary and related legislation. Editor: N.H. Health News. Home: Concord, N.H. Died Oct. 29, 1944.

HOWARD, Clifford, author; b. Bethlehem, Pa., Oct. 12, 1868; s. William and Agnes (Seidel) H.; ed. Moravian Sch., Bethlehem, Pa.; LL.B., Columbian (now George Washington) U., 1890; m. Hattie Sterling Case, 1893; 1 dau., Hildegarde. Resided in Washington, D.C., 1888-1906. Editor Am. Film Co., 1916-18. Mem. Authors' League America. Author: Twigs, Leaves and Blossoms, 1892; Thoughts in Verse, 1895; Sex-Worship, An Exposition of the Phallic Origins of Religion, 1897; Story of a Young Man (a Life of Christ), 1902; Graphology, 1904; Washington as a Center of Learning, 1904; Curious Facts, 1905; The Passover, 1910; What Happened at Olenberg, 1911; Tenatsali (dramatic poem of the Zuñi), 1912; (monograph), Suffrage for Two, 1913; Sex and Religion—A Study of their Relationship and Its Bearing on Civilization, 1925. Contbr. of fiction and essays to mags. Home: 803 N. Alexandria Av., Los Angeles. Died May 19, 1942; buried in Forest Lawn Memorial Park, Glendale, Calif.

HOWARD, Clinton Wilbur, army officer; b. Campello, Mass., Nov. 27, 1890; s. Ernest Clinton and Ida Palmer (Legge) H.; B.S., U.S. Mil. Acad., 1915; grad. Army Service Engring. Sch., 1921; M.S. and Sc.D. in aeronautics, Mass. Inst. of Tech., 1923; grad. Army Indsl. Coll., 1936, Army War Coll., 1937; rated command pilot, combat and tech. observer. Commd. 2d lt., U.S. Army, 1915, and advanced through the grades to brig. gen.; chiefly in research, experimentation and development of aeronautical equipment for the Air Corps; became comdg. gen. Air Service Command, Sacramento, Calif., June 1943. Retired as brig. gen., U.S. Army, 1946. Mgr. Markwart Industries, Inc., since 1946, Sacramento, Calif. Mem. A.A.A.S., Soc. of Automotive Engring., Inst. Aeronautical Science, Aircraft and Engine Development. Home: 3360 H St., Sacramento, Calif.; died Sept. 22, 1949; buried in Arlington National Cemetery

HOWARD, Edgar Billings, archæologist; b. New Orleans, La., Feb. 28, 1887; s. Frank Turner and Emma Cora (Pike) H.; prep. edn. St. Paul's Sch., Concord, N.H., 1900-06; Ph.B., Yale (Sheffield Scientific Sch.), 1909; M.S., U. of Pa., 1930, Ph.D., 1935; m. Elizabeth Newhall, Oct. 1, 1910; children—Edgar Billings, Frank Turner, Charles Newhall Willing, Robert Pike. Bond salesman, 1910-11; export-import business with Wharton, Sinkler & Robert Toland, 1922-28; scientific work as archæologist since 1928; research asso. U. Museum, Phila., since 1929, Carnegie Inst. of Washington, D.C., since 1934, Lab. of Anthropology, Santa Fe, N.M., 1939. Served as capt. Hdqrs. Co., 313th Inf., U.S. Army, with A.E.F., during World War; hon. mem. 1st City Troop, Phila. Former pres. Sch. Bd., Radnor Twp., Pa.; former trustee Acad. Natural Sciences, Phila. Mem. Am. Anthropol. Soc., Am. Mus. Natural Hist., Anthropol. Society Phila., Society Pa. Archæology, Archæol. Soc. of N.M., Soc. for Am. Archæology (former pres.), Museum Stone Age Antiquities, Sigma Xi, Delta Psi. Republican. Episcopalian. Clubs: Yale (Phila.); Boston (New Orleans). Writer of articles and bulletins pertaining to archeology. Home: Bryn Mawr, Pa. Died Mar. 18, 1943.

HOWARD, Edward Orson, banker; b. Skaneateles, N.Y.; s. Oscar and Cornelia (Austin) H., ed. Skaneateles (N.Y.) Acad.; m. Annie Payne Austin, Apr. 30, 1895; 1 dau., Margery (Mrs. Charles C. Brooks). Began in banking with Walker Brothers, bankers, Salt Lake City, Utah, 1890, became president 1920, now chairman of the board (name changed 1931 to Walker Bank and Trust Co.); treasurer and director Strevell Paterson Hardware Company; director Utah Idaho Sugar Company, Utah Home Fire Insurance Co., Newhouse Realty Co., Salt Lake City Union Depot & Railroad Co., Utah Fuel Co., Park Utah Consolidated Mines Company. Chairman local advisory com., Reconstruction Finance Corp.; chmn. housing committee, State Council of Defense. Trustee St. Marks Hosp., Westminster Coll. (both of Salt Lake City). Pres. Salt Lake City Chamber of Commerce, 1929-30. Republican. Clubs: Alta, Country. Office: Main and 2d S. St., Salt Lake City, Utah. Died June 30, 1946.

HOWARD, Eric, writer; b. Baltimore, Md., May 18, 1895; s. Benjamin F. and Jessie (Higginbotham) H.; student U. of Calif., 1912-15; studied lit. and psychology, Harvard and Columbia; m. Judith Bell, June 1917. Asso. editor Munsey's Mag., Argosy—All Story Weekly, until 1921. Lecturer and instr. extension div., U. of Calif., since 1923. Mem. Theatre Arts Alliance, Poetry Society of America, Am. Fiction Guild. Clubs: Harvard, P.E.N. Author: Famous Californians of Today and Yesterday, 1923. Co-Author: The Photoplay Plot Encyclopedia, 1920; also (with George Bronson Howard) The Alien (4-act play); Pretty Fast (3-act play), 1927; These Artists (3-act play), 1929. Writer of many photoplays, also stories in Story (mag.), Esquire, Prairie Schooner, Am. Spectator, Real America, etc.; author of 1500 stories in popular mag. Contbr. many biog. sketches to series, "California and Californians," edited by R. D. Hunt, 1925. Spends much of each year in Ariz. and N.M. studying Indian arts and customs. Home: 2247 Cove Av., Los Angeles, Calif. Died May 17, 1943.

HOWARD, Francis W., bishop; ordained priest R.C. Ch., June 16, 1891; consecrated bishop of Covington, July 15, 1923; apptd. asst. to Pontifical Throne, Jan. 12, 1929. Address: 1140 Madison Av., Covington, Ky.* Died Jan. 18, 1944.

HOWARD, Guy C(lemens), chemist and chemical engineer; born at Batavia, New York, August 26, 1878; son of Thomas Mentor and Frances Athalia (Rudgers) H.; B.S., University of Nebraska, 1900; A.M., Columbia, 1906; m. Mildred Jane Horan, July 5, 1916; children—John Rudgers, Elizabeth Ann. Chemist for various companies, 1901-03; head chemist Am. Smelting & Refining Co., Perth Amboy, N.J., 1903-05; chief chemist El Cobre Mines, Ltd., Santiago, Cuba, 1906, Am. Smelting & Refining Co., Salt Lake City, Utah, 1907-09; investigations in utilization of wood waste in lumber industry, Seattle, Wash., 1909-11; developments in utilization of pulp mill waste, Everett (Wash.) Pulp & Paper Co., 1911-16; chem. engr. in copper smelting plant Am. Smelting & Refining Co., Tacoma, Wash., in charge recovery sulphur products from metall. gases, 1916-20; cons. chem. engr. in utilization of industrial wastes, Seattle, Wash., 1920-27; at Marathon Paper Mills Co., Rothschild, Wis., pioneering the recovery and utilization of lignin and asso. materials since 1927, and as chemical counsellor. Mem. Am. Inst. Chem. Engrs., Am. Chem. Soc., Tech. Assn. of Pulp and Paper Industry, A.A.A.S. Republican. Conglist. Clubs: Wausau, Wausau Country (Wausau, Wis.); Chemists (New York). Contbr. to tech. jours. Address: 922 Franklin St., Wausau, Wis. Died Dec. 19, 1943.

HOWARD, Mrs. Henry (Alice Sturtevant); b. Middletown, R.I., Feb. 14, 1878; d. Eugene and Mary Rebecca (Clark) Sturtevant; ed. under pvt. tutors; m. Henry Howard, Sept. 5, 1896; children—Katharine (Mrs. Charles Townsend), Henry Sturtevant, Thomas Clark, John Babcock, Robert Sturtevant (dec.). Organizer, Jan. 1918, and was made chief of Social Service Bureau, U.S. Shipping Bd. Recruiting Service, which trained personnel for Am. Merchant Marine, World War; founder, 1921, and since pres. Am. Merchant Marine Library Assn., maintaining crews' libraries on Am. mcht. ships, also in U.S. Coast Guard vessels, life-saving stations, lighthouses and lightships. Mem. Colonial Dames of R.I., D.A.R., Garden Club of Newport, Women's Nat. Republican Club. Republican. Episcopalian. Club: Cosmopolitan (New York). Author: Seamen's Handbook for Shore Leave (pocket directory of ports of the world), 9th edit., 1945. Home: Paradise Rd., Newport, R.I. Office: 45 Broadway, New York. Died Oct. 6, 1945; buried in Berkeley Memorial Chapel, Middletown, R.I.

HOWARD, Leslie, actor. Has appeared in motion pictures "The Scarlet Pimpernel," "The Petrified Forest," "Romeo and Juliet," "It's Love I'm After," "Stand In," "Pygmalion," "Intermezzo," "Gone With the Wind." Address: Los Angeles, Calif. Died June 1, 1943.

HOWARD, Louis Orrin, mining engr.; b. Thompson, Conn., Feb. 27, 1884; s. Mart A. and Azora (Cummings) H.; A.B., Harvard, 1907, M.E., 1909; m. Muriel Burnet Crawford, Aug. 28, 1908; children—Lydia Wadsworth, Betty Burnet, Louise Orrin, Muriel Crawford, Sylvia May; m. 2d, Nellie Barker Jacobs, Nov. 25, 1925. Instr. ore treatment and metallography, Case Sch. Applied Science, Cleveland, O., 1909-11; mgr. Phila. syndicate, later organized as Radium Co. of America, Green River, Utah, 1912; asso. editor Salt Lake Mining Review, 1913-14; consulting practice, 1913-17; erected mill for Edison Tungsten Mines, Lucin, Utah, 1916; prof. mining and metallurgy, State Coll. of Wash., 1917-26, also dean Sch. of Mines and Geology; acting prof. metallurgy, S. Dak. State Sch. of Mines, Rapid City, 1926-27; same at U. of Ida., Moscow, 1928-29; cons. mining and metall. engr. since 1927. Unemployment relief work with Red Cross, County Welfare Board, and Nat. Reemployment Service as supervisor, welfare commr. and mgr. respectively, 1932-34; chief engr. Whitman County Wheat Production Control Assn., 1934-35; pvt. practice since 1936; wage, social security, unemployment and tax consultant since 1937; exec. sec. War Price and Rationing Bd., Pullman, since Oct. 1942. Mem. Sigma Tau, Sigma Gamma Epsilon, Phi Kappa Phi, Theta Xi. Republican. Episcopalian. Club: Harvard. Author: Cyanidation in the Mercur District of Utah, 1915; also 53 titles in professional jours. Home: Pullman, Wash. Died May 14, 1944.

HOWARD, Lowry Samuel, school administrator; b. Minneapolis, Minn., Feb. 20, 1891; s. John Joseph and Emma (Honstead) H.; diploma, Washington State Teachers Coll., Cheney, 1913; A.B., Stanford, 1917, A.M., 1920; U. of Calif., summer 1916; m. Gretchen Darmer, Dec. 22, 1919. Began as instr. in Wash. State Teachers Coll., 1913; student and grad. asst. Stanford, 1915-18; psychol. examiner U.S. Army, 1918; prin. Menlo (Calif.) Sch., 1919-22; asst. supt. Whittier State Sch., 1922-23, Pasadena City Schs., 1923-27; pres. Menlo Sch. and Junior Coll. (in coöperation with Stanford U.) since 1927, also sec. and treas. bd. Mem. State Mental Hygiene Com. (Calif.), N. Calif. Jr. Coll. Assn., Calif. Headmasters Assn., Phi Delta Kappa. Conglist. Clubs: Kiwanis (Palo Alto, Calif.); Commonwealth (San Francisco); Los Altos (Calif.) Country. Wrote: Story of Menlo, 1931, Getting Along in College, 1936; The Road Ahead, 1941; War Supplement to The Road Ahead, 1942. Home: Palo Alto, Calif. Died Feb. 16, 1949.

HOWARD, Nathaniel Lamson, corp. official; b. Fairfield, Ia., Mar. 9, 1884; s. Elmer A. and Mary (Lamson) H.; grad. U.S. Mil. Acad., 1907; m. Marie Blaul, June 3, 1915. Began as civil engr. C.B.&Q. Ry. Co., 1907, trainmaster, at Centerville, Ia., 1910, successively asst. supt. at Galesburg, Ill., and supt. of Burlington div., till 1916; supt. Hannibal div., 1916-17; asst. to federal mgr., C.B.&Q. Ry. Co., May-Nov. 1919, gen. supt. Mo. dist., at St. Louis, 1919-24; gen. mgr. Chicago Union Sta. Co., 1924-25; pres. C.,G.W. R.R., 1925-29; chmn. bd. and pres. North Am. Car Corp., 1930-36. Lt. col. 13th Ry. Engrs. U.S. Army, May-Aug. 1917; duty with dir. gen. of transportation in France, Aug. 1917 to spring 1918; comdr. 13th Ry. Engrs., Verdun sector; col. July 8, 1918. Decorated Officer Legion of Honor and Croix de Guerre (French). Mason (K.T., Shriner). Clubs: Commonwealth, Commercial, University, Indian Hill, Adventurers. Home: 715 Sheridan Rd., Winnetka, Ill. Died May 6, 1949; buried at Burlington, Ia.

HOWARD, Philip Eugene, publisher; b. Lynn, Mass., Apr. 1, 1870; s. Eugene (M.D.) and Susan Ella (Nash) H.; B.A., University of Pennsylvania, 1891; LL.D., Houghton College, 1937; m. Annie Slosson Trumbull, October 27, 1891 (died April 11, 1943); children—Philip Eugene, Henry Trumbull, Alice Gallaudet, Annie Trumbull. With the Sunday School Times, Philadelphia, since 1891; now pres. and treas. Sunday School Times Co.; western areas, Alliance of Reformed Chs. Throughout the World, 1910-35. Guest of British Govt. in spl. study war work in British Isles and on Western Front, 1918. Mem. Phi Delta Theta, Phi Beta Kappa. Republican. Presbyterian. Author: The Life Story of Henry Clay Trumbull, 1905; A Prayer Before the Lesson, 1911; Temptation—What It Is and How to Meet It, 1911; A History of World's Sunday School Conventions, 1912; Their Call to Service, 1915; The Many Sided David, 1917; Boy-Talks, 1920; When the Days Seem Dark, 1920; A Little Kit of Teachers' Tools, 1921; Father and Son, 1922; A New Invasion of Belgium, 1924; Living Through These Days, 1930; Collected Poems, 1943; Charles G. Trumbull, Apostle of the Victorious Life, 1944. Editor: Sunday Schools the World Around, 1907. Wrote article on History of Sunday Schools in Internat. Ency. Home: 15 Prospect Av., Moorestown, N.J. Office: 325 N. 13th St., Philadelphia 5, Pa. Died June 22, 1946.

HOWARD, Rossiter, art educator; b. Brooklyn, N.Y., June 18, 1873; s. John Raymond and Susan Raymond (Merriam) H.; grad. Phillips Acad., Andover, Mass., 1898; student, Harvard, 1901-02; studied singing and composition, New York and Boston, 6 yrs.; visited cities in Europe and studied art 10 yrs.; m. Alice Woodbury, Oct. 19, 1905; children—Mrs. Elizabeth McKee, John Tasker. Director of music, Phillips Academy and Andover Theological Seminary, 1901-04; Paris director, Bureau of University Travel, 1905-14; prof. fine arts, U. of S.D., 1915-18; ednl. dir. Army Y.M.C.A., Fort Thomas, Ky., and Camp Sherman, O., 1918; ednl. dir. Minneapolis Inst. of Arts, 1919-20; curator of ednl. work, Cleveland Museum of Art, 1921-30, curator of classical art, 1924-30, asst. dir., 1925-

30; chief of div. of Edn., Pa. Mus. of Art, 1930-33; dir. The Kansas City Art Institute, 1933-39. Research and author: The Eye and The Artist: Varieties of Vision, 1940-46. Democrat. Conglist. Contbr. and lecturer on art topics. Address: 28-21 210th Place, Bayside, N.Y. Died Jan. 1, 1950.

HOWARD, Walter Lafayette, horticulturist; b. nr. Springfield, Mo., May 12, 1872; s. Henry Tate and Nancy Elizabeth A. (Cooper) H.; B.Agr. and B.S., U. of Mo., 1901, M.S., 1903; studied U. of Leipzig, 1905; Ph.D., U. of Halle-Wittenberg, 1906; studied at East Malling Research Sta., Eng., 1930; m. May Belle Cooper, June 25, 1908; children—Thomas Henry (dec.), Robert Cooper, Edwin Lewis, Walter Egner. Asst. and asst. horticulturist, Expt. Sta., U. of Mo., 1901-03, instr. 1903-04, asst. prof., 1905-08, prof. horticulture, 1908-15; asso. prof. pomology, U. of Calif., 1915-18, prof., 1918, head div. of pomology, 1922-29, acting dir. Br. of Coll. of Agr., 1924-25, dir., 1925-37, professor emeritus since 1942. Investigated horticultural problems in France and contiguous countries, 1921-22. Secretary Missouri State Bd. of Horticulture, 1908-12; mem. Jury of Awards, San Francisco Expn., 1915. Fellow A.A.A.S.; mem. Am. Genetic Assn., Am. Pomol. Soc., Am. Soc. Hort. Science, Soc. Promotion Agrl. Science, Am. Eugenics Soc., Sigma Xi, Alpha Zeta, Sigma Kappa Zeta, Gamma Sigma Delta. Clubs: Faculty (Berkeley and Davis); Commonwealth (San Francisco). Author of Luther Burbank, A Victim of Hero Worship, 1946, and various bulls. and pamphlets. Home: 24 College Park, Davis, Calif. Died Oct. 17, 1949.

HOWARD, William Gibbs, forester; b. Medford, Mass., Feb. 17, 1887; s. Daniel Newbury and Fanny (Waterman) H.; A.B., Harvard, 1907, M.F., 1908; m. Georgia H. Walther, June 8, 1912; children—Frances Walther (dec.), Mary Katharine, Jane Waterman. Forest asst. U.S. Forest Service, 1908-09; forester N.Y. State Forest, Fish and Game Commn., 1909-11; asst. supt. State forests, N.Y. State Conservation Dept., 1911-27; dir. lands and forests N.Y. State Conservation Dept. since 1927. Fellow Soc. Am. Foresters (v.p. 1939). Republican. Mason. Clubs: Albany Country, Aurania, Harvard (New York); Rotary (Albany). Home: 68 Brookline Av. Office: N.Y. State Conservation Dept., Albany, N.Y. Died Oct. 30, 1948.

HOWDEN, Frederick Bingham, bishop, b. West New Brighton, S.I., N.Y., Dec. 10, 1869; s. William Douglas and Esther Jane (Orrell) H.; A.B., Trinity Coll., Toronto U., 1891, M.A., 1893, D.D., 1914; grad. Gen. Theol. Sem., 1894, S.T.D., 1927; m. Angelica Constance Faber, Feb. 20, 1895 (died 1923); children—Mrs. Angelica Horton, Douglas Faber, Esther Orrell, Frederick Bingham, John Faber, Margaret, William. Deacon and priest P.E. Ch., 1894; asst. St. John's Ch., Detroit, Mich., 1894-95, Calvary Ch., N.Y. City, 1895-97; rector Emmanuel Ch., Cumberland, Md., 1897-1902; archdeacon of Cumberland, 1900-02; rector St. John's Ch., Georgetown Parish, Washington, D.C., 1902-14, also rector Nat. Cathedral School; consecrated bishop of N.M. and S.W. Tex., Jan. 14, 1914. Mem. Hist. Soc. of N.M., Phi Kappa Phi. Club: Albuquerque Country. Home: Albuquerque, N.M. Died Nov. 12, 1940.

HOWE, Arthur Millidge, editor; b. St. Eleanor's, P.E.I., Can., June 28, 1867; s. William Minns and Catherine Louisa (White) H.; ed. public and private schs.; hon. LL.D., St. Lawrence Univ., 1923; m. Grace de Blois Hamilton, Sept. 5, 1893. Came to U.S., 1887; began newspaper work on Brooklyn Standard Union, 1889, later spl. writer for various New York newspapers; with Brooklyn Daily Eagle from 1893, successively exchange editor, editorial writer, mng. editor, and editor-in-chief from 1915, now emeritus. Mem. bd. mgrs., v.p. Brooklyn Assn. for Improving Condition of the Poor; mem. advisory bd. Columbia U. School of Journalism; mem. N.Y. City Board of Higher Edn., 1926-38; resigned. Mem. Mayor La Guardia's Commn. on Edn., 1940; sec. board dirs. Prospect Park South. Mem. Pilgrims Soc. Episcopalian. Home: 205 Rugby Rd., Brooklyn, N.Y. Died Oct. 13, 1947.

HOWE, Carl, ry. official; b. Berrien Springs, Mich., Jan. 11, 1870; ed. pub. schs., Buchanan and Niles, Mich.; m. Cornelia Oswald, Nov. 18, 1896; children—Oswald E., Carl, Mary E. (Mrs. Russell P. Carpenter), Mitchell B., Cornelia B., Robert L. Began as clk. local freight office M.C. R.R., 1889, and continued with same rd. successively as agt. at Chicago Heights, 1893-94, traveling freight agt., 1894-98, asst. chief clk. in office of gen. freight traffic mgr., 1898-99, chief clk. same office, 1899-1900, asst. gen. freight agt., 1900-07; mgr. N.Y.C. Fast Freight Lines, 1907-17; traffic mgr. M.C. R.R., 1917-27; v.p. Erie R.R. since 1927. Clubs: Union League, Traffic, Oak Park Country; Detroit (Mich.) Athletic. Home: 315 S. East Av., Oak Park, Ill. Office: 327 S. La Salle St., Chicago, Ill. Died Nov. 9, 1946.

HOWE, Harland Bradley, ex-judge; b. St. Johnsbury, Vt., Feb. 19, 1873; s. Worcester C. and Rosaline (Bradley) H.; ed. pub. schs. Lyndonville, Vt., and Lyndon Inst.; read law with Hon. George W. Cahoon, of Lyndon, and Hon. Henry C. Ide, of St. Johnsbury; LL.B., U. of Mich., 1894; m. Maybelle Jane Kelsey, 1900; children—Josephine E., Barbara J., Matilda A., Harriet B.; m. 2d, Mrs. Elizabeth (Crump) Johnson, 1931. Began practice St. Johnsbury, 1894; mem. Vt. Ho. of Rep., 1908. Dem. candidate for gov. of Vt., 1912, 14; became judge U.S. Dist. Court, for Vt., by apptmt. of Pres. Wilson, Feb. 19, 1915; retired Jan. 31, 1940. Home: Burlington, Vt. Died Apr. 22, 1946.

HOWE, Harrison Estell, chemist, editor; b. Georgetown, Ky., Dec. 15, 1881; s. of William James and Mary (Scott) H.; B.S., Earlham Coll., Ind., 1901; U. of Mich., 1901-02; M.S., U. of Rochester, 1913, Sc.D., 1927; LL.D., Southern Coll., 1934; Eng.D., Rose Poly. Inst. 1936, S.D. State Sch. of Mines 1939; m. May McCaren, Oct. 17, 1905; children—Mary, Betty. Chemist, Sanilac Sugar Refining Co., Croswell, Mich., 1902-04; chemist, office mgr. and editor Bausch & Lomb Optical Co., Rochester, N.Y., 1904-16; chem. engr. with Arthur D. Little, Inc., Boston, 1916; asst. to pres., Arthur D. Little, Ltd., Montreal, Can., 1916-17; mgr. commercial dept. Arthur D. Little, Inc., Cambridge, Mass., 1917-19; chmn. div. research extension, Nat. Research Council, 1919-22; editor Industrial and Engineering Chemistry, Washington, since Dec. 1, 1921. Trustee Science Service; mem. Purdue Research Foundation; chmn. Chemicals Group, and chmn. Chemicals Priority Com., Priorities Div., Office of Production Management, Feb.-July 1941, now chmn. adv. com. Chemical Sect. Cons. chemist nitrate div., Ordnance Bureau, U.S. Army, World War; col. R.O.C., C.W.S. Fellow A.A.A.S.; mem. Am. Chem. Soc., Am. Inst. Chem. Engrs. (dir., and its rep. in Am. Engring. Council 1921-32), Am. Engring. Council (treas. 1923-30); round table and gen. conf. leader Inst. of Politics, Williamstown, Mass., 1926-29. Decorated Officer Crown of Italy, 1926. Republican. Baptist. Mason (K.T.). Clubs: Cosmos, Rotary, Torch, Chemists' (New York). Author: The New Stone Age, 1921; Profitable Science in Industry, 1924; Chemistry in the World's Work, 1926; Chemistry in the Home (with F.M. Turner), 1927; Series of six Nature and Science Readers (with E. M. Patch). Editor: Chemistry in Industry, Vol. I, 1924, Vol. II, 1925. Contbr. numerous articles in scientific jours.; a leader in organizing industrial groups for research. Home: 2702 36th St. N.W., Washington, D.C. Office: 1155 16th St. N.W., Washington, D.C., and 332 W. 42nd St., New York. Died Dec. 10, 1942; buried in Ft. Lincoln Cemetery, Washington.

HOWE, John Benedict, editor; b. Utica, N.Y., Mar. 21, 1859; s. Denis F. and Elizabeth (Cogley) H.; grad. Utica Free Acad., 1875; Litt.D., Syracuse U., 1919; m. Marietta Gartlan, June 25, 1893. Editorial writer, Utica Observer, 1882-92; editor Rochester Herald, 1892-98; Syracuse Herald since 1898. Lecturer Sch. of Journalism, Syracuse U. Mem. Citizens' Com. N.Y. State Library Assn.; mem. bd. of visitors State Normal Sch., Oswego, N.Y. Catholic. Author: The Eve of Election, 1918; Howe's New Era Civics, 1922. Address: Syracuse Herald, Syracuse, N.Y. Died May 16, 1943.

HOWE, Richard Flint, mfr.; b. Green Bay, Wis., June 25, 1863; s. James Henry and Mary Gordon (Cotton) H.; A.B., Harvard, 1884; m. Abby M. Deering, Feb. 3, 1898. Entered employ Simmons Mfg. Co., Kenosha, Wis., 1884, becoming dir., sec. and gen. mgr.; v.p. First Nat. Bank, Kenosha; disposed of mfg. interests, 1900, associated with Deering Harvester Co., Chicago, 1900, later partner, dir., sec. and treas. Internat. Harvester Co., from orgn., 1901-1911, retired 1911; dir. Internat. Harvester Co., First Nat. Bank, Kenosha. Apptd. by Pres. Wilson, civilian mem. Aircraft Bd. Nov. 1917. Republican. Unitarian. Clubs: The Brook, Metropolitan, Union (New York); Tennis and Racquet (New York, Boston). Home: Jericho, L.I. Died Jan. 26, 1943.

HOWE, Will David, educator, editor; b. Charlestown, Ind., Aug. 25, 1873; s. Robert Long and Elizabeth Ellen (Carr) H.; A.B., Butler Coll., 1893; A.B., Harvard, 1895, A.M., 1897, Ph.D., 1899; m. Elizabeth Poulson, Dec. 20, 1902; children—Robert Poulson, Rebecca, Elizabeth Lucia. Prof. English, Butler Coll., 1899-1906, Ind. U., 1906-19, Columbia University, summers, 1906-16; mem. Harcourt, Brace & Howe, pub., 1919-21; editor and dir. Charles Scribner's Sons, 1921-42. Chairman board Skidmore College, Saratoga Spgs. Member edit. board of American Scholar; member Phi Beta Kappa (senator), Delta Tau Delta. Club: Century (New York City). Joint author: Rhetoric, 1908; The Howe Readers, 1909; Gate to English, 1915; Modern Student's Book of English Literature, 1924; Literature of America, 1929; American Authors and Books, 1943; Charles Lamb and His Friends, 1944. Editor: Longfellow's Poems; Lowell's Essays; Sheridan's Plays; Byron's Poems; Selections from Hazlitt; Selections from Addison and Steele. Contributor to literary and ednl. mags. and to Cambridge History of English and American Literature; editor series How to Know the Great Authors, and Modern Student's Library. Home: Mt. Kisco, N.Y.; and Silver Lake, N.H. Died Dec. 6, 1946.

HOWELL, Charles Fish, editor, author; b. S. Amboy, N.J., June 8, 1868; s. Edmund Orlando and Ann Adelia (Fish) H.; A.B., Princeton, 1891; m. Joyce Margaret Scott, June 15, 1915. On staff San Francisco Call, 1892-94; contbr. and later editor, The Argus, Chicago, 1894-1900; editor and pub. Insurance and Commercial Magazine, New York, 1900-20, Intercollegiate News, 1902-03; mng. editor The Weekly Underwriter, New York, 1919-26, editor in chief since Aug. 1926. Republican. Presbyterian. Mem. Soc. Colonial Wars, S.R. Author: Around the Clock in Europe; An Irish Ramble; The Courier. Contbr. of short stories and poems to mags. Home: 129 Columbia Heights, Brooklyn, N.Y. Office: 80 Maiden Lane, New York, N.Y. Died June 5, 1943.

HOWELL, Daniel William; b. N.Y. City, Mar. 4, 1861; s. Jesse and Julia A. (Pawling) H.; A.B., Allegheny Coll., 1888, A.M., 1892 (D.D., 1908); B.D., Drew Theol. Sem., 1891; m. Anna Mary Wilkenson, Sept. 10, 1890 (died 1948); children—Marie Julia (Mrs. George S. Nichols, dec.), William D., Jessie E. (wife of Rev. John A. Glasse), Robert Pawling. Ordained M.E. ministry, 1891; pastor Floral Park, L.I., 1891; Whitestone, 1892-93; Southold, 1894-96; Waterbury, Conn., 1897-99; Hartford, Conn., 1900-08; gen. sec. Chautauqua Literature and Scientific Circle, 1908-11; corr. sec. Gen. Deaconess Bd. of M.E. Ch., 1912-25; pastor Corning, N.Y., 1925-30, Wellsboro, Pa., 1930-31, Mount Morris, N.Y., 1931-34, Elma, N.Y., 1934-37. Official del. Ecumenical Conf. M.E. Ch., London, 1921; del. Gen. Conf. M.E. Ch., Atlantic City, N.J., 1932, Columbus, O., 1936; sec. Genesee Conf., 1928-37; retired 1937. Mem. Phi Delta Theta. Mason (32°). Author: Darff and His New England Neighbors, 1935. Home: Southold, Long Island, N.Y. Died June 17, 1949.

HOWELL, Edward Vernon, prof. pharmacy; born Raleigh, N.C., Mar. 30, 1872; s. James King and Virginia Carolina (Royster) H.; A.B., Wake Forest (N.C.) Coll., 1892; Ph.G., Phila. Coll. of Pharmacy, 1894; post-grad. work in chemistry, U. of N.C., 1897-98; unmarried. Prof. pharmacy and dean of dept., U. of N.C., since Sept., 1897; pres. Peoples Bank, Chapel Hill. Mem. Am. Pharm. Assn. (chmn. hist. sect. 1918-19, vice chmn. scientific sect.), Am. Chem. Soc., N.C. Pharm. Soc., Am. Hist. Assn., Am. Folk-Lore Soc., N.C. Folk-Lore Soc., Elisha Mitchell Scientific Soc. of U.N.C. (pres. 1913-14), Sigma Alpha Epsilon. V.p. Conf. Am. Pharm. Faculties, 1923-24; mem. exec. com. Am. Assn. Colls. of Pharmacy, 1926-27. Democrat. Baptist. Contbr. to pharm. jours. Home: Chapel Hill, N.C. Deceased.

HOWELL, Herbert P., banker; b. Coultersville, Pa., Apr. 3, 1874; s. Joseph K. and Mary E. Howell; ed. pub. schs.; m. Isabella Thorn, 1896 (died Apr. 1928); m. 2d, Beatrice Noyes Gallaher, Nov. 22, 1935. Was with Carnegie Steel Co. many years; now chmn. of bd. Commercial Nat. Bank & Trust Co. of New York; dir. Omnibus Corp., City N.Y. Ins. Co., Lehman Corp., Standard Brands, Inc.; trustee Franklin Savings Bank; dir., mem. exec. com. Gibraltar Fire and Marine Ins. Co., Baltimore Am. Ins. Co. of New York, Nat. Liberty Ins. Co. of America, Home Indemnity Co.; dir. Commercial Nat. Safe Deposit Co.; dir. and mem. finance com. Home Ins. Co.; voting trustee Internat. Match Realization Co., Ltd. Pres. New York Clearing House Assn. Trustee Grant Monument Assn. Member Am. Arbitration Assn. Nat. Panel of Arbitrators, Pa. Soc. of New York (v.p.). Clubs: Union League (bd. govs.), Bankers Club of America (chmn. exec. com., mem. bd. govs.), Recess, Manursing Island, Duquesne (Pittsburgh); Blind Brook. Home: 375 Park Av. Office: 46 Wall St., New York, N.Y. Died July 31, 1944.

HOWELL, Julius Franklin, educator, author; b. Nansemond County, Va., Jan. 17, 1846; s. Edward and Sarah (Barnes) H.; ed. Reynoldson Collegiate Inst., N.C., 1855-61; student Ill. Normal Coll., 1886, Harvard, 1891-92, Univ. of Pa., 1892; m. Ida Celsus Hinton, Sept. 17, 1870. Prin. Reynoldson Collegiate Inst., 1868-73; high schs. Austin, Ark., 1873-78, Lonoke, Ark., 1878-82, Arkadelphia, Ark., 1882-83, Morrilton, Ark., 1883-85; prof. Univ. of Ark., 1885-1898, Univ. High Sch., Fayetteville, Ark., 1898-99; pres. Mountain Home Bapt. Coll., 1899-1901; pres. Virginia Inst., 1901-02. Author: Syllabus of Egyptian History, 1897. Address: Bristol, Va.-Tenn. Died June 20, 1948.

HOWELL, Walter Rufus, business exec.; b. Milwaukee, Wis., April 3, 1888; s. Jenkin and Margaret (Anderson) H.; m. Florence McDermott, Dec. 13, 1919; children—Margaret M. (Mrs. R. W. Ramage), Florence Anne, Sarah Pauline, Walter Rufus. Dir. Bliss and Laughlin, Inc., since 1920, pres. since 1929, gen. mgr. since 1920; dir. Athey Products Corp., Chicago, Ill., Globe Steel Tubes Co., Milwaukee, Wis., Buda Co., Harvey, Ill. Clubs: Chicago Athletic Assn., Chicago, South Shore Country, Flossmoor Country. Home: 4950 Chicago Beach Drive, Chicago, Ill. Office: Harvey, Ill. Died Mar. 15, 1949.

HOWELL, William Henry, prof. physiology; b. Baltimore, Feb. 20, 1860; s. George Henry and Virginia Teresa H.; A.B., Johns Hopkins, 1881, Ph.D., 1884; hon. M.D., U. of Mich., 1890; LL.D., Trinity, 1901, U. of Mich., 1912, Washington U., 1915, U. of Edinburgh, 1923; Sc.D., Yale, 1911; m. Anne Janet Tucker, June 15, 1887; children—Janet Tucker (Mrs. Admont H. Clark), Roger, Charlotte Teresa (Mrs. Edward O. Hulburt). Asso. prof. physiology, Johns Hopkins, 1888-89; prof. physiology and histology, U. of Mich., 1889-92; asso. prof. physiology, Harvard, 1892-93; prof. physiology Johns Hopkins U., 1893-1931, dean med. faculty, 1899-1911, asst. dir. Sch. Hygiene, 1917-26, dir., 1926-31, emeritus since 1931. Chmn. Nat. Research Council, 1932-33. Mem. Nat. Acad. Sciences, Am. Philos. Soc., etc.; hon. mem. English Physiol. Soc. Author: Text-book of Physiology, 1905. Editor of An American Text-book of Physiology, 1896. Home: 112 St. Dunstan's Rd., Baltimore, Md. Died Feb. 6, 1945.

HOWELL, Williamson S., Jr., diplomat. Ambassador to Uruguay. Died May 22, 1947.

HOWER, Harry (Sloan), prof. physics; b. Parker, Pa., July 24, 1877; s. William H(enry) and Rebecca (Sloan) H.; B.S., Case Sch. Applied Science,

1899, M.S., 1907; grad. study, U. of Berlin, 1903-05; m. Sara Chester, June 23, 1909; children—Thomas Chester, Harry Sloan, Sara, William Henry II. Teacher physics, high sch., Conneaut, O., 1 yr., 1899-1900; instr. in physics, Case Sch. Applied Science, 1900-03, 1905-06; with Carnegie Inst. Tech. since 1906, prof. physics and head of dept. since 1915; cons. physicist. Designer of lenses for range lights for Panama Canal Commn., U.S. Light House Bd., U.S. Navy submarines, U.S. Army searchlight, Norwegian merchant marine, etc. Fellow Am. Physical Soc., A.A.A.S.; mem. Am. Optical Soc., Soc. Promotion Engring. Edn., Am. Ceramic Soc., Illuminating Engring. Soc., English Soc. Glass Technology, Pa. Acad. Science, Sigma Xi, Tau Beta Pi, Theta Xi. Republican. Episcopalian. Mason. Club: University. Home: 5709 Solway St., Pittsburgh, Pa. Died Oct. 10, 1941.

HOWEY, William John, developer of citrus groves; b. Odin, Ill., Jan. 19, 1876; s. Rev. William Henry and Matilda (Harris) H.; ed. pub. schs.; m. Mary Grace Hastings, Apr. 14, 1914; children—Mary Grace, Lois. Began as grower of grape fruit and orange trees, in Fla., 1905; now pres. W. J. Howey Co., Howey-in-the-Hills Juice Co., Ridge Holding Co., Orange Belt Securities Co., Howey Hotels Co.; chmn. bd. Howey-in-the-Hills Sanitarium Co.; dir. Tavares & Gulf R.R., Bankers Nat. Life Ins. Co., Howey Building & Loan Exchange, Fla. Citrus Exchange. Mem. adv. bd. Ednl. Commn. State of Fla.; mem. Tariff Com. of Fla., State C. of C. K.P., Elk. Clubs: Lake County Country (Eustis, Fla.); Orlando (Fla.) Country; Hamilton, South Shore Country (Chicago); National Arts (New York). Home: Howey-in-the-Hills, Florida. Died June 7, 1938.

HOWLAND, Charles Roscoe, army officer; b. Jefferson, O., Feb. 16, 1871; s. William Perry and Esther Elizabeth (Leonard) H.; student Oberlin (O.) Coll., 1890-91, hon. A.M., 1912; B.S., U.S. Mil. Acad., 1895; LL.B., Nat. U. Law Sch., Washington, D.C., 1909; hon. grad. Army Sch. of the Line, Fort Leavenworth, Kan., 1920; grad. Army Gen. Staff Sch., Fort Leavenworth, 1921, Army War Coll., Washington (D.C.) Barracks, 1927; Army refresher courses, 1928; unmarried. Commd. 2d lt., U.S. Army, June 12, 1895, advancing through the grades to brig. gen., Dec. 25, 1927; ret. as brig. gen. comdg. 2d Div., Feb. 28, 1935. Capt. 28th Inf., U.S. Volunteers, July 5, 1899-1901; col. of infantry Nat. Army, Aug. 5, 1917-Aug. 21, 1919, commander 343d, later 165th, Infantry; comdr. 14th Inf., 1923-26; chief of staff 3d Division, 1927; comdr. 3d Arty. Brig. to 1929; comdr. 4th Brigade, 1929-31; 3d Brigade, Ft. Sam Houston, Tex., 1932-34; 2d Div., 1934-35. Served as a.d.c. to Gen. Loyd Wheaton, 1898-1902; adj. gen., 1st Division, 4th and 7th Army Corps, 1898; a.d.c. to General Arthur MacArthur, 1903; assistant judge adv. gen., 1907-12. Organized and trained machine gun detachment, 1897; installed civil gvt., Dagupan, P.I., 1899; selected location for target range, San Francisco Area, 1903; planned and constructed Safe Protective Range, 1904; prevented spread of war south in Island of Leyte, P.I., 1906; as recorder tried Brownsville Shooting Affray Case, before Congl. Ct. of Inquiry, 1909-10; comdr., Alcatraz Island Mil. Prison (changed to Disciplinary Barracks), San Francisco Bay, Calif., 1914-17; instr. in mil. history and strategy, Army Gen. Service Schs., Fort Leavenworth, 1922-23; comdr. invading army in joint Army-Navy training exercises, May 1927; chief of staff 3d Div., 1927. Recommended for brevet promotion 6 times for gallantry in action, D.S.M., Medal of Honor; decorated 3 Silver Star citations with 2 Oak Leaf clusters; U.S. gold life saving medal; Spanish-Am. War badge; Philippine Insurrection badge; World War I Victory medal. Mem. Mil. Order of Carabao, Am. Legion, Mil. Order World War, The Pilgrim John Howland Soc., New Eng. Hist. and Genealogical Soc., Vermont and Western Reserve Hist. Socs. Conglist. Mason. Clubs: Army and Navy (Washington); University (Cleveland). Author: Digest of Opinions of the Judge Advocate General of the Army, 1912; Military History of the World War, 1923. Home: University Club, 3813 Euclid Av., Cleveland 15. Died Sept. 21, 1946; buried in Arlington National Cemetery.

HOWLAND, Hewitt Hanson, editor; b. Indianapolis, Oct. 8, 1863; s. John D. and Desdemona (Harrison) H.; grad. Indianapolis Classical Sch.; Litt.D., Wabash Coll., Crawfordsville, Ind., 1929; m. Manie Cobb. Editor and lit. adviser of The Bobbs-Merrill Co., Indianapolis, 1900-25; editor Century, 1925-31; now lit. adviser, manuscript editor and author's rep. Clubs: The Players, Dutch Treat (New York); University (Indianapolis). Author: Dwight Whitney Morrow (biography), 1930. Editor and compiler: The Lockerbie Book; The Hoosier Book of Riley Verse; Humor by Vote. Home: 117 E. 77th St. Office: 745 5th Av., New York. Died May 10, 1944.

HOWLAND, Paul, ex-congressman; b. Jefferson, O., Dec. 5, 1865; s. W. P. and Esther Elizabeth (Leonard) H.; A.B., Oberlin Coll., 1887, A.M., 1894, LL.B., Harvard, 1890; m. Jessie F. Pruden, Jan. 18, 1905. Practiced law at Jefferson, 1890-94, at Cleveland since 1894. Mem. 60th to 62d Congresses (1907-13), 20th Ohio Dist. Del. Rep. Nat. Convs., 1916, 20, 24; mem. com. on resolutions, 1916, chmn. com. on rules, 1920, 24. Mem. exec. com. Am. Bar Assn., 1918-21, chmn. com. on jurisprudence and law reform, 1928-32, pres. Cleveland Bar Assn., 1926-27. Second lt. 1st Ohio Cav. in Spanish-Am. War. Home: 1448 W. 65th St. Office: Engineers Bldg., Cleveland, O. Died Dec. 23, 1942.

HOWLAND, William, musician; b. Worcester, Mass., May 1, 1871; s. Asa Allen and Emma (Lane) H.; grad. English High Sch., Worcester, Mass., 1889; studied music in New York, London and Germany; hon. degree of Mus.Doc., 1925; m. Fredreka Shaw Barnard, June 24, 1896; children—John Barnard, Dorothy (Mrs. Robert M. Ball). Was teacher of voice and singer in chs., New York, 1889-94, Worcester and Boston, 1894-99; head of vocal dept., U. of Mich. Sch. of Music, 1900-14; v.p., dir. and head Vocal Dept., Detroit Inst. of Mus. Art, since 1914; a dir. and mus. dir., Music Festival Assn. of Detroit (inc.); founder and mus. dir., People's Choral Union, Detroit Festival Choral Soc.; bass soloist and choir dir., Temple Beth El; dir. Northwestern Choral Club; baritone soloist 2 seasons with the Bostonians. Mem. Internat. Music Teachers' Assn., Music Teachers' Nat. Assn., Mich. Music Teachers' Assn., Fine Arts Soc., Detroit. Mem. The Pilgrim John Howland Soc. (pres.), Nat. Soc. Mayflower Descendants (dep. gov.), Mich. State Mayflower Descendants (gov. two terms), Clubs: University of Michigan Union (life), Fine Arts Soc., Bohemians. Home: 590 Lakeview Dr., Birmingham, Mich. Studio: 52 Putnam Av., Detroit, Mich. Died May 1, 1945.

HOWSON, Elmer Thomas, editor; b. Folletts, Ia., May 23, 1884; s. Thomas H. and Cora (Wessels) H.; B.S., U. of Wis., 1906, C.E., 1914; m. Mae McCulloch, June 5, 1907. Began as asst. engr. C.,B.&Q. R.R., 1906, div. engr., 1909-11; engring. editor, Railway Age Gazette, 1911-19; western editor Railway Age since 1919, also editor Railway Engineering and Maintenance since its establishment, 1916, and of Railway Engineering and Maintenance Cyclopedia; v.p. Simmons Boardman Pub. Corp. since 1931; sec. Am. Builder Pub. Corp. since 1929. Mem. Am. Soc. C.E., Am. Ry. Engring. Assn. (dir.), Western Soc. Engrs. (ex-pres.), Am. Wood-Preservers Assn. (ex-pres.), Asso. Business Papers, Inc. (ex-pres), Roadmasters and Maintenance of Way Assn. (ex-pres.), Am. Ry. Bridge and Building Assn. (ex-pres.). Republican. Methodist. Clubs: Union League, Engineers, South Shore Country. Home: 6922 Paxton Av. Office: 105 W. Adams St., Chicago, Ill.* Died Sep. 1, 1944.

HOYNE, Thomas Temple, writer; b. Chicago, Nov. 2, 1875; s. Thomas Maclay and Jeanie Thomas (Maclay) H.; ed. Allen's Acad. (Chicago, and Phillips Acad., Andover, Mass.; student Williams Coll., 1893-94; U. of Chicago, 1895-98; LL.B., John Marshall Law Sch., Chicago, 1913; m. Maud Stuart Mitchell, 1914. Writer since 1895; editorial and spl. writer for Chicago Evening American and Chicago Herald and Examiner; financial editor Chicago Herald and Examiner since 1928; mem. Chicago Curb Exchange Assn. U.S. comptroller of customs in Chicago. Made original research in grain marketing, the world wheat situation, etc. Clubs: University (Chicago); Friars (New York). Author: Speculation, Its Sound Principles and Rules For Its Practice, 1922; Myself and Fellow Asses, 1923; Wall Street Remodeling the World, 1930; also pamphlets on cooperative grain marketing, the Chicago Board of Trade, etc. Home: 3270 Lake Shore Drive. Address: Chicago Herald and Examiner, Chicago. Died Dec. 17, 1946.

HOYNS, Henry, chmn. bd. and dir. Harper and Brothers; pres. Paul B. Hoeber, Inc.; trustee Kings County Savings Bank. Home: 1314 Carroll St., Brooklyn, N.Y. Office: care Harper and Brothers, 49 E. 33d St., New York, N.Y.* Died Jan. 1945.

HOYT, John Clayton, civil engr.; b. Lafayette, N.Y., June 10, 1874; s. Newton O. and Mary E. (Ford) H.; C.E., Cornell U., 1897; m. Jennie F. King, Oct. 31, 1900; 1 son, Kendall King. With Cornell Hydraulic Lab. Constrn. Co., U.S. Deep Waterways Commn. and Bur. Yards and Docks, Navy Dept., 1897-99; U.S. Coast and Geod. Survey, 1900-02; with U.S. Geol. Survey since 1902; hydraulic engr. in charge Surface Water Div., 1911-30; cons. engr. since 1931. Professional work for Geol. Survey in various states and Hawaii and Alaska. U.S. del. 13th and 14th Internat. Navigation Congress, London, 1923, Cairo, 1926; mem. Am. com. representing U.S. Dept. of Interior, World Power Conf., London, 1924; delegate to World Engring. Congress, Tokyo, Japan, 1929. Mem. Am. Soc. C.E. (dir. 1920-22; v.p. 1927-28), Washington Soc. of Engrs. (sec. 1908-15; pres. 1916), Washington Acad. Sciences (v.p. 1916), Sigma Xi. Congregationalist. Mason. Clubs: Cosmos (pres. 1921), Chevy Chase. Author: (with Nathan C. Grover) River Discharge, 1907; Droughts of 1930-34 and 1936; also of various other U.S. Geol. Survey reports and articles in tech. papers. Home: 4749 MacArthur Blvd. N.W. Office: Cosmos Club, Washington, D.C. Died June 21, 1946.

HOYT, Minerva Hamilton (Mrs. A. Sherman Hoyt), conservationist; b. on cotton plantation nr. Durant, Miss., Mar. 27, 1866; d. Joel George and Emily Victoria (Lockhart) Hamilton; ed. Wards Sem., Nashville, Tenn., and Coll. of Music, Cincinnati, O.; hon. Dr. of Botany, U. of Mexico; m. A. Sherman Hoyt; children—Charles Albert (dec.), Ruth Hamilton (Mrs. LeRoy Sanders), Julia Sherman (Mrs. Hoyt-Griswold). Conservationist and naturalist since 1898, specializing in desert flora and fauna; organizer, now pres. Internat. Desert Conservation League; suggested Internat. Peace Park between Mexico and U.S.; active in securing million acre preserve for Joshua Tree National monument in Southern California; suggested Death Valley as a nat. monument. Chmn. garden and parks com., Olympic Games, Calif., 1932. Hon. mem. Royal Hort. Soc. of Gt. Britain, Hort. Soc. of Germany, Nat. Soc. of Colonial Daughters; mem. Am. Planning and Civic Assn. Awarded Internat. gold medal, N.Y. City; gold medal, Garden Club America; Grand Centennial gold medal and $1,000 gold cup, Boston (exhibit required 2 refrigerator cars, 1 freight car and 12 airplanes); Royal Hort. Soc. gold medal and Lawrence gold medal, Spring Flower Show, Chelsea, Eng.; silver trophy, Federated Garden Clubs of State of Miss.; hon. dir. U. of Mexico; gold medal, Haverhill (Mass.) Garden Club; bronze medal Seattle (Wash.) Garden Club; also gold medals from Tacoma, Wash., Garden Club, and Pasadena, Calif., Garden Club, etc. Has made large permanent exhibits at New York Bot. Garden and Kew Gardens, Eng. Founder Music and Art Assn. of Pasadena; former pres. Los Angeles Symphony Orchestra. Clubs: Friday Morning (life), Southern Pasadena, South Pasadena Woman's (life); also hon. mem. McDowell Music and Art Club (Los Angeles), Shakespeare and Zonta clubs (Pasadena). Home: "Hillcrest," 917 Buena Vista St., South Pasadena, Calif. Died Dec. 15, 1945.

HOYT, William Dana, prof. biology; b. Rome, Ga., Apr. 16, 1880; s. (Dr.) William Dearing and Florence West (Stevens) H.; A.B., University of Georgia, 1901; M.S., 1904; Ph.D., Johns Hopkins, 1909; studied University of Heidelberg, 1909-10; research work, Naples, 1910; m. Margaret Howard Yeaton, Dec. 27, 1910 (died Sept. 26, 1943); children—William Dana, Southgate Yeaton, Robert Stephens. Tutor in biology, U. of Ga., 1901-04; fellow Johns Hopkins, 1908-09; scientific asst. U.S. Bur. Fisheries, Beaufort, N.C., 1902-09; Adam T. Bruce fellow, Johns Hopkins, 1909-10; instr. in botany, Rutgers Coll., 1910-12; fellow Johns Hopkins, 1912-15; asso. prof. biology, Washington and Lee U., 1915-20, prof. since 1920; instr. in botany, Marine Biol. Lab., Woods Hole, Mass., 1917-19. Fellow A.A.A.S.; mem. Bot. Soc. America, Am. Forestry Assn., Am. Genetic Assn., Am. Eugenic Soc., Am. Soc. Naturalists, Assn. Research Human Heredity, Va. Acad. Science, Chi Psi, Phi Beta Kappa. Democrat. Presbyterian. Club: Fortnightly. Author: Marine Algæ of Beaufort, N.C., and Adjacent Regions, 1920; also articles on life habits and physiology of algæ; proved alternation of generations in algæ. Chmn. advisory Council on State Parks and Forests, 1930-33. Home: 5 Lewis St., Lexington, Va. Died Sep. 24, 1945.

HRDLICKA, Aleš (hŭr'dlich-kȧ), anthropologist; b. Humpolec, Bohemia, Mar. 29, 1869; s. Maxmilian and Karolina H.; M.D., N.Y. Eclectic Coll., 1892, New York Homœ. Coll., 1894; Md. Allopathic State Bd., 1894; hon. Sc.D., Prague U., 1920, Brno U., 1929; investigator among insane and other defective classes, N.Y. State Service, 1894-99; asso. in anthropology, N.Y. State Pathol. Inst., 1896-99; studied in Paris U. and Anthrop. Sch., first half 1896; married 1896. Tour over European prisons, insane asylums and museums, 1896; in charge phys. anthropology of Hyde expdns. for Am. Mus. Natural History, 1899-1903; asst. curator in charge div. phys. anthropology, 1903-10, curator since 1910, U.S. Nat. Museum. Anthrop. expdns. to many countries throughout period since 1898. Author exhibits phys. anthropology and prehistoric Am. pathology, San Diego Expn., 1915-16. Asso. editor Am. Naturalist, 1901-08; founder, and editor Am. Jour. Phys. Anthrop. since 1918. Sec. gen. XIX Internat. Congress Americanists, 1915, sec. Sect. 1, anthropology, 2d Pan-Am. Scientific Congress, 1915-16; sec. com. on anthropology, Nat. Research Council, 1917-18; etc. Fellow Am. Acad. Arts and Sciences, A.A.A.S. (life); mem. Assn. Am. Anatomists, Am. Anthrop. Assn. (pres. 1925-26), Nat. Acad. Sciences, Am. Philos. Soc., Washington Acad. Sciences (pres. 1928-29), Archæol. Inst. America, Am. Assn. Physical Anthropology (pres. 1928-32; founder and life mem.); hon. and corr. member various foreign acads. and socs. Huxley medal lecturer, London, 1927. Author of numerous books and papers on anthropology and related subjects. Home: 2900 Tilden St., N.W. Address: U.S. National Museum, Washington, D.C. Died Sep. 5, 1943.

HUBBARD, Frank W., banker; b. Port Huron, Mich., Apr. 16, 1863; s. Langdon and Amanda (Lester) H.; ed. Hartford High Sch., Conn.; and Hanmer's Business Coll.; m. Elizabeth Lockwood, June 7, 1893. Engaged in banking and real estate business, Huron County, Mich., since 1886, Detroit, Mich., since 1907; pres. Hubbard State Bank (Bad Axe, Mich.), Village Homes Co. (Grosse Pointe, Mich.), Kinde State Bank, R. L. Hubbard & Co. (Caseville), Mich.; dir. Detroit Bank, Elkton State Bank. Trustee Hubbard Mem. Hosp. Democrat. Presbyterian. Mason. Clubs: Detroit, Bankers (pres. 1927), Country (Detroit); Grosse Pointe Club. Dir. Nat. War Savings for Mich., 1918-19. Home: 16900 Jefferson Av. E., Grosse Pointe. Mich. Office: 639 Penobscot Bldg., Detroit, Mich. Died Dec. 30, 1943.

HUBBARD, Henry Vincent, landscape architect; b. Taunton, Mass., Aug. 22, 1875; s. Charles Thacher and Clara Isabel (Reed) H.; A.B., Harvard, 1897, A.M., 1900, S.B. in Landscape Arch., 1901; student Mass. Inst. Tech., 1897-98; m. Theodora Kimball, June 7, 1924 (died Nov. 7, 1935); m. 2d, Isabel Fay Gerrish, June 30, 1937. Instr. landscape architecture, Harvard Univ., 1906-10, asst. prof., 1910-21, prof., 1921-29, Norton prof. regional planning, 1929-41, emeritus since 1941; chmn. council Dept. of Regional Planning, Harvard, 1929-41; mem. Pray, Hubbard & White, Boston, 1906-18; partner, Olmsted Brothers, Brookline, Mass., since 1920. A founder Landscape Architecture (mag.), 1910, and now chief editor; a founder and chief editor City Planning Quarterly,

1925-34; cons. editor, The Planners' Journal, 1935-41. Entered war service as surveyor, Camp Devens (Mass.) Survey and Constrn., Sept. 1917; successively designer cantonment br. Construction Div., U.S. Army; designer Emergency Fleet Corp., U.S. Shipping Bd.; expert with housing com. Council Nat. Defense, and asst. mgr. and acting chief Town Planning Div., U.S. Bur. Housing and Transportation (U.S. Housing Corp.); hon. disch. from army service, May 1919. Fellow, trustee Am. Soc. Landscape Architects (pres. 1931-34); mem. Boston Soc. Landscape Architects, Am. Inst. Planners; del. (and com. mem.) Nat. Conf. on Outdoor Recreation; mem. com. on subdivision layout of President's Conf. on Home Building and Home Ownership; mem. Gov. Ely's Spl. Commn. on Laws Relative to Zoning, Town Planning and Billboards; mem. Nat. Capital Park and Planning Commn. since 1932; trustee Am. Acad. in Rome since 1933. Mem. Milton Planning Bd. since 1938; planning consultant F.H.A. 1940-45, Pub. Building Adminstrn., 1941-42; mem. adv. com. to Boston Planning Bd. since 1941, planning consultant 1942-45, planning consultant Baltimore Commn. on City Plan, 1943-45; planning consultant, Providence, R.I., City Plan Commn. since 1945; mem. exec. bd. Mass. Fed. Planning Bds. since 1941 (v.p. 1942-44). Mem. Harvard Musical Association, Massachusetts Soc., Mayflower Descendants. Clubs: Union, Laurel Brook (president 1929-40), Harvard (Boston); Century Association, Harvard (N.Y.); Cosmos (Washington); Milton (Milton, Mass.). Author: Introduction to the Study of Landscape Design (with Theodora Kimball), 1917, revised edit., 1929; Our Cities Today and Tomorrow (with T. K. Hubbard), 1929. Editor: Report of U.S. Housing Corp. (Vol. II), 1919; (with Theodora Kimball) Landscape Architecture—A Comprehensive Classification Scheme, 1920; Parks and Playgrounds as Elements in the City Plan (Procs. of Nat. Conf. on City Planning), 1922, 24; Airports, Their Location, Administration and Legal Basis (with Miller McClintock and Frank B. Williams), 1930; Parkways and Land Values (with John Nolen), 1937; also articles in mags. Home: 15 Snafford Rd., Milton, Mass. Died Oct. 6, 1947; buried in Mt. Pleasant Cemetery, Taunton, Mass.

HUBBARD, John W., corp. official; b. Pittsburgh, Pa.; s. Charles White and Cleo (Winslow) H.; student Pa. Mil. Coll., Chester, U. of Pittsburgh; m. Cora M. Pack (died 1916); 1 dau., Cora W. (wife of John C. Williams, U.S. Army). Began as mfr., 1887; now chmn. bd. Hubbard & Co.; also chmn. bd. Ralston Steel Car Co.; pres. Sands Level & Tool Co., Campbell Transportation Co.; dir. New York Air Brake Co., Detroit Seamless Steel Tubes Co., Alton R.R. Co., Pittsburgh Oil & Gas Co., City Ice and Fuel Co., Teck Food Products Co., Empire Trust Co. (N.Y. City), Continental Roll & Steel Foundry Co. (East Chicago, Ind.). Episcopalian. Clubs: Duquesne, Pittsburgh Athletic, Pittsburgh Field (Pittsburgh); Lotos, New York Yacht (New York); Chicago Yacht; Longue Vue Country. Office: Granite Bldg., Pittsburgh, Pa.* Died June 3, 1947.

HUBBELL, Henry Salem, painter; b. Paola, Kan., Dec. 25, 1870; s. Willard Orvis and Maria (Gleason) H.; pupil Art Inst., Chicago, and studied in Paris with Jean Paul Laurens, Raphael Collin, and Whistler; also studied some time in Madrid, Spain; m. Rose Strong, July 30, 1895; 1 son, Henry Willard. Began as illustrator; was for some time with Woman's Home Companion. Made début in Paris Salon, 1901, with large picture, "The Bargain"; other pictures, "The Return," "The Poet" (bought by Mr. William M. Chase), "Chez Grand'mère," "The Caress," "Morning," "The Brasses" (now in Wilstach collection, Memorial Hall Mus., Phila), "Henry and Jack," "The Orange Robe," "By the Fireside," "Child and Cat" (bought by the French Govt.), "The Goldfish" (owned by Booth Tarkington), "The Samovar" (now in collection of Baron Edmond de Rothschild), "The Departure," "Black and White" (now in municipal art collection, Grand Rapids, Mich.); "Larkspurs" (bought by French Govt.); has painted portraits, including F. D. Roosevelt in Hyde Park Memorial, Sec. H. L. Ickes and 15 past secs. of Interior for Interior Bldg., also Chief Justice Harlan F. Stone and Mrs. Stone. Hon. mention, Paris Salon, 1901; medal, Paris Salon, 1904; silver medal, St. Louis Expn., 1904; 3d prize, Worcester Art Acad.; Waite bronze medal, Chicago Art Inst. A.N.A.; ex-v.p. Am. Art Assn. of Paris; mem. Paris Soc. Am. Painters, Société Internationale de Peinture et de Sculpture, Paris, Nat. Assn. Portrait Painters, Silvermine Group of Artists, Eclectic Group of Painters and Sculptors, Allied Artists America, Fla. Soc. Arts and Sciences (ex-pres.), Miami Civic Theatre (ex-pres.). Former mem. Bd. of Regents Univ. of Miami, Fla.; prof. and head of Sch. of Painting and Decoration, Carnegie Inst. Tech., Pittsburgh, 1918-21; now engaged in portrait painting. Club: Nat. Arts of New York (life mem.). Home and Studio: 740 N.E. 90th St., Miami 38, Fla. Died Jan. 9, 1949.

HUBBELL, James Wakeman, pub. utility exec.; b. Danbury, Conn., Apr. 8, 1881; s. James W. and Mary W. (Gregory) H.; A.B., Yale; m. Lucy M. Hegeman, May 3, 1926; children—Edward P., Frances. Chief engr. New York Telephone Co., Albany, N.Y., 1925-26; v.p. and gen. mgr. Upstate N.Y. Telephone Co., Albany, N.Y., 1926-34; v.p. and dir. N.Y. Telephone Co., N.Y. City, 1934-41, pres. since 1941; pres. Empire City Subway Co.; dir. Holmes Electric Protective Corp. Home: 300 West End Av. Office: 140 West St., New York, N.Y. Deceased.

HUBENY, Maximilian John (hū'bĕn-ĭ), radiologist; b. Leipzig, Germany, Oct. 12, 1880; s. Peter and Mary (Mertlick) H.; M.D., Hahnemann Med. Coll., Chicago, Ill., 1906; U. of Ill. Med. Sch., 1909; m. Daisy Twitchell, Aug. 28, 1907. Practiced in Chicago, specializing in med. application of X-ray, since 1907; dir. X-ray dept. Cook County Hosp., prof. roentgenology, Cook County Grad. Sch. of Medicine; formerly editor Radiology; former asso. editor Am. Jour. of Cancer, Italian Jour. Radiology, Cuban Jour. Radiology. Past pres. Alumni of U. of Ill. Med. Dept. Fellow A.M.A. (ex-chairman section radiology), Am. College Physicians; mem. Ill. State, Chicago, Bohemian and German med. socs., Am. Roentgen Soc., Radiol. Soc. N. Am. (ex-pres.), Chicago Roentgen Society, Am. College Radiology (ex-pres.), Phi Alpha Gamma, Alpha Mu, Omega Pi. Clubs: City (dir.), Illini, Illinois Country. Home: 4728 N. Paulina St. Office: 1835 W. Harrison St., Chicago, Ill. Died July 2, 1942.

HUBER, Edward Godfrey, pub. health adminstrn.; b. Menomonie, Wis., May 30, 1882; s. William and Emma Anna (Honegger) H.; A.B, U. of Mich., 1903, M.D., 1905; honor grad. Army Med. Sch., 1908; Dr. P.H., Harvard, 1925; m. Frances Madison, Aug. 11, 1904; 1 dau., Lucile Adelaide. Commd. 1st lieut. Med. Corps, U.S. Army, 1908, and advanced through grades to col. (temp.), 1919; with A.E.F., comdg. Base Hosp. 25, Allerey, France, 1918, Hosp. Center, Perigueux, France, 1918-19; chief of lab. service Letterman Gen. Hosp., 1919-23; comdg. officer 1st Corps Area Lab., Boston, Mass., 1923-24, asst. Corps Area surgeon, 4th C.A., 1925-27; med. inspector 2d Div., 1927-29; surgeon, Plattsburgh Barracks, N.Y., 1929-34; asst. in vital statistics, Harvard, 1924-25; commd. col. Med. Corps, U.S. Army, 1934; retired, 1935; instr. in epidemiology, Harvard Sch. of Pub. Health, 1935-36, instr. in preventive medicine and hygiene, 1936-37, asso. in pub. health adminstrn., 1937-39, asst. prof. pub. health adminstrn., 1939-42, asso. prof. pub. health practice, 1942-45; prof. pub. health practice, 1946; asst. dean 1938-42, acting dean, 1942-46, asso. dean, 1946; asst. director Div. of Adminstrn., Mass. Dept. of Pub. Health, since 1936; dir. med. div. region 5, Mass. Com. on Pub. Safety. Awarded Wellcome prize and gold medal for essay in national competition, 1927. Fellow A.A.A.S., American Acad. Arts and Sciences, Am. Med. Assn., Am. Pub. Health Assn., Am. Coll. Physicians, Mass. Med. Soc.; mem. Am. Soc. Pub. Adminstrn., Assn. Mil. Surgeons, Am. Soc. Tropical Medicine, Boston Orthopedic Club, Newton Med. Club, N.Y. Acad. Sciences, Delta Omega (nat. pres. 1929-30; nat. sec. and treas. 1942-44), Phi Rho Sigma. Republican. Mason. Clubs: St. Botolph, Harvard (Boston). Home: 45 Homewood Rd., Waban, Mass. Office: 55 Shattuck St., Boston. Died July 23, 1946; buried in Arlington National Cemetery.

HUBER, Seba Cormany, lawyer; b. Eshcol, Pa., Jan. 29, 1871; s. Benjamin G. and Naomi J. (Cormany) H.; B.S., Lebanon Valley Coll., Annville, Pa., 1892; m. Cora A. Appleton, June 29, 1905. Supt. schs., Tama, 1892-96; mayor of Tama 3 terms; county atty., Tama County, 6 yrs.; Dem. candidate for Congress, 5th Dist., Ia., 1910, 12; mem. Dem. State Central Com., Ia., 1914-16; U.S. dist. atty. for Hawaii, by appmt. of Pres. Wilson, May 1916; apptd. judge U.S. Dist. Court, Hawaii, 1934; now in practice of law. Presbyterian. Mason. Office: McCandless Bldg., Honolulu, T.H.* Died Aug. 17, 1944.

HUBERICH, Charles Henry (hū'bĕr-ĭk), lawyer; b. Toledo, O., Feb. 18, 1877; s. Conrad and Emma (Richers) H.; studied under pvt. tutors; LL.B., U. of Tex., 1897, M.L., 1898; D.C.L., Yale, 1899; univs. of Berlin and Heidelberg, 1899-1900, J.U.D., magna cum laude, Heidelberg, 1905; LL.D., Melbourne, 1907; m. Laura King Orr, June 11, 1902; 1 dau., May Bess (Mrs. Alexander D. Gibson); m. 2d, Princess Nina Mdivani, July 15, 1925. Admitted to bar, 1898; instr. and adj. prof. law and polit. science, U. of Tex., 1900-05; asst. prof. law, 1905-06, asso. prof., 1906-07, prof., 1907-12, Stanford U.; prof. law, U. of Wis., 1909-10; prof. law, summer session, U. of Chicago, 1907. Mem. Am. Bar Assn., Internat. Law Assn., Grotius Soc. (London), Internat. Verein. für Vergl. Rechtswissenschaft, Soc. de Législation Comparée, Chi Phi, Phi Delta Phi. Author: The Trans-Isthmian Canal, 1904; Die Haftflicht für Betriebsunfälle (Heidelberg dissertation), 1905; Law Relating to Trading with the Enemy, 1918; The Political and Legislative History of Liberia, 1943; and of the vols. on the commercial law of Australia, New Zealand, Canada, Newfoundland, Ceylon, Straits Settlements, British West Africa, and other British dominions in the Commercial Laws of the World (also transl. into German and French). Editor of vols. on the law of the U.S. in the same work; asso. editor of Am. edit. Contbr. numerous articles to Am., British and Continental legal periodicals. Hon. mem. Soc. Jur. de la Univ. Nacional (Bogota). Home: New York, N.Y. Offices: In Temple Chambers, London, E.C. 4, England; and 475 5th Av., New York, N.Y.

Died June 18, 1945.

HUBLEY, George Wilbur (hūb'lē), engr.; b. Pittsburgh, Pa., May 9, 1870; s. George W. and Fanny (McAlister) H.; prep. edn., high sch., Allegheny, Pa.; spl. courses in mathematics and engring. under pvt. tutors. Student with Westinghouse Electric & Mfg. Co., Pittsburgh, 1887-90; elec. supt. Citizens Traction Co., Pittsburgh, 1890-93; supt. Louisville Gas & Electric Co., 1893-1915; gen. mgr. Merchants Heat & Light Co., Indianapolis, 1915-18; administrative engr. and chief of conservation, U.S. Fuel Adminstrn. of Ky., 1918; cons. practice, Louisville, since 1918; cons. engr. Ky. State Bd. Charities and Corrections, 1920-25; engr. Public Utilities Bur., Louisville, 1923-35. Fellow Am. Inst. E.E.; mem. Am. Soc. M.E., Am. Gas Assn., Ind. Engring. Soc., Engineers and Architects Club of Louisville (ex-pres.), S.A.R. (pres. 1940). Republican. Presbyterian. Mason. Home: 2428 Longest Av. Office: Norton Bldg., Louisville, Ky.* Died Apr. 8, 1944.

HUDSON, Albert Blellock; justice Supreme Court of Can.; b. Pembroke, Ont., Aug. 21, 1875; s. Albert and Elizabeth (Blellock) H.; ed. pub. schs., Portage la Prairie, Manitoba; LL.B., U. of Manitoba, Winnipeg, 1898; m. Mary B. Russel, 1908 (died 1925); m. 2d, Marjorie G. Runciman. Called to Manitoba bar, 1899, and practiced in Winnipeg; mem. Manitoba Legislature, 1914-20; atty. gen., Manitoba, 1915-17; mem. House of Commons, Can., 1921-25; justice Supreme Court of Can. since 1936. Mem. Can. Bar Assn. Clubs: Rideau (Ottawa); Manitoba (Winnipeg). Home: 295 Metcalfe St., Ottawa, Ont., Can. Died Jan. 6, 1947.

HUDSON, Hoyt Hopewell, univ. prof.; b. Norfolk, Neb., July 6, 1893; s. Rev. Fletcher Edward and Mayme (Fitz) Randolph H.; A.B., Huron (S.D.) Coll., 1911; A.M., U. of Denver, 1913; student U. of Chicago, 1916-17; Ph.D., Cornell U., 1923; Litt.D., Huron Coll., 1938; m. Margaret Calvert Dille, Dec. 16, 1917; children—Randolph Hoyt, Michael Calvert. Teacher high schs., successively at Coeur d'Alene, Ida., Duluth, Minn., Cleveland, O., 1913-20; instr. pub. speaking Cornell U., 1920-23; asst. prof. English and pub. speaking, Swarthmore Coll., 1923-25; prof. English, U. of Pittsburgh, 1925-27; asso. prof. pub. speaking, Princeton, 1927-31; prof., 1931-33; prof. rhetoric and oratory and chmn. dept. of English, 1933-42; prof. English, Stanford Univ. since 1942. Research asso., Huntington Library, 1934. Lecturer summer schs. Cornell, 1924, 25, 29, U. of Colo., 1935, Harvard, 1937, U. of Calif. at Los Angeles, 1938, Northwestern University, 1939, 40. Mem. Modern Lang. Assn. America, Phi Beta Kappa. Mem. Soc. of Friends. Clubs: Bookfellows (Chicago). Author: First Course in Public Speaking (with J. A. Winans), 1930; Principles of Argument and Debate (with J. W. Reeves), 1941. Translator: Kant's Religion within the Limits of Reason Alone (with T. M. Greene), 1934; Thomas Moffet's Nobilis (with V. B. Heltzel), 1940; Erasmus' Praise of Folly, 1941. Editor: Poetry of the English Renaissance (with J. W. Hebel), 1929; John Hoskins' Directions for Speech and Style, 1935. Managing editor The Step Ladder, 1930, associate editor since 1931; editor Quarterly Jour. of Speech, 1933-35. Home: 578 Lowell Av., Palo Alto, Calif. Died June 14, 1944.

HUDSON, James Henry, judge; b. Guilford, Me., Mar. 21, 1878; s. Henry and Ada Medora (Lougee) H.; grad. Coburn Classical Inst., Waterville, Me., 1896; A.B., Colby Coll., Waterville, 1900; LL.B., Harvard, 1903; LL.D., Colby Coll., 1932; m. Mary Stevens McKown, Nov. 11, 1903; 1 dau., Charlotte Frances (Mrs. John Powers White). Admitted to Me. bar, 1903, and practiced in Guilford; partner Hudson & Hudson; chmn. of Selectmen, 1915-17; county atty., 1917-24; judge Probate Court, 1924-29; justice Superior Ct., 1930-33; judge of Supreme Judicial Ct. of Me. since 1933; trustee Guilford Trust Co., Colby Coll., 1933-44. Mem. Am., Me. State and Piscataquis County bar assns., Guilford Chamber Commerce, Delta Kappa Epsilon, Phi Beta Kappa. Republican. Methodist. Mason (K.T.). Club: Piscataquis Country. Home: 8 Hudson Av., Guilford. Office: Court House, Augusta, Me. Died Aug. 21, 1947.

HUFF, Joseph Bascomb, educator; b. Mars Hill, N.C., Sept. 26, 1879; s. Leonard Corder and Bregetta Bethune (Carter) H.; grad. Mars Hill Coll., 1898; A.B., Wake Forest (N.C.) Coll., 1903; A.M., U. of N.C., 1904, grad. study, 1915-16, 1922-23; m. Cornelia Vandergraff Orr, Dec. 25, 1905 (dec.); children—Leonard Orr, James Lawrence, Dorothy (dec.), Richard Edward, Joseph Bascomb, Alfred Wiley; m. 2d, Mattie Lillian Ireland, 1923; 1 son, Henry Blair. Prin. high sch., Dothan, Ala., 1905-07, Wilmington, N.C., 1907-10; dean Mars Hill Coll., 1911-22; asso. prof. English, Univ. of N.C., 1922-23; prof. English and dir. Summer Sch., Carson-Newman Coll., Jefferson, Tenn., 1923-24; pres. Wingate (N.C.) Jr. Coll., 1924-30; head of dept. English, Mars Hill Coll., since 1930. Mayor of Mars Hill, 1912-16. Democrat. Baptist. Home: Mars Hill, N.C. Died Sep. 26, 1944.

HUFF, Slaughter William, ry. official; b. Albemarle County, Va., Mar. 9, 1867; s. Samuel P. and Elizabeth (Jurey) H.; student Richmond (Va.) Coll., 1882-86; Elec. and Mech. Engring. Sch., Cornell U., 1889-91; m. Julia Evelin Graham, Oct. 5, 1892. Asst. supt. Baxter Electric Motor Co., Baltimore, Md., 1891-92; gen. mgr. Raleigh (N.C.) Street R.R. Co., 1892-94; gen. supt. Baxter Electric Motor Co., 1894-96; elec. engr. Columbia & Md. Ry. Co., Baltimore, 1896-98; developing st. ry. control and signaling apparatus, 1898-1900; master mechanic, United Ry. & Elec. Co., Baltimore, 1900-01; elec. and mech. engr. United Rys. and Elec. Co., 1901-02; gen. mgr. Va. Passenger & Power Co., Richmond, Va., 1902-08; pres. Coney Island & Brooklyn R.R. Co., 1908-14; v.p. Brooklyn Rapid Transit Co., 1914-18; pres. 3d Av. Transit Corp., N.Y. City since 1918; also pres. Westchester Electric R.R. Co., Yonkers R.R. Co., N.Y., Westchester & Conn. Traction Co., Westchester St. Transportation Co., Surface Transportation Corp. of New York. Mem. Kappa Alpha (Southern). Democrat. Home: Carmel, N.Y. Office: 2396 3d Av., N.Y. City. Died Oct. 16, 1947.

HUFNAGEL, Edward Henry (hŭf'năg-ĕl), realtor, broker; b. Mount Vernon, N.Y., Dec. 17, 1879; s. Conrad Bernhardt and Marie (Imhof) H.; ed. high sch., Mount Vernon; m. Cora Louise Kellogg, Oct. 5, 1903 (died Oct. 16, 1926); children—Dorothy Kellogg (Mrs. Clarence M. Lightner), Bernhard Minot, Frederick Fairfax, Edward Henry (dec.); m. 2d, Willa Floy MacCormack, Nov. 4, 1927. Operated as E. H. Hufnagel, Inc., jewelers, 1899-1927; organizer, 1924, and former pres. Westchester Bond & Mortgage Corp.; pres. Mount Vernon Homes, Inc.; pres., treas. Norma Chem. Co., Inc., mfrs. and distbrs. metal protective coatings; treas. Bellefontaine Holding Co.; trustee Riverside Cemetery, Norwalk, Conn.; dir. Stony Brook Sch., 1920-45. Pres. Y.M.C.A., Mount Vernon, 1920-34. Mem. Horological Inst. Am. (pres. 1924-35, treas.), Am. Nat. Retail Jewelers Assn. (pres. 1921-24), Chamber of Commerce of State of N.Y. Republican. Methodist. Mason. Club: Rotary Internat. Home: 10 Rich Av. Office: 403 N. MacQuesten Parkway, Mount Vernon, N.Y. Died Oct. 2, 1948; buried Riverside Cemetery, Norwalk, Conn.

HUGHES, Charles Colfax, educator; b. Bartholomew County, Ind., Nov. 7, 1868; s. James Sheppard and Louisa Wilcox (Gatten) H.; moved to Calif. with parents, 1876; B.A., Stanford, 1895; m. Velma Ocella Ives, 1910; children—Charles Colfax, Henry Suzzallo, Ellwood Cubberley. Teacher pub. schs., later pvt. acad., Oakland, Calif.; prin. elementary sch., Mill Valley, 1895-96, grammar sch., Alameda, 1896-99; city supt. schs., Alameda, 1899-1904; with Am. Book Co., 1904-10; city supt. schs., Eureka, California, 1910-12; superintendent schools, Sacramento, 1912-Jan. 3, 1942; elected by Board of Education, Sacramento City Schools, director of public relations and administrative advisor, Jan. 3, 1943. Member N.E.A. (life), Chamber of Commerce (honorary), State Teachers' Association California (executive board and state council of education), Northern Calif. Teachers' Assn. (pres. 1924-25). Lecturer, summers, U. of Ore., U. of Calif. (Southern Br.). Republican. Conglist. Mason (K.T., Shriner), Odd Fellow, Woodman, Elk. Clubs: Rotary, High-12, Sutter. Author of Courses of Study and School Reports, 1913-25. Home: 2031 21st St. Office: 21st and L Sts., Sacramento, Calif. Died Oct. 23, 1944.

HUGHES, Charles Evans, retired chief justice of the United States; b. Glens Falls, N.Y., Apr. 11, 1862; s. David Charles and Mary Catherine (Connelly) H.; student Colgate U., 1876-78; A.B., Brown University, 1881, A.M., 1884; LL.B., Columbia, 1884; LL.D., Brown U., 1906, Columbia, Knox, and Lafayette, 1907, Union, Colgate, 1908, George Washington, 1909, Williams Coll., Harvard, and U. of Pa., 1910, Yale, 1915, U. of Mich., 1922, Dartmouth, 1923, Amherst, Princeton, and University State of N.Y., 1924, Pa. Mil. Coll., 1928; D.C.L., New York U., 1928; Dr. honoris causa, U. of Brussels and U. of Louvain, 1924; m. Antoinette Carter (dec.), Dec. 5, 1888; children—Charles Evans, Helen (dec.), Catherine (Mrs. Chauncey L. Waddell), Elizabeth Evans (Mrs. William T. Gossett). Admitted to N.Y. bar, 1884; prize fellowship, Columbia Law Sch., 1884-87; practiced law, New York, 1884-91, 1893-1906; prof. law, 1891-93, spl. lecturer, 1893-95, Cornell; spl. lecturer New York Law Sch., 1893-1900; counsel, Stevens Gas Commn. (N.Y. Legislature), 1905; counsel Armstrong Insurance Com. (N.Y. Legislature), 1905-06; spl. asst. to U.S. atty-gen. coal investigation, 1906; nominated for office of mayor of New York by Rep. Conv., 1905, but declined; gov. of N.Y. 2 terms, Jan. 1, 1907-Dec. 31, 1908, Jan. 1, 1909-Dec. 31, 1910; resigned Oct. 6, 1910; apptd., May 2, 1910, and Oct. 10, 1910, became asso. justice Supreme Court of U.S. Nominated for President of U.S. in Rep. Nat. Conv., Chicago, June 10, 1916, and resigned from Supreme Court same day; received 254 electoral votes for the Presidency, Nov. 7, 1916, as against 277 for Woodrow Wilson, Democrat. Mem. Hughes, Rounds, Schurman & Dwight, N.Y. City, 1917-21, and 1925-30; sec. of state in cabinets of Presidents Harding and Coolidge, Mar. 4, 1921-Mar. 4, 1925; commr. plenipotentiary for U.S., Internat. Conf. on Limitation of Armament, Washington, Nov. 12, 1921, and served as chairman same; apptd. by President Coolidge mem. Permanent Court of Arbitration, The Hague, Sept. 30, 1926 (resigned 1930); chmn. U.S. delegation to 6th Pan-Am. Conf., Havana, Cuba, Jan.-Feb. 1928; U.S. del. Pan-Am. Conf. on Arbitration and Conciliation, Washington, D.C., 1928-29; elected by Council and Assembly of League of Nations as judge of Permanent Court of Internat. Justice, 1928, resigned Feb. 15, 1930; apptd. by President Hoover chief justice Supreme Court of U.S., Feb. 3, 1930, confirmed by Senate, Feb. 13, 1930, retired July 1, 1941. Spl. ambassador to Brazilian Centenary Celebration, Rio de Janeiro, 1922; chmn. N.Y. State Reorganization Commn., 1926; pres. Guatemala-Honduras Arbitral Tribunal, 1932; chancellor Smithsonian Instn., Washington, 1930-41. Fellow Brown Univ.; hon. trustee U. of Chicago. Chmn. Draft Appeals Board, N.Y. City, 1917-18; spl. asst. to atty. gen. in charge of aircraft inquiry, 1918. Pres. N.Y. State Bar Assn., 1917-18, Legal Aid Soc. (N.Y.), 1917-19, St. David's Soc. (N.Y.), 1917-18, Italy America Soc., 1918-19, N.Y. County Lawyers Assn., 1919-20; mem. Am. Bar Assn. (pres. 1924-25), Assn. Bar City of N.Y. (pres. 1927-29), Am. Soc. Internat. Law (pres. 1925-29), Am. Philos. Soc.; fellow Am. Acad. Arts and Sciences, Nat. Geog. Soc., etc. Hon. Bencher of the Middle Temple, London. Clubs: University, Union League (pres. 1917-19), Century, Lawyers', Brown, Delta Upsilon, Nassau Country. Awarded Roosevelt medal, 1928, for developing pub. and internat. law, Am. Bar Assn. Medal, 1942, for conspicuous service to jurisprudence. Author: Conditions of Progress in Democratic Government (Yale lectures), 1909; The Pathway of Peace, and Other Addresses, 1925; The Supreme Court of the United States (Columbia Univ. lectures), 1927; Our Relation to the Nations of the Western Hemisphere (Princeton Univ. lectures), 1928; Pan-American Peace Plans (Yale Univ. lectures), 1929. Home: 2223 R St. N.W., Washington, D.C. Died Aug. 27, 1948.

HUGHES, Charles Evans, Jr., lawyer; b. N.Y. City, Nov. 30, 1889; s. Charles Evans (late retired Chief Justice of United States) and Antoinette (Carter) H.; grad. Collegiate Sch., N.Y. City, 1905; A.B., Brown, 1909, LL.D., 1937; LL.B., Harvard, 1912; m. Marjory Bruce Stuart, June 17, 1914; children—Charles Evans 3d, Henry Stuart, Helen, Marjory Bruce. Editor in chief Harvard Law Review, 1911-12; admitted to N.Y. bar, 1913, and began practice at N.Y. City; with Byrne & Cutcheon, 1912-13; law sec. to Justice Benjamin N. Cardozo, 1914; with Cadwalader, Wickersham & Taft, 1914-16; mem. Hughes, Rounds, Schurman & Dwight, later Hughes, Schurman & Dwight, 1917-29 and 1930-37, and Hughes, Richards, Hubbard & Ewing, now Hughes, Hubbard & Ewing, since 1937. Solicitor General of the United States June 1, 1929-Apr. 1930 (resigned upon apptmt. of father as Chief Justice of the United States). Director N.Y. Life Ins. Co., 1930-34. Private, batt. sergt. maj. and 2d lt. F.A., U.S. Army, 1917-19. Mem. N.Y. City Charter Revision Commn., 1935-36; Gov. Lehman's Preparatory Com. on State Constitutional Conv., 1937-38. Chmn. War Com. of Bar of City of N.Y. 1942-46. Chmn. Mayor's Com. on Unity, 1944-48. Fellow Brown University; trustee of Teachers College, N.Y. City. Mem. Am. and N.Y. State bar assns., Assn. Bar City New York, N.Y. County Lawyers Assn. (pres. 1936-38), Phi Beta Kappa, Delta Upsilon. Republican. Episcopalian. Clubs: University, Century Assn., Harvard, Brown, St. Andrews Golf, Down Town (New York). Home: 5040 Independence Av., Riverdale-on-Hudson, N.Y. City 63. Office: 1 Wall St., New York 5, N.Y. Died Jan. 21, 1950.

HUGHES, Dudley Mays, congressman; b. Jeffersonville, Ga., Oct. 10, 1848; s. Daniel Greenwood and Mary Henrietta (Moore) H.; ed. U. of Ga.; m. Mary Frances Dennard, Nov. 25, 1873. Began farming 1870, has since continued on a large scale; pres. Macon, Dublin & Savannah Ry. Co. during its constrn. Mem. Ga. Senate, 1882, 1883; pres. Ga. State Agrl. Soc., 4 yrs.; commr.-gen. of Ga. at St. Louis Expn., 1904; mem. 61st and 62d Congresses (1909-13), 3d Ga. Dist. and 63d and 64th Congresses (1913-17), 12th Dist.; chmn. House Comm. on Edn., 63d Congress. Trustee U. of Ga., Ga. State Agrl. Coll.; pres. Ga. Fruit Growers' Assn. 10 yrs. Now chmn. W.S.S. Com. of 12th Dist. of Ga. Democrat. Baptist. Address: Danville, Ga. Died Jan. 20, 1947.

HUGHES, Edwin Holt, bishop; b. Moundsville, W.Va., Dec. 7, 1866; s. Rev. Thomas B. and Louisa (Holt) H.; student W.Va. U. and Ia. Coll.; A.B., Ohio Wesleyan, 1889, A.M., 1892, D.D., 1904, LL.D., 1909; S.T.B., Boston U., 1892; S.T.D., Syracuse U., 1903; LL.D., De Pauw U., 1908, U. of Me., 1919; m. Isabel Ebbert, June 8, 1892 (died 1938); children—Margaret Rebecca (dec.), Isabel (Mrs. Wm. H. Remy), Edwin Holt, Ebbert Magee, Caroline R. (Mrs. Walter S. Harban), Morris Sharp (now deceased), Anna Louise (Mrs. Mayo Soley, now deceased), Francis Montgomery. Ordained to ministry of M.E. Church, 1892; pastor Newton Center, Mass., 1892-96, Malden, Mass., 1896-1903; pres. De Pauw U., 1903-08; bishop M.E. Ch., since 1908; sr. bishop M.E. Church, and Meth. Ch., 1936-40; retired 1940; recalled Washington area, 1943, Wisconsin area, 1947; retired 1948. Former member of Indiana State Board Education; trustee Carnegie Foundation; president State Teachers' Assn. of Ind., 1904; chmn. Com. of One Hundred, religious activities, Panama Expn., 1915; pres. Board of Temperance, M.E. Ch., 1932-40; fraternal del. to English and Irish Methodisms, 1930. Chairman Emergency (War) Commission, Meth. Ch., 1941. Acting pres. Boston Univ., Apr.-Sept. 1923; acting chancellor Am. Univ., 1933. Cole lecturer, Vanderbilt U.; Mendenhall lecturer, De Pauw U.; New Era lecturer U. of Southern Calif.; Fondren lecturer, Southern Methodist University; Rich lecturer, Williamsport Dickinson College, Perkins Lecturer, Wichita Falls, Texas. Trustee De Pauw University, Ohio Wesleyan U., Am. Univ., Dickinson Coll. Mem. Joint Hymnal Commn. of Am. Methodism; chmn. Joint Commn. on Union of Am. Methodist Churches. Mem. Delta Tau Delta, Phi Beta Kappa. Author: Letters on Evangelism, 1907; Thanksgiving Sermons, 1909; The Teaching of Citizenship, 1909; A Boy's Religion, 1914; The Bible and Life, 1914; God's Family, 1926; Christianity and Success, 1928; Worship in Music (part author), 1929; Are You an Evangelist?, 1937; Evangelism and Change, 1938; I Was Made a Minister (Autobiography), 1943. Address: 691 Rollingwood Drive, Chevy Chase, Md. Died Feb. 12, 1950.

HUGHES, Hatcher, dramatist; b. Polkville, N.C., Feb. 12, 1881; s. Andrew Jackson and Martha (Gold) H.; A.B., A.M., U. of N.C., 1908; student Columbia U., 1909-11; m. Janet Ranney Cool, May 28, 1930; 1 dau., Ann Ranney. Instr. in English, U. of N.C., 1907-10; instr. in English, Columbia U., 1910-12, lecturer, 1913-17 and 1920-28, asst. prof. English since 1928. Served as capt. A.E.F., 1918-19, World War I. Author: (plays) A Marriage Made in Heaven, 1918; Wake Up, Jonathan (with Elmer Rice), 1921; Hell-Bent for Heaven (Pulitzer prize), 1923; Ruint, 1924; It's a Grand Life (with Alan Williams), 1928; The Lord Blesses the Bishop, 1932. Club: Century Assn. Home: West Cornwall, Conn. Died Oct. 17, 1945.

HUGHES, John Newton, lawyer; b. Galena, Ill., 1867; s. John and Salina (James) H.; student Upper Ia. U., 1889; U. of Chicago, 1894-95; LL.B., Northern Ill. Coll., Fulton; m. Mabel Nichols, Aug. 12, 1902; 1 son, John N. Admitted to Ia. bar, 1895; city solicitor Cedar Rapids, 1898-1906; atty. C.M.& St.P. Ry., 1909-15; solicitor for Ia. of C.,M.& St.P. Ry. Co., 1915-42, spl. atty. since 1942; gen. counsel Des Moines Union Ry. since 1942, atty. Wabash Ry. since 1921; gen. counsel Des Moines Union Ry. Co., 1921-34; dir. Des Moines Union Ry. Co. since 1921; mem. Hughes, Taylor & O'Brien, 1915-33, Hughes, O'Brien & Hughes since 1933; formerly dir. Valley Savings Bank. Trustee Morningside Coll., Sioux City. Mem. Am. Ia. State and Polk County bar assns. Democrat. Methodist. Mason, K.P. Clubs: University, Des Moines, Prairie. Home: 605 54th St. Office: Southern Surety Bldg., Des Moines, Ia. Died Dec. 4, 1947.

HUGHES, Thomas Welburn, teacher of law; b. Elgin County, Ont., Can., Jan. 17, 1858; s. Thomas and Annie (Stride) H.; ed. St. Thomas Collegiate Inst. and Hamilton Collegiate Inst., Ont., and Brandon Normal Sch., Man.; LL.B., U. of Mich., 1891, LL.M., 1892; LL.D., Oskaloosa Coll., 1916; m. Jennie Ballah, Sept. 15, 1879; children—Clarence Welburn, Chester Arthur; m. 2d, Roxie S. Austin, July 4, 1915; 1 dau., Vera Marie. Instr. law, University of Mich., 1892-98; prof. law, U. of Illinois, 1898-1910, La. State U., 1910-12; dean and prof. law, U. of Florida, 1912-15; prof. law, 1915, dean, 1915-17 and 1919-21, prof. law, 1921-28, Washburn Coll. of Law, Topeka, Kan. Mem. Phi Delta Phi, Theta Kappa Nu, Phi Kappa Phi. Author: Hughes on Evidence, 1906; Hughes on Commercial Law, 1909; Hughes on Criminal Pleading and Practice, 1910; Hughes on Criminal Law, 1913; Hughes' Pocket Digest of Evidence, 1917; Hughes on Criminal Law and Procedure, 1919; Hughes Cases on Evidence, 1920; Hughes Cases on Criminal Law and Procedure, 1921; Hughes Pocket Digest of the Law of Contracts; also pamphlets, mag. articles, etc. Home: Topeka, Kan. Died Oct. 28, 1943.

HUGHITT, Marvin, Jr., ry. official; b. Bloomington, Ill., Sept. 24, 1861; s. Marvin and Belle Barrett (Hough) H.; ed. Shattuck Sch., Faribault, Minn.; unmarried. Entered service of C. & N.W. Ry. in gen. frt. dept., 1881, div. frt. agt., 1887-93, asst. gen. frt. agt., 1893-96, gen. frt. agt., 1896-1900, frt. traffic mgr., 1900-15, gen. frt. traffic mgr., 1915-16, v.p. in charge of operation, May 24, 1916, exec. v.p. May 1, 1924, retired Dec. 1, 1925. Dir. Union Trust Co. Clubs: Chicago, Union League, Chicago Traffic, Chicago Athletic. Home: Lake Forest, Ill. Died Feb. 7, 1949.

HUHNER, Max, surgeon; b. Berlin, Germany, June 30, 1873; s. Edward and Minna (Jakmuss) H.; has resided in New York since 3 yrs. of age; ed. at Coll. City of N.Y.; M.D., Coll. Physicians and Surgeons (Columbia), 1893; studied in Europe; m. May Levy (died Dec. 11, 1936); 1 dau., Minna H. Schulz. Intern Bellevue Hosp.; attending genito-urinary surgeon, same, many yrs.; for many years chief of clinic genito-urinary dept., Mt. Sinai Hosp. Dispensary. Fellow Am. Med. Assn., Am. Urol. Assn., N.Y. Acad. Medicine; diplomate, Am. Board of Urology; mem. Soc. Med. Jurisprudence, N.Y. Urol. Assn., Med. Soc. County of N.Y., Shakespeare Assn. Author: Sterility in the Male and Female and Its Treatment, 1913; Disorders of the Sexual Function, 1916 (Spanish transl. 1920); The Diagnosis and Treatment of Sexual Disorders in the Male and Female including Sterility and Impotence, 1937; also numerous articles in med. jours. and reference works, and in periodicals, particularly on Shakespeare lit. Devised accepted test for sterility, known as The Huhner Test. Home: 88 Central Park West, N.Y. City. Died Nov. 8, 1947; buried in Cemetery of Spanish and Portuguese Synagogue.

HUIDEKOPER, Reginald Shippen (hī'dē-kō-pēr), lawyer; b. Meadville, Pa., May 24, 1876; s. Frederic Wolters and Virginia (Christie) H.; A.B., Harvard, 1898; studied law at Trinity Coll. (Oxford U.), Eng., 1898-1900, and Columbian Univ., 1900-01; admitted to bar, 1901; m. Bessie Cazenove du Pont, Jan. 24, 1917; children—Henry Shippen, Ann du Pont, Elizabeth Gardner, Peter Galloway. Practiced law, Washington, D.C.; asst. U.S. dist. atty., D.C., 1909-14; mem. Wilson, Huidekoper & Lesh, 1914-24; dir., mem. exec. com. Nat. Savings & Trust Co.; dir. St. Jo Paper Co.; trustee and v.p. Nemours Foundation; co-executor and co-trustee Estate of Alfred I. du Pont. Retired. Commissioned major, judge advocate U.S. Army, Nov. 15, 1917; lt. col., Oct. 25, 1919; over 6 months duty at G.H.Q., A.E.F., France; hon. disch., June 25, 1919. In 1917 assisted in Provost Marshal Gen.'s office in preparation of the "Rules and Regulations" and the "Forms of Proof of Claims for Exemption and Discharge" promulgated by the President to put the Selective Service Act into operation. Mem. Bd. of War Contract Adjustment, War Dept., Nov. 1, 1919-July 1, 1920. Mem. Am. Law Inst. Clubs: Alibi, Grasslands, Chevy Chase (Washington); Patuxent; Leander (England). Home: 2934 Edgevale Terrace N.W., Washington, D.C. Died Sep. 28, 1943.

HUIZENGA, Lee Sjoerds (hī'zĕng-ȧ), leprologist; b. Lioessens, Friesland, Netherlands, June 28, 1881;

s. Sjoerd Liebes and Harmke (Van Der Veen) H.; brought to U.S., 1883; student Calvin Coll. and Sem., Grand Rapids, Mich., 1902-09; M.D., Homœ. Med. Coll., New York, 1913; student N.Y. Ophthalmic Coll., 1915-16; C.P.H., Yale, 1928, Dr.P.H., 1930; married Matilda Vandyke, September 22, 1909; children—Dr. Ann Harriet, Myrtle Leonora, Hannah Eunice, Faith Lois, Philip Lee S. (adopted son). Ordained ministry Christian Reformed Church, 1909; pastor Englewood, N.J., later missionary to Navajo Indians, N.M., and med. missionary to China, by apptmt. of Foreign Missionary Bd., Christian Ref. Ch.; med. adviser to Mission to Lepers, N.Y. City; hon. sec. Shanghai Anti-Tuberculosis Assn.; has specialized in treatment of leprosy. Fellow Am. Geog. Soc., Am. Pub. Health Assn., A.A.A.S., Royal Geog. Soc. (London); mem. Internat. Leprosy Assn., Am. Soc. Parasitology, Am. Tropical Disease Assn., Far Eastern Tropical Disease Assn., China Med. Assn., Delta Omega. Author: The Navajo Indian, 1910; Unclean, Unclean, 1927; Leprosy in Legend and History (in the Chinese), 1931; Leprosy Control in Countries Bordering on the Pacific (Shanghai), 1934; Anhydrosis in Leprosy, 1934; History of Leprosy in China, 1935; John and Betty Stam—Martyrs, 1935; Legislation and Leprosy, 1937; Sensation Disturbances in Leprosy, 1937; Development of Leprosy Control Clinics, 1936; Nestorian Advance in China in the 8th Century (in Holland), 1936; Missionary Significance of the Lord's Prayer, 1938; Leonard Brink, 1939; Miss Mary Reed—Forty years a missionary to the Lepers, 1938; Hair in Leprosy 1939; Men of Note in Chinese History of Leprosy, 1939; Lu Tsu and his Relation to Other Medicine Gods in Chinese Medical Lore, 1940; Tuberculosis control, 1941. Contbr. to religious and scientific periodicals; also to Triomfen Van Het Kruis, 1913. Home: Grand Rapids, Mich. Died July 1945; buried in Bubbling Well Cemetery, Shanghai.

HUIZINGA, Henry (hī'zing-ȧ), educator, writer; b. New Groningen, Mich., Jan. 8, 1873; s. Albert Thomas and Mary (Kema) H.; grad. Hope Coll., Holland, Mich., 1893, M.A., 1896; grad. Western Theol. Sem., 1896; Ph.D., U. of Mich., 1907; m. Susan Antvelink, July 1, 1896; children—Albert Thomas, Wilhelmina Swenne (Mrs. Claire W. Lanam), Mary Joanna (Mrs. Fred Larson), John Ongole, James Devadasen, Ruth Elizabeth (Mrs. Baxter H. Webb). Ordained and sent out as missionary to India, 1896; prin. and pres. schools and colleges, Vellore, Ongole, Kurnool, India, 1896-1917; mem. Madras Government Secondary Sch. Leaving Certificate Bd. and Chief Examiner in English, 1912-15; prof. English and head of dept., Shanghai Bapt. Coll. (now U. of Shanghai), since 1917. Compiler and editor: Modern Short Stories, 1922; The World's Best Short Stories, 1924; The Best Modern Stories, 1927; The Best One-Act Plays, 1929; The Best Long Plays, 1931; The Best English Essays, Vol. I, 1934, Vol. II, 1935. Author: Missionary Education in India, 1909; The A B C Correction Code, 1930; College Composition, 1936; Grammar and Composition for Middle Schools in China, 1940; The World's Best Short Stories, New Series, 1941. "I Say Unto You", being The Sermon on the Mount according to Luke, 1942; The Gospel according to St. John in verse, 1944. Address: University of Shanghai, Shanghai, China; also 1024 Hays Park Av., Kalamazoo 30, Mich. Died Dec. 3, 1945.

HULBERT, Homer B., author; b. New Haven, Vt., Jan. 26, 1863; s. Calvin B. and Mary E. (Woodward) H.; grad. St. Johnsbury Acad., 1880; B.A., Dartmouth, 1884, M.A.; student Union Theol. Sem. 2 yrs.; m. May B. Hanna, Sept. 18, 1888; children—Helen (Mrs. Giles Blague), Madeleine, Chester, Leonard, Sheldon. In ednl. service of Korean Govt., 1886-1905; diplomatic service same govt., 1905-10; editor Korean Rev., 1900-06; lecturer. Fellow Royal Geog. Soc. Decorated by Korean Govt. Republican. Conglist. Mason. Author: The History of Korea, 1904; The Passing of Korea, 1906; Comparative Grammar of Korean and Dravidian, 1906; Omjee the Wizard, 1925; The Face in the Mist, 1926. Home: 44 Fairfield St., Springfield, Mass. Died Aug. 5, 1949.

HULBURT, Lorrain Sherman, univ. prof.; b. Albany, Wis., Mar. 8, 1858; s. Chauncey D. and Sarah E. (Searles) H.; A.B., U. of Wis., 1883, A.M., 1888; Ph.D., Johns Hopkins U., 1894, LL.D., U. of South Dakota, 1927; studied in U. of Göttingen; m. Elizabeth Dorey, Aug. 3, 1886 (died July 20, 1910); children—Edward O., Lorrain C. Prof. mathematics and astronomy, Univ. of S.D., 1887-91; fellow in mathematics, Clark U., Worcester, Mass., 1891-92; instr. and asso. in mathematics, 1892-97, collegiate prof., 1897-1926, Johns Hopkins U., now emeritus. Fellow A.A.A.S., Am. Math. Soc.; mem. Math. Assn. of America, Phi Beta Kappa, Circolo Matematico di Palmero. Club: Johns Hopkins (Baltimore). Author: Differential and Integral Calculus, 1912. Home: 4515 Garrison Blvd. Address: Johns Hopkins Univ., Baltimore, Md. Died Mar. 29, 1942.

HULBURT, Ray Garland, editor; b. Plainview, Neb., Sept. 3, 1885; s. David Sherwood and India Siloam (Rogers) H.; D.O., Am. Sch. of Osteopathy, Kirksville, Mo., 1920; m. Emma E. Kidd, June 9, 1918; children—Dayton David, Ruth Elizabeth (Mrs. Allen Beye Hamilton), and (adopted) Mary Virginia. Grew up as a farmer; began as a teacher, later engaged in newspaper writing; then identified with osteopathic editorial and pub. ednl. work; dir. statistics and information Am. Osteopathic Assn. since 1924 and editor since 1931. Mem. Am. Osteopathic Assn., Ill. Osteopathic Assn. Awarded Certificate of Honor by Osteopathic Honor Frat., Sigma Sigma Phi, 1931. Socialist. Conglist. Home: 915 Pleasant St., Oak Park, Ill. Office: 139 N. Clark St., Chicago 2, Ill. Died Apr. 15, 1947.

HULETT, Edwin Lee (hū'lĕt), chemist; b. Heuvelton, St. Lawrence County, N.Y., Apr. 30, 1870; s. Edwin Henry and Emma Catherine (Austin) H.; grad. Potsdam (N.Y.) State Normal Sch., 1896; New York U., summer sessions, 1899-1901; A.B., St. Lawrence U., 1903, A.M., 1904, LL.D., 1925; m. Minne A. Dollar, Feb. 5, 1896. Prin. high sch., Brushton, N.Y., 1896-1902; instr. chemistry, 1903-04, asst. prof., 1904-05, prof. and head dept. since 1905, head of dept. chemistry, 1905-29, St. Lawrence U.; registrar College of Arts and Sciences same, 1912-15, dean since 1915. Analyst for St. Lawrence County, N.Y., 1905-15. Mem. Am. Chem. Soc., Alpha Tau Omega. Republican. Mason. Club: Citizens'. Home: Canton, N.Y. Died Aug. 30, 1942.

HULL, David Denton, lawyer; b. at Marion, Va., Mar. 26, 1872; s. David Denton and Mary Ann Henderson (Graham) H.; B.A., Emory and Henry Coll., 1891 (valedictorian); grad. law dept. University of Virginia, 1893; married Elizabeth Duval Adams, June 16, 1923; children—Anne, Suzelle, Mary. Practiced at Pulaski, Va., 1893-1900, Bristol, 1900-08, Roanoke since 1908; gen. counsel Va. Iron, Coal & Coke Co. since 1903, also v.p. same, 1917-32, pres. since 1932; pres. Alimar Coal Corp., Hazard Coal Corp.; dir. First Nat. Exchange Bank, Roanoke, Va., Detroit and Mackinac Ry. Co.; chmn. bd. trustees Hollins College Corporation, 1925-37; trustee, Hollins Coll.; ex-pres. Roanoke Chamber of Commerce; dir. Nat. Coal Assn., 1935-43; mem. Va. Commn. Conservation and Development, 1932-41. Mem. Va. Hist. Soc., Kappa Sigma. Mem. City Planning and Zoning Commns. of Roanoke, 1928-32, Bd. of Visitors U. of Va., 1923-30. Democrat. Episcopalian. Clubs: Shenandoah, Rotary, Country (Roanoke). Home: 637 Wycliffe Av., South Roanoke. Office: 310 W. Campbell Av., Roanoke, Va. Died Aug. 30, 1945.

HULL, John Adley, army officer, lawyer; b. Bloomfield, Ia., Aug. 7, 1874; s. John Albert Tiffin and Emma Gertrude (Gregory) H.; Ph.B., State U. of Ia., 1895, LL.B., 1896; m. Norma Bowler King, Sept. 21, 1919 (divorced 1934); 1 son, John Bowler. Admitted to Ia. bar, 1896, and practiced law at Des Moines, Ia.; while serving as capt. Ia. Nat. Guard apptd. lt. col. judge adv. vols., May 9, 1898; hon. disch. Apr. 17, 1899; maj. judge adv., Apr. 17, 1899, vacated, Apr. 4, 1901; maj. judge adv., U.S. Army, Feb. 2, 1901; lt. col., Apr. 16, 1903; col., Feb. 15, 1911; apptd. judge adv. gen. with rank of maj. gen., from Nov. 16, 1924; retired with rank of maj. gen., Nov. 15, 1928; legal adviser to gov. gen., P.I., 1930-32; asso. justice Supreme Court of P.I., 1932-36. Served in World War as judge advocate, S. of S., also as dir. Rents, Requisition and Claims Service and finance officer A.E.F., in France. Awarded D.S.M. (United States); Comdr. St. Michael and St. George (Great Britain); Officer Legion of Honor (France); Order of St. Peter (Serbia); Royal Aman (Indo-China). Mem. Phi Kappa Psi. Mason. Clubs: Alfalfa, Army and Navy, Chevy Chase (Washington). Address: Army and Navy Club, Washington, D.C. Died Apr. 17, 1944.

HULL, William Edgar, ex-congressman; b. Lewiston, Fulton Co., Ill., Jan. 13, 1866; s. William Wessley and Mary (Missplay) H.; ed. high school, Lewiston, and Ill. Coll., Jacksonville, Ill. (non-grad.); m. Ella Harris, Feb. 25, 1888. Began as govt. gauger, Peoria, Ill., 1889, and operated large business; built Jefferson Hotel and Palace Theater in Peoria; hon. vice pres. and gen. mgr. Hiram Walker & Sons, Inc., distillers; postmaster of Peoria, 1898-1906; mem. 68th to 72d Congresses (1923-33), 16th Ill. Dist.; secured passage of "deep water way bill from lakes to gulf"; mem. U.S. Commn. to Pan-Am. Road Congress, Buenos Aires, Argentina, 1925. Del. Rep. Nat. Conv., 1916, 20, 24, 28, 32. Mem. bd. dirs. Ill. Highway Improvement Assn. and the original good road advocate of Ill. Mason, K.P. Clubs: Creve Coeur, Country, Mount Hawley Country, Northwestern Country, Pekin Country, Chevy Chase Country. Home: 490 Moss Av., Peoria, Ill. Died May 30, 1942.

HULLIHEN, Walter (hŭl'ĭ-hĕn), univ. pres.; b. Staunton, Va., May 26, 1875; s. Walter Quarrier and Amelia Hay (Campbell) H.; B.A., M.A., U. of Va., 1896; post-grad. study, U. of Va., 1896-97, Johns Hopkins, 1897-1900, Ph.D., 1900; U. of Leipzig, Munich, Rome, 1907-08; D.C.L., U. of the South, 1922; LL.D., Temple U., 1925; m. Maude Louise Winchester, Sept. 14, 1907; children—Louise Winchester (Mrs. C. L. Walker), Frances Hay (Mrs. J. A. Woolley). Licentiate instructor in Latin, German and mathematics, U. of Va., 1895-96; fellow in Latin, Johns Hopkins, 1899-1900; teacher Latin and Greek, Univ. Sch., Baltimore, 1902-04; prof. Latin and Greek, U. of Chattanooga, 1904-09; prof. Greek, U. of the South, Sewanee, Tenn., 1909-12, dean Coll. Arts and Sciences, 1912-20; pres. U. of Del. since 1920; mem. bd. Columbia Oil, Shale & Refining Co. (Denver, Colo.). Mem. bd. dirs. Camp Greenbrier, Inc., Alderson, W.Va., Biochem. Research Foundation, Newark, Del. Maj. inf., asst. G-3, Staff 15th Div., U.S. Army, 1918. Mem. Phi Beta Kappa, Delta Phi, Phi Kappa Phi, Chevalier Legion of Honor (France). Episcopalian. Home: Newark, Del. Died Apr. 14, 1944.

HULT, Adolf, theologian; b. Moline, Ill., Dec. 24, 1869; s. Olof and Christina (Brattlund) H.; A.B., Augustana Coll., Rock Island, Ill., 1892, B.D., 1899; student U. of Chicago, 1902-04; D.D., Wittenberg Coll., Springfield, O., and Bethany Coll., Lindsborg, Kan., 1920; m. Edna Olivia Blomgren, June 28, 1899; children—Miriam Edna (Mrs. O. I. Sohlberg), Adolf Nathanael, Evangeline Christina, Paul Luther, Stephen Blomgren. Ordained Lutheran ministry, 1899; pastor Messiah Church, Chicago, 1899-1907, Immanuel Church, Omaha, 1907-16; prof. church history, pastoral theology and hymnology, Augustana Theol. Seminary, since 1916. Dir. Bethphage Mission, Axtell, Neb. Republican. Club: After Dinner (Moline). Author: Bible Primer (Old Testament), 1919, (New Testament), 1920; The Way in Christ, 1924; Heart to Heart with You, 1925. Composer choir anthems; translator of Believer Free from the Law (Rosenius); The Theology of History, 1940; Taught of God, 1941; contbr. to anthologies and theol. jours. Home: 1739 11th Av., Moline, Ill. Address: Augustana Theol. Sem., Rock Island, Ill. Died Mar. 6, 1943

HUME, Nelson, educator; b. New York, N.Y., Jan. 12, 1881; s. Thomas Joseph and Harriet Madeleine (Kean) H.; A.B., Coll. of St. Francis Xavier, New York, 1900, M.A., 1901; Ph.D., Georgetown U., 1915; m. May Eleanor Desjardins, Dec. 15, 1923; children—Michael Hume, Stephen Hume, David Hume, Rozanne Hume. Schoolmaster, Loyola Sch., New York, 1900-04; schoolmaster Newman Sch., Hackensack, N.J., 1904-05; asst. to v.p. N.Y. Life Ins. Co., 1905-06; headmaster Hume Sch., New Rochelle, N.Y., 1906-12; asso. headmaster Newman Sch., Hackensack, N.J., 1912-13; organized Canterbury Sch., New Milford, Conn., 1913-15, headmaster since 1915, also treas. and trustee. Trustee Coll. of New Rochelle. Decorated Knight of the Order of St. Gregory the Great by Pope Pius XI, 1938. Mem. Headmasters Assn., Xavier Alumni Sodality (New York). Catholic. Clubs: Catholic Club (New York); Graduate (New Haven); Litchfield County (Conn.) University. Home: New Milford, Conn. Died June 14, 1948.

HUME, Robert Ernest; b. Ahmednagar, Bombay Presidency, India, Mar. 20, 1877; s. Rev. Robert A. (D.D.) and Abbie (Burgess) H.; B.A., Yale Univ., 1898, M.A., 1900, Ph.D., 1901; B.D., Union Theol. Sem., 1904; matriculated in U. of Göttingen, Germany; D. Théol., Strasbourg, 1932; m. Laura Caswell, March 15, 1907; children—Robert Caswell, Edward Putnam, Jane Williams. Ordained Congl. ministry, 1905; went to India as missionary A.B. C.F.M., 1907; prof. hist. of religions, Union Theol. Sem., 1914-1943, prof. emeritus since 1943. Lecturer at Bombay Univ. and Univ. of the Punjab; also at Hindu Univ., Benares; the Moslem Univ., Aligarh; Vishwas Bharati (Greater India) Univ., Bolpur; and Coll. of His Highness the Maharajah of Baroda, 1923; Indian Inst. Oxford Univ., 1938. Mem. Am. Oriental Soc., Am. Theol Soc. (pres. 1939), American Association for Advancement of Science, Phi Beta Kappa. Author: The World's Living Religions, 1924, 32nd edit., 1946 (transl. into Spanish); Treasure House of the Living Religions, 1932, 2d edit., 1933. Translator from Sanskrit; Thirteen Principal Upanishads, with an Outline of the Philosophy of the Upanishads, 1921, 3d edit., 1934. Contbr. to religious and theol. jours., India and America. His book, The World's Living Religions, the only religious book beside the Bible to be placed in "time capsule" (50 feet below ground), New York World's Fair 1939; to be opened in 6939. Home: 405 W. 118th St., N.Y. City. Died Jan. 4, 1948.

HUMMEL, George Henry; chmn. bd. P. Lorillard Co. Home: 200 Hobart Av., Summit, N.J. Address: 119 W. 40th St., New York, N.Y.* Died Aug. 27, 1946.

HUMPHREY, George Colvin, animal husbandman; b. Palmyra, Mich., Feb. 13, 1875; s. George and Sarah Celestina (Colvin) H.; B.S., Mich. Agrl. Coll., E. Lansing, Mich., 1901; m. Eva Doty, June 25, 1902 (died Mar. 12, 1941); children—Carolyn Elizabeth (dec.), George Doty, Sarah Katharine; m. 2d, Madge Herbison. Successively instr., asst. prof., asso. prof. and professor animal husbandry, professor dairy husbandry, U. of Wis., 1901-42, head dept. of animal husbandry, 1903-39, professor emeritus since 1942; continues to give active attention to practical dairy farming. Presbyterian. Mem. Am. Soc. Animal Production, Am. Dairy Science Assn., Alpha Zeta (Babcock Chapter), Alpha Sigma. Devotes spl. attention to dairy cattle improvement and research problems. Home: 407 E. Court St., Ludington, Mich. Died June 18, 1947.

HUMPHREY, Henry H., cons. engr.; b. Coolville, O., June 23, 1862; s. Shepherd and Emily (Cole) H.; A.B., Ohio U., Athens, O., 1884; A.M., 1886; M.S., Cornell U., 1886; m. Louisa D. Richardson, Sept. 12, 1887; children—William Richardson, Harry Edward, Helen, Martha Blair, Arthur Cole, Mary Louise. With U.S. Coast and Geod. Survey, summers, 1884, 85; in employ Westinghouse, Church, Kerr & Co., 1886-87; supt. Buffalo Electric Light & Power Co., 1888, Brush Electric Light Co., Buffalo, 1889-90; agt. Edison Gen. Electric Co., Omaha and St. Louis, 1891; St. Louis mgr. Gen. Electric Co., 1892; engr. and salesman St. Louis Electric Supply. Co., 1893, Laclede Power Co., St. Louis, 1894-95; mem. Bryan & Humphrey, cons. engrs., 1896-1900; cons. elec. and mech. engr., 1900-17; v.p., treas. Flad-Humphrey Engring. Co., 1917-20; gen. cons. elec. and mech. engr., 1920-35; v.p. and mgr. Evens & Howard Sewer Pipe Co., 1935-41. Designed electric part of Imperial Electric Light, Heat & Power Plant (St. Louis), complete plant of De Beers Explosives Works (Cape Town, S. Africa), mech. and elec. equipment Ry. Exchange Bldg. (St. Louis), etc. Fellow Am. Inst. E.E. (life); mem. St. Louis Inst. Cons. Engrs., Beta Theta Pi. Democrat. Methodist. Mason. Clubs: Engineers, Cornell, Circle. Retired July 1, 1942. Home: 5596 Bartmer Av., St. Louis, Mo. Died Dec. 21, 1947.

HUMPHREYS, Harrie Moreland, lawyer; b. Springfield, O., May 21, 1868; s. J(ohn) Alexander and Mary Elizabeth (Watters) H.; A.B., Wittenberg Coll., Springfield, O., 1889, A.M., 1892; married Martha Maude McGrew, June 29, 1893; 1 son, Moreland Mason. Admitted to Ohio and Colo. bars, 1891, and since practiced in Denver, with spl. attention to corp. and real property law; member law firm of Humphreys and Humphreys. Am. counsel Yorkshire Investment and Am. Mortgage Co., Ltd., of Bradford, Eng., 1893-1901; sec., dir. and counsel Mountain Holdings, Inc., 1925-41. Mem. Am. Bar Assn., Colo. Bar Assn. (pres. 1930-31, sec.-treas. 1923-30 and 1931-38), Denver Bar Assn., Beta Theta Pi. Republican. Presbyterian. Editor of Reports of the Colo. Bar Assn., vols. 26-32 and 34-40. Home: 910 Clarkson St. Office: Equitable Bldg., Denver, Colo. Died Apr. 1, 1943.

HUMPHREYS, William Jackson (hŭm'frēz), physicist; b. Gap Mills, Monroe County, W.Va., Feb. 3, 1862; s. Andrew Jackson and Eliza Ann (Eads) H.; A.B., Washington and Lee U., 1886, C.E. (valedictorian), 1888, Sc.D. (hon.), 1942, University of Virginia, 1888-89, graduated School of Physics and School of Chemistry, 1889; Johns Hopkins Univ., 1894-97, fellow in physics, 1895-96, Ph.D., 1897; m. Margaret Gertrude Antrim, Jan. 11, 1908. Prof. physics and mathematics, Miller Sch., Va., 1889-93; prof. physics and chemistry, Washington Coll., Md., 1893-94; instr. physics, U. of Va., 1897-1905; prof. meteorol. physics, U.S. Weather Bur., July 1, 1905-Dec. 31, 1935, when retired (collaborator since 1936); prof. meteorol. physics, George Washington Univ., 1911-34, now prof. emeritus. Dir. Research Sta., Mt. Weather, Va., 1905-08; mem. U.S. Naval Observatory's eclipse expdn. to Sumatra, 1901; sec. Physics of the Electron, Internat. Congress of Arts and Sciences, St. Louis, 1904. Asso. editor Jour. of Franklin Inst.; editor of Monthly Weather Review, 1931-35; spl. editor, Webster's New Internat. Dictionary, 2d edition. Fellow Am. Phys. Soc., Optical Soc. America, Astron. Soc. America, Seismol. Soc. America, A.A.A.S. (sec. sect. physics 1912-16, mem. com. on policy 1912-28; v.p., chmn. sect. B, 1917; gen. sec. 1924-28); mem. Am. Math. Soc., Am. Meteorol. Soc. (v.p. 1920-23; pres. 1928-29), Am. Acad. Arts and Sciences, Am. Philos. Soc., Am. Geophys. Union (sec. 1921-22; chmn. seismol. sect. 1922-24; chmn. 1932-35), Franklin Inst., Philos. Soc. Washington (pres. 1919), Washington Acad. Sciences (pres. 1922), Phi Beta Kappa, Sigma Xi, Raven Soc. (U. of Va.); corr. mem. Meteorol. Soc. of Hungary, State Russian Geog. Soc. Club: Cosmos (v.p. 1935; pres. 1936). Author: Physics of the Air, 1920, 2d edit., 1929, 3d edit., 1940; Weather Proverbs and Paradoxes, 1923, 2d edit., 1934; Rain Making and Other Weather Vagaries, 1926; Fogs and Clouds, 1926; Snow Crystals (with W. A. Bentley), 1931; Weather Rambles, 1937; Ways of the Weather, 1942; Fogs, Clouds and Aviation, 1943. Of Me (autobiography), 1947. Special editor (meteorology) Webster's New Internat. Dictionary, 2d edit. Contbr. Dictionary of Am. Biography and tech. jours. Address: Cosmos Club, Washington 5, D.C. Died Nov. 10, 1949.

HUN, John Gale, teacher; b. Albany, N.Y., Nov. 21, 1877; s. Edward Reynolds (M.D.) and Caroline (Gale) H.; A.B., Williams, 1899; Ph.D., Johns Hopkins, 1903; m. Leslie Crawford, June 26, 1906; children—Leslie C. (Mrs. Edward S. Morris), Elizabeth G. (Mrs. Robert G. McAllen), Carolyn G. (Mrs. Francis T. Miles). Teacher at Princeton Univ., 1903-14 (resigned); founder, 1914, and manager The Math School, Princeton, until 1917; headmaster Hun School, Princeton, since 1917. Pres. Princeton Board of Education, 1930-36. Mem. Kappa Alpha. Clubs: Nassau (Princeton); Princeton, University (New York). Author: (with C. R. MacInnes) Plane and Spherical Trigonometry, 1911. Address: Princeton, N.J. Died Sept. 15, 1945.

HUNEKE, William August (hŭn'ĕ-kē), judge; b. Cincinnati, O., Aug. 12, 1864; s. John and Christina (Ringen) H.; A.B., Baldwin-Wallace College, Berea, O., 1886; LL.B., U. of Mich., 1888; m. Grace Crook, Dec. 28, 1899; children—Bradford (dec.), Helen Josselyn, John Sherwood. In practice at Spokane, Wash., 1890-1904; judge Superior Court of Wash., 1904-Apr. 40; resigned. Pres. judge State Assn. of Superior Court Judges until 1935. Republican. Methodist. Mem. Am. Bar Assn., Wash. State Bar Assn. Home: 314 Park Pl., Spokane, Wash.* Died Apr. 11, 1946.

HUNGERFORD, Edward, author; b. Dexter, N.Y., Dec. 21, 1875; s. Charles Anson and Cora (Sill) H.; ed. Williston Sem., Easthampton, Mass.; Syracuse Univ., 2 yrs.; LL.D., St. Lawrence Univ., 1936; m. Bertha R. von Rechenberg, Sept. 26, 1906 (died Jan. 13, 1940); 1 dau., Mrs. Adrienne H. Devereaux. Reporter Rochester Herald, 1896; New York Sun, 1898-1904; editor Glens Falls (N.Y.) Times, 1904; press rep. Brooklyn Rapid Transit Co., 1904-11; adv. mgr. Wells-Fargo & Co. Express, 1912-18; dir. of publns., U. of Rochester, 1922-24; centenary dir. Baltimore & Ohio R.R., 1925-28; asst. v.p. N.Y. Central Lines, 1928; dir. Fair of The Iron Horse, Baltimore, Md., Oct. 1927; gen. dir. Rochester (N.Y.) Centennial, 1934; gen. dir. Parade of the Years Pageant, Cleveland, Ohio, summer of 1936; gen. dir. Railroads on Parade, N.Y. World's Fair, 1939. Mem. British Newcomen Soc., Psi Upsilon. Presbyterian. Clubs: Players (New York); Genesee Valley. Author: The Williamsburg Bridge, 1904; The Modern Railroad, 1911; Little Corky, 1912; Gertrude, 1913; Personality of American Cities, 1913; The Railroad Problem, 1917; Our Railroads Tomorrow, 1922; Planning Your Trip Abroad, 1923; The Copy Shop, 1925; The Story of the Public Utilities, 1927; The Story of the Baltimore & Ohio R.R., 1929; Pathway of Empire, 1935; Men and Iron, 1938; Daniel Willard Rides the Line, 1938; Locomotives on Parade, 1940; Transport for War, 1943; Railroad for Tomorrow, 1945; Men of Erie, 1946; Wells Fargo, 1948. Contbr. to mags. author and producer Wings of a Century, Century of Progress Expn., Chicago, 1933; A Century on Parade, Rochester, N.Y., 1934; Parade of the Years, Cleveland, O., 1936; Railroads on Parade, New York World's Fair, 1939; author (pageant) Wheels A Rolling, (Chicago R.R. Fair). Home: 116 East 63d St., N.Y. 17. Died July 29, 1948.

HUNT, Ernest Leroi, surgeon; b. Abington, Mass., Nov. 11, 1877; s. Washington and Mary (Nickerson) H.; desc. Enoch Hunt, Newport, R.I., 1638; student Mass. Coll. of Pharmacy, Boston, 1894-95; M.D., Harvard, 1902; m. Isabel Girling, June 4, 1907 (dec.); children—Isabel (Mrs. James A. Dawson), Ethel Dorothy (Mrs. Joseph Navas), Mildred Elizabeth (Mrs. Charles Andrew Hall); m. 2d, Charlotte Alling; 1 son, Roger Alling. Practiced in Worcester since 1903; asst. pathologist, 1903-30, and dir. div. surgery Worcester City Hospital, 1919-33; consultant surgeon Worcester City Hospital, Worcester Memorial Hospital, Worcester State Hospital, Holden Hosp., Harrington Memorial Hosp., Day-Kimball Hosp.; surgeon-in-chief to Fairlawn Hosp.; pathologist U.S. Veterans' Hosp. 89, 1922-31; chmn. and chief of staff Worcester Cancer Clinic, 1929-46. Medical member Division 4, Worcester, U.S. Selective Service, 1918; captain Medical Corp, United States Army, active service, July 1918-March 22, 1919; lt. colonel Med. Res., U.S. Army, inactive since Nov. 11, 1941; formerly asso. med. examiner 11th Worcester Dist., resigned 1942; med. div. head, Region 3, Mass. Com. Public Safety, 1941. Member governing bd. ednl. div. Worcester Y.M.C.A. (formerly Worcester Div. Northeastern U.) 1928-46; member board directors Worcester Free Pub. Library, 1938-42. Fellow Am. Coll. Surgeons, A.M.A., Mass. Med. Soc. (pres. Worcester District 1931-32; member New England Surgical Society (v.p. 1940-41), Massachusetts Medico-Legal Soc. (pres. 1926-28), N.E. Cancer Soc. (pres. 1939-40), Mass. Div. Am. Cancer Soc., Inc. (dir. 1943-48), Worcester Hist. Soc., The Gov. and Co. of Mass. Bay Colony in New England; mem. bd. dirs. Worcester chapter Am. Red Cross (chmn. 1930-35). Republican. Universalist. Mason, Odd Fellow. Clubs: Harvard (Boston & Worcester), U., Economic. Contbr. to surg. jours. Home: 20 Kenilworth Rd., Worcester; (summer) Saybrook, Conn. Office: 28 Pleasant St., Worcester, Mass. Died Jan. 17, 1948.

HUNT, Frederick Salisbury, lawyer; b. West Bend, Wis., May 22, 1868; s. George Frederick and Ann Eliza (Salisbury) H.; LL.B., U. of Wis., 1888; m. Alice Cynthia Hunt, Aug. 21, 1895; children—Lewis Salisbury, George Buttles. Admitted to Wis. bar, 1888, and began practice at West Bend; moved to Milwaukee, Wis., 1889; pres. Milwaukee Dustless Brush Co. since 1907; mem. Wis. Pub. Service Commn., 1933-39. Mem. Milwaukee Ar. Inst., Milwaukee Foundation. Officer de l'Instruction Publique (France). Democrat. Conglist. Clubs: City (dir.; pres. 1916-19 and 1928-29); University (Madison). Home: Cedar Lake, R.R. 4, West Bend, Wis. Office: 530 W. 22d St., Milwaukee, Wis Died Jan. 19, 1944.

HUNT, Livingston, naval officer; b. New Orleans, La., Nov. 3, 1859; s. William Henry and Elizabeth Augusta (Ridgely) H.; prep. edn., Hopkins Grammar Sch., New Haven, Conn.; student Harvard 1 yr., class of '81; m. Catharine Howland Hunt, July 7, 1892; 1 son, Livingston. Apptd. by President Arthur to Pay Corps, U.S. Navy, 1881; on U.S.S. New Orleans, Spanish-Am. War; promoted through grades to rank of rear adm. (by selection), July 7, 1921; retired June 1, 1923. Clubs: Clam Bake (Newport, R.I.); Army and Navy (New York). Contbr. articles on naval history. Home: 80 Catherine St., Newport, R.I. Died Jan. 18, 1943.

HUNT, Reid, pharmacologist; b. Martinsville, O., Apr. 20, 1870; s. Milton L. and Sarah E. (Wright) H.; A.B., Johns Hopkins, 1891, Ph.D., 1896; student U. of Bonn, Germany; M.D., U. of Md., 1890, Sc.D., 1925; student Ehrlich's Institut, Frankfort, 1902-04; m. Mary Lillie, d. Hannis Taylor, Dec. 12, 1908. Tutor in physiology, Coll. Phys. and Surg. (Columbia), 1896-98; asso. and asso. prof. pharmacology, Johns Hopkins, 1898-1903; chief of div. and prof. pharmacology, U.S. Pub. Health Service, 1904-13; prof. pharmacology, Med. Dept. Harvard, 1913-36; visiting prof. Peking-Union Med. Coll., 1923. Cons. pharmacologist Mass. State Dept. Pub. Health; mem. advisory bd. Hygienic Lab., U.S. Pub. Health Service. Mem. Permanent Standards Com. of League of Nations. Fellow Am. Acad. Arts and Sciences; mem. Nat. Acad. Sciences, Assn. Am. Physicians, Am. Physiol. Soc., Am. Soc. Pharmacology and Exptl. Therapeutics, A.M.A. (ex-chmn. council on pharmacy and chemistry), Am. Chem. Soc. (chmn. Northeastern sect. 2 yrs.), Leopold-Carol Akademie, Deutsch Pharmacologie Gesellschaft, Phi Beta Kappa, Alpha Omega Alpha. Pres. U.S. Pharmacopeia, 1920-30. Contbr. Am. and European med. jours. and govt. publs. Joint-Author: Non-Alkaloidal Organic Poisons, in Vol. II of Peterson, Haines and Webster's Text-Book of Legal Medicine and Toxicology, 1923; Studies in Experimental Alcoholism, 1907; Studies on the Thyroid (with A. Seidell), 1909; Effects of Various Diets Upon Resistance to Poisons, 1910; Effects of Derivatives of Choline and Analogous Compounds, 1911. Contbr. to Heffter's Handbuch der Exper. Pharmakologie, 1923. Home: 382 Commonwealth Av., Boston. Died Mar. 10, 1948.

HUNT, Seth Bliss; b. N.Y. City, Dec. 18, 1871; s. Seth Bliss and Lucy Bartlett (Thompson) H.; grad. St. Paul's Sch., Concord, N.H., 1889; m. Elisabeth Hamlin, Apr. 25, 1900. Entered employ of Standard Oil Co., 1894; v.p. Standard Oil Co. (N.J.), 1919-33, also treas. until 1933, retired. Republican. Episcopalian. Clubs: Union, N.Y. Athletic. Home: 440 Park Av., New York. Died June 22, 1948.

HUNT, William Henry, lawyer; b. New Orleans, Nov. 5, 1857; s. William H. (sec. of the Navy) and Elizabeth Augusta (Ridgely) H.; ed. Hopkins Grammar Sch., New Haven, Conn.; student Yale, class of 1878, A.M. (hon.), 1896; m. Gertrude Upshur, Aug. 31, 1882; children—Elizabeth, William H., Helen Upshur, Gertrude Livingston. Collector of customs, Mont. and Ida., 1881-85; atty.-gen. of Mont., 1885-87; mem. Mont. Constl. Conv., 1884; mem. legislature, 1889; dist. judge, 1st Jud. Dist., 1889-94; justice Supreme Court of Mont., 1894-1900; sec. Puerto Rico, May 1900-Aug. 1901, gov., Aug., 1901-July 4, 1904; U.S. dist. judge, Dist. of Mont., 1904-10; asso. judge U.S. Ct. of Customs Appeals, Jan. 1910-Feb. 1911; apptd. U.S. circuit judge, Dec. 1910; resigned Dec. 1928. Home: 1896 Pacific Av. Office: Balfour Bldg., San Francisco. Died Feb. 4, 1949.

HUNTER, George William, biologist, author; b. Mamaroneck, N.Y., Apr. 7, 1873; s. George William and Emma Louise (Cartwright) H.; A.B., Williams, 1895, A.M., 1896; fellow in zoölogy, U. of Chicago, 1896-99; post-grad. work and lecturer in methods of teaching nature study and biology, N.Y. Univ., 1907-14, Ph.D., 1918; m. Emily Isabel Jobbins, June 19, 1899; children—George William III, Cartwright, Francis Robert. Teacher of biology at Hyde Park High Sch., Chicago, 1898-99; teacher biology at DeWitt Clinton High Sch., New York City, 1899-1906, head dept. biology, 1906-19; prof. biology, Carleton Coll., 1919-20; prof. biology, Knox Coll., 1920-26; adjunct prof. biology, Pomona Colls., 1926-29; lecturer in methods in science, Claremont Coll., since 1930. Asst. Marine Biol. Lab., Woods Hole, Mass., summers, 1900-10. Ednl. dir., Washington dist., War Work Council Y.M.C.A., 1918-19. Chairman War Finance Com., Claremont, since 1942. Fellow A.A.A.S.; mem. N.E.A., American Zoölogical Society, Calif. Assn. Secondary Edn., Nat. Assn. for Research in Science Teaching, National Society for Study of Edn., Phi Delta Kappa, Theta Delta Chi. Episcopalian. Clubs: Kiwanis, University. Author: Elements of Biology, 1907; Essentials of Biology, 1911, 23; A Civic Biology, 1914; Laboratory Problems in Civic Biology, 1916; History of Y.M.C.A. War Work in the Washington District, 1919; Laboratory Manual in Biology, 1923; New Civic Biology, 1926; Teachers Manual, 1927; New Laboratory Problems in Civic Biology, 1927; Problems in Biology, (4th edition, revised, 1940); Pupil's Workbook for Problems in Biology, 1932; Teacher's Manual for Problems in Biology, 1932; The Teaching of Science at the Junior and Senior High School Levels, 1934; Life Science, A Social Biology, 1941. Co-Author: Laboratory Manual of Biology, 1903; Civic Science in the Home, 1921; Civic Science in the Community, 1922; Civic Science in Home and Community, 1923; Civic Science Manual, 1924; Problems in General Science, (4th edit, rev., 1944); Teacher's Manual And Key for Problems in General Science, 1931; Readings in Science, 1931; Workbook in General Science, 1932; A Testing Program in General Science, 1933; A Testing Program in Biology, 1933; The March of Science Series (My Own Science Problems; Science in Our Social Life; Science in Our World of Progress), 1935; Biology, The Story of Living Things, 1937; Work book and testing program for life science, 1941-42; Doorways to Science, 1947; Work book, Doorways to Science, 1947. Contbr. numerous educational and scientific articles. Address: 466 W. 10th St., Claremont, Calif. Died Feb. 4, 1948.

HUNTER, Hiram Tyram, educator; b. Mars Hill, N.C., Mar. 26, 1883; s. James Hardy and Martha Caroline (Bradley) H.; grad. Mars Hill Coll., 1908; B.A., Wake Forest Coll., 1912; M.A., Teachers Coll. (Columbia Univ.), 1917; Ed.M., Harvard Univ., 1922; honorary Ed.D., Wake Forest College, 1942; m. Glen Weaver, Aug. 7, 1912; children—Marthalou, Lucy Jane, Elizabeth Ann. Pres. Southside Institute, Chase City, Va., 1912-14; head dept. of English, Woman's Coll., Richmond, Va., 1914-16; asso. prof. edn., and head dept. of edn. Southern Meth. U., Dallas, Tex., 1917-19; prof. edn., Baylor Coll., 1919-20; prof. edn. and dir. Summer Sch., Wake Forest Coll., 1920-23; pres. Western Carolina Teachers Coll. since 1923; asst. to Dean Holmes, Grad. Sch. of Edn., Harvard, at Summer Sch., 1922. Mem. N.E.A., N.C. Edn. Assn., Phi Delta Kappa (Harvard). Democrat. Baptist. Rotarian (gov. 190th Dist. 1941-42). Home: Cullowhee, N.C. Died Oct. 9, 1947.

HUNTER, Jesse Coleman, oil prodn. exec.; b. Thurber, Erath County, Tex., Mar. 19, 1890; s. Joseph Adam and Melissa Jane (Dunham) H.; B.A., Howard-Payne Coll., Brownwood, Tex., 1910; student summer sessions, U. of Tex., 1910, 1911; m. Eloise Gillespie, June 17, 1913; 1 son, Jesse Coleman. Began as pub. sch. teacher, 1910; in banking business, Van Horn, Tex., 1914-28; engaged in oil prodn. operations, Tex., since 1926; v.p., dir. Van Horn (Tex.) State Bank since 1918; dir. Citizens Nat. Bank, Abilene. County treas., Culberson Co., Tex., 1912-23; county judge, Culberson Co., 1914-20 and 1924-28; mem. Tex. State Dem. Exec. Com., 1930-32; rep. of Gov. of Tex. on Interstate Oil Compact Commn. since 1940; mem. Petroleum Industry War Council, Washington, D.C.; mem. Petroleum Prodn. Com., Dist. 3. Pres. bd. trustees Hardin-Simmons U. Mem. Abilene C. of C. (pres. 1938), West Tex. C. of C. (dir.), C. of C. of the U.S. (mem. Southwestern Council, mem. resolutions com. Annual Meetings 1940-41), West-Central Tex. Oil and Gas Assn. (pres. 1937-38), Am. Petroleum Inst. (dir. and mem. exec. com.), Ind. Petroleum Assn. of America (dir.), Mid-Continent Oil and Gas Assn. (pres. since Dec. 1938). Democrat. Baptist. Mason. Club: Lions (Abilene). Home: 1565 Belmont Blvd. Office: 522 Mims Bldg., Abilene, Tex. Died Nov. 11, 1945.

HUNTER, Merlin Harold, prof. economics; b. Chandlersville, O., Aug. 29, 1887; s. Clement Val and Lola Belle (Taylor) H.; B.A., Muskingum Coll., 1912; M.A., Princeton, 1913; Ph.D., Cornell U., 1916; LL.D., Muskingum College, 1940; married Evangeline Groves, Dec. 24, 1918; children—John Merlin, Alonzo Linn. Instr. in economics, Ohio State U., 1914; fellow in economics, Cornell U., 1915-16; with U. of Ill. since 1916, prof. economics since 1929, acting head of dept., 1929-30, head of dept. since 1938; prof. economics, U. of Southern Calif., summer, 1930. Mem. Acad. of Polit. Science, Am. Econ. Assn., Nat. Tax Assn., Mid-west Econ. Soc. (pres. 1935-36), Alpha Kappa Psi, Pi Gamma Mu, Alpha Phi Gamma, Delta Chi, Artus. Methodist. Kiwanian. Author: Outlines of Public Finance, 1921, 26; Background of Economics (with G. S. Watkins), 1923; Outline of Economic History of the United States, 1936; Principles of Public Finance (with H. K. Allen), 1940; Personalizing Pub. Finance (with H. K. Allen), 1940; Economics, Condensed-Applied, 1942. Editor: Bulletin of the National Tax Assn., 1927-30; mem. bd. editors, Social Science. Home: 608 Pennsylvania Av., Urbana, Ill. Died May 30, 1948.

HUNTER, (Wiles) Robert, sociologist; b. Terre Haute, Ind., Apr. 10, 1874; s. W. R. and Caroline (Fouts) H.; A.B., Ind. Univ., 1896; m. Caroline M. Phelps Stokes, May 23, 1903; children—Robert, Phelps Stokes, Caroline Phelps, Helen Louisa (dec.). Organizing sec., Chicago Bur. of Charities, 1896-1902; chmn. investigating com. City Homes Assn.; supt. Municipal Lodging House; mem. Small Parks Com., resident Hull House, 1899-1902, all of Chicago; resident Toynbee Hall, London, summer 1899, and other English settlements; organized dental clinics for poor children, and a municipal lodging house for vagrants in Chicago, 1901; head-worker Univ. Settlement, New York, 1902-03; active in New York in promoting first anti-tuberculosis campaign and the movement to feed undernourished school children; chmn. first New York com. for promoting legislation to abolish child labor, 1902-06. Joined Socialist Party, 1905, and was its candidate for N.Y. Assembly and later its candidate for gov. of Conn. (1010); resigned from Socialist Party, 1914. Editorial writer, 1908-10; lecturer on economics and English, U. of Calif., 1918-22; conducted seminar on the economic and polit. causes of post-war revolutionary upheavals. Pres. Berkeley Commn. of Pub. Charities, 1921; chmn. English-Speaking Union, Santa Barbara, 1929-30; mem. spl. com. of Nat. Economic League on the Monetary Problem of the United States, 1934-1938. Episcopalian. Clubs: Social Reform of New York (pres. 1905); Faculty, Berkeley Golf, Cypress Point, Montecito. Author: Tenement Conditions in Chicago, 1901; Poverty, 1904; Socialists at Work, 1908; Violence and the Labor Movement, 1914; Labor in Politics, 1915; Why We Fail As Christians, 1919; The Links, 1926; Revolution, 1940. Home: 190 Hot Springs Rd., Santa Barbara, Calif. Died at Santa Barbara, Calif., May 15, 1942.

HUNTER, Samuel John, entomologist; b. Ireland, Nov. 11, 1866; s. Rev. James and Rebecca (Davison) H.; removed with parents to Iowa in infancy; A.B., A.M., U. of Kan., 1893; grad. student, Cornell U., 1896; investigator Marine Biol. Lab., 1901-02; m. Lida W. Campbell, June 16, 1897 (died June 1929); 1 dau., Geneva (Mrs. Edwin J. Simmons). Prin. Columbus (Kan.) High Sch., 1890-91, Atchison County High Sch., 1893-96; absent on leave, 1894, to visit zoöl. laboratories of Europe; asst. prof. entomology, 1896-99, asso. prof., 1899, asso. prof. comparative zoölogy and entomology, 1901, head dept. entomology, 1902, prof., 1906, curator entomol. collections, 1909, U. of Kan. State entomologist; mem. Kan. State Entomol. Commn., 1907, 24; collaborator Federal Bur. Entomology; mem. Nat. Com. on Unification of State and Federal Hort. Inspection Legislation; mem. City Planning Com.; mem. Nat. Com. on Real Estate Taxation. Mem. Kan. Council for Defense, World War. Pres. Eastern Kan. Teachers' Assn., 1894-95; fellow A.A.A.S.; mem. Kan. Acad. Science, Phi Beta Kappa, Sigma Xi. Author: Elementary Studies in Insect Life, 1902; An Account of Kansas Coccidæ and Their Hosts, 1903; Morphology of Artificial Parthenogenesis, 1904; Insect Parthenogenesis, 1906; Problems in Parthenogenetic Parasites, Pathogenic Parasites, 1911; etc. Chmn. Science Bull. editorial com., 1916-24. Owner (50 acres) and developer West Hills Dist. and Country Club Terrace, Lawrence. Republican. Conglist. Pres. Sportsman's Club, 1933. Home: 1145 W. Campus Rd., Lawrence, Kan. Died July 10, 1946.

HUNTINGTON, Ellsworth, geographer; b. Galesburg, Ill., Sept. 16, 1876; s. Rev. Henry Strong and Mary Lawrence (Herbert) H.; B.A., Beloit (Wis.) Coll., 1897, D.Sc.; Harvard, 1901-03, M.A., 1902, non-resident fellow, 1906-07; Ph.D., Yale, 1909; D.Litt. Clark; m. Rachel Slocum Brewer, Dec. 22, 1917; children—Charles Ellsworth, Anna Slocum, George Herbert (dec.). Asst. to pres., instr. Euphrates Coll., Harput, Turkey, 1897-1901; explored cañons of Euphrates River, 1901, and was awarded Gill Memorial by the Royal Geog. Soc. of London; research assistant Carnegie Institution, Washington, D.C., and member Pumpelly expedition to Russian Turkestan, 1903-04 (spent 1½ years in Turkestan and Persia); member Barrett expedition to Chinese Turkestan (spent 1½ years in India, China and Siberia, 1905-06) and was awarded Maunoir Medal by Geographic Society of Paris, and club medal by Harvard Travelers Club. Instructor in geography, 1907-10, assistant prof., 1910-15, and research asso., Yale, 1917-45, emeritus since 1945. Made expdn., Syrian Desert, Palestine, and Asia Minor, 8 mos., 1909, as rep. of Yale U., and spl. corr. Harper's Magazine. Research asso. of Carnegie Instn., Washington, for climatic investigations in U.S., Mex. and Central America, 1910-13. Capt., Mil. Intelligence Div., U.S. Army, 1918-19; maj. O.R.C. Asso. editor Geog. Rev., Econ. Geography, Ecology and Social Philosophy. Chmn. com. on atmosphere and man, Nat. Research Council. Attended Pan-Pacific Scientific Congress, Australia, 1923. Fellow Geol. Soc. America, A.A.A.S., Am. Acad. Arts and Sciences; mem. Assn. Am. Geographers (pres. 1923), Ecol. Soc. America (pres. 1917), Population Assn. of America (dir.), Am. Eugenics Soc. (dir., treas., pres. 1934-38), Nat. Research Council (geol. and geog. div. 1919-23, 1935; biol. and agrl. div., 1921-24); hon. mem. and medalist Geog. Soc., Phila. (Award of Merit, Council Geog. Teachers, 1943), pres. New Haven Council Religious Education, 1925-29; pres. Conn. League of Nations Association since 1941-45. Conglist. Clubs: Harvard Travelers (Boston); Ends of the Earth (New York). Author: Explorations in Turkestan, 1905; The Pulse of Asia, 1907; Asia—A Geography Reader, 1912; Palestine, and Its Transformation, 1911; The Climatic Factor, 1914; Civilization and Climate, 1915; World Power and Evolution, 1919; Red Man's Continent, 1919; Principles of Human Geography (with S. W. Cushing), 1920; Business Geography (with F. E. Williams), 1922; Climatic Changes (with S. S. Visher), 1922; Earth and Sun, 1923; The Character of Races, 1924; Modern Business Geography (with S. W. Cushing), 1924; West of the Pacific, 1925; Quaternary Climates, 1925; The Pulse of Progress, 1926; The Builders of America (with L. F. Whitney), 1927; The Human Habitat, 1927; Living Geography (with F. M. McMurry and C. F. Benson), 1932; Economic and Social Geography (with F. E. Williams and S. van Valkenberg), 1933; After Three Centuries (with Martha Ragsdale), 1934; Europe (with S. van Valkenberg), 1935; Tomorrow's Children—The Goal of Eugenics, 1935; Season of Birth, 1938; Principles of Economic Geography, 1940; Mainsprings of Civilization, 1945. Home: 38 Kildeer Road, Hamden, Conn. Address: Yale University, New Haven, Conn. Died Oct. 17, 1947.

HUNTINGTON, Ford, corp. official; b. Louisville, Ky., Nov. 1867; s. Robert Palmer and Alice (Ford) H.; A.B., Yale, 1891; unmarried. Began with Lake Shore R.R., 1891; v.p. N.Y. Telephone Co. since 1912; dir. Marine Midland Trust Co. of N.Y., Metropolitan Savings Bank of N.Y., Friendship Telephone Co., Holmes Electric Protective Co. Mem. Scroll and Key (Yale). Democrat. Episcopalian. Clubs: Knickerbocker, Racquet and Tennis, Brook. Home: 56 E. 72d St. Office: 140 West St., New York. Died Jan. 29, 1949.

HUNTINGTON, Robert Watkinson, insurance exec.; b. Norwich, Conn., Nov. 9, 1866; s. Robert Watkinson and Jane Lathrop (Trumbull) H.; B.A., Yale, 1889; m. Constance Alton Willard, May 5, 1906; children—Robert Watkinson, Mary Willard, John Willard, Sara Blair, Constance Willard, Trumbull. Began with Conn. Gen. Life Ins. Co. as clk., Nov. 1889, becoming actuary, 1893, sec., 1899, pres., 1901, and chairman board, 1936; chairman board Dime Savings Bank; director First Nat. Bank, trustee Loomis Institute; trustee Colt Request, and treas. of trustees for receiving donations for the bishop (P.E. Ch.); trustee Wadsworth Atheneum. Episcopalian. Fellow Actuarial Soc. America. Clubs: Hartford, Hartford Golf; Graduate (New Haven); Salmagundi (New York). Home: 145 Bloomfield Avenue. Office: 55 Elm St., Hartford, Conn. Died Jan. 22, 1949.

HUNTLEY, Samantha Littlefield; artist; b. Watervliet, N.Y.; d. Edgar Littlefield and Abigail Fidelia (Tilley) Littlefield; pupil of John H. Twachtman and H. Siddons Mowbray, Art Students League, New York, 1893-94 and 1896-97; student Academie Julien Paris, 1897-99; pupil of Jules Lefebvre (certificate) 1897-1900; student École des Beaux Arts, Paris (pupil Eduard Cuyer), 1898-99, École Normale d'Enseignement du Dessin (pupil Eugéne Grasset), 1899-1900; m. Frank Hall Huntley; 1 son, Grant. Instr. at Emma Willard Sch. of Art, Troy, N.Y., 1894-96, 1900-05 and 1908. Exhibited at Societe des Artistes Francais, Paris, 1898, 1900 and 1901; Nat. Acad. of Design, 1902; Soc. of Am. Artists, 1904; Boston Art Club, 1905; Detroit Museum of Art, 1911; City Art Museum St. Louis, 1911; Nat. Museum, Washington, D.C., 1928 (portrait of Dr. Charles Greeley Abbot). Represented in permanent collections: (portraits) Dr. Charles Doolittle Wolcott and Dr. Charles Greeley Abbot, Smithsonian Instn.; Daniel S. Lamont, War Dept., Washington, D.C.; Gen. John M. Schofield, Schofield Barracks, Honolulu; William F. Vilas, State Hist. Library, Madison, Wis.; Archbishop John J. Glennon, Archbishop's House, St. Louis; Frank W. Higgins, State Capitol, Albany, N.Y.; J. Townsend Lansing, John E. McElroy, Hist. and Art Soc., Albany, N.Y.; William F. Gurley, Emma Willard Sch., Troy, N.Y.; George H. Davie, Memorial Library, Kinderhook, N.Y.; John H. Vanderpoel, Vanderpoel Memorial Art Assn., Chicago; John Edgar Teeple, Chemists Club, N.Y. City; Henry Colvin, Troy (N.Y.) Savings Bank. Mem. Am. Fedn. of Arts, Am. Artists Professional League, D.A.R. Home: Kinderhook, N.Y. Died June 19, 1949.

HUNTOON, Louis Doremus (hŭn-tōōn′), mining engr.; b. Paterson, N.J., Jan. 28, 1869; s. Josiah Parmley and Sarah M. (Doremus) H.; grad. Paterson High Sch., 1887; Ph.G., N.Y. Coll. of Pharmacy, 1890; E.M., Columbia, 1895; (hon. M.A., Yale, 1908); m. Edmee B. Boynton, Oct. 7, 1903. Chemist and assayer in Colo., 1895-96; mining and metall. engr., New York, 1896-1903; asst. prof. mining and metallurgy, 1904-08, prof., 1908-11, Sheffield Scientific Sch. (Yale); cons. engr., New York, since 1911. Mem. Am. Inst. Mining and Metall. Engrs., Mining and Metall. Soc. America, Canadian Mining Inst., Sigma Xi. Home: Pleasantville, N.Y. Office: 15 Park Row, New York, N.Y., and 156 Yonge St., Toronto, Can. Died Feb. 22, 1947.

HUNTSMAN, Robert F. R., newspaper pub.; born Newark, N.J., Mar. 19, 1868; s. John F. and Zerviah Fitz (Randolph) H.; ed. pub. schs.; m. Leontine Lissignolo, Aug. 4, 1891; children—Leontine A., Dorothy H. (Mrs. Daniel C. Adams, Jr.), Florence (Mrs. Edwin Dresser). Began as reporter Newark (N.J.) Evening News, 1886; pub. Brooklyn (N.Y.) Standard Union, 1917-27; pres. R.F.R. Huntsman Corp. Republican. Presbyterian. Mason (K.T., Shriner). Club: Sphinx (pres.). Home: 835 Kensington Av., Plainfield, N.J. Died May 31, 1945.

HURBAN, Vladimir S. (hûr′bän), foreign diplomat; b. Turciansky Svaty Martin, Czechoslovakia, Apr. 4, 1883; s. Svetozar and Ida (Dobrovicova) H.; ed. Technica Coll., Vienna; m. Olga Boor, Aug. 20, 1919. Journalist, 1904-14; chief of mil. mission to U.S., 1918; mil. attaché to Czechoslovak Legation, Washington, D.C., 1919-24; chargé d'affairs, Cairo, Egypt, 1924-30; E.E. and M.P. from Czechoslovakia to Sweden, Norway and Lithuania, 1930-36, U.S. and Cuba, 1936-43; ambassador to United States 1943-46. Served as volunteer in Russian Army and Col. Czechoslovakian Legion, 1914-18. Awards: Czechoslovak Revolutionary medal, War Cross, Victory medal, Grand Cross Swedish Polar Star, Grand Cross Norwegian St. Olaf, Grand Cross Lithuanian Gedyminas, Order of the Nile, 2d class. Protestant. Address: Ministry of Foreign Affairs, Prague, Czechoslovakia. Died Oct. 26, 1949.

HURD, Harry Boyd, lawyer; b. Livingston, County, Mo., Jan. 8, 1875; s. Inscoe E. and Harriet Jane (Andrews) H.; prep. edn., high sch., Muscatine, Ia.; student Chicago Coll. of Law, 1904-06; m. Margaret Julia Frank, Dec. 25, 1902; children—Harriet Margaret, Anna Catherine, Harry Boyd, Julia Allyn. Admitted to Ill. bar, 1897, and began practice with Max Pam, of firm Moses, Pam & Kennedy, Chicago; was mem. Pam, Donnelly & Glennon, and Pam, Calhoun & Glennon; mem. Pam & Hurd, 1904-38; now member Pam, Hurd & Reichmann; dir. City Nat. Bank and Trust Co. of Chicago; Am. Steel Foundries; mem. Dawes Financial Mission to San Domingo, 1929. Republican. Clubs: Chicago, Chicago Athletic Assn., Mid-day, Bob O'Link Golf, Glenview Golf. Home: 932 Edgemere Court, Evanston, Ill. Office: 231 S. La Salle St., Chicago, Ill. Died Aug. 2, 1943.

HURD, Lee Maidment, oto-laryngologist; b. St. Charles, Minn., Dec. 23, 1873; s. Byron L. and Frances (Maidment) H.; prep. edn. Phillips Acad., Exeter, N.H.; M.D., Coll. Phys. and Surg. (Columbia University), 1895; married L. Violet Reed, 1903 (died November 24, 1944); children—Leona, Reed M., J. Anson. Practiced in New York City since 1897; emeritus professor laryngology, Univ. and Bellevue Hosp. Medical Sch. (New York U.); cons. laryngologist, Downtown, Flower-Fifth Av. hosps.; attending laryngologist, N.Y. Polyclinic Hospital. Mem. 7th Regt. N.Y. Nat. Guard 6 years. Fellow Am. Coll. Surgeons; mem. N.Y. Laryngol. Soc., A.M.A., N.Y. State and N.Y. County med. socs., N.Y. Acad. Medicine, Am. Laryngol. Assn., Am. Rhinol., Laryngol. and Otol. Soc., Am. Soc. Ophthalmology and Oto-Laryngology, Pan American Med. Assn., S.R., Soc. Colonial Wars, Nu Sigma Nu; corr. mem. San Paulo Med. Soc., Soc. of French Hospitals. Contbr. chapters on rhinology in Binnie's Regional Surgery; also over 50 monographs in med. jours. Home: "Lesurlea," Rowayton, Conn. Died May 15, 1945.

HURLEY, Charles Francis (hĕr′lē), ex-governor; b. Cambridge, Mass., Nov. 24, 1893; s. John Joseph and Elizabeth (Maher) H.; student Boston Coll., 1913 to 1915; m. Marion L. Conley, Jan. 9, 1924; children—Betty, Charles Francis, Sally (dec.), Nancy, Ellen Sarah. In real estate business, Cambridge and Boston, since 1915; receiver gen. of Mass., 1931-37; elected gov. for term, 1937-39. Mem. Cambridge Sch. Com., 1919-31. Served in U.S. Navy, World War. Mem. Charitable Irish Soc., Ancient and Hon. Arty., Am. Legion, Catholic Union of Cambridge Democrat. Catholic. Hibernian, Elk; mem. Irish Nat. Foresters, Knights of Finbar. Club: Clover (Boston). Home: 16 Ware, Cambridge, Mass. Address: 276 Commonwealth Av., Boston, Mass.* Died Mar. 24, 1946.

HURLEY, John Patrick, consular service; b. N.Y. City, Sept. 15, 1878; s. Michael and Mary (O'Neill) H.; student St. Kierans Coll., Kilkenny, Ireland, 1894-1901; C.E., Cornell U.; m. Marie Teresa Henry, Oct. 23, 1912. Asst. engr. water supply system, N.Y. City, 1907-09; highway engr., Brooklyn, 1909-14; engr. on subway constrn., N.Y. City, 1914-16; consular service since 1919; assigned to Reval, Esthonia, 1919, to Riga, Latvia, 1920, to Vienna, Austria, 1925, again to Riga, Latvia, 1929, then at Nassau, Bahama Islands, later consul gen. at Marseilles, France; now assigned to Dept. of State, Washington. Mem. Am. Soc. C.E. Catholic. Club: Crescent Athletic (Brooklyn). Address: Dept. of State, Washington, D.C.* Died Dec. 30, 1944.

HURLEY, Neil C., mfr. pneumatic tools, etc.; b. Galesburg, Ill.; s. Jeremiah and Ellen (Nash) H.; ed. St. Joseph's Acad., Brown's Business Coll., Galesburg; m. Mary Sullivan, June 28, 1906; children—Neil C., Jr., Mary Jessica, Florence Ann (Mrs. Charles Carroll). President of Hurley Machine Company, Chicago, Illinois, until 1927; now chmn. bd. and dir. Independent Pneumatic Tool Co., Chicago. Home: 914 Ashland Av., River Forest, Ill. Office: 600 W. Jackson Blvd., Chicago, Ill. Died Aug. 2, 1948.

HURST, Albert S., educator; b. Morpeth, Ont., Can., Aug. 13, 1866; s. James and Charity (Smith) H.; teacher pub. schs. of Ont., 1886-95; B.A., U. of Toronto, 1899; student Clark U., 1899-1900; M.A., Yale, 1904, Ph.D., 1905; m. Nina Sowler, Aug. 28, 1900; 1 dau., Marian Charity Ellen (Mrs. Harold J. Pierce). Came to U.S., 1899, naturalized citizen, 1912. Instr. English, Peekskill (N.Y.) Mil. Acad., 1900-02; head English dept., Bridgeport (Conn.) High Sch., 1902-05; ednl. dir., Y.M.C.A., St. Louis, Mo., 1905-06; instr. edn., Syracuse U., 1906-08, asso. prof., 1908-14, prof., 1914-20, dean Teachers Coll., 1920-30, prof. history and principles of edn. since 1930. Mem. N.E.A., Phi Kappa Phi, Kappa Phi Kappa. Republican. Methodist. Home: 1026 Ackerman Av., Syracuse, N.Y. Died Apr. 1, 1944.

HURST, Carlton Bailey; b. Bremen, Germany, Aug. 16, 1867 (parents temporarily abroad); s. late Bishop John Fletcher and Catherine (LaMonte) H.; prep. edn., Phillips Acad., Exeter, N.H.; student Harvard (editor Daily Crimson); grad. U. of Tübingen, Germany, A.M., Ph.D.; m. Harlette Hamlin, d. Rev. Geo. E. Strobridge, Aug. 1, 1892; children—John Fletcher, Carlton. Am. consul, Catania, Sicily, 1892-93, Crefeld, Germany, 1893-95, Prague, Bohemia, 1895-97; consul-gen., Vienna, Austria, 1897-1903; consul, La Guaira, Venezuela, 1904-05, Plauen, Saxony, 1905-10, Lyons, France, 1910-13; consul-gen., Barcelona, Spain, 1913-20, Habana, Cuba, 1920-27, Berlin, 1927-29, Budapest, 1929-31; retired. Founder (1915-17) and 1st hon. pres. Am. Chamber Commerce for Spain. Mem. S.A.R. Has contbd. extensively tech. and commercial information as well as travel and fiction, to Am. periodical press. Author: The Arms Above the Door, 1932. Home: 920 Coral Way, Coral Gables, Fla. Address: care Dept. of State, Washington, D.C. Died Aug. 28, 1943.

HURST, Charles Warner, publisher; b. Brooklyn, N.Y., Mar. 18, 1875; s. John Heard and Emma Clara (Warner) H.; ed. pub. schs.; m. Julia Odbert Bates, Jan. 5, 1910; children—James Ellison, Elizabeth Brittan. With Martindale-Hubbell, Inc., pubs., Summit, N.J., since 1897, pres. since 1920; dir. Summit Trust Co. Republican. Episcopalian. Clubs: Lawyers (N.Y. City); Baltusrol Golf (Baltusrol, N.J.); The Tin Whistles (Pinehurst, N.C.). Home: 10 Essex Road. Office: One Prospect St., Summit, N.J.* Died Feb. 19, 1947.

HURST, Clarence Thomas, zoölogist and archaeologist; b. Kingston, Ky., June 20, 1895; s. Alexander Lusk and Margaret Katherine (Folkerts) H.; B.Pd., Colo. State Normal Sch., Gunnison, 1920, M.Pd., 1922; A.B., Western State Coll. of Colo., Gunnison, 1923, A.M., 1923; Ph.D., U. of Calif., 1926; m. Blanche Hendricks, June 1, 1919. Pub. sch. teacher, Colo., 1916-21; teaching fellow in zoölogy, U. of Calif., 1923-24, 1925-26, tech. asst., 1924-25; asst. prof. of zoölogy, Mills Coll., 1926-28; prof. of zoölogy, Western State Coll. of Colo., since 1928, head dept. since 1928 and dean Grad. Sch. since 1930; chmn. div. of natural science and mathematics since 1937; dir. Museum of Archeol., Western State Coll., since 1935, and director Art Assn. of same, 1938-46; director field expeditions in archaeology, Museum of Archaeology, Western State Coll., since 1939; research asso. in zoölogy, U. of Calif., 1933-34. Mem. Gunnison Chamber of Commerce. Fellow A.A.A.S.; mem. Am. Assn. of Univ. Profs., Am. Soc. of Zoölogists, Colo.-Wyo. Acad. of Science (treas. 1933-40; pres. 1940-41). Colo. Archaeol. Soc. (exec. sec. and dir. since 1935), N.E.A., Colo. Edn. Assn., State Historical Society of Colorado, American Association Museums, Am. Museum of Natural History, Soc. for Am. Archaeology, N.M. Archaeol. Soc., Phi Sigma, Beta Beta Beta (mem. editorial bd.), Kappa Delta Pi, Sigma Xi. Republican. Author: Hegner's Invertebrate Nomenclature—A Dictionary of Zoölogy, 1934; Colorado's Old-Timers; The Indians Back to 25,000 Years Ago, 1946. Contbr. numerous articles on biology and anthropology to Am. and European publs. Editor of Southwestern Lore (journ. Colo. Archeol. Soc.). Home: 420 N. Main St., Gunnison, Colo. Died Jan. 17, 1949.

HUSBAND, William Walter, former second asst. sec. of Labor; b. East Highgate, Vt., Sept. 29, 1871; s. George and Mary Jane (Hogan) H.; ed. Franklin Acad. and St. Johnsbury Acad., Vt.; LL.D., Middlebury Coll., 1925; m. Agnes Marion Bullard, Nov. 17, 1903; 1 son, Richard Fenton. Reporter St. Johnsbury Caledonian, 1900-02; mng. editor Montpelier (Vt.) Daily Journal, 1902-03; clk. U.S. Senate Com. on Immigration, 1903-07; exec. sec. U.S. Immigration Commn., 1907-11; chief of contract labor div., U.S. Bur. of Immigration, 1911-13; spl. rep. U.S. Dept. of Labor, in Europe, 1913; editor Immigration Journal, 1916-17; with Am. Red Cross in Europe, 1917-19; mem. com. on repatriation of sick and wounded prisoners, Interallied Repatriation Commn., 1918-19; etc.; Am. del. to Internat. Conf. on Immigration and Emigration, Rome, 1924; chmn. of same at Havana, Cuba, 1928; commr. gen. of immigration, 1921-25; 2d asst. sec. of Labor, May 16, 1925-June 1934. Del. to Republican Nat. Convention, 1932. Received thanks of British Govt. for repatriation of sick and wounded prisoners from Germany, 1919. Republican. Club: National Press. Author: Emigration Conditions in Europe (Reports of U.S. Immigration Commn., Govt. Printing Office), 1911. Home: St. Johnsbury, Vt. Address: 3456 Macomb St., Washington. Died July 31, 1942.

HUSE, Harry Pinckney (hūs), naval officer; b. at West Point, N.Y., Dec. 8, 1858; s. Caleb and Harriet (Pinckney) H.; B.S., U.S. Naval Acad., 1878, Naval War Coll., 1916; m. Mary S. Whitelock, Sept. 15, 1886; 1 dau., Jean Stockton. Midshipman, June 4, 1880; promoted through grades to rear admiral, Aug. 29, 1916; promoted to vice admiral, retired, June 21, 1930. Pres. Naval Examining Bd., Washington, D.C., Sept. 29, 1916; comdr. Atlantic Fleet Train (flagship Columbia), Jan. 24, 1919; spl. duty, London and Paris, Dec. 13, 1919; comdr. U.S. Naval Forces in European waters, rank of vice adm., June 25, 1920; comdt. 3d Naval Dist., New York, Feb. 5, 1921; mem. Gen. Bd. of Navy, July 26, 1921-Dec. 3, 1922 (retired). Advanced 5 numbers "for eminent and conspicuous conduct in battle," while serving on bd. Gloucester, commanded landing force from Gloucester at Guanica, Puerto Rico, July 25, 1898; secured landing place for Army, hauled down Spanish flag and hoisted first American flag over Puerto Rico. Awarded Congressional Medal of Honor for "distinguished conduct in battle," engagement of Vera Cruz, April 21-22, 1914; gold life-saving medal, New York Humane Soc., for going overboard in his uniform from his flagship to rescue one of his crew. Member of Christian Science Church. Clubs: Army and Navy (Washington); New York Yacht. Author of "The Descendants of Abel Huse of Newbury (1602-1690)" Home: 2400 16th St., Washington, D.C. Died May 14, 1942.

HUSKINS, James Preston, corp. official; b. Lexington, Miss., Dec. 2, 1864; s. E. and Louisa (Pinkston) H.; ed. Miss. Agrl. and Mech. Coll.; m. Jean Dobbins, Apr. 30, 1914. Record clk., later chief clk. and cashier, Queen & Crescent R.R., 1882-87; bookkeeper, later asst. cashier Chattanooga (Tenn.) Nat. Bank, 1887-99, cashier, 1899-1905; cashier 1st Nat. Bank, Chattanooga, 1905-25; pres., 1925-33; formerly pres. Chattanooga Gas Co.; dir. sec.; treas. Signal Mountain Portland Cement Co.; also dir. many cos. Democrat. Presbyterian. Clubs: Mountain City, Fairyland Golf and Country. Home: Lookout Mountain, Tenn. Died Aug. 2, 1948; buried Forest Hill Cemetery, Chattanooga, Tenn.

HUSS, George Morehouse, civil engr.; b. Tiffin, O., July 14, 1857; s. John Thomas and Sophronia Gates (Morehouse) H.; ed. high sch., Heidelberg Coll. (Tiffin, O.), Ohio Business Coll. (Sandusky); lit. and civ. engring., Cornell U., 1875; m. Ella A. Scranton, Jan. 31, 1883; children—Grace Scranton, Helen (dec.), Marjorie (dec.), Dorothy (Mrs. W. E. Gollan), Genevieve, George M. (dec.). Civil engr. and ry. builder in West until 1890; engr. and builder Deming, Sierra Madre & Pacific Ry., in Mexico, 1890-94; cons. engr. Basra to Bagdad, and Beira Ry. in East Africa, 1894; built ry. from Haifa to Damascus, Palestine, 1895-96; pres. Northern Electric Ry., Chicago, 1897; built Cleveland, Painesville & Eastern Ry., Ohio, 1899; built rys. in Northern Wis., since 1900, establishing six towns; chief constrn. engr. M., St.P.&S.S.Marie R.R., 1906-17; built 2000 miles of ry. in western states; with U.S. R.R. Adminstrn., 1918-22, in charge additions and betterments, and as asst. dir.; mem. United States Real Estate Board, 1920-22; v.p. Mont. Ry. and Wyo. North & South R.R., 1923-24; consulting practice, and farming since 1924; expert engr. for C.B.&Q. Ry. on Miss. river dams, 1933-35; pres. G. M. Huss Land Co. Mem. Am. Soc. C.E., Am. Ry. Engring. Assn., S.A.R. Republican. Clubs: Chicago Athletic, Congressional Country, Fossils. Wrote: Syrian Letters, 1897. Contbr. on lit., tech., and farming topics. Home: Stone Lake, Wis. Died Feb. 22, 1947.

HUSTING, Berthold Juneau (hūs'ting), lawyer; b. Mayville, Wis., Mar. 6, 1878; s. John Pierre and Mary Magdalene (Juneau) H.; LL.B., U. of Wis., 1900; m. Agnes Julia Sternberger, Aug. 27, 1902; children—Suzanne Madeline (Mrs. Ralph B. Wackman), John Jakob, Constance Agnes (Mrs. J. W. Carlson). Professional baseball player, American and National leagues, 1900-02. Admitted to Wisconsin bar, 1900; in practice, Fond du Lac, Wisconsin, 1902-15, partner ex-U.S. Senator Paul O. Husting, Mayville, Wis., 1915-17, Husting & Husting, Mayville, 1915-23; U.S. dist. atty., Eastern Dist. Wisconsin, June 20, 1933-44; pres. Dodge County Bar Assn., 1945; senior member Husting & Husting, Law Offices, Mayville, Wis. Mem. county bd. Fond du Lac County, 1910-14, Dodge County, 1926-31; candidate lt. gov., 1930, U.S. Congress, 1932; del. Dem. Nat. Conv., 1932. Mem. Delta Tau Delta. Democrat. Clubs: Univ. of Wisconsin "W" (hon. mem.) (Milwaukee); Lions (hon.). Home: Mayville, Wis. Died Sept. 3, 1948.

HUSTIS, James H., railway official; b. New York, Jan. 11, 1864; ed. pub. schs. Began in office of gen. supt. N.Y.C. & H.R. R.R. Co., at N.Y. City, 1878, continued with same rd. and leased lines, in gen. office until 1891, trainmaster, asst. supt. and supt., Harlem div., 1891-1900, supt. River div., 1900-02, supt. Rome, Watertown & Ogdensburg div., 1902-06, Hudson, Putnam and Electric divs., 1906-07, gen. supt. Western dist., Apr.-Oct. 1907, asst. gen. mgr., N.Y.C. & H.R. R.R. Co. in charge Boston & Albany R.R., 1907-11, v.p., 1911-13; pres. N.Y., N.H. & H. R.R., 1913-14; made pres. Boston & Maine R.R., Aug. 15, 1914, temporary receiver Aug. 29, 1916; dist. dir. all New England railroads, U.S. R.R. Adminstrn., June 1918-June 1919; again pres. Boston and Maine R.R., 1919-26, retired. Died Sept. 18, 1942.

HUTCHESON, Grote, army officer; b. Cincinnati, O., Apr. 1, 1862; s. Ebenezer E. and Therese C. (Turpin) H.; grad. U.S. Mil. Acad., 1884; m. Rosalie E. St. George, Jan. 16, 1900 (died Feb. 20, 1942); m. 2d, Anne Holt Pegram, Dec. 11, 1943. Commd. 2d lt. 9th Cav., June 15, 1884; colonel, 1916; brig. gen. N.A., Aug. 24, 1917; maj. gen. (temp.) Aug. 27, 1918; brig. gen., regular army, July 3, 1920; maj. gen., July 19, 1924; retired July 20, 1924. Participated in campaigns in Okla., 1884-85, in campaigns against the Sioux Indians in S.D., 1890-91; duty railroad strikes, 1894; campaign against Bannock Indians, July-Sept. 1895; adj. gen., Puerto Rican expdn., 1898; adj. gen. and judge advocate Dept. of Mo., 1899-1900; with China-Relief Expdn., 1900, as adj. gen., later insp. gen. and judge advocate; participated in advance to Peking; mil. sec. to mil. gov. of P.I., 1901-02; judge adv. Dept. of the East, New York, 1903-04; mem. Gen. Staff Corps, 1904-08; duty Office Chief of Staff, 1904-08; mem. spl. mission to witness maneuvers of French Army, 1905; in Philippines, 1901-02, 1908-10, 1915-16; Mexican border, 1911-12, 1916-17; organized Recruit Depots at Ft. Sam Houston, Tex., and Ft. Thomas, Ky.; created and organized Port of Embarkation, Newport News and Norfolk, Va.; comd. 14th Div., Camp Custer, Mich., and Camp Meade, Md.; comdg. New York Gen. Intermediate Depot, reducing war activities and coördinating supply services in and around N.Y. City, 1921-23; comdg. 11th Field Arty. Brig., Schofield Barracks, Hawaii, 1923-24. Awarded D.S.M. (U.S.), "for especially meritorious and conspicuous services in administration of Port of Embarkation," 1918; also Navy D.S.M. for service, World War. Mem. Order of Dragon, Order of Carabao, Soc. Foreign Wars. Episcopalian; dir. gen. Cathedral Foundation, Washington, 1925-27. Clubs: Army and Navy (Washington, D.C.); Union League (San Francisco). Address: Saratoga, Calif. Died Dec. 28, 1948; buried in Arlington National Cemetery.

HUTCHESON, William Anderson, actuary; b. Greenock, Scotland, July 13, 1868; s. John Mitchell and Agnes (Anderson) H.; grad. Merchiston Castle Sch., Edinburgh, 1887; m. Martha Brookes Brown, Oct. 12, 1910. Began in employ Scottish Widow Fund and Life Assurance Soc., Edinburgh, 1887; asst. to actuary London Assurance Corp., 1899; asso. actuary Mutual Ins. Co., of New York, 1899-1911, actuary, 1911-17, 2d v.p. and actuary, 1917-31, v.p. and actuary, 1931-40; now retired. With War Work Council of Y.M.C.A. as chmn. Ins. Commn., World War; chmn. Com. of Actuaries of Commn. on Pensions, N.Y. City. Mem. bd. mgrs. St. Andrews Soc., 1922-24. Fellow Actuarial Soc. America (pres. 1920-22), Am. Inst. Actuaries, Casualty Actuarial Soc., Inst. of Actuaries (Eng.), Faculty of Actuaries (Scotland). Republican. Conglist. Clubs: Pilgrims, Century. Home: Gladstone, N.J. Died Nov. 19, 1942.

HUTCHINS, Frank Frazier, M.D., educator; b. Indianapolis, Feb. 9, 1870; s. Hezekiah Sharpe and Mary Elizabeth (Lemon) H.; student Butler Univ.; M.D., Indiana Medical Coll., 1892; special work several yrs., New York Post-Grad. Sch., Vienna, Berlin, Zurich, Paris and London; m. Luella McWhirter, June 12, 1907. Instr. Butler U. and Ind. Med. Coll., 1892-95; resident physician Eastern Hosp. for Insane, Richmond, Ind., 1895-1901; asst. prof. psychology and psychiatry, Central Coll. Physicians and Surgeons, Indianapolis, 1903-05; prof. mental and nervous diseases, State Coll. Physicians and Surgeons, 1906-08; prof. mental and nervous diseases, Ind. U. Sch. of Medicine, 1908-37; now emeritus; cons. City Hosp., Long Hosp., City Dispensary and Riley Memorial Hosp. for Children. Pres. Lemona Farm Stock Co.; dir. Peoples State Bank. Served as maj. and lt. col., M.C., World War; instr. Med. Officers' Training Corps, Ft. Benjamin Harrison and Ft. Oglethorpe; neuropsychiatrist 8th Div. Reg., later Base Sect. 5, France; chief neuropsychiatric service Walter Reed

Gen. Hosp., Washington, D.C.; clin. dir., neuropsychiatry U.S. Vets.' Bur., June 1922-July 1923; dean Neuropsychiatric Sch. of U.S. Vets.' Bur.; col. M.R.C., U.S. Army. Mem. Nat. Com. for Mental Hygiene. Republican. Methodist. Mem. A.M.A., Ind. State Med. Assn., Indianapolis Med. Soc., Am. Psychiatric Assn., Mil. Order of Foreign Wars, Am. Legion, Delta Tau Delta, Alpha Omega, Nu Sigma Nu. Mason (32°, Shriner). Clubs: Service, Army and Navy (Washington, D.C.). Home: 3824 N. Delaware St., Indianapolis, Ind. Died Feb. 22, 1942.

HUTCHINS, Will, artist, author; b. Colchester, Conn., June 11, 1878; s. Rev. William Tucker and Charlotte Ann (Hills) H.; B.A., Yale, 1901, B.F.A., 1909; hon. L.H.D., American University, 1941; married Lola May Evans, June 20, 1913; 1 son, Louis Whiting. Private Battery A, 1st Conn. Artillery, Spanish-Am. War; dir. edn., with Italian Army, World War. Prof. history and theory of art, Am. U., Washington, 1925. Asso. editor "Christian Art." Mem. Beta Theta Pi, Phi Beta Kappa. Democrat. Episcopalian. Club: Graduate (New Haven). Author: Jeanne D'Arc at Vaucouleurs, 1909 (verse drama); (in collaboration) The Day that Lincoln Died. Home: 2122 California St., Washington, D.C. Died Feb. 9, 1945.

HUTCHINGS, Richard Henry, physician; b. Clinton, Ga., Aug. 28, 1869; s. Richard H. and Cornelia (Greaves) H.; certificate Middle Ga. Mil. Coll., Milledgeville, Ga., 1887; student University of Georgia, 1 year; M.D., Bellevue Hospital Medical College (New York Univ.), 1891; D.Sc., Colgate Univ., 1940; m. Lillie Beall Compton, Sept. 6, 1893; children—Richard Henry, Charles Wyatt, Dorothy (Mrs. R. N. Alberts). Intern, Almshouse and Workhouse Hospital, Blackwell's Island, New York, 1891-92; entered New York State Hospital Service through competitive examination, 1892; served as asst. physician to 1903, med. supt., 1903-19, St. Lawrence State Hosp., Ogdensburg, N.Y.; med. supt. Utica (N.Y.) State Hosp., 1919-39. Prof. clin. psychiatry (emeritus), Syracuse U. Chief psychiatrist 81st Div., N.A., Camp Jackson, S.C., Sept. 1917-Jan. 1918; assigned duty, Jan. 28, 1918, at office Surgeon Gen., Div. of Spl. Hosps. and Reconstruction, representing neurology and psychiatry, rank maj. Med. R.C.; chief of Division of Neuro-psychiatry, G.H. No. 31, Plattsburg Barracks, July 1918-Feb. 1919; mem. Med. Advisory Board 37 (psychiatrist) for Selective Service System, U.S. Army, 1941; mem. bd. directors National Com. for Mental Hygiene. Member American Medical Assn., Oneida County Med. Soc. (pres. 1931), Am. Psychiatric Assn. (pres. 1938), Kappa Alpha, Alpha Omega Alpha. Clubs: Fort Schuyler, Torch (pres. 1931), Rotary. Investigated epidemic of typhoid fever, 1903, traced its origin to infected ice, a source of contagion not previously recognized; made study of the care of insane in State of Ga., at request of Gov. Harris, and filed rept. with recommendations. Author: A Psychiatric Word Book, 7th edit., 1943. Contbr. numerous articles on care and treatment of Nervous and Mental Diseases. Editor of Psychiatric Quarterly. Home: 52 Fountain St., Clinton, N.Y. Office: care Psychiatric Quarterly, 1213 Court St., Utica 2, N.Y. Died Oct. 28, 1947.

HUTCHINS, Augustus Schell, lawyer, ins. official; b. N.Y. City, Nov. 11, 1856; s. Waldo and Elizabeth (Ellsworth) H.; A.B., Amherst, 1879; LL.B., Columbia, 1880; m. Mary Josephine Johnson, Feb. 1917. Practiced at N.Y. City since 1880; mem. A. S. & W. Hutchins; chmn. bd. North River Ins. Co.; pres. Hutchins Securities Co.; dir. Crum & Forster, Internat. Ins. Co., U.S. Fire Ins. Co., Westchester Fire Ins. Co., Reserve Resources Corp., 110 William Street Corp.; dir., counsel and trustee Insurance Shares; trustee Manhattan Savings Bank. Member Chamber of Commerce of the State of New York. Dir. Mary J. Hutchins Foundation. Mem. Psi Upsilon. Club: University. Home: 1060 Fifth Av. Office: 110 William St., New York, N.Y. Died Feb. 19, 1948.

HUTCHINSON, William Spencer, prof. mining.; b. Boston, Mass., Oct. 9, 1870; s. William and Hannah Amanda (Skinner) H.; grad. Dorchester High Sch., Boston, 1888; B.S., Massachusetts Institute of Technology, 1892; m. Elizabeth E. Baker, Aug. 17, 1898 (died November 27, 1944); children—Alfred Baker (dec.), Elizabeth Baker (Mrs. Edwin Delamater Ryer), Ruth (Mrs. Jervis Jefferis Babb), William Spencer, Jr., Virginia Hope (Mrs. Bernard Joseph Corrow). Asst. to sec. Mass. Inst. Tech., 1892-93; mining engineer in Calif., Ida., and Mo., 1894-1903; practicing alone, headquarters in Boston, 1903-22; assignments in Australia, New Caledonia, Peru, Chile, Transvaal, and Southern Rhodesia, 1916-25; mem. firm Hutchinson and Livermore, 1923-39; now practicing alone as industrial minerals specialist; professor mining, Massachusetts Institute Technology, 1922-39, head department of mining and metallurgy, 1927-37, head department of mining engineering, 1937-39, now professor emeritus. Member engineering div. Nat. Research Council (1924-25 and 1928-30). Mem. Am. Inst. Mining and Metall. Engrs. (dir. 1926-28), Mining and Metall. Soc. America (mem. council 1930-34), Tau Beta Pi, Delta Upsilon, Sigma Xi. Awarded silver medal, San Francisco Expn., 1915. Republican. Conglist. Home: 45 Old Morton St., Dorchester 26, Mass. Office: 31 Milk St., Boston 9. Deceased.

HUTCHISON, George Wayland, sec. Nat. Geog. Soc.; b. Scranton, Pa., Nov. 21, 1886; s. George W. and Mary E. (Street) H.; L.H.D., S.D. Sch. of Mines, Rapid City, S.D.; m. Rose Aurelia Brooke, Oct. 4, 1910; children—John Grosvenor, Aurelia Katherine. Became associated with Nat. Geog. Soc., Dec. 1907, asst. sec., 1909, asso. sec., 1919, sec. since 1933; life trustee Nat. Geog. Soc. Mem. adv. bd. branches of Riggs Nat. Bank, Washington, D.C. Clubs: University, Columbia Country, Chevy Chase (Washington). Home: 3305 Lowell Lane. Office: 1146 16th St., Washington, D.C. Died Mar. 24, 1945.

HUTCHISON, Miller Reese, inventor, engr.; b. Montrose, Baldwin County, Ala., Aug. 6, 1876; s. William Peter and Tracie (Magruder) H.; student Marion Mil. Inst., 1889-91, Spring Hill Coll., 1891-92, University Mil. Inst., Mobile, 1892-95; B.S. in E.E., Ala. Poly. Inst., 1897, E.E., 1913; Ph.D., Spring Hill Coll., 1914; attended Ala. Med. Coll.; m. Martha J. Pomeroy, May 31, 1901. Chief elec. engr. U.S. Light House Establishment, 7th and 8th dists., during Spanish-Am. War, engaged in laying submarine mines and cables, Gulf Harbors; established Hutchison Laboratory, New York, 1899; invented and marketed many elec. and mech. appliances among which are "Acousticon" for the deaf, "Dictograph," "Klaxon Horn"; has been granted several hundred patents. Presented with spl. gold medal by Queen of Eng. for exceptional merit in the field of invention, 1902; present at Coronation Edward VII and Alexandra, Westminster Abbey, 1902; awarded gold medals, St. Louis Expn., 1904 for Acousticon and commercially operated wireless telephone. Became associated with Thomas A. Edison, 1910, in spl. work on storage batteries; apptd. chief engr. Edison Laboratory and all affiliated Edison interests, chief engr. to and personal rep. of Thomas A. Edison, 1913, and in addition adv. mgr. Edison Storage Battery Co., 1912-17; engr. adviser Thomas A. Edison, 1917-18; formed Miller Reese Hutchison, Inc., Jan. 1, 1917, to act as sole distributors Edison Storage Batteries for all govt. purposes all nations, of which became pres.; sold rights back to Edison Co., June 5, 1918, to devote entire time to govt. service for period of war; propr. Hutchison Laboratory. Hon. commr. of Dept. of Electricity, St. Louis Expn., 1904; mem. Internat. Elec. Congress, St. Louis, 1904, Internat. Engring. Congress, San Francisco, 1915; mem. Naval Consulting Bd. Mem. Am. Acad. Polit. and Social Science, A.A.A.S., Am. Inst. E.E., Am. Inst. Radio Engrs., Am. Soc. M.E., Am. Soc. Naval Engrs., Nat. Inst. Social Sciences, Navy League U.S., New York Elec. Soc., Soc. Automotive Engrs., Nat. Geog. Soc., Soc. Am. Mil. Engrs., U.S. Naval Inst., Optical Soc. Am., Kappa Alpha (Southern), Accademia Internazionale di lettre e Scienze (Napoli), Royal Soc. for Encouragement of Arts, Manufacture and Commerce (London). Awarded diploma of academic corr. by Internat. Acad. Letters and Science, Naples, 1922, also Cross of Honor "for scientific and literary achievements," by same, 1925. Address: Box 1703, 180 Central Park South, New York, N.Y. Died Feb. 16, 1944.

HYAMSON, Moses (hī'ăm-sŭn), clergyman, educator; b. Russian Poland, Sept. 3, 1862; s. Rabbi Nathan and Ellen H.; B.A., London U., 1882; LL.B., 1900, LL.D., 1912; m. Sara Gordon, 1893. Ordained rabbi, 1882; served at Swansea, 5 yrs., Bristol, 3 yrs., Dalston Synagogue, Poet's Rd., Canonbury, 10 yrs.; ecclesiastical assessor to the chief rabbi, 1901-11; acting in the chief rabbinate, 1901-13; came to the United States as rabbi Orach Chaim Congregation, New York, 1913; professor of the Codes, Jewish Theol. Seminary America, 1915-40, professor emeritus since 1940. Author: The Oral Law and Other Sermons, 1910; The Jewish Method of Slaying Animals from the Point of View of Humanity, 1923; Sabbath and Festival Addresses, 1935. Editor: (also translator) Collatio Mosaicarum et Romanarum Legum, 1913; Bachya's Duties of the Heart (introduction and first treatise), 1925 (parts 2 and 3), 1941; (parts 4 and 5), 1944; (parts 6, 7 and 8), 1945; (parts 9 and 10), and Hebrew Poems by Bar Bachya, 1947; The Mishneh Torah of Malmonides Book I, 1937, Book II, 1949; articles on religious topics. Proposed Plan for "Reform of the Calendar and the Sabbath,," 1930; The Blank Day Device in Proposed Plans for Calendar Reform, 1931. Address: 65 E. 96th St., N.Y. City 28. Died June 9, 1949.

HYDE, Arthur M., lawyer; b. Princeton, Mo., July 12, 1877; s. Ira B. and Caroline E. (Mastick) H.; A.B., U. of Mich., 1899, LL.D., 1929; LL.B., State U. of Ia., 1900; m. Hortense Cullers, Oct. 19, 1904; 1 dau., Caroline C. Practiced law at Princeton, Mo., 1900-15; mayor of Princeton, 1908-10; moved to Trenton, 1915; gov. of Mo., term 1921-25; Sec. of Agr. in cabinet of President Hoover, 1929-33; in practice of law since 1933. Trustee Mo. Wesleyan Coll. Republican. Methodist. Mason (33°, Shriner). Odd Fellow. Home: Trenton, Mo. Died Oct. 17, 1947.

HYDE, Clarence Ludlam, physician; b. Buffalo, N.Y., May 23, 1878; s. Rev. Melancthon C. and Elizabeth L. (Stoutenburgh) H.; grad. high sch., Warsaw, 1896; M.D., Homœ. Dept. U. of Mich., 1906; grad. Homœ. Hosp., Montreal, Can., 1907; m. Baca L. Chisholm, June 16, 1909; children—Cleveland Chisholm, Elizabeth Margaret. Dir. div. of tuberculosis, Dept. of Health, Buffalo, 1909-11; cons. in tuberculosis, Ernest Wende Hosp., 1909-12, Buffalo City Hosp., 1911-12; supt. J. N. Adam Memorial Hosp., Perrysburg, N.Y., 1913-20; supt. Edwin Shaw Sanatorium since 1920; cons. in tuberculosis, Akron (Ohio) City Hospital, 1921; medical director Municipal Tuberculosis Clinic (Akron, Ohio). Member American Medical Association, National Tuberculosis Assn., Am. Trudeau Soc., Phi Alpha Gamma; fellow Am. Coll. Physicians. Republican. Episcopalian. Mason (Shriner), Elk. Clubs: Exchange, Torch (Akron). Home: Edwin Shaw Sanatorium, Akron, O. Died Dec. 2, 1945.

HYDE, James Francis Clark, army officer; b. Newton Highlands, Mass., April 29, 1894; s. Frank C. and Blanche E. (Bean) H.; student Mass. Inst. of Tech., 1912-14; B.S., Colo. Coll., 1916; m. Marie S. Spink, Jan. 10, 1918; 1 son, James F. C., Jr. Commd. army engr. officer, U.S. Army, June 1916, and advanced through the grades to brig. gen., Sept. 13, 1942. Awarded World War, Army of Occupation, Defense Period, Am., European and Asiatic theater medals. Mem. Mil. Engrs., Theta Chi. Clubs: Army and Navy (Washington, D.C.); Engineer Mess (Ft. Belvoir, Va.). Home: Marlyn Apts., 39th and Cathedral, N.W., Washington, D.C. Died Aug. 7, 1944.

HYDE, Roscoe Raymond, prof. immunology; b. Cory, Ind., Mar. 23, 1884; s. John Andrew and Mary Ann (Michaelree) H.; A.B., Ind. State Teachers Coll., Terre Haute, 1908; A.B. and A.M., Ind. U., 1909; Ph.D., Columbia, 1913; m. Elsie A. Coss, Sept. 18, 1910; children—Dr. Gertrude Martina, Dr. Margaret Irene Moore, Edith Raymond. Asst. in embryology, Ind. U., 1908-09; asst. prof., later prof. and head of dept. zoölogy and physiology, Ind. Teachers Coll., 1909-19; lecturer in pathology, Terre Haute Veterinary Coll., 1912-19; fellow, Johns Hopkins, 1918-19, asso., 1919-22, asso. prof. immunology, 1922-28, asso. prof. filterable viruses and head of dept., 1928-32, prof. immunology and dir. of laboratories of filterable viruses and immunology since 1932; visiting prof., U. of Chicago, 1930; mng. editor Am. Jour. Hygiene, 1927-32. Fellow A.A.A.S., Am. Soc. Zoölogists, Am. Soc. Immunologists, Am. Soc. Geneticists, Johns Hopkins U. Club, Am. Soc. of Naturalists, Nat. Geog. Society, Sigma Xi, Delta Omega (pres. Alpha chapter). Democrat. Contbr. to scientific publs. Home: 4101 Penhurst Av. Office: N. Wolf St., Baltimore, Md. Died Sep. 15, 1943.

HYDE, William Henry, painter; b. N.Y. City, Jan. 29, 1858; s. John James H.; A.B., Columbia, 1877; studied painting in Paris under Boulanger, Lefebvre, Doucet and Harrison; m. Mary Potter, Dec. 19, 1894. A.N.A. Address: DeWitt Clinton Hotel, Albany, N.Y. Died Feb. 7, 1943.

HYLTON, Joseph Roy (hĭl'tŭn), physician; b. Grenola, Kan., Jan. 30, 1883; s. Tazewell Wesley and Mattie (Moore) H.; M.D., Bennett Med. Coll., 1906; m. Ara Louise Davis, Aug. 7, 1908, children—Roy Hollis, Helen Louise (Mrs. John D. Goodloe), Janyce Hylton (Mrs. James Michael Sullivan). Practice of medicine and surgery, Douglas, Wyo., since 1906. Dir. Farm Credit Administration of Omaha, Federal Land Bank, Bank for Coöperatives, Production Credit Corp., Intermediate Credit Corp., all for 1933-36. Chmn. Dem. State com. 9 years; Wyo. mem. advisory bd., Wyo. State Hist. Bd., 1937-40; mem. State adv. com. Farm Security Adminstrn.; examiner for draft bd. Address: Douglas, Wyo. Died Aug. 31, 1946.

HYNDS, John Arthur (hīnds), lawyer; b. Rome, Ga., June 16, 1870; s. George Henry and Ellen (Dick) H.; student Vanderbilt, 1888-90; LL.B., Vanderbilt Law Sch., 1892; m. Nell O'Donnelly, Dec. 2, 1908 (died May 16, 1935); m. 2d, Mrs. Martha Bradford Merritt, Nov. 23, 1936. Admitted to Ga. bar, 1892, and practiced since at Atlanta; mem. Brandon, Hynds & Tindall; gen. counsel and dir. Exposition Cotton Mills, The Consumers Co., City Ice Delivery Co.; gen. counsel Atlanta, Birmingham & Coast R.R., First Nat. Bank of Atlanta. Mem. City Council, Atlanta, 1902-03. Mem. Am., Ga. State and Atlanta bar assns., Chi Phi. Democrat. Methodist. Mason (Shriner), Odd Fellow. Clubs: Lawyers, Capital City. Home: 2989 Haversham Rd. Office: First Nat. Bank Bldg., Atlanta, Ga.* Died Oct. 18, 1941.

I

IDESON, Julia Bedford (ī'dĕ-sŭn), librarian; b. Hastings, Neb.; d. John Castree and Rosalie Eve (Beasman) Ideson; student U. of Tex., 1899-1900, 1901-03, certificate in library course, 1903. Librarian Houston Pub. Library since 1903; on leave as sec. Am. Art Students, Paris, 1913-14, and overseas service, A.L.A., Brest, Feb.-Oct. 1919. Mem. A.L.A. (1st v.p. 1932-33), Tex. Library Assn., Southwestern Library Assn. (pres. 1932-34), Kappa Kappa Gamma. Democrat. Episcopalian. Club: Downtown. Home: 2 Asbury St. Office: Houston Public Library, Houston, Tex. Died July 15, 1945; buried in Hollywood Cemetery, Houston.

IFFT, George Nicolas, editor; b. Butler County, Pa., Jan. 27, 1865; s. Nicolas and Eleanor Jane (Snyder) I.; A.B., Franklin and Marshall Coll., 1885, A.M.; U. of Leipzig, 1886, 1887; m. Ettie Riddle, May 23, 1891; children—George Nicholas, Mrs. Catherine Kirchhof. Newspaper reporter, various cities, Phila. to San Francisco; propr. and editor Pocatello (Ida.) Tribune, 1891-1905. Am. consul at Chatham, Ont., 1905-06, Annaberg, Ger., 1906-08, Warsaw, Russia, 1908-09, Nuremberg, Ger., 1909-14, St. Gall, Switzerland, 1914-16, Stuttgart, Germany, 1916-17; in charge Consulate Gen., Winnipeg, Can., May 21-July 18, 1917; assigned to Vardo, Norway, Sept. 5, 1917; in charge Consulate Gen., Christiania, Nov. 24, 1917-May 25, 1918; same at Christiansand, July 1,

1918-Mar. 31, 1919; consul at Bergen, 1919-24, at Nancy, France, 1924-26, at Ghent, Belgium, 1926-30; again editor Pocatello (Ida.) Tribune since 1930. Republican. Former mem. staff of Gov. Goodings, of Ida., rank of capt.; del. Trans-Miss. Cong., 1906. Presbyterian. Home: Pocatello, Ida. Died Aug. 18, 1947.

IGLAUER, Samuel (ig'lou-ĕr), otolaryngologist; b. Cincinnati, O., Dec. 28, 1871; s. Arnold and Delia (Fechheimer) I.; B.S., U. of Cincinnati, 1895; M.D., Med. Coll. of Ohio, 1898; intern and house phys. Cincinnati Hosp., 1898-99; studied Vienna Hosp., 1900; m. Helen S. Ransohoff, Apr. 19, 1906; children—Helen, Charles (dec.), Josephine. Asst. in Throat Dept., Ohio Med. Coll. Dispensary, 1901-05; laryngologist and aurist to Jewish Hospital, 1901-22, Cincinnati General Hospital, 1910-17; director of laryngology, Cincinnati Gen. Hosp., 1917-31; director of oto-laryngology, Jewish Hosp., since 1922; Cincinnati General and Children's hospitals since 1931; asso. prof. otology, rhinology and laryngology, 1904-16, prof. laryngology, 1916-30, prof. oto-laryngology since 1930, College of Medicine of U. of Cincinnati. Mem. Charter Commn., 1918. Fellow Am. Coll. Surgeons; mem. A.M.A., Ohio State Med. Assn., Am. Laryngol., Rhinol. and Otol. Soc., Am. Acad., Ophthalmology and Otolaryngology, Am. Laryngol. Soc. Ex-pres. Am. Broncho-Esophagological Soc.; mem. Cincinnati Anti-Tuberculosis League, Cincinnati Acad. Medicine, Cincinnati Oto-Laryngol. Soc., Sigma Xi. Capt. M.C. U.S. Army, 1918-19. Clubs: University, Cincinnati Country, Losantiville Country. Home: 162 Glenmary Av. Office: 707 Race St. Bldg., Cincinnati, O. Died June 23, 1944.

IGLEHART, David Stewart (ig'l'härt), pres. W. R. Grace & Co.; b. New Albany, Ind., Sept. 4, 1873; s. Ferdinand Cowle (clergyman) and Nannie Dorsey (Stewart) I.; A.B., Columbia U., 1894; m. Aida Birrell, April 29, 1909 (died Nov. 26, 1933); children—Stewart Birrell, Philip Lawrence Birrell, Wendy (Mrs. Douglas A. McCrary). With W. R. Grace and Company since 1894; representative in S.A., 1901-15; returned to New York office, 1915, pres. since 1929; also pres. Grace Line and dir. subsidiaries; director Grace National Bank. Mem. Bus. Advisory Council for U.S. Dept. of Commerce. Served as lt. 112th Regt., U.S. Army, Spanish-Am. War; capt. and aide-de-camp on staff of late Theodore Roosevelt when gov. of N.Y. Decorated with Order of the Sun (Peru); Order of Merit (Chile); Order of Merit (Ecuador); Condor de los Andes (Bolivia). Clubs: Knickerbocker, Racquet and Tennis, India House, Down Town Association (New York); Meadow Brook (L.I.); Gulf Stream Golf (Fla.). Home: Westbury, L.I., N.Y.; (winter) "La Centinela," Delray, Fla. Office: 7 Hanover Sq., New York, N.Y. Died May 14, 1946.

ILL, Edward Joseph, gynecologist; b. Newark, N.J., May 23, 1854; s. C. Fridolin and Julia (Rehman) I.; M.D., Coll. Physicians and Surgeons (Columbia), 1875; Univs. of Strassburg, Vienna and Freiburg, 1875-76; m. Clothilde Dieffenbach, Jan. 10, 1878; children—Mrs. Clothilde Scheller, Edgar A., Mrs. Edna O'Malley, Mrs. Florence K. Hensler. In practice at Newark since 1876. Formerly surgeon Woman's Hosp. and med. dir. St. Michael's Hosp.; gynecologist, supervising obstetrician and trustee St. Barnabas Hosp.; cons. gynecologist, Beth Israel Hosp., Newark, All Soul's Hosp., Morristown, N.J., Mountain Side Hosp., Montclair, N.J., Rahway Memorial Hosp., Rahway, N.J.; dir. Prudential Ins. Co. of America, Member Bd. of Education, Newark, 1878-80; trustee Newark City Home, 1880-95. Republican. Mem. Southern Surg. and Gynecol. Assn.; v.p. for N.J. of Pan Am. Med. Congress, 1893; pres. Med. Soc. State of N.J., 1907; v.p., 1893, pres. 1899, exec. council, 1901-03, Am. Assn. Obstetricians and Gynecologists; pres. Acad. Medicine, Northern N.J.; chmn. for State of N.J. of Am. Soc. for Control of Cancer; pres. Soc. for Relief of Widows and Orphans of Med. Men of N.J.; fellow Am. Coll. Surgeons (chmn. judicial com. for N.J.); hon. fellow N.J. State Med. Soc. Home: 88 Treacy Av. Office: 1004 Broad St., Newark, N.J. Died June 9, 1942.

IMES, Birney, Sr., newspaper pub.; b. Gloster, Miss., Feb. 18, 1889; s. Lemuel J. and Mary E. (Whittington) I.; ed. pub. schs., Columbus, Miss.; grad. Miss. Coll., Clinton, Miss., 1907; student army orientation course Command and Gen. Staff Sch., Ft. Leavenworth, Kan., 1943; m. Eunice Tanner, Mar. 1912; 1 son, Birney. Engaged in newspaper work since 1912; editor and publisher Commercial Dispatch, Columbus, Miss., since 1920; owner Columbus Broadcasting Co. since 1943; dir. First Columbus Nat. Bank. Exec. sec. bd. of trustees Univ. of Colls. of Miss., 1925; mem. 1st Fed. P.W.A. bd., Miss., 1933; mem. commn. to study expdn. of Hernando DeSoto in discovery of Miss. River, 1936; mem. Miss. Unemployment Commn., 1936; mem. U.S. delegation (asst. to Sec. of State Hull) to Conf. of Ministers of Fgn. Affairs of Am. Republics, Havana, Cuba, 1940; chmn. Columbus Airbase Com., 1940-41. Organizer and pres. of Columbus Rotary Club, 1922, director, 1943; Governor of Rotary International, 1928. Press rep., Inter-American Conf., Mexico City, 1945, and at United Nations Conf. San Francisco, 1945. Mem. Miss. Press Assn. (pres. 1930, mem. bd. govs. 1943), Southern Newspapers Pubs. Assn. (dir. 1943), Navy League of U.S. (dir. 1943), Miss. Automobile Assn. (dir. 1943), Columbus Chamber of Commerce (pres. 1933, dir. 1943). Apptd. col. on staff Gov. Hugh White, 1936, Gov. Thomas L. Bailey, 1944. Home: 803 College St. Office: Main St., Columbus, Miss. Died June 18, 1947.

IMMEL, Ray Keeslar (Im'l), educator; b. West Gilead, Branch County, Mich., Oct. 31, 1885; s. Daniel Aurelius and Jennie Sarah (Keeslar) I.; student Albion (Mich.) Coll., 1905-06; A.B., U. of Mich., 1910, A.M., 1913, Ph.D., 1931; m. Carrie Bell Barnard, June 24, 1910; children—Earle Barnard, Marguerite Louise, Robert Louis, Virginia May. Teacher pub. schs., Branch County, 1904-05, 06-07; asst., U. of Mich., 1909-10, 12-13; prof. oratory, Muskingum Coll., New Concord, O., 1910-12; instr. in oratory, U. of Mich., 1913-20, also extension lecturer, 1914-24, asst. prof. pub. speaking, 1920-24; dean of Sch. of Speech, U. of Southern Calif., since 1924; business mgr. Quarterly Jour. of Speech Edn., 1919-24. Mem. Nat. Assn. Teachers of Speech (treas. 1919-24; pres. 1925), Nat. Collegiate Players, Phi Beta Kappa, Tau Kappa Alpha, Alpha Phi Epsilon, Phi Kappa Phi. Democrat. Methodist. Author: The Delivery of a Speech, 1921; (with Ruth Huston Whipple) Debating for High Schools, 1928; Public Speaking for High Schools, 1931; (with Helen Loree Ogg) Speech Improvement, 1936; (with W. Norwood Brigance) Speech Making, 1938. Home: 2917 W. 78th Pl., Inglewood, Calif. Office: 3518 University Av., Los Angeles. Died Apr. 11, 1945; buried in Inglewood Cemetery, Inglewood, Calif.

INGERSOLL, Charles Henry, mfr.; b. Delta, Mich., Oct. 29, 1865; s. Orville Boudinot and Mary Elizabeth (Beers) I.; ed. pub. sch., Delta; m. Eleanor Ramsey Bond, July 5, 1898. Sec. and treas. Robt. H. Ingersoll & Bro., mfrs. watches, since 1892. Mem. exec. com. Nat. Single Tax League; pres. Mfrs. and Mchts. Taxation League, Am. Fair Trade League; treas. Nat. Pub. Ownership League, Nat. Voters' League, and mem. many other civic orgns. Democrat. Clubs: Sphinx, City, National Arts, S. Orange Field, etc. Home: South Orange, N.J. Office: 315 4th Av., New York. Died Sept. 21, 1948.

INGERSOLL, Colin Macrae, cons. engr.; born New Haven, Conn., Dec. 1, 1858; s. Colin Macrae and Julia H. (Pratt) I.; B.A., Yale, 1880; m. Theresa McAllister, May 25, 1889 (died in 1910); children—Theresa Van den Heuvel, Coline Macrae, Ralph McAllister; m. 2d, Marie Harrison, Feb. 5, 1916. Entered employ of M.P. Ry., St. Louis, 1881; became connected with N.Y., N.H. & H. R.R., 1882; had charge of double-tracking of the Shore Line, improvements on N.Y. div., and elevating the tracks through Boston; asst. to pres., in charge at Boston, 1897-1900; chief engr., 1900-06 (resigned). City engr., New Haven, 1892; chmn. Harbor Commn. of New Haven, 1895; pres. Union Freight Co., Boston, 1897-1900, Old Colony Steamship Co., 1897-1900, etc. Chief engr. Dept. of Bridges, N.Y. City, 1906-08 (erection of Manhattan and Queensboro bridges and regulation on traffic of Brooklyn Bridge); cons. practice, N.Y. City, 1908-37; retired. Mem. Alaskan R.R. Commn., investigating transportation problems in Alaska, 1912-13. Mem. Am. Inst. Cons. Engrs., Am. Soc. C.E., Delta Psi. Club: University (New York). Home: Salisbury, Conn. Died Apr. 7, 1948.

INGERSOLL, Ernest, naturalist, editor; b. Monroe, Mich., Mar. 13, 1852; s. Dr. T. Dwight and Eliza (Parkinson) I.; ed. Oberlin Coll. and Harvard Mus. of Comparative Zoölogy; m. Mary Scofield (died 1921); children—Helen, Geoffrey (dec.); m. 2d, Frances L. Buchanan (died 1929); m. 3d, Mrs. Vera Edmondson Nelson. Formerly connected with Hayden survey and U.S. Fish Commn.; later at Montreal as editor Canadian Pacific Ry. publications; lecturer zoölogy, U. of Chicago. Co-editor Standard Dictionary, New Internat. Cyclopedia, Cyclopedia Americana, and other reference books. Author: Oyster Industries, 10th Census; Friends Worth Knowing, last edit., 1901; Country Cousins; Knocking 'Round the Rockies; Crest of the Continent; Canadian Guide-Book, Part II; Down East Latch Strings, 1885; The Book of the Ocean, 1898; Nature's Calendar, 1900; Wild Life of Orchard and Field, 1902; The Life of Animals—the Mammals, 1906; Wit of the Wild, 1906; Birds in Legend, Fable and Folklore, 1923; Dragons and Dragon Lore, 1928; also The Ice Queen, An Island in the Air, and other juvenile novels. Conducted 1899-38, department of educational natural history in weekly edit. of Montreal Star. Retired, 1938. Mem. N.Y. Zoöl. Soc. and other scientific assns. Club: Explorers. Address: 404 W. 116th St., New York. Died Nov. 13, 1946.

INGERSOLL, Henry Wallace, lawyer; b. Grafton Tp., Lorain County, O., Jan. 14, 1863; s. George M. and Mary (Preston) I.; LL.B., U. of Mich., 1885; m. May Hamilton, Oct. 24, 1888; children— Mary C., Henry Hamilton (dec.), Henry Walter. In practice of law Elyria, Ohio, since 1885. Director and pres. of The Andwur Building Co., Elyria, Ohio; dir. and sec. of Telkor, Inc., Elyria, Ohio. Trustee and treasurer of Elyria (Ohio) Library. Republican. Conglist. Mason (K.T., Shriner). Clubs: Masonic, Shrine. Home: 927 Middle Av. Office: Elyria Savings & Trust Bldg., Elyria, O. Died Aug. 9, 1946.

INGERSOLL, William Harrison, mfr.; b. Delta, Eaton County, Mich., Mar. 22, 1880; s. Arthur Nichols and Agnes Nancy (Wright) I.; student Pratt Institute, Brooklyn, N.Y., 1894-97, Poly. Inst., Brooklyn, N.Y., 1902; m. Frances Mary Evans, 1909; children—William Harrison, Frances Elizabeth, Lois Dorrit. Began as elec. engr., 1903; partner Robert H. Ingersoll & Bro., mfrs. Dollar Watch, New York; while dir. and gen. marketing mgr. Ingersoll Watches in charge sales and advertising business grew to world-wide concern; pres. Positype Corp. of America, mfrs. photographic materials, New York; pres. Ingersoll Radipoint Co., manufacturers mechanical pencils, New York; v.p. and gen. marketing mgr. DeForest Radio Co., New York; mem. Ingersoll, Norvell & Babson, marketing consultants, New York; pres. Ingersoll Plastics Co., N.Y.; lecturer at various times on marketing and advertising Harvard School of Business Administration, New York University School of Commerce and Accounts, Univ. of Wis. School of Commerce and Accounts, U. of Ill. Sch. of Commerce and Accounts. Nat. dir. of pub. speaking Com. on Pub. Information, Washington, D.C., during World War. Mem. Employer's Industrial Commn. sent by govt. to study European industrial conditions; organizer original Vigilance Com., out of which developed Nat. Better Business Burs.; organizer and dir. Am. Fair Trade Assn.; served as del. from U.S. and chmn. com. on distribution and unfair competition. Internat. Chamber of Commerce, Paris. Mem. Assn. of Nat. Advertisers (dir. and mem. exec. com.). Asso. Advertising Clubs of the World (dir. and mem. exec. com.), U.S. Chamber of Commerce (chmn. com. on distribution and unfair competition), Am. Soc. Sales Execs. (charter), Am. Marketing Soc. (charter, chmn. com. on mfrs. specialty marketing), Am. Mfrs. Export Assn. (treas.), Am. Marketing Assn., Alpha Delta Sigma. Clubs: Advertising (during term as pres. membership increased from 16 to 1,100) N.Y. Sales Managers (charter), National Arts (New York); Canoe Brook (Summit, N.J.). Home: 469 Prospect St., South Orange, N.J. Office: 11 W. 42d St., New York, N.Y. Died Aug. 23, 1946.

INGHAM, Charles Samuel, teacher; b. Saybrook, Conn., Jan. 11, 1867; s. Samuel Kellogg and Lydia (Ayer) I.; A.B., Yale, 1891, post-grad., 1893-96, Ph.D., 1896; in Europe, 1897-98; m. Clara Louise Northrop, June 21, 1898; children—Katharine Louise, Travis Northrop. Teacher, Dr. Holbrook's Sch., Ossining, N.Y.; instr. Yale Coll. and Sheffield Scientific Sch., 1896-1900; house master, Washington (D.C.) Sch. for Boys, 1900-05; asst. prin., Marston's Univ. Sch., Baltimore, 1905-07; prin., Dummer Acad., S. Byfield, Mass., 1907-30; in Latin dept., Yale, since 1931. Mem. Headmasters Assn. Republican. Conglist. Home: Friendship, Me. Address: 102 Yale Station, New Haven, Conn. Died June 15, 1949.

INGHAM, Harvey, newspaper man; b. Algona, Kossuth County, Ia., Sept. 8, 1858; s. William H. and Caroline A. (Rice) I.; A.B., State U. of Ia., 1880, LL.B., 1881, LL.D., Grinnell Coll., 1915; m. Nellie E. Hepburn, Oct. 23, 1894; children—Hepburn, William H., Harvey. Editor The Upper Des Moines (weekly), Algona, Ia., 1882-1902; now editor Des Moines Register, and Evening Tribune, and v.p. of corp. Republican. Postmaster, Algona, Ia., 1898-1902. Home: 2834 Forest Drive. Office: Register and Tribune, Des Moines, Ia. Died Aug. 21, 1949.

INGHAM, John Albertson, clergyman; b. Meridian, N.Y., Jan. 13, 1868; s. Albert Constantine and Cynthia Amelia (Van Wie); A.B., Syracuse U., 1886, A.M., 1889, D.D., 1908; grad. Union Theol. Sem., 1892; m. Mary Bartlet Stebbins, Sept. 28, 1892; children—Edward Stebbins, Caroline Lawrence (Mrs. James Marshall Plumer), Albert Van Wie. Teacher of mathematics, Centenary Collegiate Inst., Hackettstown, N.J., 1887-89; ordained ministry Presbyn. Ch., 1892; asst. pastor St. Nicholas Collegiate Ch., N.Y. City, 1892-93; pastor Irvington-on-Hudson, N.Y., 1894-1910, 2d Ref. Ch., New Brunswick, N.J., 1910-20; sec. progress campaign com., Ref. Ch. in America, 1920-23; Sec. Progress Council, Ref. Ch. in America, 1923-37; stated clerk Gen. Synod. of Ref. Ch. in America, 1932-42, emeritus since 1942, treas., 1938-42. Member Presbyterian Bd. Church Erection, 1897-1910, Bd. Domestic Missions, Ref. Ch. in America, 1911-21. Mem. Am. Assn. Variable Star Observers, Phi Beta Kappa, Psi Upsilon. Republican. Home: 164 Prospect St., Leonia, N.J. Died March 20, 1944; buried in Oakwood Cemetery, Troy, N.Y.

IREY, Elmer Lincoln (ī'rē), tax consultant; born Kansas City, Missouri, March 10, 1888; son of Charles William and Elizabeth (Sandys) I.; graduate of Washington, D.C., high school, 1906; student Georgetown Law School; married Marguerite Wagner, October 30, 1912; children—Hugh Wagner, Elmer Lincoln (dec.), Robert Blair. Secretary to the president Washington Ry. and Electric Co., 1906-07; stenographer Bd. of Edn., Washington, D.C., 1907; clk. office of chief postoffice insp., 1907-17; postoffice insp., 1917-19; chief Intelligence Unit, Treasury Dept., 1919-42; chief coördinator of Treasury enforcement agencies, including Secret Service, customs, forcign funds control, narcotic service, alcohol tax enforcement and intelligence, 1937-46. Major Military Intelligence, U.S. Army Res., 1922-31. Lutheran. Mason (32°). Club: National Press (Washington, D.C.). Home: Box 263A, Sarasota, Fla. Office: Shoreham Bldg., Washington. Died July 19, 1948.

IREYS, Charles Goodrich (ī'rēz), pres. Russell-Miller Milling Co.; b. Boston, Mass., Jan. 26, 1878; s. Volney Stamps and Nellie Wheeler (Goodrich) I.; B.S., U. of Minn., 1900; m. Florence W. Wells, May 4, 1907; children—Calvin Goodrich, John Wells, Marguerite. With Russell-Miller Milling Co., Minneapolis, since 1909, v.p. and treas., 1923-39, pres. since 1939, dir. since 1909; dir. First Nat. Bank & Trust Co. Clubs: Minneapolis, Minikahda, Woodhill Country, University. Home: 401 Groveland Av. Office: 432

Midland Bank Bldg., Minneapolis, Minn. Died Feb. 19, 1943.

IRVINE, Leigh Hadley, author, editor; b. Oregon, Mo., Nov. 28, 1863; s. Clarke James and Anne K. (Johnson) I.; A.B., LL.B., U. of Mo., 1882; m. Jean Dean, Sept. 8, 1906; 1 son, Thomas M. City editor Kansas City News, 1885; on Phila. Times, also N.Y. papers, 1886; asst. mng. editor San Francisco Examiner, 1888; mng. editor Maritime World, 1889-97; Sunday editor Sacramento Union, 1898-99; editorial writer San Francisco Call, 1899-1906; mng. editor newspaper syndicate, 1906-09; mng. editor Daily Eureka (Calif.) Times, 1912-13; mgr. Humboldt (Calif.) Promotion Com., 1914; sec. San Luis Obispo Co. (Calif.) Commercial Bodies and Highway Assn., 1915; editor Progressive Business and exec. officer Progressive Bus. Club Am., since 1922; mgr. State of Wash. Anti I.W.W. movement, 1916; first sec. Japan Soc. Am. Club: Press (life charter member). Author: The Struggle for Bread, 1889; An Affair in the South Seas, 1901; Irvine's New California, 1904; The Magazine Style Code, 1906; Irvine's Cyclopedia of Diction, 1910; A History of California's Bench and Bar, 1912; By Right of Sword, 1913; History of Humboldt County, 1913; Golden Roads, on road building, 1915; The Masses in the Mirror, 1919; What Is Americanism; 1910; Too Much Law-Making, 1912; The Follies of the Courts, 1925. Editorial writer and mag. spl. writer, 1923. Address: San Luis Obispo, Calif. Died June 17, 1942.

IRVING, Isabel, actress; b. Bridgeport, Conn., Feb. 28, 1871; d. Charles Washington and Isabella Irving; m. William H. Thompson, Oct. 19, 1899 (dec.). Début as Gwendolyn Hawkins in "The Schoolmistress," with Rosina Vokes Co., Jan., 1887; with Augustin Daly's Co., 1888-94; leading woman at Lyceum Theatre, New York, and in John Drew's co. several yrs.; has played leading rôles in England also; created role of Lady Jocelyn Leigh in "To Have and To Hold," Knickerbocker Theatre, New York; later starred under the management of James K. Hackett in "The Crisis"; playing Louise in all-star cast of "The Two Orphans," management Liebler & Co., 1905; engaged by Clyde Fitch to play the comedy part in "The Toast of the Town," 1906; in "Susan in Search of a Husband," and "The Girl Who Has Everything," 1907; created title rôle in "Mater," Savoy Theatre, New York, 1908; played leading woman's rôle in "The Flag Lieutenant," Criterion Theatre, and leading part in "The Commanding Officer," Savoy Theatre, New York, 1909; comedy rôle in "Smith," with John Drew, Empire Theatre, New York, and tour, 1909-11; title rôle in "The Mollusc," with Kyrle Bellew, in Chicago, and tour, 1913; leading woman with Leo Dietrichstein in "The Concert," Belasco Theatre, New York, and tour, 1912-13; with Leo Dietrichstein in "The Temperamental Journey," Belasco Theatre, New York, 1913; comedy rôle in "Under Cover," in Chicago, and San Francisco, 1914-15; co-starred with Tom Wise and Constance Collier in "The Merry Wives of Windsor," 1916-17; played "Mistress Page," Park Theatre, New York, and tour, 1947. Played in "She Walked in Her Sleep," 1918-19, in "Civilian Clothes," 1919-20, "A Bachelor's Night," Park Theatre, 1921, "To the Ladies," 1922-23, "We Moderns," 1924, "The Bride," 1924, "A Lady's Virtue," 1925-26, "Craig's Wife," 1926-27, "The Age of Innocence," 1928-29, "Uncle Vanja," 1930; played in N.Y. City and on tour with William Gillette in John Golden's "Three Wise Fools," 1936. Home: Siasconset, Nantucket Island, Mass. Died Sept. 1, 1944; buried in Bridgeport, Conn.

IRWIN, Elisabeth Antoinette, educator; b. Brooklyn, N.Y.; d. William Henry and Josephine Augusta (Easton) Irwin; student Packer Collegiate Inst., Brooklyn, 1890-99; A.B., Smith Coll., 1903; student N.Y. Sch. of Philanthropy, 1903; A.M., Columbia, 1923; unmarried; children by adoption—Elizabeth Westwood (Mrs. Howard Gresens), Katherine, Byron, Carl. Settlement worker, 1903-05, 1909-10; free lance writer newspapers and mags., 1905-09; psychologist Pub. Edn. Assn., 1910-31; conducted exptl. classes in N.Y. pub. schs., 1920-31; dir. and trustee Little Red School House (a demonstration for pub. schs. that progressive methods may be used with large classes at small per capita cost) since 1931; dir. Asso. Exptl. Schs. Mem. Teachers Union, Progressive Edn. Assn. Author: Fitting the School to the Child (with Louis Marks), 1923. Contbr. articles to ednl. jours. Home: 23 Bank St., New York, N.Y.; also Gaylordsville, Conn. Office: 196 Bleecker St., New York, N.Y. Died 1942.

IRWIN, William Glanton, banking, mfg.; b. Columbus, Ind., Nov. 24, 1866; s. Joseph Ireland and Harriet Clementine (Glanton) I.; B.S., Butler U., 1889, LL.D., 1938. Cashier, Irwin's Bank, Columbus, Ind., 1889-1910, pres., 1910-28; pres. and dir. Irwin-Union Trust Co. since 1928; pres. Ind. Nat. Bank, Indianapolis, since Jan. 1942; president Union Starch and Refining Co. (Columbus, Ind.), Indianapolis, Columbus & Southern Traction Co., Indianapolis Gas Co.; v.p. Indianapolis Belt R.R. and Stockyards Co.; chairman of board Southern Ind. Rys.; chairman exec. committee. Am. Zinc, Lead & Smelting Co., St. Louis; co-organizer Union Tin Plate Co., Anderson, Ind., and Monessen, Pa. (now part of U.S. Steel Corp.); dir. Ind. Nat. Bank, Union Trust Co., Real Silk Hosiery Mills, Ind. Bell Telephone Co., Kingan & Co. (Indianapolis), Cummins Engine Co. (Columbus, Ind.), United Electric Coal Cos. (Chicago), Purity Stores (San Francisco). Col. on staffs of Ind. govs. Mount, Durbin, Hanly, 1897-1909; mem. Ind. State Council of Defense, 1917-19. Mem. Rep. Nat. Com., 1938-40; del. Rep. Nat. Conv., 1916, 36, del.-at-large, 1940. Trustee Butler U. since 1908, chmn. exec. com. 1922-36; pres. Butler Foundation since 1926; treas. Christian Foundation since 1922. Trustee Indianapolis Art Assn., mem. Sigma Chi. Republican. Mem. Disciples of Christ Ch. Clubs: Columbia, Athletic, University, Dramatic (Indianapolis); University (Chicago), Muskoka Lakes Golf and Country (Port Carling, Ont.); Windermere (Ont.) Golf and Country. Home: 608 Fifth St. Office: 301 Washington St., Columbus, Ind. Died Dec. 14, 1943.

IRWIN, William Henry (Will Irwin), author; b. Oneida, N.Y., Sept. 14, 1873; s. David S. and Edith E. (Greene) I.; A.B., Stanford U., 1899; Dr. Humane Letters, Knox Coll., 1940; m. Harriet Hyde, Jan. 1, 1901; 1 son, William Hyde; m. 2d, Mrs. Inez Haynes Gillmore, Feb. 1, 1916. Asst. editor, 1899, editor, 1900, San Francisco Wave; reporter, 1901, spl. writer, 1902, Sunday editor, 1902-04, San Francisco Chronicle; reporter New York Sun, 1904-06; mng. editor McClure's Magazine, 1906-07; writer Collier's Weekly, 1907-08; gen. mag. writer, since 1908. War corr. with German, Belgian and British armies for various Am. publications and London Daily Mail, 1914-15. Mem. exec. com. Commn. for Relief in Belgium, 1914-15; war corr. Saturday Evening Post, with French, Italian, British and Am. armies, 1916-18; chief Foreign Dept., Com. on Pub. Information, 1918. Pres. Am. Centre P.E.N. Club, 1929-31. Decorated Chevalier of Legion of Honor (French); King Albert medal, first class (Belgian); Médaille de la Reconnaissance (Belgian); commemorative medal of the Olympic Games (Swedish); Order of Gedeminas (Lithuanian). Clubs: Bohemian (San Francisco, Calif.); Players, Dutch Treat (New York). Formerly pres. Authors' Guild, Authors' League of America. Author: Stanford Stories (with C. K. Field), 1900; The Reign of Queen Isyl (with Gelett Burgess), 1903; The Picaroons (with Gelett Burgess), 1903; The Hamadryads (verse), 1904; The City That Was, 1907; Old Chinatown, 1908; The Confessions of a Con Man, 1909; Warrior the Untamed, 1909; The House of Mystery, 1910; The Readjustment, 1910; The Red Button, 1912; Where the Heart Is, 1912; Beating Back (with Al J. Jennings), 1914; Men, Women and War, 1915; The Latin at War, 1916; A Reporter in Armageddon, 1918; the Thirteenth Chair (play, with Bayard Veiler), 1916; The Next War, 1921; Columbine Time, 1921; Christ or Mars, 1923; Youth Rides West, 1925; How Red Is America?, 1927; Highlights of Manhattan, 1927; Herbert Hoover—A Reminiscent Biography, 1929; The House That Shadows Built, 1929; Lute Song (play with Sidney Howard), 1930; Propaganda and the News, 1936; Spy and Counterspy (with E. V. Voska), 1940; The Making of a Reporter, 1942; Spies and Saboteurs (with T. M. Johnson), 1943; also author of following pamphlets: The Babes of Belgium, The Splendid Story of Ypres, 1915. Editor: Letters to Kermit by Theodore Roosevelt, 1946. Frequent contbr. of fiction and articles to mags. Home: 240 W. 11th St., New York, N.Y., and (summer) Scituate, Mass. Died Feb. 24, 1948.

ISAACS, Lewis Montefiore; b. N.Y. City, Jan. 10, 1877; s. Myer S. and Maria (Solomon) I.; student Coll. City of New York, 3 yrs., 1891-93; Ph.B., New York U., 1897; M.A., Columbia, 1899; LL.B., 1900; m. Edith J. Rich, Nov. 28, 1904; children—Marian Brody, Lewis Myer, Hermine I. Popper. Admitted to bar, 1899, and since practiced in N.Y. City; became mem. M. S. and I. S. Isaacs, 1903, now sr. mem. Sec. Edward MacDowell Assn.; dir. Musicians' Foundation; ex-pres. Am. Branch Internat. Law Assn.; trustee West End Synagogue; ex-gov. Real Estate Bd. of N.Y.; mem. Am. Bar Assn., New York State Bar Assn., Bar Assn. City of N.Y. (former vice-pres.), Phi Beta Kappa, Delta Upsilon. Republican. Jewish religion. Clubs: Town Hall, Bohemians. Author: (with Kurt J. Rahlson) Guide to Humperdinck's Königskinder, 1912; (with same) Guide to Humperdinck's Hänsel and Gretel, 1913. Contbr. on musical topics to Ency. Americana, Bookman, etc.; composer songs, piano, orchestral, etc. Home: 24 W. 55th St. and Darien, Conn. Office: 475 5th Av., New York, N.Y. Died Dec. 12, 1944.

ISELY, Frederick B., biologist; born in Fairview, Kan., June 20, 1873; s. C. H. and Elise (Dubach) I.; grad. Hiawatha Acad., 1894; B.S., Fairmount Coll., Wichita, Kan., 1899; M.S., University of Chicago, 1909; Sc.D. (hon.), Trinity University, 1946; m. Mary E. Nickerson, May 8, 1901; children—Marion Frances, Harold Nickerson, Ralph Dubach, Frederick B. Prin. Central Sch., Hiawatha, 1899-1901; teacher biology, high sch., Wichita, 1901-06; State Prep. Sch., Tonkawa, Okla., 1906-12; scientific asst. U.S. Bur. Fisheries, summers, 1910-13; prof. biology, Central Coll., Fayette, Mo., 1912-20; instr. zoölogy, U. of Mo., summers, 1915-17; dean and prof. biology Culver-Stockton Coll., Canton, Mo., 1920-22, Texas Woman's Coll., 1922-31; prof. of biology, Trinity U., since 1931; instr. ecology, Rocky Mountain Biol. Lab., summer, 1932. Fellow A.A.A.S., Entomol. Soc. Amer., Okla. Acad. Science (sec. 1909-12), Tex. Acad. Science (v.p. 1936-37, pres. 1937-38); mem. Am. Soc. Zoölogists, Ecol. Soc. America, N. Tex. Biol. Soc. (pres. 1924-26), Phi Sigma. Presbyterian. Monographs and research papers, concerning fresh water mussels and ecology of orthoptera. Home: 2835 W. Gramercy Pl., San Antonio, Tex. Died Dec. 30, 1947.

ISHAM, Mary Keyt (ī'shăm), neurologist; b. Cincinnati, O., Aug. 20, 1871; d. Asa Brainerd and Mary Hamlin Keyt Isham; A.B., Wellesley, 1894; M.A., U. of Cincinnati, 1898; work in psychology and physiology, Univ. of Chicago, 1898-99; fellow in philosophy and psychology, Bryn Mawr, 1899-1900; M.D., Laura Memorial Med. Coll. (later absorbed into med. dept. U. of Cincinnati), 1903. Gave first course in psychology ever given at a med. coll., 1901-03; interne Presbyn. Hosp., Cincinnati, 1903-04; gen. practice, Cincinnati, 1904-09; mem. staff Columbus (O.) State Hosp., 1908-15; settled in N.Y. City, 1915; formerly instr. psychiatry N.Y. Post-Grad. Med. Sch. and Hosp., and neurologist Cornell dispensary. Fellow A.M.A., New York Acad. Medicine; mem. Med. Soc. State of N.Y., N.Y. County Med. Soc., Woman's State Med. Soc., Am. Psychiatric Assn., N.Y. Soc. for Clin. Psychiatry, N.Y. Psychoanalytic Soc., Am. Psychoanalytic Assn., etc. Presbyterian. Republican. Clubs: Women's University, Wellesley; Nat. Club of Am. Assn. of Univ. Women (Washington, D.C.). Contbr. numerous tech. articles to med. jours., also articles on med. psychology in New York Times. Author: Cosmos Limited, 1928. Home: 2207 Upland Place, Cincinnati 6, O. Died Sept. 28, 1947.

ISHAM, Norman Morrison, architect; b. Hartford, Conn., Nov. 12, 1864; s. Henry (M.D.) and Frances Elizabeth (Smyth) I.; A.B., Brown U., 1886, A.M., in course, 1890; m. Elizabeth Barbour Ormsbee, Nov. 27, 1895. Entered architect's office, 1886; in practice for himself since 1892; instr. architecture, Brown U., 1894-98; head of architectural dept., R.I. Sch. Design, 1912-20 and 1923-33, lecturer architectural history, 1920-23 and since 1933; consultant on colonial rooms Am. wing of Met. Museum, New York, 1923-24; cons. architect on Del. State House, 1930-33. Fellow A.I.A.; mem. Newport Hist. Soc., Am. Antiq. Soc., Phi Beta Kappa, Delta Upsilon, R.I. Hist. Soc., Conn. Hist. Soc., R.I. Soc. of Colonial Wars, Walpole Soc., Providence Art Club, Wren Soc. (London). Author: Early Rhode Island Houses (with Albert F. Brown), 1895; The Homeric Palace, 1898; Early Connecticut Houses (with Albert F. Brown), 1900; The Meeting House of the First Baptist Church, Providence, 1925; Early American Houses, 1928; In Praise of Antiquaries, 1931; Trinity Church, Newport, R.I., 1936; Glossary of Colonial Architecture (Walpole Society), 1939. Home and Office: Wickford, R.I. Died Jan. 1, 1943.

ITTLESON, Henry, founder and chairman of the board C.I.T., Financial Corporation, formerly Commercial Investment Trust Corporation, and subsidiaries, including Commercial Investment Trust, Inc., Canadian Acceptance Corp., Ltd., Meinhard, Greeff & Co., Inc., William Iselin & Co., Inc., Nat. Surety Corp., Nat. Surety Marine Ins. Corp., Service Fire Ins. Co. of N.Y. Home: 965 Fifth Av. Office: 1 Park Av., New York City. Died Oct. 27, 1948.

ITTNER, Martin Hill (It'nĕr), chemist; b. Berlin Heights, O., May 2, 1870; s. Conrad Smithman and Sarah Content (Hill) I.; B.Ph., Washington U., 1892, B.Sc., 1894, LL.D., 1938; A.M., Harvard U., 1895, Ph.D., 1896; D.Sc., Colgate U., 1930; m. Emilie A. Younglof, Nov. 20, 1900 (died Dec. 11, 1933); children—Irving Hill, Lois Elizabeth (Mrs. Eldon Bisbee Sullivan); m. 2d, Hildegard Hirsche, July 21, 1934; 1 son, Robert Austen. Became private asst. to Dr. Wolcott Gibbs, Newport, R.I., Nov. 1896; chief chemist Colgate & Co., New York and Jersey City, Dec. 1896-July 1928, Colgate-Palmolive-Peet Co. since July 1, 1928; also served as chem. engr. and dir. of research of both cos. Delegate of U.S. Govt. to First World Chem. Engineering Congress, London, 1936. Received Modern Pioneer award, Nat. Assn. Mfrs., 1940; Perkin medal, Soc. Chem. Industry, 1942. Mem. Am. Inst. Chem. Engrs. (pres. 1936, 37; treas. 1925-35; dir. 1925-40), Am. Chem. Soc. (chmn. nat. com. on industrial alcohol 1920-42; chmn. N.Y. sect. 1925), Soc. Chem. Industry (England), Am. Inst. Chemists, Am. Oil Chemists Soc. Franklin Inst., Assn. Harvard Chemists. Republican. Clubs: Chemists (pres. 1935-36; trustee 1932-39), Harvard (New York); Harvard (N.J.). Holder many U.S. and fgn. patents. Home: Forest Edge Farm, Glendola, N.J. Office: 105 Hudson St., Jersey City, N.J. Died Apr. 22, 1945.

IVES, Howard Chapin, civil engr.; b. Cheshire, Conn., Mar. 20, 1878; s. Howard C. and Julia (Dunham) I.; Ph.B., Sheffield Scientific Sch. (Yale), 1898; C.E., Yale, 1900; m. Mary B. Young, June 30, 1908. Civ. engr., 1899-1900; instr. in civ. engring., Worcester Poly. Inst., 1900-03; asst. prof. civ. engring., U. of Pa., 1903-06; asst. prof. railroad engineering, 1906-12, prof. 1912-25, Worcester Poly. Inst.; civil and cons. engr. since 1925. Mem. Soc. for Promotion Engring. Edn., Nat. Inst. Social Sciences, Sigma Xi; asso. mem. Am. Soc. C.E. Mason, Odd Fellow. Author: Stereotomy (with A. W. French), 1902; Problems in Surveying, R.R. Surveying and Geodesy (with H. E. Hilts), 1906; Surveying Manual, 2d edit., 1938; Field Engineering (with Wm. H. Searles), 21st edit., 1936; Seven Place Natural Trigonometrical Tables, 1929, rev., 1939; Highway Curves, 3d edit., 1941; Map Drafting and Lettering (with H. R. Saunders), 1931; Natural Trigonometric Functions to Ten Seconds of Arc, 1931, 2d edit., 1942; Mathematical Tables, 2d edit., 1934, rev. edit., 1943. Address: 226 Cliff Drive, Laguna Beach, Calif. Died Oct. 6, 1944.

IVES, James Edmund, physicist; b. London, Eng., Sept. 19, 1865; s. James Thomas Bostock and Mary Collins (Johns) I.; U. of Pa., 1888-89; Harvard U., 1894; U. of Cambridge, Eng., 1896; Ph.D., Clark U., Mass., 1901; m. Georgiana Luvanne Stone, June 25,

1903; 1 dau., Elizabeth Laura (Mrs. Ives Lowe). Asst. curator, Acad. Natural Sciences, Phila., 1887-93; instr. physics, Drexel Inst., 1893-97; scholar and fellow in physics, Clark U., 1897-1901; instr. physics, U. of Cincinnati, 1901-03; scientific expert with the DeForest Wireless Telegraph Co., New York, 1903-05; asst. prof. physics, 1905-09, asso. prof., 1909-12, U. of Cincinnati; lecturer and research asso. in physics, Clark U., 1912-21; physicist U.S.P.H.S., on duty with the Office of Industrial Hygiene and Sanitation, 1921-31, sr. physicist, 1931-36. Asso. physicist Dept. Terrestrial Magnetism, Carnegie Instn., Washington, June-Aug. 1921. In charge dept. electricity and signals of U.S. Naval Aviation Detachment, Mass. Inst. Tech., 1917; lt., 1918, capt., 1919, Signal Corps, U.S. Army; capt. Signal R.C., U.S. Army, 1921; capt. Auxiliary R.C., U.S. Army, 1926 and 1931; capt., inactive, 1935. Awarded silver medal, St. Louis Expn., 1904, for work in wireless telegraphy. Episcopalian. Fellow Am. Acad. Arts and Sciences; mem. Acad. Natural Science Phila., Am. Phys. Soc., Illuminating Engring. Soc., Optical Soc. of America, Washington Acad. of Sciences, Philos. Soc. of Washington. Clubs: Cosmos, Chevy Chase (Washington). Author: An Annotated List of Experiments in Physics, 1912; also many papers in scientific journals and reviews. Address: care Cosmos Club, Washington, D.C. Died Jan. 2, 1943.

IVES, Sumner Albert, prof. biology; b. Alfred, Me., July 23, 1882; s. Sumner Abraham and Alice (Dunbar) I.; A.B., Wake Forest (N.C.) Coll., 1903; S.B., U. of Chicago, 1909, S.M., 1918, Ph.D., 1922; m. Gladys Sharp, Jan. 29, 1909; children—Sumner Albert, Eulalia Sharp, Alice Dunbar. Prin. Siler City (N.C.) Inst., 1903-05; teacher natural sciences, Chowan Coll., Murfreesboro, N.C., 1905-09; head science dept. Ouachita Coll., Arkadelphia, Ark., 1909-12; cashier Bank of Harrellsville, N.C., 1912-17; prof. biology, Howard Coll., Birmingham, Ala., 1918-26, also dean of science, 1924-26; head of biology dept., prof. of botany and dir. Furman Biology Camp, Furman (S.C.) Univ., since 1926; curator of Furman Museum since 1934; chmn. Arboretum Com. since 1933. Mem. Ala. Home Guards, 1918. Fellow A.A.A.S.; mem. Bot. Soc. America, Am. Soc. Plant Physiologists, Southeastern Biologists, S.C. Acad. Science (pres. 1928-29), Sigma Xi. Republican. Baptist. Author of "Vascular Plants of Horry Country, S.C." Club: Kiwanis. Home: 113 Tindal Av., Greenville, S.C. Died Dec. 18, 1944.

IVEY, Alphonso Lynn (ī'vē), lawyer; b. Warren County, Ga., 1884; B.S., U. of Ga., 1908; LL.B., Columbia, 1915. Was asst. to solicitor gen. Atlanta Jud. Circuit; later practiced law in Richmond, Va.; pres. and dir. Va.-Carolina Chem. Corp. of Richmond. Home: 2222 Lake View Av., Richmond 20. Office: 401 E. Main St., Richmond 8, Va. Died Aug. 18, 1949.

IVIE, Joseph Henry, clergyman; B.A., St. Stephen's Coll., Annandale, N.Y., 1892; grad. Phila. Div. Sch., 1894. Deacon, P.E. Ch., 1894, priest, 1896; rector St. Joseph's Ch., Queens, L.I., 1894-97, Trinity Ch., Fishkill, N.Y., 1897-08, St. Bartholomew's Chapel, N.Y. City, 1908-10, St. Andrew's Ch., since since 1910. Address: 2 W. 129th St., New York. Died July 21, 1942.

J

JACK, William Blake, supt. schools; b. Portland, Me., Nov. 16, 1877; s. Charles Lewis and Eliza Andrews (Burgess) J.; A.B., Colby Coll., Waterville, Me., 1900, L.H.D., 1927; studied Columbia, summers 1912, 14, 22, 23, 24; unmarried. Sec. U.S. Consulate, Budapest, Hungary, 1900; prin. elementary sch., Wales, Mass., 1901-02; teacher of history, high sch., Portland, 1902-11, prin., 1911-22; supt. schs., Portland, since 1922. Trustee Colby Coll., Waterville, Me., since 1938. Mem. N.E.A. (dir. since 1927), Me. Teachers Assn. (pres. 1917), New England Assn. of Sch. Supts. (pres. 1929), Delta Upsilon. Republican. Conglist. Clubs: Rotary, Portland Fraternity, Economic, Torch. Home: 29 Eastern Promenade. Office: City Hall, Portland, Me. Died Jan. 8, 1943.

JACKSON, Carl Newell, univ. prof.; b. East Saugus, Mass., Oct. 23, 1875; s. Samuel and Sarah Morrill (Davis) J.; student Boston (Mass.) Latin Sch., 1888-94; A.B., Harvard U., 1898; A.M., Harvard U. Grad. Sch., 1899, Ph.D., 1901. Instr. St. Paul's Sch., Concord, N.H., 1902-05; instr. Greek, Harvard U., 1905-07, instr. Greek and Latin, 1907-10, asst. prof., 1910-20, asso. prof., 1920-25, prof., 1925-37, Eliot prof. of Greek lit., 1937-43, Eliot prof., emeritus since 1943. Mem. Am. Acad. Arts and Sciences. Home: Snowville, N.H. Died Oct. 14, 1946.

JACKSON, Clarence Martin, anatomist; b. What Cheer, Ia., Apr. 12, 1875; s. John Calvin and Adeline (Hartman) J.; B.S., U. of Mo., 1898, M.S., 1899, M.D., 1900, LL.D., 1923; grad. student, U. of Chicago, 1900-01, U. of Leipzig, 1903-04; U. of Berlin, 1904; m. Helen Clarahan, June 1898; children—Margaret, Helen, Dorothy, Mary. Instr. anatomy, 1899-1900, asst. prof. anatomy and histology, 1900-02, prof., 1902-13, jr. dean faculty of medicine, 1906-09, dean, 1909-13, U. of Mo.; prof. and dir. of dept. of anatomy, 1913-41, professor emeritus of anatomy since 1941, acting dean of the Graduate School, 1917-18, U. of Minn. Chmn. med. div. National Research Council, Washington, D.C., 1923-24. Fellow A.A.A.S.; mem. Am. Assn. of Anatomists (pres. 1922-24), Anatomische Gesellschaft, A.M.A., Phi Beta Kappa, Sigma Xi, Alpha Omega Alpha. Editor of Morris's Human Anatomy. Author: Effects of Inanition and Malnutrition upon Growth and Structure. Contbr. scientific jours. Home: 436 Harvard St., S.E., Minneapolis, Minn. Died Jan. 17, 1947.

JACKSON, Dunham, prof. mathematics; b. Bridgewater, Mass., July 24, 1888; s. William Dunham and Mary Vose (Morse) J.; A.B., Harvard, 1908, A.M., 1909; studied univs. of Göttingen and Bonn, 1909-11; Ph.D., Göttingen, 1911; m. Harriet Spratt Hulley, June 20, 1918; children—Anne Hulley, Mary Eloise. Instr. in mathematics, Harvard, 1911-16, asst. prof., 1916-19; prof. mathematics, U. of Minn., since 1919. Capt. Ordnance Dept., U.S. Army, at Washington, D.C., Nov. 1918-Aug. 1919. Fellow Am. Acad. Arts and Sciences, Am. Phys. Soc., A.A.A.S. (v.p. 1927, sec. 1941-44, Sect. A); mem. Am. Math. Soc. (v.p. 1921), Math. Assn. America (pres. 1926), Nat. Acad. Sciences, Phi Beta Kappa, Sigma Xi. Author: The Theory of Approximation, 1930; Fourier Series and Orthogonal Polynomials, 1941. Editor Trans. Am. Math. Soc., 1926-31. Contbr. to math jours. Home: 707 Essex St. S.E., Minneapolis 14, Minn. Died Nov. 6, 1946.

JACKSON, Edward, surgeon; b. West Goshen, Chester County, Pa., Mar. 30, 1856; s. Halliday and Emily (Hoopes) J.; grad. engring., at Union Coll., N.Y., 1874, A.M., 1878; M.D., U. of Pa., 1878; m. Jennie L. Price, 1878; m. 2d, Emily Churchman, 1898; children—Ethel, Robert P. (dec.), Thomas H., Herbert C. (dec.), Edward (dec.), Helen (dec.). Practiced West Chester, 1878-84, Phila., 1884-94, 1896-98; prof. diseases of eye, Phila. Polyclinic, 1888-94 and 1896-98; surgeon to Wills Eye Hosp., Phila., 1890-94 and 1896-98; practiced Denver, 1894-96, and since 1898; prof. ophthalmology, Univ. of Colo., 1905-21. Pres. Am. Bd. for Ophthalmic Examinations, 1916-17; pres. Colo. Commn. for the Blind, 1925. Am. Editor Ophthalmic Rev. (London), 1890-1915; editor Am. Jour. Ophthalmology, 1918-28. Author: Essentials of Diseases of the Eye, 1890; Skiascopy, 1895; Manual of Diseases of the Eye, 1900; Ophthalmic Year Book, 1904-17. Home: 700 Madison St. Office: Republic Bldg., Denver, Colo. Died Oct. 29, 1942.

JACKSON, Frederic Ellis, architect; b. Tarrytown, N.Y., Apr. 14, 1879; s. Frederick Harvey and Anne Blanchard (Ellis) J.; B.Arch., Cornell U., 1900, grad. student, 1901; Diplomé par le Gouvernement, l'ecole des Beaux Arts, Paris, 1909; m. Eliza Greenough Fiske, June 1, 1904 (died May 2, 1935); children—Elise Greenough (Mrs. Charles Richard Steedman), Anne Blanchard (wife of Lt. Comdr. Arthur Watson Cocroft, U.S.N.R.); m. 2d, Marianne Learned Olcott Henry, Apr. 3, 1943. Mem. firm Hilton & Jackson, architects, 1902-11, Jackson, Robertson & Adams, Providence, R.I., since 1912; instr. architecture R.I. Sch. of Design, Providence, 1912-13. Architectural works of office include: R.I. State Office Bldg., Providence County Court House, Myron Taylor Hall at Cornell U., administrn. bldg. and library, R.I. State Coll., College St. Bldg., R.I. Sch. of Design, Burrilville Town Project, R.I. Nat. Guard Hangar, Hillsgrove, R.I.; World War I Memorial, Cornell Univ. (with Charles Z. Klauder). Served with Battery A, Light Field Arty., R.I.N.G., 1910-13; capt. liaison service, U.S. Army, 1918-19. Mem. corporation R.I. Hosp., Butler Hosp., Lying-in Hosp. (Providence), Providence Dist. Nursing Assn., St. Mary's Home for Children, R.I. Hosp., Peoples Savings Bank, Providence Inst. for Savings, R.I. Sch. of Design, Coll. of Architecture Council, Cornell U., since 1940. Mem. ednl. advisory com. architecture, R.I. Sch. of Design, since 1930; vice chmn. zoning bd. of review, Providence, 1923-26. Chmn. adv. bd. Providence City Planning Commn., 1931-44; architectual adviser R.I. Home Owners Loan Corp., 1934-41; member adv. com. Met. Homes Registration Office, State Council of Defense, 1943-44; chmn. property maintenance com. Community Fund since 1941; chmn. program com. Providence Postwar Planning, 1943-44; mem. bipartisan state com. on coordination and execution of postwar planning, 1943-46; state agent R.I. chapter France Forever since 1946. Member Providence com. N.Y. Museum Modern Art since 1937. Regional dir. Cornell Alumni Assn., 1938-44; exec. com., 1942-44. Mem. nat. adv. com. N.Y. World's Fair, 1939. Trustee The Annmay Brown Memorial since 1941. Fellow A.I.A. (v.p. R.I. chapter, 1919-21, pres. 1921-23, 1935-37); dir. A.I.A. 1925-28; mem. jury of fellows 1937-41; member committee on National Capital since 1943; associate member National Academy of Design; mem. Kappa Alpha. Ind. Republican. Episcopalian. Clubs: Agawam Hunt, Art, Hope, University (Providence); Century, Cornell (New York); Edgartown Yacht (Edgartown, Mass.). Recipient silver medal 5th Congress of Pan-Am. Architects, 1940; Roger award, Providence, 1944. Home: 244 Irving Av., Providence 6. Office: Turks Head Bldg., Providence 3, R.I.* Died Feb. 9, 1950.

JACKSON, James Hathaway, physician; b. Peterboro, N.Y., June 11, 1841; s. James Caleb and Lucretia (Brewster) J.; M.D., Bellevue Hosp. Med. Coll. (New York U.), 1876; m. Katharine Johnson, Sept. 13, 1864. Business mgr. Health Instn., "Our Home on the Hillside", Danxville, N.Y., 1861-82; physician in charge Jackson Health Resort, Dansville, N.Y., 1882-1916. Address: Dansville, N.Y. Died Feb. 18, 1928.

JACKSON, Jesse Benjamin, consular service; born Paulding, O., Nov. 19, 1871; s. Andrew Carl and Lucy Ann (Brown) J.; ed. pub. schs.; m. Rosebelle Berryman, June 22, 1898 (died Jan. 11, 1928); 1 son, Virgil Allen; m. 2d, Mrs. Mary Ann Hinton, Sept. 7, 1935. Enrolling clerk, Ohio House of Reps., 1900-01; engaged in real estate and other lines of business until 1905; consul at Alexandretta, Syria, 1905-08, Aleppo, Syria, 1908-23, Leghorn, Italy, 1923-28, Fort William-Port Arthur, Canada, 1928-35; retired after 30 years' service, June 30, 1935. Active in protection of Christians in Turkey during and after World War I, and rep. all allied and neutral countries. Served in Ohio Vol. Inf., Spanish-Am. War, 1898-99. Decorated Officer of Order of Crown of Italy, 1922. Republican. Methodist. Mason. Home: 1030 Parkway Drive, Grandview, Columbus, O Died Dec. 4, 1947.

JACKSON, John Long, bishop; b. Baltimore, Md., Mar. 28, 1884; s. Edward Thornton and Helen Mary (Long) J.; A.B., Johns Hopkins U., 1905; student Virginia Theol. Sem., 1905-08, D.D., 1940; D.D., U. of the South, 1940; m. Elizabeth Eleanor Crawford, June 18, 1913; 1 daughter, Eleanor Pendleton (Mrs. John Ely Burleson). Ordained priest Protestant Episcopal Church, June 4, 1909; asst. rector Trinity Ch., Towson, Md., 1908, St. Paul's Ch., Baltimore, 1909; rector Emmanuel Ch., Harrisonburg, Va., 1910-14, St. Martin's Ch., Charlotte, N.C., 1914-40; bishop of Louisiana since May 1, 1940. Trustee U. of the South. Mem. Phi Gamma Delta. Clubs: Kiwanis (Charlotte and New Orleans); Boston (New Orleans). Home: 2136 Prytania St., New Orleans. Died Sept. 2, 1948.

JACKSON, Joseph (Francis Ambrose), editor, author; b. Phila., Pa., May 20, 1867; s. Samuel and Barbara Marie (Dougherty) J.; student Spring Garden Inst., Phila., 1882-85, Pa. Acad. Fine Arts, 1887-88; m. Harriet Holmes Fletcher, Feb. 1, 1915. Art editor Phila. Public Ledger, 1888-1902, news editor, 1904, feature writer, 1905-18; columnist Evening Ledger, 1914 and 1940-41; editor Building, 1922-25, Building Arts, 1925-26; editor and pub. Philadelphia Year Book, 1919-20; editor The Pennsylvania Architect since 1938. Mem. Phila. Building Congress. Hon. asso. Am. Inst. Architects; mem. Am. Hist. Assn., Hist. Soc. of Pa., Dickens Fellowship, Phila. City Hist. Soc. Author: Dickens in Philadelphia, 1912; Early Philadelphia Architects and Engineers, 1923; American Colonial Architecture, 1924; Development of American Architecture, 1926; America's Most Historic Highway, Market Street, Philadelphia, 2d edit., 1926; encyclopedia of Philadelphia, 4 vols., 1931-33; See Philadelphia, 1937 and 1940; Literary Landmarks of Philadelphia, 1939; also brochures, many contbns. on history of Phila., and articles in mags. Home: 113 S. 43d St. Address: 627 Weightman Bldg., Philadelphia, Pa. Died Mar. 4, 1946.

JACKSON, Joseph Henry, editor; b. Madison, N.J., July 21, 1894; s. Herbert Hallett and Marion Agnes (Brown) J.; prep. edn., Peddie Sch., Hightstown, N.J.; student Lafayette Coll., 1915-17; m. Charlotte E. Cobden, June 21, 1923; 1 dau., Marion Louise. Asso. editor Sunset Mag., 1920-23, mng. editor, 1924-26, editor, 1926-28; lit. editor San Francisco Argonaut, 1929-30, San Francisco Chronicle since 1930; broadcaster of "Bookman's Guide," over Nat. Broadcasting Co., Pacific Coast network, 1924-43. Served with Ambulance Corps, U.S. Army, 1917-18; 2d lt. inf., U.S. Army, 1918-19. Member Phi Kappa Psi. Democrat. Presbyterian. Clubs: Bohemian (San Francisco); Players (N.Y.). Author: Mexican Interlude, 1936; Notes on a Drum, 1937; Tintypes in Gold, 1939; Extra! Extra! (with Scott Newhall), 1940; Anybody's Gold, 1941. Editor: Tales of Soldiers and Civilians, 1944; Continent's End, 1944. Contbr. to newspapers, mags., revs. Mem. bd. of judges O. Henry Memorial Award, 1935 and 1942. Died July 15, 1955; buried in Oakland, Calif.

JACKSON, Josephine Agnes, physician, psychiatrist; b. Hancock County, Ill., Feb. 11, 1865; d. Luke and Mary Agnes (Brookings) Jackson; M.D., Northwestern U. Women's Med. Sch., 1896, Rush Med. Sch., U. of Chicago, 1903; unmarried; 1 dau. (adopted), Elizabeth Jackson Gregory (Mrs. Oscar Elton Sette). Interne Cook County Hosp., Chicago, 1896-97, mem. attending staff, 1898-1904; examiner N.Y. Life Ins. Co., Chicago, 1898-1904; instr. (extra-mural) in phys. diagnosis, Rush Med. Sch., 1900-04; moved to Pasadena, Calif., 1904, and engaged in coaching doctors for State Med. Bd. Examination, 1906-10; specialist in treatment of psychoneuroses, since 1910; now retired. Mem. A.M.A., Calif. State Med. Soc., Los Angeles Co. Med. Soc., Am. Medical Women's Assn. Methodist. Co-author: (with Helen M. Salisbury) Outwitting Our Nerves, 1921, 2d edit., rev. and enlarged by Dr. Jackson, 1932. Author: Guiding Your Life, 1937; also author daily syndicated column, "Outwitting Your Nerves," 1927-29. Died Dec. 31, 1945.

JACKSON, Robert Tracy, paleontologist; b. Dorchester, Mass., July 13, 1861; S. Dr. John Barnard Swett and Emily Jane (Andrews) J.; S.B., Lawrence Scientific Sch. (Harvard), 1884; Sc.D., Harvard, 1889; m. Fanny Esther Roberts, June 27, 1889; children—Esther, Dorothy Quincy (Mrs. John E. Bastille). Instr. paleontology, Harvard, 1892-99, asst. prof., 1899-1909; asso. in paleontology, Museum of Comparative Zoology, Harvard, 1911-16; curator of fossil echinoderms, Museum of Comparative Zoology, 1928-39. Fellow Am. Acad. Arts and Sciences, A.A.A.S.; mem. Am. Soc. Naturalists, Geol. Soc. America. Author: Phyolgeny of the Pelecypoda, 1890; Studies of Melonites Multiporus (with T. A. Jaggar.

Jr.), 1896; Studies of Palæchinoidea, 1896; Localized Stages in Development in Plants and Animals, 1899; Phylogeny of the Echini, 1912; Studies of Arbacia, 1927; Palæozoic Echini of Belgium, 1929; The Status of Bothriocidaris, 1929. Address: Peterborough, N.H. Died Oct. 24, 1948.

JACKSON, Samuel Morley, banker; b. Billericay, Essex County, Eng., June 21, 1864; s. George and Emma (Allen) J.; ed. Framlingham Coll., Suffolk, Eng.; m. Marie Williams, June 4, 1894; children—Marie Louise, Robert M., Emory A. Came to U.S., 1882, naturalized, 1898. Began as clk., with London & San Francisco Bank, June 1880; with Nat. Bank of Washington (Tacoma) since 1920; chmn. bd. since 1930. Pres. Tacoma Gen. Hosp., 1912-44; retired. Republican. Episcopalian. Clubs: University, Union, Tacoma Country and Golf. Home: Hickey Apts. Office: 12th St. and Pacific Av., Tacoma, Wash. Died May 26, 1945.

JACKSON, William Henry, photographer, artist, explorer; b. Keeseville, N.Y., Apr. 4, 1843; s. George Hallock and Harriet Maria (Allen) J.; ed. country school, Peru, N.Y., and public schools of Phila., Pa., and Troy, N.Y., 1850-58; m. Mary Greer, Apr. 10, 1869; 1 dau., Gracie (dec.); m. 2d, Emilie Painter, Oct. 4, 1873; children—Clarence S., Louise P. (Mrs. Kenneth McLeod), Harriet M. (Mrs. Myron Pattison). Began as photographer, Troy, N.Y., 1858; in photograph galleries, Rutland and Burlington, Vt., 1860-66 (except year with Vt. regt. in Civil War); traveled overland to Calif., 1866-67, returning to Omaha, Neb.; in photograph business, Omaha, 1868-70; official photographer U.S. Geol. Survey (Hayden Survey of Territories), 1870-78; first to take photographs in Yellowstone region; in business as W. H. Jackson Photograph and Publishing Co., Denver, Colo., 1879-97 (except photographing around the world for Harper's Weekly, 1894-96); with Detroit (Mich.) Pub. Co., 1898-1924; retired from business, 1924, moved to Washington, D.C., and began painting and writing about "Covered Wagon Days of the West"; research sec. Ore. Trail Memorial Assn., New York, since 1929. Awarded gold medal for distinguished service to Colo. and the West, by U. of Colo., 1937; also numerous medals and awards from photographic socs. Enlisted with Co. K, 12th Vt. Inf., Aug. 1862. Mem. G.A.R., Colo. Hist. Soc., N.M. Hist. Soc., Royal Photographic Soc. (London), East Orange (N.J.) Camera Club, Oregon Trail Memorial Assn. Mason. Clubs: Cosmos (Washington, D.C.); Explorers and Adventurers (New York); Colorado Mountain (Denver); Appalachian Mountain (Brattleboro, Vt.); American Alpine (New York, N.Y.). Author: The Pioneer Photographer—Rocky Mountain Adventures with a Camera (with H. R. Driggs), 1929; Time Exposure, an autobiography, 1940; also author of several descriptive catalogues of photographs of U.S. Geol. Survey of Territories and contbr. to govt. reports; contbr. to Colorado Mag. Illustrator: Oregan Trail, 1931; The Pony Express Goes Through, 1935. Home: Hotel Latham, 4 E. 28th St., New York, N.Y. Died June 30, 1942.

JACKSON, William Kenneth, lawyer; b. Denver, Tenn., Nov. 18, 1886; s. William Kendrick and Medora Elizabeth (Montgomery) J.; A.B., U. of Fla., 1904; LL.B., University of Virginia, 1908; LL.D., Univ. of Florida, 1946; married Katharine Mitchell, September 9, 1916; children—Danforth, Katharine Jackson Bass, Richard Montgomery, Joan Jackson Mason, Alexander. Recording clerk, Florida House of Representatives, 1905; admitted to Florida bar, 1908, and practiced in Jacksonville; assistant prosecuting attorney Canal Zone, and asst. attorney. Isthmian Canal Commn. and Panama R.R. Co., Panama 1909-10; pros. atty., Canal Zone, 1910-14; U.S. atty., Dist. of Canal Zone, 1914-15; v.p., gen. counsel and dir. United Fruit Co., 1922-47; pres. U.S. Chamber Commerce, 1946-47; pres. Boston Chamber of Commerce 1945-46. Mem. Goethals Meml. Commn. Trustee World Peace Found. Mem. U.S. Sect., Inter-Am. Council Commerce and Prodn., Council of U.S. Assos.; Internat. C. of C.; dir. National Foreign Trade Council. Captain, Chemical Warfare Service, U.S. Army during World War I. Mem. Am. Bar Assn., Am. Soc. Internat. Law, Fgn. Law Assn. Democrat. Home: Stonewall Farm, Dublin, N.H. Office: 1 Federal St., Boston. Died Nov. 24, 1947.

JACKSON, William Payne, army officer; b. Palmyra, Mo., Jan. 9, 1868; s. William J. and Russella (Bright) J.; grad. U.S. Mil. Acad., 1891; grad. Sch. of Electricity and Mining, Willet's Pt., N.Y., 1895; grad. General Staff Sch., Ft. Leavenworth, Kan., 1920; m. Julia Crosby Carr, Oct. 20, 1903; 1 dau., Margaret Carr. Commd. 2d lt. inf., June 12, 1891; promoted through grades to brig. gen., May 15, 1926; col., later brig. gen. N.A., Aug. 5, 1917-Aug. 15, 1919. With U.S. Internat. Boundary Commn., 1892-93; aide on staff Maj. Gen. J. Ford Kent, Santiago Campaign, Spanish-Am. War, 1898; in Philippines, 1899-1902, Alaska, 1902-04; again in Philippines, 1909-12; insp. gen., Washington, D.C., 1913-17; Mexican border duty, 1917; organized and trained 368th Inf., 92d Div., and took regt. to France, June 1918; in comd. 74th Brigade, 37th Div.; served in Argonne, St. Mihiel and Ypres-Lys campaigns; in comd. Forwarding Camp, Le Mans, Mar.-June 1919; General Staff, 1921-25; comd. 1st Arty. Dist., Boston, 1926-29; comd. 1st Inf. Brig., 1929-31; retired Jan. 31, 1932; maj. gen., retired, July 9, 1942. Decorated D.S.M. (United States); silver citation Santiago and Philippine Island service; Missouri Distinguished Citizen medal; decorated Croix de Guerre (Belgium); Officer Legion of Honor (French). Clubs: Army and Navy (Washington); Army and Navy (San Francisco); Columbus (Columbus, O.). Home: 1487 Greenwich St., San Francisco, Calif. Died Jan. 13, 1945.

JACOBS, William Plummer, publisher; b. at Clinton, S.C., Aug. 18, 1893; s. James Ferdinand and Mary Elliott (Duckett) J.; student Davidson Coll., 1910-11; A.B., Presbyterian College, 1914; LL.D., Southwestern, 1938, LL.D., 1945; m. Edna Cornelia Shockley, Oct. 25, 1916; children—William Plummer, Hugh Shockley. Pres. Presbyn. Coll., Clinton, 1935-45; chmn. bd. since 1946; pres. Jacobs Press, Clinton, Jacobs Sports Mags., Inc.; propr., Carolina Pharm. Co., Ante-Fermen Co.; founder, 1924, Clinton Bldg. & Loan Assn. Dem. presdl. elector from S.C.; 1936. Chmn. S.C. Council for Nat. Defense. Consultant Quartermaster Corps, U.S. Army, 1942-44; hearings officers National War Labor Board, 1944; member Physical Fitness Council, Federal Security Agency; chmn. Commn. on Physical Fitness in Industry, 1943-44. Donor of Jacobs Interference Trophies (football); founder Tennis Clinics, U.S. Lawn Tennis Assn.; formerly southern vice pres., U.S. Lawn Tennis Assn.; former pres. Southern Lawn Tennis Assn. Exec. dir. Print Cloth Group of Cotton Mfrs.; pres. and treas. American Cotton Mfrs. Assn., Charlotte, N.C.; member executive com. Cotton Textile Institute, spinners del. National Cotton Council; mem. Clinton (S.C.) Chamber of Commerce, Pi Kappa Phi, Phi Psi (hon. mem.), Omicron Delta Kappa, Blue Key. Democrat. Presbyterian (elder First Church). Mason. Clubs: Lakeside; Poinsett (Greenville, S.C.); West Side Tennis (L.I.): Biltmore (N.C.) Forest Country; Congressional Country (Md.). Author: Problems of the Cotton Manufacturer, 1932; The Pioneer, 1935; Tennis, Builder of Citizenship, 1940. Pub.: American Lawn Tennis, Aim, Sportfolio. Home: Clinton, S.C.; also Charlotte, N.C. Died July 25, 1948.

JACOBSON, Carl Frederick, vice-pres. Welch & Co.; b. San Francisco, Calif., Sept. 16, 1877; s. Charles and Johanna (Esborn) J.; ed. high school; m. Ella May Lewis, Jan. 1, 1901; children—Gladys Tremain, Harvey Lewis, Lauris Carlton. In import and export business with father, 1896-1900; dep. county clerk, City and County of San Francisco, 1900-02; with Am. Trust Co., San Francisco, 1902-04; with San Francisco reps. of Hawaiian and Philippine sugar factors, plantations and centrals since 1904; v.p. Welch & Co. since 1934; pres. Honolulu Plantation Co.; dir., treas., sec. Hutchinson Sugar Plantation Co., Paauhau Sugar Plantation Co.; sec. and trustee Calamba Sugar Estate (Philippine Sugar Central); sec. Hakalau Plantation Co., Kilauea Sugar Plantation Co.; Am. Rubber Co. (Philippine Rubber Producers), Pacific Farms Co.; vice pres. Philippine-Am. Chamber of Commerce. Republican. Presbyterian. Mason (Scottish Rite, Shrine), Odd Fellow. Clubs: Commonwealth (San Francisco). Home: 238 Irving St., San Mateo, Calif. Office: No. 2 Pine St., San Francisco, Calif. Died Sep. 8, 1946.

JACOBSON, Gabe, lawyer; b. Meridian, Miss., June 16, 1875; s. Julius and Bertha (Schulherr) J.; B.Sc., Miss. State Coll., 1894; LL.B., U. of Miss., 1902; unmarried. Admitted to Miss. bar, 1902, and in practice of law in State and U.S. Courts and in adminstrn. proceedings and hearings; sr. mem. Jacobson, Snow & Covington, Meridian, Mississippi, 1940; now practicing law alone in Meridian; vice-president Stonewall (Mississippi) Cotton Mills since 1936. U.S. Referee in bankruptcy, Meridian, 1910-13; former department inspector U.S. War Vets. of Mississippi. Served as 1st lt., 1st Miss. Vol. Inf., Spanish-Am. War, 1898. Former mem. Board of State Bar Examiners; mem. Miss. State Bar Assn. (pres. 1920-21), Am. Bar Assn., Rotary Internat. (past pres. Meridian Club), Phi Delta Theta. Democrat. Jewish religion. Mason (33°). Contbr. to Comml. Law Jour. and Miss. Law Jour. Home: Lamar Hotel. Office: Threefoot Bldg., Meridian, Miss. Died Aug. 9, 1944.

JAEKEL, Frederic Blair (yā'kĕl), author; b. Hollidaysburg, Pa., May 6, 1882; s. Frederick and Cora A. (Blair) J.; student Lafayette Coll., 1899-1901; B.S., Bucknell U., 1903; m. Edith Overholt McCain, Nov. 7, 1906; children—Virginia Overholt, Frederic Blair (dec.). On staff Phila. North American, 1906-07; spl. corr. Phila. Press at coronation of King George V and Queen Mary, June, 1911; spl. rep. Travel Magazine, in Holland, 1911, in Panama and Costa Rica, 1912; dramatic editor Evening Telegraph, Phila., 1917-18; editor, Bucks County Daily News, Doylestown, Pa., 1921-24; editor Camden (N.J.) Post Telegram, 1924-25; now v.p. Osmond-Laurens, Inc. Presbyterian. Fellow Royal Geog. Soc. Eng.; mem. Phi Gamma Delta, etc. Clubs: Phi Gamma Delta (New York); University, Art Alliance, and Plays and Players (Philadelphia); Country Club (Doylestown, Pa.); Nat. Press (Washington, D.C.); Authors' (London). Author: The Lands of the Tamed Turk, 1910; Windmills and Wooden Shoes, 1912; Planning a Trip Abroad, 1912. Home: Glen Echo Farm, Doylestown, Pa. Office: 1700 Walnut St., Philadelphia, Pa. Died Feb. 9, 1943.

JAMES, Alexander, artist; b. Cambridge, Mass., Dec. 22, 1890; s. William and Alice Howe (Gibbens) J.; studied painting under Abbott H. Thayer, Dublin, N.H., and Frank W. Benson, Boston; m. Frederika Paine, Aug. 31, 1916; children—Alexander Robertson, Daniel Frederick, Michael. Figure, portrait and landscape painter since 1916; instr. life drawing Corcoran Sch. Art, Washington, D.C., 1920-21. Represented by paintings in Boston Museum Fine Arts, Fogg Art Museum, Cambridge, Mass., Addison Gallery Am. Art, Andover, Mass., Met. Museum of Art, N.Y. City, Wichita (Kan.) Museum of Art, The William Rockhill Nelson Gallery, Kansas City, Mo., also in Gallery of Science and Art (1940), Internat. Business Machines Corp. Democrat. Protestant. Clubs: Century Assn., Coffee House (N.Y. City); Tavern (Boston). Home: Dublin, N.H. Address: Rehn Galleries, 683 Fifth Av., New York, N.Y. Died Feb. 26, 1946.

JAMES, Eldon Revare, prof. law; b. Newport, Ky., Nov. 21, 1875; s. Thomas and Ella (Tucker) J.; B.S., U. of Cincinnati, 1896, LL.B., 1899; S.J.D., Harvard, 1912; m. Phila W. Smith, Dec. 28, 1904. Practiced in Cincinnati, 1899-1911; instr. and prof. law, Cincinnati Law Sch. (U. of Cincinnati), 1900-12; prof. law, U. of Wis., 1912-13, U. of Minn., 1913-14; dean Law Sch., 1914-18, U. of Mo. Adviser in foreign affairs to Siamese Govt., Feb. 1918-24; judge Supreme Court of Siam, 1919-24; mem., representing Siam, Permanent Arbitral Tribunal of the Hague, 1918-35; prof. of law and librarian, Harvard Law Sch., 1923-42; spl. asst. to U.S. atty. gen., 1942; atty., legal div., Transportation Corps., War Dept., Washington, D.C., 1942-43; law librarian of Congress, 1943-46; law school consultant, Lawyers Cooperative Pub. Co., Rochester, N.Y. since 1946; apptd. M.P. of Siam, 1925. Awarded Grand Cross of Siam, 1921; Grand Cross White Elephant (Siam), 1923. Trustee Cincinnati Bur. Municipal Research, 1909-11; pres. Am. Assn. of Law Libraries, 1934-35. Mem. Am., bar assn., Am. Library Assn., Beta Theta Pi. Club: Cosmos (Washington, D.C.). Home: Edgemoor Rd. Gloucester, Mass. Office: Lawyers Cooperative Pub. Co., Rochester 3, N.Y. Died Jan. 2, 1949.

JAMES, Henry, author and trustee; b. Boston, Mass., 1879; s. William and Alice H. (Gibbens) J.; A.B., Harvard University, 1899, LL.B., 1904; LL.D., Hamilton College, New York, 1932, and Williams College, 1935; married Olivia Cutting, 1917 (divorced); married 2d, Dorothea Draper (Blagden), 1938; practiced law in Boston, Mass., 1904-12; bus. mgr. Rockefeller Inst. for Med. Research, New York, 1912-17; engaged in lit. work, also trustee. Member War Relief Commn. of Rockefeller Foundation, 1914-16; civil and mil. service, Washington, with A.E.F. and at Peace Conf., 1918-19. Overseer Harvard, 1922-28, 1929-35, fellow, 1936-47; trustee Rockefeller Inst. for Med. Research, 1929-47, Carnegie Corp., New York Pub. Library; Am. Academy in Rome, 1924-29, and 1945; chairman board Teachers Insurance and Annuity Association since 1934. Mem. American Acad. Arts and Scienes. Clubs: Century (New York); Union (Boston). Author: Richard Olney, 1923; Charles W. Eliot (Pulitzer prize biography), 1930. Editor: The Letters of William James, 1920. Home: 133 E. 64th St., New York 21. Office: 522 5th Av., New York 18. Died Dec. 13, 1947.

JAMES, Joseph Hidy, chemist; b. Jeffersonville, O., Nov. 3, 1868; s. John A. and Mary J. (Hidy) J.; B.S., Buchtel Coll., Akron, O., 1894; post-grad. work chemistry and physics, Columbia, 1897, chemistry, U. of Pa., 1898-99, Ph.D., 1899; m. Edith Mallison, Nov. 28, 1899; children—Mary Alice, Virginia, Josephine. Asst. chemistry and physics, Buchtel Coll., 1894-97; chief chemist Lake Superior Power Co., Sault Ste. Marie, 1899-1902; asst. prof. textile chemistry, Clemson (S.C.) Coll., 1902-05; asst. prof. tech. chemistry, 1905-06, asst. prof. chem. practice in charge dept. of chemistry, 1906-07, asso. prof., 1907-08, prof. chemistry from 1908 until retired, Carngeie Inst. Tech., Pittsburgh. Research and patents on acetylene storage and on oxidation products of petroleum. Mem. Am. Chem. Soc., Am. Inst. Chem. Engrs. Home: 5868 Douglas Av., Pittsburgh. Died Feb. 12, 1948.

JAMES, W. Frank, ex-congressman; b. Morristown, N.J., May 23, 1873; s. William F. and Elizabeth A. (Williams) J.; student Albion (Mich.) Coll., 1890-91; m. Jennie M. Mingay, Mar. 18, 1904; children—Anne, Frank, Newell, Jean. Treas. Houghton County, Mich., 1900-04; mayor of Hancock, 1908-09; mem. Mich. Senate, 1910-14; mem. 64th to 73d Congresses (1915-25), 12th Mich. Dist. Republican. Pvt. Co. F, 34th Mich. Regt., Spanish-Am. War. Mem. Spanish War Vets., Soc. of Santiago. Mason (32°). Home: Hancock, Mich. Died Nov. 17, 1945.

JAMES, Walter Gilbert, univ. prof.; b. Raritan, Ill., Jan. 29, 1880; s. Stephen Price and Martha Elizabeth (Lynch) J.; student Hedding Coll., Abingdon, Ill., 1898-1902; A.B., Ill. Wesleyan U., 1903; student Northwestern U. Sch. of Oratory, 1904; A.M., Northwestern U., 1907; Ph.D., Highland (Kan.) U., 1913; m. Cora B. Smith, Nov. 27, 1907; 1 son, Edwin S. Prof. public speaking, Upper Ia. U., 1905-06; prof. English and pub. speaking, Bellevue (Neb.) Coll., 1908-09; same, Highland Coll., 1910-14, pres. 1914-19; dean U. of Omaha since 1919, acting pres., 1930-31, head of English dept. since 1931, dean Sch. of Fine Arts and head dept. of speech, 1933-43, prof. emeritus since 1943. Mem. Tau Kappa Epsilon, Sigma Tau Delta. Mason. Home: 1302 S. 63d St., Omaha, Neb. Died Jan. 28, 1948.

JAMES, Warren William, judge; b. Jefferson, N.H., Mar. 23, 1884; s. William Gray and Ida Eldora (Holmes) J.; A.B., Bates Coll., 1906; student Boston U. Law School, 1908-10; m. Ethel Vivian Laughton, Oct. 13, 1911; 1 dau., Catherine Frances. Prin. Hartland Acad., Hartland, Me., 1906-08; admitted to N.H. bar, 1911; engaged in gen. practice of law in Berlin, 1911 to 1933; city solicitor Berlin, N.H., 1915-19, also 1931; solicitor for Coos County, N.H., 1919-23; asso. justice Superior Court of N.H. since 1933. Served as mem. N.H. Crime

Commn., 1925; chmn. Rep. City Com., Berlin, N.H., 1926 and 1932. Trustee Bates Coll. since 1935, chmn. board of overseers since 1937. Mem. Am. Bar. Assn., N.H. Bar Assn., College Club (Bates), Phi Delta Phi. Republican. Methodist. Mason (K.T.). Club: Rotary (Berlin). Home: 573 Second Av.. Berlin, N.H. Died Mar. 11, 1945; buried in Jefferson Hill Cemetery, Jefferson, N.H.

JAMES, Will(iam Roderick), author, artist; b. nr. Great Falls, Mont., June 6, 1892; s. William J.; no school edn.; left an orphan, adopted by fur trapper, and taught by him to write. Went to work with cow and horse outfits at 13; continued on western and Canadian ranges, also engaged in capture of wild horses in Nevada and took part in rodeos; mem. Mounted Scouts, U.S. Army, Camp Kearney, Calif., World War. Owner of 12,000 acre ranch. Author: Cowboys, North and South, 1924; The Drifting Cowboy, 1925; Smoky, 1926; Cow Country, 1927; Sand, 1929; Lone Cowboy, 1930; Sun-Up (short stories), 1931; Big-Enough, 1931; All in The Day's Riding (short stories), 1932; The Three Mustangeers, 1933; In the Saddle with Uncle Bill, 1935; Home Ranch, 1935; Uncle Bill, 1934; Young Cowboy, 1935; Scorpion (major book) 1936; Cowboy in the Making, 1937; Look-See, with Uncle Bill, 1938; Flint-Spears, 1938; The Dark Horse, 1939; Horses I've Known, 1939; My First Horse, 1939. Contbr. short stories and articles to leading periodicals since 1926. Lone Cowboy was filmed, 1933, Smoky, 1934. Illustrates his own books. Lone Cowboy was adopted by Book-of-the-Month Club, 1930, Smoky by Tex. State Textbook Commn., 1935. Awarded Newberry medal for Smoky. Home: Billings, Mont. Address: care Charles Scribner's Sons, 597 Fifth Av., New York, N.Y. Died Sep. 3, 1942.

JAMESON, Edwin Cornell, lawyer; m. Mary B. Gardner. Admitted to N.Y. bar; pres. Nat. Fire & Marine Ins. Co. of N.J., Hamilton Fire Ins. Co.; dir. Globe & Rutgers Fire Ins. Co., Am. Smelting & Refining Co., Hamilton Fire Ins. Co., Am. Home Fire Assurance Co., Pacific Fire Ins. Co., Remington Rand, Inc. Trustee Rutgers U. Mem. Soc. Colonial Wars, St. Nicholas Soc. Club: Down Town. Office: 25 Cliff St., New York, N.Y. Died Sep. 3, 1945.

JAMIESON, Robert Cary, dermatologist; b. Detroit, Mich., Sept. 18, 1881; s. Robert Andrus and Emma Louise (Thompson) J.; M.D., Detroit Coll. of Medicine and Surgery (now Wayne U.), 1903; post-graduate work, U. of Vienna, 1905-06; m. Carolyn Poppleton, June 16, 1909. Practiced in Detroit, 1903-08; on staff of Harper Hosp. since 1908; attending dermatologist Receiving Hosp. since 1916; cons. Herman Kiefer Hosp. since 1918; prof. and head dept. of dermatology, Wayne U., since 1922. Mem. Am. Med. Assn., Am. Dermatol. Assn., Am. Acad. of Dermatology, Mich. State Med. Soc., Wayne County Med. Soc. (past pres.), Phi Rho Sigma, Alpha Omega Alpha. Republican. Episcopalian. Clubs: Athletic, Bloomfield Hills Country. Home: Hotel Lenox. Office: David Whitney Bldg., Detroit, Mich. Died Apr. 24, 1946.

JAMIESON, W(illiam) D., ex-congressman; b. near Wapello, Ia., Nov. 9, 1873; s. Ira and Mary J. (Gillis) J.; ed. State U. of Ia.; LL.B., Nat. U.; m. Rena E. Moore, Aug. 1, 1936. Learned printer's trade in father's office; editor Ida Grove (Ia.) Pioneer, 1893-94, Columbus Junction (Ia.) Gazette, 1899-1901, Shenandoah (Ia.) World, 1901-16. Member Iowa Senate, 1907-11, resigned March 3, 1909; member 61st Congress (1909-11), 8th Iowa District; postmaster, Shenandoah, Ia., 1915-16. Asst. treas. Dem. Nat. Com., 1916; dir. and asst. treas. Permanent Orgn. of Dem. Nat. Com., 1917-19; dir. of finance, Dem. Nat. Com., 1919-20; now in practice of law. Editor of Window Seat, Washington, D.C., (a weekly Washington Nat. column for country papers). Mason (33°), also member Elks. Clubs: Press (Washington, D.C.). Home: The Cavalier, 3500 14th St., N.W., Washington 10. Office: Southern Bldg., Washington 5, D.C. Died Nov. 18, 1949.

JAMISON, Atha Thomas, child welfare; b. Murfreesboro, Tenn., Mar. 5, 1866; s. Robert David and Camilla (Patterson) J.; prep. edn., high sch. of Union U., Murfreesboro; partial course, Southern Baptist Theol. Sem.; D.D., Furman University, 1913; D.H.L., University of South Carolina, 1942; m. Emma C. Caldwell, 1889 (died 1900); m. 2d, Mrs. Margaret W. Caldwell, 1904; 1 dau., Sarah Caldwell (Mrs. Joel S. Bailey). Ordained Bapt. ministry, 1895; gen. sec. Y.M.C.A., Charleston, S.C., 1886-94; pastor Bapt. Ch., Camden, S.C., 1895-1900; supt. Connie Maxwell Orphanage since 1900. Pres. Baptist Young People's Union of S.C., 1896-1900, State Conf. of Social Work, S.C., 1909-18, chmn. State Bd. Correctional Adminstrn., 1914-19; pres. Bapt. State Conv., S.C., 1923-26; del. to Third Congress of Baptist World Alliance, Stockholm, Sweden, 1923; twice pres. Tri-State Conf. Orphanage Workers; del. to Third Internat. Conf. of Social Work, London, Eng., 1936. Charter mem. S.C. Child Labor Com.; v.p. Child Welfare League America; mem. bd. dirs. S.C. Department Public Welfare, 1940; vice pres. Nat. Conf. of Social Work, 1943; member Am. Assn. of Social Workers. Hon. pres. S.C. Conf. Social Work, 1937; awarded "Distinguished Citizen" by Greenwood Kiwanis, 1936; awarded plaque of "Distinguished Service" by S. C. Am. Legion, 1937; awarded plaque by Alumni of Connie Maxwell Orphanage for "service to children of his generation," 1938. Democrat. Club: Rotary (past pres.). Mason. Author: Your Boy and Girl, 1922; Thirty Years of Connie Maxwell History, 1923; The Institution for Children, 1925; Consider the Parasite, 1927; Forty Years of Connie Maxwell History, 1932. Home: Greenwood, S.C. Died Aug. 9, 1947.

JAMISON, David Lee, educator; b. Morgantown, W.Va., Oct. 15, 1867; s. John and Cinderella (Lynch) J.; B.A., U. of W.Va., 1888, LL.B., 1890; grad. study, Columbia U. Law Sch., 1890-91; U. of Chicago Div. Sch., 1894-95; grad. Rochester Theol. Sem., 1900; Th.D., Eastern Bapt. Theol. Sem., 1928; m. Janet Browse, Aug. 15, 1895; children—Donald (dec.), Mabel (dec.), Lee Browse, Gordon McLaren (dec.). Practiced law Parkersburg, W.Va., 1891-94; ordained ministry Bapt. Ch., 1895; pastor Gas City, Ind., 1895-98, Fredonia, N.Y., 1900-05, Albion, N.Y., 1905-13, Albany, N.Y., 1915-25; prof. philosophy of religion, Eastern Bapt. Theol. Sem., Phila., 1925-1941. Y.M.C.A. sec. and acting chaplain of Machine-Gun Center, Camp Hancock, World War I. Mem. Alpha Tau Omega. Republican. Mason (32°, Shriner; Grand Chaplain Masonic Order of N.Y. State, 2 yrs.). Club: St. Davids Golf (Philadelphia). Author: The Resurrection of Jesus, Considered from the Lawyer's Viewpoint, 1923; Philosophy Studies Religion, 1937. Traveled in Europe and the Orient. Home: St. Davids, Pa. Died Jan. 20, 1947; buried at Fredonia, N.Y.

JANSSEN, E. C., architect. Fellow Am. Inst. Architects since 1891. Address: 1320 Chemical Bldg., St. Louis, Mo.* Died Sep. 19, 1946.

JANSSEN, Henry (yän'sĕn), textile mfr.; b. Barmen, Germany, Feb. 8, 1866; s. Wilhelm Albert and Anna Elisabeth Helena (Benner) J.; ed. tech. schs., Germany, and evening schs., Brooklyn, N.Y.; m. Wilhelmina Raeker, Sept. 25, 1890 (died Oct. 26, 1936); children—Harry Frederick (dec.), Minnie (Mrs. John E. Livingood; dec.), Helen (Mrs. Richard C. Wetzel), Elsie (dec.). Came to U.S., 1888, naturalized, 1895. In mfg. business, Reading, since 1892; pres. Textile Machine Works, Narrow Fabric Co., Nufashond Narrow Fabric Company of Canada, Ltd., Delta Realty Co., Tulpehocken Farms, Inc., Henry Janssen Corp., Henry Janssen Foundation, North Wyomissing Heights Water Co.; v.p. Berkshire Knitting Mills, Delta Finance Co., Peoples Trust Co. Pres. br. mgrs. Reading Hospital; affiliated with various philanthropic activities through Henry Janssen Foundation. Member borough council, Wyomissing, Pennsylvania, since 1906. Mem. Am. Acad. Polit. and Social Science, Am. Civic Assn., Army Ordinance Assn., Deutscher Verein (N.Y.), German Club, Tech. Soc. of Phila., German Soc. of Pa., Nat. Assn. of Audubon Socs., Nat. Municipal League. Clubs: Automobile (Phila.); Wyomissing, Automobile, Country (Reading); Iris (Wyomissing), Berkshire Country. Home: Reading Blvd., Wyomissing, Pa. Office: P. O. Box 1382, Reading Pa. Died Jan. 28, 1948.

JAQUES, Bertha E. (Mrs. William K. Jaques) (jā'kwĕz), etcher; b. Covington, O., Oct. 24, 1863; d. John W. and Charlotta A. (Wilde) Clauson; ed. schs. in Covington, Indianapolis, Ind., and Chicago, Ill.; self-taught in etching and printing; Dr. Fine Arts, Lawrence Coll., Appleton, Wis., 1929; m. William K. Jacques, M.D., Nov. 28, 1889; 3 children (died in infancy). Etcher of landscapes. Exhibited in Paris Salon, New York, Boston, Phila. and many other cities. Represented in Congressional Library, Washington, D.C.; New York Pub. Library; Art Inst. Chicago; Worcester (Mass.) Museum, etc. Mem. Chicago Soc. Etchers, Calif. Soc. Etchers, Print Makers of Los Angeles, Friends Am. Landscape, Audubon Soc. Republican. Clubs: Cordon, Arts. Studio and Home: 4316 Greenwood Av., Chicago, Ill.* Died Mar. 1941.

JAQUITH, Harold Clarence (jā'kwĭth), educator; b. Nashua, N.H., May 25, 1888; s. Clarence E. and Carrie (Barker) J.; B.S., Trinity Coll., Conn., 1911, LL.D., 1937; M.A., Columbia U., 1914; B.D., Union Theol. Sem., 1914; LL.D., Blackburn U., 1933; m. Mary Harin, Nov. 9, 1925; children—William Harin, Elizabeth Marie. Asst. pastor First Presbyn. Ch., New York, 1912-17; asst. sec. Near East Relief, 1917-19, mng. dir. at Constantinople and Athens, 1920-29, asso. gen. sec. 1927-33 and trustee since 1931; exec. officer and nat. sec. Near East Foundation, 1930-33, now mem. nat. com. of same; dir. trustee Athens Coll.; pres. Illinois Coll., 1933-37; provost Trinity Coll. since 1938; trustee Wilbraham Acad. Served on staff Am. Mission to Poland and Am. Mission to Negotiate Peace, 1919. Awarded Order Hamediah (Turkey), 1921; Order of King George I of Greece, 1923, Croix de Guerre (Greece), 1924, Greek Red Cross Medal, 1925. Fellow Royal Geog. Soc. (London), Am. Acad. Polit. and Social Science, A.A.A.S.; mem. Phi Beta Kappa. Club: University. Author: Persistent Personality of Lincoln. Contbr. numerous articles on internat. sociol. and hist. educational subjects. Address: Trinity Coll., Hartford, Conn. Died Apr. 20, 1943.

JARMAN, Joseph Leonard, educator; b. Albemarle County, Va., Nov. 19, 1867; s. William Dabney and Catherine Goodloe (Lindsay) J.; grad. Miller Sch., Va., 1885; U. of Va., 1886-89, grad. in scientific schs.; LL.D., Hampden-Sydney Coll., 1906; m. Mary Helen Wiley, Dec. 22, 1891; children—Emerson Wiley, Elizabeth Parker, Joseph Lindsay, Helen Reeves, Wm. Dabney. Engaged in teaching since 1889; president, State Teachers Coll., Farmville, Va. 1902-46; president emeritus since July 1, 1946. Pres. Prince Edward Pub. Health Assn. Member Am. Assn. Teachers Colleges (v.p.), Va. Coöp. Edn. Assn. (dir.), A.A.A.S., Hist. Soc. Va., Phi Beta Kappa, Omicron Delta Kappa, Phi Delta Kappa. Democrat. Methodist. Home: Farmville, Va. Died Nov. 15, 1947.

JARRETT, Benjamin (jăr'rĕt), ex-congressman; b. Sharon, Pa., July 18, 1881; ed. pub. schs., Wheatland, Pa.; m. Agnes Boyle; children—Dorothy (Mrs. A. L. Brintz), Fred. Admitted to Pa. bar, 1907, and practiced in Farrell; mem. Pa. State Senate, 1911-13, Pa. State Workmen's Compensation Bd., 1919-23; mem. 75th to 77th Congresses (1937-43), 20th Pa. Dist. Home: 1209 Haywood St., Farrell, Pa.*Died Aug. 10, 1944.

JARRETT, William Paul, territorial del.; b. Honolulu, T.H., Aug. 22, 1877; ed. St. Louis Coll., Honolulu. Dep. sheriff and sheriff City and County of Honolulu 8 yrs.; high sheriff Ty. of Hawaii and warden Oahu Prison, 1914-22; del. 68th and 69th Congresses (1923-27), Hawaii. Democrat. Home: Honolulu, T.H. Died Nov. 10, 1930.

JARVIS, Chester Deacon, educationalist; b. London, Ont., Mar. 29, 1876; s. Lyman Gage and Lila (Deacon) J.; B.S.A., Ont. Agrl. Coll., 1899; Ph.D., Cornell U., 1909; m. Marion Smith, Oct. 3, 1901. Asst. supt., Internat. Correspondence Schs., 1899-1904; horticulturist, Storrs (Conn.) Agrl. Expt. Sta., 1906-13; dir. Conn. Agrl. Coll. extension service, 1913-15; specialist in agrl. edn., U.S. Bur. of Edn., 1915-21. Mem. Nat. Research Council, 1920-21. Mem. Alpha Chapter Sigma Xi. Joint Author: Trees in Winter, 1912; also bulls. relating to agr., edn., etc.; contbr. to Bailey's Standard Cyclopedia of Horticulture. Home: Grimsby, Ont., Can. Died March 27, 1948.

JARVIS, Thomas Neilson, railway official; b. Stratford, Ont., Can., May 22, 1854; s. Peter Robinson and Marion (Neilson) J. Began as clk. Grand Trunk Ry., 1872; voucher clk. Internat. Line, at Buffalo, 1875-78; bookkeeper Can. Southern Line, Buffalo, 1878-79; accountant Commercial Express Line, 1880-83; mgr. Traders Dispatch Fast Freight Line, 1883-98; gen. eastern agt., 1898-02, asst. gen. traffic mgr., Lehigh Valley R.R., 1902-03, gen. frt. agt., 1903-04, v.-p., Mar. 26, 1906-May 1, 1919; retired. Home: Ansonia Hotel. Office: 143 Liberty St., New York. Died Nov. 14, 1926.

JASTROW, Joseph (jăs'trō), psychologist; b. Warsaw, Poland, Jan. 30, 1863; s. Rev. Marcus and Bertha (Wolfsohn) J.; A.B., U. of Pa., 1882, A.M., 1885; fellow in psychology, Johns Hopkins, 1885-86, Ph.D., 1886; LL.D., Wittenberg, 1928; m. Rachel Szold, Aug. 2, 1888 (died Sept. 12, 1926); 1 son, Benno B. (adopted). Prof. psychology, Univ. of Wis., 1888-1927. In charge psychol. sect. Chicago Expn., 1893. Pres. Am. Psychol. Assn., 1900. Author: Time Relations of Mental Phenomena, 1890; Epitomes of Three Sciences (part author), 1890; Fact and Fable in Psychology, 1900; The Subconscious, 1906; The Qualities of Men, 1910; Character and Temperament, 1915; The Psychology of Conviction, 1918; Keeping Mentally Fit, 1928; Piloting Your Life, 1930; Effective Thinking, 1931; The House that Freud Built, 1932; Wish and Wisdom, 1934; Sanity First, 1935; The Betrayal of Intelligence, 1938. Editor and contbr.: The Story of Human Error, 1936. Contbr. on psychol. subjects in scientific journals and mags. Lecturer, Columbia Univ., 1910, New Sch. for Social Research (New York), 1927-33. Conducted daily syndicated articles under title "Keeping Mentally Fit," 1928-32; broadcast over Nat. Broadcasting Co. Network, 1935-38. Address: care Greenberg, 400 Madison Av., New York, N.Y. Died Jan. 8, 1944.

JAUNCEY, George Eric MacDonnell (jôn'sē), physics; b. Adelaide, Australia, Sept. 21, 1888; s. George and Agnes Binnie (Davis) J.; B.S., U. of Adelaide, Australia, 1910, D.Sc., 1922; M.S., Lehigh U., 1916; m. Ethel Sarah Turner, Jan. 16, 1913; 1 dau., Molly Horsfall. Came to U.S. 1914; asst. prof. physics, Washington U., St. Louis, 1921-24, asso. prof., 1924-30, prof. since 1930. Has made spl. researches in theory of Compton effect in X-rays and diffuse scattering of X-rays by crystals. Fellow American Physical Society, A.A.A.S.; member Sigma Xi, Phi Beta Kappa. Associate editor Physical Review, 1926-28. Author: Modern Physics, 1932 (revised 1937). Co-author: M.K.S. Units, 1940. Contbr. over 90 research papers and articles in scientific publs. on the scattering of X-rays. Home: 7310 Lindell Av., St. Louis, Mo.* Died May 19, 1947.

JAY, Pierre, banker; b. Warwick, N.Y., May 4, 1870; s. Rev. Peter Augustus and Julia (Post) J.; grad. Groton (Mass.) Sch., 1888; A.B., Yale, 1892; hon. A.M., 1917; m. Louisa Shaw Barlow, Nov. 23, 1897; children—Ellen (Mrs. Lloyd K. Garrison), Anna Maricka (Mrs. Alexander Duer Harvey), Frances, Luiza (Mrs. Jay de Vegh). With Post & Flagg, bankers, New York, 1899-1903; v.p. Old Colony Trust Co., Boston, 1903-06; bank commr. of Mass., 1906-09; v.p. Manhattan Co., New York, 1909-14; federal reserve agt. and chmn. bd. Federal Reserve Bank of New York, 1914-26; mem. Transfer Com. and deputy agent gen. for reparation payments under Dawes Plan Organization, 1927-30; chmn. bd. Fiduciary Trust Co. of New York, 1930-45, hon. chmn. since 1945. Republican. Clubs: Century, Down Town. Home: 133 E. 64th St. Address: 1 Wall St., New York, N.Y. Died Nov. 24, 1949.

JEFFERYS, Edward Miller, clergyman; b. Phila., May 4, 1865; s. Charles Peter Beauchamp and Elizabeth (Miller) J.; A.B., U. of Pa., 1886, B.D., 1889,

S.T.D., 1909; grad. Berkeley Div. Sch., 1889; m. Amy E. Faulconer, Apr. 24, 1895; children—Robert Faulconer, Charles Peter Beauchamp, Edward Miller (dec.). Deacon, 1889, P.E. Ch., priest, 1890; curate, St. Peter's Ch., Phila., 1889; asst. rector St. John's Ch., Detroit, 1890-94; rector St. Paul's Ch., Doylestown, Pa., 1894-1902, Emmanuel Parish, Cumberland, Md., 1902-06; arch-deacon Western Md., 1904-06; rector St. Peter's Church, Phila., 1906-37. Del. to Gen. Conv. P.E. Ch., 1919, 22, 25; pres. Standing Com. Diocese Pa. Chaplain U.S.A., May 1917-May 1919, in France, now maj. (chaplain) auxiliary, U.S.A. Clubs: Philadelphia, Army and Navy of Philadelphia, British Officers of Philadelphia, Corinthian Yacht (fleet chaplain); Penn Manor (Morrisville, Pa.). Author of numerous published sermons, addresses, etc. Home: Wheel Pump Lane, Chestnut Hill, Philadelphia. Died Aug. 28, 1946.

JEFFERYS, William Hamilton (jĕf'rēz), surgeon, author, missionary; b. Philadelphia, Pa., July 3, 1871; s. Charles Peter Beauchamp and Elizabeth (Miller) J.; A.B., University of Pennsylvania, 1894, A.M., 1897, M.D., 1908; D.C.L., honoris causa, 1945; m. Lucy Sturgis Hubbard, 1897 (dec.); children—Anne, Lucy Sturgis, Adelaide McCulloh, William Hamilton; m. 2d, Ann E. Prophet, 1931. Surgeon St. Luke's Hospital, Shanghai, 1901-13; professor surgery, St. John's University, Shanghai, 1905-13; editor China Med. Jour., 1902-13; supt. Phila. City Mission, 1917-43, and editor of The City Missionary. Professor of Christian mysticism, Church Training School, Philadelphia, since 1915. Pres. Am. Assn. of China, 1909-10; mem. China Med. Missionary Assn. (research, publn. and exec. coms.), Am. Soc. Tropical Medicine, London, Society of Tropical Medicine, Delta Phi Fraternity; fellow College of Physicians of Philadelphia; hon. fellow China Medical Society (China). Episcopalian. Clubs: Shanghai, Shanghai Country (China); Authors' (London); Art Alliance, Philadelphia, St. Elmo (Philadelphia). Author: The Great Mystery, 1900; Hospital Dialogue (in Shanghai dialect), 1906 (in Pekinese Mandarin), 1908; The Diseases of China, 1910; Life of Bishop Ingle, 1913; The Mystical Companionship of Jesus, 1919; The Shuffling Coolie, and Other Plays, 1913; How Can We Know the Way?, 1921; The City Mission Idea, 1922; The Mystical Assurance of Immortality, 1924; Reasonable Faith; The Discovery of God; The Key to Divine Reality, 1934; Z, A Naughty Biography. Home: 143 Grays Lane, Haverford, Pa. Died May 14, 1945.

JEFFREY, Frank Rumer, lawyer; b. Parkersburg, W.Va., Oct. 22, 1889; s. Thomas P. and Sarah (Crossfield) J.; student arts and science, George Washington U., 3 yrs., LL.B., 1913; m. Ray Rose, Nov. 13, 1919; 1 son, Frank Rumer. Formerly newspaper reporter; pvt. sec. to U.S. Senator W. L. Jones; began practice of law at Kennewick, Wash., 1914, as mem. Moulton & Jeffrey; apptd. U.S. atty. for Eastern Dist. of Wash., by President Harding, Oct. 10, 1921, resigned Mar. 2, 1925. Served 2 yrs., World War; maj. 146th F.A., 66th F.A. Brigade, A.E.F., 18 mos.; cited "for gallantry in action," Meuse-Argonne offensive. First State comdr. Am. Legion of Wash.; mem. Delta Sigma Rho, Sigma Phi Epsilon. Republican. Presbyterian. Mason (32°, Shriner), Royal Order of Jesters, Elk. Clubs: Broadmoor Golf, Rainier, Wash. Athletic, Seattle Golf. Office: Dexter Horton Bldg., Seattle, Wash. Died Feb. 10, 1940.

JEIDELS, Otto (yī'dĕlz), banker; b. Frankfort on Main, Germany, Mar. 13, 1882; s. Julius and Anna (Niederhofheim) J.; ed. Univ. of Bonn, and Univ. of Berlin (Ph.D., 1903); m. Gertrud Stargardt, Dec. 26, 1922. Came to U.S. to reside, 1938; now American citizen. Apprentice to stock broker firm, New York, 1906; with Am. Metal Co. and Affiliations in Germany, England and U.S., 1907-09; mgr., later mng. dir., Berliner Handels Gesellschaft, Berlin, 1909-38; partner Lazard Freres & Co., New York, 1939-Apr. 1, 1943; now vice-pres. Bank of America, San Francisco, and vice-chmn. gen. finance com. Decorated Companion, Order of Indian Empire. Home: 1075 California St. Office: 300 Montgomery St., San Francisco, Calif. Died June 17, 1947.

JELKS, John Lemuel, surgeon; b. Bells, Tenn., July 5, 1870; s. Lemuel Marshall (M.D.) and Nannie (Lane) J.; student U. of Ark.; M.D., Memphis Hosp. Med. Coll., 1892; m. Minnie Rollwage, Oct. 14, 1903; m. 2d, Mrs. Louise Whitmire Speegle, Jan. 25, 1940. Practiced, Memphis, since 1893; specializes in entero-proctology; asst. surgeon in chief Sons of Confed. Vets.; comdr. Tenn. Dept., United Confed. Vets. (ex-surgeon). Fellow Am. Proctologic Soc. (ex-pres.), Am. Coll. Surgeons, Nat. Gastro-Enterol. Assn.; mem. A.M.A., Southern Med. Assn., Tenn. Med. Assn., Tenn. Acad. Science, A.A.A.S., Internat. Soc. Gastro-Enterology, Am. Med. Editors and Authors. Democrat. Mem. Christian (Disciples) Ch. Mason (K.T., Shriner). Author of the theory of intestinal parasitic infection as the etiology of pellagra; contbr. chapter on Dysentery in Hirschman's Diseases of the Rectum, Sigmoid and Colon; chapter on intestinal protozoa in man, The Cyclopedia of Medicine. Home: 276 S. Pauline St. Office: Med. Arts Bldg., Memphis, Tenn. Died 1945.

JELLIFFE, Smith Ely (jĕl'ĭf), neurologist; b. New York, Oct. 27, 1866; s. William Munson and Susan E. (Kitchell) J.; A.B., Brooklyn Poly. Inst., 1898; M.D., Coll. Physicians and Surgeons (Columbia), 1889, Ph.D., 1899, A.M., 1900; post-grad. work, Europe, at various times since 1890; m. Helena Dewey Leeming, Dec. 20, 1894; children—Sylvia Canfield, Winifred, Smith Ely, Wm. Leeming (dec.), Helena; m. 2d, Bee Dobson, Dec. 20, 1917. Visiting neurologist, City Hosp., 1903-13; clin. prof. mental diseases, Fordham U., 1907-12; instr. materia medica and therapeutics, 1903-07, prof. pharmacognosy and tech. microscopy, 1897-1907, Coll. of Pharmacy, Columbia; adjunct prof. diseases of the mind and nervous system, Post-Grad. Hosp. and Med. Sch., 1911-17; cons. neurologist, Manhattan State Hosp., Kings Park Hospital. Editor Med. News, N.Y., 1900-05; asso. editor New York Med. Journal, 1905-09; mng. editor Journal of Nervous and Mental Disease, 1902-45, editor (with Dr. W. A. White) Nervous and Mental Monograph Series, 1907-45, Psychoanalytic Review, 1913-45; now retired. Mem. Am. Neurol. Assn. (pres. 1929-30), N.Y. Neurol. Soc. (pres.). N.Y. Psychiat. Society (pres.), A.M.A., Am. Psychiatric Assn., Am. Psychopathol. Society (pres.), Am. Psychoanalytic Soc. (pres.), Phila. Neurol. Soc., N.Y. Acad. Med.; corr. mem. Neurol. Soc. Paris, Acad. Medicine of Brazil. Clubs: N.Y. Athletic. Author: Essentials of Vegetable Pharmacognosy, 1895; Morphology and Histology of Plants, 1899; also "Nervous Diseases" in Butler's Diagnostics, 1902; Outlines of Pharmacognosy, 1904. Reviser: Butler's Materia Medica, 1902; Shaw on Nervous Diseases, 1903. Editor and Translator: Dubois' Psychoneuroses, 1905; Grasset-Demi Fous, 1907; Payot, Education of Will; Paranoia; the Wassermann Serum Reaction in Psychiatry; Dejerine, Psychoneuroses and Psychotherapy; Rank, Myth of the Birth of the Hero; Eppinger and Hess, Vagotonia; Silberer, Problems of Mysticism and Its Symbolism; W. Hess, Vegetive Nervous System and Psyche; also Hysteria, Tetany, Migraine, in Osler's System of Medicine, etc. Co-editor: Ency. Americana, 1904, 18; (with Dr. W. A. White) Modern Treatment of Nervous and Mental Diseases, 2 vols.; Diseases of the Nervous System, 7 edits.; Technique of Psychoanalysis; Psychoanalysis and the Drama; Respiratory Disorders in Encephalitis; Oculogyric Crises and Encephalitis. Contbr. to medical press. Home: Huletts Landing, Washington County, N.Y. Address: 64 W. 56th St., New York, N.Y. Died Sept. 25, 1945.

JENCKS, Millard Henry, coll. pres.; b. Gravesville, N.Y., Nov. 5, 1881; s. George Rufus and Estelle (Payne) J.; B.S., St. Lawrence U., 1905; D.Sc., Clarkson Coll., Potsdam, N.Y., 1941; m. Ruth Kimball, 1909; 1 son, Kimball. Teacher and prin. pub. schs., 1905-09; admitted to N.Y. bar, 1908; became asso. with Ginn and Co., 1909, partner, 1923-40; trustee St. Lawrence U., 1923-33, chmn. bd., 1939-41, acting pres., 1940-41, pres. since 1941; trustee Paul Smiths' Coll. since 1940. Dir. War Camp Community Service, Camp Upton, 1917-18. Mem. Council for Conf. on Canadian-Am. Affairs since 1935. Mem. Newcomen Soc., Alpha Tau Omega, Phi Beta Kappa. Clubs: University, Salmagundi (N.Y. City). Home: Canton, N.Y. Died Feb. 14, 1945.

JENKINS, Burris Atkins, clergyman; b. Kansas City, Mo., Oct. 2, 1869; s. Andrew T. and Sarah Henry (Baker) J.; A.B., Bethany Coll., 1891 (LL.D., 1940); S.T.B., Harvard, 1895, A.M., 1896; D.D., Kentucky Wesleyan Coll., 1903; L.H.D., Rollins Coll., Winter Park, Fla., 1930; m. Mattie Hocker, May 23, 1894; children—Katherine Baker (dec.), Burris Atkins, Paul Andrew, Logan Hocker. Ordained Christian (Disciples) ministry, 1891; pastor, Indianapolis, Ind., 1896-1900; prof. N.T. lit. and exegesis, 1898-1900, pres., 1899-1900, U. of Indianapolis; pres. Ky. U., 1901-07; pastor Linwood Blvd. Christian Ch. (now Community Ch.), Kansas City, since Sept. 1907. Also editor and pub. Kansas City Post, Jan. 1, 1919-21; pub. The Christian (weekly journal of religion) 1926-34. Author: Heroes of Faith, 1896; The Man in the Street and Religion, 1917; Facing the Hindenburg Line, 1917; It Happened Over There, 1918; The Protestant, 1918; Princess Salome, 1921; The Bracegirdle, 1922; The Beauty of the New Testament, 1925; The Drift of the Day, 1928; The World's Debt to Protestantism, 1930; American Religion as I See It Lived, 1930; Torrent, 1932; My Job—Preaching, 1932; Let's Build a New World, 1934; Hand of Bronze, 1934; Fresh Furrow, 1936; Where My Caravan Has Rested, 1939. Address: 3529 Charlotte St., Kansas City, Mo. Died Mar. 13, 1945.

JENKINS, Ralph Carlton; b. Springfield, Vermont, December 3, 1891; son of George O. and Minnie (Roby) J.; A.B., Dartmouth College, 1914; A.M., Middlebury (Vermont) College, 1918; grad. study Yale Univ., Harvard Grad. Sch. of Edn.; Ed.M., Harvard, 1933; Ph.D., New York University, 1937; m. Rose Thompson, Aug. 26, 1914 (dec. Jan. 6, 1944); children—Page Thompson, Brooks Allan, Ward Sherman. Asst. prin. Burr and Burton Sem., Manchester, Vt., 1914-16; prin. Black River Acad., Ludlow, Vt., 1916-17; supt. schs., Plymouth, Conn., 1917-20; agent Am. Book Co., 1920-22; supt. schs., Putnam, Conn., 1922-28; prin. Johnson (Vt.) Normal School, 1928-35; pres. Danbury (Conn.) State Teachers College since 1935. Mem. N.E.A. (Dept. Superintendence), New Eng. Assn. Pub. Sch. Supts., New Eng. Normal Prins. Assn., Conn. Assn. Pub. Sch. Supts. (pres. 1926), New Eng. Teacher Training Assn. (pres. 1934); dist. gov. 200th District Rotary International, 1941. Republican. Congregationalist. Mason. Club: Rotary. Author: A Practical Program for Teacher Training in Vermont (thesis), 1933; Henry Barnard, Progressive Educator of Teachers (thesis), 1937; (with Gertrude C. Warner) Henry Barnard—An Introduction, 1937. Home: Danbury, Conn. Died Oct. 2, 1946.

JENKS, Arthur Byron, congressman; b. West Dennis, Mass.; s. James H. and Emeline (Crowell) J.; ed. pub. schs., West Dennis; m. Mary E. Lucas, June 12, 1912; children—Chester W., Harvey P. Began as shoeworker, 1881; was associated with F. M. Hoyt Shoe Co.; now pres. Manchester (N.H.) Morris Plan Bank; mem. 75th to 77th Congresses (1937-43), 1st N.H. Dist. Republican. Mason. Clubs: Manchester Country (Manchester); Army and Navy (Washington, D.C.). Home: 1855 Elm St., Manchester, N.H. Died Dec. 14, 1947.

JENKS, John Story; b. Philadelphia, Pa., 1876; s. William H. and Hannah M. (Hacker) J.; student Haverford Coll., 1894-96; hon. M.A., U. of Pa., 1940; m. Isabella F. G. Morton, 1902; children—Thomas Story, Morton, Ann West (Mrs. Henry Lyne, Jr.). Clk. Girard Trust Co., 1897-99; partner Edward B. Smith & Co., bankers, 1900-08, Bertron, Griscom & Jenks, 1909-12; dir. Girard Trust Co., Ins. Co. of North America, Indemnity Ins. Co. of N. America, The Alliance Ins. Co. of Phila., Phila. Fire & Marine Insurance Company, Muskogee Company, Midland Valley Railroad Co., Kan., Okla. & Gulf Ry. Co., Okla. City, Ada, Atoka Ry. Co., Pa. Salt Mfg. Co., trustee Penn Mutual Life Ins. Co. Mem. bd. mgrs. The Western Saving Fund Soc., The Morris Arboretum. Mem. of the bd. of mgrs. University Museum (former pres.); vice-president, trustee Philadelphia Museum of Art (chmn. museum com.); trustee Thomas W. Evans Mus. and Inst. Soc., Fairmount Park Art Assn.; curator Am. Philos. Soc. since May 1943. Decorated Chevalier Légion d'Honneur (France), 1937. Mem. Am. Philos. Society. Club: Philadelphia. Home: Seminole and Chestnut Avs., Chestnut Hill. Office: 1421 Chestnut St., Philadelphia, Pa. Died Mar. 13, 1946.

JENNEY, Ralph E., judge; b. Detroit, Mich., Feb. 20, 1883; s. Royal Almond and Phernia (Hoxsey) J.; A.B., U. of Mich., 1904, LL.B., 1906; m. Gertrude O'Connor, Apr. 4, 1921; 1 son, William W. Admitted to Ore. bar, 1906, and began practice at Portland; in practice at San Diego, 1912-37; judge U.S. Dist. Court since 1937. Lt. comdr. U.S. Naval Reserve Force. Del. Dem. Nat. Conv., Chicago, 1932. Chmn. Calif. State Relief Commn., 1936-37; mem. exec. council, Nat. Civil Service Reform League; president Calif. Conf. Social Work, 1937-38; dir. and chmn. finance com. Calif. Pacific Internat. Expn.; director and 1st vice-president Los Angeles Area War Chest; dir. Los Angeles Community Welfare Federation; mem. executive com. Los Angeles Council of Social Agencies; dir. League of Nations Assn. Mem. Bd. Trustees and Fellows, Claremont Colls. Mem. Am., Calif. State and San Diego bar assns., S.A.R., Sons of Colonial Wars, Soc. of Mayflower Descendants, Beta Theta Pi, Phi Delta Phi. Democrat. Presbyterian. Mason (K.T.). Clubs: Metropolitan, California, Sunset (Los Angeles). Home: 251 S. Orange Grove Av., Pasadena, Calif. Office: Federal Building, Los Angeles, Calif. Died July 13, 1945.

JENNINGS, Herbert Spencer, naturalist; b. Tonica, Ill., Apr. 8, 1868; s. Dr. George N. and Olive Taft (Jenks) J.; B.S., U. of Mich., 1893; A.M., Harvard, 1895, Ph.D., 1896; studied Jena (Germany), 1896-97, LL.D., Clark University, 1909, University of Pa., 1940, University of California, 1943, S.D., University of Mich., 1918, U. of Pa., 1933, Oberlin Coll., 1933, University of Chicago, 1941; m. Mary Louise Burridge, 1898; 1 son, Burridge; m. 2d, Lulu Plant Jennings, 1939. Assistant professor botany, Texas Agricultural College, 1889-90; professor botany, Montana State Agrl. College, 1897-98; instr. zoölogy, Dartmouth Coll., 1898-99; asst. prof. zoölogy, U. of Mich., 1900-03; asst. prof. zoölogy, U. of Pa., 1903-05; prof. exptl. zoölogy, 1906-10, Henry Walters prof. zoölogy and dir. zoöl. lab., 1910-38, emeritus prof. since 1938, Johns Hopkins Univ.; research associate U. of Calif. at Los Angeles since 1939; visiting prof., Keio University, Tokyo, 1931-32, George Eastman visiting prof. and fellow of Balliol College, Oxford Univ., England, 1935-36; visiting prof. U. of Calif. at Los Angeles, 1939; Terry lecturer Yale, 1933; Vanuxem lecturer, Princeton, 1934; Leidy lecturer, University of Pa., 1940; Patten lecturer, University of Indiana, 1943; hon. fellow, Stanford, 1941. Specialist in research work on physiology of micro-organisms, animal behavior, and genetics. Director U.S. Fish Commn. Biol. Survey of the Great Lakes, 1901; trustee Marine Biol. Lab., Woods Hole, Mass.; biometrician, U.S. Food Administration, 1917-18; mem. Nat. Research Council, 1922-25. Asso. editor Jour. of Experimental Zoölogy, of Genetics, and of Biol. Bulletin. Pres. Am. Zoöl. Society, 1908-09, Am. Society Naturalists, 1910-11; fellow Am. Acad. Arts and Sciences, A.A.A.S.; hon. fellow Royal Micros. Soc. Great Britain; mem. Nat. Acad. Sciences, American Philosophical Soc., Philadelphia Academy Natural Sciences; Royal Society of Edinburgh; corr. member of Russian Academy of Science, Société de Biologie de Paris. Author: Anatomy of the Cat (with Jacob Reighard), 1901; Behavior of Lower Organisms, 1906; Life and Death, Heredity and Evolution in Unicellular Organisms, 1919; Prometheus—or Biology and the Advancement of Man, 1925; The Biological Basis of Human Nature, 1930; Genetics of the Protozoa, 1929; The Universe and Life, 1933; Genetics, 1935; Genetic Variations in Relation to Evolution, 1935. Contbr. of numerous papers in zoöl. and physiol. jours. Home: 10531 Wellworth Av., Westwood Village, Los Angeles 24, Calif. Died Apr. 14, 1947.

JENNINGS, Judson Toll, librarian; b. Schenectady, N.Y., Sept. 24, 1872; s. Charles Edward and Elizabeth Ann (Henry) J.; Union Coll., Schenectady, N.Y.,

1894-95; N.Y. State Library Sch., class of 1897; m. Eleanor McKelvey, Apr. 12, 1898 (died 1935); children—Elizabeth, Frances, Eleanor. With N.Y. State Library, 1889-1903; librarian Carnegie Free Library, Duquesne, Pa., 1903-06; director's asst., N.Y. State Library, 1906-07; librarian, Seattle Pub. Library, 1907-42, retired June 1, 1942. Twice pres. Pacific Northwest Library Assn.; mem. Wash. Library Assn. (pres. 1934, 35), A.L.A. (pres. 1923), Club: Seattle College. Address: Route 3, Box 224, Bellevue, Wash. Died Feb. 18, 1948.

JENNINGS, Walter Louis, chemist; b. Bangor, Me., Nov. 15, 1866; s. Stephen and Ellen Giddings (Ingalls) J.; A.B., Harvard, 1889, A.M., 1890, Ph.D., 1892; m. Alice Emily Page, July 24, 1897: children—Ruth, Frances, Alice. Asst. instr. organic chemistry, 1889-90, qualitative analysis, 1890-92, Parker fellow, 1893-94, Harvard U.; asst. prof. of chemistry, 1894-1900, prof. organic chemistry, 1900-37, dir. dept. of chemistry, 1911-37, since emeritus Worcester Poly. Inst. Fellow Am. Acad. Arts and Sciences, A.A.A.S.; mem. Am. Chem. Soc., German Chem. Soc. Mem. Mass. Medico-Legal Society, Harvard Musical Assn. Mem. Worcester Med. Milk Commn. Clubs: Bohemian, Cosmopolitan, Sigma Xi, Worcester Tennis, Worcester, Harvard, Longwood Cricket. Contbr. to scientific mags. Home: 8-A Chauncy St., Cambridge 38, Mass. Died Sep. 2, 1944.

JENSEN, Frank A., supt. schools; b. Pentwater, Mich., Feb. 16, 1879; s. Christian M. and Ella (Moran) J.; A.B., Mich. State Normal Coll., Ypsilanti, Mich., 1906; A.M., Columbia, 1913; Ph.D., U. of Mich., 1930; Ed.M., Michigan State Normal College, Ypsilanti, 1926; student University of Chicago, summers 1908-17; married Katherine Bates; children—Clyde M., Agnes T. (Mrs. Ted Bradford), Carol Gene, Richard B., William B. Teacher rural school, Oceana County, Michigan, 1900-01; superintendent schs., Kalkaska, Mich., 1906-11, Hart, Mich., 1911-14, Benton Harbor, Mich., 1914-23, Rockford, Ill., 1923-35, LaSalle-Peru Twp. High Sch., LaSalle, Ill., since 1935. Served with U.S. Army during Spanish-Am. War. Trustee Univ. of Ill. Mem. N.E.A., Nat. Secondary Prins. Assn., Nat. Soc. for Study Edn., Nat. Assn. Sch. Adminstrs., Am. Assn. Jr. Colls. Democrat. Mason. Club: Kiwanis (dist. gov. Mich. 1921-22). Author: Current Procedures in the Selection of Textbooks, 1931. Home: 1818 Second St., Peru. Ill. Office: 650 Chartres St., LaSalle, Ill. Died Mar. 30, 1947.

JENSEN, Ralph Adelbert, clergyman; b. Chicago, Ill., May 18, 1888; s. Julius A. and Carrie (Christensen) J.; student Central Coll. (Pella, Ia.), Southern Bapt. Theol. Sem. (Louisville, Ky.), 1912-15; m. Belle Samuels, 1911; children—Mrs. Kathryn Ramona MacDonald, Mrs. Carrie Muriel Carney. Ordained to ministry of Baptist Church, 1914; pastor Osceola, Neb., 1914-18, Mankato, Minn., 1918-23, Second Bapt. Ch., Chicago, 1923-28, First Ch., Long Beach, Calif., 1928-38; now exec. sec. Southern Calif. Bapt. Conv. Trustee Berkeley Bapt. Div. Sch., U. of Redlands. Y.M.C.A. sec., World War, 1917-18. Republican. Mason (32°). Address: 1201 Rossmoyne Av., Glendale, Calif. Office: 354 S. Spring St., Los Angeles, Calif. Died Mar. 11, 1946.

JEPSON, William, surgeon; b. of Am. parents at Aarhus, Denmark, June 29, 1863; s. Neils and Wilhelmina (Hostmark) J.; M.D., State U. of Ia., 1886, Jefferson Med. Coll., 1891, U. of Pa., 1891; B.S., Morningside Coll., Sioux City, Iowa, 1899; L.R.C.P. and L.R.C.S., Edinburgh, 1897; A.M., U. of S.D., 1908; LL.D., Morningside College, Sioux City, Ia., 1943; m. Beatrice Baker, Dec. 21, 1886; children—William Roscoe, Weir Agnew, Florence (Mrs. Thomas Briggs), Beatrice; m. 2d, Mary S. Ohge, Oct. 15, 1917. Began practice at Oakland, Neb., 1886; moved to Sioux City, 1886; professor surgery, Sioux City College of Medicine, 1891-1901, State University of Iowa, 1902-13; in general surgery practice, Sioux City, since 1886; president Wilmar Investment Company, Sioux Interstate Investment Co. Ex-pres. Ia. State Bd. Med. Examiners; past state chmn. Am. Soc. for Control of Cancer. Maj. Med. Corps, U.S. Army, Mexican border service, 1916-17, chief of surg. staff, Base Hosp., Camp Bowie, nr. Ft. Worth, Tex., 1918-19. Ex-pres. Tri State Med. Soc., Ia. State Med. Soc., Med. World War Vets. of Ia., Nat. Professional Men's Assn.; mem. A.M.A., Ia. Clin. Surg. Soc. (ex-pres.), Sioux Valley Med. Soc., Mo. Valley Med. Soc., Western Surg. Soc., Sigma Xi, Nu Sigma Nu, Alpha Omega Alpha; fellow Am. Coll. Surgeons, Internat. Coll. of Surgeons (Geneva). Mason (32°). Founder, Jepsonian Institute of Natural Sciences. Office: 2000 Jackson St., Sioux City, Ia. Died Nov. 7, 1946.

JERNBERG, Reinert August, theologian; b. Fredrikehald, Norway, Nov. 30, 1855; s. Peter August and Anne Margrete (Skjoldal) J.; B.A., Yale, 1884; B.D., Chicago Theol. Sem., 1887, D.D., 1910; m. Sarah Emily Libby, May 5, 1887 (died 1910); children—Prudence Emily, Arthur Reinert; m. 2d, Lenore Cummings, 1922. Ordained Congl. ministry, 1884; pastor East Berlin, Conn., 1883-85, Puritan Ch., Chicago, 1887-89, Douglas Park Ch., 1890; instr., 1885-95, prof., 1895-1916, and dir. Danish Norwegian Inst. in Chicago Theol. Sem.; prof. N.T. lit., Union Theol. Coll. (successor), Chicago, 1916-23; lecturer in N.T. Greek U. of Southern Calif., 1924-25; librarian Div. Sch. U. of Southern Calif., 1925-39. Founder, 1890, and editor 10 yrs., of Evangelisten (Norwegian weekly). Ministerial mem. Conf. Congl. Chs. Mem. Delta Kappa Epsilon. Contbr. to religious periodicals, Am. and Norwegian. Home: 1526 W. 45th St., Los Angeles, Calif. Died July 1, 1942.

JERNEGAN, Marcus Wilson (jĕr'nē-găn), prof. Am. history; b. Edgartown, Mass., Aug. 5, 1872; s. Jared and Helen Marie (Clark) J.; A.B., Brown U., 1896, A.M., 1898; Ph.D., U. of Chicago, 1906; studied U. of London, Sch. of History and Economics, 1907; m. Imogene Cameron, June 21, 1913; children—Margaret Helen, Jean Cameron. Research asst., Carnegie Instn., Washington, 1907-08; instr. Am. history, 1908-12, asst. and asso. prof., 1912-20, prof., 1920-37, U. of Chicago, prof. emeritus since 1937; prof. Harvard Summer Sch., 1927, and U. of Wash., 1937. Mem. Ill. State Council of Defense, 1918-19. Member Am. Hist. Assn., Phi Beta Kappa; corr. mem. Colonial Soc. of Mass. Club: Quadrangle. Author: History of Tammany Societies of Rhode Island, 1897; The American Colonies, 1492-1750, 1929; Laboring and Dependent Classes in Colonial America, 1607-1783, 1931; Growth of the American People, 1934. Co-author: Source Problems in United States History, 1918. Home: 5711 Kimbark Av., Chicago. Died Feb. 19, 1949.

JERVEY, Henry, army officer; b. in Va., June 5, 1866; s. Henry (M.D.) and Helen Louise (Wesson) J.; C.E., U. of the South, 1884, LL.D., 1920; grad. U.S. Mil. Acad., 1888, Engring. Sch. of Application, 1891, Army War Coll., 1916; m. Katherine Erwin, Nov. 14, 1895 (died 1929); 1 son, William Wesson; m. 2d, Henrietta Postell Jersey, Mar. 19, 1930. Add. 2d lt. engrs., June 11, 1888; promoted through grades to brigadier general, 1920; promoted major general; retired, 1930. In charge 4th Dist. Mississippi River Improvement, 1898-99; charge rivers and harbors on west coast of Fla., and defenses of Tampa Bay, 1899-1900; in Philippine Islands, 1901-03; instr. and asst. prof. U.S. Mil. Acad., 1903-05; charge rivers, harbors and defenses, Mobile Dist., 1905-10; in charge river improvements Cincinnati Dist., 1910-15; apptd. comdr. 66th Field Arty. Brigade, Camp Greene, Charlotte, N.C., Sept. 1917; chief div. of operations, Gen. Staff, Feb. 1918; comd. 41st Div., Camp Greene and Camp Mills; comd. 11th Brig. F.A., Hawaii, 1921; retired Apr. 10, 1922. Awarded D.S.M. "for especially meritorious and conspicuous services as director of operations, Gen. Staff, and as asst. chief of staff during the war"; Comdr. Legion of Honor (French); Grand Officer Order of Leopold (Belgian); Companion of the Bath (British); Order of Crown of Italy. Author: Warfare of the Future, 1917. Address: War Dept., Washington, D.C. Died Sep. 30, 1942.

JERVEY, Huger Wilkinson, lawyer, prof. law; b. Charleston, S.C., Sept. 26, 1878; s. Eugene Postell and Isabella Middleton (Wilkinson) J.; grad. high sch., 1896; student Charleston Coll., 1896-97; A.B., U. of the South, 1900, A.M., 1901, D.C.L., 1924; post-grad. work, Johns Hopkins, 1902; LL.B., Columbia Law Sch., 1913; unmarried. Prof. Greek, U. of the South, 1903-09; editor Columbia Law Rev., 1912-13; admitted to N.Y. bar, 1913; mem. Satterlee, Canfield & Stone (now Satterlee, Warfield & Stephens), 1915-28; asso. prof. law, Columbia U. Law Sch., 1923-24, prof. 1924-46, dean Law School, 1924-28, dir. Parker Sch. Advanced International Studies, since 1931; now Charles Evans Hughes professor of law, Columbia University. First lt., 304th F.A., 1917; served in France, 1917-18; maj. Gen. Staff Corps; cited by comdr. in chief "for distinguished service." Fellow A.A.A.S. Mem. Am. and N.Y. State bar assns., Assn. Bar City of N.Y., Am. Acad. Polit. and Social Science, Acad. of Polit. Science, Council on Fgn. Relations, The Pilgrims, St. Cecilia Soc., Huguenot Soc. of S.C. Episcopalian. Clubs: Century, Columbia Univ. (New York); Army and Navy (Washington). Home: 1150 Fifth Av. Address: Kent Hall, Columbia Univ., New York 27, N.Y. Died July 27, 1949.

JERVEY, James Postell, army officer; b. Powhatan County, Va., Nov. 14, 1869; s. Henry and Helen Louise (Wesson) J.; grad. U.S. Mil. Acad., 1892; m. Jean B. Webb, June 27, 1894; children—Jean P. (Mrs. A. S. Quintard), James P., Darrell E. Comd. 1st lt., engrs., June 11, 1892; promoted through grades to brig. gen., and retired, Sept. 22, 1920. Duty with Engrs'. Sch., New York Harbor, 1892-95; fortification work, Pensacola, Fla., 1895-99; instr. and asst. prof. U.S. Mil. Acad., 1899-1905; comdg. engr. co., P.I., 1905-07; dir. civ. engr., U.S. Engr. Sch., 1907-08; at Panama Canal, in charge constrn. Gatun Locks, 1908-13; dist. engr. Wheeling, W.Va., 1913-14, Norfolk, Va., 1914-17; mobilization camp and France, 1917-18; dist. engr., Wilmington, Del., 1919; dist. and div. engr., Baltimore, Md., 1920; city mgr., Portsmouth, Va., 1920-26; prof. mathematics, U. of the South, Sewanee, Tenn., since 1926. Served in Spanish-Am. War, in Philippines, in World War as div. engr. 79th Div., chief engr. 7th Corps, and asst. to chief engr. A.E.F. Awarded D.S.M.; citation by div. comdr. and comdg. gen. A.E.F. Democrat. Episcopalian. Address: University of the South, Sewanee, Tenn. Died Mar. 12, 1947.

JERVEY, J(ames) Wilkinson, ophthalmologist, laryngologist; b. Charleston, S.C., Oct. 19, 1874; s. Eugene P. and Ella M. (Wilkinson) J.; M.D., Med. Coll. State of S.C., Charleston, 1897; post-grad. study European clinics, 1908 and 1913; m. Helen Doremus Smith, Oct. 26, 1899 (died 1936); children—James Wilkinson, Mrs. Helen Ingle; m. 2d, Maude Earle Hammond, Oct. 9, 1939. Practiced in Greenville, S.C., since 1898; surgeon in charge of the Jervey Eye, Ear and Throat Hosp.; chief surgeon Piedmont & Northern Ry. Co., Southern Pub. Utilities Co.; oculist Southern Ry., etc. Fellow Am. Coll. Surg., A.M.A.; mem. South Carolina Medical Association (editor of jour., 1908-12; president 1912-13), American Laryngol., Rhinol. and Otol. Soc. (pres. 1933-34; twice chmn. southern sect.), Am. Ophthalmol. Soc., Am. Acad. Ophthalmology and Otolaryngology, Southern Med. Assn. (pres. 1937-38; chmn. eye, ear, nose and throat sect. 1915-16), S.C. Ophthalmol. and Otolaryngol. Soc. (pres. 1922-23); licentiate Am. Bd. Ophthalmology and Am. Bd. Otolaryngology. Mem. Vol. Med. Serv. Corps, Council Nat. Defense, 1918. Frequent contbr. to current med. and surg. lit. Democrat. Episcopalian. Clubs: Poinsett, Greenville Country Cotillion (pres. 1930-33), Biltmore Forest Country (Asheville, N.C.); Salamander (pres. since 1933). Home: Greenville, S.C. Died Nov. 1, 1945.

JESSE, Richard Henry, educator; b. Epping Forest, Va., Mar. 1, 1853; s. William T. and Mary (Claybrook) J.; studied, U. of Va., 1873-75, part of 1878; Europe part of 1885, 1890; U. of Munich, 1905; U. of Berlin, 1905-06; LL.D., Tulane, 1891, U. of Wis., 1904, S.C. Coll., 1905, Mo. Valley Coll., 1906, Washington U., 1907, U. of Mo., 1908; m. Addie Henry Polk, July 13, 1882. Instr. French and mathematics, Hanover Acad., 1876; prin., Washington Acad., Md., 1876-78; dean acad. dept., U. of La., 1878-84; prof. Latin, Tulane U., 1884-91; pres., U. of Mo., 1891-08; retired under Carnegie Foundn. by spl. invitation. Emeritus prof. ancient and mediaeval history, U. of Mo., since 1909; lecturer and writer, Cleveland Democrat. Baptist. Mason. Hon. mem. Columbia (Mo.) Club, Railway Club (St. Louis) and other orgns. Mem. Com. of Ten, N.E.A., 1891-92; chmn. sect. higher edn., 1898; pres. Mo. State Teachers' Assn., 1899, So. Assn. of Colls. and Secondary Schs., 1903, Nat. Assn. State Univs., 1905-06; Bapt. Congress, 1906; mem. adminstrv. bd. Congress of Arts and Sciences, awarded commemorative diploma and medal in recognition of distinguished services to edn., St. Louis Expn., 1904; del. 1st Internat. Congress of Radiology, Belgium, 1905. Author: Missouri Literature (with E. A. Allen); also pamphlets, papers in trans. various socs., addresses, etc. Address: 810 Hillcrest Av., Columbia, Mo. Died Jan. 22, 1921.

JESSUP, Walter Albert, educator; b. Richmond, Ind., Aug. 12, 1877; s. Albert S. and Anna (Goodrich) J.; A.B., Earlham Coll., 1903; M.A., Hanover, 1908; Ph.D., Columbia, 1911; LL.D., U. of Wis., 1922, Ind. U. and U. of Mo., 1928, Columbia, 1929, Northwestern, 1936, U. of Pittsburgh 1937, Hamilton Coll., 1938; Litt D., State U. of Ia., 1934; L.H.D., Boston Univ., 1936; m. Eleanor Hines, June 28, 1898; children—Richard, Bob Albert. Supt. schs., Westfield, Ind., 1900-07, Madison, Ind., 1907-09; dean Sch. of Edn., Ind. U., 1911; dean Coll. of Edn., 1912-16, pres., 1916-34, State U. of Ia.; pres. Carnegie Foundation for the Advancement of Teaching since May 1, 1934, trustee since 1933; president Carnegie Corp. of N.Y. since Nov. 1941, trustee since 1934. Chairman Committee on Manual Training and Industrial Education of Indiana Town and City Superintendants' Assn., 1908-10. Member survey coms. of Cleveland and Los Angeles pub. sch. systems; mem. survey commn., Western Reserve U., 1924-25; mem. survey commn. to evaluate secondary schs., Teachers Coll., Columbia, 1929-30. Pres. Nat. Assn. of State Univs., 1926-27; mem. Spl. Bd. of Law Sch. and Other Educators, U.S. Fed. of Justice; mem. council Am. Assn. Adult Edn. since 1929; Council on Policy and Guidance of Religious Edn. Assn.; mem. Bd. of Edn. of M.E. Ch. since 1932. Mem. Iowa Liberty Loan Advisory Committee; mem. Com. on Ednl. Policy, Am. Museum of Natural History; mem. coll. of electors, Ia. Hall of Fame; mem. citizens' sponsoring com., Am. Museum of Health; trustee Carnegie Instn. of Washington since 1938, Inst. Internat. Edn. Soc. for Advancement of Education. Member N.E.A. (Nat. Council of Edn.), Nat. Soc. for Study of Edn., Phi Beta Kappa, Phi Delta Kappa (nat. sec. 1911), Sigma Phi Epsilon, Acacia. Methodist. Mason (K.T.). Clubs: Triangle (Iowa City); Century (New York). Author: Social Factors Affecting Supervision of Special Subjects, 1911. Joint Author: Supervision of Arithmetic. Address: 522 5th Av., New York, N.Y. Died July 5, 1944.

JESTER, Beauford Halbert, governor of Tex.; b. Corsicana, Tex., Jan. 12, 1893; s. George T. and Frances (Gordon) J.; A.B., Univ. of Tex., 1916, LL.B., 1920; m. Mabel Buchanan, June 15, 1921; children—Barbara (Mrs. Howard Burris), Joan, Beauford. Admitted to bar of Tex., June, 1920, gen. practice of law, Corsicana, 1920-42; railroad commr. of Tex., hdqrs., Austin Tex., Aug. 1942-Nov. 1946; governor of Tex. since Jan. 21, 1947. Chairman Interstate Oil Compact Commission, 1948. Commd. capt. inf., 1st O.T.C., 1917; assigned to and comdr. Co.D., 357th Inf., 90th div. from orgn. to demobilization; participant in St. Mihiel and Meuse-Argonne offensives and in Army of Occupation; disch., July 1919. Mem. bd. regents Univ. of Tex., 1929-35 (chmn., 1933-35), hon. state chmn. United Service to China, Inc.; regional advisor Am. Commn. for Living War Memorials; mem. Nat. Youth Adminstrn. of Texas (dir.), Good Neighbor Foundation (hon. v.p., 1946-47), State Bar Assn. (dir. 1940-41), Navarre Co. Bar Assn. (pres. 1925-39), Texas Safety Assn., Inc., Am. Legion (hon. mem. distinguished guests com.; post comdr. Corsicana, 1923-24), Texas Resource-Use Com., 36th Div. Memorial Com., Chamber of Commerce (East Tex., Austin), 90th Div. Assn. (past pres.), 1st Officers Training Camp Leon Springs Assn. (past pres.),

Reserve Officers Assn., Sons of Republic of Texas, S.A.R., Y.M.C.A. (pres. Corsicana 1939-42), Kappa Sigma (nat. pres., 1941-43), Sigma Delta Chi. Democrat. Methodist. Mason (Shriner), Elk. Clubs: Rotary, Lions International, Rancheros Visitadores. Home: 1508 Sycamore St., Corsicana, Tex. Office: Executive Department, State Capitol, Austin 11, Texas. Died July 11, 1949.

JEWELL, Edward Alden, author; b. Grand Rapids, Mich., Mar. 10, 1888; s. Frank and Jennie Agnes (Osterhout) J.; ed. high sch., Grand Rapids, Mich., Friends' Sch., Washington, D.C.; m. Manette Lansing Carpenter, Apr. 4, 1914; 1 dau., Marcia Lansing. Reporter, Grand Rapids Herald, 1911-14; sec. to Senator William Alden Smith, Washington, 1914-15; with New York Tribune, 1915; mng. editor World Court Magazine, 1916; asso. editor Everybody's Magazine, 1916-17; Sunday editor New York Tribune, 1917-19, before and following mil. service. Commd. in Chem. Warfare Service, and trained at Camp Humphreys, Va., and Camp Kendrick, Lakehurst, N.J.; hon. disch. as 2d lt., Dec. 1918. Asso. editor Success Mag., 1923. Author: The Charmed Circle, 1921; The White Kami, 1922; The Moth Decides, 1922; Americans (Modern Art Series), 1930; Have We An American Art?, 1939; French Impressionists and Their Contemporaries, 1944; Cézanne 1944; Rouault, 1945; Van Gogh, 1946. Art editor and critic, New York Times. Home: 404 E. 55th St., N.Y. City 22. Died Oct. 11, 1947.

JEWELL, Louise Pond, author; b. Oberlin, O.; d. Chester Henry and Almeda (Gardner) Pond; grad. Adelphi Acad., Brooklyn, 1886; student Smith Coll., Mass., 2 yrs.; A.B., Oberlin, 1890; post-grad. study, Göttingen, 1894-95, Radcliffe Coll., 1897, U. of Chicago, 1899-1900, N.Y. Sch. of Philanthropy, 1907-08; m. Ogden Jewell, Dec. 16, 1903 (died 1905); adopted dau., Betty. Prin. Southold (L.I.) Acad., 1891-94 and 1895-96; prin. High Sch. Dept., Barnard Sch. for Girls, New York, 1896-97; teacher English and Latin, high schs., New York, 1898-1902; investigator under Russell Sage Foundation of citizenship training in N.Y. pub. schs., 1908-09; executrix and administrator Pond Estate, Moorhead, Miss., since 1921. Club: Phi Beta Kappa. Author: The Great Adventure, 1911; The Conqueror, 1916. Contbr. articles and short stories to mags. Home: Moorhead, Miss.; also (May-Oct.), Peconic, N.Y. Died Dec. 26, 1943.

JEWETT, Frank Baldwin, electrical engr.; b. Pasadena, Calif., Sept. 5, 1879; s. Stanley P. and Phebe (Mead) J.; A.B., Throop Poly. Inst. (now Calif. Inst. Tech.), 1898; Ph.D., U. of Chicago, 1902; D.Sc., New York U., Dartmouth, 1925, Columbia Univ. and Univ. of Wis., 1927, Rutgers University, 1928, U. of Chicago, 1929, Harvard, 1936, Univ. of Pa., 1940, Boston U., 1944; Dr. Eng., Case School of Applied Science, 1928; LL.D., Miami U., 1932, Rockford College, 1939; Norwich Univ., 1944, Yale, 1946; married Fannie C. Frisbie, Dec. 28, 1905; children—Harrison Leach, Frank Baldwin. Research assistant to Professor A. A. Michelson, Univ. of Chicago, 1901-02; instructor physics and electrical engineering, Mass. Institute of Technology, 1902-04; transmission engr. Am. Telephone & Telegraph Co., 1904-12; asst. chief engr., 1912-16, chief engr., 1916, vice-pres., 1922, Western Electric Co.; v.p. Am. Telephone & Telegraph Co., in charge development and research 1925-44; pres. Bell Telephone Laboratories, Inc., 1925-Oct. 1, 1940, chmn. bd. 1940-44. Maj. Signal Corps, U.S.R., 1917; lt. col. Signal Corps, A.U.S., Dec. 1, 1917; was advisory mem. Spl. Submarine Bd. of the Navy and mem. State Dept. Spl. Com. on Cables. Vice-chmn. Engring. Foundation, 1919-25; chmn. Div. of Engring. and Industrial Research, Nat. Research Council, 1923-27, now mem. com. on scientific aids to learning; mem. President Roosevelt's Science Advisory Board, 1933-35; mem. Nat. Defense Research Committee of Office of Scientific Research and Development; mem. coordination and equipment division, Signal Corps; consultant to Chief of Ordnance. President, Nat. Academy of Sciences, since 1939. Pres. and trustee, New York Museum of Science and Industry. Life mem. Mass. Inst. Tech. Corp.; pres. M.I.T. Alumni Association, 1939-40. Trustee Princeton U., Carnegie Instn. of Washington, Woods Hole Oceanographic Inst. Tabor Academy, Carnegie Inst. of Tech. Fellow Inst. Radio Engrs., A.A.A.S., Am. Physical Soc., Acoustical Soc. of Am., Acad. Arts and Sciences; mem. Am. Inst. Electric Engrs. (pres. 1922-23), Inst. Elec. Engrs. (Brit.), Am. Soc. for Engring. Edn., Am. Philos. Soc.; member (hon.) N.Y. Electrical Society, Delta Upsilon, Sigma Xi, Tau Beta Pi. Awarded D.S.M. (U.S.); 4th Order Rising Sun, 1923, 3d Order Sacred Treasure, 1930 (Japan); Edison medal, 1928; Faraday medal, 1935; Franklin medal, 1936; Washington award, 1938; John Fritz medal, 1939; Medal for Merit, 1946. Clubs: University, Engineers, Century Assn. (N.Y.); Short Hills (N.J.); Cosmos (Washington). Author brochures, articles and pub. addresses on physical and elec. subjects. Home: Brantwood, Short Hills, N.J. Office: 140 West St., New York, N.Y.; and 2101 Constitution Av. N.W., Washington, D.C. Died Nov. 18, 1949.

JEWETT, James Richard, univ. prof.; b. Westport, Me., Mar. 14, 1862; s. George Washington and Ann Maria (Greenleaf) J.; A.B., Harvard, 1884; holder of Harvard fellowship, 1884-87, spending time in Syria and Egypt; Ph.D., U. of Strassburg, 1891; m. Margaret Weyerhaeuser, June 28, 1894; 1 son, George Frederick. Instr. Semitic langs., Harvard, 1887-88, Brown U., 1890-91; asso. prof. Semitic langs. and Oriental history, Brown U., 1891-95; prof. same, U. of Minn., 1895-1902; prof. Arabic lang. and lit., U. of Chicago, 1902-11; prof. Arabic, Harvard, 1911-33, prof. emeritus since 1933. Fellow Am. Acad. Arts and Sciences; mem. Am. Oriental Soc., Soc. Bibl. Lit. and Exegesis, Mediæval Acad. of America. Clubs: Harvard (Boston); Harvard (New York); Faculty (Cambridge); Woods Hole Yacht, Woods Hole Golf; Crags Country (Los Angeles County, Calif.); Cliff Dwellers (Chicago). Home: Woods Hole, Mass. Address: 44 Francis Av., Cambridge, Mass. Died Mar. 31, 1943.

JIGGITTS, Louis Meredith, lawyer; b. Canton, Miss., Aug. 25, 1899; s. James Robinson and Mary Tupper (Powell) J.; student U. of Miss., 1917-18, 1919-20, 1923-24, LL.B., 1924; Rhodes scholar, Oxford U., 1920-23, B.A. in Jurisprudence, 1923; m. Lavonia Caradine, Sept. 11, 1924; children—Mary Ann, Louis Meredith. Began practice at Jackson, Miss., 1924; pros. atty., Jackson, 1926-29; reporter Miss. Supreme Court since 1929; mem. firm Powell, Harper & Jiggitts. Lecturer Jackson Sch. of Law. Served as 2d lt. inf., U.S. Army, World War; Co. C, 155th Inf., Miss. N.G., later capt.; commd. major and assigned as exec. officer, 155th Inf. Regt., 31st Div., Camp Blanding, Fla., Feb. 14, 1941, now lt. col. Trustee City Library, Jackson. Mem. Dem. Nat. Com. from 1932, until entered Army, vice-chmn., Phila., 1936. Mem. Miss. State Bar Assn., Am. Legion, Sons of Confederate Vets. (judge advocate Miss. div.), Sigma Alpha Epsilon, Sigma Upsilon. Episcopalian. Mason, K.P. Home: 920 Pinehurst St. Office: Deposit Guaranty Bank Bldg., Jackson, Miss. Died Mar. 22, 1945.

JIMENEZ OREAMUNO, Ricardo (hē-mä'näz), Costa Rican lawyer, agriculturalist, and public man; b. Cartago, 1859; s. Jesús Jiménez (pres. Costa Rica, 1863-70) and Esmeralda Oreamuno (d. Francisco M. Oreamuno, Pres. Costa Rica, 1844-50); ed. College of San Luis Gonzaga, Cartago; School of Law of San José (degree of lawyer, 1884); m. Maria Eugenia Calvo de Jiménez; children—Esmeralda, Jiménez Calvo. Minister plenipotentiary to Mexico, 1885-86; minister of fgn. affairs, treasury and pub. instr., 1889; pres. of Supreme Court of Justice, 1892; deputy to Constl. Congress from 1902-06; 1906-10 and 1922-26; pres. of same, 1909; pres. Republic of Costa Rica, 1910-14, 1914-23, and 1932-36. Awarded: Grand Official of Legation d'Honneur, and of the Order of Isabel la Católica of Spain; Merit of Chile; Vasco Núñez de Balboa of Panamá; Grand Cross of Order of Boyacá, Colombia. Mem. Real Academia Española de la lengua. Author of Instrucción Cívica (2d ed. 1926). Address: San José, Costa Rica. Died Jan. 4, 1945.

JINNAH, Mahomed Ali (jin'nä), gov. gen. of Pakistan; pres. Moslem League; b. Dec. 25, 1876. Called to bar, 1896; married; 1 dau. Enrolled lawyer Bombay high court, 1897. Practice of law, Bombay; pvt. sec. to Dadabhoy Naorojim, a founding father of India Nat. Congress, 1906. Mem. Imperial legislative Council, 1910; elected pres. All-India Moslem League, 1916, re-elected pres. spl. session, 1920, pres. Moslem League, 1934-48; pres. Pakistan Constituent Assembly, Aug. 11, 1947-Sept. 1948; gov.-gen. of Pakistan, Aug. 15, 1947-Sept. 1948. Attended Round Table Conf., 1929-30; was mem. Central Legislative Assembly and leader Moslem League Party in the House. Leader of Pakistan, which advocates establishment of separate independent Moslem States, where Moslems are a majority in their homelands, by dividing India into Hindu India and Moslem India. Address: Malabar Hill, Bombay, India. Died Sept. 11, 1948.

JOB, Thomas (jōb), playwright and prof. of drama; b. Carmarthen, S. Wales, Great Britain, August 10, 1900; s. Edwin Mansel and Emma Augusta (Beard) J.; B.A., University of Wales, 1923, M.A., 1925; m. Edith Ann Robinson, July 31, 1937; children—Thomas Mansel, Ann Bronwen. Came to United States, 1924; naturalized, 1940. Instructor Dept. of English, Carleton Coll., 1925, asst. prof. English, 1925-30, chmn. Dept. of Drama, 1930-36; hon. fellow, Yale University, 1937-39; asst. prof. Dept. of Drama, Yale, 1939-40; asso. prof. playwriting and history of dramatic lit., Carnegie Inst. Tech., since 1940. Mem. Dramatists Guild of America. Presbyterian. Author (plays): Giants in the Earth (tragedy), 1929; Barchester Towers (comedy), produced by Guthrie McClintic with Ina Claire, N.Y. City, 1937; Alas Regardless, produced by Sir Barry Jackson, Birmingham (Eng.) Repertory Theatre, 1940; Uncle Harry, produced in New York May 1942, in London, March 1944; Thérese, New York, 1945; Land's End, New York, 1946. Writer for Warner Bros., 20th Century Fox, Hollywood. Died July 31, 1947.

JOHNS, Carl Oscar, chemist; b. Sweden, Aug. 19, 1870; s. Andrew and Clara Sophia (Gabrielson) J.; came with parents to U.S., 1879; student Upsala Coll., Brooklyn, N.Y., 1894-95; A.B., Bethany (Kan.) Coll., 1899, A.M., 1902, D.Sc., 1922; Ph.B., Yale, 1904, Ph.D., 1906; m. Marie Eugenie Malmberg, 1908; children—Marie Louise, Margaret Loraine, Carl Oscar. Instr. in natural history, Bethany Coll., 1899-1902, prof. 1902-03, also treas., 1899-1903; asst. in chemistry, Sheffield Scientific Sch. (Yale), 1904-06, instr., 1906-11, asst. prof., 1911-14; organic chemist, U.S. Bur. Chemistry, Washington, D.C., 1914-15, in charge Protein Investigation Lab., 1915-20, also in charge scientific personnel, 1917-20, and of color investigation lab., 1920; lecturer in chemistry, Yale, 1920; dir. of research, development dept. Standard Oil Co. of N.J., 1920-27; dir. of research labs. and mem. bd. dirs. Standard Oil Development Co., 1927-30, chem. consultant since 1930. Chmn. Intersectional Petroleum Symposium, New York, 1924. Fellow A.A.A.S.; mem. Am. Chem. Soc. (councillor), Soc. Chem. Industry, Soc. Biol. Chemists, Am. Petroleum Inst., N.J. Chem. Soc. (dir.), Sigma Xi; pres. Washington (D.C.) Chem. Soc., 1920, Yale Chem. Soc. since 1930. Republican. Presbyterian. Club: Graduate (New Haven, Conn.). Contbr. some 80 research articles. Home: 32 Old Estate Road, Manhasset, L.I., N.Y.* Died Apr. 17, 1942.

JOHNS, Joshua Leroy, ex-congressman; b. Town of Eagle, Richland County, Wis., Feb. 27, 1881; s. William Harrison and Cynthia (Logue) J.; LL.B., U. of Chattanooga, 1906; LL.B., Yale, 1907; m. Esther M. Newman, Sept. 7, 1910 (died Apr. 1940); 1 son, Newman H.; m. 2d, Marguerite Burdon; 1 son, Richard Rowland. Asst. cashier and dir. State Bank of Richland Center, Wis., 1902-05, v.p. and dir. First Nat. Bank, Richland Center, 1905-06; admitted to Tenn. bar, 1906, Wis. bar, 1910; organizer and v.p. and dir. Farmers and Merchants Bank, Richland Center, 1913-16; practiced law in Appleton, since 1920; pres. and dir. Plumber's Woodwork Co., Algoma, Wisconsin, since 1929; vice-president Narcor Manufacturing Company, Green Bay, Wis., 1943-46, president since 1946; president Northland Lumber Co. since 1944; mem. 76th and 77th Congresses (1939-43), 8th Dist. of Wis. Col. Nat. Guard of Wis., 1928. Pres. Kiwanis Internat., 1933-34. Mem. Am. and Wis. bar assns. Republican. Episcopalian. Mason, K.P. Club: Kiwanis of Appleton. Contbr. to Kiwanis Mag. and other publs.; author of pamphlet, "Outline of U.S. Citizenship," prepared for Kiwanis Internat. Author of resolution creating "I am an American Day," presented in Congress. Home: 819 Eliza St., Green Bay, Wis. Office: Algoma, Wis. Died Mar. 16, 1947.

JOHNS, William Hingston, advertising; b. Redruth (Cornwall), Eng., Feb. 10, 1868; s. Rev. John and Mary (Hingston) J.; brought to U.S., 1873; B.S., Coll. City of N.Y., 1887; m. Florence May Wilcox, May 3, 1899; children—Ella (Mrs. Forrest Andrews), John, William H. (dec.), Janet (dec.), Talbot, Elizabeth Wilcox (Mrs. G. Wallace Ruckert). Began in employ Funk & Wagnalls, publishers, New York, 1887, later with Blair & Co., bankers; with George Batten, 1892, started George Batten Co., Inc., pres. since 1918; pres. Batten, Barton, Durstine & Osborn, Inc., 1928-36, chmn. of exec. com. since 1936, chmn. bd., 1939; v.p. and dir. Bayside Nat. Bank. Chmn. div. of advertising of Com. on Public Information, during war period. A founder, 1918, and ex-pres. Am. Assn. Advt. Agencies; elected pres. Chamber Commerce Borough of Queens, N.Y. City, 1921. Mem. Alpha Delta Phi. Republican. Episcopalian. Mason. Clubs: Union League, Bayside Yacht, Plandome Golf. Home: Bayside, L.I., N.Y. Office: 383 Madison Av., New York, N.Y. Died Apr. 17, 1944.

JOHNSON, Albert Mussey, life insurance; b. Oberlin, O., May 31, 1872; s. Albert H. and Revecca A. (Jenkins) J.; spl. work in Oberlin Coll., 1890; C.E., Cornell U., 1895; m. Bessie Morris Penniman, Nov. 19, 1896. Station agt. on Ark. Midland Ry., 1888-89; sec. and mgr. Mussey Stone Co., Elyria, O., 1897-98; sec. McDermott Stone Co., 1898; mining lead and zinc, Joplin, Mo., 1899; vice pres. Ark. Midland R.R., 1901-02; pres. Oberlin (O.) Gas & Electric Co. until 1903; treas. Nat. Life Ins. Co. of U.S.A., 1902, later v.p., pres. 1906-26, chmn. bd. since 1926; pres. 29 S. La Salle Building Corp. Clubs: Mid-Day, Chicago Athletic, Edgewater Golf. Home: 6353 Sheridan Rd. Office: 29 S. La Salle St., Chicago. Died Jan 7, 1948.

JOHNSON, Arthur Monrad, botanist; b. Fredrikstad, Norway, Jan. 19, 1878; s. Christen and Ottomine Marie (Andersen) J.; brought to U.S., 1882; A.B., U. of Minn., 1904, Ph.D., 1919, grad. study, Harvard, 1924-25; m. Eleanor Adalyn Henderson, June 22, 1915. Teacher in high schs., 1904-15; teacher summer sessions—Washington State Coll., 1908, 09, U. of Washington 1913, 14, De Pauw U., 1917, 19; fellow in botany, U. of Minn., 1916-19, instr., 1919-24; lecturer economic botany, Boston Teachers Sch. of Science, 1926; U. of Wis., 1927; lecturer U. of Calif. at Los Angeles, 1927-28, asst. prof., 1929-37, associate professor and director Botanical Garden since 1937; lecturer in art since 1940. Studied art at University of Minnesota and San Francisco Art Inst.; paintings exhibited in Minneapolis, Chicago, Brooklyn, Los Angeles, San Francisco, Sacramento; 1st prize in drawing and water-color at Odin Club Art Exhbn., Minneapolis, 1923. Mem. A.A.A.S., Am. Soc. Plant Taxonomists, Botanical Soc. of America, Am.-Scandinavian Foundation, Calif. Water-Color Soc., Theta Chi, Sigma Xi, Varsity-Village Club, Los Angeles (Westwood). Author: A Revision of the North American Species of Saxifraga, Section Boraphila (Engler), 1923; Taxonomy of the Flowering Plants, 1931. Contbr. to scientific jours. Home: 10733 Wellworth Av., Los Angeles (Westwood), Calif. Died July 19, 1943.

JOHNSON, Benjamin Alvin, judge; b. Salisbury, Md., Dec. 23, 1887; s. Rufus and Tabitha Wise (Davis) J.; A.B., Washington Coll., 1911; student Baltimore Law Sch., 1911-12; m. Ethel Frances Halloway, Oct. 20, 1915; children—Alvin Halloway (dec.), William Benjamin, Rufus Clay, Martha Jane (dec.), Frances Perdue, Mary Jane. Admitted to Md. bar, 1913; city solicitor Town of Salisbury, practicing atty. and mem. firm Long & Johnson, 1915-34; chief justice 1st Judicial Circuit Court of Md., 1934-43, now retired. Mem. bd. of gov. and visitor, Washington Coll. Mem. Kappa Alpha. Democrat. Elk. Home: 237 S. Division St., Salisbury, Md. Died Oct. 22, 1943.

JOHNSON, Bernard Lyman, editor, pub.; b. Clyde, Mich., Dec. 2, 1883; s. Lyman J. and Edith Meribah (Stevens) J.; B.S., Kalamazoo Coll., June 1906; B.S., U. of Chicago, 1907; m. Ruth Wheaton, June 20, 1908; children—Dexter Wheaton, Maxwell Allis, Melinda Elizabeth. Editor American Builder (now American Builder and Building Age, published by Simmons-Boardman Publishing Corporation), 1908-43, western editor since 1943; editor of Farm Mechanics, 1919-28. President Chicago Association Business Paper Editors, 1932-33. Member of President's Conf. on Home Building, 1931. Baptist. Mason. Author: (also joint editor) Framing, 1909; Radford's Cyclopedia of Construction (12 vols.), 1909; Details of Building Construction, 1912; Farm and Building Guide, 1915; Book of Farm Improvements, 1916; Homes for Everyone, 1919; Architectural Details, 1921; Henry Ford and His Power Farm, 1922; Saving the World from Starvation, 1923; Most Popular Homes in America, 1925; Small Homes of Charm, 1931; New Era Home Designs, 1935. Winner 1931 A.B.P. award for best editorial in a business publication. Club: Washington Athletic. Home: 1615 Ravenna Blvd., Seattle. Died Dec. 22, 1947.

JOHNSON, Charles Henry, mem. State Board of Social Welfare; b. Brooklyn, Oct. 13, 1870; s. Samuel and Marie (Holm) J.; A.B., Harvard, 1902; S.T.B., Boston U., 1902; LL.D., Alfred U., 1915; m. Elvina Peterson, Oct. 16, 1894 (died Feb. 29, 1908); 1 son, Orville Parker (dec.); m. 2d, Mrs. May B. Wallis. Organizer, 1902, and first secretary Committee on Prevention of Tuberculosis, N.Y. City; supt. St. Christopher's Home for Children, Dobbs Ferry, N.Y., 1903-06; successively supt. Albany Orphan Asylum, Leake and Watts' Home Sch. (Yonkers, N.Y.), dep. warden Sing Sing; supt. Com. Reformatory until 1916; sec. N.Y. State Bd. of Charities, 1916; was commr. of social welfare, N.Y. State. Served with Am. Relief Adminstrn., Russia, 1922. Ex-pres. bd. mgrs. N.Y. State Training School for Boys. Mem. Am. Prison Assn. (ex-pres.), Nat. Conf. Social Work, Nat. Conf. Juvenile Agencies (ex-pres.), Am. Assn. Pub. Welfare Officials (ex-pres.), N.Y. State Conf. Social Work (ex-pres.), Am. Acad. Polit. and Social Science, Legal Aid Soc. of Albany (organizer; 1st pres.), Albany Council Social Agencies (1st pres.), Y.M.C.A. (ex-pres.). Republican. Presbyterian. Mason (33°); Past Grand Master Grand Council, R. & S.M.; Grand Master of Masons, State of N.Y.; Grand Sec. Grand Lodge F. & A.M.; Past Gen. Grand Master, Gen. Grand Council R. & S.M. of U.S.; past pres. Masonic Relief Assn. of U.S. and Can. Clubs: Rotary (ex-pres.); Harvard, Nat. Republican, New York Athletic, Blizzard Men of 1888 (New York); Collectors. Author of various pamphlets and books on philanthropic and Masonic topics; also One Common Purpose (book). Home: 10 Park Av., New York. Died Oct. 28, 1948.

JOHNSON, Charles Willison, zoölogist; b. Morris Plains, N.J., Oct. 26, 1863; s. Albert Fletcher and Sarah Elizabeth (Willison) J.; ed. pub. and pvt. schs., Morristown, N.J.; m. Carrie W. Ford, Jan. 14, 1897 (died 1931). Moved to St. Augustine, Fla., 1880, continuing studies in natural history, and making large collection of insects, mollusca and fossils. Curator Mus. of Wagner Free Inst. of Science, Phila., 1888-1903; curator Boston Soc. Natural History since Mar. 1903. Especialy interested in study of mollusca and diptera, and contbr. to biol. jours. of papers relating to these spltíes.; asso. editor and mgr. The Nautilus since May, 1890. Fellow Am. Acad. Arts and Sciences, Entomol. Soc. Am. (pres. 1924), A.A. A.S.; mem. Phila. Acad. Natural Sciences, Entomol. Soc. Washington, Malacol. Soc. of London. Home: Brookline, Mass. Office: 234 Berkeley St., Boston. Died May 8, 1932.

JOHNSON, Charles Willis, chemist; b. Concord, Ind., Sept. 23, 1873; s. Frederick Angell and Marie Jane (Tustison) J.; Pharm. Chemist, U. of Mich., 1896; B.S., 1900, Ph.D., 1903; m. Parthenia Sykes, June 21, 1900 (died May 2, 1918); children—Lois Kathleen, Eloise Ruth, Frederick Francis; m. 2d, Frances Edith Hindman, June 22, 1920. Teacher in pub. schs., 1890-92; pharmacist, Ann Arbor and Detroit, 1896-98; asst. instr. chemistry, U. of Mich., 1898-1901; instr. chemistry, State U. of Ia., 1901-02; asst. prof. chemistry, 1903-04, prof. pharm. chemistry and dean Coll. of Pharmacy, 1904-39, prof. and dean emeritus since Sept. 1939, U. of Washington. Chemist State Dairy and Food Commn. of Wash., 1909-13; state chemist Dept. of Agriculture, Washington, 1913-43. Congregationalist. Mem. Am. Pharm. Assn. (pres. 1927-28), Wash. State Pharm. Assn., Kappa Psi, Sigma Xi, Rho Chi, Phi Delta Chi. Mason (K.T., 32°, Shriner). Mem. com. in charge revision of U.S. Pharmacopœia X and XI; pres. Wash. State Pharm. Assn., 1915-17; pres. Am. Conf. of Pharm. Faculties (now Am. Assn. Colls. of Pharmacy), 1923-24. Home: 4337 15th Av. N.E., Seattle. Died Jan. 4, 1949.

JOHNSON, Crawford Toy, mfr.; b. Danville, Va., May 20, 1873; s. John Lipscomb and Julia Anna (Toy) J.; B.P., U. of Miss., 1890; m. Anne Caroline Acree, Nov. 2, 1897; children—Crawford Toy, Allen Acree, John (dec.). Began as bookkeeper, Chattanooga, Tenn., 1891; dept. clk. U.S. Circuit and Dist. Court, Chattanooga, 1893-99; provision broker at Chattanooga, 1899-1901; pres. and mgr. The Birmingham Coca-Cola Bottling Co., 1902-26; chmn. bd. Crawford Johnson & Co., Inc.; pres. Chattanooga Coca-Cola Bottling Co., Augusta Coca-Cola Bottling Co., Spartanburg Coca-Cola Bottling Co., Hartsville Coca-Cola Bottling Co., Darlington Coca-Cola Bottling Co., Waynesboro Coca-Cola Bottling Co., La. Coca-Cola Bottling Co., New Orleans, Laurens (S.C.) Coca-Cola Bottling Co.; dir. First Nat. Bank, Protective Life Insurance Company, Redmont Land Company, Franklin-Crawford Realty Company, Inc., Farmers & Ginners Cotton Oil Co. (all of Birmingham, Ala.), McComb (Miss.) Coca-Cola Bottling Co. Mem. President's Economic Com., 1932. State dir. War Savings, Ala., 1917-18. Mem. Ala. State Child Welfare Bd.; director Birmingham Community Chest; trustee of Howard College, Birmingham, Ala. Delegate to Dem. Nat. Convention, 1916; mem. Birmingham Chamber Commerce (pres. 1915-16), Chi Psi, Omicron Delta Kappa, New York Southern Soc. Baptist. Mason (K.T., Shriner). Clubs: Rotary, Birmingham Country, Mountain Brook Country (Birmingham); Mountain City (Chattanooga); Bankers (New York). Home: 2935 Pawnee Rd., Birmingham, Ala.; also West Brow Rd., Lookout Mountain, Tenn. Office: 3301 11th Av. N., Birmingham, Ala. Died Dec. 9, 1942; buried at Birmingham, Ala.

JOHNSON, David Clayton, pub. utilities; b. Brooklyn, N.Y., Aug. 24, 1885; s. John Albert and Anna Mary (Jenkins) J.; M.E., Stevens Inst. Tech., 1906; m. Mary Florence Riley, Dec. 16, 1914; 1 son, David Clayton. Began as constrn. engr. Astoria Light, Heat & Power Co.; then asst. engr. to H. DeB. Parsons, cons. engr. and later engr., Humphreys & Miller; mgr. pub. utility dept. Nat. City Co., 1917-27; v.p. N.Y. Steam Corp., 1927-28, pres. since 1928; v.p. and trustee Consol. Edison Co. of New York, Inc.; dir. Brooklyn Edison Co., N.Y. & Queens Electric Light & Power Co., Consol. Telegraph & Electric Subway Co., L.I. R.R. Co., Fidelity Phenix Fire Ins. Co. Trustee Stevens Inst. Technology. Mem. Am. Soc. C.E., Am. Soc. Mech. Engrs. Clubs: Union League, West Side Tennis, Manhattan, Engineers, Bond, Rockefeller Center, Luncheon, N.Y. Athletic, Downtown Athletic (New York); Westhampton Beach Country; Quantuck Beach; National Golf. Author: Yields of Bonds and Stocks, 1923, rev. edit., 1938. Compiled Taxable-Non-Taxable Chart, Darville-Johnson Bond Yield Chart. Home: 420 Park Av. Office: 4 Irving Place, New York, N.Y. Died Dec. 19, 1942.

JOHNSON, Douglas Wilson, geologist; b. Parkersburg, W.Va., Nov. 30, 1878; s. Isaac H. and Jennie A. (Wilson) J.; Denison U., Granville, O., 1896-98; B.S., Univ. of N.M., 1901; Ph.D., Columbia, 1903, hon. D.Sc., 1929; Docteur, honoris causa, Univ. of Grenoble, France, 1924, Nancy, France, 1932, Montpelier, France, 1933; hon. D.Sc., Denison University, 1932; m. Alice Adkins, Aug. 11, 1903; m. 2d, Edith Sanford Caldwell, 1943. Teacher public schs., 1897-98; field asst., Univ. Geol. Survey, in N.M., 1899-1901, teacher in high sch., Albuquerque, N.M., 1900-01; asst. U.S. Geol. Survey, 1901, 03, 04, 05; instr. in geology, 1903-05, asst. prof., 1905-07, Mass. Inst. Tech.; asst. prof. physiography, Harvard, 1906-12; asso. prof. physiography, 1912-19, prof. since 1919, exec. officer, dept. of geology since 1937, Columbia U. Asst. N.J. Geol. Survey, 1911; dir. Shaler Memorial Expdn., 1911-12; geog. adviser U.S. Dept. State, 1919-20; cons. physiographer to Canadian govt. in Labrador boundary dispute, 1926. Maj. Intelligence Div., U.S. Army, Feb. 1918; chief of div. boundary geography, Am. Commn. to Negotiate Peace, Paris, 1918-19; exchange prof. to France, in engring. and applied science, 1923-24; pres. sect. of physical geography of Internat. Geog. Congress, Paris, 1931. Chmn. national committee United States International Geographic Union, 1933-37; president International Terrace Commission, 1934-38. Mem. Nat. Acad. Science, Geological Society America (president, 1942), American Academy Arts and Sciences, American Museum of Natural History, New York Academy Sciences, A.A.A.S., Am. Philos. Soc.; mem. Assn. Am. Geographers, Am. Geog. Soc., Nat. Research Council, Sigma Xi, Phi Beta Kappa; hon. mem. Russian Geog. Soc., Serbian Acad. Sciences, Swedish Soc. Geography and Anthropology, Geog. Soc. of Bordeaux, Geog. Soc. Belgrade, Société Belge de Géologie, Geol. Soc. China, Geol. Soc. London, Geol. Soc. Finland. Janssen medallist, Paris Geog. Soc., 1920; Elisha Kent Kane medallist, Geog. Soc., Phila., 1922, U. of Nancy medallist, 1924; A. Cressy Morrison prize, N.Y. Acad. Sci., 1924, 30; Gaudy medallist, Soc. de Geographie Commerciale de Paris, 1925; Cvijic medallist, Geog. Soc. of Belgrade, 1935; Cullum medallist, Am. Geog. Soc., 1935. Decorated Chevalier Legion of Honor (French), 1924; Order of St. Sava (Jugoslavia), 1934. Clubs: Century. Author: Lettre d'un Américain à un Allemand, 1916; Topography and Strategy in the War, 1917; Peril of Prussianism, 1917; My German Correspondence, 1917; Shore Processes and Shoreline Development, 1919; Battlefields of the World War, 1921; The New England-Acadian Shoreline, 1925; Paysages Américains et Problèmes Géographiques, 1927; Stream Sculpture on the Atlantic Slope, 1931; The Assault on the Supreme Court, 1937; The Origin of Submarine Canyons, 1939; The Origin of the Carolina Bays; also numerous scientific bulls., papers, etc. Editor of Jour. Geomorphology. Address: Columbia University, New York, N.Y. Died Feb. 24, 1944.

JOHNSON, Edgar Hutchinson, coll. prof.; b. Palmetto, Ga., Feb. 15, 1873; s. John A. and Mary (Hutchinson) J.; S.B., Emory Coll., Oxford, Ga., 1891; student Johns Hopkins, 1893-95; S.M., U. of Chicago, 1899, Ph.D., 1909; A.M., Harvard, 1903; m. Susan McMichael, Aug. 24, 1904; children—Lois McMichael (dec.), Rachel (Mrs. T. L. Ross, Jr.), Edgar Hutchinson. Professor of mathematics, Quitman College, Ark., 1891-93; adjunct prof. of mathematics, 1895, prof. history and polit. economy, 1900, v.p., 1909-16, prof. polit. economy since 1916, dean, 1916-19, Emory Coll.; dean Sch. of Business Administration, Emory U., 1919-40. Mem. Ga. Spl. Tax Commn., 1918-19, also 1929. Mem. Social Service Commn. M.E. Ch., S., 1918-26; pres. Assn. Ga. Colls., 1919; trustee Atlanta Sch. of Social Work. Mem. Phi Beta Kappa. Inventor of Leverator, a stairway elevator. Home: Emory University, Ga. Died Sep. 11, 1944.

JOHNSON, Elbert Leland, banker; b. Independence, Ia., Mar. 27, 1863; s. Emmons and Lucy Ann (Leland) J.; student State U. of Ia., 1880-82; Ph.B., U. of Mich., 1884; m. Carrie Reed, Apr. 7, 1891; children—Eleanor Reed (Mrs. George W. Williams), Mrs. Carolyn Johnson Szikszay. Loan business, Clay Center, Kan., 1885-88; mem. B. J. Johnson Soap Co., Milwaukee, Wis. (now Colgate-Palmolive-Peet Co.); banker, Waterloo, Ia., since 1889; now pres. 1st Nat. Bank, Waverly, Ia.; mem. Leavitt & Johnson Co. until 1930; dir. Fed. Reserve Bank of Chicago, 1914-30. Mem. Beta Theta Pi. Conglist. Club: Union League (Chicago). Home: 542 Lakeland, Grosse Pointe, Mich. Died May 5, 1949.

JOHNSON, Eldridge Reeves, founder Victor Talking Machine Co.; b. Wilmington, Del., Feb. 6, 1867; s. Asa S. and Caroline (Reeves) J.; ed. Spring Garden Inst., Phila.; A.E.D., U. of Pa., 1928; m. Elsie Reeves Fenimore, Oct. 5, 1897; 1 son, Eldridge Reeves Fenimore. Founder, 1894, of business, inc., 1901, as Victor Talking Machine Co. of which was pres. until 1927. Trustee U. of Pa. Mem. Am. Philos. Soc. Republican. Episcopalian. Clubs: Union League, Rittenhouse. Home: Moorestown, N.J. Address: 608 West Jersey Trust Bldg., Camden, N.J. Died Nov. 15, 1945; buried in West Laurel Hill Cemetery, Bala-Cynwyd, Pa.

JOHNSON, Franklin Paradise, anatomist, urologist; b. Hannibal, Mo., Jan. 7, 1888; s. Horace William and Lillie May (Paradise) J.; A.B., U. of Mo., 1908; A.M., Harvard, 1910, Ph.D., 1912; studied U. of Freiburg, Germany, summer, 1911; M.D., Johns Hopkins Univ., 1920; m. Juliette Omohundro, Sept. 4, 1923; children—Lillian Paradise, Virginia Martin, Louise Carter. Austin teaching fellow, Harvard Med. Sch., 1908-10; instr. histology and embryology, same sch., 1910-12; asst. prof. anatomy, 1912; asso. prof., 1913, prof., 1919-20, U. of Mo., interne New Haven Hosp., 1920-21; asst. resident in urology, 1921-22, resident, 1922-23, Johns Hopkins Hosp.; now practicing at Portland, Ore.; assistant clin. prof. urology, U. of Ore., since 1929. Member A.M.A., Am. Assn. Anatomists, Sigma Xi, Phi Beta Pi; fellow Am. Coll. Surgeons, Am. Urol. Association; diplomate Am. Bd. of Urology. Author various research papers on development of the digestive tract, embryology and histology of the liver, urethra, urol. subjects, etc.; collaborator Young's Practice of Urology, Nelson's Loose Leaf Surgery, Morris' Anatomy, 9th and 10th edits. Home: 2798 S.W. Talbot Rd. Office: Medical Arts Bldg., Portland, Ore. Died Feb. 12, 1943; buried in Riverwood Cemetery, Portland, Ore.

JOHNSON, Frederick Foote, bishop; b. Newtown, Conn., Apr. 23, 1866; s. Ezra L. and Jane E. (Camp) J.; B.A., Trinity Coll., Conn., 1894, B.D., 1897; D.D., 1906; D.D., Berkeley Div. Sch., 1906; D.D., U. of the South, 1918; m. Susan L. Beers, Feb. 4, 1899 (died 1901); m. 2d, Elisabeth L. Beers, June 26, 1915. Deacon, 1896, priest, 1897, P.E. Ch.; minister Glenwood Springs, Colo., 1897; curate St. Stephen's Ch., Colorado Springs, Colo., 1897-98; rector Redlands, Calif., 1899-1904; diocesan missionary Western Mass., 1904-05; consecrated asst. bishop of S.D., Nov. 2, 1905; elected bishop of S.D., Oct. 11, 1910; elected bishop coadjutor of Mo., May 1911, bishop of Mo., Apr. 1923; retired, 1933. Mem. Phi Beta Kappa, Delta Kappa Epsilon. Home: Newtown, Conn. Died May 9, 1943.

JOHNSON, George, clerical educator; b. Toledo, O., Feb. 22, 1889; s. Henry and Kathryn (McCarthy) J.; A.B., St. John's U. (Toledo), 1910; studied Am. Coll., Rome, Italy, 1912-14; Ph.D., Cath. U. of America, 1919; LL.D., Marquette U., 1930. Ordained priest R.C. Ch., 1914; asso. prof. edn. Cath. U. of America since 1921, head dept. of education, 1938-40; dir. dept. of edn., National Catholic Welfare Conf., Washington, D.C.; editor Catholic Educational Review; sec. gen. Nat. Cath. Ednl. Assn.; dir. Campus Sch. of Catholic U. of America. Member Assn. Am. Colls., Am. Assn. for Adult Edn., World Fedn. Cath. Ednl. Assns., Nat. Advisory Com. on Edn., 1930-32, White House Conf. on Child Health and Protection, 1939, Advisory Com. of Nat. Youth Adminstrn., 1935-43. Am. Youth Commn. of Am. Council on Edn., 1935-41, Federal Radio Edn. Com., President's Adv. Com. on Edn., 1936-38, Edn. Adv. Com. under Co-ordinator of Inter-Am. Affairs, Nat. Com. on Edn. and Defense, Joint Army and Navy Com. on Welfare and Recreation, U.S. Office of Edn. Wartime Commn., Problems and Plans Com. of Am. Council on Edn. Mem. Kappa Delta Pi. Made Domestic Prelate to Pope Pius XII, Nov. 21, 1942. Author: Bible History Series (3 vols.), 1931. Contbr. to ednl. mags. Address: The Catholic University of America, Washington, D.C. Died June 5, 1944.

JOHNSON, George E. Q., lawyer; b. Harcourt, Ia., July 11, 1874; s. John and Mathilda (Linderholm) J.; grad. Tobin Coll., Fort Dodge, Ia., 1897; LL.B., Lake Forest U., 1900; m. Elizabeth M. Swanstrom, Sept. 8, 1906; 1 son, George E. Q. Engaged in practice of law since 1900; master in chancery Circuit Court of Cook County, 1922-27; United States dist. attorney Northern Dist. Ill., 1927-32; apptd. judge U.S. Dist. Court, Aug. 17, 1932; retired Mar., 1933, and resumed practice of law, specializing in Federal Court litigation; dir. Mutual Trust Life Ins. Co. Mem. American, Illinois State and Chicago bar assns. Active in church and social work. Lutheran. Mason. Clubs: Union League, Swedish, South Shore Country. Author: Johnson, On Bankruptcy Procedure; also various mag. articles. Home: 7327 Crandon Av. Office: 105 W. Adams St., Chicago, Ill. Died Sep. 19, 1949.

JOHNSON, George Francis, shoe mfr.; b. Milford, Mass., Oct. 14, 1857; s. Frank A. (capt. U.S. Army) and Sarah J.; ed. pub. schs. Began with Seaver Bros., boot and shoe makers, Ashland, Mass.; later with A. Coburn & Co.; then became foreman of treeing and finishing depts., Lester Bros., shoe mfrs., Binghamton, N.Y.; formed partnership with Harry B. Endicott under title of Endicott, Johnson & Co., now Endicott Johnson Corp., of which is chmn. bd. Home: 1001 Park St., Endicott, N.Y. Died Nov. 28, 1948.

JOHNSON, George William, ex-congressman; born near Charles Town, West Virginia; son of George Dallas and Ann Elizabeth (Henry) J.; A.B. and LL.B., W.Va. U., 1894; m. Mary A. McKendree; children—Mildred Elizabeth, George McKendree. Practiced law at Martinsburg, W.Va., later at Parkersburg; orchardist; established Washington Jersey Farms, Wood County, W.Va.; served as city atty. Martinsburg, asst. prosecuting atty. Parkersburg and referee in bankruptcy, U.S. Dist. Court of W.Va.; gen. counsel W.Va., Pub. Service Commn.; mem. 68th and 73d to 77th Congresses (1923-25 and 1933-43), 4th W.Va. Dist. Formerly mem. bd. regents State Normal Sch., W.Va. Democrat. Episcopalian. Mason (32°). Kiwanian, Elk. Home: Parkersburg, W.Va.* Died Feb. 24, 1944.

JOHNSON, Gove G(riffith), clergyman; b. St. Louis, Mo., Sept. 20, 1869; s. George James and Maria (Nickerson) J.; A.B., Colgate, 1891, A.M., 1894, B.D., 1895, D.D., 1910; m. May Russell, Dec. 13, 1894; children—Francelia May, Grace Russell, Norma Russell, Elizabeth Sara, Gove Griffith. Ordained ministry Bapt. Ch., 1894; pastor Ballston Spa, N.Y., 1894-99, Pittsfield, Mass., 1900-02, Buffalo, N.Y., 1902-10, N.Y. City, 1910-14, Immanuel Bapt. Ch. (now Nat. Bapt. Memorial to Religious Liberty), Washington, D.C., since 1914. Mem. Delta Kappa Epsilon. Prohibitionist. Home: 4212 18th St., Washington. Died Dec. 3, 1944; buried at Hamilton, N.Y.

JOHNSON, Harold Bowtell, editor; b. Rossie, St. Lawrence County, N.Y., Aug. 9, 1880; s. John Brayton and Elizabeth (Bowtell) J.; grad. Gouverneur (N.Y.) High Sch., 1899; L.H.D., St. Lawrence U., 1925; m. Jessie Roselinda Parsons, Mar. 4, 1903; 1 son, John Brayton. Reporter Portland (Ore.) Telegram, 1900, Montana Daily Record, Helena, 1900-01, Gouverneur Free Press and Gouverneur Northern Tribune, 1901-04; reporter Watertown (N.Y.) Daily Times, 1904-07, city editor, 1907-18, editor since 1918, and pres. Brockway Co., pub. Daily Times; owner of radio stations WWNY, Watertown and WMSA, Massena, N.Y. Director, National St. Lawrence Association, Watertown National Bank; trustee Watertown Savings Bank. Trustee St. Lawrence U., Theodore Roosevelt Memorial Assn., Theodore Roosevelt House, N.Y., Edward John Noble Foundation, Jefferson County Hospital Service Corp.; dir. Auburn Theol. Sem.; mem. Synodical Council, the Synod of N.Y. Presbyterian Church; chmn. bd. trustees State Teachers Coll. Oswego, N.Y. Trustee, N.Y. State Teachers College Dormitory Authority. Member N.Y. State Soc. Newspaper Editors, Am. Soc. Newspaper Editors, Citizen's Com. on Cts., N.Y. City. Republican. Presbyterian. Clubs: Black River Valley, Jefferson County Golf. Home: 221 Flower Av. W., Watertown, N.Y.; (summer) Underbluff, Henderson Harbor, N.Y. Died May 17, 1949; buried Brookside Cemetery, Watertown, N.Y.

JOHNSON, Herbert, cartoonist; b. Sutton, Neb., Oct. 30, 1878; s. Joseph William and Mary Hollingsworth Bagley J.; Western Normal Coll., at Lincoln, Neb.; State U. of Neb., 1899-1901; spl. courses, Columbia; m. Helen L. Turner, Jan. 8, 1908; children—Herberta Hollingsworth, Katharine Turner. Asst. cartoonist, Denver Republican, 1896; head of art and engraving depts., Kansas City Journal, 1897-99; free lance cartoonist in New York, 1903-05; mgr. Sunday art dept., Phila. North American, 1906-09, cartoonist, North American, 1908-12; art editor, cartoonist, Saturday Evening Post, 1912-15, cartoonist Saturday Evening Post; retired since 1941. Mem. Soc. Illustrators, Phi Delta Theta (Neb. Alpha Chapter). Mem. Soc. of Friends. Clubs: Phila. Sketch, Union League, University. Home: Morningside Farm, Huntingdon Valley, Pa. Died Dec. 4, 1946.

JOHNSON, Herbert Spencer, clergyman; b. McMinnville, Ore., Oct. 4, 1866; s. John Wesley and Helen Elizabeth (Adams) J.; A.B., U. of Ore., 1887; A.B., Harvard, 1891; grad. Rochester Theol. Sem., 1893, Army War Coll., 1923, Infantry Sch. U.S. Army, Ft. Benning, 1924; D.D., Berea (Ky.) Coll., 1911; LL.D., Franklin Coll., 1918; m. Mary Crane, June 21, 1900; children—Elizabeth (dec.), Mary, Helen, Herbert S. Ordained Baptist ministry, 1893; pastor Pittsfield, Mass., 1893-99, Warren Av. Ch., Boston, 1899-1922, Temple Baptist Church, Los Angeles, 1934-36, Euclid Avenue Bapt. Ch., Cleveland, 1936-37, First Baptist Ch., Boston, 1938-40. Delivered addresses throughout U.S., 1905-06, in interest of Congo reform, also lobbied in U.S. Senate to secure action by Govt.; so-called Congo resolution passed by Senate, 1907, and later the Congo Free State was annexed to Belgium. Special field rep. Bapt. Five Year Program, 1915-16; speaker on Laymen's Missionary Movement programs throughout the country, 1917-18. Joined Am. Red Cross, Sept. 16, 1918; became commr. to Czechoslovakia, Apr. 1919, with mil. rank of maj.; commd. maj. Inf. O.R.C., Jan. 11, 1922. Trustee Berea Coll. Republican. Speaker for Nat. Economy League, 1932-33. Home: 15 Evans Rd., Brookline, Mass. Died Sep. 25, 1942.

JOHNSON, Hiram Warren, senator; b. Sacramento, Calif., Sept. 2, 1866; s. Grove Laurence and Annie (DeMontfredy) J.; ed. U. of Calif., leaving in jr. yr.; m. Minnie L. McNeal, 1886. Began as shorthand reporter; studied law in father's office; admitted to Calif. bar, 1888, and practiced in Sacramento; removed to San Francisco, 1902; mem. staff of pros. attys. in boodling cases, involving leading city officials and almost all pub. utility corps. in San Francisco, 1906-07; was selected to take the place of Francis J. Heney, after latter was shot down in court while prosecuting Abe Ruef, for bribery, 1908, and secured conviction of Ruef; gov. of Calif., 1911-15, reëlected for term, 1915-19 (resigned Mar. 15, 1917); a founder of Progressive Party, 1912, and nominee for V.P. of U.S. on Prog. ticket same yr.; U.S. senator from Calif., 5 terms, 1917-47. Candidate for pres., 1924. Mem. Native Sons of Golden West. Mason (K.T.). Home: 1360 Montgomery St., San Francisco, Calif. Died Aug. 6, 1945.

JOHNSON, Hugh McCain, banker; b. Lexington, Miss., Jan. 1874; s. Herbert P. and Lucy (Fultz) J.; ed. Miss. Agrl. and Mech. Coll.; m. Mary Mills, 1903. Began with First Nat. Bank, Chandler, Okla., 1893, becoming pres. 1898; became pres. First Nat. Bank, Oklahoma City, 1918; now pres. First Nat. Bank & Trust Co., Oklahoma City. Mem. Oklahoma City Chamber Commerce. Democrat. Presbyterian. Mason. Clubs: Oklahoma, Oklahoma Golf. Home: 420 West 14th St. Office: First Nat. Bank, Oklahoma City, Okla.* Died Jan. 10, 1944.

JOHNSON, Hugh S.; b. Ft. Scott, Kan., Aug. 5, 1882; s. Samuel and Elizabeth (Mead) J.; grad. Okla. Northwestern Teachers Coll., 1901; B.S., U.S. Mil. Acad., 1903; A.B., U. of Calif., 1915; J.D., 1916; m. Helen, d. Col. H. S. Kilbourne, U.S. Army, Jan. 5, 1904; 1 son, Maj. Kilbourne Johnston (U.S. Army). Advanced from 2d lt., 1903, U.S. Army, to brig. gen., 1918; resigned from mil. service, Feb. 25, 1919; brig. gen. O.R.C. V.p., general counsel and asst. gen. mgr. Moline Plow Co., 1919; organizer, and chmn. bd. Moline Implement Co., 1925-29; associated with Bernard M. Baruch, N.Y. City, 1927-33. Served as q.-m. for refugees, San Francisco fire, 1906; in Philippines, 1907-09; exec. officer Yosemite Nat. Park, 1910-12; supt. Sequoia Nat. Park, 1911; judge advocate under Gen. Pershing, Punitive Expdn., Mexico, 1916; asst. to law officer, Bur. Insular Affairs, Oct. 1, 1916-Apr. 1, 1917; dep. provost marshal gen., Washington, 1917; apptd. col. Gen. Staff, Mar. 20, 1918, brig. gen. and chief of Purchase and Supply Bur., Gen. Staff Army; mem. War Industries Bd., Apr. 1918, asst. chief of Purchase, Storage and Traffic Div., U.S. Army, July 18, 1918; comdr. 15th Brigade, 8th Div., Camp Fremont, Calif., Sept. 1-18, 1918; comdr. 8th Div., Oct.-Nov. 1918, Camp Lee, Va., Nov. 1918-Jan. 1, 1919. Originated plan for selective draft, 1917, also rules and policies of same, and was exec. in charge, 1917-18; proposed organization of Purchase, Storage and Traffic Div. of Gen. Staff, in effect Aug. 1918, to close of war. Holder of Mexican Campaign, and World War medals; awarded D.S.M. "for work on selective draft." Mem. Phi Delta Phi, Phi Beta Kappa. Democrat. Administrator NRA, June 16, 1933-Oct. 15, 1934; works progress adminstr., N.Y. City, Aug.-Oct. 1935. Editorial commentator for Scripps-Howard and many other newspapers and radio since 1934. Home: Okmulgee, Okla. Office: 1626 K St. N.W., Washington, D.C. Died Apr. 15, 1942.

JOHNSON, Irving Peake, bishop; b. Hudson, N.Y., Nov. 5, 1866; s. Rev. William Ross and Adeline (Dickinson) J.; A.B., Union Coll., Schenectady, N.Y., 1887; grad. Gen. Theol. Sem., 1891; D.D., Union Coll.; LL.D., U. of Colo.; S.T.D., Denver U.; m. Grace W. Keese, June 18, 1894; children—Norman P., Stanley Herbert. Deacon and priest Protestant Episcopal Ch., 1891; in charge St. Andrew's Ch., Omaha, Neb., 1891-94, St. Martin's Ch., South Omaha, 1894-1901; rector Gethsemane Church, Minneapolis, Minn., 1901-13; prof. ecclesiastical history, Seabury Div. Sch., Faribault, Minn., 1913-16; bishop of Colorado, 1917-39; retired. Mem. Board Corrections, Colorado, 1932-33. Editor of "The Witness," 1917-41. Mem. Phi Beta Kappa, Delta Upsilon. Home: 1771 Humboldt Av., S., Minneapolis. Died Feb. 28, 1947; buried in Lakewood Cemetery, Minneapolis.

JOHNSON, Loren Bascom Taber, psychiatrist; b. Washington, D.C., June 15, 1875; s. Joseph Taber and Edith Maude (Bascom) J.; Yale, 1894-96; M.D., Georgetown U., 1900; m. Frances Mary Oliver, Oct. 5, 1901; 1 dau., Amelia Neville (wife of Maj. David S. Barry, Jr., U.S. Army); m. 2d, Cecelia Cathrine Kennedy, Aug. 5, 1910. Began practice at Washington, 1901; now specialist in psychiatric pediatrics; psychiatrist Children's Hosp., Garfield Hosp.; asso. prof. psycho-pediatrics, Georgetown University; v.p. Fairfax & Alexandria Bldg. Assn. Mem. D.C. Bd. of Indeterminate Sentence and Parole, 1932-34. Naval cadet, Spanish-Am. War; contract surgeon, 1st lt. and capt. U.S. Vol. Med. Corps, Philippine Islands, 1900-01; psychiatrist, capt. Med. Corps, U.S. Army, World War. Fellow A.M.A.; mem. Am. Psychiatric Assn., Am. Psychopathol. Assn., Am. Psychoanalytic Assn., Washington Psychoanalytic Assn., Clinico Pathol. Soc. Washington (pres. 1924), Washington Nervous and Mental Disease Assn. (pres. 1923), Soc. Mayflower Descendants, S.A.R. Republican. Presbyterian. Clubs: Cosmos, Chevy Chase (dir.); Southwest Harbor (Me.) Country (pres.). Contbr. many med. papers. Died December 14, 1941.

JOHNSON, Lewis Edgar, banker; b. Monroe County, W.Va., Sept. 29, 1860; s. William B. and Agnes R. (Hinchman) J.; ed. pub. and pvt. schs.; grad. Eastman Business Coll., Poughkeepsie, N.Y., 1880; m. Jane Ella Johnson, May 2, 1889; children—Mary Pauline, Agnes (Mrs. Joseph B. Vernon), Ellen Langley. Hardware and furniture business, with George K. Gwinn, at Alderson, since 1883; cashier Greenbrier Valley Bank, Alderson, 1896-1900, pres. 1900-09; pres. First Nat. Bank (consolidation of Greenbrier Valley Bank and First Nat. Bank) since 1909; dir. Federal Reserve Bank of Richmond; sec. and treas. Greenbrier Milling Co.; partner Johnson & George (farming), etc. Served as county chmn. Draft Bd., World War Democrat. Presbyterian. Home: Alderson, W.Va. Died Dec. 2, 1948.

JOHNSON, Milbank, M.D., social economist; b. Columbus, Tex., Oct. 13, 1871; s. Jehu Warner and Philadelphia Wheeler (Borden) J.; B.Sc., U. of Southern Calif., 1890, LL.D., 1917; M.D., Northwestern U., 1893, LL.D., 1920; student Johns Hopkins Hosp. and European hosps.; m. Louiez Lester Lothrop, Sept. 16, 1893; children—Mrs. Louiez Webb, Mrs. Evelyn Bruner; m. 2d, Isabel Simeral, Sept. 8, 1920. Practiced at Los Angeles, Calif., 1893-1901; prof. physiology and clin. medicine, U. of Southern Calif., 1897-1901, now chmn. spl. med. research com. of the univ.; chief surgeon Southern Calif. Edison Co., 1901-13; pres. Municipal Charities Commn., Los Angeles, 1913-17; v.p. and dir. Pacific Mutual Life Ins. Co., 1917-36; dir. Am. Ins. Fed. since 1917. Pres. Western States Taxpayers Conf., 1926, Calif. Taxation Improvement Assn., 1925-26; chmn. bd. Calif. Taxpayers Assn. since 1926; dir. and mem. exec. com. Nat. Tax Assn. Mem. bd. of dirs. Pasadena Hosp. Assn. Mem. Los Angeles Bd. of Health, 1900-04; mem. Bd. of Freeholders which revised City Charter of Los Angeles, 1916; mem. exec. com. Calif. Mil. Welfare Commn., 1917-19. Pres. Southwest Museum, 1920-26. Mem. A.M.A., Southern Calif. Med. Assn., Los Angeles County Med. Soc., Calif. Conf. Social Agencies (ex-pres.), Am. Conf. Social Work, Calif. Soc. S.A.R., Phi Rho Sigma (a founder, 1890), Phi Gamma Delta. Republican. Mason (32°, K.T., Shriner). Clubs: Landmarks, Auto Club of Southern Calif. (a founder). Contbr. on social economics and med. topics. Mem. Pasadena Defense Council and Red Cross Emergency since 1942. Home: Pasadena, Calif. Office: Subway Terminal Bldg., Los Angeles, Calif. Died Oct. 3, 1944.

JOHNSON, Oscar John, coll. pres.; b. Cleburne, Kan., Oct. 8, 1870; s. Gustaf Christoffer and Louise (Ekblad) J.; student Bethany Coll., Lindsborg, Kan., 1886-87; A.B., Augustana Coll., Ill., 1896 B.D., 1899, D.D., 1917; m. Amanda Lavinia Lindberg, June 27, 1899; children—Robert Oscar Petrus, Roy Luther Cornelius, Raymond Wendell Nathaniel, Rodger Theofilus Lindberg. Ordained Luth. ministry, 1899; pastor McKeesport, Pa., 1899-1901; pres. Luther Coll., also pastor of ch., Wahoo, Neb., 1901-13; pres. Gustavus Adolphus Coll., St. Peter, Minn., 1913-42; retired July 1, 1942; v.p. Community Hosp. Commn.; mem. standing com. of Augustana Synod Constitution Alteration; mem. Augustana Synod Com. on Higher Edn. Home: St. Peter, Minn. Died Mar. 9, 1946.

JOHNSON, Paul Burney; b. Hillsboro, Scott County, Miss., Mar. 23, 1880; ed. Millsaps Coll., Jackson, Miss.; m. Corrine Venable. Admitted to bar and practiced at Hattiesburg; served as judge City Court, Hattiesburg; apptd. judge Circuit Court, 12 Jud. Dist., by Governor Noel, and elected to same office, serving 8 yrs.; mem. 66th and 67th Congresses (1919-23), 6th Miss. Dist. Dem. nominee for governor of Mississippi, 1939. Home: Hattiesburg, Miss. Died Dec. 26, 1943.

JOHNSON, Paul Rodgers, pub. utility engr.; b. Buffalo, N.Y., Apr. 12, 1888; s. William Henry and Mary Spencer (Hill) J.; student Ridley Coll., St. Catharines, Ont., 1901-07; m. Hazel Priestley, 1912; children—Rodgers Priestley, Deana and Katherine. Operator and owner of various utility properties since 1907; pres. and dir. Union Gas System, Inc., Sagamore Oil and Gas Company, Midland Industries, Inc., Crescent Oil, Inc., Union Electric Railway Co., Kansas Trails, Inc., Bradley Transportation Company, Yellow Cab & Baggage Co.; dir. Coffeyville Ice Inc., Coffeyville Creameries, Inc., Glencliff Dairy Products Co. Served with U.S.N.R.F. 1918-19. Mem. Am. Guernsey Cattle Club, Kan. Guernsey Breeders' Assn. Republican. Elk. Clubs: Independence Country, Rajah Country (Independence, Kan.). Home: Glencliff Farm, Independence, Kan.; also "Stonehaven," Parry Sound, Ont., Can. Office: Union Gas Bldg., Independence, Kan. Died Dec. 17, 1948.

JOHNSON, Philip G(ustav); b. Seattle, Wash., Nov. 5, 1894; s. Charles S. and Hanna (Gustavson) J.; student Coll. of Engring., U. of Wash., 1913-17; m. Catherine Foley, Oct. 10, 1925; children—Esther Mary, Philip G. With Boeing Airplane Co. since 1917, in engring. dept., 1917-18, in production dept.,

1918-19, supt., 1919-22, v.p. and gen. mgr., 1922-26, pres., 1926-33; pres. Boeing Air Transport, Inc., 1927; pres. Pacific Air Transport to dissolution, 1933; pres. Varney Air Lines, Inc., 1931-33; pres. Nat. Air Transport, 1931-33; pres. United Air Lines, Inc., 1931-33; voting trustee United Air Line Transport Corp., 1934-35; v.p. Kenworth Motor Truck Corp., Seattle, 1936-38, pres. since 1938; v.p. in charge operation Trans-Canada Air Lines, Montreal, 1937, now consultant; pres. Boeing Airplane Co., Seattle, Wash., since 1939; dir. various corps. Mem. Am. Soc. Mech. Engrs., Soc. of Automotive Engrs., Inst. of Aeronautical Sciences (v.p. 1940-41), Nat. Aeronautical Assn., Aerónautical Chamber Commerce, Alpha Sigma Phi. Republican. Baptist. Clubs: University, College, Rainier, Seattle Press, Seattle Golf (Seattle); Chicago Club; Bankers (New York); Washington Athletic, Bohemian, Conquistadores del Cielo. Home: Woodway Park, Edmonds, Wash. Office: Boeing Aircraft Co., Seattle, Wash. Died Sep. 14, 1944.

JOHNSON, Stanley, author, educator; b. Nashville, Tenn., Nov. 5, 1892; s. W. D. and Jessie (Bryson) J.; B.S., Vanderbilt U., 1917, M.A., 1921; m. Ruby Sparkman Akin, Sept. 7, 1927. Prof. of English, Vanderbilt U., 1921-25; prof. of journalism, U. of Tenn., 1929-42, bd. sec., 1932-37, dir. of pub. relations since 1937. Sec. Tenn. Municipal League, 1944. Charter mem. Fugitive Group (Nashville). Democrat. Author: Professor, 1925; Fugitives, 1924; Tennessee Citizenship, 1939; The Complete Reporter, 1942; Citizenship, 1944. Editor: Georgia Citizenship, 1940. Home: R. 1, Thompson Station, Tenn. Died Dec. 1, 1946.

JOHNSON, Sveinbjorn, lawyer; b. July 10, 1883; s. John and Gudbjorg J.; brought to U.S., 1887; A.B., Univ. of N.D., 1906, A.M., 1907, LL.B., 1908; spl. work, U. of Wis.; m. Esther Henryetta Slette, Sept. 16, 1917; children—Helen Barbara (dec.), Paul Sveinbjorn. Practiced at Cavalier, N.D., 1911-13; mem. O'Connor & Johnson, Grand Forks, North Dakota, 1913-21; mem. McIntyre, Burtness & Johnson until 1922; lecturer polit. science and law, Univ. of N.D., 1913-21; atty. gen. of North Dakota at first state recall election, Nov. 1921, for term ending Dec. 31, 1922; justice Supreme Court of N.D., term 1922-28, resigned, 1926, to become legal adviser and prof. law, University of Ill.; retired Aug. 31, 1944, to practice law in Chicago, firm of Johnson & Short. Apptd. by President Hoover as mem. American Commission to Iceland, June, 1930, to represent U.S. at the Parliamentary Millennial, and delivered the address in behalf of the U.S., presenting a statue of Leif Ericsson to Iceland, pursuant to a resolution of Congress; spl. counsel to Comptroller of Currency in connection with reorganization of unlicensed nat. banks, in 4th Federal Reserve Dist., in charge of Pittsburgh office, summer, 1933; spl. counsel, Office of Comptroller of the Currency, summer 1934; state dir. Office of Government Reports for Ill., 1935-42. Originated course in legislative drafting and constrn., U. of N.D., 1913. Mem. Am. and North Dakota bar assns., State Hist. Soc. North Dakota, Acad. of Polit. Science, Bókmentafjelag (Reykjavik), Phi Beta Kappa, Delta Sigma Rho, Phi Delta Theta, Gamma Eta Gamma, Pi Gamma Mu, Scabbard and Blade. Decorated Knight of the Order of the Falcon by Christian X, King of Iceland and Denmark, 1939. Lutheran. Club: Kiwanis Internat. Author: Pioneers of Freedom, A Story of the Icelanders and the Icelandic Free State (872-1262), 1930; also articles in mags. Editor: Richards' Cases on the Law of Corporations (3d edit. rev.); Grágás, a translation entitled "Ancient Laws of Iceland." Home: Champaign, Ill. Office: Conway Bldg., Chicago, Ill. Died Mar. 19, 1946.

JOHNSON, Treat Baldwin, univ. prof.; b. Bethany, Conn., Mar. 29, 1875; s. Dwight Lauren and Harriet (Baldwin) J.; Ph.B., Sheffield Scientific Sch. (Yale), 1898; Ph.D., Yale, 1901; m. E. Estelle Amerman, June 29, 1904. Instr. in organic chemistry, Sterling Lab., Yale, 1901-08, asst. prof., 1908-16, prof. 1917-25, Sterling professor chemistry, 1925-43; prof. emeritus in 1943. President Bethany Library Association, Inc.; director Bethwood Research Lab., Bethany, Conn. Mem. bd. trustees, Yale-in-China. Member Society Biol. Chemists, American Biological Society, Am. Chem. Soc., Am. Assn. Univ. Profs., Nat. Acad. Sciences, Conn. Acad. Arts and Sciences, Nat. Geog. Soc., Am. Inst. Chemists (pres. 1926-27), Nat. Research Council, Deutsche Chemische Gesellschaft, Acad. Science (Halle, Germany), Sigma Xi, Alpha Chi Sigma. Mem. ednl. advisory com. N.B.C. Radio Corp. Conglist. Clubs: Graduate (New Haven); Yale (New York). Home: "Bethwood," Amity Road, Bethany, Conn. Died July 28, 1947.

JOHNSON, Wayne, lawyer; b. Great Falls, Mont., May 30, 1892; s. Adam Forest and Laura Jane (Searight) J.; student U. of Mont., 1910-12; LL.B., Georgetown U. Law Sch., 1916; m. Gladys Royer, Sept. 8, 1920; children—Wayne, Virginia Royer, Hamilton Searight. Employed at White House, Washington, 1913-15; admitted to D.C. bar, also to N.Y. bar; began practice at Washington, 1916; spl. atty. Federal Trade Commn., Washington, 1916; with Chadbourne & Shores, N.Y. City, 1916-19; spl. atty. and solicitor of internal revenue, Washington, 1919-20; mem. Johnson & Shores, N.Y. City, since 1920; dir. Devoe & Raynolds Co., Panama R.R. Co. (govt. owned), Shevlin-Hixon Co., West Indies Sugar Corp., Lehigh Coal & Navigation Co.; dir. and gen. counsel, Columbia Gas & Electric Corp. Served as capt. F.A. U.S. Army, World War; attended French Arty. Sch., Fontainebleau. An organizer and treas. Fight for Freedom Committee. Mem. Am. and N.Y. State bar assns., N.Y. County Lawyers Assn., Assn. Bar City of New York, Sigma Chi, Phi Delta Phi. Democrat. Presbyterian. Clubs: Racquet and Tennis, Century Assn., Nat. Golf Links, Links, Links Golf (New York). In charge of petroleum matters for War Prodn. Bd. until Nov. 15, 1942, and obtained final approval for construction of 24" pipeline from Texas to New York as a war necessity. Home: 22 E. 47th St. Office: 1 E. 57th St., New York, N.Y. Died Mar. 11, 1947.

JOHNSON, William Eugene, prohibition lecturer; known as "Pussyfoot" Johnson, because of his catlike policies in pursuing lawbreakers in the Ind. Ty.; b. Coventry, N.Y., Mar. 25, 1862; s. William and Elizabeth H. (Stiles) J.; ed. U. of Neb.; m. Lillie M. Trevitt, Dec. 25, 1886 (died April 21, 1927); children—Clarence Trevitt, Clifford Lee; m. 2d, Mrs. May B. Stanley, June 16, 1928. On staff of the Lincoln Daily News, 1884-86; mgr. of the Neb. News Bureau, 1886-87; spl. feature and syndicate writer, 1887-95; asso. editor New York Voice, 1895-99; asso. editor New Voice, Chicago, 1899-1905; publicity mgr. Com. of Mfrs. in successful campaign to induce Congress to pass denatured alcohol bill, 1905-06; spl. agt. of Dept. Interior to enforce laws in Ind. Ty. and Okla., 1906-07; chief spl. officer U.S. Indian service, July 1, 1908-Sept. 30, 1911, during which time secured more than 4,400 convictions. U.S. del. 14th Internat. Anti-Alcohol Congress, Milan, Italy, 1913, Tartu, Estonia, 1926; mem. Internat. Temperance Com. of Fifty, Paris, 1919; editor New Republic, 1913-16; mng. editor 35 publs. of Anti-Saloon League, 1912-16, publicity mgr., 1916-18, dir. London office, World League Against Alcoholism; organized Anti-Saloon League of Philippine Islands; life mem. Prohibition League of India; honorary member W.C.T.U. (Australia), Devalaya Association (India), Vishwa Bharati (India); member I.O.G.T.; honorary member Hilel-e-Akdir (Turkey). Presbyterian. Mason (32°), K.T. Author: Temperance Progress in the 19th Century (with John G. Woolley), 1903; The Gothenburg System, 1903; The Federal Government and the Liquor Traffic, 1911; The Liquor Problem in Russia, 1915; Blowing Off the Froth, 1936; Prohibition in Kansas, 1935; Ten Years of Prohibition in Oklahoma, 1934; John Johnson and other Johnsons, 1941. Asso. editor Standard Ency. of the Alcohol Problem (6 vols.), 1930. Has also written about 50 brochures on various phases of the alcohol problem. Lost an eye at Prohibition meeting, Essex Hall, London, 1919, by a missile thrown by a member of a mob. Made 3 trips around the world in the interest of temperance and has delivered more than 4,000 lectures. Address: McDonough, N.Y. Died Feb. 2, 1945; buried in Sylvan Lawn Cemetery, Greene, N.Y.

JOHNSTON, Charles Haven Ladd, author; b. Washington, July 17, 1877; s. William Waring (M.D.) and Esther (Dashiell) J.; A.B., Harvard, 1899; m. Edythe M. Newlands, Apr. 4, 1903 (divorced); children—Francis Newlands, Alan Ladd; m. 2d, Berdie Abbott Mercer (widow U.S. Rep. D. H. Mercer, Omaha), 1926. Teacher dept. of English, Harvard U., 1901-02; instr. English and lecturer in mil. history, Mass. Inst. Tech., 1904-05. Hon. mem. Eugene Field Society. Author: Little Pilgrimages Among the Women Who Have Written Famous Books, 1901; Famous Cavalry Leaders, 1908; Famous Indian Chiefs, 1909; Famous Scouts, 1910; Famous Privateersmen, 1911; Famous Frontiersmen, 1913; Our Little Viking Cousin, 1916; Famous Discoverers and Explorers of America, 1917; Famous Generals of the Great War, 1919; Famous Athletes of Today, 4 vols., 1928, 30, 35; also author of many poems, including "The President," "The Lusitania Speaks" and "Christ Sits Alone." Episcopalian. Clubs: Harvard, Chevy Chase, Mil. Service Legion. Home: 4701 Connecticut Av. N.W., Washington, D.C. Died July 9, 1943.

JOHNSTON, Harry Lang, newspaper editor; b. Hollidaysburg, Pa., Apr. 1, 1873; s. William Noble and Laura (Lang) J.; ed. pub schs.; m. Annie Cherry Bunker, May 4, 1899; children—Helen Louise (Mrs. J. Lewis Hammitt, Jr.), Anna Margaret Sheldon. Began career in employ Democratic Standard, Hollidaysburg, Pa., 1889; asso. with Altoona Mirror since 1900, editor since 1908. Democrat. Baptist. Odd Fellow. Clubs: Blairmont Country, Rotary. Home: 3508 Oneida Av. Office: 1000 Green Av., Altoona, Pa. Died July 17, 1948

JOHNSTON, John Black, neurologist, educator; b. Belle Center, O., Oct. 3, 1868; s. Robert H. and Hannah M. (Clyde) J.; Ph.B., U. of Mich., 1893, Ph.D., 1899, Sc.D. (hon.), 1933; m. Juliet Morton Butler, Aug. 29, 1899; children—Stanwood (dec.), Norris. Asst. and instr. zoölogy, U. of Mich., 1893-99; asst. prof., W.Va. U., 1899-1900, prof. zoölogy, 1900-07; asst. prof., U. of Minn., 1907-08, asso. prof., 1908-09, prof. comparative neurology, since 1909, sec. faculty of medicine, 1910-13, editor-in-chief research publs., 1911-14, dean Coll. Science, Lit. and Arts, 1914-37. Charter mem. Mich. Acad. Science; fellow A.A.A.S.; mem. Am. Soc. of Zoölogists, Assn. Am. Anatomists, Am. Soc. Naturalists, Minn. Neurol. Soc. (charter mem). Mem. editorial bd. Journal of Comparative Neurology, 1908-32; chmn. com. on ednl. testing Am. Council on Edn. Author: The Nervous System of Vertebrates, 1906; The Liberal College in Changing Society, 1930; Education for Democracy, 1934; Scholarship and Democracy, 1937; also numerous articles on neurology and edn. Home: 1943 East River Rd., Minneapolis. Died Nov. 19, 1947.

JOHNSTON, Robert Story, prof. philosophy; b. Troy Center, Wis., Dec. 11, 1874; s. Robert Alexander and Ellen Augusta (Story) J.; A.B., Marquette U., Milwaukee, Wis., 1891; Jesuit Sem., Florissant, Mo., 1891-94, 1906-07; A.M., St. Louis U., 1897, grad. study, 1902-06; Jesuit Sem., Hastings, Eng., 1909-11; S.T.D., Pontifical Gregorian U. of Roman Coll., 1931. Joined Soc. of Jesus (Jesuits), 1891; ordained priest, R.C. Ch., 1905; teacher high sch., U. of Detroit, 1897-99, Coll. Liberal Arts, U. of Detroit, 1899-1901, St. Xavier High Sch., Cincinnati, O., 1901-02, high sch., Marquette U., 1907-08; prof. ethics, St. Louis U., 1908-09, prof. fundamental theology, 1911-27; prof. dogmatic and patristic theology, St. Mary of the Lake Sem., Mundelein, Ill., 1927-29, prof. grad. theology, 1929-30; pres. St. Louis U., 1930-36; prof. religion and philosophy, Marquette U., Milwaukee, since 1937; bd. dirs. Marquette U. Alumni Assn. Mem. Alpha Sigma Nu. Author: Marquette College, a Quarter Century, 1906. Address: Marquette University, Milwaukee, Wis.* Died Feb. 18, 1944.

JOHNSTONE, Ernest Kinloch, physician; b. Devon, Eng., Dec. 21, 1871; s. Charles and Mary Frances (de Beaumont) J.; brought to U.S. in infancy (father an American); ed. Trinity Coll., Glenalmond, and Wellington Coll., Eng., U. of Edinburgh and U. of Calif; M.D., U. of Calif. Med. Sch., 1898; licentiate of Royal Colleges of Physicians and Surgeons, Edinburgh and Glasgow, Scotland; hosp. work, Paris, London, Vienna and Berlin; m. Belle Shiels, 1898. Began practice at San Francisco, 1898; served as asst., chair of surgery, Post-Grad. Dept., U. of Calif., and lecturer hygiene and med. jurisprudence, same univ.; jr. demonstrator anatomy, Royal Coll. Surgeons, Edinburgh; gold medalist in clin. surgery, same. Vice-pres. San Dimas Co. Apptd. acting asst. surgeon U.S. Army, Spanish-Am. War, 1898; mustered out as maj. surgeon, U.S.V.; served through World War (with British from 1914 to entry of U.S.); chief surgeon U.S. Army Ambulance Service, with French Army, 1918-19; col. Med. Res., U.S. Army; div. surgeon 91st Div., comdg. 316th Med. Regt., 1925-36; former state pres. Res. Officers Assn. Decorations: Spanish War Medal, Philippine Insurrection Medal, Victory World War Medal, 2 stars, Silver Star Medal (U.S.); Reconnaissance Française and Médaille Commemorative (French); war service medals "as special case" (British); Veterani della Guerra (Italian). Republican. Episcopalian. Mason. Club: Army and Navy (Washington, D.C.). Author of brochures and articles on med. and mil.-med. subjects. Home: St. Francis Hotel, San Francisco. Died May 23, 1948.

JONAH, Frank Gilbert, railway official; b. Albert County, N.B., Oct. 6, 1864; ed. high sch., Moncton, N.B., and privately. Began in office of chief engr. Intercolonial Ry., 1882; asst. engr. in charge constrn. govt. lines in Nova Scotia, 1887-89; asst engr. Intercolonial Ry., 1889-90; asst. engr. St. Louis Merchants Bridge Terminal Ry., 1890-94; resident engr., St. L., Peoria & Northern Ry., 1894-99; engr. maintenance of way, C.&A.R.R., 1899-1901; chief engr., Blackwell, Enid & S.W. Ry., 1901-03; asst. engr. New Orleans Terminal Co., Mar.-June 1903; chief engr., St. L., Brownsville & Mexico Ry., 1903-04; locating engr., St.L.&S.F. R.R., 1904-05; terminal engr. N.O. Terminal Co., 1905-10; chief engr. constrn., St.L.&S.F. R.R., at St. Louis, 1910-13, chief engr., since Mar. 1, 1913; also chief engr. Ft. Worth & Rio Grande R.R., K.C., Clinton & Springfield R.R. Served as maj. 12th Regt. Ry. Engrs.; chief engr. Dept. of Light Rys., in France, Oct. 1917-Dec. 1918, with rank of lt. col. Home: 5355 Pershing Av. Office: Frisco Bldg., St. Louis. Died Dec. 7, 1945.

JONES, A(lbert) Marshall, publisher; b. Portland, Me., Mar. 5, 1872; s. William Henry and Martha Marilla (Estes) J.; A.B., Bowdoin, 1893; post-grad. work, Harvard, 1899; m. Mary Adelaide Woodward, June 29, 1899 (died Jan. 2, 1903); m. 2d, Grace Webber, Apr. 21, 1906; children—Faith Florance, Prudence Marshall (Mrs. Hamilton Gray), Beverly Marshall (Mrs. David Darling). Has been pres. Marshall Jones Co., pubs. Conceived and acted as mng. editor, The Mythology of All Races (13 vols.), secured loans for its completion from Carnegie Corp. and John D. Rockefeller, Jr., which loans were paid from sales; formed The Mythology Co., 1937. Republican. Episcopalian. Address: 136A Elm St., Andover, Mass. Died June 23, 1949.

JONES, Alfred, editor; b. Paola, Kan., July 24, 1889; s. Tilford and Anna Marie (Brown) J.; grad. Paola High Sch., 1905; m. Florence Gambati, Jan. 1, 1919. Began as printers devil, 1904; reporter Western Spirit, Paola, 1906-11; corr. Kansas City Post, 1908-12; reporter Houston (Tex.) Chronicle, 1912-14; reporter and sports editor Houston Telegram, 1914-15; mng. editor Beaumont Enterprise, 1915-22; company consolidated with Beaumont Journal, 1922, and since editor-in-chief; dir. Enterprise Co., Radio Station KRIC. Dir. Beaumont Chamber of Commerce; ex-pres. Texas Mng. Editors Assn.; mem. Am. Soc. Newspaper Editors, Asso. Press Mng. Editors Assn. Democrat. Prebyterian. Clubs: Beaumont, Rotary, Round Table. Writer of daily column in Beaumont Journal. Home: 2340 Neches St., Beaumont, Tex. Died Jan. 25, 1943.

JONES, Buell Fay, lawyer; b. Spain, S. Dak., Nov. 25, 1892; s. Even N. and Ellen (Hughes) J.; LL.B., S. Dak. U., 1914; m. Florence I. Bockler, June 21, 1914; children—Quentin B., Jamie R., Dorothy F. Admitted to S. Dak. bar, 1914, and began practice at Britton; state's atty. Marshall County, S. Dak., 1919-23; mem. Gardner & Jones, 1919-22, alone since 1922; atty. gen. S. Dak., 3 terms, 1923-29; Rep.

nominee for governor of S. Dak., 1929, gen. atty. Standard Oil Co. of Ind., 1930-40, v.p., 1945 and gen. counsel since 1940. Was mem. ex-officio S. Dak. State Game Commn., State Bd. of Pardons, etc. Organized vol. troops of cav. for World War, June 1917; entered U.S. Army as pvt., June 15, 1917; with 34th Div., at Camp Cody, N.M., later with 307th Cav.; hon. disch. as capt., Dec. 21, 1918. Mem. Am., Ill., S.Dak. and Chicago bar assns., Delta Theta Pi, Am. Legion. Republican. Presbyterian. Mason (32°, Shriner), Odd Fellow. Home: 9425 N. Hamlin Av., Evanston, Ill. Office: 910 S. Michigan Av., Chicago. Died Nov. 17, 1947.

JONES, Carter Helm, clergyman; b. Nelson County, Va., Nov. 30, 1861; s. John William (D.D.) and Judith Page (Helm) J.; descendant of Carter Braxton, signer Declaration of Independence; Richmond College; special course, U. of Va.; grad. Southern Bapt. Theol. Sem., Louisville, Ky., 1885; D.D., Washington and Lee, 1894, Baylor, 1909, Denison, 1916; m. Anne M. McCown, Apr. 7, 1886 (died Jan. 1906); children—Catherine Page (Mrs. J. G. Low), Carter Brooke; m. 2d, Mrs. Elizabeth Dabney Hutter Christian, Aug. 20, 1908. Ordained Bapt. ministry, 1884; pastor New Castle and Burk's Branch chs., Ky., 1884-85, Mechanicsville and Berea chs., Va., 1885-86, 1st Ch., Elizabeth, N.J., 1886-89, 1st Ch., Knoxville, Tenn., 1889-93, McFerran Memorial Ch., Louisville, Ky., 1893-97, Broadway Ch., Louisville, 1897-1907, 1st Ch., Lynchburg, Va., 1907-08, 1st Ch., Oklahoma City, Okla., 1908-12, 1st Ch., Seattle, Wash., 1912-18, 1st Ch., Phila., Pa., 1918-24, Second Bapt. Ch., Atlanta, Ga., 1924-28, St. Charles Av. Bapt. Ch., New Orleans, 1928-30, First Bapt. Ch., Murfreesboro, Tenn., 1930-36, Williamsburg (Va.) Bapt. Ch., 1936-41. Widely known as lecturer, commencement orator, etc. Pres. Am. Bapt. Foreign Mission Soc., 1912-15; v.p. Am. Religious Ednl. Assn., 1908-09; convention preacher Southern Bapt. Conv., Birmingham, Ala., 1891, Northern Bapt. Conv., Los Angeles, 1915; trustee Crozer Bapt. Theol. Sem.; spl. commr. Northern Bapt. Conv. to Czechoslovakia, 1922. Mem. S.A.R., Phi Delta Theta. Mason (K.T., Shriner). Clubs: Rotary, Round Table (New Orleans); Pendennis (Louisville). Author: Prophetic Patriotism, 1940. Home: Lynchburg, Va. Died May 6, 1946.

JONES, Charles Alfred, church official; b. London, Eng., Apr. 14, 1869; s. John Wells and Mary Ann (Cracknell) J.; brought to U.S. in infancy; B.A., Furman U., Greenville, S.C., 1895; D.D., 1916; Th.M., Southern Bapt. Theol. Sem., Louisville, Ky., 1904; m. Jessie Berry, Dec. 31, 1896; children—Alfred Broodus, Edwin Holmes, Charles Wells (dec.). Ordained ministry Bapt. Ch., 1891; pastor Greenville, Mullins, S.C., Belleville, Ill., later Bennettsville, S.C., until 1915; sec. Bapt. Edn. Bd. of S.C., 1915-24; gen. sec.-treas. Bapt. Gen. Bd. of S.C. since 1924. Home: 117 S. Sims Av., Columbia, S.C. Died June 4, 1942.

JONES, Charles Reading, publicist; b. on farm, nr. Phila., Pa., Nov. 9, 1862; s. Charles and Esther (Harding) J.; ed. pub. schs. Phila.; m. Bertha I. Hoar, 1882. Mem. Charles Jones and Sons, saddlery hardware, 1880-90; sec. and mgr. The Frink, Barcus and Jones Mfg. Co., saddlery and harness, Phila., 1890-93. Founder and pres. Asso. Prohibition Press; pub. Horseman's Guide, 1885-90, Harness Journal, 1886-91, The People, 1900-05; pres. Mattoon Mausoleum Co.; dir. Hillsboro Mausoleum Co. Prohibition chmn. of Pa., 1897-1905; chmn. Prohibition Nat. Com., 1905-12; v.p. World's Prohibition Confederation; dir. Christian Edn. Foundation; exec. v.p. Am. Business Men's Research Foundation; dir. Internat. Reform Federation; ex-pres. Nat. Temperance and Prohibition Council, Washington, D.C. Treas. Nat. Lincoln Chautauqua, 1914-19; financial dir. Citizen's Com. to Enforce the Landis award, 1922-29. Methodist. Mason (32°, Shriner). Home: 1456 Ridge Av., Evanston, Ill. Office: 53 W. Jackson Blvd., Chicago 4, Ill. Died Mar. 26, 1944.

JONES, Claud Ashton, rear admiral; b. Fire Creek, W.Va., Oct. 7, 1885; s. John H. and Lillian H. Jones; ed. U.S. Naval Acad., 1903-07; M.S., elec. engring., Harvard, 1912-13; Annapolis, 1911; hon. D.Sc., W.Va. U., 1942; m. Margaret Cox, Apr. 15, 1913; children—Frank C., Margaret B. Served on Indiana, New Jersey, Severn, North Carolina, Franklin, 1906-11; New York, 1913-15; engr. officer North Dakota, later Tennessee, 1916; engring. duty on elec. machinery for Tennessee at Westinghouse plant, Pittsburgh, 1917 (also asst. insp. engring. materials, Pittsburgh Dist.); attached to Indsl. Dept., N.Y. Navy Yard, 1918-20; on duty Bur. Engring., Washington, D.C., 1920-23; asst. naval attaché to American Embassies in London, Paris, Rome, Berlin, The Hague, 1923-25; on duty Bur. Engring., 1925-29; aide on staff, Comdr. Battleship Divisions, Battle Fleet with added duty as Divisions Engr. Officer, 1930; transferred to staff, Comdr.-in-Chief, Battle Fleet, as Fleet Engr. with Bur. Engring., 1931-35; insp. Groton shipyards, 1935-40; head Shipbldg. Div., Bur. Ships, 1940-42; later asst. chief; asst. chief in charge of prodn., Office of Procurement and Material to Sept. 1944; dir. Naval Engr. Exp. Sta., Annapolis, Md., 1944-46; retired, June 1946. Decorated Medal of Honor (citation for extraordinary heroism as engineer officer on board U.S.S. Memphis during Santo Domingo hurricane), Cuban Pacification medal, 1906, Mexican Service medal (Vera Cruz), Dominican Campaign medal, Victory medal (World War Services), Expert Rifleman medals; Legion of Merit, 1944; mem. Am. Soc. Naval Engrs. (past pres.), Soc. Naval Architects and Marine Engrs. (vice pres.), U.S. Naval Inst., Newcomen Soc. Home: 15 Grosscup Rd., Charleston 4, W.Va. Died Aug. 8, 1948; buried in Arlington National Cemetery.

JONES, Frank Cazenove, mfr.; b. New York, N.Y., Aug. 14, 1887; s. Frank Cazenove and Harriet Cazenove (Lamar) J.; g.g.s. Capt. Jacob Jones, comdr. U.S. sloop of war Wasp, War of 1812; student King Sch., Stamford, Conn., 1902-04, Noble and Greenough Sch., Dedham, Mass., 1904-07, Harvard, 1907-09; m. Gladys Kemp, July, 1909 (divorced); m. 2d, Helen Griffith, June 30, 1917; children—Frank Cazenove, Helen Griffith. Began as clk. for B. T. Babbit, Inc., New York, Oct. 1909; with Edgar A. Wilhelmi, Inc., New York, as treas., 1911-14; with Jones & Cammack, of New York, as partner, 1915-17; with The Okonite Co., Passaic, N.J., as treas. since 1919, pres. and gen. mgr. since 1932; pres. The Okonite-Callender Cable Co.; dir. Passaic Nat. Bank & Trust Co., Passaic, N.J.; president Community Chest, Montclair, N.J.; vice chairman Montclair chapter Am. Red Cross. Served as 1st lieutenant, 2d Plattsburg clair, N.J.; vice chairman Montclair chapter Am. Red Cross. Served as 1st lieutenant, 2d Plattsburg Officers Training Camp; trench warfare section, Engring. Div., Ordnance Dept., World War. Mem. Aztec Soc. of 1847, Bus. Adv. Council Dept. of Commerce, 1936-38. Republican. Clubs: Union, Engineers, Harvard, Downtown Athletic (New York); Montclair Golf, Montclair Athletic. Home: 237 Upper Mountain Av., Upper Montclair, N.J. Office: The Okonite Co., Passaic, N.J. Died Jan. 20, 1949.

JONES, Frederic Marshall, banker; b. Charlestown, Mass., June 21, 1874; s. Marshall and Mary Ann (Roberts) J.; A.B., Harvard, 1896; B.S. in Architectures, Lawrenee Scientific Sch., 1900; grad. study; m. Florence Osborne Harris, Oct. 30, 1907; 1 dau., Emily Harris (Mrs. Russell B. Neff). With Peabody & Stearns, architects, Boston, 1900-11; with the Third Nat. Bank & Trust Co, Boston, since 1911, president since 1926; director Holyoke Water Power Co., Springfield Fire & Marine Ins. Co., Sentinel Fire Ins. Co., Mich. Fire & Marine Ins. Co., N.E. Casualty Ins. Co., Holyoke Power & Electric Co., N.E. Fire Ins. Co., Springfield Gas Light Co., Springfield Street Ry. Co.; trustee Springfield Instn. for Savings, Springfield Cemetery, Springfield Hospital, Diocese of Western Massachusetts; member National Council Boy Scouts of America. Member Harvard Engineering Society, Newcomen Soc. Republican. Episcopalian. Clubs: Colony, University, The Club, Longmeadow Country. Home: 327 Maple St. Office: Third Nat. Bank & Trust Co., Springfield, Mass. Died Aug. 4, 1946.

JONES, F(rederick) Robertson, insurance; b. Wicomico County, Md., Jan. 4, 1872; s. John Bayley and Anne A. (Follin) J.; A.B., Western Maryland Coll., 1892, A.M., 1895; Ph.D., Johns Hopkins, 1896; m. Eleanor Dwight Cook, June 20, 1905; children—Eleanor Robertson (Mrs. Eric Paepcke), Katharine Robertson (Mrs. Hamilton Southworth). Acting prof. history and economics, Western Md. Coll., 1896-97; acting instr. economics, Johns Hopkins, 1897; instr. and asst. prof. history and sociology, Union U., 1897-1902; asso. in economics and politics, Bryn Mawr, 1902-06; asst. supt., Charity Orgn. Soc., Hartford, Conn., 1894-95; spl. rep. of U.S. Bur. of Edn. in Eng., 1897; in employ Fidelity and Casualty Co. of New York, June 12, 1906-13, asst. sec., Feb. 1910-13; sec.-treas. Workmen's Compensation Publicity Bur., 1913-29. Sec. Assn. of Casualty and Surety Execs.; hon. sec. Bureau of Personal Accident and Health Underwriters. Apptd., Oct. 1918, by Sec. of the Treas. McAdoo, mem. adv. bd. U.S. Bureau of War Risk Ins. (mil. and naval div.). Fellow Ins. Inst. of Am., Casualty Actuarial Soc. of Am.; mem. Phi Gamma Delta, Phi Beta Kappa. Club: Century (New York). Author: The History of Taxation in Connecticut, 1896; Colonization of the Middle States and Maryland, 1904; History of the United States since the Civil War, 1905; Digest of Workmen's Compensation Laws of the United States and Territories, 1913-37; Taxation of Insurance Companies for Revenue, 1915; Essential Factors of a Good Workmen's Compensation Law, 1915; Case against State-Managed Insurance under Workmen's Compensation Laws, 1916; History and Proceedings of the World's Insurance Congress (San Francisco, 1915), 1917; Dangerous Tendencies in Workmen's Compensation Laws, 1926; Workmen's Compensation Laws of the United States and Territories (editor). Also monographs and articles on hist., econ. and sociol. subjects; hist. expert 10th edit. Encyclopedia Britannica. Home: 137 E. 66th St. Office: 60 John St., New York. Died Dec. 26, 1941.

JONES, Grinnell, chemist; b. Des Moines, Ia., Jan. 14, 1884; s. Richard and Carrie Holmes (Grinnell) J.; S.B., Vanderbilt U., 1903, S.M., 1905; A.M., Harvard, 1905, Ph.D., 1908; m. Genevieve Lupton, Aug. 18, 1910; 1 son, Grinnell. Instr. chemistry, U. of Ill., 1908-12; instr. chemistry, 1912-16, asst. prof., 1916-21, asso. prof., 1921-34, prof. since 1934, Harvard. Chief chemist, U.S. Tariff Commn., 1917-19 (leave of absence from Harvard), cons. chemist same, 1919-26; detailed for several mos., 1918, to U.S. Shipping Bd. Mem. Am. Chem. Soc., Am. Acad. Arts and Sciences, Am. Assn. of Textile Chemists and Colorists, Am. Inst. of Chem. Engineers, Phi Beta Kappa, Sigma Xi, Sigma Nu, Alpha Chi Sigma, Phi Lambda Upsilon. Congregationalist. Developed fire-resistant paint, method of purifying salt water. Home: 90 Larchwood Dr., Cambridge 38, Mass. Died June 23, 1947.

JONES, Herbert Vincent, corp. official; b. Uniontown, Ala., Nov. 10, 1878; s. John Archibald and Mary Vincent (Scott) J.; A.B., Vanderbilt U., 1901; m. Eleanor Buford, December 19, 1907; children—Eleanor J. Kemper, Herbert Vincent, Edward Buford. In real estate office of A. W. Childs, Kansas City, Mo., 1902-07; mem. firm Childs & Jones, 1907-19; established Herbert V. Jones & Co., 1919, now chairman of the board of directors; director Union National Bank, Kansas City Title Ins. Co., Safety Fed. Savings & Loan Assn., Fox Midwest Theatres, Inc., Kansas City Power & Light Co.; liquidating trustee Fidelity Nat. Bank & Trust Co., Fidelity Savings Bank. Served on President Hoover's Conf. on Home Building and Home Ownership, 1932. Chmn. City Plan Commn. since orgn., 1920 until 1946; trustee Y.M.C.A.; mem. bd. trustees Vanderbilt U.; trustee William Rockhill Nelson Trust ($10,000,000 art fund), Mary Atkins Estate ($700,000 art fund); gen. chmn. Kansas City Community Chest campaign, 1937; mem. Kansas City Community Fund Com. Sponsor of Herbert V. Jones Class of Eagle Scouts, 1939. Mem. U.S. and Kansas City chambers of commerce, Kansas City Real Estate Bd. (pres. 1918-19), Phi Delta Theta. Democrat. Congregationalist. Clubs: University (pres. 1912), Kansas City, Kansas City Country (dir., pres. 1922); Cheyenne Mountain Country (Colorado Springs, Colo.). Home: 823 W. 55th St., Kansas City 2. Office: 300 Bryant Bldg., Kansas City 6, Mo. Deceased.

JONES, J. S. William, prof. mathematics; b. Chance, Md., Nov. 19, 1866; s. Benjamin J. M. and Arianna (Scott) J.; A.B., Washington Coll., Chestertown, Md., 1889, A.M., 1892; Sc.D., 1918; Litt.D., Franklin and Marshall Coll., 1928; post grad work, U. of Chicago, U. of Pa., Columbia, Cambridge (Eng.), U. of Southern Calif.; m. May L. Matthews, Sept. 7, 1896 (died Mar. 10, 1923); children—Alan Morrison (dec.), Miriam Elizabeth, Margaret Olivia (dec.), Mary Virginia; m. 2d, Ethel S. Fox, July 24, 1935. Teacher pub. schs. Somerset County, Md., 1884-86; prin. Harrington (Del.) High Sch., 1889-92; prof. mathematics Washington Coll. since 1892, acting president, 1918-19, dean, 1922-40, sec.-treas. alumni assn. since 1916. Mem. Am. Assn. Univ. Profs., Am. Alumni Council, Kappa Alpha (Southern), Omicron Delta Kappa. Home: Chestertown, Md. Died Sep. 4, 1944.

JONES, James Coulter, lawyer; b. St. Louis, Mo., Mar. 23, 1866; s. William C. and Mary A. (Chester) J.; ed. pub. schs.; m. Mamie A. Maguire, Aug. 16, 1886 (dec.); m. 2d, Clara Morgan, Aug. 3, 1907 (now dec.); m. 3d, Hazel M. Ewald, Apr. 21, 1931. Admitted to Mo. bar, 1885, and since practiced in St. Louis; specializes in ins. law; now mem. Jones, Hocker, Gladney & Grand. Active worker many yrs. in behalf of the blind; pres. bd. mgrs. Mo. Sch. for Blind (St. Louis), 1900-10; pres. Mo. Commn. for the Blind. Mem. Am. Bar Assn., St. Louis Bar Assn. (pres. 1915-17), Mo. State Bar Assn. (pres. 1917-19); chmn. legal sect. Am. Life Conv., 1919; mem. Life Ins. Lawyers Assn. (pres. 1925-27). Former pres. St. Louis Cardinal Baseball Club; hon. mem. bd. dirs. Nat. League of Baseball. Democrat. Home: 7711 Club Drive, Clayton, Mo. Office: 407 N. 8th St., St. Louis, Mo. Died July 14, 1946.

JONES, J(oseph) Addison, clergyman; b. Wales, June 1, 1873; s. John and Catherine (Williams) J.; grad. Blair Acad., Blairstown, N.J., 1896; A.B., Princeton, 1900; grad. Auburn (N.Y.) Theol. Sem., 1903; D.D., Rutgers, 1910; m. Loraine Vail, May 21, 1903 (died Sept. 4, 1927); children—Arthur Vail (dec.), John Theodore (adopted); m. 2d, Florence E. Hart, Aug. 4, 1936. Came to U.S., 1892; naturalized, 1899. Ordained ministry Presbyterian Church, 1903; pastor First Church, Perry, N.Y., 1903-05, Madison Avenue Reformed Church, Albany, N.Y., 1905-20, Reformed Ch., Poughkeepsie, 1920-45; retired, Jan. 15, 1945. Served as secertary Y.M.C.A. in France, 1918. Chaplain N.Y. State Assembly, 1914-16, N.Y. State Constl. Conv., 1916. Pres. Gen. Synod of Ref. Ch. in America, 1927 (v.p. 1917); del. World Alliance of Ref. Chs. (pres. Am. sect. 1931); v.p. World Alliance of Presbyn. and Reformed Chs., 1942. Mem. bd. supts. Theol. Sem., New Brunswick, N.J. Republican. Rotarian. Home: 3 Osborne Rd., Poughkeepsie, N.Y. Died May 7, 1949; buried Poughkeepsie Rural Cemetery.

JONES, Lewis Ralph, botanist; b. Brandon, Wis., Dec. 5, 1864; s. David and Lucy (Knapp) J.; student Ripon Coll., 1883-86; Ph.B., U. of Mich., 1889, grad. studies, 1901, 1904, Ph.D., 1904; hon. Sc.D., U. of Vt., 1910, U. of Cambridge (Eng.), 1930, U. of Wis., 1936; LL.D., U. of Mich., 1935; has also carried out investigations in lab. of Bur. of Plant Industry, Washington, under direction of Dr. Erwin F. Smith, 1899, and in Europe, 1904; m. May I. Bennett, June 24, 1890; m. 2d, Anna M. Clark, July 27, 1929. Prof. botany, U. of Vt. and botanist Vermont Expt. Sta., 1889-1910; prof. plant pathology, U. of Wis., 1910-35, emeritus prof. since 1935. Collaborator of Bureau of Plant Industry, U.S. Dept. Agriculture; ex-sec. bd. park commrs., Burlington, Vt.; ex-sec. Vt. Bot. Club; ex-pres. Vt. Forestry Assn.; fellow A.A.A.S.; ex-pres. Bot. Soc. America; mem. Nat. Acad. of Sciences, N.E. Bot. Club, Wis. Acad. Arts and Sciences, Am. Soc. Naturalists, Am. Philos. Soc.; corr. Assn. of Applied Biologists, England, Société de Pathologie Végétale et d'Entomologie Agricole de France; hon. mem. Vereinigung für Angewandte Botanik, Japanese Phytopathol. Soc.; ex-chmn. div. of biology and agr. Nat. Research Council; ex-pres. Am. Phytopathol. Soc. Conglist. Republican. Joint author of "Flora of Vermont," and author bot. reports, bulls. and contbns. to scientific jours. Editor "Phytopathology" editor Am. Jour. Botany; editor bacteriol. terms, Webster's New Internat. Dictionary. Home: 146 N. Prospect Av., Madison, Wis. Died Mar. 31, 1945.

JONES, Livingston Erringer, banker; b. Germantown, Pa., Mar. 30, 1878; s. Thomas Firth and Cornelia (Erringer) J.; prep. edn., Penn Charter Sch., Phila.; A.B., Princeton, 1899; m. Edith Bolling, May 23, 1908; children—Livingston Eric, Corneila Livingston, Peyton Bolling. With Reeves, Parvin & Co., wholesale grocers, Phila., 1899-1913; pres. Savings Fund Soc. of Germantown, 1913-22, mgr. since 1922; pres. First Nat. Bank, Phila., since 1922; dir. Fire Assn. of Phila., Reliance Ins. Co., Am. Pulley Co., Saving Fund Soc. of Germantown, Lumbermen's Ins. Co., Phila. Nat. Ins. Co.; trustee Penn Mutual Life Ins. Co. V.p. Community Fund, Associated Hosp. Service; v.p. and trustee Germantown Hosp. Republican. Episcopalian. Clubs: University, Sunnybrook Golf, Bras Coupé, Rittenhouse. Home: Crefeld St., Chestnut Hill, Phila. Office: 1500 Walnut St., Philadelphia, Pa. Died Aug. 30, 1941.

JONES, Louise Tayler, pediatrician; b. Youngstown, O., Nov. 14, 1870; d. Robert Walker and Rachel (Wick) Tayler; A.B., Wellesley, 1896; M.S., George Washington U., 1898; M.D., Johns Hopkins U., 1903; m. Edward Barton Jones, M.D., June 8, 1901. Med. practice in Washington, D.C., since 1904, pediatrician since 1909; engaged in clinics, lectures and sch. work. Dir. Red Cross unit in Serbia, 1915; physician Wellesley unit in France, 1919. Mem. Med. Women's Internat. Assn. (v.p. 1929-37), Am. Women's Hosps. (bd. mem.), Am. Med. Women's Assn. (mem. bd. and exec. com.; pres. 1928-29), A.M.A., Dist. of Columbia Med. Soc. (v.p. 1921), Am. Acad. Pediatrics, Am. Coll. Physicians, Am. Assn. Univ. Women, Women's Joint Congl. Com. (Washington, D.C.). Republican. Presbyterian. Club: Wellesley (Washington, D.C.). Contbr. articles on pediatrics to med. and scientific jours. Home: Linganore, McLean, Va.; and Washington, D.C. Deceased.

JONES, Mattison Boyd, lawyer; b. Tuttle, Ky., June 15, 1869; s. Hiram J. and Permelia W. (Black) J.; A.B., U. of Ky., 1894, grad. study, 1898-99, LL.D., 1932; grad. study, U. of Chicago, 1898; LL.D., U. of Redlands, 1941; m. Antoinette Ewell Smith, Jan. 3, 1900; 1 dau., Lillian Winifred (Mrs. Kyrill de Shishmareff). Teacher country schs., Ky., 1887-89; prin. Laurel Sem., London, Ky., 1894-95; admitted to Ky. bar, 1895; prof. mathematics and astronomy, Cumberland (Ky.) Coll., 1896-98; prof. mil. science and instr. in mathematics, U. of Ky., 1898-99; removed to Los Angeles, Calif., 1900, and practiced law there since 1900; mem. Jones & Drake, 1905-09, Jones & Evans, 1909-17, Jones, Wilson & Stephenson and Jones, Stephenson, Palmer & Moore, 1920-32; now practicing alone; prof. private corps., Law Sch., U. of Southern Calif., 1904-07, lecturer in ethics and advocacy, 1908-11; pres. First Nat. Bank, Glendale, 1931-32, now chmn. bd. Sec. Exemption Bd., 7th Dist., Los Angeles County, World War. Col. on staff gov. of Ky., 1933. Pres. board trustees Univ. of Redlands since founding, 1909 (retired 1941). Pres. Southern Calif. Bapt. Conv., 1911-13, Pacific Coast Bapt. Conf., 1910-13, Los Angeles County Bapt. Assn., 1907, Los Angeles Bapt. City Mission Soc., 1906-09; 1st v.p. Northern Bapt. Conv. of U.S., 1930, pres., 1931. Candidate for Dem. nomination for gov. of Calif. 1922; Dem. elector, Calif., 1924 and 1932. Mem. Am., Calif. and Los Angeles County bar assns. Mason (32°, K.T., Shriner; Grand High Priest of Calif. 1921-22; Grand Master of Grand Council 1927-28; past Gen. Grand High Priest of Gen. Grand Chapter R.A.M. of U.S.; awarded DeMolay Cross of Honor, 1928). Home: 727 Kenneth Rd., Glendale, Calif. Office: Pershing Sq. Bldg., Los Angeles, Calif. Died Oct. 12, 1941.

JONES, M(eredith) Ashby, clergyman; b. Lexington, Va., Nov. 7, 1868; s. John William and Judith Page (Helm) J.; student U. of Richmond, 1885-87, Washington and Lee Univ., 1889-91, Southern Baptist Theol. Sem., 1891-93; grad. student U. of Va., 1894-95; D.D., U. of Richmond; LL.D., Oglethorpe U.; m. May Turner, May 7, 1895; 1 son, Howard Turner. Ordained Bapt. ministry, 1893; pastor at Tate's Creek and Richmond, Ky., 1893-94; stated supply Charlottesville, Va., 1894-95; pastor Bardstown, Ky., 1895-98, Leigh St. Ch., Richmond, Va., 1898-1906, 1st Ch., Columbus, Ga., 1906-08, 1st Ch., Augusta, Ga., 1908-17, Ponce de Leon Av. Bapt. Ch., Atlanta, Ga., 1917-26, 2d Baptist Ch., St. Louis, 1926-32; removed to Atlanta, 1932; now gen. lecturer and preacher. Hon. chmn. Inter-racial Commn. Mem. Kappa Alpha, Phi Beta Kappa. Mason (32°, K.T., Shriner). Rotarian. Clubs: Symposium, Chi Alpha, Friars, Ansley Park Country. Columnist, "Text and Pretext," Atlanta Constitution, since 1919. Home: 39 Avery Dr., Atlanta. Died Jan. 2, 1947.

JONES, Ralph M., business exec.; b. Utica, N.Y., July 19, 1886; s. Albert G. and Julia W. (Smith) J.; student pub. schs. of Utica, N.Y.; m. Bertha F. Chaffin, June 16, 1909; children—Quentin McAdam, Alan Chaffin, Esther Louise, Helen Lea. Worked in all depts. of mill to learn knit underwear business, Utica, N.Y., 1904-08; supt. Highland Mill, Utica, 1908-16; gen. supt., later dir. Utica (N.Y.) Knitting Co., 1916-20, became v.p. mfg., 1920, now pres.; pres. and dir. Utica Duxbak Corp. since 1919; pres. Mutual Box Board Co., Commercial Warehouse Co., dir. Utica Mutual Insurance Co. Dir. Boys' Club, Utica. Chmn. Underwear Inst. since 1938; mem. Underwear Industry Com., 1939. Mem. Oneida Hist. Soc., S.A.R. Republican. Universalist. Clubs: Kiwanis, Fort Schuyler (Utica). Home: 23 South St., Utica, N.Y. Office: Utica Knitting Co., Utica, N.Y.; and 93 Worth St., New York. Died Aug. 22, 1946; buried in Forest Hill Cemetery, Utica.

JONES, Reginald Lamont, elec. engr.; b. New York, N.Y., Feb. 28, 1886; s. Albert Sinclair and Clara Evaline (Bishop) J.; B.S., Mass. Inst. of Tech., 1909, M.S., 1910, Sc.D., 1911; m. Marion Elizabeth Babcock, Oct. 2, 1917; children—Elizabeth, Reginald Lamont, Jr., Peter Babcock. On research staff Western Electric Co., 1911-14 in charge transmission research dept., 1914-23, inspection engring. dept., 1923-25; inspection mgr., Bell Telephone Lab., 1925-27, outside plant development engineer, 1927-28, director apparatus development, 1928-1944, vice pres. since Oct. 1, 1944; director Summit Trust Co. Capt. Signal Reserve Corps, U.S. Army, 1917-18. Mem. Non-Ferrous Metall. Adv. Bd., Army Ordnance Dept., Mem. Standards Council of Am. Standards Assn. Mem. Nat. panel, Am. Arbitration Assn. Pres., Summit Bd. of Edn. Trustee, Summit Cooperative Service Assn. Mem. alumni vis. com. Mass. Inst. Tech. Fellow Am. Phys. Soc., Am. Inst. of Elec. Engrs. (chmn. standards com.), A.A.A.S., Acoustical Soc. of Am.; mem. Am. Soc. Engring. Edn. Republican. Conglist. Trustee, Central Presbyn. Ch. of Summit. Club: Salmagundi (N.Y. City). Home: 190 Oakridge Av., Summit, N.J. Office: 463 West St., New York 14. Died Jan. 14, 1949; buried at West Bridgeport, Mass.

JONES, Rufus Matthew, college prof.; b. S. China, Me., Jan. 25, 1863; s. Edwin and Mary G. (Hoxie) J.; A.B., Haverford Coll., 1885, A.M., 1886, LL.D., 1922; studied in U. of Heidelberg, 1887, U. of Pa., 1893-95; A.M., Harvard, 1901, D.D., 1920; in Oxford U., 1908, Marburg, 1911; Litt.D., Penn Coll., 1898; LL.D., Swarthmore, 1922; D.Th., Marburg, 1925; LL.D., Earlham, 1929; S.T.D., Columbia, 1933; D.D., Yale, 1935; LL.D., Williams College, 1936; S.T.D., Colby College, 1937; H.LittD., Jewish Institute of Religion, 1942; L.H.D., Colgate University, 1942; married Sarah H. Coutant, July 3, 1888; 1 son, Lowell Coutant (dec.); m. 2d, Elizabeth Bartram Cadbury, Mar. 11, 1902; 1 dau., Mary Hoxie. Prin. Oak Grove Sem., Vassalboro, Me., 1889-93, instr., 1893-1901, asso. prof., 1901-04, prof. philosophy, 1904-34, Haverford Coll., now emeritus; editor Friends' Rev., 1893, The Am. Friend, 1894-1912, Present Day Papers, 1914-15. Coll. preacher. Trustee Bryn Mawr Coll. since 1896 (pres. bd. 1916-36); trustee Brown Univ., Yenching Univ. Minister Society of Friends; chmn. American Friends Service Committee European Relief, 1917-27, 1934-44; now honorary chairman; member Appraisal Commission Foreign Missions in Orient, 1931-32. Member Dominican Republic Settlement Association. Recipient of Philadelphia Award, Theodore Roosevelt Medal, 1942. Member Kant-Gesellschaft, American Philosophical Assn. Phi Beta Kappa. Author: Life of Eli and Sibyl Jones, 1889; Practical Christianity, 1899; A Dynamic Faith, 1900; A Boy's Religion from Memory, 1902; Autobiography of George Fox, 1903; Social Law in the Spiritual World, 1904; The Double Search, 1905; The Abundant Life, 1908; Quakerism, A Religion of Life, 1908; Studies in Mystical Religion, 1909; The Children of the Light, 1909; Clement of Alexandria, 1910; The Quakers in the American Colonies, 1911; Stories of Hebrew Heroes, 1911; Spiritual Reformers in the Sixteenth and Seventeenth Centuries, 1914; The Inner Life, 1916; St. Paul the Hero, 1917; The World Within, 1918; The Story of George Fox, 1919; The Remnant, 1920; Nature and Authority of Conscience, 1920; A Service of Love in War Time, 1920; Later Periods of Quakerism, 1921; The Boy Jesus and His Companions, 1922; Spiritual Energies in Daily Life, 1922; Religious Foundations, 1923; Fundamental Ends of Life, 1924; The Life and Message of George Fox, 1924; The Church's Debt to Heretics, 1925; Finding the Trail of Life, 1926; The Faith and Practice of the Quakers, 1927; New Studies in Mystical Religion, 1927; The New Quest, 1928; The Trail of Life in College, 1929; Some Exponents of Mystical Religion, 1930; George Fox: Seeker and Friend, 1930; Pathways to the Reality of God, 1931; A Preface to Christian Faith in a New Age, 1932; Mysticism and Democracy in the English Commonwealth, 1932; Haverford College—A History and an Interpretation, 1933; Re-Thinking Religious Liberalism, 1935; The Testimony of the Soul, 1936; Some Problems of Life, 1937; The Eternal Gospel, 1938; Flowering of Mysticism, 1939; Small Town Boy, 1941; Spirit in Man, 1941; New Eyes for Invisibles, 1943; The Radiant Life, 1944; The Luminous Trail, 1947; A Call to What is Vital, 1948. Home: Haverford, Pa. Died June 16, 1948.

JONES, Samuel Fosdick, surgeon; b. Cincinnati, O., Aug. 4, 1874; s. Maj. Frank J. and Frances Dering (Fosdick) J.; ed. The Hill Sch., Pottstown, Pa.; B.S., Mass. Inst. Tech., 1898; M.D., Columbia, 1902; m. Mary Catherine Cordes, Dec. 3, 1910. Began practice in N.Y. City, 1902; moved to Denver, 1906; prof. orthopedic surgery, Med. Dept. U. of Colo., 1919-31, now emeritus prof.; ex-pres. St. Lukes' Hosp. Staff of Denver; retired from active practice. Served as maj. Med. Corps, U.S. Army, Apr. 6, 1917-Jan. 13, 1919; with A.E.F. in France 8 mos. Fellow Am. Coll. Surgeons; mem. Am. Orthopedic Assn., Western Surg. Assn., New York Pathol. Soc., Soc. Mayflower Descendants, Loyal Legion, Veterans of Foreign Wars, Delta Psi; asso. mem. Calif. Inst. Tech. Republican. Episcopalian. Clubs: Denver Club, Cactus, Mile High (Denver); California (Los Angeles); University, The Athenarum (Pasadena); St. Anthony (New York); Cosmos (Washington); Santa Barbara. Home: Huntingdon Hotel, Pasadena 15, Calif. Died Mar. 24, 1946.

JONES, Thomas Clive, corp. official; b. Delaware, O., Nov. 17, 1867; s. Judge Thomas C. and Harriet A. (Williams) J.; ed. Acad. of Kenyon Coll., Gambier, O., and bus. coll., Washington, D.C.; m. Susan Baker, Feb. 12, 1889 (died Aug. 17, 1935); 1 son, Thomas Clive III. Began as teller Columbus (O.) Gas Co., 1888; sec.-treas. Delaware (O.) Gas Co., 1891-1905, pres. and gen. mgr. since 1905; v.p. and gen. mgr. Buckeye State Gas Co., Coshocton, O., 1903-06. Sec.-treas. Ohio Gas Light Assn., 1894-1902; treas. Am. Gas Inst., 1906-08; sec.-treas. Nat. Gas Assn. America, 1909-19; mem. Ohio Gas & Oil Assn. (pres. 1923-25); mem. Am. Gas Assn.; mem. Del. C. of C. Republican. Episcopalian. Mason (K.T.), Elk. Speaker and writer of technical papers on gas and its distribution. Home: 130 N. Liberty Av. Office: 68 N. Sandusky St., Delaware, O. Died May 9, 1945.

JONES, Thomas Hoyt, lawyer; b. Jackson, O., Aug. 11, 1887; s. Thomas Alfred and Grace Urla (Hoyt) J.; A.B., Ohio State University, J.D., 1911; m. Katharine Allein Brooks, Sept. 27, 1913; children—Thomas Hoyt, Brooks Morton. Admitted to Ohio bar, 1911, and since practiced in Cleveland; partner firms Blandin, Rice and Ginn, 1911-12, Blandin, Hogsett and Ginn, 1912-14, Tolles, Hogsett, Ginn and Morley, 1914-26, Tolles, Hogsett and Ginn, 1926-38, Jones, Day, Cockley and Reavis, since 1938. Pvt., World War I. Dir. and sec. Glenn L. Martin Co., Glenn L. Martin-Nebraska Co., Murray Ohio Mfg. Co.; dir. Warner & Swasey Co., Am. Greeting Publishers, Inc., Cleveland-Cliffs Iron Co., Cleveland Trust Co., Electric Controller & Mfg. Co., Foote-Burt Co., Globe Iron Co., Richman Brothers Co., Gray Drug Stores, Inc., Diamond Corp. Am. Member Cleveland Bar Assn. (pres. 1945-46), Ohio State Bar Assn., Am. Bar Assn., Phi Beta Kappa, Phi Delta Theta, Phi Delta Phi. Clubs: Union (Cleveland); Chagrin Valley Hunt (Gates Mills, O.). Home: 304 Corning Drive, Bratenahl, O. Office: 1759 Union Commerce Bldg., Cleveland 14. Died April 14, 1948.

JONES, Thomas Jesse, sociologist; b. Llanfacthraeth, Wales, Aug. 4, 1873; s. Benjamin and Sarah B. (Williams) J.; came to America, 1884; student Washington and Lee U., Va., 1891-92; A.B., Marietta (O.) Coll., 1897; A.M., Columbia, 1899, Ph.D., 1904; B.D., Union Theol. Sem., 1900; m. Carrie Schlaegel, June 18, 1901; children—Gwendolen Schlaegel, Carolyn Weller. Acting headworker, Univ. Social Settlement, New York, 1901-02; dir. research dept., Hampton Inst., Va., 1902-09; statistician in U.S. Census Bur., 1909-12; specialist in edn., U.S. Bur. of Edn., 1912-July 1919; educational director Phelps Stokes Fund, Jan. 1913-May 1946; director emeritus since May 1946. Chmn. com. on social studies in secondary schs., apptd. by N.E.A. Chmn. Edn. Commn. to West, South and Equatorial Africa, 1920-21, to East Africa, 1924. Presbyn. Clubs: Century Assn., Town Hall Club (New York City); Cosmos (Washington, D.C.). Author: The Sociology of a New York City Block, 1904; Negro Education in the United States, 1917; Educational Adaptations (ten year report of work of Phelps-Stokes Fund), 1920; Education in Africa, 1922; Education in East Africa, 1925; Four Essentials of Education, 1926; Essentials of Civilization, 1929. Address: 101 Park Av. and 464 Riverside Drive, New York, N.Y.

JONES, Walter Clinton, M.D., educator; b. Chicago, Ill., May 2, 1874; s. Henry Clinton and Naomi Lucinda (Noyes) J.; A.B., Northwestern U., 1898, A.M., 1899, M.D., 1902; scholarship in biology, summer sch., Marine Biol. Sta., Woods Hole, Mass., 1898; m. Cora Evangeline Ellis, Oct. 20, 1910 (died 1932); children—Lois Elberta (dec.); married 2d, Isabelle Doyle Hansen, August 18, 1936. Assistant in zoölogy, Northwestern U., 1898-99; asst. anatomy and pathology, Northwestern U. Med. Sch., 1900-02; asst. prof. surg. pathology, Med. Dept. U. of Ill., 1005-13; pathologist Evanston Hosp., 1913-16; prof. pathology and bacteriology, U. of Ala., 1918-19; prof. biology, Birmingham-Southern Coll., 1919-23, prof. zoölogy, 1923-30; pathologist hosp. of Tenn. Coal, Iron & Ry. Co. 1919-46, Bessemer Gen. Hosp. since 1928; cons. pathologist, Norwood Hosp., Birmingham, Ala., since 1943; pathologist, E. End Memorial Hosp., Birmingham, since 1946. Diplomate American Board of Pathology since 1939. Fellow A.M.A., Am. Coll. Surg.; mem. Med. Assn. State of Ala., Southern Med. Assn., Am. Soc. Clin. Pathologists, A.A.A.S., Ala. Acad. Science (pres. 1928-29), Birmingham Scientific Soc. (pres. 1923), N.E.A., Ala. Assn. Pathologists (pres. 1946-47), Phi Beta Kappa, Alpha Omega Alpha. Club: Optimist. Presbyterian. Author of numerous articles on med. subjects. Home: Route 2, 195 A, Birmingham, Ala. Died Oct. 27, 1948.

JORDAN, Charles Bernard, pharm. chemistry; b. Morrice, Mich., Nov. 7, 1878; s. John and Mary (McCarthy) J.; grad. Ypsilanti (Mich.) State Normal Coll., 1904; Ph.C. and B.S., U. of Mich., 1910, M.S., 1912; hon. D.Sc., Ohio Northern U., 1933; m. Helen Mary Byrnes, Aug. 20, 1907; children—Veronica Kathryn, Robert Edward, Charles Richard, Mildred Helen. Teacher pub. schs., Shiawassee County, Mich., 1897-1901; supt. schs., Morrice, 1904-08; prof. pharm. chemistry, Purdue, since 1910, dir. Sch. of Pharmacy, 1910-23, dean since 1923. Lecturer, St. Elizabeth Hosp., Lafayette, Ind., since 1915. Mem. com. of revision U.S. Pharmacopoeia since 1920, chmn. subcom. on crude drug assay since 1930. Mem. Am. Pharm. Assn. (chmn. house of delegates 1929-30), Am. Assn. Colls. Pharmacy (pres. 1918-19; chmn. exec. com., 1923-36), Am. Chem. Soc., Ind. Pharm. Assn., Ind. Acad. Science, Sigma Xi; fellow A.A.A.S. Catholic. Club: West Lafayette Country. Author: Qualitative Analysis for Students of Pharmacy and Medicine, 1928. Editor Am. Assn. Colls. of Pharmacy sect. of Jour. Am. Pharm. Assn., 1923-36. Contbr. on pharm. edn. and pharm. chemistry. Home: 409 Russell St., West Lafayette, Ind. Died Apr. 22, 1941.

JORDAN, David Francis, prof. finance; b. Watervliet, N.Y., July 21, 1890; s. Thomas Henry and Ellen (Tierney) J.; B.C.S., N.Y. Univ., 1919; m. Edith Irene Wilson, Dec. 27, 1922 (died 1924); m. 2d, Frances Marion Reinken, May 24, 1927; children—Eleanor Irene, David Francis, Nancy Ellen, Thomas Dietrich. Mem. faculty N.Y. U. since 1919, prof. finance since 1928; economist Gen. Electric Co., 1922-25. In Chem. Warfare Service, U.S. Army, 1918-19; vet. Co. G, 7th Regt., N.Y.N.G. Pres. Fedn. Coll. Catholic Clubs, 1923-24. Mem. Am. Econ. Assn., Albany Soc. of New York, Delta Mu Delta, Alpha Kappa Psi. Catholic. Author: Jordan on Investments, 1919 (22d printing 1941); Business Forecasting, 1921; Practical Business Forecasting, 1926; Economic Principles and Problems (with others), 1932; Managing Personal Finances, 1936; Problems in Investment Principles and Security Analysis, 1937. Home: 136 Shoreward Drive, Great Neck, N.Y. Office: Washington Sq., New York, N.Y. Died Aug. 20, 1942.

JORDAN, Elizabeth, editor, author, playwright; b. Milwaukee, Wis.; d. William F. and Margaretta G. Jordan; grad. Convent of Notre Dame, Milwaukee; hon. D.Litt., 1932. On editorial staff of New York World 10 yrs; asst. editor Sunday World 3 yrs.; editor Harper's Bazaar, 1900-13; lit. adviser to Harper & Brothers, 1913-18. Mem. Mayor's Com. of Women, N.Y., Big Sisters Assn., Nat. Inst. Social Sciences, Authors' League of America, Am. Com. of Mercy, Soc. of Am. Dramatists and Composers, Am. P.E.N. V.p. Notre Dame Alumnæ Assn.; mem. bd. dirs. Gramercy Park Assn. Prominent as a speaker and writer during suffrage campaign. Clubs: Colony, Cosmopolitan, Gramercy Park (pres.), all of New York; Northampton (Mass.) Country. Author: Tales of the City Room, 1898; Tales of the Cloister, 1901; Tales of Destiny, 1902; May Iverson, Her Book, 1904; Many Kingdoms, 1908; May Iverson Tackles Life, 1913; May Iverson's Career, 1914; Lovers' Knots, 1916; Wings of Youth, 1917; The Lady from Oklahoma (comedy in 4 acts, prod. 1911, 12, 13, also published in book form); Beauty Is Skin Deep (one-act play, prod. 1914, 15, 16, 17); The Story of a Pioneer (with Anna Howard Shaw); The Whole Family (with Henry James, William Dean Howells and others); The Girl in the Mirror, 1919; The Blue Circle, 1920; The Lady of Pentlands, 1923; Red Riding Hood, 1924; Miss Blake's Husband, 1925; Black Butterflies, 1926; Miss Nobody from Nowhere, 1927; The Devil and the Deep Sea, 1928; The Night Club Mystery, 1929; The Fourflusher, 1930; Playboy, 1931; Young Mr. X, 1932; Page Mr. Pomeroy, 1933; Daddy and I, 1934; The Life of the Party, 1935; The Trap, 1936; Three Rousing Cheers (autobiography), 1938; First Port of Call, 1940; Faraway Island, 1941; Young John Takes Over, 1942; Herself, 1943; Miss Warren's Son, 1944; The Real Ruth Arnold, 1945. Contributor short stories to Am. and English mags. Staff editorial writer for chain of Am. newspapers; dramatic critic of "America." Home: 36 Gramercy Park, New York, N.Y.; (country) "Spreadwings," Florence, Mass. Died Feb. 24, 1947.

JOSEPHSON, Aksel Gustav Salomon, bibliographer; b. Uppsala, Sweden, October 2, 1860; s. Jacob Axel and Hilda Augusta (Schram) J.; ed. in Sweden and N.Y. State Library Sch., Albany; m. Lucia Engberg, Apr. 27, 1899 (died May 10, 1929). Came to America, 1893, naturalized, 1898. Cataloguer, N.Y. Pub. Library (Lenox Library), 1894-96; chief cataloguer, John Crerar Library, Chicago, 1896-1923; cons. cataloguer since 1928. An organizer and officer Bibliog. Soc. Chicago and successor, Bibliog. Soc. America, also Swedish Hist. Soc. America, Swedish Ednl. League; mem. Am. Library Assn., Lärdomshistoriska Samfundet (Uppsala), Am. Assn. Advancement Science; hon. mem. Bibliog. Soc. America, Chicago Library Club. Author: Proposition for the Establishment of a Bibliographical Institute, 1905; History as Synthesis and the High School, 1930; also brochures and articles on bibliog. topics, book reviews, etc., in The Nation, 1904-14; regular contbr. letters on Swedish and English books in the Weekly Nordstjernan, New York. Compiler: Avhandlingar och program utgivna vid Svenska och Finska Akademier och Skolor, 1892-97; Bibliographies of Bibliographies, 1901, 2d edit., 1910-14; The John Crerar Library List of Books on the History of Science, 1911, Supplement, 1916; List of Books on the History of Industry, 1915. Editor: Year Book Bibliog. Soc. Chicago, 1899-1903; Papers and Bulls., Bibliog. Soc. America, 1909-11, 1914-18. Home; 133 N. Carlin St., Mobile, Ala. Died Dec. 12, 1944.

JOSLIN, Theodore Goldsmith, dir. pub. relations; b. Leominster, Mass., Feb. 28, 1890; s. Frederick Alonzo and Hannah Gammage (Hapgood) J.; grad. high sch., Leominster, 1908; m. Rowena Hawes, June 15, 1912; children—Richard Hawes, Robert Edward. With Associated Press, 1908-13; state polit. corr. Boston Evening Transcript, 1913-16; Washington corr. Boston Evening Transcript, 1916-31; sec. to President Hoover, 1931-33; Washington rep. Babson Statis. Orgn., Inc., 1933-36; pres. News-Journal Co., Wilmington, Del., 1936-39; dir. Dept. of Public Relations, E. I. du Pont de Nemours & Co., since Jan. 1, 1939. Conglist. Clubs: Nat. Press, Gridiron, Wilmington, Wilmington Country. Author: Hoover Off the Record, 1934. Home: Greenville, Del. Died Apr. 12, 1944.

JOYCE, Patrick H.; became chmn. exec. com. and pres. Chicago Great Western R.R., 1931, apptd. trustee of the railroad, 1935. Home: Antioch, Ill. Office: 309 W. Jackson Blvd., Chicago, Ill.* Died Nov. 10, 1946.

JOYCE, Thomas Martin, surgeon; b. Emmettsburg, Ia., Jan. 28, 1885; s. Matthew and Ella (Healy) J.; student U. of Notre Dame, 1903-05; M.D., U. of Mich., 1910; LL.D., U. of Portland, 1936; m. Ruth Kiernan, Oct. 5, 1915; children—Susan (Mrs. Vincent Mullins), Jane (Mrs. Richard Cole). House physician, U. of Mich. Hosp., 1910; intern St. Mary's Hosp., Rochester, Minn., 1911; 1st surg. asst. to Dr. Charles Mayo, Mayo Clinic, Rochester, Minn., 1911-14; mem. of clinic (doctors Coffey, Jones, Sears and Joyce), 1914-19; chief of surg. service, Portland Clinic, Portland, Ore., since 1920; chief of surg. service Multnomah County Hosp. since 1934; Kenneth A. McKenzie prof. of surgery and head of dept. of surgery, Med. Sch. U. of Ore., since 1934. Mem. bd. dirs. St. Vincent's Hosp. Served as chief of surg. service, Base Hosp. No. 46, A.E.F., 1917-19. Mem. Am. Bd. of Surgery, Am., Southern, and North Pacific surg. assns., Pacific Coast Surg. Soc., Am. Assn. for Study of Goiter, Portland Acad. Medicine, Residents and Ex-Residents of Mayo Clinic, Ore. State Med. Soc., Western Surg. Assn. (hon.). Republican. Roman Catholic. Home: 2823 N.W. Cumberland Rd., Portland 5, Oregon. Died April 19, 1947.

JOYES, John Warren, army officer; b. Waterloo, N.Y., Apr. 17, 1870; s. James J. and Charlotte L. (Stratton) J.; grad. 5th in class of 52, U.S. Mil. Acad., 1894; m. Georgiana M. Butler, June 14, 1904; children—John Warren, Georgiana Butler, Charlotte P. Commd. 2d lt. 5th Arty., June 12, 1894; promoted through grades to col., May 15, 1917, asst. chief of ordnance, with rank of brig. gen., 1923-27; chief of ordnance field service, 1925-27; at Army Indsl. Coll., 1927-28. In ordnance dept. of U.S. Army since 1897; served as chief ordnance officer Southern, Philippines and Western depts., 2d Corps Area, etc.; chief of nitrate div., World War, in charge government's work in fixation of nitrogen, including Muscle Shoals; toured Europe, 1919, to investigate status of nitrogen fixation; apptd. chief of tech. staff, Ordnance Office, 1921. Mem. Army Ordnance Assn., Loyal Legion. Episcopalian. Club: Chevy Chase. Home: 2405 Waterside Drive N.W. Address: care Adjutant General, U.S. Army, Washington. Died Sept. 24, 1945.

JUDAY, Chancey (jū-dā'), zoölogist; b. nr. Millersburg, Ind., May 5, 1871; s. Baltzer and Elizabeth (Heltzel) J.; A.B., Indiana U., 1896, A.M., 1897, LL.D. from the same univ. in 1933; m. Magdalen Evans, Sept. 6, 1910; children—Chancey Evans, Mary, Richard Evans. Teacher of science, high sch., Evansville, Ind., 1898-1900; biologist, Wis. Geol. and Natural History Survey, 1900-01; acting prof. biology, U. of Colo., 1903-04; instr. in zoölogy, U. of Calif., 1904-05 biologist, Wis. Geology and Natural History Survey, 1905-31; lecturer in zoölogy, 1908-31, prof. of limnology since 1931, U. of Wis.; asst. U.S. Bur. Fisheries, summers, since 1907; dir. Trout Lake Limnological Lab. since 1925; mem. Nat. Research Council, Biology and Agrl. Div., 1940-43; asso. editor, Ecological Monographs, 1940-43. Fellow A.A.A.S.; mem. Am. Soc. Zoölogists, Am. Society Naturalists, Am. Micros. Society (pres. 1923), Ecol. Soc. America (pres. 1927), Internat. Limnol. Soc., Wis. Acad. Sciences (sec.-treas., 1922-30) (pres. 1937-30), Am. Limnol. Soc. (pres. 1935-36), Phi Beta Kappa, Sigma Xi. Author: Dissolved Gases of Wisconsin Lakes, 1911; Hydrography and Morphometry of Wisconsin Lakes, 1914; Plankton of Wisconsin Lakes, 1922—all with E. A. Birge; also papers dealing with the physics, chemistry and biology of lakes. Home: 1840 Summit Av., Madison, Wis. Died Mar. 29, 1944.

JUDD, Bertha Grimmell (Mrs. Orrin R. Judd), church official; b. Buffalo, N.Y., Nov. 16, 1871; d. Rev. Julius Carl and Helen Louise (Weimar) Grimmell; grad. Brooklyn (N.Y.) Training Sch. for Teachers, 1888; hon. diploma, Colo. Woman's Coll., Denver. 1937; m. Orrin Reynolds Judd, Oct. 4, 1905; children—Orrin Grimmell, Willard Reynolds (dec.), Hila Margaret (dec.). Teacher, pub. schs., Brooklyn, 1888-93, Cleveland, 1893-1904. Vice pres. bd. auxiliary dirs., Children's Home of L.I. Baptist Assn., since 1909; mem. bd. mgrs. Woman's Am. Baptist Home Mission Society, 1920-42, president, 1937-42; pres. Women's Nat. Sabbath Alliance since 1937; mem. Council of Women for Home Missions. 1914-41 (past pres.); mem. exec. com. the Home Missions Council of North America; mem. Christian Commission for Camp Communities; mem. exec. com. Federal Council Chs. of Christ in America. 2d v.p. Northern Baptist Conv., 1942-44. Club: Cambridge. Author: Fifty Golden Years, 1927; Memoir of Rev. J. C. Grimmell. 1947. Home: 275 Clinton Av., Brooklyn, N.Y. Died Nov. 20, 1947.

JUDD, Charles Hubbard, psychologist; b. Bareilly, Brit. India, Feb. 20, 1873; s. Charles Wesley and Sarah (Hubbard) J.; came to America, 1879; A.B., Wesleyan U., 1894; Ph.D., U. of Leipzig, 1896; A.M., Yale, 1907; LL.D., Miami, 1909, Wesleyan, 1913, U. of Iowa, 1923, Colorado Coll., 1923; D.Sc., U. of Louisville, 1937; m. Ella Le Compte, Aug. 23, 1898 (died 1935); 1 dau., Dorothy; m. 2d, May Diehl, Aug. 28, 1937. Instr. philosophy, Wesleyan Univ., 1896-98; prof. psychology, New York U., 1898-1901; prof. psychology and pedagogy, U. of Cincinnati, 1901-02; instr. psychology, Yale, 1902-04, asst. prof., 1904-07, prof. psychol. and dir. Psychol. Lab., 1907-09; prof. and head dept. of edn., U. of Chicago, 1909-38, emeritus since 1938, chmn. dept. psychology, 1920-25; mem. science com. of Nat. Resources Planning Board, 1937-40; lecturer summer session U. of Ia., 1941, U. of Calif. (Berkeley), 1942; Sir John Adams lecturer U. of Calif. (Los Angeles), 1942; consultant Nat. Youth Administrn., 1938-40; consultant War Dept. and mem. faculty sch. for spl. service, 1942-43. Consultant on Social Studies Santa Barbara city schs. since 1944. Dir. Summer Sch., Yale Univ., 1906-07; Inglis lecturer, Harvard, 1928. Editor Monograph Supplements of Psyychol. Review, Studies from Yale Psychol. Laboratory, 1905-09; Elementary School Journal; School Review; Survey of the Schools of Grand Rapids; Survey of the Schools of St. Louis; also lessons in Community and National Life (pub. by U.S. Bur. of Edn. and U.S. Food Adminstrn., 1917-18. Trustee Julius Rosenwald Fund; mem. board of managers Lewis Institute. Fellow A.A.A.S.; mem. Am. Psychol. Assn. (council 1906-09, pres. 1909), Nat. Soc. Coll. Teachers of Edn. (pres. 1911, 15), North Central Assn. Colls. and Secondary Schs. (pres. 1923). Mem. staff New York Rural Sch. Survey, 1921; chmn. Am. Council on Edn., 1929-30; mem. Social Science Research Council, 1930-40; mem. staff Regents Inquiry into Cost and Character of Public Edn., State of N.Y.; mem. adv. com. of Nat. Youth Adminstrn., 1935-40, Internat. Inquiry on Sch. and Univ. Examinations, 1935, Policies Commn. of Nat. Edn. Assn., 1935-37, mem. Nat. Adv. Com. on Edn., 1937. Author: Genetic Psychology for Teachers, 1903; (transl.) Outline of Psychology, by W. Wundt (from German), 3d edit., 1907; Psychology General Introduction, 1907, 2d revised edit., 1917; Psychology Laboratory Course, 1907; Psychology Laboratory Equipment and Methods, 1907; Psychology of High School Subjects, 1915; Measuring the Work of the Public Schools, 1916; Introduction to the Scientific Study of Education, 1918; Evolution of a Democratic School System, 1918; Silent Reading, 1923; Psychology of Social Institutions, 1926; Psychology of Secondary Education, 1927; Psychological Analysis of the Fundamentals of Arithmetic, 1927; The Unique Character of American Secondary Education, 1928; Problems of Education in the United States, 1933; chapter on Edn. in Recent Social Trends, 1933; Education and Social Progress, 1934; Education as Cultivation of the Higher Mental Processes, 1936; Preparation of School Personnel, 1938; Educational Psychology, 1939; (with J. D. Russell) The American Educational System, 1940; (with W C. Reavis) The Teacher and Educational Administration, 1942; contbr. to scientific and ednl. jours. Home: Tunnel Road, Mission Canyon, Santa Barbara, Calif. Died July 18, 1946.

JUDD, James Robert, surgeon; b. Honolulu, T.H., May 20, 1876; s. Albert Francis and Agnes Hall (Boyd) J.; student Oahu Coll., 1893; A.B., Yale, 1897; M D., Coll. Physicians and Surgeons (Columbia), 1901; m. Alice Louise Marshall, Feb. 29, 1908; children—James Robert, Alice Louise. Asst., Am. Nat. Red Cross, Spanish-Am. War, 1898; began practice at Honolulu, 1903; surgeon with Am. Ambulance Corps, in France, July 1915-Oct. 1916; surgeon in chief, Juilly Hosp., France, Nov. 1915-July 1916. Exmem. Territorial Bd. of Health, and Bd. of Med. Examination, T.H.; ex-trustee Honolulu Mil. Acad. Fellow Am. Coll. Surgeons; mem. A.M.A., Alpha Delta Phi (Yale). Clubs: University, Oahu Country. Contbr. numerous articles on med. topics. Decorated Legion of Honor, France, July 14, 1920. Home: 2490 Makiki Heights. Office: 1133 Punchbowl St., Honolulu, T.H. Died June 2, 1947.

JULIAN, William Alexander, treasurer of U.S.; grad. Dodds Coll., Frankfort, Ky., 1888. Began as clk. in bank; successively shoe mfr., pres. Queen City Trust Co., vice-pres. Citizens Nat. Bank; treasurer of the U.S. since June 1, 1933. Was mem. Dem. Nat. Com. Home: Red Gables, R.F.D., Rockville, Md. Address: Dept. of Treasury, Wash. Died May 28, 1949.

JUMP, William Ashby, public official; b. Baltimore. Md., Aug. 12. 1891; s. William Ashby and Mollie (Clickner) J.; student Washington Sch. of Accounting & Bus. Adminstrn., 1917-18, Nat. U. Law Sch., 1921; m. Nellie Ruth Simering, Sept. 22, 1917; children—William Ashby, Nelson Byron. Messenger, under Civil Service, U.S. Dept. Agr., 1907-10, clk. and administrative officer, 1910-19; asst. to dir. of information, 1919-20; pvt. sec. and administrative asst. to Sec. of Agr., 1921-24; asst. dir. personnel and bus. adminstrn., U.S. Dept. of Agr., 1924-34, dir. finance since 1934, budget officer since 1922; lecturer financial adminstrn., Sch. of Social Sciences and Pub. Affairs, Am. U., 1937-40, adjunct prof. of financial adminstrn. since 1941. Alternate U.S. mem.

3d session Conf. of Food and Agr. Orgn. of U.N., Geneva, Switzerland, 1947; adviser U.S. delegation 4th session, Washington, 1948. Mem. Am. Polit. Science Assn., Am. Soc. for Pub. Adminstrn., Soc. for the Advancement of Management. Presbyterian. Mason. Grange. Home: 3247 Patterson St. N.W. Office: U S. Dept. of Agr., Washington, D.C. Died Jan. 22, 1949; buried Rock Creek Cemetery, Washington.

K

KABRICH, William Camillus (kä'brik), army officer; b. Pocahontas, Va., Sept. 19, 1895; s. William Sisiastel and Sarah Isolena (Wilburn) K.; B.S., Va. Poly. Inst., Blackburg, Va., 1917; grad. Coast Arty. Sch., 1925, Chem. Warfare Sch., 1930; S.M., Mass. Inst. of Tech., 1933; m. Beulah B. Hinkle, May 1, 1920. Commd. 2d lt., Coast Arty. Corps., U.S. Army, Aug. 15, 1917, and advanced through the grades to brig. gen., Dec. 4, 1942; transferred to Chem. Warfare Service, 1929; chief tech. div., Office of Chief, C.W.S., and comdg. gen. of C.W.S. Tech. Command, Edgewood Arsenal, Md., 1942-45; in charge of design of plants mfg. chem. agents; supervised development of smoke screen devices for large areas. Chmn. of tech. com. for control of research chem. warfare material for C.W.S. and Nat. Defense Research Com. Supervised development of chemical warfare weapons, munitions, agents and protective equipment now comdg. gen. Pine Bluff Arsenal, Arsenal, Ark. Decorated Victory, Am. Defense Service. Am. Theater of Operations medals. European Theater of Operations, African and Mediterranean Medal, Legion of Merit, Army Commendation Citation, Honorable Commander, Order of the British Empire, World War II Victory Medal, Mem. Am. Chem. Soc., Am. Inst. of Chem. Engrs., Alpha Chi Sigma. Clubs: Army and Navy, Army and Navy Country (Washington, D.C.). Home: 300 N. Mountain Av., Montclair, N.J. Died Jan. 27, 1947.

KAEDING, Charles Deering (kā'dĭng), cons. mining engr.; b. San Francisco, Calif., Aug. 5, 1880; s. Charles Van Buren and Frances Caroline (Ladd) K.; grad. Calif. Sch. Mech. Arts, San Francisco, 1900; student U. of Calif., 1900; m. Martha Vahey, 1912. Supt. Oriental Consol. Mining Co., Wunsan, Korea, 1901-03, gen. supt., 1903, asst. gen. mgr., 1903-07; mining engr. gen. practice, Central America, Mexico and Nev., 1907-11, asst. gen. mgr. Goldfield Consol. Mines Co., Nev., 1911-13; asst. supt., mines Internat. Nickel Co., Sudbury, Ont., 1913-14; v.p. and gen. mgr. Dome Mines Co., Ltd., South Porcupine, Ont., 1914-20; cons. mining engr. since 1920; pres. and dir. Sachigo River Exploration Co., Ltd.; dir. Pioneer Gold Mines of B.C., Steep Rock Iron Mines, Ltd.; mng. dir. Pacific Nickel Mines. Mem. Am. Inst. Mining and Metall. Engr., Psi Upsilon. Clubs: Wunsan Mines (Korea); Bohemian, Olympic (San Francisco). Home: Mississauga Rd., Port Credit, Ont., Can. Office: 25 King St. W., Toronto, Can. Died Sep. 9, 1942.

KAELBER, William G. (kĕl'bĕr), architect; b. Rochester, N.Y., Sept. 25, 1886; s. Charles and Anna Magdalena (Mayer) K.; Rochester Athenæum & Mechanics Institute (special classes in drawing), 1903-11; L.H.M., University of Rochester, 1943; m. Elsa Walbridge, Apr. 9, 1912 (divorced Apr. 18, 1941); children—Elsa Walbridge (Mrs. Holland Fayette Johnson), William Walbridge. Draftsman, Gordon & Madden, architects, Rochester, 1902-08, Jr. mem. firm, 1908-11; mem. Gordon, Madden & Kaelber, 1911-18, Gordon & Kaelber, 1918-32; private practice, 1932-38; partner Kaelber & Waasdorp since 1938; pres. 16 N. Goodman St., Inc. Architect, with others, Men's College, Sch. of Medicine and Dentistry, Strong Memorial Hosp. and Nurses Home, Eastman Dormitories, Eastman Sch. of Music, Eastman Theatre, Annexes and Sibley Library, Cutler Union and Munro Hall of Women's College (all Univer. of Rochester); Municipal Hosp.; Meharry Med. Coll., Nashville, Tenn.; Rochester Museum of Arts and Sciences; Rochester Pub. Library, Chmn. City Planning Commn., since 1942; mem. Rochester Zoning Bd., 1929-31, N.Y. State Bd. of Examiners of Architects 1933-46, pres. since 1946. V.p. Nat. Council Archtl. Registration Bds.; mem. N.Y. State Housing Commrs. Panel of Architects; mem. Fed. Housing Authorities Archtl. Adv. Com. Dir. Roch. Gen. Hosp. Trustee Rochester C. of C., Eastman Dental Dispensary; Allendale Sch. for Boys, Rochester Savings Bank; chairman cooperating council Coll. of Architecture, Syracuse U. Mem. Nat. Architectural Accrediting Bd. Fellow Am. Inst. of Architects; Regional Dir. A.I.A.; mem. Rochester Society Architects, (president 1939-40), Michigan Soc. Archts., N.Y. State Assn. Archts., Rochester Engring. Soc., Archaeol. Inst. Am., Rochester Mus. Arts and Sciences, Memorial Art Gallery. Republican. Member Salem Evangelical Church. Mason (Shriner). Clubs: Rochester, Genesee Valley, Country (Rochester); Century, Archtl. League of New York (N.Y. City). Home: 43 Dorchester Rd. Office: 311 Alexander St., Rochester, N.Y. Died Nov. 21, 1948.

KAGEY, Charles L. (kā'gē), lawyer; b. New Market, Va., Dec. 22, 1876; s. John H. and Emma F. (Fultz) K.; ed. Polytechnic Inst., New Market; studied law U. of Va., and awarded debaters' medal, 1898; m. Phebe M. Wanzer, Mar. 4, 1901; 1 son, Lloyd M. Began practice at Hays City, Kan., 1898; county atty. Logan County, Kan., 1899-1900; moved to Beloit, Kan., 1900; E.E. and M.P. to Republic of Finland, by apptmt. of Pres. Harding, Oct. 8, 1921-May 1, 1925; resumed practice at Beloit; removed to Wichita, Kan., Mar. 1, 1931, where has since practiced as sr. mem. Kagey, Black & Kagey. Mem. Am. Bar Assn (v.p. 1921-22), Kan. Bar Assn. (pres. 1915-16), Kan. State Hist. Soc. (pres. 1927-28; dir.); fellow Am. Geog. Soc. Mason (32°, K.T., Shriner). Republican; pres. Kansas Day Club, official Rep. organization of Kan., 1913-14. Episcopalian. Home: 351 N. Fountain. Office: Schweiter Bldg., Wichita, Kan. Died Oct. 13, 1941.

KAHN, Albert (kän), architect; b. Rhaunen, Westphalia, Germany, Mar. 21, 1869; s. Joseph and Rosalie (Cohn) K.; ed. in Germany; came to America, 1881; held Am. architect scholarship for study abroad, 1890-91; awarded hon. LL.D., University of Michigan, 1933; Dr. Fine Arts, Syracuse University, 1942; married Ernestine Krolik, 1896; children—Mrs. Lydia Winston, Edgar, Mrs. Ruth Rothman and Mrs. Rosalie Butzel. Practiced in Detroit since 1904. Architect, Burroughs Adding Machine plant, Packard Motor Car plant, Hudson and Ford Motor plants, Chrysler Corp. plant, Detroit Athletic Club, Detroit Evening News Bldg., Fisher Bldg., Detroit Free Press Bldg., General Motors Bldg., First National Bank Bldg., bldg. for N.Y. Times, Brooklyn, N.Y., also extension to New York Times Bldg., N.Y. City, Willow Run (Ford) Bomber Plant, etc. Official architect for the Aircraft Constrn. Div., Signal Corps, U.S. Army, 1917. Mem. Detroit Arts Commn. Received special award from Am. Inst. Architects for contributions in field of archtl. practice, 1942; also awards from Detroit and Phila. chapters of A.I.A. Decorated Chevalier Legion of Honor (France). Fellow A.I.A.; mem. Fine Arts Soc., Arts and Crafts Soc., Scarab Soc. Clubs: Bloomfield Hills Country, Franklin Hills Country. Home: 208 Mack Av. Office: New Center Bldg., Detroit, Mich. Died Dec. 8, 1942.

KAHN, Florence Prag, ex-congresswoman; b. Salt Lake City; d. Conrad and Mary (Goldsmith) Prag; A.B., U. of Calif.; m. Julius Kahn, Mar. 19, 1899 (died 1924); children—Julius, Conrad P. Succeeded husband as mem. 69th Congress (1925-27); also elected to 70th to 74th Congresses (1927-37), 4th Calif. Dist. Republican. Home: 2712 Webster St., San Francisco. Died Nov. 16, 1948.

KAINS, Archibald Chetwode, banker; b. London, Ont., Nov. 24, 1865; s. William King and Henrietta (Hamilton) K.; ed. London Collegiate Institute; m. Fanny George Donaldson, May 11, 1895. Began in employ Canadian Bank of Commerce, London, Ont., 1882, continuing for 25 yrs. at Montreal, New York, New Orleans, Chicago and San Francisco; examiner of clearing house banks, San Francisco, 1908-14; gov. Fed. Res. Bank, San Francisco, Nov. 1914-July 1917; pres. Am. Foreign Banking Corp., New York, 1917-21; pres. Fed. Internat. Banking Co., New Orleans, 1921, now retired. Apptd. mem. U.S. sect. of Internat. High Commn., 1916. Episcopalian. Mason (Shriner). Now citizen of Can. Home: 9 Rideau Gate, Ottawa, Can. Died Dec. 26, 1944.

KAINS, Maurice Grenville, horticulturist; b. St. Thomas, Ont., Can., Oct. 10, 1868; s. John Alexander and Emma Elizabeth (Hughes) K.; B.S., Mich. State Coll., 1895; B.S.A., Cornell U., 1896, M.S.A., 1897; m. Jean Bell Hickey, June 1, 1913; children—Maurice Eugene, Louis Stanley. Spl. crop culturist, U.S. Dept. Agr., 1897-1900; prof. horticulture, Sch. of Practical Agr. and Horticulture, Briar Cliff Manor, N.Y. (sch. now extinct), 1900-02; an editor New Internat. Cyclo., 1902-03; contbr. to Cyclo. Americana, 1904; horticulture editor Am. Agriculturist, New York, 1904-14; prof. horticulture and head of dept., Pa. State Coll., 1914-16; consultant practice since 1916; lecturer on horticulture Columbia University, 1917-19; contributing editor of Farm Knowledge, 1918-19, National Encyclopedia, 1932-33; editor Your Home (magazine), 1926-27; horticulturist, Poultry Tribune since 1934. Member Sigma Xi, Alpha Zeta. Mason. Democrat. Author: Ginseng, 1899; Making Horticulture Pay, 1909; Culinary Herbs, 1912; Plant Propagation, Greenhouse and Nursery Practice, 1916; Principles and Practice of Pruning, 1917; Home Fruit Grower, 1918; Modern Guide of Successful Gardening, 1934; Gardening Short Cuts, 1935; Five Acres and Independence, 1935; Gardening Children's Adventures, 1937; Propagation of Plants (with L. M. McQuisten), 1938; Grow Your Own Fruit, 1940; We Wanted a Farm, 1941; Food Gardens for Defense, 1942; Fifty Years Out of College, 1944; also many hort. articles. Home: Suffern, N. J. Died Feb. 25, 1946.

KALISH, Max (kă'lish), sculptor; b. Poland, Mar. 1, 1891; s. Joel and Hannah (Levinson) K.; brought to U.S. in childhood; ed. pub. schs., Cleveland; studied sculpture under H. Matzen, Cleveland Sch. of Art, 1906-10, under A. S. Calder, H. Adams, I. Konti, C. S. Pietro, Nat. Acad. Design, N.Y. City, 1910-12, under P. Bartlett, M. Injalbert, Acadamie Colorossi and Ecole des Beaux Arts, Paris, 1912-14; m. Alice B. Neuman, Nov. 20, 1927; children—Richard Alan, James A. Asso. sculptor San Francisco Expn., 1913-15; lecturer Western Reserve U., 1929-32. Represented by "Man of Steel," "Discard," Nat. Gallery of Art, Washington, D.C.; "The Christ," also "Torso," Cleveland Mus. of Art; "Laborer at Rest," Newark (N.J.) Mus. of Art; "Ecstasy," also "Laborer," Canajoharie (N.Y.) Mus. of Art; "Man of Power," Amherst Coll. Mus.; "Toil's End," Hagerstown (Md.) Mus. of Art; also in several pvt. collections, including Dr. C. A. Muncaster's collection of more than 25 works and Dr. Floyd C. Mowry's marble collection, both of Cleveland, Ohio. Created "Living Hall of Washington," 1944, collection of bronze statuettes of notables of World War II, Smithsonian Institute, Washington, D.C. Awarded Acad. Colorossi medal, 1913, Jenkins medal, 1929, Lincoln at Gettysburg memorial, 1927. President Great Neck Art Assn., Great Neck, N.Y. Mem. Nat. Sculpture Soc.; Asso. Nat. Academician. Mason (32°). Home: 8 Clover Drive, Great Neck, L.I., N.Y. Address: 939 Eighth Av., New York. Died Mar. 18, 1945; buried in Cleveland.

KALLENBACH, Walter Dustin (kăl'lĕn-băk), evangelist, lecturer; b. Everett, Mass., July 20, 1905; s. John Henry and Eva Frances (Dustin) K.; desc. Hannah Dustin; B.S., U. of Va., 1931; student Southern Bapt. Theol. Sem., 1931-32; B.D., Eastern Bapt. Theological Seminary, 1933, Th.M., 1934, graduate student, 1935; Th.D., Pikes Peak Seminary, 1936; Ph.D., Webster University, Atlanta, Ga., 1938; D.D., Eastern Sem. 1944; D.D.L., Am. Divinity Acad., 1945; m. Shelburne Wyly, May 19, 1932; children—Shelburne Brasher, Marcia Elaine. Began as musician, lost his sight as a result of hunting accident, 1927, and returned to college; began evangelistic work while student in Phila.; has held services in many of the large cities of U.S. and Canada, also in univs. and penal instns. winning many converts; pres. Northland Publishing House, St. Paul, Minn. National president, Nat. Assn. for Advancement of Blind. National councillor-at-large for American Rose Society. Member board trustees Phila. Coll. of Osteopathy, Northern Bapt. Sem., Chicago; mem. bd. dirs. Phila. Osteopathic Hosp., North Western Evangelical Sem. (Minneapolis, Minn.). Voted outstanding man in field of Christian service by Internat. Assn. of Evangelists and Christian Workers. Speaker at Easter Sunrise Service, Soldier Field, Chicago, 1941. Mem. Browning Soc., Phila. Jr. Chamber of Commerce. Am. Rose Soc., Phi Beta Kappa; hon. mem. Eugene Field Soc. of Authors and Journalists, Internat. Assn. of Evangelists. Mem. (hon.) Am. Acad. Political and Social Science. Mem. U.S. Navy League. Made Knight of the Rose by Royal Rosarians (Portland, Ore.). Baptist. Knight of Malta, Knight of Mystic Chain. Clubs: Quill (Louisville); University, Lions Internat., Exchange Internat. (hon.), Optimist Internat., Rotary (hon.); Kiwanis (hon.), Civitan. Author: The Higher Significance of the Gospel, 1938; That Men May Know, 1938; That Men May Believe, 1939; That Men May Live, 1939; That Men May See, 1940. Author of booklets: Salvation and What Follows, 1937; Message and Authorship of Hebrews, 1938; Law and Commandments, 1938; Scriptural Help for Personal Work, 1942; The Blind Man's Watch, 1944. Contbr. to religious jours. Known as America's number one blind man; has been referred to as Lion's ambassador of goodwill among service clubs, having spoken before hundreds of the clubs since 1940; also speaker on major radio networks. Author of 5-point program to aid war blind, of 10-point program for civilian blind; worked with thousands of wounded men in hospitals all over America. Home: 4506 Marvine Av., Drexel Hill, Pa. Died Nov. 16, 1946; buried in Westminster Cemetery, Philadelphia.

KANE, Grenville, railroad dir.; b. New Rochelle, N.Y., July 12, 1854; s. Pierre C. and Edith (Brevoort) K.; grad. Trinity College, Hartford, Conn., 1875; LL.B., Columbia, 1878; m. Margaret A. Wolfe, Apr. 28, 1881; children—Mrs. A. Stewart Walker, Mrs. George F. Baker, Jr., Dorothy, Mrs. Henry L. McVickar, Mrs. Garrow T. Geer. Admitted to New York bar, 1878, and began practice at N.Y. City; mem. firm Tailer & Co., bankers, 1906-22; chmn. finance com. Erie R.R., 1922-37. Dir. and mem. exec. com. Erie N.P. Ry., C.,B.&Q. Ry. Co., Colo. & Southern R.R., Chicago & Erie R.R., N.Y., Susquehanna & Western R.R. Co.; dir. City Bank Farmers Trust Co. (New York), etc. Trustee New York Pub. Library. Democrat. Episcopalian. Clubs: Grolier, Union, City Midday, New York Yacht (New York); Newport Country, Newport Reading Room (Newport, R.I.); Point Judith Country (Narragansett Pier, R.I.); Tuxedo. Home: Tuxedo Park, N.Y. Office: 50 Church St., New York, N.Y. Died July 17, 1943.

KANE, Howard Francis, obstetrician; b. Machias, Me., May 14, 1887; s. George Wesley and Cora (Leighton) K.; grad. Worcester Acad., 1905; A.B., Bowdoin, 1909; M.D., George Washington U., 1912; m. Clara Bailey, Jan. 28, 1920. Mem. house staff successively of George Washington, Children's, Columbia hosps., Washington, D.C., and New York Lying-In Hosp., 1912-16; mem. teaching staff George Washington U. Sch. of Medicine since 1916, prof. of obstetrics and gynecology since 1932; mem. attending staffs George Washington, Gallinger, Garfield hosps. Served as 1st lt. and capt. M.C., U.S. Army, with B.E.F., 1917-19; maj. Med. Res. Corps, U.S. Army, 1919-28; lieut. comdr. U.S. Naval Res., 1937-40; comdr. since 1940; consulting obstetrician United States Naval Hosp., San Diego, Calif., 1943-44; retired. Decorated Military Cross (British), 1917. Diplomate American Bd. Obstetrics. Fellow Am. Coll. Surgeons, Internat. Coll. of Anesthetists, fellow Am. Assn. Obstetricians, Gynecologists and Abdominal Surgeons; mem. A.A.A.S., Am. Legion, Mil. Order of Foreign Wars, Zeta Psi, Alpha Kappa Kappa, Sigma Xi. Republican. Conglist. Mason (K.T., Shriner). Clubs: Cosmos, Metropolitan (Washington, D.C.); Gibson Island (Md.); Columbia Country (Md.); Chevy Chase Club (Md.). Contbr. many articles to med. jours. Home: Machias, Maine. Died July 21, 1946.

KANE, Theodore Porter, officer U.S. Marine Corps; b. in Md., Feb. 6, 1869. Commd. 2d lt., U.S. Marine Corps, July 1, 1890; promoted through grades to brig.

gen., Dec. 10, 1923; retired Feb. 7, 1924. Home: Philadelphia, Pa. Address: care Girard Trust Co., Philadelphia, Pa.* Died Apr. 13, 1943.

KANE, William T., clergyman, educator; b. Chicago, Ill., Oct. 20, 1880; s. Lawrence and Elizabeth (McCarthy) K.; M.A., St. Louis U., 1905; Ph.D., D.D., Colegio de Oña, Spain, 1914. Mem. faculty, Detroit Coll., 1905-06, St. Xavier Coll., Cincinnati, O., 1906-08, St. John's Coll., Belize, Brit. Honduras, 1908-10, Creighton U., Omaha, 1916-17, Loyola U., Chicago, 1919-24; prof. philosophy and edn., St. Xavier Coll., Cincinnati, 1924-27; research work, 1927-30; librarian E. M. Cudahy Memorial Library, Loyola U., 1930-46. Served as chaplain 35th Div., U.S. Army, 1918-19, World War; cited "for bravery in action." Author: For Greater Things, 1915; Life of William Stanton, 1918; An Essay Toward a History of Education, 1935; Some Principles of Education, 1938; Catholic Library Problems, 1939; The Education of Edward Cudahy, 1941; Life of Cornelius Shine, 1945; Paradise Hunters, 1946. Address: Loyola University, Chicago. Died Dec. 29, 1946.

KAPP, Jack, pres. Decca Records, Inc.; b. Chicago, Ill., June 15, 1901; s. Meyer K. and Minnie (Leader) K.; grad. high school, Chicago, 1918; m. Frieda Lutz, August 6, 1922; children—Myra, Jonathan. Pres. Decca Records, Inc., since 1934. Home: 131 E. 64th St. Office: 50 W. 57th St., New York, N.Y. Died Mar. 25, 1949.

KARAPETOFF, Vladimir (kăr-å-pĕt'ŏf), elec. engr.; b. St. Petersburg, Russia, Jan. 8, 1876; s. Nikita Ivanovitch and Anna Joakimovna (Ivanova) K.; C.E., Inst. of Ways of Communication, St. Petersburg, 1897, M.M.E., 1902; Technische Hochschule, Darmstadt, Germany, 1899-1900; hon. Mus. Doc., N.Y. College of Music, 1934; hon. D.Sc., Poly. Inst. Brooklyn, 1937; m. Frances Lulu Gillmor, Aug. 2, 1904 (died 1931); m. 2d, Rosalie Margaret Cobb, Nov. 25, 1936. Consulting engr. for Russian Govt., and instr. elec. engring. and hydraulics in 3 colls., St. Petersburg, 1897-1902; spl. engring. apprentice with Westinghouse Electric & Mfg. Co., E. Pittsburgh, Pa., 1903-04; prof. elec. engring. Cornell U., 1904-39; prof. emeritus since 1939; visiting prof. for grad. students, Poly. Inst. of Brooklyn, 1930-32; lecturer Stevens Inst. Technology, 1939-40. Cons. engr. and patent expert to various enterprises; with J. G. White & Co., Inc., engineers and contractors, 1911-12. Inventor and patentee of several elec. devices and of five-stringed cello. Awarded Montefiore prize, 1923, and Elliot Cresson gold medal, Franklin Inst., 1927, both for kinematic models of elec. machinery. Lt. comdr. U.S. Naval Res. since 1933, assigned to engring duties for spl. service. Mem. bd. trustees, Ithaca Coll., 1932-39, chmn., 1933-36. Mem. U.S. Naval Inst., U.S. Naval Reserve Officers' Assn., International Jury Awards, Panama P.I. Expn., San Francisco, 1915; mem. advisory bd. U.S. Naval Acad., 1916. Christian. Fellow Am. Inst. E.E., A.A.A.S., Am. Physical Soc.; mem. Am. Assn. Univ. Profs. (charter), Am. Math. Soc., Math. Assn. America, Franklin Inst., Sigma Xi; hon. mem. Eta Kappa Nu, Tau Beta Pi, Phi Mu Alpha (Sinfonia), Theta Xi. Author: Ueber Mehrphasige Stromsysteme, 1900; Resistance of Ships to Propulsion (in Russian), 1st part 1902, 2d part 1911; Experimental Electrical Engineering, 2 vols., 1908; The Electric Circuit, 1910; The Magnetic Circuit, 1911; Engineering Applications of Higher Mathematics, part I, 1911; parts II to V, 1916; Rhythmical Tales of Stormy Years (poems), 1937; also numerous articles in engring. mags. and trans. Research editor of the Electrical World, 1917-26. Gave several series of public piano recitals; developed five-stringed cello and plays it in public; lecturer on engring., and on moral and psychol. topics. Chmn. com. on physics of Conf. on Electrical Insulation, National Research Council, 1928-35, chmn. com. on monographs, 1935-38. Consultant to U.S. Bd. of Economic Warfare, 1942-43; consultant to Bethlehem Steel Co. since 1944. Home: 39 Claremont Av., Apt. 84, New York 27. Died Jan. 11, 1948; buried in East Lawn Cemetery, Ithaca, N.Y.

KARELITZ, George B(oris) (kă'rĕ-lĭtz), prof. mech. engring.; b. Russia, Jan. 3, 1895; M.E. (naval architect), Imperial Poly. Inst., Petrograd, Russia, 1916; unmarried. Came to U.S., 1922, naturalized, 1928. Cons. engineer Northwest Waterways, Russia, 1918-21; jr. engr. turbine works, Westinghouse Electric & Mfg. Co., East Pittsburgh, 1923-25, research engr., 1925-30, mgr. mech. research div., 1931, mgr. marine engring. dept., S. Phila., 1931-33; asso. prof. mech. engring., Columbia, 1930-37, prof. since 1937; contract employee Bur. of Ships, Research Branch, U.S. Navy, since 1941. Served as lt. Russian Navy, 1916-18. Fellow A.A.A.S., Am. Geog. Soc.; mem. Am. Soc. M.E., Inst. Mech. Engrs. (Brit.), Am. Phys. Soc., Soc. for Promotion Engring. Edn., Mus. of Natural History, N.Y. Acad. Sciences, Tau Beta Pi, Sigma Xi. Awarded Palmes Academiques, French Acad., 1939. Club: Men's Faculty (Columbia). Author: Problems in Mechanics (with J. Ormondroyd, J. W. Garrelts), 1939. Contbr. to tech. jours. Home: 88 Morningside Dr., New York, N.Y. Died Jan. 19, 1943.

KARRER, Enoch (kăr'rĕr), research physicist; b. Rich Hill, Mo., May 23, 1887; s. Frank Xavier and Theresa (Braun) K.; A.B., U. of Wash., 1911, A.M., 1912; Ph.D., Johns Hopkins U., 1914; m. Ethel Walther, Aug. 2, 1919; children—Enoch, Aurora, Ethelda, Rathe. Research asst. with United Gas Improvement Co., Phila., 1914-18; chief searchlight sect. U.S. Bur. of Standards, 1919-21; in General Electric Co.'s research lab., Cleveland, O., 1921-26; research associate Cushing Laboratory for Exptl. Medicine, Western Reserve U., Cleveland, 1923-31; research physicist B. F. Goodrich Co., 1926-31; cons. research engr., 1031-36; economics and govt. research, Washington, D.C., 1934-35; research biophysics Smithsonian Instn., 1935; tech. consultant Am. Instrument Co., 1936; sr. physicist, U.S. Dept. of Agr. since 1936, at Southern Regional Research Lab., New Orleans, since 1941. Served as pvt. 1st sergt. Med. Corps, 345th Engrs., later master engr., 447th Engrs., U.S. Army, World War; now capt. Engrs., O.R.C. Awarded James A. Moore prize in physics, Seattle, 1913, Longstreet medal (co-winner), Franklin Inst., 1918. Mem. Washington Philos. Soc., Sigma Xi, Phi Beta Kappa, and several tech. socs. Author 70 publications in sci. field. Holder of 6 patents. Contbr. of papers to tech. jours. Home: 7003 Broad Place. New Orleans 18. Died Mar. 27, 1946; buried in Garden of Memories, New Orleans.

KASANIN, Jacob Sergi (kă-zā'nĭn), physician; b. Slavgorod, U.S.S.R., May 11, 1897; s. Isaac and Catherine (Lifshitz) K.; B.S. in med., U. of Mich., 1919, M.D., 1921, M.S. in pub. health, 1926; m. Rosalind H. Yeska, Dec. 15, 1919; 1 dau., Mary Catherine; m. 2d, Elizabeth Owen Knight, Apr. 4, 1928; children—Mark Owen, Elizabeth Merrill. Came to U.S., 1915, naturalized citizen, 1926. Asst. physician Boston State Hosp., 1923-24; med. officer Boston Psychopathic Hosp., 1924-26; dir. dept. mental hygiene, Federated Jewish Charities, Boston, 1927-28; senior research asso. Rockefeller Foundation, Boston Psychopathic Hosp., 1927-31; clin. dir. R.I. State Hosp., Howard, R.I., 1931-35; mem. staff Evans Memorial and Beth Israel hosps. and Boston Dispensary, Boston, 1929-31; dir. dept. psychiatry and attending psychiatrist, Michael Reese Hosp., Chicago, 1936-39; lecturer social psychiatry, Brown U., 1934-36, Smith Coll. Social Work, summer 1935; asst. prof. psychiatry, Rush Med. Coll., U. of Chicago, 1938-40; lecturer extension div. U. of Calif., San Francisco, 1939; chief psychiatric service, Mt. Zion Hosp., San Francisco since 1939; cons. psychiatrist, Family Service Agency, San Francisco; asst. clin. prof. psychiatry, University of Calif. Medical School since 1940; visiting consultant in neuropsychiatry, 8th Service Command, U.S. Army, 1943. Diplomate Am. Bd. Psychiatry and Neurology; Fellow A.M.A., Am. Psychiatric Assn.; mem. Am. Orthopsychiatric Assn. (past pres.); mem. N. Eng. Soc. Neurology and Psychiatry, San Francisco Psychoanalytic Soc., Northern Calif. Soc. of Neurology and Psychiatry (chmn. program com.), Calif. Acad. Med., Am. Psychoanalytic Assn. Hebrew religion. Club: Rio del Mar Country (Santa Cruz). Author: Conceptual Thinking, 1941; Language and Thought in Schizophrenia, 1944. Associate editor Diseases of Nervous System. Contbr. to Am. Jour. Psychiatry, Orthopsychiatry, and Psychoanalytic Quarterly. Home: 2960 Steiner St. Office: 2200 Post St., San Francisco. Died May 4, 1946; buried in Eternal Home Cemetery, Colma, Calif.

KASSEL, Charles (kăs'sĕl), lawyer, writer; b. Memel, East Prussia, May 29, 1877; s. Elias J. and Hannah M. Kassel; LL.B., U. of Tex., 1897; m. Della M. Lawhead, Dec. 25, 1913. Law clk., Gainesville and Sherman, Tex., and shorthand reporter until 1904; practiced at Ft. Worth since 1904. Democrat. Unitarian. Contbr. on lit., philos. and hist. subjects. Home: 1211 Clara St. Office: Fort Worth Nat. Bank Bldg., Ft. Worth, Tex. Died Aug. 9, 1943.

KAST, Miller I., architect. Mem. Am. Inst. Architects since 1909, fellow since 1934. Address: Kast & Kelker, 222 Market St., Harrisburg, Pa.* Deceased.

KAUFFMAN, Benjamin Franklin (kawf'măn), banker; b. Des Moines, Ia., Dec. 1874; s. Benjamin Franklin and Anna K.; ed. Ia. Wesleyan Coll., Mt. Pleasant, and Amherst; m. Mell Howell, Oct. 10, 1900; children—John Howell, Anna Malvina, Ray Frankin. Engaged in real estate, real estate loan and ins. business, Des Moines, 1896-1917; pres. Bankers Trust Company since 1917; dir. Bankers Trust Company, C.,St.P.,M. & O. Ry. Company, Northwestern Bell Telephone Co., Equitable Life Ins. Co. of Ia., F. W. Fitch Co., Des Moines. Mem. advisory com., Ia. Reconstrn. Finance Corp.; mem. Ia. State Banking Bd., 1934-46; pres. Ia. Bankers Assn., 1933-34; trustee Edmundson Memorial Foundation, Drake U., Iowa Meth. Hosp. (Des Moines). Mem. Ia. Nat. Guard, 1896-1900, Newcomen Soc. Republican. Methodist. Clubs: University (pres. 1935-38), Des Moines Club, Wakonda Country. Home: 3425 Grand Av., Des Moines, Ia. Died July 14, 1948.

KAUFMAN, Herbert, editor, author; b. Washington, D.C., Mar. 6, 1878; s. Abraham and Gertrude (Raff) K.; grad. Emerson Inst., of Washington, 1893 (Pinkney medalist); Johns Hopkins U., 1898 (Lee medal); m. Alta Wagstaff Rush, Aug. 1913. Formerly reporter Washington News, business mgr. Washington Times; conducted national advertising agencies in New York and Chicago, 1900-10; head of Herbert Kaufman Newspaper Syndicate, New York; served as American adviser to C. Arthur Pearson, Ltd., and William T. Stead, London, and Frank A. Munsey; editorial writer Chicago Tribune, Chicago Record-Herald and syndicate of Sunday papers, 1908-15; editorial dir. Woman's World, 1910-11; writer of Herbert Kaufman's Page, syndicated, 1916-19, Herbert Kaufman's Weekly (editorials prod. in motion pictures) since 1920. At outbreak of war cooperated with Sir Arthur Pearson, at York House, St. James, in organizing Prince of Wales Fund; contributed daily editorials to London Standard, articles to London Times and Daily Mail, and more than fifty war poems to British periodicals; prepared several series of full-page editorial appeals for Belgian Relief; assisted Herbert Hoover to organize Fed. Food Commn.; prepared for Secretary McAdoo plans for the inauguration of soldiers' ins.; spl. asst. to Secretary of Interior Franklin K. Lane, in charge of Americanization, 1918-20; in coöperation with Northcliffe publs. and under auspices of Supreme Economic Council, made survey of economic conditions in Middle Europe; purchased McClure publs. and editor and pres. McClure's Mag., 1919-21; furnished double column editorial review, nat. and internat. events, telegraphed daily for front page publ. throughout U.S.; engaged in intensive survey industrial and natural resources of America, particularly in Northwest and on Pacific Coast, 1923-25; resumed daily feature editorials, 1928; with Edward F. Hutton, organized and headed auxiliary exec. com. at end of Hoover Presidential Campaign, 1932; resumed half-page weekly editorial in U.S.A. and Canada, 1939. Author: Songs of Fancy, The Stolen Throne (with Mary I. Fish); Poems; The Winning Fight; The Dreamers; The Man Who Sneered at Santa Claus; Do Something! Be Something!; The Efficient Age; The Clock That Had No Hands and Other Essays; The Waiting Woman; Neighbors; The Song of the Guns (republ. as The Hell-Gate of Soissons, London); The Splendid Gamble, 1939. Contbr. to mags. Home: Tarrytown, N.Y. Died Sep. 6, 1947.

KAUFMAN, Kenneth Carlyle (kawf'măn), teacher, writer; b. Leon, Kan., Apr. 30, 1887; s. John and Grace Estelle (Moore) K.; grad. Southwestern State Teachers Coll., Weatherford, Okla., 1908; A.B., U. of Okla., 1916, A.M., 1919; m. Pearl Yates, Dec. 28, 1911; children—Mary Katherine, John Yates. Head of foreign lang. dept. Central High Sch., Oklahoma City, Okla., 1916-29; asst. prof. modern languages, U. of Oklahoma, 1929-35, asso. prof., 1935-37, prof. since 1937. Mng. editor Books Abroad (quarterly mag.). Mem. Am. Assn. Univ. Profs., Modern Lang. Assn. Okla. (ex-chmn.), Okla. Writers (ex-pres.), Phi Beta Kappa, Acacia. Democrat. Christian Scientist. Mason. Author: Level Land, A Book of Western Verse, 1935. Co-editor: Un Drama Nuevo, by Tamayo y Baus (with R. T. House), 1923; No Más Mostrador, by Mariano José de Larra (with Patricio Gimeno), 1927. Translator: Home At Last by Ernst Harthern (Das Land das seine Menschen Friszt), 1930; Sun and Storm by Unto Seppänen (Markku ja hänen Sukunsa), 1939; Renni the Rescuer by Felix Salten, 1940; The Good Shepherd by Gunnar Gunnarsson (Advent), 1940. Contbr. to Southwest Review, Christian Science Monitor, Dallas News, Poetry—A Magazine of Verse, Esquire, The Chicago Tribune. Editorial advisor Bobbs-Merrill Co. Lit. editor Daily Oklahoman. Home: 803 W. Brooks St., Norman, Okla. Died Apr. 29, 1945.

KAUFMAN, Louis Graveraet, banker; b. Marquette, Mich., Nov. 13, 1872; s. Samuel and Juliet (Graveraet) K.; ed. high schs., Marquette; m. Marie J. Young, Jan. 8, 1900; children—Graveraet Young, Ann Elizabeth Young, Louis G., Joan, Juliet, Marie Louise, Jane. Pres. Chatham Phenix Nat. Bank and Trust Co., 1910-31; pres. First Nat. Bank and Trust Co., Marquette, Mich.; dir. Empire State Bldg., Ins., Chicago & Erie R.R. Co. Episcopalian. Clubs: Turf and Field, Recess, South Shore Country, Bath and Tennis, Seminole Golf. Home: Marquette, Mich. Office: Empire State Bldg., New York, N.Y. Died Mar. 16, 1942.

KAWAKAMI, K. K. (kä-wä-kä-mē), author, journalist; b. Tokyo, Japan, 1875; grad. in law in Japan, 1899; in newspaper work, 1 yr.; came to America, 1901; fellow in polit. science, State U. of Ia., 1903, M.A., 1903; scholar in polit. science, U. of Wis., 1904; connected with Imperial Japanese Commn., St. Louis Expn., 1904; in journalistic work in America since 1905; m. Mildred Augusta Clarke, 1907. Traveled extensively in China, Siberia and Russia. Corr. for newspapers in Tokyo; contbr. to Am. mags. and daily press; corr. New York Herald syndicate at Conf. on Disarmament, Washington, 1921-22, at Geneva Naval Conf., 1929, London Naval Conf., 1930; in China and Japan, 1928, 32. Author: Political Ideas of Modern Japan, 1903; American-Japanese Relations, 1912; Asia at the Door, 1914; Japan in World Politics, 1917; Japan and World Peace, 1919, trans. into French, 1920; What Japan Thinks, 1921; The Real Japanese Question, 1921; Japan's Pacific Policy, 1922, trans. into French, 1923; Japan Speaks on the Sino-Japanese Conflict, 1932; Manchukuo—Child of Conflict, 1933; Japan in China, 1938, also in Japanese; History of Germany; Modern Socialism; Labour Question; Industrial Education. Washington rep. of Osaka Mainichi and Tokyo Nichi Nichi. Home: 3729 Morrison St. N.W., Washington, D.C.Died Oct. 12, 1949.

KAY, G(eorge) F(rederick) (kā), geologist; b. Virginia, Ont., Can., Sept. 14, 1873; B.A., U. of Toronto, 1900, M.A., 1902; fellow, U. of Chicago, 1903-04, Ph.D., 1914; hon. D.Sc., Cornell Coll., Mt. Vernon, Ia., 1935; LL.D., U. of Toronto, 1936. Prin. pub. schs., Ont., 1892-94; geologist, Lake Superior Power Co., 1900-02; asst. geologist, Ont. Bur. Mines, 1903; asst. prof. geology and mineralogy, U. of Kan., 1904-07; prof. geology, State U. of Ia., since 1907, head of dept. geology, 1911-34, dean College of Liberal Arts, 1917-1941; jr. geologist U.S. Geol. Survey since 1907; state geologist of Ia., 1911-34. Fellow A.A.A.S. (v.p. 1929), Geol. Soc. America, Ia. Acad. Science (pres. 1929). Contbr. on Geology and mineral resources of southwestern Oregon and Bering Coal Field; Pleistocene geology; history of Pleistocene deposits; Gumbotil; pre-Illinoian Pleistocene geology of Iowa; ages of drift sheets; mapping the Aftonian and Yarmouth interglacial horizons in Iowa; significance of post-Illinoian, pre-Iowan loess; classification and duration of the Pleistocene period. Home: Iowa City, Ia. Died July 19, 1943.

KAY, Joseph William, mfr.; b. Brooklyn, Nov. 9, 1845; s. Samuel and Mary (Spencer) K.; ed. pub. schs., New York, 1852-59; m. Sarah M. Atwell, Nov. 8, 1868. Mfr. of water meters since 1883; treas. Thomson Meter Co.; also editor and publisher Grand Army Review, 1885-90, Home and Country, 1890-97. In Co. F, 22d N.Y. State Militia, July-Aug. 1862, at Harper's Ferry, Va.; pvt. Cos. A and B, 10th N.Y. Vols., 1862-65; wounded May 6, Wilderness and June 3, 1864, Cold Harbor, Va. Coined name "Old Glory," referring to Am. flag. Author of many veteran-reference laws and changes in civil service rules in same interest. Comdr. Dept. of New York, G.A.R., 1899-1900; nat. comdr. Union Vet. Legion of U.S., 1905-06. Democrat. Home: 968 Park Pl., Brooklyn, N.Y. Office: 105 Fulton St., New York. Died May 15, 1928.

KEALY, Philip Joseph, civil engr., ex-pres. Kansas City Rys. Co.; b. Bloomington, Ill., July 2, 1884; s. Patrick J. and Mary Agnes (Ryan) K.; Lewis Inst., Chicago; U. of Ill., 1905-09; m. Josephine Dynan, 1909 (dec.); 1 dau., Coaina A.; m. 2d, Josephine Helen Crowley, 1917 (dec.); 1 son, J. Gerald; m. 3d, Joyce M. Hutchins, 1925; children—Hutchins D., Philip H. With Bd. Supervising Engrs., Chicago, 1909-10, Bion J. Arnold, Chicago, 1910-13, receivers of Traction Co., Kansas City, Mo., 1913-15; pres. Kansas City Rys., 1915-21; City mem. Board of Supervising Engrs. Chicago Traction, 1934-42, chmn. since 1942; dir. Lewis Sch. of Aeronautics, Cath. Youth Orgn. Lt. col. 3d Mo. Infantry, 1915, col., 1916-17; col. 138th Inf., U.S. Army, 1917-18. Mem. Memorial Assn. of Kansas City. Mem. Am. Soc. Civil Engrs., Am. Legion, Delta Upsilon. K.C. Club: Chicago Athletic Assn. Home: 37 Indian Hill Rd., Winnetka, Ill. Office: 231 S. La Salle St., Chicago, Ill. Died Aug. 26, 1944.

KEANE, Doris (kēn), actress; b. Mich., Dec. 1881; d. Joseph and Florence Keane; ed. pvtly. in Chicago, New York and Paris; then studied under Sargent at American Acad. of Dramatic Art, New York. Début at Garrick Theatre, New York, as Rose in "Whitewashing Julia," Dec. 2, 1903; leading lady with John Drew in "Delancy," season 1904; played in "The Hypocrites," New York and first appearance in London in the same play at Hick's Theatre, Aug. 1907; first starred in "The Happy Marriage," by Clyde Fitch; leading lady in "Arsène Lupin"; played Madame Morel in "Decorating Clementina," created in New York and London; mem. star cast in a revival of "The Lights o' London," Lyric Theatre, New York, spring of 1910; played Mimi in "Anatol," Little Theatre, New York, 1912; created rôle of La Cavallini in "Romance," Maxine Elliott Theatre, New York, Feb. 10, 1913, and subsequently became a star in same play, opening in London, Oct. 6, 1915, played consecutively over 1,000 times in London; produced "The Czarina," under management of Gilbert Miller, New York, 1922; in Eugene O'Neill's "Welded," 1924; in "Starlight," 1925; in revival of "Romance," Playhouse, London, Oct. 1926, then toured English provinces; produced "The Pirate," Belasco Theatre, Los Angeles, 1929. Address: 22 Williams St., New York, N.Y. Died Nov. 25, 1945.

KEARNY, Warren (kär'nĭ), mem. firm J. Watts Kearny and Sons; b. New Orleans, La., Feb. 14, 1870; s. J. Watts and Sarah Palfrey) K.; attended pub. schs., bus. coll. and student Tulane U., 1885-87; D.C.L., U. of the South, Sewanee, Tenn, 1928; m. Ellen Lee Sloo Johnson, Aug. 2, 1894; children—Warren Watts (dec.), Ellen Lee Sloo (dec.; wife of Col. A. Adair Watters); m. 2d, Mrs. Mary Neilson Carpender, May 17, 1940. In bus. with father, 1887, admitted to firm J. Watts Kearny & Sons, wholesale building materials, 1891, sr. mem. since death of father, 1903; U.S. collector of customs, 1931-35. Dir. Hibernia National Bank, Times Picayune Publishing Company, New Orleans North Eastern Railway, Mississippi Shipping Co., New Orleans Bd. of Trade (pres. 1918-19), Southern Education Foundation (chmn. bd.). Dir. Red Cross Motor Corps, 1918. Trustee University of the South; trustee Dillard University, Eye, Ear, Nose, Throat Hosp. (ex-pres.); mem. com. Flint-Goodridge Hosp.; treas. Waldo Burton Home for Boys; dir. Kingsley House Settlement (ex-president). Republican. Presbyterian. Mason. Clubs: Boston, Round Table (New Orleans) (bd. govs. since 1898). Home: 1915 State St. Office: 830 Union St., New Orleans. Died Nov. 8, 1947.

KEATON, James R. (kē'tŭn), judge; b. in Carter County, Ky., Dec. 10, 1861; s. Nelson T. and Mary A. K.; grad. Nat. Normal U., Lebanon, O., 1884; LL.B., Georgetown U., 1890; m. Mrs. Lucile Johnston, July 17, 1890. Went to Tex., 1884; prin. Hico High Sch., 1884-87; propr. and editor Hico Courier, 1886-88; admitted to bar, 1890; practiced in Guthrie, Okla., 1890-96; now at Oklahoma City; mem. Keaton, Wells & Johnston. Dem. and Populist nominee for del. to Congress, 1898; asso. justice Supreme Court and ex-officio judge 3d Jud. Dist. Okla., 1896-98. Mem. Okla. County Council Defense during war period and pres., 1917. Pres. Okla. State Bar and ex-officio chmn. bd. of govs., Oct. 1929-Dec. 1930; mem. exec. com. Am. Bar Assn., 1930-33 (v.p. 10th circuit, 1935-36; assembly del. to house of dels., 1940-42). Clubs: Oklahoma City, Men's Dinner. Admitted to Okla. Hall of Fame, 1937, by Okla. Memorial Assn. Life mem. Okla. Hist. Soc. Home: 508 N.W. 16th St. Office: 824 Commerce Exchange Bldg., Oklahoma City, Okla. Died Apr. 3, 1946.

KEEBLE, Glendinning, fine arts director; b. Pittsburgh, Pa., Feb. 24, 1887; s. Martin Edward and Anne (Glendinning) K.; student N.Y. Sch. of Art, 1903-08; pvt. studies, 1908-11; unmarried. Art and music editor Pittsburgh Gazette Times, 1912-23; prof. dept. of music, Carnegie Inst. Tech., 1914-24, dir. College of Fine Arts since 1924. Mem. Am. Assn. of Univ. Profs, Art Soc. of Pittsburgh, Phi Kappa Phi, Phi Mu Alpha, Tau Sigma Delta. Republican. Episcopalian. Home: 4215 Fifth Av., Pittsburgh, Pa. Died July 21, 1947.

KEEHN, Roy Dee (kēn), lawyer; b. Ligonier, Ind., Nov. 7, 1877; s. Jonathan N. and Harriet (Shobe) K.; student De Pauw U., Ind. U.; Ph.B., U. of Chicago, 1902, J.D., 1904; m. 2d, Ellen Henderson, Apr. 1922; children—Roy D., Kay, Kent. Asst. corp. counsel of Chicago, 1905-07. Served as maj. World War I; major judge advocate 33d Div., 1924-27; maj. gen. comdr. 33d Div. Ill. Nat. Guard and attached troops, 1927-41; cited and retired as lt. gen. Aug. 1942; pres. Nat. Guard Assn. of U.S., 1934-35. Chmn. Ill. Commerce Commn., 1941-42; mem. Ill. Athletic Commn. since 1942. Decorated Order of the Crown of Italy. Mem. Am., Ill. State and Chicago bar assns., Chicago, Law Inst., Art Inst. Chicago, Phi Kappa Psi, Phi Delta Phi. Clubs: University, Racquet. Home: Ken-Ro-Ka Farm, Lake Forest, Ill. Office: 208 S. La Salle St., Chicago. Died Feb. 21, 1949.

KEELER, Leonarde, criminologist; b. Berkeley, Calif., Oct. 30, 1903; s. Charles Augustus and Louise Mapes (Bunnell) K.; student U. of Calif., 1923-24; A.B., Stanford, 1930; studied under Chief of Police August Vollmer, Los Angeles, 1923-24; LL.D., Lawrence College, 1938; married Katherine Applegate, August 16, 1930. Member staff Institute for Juvenile Research, Chicago, and member staff state criminologist, Illinois, 1929-30; psychologist, Scientific Crime Detection Lab., Northwestern U., 1930, asst. prof. law in psychology and research asst. in physiology, 1933-39; asso. prof. and in charge of Lab., 1936-39; now in private practice; member Illinois Dept. Public Safety Merit Council. Awarded Jr. Assn. of Commerce medal, 1932. Mem. A.A.A.S., Internat. Assn. Identification, Chicago Academy Criminology, International Association Chiefs of Police, Chicago Society for Personality Study. Contbr. to American Jour. Police Science. Developer of a polygraph, instrument for recording blood pressure, pulse, respiration, etc. (popularly called "lie detector") for deception tests. Home: 1507 N. Dearborn Parkway. Office: Chicago. Died Sept. 20, 1949.

KEELING, Walter Angus, lawyer; b. Kosse, Tex., Nov. 22, 1873; s. B. D. and Mary Lou (Mitchell) K.; grad. high sch., Kosse, 1893; student Sam Houston Normal Inst., Huntsville, Tex., 1895, receiving first grade certificate; LL.B., U. of Tex., 1897; m. Cora Sue Scott, Oct. 1, 1908; children—Walter Scott, John Robert. Admitted to Tex. bar, 1897, and began practice at Groesbeck; asst. county atty., Limestone County, Tex., 1904-08; county atty., 1898-1902; county judge, 1908-12; mem. Dem. State Exec. Com., 1908-10; apptd. asst. atty. gen. of Tex., 1912, 1st asst. atty. gen., 1918; apptd. atty. gen. in 1921, and elected atty. gen. for term, 1922-25; voluntarily retired to resume practice of law; handled boundary cases, Okla. vs. Tex. and N.M. vs. Tex., in Supreme Court of U.S., while atty. gen; U.S. district judge for Western Dist. of Tex. since Feb. 4, 1942. Methodist. Mason (32°). Home: 3120 Wheeler St. Office: 1205 Norwood Bldg., Austin, Tex. Died Jan. 22, 1945.

KEEN, Edward Leggett, newspaper man; b. Chillicothe, O., Jan. 19, 1870; s. Rev. Samuel Ashton and Mary (Palmer) K.; B.A., Ohio Wesleyan U., 1891, M.A., 1916; m. Carrie Colvin, June 22, 1896. Began as reporter, Cincinnati Post, 1891; telegraph editor and mng. editor same until 1898; staff corr. Scripps-McRae League, in Philippines, 1898-1900; mgr. Washington Bur. United Press Assn., 1900-10, New York mgr., 1910-11, and European mgr. since 1911; v.p. United Press Assn. since 1919. Mem. Phi Beta Kappa, Phi Delta Theta. Clubs: Nat. Press (Washington, D.C.); Savage, Press (London); American (Paris) Died Oct. 7, 1943.

KEENEY, Willard F., lawyer; b. Arcola, Ill., Jan. 25, 1862; s. Daniel and Rhoda A. (White) K.; student U. of Mich., 1879-80, Law Sch., 1881-82; m. Margaret Morton, Nov. 10, 1897 (died 1920); children—Willard F., Morton, Roger B. Admitted to Mich. bar, 1883; mem. Butterfield & Keeney (now Butterfield, Keeney & Amberg), Grand Rapids, since 1887; president Clallam Lumber Company; director Peoples National Bank (Grand Rapids), Siuslaw Timber Company, Grand Rapids Chair Co. Member of bd., Police and Fire Commrs., Grand Rapids, 1903-08. Pres. and trustee High Sch. Scholarship Assn., Grand Rapids. Mem. Phi Delta Phi (legal frat.). Republican. CongList. Clubs: University, Kent Country (Grand Rapids). Home: 28 Lafayette Av. S.E. Office: 500 Michigan Trust Bldg., Grand Rapids. Mich. Died July 12, 1946.

KEEP, John Joseph, educator; b. Boston, Mass., Apr. 18, 1892; s. Maurice F. and Lucy Louise (O'Connor) K.; student Gonzaga U., 1910-11, A.B., 1918, M.A., 1919; student Sacred Heart Noviciate, Los Gatos, Calif., 1911-16, U. of Innsbruck, Austria, 1922-23, Sacred Heart Coll., Woodstock, Md., 1923-26; Ph.D., Gregorian U., Rome, 1938. Ordained priest R.C. Ch., 1925; joined Soc. of Jesus (Jesuit), 1911; dean of men, Gonzaga U., 1919-22, 1927-30, became pres. of Univ., 1930, then gen. dir. of studies of Jesuit colls. and high schs. in States of Ore. and Wash.; now pastor St. Ignatius Ch., Portland. Address: St. Ignatius Ch., Portland, Ore. Died Dec. 1947.

KEFAUVER, Grayson Neikirk, university professor and administrator; b. at Middletown, Maryland, August 31, 1900; s. Oliver Henry and Lillie May (Neikirk) K.; A.B., University of Arizona, 1921; A.M., Stanford U., 1925; Ph.D., U. of Minn., 1928; m. Anna E. Skinner, Dec. 25, 1922; children—Betty La Verne, William Henry, Robert Elwood. Began as teacher in high schs., 1921; served as vice prin. of senior high sch., prin. of elementary sch., dir. of junior high sch. and dir. of research and guidance in city school system; instr. in secondary edn., U. of Minn., 1926-28, asst. prof. edn., 1928-29; asso. prof. edn., Teachers Coll., Columbia, 1929-32; visiting prof. edn., Stanford, 1932-33; dean of sch. edn. and prof. edn., 1933-43, on leave since 1943, serving as consultant since 1944, division cultural cooperation, Dept. of State, and continuing United States delegate to conference of Allied Ministers of Education, London, 1944; acting asst. chief in charge European branch, 1944-45; Am. representative with rank of minister, Prep. Commn. for establishing U.N.E.S.C.O., 1945; member staff National Survey of Secondary Edn., 1930-32, Nat. Occupation Conf., 1933-39; co-director Stanford Lang. Arts Investigation, 1937-40; co-director, Stanford Social Edn. Investigation, 1938-43; member board trustees Menlo School and Junior College since 1937, Hood College since 1944. Fellow A.A.A.S.; mem. Am. Ednl. Research Assn., John Dewey Soc. Nat. Assn. of Colls. and Depts. of Education (v.p. 1936-37, sec.-treas. 1937-40), Nat. Assn. Coll. Teachers of Edn. (pres. 1942), Nat. Soc. for Study of Edn. (member bd. dirs. 1939-42), Progressive Edn. Assn. (v.p. 1939-42), Am. Council on Edn. (vice chmn. 1938-39), Am. Council Inst. of Pacific Relations, Liaison Committee for Internat. Edn. (chmn. 1943-44), International Edn. Assembly (chairman 1943-44) American Association School Administrs., National Association of Secondary School Principals, Acad. Polit. Science, American Acad. Political and Social Science, N.E.A., Nat. Vocational Guidance Assn., Phi Delta Kappa, Phi Kappa Tau, Pi Kappa Delta fraternities. Republican. Clubs: Commonwealth (San Francisco, California); The Athenaeum (London). Author: A Survey of Vocational Conditions in Fresno, 1926; (with Leonard V. Koos) Guidance in Secondary Schools, 1932. Co-author: Guidance in Educational Institutions, 1938; Social Education, 1938; Appraising Guidance in Secondary Schools, 1941; Foreign Languages and Cultures in American Education, 1942; English for Social Living, 1943; Education in Wartime and After, 1943. Co-author of monographs for U.S. Office of Edn. Home: Stanford University, Calif. Died Jan. 4, 1946 buried in Acacia Garden, Forest Lawn Memorial Park, Glendale, Calif.

KEFAUVER, Harry Joshua (kē-fawv'ēr), administr. occupational therapy; b. Middletown, Md., Nov. 8, 1878; s. Mahlon Calvin and Susan (Remmell) K.; A.B., U. of Md. (Md. Agrl. Coll.) 1900, A.M., 1901; post grad. work Johns Hopkins U., 1915-18; student Sch. of Mil. Psychology, Camp Greenleaf, Ga., 1918; Ph.D., George Washington U., 1924-25; m. Miriam Howard Evans, Aug. 4, 1914; 1 son, Evans Brown. Teacher and asst. prin. high schs., Md., 1904-18; mem. Md. legislature, 1908; supervisor physical edn. Pub. Athletic League of Md., 1916-18, also dir. Psycho-Ednl. Lab. High Sch. Served as 1st lt. and range officer, Md. N.G., 1905-15; 1st lt., Sanitary Corps (div. of psychology), U.S. Army, 1918, also mem. psychol. examination bd., Camp Sevier, S.C.; clin. psychologist, reconstruction service, U.S. Gen. Hosp., Oteen, N.C., 1918-19; spl. instr. occupational therapy, U.S. Public Health Service, 1919-22; specialist in occupational therapy U.S. Vets. Administrn., 1922-30, chief occupational therapy and physical therapy, 1930-44, supervisor occupational therapy since 1944. Rep. of Vets. Adminstrn. on vocational and rehabilitation programs, 1930-44, chmn. program clin. aspects of methods, value and results of occupational therapy, 25th annual meeting, Am. Occupational Therapy Assn., 1941, liaison rep. (occupational therapy) to Nat. Research Council, 1942-44. Chmn. govt. agencies at Vocational Conf. on Employment of Disabled, sponsored by Nat. Rehabilitation Assn., Washington, D.C., 1941-44. Mem. Am. Occupational Therapy Assn., Am. Legion, U. of Md., Johns Hopkins and George Washington univs. alumni assns., S.A.R. (dir. Sgt. Everhart chapter, Md. soc.), Republican. Evangl. Reformed Ch. Mason (K.T.). Author: Occupational Therapy (booklet), 1945; Progress of Occupational Therapy in the Veterans Administration (booklet), 1945. Contbr. numerous papers and articles to sci. publs. Home R.D. 2, Frederick, Md. Office: Veterans Administration, Washington, D.C. Deceased.

KEHOE, James N. (kē'hō), ex-congressman; b. Maysville, Ky., July 15, 1862; s. James and Nora K.; ed. pub. schs.; m. Hannah M. Kane, Sept. 24, 1892 (died, Oct. 28, 1910); children—Irene Marie (dec.), W. H. (dec.), James A., Mary (dec.), Ruth; m. 2d, Frances Reed Calvert, Apr. 20, 1918. Learned the printing trade, became foreman, mgr., and at 22, propr. of a printing office at Maysville; studied law, admitted to bar Ky. Court of Appeals, 1889; city atty., Maysville, 1893; master in chancery, Mason Circuit Court, 1893-1900; mem. 57th and 58th Congresses (1901-05), 9th Ky. Dist. Democrat. Pres. Bank of Maysville. Ex-pres. Hayswood Hospital. Ex-pres. Ky. Bankers Assn.; ex-v.p. Burley Tobacco Growers Credit Corp., Burley Tobacco Growers' Coöperative Assn., Ohio Valley Improvement Assn.; mem. exec. council Am. Bankers Assn. (mem. exec. com. State Bank Div.), Kentucky Bankers Association (dean, ex-pres.). Chmn. Mason County Liberty Loan Com., Am. Red Cross Soc. Home: Marysville, Ky.* Died June 13, 1945.

KEIDEL, George Charles (kī'dĕl), librarian; b. Catonsville, Md., June 16, 1868; s. Louis Julius and Emma Sophia (Brauns) K.; A.B., Johns Hopkins, 1889, Ph.D. (in French, Italian and Latin), 1895; spent summer of 1897 in Belgian and Parisian libraries, summer of 1902 in German univs. and libraries, 3 summers, 1906-08, in Library of Congress; m. Eugenia Garber, Sept. 10, 1904 (died Nov. 16, 1932). Assistant in Romance languages, 1895-97, instr., 1897-98, asso., 1898-1911, Johns Hopkins; Library of Cong. since 1911. Mem. Modern Lang. Assn. America, Md. Hist. Society, Md. Acad. Sciences, Lancaster County Hist. Society; corr. mem. Hispanic Soc. Am. German Lutheran. Author: Évangile aux Femmes, 1895; Manual of Æsopic Fable Literature, 1896; Colonial History of Catonsville, 1912-13; Dr. A. P. Garber, 1914; Catonsville Biographies, 1915 and 1921 (new series in Md. Hist. Magazine); Early Life of Professor Elliott, 1917; Catonsville Lutheran Church, 1919; Earliest German Newspapers of Baltimore, 1927; Keideliana, 2d edition, 1928; Early Maryland Newspapers, 1933; High Finance at Clifton (Civil War), 1939; Jeb Stuart in Maryland, June 1863, 1939. Contributor to Cyclopedia of Education, 1911-12, Ency. Americana, 1919; Enciclopedia Universal Ilustrada Europeo-Americana, 1926; National Year Book, 1939-41; also numerous articles in jours. of Europe and America, especially on fable lit. of the Middle Ages; specializes in local history of Maryland, bibliography of Americana. U.S. stamp collector. Home: 707 Massachusetts Av. N.E. Address: Library of Congress, Washington, D.C. Died Apr. 12, 1942.

KEIM, George de Benneville (kīm), retired banker; b. Philadelphia, Pa., Oct. 27, 1884; s. George de Benneville and Elizabeth Archer (Thomas) K.; ed. Farnum Sch., Beverly, N.J., and Peirce Sch. of Bus. Administration, Phila.; m. Crystine Fleeta Bowers, 1919. In leather business, Phila., later in banking business until retired, 1930; dir. several banks and corps.; commr. Port of New York Authority, 1930-41. Member Liberty Loan Committee, Phila., World War. Del. N.J. to Rep. Nat. Conv., 1928, 32, 36, 40; mem. N.J. State Finance Com., Hoover campaign, 1928; sec. Republican Nat. Com., 1930-36; chmn. N.J. State Rep. Finance Com., 1930; mem. N.J. Rep. State Com. for Burlington County, N.J. Appointed chmn. Commission on Historic Sites in State of N.J., 1929; chmn. N.J. U.S. Constitution Commn.; chmn. N.J. World's Fair Commn. 1938, 39, 40, 41. Trustee St. Mary's Hall, Burlington, N.J., Temple U., Phila.; mem. bd. mgrs. Burlington County Hosp. Trustee Yorktown (Va.) Sesquicentennial Assn.; chmn. N.J. Washington Bicentennial Com. Mem. Gen. Soc. Colonial Wars (gov. gen. 1930-36; ex-gov. N.J. Soc.), Soc. Colonial Wars in Commonwealth of Pa., Soc. of the Cincinnati, Order of Merit, Baronial Order of Runnemede, Pa. Soc. S.A.R., Soc. S.R. State of N.J., Colonial Soc. Pa., Fed. Huguenot Soc. in Am. (pres.-gen. 1939-40), Huguenot Soc. N.J., Huguenot Soc. S.C., Universalist Hist. Soc. (sec.), Transatlantic Soc., Nat. Security League, Soc. War of 1812, Navy League, Pan Am. Soc. U.S., N.J. Historical Society, Welcome Society. Episcopalian. Clubs: Metropolitan, Bankers, Recess, Downtown Athletic, Rockwood Hall, Circumnavigators, Union League (New York); Racquet, Corinthian Yacht, Rose Tree Fox Hunting, Philadelphia Country (Philadelphia); Seaview Golf (Absecon, N.J.); Riverton (N.J.) Country; Everglades, Bath and Tennis (Palm Beach, Fla.); Metropolitan (Washington); Maryland (Baltimore); Westmoreland (Richmond, Va.); Pendennis (Louisville, Ky.); Detroit Athletic. Home: Edgewater Park, Burlington County, N.J. Died July 19, 1943.

KEITH, Arthur, geologist; b. St. Louis, Mo., Sept. 30, 1864; s. Harrison Alonzo and Mary Elizabeth (Richardson) K.; A.B., Harvard, 1885, A.M., 1886; studied Lawrence Scientific Sch. (Harvard), 1887; m. Elizabeth Marye Smith (LL.B. and LL.M., Washington Coll. of Law), June 29, 1916. Mem. Mass. State Topog. Survey, 1886-87; asst., U.S. Geol. Survey, in Tenn. work, 1887; in charge mapping party, Tenn., 1888-95; apptd. geologist, 1895; placed in charge areal and structural geology of U.S., and of Geologic Atlas of U.S., 1907, in charge East of 100th meridian, 1913-21; making special investigation in U.S. and Canada of Appalachian mountain structure, stratigraphy, and earthquakes. Prof. grad. dept., U. of Tex., 1926. Mem. Geol. Soc. of America (pres. 1927), Nat. Research Council (chmn. div. geology and geography, 1928-31; chmn. coms. on earthquakes and fellowships), Nat. Acad. Sciences (ex-treas.), A.A.A.S., Am. Assn. Petroleum Geologists, Am. Inst. Mining and Metall. Engrs., Seismol. Soc. America, Am. Acad. Arts and Sciences, Am. Assn. Geographers, Geol. Soc. Washington (ex-pres.), Washington Acad. Sciences (ex-v.p.), Am. Geophysical Union, Chi Phi, Soc. Colonial Wars, S.R., Delta Kappa Epsilon, Hasty Pudding Club (Harvard); U.S. del. to Internat. Congress Geologists, 1913, to Internat. Geophysical Union; del. of Nat. Acad. of Sciences to Centenary of Geol. Society of France, 1930. Unitarian. Clubs: Cosmos, Chevy Chase, Harvard (Washington, D.C.); Harvard Varsity (Cambridge, Mass.); Quincy (Mass.) Yacht. Author: Geologic Atlas of U.S., Harpers Ferry Folio, 1894, and other folios, 1896-1907 (U.S. Geol. Survey); also many geol. articles. Home: 2210 20th St., Washington, D.C. Died Feb. 7, 1944.

KEITH, Arthur Leslie, univ. prof.; b. Worthington, Ind., Apr. 25, 1874; s. John Lawson and Mary Ann (Robertson) K.; A.B., U. of Neb., 1898, A.M., 1908; Ph.D., U. of Chicago, 1910; m. Mabelle Harding Homerick, June 13, 1900; children—James Lawson (dec.), Arthur Leslie (dec.), Mary Elizabeth (dec.). Instr. St. John's Mil. Sch., Salina, Kan., 1900-08; fellow in Greek, U. of Chicago, 1908-09; prof. Greek, U. of S.D., 1909-10; asst. prof. Latin, 1910-13, prof., 1913-22, Carleton Coll.; prof. Greek, U. of S.D., 1922-33, prof. of Latin since 1933. Mem. Classical Assn. Middle West and South, Am. Assn. Univ. Profs., Am. Philol. Assn., Am. Archæol. Inst., E. Tenn. Hist. Soc., N.E. Historic Geneal. Soc., Ky. Hist. Soc., Md. Hist. Soc., Eugene Field Soc., Soc. Medalists, Soc. Colonial Wars (gov. S.D., Oct. 1924-25), S.A.R., Soc. War of 1812, Phi Beta Kappa, Kappa Sigma, Eta Sigma Phi. Republican. Author: Metaphor and Simile in Greek Poetry from Homer to Æschylus, 1914. Contbr. articles in various journals. Home: Vermillion, S.D. Died Mar. 1, 1942.

KEITH, Charles S., industrial executive; b. Kansas City, Mo., Jan. 28, 1873; s. Richard H. and Anna (Boarman) K.; B.S., Fordham U., New York, 1891; m. Jane Ormsby Gregg, Apr. 25, 1895 (died Jan. 17, 1897); m. 2d, Lucille Hill, June 12, 1900; children—Richard William, Charles S., Jr. (dec.). Entered employ of Central Coal and Coke Co., miners of coal and mfrs. of lumber, in 1891, pres. and gen. mgr., 1907-36 (co. founded 1871 by father who was its head until his death, 1905); receiver Keith & Perry Bldg.; dir. Kansas City Power & Light Co. Assisted in organization, and was first pres. Southern Pine Assn., 1915-22; formerly v.p. Nat. Lumber Mfrs. Assn.; assisted in organization, and formerly pres. Southwestern Interstate Coal Operators Assn.; formerly dir. and mem. exec. com. U.S. Chamber of Commerce; formerly mayor of Kansas City, Mo. Mem. raw materials com., Council of Nat. Defense, 1917. Pres. Kansas City Commercial Club, 1914. Home: Brookside Hotel, Kansas City, Mo. Died Oct. 9. 1945.

KEITH, David, mining; b. San Francisco, Mar. 11, 1895; s. David and Mary (Ferguson) K.; student Salisbury (Conn.) Sch., 1911-12, Tome Sch. for Boys, Port Deposit, Md., 1912-14, Franklin and Marshall Coll., Lancaster, Pa., 1914-15; m. Geneva S. Savage, Dec. 16, 1916 (died Jan. 6, 1926); 1 son, David; m. 2d, Virginia Smith, Feb. 5, 1930. Began as bank teller, 1916; with Nat. Copper Bank; pres. Silver King Coalition Mines Co. since 1924. Served as 1st lt. U.S.R.C., 1916-17. Mem. Am. Legion, Phi Kappa Psi. Presbyn. Elk. Club: Alta. Home: 2285 Walker Lane, Murray, Utah. Office: David Keith Bldg., Salt Lake City, Utah. Died July 9, 1948.

KELBY, Charles Hendre, judge; b. N.Y. City, Aug. 7, 1870; s. Robert Hendre and Jennie (Corrigan) K.; B.S., New York U., 1892, LL.B., 1894; m. Lulu Buffington Richardson, Oct. 15, 1897. Practiced Brooklyn, 1894-1911; justice Supreme Court of N.Y., 2d Dist., 1911-25. Republican. Home: 923 President St., Brooklyn, N.Y. Died Aug. 1, 1944.

KELLAS, Eliza, educator; b. Mooers, N.Y.; d. Alexander and Eliza (Perry) Kellas; grad. State Normal Sch., Potsdam, N.Y., 1891; B.A., Radcliffe, 1910, post-graduate work, 1910-11; A.M., Union University; Pd.D., N.Y. State Coll. for Teachers; LL.D., Russell Sage College, Troy, N.Y.; Pd.D., Middlebury (Vt.) College, 1935. Preceptress, State Nor. Sch., Plattsburg, N.Y., 1892-1901; prin. Emma Willard School, Troy, N. Y., since Feb. 1911; pres. Russell Sage College, 1916-28. Episcopalian. Mem. Assn. Collegiate Alumnae, Radcliffe Alumnae Assn., Nat. Geog. Soc. Has traveled extensively in U.S., Can., Mexico, Europe and Iceland. Clubs: University (New York City); University (Troy, N.Y.); College (Boston, Mass.). Address: Emma Willard School, Troy, N.Y. Died Apr. 10, 1943.

KELLAWAY, Herbert John, landscape architect; b. Sevenoaks, Kent, Eng., Nov. 11, 1867; s. Joseph May and Mary Rebecca (Hyland) K.; brought to U.S., 1874; grad. Needham (Mass.) High Sch., 1886; m. Lutie F. Campbell, 1919; 1 dau., Ida Louise. Entered office of F. L. Olmsted & Co., landscape architects, Brookline, Mass., 1892; pvt. practice, Boston, since 1906; prin. works: Mystic Valley Improvements, Winchester; Hammonds' Pond Parkway, Newton and Brookline; Hitchcock Memorial Field, Amherst Coll.; Faxon Field, Quincy, and Doyle Field, Leominster; Uxbridge Field, Uxbridge; town planner Camp Devens Cantonment, World War I, and Fort Devens World War II, Ayer, Mass., Quincy housing for war workers in Fore River Shipbuilding Works, Salvation Army Fresh-Air Camp (Sharon, Mass.), Hartford Theol. Foundation Grounds (Hartford, Conn.), Newton Hosp., Leominster Hosp., Merrymount Park (Quincy), Middlebury College men's and woman's campuses, New Towne Court (U.S. slum clearance project, Cambridge), Mission Hill Project, Roxbury, Mass., Old Colony Project, South Boston, Mass.; also rose gardens, with Mrs. Harriet R. Foote Rosarian, for Mrs. Henry Ford, Dearborn, Mich., Mrs. Arthur Curtiss James, Newport, R.I., Mrs. E. S. Webster, Falmouth, Mass. Fellow Am. Soc. Landscape Architects; mem. Boston Soc. Landscape Architects, Am. S.S. Union, Am. Congl. Assn. Author: How to Lay Out Suburban Home Grounds, 1907, 2d ed., 1915. Home and Office: 41 Chase St., Newton Centre 59, Mass. Died Sept. 6, 1947.

KELLER, Henry, artist; s. Jacob and Barbara (Karcher) K.; grad. Cleveland Sch. Design (now School Art); Cincinnati Art Sch., Academy Julian, Paris, Royal Academy, Munich (given silver medal), Dusseldorf and Karlsruhe Academies. Began as theatrical lithographer. Teacher at Cleveland School of Art, 1902-48, now dean emeritus of education. Awarded Watson F. Blair prize, Chicago Art Institute; Davis prizes, Witte Museum, San Antonio, Texas; two medals for outstanding excellence and 8 medals for work exhibited at Cleveland Museum. Works included in the American-British exchange exhibition at the Tait Gallery, London, England, and in the Good Neighbor Exhibtion to the capitals of South America, 1947. Works permanently exhibited in Chicago Art Institute, Metropolitan, Whitney, Fogg, Boston, Brooklyn museums, New York Public Library, Philips Gallery, Washington, D.C.; Butler Art Museum, Youngstown, Ohio; Allen Art Gallery, Oberlin, Ohio; San Diego Museum. Associate mem. National Acad.; hon. mem. Cleveland Artists. Club: Ko Koon Art. Home: 4115 Arden-Way, San Diego 3, Calif. Died Aug. 2. 1949.

KELLER, James Albert, coll. pres.; b. Cullman, Ala., Dec. 4, 1887; s. Thomas Jasper and Nancy (Cobbs) K.; grad. State Teachers Coll., Florence, Ala., 1915; B.S., Peabody Coll. for Teachers, Nashville, Tenn., 1933; A.M., Columbia U., 1938. L.H.D., Birmingham-Southern Coll., 1935; LL.D., Ala. Poly. Inst., 1935; m. Mariglen Cornelius, July 5, 1921 (died 1948); children—Laura Jean, Margaret Anne. Prin. elementary schs., Cullman, 1909-12, Hanceville and Arkadelphia (Ala.) high schs., 1916-18; supt. Cullman Co., schs., 1919-21, Covington Co. schs., Andalusia, Ala., 1921-35; supt. of edn., State of Ala., 1935-38; president State Teachers Coll., Florence, Ala. Mem. State Planning Bd., 1935-39. President of Florence Chamber of Commerce, 1943. Served in 81st Div., U.S. Army, A.E.F., World War I. Mem. N.E.A., State Assn. Sch. Supts. (pres. 1927), Ala. Ednl. Assn. (pres. 1932), State Textbook Com. and State Com. on courses of study (chmn. 1935-39). O.P.A. adminstr., Lauderdale County, 1943-45. Mem. Phi Delta Kappa, Kappa Delta Phi, Omicron Delta Kappa, Kappa Phi Kappa. Baptist. Mason (Shriner), Rotarian (pres. 1928, and 39). Contbr. to Ala. Sch. Jour. Home: 624 N. Seminary St., Florence, Ala. Died Aug. 29, 1948.

KELLER, William Huestis, judge; b. Montgomery County, Md., Aug. 11, 1869; s. Daniel S. and Martha E. (Huestis) K.; A.B., Franklin and Marshall Coll., 1891, LL.D., 1920, LL.B., George Washington U., 1893; LL.D., Univ. of Pa., 1939; m. Anna Dickey, Oct. 18, 1893; children—Daniel S. (killed in action in France), Elizabeth D. (Mrs. Robert E. Miller), Oliver J., Martha E. (Mrs. Edmund Rowland), Mary D. Admitted to Pa. bar, 1893, and began practice at Lancaster; mem. Steinmetz & Keller, 1894-99, Coyle & Keller, 1899-1919; first dep. atty. gen. of Pa., 1915-19; judge Superior Court of Pa. since 1919, reëlected in 1929 and 1939; president judge since Jan. 7, 1935. Del. to Rep. Nat. Conv., 1908, 12. Trustee Franklin and Marshall Coll. Mem. Am. and Pa. State bar assns., Pa. Soc. S.R., Phi Beta Kappa, Phi Kappa Sigma. Republican. Mem. Evangelical and Reformed Ch. Mason. Clubs: Union League, University (Phila.); Hamilton, Lancaster. Home: 1061 Wheatland Av. Office: 124 E. King St., Lancaster, Pa. Died Jan. 17, 1945.

KELLEY, Edgar Stillman, composer, conductor, lecturer on musical topics; b. Sparta, Wis., Apr. 14, 1857; s. Hiram Edgar and Mary Clarinda (Bingham) Kelley; grad. of Stuttgart Conservatory of Music, 1880; composition under Max Seifriz, royal court conductor; Litt.D., Miami, 1916; LL.D., U. Cincinnati, 1917; m. Jessie Gregg, pianist, July 23, 1891. Spl. instr. in composition, N.Y. Coll. Music, 1896-99, lecturer on music, extension dept., New York U.; acting prof. musical theory, Yale University, 1901-02; teacher and conductor, Berlin, Germany, 1902-10; now lecturer at Cincinnati Conservatory of Music. Mem. Soc. Mayflower Descendants, Nat. Inst. Arts and Letters, Phi Beta Kappa Fraternity. Awarded International Music Society Composition fellowship, Western Coll., Oxford, O. Principal works: Music to "Macbeth"; music to "Prometheus Bound"; music for dramatic production of "Ben Hur"; "Israfel," voice and orchestra; quintette for piano and strings; string quartette; Puritania (opera); Symphony No. 1, "Gulliver"; Symphony No. 2, "New England"; orchestral suite, "Alice in Wonderland"; Chinese symphonic suite "Aladdin"; also symphonic poem entitled "The Pit and the Pendulum," which was performed at Cincinnati May Festival, 1925; "Pilgrim's Progress," musical miracle play for full chorus and orchestra; full symphonic score for talking cinema Corianton; miscellaneous choral works; various songs and piano pieces. Author: Chopin the Composer; The History of Musical Instruments; also numerous essays. Address: Western College, Oxford, O.; also (winter) Great Northern Hotel, New York, N.Y. Died Nov. 12, 1944.

KELLEY, Francis Clement, bishop; b. Vernon River, P.E.I., Can., Oct. 23, 1870; s. John and Mary

(Murphy) K.; ed. affiliated colls. of Laval U.; classics at St. Dustan's Coll., Charlottetown, P.E.I.; philosophy and theology at Nicolet (P.Q.) Sem.; D.D., Laval U., 1908; LL.D., Notre Dame U., 1907; Ph.D., Litt.D., Louvain 1927. Ordained R.C. priest, 1893; pastor, Lapeer, Mich., 1893-1907; founded Oct. 18, 1905, Catholic Ch. Extension Soc. of U.S.A., and was apptd. acting pres.; elected pres., Dec. 1905; the society established canonically by Pope Pius X, June 19, 1910, by whom was again apptd. pres. to serve 5 yrs. and reapptd. June 1917. Founder, 1906, many yrs. editor-in-chief of the Extension Magazine. Made prothonotary apostolic by Pope Benedict XV, 1915; was consecrated bishop of Oklahoma, Oct. 2, 1924; bishop of Oklahoma City and Tulsa, Okla., 1930. Capt. and chaplain 32d Mich. Vol. Inf. during War with Spain; capt. and chaplain Mich Nat. Guard 6 yrs.; col. and a.-d.-c. on staff comdr.-in-chief Spanish-Am. War Vets., 1 yr.; vice-comdr.-gen. Mil. Order Foreign Wars of U.S., 5 yrs. Vice-chmn. mng. 2d Catholic Missionary Congress, Boston, 1913. Decorated Knight of Saints Maurice and Lazarus (Italy), Grand Cross Order of Merit (Austria); Grand Cross Order of the Holy Sepulchre (Jerusalem). Clubs: University (Chicago and Tulsa, Okla.); Oklahoma Club. Author: The Last Battle of the Gods, 1907; The Flaming Cross, 1911; The City and the World; Letters to Jack, 1917; Charred Wood (novel), 1917; Dominus Vobiscum, 1922; The Story of Extension, 1922; When the Veil is Rent, 1929; The Forgotten God, 1932; Mexico, the Land of Blood-Drenched Altars, 1935; Problem Island, 1937; The Bishop Jots It Down, 1939; Sacerdos et Pontifex, 1940. Address: 1521 N. Hudson, Oklahoma City, Okla. Died Feb. 1, 1948.

KELLEY, Selden Dee, clergyman; b. Livingstone County, Mich., Aug. 6, 1897; s. William D. and Jennie (Cunningham) K.; A.B., Olivet (Ill.) Coll., 1924, D.D., 1936; student Lane Sem., Cincinnati, O., 1924-25; A.M., Boston Univ., 1931, S.T.B., 1934, S.T.M., 1936; m. Dorothy Leah Montgomery, Nov. 29, 1922; 1 son, Selden Dee. Ordained to ministry Ch. of the Nazarene, Sept. 7, 1924; pastor Fithian, Ill., 1919-24; Norwood, O., 1924-29, Malden, Mass., 1929-38, Detroit, Mich., 1938-48; radio pastor since 1931. Trustee Eastern Nazarene Coll., Wollaston, Mass., 1930-38, Olivet Nazarene Coll., Kankakee, Ill., 1925-29, and since 1948; trustee and chmn. bd. Nazarene Theol. Sem., Kansas City, Mo. since 1944, Detroit Bible Inst. since 1945. A founder Holiness Youth for Christ, 1946, The Detroit Bible Training School, 1945. Mem. Ch. of the Nazarene (del. to gen. assembly, 1928, 32, 36, 40, 44; mem. to gen. bd. 1944, pres., 1945-46, chmn. Sunday sch. dept. since 1944; mem. missionary bd. since 1944). Mem. Eastern Nazarene Coll. Hist. Soc., New England. Republican. Address: Olivet Nazarene College, Kankakee, Ill. Died Apr. 9, 1949; buried at Kankakee Memorial Gardens, Kankakee, Ill.

KELLEY, William Valentine, clergyman, editor; b. Plainfield, N.J., Feb. 13, 1843; s. Rev. Benjamin and Eliza (Valentine) K.; A.B., Wesleyan U., Conn., 1865; D.D., 1883; L.H.D., Dickinson, 1899; LL.D., Ohio Wesleyan, 1909; L.H.D., Wesleyan U., Conn., 1918; m. Eliza Whiteman, July 27, 1876. Ordained M.E. ministry, 1867; pastor Burlington, N.J., 1867, Camden, 1868-70, New Brunswick, 1870-73, Buffalo, N.Y., 1873-74, Phila., 1874-78, Newark, N.J., 1878-81, Brooklyn, 1881-92 (except Middletown, Conn., 1884), New Haven, Conn., 1892-93; editor Methodist Review, 1893-1920. Mem. Gen. Conf. 5 times; declined bishopric, 1900; fraternal del. Canadian Meth. Ch., 1906; mem. bd. mgrs. Am. Bible Soc.; v.p. M.E. Missionary Bd. and Bd. Edn. Lecturer at Yale, Hartford, Drew, Garrett and other theol. schs., also colls.; trustee Wesleyan U., Drew Theol. Sem.; pres. trustees Peking U., China; fraternal del. to M.P. Ch., 1916, M.E. Ch., S., 1918. Mem. Brooklyn Clerical Union, Victoria Inst., Philosophical Soc. of Great Britain, Psi Upsilon. Clubs: Clergy (New York); Authors' (London). Author: Ripening Experience of Life and Other Essays, 1907; Down the Road and Other Essays, 1911; The Illumined Face, 1911; Glimpses of the Soul of Gilder, 1911; With the Children, 1917; Salute to the Valiant, 1918; The Open Fire, 1920; My Gray Gull, 1926. Home: Hotel St. George, Brooklyn. Address: 150 5th Av., New York. Died Dec. 14, 1927.

KELLOGG, Abraham Lincoln, judge; b. Croton (now Treadwell), Delaware County, N.Y., May 1, 1860; s. Marvin Douglas and Hannah (Schermerhorn) K.; ed. Delaware Lit. Inst., Franklin, N.Y.; LL.D., Wittenberg Coll., Springfield, O., 1931, Alfred (N.Y.) U., 1935; m. Mary Blakeslee Lewis, June 21, 1893; 1 son, Lincoln Lewis. Admitted to N.Y. bar, 1883, and practiced at Oneonta; mem. Constitutional Conv., N.Y., 1896; county judge of Otsego County, 1908-18 (resigned); justice Supreme Court of N.Y., 6th Jud. Dist., term 1918-30; apptd. official referee of Supreme Court of N.Y., 1931; mem. conv. to revise Judiciary Article of Constn. of N.Y, 1921, and of conv. to draft rules for the Supreme Court of N.Y., 1922. Prominent as atty. for State of N.Y. in prosecuting offenders against pure food laws and tried 27 cases, winning all of them; dir. Internat. Business Machines Corp. since 1934. Pres. bd. of trustees Hartwick College; the high school, Treadwell, named in his honor. Former mem. N.G.S.N.Y. Mem. Am., N.Y. State and Oneonta bar assns. Republican. Presbyterian. Mason. Clubs: Oneonta, Oneonta Country. Home: Oneonta, N.Y.* Died Aug. 25, 1946.

KELLOGG, Edward Leland, M.D.; b. Homer, Cortland County, N.Y., Aug. 1, 1872; s. William Alvan and Chloe Irene (Churchill) K.; grad. Homer Acad. (valedictorian), 1891; student Sch. Social Economics, New York, 1891-92; M.D., Coll. Physicians and Surgeons, Columbia (Harzen prize), 1895; m. Jane Strathmeyer, July 22, 1919. Surgical intern Bellevue Hosp., New York, 1898-99; practicing physician and surgeon, New York, since 1899; resident physician and supt. Minturn Hosp., New York, 1900-03; cons. surg. and formerly dir. surgery Gouverneur Hosp.; director surgery, Manhattan General Hospital; U.S. Public Health res. sr. surgeon; chief med. exec. officer, New York Polyclinic Med. Sch.; formerly attending surgeon St. Bartholomew's Hosp.; prof. surgery N.Y. Polyclinic Med. Sch. Fellow Am. Coll. Surgeons, Internat. Coll. Surgeons, N.Y. Acad. Medicine, Nat. Gastro-enterological Soc. (hon. pres.), Pan-Am. Med. Assn. (trustee); mem. A.M.A., N.Y. State and County med. socs., Am. Soc. for the Control of Cancer, Am. Therapeutic Soc., N.Y. Gasto-enterological Soc. (past pres.); Associaca Paulista de Medicina of San Paulo, Brazil (hon.); Pan-Am. Soc., Soc. Colonial Wars, S.A.R., Colonial Soc., Americans of Royal Descent, Plantagenet Soc.; asso. mem. Am. Museum Natural History. Republican. Baptist. Author: The Duodenum, Its Structure and Function, Its Diseases and Medical and Surgical Treatment, 1933; also numerous monographs on gastro-intestinal problems. Address: 43 W. 54th St., New York 19. Died Aug. 11, 1948.

KELLOGG, Henry Theodore, judge; b. Champlain, N.Y., Aug. 29, 1869; son of Supreme Court Justice S. Alonzo and Susan Elizabeth (Averill) K.; B.A., Harvard U., 1889, LL.B., 1892; m. Katharine Miller Weed, Mar. 5, 1903. Began practice at Plattsburg, 1892; referee in bankruptcy, 1898-1903; judge County Court, Clinton County, N.Y., Jan.-June 1903; apptd. justice Supreme Court of N.Y., 4th Jud. Dist., June 25, 1903; elected to same office for term ending Dec. 31, 1917; reëlected for term ending 1931; apptd. judge Appellate Div., 3d Dept., Jan. 1, 1918; elected asso. judge Court of Appeals, Nov. 1926, for term ending 1939, having been nominated on both Rep. and Dem. tickets, resigned, 1934. Republican. Episcopalian. Address: R.F.D. 2, Peru, N.Y. Died Sep. 6, 1942.

KELLOGG, John Harvey, surgeon; b. Tyrone, Mich., Feb. 26, 1852; s. John Preston and Ann Jeanette K.; ed. State Normal Sch.; M.D., Bellevue Hosp. Med. Coll. (New York U.), 1875; studied in Europe, 1883, 89, 99, 1902, 1907, 1911, 1925; LL.D., Olivet (Mich.) Coll. and Lincoln Memorial U.; Dr. Pub. Service, Oglethorpe U., 1937; m. Ella E. Eaton, Feb. 22, 1879. Has been in practice at Battle Creek, Mich., since 1875; supt. and surgeon Battle Creek (Mich.) Sanitarium since 1876. Mem. Mich. State Bd. Health, 1878-90, 1912-16. Inventor of improved apparatus and instruments for med. and surg. purposes; discoverer of the therapeutic value of the electric light and inventor of the electric light bath; discoverer of the sinusoidal current; founder health food industries of Battle Creek. Founder and pres. emeritus, Battle Creek (Mich.) Coll.; founder and med. dir. Miami-Battle Creek Sanitarium, Miami Springs, Fla. Fellow Am. Coll. Surgeons, A.A.A.S., Royal Society Medicine (England), A.M.A., Nat. Geog. Soc.; mem. Am. Pub. Health Assn.; corr. mem. Société d'Hygiène de France. Author: Plain Facts, 1877; Home Book of Modern Medicine, 1880; Man, the Masterpiece, 1885; Art of Massage, 1895; The Stomach, 1896; Rational Hydrotherapy, 1900; Light Therapeutics, 1910; Colon Hygiene, 1912; Neurasthenia, 1915; Health Series of Physiology and Hygiene (joint author), 1915; Health Question Box, 1917; New Method in Diabetes, 1917; Autointoxication, 1918; The Itinerary of a Breakfast, 1918; The New Dietetics, 1921; Tobaccoism, 1922; The Natural Diet of Man, 1923; How to Have Good Health, 1932; also many tech. papers and articles. Editor Good Health Magazine since 1873. Founder and pres. Race Betterment Foundation, 1906. Address: Battle Creek, Mich. Died Jan. 16, 1945.

KELLOGG, Olin Clay, educator; b. Spafford, N.Y., Apr. 21, 1870; s. William S. and Olive (Churchill) K.; A.B., Syracuse U., 1892, A.M., 1893, Ph.D., 1894; studied dramatic art and oratory, New York and Phila.; m. Effie Adelia Wheelock, July 25, 1894 (died Dec. 31, 1925). Prof. of English, criticism, rhetoric and elocution, Cazenovia (New York) Seminary, 1892-96; pvt. instr. in lit. and oratory, 1896-99; sr. instr. English lang., Northwestern U., 1899-1906; prof. English lang. and lit., 1906, prof. English and forensics, 1907, prof. English and pub. speaking, 1909, prof. English lang. and lit., U. of S. Dak., 1915-41; head of 3 depts. and teacher journalism, 1915-17; staged and directed the dramatic productions of the univ., 1910-16. Extension lecturer Univ. of S.D., 1917-19; teacher, same university, summers, 1915-28. Del. to Conf. of Brit. and Am. Profs. of English, Columbia U., 1923. Mem. English-Speaking Union, Drama League of New York, Drama League America, Nat. Council Teachers of English, N.E.A., Phi Beta Kappa. One of founders Delta Sigma Rho. Contbr. dramatic criticisms, book revs., etc. Home: Vermillion, S.Dak. Deceased.

KELLY, Eugene Hill, editor; born at Sioux City, Ia., Jan. 22, 1887; s. John Charles and Martha (Hill) K.; ed. Worcester (Mass.) Academy, 1904-05, Princeton, 1905-07; m. Mary Lennon, Feb. 23, 1911; children—John Charles, Eugene F., Mary Elizabeth, Arthur L., Tone Hill, Frederick Tate. Began as carrier Sioux City Tribune 1894, served in various capacities until mgr., 1920, editor and mgr., 1933-41; dir. Troy Nat. Bank; pres. Sioux City Broadcasting Co. Mem. Am. Legion (past comdr. Monahan Post). Conglist. Mason (32°). Home: 1817 Summit Av. Office: 1817 Summit Av., Sioux City, Ia. Died May 15, 1948.

KELLY, Frank A., M.D.; b. Alpena, Mich., May 8, 1880; s. John A. and Sara Anna (Hand) K.; M.D., Detroit Homœ. Coll., 1903, U. of Mich., 1919; m. Merle Kenward Brock, June 29, 1909; children—William John, Mary Louise. Began active practice in Detroit, 1903; attending surgeon Grace Hosp. since 1903, surgeon in chief, 1938-39, chief of staff since 1939; attending surgeon Evangelical Deaconess Hosp. since 1926; cons. surgeon Receiving Hosp. since 1925, Highland Park Hosp. since 1933; mem. State Bd. of Registration in Medicine, pres. 1932. Mem. Detroit Bd. Health since 1939, pres. 1941-43. Served in U.S. Army, Spanish Am. War. Fellow Am. Coll. Surgeons; diplomate Am. Bd. Surgery (founders group); mem. Am. and Mich. State med. assns., Wayne County Med. Assn. (past pres., treas. since 1923). Republican. Mason (32°). Clubs: Country, Athletic. Home: 2906 E. Jefferson Av. Office: David Whitney Bldg., Detroit, Mich. Died Dec. 10, 1943.

KELLY, Frank V., chmn. Demo. exec. com.; b. Brooklyn, N.Y., Mar. 14, 1880; s. Frank and Ellen (Barry) K.; ed. pub. schs. and Wright's Bus. Coll; unmarried. Began as bank clerk, 1896; became building contractor and pub. adminstr., Kings County; vice pres. Fidelity and Deposit Co. of Md., Dime Savings Bank of Williamsburg. Served as sec. Dem. County Com. and Dem. State committeeman. Mem. Soc. of Old Brooklynites, St. Patrick's Soc., Friendly Sons of St. Patrick. Clubs: Montauk, Eckford (Brooklyn); Crescent-Hamilton; Lakeville Country. Home: 152 Keap St. Office: 4 Court Square, Brooklyn, N.Y. Died July 5, 1946.

KELLY, Howard Atwood, surgeon; b. Camden, N.J., Feb. 20, 1858; s. Henry Kuhl and Louisa Warner (Hard) K.; B.A., U. of Pa., 1877, M.D., 1882; LL.D., Aberdeen, 1906, Washington and Lee U., 1906, U. of Pa., 1907, Washington Coll., 1933; Johns Hopkins Univ., 1939; m. Laetitia Bredow, June 27, 1889; children—Olga Elizabeth Bredow, Henry Kuhl, Esther Warner (Mrs. Henry G. Seibels), Friederich Heyn, Howard Atwood, William Boulton, Margaret Kuhl (Mrs. Douglas Warner), Edmund Bredow, Laetitia Bredow (Mrs. Winthrop K. Coolidge). Founder of the Kensington Hosp., Philadelphia; asso. prof. obstetrics, U. of Pa., 1888-89; prof. gynecology and obstetrics, Johns Hopkins U., 1889-99, gynecology, 1899-1919, emeritus prof. since 1919; gynecol. surgeon, 1899-1919, cons. gynecologist since 1919, Johns Hopkins Hosp.; surgeon and radiologist Howard A. Kelly Hosp. since 1892; Hunterian lecturer Mansion of Lord Mayor of London, 1928; hon. curator Div. of Reptiles and Amphibians, U. of Mich. Hon. fellow Royal Coll. Surgeons (Edinburgh), Edinburgh Obstet. Soc., Glasgow Obstet. and Gynecol. Soc., Royal Acad. Medicine in Ireland, Obstetrico Gynecol. Soc. of Kiev (Russia), Obstet. Soc. of London; mem. Am. Gynecol. Soc. (pres. 1912), Chicago Gynecol. Soc., Am. Urol. Assn., Roentgenol. Soc., Seaboard Med. Assn., Va. and N.C. med. socs.; fellow Southern Surg. and Gynecol. Soc., Am. Radium Soc., Am. Coll. of Surgeons, A.A.A.S., Am. Geog. Soc., British Gynecol. Soc., Md. Acad. of Sciences (life), Natural History Soc. of Md.; mem. Nat. Assn. Audubon Socs., Phila. Acad. Natural Sciences, N.Y. Zoölogical Soc., N.Y., Bot. Gardens, Am. Mus. of Natural History, Am. Soc. Ichthyologists and Herpetologists, Assn. Française d'Urologie (Paris), Société Internationale d'Histoire de la Médecine, Philos. Soc. of Gt. Britain, British Mycol. Soc., Deutsche Gesellschaft für Pilzkunde; hon. mem. many fgn. med. socs. Comdr. Order of Leopold (Belgium), 1920; Order of Cross of Mercy (Serbia), 1922; Cross of Charity of the Kingdom of the Serbs, Croats and Slovenes, 1926. Author: Operative Gynecology (2 vols.), 1898, 1906; The Vermiform Appendix and its Diseases (with Elizabeth Hurdon), 1905; Walter Reed and Yellow Fever, 1906, 07, 23; Gynecology and Abdominal Surgery (edited with C. P. Noble), Vol. I, 1907, Vol. II, 1908; The Stereo Clynic, 84 sections, 1908—; Medical Gynecology, 1908, 1912; Appendicitis and Other Diseases of the Vermiform Appendix, 1909; Myomata of the Uterus (with T. S. Cullen), 1909; Cyclopedia of American Medical Biography (2 vols.), 1912; Some Am. Med. Botanists, 1913; Diseases of the Kidneys, Ureters, and Bladder (with C. F. Burnam—2 vols.), 1914, 1922; American Medical Biographies (with W. L. Burrage), 1920; A Scientific Man and the Bible, 1925; Gynecology, 1928; Dictionary of American Medical Biography (with W. L. Burrage), 1928; Electrosurgery (with Grant E. Ward), 1932; also some 500 scientific articles. Home: 1406 Eutaw Pl. Sanatorium: 1412-20 Eutaw Pl., Baltimore, Md. Died Jan. 12, 1943.

KELLEY, Jessie Stillman (Mrs. Edgar Stillman Kelley), music dir.; b. Chippewa Falls, Wis.; d. Andrew Kerr and Eva Nelson (Coleman) Gregg; ed. West Sch., San Francisco; studied piano with Louis Lisser, San Francisco, William Mason, New York, theory with Edgar Stillman Kelley and Gustav Hinrichs; L.H.D., Western Coll., Oxford, O.; Litt.D., Miami U., Oxford, O.; m. Edgar Stillman Kelley, July 23, 1898. Was pianist and teacher of piano, San Francisco, Calif., 1887-94, New York, N.Y., 1894-1902, Berlin, 1902-10; dir. of music, Western Coll., Oxford, O., since 1910; lecturer, Cincinnati Conservatory, since 1911. Mem. Nat. Fedn. of Music Clubs (ex-pres.; nat. chmn. legislative com.), Ohio Music Teachers' Assn. (ex-pres.). Address: Western College, Oxford, O.; and (winter) Hotel Great Northern, New York, N.Y. Died Apr. 3, 1949.

KELLY, Myra (Mrs. Allan Macnaughtan), educator, author; b. Dublin, Ireland; d. Dr. James E. and

Annie (Morrogh) Kelly; ed. Horace Mann Sch., New York, 1891-94, Teachers Coll., Columbia, 1894-99. grad. with diploma as teacher of manual training; m. Allan Macnaughtan, 1905. Teacher in pub. sch., New York, primary grades, 1899-1901; critic teacher Speyer Sch., Teachers Coll., Columbia, 1902-03. Author: Little Citizens, 1904; Isle of Dreams, 1907; Wards of Liberty, 1907; Rosnah, 1908; The Golden Season, 1909; Little Aliens, 1910. Address: Care Chas. Scribner's Sons, New York. Deceased.

KELLY, Percy R., judge; b. Arlington, Ia., July 13, 1870; s. Christopher C. and Mary Jane (Whipple) K.; B.S., Albany (Ore.) Coll., 1887; m. Margaret Dawson, Mar. 29, 1910. Admitted to Ore. bar, 1892, and practiced at Albany until 1911; dep. dist. atty., Linn County, 1894-98; state senator, 1898-1902; city atty., Albany, 1909-10; circuit judge, 1911-30; asso. justice Supreme Ct., Ore., 1930-40, chief justice, 1941-42, asso. justice since 1943. Republican. Mason, Elk, K.P. Home: 292 S. 17th St. Address: Supreme Court Bldg., Salem, Ore. Died June 14, 1949.

KELTY, Paul Ray, editor; b. Lafayette, Ore., Mar. 27, 1872; s. James Monroe and Sarah Maria (Scott) K.; ed. Lafayette pub. schs., 1879-88; m. Clara Lillian Jeter, Oct. 19, 1897; 1 son, Eugene Scott. With Portland Telegram, as telegraph editor, city editor and mng. editor, 1896-1905; city editor Los Angeles Examiner, 1905-08; news editor The Oregonian, 1908-24, editor, 1931-39; editor and pub. Eugene (Ore.) Daily Guard, 1924-27; mng. editor Eugene Register, 1928-30. Chmn. Ore. State Bd. of Parole and Probation; mem. McLoughlin Memorial Assn. Trustee Sunshine Div. of Portland Police Dept. Mem. Sigma Delta Chi. Republican. Mason (33°), hon. A.A.S.R. Home: Lafayette, Ore. Died Nov. 11, 1944.

KEMMERER, Edwin Walter, economist; b. Scranton, Pa., June 29, 1875; s. Lorenzo Dow and Martha H. (Courtright) K.; A.B., Wesleyan U., 1899, LL.D., 1926; fellow in economics and finance, Cornell, 1899-1901, Ph.D., 1903; LL.D., Occidental Coll., 1928; Dr., honoris causa, Central U., Ecuador, also from all univs. of Bolivia, 1927; D.C.S., Oglethorpe Univ., 1933; D.Sc., Rutgers Univ., 1933; LL.D., Columbia Univ., 1935; m. Rachel Dickele, Dec. 24, 1901; children—Donald Lorenzo, Ruth K. Dorf. Instr. econ. and history Purdue U., 1901-03; financial adviser U.S. Philippine Commission, 1903; chief div. of currency, P.I., 1904-06; asst. prof. polit. economy, 1906-09, prof. economics and finance, 1909-12, Cornell U.; professor economics and finance, Princeton U., 1912-28, Walker professor international finance, and director Internat. Finance Section, 1928-43, professor emeritus since June 1943; financial adviser to Govt. of Mexico, 1917, and to Government of Guatemala, 1919, 24; chmn. Commn. Am. Financial Advisers to Colombia, 1923. Mem. Kemmerer-Vissering Gold Standard Inquiry Commission for Union of South Africa, 1924-25; expert on currency and banking to Dawes Committee, 1925; chairman American Commn. of Financial Advisers to Chile, 1925; chmn. American Commn. of Financial Advisers to Poland, 1926, to Ecuador, 1926-27, to Bolivia, 1927; pres. Am. Commn. Financial Advisers to Colombia, 1930, to Peru, 1931; president American Commission, Financial Experts to China, 1929; joint chmn. Hines-Kemmerer Commn. to make econ. survey of Turkey, 1934; pres. Economists' Nat. Com. on Monetary Policy since 1937. Managing editor Economic Bulletin, 1907-10. Fellow (past v.p.), Am. Statis. Assn., fellow Am. Acad. of Arts and Sciences; mem. American Economic Association (president 1926), American Philos. Soc., Council on Foreign Relations. Awarded gold medal by Govt. of Colombia, for services to Colombia, 1923; Commander's Star, Order of Polonia Restituta, 1926; Order of Merit, First Class, Ecuador, 1927; Order of the Crown (Belgium), 1937. Trustee Wesleyan Univ. since 1936, Scranton-Keystone Junior College since 1935; Robert College (Turkey) since 1941. Director United States and Foreign Securities Corporation; U.S. and Internat. Securities Corp.; Dividend Shares; Carriers and General; Bullock Fund, Am. and Foreign Power Co. Mem. Delta Kappa Epsilon, Phi Beta Kappa. Mason. Clubs: Century, Bankers, Princeton; Nassau (Princeton); Blooming Grove Hunting and Fishing (Pa.); Bald Peak Colony (N.H.). Author: Report on the Advisability of Establishing a Government Agricultural Bank in the Philippines, 1906; Report on the Agricultural Bank of Egypt, 1906; Money and Credit Instruments in Their Relation to Gen. Prices, 1907, revised, 1909; Seasonal Variations in the Relative Demand for Money and Capital in the United States (in report of Nat. Monetary Commn.), 1910; Modern Currency Reforms, 1916; The United States Postal Savings System, 1917; Monetary System of Mexico, 1917; The A B C of the Federal Reserve System, 1918, 11th rev. edit., 1938; Six Lectures on the Federal Reserve System, 1920; High Prices and Deflation, 1920; Kemmerer on Money, 1934; Money—The Principles of Money and Their Exemplification in Outstanding Chapters of Monetary History, 1935; Inflation and Revolution: Mexico's Experience of 1912-1917, 1940; The ABC of Inflation, 1942. Papers and reports to 14 govts. are in Princeton U. Library. Home: 161 Hodge Road, Princeton, N. J. Died Dec. 16, 1945.

KEMMERER, John L., lawyer, corp. official; A.B., Amherst, 1893, M.A., 1896; LL.B., Harvard, 1896; m. Frances Mott Ream, 1906. Dir. Kemmerer Coal Co., Whitney & Kemmerer, Am. Reinsurance Co., Newmont Mining Corp.; trustee Am. Surety Co. of New York. Clubs: Recess, New York Yacht, Baltusrol Golf. Home: Short Hills, N.J. Office: 120 Broadway, New York, N.Y. Died Mar. 3, 1944.

KEMP, William Webb, educator; b. Placerville, Calif., Feb. 6, 1873; s. William and Caroline Elizabeth (Frazee) K.; B.A., Stanford, 1898; grad. student same univ., 1904-05, U. of Calif., 1905-06; research in archives of London, Eng., summer 1911; Ph.D., Columbia, 1912; m. Grace Hayes, Jan. 1, 1907; 1 dau., Marylyn Hayes Kemp; m. 2d, Nina Moses Burton, May 24, 1934. Prof. edn., and dir. summer session, U. of Mont., 1912-15; prof. Sch. of Administration and chmn. Dept. of Edn., U. of Calif., 1915-20; prof. edn. and dean Sch. of Edn., U. of Calif. since 1923; pres. San Jose State Teachers Coll., 1920-23. Lecturer Stanford U., summer, 1921, Southern Br. of Calif., 1924, Territorial Normal Sch., Honolulu, 1927, U. of Hawaii, 1927 and 35, U. of Calif., Los Angeles, 1937, 40, 41, 42, 43; U. of Mont. summer 1939; consultant Ednl. Policies Commn. of the Office of Education, 1936. Mem. bd. consultants, Nat. Survey of Education of Teachers, 1930-33, Los Angeles School Survey, 1933-34. Mem. Bd. of Edn., Berkeley, 1917-20. Mem. N.E.A., Nat. Soc. of Coll. Teachers of Edn. (pres. 1928-29), Nat. Soc. for Study of Edn., Calif. Teachers' Assn., Calif. Soc. for Study of Secondary Edn., Phi Delta Kappa. Progressive Rep. Episcopalian. Club: Commonwealth. Author: Support of Schools in Colonial New York by the Society for the Propagation of the Gospel. Joint author of Survey of Education in Hawaii. Joint author Educational Survey Inglewood High Sch. District Inglewood, Calif. Contbr. Cyclo. of Edn. and various professional mags.; mem. nat. advisory bd. Jr. Coll. Jour.; cons. editor Calif. Jour. of Secondary Edn. Home: 13 Marchant Court, Berkeley, Calif. Died May 14, 1946.

KENDALL, Henry Hubbard, architect; b. New Braintree, Mass., Mar. 4, 1855; s. Albert Asaph (M.D.) and Helen M. (Bigelow) K.; studied architecture under William G. Preston; Mass. Inst. Tech., 1872-73, Mass. Normal Art Sch., 1875-77; m. Annie B. Stearns, Nov. 29, 1881; children—Albert Stearns, Horace Bigelow, Dorothy. Asst. and prin. asst. to supervising architect, U.S. Treasury Dept., 1879-87; practiced at Boston since 1889; now mem. Kendall, Taylor & Co.; v.p. Newton Center Savings Bank. Fellow A.I.A. (pres. 1920, 21, 22); mem. Boston Soc. Architects (ex-pres.). Republican. Baptist. Clubs: Neighbors, Villagers. Home: Newton Center, Mass. Office: 221 Columbus Av., Boston, Mass. Died Feb. 28, 1943.

KENDALL, Margaret, artist.; b. Staten Island, N. Y., Nov. 29, 1871; d. Albert Stickney; pupil of J. Alden Weir, Julius Rolshoven and Sergeant Kendall; m. Sergeant Kendall. Exhibited Pa. Acad. Fine Arts, 1898-1902, Soc. Am. Artists, 1898-1902; Minneapolis, 1900; Paris Expn., 1900; Soc. Miniature Painters, 1901-04 (mem. of soc.); Boston Expn. Portraits Fair Children, 1901-03; Pan-Am. Expn. Buffalo, 1901, St. Louis Expn., 1904. Address: 26 W. 8th St., New York. Died Sept. 14, 1935.

KENDRICK, Benjamin Burks, prof. history; b. Woodland, Ga., Oct. 16, 1884; s. William Thomas and Levicie (Maddox) K.; B.S., Mercer U., Macon, Ga., 1905; A.M., Columbia, 1911, Ph.D., 1914; m. Elizabeth Shields, Nov. 24, 1909; children—Benjamin Burks, Margaret Shields (Mrs. William J. Horney, Jr.), John Whitfield, David Stewart (dec.), Janet Joanna. Prin. Norman Park (Ga.) Pub. Sch., 1905-06; teacher of history and English, Columbus (Ga.) Industrial High Sch., 1906-09; instr. of history, Columbia U., 1912-15, asst. prof., 1915-20, asso. prof., 1920-23; prof. of history, Women's Coll. of U. of N.C., 1923-30, prof. and chmn. dept. of history and polit. science since 1930; dir. and mem. exec. com. Home Industrial Bank, Greensboro, N.C. Chmn. Southern Region Com. of Social Science Research Council, 1930-35, mem. Problems and Policies com., 1933-36. Mem. Am. Hist. Assn. (mem. council and exec. com. 1941-44), Southern Hist. Assn. (v.p. 1940, pres. 1941), N.C. Hist. and Literary Soc. (v.p. 1937-38), Sigma Nu. Presbyterian. Author: The Journal of the Joint Committee on Reconstruction, 1914; The United States Since 1865 (with L. M. Hacker), 1932; The South Looks at Its Past (with A. M. Arnett), 1935. Contbr. to hist. jours. Lecturer on current topics. Home: 908 Fairmont St., Greensboro, N.C. Died Oct. 28, 1946.

KENEFICK, Daniel Joseph, lawyer; b. Buffalo, N.Y., Oct. 15, 1863; s. Michael and Mary (O'Connell) K.; grad. Central High Sch., Buffalo, 1881; m. Maysie Germain, June 30, 1891 (now dec.); children—Daniel J., Theodore G. Admitted to N.Y. bar, 1884, and began practice at Buffalo; mem. firm of Kenefick, Cooke, Mitchell, Bass & Letchworth since 1906; dir. various corps. Asst. dist. atty. Erie Co., New York, 1887-94, dist. atty., 1895-98; justice Supreme Court of N.Y., 1898-1906. Trustee U. of Buffalo. Mem. Am. and N.Y. State bar assns. Republican. Catholic. Clubs: Buffalo, Saturn, Buffalo Country. Author of City Charter of Buffalo. Home: 841 Delaware Av. Office: 1330 Marine Trust Bldg., Buffalo, N.Y.* Died Dec. 26, 1949.

KENLY, Julie Woodbridge Terry, writer; b. Cleveland, O., Mar. 26, 1869; d. Gen. Henry Whitney and Julia Woodbridge (Terry) Closson; ed. at home; m. Gen. William Lacy Kenly (U.S. Army), July 3, 1893 (died 1928); children—William Lacy (dec.), Henry Closson. Republican. Episcopalian. Author: The Vision and the Wise Woman, 1923; Strictly Personal, 1929; Green Magic, 1930; The Astonishing Ant, 1931; Children of a Star, 1932; Wild Wings, 1933; Cities of Wax, 1935; Little Lives, 1938; Voices from the Grass, 1940. Home: 2200 19th St. N.W., Washington, D.C. Died Jan. 8, 1943.

KENNA, Frank, lawyer, business exec.; b. New Haven, Conn., June 22, 1874; s. Thomas M. and Helen (Leahy) K.; LL.B., Yale, 1905; m. Vertie M. Kinney, Oct. 6, 1908; children—Roger, Elizabeth (Mrs. Theodore F. Lynch), Anita (Mrs. Edward J. Doonan), Frank, Gilbert. Admitted to Connecticut State bar, 1905; in practice New Haven, until 1928, retired; owner, dir. business ventures since 1928; mem. bd. aldermen, New Haven, 1908-10; mem. Conn. State Legislature, 1911-13; v.p. and dir. Am. Bank & Trust Co.; trustee Corporate Fiduciaries Assn.; pres. and treas. Marlin Firearms Co.; pres. Associated Realty Corp., Illustrated Current News; Marlin Industrial Division; treas. Kenro Products Co.; dir. Arms and Ammunition Inst., New Haven Taxpayers Assn., N.H. Curative Society (chmn.); incorporator, Grace-New Haven Hosp.; mem. exec. com. Interfaith Movement. Mem. Dem. State Central Com., 1912-16; Mem. New Haven Mfrs. Assn., Am. and Conn. bar assn. Democrat. Catholic. Clubs: Quinnipiack, New Haven Country, Union League, Civitan, Race Brook Country (ex-pres.); Pine Orchard Country, Centre, Conn. Sr. Golf Assn., Wilsonian Professional. Recipient of New Haven Advertising Club Gold Medal Award, 1945. Home: Oak Hill. Office: 85 Willow St., New Haven, Conn. Died Dec. 26, 1947.

KENNARD, Joseph Spencer, author; b. Bridgeton, N.J., May 20, 1859; s. J. Spencer (D.D.) and Nancy Ruth (Jeffers) K.; student Colgate, 1878-80, A.M., 1892; studied law at Columbia Coll. of Law, N.Y., and Union College of Law, Chicago, Columbia Univ., later U. of Paris; LL.B., Northwestern U., 1883; Ph.D., U. of Chicago, 1884; R. Istituto di Belle Arte, Florence, 1895-97; D.C.L., Des Moines Coll., 1902; Litt.D., U. of Paris, 1904; Dr. of Sorbonne, 1904; L.H.D., Colgate, 1906; m. Isabelle D. Brandreth, Feb. 27, 1889 (died Mar. 10, 1925); children—Joseph Spencer, Ralph Brandreth, Virginia Gladys, Elaine Muriel; m. 2d, Eva H. Young, Jan. 10, 1927. Practiced law in Chicago and New York, later in Europe, many years; commissioner to Paris Expn., 1900; lectured on art and lit., various univs. Mem. Soc. Colonial Wars, S.R., Phila. Art Club, Pan Am. League, Delta Kappa Epsilon, Am. Art Assn., Paris, Royal Inst. Fine Arts, Italy, etc. Mason. Baptist. Clubs: Authors, Andiron, Fortnightly. Author: Entro un Cerchio di Ferro, 1898; The Fallen God, 1900; Studi-Danteschi, 1901; A Liberal Education, 1901; Some Early Printers and Their Colophons, 1902; The Fanfare of the Bersigliari, 1902; De Deo Lapso Commentarius, 1902; Romanzie Romanzieri Italiani, 2 vols., 1904; La Femme dans le Roman Italien, 1905; Les Confessions d'un Octogénaire, 1905; La Paura del Redicolo, 1905; Italian Romance Writers, 1906-22; Goldoni, and the Venice of His Time, 1920; Memmo, One of the People, 1920; The Friar in Fiction; Sincerity in Art, 1923; La Religieuse, Paris, 1929; Goldoni et La Comédie Italienne, Paris, 1929; Swiss Legends, 1930; A History of the Italian Theatre for 2000 Years (2 vols.), 1931; Masks and Marionettes, 1935; A Literary History of the Italian People, 1941; Pensées Detachées, 1944; Dante and His Precursors, 1944. Address: 155 E. 49th St., New York; and 615 Candia Av., Coral Gables, Fla. 1944.

KENNEDY, Charles Rann, dramatist; b. Derby, Eng., Feb. 14, 1871; s. Edmund Hall and Annie Leng (Fawcett) K.; largely self educated; hon. LL.D., St. Mary's Coll., Calif., 1941; naturalized U.S. citizen since 1917; m. Edith Wynne Matthison, July 19, 1898. Office boy and clerk from 13 to 16, and lecturer and writer to 26; actor, press agent, writer of short stories, articles and poems and theatrical business mgr. to 1905; since engaged in dramatic writing mainly. Prof. of philosophy and (with wife) head of dramatic dept. Bennett Junior Coll., Millbrook, N.Y., also trustee; now retired. Mem. Soc. Am. Dramatists and Composers, Soc. of Authors, England. Scottish Rite Mason (33°). Author (plays): The Servant in the House, 1908; The Winterfeast, 1908; The Terrible Meek, 1911; The Necessary Evil, 1913; The Idol-Breaker, 1914; The Rib of the Man, 1916; The Army With Banners, 1917; The Fool from the Hills, 1919; The Chastening, 1922; The Admiral, 1923; The Salutation, 1925; Old Nobody, 1927; Crumbs, 1931; Flaming Ministers, 1932; Face of God, 1935; Beggar's Gift, 1935; Isles of the Blest, 1940; The Seventh Trumpet, 1941; Sonnets for Armageddon (appeared weekly in The Witness), 1943. Address: 10678 Rochester Av., Los Angeles 24, Calif. Died Feb. 16, 1950.

KENNEDY, Michael Joseph, ex-congressman; b. N.Y. City, Oct. 25, 1897; s. Michael Joseph and Margaret (Cantwell) K.; ed. Sacred Heart Parochial Sch., New York City; m. Sally Fischer, Dec. 26, 1928. Successively hotel clerk, clerk of York City Bd. of Elections, marshal of New York City for 15 yrs. Pres. Michael J. Kennedy, Inc., insurance, since 1939. Mem. 76th and 77th Congresses (1939-43), 15th Dist., N.Y. Elected leader of Tammany Hall, Apr. 1942. Democrat. Catholic. Mem. K.C., Order of Redman. Clubs: Manhattan, Elks, Sherry, New York Athletic, Owl, West Side Assn. (New York). Office: 1775 Broadway, New York, N.Y. Died Nov. 1, 1949.

KENNEDY, Robert Morris, rear admiral Med. Corps; b. Mahanoy City, Pa., June 21, 1867; s. George Washington and Elizabeth Cunningham (Morris) K. Midshipman, U.S. Naval Acad., 1885-87; M.D., U. of Pa., 1890; post grad. courses New York Polyclinic Med. Sch. and Hosp., 1893, 1901; m. Bessie Marsden Murdaugh, Aug. 3, 1898; 1 dau., Elizabeth Morris. Commd. ensign Med. Corps. U.S. Navy, June 26, 1890, and advanced through grades to rear adm., Mar. 2, 1929; asst. surgeon, June 18, 1890; passed asst. surgeon, June 18, 1893; surgeon, Oct. 20, 1901. Served in Spanish-Am. War, Philippine Insurrection, Boxer trouble in China, disturbances in Haiti and Santo Domingo, Mexican Border, World War. Comdr. Naval Hosp., San Juan, P.R., and on surg. staff Presbyn. Hosp., 1909-11; comdr. U.S. Hosp. Ship Solace, 1915-17, and naval hosps., Washington, D.C., 1917-19, Annapolis, 1922-27. Instr., Naval Med. Sch., Washington, 1911-12; insp. med. dept. activities, U.S. Navy, 1919-21 and 1929-30; pres. Bd. Med. Examiners and naval med. examining bds., 1921-22; mem. Naval Retiring Bd., 1921-22, 1927-30; retired July 1, 1931. Awarded Navy Cross; recommended for D.S.M. "for distinguished and meritorious service in World War." Fellow Am. Coll. Surgeons; mem. A.M.A., Mil. Order World War. Episcopalian. Address: Navy Dept., Washington. Died June 16, 1946; buried in Arlington National Cemetery.

KENNEDY, Willard John, v.p. Anchor Serum Co.; b. Vernon, Ont., Can., Oct. 1, 1876; s. Archibald and Jean (McInness) K.; student Ont. Agrl. Coll., Guelph, 1896-98; B.Agr., Ia. State Coll., 1899; m. Beulah Bingham, Feb. 13, 1904; children—Arloene (Mrs. Thomas W. Morony), Ronald. Instr. animal husbandry, U. of Ill., 1899-1901; prof. animal husbandry and head dept., Ia. State Coll., 1901-12, dir. of extension, 1912-14; pres. Purity Serum Co., Sioux City, Ia., 1914-24; v.p. and sales mgr. Anchor Serum Co., St. Joseph, Mo., since 1924. Pres. Animal and Poultry Foundation of America; vice chmn. and mem. exec. com. Serum and Virus Control Agency. Past. pres. Sioux City Chamber of Commerce. Mem. St. Joseph Chamber of Commerce, Am. Soc. Animal Nutrition, Alpha Zeta, Phi Kappa Phi, Pi Kappa Alpha. Ind. Republican. Mem. Christian Ch. Mason (32°). Club: Rotary (v.p. St. Joseph club; past pres. Sioux City club). Author of bulletins pub. by U.S. Dept. Agr. and Ia. Agrl. Expt. Sta.; contbr. to Chicago Daily Drovers Jour. and other agrl. jours. Trained 13 coll. livestock judging teams for Internat. Livestock Show, Chicago, and Am. Royal Show, Kansas City, 1900-12 (10 won 1st place); has judged 580 livestock shows in U.S., Can. and Scotland. Home: 1012 Ashland Court. Office: Anchor Serum Co., South St. Joseph, Mo. Died Nov. 12, 1942.

KENNEDY, William Henry Joseph, coll. pres.; b. Boston, Mass., Oct. 28, 1888; s. William Henry and Annie (Doherty) K.; ed. Boston Latin Sch., 1904-08; A.B., Harvard, 1912; student Teachers Coll. of City of Boston, 1911-12; A.M., Boston Coll., 1922, Ph.D., 1925; m. Josephine Antoinette Curran, July 30, 1919; children—William Henry, Christopher Francis, Paul Anthony. Teacher, Boston elementary schs., 1912-14; jr. master, Boston Latin Sch., 1914-20, head dept. history, 1920-22; dean, Teachers Coll. of City of Boston, 1922-28, pres. since 1930; also instr. history, Boston Coll., 1924-27, dept. architecture, Mass. Inst. Tech., 1914-28. World War I vet., 2d lt., F.A. Reserve Corps. Dir. and v.p. in charge of safety edn., Mass. Safety Council. Mem. N.E.A., Am. Hist. Assn., Archaeol. Inst. America, Am. Cath. Hist. Assn., Phi Beta Kappa. Catholic. Democrat. K.C., Am. Legion. Club: Harvard (Boston). Author: The United States, 1926, America's Story, 1926, Old World Foundations of the United States, 1927, America's Founders and Leaders, 1928 (all with Sister Mary Joseph); Today and Yesterday, 1937, Before America Began, 1937 (both with Sister Leonita and Sister Mary Joseph). Home: 31 Wellesley Park, Dorchester 24, Mass. Died Aug. 23, 1948.

KENNERLY, Wesley Travis, lawyer; b. Henry County, Tenn., Aug. 29, 1877; s. Charles M. and Sarah A. (Travis) K.; LL.B., U. of Tennessee, 1901; m. Ola D. Robertson, Mar. 15, 1906 (died Dec. 9, 1934); children—Robert Travis, Warren Wesley. Began practice at Knoxville, 1900; chairman Knox County Dem. Exec. Com., 1906-10; mem. Dem. State Exec. Com., 2d Dist. of Tenn., 1910-18 and 1922-24; city atty., Knoxville, 1912-16; U.S. atty., Eastern District of Tenn., 1917-21, mem. Kennerly & Key. Lecturer on Federal Pleading, Practice and Criminal Law, U. of Tenn.; special Justice Supreme Court of Tenn., 1939. Hon. col. staff of Gov. of Tenn., 1939-43. Del. to Dem. Nat. Convention, 1932 and 1940; Dem. elector 2d Congl. Dist., 1932. Served as 1st sergt. Co. L, 1st Tenn. Inf., Spanish-Am. War. Mem. bd. trustees U. of Tenn. Pres. Alumni Assn. of U. of Tenn., 1925-26; mem. Am. (v.p. 1921-22) and Tenn. bar assns., Knoxville Bar Assn. (ex-pres.), Am. Judicature Soc., S.R., United Spanish War Vets. (comdr. Dept. of Tenn., 1926), Tenn. Hist. Soc., East Tenn. Hist. Soc., Sons of Confederate Vets., Phi Kappa Phi, Phi Delta Phi. Methodist. Mason (K.T., Shriner), K.P., Elk. Clubs: Izaak Walton League of America, Knoxville Rod and Reel. Home: 2016 Ogden Av., Knoxville, Tenn; (summer) Kenrock Lodge on Norris Lake (Tenn.). Office: 625 Market St., Knoxville, Tenn. Died Jan. 29, 1944.

KENNEY, John Andrew, physician, editor; b. Albermarle County, Va., June 11, 1874; s. John Andrew and Caroline (Howard) K.; grad. Hampton Inst., 1897; M.D., Shaw Univ., Raleigh, N.C., 1901, LL.D. (hon.), 1938; D.Sc. (hon.) Lincoln Univ., Oxford, Pa., 1935; m. Alice Talbot, Dec. 28, 1902 (died Aug. 1912); m. 2d, Frieda Frances Armstrong, Oct. 29, 1913; children—John Andrew, Oscar Armstrong, Howard Washington, Harriet Elizabeth (Mrs. James Wallace Quisenberry). Interne Freedmen's Hosp., Washington, D.C., 1901-02; resident physician Tuskegee Inst. (Ala.), med. dir., surgeon-in-chief, John A. Andrew Memorial Hosp. and Nurses Training Sch., Tuskegee Inst., 1902-24, and 1939-44; physician Newark, N.J., 1927-35; founded Kenney Memorial Hosp., Newark, N.J., 1927, med. dir. and chief surgeon, 1927-35, deeded hosp. as gift to Booker T. Washington Commn. Hosp. Assn. rep. colored people of N.J., Christmas 1934; personal physician to Booker T. Washington, 1902-15, and to George Washinton Carver, 1902-24. Awarded C.V. Roman D.S.M. by John A. Andrew Clinic Soc., 1940. Mem. Am. Soc. Hygiene Assn. (interracial com., Montclair, N.J.), Nat. Med. Assn. (sec. 1904-12, pres. 1912), A.M.A., Med. Soc. of N.J., Essex County Med. Soc., Acad. of Medicine of Northern N.J., North Jersey Med. Soc., John A. Andrew Clin. Soc. (one of founders in 1918), Assn. Am. Med. Editors and Authors, Zeta Boulé, Beta Kappa Chi. Republican. Baptist. Clubs: Tuskegee and Hampton Alumni. Mason (Shriner). Author: Negro in Medicine, 1912. Founded Jour. Nat. Med. Assn., 1908, asso. editor and bus. mgr., 1908-16, editor since 1916. Contbr. numerous articles to med. pubs. Home: 39 Madison Av., Montclair, N.J. Died Jan. 29, 1950.

KENNY, Michael, educator; b. GlanKeen, Tipperary, Ireland, June 28, 1863; s. Dermot Shefley and Kathleen (Maders) K.; ed. Crescent Coll., Mungret Coll., Royal Irish U., A.B.; philosophy at Mungret and St. Charles Coll., La., A.M.; theology in Dublin; sociology, Ghent, Belgium, and Fordham University, N.Y. City, Ph.D.; Litt.D., Spring Hill (Ala.) College, 1930. Came to U.S., 1886, naturalized, 1892. Joined Society of Jesus (Jesuits), 1886; ordained priest Roman Catholic Ch., 1897; taught lit., philosophy, and social science at Spring-hill Coll., Ala., Loyola U., New Orleans, Creighton U., Omaha, and lectured extensively; moved to N.Y. City, 1908, as a founder of "America" (Roman Catholic weekly), and asso. editor until 1915; regent Loyola U. Law Sch. and prof. jurisprudence, legal ethics, sociology, 1915-24; prof. philosophy and social science, Spring Hill College, 1924-40. Mem. Am. Anthropol. Assn., Am. Geog. Soc., Am. Hist. Assn., Am.-Irish Hist. Soc. (vice-pres. for Ala.), Florida State Historical Soc., Conseil Historique de France. Author: Lourdes and Its Miracles; American Masonry; The People's Pope; Justice to Mexico; Ireland's Case, 1926; American Masonry and Catholic Education; The Mexican Crisis—Its Causes and Consequences, 1927; The Torch on the Hill—Centenary Story of Spring Hill College, 1931; The Romance of the Floridas (The Finding and Founding, 1512-1574), 1934; No God Next Door (Red Rule in Mexico), 1935; The Martyrs of Virginia, 1571, 1937; Martinez of Florida, Jesuit Protomartyr, 1566, 1939; GlanKeen of Borrisoleigh, 1944. Contbr. to Catholic Ency., Ency. of Universal Knowledge, Thought, Studies, Catholic World, etc. Address: Spring Hill College, Spring Hill, Ala. Died Nov. 22, 1946.

KENT, A(rthur) Atwater, mfr., inventor; b. Burlington, Vt., Dec. 3, 1873; s. Prentiss J. (M.D.) and Mary Elizabeth (Atwater) K.; ed. Worcester Poly. Inst.; hon. E.E., U. of Vt., 1924; Dr. Engring., Worcester Poly. Inst., 1926; D.Sc., Tufts Coll., 1927; m. Mabel Lucas, 1906; children—Arthur Atwater, Elizabeth Brinton (Mrs. William Laurens Van Alen), Virginia Tucker (Mrs. Kent Catherwood) and Jonathan Prentiss (adopted). Established, 1902, the Atwater Kent Mfg. Works, Philadelphia, for manufacture of telephones and small volt meters; added mfr. of the unisparker (for which John Scott Medal was awarded in 1914), panoramic sights, clinometers, fuse setters and angle of sights for the army during World War; business incorporated, 1919, as the Atwater Kent Mfg. Co., of which is pres.; started mfg. radio receiving sets, 1922. Mem. com. on general problems of radio broadcasting, 3d and 4th Nat. Radio Confs., 1924, 25; sponsored multi-station broadcasting of world's greatest musical artists, beginning Oct. 1925; sponsored Nat. Radio Audition to discover talented singer. Restored the Betsy Ross House, Phila., 1937, as it existed in Colonial Days, in recognition of which the S.A.R. presented him with a medal; acquired, restored and presented the historic Franklin Institute Building to the City of Phila. as a museum dedicated to the history of Phila., 1938, the City, in appreciation, naming it Atwater Kent Museum. Clubs: Bar Harbor (Me.); Corinthian Yacht, New York Yacht; Everglades (Fla.). Home: 801 Bel-Air Road, Los Angeles 24. Died Mar. 4, 1949; buried in Forest Lawn Memorial Park, Glendale, Calif.

KENT, Harry Llewellyn, research; b. Republic County, Kan., Nov. 27, 1879; s. George Call and Lisetta Augusta (Pfaff) K.; grad. Kan. State Normal Sch., Emporia, Kan., 1904, A.B., 1912; studied summer, Cornell U. and U. of Chicago; B.S., Kan. State Agrl. Coll., 1913, M.S., 1920, LL.D., 1931; LL.D., U. of N.M., 1939; m. Ursula Bailey Dickinson, Aug. 7, 1907; children—Harry Llewellyn, George Clarence, Lisetta Lo Ree, Ruth Margaret (dec.), Richard Franklin, Robert William. Mem. faculty, State Teachers Coll., Hays, Kan., 1904-09, State Normal Sch., Keene, N.H., 1909-11; extension work, Kan. State Agrl. Coll., 1911-13; prin. Sch. of Agr. and asst. prof. edn., same, 1913-20, also dir. Summer Sch., 1918, 19; organizer and dir. vocational edn., State of Kan., 1918-20; dir. Ft. Hays Expt. Sta., 1920-21; pres. N.M. Coll. Agr. and Mech. Arts, 1921-35; dir. administrative research, Tex. Technol. Coll., since 1937. Mem. Am. Farm Econ. Assn., N.M. Ednl. Assn. (pres. 1924), Alpha Zeta, Acacia. Republican. Presbyterian. Mason. Author: Agriculture for the Kansas Common School, 1914, 23, 31, 40. Home: 2435 22d St., Lubbock, Tex. Died Jan. 7, 1946.

KENT, Harry Watson, secretary emeritus Metropolitan Museum of Art; b. Boston, Mass., Sept. 28, 1866; s. Robert Restiaux and Eliza (Watson) K.; ed. Boston Latin Sch., Norwich (Conn.) Acad.; hon. M.A., Hamilton, 1920; hon. Dr. Arts, Brown, 1932; unmarried. Asst. sec. Met. Mus. of Art, 1905. sec. 1913-40, sec. emeritus since 1940. Writer on bibliographical, typographical and museum subjects. Clubs: Grolier, Century. Address: 15 East 69th St., New York. Died Aug. 28, 1948.

KENT, Ira Rich, publisher; b. Calais, Vt., Oct. 28, 1876; s. Le Roy A. and Blanche (Hollister) K.; prep. edn., Goddard Sem., Barre, Vt.; A.B., Tufts, 1899; m. Louise Andrews, May 23, 1912; children—Elizabeth, Hollister, Rosamond, Mary (Mrs. Arthur C. Sprague). Mem. editorial staff Youths Companion, 1900-25, ed., 1925; ed., Houghton Mifflin Co. since 1926, sec. since 1933. Trustee and mem. exec. com. Tufts Coll. since 1911, chmn. since 1935. Pres. Old West Church Association; mem. administrative board, New England Medical Center. Mem. Vt. Assn. of Boston (hon.), Vt. Hist. Soc., Theta Delta Chi, Phi Beta Kappa. Clubs: St. Botolph (Boston); Century (New York). Home: 17 Hawthorn Rd., Brookline 46, Mass. Office: 2 Park St., Boston 7. Died Nov. 9, 1945; buried at Calais, Vt.

KENT, Norton Adams, physicist; b. New York, July 28, 1873; s. Elmore Albert and Mary Abbie (Holman) K.; A.B., Yale, 1891-95; grad. work, same univ., 1897-98, Johns Hopkins, 1898-1901, Ph.D., 1901; m. Margaret Crowninshield, Mar. 27, 1906; 1 dau., Margaret Crowninshield. Asst., Yerkes Obs., Williams Bay, Wis., 1901-03; prof. physics, Wabash Coll., Ind., 1903-06; asst. prof. physics, Boston U., 1906-10, prof., 1910-42, emeritus since June 30, 1942; visiting prof. physics Mass. Inst. of Tech. since 1942. Fellow Am. Acad. Arts and Sciences; mem. Phi Beta Kappa, Sigma Xi. Republican. Conglist. Writer of research articles on various subjects in spectroscopy. Home: 1 Waterhouse St., Cambridge, Mass. Died June 5, 1944.

KENT, Raymond Asa, univ. pres.; b. Plymouth, Ia., July 21, 1883; s. Thomas Oliver and Ellen C. (Stephens) K.; A.B., Cornell Coll., Mt. Vernon, Ia., 1903; A.M., Columbia, 1910, Ph.D., 1917; LL.D., Bucknell U., 1934, Cornell Coll., 1937, U. of Maryland, 1940; m. Frances Stanton Morey, Dec. 23, 1911; children—Charles Stanton, Constance Frances, Roger Betts. Prin. graded schs., Fountain, Minn., 1904-05; supt. schs., Mabel, Minn., 1905-07, Lanesboro, 1908-09; instr. mathematics, State Normal Sch., Winona, Minn., 1909-11; supt. schs., Winona, Minn., 1911-13; sec. State Edn. Commn., St. Paul, Minn., 1913-14; prin. Univ. High Sch. and asst. prof. edn., U. of Minn., 1914-16; supt. schs., Lawrence, Kan., and prof. edn., U. of Kan., 1916-20; supt. schs., Duluth, Minn., 1920-21; dean Sch. of Edn., dir. summer session, U. of Kan., 1921-23; dean Coll. of Liberal Arts, and prof. edn., Northwestern U., 1923-29; pres. U. of Louisville since 1929; lecturer summer schs., U. of Tex., 1920, U. of Calif., 1926, and U. of Pa., 1939. Mem. Federal Advisory Com. on Emergency Aid in Edn., 1934, Ky. Liquor Control Com., 1933; pres. Ky. Assn. Colls. and Univs., 1933-34; pres. Assn. of Urban Univs., 1933-34; mem. bd. of consultants Nat. Youth Adminstrn., 1937, mem. Ky. State Textbook Commn. since 1936; mem. exec. com. Am. Printing House for the Blind; mem. Ky. Emergency Relief Commn., 1934. Mem. N.E.A. Nat. Assn. Coll. Teachers of Edn., Am. Council on Edn. (chmn. com. to Review Cooperative Test Service 1935-36, Com. on Cooperative Study in Gen. Edn. since 1938; exec. com. since 1937; chmn. Com. on Student Personnel Work since 1937); chmn. com. on Coll. standards, Ky. Assn. Colls. and Secondary Schs. since 1937; mem. Commn. on Academic Freedom and Tenure, Assn. of Am. Colleges since 1934; mem. Nat. Soc. Study of Edn., Phi Beta Kappa, Phi Delta Kappa. Methodist. Author: A Study of State Aid to Public Schools in Minnesota, 1918. Joint Author: Bulletin 47 (State Dept. of Edn., Minn.), 1913; Survey Report on School Building Program for the City of Junction City, Kan., 1922, for the City of Ottawa, Kan., 1923, for the City of Dodge City, Kan., 1923; Junior High School Manual (State of Kan.), 1923; Bobbs-Merrill Arithmetics, 1927. Editor: Higher Education in America, 1930. Collaborator of Foreign Language Equipment of 2325 Doctors of Philosophy, 1929. Editor: George H. Betts' Foundations of Character and Personality, 1937. Clubs: Rotary (pres. 1939-40), Pendennis (Louisville). Home: 1904 Lauderdale Rd. Address: University of Louisville, Louisville, Ky. Died Feb. 26, 1943.

KENT, Robert Thurston, mech. engr.; b. Jersey City, N.J., July 17, 1880; s. William and Marion Weild (Smith) K.; M.E., Stevens Inst. Tech., 1902; m. Alice Palmatier Howard, July 6, 1905; 1 dau., Marion Weild (Mrs. Charles F. Amelung). Machinist apprentice, 1898-98; erecting engr., Robins Conveying Belt Co., N.Y. City, 1902-03; designer, Link-Belt Co., Phila., 1903-04; associate editor, Electrical Review, N.Y. City, 1904-05; engring. editor Iron Trade Review, Cleveland, O., 1905-09; editor, Industrial Engring., N.Y. City, 1909-15; cons. engr., New York, 1912-17; chief engr. Myer, Morrison & Co., N.Y. City, 1917-21; cons. engr., 1921-24; supt. prison industries, N.Y. State, 1924-27 (reorganized and modernized industries and instituted wage system); gen. mgr. Bridgeport (Conn.) Brass Co., 1927-28; vice pres. and dir. engring., Divine Brothers Co., Utica, N.Y., 1928-34; cons. engr., Montclair, N.J., 1934-38; gen. mgr. Wm. Sellers & Co., Phila., 1938-40; production mgr., Control Instrument Co., Brooklyn, N.Y., 1942; cons. engr. with Stevenson, Jordan & Harrison, N.Y. City, since 1942. Served as prin.

prodn. engr., U.S. Army Ordnance Dept., 1940-41. Fellow Am. Soc. M.E., Masaryk Acad. of Work (Prague, Czechoslovakia), Delta Tau Delta. Club: Engineers (New York). Author: Power Transmission by Leather Belting, 1915; Calorific Power of Fuels (with Herman Poole), 1918; Kent's Mechanical Engineer's Handbook, 10th edit., 1923, 11th edit., 1938. Home: 3 Argyle Rd., Montclair, N.J. Office: 19 W. 44th St., New York 18, N.Y. Died May 23, 1947.

KENYON, Otis Allen, advertising; b. Baldwinsville, N.Y., Nov. 19, 1879; s. Jacob Cook and Nora (Betts) K.; student Paris Lysee Voltaire, 1899-1900, Koniglische Technische Hochschule, Berlin, 1902-03; M.E., Cornell U., 1904; m. Vivian Kenyon, Apr. 27, 1903; 1 d., Ingrid; m. 2d, Mrs. Florence Judd Bartholomew, Apr. 5, 1918; adopted step-children—Donald B. Kenyon, Elise (Mrs. Glenn M. Wiggins). Began as mem. R. R. Test Commn., World's Fair, St. Louis, Mo., 1904; chief engr. Arc Welding Machine Co., 1913-18; became asso. with Ray D. Lillibridge, Inc., technical advertising, 1918, dir. Kenyon & Eckhardt, Inc., advertising, since 1929, chmn. of bd. since Aug. 1942; chmn. bd. Kenyon Research Corp. Chmn. bd. Advt. Research Foundn., 1947, 1948, 1949. Mem. Am. Institute Electrical Engrs., Society Automotive Engineers, A.A.A.S., Am. Mus. of Nat. Hist. Sigma Xi. Clubs: Cornell, Lotos* (New York); Greenwich Country, Greenwich Riding Assn. Indian Harbor Yacht Club, Greenwich, Conn. Translated and edited: Stray Currents from Electric Railways (from the German, by C. Mischalke), 1906; Theory, Design and Construction of Induction Coils (from the French, by H. Armagnat), 1908; Handbook of Mathematics for Engineers and Engineering Students (from the French, by J. Claudel), 1906. Editor and co-author: Standard Handbook for Electrical Engineers, 1907. Invented welding system used on steel lining of Catskill Aqueduct; invented welding system for making Liberty engine cylinders, also supervised work during World War and served as mem. Shipping Board's welding com.; sold 40 welding patents after war. Home: Steamboat Rd., Greenwich, Conn. Office: 247 Park Av., New York. Died Feb. 3, 1949.

KEPHART, John William, jurist; b. Wilmore, Cambria County, Pa., Nov. 12, 1872; s. Samuel A. and Henrietta B. (Wolfe) K.; early edn. Soldiers Sch., Allegheny Coll.; LL.B., Dickinson Coll., Pa.; LL.D., Allegheny (Pa.) Coll., Dickinson Coll., Lafayette Coll., U. of Pa., Villanova Coll., St. Francis Coll., Univ. of Pittsburgh, Juniata Coll.; m. Florence M. Evans, Dec. 1, 1904; children—Alvin Evans, Henrietta F., John William. Admitted to Pa. bar, 1894, and practiced at Ebensburg; engaged in many business enterprises; county solicitor Cambria County, 1906-14; judge Superior Court of Pa., 1914-18 inclusive; justice Supreme Court of Pa., 1919-40, chief justice, 1936-40. Actively identified with ednl. affairs of Dickinson Coll. Law Sch. and Allegheny Coll. Mem. Am. Bar Assn., Am. Law Inst., Pa. Bar Assn., Alumni Assn., Dickinson Coll. (pres.). Republican. Lutheran. Clubs: Art, Clover, Union League, Hist. Soc. (Phila.); Lincoln, Whitemarsh Country. Home: Ebensburg, Cambria County, Pa. Died Aug. 6, 1944.

KEPPEL, Frederick Paul; b. Staten Island, N.Y., July 2, 1875; s. of Frederick and Frances M. (Vickery) K.; A.B., from Columbia University, 1898, Litt.D., 1929; Litt.D., U. of Pittsburgh, 1912; LL.D., U. of Mich., 1919, Hamilton, 1924, Union, 1926, U. of Toronto, 1927, U. of Melbourne (Australia), 1935, and St. Andrews (Scotland), 1939; married Helen Tracy Brown, January 31, 1906; children—Frederick Paul, Charles Tracy, David, Gordon, Francis. Asst. secretary, 1900-02; secretary 1902-10, dean college, 1910-18, Columbia Univ. Sec. American Assn. for Internat. Conciliation, 1908-18, 3d asst. sec. of war, 1918-19; dir. foreign operations, Am. Red Cross, 1919-20; commr. for U.S. Internat. Chamber Commerce, 1920-22; sec. Plan of New York, 1922-23; pres. Carnegie Corp., 1923-41; dir. Equitable Life Assurance Soc. of U.S., Guaranty Trust Co. Mem. President's Com. on War Relief Agencies, 1941. Decorated Chevalier Légion d'Honneur, France. Member Psi Upsilon, Phi Beta Kappa frats. Democrat. Episcopalian. Clubs: Cosmos (Washington); Century, University (New York). Author: Columbia University, 1913; Undergraduate and His College, 1917; Some War Time Lessons, 1920; Education for Adults, 1926; The Foundation, 1930; The Arts in American Life (with R. L. Duffus), 1933; Philanthropy and Learning, 1936. Home: Montrose, N.Y. Office: 522 5th Av., New York, N.Y. Died Sep. 8, 1943.

KER, Severn Parker (kär), steel mfr.; b. Richmond, Va., Feb. 17, 1864; s. Heber and Mary (Kinney) K.; ed. pub. schs.; m. Annie Williams Gray, Sept. 10, 1891; children—Mary Ruth (Mrs. Parker H. Cunningham), Annie Gray (Mrs. Edward H. Boyd), Severn Parker. With Smith Bros. & Co., Allegheny, Pa., 1885, title changing to The La Belle Steel Co., 1887, becoming sec. in charge of sales until merged with Crucible Steel Co., 1899; v.p. Am. Steel Hoop Co., 1899, office N.Y. City, with Carnegie Steel Co., 1901-02, Crucible Steel Co., of America, 1903-04; v.p. in charge of sales, Republic Iron and Steel Co., 1905-09; gen. mgr. Sharon Steel Hoop Co., 1909, pres. 1910-31, chmn. bd., 1931-33 (retired); dir. Sharon Steel Corp., First Nat. Bank. Republican. Episcopalian. Clubs: Youngstown (Ohio); Duquesne (Pittsburgh); Union (Cleveland, Ohio). Home: 1660 Cohasset Drive, Youngstown, O. Died July 7, 1943.

KERLEY, Charles Gilmore, pediatrist; b. Red Hook, N.Y., June 23, 1863; s. James R. and Eliza Kittle (Pitcher) K.; ed. Seymour Smith Inst., Pine Plains, N.Y.; M.D., Univ. Med. Coll. (New York U.), 1888; m. Beth McClannin, Apr. 15, 1896; children—Barbara (Mrs. Henry A. Hutchins), Priscilla (Mrs. Charles Bonner). Resident physician, Mt. Vernon (N.Y.) Infant Asylum, 1888-92; asst. and resident physician Bavarian Frauenklinik, 1892; lecturer diseases of children, 1897-1903, prof. since 1903, N.Y. Polyclinic Med. Sch.; cons. pediatrist Babies Hosp. (New York), Hosp. for Joint Diseases (New York), St. John's Hosp. (Yonkers), Tarrytown Hosp., Methodist Episcopal Hosp. (Brooklyn), Greenwich (Conn.) Hosp., Sharon (Conn.) Hosp., Vassar Hosp. (Poughkeepsie), Fitkin Memorial Hosp. (Neptune, N.J.), Wassaic (N.Y.) State Sch., Mary McClellan Hosp. (Cambridge, New York). Member Am. Pediatric Society (pres. 1907-08), N.Y. County Medical Soc. (pres. 1912), A.M.A., etc. Clubs: St. Nicholas, Hosp. Graduates. Republican. Author: Short Talks with Young Mothers, 1902, 10, 16, 25; Treatment of Diseases of Children, 1907, 1909; Practice of Pediatrics, 1914, 1918, 1924; What Every Mother Should Know, 1915; Digestive Disturbances in Infants and Children, 1924; Where Is My Mother? (fiction), 1933. Home: 10 E. 81st St., New York, N.Y. Died Sep. 7, 1945.

KERN, Howard Lewis, lawyer; b. Charles City, Ia., Feb. 4, 1886; s. Samuel Lewis and Lydia (Healey) K.; A.B., Cornell Coll., Mt. Vernon, Ia., 1907; LL.B., Harvard University, 1911; married Edna Luella Francis, Aug. 8, 1913 (dec.); children—Myrna Kern Chase, Virginia Jean. With Cravath & Henderson, New York City, 1911-13; attorney general of Puerto Rico, term 1914-21; acting governor by designation of the President during absences of gov., 1917, 18, 19; resigned Sept. 1, 1919; mem. Armstrong, Keith & Kern, N.Y. City, 1920-28; asst. gen. atty. Internat. Telephone & Telegraph Corp., and gen. atty. or gen. counsel various communications subsidiaries, 1928-41; gen. counsel Central R.R. Co. of New Jersey, N.Y. and Long Branch R.R. Co., Wharton & Northern R.R. Co., since May 1, 1941, Central R.R. Co. of Pa. Alternate Puerto Rican Delegation Democratic National Conv., 1920, 24. Pres. Presbyterian Union, Newark. Mem. Am., N.Y. State bar assns., Assn. of Am. Railroads, Assn. Bar City of New York, Pan. Am. Soc., Phi Beta Kappa. Clubs: Down Town Assn.; New York Conference of Railway Counsel. Home: 177 S. Valley Road, West Orange, N.J. Office: 143 Liberty St., New York, N.Y. Died May 12, 1947.

KERN, Jerome David, composer; b. N.Y. City, Jan. 27, 1885; s. Henry and Fannie (Kakeles) K.; grad. Newark (N.J.) High Sch., 1902; studied music under mother; piano, New York Coll. of Music, Alexander Lambert, Paolo Gallico; harmony, Dr. Austin Pierce, Albert von Doenhoff, and under pvt. tutors in Germany, 1904-05; m. Eva, d. George Draper Leale, Oct. 25, 1910; 1 dau., Elizabeth Jane. Began as composer in Eng., 1903. Mem. Am. Soc. Composers, Authors and Pubs., Dramatists' Guild, Authors' League of Am., Nat. Inst. Arts and Sciences, Soc. Authors, Playwrights and Composers (England). Specializes in application modern school harmony to lighter forms of opera. Composer: Very Good Eddie, Princess Theatre, N.Y., Dec. 1915; Theodore & Co., Gaiety Theatre, London, Eng., Sept. 22, 1916; Have a Heart, Liberty Theatre, New York, Jan. 1917; Love o' Mike, Shubert Theatre, Jan. 1917; Oh Boy, Princess Theatre, Feb. 1917; Leave It to Jane, Longacre Theatre, Aug. 1917; Miss 1917 (with Victor Herbert), Nov. 5, 1917; Oh Lady, Lady, Princess Theatre, 1918; Rock-a-Bye Baby, Astor Theatre, 1918; Head Over Heels, Cohan Theatre, 1919; She's a Good Fellow, Globe Theatre, 1919; The Night Boat, Liberty Theatre, 1920; Sally, New Amsterdam, 1920; Good Morning, Dearie, Globe Theatre, 1921; The Cabaret Girl, Wintergarden Theatre, London, 1922; The Bunch and Judy, Globe Theatre, 1922; The Beauty Prize, Wintergarden Theatre, 1923; Stepping Stones, Globe, 1923; Dear Sir, Selwyn, 1924; Sunny, New Amsterdam, 1925; The City Chap, Liberty, 1925; Criss-Cross, Globe, 1926; Lucky, New Amsterdam, 1927; Show Boat (book and lyrics by Oscar Hammerstein, II); Blue Eyes (comic opera); Sweet Adeline (musical romance), Hammerstein Theatre, 1929; Men of the Sky (musical film-drama), 1930; The Cat and the Fiddle (musical love story), Globe Theatre, 1931; Music in the Air (musical adventure in 2 acts), Alvin Theatre, 1932; Roberta (musical comedy in 2 acts), New Amsterdam Theatre, 1933; Three Sisters (musical play), London, 1934; I Dream Too Much (light opera film, for Lily Pons), 1935; Swing Time (musical comedy motion picture, starring Astaire and Rogers), 1936; When You're in Love (light opera motion picture starring Grace Moore, 1937; Joy of Living (motion picture starring Irene Dunne), 1938; Very Warm for May (musical comedy in 2 acts), Alvin Theatre, 1939; One Night in the Tropics (motion picture starring Allan Jones, Abbott & Costello) 1940; Scenario for Orchestra, world premiere by Cleveland Orchestra, Artur Rodzinski, conducting, Oct. 23, 1941; Portrait for Orchestra (Mark Twain) world premiere by Cincinnati Symphony, Andre Kostelanetz conducting, May 14, 1942; You Were Never Lovelier (motion picture starring Fred Astaire and Rita Hayworth; Cover Girl (motion picture starring Rita Hayworth and Gene Kelly), 1944; Can't Help Singing (starring Deanna Durbin), 1944; Montage for Orchestra, suite in three movements for full orchestra and two pianofortes, 1945. Home: Beverly Hills, Calif. Address: care Chappell & Co., Rockefeller Center, New York, N.Y. Died Nov. 11, 1945.

KERN, John Dwight, college prof.; b. Germantown, O., Sept. 14, 1900; s. Harry and Charlotte Elizabeth (Spring) K.; A.B., Heidelberg Coll., 1922; A.M., Harvard, 1924; Ph.D., Univ. of Pa., 1933; m. Florence Cochrane, Dec. 22, 1927 (divorced 1934); 1 son, John Dwight; m. 2d, Marion Dougherty, Oct. 3, 1936; children—Elizabeth Hunter, Charlotte Spring. Instr. of English, Rensselaer Polytechnic Inst., 1924-26; instr. of English, Temple Univ., Phila., Pa., 1926-27, prof. since 1927, chmn. dept. since 1940. Mem. Modern Lang. Assn., Am. Assn., Univ. Profs., Coll. English Assn., Nat. Council Teachers of English. Democrat. Clubs: Franklin Inn Club, Contemporary, Thirty (Philadelphia). Author: Constance Fenimore Woolson, 1934; Temple Univ. in the War, 1944; co-editor (with Irwin Griggs) This America, 1942; contbr. to Dictionary of Am. Biography. Home: Greene Manor, Greene and Johnson Sts., Philadelphia 44. Died Nov. 24, 1948.

KERN, Walter McCollough, educator; b. Fayetteville, Ind., Aug. 20, 1865; s. Lewis Davis and Virginia (Armstrong) K.; B.S., Southern Ind. Normal Coll., Mitchell, 1886; A.B., State U. of Ind., 1894, A.M., 1909; spent yr. 1911 abroad studying the German sch. system; spl. student in edn., Columbia, 1912; m. Carolyn Evans, Aug. 4, 1909. Supt. schs., David City, Neb., 1894-1901, Columbus, Neb., 1901-05; pres. State Normal and Industrial Sch., Ellendale, N.D., 1905-11; supt. schools, Walla Walla, Wash., 1912-36; mem. State Bd. of Edn., 1927-33. Served on State Vocational Edn. Commn., 1914, State Administrative Code Commn., 1920-21. Assisted in organizing and served as 1st pres. Northwest Assn. of Secondary and Higher Schs. Mem. N.E.A., Inland Empire Educators' Assn., Delta Tau Delta, Phi Beta Kappa. Republican. Conglist. Mason. Clubs: Commercial, Inquiry, Rotary. Author: A Summer Sojourn—France, 1930. Home: 1205 Alvarado, Terrace, Walla Walla, Wash.* Deceased.

KERNAHAN, A(rthur) Earl, clergyman; b. Mellette, S.D., Nov. 3, 1888; s. James and Jennie Elizabeth (Kernahan) K.; prep. edn., Upper Ia. Acad.; B.A., Upper Ia. U., 1911, D.D., 1923; S.T.B., Boston U., 1916; m. Susanna Elizabeth Gough, Sept. 20, 1910; children—Earl Gough, Mildred Ruth, Susanna Mae, Galal Joseph. Ordained ministry M.E. Ch., 1912; pastor Laurel Street Ch., Worcester, Mass., 1915-16, Northampton, Mass., 1917-18, Daniel Dorchester Memorial Ch., Boston, 1919-22; director visitation evangelism campaigns in U.S. since 1922; chautauqua lecturer. Chaplain U.S. Army in active service 7 mos., World War; formerly chaplain Res. Republican. Mason. Mem. Pi Gamma Mu. Originated "Kernahan Directed Survey," 1927, and has conducted religious surveys covering 34,000,000 people; founded visitation evangelism; introduced it into Can.; added 437,502 members to American churches. Author: Visitation Evangelism, 1925; Adventures in Visitation Evangelism, 1928; Christian Citizenship and Visitation Evangelism, 1929; Directed Survey and Visitation Evangelism, 1930; Great Sermons on Evangelism, 1934; Great Sermons for growing Disciples, 1934; Training for Church Membership; also series of 10 pamphlets on Kernahan Visitation Evangelism Campaigns, 1926. Publisher the "Kernahan Directed Survey and Visitation Evangelism Instructions," "The Christian Artisan"; "Unexpressed Christianity and Our Social Crisis"; The Messenger and His Message; Why; A Book for Young Men; What; A Book for Young Women; Sermons in Action. Home: 10510 Euclid Av., Cleveland, O. Died Sep. 16, 1944.

KERNAN, Francis Joseph, army officer; b. Jacksonville, Fla., Oct. 19, 1859; s. John A. and Elizabeth C. (Kernan) K.; grad. U.S. Mil. Acad., 1881; Army War Coll., 1914; m. Ella M. McCaffrey, Mar. 18, 1898; children—Francis Morgan, Katharine, George Morgan, Philip McCaffrey. Commd. 2d lt. 21st Inf., June 11, 1881; promoted through grades to brig. gen., Mar. 23, 1917; maj. gen. N.A., Aug. 5, 1917; major general Regular Army, Oct. 14, 1919. On staff Gen. MacArthur in the Philippines, 1898; judge advocate Dept. Santa Clara, Cuba, and at Cienfuegos, 1899; again aide to Gen. MacArthur in P.I., 1900-03; mem. Gen. Staff Corps, Washington, D.C., 1905-09; in P.I., 1909; comd. 8th Inf. Brigade, El Paso, Tex., Apr. 1917; acting asst. chief of staff, May-Aug. 1917, and drew up official instructions for Gen. Pershing (approved by Sec. of War Baker and President Wilson); apptd. comdr. Camp Wheeler, Macon, Ga., Sept. 1917; organized and comd. Service of Supply in France, Nov. 30, 1917-July 28, 1918. Mem. Am. mission to negotiate convention for treatment, exchange, etc., of prisoners of war and detained civilians with Germans, Berne, Switzerland, July 29-Nov. 11, 1918; tech. mil. adviser to Am. Commn. to Negotiate Peace, Paris, Nov. 1918-Apr. 1919; comdr. Dept. of the Philippines, Nov. 23, 1919-Mar. 6, 1922; retired, Dec. 1, 1922. Clubs: Army and Navy (Washington, D.C.); San Antonio (Tex.). Address: War Dept., Washington, D.C. Deceased.

KERR, Albert Boardman (kûr), lawyer; b. Clearfield, Pa., 1875; s. James and Julia Boardman (Smith) K.; A.B., Yale, 1897; LL.B., New York Law Sch., 1899; m. Rosamond Burr, Oct. 1913; m. 2d, Rosalie Stevens, Nov. 1933; 1 dau., Rosalie Keith Kerr. Began practice in New York City, 1899; member Sage, Kerr & Gray, 1903-05, Zabriskie, Murray, Sage, Kerr, 1905-18, Zabriskie, Sage, Kerr & Gray, 1918-21; European travel, 1921-22, 1923-31; in practice, Washington, 1922; American counsel for Royal Bank of Canada, 1905-21; chief counsel Bur. Industrial Housing and Transportation of U.S. Dept. of Labor, 1918. Chmn. Bannard Campaign Club in campaign of Otto T. Bannard for mayor of N.Y. City, 1910. Mem. Assn. Bar City of

New York. Democrat. Presbyn. Clubs: Union, Metropolitan, Yale (New York); Metropolitan (Washington); Travellers (Paris); Alpha Delta Phi, Skull and Bones (Yale); Authors' (London). Author: Jacques Coeur, Merchant Prince of the Middle Ages, 1927; The Long Crooked River, 1929; Valiant Hearts, 1931. Home: University, Va. Died June 20, 1945.

KERR, Charles, lawyer; b. Maysville, Ky., Dec. 27, 1863; s. Jesse J. and Elizabeth (Alexander) Kerr; ed. under private teachers; LL.D., Transylvania U., 1930; m. Linda Payne, Oct. 27, 1896 (died Dec. 12, 1936); children—Ellen Douglas (dec.), Charles, Margaret, Howard. Began practice at Lexington, 1886; apptd. judge Circuit Court, Lexington Dist., by Gov. A. E. Willson, 1911, elected to same office same yr. and reëlected, 1915, resigned July 1921; judge U.S. Dist. Court, Canal Zone, by apptmt. of President Harding, 1921-22; spl. asst. to atty. gen. of U.S., 1922-25; mem. Esch, Kerr, Taylor & Shipe, Washington, D.C. Counsel for Gov. before Mexican Mixed Claims Commn., 1925. Del. Rep. Nat. Conv., 1908; chmn. Rep. State Conv., Ky., 1919. Formerly law lecturer Transylvania U. and U. of Ky. Mem. Am. Bar Assn., Ky. State Bar Assn., Am. Soc. Internat. Law, English-Speaking Union, Ky. Hist. Soc. Baptist. Mason (K.T.). Clubs: Country (Lexington). Editor of History of Kentucky, 1765-1921 (5 vols.). Author of numerous legal and other publs., including Thirty Years War on the Supreme Court; History of Transylvania Law School Some Great Lawyers of Kentucky; If Spencer Roane Had Been Appointed Chief Justice instead of John Marshall. Chairman arbitration boards in wage disputes between United Brotherhood Maintenance of Way Employees and Louisville and Nashville R.R., 1927, between La. and Ark. Ry. and Ry. Employment Dept. of Am. Fedn. of Labor, 1931, between Brotherhood of Ry. and Steamship Clerks and B.&O. R.R., 1932, between Railway and Steamship Clerks and B.&M. R.R., 1932, between same orgn. and B.&O. R.R., 1933, between same orgn. and B.&M. R.R., 1933, between four brotherhoods and Southern Pacific Lines, 1934; mem. emergency board by apptmt. of President Roosevelt in Southern Pacific labor dispute, 1937. Home: Lexington, Ky. Address: Stoneleigh Court, Washington, D.C.* Died Feb. 15, 1950.

KERR, Charles Volney, mech. engr.; b. Miami County, O., Mar. 27, 1861; s. George W. and Nancy K.; Ph.B., honors in philosophy, Western U. of Pa. (now U. of Pittsburgh), 1884, Ph.M., 1888, hon. Ph.D., 1898; M.E., Stevens Inst. Tech., 1888; m. Libbie Applebee, Dec. 25, 1888; children—Clifton A. (dec.), Vida A. (dec.), Delia A., Volney A., Marion A. (dec.). Instr. mathematics and science, Pratt Inst., 1888-89; asst. prof. mech. engring., Western U. of Pa., 1889-91; prof. engring., Ark. Industrial U., Fayetteville, 1891-96; prof. mech. engring., Armour Inst. Tech., 1896-1902; engr. Westinghouse, Church, Kerr & Co., New York, 1902-04; chief engr. Kerr Turbine Co., Wellsville, N.Y., 1904-10, McEwen Bros., Wellsville, 1910-14; pres. and engr. Kerr Auxiliary Co., Chicago, 1914-16; steam turbine engr. Am. Well Works, Aurora, Ill., 1916-21, Llewellyn Iron Works, 1921-23; pres. Nat. Pump and Motor Co., 1923-24; cons. mech. engr. and inventor of Kerr pumps and blowers and Kerr steam turbine. Mem. Am. Soc. M.E. Contbr. to proceedings of socs. and mags. Home: 418 Ulysses St., Los Angeles, Calif. Died Oct. 31, 1949.

KERR, James Taggart, army officer; b. in Ohio, Apr. 22, 1859; grad. U.S. Mil. Acad., 1881; honor grad. Inf. and Cav. Sch., 1897. Commd. 2d lt. 17th Inf., June 11, 1881; promoted through grades to brig. gen., Oct. 2, 1917. Address: War Dept., Washington. Died Apr. 13, 1949.

KERR, William Jasper, educator; b. Richmond, Utah, Nov. 17, 1863; s. Robert Marion and Nancy J. (Rawlins) K.; student U. of Utah, 1882-85, Cornell U., 1890-91, and summers, 1891, 92, 93; degrees of B.S., LL.D., hon. D.Sc.; married Leonora Hamilton, July 8, 1885. Superintendent schs., Smithfield, Utah, 1885-87; del. Constl. Convs., Salt Lake City, 1887, 95; instr. physiology, geology and physics, 1887-88, instr. mathematics, 1888-90, 1891-92, Brigham Young Coll.; prof. mathematics and astronomy, U. of Utah, 1892-94; pres. Brigham Young Coll., 1894-1900; pres. Utah State Agrl. Coll., 1900-07; pres. Ore. State Agrl. Coll., 1907-32; chancellor higher edn. in Ore., 1932-35, chancellor emeritus since 1935. Chmn. bd. dirs. Northwestern Portland Cement Co. Chmn. Ore. com. Nat. Student Forum. First v.p. Land Grant Coll. Assn., 1909-10, pres., 1910-11; mem. N.E.A. (v.p. 1909-10), Nat. Council Edn., A.A.A.S. Presbyterian. Mason (33°, K.T., Shriner). Mem. Grand Council, Order of DeMolay and active member in Oregon since 1921; grand master of the Grand Council, 1944-45. Home: 1633 N.E. Knott St., Portland 12, Ore. Died Mar. 15, 1947; buried in Masonic Cemetery, Corvallis, Wash.

KETCHAM, Heber Dwight, clergyman; b. Kenton, O., Dec. 29, 1858; s. Charles Wesley and Mary Dyer (Parkison) K.; A.B., Ohio Wesleyan U., 1881, A.M., 1887; B.D., Drew Theol. Sem., 1884; D.D., Miami U., Oxford, O., 1903; m. Bertha McVay, Oct. 14, 1890; children—Maria (Mrs. Harry L. Heinzman), Bertha L. (Mrs. O. Otis Bowman), Emily Livingston (Mrs. Harold Stamm). Ordained to ministry of Methodist Episcopal Church, 1884; pastor Blanchester (O.) circuit, 1884-86, Mt. Washington and Red Bank, Cincinnati, 1886-89, Wilmington, 1889-1892, Clifton Ch., Cincinnati, 1892-95, Hillsboro, 1895-97, Piqua, 1897-1901; presiding elder Dayton Dist., 1901-06; pastor Trinity Ch., Cincinnait, 1906-09. First M.E. Ch., Knoxville, Tenn., 1909-11, First M.E. Ch., Kankakee, Ill., 1911-15, State St. M.E. Ch., Trenton, N.J., 1915-20, High St. M.E. Ch., Muncie, Ind., 1920-24, First M.E. Ch., Fairmont, W.Va., 1924-30, First M.E. Ch., Parkersburg, W.Va., since 1930. Pres. Epworth League of Ohio and Ky., 1893-96; sec. Ohio Meth. Centennial, 1898; mem. Gen. Conf. M.E. Ch., 1904. Mem. Delta Tau Delta. Chaplain W.Va. Chapter S.R. Republican. Mason (K.T., Scottish Rite). Rotarian. Author: Certainty of the Kingdom, 1905. Contbr. to church publs. Home: 1000 Juliana St., Parkersburg, W.Va. Died Feb. 12, 1944.

KETCHAM, Victor Alvin, educator; b. in Monroe Twp., Perry County, O., Aug. 7, 1883; s. Lincoln Hamlin and Mary Evaline (Norris) K.; student Ohio University, 1902-03, 1903-04; B.A., Ohio State University, 1907, LL.B., 1910; married May Clare Richards, September 6, 1911 (died December 17, 1944); 1 son, Victor Alvin. Mem. bar State of Ohio; instr. English, U. of Me., 1910-12, U. of Ill., 1912-13; asst. prof. English, Ohio State U., 1913-17, prof. English, 1917-36, prof. speech since 1936, chmn. dept., 1936-43. Mem. Am. Assn. Univ. Profs., Nat. Assn. Teachers of Speech, Ohio Society of New York, Delta Sigma Rho. Club: Faculty. Author: The Theory and Practice of Argumentation and Debate, 1914; The Course in Effective Talking, 1922; Titles of Lectures; Speech Efficiency; Persuasive Power; Tact and Skill in Argument; Extempore Speaking; The Public Address: Make a Good Speech, 1947; (lecture) The Seven Doors to the Mind. Home: 199 E. Webber Rd., Columbus, O. Died July 20, 1947.

KEY, Pierre van Rensselaer, editor; b. Grand Haven, Mich., Aug. 28, 1872; s. Francis Brute Englebert and Martha Louise (Ketchum) K.; ed. pvt. schs. and Chicago Musical Coll.; m. Gertrude Elaine Boltwood, Mar. 31, 1907. Began as asst. music critic, Chicago Times-Herald, 1898, later music and dramatic critic, Chicago American, and city editor and night editor Chicago Examiner; music editor New York World, 1907-19; now editor The Musical Digest (monthly music mag.). Contbr. weekly article on musical affairs to newspapers, U.S. and Canada, also critical revs., essays, etc., to mags. Republican. Episcopalian. Clubs: Lotos, Bohemians. Author: John McCormack—His Own Life Story, 1919; Enrico Caruso's Biography, 1922; This Business of Singing, 1937; Pierre Key's Music Year Book (published annually) and Pierre Key's Musical Who's Who (published every four years). Pub. Pierre Key's Radio Annual. Lecturer and mem. faculty Juilliard Sch. of Music, N.Y. City. Dir. of radio programs and radio commentator and speaker. Home: Park Central Hotel, 55th St. and 7th Av. Office: 119 W. 57th St., New York, N.Y. Died Nov. 28, 1945.

KEYES, Charles Rollin, geologist; b. Des Moines, Ia., Dec. 24, 1864; s. Calvin W. and Julia (Davis) K.; B.S., State U. of Ia., 1887, A.M., 1890; Ph.D., Johns Hopkins, 1892; unmarried. Asst. U.S. Geol. Survey, 1889-90; palæontologist of Mo., 1890-92; asst. state geologist of Ia., 1892-94; dir. Mo. Geol. Survey, 1894-97; geol. travel in Europe, Asia and Africa, 1897-98; pres. N.M. State Sch. of Mines, 1902-06; foreign travel, 1906-07, 1926; pres. and gen. mgr. mining cos. and other corps.; consulting mining engr. since 1890. Editor of Pan-American Geologists since 1922. Fellow Geol. Soc. America, A.A.A.S., Am. Inst. Mining Engrs., Mining and Metall. Soc. America, Ia. Acad. Sciences, St. Louis Acad. Sciences, etc. Dem. nominee for U.S. senator, 1918. Author: Geological Formations, 1892; Coal Deposits, 1893; Organization of Geological Surveys, 1894; Palæontology of Missouri, 1894; Maryland Granites, 1895; Origin and Classification of Ore Deposits, 1900; Genesis of Lake Valley Silver Deposits, 1907; Ozark Lead and Zinc Deposits, 1909; Deflation, 1910; Mid-Continental Eolation, 1911; Bibliography of Geology, 1913; Mechanics of Laccolithic Intrusion, 1922; Orogenic Consequences of a Diminishing Rate of Earth's Rotation, 1922; Astronomical Theory of Glaciation, 1925; numerous memoirs and essays; also contributor to scientific, tech. and ednl. jours. Home: 944 5th Av., Des Moines, Ia.; (winter) Avalon, Oracle Rd., Tucson, Ariz. Died May 18, 1942.

KEYES, Edward Loughborough, urologist; b. Elizabeth, N.J., May 15, 1873; s. Edward Lawrence and Sarah M. (Loughborough) K.; A.B., Georgetown (D.C.) U., 1892, Ph.D., 1901; M.D., Coll. Phys. and Surg. (Columbia), 1895; m. Emma W. Scudder, Nov. 17, 1898; children—Edward Lawrence, Emma Willard, Elizabeth Hewlett, Alexander Loughborough; m. 2d, Bessie Potter Vonnoh, June 1919. Lecturer on urology, Georgetown Med. Sch., 1902-06; adj. prof. urology New York Polyclinic Med. Sch., 1903-08; lecturer on surgery, Cornell U. Med. Sch., 1904-10; surgeon St. Vincent's Hosp., 1905-20, urologist, 1920-32; urologist, N.Y. Hosp., 1932-37; prof. urology, Bellevue Med. Sch., 1910-11, Cornell U. Med. Sch., 1911-37; urologist Bellevue Hosp., 1910-24; surgeon Gen. Memorial Hosp., 1914-17; formerly cons. urologist Memorial, Bellevue, New York, St. Vincent's hosps.; retired 1939. Maj. Med. R.C., 1917, and dir. Base Hosp. No. 1; lt. col. M.C.N.A., and col. M.C., 1918, and consultant in urology, A.E.F.; col. M.R.C., 1919. Decorated Officer Legion of Honor (France), 1935. Fellow American Coll. Surgeons; hon. fellow Royal Coll. Surgeons (London); hon. member English College Surgeons, 1936; mem. Am. Assn. of Genito-Urinary Surgeons (pres. 1912), Soc. Sanitary and Moral Prophylaxis (pres. 1913-14), A.M.A., Internat. Urol. Soc. (pres. 1927-36), Clin. Urol. Assn. (pres. 1923-24), Am. Urol. Assn. (pres. 1915), Am. Social Hygiene Assn. (pres. 1923-25), New York Acad. Medicine (v.p. 1921-23). Clubs: Century, Charaka; Southside Sportsman's (Islip, L.I.). Author: Genito-Urinary Diseases, 1903, '10; Urology, 1917; A Sea Change, 1939. Contbr. to med. jours. Home: 33 W. 67th St., N.Y. City. Died Mar. 16, 1949; buried Gate of Heaven Cemetery, White Plains, N.Y.

KEYNES, John Maynard (kānz), economist; b. Cambridge, Eng., June 5, 1883; s. Neville and Florence Ada (Brown) K.; student Eton Sch.; M.A. (and highest grad. honors), King's Coll.; Cambridge U. (Eng.); Dr. (hon.), U. of Oslo (Norway); Columbia; m. Lydia Lopokova, 1925. In Brit. govtl. service, India Office, 1906-08; mem. Royal Commn. on Indian Finance and Currency, 1913-14; with Brit. Treasury, 1915-19, prin. clerk, 1917-19, and prin. rep. at Paris Peace Conf., 1919; also dep. of chancellor of exchequer on Supreme Allied Econ. Council; mem. Com. on Finance and Industry, 1929-31; editor Econ. Jour. (Eng.); 1912-44; lecturer, King's Coll., Cambridge, many years. Created 1st Baron of Tilton, 1942. Fellow British Academy; fellow and bursar, King's College; dir. Bank of England; mem. Economic Advisory Council; chmn. Arts Theatre, Cambridge; pres. Cambridge Union Soc., 1905; chmn. Arts Council of Great Brit. Pres. Royal Econ. Soc. Awarded Order of Leopold (Belgium), Order of St. Sava (4th Class) (Serbia). Author: Indian Currency and Finance, 1913; The Economic Consequences of the Peace, 1920; Treatise on Probability, 1921; Revision of the Treaty, 1922; Monetary Reform, 1924; Laissez-Faire and Communism, 1926; Treatise on Money, 1930; Unemployment as a World Problem (with Karl Pribram and E. J. Phelan), 1931; Essays in Persuasion, 1932; Essays in Biography, 1933; Means to Prosperity, 1933; General Theory of Employment, Interest and Money, 1936; How to Pay for the War, 1940. Address: King's Coll., Cambridge; 46 Gordon Sq., London W.C. 1, Eng. Died Apr. 21, 1946.

KEYS, Noel, psychologist, univ. prof.; b. Beloit, Kan., May 13, 1893; s. William James and Alice (Dodge) K.; A.B., Coll. of Emporia, Kan., 1916; Rhodes Scholar, Oxford U., Eng., B.A., 1918; M.A., U. of Chicago, 1921; Ph.D., Columbia U., 1928; m. Marian Gratia Wiley, Aug. 11, 1928; children—Carol (dec.), Noel Wiley. Instr. in psychology, Lingnan U., Canton, China, 1919-20; asst. prof. edn., 1921-23, asso. prof. and dir. Coll. Preparatory, Lingnan U., 1923-25; asso. prof. ednl. psychology, Syracuse U., 1927-28; asso. prof. edn., U. of Calif., 1928-38, prof. since 1938; lecturer in human relations, U. of Calif., conducting "Youth and Marriage" courses on and off the campus since 1939; vis. prof., Cornell U., U. of Southern Calif., Pacific Sch. of Religion, Utah State Agr. Coll., Kansas U., Syracuse U. Served with Brit. East African Expeditionary Force, 1917-18. Fellow A.A.A.S., Soc. for Research in Child Development, Am. Psychol. Assn.; mem. Am. Assn. Marriage Counselors, Am. Ednl. Research Assn., National Conference on Family Relations, Northern California Council for Exceptional Children (pres. 1936-38), Family Relations Conf. of Northern Calif. (pres. 1942-43), Nat. Ednl. Com. of Am. Social Hygiene Assn., Phi Delta Kappa, Kappa Delta Pi, Kappa Phi Kappa. Presbyterian. Author: English Mastery Tests, 1923; The Improvement of Measurement Through Cumulative Testing, 1928; The Under-Age Student in High School and College, 1938. Contbr. to various scientific jours. Home: 828 Arlington Av., Berkeley 7, Calif. Died Apr. 9, 1948.

KEYSER, Cassius Jackson (kī'sēr), mathematician; b. Rawson, O., May 15, 1862; s. Jacob B. and Margaret Jane (Ryan) K.; B.S., Ohio Normal U., 1883; studied law, Ann Arbor, Mich., and Kenton, O., 1883-85; B.S., U. of Mo., 1892; student summer sch., U. of Mich., 1894; A.M., Columbia, 1896; Ph.D., 1902; LL.D., U. of Mo., 1914; Sc.D., Columbia, 1929; L.H.D., Yeshiva Coll., 1942; m. Ella Maud Crow, Aug. 19, 1885; m. 2d, Sarah Porter Youngman, Apr. 26, 1929. Prin. and supt. pub. schs., Ohio and Mo., 1885-90; instr. mathematics, U. of Mo., 1891-92, State Summer Schools, Kirksville, Mo., 1892; apptd. Thayer scholar in mathematics, Harvar 1892; prof. mathematics, State Normal Sch., New Paltz, N.Y., 1892-94; instr. mathematics, Smith Acad., Washington U., St. Louis, 1894-95, Barnard Coll., 1897-1900; tutor, Columbia U., 1897-1900, instr., 1900-03, adj. prof., 1903-04, Adrain prof. mathematics, 1904-27, head of dept., 1910-16, Adrain prof. emeritus since 1927, instr., summer sessions, 1900-07; prof. mathematics, U. of Calif., 1911, 15, exchange prof., 1916. Fellow A.A.A.S.; mem. Am. Math. Soc. Author: Mathematical Philosophy, etc. Asso. editor of Scripta Mathematica. Home: 50 Morningside Dr., New York, N.Y. Died May 8, 1947.

KIDD, Isaac Campbell, naval officer; b. Cleveland, O., Mar. 26, 1884; s. Isaac and Jemima (Campbell) K.; B.S., U.S. Naval Acad., 1906; attended Naval War Coll., 1936-38; m. Inez Gillmore, Apr. 29, 1911; children—Nereide (dec.), Isaac Campbell (midshipman, U.S. Navy). Became midshipman, 1902; served as passed midshipman on cruiser Columbia, which carried Marine Expeditionary Force to Canal Zone, and participated in Cuban Pacification, 1906; on U.S.S. New Jersey during round-the-world cruise of fleet, 1907-09; 1st lt., U.S.S. Pittsburgh, during Mexican disturbance, 1913-14; on staff comdr.-in-chief Pacific Fleet, 1914-16; promoted to comdr. and served as gunnery officer on U.S.S. New Mexico, later on staff of comdr.-in-chief Atlantic Fleet, during World War; exec. officer U.S.S. Utah, 1925-26;

comdg. officer U.S.S. Vega, 1926-27; on duty at Panama Canal, 1927-30, serving as capt. of Port of Cristobal, chmn. Bd. of Inspection and Survey, and actg. marine sup. Panama Canal; promoted to capt., 1930; chief of staff Base Force, U.S. Fleet, 1930-32; officer personnel assignments with Bur. of Navigation, Navy Dept., 1932-35, comdr. Destroyer Squadron One, U.S. Fleet, 1935-36; comdg. officer U.S.S. Arizona, 1938-39; selected rear admiral, 1939; chief of staff, Battleships, U.S. Fleet, 1940-41; comdr. Battleship Div., U.S. Fleet, since 1941. Served as Asso. Press corr., 1914-15, 1916; editor Proceedings, U.S. Naval Inst., 1917. Awarded Cuban Pacification Medal, 1906, Mexican Campaign Medal, 1916, World War Victory Medal with bronze star and bar, 1919. Mem. U.S. Naval Inst. Episcopalian. Clubs: New York Yacht; Los Angeles Athletic, Jonathan (Los Angeles); Pacific Coast (Long Beach, Calif.). Killed in action Pearl Harbor, Hawaii, Dec. 7, 1941.

KIDDE, Walter (kĭd), mech. engr.; b. in N.J., Mar. 7, 1877; s. F. E. and Mary O. (Lang) K.; M.E., Stevens Institute of Technology, 1897; E.D., 1935; Sc.D., Rutgers University, 1941; m. Louise Carter, October 22, 1902; children—Walter Lawrence, John Frederick, Mary (Mrs. W. E. Morgan). Practiced engineering at New York City since 1900; now pres. Walter Kidde & Co., Walter Kidde Constructors; dir. Vreeland Corp., Hudson Trust Co., of Union City, N.J., Firemen's Ins. Co. of Newark, Prudential Ins. Co.; trustee N.Y., Susquehanna & Western R.R. since 1937. Chmn. joint water com. which originated a comprehensive plan for water supply for Northern N.J., 1908; mem. N.J. advisory bd. U. S. Pub. Works Adminstrn., 1933; mem. N.J. State Highway Commn., 1922-26. Trustee Stevens Inst. Tech. (chmn. bd. 1928-35); treas. N.J. Conf. Social Work, 1917-38; v.p. N.J. Welfare Council; mem. N.J. State Sanatorium for Tuberculosis, 1914-18. Mem. Am. Soc. M.E., United Engring. Trustees (chmn. finance com.), Newcomen Soc. of Eng., N.Y. State Chamber Commerce (arbitration com.), N.J. State Chamber of Commerce (president 1935-37; vice-pres. and chmn. Cost of Govt. Com.; was chmn. State Com. to Make Zoning Effective, 1929). Episcopalian; sr. warden St. Luke's Ch., Montclair; v.p. Brotherhood of St. Andrew in U.S.A., 1900-38; mem. Nat. Council of P.E. Ch. (mem. trust fund com.). Clubs: Whitehall (New York); Essex (Newark, N.J.); Nat. Golf Links (Southampton); Yeaman Hall (Charleston, S.C.); Montclair Golf, Quantuck Beach. Home: 56 Gates Av., Montclair, N.J. Office: 140 Cedar St., New York, N.Y. Died Feb. 9, 1943.

KIEFER, Dixie, naval officer; b. Apr. 4, 1896; entered U.S. Navy, 1915, and advanced through the grades to capt., 1942; later commodore (temporary); naval aviator. Decorated Navy Cross, D.S.M. (Navy). Died in airplane crash, Nov. 11, 1945.*

KIEHNEL, Richard (kē'nĕl), architect; b. Germany, Nov. 1, 1870; s. Edward and Matilda (Spreuer) K.; grad. Sch. of Architecture, Breslau, Germany, 1891; student Sch. of Fine Arts, Breslau, 1891, Acad. of Fine Arts, Berlin, 1892, Ecole Nationale des Beaux Arts, Paris, 1902; m. Jessie Mayer, May 5, 1915. Came to U.S., 1892, naturalized, 1898. Began as archtl. designer in Chicago, 1892; in private practice, 1898-1902; designer for Eagan & Prindeville, 1902; designer and asso. of J. Milton Dyer, Cleveland, 1902-03, F. J. Oesterling, Pittsburgh, 1903-05; practiced as Kiehnel & Elliott, in Pittsburgh, 1906-28, Miami office since 1917. Awarded Gold Medal Declaration of Honor by Rollins Coll., Winter Park, Fla., 1941. Fellow A.I.A.; mem. Fla. Assn. of Architects. Mason (32°, Shriner, K.T.). Clubs: Century of Miami; Pittsburgh Architectural. Editor of Florida Architecture and Allied Arts, 1935-42. Home: 5942 Biscayne Blvd. Office: Seybold Bldg., Miami 32, Fla. Died Nov. 3, 1944.

KIEL, Henry William (kēl), ex-mayor; b. St. Louis, Mo., Feb. 21, 1871; s. Henry F. and Minnie C. (Daues) K.; ed. pub. schs. and Smith Acad.; m. Irene H. Moonan, Sept. 1, 1892; children—Mrs. Henrietta Hogan, Elmer A., Clarence V., Edna N. Learned bricklayer's trade under father and has ever since been identified with that industry; now pres. Kiel & Daues Bricklaying and Contracting Co. (established 1868); pres. Boaz-Kiel Constrn. Co. (gen. contractors); has executed many important contracts in St. Louis. Chmn. Rep. City Com.; chmn. 12th Congressional Com. of St. Louis; presdl. elector at large, Missouri, 1908; mayor of St. Louis, 3 terms, 1913-25; pres. St. Louis Bd. of Police Commrs., 1931-32; Rep. nominee for U.S. Senate, 1932; now chmn. St. Louis Public Service Co. Lutheran. Mason (32°). Mem. I.O.O.F., K.P., Moose, Royal Arcanum, Sons of Vets. Home: 1625 Missouri Av. Office: 3869 Park Av., St. Louis, Mo. Died Nov. 26, 1942.

KIELY, John J., postmaster N.Y. City since Jan. 19, 1929; mem. bd. mgrs. Citizens Savings & Loan Assn. Address: General Post Office, New York. Died Aug. 23, 1940.

KIES, William Samuel (kez), banker, retired; b. Mapleton, Minn., Dec. 2, 1877; s. Christian L. and Bertha A. (Steeps) K.; B.L., Univ. of Wis., 1899, LL.B., 1901, M.A. (hon.), 1937; m. Mabel Best, July 12, 1905; children—Margaret Kies Gibb, William S., John H. With legal department Chicago City Railway, 1901-03; trial attorney City of Chicago, 1903-05; gen. atty. C.&N.-W. Ry., 1905-10, acting as counsel in condemnation proceedings Chicago terminals of that road; gen. counsel Chicago & Western Ind. R.R. and Belt Ry. Co. of Chicago, 1910-13; spl. counsel Chicago Park Commn. and State treasurer of Illinois; removed to New York, 1913, to organize foreign trade dept. of Nat. City Bank of New York, and organized and directed fgn. branch extensions in S. America; v.p. of the bank, Sept. 1915-Jan. 1918; v.p. Am. Internat. Corp., 1916-20; organized, 1921, first Federal Foreign Banking Assn., first Edge Bill bank in U.S., and was chmn. bd. and exec. com.; organized W. S. Kies & Co., pvt. bankers, 1925. Has served on bds. of U.S. Rubber Co., Indsl. Alcohol Co., Am. Comml. Alcohol Corp., N.Y. Shipbuilding Co., Pacific Mail Co., Allied Machinery Co., Union Bag & Paper Corp., Savage Arms Corp.; now dir. and mem. exec. com., Bangor & Arostook R.R. Co., Am. Steel Export Co., W. Va. Coal & Coke Corp., Ohio River Co. A Founder, trustee, and chmn. investment com., Wis. Alumni Research Foundation. Pres. Endowment Fund Trustee of Kappa Sigma. Decorated Order of Polonia Restituta (Poland). Member Council on Foreign Relations, C. of C., State of N.Y. Phi Beta Kappa, Coif, Kappa Sigma, Delta Sigma Rho; Cloud, Megantic Fish & Game Corp. Republican. Clubs: University, India House, Sleepy Hollow, Blind Brook, Metropolitan. Has written numerous articles on foreign trade. Home: Scarborough, N.Y. Office: Graybar Bldg., New York 17. Died Feb. 2, 1950.

KILBY, Clinton Maury, physicist; b. Suffolk, Va., Nov. 1, 1874; s. Wallace and Margaret (Tynes) K.; grad. Suffolk (Va.) Mil. Acad., 1892; A.M., Randolph-Macon Coll., Ashland, Va., 1896; studied U. of Chicago, summer, 1903, Columbia, summer, 1904; Ph.D., Johns Hopkins, 1909; m. Jean McDonald Graham, June 11, 1912. Instr. mathematics, Randolph-Macon Coll., 1894-96; prin. pub. schs., 1896-98; master in mathematics and physics, Woodberry Forest Sch., 1898-1905; lecture asst. in physics, Johns Hopkins, 1908-09; instr. physics, Lehigh U., 1909-10; prof. physics and astronomy, Randolph-Macon Woman's Coll., since 1910. Fellow A.A.A.S.; mem. Am. Assn. Physics Teachers, Am. Phys. Soc., Optical Soc. America, Va. Acad. of Science, Phi Beta Kappa, Phi Delta Theta, Gamma Alpha. Democrat. Methodist. Club: Sphex. Author: Laboratory Manual of Physics, 1912; The Constellations, 1918; Definitions and Fundamentals of Physics, 1921; Introduction to College Physics, 1929, Elements of Optics, 1943; Redetermination of Wave-lengths of the Arc and Spark Lines of Titanium, Manganese and Vanadium; The Effect of Capacity and Self-induction on the Wave-lengths of the Spark Lines. Author of Genealogy of Kilby, Tynes, etc. Home: 345 Norfolk Av., Lynchburg, Va. Died March 13, 1948.

KILBY, Thomas Erby, ex-governor; b. Lebanon, Tenn., July 9, 1865; s. Peyton Phillips and Sarah Ann (Marchant) K.; ed. pub. schs.; hon. LL.D., U. of Ala., 1921; m. Mary Clark, June 5, 1894; children—Anne Horry (Mrs. Gilbert E. Porter, III), Oscar M., Thos. E. In mfg. business at Anniston since 1890; now pres. Kilby Steel Company; chmn. bd. Alabama Pipe Co. (Anniston). Mayor of Anniston 2 terms, 1905-09; mem. Ala. Senate, 1911-15; lt. gov. of Ala., 1915-19; gov. of Ala., 1919-23. Democrat. Episcopalian. Mason (32°, Shriner), K.P. Home: Anniston, Ala. Died Oct. 22, 1943.

KILGORE, Benjamin Wesley (kĭl'gōr), chemist; b. Lafayette County, Miss., Mar. 27, 1867; s. Benjamin Moon and Susan (Bruce) K.; B.S., Agrl. Coll. of Miss., 1888, M.S., 1891; spl. work in chemistry, Johns Hopkins; Sc.D., Davidson (N.C.) Coll., 1918; m. Elizabeth Carrington Dinwiddie, Aug. 10, 1898; children—Elizabeth Carrington, Benjamin Wesley, James Dinwiddie. Asst. prof. chemistry, Agrl. Coll., Miss., 1888-89; asst. chemist N.C. Agrl. Expt. Sta., 1889-97; prof. chemistry, Agrl. Coll. of Miss., and state chemist, Miss., 1897-99; state chemist N.C., 1899-1919, and since 1937; dir. N.C. Agrl. Expt. Sta., 1901-07 and 1912-25; dir. N.C. Extension Service, 1914-25; dean of agr., N.C. Coll. of Agr. and Engring., 1923-25; pres. N.C. Cotton Growers' Coöp. Assn., 1924-34; pres. Am. Cotton Exchange, 1924-26; pres. Assn. Official Agrl. Chemists in U.S., 1899-1900. Editor Progressive Farmer, 1928-30. U.S. del. to Internat. Inst. of Agr., Rome, Italy, 1924; sec. Assn. of Southern Agrl. Workers, 1899-1911. Received "award for distinguished service to Southern Agr." from Assn. of Southern Agrl. Workers, 1939; "award for distinguished service to organized agr." from Am. Farm Bureau Fed., 1939. Home: 1507 Hillsboro St. Office: N.C. Dept. of Agriculture, Raleigh, N.C. Died Dec. 27, 1943.

KILHAM, Walter H., architect; b. Beverly, Mass., Aug. 30, 1868; s. Charles H. and Maria Frances (Ober) K.; S.B., Mass. Inst. Tech., 1889; m. Jane Houston, June 16, 1896; children—Jeannette (wife of John Lewis Goldstone), Teresa, Walter H., Peter, Aline (wife of Dr. Eliot F. Porter), Lawrence. Instr. architecture, Mass. Inst. Tech., 1889-91; draftsman, 1891-93; traveled Europe as holder Rotch traveling scholarship, 1893-95; archtl. practice since 1898. Sec. Class of 1889, Mass. Inst. Tech. Fellow Am. Inst. Architects; mem. Copley Soc., Boston (pres.); Boston Soc. Architects (historiographer), Bostonian Soc., Mass. Historical Society, Society Colonial Wars, Essex Inst., Brookline Hist. Soc., Beverly Hist. Soc. Clubs: Brookline Thursday; Union of Boston. Author: Mexican Architecture of the Vice-Regal Period, 1927; Boston After Bulfinch—Architecture from 1800 to 1900, 1946. Home: 42 W. Cedar St., Boston 14. Office: 126 Newbury St., Boston 16, Mass. Died Sept. 11, 1948.

KILMER, Theron Wendell, physician; b. Chicago, Ill., Mar. 7, 1872; s. Chauncey and Antoinelle (Wendell) K.; student Coll. City of New York, 1889-92; M.D., Coll. Physicians and Surgeons (Columbia), 1895; m. Angie Ransom, Jan. 5, 1898; children—Gladys Kilmer, Theron Wendell Kilmer, Jr. Practicing medicine in New York since 1895. Asst. attending physician out-patient dept., St. Vincent's Hosp., 1895; asst. attending surgeon, St. Bartholomew's Clinic, and of Met. Throat Hosp., 1895; attending physician, diseases of children, West Side Dispensary, 1901; asso. prof. diseases of children, N.Y. Sch. Clin. Med., 1901; asso. prof. pediatric dept., N.Y. Polyclinic Med. Sch. Hosp., 1902; attending physician Halsey Day Nursery, 1902, Summer Home of St. Giles the Cripple, Garden City, N.Y., 1903; asst. attending phys. out-patient dept., Babies' Hosp., 1902; asst. attending physician Suydenham Hosp., Dispensary (dept. diseases of children), and adj. attending pediatrist to Suydenham Hosp., 1905. Lecturer, Dept. of Edn., New York, 1898-1921; medical dir. of Soc. of First Aid to the Injured, New York. Commd. surgeon (rank of maj.), 22d Regt.; Nat. Guard, N.Y., 1906. Police surgeon of Hempstead, L.I., N.Y.; mem. Nassau County Police Conf. Mem. Assn. Mil. Surgeons U.S., Nat. Assn. Police and Fire Surgeons, A.M.A., Nassau County and N.Y. State med. assns., Alpha Delta Phi; surgeon N.Y. State Assn. Chiefs of Police; associate mem. Internat. Assn. Chiefs of Police. Episcopalian. Republican. Club: Union League (N.Y.) Author: Practical Care of the Baby, 1903; Physical Examination of Infants and Young Children, 1905. Address: Hempstead, N.Y. Died July 31, 1946.

KILPATRICK, Walter Kenneth, navy officer; b. N.Y. City, Oct. 29, 1887; s. Walter Fisher and Margaret Humphrey (Holmes) K.; B.S., U.S. Naval Acad., 1908; Naval War Coll., 1922-23; Army War Coll., 1927-28; m. Ethel Studley, Nov. 30, 1925. Promoted from midshipman, 1908, through grades to rear adm., 1942; served in Asiatic, Atlantic, and Pacific fleets; comd. U.S.S. Doyen, Hatfield, Bushnell, Chester; on duty with Navy Dept. Boston, New York, Hawaii, San Francisco; flag sec. Asiatic fleet; chief of staff, 14th Naval Dist., 12th Naval Dist. Western Sea Frontier, Atlantic Fleet. Awarded Distinguished Service Medal, Legion of Merit with two stars; Nicaragua, World War, Haitian, Yangtze, Atlantic Area campaign medals. Home: 404 Roehampton Rd., Hillsborough, Calif. Died Sept. 26, 1949.

KIMBALL, Everett, coll. prof.; b. Worcester, Mass., Oct. 6, 1873; s. A.S. and Eleanor (Everett) K.; A.B., Amherst, 1896, A.M., 1899; A.M., Harvard, 1902, Ph.D., 1904; LL.D., Smith College, 1947; married Elizabeth L. McGrew, June 18, 1906; children—McGrew, Everett, Harrison. Assistant in history, Harvard, 1902-03; instructor history, Wellesley College, 1903-04; instructor history, Smith Coll., 1904-05, asso. prof., 1905-14, prof. history, 1914-19, prof. govt., 1919-42; also dir. Smith Coll. Sch. for Social Work, 1921-43; lecturer in history, Mt. Holyoke Coll., 1906-09. Editor: Bury's Students' History of Greece, 1907. Joint Editor: A History Syllabus for Secondary Schools, 1904. Author: The Public Life of Joseph Dudley, 1911; The National Government of the United States, 1919; State and Municipal Government in the United States, 1921; United States Government, 1924. Co-author of A Reference History of the World, 1920 and 1934, editor of same, 1920-41. Contbr. to Cyclo. of Am. Government, 1914, to The League of Nations, the Principle and Practice, 1919. Home: Northampton, Mass. Died July 25, 1948.

KIMBALL, James Henry, meteorologist; b. Detroit, Mich., Feb. 12, 1874; s. Charles Henry and Alice (Jordan) K.; student Mich. Agrl. Coll., 1891-94, B.S., 1912; studied U. of Mich., 1894-95; M.A., U. of Richmond, Va., 1914; Ph.D., New York U., 1926; hon. Sc.D., Mich. State Coll., 1934; unmarried. With U.S. Weather Bureau since 1895, serving in all sections of U.S. and in West Indies; now in charge New York office, U.S. Weather Bureau; meteorol. adviser, New York, for French High Commn., and instr. for flying units, 1917-18; faculty lecturer on aeronautical meteorology, New York U., 1941. Fellow Am. Meteorological Society, Inst. of Aeronautical Sciences; member New York Acad. of Sciences, Nat. Institute of Social Sciences (v.p.), D'Honneur Ligue Internationale des Aviateurs. Awarded scroll of honor with gold medal, City of N.Y.; Officers Cross Order Polonia Restituta; Chevalier Legion of Honor, France; Commandatore of the Crown of Italy. Republican. Episcopalian. Prepared first North Atlantic weather maps for transatlantic flying; cons. meteorologist for Lindbergh and subsequent Am. and European transatlantic fliers. Home: 39½ Washington Sq. Address: U.S. Weather Bureau, 17 Battery Pl., New York, N.Y. Died Dec. 21, 1943.

KIMBALL, Katharine, artist, etcher; b. Fitzwilliam, N.H., 1866; d. John Richardson and Catherine Otis (Fulham) Kimball; ed. Jersey Ladies' Coll., Channel Islands; studied art, Nat. Acad. Design, New York; Royal Coll. of Art, Sch. of Engraving, London; pupil of Sir Frank Short, R.A. Exhibited at Royal Acad., London; Royal Soc. Painters, Etchers and Engravers; Salon des Artistes Français and Salon d'Automne, Paris; Art Inst. Chicago; Anglo-Am. Exhbn., London, 1914; Pa. Acad. Fine Arts, Phila., 1925; Internat. Exhbn. Brooklyn Soc. Etchers; Canadian Nat. Exhbn., Toronto, 1924; etc. Awarded bronze medal for etching, San Francisco Expn., 1915. Represented in British Museum, Victoria and Albert Museum, London; New York Pub. Library; Boston Art Museum; Congressional Library, Washington, D.C.; Pa. Museum of Art (Phila.); Oakland (Calif.) Pub. Museum; Newark (N.J.) Pub. Library; Victoria Museum, Melbourne, Australia; Bristol (Eng.) Museum

Municipal Library and Victoria Gallery, Bath, Somerset; Bibliotheque d'art et d'archéologie, Paris. Mem. Chicago Soc. Etchers; associate mem. Royal Soc. of Painter-Etchers and Engravers. Illustrator: Okey's Paris, 1905; Gilliat Smith's Brussels, 1906; Sterling Taylor's Canterbury, 1912; Rochester (Artist Sketch Book Series), 1912; also numerous illustrations in mags. Address: care Brown, Shipley & Co., 123 Pall Mall, London, S.W. 1, England. Died Mar. 19, 1949.

KIMBALL, Philip Horatio, educator; b. Gorham, Me., Aug. 30, 1890; s. Charles Henry and Carrie Tewksbury (Fogg) K.; A.B., Bowdoin, 1911; Ed.M., Harvard, 1927; Ed.D., New York U., 1939; m. Geraldine Elaine Gerrish; 1 son, Richard Stanley. Prin., Smith Acad., Hatfield, Mass., 1911-12; instr. high sch., Westbrook, Me., 1912-13; salesman McLean, Black & Co., Boston, Mass., 1913-14; prin. high sch., Charlemont, 1914-16; headmaster high sch., Peterboro, N.H., 1916-19, Lebanon, N.H., 1919-20; prin. high sch., Brunswick, Me., 1920-24, supt. schs., 1924-27; prin. Washington State Normal Sch., Machias, since 1927. Mem. N.E.A., Supervisors of Student Teaching, New Eng. Teacher Preparation Assn. (sec. 1937; pres. 1938), Me. Teachers Assn. (v.p. 1931, pres. 1934), Cumberland County Teachers Assn. (pres.), Machias Chamber Commerce (pres.), Kappa Sigma. Republican. Conglist. Mason, Odd Fellow. Home: Machias, Maine. Died July 3, 1942.

KIMBALL, Ralph Horace, business exec.; b. Danvers, Mass., May 3, 1886; s. Frank B. and Annie F. (Goodwin) K.; grad. Salem Commercial Sch., 1904; LL.B., Nat. Law Sch., Washington, D.C., 1911, LL.M., 1912; m. Maude E. Heagy, June 24, 1911. Male stenographer Bureau of Census, 1906-08; admitted to Washington, D.C. bar and to Court of Appeals, Dist. of Columbia, 1920; U.S. Supreme Court, Wash., D.C., 1923, also N.Y. Circuit Court of Appeals, 2d Dist., 1926; confidential clerk to Interstate Commerce Commn., 1910-14; atty., 1914-22, in Interstate Commerce Commn.; atty., specializing in valuation of property, Western Union Telegraph Co., 1922-24; asst. gen. atty. law dept., 1924-41, vice pres., in charge labor relations, since Oct., 1941; dir. Western Union Telegraph Co., Teleregister Corp., Atlantic and Ohio Telegraph Co., Gold and Stock Telegraph Co., Internat. Ocean Telegraph Co., New York Mutual Telegraph Co., Southern and Atlantic Telegraph Co. Mem. Am. Bar Assn., Fed. Communications Commn. Bar Assn., Sigma Nu Phi. Mem. Protestant Episcopal Ch. Home: 320-330 Park Av., New York 22, Office: 60 Hudson St., New York 13. Died Aug. 23, 1947.

KIMBROUGH, Thomas Charles, lawyer, educator; b. nr. Carrollton, Miss., Jan. 28, 1873; s. Thomas Archibald and Janie Cameron (McKenzie) K.; Ph.B., U. of Miss., 1895; LL.B., Millsaps Law Sch., Jackson, Miss., 1898; m. Lula May Brothers, Aug. 21, 1901; children—Thomas Brothers, Renan Randle. Sec. Miss. State R.R. Commn., 1896-98; admitted to Miss. bar, 1898, and began practice at West Point; mem. Critz, Beckett & Kimbrough, 1898-1906, Critz, Kimbrough & Critz, 1906-12; judge, Circuit Court, 16th Circuit, Miss., 1914-16; prof. law, U. of Miss., since 1920, dean of Sch. of Law since 1922; dir. Columbian Mut. Life Ins. Soc. of Memphis. Trustee West Point City Schs. 12 yrs.; trustee Miss. State Teachers Coll. Mem. Am. Bar Assn. (mem. House of Delegates from Miss.), Miss. State Bar Assn. (pres.), Assn. Am. Law Schs. (exec. com.), Nat. Econ. League, Am. Law Inst.. Miss. Sons of Vets. (comdr.), Sigma Chi, Theta Nu Epsilon, Phi Delta Phi. Democrat. Baptist. Mason, Elk. Kiwanian. Contbr. to Miss. Law Jour. Home: University, Miss. Died Dec. 31, 1945.

KINCAID, William Wallace, mfr.; b. Wayne Twp., Erie County, Pa., Apr. 26, 1868; s. Rev. John S. and Margaretta (Tuttle) K.; grad. high sch., Corry, Pa., 1887; m. Clara Elizabeth Greenley, May 28, 1894. Various lines of business until 1903; an organizer, 1904, and chmn. bd. Spirella Co., corset mfrs.; officer or dir. other corps. Pres. Old Fort Niagara Assn.; dir. Niagara Frontier Planning Assn., Fla. Chautauqua (Keystone Heights, Fla.); mem. U.S. Chamber Commerce, Niagara Falls Chamber Commerce, Am. Management Assn., Niagara County Park Commn., N.Y. State Hist. Assn., Nat. Econ. League, Am. Acad. Polit. and Social Science, English-Speaking Union, Roosevelt Memorial Assn., N.E., Historic-Geneal. Soc., Pilgrim Tercentenary Memorial Soc., Civil Legion, Am. Scenic and Historic Preservation Soc., Sons of Union Vets. Del. from Pa. to Rep. Nat. Conv., 1912, to Progressive Nat. Conv., 1912. Mason. Unitarian. Clubs: City, Advertising (New York); Rotary, Niagara, Niagara Falls Country; Congressional Country (Washington). Author of pamphlets and mag. articles on business topics. Home: Ellorslie-on-Niagara, Youngstown, N.Y. Office: United Bldg., Niagara Falls, N.Y.*

KINDLER, Hans (kĭnd'lẽr), conductor; b. Rotterdam, Holland, Jan. 8, 1893; s. Carel and Jeanette (Hanken) K.; grad. Conservatory of Music, Rotterdam, Holland; Mus.D., George Washington U., 1932. First appeared as soloist at age of 15; played with orchestras in Berlin, Amsterdam, London, etc.; was mem. faculty, Scharwenka Conservatory, Berlin, also solo cellist, Opera House, Berlin-Charlottenburg; came to U.S., 1914; first and solo cellist Phila. Orchestra for 5 yrs.; became concert cellist, 1919; last World tour as cellist, 1929; conducted festivals at Library of Congress; founded Nat. Symphony Orchestra, Washington, 1931, and conductor 18 yrs., in 1935 started summer concerts at the Watergate in Washington; guest conductor N.Y. Philharmonic, Phila. Orchestra, Cleveland, Chicao (Ravinia), Los Angeles (Hollywood Bowl), Mexico City, South and Central America, Amsterdam, The Hague, Paris, Vienna; in later years also composer, symphonic works. Final concerts European tour, spring 1949, Göteborg, Stockholm, Helsinki; first American conductor behind Iron Curtain in Budapest, and Prague Music Festival, May 1949. Received Coolidge medal, 1939; Mahler medal, 1944; on Wall of Fame, N.Y. World's Fair. Decorated Officer, Order of Orange Nassau by Queen Wilhelmina. Clubs: Arts, Friday Morning Music (hon.), Federated Music Clubs (honorary); Baltimore Hamilton; Phila. Music (hon.); Cosmos. Address: 2124 Bancroft Place N.W., Washington 8. Died Aug. 30, 1949.

KINEON, George Goodhue (kĭn'ē-ŭn), physician; b. Cincinnati, O., July 19, 1879; s. Solomon Perin and Mary Graves (Goodhue) K.; prep. edn., Williston Sem., Easthampton, Mass.; M.D., Miami Coll. (now med. dept. U. of Cincinnati), 1905; unmarried. Med. dir. and supt. Ohio Hosp. for Epileptics since 1911. Chmn. Gallia County, O., Red Cross Soc., 1917, also of Draft Board, same county, 1917-18; judge of Court of Honor, Boy Scouts of America. Mem. Am., Ohio State and Gallia County med. socs., Am. Psychiatric Assn., Nat. Assn. for Study of Epilepsy, Am. Assn. for Study of Feeble Minded, Eugenics, Research Assn., L'Ligue Internationale contre l'Epilepsie. Mem. Gallia Community Assn. Episcopalian. Mason (K.T., Shriner), Elk. Clubs: Gallipolis, Rotary (past pres., also dir.); Athletic (Columbus, O.). Home: Gallipolis, O. Died Aug. 21, 1943.

KING, Caroline B(lanche), editor and author; b. Chicago, Ill.; d. Robert William and Caroline (Warren) Campion; ed. Lake View High Sch., Chicago, and under private instruction; m. J. M. McIlvaine King (dec.); 1 dau. living, Mrs. Mary Grace Ramey. Was Sunday editor of Phila. Press, 1909-13; editorial staff Evening Telegraph, 1913-17; apptd. U.S. Army, dietitian by Surgeon Gen. Gorgas, 1917 (first dietitian apptd.); lectured and conducted soldiers' cooking classes; went to France with Base Hosp. 116, Mar. 1918; asso. editor The Country Gentleman, 1924-42. Mem. Nat. Home Econ. Assn. Republican. Episcopalian. Author: Caroline King's Cook Book, 1917; Rosemary Makes a Garden; Victorian Cakes; This Was Ever In My Dream, 1947. Home: "Arborcote," Beechwood, Delaware County Pa. Died Dec. 2, 1947.

KING, Clifford William, lawyer; b. at Wolfe City, Tex., Dec. 8, 1882; s. William Gollihar and Anna Elizabeth (Craig) K.; ed. pub. schs.; studied law with Hendricks & Coffee, Miami, Tex., 1901-02; m. Jessie Brownell Orr, Dec. 14, 1906. Admitted to Tex. bar, 1903, Okla. bar, 1907, and began practice at Mangum, Okla.; asst. sec. of state, Okla., 1907; county judge Harmon County, Okla., 1909-13; asst. atty. gen. of Okla., 1914-25; rep. of Okla. before Supreme Court of U.S. in number of important revenue cases pertaining to Indian taxation, the right of the state to collect income tax from a non-resident, etc. Served as mem. Okla. Tax Code Revision Commn. and as legal adviser to Com. on Revenue and Taxation of Ho. of Rep. of Okla.; later chief atty. for Okla. Tax Commn.; now gen. counsel, Mem. Oklahoma City Chamber Commerce. Democrat. Presbyterian. Mason (32°). Home: 233 N.E. 15th St. Address: Capitol Office Bldg., Oklahoma City, Okla. Deceased.

KING, Henry Stouffer, banker; b. Baltimore, Md., Dec. 24, 1850; s. Henry S., Sr., and Susan (Johnson) K.; ed. St. Timothy's Hall, Catonsville, Md.; m. Ella Wynn, Nov. 8, 1877; children—Henry W., R. Glenn, Ralph Ashley (dec.), Roy Livingston (dec.), Edward Stouffer. Original incorporator, 1894, and first and only pres. Security Storage & Trust Co., Baltimore; original incorporator, Hopkins Place Savings Bank. Incorporator and prin. organizer Md. Asylum and Training Sch. for Feeble Minded; pres. Rosewood State Training Sch. Presbyterian. Home: (country) Riderwood, Baltimore County, Md.; (city) 2921 N. Calvert St., Baltimore, Md. Died Sep. 6, 1943.

KING, Herbert Hiram, prof. chemistry; b. Ewing, Ill., Feb. 28, 1882; s. Aaron and Viola (Harriss) K.; A.B., Ewing (Ill.) Coll., 1904, A.M., 1906; M.S., Kan. State Coll., Manhattan, Kan., 1915; Ph.D., U. of Chicago, 1918; m. Elizabeth Seargeant, Apr. 28, 1903 (died Nov. 12, 1923); children—Helen Elise, Kathryn Elizabeth; m. 2d, Grace Dickman, Jan. 30, 1926; children—Barbara Lee, Shirley Ruth. Prof. chemistry, Manchester Coll., N. Manchester, Ind., 1904-06; asst. in chemistry, Kan. State Coll., 1906-08, instr., 1908-09, asst. prof., 1909-14, asso. prof., 1914-18, prof. and head of dept. since 1918, also chemist Agrl. and Engring. Expt. Sta.; dir. State Food Lab., Manhattan. Chmn. tech. com. Kan. Indsl. Dev. Commn. Vice pres. from 5th dist. Nat. Collegiate Athletic Assn. Mem. Am. Chem. Soc. (counselor local sect.). Kan. Acad. Sci., A.A.A.S., Sigma Xi, Phi Kappa Phi, Gamma Sigma Delta, Alpha Zeta, Beta Theta Pi, Phi Lambda Upsilon. Baptist. Club: Manhattan Country. Contbr. papers on surface tension and soil chemistry. Home: Manhattan, Kan. Died Mar. 11, 1949; buried Sunset Cemetery, Manhattan, Kan.

KING, LeRoy Albert, coll. pres.; b. York, Pa., Aug. 10, 1886; s. Albert and Arabella (Stoner) K.; grad. Millersville (Pa.) State Normal Sch., 1905; B.S., Teachers Coll. (Columbia), 1910; A.M., Columbia, 1916; Ph.D., U. of Pa., 1920; m. Estella Adelle Hoffman, Aug. 24, 1915; children—John Albert, Joseph Hoffman, Jane Louise. Prof. edn. and supt. Training Sch., Central State Normal Sch., Lock Haven, Pa., 1910-14; supt. schs. in Pa., 1914-17; instr., U. of Pa., 1917-26, Prof. ednl. adminstrn., 1926-39; pres. State Teachers Coll., Indiana, Pa., since 1939; prof. edn. summer sessions State Coll. of Pa., U. of Calif., U. of Southern Calif., U. of Pittsburgh, Elizabethtown Coll.; lecturer U. of N.Dak.; dir. Bur. of Ednl. Measurements, and sec. Schoolmen's Week Ednl. Conv., U. of Pa., 1917-39, also editor proc. same. Mem. Pa. State Council of Edn., 1928-36, chmn. finance commn. Pres. Pa. Pub. Edn. and Child Labor Assn. Mem. Ednl. Research Assn., N.E.A., Pa. State Ednl. Assn., Nat. Soc. for Study of Edn., Nat. Soc. Coll. Teachers of Edn., Phi Delta Kappa, Kappa Phi Kappa, Acacia. Republican. Presbyn. Mason. Clubs: Undine Barge, Lenape, Schoolmen's (Philadelphia). Writer of Status of the Rural Teacher in Pennsylvania (Bull., U.S. Bureau Edn.), 1921; (joint) Survey of Fiscal Policies of State of Pa. in Field of Edn., 1922; Rept. on Appropriations and Subsidies (Ednl. Survey of Pa.), 1925. Participated in series of ednl. surveys, Bethlehem, 1937, Philadelphia, 1937. Contbr. to ednl. periodicals. Address: State Teachers College, Indiana, Pa. Died June 5, 1942.

KING, Lorenzo H., bishop; b. Macon, Miss., Jan. 2, 1878; s. Houston Carlton and Leah K.; A.B., Clark Coll., Atlanta, Ga., 1902; B.D., Gammon Theol. Sem., Ga., 1903, Union Theol. Sem., New York, N.Y., 1911; D.D., Wiley Coll., Marshall, Tex.; student Teachers Coll., Columbia U., 1910-11; m. Louise Marie Watts, Dec. 13, 1903; children—Walter, Lorenzo H., Jr., Earl Watts. Pastor Elberton (Ga.) Circuit, 1902-03, Covington, 1903-04, South Atlanta, 1905-08, Newman, 1909-10; teacher English, Clark U., Atlanta, 1912-13; pastor Central Ch., Atlanta, 1913-19; editor Southwestern Christian Advocate, 1920-30; New York Conf., 1930-31; then pastor St. Mark's Ch., New York, N.Y.; now bishop of Methodist Church. Pres. bd. trustees Gammon Theol. Sem.; v.p. Clark Coll. bd., Cookman bd.; pres. Claflin Coll. bd. Mason, Elk. Home: 250 Auburn Av. N.E., Atlanta, Ga. Died Dec. 17, 1946.

KING, Melvin L., architect; b. Lafayette, N.Y.; s. Russell G. and Melvina (Abbott) K.; m. Gertrude E. Gridley, 1892; children—Mabel, Russell, Helen, Harry, Ruth, Melvin L. Began as draftsman; in practice architecture, Syracuse, N.Y., since 1906. Mem. A.I.A. (ex-pres. Central N.Y. chapter), Syracuse Soc. of Architects, (ex-pres.), Syracuse chamber of Commerce (ex-pres.), Phi Sigma Delta. Republican. Methodist. Mason (Scottish Rite), Optimist. Home: 120 Wood Av. Office. 300 Denison Bldg., Syracuse N.Y.* Died Aug. 11, 1946.

KING, Paul, artist; b. Buffalo, N.Y., Feb. 9, 1867; s. Bernard and Pauline (Stephan) K.; student Art Students' League, Buffalo and New York, also in Paris and Holland; m. Cornelia Bonnell Greene, June 4, 1907; 1 son, Paul B. Awarded gold medal, Art Club, Phila.; Shaw prize and Inness prize, Salmagundi Club, N.Y., 1906; silver medal, San Francisco Expn., 1915; Phila. prize, Pa. Acad. Fine Arts, 1918; 1st Altman prize, Nat. Acad, New York, 1923; awarded Isidor prize by Salmagundi Club, 1927; National Arts Club medal, 1937. Pictures in Art Club, Phila.; Reading Art Museum; Albright Gallery, Buffalo; Nat. Gallery, Washington, D.C.; Shaw Collection, New York; New Parthenon, Nashville, Tenn.; Cabildo Art Gallery, New Orleans; Rogers Memorial Gallery, Laurel, Miss.; Athletic Club, Buffalo, New York. Served in camouflage dept. under U.S. Shipping Bd., World War. Mem. Fellowship Pa. Acad. Fine Arts, Internat. Soc. Arts, Paris; A.N.A., 1919, Nat. Academician, 1933. Republican. Mem. Ref. Episcopal Ch. Clubs: Salmagundi, Nat. Arts (New York). Address: 51 Fifth Av., New York 3. Died Nov. 25, 1947.

KING, Paul Howard; b. Arapahoe, Neb., Aug. 22, 1879; s. John S. and Agnes (Smead) K.; grad. Dowagiac (Mich.) High Sch., 1895-98, hon. alumnus U. of Mich.; m. Sarah Amelia Bidwell, Jan. 29, 1910; children—Martha Bidwell, Sarah Bidwell (Mrs. J. H. Garlick, Jr.), Elizabeth (Mrs. G. Richard Smith), Pauline. Page, Minn. Ho. of Reps., 1893-95, Mich. State Senate, 1897-99; asst. sec. Mich. Senate, 1901; journal clk. Mich. Ho. of Reps., 1903-07, chief clk., 1909-11; admitted to Mich. bar, 1904; sec. Mich. Constl. Conv., 1908; asst. to sec.-treas. Grand Rapids, Holland & Chicago Ry., 1911-14; operating receiver Pere Marquette R.R., 1914-17; referee in bankruptcy, U.S. Dist. Court, Eastern Dist. of Mich., since 1919. Sec. Rep. State Central Com., 1910; pres. Detroit Council of Churches, 1930-31; director Detroit Y.M.C.A., 1924-29. Dir. Michigan Red Cross War Fund campaign, 1917, dir. of publicity, 1918; dir. publicity 2d Liberty Loan drive. Mem. Detroit Charter Commn. and author original draft of city charter, 1917. Trustee Roosevelt Memorial Assn.; pres. Internat. Soc. for Welfare of Cripples; pres. emeritus Mich. and Nat. Soc. for Crippled Children; chmn. Mich. Crippled Children Commission; official del. from U.S. to World Congress, Workers for Crippled, Budapest, 1936, London, 1939; organized and conducted Geneva Congress, 1928; Hague Congress, 1931. Mem. Am. (chmn. com. on bankruptcy), Mich. and Detroit. bar assns.; organizer and 1st pres. Nat. Assn. of Referees in Bankruptcy, 1926-27; chmn. Nat. Bankruptcy Conference. Republican. Conglist. (moderator, Detroit Congl. Assn., 1929-31). Mason (32°), K.T. Club: Rotary (ex-pres. Detroit Club, gov. 1923-24, dir. Rotary Internat. 1924-25, mem. and chmn. extension com.) Home: 1497 W. Boston Blvd. Office: Federal Bldg., Detroit, Mich. Died May 17, 1942.

KING, Richard Hayne, pub. relations counsel; b. Lebanon, S.C., Sept. 8, 1878; s. John Julius and Mary Amanda (Ligon) K.; A.B., magna cum laude, Presbyn. Coll. of S.C., 1895; m. Louise Adger Robinson, Dec. 12, 1905; children—Louise Robinson, Mary Adger, Richard Hayne (dec.). Began Y.M.C.A. work as asst. sec., Charleston, S.C., 1898; gen. sec., Waco, Tex., 1898-1902, Charleston, 1902-17; asso. exec., later exec. of Southeastern Dept., Nat. Y.M.C.A. War Work Council and dir. War Finance campaigns, 1917-21; became exec. of internat. com. Y.M.C.A. and Nat. Council Y.M.C.A. for the South, 1921, now retired; asso. to pres. Pierce and Hedrick, Inc. Dir. Am. Red Cross campaign, S.C., 1917; chief of Am. Protective League, S.C., 1917-18. Mem. S.C. State Bd. Charities and Corrections, 1914-19; chmn. exec. com. Commn. on Interracial Coöperation, 1924-38; a founder and mem. Southern Regional Development of Southern Council on Foreign Relations; served as chmn. Playgrounds Commn. and dir. Charleston Chamber Commerce, and Charleston Museum. Trustee Y.M.C.A. Grad. Sch., Nashville, Tenn.; prin. Y.M.C.A. summer schs., Blue Ridge, N.C., 1912-26. Mem. U.S. C.V., Huguenot Soc. of S.C. Episcopalian Mason (32°, K.T., Shriner), K.P. Home 509 S. Solano Av., Albuquerque, N.M. Died Dec. 8, 1941.

KING, Stanton Henry, sailor's missionary; born Barbadoes, B.W.I., May 1, 1867; son John and Isabella (Rogers) K.; ed. Barbadoes, 1871-80, and at Mt. Hermon (Moody's School for Young Men); married Annie Emison, October 15, 1893. Served 6 yrs. in sailing ships as sailor and 6 years as enlisted man in U.S.N. Author: Dog-Watches at Sea, 1900; A Bunch of Rope Yarns, 1902. Address: Sailor's Haven, Charlestown, Mass. Died Nov. 1939.

KING, William Henry, ex-senator; b. Fillmore City, Utah, June 3, 1863; s. William and Josephine K.; ed. Brigham Young Acad., and U. of Utah; LL.B., U. of Mich., 1887; m. Annie Lyman, 1890 (died 1906); m. 2d, Vera Sjodahl, 1914. Practiced law in Utah and surrounding states; mem. Utah territorial legislature 3 terms, pres. upper body 1 term; was county atty., Utah County, city atty., Provo City; apptd. asso. judge Supreme Court of Utah, 1894; mem. 55th Congress (1897-99); declined renomination, but was elected as mem. 56th Congress to fill vacancy and served, Apr. 25, 1900-Mar. 3, 1901; choice of party for 58th and 59th Congresses (defeated), also of Dem. legislative caucus for U.S. Senate, 1905, 09; mem. U.S. Senate, 4 terms 1917-41. Del. various Dem. Nat. Convs. Mem. Ch. of Jesus Christ of Latter Day Saints (Mormon). Clubs: Alta, Commercial (Salt Lake City). Home: Salt Lake City, Utah. Died Nov. 27, 1949.

KING, William Perry, educator-editor; b. Maysville, Ky., Feb. 16, 1876; s. William Washington and Laura Ellen (Bramel) K.; student Georgetown (Ky.) Coll. and Miami U., Oxford, O.; LL.B., Cincinnati Coll. of Law, 1914; LL.D. (honorary) from Georgetown (Ky.) College; m. Amah Davis, Oct. 12, 1904; children—William Raymond, Amah Ruth. Teacher pub. schs. Mason County, Ky., 1897-1905; prin. city schs., Maysville, 1905-09; supt. schs., Bellevue, Ky., 1909-14, Newport, 1914-21; pres. Ky. Edn. Assn., 1914-15; mgr. publs. United Christian Missionary Soc., 1923-25; pres. Carr-Burdette Coll., 1925-29; in publishing business, 1929-33; executive secretary Kentucky Education Assn., 1933-48, sec. emeritus since 1948; editor Ky. School Journal, 1933-48. Represented U.S. at World Conf. on Edn. in Oxford, Eng., 1935, Tokyo, Japan, 1937. Vice chmn. of Internat. Relations Com. of N.E.A., 1938; chairman N.E.A. committee for the study of professional ethics, 1938-41; executive sec. Herman Jordan Committee of W.F.E.A., 1937-39; pres. Southern Assn. of State Secs. Mem. exec. com. Southern States Conf. on Ednl. Administrn., exec. sec. Internat. Relations Commn., World Federation of Education Associations since 1939; mem. National Educational Association, Gov's. Com. for Study of Negro Edn., State Conservation Com., Kentucky Com. to study all phases of Ky. resources and economy. Chmn. bd. dirs. Rural Editorial Service, Chicago U. Mem. Phi Sigma Sigma, Phi Delta Kappa. Mason. Club: Filson. Address: Heyburn Bldg., Louisville 2. Died Mar. 3, 1949.

KINGMAN, John J., army officer; b. Omaha, Neb.; s. Brig. Gen. Dan C. Kingman (former Chief of Engrs., U.S. Army) and Eugenia (Jennings) K.; B.S., U.S. Mil. Acad., 1904; grad. Engr. Sch., U.S. Army, 1907; m. Adelaide Lewis Warren, Aug. 22, 1911; children—Jean, Ann Warren. Commd. 2d lt. Corps Engrs., U.S. Army, 1904, and advanced through the grades to brig. gen., 1938; served in Philippines, 1907-10; on War Dept. Gen. Staff and chief of staff 90th Div., A.E.F. in France and Germany, during World War; War Dept. Gen. Staff to 1924; command 1st Engrs., 1924-26; dist. engr., Milwaukee, 1926-30; chief of River and Harbor Div., Office Chief of Engrs., 1930-33; dist. engr., Boston, 1933-36; div. engr., South Pacific div., San Francisco, 1936-38; asst. chief of engrs., 1938, until retired Nov. 1941; returned to active duty throughout World War II. Episcopalian. Address: Office Chief of Engineers, War Dept., Washington, D.C. Died July 21, 1948.

KINGMAN, Matthew Henry, Marine Corps officer; born Iowa, Mar. 1, 1890. Commd. 2d lt., Marine Corps, and advanced through the grades to col., Sept. 1938; retired, Apr. 1940; called to active duty and advanced to brig. gen., Aug. 1942. Awarded Purple Heart, Silver Star.* Died Nov. 16, 1946.

KINGSBURY, Albert, mechanical engr.; b. near Morris, Ill., Dec. 23, 1863; s. Lester Wayne and Eliza (Fosdick) K.; M.E., Cornell, 1889; studied mech. engring., Ohio State U. and Cornell; m. Alison Mason, July 25, 1893; children—Margaretta Mason, Alison Mason, Elisabeth Brewster, Katharine Knox, Theodora. Instr. in mech. engring. and physics, N.H. Coll., 1889-90; mech. engr., H. B. Camp Co., Cuyahoga Falls, O., 1890-91; prof. mech. engring., N.H. Coll., 1891-99; prof. applied mechanics, Worcester Poly. Inst., 1899-1903; mech. engr. Westinghouse Electric & Mfg. Co., E. Pittsburgh, 1903-10; consulting engr. since 1910; pres. Kingsbury Machine Works, Frankford, Phila. Fellow A.A.A.S.; mem. Am. Soc. Mech. Engrs. Contbr. to trans. of engring. socs. on subjects in mech. engring. Home: Greenwich, Conn. Died July 28, 1943.

KINGSBURY, Benjamin Freeman, university prof.; b. St. Charles, Mo., Nov. 18, 1872; s. Benjamin Barnes and Sarah Nichols (Freeman) K.; A.B., Buchtel Coll., 1893; M.S., Cornell, 1894, Ph.D., 1895; M.D., Univ. of Freiburg, 1904; D.Sc., Bowdoin Coll., Brunswick, Me., 1934; m. Marguerite Hempstead, June 22, 1904; m. 2d, Janet A. Williamson, July 2, 1929. Fellow in neurology, 1895-96, instr. histology, 1896-99, asst. prof., 1899-1902, asst. prof. physiology, 1902-08, prof. histology and embryology, 1908-41, Cornell (emeritus); guest prof. anatomy, U. of N.C., since 1941. Fellow A.A.A.S., Am. Anat. Assn.; mem. Sigma Xi, Phi Delta Theta, Nu Sigma Nu fraternities, Gamma Alpha Scientific Club. Democrat. Author: Vertebrate Histology (with S. H. Gage), 1900; Laboratory Directions in Pharmacology, 1905; Laboratory Directions in Physiology, 1906; Laboratory Directions in Histology and Histological Technique, 1910; (with O. A. Johannsen) Histological Technique, 1927. Address: Chapel Hill, N.C. Died July 8, 1946.

KINGSBURY, Jerome, dermatologist; b. Boston; s. Alden Newell and Mary Jerome K.; M.D., N.Y.U. and Bellevue Hosp. Med. Coll., 1897. Interne N.Y. hosps. special work in pathology, dermatology, obstetrics, and post grad. study, London and Paris, 1897-1900; practiced in N.Y. City since 1900; chief dept. skin diseases, Presbyn. Hosp. Dispensary, 1900-17; attending phys. N.Y. Skin and Cancer Hosp., 1912-22 and 1928-35; visiting dermatologist N.Y. City Hosp., 1920-36; prof. dermatology Polyclinic Med. School and Hosp.; dir. dermatology, Midtown Hosp.; cons. dermatologist Harlem Eye and Ear and N.Y. City hosps. Trustee Bronx Savings Bank. Trustee Northern Dispensary. Served in 7th Regt., Nat. Guard N.Y., 5 yrs.; with 1st Training Regt., Plattsburg, N.Y., 1915; 1st Medico-Mil. Train. Camp (1st lt.), Plattsburg, 1916; surgeon with 1st Provisional Regt., 1917; entered Army as capt. Med. Corps and served with A.E.F. in France; now col. Med. Res. Surgeon Veteran Corps Arty. since 1917. Mem. A.M.A., Am. Dermatol. Assn., N.Y. Dermatol. Soc., N.Y. Acad. of Medicine, Alumni Presbyn. Hosp., Alumni Skin and Cancer Hosp. (pres.), S.C.W. (surg.) S.R., Naval Order of U.S. (comdr.), Mil. Soc. War of 1812, Mil. Order World War, Soc. Am. Wars (surg. gen.), N.Y. Soc. Mil. Naval Officers World War (surg.), Res. Officers Assn. of U.S. (pres. Manhattan chapter), Vet. 1st Provisional Regt. (pres.), U.S. Revolver Assn. (life). Surgeon, N.Y. City Patrol Corp. with rank col. on staff Maj. Gen. R. M. Danford. Mem. med. advisory board and panel of specialists, Selective Service. Democrat. Mason. Licensed balloon pilot (Federation Aeronautique Internationale); has competed in nat. and internat. balloon races; formerly chmn. balloon com. Aero Club of America; charter mem. Am. Inst. Aeronautic Engrs.; mem. Early Birds. Clubs: New York Athletic, Metropolitan, Camp Fire Club of America; Army and Navy (Washington, D.C.). Address: 471 Park Av., New York, N.Y. Died July 15, 1944.

KINGSBURY, Susan Myra, social economist; b. San Pablo, Calif., Oct. 18, 1870; d. Willard B. and Helen (De Lamater) Kingsbury; A.B., College of Pacific, 1890, LL.D., 1937; A.M., Leland Stanford Jr. Univ., 1899; Ph.D., Columbia, 1905; LL.D., Mills Coll., 1937. Teacher history, Lowell High Sch., San Francisco, 1892-1900; instr. history, Vassar Coll., 1904-05; dir. investigation for Mass. Commn. on Indsl. and Tech. Edn., on relation of children to industries, 1906; prof. economics, Simmons Coll., Boston, 1906-15; Carola Woerishoffer prof. social economy and dir. Carola Woerishoffer grad. dept. of social economy and social research, Bryn Mawr Coll., 1915-1936, now emeritus. Pres. Phila. Women's University Club of Am. Assn. Univ. Women, 1936-40, chmn. com. on econ. and legal status of women, since 1934. Mem. Am. Sociol. Assn., Kappa Alpha Theta, Phi Beta Kappa. Author: (with M. Fairchild) Factory, Family and Woman in the Soviet Union, 1935. Editor: (series) Economic Relations of Women; Records of the Virginia Company of London (Library of Congress). Home: Bryn Mawr, Pa. Died Nov. 28, 1949.

KINGSLEY, Howard L., psychologist; b. Shelby, Mich., Nov. 27, 1892; s. William Dennis and Mary Jane (Barker) K.; A.B., Adrian (Mich.) Coll., 1915; A.M., U. of Mich., 1916; Ph.D., U. of Ill., 1924; m. Edith May Halliday, July 5, 1917; children—Lowell Vincent, Howard Halliday, Elaine Virginia. Prof. of psychology, Greenville (Ill.) Coll., 1916-18; instr. in edn., U. of Mich., 1918-19; prof. and dean Peniel (Tex.) Coll., 1919-20; prof. and registrar McKinney (Tex.) Jr. Coll., 1920-21; asst. in psychology, U. of Ill., 1922-24, instr., 1924-25; asst. prof. of psychology, Goucher Coll., Baltimore, 1925-27; asso. prof. of psychol., Boston U., 1927-29, prof. since 1929. Taught La. State Normal Sch., summers 1921-22, Ill. State Normal, summers, 1925-27. Fellow A.A.A.S., Am. Psychol. Assn.; mem. Eastern Psychol. Assn., Am. Assn. Univ. Profs., Nat. Soc. Coll. Teachers of Education, Rep. Club of Mass., Phi Delta Kappa, Sigma Alpha Epsilon; asso. mem. Sigma Xi. Republican. Conglist. Author: Nature and Conditions of Learning. Contbr. to psychol. jours. Home: 59 North St., Newtonville 60, Mass. Office: 84 Exeter St., Boston. Died Apr. 7, 1948.

KINGSLEY, William H.; chmn. of bd. Penn Mutual Life Insurance Co. Home: 8007 Navajo St., Chestnut Hill, Pa. Office: 6th and Walnut Sts., Philadelphia, Pa.* Died Nov. 1, 1945.

KINGSLEY, William Morgan, banker; b. New York, N.Y., Dec. 16, 1863; s. E. M. and A. W. Kingsley; A.B., New York U., 1883, A.M., 1886, LL.D., 1921; m. Susan Buek, 1890; children—Charles P., Myra, Elsa, Mabon. With Brown Bros. & Co., bankers, N.Y. City, 1883-91; mem. Kingsley, Mabon & Co., brokers, New York, 1891-1906; first vice-pres. U.S. Trust Co. of N.Y., 1906-27, pres., 1927-38, chmn. bd. since 1938. Treas. New York U., 1905-37; pres. bd. dirs. Union Theol. Sem., 1913-37; pres. and treas. Syrian Protestant Coll. to 1937; chmn. N.Y. State and pres. N.Y. City Y.M.C.A.; mem. Phi Beta Kappa and Psi Upsilon. Presbyterian. Clubs: University, City Midday, Psi Upsilon. Office: 45 Wall St., New York, N.Y. Died Sep. 7, 1942.

KINGSMILL, Harold, pres. Cerro de Pasco Copper Corp.; dir. Am. Metal Co., Homestake Mining Co., United Metals Refining Co., Grace Nat. Bank of N.Y. Office: care Cerro de Pasco Copper Corp., 40 Wall St., New York, N.Y.* Deceased.

KINGSMILL, Hugh, author; b. London, Eng., Nov. 21, 1889; s. Sir Henry Simpson Lunn; student Harrow Sch., 1903-08; New Coll., Oxford, 1908-11; M.A., Trinity Coll., Dublin, Ireland, 1913-14 and 1919; m. Dorothy Vernon, 1929; 4 children. Served in first world war, 1914-18, sub-lt., Royal Naval Div., prisoner-of-war in Germany, 1917-18; worked for some years in travel business for his father, Sir Henry Lunn; since 1927 has been author, educator and lecturer. Author (fiction): The Dawn's Delay; The Return of William Shakespeare; The Fall; (biography) Frank Harris; D. H. Lawrence; The Poisoned Crown, 1944; (with Pearson) Skye High; (with same) This Blessed Plot, 1941; (with William Gerhardi) The Casanova Fable. Home: 101 Westbourne Terrace, London, England. Address: care Alfred A. Knopf, Inc., New York 22, N.Y. Died May 1949.

KINKAID, Mary Holland (Mrs.), journalist, author; b. Wilkes-Barre, Pa., Dec. 31, 1861; d. John and Nettie S. McNeish; ed. Wilkes-Barre and Phila. schs.; m. John Kinkaid, 1891. Began newspaper work in Chicago, 1886; on staff Omaha World-Herald as editorial writer and asst. city editor, from 1888; worked in Colo. Equal Suffrage campaign, 1894; editorial writer on staff Denver Evening Times, 1894-96; asst. supt. pub. instrn., Colo., 1897-98; resigned to join staff Chicago Inter-Ocean, 1898-1901; lit. editor Milwaukee Sentinel, 1901-03; Sunday editor Los Angeles Herald, 1903-05; asso. editor Pacific Outlook. Contbr. to mags. and periodicals. Author: Walda (novel), 1903; The Man of Yesterday (novel), 1907. Address: 4537 Marmion Way, Los Angeles. Died Oct. 20, 1948.

KINLEY, David, univ. pres.; b. Dundee, Scotland, Aug. 2, 1861; s. David and Jessie Preston (Shepherd) K.; came to U.S. with father, 1872; A.B., Yale, 1884; studied Johns Hopkins, 1890-92; Ph.D., U. of Wis., 1893; LL.D., Ill. Coll., 1908, U. of Wis., 1918, U. of Neb., 1921, Yale, 1924; m. Kate Ruth Neal, June 22, 1897 (died Apr. 1931); children—Mrs. Harriet K. Brooks, Janet Fraser (Mrs. John R. Gregg). Prin. high sch., N. Andover, Mass., 1884-90; asst. Johns Hopkins, and instr. Woman's Coll., Baltimore, 1891-92; fellow and asst. in economics, U. of Wis., 1892-93; asst. prof. economics, U. of Ill., 1893-94, prof. economics, dean Coll. Literature and Arts, 1894-1906, and dir. courses in commerce, 1902-15, dean Grad. Sch., 1906-19, v.p., 1914-19, acting pres., 1919-20, pres., 1920-30. Chmn. bd. First Nat. Bank, Champaign, 1932-40. Mem. Ill. Industrial Insurance Commn., 1906-07; mem. Ill. Tax Commn., 1910, 30; del. to 4th Internat. Conf. of Am. States at Buenos Aires, 1910; minister plenipotentiary and envoy on spl. mission to Chile on delegation representing U.S. at Centennial of Chilean Independence, 1910; del. to 2d Pan-Am. Scientific Congress, Washington, D.C., 1915; special delegate to the Orient for Chicago Century of Progress Exposition, 1931; hon. mem. faculty U. of Chile; mem. permanent group com. of Pan-Am. Financial Conf., assigned to Chile; mem. com. on research, Div. of Economics and History, Carnegie Endowment for Internat. Peace, 1913-22; mem. Ill. State Commn. on State Salaries, 1919; mem. Ill. Bd. Nat. Resources and Conservation, 1917-30; mem. Ill. Advisory Committee on School Finance, 1932, Com. on Inter-governmental Debts since 1933, Com. on Am.-Scottish War Memorial in Edinburgh. Brevet col. Ill. Nat. Guard, 1920-30. Trustee Inst. of Economics, 1923-25; mem. com. Economists Nat. Com.; pres. Nat. Assn. of State Univs., 1923-24. Mem. Wis. Acad. Sciences, Arts and Letters, Alpha Kappa Psi, Phi Gamma Delta, Beta Gamma Sigma, Phi Beta Kappa; hon. mem. Am. Assn. Pub. Accountants. Clubs: Rotary (Champaign); University (Urbana); University (Chicago); University (Washington). Author: The Independent Treasury of the United States, 1893; Monograph on Trusts, 1899; Money, 1904, Chinese edit. pub.; monographs prepared for Nat. Monetary Commn. on The Use of Credit Instruments in Payments in the U.S., and The Independent Treasury of the United States and Its Relation to the Banks of the Country, 1910; Government Control of Economic Life and other Addresses, 1936; also various repts., pamphlets and mag. articles. Editor: Preliminary Studies of the War (Carnegie Endowment for Internat. Peace, Div. of Economics and History), 1913-22. Awarded Newman medal, 1930. Home: 1203 W. Nevada St., Urbana, Ill. Died Dec. 3, 1944.

KINNEY, Antoinette Brown; b. N.Y. State; d. Joseph Addison and Mary J. (Daniels) Brown; B.L., U. of Mich., 1887; m. Clesson S. Kinney, Dec. 1, 1889 (dec.); 1 son, Selwyne Perez. Organizer Utah State Federation Women's Clubs; hon. v.p. Gen. Fed. Women's Clubs; chmn. legislative com. of State and City Federation; organizer and mgr. Federation Coll. Loan Fund; past pres. League of Women Voters of Utah; and actively identified with other women's orgns. and officer or dir. various corps. Mem. Utah State Senate, 1919 and 1921; regent U. of Utah; dir. State Humane Soc.; past pres. Assn. Collegiate Alumnæ; regent D.A.R. Republican. Unitarian. Home: 14 Creighton Av., Crafton, Pa. Died Jan. 4, 1945.

KINSLEY, Albert Thomas, veterinary pathologist; b. Independence, Ia., Feb. 26, 1877; s. John and Jane Elizabeth (Footitt) K.; B.Sc., Kan. State Agrl. Coll., 1899, M.Sc., 1901; U. of Chicago, summer, 1901; Kan. City Vet. Coll., 1902-04, D.V.S., 1904; m. Anna Louisa Smith, Sept. 4, 1901; 1 son, Albert Smith. Instr. bacteriology, Kan. State Agrl. Coll., 1899-1901; pathologist and dir. museum, Kansas City Vet. Coll., 1904-18; organizer, 1909, and pres. Am. Serum Co.; became pres. Kansas City Vet. Coll.; retired, 1941. Originator of use of bacteria in vet. medicine. Pres. Kan. State Coll. Alumni Assn., 1935; del. to Internat. Veterinary Congress, London, 1930. Mem. Am. Vet. Med. Assn. (v.p. 1909-10, pres. 1921-22), Mo. Valley Med. Assn. (pres. 1909-10), Mo. State Vet. Med. Assn.; asso. mem. Jackson County (Mo.) Med. Soc. Mem. Ch. of England. Author: Veterinary Pathology, 1910; Diseases of Swine, 1914; Swine Practice, 1920. Home: 616 E. 59th St., Kansas City, Mo. Died Dec. 8, 1941.

KINSMAN, Delos Oscar, prof. economics; b. Fayette, La Fayette County, Wis., Aug. 30, 1868; s. Thomas R. and Emma (Harris) K.; grad. State Teachers Coll., Platteville, 1891; B.L., U. of Wis., 1896, Ph.D., 1900; grad. study U. of Chicago; m. Ella Williams, Dec. 28, 1892 (dec.); m. 2d, Anna Barnard, July 14, 1904; children—Georgia Bernice (Mrs. Alvin Loverud), Ellen Lenore (Mrs. Burgess Seamonson). Prin. high sch., Stockbridge, Wis., 1891-92, West Salem, Wis., 1892-94; instr., Wis. Acad., Madison, 1894-98; fellow in economics, U. of Chicago, 1898-99; hon. fellow U. of Wis., 1899-1900; expert asst. Wis. State Tax Commn., 1900-01; prof. social sciences, State Teachers College, Whitewater, 1901-16; prof. economics, Lawrence Coll., 1916-26; prof. same, American U., 1926-39, emeritus since 1939. Pres. Whitewater (Wis.) Comml. and Savings Bank, 1913-16. Drafted Wis. Income Tax Law, 1911, first successful law of its kind in U.S. Mem. Am. Econ. Assn., The Acad. of World Economics, Pi Gamma Mu. Republican. Methodist. Mason. Rotarian. Author: The Income Tax in the Commonwealths of the United States, 1903; Local Governments of Wisconsin, 1913; Essentials of Civics, 1919; Economics or the Science of Business, 1927; Man in the Making, 1934; Our Economic World, 1937. Home: 4426 Klingle St. N.W., Washington 10, D.C. Died May 2, 1948.

KINTZINGER, John W. (kĭnt'zĭng-ẽr), lawyer; b. Dubuque, Ia., Aug. 12, 1870; LL.B., State U. of Ia., 1897; m. Fannie E. Webb, July 1893; children—Helen J., John W., Robert H. Admitted to Ia. bar, 1897, since practicing in Dubuque; mem. Dubuque City Council, 1900-01; became city atty. of Dubuque, 1904; judge of Dist. Court, 19th Jud. Dist., 1911-23; justice Supreme Court of Ia., 1932-38, chief justice, 1935; now mem. Kintzinger & Kintzinger. Chmn. legal advisory bd., Dept. of War, for Dubuque County, World War. Del. Dem. Nat. Conv., 1912. Home: 563 W. 11th St. Office: Stampfer Bldg., Dubuque, Ia.* Died Apr. 3, 1946.

KIRBY, C. Valentine, art educator; b. Canajoharie, N.Y., 1875; s. Frank and Frances (Devendorf) K.; grad. high sch., Canajoharie, 1893; student Union Coll.; student Art Students' League and Chase Sch. of Art, New York, 4 yrs., also Europe; hon. A.M., Union Coll., 1922; Pd.D. (hon.), Franklin and Marshall Coll., 1937; Dr. Fine Arts, Lebanon Coll., 1937; m. Florence J. Beach, Mar. 20, 1902; 1 son, Donald Beach. Teacher of fine and industrial arts, pub. schs. of Denver, 1900-10; dir. art instrn., Buffalo, N.Y., 1911-12, Pittsburgh, 1912-20; state dir. of art, Pa., 1920-46; retired. Lecturer, univs. and Carnegie Inst. Tech.; Am. rep. and speaker Internat. Art Congress, Dresden, 1912; assisted in survey of art in Am. Industry, 1920. Mem. Am. Fedn. Arts, N.E.A., Pa. State Edn. Assn., Eastern Arts Assn., Delta Phi Delta, Psi Upsilon, S.R.; mem. yearbook com. Nat. Assn. for the Study of Edn.; mem. Am. com. 6th Internat. Art Congress, Prague, 1928. Republican. Unitarian. Mason (32°, Shriner). Club: Torch. Author: The Business of Teaching and Supervising the Arts, 1927. Co-Author: Graded Art Textbooks; Art Education in Principle and Practice. Designer of book plates; contbr. on art subjects. Home: 154 Willow Av., Camp Hill, Pa. Died Sept. 27, 1947.

KIRBY, Daniel Noyes, lawyer; b. Old Lyme, Conn., Aug. 22, 1864; s. Elias Burgess and Caroline Lydia (Noyes) K.; grad. Central High Sch., St. Louis, Mo., 1882; A.B., Washington U., St. Louis, Mo., 1886, LL.B., 1888; unmarried. Engaged in practice of law, St. Louis, Mo., since 1887; mem. firm Nagel & Kirby, and successor firms, Finkenburg, Nagel & Kirby, and Nagel, Kirby, Orrick & Shepley; since 1894. Teacher agency law, Sch. of Law., U. of Mo., 1901-11, constitutional law, 1912. Vice pres. and dir. Manufacturers Railway Co.; trustee St. Louis Refrigerator Car Co.; dir. Burch-Sulza Brothers Diesel Engine Co., Midwest Rubber Reclaiming Co. Mem. Council Am. Law Inst. since 1918. Dir. Washington U. Mem. Am. Bar Assn., Bar Assn. City of N.Y., Missouri and St. Louis bar assns. Clubs: University (New York); University, Noon Day, St. Louis Country, Bogey Golf (St. Louis). Home: 320 N. Union Av. Office: 319 N. Fourth St., St. Louis, Mo. Died June 25, 1945.

KIRBY, Robert J., warden; b. Beekmantown, N.Y., Oct. 20, 1889; s. Edward A. and Bridget Graham (Loughan) K.; student State Normal Sch., Plattsburg, N.Y., 1905-06; m. Anna Lillian Conners, Sept. 1, 1913 (died June 10, 1934); children—Irene E. (Mrs. Lloyd Eagan), Ada F. (Mrs. Charles E. Kenerson); m. 2d, Gladys Nora Kelly, Nov. 5, 1935; children—Mary G., Robert J., Gertrude S., Edward A. Attendant Dannemora (N.Y.) State Hosp., 1909-11; guard Great Meadow Prison, Dannemora, 1911-20; guard Clinton Prison, 1920-28; sergt., 1928-31; prin. keeper, Attica Prison, Attica, N.Y., 1931-41; warden, Sing Sing Prison, Ossining, N.Y., since 1941. Mem. exec. council, Boy Scouts of America for Wyoming, Genessee and Livingston counties, N.Y. Democrat. Catholic. Club: Saddle and Bridle (Attica). Home: 324 Spring St. Office: 354 Hunter St., Ossining, N.Y.* Died Jan. 15, 1944.

KIRCHWEY, George W(ashington), lawyer, criminologist; b. Detroit, Mich., July 3, 1885; s. Michael and Maria Anna (Lutz) K.; A.B., Yale U., 1879; LL.D., Yale, New York U., and U. of Cincinnati, 1908; m. Dora Child, d. Rev. Rufus Wendell, Oct. 31, 1883 (died June 30, 1926); children—Karl Wendell, Dorothy Browning, Freda, George Washington (dec.). Admitted to bar, 1882, and practiced at Albany 10 yrs.; editor of Historical Manuscripts, State of N.Y., 1887-89; dean Albany Law Sch., 1889-91; prof. law, 1891-1901, dean Sch. of Law, 1901-10, Kent prof. of law, 1902-16, Columbia U.; commr. on prison reform State of N.Y., 1913-14; warden of Sing Sing Prison, 1915-16; head of dept. of criminology, N.Y. Sch. Social Work, 1917-32; lecturer on criminology, U. of Calif., 1925. Counsel Prison Inquiry Commn. of N.J., 1917; Penal Investigating Commn. of Pa., 1918-19; federal dir. U.S. Employment Service, 1918-19; gen. dir. Pa. Com. on Penal Affairs, 1922-25, counsel, 1925. Chmn. dept. jurisprudence. Internat. Congress Arts and Sciences, St. Louis, 1904, Pres. Am. Peace Soc., 1917; dir. Am. Soc. Internat. Law, 1906-21; v.p. N.Y. Prison Assn.; pres. Am. Inst. Criminal Law and Criminology, 1917; pres. Welfare League Assn., New York; dir. Nat. Soc. of Penal Information; mem. Am. Bar Assn. Mem. Resolutions (platform) Com. of Progressive Nat. Conv., Chicago, 1912; Prog. Party candidate for judge Court of Appeals, N.Y., 1912. Mem. of Century Club. Author: Readings in the Law of Real Property, 1900; Select Cases and Other Authorities on the Law of Mortgage, 1901. Editor department of law, New International Encyclopedia, 1902-04, 1913-15. Contbr. to Encyclopedia Britannica, Encyclopedia of the Social Sciences, The Annals, and to legal and other periodicals. Home: 435 W. 119th St., New York, N.Y. Died Mar. 3, 1942.

KIRK, Arthur Dale, lawyer; b. near Hartford, Ky., Oct. 21, 1886; s. William David and Lucinda Elton (Kirk) K.; B.S., Western Ky. State Teachers Coll., 1910; m. Berenice Virginia May, Dec. 20, 1919. Asst. prin. Marksville (La.) High Sch., 1908-12; prin. Rockport (Ky.) High Sch., 1912-13; admitted to Ky. bar, 1912; county atty., Ohio County, Ky., 1916-22; U.S. commr., Federal Court, Louisville, 1925-29; state bar commr., 2d Appellate Dist., Ky., since 1936; mem. firm Cary, Miller & Kirk; v.p. and dir. Citizens Bank, Hartford, Ky.; dir. The Nat. Deposit Bank, Owensboro, Ky. Home Mutual Life Ins. Co., Louisville. Govt. appeal agt., legal advisor Selective Service Bd.; atty. Federal R.R. Adminstrn. during World War. Mem. U.S. Civil Legion (nat. pres.). Awarded Gold medal, oratory, Hartford Coll. Mem. Am., Ky. State and Daviess County bar assns., Internat. Assn. of Ins. Counsel. Republican. Methodist. Mason, Elk, Maccabee, Woodman. Clubs: Rotary Internat. (Owensboro), Owensboro Country. Home: 1729 McCreary Av. Office: 221 St. Ann St., Owensboro, Ky. Died Jan. 28, 1944.

KIRK, Charles Albert, business exec.; b. Bucyrus, O., Apr. 12, 1904; s. Albert and Florence Maybelle (Shunk) K.; A.B., Western Reserve, 1946; LL.D. (hon.), Syracuse Univ., 1946; m. Mildred Pearl Steenrod, June 27, 1928; children—Shirley Ann, Sally Kay. Salesman Internat. Bus. Machines Corp., Cleveland, O., 1927-31; mgr., Columbus, O., asst. mgr. exhibit, Century of Progress, Chicago, 1933, spl. rep. Pittsburgh, 1933-35, mgr. service bur., Chicago, 1935-37, mgr., St. Louis, 1937-40, exec. asst., New York, 1940-41, vice pres. in charge mfg., 1941-45, exec. vice pres. since 1945; dir. and mem. exec. and finance com. since 1943. Dir. Internat. Bus. Machines Co., Ltd., Can.; Internat. Bus. Machines Co. of Delaware, First Nat. Bank of Binghamton (N.Y.). Trustee New York State Inst. of Applied Arts and Scis., Robert Packer Hosp. Sponsor Readers Digest Fund for the Blind. Mem. Inter-Am. Comml. Arbitration Commn., Internat. Chamber of Commerce (mem. exec. com. U.S. Assos.), Argentine-Am. Chamber of Commerce, Peruvian-Am. Assn., Nat. Fgn. Trade Council, Nat. Safety Council, (hon. pres. Broome Co. (N.Y.) council), Am. Arbitration Assn. (mem. nat. panel of arbitrators), Am. Management Assn., Am. Acad. of Polit. and Social Scis., Am. Civic Assn. (adv. council), Nat. Conf. on Christians and Jews, Air Power League (charter), Export Advt. Assn., Office Equipment Mfrs. Inst., Acad. of Polit. Sci., Jr. Achievement (nat. adv. council), Army Air Forces Aid Soc., Army Ordnance Assn., Commn. for Ordnance Endowment for Scientific Advancement of Mil. Armament in U.S., Navy Indsl. Assn., Assn. Industries of State of New York (dir.), Grand Central Art Galleries, Mus. of Modern Art (asso.), New York State Congress of Parents and Teachers (life), New York State Hist. Assn., Sigma Nu. Democrat. Episcopalian. Clubs: Economic, Advertising, Sales Executives, Metropolitan (trustee) (New York), Binghamton Country, Binghamton (Binghamton, New York); Amrita (Poughkeepsie, New York). Home: 60 E. 67th St., New York 21. Office: 590 Madison Av., New York 22. Died June 1947.

KIRK, Charles Townsend, geologist; b. Francisco, Ind., June 22, 1876; s. David Henry and Martha Jane (Townsend) K.; B.S., U. of Okla., 1904, A.M., 1905; Ph.D., U. of Wis., 1911; m. Bessie Keller, Aug. 22, 1906; children—Ora Jane, Betty Clare, David Keller, Florence Nell. Instr. in geology, State School of Mines, Butte, Mont., 1906-08; instr. in correspondence sch., U. of Wis., 1908-10; instr. and asst. prof. geology, Hunter College, New York City, 1910-13; prof. geology U. of N.M., and state geologist, 1913-17; field geologist, U.S. Geol. Survey, 1910-11, 1934-36, 1938-39. Examinations mining, petroleum and natural gas lands and dam sites in Rocky Mountains, Mid-Continent and Spanish America since 1909. Installed Okla. Mineral Exhibit, La. Purchase Expn., St. Louis, 1904; judge of exhibits Panama Pacific International Exposition San Francisco, California, 1915. Member A.A.A.S., Geological Society of America, Am. Inst. Mining and Metall. Engrs., Am. Assn. Petroleum Geologists, N.Y. Acad. Sciences (sec. geol. sect. 1913), N.M. Geog. Soc. (sec. 1916-17), N.M. Assn. Science (pres. 1916), Tulsa Geol. Soc. (pres. 1923), Sigma Xi, Phi Kappa Phi. Democrat. Mem. Christian (Disciples) Ch. Mason (32°). Wrote: Pennsylvanian-Permian Contact through Oklahoma, 1904; Mineralization in the Copper Veins at Butte, Montana, 1912; The Geography of New Mexico, 1917; Significant Features in Western Coal Deposits; Steep Subsurface Folds versus Faults, 1926. Reviews and contbns. to scientific mags. Home: 1226 S. Newport Av., Tulsa, Okla. Died June 1, 1945.

KIRK, Raymond V., univ. pres.; b. Mount Pleasant, Pa., May 3, 1901; s. Timothy J. and Mary (Shaughnessy) K.; Ph.B., Duquesne U., 1923; Ph.D., New York U., 1933. Entered Holy Ghost Order at Ferndale, Conn., 1920, Apostolic Consecration, June 21, 1926; asst. pastor St. Mark's Ch., New York, 1926-27; instr., Duquesne U. Prep. Sch., 1927-29; organizer and first dean of Duquesne U. Sch. of Edn., 1929-40; pres. Duquesne U. since 1940. Address: Duquesne University, Pittsburgh, Pa.* Died May 27, 1947.

KIRKHAM, Harold Laurens Dundas, plastic surgeon; b. Norfolk, Eng., Mar. 24, 1887; s. Frederick William and Delphine (Laurens) K.; ed. Bedford Modern Sch. (Eng.) and Junior Local, U. of Oxford; M.D., U. of Tex., 1909; m. Frida Julia Buchel, Feb. 8, 1911 (died 1927); children—Harold Buchel, Doris Buchel (Mrs. Charles A. Brokaw); m. 2d, Margaret Shelton Shimin, Apr. 1, 1933; children—Margaret, Elizabeth. Came to U.S., 1904, naturalized, 1918. Interne, St. Joseph's Infirmary, Houston, Tex., 1909; prof. plastic surgery, Baylor U., Houston, Tex., since 1943; plastic surgeon, Southern Pacific R.R., Meth. Hosp., Jefferson Davis Hosp. (all Houston, Tex.). Serving as capt., Med. Corps V(S). U.S.N.R.; chief of dept. of plastic surgery U.S. Naval Hosp., San Diego, Calif.; organizer Med. Specialist Unit. No. 48. U.S.N.R. Diplomate Am. Bd. Surgery (Founders Group); fellow Am. Coll. Surgeons; mem. Am. Bd. Plastic Surgery, Am. Assn. Plastic Surgeons (past pres.), Tex. Surg. Soc. (past pres.), Southern Surg. Soc. Republican. Episcopalian. Clubs: Rotary, Braeburn Country (Houston). Home: 2241 Sunset Blvd., Houston, Tex. Office: 3603 Audubon Pl., Houston, Tex. Died Mar. 18, 1949; buried Forest Park Cemetery, Houston, Tex.

KIRKHAM, Stanton Davis (kûrk'hăm), author; b. Nice, France, Dec. 7, 1868; s. Maj. Murray Davis (U.S. Army) and Julia (Kirkham) Davis (adopted by grandfather, Gen. Ralph Wilson Kirkham, U.S. Army); ed. Calif. pub. schs. and Mass. Inst. Tech.; m. Mary Clark Williams, May 16, 1907; children—(by 1st marriage) Paul Davis, (by 2d marriage) Mary Clark. Traveled extensively in Mexico, S.A., Europe, Asia, Africa. Author: Where Dwells the Soul Serene, 1899; As Nature Whispers, 1900; The Ministry of Beauty, 1907; Mexican Trails; In the Open, 1908; The Philosophy of Self-Help; Resources, 1910; East and West, 1911; Outdoor Philosophy, 1912; North and South, 1913; Half-True Stories, 1916; Animal Nature, and Other Stories, 1926; Cruising, 1927; Shut-In, 1936; The Pearl Ship, 1937. Home: Canandaigua, N.Y. Died Jan. 6, 1944.

KIRKLAND, Winifred Margaretta, author; b. Columbia, Pa., Nov. 25, 1872; d. George Henry and

Emma Matilda (Reagan) Kirkland; grad. Packer Inst., Brooklyn, 1893; A.B., Vassar, 1897; grad. student in English, Bryn Mawr, 1898-1900; unmarried. Teacher of English, The Misses Shipley's Sch., Bryn Mawr, Pa., 1897-99, Bryn Mawr Sch., Baltimore, 1900-02, Baldwin Sch., Bryn Mawr, Pa., 1902-08. Episcopalian. Author: Polly Pot's Parish, 1907, Introducing Corinna, 1909; The Home-comers, 1910; Boy Editor, 1913; Christmas Bishop, 1913; The New Death, 1918; The Joys of Being a Woman, 1918; The View Vertical, 1920; Chaos and a Creed (under pseud. "James Priceman"), 1925; The Great Conjecture—Who Is This Jesus?, 1929; Portrait of a Carpenter, 1931; As Far as I Can See, 1936; Let Us Pray, 1938; Star in the East, 1938; The Man Who Gave Us Christmas, 1940; Are We Immortal?, 1941. Contbr. to various mags. Home: Sewanee, Tenn. Died May 14, 1943.

KIRKPATRICK, Thomas Le Roy, lawyer; b. Mecklenburg County, N.C., May 3, 1877; s. James Watt and Martha Ann (Griffith) K.; prep. edn., Sharon Acad.; student Erskine Coll., Due West, S.C., 1894-98; certificate of completion, U. of N.C. Law Sch., 1900; m. Eva Chalmers, Oct. 9, 1907; children—Thomas Le Roy, Carolyn Chalmers, Nancy Reynolds. Admitted to N.C. bar, 1900, and since practiced at Charlotte; alderman, Charlotte, 1907-11; v.mayor, Charlotte, 1911-17, mayor, 1915-17; chmn. Local Exemption Board, 1917-18; state senator 20th Senatorial Dist., 1933-35. Organizer and 1st pres. Wilmington, Charlotte, Asheville Highway Assn., also Citizens' Highway Assn. of N.C.; drafted Good Roads bill and successfully promoted $50,000,000 road bond issue for N.C.; chmn. bd. Bankhead Nat. Highway Assn.; pres. Chamber of Commerce, Charlotte; pres. U.S. Good Roads Assn., also mem. exec. com., representing N.C.; proponent of $50,000,000,000 bond issue for U.S. Govt. to build internat. system of interstate highways; mem. Sesquicentennial Commn., Phila., 1926. Mem. Queen City N.G., 1892-98; asst. judge advocate gen. N.C.N.G., 1905-09, rank of lt. col.; judge advocate gen., 1913-17, rank of col. Mem. Am., N.C. State and Mecklenburg bar assns., Chamber Commerce of U.S. (mem. council), Charlotte Chamber Commerce (ex-pres.). Democrat. Elder Asso. Reformed Presbyterian Ch.; supt. S.S. Mem. Woodmen of World, Modern Woodmen, Elks, Jr. Order United Am. Mechanics; served as dist. gov. Lions of N.C. and as pres. Lions Club of Charlotte, N.C.; past dictator of the Moose Lodge of Charlotte. Home: "Chal Kirk Manor," Park Rd., Charlotte, R.F.D. 2. Office: First Nat. Bank Bldg., Charlotte, N.C. Died Feb. 4, 1946.

KIRSHMAN, John Emmett, prof. economics; b. Jamestown, Mo., Feb. 8, 1883; s. John and Alvina (Gradolf) K.; Ph.B., Central Wesleyan Coll., Warrenton, Mo., 1904; Ph.M., Syracuse U., 1908; studied U. of Wis., 1908-09, U. of Ill., 1914-15; Ph.D., Harvard, 1918; m. Margaret B. Stanton, Aug. 16, 1916; 1 dau., Margaret Ann. Teacher St. Paul's Acad., St. Paul, Minn., 1904-05, Weiser (Ida.) Acad., 1905-06, Hannibal (Mo.) High Sch., 1906-07, also teacher Syracuse U., 1907-08, U. of Wis., 1908-09, Agrl. Coll., Fargo, N.Dak., 1909-14; teacher U. of Ill., 1914-15, Simmons Coll., Boston, 1916-18; statistician U.S. Shipping Bd., 1918-19; asso. prof. finance, U. of Neb., 1919-24, prof., 1924-34, prof. economics and finance since 1934, also chmn. dept. of economics; specializes in business cycles, finance, investments and corps. Mem. Am. Econ. Assn., Mid-West Econ. Assn. (pres. 1940-41), Phi Beta Kappa, Beta Gamma Sigma, Alpha Kappa Psi. Republican. Conglist. Mason. Author: Principles of Investment, 1924, revised edit., 1933. Contbr. to mags. Home: 3080 Stratford Dr., Lincoln, Neb. Died May 7, 1945; buried in College Cemetery, Iowa State College, Ames.

KIRSHNER, Charles Henry, lawyer; b. Fostoria, O., June 25, 1863; s. Henry and Rebecca (Bucher) K.; A.B., Oberlin, 1886; LL.B., Law Sch. of Cincinnati U., 1888; m. Agnes M. Fairchild, Dec. 24, 1889; children—Robert Fairchild, Mrs. Charlotte Brown, George F., Charles H. Began practice, Salina, Kan., 1888; removed to Kansas City, Mo., 1890; mem. Kirshner & Stroheker; pres. Bankers Mortgage Co. Trustee Oberlin Coll., Kidder Jr. Coll. Mem. Kansas City Bar Assn., Mo. Bar Assn. Republican. Club: The Fossils. Mason. Home: 3050 Harrison St. Office: 215 Wirthman St., Kansas City, Mo. Died Oct. 1938.

KIRSTEIN, Louis Edward, merchant; b. Rochester, N.Y., July 9, 1867; s. Edward and Jeanette (Leiter) K.; ed. business coll., Rochester, N.Y.; hon. M.A., Harvard Univ., 1933; hon. Dr. of Commercial Science, Boston U., 1938; m. Rose Stein, Jan. 23, 1896; children—Mrs. Mina Curtiss, Lincoln Edward, George Garland. Vice-pres. William Filene's Sons Co. since 1911; dir. Abraham & Straus Inc. (New York), B. Forman Co., F. & R. Lazarus & Co., R. H. White Co., Federated Dept. Stores, Bloomingdale Bros. Trustee Industrial Relations Counselors; mem. Exec. Retailer's Com. for Sec. of Treasury; chairman board Am. Retail Fedn.; vice-pres. and dir. Boston Better Business Bureau; chmn. Boston Port Authority; mem. Governing Council, Retail Trade Bd.; mem. Business Advisory Council for Dept. of Commerce, Washington, D.C.; dir. Jewish Welfare Bd.; mem. Nat. Conf. of Jews and Christians; chmn. bd. Am. Jewish Com.; pres. Asso. Jewish Philanthropies (Boston); dir. Community Fedn. of Boston (mem. allocating com.); vice-chmn. Nat. Citizens Com., Mobilization for Human Needs; mem. Mass. Commn. of Public Safety, Public Safety Com. of City of Boston; mem. national sponsoring committee of United Service Organization; mem. bd. mgrs. Boston Dispensary, Children's Hosp.; pres. Boston Pub. Library, Beth Israel Hosp.; pres. bd. West End House (Boston); dir. Boston Legal Aid Soc.; mem. visiting com. Harvard Grad. Sch. of Business Adminstrn.; mem. Com. on Semitic and Egyptian Civilizations, Harvard; mem. Zeta Beta Tau (hon.). Clubs: New Century (hon.), Harvard, University (Boston); Kernwood Country (hon.); Harmonie, Harvard (New York). Home: 333 Commonwealth Av. Office: 426 Washington St., Boston, Mass. Died Dec. 10, 1942.

KISER, Samuel Ellsworth, author, editor; b. Shippensville, Pa.; s. Samuel and Charlotte Kiser; ed. in Pa. and Ohio; m. Mildred M. Palmer; children—Palmer Ellsworth, Howard Spencer. Began writing spl. sketches for Cleveland Leader, 1896; editorial writer Chicago Record-Herald, 1900-14; editor Daily News, Dayton, O., 1917-19. Author: Budd Wilkins at the Show, and Other Verses, 1898; Georgie, 1900; Love Sonnets of an Office Boy, 1902; Ballads of the Busy Days, 1903; Charles, the Chauffeur, 1905; Thrills of a Bell Boy, 1906; Sonnets of a Chorus Girl, 1909; The Whole Glad Year, 1911; The Land of Little Care, 1913; Glorious Day, 1926; It Is To Laugh, 1927. Newspaper columnist and contbr. to mags. Home: Hazelhurst Park, New Rochelle, N.Y. Died Jan. 30, 1942.

KISSELL, Harry Seaman, realtor, banker; b. Springfield, O., Sept. 24, 1875; s. Cyrus Broadwell and Lucretia Carolina (McEwen) K.; student Wittenberg Acad., Springfield, 1888-91; A.B., Wittenberg Coll., Springfield, 1896; m. Olive Troupe, Oct. 17, 1901; children—Roger Troupe, Mary Lucretia (Mrs. Howard Bradshaw Noonan). Began as newspaper reporter, Springfield, 1896; read law 2 yrs.; began in real estate business with father, 1899, later as C. B. Kissell & Son, now president The Kissell Real Estate Company; treasurer R. T. K. Corporation; dir. and mem. exec. com. First Nat. Bank & Trust Company; director C. and L. E. Transportation Company. Chmn. Clark County War Savings Stamp Com. and dir. Am. Red Cross, 1917-20; awarded distinguished service medal of Ohio War Savings Stamp Com. Organizer and 1st chmn. Springfield Community Fund. Mem. commn. which framed present charter of Springfield. Trustee and member executive committee, Wittenberg College. Organizer and first pres. Springfield Real Estate Board; mem. Nat. Assn. of Real Estate Bds. (dir. and ex-pres.), Beta Theta Pi. Republican. Presbyterian. Mason (33°; past Grand Master and Grand Treas. Grand Lodge F.& A.M. of Ohio). Clubs: Rotary (charter mem.; ex-pres.), Men's Literary (ex-pres.). Springfield Country. Contbr. to Nat. Real Estate Journal and other trade magazines. Sponsor of Federal Home Loan Bank for relief of savings institutions holding long time mortgage paper; chmn. Federal Home Loan Bank of Cincinnati. Home: 1801 N. Fountain Blvd., Springfield, O. Offices: First Nat. Bank Bldg., Springfield, O., and U. B. Bldg., Dayton, O. Died Feb. 14, 1946.

KITCHEL, William Lloyd, lawyer; b. New Haven, Conn., Nov. 30, 1869; s. Cornelius Ladd and Alice (Lloyd) K.; A.B., Yale, 1892, B.L., 1895; m. Grace Welch Wheeler, Apr. 16, 1896; children—Lloyd, Saxton Wheeler, Alice Lloyd (Mrs. Joseph W. S. Davis), Denison. Admitted to N.Y. bar, 1895; law clerk in office of Alexander & Green, New York, N.Y., 1895-1907; associated with firm, Strong & Cadwalader (now Cadwalader, Wickersham & Taft) since 1907, mem. of firm since 1914. Mem. bd. trustees Bank of New York since 1943. Lecturer Yale Law Sch., on New York practice, 1902-07. Counsel of Village of Bronxville, N.Y., 1907-11. Mem. Assn. Bar City of New York, N.Y. County Lawyers Assn., Am. and N.Y. State bar assns., Yale Law Sch. Assn., Pilgrims of U.S., Soc. Colonial Wars in State of N.Y., Psi Upsilon, Phi Beta Kappa, Skull and Bones. Clubs: University, Yale, Down Town Association (New York); Graduates (New Haven); St. Andrew's Golf (Hastings-on-Hudson); Yeamans Hall (Charleston, S.C.); Ekwanok Country (Manchester, Vt.). Home: 33 Valley Road, Bronxville, N.Y. Died June 1, 1947.

KITCHELL, Joseph Gray, artist, writer; b. Cincinnati, Apr. 25, 1862; s. Joseph S. K.; educated in Cincinnati and New York; m. Caroline Lincoln Jacobs, Oct. 1890; 1 son, Joseph William. Introduced first bicycle (high wheel) in Cincinnati, imported from Scotland; organizer and pres. of Cincinnati Bicycle Club; dir. League of Am. Wheelmen. Photographic editor Quarterly Illustrator; publisher L'Art du Monde; invented method and apparatus for first scientific composite photograph. In 1900 produced the Kitchell Composite Madonna, a merging of the most important madonnas painted by the great masters during 300 yrs., which attracted wide attention in America and Europe; invented, 1915, and patented new method of reproducing pictures known as "Sub-Chromatic Art," examples of which were accepted by Metropolitan Museum, N.A.D., Congressional Library, British Museum, Bibliothèque Nationale, Paris. Pres. the Ethridge Co., 12 yrs. Recruited and capt. Co. F, 6th Regt. Conn. H.G.; apptd. head of personnel unit, gen. control, gun div. Ordnance Dept., Washington, with rank of capt., Nov. 1917; later headed personnel branch, engring. div. Ordnance Dept.; delivered lectures to stimulate munitions production in N.Y. dist.; made maj., Apr. 1918; pres. Commd. Officer's Exam. Bd., Gen. Staff, stationed in New York; after armistice transferred to Washington in morale br., Gen. Staff; discharged, Apr. 1919. Produced official Red Cross allegorical picture, "Thine Is the Glory," 1919, which was given to War Dept. and presented by sec. of war to Red Cross Hdqrs., Washington. Mem. Conn. State Council Defense, Army Ordnance Assn. Comdr. Military Order Foreign Wars; fellow Royal Soc. Arts (Great Britain); hon. officer, Los Angeles Police Dept. Mason. Club: Manhattan (New York City). Author: American Supremacy, 1901; Earl of Hell, 1923; 25,000 Days; also econ. features and scientific writings in mags. and newspapers. Home: Hollywood Hotel, Hollywood, Calif. Died June 1, 1947.

KITSON, Henry Hudson, sculptor; b. Huddersfield, Eng., Apr. 9, 1863; s. John M. and Emma (Jagger) K.; pupil of Bonnaissieux, Paris; m. 2d, Marie Louise Hobron, 1935. Executed: monument to Mayor Doyle, Providence, R.I.; Hayes Memorial Fountain, Providence; "The Minute Man," at Lexington, Mass.; Iowa State Monument, at Vicksburg Nat. Park; statues Gen. N. P. Banks and Patrick A. Collins, Boston; Gen. Lloyd Tilghman, Paducah, Ky.; General Lee at Vicksburg, Miss.; W. M. Hunt Memorial, Boston; Rodger Conant Statue, Salem, Mass.; Robert Burns Memorial at Boston; Endicott Memorial, State House, Boston, Mass.; Statue of Pilgrim Maiden, at Plymouth, Mass.; Haynes Memorial, at Newark, N.J.; statue of President McKinley, at Walden, N.Y.; statue of Continental Soldier, at Washington's Headquarters, Newburgh, N.Y.; Gov. Smith of Vt., St. Albans, Vt.; statue of Christ, Drexel Memorial, Phila.; Elson Memorial, New England Conservatory of Music, Boston; James Bryce, Nat. Mus., Washington, D.C.; statue of Jefferson Davis, Vicksburg, Miss.; of Gov. Kirkwood of Ia., Vicksburg; statue of Sir Richard Saltonstall and Founders Memorial, Watertown, Mass.; Minute Men Memorial and Shrine of American Liberty, Lexington, Mass.; statues of Gen. Martin L. Smith, Admiral Farragut and Admiral Selfridge, Vicksburg, Miss.; the Minute Man, Framingham, Mass.; Elizabeth Sprague Coolidge portrait relief, South Mountain Temple of Music, Pittsfield, Mass.; Franz Kneisel Memorial, Inst. Musical Art, New York City; statues of Capt. William T. Rigby, Vicksburg, Miss., also King Victor Emanuel, III, and James Viscount Bryce, Nat. Mus. of Art, Washington, D.C., The Music of the Sea, Mus. of Fine Arts, Boston; marble bust Prof. George Martin Lane, Harvard Univ.; bronze bust James Bryce, Newark Mus., Newark, N.J.; Indian Fountain, Lebanon Springs, N.Y.; Music of the Sea (statue only), Port Arthur, Tex.; Brian Boru, Irish warrior king (marble), Museum of Arts and Sciences, Pittsfield, Mass. Awarded three gold medals, Massachusetts Charitable Mechanics' Assn., gold medal of honor, Am. Art Assn., New York, 1886; decoration, Royal Order of Bene Merenti from the King of Roumania, 1889; medals, Paris Expn., 1889, Chicago Expn., 1893, Paris Expn., 1900. Mem. British Charitable Soc., Victorian Soc., Ethnographical Soc. of France, Nat. Sculpture Soc., Nat. Arts Club (New York), Copley Soc., Bostonian Soc., Boston Art Club (Boston). Address: Lee, Mass. Died June 26, 1947.

KITTELL, Albert George (kĭt-tĕl′), editor; b. Blossom, Erie County, N.Y., Apr. 2, 1881; s. Henry and Mary (Wolf) K.; student McPherson (Kan.) Coll., 1903-04; B.S., Kan. State Coll., Manhattan, 1909; m. Marie Fenton, June 21, 1911; children—Marjorie, Doris Marie. Reporter, Manhattan (Kan.) Nationalist, 1908-09; asso. editor Kansas Farmer, Topeka, 1910-14; editor Neb. Farm Jour., Omaha, 1914-24; asso. editor Capper's Weekly, 1924-28, mng. editor, 1928-32, editor since Mar. 1, 1932. Treas. Kan. Congl. Conf. Mem. Topeka Chamber of Commerce, Sigma Delta Chi. Republican. Conglist. Home: 909 Garfield Av. Address: Capper Bldg., Topeka, Kan. Died July 28, 1943.

KITTINGER, Harold D., business exec.; b. South Carrollton, Ky., 1889. Pres. and dir. H. L. Green Co., Inc., Metropolitan Stores, Ltd. of Can., London, Ont., H. D. Kittinger Co., Inc.; dir. Arnold Constable Corp., Sterling Nat. Bank & Trust Co. Home: Union League Club, 37th St. and Park Av., New York, N.Y. Office: 902 Broadway, New York 10. Died Oct. 4, 1947.

KITTREDGE, George Watson, civil engr.; b. N. Andover, Mass., Dec. 11, 1856; s. Joseph and Henrietta Frances (Watson) K.; B.S., Mass. Inst. Tech., 1877; m. Georgia Davis, Oct. 17, 1888. With Pa. Lines West of Pittsburgh, 1880-90; engr. Louisville Bridge Co., 1886-88; engr. maintenance of way and asst. chief engr., 1890-91, chief engr., 1891-1906, C.,C.,C.&St.L. Ry.; chief engr. Louisville & Jeffersonville Bridge Co., 1900-06; chief engr. N.Y.C.&H. R.R.R. and Terminal Ry. of Buffalo and of N.J. Shore Line R.R., 1906-14; chief engr. N.Y. Central R.R., 1914-27, also chief engr. Hudson River Connecting R.R., Am. Niagara R.R., 1914-27 (retired); cons. engr. since 1927. Mem. Corp. Mass. Inst. Tech., 1907-12. Fellow A.A.A.S.; hon. mem. Am. Soc. C.E. (v.p. 1917-18), Am. Ry. Engring. Assn. (ex-pres.). Home: 592 N. Broadway, Yonkers, N.Y. Died Aug. 23, 1947.

KITTS, Joseph Arthur (kĭtz), cons. engr. and concrete technologist; b. Nevada City, Calif., Apr. 14, 1881; s. James and Mary Alice (Rafford) K.; student U. of Calif., 1900-03, 1908-09; m. Alberta Waldo Hawley, Sept. 10, 1912; children—James Waldo, Mary Elisabeth, Jean Josephine. Mining, surveys and constrn., Nevada City Mines, 1900-05; engr. of constrn., Panama Canal, 1905-06; engr. and supt. constrn., C. A. Meusdorfer, Couchot & O'Shaughnessy and Union Constrn. Co., San Francisco, 1906-10; engr. of surveys, concrete tests, design and constrn., Panama Canal, 1910-15; resident and field engr. U.S. Steel Co., Sonoma County Highway Commn., Calif. Highway

Commn., Portland Cement Co., 1915-24; cons. concrete technologist, operating as Joseph A. Kitts Co., San Francisco, since 1924. Served as capt. Engr. Corps, U.S. Army, in France, 1917-19. Mem. Alpha Tau Omega (pres. Gamma Iota Asso.), Calif. Alumni Assn., Am. Concrete Inst., Am. Legion, Am. Red Cross. Awarded Roosevelt Panama Canal medal and bars; Victory medal with France bar. Author: Coordination of Basic Principles of Concrete Mixtures, 1933; Specifications for Structural Concrete, 1937. Contbr. to Concrete (Mag.). Inventor erosion control, water conservation, irrigation system, in use in exptl. project, Town Talk, Calif., since 1944. Home: Nevada City, Calif. Office: Rialto Bldg., San Francisco. Died March 1947.

KixMILLER, William, lawyer; b. Vincennes, Ind., Jan. 30, 1885; s. Simon and Wilhelmina (Alhorn) K.; student Vincennes U., 1905; Ph.B., U. of Chicago, 1908, J.D., 1910; m. May Wood, Oct. 14, 1914; children—Richard Wood, Jean Pratt. Admitted to Ill. bar, 1910; mem. KixMiller, Baar & Morris, Chicago, New York, and Washington; former pres. Commerce Clearing House. Served as prof. law, University of Florida, 1910-11, John Marshall Law Sch., Chicago, 1912, Walton Sch. of Commerce, 1913-14. Vice chmn. bd. of trustees Nat. Coll. of Edn., Evanston, Ill. Mem. Am., Ill. State and Chicago bar assns., Delta Chi. Republican. Methodist. Clubs: Union League, Sheridan Shore Yacht. Co-author: Story Case Business Law, 1915; United States Income and War Tax Guide, 1917-29; Unabridged Federal Income Tax Services, 1920-29; Consolidated United States Income Tax Laws, 1929; Board of Tax Appeals Services, 1924-29; State Inheritance Tax Services, 1924-29; Cyclopedic Tax Service since 1944. Author: Can Business Build a Great Age; We Can Have Prosperity; Foundation Guide for Payroll Taxes; Freedom From Want—An Achievement Through Revelation; Allocations and Priorities Guide. Home: 789 Michigan Av., Wilmette, Ill. Office: 11 S. La Salle St., Chicago, Ill. Died Apr. 13, 1945.

KLATH, Thormod Oscar, foreign service officer; b. Sioux City, Ia., Nov. 26, 1890; s. Olaus and Caroline Klath; student Red Wing (Minn.) Sem., 1911; LL.B., Nat. U. Law Sch., 1916, LL.M., 1917; m. Edna Marie Blomberg, Feb. 6, 1919; children—Robert Alan, Carolyn Marie. Clerk, Dept. of Interior, 1911-16, Dept. of Commerce, 1916-19; Am. trade commr., Copenhagen, Denmark, 1919-22; mgr. Chicago Dist. office, Dept. of Commerce, 1922-23, N.Y. office, 1923-24; Am. trade commr., Stockholm, Sweden, 1924-25; commercial attaché, Am. Legation, Stockholm, 1925-35, Copenhagen, 1935-37; commercial attaché, Am. Bern, Switzerland, 1940-42 and Stockholm, Sweden, since 1942. Delegate to the Congress of International Chamber of Commerce at Stockholm, 1927; observer Internat. Congress of Forestry Exptl. Stations, Stockholm, 1929; del. 23d Plenary Assembly of Internat. Parliamentary Conf. on Commerce, Warsaw, 1938. Mem. Sigma Nu Phi. Home: Sioux City, Ia. Address: Dept. of State, Washington, D.C. Died Oct. 1, 1943.

KLEBS, Arnold Carl (klēbz), physician; b. Berne, Switzerland, Mar. 17, 1870; s. Dr. Edwin Th. A. and Rose (Grossenbacher) K.; ed. primary sch. and Imperial Gymnasium, Prague, and gymnasium at Zürich, grad., 1888; univs. of Zürich, Berlin, Kiel, Wurzburg, Berne, Basel; Swiss state exam., 1894, M.D., 1895 (Basel); asst. in polyclinic (Basel); pathol. instr., Zürich; post-grad. studies at London and Paris; m. Margaret Forbes, June 1898 (died 1899); m. 2d, Mrs. Harriet K. Newell, May 21, 1909. Practiced at Chicago, 1896-1909; admitted to U.S. citizenship, 1904; in Switzerland, 1909-14, Washington, 1915-18, New York, 1918-19, 1926-27. Formerly cons. physician (tuberculosis) to Cook County (Ill.) instns., and dir. Chicago Tuberculosis Inst. Vice-pres. sect. prevention diseases, Internat. Congress Hygiene, Washington, 1912; mem. several Am. and foreign med. and scientific socs. Club: Cosmos (Washington). Editor Am. Treatise on Tuberculosis, 1909. Author: History of Variolation, 1914; Leonardo da Vinci Studies, 1916; Tuberculosis and Military Organization, 1925; Bibliography of Medical Incunabula, 1917, 18; Early Herbals (Lugano), 1925; Remèdes contre la peste (Paris), 1925, English edit. (with E. Droz), 1926; Die ersten gedurckten Pestschriften (with Karl Sudhoff), Munich, 1926; Incunabula Scientifica et Medica, 1938. Articles on med. and hist. subjects. Address: Les Terrasses, Nyon, Switzerland.

Died Mar. 6, 1943.

KLEENE, Gustav Adolph (klā'nā), college prof.; b. Peoria, Ill., May 30, 1868; s. Frederick and Elizabeth (Schaulin) K.; A.B., U. of Mich., 1891; univs. of Berlin and Tübingen, 1893-94. Columbia, 1894-95; Ph.D., U. of Pa., 1896; m. Alice Lena Cole, June 18, 1907; 1 son, Stephen Cole. Asst. in economics, U. of Wis., 1900-01; instr. economics and social science, Swarthmore Coll., 1902-03; asst. prof. economics, Trinity Coll., 1903-04, prof., 1904-38, prof. emeritus since 1938. Mem. and editor of report of Hartford Vice Commn., 1912-13. Mem. Am. Econ. Assn., Royal Econ. Soc. Author: Profit and Wages, 1916. Contbr. to econ. jours. Home: Hartford, Conn. Died July 10, 1946.

KLEIN, Eugene S., architect; b. St. Louis, Mo., Mar. 11, 1876; s. Judge Jacob and Lilly (Schreiber) K.; student, Smith Acad., St. Louis, 1894-95; A.B., Harvard, 1899; B.S. Arch., cum laude, Lawrence Scientific School, Harvard U., 1901; m. Nella M. Lambert, January 7, 1907; 1 son, Eugene Lambert. Draughtsman, Mauran Russell & Garden (Mauran Russell & Crowell), 1901-12; partner of LaBeaume & Klein since 1912. Mem. St. Louis Public Recreation Commn., 1909; project supervisor, housing div., Emergency Fleet Corp., 1918; mem. Plaza Commn., St. Louis (designed Municipal Auditorium) to Oct. 1934; supervising architect, Penal Insts. for Bi-partisan Advisory Bd., State Bldg. Commn., 1934-39; architect, 7th Constructing Quartermaster's Zone, 1941; coordinator, H. B. Deal Co., El Dorado, Ark., Anhydrous Ammonia Plant, 1942. Dir. Mercantile Library Assn. Fellow: Am. Inst. Architects. Home: 5333 Waterman Av. Office: 315 N. 7th St., St. Louis, Mo. Deceased.

KLEINSCHMIDT, Rudolph August (klīn'shmĭt), lawyer; b. Memphis, Tenn., June 26, 1878; s. August A. and Carrie (Schwing) K.; Johns Hopkins U., 1 yr.; B.L. and LL.B., U. of Mo., 1900; m. Mabel A. Diedrichsen, July 8, 1903; children—Mildred, Ralph. Practiced Oklahoma City, 1900-23, Tulsa since 1923; mem. firm of Highley & Kleinschmidt, 1901-04, asst. atty., 1904-09, gen. atty. for Okla., 1909-23, St.L. &S.F. R.R. Lecturer, Law Sch. U. of Okla., 1915-17; mem. Tulsa City Plan Commn., 1927-30; pres. of Tulsa Safety Council, 1938-40. Democrat. Mem. Am. Bar Assn. (v.p. for Okla. 1913-15), Okla. State Bar Assn. (chmn. gen. council 1914), Tulsa County Bar Assn., Sigma Chi, Phi Delta Phi. Mason (32°, Shriner). Author: Kleinschmidt and Highley's Oklahoma Form Book, 8th edit., 1946. Home: 1216 E. 28th St. Office: 218 Beacon Bldg., Tulsa 3, Okla. Died Sept. 3, 1947.

KLINE, Whorten Albert, educator; b. York County, Pa., Apr. 24, 1864; s. Daniel and Margaret A. (Ruby) K.; A.B., Ursinus Coll., Collegeville, Pa., 1893; A.M. and B.D., 1896, Litt.D., 1913, LL.D., 1943; student University of Pennsylvania, 1897-1901; unmarried. Teacher public schools, Pennsylvania, 1883-86; instr. Latin, Ursinus Academy, 1893-96; instr. Latin, Ursinus Coll., 1896-1903, prof. Latin lang. and lit. since 1903, dean since 1909. Ordained minister Ref. Ch. in U.S., 1896. Mem. Classical Assn. Middle States and Md., Phila. Bot. Club. Republican. Address: Ursinus College, Collegeville, Pa. Died Nov. 20, 1946.

KLOPP, Henry Irwin, psychiatrist; b. Stouchsburg, Pa., Jan. 1, 1870; s. Jerome and Katherine (Groh) K.; student Palatinate (now Albright Coll.), Myerstown, Pa., 1885; M.D., Hahnemann Med. Coll., 1894; D.Sc., Muhlenberg Coll., Allentown, Pa., 1927; m. Elizabeth Ladora Stump, Dec. 28, 1898; 1 dau., Mrs. Robert E. Bender. With Westboro (Mass.) State Hosp., 1895-1912; supt. and physician in chief Allentown State Homeopathic Hospital, 1912-42, superintendent emeritus since July 1, 1942; asso. prof. psychiatry Hahnemann Medical Coll., 1912-30, clinical prof. mental diseases, 1930-35, prof. mental diseases, 1935-42, professor emeritus in psychiatry since 1942; member board dirs. Lehigh Valley Child Guidance Clinic and Northampton County Branch of Pa. Assn. for the Blind, Boys Club and Family Welfare of Allentown, Case Committee of Family Welfare of Bethlehem, Pa.; special neuropsychiatric examiner U.S.P.H. Service, 1919-21. Fellow American College Physicians; mem. Am. Psychiatric Assn., Phila. Psychiatric Assn., Pa. Psychiatric Soc. (pres. 1940-41), N.E. Psychiatric Assn., Am. Inst. Homeopathy, Pa. State Homeo. Med. Soc. (pres. 1932-33), Am. Congress on Internal Medicine, and many others. Member Reformed Ch. Clubs: Contemporary, Lehigh Valley Torch. Contbr. numerous articles to med. jours. Address: Hotel Traylor, Allentown, Pa. Died Mar. 7, 1945.

KNABENSHUE, Paul (k'nä'bĕn-shōō), foreign service officer; b. Toledo, O., Oct. 31, 1883; s. Samuel S. and Salome (Natlack) K.; grad. high sch., Toledo, 1903; study under pvt. tutors, 1907-08; m. Olive Parr, Aug. 8, 1911; children—Paul Denis, Iona Macdonnell. Partner and gen. mgr. Geroe & Knabenshue, brokers, Toledo, 1903-04; vice-consul, Belfast, Ireland, 1906-11, vice and dep. consul, May-July 1911; vice and dep. consul gen., Cairo, Egypt, 1911-15, vice-consul, 1915-17, consul, 1917-19; consul, Beirut, Syria, 1919-28; consul gen., Beirut, Syria, May-Oct. 1928, Jerusalem, 1928-32; minister resident and consul gen. Bagdad, Iraq, since 1932; E.E. and M.P. to Sultan of Muscat and Oman, 1933, on 100th anniversary of the signing of Treaty of Amity and Commerce with Muscat. Mem. Sigma Lambda Nu (nat. high sch. fraternity; national pres. 1904). Home: Los Angeles, Calif. Address: Am. Legation, Bagdad, Iraq.*
Died Feb. 2, 1942.

KNAEBEL, Ernest (k'nā'bĕl), lawyer; b. Manhasset, L.I., N.Y., June 14, 1872; s. John H. and Susan Dikeman (Pray) K.; A.B., Yale Univ., 1894, LL.B., summa cum laude, 1896, LL.M., magna cum laude, 1897; m. Cornelia Park, July 10, 1900; children—Katharine Winthrop, John Ballantine, Charles Pray. Admitted to N.M. bar, 1895, N.Y. bar, 1897, Colo. bar, 1899, U.S. Supreme Ct., 1910; practiced at New York, 1897-98, at Denver, 1899-1909; asst. U.S. atty., and spl. asst. U.S. atty., Colo., 1902-07; spl. asst. to the atty. gen. U.S., 1907-08, engaged in land fraud prosecutions; organized Pub. Lands Div., Dept. Justice, Washington, 1909, and in charge of it, 1909-16; asst. atty. gen. U.S., May 9, 1911-Oct. 31, 1916; reporter of decisions Supreme Court of U.S., Oct. 31, 1916. Tendered his resignation because of ill health, Dec. 13, 1943. Retirement allowed as of Jan. 31, 1944. Edited and reported Vols. 242-321 (incl.) official reports of supreme court. Republican. Member Am. Bar Assn., Phi Beta Kappa, Phi Alpha Delta. Clubs: Lawyers' (bd. of govs.), Cosmos, Yale (all of Washington). Home: 3707 Morrison St. N.W., Washington, D.C. Died Feb. 19, 1947.

KNAPP, Fred Church, (năp), lumberman; b. Hudson, Mich., Apr. 4, 1865; s. Perry and Sarah (Church) K.; ed. pub. schs.; m. Cora Brewer, Oct. 24, 1888. Began in lumber business in Mich., 1890; moved to Portland, Ore., 1904; pres. The Knapp Co. V.chmn. Commn. of Public Docks, Portland; pres. Portland Chamber of Commerce, 1912; trustee Y.M.C.A. Republican. Baptist. Mason. Clubs: Arlington, Press, Foreign Commerce. Home: 5922 N. Willamette Blvd. Address: Henry Bldg., Portland, Ore. Died Jan. 24, 1943.

KNAPP, Kemper K., lawyer; b. Marquette, Green Lake County, Wis., Mar. 7, 1860; s. Charles and Jennette (Vine) K.; B.S., U. of Wis., 1879, LL.B., 1882, also LL.B. In practice at Chicago, since 1882; now sr. mem. law firm Knapp, Allen and Cushing. In law dept. Chicago Great Western R.R. Co., 1885-90, C.&N. Pacific R.R. Co., 1890-93; atty. Wis. Central Co., operating C.&N.P. R.R. Co., 1893-95; atty. Chicago & Calumet Terminal Ry. Co., 1893-97; atty. for receivers, C.&N.P. R.R. Co., 1895-97; gen. atty. Chicago Terminal Transfer R.R. Co., E., J.&E. Ry. Co. of Chicago, Lake Shore & Eastern Ry. Co. and Ill. Steel Co., 1897-99; gen. counsel, respectively, since 1899 of Ill. Steel Co., E.,J.&E. Ry. Co., and of Chicago Lake Shore & Eastern Ry. Co.; dir. many cos.; gen. counsel By-Products Coke Corp. (now Interlake Iron Co.), 1921—. Home: 55 E. Division St. Office: 208 S. La Salle St., Chicago, Ill.* Died 1944.

KNAPP, Shepherd, clergyman; b. N.Y. City, Sept. 8, 1873; s. Shepherd and Emma (Benedict) K.; A.B., Columbia, 1894; B.D., Yale, 1897; D.D., New York U., 1912; unmarried. Ordained Congl. ministry, 1897; pastor 1st Congl. Ch., Southington, Conn., 1897-1901; asst. pastor Brick Presbyn. Ch., N.Y. City, 1901-08; pastor Central Church (Congl.), Worcester, Mass., 1908-36. Trustee Memorial Hosp.; mem. corp. Worcester Art Museum. Y.M.C.A. sec., France, 1917-18. Mem. Am. Antiquarian Soc., Phi Beta Kappa, Alpha Delta Phi. Clubs: Bohemian, Shakespeare (Worcester); Columbia Univ. (New York). Author: History of the Brick Presbyterian Church, 1908; On the Edge of the Storm, 1921; Old Joe and Other Vesper Stories, 1922; The Liberated Bible, 1941. Home: 35 Chestnut St., Worcester 2, Mass.; and "Kettleholes," Boylston, Mass. Died Jan. 11, 1946.

KNIBBS, Harry Herbert (nĭbz), author; b. Clifton, Ont., Can., Oct. 24, 1874; s. George and Sara Augusta (Woodruff) K.; ed. Woodstock and Bishop Ridley colls., Ont., and Harvard (non-grad.); m. Ida Julia Pfeiffer, June 28, 1899. Author: First Poems, 1908; Lost Farm Camp, 1912; Stephen March's Way, 1913; Overland Red, 1914; Songs of the Outlands, 1914; Sundown Slim, 1915; Riders of the Stars, 1916; Tang of Life, 1917; Ridin' Kid from Powder River, 1919; Songs of the Trail, 1920, Partners of Chance, 1921; Saddle Songs, 1922; Wild Horses, 1924; Temescal, 1925; Sungazers, 1926; Sunny Mateel, 1927; Songs of the Lost Frontier, 1930; Gentlemen, Hush! (with Turbesé Lummis), 1933; The Tonto Kid, 1936; short stories and verse have appeared in leading publs. and anthologies. Home: 851 S. Coast Blvd., La Jolla, Calif. Died May 17, 1945.

KNICKERBOCKER, Hubert Renfro (nĭk'ĕr-bŏk-ĕr), newspaper man; b. Yoakum, Tex., Jan. 31, 1898: s. Hubert Delancey (Rev.) and Julia Catherine (Opdenweyer) K.; A.B., Southwestern U., Georgetown, Texas, 1917, Litt.D., 1941; student Columbia, 1919-20, U. of Munich (Germany), 1923-24, U. of Vienna, U. of Berlin, 1924; m. Laura Patrick, 1918 (divorced); 1 son; m. 2d, Agnes Schjoldager; 3 daughters. Reporter Newark Morning Ledger, 1920-22, New York Evening Post, 1922, New York Sun, 1922; head department journalism, Southern Methodist University, 1922-23; assistant Berlin corres. New York Evening Post and Phila. Public Ledger, 1924-25, Berlin corr., 1928-41; Moscow corr. Internat. News Service, 1925-27, Berlin corr., 1928-33; travelling corr. Internat. News Service, 1933-41; covered Italo-Abyssinian War, 1935-36, Spanish Civil War, 1936-37, Sino-Japanese War, 1937, Battle of France, 1939-40, Battle of Britain, London Blitz, 1940; Southwest Pacific, Java, Australia, New Guinea, 1942; Sicily, Italy, Normandy, France, Belgium, Germany, 1944-45; Middle East, Palestine, Turkey, 1946; chief foreign service Chicago Sun, 1941-45. The official correspondent United States Army, 1st Division, North Africa, 1942-43. Awarded Pulitzer prize for correspondents, 1939. Served with Signal Corps, United States Army, World War I. Member of Sigma Delta Chi, Kappa Alpha. Author: Fighting the Red Trade Menace, 1931; The Red Menace—Progress of the Soviet Five-Year Plan, 1931; The German Crisis, 1932; Can Europe Recover?, 1932; Will War Come in Europe, 1934; Siege of the Alcazar, 1937; Is Tomorrow Hitler's?, 1941. Address: 269 Piermont Av., Nyack, N.Y. Died July 13, 1949.

KNIGHT, Augustus Smith (nīt), physician, retired; b. Manchester, Mass., Nov. 21, 1864; s. John and Deborah (Carleton) K.; grad. Phillips Acad., Andover, Mass., 1884, Harvard, 1887; M.D., Harvard, 1891; m. Anita Merle-Smith, July 28, 1930; 1 son, Augustus Smith. Practiced in N.Y. City as med. dir. Metropolitan Life Ins. Co., 1899-1934. Pres. bd. of mgrs. N.J. State Hosp. for Mental Diseases, Greystone Park, N.J.; chmn. bd. of trustees of Somerset Hosp., Somerville, N.J.; trustee and chmn. house com. of Neighborhood House and Hosp., Inc., Keene Valley, New York. Fellow American College of Surgeons; member National Committee for Mental Hygiene (board directors); Harvard Med. Soc. of New York, Med. Soc. of N.J., Somerset County Med. Soc. (N.J.). Republican. Episcopalian. Clubs: Harvard (New York); Essex Fox Hounds (Peapack, N.J.); Keene Valley (N.Y.) Country (pres.). Home: Far Hills, N.J. Died March 21, 1948.

KNIGHT, Charles Mellen, chemist; b. Dummerston, Vt., Feb. 1, 1848; s. Joel and Fannie Maria (Duncan) K.; grad. Westbrook Sem., Deering, Me., 1868; A.B., Tufts Coll., 1873; A.M., 1878; post-grad. Harvard and Mass. Inst. Tech., 1874; hon. Sc.D., Buchtel Coll., 1897; m. May Acomb, Aug. 31, 1882 (died Oct. 31, 1930); children—Maurice Acomb, Hal Greenwood, Helen Lillian. Prof. natural science, 1875-83, physical science, 1883-1907, chemistry, 1907-13, prof. emeritus since 1913, dean, 1902-13, Buchtel Coll.; acting pres. Buchtel Coll., 1896-97; Knight Chem. Lab. named for him, 1909. Established a course in rubber chemistry, the first in any Am. coll., 1909. Universalist. Fellow A.A.A.S. (emeritus); mem. Am. Chem. Soc., Phi Beta Kappa, Zeta Psi, Phi Sigma Alpha. Contbr. on sanitary science, chemistry of rubber. Clubs: University, Chemists (hon. mem.). Home: (summer) Akron, O.; (winter) Coral Gables, Fla. Died July 3, 1941.

KNIGHT, Edward Hooker, clergyman, educator; b. Hebron, Conn., Oct. 22, 1854; s. Rev. Merrick and Abbie (Ward) K.; A.B., Amherst, 1876, A.M., 1879; grad. Hartford Theol. Sem., 1880, D.D., 1907; instr. Williston Sem., Easthampton, Mass., 1877-78; student Princeton Theol. Sem., 1880-81, U. of Berlin, 1881-82; m. Martha L. Gates, Oct. 24, 1883; children—Avis, Edith, Marian Ethel. Ordained Congl. ministry, 1883; pastor East Granville, Mass., 1882-83, West Springfield, Mass., 1883-92; prof. N.T. lang. and lit., Hartford Sch. of Religious Edn. (now a part of Hartford Sem. Foundation), 1892-1927, dean, 1904-27, dean emeritus since 1927. Mem. Soc. Bibl. Lit. and Exegesis, Phi Beta Kappa, Delta Kappa Epsilon. Republican. Club: Congregational. Author: A Guide in the Study of the Apostolic Age, 1936. Home: 71 Tremont St., Hartford, Conn. Died Feb. 28, 1948.

KNIGHT, Erastus Cole, ex-mayor; b. Buffalo, N. Y., Mar. 1, 1857; s. Theodore Columbus and Sarah Minerva (Cole) K.; grad. Buffalo pub. sch. and bus. coll.; m. Mary Elizabeth Cowles, May 14, 1881. Traveling salesman until 1880; in wholesale commn. business; sr. mem. Knight, Lennox & Co., 1880; in real estate business, 1887, also builder in firm of Jenkins & Knight, 1892; pres. E. C. & G. L. Knight, dealers in coal, since Mar. 1, 1903. Served as pvt. 74th Regt., N.Y. State Militia, participating in the defense of property at Hornellsville, N.Y., during railroad strike, 1877. Supervisor City of Buffalo, 1890-94; city comptroller, 1895-1900; comptroller State of N.Y., 1901; mayor of Buffalo, 1902-05. Republican. Presbyterian. Home: 388 Delaware Av., Buffalo, N.Y. Died Sept. 3, 1923.

KNIGHT, Eric, author; b. Menston, Yorkshire, England, Apr. 10, 1897; s. Frederic Harrison and Marian Hilda (Creasser) K.; ed. Bewerly Sch., England; art edn., Boston Mus. of Fine Arts and N.Y. Academy Design; m. 2d, Jere Knight, Dec. 2, 1932; children (by 1st marriage)—Betty, Winifred (Mrs. Charlton Mewborn, III), Jennie (Mrs. Frank Moore). Served with Princess Patricia's Canadian Light Infantry, World War I; served with U.S. Army, rank of maj., World War II. Awarded Legion of Merit (posthumously). Author: Song on Your Bugles, 1937; You Play the Black and the Red Comes Up (pseud. Richard Hallas), 1938; The Flying Yorkshireman, 1938; The Happy Land, 1940; Lassie Come-Home, 1940; This Above All, 1941; Sam Small Flies Again (The Amazing Adventures of the Flying Yorkshireman), 1942. Contbr. to Saturday Evening Post, Esquire, Story Mag. Home: Springhouse Farm, Pleasant Valley, Pa. Killed in line of duty, Jan. 14, 1943; buried in Jefferson National Cemetery, St. Louis.

KNIGHT, Frederic Butterfield, univ. prof.; b. Springfield, Mass., July 2, 1891; s. Frederic H. and Marian (Butterfield) K.; B.A., Boston U., 1913; M.A., Harvard, 1915; Ph.D., Columbia, 1920; m. Florence Brockhausen, June 16, 1922; children—Florence Butterfield, Frederic Paulsen. Was teacher in high school, Milton, Mass., 1913; supt. of schools, Ipswich, 1914-15, Danvers, 1916-19; prof. edn. and psychology, State U. of Ia., 1920-37; director div. of edn. and applied psychology, Purdue U. since 1937; former gen. editor, Education Series, Longmans, Green & Co.; dir. Gary, Ind., Sch. Survey, 1940-41, Richmond, Ind., 1942, Parkersburg, W.Va., 1944. Director Indiana State Education Committee for War Veterans. Sergeant Medical Corps, United States Army, General Hospital, Plattsburg, New York, 1918-19. Vice-president of Section Q of American Association for Advancement of Science, 1935-36. Editorial Consultant American Technical Society, 1946. Mem. S.A.R., Am. Legion, Sigma Xi, Phi Beta Kappa, Phi Delta Kappa, Beta Theta Pi. Methodist. Author: Qualities Relating to Success in Teaching, 1922; Standard Mathematical Service, 1927; High School Efficiency Book, 1928; The French Work Book, 1929; Basic Spelling Units, 1929; Basic Latin Units, 1929; (with others) 29th Yearbook of Nat. Soc. for Study of Education, 1930; The Geometry Work-Book, The Algebra Work-Book, A First Course in Educational Psychology, Basic German Units, 1931; Number Stories (I and III), 1941; Algebra—First Course, 1937; The Study Arithmetics, 1943; Mathematics and Life, 1937; Psychology of Normal People, 1946, (with others) We, The Guardians of Our Liberty, 1941; Arithmetic for the Emergency, 1942; The Refresher Book, 1943; also articles in mags. Home: West Lafayette, Ind. Died June 19, 1948.

KNIGHT, George Laurence, mech. engr.; b. Haddonfield, N.J., Feb. 20, 1878; s. George Warren and Ada Danforth (Atkinson) K.; grad. William Penn Charter Sch., 1896; E.E. (diploma, before degrees were conferred), Drexel Inst. Tech., 1900; m. Evelyn Creveling Sharp, Nov. 23, 1904 (died May 10, 1941); children—George Laurence, Richard Bunting. Began as switch operator Philadelphia Electric Co., later became draftsman N.Y. Edison Co.; with Brooklyn Edison Co., 1905-42, successively as chief draftsman, designing engr., mechanical engr., v.p. retired Mar. 1942. Trustee and sec. Bay Ridge Savings Bank since 1946. V.p. Victory Memorial Hosp. Fellow Am. Soc. M.E. (mem. and past chmn. finance com.), Am. Inst. E.E.; mem. United Engring. Trustees (chmn. finance com.). Past pres. Brooklyn Engrs. Club. Mem. and clerk of vestry Christ Ch. (Episcopal), Bay Ridge. Home: 1 Harbor Lane, Brooklyn, N.Y. Died March 27, 1948.

KNIGHT, Harry Clifford, telephone official; b. Pittston, Me., Nov. 2, 1876; s. William and Sarah (McFadden) K.; A.B., Bowdoin Coll., 1898; hon. D.Sc., 1938; hon. M.A., Yale, 1935; m. Mabel A. Bacon, Aug. 6, 1902; 1 son, Gordon C. Teacher successively at Franklin (N.Y.), Norfolk (Conn.) and Leominster (Mass.) until 1902; with Southern New Eng. Telephone Co., 1902-41, pres., 1930-41; trustee New Haven Savings Bank; director Union & New Haven Trust Co., Security Insurance Co. of New Haven. Pres. N.E. Council, 1931-32. Pres. Gen. Hosp. Soc. of Conn., 1935-44. Republican. Conglist. Clubs: Quinnipiack, Graduate, New Haven Country. Home: 389 Norton Parkway, New Haven, Conn. Died July 20, 1949.

KNIGHT, Henry Granger, chemist; b. Bennington, Ottawa County, Kan., July 21, 1878; s. Edwin Richard and Elva Maud (Edwards) K.; A.B. in chemistry, U. of Wash., 1902, A.M., 1904; student in chemistry, U. of Chicago, 1902-03, summer session, 1906; Ph.D., U. of Ill., 1917; m. Nelly Dryden, June 28, 1905; 1 son, Richard Dryden. Asst. 1900-01, instr., 1901-02, asst. prof. chemistry, 1903-04, U. of Wash.; asst. in chemistry, U. of Chicago, 1902-03, fellow-elect, 1903; prof. chemistry and state chemist, U. of Wyo., 1904-10; dir. Wyo. Expt. Sta., and Farmers' Insts., Wyoming, 1910-18, dean Coll. of Agr., 1912-18; dean and dir. Okla. Agrl. Coll., Stillwater, 1918-21; hon. fellow Cornell U., 1921-22; dir. and research chemist Expt. Sta. W.Va. U., 1922-27, dean Coll. of Agr., 1926-27; chief Bur. of Chemistry and Soils, 1927-39, chief Bur. Agrl. Chemistry and Engring. since 1939, U.S. Dept. of Agr. Chmn. Wyo. State Council Defense, 1917-18. Fellow Am. Inst. Chemists (pres. 1933-35); mem. Am. Chem. Soc., Phi Gamma Delta, Sigma Xi, Phi Beta Kappa, Alpha Zeta, Phi Lambda Upsilon, Phi Kappa Phi. Mason. Methodist. Clubs: Cosmos, Rotary. Writer of various monographs on qualitative analysis; research work on potable waters, effect of alkali upon seeds, food adulterations, Wyo. forage plants, soil nitrogen, wool, poisonous plants, effect of alkali upon cement drainage experiments, digestion experiments, soil acidity, etc. Address: 4436 Q St. N.W., Washington, D.C. Died July 13, 1942.

KNIGHT, Howard Roscoe, social worker; b. Boston, Mass., June 23, 1889; s. Frederic Harrison and Marian (Butterfield) K.; ed. Tilton Sch., 1905-07, Boston U., 1908-12 (A.B.), New York U. (part time), 1912-16; m. Pauline Helms, Feb. 18, 1917; children—Jean Marion, Howard Helms (killed in action 1944), Philip Allerton (killed in action 1944). Social worker Dept. of Recreation, Russell Sage Foundation, 1912-16, Nassau-Suffolk County Y.M.C.A., Mineola, N.Y., 1916-17; exec. sec. Matinecock Neighborhood Assn., Locust Valley, N.Y., 1917-21; acting mgr. Insular Div., Am. Red Cross, Washington, D.C., 1920-21; mem. staff Ohio Inst., Columbus, 1921-26; exec. sec. Ohio Welfare Conf., 1921-26; gen. sec. Nat. Conf. Social Work, Columbus, O., since 1926; sec.-gen. Internat. Conf. of Social Work, since 1946. Pres. Ohio Welfare Conf., 1930; sec. U.S. Com., Internat. Conf. of Social Work, 1928, 32, 36, 40. Mem. Am. Assn. Social Workers, Nat. Conf. Social Work, Am. Sociol. Soc., Am. Acad. Polit. and Social Science. Democrat. Methodist. Clubs: Columbus, Torch. Editor of Proceedings of Nat. Conf. of Social Work since 1926. Contbr. to Social Work Year Book, 1933, 35, 37. Author of booklets pub. by Russell Sage Foundation. Home: 3012 Sunset Drive. Office: 82 N. High St., Columbus, O. Died Oct. 7, 1947.

KNIGHT, L(ouis) Aston, landscape painter; born Paris, France; s. (Daniel) Ridgway and Rebecca Morris (Webster) K.; studied art under father, Jules Lefebvre and Robert Fleury, Paris; m. Carrie Ridgway Brewster, Oct. 15, 1907; children—Louis Ridgway Brewster, George William, Diane Marie Caroline. Received medal, Paris Expn., 1900; hon. mention and medals, Paris Salon, 1901, 05, 06; hors concours, Paris Salon; medals of honor at Rheims, Nantes, Cherbourg, Lyons, Geneva. Rep. Luxembourg Mus., Paris; art galleries, Toledo, O., Rochester, N.Y., Newark, N.J., New Orleans Mus., Harding Memorial Gallery (Marion, O.), Nimes, Eureux and Houfleur museums (France). Knight Legion of Honor, France, 1920, Officer, Comdr., 1927; 8 other decorations. Mem. Am. Artists Professional League (chmn. European sect.). Address: 98 Bd des Batigoolles, Paris; also Beaumont le Roger, Eure, France. Died May 8, 1948.

KNIGHT, Montgomery, aeronautical engr.; b. Lynn, Mass., Feb. 22, 1901; s. Franklin and Gertrude Boucher (Mosher) K.; B.S. in Elec. Engring., Mass. Inst. Tech., 1922; grad. student, Harvard, 1922-23, Johns Hopkins, 1924-25; m. Emily Millner, Jan. 1, 1927; children—Margaret, Ann Bowler (dec.), Montgomery, Edward. Research engr. with Army Air Corps, Aberdeen, Md., 1923-24; elec. engring. research with Westinghouse Electric & Mfg. Co., East Pittsburgh, Pa., 1925-26; aeronautical research, Nat. Advisory Com. for Aeronautics, Langley Field, Va., 1925-30; dir. Daniel Guggenheim Sch. of Aeronautics, Ga. Sch. of Tech., Atlanta, since 1930. Commd. 2d lt., Air Corps, U.S. Reserve Army, 1922-32. Asso. fellow Inst. of Aeronautical Sciences. Registered aeronautical engr., Ga. Episcopalian. Author or co-author of 16 tech. reports on aeronautical research, pub. by Nat. Advisory Com. for Aeronautics. Contbr. to tech. jours. Engaged in development of helicopter under State Engring. Expt. State of Ga. Home: 3529 Ivy Rd., Atlanta, Ga. Died July 26, 1943.

KNIGHT, Peter Oliphant, lawyer; b. Freeburg, Pa., Dec. 16, 1865; s. James William and Sarah Elizabeth (Kantz) K.; LL.B., Valparaiso (Ind.) U., 1884; Dr. Civil Law, University of Tampa, Fla., 1937; m. Lillie Frierson, Aug. 24, 1886; children—Joseph Mitchell, Peter Oliphant. Admitted to Fla. bar, 1886, and began practice at Ft. Myers; moved to Tampa, Fla., 1889; pres. Tampa Electric Co. since 1924; v.p. and gen. counsel Am. Internat. Shipbuilding Corp. (builders, Hog Island Ship Yard), 1918-20; chairman, bd. of dirs., Exchange Nat. Bank of Tampa, dir. Exchange Nat. Bank of Tampa; dir. Lyons Fertilizer Co., Tampa Union Station Co., Tampa Terminal Co.; mem. Knight & Thompson. Mayor of Ft. Myers, 1886; mem. Fla. Ho. of Rep., 1889; county solicitor Hillsborough County, Fla., 1893-99; state's atty. 6th Jud. Circuit, Fla., 1899-1902. Pres. Hillsborough County Humane Society; chairman, board of trustees, Old People's Home; trustee Old People's Home, Tampa. Mem. Am. and Fla. State bar assn., Fla. State Chamber Commerce (dir.), Tampa Bd. of Trade (dir.), S.A.R. (first pres. Tampa Chapter). Mil. Order Foreign Wars, Patriotic Order Sons of America, Phi Alpha Delta. Democrat. Episcopalian. Mason (33°), Elk, K.P. Clubs: Centro Asturiano, Centro Espanol, Italian, Circulo Cubano, Tampa Yacht and Country. Home: 325 Hyde Park Av. Office: Stoval Professional Bldg., Tampa, Fla. Died Nov. 26, 1946.

KNIGHT, Samuel, lawyer; b. San Francisco, Dec. 28, 1863; s. Samuel and Elizabeth (Stuart) K.; A.B., Yale, 1887; Yale Law Sch., 1887-88; LL.B., Columbia, 1889; m. Mary Hurd Holbrook, Oct. 8, 1895. Admitted to N.Y. bar, 1889; asst. U.S. atty., Northern Dist. of Calif., 1893-95; U.S. atty., same, 1896-97; mem. firm of Knight, Boland & Riordan; former trustee Hillsborough, San Mateo County, Calif. Maj., Judge Advocate General's Dept., U.S. Army, 1918-19. Hon. mem. central com. Am. Red Cross. Mem. San Francisco, Calif. State and Am. bar assns., Am. Soc. Internat. Law, Delta Kappa Epsilon, Skull and Bones, Phi Beta Kappa (Yale). Republican. Presbyn. Clubs: Pacific-Union, Commonwealth (San Francisco); Burlingame Country; Montecito (Santa Barbara); University (New York); Elizabethan (New Haven); Metropolitan (Washington). Home: 2234 Forest View Rd., Burlingame, Calif.; also 151 Buena Vista Rd., Santa Barbara, Calif. Office: 444 California St., San Francisco, Calif. Died Jan. 28, 1943.

KNIGHT, Thomas Edmund, judge; b. Greensboro, Ala., Oct. 13, 1868; s. William Newton and Eva (Hoppel) K.; A.B., Southern U., Greensboro, 1887; LL.B., U. of Ala., 1888; LL.D., Birmingham-Southern Coll., 1935; m. Rebecca Williams, June 7, 1895; children—Thomas Edmund, Rebecca (Mrs. James E. Odum). Admitted to Ala. bar, 1888; practiced at Selma, 1888-1926; mem. Ala. Ho. of Rep., 1892-95; judge, 4th Jud. Circuit of Ala., 1926-31; asso. justice Supreme Court of Ala. since 1931. Chmn. State Board of Examiners on Admission to the Bar in Ala., 1910-26. Mem. Sigma Alpha Epsilon. Democrat. Methodist. Mason, K.P. Home: Selma. Address: State Capitol, Montgomery, Ala. Died Apr. 11, 1943.

KNIPP, Charles Tobias (nĭp), physicist; b. Napoleon, Henry County, O., Aug. 13, 1869; s. Frederick F. and Pauline (Youche) K.; A.B., Indiana U., 1894, A.M., 1896; Ph.D., Cornell U., 1900; studied Cavendish Laboratory, Cambridge, Eng., 1910-11, 1926-27; m. Frances Winona Knause, June 25, 1896; children—Pauline Louise, Frances Mary, Julian Knause, Barbara Matilda. Instr. physics, Ind. U., 1893-1900, asst. prof. 1900-03; asst. prof. physics, U. of Ill., 1903-15, asso. prof., 1915-17, prof. experimental electricity, 1917-37, emeritus prof. experimental electricity since 1937; visiting professor of physics, Rollins College, Winter Park, Florida, 1942-1945. Member of advisory sub-committee on physics for Century of Progress Exposition, Chicago, 1933. Fellow A.A.A.S.; member American Physical Society, Am. Inst. E.E., Optical Soc. of America, Soc. for Promotion of Engring. Edn., Ill. State Acad. of Science (v.p. 1920-21, pres. 1921-22), Ind. State Acad., Sigma Xi (pres. 1930-31), Phi Beta Kappa (Indiana Univ., 1915); hon. mem. Tau Beta Pi, Eta Kappa Nu, Epsilon Chi, Synton. Republican. Presbyterian. Author monographs and articles on scientific subjects. Designer of demonstration apparatus in physics. Co-inventor, with H. A. Brown, of Alkali-vapor detector tube for use in radio; inventor of simple alpha-ray track apparatus; also of efficient mercury vapor vacuum pumps, electrodeless elec. discharge, cold-cathode rectifier. Home: Box 3808, T.S. C. W. Station, Denton, Texas. Died July 6, 1948.

KNOPF, Carl Sumner (k'nŭpf), univ. pres.; b. Columbus, O., Sept. 20, 1889; s. Albert and Dollie Jane (Williams) K.; A.B., U. of Southern Calif., 1913, A.M., 1914; B.D., Yale, 1915; Ph.D., 1931; m. Florence Nelson, Aug. 20, 1913. Asst. prof. Bible lit., U. of Southern Calif., 1916-17; prof. psychology and dir. research, Fullerton (Calif.) Junior Coll., 1917-20; sec. San Francisco area, Meth. Ch., 1920-22; asso. prof. of Biblical lit. and archeology, U. of Southern Calif., 1922-34, prof. and chmn. of dept. since 1935, dean Sch. of Religion, 1936-39, chaplain, 1936-41, dir. of religious activities, 1939; pres. Willamette Univ., Salem, Ore., since 1941; visiting prof. of Semitics, Yale Univ., 1929-30, Garrett Bibl. Inst., summer, 1939. Member advisory board Religion in Life; asso. editor of Words. Fellow Pacific Geog. Soc.; mem. So. Coast Improvement Assn (pres. 1940-41), League of Western Writers (past pres. Los Angeles chapter), Southwestern Archæol. Fed. (past pres.), Southern Calif. Acad. of Sciences (dir., past pres.), Nat. Assn. of Bibl. Instrs., Soc. Bibl. Lit., Am. Oriental Soc., Calif. Writers' Guild, Phi Beta Kappa, Phi Chi Phi, Theta Phi, Sigma Sigma, Mu Alpha Mu (Nat. pres., 1940-42). Mason (Royal Arch). Clubs: Opera and Fine Arts (gov.), Yale (Los Angeles); Nat. Travel. Author: Bible Youth in Modern Times, 1927; Comrades of the Way, 1928, rev. edit., 1936; The Student Faces Life, 1932; The Old Testament Speaks, 1933; Ask the Prophets, 1938. Contbr. features, book revs. and tech. articles to periodicals, papers and bulls. of socs. and colls.; lecturer on archeology and Bibl. lit. Apptd. lecturer in Great Britain, 1932, under Com. on Interchange of Speakers between Great Britain and America. Address: Willamette University, Salem, Ore. Died June 23, 1942.

KNOTT, Thomas Albert, prof. English; b. Chicago, Ill., Jan. 12, 1880; s. George John and Sarah Jane (Carlisle) K.; A.B., Northwestern U., 1902; student Harvard, 1909; Ph.D., U. of Chicago, 1912; m. Myra Celinda Powers, 1908; children—John Russell, Carlisle (Mrs. Karl J. Klapka). Teacher of English, Northwestern Academy, 1901-02, high school, Coshocton, Ohio, 1902-03, Bradley Polytechnic Institute, 1903-05, Northwestern University, 1905-06, Stevens Point (Wisconsin) Normal School, 1907; instructor and asso. prof. of English, U. of Chicago, 1907-20; prof. of English, State U. of Iowa, 1920-26; gen. editor Webster's Dictionaries, 1926-35; prof. of English and editor Middle English Dictionary, U. of Mich., since 1935. Served as capt., Mil. Intelligence Div., Gen. Staff, Washington, D.C., 1918-19. Fellow A.A.A.S. Mem. Modern Lang. Assn. of America, Nat. Council Teachers of English, Linguistic Society, Philol. Society, Mediaeval Acad., Mich. Acad. Sciences, Arts and Letters, Dialect Soc., Mich. Schoolmasters Club, Am. Assn. University Profs., Phi Beta Kappa, Phi Kappa Phi. Republican. Conglist. Clubs: Michigan Union, University, Quadrangle, Research (University of Michigan). Author: Elements of Old English (with S. Moore), 1919, 9th edit., 1942. General editor of Webster's New International Dictionary, 2d edit., 1934. Asso. editor Philological Quarterly, 1922-26. Contbr. articles on lang. and medieval lit. to Modern Philology, Modern Lang. Notes, Philol. Quarterly, Quarterly Jour. of Speech, Am. Speech, Manly Anniversary Studies. Home: 1504 Brooklyn Av., Ann Arbor, Mich. Died Aug. 16, 1945.

KNOTTS, Howard C(layton) (nŏts), lawyer and transportation consultant; born Girard, Illinois, Aug. 25, 1895; s. Edward Clay and Elizabeth (Routzahn) K.; student Blackburn College, Carlinville, Illinois, 1912-15; A.B., Knox College, 1916; LL.B., Harvard, 1921; m. Charlotte Ann Sterling, June 25, 1921; children—Howard Clayton, Elizabeth Ann. Admitted to Illinois bar, 1921; staff U.S. district atty., Southern Ill. Dist., 1921-23; mem. Knotts and Knotts, 1923-33; mem. firm Knotts & Dobbs since 1933; editor of Jour. of Air Law and Commerce, pub. by Air Law Inst., Northwestern U. Sch. of Law, since 1937; lecturer on air transportation, Sch. of Commerce, and on public utility law, Sch. of Law, Northwestern U.; Aviation supervisor Illinois Commerce Commn. since 1931; formerly cons. expert Bureau of Air Commerce, Dept. of Commerce and Civil Aeronautics Authority; formerly general counsel Nat. Aeronautic Assn.; counsel Am. Assn. Airport Executives. Commd. 2d lt. and pilot, U.S. Army, and served with 17th U.S. Aero Squadron, A.E.F., 1917-19; twice wounded and officially credited with 8 enemy aircraft. Awarded D.S.C., Purple Heart (oak leaf cluster), Silver Star medal (U.S.), Distinguished Flying Cross (British). Mem. Sangamon County, Ill. State and Am. bar assns.; Quiet Birdmen. Episcopalian. Mason. Club: Sangamo and Illini Country (Springfield). Author of aeronautical regulations, enactments and published articles. Home: 1303 S. 6th St. Office: 205 S. 6th St., Springfield. Ill. Died Nov. 23, 1942.

KNOX, Louis, prof. chemistry; b. Giddings, Tex., Dec. 24, 1874; s. William Alexander and Elizabeth (Williams) K.; student U. of Tex., 1892-96; B.S., U. of Texas, 1900; M.S., U. of Chicago, 1908; m. Eva Bowen, Dec. 3, 1901. Began as chemist Texas Portland Cement Co., Dallas, 1903-07; prof. chemistry, Daniel Baker Coll., Brownwood, Tex., 1903-07; head chemistry dept., The Citadel, Charleston, S.C., since Sept. 1908. Fellow, chemistry dept., U. of Chicago, 1907-08. Served as private, Hosp. Corps, U.S. Army, Puerto Rican Expedition, 1898-99. Mem. Am. Chem. Soc., St. Andrews Soc. (Charleston). Club: Charleston Rotary. Mason. Presbyterian. Address: The Citadel, Charleston, S.C. Deceased.

KNOX, Samuel Lippincott Griswold, cons. engr.; b. New York, N.Y., Nov. 28, 1870; s. Andrew and Annabel Grace (Douglas) K.; student Coll. City of New York, 1885-87; M.E., Stevens Inst. Tech., Hoboken, N.J., 1891; m. Edith Somerville Rulison, Sept. 16, 1897 (died Nov. 24, 1936); children—Nelson Rulison, Alexander Douglas. Chmn. com. of mech. design and engr. in charge drafting dept. Gen. Electric Co., 1900-02; v.p., gen. mgr. and chief engr. Bucyrus Co., S. Milwaukee, Wis., mfrs. excavating machinery, 1902-10, designing and mfg. much of machinery used in constrn. of Panama Canal, also placer gold dredges of the period; cons. engr., later v.p. and gen. mgr. Natomas Consol., of Calif., gold dredging and land reclamation, also pres. Pacific Engring. & Constrn. Co. and Pacific Dredging Co., building jetties on Pacific Coast, river correction and levee bldg., Sacramento and San Joaquin rivers, 1911-17; chmn. mech. engring. div. Nat. Research Council, Washington, D.C., also chief cons. engr. U.S. Navy Anti-Submarine Base, New London, Conn., 1917-20, devised improvement of secondary and turret guns of battleships, also apparatus for enemy airplane location; scientific attaché Am. Embassy, Rome, Italy, 1918-19; consulting engineer; president Lombard Tractor Co., 1927-28; president Knox Engring. Co., developing high efficiency steam power plants; dir. and mem. exec. com. Lamson Corp. of Del. (pneumatic tube and other service conveyors); dir., mem. exec. com. Lamson Corp. of N.Y.; dir. Boston Pneumatic Transit Co., New York Mail & Newspaper Transit Co. Fellow Am. Soc. Mech. Engrs.; mem. Pilgrims of U.S., Kappa Alpha. Episcopalian. Club: University (New York). Author: The Mailed Fist—the Background of Hitlerism. Address: 115 E. Palisade Av., Englewood. N.J. Died May 8, 1947

KNOX, (William) Franklin, Sec. of Navy, newspaper publisher; b. Boston, Mass., Jan. 1, 1874; s. William Edwin and Sarah Collins (Barnard) K.; A.B., Alma (Mich.) Coll., 1898, LL.D., 1936; LL.D., U. of N.H., 1933; Litt.D., Rollins Coll., Winter Park, Fla., 1937; LL.D., Harvard, 1942, Dartmouth, 1941, Northwestern, 1943, Williams, 1943, Colgate, 1943, Bethany Coll., 1943; m. Annie Reid, Dec. 28, 1898. Reporter, city editor, mgr. circulation, Grand Rapids (Mich.) Herald, 1898-1900; publisher Sault Ste. Marie (Mich.) News, 1901-12, Manchester (N.H.) Leader, Sept. 1912-13, Manchester Union and Leader since July 1913; also pub. Boston American, Boston Daily Advertiser and Boston Sunday Advertiser, 1927-31; gen. mgr. Hearst newspapers until Jan. 1, 1931; with Theodore T. Ellis purchased controlling interest in Chicago Daily News, becoming pub., 1931. Mem. Troop D. 1st U.S. Vol. Cav. (Rough Riders), Spanish-Am. War. Apr.-Sept. 1898; maj. on staff of gov. of Mich., 1908-10; apptd. maj. on staff of gov. of N.H., 1913. Chmn. Rep. State Central Com., Mich., 1910-12; apptd. by President Taft mem. Board of Indian Commrs., 1911. Commd. capt., F.A., U.S. Army, Aug. 14, 1917; assigned to staff of 78th Div.; promoted to maj., Dec. 1, 1917; served with 153d Arty. Brig., 78th Div., overseas May 26, 1918-Feb. 10, 1919; col. 365th F.A., Res.; now retired. Chmn. delegation from N.H. to Rep. Nat. Conv., Chicago, 1920; chmn. State Publicity Commn. of N.H., 1922-24; chmn. Nat. Campaign to Combat Hoarding, 1932. Republican nominee for Vice-President of U.S., 1936; apptd. Sec. of Navy, July 11, 1940. Conglist. Mason. Clubs: Derryfield Country (Manchester, N.H.); Army and Navy, Burning Tree (Washington, D.C.); Chicago, Commercial, Old Elm, Union League (Chicago); Advertising (New York). Home: 4704 Linnean Av. N.W. Office: Navy Department, Washington, D.C. Died Apr. 28, 1944.

KNUBEL, Frederick Hermann (nōō'bĕl), clergyman; b. N.Y. City, May 22, 1870; s. Frederick and Katharine (Knubel) K.; A.B., 1st honor, Pa. Coll., Gettysburg, 1893, D.D., 1911; A.M., Gettysburg Theol. Sem., 1895; student U. of Leipzig, Germany, 1895-96; LL.D., Thiel Coll., 1919; S.T.D., Syracuse, 1930; Litt.D., Midland Coll., 1938; L.H.D., Muhlenberg Coll., 1940; m. Christine Ritscher, June 26, 1895 (dec.); children—Frederick R., Helen M.; m. 2d, Jennie L. Christ, July 11, 1925. Ordained ministry Evang. Luth. Ch., 1896; founder, 1896, and pastor Ch. of Atonement, N.Y. City, 1896-1918. Pres. United Luth. Ch. in America since 1918. Trustee Pa. Coll., Seamen's Home; mem. bd. dirs. Presbyn. Ministers Fund. V.p. Am. Bible Soc., Am. Tract Soc.; first v.p. Lutheran World Convention; mem. Concordia Ministerial Assn., Am. Soc. of Church History, Phi Beta Kappa, Phi Gamma Delta. Contbr. on theol. topics. Editor of "Key Books," 1927. Author of Commentary on Ephesians, 1933. Home: 201 Hamilton Av., New Rochelle, N.Y. Office: 231 Madison Av., New York, N.Y. Died Oct. 16, 1945.

KNUDSEN, William S. (nōōd'sĕn), executive; b. Denmark, Mar. 25, 1879. Served apprenticeship as bicycle mechanic in Denmark; came to U.S. at age of 20; began work in shipyards, New York; in Erie Railroad shops 18 months; stockroom keeper John R. Keim Mills, Buffalo, 1902, advanced to supt.; later became an employee of Ford Motor Company in charge building of assembly plants; gen. mgr. Matthews & Ireland Mfg. Co., 1921; apptd. v.p. Chevrolet Motor Co., 1922, later pres.; exec. v.p. Gen. Motors Corp., 1933-37, with supervisory control of all Gen. Motors automobile and body mfg. activities, becoming pres. 1937; commr. advisory com. to Council of Nat. Defense, 1940; dir. gen. Office of Prodn. Management, 1941; commd. lt. gen., Army U.S. and directed prodn. for War Dept., resigned July 1945; apptd. chmn. bd. Hupp Corp., Oct. 1946. Home: 1501 Balmoral Drive, Detroit. Died April 27, 1948.

KOCH, Edward William, medical school dean; b. Lawrenceburg, Indiana, January 8, 1882; s. William and Barbara E. (Siemandel) K.; A.B., Ind. U., 1908, A.M., 1900; M.D., Rush Med. Coll., 1911; m. Rose Mary Hassmer, Apr. 21, 1917. Instr. in physiology and pharmacology, Indiana U., 1913-15; pharmacologist, Eli Lilly & Co., 1915-18; prof. pharmacology, U. of Buffalo Med. Sch., since 1918, sec. same, 1918-28, acting dean, 1928-30, dean since 1930; dean U. of Buffalo Dental Sch., 1936 to 1944. Fellow A.M.A., A.A.A.S., Indiana Acad. Science; mem. Sigma Xi, Alpha Omega Alpha, Nu Sigma Nu. Club: Saturn. Home: 506 Linwood Av., Buffalo 9, N. Y. Died Feb. 9, 1946.

KOCH, Fred Conrad, biochemistry; born in Chicago, Ill., May 16, 1876; s. Frederick and Louise (Fischer) K.; B.S., U. of Ill., 1899, M.S., 1900; Ph.D., U. of Chicago, 1912; m. Elizabeth Miller, Sept. 7, 1922. Instr. chemistry, U. of Ill., 1900-02; research chemist Armour & Co., 1902-09; asst. prof. physiol. chemistry, U. of Chicago, 1912-16, asso. professor, 1916-24, professor, 1924-40, chairman Department of Biochemistry, 1926-41. Frank P. Hixon distinguished service professor of biochemistry, 1941-42; research chemist, Armour and Company, since 1942. Member A.M.A., Soc. Biol. Chemists, Am. Chem. Soc., A.A.A.S., Exptl. Biology and Medicine, Chicago Inst. of Medicine, Association for Study of Internal Secretions, Sigma Xi, Gamma Alpha, Phi Chi, Phi Lambda Upsilon. Republican. Clubs: Quadrangle, Collegiate, Chaos, Innominates. Home: 1534 E. 59th St., Chicago 37, Ill. Office: Armour Laboratories, 1425 West 42d St., Chicago. Died Jan. 26, 1948.

KOCH, Frederick Henry (kōch), univ. prof.; b. Covington, Ky., Sept. 12, 1877; s. August William and Rebecca Cornelia (Julian) K.; A.B., Ohio Wesleyan U., 1900, Litt.D., 1936; A.M., Harvard, 1909; Litt.D., U. of N.D., 1935; m. Jean Hanigan, Mar. 24, 1910; children—Frederick Henry, George Julian, Robert Allan, William Julian. Instr. English, 1905, asst. prof., 1907, asso. prof., 1914, prof. dramatic lit., 1917-18, U. of N.D.; prof. dramatic lit., U. of N.C., 1918-31, Kenan prof. dramatic lit. since 1931, head dept. dramatic art since 1936; visiting prof., summer sessions, U. of Calif., 1910, 27, 28, 29, 30, 36, U. of Colo., 1922, 33, Columbia, 1925, 26, 35, U. of Southern Calif., 1930, 31, New York U., 1932, Northwestern U., 1934, U. of Toledo, 1934, U. of Alberta, 1937, 38, 39, 40, 41; exchange prof., U. of Manitoba, 1918. Founder of Dakota Playmakers, 1910, N.C. Bur. Community Drama, 1918 (since dir.), Carolina Dramatic Assn., 1923, Bankside Theatre, 1914, Carolina Playmakers, 1918 (since dir.), Forest Theatre, 1918 (since dir.); hon. pres. Canadian Playmakers. Originator of rural community drama by cooperative authorship; founder of native Folk-playmaking in N.C. Pres. Carolina Playmakers, Inc. Dir. Am. Nat. Theatre, 1923; v.p. Nat. Little Theatre Federation, 1923; mem. advisory council Nat. Negro Theatre, 1923; mem. council National Theatre Conf. since 1931, regional dir. since 1932; regional dir. Federal Theatre Projects for N.C., S.C. and Va., 1935; v.p. Shakespeare Assn. of America; v.p. for N.C. of Nat. Shakespeare Fed.; mem. bd. dirs. Southeastern Little Theatre Council. Mem. Advisory Council Bureau of New Plays, Inc., Nat. Theatre Conf. since 1936. Mem. Am. Folk-Song Soc. (mem. council since 1933), Nat. Council Teachers of English, Drama League of America (dir.), Am. Pageant Assn. (dir.), Am. Assn. Univ. Profs., Modern Lang. Assn. America, N.C. Lit. and Hist. Assn. (pres. 1925), N.C. Folk-Lore Soc., Roanoke Island Memorial Assn., Am. Ednl. Theatre Assn., Nat. Assn. Teachers of Speech, Sigma Chi, Omicron Delta Kappa, Phi Beta Kappa (hon. U. of N.Dak. 1935). Unitarian. Club: Town Hall (New York). Editor: Carolina Folk-Plays, 1922, 2d series, 1924, 3d series, 1928, revised and complete, 1941; Carolina Folk Comedies, 1931; Mexican Folk Plays, 1938; American Folk Plays, 1939; Folk Plays of Eastern Carolina, 1939; Alabama Folk Plays, 1943. Author: Raleigh, the Shepherd of the Ocean (a tercentenary drama), 1920; (with others) A Pageant of the North-West (communal drama), 1914; (with others) Shakespeare, the Playmaker (communal masque), 1916; A Pageant of the Lower Cape Fear (communal drama), 1921; A Century of Culture (pageant), 1937. Asso. editor, The Little Theatre Monthly. Editor of The Carolina Play-Book. Dramatic editor Southern Literary Messenger. Contbr. many articles to lit. and theatre periodicals. Home: 204 Glenburnie St., Chapel Hill, N.C. Died Aug. 16, 1944.

KOENIGSBERG, Moses (kĕn'ĭgs-bĕrg), newspaper man; b. New Orleans, La., Apr. 16, 1878; s. Harris Wolf and Julia (Foreman) K.; ed. pub. schs. and in newspaper offices; m. Virginia V. Carter, Dec. 10, 1923; 1 dau., Virginia Rose. Began writing and setting own paper at 9; as result of winning $100 essay prize was offered reporter's position on San Antonio (Tex.) Times, at 13, and became editor Texas World, Houston, same yr.; pub. San Antonio Evening Star at 16; reporter or editor New Orleans Daily States, Item, Truth, Times-Democrat, Fort Worth Record, Kansas City Journal, Kansas City Times, St. Louis Republic, Globe-Democrat, Star,

Chronicle, Chicago Times, Pittsburgh Times, New York World, Mobile Register, Montgomery Advertiser, Minneapolis Times, etc.; mng. editor Chicago American, 1903-07; pub. Boston American, 1908-09; organized and became pres. and gen. mgr. Newspaper Feature Service, 1913, King Features Syndicate, Inc., 1916; pres. and gen. mgr. Internat. News Service, Inc.; pres. Universal Service, Inc., Star Adcraft Service, Cosmopolitan News Service, Premier Syndicate; v.p. and gen. mgr. Internat. Feature Service, Inc., to 1928. Exec. dir. Song Writers' Protective Assn., 1931. Served as pvt. 2d Ala. Vol. Inf., Spanish-Am. War, 1898. Clubs: Friars, Green Room, Newspaper. Author: Southern Martyrs, 1898; The Elk and the Elephant (short stories), 1899, King News (autobiography), 1941. As one of the 5 Am. delegates to first internat. conf. of press experts, summoned by the League of Nations at Geneva, Aug. 1927, successfully led opposition to proposal for declaration of private property rights in news, contained in the League secretariat's draft law, which was unanimously excluded. Awarded Cross of Legion of Honor (France), 1928, returned insignia in protest of debt situation, 1933. Editor weekly magazine Now since 1945. Home: 160 Riverside Drive, New York, N.Y. Died Sept. 21, 1945.

KOFOID, Charles Atwood, univ. prof.; b. Granville, Ill., Oct. 11, 1865; s. Nelson and Janette (Blake) K.; A.B., Oberlin, 1890; A.M., Harvard, 1892, Ph.D., 1894; Sc.D., Oberlin, 1915, U. of Wales, 1920; LL.D., U. of Calif., 1937; m. Carrie Prudence Winter, June 30, 1894. Teacher Oberlin Acad., 1888-90; teaching fellow, Oberlin, 1890-91; instr. vertebrate morphology, U. of Mich., 1894-95; supt. Biol. Sta., U. of Ill., Havana, Ill., 1895-1900; asst. prof. zoology, U. of Ill., 1897-1900; supt. Natural History Survey of Ill., 1898-1900; asst. prof., 1900-04, asso. prof. histology and embryology, 1904-10, acting head dept. of zoology, 1905-06, prof. zoology, 1910-36, head of dept., 1910-19 and 1923-36, U. of Calif., now emeritus. Visiting prof. of biology, Tohoku Imperial U., Japan, on Rockefeller Foundation, 1930. Acting dir. San Diego Biol. Sta., 1905-06. Mem. scientific staff, Mich. Fish Commn., summer, 1894; asst. naturalist, U.S.S. Albatross, Coast of Calif., 1904; asso. naturalist, Agassiz expdn. to eastern tropical Pacific, U.S.S. Albatross, 1904-05, Smithsonian table, Naples Zool. Sta., 1909; asst. dir. San Diego Research, 1912. Hon. mention, Paris Expn., Biol. Sta., 1908-12; asst. dir. Scripps Inst. Biol., 1900-24; gold medal, St. Louis Expn., 1904. Invented plankton net, water sampler for deep sea work, self-closing plankton net for horizontal towing. Asso. editor Am. Naturalist, 1897-1908; zool. editor Jour. Applied Microscopy, 1900-04; Am. editor Internationale Revue ges Hydrobiologie, 1910; editor U. of Calif. Publs. in Zoology, 1909-36; asso. editor Jour. Morphology, 1920-24, Am. Jour. Hygiene, 1920, Zool. Acta (Stockholm), 1920, Isis, 1931. Maj., Sanitary Corps, U.S. Army, 1918-19. Fellow Nat. Acad. Sciences, Am. Philos. Soc., Phila. Acad. Natural Science, A.A.A.S., Am. Acad. Arts and Sciences, Royal Soc. Tropical Medicine and Hygiene, Calif. Acad. Sciences, Am. Pub. Health Assn.; mem. Washington Acad. Sciences, Western Soc. Naturalists, Soc. Path. Exot., Paris, Am. Soc. Tropical Medicine, Am. Soc. Naturalists, Am. Micros. Soc., Assn. Am. Anatomists, Am. Soc. Zoologists, Am. Soc. Entomologists, History of Science Society. Author: Biological Stations of Europe. Also bulls., etc., and contbr. to various Am. and European jours. on zool. subjects. Home: 2616 Etna St., Berkeley, Calif. Died May 30, 1947.

KOHN, Henry H., banker; b. in Germany, Nov. 13, 1863; s. Herman H. and Helen (Hechinger) K.; ed. high sch., Ravensburg, Germany; m. Bertha Roberts, Dec. 3, 1889; 1 dau., Helen (Mrs. George L. Hunt). Chmn. bd. (finance com.) Morris Plan Co. of New York; chmn. bd. Morris Plan Ins. Soc.; trustee City & County Savings Bank; dir. Morris Plan banks of 24 N.E. cities. Republican. Baptist. Clubs: City, Town Hall (New York); Albany, Fort Orange, Albany Country (Albany). Home: 355 State St., Albany, N.Y. Office: 420 Lexington Av., New York, N.Y.* Died Dec. 26, 1944.

KOLBE, Parke Rexford, coll. pres.; b. Akron, O., Apr. 23, 1881; s. Carl F. and Jennie (Yergin) K.; A.B., Buchtel Coll., 1901, A.M., 1902; studied U. of Göttingen, 1901-02, U. of Heidelberg, 1907 and 1910-12, Ph.D., 1912; LL.D., Temple U., 1933, U. of Akron, 1934; m. Lydia Voris, June 17, 1905. Prof. Modern langs., Buchtel Coll., 1905-13, pres. Feb. 4-Dec. 1913; pres. Municipal U. of Akron, 1913-25; pres. Polytechnic Inst. of Brooklyn, 1925-32; pres. Drexel Inst. since 1932. Mem. Federal Sch., Survey Commn. to Hawaiian Islands, 1919; head of U.S. Bur. of Edn. Survey Commn. to U. of Ariz., 1922. Past pres. Assn. of Urban Univs.; first vice chmn. Am. Council on Edn.; mem. Kurpfalz (Heidelberg), Phi Delta Theta. Republican. Universalist. Rotarian. Clubs: University (Akron, O.); University (Washington); Century (New York); Rittenhouse, Manufacturers, Bankers, Franklin Inn (Philadelphia). Author: The Colleges in Wartime and After, 1919; Urban Influences on Higher Education in England and the United States, 1928. Editor: Heine's Harzreise, 1909; Die Variation bei Otfrid, 1912. Contbr. to ednl. and philol. publs. Address: Drexel Institute of Technology, Philadelphia, Pa. Died Feb. 28, 1942.

KOLKER, Henry (Joseph) (kōl'kĕr), actor; b. Berlin, Germany; s. William and Katherine (Dürjon) K.; brought from Germany to United States, 1879; educated Catholic parochial sch., Quincy, Ill.; later by the Franciscan Brothers, Quincy; m. Margaret Bruenn. Joined German Stock Company, Pabst Theatre, Milwaukee, 1895; has supported Robert Downing, James O'Neill, Margaret Mather, Mary Mannering, Ada Rehan, Robert Edeson, Amelia Bingham, Bertha Kalich, Margaret Anglin and Mme. Nazimova; starring under the direction of Henry W. Savage in "The Great Name," 1910-11; "Our Wives," 1912-13; "Help Wanted," 1914; "Our Children," season 1914-15; starred in "Over the Phone," 1916-17; directed motion pictures; in England for Ideal Films, Ltd.; producing plays and motion pictures on Pacific Coast; appeared in "A Lady Steps In," 1932. Clubs: The Lambs, Stamford Yacht. Mem. The Players; dir. George Arliss in motion pictures, Disraeli and The Man Who Played God. Home: 1767 N. Orange Av., Hollywood, Calif. Died July 15, 1947; buried in Forest Lawn Memorial Park, Glendale, Calif.

KOLLER, Carl (kŏl'lĕr), ophthalmologist; b. Schuettenhofen, Austria, Dec. 3, 1857; grad. U. of Vienna, 1882. Ophthalmic surgeon Mt. Sinai Hosp. and other instns., New York. Mem. A.M.A., Am. Ophthal. Soc., Med. Soc. State of N.Y., N.Y. Acad. Medicine; hon. mem. Soc. of Physicians of Vienna, Soc. of Physicians of Budapest, Royal Acad. of Medicine, Rome, Am. Socs. of Physiology and Pharmacology. Introduced cocain as a local anesthetic in eye operations, 1884, thus inaugurating era of local anæsthesia, for operations in the various branches of medicine and surgery. Author of many articles pertaining to biology and ophthalmology. Awarded gold medals by Am. Ophthal. Soc., U. of Heidelberg (Germany), N.Y. Acad. of Medicine, Am. Acad. of Ophthalmology, Otology and Rhinology. Address: 68 East 86th St., New York, N.Y. Died Mar. 21, 1944.

KONKLE, Burton Alva, kŏn'k'l), author; b. Albion, Ind., Apr. 25, 1861; s. Simon Kenton and Cornelia Gale (Andrews) K.; student Lake Forest (Ill.) Coll., 1882-86, McCormick Theol. Sem., Chicago, 1889-92, U. of Chicago, Apr.-Dec. 1896; M.A., Huron Coll., 1906; m. Susie Montague Ferry, June 28, 1900; 1 dau., Winifred Ferry (Mrs. Charles E. Fischer). Teacher, pub. schs., later prin. pub. schs., Avilla and Wawaka, Ind., 1876-82; in historical work, various parts of U.S., vacations 1882-86; ordained ministry Presbyn. Ch., 1894; pastor Libertyville, Ill., 1893, Georgetown, Colo., 1894; engaged in hist. writing in vacations, 1888-97, full time, Phila., since 1897. Life mem. Hist. Soc. of Pa. Established hist. sect. of Pa. Bar Assn.; a founder of Pa. Hist. Club. Republican. Author: Life and Times of Thomas Smith of The Continental Congress, 1904; Life and Speeches of Thomas Williams (2 vols.), 1906; Life of Chief Justice Ellis Lewis, 1908; George Bryan and the Constitution of Pennsylvania, 1922; John Motley Morehead and the Development of North Carolina, 1922; History of the Presbyterian Ministers' Fund (oldest life insurance company in the world); Joseph Hopkinson, author of "Hail Columbia," 1931; The Life and Letters of Chief Justice Benjamin Chew, 1932; Life and Writings of James Wilson, Constitutionalist (6 vols.); David Lloyd and the First Half Century of Pennsylvania; Thomas Willing and the First American Financial System, 1937; Land o'Lakes, a Hoosier Tale of North, South, West and East; The Life of Nicholas Biddle; Life of Andrew Hamilton, 1676-1741, 1941. Contbr. to periodicals. Mem. Pa. Constitution Celebration Com. Home: Swarthmore, Pa. Died Oct. 24, 1944.

KONTA, Geoffrey (kŏn'tȧ), lawyer; b. St. Louis, Mo., Nov. 13, 1887; s. Alexander and Annie (Lemp) K.; A.B., Yale, 1908; LL.B., Columbia, 1911; m. Phyllis Goodhue, Nov. 30, 1912; children—Anne Marie, Phyllis. Admitted to N.Y. bar, 1910, and began practice in N.Y. City, 1911; mem. Konta, Kirchwey & Engel and predecessor firms since 1915. Mem. Am. and N.Y. State bar assns., N.Y. County Lawyers' Assn., Assn. Bar City of New York. Clubs: Yale, University, Home: East Meadow, Hempstead, L.I., and 290 Park Av., New York. Office: 7 E. 44th St., New York, N.Y. Died Nov. 24, 1942.

KONTZ, Ernest Charles, lawyer; b. Washington, D.C., Sept. 11, 1865; s. Ernest Christian and Mary Elizabeth (Trabert) K.; Ph.B., U. of Ga., 1887, LL.B., 1889; John B. Minor law class, U. of Va., 1888; m. Mary Elizabeth Thornton, Apr. 19, 1898; children—John Thornton, Mary Elizabeth (Mrs. Wm. D. Hooper, Jr.), Ernest Charles. In law practice at Atlanta, Ga., 1889-1934; also real estate investments. Auditor, recorder, City of Atlanta, 1891-92; mem. city council, 1901-02 (chmn. finance com., 1902); mem. Bd. Edn., 1910-15. Democrat. Presbyterian elder; chmn. bd. North Av. Ch. Day Sch. (sch. library named Kontz), 1908-16. Mem. exec. com. Nat. Municipal League, 1907-10. Internat. Nat. Tax Assn., 1907-11. Chmn. com. favoring councilmanic form of city govt. which defeated city mgr. charter for Atlanta, 1927; represented mayor of Atlanta at unveiling of statue of Alexander H. Stephens, at the Capitol, Washington, D.C., December 8, 1927. Member Legal Advisory Bd., World War I, 1917-18. Mem. Policy-holders Examining Com. of Northwestern Mutual Life Ins. Co., 1925-26. Pres. City Club, of Atlanta, 1928-30. Permanent pres. Class of '87, U. of Ga.; mem. Alumni Soc. of U. of Ga., Phi Kappa Soc. of U. of Ga., Kappa Alpha, Phi Beta Kappa. Mason, Odd Fellow. Club: Pioneer Schoolboys, of Atlanta. Author: Value of Public Service Franchises. His numerous pub. appeals for race, religious, sectional and polit. tolerance have been printed and widely circulated. Address: Lakemont, Ga. Died April 17, 1945.

KOUNTZE, de Lancey (kōōntz), mfr.; A.B., Yale, 1899; m. Martha Johnston; children—Martha B. (Mrs. Dudley Phelps King Wood), Helen de L. (Mrs. Jacquelin A. Swords). Chmn. bd. Devoe & Raynolds, paints, varnishes, colors, etc. Dir. Metropolitan Opera & Real Estate Co.; trustee Museum of City of N.Y. Clubs: Knickerbocker, Piping Rock, Links. Home: 760 Park Av. Office: 44th St. and First Av., New York, N.Y. Died Oct. 2, 1946.

KRAFKA, Joseph, Jr. (krăf'kȧ), prof. micro-anatomy; b. Ottumwa, Ia., Aug. 14, 1890; s. Joseph and Anna Marie (Huber) K.; B.S., Lake Forest (Ill.) Coll., 1914, M.A., 1915; Ph.D., U. of Ill., 1919; M.D., U. of Ga., 1933; m. Bessie Belle Harsch, June 25, 1916; children—Katherine, Joseph Franklyn. Prof. zoölogy, and head of dept., U. of Ga., 1919-26; prof. micro-anatomy, med. dept. same univ., since 1926. Mem. Am. Soc. Zoölogists, Entomol. Soc. America, Ga. State Acad. Science, Am. Soc. Anatomy, Sigma Xi, Phi Pi Epsilon. Democrat. Methodist. Contbr. series of papers dealing with med. history of Ga., arteriosclerosis and human embryology. Wrote text-books in histology and human embryology. Home: Lakemont Drive, Augusta, Ga. Died Nov. 5, 1946.

KRAMER, Albert Ludlow (krā'mĕr); b. Phila., Pa., Mar. 28, 1878; s. Francis D. and Mary (Leighton) K.; student Wharton Sch., U. of Pa., 1895-96; LL.B., U. of Pa., 1899; student Columbian U., Washington, D.C., 1899-1900; m. Anna Bement, 1906; children—Albert Ludlow, Marleigh (Mrs. Robert L. Gerry, Jr.); m. 2d, Alice Bishop, Sept. 7, 1932; children—Audrey, Alissa. Admitted to Pa. bar, 1899, and began practice in Phila.; asso. with Ervin & Co., bankers, Phila., 1904-08; v.p. Equitable Trust Co. of New York, 1912-13; pres. Electric Properties Co., holding company for Westinghouse Co. pub. utilities, 1914-16; formerly dir. many corps.; retired, 1916, and devotes his time to writing, lecturing and philanthropic work. Served as war work sec., Y.M.C.A., during World War. Mem. Am. Tract Soc., evangelistic com. of Greater New York Fed. of Chs. and of Federal Council of America. Republican. Presbyterian. Author (with wife, Alice Bishop Kramer): The Life in the Vine, 1936; The Unlocked Door, 1936; I Bring You Joy, 1937; Gods Reach for Man, 1938. Compiler (with wife): The Way, 1938; From Millions to Happiness, 1941. Contbr. to jours. Home: 806 Main St., Riverton, N.J. Office: 21 W. 46th St., New York. Died Aug. 8, 1948.

KRAMER, Edwin Weed, engineer; b. Louisville, Ky., Mar. 4, 1877; s. William Paul and Jean (Mobley) K.; C.E., Cornell U., 1905; m. Ruth Edwards, June 22, 1905; children—Ruth (Mrs. Joel Magnes Popper), Edwin Weed, Jean Mobley (Mrs. Samuel Harper Berry), Paul, Margaret (Mrs. David Purcell Mealiffe). Engr. with N.Y. state barge canal, 1905; construction engr., Construction Q.M. Dept., New London, Conn., 1905-07; engr. U.S. Forest Service, Missoula, Mont., and San Francisco, Calif., 1907-36; regional engr., U.S. Forest Service, San Francisco, 1929-36; mem. Calif. power bd., Federal Power Commn., 1924, regional dir. San Francisco regional office since 1936. Served as corp., U.S. Army, Spanish-Am. War. Represented Federal Power Commn. on Hoover-Young Commn. to investigate Calif. Central Valley project, 1929. Mem. Am. Soc. C.E., S.A.R. Author: Construction of Fish Dams for Water Storage in California, 1935. Co-author of reports Uses of the Stanislaus River and Uses of the American River. Prepared curves for determining Cain formula factors for arches with fixed ends. Home: 142 Capra Way. Office: 300 Phelan Bldg., San Francisco, Calif. Died Oct. 31, 1941.

KRAMER, Frederick Ferdinand, clergyman; b. Erie, Pa., July 13, 1861; s. Frederick and Elizabeth (Roehm) K.; B.A., Trinity College, Conn., 1889, M.A., 1893, S.T.D., 1913; B.D., Gen. Theol. Sem., 1891; Ph.D., U. of Colo., 1895; D.D., Seabury Divinity School, 1932; m. Ada Josephine Sprague, Oct. 29, 1891; children—Frederick Sprague, John Spalding, Paul Stevens, Elizabeth. Deacon and priest, 1891, P.E. Ch.; rector St. John's Ch., Boulder, Colo., 1891-95, All Saints Ch., Denver, 1896-1912; warden, 1912-32; became prof. O.T. and Semitic langs., Seabury Div. Sch., 1912, now retired Dep. to Gen. Conv. P.E. Ch., 1898, 1904, 10. Mem. Psi Upsilon. Author: Supremacy of the Bible, 1908; Jesus, the Light of the World, 1933; I Heard a Voice (autobiography), 1942. Translated play Death Enchained from the French, of Maurice Magre, under name, A King Against the Gods, produced by U. of Minn., 1937. Address: Faribault, Minn. Died Jan. 5, 1946.

KRAUS, René Raoul (krous), writer; b. Esseg, Austria, Nov. 3, 1902; s. Maximilian and Irène Grevelle; student Sorbonne, Paris, 1919-20; Ph.D., Vienna U., 1923; Ph.D., Berlin U., 1925. Editor Berliner Boersenzeitung, 1928-33, editor in chief Neues Wiener Journal, 1934-35; press sec. to Fgn. Sec. Stresemann, 1923-28; counsellor press dept. Austrian Govt., 1935-38; assigned to U.S., 1936-38; book and magazine writer in U.S. since 1938. Author of books written in English, French, German, Latin. Author: (books pub. in U.S.) Theodora, 1938; Private and Public Life of Socrates, 1939; Winston Churchill, 1940; Men Around Churchill, 1941; Europe in Revolt, 1942; Young Lady Randolph, 1943; Old Master (Life of Jan Christian Smuts), 1943; Winston Churchill in the Mirror, 1944. Home: Brattleboro, Vt. Died July 16, 1947.

KRAUS, Walter Max, neurologist; b. N.Y. City, Aug. 25, 1889; s. Max William and Carrie May (Adler) K.; B.A., Harvard, 1910 as of 1909; M.D., Johns

Hopkins, 1913; M.A., Columbia, 1914; studied U. of Paris Med. Sch., 1923-24; m. Marian Florance Nathan, May 5, 1917 (divorced); children—John Walter, Fancis Van Praag; m. 2d. Inès Heffes Adès, Dec. 29, 1924 (died 1931); m. 3d, Victoria Rowe, Dec. 20, 1935. Admitted to practice, N.Y., and Conn., 1913, D.C., 1938; interne Bellevue Hosp., 1914-16; instr. biology, Coll. Phys. and Surg. (Columbia), 1915-16, adjunct assistant neurologist, 1916-23; clin. assistant in neurology, Cornell Medical School Dispensary, 1917; war service Bellevue Hospital, also in Europe and at U.S. General Hospital No. 11, Cape May, New Jersey; honorably discharged as capt. Med. Corps, June 20, 1919; major Medical Reserve Corps, 1925-35; major, Medical Corps, Army of U.S., 1943. Served in various capacities with College of Phys. and Surg., Mt. Sinai, Montefiore, French and Bellevue hosps., etc.; asso. neurologist Cornell U., 1926-32; sec. Med. Bd. Montefiore Hosp., also of exec. com., 1927-30; asso. neurologist Neurol. Inst., 1929-32. Companion, Soc. of Am. Wars, Mil. Order of Fgn. Wars. Mem. Am. Assn. Advancement Science, Am. Genetic Assn., Research Council on Problems of Alcohol, New York General. and Biog. Society. Military Order World War (charter mem.), Am. Economic Assn., N.Y. Soc. Mil. and Naval Officers of World Wars, Authors League of America, Am. acad. Polit. and Social Sciences, Am. Legion. Fellow and mem. many Am. and fgn. med. socs. Club: Military-Naval (New York). Contbr. numerous articles, alone and with others, on med. subjects, reviews of books, etc. Address: The Military Naval Club, 4 W. 43d St., New York, N.Y. Died Aug. 18, 1944.

KRAUSS, Elmer Frederick, theologian; b. Kraussdale, Lehigh County, Pa., Sept. 7, 1862; s. Isaac Yeakle and Theodora Rosalie (Waage) K.; A.B., Muhlenberg Coll., Pa., 1884, A.M., 1887; D.D., 1903; grad. Phila. Luth. Theol. Sem., 1887; m. Irene E. Hartzell, Oct. 27, 1887 (died Jan. 1903); children—Irene Theodora (Mrs. D. E. Bosserman), Paul Hartzell, Harold Frederick, Ruth Sarah (Mrs. H. A. Bosch); m. 2d, Emma A. King, Sept. 20, 1904 (died Sept. 24, 1937). Ordained ministry Evang. Luth. Ch., 1887; pastor Homestead, Pa., 1887-92, Minneapolis, Minn., 1892-94, Leechburg, Pa., 1894-1900; prof. N.T. exegesis, Evang. Luth. Theol. Sem., Chicago, since 1900, acting pres., 1913-15, pres., 1915-20, dean Extra-Mural Dept., 1922-45; retired June 1945. Mem. S.A.R., Chicago br. Soc. Bibl. Research, Alliance Française of Chicago. Club: University (Chicago). Home: 60 E. 73d St., Chicago, Ill. Died May 23, 1946.

KREHBIEL, Christian Emanuel (krā'bēl), clergyman, editor; b. Summerfield, Ill., Sept. 25, 1869; s. Christian and Susanna (Ruth) K.; student Halstead Mennonite Prep. Sch., Halstead, Kan., 1887-90; grad. Kan. State Normal, 1897; student Presbyn. Theol. Sem., Bloomfield, N.J., 1898-99, Berlin Univ., Germany, 1899-1901; D.D., Bethel Coll., Newton, Kan., 1941; m. Mary Wirkler, July 27, 1902; children—Olin A., Florence (Mrs. Lynn Harmon). In editorial dept., Das Kansas Volksblatt (later Post und Volksblatt, later Der Herold); sec. Western Book and Pub. Co., Newton, Kan., 1901-20; relief worker in Russia, 1922-23; ordained to ministry of Mennonite Ch., Dec. 2, 1923; editor Christlicher Bundesbote, organ of The Gen. Conf. of Mennonite Ch. of N.A., Newton, Kans., 1930-46; organizer and pastor Lorraine Av. Mennonite Ch., Wichita, Kan., 1931-35; supt. Leisy Orphan Aid Soc., Halstead, since 1910. Mem. Gen. Conf. Mennonite Ch. (chmn. bd. pub., 1923-26, statistician, 1923-38, sec., 1926-38, pres., 1938-45, mem. Sem. Bd., since 1941, of home mission bd. since 1945); sec. Mennonite Charite, Halstead, Kan., 1908-31. Home: 2727 N. Main St., Newton, Kan. Died June 9, 1948.

KREINHEDER, Oscar Carl, pres. Valparaiso Univ.; b. Buffalo, N.Y., Nov. 10, 1877; s. Henry W. and Mary E. (Oschuetz) K.; prep. edn., Heathcote Sch., Buffalo, 1893-95, Concordia Coll., Conover, N.C., 1895-98; Concordia Sem., St. Louis, 1898-1901, D.D., 1934; LL.D., Valparaiso U., 1939; m. Hannah R. Coyner, Jan. 30, 1902; children—Edith (Mrs. John R. Shannon), Arthur C., Katherine (Mrs. Quincy Wellington), John Herbert, Jane Elizabeth. Ordained Evang. Lutheran Church, 1901; pastor Trinity Lutheran Ch., East St. Louis, Ill., 1901-03, Ch. of the Redeemer, St. Paul, 1903-20, Iroquois Av. Christ Evang. Lutheran Ch., Detroit, Mich., 1920-30; pres. Valparaiso U., 1930-39, gen. field rep. since 1939. Pres. English dist. Evang. Lutheran Synod of Mo., Ohio and Other States, 1918-28. Republican. Address: Valparaiso University, Valparaiso, Ind. Died March 26, 1946.

KREISINGER, Henry (krī'sĭng'ēr), mech. engr.; b. Radnice, Czechoslovakia, Feb. 17, 1876; s. Emanuel and Maria (Milota) K.; came to U.S., 1891; prep. edn. Lewis Inst., Chicago; B.S. in M.E., U. of Ill., 1904, M.E., 1906; m. Ella M. Zaloudek, May 6, 1905; children—Robert Henry, Helen Catharine, Elizabeth Caroline, Emily Mildred (dec.). Asst. engr. U.S. Geol. Survey, technologic br., 1904-10; fuel engr. Clinchfield Fuel Co., Spartanburg, S.C., 1910-13; fuel engr. U.S. Bur. Mines, 1913-20; research engr. Combustion Engring. Corp., New York, since 1920. Assisted in developing the use of powdered coal for steam boilers. Received Percy Nicholls award for 1943 for scientific and industrial achievements in solid fuels. Mem. Am. Soc. M.E., Am. Inst. Mining and Metall. Engrs., A.A.A.S., Sigma Xi. Awarded Chanute medal for best paper on a mech. engring. subject, Western Soc. Engrs., 1907. Republican. Free Thinker. Author of abt. 20 bulls. and tech. papers pub. by U.S. Geol. Survey and U.S. Bur. Mines; also numerous papers on engring. subjects. Home: Piermont, N.Y. Address: Combustion Engineering Company, 200 Madison Av., New York, N.Y. Died May 7, 1946.

KREUSCHER, Philip Heinrich (kroi'shēr), surgeon; b. De Witt, Neb., Nov. 18, 1885; s. Philip and Catherine K.; M.D., Northwestern U., 1909; m. Mary Veronica Miller, 1910; children—Philip H., Betty, Jane. Instr. surgery, Northwestern U. Med. Sch., 1915-19; asst. prof. surgery since 1932; clinical prof. bone and joint surgery, Loyola U., 1919-32; attending sr. surgeon Wesley Memorial Hosp. and Passavant Memorial Hosp., Chicago, since 1932; chief surgeon of Chicago Area, Carnegie-Illinois Steel Corp. Fellow Am. Coll. Surgeons, A.M.A.; mem. Ill. State Med. Soc. (pres.); Chicago Med. Soc., Chicago Surg. Soc., Chicago Pathol. Soc., Inst. of Traumatic Surgery, Am. Acad. Orthopedic Surgery, Chicago Orthopedic Club, Phi Rho Sigma. Clubs: Chicago Athletic, South Shore Country. Home: 219 Lake Shore Drive. Office: 208 S. La Salle St., Chicago, Ill. Died June 1, 1943.

KRICK, Charles Shalter, ry. official; b. Reading, Pa., Mar. 16, 1866; B.S., Lafayette Coll., 1887, Dr. Engring. (hon.). Began as rodman, Schuylkill div., Pa. R.R., July 11, 1887, successively rodman, Altoona until 1890, asst. supervisor Tyrone div., 1890-92, Phila. div., 1892-95, acting supervisor Schuylkill div., 1895-96, supervisor same div., 1896-97, middle div., 1897-1900, Pittsburgh div., 1900-03, asst. engr. Eastern and Susquehanna divs., Jan.-Aug. 1903, Phila. terminal div., 1903-06, prin. asst. engr. Phila., Baltimore & Washington R.R., 1906-10, supt. New York Terminal div., 1910-12, Manhattan div., 1912-14, supt. Phila. terminal div., 1914-15, acting gen. supt. N.J. div., 1915-16, gen. supt. same div., 1916-18, asst. gen. mgr. lines East, 1918-20, gen. mgr. Eastern region, 1920-23, vice pres. Eastern Region, 1923-36, retired, 1936, Pa. System. Home: St. Davids, Delaware County, Pa. Died July 29, 1943.

KROEGER, Frederick Charles (krā'gēr), auto mfr.; b. Winona, Minn., Apr. 27, 1888; s. Charles and Amelia (Klein) K.; B.S. in E.E., Purdue, U., 1911, hon. Dr.Engring., 1941; m. Edith T. Leverone, June 26, 1917; children—Barbara L., Marjorie R. Student engr. Gen. Electric Co., 1911-13; research engr. Remy Elec. Co., 1913-19; sales engr. Remy Elec. Div. Gen. Motors Corp., 1919-22, chief engr., 1922-25; factory mgr. Delco-Remy Div. of Gen. Motors Corp., 1925-29, gen. mgr., 1929-40; gen. mgr. Allison Div. of Gen. Motors Corp. since 1940; v.p. Gen. Motors Corp. since 1940; dir. Anderson Banking Co. Served as capt. Motor Transport Corps, U.S. Army, 1918-19. Past pres. Anderson Chamber of Commerce; dir. Ind. State Chamber of Commerce; mem. Soc. Automotive Engrs., Acacia, Tau Beta Pi. Mason. Clubs: Detroit Athletic; Indianapolis Athletic. Home: Route 17, Box 529, Indianapolis, Indiana. Office: Allison Division, General Motors Corp., Indianapolis, Ind. Died Aug. 10, 1944.

KROEH, Charles Frederick, college prof.; b. Darmstadt, Ger., Mar. 28, 1846; s. Karl August and Sophie Katharine (Ossmann) K.; came with parents to U.S., 1848; A.M., Central High Sch., Phila., 1864; D.Sc. (hon.), Stevens Inst. Tech., 1921; m. Julia Phillips, 1872; children—Jenny Rosé, Karl Frederic. Passed examination for professorship chemistry and physics same in competition, 1864; also asst. prof. German; lecturer on chemistry, 1865, mfg. chemist, 1866; asst. editor Phila. Demokrat, 1866-68, selecting and translating English news into German; instr. French and German, Lehigh U., 1868-71; prof. modern langs., Stevens Inst., 1871. Dir. School Modern Languages, 1894; chancellor Summer Schools of Long Island Chautauqua, Point of Woods, 1895. Originated method and has made specialty of teaching pupils to think directly in a foreign language. Author: The First German Reader, 1875; Die Anna-Lise, 1882; Living Method for Learning How to Think in French, 1893; The Pronunciation of French, 1884; The French Verb, 1885; How to Think in German, 1893; The Pronunciation of German, 1884; How to Think in Spanish, 1892; The Pronunciation of Spanish in Spain and America, 1888; Three Year Preparatory Course in French, 3 vols., 1897-99; Descripciones Cientificas, 1893; German Science Reader, 1907. Wrote series of articles on Modern Bee Culture, Scientific American, 1881; also various contributions on literary and other subjects in North American Review and other publications. Translator of numerous scientific reports and patents. Home: Orange, N.J. Address: Hoboken, N.J. Died Feb. 3, 1928.

KRUEGER, Ernest Theodore (krē'gēr), sociologist; b. Blue Island, Ill., Sept. 27, 1885; s. Louis Albert and Henrietta (Seyfarth) K.; A.B., U. of Ill., 1910; M.A., U. of Chicago, 1920, Ph.D., 1925; m. Margaret Enid Aldrich, Oct. 16, 1916; children—Kirwan Taylor, Marian Phyllis. Engring. constrn. work, 1911-14; prof. sociology and dean of coll., Billings (Mont.) Poly. Inst., 1914-19; asst. in sociology, U. of Chicago, 1920-24; lecturer, Chicago Recreation Training Sch., 1923, Chicago Theol. Sem., 1923-24; prof. sociology and head of dept., Vanderbilt, since 1924; prof. sociology, U. of N.C., summer 1925, 36, Pa. State Coll., summers 1926-33, U. of Ala., summers 1937, 39, U. of Mo., summer 1940, U. of Tenn., summer 1941. Mem. Am. Sociol. Soc., Am. Assn. Univ. Profs., Southern Sociol. Soc. (pres. 1935-36). Tenn. Acad. Science, Zeta Phi, Pi Gamma Mu. Conglist. Club: Freolac. Co-author: Social Psychology (with W. C. Reckless), 1931. Asso. editor Jour. Social Forces. Mem. exec. com., Am. Sociol. Soc. since 1942. Contbr. to tech. press. Home: 3100 Overlook Drive, Nashville, Tenn. Died June 19, 1945.

KRUESI, Frank E., pub. utilities exec.; b. Brooklyn, N.Y., June 19, 1885; s. John and Emily K.; ed. Union College, Schenectady, U. of Wis., 1908; m. Isobel Rogers, April 24, 1920; children—William R., Frank E., Oscar R., Paul R. Research Lab., Gen. Electric Co., Schenectady, summers 1903-06; with Commonwealth Edison Co. and subsidiaries, 1908-15; mgr. Great Lakes Power Co., Ltd., Sault Ste. Marie, Ontario, 1916-17; mgr. Frazar & Co., Seattle, 1919-26; Middle West Utilities Co., Chicago, 1926-33; pres. Wis. Power & Light Co., 1932-33; pres. Northwestern Pub. Service Co., North Dakota Power & Light Co., Central Power Co., Huron, S.D. and Grand Island, Neb., 1933-37; pres. Middle West Service Co., Chicago, 1937-45; pres. and dir. Central and South West Utilities Co. since 1946; dir. Winnipeg Electric Co., Ltd., Edison Electric Inst., American Lava Corp. Served as 1st lt. 115th Engrs., U.S. Army, 1917-19. Mem. Sigma Phi. Clubs: Union League, Electric, Chicago; Mohawk, Schenectady. Texarkana Country. Home: Texarkana, Tex., also Peacham, Vt. Office: 902 Market St., Wilmington 99, Del. Died Apr. 8, 1949; buried Vale Cemetery, Schenectady, N.Y.

KRUETGEN, Ernest J. (krĕt'gĕn), postmaster; b. Germany, Mar. 18, 1868; s. Ernest J. and Dorothy (Sass) K.; came with parents to U.S., 1880; ed. pub. schs.; m. Anna Louise Lams, Feb. 23, 1924. Founder and pres. Ernest J. Kruetgen Co.; postmaster, Chicago, since 1933. Mem. Bd. of Edn., Chicago, 1914-19; v.p. Bd. Local Improvements, Chicago, 1931; mem. Ill. State Commerce Commn., 1932; mem. Chicago Plan Commn.; trustee Century of Progress Expn., Chicago, 1933 (founder mem. and chmn. German group). Trustee Nat. Teachers Sem., Milwaukee. Mem. Art Inst. Chicago (life), Chicago Hist. Soc., Chicago Assn. Commerce, Ill. Postmasters Assn. (pres.). Nat. Saengerfest (ex-pres.), Chicago Singverein (founder, pres. 17 yrs., now hon. pres.). Mem. St. Paul's Evang. Ch. Clubs: Union League, Iroquois, German, Germania (pres. 6 terms), Lake Shore Athletic, Edgewater Golf. Home: 830 Castlewood Terrace. Office: New Post Office Bldg., Chicago 7. Died July 10, 1948.

KRUG, Henry, Jr., banker; b. St. Joseph, Mo., July 9, 1861; s. Henry and Louise (Hax) K.; ed. pvt., grade and high schs.; m. Selma Hegner, May 18, 1892. Connected with packing business under title of Henry Krug Packing Co. until plant was sold to Swift interests, 1904; chmn. bd. Am. Nat. Bank. Pres. St. Joseph Library Bd.; trustee Y.M.C.A., State Hist. Soc. of Mo.; dir. Boy Scouts of America, Northwest Mo. Assn. for the Blind. Republican. Presbyterian. Clubs: Commerce, St. Joseph Country. Donated 140 acres land to City of St. Joseph for park known as Krug Park, which father founded with gift of 20 acres, park now comprising 160 acres. Home: "Pine Ridge," Krug Park Pl. Office: Seventh and Felix Sts., St. Joseph, Mo.* Died June 19, 1946.

KRUMBEIN, Paul Otto (kroom'bīn), clergyman; b. Dresden, Germany, Dec. 3, 1875; s. Morritz and Louise (Hensel) K.; ed. in city schs. (Dresden) and ministerial courses, Germany; m. Amanda Behnke, Nov. 11, 1906 (died Aug. 4, 1925); children—Gerhard, Herbert, Irmgard, Arthur, Mary, Elsie, Gertrude, Alfred, Eleanor. Pastor various chs., 1905-10; came to U.S., 1910, naturalized citizen, 1927; successively pastor at Streeter, Lehr, North Dakota, until 1920, Walla Walla, Wash., 1920-21, Biola Calif., 1922-24, Free Evang. Luth. Cross Ch., Fresno, 1924-40 (ch. increased in membership from 875 to 2000); retired. Home: 702 Farris Av., Fresno, Calif. Died May 14, 1949.

KRUSEN, Wilmer, college pres.; b. Richboro, Pa., May 18, 1869; s. John and Elizabeth (Sager) K.; student Medico-Chirurg. Coll., Phila., Pa., 1889-90, U. of Pa., 1890-91; M.D., Jefferson Med. Coll., Phila., 1893; LL.D., U. of Pittsburgh, 1916; hon. D.Sc., Temple U., 1927, Franklin and Marshall Coll., 1933; m. Elizabeth Gilbert, June 19, 1895; children—Edward Montgomery, Francis Hammond, Carolyn Armitage (Mrs. Karl W. H. Scholz). Began as pharmacy clk., 1886; became prof. gynecology, Temple U., 1902, now med. v.p.; dir. health, Phila., 1916-20, dir. health and charities same, 1924-28; pres. Phila. Coll. of Pharmacy and Science, 1927-1941. Mem. Prison Bd., Phila. Trustee Temple U. Mem. A.M.A., Pa. State and Phila. County med. assns. Republican. Unitarian. Mason (33°). Clubs: Rotary (pres. 1932-33), Union League, Phila. Yacht. Contbr. professional journals. Home: Media, Pa. Address: Philadelphia College of Pharmacy and Science, Philadelphia, Pa. Died Feb. 9, 1943.

KUCZYNSKI, Robert René (koo-zĭn'skĭ), statistician; b. Berlin, Germany, Aug. 12, 1876; s. Wilhelm and Lucy (Brandeis) K.; ed. univs. of Freiburg, Munich, Strassburg, Berlin; m. Berta Gradenwitz, Dec. 1, 1903 (died 1947); children—Jurgen, Ursula (Mrs. L. Beurton), Brigitte (Mrs. Anthony Lewis), Barbara (Mrs. D. B. Macrae Taylor), Sabine (Mrs. Francis Loeffler), Renate (Mrs. Arthur Simpson). Mem. staff div. of methods and results, Census Office, Washington, D.C., 1900-01; dir. municipal statis. office, Elberfeld, Germany, 1904-05, Berlin-Schoeneberg, 1906-21; lecturer, Berlin Commercial High Sch., 1911-21; council mem., Brookings Inst., Washington, 1926-32; research fellow London School of Economics, 1933-38; reader in demography, U. of London, 1938-41; demographic adv., Colonial Office, London, since 1944. Author: Der Zug nach der Stadt, 1897; Loehne und Arbeitzeit in Europa und Amerika, 1913; Post-War Labor Conditions in Germany, 1925; Deutschlands Versorgung mit Nahrungsmitteln, 1926; American Loans to Germany, 1927; The Balance of Births and Deaths, vol. I, 1928, vol. II, 1931; Fertility and Reproduction, 1932; The Measurement of Population Growth, 1935; Population Movements, 1936; Colonial Population, 1937; The Cameroons and Togoland, 1939; Demographic Survey of the British Colonial Empire, 1947. Home: 12 Lawn Road, London, N.W. 3, Eng. Died Nov. 25. 1947.

KUDNER, Arthur Henry (kŭd'nẽr), advertising; b. Lapeer, Mich., Dec. 7, 1890; s. Henry Clay and Lenora B. (Cutting) K.; ed. Lapeer High Sch.; m. Madelin Thayer, Aug. 1, 1933; children—Arthur, Karyl. Began as reporter on father's newspaper, Lapeer; concert singer, 1912; reporter Detroit Free Press, 1912-13, 1915, N.Y. World, 1914; adv. writer Cheltenham Adv. Agency, 1915; adv. writer Erwin, Wasey & Co., Chicago and New York, 1916-18, chief copywriter, 1919-29, pres., 1929-35; pres. Arthur Kudner, Inc., since Oct. 1, 1935; pub. relations and advt. advisor to leading Am. corps. Writer of Red Cross and Liberty Loan advertisements, 1917. Served in R.O.T.C. and U.S. Army, 1918. Received Harvard award for best written advertisement, 1929. Mem. Business Advisory Council for the Dept. of Commerce since 1939 (exec. com. 1940; v.chmn. 1942); consultant, Advisory Commn. to Council of Nat. Defense, 1940; mem. Harriman Mission to Great Britain, 1942-43. Mem. exec. com. and chmn. com. on information N.Y. Defense Savings Staff. Mem. Am. Assn. of Adv. Agencies (chmn. of bd. 1934). Clubs: Yacht, Bankers (N.Y. City); Chicago (Chicago); Bohemian (San Francisco); Surf (Miami Beach). Contbr. to Atlantic Monthly. Home: Queenstown, Md. Office: 630 5th Av., New York, N.Y. Died Feb. 18, 1944

KUESTER, Clarence Otto (kŭs'tẽr); b. Charlotte, N.C., June 5, 1876; s. Frederick and Rixcy (Horne) K.; ed. Charlotte Graded Schs., and Maj. J. G. Baird's Private Sch. for Boys; m. Addie McDade Shaw, Dec. 21, 1896; children—Adelaide Graham and Faison Shaw (twins), Clarence Otto. Grocery clerk at age of 15; traveling salesman, 1894-1907; v.p. and mgr. Kuester-Pharr Co., 1907-12, Kuester-Lowe Co., 1912-17; mgr. new business dept. Am. Trust Co., Charlotte, 1917-18; became v.p. and business mgr. Charlotte Chamber of Commerce, 1919, now exec. v.p. and gen. business mgr.; dir. Mechanics Perpetual Bldg. and Loan Assn., Charlotte (now Home Federal Savings and Loan Association), since 1910. Sec. Mecklenburg County Draft Bd., 1917; vice chmn. County Liberty Loan campaign, World War; chmn. Draft Bd. No. 5, County of Mecklenburg, City of Charlotte, since 1940. V.p., later pres. Greater Charlotte Club, 1909-12, dir., 1912-15; hon. life mem. Charlotte Chamber of Commerce, Charlotte Jr. Chamber of Commerce. Hon. maj. United Confed. Vets. of N.C.; chmn. 150th Anniversary of Battle of Kings Mountain, 1930. Hon. v.p. (life) Charlotte Travelers Aid Soc.; hon. visiting mem. Charlotte Kiwanis Club; hon. mem. Spanish-Am. War Vets., Vets. of Fgn. Wars (Stonewall Jackson Post). Democrat. Baptist. Mason (Shriner), K.P., Moose, Elk; mem. United Commercial Travelers (past grand councillor for Carolinas). Clubs: Executives, Charlotte Country, Meyers Park Country Club, Lions (hon. life), Civitan (hon.), Rotary. Home: 427 E. Park Av., Dilworth, Charlotte, N.C. Office: 121 W. 4th St., Charlotte, N.C. Died March 12, 1948.

KUHN, Walt, artist; b. N.Y. City, Oct. 27, 1880; s. Francis and Amelia (Barbas) K.; ed. pvt. schs., N.Y. City; studied art in France, Germany, Holland, Italy and Spain; m. Vera Spier, Feb. 6, 1909; 1 dau., Brenda. Began career as cartoonist, San Francisco, 1899-1900; instr. drawing and painting, N.Y. Sch. of Art, 1908-09, Art Students League N.Y., 1926-27; art adviser to John Quinn, 1912-20. With Arthur B. Davies organized Internat. Exhbn. of Modern Art (Armory Show), 1913. Rep. in permanent collection of Addison Gallery Am. Art, Andover, Mass., Brooklyn Museum, California Palace of Legion of Honor, San Francisco, Art Institute Chicago, Columbus (Ohio) Gallery of Fine Arts, Dublin (Ireland) Museum, Los Angeles Mus., Mus. Modern Art, N.Y. City, Denver Mus., Detroit Inst. of Arts, William Rockhill Nelson Gallery (Kansas City, Mo.), N.Y. Pub. Library, Phillips Memorial Gallery, Washington, D.C., Whitney Mus. Am. Art, N.Y. City, Ency. Britannica, Norton Gallery, West Palm Beach, Fla., Univ. of Nebraska Art Galleries, Wichita (Kans.) Art Museum, Rutgers Univ., N. Brunswick, N.J., Owego Public Schools, N.Y., Fine Arts Center, Springs, John Herron Art Institute Indianapolis, Pennsylvania Academy of Fine Arts, Phila. Exhbn. Fifty Years a Painter, 1948. Most widely known works: 'The Blue Clown," "The Guide," "Jeannette," "The White Clown," "Juggler," "Trio," "Trude," "Roberto," "Apples in the Hay." Creator of ballets and pantomimes for the stage. Designer of interiors of club cars, "The Frontier Shack" on streamliner City of Denver, 1936, "The Little Nugget" on streamliner City of Los Angeles, 1937; also decorative panels in the club car "Hollywood," on the streamliner City of Los Angeles, 1941. Author of The Story of the Armory Show (brochure), 1938; author and producer of motion picture, "Walt Kuhn's Adventures in Art," 1939; "Fifty Paintings by Walt Kuhn," pub. in book form, 1940. Home: 65 University Pl. Studio: 112 E. 18th St., N.Y. City 3. Died July 13, 1949; buried Woodlawn Cemetary, N.Y. City.

KUMMEL, Henry Barnard, geologist; b. Milwaukee, Wis., May 25, 1867; s. Julius M. F. and Annie (Barnard) K.; A.B., Beloit Coll., 1889, A.M., 1892; A.M., Harvard, 1892; Ph.D., U. of Chicago, 1895; m. Charlotte F. Coe, June 20, 1899 (dec.); children—Charlotte Proctor, Lucy Barnard; m. 2d, Mrs. Anna G. Williams, Sept. 1, 1934. Instr. Beloit Coll. Acad., 1889-91; asst. in geology, Harvard U., 1891-92; fellow geology, U. of Chicago, 1892-95; asst. geologist, N.J. State Geol. Survey, 1892-98; asst. prof. physiography, Lewis Inst., Chicago, 1896-99; asst. state geologist, 1899-1902, state geologist, New Jersey, 1902-37; dir. Conservation and Development of New Jersey, 1922-37; retired, 1937; exec. officer, Forest Commn. of New Jersey, 1905-15. Asso. editor Journal of Geography, 1897-1901. Fellow Geol. Soc. Am., A.A.A.S.; pres. Assn. Am. State Geologists, 1908-13; v.p. Geol. Soc. Am., 1931. Contbr. numerous papers to geol. jours. and reports. Home: 100 Abernethy Drive, Trenton, N.J. Died Oct. 23, 1945.

KUMMER, Frederic Arnold (koom'mẽr), author, playwright; b. Catonsville, Md., Aug. 5, 1873; s. Arnold and Mary Morris (Pancoast) K.; C.E., Rensselaer Poly. Inst., Troy, N.Y., 1894; m. Clare Rodman Beecher, 1895; children—Marjorie Beecher (Mrs. Roland Young), Fredericka (dec.); m. 2d, Marion J. McLean, June 14, 1907; children—Marion McLean (Mrs. Ernest E. Wachsmuth), Frederic Arnold, Joseph Talbot Tennant. Asst. editor Railroad Gazette, 1894-96; chief engr. Am. Wood Preserving Co., 1896-98; gen. mgr. Eastern Paving Brick Co., Catskill, N.Y., 1898-1900; gen. mgr. and chief engr. U.S. Wood Preserving Co., 1900-07; lit. work since 1907. Corporate mem. Am. Soc. C.E.; mem. Soc. Am. Dramatists and Composers, Authors' League America, Chi Phi. Author: The Green God, 1911; The Brute, 1912; A Song of Sixpence, 1913; A Lost Paradise, 1914; The Second Coming (collaboration), 1916; The Painted Woman, 1917; The Web, 1919; The Battle of the Nations, 1919; Peggy-Elsie (collaboration), 1919; Pipes of Yesterday (collaboration), 1921; Plaster Saints, 1921; The Earth's Story (child's book of knowledge), vol. 1, 1922, vol. 2, 1923, vol. 3, 1924; Phryne, 1924; The Road to Fortune, 1925; Love's Greatest Mistake, 1927; Ladies in Hades, 1928; Maypoles and Morals, 1929; Gentlemen in Hades, 1930; Forbidden Wine, 1931; The Golden Piper, 1932; Red Clay, 1933; Manhattan Masquerade, 1934; Design for Murder, 1936; Death at Eight Bells, 1937; The Scarecrow Murders, The Twisted Face, The Great Road, 1938; Leif Erikson The Lucky, 1939; Courage Over the Andes, 1940; The Torch of Liberty, 1941; For Flag and Freedom, 1942; The Perilous Island, 1942; The Free State of Maryland, 1943; also author of the following plays: Mr. Buttles, 1910; The Other Woman, 1910; The Brute, 1912; The Diamond Necklace, 1912; The Painted Woman, 1913; The Magic Melody (musical comedy, with music by Sigmond Romberg), 1919; My Golden Girl (musical play, music by Victor Herbert), 1919; The Bonehead, 1920; The Voice, 1923; Song of Omar (play, with music by Harry Tierney), 1935; The Captive (grand opera with score by Gustav Strube), 1938. Wrote under pseudonym Arnold Fredericks: One Million Francs, 1912; The Ivory Snuff Box, 1912; The Blue Lights, 1915; The Little Fortune, 1915; The Film of Fear, 1917; The Mark of the Rat, 1929; The Spanish Lady, 1933. Contbr. short stories, serials, etc., to mags., and author of many motion pictures, including The Slave Market, The Yellow Pawn, Motherhood, The Ivory Snuff Box, The Belgian, etc. Home: 1501 Park Av., Baltimore, Md. Died Nov. 22, 1943.

KUNKEL, William Albert, Jr., newspaper pub.; b. Bluffton, Ind., Feb. 20, 1895; s. William Albert and Minnie Aubrey (Morgan) K.; student Culver Summer Naval Sch., 1909-10 and 1911-12, Indiana U., 1912-16, Harvard Law Sch., 1916-17; m. Lois Steen Nicholson, June 2, 1917; children—Mary Ann (Mrs. Gilmore S. Haynie), William Albert, III. Admitted to Ind. bar, 1919; oil producer, consultant on financing and organization of oil properties, 1919-30; receiver Bank of Poneto (Indiana), 1923-30, Montpelier (Indiana) State Bank, 1929-33, Citizens Trust Company, Fort Wayne, 1932-33; president Marion and Bluffton Traction Company, 1923-24; secretary Bliss Hotel Co., Bluffton, since 1921; purchased and became pub. of Fort Wayne Journal-Gazette, 1934; pres. and treas. since Oct. 15, 1935; president Northeastern Indiana Broadcasting Co., 1946; dir. Bliss Hotel Co.; sec.-treas. Kunkel & Co.; dir. Indiana State Chamber of Commerce, 1944, Fairview (Ind.) Cemetery Assn. Served as ensign, U.S. Navy, 1917-18. Del. Dem. Nat. Conv., Philadelphia, 1936. Trustee Indiana U. and Bluffton City Schs. Dir. Hoosier Salon; sec. Anthony Wayne Memorial Commn. Mem. Am. Legion, Beta Theta Pi, Sigma Delta Chi. Democrat. Methodist. Mason (32°, K.T.), K.P., Elk. Clubs: Indianapolis Athletic, Indianapolis Press; Fort Wayne Country; Bluffton Country; Quest (Fort Wayne). Home: 305 Oak St., Bluffton, Ind. Office: 701-13 Clinton St., Fort Wayne, Ind. Died Oct. 7, 1948; buried Fairview Cemetery, Bluffton, Ind.

KURN, James M., ry. official; b. Mt. Clemens, Mich., Nov. 10, 1870; s. James and Margaret (Fraser) K.; ed. pub. schs.; m. Gracia Irene McMillan, Aug. 1900; m. 2d, Nancy Clifford, Nov. 25, 1935. Began as messenger M.C. R.R., 1884, and successively telegraph operator, agt., train dispatcher and chief train dispatcher, trainmaster, supt. and gen. supt. A.T.&.S.F. Ry. to 1913; pres. Detroit, Toledo & Ironton R.R., 1913-18; apptd. 1st v.p. St.L.-S.F. Ry. Co., Mar. 1, 1918; gen. mgr. during Govt. control, and became pres. same rd., Mar. 1, 1920, apptd. receiver, Nov. 1932, apptd. trustee, Oct. 28, 1933; dir. St. Louis Federal Loan & Savings Assn., Industrial Bank & Trust Co. Republican. Episcopalian. Clubs: St. Louis, Noonday, Norwood Hills Country. Home: 56 Lake Forest, Richmond Heights, Mo.; (Florida residence) 1901 E. Gadsden, Pensacola, Fla. Office: Frisco Bldg., St. Louis, Mo. Died Jan. 13, 1945.

KURT, Franklin Thomas, educator; b. Middletown, Conn., June 30, 1872; s. Michael and Katharine (Blum) K.; Ph.B., Wesleyan U., Conn., 1895; hon. M.A. same, 1926; m. Sarah Bertha Tucker, Aug. 12, 1896; 1 son, Franklin Thorndike. Instr. chemistry and optics, 1897-99, dean, 1899-1901, N.E. Optical Inst.; instr. chemistry, 1901-03, prof. and dean, 1903-10, Boston Y.M.C.A. Evening Poly. Inst.; prin. and owner Chauncy Hall Sch., Boston, since Sept. 1900. Speaker and lecturer on scientific subjects. Mem. Soc. Chem. Industry (London), Am. Chem. Soc., Chi Psi. Republican (in nat. affairs). Episcopalian. Clubs: Boston Chamber of Commerce, Buck's Harbor Yacht, University. Home: West Newton, Mass. Office: 553 Boylston St., Boston. Died Aug. 31, 1947.

KYES, Preston (kīz), coll. prof.; b. N. Jay, Me., Jan. 24, 1875; s. Ebenezer Sylvester and Caroline Matilda (Coolidge) K.; A.B., Bowdoin Coll., 1896, A.M., 1900; Sc.D., from same, 1921; grad. student, Harvard, 1898-99; M.D., Johns Hopkins, 1900; fellow, Rockefeller Inst. for Med. Research, New York, 1902-05; asso. in Memorial Inst. for Infectious Diseases, Chicago, 1904-09; Royal Prussian Institute of Experimental Therapy, Frankfort-on-the-Maine, Germany, 1901-05; m. Martha Louise Gahan, June 28, 1904; m. 2d, Ada W. Wood, June 30, 1928. Asso. in anatomy, 1901-02, instr., 1902-04, asst. prof., 1904-06, asst. prof. exptl. pathology, 1906-12, asst. prof. preventive medicine, 1912-16, asso. prof., 1916-18, prof. 1918-40, prof. emeritus since 1940, U. of Chicago. Home: North Jay, Me. Died Dec. 27, 1949.

L

LACKEY, John Newton, clergyman; b. Mt. Blanchard, O., Jan. 17, 1875; s. Henry Hart and Lucinda (Moore) L.; A.B., Adrian (Mich.) Coll., 1901, M.A., 1909, D.D., 1914; B.D., Hartford (Conn.) Theol. Sem., 1912; m. Claribel Simmons, June 20, 1901; 1 dau., Ila Marie (Mrs. Kenilworth H. Mathus). Teacher, country schs., Hancock County, O., 1893-96; teacher La Harpe (Ill.) Sem. and pastor M.P. Ch., La Harpe, 1901-07; prof. history, Adrian Coll., 1907-10; acting pastor Presbyn. Ch., Ann Arbor, Mich., 10 mos., 1910; pastor South and Central Bapt. Chs., Hartford, Conn., since 1910. Prohibition candidate for gov. of Conn., 1915. Trustee Suffield (Conn.) Sch. Pres. Conn. Bapt. Conv., 1916-24. Mem. Sigma Alpha Epsilon. Mason (K.T.). Club: Exchange. Home: 57 Lexington Rd., West Hartford, Conn. Died Sep. 21, 1942.

LACKLAND, Frank Dorwin, army officer; b. Farquier County, Va., Sept. 13, 1884; s. Samuel and Katharine (Dorwin) L.; ed. Air Service Engring. Sch., Dayton, O., 1920-21, Air Corps Tactical Sch., Maxwell Field, Ala., 1928-29, Command and Gen. Staff Sch., Ft. Leavenworth, 1929-31; unmarried. Enlisted in Nat. Guard, Dist. of Columbia, Mar. 1903, and served in all grades to capt. up to Feb. 1911; commd. 2d lt. Inf., U.S. Army, Feb. 11, 1911; transferred to Air Service, 1920, advanced through the grades to brig. gen., wing comdr., Dec. 1939; served as maj. Signal Corps in World War. Clubs: Army and Navy (Washington, D.C.); San Antonio Country. Address: care War Dept., Washington, D.C. Died Apr. 27, 1943.

LACY, William Stokes, clergyman, educator; b. El Dorado, Ark., Oct. 31, 1874; s. Watson Eldridge and Sallie (Holcombe) L., A.B., Arkansas Coll., 1900, D.D., 1918; B.D., Union Theol. Sem., Richmond, Va., 1911; m. Sadie James, June 25, 1902; children—William Sterling, Edward Lewis, Joseph Eugene, Sarah Elizabeth (Mrs. J. Courtney White). Prin. Cameron (Ind. Ty.) Presbyn. Inst., 1900-03; prof. Greek and philosophy, Ark. Coll., 1903-08; field sec. Union Theol. Sem., 1910-11; ordained to Presbyn. ministry, 1903; pastor Belmont, N.C., 1911-15; prof. Bible, Peace Inst., Raleigh, N.C., 1915-16; pres. Ark. Coll., 1916-23 and 1932-37; executive sec. Southwestern Coll., Memphis, Tenn., 1923-30; supt. Presbyn. schs. and colls. of Miss., 1930-32. Mem. permanent advisory com. on Christian edn. of Gen. Assembly of Ark., 1917-24 and 1932-38; commr. to General Assemblies of Presbyn. Ch. of U.S., 1914, 22, 38. Trustee Belhaven Coll., Jackson, Miss., 1930-32. Mem. Ark. Ednl. Assn. Democrat. Kiwanian. Author of numerous pamphlets on church colleges; contbr. to religious and secular papers. Home: Batesville, Ark. Died Jan. 27, 1943.

LADD, Carl Edwin, educator; b. McLean, N.Y., Feb. 25, 1888; s. Arnold D. and Mary E. (Mineah) L.; Cortland (N.Y.) Normal and Training Sch., 1903-07; B.S.A., Cornell Univ., 1912, Ph.D., 1915; hon. LL.D., from University of Maine, 1941; m. Camilla

M. Cox, Mar. 9, 1912; 1 dau., Elizabeth Marie; m. 2d, Lucy Frances Clark, July 16, 1918; children—Carl Edson, Robert Daniel. Instr. in farm management, Cornell U., 1912-15; dir. N.Y. State Sch. of Agr., Delhi, 1915-17; specialist in agrl. edn., N.Y. State Edn. Dept., Albany, 1917-19; dir. N.Y. State Sch. of Agr., Alfred U., 1919-20; extension prof. farm management, Cornell U., 1920-24, dir. of extension, 1924-32; dean of N.Y. State Coll. of Agr. and N.Y. State Coll. of Home Economics, also dir. expt. stas. since 1932. Adviser in agrl. economic research, Dartington Hall, Totnes, Devon, Eng., Mar.-Sept. 1928; dep. commr. of conservation, N.Y. State Conservation Dept., Jan.-Oct. 1931 (on leave of absence from Cornell U. both periods); mem. State Defense Council since 1940. Mem. Am. Farm Econ. Assn., Am. Assn. for Advancement Science, Internat. Agrl. Econ. Conf., Acacia, Phi Kappa Phi, Epsilon Sigma Phi, Sigma Xi. Presbyterian. Mason. Author: Dairy Farming Projects, 1923. Co-editor with A. K. Getman of Wiley Farm Series; with Wylie B. McNeal of Wiley Home Economic Series; editor Wiley College Series (textbooks). Home: 201 Bryant Av., Ithaca, N.Y. Died July 23, 1943.

LADD, George Tallman, mech. engr.; b. Edinburgh, O., May 17, 1871; s. George Trumbull and Cornelia Ann (Tallman) L.; student Sheffield Scientific Sch. (Yale), 1891; M.E., Cornell, 1895; m. Florence Ewing Barrett, Sept. 2, 1910. With P.&L.E. Ry. Co., Pittsburgh, 1891-93; designer Brooks Locomotive Works, Dunkirk, N.Y., 1895-98; mech. engr. in charge engine and boiler sales, Bass Foundry & Machine Co., Ft. Wayne, Ind., 1898-1909; consulting engr., Pittsburgh, 1909-10; pres. and treas. The George T. Ladd Co., engrs., Pittsburgh, 1910-25; pres. Ladd Water Tube Boiler Co., 1925-1928; pres. and gen. mgr. United Engineering & Foundry Co., Pittsburgh, since 1928; pres. Ladd Securities Co., Ladd Equipment Co.; chmn. Pittsburgh Testing Laboratory, Woodings-Verona Tool Works; v.p. Davis Brake Beam Co., Johnstown, Pa.; dir. Columbian Enameling & Stamping Co. (Terre Haute, Ind.), United Engring. & Foundry Co., Combustion Engring. Co., Inc. (New York), Heyl & Patterson, Inc., First Nat. Bank (Pittsburgh), Pa.-Central Airlines Co., Flannery Bolt Co., Pittsburgh Steel Co., Pittsburgh Br. Federal Reserve Bank of Cleveland, Nat. Supply Co. (N.Y.), Peoples-Pittsburgh Trust Co., Tristate Industrial Assn., Follansbee Steel Corp., Westinghouse Electric & Mfg. Co., Union Switch & Signal Co. Dir. Elizabeth Steel Magee Hosp., Allegheny Gen. Hosp., Pittsburgh Chamber of Commerce; pres. Pittsburgh Diagnostic Clinic; trustee Bucknell University, Carnegie Inst., Carnegie Inst. Tech., Pittsburgh. Lt. comdr. U.S.N.R.F., in charge construction 14-inch naval railway mounts and 7-inch caterpillar mounts, which were in service in France, August 1918, with naval railway batteries, World War; was mem. advisory bd. Pittsburgh District, U.S. Fuel Administration; now mem. advisory bd. Pittsburgh Ordnance Dist. Designed and built largest water tube boilers in world, operating at Fordson Plant, Ford Motor Co., Detroit. Mem. Am. Soc. M.E., Engrs. Soc. of Western Pa. (ex-pres.), Am. Iron and Steel Inst., U.S. Naval Inst., American Geog. Soc., Pa. Soc. Mason (32°, K.T., Shriner), Republican. Clubs: Duquesne, Pittsburgh Athletic, Montour Heights Golf, Harvard-Yale-Princeton; Edgeworth (Sewickley, Pa.); Chicago Athletic (Chicago); Cornell, Yale, Lotos, Engineers' (New York); Youngstown (O.) Country Club. Home: Coraopolis Heights, Pa. Office: First Nat. Bank Bldg., Pittsburgh, Pa. Died Oct. 3, 1943.

LADD, Maynard, pediatrist; b. Feb. 24, 1873; s. Horatio Oliver and Harriett Vaughan (Abbott) L.; A.B., Harvard, 1894; M.D., Harvard Med. Sch., 1898; Mass. Gen. Hosp., 1900; m. Anna Coleman Watts at Salisbury Cathedral, Eng., June 26, 1905. Asso. in pediatrics, Harvard; cons. phys. to Children's Hosp., Boston; med. dir. preventive clinic Boston Dispensary; dep. commr. children's bureau Am. Red Cross, France, 1917-19. Fellow Am. Acad. Pediatrics; mem. Am. Pediatrics Soc. (pres. 1921-22), A.M.A., Mass. Med. Soc., N.E. Pediatric Soc. (pres. 1916-17). Decorated officier d'Academie, France, 1934. Republican. Episcopalian. Contbr. on med. topics. Home: Santa Barbara, Calif. Office: 412 Beacon St., Boston, Mass. Died Mar. 9, 1942.

LADD, William Sargeant, med. coll. dean; b. Portland, Ore., Aug. 16, 1887; s. William Mead and Mary Lyman (Andrews) L.; B.S., Amherst Coll., 1910; M.D., Columbia U., 1915; m. Mary Richardson Babbott, June 5, 1913; children—Frances Wood, William Sargent, Anthony Thornton, John. Interne, Peter Bent Brigham Hosp., Boston, 1915-17; asst. phys. Presbyn. Hosp., N.Y. City, 1917-19, 1924-31; instr. Columbia, 1917-19, 1921-24, asso. 1924-31; instr., Johns Hopkins U. and asst. in medicine Johns Hopkins Hosp., 1919-21; asst. prof. medicine, Cornell, 1931-32, professor medicine, 1932-42, associate dean Medical College, 1931-35, dean 1935-42 professor of clinical medicine since 1942, assistant visiting physician Bellevue Hospital, 1932-35; asst. attending phys. N.Y. Hosp., 1933-35, attending phys. since 1935; cons. staff Dept. of Medicine, Nassau Hosp. Association, since 1929. Director Seaboard Surety Co. Served as 1st lt. Med. Reserve Corps, 1917-18. Trustee American U. of Beirut, Syria, 1924-41, Amherst Coll., 1936-41, Memorial Hosp., N.Y., N.Y. Acad. Med. since 1934. Mem. A.A.A.S., A.M.A., N.Y. State and County med. soc., Soc. for Exptl. Biology, Soc. of Mammalogists, Harvey Soc., Alpha Omega Alpha, Alpha Delta Phi. Clubs: Century Association, University, American Alpine (pres. 1929-32), Alpine (London, Eng.); Alpine Française (hon.; Paris). Contbr. of articles to med. jours. and mountaineering mags. Home: Cold Spring, N.Y. Died Sep. 16, 1949.

LAGERQUIST, Walter Edwards (lā'gēr-kwist), finance; b. Essex, Ia., 1881; s. John and Clara Caroline (Anderson) L.; A.B., Yale, 1905, A.M., 1906, Ph D., 1911; m. Catherine Caecile Schwartz, Aug. 15, 1911; children—Philip De Bold, Walter Waldraff. Prof. economics, Beloit (Wis.) Coll., 1906-07; instr. Cornell U., 1908-11; asst. prof. economics, 1911-12, asso. prof. economics and commerce, 1912-18, prof. finance and dir. grad. div., Sch. of Commerce, 1918-25, Northwestern U.; counsellor on investments, Am. Exchange Irving Trust Co., New York, 1925-29; v.p. Irving Investors Management Co., 1929-30; chmn. bd. Brookmire Investors, Inc.; v.p. Brookmire Economic Service, Inc., 1931-32; partner Vance-Lagerquist Associates, 1933-35; v.p. Johnston & Lagerquist, Inc., 1935-41; pres. Franklin Management Co.; trustee New England Fund, General Investors Trust. Mem. Financial Commn. to Govt. of Colombia, 1930. Mem. Am. Econ. Assn., Alpha Pi Zeta, Beta Gamma Sigma, Epsilon Sigma, Alpha Kappa Psi. Author: Investment Analysis, 1921; Public Utility Finance, 1926; Balancing and Hedging an Investment Plan, 1942; also numerous articles in financial publications. Home: 255 Beacon St. Office: 111 Devonshire St., Boston, Mass. Died Feb. 22, 1944.

La GUARDIA, Fiorello H. (lȧ-gwär'dĭ-ȧ), lawyer, writer, commentator; b. N.Y. City, Dec. 11, 1882; LL.B., New York University, 1910, LL.D., 1938; LL.D., St. Lawrence University, 1938, Yale, 1940, Washington and Jefferson College, 1942; married Marie Fisher, Feb. 28, 1929. With Am. Consulate, Budapest, Hungary, and Trieste, Austria, 1901-04; consular agt. at Fiume, Hungary, 1904-06; interpreter at Ellis Island, N.Y., 1907-10; began law practice New York, 1910; dep. atty. gen. of N.Y., 1915-17; mem. 65th and 66th Congresses (1917-19), 14th N.Y. Dist., and 68th to 72d Congresses (1923-33), 20th N.Y. Dist.; mayor of New York City, term 1934-37, reëlected 2 terms, 1938-45. President Board of Aldermen of N.Y. City, 1920-21; apptd. dir. Office of Civilian Defense, May 20, 1941. Pres. U.S. Conf. of Mayors, 1936-45; chmn. Am. Sect. of Permanent Joint Defense Bd. (Canada-U.S.). Spl. Ambassador to Brazil, 1946. Dir. gen. UNRRA, Apr.-December, 1946. Commissioned U.S. Air Service, August, 1917, held rank first lt., capt., major; commanded 8th Centre Aviation Sch. and Am. Flying Force, Italian front; attached to night and day bombing squadrons there. Decorations: World War I Victory; Knight Comdr. Order of Crown of Italy, Italian War Cross; Blue Order of Jade (China); Order of Redeemer (Greece); Order of Merit (Chile); Simon Bolivar Medal (Venezuela); Medal of Honor (Haiti); Order of Honor and Merit-Commendador (Cuba); Order of St. Olav (Norway); Comdr. Legion of Honor (France); Delaware Award (Sweden); Order of Orange-Nassau (Netherlands); Lithuanian Aid Medal; Order of White Lion (Czech.); Polonia Restituta, First Class (Poland); Medal of Merit (U.S.A.); Grand Comdr. of Greek Order of Phoenix. Address: 30 Rockefeller Plaza, New York 20, N.Y. Died Sept. 20, 1947.

LAIDLAW, Harriet Burton (Mrs. James Lees Laidlaw) (lād'law), writer, speaker; b. Albany, N.Y., Dec. 16, 1873; d. George Davidson and Alice Davenport (Wright) Burton; B.Pd., N.Y. State Coll. for Teachers, 1898, M.Pd., 1899; Ph.B., Ill. Wesleyan U., 1902; B.A., Barnard Coll. (Columbia), 1902; matriculated at Columbia for Ph.D.; LL.D., Rollins College, 1930; m. James Lees Laidlaw (banker), Oct. 25, 1906; 1 dau., Louise Burton. Teacher high schs., New York, 12 yrs.; chmn. exec. council Nat. Am. Woman Suffrage Assn.; chmn. Borough of Manhattan of Woman Suffrage Party, 1909-16, and vice chmn. for N.Y. State since 1916; v.p. N.Y. State Woman Suffrage Assn., 1915; chmn. N.Y. State League of Women Voters, 1918-19; chmn. ednl. sect. N.Y. State for Federal Food Bd.; v. chmn. Woman's Pro-League Council, 1921-22; mem. Council of League to Enforce Peace; mem. exec. council City Fusion Party, 1937; chairman American Committee League of Nations Pavilion, N.Y. World's Fair, 1939, 40; mem. exec. com., nat. Congl. chmn. United Nations Assn. Mem. Citizen's Union of New York City (vice chairman and mem. exec. com.), League of Nations Assn. (exec. com., dir. chmn. Congl. com.), Univ. Women of Am. Social Hygiene Assn. (v.p. and dir.), Barnard Alumnæ, Florence Crittenden League (dir.), Am. Acad. Polit. Science, Nat. Inst. Social and Polit. Science, Nat. Soc. Colonial Dames, Hugenot Soc., Order of Daughters of Holland Dames, Order of Lords of Manors in America, Political Com. America United for World Organization. Clubs: Colony, Woman's Univ., Woman's City, Town Hall, York Club, Nat. Arts (vice chmn.), Barnard College Club. Home: Sands Point, L.I.; (winter) 60 E. 66th St., New York, N.Y. Died Jan. 25, 1949.

LAING, Gordon Jennings, educator; b. London, Ont., Can., Oct. 16, 1869; s. John Burnett and Mary (Jennings) L.; A.B., U. of Toronto, 1891, Litt.D., 1923; Ph.D., Johns Hopkins, 1896; LL.D., 1938; LL.D., U. of Western Ont., 1924, U. of Pittsburgh, 1930, La. State Univ., 1938; m. Alice C. Judson, Aug. 22, 1903. Lecturer Latin lit., Bryn Mawr Coll., 1897-99; instr. Latin, 1899-1902, asst. prof., 1902-07, asso. prof., 1907-13, prof., 1913-21, chmn. dept., 1919-21, U. of Chicago; prof. and head of the dept. of classics and dean Faculty of Arts, McGill U., 1921-23; prof. Latin, Univ. of Chicago, 1923-35, dean Div. Humanities, 1931-35, alumni dean, 1940-43; annual prof. Am. Sch. Classical Studies, Rome, 1911-12; mng. editor Classical Journal, 1905-08; asso. editor Classical Philology, 1905-21 and since 1923; gen. editor U. of Chicago Press, 1909-21 and 1923-40. Mem. Archæol. Inst. America (v.p.), Am. Philol. Assn. (ex-pres.), Classical Assn. Middle West and South (ex-pres.). Clubs: University, Wayfarers, Tavern, Quadrangle (Chicago); Lake Zurich Golf. Author: Survivals of Roman Religion, 1931. Editor: Masterpieces of Latin Literature, 1903; Selections from Ovid, 1905; The Phormio of Terence, 1908. Contbr. to philol. publs. Chmn. Nat. Groups Div., War Finance Com. of Ill., 1942-43. General Editor, United Educators, Inc., since 1944. Home: 5656 Dorchester Av. Address: University of Chicago, Chicago, Ill. Died Sept. 1, 1945.

LAING, John, coal mining; b. near Glasgow, Scotland, Aug. 24, 1865; s. Alexander and Elizabeth (MacAlpin) L.; brought to U.S., 1867; ed. pub. schs., Mercer County, Pa.; m. Margaret Slagle, Oct. 6, 1903; children—Louisa, Gertrude, Margaret. Worked in mines of Fayette County, W.Va., until 1890; assisted in organizing Sun Coal Co., Royal Coal Co. and the Lanark, Rush Run, Cunard McAlpine and Morrison coal cos., all in W.Va.; later organized and developed the Main Island Creek, McBeth, McKay and Wyatt coal cos.; pres. the Wyatt Coal Sales Co., the sales agency for all the mines in which he is interested; pres. Beckley Fire Creek Coal Co.; dir. Kanawha Valley Bank; Chief Dept. of Mines of W.Va., 1908-13. Chmn. bd. Y.M.C.A. of Charleston; pres. Union Mission. Republican. Presbyterian. Mason (32°), Elk. Home: 1325 Quarrier St. Office: Kanawha Valley Bldg., Charleston, W.Va.* Died Apr. 16, 1943.

LAING, Samuel McPherson (lăng), clergyman, educator; b. Pittsburgh, Pa., Aug. 19, 1892; s. James Alexander and Margaret (Rainey) L.; A.B., Muskingum Coll., New Concord, O., 1912, D.D., 1930; B.D., Pittsburgh Theol. Sem., 1919; m. Mary Luella Pollock, Nov. 21, 1923; children—Jane Pollock, Samuel McPherson. Teacher Assuit Coll., Egypt, 1912-16; ordained to ministry United Presbyn. Ch., 1919, pastor Russellton and Curtisville, Pa., 1919-20, Deer Creek, Pa., 1920-23, 1st Ch., Springfield, O., 1923-26, 2d Ch., Pittsburgh, 1926-36; condr. tour, Temple Tours Company, Boston, 1930; president Pittsburgh Male Chorus, 1935; president Knoxville (Tenn.) College, 1936-40; became pastor Washington Boulevard United Presbyn. Ch., Cleveland Heights, O., Nov. 1, 1940, pastor emeritus since 1943. Trustee Muskingum Coll.; dir. Assuit Coll., Egypt. Clubs: Kiwanis, Executives (Knoxville); Young Men's Literary (Springfield). Home: 1008 Quilliams Road, Cleveland Heights, O. Died Jan. 10, 1944.

LAIRD, Warren Powers, architect, educator; b. Winona, Minn., Aug. 8, 1861; s. Matthew James and Lydia (Powers) L.; ed. pub. and state normal schs., Winona, Minn., and at Cornell U.; instr. at Cornell Univ., 1886, and at U. of Pa., 1891; 6 yrs. practice and study with architects, in Minn., Boston, and New York, and 1 yr. travel and study in Europe (1882-90); Sc.D., U. of Pa., 1911, LL.D., 1932; m. Clara Elizabeth, d. Dr. Charles and Mary (Hall) Tuller, Nov. 15, 1893; children—Mary Hall (Mrs. John Dashiell Myers), Helen Powers (dec.). Prof. architecture, 1891-1932, and dean Sch. of Fine Arts, from founding, 1920-32, emeritus prof. architecture since 1932, U. of Pa. Lecturer Princeton U., 1932-33. Consulting architect of state, municipal and other pub. and pvt. bodies in many states and Can. Award of Merit, Gen. Alumni Soc. University of Pa., Founders Day, 1936. Mem. nat. advisory council Lingnan University, Canton, China; trustee, 1909-26. Mem. Pa. State Art Commn., 1928-36, 1938-41. Mem. Council of Cathedral of Washington, 1931-41; former dir. Tri-State Regional Planning Fedn. of Phila.; mem. Phila. Zoning Commission, 1929. Fellow American Inst. of Architects; an organizer, Association Collegiate Schools of Architecture, pres. 1912-21; member American Civic Assn., Phi Beta Kappa, Sigma Xi (president Pa. Chapter, 1916-17), Tau Sigma Delta; hon. mem. Soc. Architects of Uruguay, Central Soc. Architects of Argentina, Assn. of Architects of Chile, Nat. Soc. of Architects (Cuba); del. 3d Pan-Am. Congress of Architects, Buenos Aires, 1927, as rep. U.S. Govt., Univ. of Pa. and A.I.A.; chmn. architectural jury, art competition, 10th Olympics, Los Angeles, 1932; mem. permanent com. Internat. Congress of Architects, 1925-35; U. of Pa. del. to Internat. Congress Univs., Havana, 1930. Mem. bd. overseers P.E. Div. Sch. Phila. from orgn. to 1942; mem. Ch. Bldg. Commn. Diocese of Pa., Com. on Ch. Architecture of Gen. Council Lutheran Ch. of N.A., 1913-41; mem. vestry Memorial Ch. of St. Paul, Overbrook, 1898-1933 (rector's warden 1914-25). Former mem. Archeol. Inst. of Am., Coll. Art Assn., Art Teachers Assn., Scotch-Irish Soc. of Phila., Merion Civic Assn.; mem. Order of Founders, Patriots of America, S.R.; hon. mem. Art Alliance, Archtl. Alumni Soc. of U. of Pa. Clubs: University (hon.), T-Square, Lenape. Home: Bryn Mawr Gables, Bryn Mawr, Pa. Died Feb. 18, 1948; buried in West Laurel Hill Cemetery, Cynwyd, Pa.

LAKE, Everett John, ex-gov.; b. Woodstock, Conn., Feb. 8, 1871; s. Thomas A. and Martha A. (Cockings) L.; B.S., Worcester Poly. Inst., 1890; A.B., Harvard, 1892; LL.D., Conn. Wesleyan, 1921, Trinity, 1922; m. Eva Louise Sykes, Sept. 4, 1895 (deceased); children—Harold S., Marjorie S.; m. 2d, Barbara Grace Lincoln, Sept. 1940. With Hartford Lumber Co., 1893, pres. 1900-39. Mem. Conn. Ho. of Rep., 1903, Senate, 1905-06; lt. gov. of Conn.,

1907-08, gov., 1921-22. Mem. Delta Kappa Epsilon. Republican. Conglist. Mason. Home: 885 Farmington Av., West Hartford, Conn. Died Sept. 16, 1948.

LAKE, George Burt, med. editor, publisher and writer, psychiatrist; b. Topeka, Kan., Nov. 26, 1880; s. George Burt and Helen Luthera (Marsh) L.; student U. of Mich., 1898-1901; M.D., Rush Med. Coll., Chicago, 1902; grad. Army Med. Sch., Washington, D.C., 1911; m. Mary Lee Blossom, Dec. 25, 1902; children—Helen Lee Blossom (Mrs. Ray J. Cox), George Burt, Jr. Asst. surgeon Mexican Central Ry., 1902-04; general practice, Wolcottville, Ind., 1904-10, town health officer, 1907-08; special lecturer in hygiene and sanitation, Purdue U., 1908-10; editor Clinical Medicine and Surgery (now Clinical Medicine) since 1924; now also owner and pub. same; attending internist American Hosp., 1927-34; editor Bull. Med. Round Table of Chicago, 1928-34. Mem. Med. Corps, U.S. Army, 1910-24, advancing to maj.; served in campaign against Moros, Sulu, P.I., 1913, in Mexican Punitive Expdn., 1916; lt. col., camp surgeon, Camp Grant, Ill., later comdg. officer, Gen. Hosp., Indianapolis, World War; now col., Med. R.C. (inactive). Fellow A.M.A.; mem. Assn. Mil. Surgeons, Med. Round Table of Chicago (pres. 1925-27; sec. 1941), Art Inst. Chicago, Bookfellows, A.A. A.S., Miss. Valley Med. Editors Assn. (pres. 1941), Am. Physicians' Art Assn., Miss. Valley Med. Soc. (bd. dirs. 1940-41), Am. Assn. of History of Medicine, Ill. Acad. Science, Chicago Poetry Center of Poetry Soc. of London (pres. 1940). Reserve officers Assn.; asso. Coll. Physicians. Liberal Catholic priest. Clubs: Saturday Evening Club, Chicago Motor Club. Author: (verse) An Apostle of Joy, 1928; (verse) Hilltops, 1932; (verse) Eros and the Sage, 1935; A 5,000 Year Plan; Parental Therapy (with Dr. W. F. Dutton); also several hundred articles. Home: 330 Bloom St., Highland Park, Ill. Office: Medical and Dental Arts Bldg., Waukegan, Ill. Died Mar. 2, 1943.

LAKE, Kirsopp, theologian, historian; b. Southhampton, Eng., Apr. 7, 1872; s. George Anthony (M.D.) and Isabel Oke (Clark) L.; B.A., Lincoln Coll., Oxford, 1895, M.A., 1897; Arnold essay prizeman, 1902; D.D., St. Andrews Univ., 1911; Th.D., Leyden Univ., 1921; Litt.D., U. of Mich., 1926; Ph.D., Heidelberg U., 1936; m. Helen Courthope Forman; m. 2d, Silva Tipple New; children—Gerard Anthony Kirsopp, Agnes Kirsopp, John Anthony Kirsopp. Curate of Lumley, Durham, England, 1895, of St. Mary the Virgin, Oxford, 1897-1904; prof. ordinarius, U. of Leyden, Holland, 1904-13; prof. early Christian lit., Harvard, Sept. 1914-19, Winn prof. ecclesiastical history, 1919-32, prof. of history, 1932-38. Paid visits to Mt. Athos and other libraries to investigate Greek MSS., summers since 1903; dir. archaeol. expedition to Serabit, 1930, 35, to Samaria, 1932-34, to Lake Van, 1938-39. Fellow Am. Acad. Arts and Sciences. Awarded medal, British Acad., 1936. Corr. mem. Preussische Akademie der Wissenschaft. Club: Century (New York). Author: Text of the New Testament, 1898; Codex I of the Gospels, 1900; Texts from Mt. Athos, 1901; The Athos Leaves of Codex H—Paul, 1904; The Historical Evidence for the Resurrection of Jesus Christ, 1905; The Athos Leaves of the Shepherd of Hermas, 1908; Professor von Soden's Treatment of the Text of the Gospels, 1909; The Earlier Epistles of St. Paul, 1910; The Codex Simaiticus, 1911; The Stewardship of Faith, 1914, The Beginnings of Christianity, Vol. I, 1920, Vol. II, 1922, Vol. III, 1926, Vols. IV and V, 1933; Landmarks in the History of Early Christianity, 1921; The Codex Sinaiticus, Vol. II, 1921; Immortality and the Modern Mind, 1922; Religiion Yesterday and Tomorrow, 1925. Translator: The Apostolic Fathers, 1912; Eusebius, 1927; The Serabit Inscriptions (Harvard Theol. Studies), 1927; The Caesarean Text of Mark, 1928; Six Collations of N.T. MSS., 1933; Dated Greek minuscule MSS., Fasc. I and II, 1934, Fasc. III and IV, 1935, Fasc. V. and VI, 1936, Fasc. VII and VII, 1937, Fasc. IX and X, 1939, Vol. X, XI XII, XIII, 1939-41; Studies and Documents, Vols. I and II, 1934, Vols. III, IV and V, 1935, VI, VII, VIII and IX, 1936-37; Paul, His Heritage and Legacy, 1934; An Introduction to the New Testament, 1937. Home: 522 Oakley Road, Haverford, Pa. Died Nov. 10, 1946.

LAKE, Simon, naval architect, mech. engr.; b. Pleasantville, N.J., Sept. 4, 1866; s. John Christopher and Miriam M. (Adams) L.; ed. Clinton Liberal Inst., Fort Plain, N.Y., and Franklin Inst., Phila.; m. Margaret Vogel, June 9, 1890. Inventor of even keel type of submarine torpedo boats; built first experimental boat, 1894; built Argonaut 1897 (first submarine to operate successfully in the open sea); has designed and built many submarine torpedo boats for U.S. and foreign countries; spent several yrs. in Russia, Germany and England, designing, building and acting in an advisory capacity in construction of submarine torpedo boats. Also inventor submarine apparatus for locating and recovering sunken vessels and their cargoes, submarine apparatus for pearl and sponge fishing, heavy oil internal combustion engine for marine purposes, etc. Pres. The Lake Submarine Co., The Lake Engring. Co., Merchant Submarine Co., Lake Submarine Salvage Corp., Industrial Submarine Corp., Lake Torpedo Boat Co. (also consulting engineer). Mem. Soc. Naval Architects and Marine Engrs., Am. Soc. M.E., Am. Soc. Naval Engrs., Instn. of Naval Architects (London), Soc. Founders and Patriots of America, Soc. Colonial Wars, S.A.R. Mason. Clubs: Engineers (New York); Algonquin (Bridgeport, Conn.). Home: Milford, Conn.* Died June 23, 1945.

LAMAR, Clarinda Pendleton (Mrs. Joseph Rucker Lamar) (lȧ-mär'); b. Bethany, W.Va., Aug. 25, 1856; d. William Kimbrough (LL.D.) and Katherine Huntington (King) Pendleton; grad. Packer Collegiate Inst., Brooklyn, N.Y., 1876; m. Joseph Rucker Lamar, late justice Supreme Court of U.S., Jan. 30, 1879 (died Jan. 2, 1916); children—Philip Rucker, William Pendleton. Sec., 1902-10, v.p., 1910-14, pres., 1914-27, hon. pres. for life since 1927, Nat. Soc. Colonial Dames America (dedicated canopy over Plymouth Rock, 1921, and presented it to Mass. on behalf of the Society; instrumental in raising endowment for maintenance of Sulgrave Manor in Eng. and was received by their British Majesties at a garden party at Buckingham Palace, July 1925. Was chmn. for purchase, restoration, furnishing and endowment of Dumbarton House, Washington, for nat. hdqrs. of Soc.); mem. Woman's Com. and field div. Council of Nat. Defense (among 1st 9 women apptd.), 1917-18. Hon. life mem. Ga. Bar Assn. Mem. portrait com. (3 from each Colonial State) of U.S. Constitution Sesqui-Centennial Celebration; member Nat. Advisory Com. on Women's Participation in the World's Fair. Author: Life of Joseph Rucker Lamar, 1927; History National Society Colonial Dames America, 1891 to 1933, 1934; also of short stories pub. prior to 1899 in The Independent, Munsey's and Lippincott's. Home: 41 Muscogee Rd., Atlanta, Ga. Died Apr. 27, 1943.

LAMB, Charles Rollinson, architect; b. New York; s. Joseph and Eliza (Rollinson) L.; m. Ella Condie. Ex-pres. Arts Realty Co.; pres. J. & R. Lamb Corp. Splty. ecclesiastical architecture, memorial and hist. art; architect Dewey arch, erected in Madison Sq., New York, by Nat. Sculpture Soc. to commemorate home-coming of Adm. Dewey; also of Court of Honor, Hudson-Fulton Celebration, 1909. Dir. Boy Scouts of Am.; ex-v.p. Archtl. League, Nat. Sculpture Soc.; v.p. Am. Fine Arts Soc.; ex-pres. Art Students' League, Municipal Art Soc.; ex-sec. Soc. Mural Painters; trustee Nat. Arts Club; mem. S.R., S.A.R. (ex-trustee), Nat. Soc. Arts and Crafts; etc. Clubs: National Arts (bd. of govs.), Church. Home: Cresskill, N.J. Died Feb. 22, 1942.

LAMBERT, Albert Bond, mfg. pharmacist; b. St. Louis, Dec. 6, 1875; s. Jordan W. and Lily (Winn) L.; student U. of Va., 1893-95; m. B. Myrtle McGrew, Apr. 23, 1899. Pres. Lambert Pharmacal Co., since 1896; est. factories in Paris, France, and Hamburg, Germany; v.p. Lambert-Deacon-Hull Printing Co.; dir. Mechanics Nat. Bank. Commd. maj., Signal Corps, Aviation Sect., 1917. V.p. Internat. Jury, St. Louis Expn., 1904; mem. City Council, St. Louis, 1907-11. Democrat. Episcopalian. V.p. Navy League, Aero Club America. Clubs: Automobile (ex-pres.), St. Louis Country, Bellerive, Glen Echo Country, St. Louis, Noonday, Aero of St. Louis (pres.), Ridgedale Country (pres.). Home: 2 Hortense Pl. Office: 2101 Locust St., St. Louis. Deceased.

LAMBERT, Samuel Waldron, M.D.; b. New York, June 18, 1859; s. Edward Wilberforce and Martha M. (Waldron) L.; A.B., Yale, 1880, Ph.B., 1882, A.M., 1905; M.D., Coll. Phys. and Surg. (Columbia), 1885; D.Sc., Columbia, 1921; m. Elizabeth Willets, Oct. 21, 1893. Interne Bellevue Hosp., 1885-86; in gen. practice medicine, New York, since 1886; attending phys. Nursery and Child's Hosp., 1890-96, New York Lying-in Hosp., 1890-1905, New York Hosp., 1896-1909, St. Luke's Hosp., 1906-29; prof. clin. medicine, Columbia U., 1903-19; dean Coll. Phys. and Surgeons, 1904-19. Trustee Roosevelt Hosp., 1904-19. Mem. Assn. Am. Physicians, N.Y. Acad. Medicine, Med. and Surg. Soc., Am. Gastro-Enterol. Soc., Med. Soc. State of N.Y., Med. Soc. County of N.Y. Now retired from active work. Clubs: Graduate (New Haven); Union, Century, Grolier (New York). Home: 101 E. 72d St., New York, N.Y. Died Feb. 9, 1942.

LAMBERTON, John A., editor; b. Lowell, Mass., Dec. 14, 1873; s. David and Annie (Guinan) L.; student Lowell High Sch., 1886-90; m. Leah A. Lewis, Apr. 20, 1898; children—David L. (dec.), Adah G., Vivian M. (Mrs. Stanley Thomson). Reporter Lowell Sunday Arena, 1892-96, reporter, later city editor Lowell Morning Mail, 1896-1907; reporter Lowell Telegram, 1907-11; night editor Norwich (Conn.) Bulletin, 1911-14; editor Lowell Sunday Telegram, 1914-44. Formerly dir. Lowell Chamber of Commerce. Republican. Congregationalist. Mason (32°), K.P., Royal Arcanum, Knights of Malta. Clubs: Kiwanis, Temple (Lowell). Home: 51 Ruth St. Office: 27 Central St., Lowell, Mass. Died Jan. 14, 1946.

LAMBETH, William Alexander, coll. prof.; b. Thomasville, N.C., Oct. 27, 1867; s. Maj. J. H. and Clara Bell L.; M.D., U. of Va., 1892, Ph.D., 1900; grad. Harvard Sch. Phys. Training, 1893; m. Frank Irene Stallings, June, 1889. Instr. phys. edn., 1893, dir. Fayerweather Gymnasium, 1894, lecturer hygiene, 1898-1900, hygiene and materia medica, 1900-02, adj. prof., 1902-07, prof., 1907-38, U. of Va.; retired, June 1938; supt. of bldgs. and grounds, U. of Va., 1905-28, sec. gen. Athletic Assn. of same, 1897-1921. V.p. dept. phys. edn., Chicago Expn., 1893. Authority on coll. athletics in South; mem. Am. Coll. Dirs. Assn. (v.p., 1896), Va. Intercollegiate Athletic Assn. (pres., 1897-99), Nat. Collegiate Athletic Assn. (treas., 1908), etc.; mem. Am. Olympic Com. for Stockholm Olympiad, 1912; mem. track rules com. of Nat. Collegiate Athletic Assn. (mem. football rules com. 1908-21); ex-pres. Soc. Dirs. of Physical Edn.; chmn. Athletic Conf. of Southern State Univs.; mem. Am. Seismol. Soc., Raven Soc., Am. Soc. of the Royal Italian Orders, Phi Beta Kappa, Sigma Phi Epsilon; hon. mem. A.I.A. Decorated Cavalier Order of Crown (Italy), 1930, also Commendatore, 1933. Author: Trees and How to Know Them; Thomas Jefferson's Architecture, 1911; Geology of the Monticello Area; School of Athens; Food and Dietetics. Frequent contbr. to newspapers and mags. on athletic and sanitary topics; chapter on Buildings and Grounds, in "American Colleges and Universities." Clubs: Nat. Arts (New York); Colonnade (University of Va.); Art (Washington); Authors' (London). Address: Route 3, Charlottesville, Va.* Died June 24, 1944.

LAMONT, Robert Patterson, ex-sec. of Commerce; b. Detroit, Mich., Dec. 1, 1867; s. Robert and Isabella (Patterson) L.; B.S. in C.E., U. of Mich., 1891; m. Helen Gertrude Trotter, Oct. 24, 1894; children—Robert Patterson, Gertrude (Mrs. Matthew Jones), Dorothy (Mrs. Chauncey Belknap). Engineer, Chicago Exposition, 1891-92; sec. and engr. Shailer & Schinglau, contractors, 1892-97; 1st v.p. Simplex Ry. Appliance Co., 1897-1905; 1st v.p. Am. Steel Foundries, 1905-12, pres., 1912-29; Sec. of Commerce in Cabinet of President Hoover, 1930-32; pres. Am. Iron and Steel Inst., 1932-33. Commd. major N.A., Feb. 1918; chief Procurement Division Ordnance Dept., Washington, D.C., Oct. 16, 1918-Feb. 1919 with rank of col. Clubs: Century, University (New York). Home: 330 Park Av., New York. Died Feb. 19, 1948.

LAMONT, Thomas William, banker; b. Claverack, N.Y., Sept. 30, 1870; s. Thomas and Caroline Deuel (Jayne) L.; grad. Phillips Exeter Acad., Exeter, N.H., 1888; A.B., Harvard, 1892, LL.D., 1931; LL.D., Union Coll., 1921; Rochester U., 1929, Columbia U., 1932, New York U., 1934; m. Florence Haskell Corliss, Oct. 31, 1895. Reporter on New York Tribune, 1893-94; sec., treas. and vice-pres. Bankers Trust Co., 1903-09; v.p. First Nat. Bank, 1909-11; mem. firm of J. P. Morgan & Co., bankers, 1911-40; dir. J. P. Morgan & Co., Inc., since 1940, chmn. bd. since 1943; dir. U.S. Steel Corp., Lamont, Corliss & Co. Overseer, Harvard, 1912-25; rep. of U.S. Treasury on Am. Commn. to Negotiate Peace, Paris, 1919. Alternate del. Com. of (Young plan) Experts on German Reparations, Paris, 1929. Chmn. Am. group, Internat. Consortium for Assistance of China; chmn. Internat. Com. of Bankers (for adjustment of Mex. fgn. debt); trustee Carnegie Foundation for Advancement of teaching; trustee Metropolitan Museum of Art, Am. Sch. Classical Studies, Athens; pres. Markle Foundation. Clubs: Harvard, University, Union, Metropolitan, Century, New York Yacht, Down Town, Links; Mid-Ocean (Bermuda), others. Author: My Boyhood in a Parsonage, 1946; Henry P. Davison, The Record of a Useful Life, 1933. Home: Torrey Cliff, Palisades, N.Y.; also 107 E. 70th St., New York 21. Office: 23 Wall St., N.Y. City. Died Feb. 2, 1948.

LAMSON, Julius Gustavus, merchant; b. Elbridge, N.Y., Jan. 29, 1853; s. Myron Hawley and Laura Elizabeth (Rhoades) L.; ed. pub. schs. and Munroe Collegiate Inst., Elbridge; m. Katharine Tracy, Sept. 4, 1878; children—Elizabeth Almaria (Mrs. Harrie Rogers Chamberlin), Miriam Tracy (Mrs. Sydney Dryden Vinnedge), Katharine Olive (Mrs. Charles Edward Swartzbaugh). Began as clk. in store, Elbridge, 1868; clk. in store, Toledo, 1873-85; merchant since 1885 as mem. Lamson Brothers, dept. store, Toledo, incorporated, 1905, as The Lamson Brothers Co., of which is now chmn. bd. Formerly mem. Sch. Bd., Toledo. Trustee Denison U. Pres. emeritus Toledo Council of Chs.; life trustee Ohio Bapt. Conv. Republican. Club: Toledo Commerce. Home: 2056 Scottwood Av. Office: Jefferson Av., Huron and Erie Sts., Toledo, O. Died Jan. 31, 1942.

LANAHAN, William Wallace, investment banker; b. Baltimore, Md., July 24, 1884; s. Samuel Jackson and Frances (Reeder) L.; A.B., Harvard, 1907; m. Margaretta Pleasants Bonsal, 1916 (died 1921); m. 2d, Eleanor Addison Williams, 1924. Partner Alex Brown & Sons; mem. Equitable Trust Co. of Balto; trustee Income Foundation Fund, Inc.; dir. Mid Continent Petroleum Corp. Mem. N.Y. Stock Exchange. Home: Towson, Md. Died Aug. 30, 1948

LAND, William Jesse Goad, botanist; b. Alton, Ind., Dec. 2, 1865; s. James Glenn and Amanda (Goad) L.; Rome (Ind.) Acad., 1888-92; S.B., U. of Chicago, 1902, Ph.D., 1904; m. Estella Little, Feb. 8, 1890. Prin. Rome Acad., 1893-94; prin. high sch., Grand Rivers, Ky., 1894-95; supt. city schs., Ashley, Ill., 1895-1901; fellow, U. of Chicago, 1903, asst. in morphology, 1904-06, asso., 1906-08, instr. botany, 1908-11, asst. prof., 1911-15, asso. prof., 1915-28, prof. since 1928. Fellow A.A.A.S.; mem. Bot. Soc. America, Ill. Acad. Science, Am. Micros. Soc., Deutsche Botanische Gesellschaft, Tex. Geog. Society, Tex. Acad. of Science, Phi Beta Kappa, Sigma Xi, Alpha Sigma Phi. Contbr. numerous monographs, as results of original investigations in botany; bot. exploration in Mexico, 1906, 08, 10, in South Seas, especially western Polynesia, 1912. Life mem. Nat. Rifle Assn. America. Botanical exploration in tropical and neo-tropical America, 1932-34, 1935-36, 1937-38, 1939-40. Home: Brownsville, Tex.; (summer) Rome, Ind. Died Aug. 1, 1942.

LANDERS, Howe Stone, ins. exec.; b. Martinsville, Ind., Oct. 17, 1885; s. John Bothwell and Idawile

(Gardner) L.; A.B., De Pauw U., 1905; student U. of Ill., 1905; LL.B., Ind. Law Sch., 1908; m. Shirley McNutt, Mar. 26, 1919; children—Georgianna, Shirley Mary. Admitted to Ind. bar, 1908; asso. in practice with William A. Ketcham, 1908-15; mem. Ind. State Industrial Commn., 1915-19; spl. counsel U.S. Fidelity & Guaranty Co., 1919-25; atty. mgr. Met. Casualty Ins. Co., New York, 1925-31, v.p. and gen. counsel, 1931-32, pres. since 1932; v.p. and gen. counsel Commercial Casualty Ins. Co., Newark, N.J., 1931-32, pres. since 1932; also pres. Empire Properties Corp., Interstate Debenture Corp., Unified Debenture Corp., Met. Service Corp., Park Lane Hotel Co.; dir. Firemen's Ins. Company of Newark, First Reinsurance Co. of Hartford. Mem. Phi Kappa Psi. Democrat. Episcopalian. Mason. Clubs: Montclair Golf, Meridian Hills Country. Home: 332 Ridgewood Av., Glen Ridge, N.J. Office: 10 Park Place, Newark, N.J. Died Mar. 15, 1943.

LANDERS, Warren Prince; b. North Bridgewater (Brockton), Mass., July 15, 1869; s. Edmund N. and Meribah (Perkins) L.; grad. Brockton High Sch.; student Boston U., 1888-90; m. Bertha Wakefield Corliss, Sept. 16, 1890 (died Apr. 9, 1932); m. 2d, Elizabeth Griffith Donovan, Apr. 21, 1935. Ordained Congl. ministry, Dec. 2, 1891; pastor First Ch., Huntington, Mass., 1891; Middleton, 1891-98, Sutton, 1902-05, Westport, Conn., 1905-08, Gilbertville (Hardwick), Mass., 1909-13, East Congl. Ch., Milton, 1922-27, pastor ad interim, 1927-32; pastor North Reading, Mass., 1933-36; chaplain State Sanatorium, North Wilmington, 1933-39. Lecturer. Sec. Am. Com. London S.S. Conv., 1898; supt. circulation, The Congregationalist, Boston, 1898-1902; sec. Boston Layman's Missionary Movement, 1908; sec. of Mass. Total Abstinence Soc., 1913-18; sec. Allied Temperance Organizations of Mass., 1919. Editor report San Francisco C.E. Conv., 1897; Denver S.S. Conv., 1902; press sec. Cincinnati C.E. Conv., 1901; editor The Temperance Cause (monthly), Boston, 1913-18. Sec. Sutton Bicentennial, 1904; sec. and historian Brockton Centennial, 1921; chmn. Milton Com. on Centennial of First American (Granite) Ry., 1926; exec. sec. Boston com. British Congl. Pilgrimage, 1928; with Mass. Bay Tercentenary, 1928-29. Chaplain, 1914-43, emeritus since 1943, and historian Joseph Webb Lodge, A.F. and A.M., Boston; chaplain Baalis Sanford Lodge, A.F. and A.M., Brockton, 1921-22; asso. prelate since 1926, chaplain, 1926-43, emeritus since 1943, Boston Council, and Jos. Warren Commandery, Knights Templar; chaplain of Grand Lodge of Massachusetts, 1931; chaplain of Grand Council of Massachusetts since 1932. Awarded Grand Lodge Distinguished Service Medal, 1939. Mem. Suffolk South Assn. Congregational Ministers (secretary 1919-22). Club: Dickens Club of Boston, Mass. (was president 1935-36). Author: The Putnams (Magazine of History), 1917; John Davis Long (Am. Temperance Cyclo.); The Spirit of John Alden, 1920; Brockton and Its Centennial, 1921; The City of Peace (verse), 1923; Unto You This Day (verse), 1926; also sermons, including "Morris K. Jessup." Regular contbr. to daily and religious press; frequent speaker before Masonic bodies. Home: 31 Claflin Road, Brookline, Mass.; and 43 Tremlett St., Dorchester (Boston). Office: 51 Boylston St., Boston, Mass. Died Apr. 28, 1946.

LANDES, Bertha Knight, ex-mayor; b. Ware, Mass., Oct. 19, 1868; d. Charles Sanford and Cordelia (Cutter) Knight; prep. edn., high sch. and pvt. sch., Worcester, Mass.; A.B., Ind. U., 1891; m. Henry Landes, Jan. 2, 1894; children—Katherine Knight (dec.), Kenneth Knight. Resident of Seattle, Wash., since 1895; mem. City Council, Seattle, 1922-26 (pres. 1924-26), mayor of Seattle, Washington, 1926-28. Oriental tour dir. Mem. Seattle Fedn. of Women's Clubs. Republican. Conglist. Clubs: Women's City (founder), Woman's University, Soroptimist, Women's Commercial, Business and Professional Women's Club, Seattle Press (hon.). Lecturer, writer. Home: 4710 University Way, Seattle. Died Nov. 29, 1943.

LANDIS, Kenesaw Mountain, ex-judge, baseball commr.; b. Millville, O., Nov. 20, 1866; s. Abraham H. and Mary (Kumler) L.; LL.B., Union Coll. of Law, Chicago, 1891; admitted to bar, 1891; m. Winifred Reed, July 25, 1895; children—Reed Gresham, Susanne (Mrs. Richard W. Phillips). Practiced law in Chicago, 1891-1905, except for 2 years while he was private sec. to Sec. of State Gresham; U.S. dist. judge, Northern Dist. of Ill., 1905-Mar. 1, 1922 (resigned); commr. for Am. and Nat. Leagues of Professional Baseball Clubs, and Nat. Assn. Professional Baseball Leagues since Nov. 12, 1920. Republican. Clubs: Chicago Athletic, South Shore Country, Midlothian Country. Office: 333 N. Michigan, Chicago, Ill. Died Nov. 25, 1944.

LANDIS, Kenesaw Mountain. II, lawyer, writer; b. Logansport, Ind., June 3, 1910; s. Frederick and Bessie (Baker) L.; A.B., Columbia U., 1929; student Ind. U. Law Sch., 1929-31, U. of Southern Calif. Law Sch., 1931-32; m. Louise Pollock, Aug. 24, 1937. Admitted to Ind. bar, 1931, Colo. bar, 1937; with law firm Wilbur F. Denious, Denver, 1937-39; mem. law firm Landis and Landis (formerly Landis and Hanna) since 1939; pros. atty. 19th Judicial Circuit of Indiana, 1943-45, writer of syndicated newspaper column "Corn on the Cob," Chicago Sun since Jan. 1941; candidate for Congress, 1934. Home: Pottawatomie Point. Address: 214 Fourth St., Logansport, Ind. Died July 12, 1949. Buried Mount Hope Cemetery, Logansport, Ind.

LANDIS, William Weidman, coll. prof.; b. Catesville, Pa., Feb. 15, 1869; s. Isaac Daniel and Anna Mary (Davis) L.; Ph.B., Dickinson Coll., 1891, A.M., 1894; student Johns Hopkins, 1891-94, and student-asst. in mathematics, 1892-95, Sc.D., 1907. Prof. mathematics, Thiel College, Pa., 1894-95; professor mathematics and astronomy, Dickinson College since 1895. Republican. Methodist. Mem. Am. Math. Soc., Am. Math. Assn., Phi Delta Theta, Phi Beta Kappa. Mem. 5th Internat. Math. Congress, Cambridge, Eng., 1912. Contbr. Am. Math. Monthly, Popular Astronomy, Rendiconti del Circolo Matematico di Palermo. Y.M.C.A. war service, June 1918-Sept. 1919, with 3d Italian Army; was in the trenches on the lower Piave several months and in battle, Oct. 24-Nov. 4, 1918; regional dir. of all work with 3d Army about 6 months. Awarded hon. rank of maj., Cross of War, Cross of Third Army (Italian); Chevalier Crown of Italy. Home: Carlisle, Pa. Died Apr. 8, 1942.

LANDMAN, Isaac, rabbi, editor; b. Sudilkov, Russia, Oct. 24, 1880; s. Louis Hyamson and Ada (Gedaliah) L.; brought to U.S., 1890; B.A., U. of Cincinnati, 1906; rabbi, Hebrew Union Coll., Cincinnati, 1906; post-graduate work, University of Pa.; D.D., Hebrew Union College, 1943; m. Beatrice Eschner, Sept. 3, 1913; children—Amos, David, Louise. Asst. rabbi Temple Keneseth Israel, Philadelphia, 1906-16; rabbi Temple Israel, Far Rockaway, N.Y., 1917-28; editor American Hebrew, 1918-37; rabbi Congregation Beth Elohim, Brooklyn, since 1931. Organized religious services among Jewish men on Mexican border, 1916; 1st rabbi chaplain in U.S. Army on foreign soil (Mexico), 1916; organized sch. for training Jewish workers in U.S. forces at home and abroad, for Jewish Welfare Bd., 1917. Exec. sec. Nat. Farm Sch., 1906-16; corr. sec. Central Conf. Am. Rabbis, 1915-17, mem. exec. com., 1915-18; chmn. Jewish Welfare Bd. of the Rockaways, 1918; sec. Isaac M. Wise Centenary Fund, Union of Am. Hebrew Congregations in N.Y., 1919; sec. N.Y. Exec. Com. of Am. Hebrew Congs., 1919-30; rep. Union of Am. Hebrew Congregations and Central Conf. Am. Rabbis at Peace Conf., Paris, to introduce clause for universal religious liberty into Covenant of League of Nations, 1919; launched movement of good will and better understanding between Christians and Jews, 1920; del. Central Conf. Am. Rabbis at World Union for Progressive Judaism, London, 1926; organized Permanent Commn. on Better Understanding among Catholics, Protestants and Jews in America, 1927; presided at good-will conf. at the Palace of the Bishop of Tobasco, Mexico City, 1927; editor in chief Universal Jewish Encyclopedia, 1928-43. Founder Academy for Adult Jewish Education, Brooklyn, N.Y., 1931; organizer annual Institutes on Judaism for Christian Clergymen since 1935; founder of farmer colony of Jews, Utah, 1911. Mem. com. on Jewish Edn. of Union of Am. Hebrew Congregations, 1943; mem. Central Conf. Am. Rabbis, Am. Oriental Soc., New York Bd. Jewish Ministers, Assn. Reform Rabbis, Am. Acad. for Jewish Research, Jewish Hist. Soc., Religious Edn. Assn. of U.S. and Can. (v.p. 1932-39; mem. bd. dirs. since 1932), N.Y. Alumni of U. of Cincinnati (pres. 1933-34). Mason. Author: Moses Hyam Luzatto, First Hebrew Playwright, 1907; Stories of the Prophets, 1912; A Course of Instruction for Jewish Religious Schools, 1921; Christian and Jew—A Symposium on Better Understanding, 1929; Status of Adult Jewish Education, 1931; the Average Man and the Bible, 1916; (play) Man of Honor; also other plays (with brother, Dr. Michael L.). Compiler of Prayer Book for Jewish Soldiers, 1916. Address: 50 Plaza St., Brooklyn, N.Y.* Died Sep. 3, 1946.

LANDON, Hugh McKennan; b. Muscatine, Ia., June 22, 1867; s. George Washington and Emily Alice (Reeves) L.; A.B., Harvard, 1892; LL.D., Wabash (Ind.) College, 1930, Indiana Univ., 1931; Litt.D., Rose Polytechnic Institute, 1941; m. Suzette Merrill Davis, Nov. 22, 1892 (died Dec. 1918); children—Mrs. Robert F. Scott, Jr. (dec.), Mrs. Alice Rives Sawyer, Mrs. Margaret McLean Delaplane; m. 2d, Jessie (Spalding) Walker, Apr. 10, 1920 (died June 26, 1930). With Mfrs. Natural Gas Co., 1892-1902, Indianapolis Water Co., 1902-12; chmn. of bd. and chmn. exec. com. Fletcher Trust Co. since 1920; dir. State Life Ins. Co., Electric Steel Castings Co., Armstrong-Landon Co., Crown Hill Cemetery Assn., and other corps. Pres. Associated Harvard Clubs, 1907-08; pres. Harvard Alumni Assn., 1938-39; dir. Nat. Recreation Assn., Boys' Club Assn., Community Fund of Indianapolis; pres. James Whitcomb Riley Memorial Assn. Mem. Phi Beta Kappa. Democrat. Clubs: Harvard (New York); Harvard (Boston); Indianapolis Athletic. Home: The Four Winds, Spring Mill Rd. (R.R. 16). Office: Fletcher Trust Co., Indianapolis, Ind. Died Apr. 2, 1947.

LANDRUM, Robert D(allas), chemical engr.; b. Terre Haute, Ind., Feb. 8, 1882; s. James Wesley and Kate (Tolbert) L.; B.S., Rose Poly. Inst., Terre Haute, 1904, M.S., 1909, Ch.E., 1914; m. Ethel Price Sherwood, Sept. 1, 1908 (died 1935); children—Sherwood, Robert James, Kate Tolbert; m. 2d, Margaret Elizabeth Carr, 1937; 1 dau., Peggy Ann. Chemist and enameler, Columbian Enameling & Stamping Co., 1904-07; asst. prof. chemistry, U. of Kansas, 1907-10; chem. engr. Lisk Mfg. Co., Canandaigua, N.Y., 1910-13; cons. engr. Mich. Enameling Works, Kalamazoo, Mich., Gen. Stamping Co., Canton, O., 1913-14; chem. engr. and mgr. service dept. Harshaw Fuller & Goodwin Co., mfrs. industrial chemicals, Cleveland, O., 1914-22; v.p. Vitreous Enameling Co., also Vitreous Steel Products Co., Cleveland, 1922-25; gen. mgr. Ceramic Materials Div. Titanium Alloy Mfg. Co., Cleveland, 1925-32; sales mgr. Harshaw Chemical Company, Chicago, 1932-35, manager special products division, 1935-42, manager technical sales 1942 to date. Fel. A.A.A.S., Am. Ceramic Soc. (chmn. war service com., 1917-19, trustee, 1918-20, v.p., 1923-24, pres., 1924-25, trustee ex officio 1925-27); mem. Am. Chem. Soc. (sec. Cleveland sect. 1919-20), Am. Inst. Chem. Engrs., Soc. Chem. Industry, Keramos, Pi Gamma Mu, Acacia, Société de Chimie Industrielle, France. Mem. Chicago Drug and Chem. Assn. (dir. 1935-36), Chicago Assn. Commerce, Central Dist. Enamelers Club (pres. 1937-39). Republican. Methodist. Mason. Clubs: Cleveland, University, Chagrin Valley Country, Chemists' (New York). Author: Enamel, 1918; Bibliography and Abstracts of Literature on Enamels, 1929; also numerous articles and tech. papers. Mem. Nat. Tech. Salvage Advisory Com., War Prodn. Bd. Home: 3558 Bainbridge Rd. Office: Harshaw Chemical Co., 1945 E. 97th St., Cleveland 6, O. Now deceased.

LANDSTEINER, Karl (lănd'stīn-ēr), medical research; b. Vienna, Austria, June 14, 1868; s. Leopold and Fanny (Hess) L.; M.D., U. of Vienna, 1891; D.Sc., U. of Chicago, 1927; hon. D.Sc., Cambridge U., England; hon. M.D., Université Libre de Bruxelles, Belgium; D.Sc., Harvard; m. Helene Wlasto, 1880; 1 son, Earnest. Pathologist, U. of Vienna, 1909-19; mem. Rockefeller Inst. for Med. Research, 1922-39, now emeritus. Winner Nobel prize, for discovery of human blood groups, 1930; Paul Ehrlich medal, 1930; Chevalier Legion of Honor (France); Dutch Red Cross medal, 1933. Member Nat. Acad. Sciences, Royal Swedish Academy Science, Danish Academy Science, Deutsche Akademie Naturforscher (Halle, Germany), Am. Assn. Immunologists (pres. 1929), Swedish Med. Soc., Harvard Soc., Am. Philos. Soc., Société Belge de Biologie (Bruxelles), Am. Soc. of Naturalists; hon. mem. Pathol. Soc. of Gt. Britain and Ireland, Vienna Med. Soc.; fellow New York Acad. Medicine; hon. fellow Royal Soc. of Medicine (London); hon. mem. Pathol. Soc. of Philadelphia, Reale Academia delle Scienze (Modena, Italy); corr. mem. Med. Chirurgical Soc., Edinburgh. Contbr. papers on immunology, bacteriology and pathology, especially: Chemistry of Antigens; Human Blood Groups; Etiology of Poliomyelitis; Etiology of Paroxysmol Hemoglobinuria; Studies on Syphilis; etc. Home: 25 E. 86th St. Office: 66th St. and York Av., New York, N.Y. Died June 26, 1943.

LANE, Alfred Church, geologist; b. Boston, Mass., Jan. 29, 1863; s. Jonathan A. and Sarah D. (Clarke) L.; A.B., Harvard U., 1883, A.M., Ph.D., 1888; student U. of Heidelberg, 1885-87; Sc.D., Tufts Coll., 1913; m. Susanne Foster Lauriat, Apr. 15, 1896; children—Lauriat, Frederic Chapin, Harriet Page (Mrs. C. D. Rouillard). Instr. mathematics, Harvard, 1883-85; petrographer, Mich. State Geol. Survey and instr., Mich. Coll. of Mines, 1889-92; asst. state geologist of Mich., 1892-99, state geologist, 1899-1909; Pearson prof. geology and mineralogy, Tufts Coll., 1909-36, retired on account of teachers oath, elected prof. emeritus, 1936. Spl. lecturer on econ. geology, U. of Mich., 1904; first consultant in science, Library of Congress, 1929. Mem. com., apptd. by bd. overseers, to visit Harvard Observatory since 1924. Fellow A.A.A.S. (v.p. sect. E 1907), Geol. Soc. America (pres. 1931); mem. Nat. Research Council (com. on measurement of geologic time), Am. and Boston mineral socs., Am. Inst. Mining and Metall. Engrs. (pres. Boston Sect. 1918-19), Harvard Engring. Soc., Thomas Dudley Family Association (president tercentennial year), N.E. Historical and Genealogical Society; fellow Am. Academy Arts and Sciences (librarian 1929-36, vice president 1944-46), member Boston Natural History Soc., Am. Forestry Assn., Bond Astronomical Club (pres. 1933-35), Navy League, U.S. Naval Institute, Lake Superior Mining Inst. (treas. 1893); pres. Mich. Acad. Science, 1905-06, Mich. Engring. Soc., 1908-09, Lansing Law and Order League, 1904, Geol. Soc. Boston, 1919 and 1937; corr. mem. Canadian Mining Inst.; hon. mem. Geol. Soc. of Belgium; hon. life member of Harvard Engineering Society; del. Internat. Geol. Congress, 1913, 1933, 1937. With Y.M.C.A. and head dept. of mining, A.E.F. Univ., Beaune, France, 1919. Awarded Silver Beaver, Boy Scouts of America. Hon. and corporate mem. A.B.C.F.M. Mem. Mass. Civic League, Civil Liberties Union, com. of Moral and Social Welfare Suffolk North Conference, Boston Chapter United National Assn., Phi Beta Kappa, Sigma Xi. Conglist. Republican. Club: 20th Century Associates. Editor and part author books, also reports of Geol. Survey of Mich., Canada and U.S. Author: Die Korngrosse der Auvergnosen. Home: 22 Arlington St., Cambridge, Mass. Died Apr. 16, 1948.

LANE, Charles Homer, educator; b. Boston, Mass., July 17, 1877; s. John and Eliza (Wall) L.; A.B., Mt. Allison U., Sackville, N.B., Can., 1903, A.M., 1908; B.S.A., U. of Tenn., 1909; Ph.D., Research U., 1920; m. Ida West, June 6, 1907; children—Marian E., Dorothy T., Marjorie W., John E. Began as teacher, 1898-1909; editor Southern Farm Advocate, 1910-11; in charge of agrl. edn., U.S. Dept. Agr., 1911-17; regional agent for agrl. education, Fed. Bd. for Vocational Edn., 1917-20, chief agrl. edn. service, 1920-34; regional agt. agrl. edn., U.S. Office of Education, since 1934. Mem. Phi Kappa Phi, Alpha Zeta. Presbyterian. Mason. Club: Cosmos. Author: Productive Coöperative Marketing, 1928. Contbr. bulls. and articles on agrl. edn. Home: 3013 Central Av. Address: U.S. Office of Education, Federal Security Agency, Washington, D.C. Died June 25, 1944.

LANE, Edward Wood, banker; b. Valdosta, Ga., June 23, 1869; s. Remer Young and Henrietta (Brinson) L.; prep. edn., Valdosta Inst.; B.P.H., U. of Ga., 1889; m. Anna Virginia Taliaferro, Jan. 2, 1907; children—James Taliaferro, Edward Wood. Cashier Merchants Bank, Valdosta, 1889-1903; organizer Atlantic Nat. Bank, Jacksonville, Fla., 1903, and pres., 1903-28, chmn. bd. since 1928; also organizer and chmn. bd. West Palm Beach Atlantic Nat. Bank; dir. Merchants and Miners Trans. Co. Dir. Children's Home Soc. of Fla., Community Chest of Jacksonville. Mem. Fed. Advisory Council in Washington, representing 6th Fed. Res. District, 1921, 22, 23; mem. bd. of Jacksonville Branch of Fed. Reserve Bank of Atlanta, 1918-35; apptd. mem. State Bd. of Control by Gov. John W. Martin; was mem. Bd. of Govs. and treas. of Jacksonville Chamber of Commerce. Trustee U. of Fla. Endowment Corp.; co-trustee Fla. East Coast Ry. Co. Democrat. Episcopalian. Mason. Clubs: Timuquana Fla. Yacht, Civitan. Home: 3730 Richmond St. Office: 121 W. Forsyth St., Jacksonville, Fla. Died Mar. 23, 1942.

LANE, Gertrude Battles, editor; b. Saco, Me.; d. Eustace and Ella (Battles) Lane; ed. Thornton Acad., Saco, Me.; L.H.D., Colby College, 1929. Asst. editor Woman's Home Companion, 1903-12, editor, 1912-40, editorial dir. since 1940; vice-pres. Crowell Pub. Co. since 1929. Mem. Washington staff U.S. Food Adminstrn., June 1917-Dec. 1918; mem. planning com. White House Conf. on Child Health and Protection, 1930-31, President's Conf. on Home Building and Home Ownership, 1931. Unitarian. Clubs: Cosmopolitan, American Women's Assn., Town Hall, Pen and Brush, Women's Nat. Republican. Home: Harwinton, Conn. Office: 250 Park Av., New York, N.Y. Died Sept. 25, 1941; buried at Saco, Me.

LANE, James F(ranklin), coll. pres.; b. Jackson, Tenn., Feb. 18, 1874; s. Isaac and Frances Ann (Boyce) L.; A.B., Walden U., Nashville, 1896, A.M., 1899, Ph.D., 1912; student U. of Chicago, 1897-99, Harvard, summers 1900, 02, 05; m. Mary Edna Johnson, Sept. 12, 1904. Prin. Panola High Sch., 1896, Sardis, Miss., 1897-98; teacher mathematics, Lane Coll., 1897-1905, teacher edn., 1905-07, pres. since 1907. Delegate to Methodist Ecumenical Conf., London, Eng., 1901. Mem. Nat. Council Y.M. C.A., Tuberculosis Assn. (pres.), Acad. Polit. and Social Science. Republican. Mason. Methodist (colored). Author: Multum in Parvo, 1899, School Administration at the College Level, 1942; Forms of Democracy, 1932; Some Things We Saw Abroad, 1941. Home: Jackson, Tenn. Died Dec. 11, 1944.

LANE, Mills Bee, banker; b. Clyattville, Ga., Nov. 21, 1860; s. Remer Young and Henrietta (Brinson) L.; ed. high sch., Valdosta, Ga., and Vanderbilt U.; m. Mary Comer, July 11, 1906. Began in banking at Valdosta, 1881; moved to Savannah, 1891; chmn. bd. Citizens & Southern Nat. Bank; pres. Citizens & Southern Holding Co., v.p. and dir. Savannah Sugar Refining Co.; dir. Savannah Morning News, Ocean Steamship Co., Bibb Mfg. Co. (Macon, Ga.). Home: 26 Gaston St. E. Office: 22 Bull St., Savannah, Ga.* Died Aug. 6, 1945.

LANE, Rufus Herman, officer U.S.M.C.; b. Bellaire, O., Oct. 31, 1870; grad. U.S. Naval Acad., 1891. Commd. 2d lt. U.S.M.C., July 1 1893; promoted through grades to adjutant and inspector, with rank of brig. gen., Jan. 2, 1928. Served on New York during Spanish-Am. War, 1898; asst. adj. and insp. Marine Corps at hdqrs., Washington, D.C., 1903-04; adj. and insp. 1st Brigade Marines, Manila, P.I., 1906; in charge office of asst. adj. insp., San Francisco, 1908; acting asst. q.m. in charge of office at San Francisco, 1908; duty at hdqrs., Washington, D.C., 1914; apptd. adj. gen. 2d Provisional Brigade of Marines, Santo Domingo, 1916; apptd. to administer affairs of Dept. of Foreign Relations, and of Justice and Pub. Instrn., Dominican Republic, 1917; mem. staff of mil. gov. of Santo Domingo, 1918 to 1920; was head of Adj. and Insp. Dept., U.S. Marine Corps; retired, Nov. 1, 1934. Address: Falls Church, Va.* Died Apr. 20, 1948.

LANE, Stoddard, clergyman; b. Unionville, Conn., July 2, 1887; s. Charles Stoddard and Jessie (Carson) L.; grad. high sch., Mt. Vernon, N.Y., 1905; B.A., Amherst, 1909, M.A., 1910, D.D., 1934; B.D., Hartford Theol. Sem., 1913; grad. study U. of Berlin, 1914; m. Anna Hepburn, Oct. 26, 1915 (died 1916); 1 son; Stoddard; m. 2d, Estella Hitchcock, June 22, 1920; children—Barbara Hitchcock, Laura Ruth, Mary Dana. Ordained ministry, 1915; pastor Bogart Memorial Ch., Bogota, N.J., 1915-23, First Congl. Ch., Manchester, N.H., 1923-29, Plymouth Congl. Ch., Des Moines, Ia., since 1929. Served as sergt. Ambulance Service, U.S. Army, with French Army, June 8, 1917-Apr. 8, 1919. Decorated Croix de Guerre, 1918. Trustee Grinnell Coll., Chicago Theol. Sem.; chmn. Adult Edn. Council, Des Moines, and Des Moines Peace Council. Mem. Alpha Delta Phi, Phi Beta Kappa. Home: 505 Country Club Blvd., Des Moines, Ia. Died May 17, 1943.

LANE, Wallace Rutherford, lawyer; b. Whateley Mass., Aug. 12, 1876; s. John William and Mary (Haynes) L.; prep. edn., Hopkins and Williston academies; hon. A.M., Brown U., 1927; LL.B., Yale, 1900; m. Gertrude Gardner, July 2, 1901; children—Esther (Mrs. George T. Moore), Josephine (Mrs. George D. Busher), John W. Admitted to Conn. bar, 1900; practiced at Des Moines, Ia., 1901-10, also serving same period as prof. law, Highland Park Coll., and lecturer on patent, trademark and unfair competition law at Drake U. and U. of Neb.; sr. mem. Parkinson & Lane, Chicago, organized 1910 and specializing in patent, corp., trademark and unfair competition law; counsel for many mfg. and mercantile cos. Apptd. by President Coolidge, 1925, as del., representing U.S., to Internat. Conv. for Protection of Industrial Property, the meeting resulting in treaty ratified by U.S. Senate, 1930; vice chmn. Lawyers' Nat Com. to Increase Federal Judges' Salaries, 1925-26. Mem. Scarlet Fever Com. Elected trustee Brown U., 1928, Williston Acad., 1930, Hopkins Acad., 1931. Mem. Am. Bar Assn. (chmn. patent sect. 1920), Ill. State and Chicago bar assns., Bar Assn. City of New York, Am. Patent Law Assn. (pres. 1922, 23), Chicago Patent Law Assn. (pres. 1924), Yale Law Sch. Assn. (exec. council), Cum Laude Soc. (hon. 1930), Beta Theta Pi, Phi Alpha Delta, Phi Beta Kappa, Pi Gamma Mu, Book and Gavel Soc. Republican. Conglist. Clubs: Yale Univ., Brown Univ. (pres. 1928), University, Mid-Day (Chicago); Glenview Golf (Ill.); R.I. Country. Home: 1426 Chicago Av., Evanston, Ill. Office: Bankers Bldg., Chicago, Ill. Died May 24, 1946.

LANGDON, William Chauncy (lăng'dŭn), historical writer; b. Florence, Italy (Am. parents), Apr. 21, 1871; s. William Chauncy (D.D.) and Hannah Agnes (Courtney) L.; student St. John's Mil. Sch., Manlius, N.Y., 1886-88, Cornell U., 1888-90; A.B., Brown U., 1892, A.M., 1893; m. Marion Ames Hatheway, June 25, 1902; children—Margaret, William Chauncy. Teacher, 1893-1905; sec. exec. com. N.Y. State br. Am. Nat. Red Cross, 1906; sec. dist. atty.'s office, New York County (under William T. Jerome), 1907-09. Began as dramatist and dir. of pageants at Thetford, Vt., 1911, subsequently dramatizing and conducting pageants in various cities and universities of U.S. and in France, England and Belgium until 1921; asst. dir. Phila. Hist. Pageant, 1912; librettist of opera, Judith, music by George W. Chadwick. Historian Am. Telephone and Telegraph Co., 1921-36. Mem. Am. Hist. Assn., N.Y. State Hist. Assn., Newcomen Soc. of England, Soc. of Am. Historians, Am. Numismatic Soc., Socs. of Medallists of U.S., France, Belgium, Jugoslavia and Finland, Psi Upsilon, Phi Beta Kappa (hon. Brown, 1917). Episcopalian. Club: Brown Univ. (New York). Author: Every Day Things in American Life, Vol. I, 1937, Vol. II, 1941. Contbr. to Dictionary of Am. Biography. Home: Westport, Conn. Died Apr. 11, 1947.

LANGE, Dietrich (lăng'ĕ), educator, author; b. Bonstorf, Kreis Celle, Germany, June 2, 1863; s. Johann Peter Dietrich and Marie Dorothea Katharina (Ahrns) L.; came to America, 1881; student State Normal Sch., Mankato, Minn., 1883-86; A.B., U. of Minn., 1909; m. Hulda Wilhelmine Freitag, Sept. 13, 1888; children—Lorna Frances, Otto Frederick, Edna Louise. Teacher in German parochial sch., Nicolett, Minn., 1881-83; graded schs., St. Paul, 1887-89; St. Paul Central High Sch., 1889-1906; supervisor of nature study, St. Paul public schs., 1897-1906; prin. Humboldt High Sch., St. Paul, 1906-14; supt. pub. schs., St. Paul, 1914-16, prin. Mechanic Arts High Sch., St. Paul, 1916-39, dir. of nature study since Sept. 1939. Mem. Minn. Professional Men's Club, Minn. Historical Soc., Audubon Society, Wilson Ornithological Club. Unitarian. Author: Handbook of Nature Study, 1898; Our Native Birds, 1899; On the Trail of the Sioux, 1912; The Silver Island of the Chippewa, 1913; Lost in the Fur Country, 1914; In the Great Wild North, 1915; Lure of the Black Hills, 1916; Lure of the Mississippi, 1917; Silver Cache of the Pawnee, 1918; The Shawnee's Warning, 1919; The Threat of Sitting Bull, 1920; The Raid of the Ottawa, 1921; The Mohawk Ranger, 1922; The Iroquois Scout, 1923; The Sioux Runner, 1924; The Gold Rock of the Chippewa, 1925; Nature Trails, 1927; The Boast of the Seminole, 1930; On the Fur Trail, 1931; Birds of the Midwest, 1939. Writer and lecturer on education and outdoor subjects; identified with Boy Scout movement. Home: 2229 Como Av., St. Paul, Minn. Died Nov. 18, 1940.

LANGFELD, Millard, physician; b. Glasgow, Mo., Oct. 7, 1872; s. Daniel and Jette (Pretzfelder) L.; A.B., Johns Hopkins, 1893, M.D., 1898; m. Elizabeth M. Ash, Sept. 19, 1899. Practiced at Omaha since 1898; city bacteriologist since 1901; prof. medicine, John A. Creighton Med. Coll., since 1906; prof. bacteriology, John A. Creighton Dental Coll., 1904-14; vis. physician St. Joseph's Hosp., Douglas County Hosp.; mem. Milk Commn. of Omaha, 1909. Mem. Neb. Med. Soc., Omaha-Douglas County Med. Soc. Author: Introduction to Infectious and Parasitic Diseases, 1907. Home: 4205 Dodge St. Office: Brandeis Theatre Bldg., Omaha, Neb. Died June 5, 1937.

LANGHORNE, Marshall, diplomatic service; born Lynchburg, Va., May 7, 1870; s. John D. and Nannie (Tayloe) L.; grad. Va. Mil. Inst.; m. Mabel Johnson, Apr. 1916. Vice consul at Canton, China, 1901-02; consular agt., Dalny, 1903-04; dep. consul gen. Santo Domingo, 1905; sec. Am. Legation, Christiania, Norway, 1906-09; 2d sec. Embassy, Rio Janeiro, 1909-10; sec. Legation, Paraguay and Uruguay, 1910-11; chargé d'affaires at San Jose, Costa Rica, 1912-14; sec. Am. delegation to 3d Internat. Opium Conf., at The Hague, 1914; apptd. sec. of Legation, The Hague, 1914; assigned to Dept. of State, Oct. 1918; chargé d'affaires at The Hague, Jan.-Nov. 1917; resigned from service, Dec. 1918. Republican. Episcopalian. Clubs: Metropolitan, Chevy Chase. Address: Connecticut Apts., Washington. Died Dec. 20, 1942.

LANGLEY, Katherine, congresswoman; b. Marshall, N.C., Feb. 14, 1888; d. James Madison and Katherine (Hawkins) Gudger; B.L., Woman's Coll., Richmond, Va.; B.S., Emerson Coll. of Oratory, Boston; m. John W. Langley, Nov. 23, 1904; children—Katherine Gudger (Mrs. Katherine L. Bentley), John W., Susanna Madison. Formerly mem. Rep. State Central Com. of Ky.; alternate del. at large Rep. Nat. Conv., 1920, dist. del., 1924; sec. to husband many yrs.; mem. 70th and 71st Congresses (1927-31), 10th Ky. Dist. Chmn. Pike County (Ky.) Red Cross, World War. Mem. D.A.R. Republican. Baptist. Clubs: Congressional (Washington); Women's of Pikeville (ex-pres.). Home: Pikeville, Ky. Died Aug. 15, 1948.

LANGMUIR, Dean (lăng'mūr), investment counsel; b. Elmsford, N.Y., June 18, 1886; s. Charles and Sadie (Comings) L.; graduated De Witt Clinton High Sch., N.Y. City, 1904; A.B., Williams Coll., 1910 (Clark prize scholarship); m. Ethel M. Ivimey, 1911 (dec. 1945); children—Robert Vose, Evelyn; m. 2d Mary Shattuck Fisher, 1946. Accountant for Western Electric Co., 1910-11; dept. comptroller City of Schenectady, N.Y., 1912; expert accountant N.Y. Pub. Service Commn., 1912-16, New Republic, 1914-15; field investigations of corps. for banking interests, 1916-21; with Irving Trust Co., and other banks, liquidating and administering various corps., 1921-22; with Equitable Trust Co. of New York, 1922-26; in charge research, Scudder, Stevens & Clark, 1926-28; with Lazard Freres, 1929-30; v.p. in charge of research, Distributors Group, Inc., 1930-33; own investment counsel practice since 1933; trustee in liquidation Reynolds Realization Corp., pres. 1943-45; executor Estate Lester N. Hofheimer since 1943. Served as maj. U.S. Army Signal Corps.; also Bur. of Aircraft Production, 1917-18. Trustee and treas. Council Child Development Center; trustee New School for Social Research (treas.), 1929-39. Mem. Acad. Polit. Science, Am. Econ. Assn., Am. Statis. Assn., Analysts Club, Economic Research Round Table, Investment Counsel Assn. America (gov. 1940-46), Nat. Indsl. Conf. Bd., N.Y. Chamber Commerce, N.Y. Security Analysts, Menninger Foundation; Soc. of New York Hosp., Phi Beta Kappa, Phi Gamma Delta. Clubs: Players, University, India House, Am. Alpine, Appalachian Mountain. Contbr. to financial publs. Home: 148 E. 48th St. Office: 90 Broad St., New York, N.Y. Died Jan. 8, 1950.

LANGTON, James Ammon, editor; b. Smithfield, Utah, Nov. 16, 1861; s. Seth and Sarah (Kane) L.; student U. of Utah, 1882-84; B.L., Cornell U., 1895; m. Lucie Edna Cardon, Oct. 28, 1897; children—Lucie Gayle (Mrs. Grant Macfarlane), James Roscoe (dec.), Edna Kathryn (dec.), Sara Kane (Mrs. John Heber Reese). Supt. of Cache County pub. schs., 1884-86; teacher of English and psychology at Salt Lake High Sch., 1895-97; prof. of English, Brigham Coll., Logan, Utah; supt. of pub. schs., Logan; asso. editor and editor of Deseret News, Salt Lake City, Utah, since 1920. Mem. of Utah State Bd. of Edn., 1933-40; Dem. campaign speaker and writer. Mem. Phi Beta Kappa. Home: 36 F Street. Address: Desert News, 33 Richards St., Salt Lake City, Utah. Died Feb. 12, 1943.

LANGTRY, Lillie, actress; b. Island of Jersey, 1852; d. Rev. W. C. le Breton; m. Edward Langtry, 1874 (died, 1897); m. 2d, Sir Hugo de Bathe, 1899. Début Haymarket Theatre, London, 1881, as Hester Grazebrook, in An Unequal Match; made American tours, appearing as Pauline in The Lady of Lyons; Rosalind in As You Like It; has also appeared in A Wife's Peril, Nos Intimes, Esther Sandraz, As In a Looking Glass, etc.; twice leased Prince's (now Prince of Wales) Theatre, London. Became naturalized citizen of U.S., 1887. Address: 2 Cadogan Gardens, S.W., London, Eng. Died Feb. 12, 1929.

LANIER, Alexander Cartwright (lå-nēr'), engr.; b. Nashville, Tenn., June 3, 1878; s. Louis Henry and Lamiza (Cartwright) L.; B.S. in E.E., U. of Tenn., 1900, M.E., 1905; M.E.E., Harvard U., 1909; unmarried. Electrical practice, 1900-02; instr. mech. engring., U. of Tenn., 1902-05; asst. prof. elec. engring., U. of Cincinnati, 1905-08; designing elec. engr., Westinghouse Electric & Mfg. Co., East Pittsburgh, Pa., 1909-11, sect. engr. in charge design of direct current industrial motors and generators, 1911-15; prof. elec. engring. and chmn. dept., U. of Mo., since 1915, acting dean Coll. of Engring., July 1, 1939-Oct. 1, 1939. Fellow Am. Inst. Elec. Engrs.; mem. Soc. Promotion Engring. Edn. Engineers' Club (St. Louis), Kappa Sigma, Phi Kappa Phi, Tau Beta Pi, Eta Kappa Nu, Sigma Xi. Democrat. Presbyn. Home: 310 Thilly Av., Columbia, Mo. Died Feb. 26, 1942.

LANIER, George Huguley (lă'nēr'), cotton mfr.; b. West Point, Ga., Aug. 22, 1880; s. LaFayette and Ada Alice (Huguley) L.; educated high school, West Point; student Phila. (Pa.) Industrial Art and Textile Sch.; m. Marie Lamar, Feb. 26, 1904; children—Joseph Lamar, Geo. Huguley, Marie Lamar, Lucy Janett, Bruce Nichols. Began with West Point Mfg. Co., cotton mfrs., 1901, now pres.; pres. Dixie Cotton Mills, Lanett Bleachery & Dye Works; also officer or dir. many cos. Democrat. Mason, K.P. Home: West Point, Ga. Died Sept. 17, 1948.

LARDNER, John J(oseph), educator; b. Baltimore, Md., Oct. 9, 1893; s. John and Catherine (Cryan) L.; M.A., St. Mary's U., Baltimore, 1917; S.T.L., Catholic U., Washington, D.C., 1921; S.T.D., Angelico

U., Rome, 1927. Prof. philosophy, St. Mary's Sem., Baltimore, 1927-29, prof. theology and v.p., 1929-30, v.p. 1934-43, pres. since 1943; rector St. Patrick's Sem., 1930-34. Address: St. Mary's Seminary, Baltimore 10. Died Oct. 5, 1948; buried at St. Charles College, Catonsville, Md.

LARIMORE, Louise Doddridge, physician; b. New York, N.Y., Mar. 3, 1889; d. Dudley Tyng and Minnie (Morrow) Larimore; A.B., Wellesley Coll., 1910; A.M., Columbia, 1911; M.D., Women's Med. Coll. of Pa., Phila., 1915. Interne, Women's Hosp. of Phila., 1915-16; instr. in otology Women's Med. Coll., 1916; pathologist Coll. Hosp., Phila., 1916; fellow, then asst. in exptl. pathology Rockefeller Inst., pathologist Women's Hosp., New York City, 1922-23; research asst. to Dr. Haven Emerson in pub. health, 1923-24; instr., then asso. in pathology, Columbia, 1924-28; pathologist Glen Cove Hosp., 1929-30, N.Y. Infirmary for Women and Children 1927-29; pvt. practice of medicine, specializing in allergy, since 1933; pathologist Greenwich (Conn.) Hosp., 1926-46, cons. pathologist since 1946. Diplomate Am. Bd. Pathology. Fellow Am. Med. Assn., Am. Soc. Clin. Pathology, Am. Pub. Health Assn., mem. Am. Assn. for Study Neoplastic Diseases (council), Conn. Cancer Soc. (trustee), Greenwich Soc. of Artists (mem. bd.), Am. Philatelic Soc., Am. Physicians Art Assn. Holder patent on portable compound microscope. Home: 100 Lake Av., Greenwich, Conn. Died Sept. 20, 1948.

LARKIN, Adrian Hoffman, lawyer; b. Ossining, N.Y., June 6, 1865; s. Francis and Sarah E. (Hobby) L.; A.B., Princeton, 1887, A.M., 1891; m. Katherine B. Satterthwaite, Sept. 2, 1891. Mem. of law firm Larkin, Rathbone & Perry; chmn. bd. Va. Ry Co.; dir. Lanston Monotype Machine Co., Sloss Sheffield Steel & Iron Co., U.S. Industrial Alcohol Co., Brooklyn Union Gas Co. Served as mem. of the Home Defense League; mem. exec. com. and gen. counsel Nat. War Savings Com. of Greater New York; chmn. Selective Service Bd. of Instrn. for Sect. D, Draft Bd. No. 159; v. chmn. com. to secure cooperation of clubs as to food; mem. Mayor's Com. on Nat. Defense; etc. Mem. bd. dirs. Southampton Hosp. Mem. Assn. Bar City of New York, New York County Lawyers Assn. Democrat. Episcopalian. Clubs: Knickerbocker, University, Down Town Assn., National Golf Links of America, Meadow, Southampton. Home: 61 E. 82d St. Office: 70 Broadway, New York, N.Y. Died Feb. 23, 1942.

LARKIN, John Adrian, corp. official; b. New York, N.Y., Oct. 24, 1891; s. John and Ida (Rahm) L.; B.A., Princeton, 1913; m. Henrietta Rosa Kleberg, June 26, 1915; children—Henrietta Alice, Ida Louise, John A., Jr., Peter A. Admitted to N.Y. bar, 1916; engaged in practice of law, 1916-25; dir., vice chmn. Celanese Corp. of America, N.Y. City; chmn. bd. Fulton Trust Co. Episcopalian. Clubs: University, Princeton, Down Town Assn., Union League (New York), Rockaway Hunting. Home: 119 E. 81st St. Office: 180 Madison Av., N.Y. City. Died Nov. 26, 1948.

LARSEN, Alfred (Ferdinand Olaf), violinist, director; b. Nödebo, Denmark, Dec. 12, 1877; s. Lars Peter and Ane Margrethe (Christensen) L.; studied violin and other subjects in Copenhagen, also with the Danish violinist and composer, Fini Henriques; m. Caroline Dorthea Jensen, Sept. 24, 1899; stepchildren—Rudolf Ole, Agnes Margrethe. Began as soloist and teacher, Montreal, Can., 1899; conductor Montreal Amateur Symphony Orchestra, seasons 1902-03; in charge violin dept., Westmount Sch. of Music, 1904; located in Burlington, Vt., 1908, and became citizen of U.S.; founder Larsen Violin Sch.; founder, 1909, Burlington Symphony Orchestra; also Larsen String Quartette and Beethoven Piano Trio; teacher of violin and sight singing, Summer Sch., U. of Vt., 1909-10, and dir. music dept., 1910-13; prof. violin, cello and kindred subjects, Middlebury Coll., 1920-36; lecturer on music. A founder of The Danish-Am. Hist. Soc. 1932. Mason (32°). Home: 87 Hungerford St., Burlington, Vt. Died July 3, 1949.

LARSEN, Christian, educator; b. Odense, Denmark, Aug. 4, 1874; s. Hans and Marie (Frydendahl) L.; B.S., Ia. State Coll. Agr. and Mech. Arts, 1902, M.S., 1904; post-grad. course for expt. sta. workers, Cornell U., 1908; m. Elsie M. Finch, Aug. 4, 1903; children—Harald C., Alice M., Lillian D. Came to U.S., 1892, naturalized citizen, 1897. Successively instr., asst. and asso. prof., dairy dept., Ia. State Coll. Agr. and Mech. Arts, 1902-06; prof. dairy husbandry, Utah Agrl. Coll., Logan, Utah, 1906-07; prof. dairy husbandry and dir. extension, S.D. State Coll. Agr., 1907-20; dir. dairy marketing department, Illinois Agricultural Association, Chicago, 1920-23; dean of agriculture, South Dakota College Agriculture, 1923-40, dean emeritus since 1940. Chairman State Produce Commn. and U.S. Food Administration, S. D., 1917-18; capt. O.R.C., U.S. Army. First sec. S. D. State Farm Bureau; treas. S.D. State Grange. Fellow A.A.A.S.; mem. Am. Dairy Sci. Assn., Am. Farm Econ. Assn., N.E.A., Nat. Reserve Officers' Assn., S.D. Reserve Officers' Assn. (v.p.), Phi Kappa Phi, Alpha Zeta, Pi Gamma Mu. Pres. Presbyn. Brotherhood; pres. and sec. Teaching Sect. Am. Land Grant Coll. Assn. Republican. Mason (32°, Shriner). Clubs: Commercial (v.p.), Country (pres.). Author: Principles and Practices of Buttermaking, 1905; Dairy Technology, 1914; Exercises in Farm Dairying, 1918; Farm Dairying, 1919; Fundamentals of Coöperative Dairy Marketing, 1922. Contbr. research bulls. Home: Brookings, S.D. Died Aug. 24, 1948.

LARSEN, Hanna Astrup, editor; b. Decorah, Ia., Sept. 1, 1873; d. Peter Laurentius and Ingeborg (Astrup) Larsen; ed. under pvt. instrn. Asst. editor Amerika, Madison, Wis., 1901-04; editor Pacific-Posten, San Francisco, Calif., 1904-05; spl. writer San Francisco Chronicle and San Francisco Call, 1905-07; contbr. to N.Y. City newspapers and mags., 1908-12; lit. editor Am.-Scandinavian Review, N.Y. City, 1913-21, editor since 1921. Lit. sec. Am.-Scandinavian Foundation since 1921. Awarded Wasa medal (Sweden), 1931; awarded Norwegian King's D.S.M., 1933; Royal Danish Medal of Merit, 1937. Democrat. Lutheran. Author: Knut Hamsun, 1922; Selma Lagerlöf, 1935. Translator (from Danish of J. P. Jacobsen); Marie Grubbe, 1917; Niels Lyhne, 1919. Editor: Norway's Best Stories, 1927; Sweden's Best Stories, 1928; Denmark's Best Stories, 1928. Contbr. articles on lit. criticism. Home: Knollwood Park, Elmsford, N.Y. Office: 116 E. 64th St., New York, N.Y. Died Dec. 3, 1945.

LARSON, Winford Porter, prof. bacteriology; b. Poy Sippi, Wis., Mar. 7, 1880; s. Charles J. and Mary (Peterson) L.; student Milton (Wis.) Coll., 1896-97, Union Coll., at Lincoln, Neb., 1897-99; M.D., U. of Ill. Coll. of Medicine, 1904; grad. study, U. of Berlin, 1906-08, Sorbonne, Paris, 1909-10; m. Alma E. Meldal, Apr. 4, 1908; children—Lorna G., Douglas M. Instr. in bacteriology, U. of Minn., 1911-12, asst. prof. bacteriology, 1912-15, asso. prof., 1915-18, prof. and head of dept. since 1918. Mem. Soc. Am. Bacteriologists, Am. Soc. Immunologists, Assn. Pathologists and Bacteriologists, Soc. Exptl. Biology and Med., Am. Assn. Univ. Profs., Nu Sigma Nu; asso. mem. N.Y. Acad. of Sciences. Club: Minneapolis Athletic. Contbr. on bacteriology. Home: 516 9th Av. S.E., Minneapolis, Minn. Died Jan. 1, 1947.

LASKEY, John Ellsworth (lăs'kē), lawyer; b. Washington, D.C., Oct. 27, 1868; s. Robert Valentine and Virginia (Hodges) L.; grad. Central High Sch., D.C., 1888; LL.B., Columbian (now George Washington) U., 1892, LL.M., 1893; m. Pauline Ludgate, Nov. 21, 1906; children—Virginia, John. Admitted to D.C. bar, 1893. Asst. U.S. atty. for D.C., 1895-99; U.S. atty., by appmt. of Woodrow Wilson, 1914-21. Instr. criminal law, negotiable instruments and evidence, Georgetown U. Law Sch., 1910-14; lecturer criminal law, Georgetown U., since 1914. Democrat. Episcopalian. Mem. D.C. Bar Assn. (sec. 1905-07; pres. 1913-14). Clubs: Cosmos, Lawyers' (pres. 1936-38), Press, University (Washington). Home: 1657 Park Rd. Office: Albee Bldg., Washington, D.C. Died Sep. 30, 1945.

LATCHAW, D(avid) Austin (lăt'shaw), newspaper man; b. near Franklin, Pa., Jan. 2, 1861; s. Jacob and Mary (Stauffer) L.; attended Grove City (Pa.) Coll.; grad. Nat. School of Elocution and Oratory, Phila., 1885; m. Mary A. Filler, Aug. 17, 1896; stepchildren (adopted)—Frank Warren, Hortense. Teacher public schools, Venango County, Pa., 2 yrs.; sec. publishing house, 1882-86, and mgr. Kansas City br. same, 1886-87; real estate business, Kansas City, 1887-88; reporter, dramatic and music editor Kansas City Times, 1888-95; dramatic and music critic, editorial writer, Kansas City Journal, 1895-1902; same with Kansas City Star, 1902-11, night editor, 1911-22, later asso. editor, now feature writer. Clubs: City, Kansas City Country. Home: 4637 Charlotte St., Kansas City, Mo. Died Jan. 24, 1948; buried in Mount Washington Cemetery.

LAU, Robert Frederick (lou), clergyman; b. Jersey City, N.J., Dec. 21, 1885; s. Rev. Robert Julius and Katherine (Steffler) L.; grad. Trinity Sch., N.Y. City, 1904; B.A., Columbia, 1908, M.A., 1910; fellow Gen. Theol. Sem., N.Y. City, 1911-13, S.T.B., 1912; S.T.D., U. of King's Coll., Halifax, N.S., 1918; m. Helene Catherine Ricxinger, June 14, 1911 (died 1925); children—Robert John, Leicester Edwin; m. 2d, Anna Charlotte Werner, Dec. 27, 1926; 1 dau., Anna Beatrix. Deacon, 1911, priest, 1912, P.E. Ch.; asst. St. Paul's Ch., Hoboken, N.J., 1911-13; rector St. Mark's Ch., Mendham, N.J., 1913-17, St. John's Ch., Bayonne, N.J., 1918-25; asst. foreign born work, Nat. Council P.E. Ch., 1925-30; vice counselor on ecclesiastical relations, P.E. Ch., 1930-33, counselor, Dec. 1933-Apr. 1936; priest on staff of Cathedral of St. John the Divine, N.Y. City, 1935; dean Cathédrale de la Sainte Trinité, Port au Prince, Haiti, 1936-37; chaplain and instr., Rectory Sch., Pomfret, Conn., 1938-39; now rector St. Paul's Ch., Spring Valley, N.Y., and St. John's Ch., New City, N.Y. Del. to Synod of 2d Province, 1921, 22, 24; examining chaplain Diocese of Newark, 1921-25; pres. Conseil d'Avis, Missionary Dist. of Haiti; examining chaplain to the bishop of Haiti, 1936; asst. Chapel of the Intercession, Trinity Parish, New York, 1937. Mem. Alpha Chi Rho. Republican. Mason. Author: The Servers Manual, 1916; The Eastern Church in the Western World (with W. Emhardt and T. Burgess), 1928. Contbr. to symposium, Liberal Catholicism and the Modern World, edited by Frank Gavin, 1934, Am. Year Book, 1934, 35. Asst. editor of liturgics, Anglican Theol. Review 1918-21. Home: 26 S. Madison Av., Spring Valley, N.Y. Died Oct. 5, 1943.

LAUBER, Joseph (lou'bēr), artist; b. Westphalia, Germany; s. Conrad and Therese (Wigge) L.; came to U.S. at age of 9; ed. private and pub. schs.; 1st art study Cooper Inst.; studied sculpture with Karl Muller, drawing and painting in Art Students League, New York, under Shirlaw and Chase; asst. to John La Farge, then traveled abroad for observation and study; m. Ida M. Crow, Apr. 22, 1891; 1 son, Hubert Crow. Began as sculptor about 1878; assisted John La Farge in sculptural decorations of Cornelius Vanderbilt's house, 1882; painted pictures abroad, but became more identified with mural arts, executing a number of etchings, 1887-94. Has executed paintings and windows in pub. bldgs. such as Appellate Court, Ch. of the Ascension, New York, and many others; has painted a conception of Christ which has been widely noticed, also a series of apostles, St. Matthew's R.C. Ch., Brooklyn, 1926. Head of dept. of mural decoration and design, Md. Inst. of Art, Baltimore, 1912-16; instr. in arts allied to architecture, Sch. of Architecture Columbia U., 1917-34, asso. in fine arts, 1931-34. Completed his 18th Window for Trinity Luth. Ch., Lancaster, Pa., in 1947. Author of several treatises on Am. Color Windows. Mem. Nat. Soc. Mural Painters, Architectural League (v.p. 1905-07); former del. Fine Arts Federation; ex-pres. Artists' Fellowship, Inc., 1918-29. Clubs: Faculty (Columbia Univ.); Salmagundi (hon. mem., 1929; Medal of Honor, 1942). Home: 630 W. 139th St., New York. Died Oct. 18, 1948.

LAUCK, W(illiam) Jett (louk), economist; b. Keyser, W.Va., Aug. 2, 1879; s. William Blackford and Emma Eltin L.; A.B., Washington and Lee U., 1903; fellow in dept. of polit. economy, U. of Chicago, 1903-06; m. Eleanor Moore Dunlap, Oct. 1, 1908; children—William Jett, Eleanor Moore, Peter Blackford. Asso. prof. economics and polit. science, Washington and Lee U., 1905-08; in charge of industrial investigation of U.S. Immigration Commn., 1907-10; chief examiner, Tariff Bd., Washington, Oct. 1910-11; sec. Southeastern States, Nat. Citizens' League Promotion Sound Banking System, 1911-12; mng. expert and cons. statistician U.S. Commn. on Industrial Relations, 1913-15; expert witness on ry. finance for state commns., Western frt. rate case, 1915. Expert on ry. economics before arbitration bds. for Brotherhoods of Locomotive Firemen and Engrs., 1912-19; economic counsellor Canadian Commn. on Econ. Development, 1916; U.S. Pub. Health Service, 1916; statistician, U.S. Board Mediation and Conciliation, 1915-17; statistician, U.S. Shipbuilding Labor Adjustment Bd., 1917-18; asst. dir. Industrial Relations Sect., U.S. Signal Corps, 1918; sec. Nat. War Labor Bd., 1918-19; economist United Mine Workers, Com. on Industrial Orgn., United Automobile Workers and ry. and other labor orgns. in arbitration proceedings and other matters, 1919-39; investigator for U.S. Coal Commn., 1923; economist, Grain Marketing Co., Chicago, 1924-25; expert com. on branch, chain and group banking, Federal Reserve Banks, 1931; adviser, President's Orgn. for Unemployment Relief, 1931; expert H.R. spl. com. on Govt. competition with pvt. business, 1933, N.Y. Power Authority, 1935; mem. legislative drafting com., NRA, 1933; member of various special boards, and labor advisor, Coal Section, NRA, 1933-35; expert to Senate Finance Com. on revision of NRA, 1935; chmn. Pa. Anthracite Industry Coal Commn., 1937; vice chmn. Am. Assn. for Economic Freedom, 1938. Mem. Phi Beta Kappa, Kappa Sigma, Theta Nu Epsilon. Clubs: Cosmos, Chevy Chase. Presbyterian. Author: The Causes of the Panic of 1893, 1905 (winner of one-half of Hart, Schaffner & Marx econ. prize essay); The Immigration Problem (with Professor J. W. Jenks), 1911; Reports of U.S. Immig. Commn., Vols. IV-XVIII; Strikes and Lockouts and Railway Labor Arbitration, 1916 (reports for U.S. Board Mediation and Conciliation); Reports on Manufacturing and Mining, 1917 (U.S. Senate Documents); Conditions of Labor in American Industries (with Edgar Sydenstricker), 1917; The Industrial Code (with C. S. Watts), 1923. Editor: British War Experience Series; Political and Industrial Democracy (1776-1926), 1926; The New Industrial Revolution and Wages, 1929. Home: The Island, Fredericksburg, Va. Office: Mills Bldg., Washington, D.C. Died June 14, 1949.

LAUER, Conrad Newton (lou'ēr), pub. utility exec.; b. Three Tuns, Montgomery County, Pa., Nov. 25, 1869; s. Herman and Margaret Lukens (Clayton) L.; ed. pub. and pvt. schs., Montgomery County; hon. M.E., Stevens Inst. Tech., 1930; hon. LL.D., U. of Pa., 1940; m. Katherine Pierrepont Ifill, Nov. 2, 1893; children—Ida Felicia (Mrs. George Potter Darrow, Jr.), Harry Ifill. Time clerk to plant supt. Link Belt Co., 1893-1902; industrial engr., Dodge & Day (later Day & Zimmerman, Inc.), 1902-17, sec. and gen. mgr., 1917-19, treas., 1919-26, v.p., 1926-29; pres. and dir. Phila. Gas Works Co. since 1929; v.p. and dir. The United Gas Improvement Co.; dir. Cold Spring Bleachery, Bates, Inc., Baldwin Locomotive Securities Corp., Baldwin-Southwark Corp., Cramp Brass & Iron Foundries Co., Federal Steel Foundry Co., I. P. Morris & De La Vergne, Inc.; dir. and chmn. exec. com. Sharp & Dohme, Inc., Baldwin Locomotive Works. Member Am. Acad. Polit. and Social Science, Princeton Engring. Assn. (hon.), Art Club of Phila. Asso. trustee and mem. bd. of Engring. Edn., U. of Pa., since 1939. Mem. Hoover Medal Bd. of Award and John Fritz Medal Board of Award; mem. bd. mgrs. Beneficial Saving Fund Soc. Trustee Stevens Inst. Tech., Welfare Fed. Mem. Am. Soc. M.E. (ex-pres.), Am. Gas Assn. (mem. exec. com. and past pres., dir., mem. exec. bd.), Society for Advancement of Management, Franklin Inst., Newcomen Soc. of London, Pa. State Chamber Commerce, Phila. Chamber Commerce (v.p., mem. exec. com.), Pa. Acad. Fine Arts. Republican. Episcopalian. Mason. Clubs: Manufacturers, Engineers, Racquet, Poor Richard, University, Midday, Penn, Wanderers, Union League, Orpheus (Phila.); Engineers, India House (N.Y.). Author: Engineering in American Industry. Home: Penllyn, Montgomery County, Pa. Office: 1401 Arch St., Philadelphia, Pa. Died Aug. 2, 1943.

LAUGHLIN, Frank C., judge; b. Newstead, N.Y., July 20, 1859; ed. Lockport (N.Y.) Union Sch.; studied law in office; m. Mrs. Martha (Taylor) Bartlett, June 2, 1896. Admitted to bar, 1882; began practice in Buffalo, 1883; asst. city atty. and city atty. Buffalo, 1885-93; corp. counsel Buffalo, 1894-95; justice Supreme Court of N.Y., since 1895, Appellate Div. from Jan. 1900. Republican. Home: Hotel Lenox, Buffalo, N.Y. Died Jan. 18, 1943.

LAUGHLIN, George Mark, osteopathic surgeon; b. New London, Mo., Dec. 23, 1872; s. George H. and Deborah Jane (Ross) L.; B.S.D., State Teachers' Coll., Kirksville, Mo., 1894; M.S.D., 1898; D.O., Am. Sch. Osteopathy, 1900; m. Blanche Still, Apr. 11, 1900; children—Mrs. J. S. Denslow, George A. Teacher osteopathic practice and orthopedic surgery, American School of Osteopathy, 1900-18; founder, 1918, and president Laughlin Hosp.; founder, 1922, and endowed A. T. Still Coll. of Osteopathy and Surgery (now Kirksville Coll. of Osteopathy and Surgery) of which is pres. Mem. Am. Osteopathic Assn. Republican. Mem. Christian Ch. Mason, K.P., Elk, Kiwanian. Home: Kirksville, Mo. Died Aug. 15, 1948.

LAUGHLIN, George (McCully), Jr., steel mfr.; b. Pittsburgh, Pa., Feb. 25, 1873; s. George M. and Isabel B. (McKennan) L.; prep. edn., Shadyside Acad., and St. Paul's Sch., Concord, N.H.; student freshman yr. Sheffield Scientific Sch. (Yale), class of 1895; m. Henrietta Z. Speer, Jan. 10, 1895; children—George M., Katharine S. (Mrs. Erl C. B. Gould), Isabel, John S. Began with Jones & Laughlin Steel Corp., 1893, becoming v.p. and mem. exec. committee, 1923. Member Delta Psi. Republican. Episcopalian. Clubs: Pittsburgh, Duquesne, Pittsburgh Golf, Allegheny Country, Fox Chapel Golf; Racquet and Tennis (New York). Home: Woodland Rd. Address: Jones & Laughlin Steel Corp., Pittsburgh, Pa.* Died Mar. 9, 1946.

LAUGHLIN, Harry Hamilton (lawf'lin), biologist; b. Oskaloosa, Ia., Mar. 11, 1880; s. George Hamilton and Deborah Jane (Ross) L.; B.S., North Mo. State Normal Sch., 1900; M.S., Princeton, 1916, Sc.D., 1917; hon. M.D., U. of Heidelberg, Germany, 1936; m. Pansy Bowen, Sept. 13, 1902. Teacher agr., North Mo. State Normal Sch., 1907-10; supt. Eugenics Record Office (div. of Dept. of Genetics of Carnegie Instn. Washington) from its orgn., Oct. 1, 1910, until Jan. 1, 1921, in charge 1921-40; eugenics expert for Com. on Immigration and Naturalization, House of Rep., 1921-31; eugenics associate Psychopathic Lab., Municipal Court, Chicago, 1921-30; U.S. immigration agt. to Europe, Dept. of Labor, 1923-24; in charge of researches on the genetics of the thoroughbred horse since 1923; mem. Permanent Emigration Com. of Internat. Labor Office of the League of Nations, Geneva, 1925; dir. Survey of Human Resources of Conn., 1936-38. Capt. of N.Y. Home Defense Res., 1917-19. Mem. Galton Soc., Eugenics Research Assn. (sec.-treas., 1917-39); Am. Soc. Internat. Law, Am. Statis. Assn., Am. Eugenics Soc. pres., 1927-28). Mem. Internat. Commn. of Eugenics since 1921. Asso. editor Eugenical News, 1916-39; sec. 3d Internat. Congress of Eugenics, 1932; pres. Pioneer Fund, Inc., from its organization until 1941. Editor "A Decade of Progress in Eugenics," 1934. Author: Mitotic Stage Duration (Carnegie Instn.), 1918; State Institutions for the Defective, Dependent and Delinquent Classes (Bur. of Census), 1919; Eugenical Sterilization in the United States (Municipal Court, Chicago), 1922; Analysis of America's Modern Melting Pot (U.S. Govt. publ.), 1923; Europe as the Emigration-Exporting Continent and the United States as the Immigration-Receiving Nation (U.S. Govt. publ.), 1924; The General Formula of Heredity, 1933; Immigration Control, 1934; Racing Capacity in the Thoroughbred Horse, 1934; Probability Resultant, 1934; Conquest by Immigration, 1939; Current Studies on Race Conditions in the United States. Address: Kirksville, Mo. Died Jan. 26, 1943.

LAUGHLIN, Sceva Bright (lŏf'lin), univ. prof.; b. New Providence, Ia., Oct. 16, 1881; s. Preston Smith and Penelope Caroline (Martin) L.; A.B., A.M., Penn Coll., Oskaloosa, Ia., 1905; A.M., Haverford, 1906; studied Harvard, summer 1911, U. of Chicago, 1915; Ph.D., State U. of Ia., 1921; m. Lillian Catherine Goodall, Oct. 31, 1913; children—Elizabeth Jean (dec.), John Seth, William Sceva, Mary Penelope. Prin. Pleasant Plain (Ia.) Acad., 1906-07; teacher pub. schs., 1907-08; prin. high sch., Akron, Ia., 1908-10; supt. schs., Larchwood, Ia., 1910-12; English teacher Friends Boys' Sch., Ram Allah, Palestine, 1912-13; prin. Laurence Friends Acad., Gate, Okla., 1913-14, Friendswood (Tex.) Acad., 1914-15; prof. and head dept. history and social science, Culver-Stockton Coll., Canton, Mo., 1915-20; prof. and head dept. economics and sociology, Park Coll., Parkville, Mo., 1921-23, Willamette U., 1923-35; prof. of sociology and anthropology since 1935. Mem. Pacific Sociol. Soc., Fellowship of Reconciliation, Phi Delta Kappa, Pi Kappa Delta, Pi Gamma Mu (a founder and nat. chancellor). Prohibitionist. Quaker. Mem. of Grange, Farmers' Union. Author: Missouri Politics During the Civil War, 1930; Will the American Farmer Become a Peasant?, 1932; A Handbook for Thesis Writing, 1933. Editor and co-author: Beyond Dilemmas, Quakers Look at Life, 1937; Representatives of Leading Religious Denominations in Vol. XX of Who's Who and Their Family Characteristics, 1942. Home: 1705 Court St., Salem, Ore. Died Aug. 15, 1947.

LAURGAARD, Olaf (lŏr'gärd), consulting engr.; b. Ekne, nr. Trondhjem, Norway, Feb. 21, 1880; s. Oluf Christenson and Marie Cecelia (Leinhardt) L.; brought to U.S. in infancy; B.S., in C.E., U. of Wis., 1903, M.S., in C.E., 1914; m. Goldie May Sherer, Nov. 29, 1908; children—Helen, Glenn Olaf. Asst. engr. U.S. Reclamation Service, 1903-10; chief engr. Ore., Wash. & Ida. Finance Co., 1910-13; div. engr. Pacific Power & Light Co., Jan.-June 1913; project engr. State of Ore., 1913-15; cons. engineer, Portland, Ore., 1915-17; city engr. Portland, 1917-34 (in charge of expenditure of about $55,000,000 in pub. works of Portland); engr. with U.S. Bur. of Reclamation, 1934-36, services as constrn. engr. Parker Dam on Colorado River and engr. in Denver office, 1934-36; with Tenn. Valley Authority as gen. office engr. Engring. and Constrn. Depts., 1936-37, constrn. engr. on Hiwassee Dam in N.C., 1937-40; consulting engr., Portland, Ore., 1940-42, including principal engr. War Dept., U.S. Engrs. on defense projects, Anchorage, Alaska; resident plant engr., U.S. Maritime Commission on shipbuilding, Alameda, California, since 1942. Member Oregon legislature, 1917, prepared and introduced Ore. highway and irrigation codes. Mem. Ore. State Bd. Engring. Examiners, 1919-35, pres. 1919-30; pres. Nat. Council State Bds. of Engring. Examiners, 1933. Capt. Engr. Res. Corps, U.S. Army, 1918, 23. Life mem. Am. Assn. Engrs. (ex-pres. Ore. chapter); mem. Am. Soc. C.E. (life), Am. Soc. Municipal Engrs., City Ofcls., Div. Am. Road Builders Assn., Am. Soc. Mil. Engrs., Professional Engrs. of Ore. (life mem.), N.W. Soc. Highway Engrs. (past pres.), Tau Beta Pi, Chi Epsilon. Mason (32°, K.T.); mem. Elks, Woodmen of the World. Member Portland Auld Lang Syne Soc., East Bay Engineers. Clubs: Alameda Forum (Calif.), Portland City. Contbr. on engring. subjects. Home: Portland, Ore. Address: 2308 Webster St., Alameda, Calif. Died June 23, 1945.

LAUTERBACH, Jacob Zallel (law'tĕr-băk), prof. Talmud; b. Monasterzyska, Galicia, Austria, Jan. 6, 1873; s. Israel and Taube (Bandler) L.; ed. univs. Berlin and Göttingen, Ph.D., Göttingen, 1902; rabbi from Dr. Hildesheimer's Rabbiner-Seminar, Berlin, 1903; widower. Came to U.S., 1903; naturalized citizen, 1909. Prof. Talmud, Hebrew Union Coll., Cincinnati, since 1911. Office editor Jewish Ency. and contbr. numerous articles on Talmudic and rabbinic subjects; co-editor Hebrew Ency.; contbr. to Year Book of Central Conf. of Am. Rabbis, Am. Jour. Semitic Langs., Hazopeh, Jewish Quar. Rev. Member Am. Oriental Soc.; v.p. Am. Acad. for Jewish Research; mem. Com. on Jewish Classics. Author: Saadja-Al-fajjumis Arabische Psalmenübersetzung und Commentar, 1903; Midrash and Mishnah, 1916; The Three Books Found in the Temple at Jerusalem, 1918; An Introduction to the Talmud, 1925; The Pharisees and Their Teachings, 1929. Editor Hebrew Union College Annual. Author, editor and translator of A Critical Edition of the Mekilta, with an English Translation, Introduction and Notes (3 vols.), 1933; Tashlik, 1936. Also author of many brochures, etc. Research work in Palestine, 1934-35. Address: Hebrew Union College, Cincinnati, O. Died Mar. 21, 1942.

LAVELL, Cecil Fairfield (lá-vĕl'), coll. prof.; b. Kingston, Can., Nov. 28, 1872; s. Michael (M.D.) and Betsy (Reeve) L.; came to U.S., 1899; prep. edn., Kingston Collegiate Inst., 1886-90; A.M., Queen's U., Can., 1894; Cornell U., 1894-95; Ph.D., Columbia, 1911; m. Catherine Lucy Kennedy, July 7, 1900. Staff lecturer, Am. Univ. Extension Soc., Phila., 1899-1905; prof. history, Bates Coll., Lewiston, Me., 1905-06, Trinity Coll., Conn., 1906-07; professor education, dean of Department of Education, Queen's College, 1907-10; teaching fellow, Teachers College, Columbia, 1910-11; asst. professor history of edn., 1911-13; prof. history, Grinnell (Ia.) Coll., 1917-23, prof. history of thought, 1923-43. Corr. mem. Institut Historique et Heraldique de France. Club: Authors (London). Author: Italian Cities, 1905; (with Charles E. Payne) Imperial England, 1918; Reconstruction and National Life, 1919; A Biography of the Greek People, 1934; also numerous articles in mags. Home: 15 Claxton Blvd., Toronto, Canada. Died May 2, 1948.

LAVES, Kurt, astronomer; b. Lyck, Germany, Aug. 24, 1866; s. Hermann Karl and Julie (Krahnefeld) L.; grad. Kgl. Human. Gymnasium, Lyck, 1886; student U. of Koenigsberg, 1886-87, U. of Berlin, 1887-91, A.M., Ph.D., 1891; asst. in Royal Obs. of Berlin, 1892-93; m. Luise Moshagen, Aug. 25, 1896. Docent, reader, asst. and asso. in astronomy, U. of Chicago, 1893-97, instr., 1897-1901, asst. prof., 1901-08, asso. prof., since 1908. Mem. Astronomische Gesellschaft (Leipzig), Astron. and Astrophys. Soc. America, Am. Math. Soc.; fellow A.A.A.S. Home: 5611 Kenwood Av., Chicago. Died March 25, 1944.

LAW, Fred Hayes, ry. official; b. Sheridan, Ill., Nov. 10, 1876; s. Morris and Henrietta Elizabeth (Rowe) L.; grad. Sheridan High Sch., 1892; m. Frances Grace Kelley, Nov. 22, 1904; 1 son, Richard Kelley. With Ill. Central Ry. since 1897, as stenographer, rate clerk and chief clerk, St. Louis, 1897-1909, commercial agent, Pittsburgh, 1909-12, asst. gen. freight agent, Memphis, Tenn., 1912-13, St. Louis, 1913-18; mem. gen. staff at Chicago, successively as asst. gen. freight agent, gen. freight agt., asst. freight traffic mgr., asst to v.p., gen. traffic mgr., 1918-39, v.p. in charge of traffic since May 1, 1939. Episcopalian. Clubs: Chicago, Union League, Sky-Line, Traffic (Chicago); Boston (New Orleans). Home: Flossmoor, Ill. Office: 135 E. 11th Pl., Chicago, Ill. Died Mar. 30, 1942.

LAW, John Adger, mfr.; b. in Spartanburg, S.C., Sept. 19, 1869; s. of Thomas Hart and Anna Elizabeth (Adger) L.; A.B., Wofford Coll., 1887; m. Pearl Sibley, Nov. 1895; m. 2d Marjorie A. Potwin, Ph.D., July 21, 1946. Cashier Spartanburg Savings Bank, 1891-1900; pres. Central Nat. Bank, Spartanburg, 1903-33, and of Home Building & Loan Assn. until 1933; organizer, 1900, and pres., treas. Saxon Mills; pres., treas. Chesnee Mills; co-receiver Arcadia Mills; dir. Piedmont & Northern Ry. Co.; treas. Green River Corp.; pres. and treas. Lake Summit Corp. Ex-pres., mem. bd. govs. Am. Cotton Mfrs. Assn.; dir. Cotton Textile Inst.; mem. exec. com. S.C. Cotton Mfrs. Assn.; dir. and mem. com. on mfrs. Chamber Commerce, U.S. Trustee Wofford Coll., Converse Coll., Kennedy Library (all of Spartanburg). Mem. Huguenot Soc. of S.C., Newcomen Society. Democrat. Presbyterian. Home: Avon Park, Fla. and Lake Summit, N.C. Died Dec. 19, 1949.

LAW, Russell, advertising; b. Cincinnati, O., Jan. 9, 1882; s. Charles Henry and Fannie Burnet (Resor) L.; ed. Lawrenceville (N.J.) Sch.; m. Florence Gilson, July 20, 1907. Banking, Cincinnati, 1898-1901; newspaper work on The Wall Street Journal, 1911-14; started own advertising business under name of Russell Law, New York, 1914; merged with Rudolph Guenther, 1919, to form Rudolph Guenther-Russell Law, Inc.; merged with Albert Frank & Co., Sept. 2, 1932, and named changed to Albert Frank-Guenther Law, Inc.; chmn. exec. com. Albert Frank-Guenther Law, Inc., 1932-40, chmn. of bd. since 1940. Home: 26 E. 63d St. Office: 131 Cedar St., New York, N.Y. Died Dec. 22, 1942.

LAWES, Lewis E. (lawz), prison warden; b. Elmira, N.Y., Sept. 13, 1883; s. Harry Lewis and Sarah (Abbott) L.; ed. Elmira Free Acad. and New York Sch. of Social Work; hon. D.Sc., Colgate U., 1934; elected honorary member of Alpha Kappa Delta (national honorary sociology fraternity), 1944; m. Kathryn Irene Stanley, September 30, 1905 (died Oct. 30, 1937); children—Kathleen, Crystal, Joan Marie; m. 2d, Elise Chisholm, Apr. 19, 1939. Guard, Clinton Prison, 1905, transferred to Auburn Prison, 1906; guard, chief guard and chief record clerk, N.Y. State Reformatory, Elmira, 1906-14; overseer N.Y. City Reformatory, New Hampton Farms, 1914-15, supt., 1915-20; warden Sing Sing Prison, 1920-41; chief business cons. Govtl. Div., War Prodn. Bd. Served as pvt. U.S. Army, 1901-04. Pres. Wardens' Assn. America, 1922, Am. Prison Assn., 1923; hon. pres. Am. League to Abolish Capital Punishment; internat. del. to Prison Congress, England, 1925, Prague, 1930; del. Internat. Penal Conf., Berlin, 1935; dir. Boys' Clubs of America, Boys' Athletic League, N.Y. City. Independent Republican. Clubs: Point Senasqua Rod and Reel, Shattemuc Yacht, Authors, Players. Author: Man's Judgment of Death, 1923; Life and Death in Sing Sing, 1928; 20,000 Years in Sing Sing, 1932; Cell 202 Sing Sing; Invisible Stripes; Meet the Murderer, 1940; Stone and Steel, 1941; also monographs on capital punishment, prisons, penology, etc. Contbr. to mags. Lecturer and radio commentator on penal affairs. Home: Garrison-on-Hudson, N.Y. Died Apr. 23, 1947; buried in Sleepy Hollow Cemetery, Tarrytown, N.Y.

LAWLER, John J., bishop; b. Rochester, Minn., 1862; completed classical studies in Sem. of St. Francis, Milwaukee; studied philosophy College of St. Nicholas, Flanders, Belgium, theology, University of Louvain, Belgium; ordained R.C. priest, 1885, remaining at univ. for post-grad. course, 2 yrs. Prof. Scripture, Coll. of St. Thomas, St. Paul, 1 yr.; became pastor St. Luke's Ch., St. Paul, and later of Cathedral; apptd. auxiliary bishop archdiocese of St. Paul, May 1910; bishop of Lead, S.D., Jan. 29, 1916; the See (center of authority) transferred to Rapid City, Aug. 1, 1930. Home: Rapid City, S.D. Died March 11, 1948.

LAWLER, Thomas Bonaventure, author, pub.; b. Worcester, Mass., July 14, 1864; s. Thomas and Eliza L.; grad. Holy Cross Coll., Worcester, 1885, A.M., 1893, LL.D., 1910; m. Margaret A. Brennan, Apr. 12, 1899; children—Muriel, Irene (Mrs. J. K. Crimmins), Newman, Arthur. Dir. Ginn & Co., ednl. pubs. since 1906. Mem. Am. Antiquarian Soc. Clubs: Century, Salmagundi, Hudson River Country. Author: Essentials of American History, 1902; The Story of Columbus and Magellan, 1905; Primary History of the United States, 1905; Gateway to American History, 1924; Builders of America, 1927; Historia General del Mundo, 1928; Standard History of America, 1933; Elementary History of the United States, 1935; Seventy Years of Textbook Publishing, 1938. Home: 280 Van Cortlandt Park Av., Yonkers, N.Y. Office: 70 5th Av., New York, N.Y. Died July 20, 1945.

LAWRENCE, Andrew Middleton, newspaper pub. and editor; b. San Francisco; s. Clarence P. and Mary (Golding) L.; ed. Urban Acad., San Francisco; m. Minnie M. Young, Oct. 30, 1884; children—Edna G. P., Randolph L. (dec.). Began as reporter, 1884, later city editor, Washington corr. and mng. editor San Francisco Examiner, with which was connected 14 yrs.; moved to Chicago as mng. editor Hearst's Chicago American, made pub., 1903; pres. and pub. Chicago Examiner until 1915; pres. and editor San Francisco Journal, 1919; founded Chicago Journal of Commerce, 1920; mng. dir. Pacific Coast Literary and News Bur., San Francisco. Mem. Calif. Legislature, 1887-88; del.-at-large from Ill., Dem. Nat. Conv., 1904. Home: 1100 Sacramento St., San Francisco, Calif. Died Nov. 28, 1942.

LAWRENCE, Charles Kennedy, engineer; b. Washington, Pa., May 19, 1856; s. James Kennedy and Eleanor (Isett) L.; ed. Western U. of Pa. (now U. of Pittsburgh); m. Elizabeth Wolf, 18?0; children—Frank Ellmaker, Charles Kennedy, Virginia, James Kennedy, Elizabeth. Asst. engr. and div. engr., Pa. R.R., 1880-87; engr., maintenance of way, St.P., M&M. Ry., 1887; chief engr., gen. supt. lines G.N. Ry., 1888-91; asst. chief engr., Carnegie Steel Co., 1897-99; engr. of constrn., Central of Ga. Ry., 1899-1904; engr. electric zone, N.Y. C.&H.R. R.R., 1904-05; chief engr., Central of Ga. Ry., 1906-June 1, 1926 (retired). Home: 3303 Abercorn St., Savannah. Ga. Died Sep. 12, 1942.

LAWRENCE, Ellis Fuller, architect and educator; b. Malden, Mass., Nov. 13, 1879; s. Henry Abbott and Annie (Howels) L.; grad. Phillips Acad., Andover, Mass., 1897; B.S. in Architecture, Mass. Inst. Tech., 1901, M.S., 1902; traveled and studied abroad, 1905; m. Alice Louise Millet, Nov. 4, 1905; children—Henry Abbott, Denison Howels, Amos Millet. Mem. archtl. firm of MacNaughton, Raymond & Lawrence, Portland, Ore., now Lawrence & Lawrence; organized Sch. of Architecture and Allied Arts of U. of Ore., 1914, and has since served as dean. Works: Med. Sch. Bldg., Clinics Bldg., dormitories and other bldgs., U. of Ore.; park bldgs. for Portland; Masonic temples, at Salem and Eugene, Ore.; dormitories and Conservatory of Music, Whitman Coll., many chs. and residences. Hon. pres. Ore. Bldg. Congress; professional adviser Portland Auditorium competition; mem. Jury of Award Portland Auditorium, Bank of State Bldg., and Stock Exchange Bldg. (San Francisco). Victory Memorial (Hawaii); mem. exec. com. Pub. Works of Art Project; state advisory architect Home Owners Loan Corp.; has served 2 terms as mem. Portland City Planning Commn. Fellow Am. Inst. of Architects; chmn. Council of City Planning, Portland Chamber of Commerce; ex-pres. Nat. Assn. of Collegiate Schs. of Architecture; ex-v.p. and dir. Am. Inst. Architecture. Clubs: Portland City. Home: 2211 N.E. 21st Av. Office: Failing Bldg., Portland 4, Ore. Died Feb. 27, 1946.

LAWRENCE, Richard Wesley, corp. official; b. N.Y. City, May 7, 1878; s. Lewis and Mary J. (Larke) L.; student New York Law Sch., 1900-01; m. Ruth Earle, Nov. 20, 1906 (died Jan. 5, 1931); children—Ruth Earle (Mrs. Edward Ogden Wittmer), Richard Wesley; m. 2d, Mary Rutgers Sage, Feb. 24, 1938. With Weber Piano Co., 1896-1910, v.p., 1904-10; pres. Autopiano Co., 1910-16, Kohler & Campbell, New York, 1916-21; chmn. bd. of Printers Ink Pub. Co.; pres. Bankers-Commercial Corp. since 1923; director and member executive committee, Hanover Fire Insurance Company, Fulton Fire Ins. Co.; dir. Am. Piano Corp., Equitable Life Assurance Soc. of the U.S.; chmn. and dir. Aeolian-Am. Corp.; trustee Estate of Charles Kohler, N.Y. Savings Bank. Mem. New York Appeal Draft Bd., World War, New York Zoning Commn., 1915-16. Campaign chmn. New York National War Fund, 1944-45. Chmn. N.Y. Y.M.C.A. Mem. Council N.Y. Univ. Ex-pres. N.Y. State Chamber of Commerce, 1938-40. Republican. Methodist. Clubs: National Republican, New York (ex-pres.), Union League of New York; Long Island Country, Quoque Field (L.I., N.Y.). Home: 79 E. 79th St. Office: 270 Madison Av., N.Y. City. Died Oct. 7, 1948.

LAWS, Curtis Lee, pub.; b. Aldie, Va., July 14, 1868; s. John T. and Laura J. (Nixon) L.; ed. at Richmond College and Crozer Theol. Sem.; m. Grace Burnett, Apr. 25, 1894; 1 dau., Margaret B. (Mrs. John William Decker); m. 2d, Susan Bancroft Tyler, Feb. 14, 1922. Ordained Bapt. ministry, 1892; pastor 1st Ch., Baltimore, 1893-1908, Greene Av. Ch., Brooklyn, 1908-13; editor The Watchman-Examiner, New York, 1913-40; now pres. Watchman-Examiner Foundation, Inc., and pub. The Watchman-Examiner. Mem. Beta Theta Pi. Mason. Home: 51 Fifth Av. Office: 23 E. 26th St., New York. Died July 7, 1946; buried in Druid Ridge Cemetery, Baltimore.

LAWS, George William, naval officer; b. Feb. 11, 1870; entered U.S. Navy, 1887, and advanced through the grades to rear adm., 1925; retired, 1934. Decorated Navy Cross. Address: Navy Dept., Washington 25. Died June 6, 1945; buried in Naval Cemetery, Annapolis.

LAWSON, James Gilchrist, editor, author; b. Cleveland, Tenn., Sept. 10, 1874; s. James J. and Margaret (Logan) L.; student prep. course, Southern Calif. Coll. of U. of Chicago, Los Angeles; m. Camilla Martens, Nov. 14, 1914. Evangelist in Calif. and many states of U.S.; visited British Isles in 1900 and remained 8 yrs.; spl. corr. for religious papers of London, 5 yrs.; mgr. Glad Tidings Pub. Co., Chicago, 1909-22; editor Church Publishing House, pubs. of church mags., 1925-32. Mgr. Family Altar League 7 yrs. and an editor Family Altar Mag. Prohibitionist. Baptist. Compiler and Editor: The Christian Worker's Testament, 1902; Deeper Experiences of Famous Christians, 1911; Proofs of the Life Hereafter, 1912; World-Wide Reforms, 1913; Did Jesus Command Immersion?, 1915; The Precious Promise Bible, 1915; Greatest Thoughts About the Bible, 1918; Greatest Thoughts About Jesus Christ, 1919; Greatest Thoughts About God, 1920; Daily Manna, 1921; The World's Best Humorous Anecdotes, 1923; Cyclopedia of Religious Anecdotes, 1923; The World's Best Epigrams, 1924; The World's Best Conundrums and Riddles, 1924; Bible Quotation Puzzles, 1924; The World's Best Loved Poems, 1927; The Marked Bible, 1928; The World's Best Religious Quotations, 1930; That Reminds Me—, 1932; Best Loved Religious Poems, 1933; Great Sermons on World Peace, 1937; Famous Missionaries, 1939. Home: 4425 N. Monticello Av., Chicago 25, Ill. Died June 17, 1946.

LAWTHER, Harry Preston, lawyer; b. Muscatine, Ia., Jan. 27, 1859; s. Robert Ralston and Ellen (Hoopes) L.; student Washington and Lee U., 1875-76, Baylor U., 1877-78; B.L., U. of Va., 1883; m. Mary Ross, Mar. 1888; children—Andrew Ross, Harry Preston. Admitted to Tex. bar, 1883, and practiced since at Dallas. Mem. from Tex. of Nat. Conf. Commrs. on Uniform State Laws. Mem. Am. Bar Assn. (past mem. gen. council and exec. com.), Tex. State Bar Assn. (past pres.), Dallas County Bar Assn. (past pres.), Am. Law Inst., Internat. Assn. Ins. Counsel, Sigma Chi. Democrat. Mason. Home: 5124 Live Oak St. Office: Texas Bank Bldg., Dallas, Tex. Died Dec. 1, 1942.

LAZARUS, Simon; merchant; b. Columbus, O., Aug. 19, 1882; s. Fred and Rose (Eichberg) L.; student, Columbus pub. schs., 1888-96; Manlius (N. Y.) Sch., 1896-1900; m. Edna Yondorf, June 5, 1911 (dec.); children—Simon, Charles Yondorf, Rose Edna (wife of Dr. Chester C. Shinbach), Joan (wife of John S. Stark); m. 2d, Amy Weiler, Jan. 3, 1939. Associated with The F. & R. Lazarus & Co. since 1901 as stockman, salesman, buyer, supt., now pres.; vice-pres., The John Shillito Co., Cincinnati; pres. Southern Hotel Co., Columbus; dir. Federated Dept. Stores, Bloomingdale's N.Y. City. Trustee: Children's Hosp., Greenlawn Cemetery Association, Tuberculosis Soc., Mt. Carmel Hosp.; dir. Retail Merchants Assn., Columbus Better Business Bur. Elk; Red Man. Clubs: Athletic; Winding Hollow Country. Home: 172 S. Columbia Av. (9). Ohio. Office: The F. & R. Lazarus & Co., Columbus 15, Ohio. Died Dec. 21. 1947.

LAZZARI, Carolina (Antoinette) (läd'zär-rē), contralto; b. Milford, Mass., Dec. 27, 1891; d. Joseph and Maria (Ambrosoli) Lazzari; ed. Bucksport (Me.) Sem., Ursuline Acad., Milan, Italy; received musical edn. in Italy and New York. Joined Chicago Opera Company, Nov. 1917; with Metropolitan Opera Co. since 1920; also Colon Opéra, Buenos Aires, season 1921; principal rôles—Dalila, in "Samson et Dalila"; Amneris, in "Aida," and leading contralto rôles with Mme. Galli-Curci at Chicago, in "Linda di Chamounix" and others: Giglietta, in "Isabeau"; La Cieca and Laura, in "Gioconda," etc.; now teaching voice. Home-Studio: 1425 Broadway, New York, N.Y. Died Oct. 17, 1946.

LEA, Luke, ex-senator; b. Nashville, Tenn., Apr. 12, 1879; s. Overton and Ella (Cocke) L.; A.B., U. of the South, 1899, A.M., 1900, LL.D., 1915; LL.B., Columbia Univ., 1903; m. Mary Louise Warner, Nov. 1, 1906 (now dec.); children—Luke, Percy W.; m. 2d, Percie Warner, May 1, 1920; children—Mary Louise, Laura, Overton. Began practice at Nashville, 1903; organized Nashville Tennesseean, 1907, now publisher; pres. Tennessee Publishing Co.; U.S. senator, from Tenn., 1911-17. Organized and became lt. col. 114th F.A., May 1917, and col. Oct. 8, 1917; with A.E.F. in France, 10 mos.; participated in Toul sector, Aug. 23-Sept. 11; St. Mihiel offensive Sept. 12-16; Meuse-Argonne offensive Sept. 26-Oct. 8, and Woëvre sector, Oct. 11-Nov. 8, 1918. Awarded D.S.M., U.S. Mem. Alpha Tau Omega, Phi Delta Phi. Democrat. Episcopalian. Office: Tennesseean Bldg., Nashville, Tenn. Died Nov. 18, 1945.

LEACH, Raymond Hotchkiss, educator; b. Burton, O., Oct. 13, 1883; s. Frank Fowler and Emily Melissa (Sanford) L.; A.B., Oberlin Coll., 1904; grad. student, Stanford U., 1920-22, New York U., 1932-33; D.D., Coll. Emporia; LL.D., Austin Coll., 1935; m. Beatrice Harbaugh, Aug. 31, 1910; 1 dau., Dorothy Elizabeth. Teacher Mid-Pacific Inst., Honolulu, T.H., 1904-07; asst. supt. Hawaiian Pineapple Co., 1907-17; served with Y.M.C.A. in France, 1917-18; with Libby, McNeill & Libby, Calif., 1918-20; asso. prof. history and dean of men, U. of Nevada, 1922-29; sec. of university dept. Council of Ch. Board of Edn., N.Y. City, 1929-34; pres. Trinity U., Waxahachie, Tex., 1934-36; pres. College of Idaho, Caldwell, Idaho, 1937-38; engaged in research and writing since 1939. Mem. S.A.R., Phi Kappa Phi. Republican. Presbyn. Mason. Clubs: Rotary; Clergy (New York). Contbg. editor Christian Education. Home: 1781 Riverside Drive, New York, N.Y. Died May 23, 1942.

LEACOCK, Arthur Gordner (lā'kōk), educator; b. Lehman, Pa., May 27, 1868; s. John Clark and Lydia (Gordner) L.; A.B., Syracuse U., 1892; A.B., Harvard, 1893, A.M., 1894, Ph.D., 1899; m. Anne Adams Brown, Aug. 24, 1911; 1 dau., Roma Georgia. Instr. Greek, Wesleyan Acad., Wilbraham, Mass., 1894-96; instr. Latin, Wesleyan U., 1896-97; studied classical archeology, U. of Munich, 1897-98; prof. Greek, Phillips Exeter Acad., 1899-1939, now emeritus; instr. Harvard, summer, 1905. Fellow Am. Geog. Soc.; mem. Am. Classical League, Am. Philol. Assn., Classical Assn. of New Eng., Exeter Hist. Soc., Phi Beta Kappa (Syracuse), Delta Upsilon. Republican. Episcopalian. Club: Harvard (Boston). Author: De Rebus ad Pompas Sacras apud Græcos Pertinentibus Quæstiones Selectæ (doctorate thesis, Harvard, 1899), printed in Harvard Studies in Classical Philology, Vol. XI, 1900; Studies in the Life of St. Paul, 1906. Address: 70 Front St., Exeter, N.H. Died Nov. 28, 1947

LEACOCK, Stephen Butler (lē-kōk), economist; b. Swanmoor, Hampshire, England, Dec. 30, 1869; s. Walter Peter and Agnes Emma (Butler) L.; student Upper Canada Coll., Toronto, 1882-87; B.A., U. of Toronto, 1891; Ph.D., U. of Chicago, 1903; LL.D., Queens, 1919; Litt.D., Brown U., U. of Toronto, Dartmouth Coll., 1920, Bishop Coll., 1934, McGill U., 1936; m. Beatrix Hamilton, 1900 (died 1925); 1 son., Stephen Lushington. With McGill U., Montreal, since 1901, prof. polit. economy and head dept. economics since 1908; retired 1936. Mem. Anglican Ch. Club: University (Montreal). Author: Elements of Political Science, 1906; Literary Lapses, 1910; Nonsense Novels, 1911; Sunshine Sketches of a Little Town, 1912; Iron Man and Tin Woman, 1929; Charles Dickens, 1933; Mark Twain, 1932; Lincoln Frees the Slaves, 1934; Humor: Its Theory and Technique, 1934; The British Empire, 1940; Montreal, Seaport and City, 1942; How to Write, 1943. Contbr. articles to mags. Home: (winter) 3869 Cotedes Neiges Rd., Montreal; (summer) The Old Brewery Bay, Orillia, Ont., Can. Address: McGill University, Montreal, Canada. Died Mar. 28, 1944.

LEADBETTER, Frederick William (lĕd'bĕt-ēr), corp. official; b. Clinton, Ia., Sept. 15, 1875; s. Charles Hartshorne and Annie (Comings) L.; student Calif. State Coll., San Jose, Calif., 3 yrs.; m. Caroline Thuseby Pittock, Sept. 30, 1893; children—Henry Lewis Pittock, Georgiana (Mrs. Frank G. Andreae), Dorothy Vose (Mrs. Nils Teren), Elizabeth (Mrs. Ambrose Cronin, Jr.). In paper mfg., pulp and lumber business since 1895; pres. Columbia River Paper Co., Oregon Pulp & Paper Co., Calif. Oregon Paper Mills, Columbia River Paper Mills, Leadbetter Lumber & Paper Co. Served as maj., U.S. Army, World War I. Republican. Episcopalian. Clubs: Racquet and Tennis, Bankers (New York); Pacific Union (San Francisco); Santa Barbara, Valley Golf, Santa Barbara Club (Santa Barbara); Vancouver, Royal Vancouver Yacht, Vancouver Club (Vancouver, B.C.); Arlington, Waverly Golf, Multnomah Athletic (Portland, Ore.). Home: Camas, Wash. Office: Oregonian Bldg., Portland, Ore. Died Dec. 22, 1948.

LEAMY, James Patrick, judge; b. West Rutland, Vt., Jan. 16, 1892; s. James and Catherine (Clark) L.; A.B., Holy Cross Coll., Worcester, Mass., 1912; M.A., Boston Coll., 1913; LL.B., Harvard Law Sch., 1915; LL.D., Holy Cross College, 1943; married Margaret Lalor, June 17, 1929; 1 son, James Patrick Jr. Admitted to Vt. bar, 1916; in private practice, Rutland, 1916-40; U.S. commr. for Vt., 1919-31; referee in bankruptcy, Rutland, 1931-40; U.S. dist. judge, Rutland, since 1940. Democratic candidate for gov., 1932 and 34; for Congress, 1938. Trustee and sec., Rutland Hosp. Mem. Rutland County and Am. bar assns., Vt. Bar Assn. (past pres.). Democrat. Roman Catholic. K.C., Elk. Clubs: Rutland Country, Harvard (Vt.). Home: 164 Main St., W. Rutlant, Vt. Died July 22, 1949; buried St. Bridget's Cemetery, West Rutland, Vt.

LEARNED, William Setchel (lēr'nĕd), educator; b. Alpena, Mich., June 5, 1876; s. William Chandler and Adda (Setchel) L.; A.B., Brown U., 1897, A.M., 1908, Litt.D., 1939; univs. of Berlin and Leipzig, 1909-11; Ph.D., Harvard, 1912; LL.D., Lawrence Coll., 1933; LL.D., U. of Saskatchewan, 1936; m. Evelyn Blanche Williams, July 15, 1903 (died July 13, 1934); 1 dau., Annabel Frampton; m. 2d, Charlotte McMahon Smith, Mar. 7, 1936. Teacher, Cook Acad., Montour Falls, N.Y., 1897-1901; prin. University Sch., Providence, R.I., 1901-04; sr. master, Moses Brown Sch., Providence, 1904-09; research fellow, Harvard, 1912-13; staff mem. Carnegie Foundation for Advancement of Teaching, N.Y. City, since 1913. Mem. Phi Beta Kappa, Phi Delta Kappa, Delta Upsilon. Club: Century. Author: The Oberlehrer, 1914; Professional Preparation of Teachers for American Public Schools, 1920; Education in the Maritime Provinces, 1922; The American Public Library and the Diffusion of Knowledge, 1924; The Quality of the Educational Process in the United States and in Europe, 1927; Local Provision for Higher Education in Saskatchewan, 1932; The Student and His Knowledge, 1938; An Experiment in Responsible Learning, 1940; also various progress reports, study of the relations of secondary and higher edn. in Pa., 1929-37; the Graduate Record Examination, 1936-46. Home: 404 Riverside Drive, New York 25, N.Y. Died Jan. 3, 1950.

LEARY, Daniel Bell (lēr'ī), psychologist; b. N.Y. City, June 16, 1886; s. Daniel and Selina Grace (Bell) L.; B.A., Columbia, 1909; M.A., Teachers Coll. (Columbia), 1915, Ph.D., 1919. Prof. edn., Tulane, 1916-18; prof. and head of dept. psychology and edn., U. of Buffalo, since 1919. Mem. Am. Philos. Soc., Am. Sociol. Soc., Soc. Coll. Teachers of Edn., Am. Assn. Univ. Profs., A.A.A.S., Am. Psychol. Assn., Am. Assn. Applied Psychologists, N.Y. State Assn. Applied Psychologists, Phi Delta Kappa. Author: Education and Autocracy in Russia, 1919; Group-Discussion Syllabus of Sociology, 1920; Group-Discussion Syllabus of Psychology, 1920; Philosophy of Education—Outline of Fundamental Principles, 1920; Applied Psychology, an Outline and Bibliography, 1921; Philosophy and Education (Part I), 1921;

That Mind of Yours, 1927; Modern Psychology, 1928; Living and Learning, 1931; also syndicated daily newspaper articles, on edn. and psychology and reports on Russia. Contbr. to Last Twenty-Five Years of Education, 1924, Relation of the Social Sciences, 1926, Educational Psychology, 1934, Learning, also The Laws of Learning, in Readings in Psychology, 1935. Translator of several books from the Russian. Address: Townsend Hall, University of Buffalo, Buffalo, N.Y. Died Apr. 30, 1946.

LEARY, John Joseph, Jr., journalist, economist; b. Lynn, Mass., Feb. 2, 1874; s. John J. and Mary (Cronin) L.; ed. pub. and high schs., and under pvt. tutors; prepared for bar but never practiced; m. Alice Ruth Dwyer, October 6, 1896 (died October 24, 1942). Has been self-supporting since 11 years of age; began career in newspaper work with Lynn Press, 1893; night editor of the Boston Post, 1895-1903, of the Boston Journal, 1904; special writer and city editor, Boston Herald, 1905-07; financial editor and associate editor, New York Herald, 1907-12; special European correspondent and editorial adviser to James Gordon Bennett, Paris and London, 1912; staff correspondent New York Tribune, 1913-18; specialist in labor and economics, New York World, 1919-31; designated by President to make spl. survey employment exchange systems of Europe, 1931. Mem. Authors' League of America, American Academy of Political Science; fellow Royal Economic Society of Great Britain. Trustee Roosevelt Memorial Association. Mason. Clubs: National Press (Washington, D.C.); World Masonic (New York); Essex County (Massachusetts); Press (London). Author: Talks with T. R., 1920. Awarded Pulitzer prize of $1,000 in journalism, by Columbia Univ., 1920, for the most notable work of a reporter in 1919, the test being strict accuracy and terseness in dealing with the coal strike of 1919; also presented with a gold watch for same work, by Am. Federation of Labor. Voted silver button of hon. membership in their "Mutual Welfare League" by the 1,600 convicts of Sing Sing Prison, for his interest in their welfare. Address: 2025 I St. N.W., Washington, D.C. Died Jan. 4, 1944.

LEATHERS, Waller S(mith), preventive medicine and public health; b. near Charlottesville, Va., Dec. 4, 1874; s. James Addison and Bettie Elizabeth (Pace) L.; diploma of graduation in schs. of biology, geology, mineralogy and chemistry, Univ. of Va., 1892, M.D., 1895 (Alpha Omega Alpha); LL.D., U. of Miss., 1924; grad. work, Johns Hopkins, 1896, U. of Chicago, 5 summers, also Biol. Lab., L.I., summer, 1897, Marine Biol. Lab., Woods Hole, Mass., summer 1900, Harvard Med. Sch., summer 1906; LL.D., Tulane U., 1938; m. Ola Price, Nov. 14, 1906; 1 dau., Lucy Dell. Head of dept. of chemistry, Miller Sch. of Va., 1896-97; prof. biology U. of S.C., 1897-99; prof. biology, U. of Miss., 1899, prof. physiology, 1903, prof. physiology and hygiene, 1910-24; also organized and served as dean of Med. Sch., 1903-24; prof. preventive medicine and public health, Vanderbilt Univ., since 1924, asso. dean of Med. Sch., 1927, dean since 1928. Dir. pub. health of Miss., 1910; exec. officer State Bd. of Health, mem., 1917-24; mem. Miss. State Med. Assn. (pres. 1917); mem. State and Territorial Health Officers; mem. Nat. Bd. Med. Examiners (pres., 1930-34, 1936-42); mem. Tenn. Acad. of Science (pres., 1926-27). Mem. bd. scientific dirs., Internat. Health Div. of Rockefeller Foundation; mem. advisory com. on public health of Commonwealth Fund since 1920; mem. advisory health council of U.S. Pub. Health Service, 1931-35, 1937-39; mem. health and med. advisory com., American Red Cross, 1939. Mem. Acad. Tropical Medicine, 1939; Pub. Health Council of Tenn. Mem. Raven Society, University of Virginia, 1942. Chmn. Bd. of Examiners in Basic Sciences of Tenn., 1943. Fellow A.M.A. (mem. house of delegates, A.M.A., 1918-23), (sec. sect. on preventive and indsl. medicine and pub. health, 1920-23; chmn. 1923-24; council med. service and pub. relations, 1943). Fellow A.P.H.A. (chmn. com. on professional edn. since 1932; pres. 1940-41), A.A.A.S. (vice pres., 1928), Assn. of Am. Med. Colls. (pres., 1942-43), Soc. Med. Officers of Health (Eng.), Royal Sanitary Inst. (Eng.); mem. Am. Soc. of Tropical Medicine; Southern Med. Assn. (sec. sect. on pub. health, 1913-17; pres., 1922-28); Tenn. State Med. Assn.; Pub. Health Council of Tenn.; Sigma Chi, Alpha Omega Alpha, Phi Beta Kappa, Sigma Xi (charter mem.). Democrat. Methodist. Contbr. numerous scientific articles to med. jours. Home: 2004 20th Av. S. Office: Medical School, Vanderbilt University, Nashville, Tenn.
Died Jan. 26, 1946.

LEAVELL, Frank Hartwell (lĕv'ĕl), church official; b. Oxford, Miss., Mar. 11, 1884; s. George Washington and Corra Alice (Berry) L.; student Jefferson Mil. College, Washington, Miss., 1902-04; B.S., Univ. of Miss., 1909, student Harvard Law School, 1911-12; M.A., Columbia, 1925; LL.D., Miss. College, Clinton, 1935; L.H.D., Baylor University, Waco, Texas, 1945; m. Martha Maria Boone, April 5, 1917; children—Eddie Belle, Mary Martha, Frank Hartwell. Began as realtor, Hollywood, Calif., 1909; sec. Ga. State Bapt. Young People's Union, 1913-22; admitted to Ga. bar, 1915; exec. sec. Inter-Board Commn. Southern Bapt. Conv., 1922-28; sec. Dept. of Southern Bapt. Student Work, Bapt. S.S. Bd., since 1928; sec., treas., Edn. Commn. Southern Bapt. Conv., 1928-29, mem. Promotion Agency of same, 1928-30; mem. exec. com. World Bapt. Young Peoples Union, 1923-29; mem. exec. com. Baptist World Alliance since 1934; sec. Youth Com., since 1931; Tharp lecturer Bapt. Bible Inst., New Orleans, 1930; research tours Europe and Asia, 1923, 24, Europe, 1931, China, Japan, Hawaii, 1936, Europe, Near East, 1937, South America, 1939. Mem. Sigma Chi. Democrat. Rotarian. Author: Training in Stewardship, 1920; The Baptist Student Union, 1927; The Layman Measures the Minister, 1930; Baptist Student Union Methods, 1935. Author: The Master's Minority Movement, 1937. Editor in chief The Baptist Student since 1922. Home: 2121 W. Ashwood St. Office: 161 8th Av. N., Nashville, Tenn. Died Dec. 7, 1949.

Le BLANC, Thomas John (lĕ-blŏngk), prof. preventive medicine; b. Cheboygan, Mich., June 28, 1894; s. Louis John and Mary (McGurn) Le B.; A.B., U. of Mich., 1916, M.S. in pub. health, 1919; D.Sc., Johns Hopkins, 1923; m. Anna Gurklis, June 11, 1927; 1 dau., Diana. Scientist Rockefeller Inst., 1919-20; field scientist Rockefeller Foundation, 1920-21, statistician U.S. Pub. Health Service, Washington, D.C., 1924-25; head of Inst. of Human Biology, Tohoku Imperial U., Sendai, Japan, 1927-28; asso. prof., 1925-34, and prof. and head dept. of preventive medicine, Coll. of Medicine, Cincinnati, O., since 1935. Served as constrn. officer, U.S. Naval Ry. Batteries, with A.E.F., during World War. Decorated medal by Mexico for work in yellow fever; received scroll from Japanese Emperor; received citation and Silver Star (U.S.) for service at Front in World War. Mem. Am. Pub. Health Assn., Am. Soc. for Tropical Medicine. Club: Cincinnati Power Squadron of U.S. Power Squadrons. Home: 409 Warren Av., Cincinnati, O. Died Sept. 9, 1948.

LECHER, Louis Arthur (lĕk'ĕr), lawyer; b. Milwaukee, Wis., Mar. 17, 1880; s. Paul G. and Mary (Runge) L.; grad. high sch., Milwaukee, 1896; student Milwaukee Law Sch., 1901-02; read law under Judge James G. Jenkins, of U.S. Circuit Court of Appeals; LL.B., Marquette U., 1903; m. Antoinette F. Kleinsteiber, July 21, 1915; 1 dau., Sylvia Marie. Pvt. sec. to Hon. J. G. Jenkins, 1901-03; admitted to Wis. bar, 1903, later to practice before U.S. Supreme Court; now mem. firm Lecher, Michael, Spohn & Best; dir. and gen. counsel Combined Locks Paper Co., Cutler-Hammer, Inc., Phoenix Hosiery Co., Worden-Allen Co., Globe-Union, Inc., Pressed Steel Tank Co.; counsel Blackhawk Mfg. Co.; Automatic Products Co., Blatz Brewing Co., etc.; local counsel for United Shoe Machinery Co., Western Union Telegraph Co., Westinghouse Elec. & Mfg. Co., Commercial Investment Trust. Active in Liberty Loan drives and as four-minute man, World War. Pres. Milwaukee Hosp. Aux.; trustee Milwaukee U. Sch.; mem. adv. bd. Am. Legislators Assn.; mem. legal adv. com. Nat. Assn. of Mfrs.; mem. motion picture panel, Am. Arbitration Assn.; mem. Nat. Advisory Council of Jr. Achievement, Inc.; mem. board directors Associated Hosp. Service, Inc. Mem. Am. Bar Assn. (v.p. for Wisconsin 1924-25; mem. general council 1925-28; chmn. com. on commerce, 1942-46; mem. com. on federal taxation, 1924-26, 1927-39; mem. of council of section on taxation, 1939-44; mem. com. commercial law and bankruptcy 1926-27), Wis. and Milwaukee County bar assns., Am. Assn. for Internat. Conciliation, Am. Branch Internat. Law Assn., Legal Aid Soc., Am. Law Inst., Milwaukee Art Soc., Acad. of Polit. Science; hon. mem. Milwaukee Accountants Soc. Republican. Lutheran. Clubs: Milwaukee, Milwaukee Athletic, Milwaukee Country, University. Assisted in cleaning up corruption and unethical practices in bankruptcy practice in Milwaukee. Home: 4320 N. Lake Drive. Office: 110 East Wisconsin Bldg., Milwaukee, Wis. Died Feb. 25, 1948; buried in Forest Home Cemetery, Milwaukee.

Le CONTE, Joseph Nisbet (lĕ-kŏnt), mechanical engr.; b. Oakland, Calif., Feb. 7, 1870; s. Joseph and Caroline Elizabeth (Nisbet) L.; B.S., Univ. of California, 1891; M.M.E., Cornell Univ., 1892; LL.D., University of California, 1945; m. Helen Marion Gompertz, June 10, 1901 (died Aug. 26, 1924); children—Helen Malcolm, Joseph; m. 2d, Adelaide Elizabeth Graham, Feb. 16, 1929. Asst. in mechanics, U. of Calif., 1892-95, instr. in mech. engring., 1895-1903, asst. prof., 1903-12. prof. engring. mechanics, 1912-30, prof. of mech. engring., 1930-37, prof. emeritus since 1937. Collaborator with Yosemite Nat. Park Adv. Bd., 1943. Mem. Am. Soc. Mech. Engrs., Zeta Psi, Sigma Xi, Tau Beta Pi, Phi Beta Kappa. Republican. Clubs: Faculty (Berkeley, Calif.); Am. Alpine, Appalachian Mountain, Sierra. Author: Elementary Treatise on Mechanics of Machinery, 1902; Hydraulics, 1926. Contbr. over 40 tech. articles to mags. Made pioneer explorations in the high Sierra of Calif. between 1890 and 1910, including first ascents of 6 peaks between 13,000 and 14,500 feet elevation. Home: Box 1312, Carmel, Calif. Died Feb. 1, 1950.

LEDERER, Erwin Reginald, chem. engr.; b. Vienna, Austria, May 21, 1882; s. Josef Ignatius and Berta (Pekarek) L.; Chem. E., U. of Heidelberg, 1904; Ph.D., U. of Vienna, 1905; M.E., Technol. Inst., Vienna, 1905; spl. grad. work New York U., 1921; children—Elizabeth, Louise. Came to U.S., 1912, naturalized, 1919. Chemist and asst. supt. for Vacuum Oil Co. in Rumania and Austria-Hungary, 1906-12; chemist Standard Oil Co. of N.J., 1912-13; chief chemist Atlantic Refining Co., 1914-16; gen. supt. Galena Signal Oil Co., 1917-19; mgr. Atlantic Gulf Oil Corp., 1920-22; v.p. La. Oil Refining Co., 1922-25; v.p. Tex. Pacific Coal & Oil Co., 1925-35, dir. since 1935; pres. Bradford (Pa.) Oil Refining Co., 1936-41; cons. engr. Sun Oil Co. since 1941. Fellow Inst. of Petroleum (London, Eng.); mem. Am. Chem. Soc., Am. Inst. Chem. Engrs., Am. Society Automotive Engrs., Am. Soc. for Testing Material, Am. Petroleum Inst., Natural Gasoline Assn. of America (ex-pres.). Episcopalian. Clubs: Bradford, Bradford Country, Valley Hunt. Contbr. of papers to tech. jours. and assns., co-author books on petroleum technology. Home: 633 Overhill Rd., Ardmore, Pa. Office: 1608 Walnut St., Philadelphia, Pa. Died May 6, 1943

LEDOUX, Louis Vernon (lē-dōō'), author; b. New York, June 6, 1880; s. Albert Reid and Annie Van Vorst (Powers) L.; A.B., Columbia, 1902, grad. work, 1903; m. Jean Logan, 1907; children—Renée (Mrs. Thomas J. Sands), Louis Pierre. Pres. Ledoux & Co., expert chemists and assayers. Pres. Soc. for Japanese Studies; pres. Japan Society of New York; chmn. Townsend Harris Endowment Fund Committee; mem. art commission of City of New York, 1935-37; trustee of Brooklyn Museum since 1939. Club: Century Association. Author: Songs from the Silent Land, 1905; The Soul's Progress and Other Poems, 1907; Yzdra, 1909, revised edit., 1917; The Shadow of Etna, 1914; The Story of Eleusis, 1916; George Edward Woodberry—A Study of His Poetry, 1917; Japanese Figure Prints from Moronobu to Toyokuni, 1923; Landscape, Bird and Flower Prints and Surimono, 1924; The Art of Japan, 1927; An Essay on Japanese Prints, 1938; The Surviving Works of Sharaku (with H. G. Henderson), 1939; Japanese Prints of the Primitive Period, 1942; Harunobu and Shunsho, 1945. Home: Cornwall-on-Hudson, N.Y. Office: 155 6th Av., New York, N.Y. Died Feb. 25, 1948.

LEE, Albert, editor, pub.; b. New Orleans, May 11, 1868; s. Albert Lindley L.; A.B., Yale, 1891; married; children—Norman C., Barbara. Editor Yale Literary Mag., 1890-91; on staff New York Sun, 1891-94; editor Harper's Round Table, 1895-99; asso. editor McClure's Magazine, 1899; mng. editor Harper's Weekly, 1901; asso. editor, Collier's Weekly, 1901-02, mng. editor, Jan. 1903-Dec. 1911; editor Dress and Vanity Fair, July 1913-Mar. 1914; asso. editor Town and Country, Dec. 1914-Dec. 1915; mng. editor of Vanity Fair, 1915-19; mgr. foreign editions of Vogue, 1919-33; mgr. of the Vogue Paris office, 1927-28; mng. dir. Condé Nast & Co., Ltd., London, 1923-24. Club: Yale. Author: Tommy Toddles, 1896; Track Athletics in Detail, 1897; The Knave of Hearts, 1897; Four for a Fortune, 1898; He, She and They, 1899; The Pie and the Pirate, 1909; Portraits in Pottery, 1931. Plays: A Dutch Daisy; Miss Phoenix. Home: Sasqua Hills, South Norwalk, Conn. Died Dec. 10, 1946.

LEE, Blair, ex-senator; b. Silver Spring, Md., Aug. 9, 1857; s. Samuel Phillips (adm.) and Elizabeth (Blair) L.; A.B., Princeton, 1880, A.M., 1883; LL.B., Columbian (now George Washington) U., 1882, LL.M., 1883; m. Anne Clymer Brooke, Oct. 1, 1891 (died Dec. 24, 1903); children—Edward Brooke, Phillips Blair, Arthur Fitzgerald (dec.). Admitted to bar of D.C. and Md.; Dem. nominee for Congress, 6th Md. Dist., 1896 (defeated); elected mem. Md. state senate, 1905; reëlected, 1909; candidate for Dem. nomination for gov. of Md., 1911, and defeated by vote in convention of 64 to 65; elected to U.S. Senate Nov. 4, 1913, for period expiring Mar. 3, 1917. Pres. Soc. Lees of Va., 1922-34; mem. Soc. of the Cincinnati (Va.). Home: Silver Spring, Md. Died Dec. 25, 1944.

LEE, Edward Edson (Leo Edwards), author; b. Meridan, Ill., Sept. 2, 1884; s. Eugene Henry and Mary Emaline (Cannon) L.; ed. pub. schs., Utica, Ill.; m. Gladys Evaline Tuttle, Nov. 24, 1909; 1 son, Eugene Edward. Began as a factory apprentice, 1897; advertising positions with P. B. Yates Machine Co., 1913-15, with Burroughs Adding Machine Co., 1915-17, with The Autocall Co., 1917-20; writing juvenile books since 1921. Mason. Author: Jerry Todd series (16 books); Poppy Ott series (11 books); Andy Blake series (4 books); Trigger Berg series (4 books); Tuffy Bean series (5 books). Home: Cambridge, Wis. Died Sep. 28, 1944.

LEE, Edward Thomas, dean law sch.; b. Hartford, Conn.; s. Thomas and Jane (Marnell) L.; student U. of Mich., 1884-85; A.B., Harvard, 1886; LL.B., Columbian (now George Washington) U., 1894; m. Margaret Wishard Noble, 1894 (died 1925); children—Noble, Edward, Marjorie. Clk. U.S. Senate Com. on Territories, 1888-93; now dean The John Marshall Law Sch. Mem. Am., Ill. State and Chicago bar assns.; pres. Better Govt. Assn. of Chicago, 1928-31. Clubs: City, Chicago Literary, Executives. Editor of The John Marshall Law Quarterly. Home: 5615 Kenwood Av. Office: 315 Plymouth Court, Chicago, Ill. Died Dec. 14, 1943.

LEE, Edwin F., bishop, Methodist Church; b. Eldorado, Fayette County, Iowa, July 10, 1884; s. Andrew and Carrie (Anderson) L.; B.S., Northwestern U., 1909, S.T.D., 1945; D.D., Upper Ia. U., 1918, LL.D., 1939; B.D., Garrett Graduate School of Theology, 1924, D.D., 1928; M.A., University of Chicago, 1924; m. Edna Dorman, June 8, 1909. Ordained ministry M.E. Ch., 1908; pastor New Hampton, Ia., 1908-10; missionary, Batavia (Java) and pastor Wesley Ch., Kuala Lumpur (Malaya), 1910-12; Central M.E. Ch. (Am.), Manila, P.I., 1912-15, Rockford, Ia., 1915-17; asso. sec. M.E. Bd. Foreign Missions, New York, 1919-24; pastor Wesley Ch., Singapore, Straits Settlements, and supt. Singapore dist., 1924-28; missionary bishop, Malaysia and P.I., since 1928. Served as chaplain U.S. Army, 1917-19, with A.E.F. from Jan. 1918; sr. chaplain Base Sect. No. 7, and spl. rep. of sr. chaplain A.E.F., rank of capt.; (on leave) director general commn. Army and Navy Chaplains, Washington, D.C., June 1944-Dec. 1945. Del. Meth. Gen. Conf., 1928. Internat. Missionary Conf., Madras, India, 1938. Mem. Sigma

Alpha Epsilon; fellow Royal Geographic Society (London); mem. Am. Academy of Political and Social Science, American Institute of Pacific Relations (New York), Chicago Council on Foreign Relations. Decorated Officer of Acad., Order Univ. Palms (France), 1919; Cross of Mercy (Jugoslavia), 1921; King George V silver jubilee medal (British), 1935; Medal for Merit (U.S.), 1947. Republican. Mason (K.T., 32°). Address: 5 Mount Sophia, Singapore, Malaya; also 150 Fifth Av., New York 11. Died Sept. 14. 1948.

LEE, Elmo Pearce, judge; born at Coushatta, La., Feb. 10, 1882; s. Peyton A. and Pamelia J. (Herring) L.; student La. Poly. Inst. Junior Coll., 1899-1901; LL.B., La. State U., 1911; m. Katherine Galloway, Aug. 23, 1905; children—Elmo Pearce, Charles Galloway, Ruth (Mrs. Ben Roshton), Beth (Mrs. J. Selman Fortune). Admitted to La. bar, 1911, and practiced until 1943; judge 5th Circuit Court of Appeals, since 1943. Mem. Constitution Conv. of La., 1921; mem. examining com., Supreme Court of La. for Admissions to Bar, 1923-33 and 1940-43. Mem. Am. Bar Assn., La. State Bar Assn., Shreveport Bar Assn. (pres. 1943), Phi Kappa Phi. Mason. Home: 1090 E. Kings Highway. Office: Post Office Bldg., Shreveport, La Died July 26, 1949.

LEE, Frank Theodosius, clergyman; b. Kenosha, Wis., Mar. 23, 1847; s. Leonard and Sophia A. (Cook) L.; B.A., Oberlin, 1874; B.D., Yale, 1877; grad. course, 1 yr., Union Theol. Sem.; D.D., Wheaton (Ill.) Coll., 1908; m. Nellie J. Canfield, Sept. 20, 1881; 1 son, Harold Canfield. Ordained Congl. ministry, 1877; editorial staff The Congregationalist, Boston, 1878-79; pastor, Sparta and Whitewater, Wis., Muscatine, Ia., and in and about Chicago, including Lincoln Park Ch., Douglas Park Ch. and Maywood Ch., 1880-1908; dean and prof. Bibl. lit. and Christian theology, Sch. of Bible and Christian Training, Washburn Coll., Topeka, Kan., 1908-13; prof. Bible extension and instr. Bibl. lit., Atlanta (Ga.) Theol. Sem., 1913-19. An organizer and for several yrs. trustee Congl. Summer Assembly, Frankfort, Mich. Pres. Lee Family Reunion, 1896. Republican. Author: Popular Misconceptions as to Christian Faith and Life, 1900; Bible Study Popularized, 1904; Side Lights on the Bible, 1908; The New Testament Period and Its Leaders, 1913; Old Testament Heroes of the Faith, 1920. Home: Claremont, Calif. Died June 11, 1934.

LEE, George Bolling, gynecologist; b. Lexington, Va., Aug. 1872; s. Gen. W. H. F. and Mary (Tabb) L.; A.B., Washington and Lee U., 1893; M.D., College Physicians and Surgeons (Columbia), 1896; LL.D., Gettysburg (Pa.) College, 1934; m. Helen Keeney, Apr. 21, 1920. Interne Bellevue Hosp., 1896-99; practiced at N.Y. City since 1899; asso. surgeon Women's Hosp., 1900-14; former visiting gynecologist Bellevue Hosp. and Hosp. for Joint Diseases; prof. gynecology and obstetrics, Polyclinic Med. Sch. and Hosp. Served as capt. and contract surgeon, U.S. Vols., 1898; capt. Med. Officers Res. Corps, U.S. Army, 1917-18. Mem. A.M.A., Greater New York Med. Assn., Bellevue Hosp., Alumni Assn., Southern Soc. of New York, Va. Soc. of New York; fellow American Coll. Surgeons. Mem. Colonial Wars N.Y. and Va., Sons of Revolution, Sons of Confederate Vets., The Virginians, The Pilgrims of the U.S., Colonial Order of the Acorn, Mil. Order of Fgn. Wars, Washington Soc. of Alexandria, Aztec Club of 1847, Va. Hist. Soc. Democrat. Clubs: Union, Columbia Univ., Racquet, Golf, Garden City Golf, Turf and Field. Home: 20 E. 66th St., New York 21. Died July 13, 1948.

LEE, Gerald Stanley, author; b. Brockton, Mass., Oct. 4, 1862; s. Rev. Samuel Henry and Emma Chloe (Carter) L.; A.B., Middlebury Coll., 1885; student Yale Div. Sch., 1885-88; m. Jennette Barbour Perry, June 26, 1896; 1 dau., Geraldine. Ordained Congl. ministry, 1888; pastor Princeton, Minn., 1888-89, Sharon, Conn., 1890-93, West Springfield, Mass., 1893-96; substitute in dept. of rhetoric, Smith Coll., 1897-98; lecturer on lit. and the arts in modern times, since 1898; dir. (with Jennette Lee) Training School for Balance and Coördination, New York, since 1926. Member Authors' Club, London, Players, New York. Author: About an Old New England Church, 1893; The Shadow Christ, 1896; The Lost Art of Reading, 1902; The Child and the Book, 1902; The Voice of the Machines, 1906; Inspired Millionaires, 1908; Crowds—A Moving Picture of Democracy, 1913; Crowds Jr., 1914; We—A Confession of Faith for the American People; The Lonely Nation, 1917; The Air-Line to Liberty, 1918; The Ghost in the White House, 1920; Invisible Exercise, 1921; Seven Studies in Self Command, 1921; The Epidemic of Health, 1924; Rest Working, 1925; Every Man His Own Father, 1929; Heathen Rage—How We Heathen Feel About Those Who Try to Make Us True and Beautiful and Good, 1931; Recreating Oneself—A Few Adventures in Introducing Some Balancing or Floating Power Exercises, 1933; Let Yourself Up—; How To Be Half an Inch Taller All Day, 1939. Editor of Mount Tom, Little Look-Off on the World, 1905-14. Address: 88 High St., Northampton, Mass.; (summer) Monhegan Island, Me. Died Apr. 3, 1944.

LEE, Hugh Johnson, reporter, lecturer; b. Malden, Mass., Dec. 1, 1871; s. Oscar D. and Salina A. (Johnson) L.; grad. Meriden (Conn.) High School, 1891; took short course with private tutor in surveying; m. Florence A. Leonard, July 6, 1897. Supt. Boys' Club, Meriden, 1892; with R. E. Peary in Greenland, 1893-95, also summers 1896, 1897; lectured on Greenland. Reporter on Meriden Journal, 1896-1902. Apptd. June, 1902, resident missionary Cape Prince of Wales, Alaska, and supt. of the largest herd of domestic reindeer in Alaska, by Am. Missionary Assn.; apptd. Jan., 1903, U.S. commr. for Cape Prince of Wales dist., most western on Am. continent, and within sight of the coast of Siberia. Republican. Address: Wales, Alaska. Died Sept. 30, 1944.

LEE, J(ames) Beveridge, clergyman; b. Bovina Centre, N.Y., Jan. 21, 1865; s. James Boscawen (D.D.) and Jane Isabella (Campbell) L.; A.B., Hamilton Coll., N.Y., 1886; student United Presbyn. Theol. Sem., Xenia, O., 1886-88, Free and United Presbyn. Theol. Sems., Edinburgh, Scotland, 1888-89 (D.D., Hamilton, 1903); m. Mynna Greenman, Nov. 5, 1889; children—Mrs. Helen Gilbert, Meredith, Schuyler (dec.). Ordained United Presbyn. ministry, 1889; pastor Princeton, Ind., 1889-91, North Ch., Phila., 1891-94, First Presbyn. Ch., Bloomfield, N.J., 1894-99, Immanuel Ch., Milwaukee, Wis., 1899-1906; sec. for colls. with Gen. Assembly's Com. on Evangelistic Work, 1906-10; pastor St. Paul's Presbyn. Ch., Phila., 1910-15; sec. joint com. of Bds. of Edn. and Erection, having charge church bldg. at state univs., 1915-16; minister 2d Congl. Ch., New London, Conn., 1917-37; acting pastor Plymouth Congl. Ch., Coconut Grove, Fla., 1938-39, 2d Congl. Ch., Stonington, Conn., 1939-40, North Stonington Ch., 1942-44. Del. Asso. Ref. Presbyn. Ch., 1891; rep. to Eng. for International. Friendship through the Chs., 1919, 21. Trustee Theol. Sch., Bloomfield, N.J., 1895-1917, Lake Forest U., 1903-07, Ripon Coll., 1904-08. Mem. Theta Delta Chi, Phi Beta Kappa. Address: Lawers House, North Stonington, Conn.Died July 24, 1944.

LEE, Lansing B., lawyer; b. Augusta, Ga., June 20, 1887; s. John Corbett and Martha G. (Bothwell) L.; A.B., U. of Ga., 1906; LL.B., Harvard, 1910; m. Bertha Barrett, Mar. 1, 1919; children—Lansing B., Bertha B., Thomas Barrett D'Antignac (stepson). Admitted to Ga. bar, 1910; asso. firm Lamar & Callaway, 1910-14; mem. firm Alexander & Lee, 1914-24; sr. partner Lee, Congdon & Fulcher since 1924; pres. Ga.-Carolina Warehouse & Compress Co.; dir. Citizens & Southern Nat. Bank, Southern Mutual Ins. Co., Graniteville Co. Served on Augusta (Ga.) Sinking Fund Commn. since 1934. Maj. gen. staff 82d Div., A.E.F., World War. Pres. Tuttle Newton Home; trustee Augusta Free Sch., J. B. White Foundation, Gertrude Herbert Memorial Inst. of Art. Mem. Am., Ga. State and Augusta (ex-pres.) bar assns., Sigma Alpha Epsilon. Independent Democrat. Baptist. Clubs: Augusta National, Augusta Country. Home: 820 Fleming Av. Office: Southern Finance Bldg., Augusta, Ga. Died Apr. 8, 1944.

LEE, Melicent Humason, writer; b. New Britain, Conn., Jan. 11, 1889; d. William Lawrence and Florence (Cole) Humason; ed. schools of New Britain; m. Leslie W. Lee. Went to Calif. to live, 1918; has traveled in Mexico, Honduras, Costa Rica, Guatemala, Panama; lived among Indians of Southern Calif. and studied their arts, language, customs; founded Indian Arts League, 1928. Author: Pablo and Petra, 1934; Children of Banana Land (Jr. Lit. Guild award), 1936; Lah-Luck and Tuck-She, 1936; Volcanoes in the Sun, 1937; Indians of the Oaks, 1937; Marcos, a Mountain Boy of Mexico (Jr. Lit. Guild award), 1937; Our Little Guatemalan Cousin, 1937; At the Jungle's Edge, 1938; In the Land of Rubber, 1939; Chang Chee (with Jung Ho), 1939; Salt Water Boy, 1941; The Village of Singing Birds, 1942; also stories, poems and plays. Home: Encinitas, Calif.
Died Nov. 4, 1943.

LEE, Otis, prof. of philosophy; b. Montevideo, Minn., Sept. 28, 1902; s. Ernest Powers and Maude Susan (Anderson) L.; A.B., U. of Minn., 1924; B.A., Oxford Univ., Eng. (Rhodes scholar), 1924-27; Ph.D., Harvard, 1930; student Univ. of Kiel, Germany, and Univ. of Freiburg, Germany, 1933-34; m. Dorothy Demetracopoulou, Sept. 27, 1933; children—Anna Maude, Mary Hamilton, Ronald Demos, Sabra Margaret. Instr. in philosophy, U. of Mich., 1927-29; instr. and tutor in philosophy, Harvard, 1930-33, 1934-35; asso. prof. of philosophy, Pomona Coll., 1935-38; prof. of philosophy Vassar Coll., since 1938. John Simon Guggenheim fellow, 1940-41. Mem. Am. Philos. Assn., Phi Beta Kappa. Editor and contbr.: Philosophical Essays for Alfred North Whitehead, 1936. Author: Existence and Inquiry, 1949. Contbr. articles to jours. Home: Vassar College, Poughkeepsie, N.Y. Died Sept. 17, 1948.

LEE, Thomas Bailey, judge; b. Mocksville, N.C., Aug. 10, 1873; s. Rev. William Drayton (M.D.) and Sarah Ann (Bailey) L.; A.B., U. of N.C., 1894; m. Irene Teasdale, Nov. 4, 1907; children—Sarah Belle, Thomas Bailey, Mary Katherine, Eleanor Jane. Admitted to bar, N.C., 1897, Mont., 1898, Ida., 1906; began practice, Butte, Mont.; in practice, Burley, Ida., 1907-21; prosecuting attorney, Cassia County, Ida., 1908-12; judge District Court, 11th Ida. Dist., 1921-26; asso. justice Supreme Court, Ida., 1926-32, chief justice, 1931-32; dist. judge 11th Judicial Dist. of Idaho since 1935. Mem. Phi Gamma Delta, S.A.R. Republican. Mason, Elk. Club: Phi Gamma Delta (New York). Home: Burley, Ida. Deceased.

LEE, William C., army officer; b. Dunn, N.C., Mar. 12, 1895; s. Eldridge and Emma Jane (Massengill) L.; student Wake Forest (N.C.) Coll., 1913-15; B.S., N.C. State Coll., 1917; grad. company officers course, Inf. Sch., 1922, advanced course, 1933; grad. Tank Sch., Fort Meade, Md., 1930; Tank Sch., Versailles, France, 1934; grad. Command and Gen. Staff Sch., 1938; m. Dava Johnson, June 5, 1918. Commd. 2d lt., U.S. Army, 1913, and advanced through the ranks to brig. gen., 1942, major gen., Aug. 18, 1942; served in A.E.F., France, World War I; comdg. Am. parachute troops, 1941-42; comdg. airborne troops, 1942-45; retired 1945. Mem. Sigma Nu. Mason. Home: 209 W. Divine St. Address: Box 471, Dunn, N.C. Died June 25, 1948.

LEECH, Edward Towner, editor; b. Denver, Colo., June 17, 1892; s. Edward Palmer and Henrietta May (Reasoner) L.; student, U. of Colo., 1910-12; m. Pauline Bohanna, July 27, 1914; children—Edward Palmer, Robert Henry; m. 2d, Rose Loretta Roche, Apr. 15, 1931; children—Kathleen Patricia, Johanna May. Began on Denver Republican, 1909; editor Denver Express, 1916-17, Memphis (Tenn.) Press, 1917-21; founder and editor Birmingham (Ala.) Post (for Scripps-Howard Newspapers), 1921-26; editor Rocky Mountain News, Denver, 1926-31; editor and president Pittsburgh Press, Pittsburgh, Pa., since 1931. Member board Children's Hospital of Pittsburgh. Mem. Delta Tau Delta, Mason. Clubs: Duquesne, Pittsburgh Athletic Assn. Home: 78 Hoodridge Drive, Pittsburgh 16, Pa. Office: The Pittsburgh Press, Blvd. of the Allies, Pittsburgh 30, Pa.
Died Dec. 11, 1949.

LEETE, William White, clergyman; b. Windsor, Conn., Oct. 11, 1854; s. Rev. Theodore Adgate and Mary Cooley (White) L.; B.A., Amherst, 1877; B.D., Yale Div. Sch., 1880; D.D., Knox Coll., 1897; m. Sarah Elizabeth Rockwell, Apr. 4, 1883; 6 children. Ordained Congl. ministry, 1882; pastor Ridgefield, Conn., 1881-88, 1st Ch., Rockford, Ill., 1888-99; Dwight Pl. Ch., New Haven, Conn., 1899-1913; sec. for N.E. of the Congl. Ch. Bldg. Soc., 1913-25, editorial and field sec. of Congl. Ch. Extension Bds., 1925-30. Mem. Delta Upsilon, Phi Beta Kappa. Clubs: Alliance Française and other lit. and athletic clubs. Preacher and lecturer at large. Home: 1476 Chapel St., New Haven, Conn. Died May 1, 1946.

LEE, Willis Augustus, Jr., naval officer; b. Natlee, Ky., May 11, 1888; grad. Naval War Coll. senior course. Entered U.S. Navy, 1904, advanced to capt., 1936, rear adm., 1942, vice admiral Dec. 1944. Served as asst. chief of Staff to comdr. in chief, U.S. Fleet, to Feb. 1942; apptd. comdr. task force S.W. Pacific, Feb. 1942; in command when 5 Japanese ships were sunk in Naval engagement in Solomon Island, Nov. 1942. Decorated Navy Cross, Legion of Merit, Distinguished Service Medal, Died Aug. 25, 1945.

LEFAVOUR, Henry (lĕ-fā'vōōr), coll. pres.; b. Salem, Mass., Sept. 4, 1862; s. Thomas Hovey and Caroline (Wallis) L.; A.B., Williams Coll., 1883, Ph.D., 1886; U. of Berlin, 1888-90; LL.D., Williams, 1902, Tufts, 1905; m. Anna Burgess, Oct. 17, 1917 (died Jan. 15, 1941). Instr. Williston Sem., 1883-84; instr., 1884-88, prof. physics, 1888-1902, dean, 1897-1902, Williams Coll.; pres. Simmons Coll., Boston, 1902-33, now emeritus pres. and mem. corp. Chairman Mass. Emergency Public Works Commn., 1933-44. Trustee Williams Coll. since 1903, Boston State Hosp., 1908-37. Fellow Am. Acad. Arts and Sciences; mem. Colonial Soc. of Mass., Mass. Hist. Soc., N.E. Historic Geneal. Soc., Am. Antiquarian Soc. Clubs: University (New York); St. Botolph, Union (Boston). Author: Physics Lecture Notes, 1893; also various addresses and reports. Address: 119 Bay State Rd., Boston, Mass. Died June 16,1946.

LEFEVRE, Edwin (lĕ-fā'v'r), author; b. Colon, Colombia, Jan. 23, 1871; s. Henry L. (American) and Emilia (de la Ossa) L.; ed. pub. schs., San Francisco, 1880-84, Mich. Mil. Acad., Orchard Lake, Mich., 1884-87; studied mining engring., Lehigh U., 1887-90; m. Martha Moore, Jan. 22, 1902; children—Edwin, Reid. In journalism since 1890. Author: Wall Street Stories, 1901; The Golden Flood, 1905; Sampson, Rock of Wall Street, 1907; "H.R.," 1915; The Plunderers, 1916; To the Last Penny, 1917; Simonetta, 1919; Reminiscences of a Stock Operator, 1923; The Making of a Stock Broker, 1925. Mem. Am. Inst. Arts and Letter. Clubs: Century, Coffee House (New York); Nat. Press (Washington); Ekwanok Country (Manchester, Vt.). Home: Atlantic City, N.J. Died Feb. 22, 1943.

LE GALLIENNE, Richard, author; b. Liverpool, Eng., Jan. 20, 1866; s. John and Jane L.; ed. Liverpool Coll.; m. Mildred Lee, 1891 (died 1894); m. 2d, Julie Norregaard, 1897; m. 3d, Irma Hinton Perry, 1911. Engaged in business 7 yrs, but abandoned it for literature; for some time in journalism and lit. work in U.S. Editor Izaak Walton, The Compleat Angler, Hazlitt's "Liber Amoris," Hallam's "Remains." Author: My Ladies' Sonnets, 1887; Volumes in Folio, 1888; George Meredith, 1890; The Book Bills of Narcissus, 1891; English Poems, 1892; The Religion of a Literary Man, 1893; Prose Fancies, 1894; Robert Louis Stevenson and Other Poems, 1895; Retrospective Reviews, 1896; Prose Fancies, 2d series, 1896; The Quest of the Golden Girl, 1896; If I Were God; Omar Khayyam, a Paraphrase, 1897; The Romance of Zion Chapel, 1898; Young Lives, 1899; Worshipper of the Image; Travels in England; The Beautiful Lie of Rome, 1900; Rudyard Kipling, a Criticism; The Life Romantic, 1900; Sleeping Beauty, 1900; Mr. Sun and Mrs. Moon, 1902; Perseus and Andromeda, 1902; An Old Country House, 1902; Odes from the Divan of Hafiz, 1903; Painted Shadows, 1904; Little Dinners with the Sphinx, 1907; Love Letters of the King, 1908; Omar Repentant, 1908; New Poems, 1909; Attitudes and Avowals, 1910; October Vagabonds, 1910; Orestes, a tragedy, 1910; Loves of the Poets, 1911; Maker of Rainbows, 1912; Highway to Happiness, 1912; Lonely Dancer, 1913; Vanishing Roads and Other Essays, 1915; Modern Book of English Verse, 1919; Pieces of Eight, 1919; The Junk-Man, and Other Poems, 1921; A Jongleur Strayed (verse), 1922; Exaggerated Nationalism, 1936; From a Paris Scrapbook, 1938; Pieces of Eight, 1940. Compiler; The Le Gallienne Book of English Verse, 1923; Anthology of American Verse, 1925; The Romantic '90s, 1925; There Was a Ship, 1930; From a Paris Garret, 1936. Address: Mentone, A.M., France. Died Sept. 16, 1947.

LEHMAN, Clarence O(liver) (lā'măn), educator; b. Berne, Ind., Nov. 21, 1892; s. Japhet F. and Elizabeth (Neuenschwander) L.; A.B., Bluffton Coll., 1916; Univ. of Chicago, summer, 1921; A.M., Ohio State U., 1925, Ph.D., 1929; m. Carol Betzner, Aug. 28, 1920; 1 dau., Marjorie Jean. Teacher of Latin and mathematics, West Liberty (O.) High Sch., 1916-19; instr. of mathematics, N.C. State Coll., Raleigh, 1919-20; supt. of schools, Berne, Ind., 1920-24; teacher of history, 11th Av. Jr. High Sch., Columbus, O., 1925-28; dir. of training and head edn. dept., State Normal Sch., Geneseo, N.Y., 1929-39, pres. State Teachers Coll., Potsdam, N.Y., since 1939. Mem. survey staff, Pub. Schs. of New Orleans, 1938. Mem. Nat. Council, Boy Scouts America. Mem. Am. Assn. Sch. Adminstrs., Phi Delta Kappa. Republican. Presbyterian. Clubs: Rotary, Torch. Home: 6 Le Roy St. Potsdam, N.Y. Died Oct. 22, 1945.

LEHMAN, Irving (lē'măn), judge; b. N.Y. City, Jan. 28, 1876; s. Mayer and Babette (Newgass) L.; A.B., Columbia, 1896, A.M., 1897, LL.B., 1898, LL.D., 1927; LL.D., St. Lawrence University, 1936; L.H.D., Jewish Theological Seminary, 1936; LL.D., Syracuse University, 1943; m. Sissie Straus, June 26, 1901. Practiced at New York, 1898-1908; justice Supreme Court N.Y., term 1909-22; reëlected upon nomination of Democratic and Republican parties for term, 1923-36; judge Court of Appeals, term 1924-37; reëlected upon nomination of Dem., Rep. and Labor parties for term, 1938-51; elected chief judge of Court of Appeals on nomination of all parties for term 1940-46. Hon. pres. Jewish Welfare Board; hon. mem. Assn. Bar City of New York; mem. N.Y. State Bar Assn., Am. Bar Assn. Clubs: Manhattan, Harmonie, Democratic (N.Y.); Ft. Orange (Albany, N.Y.). Address: 36 W. 44th St., New York, N.Y. Died Sept. 22, 1945.

LEHMAN, Philip, investment securities; b. N.Y. City, Nov. 9, 1861; s. Emanuel L.; ed. pub. schs. Partner Lehman Bros., investment bankers, N.Y. City; mem. New York Stock Exchange; officer or dir. many corps. Home: 7 W. 54th St. Office: 1 William St., New York, N.Y.* Died Mar. 21, 1947.

LEIGH, Richard Henry, naval officer; b. Panola County, Miss., Aug. 12, 1870; s. Elbridge Gerry and Susan (Gattis) L.; grad. U.S. Naval Acad., 1891; grad. Naval War Coll., 1925; m. Minnie Hartwell Barksdale, Feb. 15, 1897. Ensign, July 1, 1891; promoted through grades to admiral, Sept. 15, 1931. Served on U.S.S. Princeton, Spanish-Am. War; comd. Pampanga, Philippine Campaign, Minneapolis, Cuban Pacification; on Oregon, Boxer troubles; in charge anti-submarine work, staff of Vice Adm. Sims, World War; chief of staff, Adm. Sims, to close of war; comd. dreadnaught Tennessee; chief of staff, U.S. Fleet; chief of Bur. of Navigation, Navy Dept.; comdr. battleships, Battle Force; comdr. Battle Force, U.S. Fleet; comdr. in chief U.S. Fleet; chmn. Gen. Board; retired for phys. disability, 1934. Naval adviser Am. delegation, Disarmament Conf. Geneva, 1933, London, 1934. Mem. Soc. Naval Engrs. Awarded D.S.M. (U.S.); decorated by British and Belgian govts., World War. Democrat. Baptist. Clubs: Army and Navy Chevy Chase (Washington); New York Yacht (New York). Home: 2316 Tracy Place, Washington, D.C. Died Feb. 4, 1946.

LEIGH, Townes Randolph, univ. prof., dean, v.p.; b. "Fair Oaks," Panola County, Miss., Oct. 26, 1880; s. Elbridge Gerry and Susie (Gattis) L.; B.S., Iuka (Miss.) Institute, 1901; A.B., Lebanon (O.) University, 1902; Ph.D., cum laude, U. of Chicago, 1915; D.Sc. (hon.), Stetson U., 1941; m. Blanche Baird Winfield, March 24, 1907. V.p.; later pres., Mary Connor Coll., Paris, Tex., 1903-08; pres. Tex. Mil. Acad., 1904-06; head dept. science, Ouachita (Ark.) Coll., 1907-09; head dept. chemistry, Woman's Coll. of Ala., Montgomery, Ala., 1910-14; fellow U. of Chicago, 1914-15; asst. prof. chemistry, Carleton Coll., Northfield, Minn., 1915-17; head dept. of chemistry, Georgetown (Ky.) Coll., 1917-20; head dept. of chemistry, U. of Fla., since 1920, dean Coll. of Pharmacy, 1923-33, dean Coll. Arts and Sciences including Sch. of Pharmacy, 1933-48, acting v.p. 1934-46; vice pres., 1946-48. State chemist, Fla., 1931. Inventor of Leigh fog screen for protection of vessels against submarines. Mem. orgn. com. Fla. Farm Chemurgic Council. Lieut. colonel Inactive Reserve. President local sector, Association Army of the U.S., 1923-25. Former mem. Res. Officers Assn. of Fla. (ex-pres. Gainesville chapter). Mem. Revision Com. U.S. Pharmacopeia XI, Am. Assn. of Colleges of Pharmacy (pres. 1931-32, mem. exec. com. 1932-34, chmn. com. on curriculum and teaching methods, 1928-31); fellow Am. Inst. Chemists; mem. Am. Council on Pharm. Edn. 1932-46. Am. Pharm. Assn., Fla. State Pharm. Assn. (hon.); Ala. Anthropol. Soc. (hon.), Am. Chem. Soc. (former dir. 4th dist.; former chmn. Fla. sect., also Lexington (Ky.) sect.; mem., com. reconsideration local Boundaries, 1935-37, Hertz Medalist, 1932), Ky. Acad. Sci. (corr.), Fla. Acad. Sci., Sigma Xi, Sigma Chi, Phi Kappa Phi (pres. Fla. chap. 1923-24), Gamma Sigma Epsilon (nat. pres. 1927-31), Sigma Tau, Alpha Epsilon Delta, Scabbard and Blade, Rho Chi, Herty medalist, 1942. Democrat. Baptist. Clubs: Antheneum (sec. 1924-25), Kiwanis (local pres. 1930), Propeller Club of U. S. Fellow Royal Soc. of Arts, London, Eng., 1949. Author of chem. and hist. pamphlets. Home: Gainesville, Fla. Died Feb. 15, 1949

LEIGHTON, Frank Thomson (lā'tŭn), naval officer; b. Tunkhannock, Pa., Sept. 2, 1885; s. James Gardner and Maria (Ackley) L.; student Phillips Andover, 1904-05; grad. U.S. Naval Acad., 1909, post-grad., 1914-15; M.S., Columbia Univ., 1916; M.Mech. Engring., Cornell, 1917; grad. U.S. Naval War Coll., 1934; m. Elizabeth Roby Ohler, Nov. 6, 1912; children—Elizabeth Roby, Marian Katharine (Mrs. Walter J. Whipple), Frank Ohler, James Gardner, David Trent. Midshipman, 1905; promoted through grades to rear adm., 1942; organized and comd. Mine Sweeping Squadron, 5th Naval Dist., 1917-18, exec. U.S.S. Savannah, 1918-19, U.S.S. Cleveland, 1919; commd. Claxton, 1919-20; asst. insp. naval machinery, N.Y. Shipbuilding Corp., Camden, N.J., 1920-23; radio material officer, 12th Naval Dist. and Trans-Pacific Circuit, 1926-29; exec. officer, Marine Engring. Dept., U.S. Naval Acad., 1931-33; comdr. Destroyer Div. 5, 1934-36; in Office Chief Naval Operations, Washington, D.C., 1936-38, 1940-42; comdr. U.S.S. Louisville, 1938-40; in Hdqrs. Comdr. in Chief, 1942; comdt. 8th Naval Dist. (Hdqrs. New Orleans) April 1942-Mar. 1943. Address: Jamestown, R.I. Died Nov. 21, 1943.

LEJEUNE, John Archer (lĕ-jŭn'), officer, U.S. M.C.; b. Pointe Coupée Parish, La., Jan. 10, 1867; s. Ovide and Laura Archer (Turpin) L.; La. State U., 1881-84; grad. U.S. Naval Acad., 1888, Army War Coll., 1910; m. Ellie Harrison Murdaugh, Oct. 23, 1895; children—Mrs. James B. Glennon, Laura T., Eugenia D. At sea as naval cadet 2 yrs.; shipwrecked on U.S.S. Vandalia, in hurricane at Apia, Samoa, Mar. 1889; commd. 2d lt. U.S. Marine Corps, July 1, 1890; promoted through grades to brig. gen., Aug. 29, 1916, maj. gen., July 1, 1918. In command marines on board Cincinnati, Spanish-Am. War, 1898; comd. battalion marines, Isthmus of Panama, 1903-04; comd. brigade, P.I., 1908-09; comd. brigade marines during capture of Vera Cruz, Mex., Apr. 1914, and of regt. marines as part of army of occupation of that city, Apr.-Dec. 1914; asst. to commandant Marine Corps, Washington, 1915-17; apptd. comdr. Marine Barracks, Quantico, Va., Sept. 27, 1917; arrived at Brest, France, June 8, 1918; duty with 35th Div., in Wesserling, Alsace sector, Vosges Mts., June 19-July 4, 1918: comd. 64th Brig., 32d Div., then in Suarce sector on Swiss border, July 5-25, 1918, 4th Brig. (marine), July 25-28, 1918, 2d Div. A.E.F., July 28, 1918-Aug. 8, 1919; participated in occupation of Marbache sector (near Metz), battles of St. Mihiel, Blanc Mont Ridge (Champagne offensive), Meuse-Argonne, march to the Rhine, Nov. 17-Dec. 13, 1918, and occupation of Coblenz bridgehead, Dec. 13, 1918-July 15, 1919; returned to U.S. in comd. 2d Div., Aug. 1919; comd. Marine Barracks, Quantico, Va., Oct. 23, 1919-June 30, 1920; maj. gen. in command Marine Corps, July 1, 1920-Mar. 5, 1929; retired; supt. Va. Mil. Inst., Lexington, 1929-37, supt. emeritus since 1937. Mem. Marine Corps Assn., 2d Div. Assn. Episcopalian. Address 540 Pembroke Av., Norfolk, Va. Died Nov. 20, 1942; buried in Arlington National Cemetery.

LELAND, Cyrus Austin, public utilities; b. El Dorado, Kan., June 16, 1887; s. Cyrus Austin and Nellie A. (Thompson) L.; B.S. in E.E., Kan. U., 1910; m. Erana Kessler, May 10, 1917; children—Cyrus Austin, III, Christine Kessler. Apprentice engineer Allis-Chalmers Co., Cincinnati, O., 1910-11; electrician and power plant foreman United Portland Cement Co., Independence, Kan., 1911-12; insp., later draftsman, estimator Kansas City (Mo.) Terminal Ry. Co., 1912-13; supt. Atchison (Kan.) Ry., Light & Power Co., 1913-17, mgr., 1920-23; constrn. engr. Kan. Power & Light Co., Topeka, 1923-25, pres., 1931-33; v.p. and gen. mgr. United Light & Power Co. of Kan., 1926-27; v.p. and gen. mgr. Des Moines (Ia.) Electric Light Co. and Ia. Power & Light Co., 1927-33; pres. Iowa Power & Light Co. since 1933; dir. United Light and Rys. Co. Served as capt. 64th Artillery, A.E.F., 1917-19. Dir. Des Moines Chamber of Commerce. Mem. Am. Inst. Elec. Engrs., Beta Theta Pi. Clubs: Des Moines, Wakonda (Des Moines, Ia.). Home: 13 W. 34th St. Office: 312 Sixth Av., Des Moines 3, Ia. Died June 10, 1949.

LELAND, George Adams, Jr. (lē'lănd), surgeon; b. Boston, Mass., May 19, 1886; s. George Adams and Alice Pierce (Higgins) L.; A.B., Harvard, 1907, M.D., 1911; m. Letitia G. Brookins, May 6, 1916; 1 dau., Letitia Adams. Asso. in surgery, Med. School Harvard U.; visiting surgeon, Mass. Gen. Hosp.; surgeon Collis P. Huntington Memorial and Palmer Memorial Hosps.; cons. surgeon Mass. Charitable Eye and Ear Infirmary, Addison Gilbert Hospital (Gloucester, Mass.); consultant N.H. Memorial Hospital (Concord). First lt., Med. R.C., assigned to Base Hosp. No. 6, July 1917; promoted to capt., Sept. 1918, detailed to Base Hosp. No. 220, as comdg. officer; hon. disch., Apr. 1919. Officier d'Academie of Pub. Instrn. and Fine Arts (France). Fellow Am. Surg. Assn., Am. Coll. Surgeons; mem. A.M.A., Am. Bd. of Surgery, New England Surg. Soc., New England Obstet. and Gynecol. Soc., New England Roentgen Ray Soc., Boston Surg. Soc., Boston Orthopedic Club. Republican. Episcopalian. Clubs: Harvard (Boston); Harvard (New York); Country (Brookline). Home: 191 Buckminster Rd. Office: 1101 Beacon St., Brookline, Boston, Mass. Died Sep. 24, 1943.

LEMON, Allan Clark, prof. ednl. psychology; b. Akron, Ia., Jan. 23, 1889; s. Eustis and Catherine (Emmett) L.; A.B., Morningside Coll., Sioux City, 1913; A.M., U. of Ia., 1921, Ph.D., 1926; m. Frankie Irene Crouch, Aug. 6, 1914; children—Emmett Dean, Lois Marian, Ralph Burton. Prin. high sch., Iowa Falls, Ia., 1913-14; supt. of schs., Culbertson, Mont., 1914-17; prof. history, Montana Wesleyan Coll., 1917-19, dean and prof. edn., 1919-24, acting pres., 1919-20; dean and prof. edn., Intermountain Union Coll., Helena, Mont., 1924-26, acting pres., 1924-25; dean and prof. psychology, Coll. of Puget Sound, 1926-31; prof. ednl. psychology, U. of Ida., since 1931. Mem. N.E.A., Mental Hygiene Assn., Nat. Vocational Guidance Assn., Phi Delta Kappa (Ia.), Pi Kappa Delta, Kappa Delta Pi, T.K.E., Kiwanis. Mason. Methodist. Author: Guidance and Placement of Freshmen, 1926; Workbook in Educational Psychology, 1941; Lessons in Mental Hygiene, 1943; Types of Problem Children, 1946. Contributor on ednl. and psychol. subjects. Mem. advisory bd. Yenching U., Peiping, China. Home: 1102 E. 6th St., Moscow, Idaho. Died Mar. 13. 1948.

LEMON, Frank Kyle, lawyer; b. Farmer City, Ill., Mar. 6, 1875; s. Richard A. and Opha Ann (Kyle) L.; LL.B., Ill. Wesleyan U., Bloomington, 1896; m. Ruthelle Keys, Oct. 12, 1910. Began practice at Clinton, 1896; mem. Moore, Warner & Lemon until 1901, Lemon & Lemon, 1902-12, Lemon & Jordan, 1931-36; practicing alone since 1936; apptd. U.S. attorney, Southern District of Illinois, 1931. Trustee Clinton Public Library. Member American and Illinois State bar assns., Phi Delta Theta. Republican. Methodist. K.P. Clubs: Rotary, Country (Clinton); Union League (Chicago). Home: 315 S. Elm St. Office: 114 Warner Court, Clinton, Ill. Died Dec. 29, 1946.

LENIHAN, Michael Joseph (lĕn'ĭ-hăn), army officer; b. Hopkinton, Mass., May 2, 1865; s. James and Catherine (Granger) L.; grad. U.S. Mil. Acad., 1887, Inf. and Cav. Sch., 1891, Army War Coll., 1917, Naval War Coll., 1921; LL.D., Holy Cross Coll., Mass., 1925; m. Mathilde O'Toole, 1891 (died Aug. 29, 1934); children—Eleanora (Mrs. Douglass Taft Greene), Catherine (Mrs. Paul James Halloran); m. 2d, Mina Ward, 1938. Commd. add. 2d lt. 25th Inf., June 12, 1887; promoted through grades to colonel, May 15, 1917; brigadier general National Army, Aug. 5, 1917; brig. gen. regular army, Oct. 11, 1925. Prof. mil. science and tactics, Seton Hall Coll., South Orange, N.J., 1893-97; in Cuba, 1899, Philippines, 1899-1902; mem. Gen. Staff Corps, 1906-10; in Hawaii, 1913-16; at Army War Coll., 1916-17; comdr. 83d Inf. Brig., Aug. 1917; comdr. 153d Inf. Brig., Nov. 1918; in France, Oct. 1917-Apr. 1919; Army instructor, Naval War Coll., 1921-24; commanded 3d Division, 1928-29; retired May 2, 1929. Decorated Comdr. Legion of Honor and Croix de Guerre with 3 palms (French); Order of the Purple Heart with Oak Leaf Cluster. Home: Hopkinton, Mass. Died 1944.

LENNOX, Patrick Joseph, univ. prof.; b. Nurney, Kildare, Ireland, Aug. 12, 1862; s. Thomas and Mary (O'Brien) L.; student Rockwell Coll. (Cashel), St. Patrick's Coll. (Carlow), University Coll. (Dublin); B.A., with honors, Royal U. of Ireland, 1886; ad eundem, Nat. U. of Ireland, 1909; Litt.D., Duquesne U., 1912; m. Lillian Clare Pakenham, Oct. 1, 1894 (died Sept. 7, 1927). Was first class exhibitioner Intermediate Edn. Bd. for Ireland, 1879, 80; supervisor exams. for same, 1906, 07; triple medalist St. Patrick's Coll., 1883; Stewart scholar in arts, Royal U. of Ireland, 1885-87; prof. Latin and French, University Coll., 1886-89; secretarial, sociol., and research work, 1889-1904; prof. English, Latin, and French, University Coll., Dublin, also prof. English and history, University Coll., Blackrock, 1904-07; came to U.S., 1907, naturalized citizen, 1917; prof. English lang. and lit., Catholic U., 1907-39; also head Dept. English, mem. and sec. Academic Senate; retired 1939, at which time he was decorated by His Holiness the Pope with the Bene Merenti medal "for long, loyal, and faithful service." Official delegate U.S. to Internat. Congress Chambers of Commerce, London, 1910; spl. agt. to investigate trade conditions abroad for Dept. of Commerce and Labor, 1910; rep. of U.S. at Internat. Congress on Alcoholism, The Hague, 1911; del. Catholic U. of America to Internat. Conf. of Profs. of English, New York, 1923; spl. leader of Irish Culture Tour under auspices of Am. Inst. of Ednl. Travel, 1938. Mem. Modern Lang. Assn. America, Am. Irish Hist. Soc. (New York), A.A.A.S., Soc. Friendly Sons of St. Patrick (Washington, D.C.). Catholic. Author: The Victorian Era in Ireland, 1887; Early Printing in Ireland, 1909; Women Writers of English in the Fifteenth Century, 1911; Addison and the Modern Essay, 1912; History of Panama, 1915. Edited and re-wrote Lessons in English Literature, 1913; joint editor of The Glories of Ireland, 1914. On editorial staff of Washington Post, 1909-29. Contributor to encyclopedias, mags. and revs. Home: 1820 G St. N.W., Washington 6, D.C. Died Dec. 15, 1943.

LENROOT, Irvine Luther (lĕn'root), judge; b. Superior, Wis., Jan. 31, 1869; s. Lars and Frederika

(Larson) L.; LL.D., George Washington, Temple, Ohio Northern univs.; stenographer in law office, 1889, court reporter, 1893; admitted to bar, 1897; m. Clara Clough, Jan. 22, 1890 (dec.); children—Katharine, Dorothy (Mrs. Robert Bromberg, dec.); m. 2d, Eleonore von Eltz, Feb. 9, 1943. Mem. Wis. Ho. of Reps., 1901, 03, 05 (speaker 1903, 05); mem. 61st to 65th Congresses (1909-18), 11th Wis. Dist. (resigned, 1918); elected mem. U.S. Senate, Apr. 2, 1918, for term ending Mar. 3, 1921, to fill vacancy occasioned by death of Paul O. Husting; reëlected for term, 1921-27; initiated Senate proposal for St. Lawrence Waterway, 1919; helped lead Senate "Reservationist" fight for acceptance of League of Nations Covenant with reservations, chiefly as to Article X; led Senate fight for U.S. adherence to World Court; declined nomination for vice pres. at Chicago Rep. Conv., 1920, which action cost him the presidency to which he would have succeeded on death of President Harding; chmn. Senate Com. on Pub. Lands, Dec. 1923-March 1924 which conducted "Teapot Dome" investigation leading to cancellation of leases of naval oil reserves, resignation of Sec. of Interior Fall; apptd. by President Coolidge Am. mem. Anglo-Am. Conciliation Commn., 1927-35; practiced law, Washington, D.C., 1927-29; apptd. judge U.S. Court of Customs and Patent Appeals, 1929. Resigned Apr. 30, 1944; dedicated war monument to service men and women, Town of Lenroot, Sawyer County, Wis., July 4, 1946. Republican. Conglist. Home: 2230 California St. N.W., Washington, D.C.; (summer) Brule, Wis. Died Jan. 26, 1949; buried in Greenwood Cemetery, Superior, Wis.

LENT, Frederick, clergyman, coll. pres.; b. Freeport, N.S., June 10, 1872; s. Shippy and Euphemia (Moore) L.; brought to U.S., 1875; B.A., Brown, 1900, M.A., 1901; B.D., Newton Theol. Instn., 1900; Ph.D., Yale, 1906; D.D. Brown, 1922; LL.D., Colgate, 1922; m. Estelle Bolles, 1896. Ordained Bapt. ministry, 1895; pastor Calvary Ch., Salem, Mass., 1896-98, Oaklawn, R.I., 1898-1901, 1st Ch., New Haven, Conn., 1903-18; instr. Bibl. lit., Brown U., 1900-01; Yale, 1903-07, 1909-10; pres. Elmira Coll., 1918-35; pres. Internat. Bapt. Sem., E. Orange, N.J., 1935-41. Trustee Bapt. Ministers' Home. Soc., 1912-41; trustee Am. Bapt. Home Mission Soc., 1912-35. Mem. Am. Oriental Soc., Phi Beta Kappa, Chi Phi. Republican. Club: Rotary. Wrote: The Life of Simon Stylites, 1914; Three Minute Talks, 1933. Home: Brockton, Mass. Died Dec. 30, 1942.

LENYGON, Francis Henry (lĕn'ĭ-gŏn), interior decorator; b. Lincoln, Eng., May 11, 1877; s. James and Elizabeth (Hawkins) L.; ed. London Polytechnic and London City and Guild Inst.; m. Jeannette Becker, Oct. 6, 1926. Founded, 1904, Lenygon & Co., London, holders of royal warrant as decorators the English Court; absorbed Morant & Co., 1912, firm becoming Lenygon & Morant, Ltd.; came to New York, 1910; now pres. Lenygon & Morant, Inc. (N.Y.); dir. Lenygon & Morant, Ltd. (London). Lecturer on English interior decoration and furniture, Met. Museum Art; lecturer in fine arts, New York U.; mem. Beaux Arts Inst., Design; hon. mem. bd. govs. Am. Inst. of Decorators; fellow Royal Soc. Arts, England, North British Acad. Episcopalian. Clubs: Metropolitan (New York); Nassau Country (L.I.); Devonshire (London). Author: Decoration and Furniture of English Mansions, 1910; Decoration in England, 1914; Furniture in England, 1914; also articles in mags. Recognized as an authority on English interior decoration. Home: 1016 Madison Av., New York, N.Y. Died June 12, 1943.

LEONARD, Adna Wright (lĕn'ărd), bishop; b. Cincinnati, O., Nov. 2, 1874; s. Adna Bradway and Caroline Amelia (Kaiser) L.; A.B., New York U., 1899; B.D., Drew Theol. Sem., 1901; Am. Sch. Archæology, Rome, 1901-03; D.D., Ohio Northern, 1909; LL.D., Coll. of Puget Sound, 1916, Univ. of Southern Calif., 1916, Syracuse U., 1930, Allegheny Coll., 1932, Am. U., 1941, S.T.D., Syracuse U., 1926; L.H.D., W.Va. Wesleyan College, 1938; m. Mary Luella Day, Oct. 9, 1901; children—Adna Wright, Phyllis Day. Ordained M.E. ministry, 1899; pastor Green Village, N.J., 1898, First Church, San Juan, P.R., 1900, Am. M.E. Ch., Rome, 1901-03 (also teacher in Meth. Theol. Sch.), Grace Ch., Piqua, O., 1903-05, Central Ch., Springfield, 1905-08, Walnut Hills Ch., Cincinnati, 1908-09, 1st Ch., Seattle, Wash., 1910-16; del. Gen. Conf. M.E. Ch., 1916; elected bishop M.E. Ch., May 1916. Pres. Gen. Bd. of Edn. of Meth Ch.; chmn. bd. trustees Am. U.; chmn. Meth. Commn. on Chaplains, Meth. Commn. on Camp Activities, Gen. Commn. on Army and Navy Chaplains. Mem. Am. Polit. Science Assn., Phi Beta Kappa, Psi Upsilon (Delta Chapter). Mason (33°, K.C.C.H., Shriner). Author: The Shepherd King; The Roman Catholic Church at the Fountain Head; Evangelism in the Remaking of the World; Hearthstone League Book of Remembrance; Ancient Fires on Modern Altars; Decisive Days in Social and Religious Progress. Home: 2480 16th St. Address: 100 Maryland Av. N.E., Washington, D.C. Killed in airplane accident in Iceland while on tour of Army camps, May 3, 1943.

LEONARD, Henry, lawyer; b. Washington, D.C., July 31, 1876; s. Charles Henry and Willa (Kain) L.; LL.B., Columbian U., 1891, LL.M., 1898; m. Ellen Warder, July 27, 1914. Practiced law, Washington, D.C., and in Colo., 1911-17 and since 1921; dir. and mem. discount com. Nat. Metropolitan Bank of Washington. Mem. Rep. Nat. Com., Rep. Post-War Adv. Council. Rep. State Com. for Colo. 2d lt. Marines, 1898; retired 1911, re-entered 1917, went on retired list again 1921; commd. lt. col., 1942; served in China, Panama, Spanish-Am. War, Boxer Rebellion, World War. Decorated Order of the Dragon (China); Purple Heart; twice promoted for "eminent and conspicuous conduct in battle." Mem. Am. and D.C. bar assns. Episcopalian. Clubs: Metropolitan (Washington); El Paso, Cheyenne Mountain Country (Colorado Springs); N.Y. Yacht, Potomac Hounds. Home: Elkhorn Ranch, Colo. Springs, Colo.; and 3038 N St. N.W., Washington D.C. Office: Investment Bldg., Washington, D.C. Died May 6, 1945

LEONARD, William Ellery, univ. prof.; b. Plainfield, N.J., Jan. 25, 1876; s. Rev. William James and Martha (Whitcomb) L.; A.B., Boston U., 1898; A.M., Harvard, 1899; fellow Boston U. in philology and lit. and student U. of Göttingen, 1900-01; U. of Bonn, 1901-02; fellow Columbia, 1902-03, Ph.D., 1904; m. Charlotte Freeman, June 23, 1909 (she died May 6, 1911); m. 2d, Charlotte Charlton, 1914 (divorced), remarried 1940. Instructor Latin, Boston University, 1898; principal high school, Plainville, Mass., 1899; instr. German, high sch., Lynn, Mass., 1904; asso. (philol.) editor, Lippincott's English Dictionary, 1904-06; instr. English, 1906-09, asst. prof., 1909-21, asso. prof., 1921-26, prof. since 1926, U. of Wis.; visiting prof. New York U., 1916-17. Mem. Mod. Lang. Assn., Nat. Inst. Arts and Letters, Wis. Acad. Letters, Arts and Sciences, Wis. Archæol. Soc., Beta Theta Pi, Phi Beta Kappa. Club: University. Author: Byron and Byronism in America, 1905; Sonnets and Poems, 1906; The Poet of Galilee, 1909; The Vaunt of Man and Other Poems, 1912; Glory of the morning (play), 1912; Æsop and Hyssop, 1913; Socrates, 1915; Poems, 1914-16; The Lynching Bee and Other Poems, 1920; Red Bird (4-act drama of the Winnebago War), 1923; Tutankhamen and After, 1924; Two Lives, 1925; The Locomotive God (autobiography), 1927; A Son of Earth (collected verse), 1928; This Midland City (verse, limited edition), 1930; Lucretius, the Man, the Poet, the Times, 1941. Translator The Fragments of Empedocles (verse), 1908; The Vale of Content (from Sudermann, in Chief Contemporary Dramatists), 1914; Lucretius (verse), 1916, reprinted in Everyman's Library, 1921; Belgium and Germany (from the Dutch), 1916; Beowulf (rhymed verse), 1923; Galgamesh, 1934. Editor: Parkman's Oregon Trail, 1910; Lucretius, the Latin Text with Notes (with Stanley B. Smith), 1942. Wrote (monographs) Bryant and the Minor Poets (chapter in Cambridge History of Am. Lit.); Beowulf and the Nibelungen Couplet, 1918; The Scansion of Middle English Alliterative Verse, 1920; La metrica del Cid (old Spanish epic versification), 1928-29; also the Recovery of the Metre of the Cid (in P.M.L.A. June 1931). Collaborator with L.A. Coerne on several cycles of songs. Contbr. to mags., tech. jours and newspapers. Address: 433 N. Murray St., Madison, Wis. Died May 2, 1944.

LEONARD, William Henry, business exec.; b. New York, 1873; ed. St. Mark's Sch., Southboro, Mass., Columbia Univ. Founder of first chlorination mill, Cripple Creek, Colo., during gold rush of 1890; cattle raiser, 1902-06; organized Denver Rock Drill Mfg Co., 1906, merged with Gardner-Governor Co., of Quincy, Ill., 1927, to form Gardner-Denver Co., dir. and chmn. bd. until 1947. Dir. U.S. National Bank, Denver, Denver Union Stockyards, Argo Oil Co., Midwest Oil Co., Saltmount Oil Co., Strayton Oil Co., Petroleum Assn. of Am. Served as capt. 1st Colo. Cavalry and in 115th U.S. Engrs., World War I. Mem. former Gov. Vivian's Indsl. Research Council of Colo., Denver mayor's bond issue adv. com., State of Colo. Rep. Finance Com., State of Colo. Selective Service Bd., World War II; head Colo. Council of Defense during World War II. Trustee Denver Univ., Colo. Sch. of Mines, Colo. Mus. Natural History, Fountain Valley Sch. of Colorado Springs. Mem. exec. com. Denver C. of C. Former pres. Denver Water Bd. Del. to Rep. Nat. Conv., 1944. Clubs: Colorado Springs Cooking (a founder), El Paso (Colorado Springs); Denver Country; Union (New York). Home: 100 Humbolt St., Denver 3. Office: 1727 E. 39th Av., Denver. Died June 29, 1947; buried in Chapel of the Will Rogers Memorial on Cheyenne Mountain, nr. Colorado Springs, Colo.

LEOPOLD, Aldo (lē'ō-pōld), forester, game manager; b. Burlington, Ia., Jan. 11, 1886; s. Carl and Clara (Starker) L.; B.Sc., Yale, 1908, M.F., 1909; m. Estella Bergere, Oct. 9, 1914; children—Aldo Starker, Lune Bergere, Adelina, Carl Aldo, Estella. Began career as forest asst., U.S. Forest Service, 1909; dep. forest supervisor, Carson Nat. Forest, 1910-11, supervisor, 1912-14, various work, 1915-16, asst. dist. forester in charge operations, 1917-24; asso. dir. Forest Products Lab., 1925-27; game survey, Sporting Arms and Ammunition Mfrs. Inst., 1928-31; cons. forester in pvt. practice, 1932; prof. of wild life management, U. of Wis., since 1933. Awarded medal by Permanent Wild Life Protection Fund, medal by Outdoor Life. Apptd. by President Roosevelt, mem. Spl. Com. on Wild Life Restoration, 1934; member Wisconsin Conservation Commission. Fellow Soc. Am. Foresters; mem. Am. Ornithologists Union, Soc. Am. Mammalogists, Cooper Ornithol. Club, Wilson Ornithol. Club, Boone and Crockett Club, Ecol. Soc. of America (pres. 1947), Am. Wildlife Soc. (pres. 1939), Sigma Xi, Phi Kappa Phi. Mem. orgn. com. The Wilderness Soc. (council mem. since 1935, vice pres. since 1945). Club: University. Author: Game Survey of the North Central States, 1931; Game Management, 1933. Contbr. to forestry, biol. and outdoor mags. Home: 2222 Van Hise Av. Office: 424 University Farm Place, Madison, Wis. Died Apr. 21, 1948.

LEOVY, Victor, lawyer; b. New Orleans, La., Mar. 9, 1867; s. Henry Jefferson and Elizabeth Adair (Monroe) L.; A.B., Davidson Coll., 1884; LL.B., Tulane U., 1888; m. Alice Galleher Sessums, May 6, 1911 (died 1926); 1 dau., Barbara Castleman (Mrs. John Dabney Miller, Jr.). Admitted to La. bar, 1888; became mem. Leovy, Blair & Leovy; now mem. Denegre, Leovy & Chaffe. Mem. Maritime Law Assn. of U.S., La. Bar Assn., Am. Bar Assn., Am. Judicature Soc., Sigma Alpha Epsilon, Order of Coif. Democrat. Presbyterian. Clubs: Boston Round Table (past pres.), Paul Morphy Chess. Home: 37 Pelham Drive, Metairie, La. Office: 724 Whitney Bldg., New Orleans. Died 1942.*

LERCH, Archer Lynn (lĕrch), army officer, Judge Advocate General's Dept.; b. Sumner, Neb., Jan. 12, 1894; s. Herman H. and Maud R. (Stevens) L.; A.B., U. of Calif., 1917; LL.B., George Washington U., 1942; grad. Infantry Sch., Fort Benning, Ga., 1922, Command and General Staff Sch., Fort Leavenworth, 1937; orders Army War Coll., revoked account declaration of emergency 1941; m. Florence M. Wentworth, Feb. 5, 1918; children—Mrs. D. W. Rush, Capt. Archer Lynn. Commissioned 2d lt. Infantry, Apr. 28, 1917, Officers Reserve Corps, U.S. Army, Oct. 25, 1917; promoted through grades to brig. gen. (temp.), December 3, 1942; major gen. (temp.), May 31, 1944; 11th Division Sch. Det., A.E.F., World War I; instructor Arkansas National Guard, 1922-24; 31st Infantry, Manila, P.I., 1924-26; assistant prof. Mil. Science tactics and adjutant, U. of Calif., Berkeley, 1926-31; asst. staff judge advocate, Honolulu, T.H., 1931-33; legal advisor to Gen. B. H. Wells, Fort Shafter, T.H., 1933-34; asst. dep. administrator, NRA, Territory Hawaii, 1934-35; also legal advisor PWA, Territory Hawaii, 1933-35; 5th Inf., Ft. Williams, Me., 1935-36; asst. prof. mil. science and tactics, U. of Fla., 1937-38; exec. officer, Judge Advocate General's Dept., Washington, 1939-40; deputy provost marshal gen., Washington, 1941-42; commandant, P.M.G. School Center, Fort Oglethorpe, Ga., and comdg. officer P.M.G. Training Center, Ft. Custer, Mich., June-Dec. 1942; asst. provost marshal gen. (brig. gen.) Dec. 1942, maj. gen., provost-marshal gen., May 31, 1944; mil. gov. of Korea since Jan. 1946. Prosecuted Grover Cleveland Bergdoll before Army court-martial, 1939; admitted to practice before bars of Fla., Korea and Supreme Court of U.S. Mem. Federal, Am. bar assns. and Nat. Bar Assn. of Korea. Mem. Mil. Order World Wars (D.C. chapt.), Army and Navy Union, Am. Legion (Geo. Washington Post); hon. mem. Internat. Assn. of Chiefs of Police, bd. of dirs. The Judge Adv. Gen. Assn. Club: Army and Navy (Washington, D.C.). Decorations: Distinguished Service Medal; Legion of Merit; Honorary Member French Foreign Legion. Mason. Methodist. Home: 6315 Broad Branch Rd., Chevy Chase, Md. Address: Munitions Bldg., Washington 25, D.C. Died Sept. 11, 1947.

LEROY, Howard Sanderson, lawyer; b. Olean, N. Y., July 18, 1891; s. Charles Hayden and Ida (Sanderson) LeR.; A.B., U. of Rochester (N.Y.), 1914; LL.B., Harvard, 1918; m. Emilia Schoenemann Redding, Feb. 28, 1920. Admitted to N.Y. bar, 1919, and practiced in N.Y. City, 1920-21; admitted to D.C. bar, 1922, and since practiced in Washington, partner Le Fevre & LeRoy, 1925-35, Culbertson & LeRoy, 1935-43; partner, Culbertson, LeRoy and Denslow, 1943-45; LeRoy & Denslow since 1945; admitted to Md. bar, 1942; with U.S. Dept. of State, as law clerk and asst. solicitor, 1918-20; asso. of former Secretary of State Robert Lansing in handling Chinese interests at Disarmament Conf., in organizing Millspaugh Financial Mission to Persia, and in preparation Chilean case for Tacna-Arica arbitration, 1921-25; Am. sec. Am.-British Arbitration Tribunal, 1925; legal adviser Am. delegation and mem. gen. secretariat of Internat. Radio-Telegraph Conf., Washington, 1927. Prof. of radio and aeronautical law at Nat. U. Law School. Del. to 2d Internt. Conf. on Comparative Law, The Hague, 1937; Am. sec. Internat. Com. on Radio (treas. and mem. exec. council); rep. Am. Bar Assn. on advisory com. to Am. Sect., Internat. Technical Committee of Aerial Legal Experts; counsel, Spanish Govt., 1939-45; Finnish Govt. since 1942; Argentine Govt.; Am. Chambers of Commerce of Brazil; mem. and sec. Registrants Advisory Bd., Dist. of Columbia, 1940-45; mem. Am. Arbitration Assn. committee for implementation of arbitrary standards approved by 7th International Conference of Am. States, 1943. Mem. national advisory council, American Peace Society, 1939 (exec. com. since 1941); del. to 1st Conf., Inter-Am. Bar Assn., Havana, 1941 (vice-treas. gen.; chmn. standing com. on communications, 1942-45), 3d Conf. Mexico City, 1944. Sec. Gen. United Nations League of Lawyers; mem. Adv. Com. American Section C.I.T.E.J.A., 1946. Member Am. Bar Assn. (chmn. com. on teaching of internat. and comparative law, 1936-37; chmn. com. on internat. aspects aeronautics and telecommunications, 1938-40; mem. council, sect. on internat. and comparative law, 1940-43); American Law Institute, Bar Association of D.C. (mem. organizing com. and first council Administrative Law Sect.), Federal Communications Bar Association, American Society Internat. Law (treas.), Friends of the Law Library of Congress (treas., mem. exec. council), mem. Past War Com., 1945-46, Rotary Internat. (chmn. Internat. Affairs, 1946-47; governor 180th Dist., 1947-48), United Nations League of Lawyers (secretary-gen. 1946-47), Alpha Delta Phi, Phi Beta Kappa, Sigma Delta Kappa (hon., Nat. Intercollegiate Flying Club (hon.). Presbyn. (National Presbyn. Ch.; v.p. bd. trustees). Clubs: Rotary (pres. 1944-45), Chevy Chase, Cosmos, Torch, Harvard (Washington, D.C.) (treas.). Author: Air Law, Outline and Guide to Law of Radio and Aeronautics, 1935, 1936; Aeronautical and Radio Law (notes and papers), 1939. Contbr. to legal periodicals. Home: Rose Hill Farm, Cooksville, Howard County, Md. Office: Washington Bldg., Washington, D.C. Died July 30, 1949. Buried Rock Creek Cemetery, Washington.

LEROY, Louis, physician; b. Chelsea, Mass., Sept. 15, 1874; s. Charles L. A. and Lizzie F. (Somerby) L.; prep. edn., Newark (N.J.) High Sch.; A.B., U. of Nashville, Tenn., 1900; M.D., Medico-Chirurgical Coll., Phila., 1896; m. Joe Carr, Jan. 11, 1922; children—Charles Louis, Joe Carr. Asst. in pathology, Medico-Chirurg. Coll., 1896; prof. pathology and bacteriology, Harvey Med. Coll. and Ill. Med. Coll., Chicago, 1899-1900; prof. pathology and bacteriology, Vanderbilt U., 1899-1905; state bacteriologist and smallpox expert to State of Tenn. since 1897; pathologist Nashville City and St. Thomas hosps., Nashville, 1896-1904; prof. practice of medicine, Coll. Physicians and Surgeons, Memphis, since 1905; prof. theory and practice of medicine, U. of Tenn., since 1911; staff physician City and Baptist Memorial hosps.; consultant med. staff, St. Joseph Hosp.; chief of staff Memphis Gen. Hosp., 1937; ex-v.p. Tenn. State Bd. of Health. Director rescue div. Am. Red Cross, from Cairo to Rosedale, in Mississippi River flood, 1937; mem. U.S. Coast Guard Auxiliary since 1940; now boatswain's mate 1st cl., U.S. Coast Guard Temporary Reserve. Medical mem. U.S. Local Bd., Memphis, for period of war; med. mem. Memphis and Shelby County Tuberculosis Commn., 1918-28. Certificated Am. Bd. Internal Medicine, 1937. Fellow Am. Coll. Physicians, 1920. Member A.M.A., Am. Congress Tuberculosis, Tenn. State Med. Soc.; fellow Am. Coll. Physicians. Asso. editor Examiner and Practitioner, New York. Author: Essentials of Histology, 1900; Smallpox Diagnosis, Treatment, etc., 1901; Pulmonary Tuberculosis. Home: 1168 Poplar Av. Office: 1210 Madison Av., Memphis, Tenn.
Died May 9, 1944.

LESLIE, Annie Louise ("Nancy Brown"), column editor; b. Perry, Me., Dec. 11, 1870; d. Levi Prescott and Annie Robinson (Lincoln) Brown; grad. high sch., Middleboro, Mass., 1888, Mt. Holyoke (Mass.) Coll., 1892; m. James Edward Leslie, Sept. 19, 1904 (now dec.). Teacher, pub. sch., White River Junction, Vt., 1893-95, Rockville, Conn., 1895-97, Mt. Clemens, Mich., 1897-1904; dramatic editor, Pittsburgh Dispatch, 1917-18; editor of "Experience" column and editorial writer, Detroit News, since 1918, also of books "Experience," "Dear Nancy," "Column Folks," "Nancy's Family," "Acres of Friends," "Column House," "Come Again," "Home Edition." Retired from active service with The News, Feb. 1, 1942. A 98-foot stone carillon tower, dedicated to Peace, erected in her honor by Experience Column contributors, on Belle Isle, Detroit park, 1940. Presented with Alumnae medal of honor for distinguished service at Mt. Holyoke College, 1942. Protestant. Home: 17400 Wisconsin Av., Detroit 21. Died Oct. 7, 1948; buried Oakview Cemetery, Royal Oak, Mich.

LESPINASSE, Victor Darwin (lĕs'pĭ-năs), surgeon; b. Aurora, Ill., Dec. 2, 1878; s. Raymond and Clara Belle (Bradley) L.; M.D., Northwestern U. Med. Sch., 1901; m. Anna L. King, June 30, 1909; children—Victoire D., Victor King. Intern Cook County Hosp., 1901-03; asso. prof. genito-urinary surgery, Northwestern U. Med. Sch.; urologist Wesley Memorial Hosp. Fellow Am. Coll. Surgeons; mem. Am. Urol. Assn., Chicago Urol. Soc. (ex-pres.), Am., Ill. State and Chicago med. socs., Englewood Med. Soc. (ex-pres.), Alpha Kappa Kappa. Awarded certificate of honor for method of blood vessel anastomosis, A.M.A., 1910; silver medal, New York meeting A.M.A., 1917; diploma for original exptl. work on spermatogenesis and sterility, A.M.A., 1920. Home: 49 E. Elm St. Office: 7 W. Madison St., Chicago, Ill.
Died Dec. 16, 1946.

LETCHER, Marion, foreign service; b. Macon County, Ala., Sept. 4, 1872; s. Francis Marion and Claudia Caroline Clanton (Howard) L.; A.B., U. of Ala., 1894; m. Marilu Ingram, Nov. 7, 1901; children—Marion Louise (Mrs. John M. Woodburn), Adele Fournier (Mrs. Donald G. Goddard), Margaret Billingslea (Mrs. Preston Watson). Pres. Douglasville (Ga.) Coll., 1900-01; supt. schs., Conyers, Ga., 1901-03; employed in Bur. of Edn., Washington, 1903-09; consul at Acapulco, Mex., 1909-11, Chihuahua, 1911-16; acting foreign trade adviser, Dept. of State, Washington, June 10, 1916; consul gen., Apr. 8, 1918; consul gen. at Christiania (now Oslo), Norway, 1918-20, at Copenhagen, Denmark, 1920-28, at Antwerp, Belgium, 1928-34; retired for disability; fgn. service officer, class II, 1924, fgn. service officer, class I, 1930. Was 1st lt. Co. A, 5th Vol. Inf., Spanish-Am. War, serving at Santiago and Baracoa, Cuba; comd. company, Sept. 5, 1898-May 3, 1899. Mem. D.C. Soc. S.A.R., Sigma Nu. Democrat. Clubs: University (Washington); Union (Rome). Address: 35 Via Ludovisi, Rome, Italy. Died July 24, 1948.

LETTS, Ira Lloyd, lawyer; b. Cortland County, N.Y., May 29, 1889; s. George Judson and Emma (Slater) L.; grad. high sch., Moravia, N.Y., 1906; student Cortland State Normal and Training Sch.; Ph.B., Brown U., 1913, M.A., 1914; LL.B., Columbia, 1917; married Madeline Houghton Greene, December 29, 1917; children—Barbara Letts Villard, Houghton (died in service, U.S. Marines, 1944), Eleanore. Began practice of law at Providence, Rhode Island, 1917; member of firm of Curtis, Matteson, Boss & Letts, 1922-27; director Tilden-Thurber Corp., Universal Optical Co., Inc., Clarke & Combs Co., Linden & Co., Panhandle Eastern Pipe Line Co., International Hydro-Electric System. Chmn. Rep. State Conv., R.I., 1922; apptd. asst. atty. gen. of U.S. by Pres. Coolidge, Mar. 1925, resigned Jan. 1927; apptd. U.S. dist. judge for the Dist. of R.I. by President Coolidge, June 1927, resigned and resumed law practice, 1935; mem. firm Letts & Quinn. Mem. Delta Kappa Epsilon. Conglist. Clubs: Hope, Turks Head, Agawam, Massasoit, Dunes. Home: Saunderstown, R.I. Address: 830 Hospital Trust Bldg., Providence, R.I. Died Nov. 24, 1947.

LEUBA, James Henry (lŭb'ȧ), psychologist; b. Neuchâtel, Switzerland, Apr. 9, 1868; s. Henri and Cecile (Sandoz) L.; B.Sc., Neuchâtel, 1887; came to U.S., 1887; Ph.D., Clark U., 1895; studied Leipzig, Halle, Heidelberg, Paris, 1897-98; m. Berthe A. Schopfer, Jan. 6, 1896; children—Clarence James, Gladys Aline. Prof. psychology, Bryn Mawr Coll., 1889-1933, emeritus since 1933. Fellow A.A.A.S. Author: The Psychological Origin and the Nature of Religion, 1909; A Psychological Study of Religion, 1912; The Beliefs in God and Immortality, 1916; The Psychology of Religious Mysticism, 1925; God or Man?—a Study of the Value of God to Man, 1933. Ready for publication, The Reformation of the Churches. Address: Yellow Springs, O. Died Dec. 8, 1946.

LEVERETT, Frank (lĕv'ĕr-ĕt), geologist; b. Denmark, Ia., Mar. 10, 1859; s. Ebenezer and Rowena (Houston) L.; B.Sc., Ia. Agrl. Coll., 1885; hon. Sc.D., U. of Mich., 1930; m. Frances E. Gibson, Dec. 22, 1887 (died July 10, 1892); m. 2d, Dorothy C. Park, Dec. 18, 1895. Teacher in pub. schs., 1878-79; taught natural sciences, Denmark Acad., 1880-83; entered U.S. Geol. Survey, May 1886, asst. geologist, 1890-1900, geologist, 1901-29; retired. Lecturer glacial geology, U. of Mich. Has specialized in glacial geology and water resources; glacial investigations in Europe, 1908. Fellow Geol. Soc. America, A.A.A.S., Geol. Soc. Washington; mem. Nat. Acad. Science, Am. Philos. Soc., Nat. Geog. Soc., Am. Forestry Assn., Wash., Ia., Mich. and Wis. academies of science, Sigma Xi and Phi Kappa Phi. Unitarian. Author: Water Resources of Illinois, 1896; Water Resources of Indiana and Ohio, 1897; The Illinois Glacial Lobe, 1899; Glacial Deposits of the Erie and Ohio Basins, 1901; Soils of Illinois, Report Ill. Bd. World's Fair Commrs.; Pleistocene Features and Deposits of the Chicago Area, Bull. Chicago Acad. Sciences; Flowing Wells and Municipal Water Supplies of the Southern Peninsula of Michigan, 1906; Water Supplies of the Eastern Portion of the Northern Peninsula of Michigan, 1906; Comparison of North American and European Glacial Formations, 1910; Surface Geology of Northern Peninsula of Michigan, 1911; Surface Geology of Southern Peninsula of Michigan, 1912; The Pleistocene of Indiana and Michigan and the History of the Great Lakes, 1915; Surface Formations and Agricultural Conditions of Northwestern Minnesota, 1915, Northeastern Minnesota, 1916, Southern Minnesota, 1918; Moraines and Shore Lines of the Lake Superior Region, 1929; Surface Geology of Northern Kentucky, 1929; Quaternary Geology of Minnesota and Parts of Adjacent States, 1932; Glacial Deposits in Pennsylvania, 1934; Pleistocene Beaches in the Huron, Erie and Western Ontario Basins, 1939; Stream Capture and Drainage Shiftings in the Upper Ohio Region, 1939. Home: Ann Arbor, Mich.
Died Nov. 15, 1943.

LEVERHULME, Viscount, gov. and dir. Lever Brothers and Unilever Limited; b. Mar. 25, 1888; s. 1st Viscount and Elizabeth Ellen Hulme; ed. Eton; Trinity Coll., Cambridge, M.A.; m. Marion Bryce Smith, 1912; 1 son, 2 daughters; m. 2d, Winifred Agnes Lee Morris, 1937. Past pres. London C. of C., Advt. Assn., Instn. Chem. Engrs., Royal Warrant Holders' Assn. and Soc. of Chemical Industry. Pres. 1935-38 Internat. Com. of Scientific Management. Knight of Justice Order of St. John of Jerusalem. Officer of the Legion of Honour; J.P., D.L. Author: Viscount Leverhulme, by his son, 1927. Address: Thornton Manor, Thornton Hough, Wirral, Cheshire, England. Died in Minneapolis, while on world tour, May 26, 1949; buried in Port Sunlight, England.

LEVERONI, Frank (lĕv-ĕr-ō'-nē), lawyer; b. Genoa, Italy, Sept. 10, 1879; s. Andrew and Katherine (Trebino) L.; brought to U.S., 1884; student Harvard U. Law Sch., 1899-1900; LL.B., cum laude, Boston U., 1903; m. Louise Fenochietti, Oct. 5, 1903; children—Beatrice, Laura, Claire, Vivian, Heloise Edna, Frank, John. Admitted to Mass. bar, 1903, later to practice in Supreme Court of U.S., and began practice at Boston; pub. administrator Suffolk County; spl. justice Boston Juvenile Court since 1906; counsel to royal consul general of Italy; trustee Home Savings Bank, Judge Baker Foundation, Infants' Hosp.; pres. Italian Cemetery Assn.; vice chmn. Mass. Child Labor Commn. Mem. Am. and Mass. State bar assns., Bar Assn. City of Boston. Knight Comdr. Order Crown of Italy. Catholic. Clubs: Harvard, Boston City. Home: 358 Arborway, Jamaica Plain, Mass. Office: 73 Tremont St., Boston. Died Aug. 1, 1948.

LEVIN, Isaac (lĕ-vēn'), physician; b. Sagor, Russia, Nov. 1, 1866; s. Salon and Etta (Brick) L.; M.D., Mil. Med. Acad., Petrograd, 1890; m. Sophie Bloch, Feb. 25, 1890; children—Ben Fenton, Charles Emmerson, Ralph Theodore. Came to U.S., 1891, naturalized citizen, 1901. Began practice, Petrograd, 1890; asso. in pathology and cancer research, Columbia, 1909-15; clin prof cancer research, New York U. since 1915; chief of cancer div. Montefiore Hosp., 1912-25; chief in radiology St. Bartholomew's Hosp., 1917-22; dir. N.Y. City Cancer Inst., 1923-30; consultant in radiology Lebanon Hosp. since 1915. Fellow A.A.A.S.; mem. A.M.A., Am. Physiol. Soc., Am. Assn. Pathologists and Bacteriologists, Soc. Exptl. Biology and Medicine, Am. Assn. Cancer Research, Am. Radium Soc., Radiological Soc. N. America, Am. Genetic Assn., Am. Med. Editors' and Authors' Assn., Harvey Soc., N.Y. Acad. Medicine, Alumni Assn. New York U. Editor Archives of Clinical Cancer Research, 1925-30. Contbr. many papers and articles in exptl. and clin. medicine. Home and Office: 57 W. 57th St., New York, N.Y.
Died June 19, 1945.

LEVISON, Jacob Bertha (lĕv'ĭ-sŭn), insurance official; b. Virginia City, Nev., Oct. 3, 1862; s. Mark and Bertha (Roman) L.; ed. pub. schs., San Francisco, Calif.; m. Alice Gerstle, July 29, 1896. Began with New Zealand Ins. Co., San Francisco, 1878; later with Hutchinson & Mann (ins. agts.) and the Anglo-Nevada Assurance Corp.; marine sec., Fireman's Fund Ins. Co., 1890-1900, 2d v.p., 1900-13, v.p., 1914-17, pres., 1917-37, chmn. of the bd. since 1937. Ex-pres. Mt. Zion Hosp., San Francisco Symphony Orchestra; pres. Ins. Federation of Calif. Republican. Clubs: Commercial, Bohemian, Family, Beresford Country. Home: 2420 Pacific Av. Office: 401 California St., San Francisco. Died Nov. 23, 1947.

LEVY, Alexander Oscar (lē'vĭ), artist; b. Bonn, Germany, May 26, 1881; s. Julius and Regina (Berger) L.; student Art Acad. of Cincinnati, 1894-99, N.Y. Sch. of Fine and Applied Art, 1902-08; m. Mayme Haas, February 18, 1904 (died 1940); 1 son, Allan James; m. 2d, Edna H. Minken, 1941. Began as artist during the Spanish American War portraying war scenes for newspapers and mags.; later entered commercial advertising field in New York and Buffalo; conducting own studios as designer, artist and stylist since 1918. Published a portfolio of Auto-Lithographs of Cartoons on World War; illustrated the West Point Year Books, 1934, 1935. Represented in print collections at Denver Art Mus., Cincinnati Art Mus., Art Inst. of Chicago, Peabody Inst. of Baltimore, Detroit Museum of Art, Toledo Museum of Art, Brooklyn Museum; The Life of St. Mary (murals), St. Mary's Ch., Batavia, N.Y., 1940; also murals and church decorations in Buffalo and Rochester. Awarded Council Prize Buffalo Soc. of Artists, 1938; hon. mention Art Mus. of Cincinnati; fellowship prize Albright Art Gallery, Buffalo; spl. hon. mention, 1936, and spl. prize, 1937, hon. mention, 1943, Buffalo Soc. of Artists. Mem. Buffalo Soc. of Artists (ex-pres.), Buffalo Soc. of Artists, Soc. for Sanity in Art of Chicago. Republican. Club: Greater Buffalo Advertising Club; "Rationalists" of Buffalo and Rochester. Pres. Society for Sanity in Art, Buffalo, Rochester and Syracuse br. Home: 41 Berkeley Place, Buffalo, N.Y. Died Jan. 21, 1947.

LEVY, Robert (lē'vĭ), otolaryngology; b. Hamilton, Ont., Can., May 30, 1864; s. Mandel and Rebecca (Elsner) L.; student U. of Denver, 1880-81; M.D., Bellevue Hosp. Med. Coll., N.Y. City, 1884; m. Rebecca Goldsmith, Aug. 27, 1889; children—Leona, Marion. Began practice at Denver, 1884; prof. otolaryngology, U. of Colo., 1889-1930, emeritus, 1930-44; cons. otolaryngologist St. Joseph's Hosp., Nat. Jewish Hosp. of Denver, Children's Hospital, St. Anthony's Hosp. Maj., Med. Corps, U.S. Army, 1918. Fellow Am. Coll. Surg.; mem. Am. Laryngol., Rhinol. and Otol. Soc. (ex-pres.), A.M.A. (ex-chmn. sect. otolaryngology), Colo. State Med. Soc. (ex-pres.), Am. Acad. Ophthalmology and Otolaryngology, Am. Laryngol. Assn., Denver Clin. and Path. Soc. (ex-pres.), Sigma Xi, Phi Delta Epsilon, Alpha Mu Pi Omega. Republican. Jewish religion. Mason (32°). Contbr. chapter on endolaryngeal operations to Loeb's Operative Surgery of Ear, Nose and Throat; also articles in med. jours. on laryngology, tuberculosis, etc. Home: 1215 Detroit St. Office: Metropolitan Bldg., Denver, Colo. Died July 1, 1945.

LEWIN, Kurt (lĕ-vēn'), univ. prof.; b. Mogilno, Germany, Sept. 9, 1890; s. Leopold and Recha (Engel) L.; ed. Kaiserin Augusta Gymnasium, 1903-08, U. of Freiburg, 1908, U. of Munich, 1909, U. of Berlin, 1909-14 (Ph.D.); m. Gertrud Weiss, Oct. 1928; children—Esther Agnes, Reuven Fritz, Miriam Anna, Daniel Meier. Came to U.S., 1932. Asst., Psychol. Inst., Berlin, 1921; privatdocent of philosophy, U. of Berlin, 1921-26, prof. of philosophy and psychology, 1926-33; visiting prof. of psychology, Stanford U., 1932-33; acting prof. of psychology, Cornell U., 1933-35; prof. of child psychology, Child Welfare Research Station, U. of Ia., 1935-44; dir. Research Center for Group Dynamics, Mass. Inst. Tech., since 1944; visiting prof., Harvard, 2d semester, 1938-39, 1939-40, Univ. of California, Berkeley, summer session, 1939. Counsellor, U.S. Department of Agriculture, Washington, D.C., since 1942; Office of Strategic Services, 1944-45; chief cons., Commission on Community Interrelations, New York, since 1944. Served as private to lt., German Army, 1914-18. Member American Psychol. Assn., Midwest. Psychol. Assn., Soc. for Psychol. Study of Social Issues (chmn.), Psychometric Soc., A.A.A.S., Phi Epsilon Pi, Sigma Xi. Author: A Dynamic Theory of Personality (translated from German by D. K.

Adams and K. E. Zener), 1935; Principles of Topological Psychology, 1936; The Conceptual Representation and Measurement of Psychological Forces, 1938; Studies in Topological and Vector Psychology I and II, Univ. Iowa; Studies in Child Welfare, 16. No. 3, 1940; Resolving Social Conflicts, 1947; also book pub. in Germany. Home: 57 Grove Hill Av., Newtonville, Mass. Died Feb. 12, 1947; buried in Mount Auburn Cemetery, Cambridge.

LEWIS, B. Palmer, Christian Science lecturer; b. New Orleans, La., Dec. 29, 1874; s. Jefferson Montgomery and Annie Eliza (Hardie) L.; student law course, U. of Md., 1906; C.S.B., Mass Metaphysical Coll., 1931; m. Mary Lorena Gourley, Dec. 26, 1931. Began as associate of father in banking and textile businesses, Ala.; later became cattleman in Mont., Northwest Territory of Can., and N.M.; has devoted entire time to practice of Christian Science since 1912; serving as Com. on Publ. for State of N.Y. since 1936; mem. bd. of lectureship of The First Church of Christ, Scientist, Boston, Mass., since 1944. Mem. advisory council Laymen's Nat. Com. Mason (32°). Contbr. articles to Christian Science publs. Home: 4 Sutton Pl. Office: 33 W. 42d St., New York, N.Y.* Died June 27, 1949.

LEWIS, Edward Mann, army officer; b. New Albany, Ind., Dec. 10, 1863; s. William Henry and Julia Frances (Snively) L.; grad. U.S. Mil. Acad., 1886; studied DePauw U. and U. of Calif.; LL.D., DePauw U., Greencastle, Ind., 1919; m. Hattie Russell Balding, June 12, 1888; children—Henry Balding, Mrs. Adelaide Palmer McMullen, Thos. Edward. Commd. 2d lt. 11th Inf., July 1, 1886; promoted through grades to col., Mar. 23, 1917; brig. gen. N.G., in federal service, July 8, 1916; brig. gen. N.A., Aug. 5, 1917; maj. gen., June 28, 1918; brig. gen. regular army, Jan. 9, 1920; maj. gen., Dec. 2, 1922. Prof. mil. science and tactics, DePauw U., 1892-96; served in Cuba as adj. 20th Inf., Spanish-Am. War, 1898; same capacity during Philippine Insurrection, 1899-1901; duty San Francisco, following earthquake and fire, 1906; prof. mil. science and tactics, U. of Calif., 1908-12; with expdn. to Vera Cruz, 1914, comdg. 19th Inf., adj. 5th Brigade and under detail as treas. Mil. Govt.; sr. insp. instr., Ill. N.G., 1915-17, and officer in charge mil. affairs at hdqrs. Northeastern Dept., Boston, 1917; apptd. comdr. 13th Provisional Div. and Camp Llano Grande, Tex., July 11, 1916; comd. 76th Inf. Brig., N.A., Aug.-Nov., 1917; comd. U.S. troops, Paris, Dec. 1, 1917-May 5, 1918; comd. 3d Brig., 2d Div. to July 13, 1918, 30th Div., July 15, 1918-Mar. 15, 1919; office of Chief of Staff, G.H.Q. and pres. Inf. Bd. to June 17, 1919; comd. Camp Gordon, Ga., to Dec. 20, 1919; comd. Douglas, Ariz. Dist., to Jan. 4, 1920; comd. 3d Div. and Camp Pike, Ark., to Sept. 15, 1921; comd. 2d Div. and Camp Travis, Tex., Sept. 15, 1921-Nov. 20, 1922; comd. 8th Corps area Nov. 1922-Aug. 1924; comd. Hawaiian Div. and Schofield Barracks, Sept. 16, 1924-Jan. 1925; comd. Hawaiian Dept., Jan. 13, 1925-Aug. 27, 1927; retired Dec. 10, 1927. Decorations: D.S.M.; Comdr. Legion of Honor and croix de Guerre with two palms (French); Comdr. Order of Leopold, Croix de Guerre (Belgian); Knight Comdr. Order of St. Michael and St. George (British); Grand Officer Order of Danilo (Montenegrin). Mem. S.R., Soc. Army Santiago de Cuba, Phi Beta Kappa. Presbyterian. Clubs: Union League (San Francisco); Faculty (U. of Calif.). Home: 89 Parkside Drive, Berkeley, Calif. Died July 27, 1949; buried in National Cemetery, Presidio of San Francisco.

LEWIS, Frank Grant, librarian; b. Gang Mills, nr. Painted Post, N.Y., July 18, 1865; s. William and Sarah Jane (Payne) Lewis; graduate of Cook Academy, 1889; A.B., Brown University, 1893 (P.B.K.); graduate Rochester Theological Seminary, 1896, D.B., 1907; grad. student U. of Chicago, 1905-07, A.M., 1906, Ph.D., 1907; m. Lena, d. Rev. Vinson Leonard and Henrietta (Russell) Garrett, Nov. 5, 1896. Ordained Bapt. ministry, Aug. 18, 1896; pastor Jefferson, Ia., 1896-98, Ambrose, O., 1898-1901; prof. theology and ch. history, Va. Union Univ., Richmond, 1901-05, also librarian; asso. in N.T., U. of Chicago, 1907-08; instr. summer quarter, same, 1908; prof. Bibl. history and interpretation, Bapt. Training Sch. (now Bapt. Inst. for Christian Workers), Phila., 1908-09; instr. in Hebrew, 1908-13, librarian, 1909-35, rank of prof., 1920-35, retired, Crozer Theol. Sem.; librarian Am. Bapt. Hist. Soc., 1912-35 (resigned), also corr. sec. Trustee Cook Acad., 1941-44. Fellow A.A.A.S.; mem. A.L.A., N.Y. Library Assn., Pa. Library Club (v.p. 1919-20; pres. 1920-21), Hist. Soc. Pa., Keystone State (now Pa.) Library Assn. (pres. 1913-14), Special Libraries Assn., Am. Peace Soc., Del. County Hist. Soc., New Eng. Historic-Geneal. Soc., World Alliance for Internat. Friendship Through the Chs., Fellowship of Reconciliation, Nat. Conf. of Jews and Christians, Bapt. Hist. Soc. (London), Bibliog. Soc. America, Inst. Am. Genealogy. Club: Photozetetics. Author: The Irenæus Testimony to the Fourth Gospel, 1908; (with Edith Maddock West) An Author, Title and Subject Index to Proceedings of Baptist Congress (vols. 1-30), 1913; How the Bible Grew, 1919; Sketch of the History of Baptist Education in Pa., 1919; Presidency of Dr. Augustus Hopkins Strong (in Rochester Theol. Sem. Anniversary Vol.), 1925; Church and State, 1928; A Critique of Conduct, 1930; (pamphlet) Scientific Money, 1938; Salyer-Ege Genealogy, 1943. Editor bibliography of a Dictionary of Religion and Ethics, 1921; Proceedings of the Delaware County (Pa.) Historical Society, 1922-29, 30; The 250th Anniversary of the First Arrival of William Penn in Pennsylvania in 1682, 1934. Compiler: (with Rittenhouse Neisser) Alphabetic Biographical Catalog of The Crozer Theological Seminary, 1855-1933, 1933. Contbr. to Crozer Quarterly, 1924-35, also articles in Library Jour., Homiletic Rev., etc. A leader in orgn. of Theol. Libraries Round Table (now Religious Books Sect.) of A.L.A. (chmn. 1916-17, 1924-26 and 1930-31), and editor of its annual list of Important Religious Books, 1925-32 (resigned). Since 1935 engaged in research and writing, chiefly genealogy and bibliography. Home: 124 Wagener St., Penn Yan, N.Y. Died Nov. 19, 1945.

LEWIS, Fred Ewing, congressman; b. Allentown, Pa., Feb. 8, 1865; s. Samuel B. and Mary A. (Rosenstiel) L.; Muhlenberg Coll., Allentown, 1881-84; studied law in office of Hon. Robert E. Wright; m. Juliet M. Hamersly, Apr. 16, 1891. Admitted to Pa. bar, 1888; organized Lehigh Telephone Co., 1900; organizer, 1904, and pres., 1904-11, Merchants Nat. Bank. Mayor of Allentown, 2 terms 1896-99, 1902-05; mem. 63d Congress (1913-15), Pa. at-large. Progressive. Home: Allentown, Pa. Died June 27, 1949.

LEWIS, Ernest Irving, Interstate Commerce economist; b. Danville, Ind., Feb. 7, 1873; s. John H. and Elizabeth (McMurry) L.; ed. country sch., 2 yrs.; m. Eleanor H. Carey, July 5, 1916; children—Volinda, Phoebe Carey. Began as printer's apprentice at 11; became newspaper reporter, spl. writer and corr., visiting leading countries of the world; polit. writer in presdl. campaigns, 1904-16; chmn. Public Service Commn. of Ind., 1917-21; mem. U.S. Interstate Commerce Commn., by apptmt. of Pres. Harding, May 3, 1921; commr. in administrative charge of valuation of common carriers, 1922-32, reapptd. by President Coolidge, Dec. 31, 1925, chairman, 1929; re-nominated by Pres. Hoover, 1932; dir. of valuation, Bur. Valuation, Interstate Commerce Commn., 1933-43; completed basic valuation of railroads and oil pipe lines of U.S. and instituted continuous inventories and property records; apptd. by President F. D. Roosevelt to Fed. Anthracite Coal Commn. to investigate 1942. Chmn. com. on valuation Nat. Assn. of Railroad and Utilities Commrs. (10 yrs.). Republican. economic conditions in anthracite coal regions of U.S., Clubs: Cosmos, Chevy Chase (Washington); Indianapolis Literary. Home: 3099 Q St. N.W., Washington, D.C. Died July 1, 1947.

LEWIS, George William, aeronautical engr.; b. Ithaca, N.Y., Mar. 10, 1882; s. William H. and Edith (Sweetland) L.; M.E., 1908, Cornell University, M.M.E., 1910; Sc.D., Norwich University; D.Eng., Ill. Inst. Tech., 1944; m. D. Myrtle Harvey, September 9, 1908; children—Alfred William, Harvey Sweetland, Myrtle Norlaine, George William, Leigh Kneeland, Armin Kessler. Instr. in engring., Cornell U., 1908-10; prof. engring., Swarthmore Coll., 1910-17; engr. in charge Clarke Thomson Research, 1917-19; sales mgr. Phila. Surface Combustion Co., 1919; exec. officer Nat. Advisory Com. for Aeronautics, 1919-24; dir. aeronaut. research Nat. Adv. Com. Aeronautics, Washington, 1924-47, research cons., 1947-48. Member Com. on Power Plants for Aircraft Nat. Adv. Com. for Aeronautics 1918; chmn. contest bd. Nat. Aeronautical Assn., 1925-38; mem. com. of judges Daniel Guggenheim Safe Aircraft Competition, 1927-29; mem. bd. judges Wright Medal Award, 1928-29, chmn. bd., 1930; mem. bd. of award Manly Memorial Medal, 1929; chmn. bd. 1931-36; mem. Guggenheim Medal Bd. of Award, 1930, chmn. 1944-45; honorary fellow, Institute of Aeronautical Sciences (vice-president, 1935-38, president, 1939), Society Automotive Engineers (v.p. 1931); mem. War Dept. Spl. Committee on Army Air Corps (Baker Bd.), 1934; American Philosophical Society, National Academy of Sciences. Awarded Daniel Guggenheim medal, 1936, Spirit St. Louis Medal 1944. Presbyn. Clubs: Cosmos, Kenwood. Home: 6502 Ridgewood Av., Chevy Chase, Md. Address: 1724 F St. N.W., Washington, D.C. Died July 12, 1948.

LEWIS, Gilbert Newton, chemist; b. Weymouth, Mass., Oct. 23, 1875; s. Frank W. and Mary B. (White) L.; U. of Neb., 1890-93; A.B., Harvard, 1896; A.M., 1898, Ph.D., 1899; univs. of Leipzig and Göttingen, 1900-01; hon. D.Sc., U. of Liverpool, 1923, U. of Wis., 1928, U. of Chicago, 1929, U. of Pa., 1938; Dr. Hon. Caus., U. of Madrid, Spain, 1934; m. Mary Hinckley Sheldon, June 20, 1912; children—Richard Newton, Margery, Edward Sheldon. Instr. chemistry, Harvard, 1899-1900, 1901-06 (on leave of absence, in charge weights and measures, P.I., 1904-05); asst. prof. chemistry, 1907-08, asso. prof., 1908-11, prof., 1911-12, Massachusetts Institute of Technology; professor phys. chemistry, University of Calif., since July 1, 1912; Silliman lecturer, Yale, 1925. Maj. U.S. Army, 1918; lt. col., 1919; chief of defense div. Gas Service, A.E.F. Decorated D.S.M. (U.S.); Chevalier Legion of Honor (French); awarded Nichols, Gibbs and Davy medals, 1929; Soc. Arts and Sciences medal, 1930; Richards medal, 1938; Arrhenius medal, 1939. Mem. American Philosophical Society, American Chemistry Society, American Physics Soc.; fellow Am. Acad. Arts and Sciences; hon. fellow London Chem. Soc., Royal Instn. of Great Britain, Indian Acad. Sciences; hon. mem. Swedish Acad., Danish Acad., Royal Soc., Franklin Inst. of Pa. Author: Thermodynamics and the Free Energy of Chemical Substances (with M. Randall), 1923; Valence and the Structure of Atoms and Molecules, 1023; The Anatomy of Science, 1926. Home: 948 Santa Barbara Rd., Berkeley, Calif. Died Mar. 23, 1946.

LEWIS, H. Edgar, corp. official; b. Pontardulais, Wales, July 24, 1882; s. William E. and Emily Ann (Williams) L.; ed. Martins Ferry (O.) High Sch.; m. Lottie May Rush (died 1918); children—Emily (Mrs. Robert W. Gillispie, Jr.), James Edgar; m. 2d, Helen Sanders, Sept. 7, 1920; 1 son, Edgar Sanders. Came to U.S. 1896; entered employ Bethlehem Steel Co., 1906, and held various positions until 1916, exec. v.p., 1916-30; chmn. exec. com. The Jeffrey Mfg. Co., 1930-36; became chmn. bd. Jones & Laughlin Steel Corp., 1936, pres., 1938; chmn. bd. and dir. British Jeffrey-Diamond, Ltd.; dir. The Jeffrey Mfg. Co., Kelsey-Hayes Wheel Co., Ltd., Ohio Malleable Iron Co., Galion Iron Works & Mfg. Co. Mem. Pittsburgh Chamber of Commerce. Republican. Episcopalian. Clubs: Metropolitan, Cloud (New York); Duquesne, Fox Chapel Golf, Pittsburgh Golf, Oakmont Country, Rolling Rock Country (Pittsburgh). Now retired. Home: 210 Tennyson Av., Pittsburgh 13. Died Dec. 5, 1948.

LEWIS, Harold C., educator; b. Des Moines, Ia., May 5, 1887; s. William E. and Hattie (Dillon) L.; ed. pub. schs.; children by 1st marriage— William Chapp, Virginia. Left school at age of 12 due to illness; spent several years in the West in construction work and on cattle ranch; entered employ of M. E. Smith, Omaha, at age of 16; later salesman; with Carson, Pirie Scott & Co., Chicago, 1909-10; with Coyne Electrical Sch. since 1919, now pres. and owner; sch. has trained about 10,000 men for various branches of U.S. Army. Mem. Ill. Assn. Commerce, Chicago Assn. Commerce. Episcopalian. Club: Electrical. Home: Oak Park, Ill. Office: 500 S. Paulina St., Chicago, Ill. Died July 13, 1946.

LEWIS, Judd Mortimer, poet-humorist; b. Fulton, N.Y., Sept. 13, 1867; s. Charles Steven and Arabella Elizabeth (Kenyon) L.; pub. schs., Cleveland, Ohio; Litt.D., Baylor U., 1920; m. Mary Bartley, Sept. 24, 1894; children—Marjorie Augusta (Mrs. E. J. Perry), Jessamine Margaret (Mrs. I. B. Sigler). Began as stereotyper with the A. N. Kellogg Newspaper Co. and later served as mgr. of the branch houses of co.; with Houston Post since 1900; v.p. and dir. Houston Post Pub. Co.; contbr. column poetry and prose humor daily in Houston Post. Widely known for "baby bureau" work. Apptd. first poet laureate, Tex., 1932. Democrat. Methodist. Life mem. Am. Folk-Lore Soc. (v.p.), Tex. Press Assn. (life; ex-pres.). Author: (verse) Sing the South, 1905; Lilts o' Love, 1906; The Old Wash Place, 1912; Toddle-Town Trails, 1914; Christmas Days, 1917; also prose humorous stories "Patsy Kildare, Outlaw," and "Jubilee's Pardner"; latter is personally syndicated and has appeared daily in numerous newspapers since 1917. Contbr. to various mags. and newspapers. Selected by Carnegie Endowment for Universal Peace to tour Orient, summer, 1929. Home: 2241 Albans Rd. Office: Houston Post, Houston, Tex. Died July 25, 1945.

LEWIS, Lawrence, lawyer, congressman; b. St. Louis, Mo., June 22, 1879; s. Thomas Addison and Melissa Ann (Lewis) L.; student U. of Colo., 1897-99; A.B., Harvard, 1901, LL.B., 1909, unmarried. Editor and mgr. Camp and Plant (weekly mag. of Colo. Fuel & Iron Co.), 1901-04; asst. instr. in English, Harvard, 1906-09; in practice of law at Denver since 1909. Mem. Colo. Civ. Service Commn., 1917-18; legal adviser to Selective Service Bd., Denver, and to adj. gen. of Colo., World War; pvt. field arty. and attended F.A. Central O.T.S., Camp Zachary Taylor, Ky. Mem. 73d to 78th Congresses (1933-45), 1st Colo. Dist. Mem. Am., Colo. State and Denver bar assns., State Hist. Soc. of Colo. (dir., sec.), Harvard Law Sch. Assn., Denver Art Museum, Am. Legion (comdr. Denver City, 1927-28), Sigma Alpha Epsilon. Democrat. Episcopalian. Mason. Clubs: University, Democratic, Rocky Mountain Harvard (ex-pres.); Harvard (New York). Author: The Advertisements of the Spectator, 1909. Home: 1673 Sherman St. Office: Equitable Bldg., Denver, Colo. Died Dec. 9, 1943.

LEWIS, Leicester Crosby, clergyman; b. N.Y. City, Mar. 30, 1887; s. George Washington and Maria Elizabeth (Sharkey) L.; A.B., Columbia, 1910, A.M., 1911; B.D., Gen. Theol. Sem. of P.E. Ch., New York, 1912; student univs. of Berlin, Tübingen and Freiburg, 1912-14; Ph.D., Univ. of Pa., 1925; S.T.D. from Columbia Univ., 1936, D.C.L., Philadelphia Divinity School, 1944; m. Beatrix Elizabeth Baldwin, June 1, 1915; children—Leicester Crosby, Richard Warrington Baldwin, Virginia Adelaide. Deacon P.E. Ch., 1911, priest, 1912; curate Christ Ch., Ridgewood, N.J., 1911-12; prof. ecclesiastical history, Western Theol. Sem. and chaplain St. Mary's Sisters, Chicago, 1913-20; master Episcopal Academy, Philadelphia, 1922-29, chaplain, 1931-32; assistant Holy Trinity Ch., Lansdale, Pa., 1922-29; dir. sch. of religious edn., St. James Ch., Phila., 1931-32; rector Ch. St. Martin-in-the-Fields, Chestnut Hill, Phila., 1932-45; vicar St. Luke's Chapel, Trinity Parish, since 1945; examining chaplain to bishop of N.Y.; pres. New York Catholic Club. Member World Conference on Faith and Order, Am. Theol. Com., Commn. on Approaches to Unity, American Society Church History, Church Hist. Soc., Am. Philos. Assn., Gesellschaft für Kirchengeschichte, Société d'Histoire Ecclésiastique de la France, Alpha Chi Rho. Founder (with S. A. Mercer) Anglican Theol. Review, 1918, and since co-editor. Contbr. monographs and articles on philosophical and religious subjects. Home: 477 Hudson St., New York, N.Y. Died Mar. 18, 1949.

LEWIS, Lee Rich, college prof., composer; b. S. Woodstock, Vt., Feb. 11, 1865; s. John Jay and Abbie Goodwin (Davis) L.; A.B., Tufts Coll., 1887, Litt.D., 1922; A.B., Harvard, 1888, A.M., 1889; diploma Conservatory of Music, Munich, 1892; m. Carrie Nichols

Bullard (composer; pseud. Carrie Bullard and Caryl B. Rich), Dec. 21, 1892; 1 son, Philip Bullard. Instr. French, Tufts Coll., 1892-95, prof. theory and history of music, 1895-1920, prof. music, asso. prof. modern langs., 1920-24, Fletcher prof. music since 1924. Chmn. music com. Medford (Mass.) 275th anniversary, 1905. Chmn. bd. of examiners in music, Coll. Entrance Exam. Bd., 1909-20; visiting instr. Harvard Summer Sch., 1915-22; vice-pres. Music Teachers' Nat. Assn., 1910-12; chmn. state music com., Mass. Tercentenary, 1930; fellow Am. Acad. of Arts and Sciences; mem. N.E.A., Internat. Music Society (sec. N. Am. Branch, 1912-19), Phi Beta Kappa, Kappa Gamma Psi, Zeta Psi. Club: University (Boston). Author: R. E. Porter (operetta), 1886; Hunt the Thimble, 1887; The Redeemer, 1887; The Consolation of Music (cantata), 1895; Sonata for Violin and Piano, 1895; Sunday School Harmonies, Number 4, 1898; Incidental Music to Milton's Comus, 1901; Melodia (with S.W. Cole), 1905; Harmonia (with S. W. Cole), 1905; School Songs with College Flavor, 1905; Incidental Music to Dekker's Fortunatus, 1906; Symphonic Prelude to Browning's A Blot on the 'Scutcheon, 1907; smaller compositions, 1914-18; Intercollegiate Inklings for symphonic orchestra, 1927; The Ambitious Listener, 1928; Masterpieces of Music, 1928; The Gist of Sight-Singing, 1929; Experiencing Music, 1929; Trumpet Concertino, 1937; Do and Don't in Harmony, 1939; 2d String Quartet, 1940; also, on French lang., Vocabulary and Grammar-Syllabus (5th edit. 1919), the first English annotation of Racine's Mithridate (1920), and Test-Compendium (1922); English Acting Version of Racine's Mithridates (with H. D. Spoerl), 1925. Editor: Zeta Psi Song Books, 1892-1904; National School Library of Song (2 vols.), 1894; Church Harmonies, New and Old, 1895; Tufts Song Book, 1906; Tufts Songs and Supplement, 1915; Assembly Praise-Book (with L. R. Maxwell), 1910; Book of Tufts Music, 1922; Orchestra-Band Series of Tufts Music since 1920. Originator of card-system of thematic cataloging applicable to all music, already embodied in a catalog of over 200,000 titles; and of patented devices, including the Strapflex Binder and Strapflex pamphlet binding processes. Editor-in-chief Tufts College Graduate, 1911-17. Address: 20 Professors Row, Tufts College, Mass. Died Sept. 8, 1945; buried in Cedar Grove Cemetery, Dorchester, Mass.

LEWIS, Lloyd Downs, writer; b. Pendleton, Ind., May 2, 1891; s. Jay and Josephine (Downs) L.; A.B., Swarthmore College, 1913; Litt.D., Northwestern University, 1947; married Kathryn Dougherty, Dec. 30, 1925. Newspaperman Phila. and Chicago, 1913-19; advertising, 1920-30; drama critic, Chicago Daily News, 1930-45, also sports editor 1936-43 mng. editor 1943-45; columnist Chicago Sun-Times since 1945. Lecturer history, U. of Chicago, 1937-38. Author: Myths After Lincoln, 1929; Chicago—The History of Its Reputation (with Henry Justin Smith), 1929; Sherman, Fighting Prophet, 1932; Jayhawker (with Sinclair Lewis), 1935; Oscar Wilde Discovers America (with Henry Justin Smith), 1936; John S. Wright, Prophet of the Prairies, 1941; It Takes All Kinds, 1947; Captain Sam Grant, 1949. Home: Little Saint Mary's Road, Libertyville, Ill. Died April 21, 1949; buried at Pendleton, Ind.

LEWIS, Mary Sybil, operatic singer; b. Hot Springs, Ark., Jan. 7, 1900; d. Joseph Lewis and Hattie (Lewis) Kidd; ed. pvt. and pub. schs., Little Rock, including 3 years in high school; m. Michael Franz Bohnen, April 14, 1927; m. 2d, Robert L. Hague, 1931. Was prima donna in Ziegfield Follies, 1920-23; made her operatic debut in "Faust," Vienna Volksopera, Oct. 15, 1923; sang at Monte Carlo, season of 1924, London same yr., and again at Monte Carlo, 1925; sang in Paris 1925; returned to U.S. and appeared in Carnegie Hall, New York, Oct. 27, 1925; debut with Metropolitan Opera Co., as Mimi, in "La Boheme," Jan. 28, 1926; sang in Berlin Staatsoper, June 1927. Principal roles: Thais, Juliet, Marguerite, Lauretta, Gilda, Manon, Nedda, Giuletta and Antonia (Hoffmann). Died Dec. 31, 1941.

LEWIS, Reuben Alexander, Jr., pub.; b. Birmingham, Ala., Aug. 29, 1895; s. Reuben Alexander and Martha Louise (Ives) L.; A.B., Washington and Lee U., 1916; spl. course, Harvard U. Grad. Sch. of Bus. Administrn., 1930; m. Sarah Stewart Briggs, Jan. 7, 1925 (divorced 1944); children—Barbara Stewart, Reuben Alexander III, Mitchell Ives; m. 2d, Catherine Mohan Richardson, Mar. 24, 1944. Reporter Birmingham Age-Herald, 1911-13, sporting editor, 1913-14; sec. Southeastern League (baseball), 1915; shipping editor, N.Y. Jour. of Commerce, 1920-21, chief Washington corr., 1921-23; asso. editor Am. Bankers Assn. Jour., 1923-28; dep. mgr. in charge trust co. div., Am. Bankers Assn., 1928-30; 2d v.p. Continental Ill. Bank & Trust Co., Chicago, 1930-37; exec. vice-pres. Metropolitan Trust Co., Chicago, 1937-41; now publisher of Finance Magazine. Member Pub. Relations Council, Am. Bankers Assn., 1939; mem. Assn. of Reserve City Bankers, 1934-37. Mem. first O.T.C., Fort McPherson, Ga., May 1917, asst. adj., 20th F.A. Brig., U.S. Army, 1918, aide de camp to comdg. gen., 1918. Mem. Phi Beta Kappa, Omicron Delta Kappa, Alpha Tau Omega. Democrat. Methodist. Clubs: Executives, Electric (Chicago); National Press (Washington, D.C.). Author: (brochures) Our Changing Investment Habits; The Big Money Makers of America; Main Street Finances Wall Street. Home: 900 N. Michigan Av. Office: 20 N. Wacker Dr., Chicago. Died May 4, 1948.

LEWIS, William Draper, lawyer; b. Philadelphia, Apr. 27, 1867; s. Henry and Fannie Hannah (Wilson) L.; B.S., Haverford, 1888; LL.B., and Ph.D., U. of Pa., 1891; LL.D., Univ. of Pa., 1926, Haverford College, 1938; m. Caroline Mary Cope, June 22, 1892. Instr. legal hist. instns., Wharton Sch., U. of Pa., 1891; lecturer on economics, Haverford Coll., 1890-96; prof. of law and dean law dept., U. of Pa., 1896-1914, prof. of law until Sept. 1924; dir. of Am. Law inst. June 1923-June 1947. Author: Federal Power Over Commerce and Its Effect on State Action, 1891; Our Sheep and the Tariff, 1891; Restraint of Infringement of Incorporeal Rights, 1904; Life of Theodore Roosevelt; also numerous articles on legal economic and historical topics for periodicals. Editor: Lewis' Edition Greenleaf's Evidence, 3 volumes, 1896; Wharton's Criminal Law, 10th edit., 2 vols., 1895; Lewis' edit. Blackstone's Commentaries, 4 vols., 1897; Digest of Decisions of United States Supreme Court and Circuit Court of Appeals, 1 vol., 1897; Pepper & Lewis' Digest of Statutes of Pennsylvania (co-editor), 3 vols., 1896, and 4 vols., 1911; Digest of Decisions and Encylopædia of Pennsylvania Laws, 23 vols.; Great American Lawyers, 8 vols., 1907-08; Pepper & Lewis' Cases on Law of Association, Part I-IX (co-editor), 1909-10; Interpreting the Constitution, 1937. Chmn. resolutions (platform) com. 1st and 2d Prog. Nat. Convs., Chicago, 1912 and 1916; Prog. candidate for gov. of Pa., 1914. Home: Awbury, Germantown, Phila. 38. Office: 3400 Chestnut St., Philadelphia 4, Pa. Died Sept. 2, 1949.

LEWIS, William Mather, educator; b. Howell, Mich., Mar. 24, 1878; s. James and Mary (Farrand) L.; student Knox Coll., Galesburg, Ill., 1896-98; A.B., Lake Forest (Ill.) Coll., 1900, LL.D., 1924; A.M., Ill. Coll., 1902; studied abroad, 1913-14; LL.D. from Norwich U., 1925, Temple U., 1927, Lehigh U., 1928, Dickinson Coll., 1933, St. John's, Maryland, 1934, U. of Rochester, 1935, U. of Pa., 1935; Columbia, 1936, Rutgers, 1939, Franklin and Marshall, 1935, Ursinus Coll., 1942; Litt.D., Knox Coll., 1930; L.H.D., Hobart, 1935, New York U., 1936; Sc.D., Rose Poly. Inst., 1940; D.Eng., Worcester Poly. Inst., 1943; Ed. D., Washington and Jefferson College, 1945; married Ruth Durand, December 20, 1906; 1 daughter, Sarah Durand (Mrs. Lewis-Betts). Instr., Ill. Coll., 1900-03, Lake Forest Coll., 1903-06; headmaster Lake Forest Acad., 1906-13; exec. sec. Nat. Com. Patriotic Socs., 1917-19; dir. savings div. U.S. Treasury Dept., 1919-21; chief of edn. service, Chamber of Commerce, U.S.A., 1921-23; pres. George Washington Univ., 1923-27; pres. Lafayette College 1927-45; director Selective Service for Pennsylvania, 1940-42; mayor Lake Forest, Ill., 1915-17; mem. Bd. of Review, 1915; pres. Bd. of Edn., 1911-13. Lecturer McCormick Theol. Sem., 1909-12; spl. lecturer Colo. Teachers Coll., 1923-26. Pres. Assn. Urban Univs., 1924-25; pres. Middle States Assn. Colls. and Secondary Schs., 1932-33; trustee Princeton Theol. Sem., Barrington Sch. (Great Barrington, Mass.); mem. bd. mgrs. Severn Sch.; bd. regents Mercersburg Acad.; mem. advisory bd. Northwestern Mil. and Naval Acad.; mem. bd. of advisers Admiral Farragut Acad.; mem. board of visitors, U.S. Naval Acad., 1940; moderator Presbyn. Synod of Pa., 1933-34; chmn. Am. Red Cross War Fund Easton Area; mem. bd. of grants, Am. Pharm. Assn., 1943; chmn. bd. Sportmanship Brotherhood, 1945. Decorated Officer French Legion of Honor; Cross of Christobal Colon (Dominican Republic); Leading Citizens Award, Exchange Club, 1941; Gold Medal, Nat. Inst. Social Sciences, for distinguished service to humanity, 1945. Member Association of American Colleges (vice pres. 1929-30; treas. 1930-31; pres. 1934-35), S.A.R., Loyal Legion, Huguenot Soc. of Pa. (pres. 1938-41), Newcomen Soc., N.Y. Hist. Soc., St. Andrews Soc., Kappa Phi Kappa, Phi Delta Theta (pres. gen. council since 1942); mem. exec. com. Nat. Inter-Fraternity Conf., 1943; mem. Phi Beta Kappa. Clubs: Alfalfa, Cosmos (Washington, D.C.); Century (N.Y.). Editor: The Voices of Our Leaders, 1917; Liberty Loan Speakers' Hand Books, 1918. Author: From a College Platform, 1932; also of articles and addresses on edn. and econ. subjects. subjects. Awarded Medal of Merit (posthumously) Home: Easton, Pa. Died Nov. 11, 1945.

LEWIS, Sir Willmott Harsant, newspaper corr.; b. Cardiff, South Wales, June 18, 1877; s. James Oliver and Marion Harsant (Butler) L.; ed. in English schs. and on continent of Europe; hon. Litt.D., Trinity College, Hartford, Conn.; m. Ethel Stoddard Noyes, June 8, 1926; 1 son, Willmott Harsant; m. 2d, Norma Bowler, June 17, 1939. Foreign corr. in Far East, covering Boxer Rebellion, Russo-Japanese War, Chinese Revolution, 1899-1910; editor Manila (P.I.) Times, 1911-17; in France during World War; mem. staff New York Tribune, Paris, 1919; with London Times since 1920, Washington corr. since Oct. 1920. Created Knight Comdr. Order of British Empire, 1931; decorated Chevalier Legion of Honor (France); awarded Brit. and Japanese war medals. Clubs: National Press (Washington); Devonshire (London); Shanghai (China); Nagasaki (Japan). Home: 2356 Massachusetts Av., Washington, Died Jan. 4, 1950.

LEWIS, W(inford) Lee, chemist; b. Gridley, Butte County, Calif., May 29, 1878; s. George Madison and Sarah Adeline (Hopper) L.; A.B., Stanford, 1902; A.M., U. of Wash., 1904; Ph.D., U. of Chicago, 1909; m. Myrtilla Mae Lewis, Sept. 1907; children—Mrs. Miriam Lee Reiss, Mrs. Winifred Lee Harwood. Asst. and instr. chemistry, U. of Washington, 1902-04; prof. chemistry, Morningside College, Sioux City, Ia., 1904-06; fellow U. of Chicago, 1907-09; instr. chemistry, Northwestern U., 1909, asst. prof., 1914, asso. prof., 1917, prof. and head of dept., 1919-24. Asst. chemist U.S. Dept. Agr., 1908-10; city chemist, Evanston, 1912-18; consulting practice; dir. dept. of scientific research Inst. Am. Meat Packers since 1924. Capt. Chem. Warfare Service, U.S. Army, 1917-18; maj. U.S.R., 1919; lt. col., 1924; col., 1933. Fellow A.A.A.S., mem. Am. Chem. Soc., Alpha Chi Sigma, Sigma Xi, Kappa Sigma, Chemists Club, Sword and Scabbard. Republican. Episcopalian. Clubs: Originalists, Chaos, Union League (Chicago); University, Rotary (Evanston). Home: 2323 Central Park Av., Evanston, Ill. Office: 59 E. Van Buren St., Chicago, Ill. Died Jan. 20, 1943.

LHÉVINNE, Josef (lĕ-vin'), pianist; b. Moscow, Russia, Dec. 14, 1874; s. Arcadie and Fanny (Lhévinne) L.; began study of piano at age of 4; pupil of Safonoff, at Moscow Conservatory; m. Rosina Bessie, 1898; children—Constantin, Marianna. Début, Moscow, 1889, A. Rubinstein conducting; winner Rubinstein prize, Berlin, 1895; made several concert tours of Europe. Am. début with Russian Symphony Orchestra, New York, Jan. 27, 1906; has toured U.S. many times—every year since 1920; also Mexico, Cuba, Panama; European trips, 1926, 29, 37; appearances with Mme. Lhévinne in two-piano recitals; mem. faculty Juilliard Graduate School. Club: Bohemian. Home: Kew Gardens, N.Y. Died Dec. 2, 1944.

LIBBY, Arthur Stephen, educator; b. Corinna, Me., Mar. 9, 1877; s. Clements Coffin and Estelle D. (Allen) L.; Ph.B., Bowdoin Coll., 1902; A.B., U. of Me., 1903; A.M., Sorbonne, Paris, 1903; A.M., Brown, 1904; Ph.D., U. of Paris, 1906; studied law depts. U. of Me. and Columbia; m. Prof. Cora M. Steele, Aug. 20, 1907. Prin. high schs. in Me., several yrs.; instr. French, Brown U., 1903-04; prof. modern langs., Converse Coll., Spartanburg, S.C., 1904-12; pres. of Southern Travel-Study Bur., Spartanburg, since 1911. Lecturer for Dept. of Edn., San Francisco Expn., 1915; traveled extensively in India, South Seas, Siberia, Africa, 1912-14; lyceum and chautauqua lecturer on travel, exploration, history and world politics since 1914; actg. prof. history and polit. science, Wofford Coll., 1917-19; dean Sch. of Commerce and prof. polit. science and internat. law, Oglethorpe U., 1919-30; founder, 1930, and pres. Libby Grad. Sch. of Business Administration and Finance (first grad. professional school of business in Southern States); founder, 1931, and pres. U. of Robert E. Lee (embracing Libby Grad. School as one of its depts.); prof. psychology at Grady Hosp. Training Sch., 1934. Served as dir. language instrn., Army Y.M.C.A., with 27th Division, and ednl. dir. and lecturer Army Camps, World War army interpreter and staff officer, rank of maj.; also speaker for Am. Red Cross and War Loan campaigns. Mem. Am. Hist. Assn.; del. from S.C. to Internat. Congress of Edn., Brussels, Belgium, 1910; founder and dir. Southern Bur. of Business Research. Lecturer economics and law, Am. Inst. of Banking. Mayor N. Atlanta, Ga., since 1924. Mem. N.E. Club, Ga. Soc. Certified Pub. Accountants, Nat. Assn. of Teachers of Marketing and Advertising, Am. Legion, Kappa Alpha, Phi Kappa Delta, Phi Beta Sigma. Democrat. Presbyn. Mason. Home: Oglethorpe University, North Atlanta, Ga. Died Sept. 24, 1948; buried in Willow Valley Cemetery, Mooresville, N.C.

LIBMAN, Emanuel, physician; b. New York, N.Y., 1872; s. Fajbush and Hulda (Spivak) L.; A.B., Coll. City of N.Y., 1891; M.D., Coll. Phys. and Surg. (Columbia), 1894; house phys. Mt. Sinai Hosp., 1894-96; post-grad. work, Berlin, Vienna, Munich, 1896-97, Berlin, 1903, 09, Johns Hopkins, 1906; unmarried. Practiced, New York since 1894; asso. pathologist, 1898-1923, attending phys., 1912-25, now cons. physician, Mt. Sinai Hosp.; cons. physician, Montefiore Hosp., Harlem Hosp., Beth Israel Hosp., Hosp. for Joint Diseases, French Hosp. (New York); Methodist-Episcopal Hosp., United Israel-Zion Hosp., Beth-El Hosp. (Brooklyn), etc. Chmn. advisory bd. Selective Draft, 1918. Mem. Am. Jewish Physicians Com. (chmn. exec. com.); mem. Council Jewish Agency for Palestine; mem. bd. govs. Hebrew Univ. (Jerusalem) v.p. Am. Friends of Hebrew U.; mem. Central Com. Union des Sociétés OSE; pres. Dazian Foundation for Med. Research. Chmn. Emergency Com. in Aid of Displaced Foreign Med. Scientists. Fellow N.Y. Acad. Medicine; mem. Am. Assn. Pathologists and Bacteriologists, A.A.A.S., Assn. Am. Physicians, Am. Soc. Advancement Clinical Investigation, Am. Coll. Physicians, Internat. Assn. Geographic Pathology, Internat. Med. Museums Assn., Pathol. Soc. N.Y., Harvey Soc., Am. Assn. Immunologists, Phi Beta Kappa, corr. mem. Société Française de Cardiologie. Contbr. papers appertaining to clin. medicine, pathology and bacteriology. Address: 180 E. 64th St., New York, N.Y.* Died June 28, 1946.

LICHTENBERG, Bernard (lĭk'tĕn-bĕrg), public relations counsel; b. Austria, Aug. 11, 1892; s. Hyman and Clara (Horodner) L.; brought to U.S., 1900; prep. education, Stuyvesant High Sch., New York; B.C.S., New York U., 1914, M.C.S., 1915; m. Minerva J. Kahn, Feb. 6, 1916; children—Ruth Elaine, Claire, Major John. With Clark Hutchinson Co., Boston, 1907, Business Book Bureau, New York, 1908; v.p. and dir. Alexander Hamilton Inst., 1909-35; v.p. and dir. Congressional Intelligence Service Corp, 1934-36; gen. mgr. Amos Parrish & Co., 1931-34; now pres. Institute of Public Relations. Hon. legion of New York Police Dept. Mem. Assn. Nat. Advertisers (pres. 1929-30, chmn. 1930-32); pres. New York U. Sch. of Commerce Alumni Assn., 1933-34; vice chmn. and dir. Better Business Bureau of N.Y.; treas. Nat. Fed. Sales Execs.; dir. Internat. Accountants Society, New York Sales Executives Club. Mem. Phi Sigma Delta (pres. 1924-26), Alpha Delta Sigma; mem.

Harvard U. Jury on Advertising Awards, 1929; official Am. representative to Cologne, Germany, Internat. Press Expn., 1929; mem. President Hoover's Nat. Survey Conf., Advertising Review Com.; mem. exec. com. United Action for Business Recovery; trustee Advertising Research Foundation. Clubs: Advertising, Economic, Sales Executives; Tavern (Chicago). Author: Advertising Principles, 1919; Advertising Campaigns (with Bruce Barton), 1926; Telling the Truth About Business, 1936; Has Business the Right to Live?, 1937; also articles in business publs. Home: 101 Central Park West. Office: Graybar Bldg., New York, N.Y. Died Oct. 3, 1944.

LICK, Maxwell John, surgeon; b. Albion, Pa., Oct. 24, 1884; s. Chauncey V. and Mary A. L.; A.B., Allegheny Coll., 1908; M.D., U. of Pa., 1912; studied abroad, 1925; m. Mary E. McLaughlin, July 1915; children—Maxwell Robert (dec.), Mary. Practicing physician in Erie, Pa., since 1912; surgeon on staff St. Vincent's and Hamot Hosps. since 1917, surgeon in chief Hamot Hosp. since 1938; surgeon to N.Y.C. R.R. and N.Y.C.&St.L. R.R. since 1917; lecturer. Member Founders Group, Am. Board of Surgery; former pres. Med. Soc. of State of Pa., Erie County Med. Soc.; fellow Am. Coll. of Surgeons; mem. A.M.A., Phi Beta Kappa, Alpha Omega Alpha, Phi Delta Theta, Phi Alpha Sigma. Republican. Methodist. Mason. Clubs: Erie, Kahkwa, Shrine. Contbr. to med. jours. Home: 149 W. 8th St., Erie. Pa.* Deceased.

LIEBER, Richard (lē'bẽr), state park builder; b. St. Johann-Saarbruecken, Germany, Sept. 5, 1869; s. Otto and Maria (Richter) L.; ed. Municipal Lyceum and Royal Lyceum, Duesseldorf, Germany; D.Sc., honoris causa, Wabash College, 1938; m. Emma Rappaport, Aug. 28, 1893; children—Otto Walther (dec.), Ralph Willard, Maria Jeannette. Came to U.S., 1891, naturalized, 1901. With Indianapolis (Ind.) Journal and Indianapolis Tribune, 1892-1900; with James R. Ross & Co., importers and jobbers, Indianapolis, 1905-18; dir. of conservation, State of Indiana, 1919-33. Councillor State of Ind. Economic Council, 1943. Mil. sec. with rank of colonel to Gov. J. P. Goodrich, 1917-21. Chmn. Indianapolis Civil Service Commn., 1909-10; pres. Indianapolis Trade Assn., 1910-12; hon. mem. nat. bd. American Gymnastic Union, 1910-23; pres. Mchts. & Mfrs. Ins. Bur., 1912-39; chmn. bd. govs. 4th Nat. Conservation Congress, 1912; chmn. Ind. State Park Commn., 1915-19; sec. Ind. State Bd. Forestry, 1917-19. Trustee Indianapolis Salvage Corps since 1917. Fellow Ind. Acad. Science; mem. Nat. Conf. State Parks (chmn. bd. since 1939), Am. Planning & Civic Assn. (v.p., dir.), Nat. Park Service (mem. advisory board on nat. parks, historic sites, buildings, and monuments also consultant), Ind. Lincoln Union (chmn. exec. com. since 1927); hon. member Assn. Park Depts., Indiana Nature Study Club. Republican. Protestant. Clubs: Columbia, Athenæum. Author: America's Natural Wealth, A Story of the Use and Abuse of Our Resources, 1942; also of annual reports, Dept. of Conservation, State of Ind., 1919-33, reports on inspections to Nat. Park Service, Dept. of Interior, 1934-43. Contbr. to Am. Planning and Civic Annual, 1935-43. Awarded Pugsley gold medal, 1932; monument erected in his honor, Turkey Run State Park, 1932. Home: 3119 N. Meridian St. Office: Electric Bldg., Indianapolis, Ind. Died Apr. 15, 1944; buried in Turkey Run State Park, Ind.

LIEBLING, Leonard (lēb'lĭng), editor, pianist; b. N.Y. City, Feb. 7, 1880; s. Max and Mathilde (de Perkiewicz) L.; student Coll. City of N.Y., 1894-98, U. of Berlin, 1900-02; m. Eda Baxter, Sept. 4, 1904. Joined staff of Musical Courier, New York, 1903, editor same since 1912; also music critic of New York American, 1923-36; music editor Radio Guide, 1937-40. Librettist: (comic operas) The Girl and the Kaiser; The Balkan Princess; The American Maid; Vera Violetta; composer of piano pieces, trio, overture, songs, etc. Wrote 5 plays which have been produced. Home: 101 W. 57th St. Office: 119 W. 57th St., New York. N.Y. Died Oct. 28, 1945.

LIEBMAN, Joshua Loth, rabbi; b. Hamilton, O., Apr. 7, 1907; s. Simon and Sabina (Loth) L.; A.B., U. of Cincinnati, 1926; rabbi, Hebrew Union Coll., Cincinnati, 1930, D.H.L., 1939; student Hebrew U. in Palestine, Harvard U. and Columbia University, 1928-30; D.D.; Litt.D. (hon.) Colby College, 1948; m. Fan Loth, July 4, 1928. Tutor German dept. U. of Cincinnati, 1925-26, Taft Teaching Fellow in philosophy, also lecturer in Greek philosophy, 1926-29; ordained rabbi, 1930; Leo W. Simon Traveling Fellowship in Philosophy, 1930-34; nat. radio preacher on Message of Israel over NBC and ABC, 1939-46; Charles W. Eliot lecturer, Jewish Inst. of Religion, New York, N.Y., 1945; Samuel Harris lecturer on lit. and life, Bangor (Me.) Theol. Sem., 1946; univ. preacher, Cornell, Dartmouth, Vassar, Wellesley, Wesleyan, Harvard, Mt. Holyoke and Smith; vis. prof. philosophy Boston U. Grad. Sch.; vis. prof. Jewish philosophy and lit. Andover-Newton Theol. Sch. Chmn. Mass. Gov.'s Com. of Clergyman for Racial and Religious Understanding; mem. Com. on Army and Navy Religious Activities, 1942-45; mem. Nat. Commn. of Edn., 1941-43; mem. Boston Civil Liberties Com., Received Simon Lazarus prize for highest academic honors and Youngerman prize for outstanding sermon, Hebrew Union Coll., 1930; Distinguished Service Medal of Phi Beta Kappa, 1947. Hon. vice chmn. United Jewish Appeal; Nat. Hillel commr. B'nai B'rith; mem. Jewish Publ. Soc. (mem. publ. com.), Jewish Acad. Arts and Sciences, Central Conf. Am. Rabbis (mem. exec. bd. 1939-41), Phi Beta Kappa, B'nai B'rith. Author: The Religious Philosophy of Aaron Ben Elijah, 1939; God and the World Crisis—Can We Still Believe in Providence, 1941; Teleology and Attributes in the Philosophy of Maimonides from the Hebrew, 1943; Peace of Mind, 1946 (Religious Book of the Month, May 1946). Contbr. articles to mags. Home: The Somerset, 400 Commonwealth Av. Office: Temple Israel, Longwood Av. at Plymouth St., Boston. Died June 9, 1948.

LIGGETT, Louis Kroh, capitalist; b. Detroit, Mich., Apr. 4, 1875; s. John Templeton and Julia A. (Kroh) L.; ed. pub. schs.; m. Musa Bence, June 26, 1895. Chmn. of bd. and dir. United Drug Co.; chmn. bd. United Mut. Fire Ins. Co.; pres. Pocasset Mfg. Co.; dir. Nat. Cigar Stands Co.; also dir. numerous corporations. Trustee Eastern States Expn.; dir. Eastern States Agrl. and Industrial League. Mem. League for Preservation of Am. Independence. Clubs: Mass. Republican, Middlesex, Algonquin, Boston Madison Square Garden, University. Home: 170 Ivy St., Brookline, Mass. Office: 43 Leon St., Boston, Mass.* Died June 5, 1946.

LIHME, C. Bai (lē'mȧ), b. Aalborg, Denmark, May 24, 1866; s. Herman L. and Adolphine (Moser) L.; grad. U. of Copenhagen, 1888; studied chemistry and metallurgy at Royal Sch. of Mines, Freiberg, and at U. of Heidelberg; m. Olga Hegeler, July 6, 1901; children—Olga H. (Mrs. C. A. Griscom, 3d), Anita H. (Princess E. J. Lobkowicz), Harold H., Edward H. Came to U.S., 1888; naturalized citizen, 1893. Chief chem. Pa. Lead Co., Pittsburgh, Pa., 1889-93; supt. Ill. Zinc. Co., Peru, Ill., 1895-1910; successively dir., sec., v.p. and pres. Matthiessen & Hegeler Zinc Co., La Salle, Ill., until 1921 (retired). Mem. Am. Chem. Soc., Am. Inst. Chem. Engineers, American Institute Mining and Metallurgical Engineers. Mason. Clubs: Metropolitan, River, Union League (New York); Watch Hill Yacht, Misquamicut (Watch Hill, R.I.); Everglades, Seminole Golf, Bath and Tennis, Gulf Stream (Palm Beach, Fla.); Sailfish Club of Fla. Home: 950 5th Av., New York, N.Y.; (summer) "Norman Hall," Watch Hill, R.I.; (winter) Palm Beach, Fla. Died Oct. 15, 1946.

LILES, Luther Brooks (lilz), lawyer; b. Helena, Ala., Mar. 31, 1890; s. Jesse Vernon and Florence (Griffin) L.; ed. Birmingham-Southern Coll., 1908-10, Yale U., 1910-12 (A.B. summa cum laude); LL.B., U. of Ala., 1914; m. Louise McCall, Dec. 24, 1918. Admitted to Ala. bar, 1914, and practiced as associate Knox, Acker, Dixon & Sterne, Anniston, 1914-18; U.S. commr. and judge Juvenile Court, 1916-18; made jr. partner Knox, Acker, Sterne & Liles, 1919; now sr. mem. Knox, Liles, Jones & Woolf; pres. Lily Ice Cream Co., Crescent Stages, Inc., Crescent Motors, Inc.; v.p. and gen. counsel M.&H. Valve and Fittings Co.; dir. Anniston Nat. Bank, Anniston Hotel Company, Calhoun Hotel Company. Director Anniston Chamber of Commerce, Alabama State Chamber of Commerce; Southeastern Motor Bus Association; v.p. Alabama Motorist Assn. Served as 2d lt. Q.M.C., U.S. Army, 1918. Mem. Am., Ala. and Calhoun County bar assns., Phi Beta Kappa, Omicron Delta Kappa, Alpha Sigma Phi. Democrat. Methodist. Mason, K.P. Clubs: Rotary, Anniston Country (past pres.). Home: 325 E. 6th St. Office: Wilson Bldg., Anniston, Ala. Died Aug. 12, 1947.

LILIENTHAL, Howard, surgeon; b. Albany, N.Y., Jan. 9, 1861; s. Meyer and Jennie (Marcus) L.; A.B. cum laude, Harvard Univ., 1883, M.D., Harvard Medical School, 1887; McLean Asylum, br. Mass. Gen. Hosp., 1886; grad. Mt. Sinai Hosp., New York, 1888; m. Mary Harriss d'Antignac, Oct. 19, 1891 (died Mar. 4, 1910); children—Mary d'Antignac (Mrs. Thompson Lawrence), Howard (dec.); m. 2d, Edith Strode, Nov. 7, 1911. Lecturer on surgery, N.Y. Polyclinic, 1888; now cons. surgeon N.Y. Polyclinic; surgeon, Mt. Sinai Hosp., 1892-1940, Bellevue Hosp., 1909-40; now retired from active practice; prof. clin. surgery, Cornell U. Med. Coll. for some years from 1917. Commd. 1st lt. Med. Reserve Corps, 1911 (resigned); maj. M.R.C., Apr. 26, 1917; lt. col., M.C., U.S. Army, June 21, 1918; dir. Base Hosp. 3, at Monpont sur l'Isle; served Meuse-Argonne and St. Mihiel as head of operating team 39, at Evacuation Hosp. 8, also base hosps. 101 and 34; hon. disch. Jan. 4, 1919; cited for D.S.M., May 1, 1921. Fellow American College of Surgeons (Founders Group), and American Board of Surgery, A.A.A.S.; member American Society Control of Cancer, A.M.A., American Surg. Association, American Soc. Thoracic Surgery (ex-pres.), N.Y. Soc. for Thoracic Surgery (ex-pres.), New York Surg. Soc. (ex-pres.), Med. Soc. Co. of N.Y. (ex-pres.), New York Acad. Medicine, Société Internat. de Chirurgie, Mil. Order World Wars (ex-surg. gen.), Am. Legion, Beta Theta Pi; corr. mem. Académie de Chirurgie. Republican. Clubs: University (Winter Park, Florida); Harvard. Author: Imperative Surgery, 1900; Thoracic Surgery, 1925. Contbr. to Binnie's Treatise on Regional Surgery, 1917, and Ochsner's Surgical Diagnosis and Treatment, 1920; more than 300 contbns. to surg. literature. Advisory editor Jour. of Thoracic Surgery. Home: 20 W. 77th St., New York 24, N.Y. Died Apr. 30, 1946.

LILLIE, Frank Rattray, zoölogist; b. Toronto, Ont., June 27, 1870; s. George W. and Emily (Rattray) L.; A.B., Univ. of Toronto, 1891; fellow Clark Univ., 1891-92, Univ. of Chicago, 1892-93, Ph.D., 1894; D.Sc., Univ. of Toronto, 1919, Yale, 1932, and Harvard University, 1938; LL.D., Johns Hopkins University, 1942; m. Frances Crane, June 29, 1895. Instr. zoölogy, U. of Mich., 1894-99; prof. biology, Vassar Coll., 1899-1900; asst. prof. zoölogy and embryology, 1900-02, asso. prof., 1902-07, prof. since 1907, chmn. dept. zoölogy, 1911-35, dean of division of biological sciences, 1931-35, U. of Chicago. Head dept. zoology, 1893-1907, assistant director, 1900-08, dir., 1908-26, pres., 1925-1942, Marine Biol. Lab., Woods Hole, Mass.; pres. Woods Hole Oceanographic Inst., 1930-39; dir. Crane Co. Mng. editor Biol. Bulletin, 1902-26; associate editor Journal Experimental Zoölogy Physiological Zoölogy. Fellow A.A.A.S. (v.p. 1914); mem. Nat. Acad. Sciences (pres. 1935-39), National Research Council (chairman 1935-36), American Philos. Soc., Acad. Nat. Sci., Phila.; Société Belge de Biologie, Société de Biologie, Paris, Am. Soc. Naturalists (v.p. 1914, pres. 1915), Am. Soc. Zoölogists (pres. Central Br. 1905-08), Assn. Am. Anatomists, Boston Soc. Natural History, Am. Philos. Soc., Royal Soc. of Edinburgh, Zoöl. Soc. of London. Clubs: Quadrangle, University (Chicago); Cosmos (Washington, D.C.); Century Assn. (New York). Contbr. to scientific jours. Home: 5801 Kenwood Av., Chicago. Died Nov. 5, 1947.

LILLIE, Gordon William (Pawnee Bill), ranchman; b. Bloomington, Ill., Feb. 14, 1860; s. Newton William and Susan A. (Conant) L.; ed. sch. Bloomington, 1866-78; m. Mary Emma Manning, Aug. 31, 1886; 1 son, Gordon William (dec.). Began career as hunter and trapper, 1878, interpreter for Pawnee tribe Indians, ranching nr. Medicine Lodge, Kan.; interpreter and mgr. Pawnee Indians with 1st Buffalo Bill Wild West Show, 1883-86; many yrs. professional showman in U.S. and Europe, known as Pawnee Bill; engaged by Bd. Trade, Wichita, Kan., to organize and lead Boomers into Okla., Apr. 1889; partner Buffalo Bill (Col. W. F. Cody), 1908-13; prop. Pawnee Bill's Buffalo Ranch, Oldtown and Indian Trading Post, since 1909; active in work among Pawnee Indians and in perpetuation of the buffalo; v.p. Fern Oil Corp. Pres. U.S. Highway 64 Assn. Nat. supervisor Mounted Troops of Am.; nat. supervisor Boy Scouts of Am.; dir. Hist. Soc. of Okla. Republican. Mason (32°, Shriner; hon. mem. temples at Phila., Pa., Little Rock, Ark., Okla. City). Lion. Author: Thirty Years Among the Pawnee Indians, 1928. Co-author: Oklahoma (with Courtney Ryley Cooper), 1926; Blazing Horizon (with Ernest Lynn), 1927; Pawnee Bill The Romance of Oklahoma (with Edwin Mootz), 1928; Stampede Range (with J. R. Johnston), 1928. Home: Oldtown, Pawnee, Okla. Died Feb. 3, 1942.

LILLY, Josiah Kirby, manufacturing chemist; b. Greencastle, Ind., Nov. 18, 1861; s. Eli and Emily (Lemon) L.; studied Asbury (now DePauw) U., 1874-76; Ph.G., cum laude, Philadelphia College of Pharmacy, 1882; m. Lily Marie Ridgely, November 18, 1882; m. 2d, Lila Allison, June 29, 1935. Entered manufacturing pharmacy with father, 1876; dir. laboratories of Eli Lilly & Co., 1882-98; became pres. and exec. head same on death of father, 1898, now chmn. bd. Pioneer in alkaloidal standardization of medicines. Dir. Indianapolis Y.M.C.A., 18 yrs. Episcopalian. Mem. Am. Pharm. Assn., Ind. Pharm. Assn., Am. Chem. Soc., Am. Mfrs. Assn., Loyal Legion. Clubs: University, Columbia, Art, Contemporary, Country. Home: Crows Nest, Indianapolis, Ind.* Died Feb. 8, 1948.

LILLY, Linus Augustine, clergyman, prof. law; b. Carrollton, Mo., Sept. 20, 1876; s. Thomas Henry and Lucinda Ann (Deaver) L.; student Creighton U., 1900-02, Florissant Sem., 1902-05; A.B., St. Louis U., 1908, A.M., 1909; LL.M., Georgetown U., Washington, D.C., 1916; studied Gregorian U., Rome, 1921. Admitted to practice in Mo., 1898; joined Soc. of Jesus (Jesuits), 1902; ordained priest R.C. Ch., 1914; with St. Louis U. since 1917, successively prof. canon law, constl. law, equity; prof. legal ethics and legal history since 1927. Mem. bd. trustees St. Louis U. Mem. Am. Soc. Internat. Law, Catholic Assn. for Internat. Peace (v.p. 1928-33), Am. Catholic Philos. Assn. Home: 221 N. Grand Blvd. Address: 3642 Lindell Blvd., St. Louis, Mo. Died Apr. 16, 1943.

LINCOLN, Jonathan Thayer, mfr.; b. Fall River, Mass., Nov. 6, 1869; s. Leontine and Amelia Sanford (Duncan) L.; A.B., Harvard, 1892; hon. A.M., Dartmouth, 1911; m. Louise Sears Cobb, June 24, 1903. Pres. Lincoln Manufacturing Co., Davis Mills. Sometime lecturer at Dartmouth Coll. on labor questions and mem. research dept. Harvard Grad. Sch. of Business Administration. Mem. Am. Econ. Assn., Am. Sociol. Soc., Asiatic Soc. of Japan, etc. Republican. Clubs: Harvard Faculty (Cambridge); Army and Navy (New York). Author: City of the Dinner Pail, 1909; The Factory, 1912; The Age of Power, 1915; The Beginning of the Machine Age in New England, 1935; also numerous articles on labor questions. Home: 6 Craigie Circle, Cambridge, Mass. Died Feb. 10, 1942.

LINCOLN, Joseph Crosby, author; b. Brewster, Mass., Feb. 13, 1870; s. Joseph and Emily (Crosby) L.; ed. Brewster and Chelsea, Mass.; m. Florence E. Sargent, May 12, 1897; 1 son, Joseph Freeman. Asso. editor League of America Wheelmen Bulletin, 1896-99; moved from Boston to New York, 1899. Author: Cape Cod Ballads, 1902; Cap'n Eri, 1904; Partners of the Tide, 1905; Mr. Pratt, 1906; The Old Home House, 1907; Cy Whittaker's Place, 1908; Our Village, 1909; Keziah Coffin, 1909; The Depot Master, 1910; Cap'n Warren's Wards, 1911; The Woman Haters, 1911; The Postmaster, 1912; Rise of Roscoe Paine, 1912; Mr. Pratt's Patients, 1913; Cap'n Dan's Daughter, 1914;

Kent Knowles, "Quahaug," 1914; Thankful's Inheritance, 1915; Mary 'Gusta, 1916; Extricating Obadiah, 1917; Shavings, 1918; The Portygee, 1919; Galusha the Magnificent, 1921; Fair Harbor, 1922; Doctor Nye, 1923; Rugged Water, 1924; Queer Judson, 1925; The Big Mogul, 1926; The Aristocratic Miss Brewster, 1927; Silas Bradford's Boy, 1928; (with Freeman Lincoln) Blair's Attic, 1929; Blowing Clear, 1930; All Alongshore, 1931; Head Tide, 1932; Back Numbers, 1933; Storm Signals, 1935; Cape Cod Yesterdays, 1935; Great Aunt Lavinia, 1936; Storm Girl, 1937; A. Hall & Co., 1938; Christmas Days, 1938; Ownley Inn (with Freeman Lincoln), 1939; Out of the Fog, 1940. Clubs: Players (New York); Franklin Inn, Arts (Phila.). Contbr. short stories, verse, etc., to various mags. Home: Villa Nova, Pa.; (summer) Chatham, Mass.* Died Mar. 10, 1944.

LINCOLN, Paul Martyn, elec. engr.; b. Antrim, Mich., Jan. 1, 1870; s. William E. and Louise (Marshall) L.; Western Reserve U., 1888-89; E.E., Ohio State U., 1892; Dr. of Engring. from same univ., 1933; m. Elizabeth R. Hague, June 30, 1897; children—Helen H. (Mrs. J. W. Reavis), Elizabeth H. (Mrs. H. L. Goodman). With Short Electric Co., Cleveland, 1892, Westinghouse Elec. & Mfg. Co., Pittsburgh, 1892-95; electrical supt. Niagara Falls Power Co., 1895-1902; with Westinghouse Elec. & Mfg. Co., 1902-19, as engr. of power division and gen. engr.; prof. elec. engring., U. of Pittsburgh, 1911-15; cons. engr. Lincoln Electric Co., Cleveland, 1919-22; dir. Sch. of Elec. Engring., Cornell U., since 1922; pres. Therm-Electric Meter Co. since 1938. Republican. Presbyterian. Fellow Am. Inst. E.E. (pres. 1914-15); mem. Am. Soc. Mech. Engrs. John Scott medal, 1902, for synchronism indicator from Franklin Inst. Mason (32°). Club: Engineers' (New York). Address: Therm Electric Meters Co., Inc., Ithaca, N.Y.

Died Dec. 20, 1944.

LINDQUIST, Rudolph Daniel, educator; b. Oakland, Calif, Nov. 27, 1888; s. John Nils and Albertina (Johnson) L.; A.B., Univ. of Calif., 1915, A.M., 1922; post grad. work, Columbia Univ., 1922; Ed.D., U. of Calif., 1936; m. Anna Eldora Carlson, Sept. 9, 1919; 1 dau., Dorothy Jean. Teacher Elko (Nev.) High Sch, 1915-18; prin. elementary schs., Berkeley, Calif., 1919-24; asso. dir. teacher training U. of Calif., 1924-25; instr. summer sessions, U. of Calif. and U. of Calif. at Los Angeles, 1924-30; dir. research, Oakland pub. schs., 1925-27, asst. supt., 1927-31; pres. Chico (Calif.) State Coll., 1931; became dir. of univ. schs. and prof. of edn., Ohio State University, 1931; dir. Cranbrook School, Bloomfield Hills, Mich., 1933-43; superintendent Santa Barbara (Calif.) City Schools since Nov. 1, 1943. Served in A.E.F., World War, 1918-19. Trustee Student Aid Foundation, University of Michigan. Lecturer, University of Michigan. Mem. N.E.A. (dept. pres. 1935-36), Dept. of Supervisors and Dirs. of Instrn. (mem. exec. com. 1941-43), Phi Delta Kappa (nat. pres., 1931-35). Independent. Episcopalian. Editor and contbr. Phi Delta Kappa. Club: University (Santa Barbara). Home: 935 Las Alturas Rd. Office: 1235 Chapala St., Santa Barbara, Calif. Died Mar. 30, 1949; buried Santa Barbara.

LINDSAY, Anna Robertson Brown (lind'zē), author; b. Washington, Feb. 20, 1864; d. Rev. Dr. William Y. and Flora (Robertson) Brown; B.A., Wellesley, 1883, M.A., 1888; Oxford University, England, 1887-88, 89; Ph.D., U. of Pa., 1892; m. Samuel McCune Lindsay, Apr. 9, 1896; children—Mrs. Flora Lindsay Magoun, Daniel England, Mrs. Eleanor Lindsay Whiteleather. Pres. Phila. Br. Assn. Collegiate Alumnæ 1894-96; trustee Wellesley, 1906-18. Author: What Is Worth While?, 1893; The Victory of Our Faith, 1895; Culture and Reform, 1896; Giving What We Have, 1897; What Good Does Wishing Do?, 1898; The Warriors, 1903; Hymn Before Election, 1905; The Warrior Spirit in the Republic of God (new edit. of The Warriors), 1906; Gloria Christi, United Study of Missions Series, Vol. VII, 1907; The Spiritual Care of a Child, 1907; The Greatest Work in the World, 1913; Hymn in War-Time, 1917; Working with Giant Power, 1924, a few later publications. Mem. American Association University Women, Phi Beta Kappa; member Pan-American Congress of Women, Lima, Peru, 1924; hon. mem. Comite Internacional de Universitarias Graduadas, Lima, 1925; member Graduate Council Wellesley Coll. Alumnæ Assn. since 1934. Student of Spanish, Columbia U., 1925-28. Clubs: Town Hall, Wellesley (New York). Home: 29 Claremont Av., New York 27. Died. Feb. 28, 1948.

LINDSAY, Arthur Hawes, corp. official; b. Fox Lake, Wis., Nov. 4, 1862; s. Edmond James and Celia (Ellis) (Hawes) L.; ed. pub. schs.; m. Alice Kingsbury, Jan. 8, 1896 (died 1920); m. 2d, Nellie E. Edwards, Sept. 16, 1924. Messenger and clk. First Nat. Bank, Milwaukee, 1878-79, Wis. Marine & Fire Ins. Co. Bank, 1879-93; teller Wis. Nat. Bank, 1893-1900; cashier Marine Nat. Bank, 1900-11, v.p., later pres., 1911-30; chmn. bd. Marine Nat. Exchange Bank, 1930-42; hon. chmn. bd. since 1942; dir. Northwestern Nat. Ins. Co., Northwestern Nat. Casualty Co., Phoenix Hosiery Co. Mem. advisory com. Milwaukee Protestant Home for the Aged. Clubs: Milwaukee. Home: 2723 E. Newton Av., Milwaukee 11. Office: 625 N. Water St., Milwaukee 1, Wis.

Died Nov. 25, 1949.

LINDSAY, George LeRoy (lind'sā), educator; b. Ashbourne, Pa., Jan. 23, 1888; s. George Alexander and Mary (Perkins) L.; A.B., Temple U., 1916; ed. Temple U. Coll. of Music, 1904-17, Mus.B., 1917, pvt. teachers, and Columbia Coll. of Music, 1904-09; hon. Mus.D., Temple U., 1936; m. Louise Downs, June 26, 1926; 1 dau., Mary Louise. Organist (various churches), and teacher of Piano, Phila., since 1906; instr. Columbia Coll. of Music, Phila., 1908-12; supervisor of music, Phila. pub. schs., 1918-25, dir. of music since 1925; spl. instr., Temple U., 1920-26, Columbia U., 1929-30, Am. Inst. of Normal Methods, 1920-25, U. of Pa., 1931-33. Dir. Music Educators Nat. Confs.; v.p. Eastern Music Educators Confs. (pres. 1935-37). Mem. N.E.A., Pa. State Edn. Assn., Phila. Teachers Assn., Sinfonia, Phi Delta Kappa and Phi Mu Alpha. Presbyterian. Mason (K.T.). Club: Philadelphia Schoolmens. Editor and author, Educational Vocal Technique, 2 vols., 1936. Editor: Educational Orchestra Folios 1 and 2, 1934, 36. Compiler (with Gartlan, Smith), Assembly Songs for Intermediate Grades. Compiler, Most Popular Operatic Songs, 1930. Editor (with McConathy and Morgan), Music: The Universal Language. Composer anthems, part songs, vocal solos, organ pieces, etc. Conductor, Phila. Home School Chorus; organizer all Phila. senior and junior musical festivals. Weekly broadcasts Phila. pub. schs. music activities. Home: 6642 McCallum St., Philadelphia, Pa. Died Aug. 25, 1943.

LINDSAY, Maud McKnight, kindergartner; b. Tuscumbia, Ala., May 13, 1874; d. Robert Burns and Sarah Miller (Winston) Lindsay; attended Deshler Female Inst., Tuscombia, Ala., 5 yrs.; kindergarten training under Mrs. Jeanne Pettett Cooper, Tuscumbia. Teacher pvt. kindergarten, Tuscumbia, 1896-98; prin. Florence (Ala.) Free Kindergarten (first free kindergarten in Ala.), 1898-1940; prin. Florence Free Kindergarten, 1898-1941; on leave of absence 2½ yrs., of which 1 yr. was spent as res. Elizabeth Peabody Settlement House, Boston; mem. faculty summer sch., New York U., kindergarten dept., 1906-10; pres. Sheffield, Ala., Free Kindergarten Assn., 1912-16; pres. Conclave Ala. Writers, 1924-25; pres. Blue Pencil Club, 1923-31; 2d v.p. Birmingham Branch League of Am. Pen Women, 1931. Presbyterian. Author: Mother Stories, 1899; More Mother Stories, 1905; A Story Garden for Little Children, 1913; Story Teller for Little Children, 1915; The Joyous Travelers (with Emilie Poulsson), 1919; Bobby and The Big Road, 1920; The Joyous Guests (with Emilie Poulsson), 1921; Little Missy, 1922; Silverfoot, 1924; The Toy Shop, 1926; The Choosing Book, 1928; Songs for Alabama, 1929; The Amazing Adventures of Ali, 1931; The Storyland Tree, 1933; Posey and the Peddler, 1938; Jock Barefoot, 1939; Fun on Childrens' Street, 1941; Songs for Alabama (booklet), pub. for benefit of Alabama Flood Sufferers, 1925. Home: 103 Park Blvd., Sheffield, Ala. Died May 30, 1941; buried in Winston Cemetery, Tuscumbia, Ala.

LINDSEY, Ben(jamin) B(arr), judge, publicist; b. Jackson, Tenn., Nov. 25, 1869; s. Landy Tunstall and Letitia Anna (Barr) L.; ed. pub. schs.; received hon. degrees from U. of Denver and Notre Dame U.; admitted to bar, 1894; m. Henrietta Brevoort, Dec. 20, 1913. Apptd. pub. guardian and administrator, Denver, 1899, under Colo. Juvenile Court law of 1899; apptd. judge Juvenile Court of Denver, 1900, elected, 1901, and served until July 1, 1927; promoter of juvenile court system and originator of some of its features, and has internat. reputation as authority upon juvenile delinquency. Author Colorado Juvenile Court laws; puts boys on their honor (boys sentenced to Industrial Sch., at Golden, Colo., go unattended, and only 5 out of several hundred have betrayed their trust); succeeded in having the first contributory delinquency law against adults passed by Colo. Legislature, holding negligent parents, employers, etc., accountable. Candidate for gov. of Colo., 1906; mem. Prog. Nat. Com., 1912. Lecturer on children's problems. Moved to California, admitted to bar, 1928; elected judge Superior Court, Nov. 1934, by largest vote ever given in similar election in California, re-elected Aug. 1940. Author: Problems of the Children; The Beast and the Jungle; The Rule of Plutocracy in Colorado; The Doughboy's Religion, 1919; Pan Germanism in America; The Revolt of Modern Youth, 1925; The House of Human Welfare; The Companionate Marriage, 1927; The Dangerous Life (autobiography), 1931; also author of The Children's Bills and the Calif. Children's Court of Conciliation Law of 1939 and appointed first judge of that court. Home: 10646 Somma Way, Bel-Air, Los Angeles, Calif. Died Mar. 26, 1943.

LINDSEY, Edward Sherman, lawyer; b. Warren, Pa., Dec. 17, 1872; s. Wilton Monroe and Emma (Sherman) L.; ed. Phillips Exeter Acad., Dartmouth Coll., 1890-91; LL.B., New York Law Sch., 1893; m. Mildred M. Crosby, May 28, 1895 (died May 31, 1937). Practiced at Warren, 1895-1920. Mem. Pa. Ho. of Rep., 1915; pres. judge 37th Jud. Dist. of Pa., 1920-22. Treasurer and asso. editor Jour. of Am. Inst. Criminal Law and Criminology. Mem. Am. Bar Assn., Pa. Bar Assn., Am. Soc. Internat. Law, Internat. Congress Americanists. Fellow A.A.A.S., Am. Geog. Soc., Selden Soc., Am. Anthropol. Assn., Am. Polit. Science Assn., Am. Sociol. Soc., Am. Hist. Assn., Am. Folk-Lore Soc., Am. Soc. Naturalists, N.Y. Acad. Sciences. Author: Indeterminate Sentence and Parole System, 1925; The International Court, 1931; and numerous articles in legal periodicals. Home: Warren, Pa. Died Apr. 25, 1943.

LINDSEY, Julian Robert, army officer; b. Irwinton, Ga., Mar. 16, 1871; s. John W. and Julia F. (Tucker) L.; grad. U.S. Mil. Acad., 1892, Gen. Staff Sch., 1920, Army War Coll., 1921; m. Hannah Broster, June 11, 1904 (died Mar. 29, 1905); 1 son, Julian Broster. Commd. 2d lt., cav., U. S. Army, June 11, 1892, and advanced through grades to col., July 1, 1920; brig. gen. (temporary), April 1918-June 1919; brig. gen., Jan. 1, 1932. Was comdg. gen. Ft. Knox, Ky.; promoted major gen. (retired). Served in China, P.I., Cuba (2d occupation), Mexico (1916-17). Awarded D.S.M. Clubs: Army and Navy, Columbia Country (Washington). Address: Army and Navy Club, Washington. Died June 27, 1948; buried at U.S. Military Academy, West Point.

LINDSTROM, Ernest W(alter) (lind'strŭm), prof. genetics; b. Chicago, Ill., Feb. 5, 1891; s. Earnst A. and Mary (Tranell) L.; B.A., U. of Wis., 1914; Ph.D. Cornell U., 1917; m. A. Cornelia Anderson, Aug. 27, 1921; children—Eugene Shipman, Cornelia Goodrich, Rosemary Vaughn. Asst. in plant breeding and investigator, Cornell U., 1914-17; asst. prof. genetics, U. of Wis., 1919-22; prof. genetics and head of dept., Ia. State Coll. Agr. and Mech. Arts, since 1922, also vice dean of Graduate College; on leave as asst. dir. European office Internat. Edn. Bd. (Rockefeller Foundation), 1927-28; on leave, visiting prof. genetics, Universidad Nacional Facultad de Agronomia, Medellin, Colombia, S.A., 1944-45. Served as 2d lt. Air Service, U.S. Army, 1917-18. Fellow Ia. Acad. Science; mem. A.A.A.S., Am. Soc. Naturalists, Bot. Soc. America, Genetic Soc. Am. (pres. 1942), Sigma Xi, Beta Theta Pi, Gamma Alpha. Contbr. to scientific jours. Home: Ames, Ia. Died Nov. 8, 1948.

LINEBERGER, Walter Franklin (lin'bĕr-gĕr), ex-congressman, cons. civil and mining engr.; b. July 20, 1883; s. John Henry and Lucy (Aynesworth) L.; ed. Rensselaer Poly. Inst. of Troy, N.Y., class, 1904; m. Florence Elizabeth Hite, June 16, 1909; children—Florence Elizabeth, Walter Franklin, Janet Hite, Anne Lorraine. Engaged in mining in Mexico 9 yrs.; mem. 67th-69th Congress (1921-27), 9th Calif. Dist. co-owner and mgr. Colosseum and Mojave Tungsten Mines, Jean, Nev. Enlisted in U.S. Army; served in France with engring. units of 1st, 32d combat divs.; wounded in action; returned to U.S., Apr. 1919. Awarded Croix de Guerre with palm (French); divisional citation for bravery under fire. Mem. Am. Soc. C.E., S.R. Home: 303 E. Valley Rd. (Montecito), Santa Barbara, Calif. Died Oct. 9, 1943.

LINTON, Frank B. A., artist; b. Philadelphia, Pa., Feb. 26, 1871; s. Edwin Ruthven and Sarah (Piper) L.; ed. Ecole des Beaux Arts and Academie Julian, Paris, France, 1890-98; studied with Thomas Eakins, Phila., 1900-09. Painted portraits of Pres. Mathis Baldwin of Baldwin Locomotive Works, Dean Ruther Weaver of Hahnemann Med. Coll. (both Phila.), Dr. Jennings of Johns Hopkins, and other notables. Awarded gold medal, Paris Salon, 1927; Officier d' Academie (France), 1927. Mem. N.Y. Soc. Pennsylvanians, Internationale Union des Beaux Arts et des Lettres (Paris). Democrat. Methodist. Club: Art. Home: 2037 De Lancey Pl., Philadelphia, Pa. Died Nov. 13, 1943.

LINTON, Robert, engineer; b. Hudson, O., May 29, 1870; s. Robert J. and Caroline S. (Doolittle) L.; A.M., Washington and Jefferson Coll., 1902, Sc.D., 1937; post-grad. work Royal Tech. Sch., Berlin, 1892-94; m. Margaret McElveen, 1896; 1 dau., Eleanor. Mining engr. with McKinney & Smith, Pittsburgh, 1890-92; in window glass mfg., 1894-1904; asst. to chmn. Am. Window Glass Co., 1904-06, with gen. supervision operations in all factories; mining engr., 1906-23, hdqrs. first Los Angeles, later New York; pres. North Butte Mining Co., 1918-23; vice-pres. and gen. mgr. Pacific Clay Products, 1923-35; in private practice since 1935. Pres. Gen. Alumni Assn. Washington and Jefferson Coll., 1917-18; dir. and mem. exec. com. Am. Mining Congress, 1920-23, bd. of govs., western div., 1939-41; president Calif. Clay Products Inst., 1928-30; v.p. Los Angeles Chamber of Commerce, 1935; mem. Calif. State Mining Board, 1929-30 and 1937-41. Fellow A.A.A.S., Am. Ceramic Soc.; mem. Am. Inst. Mining and Metall. Engrs., Am. Soc. for Testing Materials, Mining Assn. of the Southwest (v.p.), Am. Soc. C.E., Soc. Colonial Wars, S.R., Delta Tau Delta. Republican. Episcopalian. Mason (K.T.). Club: Mining (New York). Author of numerous tech. papers and articles. Home: 517½ S. Carondelet St., Los Angeles, Calif. Died Nov. 12, 1942.

LINVILLE, Henry Richardson, educator; b. St. Joseph, Mo., Aug. 12, 1866; s. Richard Baxter and Emma Smith (Richardson) L.; A.B., U. of Kan., 1893; A.B., Harvard, 1894, A.M., 1895, Ph.D., 1897; m. Adele Miln, June 9, 1908 (died Nov. 11, 1921); children—Rhoda, Gordon John (dec.), Byron Miln, Henry Richardson; m. 2d, Laura Branson, Dec. 26, 1931. Head dept. biology, DeWitt Clinton High Sch., N.Y. City, 1897-1908; head of dept. biology, Jamaica High Sch., 1908-21; pres. and exec. Teachers Union of N.Y. City, 1916-35. Pres. Am. Fedn. Teachers, 1931-34; exec. New York Teachers Guild since 1935. Mem. Sigma Xi. Author: A Textbook in General Zoölogy (with Henry A. Kelly and Harley J. Van Cleave), 1906; The Biology of Man and Other Organisms, 1923. Contbr. to ednl. publs. Died Oct. 1, 1941.

LIPMAN, Charles Bernard, plant physiologist; b. Moscow, Russia, Aug. 17, 1883; s. Michael Gregory and Ida (Birkhahn) L.; brought to U.S., 1889; B.Sc., Rutgers, 1904, M.S., 1909; M.S., U. of Wisconsin, 1909; Ph.D., University of Calif., 1910; Sc.D., honoris causa, Rutgers, 1934; m. Marion Amesbury Evans,

May 25, 1925; 1 dau., Georgia Evans. Goewey fellow, U. of Calif., 1908-09; instr. soil bacteriology, 1909, asst. prof. soils, 1910, asso. prof., 1912, prof. soil chemistry and bacteriology, 1913-21, prof. plant nutrition, 1921-25, prof. plant physiology since 1925, U. of Calif., dean of Grad. Div. since 1923. Mem. Ednl. Advisory Bd., John Simon Guggenheim Memorial Foundation; dir. Belgian American Educational Foundation. In charge administration James D. Phelan fellowships in Literature and Art (San Francisco, Calif.), 1934-39; member board of directors International House, Berkeley. Chmn. com. 6th Pacific Science Congress, 1939; pres. Calif. Chapter American-Scandinavian Foundation, 1941, 1942; mem. State Dept. Com. on Adjustment of Foreign Students, 1941, 1942; mem. War Ration Bd., Draft Bd. No. 68, Berkeley. Fellow A.A.A.S., Soc. for Research on Meteorites; Mem. Am. Chem. Soc., Am. Soc. Plant Physiologists, Soc. American Bacteriologists, California Botanical Society, California Academy Science, Society of Experimental Biology and Medicine, Sigma Xi, Alpha Zeta, Phi Sigma, Phi Beta Kappa (senator; committee on qualifications), Golden Bear, Sigma Delta Pi. Clubs: University, Bohemian (San Francisco); Athenian-Nile (Oakland); Faculty (Berkeley); Century (New York). Author numerous papers on plant physiology, plant chemistry, and plants and soils; also with soil and marine bacteria, bacteria in ancient rocks, meteorites, etc. Asso. editor Plant Physiology, Jour. of Bacteriology, Soil Science. Home: 10 Tanglewood Rd., Berkeley, Calif. Died Oct. 22, 1944.

LIPPINCOTT, Joseph Barlow, hydraulic engr.; b. Scranton, Pa., Oct. 10, 1864; s. Joshua Allen (LL.D.) and Harriet Phillips (Barlow) L.; student Dickinson Coll., 1880-82; A.B., U. of Kan., 1886, hon. C.E., 1914; m. Josephine Phillips Cook, Apr. 1890; children—Rose (dec.), Joseph Reading. With Santa Fe R.R. System, 1886-88; topographer U.S. Geol. Survey, 1888-92; asst. engr. Bear Valley Irrigation Co., 1892; in charge various irrigation investigations in Calif., 1893-94; hydrographer U.S. Geol. Survey for Calif., 1895-1902; supervising engr. for Pacific Coast dist., with U.S. Reclamation Service, 1902-06; asst. chief engr. Los Angeles Aqueduct, 1906-13; cons. engr., Los Angeles, since 1913. Consulting engr. for municipal water works in San Francisco, Fresno, Santa Barbara, Los Angeles and other Calif. towns, Denver, El Paso, Phoenix, and Los Angeles County, Hawaiian Islands, Mexico and Alaska; engr. and mgr. construction of Camp Kearney, Nat. Guard Camp, San Diego County, Calif., also Rockwell Field, San Diego, 1917-18; supervising engr. U.S. Housing Corp., Pittsburgh and Bethlehem, Pa., 1918, civil service commr. for Los Angeles; park commr. since 1910; state commr., 6th Dist. Agrl. Assn. since 1911; cons. engr., 1925, for State of Calif., Tri-County Flood Control Bd., Los Angeles County Flood Control District, 1927-28, Internat. Water Boundary Commn. between U.S. and Mex. since 1932, U.S. Army engrs. in connection with flood control work, Los Angeles County, 1939, City of Los Angeles and several cities and irrigation dists.; mem. Weather Bur. Com. of Nat. Science Advisory Bd. since 1935; architect-engineer (associated with Lippincott & Bowen) at Camp Haan and Mojave Desert Firing Center for constructing buildings and designing sewers for March Field and for Marysville Triangular Cantonment (all in Calif.), 1940-41. Awarded James R. Croes medal by American Society of Civil Engineers, 1914. Member American Society C.E. (made hon. mem. 1937). Clubs: California, Los Angeles Country (Los Angeles). Author of numerous papers and reports on water supply and irrigation topics. Home: 1256 W. Adams St. Office: 714 W. Olympic Blvd., Los Angeles, Calif. Died Nov. 4, 1942.

LIPPINCOTT, Martha Shepard, writer; b. Moorestown, N.J.; d. Jesse and Elizabeth (Holmes) Lippincott; ed. Swarthmore Coll. Began writing poetry when a school girl in 1886; since 1895, has made it life work; contbr. poems, stories, articles and book reviews to many mags., newspapers and religious papers in U.S., Can., Eng., Ireland and Scotland. Mem. Soc. of Friends; widely called "The Quaker Poetess." Author: Visions of Life, 1901; also a large number of poems and songs, among the latter of which are: Guide Thou My Bark (sacred solo), Thou Wilt Guide My Journey Through (same), That All Thy Mercies May Be Seen (quartette), Teach Me Thy Will, For Thy Own Dear Self, To My Valentine, My Love for All Eternity. Sleep Little Birdies, Faith and Trust (sacred solo), etc., and many gospel songs. Home: 6105 Jefferson St., West Philadelphia. Died Aug. 10, 1949.

LIPSEY, Plautus Iberus (lĭp'sē), clergyman, editor; b. Independence, Miss., July 5, 1865; s. John Washington and Malinda Frances (Maxville) L.; student Union U., Jackson, Tenn., 1880-82; B.A., U. of Miss., 1886; Th.M., Southern Bapt. Theol. Sem., 1889; D.D., Miss. Coll., Clinton, Miss., 1906; m. Julia Toy Johnson, Nov. 21, 1889 (dec.); children—John Johnson, Plautus Iberus, Julia Frances (Mrs. X. O. Steele), James Hollins, Crawford Hall, Mary Winston; m. 2d, Mrs. Florence Bowen Morris, June 4, 1939. Ordained Baptist ministry, 1889; pastor successively Columbus, Ind., Vicksburg, Miss., Murfreesboro, Tenn., Adairville, Ky., First Ch., Greenwood, Miss., and Clinton, Miss., until 1912; editor The Baptist Record, Jackson, Miss., 1912-41; director Bank of Clinton. First to suggest Bapt. Sem. in New Orleans; a founder Bapt. Bible Inst. and Southern Bapt. Hosp., both at New Orleans. A founder and pres. bd. trustees Miss. Bapt. Hosp., Jackson, Miss.; pres. Miss. Bapt. Conv. and of the Conv. Bd.; mem. bd. trustees of Southern Bapt. Theol. Sem., mem. Edn. Commn. of Miss. Bapt.; mem. Miss. Bapt. Orphanage Bd.; pres. bd. trustees Bapt. Bible Inst. Author: Tests of Faith and Revelation; An Interpretation. Member Delta Psi. Democrat. Home: Clinton, Miss. Died July 16, 1947.

LISLE, Arthur Beymer (lil), corp. official; b. West Newton, Mass., Dec. 26, 1871; s. Rev. William McIntyre and Anna Angell Waterman (Whiting) L.; ed. pub. schs.; m. Martha Briggs, June 2, 1896 President New England Water, Light & Power Associates, Weybosset Company; Wakefield Water Co.; also dir. or trustee many utility companies. Trustee Brown University, American University of Cairo. President Society for Preservation of New England Antiquities. Republican. Episcopalian. Clubs: Hope, Providence Art, Agawam Hunt, Turks Head, Dunes Club, East Greenwich Yacht, Union Interalliée. Home: 4365 Post Rd., East Greenwich, R.I. Office: Hospital Trust Bldg., Providence, R.I. Died Mar. 30, 1949.

LITCHFIELD, Grace Denio, author; b. N.Y. City, Nov. 19, 1849; d. Edwin C. and Grace Hill (Hubbard) Litchfield. Author: Only an Incident, 1883; The Knight of the Black Forest, 1885; Criss-Cross, 1885; A Hard Won Victory, 1888; Little Venice, 1890; Little He and She, 1893; Mimosa Leaves, 1895; In the Crucible, 1897; The Moving Finger Writes, 1900; Vita, 1904; The Letter D, 1904; The Supreme Gift, 1908; Narcissus, 1908; Baldur the Beautiful, 1910; The Nun of Kent, 1911; The Burning Question, 1913; Collected Poems, 1913; The Song of the Sirens, 1917; As a Man Sows, 1926. Home: 2010 Massachusetts Av., Washington. Died Dec. 4, 1944.

LITTAUER, Lucius Nathan, (lĭt'our), ex-congressman; b. Gloversville, N.Y., Jan. 20, 1859; s. Nathan and Harriet (Sporborg) L.; moved to New York, 1865; A.B. Harvard, 1878; D.H.L., 1927; L.L.D., Hamilton Coll., 1940; widower. Became connected with his father's glove mfg. business, 1878; succeeded to it, 1882; pres. Gloversville Knitting Co., Fonda Glove Lining Co. Member of 55th to 59th Congresses (1897-1907). Republican. Regent, Univ. of State of N.Y., 1912-14. Donor of $1,100,000 to be administered in the cause of better understanding among all mankind, 1930; donor of over $2,250,000 to Harvard Univ. for establishment of a grad. sch. of pub. administrn. and Littauer Center; builder and donor Nathan Littauer Hospital, Gloversville, N.Y. Decorated Legion d'Honneur, 1930; Médaille d'Honneur, 1930 (France). Home: 64 W. 87th St. Office: 235 4th Av., New York, N.Y. Died Mar. 2, 1944.

LITTELL, Philip, writer; b. Brookline, Mass., Aug. 6, 1868; s. Robert Smith and Harriet Anne (Moody) L.; A.B., Harvard, 1890; m. Fanny Merriam Whittemore, Nov. 6, 1894; children—Robert, Margaret (Mrs. William Platt), Whittemore. On staff of Milwaukee Sentinel, 1890-1901, New York Globe, 1910-13, New Republic, 1914-23. Club: University (New York). Author: Books and Things, 1919; This Way Out, 1928. Home: Cornish, N.H. Died Oct. 31, 1943.

LITTLE, Arthur W., printer; b. New York, N.Y., Dec. 15, 1873; s. Joseph James and Josephine (Robinson) L.; ed. pvt. schs. and business coll., New York; m. Marguerite Lanier Winslow, Apr. 19, 1897 (died Mar. 21, 1926); children—Winslow, Arthur W.; m. 2d, Charlotte Houston Fairchild, Apr. 27, 1927 (died Sept. 2, 1927); m. 3d, Mary Alice Van Nest Barney, June 30, 1928 (died Apr. 18, 1939). Joined father's company, J. J. Little & Co., printers, 1891; now chmn. bd. J. J. Little & Ives Co. Served pvt. and corpl. Co. I, 7th Regt. N.G.N.Y., 1891-98; capt. Co. D, 171st Regt. N.G.N.Y., 1898; 1st lt. Co. I, 71st Regt., 1899; capt. and a.d.c. to Gen. George Moore Smith, 1900-10; maj. insp.-gen. 1st Brigade, 1910-12. Served in World War with 15th N.Y. Inf., colored, later 369th U.S. Inf.; capt. Co. F, regtl. adj., and maj. 1st Batn., Apr. 13, 1917-Feb. 28, 1919; in all actions with Gouraud's 4th Army (French), bet. Apr. 7, 1918, and armistice, Nov. 11, 1918; wounded in action, Sept. 12, 1918. Chevalier Legion of Honor and 4 Croix de Guerre (2 palms, one gold star, one silver star); U.S. Silver Star citation for gallantry; Comdr. Order of Black Star (French); Order of Purple Heart (U.S.). Colonel 15th Inf. (colored), N.Y.N.G., Jan. 5, 1921; bvt. brig. gen., Dec. 31, 1922; resigned Apr. 8, 1925. Episcopalian. Mason (life), Elk. Mem. Business Advisory and Planning Council of U.S. Dept. of Commerce, 1933-34; mem. Industrial Advisory Board of NRA, 1934; chmn. Mayor's Advisory Bd., N.Y. City, since 1939. Mem. S.R., Sons of Vets., Am. Legion, Vets. of Foreign Wars, Nat. Farmers Union (life hon.). Home: 810 Park Av., New York, N.Y. Office: 435 E. 24th St., New York, N.Y. Died July 18, 1943.

LITTLE, Clarence Belden, banker; b. Pembroke, N.H., Nov. 18, 1857; s. George Peabody and Elizabeth Ann (Knox) L.; A.B., Dartmouth, 1881, hon. A.M., 1921; studied law in offices of Chase & Streeter, Concord, N.H., and at Harvard; m. Caroline Gore, Nov. 24, 1885; children—Viroque Mabel, George Peabody. Admitted to bar, 1883; judge Probate Court, Burleigh County, Dak. Ty., 1884-88; mem. N.D. Senate, 1889-1909 (chmn. judiciary com. entire period); chmn. Rep. State Conv., 1904; del. at large Rep. Nat. Conv., 1916; mem. Capital Issues Com., 9th Federal Reserve Dist. In banking business since 1889; now pres. First Nat. Bank, Provident Life Ins. Co. of N.D.; dir. First Bank Stock Corp., St. Paul and Minneapolis. Pres. Bismarck Library Board; trustee Dartmouth Coll. Mem. N.D. Hist. Soc. (pres.). Kappa Kappa Kappa. Unitarian. Clubs: Minnesota, Somerset (St. Paul); Minneapolis, Minikahda (Minneapolis); Union (Boston). Home: 804 Av. A West. Office: 4th and Main Sts., Bismarck, N.D. Deceased.

LITTLE, Harry Britton, architect; b. Hingham, Mass., Aug. 18, 1882; s. George Britton and Ella (Walworth) L.; A.B., Harvard, 1904; post-grad. work in architecture, same univ., 1907-08; student Atelier Duquesne, Paris, 1909-10; m. Miriam Barrett, Sept. 20, 1911; children—David Britton, Miriam. Business training with Cram & Ferguson, Boston, specializing in church architecture; practiced alone, 1916-19; mem. Frohman, Robb & Little since 1920; architects of Nat. Episcopal Cathedral, Washington, D.C.; Episcopal Cathedral, Baltimore; Trinity College Chapel, Hartford, Conn.; etc. Mem. Inst. Architects, Boston Soc. Architects. Republican. Episcopalian. Clubs: Union of Boston, Harvard Musical Assn. (Boston); Mass. Automobile; Concord Social Circle, Concord Country; Harvard (New York); University (Washington, D.C.). Home: Concord, Mass. Office: 250 Stuart St., Boston, Mass. Died Apr. 4, 1944.

LITTLE, James Lovell, architect; b. Boston, Mass., Nov. 14, 1874; s. James Lovell and Mary Robbins (Revere) L.; grad. Noble and Greenough Sch., Boston, 1893; A.B., Harvard, 1897; spl. student Dept. of Architecture, Mass. Inst. Tech., 1897-1900, Ecole des Beaux Arts, Paris, 1902; m. Leonora Schlesinger, June 2, 1902; children—Barbara, James Lovell. Began as archtl. draftsman with Guy Lowell, 1900; practiced as architect at Boston since 1904; mem. Purdon & Little, 1904-05, Little & Russell since 1915. Served as 1st lt. Signal Corps, U.S. Army, constrn. div., Oct. 1917-Aug. 1918; capt. Air Service, Aug. 1918-Mar. 1919. Former mem. Planning Bd.; Brookline. Fellow Am. Inst. Architects; mem. Boston Soc. Architects (pres. 1924-26). Club: Union (Boston). Home: 489 Boylston St., Brookline, Mass. Office: 20 Newbury St., Boston, Mass.* Died Dec. 1948.

LITTLE, Lucius Freeman, mfr.; b. Owensboro, Ky., Jan. 29, 1869; s. Lucius Powhattan and Elizabeth Elloise (Freeman) L.; student Princeton, 1893; m. Elfie Alberta Schumann, Feb. 20, 1918; children—Lucius Powhattan, Lucius Freeman (dec.), Wilbur Wilton, Alberta Freeman. An organizer, 1910, Anglo Am. Mill Co., mfrs. flour mills, pres., 1910-32; pres. Packers, Internat., and Pan-Am. meat smoking corps, Alsop Elec. Co.; mng. dir. Alsop Process, Ltd., London, Eng., 1903-10. Admitted to Ky. bar, 1893. Democrat. Methodist. Mason (K.T., Shriner), Elk. Clubs: Princeton (New York); Chicago Athletic. Home: Owensboro, Ky. Died June 27, 1946.

LITTLE, Philip, artist; b. Swampscott, Mass., Sept. 6, 1857; s. James Lovell and Julia Augusta (Cook) L.; Mass. Inst. Tech., 1875, 76; studied art sch. Museum Fine Arts, Boston, 1881-82; m. Lucretia Shepard Jackson, Jan. 10, 1883 (died Sept. 10, 1938); 1 son, Philip; m. 2d, Carolina W. King. Exhibited in art museums in U.S., in Rome, 1911, Buenos Aires, 1911, Paris Salon, 1912; dry point, Victoria and Albert Memorial, London, 1929. Honorary mention Art Institute Chicago, 1912; silver medal, Panama P.I. Expn., 1915. Curator fine arts, Essex Inst. Represented in permanent collections of Essex Inst., Salem, Mass., Walker Memorial, Brunswick, Me., Pa. Acad., Phila., Minneapolis Inst., Milwaukee Art Assn., Nashville Art Assn., R.I. School of Design, N.Y. Public Library, Dubuque Art Assn., Museum Fine Arts, Boston, Congressional Library, Peabody Museum of Science, Salem, Mass., Bibliothèque Nationale, Paris, Municipal Gallery of Modern Art, Dublin, Ireland. Donor of Annie Jeannette Staigg Jackson memorial collection of pictures by artists and of memorial pictures of Lucretia Little to Salem Y.M.C.A. Served from sergt. to maj. Mass. Nat. Guard, 1887-1901. Mason. Life mem. Portland Soc. of Arts, Nat. Arts Club, N.Y.; mem. Chicago Soc. Etchers, Am. Soc. of Etchers, Guild of Boston Artists; fellow Minneapolis Inst. Club: Union (Boston). Home: 10 Chestnut St., Salem, Mass. Died Mar. 30, 1942.

LITTLE, Richard Henry, columnist; b. Le Roy, Ill.; s. Dr. John and Helen (Humiston) L.; ed. Ill. Wesleyan Coll. of Law; m. Shelby Melton, Apr. 11, 1925. Practiced law, Bloomington; reporter Chicago Tribune, 1895, war corr., in Cuba, Hayti, Philippines, Spanish-Am. War, with armies in field, Russo-Japanese War, dramatic critic; war worker in France with A.E.F.; Berlin corr. Chicago Tribune, 1919; war corr. with Russian White Army; condr. "Line o' Type or Two" column in Chicago Tribune since 1920. Club: Saddle and Cycle. Author: The Line Book, yearly, since 1924; Better Angels, 1928. Home: 223 East Delaware Pl., Chicago. Died Apr. 27, 1946.

LITTLE, Robert Rice, clergyman; b. Wabash, Ind., Oct. 7, 1881; s. Charles and Annie L. (Thurston) L.; student Blair Acad., Blairstown, N.J., 1897-99, Williams Coll., 1899-1901, Johns Hopkins U., 1904-05; A.B., Wabash Coll., 1906; student McCormick Theol. Sem., 1906-09; D.D., Coe Coll., 1926; m. Helen Robertson, June 24, 1914; children—Charles Robertson, Frederick McHenry, Dorothy Ann. Ordained to ministry Presbyn. Ch., 1909; pastor First Ch., Winchester, Ind., 1909-13, New Castle, Pa., 1913-19, Ft. Wayne, Ind., 1919-25, Cedar Rapids, Ia., 1925-45. Director Coe Coll. Mem. Alpha Delta Phi. Home: 2662 Country Club Parkway, Cedar Rapids, Ia. Died Nov. 11, 1948.

LITTLEFIELD, Walter, author, journalist; b. Boston, Mass., Mar. 17, 1867; s. Joshua and Elizabeth (Mitchell) L.; student Harvard, 1888-93, A.B., 1920, as of 1892; taught French and ancient history, Chauncy Hall, Boston, 1890-92; m. Luigina Amalia, d. late Dr. Pagani, of Borgomanero, Italy, Oct. 30, 1893 (died May 24, 1945); children—Walter Joseph, Henry Mario. Asso. editor Norwich (Conn.) Bulletin, 1888; with N.Y. World and N.Y. Tribune, 1894-97; in editorial dept. of N.Y. Times since 1897, foreign editor emeritus since 1932 (retired, November, 1942); American correspondent Le Siècle, Paris, and has contributed to L'Événement, Paris; literary corr. Chicago Record-Herald, 1903-13. An authority on the Dreyfus case; was first to establish identity of Lt. Col. du Paty de Clam as the author of the article in L'Éclair, Sept. 14, 1896, narrating the circumstances of Dreyfus' arrest and divulging the use of secret evidence at his first trial; furnished evidence at the Camorra trial, Viterbo, Italy, showing connection between the Camorra of Naples and the Mano Nera of New York; advanced proofs to the French Ministry of Fine Arts that Leonardo da Vinci's "Mona Lisa" was not stolen from the Louvre in Aug. 1911, but concealed by an official restorer because injured. One of the 500 signers of the memorial to the Allies, Jan. 1915. Mem. La Società Dantesca (Florence), La Ligue des Droits de l'Homme (Paris), Acad. Sciences and Letters (Genoa), Dante League of America, Friends of Roumania Soc. Decorated Officer Crown of Italy, 1922, Comdr., 1932; Comdr. Order of Danilo I (Montenegro), 1922; Officer Star of Roumania, 1928. Editor: The Power of Sympathy, 1892; Letters of an Innocent Man (Dreyfus), 1898; Early Prose Writings of James Russell Lowell, 1902; Bismarck's Letters to His Wife from the Seat of War, 1870-1871, 1903; Love Letters of Famous Men and Women, 4 vols. (with the late Lionel Strachey), 1909-10; With Byron in Love, 1926. Translator: The Kaiser as He Is (Le Véritable Guillaume II), by Henri de Noussanne, 1905. Author: The Truth About Dreyfus; The Men of Silence (with Luigi Forgione), 1927; A Parisian Decameron, 1929; When France Went Mad—the Story of the Dreyfus Case, 1936. Home: "The Rafters" New Canaan, Conn. Died March 25, 1948.

LITTLEHALES, George Washington (lĭt'"l-hālz), hydrographic engr.; b. Schuylkill County, Pa., Oct. 14, 1860; s. William Henry and Margaret (Reber) L.; grad. (B.S.), U.S. Naval Acad., 1883; C.E., Columbian (now George Washington) U., 1888; m. Helen Powers Hill, Jan. 26, 1896; children—Margaret Powers (Mrs. Philip G. Vondersmith), James Hill, George Reber. Hydrographic engr. of the U.S. Hydrographic Office, 1900-1932. A founder, 1896, and was asso. editor Internat. Jour. Terrestrial Magnetism. Cons. hydrographer, dept. terrestrial magnetism, Carnegie Inst., 1904-06; prof. nautical science, George Washington U., 1913-27. Chmn. sect. of physical oceanography, Am. Geophysical Union, 1919-22; v.p. sect. of oceanography, Internat. Union of Geodesy and Geophysics, 1921-32; v.p. Am. Geophysical Union, 1926-29, chairman section of meteorology, 1929-32. Fellow A.A.A.S.; mem. Washington Acad. Sciences (v.p. 1905, 12, 13), Philos. Soc. Washington (pres. 1905), Am. Soc. Naval Engrs.; del. to Brussels Congress, 1919, for the Eestablishment of the Internat. Research Council; del. to Internat. Hydrographic Conf., London, 1919, leading to establishment Internat. Hydrog. Bur.; Pan-Pacific Scientific Conf., Honolulu, 1920; to Conf. of the Internat. Geodetic and Geophysical Union, Rome, 1922, Stockholm, 1930; to Pan-Pacific Science Congress, Tokyo, 1926; to Internat. Congress Oceanography, Marine Hydrography and Continental Hydrology, Seville, 1929. Club: Cosmos. Author: Development of Great Circle Sailing; The Methods and Results of the Survey of Lower California; Submarine Cables; The Magnetic Dip or Inclination; The Meridional Parts of the Terrestrial Spheriod, 1889; The Azimuths of Celestial Bodies, 1902; The Forms of Isolated Submarine Peaks, 1891; The Azimuth and the Hour Angle from the Latitude of the Observer and the Declination and Altitude of the Observed Celestial Body, 1903; A New and Abridged Method of Finding the Locus of Geographical Position and the Compass Error; Altitude, Azimuth, and Geographical Position, 1906; Geographical Position-Line Tables, 1915; Chart for Finding Geographical Position in Aerial Navigation, 1918; Tables of the Simultaneous Altitudes and Azimuths of Celestial Bodies, 1920; The Sumner Line of Position, furnished ready to lay down upon the chart by means of tables of simultaneous hour-angle and azimuth of celestial bodies, 1923; Finding Geographical Position in the Region of the North Pole, 1925; Mechanical Means for Finding Geographical Position in Navigation, 1929; Both the Latitude and the Longitude of the Ship Found in a Single Operation from the Observation of the Altitude and the Azimuth of a Celestial Body, 1937. He has made many researches in hydrography, oceanography and terristrial magnetism, results given in more than 100 papers; published about 3,000 charts used in the navigation of the vessels of the world. Edited the mathematical tables for the use of American seamen. Home: 2132 Le Roy Pl., Washington, D.C. Died Aug. 12, 1943.

LITTLEPAGE, Thomas Price, lawyer; b. Spencer County, Ind., Jan. 6, 1873; s. Thomas Price and Caroline C. (Barnett) L.; student Ind. State Normal, Terre Haute; LL.B. and LL.M., George Washington U.; m. Ella Tasch, Apr. 14, 1900; children—Ellen (Mrs. Willard L. Hart), John Marshall, Louise (Mrs. W. B. Fletcher, Jr.), Thomas Price, James Hemenway. Admitted to D.C. bar, 1910, and practiced since at Washington; v.p. Bank of Bowie (Md.); dir. Liberty Nat. Bank. Former pres. Washington Chamber Commerce. Republican. Mason. Clubs: Cosmos, Alfalfa, Tenuvus. Received gold medal and citation from Cosmopolitan Club "as citizen who performed most outstanding unselfish service to City of Washington during 1934." Home: Bowie, Md. Office: Investment Bldg., Washington, D.C. Died Dec. 10, 1942.

LITZENBERG, Jennings Crawford (lĭt'zĕn-bĕrg), obstetrician; b. Waubeek, Ia., Apr. 6, 1870; s. William Donny and Lydia (Crawford) L.; B.Sc., U. of Minn., 1894, M.D., 1899; studied U. of Vienna, 1909-10, later in Berlin, London, Glasgow and Dublin; m. Elizabeth Anna Fisher, June 3, 1902; children—Avis, Karl; m. 2d, Dr. Olga Hansen, Jan. 27, 1934. Gen. practice, 1900-10, specialized in obstetrics and gynecology since 1910; mem. The Nicollet Clinic. Instructor in obstetrics, U. of Minn., 1901-07, asst. prof., 1907-10, asso. prof. obstetrics and gynecology, 1910-14, prof. and head of dept., 1914-38, prof. emeritus since 1938; chief dept. obstetrics and gynecology, University Hosp.; obstetrician to Eitel and Northwestern hosps.; cons. obstetrician and gynecologist Fairview Hosp. Former mem. Am. Bd. Obstetrics and Gynecology; fellow Am. Gynecol. Soc. (2d v.p. and mem. council 1920, pres. 1940-41), Am. Assn. Obstetricians and Gynecologists and Abdominal Surgeons (pres. 1936), Am. Coll. Surgeons, A.M.A. (chmn. sect. obstetrics, gynecology and abdominal surgery 1928; exec. com. 1928-30), Hennepin County Med. Soc. (pres. 1919), Minn. Acad. Medicine (pres. 1932), Central Assn. Obstetricians and Gynecologists, Delta Upsilon, Nu Sigma Nu, Sigma Xi, Alpha Omega Alpha. Republican. Baptist. Club: Automobile. Frequent contbr. on professional topics. Home: 711 East River Rd. Office: 1009 Nicollet Av., Minneapolis 2, Minn. Died Aug. 15, 1948.

LIVELY, Frank (lĭv'lē), judge; b. Monroe County, W.Va., Nov. 18, 1864; s. Col. Wilson and Elizabeth (Gwinn) L.; grad. Concord Normal Sch., Athens, W.Va., 1882; LL.B., W.Va. U., 1885; m. Annie E. Prince, Jan. 1, 1890; children—Wm. T., Jas. P., Frank W. (dec.), Frederick, Mrs. Jenny Fontaine, Harry W. (dec.). Began practice at Hinton, 1886; pros. attorney, Summers County, W.Va., 1900-04; asst. atty. gen., W.Va., 1905-06; pardon atty., 1906-09; 1st asst. atty. gen., W.Va., 1909-20; judge Supreme Court of Appeals, W.Va., term 1920-33. Republican. Unitarian. Mason (33°, Shriner). Home: Charleston, W.Va. Died 1947.

LIVINGSTON, Arthur (lĭv'ĭng-stŭn), Italianist; b. Northbridge, Mass., Sept. 30, 1883; s. George and Alice Louise (Braman) L.; grad. high sch., Attleboro, Mass., 1900; A.B., Amherst Coll., 1904; Ph.D., Columbia, 1911; m. Lucy Evelyn Ongley, Aug. 24, 1925 (now dec.). Instr. in Italian, Smith Coll., 1908-09; asst. prof. Italian, Cornell U., 1910-11; asso. prof. Italian, Columbia, 1911-17; Italian editor Foreign Press Bureau, Com. Pub. Information, 1918-19; organized, with Ernest Poole and Paul Kennaday, Foreign Press Service, Inc., later Kennaday & Livingston, Inc., introducing and translating foreign writers (Blasco Ibanez, Luigi Pirandello, Claude Farrère, Giuseppe Prezzolini, Giovanni Papini, Guglielmo Ferrero), 1919-25; asso. prof. Romance langs., Columbia, 1925-35, prof. since 1935. Mem. Phi Beta Kappa, Phi Gamma Delta, Reale Deputazione Veneta di Storia Patria. Decorated Cavalier Crown of Italy. Universalist. Author: Sonetti di G. F. Busenello, 1911; Vita veneziana del'600. 1913; Memoirs of Lorenzo Da Ponte, 1929; (with F. Nardelli) Gabriel the Archangel (G. d'Annunzio), 1931; also 30 translations. Contbr. articles and reviews on Italian lit. and civilization. Reviewer foreign lit., N.Y. Herald, N.Y. Herald-Tribune, Nation; contbr. Ency. Italiana. Italian editor Internat. Ency.; editor and translator The Mind and Society (Pareto), 1935; Mosca, The Ruling Class, 1939. Home: 27 W. 9th St., New York, N.Y.; (summer) Atlantic, Me. Died Feb. 11, 1944.

LIVINGSTON, Burton Edward, plant physiologist; b. Grand Rapids, Mich., Feb. 9, 1875; s. Benjamin and Keziah (Lincoln) L.; B.S., U. of Mich., 1898; Ph. D., U. of Chicago, 1902; m. Grace Johnson, 1905 (divorced, 1918); m. 2d, Marguerite A. Brennan Macphilips, 1921. Asst. in plant physiology, U. of Mich., 1895-98; fellow and asst. in plant physiology, U. of Chicago, 1899-1905; soil expert U.S. Bur. Soils in charge of fertility investigations, 1905-06; staff men. dept. bot. research, Carnegie Instn., Washington, 1906-09; prof. plant physiology, Johns Hopkins U., 1909-32, prof. plant physiology and forest ecology, 1932-40, dir. lab. of plant physiology, 1913-40, emeritus prof. plant physiology since 1940. Mem. Nat. Research Council, Fellow Am. Acad. Arts and Sciences; mem. Am. Philos. Soc., Bot. Soc. America, American Soc. Naturalists (pres. 1933), Ecol. Soc. America, Am. Soc. Plant Physiologists (pres. 1934). Permanent sec. A.A.A.S., 1920-31, gen. sec., 1931-34, mem. exec. committee 1920-46, chairman exec. com., 1941-45. Author: Rôle of Diffusion and Osmotic Pressure in Plants, 1903; Distribution of Vegetation in U.S., as Related to Climatic Conditions (with F. Shreve), 1921. Editor: Physiological Researches; English edit. Palladin's Plant Physiology, 1918; Botanical Abstracts, 1918-20. Inventor: porous cup atmometer (for measuring evaporation as climatic factor); radio-atmometer (for measuring sunshine); auto-irrigator (for automatic control of soil moisture in potted plants); instruments for measuring water-supplying and water-absorbing power of soils. Writer of many tech. papers. Hales Prize Award of Am. Soc. Plant Physiologists, 1946. Home: Riderwood, Md. Died Feb. 8, 1948.

LIVINGSTONE, Colin Hamilton (lĭv'ĭng-stŭn), banker; b. St. John, N.B., Can., June 3, 1863; s. Walter Hamilton and Margaret Ellen (Fraser) L.; A.B., McGill U., Montreal, 1886; m. Anna Louise Van de Boe, July 31, 1889. Reporter, New York Herald, 1886; prof. chemistry and physics, Gramercy Park Poly., 1886-87; v.p., treas. R. Wayne Wilson Co., pubs., New York, 1890-94; sec. to U.S. Senator Stephen B. Elkins, 1895-1906; sec. to com. on interstate commerce, U.S. Senate, 1900-06; became v.p. Am. National Bank, Washington, 1903. An organizer, 1910, and pres., 1910-25, now hon. v.p. Nat Council Boy Scouts of America. Col. on staffs of 5 successive govs. of W.Va., 1898-1916. Republican. Presbyterian. Fellow Am. Geog. Soc.; mem. Archæol. Inst. America. Clubs: University, Chevy Chase, Canadian (pres.). Home: 2307 N. Albemarle St., Arlington, Va. Office: 923 15th St. N.W., Washington, D.C. Died Feb. 1, 1943.

LIVINGSTON, Sigmund, lawyer; b. Giessen, Germany, Dec. 27, 1872; s. Mayer and Dora (Blumenfeld) L.; brought to U.S., 1881, naturalized citizen; ed. pub. schs., Bloomington, Ill.; student Ill. Wesleyan U., 1890-93; LL.B., Bloomington (Ill.) Law Sch., 1894; m. Hilda Freiler, Dec. 18, 1918; 1 son, Richard M. Began practice of law in Bloomington, Ill., 1894; mem. law firm Livingston and Bach, later Sterling, Livingston and Whitmore; mem. law firm, Lederer, Livingston, Kahn and Adsit, Chicago, Ill., since 1929. Founder and chmn. Anti-Defamation League, since 1913. Mem. Am. and Chicago bar assns. Jewish religion. Clubs: Standard (Chicago, Ill.); Northmoor Country (Highland Park, Ill.). Author: Must Men Hate?, 1944. Contbr. articles to Reform Advocate, Jewish Monthly. Home: 225 Cary Av., Highland Park, Ill. Office: 160 N. La Salle St., Chicago, Ill. Died June 13, 1946.

LLOYD, Edward, VIII, naval officer; b. Baltimore, Md., July 20, 1857; s. Edward VII and Mary Lloyd (Howard) L.; ed. Bishop's Sch., Easton, Md.; grad. U.S. Naval Acad., 1878; m. Elizabeth Robinson, Oct. 12, 1887; 1 son, Edward IX. Commd. ensign, U.S. Navy, 1878, and advanced through the grades to commodore, 1911, retired, 1911. Club: Officers' (Annapolis, Md.). Home: "Wye Lodge," 203 Prince George St., Annapolis, Md. Died Feb. 5, 1948.

LLOYD, Francis Ernest, botanist; b. Manchester, Eng., Oct. 4, 1868; s. Edward and Leah (Pierce) L., both Welsh; A.B., Princeton, 1891, A.M., 1895; student at Munich, 1898, Bonn, 1901; hon. D.Sc., U. of Wales, 1933, Masaryk U., 1938; m. Mary Elizabeth Hart, May 18, 1903; children—Mary Elizabeth (dec.), Francis Ernest Llewellyn, David Pierce Caradoc. Instr. in William Coll., 1891-92; prof. biology and geology, 1892-95, biology, 1895-97, Pacific U., Ore.; adj. prof. biology, Teachers Coll. (Columbia), 1897-1906; investigator, Desert Bot. Lab., Carnegie Instn., Washington, 1906; instr. Harvard Summer Sch., 1907; cytologist, Ariz. Expt. Sta., 1907; dir. dept. of investigation, Continental-Mexican Rubber Co., 1907-08; prof. botany, Ala. Poly. Inst., 1908-12; Macdonald prof. botany, McGill U., Montreal, 1912-34, emeritus prof. botany since 1934; consultant, U.S. Rubber Company, 1919-33. Editor The Plant World, 1905-08. Bot. explorations Lumholtz expdn. to Mexico, 1890; Columbia expdn. to Puget Sound and Alaska, 1896; N.Y. Bot. Garden to Dominica, B.W.I., 1903, Java, Sumatra, F.M.S., 1919, S. Africa, 1929, 1935; Australia, New Zealand, 1935-36. Pres. bot. sect. Brit. Assn. Advancement of Science, 1933; fellow A.A.A.S. (sec.; v.p. 1923, sect. G), Royal Soc. Can. (chmn. sect. V. 1922; pres. 1933), American Society Plant Physiology (pres. 1927; Barnes life mem.), New York Academy Sciences, California Academy of Sciences, Linnæan Soc. of London; hon. fellow, Edinburgh Bot. Soc.; hon. mem. Phila. Coll. Pharmacy; mem. Bot. Soc. America, Torrey Bot. Club (asso. editor of Bull., 1899-1902; treas., 1902-06); corr. mem. Centro de Sciencios Letras e Artees, Campinas (of Brazil), also Czechoslovakian Bot. Soc.; mem. Sigma Xi, Alpha Omega Alpha, Nu Sigma Nu, Lambda Chi Alpha. Clubs: Faculty, Pen and Pencil (Montreal, Canada). Author: The Teaching of Biology (botany) in the Secondary School (American Teachers Series), 1904; The Comparative Embryology of the Rubiaceæ, 1902; The Physiology of Stomata, 1908; Guayule (a rubber plant of the Chihuahuan Desert), 1911; The Carnivorous Plants, 1942; also various other botanical papers, including studies on transpiration, stomata, tannin, rubber, cotton, growth, colloids, fluorescence, reproduction and carnivorous plants. Address: Box 842, Carmel, Calif. Died Oct. 18, 1947.

LLOYD, James Tighlman, ex-congressman; b. Canton, Mo., Aug. 28, 1857; s. Jere and Frances (Jones) L.; A.B., Christian U., 1878; m. Mary B. Graves, Mar. 1, 1881. Taught school, country and city; dep. sheriff, Lewis County, Mo., 1879-81; dep. circuit clk. and recorder, 1881-83; admitted to bar, 1882; practiced at Shelbyville, Mo., 1885-97; pros. atty., Shelby County, Mo., 1889-93; mem. 55th to 64th Congresses (1897-1917), 1st Mo. Dist.; resumed practice, at Washington, 1917. Pres. C. of C. Pres. Bd. of Edn., Washington. Mem. bd. trustees Culver-Stockton Coll., Canton, Mo. Mem. Am. and Mo. State bar assns. Home: Canton, Mo. Died Apr. 3, 1944.

LLOYD, William Allison, lawyer, agriculturist; b. Sparta, O., Sept. 9, 1870; s. James J. and Maria (Ulery) L.; B.S., Nat. Normal U., Lebanon, O., 1890 (instr. science 1891); LL.B., U. of Tex., 1893; m. Minnie Lee Rutherford, June 24, 1896; 1 dau., Leonila Marie. Admitted to Tex. bar, 1893, and practiced at Victoria, 1894-96, Georgetown, 1896-1901; editor Victoria Advocate, 1894-96; admitted to Ohio bar, 1902; admitted to bar Supreme Court of the U.S.,

1940; stock raiser and farmer in Ohio, 1901-09; collaborator Ohio Expt. Sta., 1904-09, in charge extension work 23 south eastern cos., 1909-13; dist. agt. U.S. Dept. Agr., in charge county agt. work, Central States, 1913-15, in charge 33 Northern and Western states, 1915-21; in charge extension work, Western States, 1921-28; dean of agrl. extension service, U. of Hawaii (on leave from U.S. Dept. Agr.), 1928-29; in charge extension work, Western states and territories, Hawaii and Alaska, 1929-39; principal agriculturist, office of director, 1939-40; retired from Government Service Oct. 1, 1940; made agrl. survey Am. Samoa at request of gov., 1932; visited New Zealand to study agrl. orgn., 1932; advisor Joint Prep. Commn. on Philippine Affairs, apptd. by President Roosevelt and President Quezon, 1937; now dir. information, Assn. of Land Grant Colls. and Univs., Washington, D.C. Organized Extension Work in Alaska, 1930. Asst. postmaster, Georgetown, 1897-1901. Organizer and grand dir. Epsilon Sigma Phi (awarded Service Ruby for contbn. to Am. Agr. 1933). Democrat. Clubs: University, Federal, National Press. Author of numerous bulletins of U.S. Department of Agriculture and Ohio Experiment Station. Loaned to office of Indian Affairs, Dept. of Interior, to prepare spl. report land policy for Am. Indians, 1934. Author rural recreation reserve Works Progress Project for rural playgrounds, 1935; History of Extension Work, 1939. Visited South Am. Countries, Peru, Chile, Argentine, Brazil, to study adult edn., 1940. One of introducers of sweet clover as forage plant. Home: The Sedgwick, 1722 19th St. N.W. Address: 1372 National Press Bldg., Washington. Died July 10, 1946; buried in Cedar Hill Cemetery.

LOBDELL, Charles E. (lŏb-dĕl′), lawyer, banker; b. Osawatomie, Kan., Sept. 21, 1861; s. Darius J. and Roxana C. (Godding) L.; ed. common schs.; m. 2d, Nellie E., d. D. M. and Ellen J. Ward, Sept. 12, 1900; children—Maud Avis, Charles Elmer, David Stanley, Hugh Jared; foster children—Ward, Gertrude. County attorney, Butler County, Kansas, 1885-87; mem. Kan. Ho. of Rep., 1891-99 (speaker of House 1895); dist. judge 33d Jud. Dist., 1902-11; resigned Oct. 1, 1911, to become pres. First Nat. Bank, Great Bend, Kan., also pres. Citizens State Bank (Jetmore, Kan.), and First State Bank (Tribune, Kan.); resigned bank offices to become mem. Federal Farm Loan Bd., Aug. 7, 1916; reapptd., July 1918, for term ending 1926; resigned July 1, 1923, to become fiscal agt. for Federal Land and Intermediate Credit Banks; resumed practice at Washington, 1929; sr. partner Lobdell & Co. since May 1, 1935. Mem. Am. Bar Assn., Kan. State Bar Assn. (pres. 1915), Kan. State Bankers Assn. (pres. 1916). Republican. Presbyterian. Home: 16 Koewing Place, West Orange, N.J. Office: 20 Exchange Place, New York. Died Jan. 29, 1949.

LOCKE, Charles E., educator; b. Milton, N.H., Aug. 29, 1874; s. John Elvin and Sarah (Hayes) L.; S.B. in mining engring. and metallurgy, Mass. Inst. Tech., 1896; m. Louisa Oke Stewart, June 30, 1903 (died Feb. 8, 1936). Coal mine surveyor, Wyo., 1896-97; asst. to Prof. Robert H. Richards, of Mass. Inst. Tech., in preparing book on ore dressing, 1897-1901; teacher of mining engineering, Mass. Inst. Tech., 1901-06, prof. since 1906, acting head mining dept., 1939, prof. emeritus and hon. lecturer since 1941; alumni sec. Mass. Inst. Tech. since 1930. Mem. Am. Inst. Mining and Metall. Engrs., Am. Society for Engineering Education, Am. Assn. Univ. Profs., Australasian Inst. of Mining and Metallurgy, Mining Inst. of Japan (hon. mem.), Can. Inst. Mining and Metallurgy. Conglist. Mason. Author of Text Book of Ore Dressing (with Robert H. Richards) and several ann. revs. on mining, ore dressing, and gold milling. Address: Massachusetts Institute of Technology, Cambridge 39, Mass. Died Sept. 24, 1948.

LOCKE, Edward, actor, playwright; b. Stourbridge, Worcestershire, Eng., Oct. 18, 1869; s. Joseph and Louisa (Drewry) L.; came to U.S., 1884; ed. pub. schs., Medford, Mass., and Charles Bickford Sch. of Acting, Boston; m. Martha Christian, Mar. 13, 1904; 1 dau., Edna Locke (Mrs. James O'Keefe). Mem. Am. Soc. Dramatic Authors and Composers, Authors' League Am., Actors' Equity Assn. Republican. Unitarian. Mason. Club: The Lambs. Author: (plays) The Climax, prod. 1909; The Case of Beckey, 1913; The Silver Wedding, 1914; The Revolt, 1915; The Bubble, 1915; The Land of the Free, 1916; Dangerous Years, 1919; The Dancer (adaptation), 1920; Dorothy Dixie Lee, 1920; Frieda Laughs, 1922; Mike Angelo; Swanee River; 57 Bowery, 1928; The Love Call, 1928; The Studio Girl, 1928. Address: Pineacres, East Islip, L.I. Died March 1, 1945.

LOCKE, Eugene Perry, lawyer; b. Michigantown, Clinton County, Ind., June 25, 1883; s. Maurice Eugene and Mary (Dixon) L.; LL.B., U. of Tex., 1904; m. Marie Murphy, Aug. 9, 1916; 1 son, Eugene Murphy. Admitted to Tex. bar, 1904; mem. firm Locke & Locke, 1904-26; member firm of Locke, Locke, Stroud & Randolph, 1926-39, Locke, Locke, Dyer & Purnell, 1939-45, now Locke, Locke & Purnell; practice largely identified with organization and reorganization of corps., ins., financial planning and adminstrn. of estates, firm has library of more than 20,000 vols., ranking as one of the best pvt. law libraries in U.S.; dir. Equitable Life Assurance Soc. of U.S. Pres. Philosophical Soc. of Texas, Phi Delta Theta, Order of Coif. Democrat. Presbyterian. Mason. Clubs: City, Critic, Petroleum, Dallas Country, Bankers, Lawyers (New York). Home: 2516 Maple Av. Office: First Nat. Bank Bldg., Dallas, Tex. Died Mar. 5, 1946.

LOCKEY, Joseph Byrne (lŏk′ē), prof. history; b. Jackson County, Fla., Feb. 2, 1877; s. Joseph Byrne and Tabitha Jane (Callaway) L.; B.S., U. of Nashville, 1902; M.A., Columbia, 1909, Ph.D., 1920; unmarried. Prin. pub. sch., De Land, Fla., 1902-04; prin. high sch., Pensacola, 1904-08; departmental insp. pub. instrn., Rep. of Peru, 1909-14; prof. internat. relations, George Peabody Coll. for Teachers, 1919-22; asst. prof. history, U. of Calif. at Los Angeles, 1922-25, asso. prof., 1925-29, prof. since 1929. Albert Shaw lecturer on diplomatic history, Johns Hopkins, 1929. Student 2d O.T.C., Plattsburg; commd. 1st lt. inf., Nov. 1917; assigned to 49th Inf., in France, July 1918-Feb. 1919. Mem. Am. Soc. Internat. Law, Am. Hist. Assn. (pres. Pacific Coast Branch, 1937), Miss. Valley Hist. Assn., Hist. Soc. of Southern Calif. (pres. 1938), Fla. Hist. Society; fellow Am. Geog. Soc. Author: La Enseñanza de la Aritmética, 1911; Estudios sobre la Instrucción, 1914; Pan-Americanism—Its Beginnings, 1920; James G. Blaine (in American Secretaries of State and Their Diplomacy), 1928; Essays in Pan-Americanism, 1939. Address: U of Calif. at Los Angeles 24, Los Angeles, Calif. Died Sep. 1946.

LOCKHART, Frank P., foreign service officer; b. Pittsburg, Tex., Apr. 8, 1881; s. Francis Asbury and Lida (Pruitt) L.; student Grayson Coll., Whitewright, Tex.; m. Ruby Hess, Nov. 8, 1904; children—Maurine, Frank P. Jr. Mem. Lockhart Bros., pub. Pittsburg (Tex.) Gazette, since 1900; pvt. sec. to congressman, 1902-13, to U.S. senator, 1913-14; asst. chief, Div. of Far Eastern Affairs, 1914-25, chief of division, 1925. Sent on spl. mission to Far East, by Dept. of State, 1919; tech. del. to Conf. on Limitation of Armament, Washington, 1921-22; detailed to the Spl. Conf. on the Chinese Customs Tariff, at Peking, 1925; consul gen. Hankow, China, 1925-31, Tientsin, China, 1931-35; counselor of legation, Pieping, China, Apr.-Sept. 1935, counselor of Embassy since Sept. 1935-Apr. 1940; consul general at Shanghai, 1940-42; chief, Division of Philippine Affairs, Department of State, 1942. Dir. Am. Fgn. Service Assn. Bus. mgr. Fgn. Service Jour. Address: State Dept., Washington. Died Aug. 25, 1949.

LOCKHART, Henry Jr., corp. official; b. Millerstown, Pa., Sept. 30, 1877; s. Henry and Ellen (Burns) L.; ed. Bates Acad., Millerston, Pa., and privately; m. Aletha Swift, 1903; children—Henry, IV, Meredith A., David G. With Am. Smelting & Refining Co., El Paso, Tex., 1898-99; at Monterrey, Agascalientes, Torreon, City of Mexico, Sonora (Mexico), 1900-08; banking exec., New York, 1908-17; with Goodrich Lockhart Co., New York, 1923-32; partner Blair & Co., Inc., and successor corp. Bancamerica-Blair Inc., bankers, New York, 1932-38; engaged in personal operations since 1938; chmn. bd. New York Shipbuilding Corp.; dir. Shell Union Oil Corp., Globe Steel Tubes Co., Commercial Solvents Corp., Walworth Co., Inc., North Am. Refractories Co., Interstate Co. in charge of Mission on Aeronautics (to Allies) and mem. Inter-Allied Aviation Com. during World War. Chairman board and trustee Downtown Hospital. Director and member board managers New York Botanical Gardens. Fellow American Geographical Society. Republican. Episcopalian. Clubs: Racquet and Tennis, Recess, Talbot Country, Grolier, Madison Square Garden (New York); Piping Rock (Locust Valley). Home: Longwoods, Md. Office: New York Shipbuilding Corp., Camden, N.J. Died Apr. 14, 1943.

LOCKRIDGE, Ross Franklin, Jr., writer; b. Bloomington, Ind., Apr. 25, 1914; s. Ross Franklin and Elsie Lillian (Shockley) L.; A.B., Indiana U., 1935, A.M., 1939; Diplome d'études de civilization française, Sorbonne, Paris, 1934; courses Harvard U., 1940-41; m. Vernice Baker, July 11, 1937; children—Ernest Hugh, Larry Shockley, Jeanne Marie, Ross Franklin III. Teacher, English dept., Indiana U., 1936-39; asst. prof., English dept., Simmons Coll., Boston, 1941-46. Mem. Phi Beta Kappa, Phi Gamma Delta. Author: Raintree County, 1948 (won Metro-Goldwyn-Mayer Semi-Annual Novel Award for 1947). Address: Bloomington, Ind. Died Mar. 6, 1948.

LOCKWOOD, Francis Cummins, author, univ. prof.; b. Mt. Erie, Ill., May 22, 1864; s. John Hughes and Ruth (Locke) L.; A.B., Baker U., Kan., 1892, A.M., 1895; Ph.D., Northwestern U., 1896; Litt.D., Kansas Wesleyan U., 1936; student English lit., U. of Chicago, 1897-98, Wesleyan U., Conn., 1901-02; m. Mary Pritner, Dec. 24, 1901; children—Elizabeth Pritner (Mrs. Shiras Morris, Jr.), Mary Margaret (Mrs. William McI. Thompson, Jr.). Prof. English lit., Mt. Union Coll., 1898-99, Kan. State Agrl. Coll., 1899-1902, Allegheny Coll., Pa., 1902-16 (leave of absence for study in Europe, 1909-10); prof. lit., U. of Ariz., 1916-18; dir. univ. extension div., 1919, dean. Coll. Letters, Arts and Sciences, 1920-30, acting pres., 1921-22; on sabbatic leave, Pasadena, Calif., 1926-27, Overseas Y.M.C.A. sec. on Transport Pastores and later dir. lecture service bur. of Army Ednl. Commn., Mar. 1918-May 1919. Mem. Modern Lang. Assn. America, A.A.A.S., League of Western Writers, Am. Assn. Univ. Profs., S.R., Phi Beta Kappa, Delta Tau Delta. Del. Progressive Nat. Conv., Chicago, 1912. Clubs: Old Pueblo, Literary. Author: Emerson as a Philosopher, 1896; Robert Browning, 1906; Freshman and His College, 1913; Public Speaking Today (with C. D. Thorpe), 1921; The Freshman Girl (with Kate M. Jameson), 1925; Arizona Characters, 1928; Life of Edward Everett Ayer, 1929; Pioneer Days in Arizona, 1932; with Padre Kino on the Trail and A Guide to his Mission Chain, 1933; The Apache Indians, 1938; The Old English Coffee-House, 1939; More Arizona Characters; Life in Old Tucson—1854-1864, 1943. Thumbnail Sketches of Famous Arizona Desert Riders, 1538-1946. Contbr. to mags. and revs.; lecturer on lit. and hist. subjects. Home: 601 E. First St., Tucson, Ariz. Died Jan. 12, 1948.

LOCKWOOD, Thomas B., lawyer; b. Buffalo, N.Y., Feb. 7, 1873; s. Daniel N. and Sarah (Brown) L.; A.B., Yale, 1895; student Cornell U. Law Sch., 1896-97; m. Marion Birge (dec.); m. 2d, Mildred Francis McGuire, Nov. 20, 1934. Admitted to N.Y. bar, 1897; entered Humphrey, Lockwood and Hoyt, Buffalo; dir. Mfrs. and Traders Trust Co., 1912-18; v.p. Fidelity Trust Co., 1918; trustee Erie County Savings Bank. Commr. of Parks, Buffalo, 1906-16; Dem. candidate for lt. gov. of N.Y., 1914. Donor with wife of Lockwood Memorial Library to U. of Buffalo. Trustee Union Coll., 1912-15, U. of Buffalo, State Teachers Coll., Buffalo, and Grosvenor Library, Buffalo Seminary Association; mem. council University of Buffalo, 1918. Member Buffalo Historical Soc. (trustee). Clubs: Buffalo (past pres.), Country (Buffalo); Elizabethan (New Haven). Recipient of Chancellor Medal, U. of Buffalo, 1942. Home: 844 Delaware Av., Buffalo 9, N.Y. Died Aug. 19, 1947.

LODGE, John Christian, ex-mayor; b. Detroit, Michigan, August 12, 1862; son of Dr. Edwin Albert and Christiana (Hanson) L.; graduate high school, Detroit, 1879, Michigan Military Academy, 1881; honorary LL.D., Wayne University, June 1944; unmarried. Reporter Detroit Free Press, 1889-93, city editor, 1893-96; chief clerk Wayne County Auditors, 1897-1905; secretary to Mayor George P. Codd, Detroit, 1906-07; entered lumber business, 1908; v.p. Dwight Lumber Co., mfrs. of lumber products, since 1908. Member Michigan National Guard, 1885-97; member Michigan House of Representatives, 1908-09; alderman, Detroit, 1910-18, councilman at large and president of Council, 1919-27; mayor of Detroit, 1928-29, and mem. City Council since 1932 (elected to both offices on his record without making personal campaign). Mem. Nat. Commn. for Perry's Victory Memorial. Clubs: Detroit, Yondotega, Detroit Athletic, Detroit Country, Detroit Yacht. Home: 7729 E. Jefferson Av., Detroit, Mich. Died Feb. 6, 1950.

LODGE, John Ellerton, art dir.; b. Nahant, Mass., Aug. 1, 1878; s. Henry Cabot and Anna Cabot Mills (Davis) L.; ed. Harvard, 1896-98, and abroad; m. Mary Connolly, 1911. Curator dept. Asiatic art, Boston Museum of Fine Arts, 1910-31; now director Freer Gallery of Art, Washington, D.C., and chmn. Com. on Oriental Art, Smithsonian Art Commn. since 1920. Mem. Am. Acad. Arts and Sciences, Am. Oriental Soc. Club: Somerset (Boston). Home: Nahant, Mass. Address: Freer Gallery of Art, Washington, D.C. Died Dec. 29, 1942.

LOEB, Jacob Moritz, insurance; b. Chicago, Ill., Sept. 17, 1875; s. Moritz and Johanne (Unna) L.; ed. pub. schs.; m. Rose Stein, June 1, 1897; children—Mildred Caroline (Mrs. Harry H. Asher), Hamilton Moritz, Mary Jane (Mrs. Ernest A. Grunsfeld, Jr.), John Jacob. Engaged in ins. business since age of 16; mem. ins. firm Loeb & Coffey, 1894-96, J. M. Loeb & Co., 1896-97; ins. broker, 1897-1900; mem. Eliel & Loeb, 1900-16, inc. May 1916, as Eliel & Loeb Co., and now chmn. bd. Mem. Chicago Bd. of Edn., 1913-22 (pres. 1914-17, and 1918-19); instrumental in inaugurating mil. training in pub. high schs. of Chicago. V.p. Jewish Welfare Board; mem. Am. Jewish Com. Chmn. Drive for Jewish War Sufferers, 1921 (raising $1,800,000); chmn. United Drive for $2,500,000 for philanthropic purposes, 1922; chmn. $4,000,000 United Drive, 1925. Mason; Past Master Chicago Lodge No. 437. Clubs: Standard (pres. 1921-27), Iroquois (life). Office: 175 W. Jackson Blvd., Chicago, Ill.* Died Feb. 17, 1944.

LOESCH, Frank Joseph (lĕsh), lawyer; b. Buffalo, N.Y., Apr. 9, 1852; s. Frank and Mary (Fisher) L.; LL.B., Northwestern U. (Union Coll. of Law), Chicago, 1874; LL.D., Mo. Valley Coll., Marshall, Mo., 1922, U. of Dubuque, 1929, Northwestern U., 1929, U. of Chicago, 1929, Coe Coll., 1930, Tusculum Coll., 1932; m. Lydia T. Richards, October 2, 1873 (deceased); children—Angeline L. (deceased; wife of Dr. Robert E. Graves), Winifred L. (wife of Frederick Z. Marx), Richards L., Joseph B.; m. 2d, May Browning Bausher, Feb. 7, 1925. Admitted to Ill. bar, 1874, and specialized in estate, trusts and corp. law; sr. mem. Loesch, Scofield, Loesch and Burke; counsel at Chicago for Pa. R.R. since Apr. 1886; gen. counsel Chicago Union Sta. Co. since 1913; spl. state's atty. in and for Cook County, Ill., to investigate and prosecute frauds committed at 1st direct primary, 1908-09; chief spl. asst. atty. gen. of Ill. in direct charge of spl. grand jury investigations, 1928, into murders, bombings, kidnapings and other violences and frauds in connection with elections, 1926, and primary election, Apr. 1928; 1st asst. state's atty. of Cook County, 1928-29, to carry on same work and investigations into irregularity and financial expenditures of Sanitary Dist. of Chicago for years 1922-28. Apptd. by President Hoover, May 1929, as one of 11 members of Nat. Commn. on Law Observance and Enforcement. Originated term "Public Enemy" (Apr. 1930). Mem. Chicago Bd. Edn., 1898-1902. Mem. Am. Bar Assn., Ill. State Bar Assn., Chicago Bar Assn. (pres. 1906-07), Chicago Hist. Soc. (trustee and sec. 1923-27; v.p. 1927-41), Am. Hist. Soc., Polit. Science Assn.; pres.

Crime Commn. of Chicago, 1928-37; elected life dir. U. of Dubuque, 1937. Republican. Presbyterian; commr. to Gen. Assembly of Presbyn. Ch. in U.S.A., 1914, 20. Elected hon. mem. Kiwanis Clubs of Chicago, Nov. 1937. Received medal April 1939 "Chicago (Rotary Club) Merit Award—Local," from Committee on Awards composed of eminent citizens, "for distinguished service in the common welfare as civic leader, churchman and member of the bar." Clubs: Union League (pres. 1916-17), University, Law (pres. 1922-23), Saddle and Cycle, Arts, Casino, Chicago Literary (pres. 1927-28), City, Kiwanis (hon.); Cooperstown (N.Y.) Country. Author: Acquisition and Retention of a Law Practice; Personal Experiences During the Chicago Fire; Value of Legal Novels to a Lawyer; Shall the Law Triumph?; Gleams from Glimmer Glass. Home: Drake Hotel, Chicago; (summer) Cooperstown, N.Y. Office: Otis Bldg., Chicago, Ill. Died July 31, 1944.

LOFTING, Hugh, author, illustrator; b. Maidenhead, Berkshire, Eng., Jan. 14, 1886; s. John Brien and Elizabeth Agnes (Gannon) L.; student Mass. Inst. Tech., 1904-05, London Polytechnic, 1906-07; m. Flora Small, Feb. 22, 1912 (died Mar. 1927); children—Elizabeth Mary, Colin MacMahon; m. 2d, Katherine Harrower, 1928 (died 1928); m. 3d, Josephine Fricker, May 29, 1935; 1 son, Christopher Clement. Civ. engr. until 1912; settled in U.S., 1912. Officer in British Army, 1916; in Flanders and France, 1917-18; wounded, June 1917. Author: The Story of Dr. Dolittle, 1920; The Voyages of Dr. Dolittle, 1922 (awarded Newbery medal); The Story of Mrs. Tubbs, 1923; Dr. Dolittle's Post Office, 1923; Dr. Dolittle's Circus, 1924; Porridge Poetry, 1924; Dr. Dolittle's Zoo, 1925; Doctor Dolittle's Caravan, 1926; Doctor Dolittle's Garden, 1927; Doctor Dolittle in the Moon, 1928; Noisy Nora, 1929; The Twilight of Magic, 1930; Gub Gub's Book, 1932; Doctor Dolittle's Return, 1933; Tommy, Tilly and Mrs. Tubbs, 1937; Victory for the Slain, 1942; Dr. Dolittle and the Secret Lake (published posthumously), 1948. Clubs: Players, Dutch Treat. Home: Topanga, Calif. Died Sept. 26, 1947.

LOGAN, Josephine Hancock, author; b. Chicago, Ill.; d. Col. John Lane and Emeline (Goding) Hancock; hon. Dr. Fine Arts, Boguslawski Coll. of Music, 1939; m. Frank Granger Logan, June 15, 1882; children—Rhea (Mrs. Charles A. Monroe) (dec. 1933), Stuart, Howard H. (dec. 1934), Spencer H., Waldo H. Founder (1936) and pres. Soc. for Sanity in Art, Inc. (internat. orgn. against extreme modernistic art). Trustee Chicago Galleries Assn. Donor, with husband, of Mr. and Mrs. Frank Granger Logan medal and prizes at Chicago Art Inst. and co-contbr. to Grand Central Galleries in N.Y. City. With husband, donor of research fund in pathology, surgery and exptl. medicine at U. of Chicago; also co-founder of Am. Coll. of Surgeons. Decorated by Italian Govt. for Red Cross work in World War. Hon. mem. National League of American Pen Women (past pres. and hon. pres. Chicago br.; formerly v.p.), Soc. of American Etchers; mem. Friends of Contemporary Prints, Illinois Opera Guild, Society of Midland Authors (Chicago), D.A.R., Alliance Francaise, Italy-Am. Soc., Order of Bookfellows, Field Museum, Chicago Hist. Soc., New Orient Soc. America, Am. Museum Natural History of N.Y., Chicago Council on Foreign Relations, Am. Opera Soc., Chicago Drama League, Antiquarian Soc. of Chicago Art Inst., Asso. Am. Artists, Am. Fed. of Art, Chicago Soc. of Etchers, Chicago Woman's Club (life), Renaissance Society (hon.), Assn. Chicago Painters and Sculptors (hon.), Delta Omicron, vice pres. Poetry Soc. of London, Inc. and hon. pres. Chicago Poetry Center of Poetry Soc. of London, Inc. Patroness of Poetry Week, held annually in N.Y. City; also patroness Chicago Civic Opera and Chicago Symphony Orchestra; benefactress of Art Inst. Chicago, Beloit Coll., Logan Museum and Hancock Field of Beloit Coll.; also benefactress of artists and musicians. Club: The Renaissance. Author: Lights and Shadows (verse), 1932; Heights and Depths (verse), 1935; Sanity in Art (awarded Edith Ainsfield Wolf medal by Nat. League of Am. Pen Women), 1937; Collected Poems, 1941; also articles, short stories, children's poems and many lyrics set to music by composers. Lecturer. Home: 1150 Lake Shore Drive, Chicago, Ill. Died Nov. 1, 1943.

LOGAN, William Hoffman Gardiner, oral surgeon; b. Morrison, Ill., Oct. 14, 1872; s. Robert E. and Melvina (McCoy) L.; D.D.S., Chicago Coll. Dental Surgery, 1896; M.D., Chicago Coll. Medicine and Surgery, 1905; LL.D., Loyola Univ., 1926; M.S., U. of Mich., 1930; LL.D., National Univ. of Ireland (Dublin), 1940; m. Florence, d. Dr. Truman W. Brophy, June 20, 1900; 1 dau., Jean Brophy (Mrs. Donald L. LaChance). Member attending staff of St. Joseph's, Michael Reese and Cook County hospitals; dean and prof. plastic and oral surgery, Chicago Coll. Dental Surgery since 1920. Maj. Medical Res. Corps, Aug. 1917; chief of dental div. Surgeon General's Office, Washington, D.C., Aug. 1917; commd. lt. col., Feb. 1918, col. May 1918; hon. disch. Feb. 12, 1919. Apptd. chmn. com. on legislation and enrollment and com. on dentistry, Gen. Med. Bd. of Council of Nat. Defense, 1917. Chmn. Foundation for Dental Research of Chicago Coll. Dental Surgery since 1935; mem. Gorgas Memorial Inst. of Tropical and Preventive Medicine (sec. 1929-33); mem. bd. govs. since 1933), 3d Australian Dental Congress (v.p. 1914), 7th Internat. Dental Congress (pres. 1926). Fellow Am. Coll. Surgeons (mem. bd. govs. since 1928); mem. Nat. Dental Assn. (pres. 1917-18), Ill. State Dental Soc. (pres. 1913-14), Chicago Dental Soc. (pres. 1909-10), A.M.A., Ill. State Med. Soc., Chicago Med. Soc. (pres. North Side Branch 1940-41), Am. Assn. Oral and Plastic Surgeons, Am. Bd. Plastic Surgery, Internat. Dental Federation (v.p. 1926-36; pres. since 1936), Am. Assn. Dental Schs., Omicron Kappa Upsilon, Pi Gamma Mu, Delta Sigma Delta; hon. mem. Am. Dental Soc. of Europe, Ky. State Med. Soc. Mason. Clubs: Chicago Athletic, Press, Army and Navy. Writer of many articles on dental edn., cleft palate and lip and oral surgery. Home: 179 Lake Shore Drive. Office: 55 E. Washington St., Chicago, Ill. Died Apr. 6, 1943.

LOGAN, William Newton, geologist; b. Barboursville, Ky., Nov. 5, 1869; s. Henry Elderberry and Jane Elizabeth (Points) L.; B.A., M.A., U. of Kan., 1896; Ph.D., U. of Chicago, 1900; m. Janette Cecil DeBaun, Aug. 31, 1898; children—Lois Lucene (Mrs. R. E. Esarey), Harlan DeBaun. With Kan. Geol. Survey, summers, 1893-97; supt. pub. schs., Pleasanton, Kan., 1896-98; with Wyo. Scientific expdn., 1899; prof. geology and mineralogy, St. Lawrence U., Canton, N.Y., 1900-03; with N.Y. Geol. Survey, summer 1902; prof. geology and mining engring., Miss. Agrl. and Mech. Coll., and geologist Miss. Expt. Sta., 1903-16, also geologist State Geol. Survey, 1903-16, and dean Sch. of Science, A. and M. Coll., 1913-16; asso. prof. econ. geology, Ind. U., 1916-19, prof. since 1919 and state geologist since 1919. Determined boundaries of Am. Upper Jurassic Sea ("Logan Sea"); first to suggest the biochem. theory of the origin of halloysite and other kaolin-forming minerals. Life mem. and fellow A.A.A.S.; fellow Geol. Soc. Am., Ind. Acad. Science, Royal Soc. Arts, London; mem. Am. Assn. State Geologists, Kan. Acad. Science, Miss. Acad. of Science, Sigma Xi, Phi Beta Kappa, Pi Gamma Mu; corr. mem. Soc. Geol. de France. Republican. Methodist. Kiwanian. Author: The Upper Cretaceous of Kansas, 1896; Invertebrates of Kansas Cretaceous, 1898; Brick Clays of Mississippi, 1907; Pottery Clays of Mississippi, 1909; Kaolin of Indiana, 1919; Petroleum and Natural Gas of Indiana, 1920; The Elements of Practical Conservation, 1924; Geology of the Deep Wells of Indiana, 1926; Sub-Surface Strata of Indiana; also wrote Building Stone in Indiana, Mineral Wool in Indiana, Clay Products of Indiana, Geological Map of Indiana, Rock Products of Indiana, and numerous brochures, articles, etc. General editor Handbook of Indiana Geology. Official del. 1st, 2d and 3d Internat. Conf. on Bitum. Coal. Home: Bloomington, Ind. Deceased.

LOGUE, John Terrell (lōg), corp. officer; b. Gibson, Ga., May 17, 1888; s. Joseph Henry and Ida (VanDella) L.; student U. of Ga. Med. Sch., 1909-10, U. of Ala. Med. Sch., 1910-11; m. Addie Trowbridge Eve, July 2, 1907; children—Florine Eloise, Robert Bruce, Edith Eve, John Terrell. Telegrapher, Atlantic Coast Line & Southern Ry., 1906-07; with Western Union Telegraph, 1907-08; with Postal Telegraph & Cable Co. since 1908, as operator, wire chief, chief operator, 1908-23, mgr. Jacksonville, Fla., 1923-25, supt. 1925-29, gen. mgr. Southern Div., 1929-33, v.p. since 1933; v.p. Postal Telegraph, Inc. Democrat. Presbyterian. Knights of Pythias. Home: 315 Tillou Rd., South Orange, N.J. Office: 157 Chambers St., New York, N.Y.* Died July 15, 1947.

LOMAX, John Avery (lō'măks), author; b. Goodman, Miss., Sept. 23, 1867; s. James Avery and Susan (Cooper) L.; ed. Granbury (Tex.) Coll., Weatherford Coll., U. of Tex. (B.A., 1897, M.A., 1906), U. of Chicago (1895, 1903), Harvard (M.A., 1907); m. Bess B. Brown, June 9, 1904 (died May 7, 1931); m. 2d, Ruby Terrill, July 21, 1934. Registrar U. of Tex., 1897-1903; instr. English, Tex. Agrl. and Mech. Coll., 1903-04, asso. prof., 1904-10; sec. U. of Texas, 1910-17; sec. U. of Texas Ex-Students Assn. 1910-17 and 1919-25; bond salesman Lee, Higginson & Co., 1917-19; v.p. Republic Nat. Co., Dallas, Tex., 1925-32; hon. curator of Archive of Am. Folk Song and hon. consultant, Library of Congress since 1934. Mem. Modern Lang. Assn. America (exec. com. 1916), Am. Folk Lore Soc. (pres. 1912, 13), Tex. Folk Lore Soc. (founder, fellow, ex-sec., pres. 1940-42), Tex. Acad. of Letters, Chicago Literary Soc., Tex. Philos. Soc., Phi Beta Kappa (hon.), Phi Delta Theta. Author: Cowboy Songs, 1910; Book of Texas (with H. Y. Benedict), 1916; Songs of the Cattle Trail and Cow Camp, 1918; American Ballads and Folk Songs (with Alan Lomax), 1934; Negro Folk Songs as Sung by Lead Belly (with Alan Lomax), 1937; Cowboy Songs, (revised), 1938; Our Singing Country (with Alan Lomax), 1941; The Adventures of a Ballad Hunter, 1947; The One Hundred and One Best American Ballads (with Alan Lomax and Mr. and Mrs. Chas. Seeger), 1947; asso. editor, Southwest Review, since 1943. Home: 8170 San Benito Way, Dallas, Tex. Died Jan. 26, 1948; buried Austin, Tex.

LONERGAN, Augustine (lŏn'ẽr-gan), lawyer; b. Thompson, Conn., May 20, 1874; s. Michael and Mary (Quinn) L.; LL.B., Yale, 1902; m. Lucy G. Waters; children—Ruth Ellen, Lucy Waters, Ann Yates, Mary Lee. Began practice at Hartford, Conn., 1902; was asst. corp. counsel, Hartford; mem. 63d, 65th, 66th, 72d Congresses (1913-15, 1917-21, 1931-33), 1st Conn. Dist.; in practice at Hartford. Dem. nominee U.S. Senate, 1920, 28; elected U.S. senator for term 1933-39; resumed practice of law. Chmn. in Conn. of Thomas Jefferson Memorial Foundation. Mem. Am and Conn. State bar assns. Home: 48 Forest St. Hartford, Conn.; (summer) West Chatham, Cape Cod Mass.* Died Oct. 18, 1947.

LONG, Andrew Theodore, naval officer; b. in Iredell County, N.C., Apr. 6, 1866; grad. U.S. Naval Acad., 1887; m. Mrs. Viola V. Fife, Mar. 3, 1928. Promoted ensign, July 1, 1889; promoted through grades to rear admiral, Sept. 15, 1918. Served on Minneapolis, Spanish-American War, 1898; exec. officer Dolphin, 1904-05; comdr. Mayflower, 1905-07; exec. officer Illinois, 1907-09; duty Office of Naval Intelligence, Navy Dept., 1909; naval attaché, Rome and Vienna, 1909-12; comd. Des Moines, 1912-14; supervisor naval auxiliaries, 1914-16; apptd. capt. Connecticut, Oct. 25, 1916, Nevada, Feb. 1918; naval attaché, Paris, France, staff rep., Paris; now rear adm. (perm.); comdr. div., Atlantic Fleet, 1920; dir. of naval intelligence, Navy Dept., 1920-21; chief of staff, Atlantic Fleet, 1921-22; comdr. U.S. Naval Forces in Europe, 1922-23; chief Bur. of Navigation, 1923-24; became mem. Gen. Board, Navy Dept., 1924-30, retired; dir. of Internat. Hydrographic Bur., Monte Carlo, 1930-37. Address: care Am. Security & Trust Co., Washington, D.C.* Died May 21, 1946.

LONG, Charles Grant, officer U.S. Marine Corps; b. South Weymouth, Mass., Dec. 14, 1869; s. John and Eliza (Regan) L.; grad. U.S. Naval Acad., 1889, Army War Coll., 1912; m. Edith M., d. Rear Adm. Charles J. Barclay, U.S. Navy, Sept. 1, 1903; 1 dau., Nancy Barclay. Commd. 2d lt. U.S. Marine Corps, 1891; promoted through grades to brig. gen., Nov. 1918; retired Dec. 31, 1921. Participated in campaigns in Cuba, 1898, Philippines, 1899-1900, Boxer campaign, 1900, Nicaragua campaign, 1914, at Vera Cruz, Mexico, 1915-16; served as chief of staff hdqrs., U.S. Marine Corps, Washington, 1917-20, having charge of personnel, and its distribution during the war; apptd. comdg. gen. 2d Brig., U.S. Marine Corps, Santo Domingo, D.R., Oct. 1920. Bvtd. capt. for services at Guantanamo, Cuba, 1898; mentioned in orders for spl. services as comdr. 2d Batn. Marines, at Tientsin, China, during Boxer campaign; recommended for D.S.M. for services World War but awarded Navy Cross. Home: South Dartmouth, Mass. Died Mar. 5, 1943.

LONG, Charles Ramsay, editor, pub.; b. Atlas Twp., Pike County, Ill., Nov. 4, 1872; s. Jesse Green and Caroline Farwell (Ramsay) L.; grad. Pittsfield (Ill.) High Sch., 1890; m. Hannah Hinkson, Dec. 5, 1895; children—Carolyn H. (Mrs. James Boyce), Frederick R.; m. 2d, Gertrude H. Jones, Sept. 8, 1925. In newspaper work with Chester Times for a period of fifty years; has leased newspaper to the Chester Times Publishing Company; now retired. Pres., treas. and dir. Chester Times, Inc.; dir. Chester-Cambridge Bank. Del. to Rep. Nat. Conv., 1936. Publicity dir. Liberty Loan campaign, 1917-19. Chmn. Del. County Com. of Pa. Economy League; pres. and dir. Del. County Chamber of Commerce; pres. Pa. Newspaper Pub. Assn., 2 terms, 1912-33; mem. Colonial Soc. of Pa., Ark. and Dove Soc. of Maryland, Washington Soc. of Am. Editors, Soc. War of 1812. Republican. Mason. Clubs: Union League (Phila.); Chester Rotary. Home: Wallingford, Pa. Office: Chester, Pa. Died Jan. 28, 1946.

LONG, Harriet Catherine, librarian; b. Madison, Neb., Oct. 3, 1887; d. Francis Augustus and Maggie Elizabeth (Miller) Long; B.A., U. of Neb., 1908; B.L.S., New York State Library School, 1910, M.L.S., 1925; honorary Litt.D., Willamette University, 1939. Assistant, Santa Barbara (Calif.) Free Pub. Library, 1910-13; librarian Kern County (Calif.) Free Library, 1913-15, Brumback Library, Van Wert County, O., 1916-18; war work, A.L.A., on Mexican Border, 1918, France and Germany, 1919; in charge traveling library dept. Wis. Free Library Commn., 1920-30; librarian Ore. State Library since 1930. Mem. A.L.A. (mem. exec. bd., mem. bd. on library extension), Pacific Northwest Library Assn., Am. Assn. Univ. Women, Salem Women's Club. Presbyn. Author: County Library Service, 1925. Contbr. to professional publs. Home: 1740 Saginaw St., Salem, Ore. Died July 4, 1941.

LONG, John D., officer U.S.P.H.S.; b. Mt. Pleasant, Pa., Feb. 12, 1874; s. Cyrus T. and Barbara S. (Durstine) L.; A.B., Washington and Jefferson Coll., 1894, A.M., 1897; M.D., U. of Pa., 1897; hon. Sc.D., Washington and Jefferson Coll., 1929; m. Sara S. Roberts, Oct. 11, 1899 (died 1900); 1 dau., Margaret Moore; m. 2d, Elvira Howe, June 14, 1905 (died 1919); children—Elvira H., Jean D.; m. 3d, Grace Henriques, Feb. 5, 1930; 1 dau., Grace Isabel. Asst. surgeon, United States Public Health Service, 1900, past assistant surgeon, 1905, surgeon, 1912, assistant surgeon gen., 1910-12 and 1921-25, med. dir. 1930. Dir. of health, Manila, 1915-19; prof. hygiene, U. of Philippines, 1915-19, chief quarantine officer Philippines, 1915-19; reorganized Philippine Health Service; tech. adviser Am. delegation to 5th Pan-Am. Conference, Santiago, Chile, 1923; del. Pan-Am. Union and Pan-Am. Sanitary Bur. to Conf. League of Red Cross Soc., Buenos Aires, Argentina, 1923; vice dir. Pan-Am. Sanitary Bur., 1924-27; del. of U.S. to 3d Pan-Am. Scientific Congress, Lima, Peru, 1924; loaned by U.S. Govt. as tech. adviser in pub. health to Ministry of Hygiene, Republic of Chile, for reorganization of Chilean Nat. Health Service, 1925-26; chief quarantine officer Panama Canal, 1927-28. Vice pres. for U.S. of Far Eastern Assn. of Tropical Medicine, 1925-27; del. of U.S. to 8th Pan-Am. Sanitary Conf., Lima, Peru, 1927; tech. adviser to U.S. Delegation to Sixth Internat. Conf. of Am. States, Havana, Cuba, 1928; traveling rep. Pan-Am. Sanitary Bur. since 1928; del. of U.S. to 2d Conf. on Immigration and Emigration, Havana, Cuba, 1928; del. Pan-Am. Sanitary Bur. to 7th Internat. Conf. of Am. States, Montevideo, 1933, and to 9th Pan-Am. Sanitary Conf., Buenos Aires, 1934; del. Pan-Am. Sanitary Bureau to 10th Pan-Am. Sanitary Conf., Bogota, 1938, to 8th Internat. Conf. of Am. States, Lima, 1938, to 1st Pan-Am. Conf. on Sanitary Aviation, Montevideo, 1939; del. Am. Red Cross to Red Cross Conf., Santiago, Chile, 1940; delegate of Pan-Am. Sanitary Bureau, to 11th Pan-Am. Sanitary Conference, Rio de Janeiro, Brazil, 1942; del. Pan-Am. Sanitary Bureau to Caribbean Quarantine Conference, Trinidad, B.W.I., 1943. Mem. Faculty Regional Institute of Hospitals, Lima, 1944. Retired, on account of age, from active duty with the U.S. Public Health Service, Nov. 1, 1938; continued as chief traveling rep., Pan Am. Sanitary Bureau until Jan. 31, 1949; became technical advisor, Dept. of Health, Govt. of Ecuador, Feb. 1949. Technical adviser campaigns against bubonic plague in Ecuador since 1929, Peru since 1930, Chile since 1932, Argentina since 1935, Brazil since 1935. Corresponding mem. Acad. Medicine (Lima); hon. mem. Medical Soc. (Santiago), Soc. Microbiology and Hygiene (Santiago); fellow Am. Pub. Health Assn.; mem. Assn. Mil. Surgeons, Beta Theta Pi, Alpha Mu Pi Omega. Decorated Al Merito, Chile and Ecuador; Order of Carlos Finlay, Cuba, El Sol, Peru, Vasco Nunez de Balboa, Panama. Republican. Presbyterian. Clubs: Union (Panama), Country Club (Lima), Country Club (Guayaquil). Apptd. hon. mem. Nat. Health Service (Chile), 1937. Home: Pichincha St. 332, Guayaquil, Ecuador. Died Sept. 18, 1949; interred General Cemetery, Guayaquil.

LONG, Omera Floyd, college prof.; b. Millersburg, Ky., May 10, 1870; s. James Riley and Armilda (Cheatham) L.; A.B., Ky. Wesleyan Coll., 1890, A.M., 1893; Ph.D., Johns Hopkins, 1897; m. Margaret A. Kingsley, Feb. 3, 1914; children—Margaret Appleton, Littleton, Robert Kingsley. Classical master, Friends' School, Baltimore, 1895-96; instr. Latin, 1897-1901, asst. prof., 1901-06, asso. prof., 1906-10, prof., 1910-21, John Evans prof. Latin lang. and lit. since 1921, Northwestern Univ. Mem. Am. Philol. Assn., Classical Assn. Middle West and South (ex-pres.), Am. Assn. of Univ. Prof., Archaeol. Inst. of Am., Phi Beta Kappa. Clubs: University (Evanston); Kildeer Country. Editor: Livy (selections from the first decade), 1908. Contbr. to philol. jours. Home: 827 Colfax St., Evanston, Ill. Died Nov. 27, 1945.

LONG, Ralph Herman, ch. official; b. Loudonville, O., Dec. 3, 1882; s. Thomas K. and Elizabeth (Moyer) L.; student Capital U., Columbus, O., 1904-06, D.D., 1931; grad. Evang. Luth. Sem., Columbus, 1909; grad. study University of Pittsburgh, 1925; LL.D., Wittenberg College, 1946; married Sarah Ellen Bachman, June 10, 1909; children—Robert Waldo, James Richard, Edward Victor. Ordained ministry Evang. Luth. Ch., 1909; pastor Newton Falls-Warren (Ohio) Parish, 1909-13, Zions Luth. Ch., Coraopolis, Pa., 1913-21, St. Paul's Luth. Ch., Pittsburgh, Pa., 1921-27; stewardship sec. Evang. Luth. Joint Synod of O., 1927-30; exec. dir. Nat. Luth. Council since 1930. Mem. commn. to visit Europe, 1946, for Nat. Luth. Council rehabilitation and welfare program. Served as camp pastor Camp Meade, Md., 1918. Mem. exec. com. Lutheran World Conv., Koinomia. Contributor to church publications. Home: 128 Driscoll Av., Rockville Centre, N.Y. Office: Madison Av. at 37th St., New York 16. Died Feb. 19, 1948.

LONG, Theodore Kepner, lawyer; b. Millerstown, Pa., Apr. 26, 1856; s. Abraham and Catharine (Kepner) L.; ed. State Normal Sch., Millersville; New Bloomfield (Pa.) Classical Acad.; spl. studies at Yale; LL.B., Yale Law Sch., 1878; m. Kate Carson, Nov. 25, 1885. Editor Mandan (N.D.) Daily Pioneer, 1882; compiled Long's Legislative Hand Book for Dakota, 1883; began practice of law 1884; state's atty. for dist. west of the Mo. River, Dak. Ter., 1885; atty. N.P. R.R., Bismarck, Dak. Ter., 1887; settled in Chicago, 1894. Legal adviser in formation of Ill. Life Ins. Co., 1899, and gen. counsel same, 1899-1907; assisted in organizing Western Trust & Savings Bank, 1903, and gen. counsel same, 1903-07; retired from active practice, 1908. Founded, 1914, and since president Carson Long Inst. (boys Military school, prep. and vocational instrn.), New Bloomfield, Pa. Alderman 6th Ward, Chicago, 1909-15. Mem. Chicago Bar Assn. Republican. Episcopalian. Mason, K.T., Shriner. Clubs: Union League, South Shore Country (Chicago). Home: "The Maples," New Bloomfield, Pa. Died Dec. 28, 1947.

LONG, Wendell McLean, surgeon; b. Caddo, Okla., Jan. 6, 1899; s. LeRoy and Martha (Downing) L.; A.B., Okla. U., 1922; M.D. cum laude, Harvard, 1926; grad. study Europe, 1929; m. Jamie Belle Replogle, Nov. 28, 1931; children—Lyda Louise, Wendell McLean, Jr. Surg. and gynecol. intern. Roosevelt Hosp., N.Y. City, 1926-29; attending gynecologist St. Anthony Hosp., Oklahoma City, since 1929; instr. in gynecology, U. of Okla., 1929-31; gynecologist LeRoy Long Clinic since 1929. Served in Army Training Corps, 1918. Fellow American College Surgeons, American Assn. Obstetricians, Gynecologists and Abdominal Surgeons, American Medical Association, Central Assn. Obstetricians and Gynecologists; mem. Okla. State Med. Assn. (chmn. cancer com. 1933-39), American Cancer Society (Oklahoma state chmn. 1940-45), Southern Med. Assn. (sec. 1945, v. chmn. 1946, sect. on gynecology), Okla. City Acad. Medicine, Okla. City Clin. Soc. (treas. 1935, sec. 1936, v.p. 1937, dir. 1938-39, pres. 1940), Southern Interurban Gynecol. and Obstet. Club, La. Gynecol. and Obstet. Society (hon.), Am. Board of Gynecology, Sigma Alpha Epsilon, Phi Beta Pi, Phi Beta Kappa (hon). Democrat. Methodist. Mason. Clubs: Men's Dinner, Golf and Country, Beacon. Contbr. to med. jours. Home: 6704 Avondale Drive. Office: Medical Arts Bldg., Oklahoma City, Okla. Died Dec. 27, 1946.

LONGDEN, Henry Boyer, coll. prof.; b. Vevay, Ind., Sept. 13, 1860; s. Samuel and Sarah (Boyer) L.; A.B., DePauw U., 1881, A.M., 1884, LL.D., 1925; studied U. of Chicago, 1887, Göttingen, 1888-89, Leipzig, 1890, Munich, 1898, Berlin, 1910-11; m. M. Louise Johnson, July 7, 1886; 1 son, Grafton Johnson. Asst. prof. Latin, De Pauw U., 1882-85, became prof. German lang. and lit., 1892, dir. Edward Rector Scholarship Foundn., 1918, acting pres., 1921-22, v.p., 1922, now retired. Mem. State Bd. of Edn. of Ind. Mem. Modern Lang. Assn. Am., Goethe Gesellschaft, Ind. Assn. Coll. Profs. of German (pres. 1923), Delta Kappa Epsilon, Phi Beta Kappa (ex-pres. Ind. Chapter). Republican. Methodist. Clubs: Athenaeum, Kiwanis. Mem. Univ. Senate of M.E. Ch. Home: Greencastle, Ind. Died Nov. 7, 1948.

LONGINO, Andrew Houston, ex-governor; b. Lawrence County, Miss., May 16, 1855; s. John Thomas and Annie (Ramsay) L.; A.B., Miss. Coll., Clinton, 1879; spl. summer course in law, U. of Va., 1880; m. Marion Buckley, Apr. 1887; children—Mack Buckley, S. G., James M., Annie R., Gay. Admitted to bar, 1881; clk. Circuit and Chancery courts for Lawrence County, Miss., 1876-80; mem. Miss. Senate, 1880-84; U.S. dist. atty., Southern Dist. of Miss., 1888-89; chancellor of Miss., 1894-99; gov. of Miss., 1900-04; now judge Hinds County (Miss.) Court, Jackson. Democrat. Home: Jackson, Miss. Died Feb. 24, 1942.

LONGLEY, Harry Sherman, bishop; b. Cohoes, N.Y., Sept. 10, 1868; s. John Thompson and Maria Elizabeth (Fulton) L.; B.A., St. Stephen's Coll. (now known as Bard College, Columbia Univ.), 1891, M.A., 1896, D.D., 1912; grad. Gen. Theol. Seminary, 1894, S.T.D., 1920; m. Hattie Eliza Minkler, Sept. 17, 1894; 1 son, Rev. Henry Sherman Minkler. Deacon, 1894, priest, 1895, Protestant Episcopal Ch.; curate St. Paul's Parish, Troy, N.Y., 1894-95; rector Trinity Ch., Milford, Mass., 1895-99, Christ Ch., Binghamton, N.Y., 1899-1911, St. Mark's Parish, Evanston, Ill., 1911-12; consecrated suffragan bishop of Ia., Oct. 23, 1912; elected coadjutor bishop of Ia., May 21, 1917, bishop of Ia., Dec. 27, 1929; retired Nov. 1, 1943; presiding bishop Province of Northwest, 1920-29. Dep. Gen. Conv. Protestant Episcopal Ch., Richmond, Va., 1907, Cincinnati, 1910. Mem. Kappa Gamma Chi (St. Stephen's Coll.). Scottish Rite Mason (33°); Past Grand Chaplain Grand Lodge State of N.Y. Home: 3510 Staunton Av., Charleston, W.Va. Died Apr. 5, 1944.

LONGSTRETH, Charles (lŏng'strĕth), mfr.; b. Philadelphia, Pa., 1868; s. Edward and Anna P. (Wise) L.; ed. Swarthmore Coll.; m. M. Gertrude Heyer, 1891; children—Edward, Ellanor L. Sharp. With Baldwin Locomotive Works, Philadelphia, 1886-91; gen. supt. Pa. Warehousing & Safe Deposit Co., 1891-96; v.p. 1892-1904, pres. since 1904, U.S. Metallic Packing Co., railroad supplies; pres. Am. Locomotive Sander Co., 1899-1911. Commd. lt.-comdr. U.S.N.R.F., Feb. 1917, and on active duty from Apr. 1917, until after Armistice. Mem. Am. Soc. Mech. Engrs., Am. Soc. Naval Architects and Marine Engrs., Am. Soc. Naval Engrs., Franklin Inst. Clubs: Racquet, Corinthian Yacht (Phila.); New York Yacht (New York). Author: Rules of the Road at Sea by Diagram, 1914; Elementary Seamanship and Plan for Nautical Troops, Boy Scouts, 1915. Address: 611 A Av., Coronado, Calif. Died Mar. 1, 1948.

LONSDALE, John Gerdes (lŏnz'dāl), banker and railroad executive; b. in Memphis, Tenn., April 4, 1872; s. John and Ida (Bosworth) L.; ed. Christian Brothers Coll., St. Louis; St. John's Military Acad., Manlius, N.Y.; business coll., Baltimore, Md.; LL.D., U. of Arkansas, 1939; married; children—Aileen, John G. Began in real estate business, Hot Springs, Ark., 1891, later in bond and stock brokerage business, New York and Hot Springs, as J. G. Lonsdale & Co.; an organizer of Little Rock, Hot Springs & Tex. R.R., of which was apptd. receiver, 1896, reorganizing same as the Little Rock & Hot Springs Western R.R.; mem. Logan & Bryan, stock brokers, New York, until 1915 (resigned); pres. Nat. Bank of Commerce, St. Louis, until May 20, 1929, when that institution merged with Mercantile Trust Co., St. Louis, forming Mercantile-Commerce Bank and Trust Co., of which served as pres. until Jan. 9, 1933, chmn. bd. until Jan. 1, 1937 (resigned); co-trustee St.L.-S.F. Ry. Co.; former dir. Federal Reserve Bank, 8th Dist. Past pres. Am. Bankers Assn.; former v.p. U.S. Chamber of Commerce; past pres. St. Louis Clearing House Assn. Clubs: Mo. Athletic, Noonday, Racquet (St. Louis); Bankers, Metropolitan (New York). Home: (country) Mentz Hill Rd., St. Louis County, Mo.; Park Plaza Hotel, St. Louis. Address: Frisco Bldg., 906 Olive St., St. Louis, Mo. Died June 16, 1943.

LOOMIS, Francis Butler, diplomatist, foreign trade adviser; b. Marietta, O., July 27, 1861; s. Judge William B. and Frances (Wheeler) L.; A.B., Marietta College, 1883; m. Elizabeth M. Mast, Apr. 29, 1897; children—Col. Francis Butler Loomis, Jr. (U.S. Marine Corps), Florence Isabel Loomis. Ohio State librarian, 1885-87; Washington corr., 1887-90; Am. consul at Saint-Étienne and Grenoble, France, 1890-93; editor Cincinnati Daily Tribune, 1893-96; E.E. and M.P. to Venezuela, 1897-1901, to Portugal, 1901-02; 1st asst. secretary of state, 1902; apptd. secretary of state ad interim, July 2, 1905. Active in the movement for building up American commerce in Latin America; arranged for Parcel Post conventions; opened negotiations for extradition and reciprocity treaties; made long trip up Orinoco River on U.S. man-of-war "Wilmington," 1898, for the purpose of seeking opportunities for the development of American commercial opportunities; conducted final negotiations leading to acquisition of Panama Canal Zone by U.S. Govt.; visited Santo Domingo with Admiral Dewey on the "Mayflower," and arranged for the modus vivendi, Customs collections, under U.S. supervision; special ambassador to France, to receive remains of John Paul Jones from the French Govt., June 23, 1905; apptd. (1908) spl. E.E. to Japan, to make certain representations to Japanese Govt. respecting the visit of the American Fleet in that year to Japan; U.S. commr. gen. to Turin Exposition, 1912; del. U.S. Govt. to Internat. Expn. Congress, Berlin, 1912. Decorated Grand Officer Legion of Honor (France), 1904; Order of Sacred Treasure, 1st class (Japan), 1909; Grand Cordon, Crown of Italy, 1st class, 1912; Order of Bolivar, 1st class (Venezuela). Charter mem. Am. Red Cross. Clubs: Country (Burlingame, Calif.); Pacific-Union (San Francisco, Calif.). Home: 325 Chapin Lane, Burlingame, Calif. Died Aug. 5, 1948.

LOOMIS, Frederic Morris, gynecologist, obstetrician; b. Ann Arbor, Mich., Apr. 12, 1877; s. Frank Connett and Mary (McMahon) L.; student Univ. of Mich., 1894-97 and 1908-09, A.B., 1909, M.D., 1912; m. Edith A. Prichard, Jan. 1, 1907; children—Frances Mary (Mrs. Arthur Jandrey), Jane Prichard (Mrs. Robert Sims); m. 2d, Olive Voswinkel McLellan, Oct. 26, 1919; m. 3d, Evalyn Feigenberg, Oct. 7, 1939. Salesman, 1898-1901; hard rock miner, 1901-07; editor Ketchikan Daily Miner, 1907-08; instr. anatomy and nervous anatomy, U. of Mich., 1910-11, obstetrics and gynecology, 1912-16; gynecologist and obstetrician, Oakland, Calif., 1917-49; chmn. staff Peralta Hosp., Oakland, 1933-34. Served as sergt. O. Co., 32d Mich. Vol. Inf., Spanish War. Mem. A.M.A., Calif. State and Alameda County med. socs., Bay Counties and Pacific Coast obstet. socs., Calif. Writers Club (pres. 1944-46), Sigma Xi, Alpha Omega Alpha, Gamma Alpha, Delta Upsilon. Republican. Episcopalian. Club: Claremont Country (Oakland). Author: Consultation Room, 1939; The Bond Between Us, 1942; In a Chinese Garden, 1946; The Best Medicine, 1949. Contbr. to Reader's Digest, other mags. His story "Paid in Full" (Reader's Digest) made into (Paramount) moving picture of the same title (released in 1950), and at time of his death he was directing it. Home: 516 Park Way, Piedmont 11, Calif. Died Feb. 9, 1949.

LOOMIS, Orland S., ex-atty. gen. Wis.; b. Mauston, Wis., Nov. 2, 1893; s. Morgan O. and Clara (Steen) L.; student Ripon (Wis.) Coll., 1912-14; LL.B., U. of Wis., 1917; m. Florence Ely, June 22, 1918; children—Robert M., John E., Laura Jean. Admitted to Wis. bar, 1917, and since practiced in Mauston; mem. Loomis, Roswell & Chambers; city atty. Mauston, 1922-31; mem. Wis. Assembly, 1929-30, State Senate, 1931-34 (pres. pro tem 1933-34); atty. gen. for Wis., 1937-38. Senate rep. Governor's Exec. Council, 1933-34; Senate rep. Am. Legislators Council, 1933-34; Wis. dir. Rural Electrification Coordination, 1935-36; Wis. rep. World Power Conf., 1936; chmn. 1st, 2d and 3d Progressive Party Platform Conv., 1934, 36, 38; Progressive Party candidate for governor of Wis., 1940. Chmn. Wis. Crime Control Conference, 1939. Wisconsin member Interstate Commission on Crime, 1937-41, vice-president, 1941-42. Served in Field Med. Supply Depot, U.S. Army, with A.E.F., 1918-19. Member American Legion, Veterans of Foreign Wars, Wisconsin Bar Assn., Am. Bar Assn., Phi Alpha Delta, Pi Kappa Delta, Delta Sigma Psi. Progressive. Presbyterian. Mason. Odd Fellow. Club: Kiwanis of Mauston, Wis. Home: Mauston, Wis. Office: Insurance Bldg., Madison, Wis.; and Loomis Bldg., Mauston, Wis. Died Dec. 7, 1942.

LORD, George de Forest, lawyer; b. Lawrence, Long Island, N.Y., Dec. 18, 1891; s. Franklin Butler and Josephine (Gillet) L.; grad. Westminster Sch., Simsbury, Conn., 1909; B.A., Yale, 1914; LL.B., Columbia, 1917; m. Hazen Symington, June 27, 1914; children—Edith (Mrs. Charles Garrison Meyer, Jr.), George de Forest, Jr., Edward Crary II. Teacher admiralty law, Columbia, 1919-26; practiced law with Lord, Day & Lord, N.Y. City, since 1919, partner since 1923; dir. Nat. Surety Corp., Nat. Surety Marine Ins. Co., Twenty-Five Broadway Corp.; trustee Seamen's Bank for Savings, U.S. Trust Co. of N.Y. Served as 1st lt., U.S. Army, World War I; counsel for Brit. Ministry of War Transport in U.S., World War II. Awarded Order of British Empire. Pres. Children's Aid Soc.; trustee United Charities, Pub. Library (N.Y. City). President Maritime Law Assn. of U.S. Republican. Episcopalian. Clubs: Downtown (pres.), Yale, Century, Racquet and Tennis, Turf and Field (N.Y. City); Piping Rock (Locust Valley, N.Y.). Author: Lord and Sprague Cases in Admiralty (with George C. Sprague), 1926. Author of articles, Admiralty Claims against the Government, 1919; The Foreign Ship Mortgage (with Garrard W. Glenn),

1947; Unification of Maritime Liens and Mortgages (with Garrard W. Glenn), 1949. Home: Syosset, Long Island. Office: 25 Broadway, New York 4.

Died Feb. 2, 1950.

LORD, John, educator; b. Deer Island, N.B., Can., Jan. 27, 1079; s. Charles William and Martha (Butler) L.; came to U.S., 1895; student Winchester (Tenn.), Normal Coll., 1898-99; A.B., Translyvania U., 1904, also grad. theol. dept.; A.M., Syracuse U., 1915, Ph.D., 1919; m. Inez Logan, 1907. Ednl. work in Philippines, 1907-10; instr. sociology, Syracuse U., 1915-19; head dept. of Spanish and Latin, Tex. Christian U., Ft. Worth, Tex., 1919-20, head dept. of social sciences and prof. govt. and sociology since 1920, also dean of Grad. Sch. since 1926. Mem. Phi Beta Kappa, Phi Kappa Phi. Mem. Christian (Disciples) Ch. Frequent lecturer on internat. relations. Home: Fort Worth, Tex. Died Mar. 1949.

LORING, John Alden, naturalist; b. Cleveland, O., Mar. 6, 1871; s. Lt. Benjamin William and Nellie (Cohoon) L.; ed. Owego Free Acad., zoöl. gardens, Europe, 1 yr.; unmarried. Field naturalist U.S. Biol. Survey, 1892-97; curator of animals New York Zoöl. Park, 1897-1901; field naturalist in Europe for U.S. Nat. Mus., during which time broke all previous records for field work by collecting and preserving the skins of 913 mammals and birds in 63 days; field naturalist Smithsonian-Roosevelt scientific expdn. to. Africa, 1909-10. First lt. Ordnance Dept., U.S. Army, World War. Mem. Am. Ornithologists' Union, Biol. Soc. Washington, Camp Fire Club of America. Author: Young Folks' Nature Field Book; African Adventure Stories. Also a number of articles relating chiefly to birds and mammals, in Outing Magazine, Metropolitan Magazine, Collier's Weekly, Youth's Companion. Home: Owego, N.Y. Died May 8, 1947.

LORING, Richard Tuttle, bishop; b. Newton, Mass., Feb. 7, 1900; s. Rev. Richard T. and Mary Amory (Leland) L.; A.B., Harvard, 1924; S.T.B., Episcopal Theol. Sch., 1929; (hon.) D.D., Nashotah (Wis.) House; m. Helen Dexter, June 25, 1928; children—Richard T., Christopher, Timothy. Ordained to ministry of Episcopal Ch.; rector Church of the Good Shepherd, Waban, Mass., 1929-37; chaplain Boston Psychopathic Hospital, 1932-37; lecturer Episcopal Theol. Sch., Cambridge, Mass., 1935-37; rector St. Davids Ch., Baltimore, Md., 1937-47; bishop of Springfield, Ill., since Oct. 18, 1947. Home: 821 S. Second St. Office: 197 E. Lawrence Av., Springfield, Ill. Died Apr. 16, 1948.

LORING, Victor Joseph, lawyer; b. Marlboro, Mass., Jan. 11, 1859; s. Hollis and Laura W. (Hitchcock) L.; grad. Boston Latin Sch., 1878; LL.B., Boston U., 1881; m. M. Emilie Baker, Dec. 9, 1891; children—Robert Melville, Selden Melville. Admitted to Suffolk bar, 1881, Supreme Court of U.S., 1885; in practice at Boston since 1881. Was mem. Com. of 12, Boston; mem. Rep. State Central Com. several terms; del. many local and state convs.; mem. sch. com., Wellesley, Mass., 7 yrs., and Town Counsel, 1902-07, moderator, 1918-22. Chairman of the Legal Advisory Board, Mass. Div. 33, 1917-19. Corporate mem. A.B.C.F.M.; ex-pres. Am. Federation Men's Ch. Orgns.; moderator Congl. State Assn., 1911-12; dir. Am. Congl. Assn., Congl. Ch. Union; del. Nat. Council, 1910, 13. Mem. Am., Mass. State and Norfolk bar assns., S.R. (ex-v.p.). Life mem. Y.M.C.A. Clubs: Boston City, Boston Art (v.p. 1916-17). Home: 25 Chestnut St. Office: 14 Beacon St., Boston, Mass. Died Feb. 8, 1947.

LORTON, Eugene, newspaper pub.; b. nr. Middletown, Mo., May 28, 1869; s. Riley Robert and Ellen Elizabeth (White) L.; ed. pub. schs.; m. Maud Geil, Feb. 25, 1912. Learned printer's trade at Medicine Lodge, Kan.; later published weekly newspapers at Salubria, Emmet and Boisé, Idaho; purchased Linn County Republic, Mound City, Kan., 1896; then lived in State of Wash., becoming editor Walla Walla Daily Union and founder the Walla Walla Daily Bulletin; managed campaign of Gov. Cosgrove; apptd. chmn. State Bd. of Control; purchased interest in Tulsa Daily World, 1911, becoming owner, 1917. Apptd. by President Roosevelt, mem. Internat. Joint Commn., 1933. Chmn. bd. Fourth Nat. Bank. Mem. various social and civic clubs. Episcopalian. Mason (Shriner). Home: Tulsa, Okla. Died Oct. 17, 1949; buried Rose Hill Cemetery, Tulsa.

LOTKA, Alfred James (lŏt'kȧ), mathematician; b. of Am. parents at Lemberg, Austria, Mar. 2, 1880; s. Jacques and Marie (Doebely) L.; B.Sc., Birmingham (Eng.) U., 1901, D.Sc., 1912; M.A., Cornell U., 1909; grad. study, U. of Leipzig, Germany, 1901-02, Johns Hopkins, 1922-24; m. Romola Beattie, Jan. 5, 1935. Asst. chemist Gen. Chem. Co., 1902-08; asst. in physics, Cornell U., 1908-09; examiner U.S. Patent Office 1909; asst. physicist U.S. Bur. of Standards, 1909-11; editor Scientific Am. Supplement, 1911-14; chemist Gen. Chem. Co., 1914-19; supervisor math. research, Statis. Bur. Metropolitan Life Ins. Co., 1924-33, gen. supervisor, 1933-34; asst. statistician Metropolitan Life Ins. Co. since 1934. Fellow Am. Statis. Assn. (pres. 1942), A.A.A.S., Royal Econ. Soc. Population Assn. America (pres. 1938-39), Institute of Mathematical Statistics; member Internat. Union for Scientific Investigation of Population Problems, Internat. Statis. Inst., Inter-Am. Statis. Inst., Econometric Soc., Am. Mathematical Society, American Public Health Association, Swiss Actuarial Soc., Washington Acad. Science, Sigma Xi. Club: Cornell (New York). Author: Elements of Physical Biology, 1925; The Money Value of a Man (with L. I. Dublin), 1930, revised edit. 1946; Length of Life (with L. I. Dublin), 1936; Théorie Analytique des Associations Biologiques, 1934-39; Twenty Five Years of Health Progress (with L. I. Dublin), 1937; also numerous publications in scientific and tech. jours. on math. analysis of population, math. theory of evolution, actuarial mathematics applied to problems of population and of industrial replacement. Home: Beattie Park, Red Bank, N.J. Office: 1 Madison Av., New York, N.Y.

Died Dec. 5, 1949.

LOTT, Edson Schuyler, insurance official; b. Yates County, N.Y., Nov. 10, 1856; s. Jesse T. and Sarah M. (Wheeler) L.; ed. pub. schs. and Penn Yan (N.Y.) Acad.; m. Emma A. Cowl, 1879. Began in newspaper work; later entered ins. business, becoming asst. sec., U.S. Casualty Co. of New York, 1895, sec., 1897, gen. mgr., 1901, pres., 1908-36, chmn. bd. since 1936; dir. Guardian Life Ins. Co., New Amsterdam Casualty Co. Mem. bd. govs. Nat. Council on Workmen's Compensation Ins.; trustee Workmen's Compensation Reinsurance Bureau; vice-pres. Insurance Federation of America, Insurance Society of New York, American Museum of Safety; Association of Casualty and Surety Executives; chmn. Standing Com. on Financial Responsibility for Automobile Accidents; ex-pres. International Association Accident and Health Underwriters; mem. Chamber of Commerce State of New York, American Arbitration Assn., A.A.A.S., Alliance Against Accident Fraud, Board of Casualty and Surety Underwriters, Ins. Inst. America (ex-pres.); mem. editorial bd. Internat. Ins. Ency.; mem. Permanent Commn. Internat. Industrial Congress (Paris); etc. Author of "Pioneers of American Liability Insurance" and "A Penn Yan Boy." Home: New City, N.Y. Office: 60 John St., New York, N.Y.

Died Oct. 31, 1945.

LOUGHBOROUGH, James Fairfax (lŭf'bûr-ō), lawyer; b. Little Rock, Ark., Feb. 17, 1873; s. James Moore and Mary (Webster) L.; student U. of Ark.; LL.B., U. of Ark. Law Sch., 1894; m. Mary Louise Wright, Oct. 21, 1902. Admitted to Ark. bar, 1894, and since practiced at Little Rock; mem. Cantrell & Loughborough, 1894-1905, Rose, Hemingway, Cantrell & Loughborough (now Rose, Loughborough, Dobyns & House) since 1905. Mem. Bd. Commrs. Ark. Tuberculosis Sanatorium, 1913-37; bd. dirs. Little Rock Pub. Schs., 1920-23; chmn. Bd. of Examiners by apptmt. Supreme Court on Admission to Ark. Bar, 1936-38. Mem. Am. Judicature Soc. (dir.), Am. Bar Assn. (mem. com. on jurisprudence and law reform, 1944-45), Bar Association of Ark., Little Rock Bar Association (pres. 1922). Democrat. Mason (32°). Club: Country. Home: 1920 Kavanaugh Blvd. Office: 314 W. Markham St., Little Rock, Ark. Died Mar. 11, 1945.

LOUGHLIN, Gerald Francis (lŏk'lin), geologist; b. Hyde Park, Mass., Dec. 11, 1880; s. John Francis and Adelia (Lane) L.; S.B. in geology, Mass. Inst. Tech., 1903; Ph. D., Yale, 1906; m. Grace E. French, Aug. 22, 1906; 1 dau., Beryl Frances (Mrs. W. S. Burbank). Asst. in geology, Mass. Inst. Tech., 1903-04, Yale, 1904-06; instr. geology, Mass. Inst. Tech., 1906-12; with U.S. Geol. Survey, 1912, as chief nonmetals sect., div. mineral resources, 1917-19, chief metals sect., Jan.-Dec. 1919, and chief of div. of mineral resources, 1919-23, chief of sect. of geology of metalliferous deposits, 1923-35, chief geologist, 1935-44, special scientist since 1944. Member Society of Economic Geologists, American Mineral Society, American Institute Mining and Metallurgy Engineers, Geology Society America, Geology Soc. Washington, Washington Acad. Sci., A.A.A.S. Unitarian. Club: Cosmos. Author: Clays of Conn. (Conn. Survey), 1906; Lithology of Connecticut (with J. Barrell), 1912; Gabbro and Associated Rocks Near Preston, Conn.; Geology and Ore Deposits of Tintic Utah (with W. Lindgren), 1917; Oxidized Zinc Ores of Leadville, Colo., 1919; Geology and Ore Deposits of Utah (with B. S. Butler), 1920. In charge preparation Mineral Resources of the United States (6 vols.), 1919-24; Geology and Ore Deposits of Leadville, Colo., 1926; Indiana Oolitic Limestone, Relation of Its Natural Features to Its Commercial Grading, 1929; Gold Reserves of the U.S. (with H. G. Ferguson and others), 1930; Geology and Ore Deposits of the Cripple Creek District (with A. H. Koschmann), 1935; geology and ore deposits of the Magdalena District, N.M. (with A. H. Koschmann), 1943; also papers on ore deposits, building stone and durability of concrete aggregates. Home: 3346 Runnymeade Pl., Washington. Died Oct. 22, 1946; buried in Rock Creek Cemetery.

LOUTZENHEISER, Joe L., army officer; b. Canton, O., Feb. 5, 1899; s. Oren Henry and Mary Dora (Clay) L.; grad. U.S. Mil. Acad., 1924, Army Advanced Flying Sch., 1927, Air Corps Tactical Sch., 1937, Command and Gen. Staff Sch., 1938; m. Eleanor Cook, Aug. 15, 1931; 1 son, Joe L. Commd. 2d lt., cav., U.S. Army, 1924, advancing through the grades to brig. gen., 1944; chief, operational plans div. hdqrs., Army Air Forces since 1942. Home: 2420 16th St. N.W. Office: Hdqrs. Army Air Force, Washington, D.C. Missing after air crash in Guam, Oct. 7, 1945.

LOVE, Thomas Bell, lawyer; b. Webster County, Mo., June 23, 1870; s. Thomas Calvin and Sarah Jane (Rodgers) L.; B.S., Drury Coll., Springfield, Mo., 1891, LL.D., 1919; student law dept. U. of Va.; m. Mattie Roberta Goode, June 11, 1892 (died 1946); children—Dorothy, Thomas Stafford (M.D.), Horace Goode. Practice at Springfield, 1891, at Dallas, Tex., 1899; formerly v.p. and counsel Southwestern Life Ins. Co., pres. Western Indemnity Co., both Dallas, and v.p. Internat. Travellers Assurance Co., Dallas. City atty., Springfield, 1892-94; mem. bd. mgrs. Mo. State Hosp. No. 3, 1894-97; sec. Dem. State Central Com., Mo., 1896-98, inclusive; mem. Tex. Ho. of Rep., 1902-04-06 (speaker of House, 1907); commr. ins. and banking, Tex., 1907-10; del. Dem. Nat. Conv., Baltimore, Md., 1912; unanimously elected to Dem. Nat. Com., 1920, reëlected without opposition, 1924; resigned fall of 1924 to oppose Democratic nominee for gov. of Tex.; state senator for purpose of aiding improvement of rural roads and schools, 1927-31; opposed Alfred E. Smith for President, 1928, and aided in carrying Tex. for Herbert C. Hoover; also opposed Miriam A. Ferguson, wife of impeached former Gov. James E. Ferguson, as Dem. nominee for gov., 1924 and 1932; has supported every other Dem. nominee since 1892. Apptd. asst. sec. of treasury by President Wilson, Dec. 1, 1917, and assigned to supervision Bur. War Risk Ins., and Bur. Internal Revenue, also supervision foreign enemy and neutral ins. cos.; resigned upon signing of the Armistice, Dec. 1918. Mem. Tex. Hist. Soc., Acad. Polit. Science. Clubs: Town and Gown, Agricultural, Writers' (Dallas). Methodist. Mason. Elk, Odd Fellow, Woodmen of World, Modern Woodmen of America. Home: 403 Argyle Apts. Office: Republic Bank Bldg., Dallas, Tex. Died Sept. 17, 1948.

LOVEJOY, Frank William, mfr.; b. Concord, N.H., Dec. 11, 1871; s. George Lyman and Caroline Augusta (Neal) L.; B.S., Mass. Inst. Tech., 1894; hon. D.Sc., Lawrence College, Appleton, Wis.; hon. LL.D., Colby College, Waterville, Me., St. Lawrence U., Canton, N.Y.; m. Florence I. Fuller, June 18, 1907; children—Harriet, Fuller (dec.), George Lyman (dec.), Frank W., Frederic Fuller. Chemist on La. sugar plantation, 6 mos., 1894-95; draftsman and chemist, Curtis, Davis & Co., Cambridge, Mass., 1895-97; with Eastman Kodak Co. since 1897, advancing to v.p. and gen. mgr., pres. and gen. mgr., 1934-41, chmn. bd. since 1941; dir. Security Trust Co., Rochester. Trustee U. of Rochester; life mem. corp. Mass. Inst. Tech. Mem. Am. Chem. Soc., Am. Soc. M.E., Rochester Engring. Soc., Phi Beta Epsilon. Mason. Clubs: University, Genesee Valley, Rochester Country (Rochester); Technology, Engineers', Chemists (New York). Address: Rochester, N.Y. Died Sep. 16, 1945.

LOVEJOY, J(esse) Robert, mfr.; b. Columbus, O., Nov. 10, 1863; s. Nathan Ellis and Carrie Perkins (Drew) L.; B.S., Ohio State U., 1884; m. Mary E. Gould, June 23, 1892. Apprentice, 1886, constrn. supt., 1889, Thomson-Houston Co., Lynn, Mass.; mgr. supply dept., 1892-1900, lighting, ry. and supply depts., 1900-07, gen. mgr. sales dept., 1907, v.p. since May 15, 1907, dir. since May 1922, hon. v.p., 1928, Gen. Electric Co.; also dir. several cos. affiliated with Gen. Electric Co.; chmn. bd. dirs. General Electric Employees Sec. Corp. Fellow Am. Inst. E.E., A.A.A.S.; mem. Franklin Inst., Ohio Soc. of N.Y., Phi Gamma Delta. Republican. Clubs: University, Bankers, Adirondack League (New York); Mohawk, Mohawk Golf, Fishers Island, Mt. Lake, Boca Raton. Home: 1222 Lenox Rd., Schenectady, N.Y. Died Oct. 31, 1945.

LOVELL, Earl B., civil engr.; b. Marathon, N.Y., May 2, 1869; s. Ransom Marlow and Dorcas (Meacham) L.; grad. Marathon Acad., 1886, Cascadilla Sch., Ithaca, 1887; C.E., Cornell, 1891; m. Ida L. Peck, Oct. 4, 1899 (died Sept. 20, 1932); children—Robert Marlow, Helen Louise (dec.), Esther Hope, Gordon Peck and Ruth Caroline; m. 2d, Mrs. Helen R. Shimer, June 18, 1941; 1 stepson, Rev. H. Myron Shimer. Assistant engineer, Michigan Central Railroad, 1891-93; instr. civ. engring., Lafayette Coll., 1893-96, Cornell University, 1896-98; adj. prof. civ. engring., Columbia U., 1898-1901, asso. prof., 1901-07, prof. since 1907, chmn. dept. civ. engring., 1916-34, retired. Advisory engr. and mgr. survey dept. Lawyers Title & Trust Co. (later Lawyers Title & Guaranty Co.), New York, 1907-33; pres. Earl B. Lovell, Inc., engineering and surveying, 1933-38, chairman board of directors since August 1938; chmn. Assn. of Dept. Heads, 1923-24; consulting engr. for Portland Cement Lumber Co., 1923-24. Owner "Lovell Farms," Marathon, N.Y. Pres. Assn. of City Surveyors, Greater New York, 1919-22; asso. mem. Am. Soc. C.E.; mem. Tau Beta Phi, Sigma Xi. Republican. Episcopalian. Has specialized in railroad engring and masonry constrn. Legal residence: Lovell Farms, Marathon, N.Y. Home: Surrey Strathmore Abby, 6D, White Plains, N.Y. Office: 141 Broadway, New York 6. Died Aug. 23, 1948.

LOVELL, Moses Richardson, clergyman; b. Millis, Mass., Nov. 29, 1895; s. Edmund Francis and Hester Jenkyn (Richardson) L.; A.B., Boston U., 1917; S.T.B., Harvard-Andover Theol. Sch., 1921; D.D., U. of Vermont; m. Mary Ball Blake, June 26, 1920; children—Moses Richardson, Mary Elizabeth. Ordained Congl. ministry, 1921; minister Community University Ch., Durham, N.H., 1921-26, Mt. Pleasant Congl. Ch., Washington, D.C., 1926-31, 2d Ch., Waterbury, Conn., 1931-34, 2d Ch., Holyoke, Mass., 1934-38, Central Church, Brooklyn, New York, 1938-43, Cadman Memorial Church, Brooklyn, since 1943. Founder of "The Washington (D.C.) Life Adjustment Center," 1928, Mem, Nat. Congl. Commn. on Evangelism and Devotional Life. Enlisted in U.S. Army, 1917; served at Camp Devens, Mass., and as 2d lt. instr. Citizens Machine Gun O.T.S., Augusta, Ga.; hon. disch., Dec. 21, 1918. Mem. bd. trustees Hartford Theol. Sem., Andover-Newton Theol. Sem. Mem. bd. dirs. Federal Council of Chs. in Christ, N.Y. Congl. Christian Conf. Dir. Mass. Soc. for Mental Hygiene, N.Y. City Congl. Ch. Assn., Brooklyn Music Sch. Settlement. Mem. American Palestine Committee, Protestant Welfare Agencies Council. Founder Brooklyn (New York) Life Adjustment Center, 1939. Mason (chaplain N.Y. Grand Lodge),

Royal Arcanum (chaplain Grand Council). Clubs: Cosmos (Washington, D.C.; Graduate (New Haven); Brooklyn Clerical Union; Bedford Protestant Ministers. Lecturer. Home: 125 Brooklyn Av., Brooklyn, N.Y. Died Sep. 22, 1944.

LOVELL, Ralph L., mech. engr.; b. Millbury, Mass., Aug. 2, 1865; s. William L. and Jane E. (Harris) L.; M.E., Worcester Poly. Inst., 1888; m. Miss M. L. Brackett, June 24, 1896; 1 son, Frederick H. With Gen. Electric Co., Lynn, 1888-94; with Newport News Shipbuilding Co., 1894-1904; asst. chief engr., 1904-10, chief engr., 1910-14, Fore River Shipbuilding Co., Quincy, Mass.; consulting engr. and patent expert, 1914-16; marine engr. with Theodore E. Ferris, naval architect and engr., New York, 1916-17; chief engr. U.S. Shipping Bd. Emergency Fleet Corp., Washington and Phila., 1917-19; pres. Adams, Lovell & Burlingham, consulting marine engrs., New York, 1919-22; engr. with Bethlehem Shipbuilding Corp., Elizabeth, N.J., 1924-29; began with United Dry Docks, Inc., Staten Island, N.Y., 1929, became chief engr.; chief engr. Bethlehem Steel Co., shipbuilding dir., Staten Island Works, 1938-42 (retired); now in cons. work at home. Home: 6 Greaves Place, Cranford, N.J. Died June 3, 1945.

LOVETT, Archibald Battle (lŭv'ĕt), judge; b. Sylvania, Ga., June 21, 1884; s. John F. and Maggie (Medlock) L.; student Mercer U., Macon, Ga., 1898-1901; m. Corrie Overstreet, June 20, 1908. Admitted to Ga. bar, 1907, and later to state and U.S. courts; prosecuting atty., Sylvania City Courts, 1914-18; judge Superior Cts., Ga., 1919-21; became mem. Hitch, Denmark & Lovett, 1921; later Lovett, Morris & Hitch; formerly dir. and counsel trust dept. Citizens and Southern Nat. Bank, Savannah, Savannah Sugar Refining Co.; trustee Central of Ga. Ry.; mem. advisory bd. Reconstruction Finance Com. Mayor of Sylvania, 1914-18; U.S. dist. judge, Southern District of Georgia, since October 18, 1941. Del. to Dem. Nat. convs., 1928 and 1936; chmn. Roosevelt advisory com. for Ga., 1936. Ga. chmn. Com. to Aid the Allies. V.p. Family Welfare Soc.; trustee Mercer U., Armstrong Junior Coll. Mem. Am. Bar Assn. (com. on nat. defense), Ga. Bar Assn. (pres. 1935-36), Savannah Bar Assn. (former pres.), State Bd. Vocational Edn., Ga. Hist. Soc. (past pres. and curator), English-Speaking Union (pres.), Soc. of Colonial Wars (chancellor). Phi Delta Phi, Sigma Alpha Epsilon. Democrat. Baptist (deacon). K.P. Club: Oglethorpe (Savannah). Home: 701 East 44th St., Savannah, Ga. Died Dec. 28, 1945.

LOW, Ethelbert Ide, life insurance; b. Brooklyn, N.Y., Apr. 25, 1880; s. Ethelbert Mills and Mary Louise (Ide) L.; prep. edn., Brooklyn Latin Sch. and St. Paul's Sch., Concord, N.H.; A.B., Yale, 1902; LL.B., Columbia, 1905; m. Gertrude Herrick, June 9, 1904; children—Ethelbert Herrick, Francis Hine, Gertrude. Admitted to N.Y. bar, 1905, and practiced in N.Y. City until 1924; mem. Low, Miller & Low, 1909-23, Hoes, Low & Miller, 1923-24; pres. Home Life Ins. Co., 1924-29, chairman bd. since Nov. 1929; dir. Niagara Fire Insurance Company, Continental Insurance Company, Corn Exchange Bank Trust Company, Fidelity and Casualty Company of New York. Student Central Officers Training Sch., Camp Zachary Taylor, Louisville, Ky., Aug.-Dec. 1918. Mem. Am. and N.Y. State bar assns., Assn. Bar City of New York, Chamber Commerce City of New York, S.R., Soc. War of 1812, New England Soc. of New York, Alpha Delta Phi, Phi Delta Phi, Wolf's Head (Yale). Republican. Episcopalian. Clubs: University, Yale, Down Town, Union, Brook (New York); Piping Rock, Rockaway Hunting, South Side Sportsmen's (L.I.); Angler's Club of New York. Home: 1060 Fifth Av., New York, N.Y.; and Woodmere, L.I., N.Y. Office: 256 Broadway, New York, N.Y. Died Oct. 19, 1946.

LOW, Mary Fairchild, artist; b. New Haven, Conn., 1858; d. Sidney Brown and Mary Augusta (Lines) Fairchild; ed. Sch. of Fine Arts, St. Louis, Acad. Julian, Paris, and with Carolus Duran; awarded 3 yr. scholarship St. Louis Sch. of Fine Arts; m. Frederick (William) MacMonnies, Sept. 20, 1888; children—Berthe Helene, Marjorie Eudora, Ronald (dec.); m. 2d, Will Hicock Low, Nov. 4, 1909 (died Nov. 27, 1932). Awarded medal at Chicago Expn., 1893; bronze medal, Paris Expn., 1900; bronze medal, Buffalo Exposition, 1901; gold medal, Dresden, 1902; Julia M. Shaw Memorial prize, Soc. Am. Artists, New York, 1902; gold medal, Rouen, 1903, picture bought by city of Rouen and placed in Museum of Fine Arts; gold medal, Marseilles, 1905; gold medal, Normandy Expn., Rouen, 1911. Asso. Société Nationale des Beaux Arts (Champ de Mars Salon), Paris; A.N.A.; mem. Woman's Internat. Art Club (London), Am. Woman's Art Club of Paris (pres. 1901-03), Nat. Soc. New Eng. Women, D.A.R. Home: 11 McKinley St., Bronxville, N.Y. Deceased.

LOWDEN, Frank Orren (lou'dĕn), ex-governor; b. Sunrise City, Minn., Jan. 26, 1861; s. Lorenzo O. and Nancy Elizabeth (Breg) L.; A.B., Ia. State U. (valedictorian), 1885; LL.B., Union Coll. of Law, Chicago (valedictorian), 1887; LL.D., U. of Ia., 1918, Knox Coll., 1918, Northwestern U., 1919, Lincoln Memorial U., 1919, U. of Chicago, 1921, U. of Colo., 1922, Lafayette Coll., 1923, Coll. of William and Mary, 1923, Miami U., 1924, U. of Ore., 1929, Washington and Lee, 1931; D.C.L., Syracuse U., 1924; m. Florence, d. of George M. Pullman, Apr. 29, 1896; children—Pullman, Florence (Mrs. Phillip Miller), Harriet (Mrs. Albert F. Madlener, Jr.); Frances (Mrs. Frederick R. Wierdsma). Practiced law, Chicago, 1887-1906; prof. law, Northwestern U., 1899; del. Rep. Nat. Conv., 1900, 04; mem. Rep. Nat. Com., 1904-12, and mem. exec. com., campaigns, 1904, 08; elected 59th Congress, Nov. 6, 1906, for unexpired term (1906-07) of R. R. Hitt, deceased; reëlected 60th and 61st Congresses (1907-11), 13th Ill. Dist.; gov. of Ill., 1917-21; received 311½ votes for presdl. nomination in Rep. Nat. Conv., 1920; declined nomination for v.p. by Rep. Nat. Conv. in 1924. Mem. bd. dirs. Internat. Live Stock Expn. since 1919. Pres. Holstein-Friesian Assn. America, 1921-30; trustee Carnegie Endowment for Internat. Peace, Inst. Pub. Administration; chmn. trustees Pub. Administration Clearing House, also of Farm Foundation; chmn. trustees C.,R.I.&P. Ry. Co. in bankruptcy; pres. bd. dirs. Pullman Free Sch. of Manual Training; mem. bd. dirs. Foreign Bondholders Protective Council, Inc., 1933-37. Lt. col. 1st Inf., Ill. N.G., 1898. Pres. Law Club of Chicago, 1898-99. Home: Oregon, Ill. Died Mar. 20, 1943.

LOWE, John William, missionary; b. St. Joseph, Mo., Oct. 2, 1868; s. William Ephraim and Martha Ann (Ray) L.; B.A., William Jewell Coll., Liberty, Mo., 1893, D.D., 1930; Th.M., Southern Bapt. Theol. Sem., Louisville, Ky., 1897; student Ky. Sch. of Medicine and Louisville Med. Sch., 1897-99; m. Margaret Ann Savage, Sept. 15, 1897; children—John Paul, William Alec., George Marion, Margaret Ruth, John William, Marydee, Florence Elizabeth. Missionary, Baptist Home Mission Board and teacher in public schools of Nebraska, 1889-1892. Ordained ministry Southern Baptist Church, 1893; pastor in Neb., Mo. and Ky.; missionary of the Southern Bapt. Conv., 1899-1947, now emeritus; field rep., 1937-47; opened work at Laichowfu, Shantung Province, 1902, in Manchuria, 1907, and at Tsinan, 1920; famine relief, in Central China, 1907; recalled by Fgn. Mission Bd. to assist in Seventy-five million campaign, 1919-24; treasurer Baptist Famine Relief Fund, North China, 1921; supervisor church schools of missions, Arkansas, Missouri and Oklahoma, 1927-28; dir. of med. work, Pingtu and Laichow, 1899-1909; famine relief, feeding and clothing 1000 refugee children, Pochow, Anhwei, 1932. Teacher in Bush Theol. Sem., Hwanghsien, Shantung, China; lecturer on hygiene and sanitation in govt. and mission schs. in China; now emeritus missionary Foreign Mission Bd. promoting church schools of missions and soliciting funds for relief. Mem. Internat. Com. to Promote Prohibition of Mfr. and Sale of Liquors in China. Author: Christ at the Door, 1937; Emergency World Tracts. Died May 6, 1948.

LOWE, William Baird; b. Detroit, Mich., Jan. 27, 1871; s. Thomas and Mary Ann (Poole) L.; grad. Detroit High Sch.; m. Gertrude Merrell, June 28, 1899; 1 dau., Helen Rosemary (Mrs. William James Chesbrough). Began as counter clk., Detroit Jour., 1892, advertising mgr., 1898-1901, bus. mgr., 1901-15, v.p. and gen. mgr., 1915-17; advertising counselor Detroit Free Press, 1917-23, became mng. dir., 1923 (now retired in this capacity); treas. Cerre, Inc., since 1923; dir. Free Press Co. Baptist. Clubs: Detroit; Country (Grosse Pointe); The Old Club (Ste. Claire Flats). Home: 1818 Iroquois Av. Address: Detroit Free Press Bldg., Detroit, Mich. Died Aug. 3, 1946.

LOWELL, A(bbott) Lawrence (lō'ĕl), president emeritus of Harvard University; b. Boston, Dec. 13, 1856; s. Augustus and Katharine Bigelow (Lawrence) L.; A.B., Harvard, 1877, LL.B., 1880; LL.D., U. of Ill., 1905, Williams Coll., 1908, and Columbia, Princeton, Yale, Louvain, and Dartmouth, 1909, Bowdoin, Brown, and Mo., 1914, Washington U., and Johns Hopkins, 1915; Ph.D., Frederich Wilhelm U., Berlin, 1910, Strasbourg, 1920, McGill, 1920, Cambridge, 1920, Victoria U. of Manchester, 1920; D. Litt., Oxford, 1920; D.Polit. Science, Leiden, 1920; D. honoris causa, U. of Paris, 1922; LL.D., Union Coll., 1927, U. State of N.Y., 1929, Edinburgh, 1930, Haverford and Wesleyan U., 1931, U. of Pa., 1933, Tufts, 1933; L.H.D., Boston U., 1928; m. Anna Parker Lowell, June 19, 1879 (died Mar. 23, 1930). Practiced law, Boston, 1880-97; lecturer, Harvard, 1897-99, prof. science of govt., 1900-09, pres., 1909-33, now emeritus. Sole trustee Lowell Inst., Boston, since 1900. Chmn. of exec. com. League to Enforce Peace. Mem. Am. Acad. Arts and Letters, Mass. Hist. Soc., etc. Corr. fellow British Acad.; hon. mem. Royal Irish Acad.; asso. mem. Royal Acad. of Belgium. Grand Officer of Legion of Honor (France); Comdr. Order of the Crown (Belgium). Author: Transfer of Stock in Corporations (with Francis C. Lowell), 1884; Essays on Government, 1889; Governments and Parties in Continental Europe, 1896; Colonial Civil Service (with H. Morse Stephens), 1900; The Influence of Party Upon Legislation in England and America, 1902; The Government of England, 1908; Public Opinion and Popular Government, 1913; Public Opinion in War and Peace, 1923; Conflicts of Principle, 1932; At War with Academic Traditions, 1934; Biography of Percival Lowell, 1935; What a College President Has Learned, 1938. Address: 171 Marborough St., Boston, Mass. Died Jan. 16, 1943.

LOWELL, James Harrison; b. New Bedford, Mass., May 4, 1860; s. Harrison Gray and Sarah E. (Blake) L.; ed. Ill. State Normal Sch., Normal; m. Florence E. Hard, Oct. 8, 1898; children—Wade Harrison, Blake J., Douglas Walter, Edwin Gray. Teacher, pub. schs., Calif., 1878-82; in land development business, Pasadena, Calif., 1883; in sheep business, Mont., 1884-91; in land business, Wash., 1892; sec. and mgr. Boise Land & Water Co. and Riverside Irrigation Dist., also sec. Twin Falls Land & Water Co., 1893-1903; mem. Ida. Ho. of Rep., 1903; state water commr., Ida., and pres. Payette-Boise Water Users Assn., 1903-09; mgr. Roswell Park Fruit Co., 1909-17; mgr. Gem Irrigation Dist., 1917-28; pres. Ida. Egg Producers, 1917-28, Ida. Egg Assn., 1917-43; financial dir. Coll. of Ida., 1928-38, trustee, 1903-43. Republican. Presbyterian. Odd Fellow. Elk. Kiwanian. Home: 1623 Everett, Caldwell, Ida. Died Dec. 14, 1944.

LOWER, William Edgar, surgeon; b. Canton, O., May 6, 1867; s. Henry and Mary (Deeds) L.; M.D., Western Reserve U., Med. Dept., 1891; m. Mabel Freeman, Sept. 6, 1909; 1 dau., Mary. Practiced in Cleveland since 1892; asso. surgeon, Lakeside Hosp., 1910-31; attending surgeon, Lutheran Hosp. since 1896; dir. surgery, Mt. Sinai Hosp., 1916-24; asso. prof. genito-urinary surgery, Western Reserve U., 1910-1931. A founder, dir. Cleveland Clinic Foundation since 1921; surgeon Cleveland Clinic Hosp. since 1924. Acting asst. surgeon, U.S. Army, in the Philippines, 1900; maj. Med. Reserve Corps, 1917; asst. surg. dir. Lakeside Base Hosp. Unit, U.S. Army, in service with B.E.F. in France, May-Dec. 1917, comdg. officer, Dec. 1917-May 1918; lt. col., June 1918. Mem. Am. Urol. Assn. (pres. 1914-15), Am. Assn. Genito-Urinary Surgeons (pres. 1922), Ohio State Med. Soc. (pres. 1915), Acad. of Medicine, Cleveland (pres. 1909-10), Clin. Soc. of Genito-Urinary Surgeons (pres. 1922), Interurban Surg. Soc. (pres. 1926-27), Soc. of Clin. Surgery, Société Internationale de Chirurgie Urologie; fellow A.M.A., Am. Surg. Assn., Am. Coll. Surgeons, Southern Surgical Assn. Club: Union. Author: Anoci-Association (Crile and Lower), 1914; Surgical Shock and the Shockless Operation through Anoci-Association, 2d edit., 1920; Roentgenographic Studies of the Urinary System (Lower and Nichols), 1933. Home: 12546 Cedar Rd., Cleveland Heights, O. Office: Cleveland Clinic, Euclid at E. 93d St., Cleveland. Died June 17, 1948.

LOWES, John Livingston (lōz), univ. prof.; b. Decatur, Ind., Dec. 20, 1867; s. Abram Brower and Mary Bella (Elliott) L.; A.B., Washington and Jefferson Coll., 1888, A.M., 1891; univs. of Leipzig and Berlin, 1894-95; A.M., Harvard, 1903, Ph.D., 1905; LL.D., Washington and Jefferson Coll., 1924, McGill University, 1936; Litt.D., Univ. of Me., 1925, Yale Univ., 1928, Oxford Univ., 1931, Brown Univ., 1932, Harvard, 1932; L.H.D., Tufts College, Mass., 1928; m. Mary Cornett, June 23, 1897; 1 son, John Wilber. Adj. prof. mathematics, Washington and Jefferson Coll., 1888-91; prof. English, Hanover (Ind.) Coll., 1895-1902, Swarthmore (Pa.) Coll., 1905-09; prof. English, 1909-18, dean of Coll., 1913-14, Washington U., St. Louis; prof. English, Harvard, 1918-30, Francis Lee Higginson prof. English lit., 1930-39, emeritus since 1939, also dean Grad. Sch. of Arts and Sciences, 1924-25; 1st George Eastman visiting prof., Oxford University, and fellow Balliol Coll., 1930-31. Lecturer Lowell Inst., 1918, U. of Calif., 1922, U. of Tex., 1924, University Coll. of Wales, 1926, Harris Foundation, Northwestern U., 1926, Cooper Foundation, Swarthmore Coll., 1931; Ropes lecturer comparative lit., U. of Cincinnati, 1909. Sr. fellow Soc. of Fellows; corr. fellow British Acad.; fellow Nat. Inst. Arts and Letters, Am. Acad. Arts and Sciences, Mediæval Acad. America, A.A.A.S.; mem. Am. Philos. Soc., Am. Philol. Assn., Mod. Lang. Assn. America (pres. 1933). Clubs: Saturday, Odd Volumes, Harvard (Boston); Signet, Faculty (Cambridge); Elizabethan (hon., New Haven); Round Table (St. Louis). Author: Convention and Revolt in Poetry, 1919; The Road to Xanadu, 1927; Of Reading Books and Other Essays, 1930; The Art of Geoffrey Chaucer, 1931; Geoffrey Chaucer and the Development of His Genius, 1934; Essays in Appreciation, 1936. Editor (with George Lyman Kittredge) of synonyms in New International Dictionary. Editor: Shakespeare's All's Well That Ends Well, 1912; Hamlet, 1914. Contbr. to Am. and foreign philol. and lit. jours. Home: 984 Memorial Drive, Cambridge, Mass. Died Aug. 15, 1945.

LOWNDES, Mary Elizabeth, author, head mistress; b. Wallasey, Eng., 1864; d. Richard and Anne Stuart (Byrth) Lowndes; grad. with honors Girton Coll., Cambridge Univ.; Litt.D., Trinity Coll., Dublin; unmarried. Came to America, 1909; in charge English dept., Rosemary Hall, Greenwich, Conn., 1909-10, joint headmistress, since 1911. Mem. Ch. of England. Clubs: Albemarle, Women's Univ. (London), Cosmopolitan (New York). Author: Michel de Montaigne (a biographical study), 1897; The Nuns of Port Royal, 1910. Translator: Höffding's Outlines of Psychology. Home: Greenwich, Conn. Died March 19, 1947.

LOWREY, Bill G. (lou'rĕ), ex-congressman; b. Kossuth, Miss., May 25, 1862; s. Gen. Mark P. and Sarah (Holmes) L.; prep. edn., Blue Mountain Acad.; M.A., Miss. Coll., Clinton, 1887 (LL.D., 1911); Tulane U., 1888-89; m. Marylee Booth, July 25, 1889; children—Joe J., Vernon Booth, Roswell Graves, Edwin Stovall, Leon Ray, Mary Alice, Baron Gray, Perrin Holmes. Prof. English, Blue Mountain Coll., 1888-98, pres., 1898-1911; pres. Amarillo (Tex.) Mil. Acad., 1911-16; field sec. Hillman College and Blue Mountain College, 1916-20; mem. 67th to 70th Congresses (1921-29), 2d Miss. Dist.; clk. U.S. Dist. Court, Northern District of Miss., 1929-35. Democrat. Vice-pres. Blue Mountain Coll.; pres. trustees Miss. Heights Acad.; trustee Bapt. Memorial Hosp., Memphis, Tenn. Pres. Miss. S.S. Assn., 1917-20; pres. Miss. State Bapt. Conv., 1919, 20; v.p. Southern Bapt. Conv. Author: Mississippi (with R. G. Lowrey and A. A.

Kincannon), 1937. Mason. Home: Olive Branch, Miss.* Died Sep. 2, 1947.

LOWRIE, Will Leonard, consul-gen.; b. Adrian, Mich., Mar. 8 1869; s. A. H. and Mattie Beckwith (Pease) L.; A.B., A.M., Adrian Coll., 1889; post-grad., U. of Leipzig, 1892-93; m. Amy W. Alden, Sept. 18, 1907. Newspaper and mag. corr., 1890-98; pvt. sec. to Am. minister to Brazil, 1898; vice consul gen., Rio de Janeiro, 1899; consul, Hobart, 1906, Weimar, Germany, 1906-08, Erfurt, 1908-09, Carlsbad, Austria, 1909-12; consul gen., Lisbon, Portugal, 1912-20, at Athens, Greece, 1920-24, Wellington, New Zealand, 1924-31, Frankfort-on-Main, 1931-33; assigned to dept. of State, Aug. 1, 1933; now retired. Conglist. Mem. Am. Geog. Soc., Sigma Alpha Epsilon. Club: BeHe Haven Golf. Home: 217 N. Royal St., Alexandria, Va. Died April 2, 1944.

LOWRY, Edith Belle (Edith Lowry Lambert), author; b. Austin, Minn., Nov. 11, 1878; d. Alfred and Henrietta (Hicks) Lowry; grad. Austin High Sch., 1896, Winona (Minn.) State Normal Sch., 1898; grad. Jefferson Park Hosp. Training Sch. for Nurses, Chicago, 1905; M.D., Bennett Coll. Medicine and Surgery, Chicago, 1907; m. Richard Jay Lambert, M.D., July 24, 1911. Teacher pub. schs., Minn. and Utah, 6 yrs.; practiced medicine and surgery since 1907. Mem. A.M.A., Ill. State Med. Soc., Kane County Med. Soc., Miss. Valley Med. Soc., Am. Pub. Health Assn., Am. School Health Assn. Clubs: Woman's Univ., Chicago Med. Woman's. Author: Confidences—Talks with a Young Girl, 1911; Truths—Talks with a Boy, 1911; Herself—Talks with Women, 1912; Himself—Talks with Men, 1912; False Modesty that Protects Vice by Ignorance, 1912; The Home Nurse, 1913; Teaching Sex Hygiene, 1914; Your Baby, 1915; Preparing for Womanhood, 1918; The Woman of Forty, 1919; What Does Your Child Weigh?, 1923. Served as acting chief Bureau of Hosps., Dept. Health, Chicago, during World War; dir. field investigations in child hygiene in several southern states under U.S.P.H.S., Div. Child Hygiene, 1920-23; now engaged in organizing local Civilian Defense health work, and Am. Red Cross blood donor service. Home: St. Charles, Ill. Died Mar. 8, 1945.

LOWRY, Edward George, journalist; b. Atlanta, Ga., Dec. 24, 1876; s. George P. and Sarah E. (Ragsdale) L.; ed. pvt. schs., Ga. Mil Inst. and under tutors; m. Elizabeth Lahey, Apr. 2, 1902; 1 son, Edward George. On staff Atlanta Constitution, 1900-02; Albany corr., Evening Post, N.Y. City, 1903-04, Washington corr., 1904-11, mng. editor, July 1911-13, Washington corr., 1913-14. Polit. corr. Harper's Weekly, 1909-11; extensive contbr. on post-war conditions in Europe since close of World War; resided in Europe, 1926-28. Special agent of Dept. of State attached to Am. Embassy at London (in charge German division), Aug. 1914-Nov. 1916; capt., Aviation Sect. Signal Corps U.S. Reserve, Nov. 1917-Mar. 1919; asst. mil. attaché at London Jan.-Mar. 1918; with 2d Corps A.E.F., on British front in Flanders and France until Armistice and then with Am. Army of Occupation in Germany. Awarded British Mil. Cross. Clubs: Cosmos (Washington); Century (New York). Author: Washington Close-Ups, 1921. Home: 301 Sylvan Drive, Winter Park, Fla. Died July 21, 1943.

LOWRY, Thomas Claude, univ. dean.; B.S. in Medicine, U. of Okla., 1914, M.D., 1916; dean Sch. of Medicine, U. of Okla. and prof. clin. medicine; became supt. State U. and Crippled Children's Hosp., 1920. Address: care University of Oklahoma, Norman, Okla. Died Dec. 11, 1945.

LOZIER, Ralph Fulton (lō'zhēr), b. Ray County, Mo., Jan. 28, 1866; s. Ralph M. and Fanetta (Ridgell) L.; grad. high sch., Carrollton, 1883; m. Iowa Carruthers, Feb. 24, 1892; (died Jan. 22, 1929); children—Lue C., Ralph Fulton. Was admitted to Mo. bar, 1886, and began practice of law at Carrollton; mem. 68th to 73d Congresses (1923-35), 2d Mo. Dist.; judge 7th Judicial Circuit Court, 1936. Mem. Am. Bar Assn., Mo. State Bar Assn. (pres. 1912-13). Democrat. Mem. Christian (Disciples) Ch. Mason (K.T., Shriner). Home: Carrollton, Mo. Died May 28, 1945.

LUBITSCH, Ernst (lū'bĭch), producer-director; b. Berlin, Germany, Jan. 29, 1892; s. Simon and Anna (Lindenstedt) L.; grad. high school, Berlin, Germany, 1908. Began as actor in Germany, 1911; came to U.S., 1922, to direct Mary Pickford; with Warner Bros. 3 yrs., later with Metro-Goldwyn-Mayer; entered into contract with Famous-Players-Lasky Corp., 1927. Has made following pictures: Passion; Deception; Gypsy Blood; One Arabian Night; The Marriage Circle; Kiss Me Again; Forbidden Paradise; Lady Windermere's Fan; Old Heidelberg; The Patriot; The Love Parade; Monte Carlo; Trouble In Paradise; The Smiling Lieutenant; Design for Living; Merry Widow; Angel; Bluebeard's Eighth Wife; Ninotchka, Shop Around Corner, 1939; Uncertain Feeling, 1940; To Be or Not To Be, 1941; Heaven Can Wait, 1942; Royal Scandal, 1944; Cluny Brown, 1946. Home: West Los Angeles, Calif. Address: Twentieth Century-Fox Studios, Beverly Hills, Calif. Died Nov. 30, 1947.

LUCAS, Albert Pike, painter, sculptor; b. Jersey City, N.J.; s. George Clark and Mary Elizabeth (Pike) L.; studied at École des Beaux Arts, Paris, under Hebert and Boulanger, 1882-88; pupil of Gustave Courtois and Dagnan Bouveret; unmarried. Exhibited at Salon, Paris, since 1889; also at expns. Europe and New York Academy. Awarded medal, Buffalo Expn., 1901; hon. mention, Paris Expn., 1900. Has painted portraits of many prominent persons; represented in Nat. Gallery, Washington, etc.; bust "Ecstasy" (marble), at Met. Museum of Art, New York; Art Museum, San Diego, Calif.; Milwaukee Art Inst.; Royal Academy, London; also many European exhbns. Nat. Academician; also asst. sec. of Nat. Acad. of Design since 1929. Trustee Nat. Acad. Assn. Mem. N.Y. Fedn. Arts, Nat. Sculpture Soc., Allied Artists America, N.Y. (v.p. 1931-36, pres. since 1937), Soc. Painters (pres.), N.Y. Soc. of Painters (pres.), Société Nationale des Beaux Arts, Paris; life mem. Lotos and Nat. Art clubs; mem. Salmagundi Club. Was awarded medal of honor, Allied Artists of America, 1928; Joseph S. Isador prize, 1931; anonymous prize of the Allied Artists of America, 1937. Studio: 1947 Broadway, New York, N.Y. Died Mar. 2, 1945.

LUCAS, Arthur Melville, theatrical mgr.; b. Florence, S.C., Dec. 22, 1881; s. Arthur Mellville and Cornelia Sidney (Kingman) L.; ed. pub. schs.; m. Margaret Brown Cunningham; Nov. 16, 1911; children—Jean Kingman (Mrs. Fred G. Storey, Jr.), Arthur III (dec.), John Stewart. Began in theatrical business at Savannah, Ga., 1907; now pres. Theatre Operating Co., United Theatre Enterprises, Publix-Lucas Theatres of Ga., Augusta Broadcasting Co, WSAV, Inc., Coastal Broadcasting Company (Brunswick, Ga.), Augusta Amusements, Inc., Georgia Theatres Service Corp., Community Theatres Co., Community Theatres Corp.; director First National Bank of Atlanta, N.C. Theatres Co., Atlanta Enterprises, Inc.; formerly pub. Americus Times-Recorder. Ex-chmn. state Bd. Pub. Welfare of Ga.; former mem. bd. Federal Pub. Works Admingstrn. for Ga. Mem. advisory bd. Union Soc.-Bethesda Orphanage, Savannah, Ga. Dem. Nat. elector of Ga., 1920; del. to Dem. Nat. Conv., Houston, Tex., 1928, Chicago, 1932, Phila., 1936. Ex-chmn. bd. of control Eleemosynary Instns. of Ga. Mem. Huguenot Soc. of S.C., Telfair Acad. of Art (Savannah), Spanish-Am. War Vets. Episcopalian. Clubs: Oglethorp (Savannah); Piedmont Driving, Capital City (Atlanta); Nat. Pres. (Washington, D.C.). Home: 2494 Peachtree Rd. Office: Fox Theatre Bldg., Atlanta, Ga. Died July 17, 1943.

LUCAS, John Porter, army officer; b. Kearneysville, W.Va., Jan. 14, 1890; s. Charles Craighill and Francis Thomas (Craighill) L.; B.S., U.S. Mil. Acad., West Point, N.Y., 1911; attended The Field Artillery Sch., 1920-21, advanced course, 1922-23, Command and Gen. Staff Sch., 1923-24; M.S., Colorado State Coll., 1927; student Army War Coll., 1931-32; m. Sydney Virginia Wynkoop, Aug. 23, 1917; children—John Porter, Jr., Mary Brooke. Commd. 2d lt., Cav., 1911, advanced through ranks to maj. gen. (temp.), 1941; maj. (temp.), Signal Corps, 1918, trans. to Field Artillery, 1920; assigned to command 3d Inf. Div., Fort Lewis, Wash., July 1941; later made comdg. gen. 3d Army Corps. Served with 7th U.S. Army as personal rep. of C. in C. (General Eisenhower) with combat troops during Sicilian Campaign, July-August, 1943; commanded II Corps in Sicily, Sept., 1943; comd. VI Corps during Italian Campaign Sept., 1943, to Feb. 1944; later comdr. Fort Sam Houston to July 1945. Awarded D.S.M. with oak leaf cluster, D.S.M. (Navy), Silver Star, and Order of The Purple Heart, Order of Saints Maurice and Lazarus. Mason (K.T.). Episcopalian. Home: Charlestown, W.Va. Died Dec. 24, 1949.

LUCAS, Robert H., lawyer; b. Jefferson County, Kentucky, August 8, 1888; s. Robert and Hattie (Galey) L.; grad. high sch., Louisville; student U. of Louisville; m. Gertrude Lasch, Oct. 19, 1910; 1 dau., Martha Bob. Admitted to Ky. bar, 1909, and began practice at Louisville; pros. atty. of City Court, Louisville, 1917-21; U.S. collector internal revenue, Ky., 1921-29; U.S. commr. of internal revenue, 1929-30; exec. dir. Rep. Nat. Com. since Aug. 13, 1930. Capt. Kentucky Nat. Guard, 1909-12. Chmn. Jefferson County Rep. Com., 1916-21; chmn. finance com. Am. Legion Conv., Louisville, 1929. Mem. Christian (Disciples) Ch. Home: Louisville, Ky. Office: Peoples Life Ins. Bldg., Washington. Died Oct. 13, 1947.

LUCCOCK, George Naphtali, clergyman; b. Kimbolton, Guernsey County, O., Mar. 31, 1857; s. Samuel W. and Elizabeth W. (Day) L.; A.B., U. of Wooster, 1878, A.M., 1881, D.D., 1904; D.D., Berea (Ky.) Coll., 1934; Western Theol. Sem., 1881; m. Emma Bingham, Sept 3, 1882 (died May 15, 1937); children—Tracy D., Jean T. (Mrs. F. C. Stifler), Samuel B. (dec.), Howard Rothwell (dec.), Elizabeth (dec.), Emory W., Georgia N. (Mrs. R. E. Stoddard); m. 2d, Mrs. Ella Day Krugh, Nov. 9, 1938. Ordained Presbyn. ministry, 1881; home missionary work, Kossuth, Emmett, Dickinson and Greene counties, Ia., and Westminster Ch. Des Moines, 1881-91; pastor First Ch., Bloomington, Ind., 1891-94, Met. Ch., Washington, D.C., 1894-1903, 1st Ch., Oak Park, Ill., 1903-17, College Ch., Wooster, O., 1917-27 now emeritus; winter preacher, San Mateo, Fla.; acting pastor College Union Ch., Berea, Ky., Nov. 1929-May 1930; acting pres. Berea (Ky.) Coll., Oct. 1930-May 1931; acting pastor Presbyn. Ch. and Blackburn Coll., Carlinville, Ill., Sept. 1931-May 1932; actg. pastor 1st Ch., Oklahoma City, 1934-35, at Morristown, N.J., 1935-36; supply preacher 1st Ch., Wooster, O., Sept. 1936-June 1937; supply preacher Colorado Springs, Colo., 1937, Lincoln, Neb., 1938, Ottumwa, Ia., Nov. 1938-Jan. 1939; supply pastor various chs., Danville, Ky., Indianapolis, Kansas City, Mo., since 1939. Del. World's Missionary Conf., Edinburgh, 1910; mem Gen. Assembly's com. to prepare New Intermediate Catechism; director McCormick Theology Seminary, Chicago, Ill.; director Western Theology Seminary, Pittsburgh, Pa. Member Phi Delta Theta, Phi Beta Kappa. Republican. Clubs: Century, Rotary. Writer on "Backseat Philosophy" in Presbyn. Banner and on religious subjects. Home: 829 College Av., Wooster, O. Died Feb. 23, 1943.

LUCE, Robert, ex-congressman; b. at Auburn, Me., Dec. 2, 1862; s. Enos T. and Phoebe (Learned) L.; A.B., Harvard, 1882, A.M., 1883; m. Mabelle Clifton Farnham, Sept. 21, 1885 (died Jan. 27, 1926). Mem. Mass. legislature, 1899, 1901-08; as house chmn. on election laws, author of "Luce" laws for primary elections and direct nominations; lt. gov. of Mass., 1912; mem. Mass. Constl. Conv., 1917; mem. 66th to 73d Congresses. (1919-35), 13th Mass. Dist., 75th and 76th Congresses (1937-41), 9th Mass. Dist. Republican. Pres. Luce's Press Clipping Bureau; director Boston Mutual Life Ins. Co. Clubs: Republican of Massachusetts, Middlesex, Cosmos (Washington, D.C.). Author: Legislative Procedure; Legislative Assemblies; Legislative Principles; Legislative Problems; Congress; Electric Railways; Writing for the Press; Going Abroad? Home: Waltham, Mass. Died Apr. 6, 1946.

LUCEY, Patrick Joseph (lū'sē), lawyer; b. Ottawa, Ill., May 2, 1873; s. John and Joanna (Doud) L.; grad. high sch., Ottawa, 1890; admitted to Ill. bar, 1894; m. Frances Gertrude Casey, Sept. 10, 1901; 1 dau., Frances Gertrude (Mrs. J. Allen Newton). Practiced at Streator, 1895-1912, Chicago since 1917. City atty., Streator, 1897-1901; mayor of Streator 3 terms, 1903-07, 1909-11; atty. gen. of Ill., 1912-17; mem. Pub. Utilities Commn. of Ill., 1917-21. Democrat. Clubs: Edgewater Golf, Mid-Day, Chicago Athletic Assn. Home: 442 W. Wellington Av. Office: 10 S. La Salle St., Chicago, Ill.* Died Nov. 18, 1947.

LUCKENBACH, Edgar Frederick (lŭk'ĕn-băk), ship owner; b. Kingston, N.Y., 1868; s. Lewis and Mary E. (Frey) L.; ed. pub. schs., Brooklyn; m. Andrea Marie Fenwick, Feb. 2, 1899. Pres. Luckenbach Steamship Co., Luckenbach Terminal Co., Empire Repair and Electric Welding Co. Mem. Maritime Assn. Port of New York, Chamber Commerce, Produce Exchange, Merchants Assn. Lutheran. Owned champion sloops Sue, Bobtail and Suelew. Home: Elm Court, Sands Point, L.I. Office: 120 Wall St., New York, N.Y. Died Apr. 26, 1943.

LUDLOW, Henry Hunt, army officer; b. Easton, Pa., Apr. 15, 1854; s. Dr. Jacob Rapelyea and Ann Mary (Hunt) L.; grad. U.S. Mil. Acad., 1867, torpedo course, Willet's Point, N.Y., 1885, Arty. Sch., 1888; m. Amanda J. Armistead, Apr. 14, 1904. Apptd. 2d lt., 3d arty., June 15, 1876; 1st lt., Nov. 3, 1882; capt. 6th arty., Mar. 18, 1898; maj. arty. corps, Apr. 14, 1903; lt. col. coast arty. corps, Jan. 25, 1907; col. Dec. 27, 1908. Instr. mathematics, U.S. Mil. Acad., 1879-83; prof. mil. sci. and tactics, Miss. Agrl. and Mech. Coll., 1903-06. Mem. Am. Math. Soc., A.A.A.S., Am. Geog. Soc, Am. Forestry Assn., Loyal Legion. Club: Army and Navy (N.Y.). Author: Elements of Trigonometry with Tables, 1890. Ret. by operation of law, Apr. 15, 1918. Home: 1113 Massachusetts Av. N.W., Washington. Now deceased.

LUDLUM, Clarence Allen, insurance official; b. East Jamaica, L.I., Sept. 4, 1865; s. John H. and Phebe L. (Allen) L.; ed. pub. and pvt. schs.; m. Kate M. Ayres, May 7, 1892 (died 1920); children—Mary M., Clarence A., Kate A. Railroad and Pullman Service until 1890; ins. business, 1890-1930, retired; was v.p. and dir. Home Ins. Co. of N.Y., Franklin Fire Ins. Co. of Phila., City of N.Y. Ins. Co., Harmonia Fire Ins. Co. of New York, Nat. Liberty Fire Ins. Co., Carolina Ins. Co. of N.C., Homestead Ins. Co. of Baltimore, Baltimore Am. Ins. Co., New Brunswick Fire Ins. Co. of N.J.; was also dir. Interzone Corp., Thico Securities Co., Am. Trust Co.; former pres. New York Board of Fire Underwriters, Western Underwriters Assn., Ins. Inst. of America, and dir. Chamber. Commerce of U.S., Chamber Commerce of New York; now trustee Jamaica Savings Bank; pres. Jamaica Hospital; dir. Chamber of Commerce of Borough of Queens, Soc. for Prevention Cruelty to Children. Republican. Presbyterian. Mason (32°, K.T.). Clubs: Lotos, Circumnavigators (New York); Jamaica; Pomonok Country. Home: Jamaica, L.I. Died Feb. 29, 1948.

LUDWIG, Emil (loot'vĭk), author, biographer; b. Breslau, Germany, Jan. 25, 1881; s. Herman and Valesca (Friedlander) Cohn; ed. Heidelberg U.; hon. LL.D., Rutgers U., 1931; m. Elga Wolff, 1906; children—Andrew, Gordon. Writer since 1900; began as dramatist writing plays for 12 years, mostly in verse; later began writing psychol. essays and biographies; lived in Switzerland, 1907-40; came to U.S. June 1940. Decorated Legion of Honor (French). Hon. citizen in Switzerland; Swiss Nationality since 1932. Author: (translations from German) Napoleon, 1926; Goethe, 1926 (first German edition, 1920); Bismarck, 1927; Kaiser Wilhelm, II, 1927; Genius and Character, 1927; Gothe, 1928; Son of Man, 1928; On Mediterranean Shores, 1929, July 14, 1929; Diana, 1929; Lincoln, 1930; Three Titans, 1930; Schliemann, 1931; Gifts of Life, 1931; Versailles, 1932; Hindenberg, 1935; Talks with Masaryk, 1936; Davos Murder, 1936; Cleopatra, 1937; The Nile, 1937; Roosevelt, 1938; New Holy Alliance, 1938; Quartet, 1939; Three Portraits, 1940; The Germans, 1941; Stalin, 1942;

The Mediterranean, 1942; Beethoven, 1943; Ulysses' Return, comedy, staged in Calif., 1943; The Moral Conquest of Germany, 1945; Of Life and Love, 1945. Address: Ascona, Switzerland. Died Sept. 17, 1948.

LUHRING, Oscar Raymond (lūr'ing), lawyer; b. Gibson County, Ind., Feb. 11, 1879; s. Henry W. and Martha (Boren) L.; ed. pub. schs., Ind.; B.L., U. of Va., 1900; LL.D., Nat. U., 1932; m. Margaret Graham Evans. Began practice at Evansville, 1900; mem. Ind. Ho. of Rep., 1903-04; dep. pros. atty., 1st Jud. Circuit of Ind., 1904-08, pros. atty., 1908-12; mem. 66th and 67th Congresses (1919-23), 1st Ind. Dist.; spl. asst. to sec. of labor, 1923-25; asst. atty. gen., U.S., 1925-30; apptd. asso. justice Dist. Court of U.S. for D.C., July 3, 1930. Mem. Phi Kappa Sigma, Sigma Nu Phi, Chevy Chase Club. Republican. Presbyterian. Address: District Court of the United States for the District of Columbia, Washington, D.C. Died Aug. 18, 1944.

LUKE, Thomas, pres. W.Va. Pulp Paper Co. Home: Tarrytown, N.Y. Office: 230 Park Av., New York. Died May 12, 1948.

LUKENS, Herman Tyson (lōō'-kĕns), writer; b. Phila., Jan. 29, 1865; s. James T. and Elizabeth (Jones) L.; A.B., U. of Pa., 1885, A.M., 1888; univs. of Berlin, Halle, Leipzig, Paris and Jena, Ph.D., Jena, 1891; m. Eleanor Lee Spencer, June 1897 (died 1934). Teacher biology, Northwest Div. High Sch., Chicago, 1891-94; fellow psychology, 1894-95, docent in pedagogy, 1895-98, Clark U.; lecturer on edn., Bryn Mawr Coll., 1896-97; head training teacher, State Normal Sch., California, Pa., 1898-1907; teacher in Francis W. Parker Sch., Chicago, 1907-34, retired. Author: Herbart's Psychological Basis of Teaching, 1890; The Connection Between Thought and Memory, 1895; The Fifth School Year, 1905; The Descendants of Naylor Webster, 1936; also several ednl. monographs. Now engaged in research on Descendants of Jan Lücken, of Germantown, Pa. Address: 102 E. Jacoby St., Norristown, Pa. Died Jan. 18, 1949.

LULL, Henry Morris, ry. official; b. Windsor, Vt., Mar. 31, 1875; grad. Dartmouth, 1897. With Southern Pacific Co. since 1906, advancing through various positions to chief engr., Tex. and La. Lines; now exec. v.p. Texas and La. Lines (Tex. & New Orleans R.R. Co.); v.p. in charge of operations Southern Pacific Steamship Lines; pres. Rio Bravo Oil Co.; dir. Dallas Union Terminal Co., Ft. Worth Union Passenger Station, South Tex. Commercial Nat. Bank (Houston). Home: 5303 Caroline Blvd. Office: Southern Pacific Bldg., Houston, Tex.* Died Mar. 23, 1949.

LUMSDEN, Leslie Leon (lŭmz'dĕn), U.S. Public Health Service; b. Granite Springs, Va., June 14, 1875; s. James Fife and Ann Elizabeth (Jacobs) L.; student Va. Midland and Bowling Green acads.; M.D., U. of Va., 1894; grad. student Johns Hopkins Hosp. Sch., 1894-95; m. Alfreda Blanche Healy, 1902 (died 1908); m. 2d, Flora Elizabeth Dick, Feb. 6, 1937. Commd. asst. surgeon U.S. P.H.S. (then Marine Hosp.), 1898, passed asst. surgeon, 1903, surgeon, 1912, sr. surgeon, 1928, med. dir., 1930; retired, 1939; has specialized in epidemiology of yellow fever, bubonic plague, tuberculosis, and poliomyelitis, also in rural health work; dist. dir. and research work, New Orleans, 1931-39; with Tenn. Dept. of Pub. Health, 1939-41; prof. epidemiology, Texas U. Sch. of Med. since 1943. Originated and developed full time plan of rural health service in U.S. During World War held commn. asst. surgeon gen. U.S. P.H.S. with relative rank of col. Mem. Am. Pub. Health Assn., A.M.A. Democrat. Club: Cosmos (Washington, D.C.). Author: of various U.S. P.H.S. publs. on typhoid fever, rural sanitation, rural health work, tuberculosis and poliomyelitis; also contbr. to med. jours. Home: 103 Park Pl., New Orleans. Died Nov. 8, 1946; buried in Garden of Memories, New Orleans.

LUNDBECK, G(ustaf) Hilmer; born Uppsala, Sweden, August 13, 1870; son Alfred and Caroline (Eklund) Lundbeck; came to U.S. with parents, 1881; naturalized, 1891; educated Normal School, Stockholm, Sweden, and high sch., Cambridge, Mass.; m. Clara Helsing, Nov. 28, 1893 (dec.); children—Lillian (Mrs. Lewis Luckenbach), G. Hilmer, Jr.; m. 2d, Florence C. Hammond, July 13, 1943. Mem. Nielsen & Lundbeck, fgn. exchange, 1893-1920, sole owner since 1920; U.S. mng. dir. Swedish-Am. Line, 1916-44. Hon. pres. Swedish Chamber of Commerce of U.S.; v.p. Sweden House, Inc. Trustee and v.p. Am. Scandinavian Foundation; dir. Swedish Hosp., Brooklyn, N.Y. Comdr. First Class Order of Vasa (Sweden). Club: Metropolitan (New York, N.Y.). Home: 515 Park Av. Office: 636 Fifth Av., New York, N.Y. Died June 18, 1949.

LUNDBERG, Charles J., furniture mfr.; b. Kirkland, Ill.; s. Lewis and Carrie (Johanson) L.; ed. pub. schs. and business coll.: m. Olga O. Jacobson, Sept. 28, 1898; children—Karl Wesley, Karin Phyllis. Founder, pres., Cooperative Furniture Co., Rockford World Furniture Company, The Empire, Ltd.; dir. Rockford Life Ins. Co., Commercial Nat. Bank. Alderman, Rockford, 9 yrs., purchasing agt. 5 yrs. Trustee Rockford Coll., Rockford Symphony Assn. Pres. John Erickson Rep. State League of Ill. Mem. state central com., 12th Congl. Dist.; pres. bd. of edn., Rockford; mem. Governor's Com. on Unemployment for State of Ill. Pres. Rockford Mfrs. and Shippers Assn. Lutheran. Clubs: Rotary, Rockford Country, University (life). Address: 840 Sierra Madre Blvd., San Marino, Calif. Office: Gas Electric Bldg., Rockford, Ill. Died Sep. 22, 1949.

LUNDBORG, Florence (lŭnd'bôrg), artist; b. San Francisco, Calif.; d. J. A. W. and Mehitable Mow (Peirce) Lundborg; ed. San Francisco Art Assn., and in France and Italy. Mural painter and illustrator. Awarded gold medal, San Francisco Art Assn.; bronze medal Panama-Pacific Internat. Expn., San Francisco, 1915. Mural decorations in Calif. Bldg., Panama-Pacific Internat. Expn.; "Queen of Hearts," at Henriettes, Paris; Auditorium of Wadleigh High Sch., N.Y. City; Curtis High Sch., Staten Island, N.Y.; Auditorium of Shallow High School, Brooklyn, etc.; murals in many private homes of San Francisco, Portland, Chicago, N.Y. City; murals in Met. Mus. of Fine Arts, N.Y. Illustrated the "Rubaiyat"; "Yosemite Legends"; "Honey Bee"; "Odes and Sonnets." Mem. Nat. Assn. Women Painters and Sculptors, San Francisco Art Assn., Book Club of Calif., Am. Woman's Assn. (New York). Home: 28 E. 31st St., New York, N.Y.* Died Jan. 18, 1949.

LUNDY, Elmer Johnston, lawyer; b. Gordonville, Tex., June 10, 1880; s. William Wiley and Barbara Adelaide (Burkett) L.; B.S., Dickson (Tenn.) Normal Sch., 1899; LL.B., George Washington U., 1907; m. Clara Mabel Matthews, Oct. 11, 1904 (died 1940); children—Ima Pauline (Mrs. Allen S. McMaster), Barbara Helen, James Elmer Burkett, Clara Virginia (Mrs. G. Austin Manuel), James Matthew; m. 2d, Josephine Welch McMechan, Mar. 9, 1943. Admitted to Ark. bar, 1907; in practice at Mena, Ark., 1907-16, Tulsa Okla., since 1916; dir. and treas. Royalty Corp. of Am. Mem. of State Senate, Ark., 1912-16, pres. State Senate, 1915. Mem. Okla. Bar Assn. (pres. 1939), Am. Bar Assn., Delta Theta Phi. Democrat. Methodist. Club: Tulsa. Home: 1395 E. 27th Pl. Office: 1501-1504 Hunt Bldg., Tulsa, Okla. Died Apr. 17, 1944.

LUNKEN, Edmund H. (surname changed to avoid business complications), inventor, mfr.; b. Cincinnati, O., June 20, 1861; s. Frederick and Louisa H. Lunkenheimer; ed. pub. schs., Cincinnati, and in tech. sch., Germany; m. Edith I. Hodgson, July 7, 1885 (divorced); 1 son, Eshelby Frederick; m. 2d, Kathryn French, Dec. 31, 1914; children—Homer Edmund, Charlotte Hope. With Lunkenheimer Co. (founded by father), mfrs. valves, etc., Cincinnati, many yrs., retiring as chief executive, 1923; inventor many standard devices in use in mechanical operations. Donor of tract of land Cincinnati, for aviation purposes, known as the Lunken Air Port. Protestant. Mason (32°). Home: Compton Hills Dr., Wyoming (Cincinnati), O. Died July 19, 1944.

LUNN, Arthur Constant, mathematician; b. Racine, Wis., Feb. 19, 1877; s. John C. and Emma R. (Martin) L.; A.B., Lawrence Coll., 1898; A.M., U. of Chicago, 1900, Ph.D., 1904; m. Anna J. Gowan, Sept. 27, 1900. Instr. mathematics and astronomy, Wesleyan U., Conn., 1901-02; asso. in applied mathematics, U. of Chicago, 1902-03, instr., 1903-10, asst. prof., 1910-17, asso. prof., 1917-23, prof. since 1923. Mem. Am. Phys. Soc., Am. Math. Soc., Am. Astron. Soc., Math. Assn. Am., A.A.A.S., Circolo Matematico di Palermo, Sigma Xi, Phi Beta Kappa, Gamma Alpha. Home: 5211 Kenwood Av., Chicago. Died Nov. 19, 1949.

LUNN, George Richard; b. near Lenox, Ia., June 23, 1873; s. M. A. and Mattie (Bratton) L.; B.A., Bellevue (Neb.) Coll., 1897, M.A., 1901; B.D., Union Theol. Sem., 1901; D.D., Union Coll., N.Y., 1905; m. Mabel Healy, May 7, 1901 (died 1931); children—George Richard, Mabel C., Elizabeth Healy, Raymond Healy, Eleanor Peabody; m. 2d, Anita Oliver Jensen, 1932. Ordained Presbyn. ministry, 1901; associate pastor Lafayette Avenue Ch., Brooklyn, N.Y., 1901-04, First Dutch Reformed Ch., Schenectady, N.Y., 1904-09, United People's Ch., Schenectady, 1909-15. Mayor Schenectady, 1912-Jan. 1, 1914 (first Socialist mayor elected in N.Y. State); reelected for term Jan. 1, 1916-Dec. 31, 1917; left Socialist Party, Feb. 1916; elected mayor, 3d term, Democrat ticket, 1920-22; Dem. mem. 65th Congress (1917-19), 30th N.Y. Dist.; reelected mayor for 4th term, Jan. 1, 1922-Dec. 31, 1923; resigned as mayor to become lt. gov. state of N.Y., Jan. 1, 1923; public service commr., 1925-42. Served as corporal Co. I, 3d Neb. Regt., Spanish-Am. War; past dept. comdr. N.Y. State United Spanish War Vets; comdr.-in-chief United Spanish War Vets., 1931-32. Del. Dem. Nat. Convs., 1920, 24, 28, 32, 36. Home: Rancho Santa Fe, California. Died Nov. 27, 1948.

LUTEN, Daniel Benjamin (lū'tĕn), bridge engr.; b. Grand Rapids, Mich., Dec. 26, 1869, s. Lambert and Wilhelmina (Hagens) L.; B.S. in C.E., U. of Mich., 1894; m. Edith Heath Hull, June 20, 1900; children—Granville H., Wilhelmina, Daniel B., Mary Edith. Instr. civ. engring., U. of Mich., 1894-95, Purdue U., Lafayette, Ind., 1895-1900; consulting practice, concrete bridges exclusively, 1900-32; mfr. since 1932. Home: 5024 N. Illinois St. Office: 2135 N. Illinois St., Indianapolis, Ind. Died July 3, 1946.

LUTES, Della Thompson (lūts), author; b. Jackson, Mich.; d. Elijah Bonnett and Almira Frances (Bogardus) Thompson; ed. pub. schs.; m. Louis Irving Lutes; children—Ralph Irving (dec.), Robert Brosseau. Began as dist. sch. teacher, later teacher Detroit pub. schs.; editor Am. Motherhood Mag., 1912-28; mng editor, Table Talk, 1917; editor Today's Housewife, 1919; housekeeping editor Modern Priscilla, 1923-30. Republican. Clubs: Writers, Homemakers (Detroit). Author: Table Setting and Service, 1930; The Country Kitchen, and a Book of Menus and Recipes, 1936; Home Grown, 1937; Millbrook, 1938; Gabriel's Search, 1940; The Country Schoolma'am, 1941. Contbr. to leading mags. Home: Cooperstown, N.Y. Died July 13, 1942.

LUTZ, Charles Abner (lōōts), accountant; b. Loogootee, Ill., Aug. 6, 1871; s. Gabriel and Mary Elizabeth (Shoptaugh) L.; ed. grammar school, Louisville, Ky., and Southern Business College, Louisville; m. Jennie M. Forman, Feb. 6, 1902; children—Charles Gabriel, Forman John, Virginia (Mrs. John W. Trott), Elizabeth (Mrs. Russell R. Raab). Station agent L.&N. R.R., 1887-92, clerk, bookkeeper, chief clerk, accounting dept., 1892-1901, asst. comptroller, 1901-08; chief examiner of accounts Interstate Commerce Commn., Washington, D.C., 1908-13; comptroller U.S. Express Co., N.Y. City, 1913-15; comptroller Winchester Repeating Arms Co., New Haven, Conn., 1916-18; treas. U.S. R.R. Adminstrn., Washington, D.C., 1918-20; v.p. of accounting Am. Ry. Express Co., N.Y. City, 1920-29, Ry. Express Agency, N.Y. City, 1929-41, retired. Hon. mem. Treasury and Accounting Divs., Assn. of American Railroads. Republican. Conglist. Mason. Club: Montclair (N.J.) Athletic. Home: 11 Vera Place, Montclair, N.J. Died Nov. 13, 1947.

LUTZ, Frank Eugene, biologist; b. Bloomsburg, Pa., Sept. 15, 1879; s. Martin Peter and Anna Amelia (Brockway) L.; A.B., Haverford (Pa.) Coll., 1900; A.M., U. of Chicago, 1902, Ph.D., 1907; studied Univ. Coll., London, Eng., 1902; m. Martha Ellen Brobson, Dec. 30, 1904; children—Anna, Eleanor, Frank Brobson, Laura. Entomologist, Biol. Lab. of Brooklyn Inst., 1902; asst. in zool. dept., U. of Chicago, 1903; resident investigator, Sta. for Experimental Evolution (Carnegie Instn.), Cold Spring Harbor, 1904-09; asst. curator invertebrate zoology, 1909-16, asso. curator, 1916-21; curator of entomology since 1921, also editor of tech. papers, Am. Museum Natural History, and 1925-28 in charge of Station for the Study of Insects, Tuxedo, N.Y.; lecturer Columbia U., 1937. Fellow A.A.A.S., N.Y. Acad. Sciences, Entomol. Soc. America (pres., 1927); mem. Am. Soc. Zoologists, Sigma Xi, Phi Beta Kappa, etc. Baptist. Mason. Author: Field Book of Insects, 1917; A Lot of Insects, 1941. Contbr. numerous papers on variation, heredity, assortive mating, entomology, etc. Home: Ramsey, N.J. Died Nov. 27, 1943.

LUTZ, Grace Livingston, author, see Grace Livingston Hill.

LUTZ, Philip, lawyer; b. Boonville, Ind., Aug. 28, 1888; s. Philip and Barbara (Billman) L.; A.B., Indiana U., 1912; LL.B., Indiana U. Sch. of Law, 1912; m. Lois Vane Ryse, June 17, 1914 (died Feb. 9, 1938); 1 son, John Philip; m. 2d., Marie Elizabeth Bryant, February 2, 1942. Began law practice at Boonville, 1912; pres. Boonville Bldg. & Loan Assn., Welfare Realty & Investment Co., Phil Lutz Peony Farms; v.p. La Salle Finance Co.; dir. Boonville Nat. Bank. City judge, Boonville, 1912-15; mem. Ind. House of Representatives, 1915-17; judge Warrick Juvenile Court, 1918-22; chmn. Democratic County Com., 1928, Dem. Dist. Com. of 1st Ind. District, 1928-32; Warrick County atty., 1930-32; attorney general of Indiana, 1933-37; now mem. firm Lutz, Johnson & Lutz. Former pres. and treas. Central States Probation and Parole Conf.; former chmn. bd. dirs. and mem. Interstat. Commn. on Crime for Ind.; chmn. com. on criminal law Am. Prison Assn., 1937. Hon. pres. Nat. Assn. of Attorneys General; mem. Commercial Law League America, Am. Bar Assn. (chmn. com. on criminal procedure 1935-37; chmn. com. on law enforcement 1937-38), Ind. State Bar Assn. (chmn. com. on criminal law 1933-37), Warrick County Bar Assn., Indianapolis Bar Assn. (chmn. com. on criminal law, police and prosecution 1939), Nat. Assn. Atty. Gens. (former v.p.), Boonville Chamber Commerce, Ind. Soc. of Chicago, Gamma Eta Gamma, Delta Sigma Rho. Democrat. Mem. Evang. Ch. Mason (32°), Woodman of World, Elk. Clubs: Kiwanis, Boonville Press (former pres.), Indianapolis Athletic, Indiana Democratic, Indianapolis Press. Contbr. articles on legal and pub. questions. Home: 3433 Central Av. Office: 734 Circle Tower, Indianapolis, Ind. Died May 22, 1947.

LYBYER, Albert Howe (lī'bī-ēr), univ. prof.; b. near Putnamville, Ind., July 29, 1876; s. Salem Henry and Jane Estella (Layman) L.; A.B., Princeton, 1896, A.M., 1899; grad. Princeton Theol. Sem., 1900; Ph.D., Harvard, 1909; U. of Grenoble, summer, 1904; m. Clara Sidney Andrews, July 25, 1901. Ordained Presbyn. ministry, 1900; prof. mathematics, Robert Coll., Constantinople, 1900-07; asst. in history, Harvard, 1907-09; asso. prof. medieval and modern European history, 1909-11, prof., 1911-13, Oberlin; asso. professor history, University of Illinois, 1913-16, professor since 1916; professor emeritus, 1944; prof. European history, summers, Ohio State U., 1911, U. of Calif., 1929, U. of Mich., 1930, Northwestern U., 1938. Mem. Col. House's commn. of inquiry into terms of peace, 1918; asst. in Balkan div. Am. Commn to Negotiate Peace, Paris, 1919; gen. tech. adviser to Am. Commn. on Mandates in Turkey, 1919. Fellow Royal Hist. Soc.; mem. Am. Hist. Assn., Am. Polit. Science Assn., Am. Assn. of Univ. Profs., Am. Oriental Soc., New Orient Soc. of America (pres., 1936-39), Phi Beta Kappa. Club: University. Author: The Government of the Ottoman Empire in the Time of Suleiman the Magnificent, 1913. Contbr. to Ency. Brit., Ency. of Social Sciences, Am. Year Book, World Book Ency. Annual, also to scientific publs.

Home: 808 S. Lincoln Av., Urbana, Ill. Died Mar. 28, 1949.

LYDICK, Jesse Dean (lĭ'dĭk), lawyer; b. Salem, Ill., Mar. 4, 1876; s. John Ambrose and Adelaide (Brown) L.; student Southwest Kan. Coll., Winfield, Kan., 1892-97, Okla. State U., 1897-98; m. Clara Belle George, Sept. 6, 1899; 1 son, John Marion. Reared on farm; admitted to Oklahoma bar, 1900 and began practice at Lexington; moved to Shawnee, 1905, Oklahoma City, 1920; asso. justice Supreme Court of Okla. by apptmt. of gov., Jan. 7, 1924-Jan. 7, 1925; resumed practice. Successfully defended A. L. Welch, state ins. commr. of Okla., in impeachment trial, 1915, also Lt. Gov. M. E. Trapp (later gov.) in impeachment trial, 1921, and Gov. J. B. A. Robertson, under indictment for bribery, 1922; appeared successfully for State of Okla. in Dist. Court of U.S. and Supreme Court of U.S. against Gov. Walton, 1923, 24, when the latter sought to enjoin enforcement of decree of the Senate of Okla., by which he was impeached and removed from office, successfully defended retiring bank commr. in the administration of Gov. Murray, on charge of embezzlement, 1936; in 1939-40 successfully defended Oil Workers International Union in strike at plants of Mid-Continent Petroleum Corp. throughout Oklahoma; now engaged in private practice. Democrat. Unitarian. K.P. Club: Oklahoma City Golf and Country. Mem. Sigma Nu. Office: Petroleum Bldg., Oklahoma City, Okla. Died Nov. 27, 1944.

LYDON, Richard Paul (lī'dŭn), judge; b. N.Y. City, Dec. 15, 1868; s. Patrick Henry and Ellen R. (Buckley) L.; A.B., Coll. City of New York, 1889; M.A., in Polit. Science, Columbia, 1891; student Columbia Law Sch., 1889-91; unmarried. Mem. firm Redfield, Redfield & Lydon, New York, 1896-1906, Hill, Lockwood, Redfield & Lydon, 1906-19; justice Supreme Court, 1st District, N.Y., 1919-39; Supreme Court official referee since 1939. Member of board of trustees of the Roman Catholic Orphan Asylum, Lavelle School for the Blind. Democrat. Mem. Knights of Columbus. Clubs: Metropolitan, Bankers, Lawyers', New York Athletic, Union, Long Island Country. Home: 1120 5th Av. Address: 60 Center St., New York, N.Y.* Died Mar. 6, 1946.

LYLE, Henry Hamilton Moore, surgeon; b. Connor, Ulster, Ireland, Nov. 15, 1874; s. Samuel (D.D.) and Elizabeth (Orr) L.; med. prep. edn., Cornell U., 1896; M.D., Coll Physicians and Surgeons (Columbia), 1900; m. Clara Schlemmer, May 17, 1910 (died Jan. 8, 1916); m. 2d, Jessie Benson Pickens, Apr. 16, 1919. Practiced at N.Y. City since 1900; prof. clin. surgery, Coll. Phys. and Surg., 1913-19; asst. prof. surgery, Cornell University Medical Sch., 1919-31, prof. of clinical surgery since 1931; attending surgeon at St. Luke's Hosp.; dir. of cancer service, New York Skin and Cancer Hosp.; attending surgical specialist U.S. Veterans' Bureau, Dist. No. 2; cons. surgeon to Elizabeth A. Horton Memorial Hosp., Middletown, N.Y., N.Y. State Reconstruction Home, W. Haverstraw, Cornwall (N.Y.) Hospital; consultant St. Luke's Hospital, Newburgh, N.Y. Médecin chef Am. Ambulance Hosp. B, Juilly Seine et Marne, France, 1915; chirurgien chef Ambulance Longueil Annel, Oise, France, 1916; commd. maj. O.R.C., U.S. Army, Apr. 26, 1917; active duty, May 30, 1917; organized and took abroad Evacuation Hosp. No. 2; lt. col., June 6, 1918; apptd. cons. surgeon 77th div., Sept. 1918; apptd. to field staff of the chief surgeon 1st Army, in charge of western sect. of the evacuation of wounded in the St. Mihiel drive; apptd., Sept. 30, 1918, dir. of ambulances and evacuation of the wounded for the 1st Army, Meuse-Argonne offensive; chief consultant surgeon 1st Army; mem. Gas Warfare Bd., A.E.F.; col. Oct. 23, 1918. Engagements—Oise-Aisne, Aisne-Marne, St. Mihiel, Meuse-Argonne, defensive sector. Decorated D.S. M. (U.S.); British War Medal and British Victory Medal, N.Y. State Service Medal, Liberty Service Medal of Nat. Inst. Social Services; awarded hon. testimonial for life saving by Royal Canadian Humane Assn., 1895. Fellow Am. Coll. Surgeons; mem. Am. Surg. Assn., New York Surg. Soc., Am. Soc. Clin. Surgeons, Internat. Surg. Soc. of Brussels, A.M.A., Acad. Medicine (New York), N.Y. State Soc. of Indsl. Medicine, Nat. Inst. Social Sciences, Am. Legion, Military Order of the World War, Kappa Alpha. Republican. Presbyterian. Clubs: Eclat, Charaka Club. Home: 1217 Park Av. Office: 33 E. 68th St., New York, N.Y. Died Mar. 11, 1947.

LYMAN, Charles Huntington, officer U.S. Marine Corps; b. Ravenna, O., Sept. 22, 1875; s. Charles Huntington and Rebekah (Chew) L.; grad. Naval War Coll., Newport, R.I., 1926, Army War Coll., Washington, D.C., 1927; m. Ann Blaine Irvine, July 17, 1901; children—Charles Huntington III (lt. comdr. U.S. Navy), Andrew Irvine (lt. U.S. Marine Corps). Commd. first lieutenant U.S. Marine Corps, July 1899; promoted through grades to major general, May 11, 1935. Served in Dist. of Columbia Vol. during Spanish-Am. War, with service in Cuba, 1898, Boxer uprising, China, 1900, Philippine Insurrection, Panama, 1901-03, 1909-10, Cuba, 1906-07, Alaska, 1911-12, Santo Domingo, 1921-23, China, 1928-30; apptd. comdr. gen Fleet Marine Force, U.S. Fleet, 1933; later comdg. Dept. of Pacific, U.S. Marine Corps, San Francisco, Calif.; retired, Oct. 1, 1939. Chmn. San Diego Chapter Am. Red Cross since Jan. 1940. Mason. Address: 3009 Goldsmith St., San Diego, Calif.* Died July 23, 1945.

LYMAN, Eugene William, theologian; b. Cummington, Mass., Apr. 4, 1872; s. Darwin Eugene and Julia Sarah (Stevens) L.; A.B., Amherst, 1894, A.M., 1903; B.D., Yale, 1899; Hooker fellow at univs. of Halle, Berlin, and Marburg, 2 yrs.; S.T.D., Bowdoin, 1906; D.D., Yale, 1912, Amherst, 1914; m. Bertha Burton Thayer, June 1, 1899 (died Nov. 9, 1924); children—Charles Eugene, Laura Frances; m. 2d, Mary Redington Ely, Feb. 13, 1926. Instr. Latin, Williston Sem., Easthampton, Mass., 1894-95, Lawrenceville (N.J.) Sch., 1895-96; prof. philosophy, Carleton Coll., Minn., 1901-04; prof. theology Congl. Coll. of Can., Montreal, 1904-05, Bangor (Me.) Theol. Sem., 1905-13; prof. philosophy of religion and Christian ethics, Oberlin Sch. Theology, 1913-18; prof. philosophy of religion, Union Theol. Sem., New York, 1918-40, prof. emeritus since 1940. Mem. Am. Philos. Soc., Theol. Soc., Phi Beta Kappa, Delta Upsilon. Author: Theology and Human Problems, 1910; Experience of God in Modern Life, 1918; The Meaning of Selfhood (Ingersoll lecture), 1928; (with others) Religious Realism, 1931; The Meaning and Truth of Religion, 1933; Contemporary American Theology, Vol. II (with others), 1933; The Kingdom of God and History (with others), 1938; The Gospel, the Church and Society (with others), 1938; Theology and Modern Life (with others), 1940; In Commemoration of William James (with others), 1942; Religion and the Issues of Life, 1943; also articles in theol. and philos. mags. Home: Sweet Briar College, Sweet Briar, Va. Died March 15, 1948.

LYNCH, Anna (linch), artist; b. Elgin, Ill.; d. Timothy and Anna (Ryan) Lynch; ed. pub. schs. and St. Mary's Acad., Elgin; Art Inst. Chicago; studied under Bouquereau, Simon and Mme. de Billemont-Chardon, Paris, and Charles Hawthorne, Provincetown, Mass. Miniature and portrait painter. Has exhibited in Paris Salon, at New York, Boston, Phila., Chicago, Washington, D.C., Buffalo, Pittsburgh, St. Louis, Milwaukee, Minneapolis, etc.; painted miniatures in Paris, Chicago and various other cities of the U.S. and Can. Awarded bronze medal, San Francisco Expn., 1915; Arts Club miniature prize, Chicago, 1917; Art Inst. Chicago alumni award, 1920, also honorable mention; Arché Club purchase prize; seven purchase prizes, Chicago Galleries Assn.; 1st prize for oil, Am. Pen Women (Northern Ill. br.), 1938; Mrs. Frank G. Logan miniature Sanity in Art prize, 1939; Assn. Chicago painters and sculptors, gold medal, 1940. Mem. Chicago Soc. Miniature Painters' (pres.), Pa. Soc. Miniature Painters, De Paul Art League, Perboyre Art League, Assn. Painters and Sculptors of Chicago, Chicago Galleries Assn., Arts Club of Chicago. Represented in Municipal Art Galleries of Chicago; Chicago Court House, by portrait Hon. Joseph E. Gary; portrait Hon. Arbah Waterman, Memorial Hall, Chicago; oil portrait of Mgr. Maurice D. Griffin, Am. Hosp. Assn., Chicago; oil portrait Walter Dill Scott, Scott Hall, Northwestern U., portrait Wm. E. Morgan (M.D.), Archibald Church Medical Library, Northwestern U.; miniature, oil portrait of Mrs. Walter Dill Scott, Scott Hall, Northwestern U.; Laura Davidson Sears, Acad. of Fine Arts, Elgin, Ill.; 4 miniatures of Mrs. Frank G. Logan; portrait of Rev. Mother Edmonda, Superintendent Fitzgerald-Mercy Hospital, Darby, Pennsylvania; also many private collections; has painted more than 400 portraits in oil and miniatures on ivory. Roman Catholic. Clubs: Arts, Cordon. Home: 54 S. Crystal St., Elgin, Ill. Studio: 9 E. Ontario St., Chicago. Died Jan. 8, 1946.

LYNCH, Charles F., lawyer; b. Franklin Boro, N.J., Jan. 9, 1884; s. Patrick H. and Margaret (Crawley) L.; ed. pub. schs.; studied law as clerk in offices of Michael Dunn, Paterson, N.J., and Pierce & Greer, N.Y. City; married. Admitted to N.J. bar, 1906; associated in practice with Hon. William Hughes, Paterson, N.J.; candidate on Dem. ticket for N.J. Gen. Assembly several times; apptd. 2d asst. U.S. dist. atty., Dist. of N.J., June 1, 1913, 1st asst., Sept. 1, 1914; apptd. U.S. dist. atty., June 1916; U.S. dist. judge, Dist. of N.J., by appmt. of President Wilson, 1919-25 (resigned); city counsel, Paterson, for term expiring Jan. 1, 1940. Mem. N.J. State, Passaic County and Essex County bar assns. Knight of Columbus, Elk. Clubs: Hamilton, North Jersey, Deal Golf, Spring Lake Tennis, Democratic, Newark Athletic, Sky Top. Home: 350 E. 38th St., Paterson, N.J. Office: 1110 Raymond Commerce Bldg., Newark, N.J. Died June 17, 1942.

LYNCH, Ella Frances, writer and lecturer on edn.; b. Minerva, N.Y.; d. Daniel and Margaret Cecilia (Ward) L.; ed. by parents and under tutors. Began as teacher in country schs., N.Y., later teacher at Washington Acad., Salem, N.Y.; founder, 1907, and head of Sch. of Individual Instrn., Atlantic City, N.J.; also Miss Lynch's School, Bryn Mawr, Pa. Founder Inst. of Domestic Edn., 1933; founder Internat. League of Teacher-Mothers. Lecturer on home edn. and pub. sch. reconstruction; organizer of mothers' clubs for home teaching in various countries. Chmn. Am. com. 4th Internat. Congress on Family Education, Liége, Aug. 1930. Audience with Pope Pius XI, 1930; honors from Papal Soc. of Arts and Lit. of France. Author: Educating the Child at Home, 1914; Bookless Lessons for the Teacher-Mother, 1922; Beginning the Child's Education, 1925. Contbr. to mags., U.S. and Gt. Britain. Home: Minerva, N.Y. Died Aug. 31, 1945.

LYNCH, Frank W(orthington), gynecologist; b. Cleveland, O., Nov. 5, 1871; s. Frank W. and Rebecca (Nevin) L.; A.B., Western Reserve U., 1895; M.D., Johns Hopkins, 1900; grad. study Vienna and Munich, 1910, 12; m. Rowena Tyng Higginson, Apr. 20, 1904; 1 son, Frank W. Asst. instr. and asso. in obstetrics, Johns Hopkins U. Med. Sch., 1900-04; instr. in obstetrics, Rush Med. Coll. (U. of Chicago), 1905-09, asst. prof. obstetrics and gynecology, 1909-15; prof. obstetrics and gynecology, University of California, 1915-42, professor emeritus since 1942; member of editorial board of Surgery, Gynecology and Obstetrics (abstract dept.), Am. Jour. Obstetrics and Gynecology, Western Jour. of Surgery. Mem. advisory bd. of com. on prenatal and maternal care, White House Conf.; mem. Am. Bd. Obstetrics and Gynecology. Honor guest of Pan-Pacific Surgical Congress, 1936. Fellow Am. Coll. Surgeons (bd. govs.; vice-pres. 1937-38); mem. Am. Med. Assn. (chmn. sect. on obstetrics and gynecology 1924), Am. Gynecol. Soc. (1st v.p. 1927; pres. 1933), Calif. State Med. Assn. (chmn. sect. on obstetrics and gynecology 1922), San Francisco Med. Soc., San Francisco Obstetrical and Gynecol. Soc. (pres. 1930), San Francisco Patho. Soc., Pacific Coast Surgical Soc., Pacific Coast Obstet. and Gynecol. Soc. (pres. 1931), Alpha Delta Phi, Nu Sigma Nu; mem. obstet. advisory com. Children's Bur. U.S. Dept. of Labor; mem. advisory bd. Nat. Com. on Maternal Health; hon. mem. Seattle Surg. Soc., Los Angeles Obstet. Soc., Central Assn. Obstetricians and Gynecologists; mem. exec. com. Gynecology and Obstetrics of Pan-Am. Med. Assn. Served as editor, v.p. and pres. Chicago Gynecol. Soc., 1908-14. Republican. Episcopalian. Clubs: Bohemian, San Francisco Golf. Co-Author: Pelvic Neoplasms (with A. F. Maxwell), 1922. Contbr. chapters to Am. Practice of Surgery, 1911; Oxford Surgery, 1921; Nelson's Looseleaf Surgery, 1928; Davis' Obstetrics and Gynecology, 1933; Curtis' Obstetrics and Gynecology, 1933; The Treatment of Cancer, 1937. Also contbr. on obstet. and gynecol. subjects to Am. and German med. jours. Home: 1998 Vallejo St. Office: 384 Post St., San Francisco. Died Jan. 12, 1945.

LYNCH, John David, lawyer; b. Detroit, Mich., Mar. 20, 1890; s. John and Emma (Howcroft) L.; A.B., U. of Mich., 1910, LL.B., 1912; m. Edith Louise Benson, Sept. 23, 1915; children — Edith Louise (wife of Dr. James Weaver Rae, Jr.), John David. Admitted to Mich. bar, 1912; engaged in gen. practice of law, Detroit, Mich., since 1912. Regent U. of Mich. Nat. pres. Council of Legal Fraternities, 1924-25. Mich. state dir. bldg. and loan assn., 1937-39. Special mediator Ford Motor Co. labor dispute, 1941. Mem. Detroit and Mich. State bar assns., Gamma Eta Gamma (nat. chancellor 1922-24). Mason. Clubs: Lawyers (U. of Mich.); University of Michigan (past gov.) (Detroit). Home: 1025 Yorkshire Rd., Grosse Pointe 30. Mich. Office: Penobscot Bldg., Detroit 26, Mich. Died June 22, 1946.

LYNETT, Edward James (lĭ'nĕt), editor, pub.; b. Dunmore, Pa., July 15, 1856; s. William and Catherine (Dowd) L.; ed. pub. schs. and Pa. State Normal Sch., Millersville, Pa.; m. Nellie A. Ruddy, Sept. 30, 1896 (died 1924); children—William R. (editor and publisher of The Scranton Times), Elizabeth R., Edward J., Jr. (assistant publisher). Began as solicitor for the Scranton Daily Avalanche; reporter Sunday Morning Free Press, Scranton, 1876; became publisher and proprietor of The Scranton Times, 1895 (circulation 3,000, now 55,000); dir. U.S. Lumber Co., Miss. Central Rd. Co., Internat. Corr. Schs., Internat. Ednl. Pub. Co., Internat. Textbook Co. Del. Dem. Nat. Conv. 6 times, 1900-32. Mem. Pa. State Mine Cave Commn., 1911. Trustee Univ. of Scranton, St. Patrick's Orphanage, St. Michael's Boys Industrial Sch.; vice-pres. Mercy Hosp., Maryknoll Coll. Mem. Scranton Chamber of Commerce, Am. Newspaper Pubs.' Assn., N. Am. Newspaper Alliance, Nat. Editorial Assn., Pa. Newspaper Pubs. Assn., Associated Advt. Clubs of the World, Associated Press. Catholic. Club: Scranton. Home: 841 Clay Av. Office: Times Bldg., Penn Av. and Spruce St., Scranton, Pa. Died Jan. 1, 1943.

LYNN, Robert Marshall, newspaper corr.; b. "Bloomfield," Cumberland County, Va., Jan. 12, 1871; s. Rev. James Shirley and Helen Margaret (Daniel) L.; ed. public schs. and by home study; m. Lucy Mabel Hancock, Nov. 12, 1901; 1 son, Marshall Hancock. Began as reporter Danville (Va.) Register, 1895; mng. editor Richmond (Va.) Evening Journal, 1905-15, Richmond News-Leader, 1916-22; Washington corr. News-Leader since 1922. Democrat. Baptist. Club: Nat. Press. Home: 1277 New Hampshire Av., N.W. Office: 1277 New Hampshire Av., N.W., Washington, D.C. Died Apr. 30, 1944.

LYON, Dorsey Alfred, metallurgist; b. Bureau County, Ill., July 17, 1871; s. Walter S. and Sarah S. (McKune) L.; A.B., Stanford, 1898; A.M., Harvard, 1902; D.Sc., U. of Utah, 1922; unmarried. Instr. geology and mining, 1898-99, asst. prof. mining and metallurgy, 1899-1900, prof., 1901, U. of Wash.; with U.S. Mining and Smelting Co., Midvale, Utah, 1902-03; asst. prof. metallurgy, Stanford, 1903-07; mgr. Noble Electric Steel Co., Heroult, Calif., 1907-11; cons. metallurgist, Electro-Metals Co., London, Eng., 1911-13; metallurgist, 1913-19; chief metallurgist, July 1919-July 1927, supervisor of stations, July 1917-July 1927, asst. director, Mar. 1923-July 1926, supervising engr. Intermountain Station, 1927-31, all of U.S. Bureau of Mines; dir. Utah Engineering Expt. Station, 1931-35, retired. Fellow A.A.A.S., Soc. for Promotion of Engring. Edn.; past mem. Am. Chem. Soc., Am. Mining Congress, Electrochemical Soc., Am. Inst. Mining Engrs., Delta Upsilon, Sigma Xi, Tau Beta Pi, Theta Tau, Phi Kappa Phi. Club: Rotary (Palo Alto); Commonwealth of California, Rio del Mar Country. Elk.

Episcopalian. A pioneer in electric furnace work in U.S.A. Co-Author of several bulls. of U.S. Bur. Mines, dealing with use of electric furnace in metall. work; contbr. to tech. publs. on metall. subjects. Home: 540 Harvard St., Palo Alto, Calif. Died Oct. 16, 1945.

LYON, Edmund Daniel, educator; b. Martinsburg, O., Sept. 6, 1862; s. Aaron Jackson and Olive (Weatherby) L.; A.B., Ohio Wesleyan, 1882, A.M., 1902; Ped.D., Miami U., 1908, Ohio Wesleyan, 1926; m. Camilla Gallup, Dec. 31, 1891. Supt. schs., Berea, O., 1888-93, Mansfield, O., 1893-1901, Madisonville, 1901-06; prin. Woodward High Sch., Cincinnati, 1906-12, Hughes High Sch., Cincinnati, Sept. 1912-19, Withrow High Sch., since 1919. Republican. Methodist. Mem. N.E.A., Ohio State Teachers' Assn., etc. Mason. Home: 5505 Arnsby Pl. Address: Withrow High Sch., Cincinnati. Died 1942.

LYON, Ernest, clergyman, diplomatist; b. Belize British Honduras, Oct. 22, 1860; s. Emmanuel and Ann F. (Bending) L.; A.B., New Orleans U., 1888, A.M.; spl. course at Union Theol. Sem.; D.D., Wiley U., Kittel Coll.; LL.D., Liberia Coll.; m. Marie Wright; children—Mrs. Maude A. Morris, Mrs. Anabelle Walker, Ernest Harrison, Monroe. Entered M.E. ministry, 1882; pastor La Teche, La., 1883, Mallalieu Ch., 1886, Thompson Ch., 1889, and Simpson Ch., 1891, all in New Orleans; apptd. S.S. agent for Conf., 1894; spl. agent Freedman's Aid and Southern Ednl. Soc., 1895; pastor St. Mark's Ch., New York, 1896, John Wesley Ch., Baltimore, 1901; founded Md. Industrial and Agrl. Inst. for edn. of colored youths; minister resident and consul-gen. of U.S. at Monrovia, Liberia, 1903-11; consul-gen. of Liberia at Washington, Apr. 28, 1911-13; agt. Bd. of Edn. for Liberia; again pastor John Wesley Ch., Baltimore; now pastor Ames Memorial Ch. Mgr. Summer Sch. Theology of Washington and Del. confs. of M.E. Ch. Apptd., 1896, auxiliary mem. Rep. Nat. Com., to which all matters referring to colored vote of East were referred; also of adv. bd. apptd. by Nat. Com., 1900. Chmn., colored div. Md. Council of Defense, World War; pres. Local Br. Nat. Equal Rights League. Pres. Afro-Am. Civic League of Md.; mem. Am. Acad. Polit. and Social Science, West African Soc., London, Eng. Knight, Order African Redemption, Liberia. Mason (33°). Editor Commonwealth (weekly jour.). Address: 828 N. Carey St., Baltimore. Died July 17, 1938.

LYON, F(rank) Emory, social worker; b. Lawn Ridge, Ill., Aug. 20, 1864; s. Sidney A. and Mary (Potter) L.; grad. Chicago Theol. Sem., 1891; grad. studies in sociology, U. of Wis., 1895-97; m. Jennie Charity Vredenburg, Aug. 21, 1888 (died Nov. 17, 1934). Founder, 1900, and since supt. Central Howard Assn. (prisoners' aid soc.). Apptd. by mayor of Chicago, inspr. House of Correction, 1931. Mem. Nat. Prisoners' Aid Assn. (ex-pres.), Am. Prison Assn. (dir.), Chicago Acad. of Criminology, Med. Liberty League of Chicago, Art Inst. Chicago. Asso. editor Jour. Am. Inst. Criminal Law and Criminology. Author: The Art of Living. Lecturer on sociol. topics. Home: 1421 E. 58th St. Office: 608 S. Dearborn St., Chicago, Ill. Died Apr. 2, 1943.

LYON, Frederick Saxton, lawyer; b. Chicago, Aug. 17, 1873; s. Lewis and Mary E. (Forbes) L.; student Jamestown (N.D.) Coll., 1888-1890; LL.B., U. of Minn., 1894; m. Grace A. Rood, Nov. 7, 1894; children—Leonard Saxton, Richard Forbes, Lewis Estes, Frederick William, Charles Gershom. Admitted to Minn. bar, 1894, and practiced in Minneapolis, 1896-1902, specializing in patents, trade marks and copyrights; practiced in Los Angeles since 1902; partner Townsend, Lyon, Hackley & Knight, 1905-20; sr. partner Lyon & Lyon since 1920, other partners being five sons. Mem. State Bar of Calif., Am. and Los Angeles County bar assns. Republican. Mason (32°, Shriner). Club: Los Angeles Country. Home: 724 N. Maple Drive, Beverly Hills, Calif. Office: 811 W. 7th St., Los Angeles. Died May 27, 1943.

LYON, Marcus Ward, Jr., zoölogist, bacteriologist and pathologist; b. Rock Island Arsenal, Ill., Feb. 5, 1875; s. Marcus Ward and Lydia Anna (Post) L.; Ph.B., Brown U., 1897; N.C. Med. Coll., 1897-98; M.S., 1900, M.D., 1902, Ph.D., 1913, George Washington U.; m. Martha Maria Brewer (M.S., M.D.), Dec. 31, 1902; 1 dau., Charlotte. Instr. bacteriology, N.C. Med. Coll., 1897-98; aid, later asst. curator, Div. of Mammals, U.S. Nat. Museum, Washington, 1898-1912; asst. prof. physiology, 1903-04, 1907-09, prof. bacteriology, 1909-15, Howard U., Washington; prof. bacteriology and pathology, 1915-17, prof. veterinary zoölogy and parasitology, 1917-18, George Washington U. Pathologist, Walter Reed Gen. Hosp., 1917-19; maj. Med. R.C., Sept. 1919. Fellow A.M.A., A.A.A.S.; mem. St. Joseph County Med. Soc. (past pres.), Soc. Am. Bacteriologists, Washington Acad. Sciences, Biol. Soc. Washington (sec. 1915-19), Am. Chem. Soc., Am. Soc. Parasitologists, Ecol. Society America, Am. Soc. Mammalogists (pres. 1931-33), Washington Biologists' Field Club, Am. Assn. Pathologists and Bacteriologists, Ind. Acad. Science (treas. 1928-32, pres. 1933), Am. Ornithologists' Union, Am. Soc. Clin. Pathologists, Indiana Hist. Soc., Wildlife Soc., Am. Geog. Soc., N.Y. Acad. Science, Am. Soc. Tropical Medicine, Phi Beta Kappa, Sigma Xi, Delta Tau Delta. Agnostic. Clubs: University (past pres.), Round Table, Cosmos (Washington). Author: Mammals of Indiana; also 160 papers on biol. and med. subjects. Home: 214 Laporte Av., South Bend, Ind. Died May 19, 1942.

LYON, Scott Cary, educator; b. Washington, Pa., Oct. 20, 1884; s. James Adair and Elizabeth (Barringer) L.; A.B., Southwestern Presbyn. U., 1904, A.M., 1905; A.M., Tulane U., 1909; D.Sc., Southwestern Presbyn. U., 1926; m. Malline Bradford, Dec. 22, 1909; children—William Adair, Malline Bradford. Prof. mathematics, Ala. Presbyn. Coll., 1909-10; prof. chemistry, 1910-17, prof. chemistry and biology and dean of univ., Southwestern Presbyn. U., 1917-25; prof., chair of biology, Davidson Coll., since 1926, Asst. Clarksville (Tenn.) Field Sta., Bureau of Entomology, U.S. Dept. Agr., summers, 1916-29, 1931. Pres. Tenn. Acad. Science, 1925. Fellow A.A.A.S.; mem. Am. Assn. of Economic Entomologists, Sigma Alpha Epsilon. Democrat. Presbyn. Mason, K.P., Kiwanian. Home: Davidson, N.C. Died July 24, 1942.

LYONS, Gerald Edward (lī'ŭnz), lawyer; b. Cresco, Ia., Oct. 2, 1892; s. Denis Augustus and Catharine (Fitzgerald) L.; A.B., Columbia (now Loras) Coll., Dubuque, Ia., 1913, LL.D., 1937; student U. of Minn. Law Sch., 1913-16; m. Florence Katherine Drewry, June 28, 1919; children—Mary Ellen, Gerald Edward, Thomas Judd, William Drewry. Admitted to Ia. bar, 1916, and began practice in Cresco; mem. McCook & Lyons, 1916-32; private practice, 1932-34; mem. Elwood, Lyons & Elwood since 1934; gen. counsel Farm Credit Adminstrn., Omaha, 1934-36; gen. solicitor, same, Washington, D.C., 1936-38, dep. gov., same, 1939-Mar. 1940; again practicing law in firm of Elwood, Lyons & Elwood, Cresco, Ia. Served in 313th Trench Mortar Battery, U.S. Army, with A.E.F., 1917-19. Mem. Am. Legion (former post and dist. comdr.), Delta Tau Delta. Democrat. Roman Catholic. Clubs: Cresco Country; Congressional Country (Washington, D.C.). Home: Cresco, Ia. Died Feb. 7, 1943; buried Cresco, Ia.

LYONS, John Sprole, clergyman; b. Tazewell, Va., Feb. 8, 1861; s. Rev. Jonathan and Nancy (Alexander) L.; A.B., King Coll., Tenn., 1880; grad. Union Theol. Sem., Va., 1883; D.D., Central U. of Ky., 1895; D.D., Princeton, 1926; LL.D., King Coll., 1923; m. Wallace Lillard, June 29, 1886 (died Oct. 9, 1919); children—John Sprole, Wm. Wallace; m. 2d, Anna Wooley Daniel, Aug. 4, 1922 (died Nov. 24, 1936). Ordained Presbyn. minister, 1883; pastor Lawrenceburg, Ky., 1883-90; Mt. Sterling, Ky., 1890-91, 1st Ch., San Antonio, Tex., 1891-92, 1st Ch., Louisville, Ky., 1892-1914, 1st Ch., Atlanta, 1914-36, pastor emeritus since July 1936. Moderator Synod of Kentucky, 1904; moderator Gen. Assembly Presbyn. Church in U.S., Atlanta, Ga., May 1913; also moderator of the Synod of Georgia, 1931; mem. Council Ref. Chs. in America holding the Presbyn. System since 1907, pres., 1923; mem. exec. com. of home missions, Presbyn. Ch. U.S., 1915-27; mem. Western Sect. Pan Presbyn Alliance since 1925; v.p. Alliance of Ref. Chs. Holding the Presbyn. System. Trustee Agnes Scott Coll., Decatur, Ga., Columbia Theol. Sem. (chmn. bd. since 1933), Presbyn. Coll., Clinton, S.C. Rabun Gap-Nachoochee Sch., Rabun Gap, Ga. Democrat. Mem. Sigma Chi. Mason. Traveled and studied in Europe, 1901-02, and 1923. Home: 635 Sycamore St., Decatur, Ga. Died July 11, 1942.

LYONS, Robert Edward, chemist; b. Bloomfield, Ind., Oct. 24, 1869; s. Mathew J. and Alice (Eveleigh) L.; A.B., Ind. U., 1889, A.M., 1890; student Fresenius' Labs., Wiesbaden, univs. of Heidelberg, Munich, and Berlin, and Joergensen's Inst. for Physiology of Fermentation, Copenhagen, 1892-95; Ph.D., U. of Heidelberg, 1894; m. Eleanor Joslyn, Mar. 23, 1898; 1 son, Robert Edward. Instr. of chemistry, Ind. U., 1889, asst. prof., 1890, asso. prof., 1891-92; pvt. asst. to Prof. Krafft, U. of Heidelberg, 1895; prof. chemistry and head dept., Ind. U., 1895-1938, prof. emeritus since 1938, dir. biol. station, 1900; chief chemist for Ind. State Dept. of Geology and Natural Resources, 1900-15; prof. chemistry, Central Coll. Physicians and Surgeons, Indianapolis, 1903-04; prof. chemistry, toxicology, and forensic medicine, and dir. chem. lab., Med. Coll. of Ind., Indianapolis, 1904-05; became chmn. dept. chemistry, Ind. U. Sch. of Medicine, Indianapolis, 1907, now retired; prof. in charge courses organic chemistry, U. of Wis., summer, 1907. Fellow A.A.A.S., Am. Inst. of Chemists, Ind. Acad. Science, Am. Chem. Soc. (mem. council, 1909, pres. Ind. Sect., 1908); mem. Deutsche Chemische Gesellschaft, Phi Delta Theta, Alpha Chi Sigma, Nu Sigma Nu, Sigma Xi. Local rep. of Com. of 100; chairman com. chemistry, State Council Defense. Republican. Author: Qualitative Analysis Inorganic Substances, 1897, 2d edit., 1900; Manual of Toxicological Analysis, 1899; also many articles on subs. in physiol., synthetic, organic and analyt. chemistry in Am. and German publs. Inventor of processes for amalgamation of platinum and of refractory gold; for recovery of used soap from laundry suds; for rapid polymerization and oxidation of drying oils; for light and weather proof coloring of oolitic limestone; for recovery of pectin from certain fruit and vegetable waste; for silver and gold mirror decoration; for reduction of nitro compounds. Club: Internat. Rotary. Home: 630 E. 3d St., Bloomington, Ind. Died Nov. 25, 1946.

M

MABEE, George W., business exec.; b. Ballston Spa, N.Y., 1878; ed. Yale (Sheffield Sch., 1901). Pres., treas., dir. National Folding Box Co. Home: 130 Edgehill Rd., New Haven, Conn.; and Roxbury, Conn. Office: James and Alton Streets, New Haven, Conn. Died May 11, 1948.

MacALARNEY, Robert Emmet (măk'ȧ-lär-nē), editor and writer; b. Harrisburg, Pa., Dec. 30, 1873; s. John Joseph Curtin and Elmira (Hoffman) M.; A.B., Dickinson College, 1893; Harvard, 1895-96; Litt. D. (Dickinson) 1945. m. Florence Thedford, Mar. 25, 1912; 1 daughter Rosanna Thedford. Reporter, Harrisburg (Pa.) Telegraph, 1893-95, Newark (New Jersey) Daily Advertiser, 1896-97, New York Evening Journal, and staff correspondent, 1897-1903; polit. reporter, 1903-05, city editor, 1906-11, New York Evening Post; city editor, New York Evening Mail, 1911-12; city editor, New York Tribune, 1914-16; pres. N.Y. City News Assn., 1914-16; scenario editor, Famous Players-Lasky Co., N.Y., 1916-20; production mgr. Famous Players-Lasky British Producers, Ltd., London, 1920-21; dir. and gen. production mgr. The Chronicles of America Picture Corp., 1921-23; mng. editor Ladies' Home Journal, 1923-28. Asso. prof. journalism, Columbia U., 1912-20, prof. since 1943. Dir. pub. relations, Nat. Com. on Food for Small Democracies, 1940-42. Democrat. Methodist. Mem. Authors' League America, Beta Theta Pi. Clubs: Century, Harvard. Home: The Manchester, 255 W. 108th St., New York, N.Y. Died Nov. 15, 1945.

MACAULAY, Fannie Caldwell (Frances Little), author; b. Shelbyville, Ky., Nov. 22, 1863; d. Judge James Lafayette and Mary Lettia (Middleton) Caldwell; ed. Science Hill Coll., Shelbyville; m. James Macaulay. Kindergarten teacher, Louisville, 1899-1902; supervisor normal classes, kindergartens, Hiroshima, Japan, 1902-07. Mem. Authors' Club, Kindergarten Assn. Club, Cabbage Patch Settlement, Fortnightly Club. Author: The Lady of the Decoration, 1906; Little Sister Snow, 1909; The Lady and Sada San, 1912; The House of the Misty Star, 1914; Camp Jolly, 1917. Home: 409 Fountain Ct., Louisville. Died Jan. 6, 1941.

MACBETH, Alexander Barksdale, industrialist; b. Greenville, S.C., Sept. 5, 1873; s. Alexander and Eliza (Trenholm) M.; ed. Porter Mil. Acad., 1889-92; M.E., Stevens Inst. Tech., 1897, hon. D.Eng., 1936; m. Rosemarie Newcomb, Dec. 1, 1914. Cadet engr. United Gas Improvement Co., Phila., 1898, Atlanta Gas, 1899; asst. supt. Kansas City Gas Co., 1900-10; gen. mgr. Kan. Nat. Gas Co., 1910-14; v.p. and gen. mgr. Southern Calif. Gas and Midway Gas, 1914, exec. v.p., 1925, pres., 1927-39 (retired); dir. Southern Calif. Gas, Pacific Lighting Corp., Union Oil, Union Bank and Trust Cos. Trustee, vice-pres. and treas. Calif. Inst. Tech.; trustee Stevens Inst. Tech.; dir. All-Year Club of Southern Calif., Automobile Club of Southern Calif. (v.p.). Mem. Beta Theta Pi. Clubs: Annandale, Twilight (Pasadena), California, Sunset (Los Angeles), Bohemian, Pacific-Union (San Francisco). Episcopalian. Republican. Home: 225 Grand Av., South Pasadena, Calif. Office: 810 S. Flower St., Los Angeles, Calif. Died Mar. 20, 1945.

MacCALLUM, John Archibald (măk-kăl'ŭm), clergyman; b. Gananoque, Ont., Can., Feb. 2, 1874; s. Peter and Mary (Kane) MacC.; B.A., Queen's U., Kingston, Ont., 1899; student Columbia, 1900-03; B.D., magna cum laude, Union Theol. Sem., 1903; D.D., Lafayette, 1915; m. Josephine Dickson Russell, May 30, 1904. Ordained Presbyn. ministry, 1903; minister Washingtonville, N.Y., 1903-07, 1st Ch., Chestnut Hill, Phila., 1907-10, Walnut St. Ch., Phila., since 1910. Is the 23d mem. of immediate family connection to be ordained to Presbyn. ministry. Only official rep. of Am. chs. at 13th Internat. Congress On the Lord's Day, Edinburgh, 1908. Mem. bd. Phila. Housing Assn. since 1916, pres. since 1919; mem. Phila. Nat. Council, Housing Com.; mem. bd. of dirs. Ministers' Fund; 1st pres. Com. of 100 (clergy), 1933-35 and chairman of the board of directors since 1935; pres. Union Theol. Alumni Assn., 1923-24; lecturer Inst. of Pub. Affairs, Charlottesville, Va., 1936, 37; mem. com. to Defend America by Aiding the Allies and the Fight for Freedom Com.; mem. Housing Div., Phila. Council of Defense. Trustee Temple Univ., 1918-41; trustee Mercy Hosp.; treas. and mem. bd. dirs. Berean Manual Training Sch., Phila. Member Com. on Edn. and Publicity, Women's Field Army for Cancer Control in U.S.; mem. bd. Phila. Russian War Relief, Inc., Am.-Russian Inst. for Cultural Relations with the Soviet Union; chmn. bd. of North Am. Com. to Aid Spanish Democracy, 1936-39; mem. bd. for Pa., Dogs for Defense, Inc. Clubs: Union League, Contemporary (pres. 1933-35). Author: Now I Know, 1924; The Great Partnership, 1926. Contbr. to mags., reviews and weekly papers; writer of weekly religious column. in Phila. Record. Mem. editorial bd. The Protestant (mag.). Religious adviser to Sta. WFIL and weekly broadcaster of Sunday Devotions program over this station. Home: 3925 Walnut St. Office: 3936 Sansom St., Philadelphia, Pa. Died Dec. 31, 1946.

MacCALLUM, William George, pathologist; b. Dunnville, Ont., Apr. 18, 1874; s. Dr. George Alexander and Florence O. (Eakins) MacC.; B.A., U. of Toronto, 1894; M.D., Johns Hopkins, 1897; unmarried. Asso. prof. pathology, 1900-08, prof. pathol. physiology, 1908-09, Johns Hopkins U.; prof. pathology, Columbia U., 1909-17; prof. pathology and bacteriology, Johns Hopkins U., since 1917. Contbr. to med. jours. on pathol. subjects. Fellow A.A.A.S.; mem. Assn. Am. Physicians, Nat. Acad. Sciences;

hon. fellow Royal Soc. Medicine, London, England; hon. mem. Soc. Medicorum Sverana, Stockholm, 1918. Author: Text-book of Pathology, 1916. Contbr. to Johns Hopkins Hosp. Bull., Jour. A.M.A., Jour. Experimental Medicine, etc. Home: 701 St. Paul St. Address: Johns Hopkins Hospital, Baltimore, Md.* Died Feb. 3, 1944.

MacCOY, William Logan, lawyer, banker; b. Phila., Pa., Mar. 4, 1885; s. Alexander Watt and Emma Martha (Logan) M.; grad. Haverford (Pa.) Sch., 1902; A.B., Princeton U., 1906; LL.B., U. of Pa., 1910; m. Marguerite Pascal Wood, October 16, 1912; children—Janet Morris (Mrs. Robert F. Edgar), Marguerite Wood (wife of Arthur M. Rogers, M.D.), William Logan, Jr. (lt. A.U.S. Air Corps; killed in line of duty June 19, 1943). Teacher Haverford Sch., 1906-07; admitted to Pa. bar, 1910; law clerk with Duane, Morris & Hecksher, Phila., 1910-11; successively mem. law firms of MacCoy, Evans & Hutchinson, MacCoy, Evans, Hutchinson & Lewis, MacCoy, Brittain, Evans & Lewis, until 1938; pres. and dir. Provident Trust Co. of Phila. since 1938; dir. Provident Mutual Life Ins. Co., Westmoreland Coal Co., Westmoreland Inc., Commonwealth Title Company, Goodall Rubber Company, Lyophile-Cryochem Company; manager The Philadelphia Saving Fund Soc. Served in Naval Aviation during World War; commd. ensign U.S.N.R.F. Charter trustee Princeton U., Rutgers Univ., dir. Bryn Mawr Coll., trustee Bryn Mawr Presbyn. Ch.; dir. Bryn Mawr Hosp., Big Brothers Assn., Fairmount Park Art Assn.; chmn. Phila. Co. Emergency Relief Bd., 1933-34. Mem. Phila., Pa. and Am. bar assns., Am. Inst. of Banking, Reserve City Bankers Assn., Pa. Scotch-Irish Soc., Hist. Soc. of Pa., Franklin Inst., Am. Acad. Fine Arts, Am. Acad. Polit. and Social Science. Republican. Presbyn. Clubs: Zeta Psi, Cap and Gown (Princeton); Philadelphia, Rittenhouse, Midday, Corinthian Yacht, Merion Cricket, Princeton (Phila.). Home: 69th and City Line, Overbrook, Philadelphia. Office: Provident Trust Bldg., Philadelphia. Died Jan. 11, 1948.

MacCRACKEN, John Henry, educator, publicist; b. Rochester, Vt., Sept. 30, 1875; s. Henry Mitchell and Catherine (Hubbard) M.; A.B., New York U., 1894, A.M., 1897; Ph.D., U. of Halle-Wittenberg, 1899; LL.D., Westminster Coll., 1903, New York U., 1915, Lehigh U., 1915, Pa. Coll., 1915, Rutgers Coll., 1915; Litt.D., U. of Pa., 1924; Sc.D., Lafayette Coll., 1926; m. Edith Constable, Apr. 20, 1910; children—Louise (Mrs. Robert G. Olmsted), Constable. A. Ogden Butler fellow in philosophy, 1894-95, instr. philosophy, 1896-99, asst. prof., 1899, New York U.; pres. and prof. philosophy, Westminster Coll., Mo., 1899-1903; syndic and prof. politics, New York U., 1903-15, acting chancellor, 1910-11; pres. Lafayette Coll., 1915-26. Asso. dir. Am. Council on Edn., 1930-34; chmn. Internat. Student Service Conf., 1933; del. President's Conf. on Crisis in Edn., 1933; chmn. finance com., World Conf. on Faith and Order; mem. provisional com. of the World Council of Chs.; vice chmn. Nat. Com. on Edn. by Radio, 1931-34. Dir. Brunswick Site Co.; trustee H. Constable Estate. Regional dir. S.A.T.C., 1918; del. Lausanne Conf., 1927, Oxford and Edinburgh Confs., 1937. Pres. Am. Institute of Christian Philosophy; trustee, Alborz College, Teheran, Iran; trustee American University (Cairo, Egypt); trustee Masters School (Dobbs Ferry, N.Y.), 1929. Elector, Hall of Fame. Vice-pres. for Manhattan, Huguenot Society of America; pres. Phi Beta Kappa Alumni of New York, 1929. Presbyterian. Republican. Member Psi Upsilon, Phi Beta Kappa, Tau Beta Pi, Kappa Phi Kappa fraternities. Clubs: University (New York); Cosmos (Washington); Faculty (Easton). Author: College and Commonwealth, 1920. Home: 9 E. 83d St. Office: 111 5th Av., New York. Died Feb. 1, 1948.

MacCURDY, George Grant, anthropologist; b. Warrensburg, Mo., Apr. 17, 1863; s. William J. and Margaret (Smith) M.; grad. State Normal Sch., Warrensburg, Mo., 1887; A.B., Harvard, 1893, A.M., 1894; univs. of Vienna, Paris (Sch. of Anthropology) and Berlin, 1894-98; Ph.D., Yale, 1905; m. Glenn Bartlett, June 30, 1919. Instr. anthropology, 1898-1900, lecturer and curator anthrop. collections, 1902-10, asst. prof. prehistoric archæology and curator anthropol. collections, 1910-23, research asso. with rank of prof. and curator anthropol. collections, 1923-31, now emeritus, all of Yale U. Dir. Am. Sch. of Prehistoric Research in Europe, 1921-22, and since 1924; hon. collaborator Smithsonian Instn., 1927—; trustee Lab. of Anthropology, Santa Fe, N.M.; mem. bd. mgrs. Sch. of Am. Research, Santa Fe, N.M. Fellow Galton Soc. (New York), A.A.A.S. (ex-v.p.); mem. Am. Philos. Soc., Anthrop. Soc. Paris and Brussels, Archæologist Institute America (vice pres., 1947), Am. Ethnological Society America Anthropological Assn. (sec. 1903-16; pres. 1931), Nat. Research Council since 1925, Sigma Xi; corr. mem. Inst. of Coïmbra (Portugal), Sch. Anthropology (Paris), Anthrop. Soc. Washington, Mo. Hist. Soc., Soc. des Américanistes de Paris, Numismatic and Antiquarian Soc. Phila., Anthrop. Soc. Rome, British Speleological Assn. (hon.), British Prehistoric Soc. (hon.). Life mem. Navy League, U.S. Clubs: Graduate (New Haven, Conn.); Harvard of Connecticut (president 1919-20). Author: The Eolithic Problem, 1905; Some Phases of Prehistoric Archæology, 1907; Antiquity of Man in Europe, 1910; A Study of Chiriquian Antiquities, 1911; Human Skeletal Remains from the Highlands of Peru, 1923; Human Origins—a Manual of Prehistory (in 2 vols.), 1924; Prehistoric Man, 1928; The Coming of Man, 1932; also papers on anthrop. subjects. Editor: Early Man, 1937; and Bull. of Am. School of Prehistoric Research. Address: Old Lyme, Conn. Died Nov. 15, 1947.

MacDONALD, Alexander Black, newspaperman; b. New Brunswick, Can., May 6, 1861; s. Rev. Alexander Black and Jemima (McDonald) M.; ed. pub. schs., N.B.; Litt.D., Park Coll., Parkville, Mo., 1931; m. Mary Larkin, Feb. 14, 1893; children—Donald Earl, Frank Emerson, Mary, Arthur Black, Malcolm Alexander. Came to U.S., 1890, naturalized, 1896. Reporter Kansas City (Mo.) Times, 1891-93, Kansas City World, 1893, Star, 1894-1920; on staff Country Gentleman and Ladies' Home Journal, Philadelphia, 1920-28; again with Kansas City Star since 1928. Awarded Pulitzer prize "for best reportorial feat," 1930. Baptist. Mason. Author: Hands Up, 1927. Home: 4420 Norledge Pl. Address: Kansas City Star, Kansas City, Mo. Died Apr. 9, 1942.

MACDONALD, Duncan Black, theol. prof.; b. Glasgow, Scotland, Apr. 9, 1863; s. Thomas and Margaret (Black) M.; M.A., U. of Glasgow, 1885, B.D., 1888, D.D., 1920; at U. of Berlin, 1890-91, 1893; D.D., Trinity Coll., 1909; D.H.L., Jewish Theol. Sem. of America, 1937; came to U.S., 1892; m. Mary Leeds Bartlett, June 22, 1898 (died Aug. 1929). Prof. of Semitic languages, Hartford Theol. Sem., 1892-1931. Haskell lecturer on comparative religion, U. of Chicago, 1906; spl. lecturer, Wellesley Coll., 1907-09, Episcopal Theol. Sch., Cambridge, 1912; Lamson lecturer on Mohammedanism, Hartford Theol. Sem., 1909; head of Mohammedan dept., Kennedy Sch. of Missions, Hartford, 1911-25; Haskell lecturer, Oberlin Coll., 1914, lecturer O.T., Berkeley Div. Sch., 1917, 18. Prof. emeritus Hartford Theol. Sem. and hon. cons. prof. Kennedy Sch. of Missions. Mem. Royal Asiatic Soc. Great Britain, Am. Oriental Soc.; corr. mem. Arab Acad. of Damascus. Author: Development of Muslim Theology, Jurisprudence and Constitutional Theory, 1903; Selections from Ibn Khaldun, 1905; Religious Attitude and Life in Islam, 1909; Aspects of Islam, 1911. Hebrew Literary Genius, an Interpretation, 1933; Hebrew Philosophical Genius, a Vindication, 1935. Recd. a presentation vol. from former pupils, on seventieth birthday, 1933. Discovered in Bodleian Library and published in Jour. Royal Asiatic Soc., Arabic MS. of "Story of Ali Baba and 40 Thieves," being only known Oriental form, 1910. Contbr. to eleventh edit. Ency. Britannica, Encyclopedia of Islam, and various jours. and revs. on subjects connected with Semitic, especially Mohammedan, theology, literature and history. Editor of Galland and Vatican MSS. of 1001 Nights (being completed by William Thomson, of Harvard Univ.). Address: 233 Tryon St., South Glastonbury, Conn. Died Sep. 6, 1943.

MACDONALD, George Saxe, publisher; b. Whitestone, L.I., N.Y., Sept. 10, 1866; s. Mason Allen and Mary Emma (West) MacDonald; educated pub. schs.; married to Mary Louise Brantingham, May 8, 1887 (died January 6, 1945); children—Blanché Louise (Mrs. Henry A. Lockwood), Allan Freeman. Mgr. various cycle cos., 1889-98; head of Macdonald & Co., exporters, 1898-1904; trade paper pub., 1904-17; retired, 1917-21; pres. Tobacco Trade Jour. Co., Macdonald Pub. Co., Lockwood Trade Jour. Co., 1921-43; now pres. Geo. N. Lowery Co., Haberdasher Co., Lockwood Trade Journal Co., Inc.; president Motor Boat Pub. Co., Clothier Pub. Co., 1923-29. Republican. Mem. Dutch Ref. Ch. Home: 79 Sutton Manor, New Rochelle, N.Y. Office: 15 W. 47th St., New York, N.Y. Died Mar. 18, 1945.

MacDONALD, John Alexander, osteopath; b. Alpena, Mich., Nov. 12, 1879; s. Dougald and Anna (Monahon) MacD.; student Alpena High Sch., 1897; D.O., Kirksville (Mo.) Osteopathic Coll., 1904, Mass. Coll. of Osteopathy, 1905; m. Mabel Frances Warren, Dec. 17, 1910; children—Jean, Dougald, John Alexander. Practiced osteopathy in Boston since 1905; pres. Am. Osteopathic Assn., 1929; member board of trustees, Mass. Osteopathic Hosp. Corp. (president 1936-41); mem. bd. trustees A. T. Still Research Inst. Served in Mass. 1st Corps Cadets. Mem. Alumni Assn. of Kirksville Coll. of Osteopathy and Surgery (decade dir. 1900-10; pres. 1940-41). Member Board of Governors, Academy of Applied Osteopathy. Club: New Bedford Yacht. Contbr. to Am. Osteopathic Assn. Journal. Home: 175 Bay State Rd., Boston 15, Mass. Office: 173 Bay State Rd., Boston 15, Mass. Died Mar. 31, 1947.

MacDONALD, Pirie, photographer; b. Chicago, Ill., Jan. 27, 1867; s. Dr. George and Margaret (Reilly) MacD.; m. Emile VanDeursen, 1890. Engaged as photographer since 1883; since 1900 exclusively photographer of men. Has been awarded Cramer grand prize cup, grand prize for portraiture, diamond decoration, the laurel wreath, and 7 gold and 2 silver medals by Photographers' Assn. of America; bronze trophy, Boston, spl. silver medal and later gold medal, Indianapolis, diamond medal, Omaha; gold medal, Phila., gold medal, St. Louis Expn., and medals in London, Birmingham, Belfast, Frankfort, Trier, Amsterdam, Brussels, Nancy and Paris. First and third pres. Professional Photographers Soc. of New York; mem. Chamber Syndicale Française de la Photographie; decorated Officier d'Académie, 1906; Palmes Académique, 1st class, 1920. Hon. fellow Royal Photog. Soc. (Great Britain); mem. council London Salon Photography; mem. St. Andrews Soc. Clubs: Pilgrims, Rotary, Professional Photographers of New York. Studio: 576 5th Av., New York, N.Y. Died Apr. 22, 1942.

MACDOUGALL, Hamilton Crawford, organist; b. Warwick, R.I., Oct. 15, 1858; s. Alexander and Ann Francis (Briggs) M.; ed. pub. schools, Providence, 1867-77, ed. in music under pvt. instruction of J. C. D. Parker, S. B. Whitney, B. J. Lang, of Boston, and Robert Bonner, of Providence, Dr. E. H. Turpin, of London; hon. Mus. Doc., Brown U., 1901; asso. (by exam.) Royal College of Organists, London; m. Alice Gertrude Beede, Sept. 1, 1898 (died Apr. 3, 1934); 1 son, Robert Beede; m. 2d, Elisabeth Gleason, June 22, 1936. Elected dean of the New England Chapter of the Am. Guild of Organists for 3 years, in 1908. Organist Central Bapt. Ch., Providence, 1882-95; at Harvard Ch. (Boston-Brookline), 1895-1900; prof. music, Wellesley, 1900-27, now emeritus. Mgr. Wellesley Coll. Concert Fund, 1900-38. Traveled and studied in England, Germany, and Switzerland; spl. lecturer in music at Brown U., 1908-09, 1910-12; extension lecturer, Brown U., and lecturer, Brooklyn Inst. Arts and Sciences, various years. Founder American Guild Organists (dean Mass. Chapter, 1908-09), Am. Coll. Musicians; pres. R.I. Musical Assn., 1893-94. Author: Early New England Psalmody; An Historical Appreciation, 1620-1820, 1940; Studies in Melody Playing (2 vols.); National Graded Course (7 vols); Sacred Music; Music for Women's Voices; First Lessons in Improvisation; Dramatic Pedal Studies; Operetta "Long Live the King"; etc. Organ editor The Musician, 1908-23; spl. writer for The Diapason since 1919. Home: 29 Dover Rd., Wellesley, Mass.* Deceased.

MacDOUGALL, William Dugald, naval officer; b. Auburn, N.Y., June 20, 1868; s. Clinton Dugald and Eva (Sabine) MacD.; grad. U.S. Naval Acad., 1889; m. Charlotte Sackett Stone, 1898; children—Charlotte (Mrs. Henrik de Kauffmann), Zilla (Mrs. Philip Mason Sears). Promoted ensign, July 1, 1891; lt. jr. grade, Nov. 15, 1898; lt., Mar. 3, 1899; lt. comdr., July 1, 1905; comdr., July 1, 1910; capt., June 13, 1916. Served on San Francisco, Spanish-Am. War, 1898; comd. Villalobos, 1905-06; at Naval War Coll., Newport, R.I., 1906-07; ordnance officer Virginia, 1907-08; navigator Louisiana, 1908-09; exec. officer New Jersey, 1909-10; comdr. Wolverine, 1910; duty with Gen. Bd., Navy Dept., 1910-12; comd. Nashville, 1912-13, Mayflower, 1913-14, at Naval War Coll., 1915; duty Naval Obs., 1915-16; naval attaché Am. Embassy, London, Eng., Sept 18, 1916 Dec. 1917; comd. Tacoma and North Carolina during World War; comd. Nevada, 1919-20; duty Navy Dept., 1920-21; supt. Naval Observatory, Washington, 1922-23; promoted to Rear Admiral June 8, 1923. Comdr. Train Squadron One, U.S. Fleet Base Force, Oct. 8, 1923; comdr. Battleship Div. Four, June 22, 1925, during U.S. fleet cruise to Australia and New Zealand. Comdt. Navy Yard, Portsmouth, N.H., Nov. 1925, 16th Naval Dist., Philippine Islands, Nov. 1928; comdr. Base Force, U.S. Fleet, 1930; comdt. 5th Naval Dist., Hampton Roads, Va., 1931; retired, July 1, 1932. Address: Navy Dept., Washington, D.C. Died Mar. 5, 1943.

MACE, Harold Loring, army officer; b. Lake Helen, Fla., Oct. 10, 1907; s. Loring Poole and Eleanor (Morrish) M.; student U. of Florida, 1926-28; grad. Air Corps Primary Flying Sch., 1929, Advanced Flying Sch., 1929, Tech. Sch., 1932; m. Virginia French Griggs, June 28, 1933; children—Barbara Virginia, Stephen Griggs. Commd. 2d lt., Air Res., 1929, 2d lt., Air Corps, U.S. Army, 1930, advanced through grades to brig. gen., 1944; serving overseas since Jan. 1944. Decorated Air Medal with 2 oak leaf clusters, Distinguished Flying Cross, Legion of Merit (U.S.); Croix de Guerre with Palm (Fr.); Croix de Guerre with Palm (Belgium). Mem. Sigma Phi Epsilon, Quist Birdmen. Home: 138 Stetson Av., Deland, Fla. Address: care The Adjutant General's Office, War Dept., Washington 25. Died Jan. 20, 1946; buried at Manila, P.I.

MacELWEE, Roy Samuel (măk-ĕl'wē), consulting engineer; b. Parkville, Mich., Apr. 12, 1883; s. Rev. Samuel J. and Anna Belle (Mozingo) M.; prep. edn., Hudson River Mil. Acad.; B.S., Columbia, 1907; studied several European univs.; A.M., Ph.D., U. of Berlin, 1915; m. Ellen Mohlau, 1912; m. 2d, Sarah Smyrl, 1923; children—Anne Frances, Roy Samuel, Sarah Margaret. Clerk, salesman, branch manager, Eastman Kodak Company, International Harvester and Otis Elevator companies in European cities, 1899-1914; chief clerk United States Consulate Gen., Berlin, 1915; lecturer on economics and foreign trade, port and terminal engineering, Columbia, 1916-19; prof. Sch. of Foreign Service, Georgetown U., 1919, dean, 1921-22; prof. Coll. of Charleston, 1923, S.C. Mil. Coll. (Citadel), 1927. Asst. mil. instr. Columbia U. Training Corps, 1917; commd. 1st lt. R.R. Transportation Corps of U.S. Army, Feb. 12, 1918; served as aidé to Gen. Goethals; major since 1922; lt. colonel S.P.O.R.C.; agt. Fed. Bd. Voc. Edn., 1918; 2d and 1st asst. dir. and dir. U.S. Bur. Fgn. and Domestic Commerce, Jan. 1, 1919-Mar. 31, 1921; chmn. U.S. Economic Liasion Com.; chmn. U.S. Interdepartment Com. for Commercial Aviation, 1919-21; mem. Com. for Commercial Use of Army Bases; commr. of Port of Charleston, S.C., 1923-30; v.p. (for South Carolina) Great Lakes-St. Lawrence Tidewater Assn., Nat. Rivers and Harbors Congress; dir. Atlantic Deeper Waterways Assn., Am. Bur. of Shipping; del. of U.S. to 14th International Navigation Congress, Cairo, Egypt, 1926; lecturer European univs., engring. socs., and chambers of commerce, Paris and Berlin, 1926. Mem. Soc. Terminal Engrs. (v.p.), Soc. Am. Mil. Engrs., Am. Soc. Mech. Engineers, New York Society Professional Engineers, National Society Professional Engineers, Licensed Professional Engrs. of New York, Pan-Am. Soc., Mil. Order World War Am. Legion, 40 and 8, Theta Delta Chi, Delta Phi Epsilon (co-founder and 1st nat. pres.), Navy League (chmn.) for S.C., 3 European engring. socs.;

fellow American Geographical Society. Episcopalian. Decorations: Officer Polonia Restituta (Poland); Comdr. Crown of Rumania; Chevalier Crown of Italy; Officer Order of Leopold II (Belgium); medals—Victory, D.C. Mil. Engineers. Club: University (Washington). Author: Bread Bullets, 1917; Vocational Education for Foreign Trade and Shipping, 1918; Ports and Terminal Facilities, 1919, 25; Training for Foreign Trade, 1920; Training for the Steamship Business, 1920; Port Development, 1925; Port Glossary, 1927; The Ports of Rumania, 1927; The Great Ship Canals, 1929. Translator of Delbrück's Government and the Will of the People. Co-Author: Paper Work in Export Trade, 1920; Economic Aspects of the Great Lakes-St. Lawrence Ship Channel, 1921, Wharf Management, 1921. Contbr. numerous articles to mags. Drew waterfront and port development plan for Toledo, O., Cleveland, O., Canaveral, Fla., and Turiamo, Venezuela, also fixed bridge report, Chicago, port plans for Green Bay and Marinette, Wis., Sandusky, O., Rochester, N.Y.; designed and supervised constrn. Charlotte Terminal, Port of Rochester, N.Y., etc. Home: 3726 18th St. N. Office: War Dept. Ocean Traffic Branch, Water Division, Transportation Corps, Army Supply Forces, Pentagon Bldg., Arlington, Va. Died Feb. 6, 1944.

MacEWEN, Ewen Murchison (măk-ū'ĕn), dean coll. of medicine; b. Greenwich, Prince Edward Island, Can., Sept. 16, 1885; s. William Henry and Marion Cameron (Murchison) M.; brought to U.S., 1899; student Buena Vista Coll., Storm Lake, Ia., 1902-03; and 1904-05; Parson's Coll., Fairfield, Ia., 1903-04; B.S., Coe Coll., Cedar Rapids, Ia., 1907; M.D., State U. of Ia., 1912, M.S., 1915; m. Hazel Martha Hayward, June 10, 1913; children—Helen Martha (Mrs. Frank L. Bauer), Marion Murchison (Mrs. Glenn D. Devine, Jr.). Instr. anatomy, State U. of Iowa, 1914-15, asst. prof., 1915-18, asso. prof., 1918-20, prof. since 1920, head of dept. of anatomy, 1931-40, dean of coll. of medicine since 1935; pres. First Federal Loan & Investment Co.; v.p. Ia. State Bank & Trust Co. Mem. A.M.A., Assn. Am. Med. Colls. (pres. 1943, chmn. exec. council since 1944), Am. Assn. Anatomists, Am. Assn. Phys. Anthropologists, A.A.A.S., Nu Sigma Nu, Sigma Xi, Alpha Omega Alpha. Republican. Presbyterian. Clubs: Kiwanis, Triangle. Home: 315 Fairview Av. Office: Medical Laboratory, Iowa City, Ia. Died Sept. 2, 1947.

MacEWEN, Walter, artist; b. Chicago; pupil Cormon and Tony Robert-Fleury, Paris. Represented by pictures in Art Inst. Chicago, Luxembourg, Paris, museums of Ghent, Liège, Magdeburg, Cleveland, Los Angeles, Honolulu, Corcoran Art Gallery, Washington, mus. at Budapest, Pa. Acad. Fine Arts Telfair Mus., Savannah, Ga. Decorated the hall to reading rooms in Congressional Library, Washington. Hon. mention, Salon, 1886; silver medal, Paris Expn., 1889; grand gold medal, City of Berlin, 1891; silver medal, London, 1890; medal, Chicago Expn., 1893; medal of honor, Antwerp, 1894; small gold medal, Munich, 1897; silver medal, Paris Expn., 1900; large gold medal, Munich, 1901, Vienna, 1902; Lippincott prize, Phila., 1902; Harris prize, Chicago, 1902; gold medal, St. Louis Expn., 1904; gold medal, Liège, Belgium; Proctor prize for portraiture, N.A.D., 1919. Chevalier Legion of Honor, France, Officer, 1908; Chevalier Order St. Michel, Bavaria; Officer Order of Leopold, Belgium, 1909. A.N.A.; 1st v.p. Paris Soc. Am. Painters; mem. Nat. Inst. Arts and Letters. Mem. Internat. Jury Awards, Panama P.I. Expn., 1915. Address: Century Club, 7 W. 43d St., New York; also 11 rue Georges Berger, Paris, France.* Died Mar. 20, 1943.

MACFARLANE, W. E., business mgr. Chicago Tribune; pres. Mutual Broadcasting System; v.p. WGN. Office: Tribune Tower, Chicago, Ill.* Died Oct. 8, 1944.

MACFARLAN, Will(iam) C(harles), organist; b. London, Eng., Oct. 2, 1870; s. Duncan and Eliza M.; came to U.S. with parents at 4; M.A. (hon.), Bates Coll., 1915; studied music with father and Samuel P. Warren, New York; m. Madeleine Goodwillie, June 2, 1896. Chorister, Christ Ch., New York, 1880-85; debut as concert organist, Chickering Hall, 1886, and has since given many concerts in leading cities of U.S.; organist, St. John's M.E. Ch., New York, 1885-86, St. James Ch., Danbury, Conn., 1886-87, Ch. of Messiah, New York, 1887-89, All Souls' Ch., New York, 1889-1900, Temple Emanu-el, and St. Thomas's Ch., New York, until 1912; municipal organist, Portland, Me., since 1912 (first organist engaged directly by a municipality in U.S.). Fellow Am. Coll. Musicians; a founder Am. Guild Organists (Clemson gold medal, 1897). Awarded W. W. Kimball prize by Chicago Madrigal Club, 1911, 14, 17. Composer: Message from the Cross (cantata); Little Almond Eyes (operetta); Swords and Scissors (operetta); music to patriotic hymn, "America the Beautiful"; organ pieces, etc. Address: City Hall, Portland, Me. Died May 12, 1945.

MacGILVARY, Norwood (măk-gĭl'vȧ-rĭ), painter, teacher; b. of Am. parents at Bangkok, Siam, Nov. 14, 1874; s. Rev. Daniel (D.D.) and Sophia (Bradley) MacG.; brother of Evander Bradley McGilvary; A.B., Davidson (N.C.) Coll., 1896; U. of Calif., 1896-97, Mark Hopkins Inst., San Francisco, 1897-98; pupil of Jean Paul Laurens, Académie Julian, Paris, 1904-06, also of Myron Barlow, Etaples, France; studied in galleries of Holland and Italy; m. Adeline Kaji, 1918; children—Winifred Sophia, Daniel Bradley. Figure and landscape painter; formerly illustrator for mags.; asso. prof. painting, Carnegie Inst. Tech., Pittsburgh, since 1921. Exhibited Salon, Paris; Nat. Acad. Design, New York; Pa. Acad. Fine Arts, Phila.; Corcoran Gallery, Washington, D.C.; Carnegie Inst., Pittsburgh; Art Inst., Chicago; Kansas City Museum, etc. Represented in permanent collections Nat. Gallery, Washington, D.C., by "Twilight After Rain." Silver medal, for "Nocturne," San Francisco Expn., 1915; 1st prize, Associated Artists, Pittsburgh. Mem. Am. Water Color Soc., Associated Artists of Pittsburgh (president 1944), Rehoboth Art League, Pittsburgh Art Commn. (sec.), Am. Assn. U. Profs., Sigma Alpha Epsilon, Tau Sigma Delta, Phi Kappa Phi. Clubs: Salmagundi (New York); Authors' (Pittsburgh). Home: 8 Roselawn Terrace. Pittsburgh 13, Pa. Died July 6, 1949.

MacGOWAN, John Kee, business exec.; b. Phila., Pa., Dec. 19, 1878; s. John Kee and Mary W. (Petersen) MacG.; student Girard Coll. Began as agent of St. Louis & San Francisco R.R.; became purchasing agent for Guggenheim mining interests throughout the world; partner Guggenheim Bros. for 5 yrs.; pres. Empyre Fire Extinguisher Corp., N.Y. City; dir. Auburn Central Mfg. Co., Standard Gas & Electric Co., Chicago, Central Foundry Co., N.Y. City. Republican. Episcopalian. Clubs: Metropolitan, St. Nicholas, Pilgrims, Recess (N.Y. City). Home: Miami, Fla. Died Nov. 22, 1942.

MACINTOSH, Douglas Clyde (măk'ĭn-tŏsh), theologian; b. Breadalbane, Ont., Can., Feb. 18, 1877; s. Peter and Elizabeth Charlotte (Everett) M.; A.B., McMaster Univ., Toronto, 1903; Ph.D., U. of Chicago, 1909; M.A., Yale, 1916; D.D., Colgate, 1926; LL.D., McMaster, 1932; m. Emily Powell, 1921 (died 1922); m. 2d, Hope Griswold Conklin, 1925. Minister, Bapt. Ch., Marthaville, Ont., 1897-99; instr. philosophy, McMaster U., 1903-04; ordained Bapt. ministry, 1907; prof. Bibl. and systematic theology, Brandon (Manitoba) Coll., 1907-09; asst. prof. systematic theology, 1909-16, Dwight prof. theology, Yale, 1916-32, prof. theology and philosophy of religion, 1933-42, prof. emeritus since 1942. Taught at U. of Chicago, 1919, 23. Chmn. dept. of religion, Yale Grad. Sch., 1920-38. Chaplain, rank of capt., Can. E.F., Eng. and France, 1916; Y.M.C.A. sec. with A.E.F., France, 1918. Lecturer, Nat. Council of Congl. and Christian Chs., Oberlin, O., 1934; Swander lectures, Reformed Theol. Sem., Lancaster, Pa., 1935; Foerster lecture on Immortality, U. of Calif., 1937; Dudleian lecture on Immortality, Harvard, 1941. Mem. Am. Philos. Assn., Am. Theol. Soc., bd. mgrs. Bapt. Ednl. Bd., 1936-42, Conf. on Science, Philosophy and Religion. Author: The Reaction Against Metaphysics in Theology, 1911; The Problem of Knowledge, 1915; God in a World at War, 1918; Theology as an Empirical Science, 1919; The Reasonableness of Christianity (Taylor lectures, Yale, 1924, and Bross prize, Lake Forest U.), 1925, issued as Vernunftgemässes Christentums (Gotha, Germany) 1928; The Pilgrimage of Faith in the World of Modern Thought (Stephanos Nirmalendu Ghosh lectures on Comparative Religion, U. of Calcutta, 1928), 1931; Social Religion, 1939; The Problem of Religious Knowledge, 1940; Personal Religion, 1942; Plain Man's Soliloquy, a philosophical autobiography with 90 illus. and charts, drawn by author, to be published. Editor of G. B. Foster's Christianity in Its Modern Expression, 1921; editor and contbr. Religious Realism, 1931; contbr. Humanism, Another Battle Line, 1931; Is There a God?, 1932. Contemporary American Theology, 1932; The Process of Religion, 1933; Luther, Kant, Schleiermacher (pub. in Berlin), 1939; Science, Philosophy and Religion, 1941; Liberal Theology an Appraisal, 1942; Twentieth Century Philosophers, 1943; articles to philos. and theol. jours. Asso. editor, Webster's New Internat. Dictionary 2d edit., 1934. American citizenship denied by U.S. District Court for Conn., 1929; granted by U.S. Circuit Ct. of Appeals, 1930; reversed by U.S. Supreme Ct., 1931. Address: 25 Woodlawn St., Hamden 14, Conn. July 6, 1948.

MACK, Edgar M., merchant; b. Indiana, Pa., May 17, 1877; s. D. C. and Emma K. (Wilson) M.; C.E., Lehigh U., 1904; m. Lila W. Purington, July 18, 1906; 1 dau., Martha P. With G. C. Murphy Co., 5 and 10c stores, McKeesport, Pa., as chmn. of the board dirs., dir. and vice-pres.; pres. and dir. Mack Realty Co.; dir. Union Trust Co., Pittsburgh, Pa. Mem. McKeesport Sch. Board. Club: Rotary. Home: 1501 Beech Ct. Office: 531 Fifth Av., McKeesport, Pa. Deceased.

MACK, Edwin S., lawyer; b. Cincinnati, O., Dec. 27, 1869; s. Herman S. and Jennie (Wolf) M.; student Harvard, 1887-93 (A.B., A.M., LL.B.); m. Della Adler, Oct. 9, 1900; children—Theresa (Mrs. Walter J. Goldsmith), Jean (Mrs. Roy M. Greenthal), Elizabeth (Mrs. Richard J. Kornhauser). Admitted to Wis. bar, 1893; served as law clerk and then practiced law alone, 1893-1906; partner firm Miller, Mack & Fairchild, Milwaukee, since 1906; lecturer in law, U. of Wis., 1903-05, prof. of law, 1905-06; special counsel to Wis. atty. gen., enforcing govt. food regulations, 1917. Mem. Milwaukee, Wis. and Am. bar assns., Assn. Bar of City of N.Y., Am. Law Inst., Phi Beta Kappa, Phi Alpha Delta. Club: University (Milwaukee). Author of legal and hist. studies, including "Founding of Milwaukee." Home: 2215 North Lake Drive. Office: 1504 First Wisconsin Nat. Bank Bldg., Milwaukee, Wis. Died Apr. 9, 1942.

MACK, Julian William, judge; b. San Francisco, Calif., July 19, 1866; s. William J. and Rebecca (Tandler) M.; ed. pub. sch., Cincinnati, 1872-84; LL.B., Harvard, 1887; Parker fellow, Harvard, 1887-90, at univs. of Berlin and Leipzig; m. Jessie Fox, Mar. 9, 1896 (died Nov. 30, 1938); 1 daughter, Dr. Ruth Mack Brunswick; m. 2d, Cecile B. Blumgart, September 4, 1940. Admitted to bar, 1890; professor law, Northwestern University, 1895-1902, University of Chicago, 1902-40, professor emeritus since October 1940. Civil service commr., Chicago, Jan.-May 1903; judge Circuit Ct. of Cook County, Ill., 1903-11; assigned as judge of Juvenile Ct., Chicago, 1904-07, as judge Appellate Ct., 1st Ill. Dist., 1909-11; appointed U.S. Circuit judge, 1911; assigned to U.S. Commerce Court, 1911-13 to various U.S. Circuit Courts of Appeal and U.S. Dist. Courts, 1914-41; retired September 1941. Appointed July 13, 1917, chairman section on compensation and ins. of soldiers and sailors and their dependents of Com. of Labor of Council Nat. Defense; umpire Nat. War Labor Bd.; mem. Bd. of Inquiry on Conscientious Objectors, War Dept. Pres. Palestine Endowment Funds, Inc.; hon. pres. World Jewish Congress; v.p. and chmn. bd. Survey Associates; ex-mem. bd. overseers Harvard (3d term); ex-pres. Am. Jewish Congress, Zionist Organization America; Comité des Delegations Juives, Paris, Nat. Conf. Jewish Social Work, Nat. Conf. Social Work, Friends of Russian Freedom of Chicago, Immigrants' Protective League, Infants' Welfare Soc.; ex-v.p. Children's Hosp. Soc., Soc. for Social Hygiene; ex-dir. Asso. Jewish Charities, Chicago. Mem. Am. Bar Assn., Ill. State Bar Assn., Chicago Bar Assn., Assn. Bar City of New York, Nat. Lawyers Guild. Democrat. Clubs: Harvard (ex-pres.), Chicago Literary, Law, City (Chicago); Lawyers (hon.), Metropolis (New York). Home: 24 5th Av., New York, N.Y. Died Sep. 4, 1943.

MACK, William, law editor; b. Sumter County, S.C., Oct. 24, 1865; s. Rev. Joseph Bingham and Harriet Hudson (Banks) M.; A.B., Davidson Coll., N.C., A.M., 1883, LL.D., 1907; LL.B., U. of Mo., 1887, LL.D., 1914; m. Minnie Frank Bayles, June 1, 1899; 1 son, William Bayles. Admitted to bar, 1887; sec. Am. Law Book Co. since 1900. Mem. Am. and N.Y. State bar assns., Mo. Soc., Southern Soc., N.E. Soc., Soc. Mayflower Descendants, Sigma Alpha Epsilon, Phi Beta Kappa. Mason, Royal Arcanum. Author: Digest of American State Reports, 1923; Rapalje and Mack's Digest of Railway Decisions, 1895; Encyclopedia of Forms and Precedents, 1897. Editor-in-chief Cyclopedia of Law and Procedure, 1900-12, Corpus Juris, 1914-35, and of Corpus Juris Secundum since 1936. Died Dec. 10, 1941.

MacKEACHIE, Douglas Cornell (măk-kē'chē), govt. official; b. Brooklyn, N.Y., Dec. 4, 1900; s. Samuel Stevenson and Jane Adele (Cornell) M.; grad. Ridgewood (N.J.) High Sch., 1917; student Colgate U., 1917-19; m. Martha Hoagland Bade, 1939; 1 dau., Nancy Jane. With Atlantic & Pacific Tea Co. since 1919, successively as office employe, buyer and purchasing dir., dep. dir. of purchases, Office of Production Management, Oct. 1940-Aug. 1941, dir. Aug. 1941; dep. dir. Procurement and distribution, Services of Supply, War Dept. (as civilian), Feb. 1942; commd. col. and sent overseas to be U.S.A. gen. purchasing agent for European Theatre of Operations, May 1942; pres. Atlantic & Pacific Co. of Vt. Dir. New Eng. Council. Clubs: Longwood Cricket (Brookline, Mass.); Algonquin (Boston); Metropolitan (Washington, D.C.). Home: Millbrook Pan-Am. Poets' League of N. Am., 1943. Given nat. testimonial on 70th birthday, announcing his Tetralogy for the Theatre; The Mystery of Hamlet, King of Denmark, comprising the four plays: The Ghost of Elsinore, The Fool in Eden Garden, Odin Against Christus, The Serpent in the Orchard, 1945. Edited The Journal (1898-1939) of Marion Morse MacKaye, 1946. Home Cornish, N.H. P.O. Windsor, Vt. Died Feb. 1943.

MACKELLAR, William Henry Howard (măk-kĕl'ẽr), educator; b. Greenwood, S.C., Dec. 1, 1863; s. William Pickins and Augusta (Latimer) M.; B.A., U. of the South, 1890; M.A., 1891; LL.D., Chattanooga College of Law, 1929; m. Elizabeth Anderson Hall, Oct. 3, 1893; 1 dau., Juliet Latimer. Teacher in U. of the South since 1886; head pub. speaking dept. since 1916. Commd. lt. col. Mo. N.G., 1913. Mem. Nat. Council Am. Econ. League, Am. Polit. Science Assn., Am. Acad. Polit. and Social Science, Am. Assn. Univ. Profs., Southern Polit. Science Assn., Phi Beta Kappa, Alpha Tau Omega. Democrat. Episcopalian. Mason. Club: Civitan. Home: Sewanee, Tenn. Died Oct. 1, 1946.

MACKENZIE, Donald, prof. theology; b. Ross Shire, Scotland, May 30, 1882; s. Donald and Janet (Mackenzie) M.; student Nicolson Inst., at Stornoway, 1900; M.A., U. of Aberdeen (Scotland), 1905; grad. United Free Ch. Coll., Aberdeen, 1910; student Univ. of Halle (Germany), 1909, U. of Berlin, 1909; D.D., Washington and Jefferson Coll., 1931, University of Aberdeen, 1934; m. Alice A. Murray, Sept. 7, 1910; children—Alice M. (wife of Rev. William T. Swain, Jr.), Elizabeth M., Janet C., Donald C. Came to U.S., 1928. Asst. prof. logic and metaphysics, Aberdeen U., 1906-09; ordained to ministry United Free Ch., 1910; pastor, Scotland, 1910-28; Elliott lecturer Western Theol. Sem., Pittsburgh, 1926, prof. theology, 1928-33; Sprunt lecturer Union Theol. Sem., Richmond, Va., 1933; prof. of Biblical theology, Princeton Theol. Sem. since 1933. Author: Christianity—The Paradox of God, 1933. Contbr. to religious and philos. publs. Died Oct. 19, 1941.

MACKENZIE, Philip Edward, judge of the Court of Appeal for Saskatchewan; b. London, Ont., Jan. 9, 1872; s. Philip and Elizabeth (Langley) MacK.; student Collegiate Inst., London, Ont., 1885-1889;

B.A., U. of Toronto, 1893, LL.B., 1895, LL.D., 1943; student Law Sch. Osgoode Hall, Toronto, 1893-96; m. Agnes Strickland Vickers, Sept. 24, 1902. Called to Ont. bar, June 1896; practiced law, London, Ont., 1896-1901, Kenora, Ont., 1901-10, Saskatoon, Saskatchewan, 1910-21; apptd. judge Court of Kings Bench, 1921-27; judge of Court of Appeal, since 1927. Mem. bd. of govs., U. of Saskatchewan, since 1922, chancellor since 1939. Mem. Kappa Alpha (Toronto). Clubs: Assiniboia, Wascana Golf (Regina, Sask.), Union, Victoria Golf (Victoria, B.C.). Mem. Anglican Ch. Home: 2060 Lorne St. Address: Court of Appeal for Saskatchewan, Court House, Regina, Saskatchewan, Can. Died June 19, 1946.

MACKENZIE, Thomas Hanna, clergyman; b. Sewickley, Pa., Nov. 18, 1867; s. Rev. William Adams (D.D.) and Martha J. (Hanna) M.; A.B., Monmouth Coll., 1888, A.M., 1891; D.D., Rutgers, 1912; studied Xenia and Princeton theol. sems.; m. Frances MacMillan, May 14, 1891; children—Donald, Malcolm. Ordained ministry U.P. Ch., 1890; pastor Pine Bush, N.Y., 1890-96, Ref. Ch. in America, Port Jervis, 1896-1905, Flushing, 1905-38; minister emeritus, Reformed Ch. of Flushing since 1938. Chmn. exec. com. Bd. Foreign Missions, Ref. Chs. in America since 1904; pres. Gen. Council Ref. Chs. holding Presbyn. System, 1918-20; pres. Gen. Synod Ref. Ch. in America, 1921-22; chmn. Progress Council Ref. Ch. in America, 1923-36; mem. bd. mgrs. New Brunswick Theol. Sem. since 1923; mem. bd. mgrs. Am. Tract Soc., 1924-34; mem. bd. mgrs. Am. Bible Soc. since 1928; pres. North Shore Public Nursing Assn., 1929-35; mem. bd. dirs. Associated Charities, Flushing; pres. Queens Borough Fedn. of Chs., 1936. Grand Chaplain Grand Lodge State of N.Y., F. and A.M., 1920-24. Democrat. Home: Gibson Apts., Flushing, N.Y. Died June 6, 1942.

MACKENZIE, William Adams, lawyer; b. Sewickley, Pa., Feb. 20, 1870; s. William Adams and Martha (Hanna) M.; student Monmouth (Ill.) Coll., 1889-1890; A.B., Princeton, 1892; LL.B., Albany (N.Y.) Law Sch., 1894; m. Mariella Grant, Nov. 1, 1904; children—Margaret (Mrs. John R. Hamel), Alexander Roy. Admitted to N.Y. bar, 1895, and since in practice, Syracuse, N.Y.; now mem. Mackenzie, Smith, & Mitchell; dir. L. C. Smith & Corona Typewriters Inc., Crucible Steel Co. of America, Great Lakes Steamship Co., Toledo Shipbuilding Co., New Process Gear Corp., The Syracuse Trust Co. Served as sergt., U.S. Army, Spanish-Am. War. Dir. Pebble Hill Sch., Syracuse Symphony Orchestra. Republican. Presbyterian. Clubs: Century, University (Syracuse); Princeton, Broad Street (New York); Cazenovia, Cazenovia Golf; Onondaga Golf and Country. Home: 1 Brattle Rd. Office: Onondaga County Bank Bldg., Syracuse, N.Y. Died Aug. 29, 1943.

MACKIE, Joseph Bolton Cooper (măk'ē), clergyman; b. Frankford, Phila., Pa., Sept. 5, 1882; s. Dr. Alexander J. H. and Alice Bolton (Cooper) M.; A.B., Geneva Coll., 1904; student Princeton Theol. Sem., 1904-07, M.A., Post Grad. Sch., Princeton U., 1907; D.D. (hon.), Geneva Coll., 1921; m. Marguerite McCann, Oct. 21, 1909 (died 1916); children—Horace A., Joseph R.; m. 2d, Emily Helen Dobbs, July 28, 1920; 1 dau., Edna Helen. Asst. minister First Presbyn. Ch., Germantown, Phila., 1907-09; minister, Carmel Presbyn. Ch., Edge Hill, Pa., 1909-17, Haddonfield (N.J.) Presbyn. Ch., 1917-21, Northminster Presbyn. Ch., Phila., since 1921. Moderator of Synod of Pa., Presbyn. Ch. in U.S. of Am., 1936-37; candidate for moderator Gen. Assembly, 1940; chmn. com. on Bills and Overtures, Gen. Assembly, 1940. Trustee Tennent Coll. (Phila.), Presbyn. Hosp. (Phila.), Presbytery of Phila., Nat. Temperance and Publ. Soc. (N.Y. City). Mem. Presbyn. Ministers' Social Union, St. Andrews Soc. Republican. Presbyn. Clubs: Canterbury Cleric, Twentieth Century Cleric, Union League (Phila.); Princeton (N.J.) Symposium. Address: 3504 Baring St., Philadelphia, Pa. Died Feb. 22, 1942.

MACKINTOSH, Alexander, architect; b. London, Eng., Oct. 2, 1861; s. Alexander and Elizabeth (Smith) M.; student Science and Art Dept. of Her Majesty's Council on Edn., Watt Inst. and Sch. of Arts, Edinburgh, 1885, Royal Acad., London, 1889-90; m. Jeannette E. Day, Dec. 6, 1911 (died June 9, 1945); 1 son, Alexander Day. Came to U.S., 1893, naturalized Oct. 14, 1903. Apprenticed for archtl. training 5 yrs., Inverness, Scotland; worked in Edinburgh and Glasgow, with Sir Aston Webb and other notables, London, 1888, with Francis H. Kimbell, New York, N.Y., 1893-1901; in pvt. practice of architecture, N.Y. City, 1901-Aug. 2, 1945; chief architect Garfield Court Housing project, Long Branch, N.J., 1940. Served in Troop C, Brooklyn, N.Y., Oct. 8, 1897-Nov. 3, 1903. Worked with U.S. Shipping Bd. in housing div. as project supervisor, World War I. Awarded 1st prize for design, Royal Acad., London, Lower Sch., 1889, Upper Sch., 1890. Fellow A.I.A., 1932, Royal Inst. of British Architects; A.I.A. (sec., 1903-05, pres. Brooklyn chapter, 1910-12). Mem. N.J. Soc. of Architects (Newark); St. Andrew's Soc. (N.Y.). Republican. Episcopalian. Home: 624 Woodgate Av., Long Branch, N.J. Died, Aug. 2, 1945.

MacLANE, Mary (Miss), author; b. Winnipeg, Man., May 2, 1881; d. James W. and Margaret L. M.; grad. Butte (Mont.) High Sch., 1899. Writer for New York World, Aug. 1902. Author: Story of Mary MacLane, 1902; My Friend Annabel Lee, 1903. Address: (summer) Rockland, Mass.; (winter) St. Augustine, Fla. Died Aug. 6, 1929.

MacLAREN, Malcolm (măk-lăr'ĕn), electrical engr.; b. Annapolis, Md., June 21, 1869; s. Donald and Elizabeth Stockton (Green) MacL.; A.B., Princeton, 1890, E.E., 1892, A.M., 1893; m. Angelina Post Hodge, June 1900; children—Malcolm, Angelina Hodge, Wistar Hodge, Elizabeth Green. Engr. with Westinghouse Elec. & Mfg. Co., Pittsburgh, 1893-98 and 1905-08, London, Eng., 1898-1900; chief elec. engr., British Westinghouse Electric & Mfg. Co., Manchester, Eng., 1900-05; prof. elec. engring., Princeton, 1908-37; retired. Commd. capt., Engr. R.C., Dec. 1917; maj. N.A., Apr. 1918; lt. col., Engr. R.C., July 1919; col., 1924; on duty at Washington during service. Mem. Am. Inst. Elec. Engrs. Republican. Presbyterian. Home: Princeton, N.J. Died Sep. 24, 1945.

MacLEAN, Arthur Winfield (măk-lān'), educator; b. Lowell, Mass., Nov. 25, 1880; s. Winfield S. and Emma G. (Hanson) MacL.; A.B., Boston Univ., 1903, LL.B., and J.M., from same, 1906; Litt.D., Portia College, 1936; m. Bertha L. Robinson, May 23, 1910 (divorced); children—Lowell S., Barbara, Jean; m. 2d, Mary Theresa Coleman, August 19, 1941. Admitted to Mass. bar, 1906; founder, 1908, since dean, treasurer, trustee and professor contracts since 1908 and constl. law since 1922, Portia Law School (exclusively for women), Boston; founder and dean Portia College (co-educational), Boston, 1934 (name changed to Calvin Coolidge College, 1940); founder and dean Calvin Coolidge Law School (for men), Boston, 1940; prof. real property and wills, Suffolk Law Sch., 1906-22. Mem. Am. Bar Assn., Constitutional Liberty League, Benjamin Franklin Society, Nat. Assn. of Law Schs. (pres. 1938, 39), Gamma Eta Gamma (Past High Chancellor), Pi Gamma Mu, Beta Theta Pi. Republican. Episcopalian; former sr. warden St. James P.E. Church, Cambridge, Mass. Mason. Club: Boston City. Author: Law of Real Property, 1922; Law of Wills and Administration, 1923; Constitutional Law, 1930; Law of Contracts, 1931. Address: 45 Mt. Vernon St., Boston, Mass. Died Feb. 28, 1943.

MacLEAN, James Alexander, univ. pres.; b. Mayfair, Ont., Aug. 2, 1868; s. Alexander and H. (Bateman) M.; A.B., U. of Toronto, 1892; A.M., Columbia, 1893, Ph.D., 1894; LL.D., U. of Colo., 1905; m. Mary V. Robinson, Oct. 5, 1907. Prof. polit. science, U. of Colo., 1894-1900; pres. U. of Ida., Sept. 1900-Jan. 1913, U. of Manitoba, Can., 1913-34, retired. Address: Glencoe, Ont., Can. Died Jan. 18, 1945.

MACLEAN, John Norman, clergyman; b. Antigonish, N.S., Can., July 28, 1862; s. Norman and Mary (Macdonald) M.; Pictou Acad.; Dalhousie Coll., Halifax, N.S.; B.A., U. of Man., 1890, M.A., 1893; grad. San Francisco Theol. Sem., 1893; D.D., Parsons Coll., Ia., 1910; m. Clara Evelyn Davidson, Aug. 1, 1893; children—Norman Fitzroy, Paul Davidson. Ordained Presbyn. ministry, 1893; pastor Vacaville, Calif., 1892-97, Bozeman, Mont., 1897-1902, Clarinda, Ia., 1902-09, Missoula, Mont., 1909-25; synodical exec. Presbyn. Synod of Mont., 1925-33. Elected pres. Coll. of Mont., 1913, but declined; commr. to Gen. Assembly of Presbyn. Ch. in U.S.A., 5 times; moderator Synod of Mont., 1914. Retired, 1935. Mason. Home: 217 Blaine St., Missoula, Mont. Died Dec. 30, 1941.

MacLEAN, Ray Butts, educator; born Prescott, Wis., Feb. 18, 1873; s. Alexander and Susan Eunice (Butts) MacL.; Ph.B., Hamline U., 1896; M.A., U. of Minn., 1923; Ped.D., Hamline University, 1934; m. Winona M. Lewis, Aug. 10, 1899; 1 dau., Frances. Teacher country sch., Pierce County, Wis., 1890-92; supt. schs., Appleton, Minn., 1896-98, Prescott, Wis., 1898-1900, Dodge Center, Minn., 1900-05, Wheaton, Minn., 1905-07, Fergus Falls, 1907-13; state dir. elementary schs., Minn., 1913-23; pres. State Teachers Coll., Moorhead, Minn., 1923-41. Mem. N.E.A., Minn. Edn. Assn. (pres. 1925), Phi Delta Kappa, Kappa Delta Pi. Author: (with H. E. Flynn) Minnesota and the Junior Citizen, 1936. Editor: (with others) Voices of Verse, 1933. Home: 1361 N. Cleveland Av., St. Paul. Died Aug. 10, 1947.

MACLENNAN, Francis William, mining engr.; b. Cornwall, Ont., Can., Oct. 14, 1876; s. Donald B. and Elizabeth M. (Cline) M.; E.E., McGill University, Montreal, 1898, M.E., 1900; studied Liège U., Belgium, 1898-99; LL.D., McGill University, 1931; m. Alta May Clack, Aug. 7, 1919. Engr. and assayer various mines in B.C., 1900-03, later with mines in Ore., Utah and Nev.; gen. supt. mines, Cerro de Pasco Copper Co., Peru, 1907-10; examination and reports on mines in U.S., Can. and S.A., 1910-13; with Miami (Ariz.) Copper Co. since 1913, as mine supt., 1919-38, gen. mgr., v.p. and cons. engr. since 1938. Naturalized citizen of U.S., 1920. Mem. Am. Inst. Mining and Metall. Engrs., Mining and Metall. Soc. America, Canadian Inst. of Mining and Metallurgy, Zeta Psi. Awarded William Lawrence Saunders gold medal, Am. Inst. Mining and Metall. Engrs., 1931. Clubs: California, Wilshire Country, Los Angeles Country (Los Angeles, Calif.); Arizona, Phoenix Country (Phoenix, Ariz.); Cobre Valle Country (Miami, Ariz.). Home: 406 S. June St., Los Angeles, Calif. Died June 28, 1947; buried in Forest Lawn Memorial Park.

MacLEOD, Donald Campbell, clergyman; b. Inverness County, N.S., Can., Nov. 13, 1868; s. Angus Finlay and Mary (Campbell) MacL.; A.B., Franklin Coll., New Athens, O., 1895, A.M., 1898, D.D., 1912; grad. Western Theol. Sem., Pittsburgh, 1898; m. Georgia Porter, Nov. 21, 1899. Ordained Presbyn. ministry, 1898; pastor Meadville, Pa., 1898-99, 1st Ch., Washington, D.C., 1899-1913 (successor to late Rev. T. DeWitt Talmage), 1st Ch., Springfield, Ill., 1913-18, Central Presbyn. Ch. (U.S.), St. Louis, 1918-23, Dundee Presbyn. Ch., Omaha, 1923-29; sec. Presbytery of St. Louis, 1929; pastor Lower Brandywine Presbyn. Ch., Wilmington, Del., since 1933. Democrat. Address: 1510 Delaware Av., Wilmington, Del. Died Oct. 27, 1942.

Mac LEOD-THORP, Mrs. L. E. G., artist; b. London, England; d. Robert Spring (of Aberdeen, Scotland) and Louisa (Clarke) Garden; grad. Royal Sch., South Kensington, London; pupil of N. E. Green, George Leslie (R. A.), Henry Fiske, Richard Eschke, Leandro Ramon Garrido; also studied in the Whistler School, Paris; m. Malcolm MacLeod, Mar. 14, 1890 (died Feb. 13, 1914); m. 2d, Compton P. Thorp, 1921. Removed to Calif., 1887; founder and dir. of Los Angeles Sch. of Art and Design; retired 1919. Exhibited in London, Birmingham, Nottingham, Manchester and Liverpool galleries, Eng., and Dresden, Germany. Mem. Fine Arts League, Los Angeles, Southern Calif. Acad. Science; hon. mem. Southern Calif. Art Club, Ruskin Art Club. Home: 403 S. Occidental Blvd., Los Angeles, Calif. Died June 24, 1944.

MacMILLAN, Conway, state botanist of Minn.; b. Hillsdale, Mich., Aug. 26, 1867; s. George and Josephine (Young) MacM.; grad. Univ. of Neb., 1885, A.M., 1886; grad. studies at Harvard and Johns Hopkins; m. Maud R. Sanborn, Aug. 8, 1891. Hon. commr. U.S. Dept. of Agr. to Eng., 1897; prof. botany, U. of Minn., since 1891. Mem. Am. Bot. Soc., Société Botanique de France. Author: Twenty-two Common Insects of Nebraska; The Metaspermae of the Minnesota Valley; Minnesota Plant Life; etc. Editor: Minnesota Botanical Studies; Postelsia—The Year Book of the Minnesota Seaside Station. Dir. Minn. Seaside Sta. in Straits of Fuca. Address: University of Minnesota, Minneapolis. Died June 5, 1929.

MacMILLAN, William Duncan, mathematician, astronomer; b. LaCrosse, Wis., July 24, 1871; s. Duncan D. and Mary Jane (MacCrea) MacM.; studied Lake Forest Coll., Ill., 1888-90, Sc.D., 1930; studied U. of Va., 1895; A.B., Ft. Worth U., 1898; A.M., U. of Chicago, 1906, Ph.D., 1908; Sc.D., Lake Forest Coll., 1930; unmarried. Research asst. in geology, U. of Chicago, 1907-08, asst. in mathematics and astronomy, 1908-09, instr. astronomy, 1909-12, asst. prof., 1912-19, asso. prof., 1919-24, prof., 1924-36, prof. emeritus since 1936. Maj. Ordnance Dept., U.S. Army, 1918. Fellow A.A.A.S., Royal Astron. Soc.; mem. Am. Math. Soc., Math. Assn. America, Astron. and Astrophys. Soc. Am., Société Astronomique de France. Clubs: Quadrangle, University. Author: Statics and the Dynamics of a Particle, 1927; Theory of the Potential, 1930; Dynamics of Rigid Bodies, 1936; and many scientific memoirs. Home: Marine on St. Croix, Minn. Died Nov. 14, 1948.

MacMULLEN, Wallace, clergyman; b. Dublin, Ireland, Aug. 31, 1860; s. David and Annie T. (Smith) MacM.; came to America with parents, 1862; ed. pub. schs., Brooklyn; B.D. Drew Theol. Sem., 1888; S.T.D., Wesleyan U., Middletown, Conn., 1897; m. Annie Hutchinson, 1888; m. 2d, Laura E. Neal, June 7, 1899; children—Harold Bruce (dec.), David Wallace, Paul Rice, Grace. Entered M.E. ministry, 1888; pastor Springfield, Mass., 1888-93, Grace Ch., Phila., 1893-98, Park Av. Ch., Phila., 1898-1902, Madison Av. Ch., New York, 1902-13; prof. homiletics, Drew Theol. Sem., 1913-18; supt. New York Dist. of N.Y. Conf., M.E. Ch., 1918-25; pastor Metropolitan Temple, New York, 1925-39. Mem. Bd. Foreign Missions and N.Y. City Soc., Deaconess Bd. N.Y., Bd. Edn. of N.Y. and N.Y. East Conferences; dir. Fedn. of Chs. Club: Philothean. Author: Captain of Our Faith, 1904. Address: 3681 Broadway, New York, N.Y. Died Aug. 9, 1943.

MacMURRAY, James E., manufacturer; b. Knox County, Mo., Aug. 7, 1862; s. Fletcher and Miranda (Green) MacM.; grad. law and lit. courses, Chaddock Coll., Quincy, Ill., 1884; m. Jennie A. Rubel, July 4, 1908 (died Nov. 17, 1937). Entered mfg. business at Quincy, 1890; removed to Chicago, 1899; pres. Acme Steel Co., 1890-1941, now dir; dir. Kellogg Switchboard & Supply Co., Am. Tag Co. Elected to Ill. Senate, 1920. Trustee MacMurray Coll. for Women (Jacksonville, Ill.), Garrett Bibl. Inst. (Evanston, Ill.). Republican. Methodist. Mason. Clubs: Union League, Chicago Athletic, South Shore Country, Annandale Golf, Midwick Country. Home: South Pasadena, Calif. Office: 315 Pacific S.W. Bldg., Pasadena, Calif. Died July 1, 1943.

MacNAIR, Florence Wheelock Ayscough (Florence Ayscough), writer, lecturer; b. Shanghai, China; d. Thomas Reed and Edith Haswell (Clarke) Wheelock; educated private tutors and Mrs. Quincy Shaw's School, Boston, Mass., honorary Litt.D., Acadia U., Wolfville, Nova Scotia, 1923; m. Francis Ayscough Ayscough (dec.); m. 2d, Harley Farnsworth MacNair, Sept. 7, 1935. Hon. librarian North China Br. Royal Asiatic Soc., Shanghai, 1907-22; lecturer on Chinese lit., U. of Chicago, fall 1938 and summer 1940; has lectured on Chinese art, lit. and sociology in European capitals and Am. cities. Pres. Am. Friends of China, Chicago, since 1939. Mem. Royal Asiatic Soc. of London (hon. life mem. North China branch, Shanghai), Royal Central Asian Soc., Soc. of

Women Geographers, Societe Guernesiaise (Guernsey, Channel Island), Ostasiatische Gesellschaft, English-Speaking Union. Author (under name of Florence Ayscough) Friendly Books on Far Cathay, 1916; A Chinese Mirror, 1925; Autobiography of a Chinese Dog, 1926; Tu Fu—Autobiography of a Chinese Poet, 1929; Firecracker Land, 1932; The Travels of a Chinese Poet, 1934; Chinese Women Yesterday and Today, 1937. Translator from the Chinese (with Amy Lowell) of Fir-Flower Tablets, 1921. Contbr. to mags. and jours. Home: House of the Wutung Trees, 5533 Woodlawn Av., Chicago, Ill. Died Apr. 24, 1942.

MacNAIR, Harley Farnsworth, university professor, writer on Far East; b. Greenfield, Pa., July 22, 1891; s. Dougald Evander and Nettie Adella (Farnsworth) M.; Ph.B., University of Redlands, 1912, Litt.D., 1935; A.M., Columbia, 1916; Ph.D., Univ. of Calif., 1922; m. Florence Wheelock Ayscough, September 7, 1935 (died April 24, 1942). Staff member A. K. Smiley Public Library, Redlands, Calif., 1909-12; librarian University of Redlands, 1910-12; instructor St. John's Univ., Shanghai, China, 1912-16, prof. history and govt., 1916-32, head of dept., 1919-32; also dean East China Summer Sch., 1924; engaged in famine relief in Chihli (now Hopei) province in early part of 1921; teaching fellow in political science, University of California, 1921-22; contbg. editor China Weekly Review, 1926-27, Chinese Social and Polit. Science Rev., 1926-29; mem. editorial staff The Chinese Recorder, 1926-27; hon. mem. editorial council Internat. Journal, Shanghai, 1926-27; mem. editorial bd. Far Eastern Quarterly since 1941; asso. prof. far eastern government and diplomacy, U. of Wash., 1927-28; visiting professor, U. of Chicago, summer 1928, professor far eastern history and institutions since 1928; staff member Civil Affairs Training Sch., Univ. of Chicago, 1943-45; consultant, far eastern section, Research and Analysis, Office of Strategic Services, Washington, D.C., 1943. Trustee Internat. Inst. China, 1926-27. Mem. Royal Asiatic Soc. (life; N. China branch and Korea br.), Am. Oriental Soc., Inst. of Pacific Relations (Am. council), Friends of China (member board governors) (Chicago), P.E.N. Club (Chicago chapter), Japan Society (New York); Chinese Social and Political Science Assn. (life); Am. Assn. U. Professors; Pi Kappa Delta, Alpha Pi Zeta, Pi Sigma Alpha and Delta Alpha; hon. corr. mem. Institut Litteraire et Artistique de France. Traveled extensively in Eastern Asia, 1931-32, 1934-35, 1938-39. Episcopalian. Club: Quadrangle. Author: Christian Work Among Chinese Abroad (in The Christian Occupation of China), 1922; Introduction to Western History (in collaboration), 1922; The Chinese Abroad, 1924, 33 (translated into Chinese, 1927); China's New Nationalism and Other Essays, 1925, 32; China's International Relations and Other Essays, 1926; Far Eastern Internat. Relations (with Hosea B. Morse), 1928, 31; China in Revolution, 1931; Modern Far Eastern History (syllabus), 1934; The Real Conflict Between China and Japan, 1938; With the White Cross in China, 1939; also chapters in various books, including: "The United States in the Pacific and Far East," in Survey of Am. Foreign Relations (edited by Chas. P. Howland), 1930; "China Within the Triangle," in Peace or War (edited by H. S. Quigley, 1937; "Chinese Immigration" in Vol. V (1929); "The Far Eastern Problem," in Vol. IX (1944) of Ency. Britannica. Contbr. to Ency. Social Sciences, Dictionary Am. Biography, various periodicals, etc. Editor and co-author: Short Stories for Chinese Students, 1919; Modern Chinese History (selected readings), 1923, 27; The Log of the Caroline (Captain Richard Jeffry, 1799), 1938; Voices from Unoccupied China, 1944; China (The United Nations Series), 1945; Florence Ayscough and Amy Lowell, The Correspondence of a Friendship, 1945; The Incomparable Lady: Tributes to Florence Ayscough MacNair, 1945. Reviser of articles on the Far East, in World Book Ency., 1945. Home: House of the Wu-t'ung Trees, 5533 Woodlawn Av. Office: Harper Library, U. of Chicago, Chicago, Ill. Died June 21, 1947.

MacNAIR, James Duncan, clergyman; b. Trout River, Que., Can., May 26, 1874 (father, Civil War vet.); s. James and Christina (Mitchell) MacN.; came to U.S., 1890; student Boston U. Sch. of Theology, 1898-1901, S.T.B., 1905; A.B., Boston U. Coll. of Liberal Arts, 1905, D.D., 1937; m. Grace Eunice Tibbetts, June 12, 1907. Teacher pub. sch., Burke, N.Y., 1895; agent Prudential Ins. Co., Hartford, Conn., 1895-96; asst. mgr. and mgr. E. P. Charlton Syndicate, Hartford, Conn., and Biddeford, Me., 1896-98; ordained deacon in M.E. Ch., 1902, received into E. Me. Conf., 1905; pastor Union Ch., Swans Island, Me., 1905-06; ordained elder, 1906; chaplain Craig Colony, Sonyea, N.Y., 1906-09; commd. chaplain with rank of lt. j.g., U.S. Navy, 1909; commd. lt., 1916, lt. comdr., 1919, comdr., 1919, capt., 1920; served at Naval Training Sta., Norfolk, Va., 1909, on U.S.S. Ga., 1909-11, U.S.S. Va., 1911, U.S.S. Ga., 1911-12, at Navy Yard, Mare Island, Calif., 1912-14, on U.S.S. Md., 1914-16, U.S.S. Pittsburgh, 1916, U.S.S. Ariz., 1916-17, with 6th Regt., U.S. Marines, in France, 1917-18, at Navy Yard, Boston, 1918-19, Naval Training Sta., Newport, R.I., 1919-21, Navy Yard, Phila., 1921-23, on U.S.S. Wyo. as fleet chaplain Atlantic Scouting Fleet, 1923-25, at Naval Home, Phila., 1926, Navy Yard, Phila., 1926-30; retired for physical disability, Sept. 1, 1930; commd. rear adm. and thus became senior ranking chaplain, U.S. Navy, retired, 1936; pres. Quick Maturity Bldg. & Loan Assn.; National Chaplain, 1941-42, Nat. Assn. of Legions of Honor; mem. Me. Conf. of Meth. Ch. Awarded Mexican Medal, 1914; Victory Medal, 1918; Navy Cross for extraordinary heroism in actual combat with enemy during World War, 1919. Mem. Am. Acad. of Polit. and Social Science, Pa. Historical Society, Benjamin Franklin Institute, American Legion, Military Order of the World War, Hon. Navy League, Army and Navy Union, St. Andrews Soc. of Phila., Old Guard of the City of Phila., Nat. Sojourners, Jewish Legion of Honor (hon.), Theta Delta Chi. Republican. Methodist. Mason (33°, K.T., Shriner; Legion of Honor of Lulu Temple, Phila.), Odd Fellow, Eastern Star. Clubs: Union League, Fellowship, One Hundred, Boston University Alumni, Shrine Luncheon (Phila.); Wardroom (Boston); Optimist (Upper Darby, Pa.). Author occasional articles. While on active duty was editor and mgr. of Ships' and Stations' papers. Home: 329 Brookline Blvd., Brookline, Upper Darby, Pa. Died May 4, 1946; buried in Laurel Hill Cemetery, Saco, Me.

MacNAUGHTON, James, mine mgr.; b. Can., Mar. 9, 1864; s. Archibald and Catherine (MacIntyre) M.; student Univ. of Mich., 1884-86; B.S., in civ. engring., U. of Mich., 1907 (as of 1888); m. Mary E. Morrison, August 27, 1892; children—Martha L., Mary. Pres. Calumet & Hecla Consolidated Copper Co. Mem. Am. Inst. Mining Engrs. Del. Rep. Nat. Conv., St. Louis, 1896; del. from Mich. at-large, Rep. Nat. Conv., Chicago, 1908, Kansas City, 1928. Conglist. Clubs: University (Chicago); Links (New York). Home: Calumet, Mich. Died May 26, 1949.

MacNEAL, Ward J., bacteriologist; b. Fenton, Mich., Feb. 17, 1881; s. Edward and Jane Elizabeth (Pratt), MacN.; A.B., U. of Mich., 1901, Ph.D., 1904, M.D., 1905, hon. Sc.D., 1939; m. Mabel Perry, Dec. 28, 1905; children—Edward Perry (dec.), Herbert Pratt, Perry Scott, Mabel Ruth. Asst. and fellow in bacteriology, U. of Mich., 1901-04, instr. histology, 1905-06; instr. in anatomy and bacteriology, W. Va. U., 1906-07; asst. chief in bacteriology, Ill. Agrl. Expt. Sta., 1907-11; asst. prof. bacteriology, U. of Ill., 1908-11; lecturer on pathology and bacteriology, 1911-12, prof. and asst. dir. labs., 1912-15; prof. and dir. of labs., 1915-22, prof. and dir. dept. pathology and bacteriology, 1922-24 and 1930-39, prof. bacteriology since 1939, prof. and dir. labs., 1924-30, mem. bd. trustees, 1921-24; v.chmn. Med. Bd., 1924-29, N.Y. Post-Grad. Med. Sch. and Hosp.; asst. to pres. Josiah Macy Jr. Foundation, 1931-36. Mem. Ill. State Pellagra Commn., 1909-12; mem. Thompson-McFadden Pellagra Commn., Am. Trench Fever Commn., France, 1918. Capt., Med. R.C., 1917; lt. col., M.R.C. U.S. Army, 1919; col., 1925; with A.E.F. in France to Feb. 1919. Fellow A.A.A.S.; mem. Soc. Am. Bacteriologists, Am. Assn. Pathologists and Bacteriologists (council 1929-35, pres. 1932), Assn. for Cancer Research (council 1925-33; pres. 1934), Nat. Assn. Tuberculosis, A.M.A., Soc. Exptl. Biology and Medicine, N.Y. Acad. Medicine, N.Y. Pathol. Soc. (pres. 1922-23; trustee 1925-30. 1932-37 and since 1940), N.Y. State Soc. of Pathologists (v.p. 1941, pres. 1942-45), Harvey Soc., Sigma Xi. Author: Studies in Nutrition, Volumes I to V (with H. S. Grindley), 1911-29; Pathogenic Microörganisms, 1914, 2d edit., 1920. Contbr. to Marshall's Microbiology, 1917, 20, etc. Editor Third Report Thompson Pellagra Commission, 1917. Home: 301 E. 21st St., New York 10, N.Y. Office: 303 E. 20th St., New York 3, N.Y. Died Aug. 15, 1946.

MacNEIL, Hermon Atkins, sculptor; b. Chelsea, Mass., 1866; s. J. C. and Mary (Lash) MacN.; grad. Mass. State Normal Sch., 1886, pupil of Chapu at Julian Acad. and 2 yrs. of Falguière at École des Beaux Arts; m. Carol Brooks, Dec. 25, 1895 (died June 1944); children—Claude Lash, Alden Brooks, Joie Katherine (dec.); m. 2d, Cecelia W. Muench, Feb. 1946. Taught 3 years Cornell, 3 years Art Institute, Chicago; won Roman Rinehart scholarship in sculpture, 1896-1900; awarded designer's medal, Chicago Exposition, 1893; silver medal, Paris Exposition, 1900; gold medal, Buffalo Exposition, 1901; silver medal, Charleston Exposition, 1902; commemorative medal, Louisiana Purchase Exposition, 1904; gold medal, Panama Expn., 1915; medal of honor, Archtl. League of New York, 1917; Saltus medal, 1923. Did important decorative work at Chicago, Paris, Buffalo, St. Louis and Panama expns.; the spandrels on portico of Nat. Pavilion, and exhibited groups, The Sun Vow, and Last Act of the Moqui Snake Dance, at Paris Expn., 1900; executed main cascade fountain for St. Louis Expn., 1904; mem. jury of awards, same; executed Coming of the White Man, City Park, Portland, Ore.; McKinley Memorial, Columbus, O.; Soldiers' and Sailors' Memorial, Whitinsville, Mass.; Soldiers' and Sailors' Memorial, Washington Park, Albany, N.Y.; Orville Hitchcock Platt Memorial, State Capitol, Hartford, Conn.; General Washington, Washington Arch, N.Y.; frieze—development of man in America, State Capitol, Jefferson City, Mo.; groups physical and intellectual development, Northwestern U.; Ezra Cornell Memorial, Cornell Univ.; Flushing (L.I.) War Memorial; Marquette Memorial, Chicago; The Pilgrim Fathers, Waterbury, Conn.; Burke Memorial, Seattle, Wash.; eastern pediment U.S. Supreme Court, Washington, D.C.; Ft. Sumter Memorial, Charleston, S.C.; bronze equestrian, "Pony Express," for St. Joseph, Mo.; statutes of Gen. Alfred H. Terry and Gideon Wells, Hartford, of George Rogers Clark for Memorial, Vincennes, Ind.; busts of Choate, Parkman, Roger Williams, James Monroe in Hall of Fame; bust of Chancellor Brown of New York Univ. Has works in Art Inst. Chicago; Peabody Inst., Baltimore; Cornell U.; Met. Museum of Art; Johns Hopkins U.; etc. Has made something of a specialty of Indian subjects. N.A., 1906; mem. Nat. Inst. Arts and Letters, Am. Acad. Arts and Letters, Municipal Art Soc., Nat. Sculpture Soc., Architectural League. Clubs: Century, Nat. Arts. Home: College Point, L.I. Died Oct. 2, 1947; buried Woodlawn Cemetery, Everett, Mass.

MACQUEARY, Thomas Howard, teacher; b. near Charlottesville, Va., May 27, 1861; s. Thomas H. and Sarah J. (Garland) M.; grad. Episcopal Theol. Sem., Alexandria, Va., 1886; A.B., U. of Minn., 1897, A.M., 1898; grad. student history and economics, U. of Chicago, summers 1897, 1899 and session 1900-01; m. Emma Clarkson Harris, Jan. 14, 1892. Deacon, P.E. Ch., 1885, priest, 1886; pastor Fairmont, W.Va., and Canton, O., 1887-91; tried by ecclesiastical court at Cleveland, O., Jan. 1891, for denial of miracles; suspended from P.E. ministry for 6 months; resigned, Sept. 1891, and entered Universalist ministry, but finally resigned; engaged in sociol. work; founded Unity House Social Settlement, Minneapolis, and taught in Morgan Hall Acad., Minneapolis, 1899; vice prin. Northwestern Mil. Acad., Highland Park, Ill., 1899-1900; supt. Parental Sch., Chicago, 1900-06; head asst., Yeatman High Sch. and Soldan High Sch., St. Louis, since 1906. Chautauqua lecturer. Author: The Evolution of Man and Christianity, 1889; Topics of the Times, 1891; also articles in mags. Address: Soldan High School, St. Louis. Died July 1930.

MACRAE, John, publisher; b. Richmond, Va., Aug. 25, 1866; s. John Hampden and Sheldena A. (Beach) M.; ed. pvt. and pub. schs.; m. Katharine Green, Sept. 20, 1893 (died 1913); m. 2d, Opal Wheeler, Sept. 1930. With E. P. Dutton & Co. since 1885, v.p. 1905, treas., 1914, pres. 1923. Pres. Nat. Assn. Book Publishers, 1924-27. Episcopalian. Home: 1 Gracie Square. Office: 286-302 Fourth Av., New York, N.Y. Died Feb. 18, 1944.

MacVICAR, John George, head master; b. Brockport, N.Y.; s. Malcolm and Isabella McV.; grad. Mich. State Normal Sch.; Ypsilanti, 1881; student U. of Toronto, 1882-85; B.A., U. of Rochester, 1887, M.A., 1889; m. Harriet Elizabeth Ames, June 24, 1891; children—Donald, George, Harvey Ames, Kathryn. Prin., Flat Rock (Mich.) High Sch., 1881-82; supt. pub. schs., Union City, Mich., 1885-86; founder, Montclair Acad., 1887, head master until 1925, head master emeritus, since 1925. Address: Montclair, N.J. Died May 4, 1945.

MADDEN, John Fitz, army officer; b. Sacramento, Calif., Mar. 30, 1870; s. Jerome and Margaret Eveline (Evans) M.; prep. edn., St. Matthews Hall, San Mateo, Calif.; U. of Calif., 1890-91; grad. Inf. and Cav. Sch., Fort Leavenworth, Kan., 1897, Army War Coll., Washington, 1921, Gen. Staff Sch., Fort Leavenworth, 1922, Naval War Coll., Newport, R.I., 1923; married (divorced); 1 son, John FitzPatrick. Commd. 2d lt. inf., U.S. Army, Oct. 7, 1891, and advanced through grades to colonel, Apr. 15, 1920; brig. gen. National Army, Oct. 1918-Mar. 1919; brig. gen. U.S. Army, March 6, 1931; retired account of physical disability in line of duty, March 31, 1934. Served in Spanish-Am. War, Cuban Occupation, Philippine Insurrection; chief q.m., Punitive Expdn. into Mexico, 1916; asst. q.m. 1st Div., A.E.F., and asst. to chief q.m., A.E.F., June 1917-Feb. 1919. Decorated Officer Legion of Honor (France). Episcopalian. Clubs; Army and Navy (Washington); Lambs, (New York); West Point Army Mess; Army and Navy (Manila, P.I.). Home: 89 N. Arlington Av., East Orange, N.J. Died May 19, 1946.

MADDEN, John Thomas, educator, accountant; b. Worcester, Mass., Oct. 26, 1882; s. Michael James and Mary Teresa (Lawton) M.; B.C.S., summa cum laude, New York U. Sch. of Commerce Accounts and Finance, 1911; hon. M.A., Holy Cross Coll., 1921; hon. Sc.D., U. of Newark; m. Anna Marie Callahan, Sept. 3, 1912 (died Aug. 3, 1933); children—Annette Joan (Mrs. B. J. J. Mooney), Ruth, Jane Louise, Marjorie Helen (Mrs. E. N. Burke); m. 2d, Anne G. Corrigan, Jan. 25, 1941. Certied pub. accountant, N.Y., 1911, N.J., 1926. With New York U. Sch. of Commerce since 1911, head Dept. Accounting Instrn., 1917-22, asst. dean Sch. of Commerce, Accounts and Finance, 1922-25, actg. dean 1925, dean since 1925; pres. Alexander Hamilton Inst., 1929-35; pres. Internat. Accountants Soc. since 1929. Pub. gov. N.Y. Curb Exchange; cons. Loew's Inc. on personnel problems and financial policies since 1943. Decorated Comdr. Order of Crown (Rumania); Comdr. Order of Leopold II (Belgium). Dir. Inst. Internat. Finance; mem. N.J. State Soc. Certified Public Accountants since 1927. Mem. Am. Econ. Assn., Am. Assn. Univ. Instrs. in Accounting (pres. 1921), Am. Inst. Accountants, N.Y. State Soc. Certified Pub. Accountants (dir. 1923), Nat. Assn. Cost Accountants (dir. 1938), Acad. Polit. Science, Pan-Am. Soc., Merchants Assn. N.Y. City, Am. Assn. Labor Legislation, Am. Management Assn., Am. Arbitration Assn., Foreign Policy Assn., Delta Mu Delta, Theta Nu Epsilon (nat. pres. 1925-28), Alpha Kappa Psi (nat. president 1920-21), Beta Gamma Sigma (national v.-pres. 1939; grand president 1942-45). Roman Catholic. Clubs: Accountants; Lotos. Author: Principles of Accounting, 1918; Accounting Practice and Auditing, 1919; Elementary Accounting Problems (with A. H. Rosenkampff), 1920; Foreign Securities (with Marcus Nadler), 1929; International Money Markets (with Marcus Nadler),

1934; America's Experience as a Creditor Nation (with Marcus Nadler and Dr. Harry Sauvain), 1936; Auditing (with P. E. Bacas and A. H. Rosenkampff); Money Market Primer (with M. Nadler and Sipa Heller), 1948. Pres. Am. Assn. of Collegiate Schs. of Business, 1928-29; mem. Council on Accountancy of N.Y. State Dept. of Edn. Home: 315 E. 68th St. Office: Washington Sq., New York. Died July 2, 1948; buried in Gate of Heaven Cemetery, E. Hanover, N.J.

MADDIN, Percy Downs, lawyer; b. Waco, Tex., Oct. 27, 1860; s. Dr. John Wesley and Annie (Downs) M.; B.S., Vanderbilt U., 1881, LL.B., 1882; m. Mary Belle Keith, Nov. 4, 1890; children—Samuel Keith, Percy Downs, John Keith, Mary Belle Keith. In practice at Nashville, since 1882; now mem. law firm Maddin & Maddin (son John K.); Nashville counsel for Fidelity & Deposit Co. of Md., since 1891, also for Zurich Gen. Accident Liability Ins. Co. (Chicago), Armour & Co. (Chicago), Ford Motor Co. (Detroit), John Deere Plow Co. (St. Louis), and L.&N. R.R., 1895-1910; counsel and dir. 4th Nat. Bank, Nashville, 1894-1912, Fourth & First Nat. Bank; Fourth & First Banks; dir. N.C.&St.L. Ry. since 1917, and Nashville&Decatur R.R. Co. Prof. law, Vanderbilt U., 1900-13. Pres. McKendree M.E. Ch., S., Corp.; del. Ecumenical Conf., Toronto, 1911, London, 1921; mem. Fed. Council, M.E. Ch., S., 1914-22; del. Gen. Conf. M.E. Ch., S., 1914-18; mem. Com. on Unification of Methodism, 1914-22; chmn. exec. com. and counsel for Bd. of Missions M.E. Ch., S., since 1914; commr. from M.E. Ch., S., to assemble with other representatives at Keijo (Seoul), Korea, Nov. 1930, to set up and establish the Korean Methodist Ch. Mem. Commn. on Interdenominational Relations and Church Union of M.E. Ch., South, to prepare plan for uniting Methodism in America, completed at Uniting Conf. Kansas City, Mo., 1939; del. Meth. Uniting Conf. at Kansas City. Chmn. State Legal Advisory Bd. for Tenn., 1917-19; pres. War Service League of Nashville Bar, 1917-18. Mem. Am. Bar Assn. (v.p. for Tenn., 1913, mem. gen. council, 1916-19), Internat. Law Assn., Bar Assn. Tenn. (v.p. 1909-10, pres. 1910-11), Tenn. Hist. Soc., Nashville Art Assn., Phi Delta Theta, Phi Beta Kappa (Vanderbilt Univ.). Democrat. Mason, K.P. Clubs: Belle Meade Country, Nashville Automobile. Home: 2124 West End Av. Office: American Nat. Bank Bldg., Nashville, Tenn. Died May 12, 1941.

MADDOX, Dwayne D(epew) (măd'dŏks), lawyer; b. Huntingdon, Tenn., Dec. 20, 1897; s. Pearl W. and Lou Emma (Shankle) M.; student U. of Tenn., 1915-16, Emory U., 1916-17, 1918-19, Cumberland U., 1917-18; m. Maynard Traywick, Sept. 26, 1923; children—Jacquelyn, Peggy Ann, Dwayne Depew II. Law practice at Huntingdon, 1918-20; with legal dept. Union Trust Co., Detroit, Mich., 1920-21; with firm Clark, Emmons, Bryant & Klein, Detroit, 1921-23; mem. firm Maddox & Maddox, Huntingdon, since 1923; became U.S. dist. atty., Western Tenn. Dist., 1932. Chmn. Rep. Exec. Com., Carroll County, Tenn., 1928-32; mem. Rep. Congl. Exec. Com., 8th Tenn. Dist.; Rep. nominee for U.S. senator (short term), 1934; Rep. nominee for U.S. Senate, regular term, 1936. Mem. Delta Tau Delta. Methodist. Mason; mem. Jr. Order United Am. Mechanics. Clubs: Tennessee, University. Home: Huntingdon, Tenn.* Deceased.

MADDOX, John J., educator; b. Alexandria, Ky., Apr. 5, 1876; s. John James and Visa (Gilson) M.; A.B., Nat. Normal U., Lebanon, O., 1899; A.B., Yale, 1907; M.A., Teachers Coll. (Columbia), 1912; m. Mabel Dabney, June 28, 1911; 1 dau., Mary Elizabeth. Teacher rural schs., Campbell County, Ky., 1894-98; teacher graded sch., Cold Springs, Ky., 1899-1900, Bellevue High Sch., Newport, Ky., 1900-03; supt. schs., Bellevue, Ky., and prin. high sch., Newport, 1903-06; prin. high sch., Willimantic, Conn., 1907-10; at St. Louis since 1910, successively prin. Blow Sch. (elementary), 1910-15, head asst., Harris Teachers Coll. and prin. Wyman Observation Sch., 1915-20; prin. Cleveland High Sch. (St. Louis) 1920-21, supt. schs., 1921-29; prin. Woodward Elementary School, 1929-32; prin. Cleveland High School (St. Louis) 1932-41; asst. supt. of instruction, St. Louis, since 1941. Member N.E.A. Missouri-State Teachers Assn. (pres. 1923-24). Home: 3439A Magnolia Av., St. Louis, Mo. Died Dec. 25, 1945.

MADEIRA, Percy Child (mȧ-dē'rȧ), coal mining; b. Phila., Pa., Nov. 14, 1862; s. Louis Cephas and Adeline Laura (Powell) M.; ed. Episcopal Acad., Phila.; m. Marie V. Marié, Jan. 18, 1888 (died 1893); m. 2d, Elizabeth Mason Campbell, 1896; m. 3d, Elise Donaldson Creswell, July 28, 1915. Began in office of A. Taylor Co., 1879; organized Percy C. Madeira Co., 1886, Madeira, Hill & Co., 1893; now pres. Colonial Colliery Co., Hale Coal Co., Janesville Coal Co., Madeira-Hill Coal Mining Co., Natalie Store Co., Saltsburg Colliery Co., Rockhill Coal & Iron Co., etc. Dir. Philadelphia National Bank and trustee Northwestern Mutual Life Insurance over 25 years. Member Anthracite Coal Operators Association (pres. 1916-25). Mem. 1st Troop Phila. City Cav., 1893-1901. Republican. Episcopalian. Author: Hunting in British East Africa, 1909. Retired. Home: Elkins Park, Phila. Office: Morris Bldg., 1421 Chestnut St., Philadelphia, Pa. Died Feb. 22, 1942.

MADILL, Grant Charles (mȧ-dĭl'), surgeon; b. Toulumne County, Calif., July 6, 1864; s. John Nelson and Louisa (Menken) M.; prep. ed. Ogdensburg Free Acad., Potsdam (N.Y.) State Normal Sch.; M.D., Bellevue Hosp. Med. Coll., 1886; LL.D., St. Lawrence U., 1908; New York U., 1932; m. Lucia James, Sept. 6, 1893; children—Sarah Perkins (Mrs. Philip H. Gray), Edward James. Interne Presbyn. Hosp., N.Y. City, 1886-88; chief surgeon A. Barton Hepburn Hosp., Ogdensburg, since 1888; 1st v.p. St. Lawrence County Savings Bank. Served as captain Medical Reserve Corps, United States Army, 1917-18. Regent U. of State of N.Y. Fellow Am. Coll. Surgeons; mem. A.M.A., Med. Soc. State of N.Y. (pres. 1919; trustee, 1926-35; del. to A.M.A. since 1920), St. Lawrence County Med. soc. (ex-pres.), N.Y. Acad. Medicine, A.A.A.S., Alumni Assn. New York U., Alumni Assn. Presbyn. Hosp., New York. Republican, Elk. Clubs: Century, Ogdensburg Country (Ogdensburg); Transportation (New York). Home: 92 Caroline St. Office: A. Barton Hepburn Hosp., Ogdensburg, N.Y. Died Mar. 26, 1943.

MADISON, Frank Delino, lawyer; b. San Francisco, Calif., Apr. 18, 1867; s. John Henry and Kate Nelson (Cooke) M.; ed. Hastings Law Sch., San Francisco, 1889-92; m. Grace Isabel Pierce, June 12, 1894 (dec.); children—Marshall Pierce, Margaret (Mrs. Wakefield Baker), Caroline Louise (Mrs. Charles O. Martin). In law office Pillsbury & Blanding, San Francisco, 1889-92; admitted to Calif. bar, 1892, and began practice at San Francisco; mem. Pillsbury, Madison & Sutro since 1906. Home: Pacific Union Club. Office: Standard Oil Bldg., San Francisco, Calif. Died July 30, 1941.

MAETERLINCK, Maurice (Count Polydore Marie Bernard), poet and dramatist; b. Ghent, Belgium, Aug. 29, 1862; Flemish extraction; ed. Collège Sainte-Barbe and U. of Ghent; m. Renee Dahon, 1919. Became member of Belgian bar, 1882; removed to Paris, 1887; began literary career with volume of poetry, Serres Chaudes, and a play, Princesse Maleine, 1889; l'Intruse and Les Aveugles, 2 plays pub. in Brussels, 1890; Les Sept Princesses, 1891. Major theatrical works: Pelleas et Mélisande (set to music by Debussy), Alladine et Palomides, Intérieur, La Mort de Tintagiles, Aglavaine et Sélysette, Ariane et Barbe Bleue, Soeur Béatrice, Joyzelle, L'Oiseau Bleu, La Tragédie de Macbeth, W. Shakespeare (translation), Marie-Magdeleine, Monna-Vanna, Le Miracle de St. Antoine, Le Bourgmestre de Stilmonde, La Princess Isabelle, Les Fiancailles, Le Malheur Passe, La Puissance des Morts, Marie-Victoire, l'Abbé Sétubal, Jeanne d'Arc, Les Trois Justiciers, La Nuit des Enfants, Le Jugement Dernier, Le Miracle des Mères, Rien Ne Se Perd-Tout Se Retrouve. Philosophical works: Le Trésor des Humbles, La Sagesse et la Destinée, La Vie des Abeilles, Le Temple Enseveli. Le Double Jardin. L'Intelligence des Fleurs, La Mort, Les Débris de la Guerre, L'Hote Inconnu, Les Sentiers dans la Montagne, Le Grand Secret, La Vie des Termites, La Vie de L'Espace, La Grande Féerie, La Vie des Furmis, L'Araignée, de Verre. La Grande Loi, Avant le Grand Silense, Le Sablier, L'Ombre des Ailes, Devant Dieu, La Grande Porte, L'Autre Monde ou le Cadran Stellaire. Awarded Nobel Prize, 1911. Decorated Grand Cordon de l'Ordre de Leopold, Grand Officier de la Légion d'Honneur. Address: Hotel Plaza, New York, N.Y. Died May 6, 1949.

MAGAN, Percy Tilson (mȧ-găn'), physician, coll. pres.; b. Marlfield House, Gorey, County Wexford, Ireland, Nov. 13, 1867; s. Percy and Annie Catherine (Richards) M.; ed. Arnold House, Chester, Eng., and St. George's Sch., Huntingdon; Ph.B., Battle Creek (Mich.) Coll., 1894; M.D., U. of Tenn., 1914; m. Ida Mae Bauer, June 5, 1892; children—Wellesley Percy, Shaen Saurin; m. 2d, Lillian Eshelman, M.D., Aug. 23, 1905; 1 son, Valentine O'Connor. Prof. history, Battle Creek Coll., 1891-1901, also dean of Coll., 1899-1901; dean of Emmanuel Missionary Coll., Berrien Springs, Mich., 1901-04; dean of Nashville Agrl. Normal Inst., Madison, Tenn., 1904-15; prof. medicine and dean Coll. of Med. Evangelists, Los Angeles, Calif., 1913-28; pres. same and prof. medical ethics, 1928-42, president emeritus since 1942; chmn. anatom. bd., southern division Department of Public Health, Calif.; trustee Medical Board of Los Angeles County Gen. Hosp. Fellow Am. Coll. Physicians; mem. A.M.A., Soc. Am. Bacteriologists (del. to A.M.A.), Am. Hosp. Assn., League for Conservation Pub. Health, Nat. Tuberculosis Assn., Am. Cancer Foundation, Calif. Med. Assn. (ex-v.p.), Southern Calif. Med. Assn., Los Angeles County Med. Assn. (trustee). Republican. Seventh Day Adventist. Club: University. Author: The Peril of the Republic; The Vatican and the War, 1915. Editor: Health (mag.). Contbr. to Calif. and Western Med. Mag. Home: 1738 Chelsea Rd., San Marino, Calif. Address: White Memorial Hospital, Los Angeles, Calif. Died Dec. 16, 1947.

MAGEE, Carlton Cole (ma-ge'); b. Fayette, Ia., Jan. 5, 1873; s. Rev. John C. and Jane (Cole) M.; M.Di., Iowa State Teachers Coll., Cedar Falls, 1894; M.A., Upper Iowa Univ., Fayette, 1896; m. Grace G. Griffin, Dec. 31, 1895 (dec.); children—Carl C. (dec.), Gertrude Frances (Mrs. John D. Grenko), Ted. Supt. city schs., Carroll, Ia., 1896-1901; admitted to Okla. bar, 1903, and practiced at Tulsa, 1903-20; editor Albuquerque (N.M.) Journal, 1920-22, Magee's Independent, weekly newspaper, 1922-23, N.M. State Tribune, 1923-27; editor Okla. News (a Scripps-Howard newspaper), 1927-33; inventor of parking meter. Pres. Magee-Hale Parking Meter Co., Oklahoma City, Okla., since Jan. 1, 1945. Methodist, Mason (32°, Shriner.). A leader in exposure of Teapot Dome scandals. Address: 627 Commerce Exchange Bldg., Oklahoma City, Okla. Died Jan. 31, 1946.

MAGEE, James Dysart, prof. economics; b. Morrisdale Mines, Pa., Aug. 22, 1881; s. William Archibald and Lizzie (Dysart) M.; A.B., Des Moines Coll., 1902; student U. of Chicago, 1904-06, 1909-10, A.M., 1906, Ph.D., 1913; unmarried. Office sec. Des Moines Y.M.C.A., 1902-04; asst. in mathematics, Kan. State Agrl. Coll., 1906-09; instr. in economics, Western Reserve U., 1910-13; asst. and asso. prof. economics, U. of Cincinnati, 1913-19; asso. prof. economics, New York U., 1919-22, prof. since 1922, head of dept. 1923-46. Teacher, Summer School, U. of Chicago, 1916, 19, Columbia, 1923. Fellow Royal Econ. Soc.; mem. Am. Econ. Assn., Am. Statis. Assn., Econ. Hist. Assn., Phi Beta Kappa. Author: Introduction to Economic Problems, 1922; Materials for the Study of Banking, 1923; Introduction to Money and Credit, 1926, rev. edit., 1933; Collapse and Recovery, 1934; (with E. Stein and W. E. Atkins) The National Recovery Program, 1933 (with W. E. Atkins) A Problem Approach to Economics, 1937; Taxation and Capital Investment, 1939; (with H. G. Moulton, G. W. Edwards, Cleonia Lewis) Capital Expansion, Employment, and Economic Stability, 1940; (with Emanuel Stein and William J. Ronan) Our War Economy, 1943. Office: 100 Washington Sq. E., New York 3. Died Apr. 6, 1948.

MAGEE, James M., ex-congressman; b. Evergreen, Pittsburgh, Apr. 5, 1877; s. Frederick M. and Hannah Mary (Gillespie) M.; A.B., Yale, 1899; LL.B., U. of Pa., 1902; m. 2d, Mary L. Gittings; children (by former marriage)—Mary J., Edward J. Admitted to Pa. bar, 1903, and began practice at Pittsburgh; mem. 68th and 69th Congresses (1923-27), 35th Pa. Dist.; chmn. Pa. Securities Commn., 1931-35. Resident v.p. at Pittsburgh of Am. Surety Co. of N.Y.; pres. Citizen Traction Co. (Pittsburgh); dir. Scaife Co. (Pittsburgh). Commd. 1st lt. U.S.A.S., 1917, later capt.; still later lt. col. U.S. Res. President board trustees Elizabeth Steel Magee Hosp. Clubs: Law Club of Pittsburgh, Pittsburgh Golf. Home: 631 St. James St. Office: Magee Bldg., Pittsburgh. Died Apr. 16, 1949.

MAGEE, John Benjamin (mȧ-gē'), coll. pres.; b. Albion, Ia., July 19, 1887; s. John Calvin and Jane (Cole) M.; Ph.B., Upper Ia. U., 1909, D.D., 1921; S.T.B., Boston U., 1912; m. Lillian Newhouse, Oct. 24, 1914; children—John B., Josephine G., Eloise, Jane Cole. Ordained ministry M.E. Ch., 1910; in ednl. dept. M.E. Bd. S.S., 1912-13; pastor Asbury Memorial M.E. Ch., Providence, R.I., 1913-14; v.p. East Greenwich (R.I.) Acad., 1914-16; pastor St. Albans, Vt., 1916-18; army chaplain, A.E.F., also official writer of history of Base Sect. 1, 1918-19; pastor El Reno, Okla., 1919-21, Wichita, Kan., 1921-25, Kansas City, Mo., 1925-28, Bellevue, Pittsburgh, Pa., 1928-32, First Ch., Seattle, Wash., 1932-39; pres. Cornell Coll., Mt. Vernon, Ia., since 1939. Trustee St. Luke's Hospital, Cedar Rapids, Iowa. Past president Washington State Council of Churches and Christian Education; del. Gen. Conf. M.E. Ch., 1936, 40; del. Uniting Conf., 1939. Mem. Pi Gamma Mu, Pi Kappa Delta, Phi Beta Kappa, Phi Tau Theta. Republican. Mason (32°), Past Grand Chaplain State of Washington, Royal and Select Masters, also Past Grand Prelate Knights Templar, State of Washington. Clubs: Executives, Lions. Author: Runes of the Night (verse), 1916; The Silent Shepherd, 1930; also chapter in "The Light Shines Through," 1930; Great Sermons on Evangelism, 1934; A Path to You, 1940; etc. Contbr. articles and verse to Methodist Advocate, and other periodicals, also Ministers Annual. Home: Mount Vernon, Iowa. Died Apr. 6, 1943.

MAGIE, William Francis, univ. dean; b. Elizabeth, N.J., Dec. 14, 1858; s. William Jay and Sarah Frances (Baldwin) M.; A.B., Princeton, 1879, A.M., 1882; Ph.D., U. of Berlin, 1885, LL.D.; m. Mary Blanchard Hodge, June 7, 1894. Instr., Princeton, 1879-84, prof. physics since 1885, dean, 1912-25. Mem. Am. Philos. Soc.; pres. Am. Phys. Soc., 1910. Author: Translation of Christiansen's Elements of Theoretical Physics, 1896; Revision of Anthony and Brackett's Physics, 1896; The Second Law of Thermodynamics, 1899; A Course of Lectures on Physics, 1904; Principles of Physics, 1911. Contbr. to scientific jours. Address: Princeton, N.J. Died June 6, 1943.

MAGNER, F. J., bishop; b. Wilmington, Ill., Mar. 18, 1887; s. James and Margaret (Follen) M.; student Loyola U.; Chicago; St. Mary's (Kan.) Coll., 1907; Ph.D., North American Coll., Rome, Italy, 1913; LL.D., Loyola U. (Chicago), 1941. Ordained priest R.C. Church, 1913; pastor St. Mary's Church, Evanston, Ill., 1927-41; bishop Marquette, Mich., 1941-47. Address: Marquette, Mich. Died June 13, 1947; buried in St. Peter's Cathedral, Marquette, Mich.

MAGNER, Thomas Francis, lawyer; b. Brooklyn, Mar. 8, 1860; A.B., St. Francis Xavier Coll., New York, 1880; LL.B., Columbia, 1882. Admitted to N.Y. bar, 1882, and practiced in Brooklyn. Mem. N.Y. Assembly, 1887-88; mem. 51st, 52d and 53d Congresses (1889-95), 6th N.Y. Dist.; apptd. asst. corp. counsel, New York, in charge Brooklyn Dept., Oct., 1914. Democrat. Home: 66 8th Av. Office: 190 Montague St., Brooklyn, N.Y. Died Dec. 22, 1945.

MAGNES, Judah Leon (măg'nĕs), rabbi; b. San Francisco, Calif., July 5, 1877; s. David and Sophie (Abrahamson) M.; A.B., U. of Cincinnati, 1898; rabbi Hebrew Union Coll., 1900; post-grad. studies, Berlin; Ph.D., U. of Heidelberg, 1902; m. Beatrice Lowenstein, Oct. 19, 1908. Instr. and librarian, Hebrew Union Coll., New York, 1903-04; rabbi Temple Israel, Brooklyn, 1904-06, Temple Emanu-El, New

York, 1906-10, Congregation B'nai Jeshurun, New York, 1911-12; leader Soc. for Advancement of Judaism, 1912-20. Chmn. Jewish Defense Assn., 1905; sec. Federation American Zionists, 1905-08; chmn. exec. com. Jewish Community (Kehillah) of N.Y. City, 1909-22; chancellor Hebrew Univ. Jerusalem, 1925-35, pres. since 1935. Address: Jerusalem, Palestine. Died Oct. 27, 1948.

MAGOFFIN, Ralph Van Deman (mȧ-gŏf'fĭn), coll. prof.; b. Rice County, Kan., Aug. 8, 1874; s. Thomas Clarence and Martha Elizabeth Van Deman (Gillespie) M.; A.B., U. of Mich., 1902; Ph.D., Johns Hopkins, 1908, studied Marburg, Berlin, Am. Sch. of Classical Studies in Rome 1906-07; LL.D., Washington Coll., 1922; m. Lily Buckler, June 18. 1910 (died Feb. 14, 1917); m. 2d, Kate Hampton Manning, Feb. 3, 1920; 1 son, Ralph Manning. Successively instr., asso., asso. prof. classical history and instr. archæology, Johns Hopkins, 1908-23; prof. and head dept. classics, New York U., 1923-39, prof. emeritus since 1939. Teacher summer schs. various universities; prof. in charge Sch. of Classical Studies, American Academy in Rome, 1920-21. Recorder Archæol. Inst. America, 1914-21, pres. 1921-31, honorary pres. since 1931, trustee since 1930; sec. Baltimore Society same, 1910-20, and v.p., 1920-23. Pvt., corpl., 31st Mich. Vol. Inf., Spanish-Am. War; grad. 1st course Div. Staff Officers, Army Coll., Washington, D.C., and served as capt., maj. and lt. col. Q.M.R.C. and G.S., Camp Jackson, S.C., Camp West Point, Ky., Camp Devens, Mass., and Camp Wheeler, Ga., World War. Mem. American Historical Assn., Am. Philological Assn., Am. Classical League (pres. 1926-31; hon.-pres. since 1931), Classical Assn. of Middle West and South, Classical Assn. Atlantic States, Classical Club of New York City, Classical Association of Great Britain, Spanish War Veterans, Am. Legion, Phi Beta Kappa. Omicron Delta Kappa, Eta Sigma Phi, Pi Gamma Mu; Socio Corrispondente Comitato Permanente per l'Etruria, since 1927; corr. mem. Internat. Mediterranean Research Assn. of Rome, pres. Am. nat. com. of same, since 1929. Commendatore della Corona d'Italia; Knight Order of the Saviour (Greece); Socius d. Arch. Inst. d. Deutschen Reiches; dir. Aeneid Cruise and Vergilian Pilgrimage, Bimell, Verg, 1930; national vice chairman American Hellenic Committee since 1930; advisor Master Institute of United Arts, New York. Republican. Presbyn. Mason (32°, K.T., Shriner). Clubs: Baltimore Classical; New York University. Author: The History and Topography of Praeneste, 1908; The Quinquinnales, 1913; The Roman Forum, 1928; The Lure and Lore of Archæology, 1930; 5000 Years Ago, 1937. Joint Author. A Handbook of the Economic Agencies of the War of 1917, 1917; An American Guide Book to France and Its Battlefields, 1920; Latin First Year; Miliaria in Via Latina; Lucerna Pedibus Nostris; Magic Spades, the Romance of Archæology; The Vergilian Pilgrimage and Cruise of 1930; Ancient and Medieval History, 1934. Translator: The Freedom of the Seas (by H. Grotius), 1916; The Sovereignty of the Sea (by C. V. Bynkerrhoek), 1924. Editor The Climax Series of Latin Books for High Schools; asso. editor Am. Jour. Archæology, 1924-31, Art and Archæology, 1914-25. Home: 1324 Bull St., Columbia, S.C. Died May 15, 1942.

MAGRAW, Lester Andrew, pub. utilities; born Springfield, Mass., May 7, 1883; s. Dennis Andrew and Nora (Quinn) M.; educated pub schs., Waterbury, Conn.; B.S., Worcester (Mass.) Poly Inst., 1905, D. Eng., 1948; m. Sarah de Saussure Davis, Nov. 6, 1912. With Crocker-Wheeler Co., Ampere, N.J., 1905-06; instr., Sibley Coll. of Engring., Cornell U., 1906; engr. Westinghouse Electric and Mfg. Co., at Phila., Pittsburgh, Charlotte, N.C., 1907-11; chief engr. Central Ga. Power Co., Macon, Ga., 1911-12; chief engr. Ga. Light, Power & Rys., Macon Ry. & Light Co., 1912, gen. mgr., 1912-17, treas. and gen. mgr., 1918-23, dir. 1920-28, v.p. and gen. mgr., 1923-1928; receiver Macon Atlantic Navigation Company, 1917; v.p. and gen. mgr. S.C. Power Co., 1928-30, pres., 1930-32; pres. and dir. Central Ill. Pub. Service Co. since 1932. Trustee Worcester Poly. Inst. Mem. Am. Inst. Elec. Engrs., Am. Soc. Mech. Engrs., Sigma Alpha Epsilon, Abraham Lincoln Assn. Clubs: Illini Country, Sagnamo (Springfield); Union League (Chicago); St. George's Soc., St. Andrew's Society (Charleston, S.C.). Home: 1323 Dial Court. Office: 1228 Illinois Bldg., Springfield, Ill. Died Mar. 25, 1949; buried Oak Ridge Cemetery, Springfield, Ill.

MAHAFFEY, Jesse Lynn, physician; b. Hillsdale, Pa., Apr. 13, 1879; s. John and Mary Jane (Ake) M.; student Purchase Line Acad., Pa., 1895-96; M.D., Medico-Chirurgical Coll. of Phila. (now post-grad. med. sch., Univ. of Pa.), 1902; post-grad. work in gastroenterology, New York Post-Grad. Med. Sch., New York, 1920; m. Alice Fogg, Apr. 26, 1905; children—J. Lynn, Albert F., Alice F. Teacher, Hillsdale, Pa., 1897-98; began pvt. practice of medicine (gen.), Camden, N.J., 1903; apptd. to out-patient dept. Cooper Hosp., Camden, 1905, chief of Med. Dept., 1909-29; with Dr. Schall founded and operated Bellevue Pvt. Hosp., Camden, N.J., 1916-28; mem. State Bd. of Health, 1925-31, dir. of Health, N.J., since 1931. Med. examiner Life Ins. Cos. of N.A. since 1905; chief founder of North Camden Trust Co., 1922, pres. 1922-37. Served as med. examiner Camden Local Draft Bd., World War I; chmn. health com., N.J. Civilian Defense Adminstrn. Mem. N.J. Crippled Children's Commn., Conf. of State and Provincial Health Authorities of N. Am. (pres. 1943), Gen. Alumni of Medico-Chirurgical Coll. (pres. 1938), Procurement and Assignment Bd., New Jersey; N.J. Tuberculosis League (bd. dirs.), Camden City Med. Soc. (pres. 1915), Camden County Med. Soc. (pres. 1920), Am. Pub. Health Assn., N.J. State Med. Soc., A.M.A., N.J. Sanitary, N.J. Health Officers and State and Terr. Health Officers assns. Republican. Methodist. Mason. Club: Philadelphia Medical, Tavistock Country. Home: 406 Warwick Rd., Haddonfield, N.J. Office: State House, Trenton 7, N.J. Died Nov. 1, 1948.

MAHAN, Edgar Clyde, coal operator; b. Williamsburg, Ky., Sept. 25, 1879; s. Thomas Breckenridge and Florence (Goggans) M.; A.B., Cumberland Coll., Williamsburg, Ky., 1897; m. Emily Miller, Sept. 21, 1907; children—Cynthia Miller, Emily Miller. Gen. mgr. Southern Coal & Coke Co., 1903-18, pres., 1918-41, chmn. board since 1941; pres. Southern Mining Co., Southern Collieries, Mahan Jellico Coal Co.; v.p. Fork Mountain Coal Co., J.C. Mahan Motor Co., Fidelity-Bankers Trust Co. of Knoxville; dir. Knoxville Fertilizer Co., Mahan Ellison Coal Co., High Splint Coal Co., Park Nat. Bank, Knoxville, Bank of Williamsburg (Tenn.). Trustee Cumberland Coll. Director Nat. Coal Assn. Clubs: Cherokee Country (Knoxville); Queen City (Cincinnati). Home: 3830 Lyons View Pike. Office: 531 Gay St., Knoxville, Tenn. Died Oct. 28, 1948.

MAHAN, Lawrence Elmer, mortgage banker; b. Harbor Beach, Mich., Dec. 16, 1891; s. Frank E. and Ida (Smith) M.; A.B., William Jewell Coll., 1914; m. Julia B. Miller, Feb. 22, 1922; children—Sally Ann, Patricia Jane. Pres. Real Estate Mortgage Trust Co., St. Louis, Mo., 1924-31, L. E. Mahan & Co., since 1931; chmn. bd. Mahan, Dittmar & Co., San Antonio, Tex, 1931-39; dir. Paramount Fire Ins. Co. (N.Y.), St. Louis Fire & Marine Ins. Co., Real Estate Management Co. (St. Louis). In charge mortgages and real estate taken in connection with Trading with Enemy Act during World War I. Trustee Iberia Jr. Coll.; mem. bd. dirs. Children's Home Soc. of Mo., Mo. Assn. Occupational Therapy. Founder and pres. Mortgage Bankers Assn. of St. Louis, 1926-27; mem. bd. of govs. Mortgage Bankers Assn. of America since 1926, now pres.; grand marshal Mortgage Bankers Legion, 1941. Mem Kappa Alpha. Baptist. Clubs: Bankers (N.Y.); Noonday, University (St. Louis.) Home: 4600 Maryland Av. Office: 509 Olive St., St. Louis. Died Nov. 19, 1946; buried Harbor Beach, Mich.

MAHER, Dale Wilford (mä'hẽr), foreign service officer; b. Norman, Okla., Apr. 16, 1897; s. Arthur Charles and Gertrude Eva (Marquart) M.; student Western Mil. Acad.; Alton, Ill., 1914-15, Northwestern University, 1915-16; B.S., U.S. Military Acad., 1919; graduate, United States Cavalry School, 1920; married Doreen Mary English. Vice consul, Prince Rupert, B.C., 1925-26, Calcutta, 1926-27, Batavia, 1928-30; consul, LeHavre, 1930-31, Shanghai, 1932-33, Hong Kong, 1933, Maidan, Sumatra, 1933-35, Rotterdam, 1935-36; sec. of legation, Budapest, 1935-36; consul, Cologne, 1940-41, Lyon, 1941; sec. of legation, Bern, Switzerland, 1941-45. Consul, Johannesburg, S. Africa 1946; 1st Sec. of Legation, Pretoria, Union of S. Africa 1946-47. Served as lt., U.S. Army, 1919-24. Address: Department of State, Washington, D.C. Died June 7, 1948.

MAHIN, Frank Cadle, army officer; b. Clinton, Ia., May 27, 1887; s. Frank Webster and Abbie Anna (Cadle) M.; student Nottingham (Eng.) High Sch., 1902-05, Harvard, 1905-07; m. Margaret Mauree Pickering, Sept. 25, 1913; children—Margaret Celeste (Mrs. L. E. Laurion), Anna Yeteve (Mrs. E. D. Jessup), Elizabeth Mauree (Mrs. W. A. Hamilton, Jr.), Frank Cadle. Began as stock clerk W. M. Meyer & Co., N.Y. City, 1907, later with John Wanamaker; enlisted in U.S. Army, 1910; commd. 2d lt., 1912, and advanced through the grades to brig. gen., 1941. Awarded Purple Heart. Mason. Republican. Episcopalian. Clubs: Army and Navy (Washington, D.C.); Service (Indianapolis). Address: War Dept., Washington. Died July 24, 1942; buried in Arlington National Cemetery.

MAHON, William D., (mȧ-hōn'), labor leader; b. Athens County, O., 1861; attended pub. schs. a few months; married. Entered the street car service as a driver at Columbus, O., 1888; assisted in organizing employes of that system; was elected pres., later elected sec. and business agt.; pres. Trades and Labor Council of Columbus, 2 terms; assisted in organizing Amalgamated Assn. of St. and Electric Ry. Employes at Indianapolis, 1892; eleeted pres., 1893; internat. pres. Amalgamated Assn. of St., Electric Ry. and Motor Coach Employes of America since 1893. Editor The Motorman and Conductor, 11 yrs.; apptd. by Gov. Pingree, judge State Court of Arbitration, 1898; served as presiding judge, 2 yrs. Mem. exec. com. Nat. Civic Federation; mem. St. Ry. Commn. of Detroit, 6 mos.; apptd. by Am. Fed. of Labor to investigate municipal ownership and operation of st. rys. in Europe and its effect upon the workers there, was sent to represent Am. trade unions at British Trade Union Labor Congress, Birmingham, Eng., Sept. 1916; mem. exec. council A.F. of L. since 1917, now also v.p.; served as mem. Federal Electric Ry. Commn., also mem. President Wilson's 1st Indust. Commn. Address: 1214 Griswold St., Detroit, Mich. Died Oct. 31, 1949.

MAHONEY, John C., judge; b. Cork, Ireland, Mar. 22, 1881; s. Cornelieus and Mary (Foley) M.; ed. Evening High Sch., Worcester, Mass.; studied law, Northeastern Law Sch., Harvard and Boston U.; m. Mary G. O'Connor, Nov. 25, 1914. Admitted to Mass. bar, 1914, and began practice at Worcester; mem. Mass. Ho. of Rep., 1911-13; alderman, Worcester, 1915; mayor of Worcester, term 1932-35; dir. Pub. Library, Worcester, 1924-30; apptd. judge 1st Circuit Court of Appeals, Boston, Jan. 1940; mem. Mahoney & Moynihan and spl. dist. court judge. Clubs: Lions, Wachusett Country. Home: 34 Piedmont St. Office: 390 Main St., Worcester, Mass. Died July 12, 1946.

MAHONEY, Joseph Nathaniel, inventor, cons. engr.; b. Boston, Mass., Aug. 25, 1878; s. Daniel J. and Anne (Leary) M.; ed. Mechanic Arts High Sch., Boston; Lowell Inst. course Mass. Inst. Tech.; m. Marie Hynes, 1897; children—Howard Joseph, Charles Francis, Daniel James. Began with Electric Storage Supply Co., Boston, 1894; successively with Electro-Chem. Storage Battery Co. (New York), Electric Illuminating & Power Co. (L.I. City), N.Y. Air Brake Co. (New York), Am. Electric Brake Co. (New York) until 1906; with Westinghouse Electric & Mfg. Co., Pittsburgh, Pa., 1906-18, Westinghouse Air Brake Co., Wilmerding, Pa., 1907-14, cons. engr., Sperry Gyroscope Co., Brooklyn, N.Y., 1918-29, Condit Elec. Mfg. Co., Boston. 1920-25, also other cos.; mgr. of engring., Am. Brown Boveri Electric Corp., Camden, N.J., 1926-27; pres. 1929 and 1930, Herbert E. Bucklen Corp. (Elkhart, Ind.), and Perkins Corp. (South Bend, Ind.); cons. engr. Pacific Elec. Mfg. Corp., San Francisco, 1931-32, Sperry Corp., New York, and Wright Aeronautical Corp., Paterson, N.J., since 1933. Awarded many patents, U.S. and foreign countries. Fellow Am. Institute Elec. Engrs.; mem. Am. Soc. Mech. Engrs., Am. Soc. C.E., Am. Inst. Mining and Metall. Engrs., Am. Electrochem. Soc., Inst. Radio Engrs., Soc. Automotive Engrs. Registered professional engr. State of N.Y. Contbr. to tech. publs. Home: 615 77th St., Brooklyn 9, N.Y. Died Jan. 1, 1946.

MAHONEY, William J. (mȧ-hō'nē), univ. pres.; b. Brooklyn, N.Y., Nov. 8, 1896; s. John Joseph and Margaret Mary (Lynch) M.; student St. Joseph's Coll., Princeton, N.J., 1912-16, St. Vincent's Sem., Phila., Pa., 1916-22; J.C.D., Collegium Pontificium Internationale Angelicium, Rome, Italy, 1924; A.M., Niagara U., Niagara Falls, N.Y., 1925, hon. LL.D., 1943. Ordained priest Roman Cath. Ch., 1922; prof. canon law, St. John's Sem., Brooklyn, N.Y., 1924-29, prof. of philosophy, 1929-30; prof. philosophy of edn., Niagara U., 1930-42, dean Coll. of Bus. Adminstrn., 1936-42; pres. St. John's U., Brooklyn, since 1942. Trustee St. John's U. Mem. Rochester, N.Y. Chamber of Commerce, Sigma Alpha Sigma, Delta Mu Delta. Author: De Potestate Delegata, 1924. Home: St. John's Univ., Brooklyn, N.Y. Died Apr. 28, 1947.

MAIER, Walter Arthur (mī'yẽr), college prof.; b. Boston, Mass., Oct. 4, 1893; s. Emil William and Anna Catherine (Schad) M.; prep. edn., Concordia Collegiate Inst., Bronxville, N.Y., 1906-12; A.B., Boston U., 1913; Concordia Sem., St. Louis, Mo., 1913-16; A.M., Harvard University, 1920, Ph.D., 1929; D.D., Concordia Coll., Unley, South Australia, 1943; LL.D., Houghton College, 1945; married Hulda Augusta Eickhoff, June 14, 1924; children—Walter Arthur, Paul Luther. Exec. sec. Internat. Walther League, 1920-22; prof. Semitic langs. and O.T. interpretation, Concordia Sem., since 1922. Editor Walther League Messenger, 1920-45; speaker on Lutheran Hour over Columbia Broadcasting System, 1930-31, Mutual Broadcasting System, since 1935. In relief work among German prisoners, Gallup's Island, Boston Habor, and War Prison Camp No. 1, Still River, Mass., 1917-19; camp pastor Camp Gordon, Atlanta, Ga., 1918. Served as tech. adv. to Mil. Govt. (Education and Religious Affairs Branch), Germany, 1947. Member American Oriental Society, Gamma Delta (one of founders). Awarded Billing's prize in oratory, Harvard, 1919. Independent. Lutheran. Club: Harvard. Author: The Lutheran Hour, 1931; For Better, Not for Worse, 1935, 3d edit., 1939; Christ for Every Crisis, 1935; Christ for the Nation, 1936; Winged Words for Christ, 1937; The Cross from Coast to Coast; The Radio for Christ; Peace through Christ, 1940; Courage in Christ, 1941; For Christ and Country, 1942; Victory Through Christ, 1943; America, Turn to Christ, 1944; Christ, Set the World Aright, 1945; Jesus Christ, Our Hope, 1946; Rebuilding With Christ, 1946; Let us Return Unto the Lord, 1947; He Will Abundantly Pardon, 1948; The Airwaves Proclaim Christ, 1948; 1000 Radio Voices for Christ, 1949 Day by Day with Jesus (devotional calendar issued annually), 1939-49. Home: 11 Seminary Terrace N, 5. Address: 801 De Mun Av., St. Louis 5. Died Jan. 11, 1950.

MAILHOUSE, Max, M.D.; b. New Haven, Conn., Feb. 5, 1857; s. Jacob and Caroline (Rosenthal) M., Ph.B., Yale, 1876, M.D., 1878; m. Clara L. Johnson, 1887 (died 1900); children—Grace L., Robert J.; m. 2d, Celia B. Katz, 1902 (died June 12, 1915); children—Barbara C., Virginia L. Began practice at New Haven, 1878; clin. prof. neurology, Yale U., 1907-20, now prof. emeritus; pres. Conn. Colony for Epileptics, 1910-15. Pres. Nat. Assn. for Study of Epilepsy, 1906-07, Conn. State Med. Soc., 1915-16; mem. New York Neurol. Soc., A.M.A., Assn. for Research in Nervous & Mental Disease, Am. Psychiatric Assn., Internat. Assn. for Study of Epilepsy, Conn. Psychiatric Assn. Club: Graduate. Pres. Yale Class Secs. Assn., 1916-17; mem. Yale Alumni Advisory Bd., 1916-17. Mem. Exam. Bd. for Officers of Med. R.C., 1917-18. Was sec. of first state med. exam. bd. for Conn., 1893-1900. Died Oct. 9, 1941.

MAIN, Charles Thomas, engineer; b. Marblehead, Mass., Feb. 16, 1856; s. Thomas and Cordelia (Reed) M.; S.B., Mass. Inst. Tech., 1876; Dr. of Engring., Northeastern U.; m. Elizabeth Freeto Appleton, Nov. 14, 1883; children—Charles Reed, Alice Appleton, Theodore. Asst., Mass. Inst. Tech., 1876-79; draftsman Manchester Mills, 1880-81; engr., 1882-87, supt. and engr., 1887-92, Pacific Mills; private practice as designer industrial plants since 1893; trustee Winchester Savings Bank; chmn. Chas. T. Main, Inc. Mem. Bd. Aldermen, Lawrence, Mass., 1887-89, Water and Sewerage Bd., Winchester, Mass., 1894-1905. Mem. Corp. Mass. Inst. Tech. Republican. Congregationalist. Fellow Am. Soc. Mech. Engrs. (past pres.); mem. Am. Soc. C.E., Boston Soc. C.E. (past pres.), Nat. Assn. Cotton Mfrs., N.E. Water Works Assn., Am. Acad. Arts and Sciences, Am. Inst. Consulting Engrs. (ex-pres.). Clubs: Downtown, Engineers (ex-pres.), University (Boston). Home: Winchester, Mass. Office: 201 Devonshire St., Boston, Mass. Died Mar. 6, 1943.

MAIN, John Fleming, judge; b. Mercer County, Ill., Sept. 10, 1864; s. William R. and Sarah M. (Fleming) M.; A.B., Princeton University, 1891, LL.D., 1926; student law department, U. of Mich., 1895-97, LL.D., 1937; m. Mary G. Crouch, June 29, 1892; 1 dau., Mrs. Margaret Wylde. Began practice, Aledo, Ill., 1897; removed to Seattle, Wash., 1900; prof. law, U. of Wash., 1904-09; judge Superior Court, King County, Wash., 1909-12; judge Supreme Court, Wash., since Oct. 1, 1912, chief justice, 1923-25; nonresident lecturer, Northwestern Univ. Law Sch., Chicago, summer, 1925. Republican. Presbyterian. Mason (32°). Home: 3601 E. Union St., Seattle, Wash. Office: Temple of Justice, Olympia, Wash. Died Oct. 13, 1942.

MAIER, Walter Arthur (mī'yĕr), college prof.; b. Boston, Mass., Oct. 4, 1893; s. Emil William and Anna Catherine (Schad) M.; prep. edn., Concordia Collegiate Inst., Bronxville, N.Y., 1906-12; A.B., Boston U., 1913; Concordia Sem., St. Louis, Mo., 1913-16; A.M., Harvard University, 1920, Ph.D., 1929; D.D., Concordia Coll., Unley, South Australia, 1943; LL.D., Houghton College, 1945; married Hulda Augusta Eickhoff, June 14, 1924; children—Walter Arthur, Paul Luther. Exec. sec. Internat. Walther League, 1920-22; prof. Semitic langs. and O.T. interpretation, Concordia Sem., since 1922. Editor Walther League Messenger, 1920-45; speaker on Lutheran Hour over Columbia Broadcasting System, 1930-31, Mutual Broadcasting System, 1935, 36, 37, 38, 39, 40, 41, 42, 43, 44, 45, 46. In relief work among German prisoners, Gallup's Island, Boston Harbor, and War Prison Camp No. 1, Still River, Mass., 1917-19; camp pastor Camp Gordon, Atlanta, Georgia, 1918. Served as technical advisor to Military Govt. (Education and Religious Affairs Branch), Germany, 1947. Member American Oriental Society, Gamma Delta (one of founders). Awarded Billing's prize in oratory, Harvard, 1919. Independent. Lutheran. Club: Harvard. Author: The Lutheran Hour, 1931; For Better, Not for Worse, 1935, 3d edit., 1939; Christ for Every Crisis, 1935; Christ for the Nation, 1936; Winged Words for Christ, 1937; The Cross from Coast to Coast; The Radio for Christ, Peace through Christ, 1940; Courage in Christ, 1941; For Christ and Country, 1942; Victory Through Christ, 1943; America, Turn to Christ, 1944; Christ, Set the World Aright, 1945; Jesus Christ, Our Hope, 1946; Rebuilding With Christ, 1946; Let us Return Unto the Lord, 1947; Day by Day with Jesus (devotional calendar issued annually), 1939-48. Dir. Valparaiso Univ. Home: 11 Seminary Terrace N, 5. Address: 801 De Mun Av., St. Louis 5, Mo. Died Jan. 11, 1950.

MAITLAND, Royal Lethington, lawyer; b. Ingersoll, Ont., Can., Sept. 1, 1889; s. Robert Reid and Elizabeth (Robb) M.; ed. pub. schs., Vancouver, B.C., m. Ruth Hildred, Jan. 28, 1914; children—Elizabeth Ruth (wife of Capt. Bruce Harley, M.C.), Nora Kathleen, Robert Reid (Lt., R.C.N.R.), William John (Lt., D.F.M., missing in action 1943). Pres., Vancouver Bar Assn., 1940; treas., Law Soc. of B.C., 1942-43; mem., Legislature Assembly of B.C., 1928-33 and since 1937; atty.gen. for B.C., since 1941; dir., Pacific and Gt. Eastern Ry.; leader, Progressive Party for B.C. since 1938; pres., Can. Bar Assn., 1944-45; life mem., Am. Bar Assn.; hon. mem., Washington Bar Assn. Clubs: Vancouver; Union (Victoria). Home: 4489 Angus Drive, Vancouver, B.C., Can. Died Mar. 28, 1946.

MAJOR, Duncan Kennedy, Jr., army officer; b. New York, N.Y., Apr. 2, 1876; s. Duncan Kennedy and Kate (Olwell) M.; grad. U.S. Mil. Acad., 1899; distinguished grad. Inf.-Cav. Sch., 1906; grad. Army Staff Coll., 1907, Army War Coll., 1912; m. Ruth, daughter of James Edward and Ann (Parker) Barkley. Commd. 2d lt. inf., Feb. 15, 1899; promoted through grades to brig. gen., Nov. 1, 1935. Served in Philippine Insurrection, 1899-1900, Boxer Rebellion in China, 1900, World War, 1918-19, as chief of staff 26th Div. A.E.F.; participated in Champagne-Marne defensive and Eisne-Marne, St. Mihiel and Meuse-Argonne offensive; dept. chief and chief of staff Am. Embarkation Center, La Mans, France, 1919. Was student officer L'Ecole de L'Intendance, Paris, France, 1912, Staff Sch., Langres, France, 1918, Inf. Sch., 1924; served with Gen. Staff, Dept. of War, 1921-24 and 1932-36; aide-de-camp to Gen. of the Armies of U.S., 1923; chief of staff 4th Corps Area, Atlanta, Ga., 1926-30; comd. 34th Inf., 1924-26, 29th Inf., 1930-32; rep. Dept. of War on advisory council of the dir. of Emergency Conservation Work, 1933-36; comd. 21st Inf. Brigade, 1936-38; San Francisco Port of Embarkation, 1938; now retired. Awarded D.S.M., 1919, Purple Heart, 1937. Catholic. Club: Army and Navy. Address: Seminary Rd., Route 2, Alexandria, Va. Died May 26, 1947; buried in Arlington National Cemetery.

MAJOR, Elliott Woolfolk, ex-governor; b. Lincoln County, Mo., Oct. 20, 1864; s. James Reed and Sarah T. (Woolfolk) M.; ed. dist. schs. and Watson Sem., Ashley, Mo.; m. Elizabeth Myers, June 14, 1887. Admitted to Mo. bar, 1885; mem. Mo. Senate, 11th Dist., 1897-99; atty.-gen. of Mo., 1908-12; successfully prosecuted lumber trust, beef trust and harvester trust; gov. of Mo., term Jan. 1913-Jan. 1917. Democrat. Methodist. Mem. Am. Bar Assn., Mo. State Bar Assn. Mason. Club: Country. Home: Avalon Hotel, 339 N. Taylor Av., St. Louis, Mo. Office: Federal Commerce Trust Bldg., St. Louis. Died July 9, 1949.

MALBURN, William Peabody, banker; b. Freeport, Ill.; s. John Kinney and Margaret Trimble (Morrow) M.; ed. pub. schs., Freeport; m. Helen Anna, d. Hon. Charles S. Thomas, June 7, 1898 (dec.); children—Charles Thomas, Elizabeth Brewster (Mrs. Stuart S. Smith). Mem. law firm of Thomas, Bryant & Malburn, 1906-14; asst. sec. of the treasury, by appmt. of President Wilson, 1914-17; v.p. Am. Exchange Nat. Bank, New York, now Irving Trust Co., 1919-31, Chicago Title & Trust Co., 1933-39. Author: What Happened to Our Banks, 1934; The Principles of Commercial Banking. Democrat. Episcopalian. Home: 927 W. Stephenson St., Freeport, Ill. Died Apr. 9, 1945.

MALCOLM, William Lindsay, civil engring.; b. Mitchell, Ont., Can., Feb. 2, 1884; s. George and Margaret (Milligan) M.; M.A., Queens U., Kingston, Can., 1905, B.Sc., 1907; M.C.E., Cornell U., 1934, Ph.D., 1937; m. Jessie L. Ellis, May 4, 1908; 1 son, Stewart G. W. (dec.); m. 2d, Margaret Murray, Sept. 2, 1933. City engr. Stratford, Ont., Can., 1907; asso. city engr., Guelph, 1909-10-11; asst. prof. surveying, Queens U., 1907-09, asst. prof. civil engr., 1909-14, prof. municipal engring., 1914-38; came to U.S., 1938; dir. Sch. of Civil Engring., Cornell U., since 1938. Served as capt. Canadian Engrs., C.E.F., 1914-15, major, 1915-17, lt. col., 1917-19; lt. col. Canadian Engrs. Res. since 1919. Twice mentioned in dispatches. Mem. bd. visitors Royal Mil. Coll. of Canada, 1938-41. Mem. Am. Soc. C.E., Am. Water Works Assn., Engring. Inst. of Canada, Canadian Inst. Sewage and Sanitation, Professional Engrs. of Ontario, Ontario Land Surveyors, New York State Sewage Works Assn. Presbyterian. Club: Ithaca Golf and Country. Writer of occasional articles. Home: 604 E. State St., Ithaca, N.Y. Died Jan. 18, 1948; buried Kingston, Ont., Can.

MALINOWSKI, Bronislaw Kasper (mä-lē-nôv'skĭ), anthropologist; b. Cracow, Poland, Apr. 7, 1884; s. Lucyan and Józefa (Łacka) M.; Ph.D., Polish U., Cracow, 1908; student U. of Leipzig, Germany, 1908-10; D.Sc., U. of London, 1916; D.Sc. (hon.), Harvard (Tercentenary), 1936; came to U.S., 1938; m. Elsie Rosaline Masson, Mar. 6, 1919 (died 1935); children—Józefa Marya, Wanda, Helena; m. 2d, Valetta Hayman-Joyce, June 6, 1940. Lecturer London Sch. of Econs., 1912-13; on anthropol. expdn. to New Guinea, 1914-20; reader in social anthropology, U. of London, 1924-27, prof. anthropology since 1927, on leave since 1939; visiting prof. anthropology and fellow of Timothy Dwight Coll., Yale, since 1939. Hon. fellow Royal Soc. of New Zealand; mem. Royal Acad. of Science of Netherlands, Polish Acad. of Sciences and Arts, Phi Beta Kappa, Alpha Delta Kappa, Sigma Xi. Roman Catholic. Author: The Family Among the Australian Aborigines, 1913; Primitive Religion and Social Differentiation (in Polish), 1915; Argonauts of the Western Pacific, 1922; Crime and Custom in Savage Society (translated into French and Chinese), 1926; Myth in Primitive Psychology, 1926 (Chinese transl. 1935); Sex and Repression in Savage Society, 1926 (Chinese transl. 1937, also French); The Sexual Life of Savages in N.W. Melanesia (Polish, French, Spanish, Italian, German transls.), 1929; Coral Gardens and Their Magic (2 vols.), 1935; The Foundations of Faith and Morals, 1936; also author articles in Nature, Jour. of the Royal Anthropol. Inst., Man. etc. Home: 261 Canner St., New Haven, Conn. Died May 16, 1942.

MALISOFF, William Marias, biochemist; b. Ekaterinoslav, Russia, Mar. 14, 1895; s. Mark and Hannah (Marias) E.; came to U.S., 1905, naturalized, 1911; B.S., Columbia, 1915, Ch.E., 1918; Ph.D., New York Univ., 1925; m. Sally Juster, May 19, 1919; children—Eda, Vera, Marias. Instr. Columbia, 1916-20, New York Univ., 1924-25; consultant, city of New York, 1925-29; dir. organic research, Atlantic Refining Co., Phila., 1929-34; research asso. and prof. Univ. of Pa., 1930, 1934-35; prof. biochemistry, Polytechnic Inst., Brooklyn, 1937-45, Essex Coll. of Medicine, Newark, N.J., 1945-46; dir. of research Longevity Research Foundation, New York, N.Y., since 1946; consultant U.S. Indsl. Alcohol Co., Air Reduction Co., American Molasses Co., Commercial Solvents, City of Phila., Robinson Foundation, Tobey Maltz Foundation. Served as chem. dir. milkweed project, U.S. Navy, 1944. Mem. Philosophy of Sci. Assn. (pres. since 1934), Am. Chem. Soc., A.A.A.S., Am. Assn. Sci. Workers, History of Sci. Soc., Phi Beta Kappa, Phi Lambda Upsilon. Author: A Calendar of Doubts and Faiths, 1930; Meet the Sciences, 1932; The Span of Life, 1937; The Dictionary of Biochemistry (also editor-in-chief), 1943. Editor-in-chief Philosophy of Science (quarterly) since 1934. Editorial bd. mem. Am. Rev. of Soviet Medicine. Contbr. numerous monographs and articles to scientific revs. Home: 360 West 55th St., New York 19. Office: 254 West 31st St., New York 1. Died Nov. 15, 1947.

MALLALIEU, Wilbur V(incent) (măl'lȧ-lōō), clergyman; b. Baltimore, Md., May 10, 1876; s. John Buckley and Mary (Catherine) (Amos) M.; student Baltimore City Coll., 1892-95; A.B., Dickinson Coll., Carlisle, Pa., 1899; B.D., Drew Theol. Sem., 1902; grad. study same and New York U., Free Ch. Coll., Glasgow, Scotland; S.T.D., Wesleyan U., Middletown, Conn., 1916; D.D., Dickinson Coll. Carlisle, Pa., 1935; m. Gertrude Seville, Feb. 23, 1910; 1 foster dau., Wanda (wife of Fred W. Geib, M.D.). Ordained ministry M.E. Ch., 1903; pastor Roland Park, Md., 1903-11, Union Ch., Washington, D.C., 1911-14, Summit, N.J., 1914-18; capt. Am. Red Cross, in charge home service, U.S. Gen. Hosps. No. 3 and No. 27, and Fort Wadsworth, N.Y., 1918-20; pastor Englewood, N.J., 1920-22, First M.E. Ch., Akron, O., 1922-28, First M.E. Ch., Charleston, W.Va., 1928-33, Grace Ch., Harrisburg, Pa., 1933-43; retired Oct. 15, 1943; preacher in various colleges, 1905-43. Chmn. Com. of 100, Washington, D.C., 1913; trustee Y.W.C.A., Akron and Charleston. Mem. Phi Beta Kappa, Phi Delta Theta. Home: 47 Prospect St., Madison, N.J. Died Nov. 16, 1943.

MALLET-PREVOST, Severo (măl-lā'prē-vō'), lawyer; b. Zacatecas, Mex., Oct. 8, 1860; s. Grayson and Marianita (Cosio) M.-P.; B.S., U. of Pa., 1881; m. Virginia Hopkins, d. James M. Johns, Dec. 31, 1887; m. 2d, Laeta, d. Edgar A. Hartley, July 26, 1930. Admitted to Pa. bar, 1885; removed to New York, Dec. 1885; mem. Curtis, Mallet-Prevost & Colt (now Curtis, Mallet-Prevost, Colt & Mosle), since 1897; sec. of commn. apptd. by President Cleveland to report on boundary line between British Guiana and Venezuela; counsel for Govt. of Venezuela before the Paris Arbitration Tribunal in the British Guiana boundary arbitration; agt. and sr. counsel for U.S. in arbitration with Great Britain on pecuniary claims; special assistant to attorney general of U.S. in Peralta-Reavis case, involving title to N.M. and Ariz.; former pres. Pan-Am. Soc. of U.S. Decorations: Order of Isabela la Catolica (Spain); Order of the Redeemer (Greece); Order of the Liberator (Venezuela). Home: 333 E. 57th St. Office: 63 Wall St., New York. Died Dec. 10, 1948.

MALLON, Alfred Edward, flour mfr.; b. Minneapolis, Minn., Sept. 11, 1892; s. Matthew Joseph and Frances Louise (Williams) M.; B.A., Amherst Coll., 1914; M.A., Univ. of Minn., 1915; m. Kirsten Kragh, July 1, 1925; 1 dau., Kirsten Louise. Joined Pillsbury Flour Mills, 1915, mgr. fgn. dept., 1919, dir. since 1930, vice pres. since 1933, treas. since 1940. Served in U.S. Army, 1917-18; grad. Saumur Arty. Sch., France, 1918. Mem. Nat. Fgn. Trade Council (dir.), Millers' Nat. Fedn. (dir., mem. exec. com.), U.S. Chamber of Commerce (fgn. commerce com.), Nat. Assn. Mfrs. (internat. com.), Am. Legion, Sigma Delta Rho, Phi Beta Kappa, Sigma Xi. Republican. Roman Catholic. Clubs: Minneapolis Athletic, Minneapolis Automobile. Home: 249 Interlachen Rd., Hopkins. Office: Pillsbury Bldg., Minneapolis 2. Died Nov. 29, 1947.

MALLORY, Frank Burr (măl'lôr-ĭ), pathologist; b. Cleveland, O., Nov. 12, 1862; s. George Burr and Anna (Faragher) M.; A.B., Harvard, 1886, A.M., M.D., 1890; hon. Sc.D., Tufts, 1928, Boston Univ., 1932; m. Persis McClain Tracy, Aug. 31, 1893; children—Tracy B(urr), G(eorge) Kenneth. Asst. in histology, 1890-91, pathol. anatomy, 1891-92, instr. pathology, 1894-96, asst. prof., 1896-1901, asso. prof., 1901-19, Harvard U.; prof. pathology, Harvard U. Med. Sch., 1928-32; pathologist Boston City Hospital, 1897-1932; cons. pathologist since 1932. Member Assn. of Am. Physicians, Am. Assn. of Pathologists and Bacteriologists, Am. Assn. for Cancer Research, A.M.A., Mass. Med. Soc. Am. Social Science Assn., Internat. Assn. Med. Museums; fellow Am. Acad. Arts and Sciences. Author: The Principles of Pathologic Histology, 1914; (with James H. Wright) Pathological Technique, 1897, 8th edit., 1923. Contbr. to med. jours. Died Sept. 27, 1941.

MALLOY, John Anthony, newspaper editor; b. Chicago, Ill., Jan. 18, 1896; s. John Dorsey and Anna (Clancy) M.; ed. St. James Sch. and High Sch., Chicago; student U. of Ill., 1914-15. Began as reporter on Chicago Daily News, 1918; later reporter Chicago Herald and Examiner and sports writer New York American; city editor Chicago Herald-Examiner, 1927-29; night city editor New York American, 1929-30; city editor Boston American, 1930-33; mng. editor Boston Sunday Advertiser, 1933; editor Boston American, Boston Daily Record, Boston Sunday Advertiser, 1935-38; editorial supervisor Hearst Newspapers since Jan. 1, 1939. Home: Drake Hotel. Office: 326 W. Madison St., Chicago, Ill. Died Mar. 19, 1943.

MALONEY, Francis (mȧ-lōn'ē), U.S. senator; b. Meriden, Conn., Mar. 31, 1894; s. Patrick and Grace (Hickey) M.; ed. pub. and parochial schs., Meriden; m. Martha M. Herzig, June 27, 1918; children—Robert Francis, Marilyn, Grace, Ann. Reporter for Meriden Morning Record, 1914-21. Mem. United States Naval Reserve Force, during World War. Mayor of Meriden 2 terms, 1929-33; mem. 73d Congress (1933-35), 3d Conn. Dist.; elected to U.S. Senate for term,

1935-41, re-elected, 1940. Mem. Sons of Union Vets. of Civil War, Am. Legion. Democrat. Home: 60 Park Place. Office: 3 Colony St., Meriden, Conn. Died Jan. 16, 1945.

MANCHESTER, Arthur Livingston, musical educator; b. New Gretna, N.J., Feb. 9, 1862; s. Rev. L. O. and Anne (Bray) M.; ed. Pennington (N.J.) Sem.; grad. Phila. Musical Acad. in theory; studied voice culture under various teachers; m. Etta E. Kribbs, Mar. 14, 1893; children—(by first marriage) Gerald O'Neal; (by second marriage) Frederic Arthur, Alan Kribbs, Willis Bray, Ruth Etta. Was ch. organist at 13; at 20 prin. Musical Inst. of Beaver, Pa., Female Coll. and organist and choirmaster Beaver M.E. Ch.; later organized musical dept. Clarion (Pa.) State Normal Sch., and Conservatory of Music of Martha Washington Coll., Abingdon, Va.; in charge teachers' dept., Oliver Ditson Co., 1901-04; dean Sch. of Music, Converse Coll., Spartanburg, S.C., and condr. S. Atlantic States Music Festival, Jan. 1904-June 1913; dean Sch. of Music, Southwestern U., Georgetown, Tex., 1913-18; dean Hardin Coll. Conservatory of Music, Mexico, Mo., 1918-20; condr. of Elmira, N.Y., Symphony Orchestra, and Elmira Choral Soc., 1920-23; dir. music, Weaver Coll., Weaverville, N.C., 1923-30; dir. Aeolian Choir (women's chorus), Florio Singers (women's chorus), Peoples Chorus, Asheville, N.C., Manchester Choristers (30 voices). Choirmaster Trinity P.E. Ch., Asheville, N.C., Central M.E. Ch., Florence, S.C. Mem. adv. council Yenching U. Mem. Hymn Soc. Was associate editor Étude, Phila., 4 yrs.; founder and editor The Musician, 1896-1902, The Messenger (official organ Music Teachers' Nat. Assn.), 1900-04. Pres. Music Teachers' Nat. Assn., 1900-02; a founder Am. Guild of Organists; mem. Clef Club, New York, Internat. Soc. Musicians, Asheville Music Teachers' Assn. (v.p.); chmn. Beethoven Centenary Celebration; local director of First and Second Atwater Kent Auditions; pres. music dept., Southern Ednl. Assn., 1910-12; pres. Tex. Music Teachers' Assn., 1915-18; sec.-treas. Assn. of Presidents; chmn. music dept. State Teachers' Assn.; dir. Am. Choral Alliance; hon. mem. Phi Mu Alpha, Sinfonia. Republican. Methodist. Author: Twelve Lessons in the Fundamentals of Tone Production; Special Bulletin of Status of Music Education in the United States; College Courses in Music Appreciation; Tone Production Lessons for the Choirmaster; Tonal and Physical Concepts in Singing; Music Education; A Musical America; The American Composer—A Sequence; A Study of Tone Production and Vocal Diction; The Task and Qualifications of the Teacher of Voice Culture; Cathedrals, Music and Worship; The Strange Behavior of a Studio Table. Contbr. to musical publs. Home and Studio: 61 E. Glover St., Orangeburg, S.C. Died Oct. 23, 1947.

MANCHESTER, Herbert A., clergyman; b. Hartland, N.Y., Nov. 2, 1859; s. James Harvey and Minerva (King) M.; B.A., U. of Rochester, 1887, M.A., 1890, D.D., 1913; grad. Auburn Theol. Sem., 1890; post-grad. studies, Syracuse and Harvard; m. Grace Denniston Smith, Sept. 16, 1890 (died Feb. 25, 1917); m. 2d, Mary Barbara Gersbacher, Apr. 16, 1926. Ordained Congl. ministry, 1901; pastor successively Danforth Congl. Ch., Syracuse, First Presbyn. Ch., East Boston, Mass., Union Ch., Rio Janeiro, Brazil, until 1916; sec. Mass. Bible Soc., 1916-19; pastor Union Ch., Yokohama, 1921-29, and ad interim, Central Union Ch., Honolulu, 1925. Chaplain Lake Placid Club, N.Y., 1931. Sec. Mission to Lepers, 1909-12. Mem. Japan Assn. (pres. 1926-27), Phi Beta Kappa, Delta Upsilon. Traveled around world, 1929-30. Author: Japanese Tales. Lectures on following subjects: Brazilian History, Seen in Japan, The Taj Mahal, Angkor. Home: 1512 Braeburn Rd., Altadena, Calif. Died Dec. 12, 1943.

MANDELBAUM, Samuel; judge U.S. Dist. Court, Southern Dist. of N.Y., since 1936. Address: 277 Broadway, New York, N.Y.* Died Nov. 20, 1946.

MANDEVILLE, Hubert C., lawyer; b. Ithaca, N.Y., Jan. 29, 1867; s. Edgar W. and Carrie E. (Cassidy) M.; grad. Elmira Free Acad., 1884; A.B., Union Coll. (N.Y.), 1888, L.H.D., 1923; m. Mary F. Stoops, June 8, 1892. Admitted to N.Y. bar, 1890; mem. Herendeen & Mandeville, Elmira, 1892-1918, now Mandeville, Buck, Teeter & Harpending; pres. Elmira Foundry Co., Worcester Salt Co.; chmn. board Thatcher Mfg. Co.; dir. Olean Glass Co., Chemung Canal Trust Co.; trustee Elmira Savings Bank. Pres. Bd. of Edn., Elmira, 1911; mem. N.Y. State Constl. Conv., 1915; mem. Rep. State Com., 1916-36. Pres. bd. of trustees Elmira Coll.; life trustee Union Coll., Schenectady. Mem. Am. Bar Assn., N.Y. State Bar Assn., Assn. Bar City of N.Y., Phi Beta Kappa, Psi Upsilon. Episcopalian. Mason. Clubs: Elmira City, Country (Elmira); Authors' (London). Author: Abstract Telephone Law, 1914. Home: 509 W. Church St. Office: Robinson Bldg., Elmira, N.Y.; and 40 Worth St., New York, N.Y. Died Mar. 27, 1943.

MANEY, George Alfred (mā'nē), prof. structural engring.; b. Minneapolis, Minn., Dec. 9, 1888; s. Thomas H. and Ella (Hallam) M.; C.E., U. of Minn., 1911; M.S., U. of Ill., 1914; m. Mabelle O. Draxten, Apr. 7, 1920; children—Thomas D., Elizabeth K. Draftsman Minneapolis & St. Louis R.R., 1911-12; research fellow, U. of Ill., 1913-14; instr., U. of Minn., 1914-18; served as 2d lt. C.A.C., 1918; asst. prof. structural engring., U. of Minn., until 1926; asso. prof. civ. engring., U. of Minn., 1926-27; prof. structural engring., Northwestern U., since 1928; head Dept. Civil Engring., Northwestern U. Inst. Tech., since 1939; cons. engr. on various constrn. projects, including Miss River bridge, Savanna, Ill., and Santa Fe Terminal Bldg., Dallas, Tex. Winner Wason medal of Am. Concrete Inst. for "most meritorious paper of the year 1936." Member Am. Soc. C.E., Western Soc. Engrs. Tau Beta Pi, Sigma Xi. Presbyterian. Club: University. Author: Wind Stresses in Tall Buildings (with W. M. Wilson), 1915. Made 1st gen. statement of slope deflection method, 1915, secondary stresses in steel bridges, 1922, statically indeterminate stresses (with J. I. Parcel), 1925. Home: 3751 Foster Av., Evanston, Ill. Died May 10, 1947.

MANGAN, Thomas J. (măn'găn), lawyer; b. Binghamton, N.Y., August 13, 1872; son of John H. and Catherine (Cleary) M.; B.A., Hamilton Coll., 1894, M.A., 1897, LL.D., 1942; LL.D., Manhattan College (New York City), 1925; LL.D., St. Johns Coll. (Brooklyn, N.Y.), 1927; m. Elizabeth De Lamater Everts, Aug. 2, 1906; children—Charles Everts, Dr. Catherine DeL. Maguire, William De Lamater. Admitted to N.Y. bar, 1896, since practicing at Binghamton; mem. firm Mangan & Mangan & Heath, attys. for Socony Vacuum Co. of N.Y., The Filters Company, Prudential Ins. Co., etc. Mem. Bd. of Regents U. of New York since 1919, 2d term, 1931-43, 3d term, 1943-55 (unanimously elected at joint session N.Y. legislature), vice chancellor, 1933-37, chancellor, 1937-45; chancellor emeritus since 1945. Director Catholic Charities (Inc.) of Diocese of Syracuse. Mem. N.Y. State and Broome County bar assns., Phi Beta Kappa, Delta Kappa Epsilon, Phi Delta Phi. Republican. Catholic. Club: Delta Kappa Epsilon (N.Y. City). Home: 64 Front St. Office: Mangan Bldg., 90 Chenango St., Binghamton, N.Y. Died May 19, 1947.

MANGES, Morris (măng'ĕs), physician; b. New York, May 10, 1865; s. John F. and Bertha May M.; A.B., Coll. City of New York, 1884 (Phi Beta Kappa), A.M., 1887; M.D., Coll. Phys. and Surg. (Columbia), 1887; univs. of Berlin and Vienna, 1888-89; m. Julia Hirschhorn, Jan. 1, 1906. Visiting physician Mt. Sinai Hosp., New York, 1893-1922; consulting physician, Mt. Sinai Hosp., since 1922; prof. clin. medicine, New York Poly. Med. Sch., 1898-1908, New York U., 1911-28. Consulting physician to Hosp. for Deformities and Joint Diseases, and Hebrew Orphan Asylum. Fellow New York Acad. Medicine; mem. Am. Climatol. Assn., N.Y. Pathol. Soc., Am. Gastro-Enterol. Assn., Harvey Soc., A.M.A., A.A.A.S., Archæol. Inst. of America, Oriental Inst. of U. of Chicago, Phi Beta Kappa. Club: North Shore Country. Editor: Ewald's Diseases of the Stomach, 1892. Contbr. on clin. medicine to med. jours. Address: 1185 Park Av., New York, N.Y. Died Jan. 26, 1944.

MANIGAULT, R. S., pres. and pub. News & Courier Co., Evening Post Pub. Co. Address: Charleston, S.C.* Died May 12, 1945.

MANN, Albert Clinton, ry. official; b. Effingham, Ill., Sept. 1, 1881; s. Wallace E. and Jennie A. (Cuthbertson) M.; ed. pub. schs. and business coll.; m. Elizabeth B. Dills, June 30, 1903. Began as stenographer I.C. R.R., 1900, later sec. to coal traffic mgr. and asst. purchasing agt. to 1912; purchasing agt. Central of Ga. Ry., 1912-13, I.C. R.R., 1913-18; member regional purchasing com. U.S. R.R. Administration, at Atlanta, Ga., 1918-19; v.p. Internat. Steel Corp., New York, 1919-20; v.p. I.C. R.R., in charge purchases and supplies, since Dec. 1920. Republican. Clubs: Chicago, Chicago Athletic. Home: 5844 Stony Island Av. Office: 135 E. 11th Pl., Chicago. Died Feb. 1, 1948.

MANN, Albert Russell; b. Hawkins, Pa., Dec. 26, 1880; s. William Imrie and Sarah Malinda (Lansing) M.; B.S.A., N.Y. State Coll. Agr. at Cornell U., 1904; A.M., U. of Chicago, 1916; D.Sc., Syracuse U., 1928; D.Agr., Rhode Island State Coll., 1929; LL.D., U. of Calif., 1930 and from U. of Wis., 1934; hon. D.Agr., U. of Sofia, 1939; m. Mary Douglass Judd, Aug. 23, 1906; children—Marion Lansing (Mrs. H. J. Stover), Jeanette Wilbur (Mrs. G. M. Read), Malcolm Judd, Dorothy Douglass (Mrs. A. D. R. Brown), Arthur (deceased). Assistant superintendent Boston Farm and Trades Sch., 1904; sec. to L. H. Bailey on preparation of Cyclo of American Agriculture, 1905-08; asst. prof. dairy industry, N.Y. State Coll. Agr. at Cornell U., Apr.-June 1908; sec. State Commn. Agr., Albany, N.Y., July-Oct. 1908; sec., registrar and editor, 1908-15, prof. rural social orgn., 1915-16, actg. dean, 1916-17, dean, 1917-31, N.Y. State Coll. Agr. at Cornell U., and State Agrl. Expt. Sta., 1923-31; also dean N.Y. State Coll. of Home Economics, at Cornell U., 1925-31; provost of Cornell U., 1931-37; v.p. and dir. General Education Board since 1937. Dir. agrl. edn. in Europe, Internat. Edn. Board, on leave, 1924-26. Chmn. New York State Planning Board, 1934-36. Secretary N.Y. State Food Commn., also federal food adminstr. in N.Y., 1917-18; chmn. com. on farm and village housing, President's Conf. on Home Bldg. and Home Ownership, 1930-31; mem. bd. mgrs. Bd. of Edn., Northern Bapt. Convention; trustee Cornell University, Colgate-Rochester Divinity School, Hampton Institute, Farm Foundation; member American Country Life Association (ex-pres. and dir.); vice chmn. board Agricultural Missions Foundation; hon. life mem. Assn. Land Grant Colleges and Universities (mem. exec. com., chmn. 1935-37), Nat. Land-Use Planning Com., President's Com. on Farm Tenancy (1936-37), N.Y. State Flood Control Commission. Chairman board First National Bank, Ithaca, New York Decorated Cross of the Commander II, Order of the White Rose (Finland); Agricultural Decoration of the First Class (Belgium); Officer Order of White Lion (Czechoslovakia); designated Empire State Farmer by Future Farmers of America. Fellow A.A.A.S. (v.p. and chmn. sect. 1933-34); member Sigma Xi, Alpha Zeta, Kappa Delta Rho, Phi Kappa Phi, Epsilon Sigma Phi. Baptist. Author: Beginnings in Agriculture, 1911. Contbr. article, "Agricultural Education," in Cyclo. of Social Science. Advisory editor sect. on agriculture in The Book of Popular Science; College and University Administration, Agriculture. Home: 9 Midland Gardens, Bronxville, N.Y. Office: 49 W. 49th St., New York, N.Y. Died Feb. 21, 1947.

MANN, Alexander, bishop; b. Geneva, N.Y., Dec. 2, 1860; s. Duncan Cameron and Caroline Brother (Schuyler) M.; B.A., Hobart Coll., 1881, S.T.D., 1900; S.T.B., Gen. Theol. Sem., 1886, S.T.D., 1923; LL.D., Kenyon and Allegheny colls., 1923; m. Nellie Gerrish Knapp, 1896. Deacon, 1885, priest, 1886, P.E. Ch.; asst. minister, St. James Ch., Buffalo, N.Y., 1885-86; asst. minister, 1887-1900, rector, 1900-05, Grace Ch., Orange, N.J.; rector Trinity Ch., Boston, 1905-23. Elected bishop of Washington, 1908, but declined, for reason that his work in Boston was still unfinished; elected suffragan bishop of Diocese of Newark, 1915, but declined; elected bishop of Western N.Y., 1917, but declined; consecrated bishop of Pittsburgh, Jan. 25, 1923. Pres. House of Clerical and Lay Deputies of Gen. Conv. of P.E. Ch., 1913, 16, 19, 22. Retired Dec. 31, 1943. Mem. Phi Beta Kappa. Republican. Home: 41 Pulteney St., Geneva, N.Y. Died Nov. 15, 1948; buried in Glenview Cemetery, Watkins Glen, N.Y.

MANN, Charles August, chemical engineering; b. Milwaukee, Wis., June 5, 1886; s. Peter and Friedericka (Jahns) M.; B.S. in Chem. Engring., U. of Wis., 1909, M.S., 1911, Ph.D., 1915; m. Lillian E. Shorthill, Dec. 24, 1907. Asst. pharm. chemist, U. of Wis., 1906-11; instr. chem. engring., same, 1911-16; asso. prof. chem. engring., Ia. State Coll. Agr. and Mechanic Arts, 1916-17, prof. in charge of dept., 1917-19; prof. chem. engring., U. of Minn., 1919-21, chief dept. of chem. engr. and prof. since 1921; also cons. practice. Mem. Wis. Nat. Guard 7 yrs. Mem. Am. Inst. Chem. Engrs., Am. Chem. Soc. (pres. Ames sect. 1918, Minn. sect. 1939), Inst. Food Technologists, Am. Electrochemical Soc., Am. Inst. of Chemists, Society of Chem. Industry (London), Am. Soc. for Engring. Edn., Nat. Corrosion Assn., Minn. Assn. of Professional Engrs., Wis. Acad. Science, Minn. Acad. Science, A.A.A.S., Am. Assn. Univ. Profs., Minn.-Ind. Chem. Forum, Minneapolis Garden Club, Sigma Xi, Tau Beta Pi, Phi Lambda Upsilon, Alpha Chi Sigma (pres.), Scabbard and Blade. Unitarian. Mason. Clubs: Engineers', University Campus, Kiwanis, Midland Hills Country. Organized chem. engring. courses at Ia. State Coll. and U. of Minn. Contbr. chem. engring. researches and articles. Home: 35 Barton Av. S.E., Minneapolis. Died June 25, 1949.

MANN, Charles Riborg, physicist; b. Orange, N.J., July 12, 1869; s. Charles Holbrook and Clausine (Borchsenius) M.; A.B., Columbia, 1890, A.M., 1891; Ph.D., U. of Berlin, 1895; Sc.D., Lafayette Coll., 1918; LL.D., Lawrence College, Temple University, 1933; m. Adrienne Amalie Graf, June 25, 1896; children—Riborg Graf, Adrienne. Research asst., 1896-97, asso. in physics, 1897-99, instr., 1899-1902, asst. prof., 1902-07, asso. prof., 1907-14, U. of Chicago; investigator for joint com. on engring. edn. of nat. engring. socs. and Carnegie Foundation Advancement of Teaching, 1914-18. Apptd. advisory mem. Com. on Edn. and Spl. Training, War Dept., Feb. 1918; permanent chmn. of civilian advisory board War Department, General Staff, 1919-25; dir. Am. Council on Education, 1922-34, pres. emeritus since 1934. Translated (from the German of P. Drude) Theory of Optics, 1902. Author: Manual of Advanced Optics, 1902; Physics (with George Ransom Twiss), 1905; The Teaching of Elementary Physics, 1912; A Study of Engineering Education, 1918; Report on the work of the Committee on Education and Special Training, 1919, D.S.M., 1919; Living and Learning, 1938. Home: 2440 Foxhall Rd. Office: 744 Jackson Pl., Washington, D.C. Died Sep. 10, 1942.

MANN, Charles William, pomologist; b. Pittsburgh, Pa., Jan. 4, 1879; s. William Imrie and Sarah Melinda (Lansing) M.; student U. of Pittsburgh, 1901-02; B.S.A., Cornell U., 1906, grad. study 4 mos. 1910; m. Caroline Whalen Judd, July 24, 1912; children—Douglass Lansing, William Imrie, Robert Edward. Soil scientist with Bur. of Soils, 1906-10; asst. pomologist, Bur. Plant Industry, U.S. Dept. Agr., 1910-14, pomologist, 1914-19, pomologist in charge fruit transportation and storage investigations, 1919-22, sr. pomologist since 1922. In investigations of Dept. Agr. determined methods of modified refrigeration forming basis of present practice on western railroads; granted patents on precooling process, assigned to free use of public. Fellow A.A.A.S.; mem. Am. Pomol. Soc., Am. Soc. for Hort. Science, Federal Business Assn., Alpha Zeta. Presbyterian. Club: Cornell (Los Angeles). Writer many reports and bulls. of U.S. Dept. Agr. on fruit transportation and storage. Home: S. Walnut St., San Dimas, Calif. Office: Federal Bldg., Pomona, Calif. Died Dec. 3 1943.

MANN, Kristine, physician; b. Orange, N.J., Aug. 29, 1873; d. Charles Holbrook and Clausine Christiana Riborg (Borchsenius) Mann; A.B., Smith Coll., 1895; A.M., U. of Mich., 1901; Columbia, 1905-06; M.D., Cornell, 1913. Asst. in English, U. of Mich., 1900-

01; instr. English, Vassar Coll., 1901-05, Brearley Sch., New York, 1905-08; instr. hygiene, Wellesley Coll., 1913-14; investigation of physical condition of saleswomen in New York dept. stores (under Dept. Store Edn. Assn.), 1914-16; clin. asst., Cornell U. Med. Coll., 1916-17; lecturer on health, Smith Coll., 1916-17; supervisor health of women in munition plants, Ordnance Dept., 1918-19. Dir. Health Center for Bus. and Industrial Women, 1920-24; student under Dr. C. G. Jung, Zurich; practicing psychoanalyst. Mem. A.M.A. Address: 137 E. 38th St., New York. Died Nov. 12, 1945.

MANN, Paul Blakeslee, biologist; b. Potsdam, N.Y., Dec. 20, 1876; s. Warren and Helen Elizabeth (Blakeslee) M.; grad. Potsdam State Normal and Tr. Sch., 1896; A.B., Cornell, 1902, A.M., 1903; m. Ruth Atherton Paul, Aug. 3, 1904 (died Jan. 27, 1939); 1 dau., Eleanor Atherton; m. H. Rosabell MacDonald, Feb. 1, 1940. Head of commercial dept. N.Y. Mil. Acad., 1896-97, science dept., high sch., Nyack, 1899-1901; asst. in zoölogy, Cornell U., 1902-03; teacher biology, etc., Hill Sch., Pottstown, Pa., 1903-04; teacher biology, Morris High Sch., N.Y. City, 1904-14; 1st asst. N.Y. City high schs., 1914; head biology dept. Evander Childs High School, N.Y. City, 1914-41; retired 1941; asst. prof. biol. methods, Cornell U., summers 1908-10, Coll. of City of N.Y., 1927-34; examiner Coll. Entrance Exam. Bd., zoölogy, 1914-35, biology, 1918-35; naturalist of Sea Pines Camp, 1920-37; associate in edn., Am. Museum Natural History, 1928-38; gave course in field natural history for teachers, 1933-38; chmn. Standing Com. of Science of N.Y. City and chmn. Science Council of N.Y. City, 1936-38; supervisor of science, sr. high schs., 1937, 38; on staff Dale Carnegie Inst., 1937; science com. and junior science projects for New York World's Fair, 1939. Official delegate from U.S. to 1st Internat. Congress on Ednl. Motion Pictures, Rome, Italy, 1934; chmn. nat. com. of Secondary Dept., N.E.A., on ednl. films, 1935-40, and chmn. biology com. to evaluate theatrical films for ednl. uses, 1937, chmn. steering com. for Conf. of Subject Assns. on Curriculum Change since 1942. Fellow A.A.A.S.; mem. Am. Inst. of N.Y. City (twice on bd. mgrs.), N.Y. Acad. of Sciences, N.Y. Assn. of Biology Teachers (twice pres.), Nat. Assn. Biology Teachers (v.p. 1942-43), Nat. Soc. for Study of Edn., Sigma Xi, Gamma Alpha, Pi Gamma Mu. Known as lecturer, contbr. and critic on zool. and biol. science, pedagogy and visual edn.; also on rifle shooting; former rifle coach and adviser to rifle clubs. Author: How to Tell Weather, and Cloud Plates, 1928; The Pursuit of the Vitamins, 1933. Co-author: (Mann and Hastings) Out-of-Doors, 1932, rev. 1937; (Moon and Mann) Biology for Beginners, 1933, rev. 1937; (Moon and Mann) Biology, 1938, rev. 1941; (Dull, Mann and Johnson) Gen. Sciences series: Modern Science in Our Environment, Modern Science in Our Daily Life, Modern Science in Man's Progress, also Teachers' Manual, 1942. Home: 441 W. 21st St., New York, N.Y. Died Oct. 22, 1943.

MANNER, Jane (Jenny Mannheimer), drama reader; b. New York, N.Y.; d. Sigmund (D.D.) and Louise (Herschman) Mannheimer; grad. Hughes High Sch., Cincinnati, O., 1888; B.H., Hebrew Union Coll., Cincinnati, 1888; U. of Cincinnati, 1892; Coll. of Music, Cincinnati, 1892. Dir. Cincinnati Sch. of Expression, 1892-1912; dir. drama dept., Coll. of Music, Cincinnati, 1900-07; traveled in the Orient and Europe, 1912; drama reader before colls. and clubs throughout U.S. since 1913; interpreter of Shakespeare and modern drama, also readings with music; prin. Jane Manner Speech and Drama Studio; apptd. to readership by N.Y. State Coll. for Teachers, 1919, to foster appreciation of good plays through the fine art of reading; reader Montclair Drama Festival, 1921; series, "Plays of Many Lands," Aeolian Hall, New York, 1922; Paris début in Peer Gynt, 1923; drama recitals in English of plays in repertory of Eleanora Duse and the Moscow Art Theatre, 1923, Drama Festival for Univ. of Cincinnati Alumnæ, 1931, Drama Festival, Nov. 1934, Aeolian Hall, New York; apptd. dir. speech and drama dept., School Radio Technique, Radio City, New York, May 1, 1941. Editor: The Silver Treasury, Program Anthology; compiler and editor: Junior Silver Treasury. Author of Better Speech Home Study Course, 1937. Address: 180 W. 58th St., New York, N.Y. Died May 27, 1943.

MANNHEIM, Jean (măn'hīm), artist; b. Kreuznach, Germany; s. Jean and Gertrude (Klein) M.; ed. École Delecluse, Paris; Acad. Colarossi; London Sch. of Art; m. Eunice Drennan, Aug. 31, 1902 (died Jan. 24, 1910); children—Jeanne, Eunice; m. 2d, Harriet R. Crawford, Apr. 3, 1919 (died Dec. 2, 1924); m. 3d, Olive Edwards, Nov. 12, 1935. Exhibited in Salon, Paris, Nat. Acad., New York. Gold medal, Seattle Expn.; gold and silver medals, San Diego Expn., 1915; 1st prize, Phoenix, Ariz.; 1st prize, Sacramento, Calif.; 1st prize, Ebell Club, Los Angeles, 1936; hon. mention, Ebell Club, Los Angeles, 1938; 2d prize Ebell Club, Los Angeles, 1939. V.p. Calif. Art Club. Address: 500 S. Arroyo Blvd., Pasadena, Calif. Died Sept. 6, 1945.

MANNING, Charles N., banker; b. Manchester, Ky., May 10, 1875; s. Isaac S. and Sallie T. (White) M.; ed. State Agrl. and Mech. Coll. (now U. of Ky.), Lexington, Ky., and under pvt. tutors; m. Allie M. Hunter, June 19, 1895; 1 dau., Elinor Faison. Sec. and treas. Security Trust Co., Lexington, 1899-1916, pres., sec. 1916-45, now chmn. bd.; pres. Kentucky Union Co. Trustee, treas., E. O. Robinson Mountain Fund, Frontier Nursing Service; trustee Berea College, Pine Mountain Settlement Sch., Lexington Pub. Library, Lexington Y.W.C.A. Mem. Disciples of Christ. Democrat. Club: Lexington Country, Home: 232 S. Ashland Av. Address: Security Trust Co., Lexington, Ky. Died Jan. 12, 1947.

MANNING, Edward Betts, composer; b. St. John, N.B., Can., Dec. 15, 1874; s. Edward and Sarah (Betts) M.; grad. Collegiate Sch., St. John, N.B., 1889; studied music at Columbia U. under Prof. MacDowell; also under Henry Schradieck, Brooklyn; apptd. Mosenthal Fellow (Columbia); studied also 2 years in Berlin and Paris; m. Elizabeth Matthew, July 18, 1904. Taught music in New York, 1897-1904; instr. Oberlin (O.) Coll., 1905-07; supervisor music, New York pub. schs., 1908-11; instr. Columbia U. since 1914. Composer in all forms—orchestra, chamber music, songs and piano pieces; best known compositions are, Trio op. 11; The Tryst, mezzo soprano and orchestra; Songs, Op. 4 (Breitkopf); opera, "Rip Van Winkle" (prod. N.Y., 1919). Mem. Authors' and Composers' Soc. France. Home: 501 W. 122d St., New York, N.Y. Died Mar. 8, 1948.

MANNING, Isaac Hall, physician, educator; b. Pittsboro, N.C., Sept. 14, 1866; s. John and Louisa (Hall) M.; M.D., Long Island Coll. Hosp., Brooklyn, N.Y., 1897; m. Martha Battle Lewis, April 26, 1906; m. 2d, Mary Best Jones, June 6, 1911. Prof. physiology, U. of N.C., 1901-39, prof. emeritus since 1939, also dean Sch. of Medicine, 1905-33. Pres. State Med. Soc., 1933-34. Fellow Am. Coll. of Physicians; mem. A.M.A., Phi Kappa Sigma, Alpha Kappa Kappa. Democrat. Episcopalian. Home: Chapel Hill, N.C. Died Feb. 12, 1946.

MANNING, Joseph P.; chmn. bd. Boston Elevated Ry.; pres. Joseph P. Manning Co., Metropolitan Sales Corp.; dir. Boston Edison Co., Union Savings Bank, Merchants Nat. Bank. Home: 80 Pond St., Jamaica Plain. Office: 500 Atlantic Av., Boston, Mass.* Died Jan. 23, 1944.

MANNING, Lucius Bass, mfr.; b. Tacoma, Wash., Aug. 18, 1894; s. L. R. and Lucy (Bass) M.; prep. edn., Hotchkiss Sch., Lakeville, Conn.; student Sheffield Scientific Sch. (Yale); m. Katherine Fay Whitney, Sept. 12, 1918; children—Gene Elizabeth, Meredith, Katherine. Automobile salesman, 1915-17; pres. Manning & Co., 1925-33; pres. Thermek Corp.; chmn. bd. and dir. Aviation Corp.; dir. Consolidated Air Craft Corp. In Air Service, U.S. Army, 1917-18; licensed transport pilot; lt. col. U.S. Air Corps since 1942. Club: Glen View. Home: 1500 Lake Shore Drive. Office: 105 W. Adams St., Chicago, Ill.* Died Apr. 9, 1944.

MANNING, Marie (Beatrice Fairfax) (Mrs. Herman E. Gasch), author; b. Washington, D.C.; d. M. Charles and Elizabeth (Barrett) Manning; ed. private schs., Washington, New York, and in Europe; m. Herman Eduard Gasch, June 12, 1905. Began newspaper work in London as spl. writer to N.Y. Herald, later joined regular staff, also reporter New York Evening Journal. Trustee Carnegie Library, since 1920. Clubs: The Arts, Women's National Press, Woman's City (Washington, D.C.); National Arts (New York). Author: Lord Allingham, Bankrupt, 1902; Judith of the Plains, 1903; The Prophetess of the Land of No-Smoke, 1906; Truce, 1906; Under the Sunset (in collaboration), 1906; Crete, the Beginning, 1924. Contbr. to mags. Address: 1753 P St. N.W., Washington. Died Nov. 29, 1945.

MANNING, William Ray, editor Diplomatic Documents; b. Home, Kan., Dec. 26, 1871; s. Enoch and Mariva (Stone) M.; A.B., Baker U., 1899; fellow and asst. English history, U. of Kan., 1901-02, A.M., 1902; fellow and asst. European history, U. of Chicago, 1902-04, Ph.D., 1904; studied in hist. archives at Seville, Madrid, Paris, and London, 1903; m. Mabel Marvel, May 26, 1903; children—Dorothy Carmen, Winston Marvel, Neva Pauline. Inst. economics and history, Purdue U., 1904-07; asst. prof. Am. history University of Mo. Summer Sch., 1907; asst. prof. diplomatic history, Coll. Polit. Sciences, George Washington U., 1907-10; adj. prof. Latin-Am. and English history, U. of Tex., 1910-17, asso. prof. same, 1917-19; official Dept. of State, Washington, since 1918. Lecturer on Latin-Am. history and internat. relations, American U., 1919-34. Engaged in historical research work for Carnegie Instn., summers, 1908, 09, 10; pvt. research work in archives of State Dept., Washington, summer, 1911, in archives of Relaciones Exteriores, Mexico City, summer, 1912, and in Library of Congress, Washington, summer, 1913; Albert Shaw lecturer in diplomatic history, Johns Hopkins, spring 1913. Technical adviser U.S. delegation, 3d Pan-Am. Highway Congress, Santiago, Chile, 1939. Member National Geographic Society, American Society of International Law, American Hist. Assn. (was winner, 1904, of its Justin Winsor prize, with U. of Chicago doctoral dissertion, The Nootka Sound Controversy, 1905). Author: Early Diplomatic Relations Between the United States and Mexico (Shaw lectures), 1916. Editor: Arbitration Treaties Among the American Nations, 1924; Diplomatic Correspondence of United States concerning the Independence of Latin-Am. Nations, 3 vols., 1925; Diplomatic Correspondence of the United States concerning Interamerican Affairs from 1831 to 1860, 12 vols., 1932-39. In recognition of the value of these 2 publications, decorated, National Order of Merit, Govt. of Equador, 1935. Editor: Diplomatic Correspondence of the United States concerning Canadian Relations, 1784-1860, 4 vols. (Vol. I pub. 1940). Traveled in Cuba, Haiti and Dominican Republic, winter of 1931-32, and in Mexico, spring of 1935. Home: 4701 Fessenden St. N.W., Washington, D.C. Died Oct. 28, 1942.

MANNING, William Thomas, bishop; b. Northampton, England, May 12, 1866; s. John and Matilda Manning; B.D., U. of the South, 1893, D.D., 1906, D.D., U. of Nashville, 1901; S.T.D., Columbia U., 1905, Hobart, 1908; D.D., Princeton, 1919; D.C.L., King's College, N.S., 1919; LL.D., N.Y., 1922; LL.D., Kenyon Coll., 1925; S.T.D., Russian Theol. Acad., Paris, 1946; m. Florence Van Antwerp, 1895. Deacon, 1889, priest, 1891, P.E. Ch.; rector Redlands, Calif., 1892; prof. dogmatic theology, U. of the South, 1893-95; rector Lansdowne, Pa., 1896-98, Christ Ch., Nashville, 1898-1903; vicar St. Agnes' Chapel, N.Y. City, 1903-08; asst. rector, 1904-08, rector Trinity Parish, N.Y. City, 1908-21; consecrated bishop of New York, May 11, 1921; resigned, 1946. Volunteer chaplain. Camp Upton, N.Y., Dec. 1917-Nov. 1918. Chevalier Legion d'Honneur, Grand Officer Legion d'Honneur (France); Officer Order of Crown, (Belgium); Grand Cross Order of St. Sava, (Yugoslavia); Grand Cross Order of St. John of Jerusalem, (Patriarchal); Knight Comdr. Order of Orange Nassau (Netherlands); Knight Comdr. Order of the Phoenix (Greece). Sub-Prelate, Order St. John of Jerusalem, Great Britain. Address: 8 Washington Mews, N.Y. City. Died Nov. 18, 1949; buried Cathedral St. John the Divine, N.Y. City.

MANSFIELD, Joseph Jefferson, congressman; b. Wayne, Va. (now W.Va.); s. Joseph Jefferson M., officer C.S.A. (killed in battle, 1861); ed. pub. schs.; m. Annie Scott Bruce, 1888. Settled in Tex., 1881; admitted to bar, 1886; city atty., Eagle Lake, Tex., 1888; mayor, 1889; county atty., Colorado County, Tex., 2 terms, 1892-96; county judge 10 terms and ex-officio county supt. schs.; mem. 65th to 78th Congresses (1917-45), 9th Tex. Dist. Served as adj. 4th Tex. Rgt., rank of capt. Democrat. Episcopalian. Grand Master of Masons of Tex.. 1912-13. Home: Columbus, Tex. Died July 12, 1947.

MANSHIP, Charles Phelps, newspaper pub.; b. McComb City, Miss., Nov. 28, 1881; s. Luther and Belmont (Phelps) M.; ed. Millsaps Coll., Jackson, Miss.; m. Leora Douthit, Nov. 9, 1904; children—Charles, Claude (dec.), Luther (dec.), Douglas Lewis. Began as reporter, Jackson News, 1899; city editor same, 1902-05; city editor Baton Rouge (La.) Times, 1905-09; asso. editor and business mgr. Baton Rouge State Times, 1909-17, editor and pub. since 1917; pub. Baton Rouge Morning Advocate since 1925; dir. La.&Ark. R.R., Gulf States Utilities, Baton Rouge Broadcasting Co., La. Fire Ins. Co. Pres. Southern Newspaper Pubs. Assn., 1941-43. La. del. at large to Dem. Nat. Conv., 1924; area dir. Am. Red Cross Flood Relief, 1927. Mem. Newspaper Industry Adv. Com., 1942; now mem. Adv. Com. to Office of Censorship. Mem. Associated Press (Southern advisory bd.). Asso. dir., U.S. Office of Censorship, London office, 1944; mem. bd. dirs., Am. Newspaper Pubs. Assn., 1944; Kappa Alpha. Democrat. Episcopalian. Elk. Clubs: Westdale, Golf and Country, Nat. Press (Washington); Boston (New Orleans); Bankers (New York). Home: Baton Rouge, La. Died Jan. 27, 1947.

MANSON, Daniel Edgar, pub. utility exec.; b. New Haven, Conn., Oct. 13, 1870; s. Magnus and Margaret (Mowatt) M.; B.A., Yale, 1892; m. Effie Marion Comey, Oct. 18, 1899 (died Nov. 16, 1907); children—Marion (Mrs. George Phillips Hall), John Thomas, Effie Comey (Mrs. Donald H. Butler); m. 2d, Blanche Lauriat Chandler, Jan. 28, 1927. Began as student with Thomson-Houston Electric Company, Lynn, Mass., 1892; with Dennison Elec. Mfg. Co., New Haven, 1893-95; pres. Conn. Elec. Co., 1895-97; with Westinghouse Elec. & Mfg. Co., 1897-1909; with Charles H. Tenney & Co., utility management and engring., 1909-35; dir. Rockland Light & Power Co., Concord Electric Co., Springfield Gas Light Co. Mem. Signal Corps, Conn. Nat. Guard, 1894-97. Mem. Am. Inst. E.E., Alpha Delta Phi. Republican. Conglist. Clubs: Exchange, Yale (Boston); Yale (New York), Algonquin. Home: Old Harbor Rd., Chatham, Mass. Office: 89 Broad St., Boston, Mass. Died 1942.

MANSON, John Thomas; b. New Haven, Conn., Aug. 30, 1861; s. Magnus and Margaret (Mowatt) M.; ed. pub. schs.; m. Mrs. Frank W. Benedict, Jan. 15, 1908 (died July 4, 1919); m. 2d, Mrs. Frank Dean Trowbridge, Apr. 29, 1922. Dir. Niagara Alkali Co., Equitable Life Assurance Soc. of U.S., Security Insurance Company. Trustee Princeton Theological Seminary; trustee Lafayette College; director Presbyn. Ch.; pres. Am. Bible Soc. Republican. Mason. Home: 334 Edwards St., New Haven, Conn. Died Feb. 21, 1944.

MANTLE, Burns (Robert Burns Mantle), newspaper man; b. Watertown, N.Y., Dec. 1873; s. Robert Burns and Susan (Lawrence) M.; ed. public sch. and normal coll.; m. Lydia Sears, Aug. 20, 1903; 1 daughter, Margaret Burns. Dramatic editor Denver Times, 1898-1900, Denver Republican, 1900-01, Chicago Inter Ocean, 1901-07, Chicago Tribune, 1907-08; Sunday editor Chicago Tribune, 1908-11; dramatic editor Evening Mail, New York, 1911-22; dramatic editor Daily News, N.Y., 1922-43; dramatic corr. Chicago Tribune, 1911-43; retired. Editor of Best Plays and Year Book of the Drama in Am. since 1919. Clubs: Players, Dutch Treat. Author: American Playwrights of Today, 1929; Contemporary American Playwrights, 1938. Editor: (with others) A Treasury of the Theatre, 1935. Home: Forest Hills, L.I., N.Y. Died Feb. 9, 1948; buried Fairmont Cemetery, Denver.

MANVILLE, Edward Britton, musician; b. New Haven, Conn., Dec. 25, 1879; s. Henry Lampson and Estelle Blackman (Wilson) M.; pre. edn., Hillhouse High Sch., New Haven, Conn.; student Yale, 1897-1900; student Guilmant Organ Sch., New York, 1902-03; studied piano with Prof. S. S. Sanford and Frederick Lamond; organ with Dr. Harry B. Jepson and Dr. William C. Carl; composition with Dr. Horatio W. Parker and W. R. Hedden; Mus.Dr., Detroit Inst. of Musical Art, 1920; m. Eunice Katherine Hallett, August 26, 1912; 1 daughter, Margaret Jane (Mrs. Lynn G. Stedman, Junior). Organist and dir. music, Grace Protestant Episcopal Ch., New Haven, 1897-98, 1st Congl. Ch., South Norwalk, Conn., 1898-1905, First Bapt. Ch., Franklin, Pa., 1905-12; removed to Detroit, 1912; organist and dir. music Woodward Av. Bapt. Ch., 1912-17, Woodward Av. Presbyterian Ch., 1919-31, Fort Street Presbyterian Ch. since 1937. Conductor Oil City and Franklin (Pa.) Oratorio Soc., 1910-12, Haydn Oratorio Soc. and Schubert Club, Detroit, 1914-17; mem. faculty Pa. Coll. of Music, Meadville, Pa., 1907-09, Franklin Conservatory, 1909-11, Michigan Conservatory, 1913-14, Detroit Inst. Musical Art since 1914, pres. since 1922. Commd. 1st lt. inf., U.S. Army, Ft. Sheridan, Ill., Nov. 26, 1917; served in France, Jan. 1918-Apr. 1919; instr. Officers' Specialist Centre, Langres; mem. 119th Inf. Machine Gun Co.; participated in battles including Somme offensive, Ypres-Lys, etc.; hon. disch., Apr. 12, 1919. Fellow Am. Guild Organists; mem. Mich. Music Teachers' Assn. (pres. 1926-27; dean, Mich. Chapter 1916, and 1924-26), Am. Legion (past comdr.), 40 and 8 (Grand Chef de Gare, 1937), and S.A.R. Republican. Presbyterian. Mason (32°, K.T., Shriner). Clubs: Army and Navy, Torch, The Bohemians. Composer of 3 operettas, piano and organ soli, anthems, etc. Home: 235 Montana Av., W. Address: 52 Putnam Av., Detroit. Died Aug. 23, 1944; buried in Evergreen Cemetery, New Haven, Conn.

MANVILLE, H(iram) Edward, mfr.; m. H. Estelle Romaine; children—Estelle R. (Countess Estelle Bernadotte of Wisborg, Stockholm), H. Edward. Former pres. and chairman, bd. dirs., Johns-Manville Corp.; dir. Standard Ins. Co. of N.Y., Standard Surety & Casualty Co. Clubs: Metropolitan, Union League, New York Yacht. Home: Pleasantville, N.Y. Office: 30 Rockefeller Plaza, New York, N.Y. Died Feb. 21, 1944.

MANWARING, Elizabeth Wheeler, prof. English; b. Bridgeport, Conn., June 27, 1879; d. Moses Warren and Louise Emmeline (Comstock) Manwaring; A.B., Wellesley Coll., 1902; grad. student Yale U., 1905-08, 1922-24, Ph.D., 1924. Asst. in English, Wellesley Coll., 1902-04, instr., 1907-17, asst. prof., 1917-24, asso. prof., 1924-29, prof., 1929-47. Emeritus since June 1947. Member Modern Language Association of America, Am. Assn. Univ. Profs., Am. Assn. Univ. Women, N.E. Assn. Sch. and Coll. Teachers of English, English Speaking Union. Republican. Conglist. Club: College (Boston). Author: Italian Landscape in 18th Century England, 1925; Editor (with H.R. Warfel) Of the People, 1942. Address: Wellesley Coll., Wellesley, Mass. Died Feb. 12, 1949.

MARBLE, Arthur H., banker; b. Butler, Mo., Aug. 9, 1876; s. Gilbert and Almira V. (Hall) M.; ed. Black Hills State Teachers Coll., Spearfish, S.D.; m. Hilda M. Macaulay, Dec. 13, 1913; children—Fred W., Lois F. (Mrs. Deane H. Cobb). Began in banking at Deadwood, S.D., 1889; mgr. bank dept., John Clay & Co., Chicago, since 1915; pres. Stock Growers Nat. Bank (Cheyenne, Wyo.), Montana Nat. Bank (Billings). Civilian aide to U.S. sec. of war, 1924-29. Republican. Episcopalian. Mason, Elk, K.P. Clubs: Denver; Cheyenne Country. Home: 2616 Carey Av. Office: Stock Growers Nat. Bank, Cheyenne, Wyo.* Died Feb. 16, 1945.

MARBURG, Otto, univ. prof.; b. Roemerstadt, Austria, May 25, 1874; s. Max and Adele (Berg) M.; came to United States, 1938; naturalized citizen; M.D., University of Vienna (Austria), 1899; married Malvine Knoepfmacher, September 5, 1916. Privatdozent, U. of Vienna, 1905-12, title prof., 1912-16, real prof., 1916-38, chief of the Neurological Inst., 1919-38; clinical prof. of neurology, Columbia U., since 1938. Hon. mem. Am. Neurological Assn., A.M.A. (neuropathological sect.), N.Y. and Phila. Neurological Assn. Author: Mikroskopisch-topographischer Atlas des menschlichen Zentralnervensystems, 1904 (3d edit. 1927); Die sogenannte akute multiple Sklerose, 1906; Syphilis des Nervensystems (with I. A. Hirschl), 1914; Handbuch der Neurologie des Ohres (with Alexander and Brunner), 1924-26; Die Roentgenbehandlung der Nervenkrankheiten (with Sgalitzer), 1931; Unfall & Hirngeschwulst, 1934; Injuries of the Nervous System, 1939; Hydrocephalus, Its Symptomology, Pathology, Pathogenesis and Treatment, 1940. Editor "Arbeiten aus Dem Neurologischen Institut der Universitaet Wien" from 1919; author numerous med. articles. Address: 225 Central Park West, New York 24. Died June 13, 1948.

MARBURG, Theodore, publicist; b. Baltimore, Md., July 10, 1862; s. William A. and Christine (Munder) M.; ed. Princeton Prep. Sch., 1876-79, Johns Hopkins, 1880-81, Oxford, Eng., 1892-93; École Libre de la Science Politique, Paris, 1893-95; U. of Heidelberg, summers, 1901, 03; hon. A.M., Johns Hopkins, 1902; LL.D., Dickinson Coll., 1912, U. of Cincinnati, 1917; LL.D., Rollins Coll., Winter Park, Fla., 1928; m. Fannie Grainger, Nov. 6, 1889; children—Madame A. W. L. Tjarda Van Starkenborgh Stochouwer (wife of Gov. Gen. of the Netherlands East Indies), Francis Grainger, Lt. Col. Charles Louis. U.S. minister to Belgium, 1912-14. Trustee Johns Hopkins U. Pres. Am. Soc. Judicial Settlement Internat. Disputes, 1915-16; chmn. com. foreign organization League to Enforce Peace (one of organizers); organized Municipal Art Society, Baltimore, 1900, serving as sec., pres., now chmn. exec. com.; mem. Am. Econ. Assn. (v.p. 1899-1901), Am. Polit. Science Assn., Am. Soc. Internat. Law, Phi Beta Kappa; chmn. exec. com. Am. Peace Congress, 1911; hon. pres. Md. Peace Soc., v.p. Internat. Fedn. of League of Nations Socs., 1925, and head of Am. delegation to Assembly of League of Nations Socs., Warsaw 1925, London 1926, Berlin 1927. Clubs: Century, Pilgrims, Authors (New York); Pilgrims, Authors (London); Maryland, University (Baltimore). Author: World's Money Problem, 1896; The War with Spain, 1898; Expansion, 1900; The Peace Movement Practical, 1910; Salient Thoughts on Judicial Settlement, 1911; Philosophy of the Third American Peace Congress, 1911; League of Nations, 1917; In the Hills (collection of poems), 1924; Development of League of Nations Idea, 1932; Bobbylinkapoo (poem), 1937; "The Story of a Soul" (drama), 1938. Translator: Emile Levasseur's Elements of Political Economy. Contbr. to revs. Home: 14 W. Mt. Vernon Pl., Baltimore, Md. Died Mar. 3, 1946.

MARCH, Alden, editor; b. Easton, Pa., Sept. 29, 1869; s. Francis Andrew and Mildred Stone (Conway) M.; A.B., Lafayette Coll., 1890, A.M., 1893, Litt.D., 1915; married. Taught in Keswick Acad., Va., 1890-91; on staff Phila. Press, 1891-1910, Sunday editor, 1897-1910; Sunday editor, New York Times, 1910-17; editor and pres. Phila. Press, 1917-20; day asst. mng. editor, New York Times since 1920. Mem. Delta Kappa Epsilon. Author: The Conquest of the Philippines and Our Other Island Possessions, 1899. Clubs: Century (New York). Home: 606 W. 116th St. Office: The New York Times, New York, N.Y. Died Sep. 14, 1942.

MARCH, Charles Hoyt, member Federal Trade Commn.; b. Cedar Mills, Minn., Oct. 20, 1870; s. Nelson J. and Mary Jane (Morrison) M.; ed. high schs., Litchfield, Minn.; m. Aimee Wells, Feb. 28, 1899; children—Cora, Wells, Charles Hoyt. Admitted to Minn. bar, 1893, and began practice at Litchfield; mem. firm March Bros.; atty. G.N. Ry. Organized 4th Regt. of Militia, Minn., and was made col. same; served as mayor, and pres. Library Bd., Litchfield, also as pres. Farmers & Bankers Council of Minn.; vice chairman Safety Commn. of Minn., 1918-20; member Federal Trade Commission since 1929, reappointed, 1942, present term expiring in 1949; member Special Industrial Recovery Board since June 17, 1933. Chmn. Minn. delegation to Rep. Nat. Conv., 1920, 24, 28. Mason (32°, K.T., Shriner). Home: Litchfield, Minn., and Shoreham Hotel, Washington. Address: Federal Trade Commission Bldg., 6th St. and Pennsylvania Av., Washington, D.C. Died Aug. 28, 1945.

MARCHEV, Alfred, aviation exec.; b. Zurich, Switzerland, 1896. Pres. and dir. Republic Aviation Corp.; chmn. bd. Aircooled Motors, Inc.; dir. Internat. Utilities Corp., Internat. Investment Corp., Gen. Precision Instrument Corp. Home: Hill Acres: Halesite, L.I. Office: Farmingdale, L.I., N.Y. Died Nov. 28, 1947.

MARCUSE, Milton E. (mär'kūs), pres. Bedford Pulp & Paper Co.; b. Richmond, Va., Aug. 27, 1869; s. Jonas and Rosalie (Mitteldorfer) M.; ed. pub. schs.; m. Rosa May, Oct. 24, 1924; with Myers Bros. & Co., tobacco mfrs., 1888-90; mem. firm Hasker & Marcuse, mfrs. of labels, tags and tin boxes, 1890-1901; asso. with organization of Am. Can Co., 1901-05; with Bedford Pulp & Paper Co., Inc., since 1905, now pres.; pres. Hydro-Electric Corp. of Va.; v.p. Bedford Land & Timber Corp., General Paper Co.; dir. West Disinfecting Co., N.Y., Bank of Big Island. Mem. U.S. Chamber of Commerce, Nat. Paperboard Assn., Am. Paper and Pulp Assn., Mat. Mfrs. Assn., Industrial Conf. Bd. Republican. Jewish religion; mem. B'nai B'rith. Mason, Shriner. Clubs: Jefferson, Lakeside Country. Home: Big Island, Va. Office: Bedford Pulp & Paper Co., Mutual Bldg., Richmond, Va.* Died July 26, 1946.

MARGOLD, Nathan Ross (mär'gōld), judge; born Jassi, Roumania, July 21, 1899; s. Wolf and Rosa (Kahan) Margulies; brought to U.S., 1901, father naturalized 1906; A.B., Coll. of City of N.Y., 1919; LL.B., Harvard, 1923; m. Gertrude Wiener, Apr. 2, 1927. 1 son, William Frederick. Admitted to N.Y. bar, 1923, and in general practice, New York, 1923-25, and 1928-33; assistant United States attorney, Southern District N.Y., 1925-27, and 1928; instr. law, Harvard, 1927-28; spl. counsel New York Transit Commn., 1928-29, legal adviser Indian affairs, Inst. for Government Research, 1930-31; spl. counsel Nat. Assn. for Advancement of Colored People, 1930-33; the solicitor Interior Dept., 1933-42; also chmn. petroleum administrative board, and labor policy board for the petroleum industry and Sp. Asst. Atty. Gen., 1933-35; judge Municipal Court for Dist. of Columbia since July 7, 1942. Nomination for associate Justice, District Court of U.S. for District of Columbia sent to U.S. Senate by Pres. Roosevelt on Jan. 20, 1945. Mem. Assn. of Bar City of N.Y., Am. Legion. Club: Harvard (Washington, D.C.). Coeditor (with Joseph Henry Beale): Cases on Criminal Law, 1928. Contbr. articles to legal jours. Address: Municipal Court, Washington, D.C. Died Dec. 16, 1947.

MARINONI, Antonio (mä-rē-nō'nē), educator; b. Pozzolengo, Province of Brescia, Italy, May 30, 1879; s. Luigi and Paola (Cerini) M.; grad. Liceo of Desenzano, Italy, 1898; grad. student, U. of Padua, 1899; classical and Romance langs., Yale, 1903-04, A.M., 1904; m. Rosa Zagnoni, July 30, 1908; children—Mary Stella, Paul Albert. Came to U.S., 1900; lecturer in Romance languages, Columbia, 1904-05; professor Romance languages, University of Arkansas, since 1906, also head of department. Member Modern Language Association America. Catholic. Editor: Italian Reader, 1909; Elementary Italian Grammar, 1911; Selections from G. Carducci, 1913; l'Italia (with E. H. Wilkins), 1922; España, 1926; France (with Régis Michaud), 1927; Simple Italian Lessons (with L. A. Passarelli), 1927; Andiamo in Italia, 1929; Italy Yesterday and Today, 1931. Contbr. articles to Am. and Italian mags. and revs. Active in promotion of closer intellectual relations between Italy and U.S. Cavaliere Ufficiale della Corona d'Italia, 1920. Hon. mem. dell'Accademia Fisico-Chimica of Palermo, Italy. Home: Fayetteville, Ark. Died Aug. 8, 1944; buried in Sirmione, Italy.

MARION, John Hardin, lawyer, judge; b. Richburg, S.C., Oct. 23, 1874; s. James Taylor and Janie A. (Hardin) M.; A.B., LL.B., S.C. Coll. (now U. of S.C.), 1893; LL.D., Presbyn. Coll. of S.C., Clinton, S.C., 1924; m. Mary Pagan Davidson, Dec. 31, 1902; children—John Hardin, Annie Irvine, Jean Hardin, James Taylor, Mary Davidson, Paul Blaine. Admitted to S.C. bar, 1893, and began practice at Chester; mem. S.C. Ho. of Rep., 1899-1900, Senate, 1918-22; gen. counsel Carolina & North Western Ry. Co., 1900-20; elected justice Supreme Court of S.C., Jan. 12, 1922, for term expiring Aug. 1, 1932; resigned Jan. 1, 1926; gen. atty. for Duke Power Co., P.&N. Ry. Co., and other Duke interests, Charlotte, N.C., since Sept. 1, 1927. Served as lt. 1st S.C. Inf., Spanish-Am. War; retired as lt. col. 1st Regt., S.C. Inf., Nat. Guard, 1907. Chmn. bd. trustees, Erskine Coll., 1922-30. Mem. Am. Bar Assn., N.C. Bar Assn., S.C. Bar Assn. (pres. 1926-27), Am. Judicature Soc., Phi Kappa Psi, Phi Beta Kappa. Democrat. Mem. Asso. Ref. Presbyn. Ch. Mason, K.P. Chmn. Joint Legislative Tax Commn. of S.C., and author of its report, 1921. Home: 1100 Granville Rd. Office: Power Bldg., S. Church St., Charlotte, N.C. Died May 1944.

MARK, Edward Laurens, anatomist; b. Hamlet, Chautauqua Co., N.Y., May 30, 1847; s. Charles L. and Julia (Peirce) M.; A.B., U. of Mich., 1871; Ph.D., U. of Leipzig, 1876; LL.D., U. of Mich., 1896, U. of Wis., 1904; m. Lucy Thorp King, Nov. 26, 1873; children—Kenneth Lamartine, Freedrica (Mrs. George H. Chase). Instr. mathematics, U. of Mich., 1871-72; astronomer U.S. Northwest Boundary Survey, 1872-73; instr. zoology, Harvard, 1877-83, asst. prof., 1883-86, Hersey prof. anatomy, 1885-1921, now emeritus, dir. Zool. Lab., 1900-21. Dir. Bermuda Biol. Sta. for Research, 1903-31; U.S. del. 4th Internat. Zool. Congress, 1898. Fellow Soc. Biol. Chemistry (London), A.A.A.S., Am. Acad. Arts and Sciences; life mem. Anat. und Zool. Gesellschaften; mem. Boston Soc. Natural History, Am. Philos. Soc., Nat. Acad. Sciences, Soc. Royale Zoologique et Malacol. Belgique; foreign mem. Koenigl. Boehmische Gesellschaft der Wissenschaften; hon. mem. Institut Internat. D'Embryologie (Holland); corr. mem. Peking Soc. Natural History. Author: Maturation, Fecundation and Segmentation of Limax, 1881; Simple Eyes in Anthropods, 1887; Studies in Lepidosteous, 1893. Translator: Text-Book of the Embryology of Man and Mammals from the German of O. Hertwig, 1892; Text-Book of the Embryology of Invertebrates, Part I (with W. M. Woodworth), from German of Korschelt und Heider, 1895. Edited contributions from the Zool. Laboratory, Museum of Comparative Zoology at Harvard Coll., 1884-1923 (334 numbers published), and contbr. Bermuda Biol. Sta., 1904— (168 numbers published). Socio honorario Sociedad Cubana de Historia Natural. "Felipe Poey." Contbr. to Bulletin of Museum Comparative Zoology, also chapter, "Zoology, 1847-1921," in Morison's History of Harvard University. Home: 109 Irving St., Cambridge 38, Mass. Died Dec. 16, 1946.

MARKHAM, George Dickson, insurance; b. New Haven, Conn., July 25, 1859; s. William H. and Margaret M. (Dickson) M.; A.B., Harvard, 1881; hon. A.M., 1914; LL.B., Washington U., 1891; m. Mary McKittrick, Feb. 5, 1902. In ins. business, St. Louis, since Aug. 1881; head of insurance firm of W. H. Markham & Co.; dir. and chmn. of trust com. of Mercantile-Commerce Bank and Trust Co. Advocate of fire-prevention work and reform of ins. laws. Has been pres. of St. Louis, state and national assns. of fire insurance agents; dir. Chamber of Commerce of U.S., 1931-33, representing Nat. Assn. of Ins. Agents. Was chief Bureau of Music, Louisiana Purchase Expn., 1904, and dir. of the Expn. Co.; v.p. St. Louis Symphony Soc. since 1900. Pres. Asso. Harvard Clubs, 1905; overseer of Harvard, 1907-13; v.p. Harvard Alumni Assn., 1923; pres. St. Louis Charter Revision Conf., 1908; chmn. exec. com. St. Louis Centennial, 1909; member of City Council of St. Louis, 1901-05. Trustee St. Louis Mercantile Library. Clubs: Harvard (New York and Boston); University (pres. 1911-13, 1917-22), St. Louis Country, Noonday; University (Chicago); Dublin Lake (v.p.). Home: 4961 Pershing Av., St. Louis; (summer) Dublin, N.H. Office: 1601 Railway Exchange Bldg., St. Louis, Mo. Died Mar. 12, 1947.

MARKHAM, Osmon Grant; b. Loudonville, Ashland County, O., Aug. 21, 1865; s. Rev. Lewis Augustus and Sarah (Wirt) M.; A.B., Baldwin U., 1886,

A.M., 1889; Litt.D., Baldwin, 1909; LL.D., Baker U., 1924; grad. student, U. of Chicago, 1893-94; m. Socia Buckingham, Aug. 23, 1894; 1 dau., Virginia Gatch. Teacher pub. schs., Smithton, Mo., 1886-87; prin. acad. of Baker U., 1887-93; prof. Latin, 1893-1924, dean, 1905-24, acting pres., 1921-22, Baker U.; pub. agt. Methodist Book Concern, Chicago, 1924-36, transferred to New York as pub. agt., 1936-40; retired. Mem. Kan. State Bd. Edn., 1905-11. Lay del. Gen. Conf. M.E. Ch. 6 times. Mem. Classical Assn. Middle West and South, Kan. State Hist. Soc. (dir.), Delta Tau Delta. Republican. Mason. Home: 2096 Surrey Road, Cleveland Heights, O. Died Apr. 8, 1943.

MARKHAM, Walter Tipton, vocational educator; b. Ewing, Va., Oct. 22, 1885; s. George Washington and Amanda Morrison (Robinson) M.; student Marionville (Mo.) Coll., 1905-11; A.B., Campbell Coll., Holton, Kan., 1914; student Harvard, 1923; A.M., U. of Kan., 1926; m. Daisy Ella Murphy, Aug. 16, 1910; children—Oleta Miriam, Velma Maurine. Began as a teacher, 1905; supt. pub. schs., Oneida, Kans., 1910-14, Spring Hill, 1915-17, Wetmore, 1918-22, Yates Center, 1922-32; state supt. pub. instrn., Kan., 1932-39; mem. State Bd. of Regents, 1939-43; state supervisor occupational information and guidance under the State Bd. for Vocational Edn. since June 1, 1939; chmn. Kan. State Bd. Edn., 1932-39. Mem. N.E.A., Kan. State Teachers Assn., Kan. Educators Club, Am. Vocational Assn., Phi Delta Kappa. Democrat. Methodist. Mason (Shriner), Odd Fellow, Woodman, Rotarian. Devised vocabulary test for high sch. and coll. students, 1928. Home: 1148 High Av. Office: 1001 Harrison St., Topeka, Kan. Died Jan. 18, 1946.

MARKS, Edward Bennett, music publisher; b. Troy, N.Y., Nov. 28, 1865; s. Bennett and Pauline (Spero) M.; student Coll. City, N.Y., 1888-90; m. Miriam Chuck, Dec. 15, 1897; children—Phylis Miriam, (Mrs. Edgar K. Simon), Herbert E., Edward B. Jr., salesman notion goods through New England, 1890-94; organizer and partner music pub. firm, Joseph W. Stern Co., N.Y. City, 1894-1920, owner Edward B. Marks Music Co., 1920-32, pres. Edward B. Marks Music Corp., since 1932. Mem. Music Pub. Protective Assn. (1st pres. 1935), Cooper Union Debating Soc. Mem. Pres. Roosevelt's Council for Coordination Industry, 1935-36 (mem. com. for fair trade practices, 1936). Composer of lyrics: My Mother Was A Lady, The Little Lost Child, December and May, Teacher and the Boy, Kaddish of My Ancestry. Author: They All Sang (Viking), 1934; They All Had Glamour (Messner), 1944. Home: 215 Lakeville Rd., Great Neck, Long Island, N.Y. Office: RCA Bldg., Radio City, New York, N.Y. Died Dec. 17, 1945.

MARKS, Henry Kingdon, author, neurologist; b. San Francisco, Calif.; s. Adolphe and Frances (Lambert) M.; M.D., Harvard U., 1908; student univs. of Berlin, Munich and Paris; unmarried. Interne Mass. Gen. Hosp., 1908-09; traveling fellow Rockefeller Inst. (serum research work), Berlin, 1909; physician Rockefeller Hosp., New York, 1909-10; asst. to Dr. Flexner, Rockefeller Inst., 1910-11; resident house physician Hosp. for Paralyzed and Epileptic, London, Eng., 1911-12; asst. physician Neurol. Inst., New York. Teacher anatomy of nervous system to classes of med. officers, Neurol. Inst., New York, 1913-20. Mem. Soc. Immunology and Hermatology, New York Neurol. Soc., Harvard Med. Soc., Boylston Med. Soc. (Boston), Alpha Omega Alpha. Club: Harvard (New York). Author: Peter Middleton, 1919; Undertow, 1923; Lame de Fond, 1923; Décheance, 1925; Valma, 1927; Ni Fleurs Ni Couronnes, 1929; La Fondrière, 1934. Translator: Simone's Le Désordre, 1931; Inagmire, 1935; L'Autre, 1936; L'Oriflamme, 1937. Address: Guaranty Trust Co., Paris, France.* Died Sep. 1, 1942.

MARKS, Willard Leighton, lawyer; b. Lebanon, Linn County, Ore., June 25, 1883; s. James McKinney and Mary Paulina (Blain) M.; B.Sc., Lewis and Clark Coll. (formerly Albany Coll.), Ore., 1904, LL.D., 1941; m. Beryl Fisher Turner, Apr. 16, 1907 (died 1939); children—Robert Leighton, Marian Elizabeth (wife of Lt. Col. Edward A. Martell), Helen Beryl (Mrs. William A. Dryden, Jr.), newspaper work; county clerk, 1911-14; practiced law since 1915; dep. dist. atty., Linn County, 1915-20; state senator, 1927-33 (pres. of senate, 1931-33). Mem. Ore. State Bd. of Higher Edn., which administers U. of Ore., Ore. State Coll. and other instns. of higher edn., since 1933, pres. since 1934. Served with Ore. Nat. Guard, pvt. to 2d lt., 1900-05; 1st lt., to col., Ore. Vol. Guard, 1917-18. Mem. Am., Ore. State and Linn County bar assns. Mason, K.P. (past grand chancellor of Ore.). Home: 320 W. 6th Died Nov. 17, 1947.

***MARLAND, Ernest Whitworth,** ex-governor; b. Pittsburgh, Pa., May 8, 1874; s. Alfred and Sarah (MacLeod) M.; prep. edn., Park Inst., Pittsburgh; LL.B., U. of Mich., 1893; m. Mary Virginia Collins, Nov. 5, 1903; m. 2d, Lydie Miller Roberts, July 14, 1928. Began practice at Pittsburgh; moved to Okla., and engaged largely in oil production; pres. Marland Oil Co., and various subsidiary cos. in U.S. and Mexico. Mem. 73d congress (1933-35), 8th Okla. Dist. Gov. state of Okla., 1935-39. Mason. Episcopalian. Died Oct. 3, 1941.

MARLOW, Frank William, ophthalmologist; born Abingdon, Berks., Eng., July 2, 1858; s. William and Bertha (Searle) M.; ed. St. Thomas Hospital, Royal London Ophthal. Hosp., Royal Coll. Surgeons, Apothecaries' Soc., London; M.D., Coll. of Medicine, Syracuse U., 1885; m. Laura Bisset Mills, 1889; children—Searle Bisset, John Mills, Juliet, Gertrude Honor, Frank William. Came to U.S., 1884, naturalized, 1892. Practiced ophthalmology, Syracuse, since 1881; emeritus prof. ophthalmology, Coll. of Medicine, Syracuse U.; ophthalmologist to Syracuse Memorial Hospital. Fellow Am. Coll. Surgeons, Royal Soc. Medicine; mem. A.M.A., Am. Ophthal. Soc., Ophthal. Soc. of United Kingdom, Alpha Kappa Kappa, Phi Kappa Phi, Alpha Omega Alpha. Author: The Relative Position of Rest of the Eyes, and the Prolonged Occlusion Test, 1924. Retired. Home: 200 Highland St., Syracuse, N.Y. Died Oct. 4, 1942.

***MARMON, Howard C.,** motor car designer and exec.; b. Richmond, Ind., May 24, 1876; s. Daniel W. and Elizabeth (Carpenter) M.; student Earlham Coll., 1892-94; received degree in mech. engring., U. of Calif., Berkeley, Calif.; m. Florence Myers, 1901; 1 dau., Carol Carpenter (wife of Prince Nicolas Tchkotoua); m. 2d, Martha Foster, 1911. Began as associate with father in flour mill machinery business which was absorbed by automobile industry; became vice pres. in charge engring., Marmon Motor Car Co., 1902; invented the Marmon automobile and was a pioneer in designing and producing racing cars; designed the Marmon Wasp, which won first 500-mile internat. sweepstakes on Indianapolis Speedway, May 30, 1911 (average speed of 74.61 miles per hour for the course); invented duplex downdraft manifold, widely used in building straight eights; reduced weight of 16 cylinder engine by use of aluminum parts, thus making the engine practical commercially; was a developer of Liberty airplane motor during World War I. Served as lieut. col., Army Air Corps during World War I; builder and first comdg. officer, McCook Field, Dayton, O. Mem. U.S. Commn. to Europe for selection of airplane equipment, and examination of prodn at Isotta-Fraschini Motor Car Co., Italy, 1917. Pres. Am. Soc. Automotive Engrs., 1913 and 1914 (awarded medal by Met. sect., 1931, for year's outstanding automotive design, the Marmon Sixteen). Selected as only Am. hon. mem. English Soc. Automotive Engrs., 1913. Mem. Second Presbyn. Ch., Indianapolis, Ind. Clubs: Engineers (N.Y. City); Columbia, Athletic, University (Indianapolis, Ind.). Home: Pineola, Avery County, N.C.; also Columbia Club, Indianapolis, Ind. Died April 4, 1943.

MARQUIS, Albert Nelson (mär'kwis), publisher, editor; b. Brown County, Ohio; s. Cyrenus G. and Elizabeth (Redmon) M.; left an orphan in early childhood; reared by grandparents (mother's side); ed. pub. and private schs.; LL.D., Monmouth (Ill.) Coll., 1928; m. Harriette Roseanna (Gettemy) Morgan, June 11, 1910 (died Jan. 6, 1936). Began bus. career in grandfather's gen. store, Hamersville, O.; after death of guardian conducted the business from age 18 to 21; engaged in publishing business in Cincinnati, O., as A. N. Marquis & Company; removed to Chicago, 1884; founded Who's Who in America, 1899, and sole owner till incorporation May 1, 1926, of the A. N. Marquis Company, of which was pres., 1926-37; editor-in-chief of Who's Who in America from beginning to 1940; now editor emeritus. Mem. Chicago Hist. Soc., English-Speaking Union (first pres. Chicago Branch, 1921-22 and dir. since 1922; director national organization, 1922-36), Ohio Society of Chicago (pres. 1920-21). Director Central Howard Assn.; dir. Kobe Coll. Corp. Republican. Congregationalist. Clubs: Union League; Hamilton (pres. 1919); University (Evanston). (Pres. Ashland Club, 1893-94, Illinois Club, 1906-07). Home: 1500 Forest Av., Evanston, Ill. Office: Palmolive Bldg., 919 N. Michigan Av., Chicago, Ill. Died Dec. 21, 1943.

MARQUIS, Samuel Simpson, clergyman; b. Sharon, O., June 8, 1866; s. John E. and Sarah P. M.; A.B. (with honors), Allegheny Coll., Pa., 1890, D.D., 1905; B.D., Cambridge (Mass.) Theol. Sch., 1893; LL.D., Wayne Univ., Detroit, Mich., 1937; m. Gertrude Lee Snyder, Aug. 23, 1894; children—Dorothy, Barbara Lee, Rogers I., Gertrude Lee. Deacon, 1891, priest, 1893, P.E. Ch.; rector Trinity Ch., Woburn, Mass., 1893-97, Trinity Ch., Bridgewataer, Mass., 1897-99, St. Joseph's, Detroit, 1899-1906; rector St. Paul's Ch. and dean St. Paul's Cathedral, Detroit, May 15, 1906-Dec. 1, 1915; head of sociol. dept. of Ford Motor Co., Detroit, 1915-21; rector St. Joseph's Ch., Detroit, 1921-25; rector Christ Ch., Cranbrook, Bloomfield Hills, Mich., 1925-39, now rector emeritus. Author: Henry Ford—An Interpretation. Home: 712 Fairfax Rd., Brimingham, Mich. Died June 21, 1948.

MARSDEN, Raymond Robb, civil engring.; b. Utica, N.Y., Oct. 31, 1884; s. John and Martha (Cross) M.; B.S., Dartmouth, 1908, C.E., 1909; m. Mary Gilmour Warnock, June 25, 1913 (died Mar. 1935); m. 2d, Helen Churchill, June 30, 1939. Instr. in surveying, Thayer Sch., Dartmouth, 1909-10; engr. for H. S. Ferguson, New York, in surveys, design and field engineering of paper mill and hydro-electric developments, 1910-15; design engr. Laurentide Co. and Riordan Pulp & Paper Co., Can., 1915-17; chief of design and estimating sect. Atlas Powder Co., 1917-19; prof. civ. engring., Thayer Sch. of Civ. Engring., since 1919, dean since 1925; also cons. engr.; pres. Manchester Water Co.; leave of absence from Dartmouth, 1933-34, as engr. Pub. Works Adminstrn., Concord, N.H.; dir. Works Div., N.H. Unemployment Relief Adminstrn., 1934; dir. projects and labor management Works Progress Adminstrn. for N.H., 1935 and 36; chief statistician, Vt. Statewide Highway Planning Survey, 1938; engr. Federal Works Agency, 1939; engr. Atlas Powder Co., Wilmington, Del., since 1940. Mem. Am. Soc. Civil Engrs., Phi Kappa Psi, Gamma Alpha; ex-sec. New England Sect. Soc. for Promotion Engring. Edn. Mason. Home: Manchester Depot, Vt. Died Mar. 11, 1942.

MARSH, Arthur Merwin, lawyer; b. Bridgeport, Conn., Aug. 7, 1870; s. Daniel Edwin and Sarah Florinda (Merwin) M.; grad. Bridgeport High Sch., 1888; B.A., Yale, 1892; LL.B., Harvard, 1898; m. Irene Lee Graffin, Oct. 28, 1909 (died Sept. 1, 1936); children—John Lee, Margaret (Mrs. Sheldon R. Luce). Entered law office Goodwin Stoddard, Bridgeport, 1896; admitted to Conn. Bar, 1898, and since practiced in Bridgeport; sr. partner Marsh, Stoddard & Day; dir. Bridgeport Hydraulic Co., Hicks Realty Co., University Club Co.; chmn. zoning commn., Fairfield, Conn., 1926-39. Mem. law staff Emergency Fleet Corp., Washington, World War. Mem. bd. trustees Y.M.C.A. Mem. Am. and Conn. State bar assns., Assn. of Bar of City of N.Y., Zeta Psi. Conglist. Clubs: University (Bridgeport); Yale (New York); Country Club of Fairfield; Union Interallie (Paris). Author: Questions and Answers for Bar Examinations (with C. S. Haight). Editor Harvard Law Review, 1897-98. Home: Westway Rd., Southport, Conn. Office: 886 Main St., Bridgeport, Conn. Died Nov. 22, 1942.

MARSH, Egbert, banking; b. Bridgeport, Conn., May 12, 1873; s. Daniel Edwin and Sarah Florinda (Merwin) M., prep. edn., high sch., Bridgeport; student Yale, 1892-95; m. Lucie Catlin, Oct. 14, 1896. Began with Marsh, Merwin & Lennon, Bridgeport, 1889; with Bridgeport Trust Co. (now Bridgeport-City Trust Co.) since 1901, sec., 1901-08, v.p. and trust officer, 1908-28, pres. and trust officer, 1928-30, chairman board since 1930; sec. Bridgeport Storage Warehouse Co., Turner & Seymour Mfg. Co., Lakeview Cemetery Association; director Niagara Alkali Company of New York, D. M. Read Company, Howland Dry Goods Co., Howland, Hughes Co., Waterbury. Republican. Conglist. Clubs: University, Rotary, Contemporary, Pequot Yacht, Country Club of Fairfield. Home: Willow St., Southport, Conn. Office: Bridgeport-City Trust Co., Bridgeport, Conn. Died Aug. 3, 1945.

MARSH, Francis Hedley, banker; b. Clarksburg, Ont., June 23, 1874; s. Wm. Jabez and Rosamond Matilda (Evans) M.; ed. Clarksburg public sch., Lindsay Collegiate Inst. M. Hazel Reed Peverley, 1906; 1 son, 1 dau. m. 2d, Bettie-Muriel Chapman, Feb. 20, 1933. Began in banking business at Ingersoll, Ont., mgr., Cranbrook, B.C., Cobalt, Sault Ste. Marie, Toronto and Montreal; appointed western supt. Bank of Toronto at Winnepeg, 1921, asst. gen. mgr., Toronto, 1928; gen. mgr. 1938, dir. 1941, pres. since 1942; dir. Dome Mines Ed., Excelsior Life Ins. Co. Anglican. Clubs: National, York, Granite, Toronto Golf. Office: 55 King St., W. Home: Clarksburg, Ont., Can. Died Oct. 23, 1949; buried St. Johns Churchyard, York Mills, Toronto, Ont., Can.

MARSH, George T., author, lawyer; b. Lansingburgh, N.Y., Aug. 9, 1876; s. P. James and Lelia E. (Tracy) M.; A.B., Yale, 1898; studied Harvard Law Sch., 1900; m. Eva Corliss Weeden, Sept. 30, 1915. Began practice at Providence, R.I.; mem. R.I. legislature, 1910-11; chmn. Board of Pub. Safety, Providence, 1931-35; chmn. bd. trustees R.I. State Colls. since 1939. Officer Inf. and Air Service, U.S. Army; served at Meuse-Argonne, 1918; judge advocate and mem. for U.S. Army of Aero-Convention of Peace Conf., Paris. Mem. Psi Upsilon. Democrat. Mason. Clubs: University, Hope, Art (Providence, R.I.). Author: Toilers of the Trails, 1921; The Whelps of the Wolf, 1922; The Valley of Voices, 1924; Men Marooned, 1926; Flash, the Lead Dog, 1927; Under Frozen Stars, 1928; Sled Trails and White Waters, 1929; The Heart of the King-Dog, 1929; Three Little Ojibwas, 1930; The River of Skulls, 1936; White Silence, 1938. Home: 22 Keene St., Providence, R.I. Died Aug. 10, 1945.

MARSH, Herbert Eugene, college dean; b. Hillsdale, Mich., July 25, 1874; s. Eugene B. and Sarah Ann (Way) M.; B.S., Mich. State Coll., 1908; A.M., U. of Calif., 1925; LL.D. (hon.) University of Redlands, 1942; married Elsie Wood, Oct. 25, 1899; 1 dau., Doris Gertrude (Mrs. Glenn Murdock). Teacher Mich. State Coll., 1908-12; prof. of Physics, U. of Redlands, 1912-24, 1925-34, dean of men, 1934-37, acting pres., 1937-38, dean of coll., 1938-42, head of department of physics, 1942-45, retired 1945; research, University of Calif., 1924-25. Lieut. governor, Calif.-Nev. Dist., Kiwanis International, 1941. Mem. A.A.A.S., Am. Phys. Soc., Am. Optical Soc., Assn. Physics Teachers, Tau Beta Pi, Sigma Psi. Republican. Baptist. Club: Redlands Kiwanis (pres. 1939-40). Home: 940 Campus Av., Redlands, Calif. Died March 3, 1948.

MARSH, James A., lawyer; b. nr. Lewes, Del., Oct. 25, 1879; s. Samuel P. and Emma F. (McIlvaine) M.; ed. in pub. schs. of Delaware, State Normal Sch., West Chester, Pa., and private schs.; m. Laura E. Joseph, June 17, 1902; 1 son, Joseph J. Admitted to Del. bar, 1902, and began practice at Georgetown; moved to Denver, Colo., 1909; city and county atty. of Denver, 1915-23; mem. Dem. Nat. Com. since 1934. Agency counsel R.F.C. U.S. Govt. appeal agt. for Denver, World War. Pres. Denver Bar Assn., 1926-27. Mem. Am. Bar Assn., Colo. State

Bar Assn. Democrat. Mason; former nat. officer Modern Woodmen of America. Clubs: Denver Club, Denver Athletic. Home: 760 Vine St. Office: Ernest & Crammer Bldg., Denver, Colo.* Died Mar. 24, 1946.

MARSH, James Prentiss, surgeon; b. Troy, N.Y., Oct. 25, 1862; s. Petetiah James and Eliza (Bailey) M.; student Union Coll., Schenectady, N.Y., 1881-82, A.M., 1920; M.D., Albany Med. Coll., 1885; m. Elizabeth Bailey, Nov. 14, 1893; 1 dau., Lucy Elizabeth; m. 2d, Susan Agnes Ruthven, June 24, 1924. Practiced in Troy since 1885; cons. surgeon Samaritan Hosp., also of Leonard Hosp., Troy, N.Y.; dir. Nat. City Bank, Troy. Fellow Am. Coll. Surgeons; mem. A.A.A.S., Am. Oriental Soc. Presbyterian. Address: 1285 5th Av., Troy, N.Y. Died Feb. 23, 1941.

MARSH, Spencer, Scott, chmn. bd. Nat. Newark & Essex Banking Co., Newark, N.J.; chmn. mng. com. Newark Clearing House Assn.; chmn. finance com. Princeton Theol. Sem. Home: Midwood Terrace, Madison, N.J. Office: 744 Broad St., Newark, N.J.* Died Dec. 26, 1944.

MARSH, Walter Randall, headmaster; b. Haverhill, Mass., June 16, 1867; s. George Edward and Mary Ellen (Thomes) M.; A.B., Harvard, 1889; m. Lillian Parker, Dec. 1896 (died, Dec. 1928); children—Dorothea P. (Mrs. K. C. Dolbeare), Mary E. (Mrs. L. A. Waddell); married 2d, Marion Reid, June 1941. Began as teacher in high schs. at Weymouth and Harwich, Mass., 1889-92, Phillips Exeter Acad., 1892-96, William Penn Charter Sch., Phila., 1896-1900; headmaster, Pingry School., Elizabeth, N.J., 1900-07; headmaster St. Paul's School, Garden City, L.I., since 1907. Mem. Assn. of Colls. and Prep. Schs. of Middle States and Md. (pres. 1919-20), Headmasters' Assn. (pres. 1917-18). Provisional deputy Gen. Conv. of P.E. Church, 1910, 13, deputy, 1916, 19, 34 and 40; mem. chapter corp. Cathedral of Incarnation (treas. 1933). Author: (with Charles H. Ashton) Plane and Spherical Trigonometry, 1902; Logarithmic Tables, 1902; College Algebra, 1907; (alone) Elementary Algebra, 1905. Address: Garden City, L.I., N.Y. Died Feb. 23, 1947; buried Newton Cemetery, Newton, Mass.

MARSHALL, Alfred C., pres. Detroit Edison Co.; b. Middletown, O., Sept. 26, 1872; s. William S. and Elizabeth (Miltenberger) M.; B.S. in E.E., U. of Mich., 1893, hon. M.Eng., 1932; hon. Dr. Business Adminstrn., Wayne U., 1943; m. Elizabeth Schnoor, October 16, 1901. Served as engineer Public Lighting Commn., Detroit, 1894-99; chief engr. Rapid Ry. System, 1899-1904; engr. constrn. work, Detroit Edison Co., 1904-05; gen. mgr. of Port Huron Light & Power Co., 1905-12; asst. to pres. Detroit Edison Co., 1912-13, v.p., 1913-40, president since 1940, general manager, 1923-43; director Essex County Light & Power Co., Ltd., St. Clair Edison Co., Detroit Branch, Fed. Reserve Bank of Chicago. Served as mem. Bd. of Water Commrs., Detroit, 2 times. Chmn. Commn. to Study Sewage Treatment and Disposal, Detroit. Liquidating Trustee (one of 3) Detroit Trust Co. Mem. advisory bd. Detroit Salvation Army; trustee Harper Hosp. Detroit; pres. Rackham Engring. Foundation, Detroit. Clubs: Detroit, Detroit Athletic, Detroit Golf. Home: 1930 Balmoral Dr. Office: 2000 Second Av., Detroit, Mich. Deceased.

MARSHALL, Benjamin Howard, architect; b. Chicago, Ill., May 5, 1874; s. Caleb H. and Celia F. (LeBaillie) M.; ed. Harvard Sch., Chicago; m. Mary Elizabeth Walton, Feb. 1, 1905; children—Elizabeth H., Benjamin H., Dorothy. At 19 became office boy for H. R. Wilson, architect, and at 21 was given half interest in the business, the firm becoming Wilson & Marshall; practiced alone, 1902-05; with Charles E. Fox, as Marshall & Fox, 1905-24; firm architects Blackstone Hotel, Blackstone Theatre, Edgewater Beach Hotel, Drake Hotel, Steger Bldg., Burlington Bldg. (Chicago), Northwestern Mut. Life Insurance Building (Milwaukee), Forrest Theatre (Phila.), Maxine Elliott's Theatre (N.Y.); drew plans for Victory Memorial, Chicago tribute to heroes of World War; in practice alone since 1924; architect for Warren Wright residence, Edgewater Gulf Hotel, 209 Lake Shore Drive, Edgewater Beach Apts., Lawsonia Club Hotel, Drake Tower. Home: Drake Hotel. Office: Palmolive Bldg., 919 N. Michigan Av., Chicago, Ill. Died June 22, 1944.

MARSHALL, Benjamin Tinkham, clergyman, educator; b. Boston, Aug. 12, 1872; s. Andrew and Emily Ann (Hentz) M.; A.B., Dartmouth, 1897, A.M. (hon.), 1912, D.D., 1922; post-grad. work, Columbia, 1899-1900; B.D., Union Theol. Sem., 1900; m. Laura Alice Hatch, July 11, 1900; children—Andrew, Mary Hatch, Elizabeth Ripley (dec.), Benj. T. Ordained Congl. ministry, 1900, Presbyn. ministry, 1900; pastor, Scarborough (N.Y.) Presbyn. Ch., 1900-06, First Presbyn. Ch., New Rochelle, N.Y., 1906-12; Phillips prof. Bibl. history and lit., Dartmouth Coll., 1912-17; pres. Conn. Coll., New London, 1917-28; acting pastor Piedmont Church, 1929-30, and pastor, 1930-34; acting pastor First Ch., Newton Centre, Mass., 1934-35, Plymouth Congl. Ch., Minneapolis, since Nov. 1935. Mem. Phi Beta Kappa, Delta Kappa Epsilon, Casque and Gauntlet. Home: 230 Oak Grove St., Minneapolis. Died June 30, 1946.

MARSHALL, Charles D(onnell), bridge builder; C.E., Lehigh U., 1888; m. Dora Noble; children—Elizabeth P., John N., Dorothy C., Charles Donnell, Mary M., Jane I. Pres. Union Shipbuilding Co.; dir. Hughes-Foulkrod Co., Bethlehem Steel Corp., Granite City Steel Co., Nat. Enameling and Stamping Co. Trustee Lehigh U. Home: 6300 Fifth Av. Office: Kopper Bldg., Pittsburgh, Pa.* Died May 16, 1945.

MARSHALL, Frank James, chess player; b. N.Y. City, Aug. 10, 1877; s. Alfred George and Sarah M.; ed. Montreal and Brooklyn; m. Caroline Krauss, Jan., 1905. Winner of first place without a single loss in 7 internat. chess tournaments, the chief ones being at Cambridge Springs, Pa., 1904, Nuremberg, Germany, 1906, and Budapest, Hungary, 1912; champion of the world in game of War, invented by Hudson Maxim; and the game of Saltar. Won chess championship of U.S. from Jackson W. Showalter in match Mar. 1909. First prize, New York, 1911; 1st and 2d prizes, Budapest, 1912; 1st prize, Havana, 1913; holds world's record for simultaneous play, Phila., Dec. 1915, 129 games in 6 hrs., and played 144 games in 6 hrs., Buffalo, 1917. Owner of Marshall's Chess Divan, New York. Hon. mem. clubs. Address: 57 W. 51st St., New York. Died Nov. 9, 1944.

MARSHALL, John Albert, biochemistry, dental pathology; b. Chicago, Ill., Aug. 30, 1884; s. John Sayre (M.D.) and Isabelle M. (Carter) M.; B.S., U. of Calif., 1907, M.S., 1914, D.D.S., 1916, Ph.D., 1917; post-grad. study U. of Berlin, and Tech. U., Charlottenburg, Germany, 1909-10; m. Hazel C. Knowles, May 18, 1907; children—John A., Muriel, Shirley; m. 2d, Irene Byram Kuechler, Dec. 28, 1932. Prof. biochemistry and dental pathology, U. of Calif. Served as capt. Ordnance Dept., U.S. Army, 1917-19. Mem. A.M.A., Am. Dental Assn., Internat. Assn. Dental Research, Soc. Experimental Biology and Medicine, Pacific Coast Society of Orthodontists (hon.), American Society of Orthodontists (hon.), Sigma Xi, Phi Kappa Psi, Delta Sigma Delta, Epsilon Alpha. Republican. Baptist. Mason. Club: Faculty. Author: Military Explosives (pub. by U.S. War Dept.), 1919; Manufacturing and Testing of Military Explosives, 1919; Diseases of the Teeth, 1926; (with C. N. Johnson) Operative Dentistry, 1923; Anatomy of the Rhesus Monkey (with Hartman and Straus), 1933. Contbr. research papers to Jour. Am. Dental Assn., Jour. Am. Med. Assn., Am. Jour. Physiology, etc. Asso. editor Jour. Dental Research. Address: Univ. of California, Berkeley, Calif.* Died May 7, 1941.

MARSHALL, Peter, clergyman; b. Coatbridge, Scotland, May 27, 1902; s. Peter and Janet (Muir) M.; student Coatbridge Tech. Sch. and Mining Coll., 1916-21; B.D., Columbia Theol. Sem., Decatur, Ga., 1931; D.D. (hon.), Presbyn. Coll., Clinton, S.C., 1938; m. Sarah Catherine Wood, Nov. 4, 1936; 1 son, Peter John. Came to U.S., Apr. 1927, naturalized Jan., 1938. Ordained to ministry of Presbyn. Ch., 1931; pastor Covington, Ga., 1931-33, Westminster Presbyn. Ch., Atlanta, Ga., 1933-37, New York Av. Presbyn. Ch., Washington, D.C., since 1937; chaplain U.S. Senate since Jan. 4, 1947. Mem. St. Andrews Soc. (Washington, D.C.) (pres. 1945-47), Omicron Delta Kappa. Mason (life mem. Coatbridge, Scotland). Home: 3100 Cathedral Av., Washington 8. Office: Washington 5, D.C. Died Jan. 25, 1949.

MARSHALL, Ray Gifford, newspaper man; b. Yankton, S.D., Feb. 18, 1881; s. Alvah Lyman and Anne (Litzenberg) M.; student U. of Minn., 1901-03; m. Edith Lovina Dykeman, Apr. 19, 1905. Began newspaper work at Minneapolis, 1903; city editor Minneapolis Journal, 1918-19; dir. publicity Internat. Famine Relief Commn., China, 1920-21; organized and edited Am. news service for English lang. papers in China; at request of Chinese Foreign Office investigated foreign occupation of Manchuria and Shantung and compiled report for Conf. on Disarmament, Washington, D.C.; apptd. by Chinese Cabinet as mem. Chinese delegation to Conf., 1921; was corr. and business rep. in China of United Press Assns. Established, 1923, first Am. daily cable news service in China for Chinese and English language papers; for 6 years until Aug. 1932, editor foreign services of United Press Assns. going to Philippines, China and Japan by cable and radio; later in charge of United Press business and news activities in China; became mgr. same in Japan and Manchuria, 1933; later became Pacific foreign editor United Press, San Francisco. Awarded, 1923, 4th class decoration of the Chia Ho (Bountiful Crop) for work in famine of 1921. Mem. Delta Upsilon. Democrat. Baptist. Clubs: Peking (China); Tokyo, American (Tokyo). Home: 80 Garcia Av. Office: 814 Mission St., San Francisco, Calif. Died Feb. 22, 1946.

MARSHALL, Tully (Phillips), actor; b. Nevada City, Calif., Apr. 13, 1864; s. William Lemen and Julia Mattie (Tully) Phillips; student Santa Clara (Calif.) Coll.; m. Marion Neiswanger (Marion Fairfax), June 7, 1899. Début at Winter Garden, San Francisco, Mar. 12, 1883; with stock cos. on Pacific Coast several yrs.; later with Boucicault, the elder, Fanny Davenport, Margaret Mather, Rose Wood, Mrs. D. P. Bowers, McKee Rankin, Modjeska, E. H. Sothern, Charles Frohman's cos. and others. Staged Sir Anthony Hope's "Adventure of Lady Ursula," at The Duke of York's, London, 1898; produced "The Builders," Belasco Theatre, Pittsburgh, 1907; played in "Paid in Full," Astor Theatre, New York, 1908; "The City," 1909-11; prod. "The Talker," Colonial Theatre, Cleveland, O., and starred as "Harry Lennox," 1912-13; as Jim Martin, in "The Trap," 1914; in moving pictures as star with Griffith-Fine Arts, 1915, Lasky, 1916, Famous Players-Lasky, 1917-19. Free lance, since 1920; played in "The Covered Wagon"; "Joan the Woman"; "He Who Gets Slapped"; "The Merry Widow"; "Common Clay"; "The Big Trail"; "Fighting Caravans"; "Making the Headlines"; "A Yank at Oxford"; "Arsene Lupin Returns." Died March 10, 1943.

MARSHALL, William Stanley, entomologist; b. Milwaukee, Wis., Dec. 16, 1866; s. Samuel and Emma (Hagar) M.; B.S., Swarthmore Coll., 1888; student biology, U. of Pa., 1888-89, U. of Berlin, U. of Leipzig, Ph.D., Leipzig, 1892; m. Clara A. Hughes, June 20, 1894; children—William Hughes, Richard Hughes, Samuel Hagar, Elizabeth, John. Instr. biology, U. of Wis., 1893-98, asst. prof., 1898-1905, asso. prof. entomology, 1905-33, prof., 1933-36, now prof. emeritus; dir. Marshall & Ilsley Bank, Milwaukee. Catholic. Mem. A.A.A.S., Am. Soc. Zoölogists, Am. Entomol. Soc., Wis. Acad. Sciences, Psi Upsilon. Clubs: University (Madison, Wis., and Chicago). Contbr. numerous papers on anatomy and embryology of insects in German and Am. zoöl. and entomol. jours. Address: 139 E. Gilman St., Madison, Wis. Died Mar. 17, 1947.

MARSTON, George White, merchant; b. Fort Atkinson, Wis., Oct. 22, 1850; s. George Phillips and Harriet (Marston) M.; ed. Acad. of Beloit (Wis.) Coll., 3 yrs.; U. of Mich., 1 yr.; m. Anna Lee Gunn, May 3, 1878. Moved from Wis. to San Diego, Calif., 1870; partner mercantile firm of Hamilton & Marston, 1873-78; established dry goods bus. of George W. Marston, 1878; inc. as The Marston Co. (dept. store), 1912. Trustee City Library, 1882-85; mem. City Council, San Diego, 1886-88; pres. Chamber Commerce, 1884, 99; trustee Pomona Coll., since 1888; pres. Y.M.C.A., San Diego, 30 yrs. Conglist.; corporate mem. A.B.C.F.M. Mem. Am. Civic Assn. (v.p. 1912-14), San Diego Civic Assn. (pres. 1913); pres. San Diego Museum Assn., 1923. Clubs: University, Cuyamaca. Home: 3525 7th Av. Office: 5th Av., San Diego, Calif. Died May 31, 1946.

MARSTON, Sylvanus Boardman, architect; b. Oakland, Calif., Aug. 16, 1883; s. Frank Augustine and Annie Mary (Palmer) M.; student Pomona Coll., 1901-03; B.Arch., Cornell U., 1907; m. Edith Alice Hatfield, May 26, 1910; children—Paul Hatfield, Keith Palmer, Bruce Truesdale (col. U.S. Army Air Corps). Independent practice of architecture 1908-14; mem. firm Marston-Van Pelt 1915-21, Marston, Van Pelt & Maybury 1921-26, Marston & Maybury since 1926, Pasadena, Calif. Practice includes many residences, semi-public and public buildings in So. Calif. Fellow A.I.A., pres. So. Calif. chapter 1940-41; pres. State Assn. Calif. Architects, 1939; professional advisor Los Angeles County Courts building competition. Served as physical dir. attached to French army, World War I. Mem. Nat. Arch. Accrediting Bd.; chmn. City Planning Commn., Pasadena; dir. Pasadena Art Institute, Carmelita Civic Grand Stand Assn. Mem. Gargoyle, Delta Phi. Presbyterian. Mason (32°). Clubs: Overland, University, New Century, Pasadena. Home: 560 E. California St. Office: 365 E. Green St., Pasadena 1, Calif. Died Nov. 16, 1946.

MARSTON, William Moulton, psychologist; b. Cliftondale, Mass., May 9, 1893; s. Frederick William and Annie Dalton (Moulton) M.; A.B., Harvard, 1915, LL.B., 1918, Ph.D., 1921; m. Elizabeth Holloway, Sept. 16, 1915; children—Fredericka (dec.), Moulton, Olive Ann, Byrne Holloway, Donn Richard. Asst. in psychology, Radcliffe Coll., 1915; admitted to Mass. bar, 1918; atty. for Boston Legal Aid, 1918; prof. legal psychology, Am. U., Washington, D.C., 1922-23; psychologist Nat. Com. Mental Hygiene, Staten Island sch. survey, Tex. penitentiary survey, 1924; asst. prof. psychology and dir. student clinic, Tufts Coll., 1925-26; cons. psychologist since 1925; lecturer in psychology, Columbia and New York U., 1926-29; dir. pub. service, Universal Pictures Corp., 1929; lecturer in psychology, U. of Southern Calif., 1929-30; prof. psychology, Long Island U., 1931-32; v.p. Hampton, Weeks & Marston (advertising agts.), 1931-32; lecturer psychology, New Sch. Social Science and Rand School, 1933, 34; public lecturer psychological topics since 1935. Dir. and v.p. Brunswick Sch. since 1944. Served as 2d lt., United States Army, 1918-19. Fellow A.A.A.S.; mem. Psychol. Assn., Orthological Inst. (assessor), Am. Assn. Criminal Law and Criminology, Phi Beta Kappa. Clubs: Harvard (N.Y.), Coveleigh (Rye, N.Y.), Lake Elsinore (Calif.). Author: Emotions of Normal People, 1928; The Art of Sound Pictures (with W. B. Pitkin), 1930; Integrative Psychology (with wife and C. Daly King), 1930; Venus with Us, 1932; Try Living, 1937; The Lie Detector Test, 1938; March On, 1941; F. F. Proctor, Vaudeville Pioneer (with J. H. Feller), 1943. Contributor to Am. Jour. Psychology, Abnormal and Social Psychology, Psyche, Exptl. Psychology, Encyclopedia of Psychology; Ency. Britannica, popular psychol. articles to various mags., many syndicated articles on psychology to newspapers; also short stories. Originator, writer and producer of comic strip "Wonder Woman." Discoverer of systolic blood pressure deception test (popularly called the "lie detector"), 1915. Home: Cherry Orchard, Rye, N.Y. Address: 331 Madison Av., New York. Died May 2, 1947.

MARTEL, Charles (mär-tĕl'), librarian; b. Mar. 5, 1860; ed. Gymnasium and U. of Zürich, 1872-79. Reference librarian Dept. of Arts and Letters, and curator Bibliog. Museum, Newberry Library, Chicago,

1892-97; with Library of Congress since 1897; chief classifier, 1897-1912, chief of catalogue div., 1912-30, consultant, catalogue, classification and bibliography, since 1931. Mem. Am. Library Inst., A.L.A., Am. Hist. Assn., Bibliog. Soc. America, D.C. Library Assn., Am. Forestry Assn.; fellow A.A.A.S. Contbr. to library jours. Office: Library of Congress, Washington, D.C. Deceased.

MARTIN, Arthur T., law dean; b. Hadjin, Turkey, Sept. 27, 1902; s. John Campbell (Canadian citizen) and Mary Isabel (Cameron) M.; became naturalized U.S. citizen, March 19, 1931; A.B., Oberlin College, O., 1923; J. D., Ohio State U., 1929; LL.M., Columbia, 1930; m. Alice Elizabeth Rasor, June 23, 1934. Fellow, Columbia, 1929-30; asst. prof. law, Ohio State U., 1930-34, asso. 1934-37, prof. since 1937, dean since 1940; on legal staff of the Nat. Recovery Adminstrn., 1934-35; referee Dept. of Labor, 1936-37; chmn., Administrative Law Commn. of State of Ohio, 1941-44; commr., War Prodn. Bd., 1942; arbitrator and mediator, Nat. War Labor Bd., 1942-45. Mem. Am., Ohio State, and Columbus bar assns., Am. Judicature Soc., League of O. Law Schs. (sec.-treas. since 1940), Assn. Am. Law Schs. (sec.-treas. 1942-45), Order of Coif. Clubs: Faculty, Crichton. Compiler: Cases and Other Materials on the Law of Conveyances, 1939; Cases and Materials on the Law of Real Property, 1943. Home: 1740 Arlington Av., Columbus, O. Died Feb. 7, 1946.

MARTIN, Charles Henry, ex-gov.; b. Carmi, White County, Ill., Oct. 1, 1863; s. Judge Samuel H. and Mary Jane (Hughes) M.; Ewing (Ill.) Coll., 1881-82; grad. U.S. Military Academy, 1887; LL.D., Portland (Oregon) University, 1935, Oregon State College, Corvallis, 1937; m. Louise J. Hughes, Apr. 15, 1897; children—Ellis H., Samuel H., Jane L. Commd. 2d lt. 14th Inf., June 12, 1887; 1st lt. 23d Inf., Apr. 16, 1894; transferred to 14th Inf., May 5, 1894; capt. a.-q.-m. vols., Oct. 17, 1898; capt. U.S. Army, Mar. 2, 1899; hon. discharged from vols., June 13, 1899; q.-m. by detail, Dec. 15, 1903; assigned to 2d Inf., Dec. 15, 1907; trans. to 1st Inf., Dec. 28, 1907, to 23d Inf., Jan. 28, 1910; maj. 1st Inf., Feb. 28, 1910; assigned to 18th Inf., Feb. 1, 1915; lt. col., June 3, 1916; col., May 15, 1917; brig. gen. Nat. Army, Aug. 5, 1917; major gen. N.A., Apr. 12, 1918; brig. gen. Regular Army, Oct. 10, 1921; maj. gen., Jan. 16, 1925. Served under Gen. Merritt in Philippines, 1898-1901; organized and in charge street and sanitary dept. at Manila during mil. occupation; participated in expdn. to Peking, China; mem. Gen. Staff, Washington, 1911-13; comd. 3d Inf. Regt. Ore. Nat. Guard, 1913-15; on Mexican border, 1915-17; chief instr. 1st R.O.T.C., Leon Springs, Tex., 1917; comdg. 172d Brigade, at Camp Grant, Rockford, Ill., Aug. 25, 1917; comd. 86th (Blackhawk) Div., May 1-Nov. 16, 1918, 92d Div., Nov. 19-Dec. 26, 1918, and 90th Div. (Tex., Okla. Troops), in Army of Occupation (Germany), Dec. 30, 1918-May 28, 1919; asst. chief of staff, Sept. 11, 1922-Sept. 15, 1924. Comd. Panama Canal Div. and Dept., 1925-27; retired, Oct. 1, 1927. Awarded D.S.M. for "exceptionally meritorious and distinguished service in the war." Mem. 72d and 73d Congresses (1931-35), 3d Ore. Dist; governor of Oregon, 1935-39. Democrat. Clubs: Army and Navy (Washington); Arlington, University (Portland, Ore.). Home: 2325 21st Av., S.W. Office: Hughes Bldg., Portland, Ore. Died Sep. 22, 1946.

MARTIN, Clarence Augustine, univ. prof.; b. Medina County, O., Sept. 29, 1862; s. Joseph Fleming and Sarah Emeline (Fretz) M.; student Oberlin Prep. Sch., 1 yr.; spl. student Dept. of Architecture, Cornell U., 1886-88; D.Sc., Colgate, 1918; m. Gertrude Shorb, June 30, 1896; children—Gertrude, Clarence Augustine. Assistant prof. architecture, 1895-1903, prof. since 1903, and dean Coll. of Architecture, 1908-19, acting dean, 1931-32, prof. emeritus since 1932, Cornell U. Fellow A.I.A. (ex-pres. Central N.Y. Chapter); sec.-treas. Assn. Collegiate Schs. of Architecture, 1912-25; mem. Phi Gamma Delta, Tau Beta Pi. Republican. Baptist. Author: Details of Building Construction, 1899. Home: Sarasota, Fla. Died Jan. 5, 1944.

MARTIN, George Abraham, paint mfr.; b. Montello, Wis., Nov. 7, 1865; s. Thomas Cragin and Catherine (Jones) M.; ed. pub. schs. and Chicago Atheneum Night Sch.; m. Emma Von Rehberg, June 4, 1894; 1 son, George A. In meat packing business, Chicago, 1877-81; clerical work, in 1881-86; in paint and varnish business since 1886; with The Sherwin-Williams Co. since 1891, chairman of the board since Dec. 10, 1940, also officer and director of many other companies. Mem. Ohio Soc. of N.Y. Republican. Episcopalian. Mason. Clubs: City, Union, Pepper Pike Country (Cleveland); Old Elm, Knollwood, Chicago Athletic (Chicago); Metal and Rubber (New York); Pine Valley Golf (Clementon, N.J.). Home: 12725 Lake Shore Blvd., Bratenahl Village, Cleveland. Office: 101 Prospect Av. N.W., Cleveland, O.* Died Nov. 1, 1944.

MARTIN, George Brown, ex-senator; b. Prestonsburg, Ky., Aug. 18, 1876; s. Alexander Lackey and Nannie Frances (Brown) M.; B.A., Central U. (now at Danville, Ky.), 1895; unmarried. Began practice at Catlettsburg, Ky., 1900; mem. Brown & Martin until 1909, since alone; judge, Boyd County, Ky., 1904; appointed maj. Judge Advocate General's Dept., U.S. Army, Sept. 7, 1918, but did not serve, being apptd. same day mem. U.S. Senate from Ky. (to succeed Ollie M. James, dec.), for term ending Mar. 3, 1919. Mem. Dem. State Central Com. Del. Dem. Nat. Conv., Houston, 1928; Dem. elector, Ky., 1932, 36. Member Am. Bar Assn., Ky. Bar Assn., Nat. Conf. Commrs. on Uniform State Laws, Delta Kappa Epsilon. Presbyterian. Mason. Elk. Home: Catlettsburg, Ky. Died Nov. 12, 1945.

MARTIN, George E., judge; b. Lancaster, O., Nov. 23, 1857; s. John D. and Mary Jane (Herman) M.; A.B., Wittenberg Coll., Ohio, 1877, LL.D., 1917; attended lectures, U. of Heidelberg, Germany, 2 yrs.; m. Margaret Kooken, Sept. 23, 1880. Admitted to bar, 1883; practiced at Lancaster, 1883-1904; was also pres. Hocking Valley Nat. Bank, Lancaster, 15 yrs. Presdl. elector, 1880; common pleas judge 7th Jud. Dist. Ohio, 1904-11; asso. judge U.S. Court of Customs Appeals, Washington, 1911-23, presiding judge, 1923-24; chief justice Court of Appeals, Dist. of Columbia, 1924-37; retired, Oct. 1, 1937. Clubs: University, Cosmos (Washington). Home: Lancaster, O. Address: 1661 Crescent Pl. N.W., Washington, D.C. Died April 14, 1948.

MARTIN, George Madden (Mrs. Attwood R. Martin), author; b. Louisville; d. Frank and Anne Louise (McKenzie) Madden; ed. public schs., Louisville; m. Attwood R. Martin. Author: Emmy Lou—Her Book and Heart, 1902; The House of Fulfilment (novel); Abbie Ann, 1907; Letitia—Nursery Corps, U.S. Army, 1907; Selina (novel), 1914; Emmy Lou's Road to Grace, 1916; Warwickshire Lad, 1916; Children of the Mist (dealing with Negro life), 1920; March On (novel), 1921; Made in America (novel), 1935. Contbr. articles during World War appearing in Red Cross Magazine, dealing with the families of the foreign-born drafted men; contbr. essays on the American woman to the Atlantic Monthly, also short stories, essays and polit. articles to mags. and newspapers. Wrote for Kentucky's Sesquicentennial: Jane Todd Crawford, An Epic Tale, 1942. Charter mem. Commn. on Inter-racial Cooperation; chmn. Assn. of Southern Women for Prevention of Lynching. Democrat. Episcopalian. Clubs: Woman's Arts (Louisville); Lyceum (London). Home: 1304 Eastern Parkway, Louisville, Ky. Died Nov. 30, 1946.

MARTIN, John, mining exec.; b. Stirling, Scotland, 1884; m. Elinore Mary Scott-Waring Green. Dir. Bank of Eng., 1936-46; one of H. M. Lieuts. of the City of London; pres. Transvaal Chamber of Mines, 1929, 32, 34; v.p. 1927, 1930, 31, 33, 35, 37; chmn. Rand Mines, Ltd., Crown Mines Ltd., Argus So. African Newspapers, Argus Printing and Pub. Co., Ltd., Rhodesian of the South African Economic and Wage Commn., 1926, Southern Rhodesia Railway Enquiry, 1939; dir. Transvaal gold mining and other cos.; head South African Govt. Supply Mission, Washington, 1942; chmn. Rhodesian Printing and Pub. Co., Ltd.; mng. dir. South Africa of The Central Mining and Investment Corp Ltd. Mem. British Empire Air Conf., London, 1943. Clubs: Rand Johannesburg; Pretoria; Civil Service, Capetown. Home: The Thatched House, Riviera, Johannesburg. Office: The Corner House, Simmonds St., Johannesburg, So. Africa. Died March 28, 1949.

MARTIN, Joseph, judge; b. Rockland, Brown County, Wis., May 12, 1878; s. Edward and Bridget (Farrell) M.; grad. high sch., West De Pere, Wis., 1897; student law pvtly. and spl. course, U. of Wis.; m. Mildred Eleanor Wright, Oct. 5, 1904; children—Mildred, Jean, Florence. Admitted to Wis. bar, 1903, and began practice at Green Bay; mem. Wis. Ho. of Rep., 1903-04; mem. Dem. Nat. Com. many yrs.; justice Supreme Court of Wis. Mem. Am., Wis. State and Brown County bar assns. Catholic. Home: Green Bay, Wis. Deceased.

MARTIN, Julius C(orpening), lawyer; b. Wilkes County, N.C., Oct. 2, 1861; s. Augustus Harrison and Virginia (Corpening) M.; ed. Oak Hill Acad., Mouth of Wilson, Va., 1881-82, U. of N.C., 1884-85, private law school, 1887-88; m. Helen Emilie Werres, Dec. 29, 1891; children—Harrison A., Julius, Norman. Admitted to N.C. bar, 1888, and practiced in Asheville, 1888-1924, Washington, D.C., 1924-34; counsel for Carolina Power and Light Co., Electric Bond and Share Co., Southern Ry. Co., Travelers Ins. Co., Am. Surety Co., etc.; special asst. to U.S. atty. gen., 1934-36; dir. Bureau of War Risk Litigation, U.S. Dept. of Justice, from April 21, 1936 to July 1, 1942; special asst. to the Attorney General U.S. since. Mem. N.C. State Senate, 1910-12, N.C. House of Reps., 1932-34. Mem. Am. Bar Assn., N.C. State Bar Assn., Beta Theta Pi. Democrat. Baptist. Home: 6520 Western Av. Office: Dept. of Justice, Washington, D.C. Died Feb. 9, 1949.

MARTIN, Kingsley Leverich, engineer; b. Brooklyn, N.Y., June 16, 1869; s. Charles Cyril and Mary Asenath (Read) M.; grad. Poly. Inst., Brooklyn, 1888; M.E., Stevens Inst. Tech., 1892; m. Elizabeth Saxe Johnson, Feb. 2, 1895. Asst. engr. Brooklyn Bridge, 1892-96; engr. in charge Williamsburgh Bridge, 1905; chief engr. Dept. of Bridges, N.Y. City, 1908-09; commr. of bridges, N.Y. City, 1910-11; v.p. The Foundation Co., 1911-13, Am. Writing Paper Co., 1913-15; pres. The Engineer Co. since 1916. Served in 2d Batt. Naval Militia, N.Y., Spanish-Am. War, comdr. of batt., 1911-13. Mem. Am. Soc. M.E. Home: 204 Highfield Lane, Nutley, N.J. Office: 75 West St., New York. Died May 28, 1947.

MARTIN, Lillien Jane, psychologist; b. Olean, N.Y. July 7, 1851; d. Russell and Lydia (Hawes) Martin; A.B., Vassar Coll., 1880; U. of Göttingen, 1894-98; hon. Ph.D., U. of Bonn, 1913. Science teacher, Indianapolis High Sch., 1880-89; v. prin. and head dept. science, Girls' High Sch., San Francisco, 1889-94; asst. prof. psychology, Stanford U., 1899-1909, asso. prof., 1909-11, prof., 1911-16, prof. emeritus since Aug. 1916; now cons. psychologist, San Francisco; psychopathologist and chief of mental hygiene clinic, San Francisco Polyclinic and Mt. Zion Hosp. Founder and dir. Old Age Counselling Center, S. F. Pres. Calif. Soc. Mental Hygiene, 1917-21; mem. Kongress für experimentelle Psychologie, Am. Psychol. Assn., Am. Assn. Univ. Women, Calif. League of Women Voters, Sigma Xi; fellow A.A.A.S. (ex-v.p. sect. H). Educational counselor Democratic Women's Forum, San Francisco. Clubs: San Francisco, Women's City, Century of California. Author: Zur Analyse der Untershiedsempfindlichkeit, 1899; Über Asthetische Synästhesie, 1909; Zur Lehre von der Bewegungsvorstellungen, 1910; Die Projektions Methode, 1912; Ein experimenteller Beitrag zur Erforschung des Unterbewussten, 1915; Personality as Revealed by the Content of Images, 1917; Mental Hygiene and the Importance of Investigating It, 1917; Two Years' Experience as a Clinical Psychologist, 1920; Mental Training of the Pre-School Age Child, 1923; Round the World with a Psychologist, 1927; Salvaging Old Age, 1930; Sweeping the Cobwebs, 1933; The Home in a Democracy, 1937; also various articles in psychol. and other jours. Home: Plaza Hotel, Union Square. Office: Shreve Bldg., San Francisco, Calif. Died Mar. 26, 1943.

MARTIN, Percy Alvin, university prof.; b. Jamestown, N.Y., Aug. 20, 1879; s. Albert M. and Emma (Garfield) M.; A.B., Stanford, 1902, A.M., 1903; A.M., Harvard, 1907, Ph.D., 1912; student, U. of Paris, 1903-04, univs. of Berlin and Leipzig, 1907-08; m. May Franklin, July 17, 1912; children—Ada Lord, Ruth Garfield. Prof. history and French, Whittier (Calif.) Coll., 1904-05; fellow Harvard, 1907-08; spl. lecturer Latin Am. history, same, 1915-16; at Stanford since 1908, prof. history since 1923. Lecturer on South Am. history, U. of Wash., summer 1916; research asso., U. of Calif., 1917-18; Albert Shaw lecturer on diplomatic history, Johns Hopkins, 1921; prof. Latin-Am. history, University of Wash., 1932; visiting prof. U. of Hawaii, summer 1928, Nat. U. of Mexico, summer 1933; spl. lecturer George Washington U., summer 1934; visiting prof. Univ. of Mich., summer 1936, U. of Calif. at Los Angeles, summer, 1938, U. of Brit. Columbia, summer 1940. Sec. Brazil Com. Pan-Am. Financial Conf., Washington, 1920; mem. editorial board Hispanic-American Hist. Rev., 1920-38; research asso. Carnegie Instn. of Washington, 1926. Invitado de honor to II Congreso Internacional de Historia de America, Buenos Aires, 1937. Member Am. Hist. Assn., Phi Sigma Kappa, Phi Beta Kappa; corr. mem. Instituto Historico e Geographico Brasilerio, Academia Nacional de la Historia (Buenos Aires) and many other South and Central Am. hist. socs., etc. Decorated Comdr. Order of Southern Cross (Brazil). Democrat. Club: Commonwealth (San Francisco). Author: The Republics of Latin America (with H. G. James), 1923; Latin America and the War, 1925; Simon Bolivar, the Liberator, 1931; Argentina, Brazil and Chile since Independence (with J. F. Rippey and I. J. Cox), 1935; Who's Who in Latin America, 1935, 2d edit., 1940; La Esclavitud y su abolición en el Brasil, 1936. Translator: Formação Historica do Brasil, by J. P. Calogeras, 1939. Author article on Brazil in 14th edit. Encyclopedia Britannica. Contbr. numerous Hispanic-Am. articles to publs. Address: Stanford University, Calif. Died Mar. 8, 1942.

MARTIN, Selden Osgood, corp. officer, business counsel; b. Dover-Foxcroft, Me., June 3, 1881; s. Osgood Pingree and Sarah Angelia (Lucas) M.; A.B., Bowdoin, 1903; A.M., Harvard, 1904, Ph.D., 1912; m. Ethel Jenney, 1913 (died 1918); children—Roger, Richard; m. 2d, Emily Haven Beasley, Apr. 19, 1921. Austin teaching fellow in economics, Harvard, 1904-07; mem. staff, U.S. Bur. of Corps., 1907-10; instr. econ. resources, later asst. prof. marketing, Harvard Business Sch., 1910-16; dir. Bur. Business Research, same sch., 1912-16; mgr. research dept. Am. Internat. Corp., N.Y. City, 1916-21; 1st v.p. and gen. mgr. Sonora Phonograph Co., N.Y. City and Saginaw, Mich., 1922-24, pres., 1924-27; 1st v.p. C. K. Eagle & Co., Inc., 1928-29; pres. Exhibitors Reliance Corp.; v.p. Credit Alliance Corp.; exec. dir. Industrial Advisory Com., N.Y. Federal Reserve Bank, 1934-36; trustee Richardson & Boynton Co. since 1937. Mem. Am. Econ. Assn., Am. Assn. for Labor Legislation, Metropolitan Museum Art (New York), Phi Beta Kappa, Zeta Psi, Unitarian. Mason. Clubs: Harvard, Town Hall (New York). Home: 700 Esplanade, Pelham Manor, N.Y. Office: 274 Madison Av., New York, N.Y. Died Sep. 14, 1942.

MARTIN, William Franklin, army officer; b. Ripley, O., July 19, 1863; s. Robert F. and Mary E. (Lilley) M.; grad. U.S. Mil. Acad., 1885, Engr. Sch. of Application, 1891, Army War Coll., 1913; m. Josephine Edgerton, July 20, 1892. Commd. 2d lt. 25th Inf., June 14, 1885; 1st lt. 5th Inf., June 3, 1892; capt., Mar. 2, 1899; maj. 18th Inf., June 30, 1908; trans. to 5th Inf., Mar. 20, 1909; lt. col. of inf., June 5, 1914; col. of inf., July 1, 1916; brig. gen. N.A., Aug. 5, 1917. Served in various capacities in Cuba, 1899-1900, in Philippines, 1900-03, again in Cuba, 1906-08; duty Gen. Staff, 1914-17; apptd. comdr. 174th Inf. Brigade, Camp Pike, Little Rock, Ark., Sept. 1917. Presbyterian. Club: Army and Navy (Washington). Home: Xenia, Ohio. Died Apr. 15, 1942.

MARTIN, William Joseph, college pres.; b. Columbia, Tenn., Feb. 10, 1868; s. William Joseph and Letitia Coddington (Costin) M.; A.B., Davidson (N.C.) Coll., 1888, A.M., 1894; M.D., U. of Va., 1890, Ph.D., 1894; post-grad. in chemistry, Johns Hopkins, 1891-92; LL.D., Central U. of Ky., 1913, Wake Forest (N.C.) Coll., 1913, Davidson (N.C.) Coll., 1937; m. Eloise Vernam Coite, 1894; m. 2d, Mrs. Jennie D. Vardell-Rumple, June 1897; children—William Joseph, Eloise Vernam, Jean Vardell, Mary Katherine. Prof. sciences, Presbyn. Coll., Clinton, S.C., 1888-89; student in Polyclinic Hosp. and Manhattan Eye and Ear Hosp., New York, summers 1890, 91; adj. pro. science, Davidson Coll., 1890-91; instr. chemistry, U. of Va., 1892-96; Chambers prof. chemistry, 1896-1912, bursar, 1896-99, proctor, 1908-12, pres., 1912-29, Davidson Coll., now emeritus; pres. Gen. Assembly's Training Sch., 1930-33. Moderator Gen. Assembly Presbyn. Ch. U.S., 1914; mem. exec. com. Laymen's Missionary Movement; mem. exec. com. of religious edn. and publication, permanent com. on men's work and permanent advisory com. on edn., Presbyn Ch. U.S. Democrat. Mem. Beta Theta Pi, Phi Beta Kappa (U. of Va. Chapter). Home: Davidson, N.C. Died Sep. 7, 1943.

MARTINEZ, Xavier (Xavier Tizoc Martinez y Orozco) (mär-tē'nĕs), artist; b. Guadalajara, Mexico, Feb. 7, 1869; s. Margarito Martinez Suarez and Trinidad Orozco y Zúniga; ed. Liceo de Varones, Guadalajara; grad. former Mark Hopkins Inst., San Francisco, 1895, École Nationale et Spéciale des Beaux Arts, Paris, 1899; studied under Gérôme and Carrière; m. Elsie Whitaker, Oct. 17, 1907; 1 dau., Micaela Marie. Began painting at San Francisco, 1892; prof. painting, Calif. Sch. of Arts and Crafts, Berkeley, since 1909. Gold medal, San Francisco Art Assn., 1895; hon. mention Paris Expn., 1900; gold medal and hon. mention, San Francisco Expn., 1915. Selected as one of 600 foreign born Americans who have made outstanding contributions to Am. culture, N.Y. World's Fair, 1940. Clubs: Sketch, Bohemian (San Francisco); Athenian, Nile (Oakland). Address: 324 Scenic Av., Piedmont, Calif. Died Jan. 13, 1943.

MARVELL, George Ralph (mar'vĕl), naval officer; b. Fall River, Mass., Sept. 25, 1869; s. Edward Tracy and Anna Congdon (Wilbur) M.; B.S., U.S. Naval Acad., 1889; m. Anna Nippes Wynkoop, Dec. 15, 1892; 1 son, George. Commd. lt., U.S. Navy, Mar. 3, 1899, and advanced through the grades to rear adm., June 3, 1922; vice adm. (temp.), Nov. 21, 1930; rear adm., Dec. 16, 1931; retired, Oct. 1, 1933. Mem. eclipse expdn. to Africa, 1889-90; patrol duty, Behring Sea, 1894; on Vicksburg, Spanish-Am. War, 1898; survey of Santiago, Cuba, 1899; in charge survey, Cuba and Haiti, 1906, 07, 08; head, dept. of navigation U.S. Naval Acad., 1909-12; on Helena, sr. officer Yangtse Valley, China, 1912-13; Bureau of Ordnance, Navy Dept., 1915; dir. naval dists., 1916-17; comdg. Louisiana, 1917-19, with Atlantic Fleet engaged convoying troops, 1918, and bringing back troops, 1919; insp. ordnance, Naval Ordnance Plant, S. Charleston, W.Va., 1919-21; comdg. Arizona, 1921-22; comdt. 16th Naval Dist., 1922-24; comdr. Fleet Base Force, 1924-25, at Naval War Coll., 1926-27; comdt. 14th Naval Dist. and Naval Sta., Pearl Harbor, Hawaii, 1927-30; comdg. Cruisers Scouting Force, 1930-31; mem. and chmn. General Bd., 1932-33. Mem. S.R., Sojourners. Conglist. Mason. Clubs: Army and Navy (Washington); Army and Navy (Manila). Died Nov. 12, 1941.

MARVIN, Charles Frederick, meteorologist; b. Putnam, O., Oct. 7, 1858; s. George F. and Sarah A. (Speck) M.; ed. pub. schs., Columbus, O., grad. (in mech. engring.), Ohio State U., 1883, Sc.D., 1932; instr. mech. drawing and mech. and physical lab. practice, same, 1879-83; m. Nellie Limeburner, June 27, 1894 (died Feb. 27, 1905); children—Charles Frederick, Cornelia Theresa, Helen Elizabeth; m. 2d, Mabel Bartholow, Nov. 8, 1911 (died 1932); m. 3d, Sophia A. Beuter, Nov. 12, 1932. Instr. mech. drawing, Ohio State U., 1879-83; apptd. on civilian corps of signal service, 1884, and prof. meteorology, U.S. Weather Bur.; chief U.S. Weather Bur., Aug. 1913-34; retired after 50 yrs. in U.S. Weather Bur., 1934. Conducted experiments upon which are based the tables used by Weather Bureau for deducing the moisture in the air; made important investigations of anemometers for measurement of wind velocities and pressures; invented instruments for measuring and automatically recording rainfall, snowfall, sunshine, atmospheric pressure, etc.; has made extensive studies and written on use of kites for ascertaining meteorol. conditions in the free air, the registration of earthquakes, the measurement of evaporation, solar radiation, temperature with elec. resistance thermometers, etc. Mem. nat. advisory com. for aeronautics, 1915-34, and of Nat. Research Council, 1917. First sec., and dir. sect. on meteorology, Internat. Geophysical Union organized at Brussels, July 1919. Author of various tech. papers on meteorology and the simplification of the calendar, including proposal to improve Gregorian rule for leap years by omitting 4 leap years in 500 yrs. which will keep the reckoning accurate for more than 10,000 yrs. Co-author: Moses the Greatest of Calendar Reformers. Del. Internat. Conf. on Simplification of the Calendar, Geneva, Oct. 12, 1931. Home: 5746 Colorado Av. N.W., Washington, D.C. Died June 5, 1943.

MARVIN, Walter Taylor, coll. dean; b. New York, Apr. 28, 1872; s. Walter Taylor and Eliza Rowland (Jarvis) M.; A.B., Columbia, 1893, hon. Litt.D., 1929; grad. student, 1895-97; student U. of Jena, 1893-94, Gen. Theol. Sem., New York, 1894-95, univs. of Halle and Bonn, 1897-98; Ph.D., University of Bonn, 1898; Litt.D., Rutgers University, 1942; m. Adelaide Camilla Hoffman, Apr. 14, 1903; children—Dorothy Hope, Hoffman. Asst. in Columbia, 1898-99; instr. and asst. prof., Adelbert Coll., Cleveland, 1899-1905; preceptor, Princeton, 1905-10; prof. philosophy, Rutgers U., since July 1, 1910, dean of faculty, 1921-25, dean Coll. of Arts and Sciences since 1925. Mem. of Am. Philos. Society, Am. Psychol. Assn. Club: Century. Author: Die Giltigkeit unserer Erkenntnis der objektiven Welt, 1898; Syllabus of an Introduction to Philosophy, 1899; Introduction to Systematic Philosophy, 1903; A First Book in Metaphysics, 1912; The History of European Philosophy, 1917. Co-Author: The New Realism, 1912. Address: New Brunswick, N.J. Died May 26, 1944.

MARX, Harry S., lawyer; b. Coshocton, O., Aug. 16, 1878; s. Henry and Frances P. (Stockman) M.; m. Grace A. McGowen, 1906. Began practice Chicago; moved to New York, 1909, became connected with Wells Fargo Express Co.; gen. atty. same, 1914, until orgn., 1918, of Am. Ry. Express Co. of which was gen. counsel, 1923-29; v.p. and gen. counsel Ry. Express Agency, Inc., of Dela., Railway Express Motor Transport, Inc.; v.p., gen. counsel and dir. Ry. Express Agency, Inc., of Calif. and of Va.; director, member exec. and finance coms. Expressmen's Mutual Life Ins. Co. (New York). Mem. Am. Bar Assn., Assn. Practitioners Interstate Commerce Commn., New York Law Inst., Ohio Soc. National Aeronautic Assn., Acad., Polit. Science, N.Y. State Chamber of Commerce. Clubs: Traffic, Sales Executives (New York); Ridgewood Country. Home: Ridgewood, N.J. Address: 230 Park Av., New York. Died Aug. 6, 1948.

MASARYK, Jan, government official; b. Praha, Czechoslovakia, Sept. 14, 1886; s. Thomas Garrigue and Charlotte (Guerigue) M.; ed. in Praha; LL.D. (hon.) U. of Calif.; unmarried. Came to U.S., 1907; after World War I returned to the U.S., as Chargé d'Affairs, Washington, D.C., 1919-20. Served in Fgn. Office, Praha from 1920-22, 1923-25; counselor to Czechoslovak Legation in London, 1922-23; Czechoslovak minister to Great Britain in 1925, resigned in 1938 in protest over Munich agreement. After a lecture tour in the U.S., returned to England and started shortwave broadcasts to Czechoslovakia; apptd. fgn. minister Czechoslovak Govt., London, 1940; vice-premier, 1941-45; chmn. Czechoslovak delegations to U.N.R.R.A. Conf., Atlantic City, 1943, Internat. Labour Conf., Phila., 1944, San Francisco Conf., 1945, Gen. Assembly in London and Conf. in Paris; minister fgn. affairs. Address: Ministry Foreign Affairs, Praha, Czechoslovakia. Died Mar. 10, 1948.

MASON, Edward Wilson, ry. official; b. Moberly, Mo., Mar. 23, 1877; s. John Quincy and Virginia Murdoch (Wilson) M.; ed. high sch., Tacoma, Wash.; m. Elizabeth Burroughs Pratt, Jan. 23, 1906; children—Robert Pratt, Elizabeth Anne. Began as call boy N.P. Ry., June 1893, and continued consecutively as operator, dispatcher, night chief dispatcher, chief dispatcher and trainmaster; with Western Pacific R.R. as supt. telegraph and car accountant, div. supt. and gen. supt., 1909-18; federal mgr., same rd., 1919-20, gen. mgr., Mar.-Nov. 1921, v.p. and gen. mgr. since Nov. 1921; v.p. Denver & Salt Lake R.R.; dir. of Western Pacific R.R., Denver & Salt Lake Ry., Alameda Belt Line, Central Calif. Traction Co. (mem. operating com.), Tidewater Southern Ry. Commd. maj. engrs., U.S. Army, May 1918; served with 31st Engrs. and Transportation Corps in France, June 1918-Aug. 1919; lt. col., Feb. 1919; assigned to railroad operation as div. supt. at St. Nazaire, and gen. supt. Nantes, 14th Grand Div., Transportation Corps; hon. discharged, Aug. 13, 1919. Meritorious service citation from U.S. and French govts.; Officier d'Académie (France). Republican. Protestant. Mason (32°). Club: Lake Merced Golf and Country. Home: 2321 Van Ness Av. Office: Mills Bldg., San Francisco, Calif.* Died Mar. 26, 1947.

MASON, Harold Whitney; b. Worcester, Mass., Apr. 21, 1895; s. William Lysander and Margaret Etta (Matthews) M.; B.S., Dartmouth, 1917; m. Evelyn Dunham, Mar. 17, 1918 (died Dec. 1930); 1 son, George Dunham. Vice pres. and treas. Dunham Bros. Co., Brattleboro, Vt., since 1927; dir. Dunham Brothers Co., Conn. River Power Co., New England Power Assn., Bellows Falls Hydroelectric Co., Union Mutual Fire Insurance Co. of Vt. Estey Organ Corp., Central Vt. Ry., Nat. Life Ins. Co., C. E. Bradley corporation; secretary Post-War Policy Council at Mackinac Island, Sept. 1943. Lieutenant Air Service U.S. Army, World War I; lt. colonel Army of U.S., May 1942; inactive duty because of health since Oct. 1942. Del. Rep. Nat. Conv. and presdl. elector for Vt., 1932; mem. Rep. Nat. Com. since 1936; mem. of exec. com. and sec. of Rep. Nat. Com. since 1937; sec. Rep. Nat. Conv. at Phila., 1940. Dir. New England Council. Mem. Dartmouth Alumni Council, 1942. Trustee Vermont Acad., Kurn Hattin Homes at Saxtons River, Vt.; dir. Brattleboro Memorial Hosp. Mem. Vt. Soc. Colonial wars, Vt. Soc. Sons Am. Revolution, Am. Legion, Mil. Order Fgn. Wars, Sigma Nu. Republican. Congregationalist. Clubs: Union League, Dartmouth, Links, National-Republican (New York); Union, University, St. Botolph (Boston); Metropolitan, Army-Navy Country (Washington, D.C.); Tobique Salmon (New Brunswick). Home; Brattleboro, Vt. Died Nov. 3, 1944.

MASON, Harry Howland, ex-congressman; b. McLean County, Ill., Dec. 16, 1873; s. James Alfred and Lovenia (McCollister) M.; ed. pub. schs.; m. Mabel Pennoyer, Aug. 17, 1912. Newspaper pub. in Pawnee, Ill., since 1903; now pub. Pawnee Herald (weekly); county treas. Sangamon County, Ill., 1933-34; mem. 74th Congress (1935-37), 21st Ill. Dist. Democrat. Presbyn. Clubs: 1873 Club (Springfield, Ill.); Lions (Pawnee, Ill.). Home: Pawnee, Ill. Died Mar. 10, 1946.

MASON, Herbert Delavan, lawyer; b. East Swanzey, N.H., Nov. 2, 1878; s. Herbert W. and Abbie Frances (Alexander) M.; ed. pub. schs., Glens Falls, N.Y.; LL.B., Cornell U., 1900; m. Maud Louise Richardson, June 18, 1910; 1 dau., Elizabeth Dieudonnée. Practiced law, Ithaca, N.Y., 1900-02; asso. with Hornblower, Byrne, Miller & Potter, N.Y. City, 1902-05; mem. Ivins, Mason, Wolff & Hoguet, 1905-12; removed to Tulsa 1912; mem. Mason, Williams & Lynch. Assisted as counsel Pub. Service Commn. of N.Y. City, 1907, in gen. investigation in N.Y. City and Brooklyn traction conditions; formerly mem. Bd. of Edn., Tulsa; non-resident lecturer, Okla. U.; non-resident lecturer on oil and gas law, Cornell. Trustee Cornell, 1911-26, U. of Tulsa, since 1930. President Rep. League, Tulsa. Mem. Am. Bar Assn., Assn. Bar City of New York, Okla. State Bar Assn., Tulsa County Bar Assn. (pres. 1926-30), N. H. Soc. of New York, N.Y. State Hist. Assn., Conejos Recreation Assn. (Antonito, Colo.). Phi Delta Phi, Acad. of Polit. Science. Mason. Clubs: Cornell University (New York); Town and Gown, Craftsmen's (Ithaca, N.Y.); University, Cornell of Okla. (pres.), Tulsa Polo (pres. 1926-27). Author: (with Robert Louis Hoguet) Supplement to Brightley's New York Digest (2 vols.), 1896-1907; (with William Mills Ivins) Control of Public Utilities, 1908; Mason on Highways, 3 edits. Office: Philtower Bldg., Tulsa, Okla. Died July 1947.

MASON, Jesse Henry, supt. schs.; b. Montpelier, Ind., June 13, 1889; s. Jesse and Ida May (Rhoton) M.; A.B., Ohio Wesleyan U., 1915, Ed.D., 1937; A.M., Columbia U., 1928; student Ohio State U., summers 1911, 14; m. Ruthe Wheeler, Aug. 6, 1917. Teacher elementary and high schs., 1907-13; instr. mathematics, Ohio Wesleyan U., 1915-16; high sch. prin. Ohio cities, 1916-21; supt. schs., Chillicothe, 1921-23, Marion, 1923-28, Canton since 1928. Dir. The Harter Bank & Trust Co., Citizens Savings & Loan Co. (both of Canton). Served in U.S. Army, as 1st lt. 40th Inf., World War I. Pres. Canton Welfare Fedn.; dir. Canton Y.M.C.A.; mem. N.E.A. (life), Am. Assn. Sch. Adminstrs., Phi Delta Kappa, Phi Beta Kappa. Methodist. Mason (32°). Rotarian. Address: Canton, O. Deceased.

MASON, Newton Eliphalet, rear-admiral U.S. Navy; b. Monroeton, Bradford County, Pa., Oct. 14, 1850; s. Gordon Fowler and Mary Ann M.; ed. Susquehanna Collegiate Inst., Towanda, Pa., until 1865; grad. U.S. Naval Acad., 1869; m. Dora E. Hancock, Apr. 4, 1894. After graduation served on U.S.S. Sabine, special cruise, 1869-70; promoted ensign, 1870; torpedo instrn., 1871; U.S.S. Wabash, European Sta., 1871-72; promoted master, 1872; on monitor Manhattan, 1873; U.S.S. Kansas, 1874-75; commd. lt., 1874; monitor Catskill, 1875-76; U.S.S. Ossipee, 1876-77; receiving-ship St. Louis, 1878-80; Irish famine relief ship Constellation, 1880; U.S.S. Monocacy, Asiatic Sta., 1880-83; U.S.S. Pensacola, 1883-84; on ordnance duty, Navy Yard, Washington, 1884-85; Bur. of Ordnance, Navy Dept., 1885-89; U.S.S. Petrel and monitor Miantonomah, N. Atlantic Sta., 1889-92; Bur. of Ordnance and in charge Naval Proving Grounds, Indian Head, Md., 1892-96; commd. lt.-comdr., 1896; U.S.S. Brooklyn, 1896-99 (including Spanish War); insp. ordnance League Island Navy Yard, 1899; insp. ordnance in charge Naval Torpedo Sta., Newport, R.I., 1899-1902; promoted comdr., Nov. 1899; comdg. U.S.S. Cincinnati, 1902-04; spl. duty, June-Aug. 3, 1904; chief Bur. of Ordnance, Navy Dept. with rank of rear-admiral, from Aug. 1904 to May 1911; mem. gen. bd., 1911-12; commd. capt., Sept. 30, 1904; rear-admiral, Nov. 12, 1908; retired from active service, Oct. 14, 1912. Chmn. D.C. Chapter Am. Nat. Red Cross, 1914-17; ordered to active duty, June 2, 1917; serving in Bur. of Ordnance, Navy Dept., and as mem. priorities com. War Industries Bd. of Council Nat. Defense until Jan. 1919; pres. spl. bd. on naval ordnance, Bur. of Ordnance, till Nov. 1, 1919; returned to inactive list. Was awarded Santiago medal, 1898. Mem. Pa. Commandery Mil. Order Foreign Wars, D.C. Soc. S.A.R. Address: Box 313, Coronado, Calif. Died Jan. 23, 1945.

MASON, Wallace Edward, educator; b. North Conway, N.H., June 24, 1861; s. John Edward and Lizzie (Randall) M.; A.B., Bowdoin, 1882, A.M.; studied Harvard and Clark U.; Ed.D., Rhode Island Coll. of Edn.; m. Nettie Robinson, June 30, 1887; children—Harold E., Donald R., Wallace E. Prin. high sch., Thomaston, 1886-87; admitted to Colo. bar, 1887; practiced at Cardiff, Tenn., 1888-90; prin. high sch., Orange, Mass., 1891-98, Leominster, 1898-1903; supt. schs., Charlton and Leicester, Mass., 1903-06, North Andover, 1906-11; pres. N.H. State Normal Sch., 1911-39; pres. emeritus since 1939. Rep. N.H. Legislature, 1940-41; mem. N.H. State Rep. exec. com.; chmn. Cheshire County Rep. Com, Mem. N.E.A. (state dir.), Am. Inst. Instrn. (ex-pres.), N.H. Council Edn. (ex-pres.), N.H. Schoolmasters' Club (ex-pres.), S.A.R., Alpha Delta Phi, Phi Beta Kappa. Republican. Conglist. Mason, Elk. Clubs: Keene Country, Rotary (ex-pres.), School Garden of America. Home: Keene, N.H. Died June 13, 1944.

MASSEE, W(illiam) Wellington, educator and lecturer; b. Modena, Wis.; s. William and Laura Jane (Davenport) M.; Litt.B., U. of Minn., 1901; A.M., Columbia, 1903, student in literature, 1902-06; Ph.D., Iowa Christian Coll., 1909; m. Florence Magraw; 1 dau., Mildred; m. 2d, Maude Kalberer; 1 son, William. Founder and prin. Massee Country Sch., Stamford, Conn., 1908-28; also headmaster Summer Tutoring Sch.; lecturer on lit. and geog. subjects for New York Bd. of Edn., 1904-17. Served as 1st sergt. Co. A, U.S. Vol. Signal Corps, during the Spanish-American War, in Porto Rico campaign; four-minute man, 1917-18. Mem. Spanish War Vets. (Paris). Republican. Studied and traveled in Europe, 1928-35. Broadcasted on foreign affairs, Station WBNX, New York, 1935-36. Clubs: National Arts of N.Y. City (sec.); American Playgoers (v.p.). Author: Best of Oscar Wilde, 1904; Modern Dramatists, 1905; Character Self-Measurements for Boys, 1921; also articles on ednl. and mil. subjects, and over 30 one-act plays for schools. Address: National Arts Club, 15 Gramercy Park, New York. Died Aug. 27, 1942; buried in Arlington National Cemetery.

MAST, Samuel Ottmar, biologist; b. Ann Arbor Twp., Mich., October 5, 1871; s. G. F. and Beata (Staebler) M.; certificate, State Normal Coll., Ypsilanti, Michigan, 1897, M.Pd., 1912; B.S., University of Michigan, 1899, honorary Sc.D., 1941; Ph.D., Harvard University, 1906; Johnston scholar, Johns Hopkins, 1907-08; m. Grace Rebecca Tennent, 1908; children—Louise Rebecca, Elisabeth Tennent, Margaret Tennent. Prof. biology and botany Hope College, 1899-1908; asso. prof. biology and prof. botany, Goucher Coll., Baltimore, 1908-11; asso. prof. and prof. zoölogy, Johns Hopkins, since 1911, head of dept. of zoölogy and dir. zoöl. laboratory since 1938, prof. emeritus of zoölogy, 1942. Cartwright prize, Columbia, 1909. Fellow A.A.A.S.; mem. Am. Soc. Zoölogists, Am. Physiol. Soc., Am. Soc. Naturalists Society for Study of Growth and Development, Academy of Science, Philadelphia, Phi Beta Kappa, Sigma Xi; honorary member of Beta, Beta, Beta. Author: The Structure and Physiology of Flowering Plants, 1907; Light and the Behavior of Organisms, 1911; Motor Response to Light in the Invertebrate Animals, 1936; Factors Involved in the Process of Orientation of Lower Organisms in Light, 1938; Motor Response in Unicellular Animals, 1941; also papers on responses in organisms and on growth in protozoa. Home: 415 Woodlawn Rd., Roland Park, Baltimore, Md. Died Feb. 3, 1947.

MATCHETT, David Fleming, judge; b. Newton, Jasper County, Ia., Mar. 19, 1867; s. David Jonathan and Jean (Hill) M.; grad. Washington (Ia.) Acad., 1887; B.A., Colorado Coll. 1892, LL.D., 1932; LL.B., Coll. of Law of Cornell U., 1894; LL.D., Monmouth (Ill.) Coll., 1928; m. Jennie Elizabeth Moore, June 19, 1907; children—David Fleming, Hugh M. Instr. polit. science Colorado Coll., 1894-95; admitted to Ill. bar, 1895; master in chancery Superior Court of Cook County, 1905-15; chmn. Rep. Cook County com., 1914-15; elected judge Circuit Court, 1915, and five times successively reelected; now serving term 1945-51; appointed by Supreme Court, judge Appellate Court, 1917, and has since served continuously in Second and First divisions. Chairman Legal Advisory Bd., 16th Dist., World War I. Mem. legal adv. bd., 87th Dist., World War II. Member Am., Ill. State and Chicago bar assns., Cornell Law Assn., Acad. Polit. Science, Delta Chi. Republican. Mem. U.P. Ch. and pres. Bd. of Edn. same church, 1916-46. Home: 6133 Ellis Av., Chicago, Ill. Died July 25, 1946.

MATHER, Arthur (măth'ēr), clergyman; b. Rawdon, Yorkshire, Eng., Aug. 21, 1868; s. S. J. M.; ed. Bradford Tech. Coll., and South Kensington, London; D.D., Scarritt-Morrisville Coll., 1905; m. Martha Bradley, July 14, 1891; children—Thomas Bradley, John Waterhouse. Came to America in 1899; ordained ministry M.E. Ch., S., 1901; pastor Hayti, Mo., 1901-02, Immanuel Ch., St. Louis, 1902-06, Union Ch., Louisville, Ky., 1906-07, Hardinsburg, Ky., 1908-10, Marion, Ky., 1910-12; prof. Bibl. lit., Vanderbilt Training Sch., Elkton, Ky., and pastor Petrie Memorial Ch., 1912-14; pastor Kingdom House Social Settlement, M.E. Ch., S., St. Louis, 1914-17, Kirkwood, Mo., 1918-22, Ferguson, 1922-26. Asso. editor of St. Louis Christian Advocate, 1914-17, acting editor, 1917-18. Asst. sec. Bd. of Ch. Extension, M.E., Ch., S., 1906-08; sec. St. Louis Ch. Extension and City Mission Society, M.E. Ch., South, 1916-38. Mason (33°, K.T.); Grand Chaplain, Grand Lodge A.F.&A.M. of Mo., 1917-27, Grand Corr., 1924-27, Grand Sec. since 1927, Grand Librarian since 1927, Grand Chaplain, Grand Council, R. & S. M., 1921-26, Grand Chaplain, Grand Chapter R.A.M. of Mo., 1942-43. Writer and lecturer on Masonry. Home: Maplehurst, Ferguson, Mo. Office: Masonic Temple, 3681 Lindell Blvd., St. Louis, Mo. Died Apr. 1944.

MATHER Thomas Ray (măth'ēr), prof. English; b. Rohrsburg, Pa., May 24, 1890; s. John J. and Ella May (Black) M.; A.B., Williams Coll., 1913; A.M., Harvard, 1914; Fellow in English, Princeton, 1914-15; student U. of Chicago, summer 1917; m. Ruth Evelyn Hutchins, Nov. 27, 1916; children—Thomas John, Merrilie. Instr. in history and English, Meadville (Pa.) Theol. Sch., 1915-18; instr. in rhetoric, U. of Minnesota, 1918-20; instr. in English, U.S. Naval Acad., 1921-22; instr. in English Coll. of Liberal Arts, Boston U., 1922-23, asst. prof., 1923-28, prof. and chmn. dept. of English since 1928; pres. Benton Roller Mills Corp., Benton, Pa., since 1941. Teacher, S.A.T.C., U. of Minn. during World War I. Awarded Horace F. Clark Prize Scholarship of Williams Coll. at Harvard, 1913-1914. Mem. Modern Lang. Assn. of America, Am. Assn. Univ. Profs., New England Assn. Coll. and Secondary Schs. Mason. Book reviewer for Reedy's Mirror, St. Louis, Mo., 1918-20. Editor: Types and Times in English Literature, 18th Century Vol. (with Louis Worthington Smith, editor of 4 vol. work), 1941. Home: 216 Prospect St., Belmont 78, Mass.; (summer) Benton, Pa. Office: 688 Boylston St., Boston 16, Mass. Died Aug. 26, 1947.

MATHEWS, Arthur Frank, artist; b. Wis., Oct. 1, 1860; s. Julius Chase and Pauline (Hope) M.; ed. schs. San Francisco and Oakland, Calif.; studied under Gustave Boulanger at Paris; m. Lucia Kleinhans, June 19, 1894. Architect to 1882; in Europe, studying art, 1884-89; reorganized Calif. Sch. of Design (San Francisco Art Assn.) and continued as dir. until Apr. 1906 (resigned). Exhibited Paris expns., 1889, 1898, Paris salons, 1887, 88, 89, 98, Chicago Expn., 1893, San Francisco Expn., 1915. Principal decorations: 12 panels in State Capitol, Sacramento; Oakland Library, Lane Library, and Children's Hosp., San Francisco; wall painting for State Supreme Court Room, San Francisco; decorations for Knights Templars Hall, St. Francis Hotel, Curran Theatre, San Francisco. Awarded medal of A.I.A., 1928, for mural painting. Hon. mem. Art Assn. of San Francisco and Athenian Club. Clubs: Art (Phila.); Bohemian. Home-Studio: 670 Fell St., San Francisco, Calif. Died Feb. 19, 1945.

MATHEWS, Edward Bennett, geologist; b. Portland, Me., Aug. 16, 1869; s. Jonathan Bennett and Sophia Lucinda (Shailer) M.; A.B., Colby Coll., 1891, D.Sc., 1927; Ph.D., Johns Hopkins Univ., 1894; m. Helen Louise Whitman, Sept. 12, 1900; children—William Whitman (dec.), Margaret (Mrs. Richard W. Thorpe), John B. (dec.), Roger H. (dec.). Field asst. U.S. Geol. Survey, seasons of 1891-94; instr. mineralogy and petrography, 1894-95, Johns Hopkins U., asso., 1895-99, asso. prof., 1899-1904, prof. since 1904, chmn. geol. dept., 1917-30, prof. emeritus since 1939. Asst. state geologist of Md., 1898-1917, state geologist since 1917; mem. Md. State Bd. of Forestry; dir. Maryland Weather Service; chmn. div. geology and geography, Nat. Research Council, 1919-22, and mem. advisory com. since 1933; v.p. Internat. Geol. Congress, 1922, 26, and 29, treas., 1933; chmn. advisory council U.S. Bd. of Surveys and Maps, 1920-43 and since 1929; mem. Md. State Development Commn. since 1929, Md. Water Resources Commn. since 1933. Member of Maryland-Virginia Boundary commission, 1927-31. Director Department Geology, Mining and Water Resources, 1941-43. Fellow Geological Soc. America (treas. since 1917), Washington Acad. of Sciences, Am. Acad. of Arts and Sciences, A.A.A.S.; mem. Econ. Geologists, Mineralogical Soc., Am. Inst. Mining and Metall. Engrs., Am. Geog. Soc., Assn. of Am. State Geologists (pres. 1920-23), Md. Hist. Soc., Soc. Colonial Wars. Author: Bibliography and Cartography of Md.; Maps and Map-Makers of Md.; Building Stones of Md.; Limestones of Md.; History of Mason-Dixon Line; Boundary Line Between Virginia and Maryland (with W. A. Nelson); Physical Features of Md.; Water Resources of Md.; Catalogue Published Bibliographies in Geology; and other geol. and hist. papers. Home: Lombardy Apt. 10, Baltimore, Md. Died Feb. 4, 1944.

MATHEWS, Frances Aymar, novelist, playwright; b. New York; d. Daniel A. and Sara Eayres (Webb) Mathews; ed. privately. Author: My Lady Peggy Leaves Town; Little Tragedy at Tientsin; Fanny of the 40 Frocks; Miss Carliney; Christmas Honeymoon; The Stronger Spell. Plays: Up to Him; Under the Mistletoe; Barbara; Stranger Passing By; The Prima Donna. Address: 2574 8th Av., New York. Died Jan. 13, 1923.

MATHEWS, George C., pub. utilities; b. Northwood, Ia., Feb. 22, 1886; s. John and Sarah (McKercher) M.; A.B., U. of Wis., 1908; m. Bertha Gesell, Aug. 16, 1912. Instr. Ore. Agrl. Coll., 1909-10; rate expert for R.R. Commn. of Wis., 1910-12, statistician in charge utility rate dept., 1912-16 and 1917-25, dir. securities and statis. divs., 1925-31; employed by pub. accounting firm at Chicago, 1916-17; prof. pub. utilities, Northwestern U., 1924-25; dir. securities div. and chief examiner Pub. Service Commn. of Wis., 1931-33; v.p. Middle West Utilities Co., June-Oct. 1933; apptd. mem. Federal Trade Commn., Oct. 1933, Securities and Exchange Commn., July 1934; v.p. and comptroller Northern States Power Co., Minneapolis, June 1940-Aug. 1942; vice-pres. Pub. Utility Engring. & Service Corp., 1942-Aug. 1943; Now v.p. Standard Gas and Elec. Co. Republican. Home: 693 Greenwood Av., Glencoe, Ill. Office: 231 S. La Salle St., Chicago, Ill. Died July 11, 1946.

MATHEWS, James Thomas, naval officer; b. Marion, S.C., Nov. 6, 1891; s. James Thomas and Martha Ellen (Williams) M.; B.S., U.S. Naval Acad., 1913; C.E., Rensselaer Poly. Inst., Troy, N.Y., 1918; m. Isabelle Jane Bradham, July 22, 1914; children—James Thomas (officer U.S. Navy), Laurens Bradham (officer U.S. Navy). Commd. ensign, U.S. Navy, 1913, and advanced through the grades to rear adm., 1942; served as pub. works officer, Naval Air Station, Miami, Fla., Oct. 1918-Aug. 1919; Treaty Engr., Republic of Haiti, Oct. 1919-Sept. 1920; Officer in Charge Constrn. Naval Ordnance Plant, So. Charleston W.Va., July-Nov. 1922; Pub. Works Officer, Submarine Base, New London, Conn., Mar. 1926-Sept. 1928; Navy Yard, Charleston, S.C. and 6th and 7th Naval Dists. Aug. 1930-July 1934; Bur. of Yards and Docks and Bur. of Aeronautics Sept 1934-Sept. 1937, Naval Operating Base and 11th Naval Dist., San Diego, Calif., Sept. 1937-Jan 1942, Navy Yard, Portsmouth, N.H., Feb.-Apr. 1942; superintending civil engr., Area IV, since Apr. 1942. Decorations: Legion of Merit, Mexican, Victory, Navy Expeditionary, Haitian, Defense Legion of Merit and Am. Area service medals (U.S.), Order of Honor and Merit (Haiti). Mem. American Society Civil Engineers, Society American Mil. Engrs. Home: Florence, S.C. Address: care Bureau of Naval Personnel, Navy Dept., Washington 25, D.C. Died Dec. 14, 1947.

MATHEWS, Shailer, educator, editor; b. Portland, Me., May 26, 1863; s. Jonathan Bennett and Sophia Lucinda (Shailer) M.; brother of Edward Bennett M.; A.B., Colby Coll., 1884, A.M., 1887; grad. Newton Theol. Instn., 1887; U. of Berlin, 1890-91; D.D., Colby, 1901, Oberlin, 1908, Brown, 1914, Miami, 1922, U. of Glasgow, 1928, Faculté Libre de Theologie Protestante de Paris, 1929, Chicago Theol. Sem., 1933; LL.D., Pa. Coll., 1915, U. of Rochester, 1926, Colby, 1934; m. Mary Philbrick Elden, July 16, 1890. Asso. prof. rhetoric, Colby Coll., 1887-89, prof. history and polit. economy, 1889-94; asso. prof. N.T. history and interpretation, Divinity Sch., U. of Chicago, 1894-97, prof., 1897-1905, prof. systematic theology, 1905-06, hist. and comparative theology, 1906-33, junior dean, 1899-1908, dean, 1908-33, emeritus since 1933. Lecturer on New Testament, Newton Theol. Instn., 1888-90; editor The World Today, 1903-11, Biblical World, 1913-20. Pres. The Quadrangle Club, 1902-03, Western Econ. Soc., 1911-19, Chicago Co-operative Council of City Missions, 1908-15, Chicago Bapt. Exec. Council, 1910-19; dir. religious work, Chautauqua Instn., 1912-34; pres. Federal Council Chs. of Christ in America, 1912-16, Northern Bapt. Conv., 1915, Chicago Ch. Fedn., 1929-32, Kobe Coll. Corp. since 1920; trustee Ch. Peace Union (founded by Andrew Carnegie) since 1914; was in Japan as representative of the chs. of U.S., 1915. State sec. of war savings for Ill., 1917-18, vice-director, 1918-19. Haverford Library lectures, 1907, Sarle lectures (Berkeley, Calif.), 1913, William Belden Noble lectures, Harvard, 1916, McNair lectures, U. of N.C., 1918, Slocum-Bennett lectures, Wesleyan U., 1921, Cole lectures, Vanderbilt, 1926, 1934, Ingersoll on Immortality, Harvard Univ., 1933; Barrows lectures in India, U. of Chicago, 1933-34. Clubs: Quadrangle, University. Author: Select Mediæval Documents, 1891, 1900; The Social Teaching of Jesus, 1897; A History of New Testament Times in Palestine, 1899 (rev. 1929); Constructive Studies in the Life of Christ (with E. D. Burton), 1901, revised 1927; The French Revolution—A Sketch, 1901; Principles and Ideals for the Sunday School (with E. D. Burton), 1903; The Messianic Hope in the New Testament, 1905; The Church and the Changing Order, 1907; The Social Gospel, 1909; The Gospel and the Modern Man, 1909; Scientific Management in the Churches, 1911; The Making of To-Morrow, 1913; The Individual and the Social Gospel, 1914; The Spiritual Interpretation of History, 1916; Patriotism and Religion, 1918; Dictionary of Religion and Ethics (with G. B. Smith), 1921; The Validity of American Ideals, 1922; The French Revolution (1789-1815), 1922; The Contributions of Science to Religion (with the coöperation of various scientists), 1924; The Faith of Modernism, 1924; Outline of Christianity, Volume III (with others), 1926; The Student's Gospels, 1927; Jesus on Social Institutions, 1928; The Atonement and the Social Process, 1930; The Growth of the Idea of God, 1931; Immortality and the Cosmic Process, 1933; Christianity and Social Process, 1934; Creative Christianity, 1935; New Faith for Old—an Autobiography, 1936; The Church and the Christian, 1938; Is God Emeritus?, 1940. Editor of the New Testament Handbooks; The Bible for Home and School; Social Betterment Series; Woman's Citizen's Library Series. Asso. editor: Dictionary of the Bible; Constructive Series of U. of Chicago. Died Oct. 23, 1941.

MATHEWS, William Burdette, asso. clerk Supreme Court of Appeals, W.Va.; b. Marshall County, W.Va., Aug. 27, 1866; s. Christopher C. and Esther J. (Scott) M.; A.M., Waynesburg (Pa.) Coll., 1889; LL.B., George Washington U., 1891; LL.M., 1892; LL.D., Waynesburg College, 1926; m. Elizabeth Blundon, Oct. 25, 1900; children—Mrs. Sarah Esther Gilchrist, Mrs. Elisabeth Mathews Wallace, John Ingram and Edgar Blundon (twins, both dec.). Admitted to bar, 1891; teacher, 1882-89; examiner public school teachers, Marshall County, W.Va., 1889-90; clerk 11th U.S. Census, 1890-95; sec. to speaker House of Dels., W.Va., 1897; chief clerk, office of auditor of W.Va., 1897-1902; Rep. presdl. elector, 1901; asst. atty.-gen. W.Va., 1902; clerk Supreme Court of Appeals, W.Va., 1902-37; asso. clerk since 1937; sec. W.Va. Bd. of Law Examiners since 1920. State dir. Four Minute Men, World War. Dir. Va. Joint Stock Land Bank of Charleston, Bank of Dunbar (W.Va.), Empire Savings & Loan Co., Empire Federal Savings & Loan Assn., Charleston Bldg. & Loan Assn., Title Trust & Mortgage Co., Virginian Savings & Loan Co., secretary-treasurer Roane County Development Company. Director Kanawha County Public Library, Union Mission Settlement; trustee emeritus W.Va. Wesleyan Coll.; trustee 1st Meth. Church, Charleston. Apptd., 1931, by Gov. Conley, mem. W.Va. com. for celebration of 200th anniversary of birth of George Washington; mem. President's Conf. on Home Bldg. and Home Ownership, 1931. Charter and life member American Law Inst.; mem.

Am., W.Va. and Charleston bar assns., W.Va. Hist. Soc., S.R. in W.Va. (ex-pres.). Republican. Methodist. Mem. Gen. Conf. M.E. Ch., 1900, 04; mem. Gen. Bd. Control Epworth League, 1904-08; del. 4th Ecumenical Meth. Conf., 1911. Mason (32°, K.T., Shriner); life mem. Elks. Clubs: Grandparents, Rotary (Charleston); W.Va. Soc. (Washington). Home: 1501 Quarrier St. Office: State Capitol, P.O. Box 1406, Charleston, W.Va. Died Aug. 6, 1943.

MATHEWSON, Ozias Danforth, educator; b. Wheelock, Vermont, March 10, 1864; s. Epaphras Chase and Nancy Earl (Marsh) M.; grad. Lyndon Inst., Lyndon Center, Vt., 1886; A.B., Dartmouth Coll., 1890, A.M., 1893; Pd.D., Middlebury College, Vermont, 1933; LL.D., Norwich U., Northfield, Vt., 1939; Dr. of Education U. of Vermont, 1940; Dr. of Pedagogy, Dartmouth, 1940; m. Angie M. Kelley, July 1, 1891 (died Sept. 21, 1907); m. 2d, Grace B. Hoyt, June 29, 1909; children—Miriam Rachel, Marion Rosamond, Philip Hoyt. Supt. schs., Wheelock, Vt., 1885-88; prin. Spaulding High Sch., Barre, Vt., 1890-1912; also examiner of teachers, Washington County, 1894-1908, and supt. schs., Barre, 1896-1912; prin. Lyndon Inst., 1912-43 (retired); pres. Lyndonville Realty Company; president and director Lyndonville Savings Bank & Trust Co. Town rep., 1932-34; mem. Vt. State Senate, 1936-38. Sec. Normal Sch. Commn., 1901-08; sec. and treas. Vt. State Bd. Edn., 1908-10; former Vt. mem. N.E. Council; chmn. Vt. Free Pub. Library Commn. since 1937. Trustee Lyndon Inst. since 1893 (pres. bd. trustees since 1931). Mem. Vt. State Teachers' Assn. (ex-pres.), Phi Beta Kappa, Psi Upsilon, Casque and Gauntlet. Republican. Conglist. Mason (32°), K.P. Home: Lyndon Center, Vt. Died Aug. 12, 1944.

MATHEWSON, Stanley Bernard, personnel administration; b. Augusta, Ga., Apr. 24, 1884; s. Joseph Oscar and Anna (Horton) M.; B.S., Ga. Sch. of Tech., Atlanta, 1904; m. Carmen Lee Carlyle, Jan. 1, 1921. Supt. Am. Chem. & Mining Co., 1905; asst. southern mgr. Barber-Colman Co., 1906-07; dist. mgr. Southern Bell Telephone & Telegraph Co., 1915-17; mem. bd. dirs. Carolina Pub. Service Co., 1917; mem. The Scott Co., engrs. in industrial personnel, 1919-21; exec. engr. Elwood-Myers Co., 1921-22; dir. personnel administration, Antioch Coll., 1922-28; labor investigator U.S. Coal Commn., 1923. Mem. Vocational Guidance Conf., Nat. Research Council, 1924-25; mem. Ohio Commn. on Unemployment Insurance, 1931-32; sec.-mgr. Springfield (O.) Chamber Commerce, 1928-33; Ohio dir. Nat. Reemployment Service, 1933-34; regional dir. Nat. Labor Relations Bd., 1934-35; asst. dir. Cincinnati Regional Dept. Econ. Security, 1935-37, dir., 1937-38; retired. Served as asst. dir. trade test div. com. on classification of personnel, U.S. Army, 1918; maj. A.G. Res., 1918-39. Mem. advisory com. on Internat. Labor Orgn. of League of Nations Assn.; mem. tech. bd. Nat. Occupational Research Program, 1934-40; dir. Melbourne Chamber of Commerce. Mem. A.A.A.S., American Legion, Ohio Acad. Science, Fla. Audubon Soc., Nat. Audubon Soc., Delta Tau Delta. Episcopalian. Clubs: Nine O'Clocks (Atlanta); Lake Placid (N.Y.); Top-O-Michigan (Gaylord); Melbourne (Fla.) Golf and Country; Kiwanis. Author: Restriction of Output among Unorganized Workers, 1931; Personnel Management, revised edit., 1931; Pooled vs. Individual Reserves in Unemployment Insurance, 1935; Labor, Management and the Public, 1937. Home: 629 Melbourne Av., Melbourne, Fla. Died Jan. 19, 1943.

MATHIESON, Samuel James (măth'ĕ-sŭn), clergyman; b. Dunedin, New Zealand; s. George and Mary (MacArthur) Mathieson; B.O., Drake University, 1909, D.D., 1928; student Union Theol. Sem., 1924, and U. of Chicago, summer 1908; m. Alether Wood, Feb. 3, 1920; children—Eileen Alether, Kathleen Florence (dec.), Samuel James. Came to U.S., 1906, naturalized, 1926. Ordained ministry Disciples of Christ Ch., 1909; pastor Disciples of Christ Ch., Wellington, New Zealand, 1910-14; Denton, Tex., 1920-22; asso. pastor University Ch., Des Moines, Ia., 1922-25; pastor Disciples of Christ Ch., Hollywood, Calif., 1925-29, Central Ch., Denver, Colo., since 1929. Vice-pres. Internat. Conv. of Disciples of Christ, 1929; chmn. bd. of mgrs., Disciples of Christ, 1932-33; vice-pres. Colo. Council of Churches, 1941, 42, 43. Served as chaplain with rank of capt. with Australian and New Zealand Army Corps, 1915-18. Mem. Theta Phi. Clubs: Civitan, Lakewood Country, Denver Country. Home: 832 Harrison St., Denver, Colo. Died Apr. 7, 1945.

MATSON, Carlton Kingsbury, newspaper editor; b. Kingsville, O., Aug. 8, 1890; s. Burton E. and Mary (Kingsbury) M.; A.B., Oberlin Coll., 1915; A.M., Columbia, 1917; m. Lillian Tuthill, Apr. 2, 1918; 1 dau., Elizabeth Kingsbury; m. 2d, Ruth A. Jeremiah Gottfried, 1934. Newspaper work, 1915-19; publicity dir. Cleveland Welfare Fedn. and Cleveland Foundation, 1919-20; publicity mgr. Cleveland Trust Co., 1920-21; adv. business, 1921-24; dir. Cleveland Foundation, 1924-28; chief editorial writer, Cleveland Press, 1928-30; editor Buffalo Times, 1930-32; editor Ohio state service of Scripps-Howard newspapers at Columbus, 1933-4; editor Toledo News-Bee, 1934-38; public relations dir. Libbey-Owens-Ford Glass Co., 1938-41; public relations counsel, New York City, 1941-44; editorial columnist, Cleveland Press, 1944-45; associate editor and chief editorial writer, Cleveland Press, since 1945. Address: Cleveland Press, Cleveland, Ohio. Died Dec. 13, 1948.

MATSON, Clarence Henry; b. Kirtland, O., Apr. 6, 1872; s. William Augustus and Mary Ann (Whelpley) M.; ed. Kan. Wesleyan U., Salina, 1888-91; hon. Master of Foreign Service, U. of Southern Calif., 1938; m. Loretta May Collins, June 29, 1898; children—William Archie, Marguerite Matson Walker, Elizabeth and Ted Collins. Newspaper work, Salina, 1891-97; political writer, Topeka State Journal, 1898-1907; spl. writer, Los Angeles Evening Express, 1908-12; sec. and traffic mgr. harbor dept., City of Los Angeles, 1912-20; in charge development of foreign trade and shipping, Los Angeles Chamber Commerce, since 1920 (trade increased until Port of Los Angeles first among Am. ports in export tonnage). Awarded medallion by citizens of Los Angeles in 1937 for most outstanding contribution to foreign trade. Made extensive trade survey of Japan, China, Manchoukuo and Chosen in 1936, and wrote "Trade Opportunities in the Orient." Mem. China Soc. of Southern California; v.p. Japan-Am. Soc.; mem. advisory bd. Foreign Trade Club of Southern Calif. Mem. Pacific Geog. Soc., Delta Phi Epsilon. Republican. Methodist. Mem. advisory com. Yenching U., China. Home: 1206 Chautauqua Blvd., Pacific Palisades, Calif. Office: 1151 S. Broadway, Los Angeles. Died Oct. 17, 1943; buried in Forest Lawn Memorial Park, Glendale, Calif.

MATSON, Ralph Charles, physician, surgeon; b. Brookville, Pa., Jan. 21, 1880; s. John and Minerva (Brady) M.; M.D., U. of Ore., 1902; grad. student, St. Mary's Hosp., London, Cambridge U., 1906, U. of Vienna, 1910, 23, 25, Acad. of Medicine, Dusseldorf, Germany, U. of Berlin, 1912, U. of Paris, 1924; m. Adeline Ferrari, Aug. 5, 1907 (divorced Oct. 1922); 1 adopted dau., Daphne; m. 2d, Chiara De Bona, Nov. 25, 1923. Physician and surgeon, Portland, Ore., since 1902; mem. firm Drs. Matson & Bisaillon; asso. clin., prof. of surgery and medicine, U of Ore. Med. Sch., since 1935, mem. exec. faculty since 1940, chief surgeon, Univ. State Tuberculosis Hosp., Portland, Ore.; dir. dept. of thoracic surgery, Portland Open Air Sanatorium, Milwaukie, Ore.; mem. visiting staff Good Samaritan Hosp.; chest consultant Multnomah County Hosp., and U.S. Pub. Health Service; attending specialist chest surg. center, Vets. Adminstrn. Hosp.; co-dir. tuberculosis clinic, med. dept., U. of Ore.; consulting thoracic surgeon Doernbecher Memorial Hosp. for Children; med. and surg. dir. Portland Open Air Sanatorium (all Portland); mem. med. advisory bd. Nat. Jewish Hosp., Denver, 1941; hon. 1st lt. Harvard U. Surg. Unit with B.E.F., 1916; served as capt. Royal Army Med. Corps, 1917; maj. Med. Corps, U.S. Army, chief med. examiner and tuberculosis specialist, Camp Lewis, 1917-19, chief of med. staff Gen. Hosp. No. 21, Denver, 1919-20; now lt. col. Med. Res. Corps. Del. to Internat. Union Against Tuberculosis, Washington, D.C., 1908, Rome, 1912, Lausanne, Switzerland, 1923; vice chmn. thoracic sect., 7th cruise congress, Pan-American Surg. Assn., 1938. Diplomate Am. Bd. Internal Medicine. Fellow Am. Coll. of Surgeons, Am. Coll. of Physicians, Le College International de Chirurgiens (Geneva), Am. Coll. Chest Physicians (pres. 1939); mem. Am. Assn. Thoracic Surgeons, Am. Med. Assn. of Vienna (life mem.) and Berlin, Am. Climatol. and Clin. Assn., Am. Trudeau Society, National Tuberculosis Association (former v.p.), Pan-Pacific Surg. Assn. (former v.p.), A.M.A., Portland City and County Med. Soc., Portland Acad. of Medicine, Ore. State Med. Soc., Pacific Interurban Clin. Club, Pacific Coast Surg. Soc., Internat. Artificial Pneumothorax Assn. (exec. com.), Ore. State Tuberculosis Assn., Alpha Kappa Kappa, Alpha Omega Alpha; hon. mem. Minneapolis Surg. Soc.; hon. mem. staff Lymanhurst Sch. for Tuberculosis Children, Minneapolis. Hollywood (Calif.) Academy Medicine, Sociedad Mexicano de Estudios Sobre Tuberculosis, Mex. Clubs: Arlington (Portland); Highlands Racquet (Oswego, Ore.). Contbr. of sects. or chapters to books: "Surgical Treatment of Pulmonary Tuberculosis" in Cyclopedia of Medicine, 1934; "Extrapleural Pneumolysis" in Surgical Diseases of the Chest by Graham, Ballon and Singer, 1935; "Artificial Pneumothorax" in Pulmonary Tuberculosis by Goldberg, 1935; "Operative Collapse Therapy in Treatment of Pulmonary Tuberculosis" in Internat. Clinics, Vol. II, 1934; etc. Contbr. of numerous articles on the med. and surg. aspects of tuberculosis, in English, French, Spanish and German. Editor in chief Diseases of the Chest; mem. editorial bd. Western Jour. Surgery, Obstetrics and Gynecology, Jour. Internat. Coll. Surgeons. Home: 2960 N.W. Cumberland Rd. Office: Stevens Bldg., Portland, Ore. Died Oct. 26, 1945.

MATSUDAIRA, Tsuneo, ambassador; b. Tokyo, Japan, Apr. 17, 1877; s. Katamori (Lord of Aizu); grad. Coll. of Law, Imperial U., Tokyo, 1902; LL.D., Lafayette Coll., and Rutgers Coll., 1925, U. of Mo., 1926; m. Nobu, d. Marquis Nabeshima, of Saga, 1906; children—Ichiro, Setsu, Masa, Jiro. Apptd. attaché Japanese Embassy, London, Eng., 1902, later 3d sec. and 2d sec.; on staff Treaty Revision, 1911; 2d sec. Legation, Peking, 1912-14; consul gen. at Tientsin, 1914; chief of diplomatic mission in Siberia, 1918; mem. Inter-Allied Ry. Com., Siberia, 1919; chief of European and Am. Dept. of Foreign Office, 1920; sec. gen. to Japanese Delegation to Disarmament Conf., Washington, 1921; vice minister for fgn. affairs, 1923; A.E. and P. to U.S. since Mar. 16, 1925. Decorated 2d Class Order of Rising Sun, 1920; 1st Class Order of Sacred Treasure, 1924. Address: Japanese Embassy, 1321 K St., Washington. Died Nov. 14, 1949.

MATTHES, François Emile (măth'ĕs), geologist; b. Amsterdam, Holland, Mar. 16, 1874; s. Willem Ernst and Johanna Suzanna (van der Does de Bije) M.; ed. in Holland, Switzerland and Germany; came to U.S., 1891; naturalized citizen U.S., 1896; B.S., Mass. Inst. Technology, 1895; LL.D., U. of Calif., 1947; m. Edith Lovell Coyle, June 7, 1911. With topographic branch of Geol. Survey, 1896-1914; with geologic branch, 1914-47. In charge of topographic surveys in Big Horn Mountains, Wyo., Glacier Nat. Park, Grand Canyon of Colo. River, Yosemite Valley, Mt. Rainier Nat. Park; geol. studies in Yosemite and Sequoia National Parks, Central Sierra, Nevada, California, central Mississippi Valley. Special studies: alpine glaciation; post-Pleistocene glaciation. Decorated Chevalier Order of Leopold II (Belgium), 1920; awarded silver beaver, Boy Scouts of Am., 1931; awarded Gold Medal of U.S. Dept. of Interior, Apr. 1948. Fellow Geol. Soc. Am., A.A.A.S.; mem. Assn. Am. Geographers (pres. 1933), Washington Acad. Sciences (vice-pres. 1933), Am. Geophys. Union (chmn. com. on glaciers), Internat. Commn. Snow and Glaciers (sec.), Internat. Assn. Sci. Hydrology (asst. sec.), Geol. Soc., Washington (pres. 1932), Am. Soc. Chemical Engineers (life), British Glaciological Society. Club Alpin Français (honorary); corr. mem. Appalacian Mountain Club; mem. Am. Alpine Club, Sierra Club (hon. v.p.); hon. mem. Mazamas. Wrote Glacial Sculpture of Bighorn Mountains, Wyo., 1900; Mt. Rainier and Its Glaciers, 1914; Geologic History of the Yosemite Valley, 1930; Geologic History of Mt. Whitney, 1937; various scientific reports and articles. Home: 858 Gelston Place, El Cerrito, Calif. Died June 21, 1948.

MATTHEWS, Albert (măth'ūz), writer; b. Boston, June 26, 1860; s. Nathan and Albertine (Bunker) M.; A.B., Harvard, 1882; unmarried. Engaged in etymol. and lexicog. studies. Has written various monographs in publs. Colonial Soc. of Mass., Am. Antiquarian Soc., Mass. Hist. Soc., etc.; contbr. to Dialect Notes, Dial. Nation, and other critical jours.; editor Colonial Soc. of Mass., 1905-24. Fellow Am. Acad. Arts and Sciences; mem. Am. Philos. Soc.; mem. Am. Antiquarian Soc., Am. Dialect Soc., Am. Hist. Assn., Am. Folk-Lore Soc., Am. Anthrop. Soc., Mass., Me., Va., and Wis. hist. socs., Colonial Soc. of Mass., A.A.A.S., Am. Bibliog. Soc., Am. Geog. Society. Clubs: Union (Boston); Harvard (New York and Boston). Address: 19 St. Botolph St., Boston, Mass. Died Apr. 13, 1946.

MATTHEWS, Albert, former lieut. gov., Ont.; b. Lindsay, Ont., 1873; s. George and Ann Matthews; hon. LL.D., McMaster U., 1928, U. of Western Ont., 1938, Queen's U., 1940, Univ. of Toronto, 1941; D.C.L., Acadia U., 1941; m. Margaret Maud Whiteside, Sept. 14, 1897; children—Paul W. (Wing Commander R.C.A.F.; overseas) Major-General A. Bruce, C.B.E., D.S.O., (2d Can. Div. overseas), Mrs. Charles P. Fell. Senior partner, Matthews & Co. (est. 1909), members of Toronto Stock Exchange; lt. governor, Province of Ont., Dec. 1, 1937-46; pres., Excelsior Life Ins. Co.; dir. Toronto Gen. Trusts Corp.; chmn. bd. govs., McMaster Univ.; chmn. Can. Del. 1st World Economic Conf., Geneva, 1927; nat. treas., Baptist World Alliance since 1928; Clubs: York, Arts and Letters, National, Lambton Golf. Baptist. Address: 220 Bay St., Toronto, Ont., Can. Died Aug. 13, 1949.

MATTHEWS, Arthur John, coll. pres.; b. Cazenovia, N.Y., Sept. 3, 1859; s. Patrick and Ann (King) M.; student Cazenovia Sem. and Syracuse U.; LL.D., Syracuse U., 1916; M.Pd., U. of Ariz., 1926; m. Carrie Louise Walden, 1885; children—Anna Frances (Mrs. Edgar L. Hendrix), Arthur John (dec.). Teacher country sch., N.Y., later prin. schs., West Eaton; supt. schs., Adams, N.Y., Rock Springs, Wyo., Prescott, Ariz., until 1899; pres. Territorial Normal Sch., Tempe, Ariz. (now Ariz. State Teachers Coll.), 1900-30; pres. emeritus since 1930. Mem. Ariz. State Board of Edn., 1902-30; del. to World Fedn. Edn. Assns., Edinburg, Scotland, 1925, Toronto, Can., 1927, Geneva, Switzerland, 1929. Mem. N.E.A. (state dir. 3 terms; treas. and mem. exec. com. 1918-23; ex-v.p.; mem. exec. com.), Nat. Edni. Council (exec. com.), Ariz. State Teachers Assn. (ex-pres.). Democrat. Episcopalian. Mason (32°, K.T., Shriner), K.P. (grand trustee); Grand Patron O.E.S. Clubs: Rotary, Hiram. Home: 820 College Av., Tempe, Ariz. Died July 20, 1942.

MATTHEWS, Harlan Julius, clergyman; b. Melrose, Tex., Oct. 12, 1877; s. Harlan Jackson and Arabella (Hamil) M.; B.Th., Baylor U., Waco, Tex., 1905, Southwestern Sem., Waco, 1905; m. Minnie Lee Overstreet, July 26, 1900; children—William Erwart, Mary Ruth (Mrs. Ronald G. Van Tine), Elizabeth Gertrude (Mrs. Allan Burbage, Jr.). Ordained to ministry Bapt. Ch., 1900; pastor Decatur, Tex., 1914-20, Plainview, 1920-25, Mineral Wells, 1925-30, Marshall, Tex., since 1930; v.p. Tex. Bapt. Conv., 1930-31, mem. exec. bd. since 1916, now pres.; pres. East Tex. Bapt. Encampment; chmn. Bapt. History Commn. since 1933. Sec. bd. trustees Coll. of Marshall, Marshall, Tex. Compiler: Centennial Story of Texas, 1936. Contbr. articles to religious jours. Home: 213 N. Fulton St., Marshall, Tex.
Died May 20, 1942.

MATTHEWS, Hugh, officer U.S. Marine Corps; b. Loudon County, Tenn., June 18, 1876; s. Madison Lafayette and Mary (McConnell) M.; ed. Maryville (Tenn.) Coll.; m. Mary O'Conor Higgins, Sept. 10, 1919. Commd. 2d lt. U.S. Marine Corps, Mar. 3, 1900; promoted through grades to brig. gen., Dec 26, 1929; major general April 1942, by Congressional enactment. Served in China, Philippine Isl-

Panama, Cuba, Santo Domingo; overseas with 2d Div., World War. Head of quartermaster's dept., U.S. Marine Corps, 1929-37; retired. Awarded D.S.M., Army; Navy Cross; Chevalier Legion of Honor; Croix de Guerre. Mem. Mil. Order Carabao, Mil. Order World War, Am. Legion, Nat. Sojourners. Mason. Club: Army and Navy. Home: Loudon, Tenn Died Apr. 9, 1943.

MATTHEWS, Robert David; b. Bridgend, Wales, Sept. 12, 1886; s. Richard and Catharine (David) M.; ed. British pub. schs.; m. Ethel Burge Walker, Sept. 12, 1913 (dec.); m. 2d, Gertrude Frances Black, Aug. 10, 1921; children—Richard David (dec.), Mary Constance, Natalie. Came to U.S., 1911, naturalized, 1932. With chartered accountants, Cardiff, Wales, 1902-11; with Price, Waterhouse & Co., San Francisco and Los Angeles, 1911-14; comptroller Union Oil Co. of Calif., 1914-28, v.p. of mfg., later v.p. of sales, 1928-31, exec. v.p., 1931-39; pres. Pacific States Oil Co., Los Angeles, since 1939; officer or director many companies. Fellow Soc. of Incorporated Accountants and Auditors of Great Britain; Fellow Royal Soc. of Art, Great Britain; mem. American Petroleum Inst. Episcopalian. Clubs: California, Pacific-Union (San Francisco); Midwick Country. Home: 1345 Wentworth Av., Pasadena, Calif. Office: 530 W. 6th St., Los Angeles, Calif.* Died Nov. 19, 1943.

MATTHEWS, Robert Orville, clergyman, educator; b. Sterling, N.Y., May 27, 1878; s. Andrew and Sarah M.; grad. Syracuse U., 1905; D.D., Ohio Northern U.; LL.D., Lincoln Memorial U., 1923; m. Isabelle McCutcheon, Aug. 1909; 1 son, Dudley McCutcheon. Ordained M.E. ministry, 1909; pastor St. Paul's Ch., Cincinnati, 1909-13, St. Paul's Ch., Toledo, O., 1913-17, 1st Ch., Des Moines, Ia., 1917-21; went to Europe at beginning of World War as mem. Sepakers' Commn. Am. Red Cross; spl. asst. to fed. prohibition commn. of U.S., 1921-23; pres. Lincoln Memorial U., 1923-26; now v.p. Air-Way Elec. Appliance Corp., Toledo. Republican. Mason. Mem. Phi Rho. Clubs: Kiwanis, Toledo. Home: Hotel Lorraine, 1117 Jefferson Av. Address: Air-Way Electric Appliance Corp., Toledo, O. Died Toledo, O., May 17, 1934.

MATTHEWS, William Henry, clergyman; b. McHenry, Ill., July 23, 1868; s. Joseph Jay and Cornelia Maria (Talbot) M.; B.A., Lake Forest (Ill.) Coll., 1892, M.A., 1894, LL.B., Lake Forest U., 1894; student Columbia U. Law Sch.; grad. McCormick Theol. Sem., 1898; grad. work, U. of Chicago and Chicago Theol. Sem.; D.D., Jamestown (N.D.) Coll., 1912, Fargo Coll., 1912; m. Eva Chandler, July 9, 1895; children—Paul Chandler, Ruth Elizabeth (Mrs. Carl J. A. Olsen), William Henry, Edward Talbot, Eva Standish (Mrs. Allen H. Seed, Jr.), Mark Stanley. Ordained Presbyn. ministry, 1898; pastor Marengo, Ill., 1898-1901, Central Ch., Chicago, 1901-06, First Ch., Grand Forks, N.D., 1907-17, Greenwich Ch., N.Y. City, 1918-22; gen. sec. Am. Tract Soc. since 1922-44. Now General Secretary Emeritus. Admitted to Ill. bar, 1894. Built churches at Marengo, Chicago and Grand Forks. Exchange preacher, London, England, three summers, on Carnegie Church Peace Union Foundation. Chmn. Com. on Publication and Sabbath Sch. Work, Gen. Assembly, 1912; apptd. by Gen. Assembly to attend Pan-Presbyn. Council, Aberdeen, Scotland, 1913. Made spl. visit to Bedford and Elstow, Eng., summer, 1927, to secure material for celebration of John Bunyan Tercentenary by Evang. chs. in U.S. in 1928. Contbr. to many ch. periodicals on life and works of John Bunyan, the place of Christian literature in modern life, and home mission work in the northwest. Recorded Pilgrims' Progress as a talking book for the blind, 1935. Republican. Home: Hotel Sheraton, 303 Lexington Av., New York, N.Y. Died June 18, 1946.

MATTIELLO, Joseph J. (măt′ē-ĕl-lo), chemist; b. New York, N.Y., Feb. 28, 1900; s. Celestino and Elizabeth (Bottigliere) M.; B.S., Polytech. Inst. of Brooklyn, 1925, M.S., 1931; Ph.D., Columbia U., 1936; m. Josephine Critelli, Sept. 18, 1922; children—Margaret Anne (Mrs. Harry Kimm, Jr.), Elizabeth (Mrs. Joseph Yozzo), Rosamond, Barbara. Dir., v.p., tech. dir., mem. exec. com., Hilo Varnish Corp. Consultant on protective coatings, Q.M. gen. plastics sect., research and development br., Mil. Planning Div. Received Regimental Citation and Purple Heart, World War I, Meritorious Civilian Service award, World War II. Mem. Am. Soc. Testing Materials (Marburg lecturer 1946), Nat. Paint, Varnish and Lacquer Assn. (sci. sect.), Am. Oil Chemists, Am. Chem. Soc., Am. Inst. Chem. Engrs., Am. Inst. Chemists (v.p.), Oil and Color Chemists Assn., Soc. of Chem. Industries, Assn. Research Dirs., Oil and Color Chemists Assn. of Great Britain (hon. mem.), Fedn. of Paint and Varnish Prodn., N.Y. Printing Ink Prodn., N.Y. Paint and Varnish Prodn. (past pres.), Gallows Birds Soc., Delta Kappa Pi, Phi Lambda Upsilon, Sigma Xi. Republican. Roman Catholic. Club: Sales Execs. Editor: Protective and Decorative Coatings (5 vols.); author, pubs. dealing with paints, varnish and lacquers. Home: 536A 5th St., Brooklyn, N.Y. Office: 42 Stewart Av., Brooklyn 6, N.Y. Died May 16, 1948.

MATTSON, Peter August, clergyman; b. Hvitsand, Sweden, Sept. 29, 1865; s. Mattos Johanson and Anna (Stephenson) M.; A.B., Gustavus Adolphus Coll., Minn., 1892; B.D., Augustana Theol. Sem., Ill., 1894; Ph.D., U. of Minn., 1906; D.D., Muhlenberg Theol. Sem., Pa., 1906; m. Emma Anna Olson, June 18, 1895; children—Myrtle Annette (Mrs. J. P. Kinney), Hamlin August, Violet Emma (Mrs. Carl K. Towley). Ordained to Lutheran ministry, 1894; pastor Tacoma, Wash., 1894-99, Minneapolis, 1899-1904; pres. Gustavus Adolphus Coll., 1904-11, also prof. Christianity; became pres. Lutheran Minnesota Conference, Mar. 3, 1913, now pres. emeritus. Dir. Augustana Book Concern, Bethesda Hosp., St. Paul, 6 yrs.; v.p. Lutheran Augustana Synod of N.A.; dir. Bd. of Foreign Missions and Bd. of Home Missions, Augustana Synod. Decorated by King of Sweden Knight Order of North Star, 1925, Comdr., 1929. Author: Minnen och Bilder från Bibelens Lander, 1911; Through the Land of Promise, 1919. Editor Minnesota Stats Tidning. Contbr. to newspapers and periodicals. Home: 51 9th Av. S., Hopkins, Minn. Died Apr. 4, 1944.

MAURER, Edward Rose, engineer; b. Fountain City, Wis., Feb. 18, 1869; s. John and Katherine (Moss) M.; B.C.E., University of Wisconsin, 1890; married May R. Dickens, September 1, 1892 (died, 1932); children—R. Edward, Mrs. Catherine Witter, Eugene D. Assistant engineer, C.&W. Railway, 1890; on U.S. Geol. Survey, 1891-92; asst. prof. and prof. mechanics in Engring. Coll. of U. of Wis., 1893-1935, prof. emeritus since 1935; dir. Soc. Promotion of Engring. Edn. Summer Sch. for Teachers of Mechanics, Madison session, 1927. Mem. Soc. Promotion Engring. Edn., A.A.A.S., Wis. Acad. Sciences, Arts and Letters, Am. Soc. Mech. Engrs., Wis. Engring. Soc., Sigma Xi, Tau Beta Pi, Chi Epsilon, Phi Kappa Phi, Phi Delta Theta. Club: University. Awarded Lamme medal by Society Promotion Engring. Edn., 1934. Author: Technical Mechanics, 1903 (rewritten as Mechanics for Engineers with R. J. Roark and G. W. Washa, 1945); Statics, 1904; Strength of Materials, 1904; Principles of Reinforced Concrete Construction (with F. E. Turneaure), 1907; Strength of Materials (with M. O. Withey), 1925. Asso. editor American Civil Engineers' Pocket Book, 1911. Home: 167 N. Prospect Av., Madison, Wis. Died May 1, 1948.

MAURER, Irving, educator, clergyman; b. Garnavillo, Ia., Sept. 2, 1879; s. Jacob D. and Loretta Ernstina (Wirkler) M.; B.A., Beloit Coll., 1904, B.D., M.A., Yale Div. Sch., 1909; D.D., Carleton Coll., 1924; LL.D., Coll. of Wooster, 1924; D.D., Oberlin Coll., 1925; LL.D., Colorado College, 1933; L.H.D., Yankton Coll., 1941; m. Minnie Leona Vogt, June 17, 1908; children—Irving Vogt, Mary Elizabeth (Mrs. E. Sterling Skinner), Lloyd Luther, Margaret Leona (Mrs. R. N. Gibson). Ordained to the ministry of Congl. Church, 1908; pastor West End Ch., Bridgeport, Conn., 1907-10, Plymouth Ch., Utica, N.Y., 1910-13, Edwards Ch., Northampton, Mass., 1913-18, First Ch., Columbus, O., 1918-24; pres. Beloit Coll. since Jan. 1924. Served as 2d lt. Co. L, 1st Regt., Wis. N.G., 1905, 06. Mem. bd. dirs. Chicago Theol. Sem.; ex-pres. Urban League of Columbus (coöperation between negroes and whites); mem. bd. dirs. Internat. Soc. for Crippled Children; ex-pres. Wis. Assn. for Disabled, Assn. of Am. Colls.; former pres. North Central Assn. Colls. and Secondary Schs.; mem. exec. com. Gen. Council Congl. and Christian Churches. Mem. Phi Beta Kappa, Delta Sigma Rho (Beloit), Phi Kappa Epsilon (Yale). Clubs: Faculty and Alumni Club, Kiwanis (Beloit); Apollos, University (Chicago); University (New York). Author: Prayers of College Life, 1912; My Christian Faith, 1923. Contbr. ednl. and religious articles. Home: Beloit, Wis. Died Feb. 28, 1942.

MAURER, James Hudson, labor official; b. Reading, Pa., Apr. 15, 1864; s. James D. and Sarah (Lorah) M.; ed. pub. schs., 14 mos.; m. Mary J. Missmer, Apr. 15, 1886; children—Charles H., Martha M. (Mrs. Ralph Dundore). Newsboy, farm hand, factory worker, and at 15 machinist's apprentice; joined Knights of Labor, 1880, Socialist Labor party, 1898, Socialist party, 1902; candidate of Socialist party for gov. of Pa., 1906; mem. Nat. Exec. Com., same party, 10 yrs.; mem. Pa. Ho. of Rep., 3 terms, 1910, 14, 16, introducing Workmen's Compensation Act, and other labor measures; pres. Pa. Fedn. of Labor, 1912-28; pres. Labor Age Monthly, Workers Ednl. Bur. of America; dir. Brookwood Coll., Katonah, N.Y. Became chmn. Old Age Assistance Commn. of Pa., 1917. Mem. Am. Commn. on Conditions in Ireland, 1920; made tour of Europe with Am. Seminar, 1923; mem. of Am. Fact-finding Commn. to Russia, 1927; mem. City Council, Reading, 1928-32. Socialist candidate for v.p. of U.S., 1928 and 1932, also for U.S. Senate, 1934; now retired. Author: The Far East, 1910; It Can Be Done, 1938. Home: 1355 N. 11th St., Reading, Pa. Died Mar. 16, 1944.

MAURICE, Arthur Bartlett (môr-ēs′), author; b. Rahway, N.J., Apr. 10, 1873; student Princeton. Asso. editor The Bookman, 1899-1907, editor, 1907-16; with Am. Relief for Belgium and North of France, behind German lines, 1916 to withdrawal. Author: New York in Fiction, 1901; History of the 19th Century in Caricature (with F. T. Cooper), 1904; The New York of the Novelists, 1916; Bottled Up in Belgium, 1917; Fifth Avenue, 1918; The Paris of the Novelists, 1919; A Child's Story of American Literature (with Algernon Tassin), 1923; O. Henry (for O. Henry Memorial, Asheville, N.C.); The Caliph of Bagdad (with Robert H. Davis), 1931; Magical City (text for drawings of Vernon Howe Bailey), 1935; The Riddle of the Rovers, 1942, Translator of The Flaming Crucible, and America and the Race for World Dominion. Literary editor of the New York Herald, 1922-24, New York Sun, 1924. Clubs: Players, Princeton (New York); Nassau (Princeton, N.J.); Savage (London). Home: Stamford, Conn. Died May 31, 1946.

MAURY, Magruder Gordon, newspaper man and fiction writer; b. Philadelphia, Pa., 1878; s. Thompson Brooke and Sally Taylor (Gordon) Maury; m. Jean West; 1 son—Thompson Brooke III (United States Army officer, West Point, 1934; (killed in action, 1944). Began newspaper work 1905 as reporter New Orleans Times-Democrat, later Times-Picayune; telegraph ed., Los Angeles Times, Memphis News Scimitar; city ed., Honolulu Advertiser, Star Bulletin, San Diego Union; editorial staff N.Y. Evening Sun, Herald, World, Boston American, Baltimore News; asst. mng. ed., Boston Sunday Advertiser 1924-31; prof. journalism Boston College, 1927-35; Washington corr. McGraw-Hill publications 1936-46. Served in Spanish-American War and Philippine Insurrection. Author: Seven Pearls of Shandi; also numerous sea and adventure stories. Episcopalian. Club: National Press. Home: 5031 V St. N.W., Washington. Died Nov. 22, 1948; buried with mil. honors National Cemetery, Arlington, Vr.

MAVEETY, Patrick John (mȧ-vē′tĭ), clergyman; b. Longford County, Ireland, Feb. 8, 1855; s. Thomas and Mary (Russell) M.; came to America in 1870; educated at Garrett Biblical Inst., Evanston, Ill., 1876-78; D.D. Albion (Mich.) Coll., 1907; m. Susan E. Hare, Nov. 6, 1876; children—Mrs. E. Olive Brown, Mrs. F. Blanche Brown, Mrs. Laura E. Anthony, Helen I., Mrs. P. Josephine Carpenter, Roswell H., Russell P., Donald J., Herman M. Ordained M.E. ministry, 1878; pastor Olivet, Mich., 1878-80, Bellevue, 1880-83, Cassopolis, 1883-84, Homer, 1884-87, Ovid, 1887-92, Benton Harbor, 1892-93, Hillsdale, 1893-95, Jackson, 1895-97; presiding elder Albion Dist. 1897-1903, pastor Battle Creek, 1903-07; elected corr. sec. Freedmen's Aid Soc. M.E. Ch., 1908; was sec. Dept. of Ednl. Instns., for Negroes, of the Bd. of Edn. of the M.E. Ch.; now retired after 50 years active service in ministry. Mem. Gen. Conf. M.E. Ch. 7 times. Home: 398 Main St., Battle Creek, Mich. Died Nov. 23, 1946.

MAXFIELD, Francis N(orton), clinical psychologist; b. Sandwich, Mass., Aug. 29, 1877; s. Daniel C. and Alice Rogers (Wing) M.; A.B., Haverford Coll., 1897; Ph.D., U. of Pa., 1912; m. Alice Jenkins, Aug. 3, 1904 (died Feb. 5, 1931); children—Mildred Elizabeth (Mrs. John A. Miller), William Francis; m. 2d, Rose Henline Goodman, June 1, 1932; step-dau., Dorothy Maxfield (Mrs. John R. Ervin). Teacher of mathematics and science, Oak Grove Seminary, Vassalboro, Maine, 1898-1900, Oakwood Seminary, Union Springs, New York, 1900-03, Germantown (Phila.) Friends' Sch., 1903-12, also vice prin., 1907-12; instr. in psychology, University of Pa., 1912-13, asst. prof. psychology and asst. dir. psychol. clinic, 1913-18; psychologist, Public School Clinic, Newark, N.J., 1918-20; dir. special edn., Pa. State Dept. Pub. Instrn., 1920-25; prof. clin. psychology, Ohio State U., since 1925. Fellow Am. Assn. for Advancement of Science, Ohio Acad. of Science, Am. Assn. on Mental Deficiency; mem. Am. Psychol. Assn., Nat. Com. Mental Hygiene, Progressive Edn. Association, National Society Study Education, American Genetics Assn., Am. Probation Assn., Nat. Conf. Social Work, Am. Assn. Univ. Profs., Am. Fedn. Teachers, Sigma Xi, Phi Delta Kappa. Mem. Soc. of Friends. Home: 217 S. Cassingham Rd., Bexley, Columbus 9. Address: Ohio State Univ., Columbus 10, Ohio. Died Nov. 10, 1945.

MAXON, James Matthew, bishop; b. Bay City, Mich., Jan. 1, 1875; s. Daniel and Anna (MacKenney) M.; student Gen. Theol. Sem., 1906; hon. M.A., Knox Coll., 1910; D.D., U. of South, Sewanee, Tenn., 1921; LL.D., Southwestern University, 1941; married Blanche Morris, September 10, 1903; children—James Matthew, John Burton. Deacon and priest, P.E. Ch., 1907; rector Grace Ch., Galesburg, Ill., 1907-10; pres. Margaret Coll., Versailles, Ky., 1910-17; also rector St. John's Ch., Versailles, 1912-17; rector St. Mark's, Louisville, Ky., 1917-20; rector Christ Ch., Nashville, Tenn., 1920-22. Consecrated bishop coadjutor of diocese of Tenn., Oct. 18, 1922; bishop of Tenn. since Oct. 1935; elected Chancellor of U. of the South, Sewanee, Tenn., June, 1942. Dep. Gen. Conv., 1913, 16, 19. Retired Jan. 1, 1947. Mason. Home: 2791 Central Av. Office: Diocesan House, 692 Popular Av., Memphis 7, Tenn. Died Nov. 8, 1948.

MAXSON, Ralph Nelson, prof. chemistry; b. Westerly, R.I., Dec. 2, 1879; s. Charles Albertus and Maria Margaret (Reynolds) M.; B.S., R.I. State Coll., 1902; Ph.D., Yale, 1905; m. Jessie Olivia Taylor, Dec. 27, 1905; children—William Taylor, Charles Reynolds. Asst. in instrn., Yale, 1903-05; instr. inorganic chemistry, Pa. State Coll., 1905-06, asst. prof. chemistry, 1906-09, prof. inorganic chemistry since 1909, University of Kentucky, head of chemistry dept., 1934-42. Fellow Am. Inst. of Chemists; mem. Am. Chem. Soc., Am. Assn. Univ. Profs., Ky. Acad. of Science, Photographic Soc. of America. Sigma Xi, Pi Gamma Mu. Club: Country (Petoskey, Mich.) Contbr. on inorganic and analytical chemistry to Am. Jour. Science, Jour. of Chem. Edn., Zeitschrift für Anorganische Chemie, Colloid Symposium monographs and Inorganic Syntheses. Collaborator "Modern Scientific Knowledge of Nature, Man and Society." Home: 366 Transylvania Park, Lexington, Ky. Died Nov. 18, 1943.

MAXON, William Ralph, botanist; b. Oneida, N.Y., Feb. 27, 1877; s. Samuel Albert and Sylvia Louisa (Stringer) M.; Ph.B., Syracuse Univ., 1898, Sc.D., 1922; m. Edith Hinckley Merrill, Dorchester,

Mass., June 2, 1908; 1 dau., Mary. Aid, U.S. Nat. Museum, Washington, 1899; later asst. curator, asso. curator and curator, U.S. Nat. Herbarium, 1937-46; now asso. in Botany, U.S. Nat. Museum. Has specialized in study of the Pteridophyta, mainly of tropical America. Fellow Am. Assn. for the Advancement of Science, American Acad. Arts and Sciences; member Bot. Soc. of Washington, Biol. Soc. of Washington, Washington Academy of Sciences, D.K.E., Sigma Xi. Unitarian. Club: Cosmos. Author series of papers entitled "Studies of Tropical American Ferns" in Contbns. U.S. National Herbarium; also "Ferns as a Hobby," "Pteridophyta of Porto Rico," and numerous other articles and repts. upon ferns. Home: 2333 20th St. Address: Smithsonian Institution, Washington, D.C. Died Feb. 25, 1948.

MAXWELL, Archibald McIntyre, oil exec.; b. Knoxville, Tenn., Apr. 22, 1895; s. James Lee and Susan (Weir) M.; A.B., Cornell Univ., 1918. Enlisted in U.S. Navy, 1918, and served for 23 months; then entered employ of Standard Oil Co. of N.J., serving an apprenticeship in the refinery forces at Eagle Works for 6 months; transferred to Fuel Oil and Asphalt Div. of the Jersey Co., holding the position of asst. mgr. until July, 1924, at which time he was made vice-pres. in charge of sales of the Ethyl Gasoline Corp. at the time of its formation, representing the Jersey Co. as dir. on the Ethyl Gasoline Corp.'s bd.; vice-pres. and dir. of the Standard Oil Co. of Ohio since Mar. 1929; Sohio Petroleum Company, Solio Pipe Line Company; dir. Fleet-Wing Oil Corp., Atlas Supply Co. Mem. Asphalt Institute (dir.), Phi Delta Theta. Clubs: Whitehall, Cloud (New York City); Racquet (Washington, D.C.); Tavern, Union, Kirtland Country (Cleveland). Home: 2466 Coventry Rd., Cleveland Heights. Office: Midland Bldg., Cleveland, O. Died April 18, 1949; buried Owensburo, Ky.

MAXWELL, Francis Taylor, mfr.; born Rockville, Conn., Jan. 4, 1861; s. George and Harriet (Kellogg) M.; desc. Col. Hugh Maxwell, from Scotland to Mass., 1733; high sch. edn.; m. Florence Russell Parsons, Nov. 18, 1896; children—Helen, Priscilla, Harriett Kellogg. Began at 17 with Hockanum Co., Rockville; then pres. Hockanum Mills Co. until retirement, 1934; mem. bd. dirs. Mechanics & Traders Ins. Co., Charter Oak Fire Ins. Co., N.Y., N.H.&H. R.R., N.E. Steamship Co., Hartford & New York Transportation Co., Travelers Ins. Co., Travelers Indemnity Co., Travelers Fire Ins. Co., Nat. Fire Ins. Co., Colonial Securities Co. (Hartford), Rockville Mut. Fire Ins. Co., Rockville Water & Aqueduct Co.; also trustee Savings Bank of Rockville; Conn. Pres. Rockville Public Library, City Hosp. Col. on staff of Gov. Bulkeley, 1892; mem. Rockville council, 1896; chmn. ins. com. Conn. Ho. of Rep., 1899; chmn. edn. com. Conn. Senate, 1901; del. Rep. Nat. convs., 1900, 04, 16; a presidential elector 5 times, 1900, 04, 16, 20, 28; district mem. U.S. Labor Bd., World War. Conglist. Mem. Met. Mus. of Art, Royal Soc. Arts (London), S.A.R., Conn. Soc. Colonial Wars. Clubs: Union League, Metropolitan (New York). Home: Rockville, Conn. Died March 23, 1943.

MAXWELL, George Hebard, lawyer, author, irrigationist; b. Sonoma, Calif., June 3, 1860; s. John Morgan and Clara Love (Hebard) M.; ed. pub. schs. Sonoma and San Francisco, and St. Mathew's Hall, San Mateo, Calif.; m. Katharine Vaughan Lanpher, Oct. 28, 1880; children—Ruth, Donald H.; m. 2d, Lilly Belle Richardson, June 3, 1935. Official stenographer, U.S. Circuit Court, and Superior Courts of Calif., 1879-82; admitted to bar, Aug. 3, 1882; mem. firm Mesick & Maxwell; practiced law until 1899. Organized Nat. Reclamation Assn., 1899, became exec. chmn. campaign for inauguration of a nat. irrigation policy, accomplished by passage of Nat. Reclamation Act, approved June 17, 1902; the following year organized 1st Water Users Assn. under that act, in Salt River Valley, Ariz., thereby securing constrn. of the Roosevelt Dam by U.S. Reclamation Service; inaugurated, 1903, and for 14 yrs. thereafter conducted campaign for adoption of nat. policy for river regulation and flood control embodied in the Newlands river regulation amendment to the River and Harbor Bill passed Aug. 3, 1917. Exec. dir. Pittsburgh Flood Commn., 1908-11, La. Reclamation Assn., 1912-13. Organized Am. Homecroft Soc., Mar. 1907; now exec. dir. Nat. Reclamation Assn., Nat. Flood Prevention and River Regulation Commn., Am. Homecroft Soc., Am. Soc. for Nat. Service, Ohio Water and Soil Resources Commn.; mem. Ohio State Water Conservation Bd. and conservation com. of The Ohio Mfrs.' Assn. Clubs: Pacific Union (San Francisco); Cosmos (Washington, D.C.); Scribes (Los Angeles). Life mem. Mass. Hort. Soc. Editor Maxwell's Talisman. Author: The First Book of the Homecrofters; Our National Defense—the Patriotism of Peace; Golden Rivers and Treasure Valleys; The Nation's Greatest Asset—A Balance Wheel for Industry; The End of Unemployment. Residence: Phoenix, Ariz. Family Home: Sonoma, Calif. Address: Maryland Bldg., Washington. Died Dec. 1, 1946.

MAXWELL, George Lawrence, educator; b. Woodland, Calif., July 11, 1896; s. George Lawrence and Katherine Elizabeth (Mock) M.; A.B., U. of Calif., 1917, A.M., 1925; B.D., Pacific Sch. of Religion, Berkeley, Calif., 1925; student Columbia Univ. and Union Theol. Sem., New York, N.Y., 1925-27; m. Eva E. Banton, July 10, 1917; 1 son, Robert. Sec. Young Men's Christian Assn., U. of Calif., 1919-23; field dir., survey of Brooklyn and Queens Y.M.C.A., New York, N.Y., 1927-28; field sec., Nat. Council on Religion in Higher Education, New York, N.Y., 1928-29; asso. prof. edn. and religion, dir. religious activities, U. of Denver, 1929-34; state dir. edn., Colo. Work Projects Adminstrn., 1934-36; asst. dir. edn. div., W.P.A., Washington, D.C., 1936-39; asst. sec., Educational Policies Commn. Nat. Edn. Assn., Washington, D.C., 1939-44; dean of adminstrn. and prof. edn., U. of Denver, Denver, Colo., since 1944; staff mem. Laymen's Foreign Missions Inquiry in Japan. Inst. of Social and Religious Research, 1931; staff mem. summer workshop of Commn. on Teacher Edn. U. of Chicago, 1940, summer workshops Phila. pub. schs., 1941 and 1942. Served as 2d lt., advancing to capt., U.S. Marine Corps, 1917-19; with A.E.F., France. Fellow Nat. Council on Religion in Higher Edn. Am. Assn. for Adult Edn. (exec. council): mem. Phi Beta Kappa, Phi Delta Kappa, Kappa Delta Pi, Alpha Kappa Lambda. Author (with others): Japan—Fact Finders' Report of Laymen's Foreign Missions Inquiry, 1933; Learning the Ways of Democracy, 1940; Education for All American Youth, 1944. Associate editor Adult Education Bulletin. Mem. bd. advisory editors National Parent-Teacher. Home: 2255 S. Columbine St., Denver 10, Colo. Died Jan. 3, 1947.

MAXWELL, Lee Wilder, publisher; b. Hicksville, O., July 24, 1881; s. Isaac Miller and Celestia (Crary) M.; prep. edn., high sch., Clyde, Ill.; Ph.B., U. of Chicago, 1905; m. Anne Payne Wells, 1907; children—Anne, Lee Wilder. With Chicago office Frank A. Munsey Co., 1907-10; western mgr. The Outlook, 1910; gen. mgr. Associated Sunday Mags., New York, 1910-13; with Crowell Pub. Co. since 1913, v.p. and gen. mgr., 1920-23, president 1923-34, chairman of board, 1934-37; Liberty Loan and American Red Cross organizer, World War I. Mem. Chi Psi. Republican. Episcopalian. Club: Ekwanok. Home: 300 Park Av., N.Y., City. Office: Chrysler Bldg., New York, N.Y. Died Oct. 4, 1948.

MAXWELL, William Allison, Jr., corp. official; b. Ardmore, Pa., Jan. 25, 1879; s. William Allison and Kate (Hicks) M.; student Haverford Coll. Grammar Sch., 1895-97, Pa. State Coll., 1897-99; m. Jane Weaver, Apr. 19, 1906 (dec.); m. 2d, Cecelie Hazel Grant, Apr. 28, 1941. With Homestead Steel Works, Carnegie Steel Co., 1902-05, supt. open hearth, North Sharon Works, 1905-09, asst. supt. open hearth, Ohio Works, 1909, Homestead Steel Works, 1909-14, supt. open hearth, 1914-19; asst. gen. supt., Johnstown Works, Midvale Steel & Ordnance Co., 1919-20; gen. supt. Inland Steel Co., Indiana Harbor, Ind., 1920-27; v.p. Colo. Fuel & Iron Corp., Denver, 1927-38, pres. since 1938; pres. Colo.&Wyo. Ry. Co., Calif. Wire Cloth Corp. Served as corp., Co. I, 9d Pa. Vol. Inf., 1898. Mem. Am. Iron and Steel Inst., Am. Inst. Mining and Metall. Engrs., Sigma Chi. Republican. Mason (Shriner). Clubs: Denver, Denver Country, Mile High (Denver); Cherry Hills (Englewood, Colo.). Home: 225 Vine St. Office: Continental Oil Bldg., Denver, Colo. Died Oct. 30, 1946.

MAY, Charles Henry, ophthalmologist; b. Baltimore, Aug. 7, 1861; s. Henry and Henrietta M.; student Coll. City of New York, 1875-77; spl. studies chemistry, 1877-79; M.D., Coll. Phys. and Surg. (Columbia), 1883; took both 1st Harsen prizes ($500 and $150 with medal), 1883; study in eye abroad, 1887; m. Rosalie Allen, Nov. 7, 1893. Lecturer diseases of eye, New York Polyclinic, 1887-90; instr. ophthalmology and chief of clinic, Columbia, 1890-1903; dir. and visiting surgeon, eye dept. Bellevue Hosp., 1915-25; ophthalmic surgeon, Mt. Sinai Hosp.; cons. ophthalmic surgeon to Bellevue, French and Monmouth hosps. Mem. Am. Acad. Ophthalmology, Am. Ophthalmol. Soc., N.Y. Acad. Medicine, A.M.A., N.Y. State and County med. socs.; fellow Am. Coll. Surgeons. Author: Manual of Diseases of the Eye, 1900, 17th edit., 1941; also 10 translations into foreign langs. Contbr. to New Internat. Ency., and Reference Handbook of Med. Sciences. Introduced improved system of illumination in electric ophthalmoscopes in 1914, now universally adopted. Address: 70 E. 66th St., New York, N.Y. Died Dec. 7, 1943.

MAY, James Vance, physician; b. Lawrence, Kan., July 6, 1873; s. Vance W. (M.D.) and Eleanor (Shearer) M.; A.B., U. of Kan., 1894; M.D., U. of Pa., 1897; m. Ada L. Arms, 1905; children—Dorothy Louise, James V. Resident phys., Phila. Hosp., 1897-98; asst. physician Brigham Hall Hosp., Canandaigua, N.Y., 1899-1900; acting asst. surgeon U.S. Army, 1900-02 (1½ yr. in P.I.); asst. physician, Central Islip (N.Y.) State Hosp., 1902, asst. physician and 1st asst. physician, Binghamton (N.Y.) State Hosp., 1902-11; med. supt., Matteawan (N.Y.) State Hosp., 1911; med. mem. N.Y. State Hosp. Commn., 1911-16; supt. Grafton (Mass.) State Hosp., 1916-17; supt. Boston State Hosp., 1917-36; commr. of mental diseases, Commonwealth of Mass., 1933-34. Lecturer on mental hygiene, Sch. of Pub. Health, Harvard, 1933-36. Served as first lieutenant, later captain and major Med. Reserve Corps, U.S. Army. Member Nat. Com. for Mental Hygiene, Internat. Com. for Mental Hygiene (mem. council). Trustee Boston School of Occupational Therapy. Diplomate of Am. Bd. Psychiatry and Neurology. Fellow A.M.A., Am. Psychiatric Assn. (pres. 1932-33), Mass. Psychiatric Soc. (pres. 1927-28), Am. Acad. of Arts and Sciences; mem. N.E. Soc. of Psychiatry (pres. 1933-34), Am. Legion, United Spanish War Vets., Pi Gamma Mu; corr. mem. Royal Medico-Psychol. Assn. of Great Britain, Verein für Psychiatrie und Neurologie (Vienna); hon. mem. Verein für angewandte Psychopathologie und Psychologie (Vienna); foreign asso. mem. Société Médico-Psychologique, Paris. Mem. Old South Ch. Mason (32°). Author: Mental Diseases, A Public Health Problem, 1922. Numerous contbns. to med and psychiatric lit. Died Dec. 24, 1947.

MAYER, Elias, lawyer; b. Chicago, Ill., Nov. 4, 1877: s. Solomon and Helena (Sinsheimer) M.; A.B., Harvard Univ., 1900; LL.B., Northwestern U., 1903; m. Lucile B. Marks, June 1, 1909 (divorced, 1934); children—Robert E., Elinor L. Admitted to Ill. bar, 1903; with Julian W. Mack until July 1903; practiced alone, 1903-04; mem. Stein, Mayer, Stein & Humes, 1904-06, Stein, Mayer & Stein, 1906-19, Stein, Mayer & David, 1919-28, practicing alone since 1932; pres. Gen. Am. Tank Car Corp., 1928-31. Dir. Jewish Charities of Chicago. Mem. Am., Ill. State and Chicago bar assns., Art Inst. Chicago, Theta Delta Chi, Phi Alpha Delta. Clubs: Standard, Tavern, Press, Northmoor Country. Home: Deerfield, Ill. Office: 33 S. Clark St., Chicago, Ill.* Died May 3, 1945.

MAYER, Lucius W., cons. mining engr.; b. New York, N.Y., Apr. 28, 1882; s. Gerson and Rosa (Wolf) M.; student Rensselaer Poly. Inst.; E.M., Columbia U., 1904; m. Mildred Mack, Apr. 19, 1910 (now dec.); 1 son, Chester Mack; married 2d, Dorothy P. Saks, September 17, 1943. With Stratton Independence Mining Co., Ltd., Cripple Creek, Colo., 1904-05; with Federal Lead Co., Flat River, Mo., 1906-07; investigating mining methods in Europe for Am. Smelters Securities Co., 1907; asso. with A. Chester Beatty in general consulting work from 1908-16; cons. engr. for Eugene Meyer Jr. & Company, 1916; partner in firm Rogers, Mayer & Ball since 1917. Dir. Air Express International Agency, Incorporated. Mem. Am. Inst. Mining and Metall. Engrs., Mining and Metall. Soc. America. Clubs: City Midday, Mining, Columbia Yacht (N.Y. City). Author: Mining Methods in Europe, 1907; Financing of Mines, 1916. Lecturer and contbr. papers on mining. Home: 111 E. 56th St. Office: 26 Beaver St., N.Y. City. Died June 11, 1947.

MAYNARD, Edwin Post (mā'nărd), banker; b. Brooklyn, N.Y., July 12, 1864; s. Theodore and Matilda (Trask) M.; ed. pub. sch.; m. Glorianna Conklin Stratton, Nov. 4, 1891; children—Edwin Post, Richard S. Began with Annidown Lane & Co., drygoods commn., N.Y. City, 1879; asst. bookkeeper, advancing to comptroller Brooklyn Savings Bank, 1882-1912, pres., 1912-13; pres. Brooklyn Trust Co., 1913-27, chmn. bd., Dec. 1, 1927-Jan. 1947. Dir. N.Y. Telephone Co., Equitable Life Assurance Soc. of U.S., Brooklyn Trust Co. Trustee Brooklyn Savings Bank. Republican. Presbyterian. Clubs: City Midday, Rembrandt, Bankers (Brooklyn); Apollo, Quantuck Beach; Highland Park (Lake Wales, Fla.). Home: Hotel Bossert. Office: 177 Montague St., Brooklyn, N.Y. Died Nov. 10, 1949; buried in Green-Wood Cemetery.

MAYNARD, John Blackwell, army officer; b. Portsmouth, Va., Aug. 12, 1887; s. Harry Lee and Mary Eleanor (Brooks) M.; B.S. in C.E., Va. Poly. Inst., 1907; student Colo. Sch. of Mines, 1907-08, Coast Arty. Sch., 1912, Coast Arty. Sch. (Advanced), 1928, Field Arty. Sch., 1917, 18, Chem. Warfare Sch., 1924, Command and Gen. Staff Sch., 1923-24, Army War Coll., 1928-29; m. Lucy Talbott Dorsey, Oct. 19, 1911; children—John Blackwell, Mary Eleanor (Mrs. Charles Murray Henley), Charles Dorsey, Harry Lee. Commd. 2d lt., Coast Arty. Corps, Sept. 25, 1908; promoted through grades to brig. gen., U.S. Army, Apr. 5, 1941. Mem. Mil. Order World War, Sigma Nu, Omicron Delta Kappa. Mason. Home: Denbigh, Va. Died Feb. 2, 1945; buried in Arlington National Cemetery.

MAYNARD, Reuben Leslie, lawyer; b. North Litchfield, N.Y., Sept. 15, 1862; A.B., Hamilton Coll., 1884, A.M., 1887; studied Friedrich Wilhelms U., Berlin, 1889-90; LL.B., Cornell U., 1891; LL.D. (honorary) Hamilton College, 1943; married Mary Kirk Rider, Aug. 16, 1916. Principal Deposit Academy and Supt. Deposit (N.Y.) Union Free Schools, Sept. 15, 1884-June 30, 1888; admitted to N.Y. bar, 1891, and began practice at N.Y. City; mem. Maynard & Tolles, 1896-1901, alone since 1901; 1st asst. dist. atty., N.Y. County, 1910-12, under Dist. Atty. Charles S. Whitman. Trustee Hamilton Coll. since 1910. Member Am. and N.Y. State bar assns., Bar Assn. City of N.Y., Met. Museum of Art, Soc. Med. Jurisprudence, Nat. Inst. Social Sciences (vice-pres. and counsel), Am. Scenic and Historic Preservation Soc. (v.p., counsel), Hamilton Coll. Alumni Assn. (ex-pres.), Delta Kappa Epsilon, Theta Nu Epsilon, Phi Delta Phi. Republican. Presbyterian. Mason (32°). Clubs: Union League (chmn. com. on polit. reform, 1913-20), Nat. Republican (sec. 1906-08), Quill (pres. 1916-17), Bankers of America, Pilgrims, Sleepy Hollow Country. Home: 60 E. 96th St. Office: 141 Broadway, New York, N.Y. Died Sept. 25, 1945.

MAYO, George Elton, univ. prof.; b. Adelaide, Australia, Dec. 26, 1880; s. George Gibbs and Hetty Mary (Donaldson) M.; Westminster classical scholar, St. Peter's Coll., Adelaide, 1894-95; Adelaide Univ., 1898-99, B.A., 1910, M.A., 1919; hon. M.A., Harvard, 1942; m. Dorothea McConnel, Apr. 18, 1913; children—Patricia Elton (Mrs. Walter Goetz), Ruth Elton (Mrs. Guy Vincent). Lecturer in logic and psychology, Queensland U., 1911, prof., 1919-23; research associate, U. of Pa., 1923-26; asso. prof. industrial research, Harvard, 1926, professor, 1929-47, professor emeritus since September 1947. Roby Fletcher prizeman (Adelaide), 1906, David Murray research scholar, 1911. Fellow American Academy Arts and Sciences. Author: Democracy and Freedom,

1919; The Human Problems of an Industrial Civilization, 1933, 2d edition 1946; The Social Problems of An Industrial Civilization, 1945. Address: Polesden Lacey, near Dorking, Surrey, Eng. Died Sept. 7, 1949.

MAYO, William Benson, mech. engr.; b. Chatham, Mass., Jan. 7, 1866; s. Andrew Benson and Amanda (Nickerson) M.; ed. pub. schs. and pvt. training; m. Susan Harratt Dana, Jan. 8, 1891. With Hooven-Owens-Reutschler Co., steam engines, mfrs., Hamilton, O., 25 yrs., chief engr. 10 yrs., gen. mgr., v.p. 10 yrs.; chief engr. Ford Motor Co. 1913-33; gen. mgr. Dept. of Street Rys., City of Detroit 2 yrs.; chmn. exec. bd. Detroit Motorbus Co.; pres. Chicago, Duluth and Georgian Bay Transit Co.; v.p. General Machinery Co. of Hamilton, O.; dir. United Aircraft Co., Hartford, Conn.; also officer or dir. other cos. Trustee Antioch College for 8 yrs. Mem. Am. Soc. Mech. Engrs., Detroit Engring. Soc., Detroit Aviation Soc. (pres.), Mich. State Board Aeronautics (pres.). Episcopalian. Mason, Elk. Clubs: Detroit, Detroit Athletic, Recess, Country; Bloomfield Hills Golf (Birmingham, Mich.); Engineers' (New York). Home: 1457 Seminole Av., Detroit, Mich.* Died Jan. 31, 1944.

MAZET, Robert (má-zĕt'), lawyer; b. Pittsburgh, Pa., May 15, 1857; s. William and Malcena M.; ed. Pittsburgh High Sch.; LL.B., Columbia, 1879; m. Elsie Sawyer Moore, Nov. 11, 1899 (dec.); children—Robert Mazet, Horace S.; m. 2d, Frances Cullen, Mar. 25, 1916. Law practice since 1880; dep. atty. gen. State of N.Y., 1898. Mem. of N.Y. Assembly, 1897-99; mem. Com. of N.Y. Legislature, 1897, to investigate trusts; chmn. Mazet Com., 1899, to investigate govt. of N.Y. City; chmn. Bd. of Transfer Tax Appraisers, 1901-05. Republican. Commd. maj. 7th Regt., Nat. Guard N.Y.; maj. 107th Inf., U.S. Army, Aug. 5, 1917; lt. col., 1918; comd. 107th Inf., 27th Div., A.E.F., in Flanders, July-Aug. 1918; hon. discharged, Oct. 31, 1918. Mem. Pa. Soc. Mil. Order of Foreign Wars (judge advocate N.Y. Commandery), Soc. of World War, Pa. Soc. of New York (sec., treas.), Soc. of War Veterans of 7th Regiment (pres.), Chi Phi. Address: 270 Broadway, New York, N.Y. Died Dec. 25, 1945.

MAZYCK, William Gaillard (mă'zĭk), insurance; b. Cordesville, S.C., Oct. 12, 1846; s. Alexander Harris and Emma Anna (Gaillard) M.; educated Charleston private schools; m. Henrietta Vallée Ronan, Oct. 12, 1869 (now dec.); children—Marion (dec.), Ethel, Vallée, William Gaillard. Q.m. and adj. 2d Batt. S.C. Vols. In ry. service 28 yrs. from apprentice in mach. shop to treas.; with Charleston Daily News, 1871-72; sec. Equitable Fire Ins. Co., since orgn., now also v.p. Formerly sec. and treas. Elliott Soc. of Science and Art; sec., treas., life mem. Agrl. Society of S.C.; sec. and treas. St. George's Soc.; hon. v.p. Huguenot Soc. of S.C.; former librarian Charleston Library Soc.; mem. S.C. Soc. (life), St. Andrews Soc. (life), Conchological Soc. of Great Britain. Hon. curator conchology, Charleston Museum; hon. historian Charleston Chamber of Commerce; mem. Am. Malocological Union. Democrat. Episcopalian. Mason (32°, K.C.C.H., K.T.). Contbr. on conchology, and articles in scientific mags. Address: 56 Montagu St., Charleston, S.C. Died July 24, 1942.

McADIE, Alexander George (măk'á-dē), meteorologist; b. N.Y. City, Aug. 4, 1863; s. John and Anne (Sinclair) M.; A.B., Coll. City of New York, 1881, A.M., 1884; A.M., Harvard, 1885; hon. M.S., Santa Clara Coll.; m. Mary Randolph Browne, Oct. 7, 1893. In Physical Lab., U.S. Signal Office, 1886-87; fellow in physics and lecturer in meteorology, Clark U., Worcester, Mass., 1889-90; Weather Bur., Washington, 1891-95; local forecast official, New Orleans, 1898; forecast official, San Francisco, 1899; prof. meteorology, U.S. Weather Bur., 1903-13; A. Lawrence Rotch prof. meteorology, Harvard U., and dir. Blue Hill Obs. since 1913. Hon. lecturer U. of Calif. Lt. comdr. U.S.N.R.F. and sr. aerographic officer overseas, 1918. Mem. Astron. Society Pacific (pres. 1912), Seismol. Soc. America (pres. 1914), Am. Antiquarian Soc.; fellow Am. Acad. Arts and Sciences. Author: Principles of Aerography; Climatology of California; Rainfall of California; The Fogs and Clouds of San Francisco; The Winds of Boston; The Ephebic Oath; Wind and Weather; Cloud Atlas; Making the Weather; War Weather Vignettes; Man and Weather; Clouds, Airgraphics, Fog; also bulletins and pamphlets on meteorol. subjects, especially lightning, frost, fog and scientific units. Home: 3533 Chesapeake Av., Hampton, Va. Address: Blue Hill Observatory, Milton, Mass. Died Nov. 1, 1943.

McAFEE, Cleland Boyd, clergyman; b. Ashley, Mo., Sept. 25, 1866; s. Rev. John Armstrong (pres. Park Coll.) and Anna Waddle (Bailey) M.; A.B., Park Coll., 1884, A.M., 1888; grad. Union Theol. Sem., 1888; Ph.D., Westminster Coll., Mo., 1892; D.D., Park, 1897; LL.D., Tusculum, 1921; LL.D., Hanover Coll., 1929; S.T.D., Syracuse, 1930; m. Harriet Brown, Aug. 10, 1892; children—Ruth Myrtle (Mrs. Geo. W. Brown), Katherine Agnes (Mrs. A. G. Parker), Mildred Helen. Ordained Presbyn. ministry, 1888; prof. mental and moral philosophy, Park Coll., 1888-1901; pastor Forty-first St. (now First) Ch., Chicago, 1901-04, Lafayette Av. Ch., Brooklyn, 1904-12; prof. systematic theology, McCormick Theol. Sem., Chicago, 1912-30; sec. Presbyn. Bd. Fgn. Missions, 1930-36, now sec. emeritus; lecturer various instns.; substitute prof. systematic theology, McCormick Theol. Sem., Chicago, 1939-40; teaching ministry, Pacific Coast and Central West, 1940-44. Lecturer on Joseph Cook Foundation, in Syria, Egypt, India, Siam, China, Korea, Japan, 1924-25. Moderator Gen. Assembly Presbyn. Ch., U.S.A., 1929-30. Author: Where He Is, 1898; Faith, Fellowship and Fealty, 1902; The Growing Church, 1903; Mosaic Law in Modern Life, 1906; Studies in the Sermon on the Mount, 1910; The Greatest English Classic, 1912; Psalms of the Social Life, 1917; Christian Faith and the New Day, 1919; The Christian Conviction, 1926; Changing Foreign Missions, 1927; Ministerial Practices, 1928; The Christian Message and Program, 1929; The Ruling Elder, His Opportunities and Duties, 1930; The Uncut Nerve of Missions, 1932; The Foreign Missionary Enterprise and Its Sincere Critics, 1935; Studies in the Philippines, 1943. Director religious work department Y.M.C.A., with A.E.F., 1919. Home: Four Aces, Jaffrey, N.H. Office: 156 5th Av., New York, N.Y. Died Feb. 4, 1944.

McAFEE, Joseph Ernest, community service; b. Louisiana, Mo., Apr. 4, 1870; s. John Armstrong and Anna Waddle (Bailey) M.; A.B., Park Coll., Mo., 1889; student Union Theol. Sem., 1889-90, Auburn Theol. Sem., 1891-93 (certificate of graduation), Princeton Theol. Sem., Princeton U., 1895-96, B.D., 1896; m. Adah Elizabeth Brokaw, July 26, 1898; 1 dau., Janet Brokaw (Mrs. Erle B. Ayres). Asst., Park Coll., 1890-91, and 1893-96, prof. Greek, 1896-1900, chaplain and prof. history of religion and ethics, 1900-06; asso. sec. Board of Home Missions Presbyn. Ch. in U.S.A., 1906-14, sec., 1914-17; sec. Am. Missionary Assn., 1918-20; community counselor extension div., U. of Okla., 1921-23; dir. community service, Community Ch., New York, 1924-32. Author: Missions Striking Home, 1908; World Missions, from the Home Base, 1911; Religion and the New American Democracy, 1917; A Mid-West Adventure in Education, 1937; College Pioneering, 1938; (booklets) Community Types and Programs; Religion Without a Church; Organizing the Community for Good Will; You Are a McAfee; historical papers of Park College; also bulls. on community extension, community house, town govt., beautification, etc. Contbr. on social and religious subjects. Home: 15 Vandeventer, Princeton, N.J. Died Mar. 14, 1947.

McALISTER, John Barr, physician; b. Carroll County, Md., Jan. 31, 1864; s. James and Jane A. (Barr) M.; A.B., Pa. Coll., 1884; M.D., U. of Pa., 1887; m. Helen Motter, Jan. 20, 1909. Practiced in Harrisburg, Pa., since 1887; med. dir. Harrisburg Hosp. Trustee Pa. Coll., Gettysburg Coll. (pres. bd.). Mem. A.M.A., Am. Coll. Physicians, Med. Soc. State of Pa. (pres. 1915-16), Dauphin County Med. Soc. (ex-pres.), Harrisburg Acad. Medicine (ex-pres.), Phi Beta Kappa. Republican. Presbyterian. Clubs: Harrisburg, Country. Home: 232 N. 3d St. Office: 234 N. 3d St., Harrisburg, Pa. Died July 22, 1948.

McALLISTER, Addams Stratton (măk-ăl'ĭs-tẽr), engineer; b. Covington, Va., Feb. 24, 1875; s. Abraham Addams and Julia Ellen (Stratton) M.; B.S. (1st honors), Pa. State Coll., 1898, E.E., 1900; M.M.E. (1st honors), Cornell U., 1901, Ph.D., 1905; m. Homé C. Stephens, Jan. 28, 1922; children—Julia Adeline, Homé Stephens, Lydia Addams, Addams Stratton, Sarah Billopp. Served as elec. engr. with Berwind-White Coal Mining Co., 1898, Westinghouse Electric & Mfg. Co., 1899; asst. in physics, Cornell U., 1901, instr., 1902-03, acting asst. prof. elec. engring., 1903-04; asso. editor Electrical World, 1905-12, editor, 1912-15; professorial lecturer on elec. engring., Pa. State Coll., 1909-14. Was mem. Engring. Council's War Com. of Tech. Socs. of U.S. Naval Consulting Bd.; sec. Am. Engring. Service of Engring. Council; mem. divisional com. on lighting of com. on labor of advisory commn. Council Nat. Defense; chmn. elec. engring. service com., and bd. examiners, etc. of Am. Inst. E.E. Became associated with progress sect. of control bureau, Ordnance Dept., Washington, and later head of reports branch of progress sect., Apr. 1918; sec. bd. of army ordnance officers to review the arty. program, 1918. Elec. engr. Nat. Bur. Standards, 1921; acting sec. Am. Engring. Standards Com., 1921; liaison officer Bur. of Standards and Federal Specifications Bd. with Am. Engring. Standards Com., New York, 1922-23; engr.-physicist Bur. of Standards, Washington, since 1923, chief div. of specifications, 1929, asst. dir., 1930-45; technical liaison officer, Department of Commerce and Federal Specifications Exec. Com., 1939-45; secretary Sect. Com. on Rating of Elec. Machinery, 1921-28; mem. U.S. Nat. Com., Internat. Electrotech. Commn., 1924-27; mem. council, Am. Standards Assn., 1930-45; pres. A. A. McAllister & Sons, Pounding Mill Water Supply Co.; pres. McAllister & Bell, Covington, Va. Fellow A.A. A.S.; member Illuminating Engineering Society (dir. 1910-11; pres. 1914-15; chmn. N.Y. Sect. 1917-18; chmn. edit. and pub. com., 1920-22); fellow Am. Inst. E.E. (mgr. 1914-17, v.p. 1917-18, chmn. pub. com., 1921-22); mem. Nat. Geneal. Soc. (pres. 1924-28), Geneal. Soc. Pa., Huguenot Soc. Pa., Hist. Soc. Pa., Baronial Order of Runnymede (a surety and mem. Court of Eligibility, 1923-28), Abracadabra Club of Washington (pres. 1932-34), N.Y. State Soc. of Washington, First Families of Va., Virginia Soc. of Washington, Southern Soc. of Washington, Huguenot Soc. of Washington (dir. 1932-35), Phi Kappa Phi, Sigma Xi, Eta Kappa Nu, Tau Beta Pi. Genealogist of Nat. Soc. Americans of Royal Descent, 1929-45. Clubs: Federal (hon.), Cleveland Park of Washington (pres. 1930). Author: Alternating Current Motors (4 editions), 1906; Standard Handbook for Electrical Engineers (3 edits.), 1907; The Descendants of John Thomson, 1917. Directed compilation of the Nat. Directory of Commodity Specifications (pub. by the U.S. Dept. of Commerce), 1925, 32, 45; Standards Year Book, 1927-33; Directory of Commercial Testing and Coll. Research Laboratories, 1927; Standards and Specifications in the Wood-Using Industries, 1927; Standards and Specifications of Non-Metallic Minerals, 1930; Standards and Specifications for Metals and Metal Products, 1933; Directory of Federal Government Testing Laboratories, 1929, 35. Contbr. about 100 original articles on engring. subjects to tech. press; inventor alternating current machinery. First to propound and formulate the law of conservation as applied to illuminating engring. calculations. Home: Rosedale, Covington, Va. Died Nov. 26, 1946.

McALLISTER, Frank Winton, lawyer; b. Monroe County, Mo., Jan. 26, 1873; s. William Horace and Sarah Palmer (Caldwell) M.; ed. high sch., Nelson, Saline County, Mo.; m. Amber Katherine Smith, June 1, 1911. Began practice at Paris, Mo., 1895; city atty., 1896-1900; pros. atty. Monroe County, Mo., 1901, 02; mem. Mo. Senate, 1905-12 (pres. 1911, 12); atty. gen. of Mo., 1917-20, inclusive. Mem. Mo. Council Defense, 1917-18; chmn. State Legal Com., to aid soldiers and sailors and their families. Mem. exec. com. Mo. State Council of Defense since Jan. 1942. Democrat. Mason, Odd Fellow. Home: 6015 Morningside Drive. Office: Rialto Bldg., Kansas City, Mo. Died June 11, 1948.

McALLISTER, Sydney G., mem. exec. com. Internat. Harvester Co. Joined company as office boy, McCormick Works, 1897; became asst. supt. of its harvester plant, Hamilton, Ont., 1903; following various promotions was sent to Europe as asst. inspector gen. of mfg., 1914; inspector gen., company's European mfg. operations, 1919, and chmn. company's European advisory council, 1925; recalled to U.S., 1931, and made v.p. in charge of mfg. and engring. depts.; elected 1st v.p., May 1934, pres. May 1, 1935, now mem. exec. com. and dir.; also dir. Harris Trust & Savings Bank, Ill. Bell Telephone Co., Crane Co., Chicago. Trustee Illinois Inst. Tech., Chicago. Home: 2754 Deere Park Drive, S.E., Highland Park, Ill. Office: 180 N. Michigan Av., Chicago 1, Ill. Died Dec. 25, 1946.

McALPINE, Charles Alonzo (măk-ăl'pĭn), clergyman; b. at Mansfield, Mass., Feb. 7, 1874; s. Charles Alonzo and Eliza Jane (King) McA.; grad. high sch., Mansfield, 1890; Worcester Acad., 1898; A.B., cum laude, Harvard, 1901; grad. Rochester Theol. Sem., 1904; B.D., Colgate-Rochester Divinity Sch.; m. Lunetta M. Briggs, Sept. 7, 1904; children—Paul Theodore, Halcyon Delight, Louise Rae, Elizabeth Marie. Ordained Bapt. ministry, 1904; pastor Bronson Av. Ch., Rochester, N.Y., 1904-07; sec. Bapt. Missionary Conv., N.Y., 1907-13; field sec. Pacific Bapt. Theol. Union, 1915-16; dir. Daily Vacation Bible Schs., Northern Bapt. Conv., 1916-18; dir. publicity, Northern Bapt. Laymen, 1918-19; dir. adv. Gen. Bd. of Promotion, N.B.C., 1919-21; dir. publicity Am. Bible Soc., 1920-21; became pres. Ch. Service, Inc., 1922; acting sec. Am. Bible Soc., 1927-28; extension dir. Bapt. Inst. for Christian Workers, 1928-29; pastor Lefferts Park Baptist Church, Brooklyn, New York, 1930-37; minister at large, 1937-41; acting pastor Fulton Av. Bapt. Ch., New York, 1941-42; pastor Ascension Baptist Ch., New York, since 1943; chaplain Brooklyn State Hosp. since 1940; lecturer on religious publicity. Mem. Pi Eta. Member Board of Managers, Board of Education and Publication, Northern Baptist Convention. Republican. Mason. Author: Hogan and Hogan, 1914; The Pulpit Committee, 1916; Says Hogan, 1917; The Readers Bible, 1936; The Life and Teachings of Jesus Christ, 1937; Through the Bible in a Year, 1939; The Bible Log, 1942; also weekly feature articles in various pubs. under general title, "I Was Wondering," 1919-31, and miscellaneous articles in religious press. Editor of The Church Messenger, 1923-28. Home: 305 E. 161st St. Address: 150 Nassau St., New York 7, N.Y. Died Aug. 5, 1945.

McANDREWS, James, ex-congressman; b. Woonsocket, R.I., Oct. 22, 1862; s. James and Catherine (Brennan) McA.; ed. pub. and pvt. schs., Chicago; m. Louise Klaus, Aug. 21, 1905; children—Catherine Louise, James Thomas, William Joseph. Formerly building commr. of Chicago; mem. 57th Congress (1901-03), 4th Ill. Dist., 58th Congress (1903-05), 5th Ill. Dist., 63d to 66th Congresses (1913-21), 6th Ill. Dist. and 74th to 76th Congresses (1935-41), 9th Ill. Dist. Democrat. Club: Post and Paddock (Arlington Park, Ill.). Home: 2440 Lake View Av., Chicago, Ill. Died Aug. 31, 1942.

McAULIFFE, Joseph John, editor; b. St. Louis, Mo.; s. Daniel and Bridget (Cleary) M.; St. Louis U., 1889-94; m. Irene Murray, Aug. 23, 1910; 1 dau., Mary Irene. Began as reporter St. Louis Post-Dispatch, Sept. 23, 1897; became state polit. reporter and legislative corr., 1900; asst. city editor, 1909-10, chief copy editor, 1911-12; joined staff of Globe-Democrat as city editor, Oct. 26, 1913, mng. editor since Feb. 26, 1915. Mem. Mo. Hist. Soc., Asso. Press Mng. Editors Assn. Clubs: Missouri Athletic, Chamber of Commerce. Home: 4372 W. Pine Blvd. Office: Globe-Democrat, St. Louis, Mo. Died July 9, 1942.

McAULIFFE, Maurice Francis, bishop; b. Hartford, Conn., June 17, 1875; s. Daniel and Catherine (Noonan) McA.; student Mt. St. Mary's Coll., Emmitsburg, Md., 1894-95; A.B., Seminary of St. Sulpice, Paris, France, 1897; student Catholic Sem., Eichstaett, Germany, 1897-1900; D.D. from Rome, 1926; LL.D., Mt. St. Mary's Coll., 1922. Pres. St.

Thomas Sem., Hartford, 1921-34; bishop atts. of Hartford, 1926-34, bishop of Hartford since Apr. 23, 1934. Home: 140 Farmington Av., Hartford, Conn. Died Dec. 15, 1944.

McAVITY, Malcolm (măk'ă-vĭt-ĭ), Pres. Consolidation Coal Co.; b. St. John, N.B., Can., Mar. 14, 1899; s. John A. and Mary Elizabeth (Humphrey) McA.; ed. Rothesay Collegiate Sch., Royal Mil. Acad.; m. Frances Hazen, Jan. 1, 1915 (now deceased); children—John, Douglas, Peter; m. 2d, Frances Bergen, Feb. 18, 1939. Production mgr. T. McAvity & Sons, Can., 1910-14; pres. Malcolm McAvity & Co., import and export, London and Montreal, 1919-26; pres. Rochester & Pittsburgh Coal Co., Can., 1926-32, also v.p. parent company, U.S., 1929-32; pres. Empire Coal Co., Can., 1932-39; v.p. Consol. Coal Co., Inc., N.Y. City, 1939-41, pres. since 1941; also pres. Empire-Hanna Coal Co., Can., 1939-41, chmn. bd. since 1941. Served on Gen. Staff, Canadian Corps, overseas, 1914-19; decorated C.B.E., D.S.O. Clubs: Mount Royal, Royal Montreal Golf (Montreal); National (Toronto); University (N.Y. City); Union (Cleveland); Round Hill Country (Greenwich, Conn.). Episcopalian. Home: Rockwood, Calhoun Drive, Greenwich, Conn. Office: 30 Rockefeller Plaza, New York, N.Y. Died Apr. 30, 1944.

McBRIDE, Allan Clay, army officer; b. Frederick, Md., June 30, 1885; grad. St. John's Coll., Md., 1908; commd. 2d lt., F.A., Sept. 1908, and advanced through the grades to brig. gen., Dec. 1941; became comdr. 12th F.A., Ft. Sam Houston, Tex., 1939; inspector gen. hdqrs. Third Army, San Antonio, Tex., 1940; assigned to hdqrs. Philippine Dept., Manila, P.I., as plans and training officer, Feb. 1941; in Philippine Islands, when hostilities broke out and is now believed prisoner of war in hands of Japanese. Awarded Distinguished Service Medal, Nov. 1942.* Died May 9, 1944.

McBRIDE, Malcolm Lee, merchant; b. Cleveland, O., Aug. 22, 1878; s. John Harris and Elizabeth (Wright) McB.; grad. Univ. Sch., Cleveland, 1896; A.B., Yale, 1900, hon. A.M., 1920; m. Lucia McCurdy, June 6, 1905; children—Lucia, John Harris, Malcolm Rhodes. With The Root & McBride Co., wholesale dry goods merchants, since 1900, v.p. and treas., 1909-29, pres. since 1929; dir. Central Nat. Bank. Mem. Troop A, Cleveland, 1902-05. Mem. 1st Cleveland Charter Com., 1912; mem. Cleveland Foundation since 1918, chmn. since 1922. Mem. Alpha Delta Psi, Scroll and Key. Clubs: Union, Mayfield, Chagrin Valley Hunt (Cleveland); Yale (N.Y. City). Home: 1583 Mistletoe Drive. Office: 1250 W. 6th St., Cleveland, O. Died Dec. 20, 1941.

McBRIDE, Robert Edwin, physician; b. Thibodaux, LaFourche Parish, La., Feb. 21, 1873; s. Robert R. and Ada E. (Thibodaux) M.; M.D., Tulane U., 1896; m. Genevieve Edmondson Williams, May 12, 1898; children—Mary Ethel, Robert Edwin, James Monroe, Paul Cooke, Genevieve Williams, Ada Thibodaux, Lucy Stewart, Margaret Theresa, Catherine Olive. Practiced at Houma, La., 1896-1904, at Las Cruces, N.M., since 1904; med. dir. McBride Hosp. County supt. public edn., 1917-21. Was editor N.M. Med. Journal and editor in chief Southwestern Medicine. Ex-regent Agrl. Coll. of N.M. Sec. N.M. Med. Assn., 1907-08, 1910-20; fellow A.M.A.; formerly sec. County Bd. of Edn., Dona Ana County; formerly sec. Bd. of Med. Examiners of State of N.M.; fellow A.A.A.S., Am. Coll. Physicians. Republican. Episcopalian. Lt. col., Med. Corps, N.M. Nat. Guard, retired. Dist. gov. Rotary Internat., 1930-31. Home: Las Cruces, N.M. Died Jan. 17, 1947; buried in Las Cruces, N.M.

McCAFFERY, Richard Stanislaus (măk kăf'fĕr-ĭ), mining engr.; b. New York, N.Y., June 2, 1874; s. Michael J. A. (A.M., LL.D.), and Mary (Treacy) McC.; E.M., Sch. of Mines (Columbia), 1896; m. Kathleen Kirwan, Jan. 27, 1897; children—Arthur L., Miriam, Richard S., Agatha G., Philip, John K. Supt. Copper Corp. of Chile, Chanaral, Chile, 1900; supt., 1901-02, mgr., 1905-07, Santa Fe Gold & Copper Mining Co., San Pedro, N.M.; mgr. Salt Lake Copper Co., Utah, 1905-07; general supt. Tintic Smelting Co., Silver City, Utah, 1908; prof. mining and metallurgy, U. of Ida., 1909-14; prof. mining and metallurgy, U. of Wis., 1914-41; now consulting metall. and mining engineer. Member. American Institute Mining Engrs., Canadian Mining Inst., Am. Chem. Soc., Iron and Steel Inst., Soc. Promotion Engring. Edn., Am. Foundrymens' Assn., N.Y. Acad. Sciences; Sigma Psi, Tau Beta Pi. Democrat. Catholic. Home: 235 E. 22d St. Office: 163 W. 94th St., New York, N.Y. Died June 12, 1945.

McCAIN, C(harles) Curtice, ry. official; b. Minneapolis, Minn., Sept. 18, 1856; s. John Curtice and Sarah Ann (Dailey) M.; pub. sch. edn.; m. Maria Bradley Shaw, Apr. 8, 1886; children—Curtice Shaw, H. Berrien. Clerk and chief clerk Trunk Lines Assn., New York, 1877-87; auditor Interstate Commerce Commn., Washington, 1887-95; commr. Assn. of Lake Lines, Buffalo, 1895-1907; chmn. Trunk Line Assn., Oct. 1, 1907-May 1918; sec. Eastern Freight Traffic Com. U.S. R.R. Adminstrn., May 1918-March 31, 1919; appointed mgr. Eastern Freight Inspection Bur., Apr. 1, 1919; mem. Official Classification Com., 1920-34 (retired on account of ill health). Republican. Episcopalian. Author: Compendium of Transportation Theories, 1890; (pamphlet) Changes in Freight Rates for Fifty Years, 1894; (pamphlet) Diminished Purchasing Power of Railway Earnings, 1908. Home: East Orange, N.J. Died July 14, 1942.

McCAIN, John Sidney, naval officer; b. Carroll County, Miss., Aug. 9, 1884; s. John Sidney and Elizabeth Ann (Young) McC.; student U. of Miss., 1901-02; grad. U.S. Naval Acad., 1906, Naval War Coll., 1929; flight instrn. (naval aviator), Naval Air Station, Pensacola, Fla., 1935-36; m. Katherine Vaulx, Aug. 9, 1909; children—John Sidney, James Gordon, Katherine Vaulx. Commd. ensign, U.S. Navy, 1906; promoted through grades to rear adm., 1941, vice admiral, July 1943; chief Bureau of Aeronautics, Sept. 1942-July 1943; dep. chief naval operations for air, July 1943; comdr. Carrier Task Force 38. Witnessed the Japanese surrender on board U.S.S. Missouri, Sept. 2, 1945. Mem. Phi Delta Theta. Mason. Clubs: Army and Navy, Army and Navy Country (Washington); Jonathan (Los Angeles). Home: Carrollton, Miss. Died Sept. 6, 1945.

McCAIN, Paul Pressly, M.D.; b. Due West, S.C., June 26, 1884; s. John Iranaeus and Lula Jane (Todd) McC.; A.B., Erskine Coll., Due West, 1906; M.D., U. of Md., 1911; LL.D., U. of N.C., 1936; m. Sadie Lou McBrayer, Oct. 17, 1917; children—Sarah Louise, Paul Pressly, Lillian Irene, John Lewis, Jane Todd. Interne Bay View Hosp., Baltimore, Md., 1911; resident physician Gaylord Farm Sanatorium, 1912-13; chief of med. service and asst. supt. N.C. Sanatorium, 1914-23, supt., med. dir. and dir. extension dept. since 1924; supt. Western N.C. Sanatorium since 1936; supt. Eastern N.C. Sanatorium since 1941. Trustee Flora Macdonald Coll., Red Springs, N.C. Diplomate American Board Internal Medicine; fellow Am. College Physicians; member subcommittee on tuberculosis National Research Council; member Clin. and Climatol. Assn., Nat. Tuberculosis Assn. (dir., mem. exec. com., 1936-39, v.p. 1938-39, pres. 1940-41), Southern Tuberculosis Conf. (pres.), N.C. Tuberculosis Assn. (dir.; exec. com.), N.C. Med. Soc. (pres. 1935), Sigma Xi. Awarded Moore County medal, N.C. Med. Soc., 1928. Democrat. Presbyterian. Kiwanian. Member editorial bd. N.C. Med. Jour. Address: Sanatorium, N.C. Died Nov. 25, 1946; buried in Bethesda Cemetery, Aberdeen, N.C.

McCALL, Thomas, lawyer; b. Malvern, O., June 14, 1889; s. William Hosea and Ellen (Freaner) McC.; A.B., cum laude, Harvard, 1912; m. Margaret Aliona Dole, Oct. 2, 1916; children—Thomas Dole, Margaret Frances, Dorothy Freaner. Admitted to Ill. bar, 1915, N.Y. bar, 1924; asst. state's atty., Chicago, 1915; moved to New York, 1923; mem. firm Dawson, McCall & Dawson until 1925, later with Swiger, Scandrett, Chambers & Landon; apptd. asst. U.S. atty., Southern Dist. of N.Y., Jan. 1934. Legal adviser Draft Bd. 14, Chicago, World War. Democrat. Episcopalian. Home: 18 Jacobus Pl. 63. Address: Office U.S. Atty., New York 7. Died March 8, 1946; buried Mt. Hope Cemetery, Mt. Hope, Westchester County, N.Y.

McCALLIE, Spencer Jarnagin, educator; b. Chattanooga, Tenn., Aug. 24, 1875; s. Thomas Hooke (D.D.) and Ellen Douglas (Jarnagin) Mc.C.; B.A., Southwestern Presbyn. U., 1897, M.A., 1901; studied Cornell U., summer 1901; U. of Chicago, 1903-05; Ped.D., Davidson Coll., 1925; Litt.D., Erskine Coll., 1939; LL.D., University of Chattanooga, 1945; m. Alice Bradford Fletcher, August 15, 1906 (died Nov. 1918); children—Mary Fairfax, Spencer Jarnagin, Thomas Hooke, Alice Fletcher, Ellen Douglas; m. 2d, Katharine Pierce, May 26, 1920; 1 son, David Park. Teacher public schools, 1897-98; head science department Chattanooga High School, 1898-1901; supt. schs., Cleveland, Tenn., 1901-03; associated with brother, James P., 1905, in founding McCallie Sch. (prep. sch. for boys), Chattanooga, of which is now president of board of trustees and teacher, formerly trustee. Ex-pres. Chattanooga Chamber of Commerce. Awarded Citation for Public Service, 1947. Member Selective Service Draft Board No. 4, Chattanooga. Member Headmasters Association, Pvt. Sch. Assn. of Tenn. (past pres.), Mid-South Assn. of Pvt. Schs. (ex-pres.); Pvt. Sch. Assn. of Central States; charter mem. Southern Commn. on Accredited Schs.; mem. Sigma Alpha Epsilon, Omicron Delta Kappa. District governor of Kentucky-Tennessee District, Kiwanis Internat., 1925; Kiwanis Service Award. Civic Leadership, 1943. Democrat. Presbyterian. Clubs: Kiwanis (ex-pres), Lookout Schoolmasters' (ex-pres). Address: The McCallie School, Chattanooga, Tenn. Died Oct. 18, 1949.

McCALLUM, Francis Marion (măk-kawl'ŭm), urologist; b. Decatur, Ill., June 10, 1867; s. George L. and Mary Elizabeth (McMikell) McC.; M.D., Edsworth Med. Coll., St. Joseph, Mo., 1892; grad. study, Jefferson Med. Coll., 1910; m. Juanita Johnson, Apr. 15, 1901; 1 dau. (adopted), Lucille. Began practice, 1892; asst. surgeon St. Margaret's Hosp., 1892-97; asst. surgeon 5th Mo. Vols., Apr.-Nov. 1898; acting asst. surgeon U.S. Army, 1898-99, capt. and asst. surgeon, U.S. Vols., 1899-1902; asst. surgeon U.S. Army, 1902-10; organizer urology dept., Kansas City Gen. Hosp., 1910, chief of dept. since 1911 (ex-v.p. of hosp. staff); mem. staff St. Joseph and Menorah hosps. Mem. Mo. State Bd. of Health, 1929-33, pres., 1930-32; mem. White House Conf. on Child Health and Protection. Fellow Am. Coll. Surgeons; mem. A.M.A., Am. Med. Authors Club, Am. Neisserian Med. Soc., Phi Beta Pi. Citation for meritorious service in battle, P.I., Mar. 16, 1899. Republican. Presbyterian. Mason (Shriner). Home: 5116 Baltimore St. Office: Argyle Bldg., Kansas City, Mo.* Deceased.

McCAMANT, Wallace (mak-kăm'ănt), lawyer; b. Hollidaysburg, Pa., Sept. 22, 1867; s. Thomas and Delia (Rollins) M.; Ph.B., Lafayette Coll., Pa., 1888; m. Katherine S. Davis, Apr. 25, 1893; children—Davis (dec.), Thomas. Admitted to bar, Lancaster, 1890; removed immediately to Portland, Ore.; master in chancery U.S. Court for Dist. of Ore., 1894-1917; asso. justice Supreme Court of Ore., Jan. 9, 1917-June 4, 1918; del. Rep. State convs. of Ore., 1892, 94, 96, 98, 1900; del. Rep. nat. convs., 1896, 1900, 20. Pres. Gen. Nat. Soc. S.A.R., 1921-22; mem. Ore. and Am. bar assns. Presbyterian. Mason (33°). Clubs: Arlington, University. Home: 1046 S.W. King Av. Office: American Bank Bldg., Portland, Ore. Died Dec. 17, 1944.

McCAMPBELL, Leavelle, pres. McCampbell & Co.; b. Chicago, Ill., May 28, 1879; s. Amos Goodwin and Sarah L. (Bryant) McC.; ed. pub. schools, Louisville, Kentucky; LL.D., Presbyn. College, Clinton, S.C.; m. Matilda Goldsborough Robinson, Jan. 10, 1906; m. 2d, Gertrude Bachelor Gore, Apr. 14, 1915. Pres. McCampbell and Co., N.Y. City; chmn. bd. Graniteville Co., Graniteville, S.C. Clubs: Merchants (pres.), The Links (New York); Links Golf (Searington, L.I.); Pendennis (Louisville, Ky.); Biltmore Forest Country (Biltmore, N.C.). Home: 480 Park Av. Office: 40 Worth St., New York, N.Y. Died Feb. 14, 1946.

McCANDLISS, Lester Chipman (măk-kăn'dlĭs), univ. prof.; b. Anderson, Ind., June 16, 1886; s. Harry E. and Harriet (Barr) McC.; B.S. in C.E., Purdue U., 1909; m. Abby McNamee, Oct. 12, 1910; children—Alfred Neal, John Harry. Transitman C.,B.&Q. R.R., 1909-11; estimator Carmichael Construction Co., Akron, O., Feb.-Sept. 1911; bldg. supt. Second Nat. Bldg. Co., Akron, 1911-12; with U. of Pittsburgh since 1912, beginning as instr., prof. and head civil engring. dept. since 1929. Served as 1st lt., later capt., 15th U.S. Engrs., with A.E.F., 1917-19. Mem. Am. Soc. Civil Engrs., Phi Gamma Delta, Sigma Tau, Scabbard and Blade. Republican. Mason (32°). Clubs: Pittsburgh Motor (pres.); Faculty (Univ. of Pittsburgh). Home: 741 S. Linden A., Pittsburgh, Pa. Died Oct. 31, 1945.

McCANN, T(homas) Addison, M.D.; b. Dresden, O., Sept. 25, 1858; s. Thomas Addison and Jane (McKee) McC.; prep. edn. high sch., Dresden; student Denison U. and Ann Arbor Med. Coll.; M.D., Hahnemann Med. Coll., Phila., Pa., 1891; m. Jeannette Kratochwill, Feb. 21, 1899; children—Harriette K. (Mrs. George Roudebush), Thomas A., Jane (Mrs. Carl Linxweiler), Richard L. (dec.), Joseph K. Practiced at Dayton, 1891-1938; surgeon Miami Valley Hosp., 1895-1938; surgeon Gen. Motors Corp.; mem. Ohio State Med. Examining Bd., 1910-38. Now retired. Recruiting officer World War I. Trustee New York Homœ. Med. Coll. Mem. Am. Inst. Homœopathy (ex-pres.), Ohio State Homœ. Med. Assn. (ex-pres.), Dayton Soc. Homœopathy (ex-pres.), Sigma Chi. Democrat. Baptist. Mason (Shriner). Home: 111 Ravenwood Av., Dayton, O. Died Nov. 7, 1943.

McCARN, Jeff, lawyer; b. Marshall, Ark., Aug. 7, 1861; s. Cornelius Alexander and Dulcenia Linton (Thomas) M.; cowboy on Tex. ranch 8 yrs.; student Coggin High School, Brownwood, Tex., 1886-88, Vanderbilt U., 1888-94, LL.B., 1894; m. Mary D. Allison, Oct. 9, 1895; children—Corneille, Andrew Allison, Mary D. In practice at Nashville, Tenn., since 1894; atty. Com. of 100 (organized to suppress lawlessness in Nashville), 1903; dist. atty. gen., Nashville, 1908-10; successfully prosecuted slayers of Senator E. W. Carmack, 1909; independent candidate for judge of Criminal Ct., 1910, vote largest ever polled for any independent candidate in Davidson County (defeated by liquor and gambling interests); U.S. dist. atty., H.T., Nov. 6, 1913-Dec. 21, 1915 (resigned); in practice at Nashville since 1915. State committeeman for Tenn. of Nat. Constl. Dem. Com.; state chmn. for Tenn. of Anti-Smith Democratic State Hdqrs. Methodist. Mem. Delta Kappa Epsilon. Home: 808 Campbell Av. Office: Nashville Trust Bldg., Nashville, Tenn. Died May 12, 1942.

McCARRENS, John S. (măk-kăr'ĕnz), v.p. and gen. mgr. Cleveland Plain Dealer; b. Freeport, Pa., July 27, 1869; s. Dennis A. and Annie (McGinley) McC.; ed. schs. Bradford, Pa., and Limestone, N.Y.; Niagara U., 1893; married Mary Sweeney, June 24, 1896; children—Margaret, John, Alice, Arthur. Salesman and advt. mgr., then advt. writer and dir., 1900-14; newspaper business mgr., 1914-33; v.p. and gen. mgr. Plain Dealer Pub. Co. since 1933; pres. Art Gravure Corp. of O., United Broadcasting Corp.; v.p. Forest City Pub. Co.; v.p. Am. Newspaper Pub. Assn., 1937-39, pres., 1939-40. Catholic. Clubs: Union, Mid-Day, Shaker Country. Home: 21301 Shaker Blvd., Shaker Heights, O. Office: Plain Dealer Pub. Co., Cleveland, O. Died July 24, 1943.

McCARROLL, Russell Hudson, chem. and metall. engr.; b. Detroit, Feb. 20, 1890; s. John and Emily (Roberts) McC.; B.S. in Chem. Engring., U. of Mich., 1914, M.S. in Engring. (hon.), 1937; m. Muriel C. Channer, Sept. 30, 1916; children—Charlotte Jane (Mrs. Charles R. Vincent, Jr.), Marjorie. With Solvay Process Co., Detroit, 1914-15; connected with dept. of chem. and metall. engring., Ford Motor Co., Dearborn Mich., since 1915, in charge of dept. since 1921; became exec. engr., in charge of research, metall. engring., chem. engring. and automotive engring., Ford Motor Co., 1944, now director of chemical and metallurgical engineering and research. Mem. tech. adv. com. automotive div., O.P.M.; mem. sr. tech. adv. com. steel div., O.P.M. Mem. Am. Soc. for Metals, Am. Chem. Soc.,

Iron and Steel Inst. (London), Soc. of Automotive Engrs., Inc. (mem. tech. bd.; mem. exec. com.; chmn. engring. materials com.), Engring. Soc. Detroit (sec.), Am. Foundrymen's Assn. (bd. dirs.), Soc. for Promotion of Engring. Edn., Detroit Bd. of Commerce Research Com., Tau Beta Pi (trustee). Episcopalian. Clubs: Dearborn (Mich.) Country (past sec.-treas. and pres.); Detroit Athletic; Orchard Lake Country (Birmingham, Mich.). Contbr. of articles to professional journals. Granted more than 20 metallurgical and engineering patents; has given special attention to experiments designed to widen indsl. uses of farm produced materials. Home: 205 River Lane. Office: Ford Motor Company, Engineering Laboratory, Dearborn, Mich. Died March 31, 1948.

McCARTAN, Edward, sculptor; b. Albany, N.Y., Aug. 16, 1879; s. Michael and Anna (Hyland) M.; ed. Albany High Sch., Art Students' League (New York), Ecole des Beaux Arts (Paris); unmarried. Exhibited at Salon (Paris), Nat. Acad. Design (New York), Pa. Acad. Fine Arts, Art Inst. Chicago, etc. Awarded Helen Foster Bennett prize, N.A.D., 1912; Widener gold medal, Pa. Acad. Fine Arts, 1916; medal of honor, Archtl. League of N.Y., 1923; Concord Art Assn., 1925; James E. McClees prize, Pa. Acad. Fine Arts, 1931, George D. Pratt prize, Grand Central Galleries, 1931. Works on permanent exhbn., Met. Museum (N.Y.) Albright Gallery (Buffalo), St. Louis Museum, Fogg Museum (Cambridge), Brookgreen (S.C.) Gardens. National Academician since 1925. Trustee Fontainebleau School of Fine Arts. Member of American Academy of Arts and Letters. Mem. American Society of Painters, Sculptors and Gravers, Am. Inst. Architects (hon.), Concord Art Assn. (pres.), Nat. Sculptors' Soc., National Institute Arts and Letters, Beaux Arts Institute of Design. Clubs: Century Assn., National Arts, Coffee House. Awarded Medal of Honor, Allied Artists of America, 1933. Home: 225 E. 67th St., N.Y. City. Died Sept. 20, 1947; buried St. Agnes Cemetery, Albany, N.Y.

McCARTER, Henry, artist, illustrator; b. Norristown, Pa., July 5, 1864; ed. Philadelphia, and Paris, France, under Thos. Eakin, late Puvis de Chavannes, Alexander Harrison, Rixens, Toulouse, Lautrec, Léon Bonnât. Illustrated for Scribner's, Century, Collier's, and other mags. Instr. Pa. Acad. Fine Arts, Phila., Art Students' League, New York. Bronze medal, Buffalo Expn., 1905; silver medal, St. Louis Expn., 1904; gold medals San Francisco Expn., 1915; Beck prize, Pa. Acad. Fine Arts, 1906; 1st prize, Phila. Art Week, 1924; Joseph Pennell gold medal, Pa. Acad. Fine Arts, 1930; gold medal, Art Club of Phila., 1936; Temple gold medal, 1939; Fellowship gold medal, Pa. Acad. Fine Arts, 1941. Represented in permanent exhibits Pa. Acad. Fine Arts, Pa. Art Museum. Address: Pa. Academy of Fine Arts, Philadelphia. Died Nov. 20, 1942, buried Church of the Messiah, Gwynedd, Pa.

McCARTHY, Charles Hallan (mȧ-kär'thĭ), univ. prof.; b. Franklin, N.J., Feb. 14, 1860; s. Charles and Mary (Hallan) McC.; Ph.D., U. of Pa., 1898; m. Evelyn McKenna, Nov. 17, 1887 (dec.); children—Charles Stephen, Florence Marie McC. Webster, Edwin Justin, Evelyn Cecelia (dec.). Instr. and prof. history and civil govt., Catholic High Sch., Phila., 1890-1903; lecturer Am. and English history, Inst. of Pedagogy of Catholic U. of America, New York, 1902-04; asst. prof. Am. history, Cath. U. of America, 1904-07, asso. prof., 1907-09, prof. since Nov. 1909. Received Medal "Benemerenti" from Pope Pius XII, 1940. Pres. Am. Catholic Hist. Assn., 1922-23. Author: Lincoln's Plan of Reconstruction; Civil Government in the United States; Columbus and His Predecessors; A History of the United States for Catholic Schools; also edited and revised several works, 1901. Home: 2127 P St. N.W., Washington, D.C. Died Dec. 22, 1941.

McCHESNEY, Wilbert Renwick, coll. pres.; b. nr. Wampum, Lawrence County, Pa., July 7, 1871; A.B., Franklin (O.) Coll., 1892, A.M., 1893, Ph.D., 1908; D.D., Tarkio (Mo.) Coll., 1915; LL.D., Cedarville Coll., 1940; m. Martha Lulu Morton, July 17, 1895 (died Apr. 25, 1939); children—infant son (dec.), Robert (dec.), Frances (dec.); married 2d, Mary Ellen Turner, June 5, 1943. Began teaching at Franklin Coll., 1890; with Cedarville Coll. since 1894, pres, 1915-40, also trustee; dean Ref. Presbyn. Theol. Sem., Cedarville. Mem. 90th, 91st, 93d, 94th and 95th Gen. Assemblies, Ohio. Republican. Lecturer. Home: Cedarville, O. Died June 13, 1944.

McCLELLAN, Bryon Charles, oil exec.; b. Long Branch, N.J., Oct. 2, 1869; s. Ermonteen and Elizabeth (Pinkerton) McC.; ed. pub. schs.; m. Pearl Thornton, Sept. 26, 1904. Started as machinist, and later construction engr. and salesman; v.p. Chalmette Laundry, 1904, pres., 1916; pres. Laundry & Dry Cleaning Service, Inc., 1924, chmn. bd., 1925; chmn. bd. Shreveport Laundries, Inc., 1925; chmn. bd. Nat. Linen Service Corp., 1925; chmn. bd. Atlanta Laundries, Inc., 1925; pres. Chalmette Petroleum Corp., New Orleans, La., since 1927; treas. Union Products Co. and Rudolph Ramelli, Inc., 1927; dir. Crescent City Laundries, Inc., Shreveport Laundries, Inc., Nat. Linen Service Corp., Atlanta Laundries, Inc., Union Products Co., Rudolph Ramelli, Inc., Hibernia Nat. Bank, Standard Fruit & Steamship Co.; chmn. bd. and dir. Shreveport Laundries, Inc., Nat. Linen Service Corp.; pres. and dir. Crescent City Laundries, Inc., Chalmette Petroleum Corp.; Union Brewery, Inc.; treas. and dir. Ramelli Coal Co., Inc.; dir. Hibernia Nat. Bank, Dixie Homestead, Standard Fruit & Steamship Lines. Clubs: Metairie Golf, Colonial Country, Crescent, New Orleans Athletic. Home: 20 Audubon Pl. Office: 2207 American Bank Bldg., New Orleans, La.* Died Mar. 5, 1946.

McCLELLAND, Charles P., judge; b. Scotland, Dec. 19, 1854; s. William and Nicholas (Paul) McC.; came to the United States in 1871; LL.B., New York U., 1882; LL.D., MacMurray Coll., 1941; m. Meta Jenette Babcock, Sept. 6, 1879; children—George William, Myra Belle (Mrs. Clarence P. Fields), Rev. Clarence Paul, Meta Josephine (Mrs. Louis De Voursney Day). Practiced, N.Y. City; mem. N.Y. Assembly, 1885, 86, 91, Senate, 1892, 93, 1903; spl. dep. collector of customs, 1886-90; judge of U.S. Customs Court, by appmt. of President Roosevelt, Oct. 1903-39 and designated presiding judge, Dec. 8, 1934. Mem. Dobbs Ferry (N.Y.) Bd. of Edn. 32 yrs. (pres. 28 yrs.); mem. bd. mgrs. Poughkeepsie Hosp. for Insane, 1886-96; mem. 1st Greater New York Commn. Mem. St. Andrews Soc., Burns Soc. Democrat. Methodist. Mason. Home: Dobbs Ferry, N.Y. Office: 201 Varick St., New York, N.Y.* Died June 6, 1944.

McCLELLAND, William, bishop; b. Phila., Pa., Jan. 22, 1883; s. Alfred Lee and Marion Taylor (MacDongall) McC.; A.B., Harvard, 1911; A.M., U. of Pa., 1914; student Phila. Divinity Sch., 1911-14, D.D., 1939; m. E. Rozelle Connelly, June 16, 1914; children—William, James Alfred. Ordained P.E. Ch.; curate, St. Matthews Ch., Francisville, Phila., 1914-16; rector St. Lukes Ch., Bustleton, Phila., 1916-24; rector Dorchester Parish, Dorchester County, Md., St. Stephen's Parish, East New-Market, Md., St. Pauls Parish, Vienna, Md., 1924-39; bishop of Easton, Md., since June 2, 1939. Trustee, U. of the South. Mem. bd. Evangelical Edn. Soc. Mem. Grange. Mason. Clubs: Harvard (N.Y. City); Chesapeake Bay Yacht (Easton, Md.). Home: The Bishop's House, Easton, Md. Died April 16, 1949.

McCLENNEN, Edward Francis, lawyer; b. Passaic, N.J., Dec. 19, 1874; s. Edward Davenport and Laura Frances (White) M.; LL.B., Harvard, 1895; m. Mary Crane, Aug. 28, 1911; children—Mary (Mrs. Bernhard Knollenberg), Persis (Mrs. Chester T. Lane), Louis, Joshua, James W., Alan, Margaret L. Admitted to Mass. bar, 1896; member Warren & Brandeis, 1895-97, Brandeis, Dunbar & Nutter, 1897-1916, Dunbar, Nutter & McClennen, 1916-29, Nutter, McClennen & Fish since 1929; spl. asst. to atty. gen., U.S., 1914-23 and 1939-40; special master U.S. Supreme Court in the Lake Michigan water diversion suits, 1932-33; spl. asst. to atty. gen. U.S. in U.S. v. N.P. Ry. Co., 1939-40. Mem. The Am. Judicature Soc., Am. Law Inst., Am. Bar Assn., Mass. State Bar Assn., Bar Assn. City of Boston (v.p. 1936-39), Acad. of Polit. Science, Harvard Law Sch. Assn., Cambridge Hist. Soc., Bostonian Soc. Unitarian. Clubs: Cambridge, Union (Boston); Harvard (New York); Eastward Ho Country. Chmn. Selective Service Bd. 48, Cambridge, Mass. Home: 35 Lakeview Av., Cambridge 38, Mass. Office: 220 Devonshire St., Boston 10, Mass. Died July 2, 1948.

McCLENNY, George L., state supt. public instruction. Address: State Capitol, Topeka, Kan.* Died 1947.

McCLINTIC, George Warwick, judge; b. Pocahontas County, W.Va., Jan. 14, 1866; s. William H. and Mary (Mathews) McC.; A.B., Roanoke Coll., Salem, Va., 1883; LL.D., 1928; LL.B., U. of Va., 1886; m. Mary Ethel Knight, Oct. 17, 1907; 1 dau., Elizabeth K. Practiced at Charleston, 1888-1921; mem. Ho. of Delegates, W.Va., 1919-21; judge U.S. Dist. Court, Southern Dist., W.Va., by apptmt. of Pres. Harding, since Aug. 4, 1921. Republican. Presbyterian. Mason (K.T., Shriner); Grand Master Grand Lodge of Masons of W.Va., 1905-06. Home: 1598 Kanawha St. Office: Federal Bldg., Charleston, W.Va. Died Sep. 25, 1942.

McCLINTIC, James V., ex-congressman; b. Bremond, Tex., Sept. 8, 1878; s. G. V. and Emma C. M.; educated Adran Univ. (now Texas Christian University), Georgetown Law School. Admitted to Oklahoma bar; city clk., Snyder, Okla., later county court clk., Kiowa County; served as mem. Okla. Ho. of Rep. and Senate; mem. 64th to 73d Congresses (1915-35), 7th Okla. Dist.; now Congressional liaison official for readjustment div. of War Dept. Home: Snyder, Okla. Address: Chastleton Hotel, Washington, D.C. Died Apr. 22, 1948.

McCLINTOCK, Walter, ethnologist; b. Pittsburgh, Pa., Apr. 25, 1870; s. Oliver and Clara C. (Childs) M.; B.A., Yale, 1891, hon. M.A., 1911; unmarried. Spent 1896-1909 with Blackfeet tribe of Indians, in Mont.; adopted as son of Chief Mad Wolf and collected many valuable ethnol. materials, especially photographs, moving pictures, songs, legends, etc.; made a mem. of Blackfeet tribe by ceremonials. McClintock Peak, Glacier Nat. Park, named by nat. govt., Feb. 7, 1912. Lectured before scientific and educational institutes in U.S., Great Britain and Germany, 1907-13; fellow in ethnology, Southwest Mus. Los Angeles; curator Yale University Library. Author: The Old North Trail; Leben, Bräuche, Legenden der Schwarzfuss-Indianer; Medizinal and Nutsflanzen der Schwarzfuss-Indianer; Old Indian Trails; Tragedy of the Blackfoot; Blackfoot Culture; The Blackfoot Tipi; The Beaver Bundle; Dances of the Blackfoot; The Warrior Societies; Painted Tipis and Picture Writing; Swan Song of the Red Warrior. Contbr. to mags. Clubs: Yale Faculty, Graduate (New Haven); Yale (New York); University (Pittsburgh, Pa., and Pasadena, Calif.). Address: The Ruskin, Pittsburgh 13, Pa. Died March 24, 1949; buried Allegheny Cemetery, Pittsburgh.

McCLOSKEY, James Paul, bishop; b. Philadelphia, Pa., Dec. 9, 1870; s. Paul and Ann (Brolley) M.; student La Salle Coll., Phila., 1886-88, St. Charles Sem., Phila., 1888-98, LL.D., 1917; D.D., La Santa Sedo, Rome, Italy, 1917. Ordained priest, R.C. Ch., 1898; asst. rector, Phila., 1898-1903; sec. to bishop of Vigan and prof. and vice-rector Vigan Sem., P.I., 1903-05; rector West Conshohocken, Pa., 1905-09; sec. to vicar gen. Jaro Diocese, P.I., 1909-16; rector, Media, Pa., 1916-17; bishop Zamboanga Diocese, P.I., 1917-20, Jaro Diocese since 1920. Home: Jaro, Iloilo, P.I.* Died Apr. 9, 1945.

McCLUNG, Clarence Erwin, zoölogist; b. Clayton, Calif., Apr. 5, 1870; s. Charles Livingston and Annie Howard (Mackey) McC.; Ph.G., U. of Kan., 1892, A.B., 1896, A.M., 1898, Ph.D., 1902; grad. student, Columbia, 1897, U. of Chicago, 1899; Sc.D., U. of Pa., 1940; Franklin and Marshall College, 1941; m. Anna Adelia Drake, Aug. 31, 1899; children—Ruth, Cromwell and Della Elizabeth. Assistant professor zoölogy, U. of Kan., 1897-1900, asso. prof., 1900-06, prof., 1906-12, head of dept. and curator vertebrate paleontol. collections, 1902-12, acting dean, School of Medicine, 1902-06; prof. zoölogy and dir. zoöl. lab., U. of Pa., 1912-40, emeritus prof. since 1940; visiting prof. Keio U., Tokyo, 1933-34, U. of Ill., 1940-41; acting head zoölogy dept., Swarthmore Coll., 1943. Mem. embryol. staff, Woods Hole Mass., 1893, and since 1914 (trustee); head of scientific expdns. to Ore., Wash., Western Kan., Japan, China, Java, Ceylon, South America and South Africa. Chmn. div. biology and agr., Nat. Research Council, Washington, 1919-21 (fellowship bd.); mem. advisory bd., Wistar Inst., Morris Arboretum. Republican. Conglist. Fellow A.A.A.S. (v.p. sect. F, 1926); mem. Am. Zoöl. Soc. (pres. 1910, 14), Am. Philos. Soc., Am. Soc. Naturalists (pres. 1927), Acad. Natural Sciences (research associate), Philadelphia, National, Washington and Kansas academies of science, American Association of Anatomists, Union of American Biol. Socs. (pres. 1922-30), Sigma Xi (pres. 1919-21), Tri Beta (pres. 1936); fgn. mem. La Sociedad de Biologia de Montevideo. Author of Microscopical Technique, Chromosome Theory of Heredity (General Cytology); also tech. papers on cytology, sex-determination, paleontology, etc. Mng. editor Journal of Morphology; mem. bd. editors Acta Zoölogica, Cytologia; pres. bd. trustees (1925-33) and seci-editor Biol. Abstracts. Clubs: Cosmos, Lenape; University (Ill.). Home: Swarthmore, Pa. Died Jan. 17, 1946.

McCLURE, Martha, Rep. nat. committeewoman for Ia. Home: Mount Pleasant, Ia.* Died Aug. 18, 1945.

McCLURE, Nathaniel Fish, retired army officer; b. Crittenden, Ky., July 21, 1865; s. Ezra K. and Nannie (Dickerson) McC.; B.S., U.S. Mil. Acad., 1887; distinguished grad. Army Sch. of the Line, 1909; grad. Army Staff Coll., 1910, Army War Coll., 1917; m. Mamie Chapin, July 14, 1890. Commd. 2d lt. cav. U.S. Army, June 12, 1887, and advanced through grades to brig. gen. Nat. Army, Dec. 17, 1917-Nov. 11, 1918; brig. gen. U.S. Army, retired, June 21, 1930. In Porto Rico, 1899-1900; in Philippines, 1901-03; instr. Army Service Schs., 1913-16; campaign, Northern Mexico, 1916; comdg. Camp No. 1, St. Nazaire, France, 1917-18, Base Sect. No. 5, S.O.S., Brest, France, Feb. 3-May 13, 1918; commanded 69th Inf. Brig. for 2 mos. and 35th Div. for 5 weeks; in line of battle with Div. and Brig. for 3 mos.; duty Office Chief of Staff, Washington, D.C., 1918-19; asst. comdt. U.S. Disciplinary Barracks, Fort Leavenworth, Kan., 1920-22; with Signal Corps, 1923-26; retired as col., July 21, 1929. Mem. Mil. Order Carabao, Assn. Grads. U.S. Mil. Acad., U.S. Cav. Assn., Am. Legion, United Vets. Foreign Wars, Mil. Order World War. Democrat. Presbyterian. Clubs: Army and Navy (Washington); Sierra (San Francisco); Union League (Chicago). Author: Class of '87; United States Military Academy, 1939. Address: 2660 Woodley Road, Wardman Park Hotel, Washington, D.C. Died June 26, 1942.

McCLURE, Samuel Grant, editor, pub.; b. Wayne County, O., Aug. 9, 1863; s. Alfred and Ellen (Gailey) McC.; A.B., College of Wooster, 1886, A.M., 1889; m. Louise Truesdell, Sept. 30, 1892; children—Robert Emerson, Elinor (Mrs. Jacob Deane Funk). Began as editorial writer, later state corr. Cleveland Leader, 1887-96; pub. and gen. mgr. Ohio State Journal, Columbus, O., 1896-1906; owner and pub. Youngstown Telegram, 1906-22, Glendale (Calif.) Evening News, 1926-28; pres. So. Calif. Newspapers Associated, 1928-32; now owner and pub. Santa Monica Outlook. Mem. Metropolitan Water District Board, 1931-33, 1941-47. Dir. Mahoning County (O.) Food Conservation, World War. Dir. All-year Club. Mem. Phi Gamma Delta. Republican. Presbyterian. Mason. Home: 2101 La Mesa Drive. Office: The Outlook, Santa Monica, Calif. Died Dec. 25, 1948.

McCLURE, Samuel Sidney, editor; b. County Antrim, Ireland, Feb. 17, 1857; A.B., Knox Coll., 1882, A.M., 1887 (L.H.D., 1907); m. Harriet Hurd, Sept. 4, 1883 (died May 29, 1929). Editor and mgr. The Wheelman, for Pope Mfg. Co., 1882-83; with the De Vinne Press, New York, 1883-84; established the McClure Syndicate (1st newspaper syndicate in U.S.).

1884; founded McClure's Magazine, 1893, of which is editor. Trustee Knox Coll. since 1894. Awarded Order of Merit, Am. Acad. Arts and Letters, 1944. Clubs: Union League (N.Y.); Brit. Empire, Authors' (London); Cosmos (Washington, D.C.). Author: My Autobiography, 1914; Obstacles to Peace, 1917; The Science of Political and Industrial Self-Organization, and the Influence of Human Organization upon History, 1934; The Achievements of Liberty, 1935; What Freedom Means to Man, 1938. Has made close studies of nations and forces of modern civilization; spent 2 yrs. in Italy studying Fascism. Mem. Phi Beta Kappa. Home: Brookfield Center, Conn. Address: Union League Club, 38 E. 37th St., New York. Died March 21, 1949.

McCOLLESTER, Lee Sullivan (māk-kŏl'ĕs-tẽr), clergyman; b. Westmoreland, N.H., June 5, 1859; s. Sullivan Holman and Sophia Fanny (Knight) McC.; A.B., Tufts Coll., 1881, B.D., 1884, D.D., 1899; D.D., Meadville Theol. Sch., 1939; m. L.A. Wright, Aug. 21, 1884 (died Aug. 1, 1885); m. 2d, Lizzie S. Parker, May 1, 1889 (died Apr. 1, 1929); children—Parker, Mrs. Catherine Gallaher. Ordained Universalist ministry, 1884; pastor, Claremont Ch., 1884-88, Ch. of Our Father, Detroit, 1889-1912; dean Crane Theol. Sch., Tufts Coll., 1912-33, dean emeritus since 1933 (chaplain since 1919); acting pastor Universalist Ch., Lynn, Mass., 1927. Trustee Universalist Gen. Conv. since 1906, chmn., 1911-23, pres. 1915-19; pres. Mich. Universalist Conv., 1895-1905; librarian Universalist Historical Society (president since 1942). Trustee Buchtel College, Dean Academy. Chaplain general S.A.R., 1918-21; chaplain Michigan Society Colonial Wars; member Japan Society of Boston, Boston Browning Society (v.p. 1924), American Academy of Arts and Science, Phi Delta Theta, Phi Beta Kappa (pres. Mass. Delta 1920). Mason (32°, K.T.). Clubs: New England, University, Boston City, Puddingstone, Ministers', Twentieth Century (v.p. 1931-32), Harvard Faculty, Claremont, Country. Author: Passing of the Old Homestead; A New Emphasis on Four American Affirmations; A Revised American Creed for the College Student; "Religion, Learning and Men of the Free Spirit," Tufts Papers on Religion. Newspaper contbr. Home: 209 Broad St., Claremont, N.H.* Died Dec. 26, 1943.

McCOLLUM, Earl, newspaper publisher; b. Henry County, Ia., June 7, 1889; s. James M. and Mary Geneva (Willeford) McC.; student pub. schs.; m. Christine E. Moler, Jan. 22, 1921; children—Betty Jeane, Mary Lucille. Began as office boy, Kansas City Star, 1903; now pres. Kansas City Star Co. Mason. Club: Kansas City. Home: 1216 W. 63d Terrace. Office: Kansas City Star, Kansas City, Mo. Died Feb. 5, 1947.

McCOMBS, Carl Esselstyn (măk-kōmz), public health; b. Clayton, N.Y., Feb. 11, 1883; s. George Mason and Alice Annette (Weaver) McC.; A.B., Union Coll., Schenectady, N.Y., 1904; M.D., Cornell U. Med. Coll., 1909; m. Alice Losea, Apr. 5, 1911. House surgeon Harlem Hosp. N.Y. City, 1909-11; practiced medicine at Schenectady, 1911-12; with Bur. Municipal Research and Institute Public Adminstrn. since 1912, mgr. since 1928. Has made various state, county and municipal surveys of pub. health and welfare adminstrn., among them: states of New York, New Jersey, Delaware, Virginia, Colo., Maine, Mass., Conn., New Hampshire, R.I., S. Dakota, Oregon; cities of New York, San Francisco, Montreal, Wilmington, Pittsburgh, Denver Indianapolis, Charleston, Springfield, Rochester, Reading, New Orleans, Columbus, Providence and Newport, R.I., etc. Member research staff New York Commn. for Revision of the Tax Laws, 1933-35; mem. research staff of Westchester County (N.Y.) Commission on Government, 1934-35. Mem. advisory com. medicine and pub. health, New York World's Fair, 1939. Mem. Am. Pub. Health Assn., Am. Hospital Assn., Am. Pub. Welfare Assn., Pub. Health Assn. of N.Y. City, Phi Beta Kappa, Chi Psi, Phi Alpha Sigma. Republican. Author: City Health Administration, 1927; also spl. reports and memoranda on health, welfare and personnel adminstrn. N.Y. State and City, 1933-41. Contbr. Am. Jour. Pub. Health, Nat. Municipal Rev., Am. City, Modern Hosp. Home: Chappaqua, N.Y.; and Brookfield Center, Conn. Office: 684 Park Av., New York, N.Y. Died May 6, 1949.

McCONATHY, Osbourne (măk-kŏn'ȧ-thĭ), prof. music; b. Bullitt County, Ky., Jan. 15, 1875; s. William Jacob and Cynthia (Osbourne) McC.; ed. pub. schs.; studied music under pvt. teachers; Mus. D., Am. Conservatory Music, Chicago, 1937; m. Alice Mary Brown, July 9, 1907; children—Osbourne William, Elizabeth, James Stewart. Supervisor of music, pub. schs., Louisville, 1893-1903, Chelsea, Mass., 1903-13; prof. music methods and dir. dept. of pub. sch. and community music, Northwestern U., 1913-25; instr. at summer sessions of following univs.: Harvard, Columbia, Syracuse, Western Res., Calif. (Berkeley and Los Angeles), Southern Calif. at Los Angeles, Neb., Utah, Idaho; also Utah State Agr. Coll. (Logan, Utah), and Trenton, N.J., San Francisco, Calif., and Eastern Tenn. state teachers colleges. Editor music publs. of Silver, Burdett & Co., New York; supt. Eastern session Am. Inst. Normal Methods, Boston, since 1909. Music dir. Louisville annual music festivals, 1900-03; asso. conductor North Shore music festivals, 1914-25. Mem. N.E.A. (pres. music sect. 3 terms), Music Educators Nat. Conf. (pres. 1919; mem. ednl. council), Music Teachers Nat. Assn. (pres. 1922), Ill. State Music Teachers Assn. (pres. 1924, 25), N.Y. Southern Soc. Mem. Ky. N.G. 3 yrs. Democrat. Episcopalian. Mason. Clubs: Town Hall, Southern (New York). Co-author: The Progressive Music Series (14 books issued), 1914; Music in Secondary Schools, 1917; A Book of Choruses, 1923; The Symphony Series, 1925; The Music Hour Series, 1927; The Oxford Piano Course, 1927; An Approach to Harmony, 1927; Ditson School and Community Band Series, 1928; The Catholic Music Hour, 1929; Music in the Jr. High School, 1930; The Junior Band Series, 1931; Music of Many Lands and Peoples, 1932; Music in Rural Education, 1933; Pieces We Like to Play, 1934; Gregorian Chant Manual, 1935; Music Highways and Byways, 1936; All-Wagner Orchestra and Choral Program, 1938; Music the Universal Language, 1941; Music in the Sr. High School, 1941; Carl Fischer Piano Course, 1941; New Music Horizons, 1944. Six books and two manuals now available. Editor: The School Song Book, 1909. Home: Box 52, Pattenburg, N.J. Died April 2, 1947.

McCONAUGHY, James Lukens (mȧ-kŏn-ȧ-hē), governor; b. N.Y. City, October 21, 1887; s. James and Eleanor (Underhill) M.; B.A., Yale, 1909; M.A., Bowdoin Coll., 1911, Dartmouth Coll., 1915, Wesleyan U., 1925; Ph.D., Columbia, 1913; LL.D., Williams Coll. and Trinity Coll., 1926, Middlebury (Vt.) Coll., 1930, Dartmouth Coll., 1931, Amherst Coll., 1934, Rutgers University and Yale University, 1938, Wesleyan University, 1943; L.H.D., Muhlenberg University, 1934, Knox Coll., 1937; m. Elizabeth Townsend Rogers, June 30, 1913; children—James L., Pierce Rogers, Phoebe. Prof. edn. and English, Bowdoin, 1909-15; prof. edn., Dartmouth, 1915-18; pres. and prof. edn., Knox Coll., Galesburg, Ill., 1918-25; pres. Wesleyan University, Middletown, Conn., 1925-43. Lt. gov. State of Conn., 1939-40, gov. since 1947. President United China Relief, 1942-46. Deputy dir. Office Strategic Services, Washington, D.C., 1943-45. Chmn. Navy Civilian Adv. Com., 1946. Trustee The Northfield Schools and Vassar College, Pratt Institute. Member Association Am. Colls. (pres. 1937), N.E. Assn. of Colls. and Secondary Schools (pres. 1938). Mem. Beta Theta Pi, Phi Beta Kappa. Clubs: University, Century Assn. (New York). Republican. Conglist. Author: The School Drama, 1913. Home: Cornwall, Conn. Office: State Capitol, Hartford, Conn. Died March 7, 1948.

McCORD, Joseph, author; b. Moline, Ill., July 21, 1880; s. Joseph Smith and Sara Anna (Christy) McC.; prep. edn. Ia. City Acad., Iowa City, Ia., 1894-98; A.B., State U. of Ia., 1901; m. Clara Kingswell Wheeler, Sept. 4, 1907; 1 son, Joseph. Began as draftsman, 1901; mineral explorations, Mich. and Minn. Iron Ranges, Mich. Copper Country, 1902-11; rep. of Gulland of London, diamonds, 1911-14; steel mfg. Phila. and Baltimore, 1914-26; newspaper work with Baltimore News, Baltimore American, Baltimore Post, Brooklyn Daily Eagle, 1926-32; author since 1932. Mem. Authors Guild, Authors League of America. Republican. Mason. Author: Silver Linings, 1932; Bugles Going By, 1933; Dream's End, 1934; Dawns Delayed, Heart's Heritage, With All My Heart, 1935; One Way Street, Dotted Line Honeymoon, Magnolia Square, 1936; Flanders' Folly, The Prodigal Moll, The Return of Joan, 1937; The Piper's Tune, Redhouse on the Hill, 1938; A Husband for Hiliary, Sweet for a Season, 1939; Dreams To Mend, 1940; His Wife The Doctor, 1941; And The Walls Came Tumbling, 1941. Home: Boonsboro, Washington County, Md. Address: Care M. S. Mill, Agent, 286 5th Av., New York, N.Y. Died Jan. 27, 1943.

McCORMAC, Eugene Irving (măk-kôr'măk), coll. prof.; b. Boone County, Ill., Mar. 12, 1872; s. William H. and Catherine (Conry) M.; B.S., Upper Ia. U., 1896; Ph.D., Yale, 1901; m. Leila M. Graves, Sept. 26, 1906. Asst. prof. Am. history, 1910, asso. prof., 1914, prof. since 1919, U. of Calif. Mem. Am. Hist. Assn. Club: Faculty. Author: White Servitude in Maryland, 1904; Colonial Opposition to Imperial Authority During the French and Indian War, 1911; Two Ideals of Government in American History, 1913; James K. Polk, 1922; also lives of McLane and John Forsyth, in American Secretaries of State (Vol. IV). Home: 1404 Hawthorne Terrace, Berkeley, Calif. Died Jan. 9, 1943.

McCORMACK, Arthur Thomas, physician; b. near Howardstown, Nelson County, Ky., Aug. 21, 1872; s. Joseph N. and Corinne (Crenshaw) McC.; B.A., Ogden Coll., Bowling Green, Ky., 1892; M.D., Columbia, 1896; student U. of Va.; hon. M.A., Bethel Coll., Russellville, Ky., 1900; D.P.H., Detroit Coll. Medicine and Surgery, 1925; D.Sc., Berea (Ky.) Coll., 1926; LL.D., Transylvania U., 1930; m. Mary Moore Tyler, Dec. 15, 1897; children—Joseph Nathaniel (dec.), Lucy Norton (dec.), Arthur Thomas (dec.), Mary Wilbur; m. 2d, Mrs. Jane Teare Dahlman, Oct. 16, 1924. Began practice at Bowling Green, 1897; health officer, Warren County, Ky., 1897-1900; asst. state health officer, 1898-1912, state health commr. since 1912, also mem. Bd. of Health, Ky.; surg. gen. Ky. N.G., 1900-08; lt. Med. Reserve Corps, U.S. Army, 1911-17; maj., 1917; organized Base Hosp. No. 59, and sent by Gen. Gorgas to Panama to succeed him as chief health officer; completed building of Ancon Hosp.; controlled epidemic of cerebro-spinal meningitis on Japanese S.S. Anyo Maru and was thanked by Mikado; spl. consl. U.S.P.H.S. State flood relief dir. for 1937 flood. Founder, 1901, editor Ky. Med. Jour.; organizer and dean Sch. of Pub. Health, Ky. State Bd. Health; mem. Gorgas Memorial Inst.; mem. Nat. Health Council, Fellow Am. Coll. Surgeons; mem. and officer Am., Ky. and Jefferson County med. assns., Med. Vets. of World War (sec., ex-pres.), Assn. Mil. Surgeons, Nat. Tuberculosis Assn., Conf. of State and Provincial Health Authorities of N.A. (pres.), Ky. Conf. Social Work (pres.), Am. Pub. Health Assn. (ex-pres.), Southern Med. Assn. (ex-pres.). Democrat. Presbyterian. Mason, Odd Fellow, K.P., Elk. Author: Course in Physical Education for the Common Schools of Kentucky, 1920. Home: Brown Hotel. Office: State Board of Health, 620 S. 3d St., Louisville. Died Aug. 7, 1943; buried Fairview Cemetery, Bowling Green, Ky.

McCORMACK, John, tenor; born in Athlone, Ireland, June 14, 1884; ed. Summer Hill Coll., County Sligo, Ireland; studied voice under Signor Sabatini, Milan; Litt.D., Holy Cross Coll., Mass., 1917; m. Lily Foley, July 2, 1906; children—Cyril Patrick, Gwendolyn (Mrs. Edward Pyke), Kevin Foley (adopted). First prize at Dublin Mus. Festival, 1904; after 2 yrs. study in Italy, made London début as "Turiddu" in "Cavalleria Rusticana," Oct. 15, 1907; shortly afterwards sang in "Rigoletto" with Mme. Tetrazzini; engaged with Manhattan Opera Co., 1909, and later with Chicago-Phila. Opera Co., Chicago Grand Opera Co., Met. Opera Co., Monte Carlo Opera Co.; appeared as guest at Champs Elysees, Paris, and with Boston Grand Opera Co. Principal rôles: "Rodolfo" in "La Bohême," "Faust," "Pinkerton" in "Butterfly," "Don Ottavio" in "Don Giovanni," etc.; especially noted as concert singer. Became naturalized citizen of U.S., 1919. Knight Comdr. Order of St. Gregory the Great, and Knight Comdr. Order of Holy Sepulchre, by Pope Benedict XV, 1921; Chevalier Legion of Honor (France), 1924. Clubs: Lotos, Lambs, Columbia Yacht (New York); American, R.A.C. (London); Corinthian (Dublin). Made Freeman of City of Dublin, 1923; given title of Count by Pope Pius XI, 1928. Awarded The Laetare medal by U. of Notre Dame, 1933. Died Sept. 16, 1945.

McCORMICK, Donald, pres. Dauphin Deposit Trust Co.; b. Harrisburg, Pa., Oct. 29, 1868; s. James and Mary W. (Alricks) McC.; B.A., Yale, 1890. With Dauphin Deposit Trust Co., 1905-12; pres. Dauphin Deposit Trust Co. since 1912. Republican. Presbyn. Home: 101 N. Front St. Office: Dauphin Deposit Trust Co., 213 Market St., Harrisburg, Pa.* Died May 15, 1945.

McCORMICK, Howard, artist; b. Hillsboro, Ind., Aug. 19, 1875; s. Isaac Newton and Sarah Elizabeth (Bryce) McC.; ed. pub. schs., Newcastle and Indianapolis, Ind.; art education, Indianapolis School of Art, New York School of Art and Julian Acad., Paris, France; m. Josephine Newell, May 16, 1911; children—Newell, Sally, Nancy. Painter and wood engraver. Prin. works: Habitat Indian groups (Hopi, Apache, Navajo), Am. Museum, N.Y. City; New Jersey Indians, N.J. State Museum, Trenton; Am. Red Cross war models, at Washington, D.C., hdqrs.; Gesso painting, prize purchase, John Herron Inst., Indianapolis; mural decorations, Museum of Science and Industry, N.Y. City, and 6 murals at Trenton, also mural decorations for George W. Perkins, Riverdale, N.Y., and Frank J. Marion, Stamford, Conn.; 2 murals Library of Mayo Clinic, Rochester, Minn.; 2 murals Grammar Sch. Assembly Room, Leonia, N.J. A.N.A. (engraver), 1928. Club: Salmagundi. Home: 165 Leonia Av., Leonia, N.J. Died Oct. 13, 1943.

McCORMICK, John Francis, clergyman, educator; b. Chicago, Ill., Mar. 3, 1874; s. Patrick J. and Ann (Cranly) McC.; student St. Ignatius Coll. (Chicago), 1887-91, St. Stanislaus Sem. (Florissant, Mo.), 1891-95, St. Louis U., 1895-98, 1903-07. Teacher of classics, St. Louis U., 1898-1900, St. Mary's Coll., Kan., 1900-03; ordained priest R. C. Ch., 1906; v.p. St. Ignatius Coll., Cleveland, O., 1908-09, Marquette U., Milwaukee, Wis., 1909-11; prof. philosophy, St. Xavier Coll., Cincinnati, 1911-19; pres. Creighton U., 1919-25; head dept. of philosophy Marquette U., 1925-32; head dept. of philosophy, Loyola U., Chicago, 1932. Author: Scholastic Metaphysics, 1928, part II, 1930; St. Thomas and the Life of Learning, 1937. Address: Loyola University, Chicago, Ill. Died July 14, 1943.

McCORMICK, Vance Criswell, newspaper pub.; b. Harrisburg, Pa., June 19, 1872; s. Henry and Annie (Criswell) M.; Ph.B., Yale, 1893, M.A., 1907; LL.D., Dickinson Coll., 1934; m. Gertrude Howard Olmsted, Jan. 5, 1925. Publisher The Patriot (morning newspaper) and Evening News, Harrisburg. Mem. City Council, Harrisburg, 1900-02; mayor, 1902-05; Dem. candidate for gov. of Pa., 1914; chmn. Dem. Nat. Campaign Com., 1916. Chmn. War Trade Bd., 1917-19; mem. war mission to Great Britain and France, 1917; adviser to the President, Am. Commn. to Negotiate Peace, Paris, 1919. Dir. Federal Reserve Bank, 1916. Mem. Yale corp., 1913-36; trustee, mem. exec. com. Pa. State Coll. Mem. Delta Psi. Presbyterian. Clubs: Philadelphia (Phila.); University, Yale, St. Anthony (New York); Metropolitan (Washington, D.C.); Yeaman's Hall (Charleston, S.C.). Home: Harrisburg, Pa. Died June 16, 1946.

McCOURT, Walter Edward, geologist; b. Brooklyn, N.Y., Feb. 2, 1884; s. William Menzie and Elizabeth Wilson (McKeon) McC.; A.B., Cornell, 1904, A.M., 1905; m. Edna Wahlert, Aug. 4, 1910; 1 son, Andrew. Asst., fellow and instr. geology, Cornell U., 1902-06; instr. geology, asst. prof., asso. prof., 1906-15, prof. since 1915, dean Schs. of Engring. and Architecture, 1920-28, asst. chancellor since 1928, dean Coll. of Liberal Arts, 1931-32, 1937-39 and 1940-41, Washington University. Geologist New York State Agriculture Expt. Station, summer 1903; asst. geologist

N.Y. State Museum, summer 1904; asst. geologist, N.J. Geol. Survey, summers 1905-06; geologist Mo. Geol. Survey, summers 1910-12; prof. geology, summer sessions U. of Colo., 1913-29, and dir. U. of Colo. Mountain Lab., 1920-29; mem. bd. mgrs. Mo. Bur. of Geology and Mines, 1930-33. Fellow A.A.A.S., Geol. Soc. America; mem. Am. Inst. Mining and Metall. Engrs. (dir. 1938-1941), Soc. Econ. Geologists, Sigma Xi. Clubs: University, Noonday, Town and Gown, Round Table. Author tech. papers and repts. Home: 6228 Pershing Av. Address: Washington University, St. Louis, Mo. Died May 30, 1943.

McCOWN, Edward C., clergyman; b. Fayetteville, Tenn., Feb. 10, 1875; s. Samuel S. and Margaret Jane (Wyatt) McC.; student Muskingum Coll. (New Concord, O.), Cedarville (O.) Coll.; A.B., Westminster Coll., New Wilmington, Pa.; grad. Pittsburgh Theol. Sem., 1904; D.D., Sterling (Kan.) Coll., 1920; m. Pearl Neely, Oct. 11, 1904; children—Mary Margaret, Joseph Neely, Virginia. Ordained ministry U.P. Ch., 1904; pastor Mt. Lebanon Ch., Pittsburgh, 1904-43, pastor emeritus since 1943. Trustee Westminster Coll. Mem. Home Mission Bd., U.P. Ch., also of Evangelistic Com. and Com. on Union of All Presbyn. Bodies; elected moderator Gen. Assembly United Presbyterian Church, 1935. Republican. Home: 243 Washington Rd., South Hills Branch, Pittsburgh. Died Nov. 14, 1946; buried Mt. Lebanon Cemetery, Pittsburgh.

McCOY, Herbert Newby, chemist; b. Richmond, Ind., June 29, 1870; s. James W. and Sarah N. McC.; B.S., Purdue U., 1892; M.S., 1893, hon. D.Sc., 1938; fellow U. of Chicago, 1896-98, Ph.D., 1898; m. Ethel M. Terry, June 13, 1922. Technical chemist, Chicago, Ill., 1893-94; prof. chemistry and physics, Fargo (N.D.) Coll., 1894-96; assistant in chemistry, U. of Chicago, 1898-99; asst. prof., U. of Utah, 1899-1901; instr., 1901-03, asst. prof. chemistry, 1903-07, asso. prof., 1907-11, prof., 1911-17, U. of Chicago; sec. Carnotite Reduction Co., Chicago, 1915-17, pres., 1917-23; v.p. Lindsay Light & Chem. Co. since 1919. Mem. Am. Chem. Soc., Am. Electrochem. Soc., Am. Phys. Soc., Institute of Chem. Engrs. Awarded Willard Gibbs medal, 1937. Clubs: Quadrangle, Chemists (Chicago); Chemists (New York). Author: (with Ethel M. Terry) Introduction to General Chemistry, 1919; A Laboratory Outline of General Chemistry, 1919. Contbr. numerous papers on phys. chemistry, radioactivity and rare earths. Home: 1226 Westchester Place, Los Angles 6, Calif. Office: care Lindsay Light & Chemical Co., West Chicago, Ill. Died May 7, 1945.

McCOY, Horace Lyman, insurance; b. Portland, Ore., Feb. 5, 1888; s. Newton and Mary Frances (Lyman) McC.; student Pacific U., Forest Grove, Ore., 1907-09; A.B., U. of Washington, Seattle, Wash., 1912; LL.B., U. of Ore., 1915; m. Evelyn Elizabeth Orr, June 29, 1918; 1 son, Horace Lyman. Admitted to bar, Ore., 1915, and engaged in practice of law, Portland, Ore., 1915-18; dir. of insurance U.S. Veterans Adminstrn. since 1931. Served with U.S. Army, 1918-19; hon. disch. with rank 1st lt., Adj. Gen.'s Dept., 1919. Mem. Delta Upsilon, Phi Alpha Delta. Club: Federal. Home: 24 E. Woodbine St., Chevy Chase, Md. Office: Veterans' Administration, Washington, D.C. Died Feb. 4, 1946.

McCREA, Charles Harold, business executive; b. Logansport, Ind., Apr. 25, 1890; s. Walter and Mary Ann (Yeider) McC.; B.S., Purdue U., 1912, C.E., 1916; m. Mary Jette Edwards, Feb. 24, 1923; children—Mary Pleasants, Charles Harold, Richard Edwards. Mem. engr. corps, Pennsylvania R.R., during college vacations, 1908-12; bridge engr., Erie R.R., 1912-13; with Nat. Malleable and Steel Castings Co., Cleveland, O., since 1913, special engr., 1913-19, dist. sales mgr., 1919-30, sales mgr., 1930-37, works mgr., 1937-42, 1st vice pres., 1942, pres. and dir. since 1942; dir. and mem. exec. com. Interlake Iron Corp.; director Railway Business Association. Served as captain and adjutant, 46th Inf., 9th Div., U.S. Army, 1917-19. Dir. Malleable Founders Soc. Mem. Soc. Automotive Engrs., Am. Soc. C.E., Sigma Nu. Mason. Clubs: Union, Pepper Pike, Canterbury Golf (Cleveland); Chicago; Detroit (Mich.) Athletic; Missouri Athletic (pres. 1927; life mem.) (St. Louis). Home: 2691 Wadsworth Rd., Shaker Heights, O. Office: 10600 Quincy Av., Cleveland, Ohio. Died Aug. 24, 1946.

McCREA, Nelson Glenn, coll. prof.; b. Brooklyn, N.Y., Sept. 18, 1863; s. Robert Glenn and Mary Jane (Turner) M.; grad. Poly. Inst. Brooklyn, 1880; A.B., Columbia, 1885, A.M., 1886, Ph.D., 1888, Litt.D., 1929; unmarried. Tutorial fellow in Latin, Columbia, 1888-89, tutor in Latin, 1889-95, instr., 1895-1900, adj. prof., 1900-03, prof., 1903-11, Anthon prof. Latin lang. and lit., 1911-37, prof. emeritus in residence 1937-42; member University Council, 1931-37, chmn. Council on Research in the Humanities since 1933; annual prof., American Sch. Classical Studies in Rome (Am. Acad.), 1921-22; acting sec.-treas. Coll. Entrance Exam. Board, 1907-08 and Oct. 1915-Feb. 1916. Fellow A.A.A.S. (v.p. 1938); mem. Am. Philol. Assn., Archæol. Inst. America, Classical Assn. Atlantic States, Classical Assn. N.E., Classical Assn. Middle West and S., Brit. Classical Assn., N.Y. Classical Club (pres. 1912-14), Am. Classical League (council 1919-21), Am. Assn. Univ. Profs., Delta Upsilon; sec.-treas. Phi Beta Kappa Alumni in N.Y., 1903-21, pres. 1923-24; senator, United Chapters Phi Beta Kappa, 1925-34. Republican. Episcopalian. Clubs: Century, Columbia University. Author: Literature and Liberalism, with Other Classical Papers, 1936. Home: 430 W. 119th St., New York 27, N.Y. Died May 31, 1944.

McCREADY, Robert Thompson Miller, lawyer; b. Sewickley, Pa.; s. Robert (M.D.) and Rachel Catharine (Miller) McC.; ed. prep. dept. Allegheny Coll., Meadville, Pa., and at Ohio Wesleyan U.; A.B., Princeton, 1890; LL.B., New York Law Sch., 1893; m. Margaret Courtney, Mar. 14, 1900; children—Robert, Mary Courtney, James Miller, Margaret, Rachel Catharine. Admitted to Pa. bar, 1893, and since practiced at Pittsburgh. Mem. Am. Bar Assn., Phi Beta Kappa, Phi Delta Theta. Clubs: Keystone Athletic (Pittsburgh); Edgeworth Club; Princeton (New York). Home: Sewickley Heights, Pa. Office: Union Bank Bldg., Pittsburgh, Pa. Died Jan. 2, 1942.

McCULLOCH, Catharine Waugh (mȧ-kŭl-ŏk), lawyer; b. Ransomville, N.Y., June 4, 1862; d. Abraham Miller and Susan (Gouger) Waugh; grad. Rockford (Ill.) Coll., A.B. and A.M., 1888; LL.B., Union Coll. of Law, Chicago, 1886; LL.D., Rockford Coll., 1936; m. Frank Hathorn McCulloch, May 30, 1890; children—Hugh Waugh, Hathorn Waugh, Frank Waugh, Catherine W. McCulloch Spray. Admitted to bar, Supreme Ct. of Ill., 1886, Supreme Ct. of U.S., 1898; member of firm of McCulloch and McCulloch. Was twice elected justice of the peace, Evanston, Ill.; Democratic nominee for presidential elector, 1916; master in chancery Superior Ct. Cook County, 1917-25. Mem. bd. trustees Chicago Church Federation, Chicago Commons, Illinois Anti-Saloon League, Illinois Temperance Conference, Mem. American, Ill. State, Illinois Woman's and Chicago bar associations, Nat. Lawyer's Guild, W.C.T.U., League of Women Voters, honorary member, The Zonta, Civil Liberties Union, Woman's League for Peace and Freedom. Congregationalist. Clubs: Chicago Woman's, Woman's City, Business and Professional Woman's, Evanston Woman's, Rockford College Assns. Apptd. by Ill. Bar Assn., 1940, "senior conseller in recognition of more than 50 years hon. service at the bar." Author: (with husband) Law of Will Contests in Illinois. Home: 2236 Orrington Av., Evasnton, Ill. Office: 231 S. La Salle St., Chicago, Ill. Died Apr. 20, 1945.

McCULLOCH, Charles Alexander, officer corps.; b. Chicago, Ill., Dec. 2, 1875; s. William W. and Agnes (Alexander) McC. Circulation mgr. Chicago Evening Post, 1892-98; gen. mgr. Frank Parmelee Transfer Co., 1898-1919, pres., 1919-28; vice-pres. Yellow Cab Mfg. Company, 1918-26; chmn. bd. and treas. John R. Thompson Co. until 1932; formerly dir. of Balaban & Katz Corp., Paramount Publix Corp., First Nat. Bank of Chicago, Omnibus Corp., Chicago Motor Coach Co., Chicago, Corp.; receiver, Middle West Utilities Co.; formerly director of Commonwealth Edison Company; First Nat. Bank of Chicago; dir. and mem. exec. com. The Texas Co., trustee Field Mus. Nat. Hist.; trustee Northwestern Univ. Mason. Mem. Royal League. Clubs: Chicago Athletic, Post and Paddock; New York Athletic; Bath (Miami Beach, Fla.); Bath and Indian Creek (Miami Beach, Fla.). Home: 179 Lake Shore Drive; (winter) 21 La Gorce Circle, La Gorce Island, Miami Beach, Fla. Address: The Texas Co., 332 S. Michigan Av., Chicago, Ill. Died Jan. 24, 1946.

McCULLOCH, Frank Hathorn (mȧ-kŭl'ŏk), lawyer; b. Winnebago County, Wis., Jan. 14, 1863; s. Hathorn and Charlotte M. (Brown) McC.; desc. Hathorn McCulloch who came to U.S. in 1802, later settling in N.Y. State; ed. pub. schs.; LL.B., Union Coll. of Law, Chicago, 1886; m. Catharine G. Waugh, May 30, 1890; children—Hugh Waugh, Hathorn Waugh, Catharine M. Spray, Frank Waugh. Admitted to bar, June 1886; mem. firm McCulloch and McCulloch. Trustee Chicago Commons. Member Illinois and Chicago bar assns., National Lawyers Guild, Wisconsin Society of Chicago. Democrat. Conglist. Clubs: Union League, Congregational, Law Club (Chicago); University (Evanston). Author: (with Catharine Waugh McCulloch) Law of Will Contests in Illinois. Home: 2236 Orrington Av., Evanston, Ill. Office: 231 S. LaSalle St., Chicago. Died July 25, 1947.*

McCULLOUGH, Myrtle Reed, author; b. Chicago, Sept. 27, 1874; d. H. V. and Elizabeth A. Reed; grad. West Div. High Sch., Chicago, 1893; m. James Sydney McCullough, Oct. 22, 1906. Mem. Ill. Woman's Press Assn. Club: Little Room. Author: Love Letters of a Musician, 1899; Later Love Letters of a Musician, 1900; The Spinster Book, 1901; Lavender and Old Lace, 1902; Pickaback Songs, 1903; The Shadow of Victory, 1903; The Master's Violin, 1904; The Book of Clever Beasts, 1904; At the Sign of the Jack o' Lantern, 1905; A Spinner in the Sun, 1906; Love Affairs of Literary Men, 1907; Flower of the Dusk, 1908; Old Rose and Silver, 1909. Address: 5120 Kenmore Av., Chicago. Died Aug. 17, 1911.

McCULLOUGH, Willis, pres. Collins & Aikman Corp. Home: Stamford, Conn. Office: 200 Madison Av., New York, N.Y.* Died Dec. 7, 1948.

McCUNE, George Shannon, educator; b. Pittsburgh, Pa., Dec. 15, 1873; s. Alonzo and Vienna Catherine (Shannon) McC.; A.B., Park Coll., Parkville, Mo., 1901; A.M., Park Coll., 1903; D.D., Coe Coll., 1914; LL.D., Huron (S.D.) Coll., 1927; m. Helen Bailey McAfee, June 14, 1904; children—Anna Catherine (Mrs. B. W. Kingdon), George McAfee, Helen Margaret (Mrs. Kermit H. Jones), Shannon Bailey. Prof. Latin lang. and lit., Park Coll., 1901-02; prin. acad. and prof. edn., Coe Coll., 1902-05; supt. schs., Pyeng Yang, Korea 1905-08; pres. Union Christian Coll., Pyeng Yang, 1908-09; gen. supt. schs. of N. Korea and pres. Sin Sung Sch., 1909-21, also lecturer on religion and edn. in Korea, and lecturing in U.S.; pres. Huron Coll., 1921-27 (raised endowment to $900,000); pres. Union Christian Coll., Korea, 1927-36; mem. faculty Moody Bible Inst., Chicago, since 1937. Served as pres. Federal Council Churches in Korea and pres. Gen. Bd. Edn., Presbyn. Ch. of Korea; chmn. of com. that organized ednl. system of Korea; organizer and first pres. of Ednl. Assn. of Korea; exec. secretary Korean Nat. Christian Council; chmn. bd. Korean Nat. Christian Endeavor. Adviser to Washington Disarmament Conf.; mem. Internat. Council Y.M.C.A.; mem. Internat. Missionary Council, Jerusalem, 1928; del. to Internat. Rotary convs., St. Louis and Cleveland; pres. Assn. Colls. of S.D., 1926-27; vice moderator synod of S.D., 1926-27. Chmn. Sino-Korean League; mem. bd. dirs. Winona Assembly; pres. Union Christian Coll. Press. Mem. Internat. Lecturers' Assn., Pi Kappa Delta, Theta Alpha Phi, Pi Gamma Mu; life mem. Heijo Golf Assn. Republican. Clubs: University, Rotary. Author: Christian Psychology, 1914; The Revelation (in Korean lang.), 1916; Four Portraits of Christ (in the Korean), 1918; Solve Your Problems with Jesus, 1932; Shinto Is A Religion, 1937. Died Dec. 5, 1941.

McCUNE, Henry Long, lawyer; b. Ipava, Ill., June 28, 1862; s. Joseph L. and Martha E. (Quillin) McC.; Ill. Coll., 1877-78; B.S., U. of Ill., 1883; LL.B., Columbia, 1886; m. Helen A. McCrary, Dec. 6, 1888 (now dec.); children—Joseph McCrary, Helen Elizabeth (Mrs. Irvine O. Hockaday); m. 2d, Mrs. Marie Powers Tureman, Jan. 6, 1934. Began practice at Oswego, Kan., 1886; removed to Kansas City, Mo., 1890; mem. McCune, Caldwell & Downing; gen. counsel and dir. Prescott, Wright, Snider Co.; gen. counsel Central Surety & Ins. Corp., Kan. Gas & Electric Co.; judge Circuit Court, Kansas City, Mo., 1905-09; mem. charter com. Kansas City, 1925; mem. City Council, Kansas City, 1925-29. Mem. Bd. of Edn., Kansas City, 1910-16. Established McCune Home for Boys, Kansas City. Mem. advisory com. Kansas City "Ten-Year Public Improvement Plan." Mem. Am., Mo. State and Kansas City bar assns., Phi Beta Kappa, Sigma Chi, Phi Delta Phi. Republican. Conglist. Clubs: University, Kansas City Country. Editor: McCrary on Elections. Home: 5235 Oak St. Office: Fidelity Bank Bldg., Kansas City, Mo. Died Feb. 7, 1943.

McCUTCHEON, John Tinney, cartoonist; b. near South Raub, Tippecanoe County, Ind., May 6, 1870; s. John Barr and Clara (Glick) McC.; brother of George Barr and Ben Frederick M.; lived on farm until 1876; removed to Lafayette; B.S., Purdue, 1889, D.H.L., 1926; LL.D., Notre Dame University, 1931; D.H.L., Northwestern University, 1943; married Evelyn Shaw, Jan. 20, 1917; children—John T., Evelyn (dec.), Shaw, Barr. With Chicago Record, 1889-1901, Chicago Record-Herald, 1901-03, Chicago Tribune since July 1, 1903. His first political cartoon work was in the campaign of 1896. Started on trip around the world on dispatch boat McCulloch, in Jan. 1898; was on board that vessel during war against Spain, and in battle of Manila Bay, 1898. In 1899 made tour of spl. service in India, Burma, Siam and Cochin-China; also tour on spl. service to Northern China, Korea and Japan, returning to Philippines in Nov. for fall campaign. Attended the mil. expdns. of occupation until the following April, when he was sent to the Transvaal; joined the Boers in interest of his paper. Furnished political cartoons for Chicago Record during 1900 campaign; 5 months trip, Caucasus, Persia, Turkestan, Chinese Turkestan; on trip to Africa, hunting big game, 1909-10; contbr. articles and cartoons for Chicago Sunday Tribune; at Vera Cruz and other parts of Mexico, 1914; with Belgian and German armies, 1914; in France, Saloniki and the Balkans, 1915, 16; retired from active work April 1946. Crossed Gobi Desert, 1925; expdn. over Andes and down Amazon, 1929; crossed Atlantic (Rio to Germany) on Graf Zeppelin, 1935. Member Chicago Zoological Society; fellow Royal Geog. Soc. Clubs: Chicago, Arts, Onwentsia, Shoreacres, Commercial (Chicago); Players. Author: Stories of Filipino Warfare, 1900; Cartoons by McCutcheon, 1903; Bird Center Cartoons, 1904; The Mysterious Stranger and Other Cartoons, 1905; Congressman Pumphrey, the People's Friend, 1907; In Africa, 1910; T. R. in Cartoons, 1910; Dawson '11, Fortune Hunter, 1912; The Restless Age; An Heir at Large. Winner Pulitzer prize for cartoons, 1931. Home: 2450 Lake View Av., Chicago; (summers) 1272 Green Bay Rd., Lake Forest, Ill.; (winter) Treasure Island, Bahamas. Died June 10, 1949.

McDANIEL, Arthur Bee, army officer; b. San Antonio, Tex., Aug. 31, 1895; s. Arthur Shaw and Leila Grayson (Ervin) McD.; LL.B., U. of Tex., 1917; grad Command and Gen. Staff Sch., 1936, Army War Coll. 1939; m. Leah Glenn Burpee, Dec. 26, 1933. Commd 2d lt., U.S. Army, Aug. 15, 1917, Inf., and advanced through the grades to brig. gen., March 27, 1942 trans. to Air Corps, 1922; mem. Pan Am. Goodwil Flight through Central and S.A., 1926-27; now comdg gen. III Reconnaissance Command, Army Air Forces Decorated Distinguished Flying Cross (U.S.); Order of the Sun (Peru); Order of the Liberator (Venezuela) Order of Merit (Chile); Order of the Condor (Bolivia). Mem. Sigma Alpha Epsilon. Club: Birmingham Country. Home: 811 N. Alamo St., San Antonio Tex. Died Dec. 26, 1943.

McDANNALD, Clyde Elliott, ophthalmologist; b. Warm Springs, Va., Mar. 27, 1876; s. John P. and

Sarah H. (McClintic) McD.; student Va. Poly. Inst., 1892-94; M.D., U. Coll. of Med. (now consol. with Va. Med. Coll.), 1898; certificate, N.Y. Postgrad. Med. Sch. and Hosp., 1900; m. Evelyn Tunison, Sept. 21, 1918; children—Clyde Elliott, Ann Pettus. Interne, Va. Hosp., Richmond, 1898-99; jr., later sr. asst., Metropolitan Hosp., N.Y. City, 1900-01; staff, Bloomingdale Hosp. (psychopathic dept. N.Y. Hospital), White Plains, 1902-03, 1906-07, N.Y. Lying-In Hosp., 1903-04; interne house staff, N.Y. Eye and Ear Infirmary, 1905-08, clin. asst., 1908-11, asst. surgeon, eye division, 1911-21, surgeon since 1921, now consulting surgeon; instructor opthalmology, Bellevue Med. Coll. (New York U.), 1915-19; cons. ophthalmologist, N.Y. Lying-In Hosp., 1914-32, New York Hosp. (asso. Cornell U. Med. Sch.), since 1932; now consulting surgeon, N.Y. Polyclinic Med. Sch. and Hosp.; cons. ophthal., Park East Hosp., N.Y. Central Ry., 5th Avenue Coach Co. (all N.Y.). Served as mem. Med. Exam. Bd., Selective Service, U.S. Army, 1917-18. Fellow Am. Coll. Surg., N.Y. Acad. Med.; mem. A.M.A., Am. Acad. Ophthal. and Otolaryngology, N.Y. County and N.Y. State med. socs., N.Y. Ophthalmological Soc., Am. Ophthalmol. Soc., N.Y. Central Lines Surgeons, and to the alumni assns. of N.Y. Eye and Ear Infirmary, Metropolitan Hosp., N.Y. Lying-In Hosp. Mem. S.A.R. Mason (Shriner). Club: Virginians (N.Y. City). Home: 116 E. 63d St. Office: 100 W. 59th St., New York 19, N.Y. Died Aug. 13, 1949.

McDERMOTT, Arthur Vincent, lawyer; b. Brooklyn, N.Y., Aug. 27, 1888; s. Michael F. and Mary (Campbell) McD.; student Columbia Coll., 1906-08; LL.B., New York Law Sch., 1912; m. Genevieve Markey, June 4, 1919. Admitted to bar, 1913; engaged in general practice of law, N.Y. City, since 1913; member of firm of Burke & Burke, 72 Wall St., 1st dep. comptroller, City of N.Y., 1938-40; dir. Selective Service System, New York City, 1940-47. Judge advocate gen., N.Y. Nat. Guard, 1919-40; brig. gen. 1947; captain regimental operations officer, 106th Inf., A.E.F., World War I; recalled to active service with U.S. Army Sept. 1940. Awarded Medal of Merit, Columbia University, 1941; annual medal St. Nicholas Society of New York, 1943. Decorated Distinguished Serv. Med. (U.S.), Military Cross (Brit.), Silver Star, Purple Heart, 2 citations for gallantry (U.S.) N.Y. State Conspicuous Service Cross. Trustee Andrew Freeman Home for Aged. Mem. Brooklyn and N.Y. State bar assns., Judge Advocates Assn., Am. Legion, Mil. Order World War, N.Y. Soc. Mil. and Naval Officers, Theta Delta Chi. Republican. Clubs: Montauk, Municipal (Brooklyn); Columbia University (New York); Ship Lore and Model (Brooklyn). Home: 995 Fifth Ave. Office: 72 Wall St., New York, N.Y. Died Dec. 18, 1949.

McDONALD, Allen Colfax, ex-mayor; b. nr. Laura, O., Nov. 29, 1869; s. William and Keren H. (Burns) McD.; student Earlham Coll., Richmond, Ind., 1889-90; LL.B., Georgetown U., 1897, LL.M., 1898; m. Mary A. Murray, Aug. 3, 1893 (died June 14, 1932); 1 dau., Mary Frances (Mrs. John Hobart Sutton). Began practice at Dayton, O., 1899; dir. Dayton Morris Plan Bank. Mem. Ohio Ho. of Rep., 1901-04, 1923-26; city commr. and mayor of Dayton, 1926-33; in law practice since 1933. Republican. Presbyn. Mason, Odd Fellow, K.P., Eagle, Moose; mem. Jr. Order United Am. Mechanics. Clubs: Optimist, Triangle. Home: 1612 Grand Av. Office: Davies Bldg., Dayton, O. Died Jan. 15, 1942.

McDONALD, A(ngus) D(aniel), railway pres.; b. Oakland, Calif., Apr. 14, 1878; student U. of Notre Dame, Ind., LL.D.; m. Mary Josephine, dau. Joseph B. MacDonald. Began with accounting dept. S.P. System, Houston, Tex., Jan. 8, 1901; with same system, San Francisco, Calif., 1904-07; auditor Los Angeles Pacific Co., at Los Angeles, 1907-08, Pacific Electric Co., Los Angeles, 1908-10; auditor S.P. Co., at San Francisco, 1910-13; became dep. comptroller S.P. System, at New York, 1913, later v.p. and comptroller, vice chmn. exec. com., 1925, pres. Tex. & N.O. R.R. Co. (operating S.P. lines in Tex. and La.), 1926, duties extended to include gen. control S.P. Steamship Lines, 1929, pres. S.P. Co. since Aug. 1, 1932. Trustee U. of Notre Dame. Knight Mil. Order of Malta, 1931. Catholic. Clubs: Bohemian, Pacific Union, Pacific Ry. Club, Transportation, Olympic, Golf (San Francisco); Stock Exchange Luncheon, Traffic, Metropolitan, St. Andrews Golf (New York); Congressional Country (Washington, D.C.). Died Nov. 15, 1941.

McDONALD, Jesse Fuller, ex-governor; b. Ashtabula, O., June 30, 1858; s. Lyman M. and Caroline (Bond) McD.; ed. country dist. sch. and acad.; hon. E.M., Colo. Sch. of Mines, 1905; m. Flora Collins, Apr. 1890 (died 1918); m. 2d, Mrs. Madeline Harrington, 1924. Reared on farm; went to Leadville, Colo., 1879; practiced civ. and mining engring., 1878-88; devoted attention to own mining interests from 1888 until retired; owner Penrose and Harvard mines; was mgr. Down Town Mines Co., Leadville. Mayor of Leadville, 1899-1905; elected state senator, 1902; elected lt. gov. of Colo., Nov. 1904, and presided over Senate and joint sessions of 15th Gen. Assembly; gov. of Colo., 1905-06; chmn. Rep. State Central Com., 1910-14, and 1931-34. Mem. Am. Inst. Mining and Metall. Engrs., Colo. Mining Assn. (pres.), Am. Mining Congress (gov. Colo. Chapter). Scottish Rite Mason (32°). Home: 354 Humboldt St., Denver, Colo. Died Feb. 25, 1942

McDONALD, William James, real estate; b. Burke, N.Y., Oct. 14, 1870; s. James W. and Mary Ann (Percy) McD.; educated public school Burke, N.Y. married Maud Severance, June 7, 1891; 1 daughter, Vera M. (Mrs. Winthrop Richardson Scudder). Engaged in business as realtor, Boston, Mass., since 1894; participated in development of Park Square section of Boston, in construction of Park Square Bldg., Metropolitan Theatre and Office Bldg., and numerous other development projects in Boston; pres. and dir. Boston Port Development Co.; Motor Park Inc.; dir. East Boston Co., Eastern Shipbuilding Co. Dir. Mass. Real Estate Exchange. Mem. Maritime Assn. Chamber of Commerce, Back Bay Assn. Club: Metropolitan Driving (Boston). Home: 534 Beacon St. Office: One Court St., Boston. Died Aug. 2, 1948.

McDONOUGH, Frank Wheatley, editor; born at West Des Moines, Ia., Oct. 20, 1905; s. Stephen Joseph and Margaret (Wheatley) McD.; student Creighton U., Omaha, Neb., 1924-25; B.C.S., Drake U., 1928; m. Jane Joan Heflen, June 23, 1930; children—Frank William, Joan Marie, Stephen Joseph. Editor, Better Homes and Gardens mag. since 1938. Mem. Sigma Delta Chi. Catholic. Home: 741 55th St. Office: Meredith Publishing Co., Des Moines, Ia. Died Mar. 3, 1950.

McDOWELL, Charles Samuel, Jr., lawyer; b. Eufaula, Ala., Oct. 17, 1871; s. Charles Samuel and Maggie (McKay) M.; student U. of Ala., 1888-89; m. Caroline Dent, Oct. 15, 1902; 1 dau., Caroline Joy. Admitted to Ala. bar, 1896, and since in practice at Eufaula. Probate clerk, Barbour County, Ala., 1895-97; supt. edn., Barbour County, 1897-1901; chmn. Dem. County and mem. State Exec. Coms., 1898-99; mayor of Eufaula, 1908-12; del. Dem. Nat. Conv., 1912, 24, 36; mem. Ala. State Senate, 1919-23, 1930-34, pres., 1923; lt. gov. Ala., 1923-27. Capt. Eufaula Rifles, 1899-1903; mem. mil. staff of Govs. Samford, Jelks and Henderson, with rank of col. Trustee U. of Ala., Ala. Normal Schs., Ala. Poly. Inst. Mem. Am. Bar Assn., Ala. Bar Assn. (pres. 1915-16), Delta Kappa Epsilon, Phi Beta Kappa. Elder Presbyterian Ch.; moderator Presbyn. Synod, 1916-17. Mason, K.P., Elk, Woodman. Candidate for gov. of Ala., 1926. Bridge across Chattahoochee River at Eufaula, named "McDowell Bridge" in his honor. Home: Eufaula, Ala. Died May 22, 1943.

McDOWELL, Rachel Kollock, journalist; b. Newark, N.J., Jan. 11, 1880; d. William Osborne and Josephine Rebecca (Timanus) McDowell; ed. private, high and normal and training schs., Newark. Reporter, Newark Evening News, 1902-08; religious news editor, New York Herald, 1908-20, and New York Times, since 1920; weekly radio broadcaster, 1935-40; founded Pure Language League, Margaret Coult Memorial Assn., v.p., since 1930; held two audiences with Pius XI. Presbyterian. Mem. Daughters of Am. Women, Women's Press Club of N.Y. City, N.J. Woman's Press Club, Nat. Religious Publicity Council. Received two blessings in writing from Pope Pius XI. Presbyterian. Mem. Pen and Brush Club, D.A.R., Women's Christian Temperance Union. Author: My Audience with the Holy Father; One Woman's View; Reasons for My Faith; Pacific Presbyterianism as I Saw It. Weekly contbr. to Presbyterian; contbr. to other religious periodicals. Received citation from Nat. Council of Press Women, 1939 and 1942, from N.J. Women's Press Club, 1943. Home: Times Square Hotel. Office: The New York Times Bldg., New York, N.Y. Died Aug. 30, 1949.

McELFRESH, William Edward (măk'ĕl-frĕsh), physicist; b. Griggsville, Ill., Oct. 5, 1867; s. Greenbury Riggs and Elvira (Morgan) McE.; A.B., Ill. Coll., 1888; A.B., Harvard, 1895, A.M., 1896, Ph.D., 1900; m. Georgiana Frances Adams, June 25, 1903; 1 dau., Frances Adams (Mrs. William G. Perry). Asst. in physics, 1896-1901, Austin teaching fellow, 1901-02, Harvard; instr. physics, Radcliffe Coll., 1897-1901; instr. physics, Williams Coll., 1901-03, asst. prof., 1903-05, Thomas T. Read prof., 1905-36, prof. emeritus since 1936. Fellow A.A.A.S., Am. Physical Soc. Conglist. Author: Directions for Laboratory Work in Physics, 1906. Home: Williamstown, Mass. Died June 2, 1943: buried in Williams Coll. Cemetery.

McENERNEY, Garret William (mă-kĕn'ĕr-nĭ), lawyer; b. Napa, Calif., Feb. 17, 1865; s. John and Margaret (Gunoude) McE.; B.S., St. Mary's Coll., San Francisco, 1881; (D.C.L., Catholic U. of America, 1915); studied law at Napa, 1882-86; m. Elizabeth Hogan, Aug. 20, 1896 (died Sept. 25, 1900); m. 2d, Genevieve, d. of Will S. and Mary Josephine Armstrong Davis Green, Apr. 14, 1903 (died June 7, 1941). Practiced San Francisco since 1886; atty. for state and San Francisco bds. of health, 1896-99; counsel for U.S., representing archbishop and bishops of Calif. in arbitration between U.S. and Mexico at The Hague, in relation to the Pious Fund of the Californias, 1902; promoted passage by legislature, after San Francisco earthquake and fire, 1906, and defended validity in courts, of the "McEnerney Act" to permit owners of real property to restore their record titles which were lost by destruction of the pub. records. Regent U. of Calif. since 1901. Democrat. Catholic. Home: 1998 Broadway. Office: Hobart Bldg., San Francisco, Calif. Died Aug. 3, 1942.

McEWEN, James Henry, hosiery mfg.; b. Matthews, N.C., June 27, 1894; s. James Walter and Margaret (Freeman) M.; A.B., Davidson (N.C.) Coll., 1914; grad. student U. of N.C., 1915; m. Iris Leola Holt, Dec. 27, 1917; children—James Henry, Jr., Iris Holt. Prin. Burlington High Sch., 1915-17; supt. Star Hosiery Mills, Spartanburg, S.C., 1919-20; sec. and treas. Charlotte (N.C.) Knitting Co., 1921-24; organized McEwen Knitting Co., 1925, becoming v.p. and treas.; merged with May Hosiery Mills to form May McEwen Kaiser Co., 1940, pres. since that date; organized Grabur Silk Mills, Burlington, N.C., 1935, and Dothan (Ala.) Silk Hosiery Mills, 1938, pres. both companies; pres. Charles V. Sharpe, Inc., since 1928, Holt Bros. Knitting Company since 1929; president Sidney Knitting Mills; director Security National Bank, Graham, N.C. since 1944. Served in United States Navy, 1917-18. Pres. Elon College Foundation, Inc. since 1943; pres. Burlington Community Foundation, Inc. since 1943; dir. N.C. State Textile Foundation since 1944; mem. N.C. State Bd. of Correction and Training since 1944; trustee Elon Coll., Christian Orphanage, Elon, N.C.; treas Burlington City Library since 1932; pres. Burlington C. of C., 1934-35. Mem. Nat. Assn. Mfrs. (mem. spl. coms. on indsl. relations and edn.), Southern Hosiery Mfrs. Assn. (v.p. 1938-39; pres. 1940-41); dir. Nat. Assn. Hosiery Mfrs., 1936-40. Mem. Southern Soc. of N.Y., Am. Legion. Club: Burlington Country. Home: 907 W. Davis St, Office: May McEwen Kaiser Co., Burlington, N.C. Died Oct. 8, 1946.

McFARLAND, J(ohn) Horace, master-printer; b. McAlisterville, Juniata County, Pa., Sept. 24, 1859; s. Col. George F. and Adeline D. (Griesemer) McF.; ed. pvt. sch., Harrisburg, 1867-71; further edn. in printing office and continued pvt. reading and study; L.H.D., Dickinson Coll., 1924; m. Lydia S. Walters, May 22, 1884; children—Helen Louise, Katharine Sieg (dec.), Robert Bruce. After learning printing business, established for self, Jan. 1, 1878; moved and established Mt. Pleasant Press, 1889, inc., 1891, as J. Horace McFarland Co. of which is now pres.; also pres. McFarland Publicity Service. Printer of and contbr. to American Gardening, 1890-93; printer of and contbg. photographs and articles to Country Life in America, 1901-04, and to Country Calendar, Suburban Life and Countryside mags. during their existence. Editor "Beautiful America" dept. of the Ladies' Home Journal, 1904-07. Lecturer on civic, scenic and horticultural topics, especially on roses. Secretary Municipal League of Harrisburg, 1907-45; mem. Harrisburg Park Commn., 1905-13; pres. Harrisburg Board of Trade, 1912-13, Am. League for Civic Improvement, 1902-04, Am. Civic Assn., 1904-24, v.p. Nat. Municipal League, 1912-28. Conducted campaign for preservation Niagara Falls since 1905, for preserving and developing national parks since 1911, and for roadside development since 1925. Am. mem. Niagara Bd. of Control since 1926; apptd. by President Franklin D. Roosevelt mem. Nat. Park Trust Fund Bd., 1935. Treas. commn. on living conditions of war workers, Dept. of Labor, 1918-19; mem. com. on zoning, Dept. of Commerce, 1921-37; chmn. State Art Commn. of Pa. since 1927. Pres. Central Pa. Typothetæ, 1921-22; pres. Am. Rose Soc., 1930-32, Harrisburg Music Foundation, 1929-33; trustee Dickinson Coll. Mem. Am. Assn. Nurserymen (chmn. Am. joint com. on hort. nomenclature since 1916; chmn. com. on hort. quarantine since 1920). Garden Club of America, Royal Hort. Soc. (London), Council Pa. Hort. Soc., Am. Inst. Graphic Arts, and other tech. and philanthropic socs. Methodist. Republican. Clubs: Cosmos (Washington); Eclectic (Harrisburg). Author: Photographing Flowers and Trees, 1902; Getting Acquainted with the Trees, 1904; Laying Out the Home Grounds, 1915; My Growing Garden, 1915; The Rose in America, 1923; Modern Roses, 1930; Modern Roses II, 1940, III, 1948; Roses of the World in Color, 1936. Co-author: How to Grow Roses, 1930 (rev. 1937); What Every Rose Grower Should Know, 1931; Garden Bulbs in Color, 1938. Ed.: The Am. Rose Annual, 1916-43; The American Rose Magazine, 1933-42; Pennsylvania Gardens, 1937-38; assisted in illustrating, as well as printing, also contbr. Bailey's Standard Cyclopedia of Horticulture. Contbr. to N.Y. Times and other metropolitan dailies; also Flower Grower, Horticulture Illus., House and Garden, Farm Journal, Country Gentleman, Organic Gardening. Developed Breeze Hill Gardens for testing roses and ornamental plants from 1912; spcl. Victory garden effort from 1942. Awarded George Robert White medal of honor for horticulture by Massachusetts Hort. Soc., 1933; Am. Rose Soc. gold medal for "unstinted effort for the advancement of the rose in America," 1933; Arthur Hoyt Scott Award, for horticultural promotion, 1938; Pugsley Gold Medal Award of Am. Scenic and Hist. Preservation Soc., for Niagara protection effort, 1937; Jane Righter medal of Garden Club of America, 1942; Dean Hole Memorial medal of Nat. Rose Soc. (Eng.), 1942. Home: Breeze Hill, 2101 Bellevue Rd. Office: Mt. Pleasant Press, Harrisburg, Pa. Died Oct. 2, 1948.

McFARLAND, Joseph, pathologist; b. Phila., Pa., Feb. 9, 1868; s. Joseph and Susan E. (Grim) M.; acad. edn. Lauderbach Acad., Phila., M.D., U. of Pa., 1889, Medico-Chirurg. Coll., 1898; studied Heidelberg and Vienna, 1890, Berlin and Halle, summer of 1895, Pasteur Inst., Paris, summer of 1903; Sc.D., Ursinus Coll., Pa., 1913; m. Virginia E., d. Gen. William B. Kinsey, Sept. 14, 1892; children—Helen Josephine, Katharine A., Ruth, Joseph. Prof. pathology and bacteriology, Medico-Chirurg. Coll., 1896-1916; prof. pathology, Woman's Med. Coll. Pa., 1911-13; prof. pathology, U. of Pa., 1916-40, now emeritus; prof. gen. pathology, Temple U., Dental Sch. since 1940; visiting prof. pathology, Jefferson Med. Coll., 1943. Maj. M.C., U.S. Army; chief of lab. service, Base Hosp., Camp Beauregard, Alexandria, La., 1918, at General Hosp. 9, Lakewood, N.J., Apr.-Nov. 1918, General Hosp. 14, Ft. Oglethorpe, Ga., Nov. 1918; dir. laboratory instruction in

M.O.T.C. at Camp Greenleaf, Nov. 1918. Fellow Am. Coll. of Physicians, Coll. Physicians of Phila., A.M.A., Acad. of Natural Science Phila., Acad. of Stomatology; mem. Med. Soc. State Pa., Phila. County Med. Soc., Am. Assn. Pathologists and Bacteriologists, Soc. Clin Pathologists. Author: Pathogenic Bacteria, 9 edits., 1890-1910; Text-book of Pathology, 2 edits., 1904, 09; Biology, General and Medical, 5 edits., 1910-26; The Breast (with Dr. John B. Deaver), 1917; Fighting Foes Too Small to See, 1923; Surgical Pathology, 1924; also many contbns. to med. lit. in English and German. Home: 542 W. Hortter St., Mt. Airy, Philadelphia. Died Sept. 22, 1945; buried in Arlington National Cemtery.

McFARLANE, Arthur Emerson, author; b. Islington, Ont., Can., Feb. 25, 1876; s. Walter and Mary Ann (Johnston) M.; B.A., U. of Toronto, 1898; m. Margaret E. Hunter, Jan. 8, 1904. Mem. Delta Upsilon Frat. Contbr. to mags. Author: Redney McGaw, 1909; Great Bear Island, 1911; Behind the Bolted Door, 1915. Address: Greenwich Settlement House, New York. Died Apr. 11, 1945.

McGAVICK, Alexander Joseph (mȧ-găv'ĭk), bishop; b. Fox Lake, Ill., Aug. 22, 1863; s. James and Catherine (Watt) M.; A.M., St. Viator's Coll., Kankakee, Ill., 1887. Ordained R.C. priest, 1887; apptd. asst. pastor All Saints Ch., Chicago, 1887; apptd. pastor St. John's Ch., 1897; on account of work there, was made auxiliary bishop of Chicago, and was consecrated May 1, 1899, titular bishop of Marcopolis; apptd. pastor of Holy Angels Ch., Oakwood Blvd., Chicago, 1900; bishop of La Crosse, Wis., since Nov. 21, 1921. Author: Some Incentives to Right Living, 1909. Home: 1419 Cass St., La Crosse, Wis. Died Aug. 25, 1948

McGEOCH, John Alexander (mȧ-gē'ōō), univ. prof.; b. Argyle, N.Y., Oct. 9, 1897; s. Alexander and Agnes (Foster) McG.; A.B., Westminster Coll., New Wilmington, Pa., 1918; A.M., Colo. Coll., 1919; student U. of Calif., 1919-20, Columbia U., summer, 1921; Ph.D., U. of Chicago, 1926; hon. A.M., Wesleyan U., 1936; m. Grace Oberschelp, June 13, 1924 (died Sept. 7, 1937); m. 2d, Frances Hady, Dec. 26, 1939; step-children—Joan Hady, John Hady. Instr. in psychology, Washington U., St. Louis, 1920-22, asst. prof., 1922-26, asso. prof., 1926-28; prof. psychology, U. of Ark., 1928-30; prof. psychology and chmn. dept., U. of Mo., 1930-35, Wesleyan U., Conn., 1935-39; head dept., U. of Ia., since 1939; visiting prof., Clark U., 1936-37, Univ. of N.D., summer, 1928, U. of Ill., summer, 1930, Stanford U., summer, 1934. Served as civilian in Chem. Warfare Service, 1918. Fellow A.A.A.S. (sec. Sect. I, 1934-36; mem. council, 1939-41); mem. Am. Psychol. Assn. (mem. council, 1936-39), Midwestern Psychol. Assn. (sec.-treas. 1932-34; pres. 1935), Soc. Exptl. Psychologists, Nat. Inst. Psychology (president 1941), Am. Assn. Univ. Profs., Phi Beta Kappa, Sigma Xi. Episcopalian. Clubs: Triangle, Univ. of Iowa. Contbr. chapters in Readings in General Psychology, 1929; Psychology: A Factual Textbook, 1935; Introduction to Psychology, 1939; also to psychol. jours. Editor: Psychological Bulletin since 1935; Longmans, Green Psychology Series since 1937. Cooperating editor: Am. Journal of Psychology since 1939, Journal of Psychology since 1935. Home: 615 Templin Rd., Iowa City, Ia. Died Mar. 3, 1942.

McGIFFERT, James, prof. mathematics; b. Stockport, N.Y., June 1, 1863; s. James D. McG.; C.E., Rensselaer Poly. Inst., 1891; student Johns Hopkins, 1891-92; A.B., Harvard, 1896, A.M., 1897; Ph.D., Columbia, 1927; m. Cora Emily Medway. Instr. mathematics, Rensselaer Poly. Inst., 1892-1900, asst. prof., 1900-10, asso. prof., 1910-20, prof. since 1920, prof. of grad. mathematics since 1930, counselor and adviser of mathematics dept. since 1935. Pres. Troy Soc. for Spoken English. Mem. Am. Math. Soc., Math. Assn. of America, A.A.A.S., Sigma Xi, Tau Beta Pi, Theta Nu Epsilon. Republican. Presbyterian. Author: Plane and Solid Analytic Geometry, 1928; College Algebra, 1934; also pamphlets, Problems in Mensuration, Mathematical Short Cuts. Contbr. to math. jours. Mem. editorial bd. National Mathematics Magazine. Lecturer. Home: 169 8th St., Troy, N.Y. Died June 18, 1943.

McGIFFERT, Julian Esselstyn, mfr.; b. Greenport, N.Y., Dec. 11, 1885; s. James Brier and Clara (Esselstyn) McG.; B.A., Princeton, 1906; m. Eloise Shilton Howe, May 17, 1911; children—James Brier, Sidney (Mrs. W. W. Watt), John Ireland Howe, Barbara (Mrs. Edgar Lockwood, Jr.), Robert Carnahan. Started business career as copywriter with Frank Presbrey Co., N.Y. City, 1906-08; advt. solicitor, Town & Country, 1908-09; partner, Clarke Advt. Directorate, 1909-11; account exec. C. Ironmonger Advt. Agency, 1911-14, 1915-17; sales promotion mgr., W. A. Hathaway Co., N.Y. City, 1914-15; New York mgr. McLain-Hadden-Simpers Co., Phila. and New York, 1917-19; sec. and account exec. McLain-Simpers Orgn., later The Simpers Co., Phila., 1919-30; sales mgr. Individual Drinking Cup Co., Easton, Pa., 1930-36; v.p. and dir. Dixie-Vortex Co. (name later changed to Dixie Cup Co.), paper cups and food containers, Easton, 1936-43., pres. since 1943. Republican. Presbyterian. Clubs: Northampton County Country, Pomfret (Easton); Princeton (New York); Elm (Princeton). Home: 113 Parker Av. Office: Dixie Cup Co., Dixie Av. and 24th St., Easton, Pa. Died Dec. 24, 1947; buried Bolton Rural Cemetery, Lake George, N.Y.

McGILL, James Henry, manufacturer; b. near Hebron, Ind., Nov. 13, 1869; s. Charles A. and Mary Frances (Brownell) McG.; student Valparaiso Normal Sch. and Bus. Inst. (now Valparaiso (Ind.) Univ.), 1887-88; m. Fannie R. Skinner, Dec. 21, 1897. Owned and operated students' supply store, Valparaiso, Ind., 1888-91; in retail sales dept., Electric Supply Co., Chicago, Ill., 1891; traveling salesman for various electric supply or mfg. cos., 1895-1905; organized Northwestern Independent Telephone Co., Valparaiso, Ind., 1895, pres., 1895-1926, when company was sold to Am. Telephone and Telegraph Co.; established McGill Mfg. Co., Inc., Valparaiso, Ind., 1905, pres., 1905-40, chairman of board since 1940. Comptroller Nat. Citizens Polit. Action Com., 1944-46. Mem. Nat. Popular Govt. League (pres. since 1945), People's Lobby, (pres. since 1947). Pub. Ownership League (ex-exec. committeeman), Progressive Citizens of Am. (dir.). Home: 411 N. Washington St. Office: care McGill Mfg. Co., Valparaiso, Ind. Died Apr. 26, 1948.

McGILL, John Thomas, chemist; b. Monroe County, Tenn., Oct. 13, 1851; s. Robert and Elizabeth (Hogg) McG.; B.S., Vanderbilt U., 1879, Ph.D., 1881, Ph.G., 1882; U. of Berlin, 1885-86; m. Lizzie Allen, July 6, 1893; children—Elsa (Mrs. J. F. Daley), Allen Lenoir. Fellow, Vanderbilt U., 1879-81, instr., 1881-86, adj. prof. chemistry, 1886-1900, prof. organic chemistry and dean of the dept. of pharmacy, 1903-19, prof. organic chemistry emeritus since 1919. Fellow A.A.A.S.; mem. Am. Chem. Soc., Tenn. Hist. Soc., Phi Beta Kappa (sec. Vanderbilt Chapter since its orgn., 1901, and of the South Central District, 1925-37), president Am. Conf. Pharm. Faculties, 1907-08, Tenn. Acad. Science, 1918-19, sec.-treas., 1925-39, hon. pres. since 1939. Author: Introduction to Qualitative Chemical Analysis, 1889; Laboratory Experiments in General Chemistry, 1892; Investment in Universities (pamphlet), 1895. Report to Supreme Court U.S. in Cause State of Georgia vs. Ducktown Copper Co., 1916. Address: Vanderbilt University, Nashville, Tenn. Died Apr. 11, 1946.

McGINNIES, Joseph A.; b. Ireland, Nov. 7, 1861; s. William and Eliza (Lightbody) M.; brought to U.S. in infancy; ed. grade and high schs., Ripley, N.Y.; m. Anna B. Brockway, May 3, 1886; 1 dau., Clara Elizabeth (Mrs. Park J. Johnson). Began as clk. in pharmacy, Ripley; purchased store at 21, conducted pharmacy and gen. store 25 yrs.; sales mgr. Chautauqua and Erie Coöperative Grape Assn., Inc. Supervisor of Ripley 32 yrs.; clk. Bd. of Supervisors, Chautauqua County, 35 yrs.; mem. N.Y. Assembly since 1916 (speaker of House 10 yrs.). Trustee Chautauqua Instn., Cornell Agrl. Coll. Republican. Presbyterian. Mason (32°, K.T., Shriner); Odd Fellow, Grange, K.P. Clubs: Jamestown Automobile, Shorewood Country; National Republican (New York); Lake Placid (N.Y.) Club: Rotary. Home: Ripley, N.Y. Died Oct. 31, 1945.

McGINNIS, Felix Signoret, ry. official; b. Los Angeles, Calif., Jan. 25, 1883; s. Edward T. and Rose (Signore) McG.; ed. high sch., Los Angeles; m. Clara Leonardt, June 1917. Began as office boy Los Angeles freight office, S.P. Co., 1900; trans. to city ticket office, 1901; city passenger agt., Los Angeles, 1912-15; commercial agt., Pasadena, 1915-16; gen. passenger agt., Los Angeles, 1916-23; asst. passenger traffic mgr., Los Angeles, 1923-25, passenger traffic mgr., hdqrs. San Francisco, 1925-29—all S.P. Co.; v.p. S.P. System passenger traffic since Oct. 1, 1929, with hdqrs. at San Francisco, Calif., and Houston, Tex., having passenger jurisdiction over Pacific Lines, Tex. and N.O. Lines, S.P. Lines in Mexico and S.P. Steamship Lines; dir. S.P. Golden Gate Ferries. Republican. Catholic. Clubs: Pacific Union, Bohemian, Family, Transportation, Olympic, Commonwealth (San Francisco); California, Los Angeles Turf, Inc. (dir.), Los Angeles Country (Los Angeles); Menlo Circus (Menlo Park, Calif.); Menlo Country (Atherton, Calif.). Home: 2150 Washington St., San Francisco; and "Fair Winds," Menlo Park, Calif.; (summer) Brockway, Lake Tahoe, Calif. Office: 65 Market St., San Francisco, Calif.* Died Mar. 17, 1945.

McGLACHLIN, Edward Fenton (măk-glăk'lĭn), army officer; b. Fond du Lac, Wis., June 9, 1868; s. Edward Fenton and Mary Eliza (Lawrence) McG.; grad. U.S. Mil. Acad., 1889; course in submarine mining Engr. Sch. of Application, 1893; Arty. Sch., 1896; Sch. of Fire for Field Arty., 1912; Field Officers' Course, Army Service Schs., 1916; Army War Coll., 1917, 22; m. Louisa Harrison Chew, Nov. 26, 1892; children—Fenton Harrison (dec.), Helen Olcott (wife of John E. Hatch, U.S. Army), Elizabeth (wife of Joseph C. Odell, U.S. Army). Additional 2d lt. 3d Arty., June 12, 1889; promoted through grades to col., July 1, 1916, 8th and 10th Field Arty.; brig. gen. N.A., Aug. 5, 1917; maj. gen., Apr. 12, 1918; permanent brig. gen., Jan. 13, 1920; maj. gen., Apr. 1, 1922. Spl. mention for gallantry, Battle of Bud Dajo, Jolo, P.I., 1906; comdr. Recruit Depot, Ft. McDowell, Calif., 1909-11; commandant Sch. of Fire for Field Arty., 1914-16; comdr. 165th F.A. Brig. (90th Div.), Aug.-Dec. 1917, 57th F.A. Brig. (32d Div.), Dec. 1917-Mar. 1918, 66th F.A. Brig. and chief of arty., 1st Army Corps, Mar.-May 1918; comdr. army arty. and chief of arty., 1st Army, May-Nov. 1918; comdr. 1st Div., Nov. 19, 1918-Sept. 30, 1919, 7th Div., Sept. 30, 1919-June 30, 1921; comdt. Army War Coll., July 13, 1921-June 30, 1923; retired Nov. 2, 1923. Awarded D.S.M., silver star. Comdr. Legion of Honor; Croix de Guerre. Club: Army and Navy (Washington). Address: Army and Navy Club, Washington, D.C. Died Nov. 9, 1946.

McGOVERN, Francis Edward, ex-governor; b. near Elkhart, Wis., Jan. 21, 1866; s. Lawrence and Ellen (Wren) M.; B.L., U. of Wis., 1890; unmarried. Prin. and supt. schs., Brodhead, Wis., 1890-93; prin. High Sch., Appleton, Wis., 1893-97; admitted to bar, 1897, and practiced at Milwaukee. First asst. dist. atty., Milwaukee County, 1901-05; dist. atty., 1905-09; governor of Wis., 2 terms, 1911-15, 1913-15. Commd. maj. U.S.A., Aug. 12, 1918; judge adv. 18th Div., then at Camp Travis, Tex., and Camp Grant, Ill.; promoted to rank of lt. col., June 12, 1919; discharged, Feb. 2, 1920, to accept apptmt. as gen. counsel U.S. Shipping Bd. and Emergency Fleet Corp., Washington; resigned, June 15, 1920, to resume practice of law. Mem. Wis. bar assn., Milwaukee Bar Assn. (pres. 1923), Phi Beta Kappa. Former trustee and dir. Milwaukee Art Inst.; pres. Milwaukee Seven Arts Soc.; dir. Wis. Conf. Social Work of Wis. Assn. for Disabled, County Chapter Am. Red Cross; dist. comdr. Am. Legion (Wis. Dept.); mem. Mil. Order Foreign Wars. Mason (32°). Clubs: City, Milwaukee Athletic, Kiwanis (hon.). Home: 2333 North 56th St. Office: 108 West Wells Street, Milwaukee, Wis. Died May 16, 1946.

McGOVNEY, Dudley Odell (mȧ-gŭv'nē), prof. law; b. Huntington, Ind., June 23, 1877; s. Samuel Taylor and Florence Louisa (Wright) M.; A.B., Ind. U., 1901; A.M., Harvard, 1904; LL.B., Columbia, 1907; m. Laura Woodburn, Apr. 22, 1902; children—Richard Burritt, Margarita, Ruth. Instr. govt., Insular Normal Sch., Manila, P.I., 1901-03; instr. polit. science, Ind. U., summer, 1907; instr. law, U. of Ill., 1907-08; prof. law, 1908-14, dean law dept., 1913-14, Tulane U.; prof. law, U. of Mo., 1914-16; dean Coll. of Law, State U. of Ia., 1916-21, prof. of law, 1921-25, State U. of Ia.; prof. law, Sch. of Jurisprudence of Calif., 1925-47, prof. emeritus, 1947; prof. of law Hastings College of Law, U. of Calif., San Francisco, since 1947. Formerly lecturer summer sessions law depts. of Columbia U. and univs. of Chicago, Wis. and Mich.; visiting prof. law, Yale U. Sch. of Law, 1927-28. Corporal Co. H, 159th Ind. Vols., Spanish-Am. War. Mem. Assn. Am. Law Schs. (exec. com., 1912-15), Phi Beta Kappa, Sigma Chi, Phi Delta Phi, Order of the Coif. Mem. Conf. on Law of Contracts and of the Law of Corps., Am. Law Inst. Author: Civil Government in the Philippines, 1903; Stories of Long Ago in the Philippines, 1906; Cases on Constitutional Law, 1929 (2d edit. 1935, with supplement, 1946); The American Suffrage Medley (published posthumously), 1949. Contributor on legal topics. Home: 1598 Le Roy Av., Berkeley 8, Calif. Died Oct. 16, 1947.

McGOWEN, James Greer (mȧ-gou'ĕn), judge; b. Nesbitt, Miss., Sept. 19, 1870; s. James Greer and Mary (Dean) McG.; student U. of Miss. 1 yr.; course at business coll.; m. Lucia Lamar Richmond, Nov. 8, 1893. Admitted to Miss. bar, and began practice at Water Valley; mem. Miss. Ho. of Rep., 1904-08; city atty. Water Valley, 1906-13; chancellor 3d Dist. of Miss.; 1913-25; asso. justice Supreme Court of Miss. since Jan. 5, 1925, reëlected, 1932, for term ending Jan. 1, 1941. Mem. bd. trustees Grenada (Miss.) Coll. since 1915; trustee, Millsaps Coll., Jackson, Miss. Mem. M.E. Ch., S.; del. Gen. Conf., 7 times, 1914-34; del. to Ecumenical Conf. World Methodism, Atlanta, Ga., 1932; mem. Commn. on Unification of Chs., North and South, 1916-20; del. Uniting Conf. Methodists, 1939; del. Gen. Conf. Southeastern Jurisdiction Meth. Ch., Asheville, N.C., 1940; chmn. com. Am. Bar Assn. to study federal legislation as related to liberties of Am. citizens. Mason (K.T.), Odd Fellow, K.P., Woodman, Maccabee. Address: New Capitol, Jackson, Miss.* Died 1941.

McGRAW, James H., publisher; b. Panama, Chautauqua County, N.Y., Dec. 17, 1860; grad. (valedictorian), State Normal Sch., Fredonia, N.Y., 1884; m. Mildred F. Whittlesey, 1887; children—Harold W., James H., Curtis W., Donald C., Mrs. John E. Osmun. Taught dist. sch. at 18; taught sch. at Corfu, N.Y.; entered pub. business, 1885, with Am. Ry. Pub. Co. Hon. chmn. McGraw-Hill Pub. Co., Inc.; chmn. McGraw-Hill Co. of Calif. Mem. Am. Soc. Mech. Engrs., Internat. Benjamin Franklin Soc., English Speaking Union, Illuminating Engring. Soc., Acad. of Polit. Science, Am. Transit Assn., Elec. and Gas Assn. of N.Y., Nat. Geographic Soc., Elec. Club of San Francisco. Clubs: Engineers, Railroad, Republican, Union League (New York). Office: 330 W. 42d St., New York. Died Feb. 21, 1948.

McGREGOR, Robert Gardner, clergyman; b. Glasgow, Scotland, Nov. 30, 1870; s. Robert Gardner and Marion (Dickson) McG.; brought to U.S., 1872, naturalized, 1892; A.B., Hamilton Coll., 1897, A.M., 1900, D.D., 1912; student Columbia, 1898-99; B.D., Union. Theol. Sem., New York, 1900; m. Lena Lydia Miller, Oct. 25, 1902; children—Louise (Mrs. Geoffrey John Hamilton), Robert Gardner, Jr., Rumsey Miller, Janet (Mrs. Talbot Curtin). Ordained to ministry of Presbyn. Ch., 1900; Master, Hill Sch., Pottstown, Pa., 1900-01; pastor St. Cloud Presbyn. Ch., Orange, N.J., 1901-06, North Av. Presbyn. Ch., New Rochelle, N.Y., 1906-40, pastor emeritus since 1940; interim pastor, Westminster Presbyterian Church, Lincoln, Nebraska, since 1943. Member New Rochelle Board of Education, 1908-14; member Foreign Missionary Board, Presbyterian Church U.S.A., 1917-43. Religious sec. in various camps in World War, 1918. Director of The Central National Bank, New Rochelle, N.Y., 1922-37. Trustee Hamilton College since 1910. Member Alpha Delta Phi. Republican. Club: Wykagyl Country (New Rochelle); Lake Placid Club. Author: Modern Missions in Chile and Brazil (with others), 1926. Home: Lake Placid Club, N.Y. Deceased.

McGROARTY, John Steven (má-grōr'tĭ), ex-congressman, author; b. Luzerne County, Pa., Aug. 20, 1862; s. Hugh and Mary M. McG.; ed. Harry Hillman Acad., Wilkes-Barre, Pa.; Litt.D., U. of Calif., 1925; LL.D., U. of Santa Clara, 1927; m. Ida Lubrecht, Nov. 19, 1890. Treas. Luzerne County, Pa., 1890-93; admitted to bar, 1894, and practiced 2 yrs.; left Pa., 1896, and settled in Los Angeles, 1901; mem. 74th and 75th Congresses (1935-39), 11th Calif. Dist. Author: Poets and Poetry of Wyoming Valley, 1885; Just California, 1903; Wander Songs, 1908; The King's Highway, 1909; California—Its History and Romance, 1911; The Mission Play, 1911; La Golondrina (a drama of Calif.), 1923; Osceola (drama), 1927; Babylon (drama), 1927. Elected poet laureate of Calif. by State Legislature, 1933. Home: Tujunga, Calif. Died Aug. 7, 1944.

McGUGIN, Harold (má-gŭg'ĭn), ex-congressman; b. Liberty, Kan., Nov. 22, 1893; s. William and Caroline (Bickell) McG.; student Washburn Law Sch., Topeka, Kan., 1912-14; grad. study, Inns of Court, London, Eng., 1919; m. Nell Bird, Feb. 27, 1921. In practice of law at Coffeyville, Kan., since 1914. Served as 2d lt., Adj. General's Office, U.S. Army, in France, February 1917-July 1919; now lt. col. A. C., Military Government France. Mem. Kansas House of Rep., 1927 (author of bill repealing Kan. anticigarette law); mem. 72d and 73d Congresses (1931-35), 3d Kan. Dist. Mem. Am. Legion. Republican. Mason, Odd Fellow. Home: Coffeyville, Kan. Died Mar. 7, 1946.

McGUIRE, John A. (má-gwīr), editor, pub.; b. Warren County, Ia., Apr. 20, 1869; s. Michael and Mary (McGonigle) McG.; ed. pub. schs.; m. Eleanor Youngblodt, Nov. 27, 1896; children—Mrs. Gertrude Foy, Harry Aloysius; m. 2d, Dooie Lena Carper, July 31, 1909; 1 dau., Virginia Mae. Began learning printing trade at 13; founder, Cycling West (mag.), Denver, Colo., and pub., 1893-98; founder, 1898, owner and editor until 1931, Outdoor Life Magazine; formerly pres. and mgr. McGuire Printing Co. Pres. for Colorado of Liberty Highway. Member American Museum Natural History, Colorado Museum Natural History (Trustee), Quetico-Superior Council (mem. advisory board), Nat. Econ. League (Nat. Council). Catholic. Clubs: Campfire (Chicago); Boone and Crockett (New York). Engaged in 22 big game hunting and scientific collecting expdns.; species of caribou (Rangifer mcguirei) and a sailfish of Fla. waters (Istiophorus mcguirei) named in his honor; pioneer in idea of giving protection to bears of U.S. Author: In the Alaska-Yukon Gamelands, 1920. Home: 173 N. N. Mansfield Av., Los Angeles, Calif. Died Feb. 28, 1942.

McGUIRE, Joseph Hubert, architect; b. N.Y. City, Jan. 21, 1865; s. Joseph and Catharine (Rorke) McG.; ed. City Coll. and St. F. Xaviers Coll., 1882-85, Met. Art Schs., 1886-88, École des Beaux Art, Paris, 1888-91; m. Harriet Mein, June 7, 1899; children—Joseph Mein, Hubert Amer (dec.), Alan Steel, Catharine (Mrs. Charles G. Reichert). Practiced in New York City since 1892. Designer of Catholic Cathedral, Richmond, Va.; Holy Trinity Church and St. Rose of Lima Church, New York City; St. Elizabeth's Hospital, New York City; also schs., pvt. residences, etc. Served in France as Sec. Knights of Columbus 9 mos., World War. Former mem. Bd. of Edn., New Rochelle, N.Y. Mem. Am. Inst. Architects, and New York Chapter same, Soc. of Beaux-Arts Architects, U.S. Catholic Hist. Soc., Friendly Sons of St. Patrick. Ind. Democrat. Clubs: Centre, Catholic (New York); Wykagyl Country (New Rochelle, N.Y.). Wrote: (brochures) Let's Go, 1919; Freezing with the Turks, 1931; Before the Gay Nineties, 1932; etc. Home: 124 Pelhamdale Av., Pelham, N.Y.; and Southampton, L.I., N.Y. Died Apr. 28, 1947.

McGUIRE, Murray Mason, lawyer; b. Richmond, Va., Jan. 19, 1872; s. John Peyton and Clara Forsythe (Mason) McG.; student U. of Va., 1890-93 and 1895-96 (law session); m. Mary Van Benthuysen, June 14, 1894 (died 1939); married 2d, Mrs. Mayo Cabell (nee Clara Winston Cabell), March 14, 1942. Teacher, St. Alban's School, Radford, Virginia, 1893-95, McGuire's University School, Richmond, (part time) 1896-98; admitted to Virginia Bar, 1896, and since in practice at Richmond; partner McGuire, Riely, Eggleston & Bocock. Mem. bd. of trustees, Episcopal Theol. Sem., Alexandria, Va.; member advisory committee to board regents Gunston Hall; member City of Richmond, Virginia, State and American bar assns., American Law Inst., N.Y. Southern Soc., Assn. for Preservation of Va. Antiquities (advisory com.), Va. Hist. Soc., Soc. of The Virginians (N.Y. City), Soc. of Colonial Wars in the State of Va., Delta Kappa Epsilon, Phi Delta Phi, Phi Beta Kappa. Democrat. Episcopalian. Clubs: Colonnade (U. of Va.); Commonwealth (Richmond); Farmington Country (Charlottesville, Va.). Home: Prestwould Apts. Office: Mutual Bldg., Richmond, Va. Died Sep. 10, 1945.

McGUIRE, Stuart, surgeon; b. Staunton, Va., Sept. 16, 1867; s. Hunter Holmes (M.D., LL.D.) and Mary (Stuart) McG.; Richmond Coll.; M.D., U. of Va., 1891; LL.D., Richmond Coll., 1916; m. Ruth I. Robertson, Aug. 1919. Ex-pres. Med. Coll. of Va.; surgeon in charge, St. Luke's Hosp.; cons. surgeon Med. Coll. Hospital. Lt. col., M.C., U.S. Army, comdg. officer Base Hosp. 45, A.E.F.; retired as colonel, World War I. Ex-president Richmond Acad. Medicine, Medical Soc. of Virginia, Tri-State Med. Assn., Southern Surg. and Gynecol. Assn., Southern Med. Association; member Phi Beta Kappa. Phi Kappa Sigma, Alpha Omega Alpha. Awarded D.S.M. (U.S.); Medal of Honor (France). Clubs: Westmoreland, Commonwealth. Author: Principles of Surgery, 1908; The Profit and Loss Account of Modern Medicine, 1915. Address: 2304 Monument Av., Richmond, Va. Died Oct. 27, 1948.

McHANEY, Edgar La Fayette, judge; b. Gibson, Tenn., Nov. 6, 1876; s. William W. and Mary Ellen McH.; A.B., Southern Normal U., Huntington, Tenn., 1899; LL.B., U. of Ark., 1904; m. Gail Myers, Apr. 20, 1904; children—Miriam Ellen, Virginia, Edwin L., Gailon Myers, James Monroe, Betty Ann. Supt. schs., De Witt, Ark., 2 yrs. Piggott, 1 yr.; settled in Little Rock, 1902; dep. sec. of state, Ark., 1902-08; admitted to Ark. bar, 1904; mem. Ark. Ho. of Rep., 1921; apptd. asso. justice Supreme Court of Ark., Feb. 12, 1927, for term ending Jan. 1, 1930; elected, 1928, present term expires 1955. Democrat. Baptist. Mason. Club: Little Rock Country. Home: 3003 Arch St. Address: State Capitol, Little Rock, Ark. Died May 24, 1948.

McHUGH, John, banker; b. Belleville, Ont., Can., Aug. 29, 1865; ed. pub. schs. Came to U.S., 1891; formerly pres. First Nat. Bank, Sioux City, Ia.; formerly chmn. bd. Discount Corp. of New York; formerly chmn. exec. com. Chase Nat. Bank of City of New York; dir. and mem. exec. com. Air Reduction Co., Am. Express Co., Am. Express Co., Inc., Technicolor, Inc., Technicolor Motion Picture Corp.; dir. Congoleum-Nairn, Inc. Club: Union League. Home: Chappaqua, N.Y. Died Aug. 1, 1948.

McILHENNY, Edward Avery; b. Avery Island, La., Mar. 29, 1872; s. Edmund and Mary Eliza (Avery) McI.; student Wyman's Inst., Alton, Ill., 1885-87, Holbrook Sch., Ossining, N.Y., 1887-90, Lehigh U., 1890-92; m. Mary Matthews, June 9, 1900; children—Rosemary (Mrs. Harold Gray Osborn), Pauline (Mrs. Fisher Edward Sammons), Leila (Mrs. Alfred Whitney Brown). Pres. McIlhenny Co., Petite Co., Jungle Gardens, Inc., Jan Jean Lafitte Co. Mem. Nat. Assn. Audubon Socs., Am. Game Protective Soc., Am. Geog. Soc., Am. Mus. Natural History, Am. Ornithologists' Union, Am. Genetic Soc., Am. Soc. Mammalogists, Game Conservation Soc., The Agassiz Assn., Hort. Soc. of N.Y., Fla. State Hort. Soc., Philharmonic Soc. (New Orleans, La.), Washington (D.C.) Biol. Soc., Phi Delta Theta. Clubs: Arctic, Explorers' (New York); Boston (New Orleans, La.); Camp Fire (Chicago, Ill.). Naturalist Peary Relief Expdn., 1893; head own Arctic expdn., 1897-99; big game hunter. Propr. game refuge housing many species of animals, songbirds and waterfowl, exptl. gardens testing and propagating imported plants. Has written much on subjects of game hunting and exploration. Address: Avery Island, La. Died Aug. 8, 1949.

McILVAINE, William Brown, lawyer; b. Peoria, Ill.; s. George H. and Priscilla J. (McClure) McI.; A.B., Princeton, 1885, A.M., 1888; m. Julia LeMoyne, Oct. 1891; children—Romaine LeMoyne (Mrs. Blanchard Randall, Jr.), Madeleine LeMoyne (Mrs. David B. McDougal), Priscilla (Mrs. Benjamin H. Brewster, III), William B. Read law in offices of John P. Wilson and Nathan G. Moore; admitted to bar, 1888; mem. firm of Wilson & McIlvaine. Mem. Am., Ill. State and Chicago bar assns., Chicago Law Inst., Art Inst. Chicago (life), Field Museum of Natural History (life). Republican. Vestryman Christ Ch., Winnetka, Ill. Clubs: University, Law, Indian Hill. Home: 1029 Green Bay Rd., Winnetka, Ill. Office: 120 W. Adams St., Chicago, Ill. Died May 6, 1943.

McINTOSH, Burr (William), lecturer, actor; born Wellsville, O., 1862; ed. Lafayette Coll., 1880-82, Princeton, 1882-83. Engaged in coal bus., Pittsburgh, 1884; reporter Phila. News, 1884-45. Debut on stage, Bartley Campbell's "Paquita," N.Y. City, Aug. 31, 1885; appeared in numerous plays; original "Taffy" in "Trilby," 1895; rep. Leslie's Weekly and syndicate, Spanish-Am. War, Cuba, 1898; started Burr McIntosh Studio, N.Y. City, 1900, and Burr McIntosh Monthly, Apr. 1902; official photographer Taft Philippine expdn., 1905; toured U.S. in "The Gentleman from Mississippi," 1909; lecture tour, patriotic topics, 1917; Y.M.C.A. entertainer, France and Germany, 1918-19. Syndicate corr.; lecturer. Author: The Little I Saw of Cuba, 1898. Home: New York City. Died Apr. 28, 1942.

McINTOSH, Walter Kenneth, corp. exec.; b. Burlington, Ia., Mar. 14, 1878; s. John Finley and Minnie I. (Fleming) McI.; LL.B., Chicago-Kent Coll. Law, 1903; m. Mary Josephine Kasper, Sept. 28, 1940; children—Mary Retlaw, Peter. Stenographer with The Liquid-Carbonic Corp., 1902, pres., 1923-29, chmn., 1929-47, chmn. bd. dirs. since Jan. 1947. Admitted to Ill. bar, 1903. Mem. Delta Chi. Club: Union League. Home: 521 N. Euclid Av., Oak Park, Ill. Office: 31st St. and Kedzie Av., Chicago. Deceased.

McINTOSH, William M., Publisher; b. Stratford, Ont., Mar. 13, 1876; s. David and Isabella (McKay) McI.; m. Clara Edith Mason, Oct. 19, 1907. Began on The Beacon, Stratford, Ont., 1892; successively advertising dir. on Cincinnati Post, business mgr. Kentucky Post (Covington), business mgr. Fort Worth Press, gen. mgr. Fort Worth Record; editor and pub. San Antonio Light since 1924. Mem. Nat. Council Boy Scouts of America; received Silver Beaver award. Mem. San Antonio Petroleum Club, San Antonio Country Club (bd. govs.), Rotary Club. Presbyterian. Mason (33°, K.T., Shriner, Knight Red Cross of Constantine). Mem. Order of the Alamo, Circus Fans Assn., of America; Texas Newspaper Publishers Assn., Texas Press Assn. Chamber of Commerce (dir.). Address: San Antonio Light, San Antonio, Tex. Died July 29, 1946.

McINTYRE, Alfred Robert (măk'ĭn-tīr), publisher; b. Hyde Park, Mass., Aug. 22, 1886; s. James W. and Harriette Frances (Bradt) McI.; A.B., Harvard, 1907; m. Helen Palmer Horner, Apr. 11, 1923; children—Henry Pierre, Ann Elizabeth. With Little, Brown & Co., Boston, since 1907, became partner, 1911, v.p. and gen. mgr., 1913, pres. since 1926. Pvt. U.S. Inf., Sept. 1917, later regtl. sergt. 301st Inf., with service in France. V.p. Nat. Assn. Book Publishers, 1921-22 and 1925-28. Director Grosset & Dunlap and Bantam Books (N.Y.). Club: Somerset, Union, St. Botolph (Boston); Century, University (N.Y.); York Harbor Reading Room, York Colf and Tennis (York, Me.). Home: 13 Louisburg Sq. Office: 34 Beacon St., Boston, Mass. Died Nov. 28, 1948.

McINTYRE, Frank, army officer; b. Montgomery, Ala., Jan. 5, 1865; s. Denis and Mary (Gaughan) McI.; student U. of Ala., 1880-82; grad. U.S. Mil. Acad., 1886; U.S. Inf. and Cav. Sch., 1887-89; m. Marie Dennett, July 12, 1892; children—James Dennett, Frank (dec.), Edward, Marie Dufilho, Margaret Dennett (dec.), Nora. Commd. 2d lt., July 1, 1886; promoted through grades to brig. general, chief Bur. of Insular Affairs, Aug. 24, 1912; maj. gen. (temp.), Oct. 6, 1917. Served on Rio Grande River and various stations in Texas; instr. mathematics, West Point, 1890-94; at Ft. Wayne, Mich., 1894-98; comd. co. in Porto Rican expdn., 1898; in P.R. on staff of Gen. Guy V. Henry until 1899; in P.I., 1899-1902; mem. gen. staff, 1903-05; with Bur. Insular Affairs since 1905, chief, Aug. 24, 1912-July 10, 1918; asst. chief of staff, July 10, 1918-Dec. 31, 1919; again chief Bur. Insular Affairs, Jan. 1, 1920-Jan. 5, 1929; maj. gen. regular army, Aug. 17, 1928, with rank from Oct. 6, 1917; retired Jan. 5, 1929. Awarded D.S.M., Feb. 13, 1919, "for exceptionally meritorious and conspicuous service to U.S. Government"; Comdr. Legion of Honor, France, 1919; Knight Commander of the Bath, Great Britain, 1919; Czecho-Slovak war cross, 1919; Grand Cordon of the Striped Tiger, China, 1919. Catholic. Clubs: Army and Navy (Washington and New York). Home: 1615 S. Hull St., Montgomery, Ala. Died Feb. 16, 1944.

McINTYRE, Marvin Hunter, sec. to the President; b. LaGrange, Ky., Nov. 27, 1878; s. Thomas Jackson and Margaret Hunter (Poynter) McI.; student Vanderbilt U.; m. Gertrude Kennedy, 1910; children—Marie (Mrs. Frederick Hayes Warren, 2d), Logan Kennedy. With railroad cos. and with banking firms, 1901-08; in newspaper work, 1908-18; spl. asst. to Sec. of Navy in charge pub. relations, 1918-22; Washington rep. motion picture newsreel cos., 1922-32; business mgr. and publicity rep. Gov. Roosevelt's Presidential campaign, 1932; mem. secretariat of President Roosevelt since 1933. Mem. Sigma Chi. Democrat. Methodist. Clubs: National Press, Columbia Country, Washington Country, Army and Navy Country, Burning Tree. Home: 3106 34th St. Address: White House, Washington, D.C. Died Dec. 13, 1943.

McINTYRE, William H., capitalist; b. New York, Jan. 7, 1865; ed. pub. schs. Since leaving school has been connected with Equitable Life Assurance Soc. of U.S., becoming 4th v.p. and dir. Trustee and v.p. Mercantile Safe Deposit Co.; pres. San Antonio & Aransas Pass Ry.; dir. Brooklyn City and Newtown R.R., Casualty Co. of Am., Coney Island & Brooklyn R.R., Conried Met. Opera Co., Fidelity Trust Co. of Newark, Mo. Safe Deposit Co. (St. Louis), Security Safe Deposit Co. (Boston), Union Nat. Bank (Newark), Mercantile Burglar Alarm Co. Address: 120 Broadway, New York. Died Sept. 9, 1947.

McKAY, Claude, writer; b. Sunny Ville, Jamaica, W.I., Sept. 15, 1890; s. Thomas Francis and Ann Elizabeth (Edwards) McK.; student Tuskegee (Ala.) Normal and Industrial Inst., 1912, Kan. State Coll., 1912-14. Came to U.S., 1912. Worked as waiter and porter, 1915-18; asso. editor and contbr. Liberator mag., 1919-22. Author: Songs of Jamaica, 1911; Constab Ballads, 1912; Spring in New Hampshire, 1920; Harlem Shadows, 1922; Home to Harlem, 1927; Banjo, 1929; Gingertown, 1931; Banana Bottom, 1933; A Long Way From Home (a travel autobiography), 1937; Harlem: Negro Metropolis, 1940. Died May 22, 1948.

McKAY, Kenneth Ivor (măk-kā'), lawyer; b. Tampa, Fla., Jan. 21, 1881; s. John Angus and Mary Jane (McCarty) McK.; student Tampa Business Coll., 1898-99; LL.B., Washington and Lee U., Lexington, Va., 1904; m. Olive Petty, Nov. 21, 1917; children—Kenneth Ivor, Shirley Louise, Herbert Gifford, Howell Angus. Admitted to Fla. bar, 1904, and since practiced in Tampa; sr. partner McKay, Macfarlane, Jackson & Ferguson; member board directors Lykes Brothers, Incorporated, Lykes Brothers S.S. Company, Incorporated, Tampa Interocean S.S. Co., Blocks Terminal, Inc., Berriman Bros., Inc., J. W. Roberts & Son. Chairman board of trustees U. of Tampa. Mem. Am., Fla. State and Hillsborough County bar assns., Am. Judicature Soc., Phi Kappa Sigma. Democrat. Episcopalian. Elk. Clubs: Rotary, Tampa Yacht & Country Palma Ceia Golf, Centro Espanol. Home: 705 S. Newport Av. Office: First Nat. Bank Bldg., Tampa, Fla. Died Aug. 6, 1945.

McKAY, Oscar Reed, clergyman; b. Mason, Ill., Nov. 1, 1861; s. Rev. Uriah and Mary Adelaide (Billingsley) McK.; A.B., Colgate U., 1887, D.D., 1913; grad. Colgate Div. Sch., 1890; m. Mary Gertrude Lankton, Sept. 3, 1890; 1 son, Ralph Lankton. Ordained Bapt. ministry, 1890; pastor Sayre, Pa., 1890-91; missionary teacher in Ongole, India, 1891-94; pastor successively Warsaw, N.Y., Lafayette and Bluffton, Ind., until 1921; dir. religious edn. for Ind. under Ind. Bapt. Conv., 1921-25; asso. pastor First Bapt. Ch., Indianapolis, 1925-33. Pres. Ind. Bapt. Conv., 1914, 15; v.p. Am. Bapt. Foreign Missionary Soc., 1917. Pres. Am. Red Cross, Wells County, Ind., World War. Mem. Phi Beta Kappa. Republican. Mason, Odd Fellow. Home: 55 N. Arlington Av., Indianapolis, Ind. Died Dec. 10, 1942.

McKAY, William M., state health commr.; b. Huntsville, Utah, Sept. 3, 1887; s. David and Jeannette (Evans) McK.; student U. of Chicago, 1918-22; M.D., Rush Med. Coll., Chicago, 1924; post-grad. work in pub. health, Columbia, 1936-37; m. Maralda Allen, Oct. 15, 1913; children—Helen, Eloise, William, Ruth, Ann, Janet. Practiced surgery and medicine, Ogden, Utah, 1924-36; became state epidemiologist for Utah; 1937; now state health commr. for Utah. Mem. exec. council Salt Lake area Boy Scouts of America. Mem. Salt Lake County Med. Soc., Utah State Med. Assn., Utah and Am. pub. health assns. Mem. Church of Jesus Christ of Latter Day Saints (pres. Zurich Conf., Germany, 1908-10; mem. high council of Ogden Stake, 1910-12, stake supt. Sunday schs., 1912-18; mem. gen. bd. Deseret Sunday Sch. Union; mem. Ogden Tabernacle Choir; mem. Salt Lake Oratoria Soc.). Home: 1254 E. Fifth South St. Office: Utah State Dept. of Health, State Capitol, Salt Lake City, Utah.* Died Apr. 13, 1947.

McKEAG, Anna Jane, college prof.; b. W. Finley, Pa., Mar. 13, 1864; d. Moses and Jane (Tannehill) M.; B.A., Wilson Coll., Chambersburg, Pa., 1895; Ph.D., U. of Pa., 1900; LL.D., Lafayette Coll., 1912; Ed.D., Wilson Coll., Penn., 1932; hon. fellow in philosophy, Clark Univ., 1903-04; unmarried. Teacher in pub. and pvt. schs., Pa. and Ohio, 1881-92; instr., 1892-94, prof. philosophy, 1894-1902, dean, 1901-02, Wilson Coll., Chambersburg, Pa.; instr. in pedagogy, 1902-03, asso. prof., 1903-09, prof. edn., 1909-11, Wellesley (Mass.) Coll.; pres. Wilson Coll., 1911-15; prof. history and principles of edn., Wellesley Coll., 1915-32, emeritus. Presbyterian. Mem. Presbyn. Bd. of Christian Edn. of U.S.A., 1929-36, N.E. Soc. Coll. Teachers of Edn. (pres. 3 terms), N.E. Assn. Colls. and Secondary Schs. (pres. 1924). Author: The Sensation of Pain and the Theory of the Specific Sense Energies, 1902. Collaborator on Journal of Educational Psychology, 1910-20. Home: 15 Appleby Rd., Wellesley, Mass. Died Nov. 23, 1947.

McKEAN, Thomas, author, playwright; b. Phila., Apr. 29, 1869; s. Thomas and Elizabeth (Wharton) McK.; B.S., Trinity Coll., Conn., 1892; m. Katharine Johnstone Bispham, Nov. 25, 1896. Author: The Mermaid, 1907; The Master Influence, 1907; The Punishment, 1909; The Mercy of Fate, 1910; The Wife Decides, 1911. Home: 1900 Rittenhouse Sq. Office: Drexel Bldg., Philadelphia. Died Feb. 7, 1942.

McKECHNIE, Robert Edward (măk-kĕk′ nĭ), surgeon; b. Brookville, Ont., Apr. 25, 1861; s. William and Mary (Bell) McK.; student Prince of Wales Coll., Charlottetown, Prince Edward Island, 1875-79; M.D., C.M., McGill Med. Coll. (gold medalist), 1890; m. Helen Albina Russel, 1891; 1 son, Eberts Mills (deceased). Began gen. practice, 1891; mem. surgical staff, Vancouver Gen. Hosp., since 1903, St. Paul's Hosp., since 1930. Chancellor, U. of Brit. Columbia, since 1918; elected mem. Provincial Legislature, 1898-1900, served as pres. of exec. council. Mem. Canadian Med. Assn. (past pres.), Brit. Columbia Med. Assn. (past pres.), Dominion, Provincial and Vancouver med. assns. Club: Vancouver. Mason. Mem. Liberal Party. Mem. Anglican Ch. Home: 3538 Osler Av. Address: 718 Granville St., Vancouver, British Columbia, Can. Died 1944.

McKEE, John Dempster, banker; b. San Francisco, Calif., Sept. 29, 1865; s. John and Sara Ann (Dempster) McK.; prep. edn., University Mound Coll. and Berkeley Gymnasium; student U. of Calif. (non-grad.); m. Anita Isabel Boole, Nov. 6, 1890; children—Paul Boole, Donald (dec.). Began as clk. with Tallant Banking Co., San Francisco, 1885, later with Mercantile Nat. Bank and Mercantile Trust Co.; chmn. bd. Am. Trust Co. since 1920; pres. Honolulu Plantation Co., The McKee Co.; also officer or dir. various other cos. Trustee William G. Irwin Charity Foundation; trustee Musical Assn. of San Francisco. Republican. Presbyterian. Clubs: Bohemian, Family, Pacific-Union, and many others. Home: 3456 Washington St. Office: Russ Bldg., San Francisco. Died Feb. 5, 1948.

McKEE, Oliver, Jr., newspaperman; born in East Orange, N.J., Dec. 2, 1893; s. Oliver and Julia L. (Wilbur) McK., Taft Sch., Watertown, Conn., 1908-11; B.A., Yale, 1915; grad. 5th class, Sch. Military Government, Charlottesville, Va.; m. Virginia Wilkins, Jan. 7, 1922; 1 son, Oliver III. Reporter Hartford Times, 1915, Washington staff New York World, 1916-17; editorial staff Boston Evening Transcript, 1919-24, Washington corr., 1924-40; with Washington Evening Star, 1940-43; spl. asst. to asst. sec. of state for pub. affairs since 1946. Served at Plattsburg O.T.C., 1915; pvt. Troop B, 5th Conn. Cav., Mexican border, 1916; 2d lt. Cav. Res., 1917; 1st lt. 115th F.A. (formerly 1st Tenn. Inf.), 30th Div.; overseas with 310th F.A., 79th Div.; capt. and major F.A. Res., U.S. Army, 1919-40; commd. maj., specialist, Res. U.S. Army, July 10, 1943; Civil Affairs Div., Chief of Staff, Supreme Allied Comd., London, Nov. 1944; with hdqr. 1st Army Jan. 1944-May 1945; after V-E day transferred to Supreme Hdqrs. Allied Expeditionary Forces, G-5 div.; promoted to lt. col.; inactive duty, 1946. Former member Yale Alumni Advisory Bd. Mem. Am. Legion, Zeta Psi, Chi Delta Theta. Republican. Episcopalian. Clubs: National Press, Yale (pres. 1935-37), Overseas Writers (Washington); Elizabethan (New Haven). Contbr. to mags.; also to Encyclopædia Britannica and Dictionary of American Biography. Home: 1613 30th St. Address: Department of State, Washington, D.C. Died June 2, 1948.

McKEEL, Ben S., insurance exec.; b. Raleigh, N.C., 1898; ed. Univ. of N.C., 1920. Vice Pres. and dir. Hanover Fire Ins. Co.; dir. Fulton Fire Ins. Co. Home: 35 Edgewood Lane, Bronxville. Office: 111 John St., New York 8. Died Nov. 26, 1948.

McKEEN, Benjamin, railway official; b. Terre Haute, Ind., Jan. 23, 1864; s. William Riley and Ann (Crawford) M.; attended Worcester Poly. Inst., 1881-82; M.E., Rose Poly. Inst., Terre Haute, 1885; m. Anna Massie Strong, Oct. 20, 1891; 1 dau., Mary Josephine. Entered service of Terre Haute & Indianapolis R.R. (now Pa. R.R.), Sept. 25, 1885, as draftsman; later rodman and resident engr., 1886-87, engr. maintenance of way, Logansport div., 1887-94; supt. Peoria and St. Louis divs. of same railroad, 1894-1901; supt. Chicago terminal div., Pa. Lines W. of Pittsburgh, with office at Chicago, 1902-03; gen. mgr. Vandalia R.R., St. Louis, 1903-12; apptd. gen. mgr. Pa. Lines West of Pittsburgh, Jan. 1, 1913, v.p. same, 1917-20, v.p. Southwestern Region, 1920, v.p. Pa. R.R. System, 1925-34 (retired); dir. Miss. Valley Trust Co. Mem. Am. Soc. C.E. Home: 4959 Hortense Pl., St. Louis. Died Dec. 1947.

McKEEVER, Emmet G., pres. Pan-American Petroleum & Transport; vice chmn. of the bd. of Pan-American Production Co.; Pan-American Gas Co.; Pan-American Refining Corp.; Mexican Petroleum Corp. of Ga., chmn. of bd. of Pan-American Pipe Line Co., pres. of The American Oil Co., Lord Baltimore Filling Stations, Inc. and Mexican Petroleum Corp; dir. Petroleum Heat and Power. Office: 122 E. 42nd St., New York, N.Y. Died July 9, 1947.

McKELVEY, John Jay (măk-kĕl′vē), legal author; b. Sandusky, O., May 24, 1863; s. John and Jane (Huntington) M.; A.B., Oberlin Coll., 1884; A.M., LL.B., Harvard, 1887; m. Mary C. Mattocks; children—Mrs. Mary Alice Barbour, Mrs. Constance Brown, Mrs. Ruth Moore. Mrs. Jane Hersey; m. 2d, Louise E. Brunning; children—Louise, (Mrs. John L. Holsapple), John Jay and Robert Adams. Admitted to the New York bar, 1888, and in practice at N.Y. City. 1910-12. In Europe and S. Am., as pres. and counsel organizing financing and construction of first Uruguay section of Pan American Transcontinental Railway. Trustee Barnard School for Boys, Harvard Law Review Assn. Member American and New York Harvard Law Review Assn. Mem. Am. and N.Y. State bar assns., Assn. Bar City of New York, Am. Museum of Natural History, Metropolitan Museum of Art, N.Y. Zoölogical Society. Clubs: Lawyers, Harvard. Author: Principles of Common Law Pleading, 1894, 1917, 1925; Handbook of the Law of Evidence, 1898, 1907, 23, 32, 44; McKelvey's Revision Throckmorton's Cases on Evidence, 1923; McKelvey's Cases on Evidence, 1932. Founder and 1st editor-in-chief of Harvard Law Rev. Home: Quaker Road, Chappaqua, N.Y. Office: 36 W. 44th St., New York. Deceased.

McKENNEY, Frederic Duncan, lawyer; b. Washington, D.C., Mar. 11, 1863; s. James Hall and Virginia Dorcas (Walker) M.; student Columbian (now George Washington) U., 1 yr.; A.B., Princeton, 1884, A.M., 1887; LL.B., Columbian, 1886, LL.M., 1887; m. Kathleen Handley, July 10, 1899 (died Apr. 23, 1938); children—Virginia, Frederica. Admitted to D.C. bar, 1886, Supreme Court of U.S., 1889; mem. McKenney & Flannery, now McKenney, Flannery & Craighill, gen. practice. Mem. Am. Bar Assn., Am. Soc. Internat. Law, etc. Episcopalian. Clubs: University (New York); Metropolitan (Washington). Home: 3133 Connecticut Av., Washington. Died June 27, 1949; buried Oak Hill Cemetery, Washington.

McKENNEY, Robert Lee, editor, pub.; b. Butler, Ga., Apr. 11 1865; s. Joshua and Sarah Sophronia (Walton) McK.; ed. pub. schs.; m. Mary Odessa Roush, Jan. 26, 1898; children—Margaret, Louise. Began as pub. and pres. Macon (Ga.) News, 1894, editor, 1899-1930 (retired); apptd. dist. chmn. NRA Compliance Bd. Chmn. four-minute speakers, Macon dist., World War; dir. Ga. State Fair Assn., 1908-28. Mem. Philharmonic Soc. (pres.). Grand Opera Assn. of Macon (pres.). Democrat. Methodist. Club: Kiwanis (pres. 1926; trustee). Home: 2583 Vineville Av., Macon, Ga.; (winter) 1047 Astruria Av., Coral Gables, Miami, Fla. Died Nov. 13, 1947; buried Riverside Cemetery, Macon, Ga.

McKENZIE, Aline, religious educator; b. Meridian, Miss., July 25, 1882; d. John and Lucy (Kimbrough) McKenzie; educated Moffett-McLauren Institute, Cincinnati Conservatory of Music, Bible Teachers College (N.Y.), Nat. Y.W.C.A. Training Sch. (N.Y.); hon. Dr. R.Ed., Queen's College, Charlotte, N.C., 1929. First inducted deaconess, Presbyn. Ch. U.S., Meridian, Miss., Oct. 25, 1914; served 1st Ch., Meridian, 1914-18, 1st Ch., Charlotte, N.C., 1918, 1st Ch., Durham, 1919-40; inst. in religious leadership edn., Children's Div. S. Atlantic States since 1940. Pres. Christian Workers Assn. Presbyn. Ch. U.S., 1925-27; pres. dirs. Religious Edn. Assn. Southern Presbyn. Ch., 1934-36; toured Europe, Asia, Africa, 1926 and 1930; visited Grenfell missions, Labrador, 1934. Mem. Pi Gamma Mu, 1928. Club: Local Business and Professional Women's (pres. 1924). Home: Village apts., Chapel Hill, N.C. Died Oct. 12, 1948.

McKENZIE, Kenneth, univ. prof.; b. Cambridge, Mass., July 24, 1870; s. Alexander and Ellen Holman (Eveleth) M.; A.B., Harvard, 1891, A.M., 1893, Ph.D., 1895; postgrad. work in Europe at various times; hon. Doctor, U. of Padua, 1922; m. Aimée G. Leffingwell, July 30, 1908. Instr. modern langs., Union Coll., N.Y., 1895-98; prof. Romance langs., W.Va. U., 1898-1900; instr. Romance langs., 1900-05, asst. prof. Italian, Yale, 1905-15; prof. Romance langs. and head of dept., U. of Ill., 1915-25; prof. Italian, Princeton, 1926-38, prof. emeritus since 1938; instr. at Columbia U. Summer Sch., 1914-15, U. of Calif., summer session, 1931. Mem. Modern Lang. Assn., Assn. Mod. Lang. Teachers Central West (pres. 1918), Dante Soc., Am. Assn. Teachers of Italian (pres. 1924), Phi Beta Kappa. Cavaliere della Corona d'Italia; corr. mem. R. Instituto Lombardo; fellow Mediaeval Acad. of America. Has published Concordanza delle Rime di Francesco Petrarca, 1912; Il Ventaglio by Carlo Goldoni, transl., 1910; Il Bestiario Toscano, 1912; Symmetrical Structure of Dante's Vita Nuova, Italian Bestiaries, Italian Fables in Verse, A Sonnet Ascribed to Davanzati, in Publs. of Modern Lang. Assn.; Ysopet-Avionnet, 1921; and editions of Alfred de Musset, Victor Hugo, Sardou, Molière, La Fontaine, and Dante's Vita Nuova; Conferenze sulla letteratura americana, 1922; Elementary French Grammar (with A. Hamilton), 1923; Selections from Silvio Pellico, 1924; Antonio Pucci, Le Noie, 1931. Writer scientific articles for Modern Philology, Modern Language Notes, Annual Reports of Dante Soc., Romanic Rev., Italica, Giornale Storico d. Letteratura Ital., Speculum, Enciclopedia Italiana, and various memorial volumes. Gen. editor Century Modern Lang. Series. Dir. Italian Br. Am. Univ. Union in Europe, 1918-19; Am. exchange prof. in Italy, 1921-22. Home: New Haven, Conn. Died Nov. 3, 1949.

McKEON, John J., investment banker; b. Mount Carmel, Conn., Oct. 12, 1877; s. Daniel and Bridget Elizabeth (Bagley) M.; ed. pub. schs. and business sch.; m. Anna Augusta Hoye, July 14, 1909; children—John J., Stephen C., Elizabeth M., Frederick T., Frank D. Senior partner Charles W. Scranton and Co. Mem. N.Y. Stock Exchange. Dir. Security Ins. Co., Aetna Life Ins. Co., Pullman Co., Scovill Mfg. Co., Acme Wire Co., Creist Mfg. Co., Kerite Co. Trustee New Haven Savings Bank. Mem. Conn. Chamber of Commerce (dir.), New Haven Chamber of Commerce, New Haven Employees Retirement Bd., mem. New Haven Sinking Fund Commn.; dir. Grace-New Haven Community Hosp., Hosp. of St. Raphael, St. Francis Orphan Asylum, Quinnipiack Council Boy Scouts of Am.; mem. adv. bd. Albertus Magnus Coll., Nat. Council, Boy Scouts of Am. Clubs: Quinnipack, New Haven Country; Bankers (New York). Home: 131 Edgehill Rd. Office: 209 Church St., New Haven, Conn. Died Nov. 10, 1948.

McKERNON, Edward, journalist; b. Cambridge, N.Y.; s. Rev. Edward John and Mary Jane (Proudfit) McK.; grad. Troy Conf. Acad., Poultney, Vt., 1892; m. Josephine Marion West, June 10, 1896. Reporter and night editor Springfield (Mass.) Union, 1892-94; independent newspaper work, Springfield, 1894-98; owner and editor Mohawk Valley Register, Ft. Plain, N.Y., 1898-1901; with Associated Press, 1903-28, as an editor, at Boston, Mass., 1903-05, transferred to N.Y. City, 1905, and advanced to day mgr., news editor and foreign news editor; apptd. news editor for New Eng., Jan. 1913; head of Boston Bur., Sept. 1913-Apr. 1921; supt. Eastern Div., at New York, 1921-28; pub. Rochester (N.Y.) Journal and Washington corr., 1928-29; editor publs. of Regional Plan Assn., New York, since 1929; consultant to Nat. Resources Com. since 1934. Decorated Order of the Bust of the Liberator by Venezuelan Govt., 1912. Episcopalian. Mem. S.A.R. Home: Washington (Salt Point P.O.), N.Y. Office: 400 Madison Av., New York, N.Y. Died May 22, 1943.

McKIM, Judson J(ackson), dir. ednl. and religious radio programs; b. Bradford, Ia., Nov. 12, 1877; s. Sidney T. and Ella Nora (Robeson) McKim; grad. Normal Dept., Cornell, 1896, Ph.B., 1902, A.M., 1906; grad. Geo. Williams Coll., Chicago, 1903, B.S., 1912, M.S., 1924; LL.D. (hon.) Cornell, 1940; student Yale Univ. Divinity Sch., 1916, Washington Coll., St. Louis, 1913, Univ. of Cincinnati, 1926; m. Jessie Wood, June 6, 1904; children—Clare (Mrs. J. David Roy), Ruth (Mrs. Arthur D. Moor). Y.M.C.A. sec., Cedar Rapids, Ia., 1899-1900, Scranton, Pa., 1902-03, Newcastle, Pa., 1903-04, Scranton, Pa., 1904-07, St. Louis, 1907-13, New Haven, Conn., 1913-22, Cincinnati, 1922-42; dean Y.M.C.A. Professional Training Summer Sch., Hollister, Mo., 1908-09; assisted in establishing Y.M.C.A. course Yale Divinity Sch., 1916, lecturer, 1916-22; dir. ednl. and religious radio programs radio sta. WKRC, Cincinnati, since 1943. Ordained lay elder Methodist Ch., N.Y. East Conf., 1918 (served exec. positions various confs., mem. ch. book concern, 1936-42, mem. exec. com., 1936-40). Mem. Cincinnati Radio Council (vice pres.). Mason. Clubs: Rotary,

Torch, Cosmic. Author: The Operation and Management of the Local Y.M.C.A., 1927; Basic Concepts in the Religious Work Program of the Y.M.C.A., 1931; The Task of the Secretary as an Administrator, 1934; How Religion Functions in the Local Y.M.C.A.; A Cincinnati Symposium, 1938; The Formal Wedding, 1947. Collaborator: Christian Work as a Vocation, 1922; The Handbook of Association Administration, 1933; Christian Emphasis in Y.M.C.A. Program, 1944. Editor house organ bulls., Y.M.C.A. for 10 yrs. Home: 2754 Observatory Rd., Cincinnati 8. Office: Hotel Alms, Cincinnati 6. Died Mar. 12, 1948.

McKINNEY, Colin Pierson, judge; b. Ripley, Tenn., May 23, 1873; prep. edn., Bingham Mil. Acad., Asheville, N.C.; studied law U. of Va.; m. Mayme Bullock. Chancellor 9th Chancery Div. of Tenn., 1910-18; justice Supreme Court of Tenn. since 1918. Presbyterian. Address: 405 7th Av. N., Nashville, Tenn.* Died Apr. 29, 1944.

McKINSTRY, Helen (May), coll. president; b. Winnebago, Minn.; d. Henry and Alice Denison (Packer) McKinstry; grad. Dept. Hygiene, Wellesley Coll., 1900; B.S., New York U., 1928, A.M., 1932; LL.D. (Skidmore); unmarried. Dir. phys. edn., Wolcott Sch., Denver, Colo., 1900-06, Springfield (Mass.) High Sch., 1906-10, Pratt Inst., Brooklyn, N.Y., 1910-17, Central Branch, Y.W.C.A., New York, 1917-29; organizer and director Central School of Hygiene and Physical Education, N.Y. City, 1919-29; organizer and dir. Sch. of Physical Education Russell Sage Coll., Troy, N.Y., 1929-43; acting pres. Russell Sage Coll., March 1942-Dec. 1943; pres. since Dec. 1943. Trustee Heckscher Foundation for Children, New York, 1922-30; mem. Nat. Council on Physical Fitness since 1945. Mem. adv. com. New York State War Council since 1942. Member N.E.A., Am. Assn. for Health and Physical Edn., Acad. of Physical Edn., Bus. and Professional Women's Club (Troy). Republican. Episcopalian. Clubs: American Woman's Assn., Woman's University (New York); Wellesley (Troy). Home: East Acres, Troy, N. Y. Died June 11, 1949; buried Woodland Cemetery, Stamford, Conn.

McKISICK, Lewis, v.p. and sec. Western Union Telegraph Co.; b. Memphis, Tenn., Nov. 17, 1866; s. Lewis David and Elizabeth (Topp) McK.; grad. U. of Calif., 1890; m. Agnes L. Dornin, June 11, 1896; 1 dau., Helen A. With Western Union Telegraph Co., in various capacities and various places since 1890, beginning as bookkeeper and operator at San Jose, Calif., now v.p. and sec. since 1931. Mem. Delta Kappa Epsilon. Home: Gramercy Park Hotel. Office: 60 Hudson St., New York. Died Jan. 6. 1942.

McKISSICK, J(ames) Rion (măk-kĭz'ĭk), editor, educator; b. Union, S.C., Oct. 13, 1884; s. Col. Isaac Going and Sarah (Foster) McK.; A.B., S.C. Coll., 1905; grad. student, Coll. of Charleston, 1905-06; student Harvard Law Sch., 1906-09; M.A. in journalism, U. of Wis., 1933; LL.D., Furman U., 1934, Coll. of Charleston, 1938, Erskine Coll., 1939; m. Caroline Virginia Dick, May 18, 1927. Reporter Union Progress, and business mgr. Union Times, 1905; reporter Richmond Times Dispatch, 1909-10, asst. editor, 1910-11, chief editorial writer, 1911-14; admitted to S.C. bar, 1914, practicing at Greenville; contbg. editor Greenville News, 1916, editor, 1916-19; editor Greenville Piedmont, 1919-26; lecturer on S.C. history, Furman U., 1926-27; dean Sch. of Journalism, U. of S.C., 1927-36, now pres. Mem. of Staff of Gov. Richard I. Manning; code commr. of S.C., 1916-18; mem. Dem. State Exec. Com., 1920-28; del. Democratic Nat. Conv., 1924; mem. State Rural Electrification Authority. Trustee Greenville Woman's Coll., 1923-32, Univ. of S.C., 1924-27. Mem. bd. of visitors, U.S. Naval Academy, 1943. Member S.C. Hist. Soc., S.C. Hist. Assn., Alumni Assn. Univ. of S.C. (past pres.), S.C. Press Assn. (past pres.), Citizens Ednl. Assn. (past pres.), Am. Assn. Teachers of Jour. S.C. Edn. Assn., Newcomen Soc., Kappa Alpha, Phi Beta Kappa, Tau Kappa Alpha, Sigma Upsilon, Omicron Delta Kappa, Sigma Delta Chi. Baptist. Made Mason at sight by grandmaster of S.C., 1937; 32d degree, Scottish Rite. Club: Kosmos. Home: U. of S.C. Campus, Columbia, S.C. Died Sept. 3, 1944; buried on campus of University of S.C.

McKNIGHT, Anna Caulfield (Mrs. William F. McKnight), art lecturer; b. Grand Rapids, Mich.; d. John and Esther (Egan) Caulfield; ed. pvt. schs. (Grand Rapids), Sacred Heart Acad. (Detroit), Radcliffe Coll., and traveled and studied in Europe and Orient 10 yrs.; m. William F. McKnight, Aug. 20, 1907 (dec.). Upon death of husband succeeded him as pres. White River Timber Co., pres. Miami Lumber Co., and as sec. and treas. Dickie Mining Co. Mem. Dept. of Fine Arts, Paris Expn., 1900; during stay in Paris, 1929-40, lectured at Louvre Museum, Union Interalliée, Am. Women's Club, Am. Library, Am. Students' and Artists' Center; was named Officier de l'Instruction Publique by French govt., and elected v.p. Am. Artists Professional League of Paris; also lectured in London and in U.S.; in Washington, D.C., for Pres. McKinley, Cabinet and guests, at French Embassy for Ambassador Cambon and members of Diplomatic Corps. at Congressional Club; at Brooklyn Inst. of Arts and Sciences, Nat. Arts Club (New York), Copley Soc., Boston Art Club, Pittsburgh Art Soc., Providence Art Club, Hartford Art Soc., Art Inst. Chicago, Vassar Coll.; also before leading women's clubs of U.S.; gave art address at Denver Biennial. Apptd. by govs. of Mich. delegate to following congresses in Washington: Nat. Civic Fedn., 1911-12, Am. Civic Assn., 1912, Nat. Conservation Congress, 1913, Nat. Rivers and Harbors Congress, 1913, Industrial Fedn. Conv., 1914-15, 2d Pan-Am. Congress, 1915; Panama P.I. Congress, San Francisco, 1915; Art Congress, Paris, 1921, 37, 38. Wartime speaker for Mich. Unit of Women's Council Nat. Defense, Liberty Loan Drive, and Food Conservation. Organizer and hon. pres. Alliance Française, also Drama League of Grand Rapids; former chmn. Women's City Club of Grand Rapids for entertaining distinguished guests; former dir. Mich. State Fedn. Women's Clubs. Mem. women's com. Grand Rapids Symphony Orchestra. Mem. Women's Nat. Assn. Commerce, Fedn. Alliance Française of N.Y. (life), Am. Fedn. of Arts, Drama League of America, Am. Civic Assn., League of Women Voters, Internat. Council of Women (Paris), Univ. of Mich. League (life), Humane Soc., St. Cecilia Soc., Art Assn. of Grand Rapids. Clubs: Ladies Literary (life mem.; pres. 3 terms, during which time club was addressed by U.S. presidents Taft, Theodore Roosevelt and Wilson), Civic Players, Mary Katherine Guild, Women's City (Grand Rapids); Paris Group of N.Y.; Comité France-Amerique, Lyceum de France, Les Amis du Livre Français, Union des Etrangers Catholiques, Les Amitiés Internationales, American Women's (Paris). During residence in Rome was received in pvt. audience by Pope Leo XIII, and audience by Pope Benedict XV and Pope Pius XI. Home: 71 N. Lafayette Av., Grand Rapids, Mich. Died June 18, 1947; buried in Woodlawn Cemetery, Grand Rapids, Mich.

McKOWNE, Frank A. (măk-kou'ăn), hotel exec.; b. Brockport, N.Y., Oct. 30, 1889; s. James R. McKowne and Mary Jane (Pendergast) McK.; LL.B., U. of Buffalo, 1910; m. Lura Renaker Shepard, June 17, 1922; children—Shirley Jane, Frances Shepard. Admitted to N.Y. bar, 1910; asst. to corp. counsel, City of Buffalo, 1910-13; asst. to Ellsworth M. Statler, hotel exec., 1913-16; asst. sec. Hotels Statler Co., Inc., 1916-19, sec.-treas., 1919-28, pres., 1928-46; dir. Marine Midland Trust Co.; American Hotel Assn. Directory Corp. Chevalier, Legion of Honor (France). Mem. Delta Chi. Clubs: Buffalo, Buffalo Country, Winged Foot, Tavern, N.Y.; Lake Placid. Home: 655 Park Av., New York 21. Died May 7, 1948.

McLANAHAN, Austin (măk-lăn'ȧ-hăn), banker; b. Chambersburg, Pa., Oct. 31, 1871; s. Johnston and Rebecca Anne (Austin) McL.; A.B., Princeton, 1892, LL.B., U. of Md., 1897; m. Romaine Le Moyne, Nov. 6, 1902; children—Jean Romaine (Mrs. Francis C. Taliaferro), Anne Austin (Mrs. John A. Leutkemeyer). With Alex Brown & Sons, 1894-1922, mem. firm, 1902-22; pres. Savings Bank of Baltimore since 1922; dir. First Nat. Bank. Pres. Export and Import Bd. of Trade, Baltimore, 1920-22. Served as maj. A.R.C., France, World War. Trustee Sheppard & Enoch Pratt Hosp. Presbyterian. Club: Maryland (Baltimore). Home: 4801 Green Spring Av. Office: Savings Bank of Baltimore, Baltimore, Md.* Died Apr. 3, 1946.

McLARTY, Norman Alexander, sec. of state of Can.; b. St. Thomas, Ont., Can., Feb. 18, 1889; s. Dr. Duncan and Hattie (Allan) McL.; B.A., U. of Toronto, 1910; student Osgoode Hall, 1910-13; m. Dorothy McColl, June 17, 1914; children—Barbara Monica, Sheila Beryl. Called to Ont. bar, 1913; practiced in Medicine Hat, 1913-22; King's counsel of Ont., 1935; mem. Parliament, 1935; postmaster gen. of Can., 1939; minister of labor of Can., 1939-41; sec. of State of Can., Dec. 1941-45. Member Bar Assn. of Can., Upper Can. Law Soc., Psi Upsilon. Clubs: Essex Golf (Windsor, Ont.); Windsor (Windsor); Rideau, Royal Ottawa Golf, County (Ottawa). Mem. Liberal Party. Presbyterian. Address: 153 Gilmour Street, Ottawa, Can. Died Sept. 16, 1945.

McLAUGHLIN, Andrew Cunningham (măk-lŏf'lĭn), univ. prof.; b. Beardstown, Ill., Feb. 14, 1861; s. David and Isabella (Campbell) McL.; A.B., U. of Mich., 1882, LL.B., 1885 (A.M., 1896, LL.D., 1912); m. Lois Thompson, d. James B. Angell, 1890 (dec.); children—James Angell, Rowland Hazard (deceased), David Blair (dec.), Constance Winsor (Mrs. Donald R. Green), Esther Lois (Mrs. Elmer W. Donohue), Isabella Campbell (Mrs. Rockwell R. Stephens). Instr. of Latin, U. of Mich., 1886-87, instr. history, 1887-88, asst. prof., 1888-91, prof. Am. history, 1891-1906; prof. history, U. of Chicago, 1906-29, head of history dept., 1906-27; now emeritus. Dir. Bur. of Historical Research, Carnegie Institution, Washington, 1903-05; asso. editor, 1898-1914, mng. editor, 1901-05, Am. Hist. Review. Mem. Am. Hist. Assn.; corr. mem. Mass., Wis., and Mo. hist. socs.; Author: Lewis Cass (Am. Statesmen series), 1891; History of Higher Education in Michigan, 1891; Civil Govt. in Mich., 1892; A History of the Am. Nation, 1899, revised edit., 1913; The Confederation and the Constitution, 1905; The Courts, the Constitution and Parties, 1912; America and Britain, 1918; Steps in the Development of American Democracy, 1920; Foundations of American Constitutionalism, 1932; A Constitutional History of the U.S., 1935. Editor: Cooley's Principles of Constitutional Law (3d and revised edit.), 1898; The Study of History in Schools, 1899; Cyclopedia of Am. Government (with A. B. Hart), 1913. Home: 5609 Woodlawn Av., Chicago, Ill. Died Sep. 24, 1947.

McLAUGHLIN, Dorsey Elmer; b. Titusville, Pa., May 27, 1863; s. James Milton and Mina (Kellogg) McL.; ed. pub. schs., Titusville, Pa.; m. Catherine J. Hamilton, Jan. 25, 1919; children—Dorsey H., Marian. Successively with Acme Oil Co., Northern Dakota Elevator Co. and N.P. Ry. Co., 1877-1903, with Pacific Coast Steel Co., 1903-37, pres. 1927-37; pres. Hot Springs Ranch, Inc., Spring Hill Corp.; vice-pres. Pacific Coke & Coal Co.; trustee under will of Elliott M. Wilson. Republican. Home: Hillsborough, San Mateo County, Calif. Office: Mills Tower Bldg., San Francisco. Died Feb. 17, 1945.

McLAUGHLIN, George Dunlap, chemist; b. Retort, Center County, Pa., Aug. 23, 1887; s. George Edmund and Adda (Roche) McL.; grad. high sch.; hon. M.S., U. of Cincinnati, 1924; m. Emilie Sophia Gnauck, June 7, 1915. Chief chemist Leas & McVitty, Inc., Phila., Pa., 1907-11, Kullman, Salz & Co., San Francisco, 1912-19; research asso. in physiology, U. of Cincinnati, 1919-20; prof. of leather research and dir. research lab., Tanners Council of America, same univ., 1921-30; dir. B. D. Eisendrath Memorial Lab., Racine, Wis., since 1931. Awarded Fraser Muir Moffat gold medal by Research Foundation of Tanners Council for researches in tanning, 1937. Fellow A.A.A.S., Am. Inst. Chemists; mem. N.Y. Acad. Sciences, Am. Chem. Soc. (pres. Cincinnati sect. 1925), Am. Leather Chemists Assn. (pres. 1933-34), Wisconsin Acad. Science, Sigma Xi (pres. Cincinnati sect. 1929-30). Democrat. Contbr. papers concerning physical chemistry of proteins and the chemistry, bacteriology and histology of tanning. Home: 3429 N. Main St. Office: B. D. Eisendrath Memorial Lab., Racine, Wis. Died Oct. 15, 1945.

McLAUGHLIN, Thomas H., bishop; b. New York, N.Y., July 15, 1881; s. John and Margaret (Byrne) McL.; prep. edn., St. Francis Xavier High Sch.; A.B., St. Francis Xavier Coll., 1901; S.T.D., Imperial Royal U., Innsbruck, Austria, 1908. Ordained R.C. priest, 1904; chaplain Innsbruck and Fennberg, Austria; asst. St. Michael's Ch., Jersey City, N.J., 1908; prof. of philosophy and theology, Seton Hall College and Immaculate Conception Sem., S. Orange and Darlington, N.J., 1908-36; pres. Seton Hall Coll. and rector Immaculate Conception Sem.; became auxiliary bishop, Newark, N.J., 1935, bishop of Paterson, 1938; examiner clergy, 1910; diocesan official since 1923; became consultor Newark Diocese, 1923, vicar gen., 1933. Mem. Cath. Ednl. Assn., Cath. Philos. Assn., Cath. Hist. Assn., Irish Hist. Assn., Collectors League of N.J. Address: 178 Derrom Av., Paterson, N.J. Died Mar. 17, 1947.

McLELLAN, Asahel Walker, pres. Alden Mills; b. New Orleans, La., Aug. 10, 1868; s. Alden and Sarah Jane (Cooper) McL.; student grade and high schs.; m. Helen DeGrange, June 3, 1896. Began as clerk in hardware store, 1885. With New Orleans Nat. Bank, The Lottery Bank, 1885-88. Organized Alden Mills, 1890, and has been pres. since that time. Mem. exec. com. Am. Cotton Mfrs. Assn. since 1914, v.p., 1923-24, pres., 1924-25; reptd. cotton mfrs. on Return Visit Com. to West Coast of South America, after Latin-America Industrial Congress in Washington, 1916. Served as mem. Cotton Com. to visit Europe immediately after World War, 1919, to systematize cotton business. Clubs: Boston, Louisiana (New Orleans); New York Athletic. Home: 22 Auburn Pl. Office: 2308 Chartres St., New Orleans, La. Died Apr. 26, 1943.

McLENNAN, Donald Roderick, insurance; born at Duluth, Minn., Oct. 27, 1873; s. William L. and Julia (MacLeod) McL.; ed. grammar and high schs. and business coll., Duluth; m. Katherine Cole Noyes, Feb. 14, 1906; children—Jane, Donald Roderick, Jr., Margaret, Katherine, George Noyes, William Lillingstone. Began as bank clk., Duluth, 1888; clk. Bd. of Trade, 1889-91; clk., salesman and asst. buyer, Duluth Shoe Co., 1891-94; clk. Stryker, Manley & Buck, insurance, 1894; partner, 1895, C. H. Graves & Co., insurance, real estate and loans; consol. with Stryker, Manley & Buck, and became v.p. Graves-Manley Agency; pres. Manley-McLennan Agency, successor to Graves-Manley Agency; removed to Chicago, 1905, forming ins. firm of Burrows, Marsh & McLennan, now Marsh & McLennan, Inc., with offices in Chicago, New York, San Francisco, and other cities; dir. Marsh & McLennan, Inc., Am. Sugar Refining Co., Evergreen Mines Co., Armour & Co., First Nat. Bank of Lake Forest, Manley-McLennan Agency, Pa. R.R., Peoples Gas Light & Coke Co., Continental Ill. Nat. Bank & Trust Co., Pullman Co., Pullman, Inc., Chicago Corp., Empire Securities Co. Republican. Presbyterian. Clubs: Chicago, Mid-Day, Commercial, Onwentsia, Old Elm, Attic, Links, Recess (New York). Home: Lake Forest, Ill. Office: 164 W. Jackson Blvd., Chicago, Ill. Died Oct. 14, 1944.

McLEOD, Frank Hilton, surgeon; b. Richmond County, N.C., Feb. 26, 1868; s. Samuel Johnson and Caroline Elizabeth (Smith) McL.; student Wofford Coll., Spartanburg, S.C.; M.D., U. of Tenn., 1888; post-grad. study New York Polyclinic; LL.D., U. of S.C., 1935; m. Florence Allen, Apr. 26, 1893 (died Aug. 1, 1899); m. 2d, Caroline Nelson, Oct. 5, 1904; children—Frank Hilton, James Carlisle. Began practice at Florence, 1891; established, 1906, The Florence Infirmary, now The McLeod Infirmary, of which he is dir. and surgeon in chief; regent State Hospital, 1918-24. Ex-pres. Tri-State Med. Soc., S.C. State Med. Assn., councilor Southern Med. Assn., 1929-35; Pee Dee Med. Soc., Florence County Med. Soc.; fellow Am. Coll. Surgeons. Sullivan Award, University of South Carolina, 1928. Democrat. Methodist. Mason. Editor Jour. S.C. Med. Assn., 1904. Home: Florence, S.C.* Died Oct. 26, 1944.

McMAHON, Amos Philip (măk-mä'ŭn), coll. prof.; b. Warren, O., Aug. 14, 1890; s. Amos Nelson and Ellen Mary (Sheppey) M.; A.B., Harvard, 1913, A.M., 1914, Ph.D., 1916; Sheldon traveling fellow (Harvard), 1916-17; m. Audrey Alden, April 11, 1922. In pub. business, 1917-26; asso. prof. of fine arts, N.Y. Univ., 1926-28, prof. since 1928; chmn. fine arts dept., Washington Sq. Coll. of N.Y. Univ. since 1928. Mem. Internat. Instn. of Edn., College Art Assn. Mediæval Academy of America, American Institute of Archæology, Phi Beta Kappa. Republican. Episcopalian. Clubs: Harvard, Grolier (New York). Author: Life and Times of Miguel Hidalgo y Costilla (with A. H. Noll), 1910; The Meaning of Art, 1930; The Art of Enjoying Art, 1938; Preface to an American Philosophy of Art, 1945. Contbr. numerous articles to jours. Home: 27 Washington Square N., New York, N.Y. Died June 21, 1947.

McMAHON, Thomas F., labor leader; b. Ballybay, County Monaghan, Ireland, May 2, 1870; s. James and Bridget (Shreenan) McM.; ed. in Nat. Sch., Ireland; m. Catherine E. Murray, Oct. 15, 1891. Actively identified with labor movement for many years; ex-pres. United Textile Workers of America. Home: Edgewood, R.I.* Died Apr. 22, 1944.

McMAIN, Eleanor Laura, settlement worker; born Parish of E. Baton Rouge, La., Mar. 2, 1868; d. Jacob West and Jane Josephine (Walsh) McMain.; grad. Free Kindergarten Training Sch., New Orleans, 1900; extension courses U. of Chicago and Columbia U.; unmaried. Head worker Kingsley House Social Settlement, New Orleans, since Oct. 1, 1900; started the first playground opened in New Orleans, inaugurated children's gardens and vacation schs.; conducting pub. recreation centre and settlement activities, with roll of 1,350 members; was instr. sociology, H. Sophie Newcomb Memorial Coll.; dir. Home Service Inst., New Orleans, during war period. Mem. bd. Child Welfare Assn. Episcopalian. Address: Kingsley House, 1600 Constance St., New Orleans. Died May 26, 1934.

McMANAMY, Frank (mak-măn'ă-mĭ), retired interstate commerce commr.; b. Fallen Timber, Pa., Sept. 3, 1870; s. William N. and Sarah A. (Grey) McM.; ed. normal schs., Pa., and Traverse City (Mich.) Business Coll.; m. Anna May Kobe, June 12, 1895. U.S. asst. chief insp. of locomotives, Washington, D.C., 1911-13, chief insp., 1913-18; asst. dir. transportation U.S. R.R. Administration, 1918-20; chmn. com. on design of standard locomotives and cars of U.S.R.R.A., and in charge constrn. and maintenance of all ry. equipment during federal control of rys., 1920-23, mem. Interstate Commerce Commn., 1923-38, chmn., 1930-38. Mem. Am. Soc. M.E., Am. Ry. Assn. (hon.), Traveling Engrs., Brotherhood of Locomotive Firemen and Enginemen, Air Brake Assn. (hon.). Democrat. Mason (Shriner). Clubs: Cosmos, Columbia Country. Home: 230 Anita Av., Daytona Beach, Fla. Died Oct. 3, 1944.

McMANUS, Charles Edward, chmn. of bd. and pres. Crown Cork & Seal Co. Home: Green Gables, Spring Lake, N.J. Office: 60 E. 42d St., New York, N.Y.* Died July 1946.

McMASTER, LeRoy, chemist; b. Mt. Pleasant, Md., Mar. 26, 1879; s. John Lincoln and Susan Catharine (Barrick) McM.; Ph.B., Dickinson Coll., 1901, M.A., 1902, ScD. (hon.), 1931; Ph.D., Johns Hopkins, 1906; m. Anna B. Jones, June 12, 1902; m. 2d, Ernestine T. Schafer, Feb. 7, 1923. Instr. chemistry, Dickinson Coll., 1901-04; fellow Johns Hopkins, 1905-06; instr. chemistry, Washington U., 1906, asst. prof., 1912, prof. since 1914, head of dept. since 1920, Eliot prof. since 1921. Mem. Am. Chem. Soc., Soc. Chem. Industry (London), Phi Beta Kappa, Alpha Chi Sigma, Beta Theta Pi, Sigma Xi, Tau Pi Epsilon, Tau Beta Pi. Democrat. York and Scottish Rite Mason (K.T., Shriner). Home: Gatesworth Hotel. Address: Washington Univ., St. Louis 5, Mo. Died Sept. 1, 1946; buried Valhalla Cemetery, St. Louis.

McMEIN, Neysa (mac-mein), artist; b. Quincy, Ill.; d. of Harry Moran and Isabelle Lee (Parker) McMein; ed. high sch., Quincy, and Art Inst. Chicago; m. John Gordon Baragwanath, May 18, 1923; 1 dau., Joan. Has specialized in portraits and in cover designs, Saturday Evening Post, Woman's Home Companion, Collier's, McCall's; made 14 war posters for U.S. and France. Y.M.C.A. entertainer and lecturer in France, 1918. Republican. Author short stories, articles, and moving picture play. Home-Studio: 131 E. 66th St., New York, N.Y. Died May 12, 1949; buried Rhinebeck, N.Y.

McMENAMIN, Hugh L. (măk-mĕn'ă-mĭn), monsignor R.C. Church; b. Freeland, Pa., Sept. 11, 1871; s. Hugh and Anne (O'Donnell) McM.; A.B., Regis Coll., Denver, Colo., 1897, LL.D., 1932; S.T.B., St. Mary's Sem., Baltimore, 1900. Ordained priest R.C. Ch., 1900; asst. rector St. Mary's Ch., Colo. Springs, 1900-04, asst. rector Cathedral, Denver, 1904-08, rector since 1908 (builder of $1,000,000 plant); made domestic prelate to His Holiness the Pope, 1933. Diocesan consultor and mem. Diocesan Sch. Bd. for many yrs. Mem. Denver Red Cross (exec. com.), Anti-Tuberculosis Soc., Knights of Columbus. Wrote "Pinnacle Glory of the West." Contbr. religious jours. Address: Cathedral, Denver, Colo. Died July 27, 1947.

McMENAMY, Francis Xavier, univ. pres.; b. St. Louis, Sept. 22, 1872; s. Bernard A. and Mary Ann (Bowles) M.; student St. Louis U., 1885-92; studied theology at St. Stanislaus Sem., Florissant, Mo. Joined Soc. of Jesus, 1892; ordained priest R.C. Ch., 1907; prof. classics, Marquette U., Milwaukee, 1899-1904; prof. philosophy, St. Louis U., 1909-11; v.p. Creighton U., 1911-14, pres., 1914-19; provincial, Mo. Province Soc. of Jesus, 1919-26. Address: St. Stanislaus, Brooklyn Sta., Cleveland. Died Jan. 20, 1949.

McMILLAN, James Thayer, business exec.; b. Detroit, Michigan, April 20, 1885; s. William Charles and Marie Louise (Thayer) McM; student Westminster School, Simsbury, Connecticut, 1899-1904, Yale, 1905-07; married Anne Russel, Oct. 15, 1907; children—Helen Russel (wife of Dr. Frederic Schreiber), Marie Louise (Mrs. Henry T. Bodman), James, Elsie (Mrs. Edward B. Caulkins, Jr.), Lt. (j.g.) William Charles, Anne. Began as apprentice with Detroit & Cleveland Navigation Co., 1907; served in engring. and navigating depts. aboard company's steamers; asst. to gen. mgr., 1909, gen. supt., 1910-21, v.p. in charge of operations, 1921-27, pres. since 1930; v.p. F. P. Co.; dir. Ferry Morse Seed Co., Grand Trunk Western Ry. Co., Packard Motor Car Co., Detroit Bank. Served as capt. in Motor Transport Corps, U.S. Army, 1918. Trustee Charles Godwin Jennings Hosp. Member Society of Colonial Wars, Sons of the American Revolution, American Legion, Delta Kappa Epsilon. Republican. Presbyterian. Mason (32°, K.T., Shriner). Clubs: Detroit, Detroit Athletic, University, Yondotega, Detroit Country; Newcomen Society; Huron Mountain Club, St. Clair Flats Shooting Club, Old Club, Grosse Pointe, Fontinalis. Home: 16006 Essex Blvd., Grosse Pointe Park, Mich. Office: Free Press Bldg., Detroit 26, Mich. Died Sep. 4, 1946.

McMILLAN, Robert Johnston, judge; b. Galveston, Tex., Aug. 21, 1885; s. William Blair and Fannie Goode (Howard) McM.; LL.B., U. of Tex., 1906; m. Susie Spyker Shelton, Nov. 10, 1908; children—Sam Shelton, William Blair. Admitted to Tex. bar, 1906, and began practice at San Antonio; became judge U.S. Dist. Court, Western Tex. Dist., 1932. Republican. Presbyn. Home: 111 Park Lane Dr. Office: Federal Bldg., San Antonio, Tex. Died Oct. 1941.

McMILLIN, Lucille Foster, civil service commr.; b. Shreveport, La.; d. James Martin and Ellen (Long) Foster; ed. by pvt. tutors and at Mary Baldwin Sem., Staunton, Va.; Dr. Humane Letters, Lincoln Memorial Univ., 1936; m. Congressman Benton McMillin, of Carthage, Tenn. (then serving his 10th term); 1 dau., Ellinor (Mrs. Joseph Doty Oliver, Jr.). Was first lady of Tenn. during the two terms of her husband's office as gov., 1899-1903; spent 7 years in Peru during her husband's mission there as U.S. minister and 2 years in Guatemala, 1913-22; nat. com. woman from Tenn., 2 terms; apptd. by Cordell Hull, then chmn. Nat. Dem. Com., as regional dir. of Dem. women of southern states, 1924. Mem. U.S. Civil Service Commn., Washington, D.C., since 1933. Past pres. of the Pres. James K. Polk Assn., State Fedn. Womens Clubs of Tenn. Mem. Delta Delta Delta. Presbyn. Author: Women in the Federal Service; The First Year; The Second Year. Home: 2400 16th St., Washington, D.C. Died Feb. 25, 1949.

McMULLEN, Richard Cann, governor; b. Glasgow, Del., Jan. 2, 1868; s. James and Sarah Louise (Boulden) McM.; ed. pub. schs. and Goldey Coll., Wilmington, Del.; m. Florence E. Hutchinson, of Delaware City, Del., Jan. 17, 1895; children—Laura Boulden (wife of Captain James W. Whitfield, U.S. Navy), Richard Hutchinson, Florence Rebecca (Mrs. Irvin Spencer Taylor). In leather mfg. business since 1888, Charles Mullen, later Mullen & Pierson, Daniel Pierson, Amalgamated Leather Cos.; supt. and v.p. Standard Kid Mfg. Co., 1917-29, later Standard Div. of Allied Kid Co.; v.p. Allied Kid Co. since 1929. Served as mem. Wilmington City Council, and mem. Del. Pub. Utility Commn.; elected gov. of Del. for term, 1937-41. Mem. S.A.R., Dem. League. Democrat. Methodist. Mason, Odd Fellow, Red Man, Ancient Order United Workmen. Clubs: Kiwanis, Monarch. Home: 1007 Rodney St. Office: 4th and Monroe Sts., Wilmington, Del. Died Feb. 18, 1944.

McMURDY, Robert, lawyer; b. Frankfort, Ky., Mar. 8, 1860; s. Rev. Dr. Robert and Marcella E. (Russell) McM.; LL.B., U. of Mich., 1880, hon. LL.M., 1895; m. Lillian May Harter, July 16, 1891 (dec.); m. 2d, Jeannette Sherman Lyon, 1918. In practice, Chicago, since 1881; master in chancery, Circuit Ct. of Cook County, 1890-92; mem. Ill. Ho. of Rep., 1893; mem. Ill. Practice Commn., 1900; Rep. presdl. elector, 1904; judge Ill. Ct. of Claims, 1913. Lecturer on med. jurisprudence, Hahnemann Med. Coll., 1890-92, on legal ethics, John Marshall Law Sch., 1910-32, pres. of faculty since 1915. Trustee Fisk U., 1916-27; chmn. trustees Provident Hosp., 1916-25. Pres. Chicago Law Inst., 1898, Ill. State Bar Assn., 1913-14; founder, 1890, and 1st pres. Hamilton Club, Chicago; pres. Sigma Phi Fraternity, 1893. Author: The Upas Tree (lawyer's novel), 1912; The Modern Chesterfield, 1916. Home: 1503 Scott Av., Winnetka, Ill. Office: 69 W. Washington St., Chicago, Ill. Died Dec. 2, 1941.

McMURRY, Lida Brown, author; b. Kiantone, Chautauqua County, N.Y., Feb. 6, 1853; d. Russell McCary and Electa Louisa (Sherman) Brown; grad. Ill. Normal U., 1874; m. William P. McMurry, Aug. 7, 1878; children—Fred Russell, Karl Franklin. Primary teacher pub. schs., Normal, Ill., 1884-91; primary training teacher, State Normal U., 1891-1900, Northern Ill. State Teacher's Coll., DeKalb, Ill., 1900-17. Hon. mem. Kappa Delta Pi, Delta Kappa Gamma. Presbyterian. Author: Classic Stories for the Little Ones, 1892; Robinson Crusoe for Boys and Girls, 1893; (with Mrs. Agnes Cook Gale) Songs of Mother and Child (collection), 1902; Our Langauge Book (No. 1), 1905; Fifty Famous Fables, 1910; Tell Me a Story, 1912; (with Dr. C. Alphonso Smith) Smith-McMurry Language Series, 1919. Compiler "Treetop and Meadow" and "Sunshine" (poems for children). Home: Polo, Ill. Deceased.

McMURRAY, Orrin Kip, educator; b. San Francisco, Calif., Nov. 25, 1869; John P. and Margaret (Farrell) McM.; Ph.B., U. of Calif., 1890; LL.B., Hastings Coll. of Law (U. of Calif.), 1893; LL.D., U. of Southern Calif., 1926; m. Amy C. Hickox, Mar. 22, 1899; children—Margaret M., Katharine (Mrs. John F. Finn), John P. Practiced in San Francisco, 1893-1904; prof. law, U. of Calif., since 1907, dean Sch. of Jurisprudence, 1923-26; taught in law depts. of Columbia U., U. of Mich. and Stanford U. Mem. Am. Bar Assn., Am. Law Inst., Zeta Psi, Phi Delta Phi. Club: Faculty. Contbr. to Calif. Law Review, etc. Home: 2357 Le Conte Av., Berkeley, Calif.* Deceased.

McMURTRIE, Douglas Crawford (măk-mûr'trē), typographer; b. Belmar, N.J., July 20, 1888; s. William and Helen (Douglass) McM.; prep. edn. Hill Sch., Pottstown, Pa.; studied Mass. Inst. Tech., 1906-09; m. Adele Koehler, Feb. 20, 1915; children—Havelock Heydon, Helen Josephine, Baskerville. Editor Am. Jour. of Care for Cripples, 1912-19; dir. Columbia U. Printing Office, 1917-19; pres. Arbor Press, 1919-21; gen. mgr. Condé Nast Press, Greenwich, Conn., 1921-23; pres. Douglas C. McMurtrie, Inc., N.Y. City, 1924-26; editor Ars Typographica, 1925-26; dir. of typography, Cuneo Press, Chicago, 1926-27; dir. of typography, Ludlow Typograph Co., Chicago, since 1927. Pres. Fedn. of Assns. for Cripples, New York, 1915-19; dir. Red Cross Inst. for Crippled and Disabled Men, New York, 1917-18, trustee 1919-26; v.p. Continental Typefounders Assn., 1925-26; pres. John Calhoun Club, Chicago, since 1929; editor Bulletin Chicago Hist. Soc. since 1934; nat. editor Am. Imprints Inventory, 1937-41; chmn. invention of printing anniversary com., Internat. Assn. of Printing House Craftsmen, 1939-40, chmn. educational commission since 1940; sec. National Council on Business Mail since 1942. Mem. Bibliographical Soc. (London), Bibliog. Soc. America, Am. Inst. Graphic Arts, Gutenberg Gesellschaft, Deutscher Buchgewerbeverein, Am. Hist. Assn., Southern Hist. Assn., Miss. Valley Hist. Assn. Author: Bibliography of the Education and Care of Crippled Children, 1913; Re-education for Disabled Soldiers, 1918; The Disabled Soldier, 1919; The Corrector of the Press in the Early Days of Printing, 1922; American Type Design, 1924; Plantin's Index Characterum, 1924; Printing Geographical Maps with Movable Types, 1925; Alphabets, 1926; Jean Guttemberg, 1926; The Fichet Letter, 1927; First Printers of Chicago, 1927; The Golden Book, 1927; Type Design, 1927; Book Decoration, 1928; Initial Letters, 1928; The Pacific Typographical Society, 1928; Early Printing in New Orleans, 1929; Modern Typography and Layout, 1929; New York Printing, 1693, 1929; Jotham Meeker, Pioneer Printer of Kansas, 1930; Printers' Marks, 1930; Beginnings of Printing in Utah, 1931; Early Printing in Michigan, 1931; Early Printing in Wisconsin, 1931; Early Printing in Tennessee; 1933; Beginnings of the American Newspaper, 1935; Beginnings of Printing in Virginia, 1935; General Epistle of the Latter Day Saints, 1935; Letters of Peter Timothy, 1935; Nevada Mining Laws, 1935; Rates of Exchange in Pennsylvania in 1706, 1935; Six New York Imprints, 1935; Three Printed New Hampshire Documents of 1699, 1935; History of Printing in the United States, 1936; Issues of the Brooklyn Press, 1936; Mississippi Banking Law of 1809, 1936; Beginnings of Printing in Arizona, 1937; The Book—the Story of Printing and Bookmaking, 1937; Indiana Imprints, 1937; Montana Imprints, 1937; Eighteenth Century North Carolina Imprints, 1938; Some Facts Concerning the Invention of Printing, 1939; Wings for Words: the Story of The Gutenberg Documents, 1941; Louisiana Imprints, 1942; Early Printing in Wyo. and the Black Hills, 1943; (with A. H. Allen) Early Printing in Colorado, 1935; Check Lists of Kentucky Imprints, 1787-1820, 1939; (as editor) A History of California Newspapers, 1927; A House Divided Against Itself, 1936; Lincoln's Religion, 1936; Lincoln Group Papers, 1936; Overland to California, 1937; The invention of Printing: a Bibliography, 1942. Known principally as an authority on typography and the history of printing; also an authority on provision for crippled children and disabled soldiers. Home: 950 Michigan Av., Evanston, Ill. Office: 2039 N. Magnolia Av., Chicago 14, Ill. Died Sep. 29, 1944.

McNAB, Archibald Peter, lt. gov. of Saskatchewan; b. Glengarry County, Ont., May 29, 1864; s. Malcolm and Margaret (McCrimmon) McN.; ed. pub. school, Glengarry County, Ont.; m. Edith Todd, 1892; children—Edgar James, Spencer Campbell, Ernest Archibald, John Allan, Verna Kathleen (Mrs. Wm. J. Harman), Edith Jean (wife of Dr. Robert Vivian Little). Began as homesteader in Manitoba, 1882; mem. legislature, Saskatoon, 1908-26; minister of municipal affairs, Saskatchewan, 1908-12; min. of pub. works, 1912-27; mem. Saskatchewan Local Govt. Bd., 1926-30; lt. gov. of Saskatchewan since Oct. 1936. Owner McNab Flour Mill, Humboldt, Saskatchewan. Liberal. Presbyterian. Clubs: Assiniboia, Wascana Golf, Regina Golf, Canadian (Regina).

Home: Dewdney Av., Regina, Saskatchewan, Can. Died Apr. 29, 1945.

McNABB, Joe Hector, business exec.; b. St. Thomas, Ont., Can., 1887; married; two children. Pres., treas. and chmn. bd., Bell & Howell Co.; pres. and dir. Cases, Inc.; dir. Nat. Security Bank (Chicago), Carrier Corp., Lincoln Security National Bank. Dir. Ill. Mfrs. Assn., Nat. Metal Trades Assn.; member Soc. Motion Picture Engrs. Mason (Shriner). Home: 950 Hill Rd., Winnetka, Ill. Office: 7100 McCormick Rd., Chicago 45. Died Jan. 5, 1949.

McNAIR, Lesley James, army officer; b. Verndale, Minn., May 25, 1883; s. James and Clara (Manz) McN.; B.S., United States Military Academy, 1904; LL.D., Purdue University, 1941; m. Clare Huster, June 15, 1905; 1 son, Douglas Crevier (died in Guam, Aug. 1944). Commd. 2d lt., June 15, 1904, advanced through grades to maj. gen., 1940, lt. gen., June 1941; apptd. comdr. Groud Forces, U.S. Army, Mar. 1942; wounded in action N. Africa, Apr. 1943; with Funston Expdn. to Vera Cruz, Mexico, 1914. Pershing Expdn. in Northern Mexico, 1916-17; with A.E.F. in France, 1917-19. Awarded D.S.M., 1918; officer Legion of Honor (France). Killed in action on Normandy front July 27, 1944.

McNAMEE, Graham (măk'nȧ-mē), radio broadcasting; b. Washington, D.C., July 10, 1888; s. John Bernard and Annie (Liebold) McN.; student Irving Sch. and Cretin High Sch., St. Paul, Minn.; m. Ann Lee Sims, Jan. 20, 1934. Made debut at Aeolin Hall, N.Y. City, as baritone, 1920; sang in most large cities in America and most large churches in N.Y. City; began in radio work, 1923, specializing in sports broadcasts; now known for commercial and special broadcasts. Roman Catholic. Clubs: Lakeville, National Press, Saints and Sinners. Author: You're on the Air, 1928. Contbr. to Saturday Evening Post, Am. Mag. and several radio mags. Home: 25 Central Park W. Office: care Nat. Broadcasting Co., New York, N.Y.* Died May 9, 1942.

McNAMEE, William John, Jr., govt. official; b. Brooklyn, N.Y., Apr. 22, 1912; s. William John and Ethel Mary (Henderson) McN.; B.S., Columbia, 1933; m. Marion Eloise Wells, Mar. 27, 1937; children—Ann, Margaret, Elizabeth, Martha, William. Org. analyst, Farm Credit Administrn., Washington, D.C., 1934-37; field investigator and auditor, Federal Farm Mortgage Corp., 1937-39, head accountant 1939-43; asst. budget officer and budget officer, Rubber Development Corp., 1943-45, v.p. and dir. since 1945; asst. budget dir. R.F.C. since 1946. Mem. Beta Gamma Sigma. Home: 3734 Kanawha St. N.W. Office: 811 Vermont Av., N.W., Washington 25, D.C. Died May 5, 1949; buried Valhalla, Staten Island, N.Y.

McNARY, Charles Linza (măk-nâr'ĭ), senator; b. on farm near Salem, Ore., June 12, 1874; s. Hugh Linza and Margaret (Claggett) M.; Leland Stanford Jr. U., 1896-98; also under pvt. tutors; m. Jessie Breyman, Nov. 19, 1902; m. 2d, Cornelia W Morton, Dec. 29, 1923. Admitted to Ore. bar, 1898; practiced with John H. McNary, 1898-1913; justice Supreme Ct. of Ore., 1913-15; chmn. Rep. State Central Com., 1916-17; apptd. U.S. senator, June 1, 1917, for unexpired term (1917-19) of Harry Lane, deceased; elected to same office, 5 terms, 1919-48; minority leader of Senate since 1933. Republican vice-presidential candidate in National election, 1940. Baptist. Mason, Odd Fellow, Elk. Home: Salem, Ore. Died Feb. 25, 1944.

McNAUGHER, John (măk-naw'ẽr), theologian; b. Allegheny, Pa., Dec. 30, 1857; s. Joseph and Jessie (White) M.; A.B., Westminster Coll., 1880; grad. Xenia (O.) Theol. Sem., 1884; post-grad. course Edinburgh, Scotland; D.D., Westminster, 1889; LL.D., Monmouth, 1906; Litt.D., Muskingum Coll., New Concord, O., 1937; LL.D., U. of Pittsburgh, 1938; m. Ella M. Wilson, Apr. 26, 1888. Ordained United Presbyn. ministry, 1885; pastor Fredericksburg, O., 1885-86; professor The John McNaugher Chair of New Testament literature and exegesis, Pittsburgh Theol. Sem., 1887-1945, prof. emeritus since 1945, pres. of faculty, 1909-45, president emeritus since 1943. Member Board of Publ., 1898-1945; member Presbyn. Alliance Commn. since 1896; del. Pan-Presbyn. Council, Liverpool, 1904, New York, 1909, Pittsburgh, 1921, Cardiff, 1925, Boston, 1929, Belfast, 1933, Montreal, 1937. Pres. Alliance of Reformed Churches throughout World Holding the Presbyterian System, 1921-25; chmn. Comn. on Confessional Statement, 1919-23; moderator Gen. Assembly United Presbyn. Ch., 1929-30. Author: United Presbyterian Church—Its History and Mission, 1899; The History of Theological Education in the United Presbyterian Church and Its Ancestries, 1931; Quit You Like Men, 1940, Yesterday, Today and Forever, 1947; (also author of brochures); The Virgin Birth; Authorship of Hebrews; The Resurrection of Jesus; also contbr. to the religious press. Editor The Psalms in Worship; Bible Songs, 1901; Psalter Hymns, 1911; The Psalter of the United Presbyterian Church (new version), 1912; Bible Songs, No. 4, 1917; Evangelistic Songs, No. 2, 1919; Children's Praise, No. 2, 1921; The Psalter Hymnal, 1927; Bible Songs Hymnal, 1927. Home: 321 Lafayette Av., Pittsburgh. Died Dec. 12, 1947.

McNEAL, Thomas Allen, editor; b. Marion County, O., Oct. 14, 1853; s. Allen and Rachel (Brownlee) McN.; ed. Ohio Central, Oberlin and Hillsdale colls. to junior yr.; farmed and taught sch. alternately; settled at Medicine Lodge, Kan., 1879; m. Anna Belle McPherson, Aug. 26, 1884 (died June 11, 1920). One of editors of Medicine Lodge Cresset, 1879-84; established Kansas Breeze, 1894, later consol. it with the North Topeka Mail as Farmers Mail and Breeze, of which is editor; asso. editor Topeka Daily Capital. Mem. Kan. Legislature, 1885-86-87; mayor Medicine Lodge, 1890. Republican. Apptd. gov.'s sec., Jan. 9, 1905; state printer, Kan., 1905-11; mem. State Text Book Commn., 1915-23. Author: Tom McNeal's Fables, 1901; When Kansas Was Young, 1922; Stories by Truthful James, 1925. Home: 701 Taylor St., Topeka, Kan. Died Aug. 7, 1942.

McNEAR, George Plummer, Jr. (măk-nâr), pres. Toledo, Peoria & Western Railroad; b. Petaluma, Calif., June 15, 1891; s. George Plummer and Ida Belle (Denman) McN.; prep. edn., Hitchcock Mil. Acad., San Rafael, Calif., 1904-08; student U. of Calif., 1908-09; M.E. Cornell U., 1913; m. Elizabeth G. Mackenzie, June 28, 1917; children—George P., III, Clinton M., James Graham, Elizabeth H., John W. Engaged in engring. and constrn. work, successively with N.Y. Central R.R. Co., E. I. duPont de Nemours & Co., Westinghouse, Church, Kerr & Co., 1913-17; then with Guaranty Trust Co. of New York, in buying dept., 1919-23, investigator of investments, 1923-26; gen. mgr., later pres., Toledo, Peoria & Western R.R. since 1926; pres. The Prairie Schooner Co. Served as 1st lt. Engr. Corps, U.S. Army, in France, Jan. 1918-May 1919. Mem. Tau Beta Pi, Alpha Delta Phi. Presbyn. Clubs: Peoria Country, Crève Coeur. Home: 202 Moss Av., Peoria, Ill.* Died Mar. 10, 1947.

McNEW, John Thomas Lamar, civil engr., educator; b. Belcherville, Tex., Jan. 20, 1895; s. Edgar Ogletree and Sarah Elizabeth (Taylor) McN.; B.S., A. and M. Coll of Tex., 1920, M.S., 1926; C.E., Ia. State Coll., 1925; m. Edna Ethel Murphy, May 27, 1920; children—Edna Elizabeth (Mrs. Don Dale Little), John Thomas Lamar. Instr., asst. prof., asso. prof. civil engring. A. & M. Coll. of Tex., 1920-25; engaged in municipal and highway engring. with various cities and counties, 1920-28; prof. highway engring., A. & M. Coll. of Tex., 1925-40, head dept. civil engring., 1940-43, vice pres. for engring. since 1944, dir. engring. extension service since 1945. Served in U.S. Army, France and Germany, as 2d lt. Corps of Engrs., 1918-19; lt. col. Corps of Engrs. as airport engr. China-Burma-India Theatre, World War II; lt. col. engrs., O.R.C. U.S. Army. Vice chmn. A. & M. Coll. of Texas. Development Fund Bd. Mem. Am. Soc. C.E. (sec.-treas. Tex. sect. 1928-37, pres. 1938, nat. dir. dist. 15 (La., Tex., Mex. and N.M.), 1942-45, vice pres. zone 4, 1946-48, chmn. com on engring. edn., 1946, Am. Soc. Engring. Edn., Am. Soc. M.E., Texas Soc. of Professional Engrs. (past dir.). Democrat. Baptist. Club: Kiwanis. Contbr. miscellaneous professional papers and discussions to pubs. of Am. Soc. C.E. Home: 100 Hereford St., College Station, Tex. Died Dec. 21, 1946.

McPHERSON, Aimee Semple, evangelist; b. near Ingersoll, Ont., Can., Oct. 9, 1890; ed. public schs. and acad. Began as evangelist at 17; traveled as evangelist in U.S., Can., Eng., Australia, etc.; settled at Los Angeles, Calif., 1918; founded Echo Park Evangelistic Assn., 1921, and pres. same; built Angelus Temple Church of the Foursquare Gospel; built class "A" Inst., 1925. Owner of radio station KFSG. Baptist. Mem. W.C.T.U., Los Angeles C. of C. Author: The Bridal Call, 1915; Divine Healing Sermons, 1920; The Second Coming of Christ, 1920; This is That (sermons). Address: 1100 Glendale Blvd., Los Angeles. Died Sept. 27, 1944.

McPHERSON, Charles (măk-fẽr'sŭn), lawyer; b. Calhoun County, Mich., Dec. 2, 1873; s. William and Katherine (Walker) McP.; Ph.B., Albion (Mich.) Coll., 1895; m. Glenna Frances Mixer, May 17, 1926. Admitted to Mich. bar, 1898, and since practiced at Grand Rapids; mem. McPherson, Harrington, Waer & Cary; gen. atty. Pere Marquette Ry. Co., 1903-10; gen. counsel Am. Pub. Utilities Co., 1913-23; an executor and trustee Estate of Charles F. Ruggles. Mem. Am., Mich. State and Grand Rapids bar assns., Delta Tau Delta. Republican. Presbyn. Club: Peninsular. Home: Ada, Mich. Office: Peoples National Bank Bldg., Grand Rapids, Mich. Died Feb. 8, 1945.

McPHERSON, Isaac V., ex-congressman; born Douglas County, Mo., Mar. 8, 1868; ed. Marionville (Mo.) Coll.; m. Bessie Barnette, 1891. Admitted to Mo. bar, 1891, and began practice at Aurora; pros. atty. Lawrence Co., Mo., 1901-02; mem. Mo. Ho. of Rep., 1903-04; mem. 66th and 67th Congresses (1919-23), 15th Mo. Dist.; Republican. Home: Aurora, Mo. Died Oct. 1932.

McREYNOLDS, James Clark, jurist; b. Elkton, Ky., Feb. 3, 1862; s. Dr. John O. and Ellen (Reeves) McR.; B.S., Vanderbilt U., 1882; grad. law dept., U. of Va., 1884; unmarried. In pvt. practice, Nashville, Tenn., many yrs.; asst. atty. gen. U.S., 1903-07; thereafter practiced in N.Y. City; atty.-gen. of U.S. in cabinet of President Wilson, 1913-14; apptd. asso. justice Supreme Court of U.S., Aug. 1914, and took seat on bench at opening of following Oct. term; retired Feb. 1, 1941. Home: 2400 16th St. N.W., Washington, D.C. Died Aug. 24, 1946.

McREYNOLDS, John Oliver, M.D.; b. Elkton, Ky., July 23, 1865; s. Richard Bell and Victoria Campbell (Boone) McR.; B.S., Ky. (now Transylvania) U., 1890, M.S., 1900, LL.D., 1904; student Bellevue Hosp. Med. Coll. (New York U.); M.D. (highest honors in class of 116), Coll. of Physicians and Surgeons (now U. of Md.), Baltimore, 1891; Sc.D., Transylvania U., 1934; 1st asst. resident physician Baltimore City Hosp., 1891-92; attended eye and ear clinics, Chicago, New York, London, Paris, Berlin and Vienna, making many trips to Europe; m. Katherine, d. Judge George E. Seay, Nov. 27, 1895. Prof. mathematics and natural science, Burritt Coll., Tenn., 1886; teacher mathematics and astronomy, Dallas High Sch., 1887-88; began practice at Dallas, 1892; pres. McReynolds Clinic (mem. board govs.); holds certificate of American Board of Ophthalmic Examinations and Am. Bd. of Oto-Laryngology. Maj. Med. Corps, U.S. Army (A.S. Div.) and surgeon 18th Corps Area; colonel M.R.C. Decorated Comdr. Order of Carlos Finlay, Cuba, 1934; also decorated by the government of Venezuela. Past pres. 4th Pan-American Medical Congress and pres. of Pan-Am. Med. Assn.; fellow Am. Coll. Surg. (bd. of govs.; representative to 3d Pan-Am. Med. Congress, Mexico City, 1931), Am. Acad. Ophthalmology and Oto-Laryngology (1st v.p.; chmn. sect. on ophthalmology; life mem.), Am. Laryngol., Rhinol. and Otol. Soc. (v.p.; chmn. western sect.), A.M.A. (v.p.; chmn. sect. ophthalmology); mem. Tex. State Med. Assn. (pres.), Dallas County Med. Soc. (pres.), Med. Vets of World War (pres.), Air Service Med. Assn. of U.S. (pres.), Flight Surgeons Assn. of U.S. (pres.), Assn. Mil. Surgeons of U.S., Zeta Chapter Phi Chi of U. of Tex. (hon.), Oxford Ophthal. Congress; hon. mem. Ophthal. Soc. of Mexico, National Academy of Medicine of Mexico. Episcopalian. Clubs: Dallas Country; Authors' (London). Author of papers and monographs on med. subjects. Home: Dallas Country Club. Office: Texas Bank Bldg., Dallas, Tex. Died July 7, 1942.

McROBERTS, Harriet (Pearl) Skinner, author; b. Creston, Ia.; d. Rev. Anson and Lydia J. (Morgan) Skinner; ed. Lewis Acad., Wichita, Kan., and pvt. instrn. in music; m. Samuel McRoberts, Sept. 1, 1906. Life dir. Am. Bible Soc.; founder Kashmir Fellowship; hon. v.p. Am. Tract Soc.; v.p. Heartsease Home for Women and Babies. Mem. D.A.R. As Harriet Pearl Skinner, contbr. of essays to musical publs., children's stories to denominational and juvenile publs., also sketches, reviews, juvenile serial stories, etc., to newspapers. Author: Boys Who Became Famous Men, 1905; A Christian Crieth Unto Israel, 1919; Every Christian, 1921. Home: Mt. Kisco, N.Y. Died June 21, 1946.

McSURELY, William Harvey (măk-shûr'lĭ), judge; b. Oxford, Butler County, O., Jan. 27, 1865; s. Rev. William Jasper (D.D.) and Hulda (Taylor) McS.; A.B., U. of Wooster, 1886; (LL.D., from same univ., 1921); m. Mary Elizabeth Cadman, Oct. 18, 1892; children—Marion (Mrs. Alfred Schnoor), William Cadman. Admitted to Ill. bar, Mar. 29, 1889; mem. firm of Norton, Burley & Howell, Chicago, 1895, succeeded, 1897, by Burley & McSurely; mem. Ill. Gen. Assembly, 5th Senatorial Dist., 1905-06; elected judge Superior Court of Cook County, Ill., Apr. 1907; chief justice superior Court, 1911-12; apptd. to Appellate Court, First Dist., Ill., 1912; presiding justice Appellate Court. Presbyn. Mem. Am., Ill. State and Chicago bar assns., Chicago Historical Society, Ohio Soc., Art Inst. Chicago, Sigma Chi, Phi Beta Kappa. Clubs: Union League (pres. 1913-14), University, Flossmoor Country, Law. Home: 5415 Hyde Park Blvd. Office: 30 N. Michigan Av., Chicago. Died May 27, 1943; buried in Rosehill Cemetery, Chicago.

McSWEENEY, Henry, pres. United States Potash Co. Address: 30 Rockefeller Plaza, New York, N.Y.* Died Mar. 5, 1946.

McVAY, Charles Butler, Jr., naval officer; b. Edgeworth, Pa., Sept. 19, 1868; s. Charles Butler and Annie Huntington (Jones) McV.; grad. U.S. Naval Acad., 1890. Ensign, July 1, 1892; promoted through grades to rear admiral, Jan. 6, 1923. Served on Amphitrite, Spanish-Am. War, 1898; navigator Hartford, 1905; at U.S. Naval Acad., 1905-07; navigator Alabama, 1907-08; comd. Yankton, 1908-10; at U.S. Naval Acad., 1910-12; chief of staff, Asiatic Fleet, 1912-14; asst. to Bur. of Ordnance, Navy Dept., 1914-16; at Naval War Coll., Newport, R.I., 1917; commanded Saratoga, 1917; apptd. comdr., New Jersey, Aug. 1917, Oklahoma (war zone), 1918; chief of Ordnance, 1920-23; comdr. Yangtze Patrol, 1923-25; mem. Gen. Bd. and budget officer, Navy Dept., 1925-29; became comdr.-in-chief Asiatic Fleet, with rank of admiral, Sept. 9, 1929; then mem. Gen. Board; retired, Oct. 1, 1932; commd. admiral by act of Congress, June 1942. Address: 2131 Bancroft Place N.W., Washington. Died Oct. 28, 1949; buried in Arlington National Cemetery.

McVAY, Charles Butler, Jr., naval officer; b. Edgeworth, Pa., Sept. 19, 1868; s. Charles Butler and Annie Huntington (Jones) McV.; grad. U.S. Naval Acad., 1890. Ensign, July 1, 1892; promoted through grades to rear admiral, Jan. 6, 1923. Served on Amphitrite, Spanish-Am. War, 1898; navigator Hartford, 1905; at U.S. Naval Acad., 1905-07; navigator Alabama, 1907-08; comd. Yankton, 1908-10; at U.S. Naval Acad., 1910-12; chief of staff, Asiatic Fleet, 1912-14; asst. to Bur. of Ordnance, Navy Dept., 1914-16; at Naval War Coll., Newport, R.I., 1917; commanded Saratoga, 1917; apptd. comdr., New Jersey, Aug. 1917, Oklahoma (war zone), 1918; chief of Ordnance, 1920-23; comdr. Yangtze Patrol, 1923-25; mem. Gen. Bd. and budget officer, Navy Dept., 1925-29; became comdr.-in-chief Asiatic Fleet, with rank of admiral, Sept. 9, 1929; then mem. Gen. Board; retired, Oct. 1, 1932; commd. admiral by act of Congress, June 1942. Address: 1527 4th St., New Orleans. Died Oct. 28, 1949; buried in Arlington National Cemetery.

McWHORTER, Ernest D. (măk-hwôr'tẽr), naval officer; b. in Miss., Sept. 23, 1884. Entered U.S. Navy, May 3, 1911; promoted through grades to rear adm., Dec. 1940; comdr. Naval Air Force in U.S. Occupation of N. Africa, Nov. 1942.† Died Jan. 31, 1950.

MEAD, Albert Davis, biologist; b. Swanton, Vt., Apr. 15, 1869; s. Charles Davis and Phœbe Minerva (Harrington) M.; A.B., Middlebury Coll., 1890; A.M., Brown, 1891, LL.D., 1939; Ph.D., U. of Chicago, 1895; Sc.D., U. of Pittsburgh, 1912, and Middlebury Coll., 1916, R.I. State College, 1927; m. Ada Geneva Wing, July 2, 1902. Asso. prof. comparative anatomy, 1895, prof., 1901, prof. biology, 1909, vice-pres., 1925-36, acting pres., 1931, prof. emeritus since 1936, Brown Univ. Trustee Middlebury Coll., 1933, Wellesley College, 1934-45, R.I. Sch. Design, 1923-39; trustee, 1901-34 and president, 1934-40; Rhode Island Hospital. Member American Soc. Naturalists, Am. Soc. Zoölogists, A.A.A.S., Phi Beta Kappa, Sigma Xi; fellow Am. Acad. Arts and Sciences. Address: 283 Wayland Av., Providence, R.I. Died Dec. 8, 1946.

MEAD, Daniel Webster, engr.; b. Fulton, N.Y., Mar. 6, 1862; s. Washburn and Adelia A. (Shufelt) M.; B.C.E., Cornell University, 1884; LL.D., University of Wisconsin, 1932; married Katie Ross Gould, Nov. 30, 1886 (died Apr. 25, 1944); children—Hazel Marguerite, Ruth Claudia (dec.), Harold Washburn, Ross Webster (dec.), Paul Gould (dec.), Franklin Braidwood. With U.S. Geol. Survey, 1884-85; city engr., Rockford, 1885-87; chief engr. and gen. mgr., Rockford Constrn. Co., 1888-96; cons. engr. on hydraulic works and power plants since 1896; prof. hydraulic and sanitary engring., U. of Wis., 1904-32, professor emeritus since 1932; cons. engr. Mead & Hunt (Madison); mem. Mead & Scheidenhelm (New York). Built water works at Rockford, Illinois, Fort Worth, Texas, Danville, Illinois, Moline (Ill.) filter, Kilbourn (Wis.) hydro-electric plant (10,000 h.p.), Prairie du Sac (Wis.) hydro-electric plant (20,000 h.p.), etc. Mem. Red Cross commn. to China on flood protection of Huai River, 1914; cons. engr. Miami Conservancy Dist., 1913-20 (expenditure $30,-000,000); mem. Colorado River Board, apptd. by President Collidge to pass on Boulder Canyon project, 1928. Awards: Fuertes medal, Cornell U., 1911; Octave Chanute medal, Western Soc. Engrs., 1913; Norman medal, Am. Soc. C.E., 1936; Washington award, Western Soc. Engrs., 1939; awarded citation as "Pioneer Hydrologist" by the Hydrology Conference, Pa. State College, 1941. Fellow Am. Inst. Electrical Engrs., Am. Pub. Health Assn.; hon. mem. Am. Water Works Assn., Am. Soc. Civil Engrs. (pres. 1936), Ill. Soc. Engrs., Canadian Institute Engrs. (hon.), Western Soc. Engrs., member Am. Soc. Mech. Engrs., New Eng. Water Works Assn., Am. Inst. Consulting Engrs., Wis. Engring. Soc., A.A.A.S., Tau Beta Pi, Sigma Xi, Phi Kappa Phi; nat. hon. mem. Triangle, Chi Epsilon. Clubs: Union League (Chicago); University, Madison (Madison). Author: Notes on Hydrology, 1904; Water Power Engineering, 1908; Contracts, Specifications and Engineering Relations, 1916; Hydrology, 1919; Hydraulic Machinery, 1933; also numerous papers read before scientific socs. and bulls. of U. of Wisconsin. Home: 120 W. Gorham St. Office: 550 State St., Madison, Wis. Died Oct. 13, 1948; buried Forest Hill Cementery, Madison, Wis.

MEAD, George Jackson, aeronautic engr.; b. Everett, Mass., Dec. 27, 1891; s. George Nathaniel Plummer and Jenny (Leman) M.; prep. edn., St. George's Sch., Newport, R.I., and Choate Sch., Wallingford, Conn.; student Mass. Inst. Tech., 1911-15; hon. D.Sc. Trinity Coll., Hartford, Conn., 1937, Williams Coll., 1940; m. E. Cary Hoge, May 18, 1921; children—George Nathaniel Jackson, Mary Randolph, Peyton H., Charles Cary, William Randolph. Experimental engr. Wright Martin Aircraft Corp., 1916-19; engr. in charge power plant labs., U.S. Air Service, Dayton, O., 1919; chief engr. Wright Aeronautical Corp., 1920-25; engring. founder and v.p. Pratt & Whitney Aircraft Co., 1925-30; v.p., mem. exec. com. and chmn. tech. advisory com. United Aircraft & Transport Corp., 1930-34; cons. engr. United Aircraft Corp., 1934-35, v.p., dir. and mem. exec. com., 1935-June 1939. Mem. and vice-chmn. Nat. Advisory Com. for Aeronautics, Oct. 1939-Feb. 1944; asst. to Sec. of Treasury, May 22-June 4, 1940; dir. Aeronautical Sect., National Defense Commn., June 4-Nov. 1, 1940; spl. asst. to William S. Knudsen, Nov. 1, 1940-Mar. 1941. Chmn. exec. com. Hartford Hosp., 1942-47. Mem. Soc. Automotive Engrs.; hon. fellow Inst. of Aeronautical Sciences; fellow Royal Aeronautical Soc., England. Republican. Conglist. Clubs: Engineers (New York); Hartford, Hartford Golf; Cosmos Club, Washington, D.C. Home: Mountain Rd., West Hartford, Conn. Office: P.O. Box 6, West Hartford, Conn. Died Jan. 20, 1949.

MEAD, George Whitefield, clergyman; b. Norwalk, Ohio; son Joel E. and B. Ann (Lewis) M.; Ph.B., Oberlin College, 1891; Princeton University and Theol. Seminary, 1891-92; Union Theol. Seminary, 1892-95; New York Univ., 1894-96; Ph.D., Heidelberg U., 1903; D.D., Berea (Ky.) Coll., 1919; m. Jenny Gladiss von Oetinger, Sept. 4, 1896 (died 1932); children—George Whitefield, Alfred Reginald; m. 2d, Martha Elizabeth Norburn, April 3, 1941. Ordained Presbyn. ministry, 1894; asst. pastor Madison Av. Ch., New York, 1894-98; pastor First Ch., Newport, R.I., 1898-1906, Second Wilkinsburg (Pa.) Ch., 1906-10; recuperating health in N.Y. and N.J., 1910-12; lit. work, lecturer, New York, 1912-17; actg. prof. English lang. and lit., Berea (Ky.) Coll., 1917-19; World War work in South; pastor First Ch., Bel Air, Md., 1919-26; pres. Fla. Chautauqua, Keystone Heights, Fla., 1926-30; prof. economics and sociology, Tusculum Coll., Greeneville, Tenn., 1929-38. Commr. Gen. Assembly, Phila., 1901; moderator Boston Presbytery, 1903. Chaplain Res. U.S. Army. Member S.A.R., Am. Econ. Assn., Am. Sociol. Society, Pi Kappa Delta. Club: Lake Placid (New York). Author: Modern Methods in Church Work, 1897; Modern Methods in Sunday-school Work, 1903; The Great Menace—Americanism or Bolshevism? 1920. Home: 16 Stuyvesant Road, Asheville, N.C. Died Dec. 18, 1946; buried, Rock Creek Cemetery, Washington, D.C.

MEAD, Gilbert Wilcox, educator; b. Pittsburgh, Pa., May 7, 1889; s. Rev. Wesley Gilbert (Ph.D.) and Carolyn Switzer (Wilcox) M.; diploma Southwestern Pa. Normal Sch., 1905; B.A., Allegheny Coll., 1911, Litt.D., 1934; M.A., Columbia, 1916 grad. student, 1916-18; LL.D., Birmingham-Southern Coll., 1933; traveled and studied in Eng. and France; m. Iva Madeline Clark, Aug. 18, 1914; children—John Clark, Gilbert Wilcox, Francis Hudson, Robert Wesley (dec.). Teacher county sch., Allegheny County, Pa., 1905-07; prin. and supervisor schs., Bergenfield, N.J., 1911-15; English master Buckley Sch., New York, 1915-17; instr. in English and comparative lit., Columbia, 1917-23; spl. lecturer Hunter Coll., 1917-23; head dept. of English, Westminster Coll., Pa., 1923-25; dean Birmingham-Southern Coll., 1925-33; pres. Washington Coll., Chestertown, Md., since 1933. Pres. Dixie Intercollegiate Athletic Conf., 1930-32; mem. Md. State Library Commn., Md. Commn. on State Mental Insts., Chesapeake Biol. Lab. (exec. com.); chmn. dist. council and v.p. area council Boy Scouts of America. Member bd. Grants Am. Foundation for Pharm. Edn.; rep. Assn. Am. Colls. in Am. Council on Edn.; mem. exec. com. Maryland Conf. Postwar Edn. Fellow Royal Soc. Arts, Sons Am. Revolution. Decorated Yorktown medal, Soc. of Cincinnati, 1940, Silver Beaver, Nat. Council Boy Scouts Am., 1943. Mem. Southern Conf. Liberal Arts Coll. Deans (sec. 1930-33), Ala. Colls. Assn. (pres.), Southern Intercollegiate Athletic Assn. (v.p.), Ednl. Assn. M.E. Ch. South, Nat. Interfraternity Conf. (exec. com., sec., chairman, 1947-48), Middle States Assn. Colls. (exec. com., representative on American Council on Education), Phi Beta Kappa, Phi Gamma Delta (national officer), Tau Kappa Alpha, Omicron Delta Kappa, Kappa Phi Kappa (nat. pres. 1937-39). Episcopalian (vestryman). Clubs: Rotary, Chester Yacht and Country. Contbr. literary and critical articles. Lit. editor Birmingham News-Age Herald, 1928-33. Home: Chestertown, Md. Died March 25, 1949.

MEADE, Frank B., architect; b. Norwalk, O., Jan. 6, 1867; s. Alfred Newman and Martha Althea (Morse) M.; ed. Case Sch. of Applied Science, Cleveland, O.; student Mass. Inst. of Tech., 1885-88; m. Dora Rucker, Nov. 3, 1898. Architect since Oct. 1893. Fellow A.I.A.; mem. Loyal Legion of America, Sigma Chi. Club: Hermit (Cleveland, O.). Home: 2057 E. 100th St., Cleveland, O. Died March 21, 1947.

MEANS, George Hamilton, dentist; b. Henderson, Ky., Feb. 9, 1886; s. George Hamilton and Virginia (Lively) M.; D.D.S., U. of Louisville Sch. of Dentistry, 1905; m. Frankie Duvall McDonald, Dec. 18, 1912. Began practice at Midway, Ky., 1905; moved to Louisville, 1909; mem. Louisville inlay unit, 1920; chmn. Louisville X-ray unit, 1923; clin. demonstrator, dental dept., U. of Louisville, 1921-23, asso. prof. operative dentistry, 1923-25, prof. since 1927; dir. Louisville Free Dental Clinic, 1924-26. Fellow Am. Coll. Dentists; mem. Am. Dental Assn. (chmn. exhibits 1925, Kentucky chmn. Dental Relief since 1932), Ky. State Dental Assn. (pres. 1929; editor of program 1925-27; historian 1931; chmn. exec. com. 1937), Bluegrass Dental Assn., Louisville Dist. Dental Soc. (pres. 1926), Alumni Assn. U. of Louisville (vice-pres.), Psi Omega, Omicron Kappa Upsilon (pres. Omicron Chapter 1929-30). Republican. Methodist. Mason, Elk. Home: 1848 Tyler Parkway. Office: 1380 Bardstown Rd., Louisville, Ky. Died Nov. 9, 1941.

MEANS, Philip Ainsworth, historian; b. Boston, Mass., Apr. 3, 1892; s. James and Helen Goodell (Farnsworth) M.; B.A., Harvard, 1915, M.A., 1916; m. Louise Munroe, Apr. 18, 1934. Traveled extensively in Europe prior to 1913; mem. Yale Peruvian Expdn., 1914-15; hon. collaborator in archeology, U.S. Nat. Museum, 1916-19, traveled in Peru and Bolivia, 1917-18, for Smithsonian Instn., Museum of Am. Indian, Heye Foundation, and Am. Geog. Soc.; traveled in Peru, 1919, on research for Wonalancet Co., and spl. investigator for same in Nashua and Piura (Peru), 1918-20; dir. Nat. Museum of Archeology, Lima, Peru, 1920-21; asso. in anthropology, Peabody Museum, Harvard U., 1921-27. Traveled in Latin-Am. countries, 1914-26 and 1933-34; in Germany, Scandinavia and Iceland, 1937. Fellow A.A.A.S.; mem. Institute of Andean Research (Council), Am. Anthropol. Assn., Am. Antiquarian Soc., Instituto Arqueologico del Cuzco, Connecticut Acad. Arts and Sciences, Hakluyt Soc. (London), Conn. Hist. Soc., New York Historical Society, Mediaeval Academy of America; corr. member National Academy History, Quito, Ecuador. Decorated Official Order of the Sun (Peru). Clubs: Harvard, University (New York); Harvard (Boston); Cosmos (Washington, D.C.); Faculty (Cambridge, Mass.); Explorers (New York); Nacional (Lima, Peru). Author: A History of the Spanish Conquest of Yucatan and of the Itzas, 1917; A Survey of Ancient Peruvian Art, 1917; Racial Factors in Democracy, 1918; La Civilización precolombina de los Andes, 1919; Aspectos cronológicos de las civilizaciones andinas, 1921. Editor Relación of Pedro Sancho (Cortes Soc.), 1918; Relación de Pedro Pizarro (Cortes Soc.), 1921; Memorias Antiguas of F. Montesinos (Hakluyt Soc.), 1921; A Study of Ancient Andean Social Institutions, 1925; Biblioteca Andina, Part I, 1928; Ancient Civilizations of the Andes, 1931; Fall of the Inca Empire, 1932; A Study of Peruvian Textiles, 1932; The Spanish Main, 1935; The Incas: Empire Builders of the Andes, 1938; Tupak of the Incas (a book for children), 1942; Newport Tower, 1942; articles on pre-Columbian Andean art in mags. and museum bulletins in this country and in Peru, 1940-41; also numerous sociol. papers in English and Spanish and many book reviews for the N.Y. Times, etc. Home: Pomfret, Conn. Died Nov. 24, 1944.

MEANS, Rice William; b. St. Joseph, Mo., Nov. 16, 1877; s. George W. and Sarah D. (McDonald) M.; student Sacred Heart Coll., Denver, Colo.; LL.B., U. of Mich., 1901; m. C. Frances Dickinson, Apr. 23, 1902. Began practice at Denver, 1901; county judge, Adams County, Colo., 1902-04; mgr. of safety and excise, City and County of Denver, 1923 (resigned); atty. City and County of Denver, 1923-24; mem. U.S. Senate from Colorado, 1924-27. Enlisted in Colo. Nat. Guard, 1895, 2d and 1st lt. 1st Colo. Inf., 1898-99; comd. co. of scouts, Philippine campaign, 1899; recommended for Medal of Honor and promotion by Maj. Gens. Greene and Bell; capt. Colo. Nat. Guard, 1903; commd. lt. col. inf., U.S. Army, June 22, 1917; grad. Field Officers' Sch., Langres, France; comd. 4th U.S. Inf. in Meuse-Argonne campaign, later comd. 157th Inf.; hon. disch. May 15, 1919. Awarded D.S.C., 1925, for acts of bravery in the Philippine Campaign prior to and during capture of City of Manila. Mem. Soc. Army of the Philippines (comdr. in chief 1913), Vets. Foreign Wars of U.S. (comdr. in chief 1914-15), United Spanish War Vets. (comdr. in chief 1926). Republican. Methodist. Home: 2081 Fairfax St., Denver, Colo. Died Jan. 30, 1949.

MEANS, Stewart, clergyman; b. Steubenville, O., Aug. 4, 1852; s. Thomas and Ann J. (Stewart) M.; student Kenyon Coll., 1869-72, Union Theol. Sem., 1872-75, Episcopal Theol. Sch., 1875-76; A.M. (hon.), Kenyon; D.D., Trinity, and Yale, 1904; m. Katharine Elizabeth Gower, May 10, 1887. Deacon, P.E. Ch., 1875, priest, 1876; rector Bayonne, N.J., 1876-79, Middletown, O., 1879-81; asst. minister St. Ann's, Brooklyn, 1882-83; rector St. John's, New Haven, 1883-1923. Author: St. Paul and the Ante-Nicene Church; Parish Sermons; Faith—An Historical Study, 1933. Translator: Harnack's Apostles' Creed. Home: Hamden, Conn. Died March 11, 1940.

MEARS, Eliot Grinnell, economist, author; b. Worcester, Mass., Feb. 1, 1889; s. David Otis and Mary Chapin (Grinnell) M.; grad. Albany (N.Y.) Acad., 1905, post-grad. work 1 yr.; A.B., Harvard, 1910, M.B.A., 1912; LL.D., Grinnell Coll., 1932; m. Gladys Chute, June 10, 1914; children—Helen (Mrs. Weldon B. Gibson), Dorothy Chute (Mrs. Oliver I. Allen), Julianne. Sec. and instr. in pub. utilities operation, Harvard Grad. Sch. Business Administration, 1912-16; efficiency engr., Day & Zimmerman, Phila., 1913; with U.S. Bur. Foreign and Domestic Commerce, 1916-20, organizer and chief of Trade Commr. Div., chief of Commercial Attaché Div., acting chief European Div. and Am. trade commr. in Near East; commercial attaché to American High Commissioner in Turkey, 1919-20; member faculty Western Summer School for Commercial Organization Executives, Stanford University, 1923, 24; executive sec. Survey of Race Relations 1924-36; acting prof. and lecturer economics, same univ., 1921-25, prof. geography and internat. trade, Grad. Sch. of Business, since 1925, and dir. summer quarter 1932-1942; War Shipping Administration, 1942. Economic mem. Am. Mil. Mission to Armenia and Transcaucasia, under Maj. Gen. J. G. Harbord, U.S. Army, 1919. Permanent sec. Pan-Pacific Commercial Conf., Honolulu, 1922; member Institute of Pacific Relations Conference, Honolulu, 1927; visiting prof. Institute Universitaire de Hautes Etudes Internationales, Geneva, 1929-30, lecturer, 1938; del. Internat. Chamber of Commerce, Amsterdam, Holland, 1929; delivered address at inauguration Greek Centenary, Athens, 1930; Carnegie visiting professor to Univs. of Glasgow, Edinburgh, Vienna, Istanbul, Athens, Jerusalem, American Near East Colleges, 1930. Official delegate Pan-American Institute of Geography and History, Lima, Peru, 1941. Director Hoover Library on War, Revolution, and Peace. Member Institute of World Affairs (executive committee), American Geog. Soc., Am. Econ. Association, American Statistical Assn., Inst. of Pacific Relations, Council on Foreign Relations, Inc., P.E.N., Calif. Hist. Soc., Assn. of Am. Geographers, Assn. Pacific Coast Geographers (pres), Sociedad Geográfica de Lima, N.Y. Acad. of Sciences, Am. Geophysical Union. Fellow Royal Soc. of Arts, Royal Economic Society, A.A.A.S., California Academy Sciences. Decorated Officer Order of the Redeemer (Greece). Conglist. Clubs: Bohemian Commonwealth, Harvard (San Francisco); Cosmos (Washington); Royal and Ancient (St. Andrews, Scotland). Author: Modern Turkey, 1924; Principles and Practices of Cooperative Marketing (with M. O. Tobriner), 1926; Resident Orientals on the American Pacific Coast, 1927; San Francisco's Trans-Pacific Shipping,

1929; Greece Today, 1929; Maritime Trade of Western United States, 1935; Pacific Ocean Handbook, 1944; A Trade Agency for One World, 1945; consulting editor World Affairs Interpreter; contbr. economic geog. and scientific jours., monographs, biennial confs. Inst. of Pacific Relations, 1927, 29, 33. Home: 593 Gerona Rd., Stanford University, Calif. Died May 27, 1946; buried, Essex, Mass.

MECHAU, Frank Jr. (May-show), painter, educator; b. Glenwood Springs, Colorado, January 26, 1904; s. Frank Albert and Alice Bluegown (Livingston) M.; student Denver University, 1923-24, Art Institute Chicago, 1924-25; studied museums of New York City, 1925-29; Europe, 1929-31; married Paula Ralska, 1925; children—Vanni, Dorik, Duna, Michael. Began as painter and art instr., 1931; lectured Kirkland Sch. of Art, Denver, 1931; operated own art sch., 1931-33; dir. art, San Luis Sch., Colorado Springs, Colo., 1934-35; painting instr., Colorado Springs Fine Arts Center, 1937-38; dir. art classes Columbia U., 1939-44, associate professor architecture and dir. of drawing, painting and sculpture. War artist-correspondent for Life Magazine, 1943. Awarded Guggenheim Fellowship, 1933, 34, 38; Norman Waite Harris bronze medal, Chicago Art Inst., 1936; Altman gold medal and cash award for landscape. Rep. in Museum of Modern Art (2 mural sketches), Detroit Inst., Cincinnati Museum, Met. Museum, Denver Museum, Encyclopedia Britannica col. of Contemporary American Art. Murals for Post Office, Washington, D.C., Colorado Springs, Fine Arts Center, Colorado Springs Post Office, also in Glenwood Springs, Colo., Ft. Worth and Brownfield, Tex., Ogalla, Neb., and Denver Fine Arts Library. Association National Academy Design; A.N.A. Lectured at U. of Neb., Met. Museum of Art (N.Y.); Sch. Art League of N.Y., Belle Harbor Inst. Museum of Modern Art, N.Y.C., Philadelphia Museum of Art. Juror for Rosenwald Foundation, 1941, 42, 43; juror for Pa. Acad., 1942. Home: Redstone, Colo. Address: Columbia University, New York, N.Y. Died Mar. 9, 1946.

MECHEM, Merritt Cramer, lawyer, ex-governor; b. Ottawa, Kan., Oct. 10, 1870; s. Homer Clark and Martha Shannon (Davenport) M.; student Ottawa U.; m. Eleanor Frances O'Heir, Feb. 12, 1910. Dist. atty., 1905-07; mem. Territorial Council of N.M., 1909; apptd., by President Taft, asso. judge Territorial Supreme Court, 1909; elected dist. judge, 1911, for term expiring 1924; gov. of N. Mex., 1920-22; resumed law practice; mem. Mechem and Hannett since Jan. 1, 1934. Pres. N.M. State Bar Assn., 1931. Republican. Home: 1208 E. Marquette Place. Office: First Nat. Bank Bldg., Albuquerque, N. Mex.* Died May 24, 1946.

MECHLIN, Leila (mĕk'lĭn), art critic; b. Washington, D.C., May 29, 1874; d. Frederick S. and Cornelia S. (Hyatt) M.; ed. pub. schs. and Corcoran Sch. of Art, Washington; hon. M.A., George Washington Univ., 1921; Dr. of Fine Arts, U. of Neb., 1927; unmarried. Fellow Royal Soc. of Arts (London), 1940. Art critic Washington Evening Star since 1900; editor The American Magazine of Art (formerly Art and Progress), 1909-31. Sec. Am. Fed. of Arts, 1912-33; sec. Washington Soc. Fine Arts since 1907. Writer and lecturer on art. Episcopalian. Home: 1402 21st St., Washington 6, D.C. Died May 6, 1949.

MEDALIE, George Zerdin (mē-dăl'yȧ), lawyer; b. New York, N.Y., Nov. 21, 1883; s. Aaron and Rachel (Zerdin) M.; B.A., Columbia, 1905, LL.B., 1907; m. Carrie Kaplan, June 30, 1910; children—Arthur Hamilton, Gladys M. Heldman. Began practice in N.Y. City, 1907; asst. dist. atty., New York Co., 1910-15; mem. firm Wasservogel & Medalie, 1916-20; practiced alone, 1920-31; U.S. atty. Southern Dist. of N.Y., 1931-33; special asst. atty. gen. in charge prosecution of election frauds, 1926-28, in Office of Sec. of State of New York, 1928. Rep. candidate for U.S. Senate, New York, 1932. Pres. Fedn. of Jewish Philanthropies of New York, 1941-45; member executive, administrative committees Amer. Jewish Com. V.p. Greater N.Y. Fund. Member board of visitors Columbia U. Law School; pres. Alumni Assn. Columbia U. Law School, 1940-1942. Member American and N.Y. State bar associations, Bar Association City of New York, N.Y. County Lawyers Association (pres. 1938-40; dir.). Republican. Mason, K.P., Elk. Clubs: Nat. Republican, Harmonie, Bankers, Lotos, Columbia University. Home: 225 W. 86th St. Office: 70 Pine St., New York 5, N.Y. Died Mar. 5, 1946.

MEEKER, Arthur, business exec.; b. Chicago, Ill., Apr. 11, 1866; s. Arthur B. and Maria L. (Griggs) M.; B.S., Sheffield Scientific Sch. (Yale), 1886; m. Grace Murray, 1892; children—Mrs. Katharine Gray, Mrs. Grace Lloyd, Arthur, Mrs. Mary Cramer. Chmn. Arcady Farms Mfg. Co.; chmn. of bd. Nat. Aluminate Corp., Chicago. Presbyn.* Clubs: The Links (New York); Chicago, Saddle and Cycle, Casino (Chicago). Home: 1100 Lake Shore Drive. Office: 223 W. Jackson Blvd., Chicago, Ill.* Died Feb. 5 1946.

MEEKER, Frank Leroy, lawyer; b. Marshalltown, Ia., July 23, 1869; s. John Franklin and Sarah Tildon (Pierce) M.; grad. high sch., Marshalltown, 1888; B.A., Grinnell Coll., 1892; read law in office of father; m. Caroline Sipher, Oct. 11, 1899; children—Marcia, Mahlon Morgan. Admitted to Ia. bar, 1894, and began practice at Marshalltown; mem. firm Meeker & Meeker until death of father, 1908, since alone; specialized in probate practice; also largely identified with real estate business, acquiring holdings in Fla., Mo., and N.D., and S.D.; sec. Ia.-Fla. Land Co. Presented a permanent camp site, at Pine Lake, Eldora, Ia., to Marshall County Y.M.C.A. and Y.W.C.A. Trustee Iowa Children's Home, Y.M.C.A. Mem. Ia. State Bar Assn., Marshall County Bar Assn. (pres. 1931), Marshalltown Chamber Commerce. Republican. Conglist. Clubs: Lions (2d pres.; elected dist. gov. of 9th Dist., Ia. and Neb., May 1925; apptd. Internat. Counsellor of Lions Club for service rendered by those Lions who have held the office of dist. gov. in Lions Internat.), Elmwood Country Club. Home: Marshalltown, Ia.* Died Oct. 14, 1944.

MEEKER, George Herbert, chemist; b. Phillipsburg, N.J., Aug. 13, 1871; s. George Edward and Hannah M. (Kelly) M.; B.S. (chemistry), Lafayette Coll., Pa., 1893, M.S., 1895, Ph.D., 1898; Pharm.D., Medico-Chirurg. Coll., Phila., 1906; D.D.S., 1907; spl. chem. research in Munich, 1909-10; LL.D., Ursinus Coll., Pa., 1905, Lafayette, 1925; Sc.D., Villanova, 1913, U. of Pa., 1940; m. Annie Uhler Hunt, 1900. Chemist for various cos., 1893-95; prof. physics, chemistry, metallurgy and toxicology, Medico-Chirurg. Coll., Phila., 1897-1916; established 1907, dean Dept. Pharm. Chemistry, same to 1916; prof. chemistry, Sch. Medicine, 1916-40, est., 1918, dean Grad. Sch. Med., U. of Pa., 1918-41, now emeritus; dir. Graduate Hospital, 1924-28. Toxicologist and expert chemical witness in many prominent cases. Franklin Inst. medallist, 1906; inventor of mech., elec. and chem. devices. Fellow A.A.A.S., Am. Inst. Chemists; mem. Am. Chem. Soc., Pa. Med. Soc. (hon.), Franklin Inst., Delta Upsilon, Phi Rho Sigma, Psi Omega. Clubs: Union League, Medical, Æsculapian (hon.). Mason (K.T., Shriner). Home: 4701 Pine St., Phila., Pa. Died Sept. 4, 1945.

MEEKINS, Isaac Melson, judge; b. Tyrrell County, N.C., Feb. 13, 1875; s. Jeremiah Charles and Mahalah Elizabeth (Melson) M.; prep. education, Horner Military School, Oxford, N.C.; A.B., Wake Forest (N.C.) Coll., 1896, LL.D., 1932; m. Lena Allen, June 4, 1896. Admitted to N.C. bar, 1896, and began practice at Elizabeth City; mayor of Elizabeth City, 1897; city atty., 1898, postmaster, 1903-08; asst. U.S. atty., 1910-14; mem. Rep. State Com. N.C., 1900-18; widely known as popular speaker; gen. counsel for alien property custodian, Washington, D.C., 1921-22; apptd. gen. counsel and mgr. Enemy Ins. Cos., 1922; dist. judge U.S. Court, Eastern Dist. of N.C., by apptmt. of President Coolidge, since Jan. 17, 1925. Endorsed by Rep. State Conv., Raleigh, N.C., March 1936 as nominee for President of U.S. by Rep. Nat. Conv., Cleveland, O. Mem. Am. and N.C. bar assns. Missionary Baptist. Mason (32°). Home: Elizabeth City, N.C. Died Nov. 21, 1946.

MEEM, Harry Grant, banker; b. Georgetown, D.C., August 14, 1870; s. Peter Gilbert and Mary Eleanor Eastbourne (Ritter) M.; grad. Central High School, Washington, 1890; m. Louise Hill, June 26, 1918; children—Ann Meem McLean, Eleanor Meem Jamison (Mrs. Cecil A. Jamison). With Washington Loan & Trust Co., Washington, D.C., since 1891, asst. treas., 1904-07, treas., 1907-17, v.p., 1917-31, pres. since 1931. Directed Liberty Loan drive for bank, devised instalment purchase method and effected sale of one-eighth of City's total, during World War. Dir. and 1st v.p. Equitable Cooperative Bldg. Assn.; trustee endowment fund Am. Nat. Red Cross, Army and Navy Memorial Aid; pres. and trustee John Dickson Home. Mem. Board of Trade, Chamber of Commerce of U.S., Soc. of Natives, Columbia Hist. Soc., Soc. of Oldest Inhabitants, Chevy Chase Club. Home: 2730 34th Pl. N.W. Office: Washington Loan & Trust Co., 9th and F Sts. N.W., Washington, D.C. Died Jan. 20, 1949.

MEGAN, Charles P. (mē'gȧn), lawyer; b. Stratford, Ont., Can., Aug. 24, 1876; s. Peter and Mary Jane (Graydon) M.; ed. Stratford Collegiate Inst., 1887-91; B.A., U. of Toronto, 1895, M.A., 1896; LL.D., De Paul U., 1933; m. May E. Magan, July 1, 1909; children—Charles Graydon, Thomas I., Frances Patricia. Naturalized as citizen of the United States, 1904. Taught in Regiopolis College, Kingston, Can., 1896-98; taught in evening schs., Chicago, 1898, and in Englewood High Sch., 1899-1902; asst. supt. schs. of Chicago, 1902-12; admitted to bar, 1910; practiced law since 1912; member of firm Tolman, Megan & Bryant, state counsel for Home Owners' Loan Corp., 1934, regional counsel, 1934-35; chairman State Adjustment Board, NRA, 1935; trustee C.&N.W. Ry. by apptmt. Federal Court, 1935-39. Mem. Appeal Bd., Selective Service System, since 1940; mem. Ill. State Board Law Examiners, 1928-35, and since 1939; chmn. Nat. Conf. of Bar Examiners, 1933-35. Mem. American and Illinois (pres. 1935-36) bar associations, Chicago Bar Assn. (pres. 1931-33, gen. counsel 1935), Am. Law Inst., Order of the Coif, Phi Delta Phi. Democrat. Catholic. Clubs: Chicago Literary (pres. 1928-29), Law Club of Chicago, Legal Club of Chicago, Cliff Dwellers, Chicago Classical (pres. 1936-38), University, Quadrangle. Mem. bd. of editors Am. Bar Assn. Jour., 1933-43. Author: Murder in the Tower; also numerous essays and addresses. Home: 4640 Ellis Av. Office: 30 N. La Salle St., Chicago, Ill. Died June 14, 1947.

MEHAFFY, Tom Miller (mē-hăf'fĭ), judge; b. near Ripley, Miss., Oct. 3, 1859; s. Thomas L. and Ruth B. (Bradley) M.; attended sch. about 10 mos. between ages of 7 and 21; ed. by pvt. study at home; m. Anna A. Poe, June 15, 1884 (died May 21, 1917); children—Bertha (dec.), James W. (dec.), Tom M. (dec.), John (dec.), Blanch (dec.), Charles, Carl, Helen, Pat, Lucile; m. 2d, Mabel Holland, Jan. 10, 1920; 1 dau., Mary. Admitted to Ark. bar, 1888, and began practice at Benton; mayor of Benton, 1888-89; mem. Ark. Ho. of Rep., 1889-91, Senate, 1892-96; moved to Little Rock, 1905; atty. for Iron Mountain R.R., 7 yrs.; mem. Bd. of Edn., 9 yrs.; del. Constl. Conv. of Ark., 1917 (elected pres. same); asso. justice Supreme Court of Ark., Jan. 1, 1927, by apptmt. of governor, to fill vacancy occasioned by death of son, James W.; elected to fill balance of term, 1928, and reelected Nov. 1934, for term of 8 yrs., beginning Jan. 1935. Democrat. Methodist. Mason (32°, Shriner). Clubs: Shrine, Spring Lake. Home: 2102 Louisiana St. Address: Capitol Bldg., Little Rock, Ark.* Died Oct. 20, 1944.

MEINZER, Oscar Edward, geologist; b. near Davis, Ill., Nov. 28, 1876; s. William and Mary Julia (Meinzer) M.; A.B., magna cum laude, Beloit Coll., 1901 (Phi Beta Kappa), D.Sc., 1946; studied U. of Chicago, 1905-07; Ph.D., 1922; m. Alice Breckenridge Crawford, Oct. 3, 1906; children—Robert William (adopted), Roy Crawford. Prin. public schools, at Frankfort, South Dakota, 1901-03; prof. physical sciences, Lenox Coll., Hopkinton, Ia., 1903-05; instr. geology, Corr. Sch., U. of Chicago, 1906-08; with U.S. Geol. Survey, 1906 to retirement, 1946, devoting time chiefly to investigations of underground water; geologist in charge div. of ground water, 1912-46; in charge desert watering-place survey, 1917-18; del. to Edinburgh Assembly of Internat. Union Geodesy and Geophysics, 1936; U.S. rep. on Exec. Com. Internat. Assn. Hydrology since 1933; pres. Internat. Commn. on Subterranean Water since 1936. Fellow Geological Soc. Am., A.A.A.S. (mem. council since 1946); mem. Wash. Acad. Scis. (v.p. 1932-33, pres. 1936-37), Geol. Soc. Wash. (pres. 1930-31), Soc. of Econ. Geologists (councilor 1937-40, v.p. 1944, pres. 1945), National Research Council (division foreign relations 1930-33), Am. Geophysical Union (first chairman section on hydrology, 1930-33, president since 1947), Pi Gamma Mu, Sigma Xi; 30-year veteran Boy Scouts America. Presbyterian (elder, 1937-45). Club: Cosmos. Author: Outline of Ground-Water Hydrology; Occurrence of Ground-Water in the United States; Large Springs in the United States; Plants as Indicators of Ground-Water; Compressibility and Elasticity of Artesian Aquifiers; Outline of Methods for Estimating Ground-Water Supplies; History and Development of Ground-Water Hydrology; Our Water Supply; Hydrology (with others); Hydrology in Relation to Economic Geology; asso. editor Economic Geol. Commd. as capt. engrs., Oct. 23, 1918, but prevented from active duty by close of war. Awarded Bowie Medal Am. Geophys. Union, 1943; gold medal and button award for distinguished service in sci. work Dept. of Interior, 1948. Home: 2923 South Dakota Av. N.E., Washington 18. Died June 14, 1948; buried Ft. Lincoln Cemetery, Washington.

MEKEEL (Haviland) Scudder (mē-kĕl'), anthropologist; b. St. Louis, Mo., Apr. 30, 1902; s. I. A. and Elizabeth May (Schureman) M.; student Calif. Inst. Tech., 1920-21, Princeton U., 1921-24, Université de Strasbourg, France, 1925-26; B.S., Harvard, 1928; A.M., U. of Chicago, 1929; Ph.D., Yale, 1932; m. Velma Lucile Brown, Apr. 30, 1925; children—Joyce Haviland, Judith Abbott, Peter Schureman. Research asst., Inst. Human Relations, Yale, 1929-33; fellow Social Science Research Council, 1932-34; fellow in psychology, Harvard, 1933-35; field rep. of Commn. of Indian Affairs and dir. applied anthropology, U.S. Bureau of Indian Affairs, 1935-37; acting dir. special socio-economic unit, Soil Conservation Service, U.S. Dept. of Agr., 1936; dir. Lab. of Anthropology, Santa Fe, N.M., 1938-42; on leave, 1940-42; asso. prof. of sociology and anthropology, U. of Wis., since 1940; on leave, 1943-44; consultant, Julius Rosenwald Fund, 1943-44; lecturer U. of N.M., 1938-40. Mem. gov. bd. Internat. Com. for Mental Hygiene, since 1947. Fellow A.A.A.S. (mem. council); mem. Am. Anthrop. Assn., Am. Folklore Soc., Inst. of Pacific Relations, Am. Sociol. Soc., Am. Orthopsychiatric Assn., Am. Ethnol. Soc., Chicago Psychoanalytic Soc., Sigma Xi, Alpha Kappa Delta. Author: Americans and Their Prejudices, 1946. Contributor to (books) Walapai Ethnography, 1936; Explorations in Personality, 1938; Marriage and Family, 1942; Education and the Cultural Process, 1943; also to professional jours. Home: 3518 Blackhawk Drive. Address: Sterling Hall, University of Wisconsin, Madison, Wis. Died July 23, 1947.

MELCHER, Columbus Rudolph (mĕl'chẽr), prof. modern langs.; b. Vevay, Ind., Apr. 7, 1863; s. John and Susan Elizabeth (Chatelain) M.; A.B., Hanover (Ind.) Coll., 1885, A.M., 1899; univs. of Munich and Leipzig, 1886-88; LL.B., Univ. of Louisville, 1896; Univ. of Chicago, 1900-01; LL.D., Hanover (Indiana) College, 1935; m. Mary Shannon Taylor, Aug. 9, 1893; 1 dau., Ruth Taylor. Prin. high sch., Vevay, Ind., 1885-86; supt. schs., Carrollton, Ky., 1889-95; prin. Reynolds Presbyn. Acad., Albany, Tex., 1901-02; prof. ancient and modern langs., Hanover Coll., 1902-07; asst. prof. modern langs., 1907, asso. prof., 1908; prof., 1910, dean of men, 1914, head dept. German lang. and lit., 1917-33, U. of Ky., now emeritus; visiting prof. German, Centre Coll., 2d semester, 1933-34. Pres. Bd. of Edn., Lexington, 1913-16. Mem. Ky. Acad. Science, Ky. Ednl. Assn., Am. Assn. Univ. Profs., Modern Lang. Assn. America, Delta Tau Delta, Omicron Delta Kappa. Pres. Conf. of Deans of Men, 1925-26. Presbyterian. Mason (K.P.). Home: 129 Barberry Lane, Lexington 10, Ky. Died March 23, 1947; buried, Lexington, Ky.

MELINE, Frank L. (mĕ-lēn'), realtor; b. Jacksonville, Ill., Aug. 5, 1875; s. Joseph and Mary (Lomelino) M.; ed. pub. sch. and business coll., Jacksonville; m. Alma Wellman, Nov. 28, 1901; 1 son, Frank Wellman (dec.). Sec. and owner The Hollywood Laundry, Calif. Laundry, Beverly Hills Laundry, Modern Way Laundry (all inc.); owner City Dye Works, Calif. Paper Box & Printing Co., Inter-City Ins. Co.; now retired. Republican. Protestant. Clubs: Los Angeles Athletic, Hollywood Athletic, Bel Air Country. Home: 331 N. Rockingham Rd., W. Los Angeles, Calif. Office: 9405 Brighton Way, Beverly Hills, Calif. Died Aug. 17, 1944.

MELLER, Harry Bertine, research engr.; b. Altoona, Pa., May 26, 1878; s. Charles William and Annie (Adams) M.; U. of Pa., 1906-07, 1908-09; Mich. Coll. of Mines, Houghton, 1907-08, 1909; Engr. of Mines, U. of Pittsburgh, 1910; Sc.D., U. of Toledo, 1938; m. Mary Alice Rothrock, Apr. 8, 1901. Clerk Pa. R.R. Co., Altoona, Pa., 1895-1900; clk. of faculty, dept. of medicine, U. of Pa., 1900-04; sec. same, 1904-07; instr. mining, 1910-11, asst. prof., 1911-12, prof., 1912-24, vice-dean, 1912-14, dean, 1914-23, School of Mines—all of University of Pittsburgh; head of air pollution investigation, Mellon Inst., U. of Pittsburgh, since 1923; chief Bur. of Smoke Regulation of City of Pittsburgh, 1920-38. Managing dir. Industrial Hygiene Foundation America (formerly Air Hygiene Foundation) since 1935. Enlisted Company C, 5th Regt. Nat. Guard Pa., 1897; with same company and regt. Pa. Vol. Inf., May-Oct. 1898; successively 2d lt., 1903-04, 1st lt., 1904-05, capt., 1905-07, Co. L, 3d Regt., Nat. Guard Pa.; capt. Air Service U.S. Army, 1917-19. Republican. Mem. A.A.A.S., Am. Pub. Health Assn., Phi Delta Theta, Sigma Gamma Epsilon, Alpha Omicron. Mason. Home: Schenley Apts. Office: Mellon Institute, Pittsburgh, Pa. Died June 27, 1943.

MELLON, Thomas Alexander, corp. official; b. Pittsburgh, Pa., Nov. 19, 1873; s. Thomas Alexander and Mary (Caldwell) M.; ed. acad. in Pittsburgh and took regular course with engring. firm; m. Helen Wightman, Nov. 15, 1899; children—Thomas Alexander (dec.), Elisabeth Wightman, Edward Purcell, Helen Sedgley. Water works constrn. since 1895, also has been largely identified with housing problems, railroad construction and building of industrial plants, bridges, office buildings. Presbyterian. Mason (32°, K.T., Shriner) Clubs: Duquesne, Pittsburgh, Allegheny Country, Pittsburgh Field, Pittsburgh Golf, Fox Chapel Golf, Rolling Rock, Rolling Rock Hunt (all of Pittsburgh or Pa.); Congressional Country (Washington, D.C.); Henrys Lake Club (Idaho). Home: 401 N. Negley Av. Office: 210 E. Park Way N.S., Pittsburgh 12. Died April 15, 1948.

MELLON, William Larimer, banker; b. Pittsburgh, Pa.; s. James Ross and Rachel H. (Larimer) M.; ed. Pa. Mil. Coll., Chester, Pa.; LL.D., Pa. Mil. Coll., 1928; m. Miss Taylor. Began with Mellon Bros., real estate and building supplies, Pittsburgh; entered street ry. business and became pres. Monongahela St. Ry., Pittsburgh; chmn. bd. Gulf Oil Corp. and other oil cos.; v.p. Nat. Union Fire Ins. Co.; dir., v.p. Mellon National Bank and Trust Co., Standard Car Finance Corp., Union Spring & Mfg. Co. Pres. & dir. Ligonier Transportation Co., Ligonier Valley R.R. and various other corps. Clubs: Pittsburgh, Duquesne, etc. Home: Forbes St. and Darlington Rd. Office: Gulf Bldg., Pittsburgh 19, Pa. Died Oct. 8, 1949.

MELONEY, Marie Mattingly, editor; b. Bardstown, Ky.; d. Cyprian Peter (M.D.) and Sarah (Irwin) Mattingly; ed. privately; hon. Dr. of Humane Letters, Russell Sage Coll.; hon. M.S. and Bus. Adminstrn., Bryant College; m. Col. William Brown Meloney, author, June 6, 1904 (died Dec. 7, 1925); 1 son, William Brown. Mem. staff Washington (D.C.) Post, 1900, Denver Evening Post, 1900; mem. U.S. Senate Press Gallery and Washington corr., 1900-01; staff N.Y. Sun, 1901-04; editor Woman's Magazine, 1914-20, also asso. editor of Everybody's, 1917-20; editor The Delineator, 1920-26; editor Sunday Magazine, N.Y. Herald Tribune, since 1926, and of This Week Magazine since 1934. Decorated, 1917, Médaille de Charleroi, for service in behalf of Belgian children; 1919, Ordre de la Reine Elisabeth for distinguished service to Belgian cause in U.S.; Order of the Crown of Belgium, 1928; Officier Légion d'Honneur, Médaille d'Honneur des Assurances Sociales, and gold medal for state service—all from France; Polonia Restituta (Poland) for helping build cancer hospital in Warsaw. Organizer Marie Curie Radium Com. (for purchase of gramme of radium); organizer and chairman, New York Herald Tribune Forum on Current Problems for women's clubs and colleges. Lecturer at Harvard and St. Lawrence universities. Director The Child Foundation, American Child Health Assn.; founder and v.p. Better Homes in America; originated plan for Junior Red Cross, 1916-17; mem. Nat. Inst. Social Sciences, Nat. League Business and Professional Women. Clubs: P.E.N., New York Newspaper Women's, Colony. Inaugurated weights conference called by Am. Med. Assn., 1926; also conference of members of Am. Psychiatric Assn. on "Why Men Fail." Wrote introductions to The Log Cabin Lady (biography), 1922; also introductions to biography and autobiography of Pierre and Marie Curie, 1923; What Man Can Not Destroy, 1940. Home: South Quaker Hill, Pawling, N.Y. Office: 420 Lexington Av., New York, N.Y. Died June 23, 1943.

MELTON, LeRoy; b. nr. Westfield, Ill., Jan. 24, 1881; s. Benjamin Allen and Sarah A. (Faris) M.; Westfield Coll., 1898-1901; B.C.S., Greenville Coll., 1904; m. E. Leona Ferguson, Feb. 2, 1902; children—Mrs. Ethel Adine Melton McDowell, Charles O., Ralph Allen. Teacher public schools; dir. commercial dept., Westfield Coll., 1905-08; dir. School of Commercial Science, Greenville Coll., 1908-18; nat. sec. Farmers' Equity Union (cooperative marketing), 1918-22, pres., 1922-48, pres. emeritus since 1948, editor Equity Union Exchange since 1918. Free Methodist. Writer and lecturer on coop. marketing. Home: Greenville, Ill. Died Mar. 7, 1950.

MELTON, Wightman Fletcher, editorial writer; b. Ripley, Tenn., Sept. 26, 1867; s. Rev. Isaac Quimby and Fanny Louise (Ellis) M.; grad. Peabody Coll. for Teachers, Nashville, Tenn., 1889; A.B., Blount Coll., Blountsville, Ala., 1890; Ph.D., State Normal Coll., Troy, Ala., 1894; Ph.D., Johns Hopkins, 1906; m. Oliver Keller, Sept. 19, 1889; children—Oliver Quimby, Mrs. Emily McNelley, Keller Fletcher. Began teaching at Blountsville, 1889; pres. Fla. Conf. Coll., Leesburg, Fla., 1892-95; v.p. Nashville (Tenn.) Coll. for Young Ladies, 1895-97; pres. Tuscaloosa (Ala.) Female Coll., 1897-1903; student and fellow by courtesy, Johns Hopkins, 1903-06; head dept. of English, Baltimore City Coll., 1906-08; prof. English lang. and lit., Emory U., 1908-24; prof. extension, English, Oglethorpe U., 1931-43; div. of information and publs., State Dept. Edn., 1935-39; with Griffin News since 1924. Inaugurated teaching of journalism in Ga. Official examiner of teachers, Blount County, Ala., 1890, Alachua County, Fla., 1891; mayor of Oxford, Ga., 1912-18; asso. field dir. Am. Red Cross, Ft. McPherson and Camp Jesup, Ga., 6 mos., 1918. Mem. Poetry Soc. of America, Poetry Soc. of England, Poetry Soc. of Ga., Poetry Soc. of Miss., Ark. Authors and Writers Soc. (hon.), N.Y. Craftsman Poetry Group (hon.), Atlanta Writers' Club (pres.), Burns Club of Atlanta (dir.), Kappa Alpha. Democrat. Mason. Mem. M.E. Ch., S. Author: The Preacher's Son, 1894; The Rhetoric of John Donne's Verse, 1903; Chimes of Oglethorpe (poems), 1933. Editor: Ruskin's Crown of Wild Olive, and Queen of the Air, 1908; Lanier Memorial Poems of Trees, Vols. I to VIII, 1932-40; Versecraft, 1931-33; Bozart and Contemporary Verse, 1933-35. Curator State Museum of Ga., 1943. Poet Laureate of Ga., 1943. Home: 1205 Emory Drive, Atlanta, Ga. Died Nov. 10, 1944.

MELVILLE, Rose, actress; b. Terre Haute, Ind., Jan. 30, 1873; d. Rev. Jacob and Caroline (Puett) Smock; ed. Convent of St. Mary's of the Woods and Franklin Coll., Ind.; m. Frank Minzey, June 12, 1910. Début 1891; created rôle of Sis Hopkins in "Zeb," 1893; "Little Christopher," 1895; played leading rôle in "The Prodigal Father," 1896-97, "By the Sad Sea Waves," 1898; starring as Sis, in "Sis Hopkins," in own co. since 1899. Home: South Bend, Ind. Died Oct. 8, 1946.

MELVIN, Ridgely Prentiss, judge; b. Denton, Md., Nov. 4, 1881; s. George Thomas and Maria Louise (Hopkins) M.; A.B., St. John's Coll., Annapolis, Md., 1899, A.M., 1900; LL.B., U. of Md. Law Sch., 1902; m. Augusta Somervell Burwell, Oct. 24, 1914; children—Augusta Burwell, Ridgely Prentiss, Mary Burwell, Elizabeth Somervell, John Burwell. Admitted to Md. bar, 1903, and since engaged in gen. practice of law at Annapolis; city counselor of Annapolis, 1907-15; counsel to county commrs. of Anne Arundel County, 1910-25; mem. County Bd. Edn., 1922-30; mem. Jud. Council of Md., 1922-34; Maryland State Press Association, 1920-26; member Maryland House of Dels., 1918-20; mem. Md. Senate, 1930-38; asso. judge Fifth Jud. Circuit Md., 1938-42; chief judge Fifth Jud. Circuit and mem. of Court of Appeals, Md., since 1942. Served as food adminstr. Anne Arundel County, 1918; chmn. Red Cross Chapter. Mem. legal adv. com., dist. gov. of Rotary, 1927-28. Mem. Am., Md. State and Anne Arundel County bar assn., Am. Judicature Soc., Phi Kappa Sigma. Democrat. Episcopalian (vestryman, mem. exec. council Diocese Md.). Home: Annapolis, Md. Died Dec. 14, 1945.

MENSEL, Ernst Heinrich, philologist; b. Lunden, Ger., Mar. 12, 1865; s. Johann Jakob and Margarete (Siercks) M.; prep. edn. Germany; A.B., Carthage Coll., 1887, A.M., 1890, Litt.D., 1920; Ph.D., U. of Mich., 1896; m. Sarah L. Hyde, June 11, 1890 (died Aug. 21, 1914); children—Ernst Edmund, Margaret Lucinda, John Hyde, Mary Elizabeth, Sarah Harriet, Gertrud Hyde; m. 2d, Ann Elizabeth Chaney, July 26, 1935. Instr. ancient langs., 1886-88, prof. ancient langs. and German, 1888-92, Carthage Coll.; instr. German, U. of Mich., 1892-98, asst. prof., 1898-1901; prof. Germanic langs. and lits., Smith Coll., 1901-33, emeritus. Lecturer on Germanic philology, Harvard, 1904-05. Lutheran. Mem. Modern Lang. Assn. America, Linguistic Soc. Am. Author: Die erste deutsche Romeo-Übersetzung, 1933. Contbr. articles on Germanic philology and edn. and of reviews to many scientific jours. Home: 262 Bridge St., Northampton, Mass. Died Sept. 6, 1942.

MENVILLE, Raoul Louis, univ. dean emeritus; b. Napoleonville, La., Nov. 23, 1885; s. Charles Marie and Arabella (Gouaux) M.; B.S., La. State U., 1905, M.S., 1912; student U. of Chicago, summer, 1924, Ph.D., Ohio State U., 1929; m. Mae Eleanor Friedman, June 19, 1907; children—Mae Eleanor (Mrs. Lawrence V. George), Raoul Louis, Charles Alcide, Elaine Elizabeth (Mrs. Karl M. Shuman). Asst. chemist La. State Expt. Sta., 1905-06; instr. in chemistry, La. State U., 1906-12, asst. prof., 1912-20, associate professor, 1920-27, professor 1927-37, dean of college of chemistry and physics and head of department of chemistry, 1937 to 1944; dean emeritus, Sept. 1, 1944. Fellow A.A.A.S., member American Chemical Society, Louisiana Academy of Sciences, La. Teachers Assn., Sigma Xi, Alpha Chi Sigma, Phi Lambda Upsilon, Phi Kappa Phi, Omicron Delta Kappa, Theta Kappa Phi. Democrat. Roman Catholic. K.C. Home: 910 S. 18th St., Baton Rouge, La. Died Mar. 27, 1946.

MEREDITH, Albert Barrett (mĕr'ĕ-dĭth), prof. edn. emeritus; b. Gorham, N.H., February 2, 1871; s Rev. William Henry and Susan (Barrett) M.; grad. Classical High Sch., Lynn, Mass., 1889; Boston U., 1891-93; B.A., Wesleyan U., Conn., 1895, M.A., 1916, LL.D., 1921; studied Harvard, summers, 1896, 1898, 1900, 1901, Teachers Coll. (Columbia), 1910-11; Pd.D., Muhlenburg Coll., Allentown, Pa., 1918, L.H.D., Upsala Coll., East Orange, N.J., 1918; LL.D., Boston University, 1930; Litt.D., Rutgers U., New Brunswick, N.J., 1937; m. Adelaide Spencer (A.B., Wellesley), June 29, 1899; 1 son, Spencer Barrett. Teacher Holbrook Military School, Ossining, N.Y., 1895-97; vice prin. high sch., Plainfield, N.J., 1897-1901; supt. schools, Nutley, N.J., 1901-11; county supt. schs., Essex County, N.J., 1904-12; asst. commr. edn., N.J., in charge of secondary edn., 1912-20; commr. of education, State of Conn., 1920-30; prof. of edn. and head dept. sch. adminstrn., New York U., 1930-41; chmn. grad. div. School of Education, 1931-41; coordinator Civilian Defense Training, State of New York, 1941-43; administrative assistant to commr. of edn., N.Y. State Dept. of Edn., 1943. Lectured at State University of New Jersey, New York Univ., Yale Univ., etc. Asso. ednl. dir. Y.M.C.A., Camp Dix, N.J., 1918; mem. staff on edn. and spl. training, Plans Div. of Gen. Staff, U.S. Army, Washington, D.C., 1918. Made secondary school surveys of St. Paul, St. Louis, and school surveys of Cincinnati, Niagara Falls (New York) and Buffalo, administrative and financial survey, Puerto Rico, 1925; consultant Nat. Secondary Sch. Survey, 1929, and dir. many surveys. Mem. Commn. of 7 on higher edn. in Calif., Carnegie Foundation of Teaching, 1932; mem. Ednl. Adv. Com., Surveys of Fall River, Mass., 1933, Phila., 1937; member Advisory Com., Peabody Museum (Yale); trustee Wesleyan (Conn.) University, 1928-38; Drew University since 1935; Centenary Junior College (Hackettstown, N.J.) since 1932, Teachers College (Columbia), 1922-24, Conn. State College, 1921-30. Chmn. Am. Council on Edn., Washington, D.C., 1931; ednl. advisor N.J. State Bd. of Regents (higher education), 1931-38; Bd. Edn., Hartford, Conn., 1934-35; mem. bd. dirs. National Society for Prevention of Blindness (N.Y.). Member N.E.A., Nat. Council Education, Nat. Conf. on St. and Highway Safety, Nat. Soc. for Study of Edn., Phi Beta Kappa, Theta Delta Chi. Republican. Methodist. Clubs: N.Y. Schoolmasters' (pres. 1914). Author: (with John H. Greenan) Problems of American Democracy; (with Vivian Hood) Geography, History and Civics of New Jersey; also various monographs on teaching high school subjects, and on school administration. Home: "Westlook," Wakefield, N.H. Died Apr. 12, 1946.

MEREDITH, James Alva, lawyer; b. Alma, Tyler County, W.Va., Jan. 27, 1875; s. Absalom P. and Catherine (Riley) M.; Normal and Classical Acad., Buckhannon, W.Va., 1895; A.B., LL.B., W.Va. U., 1900; m. Gillian Jamison, Sept. 17, 1902; 1 son, Jamison. Began practice at Middlebourne, W.Va., 1900; moved to Fairmont, 1903; apptd. judge Supreme Court of Appeals, W.Va., to fill vacancy caused by resignation of Judge Charles W. Lynch, Jan. 2, 1922, later nominated for same office by Rep. State Conv., to fill unexpired term, but defeated in election; re-apptd. mem. Supreme Court of Appeals, Dec. 18, 1922, to fill vacancy occasioned by resignation of Judge Harold A. Ritz, term expiring Nov. 1924; now mem. Meredith & Bell; counsel for Monongahela West Penn Public Service Co. Member Joint Legislative Com. on Revision W.Va. Code. Mem. Am. and Marion County bar assns., W.Va. Bar Assn. (pres. 1932-33). Methodist. Mason (32°, K.T., Shriner). Home: Fairmont, W.Va. Died Apr. 18, 1942.

MERIVALE, Philip (mĕr'ĭ-văl), actor; b. Rehutia, Manickpur, India, Nov. 2, 1886; s. Walter and Emma Magdalene (Pittman) M.; ed. St. Edward's Sch., Oxford, 1899-1903; m. Viva Birkett, July 23, 1912 (died in 1934); children—Rosamund, Valentine, John Herman and Philip David Birkett; married 2d, Gladys Cooper. Began as an office boy, London, England, 1904; became a member of F. R. Benson's Shakespearean Co., 1906; joined Fred Terry and Julia Nielson's Company, came to U.S. in The Scarlet Pimpernel, 1910; with Sir Herbert Tree at His Majesty's, 3 yrs.; returned to U.S. with Mrs. Patrick Campbell in Pygmalion. Principal roles: Prince Albert in "The Swan," Hannibal in "The Road to Rome," Sirki in "Death Takes a Holiday," Bothwell in "Mary of Scotland," Washington in "Valley Forge"; played roles of Canio, Othello, Macbeth, Prospero, in Shakespearean productions. With Royal Flying Corps, World War. Clubs: Garrick, Green Room (London); Players, Coffee House (New York, N.Y.). Author: The Wind Over the Water; Knut at Roeskilde; The Peace of Ferrara. Address: 750 Napoli Drive, Pacific Palisades, Calif. Died Mar. 12, 1946.

MERLE-SMITH, Van Santvoord, banker; b. Seabright, N.J., June 22, 1889; s. Wilton and Zaidee (Van Santvoord) M.; A.B., Princeton, 1911; LL.B., Harvard, 1914; m. Kate Grosvenor Fowler, June 20, 1916; children—Van Santvoord, Nancy, Fowler, Margaret. Began law practice, New York, 1914; mem.

Dick & Merle-Smith, investment bankers; member advisory committee New York Trust Co. Fortieth St. office; director Hudson River Day Line, Lincoln Warehouse and Safe Deposit Co., Mississippi Land Co. On secretariat of Peace Conf., Paris, 1919; 3d asst. sec. of state of U.S., 1920-21. Enlisted in Troop C, Squadron A, N.Y. Cav., 1914; promoted through grades to maj., 165th Inf., U.S. Army, 1919; service on Mexican border, June 1916-Mar. 1917; sailed for France, Nov. 4, 1917; participated in battles at Luneville, Baccarat, Espérance-Souain, Champagne-Marne defensive, Aisne-Marne offensive, St. Mihiel offensive, Essey-Pannes, Meuse-Argonne offensive; with Army of Occupation; wounded at Luneville and at Villers-sur-Fère; hon. disch., May 7, 1919. Awarded D.S.C. Trustee Hill Sch., Bd. of Nat. Missions, Presbyn. Ch. in U.S.A.; trustee and treas. Church Extension Com. of Presbytery of New York. Republican. Presbyterian. Clubs: Metropolitan (Washington); Knickerbocker, University, Princeton, New York Yacht, Seawanhaka. Home: Oyster Bay, L.I., N.Y. Office: 30 Pine St., New York, N.Y. Died Nov. 9, 1943.

MERRELL, Edgar Sanford Keen, judge; b. Lowville, N.Y., May 21, 1865; s. Eliada Sanford and Emeline A. (Clark) M.; prep. edn., Lowville Acad.; B.S., St. Lawrence U., N.Y., 1887; degree LL.D., conferred by same university, 1929; m. Johanna F. Voshage, Sept. 22, 1891; children—Charlotte Emeline (Mrs. Stanley B. Miller), Nathaniel Eliada. Admitted to bar, 1889, and practiced at Lowville until 1910; county judge and surrogate, Lewis County, N.Y., 1902-09; justice Supreme Court, N.Y., since Jan. 1, 1910; assigned as asso. justice Appellate Div., 4th Dept., May 1913, to 1st Dept., May 7, 1918; redesignated as asso. justice 1st dept., Appell. Div., May 1923; reëlected as Justice Supreme Court, 5th Jud. Dist., Nov. 1923; redesignated as asso. justice Appell. Dept., 1st Div., Jan. 1, 1924, and Jan. 1, 1929; retired on account of age limitation, Dec. 31, 1935. Democrat. Trustee Lowville Acad. Episcopalian. Mason. Mem. Phi Beta Kappa. Clubs: Roaring Brook Fish and Game; Ft. Schuyler (Utica, N.Y.). Address: 48 Collins St., Lowville, Lewis County, N.Y. Died Dec. 5, 1942.

MERRIAM C(linton) Hart, naturalist; b. N.Y. City, Dec. 5, 1855; s. Hon. Clinton L. and Caroline (Hart) M.; student Sheffield Scientific Sch. (Yale), 1874-77; M.D., College Physicians and Surgeons (Columbia), 1879; m. Virginia Elizabeth Gosnell, Oct. 15, 1886 (died Dec. 7, 1937); children—Dorothy (Mrs. Henry Abbot), Zenaida (Mrs. M. W. Talbot). In med. practice, 1879-85; chief of U.S. Biol. Survey, 1885-1910; resigned to conduct biol. and ethnol. investigations under a spl. trust fund established by Mrs. E. H. Harriman, 1910-39. Naturalist, Hayden's survey, 1872; asst. U.S. Fish Commn., 1875; visited Arctic seal fishery from Newfoundland, 1883, as surgeon S.S. Proteus; visited Alaska, 1891, as U.S. Bering Sea Commr., and investigated the fur seal on Pribilof Islands; has conducted many biol. explorations in Far West. Chmn. U.S. Geographic Bd., 1917-25. Fellow American Ornithologists' Union (pres. 1900-02), A.A.A.S.; a founder and mem. board of trustees Nat. Geog. Soc. since 1888; mem. Nat. Acad. of Sciences, Am. Philos. Soc., Am. Soc. Naturalists (pres. 1924-25), Washington Acad. Sciences, Biol. Soc. Washington (pres. 1891, 92), Anthropol. Soc. Washington (pres. 1920, 21), Am. Soc. Mammalogists (pres. 1919-21); foreign mem. Zoöl. Soc. London. Author: The Birds of Connecticut, 1877; Mammals of the Adirondacks, 1882-84; Results of Biol. Survey of San Francisco Mountain Region and Desert of Little Colorado in Arizona, 1890; Biological Reconnaissance of Idaho, 1891; Geographic Distribution of Life in North America, 1892; Trees, Shrubs, Cactuses and Yuccas of Death Valley Expedition, 1893; Laws of Temperature Control of Geographic Distribution of Terrestrial Animals and Plants, 1894; Monographic Revision of the Pocket Gophers (Geomyidæ), 1895; Revision of the American Shrews, 1895; Synopsis of Weasels of North America, 1896; Biological Survey of Mount Shasta, Calif., 1899; Life Zones and Crop Zones of the United States, 1898; Indian Population of California, 1905; Distribution and Classification of the Mewan Indians of California, 1907; Totemism in California, 1908; The Dawn of the World, 1910; Review of the Grizzly and Big Brown Bears of America, 1917; G. K. Gilbert, Geologist, 1918; The Acorn, a Neglected Source of Food, 1918; A California Elk Drive, 1921; Earliest Crossing of the Deserts of Utah and Nevada to Southern California—Route of Jedediah H. Smith in 1826, 1923; First Crossing of the Sierra Nevada—Jedediah Smith's trip from California to Salt Lake in 1827, 1923; The Name of Mount Rainier, 1924; Baird, the Naturalist, 1924; Source of the Name Shasta, 1926; The Buffalo in Northern California, 1926; Classification and Distribution of the Pit River Indian Tribes of California, 1926; William Healey Dall, 1927; Annikadel History of the Universe as told by the Modesse Indians of Calif., 1928; also about 400 papers on zoöl., bot. and ethnol. subjects. Home: 2590 Cedar St., Berkeley, Calif. Died Mar. 19, 1942.

MERRIAM, John Campbell, palæontologist, educator, administrator; b. Hopkinton, Ia., Oct. 20, 1869; s. Charles Edward and Margaret Campbell (Kirkwood) M.; B.S., Lenox Coll., Ia., 1887; Ph.D., U. of Munich, 1893; Sc.D., Columbia, 1921, Princeton, 1922, Yale, 1922, U. of Pa., 1936, U. State of N.Y., 1937; Ore. State Coll., 1939; LL.D., Wesleyan U., 1922, U. of Calif., 1924, New York U., 1926, U. of Mich., 1933, Harvard U., 1935, George Washington U., 1937, U. of Ore., 1939; m. Ada Gertrude Little, Dec. 22, 1896 (died Apr. 13, 1940); children—Lawrence Campbell, Charles Warren, Malcolm Landers; m. 2d, Margaret Louise Webb, Feb. 20, 1941. Instr. palæontology and hist. geology, 1894-99, asst. prof., 1899-1905, asso. prof., 1905-12, prof., 1912-20, dean of faculties, 1920, U. of Calif.; chmn. Nat. Research Council, 1919; pres. Carnegie Instn., Washington, 1920-38, emeritus since 1939. Regent Smithsonian Inst. since 1923. Fellow Am. A.A.A.S. (pres. Pacific Div., 1919-20), Geol. Soc. America (pres. 1910), Am. Palæontol. Soc. (pres. 1917); mem. Nat. Acad. Sciences (Washington), Am. Philos. Soc., Washington Acad. Sciences; Calif. Acad. Sciences, Phila. Acad. Sciences, Am. Acad. Arts and Sciences, Am. Assn. Univ. Profs., Commission du Parc National Albert; corr. mem. London Zoöl. Soc., Chr. Michelsens Institute (Bergen, Norway); hon. mem. Soc. de Geog. e Hist. de Guatemala, Acad. Nacional Cient. Antonio Alzate de Mex., La Asociacion Conservadoro de los Monumentos Arquelogicos de Yucatan, Soc. de Geog. e Hist. de Michoacán, Mexico. Pres. executive com. Pan-American Institute of Geography and History, 1935-38; chmn. research committee California State Council of Defense, 1917-20. Congregationalist. Republican. Author: Primitive Characters of the Triassic Ichthysauria, 1904; The Thalattosauria, a Group of Marine Reptiles from the Triassic of California, 1905; Cave Exploration, 1906; Triassic Ichthysauria (with special reference to the American forms), 1908; The Occurrence of Human Remains in California Caves, 1909; The Occurrence of Twisted Horned Antelopes in the Tertiary of Northwestern Nevada, 1909; The story of the Calaveras Skull, 1910; Synopsis of Lectures in Palæontology, 1910; The Relation of Palæontology to the History of Man (with particular reference to the Am. problem), 1910; The Fauna of Rancho La Brea, Part I, Occurrence, 1911; Part II, Canidæ, 1912; The Horses of Rancho La Brea, 1913, Discovery of Human Remains in an Asphalt Deposit at Rancho La Brea, 1914; Extinct Faunas of the Mojave Desert (their significance in a study of the origin and evolution of life in America), 1915; Relationships of Pliocene Mammalian Faunas from the Pacific Coast and Great Basin Provinces of North America, 1917; Science in Mobilization, 1917; The Beginnings of Human History Read from the Geological Record; The Emergence of Man, 1919; The Function of Educational Institutions in Development of Research, 1920; Earth Sciences as the Background of History, 1920; The Research Spirit in the Everyday Life of the Average Man, 1920; Common Aims of Culture and Research in the University, 1922; The Place of Education in a Research Institution, 1925; The Responsibility of the Federal and State Governments for Recreation, 1926; International Coöperation in Historical Research, 1926; Medicine and the Evolution of Society, 1926; Inspiration and Education in National Parks, 1927; The Place of Geology Among the Sciences, 1929; Institutes for Research in the Natural Sciences, 1929; Significance of the Border Area between Natural and Social Sciences, 1929; The Living Past, 1930; The Unity of Nature as Illustrated by the Grand Canyon, 1931; The Felidae of Rancho La Brea (with Chester Stock), 1932; Spiritual Values and the Constructive Life, 1933; Responsibility of Science to Government, 1934; Ultimate Values of Science, 1935; Science and Human Values; Time and Change in History, 1936; The Most Important Methods of Promoting Research, as Seen by Research Foundations and Institutions; Geography and History Among the Sciences, as Influencing Research in the Americas, 1937; Application of Science in Human Affairs; Influence of Science upon Appreciation of Nature; Some Aspects of Cooperative Research in History, 1938; Contribution of Geology to Shaping of Ideas on the Meaning of History; Science and Belief; The Development of Cultural and Social Values through the Relation of Science to Other Major Fields of Activity, 1939; also numerous other papers on palæontology, hist., geology and problems of research in their relation to edn. Clubs: Cosmos (Washington); Century Association (New York); Commonwealth Club of California (San Francisco). Address: Carnegie Institution of Washington, Washington, D.C.* Died Oct. 30, 1945.

MERRICK, Frank Anderson, v. chmn., Westinghouse Electric & Mfg. Co.; b. Lambertville, N.J.; s. Stephen W. and Mary Elizabeth (Walton) M.; E.E., Lehigh U., 1891; Engr. D., 1933; m. Louise Finney, 1893; children—John F., Lester F., Sara. With Thomson Houston Electric Co. and Gen. Electric Co., 1891-96, Blood & Hale, Boston, 1896-98; with Steel Motors Co., Johnstown, Pa., mgr. and chief engr., 1898-1902; with Westinghouse Electric & Mfg. Co., East Pittsburgh, Pa., 1902; supt. Canadian Westinghouse Co., Ltd., 1903, then mgr. works, v.p. and gen. mgr.; gen. mgr. New England Westinghouse Co., Chicopee Falls, Mass., mfg. rifles and machine guns, 1917-18; special rep. Westinghouse Internat. Co., London, Eng., 1919-21; v.p. and gen. mgr. Canadian Westinghouse Co., 1921-25; v.p. and gen. mgr. Westinghouse Electric & Mfg. Co., 1925-29, pres., 1929-38, vice chmn. since Feb. 1938. Awarded Imperial Decoration Third Order of the Rising Sun (Japan), 1935. Episcopalian. Home: 95 Arkledun Av., Hamilton, Can.; and Schenley Hotel, Pittsburgh. Office: Westinghouse Electric & Mfg. Co., Pittsburgh, Pa. Died Oct. 26, 1944.

MERRICK, George Edgar, real estate; b. Springdale, Pa., June 3, 1886; s. Solomon Greasley and Althea (Fink) M.; ed. Rollins Coll., Winter Park, Fla., and New York Law Sch.; m. Eunice I. Peacock, Feb. 1916. In real estate business since 1911; began 1921, upon development of Coral Gables (a $100,000,000 enterprise). Originated and made possible by promotion and gifts founding of U. of Miami, and regent since its beginning. Pres. George E. Merrick, Inc., real estate, since 1934; postmaster of Miami since 1940. Commissioner, Dade County, 1915-17; chairman Dade County Planning Council, 1935-39; chairman Dade County Zoning Commn., 1937-39. Dir. Fairchild Tropical Garden. Decorated Don of Order of Isabella de Catolica, 1927. Mem. Christian Science Church. Author: Songs of the Wind on a Southern Shore, 1920. Home: 907 Coral Way, Coral Gables, Fla. Died Mar. 26, 1942.

MERRILL, Edwin Godfrey, banker; b. Bangor, Me., Nov. 21, 1873; s. Isaac Hobbs and Ada Frances (Godfrey) M.; A.B., magna cum laude, Harvard, 1895; LL.D., U. of Maine, 1928; m. Adelaide Isabel Katte, Jan. 21, 1902; children—Edwin Katte, Dudley, Adele Katte (Mrs. Charlton MacVeagh), Priscilla Godfrey (Mrs. F. R. Murad), Elizabeth (Mrs. E. B. Katte). With Merrill & Co., bankers, Bangor, 1896-98, Kountze Bros., N.Y., Feb.-Sept. 1898, Estabrook & Co., N.Y., 1898-1901; mng. partner Merrill & Co., Bangor, 1901-03; organizer and pres. Merrill Trust Co., 1903-09; pres. Veazie Nat. Bank, 1905, till absorption by Merrill Trust Co., 1908; v.p. Central Trust Co. of New York, 1909-10; pres. Union Trust Co. of New York, 1910-18, till consolidation with Central Trust Co.; v.p. and vice chmn. bd. of trustees of Central Union Trust Co., 1918-19; pres. and trustee New York Life Ins. & Trust Co., 1920-22, till consolidation with The Bank of New York; pres. and trustee Bank of N.Y. & Trust Co. (now Bank of N.Y.), 1922-31; chmn. bd., 1931-48; hon. chmn. Bank of N.Y. and Fifth Av. Bank (merged) since 1948; trustee Greenwich Savs. Bank; also treas. and trustee Federal Hall Memorial Associates, Inc.; dir. Globe & Rutgers Fire Ins. Co., N. Am. Reassurance Co. (chmn. bd.), Parish Safe Deposit Co., N.Y. Clearing House Building Co., The European General Reinsurance Co., Ltd., London, North Am. Fire & Marine Reins. Corp. (chmn. bd.), North Am. Casualty & Surety Reins. Corp. (chmn. bd.), Sun Indemnity Co. of N.Y., Patriotic Ins. Co. of America, Sun Underwriters Ins. Co. of N.Y., Am. Home Fire Assurance Co.; U.S. dir. Atlas Assurance Co., Ltd., of London, (chmn. bd.) Western Union Telegraph Co.; mem. United States Board of Caledonian Ins. Co. of Edinburgh. Republican. Episcopalian. Trustee Community Service Soc., New York; treas. and trustee Children's Aid Soc.; mem. bd. mgrs. St. Luke's Hosp. Mem. Chamber of Commerce. Clubs: Harvard, Down Town, Union, Century. Home: Bedford Hills, N.Y. Office: 48 Wall St., New York, N.Y. Died Jan. 16, 1950.

MERRILL, John Fuller Appleton, lawyer; b. Portland, Me., Feb. 10, 1866; s. Col. Charles B. and Abba I. (Little) M.; A.B., Yale, 1889; studied law in office of Judge William L. Putnam, of Portland, and at Harvard Law Sch.; m. Elizabeth Payson Goddard, June 7, 1910. Admitted to Me. bar, 1892, and since practiced in Portland; mem. Common Council, Portland, 1 yr., Bd. of Aldermen, 2 yrs.; mem. Me. Senate, 1907; mem. Police Examining Bd., Portland, about 5 yrs.; judge Municipal Ct., of Portland, 1911-15; U.S. atty., Dist. of Me., Mar. 1915-July 1922; spl. asst. to atty. gen. of U.S., July 1, 1922-Jan. 1, 1923; became receiver First Nat. Bank of Portland, 1933. Mem. Am. Bar Assn., Cumberland Bar Assn. Trustee Children's Hosp. Chancellor Episcopal Diocese of Me. Democrat. Episcopalian. Home: 157 High St. Office: Clapp Memorial Bldg., Portland, Me. Died Jan. 2, 1944.

MERRILL, John Leonard, chmn. bd. All Am. Cables and Radio, Inc.; b. Orange, N.J., Sept. 17, 1866; s. John L. and Elizabeth Tappan (Balch) M.; ed. pvt. and pub. schs.; m. Grace Towner, Oct. 16, 1899. With Mexican, and Central, and S. Am. Telegraph companies (now All America Cables and Radio, Inc.), since 1884, auditor, both cos., 1891, 2d v.p., 1915-18, president, 1918-39, chairman of the board since 1939. Mem. City Council, East Orange, N.J., 1910-12. Member General Society of Colonial Wars (elected sec. general, 1915, vice gov.-gen., 1918-21; dep. gov.-gen. 1927), Soc. Colonial Wars in N.J. (gov. 1916), Huguenot Society America, Huguenot Soc. of N.J. (pres. 1923-25), Revolutionary Memorial Soc., Pilgrims of U.S., S.R. of N.Y., Order of Founders and Patriots (dep. governor-general 1925; governor-general 1927), N.J. Order Founders and Patriots (governor 1924-25); Soc. of War of 1812 (v.p. N.J. Soc. 1927); hon. pres. Pan Am. Soc., Venezuelan Chamber Commerce of U.S.; an incorporator of Am. Red Cross; hon. pres. Argentine Am. Chamber of Commerce, Mexican Chamber of Commerce, Columbian Am. Chamber of Commerce. V.p. and mem. corp. New York Bot. Garden. Home: 45 Park Av. Office: 67 Broad St., New York, N.Y. Died Dec. 18, 1949.

MERRILL, Thomas Emery, army officer; b. Cincinnati, O., June 1, 1875; s. William Emery and Margaret Ellen (Spencer) M.; student Washington and Lee U., 1891-94; grad. U.S. Mil. Acad., 1898; m. Mary Ryan Malone, Sept. 2, 1930; children—Marian, Jean. Commissioned 2d lt. artillery, 1898; promoted through the grades to brig. gen., 1933; served through Spanish-Am. War, Philippine Insurrection, Pershing Expdn. into Mexico and World War; retired from active service, June 30, 1939. Mem. Am. Theosophical Soc. Home: 651 Spazier St., Pacific Grove, Calif. Address: War Dept., Washington, D.C. Died Aug. 18, 1943.

MERRIMAN, Roger Bigelow, teacher of history; b. Boston, May 24, 1876; s. Daniel and Helen (Bigelow)

M.; student Harvard, 1892-96, 1896-97, 1899-1900, and as John Harvard fellow in Europe, 1900-02, A.B., 1896, A.M., 1897, Ph.D., 1902; Balliol Coll., Oxford Univ., Eng., 1897-99, B.Litt., 1899, D.Litt. from same univ., 1922; LL.D. from Glasgow Univ., 1929; Litt.D., Cambridge University, 1935; L.H.D., Hobart College, Geneva, N.Y., 1942; m. Dorothea Foote, June 2, 1904; children—Roger Bigelow, Daniel, Frances Eliot (dec.), Dorothea Foote (Mrs. E. A. H. Sims), Helen Prudence (Mrs. Mason Fernald). Instr. in history, 1902-08, asst. prof., 1908-18, prof., 1918-29, Gurney prof. of history and polit. science since Sept. 1, 1929, Harvard U. Master of Eliot House, Harvard, 1931-42. Harvard U. exchange prof. at the Sorbonne, 1925-26; David Murray lecturer, U. of Glasgow, 1937. Capt. U.S. Army, May-Dec. 1918. Decorated Chevalier de la Légion d'Honneur, 1936. Republican. Fellow Am. Acad. Arts and Sciences; v.p., Mass. Hist. Soc., Royal Hist. Soc.; corr. mem. Academia de la Historia, Madrid. Clubs: Somerset (Boston); Athenæum (London). Author: Life and Letters of Thomas Cromwell (2 vols.), 1902; Gómara's Annals of Charles V, 1912; Rise of the Spanish Empire (4 vols.), 1918, 25, 34; Six Contemporaneous Revolutions, 1938; Suleiman the Magnificent, 1944. Contbr. to current hist. revs. Home: 175 Brattle St., Cambridge, Mass. Died Sept. 7, 1945.

MERRITT, Abraham, editor and author; b. Beverly, N.J., Jan. 20, 1884; s. William Henry and Ida Priscilla (Buck) M.; student Phila. (Pa.) High Sch.; m. Eleanore Ratcliffe (dec.); m. 2d, Eleanor Humphrey Johnson; 1 dau., Ida Eleanor. Began as reporter Phila. Inquirer, 1902, later night city editor; became asst. editor The American Weekly, editor since 1937. Clubs: Players and Lotos (New York). Author: The Moon Pool; The Ship of Ishtar; Seven Footprints to Satan; The Face in the Abyss; The Woman of the Wood; Dwellers in the Mirage; Burn Witch Burn; Creep Shadow!; also various archeological and botanical studies and papers upon witchcraft and modern survivals of ancient cults. Home: Hollis, L.I., N.Y. Address: The American Weekly, 235 E. 45th St., New York, N.Y. Died Aug. 1943.

MERRITT, Ernest George, physicist; b. Indianapolis, Ind., Apr. 28, 1865; s. George and Paulina Tate (McClung) M.; student Purdue U., 1881-82; M.E., Cornell U., 1886; grad. student, Cornell, 1888-89, U. of Berlin, 1893-94; m. Bertha A. Sutermeister, Apr. 10, 1901; children—Louise S. (Mrs. Ralph H. Brandt), Julia S. (Mrs. J. G. Hodge), Virginia S. (Mrs. J. T. Emlen, Jr.), Grace S. (Mrs. Jürg Waser), Howard S. Instr. in physics, 1889-92, asst. prof., 1892-1903, professor, 1903-35, head of department, 1918-35, and professor emeritus since 1935, dean of Graduate School, 1909-14, Cornell Univ. Engaged in anti-submarine devices at U.S. Naval Exptl. Sta., New London, Conn., 1917-18. Mem. Nat. Acad. Sciences; fellow Am. Acad. Arts and Sciences, Am. Physical Soc. (pres. 1914-15), A.A.A.S., Sigma Xi, Tau Beta Pi, Phi Kappa Phi, Gamma Alpha, Phi Kappa Psi. Asso. editor Physical Review, 1893-1913. Contbr. to scientific jours. on investigations in physics especially on the subjects of luminescence and radio. Engaged in European relief, 1946-48. Address: 1 Grove Pl., Ithaca, N.Y. Died June 5, 1948

MERRITT, Matthew J., ex-congressman; b. New York, N.Y., Apr. 2, 1895; s. Howard N. and Augusta C. (Port) M.; grad. high sch., New York; pvt. study in economics and finance; m. Grace Ferry, of Jamaica, L.I., 1930; 1 son, Matthew. With New York Loan Agency of R.F.C., 1933; mem. 74th to 78th Congresses (1935-45), N.Y. at large. Served as sergt., U.S. Army, World War I; major, Res. Corp. Mem. Am. Legion. Democrat. Elk (past Exalted Ruler, past pres. of past Exalted Rulers Assn., past v.p. N.Y. State Assn., dist. dep. S.E. Dist. since 1934). Home: Malba, L.I., N.Y. Office: 49 Wall St., New York, N.Y.* Died Sep. 29, 1946.

MERSEREAU, George Jefferson (mẽr'sẽr-ō), lawyer; b. Owego, N.Y., Nov. 20, 1875; s. George Jefferson and Lucy Adeline (Steele) M.; LL.B., Cornell U., 1899; m. Mary Edna Beaham, Jan. 25, 1917. Admitted to N.Y. bar, 1899, Mo. bar, 1900; asso. with Lathrop, Morrow, Fox & Moore, 1900-10, mem. firm, 1910-28, name changed to Lathrop, Crane, Reynolds, Sawyer and Mersereau, 1928, and since mem. firm; asst. atty. of Mo. and Ia. for A.,T.&S.F. Ry. Co., 1913-34, solicitor since 1934. Trustee Elmira (N.Y.) Coll. Mem. Am., Mo. and Kansas City bar assns., Lawyers Assn. of Kansas City, Sons of the Revolution (ex-pres. Kansas City Chapter), Chi Phi. Republican. Episcopalian. Clubs: University, Kansas City Country (Kansas City); Cornell, Lawyers (N.Y.). Legal residence: "The Walnuts," 51st and Wornall Road, Kansas City, Mo. Office: Fidelity Bldg., Kansas City, Mo. Died Nov. 5, 1947.

MERSHON, William Butts, lumberman, retired; b. at Saginaw, Mich., Jan. 16, 1856; s. Augustus Hull and Helen (Johnson) M.; Saginaw High Sch. to 17; m. Catherine Morse, Jan. 9, 1889; children—Wm. Briggs, Edward Lowry, Marion (Mrs. C. H. Sayre), John Morley. Began mfg. and dealing in lumber in Saginaw, Mich., 1876; salt manufacture added 2 yrs. later; consolidated in 1900 and Mershon-Schuette-Parker Co. formed, of which was pres. until retired, 1905; pres. W. B. Mershon & Company. Alderman of East Saginaw, 2 yrs.; mayor of Saginaw, 1894-95; mem. Park and Cemetery Commn. 5 yrs., State Forestry Commn. 2 yrs., State Tax Commn., 1912. Mem. 3d Regt. Mich. Nat. Guard, 6 yrs. Mem. Am. Ornithologists' Union, Mich. Forestry Assn. Clubs: Boone and Crockett (New York); East Saginaw, Saginaw Country; Warren Country (Ariz.). Author: The Passenger Pigeon, 1907; Recollections of My Fifty Years Hunting and Fishing, 1923. Sportsman, salmon angler; contbr. shooting and fishing articles to mags. and periodicals. Address: 1501 N. Michigan Av., Saginaw, Mich. Died July 12, 1943.

MERTON, Holmes Whittier, vocational counselor; b. Lebanon, O., Apr. 5, 1860; s. Alesha Sivartha and Josephine (Evans) M.; ed. under pvt. tutors; m. Caroline E. Dodge, Oct. 17, 1894. Began as lecturer on mental and physical life of man, 1880; delivered about 2,500 lectures in Providence, Boston, etc.; mem. Helmer & Merton, pubs.; pres. and founder Merton Inst. (vocational counseling); sec.-treas. and gen. mgr. Merton Music Co.; sec.-treas. Merton's First Aid Chart Co.; mem. faculty Pace Inst. Pvt. Slocum Light Guard, Providence, 3 yrs. Author: Descriptive Mentality of Head and Face, 1886; Life and Healing, 1894; Heliocentric Astrology and Astronomy, 1899; Merton's First Aid Charts, 1911; Social Harmonism, 1914; Johnson's First Aid Chart, 1915; How to Choose the Right Vocation, 1917; Merton Course in Vocational Counseling and Employee Selection, 1919; taught at the Merton Institute, Inc., New York. Part Author: Physiological Charts of Life, 1881; Helmer-Merton's Anatomical Charts, 1901; Miller-Merton Vocal Atlas, 1912; Domestic Medicine, 1913. Home: Stamford, Conn. Office: 36 W. 44th St., New York. Died Jan. 18, 1948.

MESERVE, John Bartlett, (mĕs-ẽrv'), lawyer; b. Waterloo, Ind., Nov. 17, 1869; s. True Whitcher and Atline Nancy (Stearns) M.; grad. Dickinson County High Sch., Chapman, Kan., 1892; m. Elizabeth Myrtle Broughton, Dec. 28, 1898; 1 dau., Naomi Helen (Mrs. Glenn Arthur Campbell). Admitted to Colo. bar, 1895, and began practice at Las Animas. Mem. Colo. Ho. of Rep., 1903; pres. bd. of freeholders which framed municipal charter of Tulsa, Okla., 1908; asst. U.S. atty. for Eastern Dist. of Okla., 1908-13; municipal counsellor, Tulsa, 1915-17; asst. counsel U.S. Shipping Bd., Washington, D.C., 1924-25. Mem. Am. and Okla. state bar assns., Okla. Soc. S.A.R. (state pres. 1928), Okla. State Hist. Soc. (dir.), N.H. State Hist. Soc., Soc. Colonial Wars. Republican. Episcopalian. Mason (K.T., Shriner). Club: Tulsa. Contbr. many hist. and biog. sketches to eastern mags. Home: Ambassador Hotel. Office: Kennedy Bldg., Tulsa, Okla. Died Jan. 1, 1943.

MESSNER, Julian, book publisher; b. New York, N.Y., Sept. 25, 1890; s. Emil M. and Betty (Shuster) M.; ed. Columbia U.; m. Kathryn Grossman, May 10, 1929. For some years with banking firm of Ladenburg, Thalmann & Co., and with the Grand Lake Co., paper bag mfrs.; with Boni and Liveright, book pubs., 1918-33, becoming v.p.; formed book publishing firm of Julian Messner, Inc., 1933. Home: 502 Park Av. Office: 8 W. 40th St., New York 18, N.Y. Died Feb. 8, 1948.

METCALF, Clell Lee, entomologist; b. Lakeville, O., Mar. 26, 1888; s. Abel Crawford and Catherine (Fulmer) M.; A.B., Ohio State U., 1911, A.M., 1912; D.Sc., Harvard, 1919; m. Cleo Esther Fouch, Dec. 31, 1908; children—Robert Lee, James Richard. Asst., Ohio State U., 1911-12; asst. entomologist, N.C. Dept. Agr., 1912-14; asst. prof. entomology, Ohio State U., 1914-19, prof., 1920-21, prof. entomology and head of dept., U. of Ill., since 1921; chairman div. of biological sciences, 1936-38, secretary of the same since 1938; consulting entomologist, Maine Expt. Station, summers 1915-17; teacher of biology, Cornell U., summers, 1918, 19; field entomologist, New York State Museum, summer, 1929. Chairman board of directors University Y.M.C.A.; vice pres. Illini Pest Control and Service Company. Fellow Entomol. Soc. America (sec.-treas. 1921-25; v.p. 1926; pres. 1934), A.A.A.S.; mem. Am. Assn. Econ. Entomologists (v.p. 1940), Am. Assn. Univ. Professors, Illinois Academy Science, Eugene Field Society, Sigma Xi (pres. Ill. Chapter, 1937-38), Gamma Alpha. Methodist. Clubs: Rotary, Chaos, Dial, Urbana Golf and Country (bd. mgr. since 1933). Author: Destructive and Useful Insects (with W. P. Flint), 2d edition, 1939; Key to the Principal Orders and Families of Insects (with Zeno Payne Metcalf), 1928; Fundamentals of Insect Life (with W. P. Flint), 1932; Insects—Man's Chief Competitors (with W. P. Flint), Century of Progress Series, 1932. Contbr. bulls. and articles on biology and entomology. Home: 704 Pennsylvania Av., Urbana, Ill. Died Aug. 21, 1948.

METCALF, Haven, plant pathologist; b. Winthrop, Me., Aug. 6, 1875; s. George Shepard and Prudence (Grant) M.; A.B., Brown, 1896, A.M., 1897; studied Harvard, 1899; U. of Neb., 1901-02, Ph.D.; m. Flora May Holt, June 28, 1899 (died Apr. 26, 1935). Instr. in botany, Brown U., 1896-99; prof. of biology, Tabor Coll., 1899-1901; instr. bacteriology, U. of Neb., 1901-02; prof. botany, Clemson Agrl. College, S.C., 1902-06; pathologist, 1906-07, in charge div. of forest pathology since 1907, U.S. Dept. Agr. Asso. editor of Phytopathology, 1910-14. Mem. Sigma Xi, Delta Upsilon; fellow A.A.A.S., Bot. Soc. America, Am. Phytopathol. Soc. (ex-pres.), Soc. Am. Bacteriologists, Soc. Am. Foresters, Bot. Soc. of Washington (ex-pres.), Am. Shade Tree Conf. (ex-pres.), Washington Acad. Sciences; U.S. del. Internat. Conf. on Phytopathology, Holland, 1923. Author of publs. on botany, plant pathology and bacteriology. Mason (K.T.). Clubs: Cosmos, Washington Country. In 1908, introduced from Italy, Colusa rice, now extensively grown in Calif. Home: 1841 Summit Pl., N.W. Office: U.S. Dept. Agr., Washington, D.C. Died May 23, 1940.

METCALF, Jesse Houghton, ex-senator; b. Providence, R.I., Nov. 16, 1860; s. Jesse and Helen A. (Rowe) M.; private schs. and Yorkshire Coll., Eng.; m. Louisa D. Sharpe. Agent Wanskuck Mills, 1885-1913, pres. since 1913; dir. Providence Washington Ins. Co.; mem. R.I. House of Rep., 1907; elected mem. U.S. Senate, 1924, reelected 1930, for term ending 1937. Mem. Providence Chamber Commerce. Trustee Brown U. Unitarian. Clubs: New York Yacht, Union League (New York); Hope, Squantum, Agawam Hunt, Turks Head, R.I. Yacht. Home: Woodward Rd. Office: 15 Westminster St., Providence, R.I. Died Oct. 9, 1942.

METCALF, John Calvin, univ. prof.; b. Christian County, Ky., Aug. 7, 1865; s. Dr. John Calvin and Victoria Jackson (Willis) M.; A.M., Georgetown (Ky.) College, 1888; grad. student, U. of Chicago; A.M., Harvard U., 1905; Litt.D., Georgetown Coll., 1913, Baylor Univ., 1920, Univ. of Kentucky, 1942; LL.D., University of Richmond, 1922; m. Ruth Cooper Sharp, June 16, 1891 (died 1925); 1 son, Victor Sharp (dec.); m. 2d, Edmonia Carrington Lancaster, Feb. 14, 1929. Prof. Latin, Soule Coll., Murfreesboro, Tenn., 1890-94; prof. modern langs., Mercer U., 1894-95; prof. English, Georgetown Coll., 1895-1904; prof. English, 1904-17, dean, 1914-17, U. of Richmond; Linden Kent prof. English lit., U. of Va., 1917-40, dean Grad. Sch., 1923-37. Received Raven Soc. (U. of Va.) award, 1938; Sullivan award, 1940; volume of Humanistic Studies by his colleagues published in his honor, 1941. Member Modern Language Association of America, Kappa Alpha, Omicron Delta Kappa, Phi Beta Kappa, Sigma Nu. Trustee Univ. of Richmond. Clubs: Colonade (Univ. of Va.); Authors' (London). Author: History of English Literature, 1912; History of American Literature, 1914; "The English in the South," in The South in the Building of the Nation; "George Cary Eggleston," and "Philip Alexander Bruce," in Library of Southern Literature; The Stream of English Biography, 1930; Virginia Authors, Books and Imprints in Richmond Bi-centennial volume, 1938; De Quincey—a Portrait, 1940. Editor: Macbeth, 1911, Addison's Spectator (selections), 1910; Readings in American Literature (joint editor), 1918; The Literary World (3 vols.), 1919; Sonnets and Other Poems, by Henry Aylett Sampson, 1920; The Enchanted Years, A Book of Contemporary Verse (with J. S. Wilson), 1921; Centennial Volume of University of Virginia, 1922. Literary editor of the Library of Southern Literature, Vol. XVII, 1923; Coleridge's Biographia Literaria, 1926. Advisory editor, Va. Quarterly Reivew. Address: University of Virginia, Charlottesville, Va. Died Sep. 9, 1949.

METZENBAUM, Myron Firth (mĕt'zĕn-boum), surgeon; b. Cleveland, O., Apr. 1, 1876; s. Joseph and Fannie (Firth) M.; B.S., Adelbert Coll., Cleveland, 1897; M.D., Western Res., 1900; grad. study, Vienna Med. U., 1900, 23, U. of Paris, 1927, Berlin and London, 1927; m. Elsa Fuldheim, 1912; children—Louise, Jane. Intern St. Alexis Hosp., Clev land, 1900; lecturer on anatomy, Western Reserve Univ., 1902-05; ear, nose and throat, and oral surgery and reconstructive surgery of head and neck. Fellow Am. Coll. Surgeons; Diplomat Am. Board Otolaryngology, Am. Board Plastic Surgery (founders group); mem. A.M.A., Am. Acad. Otolaryngology, Cleveland Otolaryngol. Club, Acad. Medicine of Cleveland, European Congress of Reconstructive Surgery, Am. Soc. of Plastic and Reconstructive Surgery. Awarded medal U.S. Govt. for research in radium, St. Louis Expn., 1904. Established Cleveland's present ambulance system under Police Dept., 1909, which was adopted throughout country. Contbr. many papers on radium, anesthesia, nose, throat and larynx surgery and reconstructive nasal surgery. Developed and introduced the method of administering ether-air or drop ether anesthesia, 1900; pioneer in use of scopolamin (twilight sleep) in gen. surgery; author of surgical method for resetting the dislocated cartilage of the nose in young children and the dry method for the treatment of sinus infections in children. Home: 2765 Euclid Heights Blvd. Office: 10515 Carnegie Av., Cleveland, O. Died Jan. 25, 1944.

METZGER, Irvin Dilling (mĕtz'kẽr), ophthalmologist; b. New Enterprise, Pa., Apr. 12, 1873; s. Jacob Burket and Catherine (Dilling) M.; B.E., Juniata Coll., Huntingdon, Pa., 1894, Ed.M., 1896, honorary D.Sc., 1940; M.D., Hahnemann Medical College, Philadelphia, 1904, hon. A.M., 1937; Oculi et Auris Chirurgus, New York Ophthalmic Hospital College, 1910; grad. study University of Vienna and London, 1913-14; D.Sc. (hon.), University of Pittsburgh, 1936; m. Dorothy Thompson, Aug. 6, 1919; 1 son, James Thompson. Supt. pub. schs., Hollidaysburg, Pa., 1895-1900; in gen. practice, Tyrone, Pa., 1904-09, eye, ear, nose and throat practice, 1910-13; practice confined to ophthalmology, Pittsburgh, Pa., since 1914. Served as capt., Med. Corps, U.S. Army, Base Hosp., Camp Taylor, Louisville, Ky., 1918-19. Administrative officer, Pa. State Bd. Med. Edn. (pres. bd.) and insp. med. schs. and hosps. 1915 to 1944. Pres. Fed. State Med. Bds. of U.S., 1935-36; mem. Am. Inst. Homœopathy (pres. 1929-30), Ophthal., Otol. and Laryngol. Soc. (pres. 1927-28), Pa. Homœo. Med. Soc., Philos. Soc., Fellowship Soc., Pi Epsilon Rho. Republican. Baptist. Mason (33°, Shriner). Clubs: University, Agora, Quiz. Writer of med. bulls. for State of Pa. Contbr. to Jour. Am. Inst. Homœopathy, etc. Home: 450 S. Atlantic Av. Office: 5230 Center Av., Pittsburgh, Pa. Died April 1, 1947.

MEUSER, Edwin Henry, clergyman; b. Columbus, O., Sept. 22, 1897; s. William and Elizabeth (Miller) M.; B.A., Capital U. (Coll.) Columbus, 1917; M.A., Am. U., 1927; m. Naomi E. Waltner, June 11, 1924; children—Janet Ruth, William Waltner, David Edwin. Pastor St. Paul's Lutheran Church, Bridgeport, O., 1920-24, St. Matthew's Church, Washington, 1925-37; exec. sec., Bd. of Am. Missions, Columbus, O., since 1937; dir. Fla. Missions of Am. Lutheran Ch., since 1948. Honorary degree, D.D., conferred by Capital U. Seminary, 1944. Author: Graded Lesson Leaves, Lutheran Joint Synod of Ohio. Statistical Yearbook. 1926-30. Address: 585 N.E. 123rd St., N. Miami, Fla. Died Nov. 12. 1949; buried Forest Lawn Memorial Park, Columbus, O.

MEYER, Adolf (mī'ẽr), psychiatrist, neurologist; b. Niederweningen, nr. Zürich, Switzerland, Sept. 13, 1866; s. Rudolf and Anna (Walder) M.; ed. Gymnasium, Zürich; Swiss Staatsexamen for practice of medicine, 1890; post-grad. studies at Paris, London, Edinburgh, Zürich, Vienna and Berlin, 1890-92; M.D., of Zürich, 1892; LL.D., Glasgow Univ., 1901, Clark U., 1909; Sc.D., Yale, 1934; Harvard, 1942; m. Mary Potter Brooks, Sept. 15, 1902; 1 dau., Julia Lathrop. Came to U.S., 1892. Hon. fellow, then docent in neurology, U. of Chicago, 1892-95; pathologist to Ill. Eastern Hosp. for the Insane, Kankakee, 1893-95; pathologist and later dir. of clin. and lab. work, Worcester (Mass.) Insane Hosp. and docent in psychiatry, Clark U., 1895-1902; dir. Pathol. (psychiatric) Inst., N.Y. State Hosps., 1902-10; prof. psychiatry, Cornell U. Med. Coll., 1904-09; prof. psychiatry, Johns Hopkins, and dir. Henry Phipps Psychiatric Clinic, Johns Hopkins Hosp., 1910-41, prof. emeritus since 1941; Salmon memorial lecturer, 1932; Maudsley lecturer, 1933; guest lecturer Acad. of Neurology and Psychiatry, Kharkow, U.S.S.R., 1933; Thomas Salmon medal for distinguished service in psychiatry, 1942. Hon. pres. Nat. Com. for Mental Hygiene and president Internat. Com. for Mental Hygiene since 1937; hon. vice-pres. Conf. on Method in Philosophy and the Sciences; hon. mem. Boston Soc. Neurology and Psychiatry, Royal Medico-Psychological Assn., New York Psychiatric Society (pres. 1905-07); New York and Washington psychoanalytic societies, mem. Assn. Am. Physicians, Am. Neurol. Assn. (pres. 1922), Am. Psychiatric Assn. (pres. 1927), Academie der Naturforscher zu Halle, Am. Inst. Criminal Law and Criminology, A.A.A.S., N.Y. Acad. Sciences, Assn. for Research in Nervous and Mental Diseases, Am. Orthopsychiatric Assn., Am. Psychopathol. Assn. (pres. 1912, 16), American Psychological Assn., Assn. of Anatomy, Harvey Society, New England Soc. Psychiatry; corr. mem. Société de Neurologie, Société de Psychologie and Société Medico-psychologique (Paris), Sociedad Neurologia y Psiquiatria (Buenos Aires). Extensive contbr. on neurology, pathology, psychiatry, mental hygiene, etc. Zwinglian Protestant. Clubs: Century (New York); Cosmos (Washington). Address: 4305 Rugby Rd., Baltimore 10, Md. Died Mar. 17, 1950.

MEYER, Alfred Henry, dean; b. Quincy, Ill., May 28, 1888; s. John Henry and Sophia Emilie M.; Mus. B., Oberlin Conservatory of Music, 1910; A.B., Oberlin Coll., 1913; student Harvard U., 1915-17, N.E. Conservatory of Music, 1915-17; m. Antoinette Van Cleve, June 17, 1915; children—Alfred Van Cleve, Antoinette Hunter, Kathryn Houston. Prof. history and theory of music since 1913; at Tarkio (Mo.) Coll., 1913-15, State Coll. of Wash., 1917-23, Wheaton (Mass.) Coll., 1923-24, Wellesley Coll., 1923-25, Boston Conservatory of Music, 1924-40, Boston U. since 1929, N.E. Conservatory of Music, 1933-39, dean Coll. of Music, Boston U., since 1941; asst. music reviewer Boston Transcript, 1924-34; organist First Bapt. Ch., Boston, 1930-42; Auburndale Congregational Ch. since 1942. Lecturer Mass. Univ. Extension, 1928-43. Mem. Phi Beta Kappa. Home: 80 Beaumont Av., Newtonville, Mass. Died Dec. 29, 1944.

MEYER, B. G., pres. Gen. Cigar Co., Inc.; b. N. Y. City, Nov. 22, 1882; s. Max and Bertha (Berlyn) M.; student pub. schs. of N.Y. City; m. B. Marqusee, Oct. 21, 1907; children—Marjorie (Mrs. Lawrence F. Picker), Max. Started with Meyer & Mendelsohn, N.Y. City, 1898; v.p. Gen. Cigar Co., Inc., N.Y. City, 1917-37, pres. since 1937. Jewish religion. Club: Inwood Country. Home: Lefferts Rd. and Macy Channel, Hewlett, L.I., N.Y. Office: 119 W. 40th St., New York, N.Y. Died Aug. 26, 1949.

MEYER, Charles F.; b. Boston, Mass., 1864; s. Charles E. and Henrietta L. (Quimby) M.; ed. Roxbury Latin Sch.; m. Myra Comstock. Began with Standard Oil Co., at Boston, 1886; v.p. Standard Oil Co. of N.Y., 1920-28, pres., 1928-31; retired, Feb. 1, 1932. Mason. Clubs: India House, Metropolitan (New York); Byculla, Royal Bombay Yacht (India). Home: Rancho Santa Fe, Calif. Office: 26 Broadway, New York, N.Y. Died Oct. 13, 1948.

MEYER, J(ohn) Franklin, physicist; b. Spring Mills, Pa., Mar. 11, 1875; s. Jacob Sheller and Susan Catherine (Bitner) M.; A.B., Franklin and Marshall Coll., Lancaster, Pa., 1894; A.M., 1897, Sc.D., 1918; grad. study Johns Hopkins, 1897-1900; Ph.D., U. of Pa., 1904; m. Ella Jane Mather, July 12, 1909; 1 son, Theodore Franklin. Asst. prof. physics, U. of Pa., 1902-07; prof. physics, Pa. State Coll., 1907-09; research engr., Westinghouse Lamp Co., 1909-13; physicist Nat. Bur. of Standards, 1913-41; retired; lecturer in elec. engring., George Washington U., 1922-27. Mem. advisory council Franklin and Marshall College; trustee Catawba College. Mem. Optical Society of America, International Electrotech. Am. Inst. Elec. Engrs., Illuminating Engring. Soc., Optical Soc. of America, Internat. Electrotech. Commn., Phi Beta Kappa, Sigma Xi, Phi Gamma Delta, Acacia. Mem. Evang. and Ref. Ch. Mason. Club: Cosmos. Contbr. to Physical Rev., Elec. World, Jour. of Franklin Inst., pubs. of Bur. of Standards, etc. Home: 3727 Jocelyn St. N.W., Washington, D.C. Died Oct. 30, 1944.

MEYER, Julius Paul, ocean transportation; b. Hoboken, N.J., Nov. 1, 1871; s. Juergen Frederick Henry and Mathilde (Teubner) M.; ed. Hoboken Acad. and for 5 yrs. under tutors and pvt. schs. abroad; m. Minnie Auguste Spies, Nov. 3, 1897. Began with firm of Kunhardt & Co., gen. agts. Hamburg-Am. Line of Steamers, 1888; with Hamburg-Am. Line since 1889, mem. New York bd. dirs., 1912-17, resident dir. and gen. rep., 1920-31 (co. resumed operations after World War under agreement for joint service with Harriman group until 1920, operating under own name since 1926), retired from active business, 1931. Trustee German Soc. of City of N.Y., Central Savings Bank, Seaman's Mission at Hoboken, Germanistic Soc. America (hon. pres.); dir. Bd. of Trade of German-Am. Commerce. Lutheran. Home: 755 Park Av., New York, N.Y. Died July 9, 1945.

MICHAEL, Arthur, chemist; b. Buffalo, N.Y., Aug. 7, 1853; s. John and Clara M.; student univs. of Berlin and Heidelberg, Ecole de Médecine de Paris; A.M. (hon.) Tufts, 1882, Ph.D., 1890, LL.D., 1910; LL.D., Clark U., 1909; m. Helen C. Abbott, June 1889. Prof. chemistry, Tufts Coll., 1882-89 and 1894-1907, prof. emeritus, 1907-12; prof. organic chemistry, Harvard, 1912-36, emeritus since 1936. Mem. Nat. Acad. Sciences. Author of numerous investigations on subjects in pure chemistry. Home: Newton Center, Mass. Died Feb. 8, 1942.

MICHAEL, Moina Belle, educator; b. Good Hope, Ga., Aug. 15, 1869; d. John Marion and Alice Sherwood (Wise) Michael; ed. Teachers Coll., Athens, Ga., and Columbia U. Teacher pub. schs., Ga., many yrs.; social dir. Winnie Davis Hall and gen. sec. Y.W.C.A. of Ga. State Teachers Coll. since 1913. Pres. Ga. Council of Deans of Women and Social Dirs. of Schs. and Colleges of Ga., 1915-20; mem. Bi-Centennial Commn. of Ga., 1933. Served with Am. Com. of World War, Rome, Italy, 1914; with Y.M.C.A. Overseas Hdqrs., Columbia U., 1918. Mem. D.A.R., Daughters of Confederacy; hon. mem. Spanish-Am. War Vets. Auxiliary. Democrat. Baptist. Originated Flanders Field Memorial Poppy commemoration, Nov. 1918. Awarded D.S.M. by Am. Legion Auxiliary, Boston, 1930; "Distinguished Citizen" citation, Ga. legislature, 1931. Address: Athens, Ga. Died May 10, 1944.

MICHAELIS, Leonor (mī-kā'lĭs), med. research; b. Berlin, Germany, Jan. 16, 1875; s. Moriz and Hulda (Rosenbaum) M.; student U. of Berlin, 1893-96 (M.D.), Freiburg, 1896-97; m. Hedwig Philipsthal, Apr. 12, 1905; children—Ilse, Eva M. Became asst. to Prof. Paul Ehrlich, then at Berlin, 1898-99; asst. Municipal Hosp., Berlin, 1899-1902; oberarzt with Inst. for Cancer Research, Berlin, 1902-06; dir. lab., Berlin Municipal Hosp., 1906-22; privat-docent U. of Berlin, 1905, prof., 1908; prof. biochemistry, Med. Sch., Nagoya, Japan, 1922-26; resident lecturer Johns Hopkins U., Baltimore, 1926-29; mem. Rockefeller Inst. Med. Research, 1929-40, now mem. emeritus. Fellow A.A.A.S., N.Y Academy of Science; member American Society Biological Chemists, American Chem. Soc., National Academy of Sciences. Author: Compendium der Entwicklungsgeschichte des Menschen mit Berücksichtigung der Wirbeltiere, 1898; Einführung in die Farbstoffchemie für Histologen, 1900; Dynamik der Oberflächen, 1909; Einführung in die Mathematik für Biologen u. Chemiker, 1912; Die Wasserstoff-Ionen-Concentration, 1914; Praktikum d. Physikalischen Chemie insb. der Kolloid-Chemie, 1920; Oxydations-Reductions-Potentiale, 1929. Home: 325 E. 79th St. (21). Office: Rockefeller Institute for Medical Research, New York 21, N.Y. Died Oct. 9, 1949.

MICHAELS, Charles Frederick (mī'kẽlz), chmn. bd. McKesson & Robbins, Inc.; b. San Francisco, Calif., Dec. 22, 1869; s. Henry and Louisa (White) M.; ed. pub. schs.; m. Kathryn Tuohy, Feb. 7, 1907. Treas. Langley & Michaels Co., 1897-1907, v.p., 1907-20, pres., 1920-29; exec. v.p. and dir. McKesson & Robbins, Inc., 1929-39, pres., 1939-41, chmn. bd. since 1941; dir. Pacific Lighting Co. Pres. San Francisco Chamber of Commerce, 1914. Pres. Menlo School and Junior Coll. since 1925. Clubs: Pacific Union, Bohemian (San Francisco); California (Los Angeles); Menlo Country (Redwood City). Home: Isabella Av., Atherton, Calif. Office: 50 First St., San Francisco, Calif.; and 155 E. 44th St., New York, N.Y.* Died Feb. 20, 1944.

MICHAELSON, M. Alfred, congressman; b. Kristiansand, Norway, Sept. 7, 1878; s. Martin and Olivia (Syvertsen) M.; brought to U.S. at age of 7; ed. pub., high and normal schs., Chicago; m. Lillian H. Gramm, Nov. 28, 1906. Teacher pub. schs., Chicago, 1898-1914; mem. City Council, Chicago, 1914-18; mem. Ill. Constl. Conv., 1920; mem. 67th to 71st Congresses (1921-31), 7th Ill. Dist.; chmn. bd. Madison and Kedzie State Bank. Republican. Lutheran. Mason (Shriner). Home: 3022 Palmer Sq., Chicago. Died Oct. 26, 1949.

MICHEL, Ernest A(dolph) (mĭch'ĕl), lawyer; b. Appleton, Minn., Oct. 5, 1887; s. Ernest A. and Caroline (Schmidt) M.; grad. high sch., Appleton, Minn.; studied in law office, 1906-09; m. Arloine Forbes, June 23, 1915; children—Maxine Caroline, William Forbes. In practice of law at Marshall, Minn., 1909-18, Minneapolis since 1918; now mem. Davis, Michel, Yaeger & McGinley. Mem. Am., Minn. State and Hennepin County bar assns. Episcopalian. Club: Minneapolis Auto. Home: R. 4, Anoka, Minn. Office: 610 Baker Bldg., Minneapolis, Minn. Died Aug. 4, 1947.

MICHELSON, Charles (mī'kĕl-sŭn), editor, writer; b. Virginia City, Nev.; s. Samuel and Rosalie (Przlubska) M.; m. Lillian Sterritt, 1896; 1 child, B. C. Was reporter San Francisco Post, San Francisco Examiner, San Francisco Call; war corr. New York Journal, 1896; editorial writer New York American; mng. editor San Francisco Examiner, 1906-08, Chicago Examiner, 1908-09, Chicago American, 1909-14; later Washington corr. Chicago Herald; chief Washington corr. N.Y. World, 1917-29; dir. of publicity, Dem. Nat. Com., 1929-40; dir. of public relations NRA, 1933-34. Contbr. to magazines. Clubs: Gridiron, Nat. Press, Golf (Washington); Lotos (New York). Home: The Westchester. Office: Mayflower Hotel, Washington, D.C. Died Jan. 9, 1947.

MICHELSON, Miriam (Miss), author; b. Calaveras, Calif., 1870; d. Samuel and Rosalie (Przlubska) Michelson. Wrote for "Arthur McEwen's Letter," San Francisco, 1894; dramatic critic and spl. writer for San Francisco and Phila. newspapers. Contbr. short stories in leading mags. Author: In the Bishop's Carriage, 1904; The Madigans, 1904; A Yellow Journalist, 1905; Anthony Overman, 1906; Michael Thwaites's Wife, 1909; The Awakening of Zojas, 1910; The Duchess of Suds, a romantic comedy, 1911; The Superwoman, 1912; The Country of Two Kings, 1921; Petticoat King, 1929; The Wonderlode of Silver and Gold, 1934. Home: 1998 Vallejo St., San Francisco, Calif. Died May 28, 1942.

MIDDELSCHULTE, Wilhelm (mĭd'dĕl-shōōl-tē), organist; b. Dortmund, Westphalia, Germany, Apr. 3, 1863; s. Heinrich and Wilhelmina (Köhling) M.; played ch. service at 12; mus. edn. Royal Acad. Ch. Music, Berlin, under Haupt, Loeschorn, and Julius Alsleben; LL.D., U. of Notre Dame, 1922; m. Annette Musser (organist), June 29, 1896 (Dec.); m. 2d, Florence Knox Michael, Oct. 5, 1929. Organist St. Lucas Ch., Berlin, 1888-91; organist Cathedral of the Holy Name, Chicago, 1891-95, Thomas Orchestra (now Chicago Symphony Orchestra), 1894-1917, St. James' (R.C.) Church since 1899; dir. and prof. organ and mus. theory, Wis. Conservatory of Music, Milwaukee, since 1899; prof. organ and theory, Detroit Conservatory of Music; prof. of organ, U. of Notre Dame (summers), since 1919, Rosary Coll. (River Forest, Ill.). Organ soloist Cincinnati May Festival, 1900-02; has given recitals in prin. cities of Germany and U.S. and recognized as authoritative interpreter of Bach's organ works. Upon invitation of the Prussian ministry of art and science, held a master course in organ playing in Berlin, May and June, 1925, 27. Mem. Am. Guild of Organists. Compositions: Passacaglia in D Minor; Toccata; canons and fugue on a German choral; concerto on theme by J. S. Bach; canonical fantasie on Bach, and fugue on 4 themes by Bach; Chromatic Fantasie and Fugue in C Minor; (transcriptions for organ) Bach's Chaconne in D minor; Bach's Aria in G major, with 30 variations (socalled Goldberg Variations); Busoni's Fantasia Contrappuntistica. Home: 7348 Lafayette Av., Chicago, Ill. Died May 4, 1943.

MIDDLETON, Stanley Grant, portrait painter; b. Brooklyn, N.Y., June 8, 1852; s. John N.B. and Louisa Frances M.; ed. Polytechnic Inst., Brooklyn; m. Annie H. Reese, June 29, 1904. Hon. mention Buffalo Expn., 1901; Charleston (S.C.) Expn., 1901. Portrait of Andrew D. White in perm. collection, National Gallery, Washington, D.C.; ex-speaker Lynn Boyd, Capitol Bldg., Washington, D.C.; George H. Daniels, Lotos Club, New York; Prof. Albert S. Bickmore, Am. Mus. Natural History, New York; Col. W. B. Jordon, Library at West Point, N.Y.; James J. Walker, mayor of N.Y. City; Carter Glass, Harvard U.; Woodrow Wilson, Princeton Library; Maj. Gen. Fredrick Steele, Cullum Hall, West Point, N.Y.; etc. Fellow Am. Mus. Natural History; mem. Artists' Fund. Episcopalian. Mem. Royal Arcanum. Clubs: Lotos, Salmagundi. Home-Studio: 1 W. 67th St., New York. Died Sept. 20, 1942.

MIDGLEY, Thomas, Jr., research chemist; b. Beaver Falls, Pa., May 18, 1889; s. Thomas and Hattie Lena (Emerson) M.; M.E., Cornell U., 1911; D.Sc., Coll. of Wooster, 1936; m. Carrie M. Reynolds, Aug. 3, 1911; children—Thomas 3d, Jane (Mrs. Edward Z. Lewis). With Nat. Cash Register Co., 1911; research work on automobile tires, 1912-14; supt. Midgley Tire & Rubber Co., Lancaster, O., 1914-16; worked with Charles F. Kettering, Dayton, O., and later with Gen. Motors Research Corp., 1916-18; head fuel div. Gen. Motors Research Corp., 1918-23; gen. mgr. Gen. Motors Chem. Co., 1923; v.p. Ethyl Corp. since 1923 and Kinetics Chemical, Inc., since 1930; dir. Ethyl-Dow Chem. Co. since 1933. Awarded Nichols medal, Am. Chem. Soc., 1923, Perkins medal, 1937; Longstreth medal, Franklin Inst., 1925; Priestly medal, Am. Chem. Soc., 1941; Willard Gibbs Medal, 1942. Vice-pres. Ohio State

U. Research Foundation since 1940; vice-chmn. Nat. Inventors Council since 1940. Pres. Am. Chemical Soc. (chmn. bd. dirs.); mem. Nat. Acad. Sciences, Sigma Xi, Phi Kappa Phi, Tau Beta Pi, Alpha Chi Sigma, Atmos. Writer many technical papers. Discovered tetraethyl lead as gasoline anti-knock compound; also certain organic fluoride compounds for refrigerants which are nontoxic and noninflammable. Holder of many patents. Home: Worthington. O. Office: Ethyl Corp., Detroit, Mich. Died Nov. 2, 1944.

MIGHELS, Ella Sterling (pen-name Aurora Esmeralda), author; b. in mining camp nr. Folsom, Calif., May 5, 1853; d. Sterling B. F. and Rachel Hepburn (Mitchell) Clark; ed. Nev., and Sacramento, Calif.; m. Adley H. Cummins, 1872 (died 1889); m. 2d, Philip Verrill Mighels, 1896 (died 1911); 1 dau., Viva Cummins (died 1905). Lived in London 4 yrs., returning to U.S., 1901; commr. from San Francisco to Chicago Expn., 1893. Founder Soc. of Calif. Lit., 1913; founder of philosophy, 1910, under title of "Ark-adian Brothers and Sisters of California," based on the kindness of the miners to the children in Aurora Esmeralda. Methodist. Author: The Little Mountain Princess, 1880; Story of the Files, 1893; The Full Glory of Diantha, 1909; Society and Babe Robinson, 1914; Fairy Tale of the White Man, 1915; Literary California, 1919; Wawona, 1921; Life and Letters of a Forty Niner's Daughter, 1929. Legislature of Calif., in 1919, conferred upon her the title of "First Literary Historian of California," in recognition of work in preserving the history of early writers of the state. Home: 1605 Baker St., San Francisco. Died Dec. 10, 1934.

MIKELL, Henry Judah (mī'kĕl), bishop; b. Sumter, S.C., Aug. 4, 1873; s. Thomas Price (M.D.) and Rebecca (Moses) M.; B.A., U. of the South, 1895, M.A., 1898, B.D., 1898, D.D., 1918; D.D., U. of Nashville, 1910; LL.D., Oglethorpe University, Atlanta, 1928; m. Henrietta Campbell Bryan, Nov. 8, 1905; 1 dau., Henriette Campbell Bryan. Deacon, 1898, priest, 1899, Protestant Episcopal Ch.; rector Ch. of the Holy Communion, Charleston, 1899-1908, Christ Ch., Nashville, Tenn., 1908-17; consecrated bishop of Atlanta, Nov. 1, 1917. Chancellor Univ. of the South, Sewanee, Tenn. Deputy to Gen. Conv. P.E. Ch., 1901, 13, 16; pres. Fourth Province of P.E. Ch. Trustee U. of the South, George Peabody Coll. for Teachers, Nashville (chmn. bd.). Mem. (Southern) Kappa Alpha, Phi Beta Kappa. Democrat. Mason (32°). Home: 108 E. 17th St. Address: St. Philip's Cathedral, Atlanta, Ga. Died Feb. 20, 1942.

MIKELL, William Ephraim (mī'kĕl), professor of law; born in Sumter, South Carolina, January 29, 1868; son Thomas Price and Rebecca (Moses) Mikell; B.S., South Carolina Military Coll., Charleston, 1890; U. of Va. Law Sch., 1894; LL.M., U. of Pa., 1915, J.U.D., 1929; LL.D., U. of S.C., 1921; D.C.L., U. of the South, Tenn., 1921; m. Martha Turner McBee, Apr. 12, 1894; children—William E., Mary McBee, Thomas Price. Practiced at Sumter, S.C., 1895-96; prof. law, U. of Pa., 1898-1938, prof. emeritus since 1938, dean faculty, 1914-29. Democrat. Episcopalian. Mem. Am. Law Inst., Kappa Alpha (S.), Phi Delta Phi, Order of the Coif. Author: Mikell's Cases on Criminal Law, 1903; Mikell's Cases on Criminal Procedure, 1910. Wrote: Life of Chief Justice Taney, in "Great American Lawyers"; Limitations of the Treaty-Making Power of the Federal Government, pub. in Univ. of Pa. Law Review. Editor: third edit. Clark's Criminal Law, 1915; 2d edit. Clark's Criminal Procedure, 1917. Author of proposed Penal Code for Pennsylvania, 1917. Co-reporter on Code of Criminal Proc. for Am. Law Inst. Home: 209 E. Johnson St., Germantown, Philadelphia, Pa. Died Jan. 20, 1945.

MILBANK, Albert Goodsell, lawyer, corp. officer.; b. New Haven, Conn., July 15, 1873; s. Albert Journeay and Georgiana (Goodsell) M.; grad. Cutler Sch., New York, 1892; A.B., Princeton Univ., 1896; LL.B., New York Law Sch., 1898; m. Marjorie E. Robbins, Jan. 28, 1902 (died Oct. 11, 1933); children—Robbins, Samuel Robbins. Admitted to N.Y. bar, 1898 and began practice in N.Y. City; mem. of firm of Milbank, Tweed, Hope and Hadley; chairman of the board of the Borden Company. Associate chairman with John D. Rockefeller, Jr., in United War Work Campaign, 1918; trustee and v.p. Community Service, Soc. of N.Y.; mem. bd. dirs. Welfare Council N.Y. City and Greater New York Fund (mem. Members' Council); pres. Milbank Memorial Fund; dir. New York War Fund; vice president of National Institute Soc. Scis.; trustee emeritus, Princeton University; trustee The Pierpont Morgan Library; Mem. Am. and N.Y. State Bar Assns., N.Y. County Lawyers Assn., Assn. Bar City of N.Y. Decorated Order of St. Sava by Kingdom of Serbs, Croats and Slovenes, Hon. Comdr. of Most Excellent Order of British Empire, Civil Div., 1st Annual Award Medal by Welfare Council of New York City for distinguished service to the community, 1946. Republican. Episcopalian. Clubs: University, Down Town, Church, Century, Princeton, Huntington Country, Tiger Inn of Princeton. Home: Lloyd Harbor, Huntington, L.I., N.Y.; also 168 E. 74th St., New York 21. Office: 15 Broad St., New York 5, N.Y. Died Sept. 7, 1949.

MILDEN, Alfred William (mĭl'dĕn), prof. Greek; b. Whitevale, Ontario, Can., Mar. 11, 1868; s. George and Catherine (Lougheed) M.; B A., with honors in classics, University of Toronto (Can.), 1888; fellow in Greek, Johns Hopkins University, 1898-99, Ph.D., 1899; m. Minnie Brown, of Cornwall, Ont., Sept. 2, 1903; children—Gertrude Brown, Alfred Reynolds (dec.), Dorothy Maude. Classical master Barrie Collegiate Inst., Ont., 1889-96; prof. classics, Emory and Henry Coll., Emory, Va., 1900-10; prof. Greek, U. of Miss., since 1910, dean College of Liberal Arts, 1920-36, dean emeritus since 1936, head dept. of classics since 1937; mem. faculty George Peabody Coll., summers, 1924, 26. Dir. War Aims at U. of Miss., World War. Naturalized citizen of U.S., 1923. Lay del. to Gen. Conf. of M.E. Ch., S., 1934, 1938. Member Am. Philol. Assn., Am. Assn. Univ. Profs., Classical Assn. Middle West and South (exec. com.), State Assn. Miss. Colls. (pres. 1931-32), Nat. Com. of 100 of Phi Beta Kappa, Alpha Tau Omega. Democrat. Methodist. Rotarian. Contbr. on classical topics, chiefly with reference to Herodotus. Author: Limitations of the Predicative Position in Greek. Home: University, Miss. Died Feb. 16, 1944.

MILES, Emma Bell, writer; b. Evansville, Ind., Oct. 19, 1879; d. B. T. and Martha Ann (Mirick) Bell; ed. pub. schs. and St. Louis Art Sch.; m. G. F. Miles, Oct. 30, 1901. Contbr. to the current mags. Author: The Spirit of the Mountains, 1905. Address: Albionview, Tenn. Died March 19, 1919.

MILES, L(ouis) Wardlaw, coll. prof.; b. Baltimore, Md., Mar. 23, 1873; s. Francis Turquand and Jeanie (Wardlaw) M.; grad. University Sch., Baltimore, 1891; B.A., Johns Hopkins, 1894; M.D., U. of Md., 1897, LL.D., 1919; Ph.D., Johns Hopkins, 1902; m. Katharine Wistar Stockton, Jan. 25, 1908; children—Francis Turquand, Sarah Bache (Mrs. Charles P. Kindleberger), Samuel Stockton (killed in action, Aug. 1942), Jeanie Wardlaw (Mrs. William H. Walker, II). Master in German, Country Sch. for Boys, Baltimore, 1903-04; instr. in English, Princeton U., 1905, preceptor, 1905-17; headmaster Gilman Country Sch., 1919-26; lecturer St. John's Coll., Annapolis, 1926-27; collegiate prof. of English, Coll. of Arts and Sciences, Johns Hopkins, 1927-42, emeritus professor since 1942. Served as captain 308th Infantry, 77th division, A.E.F., World War; awarded the Congressional Medal. Mem. Alpha Delta Phi, Phi Beta Kappa, Omicron Delta Kappa. Democrat. Episcopalian. Club: Nassau (Princeton, N.J.). Author: History of the 308th Infantry, 1927; The Tender Realist and Other Essays, 1930. Address: 506 Woodlawn Rd., Baltimore, Md. Died June 27, 1944.

MILES, Vincent Morgan; b. Marion, Va., Oct. 16, 1885; s. George W. and Martha (Morgan) M.; student Univ. of Va., 1902-03; LL.B., Washington and Lee Univ., 1906; m. Evelyn Trezevant Williams, Feb. 8, 1910; 1 son, Vincent Morgan. Began practice at Ft. Smith, Ark., 1907; city atty., Ft. Smith, 1909-13; moved to Little Rock, 1914; mem. Rose, Hemingway, Cantrell, Loughborough & Miles, 1914-17, Pryor & Miles, 1919-30; Miles, Armstrong and Young, 1930-1935. Member Democratic National Committee, 1914-16 and 1920-32; regional adviser 8th Region, Federal Emergency Adminstrn. of Pub. Works, also chmn. Dist. 6; mem. Social Security Bd., 1935-37; special asst. to atty. gen., Dept. of Justice, 1937-38; solicitor of Post Office Dept. since 1938. Joined 1st O.T.C., at Ft. Logan H. Roots, Arkansas, April 1917; commd. captain inf., Aug. 15, 1917; landed in France, July 1918; asst. Gen. Staff officer, 4th A.C., from St. Mihiel offensive until armistice; Superior Provost Court with Corps. in Germany, Army of Occupation, 2 mos.; hon. discharged Mar. 1919. Mem. Am. Bar Assn., Sigma Alpha Epsilon. Episcopalian. Clubs: Army and Navy Country. Home: 1312 South 22d St. Arlington, Va. Office: Post Office Dept., Washington, D.C. Died Aug. 20, 1947; buried in Arlington National Cemetery.

MILEY, John Henry, lawyer; b. Bastrop, Tex., Feb. 23, 1878. s. Andrew Barnwell and Avarilla (Dollahite). M.; B.S., C.E., Agrl. and Mech. Coll., College Sta., Tex., 1896; m. Cora May Brown, June 12, 1907; children—Cora A. Harney (by 1st marriage), William H. (by 2d marriage). Began practice at Bastrop, 1899; removed to Shawnee, Okla., 1910; mem. Burford, Miley, Hoffman & Burford, Oklahoma City, 1919-31, Miley, Hoffman, Williams, France & Johnson since 1931. Spl. asst. to atty. gen. of U.S., 1913-15; asst. atty. gen. of Okla., 1915-16; justice Supreme Court of Okla., Apr. 1917-Jan. 1919. Democrat. Episcopalian. Home: 733 E. 19th St. Office: First National Bldg., Oklahoma City, Okla.*Died Oct. 1944.

MILLAR, Preston S(trong), electrical testing; b. Andover, New Jersey, March 9, 1880; s. George and Anna Catherine (Bowers) M.; educated in preparatory school; m. Lily Bradford Baylies, Mar. 31, 1906; children—Bradford Preston, Katherine LeBaron, Robert Visscher. Began electrical testing at Harrison, N.J., 1897; various positions in Elec. Testing Labs., including pres. and dir., 1929-42; pres. and dir. Elec. Testing Laboratories, Inc., since 1942; sec. Assn. of Edison Illuminating Cos., 1919-42; sec. and treas. Utilities Coördinated Research, Inc., 1934-43; pres. Illuminating Engineering Society, 1913, Medalist, 1945; president United States National Committee, International Commission on Illumination since 1936; president American Council of Commercial Labs., 1937-39; pres. New York Elec. Society, Inc., 1943-44; v.p. Nat. Soc. for Prevention of Blindness. Authority on electric lighting; introduced silhouette concept in street lighting. Mem. War Com. of Tech. Socs. and chmn. Com. on War Service of Illuminating Engring. Soc., World War I; also active in tech. com. work; lighting adviser Westchester County OCP, World War II. Fellow Am. Physical Soc., A.A.A.S.; mem. Am. Inst. E. E., Illuminating Engring. Soc., Am. Optical Soc., Assn. Consulting Chemists and Chem. Engrs., Am. Soc. for Testing Materials. Clubs: Engineers (New York and Boston). Contbr. Illuminating Sect. of Standard Handbook for Elec. Engrs.; also many papers in procs. of tech. socs. Home: The Buckingham, Scarsdale, N.Y. Office: 79th St. and East End Av., New York, N.Y. Died June 17, 1949.

MILLAR, Ronald, editor; b. Chadron, Neb., Aug. 29, 1890; s. Stocks and Margaret (Richards) M.; A.B., Dartmouth Coll., 1913; m. Lucille (Magorian) M., Feb. 10, 1914; children—Ronald Lewis, Elizabeth Marie, Muriel Monica. Reporter, book reviewer, asst. editor, editorial writer, Rocky Mountain News, Denver, Colo., 1913-17; with Chicago Evening Am., 1917-19; helped plan, prepare first edition Compton's Pictured Encyclopedia, 1917-22, asst. editor, 1922-25; mng. editor Liberty Mag., 1925-26, exec. editor, 1927-28; free lance writer, 1928-31; asso. editor Compton's, 1931-42, mng. editor since 1942. Mem. A.A.A.S., Am. Geog. Soc., Alpha Delta Phi. Club: Physics (Chicago). Author: Sunrays and Health, 1930. Contbr. of articles to Compton's Pictured Encyclopedia. Home: 1251 Columbia Av. Office: 1000 N. Dearborn St., Chicago, Ill. Died May 26, 1946.

MILLARD, Charles Dunsmore, ex-congressman; b. Tarrytown, N.Y., Dec. 1, 1873; student Brown U., 1893-95, later New York U.; m. Ethel Lee Williams, July 15, 1902; 1 dau., Ethel Lee. Admitted to N.Y. bar, 1898, and began practice in N.Y. City; mem. Westchester County Bd. of Supervisors, 1907-30 (twice chmn.); supervisor Town of Greenburg; mem. Rep. State Com.; mem. 72d to 75th Congresses (1931-39), 25th N.Y. Dist., resigned, 1937; surrogate of Westchester County, since Jan. 1, 1938. Mem. Westchester County Bar Assn. Home: Tarrytown, N.Y. Died Dec. 11, 1944.

MILLARD, Charles Sterling (mĭl-lärd'), ry. official; b. Louisville, Ky., May 3, 1874; s. Charles Sterling and Lydia Morgan (Gilbert) M.; Ph.B., Sheffield Scientific Sch. (Yale), 1896; m. Elizabeth Ekin, Nov. 5, 1901; children—Charles S., William E., Elizabeth. Began as asst. Engr. Corps, P.&E. R.R., 1897; div. engr. D.L.&W. R.R., 1901; engr. maintenance of way, Peoria & Pekin Union Ry., 1901, P.&E. Ry., 1903; engr. tracks and roadway, C.C.C.&St.L. Ry., 1910, supt. Mich. div., 1912, St. Louis div., 1916, asst. gen. supt., 1918, gen. mgr., 1924, now v.p. and gen. mgr.; officer and director various other companies. Mem. American Soc. Civil Engineers. Republican. Presbyterian. Clubs: Camargo, Queen City, Commonwealth (Cincinnati); Yale (New York). Home: 2306 Grandview Av. Office: 230 E. Ninth St., Cincinnati, Ohio. Died June 5, 1942.

MILLARD, Douglas, business exec.; b. Cleveland, O., Sept. 29, 1879; s. Addison and Mary (Weeks) M.; grad. Evanston (Ill.) High Sch.; m. Elizabeth Wilson, July 25, 1935; children—(by previous marriage) Douglas, Gordon Leonard. Clerk, Franklin MacVeagh & Co., Chicago, Ill., 1898-1900; removed to Colo., 1900; entered real estate business, 1900; ranchman, 1902-06; pres. Adams Cattle Co., and mgr. Bartlett Ranch, Vermejo Park, N.M., 1918-26; with The Colo. Fuel and Iron Corp. since 1906, vice pres., sales, since 1919. Chmn. advisory com. Colo. and N.M. div., Solid Fuel Coordinator for War. Vice-pres. and dir. Colo. and N.M. Coal Operators Assn. (Denver, Colo.); dir. Nat. Coal Assn. (Washington, D.C.). Mem. Newcomen Soc. (Internat.). Clubs: Denver, Country, Mile High (Denver). Home: 819 E. 8th Av. Office: Continental Oil Bldg., Denver, Colo. Died Sep. 9, 1946.

MILLARD, Paul Adsworth, clergyman; b. Red Oak, Mo., Aug. 19, 1892; s. Pleasant Anderson and Margaret Martha (Moberly) M.; student Drake U., 1915-17; D.D., from Minnesota Bible University, 1937; LL.D., 1935; m. Leah S. Walker, Oct. 28, 1913 (she died February 20, 1941); children—Donna Leah, Patricia Allene; m. 2d, Carmen Sylvia Sietsema, Nov. 5, 1943. Ordained ministry Disciples of Christ Ch., 1913; song evangelist, 1910-13; pastor Disciples of Christ Ch., Scranton, Ia., 1913-17; pastor Ch. of Christ, Worthington, Minn., since 1918; pres. and trustee Minn. Bible U. since 1936. Served in Minn. Nat. Guard, 1918-28. Republican. Editor of Minn. Bible Coll. News. Author: The Holy Spirit—His Personality and Work, 1938; Silver Sickles for the Golden Harvest, 1939; The Divine Plan of the Ages, 1937; Bible Ammunition for Christian Soldiers, 1939; The Apostles' Doctrine, 1940. Home: Worthington, Minn. Address: 1507 University Av., S.E., Minneapolis, Minn.* Died Feb. 3, 1945.

MILLARD, Thomas Franklin Fairfax (mĭl'ärd), author; b. Phelps County, Mo., July 8, 1868; s. Alvin Marion and Elizabeth E. M.; ed. Missouri School of Mines and Metallurgy, and Univ. of Mo., 1883-87; LL.D. from Univ. of Mo., 1929; unmarried. Reporter and editor of several newspapers, St. Louis, 1895-97; war corr. for Scribner's Mag., N.Y. Herald, World, London Daily Mail, etc., in Græco-Turkish, Boer, Spanish-Am. wars, Chinese Boxer uprising, Russo-Japanese War, The World War, Japan-China War, etc. Founder and editor The China Press, Shanghai, China, 1911-17; founded Millard's Review, Shanghai, June 9, 1917. Unofficial adviser to Chinese delegation to Paris Peace Conf., 1919, to sessions League of Nations, at Geneva, 1920, 21 and 22, to Conf. on Pacific Ocean and Far Eastern Questions, Washington, D.C., 1921. Member Beta Theta Pi, Zeta Phi. Clubs: Authors' (London); Lambs (New York); Nat. Press (Washington). Author: The New Far East, 1906; America and

the Far Eastern Question, 1909; Our Eastern Question, 1916; Democracy and the Eastern Question, 1919; Conflict of Policies in Asia, 1924; China—Where It Is Today and Why, 1928; The End of Exterritoriality in China, 1931. Official adviser to the Chinese Govt., 1929-35. Decorated Order of the Jade (China), 1936. Address: American Club, Shanghai, China.
Died Sep. 7, 1942.

MILLAY, Kathleen (Kalloch), author; b. Union, Me.; d. Henry Tolman and Cora L. (Buzzelle) Millay; grad. Hartridge Sch., Plainfield, N.J., 1917; student Vassar Coll., 1917-20; m. Howard Irving Young, Dec. 17, 1920. Author: (novels) Wayfarer, 1926; Against the Wall, 1929; (fairy tales) The Very Little Giant, 1934; Whirligiggle and the King's Beard, 1934; Plup Plup's Housewarming, 1935; (verse)—The Evergreen Tree, 1927; The Hermit Thrush, 1929; The Beggar at the Gate, 1931; Of All the Animals!, 1932; (plays) Persephone, 1932; Black of the Moon, 1934; The Man Who Became a Bird, 1935; Hollywood Wife, 1939; (short stories) Windy Tuesday, After Tomorrow, Judy Listens In, Harem Scarem, Mad Money, Grafted Fruit, Nobody's Business, Mr. Nightingale, Thaw Country, etc., 1935, 1936. Address: New York, N.Y. Died Sep. 21, 1943.

MILLER, A. Blanchard, farming and land development; b. Richlands, N.C., Sept. 5, 1878; s. Joseph K. and Eliza (Blanchard) M.; ed. Pomona Coll., Claremont, Calif.; unmarried. Pres. Fontana Farms Co., ranchers and subdividers; pres. Fontana Union Water Co., Fontana Domestic Water Co., Fontana Power Co., B.B. Co. Regent U. of Calif. Republican. Elk. Clubs: Jonathan (Los Angeles); Newport Harbor Yacht (Balboa, Calif.). Home: Fontana, Calif. Died Apr. 13, 1941.

MILLER, Alice Duer, author; b. New York, N.Y., 1874; d. James G. K. and Elizabeth (Meads) Duer; grad. Barnard Coll., 1899; m. Henry Wise Miller, Oct. 5, 1899. Author: The Modern Obstacle, 1903; Calderon's Prisoner, 1904; Less Than Kin, 1909; Blue Arch, 1910; Are Women People?, 1915; The Charm School, 1919; The Beauty and the Bolshevist, 1920; Manslaughter, 1921; Priceless Pearl, 1924; Are Parents People?, 1925; Reluctant Duchess, 1925; The Springboard (play), 1927; Forsaking All Others, 1930; Gowns by Roberta, 1933; Come Out of the Pantry, 1933; Death Sentence, 1934; The Rising Star, 1935; Five Little Heiresses, 1935; Not For Love, 1937; And One Was Beautiful, 1937; The White Cliffs, 1941. Address: 450 E. 52d St., New York, N.Y. Died Aug. 22, 1942.

MILLER, Amos Calvin, lawyer; b. Marshalltown, Ia., Dec. 16, 1866; s. Wells W. and Mary (Caswell) M.; A.B., Oberlin (O.) Coll., 1889; LL.B., Chicago-Kent Coll. Law, 1891; m. Jeanne Gilbert, Dec. 1, 1891; children—Gilbert A., Wells W., Norman. Admitted to Ill. bar, 1891, and began practice at Chicago; mem. Lackner, Butz & Miller, Chicago, 1895-1912, Miller, Gorham & Wales (now Miller, Gorham, Wescott & Adams) since 1912; an organizer, 1st v.p. and counsel 25 yrs. Firestone Tire & Rubber Co.; dir., mem. exec. com. Chicago Title & Trust Co. Mem. Ill. Constl. Conv., 1920-22; mem. Cook County Judicial Advisory Council since 1928. Trustee Oberlin Coll., formerly member exec. com.; trustee, member executive committee Century of Progress Exposition, 1933-34. Mem. Am. Bar Assn., Ill. State Bar Assn. (pres. 1931-32), Am. Law Inst., Chicago Bar Assn. (pres. 1918-19), Law Club (pres. 1921), Chicago Law Inst., Legal Club, Art Inst. Chicago, Lincoln Centennial Assn., Ill. State Hist. Soc., Chicago Hist. Soc. Republican. Mason. Clubs: University, Union League, Mid-Day (Chicago); Glen View (Golf, Ill.); Sheridan Shore Yacht (Wilmette); Los Angeles (California) Country. Home: 2829 Sheridan Pl., Evanston, Ill. Office: One N. La Salle St., Chicago 2, Ill. Died Oct. 18, 1949.

MILLER, Benjamin LeRoy, geologist; b. Sabetha, Kan., Apr. 13, 1874; s. Jacob J. and Mary (Moorhead) M.; student Morrill (Kan.) Coll., 1889-90, Washburn Coll. (Topeka), 1891-92; A.B., U. of Kan., 1897; U. of Chicago, summer, 1898; Ph.D., Johns Hopkins University, 1903; honorary Sc.D., Moravian College, 1941; m. Mary A. Meredith, Sept. 15, 1904 (died May 30, 1930); children—Ruth Meredith (Mrs. Otto H. Spillman), Ralph LeRoy. Teacher pub. schs. of Kan., 1894-95; asst., Kan. U. Geol. Survey, summer, 1896; prof. biology and chemistry, Penn Coll., Oskaloosa, Ia., 1897-1900; spl. asst. Ia. Geol. Survey, summer, 1899; asso. in geology, Bryn Mawr Coll., 1903-07; prof. geology, Lehigh U., since 1907. Geologist, Md. Geol. Survey, 1900-11; asst., 1904-07, asst. geologist, 1907-13, U.S. Geol. Survey; asso. geologist, Pa. Geol. Survey, since 1919. Spl. consulting editor Engring. and Mining Jour., 1920-22. Fellow A.A.A.S., Mineralogical Soc. America, Geol. Soc. America, Ia. Acad. Sciences, Geol. Soc. London; mem. Am. Inst. Mining and Metall. Engrs., Soc. Econ. Geologists, Seismological Soc. America, Am. Meteorol. Soc., Am. Assn. Univ. Profs., Pa. Acad. Science (pres. 1925-26), Sigma Xi, Tau Beta Pi. Mem. Soc. of Friends. Has written numerous reports on geol. survey results, pub. by U.S. Geol. Survey and state geol. surveys of Iowa, Md., Va., N.C. and Pa.; articles on econ. geology in tech. jours., especially on limestones, cement, graphite and other non-metallic products; articles on stratigraphic geology of Eastern Pa. in geol. periodicals; reviews of Am. geog. lit. in Annuelle Bibliographie, Annales de Géographie, 1902-06; also collaborator with Dr. George B. Shattuck in "Geology and Geography of the Bahama Islands," in Bahama Islands, 1905; Geology of Mining Districts of South America and Central America; Mineral Deposits of South America (with Dr. J. T. Singewald, Jr.), 1919. Rotarian. Home: 429 N. New St., Bethlehem, Pa. Died Mar. 23, 1944.

MILLER, Benjamin M., ex-governor; formerly asso. justice Supreme Court of Ala.; b. Oak Hill, Wilcox County, Ala., Mar. 13, 1864; s. Rev. John and Sara (Pressly) M.; A.B., Erskine Coll., S.C., 1884; grad. in law, U. of Ala., 1888; m. Otis Duggan, Sept. 21, 1892; children—Benjamin M., Margaret (Mrs. Roy Childers). Prin. Lower Peach Tree High Sch., 1884-87; admitted to Ala. bar, 1888, and practiced at Camden, 1889-1904; judge 4th Judicial Circuit, 1904-21; associate justice Supreme Court of Ala., 1921-28; gov. of Ala., 1931-35. Elected mem. Ala. Legislature while a student at U. of Ala., 1888-89. Mem. Wilcox Mounted Rifles, 1887-89. Chmn. Dem. Exec. Com., Wilcox County, 1901-02. Mem. Kappa Alph; mem. Associate Reform Presbyn. Ch. K. of P. Home: Camden, Ala. Deceased.

MILLER, Bert H., U.S. senator; b. St. George, Utah; s. Arnold D. and Mary J. (Laub) M.; grad. Brigham Young U., 1901; LL.B., Cumberland U., 1902; m. Carolin H. Miller, July 1, 1916; children—Lee Francis, Patricia Ann. Law practice, St. Anthony, Ida., 1903; pros. atty. Fremont County, Ida., 1911-13; atty. gen. of Idaho, 1933-37; atty. Wage and Hour Div. Dept. of Labor, headquarters Seattle, 1939-40. Attorney General of Idaho, 1941-45; justice Supreme Court of Idaho, 1945-48; elected U.S. senator, Nov. 1948; served Jan.-Oct. 1949, for term ending 1955. Democrat. Home: Boise, Idaho. Office: Washington, D.C. Died Oct. 8, 1949; buried Morris Hill Mausoleum, Boise.

MILLER, Carroll, mem. Interstate Commerce Commn.; b. Richmond, Va., Mar. 18, 1875; s. William Gardner and Emma Hazletine (Wiglesworth) M.; ed. Richmond (Va.) Coll., 1891-92; M.E. Stevens Inst. of Tech., Hoboken, N.J., 1896; m. Mary Emma Guffey, Oct. 28, 1902; children—William Gardner III, John Guffey, Carroll, Joseph F. Guffey. Engr. Ill. Steel Co., Chicago, 1896-97; Humphreys & Glasgow, London, Eng., 1897-98, United Gas Improvement Co., 1898-1901; cons. engr. with George O. Knapp (pres. Peoples Gas Light & Coke Co. of Chicago), 1901-07; cons. engr., Pittsburgh, Pa., 1907-09, chief engr. Providence (R.I.) Gas Co., 1909-14; gen. mgr. Western United Gas & Electric Co., Aurora, Ill., 1914-18, Phila. Co., Pittsburgh, Pa., 1918-19; vice-pres. Guffey-Gillespie Oil Co., 1919-21; v.p. Thermatomic Corp. and Thermatomic Carbon Co., 1921-29, pres., 1929-33; mem. Interstate Commerce Commn. since 1933, chmn., 1937. Mem. Am. Gas Assn., Guild of Gas Mgrs. of Boston, Soc. of Gas Lighting of N.Y., Beta Theta Pi. Democrat. Episcopalian. Clubs: Pittsburgh, Duquesne, University (Pittsburgh). Home: Wolf Creek Farm, Slippery Rock, Pa.; and 2929 Benton Pl. N.W., Washington, D.C. Address: Interstate Commerce Commn., Washington, D.C. Died Dec. 24, 1949.

MILLER, Charles Addison, lawyer; b. Utica, N.Y., Dec. 29, 1867; s. Addison C. and Cynthia J. (Brayton) M.; A.B., Harvard U., 1890; LL.D. from Hamilton Coll., 1930, Union Coll., 1933; m. Emily J. Elliott, June 19, 1890; 1 dau., Cynthia Anne. Admitted to bar, 1892, and since in practice at Utica; sr. partner of the firm of Miller, Hubbell & Evans; pres. The Savings Bank of Utica, 1907-32; mgr. New York Agency RFC, Feb.-July 1932; pres. RFC, Aug. 1932-Mar. 1933. Pres. N.Y. State Savings Bank Assn., 1909; v.p. N.Y. State Bar Assn., 1910. Trustee Hamilton Coll. Clubs: University, Century (New York); Fort Schuyler (Utica). Republican. Episcopalian. Home: Barneveld, N.Y. Office: Utica, N.Y., and 14 Wall St., New York, N.Y. Died Nov. 22, 1944.

MILLER, Edwin Lee, surgeon; b. Stafford, Kan., Feb. 8, 1887; s. Stonewall and Catherine (Cramer) M.; A.B., U. of Mo., 1908; M.D., Harvard Med. Sch., 1911; m. Faith Pearse, Sept. 24, 1910; children—William Stonewall, John Pearse, Richard Cramer. Practicing surgeon since 1911; attending surgeon, St. Lukes Hosp., since 1914, St. Mary's Hosp., 1924-36; chief of surgical staff, Kansas City Gen. Hosp., 1936-41; cons. surgeon, Mo. Pacific Railway. Served as 1st lt., M.C., U.S. Army, 1918. Received Certificate, Distinguished Alumni Award of Merit, U. of Mo., 1938. Fellow Am. Coll. Surgeons; mem. Mo. Med. Soc. (pres. 1935-36), Western Surg. Soc., Am. Med. Assn., Southern Med. Assn., Am. Surg. Bd., Beta Theta Pi, Phi Beta Kappa, Phi Beta Pi. Democrat. Methodist. Address: 5432 Wyandotte St., Kansas City, Mo. Died Oct. 6, 1943.

MILLER, Fred W., army officer; b. Manchester, Ia., May 10, 1891; commd. 1st lt. inf., July 1920, and advanced through the grades to brig. gen., June 1942; maj. gen., Oct. 1942; became operations and training officer, G-3, Seventh Corps Area, Omaha, Neb., Aug. 1940; operations and training officer, G-3, VIII Army Corps, hdqrs. Brownwood, Tex., July 1941, later assigned to Inf. Div.; assumed command, 93d Inf. Div., Oct. 1942; retired as major gen., June 1944.*† Deceased.

MILLER, Glenn, orchestra leader; b. Clarinda, Ia.; s. Lewis Elmer and Mattie Lou (Cavender) M.; ed. Ft. Morgan (Colo.) High Sch. and U. of Colo.; m. Helen Burger, Oct. 6, 1928. Trombone player and arranger for various orchestras; organized Glenn Miller Orchestra, 1938; played on Chesterfield radio program; served as band leader Army Air Forces. Mem. Sigma Nu. Composer of "Moonlight Serenade" and other popular songs. Address: "Cotswold," Byrne Lane, Tenafly, N.J. Reported missing on flight from England to Paris, Dec. 1944.*

MILLER, Gray, tobacco exec. Chmn. bd. and dir. British American Tobacco Co., Ltd.; dir. Imperial Tobacco Co. of Can., Ltd. Office: Imperial Tobacco Co. of Canada, Ltd., 3810 Antoine St., Montreal, Canada. Died May 1947.

MILLER, Helen Richards Guthrie, humanitarian; b. Zanesville, O., Sept. 2, 1862; d. Stephen Hand and Mary Annette (Strong) Guthrie; ed. Putnam Sem., Zanesville; spl. work at U. of Nev., Stanford U., U. of Mo., also in Leipzig, Prague, Paris and London; m. Walter McNab Miller (M.D.), Jan. 10, 1889; children—Guthrie McNab, Charles Edward. Organizer, 1898, and pres. Red Cross, Reno, Nev.; organizer and pres. 1st woman's club in Nev.; organized work for pure food in Gen. Fedn. of Women's Clubs and was chmn. Pure Food Com., 1904-08, until after passage of federal pure food and drug act and Mo. food and drug act; mem. Gov.'s Commn. on Tuberculosis, 1910-11, and editor of report to gov.; chmn. Pub. Health Com. and mem. Exec. Bd. State Conf. Charities. Pres. Mo. Equal Suffrage Assn.; 1st v.p. Nat. Am. Woman Suffrage Assn.; chmn. Hoover registration woman's com. Council Nat. Defense; spl. agt. Missouri food adminstr.; dir. health edn., Mo. Tuberculosis Assn.; chmn. dept. of pub. welfare Gen. Fedn. Women's Clubs; del. at large Mo. Constl. Conv., 1922. Special consultant U.S. P.H. Service; pres. Association Women in Public Health, 1920-28; asso. dir. div. of publication and promotion Am. Child Health Assn.; mem. White House Conf. on Child Health and Protection; mem. Com. on Costs of Medical Care; mem. bd. Nat. Com. on Prisons and Prison Labor; sec. Motion Picture Research Council; chmn. Pub. Welfare Dept., Columbia League of Women Voters; vice chmn. Columbia Recreation Commn.; Member National Bd. Children's Federation. Episcopalian. Mem. Kappa Kappa Gamma. Clubs: Wednesday (St. Louis); Fortnightly, Town (pres.); Saturday's Children.‡ Died June 22, 1949.

MILLER, Hilliard Eve, gynecologist; b. Cowan, Tenn., Sept. 25, 1893; s. Charles Jewett and Elizabeth (Johnston) M.; student Sewanee Mil. Acad., 1908-10, U. of the South (both of Sewanee, Tenn.), 1910-12; M.D., Tulane U., New Orleans, 1916; m. Veva Penick, Oct. 31, 1917; children—Veva Penick, Hilliard Eve., Jr. Interne Charity Hosp., New Orleans, 1916; house surgeon New York Lying-In Hosp., New York, 1917; instr. gynecology and obstetrics Tulane U. Med. Sch., 1917-24, asst. prof. gynecology, 1924-36, prof. and head dept. of gynecology since 1936; prof. and head dept. of gynecology, Grad. Sch., Tulane U.; chief dept. of gynecology, Touro Infirmary; sr. gynecologist, Tulane Div., Charity Hosp.; cons. gynecologist, Flint-Goodridge Hosp. Served as 1st lt., Med. Corps, U.S. Army, 1917. Trustee Isaac Delgado Memorial Fund. Fellow Am. Coll. Surgeons, Southern Surg. Assn.; mem. Nat. Bd. Obstetrics and Gynecology, A.M.A., Am. Gynecol. Soc., South Eastern Surg. Congress, Southern Med. Assn., La. State Med. Soc., Orleans Parish Med. Soc., New Orleans Gynecol. and Obstet. Soc., La. State Gynecol. and Obstet. Soc., Am. Gynecol. Club (pres.), Phi Delta Theta, Phi Chi. Democrat. Episcopalian. Mem. Knights of Momus; Mystic and Neptune Clubs. Clubs: Boston, Louisiana, Country. Wrote chapters for Curtis Gynecology and Obstetrics and Davis Gynecology and Obstetrics; also about 20 papers read before med. socs. and pub. in med. jours. Home: 325 Walnut St. Office: Medical Arts Bldg., New Orleans, La. Died Apr. 20, 1945.

MILLER, James Alexander, physician; b. Roselle, N.J., Mar. 27, 1874; s. Charles Dexter and Julia (Hope) M.; A.B., Princeton, 1893, A.M., 1894, Sc.D., 1936; M.D., Columbia U., 1899; ScD., 1930; D.P.H., N.Y. Univ., 1937; m. Marion Hunt, June 4, 1902; children—Mrs. Richard S. Meredith, Mrs. Daniel A. Lindley. Practiced in N.Y. City since 1899; prof. clin. medicine, College of Physicians and Surg. (Columbia), 1913-45; cons. physician tuberculosis div. Bellevue Hospital; consulting physician, Trudeau Sanatorium, and Sprain Ridge Hospital (Yonkers, N.Y.); consultant Tuberculosis Woman's Hospital. Served as maj. Am. Red Cross in France, and as med. dir. Rockefeller Tuberculosis Commn. in France, 2 yrs. Ex-pres. Nat. Tuberculosis Assn., New York Tuberculosis Assn. Mem. bd. Community Service Soc. (New York); mem. Am. Medical Assn., Assn. Am. Physicians, Alumni trustee, Columbia University, Am. Clin. and Climatol. Assn., New York Acad. Medicine (ex-pres.), Am. Coll. Physicians (ex-pres.). Decorated Chevalier Légion d'Honneur (France), Jan. 1, 1919. Republican. Presbyterian. Club: Century (New York). Contbr. to medical journals, also popular magazines. Home: 133 E. 64th St., New York, N.Y. Died July 29, 1948.

MILLER, Jesse I(sidor), lawyer; b. Lexington, Ky., July 12, 1891; s. Isidor Jacob and Jennie (Faller) M.; A.B., U. of Ky., 1912, M.A., 1913, LL.B., 1914; m. Florence B. Glaser, July 15, 1923; children—Jesse I., Jane Elsie. Admitted to Ky. bar, 1913; practiced law at Lexington, 1913-17, Washington, D.C., 1920-33, 1934-41 and since 1946; asst. solicitor Bur. Internal Revenue, 1919-20; spl. rep. U.S. Govt. for Nicaraguan presdl. elections, 1920; exec. dir. National Labor Bd., 1933-34; civilian advisory representative on War-Justice Dept. to plan for treatment of enemy aliens. Served as pvt. and sergt. Hdqrs., 38th Div., 1917-18; lt. and capt. U.S. Army, 1918-19; aide-de-camp, Maj. Gen. E. H. Crowder, provost marshal gen., 1918-19; maj., judge adv., 1919-20. Col. U.S. Army, 1942-46; asso. dir. Sch. Mil. Govt., dir. Mil. Govt., div. Provost Marshall Gen's. Office. Awarded Legion of Merit (declined). Mem. Am. Bar Assn., Delta Chi. Democrat. Jewish religion. Clubs: Woodmont Country (Bethesda, Md.): Loudoun Golf and Country (Purcellville, Va.); Army and Navy (Washington). Author: Spirit of Selective Service (with Maj. Gen. E. H. Crowder), 1919; also articles on federal taxation and labor relations. Home: 14 Oxford St., Chevy Chase, Md. Office: Woodward Bldg., Washington, D.C. Died Nov. 9, 1949.

MILLER, John D., lawyer; b. Hunter, Greene County, N.Y., Dec. 6, 1856; s. Abram D. and Lydia (Douglas) M.; ed. common and night schs.; m. Jennie M. Blandin, Jan. 20, 1882; children—Harry L. (dec.), Allan D., Myron B., Walter L. Admitted to Pa. bar, 1891, and practiced in Susquehanna County, Pa., also operating dairy farms; assisted in organizing local co-operative marketing assns. among dairymen; gen. counsel, Dairymen's League, Inc., and Dairymen's League Co-operative Assn., Inc., since Jan. 1, 1917, v.p., 1918-35; author amendments to state anti-trust acts authorizing farmers to combine for marketing purposes; also prepared first draft and assisted in preparing Capper-Volstead Co-operative Marketing Law, 1922 Dir. and mem. exec. com. Central Bank for Coöperatives, 1934-44; dir. Federal Prison Industries, Inc., 1934-Mar. 1937. Mem. Nat. Cooperative Milk Producers' Fedn. (life dir.; pres. 1922-28), Nat. Coöperative Council (pres. 1932-42, now emeritus). Am. Inst. of Co-operation (dir.). Del. from U.S. to World's Dairy Congress, England, 1928. Mem. Am. Bar Assn., Bar Assn. Susquehanna County. Democrat. Methodist. Mason. Odd Fellow. Home: Thompson, Susquehanna County, Pa. Office: 11 W. 42d St., New York, N.Y. Died Nov. 26, 1946.

MILLER, John Maffit, Jr., banker; b. Lynchburg, Va., Mar. 31, 1868; s. John Maffit and Mary Elizabeth (Norvell) M.; ed. grammar schools; m. Nannie Louis Otey, June 7, 1887 (died Jan. 6, 1935); children—Otey Norvell, Rush Floyd, Mallie Floyd (Mrs. James Douglas Cook), Gertrude Kinckle (Mrs. Guthrie Smith), Nannie Matthews, Peter Otey, Virginius Newton, Louis, Mary Elizabeth (Mrs. Stuart L. Crenshaw). Began as clerk with Lynchburg National Bank, 1883; cashier First National Bank, Buchanan, Va., 1890-93; national bank examiner, 1893-95; cashier Merchants & Farmers National Bank, Charlotte, N.C., 1895-1902; cashier, v.p., pres. and chmn. bd. respectively First Nat. Bank (now First and Merchants Nat. Bank), Richmond, since 1902; pres., dir., First National Bank Building Corp.; chairman board Dan River Mills, Inc., Danville, Virginia; director and mem. exec. com. Life Ins. Co. of Va.; director Newport News Shipbuilding and Dry Dock Co.; dir. R.F.&P.R.R. Co., Craddock-Terry Shoe Co., Indstl. Cotton Mills Co.; dir. 1st and Merch. Nat. Bk., Richmond Terminal Co., Tredegar Co. Trustee Cripple Children's Hospital, Virginia Museum of Fine Arts, Va. Cancer Foundation. Democrat. K.C. Club: Commonwealth. Home: 3204 Hawthorne Av. Address: First and Merchants National Bank, Richmond 17, Va. Died Oct. 9, 1948.

MILLER, Julian Sidney, newspaper editor; b. Fairfield County, S.C., Nov. 27, 1886; s. Robert Grier (D.D.) and Roberta (Emmons) M.; student U. of N.C., 1902-03; A.B., Erskine Col., Due West, S.C., 1906, LL.D., 1930; m. Fannie Belle Faulkner, Jan. 13, 1913; children—Samuel Grier, Frances Isabelle, Roberta Rosemary, Julian Sidney, Robert Brice. Mem. editorial staff Charlotte Observer, 1906-15; editor in chief Charlotte News, 1915-32; asso. editor Charlotte Observer, 1933-35, editor in chief since 1935. Dir. of pub. relations for federal relief in N.C., 1932; chmn. Governor's Commn. on Edn., N.C., 1938-39; v.p. N.C. Press Assn., 1939; pres. Charlotte Community Chest, 1938-40; pres. N.C. Conf. on Social Service; mem. promotion com. Southern Conf. on Human Relations in Industry; mem. N.C. Sch. Commn.; mem. State Bd. of Edn. of N.C. since 1943; chmn. Celebration of President's Birthday Com. (N.C.), 1941-43. Trustee Erskine Coll. Mem. Am. Soc. Newspaper Editors (dir. 1942-43), Newcomen Soc. of Eng. (N.C. chapter); hon. mem. Omicron Delta Kappa (Davidson Coll.). Democrat. Ref. Presbyn. Clubs: Rotary, Variety Clubs of America, Executives (v.p. 1939). Home: Sardis Rd. Office: 600 Tyron St., Charlotte, N.C.* Died July 28, 1946.

MILLER, Kelly, univ. dean; b. Winnsboro, S.C., July 23, 1863; s. Kelly and Elizabeth M.; grad. Howard U., 1886, A.M., 1901, LL.D., 1903; post grad. work in mathematics and physics, Johns Hopkins, 1887-89; m. Annie May Butler, July 17, 1894. Entered govt. service as result of civil service exam. while student Howard U.; taught mathematics, Washington High Sch., 1889; prof. sociology, 1890-1926, also dean Coll. Arts and Sciences, Howard U. Home: 2225 4th St. N.W., Washington. Died Dec. 29, 1939.

MILLER, Louise Klein; b. nr. Centerville, O., Aug. 7, 1854; d. William and Ann (Cline) Miller; grad. High Sch. and Dayton Normal Sch.; grad. Cook County Normal Sch., Chicago, 1893; studied agr., horticulture and forestry, Cornell U.; unmarried. Began as teacher, Dayton; was supervisor nature study, E. Saginaw, Mich., and Detroit; teacher Sch. of Agr. and Horticulture, Briar Cliff, N.Y.; dean Lowthorpe Soc. of Horticulture and Landscape Gardening for Women, Groton, Mass.; curator of sch. gardens, Cleveland, Mar. 1904, also Memorial Garden; was landscape architect Bd. of Edn., Cleveland, now at Blossom Hill Sch. Fellow A.A.A.S., Am. Geog. Soc.; mem. Sch. Gardening Assn. America, Astron. Soc., Woman's Aeronautical Assn. (hon. life), Am. Pen Women (hon. life), Women's Nat. League of Justice to the Indians (trustee), Am. Forestry Assn., Ia. State Audubon Soc. (hon.), Cleveland Bird Club (dir.). Member at large Indian Assn. of America, Inc. (totem Blue Bird; Indian name O wa issa). Awarded degree of Doctor of Indian Philosophy. Unitarian. Clubs: Garden Club of Cleveland, Garden Club of America (mem. council), Garden Club of Ohio, Cleveland, Zonta, Women's Rotary, Business and Professional Women's (dean), Cornell Women's, Cleveland Writers' (hon. life). Author: Children's Gardens, 1904; Philosophy of Gardening; As I Did It; As I See It; Why Grow Old. Advisory editor of "Your Garden" (mag.). Home: Hotel St. Regis, Cleveland, O. Died Oct. 24, 1943.

MILLER, Lucius Hopkins, educator, author; born Roselle, N.J., Sept. 25, 1876; s. Charles Dexter and Julia Dunham (Hope) M.; A.B., Princeton, 1897, A.M., 1899; student Union Theol. Sem., 1905; studied U. of Heidelberg, 1911-12, U. of Berlin, 1912; m. Mae Coffeen, June 5, 1905. Teacher Syrian Protestant Coll., Beirut, Syria, 1899-02, The Hill Sch., Pottstown, Pa. (part of time), 1903-05; asst. prof. Bibl. instrn., Princeton, since 1905. Made a sociol. study of the Syrian community of Greater New York, 1902-03, under auspices of Ch. Fedn. Soc. of New York. Mem. adv. bd. Nat. Vacation Daily Bible Schs. movement. Mem. Soc. Bibl. Lit. and Exegesis, Internat. Soc. Apocrypha (v.p.). Clubs: Princeton (New York and Phila.); Cap and Gown (Princeton). Author: Bible Stories, 1901; The Life of Jesus, the Christ, 1902; Our Knowledge of Christ, 1914; Bergson and Religion, 1916; also numerous articles and revs. Home: 12 Edgehill St., Princeton, N.J. Died Feb. 1, 1949.

MILLER, Roger; b. at Morristown, Tenn., May 1, 1886; s. John S. and Orlena (Miller) M.; ed. high sch., Morristown, Tenn.; m. Helen Topping, June 16, 1910; children—John Wallace (dec.), Frederick Eugene. Newspaper work, Knoxville, Chattanooga, Morristown; commercial orgn. sec., beginning at Morristown, 1907; organized and directed Southern Aeronautical Congress, at Macon, Ga., 1919, Dixie Nat. Tractor Expn., Macon, 1919, Southern Nat. Motor Truck Demonstration, Macon, 1920; Macon Centennial Celebration, 1923; mgr. Chamber of Commerce, Macon, 1918-24; same Asheville, N.C., 1924-28; vice-pres. Grove Park Inn, Inc. (Asheville), 1929-32; mgr. Southwestern Div. U.S. Chamber of Commerce, 1933-43. Chmn. advisory bd. Southern Expn., New York, 1925. Accredited with having originated nat. "Own Your Home" movement, 1912. Organized Rhododendron annual festival at Asheville; secretary-treasurer Southwestern Chamber of Commerce Institute, Dallas, Tex., 1941-43. Mem. Nat. Assn. Commercial Orgn. Secs. (v.p. 1923-24; pres. 1928-29), Southern Commercial Secs. Assn. (pres. 1922-23), Ga. Assn. Commercial Secs. (pres. 1920-21), Am. Acad. Polit. and Social Science, Am. Sociol. Soc., Am. Hist. Assn., O. Henry Memorial Assn. (pres. 1925-33), Am. Forestry Assn.; pres. Nat. Sch. for Orgn. Execs., Northwestern U., 1925-29. Episcopalian; pres. Trinity Church Men's Club. Club: Rotary (president Asheville 1928-29). Home: Arrowhill Farm, Talbott, Tenn. Office: Chamber of Commerce, Morristown, Tenn. Died Jan. 26, 1944.

MILLER, Richard E., artist; b. St. Louis, Mo., Mar. 22, 1875; s. Richard L. and Essie (Story) M.; student St. Louis Sch. of Fine Arts, 1885-89; studied Julian Acad., Paris, 1899-1901; m. Harriet Adams, Nov. 1907. First picture exhibited, Paris, France, awarded gold medal, Salon, 1901; second gold medal, Salon, 1904; medal, Buffalo Expn., 1901, St. Louis Expn., 1904, Liege, Belgium, 1905, Portland (Ore.) Expn., 1905; Temple gold medal, Pa. Acad. Fine Arts, 1911; Potter Palmer gold medal and $1,000 prize, Art Inst. Chicago, 1914; Thomas B. Clarke prize, N.A.D., 1914; gold medal of honor, San Francisco Expn., 1915. French Govt. purchased Salon pictures, 1908, 09, 14, for Luxembourg Galleries. Decorated Knight Legion of Honor (France), 1906. N.A., 1915. Awarded gold medal Allied Artists of America. Home: Provincetown, Mass. Died Jan. 23, 1943.

MILLER, Sydney Robotham, physician; b. Newark, N.J., 1883; s. Fred H. and Annie (Robotham) M.; B.S., N.Y. Univ., 1905; M.D., Johns Hopkins, 1910; m. Ella Wood Miller, Sept. 7, 1911; children—Sydney R., Donald Barker, Walter Baetjer, Mary Ellison. Practiced at Baltimore, since 1914; asso. in clin. medicine, Johns Hopkins Med. Sch., since 1916; asso. prof. medicine, U. of Md., since 1920. Mem. A.M.A., Am. Coll. Physicians (pres. 1930-31), Am. Climatol. and Clin. Assn., Southern Med. Assn., Alpha Omega Alpha, Zeta Psi, Phi Beta Kappa. Presbyterian. Republican. Contbr. to med. jours. Home: 108 St. John's Rd. Office: 1115 St. Paul's St., Baltimore, Md.* Died May 25, 1949.

MILLER, W. Leslie, lawyer; b. North Benton, O., May 1, 1890; s. George Pow and Effie Maria (Lazarus) M.; B.A., Mt. Union Coll., Alliance, O., 1913; J.D., U. of Mich., 1916; studied elocution, Wooster U., Wooster, O., summer 1913; m. Ruth E. Sherer, Nov. 11, 1919; children—Richard Sherer, Barbara Jean, William Leslie, Jr. Admitted to Mich. bar, 1916; tax atty. for Pere Marquette R.R., 1916; asso. with legal firm, Clark, Emmons, Bryant and Klein, Detroit, Mich., 1917-27; then partner, Bryant, Lincoln and Miller, Detroit (later changed to Bryant, Lincoln, Miller & Bevan, subsequently to Miller, Bevan Horwitz & Des Roches); sr. partner Miller, Des Roches & Stern, since June 1, 1942; formed and established legal dept. of Detroit Automobile Club (now Automobile Club of Mich.), 1919-20; sec.-treas. and atty., Huck Mfg. Co.; sec. and atty., Huxon Holding Corp.; mem. bd. dirs., Kendrick Mfg. Co.; has served on committees of local, state and Am. Bar Assns.; chmn. bd. Adv. Council, sect. of Corp., Banking and Mercantile Law of Am. Bar Assn.; mem. Resolutions Com, J.A.B.A.; former president Commercial Law League of Am., 1936. Served as 2d lt. Signal Corps and 1st lt. Aviation Corps, World War I, contracting officer for govt. renegotiation and settlement of contracts for the air service. Mem. Am., Mich. and Detroit Bar Assns., Order of the Coif, Sigma Alpha, Alpha Epsilon, Phi Alpha Delta. Clubs: Detroit Athletic, Lochmoor Golf, Players. Mason. Home: 695 Lincoln Rd., Grosse Pointe City, Mich. Address: 2388-99 Nat. Bank Bldg., Detroit 26, Mich. Died April 1948.

MILLER, Walter, educator; b. Ashland County, O., May 5, 1864; s. Samuel G. and Harriet (Romich) M.; A.M., U. of Mich., 1884; U. of Leipzig, 1884-85, 1889-91; Am. Sch. of Classical Studies, Athens, Greece, 1885-86; LL.D., U. of Ark., 1916; Litt.D., U. of Mich., 1932; m. Jennie Emerson (A.B., U. of Mich., 1884), Sept. 13, 1888; children—Edith (wife of Rev. Wm. Crowe), Marjorie (dec.). Instr. Greek, 1886-87, Latin and Sanskrit, 1887-88, acting asst. prof., 1888-89, U. of Mich.; asso. prof. Greek, U. of Mo., 1891-92; prof. classical philology, Stanford, 1892-1902; prof. Greek, 1902-07, dean Acad. Colls., and prof. classical philology, 1907-11, Tulane U. of La.; prof. Latin, U. of Mo., 1911-29, prof. classical languages and archæology, 1929-36, dean of the Graduate School, 1914-30, emeritus since 1936. Associate editor The Classical Journal, 1905-33, editor-in-chief and business manager, 1933-35; editor-in-chief of the Standard American Encyclopedia, 1937. Professor Latin, Summer School of the South, Knoxville, Tenn., 1905-09; lecturer, U. of Chicago, summer 1909, U. of Colo., 1920; conductor Bur. of U. Travel many times since 1902; annual prof. Am. Sch. Classical Studies, Athens, 1925-26; dir. summer sessions, 1925, 1926; visiting prof. Southwestern, Memphis, Tenn., 1938-39; visiting prof. Latin and Greek, Washington U. (St. Louis), 1940-41. Y.M.C.A. service in France, 1917; regional dir. Y.M.C.A., in Italy, 1918. Mem. Classical Assn. of Middle West and South (ex-pres.), Am. Philol. Assn., Archæol. Institute America, Phi Beta Kappa, Eta Sigma Phi, Phi Mu Alpha, Sigma Phi Iota. Presbyterian. Author: Latin Prose Composition for College Use, 1890, revised edit. 1909; Cicero, De Officiis (Loeb Classical Library), 1913; Xenophon, Cyropædia (Loeb Classical Library), 1914; Dædalus and Thespis, 1929; Greece and the Greeks, 1941; Homer's Iliad, translated line for line in English dactylic hexameters (with Wm. Benjamin Smith), 1944; also various contbns. to scientific and other jours. on classical philology, Greek archæology, etc. Home: 1516 Wilson Av., Columbia, Mo. Died July 28, 1949.

MILLETTE, John W. (mĭl-lĕt'), aurist, oculist; b. St. Paris, O., June 16, 1869; s. Joseph Warren and Nancy (Neher) M.; B.A., Ohio Northern U., 1889; B.L., Ohio Wesleyan U., 1895, B.S., 1897, M.S., 1903; A.M., Wittenberg Coll., Springfield, O., 1898; M.D., Ohio Med. U. (Ohio State U.), 1903; grad. study, Royal Ophthalmic Hosp., London, and U. of Vienna, 1903-04; m. Cora Hartman, Dec. 25, 1889 (died Oct. 13, 1898); m. 2d, Minnie Florence Roop, June 16, 1903; 1 dau., Nancy Margaret Roop. Supt. schs., Dunkirk, O., 1889-93, New Carlisle, O., 1895-1900; began med. practice specializing in eye, ear, nose and throat, Dayton, O., 1905; mem. staff St. Elizabeth Hosp. since 1906; cons. aurist and oculist Nat. Mil. Home, Ohio, since 1913. Fellow Am. Coll. Surgeons; mem. A.M.A., Am. Acad. Ophthalmology and Oto-laryngology, A.A.A.S., Ohio State Med. Assn., Montgomery County Med. Soc., Dayton Acad. Medicine, Chicago Ophthal. Soc., Nu Sigma Nu. Methodist. Mason (32°, K.T., Shriner). Clubs: Torch, Miami Valley Golf. Contbr. to med. jours. Home: 58 Cambridge Av. Office: 117 S. Main St., Dayton, O. Died Dec. 28, 1943.

MILLHAUSER, DeWitt (mĭl'hou-zẽr), radio exec.; b. N.Y. City, August 7, 1884; s. Napthali and Elizabeth (Millhauser) M.; ed. high sch. N.Y. City; m. 2d, Margaret Schaffner, May 7, 1930; 1 dau. (by previous marriage) Margaret Joan. With Speyer & Co., bankers, N.Y. City, 1899-1937, partner, 1920-37, retired, Dec. 31, 1937; chmn. finance com., dir. Radio Corp. of America; dir. RCA Communications, Inc., American Bemberg Corp., North Am. Rayon Corporation, Hart, Schaffner & Marx, Nat. Broadcasting Co.; mem. Provident Loan Soc., New York. Mem. International Com. Bankers on Mexico. Mem. Bibliophile Society. Republican. Clubs: Rockefeller Center Luncheon, Harmonie, Century Country. Home: 570 Park Av., New York 21; also Lincoln Av., Harrison, N.Y. Office: 30 Rockefeller Plaza, New York 20, N.Y. Died Apr. 14, 1946.

MILLIKEN, Gerrish H., corp. officer; b. Dover, N.H., Aug. 1877; s. Seth Mellen and Margaret L. (Hill) M.; Ph.B., Yale, 1898; LL.D., Presbyterian Coll., 1938; m. Agnes M. Gayley, 1913. Pres. Deering, Milliken & Co. Inc., New York; trustee Atlantic Mutual Ins. Co., dir. Nat. City Bank, New York Life Ins. Co., Mercantile Stores Co., Monarch Mills, Spartan Mills, Pacolet Mfg. Co., Gaffney Mfg. Co., Judson Mills and many other corps. Mem. N.Y. State Chamber Commerce (v.p., 1925-29). Republican. Presbyterian. Clubs: Yale, Union League, University, Merchants, Jekyll Island, Yeamans Hall,

Squadron A, Blind Brook, Nat. Golf Links, Piping Rock. Home: 723 Park Av., New York 21. Office: 240 Church St., New York 13. Died June 11, 1947.

MILLIMAN, Elmer Edward, organization exec.; b. Mount Morris, N.Y., Nov. 22, 1890; s. John E. and Mary E. (Ward) M.; student Rochester (N.Y.) Inst. of Tech., 1907-10; m. Esther D. Gumaer, June 7, 1919; children—John Richard, Elmer Edward. Electrician, N.Y. Telephone Co., 1910; foreman constrn. maintenance D.L.&W. R.R., 1910-18; gen. chmn. D.L.&W. R.R. System Brotherhood Maintenance of Way Employes, 1919-22; internat. sec.-treas. Brotherhood Maintenance of Way Employes, 1922-40, internat. pres. since 1940, vice-pres., mem. exec. com. and bd. dirs. Union Labor Life Ins. Co.; chmn. bd. Labor Cooperative Pub. Co., Washington, D.C. Mem. A.F. of L. (pres. workers edn. bur., sec. permanent com. on edn., mem. internat. labor relations com. and chmn. consumers' cooperatives com., del. to British Trade Union Congress, Eng., 1932). V.p. Catholic Conf. on Industrial Problems. Clubs: Economic, Rtoary (Detroit, Mich.). Home: 15419 Warwick Rd. Office: 61 Putnam Av., Detroit 2, Mich. Died Dec. 31, 1946.

MILLING, Robert Edward, lawyer; b. Winnfield, La., Apr. 16, 1861; s. Thomas David and Mary Edna (Teddlie) M.; student La. State U.; Ph.B., Cooper Inst., Lauderdale County, Miss., 1882; m. Ida Roberts, Apr. 11, 1883; children—Christine, Roberts Clay, Thomas DeWitt, Ida, Wear Francis, Odelle, Alice, Robert Edward, Dixie. Admitted to La. bar, 1885, and began practice at Winnfield; dist. atty., 4th jud. dist., La., 1888-96; moved to Franklin, La., 1896, New Orleans, 1913; mem. firm Milling, Godchaux, Saal & Milling. Democrat. Methodist. Mason, K.P. Club: Boston. Home: 1468 Nashville Av. Office: Whitney Bldg., New Orleans, La. Died July 15, 1947.

MILLIS, Harry Alvin (mĭl'lĕs), economist; b. Paoli, Ind., May 14, 1873; s. John and Maria (Bruner) M.; A.B., Ind. U., 1895, A.M., 1896; Ph.D., U. of Chicago, 1899; LL.D., Lawrence Coll., Ind. U., and U. of N.C.; m. Alice M. Schoff, 1901; children—Savilla, John S., Charlotte Melissa. Prof. economics and sociology, U. of Ark., 1902-03; asst. and asso. prof. economics, Stanford U., 1903-12; prof. and head of dept. economics, U. of Kan., 1912-16; prof. economics, U. of Chicago, since 1916 and chmn. dept. 1928-38. Director investigations, Rocky Mountain and Pacific states, U.S. Immigration Commn., 1908-10; dir. investigations Ill. State Health Ins. Commn., 1918-19; chmn. trade bd. and chmn. bd. of arbitration men's clothing industry, Chicago, 1919-23, 1937-40 and since 1945; mem. Nat. Labor Relations Bd., 1934-35, chmn., 1940-45, mem. since 1945. Mem. Am. Econ. Assn. (pres. 1934). Club: Quadrangle. Author: The Japanese Problem in the United States, 1915; Sickness and Insurance, 1926; Labor Economics (with R. E. Montgomery), vols. I and II, 1938, vol. III, 1945; also various reports. Home: 5710 Blackstone Av., Chicago, Ill. Died June 25, 1948.

MILLIS, Harry Lee, newspaper editor; b. Sikeston, Mo., Oct. 26, 1888; s. Rev. Van Jefferson and Mattie Ann (Williams) M.; student Centenary Coll., Palmyra, Mo., 1905-06, Southwestern U., Georgetown, Tex., 1907-09; m. Ella A. Barclay, Dec. 30, 1912; 1 son, Harry Lee. Began as printer's apprentice, 1902; editor and pub. Center (Mo.) Herald, 1905, Hutto (Tex.) Enterprise, 1906, Troy (Tex.) Enterprise, 1908, Bowie (Tex.) Blade, 1910; commercial and religious editor Houston Post, 1909-17, night editor, 1917-18, editorial writer, 1919-27, chief editorial writer, 1927-31, editor since 1932; owner Star Press (pub. community newspapers). Mem. Texas Meth. Centennial Commn., 1934; del. Tex. Meth. Conf., 1931, 32, and 33; v.p. Southwestern U. Ex-Students Assn., 1926; mem. nat. council Nat. Econ. League. Mem. Tex. Editorial Assn., Tex. Press Assn., Am. Soc. Newspaper Editors. Independent Democrat. Methodist (chmn. bd. publicity First Ch. of Houston). Club: Elks. Home: 712 Arlington St. Office: The Post, Houston, Tex. Died Aug. 20, 1942.

MILLIS, William Alfred, ex-coll. pres.; b. Paoli, Ind., June 17, 1868; s. John and Maria (Bruner) M.; A.B., Ind. U., 1889, A.M., 1890; LL.D., Franklin Coll., Ind., 1908; D.D., Hanover (Ind.) Coll., 1927; m. Laura Clark, Aug. 27, 1889; children—Laura Eloise (dec.), Fred, Robert J.; m. 2d, Harriett Harding, June 9, 1921. Supt. schs., Paoli, Ind., 1889-94, Attica, 1894-1900, Crawfordsville, 1900-08; dean Winona Summer Sch., 1895-1902; lecturer on edn., 1900-01, prof. edn., 1907-08, Wabash Coll.; lectured on edn., Ind. U., 1904-05; pres. Hanover Coll., 1908-29. Presbyn. minister; moderator of Synod of Indiana, Presbyn. Ch., U.S.A. Lecturer on ednl. and social problems. Dir. McCormick Theol. Sem. Dir. ednl. exhibits for Ind. at St. Louis Expn., 1904. Mem. N.E.A., Nat. Soc. for Scientific Study of Edn., Delta Tau Delta, Phi Beta Kappa, etc. Author: Teaching of High School Subjects; Talks to College Students; The History of Hanover College. Home: Kennedy Pl., Crawfordsville, Ind.

MILLS, Charles Smith, clergyman; b. Brockton, Mass., Jan. 17, 1861; s. Rev. Charles Lewis and Rebecca Bartlett (Smith) M.; A.B., Amherst, 1882, D.D., 1907; Hartford Theol. Seminary, 1882-84, Andover Theol. Seminary, 1884-85, grad. 1885; D.D., Oberlin, 1901; m. Alice Morris, June 17, 1885 (died May 21, 1937); children—Margaret Morris (dec.), Charles Morris. Ordained Congl. ministry, July 2, 1885; pastor Springfield, Vt., 1885-88, First Ch., N. Brookfield, Mass., 1888-91, Pilgrim Ch., Cleveland, O., 1891-1905, Pilgrim Ch., St. Louis, 1905-12, First Ch., Montclair, N.J., 1912-20. Trustee Oberlin Coll., 1896-1917, Hartford Theol. Sem., 1906-17; pres. Congl. Home Missionary Soc., 1906-10; mem. Congl. Commn. of Nineteen on Polity, 1910-13; mem. Congl. Commn. on Missions, 1915-20 and 1928-34, chmn., 1929-31; chmn. Pilgrim Memorial Fund Commn., 1917-20, gen. sec., 1920-28; trustee Annuity Fund for Congregational Ministers, 1913-20 and since 1928, gen. sec., 1920-28, pres., 1928-39; trustee and pres. Retirement Fund for Lay Workers (Congregational), 1930-39; dir. Congl. Board Ministerial Relief, 1913-20 and 1928-34, gen. sec., 1920-28, and mem. administrative com., 1928-34; dir. Congl. Home Bds., 1928-34; mem. Corp. for Nat. Council of Congl. Chs. since 1918, sec., 1920-23; acting pastor First Ch. of Christ, Hartford, 1928-30; pres. Hartford Fed. Chs., 1934-38. Mem. Soc. Mayflower Descendants, Phi Beta Kappa, Alpha Delta Phi, S.A.R. Clubs: Thorndike (Jaffrey, N.H.); University, Winter Park Country (Winter Park, Fla.); Am. Guernsey Cattle Club. Home: "Brechinwood," Jaffrey, N.H. Died Mar. 3, 1942.

MILLS, Charles Wilson, M.D.; b. South Williamstown, Mass., Sept. 1, 1879; s. Charles A. and Clara J. (Paige) M.; B.A., Williams Coll., 1902; M.D., Johns Hopkins, 1908; m. Mary Durborow, Apr. 19, 1911; children—Ruth Durborow, Margaret Abbot (Mrs. R. Y. McElroy), Charles W. Med. house officer Johns Hopkins Hosp., Baltimore, Md., 1908-09; asso. physician Loomis (N.Y.) Sanatorium, 1910-17; acting med. dir. Cragmor Sanatorium, Colorado Springs, Colo., 1917-18; in practice at Tucson, Ariz., since 1920; one of organizers Desert Sanatorium of Southern Ariz.; medical staff, Tucson Medical Center, and St. Mary's Hospital. Served in Vol. Med. Service Corps, World War I; member Examining Bd., Selective Service, Colorado Springs; chmn. med. advisory board, Selective Service, Arizona, 1940-45. Member of Committee of Expert Consultants on Dust Diseases, Arizona Industrial Commission, 1943-45. Fellow Am. Coll. Physicians; member Am. Clinical and Climatological Association, Nat. Tuberculosis Assn. (dir.-at-large 1933-36), Trudeau Soc., Am. Coll of Chest Physicians, Southwestern Medical Association, A.M.A., Arizona State and Pima County medical societies, Alpha Omega Alpha, Phi Beta Kappa, Nu Sigma Nu, Phi Gamma Delta. Episcopalian. Contbr. of many papers on tuberculosis and other subjects to med. jours. Home: El Encanto Estates, Tucson. Office: 123 S. Stone Av., Tucson, Ariz. Died Sep. 29, 1945.

MILLS, Earl Cuthbert, fraternal order official; b. Newton, Ia., Dec. 28, 1870; s. Levi and Margaret (Cuthbertson) M.; B.S., Highland Park Coll., Des Moines, Ia., 1893, hon. M.S., 1899; LL.B., Drake U., 1900; m. Jessie Lamb, June 17, 1897. Supt. pub. schs., Eldon, Ia., 1893-98; in practice of law at Des Moines since 1900; mem. Spurrier & Mills, 1900-10, Parsons & Mills, 1910-35, now Mills, Hewitt & Diltz; gen. counsel Ia. State Traveling Men's Assn., Ia. Bankers Assn. Mem. School Board, Des Moines, 6 yrs., pres., 2 yrs. Mem. Delta Theta Phi. Republican. Episcopalian. Mason (33°; Past Imperial Potentate of Shrine of North America). Club: Des Moines University. Home: 5120 Shriver Av. Office: Southern Surety Bldg., Des Moines, Ia. Died Apr. 16, 1947.

MILLS, John, engineer; b. Morgan Park, Ill., Apr. 13, 1880; s. John and Sarah Elizabeth (Ten Broeke) M.; A.B., U. of Chicago, 1901; A.M., U. of Neb., 1904; B.S., Mass. Inst. of Tech., 1909; m. Emma Gardner Moore, June 1, 1909; children—John, Marion, Theodora Ten Broeke. Fellow in physics, U. of Chicago, 1901-02, U. of Neb., 1902-03; instr. physics, Western Reserve U., 1903-07, Mass. Inst. Tech., 1907-09; prof. physics, Colo. Coll., 1909-11; with engring. dept. Am. Telephone & Telegraph Co., 1911-15; with research dept. Western Electric Co., 1915-21, asst. personnel dir., 1921-23, personnel dir., 1923-24; dir. of publ., Bell Telephone Labs., Inc., 1925-45; administrative asst., Calif. Inst. Tech. since 1946. Fellow Am. Phys. Soc., Am. Inst. Elec. Engrs., Institute Radio Engineers; mem. Phi Beta Kappa, Sigma Xi, Delta Upsilon. Author: Electricity, Sound and Light, 1907; Introduction to Thermodynamics, 1909; Alternating Currents, 1911; Radio-Communication, 1917; Realities of Modern Science, 1919; Within the Atom, 1921; Letters of a Radio Engineer to His Son, 1922; Magic of Communication, 1923; Signals and Speech in Electrical Communication, 1934; A Fugue in Cycles and Bels, 1935; Electronics, Today and Tomorrow, 1944; The Engineer in Society, 1946. Inventor of several methods for wire and radio-telephony; conceived and supervised design of Bell Telephone Exhibits at the world's fairs in Chicago, 1933; San Diego, 1935; Dallas, 1936; San Francisco, 1939-40; and New York, 1939-40. Home: 300 Susquehanna Rd., Rochester 10, N.Y. Died June 14, 1948.

MILLS, Weymer Jay, author; b. Jersey City, N.J., Aug. 26, 1880; s. Mortimer and Lilly Wilcox (O'Reilly) M.; ed. by pvt. tutors; m. Dorothy, niece Sir Herbert Warren. Editor: Some of the Papers of Philip Freneau, an ancestor, 1900; Glimpses of Colonial Society and Life at Princeton College by One of the Class of 1763; The Letters of William Paterson, Governor of New Jersey, to John Macpherson, Aaron Burr, and Henry Lee, Junior, 1903; Family Papers Relating to New York's Early Social History. Author: Historic Houses of New Jersey, 1902; Through the Gates of Old Romance, 1903; Caroline of Courtland Street (novel), 1905; The Ghosts of Their Ancestors, 1906; The Van Rensselaers of Old Manhattan; The Girl I Left Behind Me, 1910; Old Loves, 1912; The Eighteenth Century in Silhouette (Oxford Press); Seventeenth and Eighteenth Century Pictures; The Connoisseur, 1914. Editor of decorations, Vogue Mag., 1920-23. Home: Giardino Vecchio, 6 Via della Liggia, Quarto dei Mille, Genoa, Italy; Castello Plars, Merano, Italy; Old Sun House, Cheyne Row, London, Eng. Died May 25, 1938.

MILLS, William Fitz Randolph; b. N.Y. City, Sept. 8, 1856; s. James Bishop and Sarah Martin (Crowell) M.; ed. pub. schs.; m. Corwina Rouse, Jan. 25, 1881 (dec.); children—Edith Randolph, William F. R., Mrs. Jessie Painter, Harold G., and 4 dec. Entered fire ins. business, N.Y. City, 1871; removed to Denver, Colo., 1889; pres. Western Steam Laundry Co.; mayor of Denver, 1918-19; was gen. mgr. Denver Municipal Water Works; chmn. Denver Compliance Bd.; sec. The Community Chest. V.p. and sec. Denver Chamber of Commerce (elected hon. mem.); v.p. Federated Charities of Denver; sec. and mgr. Denver Convention League; pres. Denver Tourist Bur. Mem. A.A.A.S., Colo. Scientific Soc. Republican. Universalist. Now retired. Club: Rotary (hon.). Home: 1253 Race St., Denver, Colo. Died Nov. 16, 1942.

MILLS, William Hayne, clergyman, educator; b. Winnsboro, S.C., Sept. 12, 1872; s. William Wilson and Sarah Edith (Smith) M.; A.B., Davidson (N. C.) Coll., 1892; B.D., Columbia (S.C.) Theol. Sem., 1897; m. Emma Louise Pressley, Apr. 18, 1899; children—Edith Louise, William, Mary Leighton, Annie Pressley (dec.), Eleanor Geddes (dec.). Ordained ministry Presbyn. Ch. in U.S., 1898; pastor Clarendon and Williamsburg counties, S.C., until 1902; home missionary under Synod of S.C., 1903-06; pastor Presbyn. Ch., Clemson Coll., S.C., 1907-18; prof. rural sociology, Clemson Agrl. Coll., since 1918, also specialist in rural orgn. and agrl. economics for same coll. In charge dept. rural economics and sociology, A.E.T., U. of Beaune, France, 1919. Specialist and consultant in Farmers' Mut. Fire Ins. in N.C. and S.C. Trustee Penn Normal Industrial and Agrl. Sch., St. Helena Island, South Carolina. Mem. Kappa Sigma, Phi Beta Kappa. Democrat. Chief author of Reports on the Country Church, to Presbyn. (South) Gen. Assembly, 1924, 25. Wrote: (bull.) South Carolina Agriculture and Industry, 1925; The Taxation System of South Carolina, 1926. Joint editor of History of the Presbyterian Church in South Carolina Since 1850, 1927; South Carolina: The Comfortable State, 1926-27; Twelve Great South Carolina Farmers; The One-Crop System in the Cotton Belt; History of the Agriculture of South Carolina, 1669-1940. Home: Clemson College, S.C. Died Mar. 29, 1942.

MILROY, William Forsyth (mĭl-roi'), physician; b. York, N.Y., Dec. 28, 1855; s. James and Sarah Ann (Cullings) M.; grad. State Normal Sch., Geneseo, N.Y., 1879; student U. of Rochester; dept. of biology, Johns Hopkins, 1 yr.; Coll. Physicians and Surgeons, Baltimore, 1 yr.; M.D., Coll. Phys. and Surg. (Columbia), 1882; intern City and Maternity hosps., New York, 1882-84; m. Lillian Barton, Apr. 27, 1886; children—Mrs. Isabelle Sarah Dunn, Mrs. Katharine Jean Uhl. In practice at Omaha, 1884-1933; former mem. faculty Omaha Med. Coll. and prof. clin. medicine and physical diagnosis, Coll. of Medicine, U. of Neb., also visiting physician Immanuel, U. of Neb. and Douglas County hosps. First pres. Douglas County Med. Soc., 1890; pres. Mo. Valley Med. Soc., 1907, Neb. State Med. Assn., 1917; mem. Am. Therapeutic Soc. (v.p. 1923), Am. Coll. of Physicians, Delta Kappa Epsilon, Alpha Omega Alpha. Republican. Presbyterian. Home: 7965 W. 4th St., Los Angeles, Calif. Died Sep. 21, 1942.

MILTON, William Hall, ex-senator; b. Jackson Co., Fla., Mar. 2, 1864; s. Maj. William Henry and Lucy Hall (Hearn) M.; ed. Agrl. and Mech. Coll., Auburn, Ala.; admitted to bar, 1890; m. Sarah S. Baker, Nov. 23, 1893. City clerk, Marianna, 1885-93; mem. Fla. Ho. of Rep., 1889; Dem. presdl. elector, 1892; apptd. U.S. surveyor-gen. of Fla. by Pres. Cleveland, 1894; mayor of Marianna, 1898-99; pres. bd. of mgrs., State Reform Sch., Marianna, 1897-1913; apptd. U.S. senator, Mar. 27, 1908, for unexpired term (1908-09) of William James Bryan, dec. U.S. commr. since 1923. Was mem. Fla. Repeal Conv. V.p. Ga. Soc. of the Cincinnati. Episcopalian. Mem. local exemption bd., Jackson County. Mem. State Welfare Bd. of Fla. Sec.-treas. Marianna Federal Savings and Loan Assn. Home: Marianna, Fla. Died Jan. 4, 1942.

MINER, James Burt, prof. psychology; b. Berlin, Wis., Oct. 6, 1873; s. Horace and Loduska Almeda (Montague) M.; B.S., U. of Minn., 1897, LL.B., 1899, M.S., 1901; Ph.D., Columbia, 1903; m. Jessie Lightner Schulten, June 30, 1908; 1 son, Horace Mitchell. Formerly mem. faculty U. of Illinois, University of Ia., U. of Minn., Carnegie Inst. Tech.; first exec. sec. and acting dir. Research Bur. for Retail Training, Pittsburgh; head dept. of psychology, U. of Ky., since 1921, also dir. University Personnel Bureau since 1930. Fellow A.A.A.S., Am. Assn. Applied Psychology; mem. Am. Psychol. Assn., Southern Soc. for Philosophy and Psychology (pres. 1925-26), Phi Beta Kappa, Sigma Xi, Zeta Psi, Phi Delta Kappa, Delta Sigma Rho, Alpha Delta Sigma (v.p. 1929-30); chmn. Clin. Sect., Am. Psychol. Assn., 1931. Conglist. Translator: Principles of Experimental Psychology by Henri Piéron. Author: Deficiency and Delinquency, an Interpretation of Mental Testing. 1918. Home: 114 Waller Av., Lexington, Ky. Died Mar. 24, 1943.

MINICK, James William (mĭn'ĭk), architect; b. Carlisle, Pa., Sept. 14, 1898; s. John Drawbaugh and

Emma Grace (Baer) M.; ed. Harrisburg (Pa.) Tech. Sch., 1916-17, Pa. State Coll., 1918-20, Carnegie Inst. Tech., Pittsburgh, Pa. (A.B. in architecture), 1920-22; m. Leah Gertrude Kennedy, Oct. 16, 1924; 1 son, Dean Kennedy. Successively archtl. draftsman, chief draftsman and designer in offices at Pittsburgh, Harrisburg, Pa., and Miami, Fla., 1917-28; mem. firm Jamison & Minick, Harrisburg, 1928-32; practiced alone, 1932-41; mem. Gravell & Minick, architects-engrs., since 1941. Designs include: Gymnasium, Sci. Bldg., Training Sch. at State Teachers Coll., Shippenburg, Pa.; Main Infirmary Bldg. at State Sanatorium for Tuberculosis, Mont Alto, Pa.; Naval Supply Depot, Mechanicsburg, Pa. Chief of tech. adv. bd. Civil Works Adminstrn. of Pa., 1932-34; sec. Pa. State Bd. of Examiners of Architects, 1937-39. Mem. Am. Inst. of Architects (sec. Central Pa. Chapter, 1935-37; treas., 1933-35; pres. 1938-40), Pa. Assn. of Architects (sec. 1940-41), Theta Xi. Democrat. Lutheran. Mason. Clubs: Harrisburg Country, West Shore Country. Home: Camp Hill, Pa. Office: Front and Harris Sts., Harrisburg, Pa. Died Dec. 23, 1949.

MINIGER, Clement Orville (mĭn'ĭg-ẽr), chmn. bd., Electric Auto-Lite Co.; b. North East, Pa., Nov. 11, 1874; s. Samuel O. and Clementine (Sherman) M.; student Fostoria (O.) High Sch.; m. Eleanor Couldwell, 1904 (died 1931); 1 dau., Eleanor (Mrs. Eleanor M. Jones); m. 2d, Mrs. Thomas A. DeVilbiss, Oct. 7, 1933. Began as coal mining operator, later traveling salesman; organized Electric Auto-Lite Co., 1911, pres. and gen. mgr., 1914-34, chmn. bd. since 1934; dir. Bendix Aviation Corp., City Auto Stamping Co., Monroe Auto Equipment Co., Bingham Stamping Co., Textileather Corp., Air-Way Elec. Appliance Corp., Willys-Overland Motors, Inc. Served as v.p. in charge of war material production, Willys-Overland Co., World War. Chmn. spl. sales com. Toledo Community Chest, 1922-30. Trustee Toledo Mus. of Art, Toledo Hosp., Women's and Children's Hosp., Toledo Y.M.C.A., Boys' Club of Toledo. Mem. and trustee Toledo Zoöl. Soc. Republican. Episcopalian. Mason (32°, K.T.), Elk. Clubs: Toledo, Inverness, Toledo Yacht, Toledo Country, Maumee River Yacht (Toledo); Detroit Athletic, Question (Detroit). Home: Perrysburg, O. Office: Electric Auto-Lite Co., Toledo, O. Died Apr. 23, 1944.

MINOR, Anne Rogers (Mrs. George Maynard Minor); b. East Lyme, Conn.; d. James Chapman and Nancy (Beckwith) Rogers; ed. pub. and pvt. schs., and under tutors; studied art; m. George Maynard Minor, 1897; 1 son, George Rogers. Served as pres.-gen. D.A.R. for the constitutional term of 3 years, 1920-23; elected hon. pres.-gen. 1923. Mem. Conn. Soc. Colonial Dames America, Daughters of Founders and Patriots, Daughters of 1812, Daughters of Am. Colonists, etc. Dir. Conn. State Farm for Women; trustee Conn. Coll. for Women (New London, Conn.), Am. Internat. Coll. (Springfield, Mass.). Landscape painter. Has pictures in notable collections. Home: Waterford, Conn. Died Oct. 24, 1947.

MINOR, Benjamin Saunders, lawyer; b. Comorn, Va., July 21, 1865; s. John T. and Sarah A. (Saunders) M.; B.L., U. of Va., 1886; m. Virginia Mason, Dec. 19, 1898; m. 2d, Neenah Laub, Nov. 8, 1944. Admitted to D.C. bar, 1887; member firm of Minor, Gatley and Drury; represented for many years Washington Gas Light Company, National Savings and Trust Co., Metropolitan Life, and Prudential Ins. Cos., also various foreign embassies; receiver of Washington Post Co.; co-receiver and operator Anacosita and Potomac St. Ry Co.; reorganized Washington Am. League Baseball Club and sec. for 15 yrs., later pres. Decorated Legion of Honor (France). Mem. Am. and D.C. bar assns., Lawyers Club, Washington Bd. of Trade, Beta Theta Pi. Democrat. Episcopalian. Clubs: Metropolitan of Washington, Chevy Chase (Md.). Home: 2415 California St. N.W. Office: 312 Colorado Bldg., 14th and G Sts., Washington 5, D.C. Died Sep. 26, 1946.

MINOR, H. Dent, lawyer; b. Macon, Miss., Mar. 9, 1868; s. Henry Augustine and Mary Anne (Dent) M.; B.S., Miss. State Coll., 1887; LL.B., U. of Va., 1890; also U. of Va. diplomas in Latin and French; m. Florence M. Fryser, Apr. 28, 1897 (died Mar. 16, 1903); children—Mary Lane (dec.), Dent, Jr. (dec.). Mem. editorial staff Am. and English Ency. of Law, Northport, L.I., N.Y., 1890-92; admitted to Tenn. bar, 1894, to bar of U.S. Supreme Court, 1907; gen. law practice Memphis, Tenn., 1894-1909; chancellor, Memphis, 1909-10, resigned; gen. atty. Ill. Central R.R. Co., Southern Lines, 1910-38; retired; mem. law firm Burch, Minor & McKay since 1911. Pres. John Gaston Hosp. Mem. Am., Tenn. and Memphis bar assns., Sigma Chi, Phi Beta Kappa. Methodist. Clubs: Tennessee (pres. 1917-19 and 1926-28), Memphis Country, Down Town (Memphis). Editor: Wood on Railroads, Minor's Edit., 1894. Author of present charter of Memphis, establishing commn. form of govt. Writer of legal articles. Home: "Briarfield," R.F.D. 4. Office: Exchange Bldg., Memphis, Tenn. Deceased.

MINOT, George Richards, (mī'nŏt), physician; b. Boston, Mass., Dec. 2, 1885; s. James Jackson and Elizabeth (Whitney) M.; A.B., Harvard, 1908, M.D., 1912, S.D. (hon.), 1928; m. Marian Linzee Weld, June 29, 1915; children—Marian Linzee, Elizabeth Whitney, Charles Sedgwick. House officer Mass. Gen. Hosp., Boston, 1912-13; asst. resident physician Johns Hopkins Hosp., 1913-14; asst. in medicine and research fellow Physiol. Lab., Johns Hopkins Med. Sch., 1914-15; mem. staff, Mass. Gen. Hosp., 1915-23, now mem. bd. of consultation; asso. in medicine, Peter Bent Brigham Hosp., 1923-28, now cons. physician; chief of med. service Collis P. Huntington Memorial Hospital, 1923-28; professor medicine, Harvard, 1928-48. Visiting physician, Boston City Hosp., 1928-; dir. Thorndike Memorial Lab. (Harvard) of Boston City Hosp. to 1948, consultant physician since 1948. Served as contract surgeon several weeks, U.S. Army, 1917, 18. Hon. fellow Royal Coll. Physicians, Edinburgh, Royal Coll. Physicians (London), N.Y. Acad. Medicine, Inst. of Medicine of Chicago, Royal Soc. of Medicine, London; v.p. étranger Société Française d'Hematologie, 1938-39; fellow Am. Philos. Soc., Phila., Am. Coll. Physicians; mem. A.M.A., Assn. Am. Physicians (pres. 1937-38), Am. Soc. Clin. Investigation, Am. Acad. Arts and Sciences, American Clin. and Climatol. Assn. (pres. 1932-33), Nat. Acad. Sciences, Med. Library Assn. Am. (v.p. 1938-39), Phi Beta Kappa, Alpha Omega Alpha, Sigma Chi; hon. mem. Royal Acad. Med. (Belgium) since 1939; hon. mem. Kaiserlich Leopold Caroline Deutsche Akademie der Naturforscher (Halle), Society Biol. Chemists (India), Finland Soc. of Internal Medicine (Helsingfors). Awarded Kober gold medal, Assn. Am. Physicians, 1928; Charles Mickle fellowship, Univ. of Toronto, 1928; Cameron prize, University of Edinburgh, 1930; gold medal, Nat. Inst. Social Sciences, 1930; gold medal and award, Popular Science Monthly, 1930; Moxon medal, Royal Coll. Physicians, London, 1933; John Scott medal of City of Phila., 1933; gold medal of Humane Soc. of Mass., 1935; awarded, jointly with Wm. P. Murphy and George H. Whipple, the Nobel prize in medicine for 1934, for work on liver treatment of the anemias; scroll award of Associated Grocery Mfrs. of America, 1936. Gordon Wilson lecturer and medalist Am. Clin. and Climatol. Assn., 1939. Trustee Brookline (Mass.) Public Library since 1941. Unitarian. Author: Pathological Physiology and Clinical Description of the Anemias (with William B. Castle), 1936. Contbr. about 160 papers, chiefly on the blood. Discovered, in 1926, the curative effect of liver on pernicious anemia. Address: 311 Beacon St., Boston; or Thorndike Memorial Lab., Boston City Hosp., Boston, Mass. Died Feb. 25, 1950.

MINOT, John Clair, editor; b. Belgrade, Me., Nov. 30, 1872; s. George Evans and Effie (Parcher) M.; 10th in descent from George Minot who came from Eng. to Dorchester in 1630; A.B., Bowdoin Coll., 1896, hon. Litt.D., 1925; m. Marion Bowman, Feb. 20, 1912; 1 son, John Hallowell. Was asso. editor of Kennebec Journal, Augusta, Me., 1897-1909, Youth's Companion, Boston, 1909-18, with cinema work of Y.M.C.A. in France, 1918-19; lit. editor Boston Herald, 1919-38. Lecturer on current lit., Boston U., 1920-26. Republican. Conglist. Mem. Delta Kappa Epsilon (pres. 1935). In Masonry has been at head of Lodge, Chapter and Commandery. Mem. bd. overseers Bowdoin Coll.; trustee Nasson Inst. Mem. Phi Beta Kappa. Author: History of Belgrade; Centennial History of Augusta; History of Theta of D.K.E., 1844-1904; The Story of Bowdoin, 1896; Tales of Bowdoin, 1901; Bowdoin Verse, 1907; Under the Bowdoin Pines, 1907; The Best Animal Stories I Know, 1929; The Best Bird Stories I Know, 1930; The Best College Stories I Know, 1931; The Best Stories of Exploration I Know, 1932; Rhymes of Freckle Days, 1933; Tales of Freckle Days, 1934; The Best Stories of Heroism I Know, 1934; also verse, stories, articles and lectures. First radio speaker on books, 1922. Died Oct. 3, 1941.

MINOT, Joseph Grafton; b. N.Y. City, Jan. 13, 1858; s. Charles Henry and Maria Josephine (Grafton) M.; ed. pvt. schs., Boston, Harvard Law Sch., Mass. Inst. Tech.; m. Honora Elizabeth Temple Winthrop, 1890. Pres. Indsl. Sch. for Crippled and Deformed Children, Boston. Mem. Mass. Hist. Soc., Am. Antiquarian Soc., Bostonian Soc. (dir.). Author: A Genealogical Record of the Minot Family in America and England, 1897. Home: 100 Beacon St., Boston. Died June 19, 1939.

MINTER, William Ramseur, clergyman; b. Sedalia, S.C., July 9, 1873; s. John Russell and Fannie Dodson (Ramseur) M.; A.B., Davidson (N.C.) Coll., 1892, D.D., 1913; student McCormick Theol. Sem., 1893-94; B.D., Columbia (S.C.) Theol. Sem., 1897; m. Harriet Maria Smith, Dec. 21, 1898; children—William Smith, Catherine Christina, John Perrin, David Ramseur. Ordained ministry Presbyn. Ch. in U.S., 1897; pastor Rutherfordton and Shelby, N.C., until 1905; prin. Westminster (N.C.) Sch., 1905-07; pastor Lincolnton, N.C., 1907-15, Austin, Tex., 1915-40. Chaplain 1st N.C. Nat. Guard, 1915. Trustee Presbyn. Theol. Sem., Austin, Davidson Coll., Barium Springs (N.C.) Orphans' Home. Mem. Sigma Alpha Epsilon. Moderator Synod of Texas, 1928. Author: Travel Letters, 1909. Home: Palestine, Tex. Died Sep. 26, 1943.

MIRZA, Youël Benjamin (mẽr'zä), author; b. Nazie, Persia, Dec. 23, 1888; s. Moshi and Rachel (Nweeya) M.; A.M., Johns Hopkins University, 1914, Ph.D., from same, 1920; m. Althea Emily Brown, July 29, 1922; 1 son, David Brown. Came to U.S., 1903, naturalized citizen. Enlisted in U.S. Navy, June 6, 1917; served at office of Naval Intelligence, Washington, D.C., also saw foreign service. Asst. prof. history Earlham Coll., Richmond, Ind., 1923-24. Mem. Am. Legion. Mem. Soc. of Friends. Club: Johns Hopkins (Baltimore). Author: Iran and the Iranians, 1913; When I Was a Boy in Persia, 1920; Myself When Young, 1929; Children of the Housetops, 1931; Son of the Sword, 1934; The Young Tentmaker, 1935; The Rug That Went to Mecca, 1939; Stripling, 1940. Home: 1614 Manor Place, Dayton, O. Died Sept. 29, 1947.

MITCHELL, Charles Bayard, bishop; b. Allegheny City, Pa., Aug. 27, 1857; s. Rev. Daniel Patrick and Anna E. (Baker) M.; A.B., Allegheny Coll., 1879, A.M., 1882, Ph.D., 1892, D.D., 1000, LL.D., 1911, L.H.D.. 1917; m. Clara Aull, July 6, 1882. Ordained M.E. ministry, 1882; pastor Burton, Marion and Leavenworth, Kan., until 1886; Pittsburgh, 1886-88, Plainfield, N.J., 1888-92, Kansas City, 1892-97, Minneapolis, 1897-1901, First Ch., Cleveland, 1901-08, St. James', Chicago, 1908-16; bishop M.E. Ch., May 20, 1916-May 1924; served Ch. in St. Paul Area, comprising States of Wis., Minn. and S.Dakota; apptd. to adminster M.E. Ch. in P.I. for 4 yrs. Del. 3d Ecumenical Conf., London, 1901, 4th Conference, Toronto, 1911; del. Gen. Conf. 1904, 08, 16; del. World's Sunday Sch. Conv., Zürich, 1913; fraternal del. to Japan Meth. Conf., 1927. Mem. Phi Beta Kappa, Delta Tau Delta. Mason (33°); Grand Prelate Grand Encampment of K.T. of U.S. Author: Bundle of Letters from Three Continents; The Noblest Quest; The Way of a Man. Spl. preacher to A.E.F. in France for Y.M.C.A., during spring and summer, 1919; retired 1928. Home: 456 La Loma Rd., Pasadena, Calif. Died Feb. 23, 1941.

MITCHELL, Charles Tennant, mfr.; b. Cadillac, Mich., May 31, 1880; s. William Whittier and Ella (Yost) M.; ed. Lawrenceville (N.J.) Sch., Phillip's Acad., Andover, Mass.; m. Mary Gleason, Aug. 17, 1916; children—William Whittier, Katherine Ellen. Pres. Cobbs & Mitchell (Douglas fir), Portland, Ore., William W. Mitchell Co. (timber), Valley & Siletz R.R. Co.; dir. Cadillac Malleable Iron Co., Ann Arbor Ry. Co., Cadillac-Soo Lumber Co.; trustee Mitchell-Diggins Iron Co. Chief of Am. Protective League, Northern Mich. Dist., World War; mem. Park Bd., Cemetery Bd. Mem. Nat. Lumber Mfrs. Assn., Maple Flooring Mfrs.' Assn. (v.p. 1912-22), Mich. Hardwood Mfrs.' Assn. (ex-pres.). Republican. Elk. Club: Cadillac Country. Home: Cadillac, Mich. Died Nov. 17, 1948; buried Cadillac, Mich.

MITCHELL, G. P., church official, retired; b. of Am. parents, Ont., Can., Dec. 12, 1856; s. J. E. and Eliza (Potts) M.; ed. pub. schs.; spent 5 yrs. at Shurtleff Coll., Alton, Ill., after 40 yrs. of age, and grad. B.A., 1907; D.D., same coll., 1915; m. Nettie May Clark, Sept. 26, 1883; children—Hazel M. E., Phillip D. Ordained Bapt. ministry, 1891; pastor successively at Plainfield, Ill., Ovid, Mich., Grand Rapids, Mich., Shenandoah, Ia.; missionary and exec. sec. Ia. Bapt. Conv., 1913-26 (retired). Mem. bd. trustees Des Moines U. and Northwestern Bapt. Hosp. Assn., St. Paul, Minn., many yrs.; mem. Bd. Promotion and Missionary Cooperation, Northern Bapt. Conv., 7 yrs.; del. from Ia. Bapt. Conv. to Bapt. World Alliance Meetings, Stockholm, Sweden, July 1923. Author: An Adventure With Chance, 1935. Editor: A Century of Iowa Baptist History. Home: 1622 W. 11th St., Des Moines, Ia.* Died Aug. 1943.

MITCHELL, George T., lawyer; b. Pontotoc, Miss., Sept. 1, 1874; s. Charles Baldwin and Virginia (Dennis) M.; student Miss. Agrl. and Mech. Coll., 1891-92; LL.B., U. of Miss., 1895; m. Jennie Preston Summers, Nov. 17, 1897; children—Virginia Preston, Charles Summers. Admitted to Miss. bar, 1895, and began practice, Pontotoc; dist. atty., 1st Miss. Dist., 1904-10; atty. gen. of Miss. since 1929, term expiring 1932; U.S. dist. atty. Northern Dist. of Miss. since Aug. 7, 1937. Mem. Sigma Alpha Epsilon. Democrat. Presbyterian. Mason. Club: University. Home: Tupelo, Miss. Died Feb. 23, 1945.

MITCHELL, Hal E., newspaper editor; b. St. Joseph, Mo., Apr. 14, 1869; s. Robert Chalmers and Frances (Hulburd) M.; grad. Shattuck Mil. Sch., Faribault, Minn., 1889; student Oberlin Coll., 1889-92; m. Lucy Lancaster Davidson, Oct. 30, 1895; children—Frances Louise, Elsie L., Bruce D. Mng. editor Lincoln Daily Call, 1895-97; mng. editor Duluth News Tribune, 1900-13; night editor Milwaukee Sentinel, 1914-16; night editor Detroit Free Press, 1917-26, mng. editor, 1926-31. Republican. Episcopalian. Mason, Elk. Home: 365 Fisher Road, Grosse Pointe, Mich. Died July 27, 1947.

MITCHELL, Harry Luzerne, pub. utility official; b. Warren, Pa., Jan. 11, 1883; s. Willis A. and Sarah Oliphant (Gemmill) M.; ed. Warren High Sch.; m. Edith M. Davidson, Sept. 19, 1908; children—Charles D., Caroline S., Margaret D. Began as clk. with cos. of West Penn System, 1902; has held exec. positions in various ry. and power operating cos. of same; pres. West Penn Power Co., West Penn Rys. Co., W.Va. Power & Transmission Co., Allegheny Pittsburgh Coal Co., Windsor Power House Coal Co., Potomac Transmission Co.; director Beach Bottom Power Co., Monongahela Power Co.; trustee Dollar Savings Bank, Pittsburgh, dir. Colonial Trust Co., Pittsburgh, Second Nat. Bank, Connellsville, Pa. Republican. Presbyterian. Clubs: Oakmont Country, Fox Chapel Golf, Duquesne (Pittsburgh); Pike Run Country (Jones Mills, Pa.); Pleasant Valley Country (Connellsville, Pa.). Home: 6334 Forbes St. Office: 14 Wood St., Pittsburgh, Pa. Died Sept. 10, 1948.

MITCHELL, Howard Hawks, prof. mathematics; b. Marietta, O., Jan. 14, 1885; s. Oscar Howard and Mary Hoadley (Hawks) M.; Ph.B., Marietta (O.) College, 1906; Sc.D. from same college, 1935; Ph.D., Princeton Univ., 1910; m. Emma Vestine White, Sept. 18, 1912. Fellow in mathematics, Princeton, 1908-10; instr. mathematics, Yale, 1910-11; instr. mathematics, 1911-14, asst. prof., 1914-21, prof. since 1921,

U. of Pa. Editor Trans. Am. Math. Soc., 1925-30. Served as ballistician at Aberdeen Proving Grounds, World War, 1918. Mem. Am. Math. Soc. (v.p. 1932-33), A.A.A.S. (v.p. 1932), Am. Philos. Soc., Phi Beta Kappa, Sigma Xi, Delta Upsilon. Home: Merion, Pa. Died Mar. 13, 1943.

MITCHELL, Howard Walton, lawyer; b. Pittsburgh, Pa., Apr. 5, 1867; s. Joseph and Adelaide V. (McKee) M.; B.S., Pa. State Coll., 1890; LL.D., U. of Pittsburgh, 1915; m. Anna Cameron, June 11, 1896 (died Sept. 24, 1908). Began practice of law at Pittsburgh, 1893; mem. firms Lyon, McKee & Mitchell, 1897-1907, McKee, Mitchell & Patterson, 1907-08, McKee, Mitchell & Alter, 1908-19; apptd. judge Orphans' Court, 5th Jud. Dist. of Pa., by Gov. William C. Sproul, July 10, 1919, and elected to same office, Nov. 1919, for term ending, 1929, reëlected for terms ending 1939 and 1949. Pres. bd. Pa. State Coll., 1914-29 (acting pres. of the coll., 1920-21); pres. bd. trustees, Pittsburgh Y.M.C.A. and Athalia Daly Home (Pittsburgh); trustee Presbyn. Hosp., Henry C. Frick Ednl. Commn. Moderator of Gen. Assembly United Presbyn. Ch. of N.A. Mem. Am., Pa. State and Allegheny County bar assns., Beta Theta Pi. Republican. United Presbyn. Clubs: Duquesne, University, Oakmont Country. Home: 1090 Devon Rd., Pittsburgh, Pa. Died Oct. 11, 1943.

MITCHELL, James McCormick, lawyer; b. Washington, D.C., Sept. 6, 1873; s. Rev. Samuel S. and Theresa E. (Wierman) M.; A.B., Princeton, 1894, A.M., 1897, LL.D., 1945; LL.B., U. of Buffalo, 1897; m. Lavinia Austin Avery, Dec. 5, 1906; children—Margaret (Mrs. Robert Fisher), Ruth Avery (Mrs. David A. Thompson), Austin Avery. Admitted to New York bar; practiced law at Buffalo, N.Y., since 1897; mem. of the law firm Bissell, Carey & Cooke, 1902-06, Kenefick, Cooke, Mitchell & Bass, 1906-29, Kenefick, Cooke, Mitchell, Bass & Letchworth since 1929. Dir. Buffalo C. of C., 1928-31; trustee Buffalo Bd. of Trade; life mem. Buffalo Fine Arts Acad., mem. Grad. Council, Princeton U., 1918-23, 1932-37; chmn. Council, U. of Buffalo; trustee 1st Presbyn. Ch. (pres. 1920-24, 1931-35). Mem. Am. Bar Assn., N.Y. State Bar Assn. (v.p. 1929, pres. 1943), Erie County Bar Assn., Assn. Bar City of New York, Am. Arbitration Assn., Am. Acad. Polit. and Social Science (life), Acad. Polit. Science, Am. Soc. Internat. Law, Am. Polit. Science Assn., Am. Econ. Assn., Am. Law Institute (life); The Newcomen Society. Republican. Clubs: Buffalo (pres. 1918), Saturn (dean 1924), Buffalo Country (pres. 1937-38), Thursday, Buffalo Tennis and Squash (pres. 1918); University, Princeton (New York); Yeamans Hall (Charleston, S.C.). Home: 70 Oakland Pl. Office: Marine Trust Bldg., Buffalo, N.Y. Died Oct. 14, 1948.

MITCHELL, Margaret, author; b. Atlanta, Ga.; d. Eugene Muse and Maybelle (Stephens) Mitchell; student Washington Sem., Atlanta, 1914-18, Smith Coll., 1918-19, hon. M.A., 1939; m. John R. Marsh, July 4, 1925. Feature writer and reporter Atlanta Journal, 1922-26. Awarded Nat. Book Award, Am. Booksellers Assn., 1936; Pulitzer prize, 1937; Carl Bohnenberger Memorial Award, 1938; gold medal, New York Southern Soc., 1938. Mem. Atlanta Hist. Soc., Huguenot Soc. of S.C. Democrat. Author: Gone with the Wind, 1936. Home: 1268 Piedmont Av., N.E., Atlanta 5, Ga. Died Aug. 16, 1949; buried Oakland Cemetery, Atlanta, Ga.

MITCHELL, Samuel Chiles, univ. prof.; b. Coffeeville, Miss., Dec. 24, 1864; s. Morris Randolph and Grace Anne (Chiles) M.; M.A., Georgetown (Ky) Coll., 1888; student U. of Va., 1891-92; Ph.D., U. of Chicago, 1899; LL.D., Brown U., 1910, Baylor U., 1913, U. of Cincinnati, 1914; m. Alice Virginia Broadus, June 30, 1891; children—Broadus, Morris Randolph, Terry, Mary Adams, George Sinclair. Prof. history and Greek, Miss. Coll., 1889-91; prof. Latin, Georgetown Coll., 1891-95; prof. history, U. of Richmond, 1895-1908; lecturer on history, Brown U., 1908-09; pres. U. of S.C., 1908-13; pres. U. of Del., 1914-20; prof. history, U. of Richmond, 1920-45. Trustee Jeanes Fund. Mem. Phi Beta Kappa, Phi Gamma Delta. Baptist. D.C.L. conferred by U. of S.C., 1942; Litt.D., Med. Coll. of Va., 1943. Editor vol. on social life in "The South in the Building of the Nation," and contbr. to various publs. Address: University of Richmond, Richmond, Va. Died Aug. 20, 1948.

MITCHELL, Sidney Zollicoffer, ex-chmn. bd. Electric Bond & Share Co.; b. Dadeville, Ala.; grad. U.S. Naval Acad., 1883. Served in U.S. Navy, 2 yrs., left the Naval service in 1885; entered employ Edison Electric Light Co., Goerck St. factory, New York; apptd. organizer electric light plants for Edison Co. in Northwest, hdqrs. Seattle, 1885; head of Electric Bond & Share Co. and dir. many cos., 1905-33; now retired. Office: 80 Broadway, New York, N.Y. Died Feb. 17, 1949.

MITCHELL, Steele; pres. Adams Express Co. Office: 25 Broad St., New York, N.Y. Died Dec. 2, 1940.

MITCHELL, Sydney Bancroft, library science; b. Montreal, Can., June 24, 1878; s. James and Sarah (Cooper) M.; B.A., McGill U., 1901, M.A., 1904; student New York State Library School, Albany, New York, 1903-04; Litt.D., Occidental Coll., 1945; m. Rose Frances Michaels, Dec. 28, 1908. Came to U.S., 1908, naturalized 1922. In charge reading room McGill U., 1902-03, cataloguer, 1904-08; chief of order dept., Stanford U., 1908-11; head of accessions dept., U. of Calif. Library, 1911-19, asso. librarian, 1919-26, also asso. prof. library sci., 1922-26; prof. library science Univ. of Mich., 1926-27; director School of Librarianship and prof. librarianship, U. of Calif., 1927-44, dean of school and prof. librarianship, 1944-46, emeritus since 1946. Member American Library Association, California Library Association (pres. 1938-39), Calif. Horticultural Soc. (pres. 1933-45). Awarded W. R. Dykes medal for best new American iris, 1927. Awards: American Iris Society Medal for Hybridizing 1943, and (English) Iris Society Foster Memorial, 1944. Author: Gardening in California, 1923; Adventures in Flower Gardening, 1928; From a Sunset Garden, 1932; Your California Garden and Mine, 1947. Contbr. on librarianship to professional mags. and on gardening to Sunset and other periodicals. Home: 633 Woodmont Av., Berkeley, Calif. Died Jan. 23, 1948.

MITCHELL, Wesley Clair, economist; b. Rushville, Ill., Aug. 5, 1874; s. John Wesley and Lucy Medora (McClellan) M.; A.B., U. of Chicago, 1896; grad. student same 1896-97, 1898-99, Ph.D., 1899; univs. of Halle and Vienna, 1897-98; M.A., Oxford; LL.D., University of Chicago, Columbia, U. of California, Princeton U.; D.Litt., Harvard; D.Sc., University of Pennsylvania; Dr. Honoris Causa, Univ. of Paris; Dr. of Humane Letters, New Sch. for Social Research; married Lucy Sprague, May 8, 1912; children—John McClellan, Sprague, Marian, Arnold. In Census Office, Washington, 1899-1900; instr. economics, U. of Chicago, 1900-02; asst. prof. commerce, 1902-08, prof. polit. economy, July 1902-12, U. of Calif., lecturer, Columbia U., 1913-14, prof. economics, 1914-19 and 1922-44; lecturer New School for Social Research, 1919-21. Chief price sect., War Industries Bd., 1918-19. Lecturer, Harvard, 1908-09; George Eastman visiting prof. Oxford U., 1930-31; Hitchcock prof., U. of Calif., 1934; Messenger lecturer Cornell Univ., 1935. Francis A. Walker medal (1st award), Am. Econ. Assn., 1947. Awarded gold medal, Nat. Inst. Social Sciences; Dir. of Research, Nat. Bur. of Econ. Research, 1920-45; chmn. Social Sci. Research Council, 1927-30; chmn. President's Research Com. on Social Trends, 1929-33; men. Nat. Planning Bd., Federal Emergency Admn. of Public Works, 1933; member National Resources Board, 1934-35; dir. New School for Social Research, 1919-31, Bur. of Ednl. Expts. Clubs: Century (New York City); Faculty (Berkeley); Cosmos (Washington, D.C.). Honorary fellow Royal Statistical Society; fellow Am. Statis. Assn. (past pres.), Royal Econ. Soc., Econometric Soc. (past pres.); mem. Am. Econ. Assn. (past pres.), Institut International de Statisque, Acad. Polit. Science (pres. 1935-38), Am. Philos. Soc., Am. Acad. Arts and Sciences, Stable Money Assn., A.A.A.S. (v.p., chairman sect. K, 1933, pres. 1938); corr. mem. Manchester Statis. Society, Institut de Science Economique Appliquee. Author: A History of the Greenbacks, 1903; Gold Prices and Wages Under the Greenback Standard, 1908; Business Cycles, 1913; Business Cycles, The Problem and Its Setting, 1927; The Backward Art of Spending Money, 1937. Editor: History of Prices During the War: Business Cycles and Unemployment, 1923. Co-Author: Income in the United States—Its Amount and Distribution, 1921; Recent Economic Changes, 1929; Recent Social Trends, 1933; Measuring Business Cycles, 1946. Home: 2 Horatio St., New York 14, N.Y. Died Oct. 29, 1948.

MITCHELL, Willard A., lawyer; b. Chateaugay, N.Y., Feb. 5, 1868; s. James and Amelia (Rockwell) M.; grad. Chateaugay Acad., 1882; A.B., U. of Vt., 1887; student law, Columbia, 1888-89; m. Lilian I. Miles, Dec. 21, 1893. Admitted to N.Y. bar, 1890, and began practice at N.Y. City; executor and trustee of estates and counsel and dir. corps.; dir. and gen. counsel Chicago Pneumatic Tool Co.; dir. and secretary United Zinc Smelting Corp. Mem. N.Y. State Bar Assn., N.Y. County Lawyer's Assn., Assn. Bar City New York, S.R., Phi Beta Kappa, Delta Psi. Republican. Episcopalian. Clubs: Lawyers, Seawane, Atlantic Beach, Regency. Home: 1040 Park Av. Office: 141 Broadway, New York, N.Y. Died Dec. 20, 1942.

MITSCHER, Marc Andrew, naval officer; b. Hillsboro, Wis., Jan. 26, 1887; grad. U.S. Naval Acad., 1910; commd. ensign U.S. Navy, 1910, and advanced through the grades to rear admiral, 1941, vice admiral, 1944; connected with naval aviation since Oct. 1915; served as pilot on first Navy trans-Atlantic flight, 1919; in command Naval Air Station, Anacostia, D.C., 1922-25; exec. officer, U.S.S. Langley, 1929-30; with Bureau of Aeronautics, Navy Dept., 1930-33; chief of staff to comdr. Aircraft, Base Force, U.S.S. Wright, flagship; served as exec. officer Saratoga and 2 yr. tour of duty in Bur. of Aeronautics, then returned to the Wright as comdg. officer; asst. chief Bur. of Aeronautics, 1939-41; comdg. officer, U.S.S. Hornet, 1941-42 (the Hornet was the Shangri-La from which the American planes, under command of Maj. Gen. James Doolittle, took off on Apr. 18, 1942, to bomb mil. objectives in Tokyo and 4 other Japanese cities); in command of carrier Midway during battle of Midway, June 1942; comdr. air, Solomon Islands, Apr.-July 1943; comdr. Task Force 58 Pacific Fleet, 1944 (during operations against the Marshall Islands, Truk and Tinian-Saipan); chief of naval operations for air, 1945; Awarded Navy Cross, Distinguished Service Medal, and The Gold Star in lieu of the second Distinguished Service Medal, Mexican Service medal, Victory Medal, Escort Clasp; American Defense Service Medal, Fleet Clasp; The Asiatic-Pacific Area Campaign medal; NC-4 Medal; Order of Tower and Sword with grade of official by Portugal (connection with NC-4 flight, May 6, 1919) cited for third Distinguished Service Medal, 1944. Home: 229 East Park Place, Oklahoma City, Okla. Died Feb. 3, 1947; buried in Arlington National Cemetery.

MITTON, George W., chmn. bd. Jordan Marsh Co., Boston dept. store; dir. Allied Stores Corp., N.Y. City. Home: 135 Fisher Av., Brookline, Mass. Office: 450 Washington St., Boston, Mass. Died Nov. 14, 1947.

MOEHLENPAH, Henry A., banker; b. Joliet, Ill., Mar. 9, 1867; s. Frederick and Elizabeth (Brady) M.; Northwestern U., 1890-94; m. Alice Hartshorn, Oct. 15, 1896. Began in banking business, Joliet, 1888; pres. of Citizens Bank (Clinton), Wis. Mortgage & Securities Co. (Milwaukee, Wis.); mem. Fed. Res. Bd., Washington, 1919-21; became pres. Bankers Finance Corp., 1921; now supervisor Eastern dist., Aetna Life Ins. Co. Dem. nominee for Congress, 1st Dist., Wis., 1906, for lt. gov., 1908, for presdl. elector, 1916, for gov. 1918. Mem. Wis. Bankers' Assn. (pres. 1913-14, since 1935), Phi Kappa Sigma. Methodist. Clubs: City, Kiwanis. Mem. Knights of Pythias. Author of many pub. articles and addresses on financial matters. Home: 839 N. Marshall St. Office: 735 N. Water St., Milwaukee, Wis. Died Nov. 9, 1944.

MOENKHAUS, William J., univ. prof.; b. Huntingburg, Ind., Jan. 6, 1871; s. William and Fredricka (Ramsbrook) M.; grad. Ind. State Normal Sch., Terre Haute, 1892; A.B., Ind. U., Bloomington, 1894, A.M., 1895; studied Harvard, 1896-99; U. of Chicago, 1899-1901, Ph.D., 1903; m. Sara Katherine Rettger, Sept. 10, 1901; children—William Ernest, Charles Augustus. Asst. dir. State Museum, Sao Paulo, Brazil, 1897-98; asst. prof. zoölogy, 1901-04, asso. prof. physiology, 1904-05, jr. prof., 1905-08, prof., since 1908, Ind. U. Fellow A.A.A.S., Ind. Acad. Science; mem. Am. Soc. Naturalists, Am. Soc. Zoölogists, Phi Gamma Delta, Phi Beta Kappa, Sigma Xi. Contbr. to scientific jours. on exptl. biology. Home: Bloomington, Ind. Died June 8, 1947.

MOERK, Frank Xavier, chemist, educator; b. Phila., July 3, 1863; s. Ernest Gottlieb and Maria (Fehrenbach) M.; ed. German pvt. schs., Wilmington, Del., Phila. Coll. Pharmacy, Ph.G., 1884; m. Katharine Nicolai, March 22, 1888. Clerk in retail drug store, 1877-84; asst. chem. laboratory, 1884-92; asst. to chair theoretical chemistry, 1886-99, prof. analytical chemistry since 1899, Phila. Coll. Pharmacy. Mem. Am. Chem. Soc., Pa. State Pharm. Assn., Phila. Coll. Pharmacy, Am. Pharm. Assn., German Chem. Soc. Lutheran. Author: Notes on Qualitative Analysis, 1901 01; Qualitative Chemical Analysis, 1905 X1. Residence: 646 E. Chelten Av., Germantown. Office: 145 N. 10th St., Philadelphia. Died Nov. 19, 1945.

MOFFAT, David William (mŏf'făt), judge; b. Salt Lake City, Utah, Mar. 26, 1870; s. Joseph Smith and Mary Jane (Brown) M.; edn. Univ. of Utah, 1891-94; U. of Chicago, 1903-05; m. Sarah Elizabeth Howe, Jan. 1, 1896; children—David Howe, Dean Alexander. Successively farmer, rancher, teacher, surveyor, lawyer, city atty., dist. judge; justice Utah Supreme Court since 1932, chief justice, 1939-42; legal adviser to Draft Bd., 1917-18. Mem. Salt Lake Bd. No. 2, Selective Service Bd. of Appeals. Mem. Nat. Council Boy Scouts of America (mem. exec. com. of Salt Lake Council; has served in Boy Scouts for period of 26 years). Pres. Alumni Assn. U. of Utah; mem. Am. Bar Assn., Utah State Bar Assn., Western States Probation and Parole Assn., Utah Peace Officers Assn. Democrat. Mormon. Clubs: University, Country, Lions. Home: 286 Vine St., Murray City, Utah. Office: State Capitol, Salt Lake City, Utah. Died Mar. 4, 1944.

MOFFAT, J(ay) Pierrepont, diplomat; b. Rye, N.Y., July 18, 1896; s. R. Burnham and Ellen Low (Pierrepont) M.; prep. edn., Groton (Mass.) Sch.; student Harvard University, 1915-17; LL.D., University of Toronto, Tufts College, Queen's College, 1941; m. Lilla Cabot Grew, July 27, 1927; two children. Private sec. to Am. minister, The Hague, Netherlands, 1918-19; 3d sec. of legation, Warsaw, Poland, 1919-21; 2d sec. of legation, Tokyo, Japan, 1921-23, Constantinople, Turkey, 1923-25; 1st sec. of legation, Berne, Switzerland, 1927-31; chief of Div. of Western European Affairs, Dept. of State, 1932-35; consul gen. Sydney, Australia, 1935-37; chief of Div. of European Affairs, Dept. of State, 1937-40; U.S. minister to Canada since June 1940. Attached to Am. delegations to Preparatory Disarmament Commn., 1927, 29, Internat. Conf. for Abolition of Import and Export Prohibitions and Restrictions, 1928, Internat. Conf. for Revision of Geneva Red Cross Conv. of 1906, 1929. Clubs: Metropolitan, Burning Tree, Alibi (Washington); Union (New York). Home: Hancock, N.H. Address: American Legation, Ottawa, Can. Died Jan. 24, 1943.

MOFFATT, Fred Cushing, stock broker; b. New York, N.Y., Oct. 16, 1889; s. John M. and Jessie (Spear) M.; ed. grammar sch., Dunmore, Pa.; m. Margaret Fisher, Oct. 15, 1926. In securities business under own name since 1923. Dir. New York Curb Exchange; pres. and dir. New York Curb Exchange Securities Clearing Corp.; dir. New York Curb Exchange Realty Associates, Inc. Republican. Home: 393 Ryder Rd., Manhasset, L.I., N.Y. Office: 86 Trinity Place, New York, N.Y. Died Dec. 16, 1949.

MOFFATT, James, prof. ch. history; b. Glasgow, Scotland, July 4, 1870; s. George and Isabella (Morton) M.; M.A., Glasgow U., 1889; B.D., 1894, D.Litt., 1909; D.D., St. Andrews U., 1901; M.A., Oxford, 1915, D.D., 1927; LL.D., Dickinson Coll., Carlisle, Pa., 1928; m. Mary Reith, Sept. 29, 1896; children—George Stuart (dec.), Eric Morton, Margaret Skelton, James Archibald Reith. Came to U.S., 1927. Minister of United Free Ch. of Scotland, 1896-1912; Yates prof. Greek, Mansfield Coll., Oxford, 1911-15; prof. ch. history, United Free Ch. Coll., Glasgow, 1915-27; Washburn prof. ch. history, Union Theol. Sem., N.Y. City, since 1927; Jowett lecturer, London, 1907; Cunningham lecturer, Edinburgh, 1914; Hibbert lecturer, London, 1921. Author: Historical New Testament, 1901; Primer to Novels of George Meredith, 1909; Introduction to Literature of New Testament, 1911; Theology of the Gospels, 1912; Approach to the New Testament, 1921; Hebrews-Internat. Critical Commentary, 1924; Everyman's Life of Jesus, 1924; The Bible in Scots Literature, 1925; Presbyterianism, 1928; Love in the New Testament, 1929; The Day Before Yesterday, 1930; Grace in the New Testament, 1931; First Five Centuries of the Church, First Corinthians, 1938; The Books of the Prophets, 1939. Home: 606 W. 122d St., New York, N.Y.* Died June 27, 1944.

MOFFETT, Thomas Clinton, clergyman; b. Madison, Ind., July 29, 1869; s. Samuel Shuman and Maria J. (McKee) M.; B.S., Hanover (Ind.) Coll., 1890; M.A., 1894, D.D., 1910; studied Union Theol. Sem., 1891; studied Free Ch. Coll., Edinburgh, Scotland, unmarried. Ordained Presbyn. ministry, 1893; pastor Flagstaff, Ariz., Raton, N.M., and Portland, Ore., 1893-1901; gen. missionary for Ariz., 1901-06; supt. Indian work, Presbyn. Bd. Nat. Missions, New York, 1906-28; sec. Commn. on the Indians of Latin America. Author: The American Indian on the New Trail, 1914; The Bible in the Life of the Indians. Home: 15 Gramercy Park, New York, N.Y. Died Nov. 13, 1945.

MOHOLY-NAGY, Laszlo George (mō-hō'lī-nădj), painter, author, photographer, cinema dir.; b. Borsod, Hungary, July 20, 1895; s. Leopold Gustave and Carola Aester Moholy-Nagy; grad. in law, U. of Budapest, 1915; m. Sibyl Dorothy Peech, 1933; children—Hattula Sibylle Carola, Claudia Eve. Came to U.S., 1937, naturalized, 1946. Painter, photographer and writer since 1920; prof. teaching basic elements of art, and head of metal workshop, Bauhaus, Weimar and Dessau, Germany, 1923-28; dir. New Bauhaus, Chicago, 1937-38; pres. Inst. of Design, Chicago since 1939. Made first photograms (photographs without camera), Berlin, 1921; did experimental work with light and color in painting, photography and film, Berlin, 1928; made stage settings for Piscator's theatre and the State Opera, Berlin; produced books with photographs, films and special effects for films, London, 1935-37. Had one-man show of photographs, Royal Photographic Soc.; exhibited painting and sculpture, London and many other cities in Eng.; at Museum of Non-objective Painting and Museum of Modern Art, N.Y. City, 1942. Represented in Budapest and Berlin National Galleries and private collections in Europe and U.S. Lecturer at Cambridge and Oxford universities art societies. Served as artillery officer in Austro-Hungarian Army, World War I. Hon. mem. Cambridge and Oxford univs. art assns. and British Designer Inst.; dir. of Am. Designer's Inst., Congrès Internationale Architecture Moderne. Received Signum laudis, silver and bronze fortitude, etc., medals. Author: Horizont, 1921; (with L. Kassák) Book of New Artists, 1921; Painting, Photography, Motion Picture, 1924; From Material to Architecture, 1928; The New Vision, 1930, 2 edit., 1938, 3 edition 1946; Vision in Motion, 1946. Editor of "id" (Institute of Design) books, 1946; (with Walter Gropius) 14 Bauhaus Books, 1924-28. Book illustration in photography: 60 photographs by L. Moholy-Nagy, 1930; Telehor, 1936; (with Mary Benedetta) Street Markets of London, 1936; (with J. Ferguson) Eton Portrait, 1937; (with John Betjeman) Oxford University Chest, 1938. Films: Still Life (Berlin), 1926; Marseille Vieux Port, 1929; Light Display, Black, White and Gray, 1930; Sound ABC, 1932; Gypsies, 1932; Architecture Congress, Athens, 1933; Lobster, 1935; special effects for H. G. Wells' "Things to Come," 1935; New Architecture at the London Zoo, 1936; Design Workshops, 1942; Do Not Disturb, 1945. Portfolio of lithographs, 6 constructions, 1923. Lectured in most of the larger cities of Europe and U.S. Contbr. of articles to art, architectural and photographic magazines of Europe and U.S. Home: 2622 Lakeview Av. Address: 632 N. Dearborn St., Chicago, Ill. Died Nov. 24, 1946.

MOISSEIFF, Leon S(olomon) (mō'sĕf), cons. engr.; b. Riga, Latvia, Nov. 10, 1872; s. Solomon and Anna (Bloch) M.; student Emperor Alexander Gymnasium, Riga, 1880-87, Baltic Poly. Inst., Riga, 1889-91; C.E., Columbia, 1895; m. Ida Assinofsky, 1893; children—Liberty (wife of Dr. Harry Weiss), Siegfried, Grace (wife of Hancel Bechtel Smith). Came to U.S., 1891, naturalized, 1896. Civil engr. pvt. engring. firm, 1895-97; asst. engr. and engr. of design Dept. of Bridges, N.Y. City, 1897-1915; engr. of design, Delaware River Bridge, Phila., 1920-26; cons. engr. George Washington and Bayonne bridges, N.Y. City, 1927-31, Ambassador Bridge, Detroit, 1928-30, Maumee River Bridge, Toledo, 1929-32, Triborough Bridge, N.Y. City, 1934-36, East River bridges, N.Y. City, 1934-37, Bronx-Whitestone Bridge, N.Y. City, 1936-39, Tacoma Narrows Bridge, 1938-40, Mackinac Straits Bridge Authority, 1938-40; mem. board of engineers, Golden Gate Bridge, 1929-37, and San Francisco-Oakland Bay Bridge, 1931-37; cons. engr. Commissariat of Transportation, Russia, 1929-32; cons. engr. Century of Progress Expn., Chicago, 1933. Awarded gold medal, Franklin Inst., 1933; Norman medal, Am. Soc. C.E., 1934; James Laurie prize, Am. Soc. C.E., 1939; awarded Columbia U. Egleston medal for distinguished achievement in engring., 1939, Modern Pioneer award for achievement in the field of science and invention, Nat. Assn. Mfrs., 1940. Mem. Am. Soc. C.E. (life), Am. Soc. Testing Materials, Am. Ry. Engring. Assn., American Welding Society, Structural Steel Welding Com., Com. on Specifications for Welding Bridges, Joint Com. on Design of Structural Members, Alloy Steel Com., Com. on Design of Lightweight Structural Alloys (chmn.), Sigma Xi, Zeta Beta Tau. Compiler and translator, Considère's Experimental Researches on Reinforced Concrete, 1906. Author of articles "Deflection Theory for Design of Suspension Bridges," "Towers, Cables and Stiffening Trusses, Delaware River Bridge," "High Structural Steels for Bridges," "Hudson River Bridge Towers," "Investigation of Cold Drawn Bridge Wire," "Suspension Bridges Under Action of Lateral Forces," "Evolution of High Strength Steels in Structural Engineering," "Theory of Elastic Stability Applied to Structural Design," "Design Specifications for Bridges and Structures of Aluminum," 1940. Home: 530 West End Av. Office: 99 Wall St., New York, N.Y. Died Sep. 3, 1943.

MOLDENHAWER, Julius Valdemar, clergyman; b. Tavastehus, Finland, 1877; s. Carl Julius and Maria (Fogh) M.; A.B., Southwestern Coll., Memphis, Tenn., 1897; grad. Union Theol. Sem., N.Y. City, 1900; D.D., Western Reserve U., 1922, Hamilton Coll., 1930; Litt.D., Southwestern, 1939; m. Alice Frances Sprague, 1899. Came to U.S., 1879, naturalized, 1905. Ordained ministry Presbyn. Ch., 1900; pastor Margaretville, N.Y., 1900-02, Salem, N.Y., 1902-05, Second Ch. Albany, N.Y., 1905-19, Westminster Ch., Albany, N.Y., 1919-27, First Ch., N.Y. City since 1927. Trustee Mackenzie Coll. (Sao Paulo, Brazil); dir. Union Theol. Sem.; mem. bd. mgrs. Presbyn. Hosp., N.Y. City; trustee Sailors Snug Harbor. Author: Fairest Lord Jesus, 1937; The Voice of Books, 1940. Home: 43 5th Av. Office: 12 W. 12th St., New York, N.Y. Died Mar. 31, 1948.

MOLITOR, David Albert, civil engr.; b. Detroit, Aug. 16, 1866; s. Edward Philip and Catherine L. (Jung) M.; student Washington U., St. Louis, 1883-87; B.C.E., C.E., George Washington U., 1908, E.D., 1932; m. Mabel H. White. Engr. on design and constrn. strategical Ry. Weizen-Immendingen, Baden, 1887-90; asst. engr. Miss. Bridge, Memphis, in charge of erection of superstructure, 1890-92; entered Engring. Dept. U.S.A., under Gen. O.M. Poe, serving in various capacities as designing and suptg. engr., 1892-98, on works connected with Sault Ste. Marie Falls Canal and the Channels through the Great Lakes; conducted precise leveling operations for U.S. Bd. of Engrs. on deep waterways, St. Lawrence River, 1898-99; in pvt. business as cons. engr., chem. and bacteriol. lab., etc., 1899-1906; designing engr. Panama Canal, at Washington, 1906-08, visited Isthmus, May 1907; prof. civ. engring., Cornell U., 1908-11; practicing bridge and gen. engring., Kansas City, 1911-12; chief designing engr., Toronto Harbor Commrs., 1913-16; cons. practice, Detroit, 1916-23; structural engr. with Albert Kahn, 1924-32; structural engr. U.S. supervising architect, 1932-38; structural engr. private practice since 1938. Life mem. Am. Soc. of C.E. Mason. Author: Hydraulics of Rivers, Weirs and Sluices, 1908; Kinetic Theory of Engineering Structures, 1911; Structural Engineering Problems and Practical Chimney Design, 1937; also many professional papers and monographs. Address: New Center Bldg., Detroit. Died Nov. 1939.

MOLLOY, Thomas Marcus, coast guard officer; b. Worcester, Mass., June 4, 1874; s. John and Mary (Carey) M.; B.S., Worcester Poly. Inst., 1897; m. Caroline Emily Ainslie, June 24, 1909; children—Marian Ainslie (wife of Dr. Gaudens Megaro), Eleanor Virginia (wife of Dr. Julius S. Prince), Robert Thomas. Cadet, U.S. Revenue Cutter Service (now U.S. Coast Guard), 1897; commd. 3d lt., 1899, and advanced through the grades to rear adm.; served in northern coast patrol, 1917; overseas duty, Oct. 1917-Jan. 1919; retired, 1938, recalled to active duty, 1941, assigned on staff of comdt., U.S. Coast Guard Hdqrs., Washington, D.C. Decorated Navy Cross. Pres. Coast Guard Welfare Assn. Mem. Worcester Poly. Inst. and Coast Guard Acad. alumni assns., U.S. Naval Inst., Am. Soc. Naval Engrs., Mil. Order World Wars, Am. Legion. Home: North Colebrook, Conn.; also 2015 Belmont Road N.W., Washington. Office: U.S. Coast Guard Hdqrs., 1300 E St. N.W., Washington 25. Died Oct. 11, 1945; buried in Arlington National Cemetery.

MONAGHAN, Frank J. (mŏn'ă-hăn), clergyman, bishop; b. Newark, N.J., Oct. 30, 1890; s. Thomas P. and Anna (Daly) M.; A.B., Seton Hall Coll., South Orange, N.J., 1911, A.M., 1913; S.T.D., North Am. Coll., Rome, 1915; LL.D., St. Peter's Coll., Jersey City, N.J., 1934. Ordained priest R.C. Ch., 1915; curate St. Paul of the Cross Parish, Jersey City, 1915-26; teacher dogmatic theology Immaculate Conception Sem., Darlington, N.J., 1926-33; pres. Seton Hall Coll. and dir. Aquinas House of Studies, South Orange, 1933-36; consecrated bishop, June 29, 1936; coadjutor bishop of Ogdensburg, N.Y., 1936-39; succeeded to the See of Ogdensburg Mar. 20, 1939. Made Papal Chamberlain, 1934. Address: 624 Washington St., Ogdensburg, N.Y. Died Nov. 13, 1942.

MONAGHAN, James, lawyer; b. near St. Louis, Mo., Sept. 21, 1854; s. J. J. and Rebecca (Murdagh) M.; descended from first settlers of Germantown, Pa., also by tradition from Oliver Cromwell; C.E., Lafayette Coll., Pa., 1876; m. Anna Jackson, June 7, 1882; children—Florence Jackson (Mrs. Herbert S. Thatcher) Gertrude, Hanna Darlington, James. Admitted to Pa. bar, 1878; apptd. Supreme Court reporter by Gov. Pattison, 1892; asso. librarian Pa. Supreme Court, 1921. Charter mem. Pa. State Bar Assn., Chester County Hist. Soc.; former vice-pres. Phila. Ethical Soc., mem. Federal Union; former mem. Am. Acad. Polit. and Social Science, Phila. Browning Soc., Friends of Lafayette; hon. mem. Inst. Am. Genealogy. Editor: Chester County Reports, 2 vols.; Monaghan's Supreme Court Reports, 2 vols.; Pa. Supreme Court Reports, 19 volumes; Appellate Practice, 1 vol.; Cumulative Ann. Digest of Pennsylvania Law Reports (25 vols. combined in 7 vols.), 1899-1937. First editor Pa. County Court Reports and Pa. District Reports. Author of monographs: Lafayette at Brandywine; Falstaff's Forbears; Bayard Taylor, Poet and Patriot, and essays on anti-slavery; Woolman, Audubon and Thoreau. Home: (summer) Nantucket, Mass.; (winter) Buck Hill Falls, Pa. Died Apr. 3, 1949.

MONAGHAN, Peter Joseph, lawyer; b. Detroit, Mich., Jan. 7, 1881; s. Peter J. and Hannah (Kiley) M.; A.B., A.M. and LL.D., U. of Detroit; LL.B., Detroit Coll. of Law; m. Alma Noeker, June 23, 1908 (died Feb. 11, 1931); children—Peter J., Joseph N., Philip. Admitted to Mich. bar, 1902; in practice at Detroit since 1902; now mem. firm Monaghan, Crowley, Clark & Kellogg; dean U. of Detroit, 1927-32; dir. Nat. Bank of Detroit, Fisher & Co. Trustee U. of Detroit. Mem. Am., Mich. State and Detroit bar assns. Democrat. Catholic. K.C. Clubs: Detroit, Detroit Athletic, Bloomfield Hills Country. Home: 19346 Berkeley Drive. Office: Nat. Bank of Detroit Bldg., Detroit, Mich. Died Aug. 14, 1942.

MONRO, William Loftus, glass mfr.; b. Pittsburgh, Pa., Oct. 20, 1866; s. George Nugent and Sarah Ann (Morgan) M.; A.B., Harvard, 1889; m. Violet Kennedy Bedell, Sept. 27, 1892; children—William Loftus, Charles Bedell, George Nugent III. Admitted to Allegheny County Bar, 1891, engaged in practice until 1906; organized Pittsburgh Window Glass Co., Washington, Pa., 1901, pres. to 1906; elected sec. and treas., Federated Window Glass Co., Columbus, O., 1902; became gen. mgr., Am. Window Glass Co., Nov. 1906, pres. and dir. since 1919; pres. and dir. Am. Window Glass Machine Co., 1919-29, Window Glass Machine Co., 1919-33, Western Pa. Natural Gas Co. since 1919, Empire Machine Co., 1919-33, Am. Photo Glass & Export Co., 1921-41; dir. 14th St. Bank, 1917-34, Duquesne Light Co., 1923-26, Phila. Co., 1923-26, Reliance Life Ins. Co. since 1924, Equitable Gas Co., 1924-28, Westinghouse Air-brake Co. since 1924 (mem. exec. com. since 1927), Pittsburgh Rys. Co. since 1926, Union Switch & Signal Co. since 1926 (mem. exec. com. since 1932), Pa. Mfrs. Assn. Fire Ins. Co. since 1931, Pa. Mfrs. Casualty Ins. Co. since 1924, Pa. Central Airlines, 1936-37; trustee Dollar Savings Bank of Pittsburgh since 1925. Mem. bd. mgrs. Children's Hosp. of Pittsburgh since 1923. Dir. Chamber Commerce, 1918-40. Mem. bd. corporators Allegheny Cemetery Assn. since 1938. Mem. Am. Tariff League, 1927-42 (pres. 1930-42), Window Glass Mfrs. Assn. (pres. and dir. 1928-37). Mem. adv. bd. Pittsburgh Ordnance Dist., U.S. War Dept., since Sept. 1926. Chmn. war service com. Nat. Assn. Window Glass Mfrs. and chmn. com. on glass industries, War Savings Campaign, World War I. Mason. Republican. Sr. warden and vestryman P.E. Church of the Ascension. Clubs: Duquesne, Pittsburgh Athletic, University, Longue Vue; Oakmont Country; Harvard Club of Western Pa. Author: Window Glass in the Making, 1926. Home: 5840 Wilkins Av. Office: Farmers Bank Bldg., Pittsburgh, Pa. Died July 27, 1945.

MONROE, Anne Shannon, writer; b. Bloomington, Mo.; d. William A. (M.D.) and Sarah Louise (Hall) Monroe. Contbr. serials to Saturday Evening Post: A Woman Wins, Making a Business Woman, Making Business Men; also writes for Ladies' Home Journal, Delineator, Good Housekeeping, etc. Democrat. Clubs: Southern California Woman's Press; Zonta, Mazamas (Portland, Ore.). Author: Eugene Norton, 1900; Making a Business Woman, 1912; Happy Valley—A Story of Oregon, 1916; Behind the Ranges, 1925; Singing in the Rain, 1926; The Hearth of Happiness, 1929; The World I Saw, 1929; Feelin' Fine, 1930; God Lights a Candle, 1933; Walk with Me, Lad, 1934; Mansions in the Cascades (with Elizabeth Lambert Wood), 1936. Home: Bryant Hill, Lake Grove, Oregon. Died Oct. 18, 1942.

MONROE, Paul, prof. edn.; b. North Madison, Ind., June 7, 1869; s. Rev. William Y. and Juliet (Williams) M.; B.S., Franklin (Ind.) Coll., 1890; Ph.D., U. of Chicago, 1897; student U. of Heidelberg, 1901; LL.D., U. of Peking, 1913, Franklin Coll., 1918; Litt.D., Columbia, 1929, U. of Dublin, 1933; LL.D., U. of Brazil, 1939; m. Emma Ellis, 1891; children—Juliette (dec.), Ellis, Jeanette. Fellow of sociology, U. of Chicago, 1895-97; hon. fellow Educational Inst. of Scotland, 1925, Hungarian Academy Science, 1930. Instr. hist., Teacher Coll., Columbia, 1897-99, adjunct prof. edn., 1899-1902, prof., 1902, dir. Sch. of Edn., 1915-23, Barnard prof. edn., 1925-38, prof. emeritus since 1938; dir. Internat. Inst. of Teachers Coll. since

1923; became pres. Robert Coll., Istanbul, Turkey, 1932; pres. Am. Coll. for Girls, Istanbul, 1932-35. Lecturer in edn., U. of Calif., 1905, Yale, 1906-07; survey educational system of Philippine Islands, 1913, 25, Porto Rico, 1926, Iraq, 1933. Mem. bd. trustees China Foundation for the Promotion of Edn. and Culture, Chungking, China; mem. bd. trustees Internat. Coll. of Smyrna (now at Beirut, Syria), Am. Sch. of Sofia, Lingnan Univ., Canton; mem. bd. trustees Internat. Coll. for Girls, Istanbul. Pres. China Inst. in Am.; pres. World Fedn. of Edn. Assns., 1931-33, 1935-43; director Internat. Inst. Conf. on Examination, Eastbourne, England, 1931, Folkstone, England, 1935, Dinard, France, 1939. Awarded scientific medal "of highest degree" by Persian Government, 1929; decorated Order of Polonia Restituta (Poland), 1930; Order of the Jade (China), 1937; Order of the Sacred Treasury (Japan), 1937. Club: Century. Author: Source Book in the History of Education for the Greek and Roman Period, 1901; Thomas Platter and the Educational Renaissance of the Sixteenth Century, 1904; Text-Book in the History of Education, 1905; Brief Course in the History of Education, 1907; Principles of Secondary Education, 1914; China—A Nation in Evolution, 1928; Essays on Comparative Education, Series No. 1, 1927, No. 2, 1932; Founding of the American Public School System, 1940; also articles in tech. publications. Editor dept. of edn., Internat. Encyclopedia, Internat. Year Book and Nelson's Ency. Editor in chief Cyclopedia of Education, Vols. I-V, 1910-13; editor Brief Course of Ednl. Texts, Home and School Series, 1914; Technical Art Series, 1914. Home: Garrison-on-Hudson, N.Y. Died Dec. 6, 1947; buried Sleepy Hollow Cemetery, Tarrytown, N.Y.

MONSKY, Henry (mŭn'skĭ), lawyer; b. Omaha, Neb., Feb. 4, 1890; s. Abraham and Betsy (Perisnev) M.; LL.B., cum laude, Creighton U. (Omaha), 1912; D.H.L. (hon.), Dropsie College, Philadelphia, 1942; m. Sadie Lesser, May 2, 1915; children—Joy, Hubert, Barbara; m. 2d, Mrs. Albert (Daisy) Rothschild, Nov. 3, 1937; 1 step-dau., Babette Rothschild. Admitted to Neb. bar, 1912, practicing in Omaha, Neb.; mem. firm Monsky, Grodinsky, Marer & Cohen (Omaha). Consultant to U.S. delegation, United Nations Conf. Internat. Orgn., San Francisco, April 1945. President of Omaha B'nai B'rith Lodge, 1912; president Dist. Grand Lodge No. 6, 1921, member exec. com. B'nai B'rith Supreme Lodge, 1923-38, pres. Supreme Lodge since 1938; mem. bd. trustees Father Flanagan's Boys' Home since 1925; founder Omaha Community Chest and Welfare Fedn., 1921, 1st v.p., 1921, pres. 1929, mem. bd. govs. since 1921; mem. bd. trustees Nat. Bd. of Community Chests and Councils, 1935; elected Family Welfare Assn. of America, 1935; past pres. Neb. Conf. on Social Work; pres. Omaha Council Boy Scouts of America, 1927, mem. Nat. Council; mem. Bd. Nat. Council of Jewish Fedns. and Welfare Funds, 1939; pres. Jewish Community Center and Welfare Fedn., 1941-42; mem. voluntary participation com. Office Civilian Defense; mem. nat. Jewish com. on scouting, and of nat. adv. council Girl Scouts; mem. exec. com. Am. Jewish Joint Distrbn. Com.; mem. bd. dirs. Council of Jewish Fedns. and Welfare Funds; mem. nat. Army and Navy com. Jewish Welfare Bd.; mem. nat. council Am. Friends of Hebrew U. in Palestine; convenor, Am. Jewish Assembly; chmn. Am. Jewish Conference; hon. chmn. United Palestine Appeal, United Jewish Appeal. Mem. bd. govs., Dropsie Coll., Phila. Mem. Am., Neb. and Omaha bar assn., Am. Judicature Soc., Zeta Beta Tau. Chmn. Exec. Com. U.S. Attorney General's Nat. Conf. for Prevention and Control of Juvenile Delinquency, chmn. of Continuing Com. said Conf. Republican. Jewish religion. Mason. Elk. Club: Highland Country (Omaha). Editor: Nat. Jewish Monthly. Contbr. to welfare publs. Home: Blackstone Hotel. Office: 737 Omaha Nat. Bank Bldg., Omaha, Neb. Died May 2d, 1947.

MONTAGUE, James Jackson, newspaper wrtier; b. Mason City, Ia., Apr. 16, 1873; s. J.V.W. and Martha (Jackson) M.; ed. high sch., Portland, Ore.; m. Helen L. Hageny, Aug. 18, 1898 (died Jan., 1937); children—Richard, Doris, James Lee. Formerly reporter and asst. editor Portland Oregonian; nat. conv. and Washington corr. Universal News Service, 1912-16; reported Peace Conf., Paris, France, for newspaper syndicate, 1918-19; widely known as writer of verse. Club: Pelham Country. Author: More Truth Than Poetry, 1920. Home: 204 Drake Av., New Rochelle, N.Y. Died Dec. 16, 1941.

MONTGOMERY, Charles Carroll (mŭnt-gŭm'ẽr-ĭ), jurist; b. Lincoln, Neb., Apr. 6, 1876; s. Carroll Sinclair and Anna Martha (Gray) M.; Shattuck Mil. Sch., Faribault, Minn., 1891-92; A.B., U. of Wis., 1897, LL.B., 1900; m. Mona Martin, Sept. 1, 1903; children—Charles Carroll, Helen Mona. Began in office Jones & Stevens, Madison, Wis., 1900; moved to Omaha, 1901, to Los Angeles, Calif., 1909; mem. Groff & Montgomery, 1909-14, later practiced alone; city atty., Sierra Madre, Calif., 1912-18. Served as prof. constl. law, Creighton U., Omaha; formerly prof. equity and other subjects; instr. federal practice, Law Sch. of U. of Southern Calif.; master U.S. Dist. Court, 1922-27; formerly judge Superior Court of Los Angeles County, Calif.; now mem. Montgomery & Montgomery. Mem. Am. Bar Assn., Calif. Bar Assn., Delta Tau Delta, Phi Alpha Delta. Democrat. Episcopalian. Author: Montgomery's Manual of Federal Procedure. Home: 201 S. Alexandria. Address: 918 Pershing Square Bldg., Los Angeles, Calif.* Died Feb. 20, 1943.

MONTGOMERY, Fletcher H., mfr.; b. N.J., May 31, 1880; s. James and Mary Elizabeth (Anderson) M.; student Horace Mann Sch., New York, 1894-96, Wesleyan Acad., Wilbraham, Mass., 1897-98; m. Ruth Grey Hebard, Nov. 27, 1906; children—James H., Ruth (dec.), Jane. Began as office boy, Baker, Carver & Morell, New York, 1898; with Crofut & Knapp, Norwalk, Conn., 1899-1917; became pres. Knox Hat Co., 1917; pres. Hat Corp. of America and all its subsidiaries, U.S. Hat Machinery Corp., Dunlap & Co. Republican. Methodist. Home: Stamford, Conn. Office: 417 5th Av., New York, N.Y. Died Oct. 15, 1948.

MONTGOMERY, George Redington, clergyman; b. Marash, Turkey, June 17, 1870; s. Giles Foster and Emily (Redington) M.; A.B., Yale, 1892, LL.B., 1894, B.D., 1900, Ph.D., 1901; U. of Berlin, 1897-98; m. Emily E. Emerson, June 23, 1902 (died, May 30, 1903); 1 son, Roger Emerson; m. 2d, Helen M. Perkins, Aug. 5, 1907; children—Marshall Hugh, Giles Newton. Ordained Congl. ministry, 1901; pastor Olivet Ch., Bridgeport, Conn., 1901-04; prof. philosophy, Carleton Coll., 1904-05; asst. minister Madison Sq. Presbyn. Ch., New York, 1906-16; spl. asst. to Am. ambassador at Constantinople, 1916; in air service, Paris, 1917; sec. of Paris div. Y.M.C.A., 1918; attached to Peace Conf., Dec. 1918; tech. adviser to Commn. on Mandates in Turkey, 1919; asst. prof. French, Yale U., 1919-20; dir. The Armenia America Soc., 1920-23; asst. sec. Federal Council of Chs., since 1922. Special corr. London Daily Graphic, in Turkey, and war corr. London Standard, during Graeco-Turkish War; lecturer, Yale, 1900-04, New York Univ., 1911-18. Mem. Am. Philos. Soc., Am. Psychol. Assn. Author: Talking English, 1898; The Place of Values, 1903; The Unexplored Self, 1910. Translated Leibnitz's Metaphysics, 1901. Home: Noroton, Conn. Died Nov. 29, 1945.

MOODY, Herbert Raymond, chemist; b. Chelsea, Mass., Nov. 19, 1869; s. Luther Richmond and Mary Emily (Sherman) M.; S.B., Mass. Inst. Tech., 1892; A.M., Columbia, 1900, Ph.D., 1901; m. Edna Wadsworth, Aug. 20, 1895. Asst. labs. of Chelsea High Sch., 1887-88; asst. gen. chemistry, Mass. Inst. Tech., 1892-94, instr. analyt. chemistry, 1894-95; instr. science, Gilbert Sch., Winsted, Conn., 1895-99; prof. chemistry, Hobart Coll., 1901-05; prof. chemistry, Coll. City of N.Y., 1905-20, prof. chem. engring., 1921, prof. chemistry and dir. of dept. 1922-38, now prof. emeritus. Chief of tech. br., chem. div. of War Industries Bd., Washington, 1917-18; asst. in dept. of adminstrn. NRA, part of 1934. Mem. Div. Chemistry and Chem. Tech. of Nat Research Council, 1936-41. Mem. Am. Chem Soc., London Soc. Chem. Industry, London Chem. Soc., Societe de Chimie Industrielle, Phi Beta Kappa; fellow Am. Inst. of Chemistry. Club: Cosmos (Washington). Author: Reactions at the Temperature of the Electric Arc, 1901; College Text-book of Quantitative Analysis, 1914; Chemistry of the Metals, 1923. Home: Vienna, Va. Office: Nat. Research Council, Washington, D.C. Died Oct. 20, 1947.

MOODY, Nelson Kingsland, petroleum producer; b. Titusville, Pa., Jan. 20, 1877; s. George Owen and Emma (Kingsland) M.; grad. high sch., Titusville, 1894, Lawrenceville (N.J.) Sch., 1895; M.E., Cornell U., 1899; m. Mary Stirling Hoag, Nov. 22, 1906; children—Mary Hoag, Nelson Kingsland. With Carter Oil Co., W.Va., 1899-1906; became connected with South Pa. Oil Co., 1906; mng. dir. Romano-Americano Co., Bucharest, Roumania, 1906-09; started with Prairie Oil & Gas Co., 1910, becoming pres. in 1923; now pres. Sinclair Prairie Oil Marketing Co., Amarillo (Tex.) Oil Co., Southwestern Development Co., Canadian River Gas Co.; pres. and dir. Red River Gas Co. Mem. Am. Petroleum Inst. Republican. Presbyn. Home: 1165 E. 24th Pl., Tulsa, Okla. Died Dec. 30, 1944.

MOODY, Paul Dwight, clergyman, educator; b. Baltimore, Md., Apr. 11, 1879; s. Dwight L. (evangelist) and Emma C. (Revell) M.; B.A., Yale, 1901, hon. D.D., 1924; student New Coll. (Edinburgh, Scotland), Glasgow Free Ch. Coll., Hartford (Conn.) Theol. Sem.; married Charlotte May Hull, Apr. 14, 1904; children—Charlotte (Mrs. J. V. Emerson), Margaret Emma (Mrs. Chas. M. Rice). Ordained Congl. ministry, 1912; pastor South Sh., St. Johnsbury, Vt., 1912-17; asso. pastor Madison Av. Presbyn. Ch., N.Y., 1919-21; pres. Middlebury (Vt.) Coll., Aug. 1921-June 1942; assoc. pastor First Presbyn. Ch., N.Y., since 1942. Chaplain 1st Vt. Inf., 1916-17, 103d U.S. Inf., 1917-18; G.H.Q. chaplain A.E.F., 1918-19; asst. and successor to Bishop Brent, sr. chaplain A.E.F.; dir. Gen. Com. on Army and Navy Chaplains, 1940-41. Chevalier Legion of Honor (French); comdr. Order of Isabella the Catholic (Spanish). Mem. Alpha Delta Phi. Republican, Club: Century (New York). Home: 12 W. 12th St., New York, N.Y. Died Aug. 18, 1947.

MOON, Carl, artist, writer; b. Wilmington, O., Oct. 5, 1879; s. Sylvester Bronston (M.D.) and Lucy (Gudgeon) M.; grad. high sch., Wilmington; m. Grace Purdie, June 5, 1911; children—Francis Maxwell, Mary Caryl. In photographic business, Albuquerque, N.M., 1904-07, and began making first collection of photographs and paintings of Pueblo Indians there; in charge of art business Fred Harvey, hdqrs. Grand Canyon, Ariz., 1907-14; made historic collection of pictures of Am. Indians for Am. Museum Natural History, New York, and for the Harvey collection at Grand Canyon; Indian prints in collections of Congressional Library; Indian prints and paintings in Montclair (N.J.) Museum; settled in Pasadena, Calif., 1914. Member Ohio Nat. Guard, 1896, 97, California Reserves, 1917, 18. Clubs: Pasadena Society of Artists, Calif. Writers Guild (dir.), Pasadena Library (pres. 1931-32), Vagabonds (hon.). Rep. Christian Scientist. Mason. Author and illustrator: Lost Indian Magic (with wife), 1918; Wongo and the Wise Old Crow (with same); The Flaming Arrow, 1927; Painted Moccasin, 1931; Tah-kee, 1932. Illustrated all books by both Mrs. Moon and himself. Illustrated Wongo and the Wise Old Crow, Indian Legends in Rhyme, Chi-Wee, Chi-Wee and Loki, Nadita (by Mrs. Moon). Executed studies of Indians of the Southwest, in Huntington Library; 26 oil paintings of Indians of Southwest for The Smithsonian Instn., Washington, D.C. Home: 565 N. Mentor Av., Pasadena, Calif. Died June 24, 1948.

MOON, Don P., naval officer; b. Kokomo, Ind., Apr. 18, 1894; s. Barnabas C. and Ellen Pearl (Bennett) M.; B.S., U.S. Naval Acad., 1916; student U.S. Naval Acad. Post Grad. Sch., 1920-21; S.M., U. of Chicago, 1922; student U.S. Naval War Coll., jr. course, Newport, R.I., 1932-33, sr. course, 1937-38; m. Sibyl Peaslee Hall, Sept. 28, 1920; children—Meredith Whittier, Don Pardee, David Peaslee, Peter Clayton. Commd. ensign, U.S.N., 1916, advancing through the grades to rear adm., 1944; served in U.S.S. Arizona, 1916-20, U.S.S. Colorado, 1923-25, U.S.S. Nevada, 1926, U.S.S. John Ford (destroyer), 1934-37; in design sect., in charge patent sect., Bureau of Ordnance, 1927; officer in charge drafting room Naval Gun Factory, 1928-29; destroyer squadron gunnery officer, Pacific, 1929-32; comdr. destroyer div., Pacific and Atlantic Fleets, 1940-41; comdr. destroyer squadron, Atlantic Fleet, operating in connection with N. African invasion, part of time in British Home Fleet and in support of Russian Convoys, 1941-42; in planning sect. of comdr. in chief, U.S. Fleet, 1943; commd. rear adm. and assigned sea duty, 1944. Decorated World War Victory medal with bronze star, Am. Defense medal with numeral A, Am. Theater medal, European Theater medal with numeral 2 and 2 bronze stars, Commendation Ribbon, Order of Alexandrov (Russia). Mem. Naval Acad. Alumni Assn., Naval Inst. (since 1916). Home: 818 W. Sycamore St., Kokomo, Ind. Died Aug. 5, 1944.

MOON, Grace, author; b. Indianapolis, Ind.; d. Francis Baillie and Mary Bragdon (Du Souchet) Purdie; ed. under pvt. tutors, also U. of Wis. (non-grad.), and Art. Inst. Chicago 2 yrs.; m. Carl Moon, June 5, 1911; children—Francis Maxwell, Mary Caryl. Has made paintings of Indian children to be seen in many pvt. collections. Mem. D.A.R., Pi Beta Phi, Calif. Writers Guild (dir.). Clubs: Zonta Internat. (pres. Pasadena club 1931-32), Library. Author: Indian Legends in Rhyme, 1916; Lost Indian Magic, 1918; Wongo and the Wise Old Crow, 1922 (last two with husband); Chi-Wee, 1925; Chi-Wee and Loki, 1926; Nadita, 1927; The Runaway Papoose, 1928; The Magic Trail, 1929; The Missing Katchina, 1930; The Arrow of Teemay, 1931; Far Away Desert, 1932; Book of Nah-Wee, 1932; Tita of Mexico, 1934; Shanty Ann, 1935; Singing Sands, 1936; White Indian, 1937; Solita, 1938; Daughter of Thunder, 1942. Contbr. verse and stories to mags. Home: 565 N. Mentor Av., Pasadena, Calif. Died Sep. 6, 1947.

MOORE, Allen, II, coll. pres.; b. Stanberry, Mo., Feb. 19, 1886; s. Allen and Emma Julian (Dryden) M.; grad. Chillicothe (Mo.) Normal Sch., 1904; B.S., Valparaiso U., 1906; m. Helen Margaret Huey, July 18, 1919; children—Mary Ann, Martha Amma, Allen Moore III. Took over management of Chillicothe Normal Sch., 1907, on death of father, founder of same; name changed, 1909, to Chillicothe Business Coll., of which is pres.; dir. Chillicothe State Bank, Mutual Savings Life Ins. Co., St. Louis, Missouri. County chmn. Red Cross Drive, Livingston County, 1918; mem. State Com. Y.M.C.A.; mem. National Council of Business Schools, National Business Educational Assn., Missouri State Teachers Assn., Central Commercial Teachers Assn., Southwestern Private Commercial Schs. Assn., (dir.) Mo. Private Bus. Schs. Assn. (dir.), Chillicothe Chamber Commerce. Democrat. Methodist. Clubs: Rotary (gov. 134th Dist. Rotary Internat. 1940-41), Chillicothe Country. Home: 665 Elmdale Road, Chillicothe, Mo. Died July 13, 1945.

MOORE, Charles; b. Ypsilanti, Mich., Oct. 20, 1855; s. Charles and Adeline (MacAllaster) M.; prep. edn., Phillips Acad., Andover, Mass.; A.B., Harvard, 1878, hon. Art.D., 1937; Ph.D., George Washington U., 1890, LL.D., 1923; LL.D., Miami U., 1930; m. Alice Williams Merriam, 1878 (died 1914); children—MacAllaster, James Merriam. Newspaper work in Detroit and Washington, 1878-95; polit. sec. to U.S. Senator James McMillan, 1889-1903; clerk U.S. Senate Com. on D.C., 1891-1903; sec. Union Trust Co., Detroit, 1904-06; chmn. Submarine Signal Co., Boston, 1906-08; sec. Security Trust Co., Detroit, 1908-14. Acting chief Div. of Manuscripts, Library of Congress, 1918-27. Apptd. by President Taft original mem. Nat. Commn. of Fine Arts, 1910, reapptd. by 6 successive Presidents (chmn. 1915-37). Visited Brit. univs. on World War mission arranged by London U., 1918; mem. commn. to plan Am. war cemeteries in Europe, 1923. Overseer Harvard Coll., 1924-30. Life mem. Am. Hist. Assn. (treas. 1917-30); v.p. Wakefield Nat. Memorial Assn.; mem. Am. Inst. Arts and Letters, Acad. Arts and Letters of Cuba, Nat. Sculpture Soc., Am. Planning and Civic Assn., Phi Beta Kappa; hon. mem. A.I.A., Am. Soc. Landscape Architects, N.Y. Archtl. League, Institut François de Washington; Incorporator and life member Am. Acad. in Rome; pres. Detroit City Planning Com., 1912-19. Gold Medal of Honor, Am. br. Société des Architectes Diplomés par le Gouvernement Français, 1924; Chevalier Legion of Honor (France), 1928; gold medal Nat. Com. of Fine Arts, 1935; Friedsam fellowship gold medal award, New York Archtl. League, 1937; Carnegie Corp. award for services to the arts in America, 1937. Clubs: Harvard (Seattle); Witenagemote (Detroit); Cosmos (Washington); Century, Harvard (N.Y.). Author: Charities of Dist. of Columbia, 1897; The Gladwin Manuscripts, 1897; The Northwest Under Three Flags, 1900; History of Michigan, 1915; Daniel H. Burnham, Architect, Planner of Cities, 1921; The Family Life of George Washington, 1926; Life and Letters of Charles Follen McKim, 1929; Washington Past and Present, 1929; Wakefield, Birthplace of George Washington, 1932. Editor: The Plan of Chicago, by D. H. Burnham and E. H. Bennett; Plan for the Improvement of Washington, by D. H. Burnham, C. F. McKim, Augustus Saint-Gaudens, F. L. Olmsted; Filtration of the Washington Water Supply; The Restoration of the White House; George Washington's Rules of Civility; Lincoln's Gettysburg Address and Second Inaugural; Annual Reports Nat. Com. Fine Arts. Home: "Moorelands," Gig Harbor, Wash. Died Sep. 26, 1942.

MOORE, Charles J(ames), prof. of chemistry; b. Flint Hill, Va., Aug. 9, 1875; s. John Randolph and Elizabeth Jane (Green) M.; B.S., Va. Mil. Inst., 1895; Ph.D., U. of Va., 1901; A.M., Harvard, 1909; m. Sophie Schwartz, June 25, 1919; children—Elizabeth Jane, Charles James. Instr. mathematics, Horner Sch., N.C., 1896-98; prof. chemistry and geology, Western Md. Coll., 1901-02; instr., U. of Ga., 1902-04, adjunct prof., 1904-07; Austin teaching fellow, Harvard, 1908-12; instr. chem., New York U., 1912-14; asst. prof. chem., Hunter Coll., 1914-17, asso. prof., 1917-20, prof., 1921-45, emeritus since 1945; chief. chem. Bur. Soils, U.S. Dept. Agr., 1920-21. Awarded Jackson-Hope medal. Fellow A.A.A.S.; mem. Am. Chem. Soc., Alpha Chi Sigma. Episcopalian. Republican. Researches: aliphatic metal amines, colloidal materials in soils, purification of mercury, atomic weight of phosphorus. Author: Logarithmic reduction tables for analytical chemists, 1913. Exercises in organic chemistry. Lecture table demonstrations of common gases. Home: York Harbor, Me. Died Jan. 25, 1950.

MOORE, Edward Caldwell, theologian; b. West Chester, Pa., Sept. 1, 1857; s. William Eves (D.D., LL.D.) and Harriet Francina (Foot) M.; A.B., Marietta Coll., 1877; grad. Union Theol. Sem., 1884; univs. of Berlin, Göttingen and Giessen, 1884-86; Ph.D., Brown U., 1891; D.D., Yale, 1909; LL.D., Grinnell Coll., 1920; D.Th., U. of Giessen, 1926; m. Eliza Coe Brown, Nov. 9, 1887; children—Dorothea May, John Crosby Brown, Elizabeth Ripley. Was ordained to Presbyterian ministry, 1884; pastor Yonkers, N.Y., 1886-89, Central Congl. Ch., Providence, R.I., 1889-1901; Parkman prof. theology, 1901-29, Plummer prof. Christian morals, 1915-29, Harvard, now emeritus. Preacher to the university and chmn. Board of Preachers, 1905-28; lecturer Mansfield Coll., Oxford, Eng., 1894 and 1913, Andover Theol. Sem., 1900, Yale Div. Sch., 1906, Lowell Inst., Boston, 1903. Mem. Prudential Com. A.B.C.F.M., 1899-1914 (chmn. 1905-14; pres. 1914-25). Fellow Am. Acad. Arts and Sciences; mem. Am. Hist. Assn., Colonial Society of Mass. Mem. Am. Commn. for Relief in Near East, 1919. Clubs: Authors' (London, Eng.); Century (New York City); Harvard (Boston); Faculty (Cambridge). Author: The New Testament in the Christian Church, 1904; History of Christian Thought Since Kant, 1912; The Spread of Christianity in the Modern World, 1919; West and East, 1919; The Nature of Religion, 1936. Editor (with A. T. Davison), The Harvard University Hymn Book, 1925. Address: 21 Kirkland St., Cambridge, Mass. Died Mar. 26, 1943.

MOORE, Edward James, physicist; b. Chili, N.Y., June 13, 1873; s. Thomas and Margaret (Hill) M.; A.B., Oberlin, 1903, A.M., 1906; grad. student in physics, U. of Chicago, 1908-10, fellow, 1909-10, Ph.D., 1913; m. Amelia May Eade, July 12, 1905; children—Margaret Carolyn, Edward James. Began as tutor mathematics, Oberlin, 1903, and advanced to asso. prof. physics, 1910; prof. physics, U. of Buffalo, since Sept. 1919, dean Grad. Sch. Arts and Sciences, 1939-46; dean emeritus since 1946. Fellow Am. Assn. for Advancement of Science; member Am. Physical Soc., Am. Assn. Univ. Profs., Sigma Xi. Conglist. Has specialized in molecular physics and the electron theory. Contbr. on tech. topics. Perfected, with J. A. Demuth, an autographic system for recording employees' time, known as the "Symbol System." Home: Getzville, N.Y. Died March 11, 1948.

MOORE, Edward Small; b. Chicago, Ill., Jan 6, 1881; s. Wm. Henry and Ada (Small) M.; student Yale; m. Jean McGinley, Apr. 26, 1905; children—Edward Small, Jean, Marion; m. 2d, Evelyn Nickels Thompson, Nov. 17, 1934. Began with C.,R.I.&P. Ry., Chicago, 1903; with same at Cedar Rapids, Ia., 1904; with St.L.&S.F. R.R., at St. Louis, 1905-08; 2d asst. to the pres., 1908-09, v.p., Dec. 1, 1909-Apr. 15, 1915, C.,R.I.&P. Ry.; v.p. Am. Brake Shoe and Foundry Co., June 22, 1915-Aug. 1917; dir. divisional administration, Am. Red Cross, nat. hdqrs., Aug. 1917-Jan. 1918; maj., Air Service, Aircraft Production, Jan. 1918-June 1919; v.p. Finance & Trading Corp., Chicago, 1919-21; v.p. Beech-Nut Packing Co., New York, 1921-22; dir. Am. Can. Co., Nat. Biscuit Co. Clubs: Racquet and Tennis, The Links, Links Golf, Chicago (Chicago). Home: Circle M Ranch, Sheridan, Wyo.* Died Sep. 26, 1948.

MOORE, George Andrew, eye surgeon; b. Long Society, Conn., Aug. 24, 1871; s. James and Bridget Magdaline (Kilkenney) M.; M.D., Coll. Physicians and Surgeons, 1910; post. grad. work every winter for about 20 yrs., studying in Edinburgh, London, Paris and various cities in U.S.; m. Marion Ross Paine, Apr. 24, 1894. Due to self study passed examination and was registered to practice medicine, 1901; in practice eye surgery since 1902. Chmn. 2 advisory bds., World War; 4 minute speaker; dir. war savings effort. Chmn. bd. trustees Monson State Hosp. since 1910. Certified by Am. Bd. Ophthalmology, 1918. Fellow Am. Coll. Surgeons; mem. Am. Acad. Ophthalmology, A.M.A., Mass. Med. Soc., Brookfield Med. Club. Democrat. Home: 92 Thorndike St. Office: 483 N. Main St., Palmer, Mass. Died Oct. 6, 1945.

MOORE, George F., army officer; b. July 31, 1887; B.S., Agrl. and Mech. Coll. of Tex., 1908. Commd. 2d lt., Coast Arty. Corps, Sept. 25, 1909; promoted through grades to col., Oct. 1, 1938; temp. rank of maj. gen. since Dec. 1941; fought in Bataan Campaign, P.I., 1941-42; prisoner of war of Japanese Govt.; with Gen. Wainwright, released, Aug. 1945. Awarded D.S.M., Nov. 1942. Address: Care War Department, Washington 25, D.C.* Died Dec. 2, 1949.

MOORE, Grace, soprano; b. Jellicoe, Tenn., Dec. 5, 1901; ed. pub. schs.; studied music in Washington, D.C., and later under masters in Europe and America; m. Valentin Parera, July 15, 1931. Appeared with Martinelli in concert, at Washington, D.C., while attending school; ran away from school and joined a traveling concert co. in N.Y. City; sang in N.Y. City in Irving Berlin's "Music Box Review," 1923; appeared in Broadway musical successes and later sang in Paris and Nice; was with Opera Comique, Paris; joined Metropolitan Opera Co. and made début in "La Boheme," Feb. 7, 1928; revived French opera "Louise" by Charpentier, Metropolitan Opera, 1939; starred in film of same name; starred in singing motion pictures "Jenny Lind," "New Moon," "One Night of Love," "Love Me Forever," "I'll Take Romance." Decorated Chevalier Legion of Honor (France), 1939; also received decorations from Norway, Sweden, Denmark, Belgium, Cuba and Mexico. Died in plane crash, Copenhagen, Denmark, Jan. 26, 1947; buried, Forest Hills Cemetery, Chattanooga, Tenn.

MOORE, Henry Frank, biologist; b. Phila., June 4, 1867; s. John P. and Emma C. (Frank) M.; A.B., Central High Sch., Phila., 1885; Ph.D., U. of Pa., 1895; m. Annie Florence Dennis, Apr. 13, 1903. Naturalist, Internat. Fishery Commn., 1893-95; chief naturalist, Steamer Albatross, 1896-1903; sci. asst., 1903-11, in charge of sci. inquiry, 1911-15, and dep. commr., 1915-23, U.S. Bureau of Fisheries. Recipient of various awards for investigations; U.S. del. and v.p. 5th Internat. Fishery Congress, Rome, 1911. Fellow A.A.A.S.; hon. mem. Société Internationale Protectrice des Pêcheurs d'Éponges; mem. Am. Geophys. Union, N.C. Forestry Assn., Acad. Natural Science (Phila.), Psi Upsilon. Writer on zoölogy and fisheries. Mem. Inter-departmental Bd. on Internat. Ice Patrol, 1915-23; mem. Nat. Research Council, 1917-25, Internat. Com. on Marine Fishery Investigations (chmn.), 1919-23. Home: Linville Falls, N.C. Died Jan. 8, 1948.

MOORE, Harry Hascall, writer and educator; born at Ann Arbor, Mich., June 3, 1881; son of George L. and Mary E. (Hascall) M.; A.B., Reed Coll., Portland, Ore., 1917; A.M., George Washington U., 1923; Ph.D., Brookings Grad. Sch. of Econs. and Govt., 1926; unmarried. With various business firms, Cleveland, O., and other cities, 1899-1902; with Y.M.C.A. in various capacities, 1903-11; exec. sec. Ore. Social Hygiene Soc., 1911-17; sec. com. on civilian coöperation for combating venereal disease, Council Nat. Defense, 1917-18; dir. edn. div. venereal diseases, U.S. Pub. Health Service, 1918-26, pub. health economist, div. scientific research, 1926-27; dir. studies Com. on Costs of Med. Care, 1927-33; dir. study of surveys, Regents' Inquiry into cost and character of pub. edn., State of N.Y., Dec. 1935-May 1936; asso. dir. Am. Youth Commn., 1936-37; dir. Research Council on Problems of Alcohol, 1938-46. Secretary Nat. Com. for Teaching Citizenship, 1919-22; dir. Disarmament Edn., Com., 1920. Author: The Social Emergency (co-author), 1914; Keeping in Condition, 1915; The Youth and the Nation, 1917; Public Health in the United States, 1923; American Medicine and the People's Health, 1927; also collaborated in preparation of "Report of the President's Research Committee on Recent Social Trends," 1933. Editor: We are the Builders of a New World, 1934; Survival on Suicide, 1948. Contbr. to ednl., pub. health and sociol. jours. Home and office: Bronxville, N.Y. Died Dec. 27, 1949.

MOORE, Herbert McComb, clergyman, educator; b. Macomb, Ill., Aug. 17, 1876; s. Josiah and Jennie (Lindsay) M.; B.A., Lake Forest, 1896; grad. McCormick Theol. Seminary (now Presbyterian Theol. Sem. of Chicago), 1899; grad. study U.P. Sem., Edinburg, Scotland (now United Free Church Sem.), 1899-1900; D.D., U. of Pittsburgh, 1921; m. Abigail Donohue, Dec. 1902; 1 son, Charles Herbert. Ordained Presbyn. ministry, 1901; pastor Goldfield, Colo., 1901-03, Grace Ch., Milwaukee, Wis., 1903-06, Appleton, Wis., 1906-12; univ. pastor Presbyn. Ch., Ithaca, N.Y., 1913-17; sec. Y.M.C.A., Chaumont and Lormont, France, 1917-18; Harbison Foundation sec. Y.M.C.A.; mem. Dean's Council, U. of Pittsburgh, 1918-20; pres. Lake Forest Coll. since 1920. Mason. Clubs: University (Chicago), Onwentsia. Home: Lake Forest, Ill. Died May 7, 1942.

MOORE, Jere, pres. Greenville and Tusculum Coll. since May, 1883; b. Tusculum, Tenn., Nov. 25, 1845; s. Anthony and Nancy Paxton (Holt) M.; D.D., Greenville and Tusculum Coll., 1871; grad. Lane Theol. Sem., Cincinnati, 1874; m. Bell R. Mathes, Dec. 10, 1874. Ordained and still active as Presbyn. minister. Address: Tusculum, Tenn. Died March 23, 1946.

MOORE, John Bassett, lawyer; b. Smyrna, Del., Dec. 3, 1860; s. Dr. John A. and Martha A. (Ferguson) M.; grad. U. of Va., 1880; LL.D., Columbian, 1899, Delaware Coll., 1900, Yale, 1901, U. of Chile, 1910, Brown U., 1914, McGill U., 1921, U. of State of N.Y., 1923, U. of Pa., 1924, Columbia U., 1927 Washington Coll., 1932; m. Helen Frances Toland, Apr. 9, 1890. Studied law, Wilmington, Del., 1880-83; admitted to bar, 1883; law clerk Department of State, 1885-86; 3d asst. sec. of state, 1886-91; prof. internat. law and diplomacy, Columbia, 1891-1924, also chmn. administrative bd. Legislative Drafting Fund, 1911-15. Asst. sec. of state, Apr.-Sept. 1898; sec. to Conf. on Samoa, 1887; sec. to Conf. on North Atlantic Fisheries, 1887-88; sec. and counsel Spanish-Am. Peace Commn., Paris, 1898; agt. of U.S. before U.S. and Dominican Arbitration Tribunal, 1904; U.S. del. 4th Internat. Am. Conf., Buenos Aires, 1910; spl. plenipotentiary to Chilean Centenary, 1910; mem. Internat. Commn. of Jurists, 1912-22; counselor Dept. of State, with power to sign as sec. of state, 1913-14. Mem. Permanent Court of Arbitration, The Hague, 1912-38; judge Permanent Court of International Justice, 1921-28 (resigned); del. Pan-Am. Financial Congress, 1915, and vice-chmn. Internat. High Commn. then organized; ambassador extraordinary, U.S. del. and pres., Internat. Conf., The Hague, 1922-23, on Rules for Aircraft and Radio in Time of War. Dir. and mem. exec. com., Equitable Life Assurance Soc. Hon. mem. Institut de Droit Internat., Acad. of Polit. Science in City of N.Y., Del. State Soc. of the Cincinnati; mem. Institut Colonial Internat., American Philosophical Soc., Pan-Am. Soc. of U.S. (hon. pres., past pres.), Hispanic Soc. America (hon. pres.); Am. Military Inst. (life), Friends of Old Drawyers, Del. (life); hon. v.p. Am. Soc. of Internat. Law; hon. mem. Coll. of Lawyers of Costa Rica; corr. mem. Mass. Hist. Soc., Royal Acad. History of Spain, Instituto da Ordem dos Advogados Brazileiros; mem. Royal Acad. Sciences of Netherlands, Instituto de Las Españas, corr. mem. Instituto Sanmartiniano; pres. of Am. Polit. Science Assn., 1913-14, Mohonk Conf. on Internat. Arbitration, 1914, 15; mem. Pa. Hist. Soc.; fellow Am. Acad. Arts and Sciences, A.A.A.S.; incorporator Am. Nat. Red Cross; mem. central com. and exec. com. N.Y. County Chapter, 1914-20. Awarded Roosevelt Distinguished Service medal, 1927; Grand Cross Royal Order of Isabel the Catholic (Spain), 1921; White Grand Cordon with Red Borders of the Order of the Jade of China, 1938; gold insignia Pan-American Soc., 1941; insignia National Order of Southern Cross (Brazil), 1945. Clubs: Century, Bar Association (New York); Cosmos, Metropolitan (Washington, D.C.); Authors (London, England). Author: Report on Extraterritorial Crime, 1887; Report on Extradition, 1890; Extradition and Interstate Rendition (2 volumes), 1891; American Notes on the Conflict of Laws, 1896; History and Digest of International Arbitrations (6 volumes), 1898; American Diplomacy, Its Spirit and Achievements, 1905; Digest of International Law (8 vols.), 1906; Four Phases of American Development—Federalism, Democracy, Imperialism, Expansion, 1912; Principles of American Diplomacy, 1918; Internat. Law and Some Current Illusions and Other Essays, 1924; Pending Neutrality Proposals, Their False Conceptions and Misunderstandings, 1936. Editor: The Works of James Buchanan (12 vols.), 1908; International Adjudications, Ancient and Modern, together with mediatorial repts., advisory opinions and the decisions of domestic commns. on internat. claims, with hist. and legal commentaries (8 vols.), 1937. Home: 960 Park Av., New York 28, N.Y. Address: care Chase Nat. Bank, 11 Broad St., New York. Died Nov. 12, 1947.

MOORE, John C(handler), jeweler; m. Corinne de Bébian. Chmn. bd. dirs. Tiffany & Co. Clubs: Union, Union League, Colony, Piping Rock. Home: 15 E. 70th St. Office: 727 Fifth Av., New York, N.Y.* Died Dec. 21, 1946.

MOORE, John Milton, clergyman; b. Butler County, Pa., June 29, 1871; s. Samuel H. and Catharine J. (Patterson) M.; A.B., Grove City (Pa.) Coll., 1894, D.D., 1913; grad. Crozer Theol. Sem., Chester, Pa., 1897; m. Clara Mary Ross, May 2, 1894 (died May 9, 1926); children—Paul Ross (died Jan. 19, 1943), Helen Ruth Winters; m 2d, Helen Mabel Heffly, June 28, 1928. Ordained ministry Baptist Church, 1897; pastor Wilkinsburg, Pa., 1897-1903, Centennial Church, Chicago, 1904-06; secretary Department of Missionary Education, Northern Bapt. Conv., 1907-17; advisory pastor 1st Ch., Montclair, N.J., 1915-16; pastor Marcy Av. Ch., Brooklyn, N.Y., 1917-26; gen. sec. Federal Council Chs. Christ in America, 1927-31; interim pastor First Bapt. Ch., Evanston, Ill., 1931; pastor First Bapt. Ch., Bridgeport, Conn., 1931-36; interim pastor 1st Ch., Oak

Park, Ill., 1936. Mem. bd. Am. Bapt. Home Mission Soc., 1918-28; chmn. administrative com. Federal Council Chs. of Christ in America, 1920-24; pres. Brooklyn Fedn. of Chs., 1924; Am. rep. Conf. on Politics, Economics and Citizenship, Birmingham, Eng., 1924; pres. Greater New York Fedn. of Chs., 1926. Author: Things That Matter Most; The Challenge of Change; On the Trail of Truth. Mem. editorial bd. An Outline of Christianity. Decorated Cross of the Holy Sepulchre. Club: University of Winter Park, Fla. (pres. 1938-39 and 1942-43). Address: Winter Park, Fla. Died Feb. 10, 1947.

MOORE, John Monroe, bishop; b. Morgantown, Ky., Jan. 27, 1867; s. Joseph A. and Martha Ann (Hampton) M.; A.B., Lebanon (O.) Coll., 1887; student Yale, 1891-94, Ph.D., 1895, D.D., 1925; univs. of Leipzig and Heidelberg, 1894-95; D.D., Central Coll., 1908; LL.D., Southwestern U., Georgetown, Tex., 1926; Litt.D., Wesleyan Univ., Middletown, Conn., 1935; LL.D., Southern Methodist U., Dallas, 1938; m. Bessie Harris, Mar. 25, 1901. Licensed to preach in M.E. Ch., S., 1887; ordained deacon, 1894, elder, 1898; pastor Marvin Ch., St. Louis, 1895-98, Travis Park Ch., San Antonio, Tex., 1898-1902, First Ch., Dallas, Tex., 1902-06; mng. editor Christian Advocate (gen. organ M.E. Ch., S.), 1906-09; pastor St. John's Ch., St. Louis, 1909-10; sec. home missions of M.E. Ch., S., Nashville, Oct. 1, 1910-May 1918; elected bishop, May 14, 1918, and apptd. bishop in charge of work in Brazil, 1918-22; bishop in charge Okla. and east half Texas, 1922-26, in charge west half of Texas and New Mexico, 1926-30, Georgia and Florida, 1930-34, Missouri and Arkansas, 1934-38, officially retired, 1938. Secretary College of Bishops, 1927-37, sr. bishop, Feb. 1937-May 1938. Chmn. Gen. Bd. Missions, 1934-38. Editor Daily Christian Advocate (organ General Conf.), 1910. Mem. Joint Hymnal Commn. to prepare Methodist Hymnal, 1904-06, and mem. Revision Commn. of same, 1931-34; mem. Gen. Conf. of M.E. Church, S., 1906, 14, 18; mem. Joint Commn. on Unification of M.E. Ch., S., and M.E. Ch.; was mem. Lausanne World Conf. on Faith and Order; mem. of Oxford Universal Council on Life and Work, 1937, Edinburgh World Conf. on Faith and Order, 1937; fraternal messenger to Meth. Ch. of Great Britain, July 1937; chmn. exec. com. Federal Council Chs. of Christ in America, 1924-28; mem. 6th Ecumenical Conf. of Methodism, Atlanta, Georgia, 1931. Chmn. dept. schs. and colls. M.E. Ch., 1934-38; chmn. bd. trustees Southern Methodist Univ., Dallas, Tex., 1932-38. Author: Etchings of the East, 1909; The South Today, 1916; Brazil—An Introductory Study, 1920; Making the World Christian, 1922; The Long Road to Methodist Union, 1943. Methodism in Belief and Action, 1946; Life and I, 1948. Address: 4311 Rawlins St., Dallas, Tex. Died July 30, 1948.

MOORE, John William, ex-congressman; b. Morgantown, Ky., June 9, 1877; s. Jerome T. and Nancy (Albinnie) M.; ed. pub. schs. and commercial coll.; m. Kathryn Helm, Dec. 28, 1907; children—Nancy Helm, Martha Belle. Began as clk. Morgantown Deposit Bank, 1898; with T. J. Moss Tie Co., 1899-1919 except 2 yrs.; cashier Morgantown Deposit Bank, 1920-25; mem. 69th and 70th Congresses (1925-29), and reëlected to 71st and 72d Congresses (1929-33), 3d Ky. Dist.; now asst. to comptroller, Federal Housing Adminstrn., Washington, D.C. Democrat. Presbyterian. Home: Morgantown, Ky. Address: 1914 Connecticut Av., Washington, D.C. Died Dec. 11, 1941.

MOORE, Joseph Haines, astronomer; b. Wilmington, O., Sept. 7, 1878; s. John Haines and Mary A. (Haines) M.; A.B., Wilmington Coll., 1897; Ph.D., Johns Hopkins U., 1903; m. Fredrica Chase (B.A., Vassar, 1904), June 12, 1907; children—Mary Kathryn, Margaret Elizabeth. Asst., 1903-06, asst. astronomer, 1906-09, Lick Obs.; acting astronomer in charge of the D. O. Mills Expdn. to Chile, 1909-13; asst. astronomer, 1913, asso. astronomer, 1918-23, astronomer since 1923, asst. dir., 1936-42, dir., 1942-46, Lick Observatory; mem. five Lick Observatory Eclipse Expeditions, 1918-32. Republican. Mem. Soc. of Friends (Quaker). Fellow A.A.A.S. (v.p. and chmn. sect. D, 1931), Royal Astron. Soc., Calif. Acad. Science; mem. Nat. Acad. Science, Am. Astron. Soc. (v.p. 1942), Astron. Soc. Pacific (pres. 1920 and 28); mem. com. 30, Internat. Astron. Union. Author of various astron. papers. Address: 6138 Swainland Rd., Oakland 11, Calif. Died March 15, 1949.

MOORE, Nathan Grier (mōōr), lawyer; b. Indiana County, Pa., Jan. 26, 1853; s. Rev. John and Anna Eliza (White) M.; grad. Lafayette Coll., 1873; LL.D., Wooster Coll., 1922; m. Anna Walker, July 28, 1881; children—Mary W. (Mrs. Edward R. Hills), Marjorie (Mrs. John Coleman Bagby). Admitted to bar, 1878; practiced at Peoria, 1878-85; since in Chicago, first in law firm of Wilson & Moore, 1885-88, Wilson, Moore & McIlvaine, 1888-1919, Cutting, Moore & Sidley, 1919-35. Trustee Lafayette Coll. Vice moderator of Gen. Assembly Presbyn. Ch. in U.S.A., 1921; mem. Peace Commn. of 15, 1925, com. of 15 to raise capital for pension fund, 1926, Loyalty Commn., 1929; dir. Presbyterian Theol. Sem., Chicago; v.p. Chicago Presbyn. Ch. Extension Bd. Mem. Am., Ill. State and Chicago bar assns. Republican. Clubs: Union League, University. Author: The Theory of Evolution—an Inquiry; Man and his Manor. Home: 329 Forest Av., Oak Park, Ill. Died Aug. 16, 1946.

MOORE, (William) Underhill (mor), b. New York, N.Y., May 25, 1879; s. William Oliver and Katharine (Underhill) M.; A.B., Columbia, 1900, A.M., 1901, LL.B., 1902; m. Henelia M. Wilhelmi, Sept. 1908; children—Alwine Jane, Kent. Practiced law at N.Y. City, 1902-07; prof. law, U. of Kan., U. of Wis. and U. of Chicago; prof. law, Columbia U., 1916-29, Sterling prof. law, Law Sch. and Inst. of Human Relations (Yale), 1929-47, Sterling prof. emeritus, Yale, since 1947. Cons. practice, Madison, Wis., 1908-14, N.Y. City, 1916-27, and since 1947. Sole arbitrator in dispute arising from failure of Credit Anstalt, between Internat. Acceptance, Brown Brothers, Chase, Irving Trust, N.Y. Trust and other N.Y. banks, on one hand and S. M. v. Rothschild and Amstelbank of the Netherlands, on the other, 1935; spl. mediation rep. of the public Nat. War Labor Bd. since 1942. Pvt. 71st N.Y. Vols., in Cuba, Spanish-Am. War. Sec. Wis. State Bar Assn., 1912. Mem. bars of N.Y., Kan., Wis. and Ill., Assn. Bar City of New York, A.A.A.S., Assn. for Symbolic Logic, Am. Sociol. Soc., Am. Statis. Assn., Sigma Chi, Phi Delta Phi. Author: Cases on Bills and Notes, 1910, 22, 31, 41; monographs on exptl. work in Sociology of Law; editor Bills and Notes (Norton), 1914; A Statement of Accounting Principles (with T. H. Sanders, H. R. Hatfield), 1938; My Philosophy of Law, 1941; Law and Learning Theory, 1943. Contbr. to law revs., etc. Died Jan. 26, 1949.

MOORE, Walter Bedford, mfr., philanthropist; b. York, S.C., Oct. 7, 1863; s. Eli Peyton and Elizabeth Ann (Neely) M.; student Kings Mountain Mil. Sch., York, 1876-79; m. Annie Lee Adickes, Oct. 22, 1884; children—Walter Bedford, Marie (Mrs. Joseph Everett Hart). Began as clk., 1879; merchant, 1885-89; mfr. of buggies, 1889-95; insurance business, 1895-97; gen. merchant and factor, 1897-1905; cotton textile mfr., with 3 mills at York, 1905-28; pres. Peoples Bldg. & Loan Assn.; dir. and pres. York Depository. Pioneer builder of telephone systems in the Carolinas, starting 1893. Served as maj. in S.C. Nat. Guard. Mayor of York several terms; mem. sub-com. Nat. Council of Defense, 1917; trustee Church Home Orphanage, York; trustee Voorhees Normal and Industrial Sch., Denmark, S.C., St. Mary's Coll., Raleigh, N.C. Mem. Southern Spinners Assn. (pres. 1910-25), S.A.R. Awarded medal for sale of Liberty Bonds, 1918. Democrat. Episcopalian (mem. Com. on Eucharist, Province of Sewanee). Mason. Club: Crustbreakers (ex-pres.). Donor of bldgs. and land of P.E. Ch. Home Orphanage; parish house and social center P.E. Ch. at Clemson Coll., S.C.; chapel at Voorhees Normal and Industrial Sch.; rectory for church at Myrtle Beach, S.C.; endowment to Prot. Episc. Soc. for the Advancement of Christianity in Upper S.C. Home: York, S.C. Died Mar. 12, 1947.

MOORE, William Emmet (mōōr), newspaper editor; b. La Grange, Mo.; s. William Pike and Catherine Linn (Threlkeld) M.; ed. Whipple Acad., Jacksonville, Ill., and U. of Mo., LL.D., 1941; unmarried. Reporter Quincy (Ill.) Herald and Journal, 1899-1901, Chicago American, 1901-04; city editor Chicago Inter Ocean, 1904-07; mem. staff New York Herald, 1907-08; night editor Chicago Inter Ocean, 1909-12, mng. editor, 1912-14; editorial writer, Chicago Daily News, 1914; city editor and mng. editor New York Tribune, 1915-17; with the Baltimore Sun since 1922; mng. editor of The Sun, chief news editor of The Sun and The Evening Sun, and v.p. of the company. Private Ill. Vol. Inf., Spanish-Am. War; capt. Signal Corps, U.S. Army, Oct. 1917-Oct. 1919; served in France on General Pershing's Headquarters staff; awarded Victory medal with battle clasps for Aisne-Marne, Marne-Vesle and St. Mihiel campaigns, G. H. Q. citation, and Chateau-Thierry, (French) Medal. Mem. Phi Delta Theta, Phi Beta Kappa, Mil. Order of World War, Am. Legion. Clubs: University (Baltimore); National Press, University (Washington); Authors' (London). Author: Democratic Campaign Text Book, 1920; U.S. Official Pictures of the World War, 1920. Home: 100 University Parkway West. Office: The Sun, Baltimore, Md. Died Dec. 27, 1941.

MOORE, William Garrett, banker; b. Haddonfield, N.J., Jan. 8, 1874; s. Henry D. and Mary J. (Smith) M.; grad. Rittenhouse Acad., 1890; B.S., U. of Pa., 1894; m. Martie Doughty, June 4, 1896; m. 2d, Emma McDevitt, June 6, 1901; children—Helen (Mrs. A. P. Ellis), and John D. (1st marriage), Katherine (Mrs. C. Franklin Fritz), Elizabeth (Mrs. Stanley W. Rusk) (2d marriage). President of Guanajuato Reduction & Mines Company and Empire Lumber Company; formerly director Camden (N.J.) Safe Deposit and Trust Company. Chairman rural dist. Eastern sect. U.S. War Work Campaign. Organizer and chmn. for 15 yrs., County Y.M.C.A., Camden County; organizer and pres. for many years Musical Club of U. of Pa. Ex-pres. Presbyn. Social Union of Phila. Former mem. bd. of edn, now mem. bd. trustees Gen. Assembly of the Presbyn. Ch. U.S.A.; elder of First Presbyn. Ch. of Haddonfield, N.J.; del. of General Assembly to Alliance of Churches holding the Presbyn. System Cardiff, Wales, 1925, Boston, 1929; formerly trustee Princeton Theol. Sem. Chmn. and dept. dir. Haddonfield Unemployment Relief, 1931-33. Mem. S.A.R. Republican. Mason (32°, K.T., Shriner). Clubs: Union League, Orpheus (ex-pres.), Pen and Pencil (Phila.); Travistock Country. Home: 257 Kings Highway, W., Haddonfield, N.J. Office: 103 N. 7th St., Camden, N.J. Died May 17, 1944.

MOOREHEAD, Frederick Brown (mōr'hĕd), oral and plastic surgery; b. Mineral Point, Wis., Oct. 14, 1878; s. James and Mary Jane (Brown) M.; B.S., U. of Chicago, 1904; M.S., U. of Mich., 1913; M.D., Rush Med. Coll. (U. of Chicago), 1906; m. Marguerite Mary Hirst, Oct. 29, 1901; children—Chester Hirst, Dorothy Marguerite; m. 2d, Margery Maxwell, 1931. Practiced at Chicago since 1900; prof. oral and plastic surgery Rush Med. Coll., U. of Chicago; prof. oral and plastic surgery, U. of Ill.; attending oral and plastic surgeon, Presbyterian Hosp. Chicago; consulting plastic surgeon, Illinois Central R.R. System. Member A.M.A., Illinois State Med. Society, Chicago Med. Soc., Chicago Inst. Medicine, Chicago Pathol. Soc., Am. Assn. of Plastic Surgeons (pres. 1926-27), Chicago Hist. Soc., Delta Sigma Delta, Nu Sigma Nu. Republican. Presbyterian. Clubs: University, Tavern. Author: Pathology of the Mouth, 1923; also numerous monographs on pathology and plastic surgery. Home: 2150 Lincoln Park W. Office: 25 E. Washington St., Chicago, Ill. Died Aug. 29, 1944.

MOORHEAD, Harley G., postmaster Omaha, Neb.; b. Dunlap, Ia., Sept. 3, 1876; s. George P. and Annis (Bowerman) M.; Ph.B., Oberlin (O.) Coll., 1899, LL.D., 1924; LL.B., Columbia, 1902; m. Bertha Wallin, Apr. 24, 1907; children—Harley G., George Chadbourne (dec.). Admitted to Neb. bar, 1902, and since practiced in Omaha; mem. Moorhead and Brumbaugh since 1936; postmaster Omaha since 1936. Mem. Omaha Chamber of Commerce; mem. Met. Utilities Bd., 1931-33, Bd. of Commrs. of Insanity, 1933-36; election commr. in charge elections and registrations, 1913-23; jury commr., 1915-23; chmn. Compliance Bd., NRA, 1934-35; pres. Milk Fund, 1933-38; mem. Selective Draft Board during World War. Mem. State and Omaha bar assns., Nat. Assn. of Postmasters, Phi Gamma Delta, Phi Delta Phi. Democrat. Conglist. Mason, Elk. Clubs: Rotary (pres. 1915-16), Omaha Athletic (Omaha). Home: 5210 Burt St. Office: Post Office, also 307 Patterson Bldg., Omaha, Neb. Died May 1944.

MORA, Jo(seph Jacinto) (mô'rä), sculptor, painter; b. Montevideo, Uruguay, Oct. 22, 1876; s. Domingo and Laura (Gaillard) M.; came to U.S. in childhood; ed. Allston (Mass.); grad. Pingry Acad., Elizabeth, N.J., 1894; studied art at Art Students' League, and Chase's Sch., New York, and Cowles Art School, Boston; m. Grace Alma Needham, Jan. 6, 1907; children—Joseph Needham, Grace Patricia. Employed as artist for Boston Traveler, 1897; then by Boston Herald until 1900; left newspaper work to get out books for Dana, Estes & Co.; traveled in West and Southwest, making ethnol. studies of Hopi and Navajo Indians, 1903-07; mem. Jury Award, Panama Expn., 1915. Author and Illustrator: The Animals of Æsop, 1900; wrote "Animaldom" in Boston Sunday Herald and its Syndicate associates, 1907. Editor and Illustrator: Reynard the Fox, 1901; Andersen's Fairy Tales, 1902. Illustrator: Laura E. Richards' Hurdy Gurdy, 1902; Animal Football Calendar for 1903. Executed monument to "Cervantes," Golden Gate Park, San Francisco; 8 heroic figures, Realty Syndicate Bldg., Los Angeles; archtl. sculpture for Portland (Ore.) Post Office and Court House; Archbishop Reardon Memorial, K.C. Hall, and Bret Harte Memorial, Bohemian Club, San Francisco; doughboy monument, San Rafael, Calif.; Serra Sarcophagus, San Carlos Mission, Carmel, Calif.; heroic pediment, S.F. Stock Exchange; heroic figures, Scottish Rite Temple, San Jose, Calif.; heroic pediment group, Don Lee Bldg., San Francisco, and Pacific Mutual Bldg., Los Angeles; federal 50 cent piece, Calif. Diamond Jubilee; 4 heroic bronzes for Marland Estate, Ponca City, Okla.; stone sculptural work for home of Earle C. Anthony, Los Angeles; sculpture and memorial fountain, Courthouse, Salinas, Calif.; sculpture for Auditorium, King City, Calif.; murals for Hotel Canterbury, San Francisco; murals for Fable Room, Drake-Wiltshire Hotel, San Francisco; 100 foot diorama, "The Portola Expdn.," Golden Gate Internat. Expn., 1939; 13 biog. dioramas of Will Rogers, Will Rogers Memorial, Claremore, Okla.; diorama for Sutter's Fort Hist. Museum, Sacramento; triple equestrian group (half life) "La Novia," Hotel Del Monte, Calif. Wrote, illustrated Trail Dust and Saddle Leather; Californios, 1947. Mem. Nat. Sculpture Soc. Enlisted in U.S. Army, 1918, F.A.C.O. T.S., Camp Zachary Taylor, Ky.; commd. maj. of Field Arty., O.R.C. Clubs: Bohemian, Family, Author of The Jo Mora Maps. Home: Pebble Beach, Calif. Died Oct. 10, 1947.

MORAN, Daniel James (mō-răn'), pres. Continental Oil Co.; b. Cygnet, O., May 31, 1888; s. Martin and Helen (Cusack) M.; B.S., U. of Dayton, 1907; grad. study Case Sch. of Applied Science; m. Marie Elizabeth Farasey, May 28, 1921; children—Francese, Daniel James. Began with The Buckeye Oil Co., 1905; later engr. The Tex. Oil Co., advancing to v.p., dir. and mem. exec. com., was also v.p. The Texas Co. of Mexico; now pres., dir. and mem. exec. com. Continental Oil Co. and pres. and dir. subsidiaries and affiliated cos. Catholic. Clubs: Ponca City (Okla.) Country, Metropolitan, Racquet and Tennis (New York); Houston, River Oaks Country, Ramada (Houston). Address: Oil & Gas Bldg., Houston, Tex. Died April 3, 1948.

MORE, Brookes (mōr), poet, business exec.; b. Dayton, O., Mar. 29, 1859; s. Enoch Anson and Katharine Hay (Elmer) M.; ed. St. Louis pub. schs.; m. Bedelia Margaret Madden, Feb. 19, 1898; children—Katharine Hay (Mrs. Wilmon Brewer), Trenchard, Pres. The Cornhill Publishing Co., Boston, since 1922. The Jordan & More Press, 1933-39. Mem. Am. Poetry Assn., (pres. 1922-25), N.E. Poetry Club, Boston Classical Club, also member of the Boston Authors Club. Republican. Unitarian. Author: The Convent Legend, 1916; Silence and True Love, 1916; Great War Ballads, 1916; Songs of a Red Cross Nurse, 1918 reprinted as Sweet Maggie McGee, 1923;

Gods and Heroes (from Ovid), 1916; The Beggar's Vision, 1921; The Lover's Rosary, 1918; The Ring of Love, 1923; Hero and Leander, 1926; Myrtella, 1927; Bootleg Charlie, 1927; Adventured Values, 1929. Translator: Gods and Heroes (from Ovid), 1916; Ovid's Metamorphoses, book 1, 1922, books 2 and 3, 1923, books 1 to 5, 1933, books 6 to 10, 1941. Home: Great Hill, Hingham, Mass. Died June 9, 1942; buried at Hingham, Mass.

MORE, Louis Trenchard, educator; b. St. Louis, Apr. 9, 1870; s. Enoch Anson and Katharine Hay (Elmer) M.; ed. pub. schs., St. Louis, Washington U., B.S., 1892; scholarship, 1893, fellowship, 1894, Ph.D., 1895, Johns Hopkins; L.H.D., Kenyon, 1940; m. Eleanor F. Herron, Mar. 17, 1903 (died 1931); children—John Herron, Catherine Elmer. Instr. physics, Worcester Poly. Inst., 1896; instr. and adj. prof. physics, U. of Neb., 1896-1900; prof. physics since 1900, dean, 1910-13, and dean and fellow of Grad. Sch. since 1916, emeritus, 1940, U. of Cincinnati. Vanuxem lecturer Princeton Univ., 1925; William Vaughn Moody lecturer U. of Chicago. Taft Memorial lecturer Univ. of Cincinnati, 1941. Fellow of the A.A.A.S.; late fellow American Physical Society, Am. Philosophical Association, History of Science Society, Société Française de Physique. Phi Beta Kappa, Sigma Xi. Internat. Congress of Electricians, La. Purchase Expn., 1904. Vice-pres. of Cincinnati Inst. Fine Arts; dir. Cincinnati Orchestra Association. Clubs: Literary, Commonwealth. Contbr. to technical publications on light, electricity and magnetism, ionization and sound; also essays on theories of modern physics and on philosophy. Author: The Limitations of Science; The Dogma of Evolution; Life of Isaac Newton; Life and Works of Robert Boyle. Contributor Humanism in America; Irving Babbitt, Man and Scholar. Home: 317 Pike St., Cincinnati, O. Died Jan. 16, 1944.

MOREAUX, Amable Oil (môr-ō'), exec. dir. Great Lakes-St. Lawrence Tidewater Assn.; b. Heron Lake, Minn., Dec. 28, 1874; s. Isadore Amable and Anna Marie (Tweeton) M.; ed. pub. schs. Luverne, Minn.; m. Nellie Mae Brown, Nov. 6, 1919; 1 son, Charles Mabe. Owner and editor Rock County Herald, Luverne, since 1909; exec. dir. and v.p. at large Great Lakes-St. Lawrence Tidewater Assn., Washington, D.C., having written much in promotion of the project; pres. Rock County Bldg. & Loan Assn. Chmn. Minn. Great Lakes-St. Lawrence Tidewater Commn.; treas. Rock County chapter Am. Red Cross since 1917. Mem. Minn. State Editorial Assn. (pres. 1918), 2d Dist. Editorial Assn. (1st pres. 1910), Nat. Editorial Assn. Republican. Methodist. Mason (K.T., Shriner), Elk. Club: National Press (Washington, D.C.). Home: Luverne, Minn. Died June 26, 1942.

MOREHEAD, John Henry, ex-congressman; b. Lucas Co., Ia., Dec., 3, 1861; s. Andrew and Frances (Cooper) M.; ed. pub. schs.; m. Minnie Weisenreder, Neb., Feb. 14, 1885; children—Dorothy L. (dec.), Edwin J. Removed to Neb., 1884; taught sch. and later engaged in mercantile business at Barada, Neb.; county treas., Richardson County, 1896-99; mayor Falls City, 1900; mem. Neb. Senate, 1910-11; pres. pro tem of Senate and lt.-gov., 1910-11; gov. of Neb., terms 1913-15, 1915-17; mem. 68th to 73d Congresses (1923-35), 1st Neb. Dist. Nominated for U.S. Senate, 1918, for gov. for 3d time, 1920. Democrat. Stock raiser, farmer and banker. Presbyterian. Home: Falls City, Neb. Died May 31, 1942.

MOREHOUSE, Frances M(ilton) I(rene), writer; b. Annawan, Ill.; d. Lewis Cass and Kate H. (Wardall) Morehouse; A.B., U. of Ill., 1910, A.M., 1914; Ph.D., U. of Manchester (Eng.), 1926. Teacher, U. of Ill. Acad., 1910-11; instr., Ill. State Normal U., 1911-17, U. of Minn., 1917-20, 1921-24; visiting lecturer, U. of Manchester, 1920-21; instr., Columbia, 1924-25; instr. history, Hunter Coll., N.Y. City, 1926, asst. prof., 1928, asso. prof., 1939-42; taught summers, Univs. of Minn., Ore., Columbia. Mem. Phi Beta Kappa, Pi Lambda Theta, Phi Kappa Phi, Alpha Delta Pi. Baptist. Author: Discipline of the School, 1913; The Antiphony, 1916; Life of Jesse W. Fell, 1916. Joint author: American Problems (with Sybil F. Graham), 1923; The American Nation Yesterday and Today (with C. R. Lingley and R. M. Tryon), 1930; The American People and Nation, 1936. Writer and lecturer on history and edn. Home: Shafer, Minn. Died Mar. 21, 1945.

MORELAND, John Richard, writer; b. Norfolk, Va., Nov. 28, 1880; s. Richard Rogers and Agnes (Bready) M.; ed. pub. and high schs., Norfolk; unmarried. Founder of the Lyric (magazine of verse), 1920, and editor 3 years; advisory editor The Kaleidoscope; mem. adv. bd. The American Family (magazine). Member Poetry Society America; hon. member Poetry Society, Alabama; Poetry Society, Spring Hill, Alabama. Presbyterian. Author: Red Poppies in the Wheat, 1921; The Sea and April, 1928; Blowing Sand; Newry, 1930; The Moon Mender, 1933; From Dingle to Derry, 1936; A Blue Wave Breaking, 1938; A World Turning, 1940; What of the Night?, 1942; Bridle for a Unicorn, 1944; Shadow at My Heel, 1946. Works in more than 100 anthologies and compilations, and more than 100 lyrics have been set to music. Contbr. verse to leading Am. and Brit. mags Home: 522 Spottswood Av., Norfolk, Va. Died Nov. 12, 1947.

MORELAND, William Hall, bishop; b. Charleston, S.C., Apr. 9, 1861; s. Edward McCreight and Caroline (Hall) M.; grad. Holy Communion Ch. Inst., Charleston, S.C., 1877; B.S., B.Litt., A.M., U. of the South, 1881; grad. Berkeley Div. Sch., Conn., 1884; D.D., U. of the South, 1899, Berkeley, 1900; m. Harriet E. Slason, Sept. 6, 1893; children—Helen Hall, William Hall, Ruth (dec.), Harriett Tilden, Edward Philip, John Nichols. Deacon, 1884, priest, 1885, P.E. Ch.; asst. rector Christ Ch., Hartford, Conn., 1884-85; rector Ch. of Good Shepherd, Nashua, N.H., 1885-93, St. Luke's, San Francisco, 1893-99; consecrated bishop of Sacramento, Jan. 25, 1899; acting rector Christ Ch., Hackensack, N.J., 1935-37; now retired. Author: What Is Christianity?, 1887; The Church, or the Churches—Which?, 1894. Address: Delray Beach, Fla. Died Oct. 27, 1946.

MORELAND, William Haywood, law educator; b. Norfolk, Va., Sept. 17, 1879; s. Robert William and Margaret Ann (Haywood) M.; LL.B., Washington and Lee University, 1906; LL.D., Hampden-Sydney College, 1933; married B. T. Moreland, December 21, 1909. Practiced at Norfolk, 1906-14; became prof. law, Washington and Lee U., 1914, now dean Sch. of Law. Home: Lexington, Va. Died Mar. 30, 1944.

MORELL, Parker (môr-ĕl'), author; b. Bogota, N.J., June 14, 1906; s. Alfred and Elizabeth Cousins (Parker) M.; student architecture, Mass. Inst. Tech., 1924-28; Litt.B., Columbia, 1929; m. Madeleine Blabon Wagner, Oct. 8, 1937. Writer for Universal Pictures, Hollywood, Nov. 1934-Mar. 1935. Republican. Episcopalian. Author: Diamond Jim Brady, 1934; Lillian Russell: The Era of Plush, 1940. Contbr. to Cosmopolitan Mag., Saturday Evening Post, Ladies' Home Journal, Reader's Digest, Am. Mag., etc. Home: Bryn Mawr, Pa. Died Mar. 17, 1943.

MORGAN, Charles Eldridge, 3d, lawyer; b. Phila., Pa., May 27, 1876; s. Charles E. and Lillie (Merrick) M.; A.B., Harvard, 1898; LL.B., U. of Pa., 1901; m. Theresa Hamilton Fish, Oct. 28, 1916.; (died Jan. 6, 1946); children—John Thackeray Fish, Daphne Merrick. Began practice at Phila., 1901; mem. Morgan, Lewis & Bockius. Mem. Soc. of the Cincinnati. Republican. Episcopalian. Home: Newtown, Bucks County, Pa. Office: Fidelity-Philadelphia Trust Bldg., Philadelphia, Pa. Died Apr. 13, 1947; buried in Indian Field, Newtown, Bucks County, Pa.

MORGAN, Daniel Edgar, judge; b. Oak Hill, O., Aug. 7, 1877; s. Elias and Elizabeth Jane (Jones) M.; Marietta (O.) Coll., 1893-95; A.B., Oberlin Coll., 1897; LL.B., cum laude, Harvard, 1901; m. Ella A. Mathews, Apr. 22, 1915 (died July 1923); 1 dau., Nancy Olwen; m. 2d, Wilma Ball, Jan. 16, 1926. Began law practice at Cleveland, 1901. Mem. City Council, Cleveland, 1910-12; mem. Ohio State Senate, 1929; city manager of Cleveland, 1930-31; apptd. judge Court of Appeals, 8th Ohio Dist., to fill vacancy, May 1939, elected, Nov. 1940, to fill the unexpired term; reelected 1944. Mem. Charter Commn. of Cleveland, 1913. Mem. Alpha Tau Omega. Republican. Clubs: Union, University, City. Home: 2605 E. Overlook Rd., Cleveland Heights 6, O. Address: County Court House, Cleveland, O. Died May 1, 1949.

MORGAN, DeWitt Schuyler, supt. of schs.; b. Middle Point, Ohio, June 27, 1890; s. Peter Schuyler and Agnes (Foster) M.; student Northeastern Ohio Normal Coll., Canfield, O., 1907-09, Cedarville (O.) Coll., 1909-11; A.B., Henry Kendall Coll. (U. of Tulsa), 1912; A.M., University of Wisconsin, 1916; honorary LL.D., De Pauw U., 1937, Butler U., 1940, Wabash College, 1943; married Marie Elizabeth St. Clair, December 30, 1915; children—Robert DeWitt, Donald Pryse. Sec. to pres. Henry Kendall Coll., 1912-14; asst. in history, U. of Wis., 1914-16; teacher of history, Arsenal Tech. Schs., Indianapolis, Ind., 1916-18, head dept. social studies, 1918-30, prin., 1930-37; supt. Indianapolis Pub. Schs. since 1937; lecturer summer sessions of Ind., Calif., Columbia, Ohio State, Chicago univs. Pres. North Central Assn. Secondary Schs. and Colls., 1941; pres. Nat. Council of Social Studies, 1931-32; chairman Yearbook Commission; Am. Assn. School Adminstrs., 1941-43; mem. Phi Delta Kappa. Presbyterian. Mason (Scottish Rite). Clubs: Rotary, Literary, Contemporary. Author: Living and Working Together, 1923; Civics and Industry (with O. S. Flick), 1930; Guidance at Work (with M. H. Stuart), 1930; This Government (with H. J. Eckenrode and J. J. Corson), 1938. Editor: Second Year Book Nat. Council for Social Studies, 1932. Contbr. to ednl. jours. Home: 4504 Broadway. Office: 150 N. Meridian St., Indianapolis 4, Ind. Died Feb. 27, 1944.

MORGAN, Ephraim Franklin, ex-governor; b. Marion County, W.Va., Jan. 16, 1869; s. Marcus and Jennie (Wymer) M.; Fairmont (W.Va.), State Normal Sch., 1889-90; LL.B., W.Va. U., 1897; m. Alma Bennett, Sept. 1902. Began practice of law at Fairmont, 1898; city atty., Fairmont, 1901-02; judge Intermediate Court, Marion County, W.Va., 1907-12; mem. Pub. Service Commn. W.Va., 1915-20; gov. of W.Va., term 1921-24; solicitor Dept. of Commerce, 1927-33. Mem. Co. E, 1st Va. Inf., Spanish-Am. War. Republican. Methodist. Mason (32°), K.P., Moose, Woodman. Home: The Mayflower, Washington, D.C. Died Jan. 15, 1950.

MORGAN, John Hill, lawyer; b. N.Y., June 30, 1870; s. James Lancaster and Alice M. (Hill) M.; St. Paul's Sch., Concord, N.H.; A.B., Yale, 1893, LL.B., cum laude, 1896, M.A., 1929; LL.D., Washington and Lee, 1932; m. Lelia A. Myers, Nov. 10, 1903; 1 dau., Lelia A. P. (Mrs. E. R. Wardwell). Mem. firm Rumsey & Morgan, retired, 1936; trustee Brooklyn Savings Bank, 1910-36; dir. Bank of America, 1925-32. Mem. N.Y. Assembly, 1900-03. Vet. 23d Regt., N.Y.N.G.; mem. 1st Prov. Regt. N.Y.G., 1917. Trustee Brooklyn Inst. Arts and Sciences, New York Hist. Soc.; gov. com. Brooklyn Museum. Hon. curator of Am. Painting, Yale Sch. of Fine Arts. Mem. Wolf's Head, Elizabethan Club, Psi Upsilon (all Yale University); associate fellow Calhoun College (Yale University). Member of the American Antiquarian Society. Republican. Episcopalian. Clubs: Union, The Brook (New York). Author: Early American Painters, 1921; A Sketch of the Life of Gilbert Stuart, 1925; Paintings by John Trumbull at Yale University, 1926; Two Early Portraits of George Washington, 1927; John Ramage, 1930; (with Mantle Fielding) Life Portraits of George Washington and Their Replicas, 1931; (with H. W. Foote) An Extension of Lawrence Park's List of the Work of Joseph Blackburn, 1937; Gilbert Stuart and His Pupils, 1939; John Singleton Copley, 1939; John Watson, Painter, Merchant and Capitalist of Early New Jersey, 1941. Home: Mill Streams, Farmington, Conn. Died July 16, 1945.

MORGAN, John Jacob Brooke, prof. psychology; b. Norristown, Pa., Aug. 23, 1888; s. George Custer and Inez (Brooke) M.; A.B., Taylor U., Upland, Ind., 1911; A.M., Columbia, 1913, Cutting traveling fellow, Ph.D., 1916; B.D., Drew Theol. Sem., Madison, N.J., 1914; m. Rose Davis, Mar. 23, 1913; children—Burton Davis, James Newton; married 2d, Sarah Smith, June 22, 1934; 1 daughter, Nancy Wynn. Instructor in psychology, Princeton University, 1916-17; asst. professor psychology, Univ. of Minn., 1919-20; grading and testing specialist, ednl. dept., U.S.A., 1920-21; dir. psycholog. clinic, State U. of Ia., 1921-24; asso. prof. psychology, Northwestern U., 1925-33, prof. since 1933. Capt., chief psychol. examiner, Camp Hancock, 1917-19. Fellow A.A.A.S., Am. Assn. Applied Psychology; mem. Am. Psychol. Assn., Mid-Western Psychol. Assn. (pres. 1934), Ill. Assn. Applied Psychology; Sigma Xi, Alpha Pi Zeta. Republican. Methodist. Mason. Author: The Psychology of the Unadjusted School Child, 1924, rev. edit., 1936; (with A. R. Gilliland) An Introduction to Psychology, 1927; The Psychology of Abnormal People, 1928, rev. edit., 1936; General Psychology for Professional Students (with Gilliland and Stevens), 1930; Strategy in Handling People (with Ewing T. Webb), 1930; Child Psychology, 1931, rev. edit., 1942; Workbook in Abnormal Psychology, 1931; Making the Most of Your Life (with E. T. Webb), 1932; Keeping a Sound Mind, 1934; Psychology: A General Textbook, 1941; Workbook in General Psychology, 1941; also monograph, The Overcoming of Distractions and Other Resistances (Archives of Psychology), 1916; and articles in psychology journals. Home: 3015 Simpson St. Address: Northwestern University, Evanston, Ill. Died Aug. 17, 1945.

MORGAN, J(ohn) Pierpont, banker; b. Irvington, N.Y., Sept. 7, 1867; s. John Pierpont and Frances Louise (Tracy) M.; A.B., Harvard, 1889; LL.D., Trinity Coll., Conn., 1918, Cambridge U. (England), 1919, Harvard, 1923, Princeton U., 1929; D.C.S., New York Univ., 1922; D.C.L., Oxford Univ. (Eng.), 1930; m. Jane Norton Grew, Dec. 11, 1890 (died Aug. 14, 1925). Chmn. of the board J. P. Morgan & Co., Inc.; chmn. bd. U.S. Steel Corp. until 1932, now director; director Pullman Company, Discount Corp. of New York, etc. Apptd. mem. com. to deal with German reparations, 1929. Trustee Metropolitan Museum of Art, N.Y. Public Library, Cooper Union; member joint administrative board of New York Hosp., Cornell Medical Coll. Assn.; governor Peabody Donation Fund. Officer, 1919, Comdr., 1920, Legion of Honor (France); Grand Officer Order of Leopold II (Belgium), 1920; Grand Officer of Order of the Crown of Italy, 1927; First Order of the Sacred Treasure (Japan), 1927; hon. freedom of the Goldsmiths' Company (England), 1919; Grand Cross Order of St. Gregory the Great (Pope Pius XI), 1938. Clubs: Century, University, Harvard, Union, Union League, Racquet and Tennis, New York Yacht, Brook (New York); Somerset (Boston); Metropolitan (Washington); Larchmont Yacht; Athenæum, Garrick, Whites (London). Home: Matinicock Point, Glen Cove, N.Y.; 12 Grosvenor Sq., London, W., and Wall Hall, Watford, Eng. Office: 23 Wall St., New York, N.Y. Died Mar. 13, 1943.

MORGAN, Thomas Hunt, zoölogist; b. Lexington, Ky., Sept. 25, 1866; s. Charlton H. and Ellen Key (Howard) M.; B.S., State Coll. of Ky., 1886, M.S., 1888; Ph.D., Johns Hopkins, 1890; LL.D., Johns Hopkins, 1915, U. of Ky., 1916, McGill U., 1921, U. of Edinburgh, 1922, U. of Calif., 1930; hon. Sc.D., U. of Mich., 1924; Ph.D., Heidelberg U., 1931; hon. M.D., U. of Zurich, 1933; Docteur Honoris Causa, U. of Paris, 1935; m. Lilian V. Sampson, 1904; children—Howard Key, Edith Sampson, Lilian Vaughn, Isabel Merrick. Prof. biology, Bryn Mawr, 1891-1904; prof. exptl. zoölogy, Columbia, 1904-28; dir. William G. Kerckhoff Labs. Biol. Sciences, Calif. Inst. Tech., since 1928. Fellow A.A.A.S. (pres. 1929-30); mem. Nat. Acad. Science (pres. 1927-31), Am. Soc. Naturalists, Am. Soc. Zoölogists, Soc. Exptl. Biology and Medicine, N.Y. Acad. Sciences, Royal Soc. London; corr. mem. or fgn. asso. numerous European socs. Author: Regeneration, 1901; Evolution and Adaptation, 1903; Experimental Zoölogy, 1907; Heredity and Sex, 1913; Mechanism of Mendelian Heredity, 1915; Critique of the Theory of Evolution, 1916; The Physical Bases of Heredity, 1919; The Theory of the Gene, 1926; Experimental Embryology, 1927; The Scientific Basis of Evolution, 1932; Embryology and Genetics, 1933; also monographs and papers on biol. and embryol. subjects. Awarded Nobel prize, 1933, for discoveries concerning the laws and mechanism of heredity. Address:

1149 San Pasqual St., Pasadena, Calif. Died Dec. 4, 1945.

MORGAN, Wallace, illustrator; b. New York, N.Y., July 11, 1873; s. William Penn and Frances Ann (Wallace) M.; grad. Albany (N.Y.) High Sch., 1891; student Acad. of Design Art Sch., New York, 1892-98; unmarried. Illustrator art dept. New York Herald, 1898-1908; illustrator for books and mags. since 1908; former instructor illustration class Art Students League of New York, N.Y. Soc. Illustrators. Commd. capt. Engr. Corps, Feb. 1918, and appointed official artist with the army; served a year in France with A.E.F.; made many drawings for historical record of the war. Mem. Soc. of Illustrators (pres. 1929-36; hon. pres. since 1946), Artist Guild, Nat. Inst. of Arts and Letters. Clubs: Players, Century, Coffee House, Dutch Treat (New York). Asso. Nat. Acad. Design since 1946. Home: 162 E. 80th St. Studio: 26 E. 95th St., New York. Died April 28, 1948.

MORGAN, William Fellowes, warehouseman; b. Staten Island, N.Y., Sept. 24, 1860; s. David Pierce and Caroline (Fellowes) M.; A.B., Columbia, 1880; E.M. Sch. of Mines (Columbia), 1884; m. Emma Leavitt, Jan. 22, 1885. In stock brokerage business, 1884-87, cold storage business since 1887; chmn. bd. Merchants' Refrigerating Co.; dir. Chem. Bank & Trust Co.; trustee Bank for Savings; dir. Savannah Sugar Refining Corp. Mem. Gen. Assembly of New Jersey, 1905 and 1907. Mem. 7th Regt. Nat. Guard N.Y., 1882-84; apptd. mem. Gen. Ward's staff, 1st Brigade, 1884. Pres. Merchants' Assn. of New York, 1915-22; dir. Church Life Ins. Co. (pres. 1932-41); Church Properties Fire Ins. Co. (pres. 1929-41); trustee Church Pension Fund (pres. 1931-40); pres. Y.M.C.A. of New York, 1905-19; alumni trustee Columbian U., 1910-16; trustee American U. (Beirut, Syria), Wells Coll., Aurora, N.Y. Mem. A.A.A.S., N.Y. Acad. of Sciences, Delta Psi. Episcopalian. Clubs: Union, Garden City Golf, Jeckyl Island. Home: 510 Park Av., New York, N.Y. Died May 2, 1943.

MORGAN, William Gerry, physician; b. Newport, N.H., May 2, 1868; s. Gerry and Mary (Strong) M.; A.B., Dartmouth, 1890; M.D., U. of Pa., 1893, post-grad. work, New York; m. Cora Boyd, Nov. 27, 1895. Began practice at Southport, Conn., 1894; settled at Washington, D.C., 1899; prof. diseases of digestive tract, Georgetown U., since 1904, dean of Sch. of Medicine, 1931-35; also regent of univ.; an asso. editor Tice System of Practice of Medicine; asso. editor Lippincott's Am. System of Medicine and Principles and Practice of Physical Therapy. Chmn. D.C. Advisory Draft Bd., also lt. (j.g.) Navy R.C., World War, retired, 1922; maj. M.R.C., U.S. Army from 1922, retired, 1932. Pres. Am. Congress of Internal Medicine, 1922. Fellow and master American College Physicians (regent 1918-30, gov. 1930-33, sec. gen. 1933-37, v.p. 1937); mem. A.M.A. (Ho. of Delegates 1920-25; pres. 1930-31), Am. Gastroenterol. Assn. (pres. 1913), Am. Therapeutic Assn., Clinico-Pathol. Soc. (pres. 1919), D.C. Med. Soc. (pres. 1919), N.Y. Acad. Medicine, Washington Acad. Sciences (v.p. 1919), Southern Med. Soc. (councillor), Va. Med. Soc., Wash. Hist. Soc., Am. Archeol. Assn., Assn. Mil. Surgeons, Med. Vets. of World War, Internat. Med. Club (pres. 1930; mem. U.S. Annual Assay Commn., 1922,1924), Internat. Gastro-entrology Soc. (U.S. del. to Brussels 1935), Psi Upsilon. Republican. Author of Functional Diseases of the Alimentary Tract, The History of the American College of Physicians. Clubs: Metropolitan, Cosmos, Congressional. Home: 3737 Fessenden St. N.W. Office: 1801 Eye St., N.W. Washington. Died July 7, 1949; buried Rock Creek Cemetery, Washington.

MORGAN, William McKendree, judge; b. Adams County, Ill., Dec. 2, 1869; s. John Milton and Mary (Gooding) M.; ed. Kan. Normal Coll., Ft. Scott, and Harper (Kan.) Normal Sch. and Business Coll.; LL.M., Georgetown U., 1899; m. Emma M. Friedline. July 22, 1895; children—Mrs. Pearl Smith, Arthur P. (dec.), Mrs. Grace Thiel. Admitted to Ida. bar, 1894, and practiced in Moscow; mayor of Moscow, 1906-08; mem. Ida. Ho. of Rep., 1897-99, 1911-13; justice Supreme Court of Ida., 1915-21, and 1933-45. Democrat. Address: State House, Boise, Ida. Died Oct. 16, 1942.

MORGAN, William Thomas, prof. European history; b. Dell Roy, O., May 19, 1883; s. Thomas William and Mary (Davies) M.; Ph.B., Ohio U., 1909; univ. scholar, Harvard, 1909-10, A.M., 1910, Adams Woods fellow, 1911-12; Cutler fellow, Yale, 1914-16, Ph.D., 1916; research in European archives and libraries, 1915, 1923-24, 1929-30, 33, 36, 1939; Am., 1934, 1938, 1943, 1945; m. Chloe Siner, Aug. 9, 1916; children—John Siner (dec.), Katherine Lenore. Instr European history, Columbia, 1916-19; asst. prof. same, Ind. U., 1919-20, asso. prof., 1920-28, prof. since 1928; teacher in summer sessions, State U. of Iowa, 1926, Boston U., 1927, U. of Mich., 1928, Duke Univ., 1935. Fellow Royal Hist. Society (London); member American Historical Association, Miss-Hist. Assn., Miss. Valley Hist. Assn., Phi Beta Kappa, Acacia. Herbert Baxter Adams prize essayist, Am. Hist. Assn., 1919. Episcopalian. Author: English Political Parties and Leaders in the Reign of Queen Anne, 1920; A Syllabus in Modern European History, 1920; A Guide to the Study of English History, 1926; A Bibliography of British History, 1700-1715, Vol. I, 1934, Vol. II, 1937, Vol. III, 1939 (with Mrs. Chloe Siner Morgan), Vol. IV, 1942, Vol. V (with Mrs. Chloe Siner Morgan), 1942. Contbr. 50 articles to Polit. Science Quarterly, South Atlantic Quarterly, Contemporary Review, Am. Hist. Rev., Jour. Modern History, and other periodicals; also M.S. vols. ready for publication on Early 18th Century British Elections; The British Navy; History of English Political Parties to 1855. Home: 816 Atwater Av., Bloomington, Ind. Died June 9, 1946; buried in Hull Cemetery, near Terre Haute, Ind.

MORGENTHAU, Henry (môr'gĕn-thaw), former ambassador; b. Mannheim, Germany, Apr. 26, 1856; s. Lazarus and Babette (Guggenheim) M.; came to U.S., 1865; ed. Pub. Sch. No. 14 and Coll. City of New York; LL.B., Columbia, 1877; LL.D., Constantinople Coll. for Girls, Turkey, 1915, Oberlin Coll., Temple U., 1925, U. of Athens, Greece, 1925, Syracuse U., 1935; m. Josephine Sykes, May 10, 1883; children—Mrs. Helen Fox, Mrs. Alma Wiener, Henry, Jr. (ex-sec. of treasury), Mrs. Ruth Knight. Mem. law firm Lachman, Morgenthau & Goldsmith, New York, 1879-99; pres. Central Realty Bond & Trust Co., 1899-1905; pres. Henry Morgenthau Co., 1905-13; director Underwood Corporation; dir. Equitable Life Assurance Soc. of U.S., 1915-21; pres. Herald Square Realty Co. Chmn. finance com. Dem. Nat. Com., 1912 and 1916; ambassador to Turkey, Sublime Porte, 1913-16; in charge of interests in Turkey of Great Britain, France, Italy, Russia, Belgium, Montenegro, San Marino, Servia, Switzerland, 1914-16; mem. mission apptd. by Pres. Wilson, June 1919, to investigate conditions in Poland. Nominated as ambassador to Mexico, Mar. 1920. Chmn. of Greek Refugee Settlement Commn. created by League of Nations, 1923; del. to Wheat Conf. Geneva, 1933; tech. expert to Monetary and Economic Conf., London, 1933. An incorporator Am. Nat. Red Cross; v. chmn. Near East Relief, inc. by Act of Congress, 1919-21. Dir. Inst. of Internat. Edn.; pres. Economic Club, 1919-20, and pres. Bronx House Settlement; dir. Mt. Sinai Hosp. Mem. New York County Lawyers Assn. Decorated Grand Officer Legion of Honor (France), 1919; Hon. Knight of Grand Cross Civil Div. Order of British Empire, 1920; Order of the Holy Savior of Greece. Author: Ambassador Morgenthau's Story (also pub. in Eng. under title of Secrets of Bosphorus, and transl. into French and other languages), 1918; All in a Lifetime, 1922; My Trip Around the World, 1928; I Was Sent to Athens, 1929. Home: 1133 Fifth Av., New York, N.Y., and Mizzentop, Bar Harbor, Me. Died Nov. 25, 1946.

MORIN, John M., ex-congressman; b. Phila., Pa., April 18, 1868; s. Martin Joseph and Rose (Joyce) M.; ed. pub. schs. and business coll.; m. Eleanor C. Hickey, 1897; 10 children. In glass factory and steel mills, Pittsburgh, to 1889; with D. J. Hennessy Mercantile Co., Missoula, Mont., 1889-93; returned to Pittsburgh, 1893. Mem. Pittsburgh Common Council, 1904-06; mem. Rep. State Conv., Pa., 1905-12; dir. pub. safety, Pittsburgh, 1909-13; mem. 63d Congress (1913-15), Pa. at large, and 64th to 68th Congresses (1915 to 1925), 31st District, and 69th and 70th Congresses (1925-29), 34th Dist.; mem. U.S. Employees' Compensation Commn. since Apr. 1929. Catholic. Home: 1726 Massachusetts Av. N.W. Office: Old Land Office Bldg., Washington, D.C. Died Mar. 3, 1942.

MORLEY, Sylvanus Griswold, archeologist; b. Chester, Pa., June 7, 1883; s. Benjamin Franklin and Sarah Eleanor Constance (de Lannoy) M.; C.E., Pa. Mil. Coll., 1904; A.B. Harvard, 1907; research fellow in Central Am. Archeology, Harvard, 1907-08, A.M., 1908; (hon.) Ph.D., Pa. Mil. Coll. 1921; m. Alice Gallinger Williams, Dec. 30, 1908 (divorced); 1 dau., Alice Virginia; m. 2d, Frances Louella Rhoads, July 14, 1927. Engaged in field work in Central Am. and Mexico for School of Am. Archeology, 1909-14; research asso. Carnegie Instn. of Washington, 1915-17; asso., same, 1918; in charge Carnegie Instn. archeol. expdns. to Central America; dir. Chichen Itza Project, 1924-40. Entered service of Office of Naval Intelligence as ensign, Apr. 6, 1917; retired as lt. j.g., Mar. 1919. Specializes in Maya hieroglyphic writing and gen. problems in Middle Am. archeology. Hon. fellow Royal Anthropological Inst., Great Britain; Order of the Quetzal, Guatemala, 1939. Member Society for American Archaeology, Am. Philos. Soc. Republican. Catholic. Mason (32°, Shriner). Club: Century Association. Author: Introduction to Study of Maya Hieroglyphs, 1915; Inscriptions at Copan, 1920; Guide Book to the Ruins of Quirigua, 1935; The Inscriptions of Peten, 1937, 38; The Ancient Maya; also bulls. and articles in the Am. Anthropologist, Jour. Am. Archeology, Jour. Am. Museum, Nat. Geog. Magazine, Scientific American, etc. Home: Hacienda Chenku, Merida, Yucatan, Mexico; and Quinta San Jose, Santa Fe, N.Mex. Address: Apartado Postal, 385, Marida, Yucatan, Mexico. Died Sept. 2, 1948; buried Santa Fe, N.M.

MORRILL, Albert Henry (môr'ĭl), chain store exec.; b. Cincinnati, O., June 20, 1875; s. Henry Albert and Anna (McGuffey) M.; A.B., Dartmouth Coll., 1897; LL.B., Cincinnati Law Sch., 1900; m. Lily Logan, June 28, 1905; children—Logan, Elizabeth Drake Holladay. Admitted to Ohio bar, 1900, and practiced since at Cincinnati; formerly member Nichols, Morrill, Wood, Max & Ginter; pres. The Kroger Grocery & Baking Co., chain store operators, since Apr. 1930; pres. The Piggly Wiggly Corp.; dir. The Commercial Nat. Bank & Trust Co., Pittsburgh, Cincinnati, Chicago & St. Louis R.R. Dir. Community Chest, Cincinnati Y.M.C.A.; trustee Children's Home of Cincinnati. Served with Artillery Corps, U.S. Army, 1918. Mem. Am., Ohio State and Cincinnati bar assns., Alpha Delta Phi, Phi Delta Phi. Republican. Episcopalian. Clubs: Queen City, Commercial, Camargo, Cincinnati Country, Farmington Country, Farmington Hunt (Charlottesville, Va.). Home: Montgomery, Ohio; (summer), Enniscorthy, Keene, Va. Office: 35 E. 7th St., Cincinnati, Ohio. Died Sep. 13, 1942.

MORRILL, Albro David, biologist; b. Tilton, N. H., Aug. 29, 1854; s. Smith and Mary (Clark) M.; B.S., Dartmouth, 1876, M.S., 1879; U. of Mich., 1876-77; A.M. (hon.) Belmont Coll., College Hill, O., 1886; m. Lena E. Carver, Dec. 23, 1879. Science teacher, Lewistown, Pa., 1878-83; prof. chemistry, physics and higher mathematics, Belmont Coll., 1883-88; prof. biology and geology, Ohio U., Athens, 1888-92; prof. chemistry and biology, 1892-96, biology, since 1896, Hamilton Coll. Fellow A.A.A.S.; mem. Am. Soc. Naturalists, Am. Soc. Zoölogists, Boston Soc. Natural History. Republican. Presbyterian. Home: Clinton, N.Y. Died June 8, 1943.

MORRILL, John Adams, judge; b. Auburn, Me., June 3, 1855; s. Nahum and Anne Isabella (Littlefield) M.; A.B., Bowdoin Coll., 1876, A.M., 1879; LL.D., Bowdoin Coll., 1912, U. of Me., 1920; m. Isabella Olive Littlefield, Nov. 1, 1888; children—Dorothy Isabella, Olive Anna. Admitted to bar, 1880; apptd. by Me. legislature, Mar. 21, 1901, and reappointed Apr. 4, 1913, sole commr. to revise and consolidate pub. laws of state, and prepared 5th and 6th revisions of pub. laws of Me.; judge of probate, Androscoggin County, 1913-18; asso. justice Supreme Judicial Court of Me., 1918-26; active retired justice of Supreme Judicial Court, 1926-33. Mem. State Bd. Examiners of applicants for admission to the bar, 1900-08; del. Universal Congress Lawyers and Jurists, St. Louis, 1904. Mem. bd. overseers Bowdoin Coll., 1888-1925, bd. of trustees, 1925-28. Mem. Me. State Bar Assn. (pres. 1917), Me. Hist. Soc. Home: Auburn, Me. Died Aug. 24, 1945.

MORRILL, Warren Pearl, hosp. consultant; b. Benton Harbor, Mich., Jan. 20, 1877; s. Roland and Ellen (Pearl) M.; Ph.B., U. of Mich., 1898; M.D., Johns Hopkins, 1908; m. Helen Wallace, Oct. 18, 1899; children—Ellen (Mrs. Reid R. Bronson, D.D.S.), Joanna (Mrs. Edward Timke), Helen (Mrs. Arthur E. Oliver, dec.). Superintendent Sydenham Hospital, Baltimore, Md., 1909-12, Winnipeg General Hospital, 1912-13; general practice of medicine, Benton Harbor, Mich., 1913-17; superintendent University Hospital, Augusta, Georgia, 1919-20, Shreveport (La.) Charity Hosp., 1920-24, Columbia Hosp. for Women, Washington, D.C., 1925-29, Me. Gen. Hosp., Portland, 1929-30; field rep. Am. College Surgeons, 1931, survey of state instns., Tex. and Conn., 1932-33. Served as pvt., inf., Spanish-Am. War; 1st lt., Med. R.C., 1911-17; capt. Med. Corps., Dec. 1916 to Dec. 1917, maj., Jan.-Nov. 1918; lt. col. Med. Corps, U.S. Army, A.E.F., Nov. 1918-Aug. 1919; col. Med. Res. U.S. Army (inactive). Mem. A.M.A., Am. Hosp. Assn., Heroes of '76, S.A.R. Mason (K.T.), K.P. Clubs: Army, Navy and Marine Corps Country (Ft. Meyers, Va.); Sojourner. Author: The Hospital Manual of Operation. Editor: Hospital Abstract Service; Medical Abstract Service. Dir. of research Am. Hosp. Assn. Address: 18 E. Division St., Chicago 10, Ill. Died Sep. 27, 1947.

MORRIS, Benjamin Wistar, III, architect; b. Portland, Ore., Oct. 25, 1870; s. Benjamin Wistar, II (missionary bishop of Ore. and Wash., 1869, and bishop of Ore. until 1906) and Hannah (Rodney) M.; St. Paul's Sch., Concord, N.H.; Trinity Coll., Conn.; Ph.B., Columbia Univ., 1894, hon. Litt.D., 1929; École des Beaux Arts, Paris, 1894-96; hon. M.A., Trinity, 1906; m. Alice Fenwick Goodwin, Feb. 13, 1901; children—Mary Wistar (Mrs. R. B. O'Connor), Benjamin Wistar, IV (lt. U.S.N.R.). Asst. to Carrere & Hastings, in preparation of competitive drawings for New York Pub. Library, etc., for 4 yrs.; about 1900 partnership of 1 yr., Morris, Butler & Rodman, architects; then alone until 1910; mem. La-Farge & Morris, 1910-15; sr. partner Morris & O'Connor since 1930. Architect of '79 and Patton halls, Princeton U.; Conn. State Arsenal and Armory; Junius S. Morgan Memorial, Hartford; Ætna Fire and Phœnix Fire and Life Ins. buildings; State Savings Bank and Mechanics Savings Bank, Hartford; Conn. Mut. Life Ins. Co. Bldg.; Westchester County Court House, White Plains, N.Y.; Cunard Bldg., Seamen's Bank for Savings and Bank of New York & Trust Co. (New York); Hartford (Conn.) Trust Co. Bldg.; Lincoln Nat. Life Ins. Co. Bldg.; also plan for Metropolitan Opera House and Metropolitan Square, Annex to Pierpont Morgan Library, Union League Club, Continental Bank & Trust Co. (New York), etc. Architectural advisor School of Architecture, Princeton U., 1921-23; member Art Commn. City of New York, 1923-25. Chmn. bd. Beaux Arts Inst. of Design, 1922-35; fellow A.I.A. (dir.), Royal Soc. of Arts of London, 1940; mem. Society Beaux Arts Architects, New York Chapter A.I.A. (pres. 1924-25), Architectural League of New York, Psi Upsilon. Mem. Nat. Commn. of Fine Arts, 1927-31; Nat. Acad. Design, Nat. Inst. Arts and Letters. Gold medallist Archtl. League New York, 1918; Medal of Honor, New York Chapter A.I.A., 1922. A.N.A. Pres. Westchester County Soc. for Prevention of Cruelty to Children, 1932-33; trustee Metropolitan Museum of Art since 1935. Episcopalian. Club: Century. Joint architect for interior plan and decoration of S.S. Queen Mary. Home: Mt. Kisco, N.Y. Office: 101 Park Av., New York, N.Y. Died Dec. 4, 1944.

MORRIS, Dave Hennen, former ambassador, lawyer; b. New Orleans, La., Apr. 24, 1872; s. John A.

and Cora (Hennen) M.; A.B., magna cum laude, Harvard, 1896; LL.B., New York Law School, 1901; A.M., Columbia, 1909; hon. Docteur, University of Brussels, 1935; honorary M.D., University of Ghent, 1937; LL.D., University of Syracuse, 1935, Tufts College, 1940, Colby College, 1943; m. Alice Vanderbilt Shepard, June 19, 1895; children—Lt. Col. Dave H., Louise (Mrs. Dudley H. Mills), Lawrence, Noel (dec.), Emily H. (Mrs. Hamilton Hadley), Alice V., II (Mrs. Walter Knight Sturges). Practiced N.Y. City, 1901-33; U.S. ambassador to Belgium and minister to Grand Duchy of Luxembourg, 1933-37; formerly v.p. St. Louis Southwestern Ry. Co.; formerly pres. Automobile Club of America; consultant to treasury dept.; govt. appeal agt. during World War; one of five founders Aero Club of America; vice-pres. and treas. Research Corp. Hon. chmn. bd. trustees Y.W.C.A. Retirement Fund; treas. Internat. Auxiliary Lang. Assn.; trustee and v.p. New York Post-Grad. College and Hosp. of Columbia U.; trustee Barnard Coll. of Columbia University; trustee Nat. Foundation for Education in Am. Citizenship; pres. Diplomatic Affairs Foundation, Belgian War Relief Soc., Inc., Belgian-Am. Associates, World Religious Edn. Assn., dir. American Society of French Legion of Honor, Inc.; chmn. bd. Josiah Macy Jr. Foundation; dir. Edwin Gould Foundation; former pres. Buhl Com. of Brussels for Victims of War; director C.R.B. Educational Foundation; chmn. exec. com. N.Y. Orthopædic Dispensary and Hosp.; dir. Legal Aid Soc; former mem. com. to visit Grad. Sch. of Edn. and Music Dept. of Harvard Coll.; former Bronx Park commr., N.Y. City. Decorated with Grand Cordon, Order of Leopold I, by King of Belgium; Grand Cordon, Order of the Oak Leaves, by Grand Duchess of Luxembourg; Officer Legion of Honor by President of French Republic. Mem. Bar Assn. City of New York, Economic Club of N.Y. (director), Phi Beta Kappa Associates (president), Alpha Delta Phi, Phi Beta Kappa (New York chmn. campaign Defense Fund), Alpha Kappa Delta (hon.). Apptd. by gov. of Ky. aide de camp, with grade of col., 1935. Democrat. Presbyterian. Clubs: Union, Metropolitan, University, Harvard, City Midday, The Creek, New York Yacht; Boston Club (New Orleans); Faculty (Harvard); Union (hon. pres.), American (hon. pres.), Fondation Universitaire, Cercle Noble (Brussels). Home: 19 E. 70th St., New York, N.Y. Address: 420 Lexington Av., New York, N.Y. Died May 4, 1944.

MORRIS, Florance Ann, artist; b. Nevada, Mo., Mar. 5, 1876; d. Luther Vernile and Elizabeth Ann (Montooth) Baker; student Mo. pub. and pvt. schs.; pupil of Warren E. Rollins, A. J. Hammond, L. Brezoli; studied in Paris, Antwerp and Florence; m. Richard E. Morris, Feb. 3, 1895; 1 dau., Mary Katharine (Mrs. R. L. Villard). Works: "The Papoose," Museum of Art and Archeology, Santa Fe; portrait of Gov. Richard C. Dillon, N.M. State Museum; "Shasta Tribe," Sorbonne, Paris; "Ancient Acoma," Woman's Club Bldg., Paris; "Zuni Water Carriers," Roswell, N.M.; portrait of Will Rogers, Claremore (Okla.) Library; Dean Walter Williams, U. of Mo.; Sir Harry Lauder, Roswell (N.M.) Museum; Dr. V. A. C. Stockard, P.E.O. Memorial Library, Mt. Pleasant, Ia.; New Mexico Landscape, Carnegie Library, Roswell, N.M. Awarded 1st prize Tri-State Fair, N.M., 1925, French medal, 1930. Mem. N.M. Archeol. Soc., Am. Fed. of Arts, W.C.T.U., P.E.O. Democrat. Southern Methodist. Clubs: Boston Art (Boston); Woman's, Reading (Roswell, N.M.). Home: Roswell, N.M. Died Sept. 3, 1947; buried in South Park Cemetery, Roswell, N.M.

MORRIS, George, newspaper corr., writer; b. Fayette County, Tenn., Jan. 30, 1886; s. Walter and Mary Etta (Parker) M.; B.A., Union U., Jackson, Tenn., 1906, LL.D., 1928; m. Karen McGehee, July 23, 1907; 1 son, George. Asso. editor Nashville Banner, 1914-16; Washington corr. same newspaper, and sec. to Senator John K. Shields, 1916-17; editor Memphis News-Scimitar, 1918-26; editor Memphis Evening Appeal, 1926; vice-pres. Memphis Commercial Appeal, Inc., 1927-30, pres. and editor, 1931-32, asst. pub., 1933-37; Washington columnist and correspondent since 1937. Del. to Dem. Nat. Conv., 1932. Pres. Memphis Chamber of Commerce, 1925. Mem. Kappa Sigma. Named by Carnegie Peace Foundation as one of group of editors to study conditions in Europe, 1927. Democrat. Episcopalian. Club: National Press. Home: "Etowah Farm," Harwood, Md. Address: Scripps-Howard Newspaper Alliance, Washington, D.C. Died Apr. 24, 1944.

MORRIS, Harrison Smith, author; b. Phila., Pa., Oct. 4, 1856; s. George W. and Catharine (Harris) M.; ed. pub. and pvt. schs.; m. Anna Wharton, June 2, 1896; 1 dau., Mrs. Catharine Morris Wright. Mng. dir. Pa. Acad. Fine Arts, 1893-1905; editor Lippincott's Magazine, 1899-1905; art editor Ladies' Home Journal, 1905-07; was chmn. com. on ways and means Nat. Acad. Design, N.Y.; pres. Wharton Steel Co., 1909-17. Commr.-gen. U.S. to Roman Art Exposition, 1911. Mem. Nat. Inst. Arts and Letters (former v.p.; treas.), Am. Philos. Soc., Phi Beta Kappa; pres. Contemporary Club, Phila., 1915; pres. Art Assn., Newport, 1916-47; Am. sec. Keats-Shelley Memorial, Rome, Italy. Trustee Wagner Inst.; former mem. Bd. of Edn., Phila. Elector of Hall of Fame. Clubs: Franklin Inn, Sketch (Phila.); Salmagundi, Players, Lotos (N.Y. City); Corinthian Yacht and Conanicut Yacht. Author: A Duet, in Lyrics, poems (with J. A. Henry) 1883; Tales from Ten Poets, 1893; Madonna and Other Poems, 1894; Lyrics and Landscapes, 1908; Masterpieces of the Sea, biography of William T. Richards, 1912; Hannah Bye (a novel), 1920; Walt Whitman (biography, pub. in Italian), 1920, also in English with additions, 1929; The Landlord's Daughter (novel), 1923; Martial Notes (verse), 1929; Confessions in Art, 1929. Editor: In the Yule Log Glow, 1892; Where Meadows Meet the Sea, 1892; also wrote a continuation and completion of Lamb's Tales from Shakespeare, 1893; Odes, 1938. Contbr. verse and prose to mags. Cavaliere di Grande Groce decorato del Grande Cordone dell'Ordine della Corona d'Italia. Home: Pear Hill, 1600 Chelten Av., Philadelphia 26, Pa.; (summer) Horsehead, Jamestown, R.I. Died April 12, 1948.

MORRIS, Henry Crittenden, lawyer; b. Chicago, Ill., Apr. 18, 1868; s. John and Susan (Claude) M.; A.B., Lombard Coll., 1887, A.M., 1890; LL.B., Chicago Coll. Law, 1889; grad. study France and Germany; hon. A.M., Buchtel Coll. (U. of Akron), 1909; m. Grace Mühlenberg Hills, Sept. 10, 1917. U.S. consul at Ghent, Belgium, 1893-98. Sec. to Chief Justice Fuller, 1905, in Muscat Dhows arbitration before International Permanent Court at The Hague. Chmn. 6th Ward Chicago Red Cross and 3d Liberty Loan Campaigns, 1917-18. Trustee Lombard College, 1900-15; pres. Young People's Christian (Universalist) Union of Ill., 1891-92; mem. Board Foreign Missions, Universalist Church, 1920-29; mem. Universalist Nat. Memorial Church, Washington, D.C. (mem. building com. 1929-30; mem. bd. management 1939-43); mem. Fedn. of French Alliances (v.p. 1921-22; dir. 1925-28). Decorated Chevalier French Legion of Honor, 1937. Mem. Am. Bar Assn., Am. Peace Soc. (dir. (1918-47), Am. Soc. of Internat. Law, Am. Hist. Assn., Am. Polit. Sci. Assn., Am. Soc. of French Legion of Honor, Am. Acad. Polit. and Social Science, Chicago Bar Assn., Ill. Hist. Soc., Chicago Hist. Soc., Chicago Peace Soc. (pres. 1914-21), Art Inst. Chicago, English-Speaking Union, Library of Internat. Relations, Institut Français of Washington, D.C. (1st v.p.), Pi Gamma Mu; mem. Hamilton Club of Chicago (sec. 1908-09, dir. 1909-10, 1912-14, 1st v.p. 1910-11). Republican. Clubs: Alliance Française of Chicago (dir. 1910-44, pres. 1921-23), University, Arts, Archaeological Soc. (Washington). Author: The History of Colonization from the Earliest Times to the Present Day, 1900; History of the First National Bank of Chicago, 1902. Home: Hyde Park Hotel, Chicago, and 3006 Albemarle St., Washington, D.C. Address: 5100 S. Woodlawn Av., Chicago 15. Died July 25, 1948.

MORRIS, James Craik, bishop; b. Louisville, Ky., June 18, 1870; s. John Hite Morton and Fanny (Craik) M.; B.Litt., U. of the South, Sewanee, Tenn., 1890, M.A., 1891, D.D., 1915; LL.B., Louisville Law Sch., 1892; General Theol. Seminary, 1893; m. Edith Garland Tucker, Oct. 31, 1900; children—Edith Nelson, Mary Leith, James Craik. Deacon and priest, P.E. Ch., 1896; asst. St. Matthew's Cathedral, Dallas, Tex., 1896-98; curate St. James Ch., Brooklyn, N.Y., 1898-1901; dean St. Mary's Cathedral, Memphis, Tenn., 1901-16; rector Grace Ch., Madison, Wis., 1916-20; consecrated bishop of Panama Canal Zone and Parts Adjacent, Feb. 1920; became bishop of Diocese of La., Sept. 24, 1930; retired Mar. 1, 1939. Mem. Soc. of The Cincinnati, Phi Beta Kappa, Alpha Tau Omega. Home: Sewanee, Tenn. Died May 5, 1944.

MORRIS, John Baptist, bishop; b. Hendersonville, Tenn., June 29, 1866; s. John and Annie (Morrisey) M.; ed. St. Mary's Coll., Ky., and N.A. Coll., Rome, Italy. Ordained R.C. priest, 1892; pastor St. Mary's Cathedral, Nashville; vicar-gen. Diocese of Nashville, 1900-06; consecrated coadjutor bishop of Little Rock, June 11, 1906; became bishop of Little Rock, Feb. 21, 1907; made asst. to Pontifical Throne, May 7, 1931. Fellow Am. Geog. Soc. Home: Little Rock, Ark. Died Oct. 22, 1947.

MORRIS, Lewis Spencer, chmn. bd. Fulton Trust Co. of N.Y.; b. NY City, Aug 21, 1884; s. Henry Lewis and Ann Rutherford (Russell) M.; student Princeton; m. Emily Pell Coster, Apr. 6, 1907. Mem. firm Morris & McVeigh, N.Y. City; chmn. bd. Fulton Trust Co. of N.Y.; v.p. and trustee Bank for Savings; trustee Bank of New York; dir. Fulton Safe Deposit Co., Parish Safe Deposit Co., Northern Ins. Co. Pres. Soc. for Relief of the Destitute Blind; trustee N.Y. Soc. Library; dir. Burke Relief Foundation. Republican. Episcopalian. Clubs: Tuxedo, Knickerbocker, Down Town, Brook, Racquet and Tennis, Princeton, Century, National Golf Links of America (N.Y. City); Shinnecock Hills Golf. Home: 116 E. 80th St. Office: 149 Broadway, New York, N.Y. Died Nov. 28, 1944.

MORRIS, Oscar Matison, prof. horticulture; b. Donophan County, Kan., June 26, 1874; s. Sylvester Edward and Clarissa Adeline (McCulloch) M.; B.S., Okla. Agrl. and Mech. Coll., 1896; Cornell U., 1897-98; M.S., State Coll. of Wash., 1915; m. Leona Jane Hall, July 11, 1901; children—Howard V., William E. Asst. in horticulture, 1898-1902, instr. in same, 1902-06, asst. prof., 1906-08, prof. horticulture and botany, 1908-10, Okla. Agrl. and Mech. Coll.; asst. prof. horticulture, 1910-11, prof. since 1911, State Coll. of Wash. Mem. Am. Pomol. Soc., Am. Soc. for Hort. Science, Phi Kappa Phi, Alpha Zeta, Sigma Xi. Republican. Methodist. Home: Pullman, Wash. Died Nov. 13, 1943.

MORRIS, Robert Hugh, clergyman; b. Bluffton, Ga., Aug. 9, 1876; s. Rev. William Jefferson and Iowa (Singleton) M.; Southwestern Ga. Mil. Sch., Cuthbert, Ga.; Emory Coll., Oxford, Ga., 1898; M.A., Princeton, 1905; grad. Princeton Theol. Sem., 1906; D.D., Northwestern, 1909; LL.D., Coe Coll., Cedar Rapids, Ia., 1929; m. Lydia Addy, Oct. 3, 1906; children—Robert Hugh, Mary, William James. Ordained Presbyn. ministry, 1901; pastor Ocala, Fla., 1901-02; stated supply Barnesville, Ga., 1902-03; pastor Elmer, N.J., 1904-06, Oak Lane Ch., Phila., 1906-08, 1st Ch., Evanston, Ill., 1908-11, Central N. Broad Ch., Phila., 1911-17, First Ch., Stamford, Conn., 1917-21, First Ch., Haddonfield, N.J., since May 1, 1921. Declined calls to Can. and England. Mason, Odd Fellow, K.P. Author: Good Man or God-Man, 1912; Sleeping Through the Sermon, 1916; The Fifth Horseman, 1923; Pan's Pipes and the Lyre of Orpheus, 1925; The Prince and the Pig's Gate, and Other Tales, 1928; A Communicant's Catechism, 1936. Home: Haddonfield, N.J. Died Oct. 19, 1942.

MORRISON, Robert John, surgeon; b. Brooklyn, N.Y., Jan. 1, 1857; s. Murdock and Jennette James (Thompson) M.; M.D., L.I. Coll. Hosp., 1891; m. Sarah Eldridge Perry, Sept. 15, 1881; children—Russell P., Mrs. Alma Bara. Practiced in Brooklyn since 1891; surgeon 1st division Williamsburgh Hosp. since 1905; surgeon in chief Batterman Clinic, Brooklyn. Fellow Am. Coll. Surgeons; mem. Assn. Physicians of L.I. (ex-pres.), Alumni St. Mary's Hosp. (ex-pres.), Kings County Med. Soc. Baptist. Address: 1173 Dean St., Brooklyn, N.Y. Died June 8, 1942.

MORRIS, Robert Tuttle, surgeon; b. Seymour, Conn., May 14, 1857; s. Gov. Luzon Burritt and Eugenia Laura (Tuttle) M.; student Cornell U., 1876-79; M.D., Coll. Phys. and Surg. (Columbia), 1882; (hon. A.M., Centre Coll., Ky., 1891); m. Mrs. Aimée Reynaud Mazergue, June 4, 1898; 1 dau., Eugenia Reynaud; m. 2d, Mary Hannah Best, May 1, 1922; 1 dau., Mary. Prof. surgery, New York Post-Grad. Med. Coll., 1898-1917 (emeritus). Pres. Am. Assn. Obstetricians and Gynecologists, 1907; pres. Am. Therapeutic Assn., 1916; fellow Am. Coll. Surgeons. Clubs: Cornell, Alpha Delta Phi, Campfire. Author: How We Treat Wounds Today, 1886; Lectures on Appendicitis, 1895; Hopkins's Pond, 1896; Dawn of the Fourth Era in Surgery, 1910; To-morrow's Topics Series 1915; Microbes and Men; A Surgeon's Philosophy; Doctors versus Folks; The Way Out of War, 1918; Nut Growing, 1921; Editorial Silence, 1927; Fifty Years a Surgeon, 1934; also various monographic repts. on original investigations. Home: Stamford, Conn. Died Jan. 9, 1945.

MORRIS, Roland Sletor, lawyer; b. Olympia, Wash., Mar. 11, 1874; s. Thomas Burnside and Sarah Arndt (Sletor) M.; grad. Lawrenceville (N.J.) Sch., 1892; A.B., Princeton, 1896; LL.B., U. of Pa., 1899, LL.D., Temple U., 1921, Princeton U., 1921, U. of Pa., 1932, D.C.L., U. of Del., 1929; D.H.L., Hobart, 1933; m. Augusta Shippen West, Apr. 20, 1903; children—Sarah Morris Machold, Edward Shippen. Began practice in Phila., 1899; mem. Duane, Morris & Heckscher since 1904; prof. internat. law, U. of Pa., since 1924, dir. Mutual Life Ins. Co. of N.Y., Franklin Fire Ins. Co. Ambassador E. and P. to Japan, 1917-21, on special mission to Siberia, Sept.-Nov. 1918, Jan.-Mar. 1919, and July-Oct. 1919. Trustee, Carnegie Endowment for Internat. Peace Millbank Fund, Brookings Instn.; mem. Bd. City Trusts; mem. Fgn. Bondholders Protective Council; regent Smithsonian Instn. Del. to Dem. Nat. convs., 1904, 08, 12, 28, chmn. Dem. Finance Com. of Pa., 1908, 16; state chmn. Dem. party in Pa., 1913-16. Elected life trustee Princeton, 1934. Mem. Am. Philos. Soc. (ex-pres.), Oriental Soc., Am., Pa. and Phila bar assns. (ex-chancellor); ex-pres. Phila. br. English-Speaking Union. Episcopalian. Clubs: Philadelphia, Princeton, Contemporary, University Barge (Phila.); Century (N.Y.). Chancellor Diocese of Pa. Home 2113 Spruce St. Office: Land Title Bldg., Philadelphia, Pa. Died Nov. 23, 1945.

MORRIS, William Alfred, univ. prof.; b. nr. Dallas, Ore., May 24, 1875; s. John and Mary Elizabeth (Farley) M.; A.B., Leland Stanford Jr. U., 1901 (Carnot medalist); Ph.D., Harvard, 1907; research work, London, 1907, 20, 23, 29, 37; m. Miriam Belt Huelat, Sept. 1, 1904. Teacher pub. schs., Wash., Ore., 1895-97; teacher history and Latin, Portland High Sch., 1901-04; Austin fellow and Tappan fellow, Harvard, 1904-06; asst. in history, Harvard and Radcliffe, 1906-07; instr. hist., 1907-10, asst. prof., 1910-12, U. of Wash.; asst. prof. English history, 1912, associate professor, 1918, professor, 1922-45; professor emeritus since 1945, University of Calif. Special lecturer, King's Coll., U. of London, 1921; dir. Medieval Acad. America research project, The English Government at Work, 1936. Fellow Royal Hist Soc.; mem. Am. Hist. Assn., Medieval Acad. America, Am. Assn. Univ. Profs., Phi Beta Kappa. Republican. Episcopalian. Author: The Frankpledge System, 1910; The Old English County Court, 1926; The Medieval English Sheriff, 1927; Constitutional History of England to 1216, 1930. Editor (with J. F. Willard) and contbr., The English Government at Work, 1327-1336, Vol. I, 1940. Home: Sequoia Apts., 2441 Haste St., Berkeley, Calif. Died Feb. 20, 1946.

MORRIS, William Thomas, pres. Am. Chain & Cable Co., Inc.; b. W. Pittston, Pa., July 20, 1884; s. Thomas J. and Jane (Reese) M.; student pub. schs.; m. Jessie Mae Forker, June 24, 1904. Pres. and dir. Am. Chain & Cable Co., Inc., Bridgeport, Conn., since 1936; pres. & dir. Centennial Development Co., Inc., Sormir Petroleum Corp., Colony Management Inc., American Fabrics Co., Magazine Repeating Razor Co., Mich. Chemical Corp., Pa. Woven Wire Co.; dir. Dominion Chain Co., Ltd., Parsons Chain Co., Ltd., British Wire Products, Ltd.

Mason. Clubs: Cloud, Question, Advertising (New York); Cornell, Madison Square Garden, Siegniory; Union League, Annapolis Yacht. Address: Bridgeport, Conn. Died Feb. 6, 1946.

MORRISON, Charles Munro, newspaper editor; b. Jefferson County, Ill., Nov. 23, 1881; s. William David and Melisse (Garrison) M.; student McKendree Coll., Lebanon, Ill., 1898-99, 1901; m. Dana Rae Maxey, October 26, 1901; children—Alice Morrison Wilmsen, Maxey Neal. Asst. school prin., Mt. Vernon, Ill., 1901-02; prin. high sch., Fairfield, Ill., 1902-07; successively reporter, Sunday editor, political editor, editorial writer and asst. mng. editor St. Louis (Mo.) Republic, 1909-19; asso. editor St. Louis Globe-Democrat, 1919-21; chief editorial writer, Phila. (Pa.) Pub. Ledger, 1921-26; also chief editorial writer, New York Evening Post, 1924-26; dir. of editorial pages and asso. editor Phila. Pub. Ledger and Evening Ledger, 1926-29, acting editor, 1929-30, editor, 1930-42; v.p. and sec. Pub. Ledger, Inc., 1936-42; sec. Commonwealth of Pa. since 1943. Member American Society Newspaper Editors, American Academy Polit. and Social Sciences. Clubs: Union League, Racquet, Camp and Trail (Phila.); National Press (Washington). Home: Mearns Rd., Ivyland, Pa. Address: 1608 Walnut St., Philadelphia, Pa. Died Jan. 14, 1950.

MORRISON, Frank, sec. emeritus Am. Fedn. of Labor; b. Frankton, Ont., Nov. 23, 1859; s. Christopher and Eliza (Nesbitt) M.; LL.B., Lake Forest U. Law Sch., Chicago, Ill., 1894, grad. Study, 1895; m. Josephine Curtis, June 11, 1891; 1 dau., Esther; m. 2d, Alice S. Boswell, Aug. 11, 1908; 1 son, Nesbitt. Began as printer, 1873; sec. Am. Fedn. of Labor, 1897-1939, also treas.; retired Dec. 31, 1939 (elected sec. emeritus). Mem. Chicago Typo. Union No. 16; mem. exec. com. Federal Council Chs. of Christ in America, Nat. Bd. Trustees Near East Relief. Home: 1216 Decatur St. N.W. Office: A. F. of L. Bldg., Washington, D.C. Died March 12, 1949.

MORRISON, Henry Clay, theologian; b. Bedford, Ky., Mar. 10, 1857; s. James S. and Emily (Durham) M.; ed. Ewing Inst., Perryville, Ky. and Vanderbilt U.; D.D., Ohio Northern U., Ada, O.; m. Geneva Pedlar, 1895. Ordained M.E. ministry. Pres. Asbury Coll., Wilmore, Ky., many years; pres. Pentecostal Pub. Co.; editor Pentecostal Herald. Del. Ecumenical Conf., London, Eng. Evangelist. Address: Wilmore, Ky. Died March 24, 1942.

MORRISON, Henry Clinton, univ. prof.; b. Oldtown, Me., Oct. 7, 1871; s. John and Mary Louise (Ham) M.; A.B., Dartmouth, 1895; M.S., N.H. Coll., 1906; LL.D., U. of Me., 1914; L.H.D., U. of N.H., 1931; m. Marion Locke, July 29, 1902; children—John Alexander, Hugh Sinclair, Robert Drew. Prin. high sch., Milford, N.H., 1895-99; supt. schs., Portsmouth, 1899-1904; state supt. pub. instrn., N.H., 1904-17; asst. sec. State Bd. of Edn. of Conn., 1917-19; prof. edn. and supt. laboratory schs., U. of Chicago, 1919-28, then prof. edn., now retired. Pres. N.H. Teachers Assn., 1903; pres. Am. Inst. Instrn., 1908-09; mem. Ednl. Finance Com., 1921-23; fellow A.A.A.S. Author: The Financing of Public Schools in Illinois, 1924; Practice of Teaching in the Secondary School, 1926, revised edit., 1931; School Revenue, 1930; Management of School Money, 1932; The Evolving Common School, 1933; Basic Principles in Education, 1934; School and Commonwealth, 1937; Curriculum of the Common School, 1940; American Schools: A Critical Study of Our School System, 1943. Lecturer and consultant. Home: 5739 Blackstone Av., Chicago, Ill. Died Mar. 19, 1945.

MORRISON, Ralph Waldo; b. Howell Co., Mo. Sept. 7, 1878; s. Joseph and Julia (McCann) M. student West Plains Coll., 1900; m. Leo Louise Chartrand, of St. Louis, Mo., Mar. 1903. Fgn. sales mgr. St. Louis Car Co., St. Louis, 1903-11; in utility business, 1911-25; operating in investment, ranching and banking business, 1925-34; pres. Pan-Am. Hotel Co.; pres. Texas-Mexican Ry. Co., 1939-48; owner St. Anthony Hotel, San Antonio; organized Central Power & Light Co.; dir. Central and Southwest Utilities. Mem. Am. del. to Econ. Conf., London, 1933; apptd. mem. Federal Reserve Bd., Jan. 27, 1936, resigned, May 20, 1936. Mem. The Council on Fgn. Relations. Democrat. Mason (32°). Clubs: Country (San Antonio); Press, Jefferson Island (Washington, D.C.). Home: 239 W. Mistletoe Av. Office: Alamo Nat. Bldg., San Antonio, Tex. Died April 3, 1948.

MORRISON, Thomas, steel mfr.; b. in Scotland, Dec. 5, 1861; m. Elizabeth Park. Served apprenticeship as machinist and engr. in Scotland; came to U.S., 1886; became identified with Carnegie Steel Corp.; was made Supt. Duquesne Works, 1891, Edgar Thompson Works, 1895; dir. Internat. Nickel Co. of Canada, Ltd. Home: Spring Lake, N.J. Died Oct. 26, 1946.

MORRISON, William Brown, coll. prof.; b. Lexington, Va., June 12, 1877; s. James Davidson and Laura (Chapin) M.; A.B., Washington and Lee U., 1897; D.Litt., Austin Coll., Sherman, Tex., 1917; M.A., U. of Okla., 1925; m. Christine Barton, Dec. 25, 1902; children—James Davidson, Ross Williams, Natalie Virginia, Elizabeth Chapin, William Barton. Teacher Latin, Rockville (Md.) Acad., 1897-1900; prin. high sch., Beaumont, Tex., 1902; teacher Latin, Durant (Okla.) Coll., 1902-04; prin. Williamson (W.Va.) Presbyterial Academy, 1904-07; editor Williamson (W.Va.) Enterprise, 1907-10; president Okla. Presbyn. Coll. for Girls, Durant, Okla., 1910-20; prof. history, Southeastern State Coll., since 1922, acting pres., 1937, acting dean, 1938. Trustee Austin Coll. Mem. for Okla. of Advisory Com. of Edn., Presbyn. Ch. in U.S. Mem. Classical Assn. Middle West and South, Phi Alpha Theta. Democrat. Mason (K.T.), K.P., Woodman. Club: Lions. Author: An Oklahoman Abroad, 1928; The Red Man's Trail, 1931; Out in Oklahoma (verse), 1934; Military Posts and Camps in Oklahoma. 1936. Home: Durant, Okla. Died Mar. 20, 1944.

MORROW, Lester William Wallace, editor, educator; b. Hammond, W.Va., Aug. 7, 1888; s. Daniel Lickard and Alice Bell (Shinn) M.; grad. Marshall Coll., Huntington, W.Va., 1907; M.E., Cornell U., 1911; m. Esther K. Morrow, Aug. 14, 1913; children—John Lockard, Anne Virginia, George Luther. Instr. in elec. engring., Cornell U., 1912-13; prof. elec. engring. and dir. Sch. of Elec. Engring., U. of Okla., 1913-18; was mem. Bur. of Standards, Okla., and sec. Okla. Utilities Assn.; asst. prof. elec. engring., Yale, 1918-22; also asso. editor Electrical World, 1922-24, mng. editor, 1924-28, editor, 1928-36; gen. mgr. Fibre Products Div., Corning Glass Works, 1936-37; editorial dir. McGraw-Hill Pub. Co., 1938-41; prof. engring. adminstrn., Rutgers U., since 1941. Asst. dir. Signal Officers' Sch., Yale, 1918-20. Fellow Am. Inst. E.E.; mem. Am. Soc. M.E., Am. Electrochem. Soc., Sigma Tau, Sigma Xi, Epsilon Xi, Acacia. Vice-pres. Thomas Alva Edison Foundation. Republican. Presbyterian. Clubs: Cornell Univ. (New York); Graduate (New Haven). Home: Colonial Gardens, New Brunswick, N.J. Died Nov. 15, 1942.

MORROW, Walter Alexander, editor; b. Crawfordsville, Ind., Mar. 25, 1894; s. Ellery Herbert and Theodosia (Imlay) M.; student U. of Okla., 1913-16; m. Blanche Teape, Apr. 8, 1916; children—Scott Imlay, Richard Montrose. Began as reporter The Daily Oklahoman, Oklahoma City, 1918; successively city editor, news editor, and asst. mng. editor of The Oklahoman; mng. editor The Memphis (Tenn.) Press, 1924-25; editor The Lansing (Mich.) Capital-News, 1926-28; on staff The (N.Y.) World-Telegram, 1928-29; city editor and news editor Buffalo Times, 1929-30; feature writer The Cleveland Press, 1930-31; editor The Akron Times-Press, 1931-37; editor-in-chief southwestern group Scripps-Howard Newspapers, 1937-38; editor, The Columbus (O.) Citizen, 1942. Vice pres. American Retail Federation, Washington, D.C., 1943-44, president, 1945. Mem. Phi Gamma Delta, S.A.R., National Press Club. Home: 2700 Connecticut Av. N.W. Office: 1627 K St. N.W., Washington. Died July 14, 1949; buried at Rose Hill Cemetery, Oklahoma City.

MORSCHAUSER, Joseph, judge; b. Hyde Park, N. Y., Mar. 30, 1863; s. Joseph and Henrietta (Rottman) M.; ed. common schs. and under pvt. tutor; m. Katherine W. Bauer, Jan. 27, 1889; 1 son, Joseph. Admitted to N.Y. bar, 1884, and practiced in Poughkeepsie; justice of the peace, 1886-92; civil service commr. Poughkeepsie, 1889-90; recorder, 1899-1902; city judge, 1902-06; justice Supreme Court of N.Y., 9th Dist., 2 terms, 1907-33. Republican. Roman Catholic. Home: Poughkeepsie, N.Y. Died Nov. 3, 1947.

MORSE, Arthur Henry, gynecologist; b. Salem, Mass., Dec. 13, 1880; s. James Henry and Susan Augusta (Ballard) M.; B.A., Tufts Coll., 1902; M.D., Johns Hopkins U., 1906; hon. M.A., Yale, 1921; m. Evanita Von Schlieder, Dec. 14, 1926; children—J. Harvey-Lander, Arthur Henry II. Resident pathologist R.I. Gen. Hosp., Providence, 1906-07; resident obstetrician and instr. in obstetrics, Johns Hopkins, 1910-11; resident surgeon Union Memorial Hosp., Baltimore, 1912-13; instr. in obstetrics and gynecology, U. of Calif., 1913-15, also asso. gynecologist Univ. Hosp., San Francisco; asst. prof. obstetrics and gynecology, Yale, 1915-20, also asst. obstetrician and gynecologist, New Haven Hosp., 1915-19, obstetrician and gynecologist, 1919-20; asst. clin. prof. obstetrics and gynecology, Yale, 1920; clin. prof. obstetrics and gynecology, New Haven Hosp., 1920-21, prof. and obstetrician and gynecologist in chief since 1921. Diplomate Am. Board Obstetrics and Gynecology. Fellow Am. Coll. Surgeons, A.M.A., Am. Gynecol. Soc.; mem. A.A.A.S., Soc. for Exptl. Biology and Medicine, New Eng. Surg. Soc., Phi Beta Kappa, Sigma Xi, Delta Upsilon, Nu Sigma Nu, Alpha Omega Alpha. Episcopalian. Club: Graduate, Faculty. Home: 141 Deepwood Drive, Hamden, Conn. Address: New Haven Hosp., New Haven, Conn. Died Jan. 26, 1950.

MORSE, Charles Wyman, financier; s. Benjamin W. Morse; A.B., Bowdoin Coll., 1877; m. Hattie Bishop Hussey, Apr. 14, 1884 (died July 30, 1897); m. 2d, Mrs. Clemence Cowles Dodge, June 18, 1901. Engaged with father in shipping at Bath, Me., 1877; removed to Brooklyn, 1880 and engaged in ice business extensively, est. large branches at Phila. and Baltimore; now largely engaged in steamship transportation; 1st v.p. The Butterick Co.; dir. Mallory Steamship Co., Met. Steamship Co., N.Y. & Cuba Mail Steamship Co. (Ward Line), Clyde Steamship Co., Eastern Steamship Co., Hudson Navigation Co., Boston Ins. Co., Title Ins. Co. of N.Y., New York Mortgage & Security Co., Wall St. Exchange Bldg. Assn. (v.p.), Fifth Av. Estates, Century Realty Co., William Campbell Wall Paper Co. Clubs: Metropolitan, Union League, University. Residence: 724 5th Av. Office: 41 Wall St., New York. Died Jan. 12, 1933.

MORSE, Edwin Kirtland, engr.; b. Poland, Mahoning County, Ohio, July 3, 1856; s. Henry Kirtland and Mary A. (Lynn) M.; A.B., Yale, 1881; m. Caroline U. Shields, Sept. 25, 1884; m. 2d, Elizabeth Wood, Apr. 12, 1914. In various depts. of brother's bridge works at Youngstown, O., and gen. agt. for the co. at Chicago, to 1887; went to Sydney, Australia, 1887, and contracted for erection of superstructure, under firm head of Ryland & Morse, Hawkesbury Bridge, at Dangar Island (7 spans, 415 ft. each, the largest bridge in the southern hemisphere); returned to Pittsburgh, 1889; cons. engr. since 1892. Built substructures for Buffalo, Rochester & Pittsburgh R.R. Bridge, and Carnegie's Railroad, both across Allegheny River; foundations for hot metal bridges at Port Perry and Homestead, across Monongahela River for Carnegie Steel Co., substructures for Jones & Laughlin Steel Co.'s bridge across Monongahela River; 3 suspension bridges across Ohio River with channel spans 700 to 800 ft. each; consulting engr., chmn. engr. com. of Flood Commn. Transit commr. for city of Pittsburgh, 1916-20; cons. engr. City of Pittsburgh for study of flood control, wharf walls and river terminals; apptd. mem. Water and Power Resources Bd., by Gov. John S. Fisher, Nov. 9, 1927, reapptd., 1931, by Gov. Gifford Pinchot. Mem. Am. Inst. Cons. Engrs., Inc., Am. Soc. C.E. (dir.); ex-pres. Engrs. Soc. of Western Pa. Cons. engr. Allegheny County Authority. Club: Duquesne. Home and Office: 401 S. Graham St., Pittsburgh, Pa. Died May 28, 1942.

MORSE, Josiah, psychologist; b. Richmond, Va., Feb. 17, 1879; s. Jacob and Huldah (Bear) M.; A.B., Richmond Coll., 1899, A.M., 1900; Ph.D., Clark U., 1904; m. Etta Ferguson, Sept. 25, 1907; children—Josiah M., Vivian R., Stanley B., Henry F. Lecturer Clark U. and instr. Clark Coll., 1904-05; instr. psychology and edn., U. of Tex., 1905-06; research asst., Clark U., 1906-07; prof. philosophy and edn., Peabody Coll. for Teachers, 1908-11; prof. philosophy and psychology, Univ. of S.C., since 1911. Mem. bd. of trustees Southern Edn. Foundation. Ex-pres. Southern Psychol. and Philos. Assn.; mem. Am. Psychol. Assn.; fellow Am. Assn. for the Advancement of Science; chmn. Univ. Commn. on Race Questions; v.p. Nat. Consumers' League. State dir. Am. Red Cross; field dir. A.R.C., Camp Jackson, World War. Chmn. Southern Region (Joint Distribution Com.), 1940. Mem. Phi Beta Kappa, Omicron Delta Kappa. Author: Pathological Aspects of Religions, 1906; The Psychology and Neurology of Fear, 1907. Co-author: The Moral Life, 1911; The Elements of Character, 1912; Behaviorism—A Battle Line. Contbr. to jours., mags. and newspapers on psychol., ednl. and civic topics. Home: 811 Sumter St., Columbia, S.C. Died Mar. 22, 1946.

MORSE, Perley, accountant; b. Litchfield, Bradford County, Pa., Jan. 9, 1869; s. George W. and Mary (Brink) M.; ed. Arlington Acad., Washington, D.C.; Certified Pub. Accountant U. of State of N.Y., 1904; m. Mary Bremner, July 25, 1893; children—George Perley, Stanley. Engaged as accountant since 1894; sr. mem. Perley Morse & Co., conducted important investigations for Federal Govt. in war and other matters; also for State of N.Y.; banks, etc. Discovered that Bolo Pasha received $2,000,000 of German money in U.S. for German propaganda through purchase of French newspapers. Vice-pres. and dir. Addressograph-Multigraph Corp. Apptd. mem. N.Y. State Recovery Bd., 1933 (v. chmn.); apptd. chairman Selective Service Draft Board No. 762, Ramapo Township, Rockland County, N.Y., Oct. 1940. Mem. Order Founders and Patriots, S.R. (1st vice-pres.), General Society of Colonial Wars, N.Y. Hist. Society. Clubs: Lawyers', Metropolitan, City (vice pres.). Mason. Author: The ABC of the Government of the U.S. (adopted as text book on civics by N.Y. City Bd. Edn.), 1916; Business Machines, 1931. Decorated Pro Georgiæ Libertate (Nat. Govt. of Georgia). Home: Suffern, N.Y., Metropolitan Club, New York. Office: 165 Broadway, New York, N.Y. Died Apr. 25, 1942.

MORTON, Howard McIlvain, oculist, aurist; b. Chester, Pa., May 23, 1868; s. Charles J. and Annie E. (Coates) M.; B.S., Lafayette Coll., 1888, M.S., 1891; M.D., U. of Pa., 1891; post-grad. work Royal Ophthalmic Hosp., London, and Charite Hosp., Berlin; m. Lucretia Jarvis, Dec. 9, 1891. Interne, St. Luke's Hosp., Bethlehem, Pa., 1891; practiced at Minneapolis, Minn., since 1891; prof. diseases of eye and ear, Hamline U., 1893-95; formerly oculist and aurist, Minneapolis City and Swedish hosps.; chief dept. eye surgery, Minneapolis Gen. Hosp.; chief eye and ear surgeon, Wells Memorial Clinic and St. Barnabas and Fairview hosps.; now retired. Mem. Internat. Congress Ophthalmologists. Mem. A.M.A., Minn. State Med. Assn., Hennepin County Med. Soc., Am. Acad. Ophthalmology and Oto-Laryngology, Minn. Acad. Ophthalmology and Oto-Laryngology (1st pres.), Assn. Mil. Surgeons of U.S., Internat. Soc. for Prevention of Blindness, Am. Legion; fellow Am. Coll. Surgeons; dep. gov. gen. Nat. Soc. Sons and Daughters of the Pilgrims. Republican. Episcopalian. Maj. Med. Corps, U.S.A., during World War; lecturer Army Sch. of Ophthalmology, Ft. Oglethorpe, Ga. Clubs: Minneapolis, Skylight (Minneapolis); University (St. Paul). Author: Visual Neurology (text book); also Perimetry (monograph in Am. Ency. of Ophthalmology); also over 100 articles in tech. jours. Inventor of Morton perimeter and other instruments. Address: Vincentown, N.J. Died July 19, 1939.

MORTON, Joseph, foreign correspondent; b. Buchanan County, Mo., June 30, 1911; s. Joseph and Pearl Jane (King) M.; student Wentworth Mil. Acad.,

1927-28, St. Joseph's Jr. Coll., 1930-31, St. Benedict's Coll., 1932-33, U. of Neb., 1933-34; m. Letty Aleene Miller, Nov. 10, 1934. Telegraph editor Omaha (Neb.) Bee-News, 1937; editor for Asso. Press, Lincoln, Neb., and Cleveland, O., 1937-40, editor A.P. feature service, N.Y. City, 1940-42, A.P. fgn. corr. since 1942. Only corr. present at entrance Am. forces, Dakar, French W. Africa, 1942; aboard battleship Richelieu from Dakar to N.Y. City, 1942; aboard Am. bomber, first raid on Rome, 1943. Editor of A.P. war background maps. Author of articles on conditions at Dakar, French W. Africa, 1942-43. Mem. Beta Theta Pi. Home: 33 Washington Square, W. Office: Associated Press, New York, N.Y. Died Jan. 24, 1945.

MOSBY, Charles Virgil (mōz'bĭ), med. pub.; b. Nevada, Mo., Aug. 18, 1876; s. John Smith and Mary Frances (Hilliard) M.; student Beaumont Med. Coll., 1897-99; M.D., St. Louis Coll. Physicians and Surgeons, 1900; hon. D.Sc., Bates Coll., 1938; m. Margaret Cavanaugh, Apr. 10, 1901; children—Charles Virgil, Highland Mary (wife of Dr. Wood); Don E. (adopted). Pub. med. books and jours. since 1906; chmn. bd. dirs. C. V. Mosby Co.; pubs. of Am. Jour. Obstetrics and Gynecology, Am. Heart Jour., Am. Jour. Thoracic Surgery, Jour. of Laboratory and Clin. Medicine, Am. Jour. Orthodontics and Oral Surgery, Am. Jour. Syphilis and Venereal Diseases, Jour. of Pediatrics, Surgery, Jour. of Allergy. Democrat. Conglist. Author: Making the Grade, 1926; also Little Journeys to the Homes of the Great (7 vols.), 1917-20. Home: 425 Fairlawn Av., Webster Groves, Mo. Office: 3525 Pine Blvd., St. Louis. Died Nov. 9, 1942; buried in Oak Hill Cemetery, Webster Groves, Mo.

MOSCHCOWITZ, Paul (môsh'kô-wĭtz), artist; b. Giralt, Hungary, Mar. 4, 1875; s. Morris and Rose (Baumgarten) M.; ed. pvt. tutors in Hungary, pub. schs., 1883-90, evening high sch., 1890-94, New York; Art Students' League, New York, 1894-98, Académie Julian, Paris, 1899; m. Madeline M. Raab, July 15, 1905; 1 dau., Mildred. In professional work as artist since 1893; work largely in portraiture and mural decoration. Has been instr. at Art Students' League, New York; now instr. at Pratt Institute, Brooklyn. Tiffany gold medal for drawing, 1894, Saltus prize, 1897; exhibited in Paris Salon, 1899; silver medal, St. Louis Expn., 1904. A.N.A. Died Jan. 4, 1942.

MOSCOWITZ, Grover M., judge; b. Hot Springs, Ark., Aug. 31, 1886; s. Morris and Bertha (Less) M.; LL.B., New York U., 1906; m. Miriam H. Greenebaum, Apr. 4, 1911; children—Alva M. (Mrs. Raymond Zeitz), Grover M., Marion Sue (Mrs. Joseph P. Landes), Warren S. Admitted to N.Y. bar, 1907; began practice in Brooklyn; special deputy attorney general New York in charge of prosecution of election frauds, Brooklyn, 1909, 10, 22, 25; U.S. district judge, Eastern District of New York, by appointment of President Coolidge, since December 16, 1925. Mem. Legal Advisory Bd., World War. Mem. Am., N.Y. State and Brooklyn bar assns., Zeta Beta Tau. Mason (32°, Shriner), K.P. Address: Federal Bldg., Brooklyn, N.Y. Died Mar. 31, 1947.

MOSELEY, Hal Walters; univ. prof.; b. Russellville, Ky., July 14, 1888; s. James Henry and Sadie Carlyle (McCarty) M.; B.S., Bethel Coll. (Russellville, Ky.), 1908, M.S., 1910; M.A., Tulane U., 1914; grad. student, U. of Chicago, summers, 1918, 1919, 1921; m. Mamie Dell Wagner, Sept. 9, 1914; 1 dau., Mamie Dell (Mrs. Norman E. Nelson); m. 2d, Myrtle Todd Moore, June 5, 1937; 1 stepson, Aubrey Lee Moore. Prof. chemistry and physics, Okla. Bapt. Coll., 1908-11; instr. chemistry, Peabody Coll., summer, 1914; instr., asst. prof., asso. prof., prof. chemistry, Tulane U., 1911-38, W. R. Irby prof. chemistry since 1938, chmn. dept., 1918-28, head since 1928. Fellow A.A.A.S., Am. Inst. of Chemists, New Orleans Acad. of Sciences (pres. 1938-39); mem. Am. Chem. Soc. (pres. La. sect. 1923-25 and 1931-33; now mem. nat. council), Am. Assn. Univ. Profs. (mem. council 1933-36), Phi Gamma Delta, Alpha Chi Sigma, Sigma Xi, Phi Phi, Kappa Delta Phi. Democrat. Baptist. Clubs: Round Table, Audubon Golf (New Orleans, La.). Contbg. editor Jour. of Chem. Edn.; articles on chemistry in various jours. Home: 1512 Pine St., New Orleans, La. Died Aug. 25, 1941.

MOSES, Andrew, army officer; b. Burnet County, Tex., June 6, 1874; s. Norton and Lucy Ann (Lewis) M.; student U. of Tex.; B.S., U.S. Mil. Acad., 1897, Sch. of Submarine Defense, 1906, Army War Coll., 1921; m. Jessie Fisher, Sept. 24, 1897; 1 dau., Kathleen (wife of Frank Fenton Reed, U.S. Army). Commd. add. 2d lt., inf., U.S. Army, June 11, 1897, 2d lt. arty., Mar. 8, 1898, and advanced through grades to col., July 1, 1920; brig. gen., Sept. 19, 1929; major general, December 1, 1935. Member General Staff, Nov. 14, 1914-Aug. 16, 1917; brig. gen. (temp.), June 26, 1918-Mar. 15, 1920; comdg. 156th Brigade F.A. (81st Div.) in U.S. and France; chmn. joint bd. for redelivery of troop transports, 1919-20; comdt. cadets, Agrl. and Mech. Coll., Tex., 1907-11, also Nat. Guard and organized reserves duty in various states; dir. Army War Coll., 1921-23, 1928-29; comdg. Coast and Antiaircraft Arty. Defenses, Panama Canal, 1930-31; asst. chief of Staff, War Dept., Oct. 8, 1931-Oct. 7, 1935; on duty Army Group, Washington, D.C., Oct. 8, 1935-Feb. 6, 1936; comdg. Hawaiian Div. and Schofield Barracks, Mar. 11, 1936-July 30, 1937; comdg. Hawaiian Dept., 1937-38; retired June 30, 1938. Awarded D.S.M. Mem. Am. Legion, Mil. Order World War. Mason. Club: Army and Navy (Washington). Address: 5830 Chevy Chase Parkway, Washington. Died Dec. 22, 1946; buried in Arlington National Cemetery.

MOSES, George Higgins, ex-senator; b. Lubec, Maine, Feb. 9, 1869; s. Rev. Thomas Gannett and Ruth (Smith) M.; A.B., Dartmouth, 1890, A.M., 1893; LL.D., George Washington, 1921, Dartmouth, 1928; Litt.D., Lincoln Memorial, 1929; m. Florence Abby Gordon, Oct. 3, 1893; 1 son, Gordon. Pres. Monitor and Statesman County, Concord, 1898-1918; pvt. sec. to gov. of N.H., 1889-91, 1905; sec. to chmn. Rep. State Com., 1890; sec. State Forestry Commn., 1893-1906; mem. Bd. of Edn., Concord, 1902-03, 1906-09, 1913-16; del. at large Rep. Nat. Conv., 1908, 16, 28 (permanent chmn.), 32, 36, 40; E.E. and M.P. to Greece and Montenegro, 1909-12. Elected U.S. senator from N.H., Nov. 5, 1918, for unexpired term, ending 1921; reëlected for terms, 1921-33; pres. pro tempore of the Senate, Mar. 6, 1925-Mar. 4, 1933; chmn. Rep. Senatorial Campaign Com., 1924-30; pres. New Hampshire Constitutional Convention, 1938. Conglist. Clubs: Passaconaway, Athenian; Army and Navy. Nat. Press (Washington); Lotos (New York); Union (Boston). Home: Concord, N.H. Died Dec. 20, 1944.

MOSES, Horace Augustus, mfr. paper; b. Ticonderoga, N.Y., Apr. 21, 1862; s. Henry H. and Emily J. (Rising) M.; grad. Troy Conf. Acad., Poultney, Vt., 1881; m. Alice Elliott, 1895. Engaged in paper mfg. since 1881, beginning with Agawam Paper Co.; organized Mittineague Paper Co., 1892; consolidated same with Woronoco Paper Co., 1911, into Strathmore Paper Co., of which is chairman of board; president West Springfield Trust Co.; chmn. bd. Rising Paper Co.; dir. Premoid Products, Old Colony Envelope Co. Largely interested in developing closer relationship between city and country and improving position of farmer. Hon. pres. Hampden County Improvement League; hon. pres. Jr. Achievement, Inc.; honorary pres., N.Y. State Historical Assn., 1945. Trustee Boston U., Wesleyan Univ., Deerfield Acad., Service League Foundation, N.Y. State Hist. Assn., Trinity M.E. Ch., Springfield; mem. bd. dirs. Life Extension Inst., Eastern States Expn., Eastern States Farmers' Exchange, Eastern State Cooperative Milling Corp., Springfield Y.M.C.A. Republican. Mason. Clubs: Rotary, University, Colony, Longmeadow Country (Springfield); Republican Club of Massachusetts; Union League (New York). Home: Russell, Mass., also 55 Riverview Terrace, Springfield 8. Office: West Springfield, Mass. Died Apr. 22, 1947.

MOSES, John, U.S. senator; b. Strand, Norway, June 12, 1885; s. Henrik B. and Isabelle Desiree (Eckersberg) M.; high school and junior college edn., Oslo, Norway; A.B., U. of N.D., 1914, J.D., 1915; m. Ethel Lilian Joslyn, June 29, 1918; children—John Ramsey, James Joslyn, Mary Jean, Robert Henrik. Came to U.S., 1905, naturalized, 1914. Clerk, Oslo, Norway, 1902-05; section and farm laborer, Benson, Minn., 1905-06; clerk, later freight claim investigator, Great Northern Ry., St. Paul, Minn., 1906-11; sec. Valley City (N.D.) Teachers Coll., 1911-12; admitted to N.D. bar, 1915, and practiced in Hazen, N.D., 1915-38; states atty., Mercer County, 1919-23, 1927-33; pres., Union State Bank, Hazen. Dem. candidate for atty. gen. of N.D., 1934, gov., 1936; elected gov. of N.D., 1938, for term 1939-41, re-elected, 1940, for term 1941-43; re-elected, 1942, for term 1943-45; elected U.S. senator for term, 1945-51. Decorated Comdr. Order of St. Olaf by King Haakon of Norway, 1940. Mem. Am. Bar Assn., N.D. State Bar Assn., N.D. State Hist. Soc. (dir.), Sigma Nu. Lutheran. Mason (Shriner; Grand Master Grand Lodge, A.F. & A.M. of North Dakota, 1941-42). Elk. Home: Hazen, N.D. Office: State Capitol, Bismarck, N.D. Died Mar. 3, 1945.

MOSHER, Esek Ray (mō'zhēr), educator; b. Dexter, Mich., Apr. 15, 1882; s. Roswell Curtis and Margaret Emily (Kane) M.; B.A., U. of Minn., 1903; A.M., Western Reserve U., 1907; Ed.M., Harvard U., 1921, Ed.D., 1924; m. Eleanor Marie Schmidt, Aug. 23, 1911; children—Paul Ray, Thomas Edward. Prof. of mathematics and commandant, State Manual Training Sch., Ellendale, N.D., 1904-06; supervisor of instrn., Evening Sch. System, Cleveland, O., 1906-07; prof. mathematics, State Normal Coll., Dillon, Mont., 1907-21, v.p., 1912-21, acting pres., 1919; prof. of ednl. psychology, State Teachers Coll., Salem, Mass., 1921-23; prof. of edn., U. of N.C., 1923-32, dir. of training, 1926-32; asso. prof. of edn., Coll. of the City of N.Y., 1932-37, prof. since 1937, acting dean, Sch. of Edn., 1939-40, dean since 1940. Mem. N.E.A., Am. Assn. Univ. Profs., Phi Delta Kappa. Mason. Author articles on ednl. subjects. Home: 35 Hamilton Place, New York, N.Y. Died Oct. 30, 1944.

MOSHER, William Eugene, univ. prof.; b. Syracuse, N.Y., Nov. 26, 1877; s. George A. and Laura (Coleman) M.; A.B., Oberlin, 1899 (LL.D.); student U. of Berlin, 1902-03; Halle, 1903-04, Ph.D.; private study, Berlin, 1905-06; m. Laura M. Camp, June 20, 1905; children—Horace B., William E., Richard T., Frederick C., Henry C. Instr., 1904-05, prof. German lang. and lit., 1905-18, Oberlin Coll.; with Bur. Municipal Research, New York, 1918-24; spl. agent U.S. Dept. Labor, 1918; mem. staff employment management courses under War Industries Bd., 1918-19; asso. dir. of staff of Joint Commn. on Reclassification of Salaries, Washington, 1919-20; made survey of employment policy, Post-Office Dept., Washington, 1921; staff N.Y. Legislative Commn. on Taxation and Retrenchment, 1922-24; sec. Com. on Civil Service of Nat. Municipality League and Govt. Research Conf., 1922-23; now prof. polit. science and dean Maxwell Grad. Sch. of Citizenship and Public Affairs, Syracuse University. Dir. Research Legislative Commn., public utility laws, N.Y., 1929. Dir. electric rate survey Federal Power Commission, 1934-35, consultant to same, 1935; consultant Foreign Econ. Adminstrn., 1943-44 and to State Dept., 1944. Member of Political Science Assn. (member council 1929-31, 1st vice-president 1937), National Municipal League (honorary vice-president), Govt. Research Assn. (chmn. exec. com. 1939-40), Am. Soc. Pub. Adminstrn. (pres. 1940), City Managers Assn., Nat. Assembly Civil Service Commission, Am. Assn. Univ. Profs., Oberlin Alumni Assn. (pres. 1932-35). Conglist. Author: Albrecht von Hallers Usong, 1905; Willkommen in Deutschland, 1906; (with Dr. F. G. Jenney) Deutsches Lern und Lesebuch, 1913. Author: (with F. G. Crawford) Public Utility Regulation, 1933. Co-author and editor of Electrical Utilities Crisis in Public Control, 1929; (with James C. Bonbeight), Public Regulation of Private Electric and Gas Utilities (for World Power Conf.); (with D. Kingsley) Public Personnel Administration, 1935. Ed. and contr. to Pub. Relations of Pub. Pers. Agencies, 1941. Editor and contbr. Introduction to Responsible Citizenship; contbr. to H. C. Metcalf's "Business Management as a Profession"; also reports and articles on civil service and utility regulation. Editor of Repts. Electric Rate Survey. Home: 310 Berkeley Drive, Syracuse, N.Y. Died June 1, 1945.

MOSS, Leslie Bates, clergyman; b. Minneapolis, Minn., Apr. 1, 1889; s. Charles H. and Nellie (Bates) M.; B.S., Denison U., 1911, D.D., 1935; student Newton (Mass.) Theol. Inst., 1912-14; M.A., Harvard, 1915; Litt.D., Fla. Southern Coll., Lakeland, Fla., 1942; m. Marion F. Venn, June 2, 1915. Ordained Bapt. minister, 1915; ednl. missionary, Am. Bapt. Foreign Mission Soc., U. of Nanking, China, also dean Junior Coll., 1915-20; alumni sec., Denison U., 1921-22; sec. China Union Universities (N.Y. office), 1922-24; sec. Fgn. Missions Conf. of N.A., 1924-40; exec. dir. Ch. Com. on Overseas Relief and Reconstrn., 1940-46; executive, Church World Service, since May, 1946, coordinating overseas relief program of maj. Protestant denominations; it also acts as church liaison with govt. and govt. agencies in this field. Mem. board trustees Shanghai Am. Sch. Phi Beta Kappa, Phi Delta Kappa. Author: Adventures in Missionary Cooperation, 1930; Brushing Elbows, 1937; Who Holds the Key, 1938; The Church Builds for Tomorrow, 1939; Strength for Giants, 1940; Alert, 1941. Contbr. numerous articles in nat. ch. and secular publs. Commentator on Blue Network program, This World of Ours and other radio series, 1936-45. Home: 10 Lester Place, White Plains, N.Y. Office: 214 E. 21st St., New York 10, N.Y. Died Apr. 2, 1949; buried Gibbon, Neb.

MOSS, Louis John, lawyer; b. Hungary, Feb. 12, 1884; s. Michael and Jennie (Friedman) M.; brought to U.S., 1887; A.B., Coll. of the City of N.Y., 1903; LL.B., St. Lawrence U., 1907; m. Bryna Finegold, Jan. 15, 1922; children — Esther Myra Jamieson, Judith, Henry Samuel. Admitted to N.Y. bar, 1907, and since in practice in Brooklyn; mem. firm Moss & Merrell, 1921-25, resumed individual practice, 1945. Mem. Draft Board during World War; now mem. legal advisory bd. under Selective Service Act. Mem. exec. com., Temple of Religion, N.Y. World's Fair, 1939-40. Mem. Brooklyn Bar Assn. (com. on ethics), United Synagogue of America (pres., mem. exec. com. of Am. Jewish Com.), Jewish Edn. Com. of N.Y. (exec. com.), Brooklyn Region Zionist Orgn. of America (hon. pres.), United Palestine Appeal (adminstrn. com.), Synagogue Council of America (adminstrn. com.), Brooklyn Jewish Community Council (v.p.). Mem. exec. bd. Nat. Conf. of Christians and Jews. Democrat. Jewish religion (trustee Congregation Baith Israel). Home: 319 St. Johns Pl. Office: 32 Court St., Brooklyn, N.Y. Died Mar. 18, 1948.

MOSS, William Washburn, judge; b. Stonington, Conn., Mar. 10, 1872; s. William Chesbrough and Alice (Washburn) M; A.B., Brown U., 1894; A.M., 1895; LL.B., Harvard Univ., 1899; m. Julia Trent Howard, June 19, 1906; children—Alice Washburn (Mrs. Waldemar Arent Backlund), Mary Louise (Mrs. Donald Pitkin Tucker), Margaret Lynne (Mrs. Paul Coyte Pape), Peyton Howard, William Washburn. Admitted to R.I. bar and Mo. bar, 1899; practiced law in Kansas City, 1899-1902; returned to R.I., 1902 and practiced law in Providence, 1902-34; asst. atty. gen. of R.I., Jan. 1, 1933-Jan. 1, 1935; asso. justice of the R.I. Supreme Court since Jan. 1, 1935. Mem. Providence Sch. Com., 1910-18 and 1919-20; pres. Providence Chamber of Commerce, 1930-32. Mem. Am. and R.I. bar assns., Am. Law Inst., Soc. of Mayflower Descendants, Soc. of Colonial Wars, Soc. of Founders and Patriots, Phi Beta Kappa, Delta Upsilon. Democrat. Episcopalian. Clubs: Providence Art, British Empire, Turks Head, Churchman's (Providence). Home: 27 Angell St. Address: County Court House, Providence, R.I. Died Dec. 15, 1949.

MOSSMAN, Frank E. (mŏs'măn), coll. pres.; b. Urbana, Benton County, Ia., Aug. 26, 1873; s. David C. and Mary E. (Cross) M.; grad. Tilford Collegiate Acad. (Ia.), 1893; A.B., Morningside Coll., Sioux City, Ia., 1903, M.A., 1905; U. of Chicago, 1904-05; D.D., Upper Ia. U., 1909; LL.D., Southwestern College, Winfield, Kan., 1929; m. Zoa H. Foster, Mar. 27, 1895; children—Mereb E., Nina Benita, Hobart Foster, Frank Homer. Pres. Southwestern Coll., Winfield, Kan., 1905-18, Morningside Coll., 1918-31; again pres. Southwestern Coll., June 1, 1931, emeritus since June 1, 1942. Mem. Gen. Conf. M.E. Ch. 8 times

Republican. Mason (32°). Rotarian. Home: Winfield, Kan. Died June 12, 1945.

MOTE, Carl Henry (mōt), lawyer; b. Randolph County, Ind., June 25, 1884; s. Oliver P. and Emma Alice (Thomas) M.; Quaker ancestry; student Ind. U., 1902-04; A.B., De Pauw U., 1907; student Ind. Law Sch., 1910-12; m. Mary Hook, Nov. 14, 1914 (divorced Feb. 2, 1932); children—Carl H., Jr., David, Martha; m. 2d, Blanche Shaw, Apr. 2, 1936 (divorced 1941). Served as supt. of schools, Parker City, Ind., 1907-08; prin. high sch., Union City, Ind., 1908-09; city editor Muncie (Ind.) Star, 1909-10; reporter Indianapolis Star, 1910-11; editor Indianapolis Sun (now Times), 1911-13; spl. asst., Ind. Legislative Bur., 1913-16; chmn. Gov.'s Legislative Council, 1917; sec. Pub. Service Commn., Ind., 1917-20; admitted to Ind. bar, 1921, and began practice at Indianapolis; pres. Northern Ind. Telephone Co., Commonwealth Telephone Corp.; atty. and chief counsel for numerous pub. utility cos. in reorgn. and mergers since 1921; chief counsel in consol. electric and heating properties, Indianapolis, 1926-27. Pres. Nat. Farmers Guild, since 1944. Candidate for Rep. nomination for U.S. Senator, 1944. Mem. Indianapolis Bar Assn., Am. Hist. Assn., Ind. Soc. of Chicago, Delta Tau Delta, Theta Delta Chi. Mason (32°). Clubs: Woodstock, Contemporary (Indianapolis). Author: Industrial Arbitration, 1914; (with John A. Lapp) Learning to Earn, 1915; The New Deal Goose Step, 1939. Editor and publisher, America Preferred, 1943. Home: 5685 Central Av., Indianapolis, Ind. Died Apr. 29, 1946.

MOTHERWELL, Robert Burns, II (mŭth-ẽr-wĕl), banker; b. Logan, O., Nov. 22, 1884; s. Robert Burns and Louise (Reich) M.; student Western Reserve U., Cleveland, O., 1903-07; studied law, U. of Ore., 1908, 09; m. Margaret Lillian Hogan, Mar. 4, 1914; children—Robert Burns, III, Mary-Stuart. Settled in Aberdeen, Wash., 1910; officer and dir. Aberdeen State Bank, 1910-17; dep. bank commr., State of Wash., 1917-19; asst. chief examiner Fed. Reserve Bank of San Francisco, 1919-20; mgr. Fed. Reserve Bank, Salt Lake City, 1920-25; mng. dir. Los Angeles Br. Fed. Reserve Bank of San Francisco, 1925; v.p. Wells Fargo Bank and Union Trust Co. of San Francisco, 1927-35, pres. since Jan. 10, 1935. Mem. Phi Delta Phi. Episcopalian. Clubs: Pacific Union, San Francisco Golf (San Francisco). Home: Middlefield Farm, Indian Valley, Novato, Calif. Office: Wells Fargo Bank and Union Trust Co., San Francisco, Calif.* Died Aug. 29, 1944.

MOTT, James Wheaton, congressman; b. Clearfield County, Pa., Nov. 12, 1883; s. William Sunderland (M.D.) and Willetta May (Bunn) M.; student U. of Ore., 1902-04, Stanford, 1906-08; A.B., Columbia, 1909; LL.B., Willamette U., 1917; m. Ethel Lucille Walling, Dec. 14, 1919; children—Frances Anne, Dorothy May, Beverly Jane. In practice of law at Astoria, Oregon, 1917-29; city attorney, Astoria, 1920-22; moved to Salem, Oregon, 1929; corporation commr. of Ore., 1931-32. Served in U.S. Navy, 1918. Mem. Ore. Ho. of Rep., 1922, 24, 26, 30; mem. 73d to 78th Congresses (1933-45), 1st Ore. Dist. Mem. Ore. State and Marion County bar assns., Am. Legion, Forty and Eight, Sons of Am. Revolution, Sigma Chi, Acacia. Republican. Presbyterian. Elk, Grange. Club: University (Washington, D.C.). Home: Salem, Ore. Died Nov. 12, 1945.

MOTT, John Griffin, lawyer; b. Los Angeles, Calif., Aug. 3, 1874; s. Thomas D. and Ascension (Sepulveda) M.; ed. St. Vincent's Coll., Los Angeles; B.L. and LL.B., Notre Dame U.; M.L., Catholic U. of America; m. Lila Jean Fairchild, Feb. 23, 1905. Practiced at Los Angeles since 1896, first as mem. firm Mott & Dillon; for many years member Mott, Vallée & Grant (now Mott & Grant); specialized in probate and corporation law; dir. Citizens Nat. Trust & Savings Bank; chmn. bd. Associated Telephone Co.; v.p. and dir. Nat. Title Ins. Co.; pres. Crags Land Co. Led in movement to consolidate a part of San Pedro with Los Angeles, also in campaign to finance constrn. of Owen River Aqueduct, and in numerous civic activities. Mem. Am. Bar Assn., State Bar of Calif., Los Angeles County Bar Assn. (pres. 1925), S.R., Native Sons of Golden West. Mem. Bur. of Catholic Charities. Del. Rep. Nat. Conv., Chicago, 1916, Cleveland, 1936, and Philadelphia, 1940. Clubs: California, Crags Country. Home: 2629 Portland St. Office: Citizens Nat. Bank Bldg., Los Angeles, Calif. Died July 23, 1942.

MOTT, Omer Hillman, pub., author; b. Buffalo, N.Y., Apr. 30, 1891; s. Lawrence Mansfield and Catherine Worthington (Hillman) M.; A.B., St. John's Coll., 1913; M.A., Columbia, 1917, Ph.D., 1927; research, Oxford, Eng., 1925; m. Betty Ruth, Dec. 2, 1942. Began as teacher, 1918; Instructor Greek, St. John's University, Minn., 1918-20; professor classical languages and head of department, Belmont, N.C., 1921-24; lector in theology, Fort Augustus Abbey, Inverness-shire, Scotland, 1924-25; tutor in Sanskrit, dept. of Indo-Iranian langs., Columbia, 1926-28. Mem. editorial bd. The Living Age; lit. editor U.S. Law Rev. and N.Y. Law Review, 1939-41. Trustee The Arden Sch., S.I., N.Y. Mem. Royal Asiatic Soc. of Gt. Britain and Ireland, Agrégé de la Société Mabillon, Am. Catholic Philos. Assn. Club: Richmond County Country (S.I., N.Y.). Author: A Compendium of Beuronese Art, 1917; Religious Inquiries—A Prolegomenon to Theological Reconstruction (with Robert Leet Patterson), 1938; Utility as the Norm of Law, 1941. Address: Country Club, Dongan Hills, N.Y. Deceased.

MOTT, William Elton, civil engr.; b. Burlington, N.J., Jan. 24, 1868; s. Richard Field and Susan (Thomas) M.; U. of Pa., 1884-85; S.B. in C.E., Mass. Inst. Tech., 1889; m. Amy Coughlin, Aug. 20, 1891 (died Dec. 11, 1905); children—Margaret Burling, Katharine; married 2d, Oli Coughlin, Dec. 26, 1911 (died Aug. 12, 1945). Instructor civil engineering, Massachusetts Institute Tech., 1889-90; instr. and asst. prof. civ. engring. Cornell U., 1892-1905; asso. prof. hydraulic engring., Mass. Inst. Tech., 1905-09; prof. civ. engring., 1909-17, dean and dir. Coll. of Engring., 1917-32, Carnegie Inst. Tech., Pittsburgh, Pa.; retired Jan. 1933. Pres. Library Co. of Burlington, Asso. Charities; dir. Bur. Savings Inst., Burlington Coll. Asso. mem. Am. Soc. C.E.; mem. A.A.A.S., Soc. Promotion Engring. Edn., Am. Forestry Assn., Theta Xi, Sigma Xi, Tau Beta Pi. Republican. Episcopalian (vestryman, St. Mary's Ch.). Home: 315 Wood St., Burlington, N.J. Died Oct. 5, 1945.

MOULTON, Charles Robert, chemist; b. Clifton, Pa., Sept. 16, 1884; s. Charles Lewis and Maria Ross (Harper) M.; academic certificate, Lewis Inst., Chicago, 1903; B.S. in Chem. Engring., U. of Ill., 1907; M.S. in Agr., U. of Mo., 1909, Ph.D., 1911; m. Edith Ione Lehnen, June 24, 1911; children—Ruth Elizabeth, Marjorie. Asst. agrl. chemistry, 1907-10, instr. in agrl. chemistry, 1910-11, asst. prof., 1912-18, asst. in animal nutrition, Inst. of Animal Nutrition, 1917-18, prof., 1918-22, U. of Mo.; dir. Dept. of Nutrition, Inst. of Am. Meat Packers, 1923-33; lecturer Inst. of Meat Packing, Univ. of Chicago, 1926-32; lecturer Schs. of Speech and Edn., Northwestern Univ., 1933-37; cons. chemist since 1935; curator dept. of chemistry, Museum of Science and Industry, Chicago, 1937-40; lecturer Ill. Inst. of Tech., 1941-42; personnel dir., metallurgical lab., U. of Chicago, 1942-43, research asso., 1942-43; technical adviser, Chicago O.S.R.D. Patent Group, 1943-46; asst. dir., Chicago Patent Group, Argonne Natl. Lab., since 1946; tech. editor Meat Mag., 1934-35, mng. ed., 1935-37, ed., 1937-40; consulting ed., The National Provisioner, 1941-42. Fellow A.A.A.S., American Public Health Association; member American Chem. Soc., Am. Inst. Nutrition, Inst. Food Technologists, Am. Soc. Animal Production, Research Council, Sigma Xi, Phi Lambda Upsilon, Alpha Chi Sigma, Gamma Sigma Delta. Author: Meat Through the Microscope; also sect. on meat, meat products, poultry, eggs, fish in Vol. IX of Allen's Commercial Organic Analysis. Editor and joint author "The Service of Science in the Packing Industry"; also jt. author (with H. P. Armsby) of "The Animal as a Converter of Matter and Energy." Home: 5602 Dorchester Av. Office: Argonne National Laboratory, Chicago, Ill. Died Dec. 4, 1949.

MOULTON, Sherman Roberts, judge; b. N.Y. City, June 10, 1876; s. Clarence Freeman and Annie Jane (Roberts) M.; A.B., Dartmouth, 1898; LL.B., Harvard, 1901; LL.D., Boston U., 1942; D.C.L., U. of Vermont, 1945; m. Stella Allen Platt, June 20, 1906; 1 son, Horace Platt. Admitted to Vt. bar, 1901, U.S. Dist. Court, Vt., 1902, U.S. Circuit Court of Appeals, 1903; asst. atty. Rutland R.R. Co., 1902-03; mem. Cowles & Moulton, Burlington, 1903-11, Cowles, Moulton & Stearns, 1911-12, alone, 1912-19; exec. clk. to Gov. Charles W. Gates, 1915-17; reporter of decisions, Supreme Court of Vt., 1916-19; mem. Vt. Senate, 1919; judge Superior Court of Vt., 1919-26, chief judge, 1926; asso. justice, Supreme Court of Vt., 1926-38, chief justice, 1938-49; retired Apr. 1, 1949. Mem. Vt. Commn. on Uniform State Laws, since 1940. Mem. American and Vermont bar associations, Alpha Delta Phi, Phi Beta Kappa, Casque and Gauntlet. Republican. Conglist. Mason. Home: 178 S. Prospect St., Burlington, Vt. Died June 16, 1949; buried Moulton Family Cemetery, Randolph, Vt.

MOULTON, Warren Joseph, theologian; b. Sandwich, N.H., Aug. 30, 1865; s. Gilman and Lydia Ann (Dearborn) M.; student Boston U., 1884-85; B.A., Amherst, 1888, M.A., 1893, D.D., 1908; B.D., Yale, 1893, Hooker fellow, 1893-95; studied U. of Göttingen, 1895-98, Ph.D., 1898; LL.D., U. of Maine, 1921; m. Helen Winifred Shute, June 21, 1900. Teacher Semitic and Bibl. Dept., Yale, 1898-1902; ordained Congl. ministry, 1899; traveled, mainly in Palestine and Middle East, 1902-03; pastor, mainly at Athol, Mass., 1903-05, asso. prof. N.T. lang. and lit. and corr. sec., 1905-08, Hayes prof. N.T. lang. and lit., 1908-33, pres., 1921-33, pres. emeritus since 1933, Bangor Theol. Sem. Resident dir. Am. Sch. of Oriental Research in Jerusalem, 1912-13, hon. lecturer at same sch., 1935-36, treas. of Am. Schools of Oriental Research (Jerusalem and Baghdad), 1936-46; pres. Conf. of Theol. Seminaries and Colleges of U.S. and Canada, 1932-34; gov. of 38th Dist. of Rotary Internat., 1933-34; pres. Interdenominational Commn. of Maine since 1934; pres. Maine Sea Coast Mission, pres. Penobscot Co. Assn. for the Blind since 1940; pres. board managers of Bangor Public Library since 1934; trustee of the Alfred Quimby Fund for the town of Sandwich, N.H. Member Archæological Institute of America, Phi Bet Kappa, Theta Delta Chi, Soc. Bibl. Lit. and Exegesis (pres. 1917), Palestine Exploration Fund, The Palestine Oriental Society. Clubs: Rotary, 20th Century, Executives (Bangor). Contributor Hastings' Dictionary of the Bible, Dictionary of Christ and the Gospels, Yale Bicentennial Bibl. and Semitic Studies, Ency. of Religion and Ethics, Papers of Am. School of Oriental Research in Jerusalem, Annual of Am. Schools of Oriental Research, and jours. Editor Annual of Am. Sch. of Oriental Research, 1921-22. Address: Hannibal Hamlin House, 15 5th St., Bangor, Me. Died May 7, 1947.

MOUNT, Arnold John, banker; b. Mayfield, Calif., Oct. 7, 1884; s. William and Huldah (Dietz) M.; ed. pub. schs.; m. Marion Leigh Seybolt, Aug. 5, 1908; children—John Arnold, Barbara Leigh, Mary Elizabeth. Began with Bank of Palo Alto, 1900; chmn. bd. The Bank of Commerce, Oakland, Calif. Republican. Mason. Club: Claremont Country (Oakland, Calif.). Home: 25 Oakridge Road, Berkeley, Calif. Office: Washington, 16th and San Pablo, Oakland, Calif. Died Dec. 17, 1942.

MOUSER, Grant Earl, Jr. (mou'zẽr), ex-congressman; b. Marion, O., Feb. 20, 1895; s. Grant Earl and Della (Ridgway) M.; Ohio Wesleyan University, 1913-14; LL.B., Ohio State U., 1917; grad. Army Med. Sch., 1918; m. Hilda Gorham, Nov. 7, 1918; children—Gwendolen Shethar, Grant Earl III, Harold Gorham. Admitted to Ohio bar, 1917, and began practice at Marion, 1920, as mem. firm Justice, Young & Mouser; now Mouser & Mouser. City solicitor, Marion, 1924-27; spl. counsel, office of atty. gen. of Ohio, 1927-29; atty. for Ohio State Highway Dept., 1927-28; mem. 71st and 72d Congresses (1929-33), 8th Ohio Dist. With Western Reserve U. Coll. Ambulance Unit, Aug. 1917 to Aug. 30, 1919; 2d lt., Med. Corps, U.S. Army, 1918. Mem. Am. Legion (past comdr. post), Phi Delta Phi, Phi Gamma Delta. Republican. Presbyn. Mason, Elk, Eagle. Home: 527 E. Church St. Office: 133 E. Center St., Marion, O. Died Dec. 21, 1943.

MOWBRAY, Albert H(enry) (mō'brā), coll. prof.; b. San Francisco, Calif., Mar. 30, 1881; s. Robert Henry and Julia Amanda (Brown) M.; A.B., U. of Calif., 1904; m. Elizabeth Gray, Mar. 23, 1913; children—Mary Elizabeth, Albert Gray. Actuarial clerk, N.Y. Life Ins. Co., 1905-07; actuary, N.C. State Ins. Dept., 1907-08, Calif. State Ins. Dept., 1908-10, Liberty Mutual Ins. Co., Boston, 1913-18, Indsl. Commn. N.Y., 1918-20, Nat. Council on Compensation Ins., 1920-23; cons. actuary, 1910-13, since 1923; instr. ins., U. of Calif., 1910-11, asso. prof., 1923-28, prof. since 1928. Actuarial cons., Com. on Econ. Security, 1935; mem. Adv. Council on Social Security Act, 1937-39; consulting actuary, California State Insurance Department. Fellow: Actuarial Soc. America, Am. Statis. Soc., Ins. Inst. America, A.A.A.S., Casualty Actuarial Soc. (pres. 1920-22); mem. Am. Assn. Univ. Profs., Am. Math. Soc., Am. Econ. Soc., Phi Beta Kappa, Sigma Xi, Phi Kappa Sigma. Club: Faculty. Author: Insurance, Its Theory and Practice in the United States, 1930, 37, 46. Home: 866 San Luis Rd., Berkeley 7, Calif. Died Jan. 7, 1949.

MOWER, Charles Drown, naval architect; b. Lynn, Mass., Oct. 5, 1875; s. Charles F. and Juliet (Drown) M.; ed. Lynn public schools; m. Frances Hollingsworth Petrikin, December 7, 1915; 1 son, Charles Petrikin. In office of Arthur Binney, naval architect, in Boston, as draughtsman, 1895-98; with B.B. Crowninshield, naval architect, 1898-99; left in 1899 to become designing editor of The Rudder, New York yachting mag.; official measurer New York Yacht Club, seasons of 1903, 04; measured yachts Shamrock III and Reliance for Am. cup races, 1903. With Navy Dept., 1917-19; pvt. practice since 1919. Republican. Author: How to Build a Motor Launch, 1900; How to Build a Knockabout, 1901; How to Build a Racing Sloop, 1901; How to Build a Cruiser, 1903. Home: Pelham Manor, N.Y. Office: 110 E. 42d St., New York. Died Jan. 17, 1942.

MOYER, James Ambrose (moi'ẽr), educator, engineer; b. Norristown, Pa., Sept. 13, 1877; s. Isaac Kulp and Jane Hunsicker (Grater) M.; E.B., State Teachers College at Westchester, Pa., 1893; S.B., Lawrence Scientific Sch., Harvard, 1899; A.M., Harvard, 1904; m. Dorothy Tremble, May 18, 1922; 1 dau., Jane Modella. Draftsman, 1899-1900; instr. in Harvard, 1901-04, in Harvard Engring. Camp, 1902-04; mech. engr. and chief computer, Gen. Electric Co., 1905-07; gen. engr. Westinghouse, Church, Kerr & Co., New York, 1907-08; asst. prof. mech. engring. in charge mech. and hydraulic labs., U. of Mich., 1908-11; jr. prof. mech. engring., U. of Mich., 1911-12; prof. mech. engring. in charge of dept., Pa. State Coll., 1912-15; dir. Pa. Engring. Expt. Sta. and of univ. extension dept. of Pa., 1913-15; dir. Univ. Extension Mass. Dept. of Edn. since 1915. Pres. Nat. Commn. on Enrichment of Adult Life (N.E.A.); New Eng. rep. U.S. Dept. of Interior, 1917-20; chmn. U.S. com. of scientists on war inventions, 1918-19. Pa. del. First Nat. Conf. on Univ. Extension; past pres. Nat. Assn. Univ. Extension; mem. advisory com. on edn., U.S. Navy; mem. commn. of U.S. Dept. of Interior on edn. by radio broadcasting; advisory bd. Nat. Home Library Foundation; edn. advisory com. World Wide Broadcasting Corp.; v.p. Nat. Acad. Visual Instrn., Am. Assn. for Adult Edn.; sec. Internat. Elec. Congress; mem. visiting com. Univ. Extension, Harvard; mem. state advisory com. on Higher Edn. in Conn.; mem. Survey Commn. on Noncollegiate Tech. Edn., 1928-31; mem. Mass. Com. Pub. Safety (recreation chmn.). Fellow Royal Acad. (London), A.A.A.S., Am. Inst. Genealogy; mem. Am. Acad. Polit. and Social Science, Verein deutscher Ingenieure, Franklin Inst., Am. Soc. M.E., Assn. Internationale du Froid (Paris), Nat. Council of Safety, Engrs. Soc. Pa. Soc. Automotive Engrs. (chmn. New Eng. sect. and mem. nat. council), League of Nations Assn. (dir.), Am. Assn. Refrigerating Engrs., Am. Inst. E.E., Soc. Promotion Engring. Edn., Boston Adult Edn. Council (dir.), Mass. Youth Council, Assn. Harvard Engrs., Lawrence Scientific Assn., Nat. Edn. Assn., Pi Gamma Mu (pres. Boston chapter), Phi Sigma Kappa, etc. Presbyterian. Clubs: City, Harvard, Schoolmasters (Boston); Union (Ann Arbor); Authors' (London). Author: Elements of Descriptive Geometry, 1904; Descriptive Geometry for Engineers, 1905; Internal Combustion Motors, 1905; Steam Turbines, 1905; Power Plant Testing, 1911; Engineering Thermodynamics (with J. P. Calderwood and A. A. Potter), 1915; Gasoline Automobiles, 1921; Marine Steam Turbines, 1922; Oil-burning Boilers, 1923; Practical Radio (with J. F. Wostrel), 1924; Radio Construction and Repairing, 1926; Refrigeration, 1928; Radio Receiving Tubes, 1929; Industrial Electricity, 1930; Radio Handbook, 1931; Air Conditioning, 1933; Oil Fuels and Burners, 1937; Welding, 1942. Editor Bull. of Dept. of Edn.; Enrichment of Adult Life; contbr. to ednl. and engring. jours. Home: 382 Kenrick St., Newton 58, Mass. Address: State House, Boston; and Pa. Bldg., Philadelphia, Pa. Died Nov. 29, 1945.

MOYLE, James Henry (moil), lawyer; b. Salt Lake City, Utah, Sept. 17, 1858; s. James and Elizabeth (Wood) M.; grad. U. of Utah, 1879; LL.B., U. of Mich., 1885; m. Alice E. Dinwoodey, Nov. 17, 1887; children—Henry Dinwoodey, James Hubert (dec.), Alice Evelyn, Walter Gladstone, Gilbert Dinwoodey, James Douglas, Richard Granville (dec.), Sara Virginia. In practice at Salt Lake City since 1885; county atty. Salt Lake County, 1886-90; mem. Utah Ho. of Rep., 1888; trustee 4 yrs., pres. 2 yrs., State Indust. Sch.; chmn. Dem. State Com., 1898 and 1910; Dem. nominee for gov. of Utah, 1900, 04; Dem. and Prog. Republican nominee for U.S. Senate, 1914; asst. sec. U.S. Treasury, Washington, 1917-21; commr. of customs, 1933-39; asst. to sec. of treasury, Sept. 1939-July 1940. Mem. Dem. Nat. Com., 1916-32; pres. Eastern States Mission of the Ch. of Jesus Christ of Latter Day Saints, 1929-33; retired, July 19, 1940. Mem. Am. Anthropol. Assn., Am. Archæol. Assn., A.A.A.S. Home: 73 Fourth East St., Salt Lake City, Utah. Died Feb. 19, 1946.

MOYNIHAN, P. H., ex-congressman; b. Chicago; ed. pub. schs. Engaged in printing and pub. business; now v.p. Calumet Coal Co.; served 4 terms as alderman, Chicago; chmn. and mem. Ill. State Commerce Commn., 8 yrs.; mem. 73d Congress (1933-35), 2d Ill. Dist. Republican. Address: 9022 Commercial Av., Chicago. Died May 20, 1946.

MUDD, William Swearingen, newspaper pub.; b. Birmingham, Ala., Nov. 24, 1885; s. Joseph Paul and Eula (Anglin) M.; B.S., U. of Ala., 1906; LL.B., U. of Va., 1908; m. Nellie Nabers, Nov. 24, 1908; children—William Swearingen, Anne Earle. Admitted to Ala. bar, 1908, and practiced until 1913; actively identified with real estate, theatre, newspaper and hotel business since 1913; pres. Tuscaloosa (Ala.) News, Gadsden (Ala.) Times, Rome (Ga.) News Tribune; chmn. bd. Etowah Hotel Co. Mem. Phi Delta Theta, Phi Delta Phi. Democrat. Presbyterian. Mason (32°). Author: The Old Boat Rocker, 1935; also The Prodigal Has Returned—and How? (short story). Home: 924 Essex Road, Birmingham, Ala. Died Sep. 19, 1942.

MUDGE, Alfred Eugene (mŭj), lawyer; b. Brooklyn, N.Y., Jan. 20, 1882; s. Alfred Eugene and Mary G. (Ten Brook) M.; A.B., Cornell U., 1904; LL.B., N.Y. Law Sch., 1905; m. Alice May Horton, Nov. 1, 1910; children—Eugene T., Gilbert H., Elizabeth D.; m. 2d, Marjorie Reeves Young, June 15, 1932. Admitted to N.Y. bar, 1905; in practice in N.Y. City, 1905-15; mem. Rushmore, Bisbee & Stern, 1915-33, succeeded by Mudge, Stern, Williams & Tucker, 1934. Trustee Inst. Arts and Sciences, Bur. of Charities, Y.W.C.A., Brooklyn Hosp.—all of Brooklyn. Republican. Clubs: University, Cornell (New York); Huntington Crescent. Home: 2 Montague Terrace, Brooklyn; and Northport, L.I. Office: 20 Pine St., New York, N.Y. Died Aug. 23, 1945.

MUDGE, Edmund Webster, mfr.; b. Phila., Pa., Jan. 12, 1870; s. Thomas Henry and Mary Emma (Shephard) M.; ed. Friends Sch. and Woods Town (N.J.) Acad.; m. Pauline Seeley, Apr. 4, 1899; children—Mary Louise (dec.), Edmund Webster, Leonard Seeley. Engaged in mfr. of iron and steel, at Pittsburgh, since 1887; head of Edmund W. Mudge & Co.; dir., chmn. finance com. Edgewater Steel Co., Fidelity Title & Trust Co.; dir. Nat. Steel Corp., Mudge Oil Co., Hanna Furnace Corp., Mich. Steel Corp., Stoner-Mudge, Inc. Mem. Pa. Council Nat. Defense, World War. Mem. bd. dirs. Allegheny Gen. Hosp. (exec. com.). Trustee Episcopal Diocese of Pittsburgh, Trinity Cathedral, Y.M.C.A. Republican. Clubs: Pittsburgh, Duquesne, University, Pittsburgh Athletic Association, Longue Vue, Fox Chapel, Rolling Rock (Pittsburgh); Union (Cleveland); Union League (Philadelphia). Home: 1000 Morewood Av. Office: Grant Bldg., Pittsburgh, Pa. Died July 1, 1949.

MUDGE, Lewis Seymour, church official; b. Yonkers, N.Y., Aug. 24, 1868; s. Rev. Lewis Ward (D.D.) and Elizabeth (Seymour) M.; B.A., magna cum laude, Princeton U., 1889, fellow exptl. science, 1889-90, M.A., 1890; instr. mathematics, Princeton, 1892-94; grad. Princeton Theol. Sem., 1895; D.D., Franklin and Marshall, 1910; LL.D., Lafayette Coll., and U. of Dubuque, 1923; m. Caroline Denny Paxton, Feb. 11, 1896 (died Sept. 22, 1922); m. 2d, Anne Evelyn Bolton, Dec. 17, 1925; 1 son, Lewis Seymour, Jr. Ordained Presbyn. ministry, 1895; pastor First Ch., Beverly, N.J., 1895-99, First Ch., Trenton, 1899-1901, First Ch., Lancaster, Pa., 1908-14, Pine Street Ch., Harrisburg, 1914-21; moderator Synod of Pa., 1913-14; mem. Bd. of Edn. of Presbyn. Ch., 1900-03; mem. Gen. Bd. of Edn., 1918-20; mem. exec. commn. Presbyterian Church, 1920-21; stated clerk of General Assembly Presbyn. Ch. U.S.A., 1921-38; stated clerk emeritus since 1938; sec. Gen. Council Presbyn. Gen. Assembly U.S.A., 1923-38; sec. Dept. of Ch. Co-operation and Union, 1923-38, mem., 1923-43; mem. Joint Com. on Organic Union with Protestant Episcopal Ch. since 1937 (chmn. drafting com.); mem. Joint Com. on Reunion with Southern Presbyn. Ch. (chairman drafting com.); moderator Gen. Assembly, 1931-32; acting gen. sec. Bd. of Christian Edn., 1938-40; sec. Sesquicentennial Fund for Christian Edn. ($10,000,000 raised), 1938-41; lecturer on ecclesiastical theology, Princeton Theol. Sem., since 1935. Sec. Joint Com. on Organic Union of Presbyn. Ch. in U.S.A. and Presbyn. Ch. of N. America, 1930-34; sec. spl. commn. apptd. by Presbyn. Gen. Assembly, 1924, for "purity, peace, unity and progress"; trustee of Presbyterian Gen. Assembly since 1921. Speaker under Y.M.C.A. at mil. camps, World War. Mem. exec. com. Federal Council Churches of America; mem. Commn. on Church Unity and Race Relations; vice-pres. trustees Princeton Theol. Seminary; trustee Wilson Coll., Chambersburg, Pa.; chmn. bd. dirs. Presbyn. Ministers' Fund for Life Ins.; president Presbyn. Historical Society; mem. continuation coms. of Faith and Order and of Life and Work conferences; mem. Provisional Com., World Council of Churches; official representative of Ch. at Lausanne, 1927, Edinburgh, 1937, Oxford, 1937, Utrecht, 1938 (when World Council of Churches was organized), and at other nat. and internat. conferences in America and Europe; member World Alliance of Presbyn. Chs. Preacher 1st Presbyn. Ch., Philadelphia, since 1939. Mem. Soc. Founders and Patriots, Phi Beta Kappa. Republican. Clubs: Cleric, Phi Alpha, Adelphoi. Editor, 1921-38, of The Constitution, The Digest. Co-author: Manual of Law of Presbyn. Church U.S.A.; author pamphlets and papers on ecclesiastical law and procedure, published addresses and sermons. Home: New Gulph and Pennswood Roads, Bryn Mawr, Pa. Office: Witherspoon Bldg., Phildelphia, Pa. Died Apr. 29, 1945.

MUEHLING, John Adam (mül'ĭng), publisher; b. Conestoga, Ont., Can., Nov. 26, 1862; s. Adam and Mary (Wagner) M.; ed. pub. schs., Bridgeport, Ont.; m. Martha Green, Feb. 7, 1885; children—Percival (dec.), Lawrence Green (dec.). Came to U.S., 1883, naturalized, 1893. Began as printers' apprentice and advanced through depts. of printing and publishing; pub. Grand Rapids (Mich.) Post, 1898-1900; printer and book binder, 1900-02; alderman and county supervisor, Grand Rapids, 1900-02; treas., business mgr. Sault Ste. Marie (Mich.) Evening News, 1902-12, Manchester (N.H.) Union and Manchester Leader, 1913-40, editor and pub. same, 1925-40; retired. Major on staff of Gov. J. H. Bartlett, 1918-20. Trustee N.H. Sanatorium, Glencliff, since 1927. Mem. N.E. Senior Golfers Assn. Republican. Lutheran. Mason (32°, K.T., Shriner), Elk. Clubs: Derryfield, Manchester Country. Home: 2143 Elm St., Manchester, N.H. Died Apr. 19, 1944.

MUELLER Adolph (mū'lẽr), mfr.; b. Decatur, Ill., May 8, 1866; s. Hieronymus and Fredericka (Bernhardt) M.; prep. edn., high sch. Decatur; student U. of Ill., 1884-86; m. Minnie Bachman, June 14, 1893; children—William Everett, Charles Philip (dec.), Charlotte (Mrs. Frederic E. Schluter). Chmn. bd. Mueller Co., plumbing, water and gas brass goods, Decatur since 1902; pres. Mueller, Ltd. (Sarnia, Ont., Can.); pres. Columbian Iron Works, Chattanooga, Tenn.; dir. Millikin Nat. Bank (Decatur). Republican. Christian Scientist. Mason. Clubs: Decatur, University, Decatur Country. Mem. Com. of One Hundred Club, Miami Beach, Fla. Home: 4 Millikin Pl. Office: 512 W. Cerro Gordo St., Decatur, Ill. Died May 14, 1944.

MUHLFELD, George O. (mīl'fĕld), vice chmn. Stone & Webster, Inc., engring., pub. utilities; also director Stone & Webster Engring. Corp.; dir. and mem. exec. com. Stone & Webster Securities Corp. Home: Highview Rd., Tenafly, N.J. Office: 90 Broad St., New York, N.Y. Died July 8, 1948.

MULHERIN, William Anthony (mŭl-hẽr'ĭn), physician; b. Augusta, Ga., July 3, 1872; s. William Andrew and Mary Anne (Roche) M.; A.B., Spring Hill Coll., Mobile, Ala., 1891, A.M., 1893; post-grad. Johns Hopkins, 1897; M.D., Harvard, 1901; hon. Dr.Sci., U. of Georgia, 1929; m. Hattie Fargo Butler, Sept. 21, 1904; children—Philip Anthony, William Butler (dec.), Charles McLaughlin, Virginia McLaughlin (dec.), William Anthony, Jr. Interne St. Vincent's Hosp., Worcester, Mass., 1901-03; apptd. asso. prof. pediatrics, U. of Ga., 1905, prof. clin. pediatrics since 1923; cons. pediatrician University and Children's hosps. (chmn. med. advisory bd.); apptd. "essential prof." of pediatrics, U. of Ga., 1917, precluding entrance into war; mem. Ga. State Bd. of Health; chmn. Richmond County Board of Health. Dean emeritus Southern Pediatric Seminar; fellow Am. Acad. Pediatrics, one of 5 to organize pediatric sect. of Southern Med. Assn., 1916, sec. of sect., 1919, chmn., 1920; v. chmn. pediatric sect. A.M.A., 1920, chmn. of sect., 1929, also mem. Abraham Jacobi com. of sect., 1922, and mem. com. to study teaching of pediatrics in Am. univs., 1925, and report to sect. with suggestions as to betterments; pres. Ga. State Med. Assn. Organized pediatric socs. in 16 Southern states and D.C., also the Southern Pediatric Seminar; mem. Am. Pediatric Soc. Mem. Phi Kappa Psi, Phi Rho Sigma. Democrat. Catholic. Contbr. to professional jours. Mem. Pres. Hoover's Conf. on Child Health and Protection. Home: 2068 Walton Way. Office: 1211 Greene St., Augusta, Ga.* Died Apr. 1945.

MULHERON, Anne Morton (mŭl-hẽr'ŭn), librarian; retired; b. Detroit, Mich., Nov. 20, 1883; d. John J. (M.D) and Anne (Morton) Mulheron; prep. edn., Liggett Sch. and Detroit Cent. High Sch.; A.B., U. of Mich., 1906; student Western Res. Library Sch., 1907-09, N.Y. State Library Sch., Albany, N.Y., 1916. Began as high sch. librarian, Cleveland, O., 1906; head of open shelf dept. Detroit (Mich.) Pub. Library, 1911; teacher mission sch., Honolulu, T.H., 1913-15; head of order dept. Los Angeles Pub. Library, 1916; war work with A.L.A., at Camp Cody and Ft. Bayard, N.M., and in France, 1918-19; head of sch. dept. Library Assn. of Portland, Ore., 1919-20, librarian, 1920-37; visiting instr. summer school, State System of Higher Edn., 1938-41; member School Board, 1940-42. State chmn. F. D. Roosevelt Library, Inc.; mem. bd. mgrs. Ore. Inst. Tech., 1938-44; pres. Civic Theatre, Portland, 1931-33; mem. bd. Boys' & Girls' Aid Soc., 1940-46; mem. budget com. Community Chest, 1937-42. Mem. A.L.A. (2d v.p., 1926-27), Pacific Northwest Library Assn. (pres. 1926-27), Portland League of Women Voters (pres. 1934-35), Portland Red Cross (v.p. 1935-39; chmn. Jr. Red Cross, chmn. nutrition since 1945), Am. Assn. Univ. Women (pres. 1938-40), Kappa Alpha Theta. Republican. Episcopalian. Home: 3730 S.W. Greenleaf Dr., Portland 1, Ore. Deceased.

MULHOLLAND, Frank L., (mŭl'hŏl-lănd), lawyer; b. Disco, Mich., Apr. 20, 1875; s. Rev. Robert N. and Alice M. (Ostrander) M.; A.B., Albion (Mich.) College, 1896, LL.D., 1927; LL.B., Law Dept. U. of Mich., 1899; m. Maude M. Rutter, Sept. 19, 1900; children—Clarence M., Mrs. Marion A. Cubbedge, Mrs. Margaret C. Hankins. Mem. Mulholland Robie & McEwen; counsel for defendants in Danbury Hatters case; Buck Stove and Range case; Gompers, Morrison, Mitchell Comtempt cases; Duplex Printing Press Co. case; Ark. Full Crew case; Railway Pension case; etc. Co-author of Railway Labor Act of 1934; counsel Railway Labor Executives Assn.; general counsel Railway Employes' Dept., A. F. of L. Lecturer and organizer for War Dept. Commn. on Training Camps, 1917; lecturer for Mil. Entertainment Council, 1917; mem. Publicity Commn. to Western Battle Fronts, 1918; commd. capt. in France, assigned to Red Cross, 1918. Trustee Toledo Univ., 1910-12, Albion Coll., 1930-35. Mem. Toledo Chamber Commerce (pres. 1912-13), Delta Tau Delta. Republican; nominee for Congress, 1916, 34. Methodist. Mason, K.P., Elk. Club: Rotary (pres. 1913-14); pres. Rotary Internat., 1914-15. Home: 2425 Meadowood Drive. Office: Nicholas Bldg., Toledo, O. Died June 7, 1949.

MULLALY, Charles J., clergyman, author; born Washington, D.C., September 19, 1877; s. Charles W. and Catherine (Croghan) M.; ed. Immaculate Conception Sch., Gonzaga High Sch. and Gonzaga Coll., Washington, D.C.; Jesuit scholasticates, Frederick and Woodstock, Md., and Tortosa, Spain. Joined Soc. of Jesus, 1895; instr. Latin and Greek, Fordham Prep. Sch., 1903-06, and headmaster, St. John's Hall, Fordham U., 1906-08; ordained R.C. priest, 1911; European corr. for America, weekly review, 1909-12; prof. Gonzaga Coll., Washington, D.C., 1912-13; dean of discipline, Fordham U., 1914-16; pastor Reading, Jamaica, B.W.I., 1916; asst. editor "The Messenger of the Sacred Heart," 1917-20, editor, 1920-41; national director Apostleship of Prayer (assn. numbering 6,000,000 Catholics in the U.S.), 1920-41; spiritual director of Jesuit students, Novitiate, Wernersville, Pa. Trustee Fordham University; consultor of Permanent Organization for National Eucharistic Congresses. Mem. bd. dirs. Xavier Free Publication Soc. for the Blind, Loyola House of Retreats (Morristown, N.J.), Shrine of Our Lady of Martyrs (Auriesville, N.Y.). Vice-pres. Cath. Press Assn., 1921-22, treas., 1938-39. Author: Spiritual Reflections for Sisters, Vol. 1, 1936, Vol. 2, 1938; The Priest Who Failed, 1936; Could You Explain Catholic Practices?, 1937; The Bravest of the Virginia Cavalry, 1937; also pamphlets. Contbr. to The Cath. Encyclopedia, and foreign and Am. reviews. Home: Jesuit Novitiate, Wernersville, Pa. Died Oct. 25, 1949.

MULLALLY, Thornwell (mŭl'lăl-ĭ), lawyer; b. Columbia, S.C.; s. Francis P. and Elizabeth Keith (Adger) M.; student Adger Coll., S.C., U. of S.C.; grad. Hopkins Grammar Sch., New Haven, Conn., 1888; A.B. with honors, Yale, 1892, awarded Thomas Glasby Waterman scholarship prize jr. and sr. yrs.; law study U. of Va.; LL.B., New York Law Sch., 1894; unmarried. With law firm Betts, Atterbury, Hyde & Betts, N.Y. City, 18[illegible]-93; admitted to N.Y. bar, 1894; with Alexander & Green, N.Y. City, 1893-94; mem. firm Atterbury & Mullaly, 1894-1906; asst. to pres. Market St. Rys. (st. ry., San Francisco, Calif.), 1906-17, in charge during San Francisco earthquake and fire, 1906, safeguarding company's property and maintaining valuable service to stricken city, rapidly restored street car transportation (mem. Committee of 50 and Transportation Committee of provisional govt.); chairman committee for removal all debris; specializing in corp. and business law since 1919. Mem. Squadron A, Cav., N.G.N.Y., 1894-99; organizer and comdr. San Francisco Cav. Troop, 1915-17; organizer 2d Calif. F.A. and commd. lt. col. of regt., Aug. 3, 1917, mustered into federal service as 144th F.A., U.S. Army, of which served as col. Oct. 13, 1917-Jan. 3, 1919; also comdr. 65th F.A. Brig. for a time in France; commd. col. F.A., O.R.C., 1919; commd. brig. gen. O.R.C., Dec. 23, 1921, brig. gen. Aux. Res., Dec. 23, 1926; comdr. 188th Arty. Brig., 1923-26; recommd. brig. gen. Aux. U.S. Army, 1926, 1936; brig. gen. Inactive Service since 1936; awarded

D.S.M. for services with 144th F.A. Mem. bd. dirs. Panama-Pacific Internat. Expn., 1915, chmn. spl. events com., mem. concessions com., and in charge opening day ceremonies; mem. Advisory Commn. for San Francisco, and mem. State Participation Comm., Golden Gate Internat. Expn., 1939; organizer and grand marshal "Preparedness Day Parade," San Francisco, 1916. Mem. Assn. Bar City of New York, Assn. Army of U.S. (an organizer; 1st nat. comdr.), Assn. Ex-mems. Squadron A, Am. Legion, Vets. of Foreign Wars; hon. mem. Spanish War Vets. Presbyn. Clubs: Bohemian, Army and Navy (hon.), Press (San Francisco); Burlingame Country; Monterey Peninsula Country; University (New York). Was editor Yale Lit. Mag. and mem. Scroll and Key (Yale). Home: 1175 Greenwich Terrace. Office: Crocker First Nat. Bank Bldg., San Francisco, Calif. Died Mar. 16, 1943.

MULLENIX, Rollin Clarke, zoölogist; b. Ironton, Wis., Nov. 26, 1869; s. William Cox and Cynthia Ann (Bates) M.; A.B., Wheaton (Ill.) Coll., 1895, A.M., 1897; Ph.D., Harvard, 1908; m. Mary Walker, June 25, 1895; children—Carlos Walker, Ralph Bernard. Prof. biology and chemistry, Wheaton Coll., 1895-1905; scholar of Harvard Club of Chicago, at Harvard U., 1905-07; research student, Harvard, 1907-08; prof. biology, Yankton (S.D.) Coll., 1908-11; prof. zoölogy, 1911-35, prof. emeritus, since 1935, Lawrence Coll., Wis. Fellow A.A.A.S.; mem. Am. Soc. Zoölogists, Am. Genetic Assn., Ethical Soc. of Chicago. Conglist. Awarded Bowdoin prize and bronze medal by Harvard U. in 1909 for essay, The History and Present Status of the Neurone Theory; author of Peripheral Terminations of Eighth Cranial Nerve in Vertebrates. Home: Oracle, Ariz. Died June 8, 1949.

MULLER, Edouard, business exec.; b. La Tour de Peilz, Switzerland, Feb. 16, 1885; s. Edouard Johann and Philippine (Denereaz) M.; ed. Indsl. Coll., Vevey, Switzerland; High Sch. of Commerce and Economic Science, Zurich; hon. Dr. Econ. Sci., U. of Lausanne; LL.D., Lincoln Memorial U., Harrogate, Tenn., 1944; L.H.D., Washington and Jefferson Coll.; m. Jeanne Levillain, Mar. 1910 (dec.); m. 2d, Elsie Ellen Margery Hemmeler, Oct. 7, 1930; children—André, Roland (dec.), Micheline Françoise, Christiane, Joanne Ellen, Elyette Lucienne Nadine. Apprentice, Crédit du Léman Bank, Vevey, Switzerland, 1902; fgn. corr. and sec. to management Nestlé and Anglo-Swiss Condensed Milk Co., Ltd., London, Eng., 1903-06, became mgr. chocolate export dept., 1906; became mgr. Middle East agencies Nestle and Anglo-Swiss Holding Co., Ltd., 1910, mgr. central orgn. for Europe and Latin America, 1919, gen. mgr., Vevey, 1926, mng. dir., 1930, vice chmn., 1937, now chmn. bd. and pres.; chmn. and pres. Unilac, Inc., of Panama City and Stamford, Conn., since 1939; dir. allied and subsidiary companies of Nestleé-Unilac group, also of Crédit Suisse, Swiss Gen. Ins. Co. (both Zurich), Garber & Co. (Thoune), Lamont, Corliss & Co. (New York). Permanent del. to Internat. Red Cross Com. since 1917. Internat. agent for prisoners of war, with Eastern Army (apptd. by Swiss govt.), 1917-18. Recipient decorations from Turkey, Greece, France, Spain, Portugal, Cuba. Hon. citizen of Town of Vevey, Switzerland. Member (hon.) Nouvelle Société Helvétique, French Red Cross A.D.F., Greek-Swiss League (past v.p.), Swiss Benevolent Soc. of N.Y., Swiss Soc. of Greater N.Y., Belgian Soc. of Study and Expansion, N.Y. State Chamber of Commerce. Clubs: Woodway Country (Stamford); Bankers of America (New York). Author: Swiss Diplomatic Representation in Middle East; La Position Economique de la Suisse; Le Rôle de la science dans l'Industries; Schokolandenindustrie; Kondensmilchindustrie, and other publs. Home: Villa Mycena, 36 Route de St. Maurice, Tour de Peilz, Switzerland; also Davenport Dr., Southfield Point, Stamford, Conn. Office: Unilac, Inc., 1 Atlantic St., Stamford, Conn. Died Sept. 27, 1948.

MULLER, George P. (mū'lẽr), surgeon; b. Phila., Pa., June 29, 1877; s. Philip R. and Frances (Hughes) M.; A.B., Central High Sch., Phila., 1895; M.D., U. of Pa., 1899; m. Helen Ramsay, Sept. 20, 1905; children—George R., Helen R., Philip, John. Practiced at Phila. since 1899; interne Lankenau Hosp., 1899-1902; successively asst. instr. surgery, instr., asso. and prof. clin. surgery, U. of Pa. Sch. of Medicine until 1933; prof. of surgery, Grad. Sch. of Medicine, U. of Pa., 1919-33; prof. of surgery, Jefferson Med. Coll. since 1936; served as surgeon to various hosps., now to Misericordia, Jefferson hosp. Contract surgeon, also member Advisory Board and of Medical Corps, U.S. Army, World War; honorary discharge as maj., June 30, 1919. Fellow American College Surgeons; mem. A.M.A., Am. Surg. Assn., Clin. Surg. Soc., Interurban Surg. Soc., Am. Assn. Thoracic Surgery, Phila. Acad. Surgery, Phila. Coll. Physicians, Phila. County Med. Soc., Alpha Mu Pi Omega. Republican. Catholic. Club: Phila. Country. Contbr. abt. 50 papers, chiefly on surg. subjects; also articles in text books. Revised Davis' Applied Anatomy. Died Feb. 18, 1947.

MULLER, James Arthur (mŭl'ẽr), clergyman, educator; b. Phila., Pa., Dec. 23, 1884; s. Robert Jules and Susanna (Speidel) M.; student Central High Sch., Phila., 1899-1903; A.B., Princeton, 1907, Ph.D., 1915; A.M., Harvard, 1910; B.D., Episcopal Theol. Sch., Cambridge, Mass., 1910; studied in Europe, 1912-14; Litt.D., Occidental College, 1943; married Gulli Lindh, December 23, 1919. Deacon, 1910, priest, 1911, P.E. Ch.; fellow in history, Princeton U., 1910-11; curate Trinity Ch., Princeton, 1911-12; fellow in ch. history, Episcopal Theol. Sch., 1912-15, instr. in ch. history, 1915-17; minister-in-charge Ch. of Our Redeemer, Lexington, Mass., 1914-17; prof. history, Boone U., Wuchang, China, 1917-19; asst. minister Ch. of Epiphany, New York, 1920-21; prof. history, St. Stephen's Coll., 1921-23; lecturer in ch. history, General Theol. Sem., 1923; prof. ch. history and lecturer in liturgics and polity, Episcopal Theol. Sch., since 1923. Registrar of diocese of Massachusetts since 1942. Mem. Liturgical Commn. of P.E. Ch., 1933-40. Mem. Am. Soc. Ch. History, Church Hist. Soc., Am. Hist. Assn., Anglican Soc., Phi Beta Kappa; fellow Royal Hist. Soc., London. Club: Parsons. Travelled in India and Burma, 1930. Author: Stephen Gardiner and the Tudor Reaction, 1926; revised edit. of George Hodges' The Episcopal Church, 1932; The Letters of Stephen Gardiner, 1933; Apostle of China, A Life of Bishop Schereschewsky, 1937 (Chinese transl. by H. S. Wei, 1940); History of the Episcopal Theological School, 1943. Asso. editor Historical Mag. of the P.E. Ch. since 1932. Home: 4 St. Johns Rd., Cambridge, Mass. Died Sept. 5, 1945.

MULLER-URY, Adolfo (mŭl'lẽr-ū-rĭ), portrait painter; b. Airolo, Switzerland, Mar. 28, 1864; s. Louis and Genoveffa (Lombardi) M.; ed. pub. schs. and Sarnen, where was prepared for univ. and also began study of art; pupil of Deschwanden (painter) at Stans, Switzerland, then to Munich Acad., to Paris as pupil of Cabanel, 1881-83, and to Rome, where studied and worked, 1883-85; unmarried. Came to America, 1888. At Rome painted portraits of Cardinals Hergenrother, Hohenlohe, Pope Pius X, Cardinal Merry del Val, and Bishop Kennedy, 1907; and 2 portraits of Pope Benedict XV, 1920; also many religious pictures; in Switzerland portraits of President Ruchonnet, Federal Councillor Hammer, etc.; at London, Lord and Lady Strathcona, Lord Mount Stephen, etc.; in New York portraits of President McKinley, General Grant, Senator and Mrs. Depew, Senator Hanna, J. Pierpont Morgan, James J. Hill, etc.; at Neue Palais, Potsdam, life-size portrait of Emperor William, 1909; painted portrait of Mrs. Woodrow Wilson, 1916, now in The White House; of President Wilson delivering the "war speech" before Congress, Apr. 3, 1917; portrait of President Wilson opening Congress, presented the League of Nations, at Geneva, by Lord Duveen, 1935; portrait of Cardinal Mercier, when visiting U.S., for Catholic Univ., Washington; portrait of Pope Pius XI, 1922, again, 1931, for Vatican New Gallery (gold medal); also portrait of Henry Robinson, Henry E. Huntington: portrait of G. Motta, pres. of Switzerland, for his home town Bellinzona; portrait of Lord Duveen, 1939; portrait of Archbishop Francis Spellman of New York for Fordham U., 1941; portrait of Pope Pius XII for Archbishop Spellman 1942; portrait of Archbishop Rummel, New Orleans, 1943; Jessica Dragonette, soprano. Decorated Knight of St. Gregory (Pope Pius XI), 1923. Catholic. Visits Europe every year and has studio in London. Club: Nat. Arts, Lotos. Home: 33 W. 67th St., New York, N.Y. Died July 7, 1947.

MULLIN, Francis Anthony, clergyman, librarian; b. Dubuque, Ia., Dec. 31, 1892; s. James and Mary Ann (Kingsley) M.; A.B., Loras Coll., Dubuque, Ia., 1914; student St. Mary's Sem., Baltimore, 1915-19; A.M., U. of Iowa, 1925; Ph.D., Cath. U. of America, 1932; A.M. in Library Science, U. of Mich., 1936. Ordained to priesthood, Roman Cath. Church, 1919; curate, Cathedral, Dubuque, Ia., 1919-21; instr., Loras Acad., 1921-24; prof., Loras Coll., 1926-30, 1932-34; dir. of library, Cath. U. of America since 1936. Mem. Am. Library Assn., Cath. Library Assn., Ia. State Hist. Soc., Medieval Acad. of America, Ia. Cath. Hist. Assn. Author: The Work of Cistercians in Yorkshire, 1932. Address: Library, Catholic University of America, Washington 17, D.C. Died Jan. 2, 1947.

MULLINNIX, Henry Maston, naval officer; b. July 4, 1892; entered U.S. Navy, July 3, 1912; advanced through the grades to capt., July 1941, rear admiral, Aug. 1943; served as engr. on destroyer, World War I; comd. U.S.S. Albermarle, 1941; comdr. Atlantic Patrol Wing in anti-submarine and convoy escort work, 1942; command of aircraft carrier Mar. 1943. Home: Stockton, Calif. Reported missing in action. Nov. 1943.*

MUMFORD, George Saltonstall, mining; b. Rochester, N.Y., Aug. 18, 1866; s. George E. and Julia (Hills) M.; A.B., Harvard, 1887; m. Isabella Lee, December 7, 1895; children—George Saltonstall, Junior, Isabella Lee, Junior (Mrs. Sydney P. Clark). Began with the C.&C. Electric Company, mfrs., New York, N.Y., and continued 7 yrs.; sub-manager Union Safe Deposit Vaults, Boston, 4 yrs.; sec. City Trust Co., 8 yrs.; pres. Commonwealth Trust Co., 1909-23; pres. Atlantic Nat. Bank, Boston, 1923-32; now chmn. bd. Calumet & Hecla Consol. Copper Co.; dir. Haverhill Gas Light Co. Treas. exec. com., Boston Tuberculosis Assn.; treas. Florence Crittenton League of Compassion. Club: Somerset (Boston). Home: Chestnut Hill, Mass. Office: 12 Ashburton Pl., Boston, Mass. Died July 15, 1946.

MUMPER, Norris McAllister, govt. official; b. Cincinnati, O., Oct. 31, 1891; s. William Norris and Mary Alice (Hewlings) M.; B.S., Dickinson Coll., Carlisle, Pa., 1912; student Columbia, 1912-14; m. Helen Easton, Sept. 12, 1914 (div.); 1 son, William Norris II; m. 2d, Evelyn Throsby Petit, Dec. 20, 1946. Salesman with Columbia Phonograph Co., 1914-16, Bertron, Griscom, bonds, 1916-17; studio mgr. Great Authors Pictures, Inc., and Zane Grey Pictures, Inc., 1919-22; with Milnor Inc., importers from Europe and Orient, 1923-29; retired to handle personal investments in oil production and refining, 1929-38; foreign sales mgr. Vultee Aircraft, 1938-41; with Am. Republics Aviation Div. of Defense Supplies Corp., U.S. Govt. (elimination of German airlines in Latin America), 1941-42; dir. aviation Office of Coordinator of Inter-Am. Affairs, 1942-46. Served as regtl. adj., 309th F.A., 78th Div., U.S. Army, during World War I; participated in engagements St. Mihiel, Meuse-Argonne, Verdun. Mem. Phi Kappa Psi. Club: University (Los Angeles). Contbr. tech. articles on aviation subjects to periodicals in U.S. and Latin America. Home: 261 S. San Rafael Av., Pasadena, Calif. Died Sept. 2, 1948.

MUNDY, William Nelson, physician; b. Jersey City, N.J., May 7, 1860; s. William Nelson and Margaret Jane (Harris) M.; student prep. dept. Coll. City of New York, 1 yr.; M.D., Eclectic Med. Inst., Cincinnati, 1883; post-grad. work, New York, 1887-93; m. Maggie Waltermire, July 12, 1883; children—Carll Seymour, Giles Justin. Began practice, Forest, O., 1883; specialist in diseases of eye, ear, nose and throat; prof. pediatrics, Eclectic Med. Coll., Cincinnati, 1906-13. Mem. and clerk Bd. of Edn, Forest, 1890-1911 and 1918-22; mem. City Council, Forest, 2 terms. Presbyterian. Mem. Nat. Eclectic Med. Soc. (sec. 1909-23; ex-pres.), Ohio State Eclectic Med. Soc. (sec. 1893-1917), S.A.R. Past Grand Patriarch and Past Grand Rep. of Grand Encampment, I.O.O.F. of Ohio; Past Comdr. Patriarchs Militant of Ohio. Author: Diseases of Children, 1902. Home: Forest, O. Died Feb. 28, 1946.

MUNGER, Royal F(reeman), newspaper writer; b. Chicago, Ill., July 25, 1894; s. Edwin Alston and Alemena (Silke) M.; ed. Harvard Sch. for Boys, 1911-12; Wendell Phillips High Sch., Chicago, 1912-14; student U. of Chicago, 1914-17 and 1919-20, Ph.B., 1937, for thesis on economics; m. Mia Stanton, Oct. 9, 1920; children—Edwin Stanton, John Robin, Roger Poindexter. With Chicago Daily News since Aug. 1921, successively as reporter, financial reporter, investment editor, vocational adviser, and financial editor; also wrote financial comment for Chicago Assn. Commerce, 1923-28. Pvt. U.S. Marine Corps, Apr. 6, 1917, 1st lt. U.S. Army, Nov. 27, 1917; wounded at Attigny, France, Oct. 12, 1918; hon. disch. as 1st lt. inf., June 30, 1919; capt. O.R.C., 1925; maj. Ill. Nat. Guard, 1935-37; lt. col. and div. signal officer, 1937-41; later col. Ill. Reserve Militia and dir. Public Relations, Chicago Ordnance District; later capt., U.S. Marine Corps, on active duty. Trustee park district, La Grange. Member La Grange Post American Legion, Delta Upsilon. Republican. Mason. Author: The Rise and Fall of Samuel Insull; A Square Deal for Labor. Home: 5605 Dorchester Av. Address: Chicago Daily News, 400 W. Madison St., Chicago, Ill. Reported missing in action, Mar. 25, 1944; declared legally dead by Marine Corps.

MUNSON, Edward Lyman, medical officer U.S. Army; b. New Haven, Conn., Dec. 27, 1868; s. Lyman E. (U.S. judge) and Lucy A. (Sanford) M.; A.B., Yale, 1890, M.D., 1892, A.M., 1893; m. Martha Schneeloch, May 29, 1893; children—Katharine, Edward L. Was asst. surgeon U.S. Navy (resigned); capt. asst. surgeon U.S. Army, May 12, 1898; maj. surgeon, July 11, 1906; lt. col. surgeon, May 9, 1915; col., May 15, 1917; apptd. brig. gen., Oct. 3, 1918. Was prof. hygiene, Army Med. Sch., Washington. Was on Gen. Shafter's staff in expdn. against Santiago; asst. to surgeon-gen. U.S. Army, 1898-99, 1901-02, 1915-17 and since June 1, 1931, with rank of brig. general; asst. to chief surgeon, P.I., 1902-03; acting commr. pub. health, P.I., 1903-04; adviser to Philippine govt. in hygiene and sanitation, 1914-15, and 1922-24; prof. mil. hygiene, Army Service Schools, 1908-12; asst. to Surgeon Gen. in charge all training of med. dept. personnel U.S. Army, 1917-18; chief of morale br., Gen. Staff, 1918; comdg. Camp Greenleaf, Chickamauga Park, Ga., 1918; retired 1932. Served as prof. preventive medicine, George Washington U. Appointed prof. dept. of preventive medicine, U. of California, 1932, retired as prof. emeritus, 1939. In charge medical service U.S. Relief Mission, earthquake area of Japan, 1923. Inventor of several articles of equipment adopted and now in use in U.S. Army. Awarded D.S.M., 1919. "for exceptionally meritorious and conspicuous service," in connection with med. dept. and General Staff U.S. Army; Companion Order of the Bath (British), 1919; Order of Red Cross (Japanese), 1923. Fellow Am. Coll. Surgeons; mem. A.M.A., Assn. Mil. Surgeons of U.S. Army. Clubs: Army and Navy (Washington and Manila); Zeta Psi (New York); Elihu (New Haven); Bohemian (San Francisco). Author: Theory and Practice of Military Hygiene, 1902; A Study in Troop Leading and Sanitary Service in War, 1910; Sanitary Tactics, 1911; vol. on hospitals, in Photographic History of Civil War, 1911; The Soldier's Foot and the Military Shoe, 1912; The Management of Men, 1921. Contbr. to current literature on gen. and mil. hygiene. Editor: Military Surgeon, 1915-18. Home: 24 Huntington St., New Haven, Conn. Died July 7, 1947; buried in Arlington National Cemetery.

MURCHIE, Robert Charles, lawyer; b. Creetown, Scotland, Jan. 22, 1885; s. William Agnes Janet (Kellie) M.; ed. high sch.; LL.B., U. of Mich., 1909; m. Marguerite M. Varick, June 12, 1920 (died Jan. 31, 1944); m. 2d, Hazel Kane, June 30, 1945. Entered office of United States Senator Henry F. Hollis, 1909; mem. Remick & Hollis, 1910-12, Hollis & Murchie, 1912-19, Murchie & Murchie, 1919-29, Murchie, Murchie & Blandin, 1929-41, Murchie & Murchie since 1941; county solicitor Merrimack County, N.H., 1913-17; special asst. atty. gen. U.S., 1920. Commd. maj., O.R.C., June 1, 1917; in active service, July 2, 1917-Feb. 14, 1919; adj. 152d Inf. Brigade, N.A.; grad. Army Gen. Staff College, A.E.F. Mem. Gen. Court of N.H., 1917; sec. Dem. State Com., 1912-17; mem. Dem. Nat. Com., 1916-28; Dem. candidate for U.S. Senate, 1926; chmn. Dem. State Com., 1932-38. Mem. Am. and N.H. bar assns., Bar Assn. City of Boston. Elk. Home: 113 School St. Office: 4 Park St., Concord, N.H. Died May 28, 1947.

MURDOCK, George John, inventor; b. New Berlin, N.Y., Apr. 17, 1858; s. Chester and Elizabeth (Armstrong) M.; acad. and engring. edn.; m. Jeanette P., d. Thomas W. Waterman (law author), April 23, 1883; 2 children living. Studied mech. and elec. science and engring.; discovering in 1879 that electric lamp carbons when isolated from atmospheric air were of much longer life, he took out in 1883 the first patent in the U.S. on the enclosed form of arc lamp which is now commonly used throughout the civilized world; prior to 1885 had developed a complete system of electric lighting, including dynamo, regulator for arc lamps, arc lamps, and other accessories; other patented inventions have followed including bolt machines, files, and holder button, and button fastener (with A. L. Lesher), an exhaust turbine, an electric surface gage, magnetic drill holder, electric ry. signal indicator, and many other tools, and instruments that have come into common use; constructed, 1903, first gasoline tank with a rubber composite cover; inventor of self-sealing fuel tanks for war airplanes of the type used by the U.S. and foreign govts. in World War; since war chiefly engaged in research and development. Elected to membership in many Am. and foreign socs. Contbr. to tech. press on subjects relating to electricity and mechanics. Address: 213 W. Market St., Newark, N.J. Died July 25, 1942.

MURDOCK, John Samuel, judge; b. Pittsfield, Mass., Dec. 25, 1871; s. Thomas and Jane (Dumlop) M.; A.B., Brown U., 1896; LL.B., Harvard, 1899; m. Nettie S. Goodale, Oct. 9, 1901. Admitted to R.I. bar and began practice at Providence; became mem. firm Murdock & Tillinghast, 1911; served as U.S. dist. atty. of R.I.; v.p. Southern N.E. Ry. Co. Mem. Commn. on Banking Laws of R.I., 1908, Commn. on Revision of Statutes of R.I., 1909; asso. justice Supreme Court of R.I., Apr. 22, 1929-35. Mem. Am. Bar Assn., R.I. Bar Assn. (pres.), Providence Bar Club. Republican. Clubs: University, A.E. Club. Home: 89 Keene St., Providence, R.I.* Died Dec. 18, 1946.

MURDOCK, Victor, editor; b. Burlingame, Kan., Mar. 18, 1871; s. Marshall M. and Victoria (Mayberry) M.; ed. common schs. and Lewis Acad., Wichita, Kan.; m. Miss M. P. Allen, 1890; children—Marcia (Mrs. Harvey Delano), Katherine (Mrs. Howard Fleeson). Managing editor Witchita Daily Eagle, 1894-1903, editor in chief since 1924. Elected to 58th Congress, 1903, to fill vacancy; reëlected 59th to 63d Congresses (1905-15), 8th Kansas District; apptd. mem. Federal Trade Commission, Washington, Sept. 6, 1917, reapptd., term ending 1925 (chmn., 1919-20, 1922-23), resigned 1924. Apptd. mem. Meat Commn. U.S. Govt., Apr. 1918. Chmn. Prog. Nat. Com., 1914-16. Club: University (Washington). Author: China, the Mysterious and Marvelous, 1920; Folks, 1921; Constantinople, 1926. Home: 204 S. Rutan Av., Witchita, Kan. Died July 8, 1945.

MURPHREE, Thomas Alexander, judge; b. Blount County, Ala., Dec. 1, 1883; s. Lindsey Sylvester and Martha (Hendricks) M.; B.S., U. of Ala., 1910, LL.B., 1911; m. Helen Rosa Randolph, Apr. 25, 1914; 1 dau., Florence. Admitted to Ala. bar, June 7, 1911, and practiced in Birmingham, 1911-38; U.S. dist. judge, Northern Dist. Ala., since May 30, 1938. Mem. Kappa Sigma, Omicron Delta Kappa. Club: Birmingham Country. Democrat. Episcopalian. Home: 73 Country Club Blvd. Office: Federal Bldg., Birmingham, Ala. Died Sept. 5, 1945; buried Oak Hill Cemetery, Birmingham, Ala.

MURPHY, Frank, justice U.S. Supreme Court; b. Harbor Beach, Mich., Apr. 13, 1890; s. John T. and Mary (Brennan) M.; A.B., U. of Mich., 1912, LL.B., 1914; graduate study Lincoln's Inn, London, and Trinity Coll., Dublin; LL.D., Univ. of Santa Tomas, Manila, 1934, Fordham U., 1935, Univ. of Philippines, Loyola Univ., 1936; Univ. of Detroit, Duquesne U., 1937, St. John's Univ., Brooklyn, N.Y., 1938, N. Mex. State Coll., La. State Univ., St. Bonaventure College (New York), Univ. of Mich., John Marshall College, St. Joseph's Coll., Philadelphia, 1939, Tulane Univ., 1941, Creighton Univ. and Wayne Univ., 1942. Admitted to Mich. bar, 1914; law clerk Monaghan & Monaghan, Detroit, and teacher of law, night sch., 1914-17; chief asst. U.S. atty., Eastern District of Mich., 1919-20; private practice, 1920-23; instructor law, Univ. of Detroit, 1922-27; judge, Recorder's Court, Detroit, 1923-30; mayor of Detroit, 1930-33, resigning May 1933, to accept apptmt. as gov.-gen. of Philippine Is.; U.S. 1st high comr. to Philippines, 1935-36; elected gov. State of Mich., 1936; apptd. atty. gen. of U.S., 1939; apptd. asso. justice U.S. Supreme Court, Jan. 1940. Served as 1st lt., capt., infantry, U.S. Army, A.E.F., and with Army of Occupation in Germany, World War I; lt. col., Armored Force, World War II. First pres. U.S. Assn. of Mayors, 1933. Democrat. Catholic. Address: U.S. Supreme Court, Washington. Died July 19, 1949.

MURPHY, Fred Towsley, surgeon; b. Detroit, October 23, 1872; s. Charles Edmund and Helen P. (Towsley) M.; grad. Phillips Acad., 1893; A.B., Yale, 1897, hon. A.M., 1914; M.D., Harvard, 1901; m. Cornelia Brownell Gould, Aug. 8, 1904 (died, 1907); children—Charles Barney Gould, Helen Towsley Gould (dec.); m. 2d, Esther Longyear McGraw, July 23, 1929 (died, Jan. 28, 1934); m. 3d, Mary Swift Alger, Jan. 18, 1937. Asst. in anatomy, Harvard Med. Sch., 1903-04; asst. surgeon at Infants' Hosp., Boston, 1904-08; Austin teaching fellow in surgery, Harvard Med. Sch., 1905; surgeon to out patients, Mass. Gen. Hosp., 1907-11; visiting surgeon to clinic, Harvard Med. Sch., 1909-11; asst. in surgery, Harvard Med. Sch., 1910-11; prof. surgery, Washington U., 1911-19; surgeon in chief Barnes Hosp., St. Louis Children's Hosp., and cons. surgeon St. Louis City Hosp., 1914-19; now at Detroit. Dir. Parke Davis & Co., Standard Accident Co., Detroit Trust Co., Detroit and Canada Tunnel Co. Director and comdg. officer Base Hosp. 21; in France, 1917, 18; attached to A.E.F. Gen. Hdqrs., 1918, and later dir. med. and surg. dept. of Am. Red Cross, representing the chief surgeon A.E.F., with rank of col. Awarded D.S.M. Trustee Phillips Acad.; formerly mem. Yale Corp.; pres. Merrill-Palmer School. Republican. Mem. A.M.A., Soc. Clin. Surgery, Am. Surg. Assn., Mass. Med. Soc. Clubs: Country, Yondotega. Home: 17620 E. Jefferson Av., Grosse Pointe, Mich. Address: Penobscot Bldg., Detroit, Mich. Died Jan. 10, 1948.

MURPHY, Henry Constant, banker; b. Woodstock, Ill., Dec. 3, 1873; s. John J. and Elizabeth A. (Donnelley) M.; prep. edn. high sch. (Woodstock) and Notre Dame (Ind.) Prep. Sch.; Ph.B., U. of Chicago, 1895; m. Katherine K. Speed, Apr. 26, 1900; 1 son, John Speed (dec.). Polit. and dramatic editor Chicago Journal, 1895-97; owner and mgr. Marion (Ind.) News, 1896-98, Evansville Courier, 1897-1920; resided at Asheville, N.C., and N.Y. City, 1920-23, Chicago since 1923; chmn. bd. Upper Av. Nat. Bank, Chicago; chmn. 1st Nat. Bank, Woodstock, Ill.; dir. Clark Equipment Co., Internat. Cellucotton Products Co. Clubs: Chicago Athletic, Knollwood Country; Evansville Country; California (Los Angeles). Home: 181 Lake Shore Drive. Office: 919 N. Michigan Av., Chicago, Ill. Died Feb. 28, 1947.

MURPHY, Hermann Dudley, artist; b. Marlborough, Mass., Aug. 25, 1867; s. Daniel Francis and Ellen Frances (Ladd) M.; student Chauncy Hall School, Boston, 1880-85, Museum of Fine Arts, Boston, Acad. Julian, Paris; pupil of Jean Paul Laurens, and Benjamin Constant; m. Caroline S. Bowles, 1895; children—Dudley, Bowles, Carlene Bowles; m. 2d, Nelly Littlehale Umbstaetter, 1916. Artist of Nicaragua Canal Constrn. Co.'s expdn., 1887-88; illustrations for newspapers, mags., books, etc., 1888-94; exhibited in salon, Champs de Mars, 1895, and 1896. Mem. faculty architecture, Harvard, 1902-37; member Art Commission of Massachusetts, 1916-43. Represented in permanent collections of Albright Gallery (Buffalo), Museums of Fine Arts (Boston), Art Inst. Chicago, Cleveland Museum of Art, Nashville Art Assn., Art Museum (Dallas, Tex.), Springville (Utah) Art Assn., Buck Hill Art Assn. Bronze medals, Buffalo Expn., 1901; silver and bronze medals, St. Louis Expn., 1904; silver medal for landscape and silver medal for water color, San Francisco Expn., 1915; Chas. Peterson prize Art Inst. Chicago, 1922; Logan prize, Sanity in Art Exhbn., 1939. Actg. asst. to officer in charge of draft in Mass., 1917; insp. camouflage, U.S. Shipping Bd., 1918. Mem. Boston Water Color Club, Copley Soc., Boston, Boston Water Color Soc., Guild of Boston Artists; A.N.A., 1931, N.A., 1935. Clubs: Nat. Arts (New York); Winchester Boat (hon.); Royal Canoe of England (hon.). Holder sailing championship, Am. Canoe Assn., 1902, 09, 10, 31. Home: Lexington, Mass. Died Apr. 16, 1945.

MURPHY, J. Edwin, journalist; b. Baltimore, Md., Apr. 16, 1876; s. John C. P. and Emily R. (Mullan) M.; A.B., Loyola Coll., Baltimore, 1893; m. Mary Julia Austin, June 16, 1908. Reporter on various Baltimore newspapers, 1894-1908; city editor, later mng. editor Baltimore News, 1908-13; mng. editor New York Press, 1913-14, Washington Times, 1915-16; news editor Baltimore Evening Sun, 1917-19, mng. editor, 1919-39; retired. Vice-pres. A.S. Abell Co., pubs. The Sun and the Evening Sun, Baltimore. Home: 4305 Norwood Road, Guilford, Baltimore, Md. Died Mar. 29, 1943.

MURPHY, John Donahoe, tax consultant; b. Pittsfield, Mass., Oct. 13, 1885; s. John Joseph and Anne (Donahoe) M.; B.A., Williams Coll., 1907; m. May Coogan Castello, July 19, 1911; children—Richard, Katherine (Mrs. Harry G. Ommerle), Eleanor (Mrs. Carl W. Dudley), Eugene. Teacher Pittsfield High School, Pittsfield, Mass., 1907-11; jr. master High Sch. of Commerce, Boston, 1911-16; chief deputy collector of Internal Revenue, Boston, 1916-17; spl. lecturer on federal taxation, Boston U. Sch. of Business Adminstrn., 1917-18; chief of revenue agents U.S. Treasury, Washington, 1918; partner Lewis, Murphy & Co., accountants and tax consultants, 1919-26; sr. partner Murphy, Lanier & Quinn, New York, Chicago, Cincinnati and Washington, since 1926. Democrat. Roman Catholic. Clubs: Williams, Players (New York). Home: 419 E. 57th St., New York 22. Office: 295 Madison Av., New York 17. Died Aug. 2, 1949; buried St. Joseph's Cemetery, Pittsfield, Mass.

MURPHY, John Thomas, roentgenologist; b. Toledo, O., Aug. 15, 1885; s. Thomas J. and Ella (Weaver) M.; M.D., Univ. of Toledo, 1906; m. Lela Schuller, Feb. 2, 1907; 1 dau., Helen; m. 2d, Pauline Feil, Sept. 12, 1916; children—Jeanne, John Thomas, Patricia. Began practice, 1906; dir. Roentgenology, St. Vincent's Hosp., Toledo, since 1919. Mem. Am. Roentgen Ray Soc. (pres. 1933), Radiol. Soc. of N. America, Am. Coll. of Physicians, Am. Coll. Radiology (pres. 1935), A.M.A., A.A.A.S. Catholic. Elk, K.C. Clubs: Toledo, Catawba Cliffs Beach. Home: 2103 Scottwood Av. Office: 421 Michigan St., Toledo, O. Died June 15, 1944.

MURPHY, Samuel Wilson, corp. official; b. Brooklyn, N.Y., Aug. 27, 1892; s. William Gordon and Mary (Hett) M.; A.B., Wesleyan U., 1913; LL.B., Columbia University, 1916; m. Lottie Cort Black, February 20, 1918; children—Ruth Black (Mrs. H. F. Shattuck, Jr.), Samuel Wilson. Admitted to New York bar, 1916, asso. with firm of Hornblower, Miller & Potter, 1916, Geller, Rolston & Blanc, 1916-19, Simpson, Thacher & Bartlett, 1919-23; atty. with Electric Bond & Share Co., 1923-32, gen. atty., 1932-34, v.p., 1934-35 and 1937-41, pres. since 1941; mem. Reid & Murphy, 1935-37. Mem. U.S. Naval Forces, 1917-18. Mem. Bd. of Edn. South Orange-Maplewood Sch. Dist. Mem. Delta Kappa Epsilon, Phi Beta Kappa, Delta Sigma Rho. Republican. Methodist. Clubs: University (New York); Metropolitan (Washington); Rock Spring (West Orange, N.J.). Home: 237 Raymond Av., South Orange, N.J. Office: 2 Rector St., New York, N.Y. Died Nov. 19, 1944.

MURPHY, Walter, lawyer; b. Salisbury, N.C., Oct. 24, 1872; s. Andrew and Helen Webb (Long) M.; LL.B., U. of N.C., 1894, LL.D., 1925; m. Maude Horney, Mar. 18, 1903; children—Spencer, Elisabeth. In practice law at Salisbury since 1894; mem. N.C. Ho. of Rep., 1897-99, 1903-09, 1913-16, 1917-19, 1921-29 (speaker House 1914-15, 1917-19), and since 1933; city atty., Salisbury, 1903-08; dir. N.C. Bank & Trust Co., Yadkin R.R. Mem. N.C. State Budget Commn.; chmn. legislative com. for N.C. on adult illiteracy; chmn. Powan County Pension Bd. Sec. Dem. State Conv., N.C., 1904, 12, 32; mem. Dem. Exec. Com., N.C., 1906-24; Dem. elector at large for N.C., 1908; del. Dem. Nat. Conv., 1908, 32. Served in U.S. Navy on U.S. Monitor Nantucket, Spanish-Am. War. Mem. exec. com. trustees U. of N.C. since 1901; pres. N.C. Woodrow Wilson Memorial; v.p. Thomas Jefferson Memorial Foundation; dir. N.C. Tuberculosis Hosp., 1907-14. Mem. Am. and N.C. State bar assns., N.C. Hist. Soc., Nat. Legislative Assn., Alumni Assn. U. of N.C. (pres.), Sigma Nu. Episcopalian. Mason (Shriner). Delivered address at unveiling of N.C. memorial on Gettysburg Battleground, 1928. Home: 229 W. Bank St. Office: Pilot Life Ins. Bldg., Salisbury, N.C.* Died Jan. 12, 1946.

MURPHY, Walter Patton, ry. equipment mfr.; b. Pittsburgh, Pa., Jan. 26, 1873; s. Peter Henry and Jane Elizabeth (Patton) M.; hon. M.A., Trinity Coll., Hartford, Conn.; unmarried. Began in railroad service, St. Louis, Mo., 1892; in ry. supply business since 1898; pres. Standard Ry. Equipment Mfg. Co. Organizer Walter P. Murphy Foundation (charitable corp.). Fellow Royal Soc., London. Clubs: Metropolitan (Washington); New York Yacht (New York); Chicago; Pacific-Union (San Francisco); American Royal Thames Yacht (London). Home: Lake Forest, Ill. Office: 310 S. Michigan Av., Chicago, Ill. Died Dec. 16, 1942.

MURPHY, William Charles, Jr., newspaper man; b. Crawfordsville, Ind., Apr. 10, 1898; s. William Charles and Jane Alice (Maloney) M.; A.B., Wabash Coll., 1919; A.M., Catholic U. of America, 1920; m. Irene Cecelia Gainer, Jan. 11, 1922 (died 1923); 1 dau., Mary Jane (Mrs. Thomas C. Fraser); m. 2d, Maybelle Margaret Gainer, July 9, 1924; 1 son, William Gainer. Began as reporter Washington (D.C.) Post, 1920; with Nat. Catholic Welfare Conf. News Service, 1923-26; chief of Capitol staff United States Daily, 1926-29; with Washington Bureau, New York World, 1929-31; correspondent United Press, Universal Service, Washington, 1931; with Washington Bur. Phila. Public Ledger, 1931-34, chief Washington Bur., 1934; dir. of publicity, Am. Liberty League, Washington, D.C., 1934-37; chief of Washington Bur., Phila. Inquirer, 1937-45; dir. publicity, Republican National Com., since 1945. Served as 2d lt., F.A., U.S. Army, 1918. Mem. Delta Tau Delta, Sigma Delta Chi. Catholic. Clubs: National Press (pres. 1934), Gridiron, Washington Golf & Country (Washington). Contbr. to Saturday Evening Post, Am. Mercury, Commonweal, North Am. Review. Home: 3606 Van Ness St., N.W. Office: 1337 Connecticut Av., N.W., Washington. Died Nov. 27 1949; buried Arlington National Cemetery.

MURPHY, William F., bishop; b. Kalamazoo, Mich., May 11, 1885; s. William and Mary (Gibson) M.; student St. Jerome Coll., Kitchner, Ont., 1900-02, Assumption Coll., Sandwich, Ont., 1902-04 S.T.D., Propaganda Coll., Rome, Italy, 1908; J.C.L., Apollinaris Coll., Rome, 1909; hon. LL.D., U. of Detroit, 1930. Ordained priest Roman Catholic Ch. Rome, June 1908; curate St. Thomas Ch., Ann Arbor, Mich., 1910-12, Holy Cross Ch., Marine City Mich., 1912-19, St. Peter and Paul Cathedral, Detroit, 1919-21; pastor St. David Church, Detroit (organized parish), 1921; domestic prelate, July 11 1934; consecrated 1st Bishop of Saginaw, May 17 1938. Mem. Mich. Hist. Commn. Home: 1555 Wash ington St. Address: 124 N. Hamilton St., Saginaw, Mich. Died Feb. 7, 1950.

MURPHY, William Mansuetus, prof. edn.; b. Boston, Mass., Feb. 19, 1878; s. William and Hannah (Donovan) M.; B.S., summa cum laude, Tufts, 1920, A.M., 1921; Ed.M., Harvard, 1922, Ed.D., 1923; unmarried. Admitted to Mass. bar, 1901, bar of U.S. Dist. Court, 1918; practiced, Boston, Mass., 1901-18; teacher, East Boston High Sch., 1922-25; prof. edn., Marquette U., 1925-29; prof. and head dept. edn., De Paul U., since 1929, dean of instrn. since 1930. Member American Association University Professors, National Society College Teachers of Education, Wis. Teachers Assn., Nat. Edn. Assn., Tufts College Teachers' Assn., Harvard Univ. Teachers' Assn., Milwaukee Schoolmasters' Club, Mass. Charitable Irish Soc., Phi Beta Kappa, Phi Delta Kappa, Pi Gamma Mu, Phi Beta Epsilon. Catholic. Research in interrelationship of common law and secondary education. Home: Arlington, Mass. Address: 1406 Chicago, Av., Evanston, Ill. Died Oct. 21, 1943.

MURRAY, David Ambrose, coll. prof.; b. Montgomery County, N.Y., Mar. 23, 1861; s. Andrew Keachie and Margaret Martin (Gordon) M.; grad. Coe Collegiate Inst. (now Coe Coll.), 1879; A.B., Monmouth Coll., Ill., 1885, L.H.D., 1940; A.M., Princeton, 1887; grad. Princeton Theol. Sem., 1888; D.D., Coe Coll., 1902; m. Annie Louise Ardagh Foster, Oct. 11, 1905; children—Margaret Elizabeth, Andrew Foster, David Thompson, Raymond Gorbold, William Henry Thomas. Ordained Presbyn. ministry, 1888; teacher in govt. schs., Kyoto and Osaka, Japan, 1888-92; pastor, Chicago, 1893-94, Perry, Ia., 1894-95, Ottumwa, 1896-1902; missionary in Japan, 1902-22; founded Osaka Theol. Sem., 1902, prin., 1902-10; in charge work in Ise Province, of Bd. of Fgn. Missions Presbyn. Ch. in U.S.A., 1911-19; prof., Meiji Gakuin Theol. Sem., Tokyo, 1919-21; mgr. Christian Lit. Soc. of Japan, 1921-25; prof. Biblical literature, Monmouth Coll. since 1925. President Santa Monica Y.M.C.A. since 1934. Author: Inductive English Lessons, 1890; Atoms and Energies, 1901; Kojin Dendo (Studies for Personal Workers), 1905; Ten No Tomo (Friend from Heaven), 1907; Sukui No Michi (Way of Salvation), 1907; Christian Faith and the New Psychology, 1911; The Supernatural, 1917; His Return, 1925; The Real Meaning of Genesis, 1930; Studies in the Beliefs of Our Religion, 1931; Jehovah, Friend of Men, 1936; Vignettes of Life, 1941; I Believe in God, 1941. Editor of Christian Movement in Japan, 1920-21. Home: 401 Marguerita Av., Santa Monica, Calif.
Died Sep. 29, 1949.

MURRAY, Eugene, pres. Fidelity Trust Co., Pittsburgh; pres. First Nat. Bank, Sewickley, Pa.; dir. Nat. Union Fire Ins. Co., Union Title Guaranty Co. Home: Sewickley Heights, Sewickley, Pa. Office: 341 Fourth Av., Pittsburgh. Died June 7, 1948.

MURRAY, George Welwood, lawyer; b. Edinburgh, Scotland, Mar. 8, 1856; s. Welwood and Lily (Gourlay) M.; ed. pub. and pvt. schs.; LL.B., Columbia, 1876, LL.D., 1930; m. Caroline C. Church, July 29, 1878 (died 1917); 1 dau., Lily Sylvester (wife of Prof. Adam Leroy Jones); m. 2d, May I. Ditto, May 29, 1920. Admitted to N.Y. bar, 1877; counsel law firm of Milbank, Tweed & Hope (formerly Murray, Aldrich & Webb); consulting counsel Montclair Trust Co.; dir. Montclair Trust Co., Albany & Susquehanna R.R. Co., Equitable Life Assurance Soc. Mem. bd. dirs. and chmn. legal research com. The Commonwealth Fund; trustee Community Chest of Montclair. Dir. Laura Spelman Rockefeller Memorial during its existence; hon. pres. Assn. for the Protection of the Adirondacks. Treas. and mem. of council Am. Law Inst.; mem. Am. Bar Assn., N.Y. State Bar Assn., Assn. Bar City of New York. Clubs: Century, Broad Street (New York); Cosmos (Washington, D.C.). Home: 77 S. Mountain Av., Montclair, N.J. Office: 15 Broad St., New York. Died Apr. 25, 1943; buried in Mount Hebron Cemetery, Montclair, N.J.

MURRAY, Maxwell, army officer; b. West Point, N.Y., June 19, 1885; s. Gen. Arthur and Sarah Wetmore (de Russy) M.; B.S., U.S. Mil. Acad., 1907; student Mass. Inst. of Tech., 1919-20, Coast Arty. Sch., 1911-12, Field Arty. Sch., 1924-25, Command and Gen. Staff Sch., 1925-26, Army War Coll., 1928-29; m. Phyllis Muriel Howard, Nov. 18, 1911; children—Arthur Maxwell, Anne Howard (Mrs. Robert W. Van de Velde). Commd. 2d lt., U.S. Army, June 15, 1907; promoted through grades to brig. gen., Dec. 1, 1938; advanced to maj. gen., 1941; capt., maj., lt. col. 5th F.A., 1st Div., A.E.F., 1917-18; comdr. Camp Bragg (N.C.), 1918-19; asst. to chief field arty., 1920-24; asst. and aide to Dwight F. Davis, gov. gen. P.I., 1929-32; mem. Field Arty. Bd., 1932-36; comdr. 5th F.A. and Madison Barracks (N.Y.), 1936-38; asst. comdr. Field Arty. Sch. (Fort Sills, Okla.), 1938. Awarded D.S.M., Silver Star, U.S. Treasury Life Saving Medal (U.S.); Croix de Guerre (France). Club: Army and Navy (Washington, D.C.). Home: 2710 36th St., Washington, D.C.* Died Aug. 4, 1948.

MURRAY, Sidney Eugene, lawyer; b. Lone Elm, Henderson County, Tenn., July 19, 1875; s. John Leonadus and Addie (Neely) M.; ed. pub. schs.; m. Eddie Mai Hilliard, July 11, 1906; children—Addie Louise, Mary Elizabeth, Eddie Mai, Jean. Admitted to Tenn. bar, 1895; mem. Tenn. Ho. of Rep., from Carroll County, 1905-09; mem. Rep. Nat. Conv., 1908, 20; mem. Rep. State Exec. Com., 1914-22; nominee for Congress, 8th Tenn. Dist., 1910; became U.S. dist. atty., Western Dist. of Tenn., Nov. 1921. Mem. Christian (Disciples) Ch. K.P. Died May 24, 1943.

MUSSELMAN, Clarence Alfred, publishing exec.; b. Dec. 16, 1872; s. Edwin I. and Clara (Collom) M.; ed. Episcopal Acad., Philadelphia, Pa.; m. Mabel Moon, Nov. 11, 1902; 1 dau., Mary Moon (Mrs. Kenneth Davis Acton). One of founders of Chilton Co., pioneer automotive business publishers, 1899, which company later merged with United Publishers; became vice pres. and dir., also pres. of automotive div., Chilton Co., later being pres., then becoming chmn. bd., 1945. Mem. bd. dirs. Nat. Publishers Assn., 1938, 1941, 1944 (resigned for reasons of health, 1945). Clubs: Union League, Philadelphia Country, Poor Richard (Phila.). Home: 260 Sycamore Av., Merion, Pa. Died Jan. 3, 1946.

MUSSER, John, prof. history; b. Huntingdon, Pa., Nov. 14, 1887; s. Cyrus John (D.D.) and Nettie Edith (Mowry) M.; grad. Mercersburg (Pa.) Acad., 1905; student Franklin and Marshall Coll., 1905-07; A.B., U. of Pa., 1909, Harrison scholar, 1909-10, Harrison fellow, 1911-12, A.M., 1910, Ph.D., 1912; m. Grace Winter Greene, Sept. 6, 1919; children—Robert John, Nancy Louise. Asst. hist. U. of Pa., 1912-14; acting assistant prof. history, Swarthmore, 1914-15; instr. in history, New York U., 1916-19, asst. prof., 1919-22, asso. prof., 1922-24, prof. since 1924; administrative chmn. dept. of history, Washington Sq. Coll., since 1925, sec. of faculty of Grad. Sch., 1925-36, exec. sec., 1928-36, dean, 1936-43, dean emeritus since 1943. Mem. Phi Beta Kappa, Phi Kappa Psi, Phi Eta. Democrat. Mem. Ref. Ch. in U.S. Club: Seaside Park Yacht. Author: The Establishment of Maximilian's Empire in Mex., 1918. Home: 106 D St., Seaside Park, N.J. Died March 21, 1949.

MUSSER, John Herr, physician, educator; b. Phila., Pa., June 9, 1883; s. John Herr and Agnes Gardiner (Harper) M.; B.S., U. of Pa., 1905, M.D., 1908; m. Marguerite Hopkinson, Jan. 7, 1911; children—Frances Avegno, John Herr, III. Asst. editor Am. Jour. Med. Sciences, 1911-20, editor, 1920-24; asso. in medicine, U. of Pa. Med. Sch., 1914-20, asst. prof., 1920-24; was physician Phila. Gen. Hosp., Howard Hosp., and asso. phys. Presbyn. Hosp.; prof. medicine, Tulane U. of La., since Jan. 1, 1925; physician Charity Hosp.; pres. Louisiana State Board of Health, 1940-42. Major Med. Corps, U.S. Army, World War, in U.S. one year, France one year; colonel Med. Reserve Corps since 1938. Member American Medical Assn. (v.p. 1933-34), Assn. Am. Physicians, Coll. of Physicians Phila., Am. Climatol. and Clin. Assn., Am. Soc. for Clin. Investigation, Am. Coll. Physicians (pres. 1929-30), Psi Upsilon, Democrat. Presbyterian. Clubs: Boston, Round Table, Metairie Golf. Editor: Internal Medicine, 1932, 4th edit., 1945. Editor New Orleans Med. and Surg. Jour. Home: 1427 2d St. Office: 1430 Tulane Av., New Orleans 13, La. Died Sep. 5, 1947.

MUSSEY, Henry Raymond (mŭz'ē), prof. economics; b. Atkinson, Ill., Dec. 7, 1875; s. William Alvord and Louisa (Nowers) M.; student Geneseo (Ill.) Collegiate Inst., 1891-93; A.B., Beloit Coll., 1900; Ph.D., Columbia, 1905; m. Mabel Hay Barrows, June 28, 1905; 1 son, June Barrows; m. 2d, Sally Kennard Corbett, July 15, 1934. Engaged in teaching at various schs., 1893-96, 1901; asst. prof. economics, New York U., 1903-05; asso. prof. economics, Bryn Mawr Coll., 1905-07; asst. prof. sociology, U. of Pa., 1907-09; asst. and asso. prof. economics, Columbia, 1909-18; prof. economics, Wellesley Coll., 1922-29 and since 1931; mng. editor of the Nation (mag.), 1918-20 and 1929-30. Mem. Phi Beta Kappa, Sigma Chi. Home: 6 Appleby Road, Wellesley, Mass.* Died Feb. 10, 1940.

MUTCH, William James, coll. prof.; b. Hillsboro, Wis., Feb. 7, 1858; s. James and Jane (Tough) M.; B.A. and B.Litt., U. of Wis., 1882, M.A., 1891; B.D., Yale, 1885, Ph.D., 1894; m. Rosa Prevey, Jan. 28, 1886; children—Helen (Mrs. H. A. Clark, dec.), James C., W. Warren. Ordained Congl. ministry, 1885; pastor Howard Av. Ch., New Haven, Conn., 1885-1907; prof. philosophy and religion, Ripon Coll., 1907-25; mem. and institute condr. Am. Inst. Religious Edn., 1901; lecturer on religious education, Yale U., 1901-04. Mem. Brit. Inst. of Philos. Studies. Author: Christian Teachings, 1899; History of the Bible, 1912; How to Interest, 1906; Samuel, Saul and David, 1907; Graded Bible Stories, 1914; The Testing of a Soul, 1899. Contbr. to mags. and to Nelson's Sunday School Ency., Ency. of Religion and Ethics, etc. Home: Ripon, Wis. Died Nov. 24, 1947.

MYERS, Clyde Hadley, plant breeder, teacher; b. Randolph, Ill., Feb. 6, 1883; s. John J. and Justina L. (Hadley) M.; B.S., Ill. Wesleyan U., 1907; M.S., U. of Ill., 1910; Ph.D., Cornell U., 1912; m. Fleda DeVere Straight, June 28, 1910; children—John Straight, Marylee. Asst. in plant breeding, U. of Ill., 1907-10; instr. plant breeding, 1911-12; asst. prof., 1912-13; prof. since 1914, Cornell U. Special representative Internat. Education Board of U. of Nanking, China, 1926, 1931. Mem. A.A.A.S. (Fellow), Am. Soc. Agronomy, Am. Genetic Assn., Sigma Xi, Phi Kappa Phi, Gamma Alpha, Tau Kappa Epsilon. Republican. Protestant. Mason. Club: Savage Club (Ithaca). Specializes in breeding of vegetable crops; teaches plant breeding; author papers on plant breeding in various journals. Home: 614 Wyckoff Road, Ithaca, N.Y. Died Aug. 5, 1944.

MYERS, Diller S., army officer; b. Ill., Nov. 21, 1887; commd. 2d lt. Inf., Ill. Nat. Guard, July 1912; 1st lt. Fed. service, June 1914, and advanced to lt. col. Sept. 1918; col. Officers Reserve Corps, 1919; col. Calif. Nat. Guard, 1924, made brig. gen. of the line, Aug. 1938; entered Fed. service, Mar. 1941; now in command of 65th Inf. Brigade, 33d Div., in training, Camp Forrest, Tenn. Awarded Silver Star, World War I. Address: War Dept., Washington, D.C.*
Died May 12, 1947.

MYERS, Gustavus, author; b. Trenton, N.J., Mar. 20, 1872; s. Abram and Julia (Hillman) M.; ed. various schs., Phila. and New York, specializing in original hist. research; m. Genevieve Whitney, Dec. 23, 1904. Author: History of Public Franchises in New York City, 1900; History of Tammany Hall, 1901, 1917; History of the Great American Fortunes, 1910; Beyond the Borderline of Life, 1910; History of the Supreme Court of the United States, 1912; History of Canadian Wealth, 1914; German Myth, 1918; Ye Olden Blue Laws, 1921; The History of American Idealism, 1925; America Strikes Back, 1935; History of the Great American Fortunes (revised edit.), 1936; The Ending of Hereditary American Fortunes, 1939; awarded fellowship by the John Simon Guggenheim Memorial Foundation, 1941, to write book, Sources of Bigotry in the United States (published 1943). Contbr. to mags. Club: Authors (New York). Home: 2740 Marion Av., Bronx, New York, N.Y. Died Dec. 7, 1942.

MYERS, Henry L., lawyer; b. Cooper County, Mo., Oct. 9, 1862; s. Henry M. and Maria M. (Adams) M.; ed. pvt. schs., Cooper Inst. and Boonville (Mo.) Acad.; m. Nora S. Doran, July 10, 1896; 1 dau., Mary A. (Mrs. J. C. Donnally). Practiced law at Boonville and West Plains, Mo., 1885-93, Hamilton, Mont., 1893-1907. Pros. atty. Ravalli County, Mont., 1895-99; mem. Mont. Senate, 1899-1903; dist. judge, 4th Jud. Dist., Mont., 1907-11; U.S. senator, Mont., terms 1911-17, 1917-23; apptd. asso. justice, Supreme Court of Mont., Jan. 1, 1927; retired Jan. 1, 1929, and resumed practice of law. Episcopalian. Mason. Author: The United States Senate; What Kind of Body? Home: Billings, Mont. Deceased.

MYERS, Howard, publisher, editor; b. Philadephia, Pa., November 4, 1894; s. Martin and Clara (Rau) M.; ed. N.Y. Univ., 1913-14; N.Y. Sch. Fine and Applied Arts, 1914-15; m. Louise Weigand, Jan. 4, 1917; children—Barbara King, Howard, Mary. With Conde Nast Publs., 1915; mgr. housing dept., Nat. Lead Co., 1915-19; v.p., The Architectural Forum, 1919-25, president, 1925-29; pres. National Trade Jours., 1929-30; pub. and editor, The Architectural Forum since 1930; dir. Citizens' Housing Council. Chmn. archtl. adv. com. Fed. Pub. Housing Authority; gov. N.Y. Bldg. Congress; dir. Nat. Pub. Housing Conf. Mem. Am. Design Award Jury, Beaux-Arts Inst. of Design (dir.), Archtl. League of N.Y. Clubs: Manhattan (N.Y.), Tavern (Chicago). Home: 125 E. 57th St. Office: 350 Fifth Av., New York 1, N.Y. Died Sept. 18, 1947.

MYERS, Jefferson, ex-commr. U.S. Shipping Bd.; b. Scio, Ore., Aug. 8, 1863; s. David and Mary Priscilla (MacDonald) M.; A.B., Willamette U., 1893; m. Helene P. Rowe, Feb. 14, 1913. Educated in law and admitted to practice in several states and U.S. Supreme Court. Actively interested for many years in farming and stock raising, banking, etc.; mem. Ore. State Senate and Ho. of Rep., 1885-95; state treas., Ore., 1924-25; apptd. mem. U.S. Shipping Bd., 1926. Formerly col. Ore. Nat. Guard. Pres. Lewis and Clark Centennial Expn., Portland, 1904. Mem. Bd. of Regents Ore. State Agrl. Coll. Mem. Ore. State Grange, Nat. Grange. Democrat. Presbyterian. Mason (32°, Shriner). Home: 1731 N.E. 12th St., Portland, Ore. Died Dec. 29, 1943.

MYERS, John Quincy, physician; b. Wilkes County, N.C., Sept. 25, 1877; s. Trelius C. and Julia Ann (Brown) M.; 18th generation in descent from Joseph Myers (English); student Davidson Coll. and N.C. Med. Coll., 1901-04, M.D., 1904; post-grad. work N.Y. Polyclinic, Johns Hopkins, Mayo Clinic, Rochester, Minn., etc.; m. Elizabeth Crosland, 1906 (died Jan. 21, 1929); children—John Quincy, Wm. Turrelius, Elizabeth. Practiced at Charlotte since 1909; founder and propr. Tranquil Park Sanitarium. Mem. Draft Bd., Charlotte, World War; pres. State Bd. Med. Examiners, 1914-20; pres. N.C. Bd. U.S. Pension Examiners; apptd. to Board of Med. Examiners for State of N.C. by Nat. Board of Examiners of The Life Extension Inst., N.Y., 1933; Organizer and 1st sec. N.C. Hosp. Assn.; med. referee Life Extension Inst., Met. Life Ins. Co., North Western Life Ins. Co. Capt. Med. O.R.C. Mem. A.M.A. (N.C. del., 1919-39; com. on rules since 1939), Med. Soc. State of N.C. (pres. 1926-27), Mecklenburg Med. Assn., Wilkes County Med. Soc., Pi Gamma Mu; elected med. mem. Nat. Council Traveling Salesmen's Assn., for Charlotte, Dec. 17, 1923; fellow Hotel Physicians Assn. of America. Republican. Deacon 1st Bapt. Ch. Mason (32°, Shriner). Clubs: Charlotte Executive, Myers Park Country. Chmn. Charlotte Med. Com., Procurement and Assignment Service, U.S. Manpower Commn., since 1942. Home: Selwyn Hotel, Charlotte, N.C. Died Dec. 3, 1944.

MYERS, Lewis Edward, public utilities; b. Pittsburgh, Pa., July 14, 1863; s. Joseph and Ella (Schamberg) M.; prep. edn. Episcopal Academy; Western U. of Pa. (now U. of Pittsburgh), 1877-80; m. Caroline Livingston, June 3, 1900. Began with Edison Electric Co., Pittsburgh, 1882, later at Phila.; in charge Chicago office of Detroit Elec.

Works, 1887-89; organizer and chmn. bd. The L. E. Myers Co., builders and operators public utilities, since 1888; pres. Michigan Gas & Electric Co., Ironwood & Bessemer Railway & Light Co., Ashland Light, Power & Street Railway Co., Bituminous Products Co., Booth Elec. Furnace Co., Ashland County Land Co., Compania Cubana L. E. Myers, Marquette County Gas & Electric Co., L. E. Myers Construction Co., L. E. Myers Co. of Ontario, Southwest L. E. Myers Co.; also officer and dir. many other corps. Apptd. Aug. 1917, chmn. State Council of Defense for Cook County (Chicago). Vice chmn. Governor's Com. on Unemployment and Relief; pres. Allendale Farm for Boys; chmn. Salvation Army Bd., South Side Boys' Club, Chicago Civic Hosp. Assn.; dir. Boys Club Fedn. of America. Ex-president Board of Education, Chicago. Mem. Western Society Engineers, Edison Pioneers. Mason (32°). Clubs: Engineers', Electric, Tavern, Lake Shore Athletic (Chicago); Lake Geneva Country, Butterfield Country. Home: Blackstone Hotel, Chicago, Ill.* Died Feb. 5, 1945.

MYERS, Victor Caryl, biochemist; b. Buskirk Bridge, N.Y., Apr. 13, 1883; s. Dr. Adam Young and Mary Evelyn (Defandorf) M.; B.A., Wesleyan U., 1905, M.A., 1907, D.Sc., 1930; Ph.D., Yale Univ., 1909; m. Marion Christine Smith, Sept. 7, 1910. Adj. prof. physiol. chemistry, and exptl. physiology and dir. of these labs., Albany Med. Coll. (Union U.), 1909-11; with New York Post-Grad. Med. Sch. and Hosp. as lecturer on chem. pathology, 1911-12, prof. pathol. chemistry, 1912-22, acting dir. labs., 1917-19, prof. biochemistry and dir. dept., 1922-24; prof. and head biochemistry, State U. of Ia., and pathol. chemist to Univ. hosps., 1924-27; prof. biochemistry and director of department, School of Medicine, Western Reserve University, since 1927; visiting biochemist, Cleveland City Hospital, since 1927; secretary Medical Faculty, 1929-44; asso. editor Jour. of Lab. and Clin. Medicine and Gastroenterology; associate editor, Cyclopedia of Medicine; sectional editor Biology Abstracts. Mem. council on dental therapeutics American Dental Association. Maj. Sanitary Corps, O.R.C., U.S. Army, 1924-34. Fellow A.A.A.S.; associate fellow A.M.A., New York Academy Medicine; mem. American Society Biology Chemists (sec. 1919-23; councilor 1924), Fedn. Am. Socs. Exptl. Biology (exec. sec. 1922), Soc. Exptl. Biol. Medicine (councilor, 1921-23; sec.-treas., mng. editor, 1923-24, chmn. Ia. br. and v.p., 1927), Am. Physiol. Society, American Institute of Nutrition, American Gastroenterol. Association, Harvey Society, Am. Chem. Soc., Cleveland Acad. Medicine (chmn. sect. experimental medicine, 1929), Soc. de Chim. Biologie, Internat. Assn. of Dental Research, S.R. of State of N.Y., Delta Kappa Epsilon, Phi Beta Kappa, Sigma Xi; hon. mem. Des Moines Acad. of Medicine, St. Louis Medical Society. Methodist. Club: University (Cleveland). Author: Essentials of Pathological Chemistry, 1913; Practical Chemical Analysis of Blood, 1921, 24; Laboratory Directions in Biochemistry, 1942. Home: 21059 Claythorne Rd., Shaker Heights, O. Summer Residence: 329 Washington Terrace, Middletown, Conn. Address: School of Medicine, Western Reserve U., Cleveland, O. Died Oct. 7, 1948.

MYERS, William Shields, chemist; b. Albany, N.Y., Dec. 15, 1866; s. Benjamin F. and Elizabeth (Shields) M.; desc. of Christian Myers, who came to N.Y. from Huguenot France, 1710; educated Albany Acad., 1881-85; B.Sc., Rutgers University, 1889, M.Sc., 1894, D.Sc., 1908; studied at Munich, Berlin, under von Hofmann, and at London, under Sir William Ramsay, 1890-92; m. Annie Tayler Lambert, September 11, 1889; 1 son, W. Lambert, Assistant chemist, N.J. Experiment Station, 1888-89; chemist, Lister Chemical Works, 1892-93; instr. and later asso. prof. chemistry, Rutgers Coll., 1893-1901; dir. Chilean Nitrate Com. for U.S. and Colonies, 1901-26, agr. consumption of Chilean nitrate in U.S. increasing nearly forty fold under his adminstrn., compared to increase of threefold in gen. fertilizer consumption in U.S. during same period; first to use motion pictures in presenting qualities and character of Chilean nitrate to North Am. farmers (leading woman was Claudette Colbert, in this, her first picture work). Chmn. Com. on Survey of Coll. of Agr., Rutgers U.; pres. Rutgers League of N.J.; author of bill which organized dept. ceramics in Rutgers Coll., which passed N.J. Legislature, 1902, securing first annual income from the state for the coll.; trustee Rutgers Coll., 1902-07 and since 1912; mayor New Brunswick, N.J., 1904-06 (cut down number of saloons by 20 per cent and cut city tax rate by 10 per cent). Mem. jury award, Jamestown Expn., 1907. Trustee Okolona (Miss.) Sch. Bd., 1913-18; member mng. com. N.J. State Coll. Agr. since 1920; spl. consul of Chile in U.S. since 1918; trustee Central High Sch., Banbridge, N.Y. Life fellow Chem. Soc., London, 1891; life mem. Soc. Chem. Industry of Great Britain; mem. Am. Chem. Soc., A.A.A.S., Chi Phi. Ind. Republican. Clubs: University, Chemists (charter mem.), Canadian, British Schools and Universities (New York); Authors' (London). Contbr. papers to Chem. Soc. of London, Am. Chem. Soc., tech. jours. on water, soils and clays of N.J. Editor and pub. of monographs on scientific fertilization, water transportation and freights. Joint author, with late Prof. E. B. Voorhees, of plan for systematic development of agrl. edn. in Mexico, accepted by govt. Spent 6 months in Europe in a study of crop production and soils, Britain, France, Germany, Italy and Denmark, 1926. Delivered anniversary address, Aug. 1929, at unveiling of Clinton-Sullivan monument on the Old Frontier of New York Colony and Indian Territory, at junction of the Susquehanna and Unadilla Rivers, first point of invasion of Indian Territory by Am. troops. Leader in centralization movement of rural schs. of southern tier of counties of N.Y., Jan.-June 1931; made survey of orgn. and procedure of 10 northeastern colls., 1931; asso. of late Myron T. Herrick in promoting agrl. co-operative socs. Wrote "Some Causes of the Depression and Some Aids to Convalescence" for Sunday Times, New Brunswick, N.J.; author of Bureaucrats Song In Washington and Out; The Cult of Incompetence; Philosophies of Governments, Christian and Barbarian, 1939. Founder (with L. F. Loree) Jour. of Soil Science. Home: "Stonehenge," Bainbridge, N.Y. Died Jan. 10, 1945.

MYERSON, Abraham (mī'ēr-sŭn), neurologist, psychiatrist; b. Yanova, Russia, Nov. 23, 1881; s. Morris Joseph and Sophie (Segal) M.; grad. English High Sch., Boston, 1898; M.D., Tufts, 1908; m. Dorothy Marion Loman, Mar. 9, 1913; children—Paul Graves, David John, Anne. Began practice at Boston, 1908; resident neurologist Alexian Bros. Hosp., St. Louis, 1912-13; also instr. in neuropathology, St. Louis U. Sch. of Medicine; asst. physician Boston Psychopathic Hosp., 1913-14; pathologist and clin. dir. State Hosp., Taunton, Mass., 1914-18; chief med. officer, out patient dept., Boston Psychopathic Hosp., 1918-20; cons. neurologist Boston City Hosp.; former chief of neuropsychiatry, Beth Israel Hosp.; cons. neuropsychiatrist Washingtonian Hosp.; cons. psychiatrist McLean Hosp.; cons. neurologist Boston Psychopathic Hosp.; prof. neurology emeritus Tufts Coll. Med. Sch.; former clinical prof. of psychiatry, Harvard; director research Boston State Hospital; member Com. on Research in Mental Health, Commonwealth of Mass.; trustee Assoc. Jewish Philanthropies Diplomate Am. Bd. Psychiatry and Neurology. Member A.M.A., Am. Neurol. Assn., Am. Psychiatric Assn., Am. Psychopathol. Assn., Phi Delta Epsilon. Author: The Nervous Housewife, 1920; Foundations of Personality, 1921; Inheritance of Mental Diseases, 1925; When Life Loses Its Zest, 1926; Psychology of Mental Disorders, 1927; The German Jew—His Share in Modern Culture (with Isaac Goldberg), 1933; Social Psychology, 1934; Eugenical Sterilization, 1936; book published posthumously, 1950; also many papers and articles on mental and nervous diseases. Home: 33 Taylor Crossway, Brookline, Mass. Office: 171 Bay State Rd., Boston, Mass. Died Sept. 3, 1948.

N

NACHTRIEB, Henry Francis, animal biologist; b. near Galion, O., May 11, 1857; s. Christian and Friedericka (Diether) N.; German Wallace Coll., Berea, O., 1874-77; B.S., U. of Minn., 1882; Johns Hopkins, 1882-85; m. Anna Eisele, June 21, 1886. With U. of Minn., 1886, prof. animal biology and head of dept., 1887; state zoölogist, Minn., 1889-1912. Edited Reports of the Geological and Natural History Survey of Minnesota, Zoölogical Series, 1892-12; published papers on Echinoderms and Polyoden Spathula. Fellow A.A.A.S.; mem. Am. Soc. Naturalists, Am. Soc. Zoölogists, Am. Assn. Anatomists, Am. Genetic Assn., Phi Beta Kappa, Sigma Xi, Psi Upsilon. Home: 2317 Pleasant Av., Minneapolis. Died July 25, 1942.

NAEGELE, Charles Frederick (nā'gĕ-lē), artist; b. Knoxville, Tenn., May 8, 1857; s. Charles and Christina (Russ) N.; studied art under C. Myles Collier, William Sartain and William M. Chase; m. Lisette Stivers, Aug. 17, 1884; children—Evelyn (Mrs. Lewe Sessions), Charles. Has painted portraits of Gov. Roswell P. Flower, Memorial Library, Watertown, N.Y.; Col. George W. Flower, City Hall, Watertown; Dr. Tod Helmuth, Flower Hosp., N.Y. City; James T. Woodward, Clearing House, N.Y. City; Col. Sam Tate, school auditorium, Tate, Ga.; Gov. Henry McDaniel, Chief Justice Henry Lampkin and Deverly D. Evans, State Capitol, Atlanta, Ga.; Gov. William D. Jelks, State Capitol, Montgomery, Ala.; Mrs. Nellie Tayloe Ross, dir. U.S. Mint; Miss Martha Berry, Berry School, Rome, Ga.; Hon. and Mrs. Robert F. Maddox, of Atlanta, Ga.; Hon. J. Jack Spalding, of Atlanta, Ga. Painting entitled "Recognition" (7'x12'), in Baptistry of the Christian Church, Atlanta, Georgia. Awarded gold medal for medal commemorating 400th anniversary of Columbus' discovery of America, for Com. of 100 Citizens, N.Y. City, 1892; Gold medal for painting, Divinity of Motherhood, Boston, Mass., monogram for Salmagundi Club, George Innis diploma, Salmagundi Club award diploma; Silver medal, portrait of Mrs. Naegele, Charleston, S.C. Painting "Motherlove" is hung in Nat. Gallery, Washington, D.C. Mem. Am. Social Science Assn., Artists Fund Soc. of N.Y. City. Clubs: Lotos (New York); Allied Arts (Birmingham). Originator of method of encouraging public collection of pictures; originated and installed new method for indexing the library, at the Salmagundi Club, N.Y. City. Address: Artcrest, Marietta, Ga.* Died Jan. 27, 1944.

NAIDEN, Earl L. (nād'ĕn), army air corps officer; b. Woodward, Ia., Feb. 2, 1894; s. Henry Richard and Carra (Sanks) N.; ed. Swarely's Prep. Sch., Washington, D.C., 1910-11; B.S., U.S. Mil. Acad., 1915; grad. Command and Gen. Staff Sch., 1920, Army War Coll., 1927, École Supérieure de Guerre, Paris, 1929. Commd. 2d lt., Cav., U.S. Army, 1915, entered aviation 1916, and advanced through the grades to brig. gen., 1942; served in France, Italy, and Eng., World War I. Decorated Black Star; Purple Heart; World War and Mexican Border medals.† Deceased.

NASH, Bert Allen, prof. ednl. psychology; b. Topeka, Kan., Oct. 28, 1898; s. John Winton and Addie Gertrude (Allen) N.; A.B., Washburn Coll., Topeka, 1921; student U. of Kan., 1922-23, Ph.D., Ohio State U., 1928; m. Mina Ruth Bushong, June 1, 1923; children—Barbara Joanne, Robert Alan. Teacher and prin., Rock Creek (Kan.) High School, 1921-22; asso. prof. of psychology, Emporia State Teachers Coll., 1923-26, prof., 1928-30; instr. psychology, Ohio State U., 1926-28; prof. of ednl. psychology, U. of Kan., since 1930; dir. Ednl. Clinic and Reading Lab., U. of Kan.; adminstr. Army Svc. Forces at U. of Kan., 1943-44; cons. Kan. Receiving Home for Children (diagnostic center), Atchison, Kan. Served in S.A.T.C., 1918. Member Governor's Advisory Com. on State Instns. Fellow Am. Psychol. Assn., Mid-West Psychol. Assn., Kansas Psychol. Assn. (pres. 1934), Kan. Mental Hygiene Soc. (pres. 1933-38), Kansas Council for Children (president 1944-45). N.E.A., A.A.A.S., American Legion, Sigma Xi, Phi Delta Kappa, Psi Chi. Republican. Methodist. Clubs: Kiwanis (pres. Lawrence Club 1937; lieut. gov. Div. V., 1939); University (pres. 1944). Editor of Kan. Mental Hygiene Soc. Bull., 1933-38; contbg. editor of Mental Hygiene in Modern Education. Contbr. to ednl. jours. Home: 725 Ohio St., Lawrence, Kan. Died Feb. 18, 1947.

NASH, Charles Sumner, theologian; b. Granby, Mass., Feb. 18, 1856; s. Lorenzo Smith and Nancie Swinington (Knight) N.; A.B., Amherst, 1877, A.M., 1891; instr. Robert Coll., Constantinople, Turkey, 1877-80; B.D., Hartford Theol. Sem., 1883, post-grad. student, 1883-84; D.D., Amherst, 1897; m. Marie Louise Henry, May 15, 1889; children—Charles Sumner (dec.), Katharine Louise (dec.). Ordained Congl. ministry, 1884; pastor First Ch., E. Hartford, Conn., 1884-90; instr. elocution and Bibl. theology, Hartford Theol. Sem., 1890-91; prof. homiletics and pastoral theology, 1891-1911, pres. and prof. ch. polity, 1911-20, pres. emeritus and prof. church polity, 1920, Pacific Theol. Sem. (now Pacific Sch. of Religion), Berkeley, Calif. Carew lecturer, Hartford Theol. Sem., 1908-09. Asst. moderator, Nat. Council Congl. Chs., 1910-13. Mem. Religious Edn. Assn., Amherst Chapter Delta Kappa Epsilon. Republican. Clubs: Authors' (London); Outlook, Sierra, Faculty (Berkeley). Author: Congregational Administration (Carew Lectures), 1909; Our Widening Thought of God, 1914. Address: Pacific School of Religion, Berkeley, Calif. Died Nov. 22, 1926.

NASH, Charles W., automobile mfr., b. De Kalb County, Ill.; s. David L. and Anna (Cadwell) N.; ed. pub. schs.; m. Jessie Hallack, Apr. 23, 1884. Farmer until 1891; entered employ of Flint (Mich.) Road Cart Co., as trimmer, 1891, advanced to supt. and v.p. and gen. supt. of its successor, the Durant-Dort-Carriage Co.; pres. and mgr. Buick Motor Car Co., 1910-16; pres. Gen. Motor Co., 1912-16; organizer, and pres. The Nash Motors Co., 1916-32, chmn. bd. since 1932, name changed to Nash-Kelvinator Corp., 1937; dir. C.&N.W. Ry. Co. (Chicago), C.,St.P.,M.&O. Ry. Co. Republican. Mason, Elk. Home: Beverly Hills, Calif. Died June 6, 1948.

NASH, George Williston, educator; b. Janesville, Wisconsin, December 22, 1868; s. Newman C. and Jennie Elizabeth (Williston) N.; B.S., Yankton Coll., 1891, M.S., 1895; studied U. of Leipzig, 1894-95, U. of Minn. (mathematics, astronomy); 1896-97; LL.D., Yankton, 1911, Colo. College, 1922, Drury Coll., 1923; m. Adelaide M. Warburton, Nov. 17, 1903; children—Newman Curtis, Margaret Adelaide. Joint publisher Sioux Valley News, Canton, S.D., 1887-88; teacher mathematics, Augustana Coll., Canton, S.D., 1891-92; prin. Yankton Coll. Acad., 1893-97; prof. mathematics and astronomy, Yankton Coll., 1897-1902; state supt. pub. instrn. of S.D., 1903-05; pres. Northern Normal and Industrial Sch., Aberdeen, S.D., 1905-14, State Normal Sch., Bellingham, Wash., 1914-22; pres. Congl. Foundation for Edn., 1922-25; pres. Yankton Coll., 1925-40, pres. emeritus since 1940. Mem. bd. dirs. Chicago Theol. Sem. Pres. S.D. Ednl. Assn., 1912; was mem. Wash. State Bd. Edn. and Joint Board of Higher Curricula. Pres. Bellingham Community Chest; elector N.Y. Univ. Hall of Fame, 1945. Life mem. N.E.A.; mem. S.D. Edn. Assn., Pi Gamma Mu, S.A.R. Republican. Congregationalist. Mason (32°). Clubs: Collegiate, Beadle, Music, 20th Century, Hobby; Rotary Internat. (dist. gov. 19th Dist., 1934-35; mem. youth service com., 1935-36). Home: 419 Cedar St., Bellingham, Wash. Died June 30, 1944.

NASH, John Henry, master printer; b. Woodbridge, Can., Mar. 12, 1871; s. John Marvin and Catherine (Cain) N.; ed. high sch., Toronto, Can.; hon. M.A., Mills Coll., 1923; Litt.D., U. of Ore., 1925; LL.D., U. of San Francisco, 1931; m. Mary Henrietta Ford, Oct. 3, 1901. Came to U.S., 1894, naturalized, 1922. Learned printers' trade in Can.; moved to San Francisco, 1895, and has devoted attention to making fine books; lecturer, U. of Ore., 1926-39, prof. typography since 1940. Republican. Mason. Clubs: Family, Book Club of Calif.; Caxton (Chicago); Philolexian of Columbia Univ. (hon.), Grolier (New York). Frequently called upon to speak upon the finer aspects of printing. Home: 2915 Piedmont Av., Berkeley, Calif. Address: U. of Oregon, Eugene, Ore.* Died May 24, 1947.

NASH, Philip Curtis, educator; b. Hingham, Mass., Aug. 28, 1890; s. Louis Philip and E. Harriot (Curtis) N.; A.B., Harvard, 1911, M.C.E., 1912; D.Eng. (hon.), Case Sch. Applied Science, 1937; LL.D., Northeastern, 1938; Antioch, 1944; m. Frances Erma Nightingale, June 16, 1913; children—Curtis Eliot, Erma Harriet, Jeanne Lillian. Asst. engr. Boston Transit Commn., 1912-17; prof. civ. engring., Northeastern Univ., Boston, 1919-21; dean Antioch Coll., 1921-29; exec. dir. League of Nations Assn., 1929-33; pres. University of Toledo since 1933. Moderator Am. Unitarian Assn., 1942-44. Pres. Association of Urban Universities, 1945. Served as 1st lieut. and capt. 1st Replacement Regt. Engrs., Washington Barracks, D.C., and dir. Mil. Trade Schs. there. Pres. Ohio College Assn., 1938. Mem. Phi Beta Kappa, Delta Upsilon. Club: Toledo. Unitarian. Home: 3031 Bancroft St., Toledo, O. Died May 6, 1947.

NASON, Arthur Huntington, univ. prof, retired; b. Augusta, Me., Feb. 3, 1877; s. Charles H. and Emma (Huntington) N.; A.B., Bowdoin, 1899, A.M., 1903; grad. student Columbia, 1903-05, Ph.D., 1915; m. Edna Walton Selover, June 4, 1915. Teacher of English in secondary schools and Bowdoin Coll., 1899-1903; mem. dept. of English since 1905, prof. English, 1916-42, emeritus since 1942, New York University; dir. New York Univ. Press, 1916-33; instr. in English, Union Theological Seminary, 1910-27; fellow in Am. Lit., Sarah Lawrence Coll., 1928-30. Mem. Modern Lang. Assn. America, Modern Humanities Research Assn. (sub.-sec. 1924-28), Delta Kappa Epsilon, Phi Beta Kappa; mem. council Phi Beta Kappa Alumni in New York, 1935-37; asso. mem. Scabbard and Blade; a founder, 1907, and bus. mgr., Andiron Club of N.Y. City and mng. editor of its publs. to 1941, first hon. mem. since 1942. Chairman Registrants' Advisory Board 86, The Bronx, N.Y. City, 1940-41. Club: New York Univ. Faculty (pres. 1933-34). Author: Heralds and Heraldry in Jonson's Plays, 1907; James Shirley, Dramatist, 1915; Efficient Composition, 1917; and other text-books. Home: 304 Brunswick Av., Gardiner, Me. Died Apr. 22, 1944.

NAST, Condé, publisher; b. N.Y. City, Mar. 26, 1874; s. William F. and Esther (Benoist) N.; A.B., Georgetown, 1895, A.M., 1896; LL.B., Washington U., 1898; m. Clarisse Coudert, Aug. 20, 1902; m. 2d, Leslie Foster, Dec. 28, 1928. Advertising mgr., 1900-05, business mgr., 1905-07, Collier's publs.; with Theron McCampbell, organized Home Pattern Co., 1904; joint pub. with Robert J. Collier of The Housekeeper, 1911; pres. and pub. Vogue since 1909, also House and Garden, Glamour, Vogue Patterns, Hollywood Patterns; pres. Condé Nast Press. Clubs: Racquet and Tennis, Deepdale, Sands Point, National Golf. Home: 1040 Park Av. Office: Graybar Bldg., 43d St. and Lexington Av., New York, N.Y. Died Sep. 19, 1942.

NATHAN, Maud, social worker; b. New York, N.Y.; d. Robert Weeks and Ann Augusta (Florance) Nathan; ed. Mrs. Ogden Hoffman's Sch., Gardiner Inst., New York, and Green Bay (Wis.) High Sch.; m. Frederick Nathan, 1880; 1 dau., Annette Florance (dec.). Was speaker before Internat. Congress of Women in London, 1899, Berlin, 1904, Internat. Peace Congress, New York, 1907, Internat. Conf. of Consumers' Leagues, Geneva, Switzerland, 1908; del. Internat. Congress for Labor Legislation, Lucerne, 1908; has occupied pulpits in New York, Chicago, and Boston; was active in 3 municipal campaigns in New York; contbr. to mags. and newspapers. Del. internat. Woman Suffrage Conv., Stockholm, 1911; Internat. Woman Suffrage Conv., Budapest, 1913; Internat. Conf. Consumers' Leagues, Antwerp, 1913; Internat. Peace Congress, The Hague, 1913; del. and speaker at Internat. Woman Suffrage Alliance Conv., Geneva, Switzerland, 1920; speaker at Nat. Univ., Pekin, China, 1921, also at Girls' Normal Sch., Canton, China; del. and speaker Internat. Women's Suffrage Congress, Rome, Italy, 1923. Rep. of D.A.R. at opening of Peace Palace, The Hague, 1913, and presented peace flags. Pres. Consumers' League of New York, 1897-1917, hon. pres. since 1917; ex-v.p. of Nat. Consumers' League; ex-1st v.p. N.Y. Fedn. of Women's Clubs; former v.p. Nat. Inst. Social Sciences (awarded medal); hon. v.p. Woman's Roosevelt Memorial Assn.; hon. v.p. N.Y. sect. of Council of Jewish Women; mem. English-Speaking Union, Red Cross; former mem. D.A.R. Hebrew. Clubs: Barnard (New York); Authors League of America. Author: The Story of An Epoch-Making Movement, 1926; Once Upon a Time and Today, 1933. Home: 225 W. 86th St., New York, N.Y.; also Morris, Conn. Died Dec. 15, 1946.

NAYLOR, Joseph Randolph, merchant; born Wheeling, W.Va., Aug. 27, 1878; s. John Sargent and Anna (Wendelken) N.; grad. Linsly Inst., Wheeling, W.Va., 1895; A.B., Washington and Jefferson Coll., 1898, A.M., 1901; LL.B., U. of Va., 1901; m. Reita Caldwell, June 1, 1905 (died Aug. 22, 1925); children—Joseph Randolph, Anna Elizabeth Metcalfe; m. 2d, Mrs. Inez Leslie Murdock, Aug. 12, 1929. Instr. Linsly Inst., 1898-99; admitted to W.Va. bar, 1901, and practiced at Wheeling until 1906; mem. since 1906 John S. Naylor & Co., wholesale dry goods, notions, etc., inc., 1908, as John S. Naylor Co., of which was sec.-treas., 1908-17, v.p., 1917, pres. since 1918; dir. Pittsburgh Br. Federal Reserve Bank of Cleveland, 1924-30, chmn. bd., 1926, 29; pres. Nat. Exch. Bank, Wheeling, 1929-42. Mem. W.Va. House Representatives, 1903-07. Vice chmn. board of trustees, Washington and Jefferson College. Member Wheeling Landscape Commission, West Virginia Chamber of Commerce, Wheeling Chamber of Commerce, Phi Gamma Delta, Phi Delta Phi. Republican. Clubs: Rotary Internat. (ex-gov. 24th dist.), Twilight, Fort Henry; Wheeling Country. Home: Bethany Pike. Office: 1401 Main St., Wheeling, W.Va. Died March 8, 1948.

NAYLOR, William Keith, author, army officer; b. Bloomington, Ill., Nov. 24, 1874; s. William Alexander and Genevieve Charlotte (Hay) N.; grad. Mich. Mil. Acad., 1894; LL.B., U. of Minn., 1898; admitted to Minn. bar; distinguished grad. Inf. and Cav. Sch., Ft. Leavenworth, Kan., 1904; grad. Staff Coll., Ft. Leavenworth, 1905, 21, Army War Coll., Washington, 1910, 23; m. Margaret Wagner, dau. Col. A. L. Wagner, U.S. Army, Dec. 27, 1904; children—Margaret (wife of 1st lt. Dwight L. Adams, U.S. Army), William K., Alexander Hay. Vol. 14th Minn. Inf., May 8, 1898, and commd. 2d lt.; hon. discharged, vol. service, July 24, 1898; commd. 2d lt. regular army, July 9, 1898; promoted through grades to col., July 1, 1920; served in World War as col. N.A., and brig. gen. U.S. Army. With 9th Inf. in Philippines, 1898-99; China Relief Expdn., 1900; later instr. strategy and mil. history, service schs., about 5 yrs.; chief of staff 33d Div. that participated in Somme offensive; in Meuse-Argonne with 3d Corps; promoted, and assigned as chief of staff of corps; after return to U.S., again apptd. instr. strategy and mil. history, Service Schs., later dir. Staff Sch. and dir. War Plans Div. of Army War Coll.; asst. chief of staff and dir. mil. intelligence, gen. staff, 1922-24; commander 15th Infantry in China, 1924-26; appointed commander Infantry Post, Boston Harbor, and 13th Inf., Oct. 16, 1926; apptd. chief of staff 2d Corps Area, Governor's Island, N.Y., May 27, 1929; completed tour as chief of staff, May 26, 1933, and detailed in charge of Corps Area; apptd. prof. mil. science and tactics, U. of Ill., July 1, 1933; promoted brig. gen. regular army, Dec. 1, 1933; apptd., in command Ft. Benjamin Harrison, Ind., Dec. 8, 1933; retired November 30, 1938. Decorated Silver Star with oak leaf cluster, "for gallantry in action" at Tientsin, China, July 13, 1900, and in Meuse-Argonne Offensive, Sept. and Oct. 1918; Distinguished Service Medal (U.S.). Comdr. Order of St. Michael and St. George (British); Comdr. Crown of Italy; Officer Legion of Honor and Croix de Guerre (French). Mem. Mil. Order of the Dragon, Delta Chi. Republican. Mason (32°). Club: Army and Navy (Washington). Author: Principles of Strategy, 1922 (adopted as official textbook by Japan); Marne Miracle, 1924; The Principles of War, 1923. Address: War Dept., Washington, D.C. Died Aug. 3, 1942.

NAZIMOVA, Alla (Mrs. Charles Bryant), actress; b. Yalta, Crimea, Russia, June 4, 1879; d. Jacob and Sofia N. Taken to Montreux, Switzerland, and early learned to speak the German and French langs., also to play the violin; returned to Russia at 10 and studied music at St. Petersburg Conservatory; at Odessa, and dramatic art at Philaem Soc. at Moscow. Began as leading woman in Kostroma, Russia; later in stock cos., and appeared at St. Petersburg in prominent roles, 1904; début in New York as Lia, in Russian-language, in "The Chosen People," at the Herald Square Theatre, March 10, 1905; studied the English language and later played leading parts in "Hedda Gabler," "A Doll's House," "Comptess Coquette," "The Master Builder," "Little Eyolff," "The Comet," "Bella Donna," "War Brides," "Ception Shoals," etc. Made first motion picture, "War Brides," 1916. Address: 8080 Sunset Boul., Hollywood, Calif. Died July 13, 1945.

NEAGLE, Pickens (nē'g'l), lawyer; b. Gaston County, N.C., Sept. 10, 1861; s. John Liddell and Martha Lavinia (Stone) N.; A.B., C.E., Union Coll., Schenectady, N.Y., 1884, A.M., 1894; LL.B., Columbian (now George Washington) U., 1886; unmarried. Became connected with legal div. of Navy Dept., 1887, sr. mem. solicitors' staff, 1908-21, solicitor, 1921-33; now in pvt. practice. Episcopalian. Home: 1821 Biltmore St. N.W. Office: 910 17th St. N.W., Washington, D.C. Deceased.

NEAL, George Ira, lawyer; b. Milton, W.Va.; s. Andrew Dickerson and Malinda (Newman) N.; LL.B., W.Va. U., 1888; m. Eunice Earp, Dec. 5, 1912; children—Virginia (dec.), Irene, George I. Admitted to W.Va. bar, 1889; and has since practiced at Huntington; became U.S. atty, Southern Dist. of W.Va., 1933; formerly mayor of Huntington; was Dem. nominee for Congress. Mem. Huntington Chamber of Commerce (pres.). Democrat. Baptist. Club: Rotary (pres.). Home: 1112 Sixth St. Office: Guaranty Bank Bldg., Huntington, W.Va. Died Feb. 3, 1946.

NEAL, William Joseph, farmer and govt. official; b. Meredith, N.H., Aug. 3, 1905; s. William Howard and Lucy M. R. (Neal) N.; ed. pub. schs., Meredith, N.H.; U. of New Hampshire, 1923-25; m. Barbara Louise Watson, June 18, 1033; children—Mary Eliza beth, William Sumner, James Edgar, John Raymond. Engaged in farming and pure bred livestock business since early years; secy.-treas. American Devon Cattle Club since 1924; active in leadership of farm organizations since 1925; held local public offices, 1927-35; mem. N.H. legislature, 1933-35; supervisor Federal Farm Census in N.H., 1935; postmaster, Meredith, N.H., 1935-42; Dem. candidate for governor of N.H., 1942; dep. adminstr. Rural Electrification Adminstrn., Washington, D.C., since 1943. Chmn. agrl. adv. com. and mem. exec. com. N.H. Council of Defense, 1941-43. Sec. Union Grange Fair Assn., Plymouth, N.H., since 1936; master N.H. State Grange, 1937-43; pres. N.H. Electric Cooperative, Plymouth, N.H., 1939-43; Patron of Husbandry Nat. Grange. Home: Meredith, N.H. Office: U.S. Dept. Agriculture, Washington 25. Died Oct. 26, 1949.

NEEDHAM, Charles Willis, educator, lawyer; born Castile, N.Y., Sept. 30, 1848; s. Charles Rollin Needham; ed. Castile, N.Y.; LL.B., Albany Law Sch., 1869; LL.D., U. of Rochester, 1901, Georgetown Coll., Ky., 1901; m. Caroline M. Beach, Nov. 2, 1870 (died 1912). Practiced law at Chicago, 1874-90, Washington, 1890-97; prof. law, Columbian (later George Washington) U., 1897, organized and elected dean Sch. of Comparative Jurisprudence and Diplomacy, 1898, pres., 1902-10 (resigned); with approval of trustees applied for amendment by Congress to the Univ. Charter, enlarging its powers, making it non-sectarian, and changing name to George Washington U.; served as gen. solicitor Interstate Commerce Commn. Lecturer upon legal ethics, constitutional law, interstate commerce law, Washington Coll. of Law and Am. Univ. to 1928. Del. Congrès International de Droit Comparé, 1900, Congrès Internat. des Chemins de Fer, Congrès Internat. d'Assistance Publique et de Bienfaisance Privée, Paris; speaker upon jurisprudence, Congress of Arts and Sciences, St. Louis Expn., 1904, and upon Free School Day, Jamestown Expn., 1907. Mem. Am. Bar Assn., Am. Inst. Law, Am. Econ. Assn. Clubs: Cosmos (Washington); Fine Arts (New York). Author: Cases on Foreign and Interstate Commerce Law (2 vols.). Contbr. to periodicals. Home: La Salle Apts., Washington. Died June 15, 1935.

NEEDHAM, James Carson; b. Carson City, Nev., Sept. 17, 1864, in an emigrant wagon (parents en route to Calif.); s. Charles E. and Olive L. (Drake) N.; Ph.B., U. of Pacific, 1886; LL.B., U. of Mich., 1889; m. Dora Deetta Parsons, July 1, 1894; children—Mildred (Mrs. Edward Thomas Taylor, Jr.), Chauncey Everett, Nathalie (Mrs. Maynard P. Garrison). In practice at Modesto, Calif., 1889-1913, San Diego, 1913-16, Modesto, 1916-18. Mem. 56th to 62d Congresses (1899-1913), 6th Calif. Dist.; judge Superior Court, Jan. 1, 1919-Feb. 1, 1935. Republican. Member Phi Kappa Psi. Pres. Covered Wagon Baby Club (over 100 persons who were born in covered wagons before the building of Union Pacific R.R., prior to 1869). Home: 1105 15th St., Modesto, Calif. Died July 11, 1942.

NEFF, Elmer Hartshorn, mech. engr.; b. Clio, Mich., Mar. 6, 1866; s. Henry Clinton and Emily (Hartshorn) Neff; B.S. in Mechanical Engring., University of Michigan, 1890, M.E., 1901, awarded citation, 1941; m. Isabella Cottrell, June 28, 1894; 1 dau., Dorothy Isabel (wife of Prof. Walter Andrew Curry). Erecting engr., Edw. F. Allis Co., Milwaukee, Wis., 1890-91; designer, Gisholt Machine Co., Madison, Wis., 1891-92; with Westinghouse interests, Pittsburgh, Pa., 1893; instr. in mech. engring., Purdue U.; with Brown & Sharpe Mfg. Co., Providence, R.I., since 1896, mgr. N.Y. Co., 1897-1937. Served as mem. first N.J. State Park Commn.; mem. Montclair (N.J.) Bd. Edn., 5 yrs. Mem. Essex Co. (N.J.) Republican Com. over 30 yrs.; mem. Upper Montclair Rep. Club. An organizer of Machinery Club (N.Y. City) and of Montclair (N.J.) Soc. Engrs. Mem. S.A.R. Conglist. Mason. Clubs: Commonwealth (Upper Montclair); University of Michigan, Railroad-Machinery (New York). Home: 69 Oakwood Av., Montclair, N.J. Died Jan. 26, 1946.

NEFF, Frank Chaffee, pediatrics; b. Winchester, Ind.; s. Andrew Jackson and Ann (Chaffee) N.; student State U. of Iowa, 1893-96; M.D., Univ. Med. College, Kansas City, Mo., 1897; hon. D.Sc., Kansas Wesleyan Coll., 1931; m. Josephine Cole; children—Mrs. Frances Elizabeth Link, Warren Cole, Frank Chaffee. Interne Kansas City Gen. Hosp., N.Y. Infant Asylum, King's County Hosp., Brooklyn; asst., Charite Children's Clinic, Berlin, 1909; began practice at Kansas City, Mo., 1901, practice limited to diseases of children since 1910; emeritus prof. pediatrics, Sch. Med., U. Kan. Mem. A.M.A. (sect. on diseases of children), Am. Acad., Bd. Pediatrics, Am. Pediatric Soc., Mo. State Med. Assn., Jackson County Med. Soc., Sigma Xi, Alpha Omega Alpha, Phi Kappa Psi. Phi Beta Pi. Contbr. to various med. books and current jours. Home: 6027 McGee St. Office: 315 Alameda Rd., Kansas City, Mo. Died Dec. 3, 1947.

NEILER, Samuel Graham (nā'lẽr), elec. and mech. engr.; b. Erie, Pa., Nov. 14, 1866; s. Samuel E. and Lovina (Jackson) N.; spl. student, Mass. Inst. Tech., 1884-86; mech. engring. course, U. of Minn., 1888-89; m. Mary A. Gowdy, May 14, 1901; 1 son, Richard. Asst. mech. engr., M.,St.P.&S.S.M. Ry., 1889-90; engr. at Boston office of Thomson-Houston Electric Co., 1891-92; asst. elec. engr., World's Fair, Chicago, 1892-94. Mem. Pierce, Richardson & Neiler, cons. and designing engrs., 1895-1911, pres., 1911-13; mem. Neiler, Rich & Co. since 1913; also mem. firm Fugard, Olsen, Urbain & Neiler. Mem. of Internat. Jury of Awards St. Louis Expn., 1904; mem. com. on elect. generation, Century of Progress, Chicago, 1933. Life mem. Am. Inst. of E.E., Am. Soc. M.E., Am. Soc. Heating and Ventilating Engrs.; mem. Franklin Inst., A.A.A.S., Inst. of E.E. of Gt. Britain, Nat. Dist. Heating Assn., Am. Soc. Civil Engrs., The Electric Assn. of Chicago (v.p. and dir.). Republican. Episcopalian. Club: Union League. Home: 737 N. Oak Park Av., Oak Park, Ill. Office: 431 S. Dearborn St., Chicago, Ill.; and 520 N. Michigan Av., Chicago, Ill. Deceased

NEILL, Charles Patrick (nēl), ex-U.S. commr. of labor; b. Rock Island, Ill., Dec. 12, 1865; s. James and Julia (Walsh) N.; student U. of Notre Dame, Ind., 1885-88; U. of Tex., 1888-89; A.B., Georgetown

U. (D.C.), 1891; Ph.D., Johns Hopkins, 1897; LL.D., Notre Dame, 1908; m. Esther Waggaman, June 6, 1901; children—Charles W., Thomas T., James K., Richard N. (dec.). Instr. U. of Notre Dame, 1891-94; instr., asso. prof. and prof. polit. economy, Catholic U., Washington, 1897-1905; U.S. commr. of labor, Feb. 1, 1905-Mar. 1913; commr. labor statistics, Dept. of Labor, Mar.-May 1913; with Am. Smelting & Refining Co., New York, 1913-15; manager Bureau of Information of Southeastern Railways, Washington, 1915-39. Was v.p. Board of Charities, D.C., 1900-1908; asst. recorder Anthracite Strike Commn., 1902; recorder Arbitration Bd., Birmingham, 1903; mem. U.S. Immigration Commn., 1907-10; mem. U.S. Coal Commn., 1922-23. Fellow Am. Econ. Assn.; mem. Internat. Inst. Statistics, Internat. Com. on Social Insurance; pres. Am. Statis. Assn., 1916-17. Clubs: Cosmos (Washington); Seigniory Club (P.Q., Can.). Home: 3556 Macomb St., Washington, D.C. Died Oct. 2, 1942.

NEILL, Paul, newspaper editor; b. Joplin, Mo., Apr. 16, 1892; s. Thomas Franklyn and Mary (McCullough) N.; A.B., U. of Wash., 1917; m. Isabel Perry, May 25, 1921. Began as reporter Yakima (Wash.), 1917; successively reporter Seattle Daily Times, Seattle Post-Intelligencer, Spokane Daily Chronicle; editor Yakima Morning Herald, 1921-38, Yakima Daily Republic since May 9, 1938. Served as regimental sergt. maj., U.S.G.H.Q., Chaumont, France, World War. Mem. Am. Legion, Sigma Delta Chi, Alpha Tau Omega. Granted Certificate of Merit (U.S.) and Order of Purple Heart for service in World War. Republican. Presbyterian. Clubs: Rotary, Riverside Golf. Home: 212 N. 21st Av. Address: Yakima Daily Republic, Yakima, Wash. Died Mar. 9, 1940.

NEILSON, Nellie, coll. prof.; b. Phila., Pa., Apr. 5, 1873; d. William George and Mary (Cunningham) Neilson; A.B., Bryn Mawr Coll., 1893, A.M., 1894, Ph.D., 1899; L.H.D., Smith Coll., 1938; Litt.D., Russell Sage Coll., 1940; resident fellow in history, Bryn Mawr Coll., 1894-95, Coll. Alumnæ Assn. fellowship, 1895-96, reader in English, 1900-02, instr. history, 1902-03, prof. history, Mt. Holyoke Coll., 1903-39; emeritus prof. since 1939. Mem. British Record Society, American Historical Association (president), Selden Society. Fellow Mediæval Academy of America, Royal Historical Society. Episcopalian. Author: Economic Conditions on the Manors of Ramsey Abbey, 1899; Customary Rents (Oxford Studies in Social and Legal History), 1910; collaborator in Survey of the Honour of Denbigh (Brit. Acad., Records of Social and Economic History), 1914; The Terrier of Fleet, Lincolnshire (same), Vol. IV, 1920; The Cartulary of Bilsington, Kent (same), Vol. VII, 1927. Editor Year Book 10, Edward IV (Vol. 47), for Selden Soc., 1930; Mediæval Agrarian Economy, 1936; Royal Forests, in "English Government at Work, 1327-1336" (Mediæval Acad.), 1940; chapter on English agrarian society, Middle Ages, in Cambridge Econ. History of Europe, Vol. I, 1941; "Early Pattern of the Common Law (Am. Hist. Review, Jan. 1944)"; The Register of Stoneleigh Abbey (published posthumously). Contbr. hist. articles and revs. Address: Open Fields, South Hadley, Mass. Died May 26, 1947; buried in West Laurel Cemetery, Philadelphia.

NEILSON, William Allan, coll. pres.; b. Doune, Scotland, Mar. 28, 1869; s. David and Mary (Allan) N.; M.A., U. of Edinburgh, 1891; M.A., Harvard, 1896, Ph.D., 1898, LL.D. from same univ., 1935; LL.D., Brown and Amherst, 1918, Edinburgh, 1928, Dartmouth, Princeton and Oberlin, 1937, Mt. Holyoke, 1938, McGill U., 1938, Smith, 1941; L.H.D., Williams, 1925, Kenyon and Middlebury, 1940, U. of Vermont, 1941; Litt.D., Yale, 1927; m. Elisabeth Muser, June 25, 1906; children—Allan (dec.), Margaret, Caroline. Teacher in Scotland and Toronto, Can., 1891-95; asso. in English, Bryn Mawr Coll., 1898-1900; instr. Harvard, 1900-04; adj. prof. English, 1904-05, prof. English, 1905-06, Columbia Univ.; prof. English, Harvard Univ., 1906-17; pres. Smith Coll., 1917-39. Exchange prof., U. of Paris, 1914-15. Decorated by govts. of France and Spain. Fellow Am. Acad. of Arts and Sciences, Medieval Acad. Am., Mass. Hist. Society, Am. Philos. Soc. Overseer, Harvard, since 1942. Clubs: Tavern, Century, Town Hall, Harvard (N.Y.). Author: Origins and Sources of The Court of Love, 1899; Essentials of Poetry, 1912; The Facts About Shakespeare, 1913; Burns, How to Know Him, 1917; A History of English Literature, 1920, Intellectual Honesty, 1940. Editor: Milton's Minor Poems, 1899; Shakespeare's Complete Works (Cambridge Poets), 1906, rev., 1942; The Types of English Literature, series beginning 1907; The Chief Elizabethan Dramatists, 1911; Roads to Knowledge, 1932; We Escaped, 1941. Co-editor: The Tudor Shakespeare, 1911; Chief British Poets of the 14th and 15th Centuries, 1916. Asso. editor of The Harvard Classics, 1909; Harvard Classics Shelf of Fiction, 1917; Selections from Chaucer, 1921. Editor-in-chief Webster's New Internat. Dictionary, 2d Edition, 1934. Contbr. articles for tech. jours. and lit. mags., and for Cambridge History of English Literature, Vol. VI, 1910. Home: Falls Village, Conn. Died Feb. 13, 1946; buried at Smith College, Northampton, Mass.

NELSON, George Bliss, judge; b. Amherst, Wis., May 21, 1876; s. James J. and Juniata P. (Andrews) N.; B.L., U. of Wis., 1898; LL.B., George Washington University, 1902; LL.D., Nashotah House, 1941; married Ruth Weller, April 16, 1912; children—James J., Reginald W., George B. Admitted to Wisconsin bar, 1904, practicing at Stevens Point until 1930; dist. atty. Portage County, 1906-12; apptd. justice Wis. Supreme Court, Sept. 25, 1930, elected for 10 yr. term, 1935. Mem. bd. of Regents of Normal Schs., Wis., 1910-20. Mem. Am. and Wis. State bar assns., Order of Coif, Theta Delta Chi, Phi Delta Phi. Episcopalian. Mason (32°), Shriner, Elk. Clubs: Madison Literary, Town and Gown, Rotary (hon.). Home: 822 Miami Pass, Madison, Wis. Died Jan. 10, 1943.

NEMMERS, Erwin Plein, lawyer, publisher; b. Kenosha, Wis., Jan. 14, 1879; s. Michael Ludwig and Barbara Rosa (Plein) N.; A.B., Marquette Coll., 1898; A.M., Georgetown U., 1899, Ph.D., 1900, LL.B., 1901, LL.M., 1902; m. Mechthild Henrietta Esser, April 25, 1915; children—Erwin E., Frederic E. Admitted to Wis. state bar, 1901, U.S. Supreme Ct. bar, 1902, and practiced in Milwaukee, Wis., since 1902; counsel and dir. Marquette Bldg. & Loan Assn. since 1912; atty. Northwestern Mutual Life Ins. since 1925; sr. partner M. L. Nemmers Pub. Co. (Catholic Ch. Music) since 1929. Awarded grad. scholarship to Georgetown U. by Marquette U., 1899. Mem. Am., Wis., Milwaukee bar assns., Marquette Alumni Assn. (past pres.), Catholic Knights of Wis. Roman Catholic. Home: 2936 N. Hackett Av., Milwaukee, Wis. Died Dec. 22, 1944.

NESBITT, Frank Watterson (nĕz'bĭt), lawyer; b. Wheeling, W.Va., Apr. 4, 1870; s. Thomas Wilson and Rebecca (Watterson) N.; Ph.B., Wooster (O.) Coll., 1892; LL.B., U. of Va., 1895; m. Della M. Goodwin, Oct. 20, 1897; 1 son, Russell Goodwin. City solicitor, Wheeling, 1897-1900; pros. atty. Ohio County, W.Va., 1901-04; judge 1st Jud. Circuit of W.Va., 1905-13; sr. mem. Nesbitt, Goodwin & Nesbitt; div. counsel of B.&O. R.R. since 1915; solicitor of 14th Dist. of Pa. R.R. System. Mem. Am. and W.Va. bar assns. Republican. Methodist. Mason, Elk. Clubs: Ft. Henry, Wheeling Country. Home: McClure Hotel. Office: Riley Law Bldg., Wheeling, W.Va. Died Nov. 4, 1945.

NESTOR, Agnes; b. Grand Rapids, Mich.; d. Thomas and Anna (McEwen) N.; ed. parochial and pub. schs., Grand Rapids; LL.D., Loyola Univ., Chicago, 1929. Began as glove worker, with Eisendrath Glove Co., Chicago, 1897; gen. sec.-treas., 1906-13, gen. pres., 1913-15, v.p. since 1915, Internat. Glove Workers' Union of America; mem. bd. Nat. Women's Trade Union League; pres. Chicago Women's Trade Union League; apptd. by Pres. Wilson as mem. Fed. Commn. to consider nat. aid for vocational edn., 1914; apptd. by gov. of Ill. mem. Indsl. Survey Commn., Jan. 1918; mem. Woman's Com., subsidiary to Council of Nat. Defense, and made chmn. dept. of women in industry; mem. adv. council to sec. of Labor in war labor legislation. Mem. Labor Mission, visiting Great Britain and France, Apr. 1918; mem. Governor's Commn. on Unemployment and Relief, 1930; mem. bd. Joint Emergency Relief Fund of Cook County, 1931; mem. bd. trustees Century of Progress Expn., Chicago; mem. adv. council U.S. Employment Service; mem. local adv. com., Div. of Unemployment Compensation and Employment Service for Chicago Metropolitan Area; mem. Chicago Recreation Commn., 1934; mem. adv. com. of Chicago Plan Commn., 1939. Roman Catholic. Home: 4840 N. Hermitage Av. Office: 630 S. Ashland Boul., Chicago. Died Dec. 8, 1948.

NESTOS, Ragnvald Anderson (nĕst'ŏs), ex-governor; b. Voss, Norway, Apr. 12, 1877; s. Andres R. and Herborg (Saue) N.; came to U.S., 1893, naturalized citizen, 1898; grad. Mayville (N.D.) State Normal Sch., 1900; Ph.B., U. of Wis., 1902; LL.B., U. of N.D., 1904; unmarried. Began at Minot, N.D., as mem. Johnson & Nestos, 1904, now mem. Nestos & Herigstad. Mem. N.D. Ho. of Rep., 1911-12; state's atty., Ward County, N.D., 1913-16; candidate for Rep. nomination for U.S. Senate, 1916; elected gov. of N.D. against candidate of Non-Partisan League, at recall election, as independent candidate, Oct. 28, 1921, for term ending Jan. 2, 1923; reëlected as Republican for term, 1923-25. Del. Rep. Nat. Conv., 1932, mem. Platform Com.; mem. regional exec. com. and nat. rural com., Boy Scouts of America. Mem. Am. and N.D. State bar assns., Phi Delta Theta, Delta Sigma Rho. Lutheran. Rotarian. Chautauqua and lyceum lecturer. Home: 420 Second St., Minot, N.D. Died July 15, 1942.

NETHERWOOD, Douglas B(lakeshaw), army officer; b. Birmingham, Eng., Feb. 4, 1885; s. Tom and Ann (Wood) N.; brought to U.S., 1887, naturalized, 1910; B.S. in Mech. Engring., Agr. and Mech. Coll. of Tex., 1908; M.B.A., Harvard Grad. Sch. of Business Adminstrn., 1927; grad. Army Industrial Coll., 1925, Air Corps Tactical Sch., 1932, Army War Coll., 1936; m. Harriet V. C. Browne, April 30, 1919; children—Douglas Blakeshaw, Francis Bowne, William Draper, Elisabeth Grant. Enlisted in U.S. Army, 1908; commd. 2d lt. Coast Arty. Corps, 1911, and advanced through the grades to brig. gen. (temp.), Oct. 1940; detailed to Signal Corps for flying training, Dec. 1913; made first solo flight, San Diego, Calif., Feb. 7, 1914; comd. Aviation Repair Dept., Dallas, Texas, Nov. 1917-Mar. 1921; comd. Borinquen Field, Puerto Rico. Awarded Victory medal. Mem. Early Birds. Clubs: Army and Navy (Manila, P.I.). Home: 4936 Rodman St. N.W., Washington, D.C.* Deceased.

NETERER, Jeremiah, judge; b. nr. Goshen, Ind., 1862; B.L., Law Sch., Valparaiso Univ., 1885; twice married; 4 children. Admitted to state bars Ind. and Kan., 1885, Wash. State, 1890; settled in Bellingham, Wash., 1890; elected city atty., 1893; chmn. Dem. State Conv., 1898; chmn. bd. regents State Normal Sch., Bellingham, beginning 1899-1913; was mem. bd. overseers, Whitman Coll. many yrs.; became judge Superior Court, Whatcom County, Wash., 1901; del. Dem. Nat. Conv., Baltimore, 1912; U.S. dist. judge, Western Dist. of Wash., 1913-34; retired June 1, 1934, but is continuing in service by assignment in the District Court, and Circuit Court of Appeals, 9th Circuit. Mem. Am. Bar Assn.; asso. mem. Maritime Law Assn. of U.S.; mem. Order of Coif. Conglist. Grand Master, Grand Lodge F. and A.M. of Wash., 1910-11. Home: 2702 Broadway N., Seattle, Wash. Died Feb. 2, 1943.

NEUBERG, Maurice J(oseph), educator; b. Katowitz, Germany, Aug. 15, 1888; s. Charles H. and Pearl N.; A.B., Wheaton (Ill.) Coll., 1915; B.D., Drew Theol. Sem., 1917; A.M., Columbia University, 1918; Ph.D., U. of Chicago, 1925; m. Buelah E. Rhodes, Aug. 1, 1928; children—Barbara Jane, Vivian Lucile. Clergyman M.E. Ch. and teacher pub. schs. in New Jersey and Maine, 1915-18; research asso. Interchurch World Movement, 1919-20; asst. prof. edn. and psychology, U. of Okla., 1920-22; prof. edn., Chicago Normal Coll., 1925-26; same, and head of dept., Ill. Wesleyan U., 1926-27; prof. edn. and dir. personnel, Wittenberg Coll., since 1927; on leave to work for U.S. Government as Civilian Administrator of the Engineering Maintenance Officers Training School, F.A.D. Taberson Field, Fairfield, O. Chmn. research com. Nat. Lutheran Ednl. Conf. Fellow A.A.A.S., Assn. Applied Psychologists, Am. Psychol. Assn.; mem. Am. Assn. Univ. Profs., Ohio Colls. Assn. (com. on tech. research), Am. Personnel Assn., Eugene Field Soc. (hon.), Kappa Phi Kappa, Kappa Delta Pi, Psi Chi. Club: Torch. Author: Right Living (2 vols.), 1925; Introduction to Guidance, 1930; Principles of Vocational Choice, 1934. Editor: Guidance Program Manuals, 1931-32. Organized guidance programs in Miami and Montgomery Counties, Ohio, 1930-32; then in pub. schs. of Dayton, O. Home: St. Paris Pike, R.R. No. 2, Springfield, O. Died Feb. 10, 1944.

NEUMANN, A(rnold) J(ohn) Robert, clergyman; b. Trebnitz, Germany, Dec. 1, 1872; s. Julius Robt. and Fanny Louisa (Pichon de la Tremouille) N.; grad. Gymnasium, Sondershausen, 1891; students univs. Halle, Basel and Göttingen; A.M., Carthage (Ill.) Coll., 1903; D.D., Midland (Neb.) College, 1912; Litt.D., Wittenberg Coll., Springfield, O., 1922; m. Emma Geisendorfer, Nov. 23, 1897; children—Robert L., Arthur M., Prosper F., Kenneth B., Mary Louise. Came to U.S., 1895, naturalized citizen, 1901. Ordained ministry Evang. Luth. Ch., 1897; pastor, Chicago, 1895-96. Pittsfield, Illinois, 1897-98, Bethany Ch., Burlington, Ia., 1898-1929; head Dept. of Bible, Religious Edn. and French and German Langs. Carthage Coll. since 1929, Supt. Luth. Lit. Bd. and editor since 1899; pres. Wartburg Synod Evang. Luth. Ch. in Am., 1919-31. Trustee Chicago Sem.; mem. Am. Soc. of Oriental Research, Am. Geog. Soc., Modern Lang. Assn. of Am. Am. Philol. Soc., Pi Gamma Mu Fraternity and Alpha Mu Gamma. Dem. Author: "I Believe," Sermons on Creed, 1918; The Sacrament of the Altar, 1916; The Path of the Cross, 1917; Handbook of Religious Instrn; The Voice from the Cross; Two Worlds and One God; The Personality Ideal; Essentials of the Word; A French Teacher's Course; (brochure) The Wisdom of Job and the Social Distress of Today; The Lutheran Tract Society; A System of Religious Education, 1938; The Present Call, Timely Sermons on Special Texts, 1940; The Book of Job (a Metrical Translation with Annotations). Has been contributor to every volume of the series of sermons entitled "In the Kingdom of Grace." Editor: German paper of the General Synod, of the Year Book of United Luth. Ch. in America; and of Luther's Small Catechism with Prooftexts. Home: Carthage, Ill. Died Dec. 3, 1946.

NEVE, Juergen Ludwig (nĕ'vĕ), theologian; b. Schleswig, Germany, June 7, 1865; s. Johann Ludwig and Christine (Jacobsen) N.; grad. Breklum, Schleswig, 1886; studied U. of Kiel, 1886-87; Dr. Theology, U. of Kiel, 1924; D.D., Carthage (Ill.) Coll. and Wittenberg Coll., Springfield, O., 1902; m. 2d, Martha Flemming, Aug. 23, 1895; children—(by 1st marriage) Carl, (by 2d marriage) Marie (wife of Rev. Dr. W. Allbeck), Elizabeth (wife of Rev. O. Smith), Herbert T., Arthur F.; m. 3d, Charlotte Mangelsdorf, Aug. 31, 1935. Ordained Evang. Luth. ministry, 1888; prof. ch. history, Chicago Theol. Sem., 1887-92; pastor, Chester, Ill., and editor Lutheran Zionsbote, 1892; prof. ch. history and symbolics, Western Theol. Sem., Atchison, Kan., 1898-1909; prof. symbolics and history of doctrine, Hamma Divinity Sch., Wittenberg Coll., since 1909. Author: Free Church in Comparison with State Church, 1900; Traits of the American People, 1902; Brief History of the Lutheran Church in America, 1903, second and enlarged edition, same, 1915, prepared for 3d edit. by Rev. Dr. W. D. Allbeck, 1934; Altered and Unaltered Augsburg Confession, 1910; The Augsburg Confession, Its History and Interpretation (for laymen), 1914; Introduction to the Confessions of the Evang.-Luth. Church, 1917, 26; The Lutherans in the Movements for Church Union, 1921; Story and Significance of Augsburg Confession (on 400th anniversary); Churches and Sects of Christendom, 1940; History of Christian Thought (with Dr. O. W. Heick), 2 vol. work: vol. 1, 1943. Address: 1015 N. Fountain Av., Springfield, Ohio. Died Aug. 12, 1943.

NEVILLE, Edwin Lowe (nĕv'ĭl); b. Cleveland, O., Nov. 16, 1884; s. Richard and Agnes (Lowe) N.; A.B., U. of Mich., 1907; m. Betsey Coe Baird, 1922; children—Richard, Edwin. Began as student interpreter, in Japan, Aug. 1907; consul at Antung, China, 1913-14, Taihoku, Formosa, 1914-16, Nagaaki, Japan, 1916-20; assigned to Div. Far Eastern Affairs, Dept. of State, 1920; with Conf. on Limitation of Armament, 1921; del. to Internat. Narcotics Conf., Geneva, 1924; sec. of Embassy, chargé d'affaires, Tokyo, 1925; apptd. consul gen., Tokyo, 1925; counselor of Embassy, Tokyo, 1928, chargé d'affaires, 1928-29, and at different times during 1930, 31, 32, 34, 35; minister to Siam, 1937-40; retired. Special visiting lecturer, U. of Mich., 1941. Mem. Ch. of Disciples. Mason Clubs: Cosmos, Nat. Press, University (Washington) Address: Center Conway, N.H. Died Apr. 7, 1944.

NEVILLE, Robert Henry, banker; b. Yonkers, N.Y., Dec. 27, 1858; s. Robert and Catherine (Farley) N.; ed. pubs. schs., Yonkers, and Columbia Grammar Sch., N.Y. City; m. Fannie Wheeler Sands, Nov. 7, 1889 (died Mar. 1, 1926). In banking business at Yonkers since 1887; pres. Peoples Savings Bank; treas. Vernash Realty Corp. Has served as civil service commr., pres. bd. of assessment and dep. city treas. of Yonkers. Democrat. Episcopalian. Club: City. Home: 10 Lamartine Terrace. Office: 12 S. Broadway, Yonkers, N.Y. Deceased.

NEVIN, Arthur Finley (něv'ĭn), composer; b. Vineacre, Edgeworth, Pa., Apr. 27, 1871; s. Robert P. and Elizabeth (Oliphant) N.; (brother of late Ethelbert Nevin); gen. edn. at Sewickley Acad., Pa., and Park U., Allegheny, Pa.; musical edn., N.E. Conservatory of Music, Boston, and under Profs. Klindworth and Boise, Berlin, Germany; Mus.D., U. of Pittsburgh, 1935; married. Prof. music, U. of Kan., 1915-20; dir. municipal music and dramatic art, Memphis, Tenn., 1921-22; asst. sec. Nat. Music Week Com., 1925-26. Composer of songs, piano and orchestral works, etc. Composer: "Poia," N.Am. Indian opera, prod. Royal Opera, Berlin, Apr. 1910; "Daughter of the Forest," prod. Chicago Opera Assn., 1918. Address: care Ascap, 30 Rockefeller Plaza, New York, N.Y. Died July 10, 1943.

NEVIN, Gordon Balch, organist, composer; b. Easton, Pa., May 19, 1892; s. George Balch and Lillias Clara (Dean) N.; studied piano under Charles Maddock (Easton), organ under J. Warren Andrews (New York), theory under J. Fred Wolle (Bethlehem, Pa.); m. Jessie Harrie Young, June 30, 1915; children—Jean Lillias, Ruth Elizabeth. Organist and teacher, Easton, Pa., 1909-14, Johnstown, 1914-15; organist, Cleveland, O., and teacher at Hiram Coll., 1915-17; musical arranger for Ernest M. Skinner Co., Boston, 1917-18; organist and teacher at Greensburg, Pa., 1918-20, at Johnstown, Pa., 1920-32; prof. organ and composition, Westminster Coll., New Wilmington, since 1932. Mem. Am. Soc. Composers, Authors and Publishers. Republican. Presbyterian. Mason. Author: Primer of Organ Registration, 1919; Swell Pedal Technique, 1921; First Lessons at the Organ, 1923; The Harp and Chimes in Organ Playing, 1939. Composer of a sonata, 3 suites and about 20 single numbers for the organ, 23 songs, 18 part songs (secular); anthems, also an operetta, "Following Foster's Footsteps," etc. Has given over 200 recitals in Eastern cities. Home: New Wilmington, Pa. Died Nov. 15, 1943.

NEWBERRY, Truman Handy, ex-secretary of navy, ex-senator; b. Detroit, Mich., Nov. 5, 1864; s. John S. and Helen Parmelee (Handy) N.; Ph.B., Yale, 1885, hon. A.M., 1910; m. Harriet Josephine Barnes, February 7, 1888 (died Jan. 18, 1943); children—Mrs. Carol Lord, Barnes, Phelps. Superintendent of construction, p.m. and general freight and passenger agent, Detroit, Bay City & Alpena Ry., 1885-87; pres. and treas. Detroit Steel & Spring Co., 1887-1901; dir. Packard Motor Car Co. since 1903; chmn. bd. dirs. Detroit Steel Casting Co. since 1937; director Detroit Trust Co., Cleveland-Cliffs Iron Co., Grace Hosp. Asst. sec. of navy, 1905-08, sec. of navy, in cabinet of President Roosevelt, Dec. 1, 1908-Mar. 6, 1909; mem. U.S. Senate from Mich., term 1919-25, resigned 1922. One of organizers Mich. State Naval Brigade, serving as landsman, 1895, lt. and navigator, 1897-98; commd. U.S. Navy as lt. (jr. grade), May, 1898, and served on U.S.S. Yosemite through Spanish-Am. War; col. and a.d.c. to the to the gov., Mich. Nat. Guard 1899. Lt. comdr. U.S. Naval Fleet Reserve, June 6, 1917, and asst. to comdt. 3d Naval Dist., N.Y Republican. Presbyterian. Clubs: Union, University, New York Yacht, St. Anthony (New York); Chicago, Yondotega, Detroit, Country Club, Detroit Boat, Bloomfield Country (Detroit); Grosse Pointe, Grosse Pointe Hunt (Grosse Pointe). Author: Log of the U.S.S. Yosemite, 1899. Home: 123 Lake Shore Road, Grosse Pointe Farms, Mich. Office: Buhl Bldg., Detroit, Mich. Died Oct. 3, 1945.

NEWBOLD, Fleming, v.p. and mgr. Washington Evening Star; b. Dayton, O., Apr. 11, 1873; s. Charles and Frances Kemper (Lowe) N.; ed. pub. schs., Washington, D.C.; married to Ethel Seckendorff, November 21, 1906; children—Janet (Mrs. James S. Bush), Nancy (Mrs. Morris Legendre). Began with Washington Evening Star, 1890; business mgr. and dir. Evening Star Newspaper Co. since 1910, v.p., later made pres.; dir. Merchants Transfer & Storage Co., The Riggs Nat. Bank, Columbia Planograph Co. Episcopalian. Clubs: Metropolitan, Chevy Chase. Office: Evening Star Bldg., Washington, D.C. Died Jan. 31, 1949; buried in Rock Creek Cemetery, Washington.

NEWCOMB, Harry Turner, lawyer, railroad exec., retired; b. Owosso, Mich., Jan. 4, 1867; s. Henry Martyn and Lucia (Turner) N.; educated Ludington, Mich., 1873-81; LL.B., Columbian (now George Washington) U., 1891; LL.M., 1892; m. Lucy Theodora Comstock, Oct. 11, 1893; children—Comstock (dec.), Ellsworth (Mrs. Hubert Alan Kenny, Junior), Winifred Wheeler (Mrs. A. D. A. Crawford), Josiah Turner, Lucy Lamson (Mrs. A. Morgan de Treville), Maryland (Mrs. Edmund F. Kressy), Holly (Mrs. John B. H. Luckett), Simone (Mrs. Alfred Rowe Clark), Harrie Janet (Mrs. Theodore Lyman Crockett), Harry Turner. Began business career by entering service with the Chicago, Milwaukee & St. Paul R.R. as clerk in general offices, 1882; with Interstate Commerce Commn., 1888-95; chief transportation U.S. Dept. Agr., 1895-99; expert chief, div. of agr. U.S. Census, 1899-1901; editor Railway World, 1901-02; lecturer on statistics, Columbian U., 1896-1901. Was counsel for Phila. & Reading Coal & Iron Co. before Anthracite Coal Strike Commn., 1902-03. With Prof. Henry C. Adams, was employed by com. on interstate commerce of U.S. Senate to digest the testimony taken by that com. prior to the enactment of the Hepburn law and to report as experts on certain points not fully covered by the testimony; sr. mem. law firm Newcomb & Frey, Washington, 1907-17; in practice N.Y. City, 1918-20; gen. solicitor, D. & H., Co., 1921-26, gen. counsel of same co., 1926-34; also v.p. and gen. counsel Delaware and Hudson R.R. Corp., Apr. 1, 1930-Dec. 31, 1934; gen. counsel Hudson Coal Co., Champlain Transportation Co., Chateaugay Ore and Iron Co., Lake George Steamboat Co., etc. Trustee and treas. Am. Inst. City of New York, 1929-39; chmn. administrative com. Council for Tariff Reduction. Fellow A.A.A.S. (ex-v.p.); mem. Am. Bar Assn., Assn. Bar City of New York, Nat. Inst. of Social Sciences, Soc. Colonial Wars, Pi Gamma Mu. Clubs: Metropolitan (New York); Cosmos (Washington); George Washington University. Author: Railway Economics, 1898; The Postal Deficit, 1900; Constitutionality of the Delegations in the Interstate Commerce Law, 1910; also many articles on legal questions, rys., trusts, pub. ownership, labor problems, civil service, etc., in mags. and revs. Home: Holly Farms, New Preston (P.O.), Conn. Died Oct. 7, 1944.

NEWCOMB, James Farmer, business exec.; b. Dennis, Mass., May 5, 1880; s. John Ellsworth and Lucy Evelyn (Foster) N.; m. Emma Marie Kellogg, June 11, 1910 (died July 1, 1924). Salesman John H. Gresham, 1897-1912; James F. Newcomb & Co., 1912-16; established James F. Newcomb Co., Inc., New York, N.Y., 1916, pres. and dir. since 1916. Served as chmn. joint com. govt. relations of Comml. Printing Industry, 1943-45. Mem. Printing Industry of Am., Inc. (pres. since 1945); New York Employing Printers Assn. (dir.). Republican. Methodist. Clubs: Athletic (New York); Seignory (P.Q., Can.). Home: 390 West End Av., New York 24. Office: 345 Hudson St., New York 14, N.Y. Died June 15, 1948.

NEWCOMB, Josiah Turner, lawyer; b. Owosso, Mich., June 19, 1868; s. Henry Martyn and Lucia (Turner) N.; A.B., Williams, 1892; A.M., George Washington, 1925, Ph.D., 1929; m. Sophie De Wolfe, 1892 (died 1894); m. 2d, Louise Stetson, 1900; children—Mary (Mrs. Alexander Henry Higginson), Louise (Mrs. William Chase Gilman), Helen Silliman (dec.), Henry Martyn, Wyllys Stetson, Josiah Turner. Mem. editorial staff New York Evening Post, 1895-1902; admitted to N.Y. bar, 1902, and began practice at N.Y. City; spl. counsel Electric Bond and Share Co., 1917-27; counsel for joint com. of Nat. Utility Assns., Washington, 1927-32, now retired. Mem. N.Y. State Assembly, 1902-05, N.Y. State Senate, 1908-12; del. to Rep. Nat. Conv., 1912. Home: R.D. 3, Poughkeepsie, N.Y. Died Jan. 3, 1944.

NEWCOMET, Horace Edgar (nū'kŭm-ĕt), ry. official; b. Phila., Pa., Apr. 27, 1874; s. Henry W. and Elizabeth K. (Stell) N.; prep. edn. Friend Sch., Phila., and Lauderbach Acad.; student U. of Berlin 2 yrs., U. of Pa., 4 yrs.; m. Louise Worthington, Oct. 4, 1899; children—Walborn W., Edith Louise (Mrs. J. B. Clow). With Pa. R.R. since Feb. 1896; consecutively asst. on engr. corps, Chicago div., Cleveland and Pittsburgh div., and acting asst. engr. Cincinnati div. to 1899; asst. engr. Cincinnati div., 1899-1901; div. engr. maintenance of way various divs.. 1901-06; acting engr. and div. engr. maintenance of way, Cleveland div., 1906-13; supt. Louisville div., 1915-18, Logansport div., 1918-20, Cleveland and Pittsburgh div., 1920-23; gen. supt. Lake div., 1923-26; gen. mgr. Western Region Pa. R.R., at Chicago, 1926-29, v.p. same since June 16, 1929; also pres. Indianapolis Union Ry. Co. since Oct. 3, 1929; pres. Western Warehousing Co. (Chicago), Dayton Union Ry. Co., Union Depot Co. (Columbus, O.), Mackinac Transportation Co., Terre Haute & Peoria R.R. Co.; v.p. and dir. Calumet Western Ry. Co., Central Ind. Ry. Co., Chicago Union Station Co., Fort Wayne Union Ry. Co., Mo. & Ill. Bridge & Belt R.R. Co.; dir. Belt Ry. Co. of Chicago, Cincinnati Union Terminal Co., Detroit Union R.R. Depot & Station Co., Fort Street Union Depot Co., Green Real Estate Co., Indianapolis & Frankfort R.R. Co., Little Miami R.R. Co., Louisville Bridge & Terminal Ry. Co., Peoria & Pekin Union Ry. Co., Pittsburgh, Ft. Wayne & Chicago Ry. Co., South Chicago & Southern R.R. Co., Terminal R.R. Assn. of St. Louis, The Willett Co., The Willett Co. of Ind., Travelers Aid Soc. of Chicago. Clubs: Union League, Chicago (Chicago). Home: 70 Cedar St., Chicago. Office: Union Station, Chicago, Ill. Died Jan. 14, 1944.

NEWELL, Franklin Spilman, obstetrician; b. Roxbury, Mass., Apr. 30, 1871; s. James W. and Elizabeth (Spilman) N.; desc. Abraham Newell, Roxbury, 1636; A.B., Harvard, 1892; M.D., Harvard Med. Sch., 1896; unmarried. Practiced in Boston since 1897; with Harvard Med. Sch., 1897-1930, prof. of clin. obstetrics emeritus since 1930; cons. obstetrician Boston Lying-in Hospital; mem. bd. of consultation Mass. Gen. Hosp. Fellow Am. Coll. Surgeons; mem. Am. Gynecol. Soc., A.M.A., Mass. Med. Soc., Obstet. Soc. of Boston, Boston Med. Library Assn. Unitarian. Clubs: Harvard, Somerset, Tennis and Racquet, The Country. Home: 925 Boylston St. Office: 221 Longwood Av., Boston. Died Mar. 4, 1949.

NEWELL, G(eorge) Glenn, artist; b. Berrien County, Mich.; s. George Hicks and Huldah (Phillips) N.; A.B., Albion (Mich.) Coll., 1891, LL.D., 1936; grad. Teachers Coll. (Columbia); student Nat. Acad. Design, 1897-99; m. Louisa E. West, Sept. 12, 1901. Represented in Nat. Gallery (Washington, D.C.), Youngstown (O.) Museum, Dallas (Tex.) Museum, Detroit Museum of Art, Mich. State Teachers Coll., Albion Coll.; Lotos Club, Nat. Arts Club, Salmagundi Club (all of New York); Paramount (N.Y. and Brooklyn); also in theatres and private collections. Awarded first prize Salmagundi Club, 1906; Speyer prize, Nat. Acad. Design, 1923; prizes, Nat. Arts Club, 1925; gold medal, Allied Artists of America, 1927; 1st prize, National Artists, 1929; prize ($2,000) in nat. ranch life competition, 1929. President Allied Artists of America, 1919-26, New York Society Painters, 1928-35, Jeffersonian Society of Dutchess County, N.Y., since 1934; member American Water Color Society, New York Water Color Club, Delta Tau Delta. Nat. Academician. Lecturer on art. Mason, K.P. Clubs: Lotos, National Arts Salmagundi (New York). Home: Dover Plains, Dutchess County, N.Y. Address: 47 5th Av., New York, N.Y.* Died May 7, 1947.

NEWELL, Jake F. (John Franklin), lawyer; b. Cabarrus County, N.C., Feb. 15, 1869; s. William Greene and Elizabeth Caroline (Hudson) N.; A.B., Rutherford (N.C.) Coll., 1896; student law and English, U. of N.C., 1898-99; m. Frances Moody Black, Dec. 30, 1915. Reporter for Charlotte Observer, 1892-95; admitted to N.C. bar, 1899; began practice at Charlotte, 1901. Rep. nominee for Congress, 1904, 14, 20, for atty. gen. of N.C., 1908, for U.S. senator, 1932. Led the Republican fight against repeal of the 18th Amendment to U.S. Constitution, North Carolina voting overwhelmingly against repeal in election, Nov. 7, 1933. Chmn. N.C. Rep. State Exec. com., 1938-42. Mem. Jr. Order United Am. Mechanics. Elected Pres. Mecklenburg Co. (Charlotte) Bar Asso. for year 1945. Methodist. Home: 819 Sunnyside Av. Office: Law Bldg., Charlotte, N.C. Died Aug. 9, 1945.

NEWELL, Robert Brewer, banker; b. Hartford, Conn., Sept. 11, 1879; s. William Henry and Ellen Louise (Brewer) N.; B.A., Wesleyan Univ., Middletown, Conn., 1902; m. Helen C. Lincoln, Dec. 17, 1907; children—Katharine Lincoln (Mrs. Woodruff Johnson), Elizabeth (Mrs. Richard H. Butler), Robert Lincoln (Ensign U.S.N.R.). With Phoenix Nat. Bank, Hartford, Conn., 1902; with State Bank, 1903-07, State Savings Bank, 1907-17; vice-pres. Fidelity Trust Co., 1917-23; vice-pres. U.S. Security Trust Co., 1923-26, pres., 1926-27; pres. Hartford Nat. Bank & Trust Co. since 1927; mem. board of dirs. Standard Fire Ins. Co., Kellogg & Bulkeley; mem. bd. trustees Society for Savings. Trustee Wesleyan Univ.; dir. Hartford Hosp. Mem. Hartford Chamber of Commerce. Trustee Am. Sch. for Deaf, Hartford. Mem. Beta Theta Pi. Republican. Methodist. Clubs: University, Hartford, Hartford Golf. Home: 7 Woodside Circle. Office: 777 Main St., Hartford. Conn. Died Sep. 15, 1947.

NEWELL, Wilmon, entomologist; b. Hull, Ia., Mar. 4, 1878; s. William J. and Elizabeth A. (Anderson) N.; B.S., Iowa State Coll., 1897, M.S., same, 1899; D.Sc., 1920; D.Sc., Clemson Coll., 1937; m. Helen M., d. Dr. and Mrs. O. P. Mabee, of Galesburg, Ill., Feb. 12, 1907. Asst. entomologist, Ia. Agricultural Expt. Sta., 1897-99, Ohio Agrl. Expt. Sta., 1899-1902; asst. entomologist and apiarist, Tex. Agrl. Expt. Sta., 1902-03; state entomologist of Ga., 1903-04; entomologist, La. Agrl. Expt. Sta. and sec. and entomologist State Crop Pest Commn. of La., 1904-10; entomologist, Tex. Agrl. Expt. Sta. and state entomologist, 1910-15; plant commr. Fla. State Plant Bd. since 1915; dean Coll. of Agr., 1921-38, dir. Expt. Sta. and Agrl. Extension Div., U. of Fla. since 1921, provost for agriculture since 1938; administrator of Florida State Soil Conservation; chmn. Fla. State Land-Use Planning Com. since 1940; chmn. advisory com. on agr., Fla. State Defense Council since 1941. Fellow A.A.A.S.; mem. Entomol. Society of America, Assn. Econ. Entomologists (pres. 1920), Assn. of Southern Agrl. Workers (pres. 1929-30), Soil Science Soc. America, Kappa Sigma, Alpha Zeta, Phi Kappa Phi, Gamma Sigma Delta. Mason (Shriner). Pres. Gainesville Rotary Club, 1920-21. Home: 504 E. Church St., Gainesville, Fla. Died Oct. 25, 1943.

NEWEY, Frederick John, lawyer; b. Wolverhampton, Eng., Sept. 4, 1872; s. William Newey; mother died in his infancy; LL.B., Lake Forest U., 1899; m. Gertrude E. Newton, June 1901; children—Harriet Adelaide, Kathryn Brooks, Helen, Frederick John (dec.). Admitted to Ill. bar, 1899, and joined William W. Wheelock and George B. Shattuck, forming the law firm of Wheelock, Shattuck & Newey; now mem. firm of Newey, Mackenzie & Abrahamson. Mem. Am. and Ill. State bar assns., Chicago Bar Assn. (grievance com., 1923-24; com. on admission,

1929-31; professional ethics com., 1943-44), English-Speaking Union, Delta Chi. Clubs: Union League, Law, Congregational (pres. 1934-35), Exchange (pres. 1928). Home: 436 Lake Av., Wilmette, Ill. Office: 140 S. Dearborn St., Chicago, Ill. Died Jan. 10, 1944.

NEWFANG, Oscar (nū′făng), writer; b. Columbus, O., Jan. 24, 1875; s. Adam and Mary (Schmelz) N.; student Capital U., Columbus, 1890-93; m. Mary E. Jefferson, May 22, 1902; children—Florence Jefferson, Edward Carl, Dorothy May. Credit mgr. Shoe & Leather Nat. Bank, N.Y. City, 1902-04, Citizens Central Nat. Bank, N.Y. City, 1905-13; credit mgr. and asst. treas. Julius Forstmann & Co., woolen mfrs., 1914-33. Mem. com. to study orgn. of peace, N.Y. Democrat. Author: A World Government Needed (pamphlet), 1918; The Development of Character, 1921; The Road to World Peace, 1924; Harmony Between Labor and Capital, 1927; The United States of the World, 1930; Capitalism and Communism, 1932; Economic Welfare, 1936; World Federation, 1939. Contributor to World Order. Home: 38 Circle Driveway, Hastings-on-Hudson, New York. Died Feb. 14, 1943.

NEWFIELD, Morris, rabbi; b. Homonna, Hungary, 1869; s. of Simon Sabbatai and Lena (Klein) N.; ed. Royal Gymnasium, Homonna and Budapest, Hungary; B.D., Theol. Coll., Budapest, 1889; M.A., U. of Budapest, 1895; B.A., U. of Cincinnati; rabbi, Hebrew Union Coll., Cincinnati, 1895; Litt.D., U. of Alabama, 1921; D.D., Hebrew Union Coll., 1939; m. Leah Ullman, Jan. 29, 1901; children—Semon U., Emma U., Mayer U., Lena J., Lincoln, John. Rabbi Temple Emanu-El, Birmingham, 1895—. Treas. Central Conf. of Am. Rabbis, 1923-29, v.p., 1929, pres., 1931-33; mem. exec. bd. Union of Am. Hebrew Congregations, 1925-38; pres. Alumni Assn. Hebrew Union Coll., 1907-08; mem. bd. Court of Domestic Relations and Juvenile Delinquency, Birmingham, 1915-32. Supervisor Jewish Welfare Bd., Camp McClellan, World War. Founder of Free Kegten and its sec. for a number of yrs.; an organizer and dir. Associated Charities, Birmingham; sec. and mgr. Citizens' Relief Com., following Virginia Mine disaster, distributing $30,000 to the sufferers and conducting relief extending over a period of 4 yrs.; pres. Ala. Tuberculosis Assn., 1919-21; v.p. Jefferson Anti-Tuberculosis Assn.; dir. Birmingham Humane Soc., Kindergarten Soc. Mem. bd. of govs. of Hebrew Union Coll. since 1938. Prof. Hebrew and Semitics, Howard Coll. (Bapt.), Birmingham, 1914-20; supervisor of synagogues in Ala. and Fla. Awarded B'nai B'rith bronze tablet, 1939, for "meritorious service in promoting amity and good will between the Jew and his neighbor." Pres. Ala. Sociol. Congress, 1913-21 and 1925-27; pres. Birmingham Social Workers, 1913-15. Chmn. Home Service of Jefferson County Chapter Am. Red Cross since 1918, and of Jefferson County Chapter Am. Red Cross, 1933-36; founder, and pres. Ala. Jewish Religious Teachers' Assn., 1914-16; pres. Fedn. Jewish Charities since 1924; dir. Community Chest, Birmingham, 1928-37; v.p. World Union of Liberal Judaism since 1932; mem. Federal Advisory Bd. on Better Housing. Mason (33°). Clubs: Hillcrest Country Club, Rotary. Author: (monograph) The Book of Ecclesiastes, 1895; also numerous published sermons, addresses and articles on lit. and philosophy. Died May 7, 1940. Home: 2150 S. 15th Av., Birmingham, Ala.

NEWGARDEN, Paul W., army officer; b. Phila., Pa., Feb. 24, 1892; s. George Joseph and Margaret (Woolever) N.; B.S., U.S. Military Acad., 1913, distinguished grad. Command and Gen. Staff Sch., 1926, Army War Coll., 1932; m. Priscilla Quinby, Dec. 28, 1927. Commd. 2d lt., Inf., 1913 and advanced through the grades to maj. gen. (temp.), 1942; Instr. of tactics, U.S. Mil. Acad., 1917-21; with Inspector General's Dept., 1925; comdr. bat., 20th Inf., 27th Inf., 18th Inf.; exec. officer, 18th Inf., 1936, gen. staff, G-3, 6th C.A., 1936-40; comdr. 41st Armored Inf., 1941; combat comdr. A., 2nd Armored Div., 1942; comdr. 10th Armored Div., since 1942; organized and trained 41st Armored Inf., 1941-42, 10th Armored Div., 1942-43. Distinguished pistol shot; nat. junior saber champion, 1919. Clubs: Army-Navy, Country (Washington, D.C.).† Died July 14, 1944.

NEWHALL, Charles Watson, educator; b. Galena, Ill., Feb. 7, 1872; s. Francis Bates and Clara Patience (Bennett) N.; grad. Shattuck Sch., Faribault, Minn., 1890; A.B., Johns Hopkins, 1893; grad. work, Harvard and Univ. of Chicago; Pd.D., Dartmouth, 1933; m. Evangeline Abbotf, July 6, 1899; 1 son, Charles Watson. Teacher, Shattuck Sch. since 1893; headmaster since 1915. Pres. Assn. of Mil. Schs. and Colls. of U.S. Mem. Beta Theta Pi. Republican. Episcopalian. Mason. Clubs: Rotary (Faribault); University (Chicago). Address: Shattuck School, Faribault; Minn. Died June 10, 1944.

NEWHALL, Thomas, born in Philadelphia, Pennsylvania, Oct. 17, 1876; s. Daniel Smith and Eleanor (Mercer) N.; student Haverford (Pa.) Sch., 1884-93; m. Honora Guest Blackwell, May 28, 1898; children—Blackwell, Campbell, Charles Mercer. Began with Chester (Pa.) Pipe & Tube Co., 1893; with John Wanamaker, Phila., 1898; pres. Newhall & Co., Baltimore, 1900-07; partner E. B. Smith & Co., Phila., 1910-20; pres. Phila. & Western Ry., 1910-22; partner Drexel & Co., Phila., 1922-36, J. P. Morgan & Co. (N.Y. City), Morgan, Grenfell & Co. (London), and Morgan & Cie (Paris), 1929-36; financial v.p. Penn Mutual Life Ins. Co., 1937-43; dir. The Pa. R.R. Co.; dir. Pa. Co., 1938-45. Trustee Estate of H. H. Houston, Phila. Lieut. comdr. U.S.N.R.F., World War I; with mining squadron, A.E.F. Republican. Episcopalian. Clubs: Philadelphia, Union League; Metropolitan (Washington). Home: Green Hill Farms, Overbrook, Pa. Died May 9, 1947.

NEWHART, Horace, otolaryngologist; b. New Ulm, Minn., Dec. 9, 1872; s. Jude and Sarah (Parker) N.; student Carleton Coll., Northfield, Minn., 1891-93; A.B., Dartmouth, 1895; M.D., U. of Mich., 1898; post-grad. work Vienna, 1898-99, 1905, 08, 12; certificate of Am. Board of Otolaryngology, 1925; m. Anne Hendrick, Sept. 4, 1904; 1 son, Ellwood Hendrick. Practiced at Minneapolis, Minn., since 1901; became asso. with U. of Minn., 1912; prof. emeritus, otolaryngology, U. of Minn. Med. Sch.; also same U. of Minn. Graduate School; staff member University, Northwestern, Abbott and St. Barnabas hospitals and Glen Lake Sanatorium; consulting otologist Minneapolis pub. schs., since 1925. Fellow Am. Coll. Surg., Am. Acoustical Soc.; mem. A.M.A., Hennepin County Med. Soc., Am. Otol. Soc. (pres. 1939-40), Am. Laryngol. Assn., Am. Laryngol., Rhinol. and Otol. Assn., Am. Acad. Ophthalmology and Otolaryngology (pres. 1924-25), Am. Soc. for the Hard of Hearing (pres. 1927-28), Minneapolis Society for Hard of Hearing (pres. 1925-29), Minn. Acad. Ophthalmology and Otolaryngology, Minn. Acad. Medicine, Phi Beta Kappa, Sigma Chi, Phi Rho Sigma. Clubs: Minneapolis, Minikahda, Lafayette, Campus. Contbr. numerous articles on med. topics, especially on diseases of the ear and the conservation of hearing. Home: 212 W. 22d St. Office: Medical Arts Bldg., Minneapolis 2, Minn. Died July 9, 1945.

NEWLIN, Ora Allen, evangelist; b. Jasper County, Ill., Sept. 18, 1875; s. Absalom L. and Nettie (Sowers) N.; grad. Brown's Business Coll., Decatur, Ill., 1895; grad. theol. dept. Findlay (O.) Coll., 1900; D.D., Defiance (O.) Coll., 1917; m. Lena May Sheets, June 26, 1900; children—Clyde Kenneth (dec.), Dwight Wendell (dec.), Ruth Elizabeth. Founder, 1902, pres. until 1909, Collegiate Inst., Fort Scott, Kan.; ordained ministry Presbyn. Ch. in U.S.A., 1900; engaged in evangelistic work since 1909; pres. Interdenominational Evangelistic Assn., 1924-25, and since 1927; chmn. Winona Bible Conf.; mem. bd. dirs. Winona Lake Instns.; moderator North Florida Presbytery, 1941; commr. to Gen. Assembly Presbyn. Ch., U.S.A., 1942. Served as Y.M.C.A. sec., World War. Mem. Internat. Lyceum and Chautauqua Assn. Republican. Author: Strangers to God, 1917; Great Things of the Bible, 1919; The Hoosier Pen (poetry), 1935. Lecturer. Home: San Mateo, Florida. Died Apr. 16, 1943.

NEWMAN, Jacob Kiefer, banker; b. New Orleans, La., Jan. 31, 1872; s. Isidore and Rebecca (Kiefer) N.; student Cornell U., 1888-92; m. Mae Polack, May 31, 1900; children—Sophie Mae (Mrs. Samuel L. Gerstley), Alice Louise (Mrs. Nicolai Berezowsky), Jacob Kiefer, Melvin. Pres. New Orleans Carrollton R.R., Light & Power Co., 1895-1902; mem. firm Isidore Newman & Son, pvt. bankers, New Orleans, 1900-22; pres. Am. Cities Ry. & Light Co., 1906-11; pres. Newman, Saunders & Co., bankers, N.Y. City, since 1922; pres. City Utilities Co. since 1924; dir. Nat. Power & Light Co. Dir. Isidore Newman Manual Training Sch., Jewish Orphans Home, Audubon Park Commn. (all of New Orleans), Jewish Welfare Bd., N.Y. City. Democrat. Jewish religion. Home: 270 Park Av. Office: 32 Broadway, New York, N.Y.* Died Apr. 5, 1943.

NEWSOM, William Monypeny, stock brokerage; b. Columbus, O., July 7, 1887; s. Logan Conway and Sally (Monypeny) N.; grad. Hill Sch., Pottstown, Pa., 1906; Ph. B., Yale, 1909; m. Frances Billings, May 15, 1915; 1 dau., Sally. Mgr. N.E. div. Breakwater Co., builders of govt. breakwaters, 1909-13; with Parkinson & Burr, stock brokers, New York, 1913-14; asst. to mgr. military and promotion depts. Remington Arms Co., 1915; sec. and treas. Sundstrand Adding Machine Sales Co., 1916-25; with Watson & White, brokers, 1927; mem. Berg, Eyre & Kerr, 1928-38, Hubbard Bros. & Co., 1938-39, Lawrence Turnure & Co. members N.Y. Stock Exchange since 1939. Served as 1st lt. Mil. Intelligence Div., U.S. Army, 1917-18. Fellow Am. Museum of Natural History (New York), Royal Geog. Soc. (London), Am. Geog. Soc.; mem. Am. Soc. Mammalogists. Protestant. Clubs: Explorers, Beaverkill Trout. Author: White-tailed Deer, 1926. Contbr. to Forest and Stream, Outdoor Life, Field and Stream. Home: 224 E. 61st St. Office: 50 Broadway, New York, N.Y. Died Feb. 1, 1942.

NEWTON, Cleveland Alexander, lawyer; b. Wright County, Mo., Sept. 3, 1873; s. John and Rebecca E. N.; student Drury Coll., Springfield, Mo., 1895-1900; LL.B., U. of Mo., 1902; m. Meta Mitchell, June 7, 1907; 1 son, John A. Began practice at Hartville, Mo., 1902; elected to Mo. Ho. of Rep., 1902, re-elected, 1904; asst. U.S. atty. Western Dist. of Mo., 1905-07; asst. circuit atty., St. Louis, 1907-11; asst. atty. gen. of U.S., Washington, D.C., 1911-13; resigned to engage in practice at St. Louis; mem. 66th to 69th Congresses (1919-27), 10th Mo. Dist.; gen. counsel Miss. Valley Assn., 1928-43. Home: 6188 McPherson Av., St. Louis, Mo. Died Sep. 17, 1945.

NEWTON, John Henry, naval officer; b. Pittston, Pa., Dec. 13, 1881; s. John Henry and Elizabeth (Moon) N.; A.B., U.S. Naval Acad., 1905; m. Elise Barr Curry, Apr. 28, 1915; 1 son, John Henry. Commissioned ensign U.S. Navy, 1907, and advanced through the grades to vice adm., 1943; comdr. S. Pacific Force, S. Pacific area. Decorated Navy Cross and Legion of Merit. Presbyterian. Home: Carbondale, Pa. Died May 2, 1948.

NEWTON, Joseph Fort, clergyman; b. Decatur, Tex., July 21, 1880; s. Lee and Sue G. (Battle) N.; student Hardy Inst. (now defunct) and Southern Bapt. Theol. Seminary, Louisville, Ky.; Litt.D., Coe Coll., Cedar Rapids, Ia., 1912; D.D., Tufts Coll., 1918; LL.D. from Temple Univ. in 1929; m. Jennie Mai Deatherage, June 14, 1900; children—Joseph Emerson, David (dec.), Josephine Kate. Ordained Bapt. ministry, 1893; pastor 1st Bapt. Ch., Paris, Tex., 1897-98; asso. pastor non-sectarian ch., St. Louis, 1898-1900; founder, and pastor People's Ch., Dixon, Ill., 1901-08; pastor Liberal Christian Ch., Cedar Rapids, Ia., 1908-16, The City Temple, London, Eng., 1916-19, Church of the Divine Paternity, New York, 1919-25, Memorial Church of St. Paul, Overbrook Philadelphia, 1925-30, St. James Church, Philadelphia, 1930-35; Church of St. Luke and Epiphany, Phila., 1938. Served as Grand Chaplain Grand Lodge of Masons of Iowa. Author: David Swing, Poet Preacher, 1909; Abraham Lincoln, 1910; Lincoln and Herndon, 1910; The Eternal Christ, 1912; Sermons and Lectures, 1912; The Builders, A Story and Study of Masonry, 1914; Wesley and Woolman, 1914; What Have the Saints to Teach Us? 1914; The Ambassador, 1916; The Mercy of Hell, 1918; The Sword of the Spirit, 1918; The Theology of Civilization, 1919; Some Living Masters of the Pulpit, 1922; Preaching in London, 1923; The Men's House, 1923; Preaching in New York, 1924; The Truth and the Life, 1925; The Religion of Masonry, 1926; God and the Golden Rule, 1927; Altar Stairs, 1928; The New Preaching, 1929; Things I Know in Religion, 1930; The Angel in the Soul, 1931; The Sermon in the Making, 1932; Living Every Day, 1937; We Highly Resolve, The Stuff of Life, 1939; His Cross and Ours, 1940; Living Up to Life, 1941; Live, Love and Learn, 1943; Where Are We In Religion?, 1944; River of Years (autobiography), 1946; The One Great Church, 1947; Life Victorious, 1948. also many pamphlets on patriotic and Masonic topics, and numerous addresses and sermons. Address: 330 S. 13th St., Philadelphia, Pa. Died Jan. 24, 1950.

NICHOLS, Isabel McIlhenny (Mrs. H. S. Prentiss Nichols); b. Wilmington, N.C.; d. John (pioneer gas engr., philanthropist) and Bernice (Bell) McIlhenny; ed. schs., Columbus, Ga., and Mary Baldwin Sem., Staunton, Va.; L.H.D., Tennent Coll. of Christian Edn., 1938; m. Henry Sargent Prentiss Nichols, lawyer, June 4, 1895. Apptd. by gov. of Pa. as mem. State Council Edn.; by mayor of Phila. as mem. Phila. Art Jury; by mayor as mem. committee to assign city scholarships to Sch. of Design; v.p. Board of Christian Education by appointment of General Assembly Presbyn. Ch. U.S.A.; dir. Southeastern Chapter Am. Red Cross; dir. Emergency Aid of Pa.; dir. Germantown and Chestnut Hill Improvement Assn.; trustee Wilson Coll. for Women, Chambersburg, Pa.; v.p. Woman's Bd. Pa. Museum Sch. Industrial Art, Germantown Hort. Soc., Law Enforcement League of Phila., Independent Rep. Com. of 35; mem. Phila. Com. of 70, Woman's Nat. Com. of 100 for Law Enforcement, Pa. League of Women Voters, Advisory Bd. Fairmount Bird Club; corr. sec. Phila. Home for Incurables; chmn. Advisory Com. for Phila. of Nat. War Work Council Y.W.C.A.; mem. English-Speaking Union-Transatlantic Soc. (bd. govs.), Hist. Soc. of Pa., Athenæum of Philadelphia; sec. Civic Safety Fund Assn. Received annual award of the Southern Soc. of New York from Mary Baldwin Coll., 1937. Clubs: Acorn, Sedgeley, New Century (pres. 1913-21), Rep. Women of Pa. (Phila.); Women's (Germantown); hon. mem. Modern (Phila.), Woman's (Narberth), and Neighbors (Hatboro). Home: The Barclay, Rittenhouse Square East, Philadelphia, Pa.; (summer) 115 S. Newton Av., Chelsea; Atlantic City, N.J. Died Nov. 15, 1941.

NICHOLS, Jesse Clyde; b. Olathe, Kan., Aug. 23, 1880; s. Jesse Thomas and Josie (Jackson) N.; A.B., U. of Kan., 1902; A.B., Harvard, 1903 (Beta Theta Pi, Phi Beta Kappa); m. Jessie Eleanor Miller, June 28, 1905; children—Eleanor, Miller, Clyde. Engaged in development of Country Club Dist. (5,000 acres), Kansas City; dir. Commerce Trust Company, Kansas City Title Insurance Company, Business Men's Assurance Co., Kansas City Fire & Marine Ins. Company, Plaza Bank of Commerce. Member Kansas City Board of Education 8 years. Chairman or vice chairman all local money-raising campaigns, World War I. Head Miscellaneous Equipment Div. of National Defense Council, O.P.M., 13 mos., 1940-41; cons. Pub. Bldgs. Adminstrn., Washington, D.C., 6 mos. Mem. Nat. Conf. on City Planning (dir.), Am. City Planning Inst. (hon.), Am. Inst. Architects (hon.), Am. Soc. Landscape Architects, Nat. Conf. for State Parks, Am. Civic Planning Assn.; pres. Nat. Conf. of Subdividers of High Class Residential Property; mem. bd. govs. Kansas City Art Inst.; vice pres. Mo. River Navigation Assn. Apptd. by Presidents Hoover, Coolidge and Roosevelt to membership in Nat. Capital Park and Planning Com., has served 22 years. Chmn. board of trustees Midwest Research Institute. Mem. Harvard Commn. on Univ. Resources; chm. trustees of William R. Nelson fund of $12,000,000 for purchase of objects of art. Mem. business advisory council, Dept. of Commerce of U.S. Democrat. Clubs: University, Kansas City, Mission Hills Country, Kansas City Country, Indian Hills Golf. Author numerous pamphlets on city planning; developing residential properties and outlying shopping centers; river navigation; fgn. trade possibilities; indsl. research; also speaker on same subjects. Leader in work for good roads and appropriate highway development throughout Middle West. Elected "Kansas City's Man of the Year" by Metro Club of Kansas City, 1940. Home: 1214 W. 55th St. Office: 310 Ward Parkway, Kansas City, Mo. Died Feb. 16, 1950.

NICHOLS (Jack) John Conover, former congressman; b. Joplin, Mo., Aug. 31, 1896; s. John Adams and Mary (Conover) N.; student Teachers Coll., Emporia, Kan., 1915-16; m. Marion E. Young, Mar. 30, 1921; children—Nina Jean, Dan. Admitted to Okla. bar, 1926; mem. firm Clark and Jack Nichols, Eufaula, since 1926; mem. 74th to 78th Congresses (1935-45), 2d Okla. Dist.; resigned from Ho. of Rep., July 3, 1943, to become vice-pres. Transcontinental and Western Air, Inc., Kansas City, Mo. Pres. Syfo Water Co., Washington, D.C. Served in O.T.C., Little Rock, Ark., 1917, and as pvt., U.S. Army, Camp Trevis, Tex., World War I. Mem. Am. Legion. 32° Mason (Shriner). Clubs: Elks, Jesters, Burning Tree, Conquistadores del Cielo (Washington, D.C.). Democrat. Eufaula, Okla. Killed in airplane accident in Egypt.

NICHOLS, John Grayson, govt. official; b. Marion N.C., Sept. 5, 1892; s. Joseph Grayson and Alma Eliza (Elliott) N.; grad. Marion High Sch., 1908; student U. of N.C., 1908-09; m. Tempie Parker Harris, June 24, 1925; (divorced 1939); 1 son, John Grayson. Asst. cashier Mitchell County Bank, Bakersville, N.C., 1908-09, Commercial Bank, Rutherfordton, N.C., 1909-14; asst. bank examiner Banking Dept., State of N.C., 1914-18, chief bank examiner, 1919; v.p. Am. Trust Co., Charlotte, N.C., 1919-23; exec. v.p. Page Trust Co., Aberdeen, N.C., 1923-33; special rep. Comptroller of Currency in reorganization of nat banks, Washington, D.C., Mar.-Oct. 1933; chief, div of examination, Federal Deposit Ins. Corp., Washington, D.C., since Oct. 1933. Cadet pilot Naval aviation, Company 22, M.I.T., 1918. Democrat. Baptist. Died Nov. 10, 1941.

NICHOLS, Spencer Van Bokkelen, publicist; b. N.Y. City, July 30, 1882; s. Allan and Elizabeth Morris (Van Bokkelen) N.; law, University of N.C.; spl. courses in internat. law, Columbia and Yale; m. Virginia Center Ward, July 30, 1918; children—Spencer Van Bokkelen, Virginia Center. Apptd. asst. sec. of State by President Wilson, 1913; associated with Schermerhorn Estate; v.p. Hamilton & Wade, ins. advisors; trustee of estates. Long active as layman P.E. Ch. and in boys' work, prison reform, rescue missions, forwarding Boy Scout and Big Brother movements; former traveling sec. Delta Kappa Epsilon. Served as officer U.S. Navy, 1917-20, duty U.S. Naval Acad.; aide to Rear Adm. H. F. Bryan; mem. staff of Adm. Caperton; mem. mission to S. Am. Republics, 1918. Trustee, dir., member or hon. mem. numerous socs., among them, League of Nations Assn. (chmn. of board and chmn. of exec. com.), Woodrow Wilson Foundation, Nat. Peace Conference, Am. Colony Charities Assn. of Jerusalem (sec.), Naval Hist. Soc. (sec.), N.Y. Hist. Soc., Am. Geog. Soc., Naval Inst., Am. Bookplate Soc., Am. Merchant Marine Library Assn., Soc. for Nautical Research (London), Naval Records Soc. (London), Delta Kappa Epsilon, etc. Democrat. Warden and vestryman Grace Episcopal Ch., Norwalk, Conn., Trinity Church, N.Y. City; treas. Church Army in U.S.A.; mem. Permanent Com. on Archives, Diocese of Conn.; N.Y. chmn. St. Luke's Internat. Hosp., Tokio. Clubs: Century, D.K.E., Grolier (gov.), Church (N.Y.); Samuel Pepys and First Edition clubs (London). Author of various works, including Volcanic Action, 1910; Fiona Macleod, William Sharp, 1913; Toby Jugs, 18th Century, 1913; John Rogers, Sculptor, 1913; John Dryden, Master, 1914; Samuel Pepys, the Man, 1913; A Pepysian Admiral, 1914; Disraeli, Political Novelist, 1915; The Significance of Anthony Trollope, 1925; Nelson (play), 1929. Also wrote Woodrow Wilson, Internationalist, Has the League Failed?, The Machinery of Peace, Moral Disarmament, Tariffs-Intergovernmental Debts, The Psychology of the American People Toward the Administration's Foreign Policy, The Non-Political Aspects of the League of Nations. Contbr. on lit. subjects, also verse, short stories and editorials. Book collector. Public speaker on League of Nations, World Court and internat. subjects. Home: 192 E. 75th St. Office: 52 William St., New York, N.Y. Died June 30, 1946.

NICHOLS, Walter Franklin, cattle raising; b. Hulington, O., Nov. 16 1882; s. James Albert and Amanda (Melissa) N.; ed. pub. schs.; m. Grace Short, June 20 1907; 1 son, James Albert. Began in wholesale and retail hardware business with Brother, as Nichols Hardware Co., 1900, sec. and treas.; rancher and cattle raiser, as Nichols Bros. Flying V. Ranch, 20,000 acres, since 1910. Democrat. Mason (32°, Shriner), K.P. Home: Route 1, Catoosa, Okla. Office: 123½ E. 1st St., Tulsa, Okla. Died Mar. 27, 1946.

NICHOLS, William Wallace, engineer, mfr.; b. N.Y. City, Nov. 17, 1860; s. Edward Erastus and Anna Maria (MacAuley) N.; student Colorado Coll.; Ph.B., Yale, 1884, M.E., 1886; m. 2d, Mary Emily Miller, June 26, 1912; 1 dau., Marian (by 1st marriage). With motive power dept. C.,C.,C.&St.L. Ry., 1885-86; with C.,B.&Q. Ry. as engr. of tests, asst. master mechanic and supt. telegraph, 1886-90; supt. Chicago Telephone Co., 1890-93; instr. mech. engring., Yale, 1894-1900; works mgr. Baltimore Copper Works, 1900-04; with Allis-Chalmers Co. as vice president, 1904-13, became assistant to president, 1913. Served as chmn. American Industrial Commn. to France, 1916; chmn. Am. Industrial Commn. to Mexico, 1924. Trustee Arbitration Foundation, Inc.; dir. Am. Arbitration Assn. Member Inter-Am. High Commission, Nat. Industrial Conf. Board, Am. Engineering Standards Com., Am. Iron & Steel Inst., Am. Soc. Mech. Engrs., Acad. Polit. Science, Am. Mfrs. Export Assn. (ex-pres.), Mexican Chamber of Commerce in U.S. (hon. v.p., dir.), Elec. Mfrs.' Club (ex-pres.), Edgemont Assn. (ex-pres.), Berzelius Soc., Mexico Soc. (dir.), Machinery Builders Soc. (ex-pres.), Acad. Polit. Science, Seniors' Golf Assn., Sigma Xi. Republican. Episcopalian. Clubs: Machinery, Engineers', Scarsdale Golf. Contbr. many articles on engring. edn., foreign trade and business conduct. Home: Scarsdale, N.Y. Office: 50 Church St., New York, N.Y. Died Aug. 14, 1948.

NICHOLSON, George Robert Henderson, educator; b. Wainfleet, Lincolnshire, Eng., Nov. 18, 1885; s. Robert and Rachel Jane (Henderson) N.; grad. Kingswood Sch., Bath, Eng., 1904; B A., Manchester Univ., 1907, M.A., 1908; Pd.D., Colgate Univ., 1937; m. Elizabeth Ward Chase, June 17, 1921; stepsons—Charles Ward Chase, Warren Doty Chase. Housemaster Kingswood Sch., Bath, 1907-14; came to U.S., 1914; pvt. tutor, 1914-16; founder, 1916, and since headmaster Kingswood School (inc. as Kingswood Acad. of which is trustee). Mem. Headmasters Assn., Country Day Sch. Headmasters' Assn. (pres. 1935-36), Progressive Edn. Assn., N.E. Assn. Schs. and Colleges. Address: Kingswood School, West Hartford, Conn. Died Nov. 27, 1947.

NICHOLSON, Meredith, author, diplomat, lecturer; b. Crawfordsville, Ind., Dec. 9, 1866; s. Edward Willis and Emily (Meredith) N.; ed. pub. schs., Indianapolis; hon. A.M., Wabash Coll., 1901, Butler Coll., 1902; Litt.D., Wabash, 1907; LL.D., Indiana U., 1928, Butler Coll., 1929; m. Eugenie Kountze, June 16, 1896 (died 1931); children—Elizabeth Kountze (Mrs. Austin H. Brown), Eugenie (dec.), Meredith, Charles Lionel; married 2d, Mrs. Dorothy Wolfe Lannon, September 20, 1933 (divorced December 24, 1943). E.E. and M.P. to Paraguay, 1933-34, to Venezuela, 1935-38, to Nicaragua, 1938, resigned, March 1941. Elected mem. Indianapolis Common Council through reconstruction efforts of civic bodies, 1928, term 1928-30; Dem. dist. chmn.; mem. Dem. State Com., 1930-32. Mem. Nat. Inst. Arts and Letters, Military Order Loyal Legion, S.R., Phi Beta Kappa, Phi Gamma Delta. Episcopalian. Democrat. Clubs: Athletic (Indianapolis); National Press (Washington, D.C.). Author: Short Flights (poems), 1891; The Hoosiers (published in "National Studies in American Letters"), 1900; The Main Chance, 1903; Zelda Dameron, 1904; The House of a Thousand Candles, 1905; Poems, 1906; The Port of Missing Men, 1907; Rosalind at Red Gate, 1907; The Little Brown Jug at Kildare, 1908; The Lords of High Decision, 1909; The Siege of the Seven Suitors, 1910; A Hoosier Chronicle, 1912; The Provincial American (Essays), 1913; Otherwise Phyllis, 1913; The Poet, 1914; The Proof of the Pudding, 1916; The Madness of May, 1917; A Reversible Santa Clause, 1917; The Valley of Democracy (essays), 1918; Lady Larkspur, 1919; Blacksheep! Blacksheep!, 1920; The Man in the Street (essays), 1921; Play: Honor Bright (with Kenyon Nicholson), 1921; Best Laid Schemes (short stories), 1922; Broken Barriers, 1922; The Hope of Happiness, 1923; And They Lived Happily Ever After, 1925; The Cavalier of Tennessee, 1928; Old Familiar Faces (essays), 1929. Special contbr. to Indianapolis News, 1943. Home: Indianapolis, Ind. Address Indianapolis Athletic Club, Indianapolis, Ind. Died Dec. 20, 1947.

NICHOLSON, Thomas, bishop; b. Woodburn, Ont., Can., Jan. 27, 1862; s. James and Hannah (Burkholder) N.; grad., Toronto (Can.) Normal Sch., 1883; A.B., Northwestern U., 1892, A.M., 1895; S.T.B., Garrett Bibl. Inst., 1892; D.D., Ia. Wesleyan, 1898, Garrett, 1906, Wesleyan, 1909; LL.D., Cornell Coll., 1907, Northwestern U., 1912, Allegheny Coll., 1915; m. Jane Boothroyd, Aug. 20, 1885 (died May 10, 1915); m. 2d, Evelyn C. Riley, June 19, 1917. Taught in various pub. and high schs., 1878-83; entered M.E. ministry, 1884; on various charges in Mich., 1884-89, at Big Rapids, Mich., 1893-94; prof. philosophy and Bibl. lit., and prin. acad. of Cornell Coll., 1894-1903; pres. and prof. philosophy, Dak. Wesleyan U., 1903-08; gen. corr. sec. Bd. of Edn., M.E. Ch., 1908-16; elected bishop M.E. Ch., May 1916; resident bishop in Chicago, 1916-24; resident bishop, Detroit, 1924-32. President of Anti-Saloon League of America, 1921-32. Lecturer on the English Bible in many states. Chmn. exec. com. Ia. State Teachers' Assn., 1899; pres. S.D. State Teachers' Assn., 1908; chmn. State Conf. Charities and Corrections, also of com. which named list of accredited high schs. and pub. State High Sch. Manual, which he edited. Founder and first pres. Council of Ch. Bds. of Edn.; one of organizers Assn. of Am. Colls. Mem. Internat. Y.M.C.A. Com.; mem. exec. com. Federal Council of Churches; pres. Bd. of Sunday Schs. M.E. Ch.; pres. Bd. Hosps., Homes and Deaconess Work; trustee Northwestern U., Meharry Med. Coll., U. of Chattanooga, etc. Del. to Gen. Conf., 1908, 12, 16; del. to Ecumenical Meth. Conf., Toronto, Can., 1911; fraternal del. of M.E. Ch. U.S.A. to Irish Wesleyan Conf., Belfast, to British Wesleyan Conf., Bristol, Eng., 1923, and to United Ch. of Can., 1930; del. to Internat. Missions Conf., Oxford, Eng., 1923, and to Budapest, 1927. Mem. com. to organize Korean Methodist Ch., 1930. Granted retired relation by Gen. Conf., 1932. Address: Mount Vernon, Ia. Died Mar. 4, 1944.

NICHOLSON, Vincent DeWitt, lawyer; b. Azalia, Ind., May 2, 1890; s. Samuel Edgar and Rhoda Elma (Parker) N.; A.B., Earlham Coll., Richmond, Ind., 1910; George Washington U. Law Sch., 1911-12; LL.B., Harvard U. Law Sch., 1916; m. Rebecca Carter, May 8, 1920; children—Carolyn, John Edgar, Francis Tim, Christopher. In law practice with Stetson, Jennings & Russell, New York, 1916-17; with law firm of Taylor, Robey & Hoar, and mem. of Taylor, Hoar & Nicholson, Phila., 1920-34; atty. with N.R.A., Dec. 1934-May 31, 1935; gen. counsel, Rural Electrification Adminstrn., June 1935-July 1, 1941, asso. solicitor in charge of rural electrification, Office of the Solicitor, Dept. of Agr., since July 1, 1941; first deputy adminstr. of Rural Electrification Adminstrn. since June 6, 1942. War relief work as exec. sec. Am. Friends Service Com. Phila. 1917-18; Am. Red Cross 1918-19. Mem. Am. Bar Assn., Federal Bar Assn., Sigma Phi Epsilon. Democrat. Mem. Soc. of Friends (Quaker) Author: Pennsylvania Law of Real Estate (3 editions, 1924, 1926, 1928). Contbr. articles in law publications. Home: 1307 Noyes Dr., Silver Spring, Md. Address: Dept. of Agriculture, Washington, D.C. Died Nov. 5, 1945.

NICKLAS, Charles Aubrey, corp. official; b. Turin, N.Y., July 7, 1886; s. Frederick Charles and Cora (Erlenbach) N.; student Coll. City of N.Y., 1900-04, Wagner Free Inst. (Phila.), 1905-06; C.P.A., N.Y. Univ., 1912; m. Mary Spottswood, Oct. 5, 1915; children—Mary Spottswood, Helen, Charles Aubrey. Clerk on constrn. work, 1904-06; chief clk., later sec.-treas., Empire Engring. Corp., 1906-17, sec. and treas., 1917-24, v.p. since 1924; chmn. bd. Empire Constrn. Co. since 1931 (dir., mem. exec. com.); asso. with Boyce, Hughes & Farrell, c.p.a.'s as spl. partner, since 1915; pres., dir. and mem. exec. Com. The Little Empire Corp.; chmn. bd., dir. and mem. exec. com. George W. Rogers Constrn. Co.; chmn. bd. and mem. exec. com. Northern Constrn. Co., Inc.; pres. Garrison Park Corp.; dir. Hytian Am. Sugar Co., Hytian Corp. of America, Greenwich Gardens, Inc., Setay Co., Inc., First Nat. Bank (Spring Lake, N.J.). Trustee and treas. St. Luke's Home for Aged Women; trustee Trinity Sch. for Boys, New York P.E. Pub. Sch. Mem. Am. Inst. of Accountants, N.Y. State Soc. of C.P.A.'s., Am. Soc. of C.P.A.'s, Soc of C.P.A.'s of State of N.J.., Am. Arbitration Assn., Gen. Contractors Assn. Episcopalian (vestryman Trinity Ch.) Clubs: Railroad-Machinery, Downtown Athletic, Nat. Republican (New York). Home: Spring Lake, N.J. Office: 6 Church St., New York, N.Y. Died Mar. 7, 1942.

NIEDRINGHAUS, (George) Hayward (nē′dring-hous), pres. Granite City Steel Co.; b. St. Louis, Mo., May 11, 1891; s. George Wallace and Fanita (Hayward) N.; ed. Smith Acad., St. Louis, and Lake Placid (N.Y.) Sch. for Boys; m. Lorna Tweedy, Sept. 18, 1917; 1 dau., Joan Hayward. Began as laboratory assistant Granite City (Ill.) Steel Co., 1911, personnel dir., 1916-17, works mgr., 1920-23, mng. dir., 1924, vice president and general manager, 1925-28, pres. and gen. mgr. since 1929; pres. Granite City Culvert Co., Granite City, St. Louis & Eastern Belt Line. Vice president and director of William F. Niedringhaus Investment Company, West Calumet Mining Co., Black Mountain Land Co.; chmn. bd. and dir First Granite City Nat. Bank; dir. and mem. exec. com. Nat. Enameling & Stamping Co.; dir. Miss. Valley Trust Co., St. Louis Shipbuilding & Steel Co., Granite City Realty & Investment Co., St. Louis Dry Dock Company, American Zinc, Lead & Smelting Co., Am. Iron and Steel Institute, Paducah Marine Ways, Inc. Served as private to sergeant, 6th Air Squadron, U.S. Army, 1917-18. Served as member iron and steel industry advisory com.; mem. Com. for Econ. Development, St. Louis and Madison County. Mem. Nat. Council Boy Scouts of Am.; mem. St. Louis Chamber Commerce, Iron and Steel Inst. of Great Britain, Nat. Assn. Mfrs., Army Ordnance Assn., Newcomen Soc. England. Republican. Episcopalian. Clubs: Round Table, Racquet, Noonday, Deer Creek, St. Louis Country, Links (New York). Home: Clayton, Mo. Office: Granite City, Ill. Died July 7, 1949.

NIELDS, John P., judge; b. Wilmington, Delaware, August 7, 1868; s. Benjamin and Gertrude (Fulton) N.; prep. edn., Haverford Coll., Pa.; A.B., Harvard, 1889; Harvard Law Sch., 1890, 92; m. Mary Blanchard Craven, Jan. 23, 1907; 1 dau., Ann. In practice at Wilmington since 1892; apptd. U.S. atty. for Dist. of Del. by President Roosevelt, 1903, reapptd. 1907, and by President Taft, 1912; U.S. dist. judge, Dist. of Delaware, since 1930. Attended Plattsburg Training Camp, 1915; capt. U.S. Army, 1918. Pres. Wilmington Pub. Library; hon. pres. Wilmington Boys' Club. Mem. Am. and Delaware bar assns.; chancellor and chmn. membership com. Soc. of Colonial Wars; chmn. membership com. Del. Hist. Society; mem. Loyal Legion; hon. mem. Soc. of The Cincinnati. Republican. Episcopalian. Clubs: Wilmington, Wilmington Country; Harvard. Editor Harvard Law Review and Phi Delta Phi Law School. Home: Aston, R.D. 1, Wilmington, Del. Died Aug. 26, 1943.

NIELSEN, Alice, prima donna; b. Nashville, Tenn., 1876; d. Erasmus Ivarius and Sarah A. Nielsen; musical edn. San Francisco, under Mlle. Ida Valerga; m. Benjamin Nentwig; m. 2d, LeRoy R. Stoddard, Dec. 21, 1917. First stage appearance with opera company at Oakland, Cal., as Yum Yum in "The Mikado," after Tivoli engagement joined the Bostonians, 1896, and took the role of Annabel in "Robin Hood," the following season played leading part Maid Marion; also prin. soprano role in "The Serenade"; stellar début Grand Opera House, Toronto, Sept. 14, 1898, in "The Fortune Teller"; later starred in "The Singing Girl"; played in "The Fortune Teller," London, 1902; studied for grand opera, Rome; 1st appearance in grand opera at Bellini Theatre, Naples, Italy, as Marguerite, in "Faust"; later appeared at San Carlo Opera House, Naples, in "La Traviata," Covent Garden, London, in "Don Giovanni" and "The Marriage of Figaro"; prima donna at Covent Garden, London, in "La Bohême" and "Rigoletto," 1905; New Waldorf Theatre, London, alternating with Eleanor Dusé in the drama, 1906; toured U.S. in grand opera, with Don Pasquale Co., 1906, San Carlo Co., alternating with Lillian Nordica, 1907-08, Boston Opera Co., 1910-11; several yrs. with Met. Opera Co. Died March 8, 1943.

NILES, Alva Joseph, brig. gen.; b. Whitehall, Ill., Apr. 5, 1882; s. Albert George and Sarah Ruth (Pruett) N.; student Winfield Coll., 1899-1901; m. Ethel M. McNeal, Jan. 3, 1906; children—Joe Allen, Mary Louise. Treas. sch. land funds, Okla. Ty., 1903-05; adj. gen. Okla. Ty., 1906-07; pres. Farmers & Merchants Bank, Mountain View, Okla., 1908-09, 1st Nat. Bank, Sentinel, 1911-12, Citizens State Bank, Okemah, 1912-14; oil producer, Tulsa, Okla., 1915; organizer, 1919, pres., 1919-23, Security (now Tulsa) Nat. Bank; oil production and investment business since 1923; pres. Trevino Oil Corp. of Texas. Served as pvt. U.S. Vols., Spanish-Am. War (enlisted at age of 16); in State-Federal Nat. Guard Service, 1900-17, advanced from capt. to brig. gen. and adj. gen., 1906; brig. gen. and judge adv. Okla. Nat. Guard, and ex-officio U.S. disbursing officer, 1908-12; company and bn. comdr., Mexican border service, 1916-17; maj. and insp. gen. U.S. Army, France, World War; participated in Meuse-Argonne engagements and defensive operations Toul sector; col. O.R.C., 1921-23; apptd. brig. gen., 1923; organized and commanded 70th F.A. Brig., Federal Nat. Guard, Okla., Colo., N.M. and Ariz., 1923-26. Chmn. and mgr. Rep. Campaign Com., Okla., 1910; treasurer of Rep. Nat. Com. for Oklahoma, 1920. Mem. board advisers Castle Heights Mil. Acad.; formerly mem. bd. regents U. of Tulsa, Okla. Mil. Acad. (Claremore); mem. Am. advisory council, Yenching U., Peiping, China. Awarded Distinguished Service medal. Member national advisory com. Am. Legion Marksmanship; mem. exec. com. Nat. Guard Assn. America, 1907-10; dir. and life mem. Nat. Rifle Assn. America, 1906-10; past president Tulsa (Oklahoma) Chamber of Commerce. Mem. Am. Bankers Assn., Okla. Bankers Assn., United Spanish War Vets. (an organizer; Okla. state comdr. 1905-08), Am. Legion (del. to St. Louis meeting, May 1919, when Am. Legion was organized, and mem. com. on preamble), Joe Carson Post Am. Legion No. 1 of Tulsa (an organizer and past post comdr.), Mil. Order World War, Mil. Order Foreign Wars (vice comdr. Okla. Dept.). Republican. Presbyterian. Mason (33°, Shriner), Elk. Clubs: City, Scottish Rite (Tulsa); Tulsa (Okla.) Country; Virginia Country (Long Beach, Calif.); La Grulla Gun, Baja California (Mexico); Casa Blanca Country (Laredo, Tex.); Casino Mexicano (Nuevo Laredo, Mexico). Home: 1500 S. Frisco St., Tulsa 5, Okla. Died Jan. 19, 1950.

NILES, Walter Lindsay, physician, educator; b. Lebanon, N.Y., Jan. 2, 1878; s. Isaac Newton and Harriet (Lindsay) N.; grad. high sch., Norwich, N.Y., 1896; M.D., Cornell U., 1902; m. Louise Vezin, May 20, 1908; children—Harriet Lindsay, Nelson Robinson. Practiced at N.Y. City since 1904; prof. clin. medicine, Cornell U. Med. Coll., since 1916, dean 1919-28; consulting physician Bellevue Hosp. since 1930; consulting physician Memorial, Southampton, Jamaica, Nassau hosps., New York Infirmary for Women and Children; attending physician New York Hosp., also mem. joint administration bd. same and Cornell Med. Coll. Assn. Mem. Assn. Am. Physicians, Am. Climatol. and Clin. Assn., Harvey Soc., N.Y. Acad. of Medicine, Alpha Omega, Phi Alpha Sigma. Clubs: Links, Century, Cornell, National Golf Links, Shinnecock Hills Golf; Meadow (Southampton, L.I.); Piping Rock, Deepdale. Died Dec. 22. 1941.

NILSSON, Victor (nĕls'sŭn), author; b. near Trelleborg, Sweden, Mar. 10, 1867; s. John and Bertha (Hansson) N.; Higher Latin Coll., Gothenburg, Sweden; Cand. Ph., U. of Minn., 1894, Ph.D., 1897 (1st person to obtain doctor's degree in America with Scandinavian langs. and lit. as major line of study); unmarried. Came to America, 1885, naturalized, 1897. Editorial writer in English and Swedish, Minn., since 1885; librarian East Side Branch of Minneapolis Public Library, 1891-1903; European corr. and music critic Minneapolis Times, 1897-1900; founder and pub. Musiktidning, 1906-10; music critic and music editor Minneapolis Journal, 1907-08 and 1910-38; editor The Progress-Register (weekly) since 1906, owner and pub. since 1919; corr. Musical America, 1929-35. Mem. bd. Am. Inst. Swedish Arts, Lit. and Letters since 1930. First v.p. Hennepin County Publishers Assn. Knighted by King Gustaf of Sweden with Royal Order of Vasa, 1st class, 1919, Order of the North Star, 1929. Republican. Unitarian. Charter member and frequently festival secretary of The American Union of Swedish Singers; hon. member United Singers of the Red River Valley, De Svenske Chorus of Sweden; charter mem. Swedish Soc. of Minneapolis and St. Paul (pres. 1933-35). Author: Förenta Staternas Presidenter, 1894; Loddfáfnismál, an Eddic Study, 1898; History of Sweden, 1899; Sångarfärden till Sverge, 1910; A Bayreuth Pilgrimage, 1925; A Pilgrimage to Bonn and Its Beethoven House, 1927; Absaroka, 1938. Contbr. of chapter on music in Delaware Tercentenary book, 1938. Lecturer upon and translator of Strindberg, Lagerlöf, Hamsun and Fröding. Recording sec. Gunnar Wennerberg Monument Assn., 1912, Jenny Lind Memorial Foundation, 1934. Home: 551 Newton Av. N. Office: 305 S. Fifth St., Minneapolis, Minn. Died Apr. 7, 1942.

NIMMONS, George Croll, architect; b. Wooster, O., July 8, 1865; s. John Wesley and Rebecca S. N.; A.B., Univ. of Wooster, 1887; traveled and studied architecture in Europe; later attended Art Inst. Chicago; m. Justine V. Wheeler, 1898; children—Paul Wesley, Marie Josephine (dec.), Nancy. Began as draftsman in office of D. H. Burnham & Co., 1887, and later engaged in practice on own account; with William K. Fellows in firm of Nimmons & Fellows, 1898-1910; alone 1910-17; served as head of George C. Nimmons & Company, 1917-33, now firm Nimmons, Carr & Wright. Fellow A.I.A.; mem. Municipal Art League, Art. Inst. Chicago, Phi Kappa Psi. Awarded gold medal for commercial industrial bldgs., by A.I.A., 1921. Ex-pres. Illinois Chapter A.I.A. Republican. Episcopalian. Clubs: University, Chicago Athletic Assn., Cliff Dwellers, Quadrangle, Olympia Fields Country, Flossmoor Country, South Shore Country. Home: Flossmoor, Ill. Office: 333 N. Michigan Av., Chicago, Ill. Died June, 1947.

NISBET, Charles Richard (nĭz'bĕt), clergyman; b. Macon, Ga., July 24, 1871; s. James Taylor and Mary Seymour (Wingfield) N.; prep. edn., high sch. (Atlanta, Ga.) and Moreland Park Mil. Acad.; student U. of Ga.; admitted to Ga. bar, 1894; student Princeton Theol. Sem., 1895-96, 1897-98; D.D., Southwestern Presbyn. U., Clarksville, Tenn. (now at Memphis), 1909; m. Ola May Jones, Feb. 15, 1899 (died July 19, 1929); children—Mary Elizabeth (Mrs. Samuel Clinton Marty), Charles Richard; m. 2d, Mrs. Freda Dotger Burch, June 8, 1931. Began preaching at Bainbridge, Ga., 1898, later at Kirkwood, Ga.; ordained ministry Presbyn. Ch. in U.S., 1898; pastor successively Westminster Presbyn. Ch., Atlanta, Woodland Street Presbyn. Ch., Nashville, Tenn., and Trinity Presbyn. Ch., St. Louis, until 1911, Central Presbyn. Ch., Kansas City, Mo., 1911-27, Caldwell Memorial Presbyn. Ch., Charlotte, N.C., since 1927. Pres. Council of Chs. Greater Kansas City, 1926-27; trustee Synodical Coll., Fulton, Mo. (pres. bd.); trustee Davidson Coll., Queens Coll. Mem. Christian Ministers' Assn. of Charlotte and Mecklenburg County, N.C. (pres.), Chi Phi. Democrat. Mason, K.P. Clubs: Goodfellows, Charlotte Country, Mission Hills Golf and Country. Home: 1614 Park Drive, Charlotte, N.C.* Died June 26, 1943.

NIX, James Thomas, surgeon; b. Greenville, S.C., May 31, 1887; s. James Thomas and Evelyn Beatrice (Fleming) N.; B.S., Tulane U., New Orleans, 1906, M.D., 1910; A.M., Loyola U., New Orleans, 1918, LL.D., 1924; m. Vera Irene Malter, Dec. 8, 1913; children—Rosary Vera, James Thomas. Interne Charity Hosp., New Orleans, 1908-10; practicing surgeon, New Orleans, since 1910; asst. surg. staff of Rudolph Matas, M.D., Tulane U., 1911-15; senior on surg. staff Hotel Dieu, New Orleans, since 1911, pres. 1929; dir. J. T. Nix Clinic since 1918; prof. of surgery Loyola Post Grad. Sch. of Medicine, 1916-18; prof. gen. surgery, Loyola U. Sch. of Dentistry, since 1926; sr. on surg. staff Charity Hosp., 1931-42; clin. prof. surgery, Sch. of Medicine, La. State U., since 1940; adviser Catholic Hospital Association of America since 1933; dir. Oscar Allen Tumor Clinic, Charity Hosp., 1933-42; medical director, Higgins Industries and Higgins Corporation, New Orleans, 1942-44. Hon. life fellowship, Case Records Award, Am. Coll. of Surgeons, 1930. Chmn. hon. advisory com. La. State Hosp. Bd., 1937; chmn. health com., 8th Nat. Eucharistic Congress, New Orleans, 1938. Mem. Founders Group, Am. Bd. of Surgery. Served as 1st lt. Med. Reserve Corps, U.S. Army, 1918-19. Decorated Knight of St. Gregory, 1929; Knight Comdr. of Holy Sepulchre, 1930. Fellow Am. Coll. Surgeons, S.E. Surg. Congress; mem. A.M.A., Cath. Hosp. Assn., Southern Med. Assn., La. State Med. Soc. (2d v.p. 1931, 1st v.p. 1932), Orleans Parish Med. Soc. (v.p. 1930, pres. 1937), Cath. Physicians Guild of New Orleans (pres. 1936-38), New Orleans Grad. Med. Assembly, Société Internationale de Gastro-Enterologie, Internat. Cancer Congress (1939), Phi Beta Pi, Beta Theta Pi, Blue Key; hon. mem. Ill. Clin. Club, Lafourche Valley Med. Soc. of La., 7th Dist. Med. Soc. of La., Theta Beta; hon. lay mem. Oblate Brothers of Mary Immaculate. Member and corr. Academician of Institute of Coimbra, Portugal, since 1941. Democrat. Roman Catholic. Clubs: Round Table, Southern Yacht, Country (New Orleans). Author: The Unborn, 1924; (verse) Reflections, 1927; Mother-love, 1928; A Surgeon Reflects, 1940. Contbr. to med. jours. Home: 2140 S. Carrollton Av. Office: 1407 S. Carrollton Av., New Orleans. Died May 17, 1945; buried in Metairie Cemetery, New Orleans.

NOBLE, Eugene Allen, educator; b. Brooklyn, N. Y.; s. William Richard and Margaret J. (Hayes) N.; Ph.B., Wesleyan U., Conn., 1891; studied Northwestern Univ.; L.H.D., Dickinson Coll., Pa.; S.T.D., Wesleyan Univ.; LL.D., Hamilton Coll. and Univ. of Pittsburgh; m. Lillian White Osborn, Nov. 19, 1893; m. 2d, Mrs. T. K. Lownes, Aug. 6, 1930. Head master Centenary Collegiate Inst., Hackettstown, N.J., 1902-08; pres. Goucher Coll., Baltimore, 1908-11, Dickinson Coll., Carlisle, Pa., 1911-14; exec. sec. Juilliard Musical Foundation, New York, 1922-37, retired. Mem. Alpha Delta Phi, Phi Beta Kappa. Clubs: Graduate, City, Alpha Delta Phi, University (New York). Writer on ednl. and other topics. Home: 1 Beekman Pl., New York; and Narragansett, R.I. Died June 28, 1948.

NOBLE, Marcus Cicero Stephens, prof. pedagogy; b. Louisburg, Franklin Co., N.C., Mar. 15, 1855; s. Albert Morris and Mary Ann (Primrose) N.; preparatory edn. Bingham Sch., now at Asheville, N.C.; student Davidson Coll., 1875-76, U. of N.C., 1877-79, Pd.D.; m. Alice J. Yarborough, Aug. 26, 1885; (dec.); children—Alice, Marcus C. S. Instr. and comdt. cadets, Bingham Sch., 1880-82; first supt. pub. schs., Wilmington, N.C., 1882-98; prof. pedagogy, U. of N.C., 1898-1934, also dean Sch. of Edn., 1913-1934; Kenan prof. emeritus in edn., 1934; pres. Bank of Chapel Hill, N.C. Mem. first bd. dirs. State Normal and Industrial Coll., N.C., 1891-98; mem. State Bd. Examiners, N.C., 1897-1904; trustee State Agrl. and Tech. Coll. (colored) since 1899 (pres. bd. since 1907); mem. N.C. Hist. Commn. since 1907, chmn. since 1932. Mem. N.C. Teachers' Assembly (pres. 1913-14). Mason, Odd Fellow, K.P. Editor: Williams' Beginner's Reader, 1885; Davies' Standard Arithmetic, 1886; N.C. Edition Maury's Manual of Geography, 1890; The Teaching of County Geography; A History of the Public Schools of North Carolina; The Battle of Moore's Creek Bridge, 1776. Contbr. numerous articles on N.C. history. Home: Chapel Hill, N.C. Died June 1, 1942.

NOBLE, Raymond Goodman; born at South Windsor, Connecticut, Nov. 30, 1873; son of Hezikiah B. and Elizabeth A. (Stoughton) N.; ed. Connecticut Literary Institute, Suffield, Connecticut; m. Dorothy Couthouy Gage, Jan. 23, 1926 (died Mar. 26, 1934). Retired; was formerly a mem. mgrs. com. of Union Carbide & Carbon Corp.; pres. Nat. Carbon-Eveready S.A. (Monterey, Mexico), National Carbon-Argentina Ltd.; vice-pres. Nat. Carbon Co. Fed. Inc. U.S.A. (Shanghai, China), Union Carbide Sales Co., also dir. foreign dept. of all cos. owned or controlled by same and by Union Carbide & Carbon Corp., of New York, including Nat. Carbon Co., Prest-O-Lite Co., Oxweld Acetylene Co., Carbide & Carbon Chem. Corp., Electro-Metall. Co., Haynes Stellite Co., etc. Republican. Conglist. Mason. Clubs: Union League (New York); Hartford, Hartford Golf (Hartford, Conn.); Lake Placid (Adirondocks, N.Y.); Everglades (Palm Beach, Fla.). Home: S. Windsor, Conn. Died July 31, 1945.

NOBLE, Urbane Alexander, banking; b. Edwards, N.Y., Nov. 16, 1877; s. David and Jurane J. (Hill) N.; ed. Potsdam Normal Sch., 1893-99; M.D., Columbia U. Coll. Physicians and Surgeons, 1904; m. Clara J. Simpson, Apr. 19, 1906; children—John, Elizabeth (Mrs. Charles E. Scott), Jane. Engaged in teaching sch., 1895-99; in private practice as physician and surgeon, 1904-09; asso. with Cleland-Simpson Co., dept. store, Scranton, Pa., since 1909, dir. since 1909, pres. since 1936; pres. and dir. Miss. R.R. and of U.S. Lumber Co. (both since May 1942); dir. First Nat. Bank of Scranton since 1932, pres. since 1936; dir. Scranton Lackawanna Trust Co., Hudson Coal Co.; chmn. bd. Simpson Real Estate Corp. Trustee Scranton-Keystone Jr. Coll. Republican. Presbyterian. Clubs: Scranton, Country, Rotary of Scranton. Home: 520 Clay Av. Office: First Nat. Bank, Scranton, Pa. Died Oct. 10, 1946.

NOCK, Albert Jay, author, educator; A.B., Litt.D. St. Stephen's Coll. (now part of Columbia U.). Vis. prof. Am. history and politics, St. Stephen's Coll., since 1930. Author: (with Francis Neilson) How Diplomats Make War, 1915, 2d edit., 1916; Myth of a Guilty Nation (pseud. Historicus), 1922; Jefferson, 1926; On Doing the Right Thing and Other Essays, 1928; (with C.R. Wilson) Francis Rabelais, the Man and His Work, 1929; The Book of Journeyman (pseud. Journeyman), 1930; Theory of Education in the United States (pseud. Journeyman), 1932. Editor: Selected Works of Charles F. Browne ("Artemus Ward"), 1924; (with Catherine Rose Wilson) Francis Rabelais, Urquhart-Le Matteaux translation (2 vols.), 1931. Contbr. to New Republic, Atlantic Monthly, etc. Formerly editor The Freeman. Address: St. Stephen's Coll., 16 Gramercy Park, New York. Died Aug. 19, 1945.

NOEL, James W(illiam), lawyer; b. Melmore, O., Nov. 24, 1867; s. William Percival and Caroline (Graves) N.; B.S., Purdue, 1892; LL.B., Indiana Law Sch., 1895; m. Cornelia Horton Humphrey, June 25, 1895 (died Sept. 11, 1895); m. 2d, Anne Madison, June 29, 1899 (died Feb. 28, 1924); m. 3d, Genevieve Thurman Downing, Apr. 15, 1925. In practice of law at Indianapolis, Ind., since 1895; mem. of law firm of Noel, Armstrong & Woodard. Special atty. for City of Indianapolis (investigations resulted in overthrow of administration), 1903; spl. asst. to Atty. Gen. Wickersham in prosecution of dynamite conspiracy cases, Indianapolis, resulting in conviction of 40 conspirators; spl. atty. for State of Calif. in trial of Matthew A. Schmidt for murder in Los Angeles Times explosion, 1915; gen. counsel Ind. Coal Commn., 1920. Mem. Ind. Ho. of Rep., 1899 (author of Ind. St. Ry. Charter, Pharmacy Law, Park Commn. Law). Author of law providing uniform system of public accounts and annual audit (considered a model law). Trustee Purdue since 1917, v.p. bd., 1925-42, pres. since 1942; dir. Purdue Research Foundation. Mem. American Ind. State and Indianapolis bar assns., American History Soc., Ind. Hist. Soc., Nat. Econ. League, Internat. Law Assn., Indianapolis Bd. of Trade, Indianapolis Chamber Commerce, Sigma Nu (vice-regent 1898). Republican. Methodist. Scottish Rite Mason, Knight of Pythias (judge adv. gen. Sons of Vets. 1899). Clubs: Columbia, Indianapolis Literary, Indianapolis Country. Author: Report on State Finances and Investigation of Indiana Insurance Companies, 1907-08. Home: 80th St. and Lafayette Rd., R.R. 1, New Augusta, Ind. Office: 130 E. Washington St., Indianapolis, Ind. Died Apr. 6, 1944.

NOELTE, Albert (nōl'tē), composer; b. Starnberg, Bavaria, March 10, 1885; s. Hermann and Marie (Schaaf) N.; came to U.S., 1900; ed. Latin Sch., N.E. Conservatory, Boston and Munich Univs.; study of music in Munich under Felix Mottl, and Richard Strauss; m. Shirley Dean Shank, March 31, 1930. Began career as violinist, later composer; music critic in Boston; now chmn. of the theory dept., Northwestern U. Sch. of Music; dir. of theory dept., Civic Orchestra, Chicago. Mem. Internat. Soc. of Contemporary Composers. Clubs: Cliff Dwellers, Chicago Arts. Composer of songs, piano pieces, a Mass, a Suite for Strings and Timpani, a Suite for 26 Wind Instruments and Percussions, a considerable number of symphonic and choral works, and two operas. Home: Hotel Belmont, Chicago, Ill.* Died Mar. 1946.

NOLAND, Lloyd, surgeon; b. Gordonsville, Va., July 25, 1880; s. Cuthbert Powell and Rosalie (Haxall) N.; grad. Central High Sch., Washington, 1898; M.D., Baltimore Med. Coll., 1903; m. Margaret Gillick, Nov. 7, 1907. Began practice, Baltimore, 1903; exec. officer to chief sanitary officer, Isthmian Canal Commn., 1904-05; chief of surg. clinic, Isthmian Canal Hosp., Colon, 1906-13; commd. asst. surgeon Med. Reserve Corps, U.S. Navy, 1913-21; supt. dept. of health, and chief surgeon, Tenn. Coal, Iron & R.R. Co., since 1913. Democrat. Episcopalian. Mem. A.M.A. (chmn. sect. on surgery, 1941; mem. Judicial council since 1942), Am. Pub. Health Asso., Canal Zone Med. Asso., Medical Assn. State of Ala. (past pres.), Southern Med. Assn.; fellow Am. Coll. Surgeons, Southern Surg. Assn. (past pres.). Clubs: Mountain Brook Country, Army and Navy. Home: 3240 Sterling Road, Birmingham, Ala. Office: Employees Hospital, Fairfield, Ala. Died Nov. 27, 1949.

NOLLEN, Henry Scholte, life ins.; b. Pella, Ia., Sept. 26, 1866; s. John and Johanna Sarah (Scholte) N.; B.S., Central Univ. (now Coll.), Pella, 1885; LL.D., Drake Univ., Des Moines, 1933; m. Bessie Sarah Snow, May 17, 1892 (died Aug. 1905); m. 2d, Pearl Hamilton, Nov. 7, 1916. Began as bookkeeper Pella Nat. Bank, at age of 10; prof. mathematics Central U., 1886-87; successively with Des Moines Electric Light Co., Citizens Nat. Bank (Des Moines), Sickles & Co., wholesale implements, United Gas Improvement Co. of Phila. until 1893; auditor, later sec. and trustee Banker's Life Assn. of Des Moines, 1893-1913, reorganizing the Assn. from an assessment to a legal reserve basis; v.p. Equitable Life Ins. Co. of Ia., 1913-21, pres., 1921-39, chmn. of bd., 1939-41, trustee since 1941; pres. and dir. Pella (Ia.) Nat. Bank. Trustee Des Moines Pub. Library, 1909-19; chmn. bd. trustees Des Moines Water Plant, 1919-37, and since 1939; patron mem. bd., formerly v.p. Des Moines Assn. Fine Arts; mem. bd. Des Moines Civic Music Assn., pres., 1938-40; mem. Des Moines Chamber Commerce, U.S. Chamber Commerce, Iowa State Hist. Soc., Ia. Acad. Science, Archeol. Inst. America (former pres.), Des Moines Assn. Life Underwriters, Assn. Life Ins. Presidents (chmn. 1925 conv.); fellow A.A.A.S., Am. Geol. Soc.; mem. Phi Beta Kappa (hon. Drake U.). Republican. Episcopalian. York and Scottish Rite Mason (33°, K.T.); Red Cross of Constantine; C.B.C.S.; chairman Masonic Service Com. of Grand Lodge of Ia. since 1920, grand treas., 1940-41. Clubs: Grant (ex-pres.), Des Moines, Prairie (ex-pres.), Rotary, University, Garden, Wakonda Golf and Country. Widely known as lecturer on life insurance and other subjects. Contbr. to mags. Home: 402 29th St. Address: Equitable Life Ins. Co. of Iowa, Des Moines, Ia. Died Apr. 24, 1942.

NOLTE, Charles Beach (nōl'tē), pres. Crane Co.; b. Mattoon, Ill., Dec. 28, 1885; s. Richard Beach and Anna Turner (Miller) N.; B.S. in M.E., U. of Ill., 1909; m. Maude Alice Bacon, Nov. 8, 1911; children—Margaret Alice, Richard Bacon. Mech. engr. Engring Expt. Sta., Univ. of Ill., May-Oct. 1909; engr. Robert W. Hunt Co., engrs., Chicago, 1909-12, mgr., 1912-23, v.p. and gen. mgr., 1923-30, pres. and gen. mgr., 1930-35; also mem. bd. dirs. R. W. Hunt Co., engrs.; pres. and dir. Crane Co. since Mar. 1935; also pres. and dir. Crane Co. of Mex., Crane, Ltd., Montreal, Crane Export Corp., Crane Enamelware Co., Canadian Potteries, Ltd., Warden King, Ltd.; chmn. Trenton Potteries Co. Mem. Am. Soc. M.E., Am. Soc. Civil Engrs., Am. Soc. for Testing Materials, Am. Ry. Engring. Assn., Western Society Engineers. Republican. Presbyterian. Clubs: Chicago, Union League, University, Chicago Engineers, South Shore Country. Home: 6718 South Shore Drive. Office: 836 S. Michigan Av., Chicago, Ill. Died Apr. 29, 1941.

NOLTE, Louis Gustavus, surgeon; b. Milwaukee, Wis., Dec. 19, 1862; s. Simon and Pauline (Esche) N.; student Concordia Coll., Ft. Wayne, Ind.; M.D., Coll. Physicians and Surgeons (Columbia), 1886; m. Wilhelmina Widmayer, Oct. 17, 1888. Asst. to Dr. Nicholas Senn, Milwaukee, when he made his famous experiments in intestinal surgery, and succeeded to his practice when he removed to Chicago, 1892; county physician and police surgeon, Milwaukee, 1888-93; surgeon Johnston Emergency Hosp. (one of founders and later trustee); surgeon Trinity Hosp.; cons. surgeon Milwaukee County Hosp.; prof. principles and practice of surgery, med. dept. Marquette Univ., Milwaukee; surgeon Evang. Deaconess' Hosp.; surgeon Misericordia Hosp. Fellow Am. Coll. Surgeons, A.M.A.; mem. Wis. Surg. Assn., Wisconsin, Brainard, Milwaukee and Northwestern med. socs., Milwaukee County Med. Soc. (hon. mem., ex-pres.), Old Settlers Club of Milwaukee, A.A.A.S., Milwaukee Acad. Medicine (hon.), Milwaukee Soc. Clin. Surgery (hon.), Alumni Assn. College Physicians and Surgeons (Columbia), Columbia U. Alumni Assn. of Wis. (pres.), Alpha Kappa Kappa. Mason (32°, K.T.). Contbr. on med. subjects. Mem. Vol. Med. R.C. Home: 1523 N. Cass St. Office: 1207 N. Third St., Milwaukee, Wis. Died Feb. 15, 1942.

NORCROSS, Cleveland, administrator; b. Denver, Colo., Jan. 28, 1912; s. Theodore White and Christine Seruah (Cleveland) N.; B.S., Univ. of Pa., 1934; m. Helen Elizabeth Curley, Nov. 28, 1934; children—Frederick Cleveland, David Rogers. Mgr. various depts. R. H. Macy & Co., New York, 1934-37; personnel asst., Office Dir. Personnel, Home Owners Loan Corp. (U.S. govt.), 1937-40; administrative officer, exec. asst., exec. sec., contracting officer, Office Scientific Research and Development, Washington, D.C., 1940-47; asst. dir. Am. Inst. of Physics since July 1947. Awarded Presidential Certificate of Merit, 1948. Mem. Sigma Phi Epsilon. Club: Kenwood Golf (Bethesda, Md.). Home: 31 Mitchell Rd., Port Washington, N.Y. Office: 57 E. 55th St., N.Y. City. Died March 21, 1949.

NORDHOFF, Charles Bernard (nôrd'hŏf), author; b. of Am. parents, London, Eng., Feb. 1, 1887; s. Walter and Sarah Cope (Whitall) N.; brought to U.S. in childhood; A.B., Harvard, 1909; m. Pepé Teara, 1920 (divorced); children—Sarah, Margaret, Jane, Charles, Mary, James; m. 2d, Laura Grainger Whiley, 1941. Brought up on father's ranch in California. Went to France, 1916, as driver in American Ambulance; enlisted in Foreign Legion and was detached to Lafayette Flying Corps; trans. to U.S. Air Service as 2d lt. and promoted 1st lt.; hon. disch. Mar. 1919. Served 1917-19 as pilot French-U.S. Air Services. Author: The Fledgling, 1919; The Pearl Lagoon, 1924; Picaro, 1924; The Derelict, 1928. Author (with James Norman Hall): The Lafayette Flying Corps., 1920; Faery Lands of the South Seas, 1921; Falcons of France, 1929; Mutiny on the Bounty, 1932; Men Against the Sea, 1934, Pitcairn's Island, 1934; The Hurricane, 1935; The Dark River, 1938; No More Gas, 1940; Botany Bay, 1941; Men Without Country, 1942; The High Barbaree, 1945. Contributors, stories and articles to Atlantic, Harpers, and other mags. Address: Hope Ranch, Santa Barbara, Calif.; also Tahiti. French Oceania. Died Apr. 10, 1947.

NORLIN, George, educator; b. Concordia, Kan., Apr. 1, 1871; s. Gustav Wilhelm and Valborg (Fahnehjelm) N.; A.B., Hastings Coll., 1893; Ph.D., U. of Chicago, 1900; The Sorbonne, Paris, 1902; LL.D., Colo. Coll., 1920, U. of Mo., 1921; Litt.D., Columbia, 1932; L.H.D., U. of Denver, 1934; D.Eng., Colo. State Sch. of Mines, 1935; m. Minnie Covert Dutcher, June 21, 1904; 1 dau., Agnes Rebecca. Professor Greek, Hastings Coll., 1893-96; fellow in Greek, U. of Chicago, 1896-99; prof. Greek, U. of Colo., 1899-1939, acting pres., 1917-18, pres., 1919-30; research prof. of humanities since 1930. Theodore Roosevelt professor American life and institutions, University of Berlin, 1932-33; Weil lecturer Univ. of N.C., 1934. Elector, Hall of Fame. Former trustee Carnegie Foundation for the Advancement of Teaching. Mem. Phi Beta Kappa, Phi Gamma Delta, and of various learned and ednl. socs. Contbr. to popular and scientific publs. Clubs: University, Mile High, Cactus (Denver); Boulder, Kiwanis. Author: Integrity in Education and Other Papers; Fascism and Citizenship; Hitlerism—Why and Whither; Nationalism in Education; Things in the Saddle, 1940; also editor and translator into English of works of Isocrates. Home: Boulder, Colo. Died Mar. 30, 1942.

NORMAN, Fred, ex-congressman; b. Martinsville, Ill., Mar. 21, 1882; s. Tilghman Ashurst Howard (M.D.) and Pauline (Bartholdt) N.; grad. Martinsville High Sch., 1897; m. Alice Derry, Dec. 28, 1906; children—Howard Addison, Evelyn Pauline (Mrs. Harry E. Carlson). Sec. Raymond Overland Co., 1919-21; organized Fred Norman Co., 1922, and since pres. Mem. Raymond City Council, 1916-18, Wash. House of Reps., 1919-20, State Senate, 1925-35; mem. 78th Congress (1943-45), 3d Wash. Dist. Dir. White Pass Cross State Highway Assn.; pres. Southwest Wash. Good Roads Assn. Republican. Elk, Eagle, Odd Fellow, Rebeckah. Home: 449 11th St. Office: 405 1st St., Raymond, Wash. Died Apr. 18, 1947.

NORMAN, Montagu Collet, banker; b. 1871. Served with British army in S. Africa, 1900-02. Dir. Bank of England since 1907, dep. gov., 1918-20, gov., 1920-44. Decorated Companion Distinguished Service. Address: Thorpe Lodge, Campden Hill, W. 8, Eng.* Died Feb. 4, 1950.

NORRIS, Charles Gilman, author; b. Chicago, Ill., Apr. 23, 1881; s. Benjamin Franklin and Gertrude G. (Doggett) N.; Ph.B., U. of Calif., 1903; m. Kathleen Thompson (now the well known author), Apr. 30, 1909; children—Frank, Josephine (dec.), Gertrude (dec.). Asst. editor Country Life in America, 1903, Sunset Mag., 1905; asst. editor Am. Mag., 1908-13. Entered R.O.T.C. at Madison Barracks, N.Y., Apr. 1917; grad. capt. inf.; assigned to 153d Depot Brigade, Camp Dix, N.J.; maj. inf., Aug. 1918; resigned, Dec. 1918. Mem. Phi Gamma Delta. Clubs: Players, Dutch Treat (New York); Bohemian (San Francisco); Menlo Country (Menlo, Calif.). Republican. Episcopalian. Author: The Amateur, 1915; Salt, or the Education of Griffith Adams, 1917; Brass, 1921; The Rout of the Philistines (poetic drama—"grove play" of Bohemian Club), 1922; Bread, 1923; Pig Iron, 1925; Zelda Marsh, 1927; A Gest of Robin Hood ("grove play" of Bohemian Club), 1929; Seed, 1930; Zest, 1933; Hands, 1935; Ivanhoe ("grove play" of Bohemian Club), 1936; Bricks without Straw, 1938; Flint, 1944; also numerous short stories in mags. Home: 1247 Cowper St., Palo Alto, Calif. Died July 25, 1945.

NORRIS, George Washington, lawyer, banker; b. San Francisco, Calif., July 5, 1864; s. Joseph Parker and Mary Elizabeth (Garesche) N.; student U. of Pa., 1 yr.; m. Sarah Fox, June. 10, 1891. Law practice in Phila., 1886-94; mem. Edward B. Smith & Co., bankers, 1894-1911; dir. Dept. Wharves, Docks and Ferries, Phila., 1911-15; v.chmn. Federal Reserve Bank, Phila., 1916; Federal Farm Loan commr., 1916-20; gov. Federal Reserve Bank, Philadelphia, 1920-36; mem. bd. mgrs. Girard Trust Co., Beneficial Saving Fund Soc. (chmn.); dir. Phila. Belt Line R.R. Co. Democrat. Home: Gwynedd Valley, Montgomery County, Pa. Died May 13, 1942.

NORRIS, George William, U.S. senator; b. on farm, Sandusky County, Ohio, July 11, 1861; worked out for farmers, summers, and attended sch. winters; afterwards taught sch. in order to earn the means for higher edn.; attended Baldwin U., Ohio, and Northern Ind. Normal Sch.; studied law while teaching and later finished law course at Valparaiso U.; admitted to bar, 1883, but taught 1 yr. in order to get means to purchase a law library; moved to Neb., 1885; m. Pluma Lashley, 1890 (died 1901); children—Mrs. Hazel Robertson, Mrs. Marian Nelson, Mrs. Gertrude Rath; m. 2d, Ella Leonard, 1903. Prosecuting attorney 3 terms; judge 14th Neb. Dist., 1895-1902; mem. 58th to 62d Congresses (1903-13), 5th Neb. Dist.; U.S. Senator, 5 terms, 1913-43 (re-elected, 5th term as Independent Republican). Led fight in Ho. of Rep. which overthrew "Cannonism"; secured the enactment of the Anti-Injunction Act and the Muscle Shoals Act; father of the Twentieth Amendment to the Constitution, and of the unicameral legislature in the state of Neb.; chmn. National Progressive League for Roosevelt as President, 1932. Republican. Address: McCook, Neb. Died Sept. 2, 1944; buried in Memorial Park, McCook, Neb.

NORRIS, George William, physician; b. Phila., Jan. 1, 1875; s. William Fisher (M.D.) and Rosa Clara (Buchmann) N.; B.A., U. of Pa., 1895, M.D., 1899; unmarried. Practiced, Phila., 1899-1932, was prof. clin. medicine, U. of Pa.; chief of medical service "A," Pennsylvania Hospital. Colonel Med. Corps, U.S. Army, World War, later col. Med. O.R.C. Trustee of Mutual Assurance Co. of Phila. Fellow Coll. Physicians of Phila.; mem. Am. Philos. Soc., Assn. Am. Physicians, A.M.A., Phila. Pathol. Soc., Acad. Natural Sciences, Phi Kappa Sigma Fraternity. Club: Philadelphia. Author: Studies in Cardiac Pathology; Blood Pressure, Its Clinical Applications; also articles on "Pneumonia," in Osler's Modern Medicine, and numerous contbns. in med. jours. Co-author of Norris & Landis Diseases of the Chest and the Principles of Phys. Diagnosis. Address: Dimock, Pa. Died Apr. 7, 1948.

NORRIS, Harry Waldo, zoölogist; b. Pittsfield, N.H., Sept. 11, 1862; s. Moses Leavitt and Lydia Ann (Joy) N.; A.B., Iowa (now Grinnell) Coll., 1886, A.M., 1889, Sc.D., 1924; Cornell U., 1888-90; U. of Neb., 1890-91; U. of Freiburg, 1901-02; m. Harriet Victoria Ruliffson, June 14, 1893; children—Waldo Willard, Genevieve Eugenia, Selden Harmon. Inst. natural history, Grinnell Coll., 1888, prof. biology, 1891-1903, prof. zoölogy, 1903-31, research prof. zoölogy, 1931-41, emeritus prof. zoölogy since 1941; exchange lecturer, Harvard University, 1913-14. Congregationalist. Fellow A.A.A.S., Iowa Academy Science; mem. Am. Micros. Soc., Am. Soc. Naturalists, Am. Assn. Anatomists. Author: (with M. L. Macy) Physiology for High Schools, 1899; The Plagiostone Hypophysis, General Morphology and Types of Structure, 1941. Engaged in research on comparative anatomy of nervous system; contbr. scientific jours. and procs. of socs. Home: Grinnell, Ia.* Died Jan. 15, 1946.

NORRIS, Philip Ashton, banker, mfr.; b. Hopkins County, Tex., Jan. 19, 1863; s. George W. and Susan Trigg (Arbery) N.; ed. pub. schs.; m. Alice McCormick, Nov. 11, 1890; children—Ada, Margaret; m. 2d, Josephine Sparks, June 21, 1905; children—Marjorie Elizabeth, Frank Crawford, Philip Ashton, John Calhoun, Harry Ashton, (deceased), Tom Randolph, Susan Josephine. Began work as printer's devil, then clerk in general store; bookkeeper First Nat. Bank, Greenville, Tex., 1883-86; cashier First Nat. Bank of Commerce, Tex., 1890-1904; gen. mgr. Shawnee (Okla.) Cotton Oil Co., 1904-12; pres. First Nat. Bank, Ada, Okla., since 1912; also pres. Choctaw Cotton Oil Co. (Ada, Okla.), Sulphur Springs (Tex.) Cotton Oil Co., Honey Grove (Tex.) Cotton Oil Co., Mount Pleasant (Tex.) Oil Mill, Lamar Cotton Oil Co. (Paris, Tex.), Greenville (Tex.) Cotton Oil Co., Lamesa (Tex.) Cotton Oil Co.; dir. various other cos. Fuel administrator for Okla., mem. Council of Nat. Defense, Am. Red Cross during World War. Democrat. Episcopalian. Mason (32°). Club: Oak Hills Country. Home: Ada, Okla. Died Nov. 26, 1942.

NORRIS, Richard Cooper, physician; b. Havre de Grace, Md., Nov. 9, 1863; s. Rev. Richard and Sarah Amanda (Baker) N.; A.B., Dickinson Coll., 1884, A.M., 1887; M.D., U. of Pa., 1887; m. Anna M.

Berger, Apr, 24, 1890 (dec.); m. 2d, Grace E. Vogt, Oct. 14, 1903. Prof. obstetrics, Grad. Sch. Medicine, U. of Pa.; surgeon M.E. Hosp., 1890, Phila. Hosp. since 1892; surgeon-in-charge Preston Retreat since 1894. Mem. Am. Gynecol. Soc., Coll. Physicians Phila., Phila. Obstet. Soc., Phila. Co. Med. Soc. Author: American Text Book of Obstetrics, Syllabus Obstetrical Lectures. Editor: Atlas of Gynecology. Contbr. to current and med. mags. Address: 500 N. 20th St., Philadelphia. Died Sept. 4, 1937.

NORTHCOTT, Elliott, judge; b. Clarksburg, W.Va., Apr. 26, 1869; s. Gen. Robert Saunders and Mary (Cunningham) N.; ed. Northwestern Acad, (Clarksburg), McCabe's Univ. Sch. (Petersburg, Va.), Law Sch., U. of Mich., spl. course, 1890-91; m. Lola Beardsley, Sept. 1, 1893; 1 son, Gustavus Andrew. Admitted to bar, 1891, city atty., Huntington, 1897-98; asst. U.S. atty., Southern Dist. of W.Va., 1898-1905; U.S. atty. same, 1905-09; E.E. and M.P. to Colombia, 1909-11, to Nicaragua, Feb.-Dec. 1911, to Venezuela, 1911-13; again apptd. U.S. dist. atty. Southern Dist. of W.Va., 1922; judge U.S. Circuit Court of Appeals, 4th Circuit, 1927-39, retired Oct. 15, 1939. Mem. Republican State Exec. and Central coms., 1900-08; chmn. speakers' bureau Republican State Committee, 1900; chmn. Republican State Com. campaign of 1904. Mem. Bd. of Regents, W.Va. Normal Schs., 1905-09. Apptd. mem. Pub. Service Commn. of W.Va., 1915, and later chmn. same. Mason (33°). Club: Guyandotte. Home: Le Sage, W.Va.* Died Jan. 3, 1946.

NORTON, Edwin Clarence, educator; b. Bradford, Pa., July 5, 1856; s. Rev. William Wallace and Frances Beach (McCoy) N.; A.B., Amherst, 1879; studied Johns Hopkins, 1880, Yale, 1881-83; M.A., Yale, 1900; studied Oxford U., Eng., 1904, Columbia, 1914; Ph.D., Carleton Coll., Northfield, Minn., 1896; D.D., Pacific Sch. of Religion, 1910; m. Frances Lee Rice, June 26, 1884; children—Katharine Rice, Philip (dec.), Dorothy (dec.), Theodore Edwin (dec.). Prin. pub. schs. Alexandria and Waseca, Minn., 1880-81; prof. Greek, Yankton (S.D.) Coll., 1883-87; prin. Prep. Dept., Pomona Coll., Claremont, Calif., 1888-90; apptd. dean Pomona Coll. and prof. Greek lang. and lit., 1890, dean emeritus since 1923. Ordained ministry Congl. Ch., 1884; pres. and moderator Southern Calif. Congl. Conf., 1911-12. Mem. Delta Upsilon, Phi Beta Kappa. Home: Claremont, Calif. Died Oct. 6, 1943.

NORTON, Roy, author; b. Kewanee, Ill., Sept. 30, 1869; s. Frank Elisha and Frances Ellen (Way) N.; ed. Clarinda Academy, took special course mining engineering; practiced law in Ogden, Utah, 1889-90; mined on Pacific Coast, in western states, 1890-92, and in Alaska, 1897-98; crossed Alaska diagonally with dog teams, 1901; founded San Bernardino (Calif.) Sun, 1892; editor San Jose Herald, 1899; on editorial staff Seattle Star, Portland (Ore.) Journal, San Francisco Chronicle; mng. dir. Golconda Mine, Ore., 1903-05; engring. work, Cuba, 1905-06; explored Sinai, Peninsula and Northern Arabia, 1920; engring. in Northern Africa, 1922-26; built first golf course on Sahara Desert at Biskra, designed course at Tunis. Fellow Royal Geog. Society (London); Oxford pamphleteer. Clubs: Authors' (London); The Players (New York). Author: Guilty (with William Hallowell), 1903; The Vanishing Fleets, 1907; The Toll of the Sea, 1909; Mary Jane's Pa, 1909; The Garden of Fate, 1910; The Plunderer, 1911; Captains Three, 1912; The Mediator, 1913; The Moccasins of Gold, 1913; The Boomers, 1914; The Man of Peace, 1915; The Flame, 1915; The Unknown Mr. Kent, 1916; The Scamps, 1917; Drowned Gold, 1919; Mixed Faces, 1921; The Land of the Lost, 1924; Caves of Treasure, 1925; The Shaman, 1926; The Benevolent Liar, 1927; The Liberator, 1928; The Crusader's Casket, 1928; The Lone Rider, 1932; Frozen Trail, 1932; Below the Rio Grande, 1933; The Lone Rider, 1934; The Cañon of Gold, 1935; The Blossom Belle, 1936; also short stories in mags. With Thomas F. Hanshew, wrote play, "Whistling Sandy." Literary work published in 7 languages. Home: 239 Rose St., Freeport, Long Island, N.Y. Died June 28, 1942.

NORTON, Thomas Herbert, chemist, editor; b. Rushford, N.Y., June 30, 1851; s. Rev. Robert and Julia Ann Granger (Horsford) N.; desc. Thos. Norton, a founder of Guilford, Conn., 1639; A.B., Hamilton (valedictorian), 1873, Sc.D., 1895; Ph.D., University of Heidelberg, 1875, Dr. Natural Science, 1936; grad. student Univs. of Berlin and Paris, 1876-78; m. Edith Eliza Ames, Dec. 27, 1883 (died Oct. 30, 1929), 1 son, Robert Ames. Was manager of large chem. works, Paris, France, 1878-83; prof. chemistry, U. of Cincinnati, 1883-1900; traveled 12,000 miles on foot through Europe and Asia, the first to traverse Greece and Syria in this manner. Apptd. by President McKinley, May 1900, to establish the U.S. consulate at Harput, Turkey; sent by U.S. Govt. to investigate conditions in Armenia, 1904, to Persia, 1904-05; Am. consul at Smyrna, Turkey, 1905-06; at Chemnitz, Saxony, 1906-14. Detailed under Dept. of Commerce to report on chem. industries of Europe, 1911-12; to further development of Am. chem. industries, especially dyestuffs, 1915-17; editor of The Chemical Engineer, 1917-18. Chemist with E. I. du Pont de Nemours & Co., 1917-20; editor Chemicals, 1920-29; research chemist Am. Cyanamid Co. since 1930. Awarded Lavoisier medal by La Société Chimique de France, 1937. Fellow A.A.A.S. (sec. council, 1892; gen. sec., 1893; v.p., 1894), Chemical Society (London); mem. Washington Acad. Sciences, New York Acad. Sciences, Am. Chem. Soc. (councilor 1897-99), Nat. Inst. Social Sciences, Internat. Inst. of China (sec. of council), Soc. Chem. Industry, Soc. Chimique de France, Deutsche Chem. Gesellschaft, Russian Chem. Society, Delta Kappa Epsilon, Phi Beta Kappa, Sigma Xi, S.A.R., S.R., Soc. War of 1812, Soc. Colonial Wars, English-Speaking Union, Hamilton Coll. Alumni Soc. (pres. New England Assn., 1917-20). Republican. Presbyterian. Author: Report on Chemical Industry, Paris Exposition, 1878; Utilization of Atmospheric Nitrogen, 1912; Chemical Industries of Belgium, Holland, Norway and Sweden, 1913; Dyestuffs for American Textile Industry, 1915; Cottonseed Industry in Foreign Countries, 1915; The Dyestuff Census, 1916; Training Materials of Latin America, 1917; Reflections at the 70th Milestone, 1921; also many papers on chem. tech. and econ. subjects in Am. and European jours. As genealogist, compiler of Ancestry of Gov. Wm. Leete (2,000), 1934, and personal ancestry (6,390), 1935 Died Dec. 2, 1941.

NORTON, William Harmon, geologist; b. Willoughby, O., Apr. 3, 1856; s. Rev. Roderic and Caroline (Pardee) N.; A.B., Cornell Coll., Iowa, 1875, A.M., 1878; LL.D., State U. of Ia., 1911; m. Mary Florence Burr, (prof. mathematics Cornell Coll., 1886-1919), Aug. 27, 1883. Tutor Latin and Greek langs., 1875-77, adj. prof., 1877-81, prof. Greek lang. and lit. and geology, 1881-90, curator museum, 1882-1923, prof. geology, 1890-1923, Cornell Coll. Spl. asst. Ia. Geol. Survey, 1892-1932; asst. U.S. Geol. Survey, 1903-13. Mem. board trustees Cornell College, 1917-40, also mem. exec. com., 1934-40. Fellow Geol. Society America; pres. Iowa Acad. Sciences, 1900; pres. science sect. N.E.A., 1902; mem. Sigma Xi Fraternity, Phi Beta Kappa. Methodist. Republican. Author: Artesian Wells of Iowa (Vol. VI, Iowa Geol. Survey, 1897); Norton's Elements of Geology, 1905; Underground Water Resources of Iowa (U.S. Geol. Survey), 1913; Deep Wells of Iowa (Vol. XXXIII, Ia. Geol. Survey), 1927, and (Vol. XXXVI, Ia. Geol. Survey), 1935; The Church and Social Action, 1936; also various geol. and ednl. papers. Address: Mt. Vernon, Ia. Died May 3, 1944.

NORTON, William Warder, pres. W. W. Norton & Co., Inc.; b. Springfield, O., Sept. 17, 1891; s. Percy and Emily (Warder) N.; ed. St. Paul's School, Ohio State U.; m. Mary Dows Herter, June 6, 1922; 1 dau., Anne. Pres. W. W. Norton & Co., Inc., publishers, N.Y. City, since 1924. Ensign (s.c.) USNRF, 1917-18. Chmn. New School Association, 1920-22; treasurer American Friends of Spanish Democracy. 1936-38. Comdr. Willard Straight Post, Am. Legion, 1920-22; chmn. Joint Bd. of Publishers & Booksellers, 1932-33; pres. Nat. Assn. of Book Publishers, 1933-35. Chmn. Council on Books in Wartime, Inc., 1942-44; chmn. Editions for Armed Services, 1942-44. Clubs: Century, The Players, P.E.N. Home: 1 Lexington Av. Office: 70 Fifth Av., New York, N.Y. Died Nov. 7, 1945.

NORTONI, Albert Dexter, lawyer; b. New Cambria, Mo., Jan. 26, 1867; s. Dr. Edward Warren and Hannah T. (Howell) N.; ed. in common schs. and by pvt. instrn.; m. Maggie L. Francis, Dec. 22, 1892 (died Sept. 30, 1894); m. 2d, Emma T. Belcher, July 3, 1906. Practiced in Macon, Linn and Chariton counties, Mo., and at St. Louis; city atty., New Cambria, 2 terms; pvt. sec. to Congressman C. N. Clark, 1 term; Republican nominee for probate judge of Macon Co., 1894 (declined); defeated for Mo. Senate, 1896, and for circuit judge, 2d Circuit, 1898; apptd., Jan. 1, 1903, asst. U.S. dist. atty., and moved to St. Louis; judge St. Louis Court of Appeals, 1905-16; resigned and resumed practice; v.p. and gen. counsel Continental Life Ins. Co., Continental Securities & Holding Co.; dir. and counsel Grand Nat. Bank, St. Louis Building & Loan Assn., St. Louis Agency Co.; v.p. and counsel Radio Amplifiers Co., Inc.; dir. Export Cooperage Co. Curator Univ. of Mo., 1913-19, and of Forest Park Coll., St. Louis; mem. Mo. Code Commn., 1914-15; served as mem. mng. com. Sch. of Mines and Metallurgy, Rolla, Mo., 1913-19. Progressive candidate for gov. Mo., 1912, and mem. exec. com. Progressive Nat. Com.; del. at large Progressive Nat. Conv., 1912 (platform com.) and chmn. Mo. Nat. delegation, 1916; dir. Progressive Bur. Dem. Nat. Com., 1916; dir. Non-Partisan Assn. for League of Nations of World Court. Mem. Mo. and St. Louis bar assns., Soc. Colonial Wars, S.R. (pres. St. Louis chapter, 1928; v.p. State Soc. and mem. State Bd. Mgrs.), N.E. Soc. of St. Louis (pres. 1922-23). Presbyterian. Clubs: Noonday, Sunset Hills Country, Glen Echo. Home: 4473 McPherson Av. Office: Boatmen's Bank Bldg., St. Louis. Died Oct. 1938.

NORVAL, Theophilus Lincoln, judge; b. London Mills, Ill., Aug. 26, 1847; s. Oliver and Mary J.N.; student Hedding Coll., Abingdon, Ill.; LL.B., Univ. of Mich., 1871; admitted to Mich. bar, 1871; m. Ella Godfrey, Feb. 5, 1875; children—Winifred, Merle (dec.). Practiced at Seward, Neb., 1872-83; mem. Neb. Senate, 1878; judge Dist. Court, 1883-89; justice Supreme Court of Neb., 1889-1901; presdl. elector, 1904. Republican. Address: Seward, Neb. Died Feb. 9, 1942.

NORWOOD, John Wilkins, banker; b. Hartsville, S.C., Mar. 18, 1865; s. George Alexander and Mary Louisa (Wilkins) N.; student Wake Forest, N.C. Coll., 1881-82, 1883-84; S.C. Mil. Acad., 1882-83; m. Vina, d. Col. John B. Patrick, 1887; m. 2d, Lidie, d. James Y. Goodlett, 1891; children—George, Laura Cleveland; m. 3d, Fannie Conyers, 1906; children—John Wilkins, Benjamin King, Oliver, Frances. Began as clk. in cotton office of G. A. Norwood & Co., Charleston, 1884; cashier Peoples Bank, Greenville, 1887-88; organizer, 1887, and pres. until 1892, Greenville Savings Bank; organizer, 1892, and pres. until 1902, Atlantic Nat. Bank, Wilmington, N.C.; pres. Wilmington Sav. & Trust Co., 1894-1910, v.p., 1910-41; organizer, 1898, pres. until 1908, Blue Ridge Nat. Bank, Asheville, N.C.; pres. City Nat. Bank, Greenville, 1903-06; organizer, Norwood Nat. Bank, Greenville, 1907, pres. until 1925, then chmn. bd.; chmn. bd. S. Carolina Nat. Bank, a consolidation of Bank of Charleston, N.B.A., of Charleston, the Carolina Nat. Bank of Columbia, and the Norwood Nat. Bank of Greenville until 1933; formerly v.p. and chmn. bd. Carolina Nat. Bank, Anderson, S.C., now dir.; dir. Brandon Mills, Liberty Life Ins. Co., chmn. Greenville County Highway Commn., 1915-19; mem. Federal Advisory Council of Federal Reserve System, 5th Dist., 1915-18. Trustee Greenville Pub. Library. Democrat. Unitarian. Home: 111 Belmont Av., Greenville, S.C.* Died July 10, 1945.

NOVAK, Frank John, Jr. (nō'văk), laryngologist; b. Chicago, Ill., July 3, 1888; s. Frank J. (M.D.) and Anna (Prachar) N.; grad. Lewis Inst., Chicago, 1908; student U. of Chicago; M.D., U. of Ill., 1914; m. Antoinette D. Horvath, Feb. 5, 1916; children—Frank J., Olga Vivian. Practiced at Chicago since 1914; attending otolaryngologist Henrotin Hosp. Served as lt. col. Med. Res. Corps. Cons., Chicago Tumor Inst. Mem. Am., Ill., and Chicago med. assns., Am. Acad. Otolaryngol., Am. Laryngol., Rhinol. and Otol. Soc., American Otol. Soc., Chicago Laryngol. Soc., Kansas City Otolaryngol. Society (hon. member), Med. Round Table of Chicago, Phi Kappa Sigma. Republican. Author of various brochures and papers on med. subjects. Evacuation coordinator for State of Ill., Ill. State Council of Defense. Home: 156 Lawton Rd., Riverside, Ill. Office: 30 N. Michigan Av., Chicago, Ill. Died July 25, 1948.

NOWELS, Trellyen Ernest, newspaper man; born Rensselaer, Indiana, March 7, 1875; son Ezra Crane and Sarah Jane (Busey) N.; student Tillotson Acad., Trinidad, Colo., 1891-95; student Colorado Coll., 1896-99, hon. M.A., 1930; m. Bertie M. Wright, June 18, 1906; children—Trellyen Ernest, Margaret Jane, Richard Wright. Began as newspaper reporter, 1901, successively sporting, news, city, and mng. editor, Colo. Springs Gazette, Evening Telegraph, Sunday Gazette and Telegraph; gen. mgr., treas., pres. Gazette and Telegraph Co.; sec. and dir. Mackinnie Oil & Drilling Co.; dir. First Federal Loan Association of Colorado Springs; director Exchange National Bank. Member Republican State Central Committee of Colorado and Republican Central Committee of El Paso County (ex-chmn.). Pres. Colo. Press Assn., 1933-34; member official Colo. State Publicity Commn.; member Phi Gamma Delta. Republican. Conglist. Elk. Clubs: El Paso; Cheyenne Mountain Country Club. Home: 1528 Wood Av. Office: 18 E. Pikes Peak Av., Colorado Springs, Colo. Died Feb. 20, 1949.

NOXON, Frank Wright, economist; b. Syracuse, N.Y., March 25, 1873; s. late Justice James and late Sarah Matilda (Wright) N.; student Syracuse U., 1890-92, Ph.B., 1911; Harvard, 1893-94. Reporter Syracuse Herald, 1892-93; dramatic critic Boston Record, 1893-1900; mng. editor Providence News, 1900, Boston Republic, 1902-03, Boston Traveller, 1903-05; sec. to Henry M. Whitney, 1905; editorial writer Boston Herald, 1906-07; course lecturer, Boston Pub. High Sch. of Commerce, 1907-08; sec. Ry. Business Assn., 1908-32; del. Internat. Ry. Congress, London, 1925, Madrid, 1930; mem. Conf. Statisticians in Industry of Nat. Industrial Conf. Bd. (New York); lay chmn. Pastors' Citizenship Survey (national all protestant denominations) since 1936; exec. Pressure Group for Employment Stability since 1941. Mem. Washington Soc. of Alexandria, Va. (spokesman 1929, presenting English-Speaking Union, London, replica of Mt. Vernon andirons); mem. Alexandria (Va.) Chamber of Commerce (pres. 1930-31), Delta Upsilon (chmn. quarterly com. 1922-25). Elder 2d Presbyn. Ch., Alexandria, Va., since 1932; leader Westminster Men's Bible Class, 1927-32; Commissioner Gen. Assembly So. Presbyn. Ch., 1934, 41, 43, Synod of Va., 1934, 36, 38, 41, Potomac Presbytery, 1934-43 (moderator 1938). Clubs: Delta Upsilon of N.Y. (pres. 1916); Author: Are We Capable of Self-Government?, 1917; Excess Prophets, 1920; Religion in Red Russia, 1931; Economy in Public Expenditure, 1932; Proposed Railway Remedies, 1933. Contbr. to various periodicals. Home: 204 Myrtle St. Office: Westminster Bldg., Alexandria, Va. Died 1945.

NOYES, Alexander Dana (nois), newspaper man; b. Montclair, N.J., Dec. 14, 1862; s. Charles H. and Jane R. (Dana) N.; A.B., Amherst, 1883, A.M., 1886, LL.D., 1920. On city staff New York Tribune, 1883-84; editorial staff New York Commercial Advertiser, 1884-91; financial editor New York Evening Post, 1891-1920; financial editor of New York Times since Oct. 1920. Lectured, economic course, Harvard, U. of Illinois, and in New York U. Mem. Am. Economic Assn., Amherst Assn., Delta Upsilon. Clubs: Century, Economic (New York). Author: Thirty Years of American Finance, 1898; Forty Years of American Finance, 1909; Financial Chapters of the War, 1916; The War Period of American Finance, 1926; The Market Place, 1938. Wrote: The Evening Post's Free Coinage Catechism, of which 2,000,000 copies were circulated in 1896, and various other monographs on the financial question; contbr. to newspapers and mags., U.S. and abroad. Home: 1 W. 64th St. Office: New York Times, New York, N.Y. Died Apr. 22, 1945.

NOYES, Frank Brett, newspaper man; b. Washington, July 7, 1863; s. Crosby Stuart and Elizabeth S. (Williams) N.; prep. dept. Columbian Coll., D.C.; A.M., Yale; LL.D., Univ. of Pa., George Washington, U. of Maryland; m. Janet Thruston Newbold, Sept. 17, 1888 (dec.); children—Frances (Mrs. Edward H. Hart; dec.), Newbold (dec.), Ethel (Mrs. Noyes Lewis) (dec.). Manager Washington Star, 1881-1901; editor Chicago Record-Herald, 1902-09; president Evening Star Newspaper Company, Washington, 1910-47, chmn. bd., 1948. Director, executive committee from 1894, pres., 1900-38, hon. pres. since 1943, the Associated Press. Clubs: Metropolitan, Chevy Chase. Home: 2339 Massachusetts Av. Office: The Evening Star, Washington. Died Dec. 1, 1948.

NOYES, Newbold, newspaperman; b. Washington, D.C., Jan. 19, 1892; s. Frank Brett and Janet (Thruston) N.; grad. Westminster School, Simsbury, Conn., 1910; A.B., Yale, 1914; m. Alexandra Ewing, Nov. 27, 1915 (divorced 1934); children—Newbold, Crosby Stuart, Thomas Ewing; m. 2d, Lelia Gordon Dickey, 1934. Began as reporter Evening Star, Washington, 1914, asso. editor since 1919; dir. North Am. Newspaper Alliance, 1925, v.p., 1926-27, later pres., now mem. exec. com.; v.p. M. A. Leese Radio Corp.; dir. Am. Security & Trust Co., Evening Star Newspaper Co. First lt. inf., U.S. Army, during World War. Decorated Croix de Guerre (France), 1918; Chevalier Legion of Honor (France), 1933; Chevalier Order of the Crown (Belgium), 1939; Comdr. Order of the White Rose of Finland. Director Washington Council of Social Agencies (ex-pres.), Washington Community Chest (pres. 1933-34), Asso. Charities, Garfield Hosp. Mem. Associated Press, S.A.R., Alpha Delta Phi. Episcopalian. Clubs: Metropolitan, Chevy Chase, University (Washington); Elihu (New Haven, Conn.); Lotos, Brook, Yale (New York). Author: Echo and Other Poems, 1917. Contbr. verse and short stories to mags. Home: 1239 Vermont Av. Office: Star Bldg., Washington, D.C. Died Apr. 16, 1942.

NOYES, Theodore Williams, newspaperman; b. Washington, Jan. 26, 1858; s. Crosby Stuart and Elizabeth S. (Williams) N.; A.B., Columbian (now George Washington) U., 1877, A.M., 1877, LL.B., 1882, LL.M., 1883, LL.D., 1917; m. Mary E. Prentice, Aug. 1886 (dec.); children—Ruth (wife of Luther Sheldon, Jr., officer U.S.N.), Elizabeth Crosby (wife of Smith Hempstone, officer U.S.N.), Theodore Prentice (dec.). Reporter on Washington Star, 1877-81; practiced law in S.D., 1883-87; asso. editor-in-chief, Washington Evening Star, 1887-1908, editor-in-chief since 1908. Treas., 1902-06, pres. 1906-10, Evening Star Newspaper Co. Trustee Columbian (now George Washington) U. since 1889; pres. bd. trustees Washington Pub. Library since 1896; pres. Washington Bd. of Trade, 1897-99. Pres. Assn. Oldest Inhabitants of Washington, D.C., since 1908. Author: The National Capital, 1893; Newspaper Libels, 1894; Notes on Travel, 1894; War of the Metals, 1899; Conditions in the Philippines, 1900; Oriental America and Its Problems, 1903; Fiscal Relations between the United States and the District of Columbia, 1916; Representation of the District of Columbia in Congress, 1916; The Presidents and the National Capital, 1917; Americanize Washington as a Wise Measure of War Preparedness, 1917; The World's Great Waterfalls, 1926. Home: 1730 New Hampshire Av., Washington 9, D.C. Died July 4, 1946.

NOYES, William Albert, chemist; b. nr. Independence, Ia., Nov. 6, 1857; s. Spencer W. and Mary (Packard) N.; A.B. and S.B., Ia. (now Grinnell) Coll., 1879; Ph.D., Johns Hopkins, 1882; LL.D., Clark U., 1909; Chem.D., U. of Pittsburgh, 1920; hon. D.Sc., Grinnell Coll., 1929; m. Flora E. Collier, Dec. 24, 1884 (dec.); children—Helen Mary (dec.), Ethel (dec.), William Albert, Jr.; m. 2d, Mattie L. Elwell, June 18, 1902 (dec.); 1 son, Charles Edmund; m. 3d, Katharine Haworth Macy, Nov. 25, 1915; children—Richard Macy, Henry Pierre. Prof. chemistry U. of Tenn., 1883-86; Rose Poly. Inst., 1886-1903; chief chemist Nat. Bureau of Standards, 1903-07; prof. chemistry and dir. Chemical Lab., U. of Ill., 1907-26 (emeritus). Editor Journal Am. Chemical Soc., 1902-17, Chemical Abstracts, 1907-09, Scientific Monographs, Am. Chem. Soc., since 1919, Chemical Reviews, 1924-26; sec. State Bd. of Nat. Resources and Conservation since 1917. Awarded Nichols medal, 1908, Willard Gibbs medal, 1919, Priestley medal, 1935. Fellow Am. Acad. of Arts and Sciences; mem. Nat. Acad. of Sciences, Am. Philos. Soc., Am. Chem. Soc. (sec. 1903-07, pres. 1920); chmn. chem. sect. A.A.A.S., 1896 and 1918. Author: Organic Chemistry for the Laboratory, 1897; Elements of Qualitative Analysis, 1888; Organic Chemistry, 1903; Kurzes Lehrbuch der organischen Chemie (translation), 1907; Text-book of Chemistry, 1913; Laboratory Exercises in Chemistry, 1917; College Textbook of Chemistry, 1919; Building for Peace, 1923; Building for Peace, II; Pour la Paix (translation), 1924; Organic Chemistry, 1926; Modern Alchemy (with W. Albert Noyes, Jr.), 1932; also many scientific, economic, internat. and religious papers. Died Oct. 24, 1941.

NUELSEN, John Louis (nūl'sĕn), bishop; b. of Am. parents, Zürich, Switzerland, Jan. 19, 1867; s. Henry and Rosalie (Muller) N.; prep. edn. in Germany; B.D., Drew Theol. Sem., 1890; M.A., Central Wesleyan Coll., 1892; univs. of Berlin and Halle, 1892-93; D.D., U. of Denver, 1903; LL.D., Neb. Wesleyan U., 1910, and Baldwin-Wallace College, Berea, O., 1935; Th.D., Berlin, 1922; m. Luella E. Ströter, Sept. 8, 1896; children—Albert Ernest, Henry Erwin, John Louis, Marie Louise. Ordained M.E. ministry, 1889; pastor Sedalia, Mo., 1890; prof. ancient langs., St. Paul's Coll., Minn., 1890-92; prof. exegetical theology, Central Wesleyan Sem., Warrenton, Mo., 1894-99, Nast Theol. Sem., Berea, O., 1899-1908; became bishop M.E. Ch., 1908, and in charge M.E. Church in Continental Europe, 1912; retired 1940. Editor Deutsch Amerikanische Zeitschrift für Theologie und Kirche (Berea, O.), 1897-1908; Am. corr. Theologischer Literatur-Bericht (Germany); contbr. to Realencyklopädie für Theologie und Kirche, Leipzig; associate editor Internat. Standard Bible Ency., Washington. Club: Rotary of Zürich. Author: Die Bedeutung des Evangeliums Johannes, 1903; Das Leben Jesu im Wortlaut der vier Evangelien, 1904; John Wesley, Ausgewählte Predigten, 1905; Luther the Leader (Men of the Kingdom Series), 1906; Kurzgefasste Geschichte des Methodismus, 1907 and 29; Recent Phases of German Theology, 1908; Methodismus und Weltmission, 1913; Reformation und Methodismus, Zürich, 1917; Jean Guillaume de la Fléchère, 1929; Die Ordaination im Methodismus, 1935. Mem. exec. com. Central Bur. for Relief of Evangelical Chs. of Europe. Home: 46 Green Village Rd., Madison, N.J.* Died June 26, 1946.

NUGENT, Daniel Cline, merchant; b. Belmont, Can., Nov. 20, 1855; s. Thomas and Eleanor (Morgan) N.; ed. London (Can.) High Sch.; m. Carrie Casey, June 30, 1885. Began in mercantile business with Byron Nugent, Mt. Vernon, Ill., 1871; mem. firm of B. Nugent & Bro.; now retired. Clubs: St. Louis, St Louis Country, Sunset Hill Country. Home: Hotel Chase, St. Louis. Died Jan. 16, 1926.

NUGENT, James Alexander (nū'jĕnt), educator; b. Jersey City, N.J., June 19, 1879; s. John and Margaret (Lynch) N.; A.B., St. Peter's Coll., Jersey City, 1898, A.M., 1899; LL.D., Seton Hall Coll., 1924; Ph.D., Fordham U., 1926; m. Eleanor Farley, Dec. 31, 1913; children—Margaret, Eleanor, Dorothy. Teacher N.Y. and N.J. schs., 1900-14; prin. schs. Jersey City, 1914-23, asst. supt., 1923-24, supt. since 1924. K.C. Clubs: N.J. Schoolmasters', N.Y. Schoolmasters', Rotary of Jersey City (past pres.). Home: 269 Armstrong Av. Address: 2 Harrison Av., Jersey City, N.J.* Died Dec. 24, 1946.

NUTT, Joseph Randolph; b. Uniontown, Pa., Mar. 9, 1869; s. Adam C. and Charlotte Frances (Wells) N.; ed. pub. schs.; m. Elizabeth Hasbrouck, Nov. 27, 1907; children—(by 1st wife), Robert Hay, (by 2d wife), Joseph R., Frances, David C. Began in banking business at Akron, O., 1897; moved to Cleveland, 1901; became sec. and treas. Sav. & Trust Co.; that company consolidated, forming Citizens Sav. & Trust Co., became v.p. and later pres.; pres. Union Trust Co., 1920-30, chmn. bd., 1929-32; dir., N.Y.C.&St.L. R.R., Goodyear Tire & Rubber Co. Treas. Republican Nat. Com., 1928-33. Christian Scientist. Mason (32°). Club: Union. Home: 2285 Coventry Rd. Office: Terminal Tower, Cleveland, O. Died Dec. 18, 1945.

NUTT, Robert Lee, ry. official; b. Rowan Co., N.C., Apr. 8, 1873; s. Richarrd T. and Elizabeth (Nutt) N.; ed. Wake Forest Coll.; m. Juliet C. McLure, of Chester, S.C., 1895. Began as clk. in office of gen. mgr. Seaboard Airline Ry., Oct. 1892, and has continued with same rd., successively, clk. to gen. auditor, 1893-95, chief clk. to auditor of receipts, 1895-1900, cashier, 1900-01, asst. treas., 1901-06, treas., 1906-18, sec. and treas., 1918-20, v.p., sec. and treas., 1920-27, chmn. bd. since 1927. Democrat. Presbyn. Clubs: Recess, Metropolitan, Army and Navy of America, Hudson River Country, Broad Street (New York); Everglades (Palm Beach, Fla.); Princess Anne Country (Norfolk, Va.). Home: 1165 Park Av., New York. Died Apr. 18, 1943.

NUTTALL, Leonard John, Jr.; b. Salt Lake City, Utah, July 6, 1887; s. Leonard John and Christina (Little) N.; student Brigham Young U. 2 yrs.; grad. Teachers Coll. (Columbia), 1911, M.A., 1912; studied summers, U. of Chicago, Teachers Coll.; Ph.D., Columbia Univ., 1930; m. Fannie Burns, 1911; children—Drayton B., Lyal (dau.), Ralph Leslie, Doris, Hubert Vernon, Wendell, Leonard John, Ned A., Janeth, Barbara, Richard D., Jerry. Prin. elementary school, Pleasant Grove, Utah, 1906-08; critic teacher Brigham Young University Training School, 1908-09; teacher high school, Payson, 1911-15; prin. high school, Spanish Fork, Utah, 1915-16; supt. schs., Iron County, Utah, 1916-19, Nebo Dist., Utah County, 1919-22; dir. Training Sch., Brigham Young U., 1922-24; prof. edn. same univ., 1922-30, dean Coll. of Edn., 1924-30, acting pres., 1926-27; prof. of edn. and dir. of training schs., U. of Utah, 1930-32; supt. Salt Lake City Schools since 1932. Mem. N.E.A. (Utah state dir. 1922-24), Utah Ednl. Assn. (pres. 1922-23). Mormon. Democrat. Home: 433 Douglas St. Address: 440 East First South St., Salt Lake City, Utah. Died Apr. 18, 1944.

NUTTING, Mary Adelaide, prof. nursing edn.; b. Can., Nov. 1, 1858; d. Vespasian and Harriet Sophia (Peaslee) Nutting; prep. edn., pvt. schs. and at home; grad. Johns Hopkins Hosp. Sch. of Nursing, 1891; M.A. (hon.), Yale, 1922. Came to U.S., 1889. Asst. supt. nurses, Johns Hopkins Hosp., 1893-94, prin. Sch. of Nursing and supt. nurses, 1894-1907; prof. institutional adminstrn., Teachers Coll., Columbia, 1907-10, prof. nursing and health, 1910-25, emeritus prof. nursing edn. since 1925. Chmn. com. on nursing, Council Nat. Defense, 1917-18. Mem. Am. Nurses Assn. (hon.), Nat. League Nursing Edn., Internat. Council Nurses; hon. pres. Florence Nightingale Internat. Foundn., London, Eng., 1934. Awarded Liberty medal Nat. Inst. Social Sciences. and Am. Social Science Assn., 1918. Clubs: Cosmopolitan, Women's Faculty, Columbia University. Author: A History of Nursing, 2 vols. (with L. L. Dock), 1907; A Sound Economic Basis for Schools of Nursing, 1926; also Govt. bulls. Former contbr. to professional jours. Home: 500 W. 121st St., New York. Died Oct. 3. 1948.

NUTTING, Perley Gilman, physicist; b. at Randolph, Wis., Aug. 22, 1873; s. Charles and Cordelia (Gilman) N.; Carleton College, Northfield, Minn., 1891-92; A.B., Stanford, 1897; M.S., U. of Calif., 1899; studied U. of Göttingen, 1901-02; Ph.D., Cornell U., 1903; m. Edith Eva Lightfoot, Oct. 12, 1906; m. 2d, Julia E. Stouffer, Apr. 7, 1928. Asst. physicist, 1903-09, asso., 1909-12, Bureau of Standards, Washington; physicist and asst. dir. research lab., Eastman Kodak Co., Rochester, N.Y., 1913-16; dir. Westinghouse Research Lab., East Pittsburgh, Pa., 1916-21, cons. engr., 1921-24; geophysicist U.S. Geol. Survey since 1924. Asst. professor physics, George Washington University, 1907-09. Author: Outlines of Applied Optics, 1911; Visibility of Radiation, 1911; New Precision Colorimeter, 1912; Organized Knowledge and National Welfare, 1917; Factors in Achievement, 1919. Author 173 papers in the fields of optics and geophysics. Address: 3216 Oliver St., Washington. Died Aug. 8, 1949; buried Rock Creek Cemetery, Washington.

NUVEEN, John (nū-vēn'), investment banking; b. Denmark, August 26, 1864; of Dutch ancestry; son John and Margaret C. (Reimer) N.; brought to Chicago, 1866; ed. Kalamazoo, Mich. West Division High Sch. and Souder's Business Coll., Chicago; m. Ida E. Strawbridge, June 18, 1895 (died Jan. 23, 1910); 1 son, John; m. 2d Anna M. Strawbridge, June 21, 1912 (died March 10, 1945). Engaged in dry goods business with father in Chicago, later was sec. Chapman & Smith Co., wholesale grocers, until 1898; founded, 1898, investment banking business under firm name of John Nuveen & Co., of which is sr. partner; v.p. Columbian Bank Note Co. State pres. Bapt. Young Peoples Union of Ill., 1893-95; pres. Cook County S.S. Assn., 1916-18; pres. Chicago Bapt. Social Union, 1925-26; pres. Amer. Bapt. Publ. Soc., 1926-36, now hon. pres.; sec. and mem. bd. of trustees Y.M.C.A., Chicago; trustee George Williams Coll., Chicago, Kalamazoo (Mich.) Coll., Pacific Garden Mission, Chicago. Baptist. Republican. Clubs: Union League, The Attic, Mid-Day, Quadrangle (Chicago); Muskegon Country, White Lake (Mich.) Yacht, White Lake Golf; Knapp Island Gun Club, Everglades (Palm Beach, Fla.). Home: 5300 S. Hyde Park Blvd., Chicago 15, Ill.; (summer) Wabaningo, White Lake, Mich.; (winter) 260 S. Ocean Blvd., Palm Beach, Fla. Office: 135 S. La Salle St., Chicago 3, Ill. Died Nov. 14, 1948.

NYE, Edgar Hewitt (nī), landscape painter; b. Richmond, Va., Apr. 30, 1879; s. Lt. Col. William Edgar and Frances (Hewitt) N.; student Corcoran Art Sch., Washington, D.C., 1892-1900; art study Oxford and London, Eng., 1907-09, St. Ives and Newlin, Eng., 1910-14; m. Elizabeth Quackenbush, Sept. 16, 1922. Made numerous trips abroad, 1902-14; has exhibited with West Country Painters and at Plymouth Gallery, Eng. Mem. Soc. Washington (D.C.) Artists, Washington Water Color Club, Landscape Club of Washington. Hon. mention, Washington Soc. of Artists, 1926, 1st prize for landscape, same 1927, 1st prize for figure, 1933, hon. mention, landscape, 1937; purchase prize Washington Independent Show, 1934. Two paintings owned by Phillips Memorial Galler, Washington, D.C. Home: 1008 Taylor St. N.E., Washington, D.C. Died Nov. 30, 1943.

O

OBENAUER, Marie Louise (ō'bē-now-ẽr), b. Saginaw, Mich.; d. Henry G. and Emma (Lippert) Obenauer; A.B., U. of Mich. Formerly econ. cons., lit. critic and 2d editorial writer, St. Paul Globe, also editor Courant, St. Paul; served as chief Woman's Div., U.S. Bur. Labor Statistics, Washington, also as chief woman administrative examiner, Nat. War Labor Board; dir. living conditions investigation of U.S. Coal Commn., 1922-23; dir. nation-wide Home Equipment Survey and Better Equipped Home campaign, for Gen. Fed. Women's Clubs; dir. Industrial Survey and Research Service. Founder mem. and joint chmn. bd. of govs., Home Owners Protective Enterprise; charter mem., trustee and editor Am. Synergics. Mem. Rep. Program Com., 1938-40. Mem. American Woman's Association, Women's National Republican Club, Nat. Assn. of University Women. Author: The Woman Power of the Nation; Is It Time to Change Faith in our American Way of Life?, also numerous brochures, articles and govt. bulletins on women in industry, conditions of life among wage-earners, effect of the tariff and kindred subjects. Joint author: Profit Without Honor. Address: 6808 Meadow Lane, Chevy Chase, Md. Died Jan. 7, 1947; buried, Detroit, Mich.

OBERHANSLEY, Henry Ernest (ō-bẽr-hăns'lē), educator; b. Payson, Utah, Apr. 12, 1885; s. Herman and Amelia (Smith) O.; A.B., Brigham Young U., 1915; M.A., University of California, 1930; married Salome Barney, December 18, 1917; children—

Victor Curtis, Russell John. Teacher, Provo City Schools, 1908-09; prin. grammar grades, Payson, Utah, 1912-14; head dept. agr., Payson High Sch., 1915-16; prin. high school, Parowan, Utah, 1916-18; asst. state leader Boys and Girls Clubs, Utah, 1918-21; with Utah State Agr. Coll. since 1918, successively instr., asst. prof., asso. prof. and head dept. of edn. to 1929, dir. Branch Agrl. Coll. since 1929; pres. Cedar City Home Bldg. Soc.; dir. Cedar Finance Co. County chmn. Am. Red Cross since 1938. Member Ch. of Jesus Christ of Latter Day Saints; mem. central com. City Coordinating Council; mem. exec. com. Utah Citizens Council for the Study of Peace. Mem. N.E.A., Utah Ednl. Assn., Cedar City Chamber of Commerce (dir.), Phi Kappa Phi, Phi Delta Kappa, Phi Kappa Iota. Club: (past pres.) Rotary. Author: The Construction and Organization of a Course in Agriculture for Secondary Schools, 1930. Home: Cedar City, Utah. Died Apr. 6, 1945.

OBICI, Amedeo, business exec.; b. Oderzo, Province of Treviso, Italy, July 15, 1877; s. Pietro Lodovico and Luigia Charlotte (Sartor) O.; student pub. sch. and night sch.; m. Louise Musante, May 12, 1916. Came to U.S. at age of 11, and shortly after secured job at peanut stand; various positions in peanut business, and in 1906, with M. Peruzzi, organized Planters Peanut Co and became pres. and mgr.; incorporated in 1908 and name changed to Planters Nut & Chocolate Co., Wilkes-Barre, Pa., with branches N.Y. City, Chicago, Phila., Boston, Suffolk (Va.), San Francisco (Toronto (Can.), Atlanta, Dallas, Detroit, Kansas City, Memphis, Milwaukee, Minneapolis, Newark, Pittsburgh and St. Louis. Dir. Suffolk Hotel Corp. Mason (32°, Shriner), Elk, Moose. Clubs: Rotary, Italo-American of Wilkes-Barre. Home: Driver, Va. Office: Wilkes-Barre, Pa. Died May 21, 1947.

O'BOYLE, Francis Joseph, clergyman, educator; b. London, Ont., Can., Oct. 9, 1870; s. Andrew and Julia (Delaney) O.; A.B., Detroit Coll., 1889; post-grad. studies, Florissant, Mo., 1889-92, St. Louis U., 1892-95, 1900-04. Joined Soc. of Jesus (Jesuits), 1889; ordained priest R.C. Ch., 1903; prof. Latin and Greek, St. Xavier Coll., Cincinnati, 1905-06; prof. classical literature, 1895-1900, chancellor and dir. studies, 1906-07, dean schs. of Divinity and Philosophy, 1914-22, also prof. moral theology, 1910-40, St. Mary's Coll. of St. Louis U.; prof. moral theology, West Baden Coll., West Baden Springs, Ind., since 1940. Address: West Baden Springs, Ind. Died June 2, 1949.

O'BRIEN, Dennis Francis, lawyer; b. North Brookfield, Mass., Jan. 20, 1876; s. Charles and Ellen (Driscoll) O'B.; A.B., Brown U., 1898; LL.B., Georgetown U., 1901; m. Mary Rita Brennan, Oct. 12, 1904 (now dec.); children—Paul Dennison, Kenneth A., M. Denise, Robert Driscoll. Admitted to bar, Dist. of Columbia, 1901; began practice at Providence, R.I., 1902; mem. Sheahan & O'Brien, 1902-05, alone, Providence, 1905-06, N.Y. City, 1906-10; mem. O'Brien & Malevinsky, 1910-13, O'Brien, Malevinsky & Driscoll, 1913-33, O'Brien, Driscoll & Raftery since 1933; until the death of Douglas Fairbanks, Sr., was gen. counsel and v.p. Douglas Fairbanks Pictures Corp., and Elton Corporation; general counsel and vice-president The Pickford Corp., Mary Pickford Co., United Artists Corp., United Artists Theatre Circuit, Inc., George M. Cohan Productions, Sam H. Harris Theatrical Enterprises. Former trustee of Brown Univ., Providence, R.I. Mem. Alpha Tau Omega. Clubs: Brown University (New York); Hudson River Country (Yonkers); Misquamicut Country (Watch Hill, R.I.). Catholic. Home: 125 Alta Av., Yonkers, N.Y.; (country) "Sunnylands," Westerly, R.I. Office: 152 W. 42d St., New York 18, N.Y.* Died Oct. 2, 1946.

O'BRIEN, Edward Francis, editor, pub.; b. Adams, Mass., Apr. 25, 1876; s. William and Louise Ruth (Stark) O'B.; desc. John and Priscilla Alden, and 3 other Mayflower passengers; ed. high sch. and self instructed; m. Elsa de Lila, 1904 (died 1904); m. 2d, Mildred Josephine Correard, 1907. Newspaper work in various cities, until 1898; mem. 14th N.Y. Inf., Spanish-Am. War; in Philippines as mem. 22d U.S. Inf., 1898-1901; War Dept. clerk, Manila, 1901-02; editor Manila Daily Freedom, 1902-03; pub. Manila Sun, 1903-05; prosecuted for polit. writings and pardoned after serving 4 mos. of 6 mos. sentence, telegraph editor N.Y. Tribune, 1906-11; editor Havana Daily Post, 1911-12; founder, 1913, and editor Times of Cuba (monthly); founder Habana, 1928; merged as Pan-Am. Review (P.A.R.), 1933. Member Soc. Mayflower Descendants, S.A.R., Descendants of Robert Bartlett of Plymouth, Mass., United Spanish War Vets. Mason (33°, K.T., Shriner, Jester), Elk. Clubs: American, Country, British, Propeller (Havana); Circumnavigators, Philippine (New York). Address: P.O. Box 329, Havana, Cuba. Died Jan. 18, 1945; buried at Adams, Mass.

O'BRIEN, Ernest Aloysius, judge; b. Deroit, Mich., July 1, 1880; s. James and Mary Ann (Brennan) O'B.; ed. Detroit Coll., 1895-1901; LL.D., Detroit Coll. of Law, 1906; m. Elizabeth Dee, Sept. 16, 1909; children—Ernest Dee, John James, Paul (dec.). Admitted to Mich. bar, 1906, and began practice at Detroit; mem. Monaghan, Monaghan, O'Brien & Crowley, 1912-20, Van Dyke, O'Brien & Wheat, 1920-25, O'Brien & August, 1925-30; judge Circuit Court of Mich., 1928; mem. O'Brien, McLeod & August, 1930-31; judge U.S. Dist. Court, Eastern Dist. of Mich., since Apr. 1931. Legal adviser Draft Bd., World War, also in charge Knights of Columbus war activities. Mem. Bd. of Control Mich. State Pub. Schs., Jefferson Diagnostic Hosp. and Clinic; mem. bd. dirs. Detroit Community Fund; pres. Bur. Catholic Welfare of Detroit. Mem. Am. and Mich. State bar assns., Bar Assn. City of Detroit, Detroit Hist. Assn., Delta Theta Phi. Knight Comdr. of St. Gregory; past state deputy K.C. Republican. Clubs: Detroit Athletic, Detroit Yacht, St. Clair Golf, Beechwood Golf and Country (Ont., Can.). Home: 1001 E. Jefferson Av. Address: New Federal Bldg., Detroit, Mich. Died Oct. 9, 1948.

O'BRIEN, Frank Michael, newspaper editor; b. Dunkirk, N.Y., Mar. 31, 1875; s. Michael and Ann (Cryan) O'B.; student St. Joseph's Coll., Buffalo, N.Y., 1884-91; Dr.Litt., Manhattan Coll., N.Y. City, 1938; m. Marion Mousley, Dec. 12, 1910; 1 son, Frank Michael. City editor Buffalo (N.Y.) Express, 1896-1904; reporter The Sun, New York, 1904-05; sec. to mayor of New York, 1906-10; editorial and spl. writer, N.Y. Press, 1912-15; editorial writer The Sun, 1916-18, N.Y. Herald, 1918-24, The Sun, 1924-26, editor of The Sun since Dec. 1, 1926. Awarded Pulitzer prize for best editorial article, "The Unknown Soldier," printed in 1921. Catholic. Author: The Story of The Sun, 1918; New York Murder Mysteries, 1932; also numerous short stories. Home: 29 Washington Sq., New York, N.Y. Office: The Sun, New York, N.Y. Died Sep. 22, 1943.

O'BRIEN, Howard Vincent, author; b. Chicago, Ill., July 11, 1888; s. William Vincent and Mary Ellen (McGrath) O'B.; B.A., Yale, 1910; m. Louise Waller, Dec. 28, 1912; children—Bayne, Jean (Mrs. J. M. Lowman), Donel (killed in action, Feb. 10, 1944). Editorial staff Printers' Ink, 1911; founder, editor of "Art" (mag.), 1911-14; mem. David C. Thomas Co. (advertising), also The Buchen Co., Chicago; literary editor Chicago Daily News, 1928-32, columnist since 1932. Served as 1st lt. Field Artillery, A.E.F., World War I, Dec. 1917-Feb. 1919. Mem. Zeta Psi Fraternity, Wolf's Head (Yale). Author: New Men for Old, 1912; Thirty, 1914; Trodden Gold, 1922; The Terms of Conquest, 1923; (pseud. Clyde Perrin), The Thunderbolt, 1923; The Green Scarf, 1924; What a Man Wants, 1925; Wine, Women and War, 1926; P.S., 1928; Four and Twenty Blackbirds, 1928; An Abandoned Woman, 1930; Folding Bedouins, 1936; Notes for a Book About Mexico, 1937; Memoirs of a Guinea Pig, 1942; So Long, Son, 1944. Translator: When Tytie Came (from the French), 1920. Contbr. to mags. Home: 790 Bryant Av., Winnetka, Ill. Address: care Chicago Daily News, Chicago, Ill. Died Sep. 30, 1947.

O'BRIEN, Thomas Henry, mining exec.; b. Dannemora, Clinton Co., N.Y., Feb. 21, 1869; s. Michael and Mary (Collins) O'B.; student pub. schs.; m. Margaret O'Connor, Apr. 24, 1916 (dec.). Mining business since 1890; with Phelps Dodge Corp. in various capacities, 1904-19; gen. mgr. Inspiration Consol. Copper Co., 1920-46, v.p. since 1936, dir.; pres. Warrior Coöp. Mercantile Co.; chmn. bd. dirs. Valley Nat. Bank, since Mar. 1940. Del. Constl. Conv. of N.M., 1910. Mem. Am. Inst. Mining and Metall. Engrs., Am. Mining Cong., etc. Club: California (Los Angeles). Home: Inspiration, Ariz. Died June 25, 1947.

O'BRIEN, William Austin, M.D.; b. Fairbury, Ill., Feb. 28, 1893; s. John Francis and Mary Frances (Harrington) O'B.; student St. Bede Coll., Peru, Ill., 1906-08, Notre Dame U., 1908-09; M.D., St. Louis Univ. Sch. of Medicine, 1914; grad. work, U. of Minn., 1921-23; m. Dorathy Daniel Beharrell, Mar. 3, 1919 (died Mar. 10, 1934); children—William Austin, Margaret Jean; married 2d, Virginia Mary Benton, Nov. 28, 1935; children—Kathleen Ann, Patrick James, Michael Paul, Mary Virginia. Intern Mount St. Rose Hospital, St. Louis, Missouri, 1912, St. John's Hospital, 1913-15; private practice, Detroit, 1915-17; active military duty, Medical R.C., 1917-19; again practiced, Detroit, 1919-21; instr. pathology, U. of Minn., 1923-27, asst. prof., 1927-29, asso. prof. pathology and preventive medicine, 1929-40, prof. preventive medicine and pub. health, 1940-44; professor public health since 1944; also mem. committee for course in med. technology and member committee on div. of inter-departmental instrn., med. rep. Center for Continuation Study since 1936; pathologist Univ. hosps., 1923-38, dir. Dept. Post-grad. Med. Edn., U. of Minn., since 1938. State chmn. for Minn. and mem. bd. directors of American Cancer Society; mem. A.M.A., Minn. State Med. Assn., Hennepin County Med. Soc., Minn. Pathol. Soc., Radio spokesman for Minn. State Med. Assn. on Sta. WCCO once a week since 1928; radio spokesman, Minn. Hosp. Assn., since 1938, Minn. Dental Assn., since 1936, WCCO; staff mem. Sch. of Air Sta. KVOM, U. of Minn. since 1940. Med. editor Newspaper Enterprise Assn., 1945. Home: 1589 Northrop St., St. Paul, Minn. Address: University of Minnesota, Minneapolis 14, Minn. Died Nov. 15, 1947.

O'BRIEN, William Smith, lawyer and state official; b. Barbour County, W.Va., Jan. 8, 1862; s. Emmet Jones and Martha Anne (Hall) O.B.; student Weston (W.Va.) Acad.; LL.B., W.Va. Univ., 1891; m. Emma White, Oct. 14, 1896; children—Perry Emmet, Daniel Pitt, Mary Martha, William Talbot. Admitted to W.Va. bar, 1891, and began practice at Buckhannon, 1892; mem. firm O'Brien & Hall since 1920; secretary of state of W Va. since 1933. Formerly capt., W.Va. Nat. Guard; formerly teacher and editor; judge Twelfth Jud. Circuit, W.Va., 1913-20; mem. 70th Congress (1927-29), 3d W.Va. Dist. Democrat. Methodist. Mason, K.P. Home: Buckhannon, W.Va. Died Aug. 10, 1948.

OCKERSON, John Augustus, civil engr.; b. Skane, Sweden, Mar. 4, 1848; s. Jons and Boel Jons (Dotler) Akerson; came to U.S., 1851; B.S., C.E., Univ. of Ill., 1873 (D.Eng., 1903); m. Helen M. Chapin, Nov. 3, 1875 (died 1886); 2d, Clara W. Shackelford, June 4, 1890. Served in Civil War in 132d Ill. Inf. and 1st Minn. Heavy Arty., in milling business in Minn., 1865-68; recorder and later asst. in field and office on survey Great Lakes, 1871-79; asst. engr. location and constrn. A.,T. & S.F. R.R., 1872; U.S. asst. engr. Eads jetties, 1876, survey Miss. River, 1879-87; mgr. and engr. gold and silver mine in Colo., 1888-89; chief asst. engr., 1889-98, and since Aug. 4, 1898, mem. Miss. River Commn.; cons. engr. Chief Dept. Liberal Arts, St. Louis Expn., 1904; mem. Internat. Jury of Awards, Paris Expn.; del. Internat. Congress of Navigation, 1900, Milan, 1905, St. Petersburg, 1908, Phila., 1912, Congress of Merchant Marine, Paris. Decorated Officer Public Instruction Meritede Agricole (France); Knight Crown of Italy; Knight Order of Vasa (Sweden); comdr. Order of the Vasa (Sweden), Knight Crown of Germany; Knight Crown of Belgium; Order of Double Dragon (China). Mem. Am. Soc. C.E. (pres., 1912), St. Louis Engrs. Club (twice pres.), Nat. Geog. Soc. Clubs: Noonday, Bellerive. Author numerous papers on topog. and engring. subjects. Home: 5305 Delmar Av. Office: International Life Bldg., St. Louis. Died March 22, 1924.

O'CONNELL, John Joseph, judge; b. Pittsburgh, Pa., Sept. 8, 1894; s. Edward and Mary (Murphy) O'C.; student St. John the Baptist Parochial Sch., Pittsburgh, Pa., 1900-08; B.S., Duquesne Univ., 1928, LL.B., 1931; m. Marie V. Shea, June 22, 1927. Engaged in bus., Pittsburgh, 1912-31; admitted to Pa. bar, 1931, asso. with Marshall, O'Brien and Nevin in gen. practice of law, Pittsburgh, 1931-36, asst. solicitor Allegheny County, Pa., 1936-43, solicitor, 1944-45; judge U.S. Circuit Court of Appeals, 3d circuit, since Oct. 1945. Former sec. and treas. Am.-Connellsville Fuel Co., Am. Coke Corp., affiliated and subsidiary cos.; former auditor Century Wood Preserving Co. and subsidiary cos.; former sr. accountant Arthur Young & Co. Served in U.S. Navy, 1918-19. Mem. Allegheny County Bar Assn., Am. Legion. Democrat. Roman Catholic. A.O.H., K.C. Home: 311 LaMarido St., Pittsburgh 26. Office: U.S. Post Office and Courthouse, Pittsburgh 19, Pa. Died Dec. 16, 1949.

O'CONNELL, Joseph Francis, lawyer, educator; b. Boston, Mass., Dec. 7, 1872; s. James and Elizabeth (O'Connell) O'C.; A.B., Boston Coll., 1893; LL.B., Harvard University, 1896; m. Marisita R. Lenahan, November 23, 1910; children—Joseph F., Lenahan, Frederick P., Finbarr D., Marisita A., Brendan, Kevin, Meta, Conleth, Lelia, Declan, Diarmuid. Practicing in Boston since 1897; mem. J. F. & J. E. O'Connell; vice-president and lecturer on admiralty law, wills and probate law, Suffolk Law School, 1920-25; trustee of Hibernia Savings Bank; director Pilgrim Trust Company; manager for trustees of George Robert White Fund; director Fraternal Credit Union. Mem. U.S. Ho. of Rep., 1906-10; mem. Mass. Constl. Conv., 1918-20; commr. Uniform State Laws, from Mass., since 1914; v.p. Nat. Commn. on Uniform State Laws, 1923-24, and chmn. Com. on Laws of Commercial Arbitration; mem. Bd. of Arbitration on dispute between U.S. Housing Corp. and cities of Portsmouth and Norfolk, Va., concerning Ferries taken over by U.S. during World War; mem. Charter Revision Commn. City of Boston, 1923; mem. Nat. Safety Council called by Sec. Hoover, 1926-27. Trustee Middlesex U. Mem. Am. Bar Assn. (exec. com.; house of delegates; mem. com. jurisprudence and law reform), American Law Institute, Internat. Law Association, American Judicature Society (director), Bar Assn. City of Boston, American Irish Hist. Soc. (v.p.). Democrat; candidate for nomination for U.S. Senate, 1930. Moose. Clubs: Harvard, University of Boston (bd. govs.); Harvard (New York). Home: 155 Kilsyth Rd. Office: 31 Milk St., Boston, Mass. Died Dec. 10, 1942.

O'CONNELL, William Henry, cardinal; b. Lowell, Mass., Dec. 8, 1859; A.B., Boston Coll., 1881; entered N.Am. Coll., Rome, Italy, 1881. Ordained priest, Rome, June 8, 1884; apptd. rector N.Am. Coll., Rome, Nov. 21, 1895; named domestic prelate, June 9, 1897; apptd. bishop of Portland, Me., Apr. 22, 1901; consecrated bishop, St. John Lateran, Rome, May 19, 1901; installed in Cathedral of Portland, July 4, 1901; named asst. at Pontifical Throne, Jan. 1905; papal envoy to Japan, 1905; named archbishop of Constance and coadjutor with succession of Boston, Mar. 1906; succeeded to the See of Boston on death of Archbishop Williams, Aug. 30, 1907; elevated to the cardinalate, Nov. 27, 1911. Awarded Grand Cordon of Sacred Treasure (Japan), Grand Medal of Merit (Lebanese) and grand crosses of Order of Malta, Crown of Italy, Constantinian Order of St. George, Holy Sepulchre, Legion of Honor. Home: 2101 Commonwealth Av., Brighton, Mass. Died Apr. 22, 1944; buried on St. John's Seminary grounds, Brighton, Mass.

O'CONNOR, George H(enry), title insurance; b. Washington, Aug. 20, 1873; s. Capt. (U.S. Army) Patrick Edward and Ellen Mary (McCarthy) O.; student St. Johns Academy, Alexandria, Va., 1888-91; LL.B., Nat. U. Law Sch., 1894, LL.M., 1895; spl. student Georgetown U., 1895, hon. A.M., 1915; m. Blanche Higgins, Jan. 20, 1905; children—Helen Louise, George Henry. Admitted to Dist. of Columbia bar, 1895, bar of Supreme Court of U.S., 1918;

practiced in Washington, D.C.; sec. and treas. Dist. Title Ins. Co., 1900-07, v.p. and title officer, 1907-41, pres. since 1941; also v.p. and title officer Lawyers Title Ins. Co. and Washington Title Ins. Co. to 1941, pres. since Jan. 5, 1941. Served on many civic coms., presdl. inaugural coms. and Community Chest Com. Del. to Nat. C. of C.; mem. D.C. Unemployment Compensation Bd., Trustee Catholic Charities of Washington, St. Vincent's Home and Sch., Group Hosp. Association. Member American Bar Association, Bar Association of District of Columbia, American Title Assn., White House Corrs. Assn., Washington Bd. of Trade. Roman Catholic. Mem. K. of C.; Friendly Sons of St. Patrick (Washington, D.C.). Clubs: Alfalfa, National Press, University, Lawyers, Rotary, Calvert; Wellwood Country and Yacht (Charlestown, Md.). Former contbr. to Washington Daily News. Home: 3313 Cleveland Av. Office: 1413 I St., Washington. Died Sept. 28, 1946; buried in Mt. Olivet Cemetery, Washington.

O'CONNOR, J. F. T., judge; s. Edward and Honora (Lane) O'C.; A.B., U. of N.D., 1907, LL.B., 1908, LL.D., 1934; LL.B., Yale, 1909, M.A., 1910; LL.D., Southern Methodist U., 1935, John Marshall Coll., 1937, College of the Pacific, 1938, Univ. of the West, 1938, Southwestern Law Coll., 1939. Instr. in rhetoric, Yale, 1909-12; admitted to N.D. bar, 1908, and practiced at Grand Forks, N.D., until 1925; mem. firm O'Connor & Johnson, 1912-21, O'Connor & Peterson, 1921-25; spl. lecturer on evidence and pleading, Law Dept. of U. of N.D., 1918-24; moved to Los Angeles, Calif., 1925; partner in firm with Senator William G. McAdoo, 1925-30; asso. in practice with ex-Judge C. J. Mulvane and ex-Asst. Atty. Gen. of the U.S.A.G. Divet, 1930; admitted to practice U.S. Supreme Court, 1933; comptroller of the currency, 1933-38; U.S. Dist. Judge, Southern Dist. of Calif. since 1940; organizer, vice chmn. Fed. Deposit Ins. Corp.; ex-officio mem. bd. govs. Federal Res. System. Chmn. Hollywood Polish Relief Com.; chmn. Calif. com. for Franklin D. Roosevelt Library, Inc.; mem. com. Warm Springs Foundation. Apptd. mem. com. on reclassification of court personnel, and member committee for redefinition of a felony by Chief Justice Harlow Stone. Member North Dakota House of Rep., 1915-19; fusion (Dem.-Rep.) candidate for gov. of N.D., 1920, for U.S. Senate, 1922. Mem. N.D. Nat. Guard, 1905-08; apptd. col. on staffs of govs. of N.D., Miss., Ky. Mgr. Roosevelt primary campaign in Calif., 1932; del. Dem. nat. convs., 1916, 24. Mem. Am. and Los Angeles bar assns., State Bar of Calif., Phi Alpha Delta, Phi Delta Theta, Delta Sigma Rho (pres. 1910-14). K.C., Elk. Club: Breakfast, Jonathan. Author of "Banks Under Roosevelt." Winner Palmer diamond medal for debate, 1906; N.D. state oratorical contest, 1907; Townsend oratorical contest, Yale, 1909; mem. Yale debating team, 1909, N.D. Hall Fame. Rep. Calif. orgn. at meeting of United Service Orgns., Washington, D.C., 1941. Home: 10331 Wilshire Blvd. Office: Federal Bldg., Los Angeles. Died Sept. 29, 1949.

O'CONNOR, James Francis, congressman; b. nr. California Junction, Ia., May 7, 1878; s. Patrick and Bridget (O'Brien) O'C.; LL.B., U. of Neb., 1904; m. Kate Adams, Apr. 7, 1899; children—Geneva (Mrs. M. J. Forney), Miles J. Admitted to bar, practiced law in Mont.; served as judge 6th Judicial Dist., Mont.; mem. Mont. Ho. of Reps., 1917-18 (speaker); spl. counsel Federal Trade Commn., Washington, D.C., 1918; mem. 75th to 78th Congresses (1937-45), 2d Mont. Dist. Mem. Livingston Chamber of Commerce; pres. Livingston Roundup Assn.; former pres. Park County High Sch. Bd. Democrat. Catholic. Elk. Home: Livingston, Mont. Died Jan. 14, 1945.

O'DAY, Mrs. Caroline Goodwin, congresswoman; b. Perry, Ga., June 22, 1875; d. Sidney Prior and Elia (Warren) Goodwin; ed. Lucy Cobb Inst., Athens, Ga.; art study in Paris, Munich and Holland, 8 yrs.; m. Daniel O'Day, Apr. 30, 1902 (now dec.); children—Elia Warren, Daniel, Charles. Exhibited paintings at Paris Salon, 1899 and 1900; congresswoman, 74th to 77th Congresses (1935-43), New York State at large. President Rye School Board. Director New School for Social Research, Henry Street Settlement. Vice chmn. Dem. State Com., N.Y., 1916; del. to Dem. Nat. Conv., 1924, 28, 32, 36. Mem. Women's Trade Union League. Episcopalian. Clubs: Cosmopolitan, Women's City. Home: "Sunbright," Rye, N.Y. Died Jan. 4, 1943.

ODDIE, Tasker Lowndes (ŏd'dē), ex-senator; b. Brooklyn, Oct. 24, 1870; s. Henry Meigs and Ellen Gibson (Prout) O.; ed. pub. schs., E. Orange, N.J.; LL.B., New York U., 1895; D.Eng., Colo. Sch. of Mines, 1934; m. Daisy Rendall, Nov. 30, 1916. Sec., manager Woodbridge Co., real estate, New York, 1896-98; went to Nevada, 1898 and engaged in mining operations; one of original locators and in charge of early development of Tonopah Mines; dist. atty. Nye County, Nev., 1900-02; mem. Nev. Senate, 1904-08; gov. of Nev., term 1910-14; U.S. Senator, 2 terms, 1921-33. Republican. Episcopalian. Mason (32°, K.T., Shriner), Elk. Life mem. Am. Inst. Mining and Metall. Engrs., Gold Mining Assn. of America (pres.). During war was mem. Nev. State Council Defense (chmn. highways transport com.), chmn. Nev. dist. of War Resources Com. coöperating with resources and conversion sect. of War Industries Bd. Home: Riverside Hotel, Reno, Nev.; and 1201 Greenwich St., San Francisco. Died Feb. 17, 1950.

ODELL, Albert Grove (ō-dĕl'), psychiatrist; b. Canoga, N.Y., Aug. 8, 1878; s. Franklin P. and Jennie L. (Gould) O.; M.D., Syracuse U., 1904; m. Anna M. Hopper, Apr. 12, 1909 (died 1939); m. 2d, Sybil M. Mather, July 2, 1942. Teacher pub. schs., 1895-1900; gen. med. practice, West Henrietta, N.Y., 1905-11; mem. staff The Sanitarium, Clifton Springs, N.Y., since 1911; cons. psychiatrist Newark (N.Y.) State Sch. Trustee Baxter (Tenn.) Sem. (pres. bd.), Bennett Coll. (Greensboro, N.C.), Meth. Home for Children (Williamsville, N.Y.), Harpst Home for Children, Cedartown, Ga. Pres. Lay Conf. (Central N.Y.) of Meth. Ch., 1932-39; del. to Gen. Conf. of Meth. Ch., 1928, 32, 36, 40, 44; del. Uniting Conf., 1939. Fellow Am. Psychiat. Soc., Am. Assn. for Study of Mental Deficiency; mem. A.M.A., Med. Soc. State of N.Y., Phi Beta Pi, Neuron Club of (Central N.Y.) of Meth. Ch., 1932-39; conf. leader, 1939-47; del. to Gen. Conf. of Meth. Ch., 1928, 32, 36, 40, 44; del. Uniting Conf., 1939. Trustee Peirce Free Library. Diplomate Nat. Bd. Neurology and Psychiatry. Fellow Am. Psychiat. Soc., Am. Assn. for Study of Mental Deficiency; mem. A.M.A., Med. Soc. State of N.Y., Phi Beta Pi, Neuron Club of Central N.Y. Methodist. Mason (K.T.); member Modern Woodmen of America. Contributor to med. jours. Home: 16 Pleasant St. Address: The Sanitarium, Clifton Springs, N.Y. Died May 19, 1947; buried in Woodlawn Cemetery, Syracuse, N.Y.

ODELL, George Clinton Densmore, educator, author; b. Newburgh, N.Y., Mar. 19, 1866; s. Benjamin Barker and Ophelia (Bookstaver) O.; ed. Siglar Prep. Sch.; B.A., Columbia, 1889, M.A., 1890, Ph.D., 1893; unmarried. Connected with dept. of English, Columbia U., since 1895, succeeding Brander Matthews as prof. dramatic lit., 1924-39, Brander Matthews prof. emeritus dramatic lit. since July 1939. Fellow N.Y. State Historical Association; honorary member New York Historical Society (gold medalist for achievement in history). Republican. Clubs: Century, Players, Columbia Univ. Club. Author: Shakespeare from Betterton to Irving (2 vols.), 1920; Annals of the New York Stage (14 vols.), 1927-45 (to comprise 16 vols.). Compiler: Simile and Metaphor, in the English and Scottish Ballads, 1893. Editor sch. edits. of Julius Cæsar and Henry V. Home: Hotel Seymour, W. 45th St., New York, N.Y. Died Oct. 17, 1949.

O'DONNELL, J(ohn) Hugh, univ. pres.; b. Grand Rapids, Mich., June 2, 1895; s. Edward J. and Sarah A. (O'Grady) O'D.; B.Litt., U. of Notre Dame, 1916; Ph.D., Catholic U. of America, 1922. Entered Congregation of Holy Cross, 1917; ordained priest, Grand Rapids, Mich., Dec. 28, 1921; assigned to U. of Notre Dame, 1922, prefect of discipline and dir. student welfare, 1923-30; pres. St. Edward's U., Austin, Tex., 1931-34; v.p. U. of Notre Dame and chmn. faculty bd. in control of athletics, 1934-40. acting pres., Jan.-July 1940, pres., July 1940-46. Active in Catholic Students' Mission Crusade (predecessor of Catholic Youth Movement). Active mem. Am. Catholic Hist. Assn. (mem. exec. council 2 terms). Contbr. to Catholic Hist. Review. Address: U. of Notre Dame, Notre Dame, Ind. Died June 12, 1947; buried in Community Cemetery, University of Notre Dame.

OESTERLE, Joseph Francis (ŏs'tĕr-lē), coll. prof.; b. Philadelphia, Pa., Oct. 18, 1888; s. Herman George and Anna Marie (Dwight) O.; student Phila. Coll. Pharmacy, 1904-07; B.S., U. of Wis., 1913, grad. student, 1917-18, 1921-29, research asst., 1921-29, Ph.D., 1929; m. Helen Barbara Shaeffer, Sept. 19, 1922; children—David Swenk Tim, Joseph George Francis, Ellen Ann, John Harry, Mary Frances. Metall. engr. with Tacony Iron Co., Phila., 1907-09, test dept., Pa. R.R., 1909-11, 1913-16; Ill. Steel, Gary, Ind., 1916-17; associate physicist Bur. Standards, Washington, as enlisted personnel Chem. Warfare, 1918, civilian personnel, 1918-21; with Coll. of Engring. dept. mining and metallurgy, U. of Wis., since 1921, successively asst. prof., asso. prof. and prof., 1929-43, chmn. dept. since 1940; cons. engr. on ordnance materials. Mem. Boy Scouts of America (Silver Beaver award). Mem. Am. Soc. for Metals (formerly on nat. publ. com.), Am. Inst. Mining and Metall. Engrs. (v. chmn. mineral industry edn. div.), Soc. for Promotion of Engring. Edn. (chmn. div. mineral tech.), Am. Foundrymen's Assn. (engring. edn. com.), Alpha Chi Sigma, Gamma Alpha, Alpha Phi Omega, Sigma Xi. Roman Catholic. K.C. Co-author: Elements of Ferrous Metallurgy. Home: 2411 Monroe St., Madison, Wis. Died Dec. 1943.

OGDEN, Edward William; b. Rutherford, N.J., Nov. 26, 1870; s. William and Adele (Chavannes) O.; ed. Peekskill (N.Y.) Mil. Acad.; m. Mary Wilson, Dec. 3, 1902. Formerly pres. Knoxville Lithographing Co., v.p. Journal and Tribune (Knoxville), Greenwood Advt. Co.; resigned, Oct. 1917, and spent 13 mos. in France, with Am. Red Cross; now devoting attention principally to community welfare work. Ex-pres. State Council Social Agencies; ex-pres. Tenn. Conf. of Social Work; ex-v.p. Knoxville Morris Plan Bank. Club: Cherokee. Home: 715 Walnut St., Knoxville, Tenn. Deceased.

OGDEN, Henry Neely, civil engr.; b. Dexter, Me., Apr. 30, 1868; s. Charles Talcott and Anna (Bennett) O.; ed. Episcopal and Cheltenham acads., Phila.; C.E., Cornell, 1889; m. Mary G. Smith, Dec. 26, 1895; children—Katharine, Priscilla Campbell, John Bennett, William Hall, Robert Neely (dec.), Ruth Patterson. Made study of sewerage in Europe, 1897; engr. in charge of the sewer system of Ithaca, New York; was the designer of the plans for the stone arch 64 ft. span and retaining wall 30 ft. high, Cornell U.; prof. civ. engineering, 1896-1906, prof. sanitary engring. since 1906, professor emeritus since 1938, Cornell University. Engineer to New York State Board of Health, 1906-13. Member Public Health Council State of N.Y. since 1913. Mem. Am. Soc. C.E., Sigma Xi. Author: Sewer Design, 1899; Sewer Construction, 1908; Rural Hygiene, 1910. Consulting engr. Home: 416 Hanshaw Rd., Ithaca, N.Y. Died Sep. 29, 1947.

OGDEN, Herschel Coombs, newspaper pub.; b. Worthington, W.Va., Jan. 12, 1869; s. Presley Benjamin and Mary Ellen (Coombs) O.; grad. State Normal Sch., Fairmont, W.Va., 1883; A.B., W.Va. U., Morgantown, 1887; LL.D., Bethany Coll.; hon. D.C.L., W.Va. Wesleyan Coll.; hon. D.C.L., W.Va. U., 1938; m. Mary Frances Moorehouse, Oct. 15, 1890. Established Wheeling News, 1890; bought Wheeling Intelligencer 1904; pres. News Publishing Co., Intelligencer Publishing Co., Parkersburg Sentinel Co., Parkersburg News Co., Fairmont Newspaper Publishing Co., Elkins Inter-Mountain, Welch Daily News, Williamson Daily News, Hinton Daily News, Point Pleasant Register, and Washington (N.C.) News. Republican. Episcopalian. Clubs: Masonic, Press, Wheeling Country, Fort Henry. Home: Wheeling, W.Va. Died Jan. 31, 1943.

OGILBY, Remsen Brinckerhoff (ō'gĭl-bĭ), coll. pres.; b. New Brunswick, N.J., Apr. 8, 1881; s. Charles FitzRandolph and Agnes (Brinckerhoff) O.; A.B., Harvard, 1902, A.M., 1907; Gen. Theol. Sem.; B.D., Episcopal Theol. Sch., Cambridge, 1907; LL.D., Wesleyan, 1921; Litt.D., Columbia, 1923; m. Lois M. Cunningham, Aug. 26, 1919; children—Peter Brinckerhoff, Lyman Cunningham, Alexander. Master, Groton School, 1902-04. Deacon, 1907, priest, 1908, P.E. Church; curate St. Stephen's Ch., Boston, 1907-09; headmaster Baguio Sch., P.I., 1909-18; chaplain U.S. Army, 1918-19; master St. Paul's School, Concord, N.H., 1919-20; pres. Trinity Coll., Hartford, Conn., since 1920. Dir. Hartford Hosp. Trustee Watkinson Memorial Library, Lenox (Mass.) School, Salisbury (Conn.) Sch. Mem. Classical Assn. of New Eng., New England Assn. Schs. and Colls. Clubs: University (Hartford); University (Boston); Harvard, Century (New York); Authors' (London). Home: 115 Vernon St., Hartford, Conn. Died Aug. 7, 1943.

OGLEBAY, Crispin (ō-g'l-bā'), mining, shipping, mfg.; b. Wheeling, W.Va., Oct. 10, 1876; s. James Hill and Annie D. (List) O.; prep. edn., St. Paul's School, Concord, N.H.; A.B., Yale University, 1900; Litt.D., Bethany College, Bethany, West Virginia, 1941, University of West Virginia, 1942; unmarried. Began as clk. Swift Packing Co., Kansas City, Mo., 1901; shipping clk. J. G. Peppard Seed Co., Kansas City, 1902; sec. Hoffman Hinge & Foundry Co., Cleveland, 1903-06; pres. Ferro Machine & Foundry Co., Cleveland, 1906-20, chmn. bd. and dir., 1920-46; chairman board, dir. Oglebay, Norton & Co., pres. and dir. The Atwater Dock Co., Brule Smokeless Coal Co., Columbia Transportation Co., Fairport Machine Shop, Inc., Fortune Lake Mining Co., North Shore Land Co., Pringle Barge Line, Saginaw Dock and Terminal Co., St. James Mining Co., Toledo, Lorain & Fairport Dock Co.; v.p. and dir. Castile Mining Co., Montreal Mining Co., Ferro Engring. Co., Standard Box Co., Reserve Mining Co., Lake Superior Land Company, Northern Land Co.; director Wheeling Steel Corporation, Richwood Sewell Coal Company, Bristol Equipment Company. Director Cleveland War Chest, Trustee, member exec. com. Western Res. Univ.; trustee Oglebay Inst. (Wheeling, W.Va.), Cuyahoga County Conservation Council, The Play House Foundation (Cleveland), Cleveland Museum of Natural History, Nat. Recreation Assn., Alpha Delta Phi, Scroll and Keys. Republican. Episcopalian. Clubs: Tavern, Union, Mid-Day (Cleveland); Fort Henry (Wheeling, W.Va.); Yale, Jockey, Links (New York); Duquesne (Pittsburgh); Chagrin Valley Hunt (dir.) (Gates Mills). Home: Gates Mills, O. Office: Hanna Bldg., Cleveland. Died Oct. 23, 1949.

O'GORMAN, James A., ex-senator; b. New York, N.Y., May 5, 1860; s. Thomas and Ellen (Callan) O'Gorman; educated Coll. of City of New York; LL.B., New York U., 1882; LL.D., Villanova Coll., 1904, Fordham U., 1908, New York U., 1909, Georgetown U., 1911; m. Anne M. Leslie, Jan. 2, 1884. Admitted to bar, 1882; justice Dist. Court of New York, 1893-1900; justice Supreme Court of N.Y., 1900-14; elected U.S. senator, Mar. 1911, for term 1911-17, and resigned from bench, Mar. 31, 1911; resumed practice of the law, 1917; apptd. official referee N.Y. Supreme Court, 1934. Trustee New York U., 1920-27, Coll. of New Rochelle. Pres. N.Y. County Lawyer Assn., 1923-24; mem. Am. Bar Assn., N.Y. State Bar Assn., Assn. Bar City of N.Y., Am. Law Inst., N.Y. Law Inst. Clubs: Lawyers (pres. 1932-33), Nat. Democratic, Catholic, New York Athletic. Home: 1148 5th Av. Address: County Court House, New York, N.Y. Died May 17, 1943.

O'HARA, Joseph Alphonsus, health officer; b. New Orleans, La., Jan. 23, 1869; s. Joseph and Anna (Norris) O'H.; M.D., Tulane U., 1900; m. Mary T. Cosgrove, Jan. 6, 1896; children—William Joseph, Ruth B. (Mrs. Hugh J. Le Blanc). Began as druggist, 1890; coroner's phys., New Orleans, 1904-24; pres. and exec. officer La. State Bd. of Health since 1928; prof. preventive medicine and pub. health, La. State U., since 1928; pres. bd. East La. Hosp. for Insane since 1928. Pres. La. State Med. Assn., 1938,

Soc. Mental Hygiene for La., 1937-38, La. Democratic Assn., 1932; dir. La. Med. Center, New Orleans. Catholic. Author of med. papers and contbr. articles to med. jours. Home: 2311 St. Charles Av., New Orleans, La. Died Feb. 25, 1948.

O'HARRA, Margaret Tustin (Mrs. I. Harrison O'Harra), social worker; b. Lewisburg, Pa., Jan. 23, 1866; d. Francis Wayland (Ph.D.) and Maria (Probasco) Tustin; A.B., Bucknell U., 1883; A.M., 1891, Dr. Humanities, 1935; m. I. Harrison O'Harra, 1902 (died June 1937); 2 children—Ernest Tustin, Margaret (Mrs. L. T. Koons). Teacher, Bucknell U., 1883-87. Sch. dir., West Phila., 1904-13. Vice chmn. canteen dept. Am. Red Cross and Liberty Loan Com., World War. One of founders Playground Assn. of Phila.; an incorporator of Public Edn. Assn.; v.p. State Federation of Pa. Women 4 yrs. (mem. edn. com. 4 yrs.); apptd. by gov. of Pa. vice-pres. Home and Sch. League for Phila.; mem. nat. com. on marriage and the home, Federal Council Chs. of Christ in America; apptd. by Court of Common Pleas as visitor for children, 1924-27; mem. Am. Bapt. Home Mission Bd.; mem. social service com. Northern Bapt. Conv. (mem. hist. bd.); dir. State Mission Soc. of Pa. Mem. advisory bd. Rep. Women of Phila. County. Founder Bucknell Alumnæ Club of Phila. (hon. pres. 1928); mem. Am. Assn. Univ. Women, English-Speaking Union, Trans-Atlantic Soc., D.A.R., Colonial Dames of America, Phila. Art Alliance (dir. jr. work). Republican. Clubs: Civic (v.p.), College, New Century, City, Print. Writer of biographies of Mrs. Henry W. Peabody, Mrs. Helen Barrett Montgomery, Mrs. George Coleman, etc. Home: Fairfax Apts., Locust at 43d St., Philadelphia, Pa.*Died Nov. 20, 1942.

O'KEEFE, Arthur Joseph, ex-mayor; b. New Orleans, La., Nov. 8, 1876; s. Arthur and Sarah (Hanley) O'K.; grad. St. Alphonsus High Sch., New Orleans, 1892; m. Mamie McDonald, Nov. 14, 1901; children—Arthur J., Mae Lucile (Mrs. Conrad H. Foerester), John Harold, William Donald, Helen (Mrs. Louis J. Healy), Lorraine (Mrs. Francis J. Codina), Dorothy. Formerly engaged as coffee importer and roaster, also in banking and ins. business; now head of firm Arthur J. O'Keefe, teas and coffees; active vice pres. Am. Bank & Trust Co.; dir. Lafayette Fire Ins. Co., Mut. Building & Loans Assn. Mem. La. State Senate, May-Aug. 1908 (resigned); alderman City Council, 1908-12; city treas. New Orleans, 1912-20; commr. Pub. Finance, 1925-26; mayor of New Orleans, term May 1926-May 1930. K.C., Elk, Moose, Woodman. Democrat. Clubs: Choctaw (pres.), Young Men's Gymnastic. Home: 1018 St. Mary St. Office: American Bank Bldg., 1904 Magazine St., New Orleans. Died Nov. 13, 1943.

O'KEEFFE, Arthur, pres. grocery chain; b. Boston, Mass., Apr. 17, 1899; s. Michael and Margaret (McNamara) O'K.; student Boston U., 1916-17; C.P.A., Mass., 1922; m. Mary Adelaide Watson, Oct. 21, 1922; children—Richard Michael, Marcia, Adelaide Teresa. Began as accountant for Lewis Murphy & Co., Boston, 1918; with M. O'Keeffe, Inc., 1923; merged into First Nat. Stores, Inc., 1925; advanced through various positions in latter to pres., 1934, and so continues; firm operated more than 2,600 stores in New Eng. and N.Y., 1934. Former chmn. exec. com. Nat. Assn. Food Chains. Dir. Boston Bruins, Erie Soc. of Boston, Newton Community Fund. Trustee Suffolk Instn. for Savings for Seamen, St. Elizabeth's Hosp., Boston Coll. Sch. of Bus. Adminstrn. Catholic, Knight of Malta. Clubs: Charles River Country (Newton Center, Mass.), Oyster Harbours (Oysterville, Mass.), Clover (Boston). Home: 111 Hammondswood Rd., Chestnut Hill, Mass. Office: 5 Middlesex Av., Somerville, Mass. Died July 25, 1948.

OKIE, R. Brognard, architect; b. Camden, N.J., June 26, 1875; s. Dr. Richardson B. and Clara (Mickle) O.; student Haverford Coll., 1893-94; B.S. in Arch., U. of Pa., 1897; m. Christine Laurence Thomas, Oct. 15, 1903; children—Jeanie Laurence (Mrs. Robert Huston Brinkerhoff), Charles Thomas. In gen. practice of architecture since 1897. Prin. works include: reproduction of High Street for the Sesqui-Centennial, 1925-26; restoration of the Betsy Ross House, Phila.; re-creation of William Penn's Manor House; restoration of Silver Spring Ch., and of Paxton Presbyn. Ch., Pa. Fellow A.I.A. Vestryman, Old Saint David's Ch., Radnor, 1903-41. Home: Hillside Farm, Devon, Pa. Address: 306 S. Smedley St., Philadelphia, Pa. Died Dec. 27, 1945.

OLANDER, Victor A. (ō'lănd-ēr), trades unionist; b. Chicago, Ill., 1873; m. Elizabeth Grace Cervenka, 1902; children—Mrs. Grace Elizabeth Smedstad, Ruth Helen. Sec.-treas. Ill. State Federation of Labor since 1914; was a sailor for a number of yrs. until elected sec. of Sailors' Union of Great Lakes; sec.-treas. Seamen's Internat. Union of America, 1925-36; mem. Joint Com. A. F. of L. and Am. Bar Assn., 1927. Dir., sec. Radio Station WCFL, Inc., to 1946. Member National War Labor Bd., State Council of Defense, Ill., and of Draft Appeal Bd., 1917; mem. Ill. Emergency Relief Commn., 1932-35; apptd. mem. NRA Dist. Recovery Bd. for Ill. and Wis., 1933; mem. bd. Unemployment Compensation, Free Employment Advisors, and other public coms. Delegate, A.F. of L. Home: 1336 N. Mason Av. Office: 666 Lake Shore Dr., Chicago, Ill. Died Feb. 5, 1949.

O'LAUGHLIN, John Callan (ō-lŏk'lĭn), publisher; born Washington, D.C., January 11, 1873; son John and Mary (Osborne) O'L.; public school education; course in European diplomacy, Columbia U.; hon. M.A., LL.D., Villanova Coll.; m. Mabel Hudson, July 15, 1896. With Washington bur. N.Y. Herald, 1893-1902; went to Venezuela, 1902, and reported blockade of that country by Great Britain, Germany and Italy; mem. European staff Associated Press, 1903-04; in Russia during Russo-Japanese War; on staff the Chicago Tribune, 1905-14, Washington corr., 1909-14; Washington corr. of Chicago Herald, 1914-17; v.p. Lord & Thomas, Chicago, 1917; pub. Army and Navy Journal; specializes in national defense and foreign affairs. Secretary of United States Commission to Tokyo Expn., 1908, 11; first asst. sec. of state, Jan. 19-Mar. 5, 1909; declined office of asst. secretaryship of treasury and minister to Argentine; acted as sec. to Theodore Roosevelt in Africa and Europe. During World War I as rep. of Chicago Herald and other papers, took Christmas ship laden with 6,000,000 gifts to war orphans in Europe. Del. Progressive Nat. Conv., 1912; exec. sec. policy com. of Rep. party, 1920; asst. to chmn. Rep. Nat. Com., 1933-34; chmn. Goethals Memorial Com.; vice-chmn. U.S. Goethals Memorial Commn. Chmn.; mem. and later coordinator of Selective Service Board of Appeals, District of Columbia, since 1941. Member board visitors United States Naval Academy, 1932. Commissioned major, Jan. 25, 1918, and assigned as aide to Major General Goethals, acting q.m. general United States Army; subsequently served in France with intelligence sect. General Staff, and later as sec. for the U.S. Inter-Allied Munitions Council; col. O.R.C., 1921-35. Catholic. Clubs: Chevy Chase, Gridiron (Washington). Author: With Roosevelt from the Jungle Through Europe, 1910; Imperiled America, 1916. Address: Army and Navy Journal, Washington. Died March 14, 1949; buried in Arlington National Cemetery.

OLDER, Clifford, cons. engr.; b. Lincoln, Adams County, Wis., Nov. 17, 1876; s. Milton DeWitt and Elizabeth Ann (Clark) O.; B.S. in C.E., Univ. of Wis., 1900; m. Kitty May Drake, May 28, 1903; children—Fern Elizabeth, Kitty Beatrice, Clifford Dewilton, David Drake, Grenfell. Asst. engr. with Pa. R.R., 1900-01, Wabash Pittsburgh Terminal R.R., 1901-02; div. engr. C.&A. R.R., 1902-06; bridge engr. Ill. State Highway Dept., 1906-17; chief state highway engr. of Ill., 1917-24 (handling road constrn. involving outlay of over $100,000,000); conducted Bates test road research; now cons. engr. Mem. design com. U.S. Research Council. Mem. Am. Soc. C.E., Western Soc. Engrs. Republican. Methodist. Mason. Home: 1026 Elmwood Av., Wilmette, Ill. Died Nov. 28, 1943; buried in Silver Lake Cemetery, Portage, Wis.

OLDFATHER, William Abbott, coll. prof.; b. Urumiah, Persia, October 23, 1880; s. Jeremiah M. and Felicia Narcissa (Rice) O.; A.B., Hanover (Ind.) Coll., 1899, LL.D., 1933; A.B., Harvard U., 1901, A.M., 1902; Ph.D., Munich, 1908; m. Margaret Agnes Giboney, Sept. 22, 1902; children—Margaret, Helen. Instr. classics, 1903-06 and 1908, asst. prof. Latin, 1908-09, and registrar Coll. of Liberal Arts, 1904-06, Northwestern U.; asso. prof. classics, 1909-15, prof. since 1915, head of dept., 1926-31, chmn. since 1931, chmn. div. of langs. and lit., 1935-42, Univ. of Ill.; Sather prof. U. of Calif., 1934; prof. of classics, ancient history, summer sessions, Columbia, 1924, 31, U. of Chicago 1923, U. of Calif. at Los Angeles, 1925, U. of Colo., 1929, 30, Stanford Univ., 1935; visiting prof., Am. Sch. of Classical Studies, Athens, 1937, Columbia, 1938. Mem. advisory council Am. Council of Learned Socs.; fellow A.A.A.S. (chmn. sect. on philology, v.p. 1925), Am. Acad. Arts and Sciences since 1934; mem. Am. Philol. Assn. (pres. 1937-38), Archæol. Inst. America, Am. Hist. Assn., Classical Assn., Am. Assn. Univ. Profs. (charter mem.; mem. council 1924-27 and 1934-37), Nat. Research Council, Classical League, Linguistic Soc. America (v.p. 1928), Mediæval Academy, American Committee for Democracy and Intellectual Freedom (mem. exec. com. 1941; mem. council for democracy since 1942), Phi Delta Theta, Phi Beta Kappa, Phi Eta, Phi Kappa Epsilon, Eta Sigma Phi, Phi Kappa Phi. Club: University. Author: Lokrika, 1908; The Defeat of Varus, 1915; Index Verborum to Seneca's Tragedies, 1918; Bibliography to Epictetus, 1927; Pufendorf's Elementa Jurisprudentiæ, 1930, and De Jure Naturæ at Gentium, 1934; Index to Apuleius, 1934; Index to Cicero's Letters, 1938; Supplement to Bibliography to Epictetus, 1945. Editor: Ysopet-Avionnet, 1920; Greek Tacticians, 1923; Epictetus, 1926, 28; L. Enler's Elastic Curves, 1933; Studies in the text tradition of St. Jerome's Vitae Patrum, 1943; the text tradition of Avianus, 1945. Editor Univ. of Ill. Studies in Language and Literature since 1915. Contbr. on classical subjects. Address: 804 W. Green St., Urbana, Ill. Died May 27, 1945.

OLDHAM, Robert Pollard, lawyer; b. Marietta, O., May 19, 1877; s. Francis Fox and Betty Washington (Lovell) O.; A.B., U. of Cincinnati, 1908; LL.B., Harvard, 1901; m. Mary Belle Strickland, Jan. 1, 1902 (died Jan. 22, 1923); children—Frances Lovell, Robert Pollard, Mary; m. 2d, Alice Pickering, June 27, 1926. Admitted to Wash. bar, 1902, and began practice at Seattle; mem. firm Bausman, Oldham, Jarvis & Wampold since 1910. Wash. State chmn. Liberty Loan Campaigns, World War. Chmn. Wash. delegation to Dem. Nat. Conv., 1924. Mem. Sigma Alpha Epsilon. Clubs: University, Rainier. Home: 928 13th Av. N. Office: Hoge Bldg., Seattle, Wash. Died Dec. 8, 1941.

OLDS, Robert, army officer; b. Woodside, Md., June 15, 1896; s. Henry W. and May Clendening (Meigs) O.; ed. Central High Sch., Washington, D.C., and private tutors; grad. Air Corps Tactical Sch., 1928, Command and Gen. Staff Sch., 1935; m. Eloise Wichman, Oct. 22, 1921 (died 1926); children—Robin, Stevan Meigs; m. 2d, Marjorie Marvin, 1928 (divorced); m. 3d, Helen Post Sterling 1933 (divorced); children—Sterling Meigs, Frederick Sterling. Joined Aviation Sect. of Signal Corps, Jan. 1917; rated Reserve mil. aviator, May 1917; commd. 1st lt., Signal Officers Reserve Corps, June 1917; comd., 17th Aero Squadron, San Antonio, Tex., 1917; instr. Scott Field, Belleville, Ill.; Ellington Field, Houston, Tex., later officer in charge of flying; arrived in France with A.E.F., Sept. 1918, assigned officer in charge of training at Clermont-Ferrand instrn. center, then on staff 2d Army Air Service comdr. at Toul; with Hawaiian Dept., 1919-22, War Plans Div., Office of Chief of Air Corps, Washington, D.C., 1922-26; promoted to major, 1935; rated command pilot, mil. airplane pilot, combat observer; asst. to chief inspector, later chief of inspection sect., G.H.Q., Air Force, 1935-37; as comdg. officer 2d Bombardment Group, Langley Field, Va., piloted Flying Fortress No. 10, on non-stop transcontinental flights; comd. 6 Flying Fortresses on group flight to Buenos Aires and return, Feb. 1938; flight leader on flight of 7 Flying Fortresses to Rio de Janeiro, Nov. 1939; promoted to col., Oct. 1940; command of Air Corps Ferrying Command, delivering bombers to Eng., since June 1941. Awarded bronze trophy of Internat. League of Aviators, 1941; also Victory medal, Mackay trophy, Harmon trophy. Decorated Distinguished Flying Cross (U.S.); Officer of Southern Cross (Brazil). Episcopalian. Mem. Order of Daedalians. Clubs: Columbia Country, Army and Navy (Washington, D.C.). Contbr. on flying to jours. Address: War Dept., Washington, D.C. Died Apr. 28, 1943.

O'LEARY, James A., congressman; b. New Brighton, Staten Island, N.Y., Apr. 23, 1889; ed. St. Peter's Sch., Augustinian Acad. and Westerleigh Collegiate Inst., Staten Island; studied law; widower; 3 children. Was with North Shore Ice Co., later became gen. mgr.; also official other Staten Island cos.; mem. 74th to 78th Congresses (1935-45); 11th N.Y. Dist.; apptd. chmn. Committee on Expenditures in the Executive Depts. of the House, 77th Congress. Democrat. Home: W. New Brighton, Staten Island, N.Y. Died Mar. 16, 1944.

O'LEARY, John William, mfr.; b. Chicago, Ill., July 9, 1875; s. Arthur John and Emma S. (Hunt) O'L.; ed. pub. schs. and Armour Inst. Tech., Chicago; M.E., Cornell U., 1899; m. Alice Estelle Smith, 1901; children—Alice Estelle, Lillian Emma, Dorothy Rose, Janet Edna, John William. Identified since beginning of active career with business established by father, and now director Kelly Steel Works, mfrs. iron and steel products; now member executive committee Machinery and Allied Products Institute.; director C.G.W. Ry. Co. Chmn. Industry Members War Labor Board (6th region). President American Enterprise Assn., Inc. Member Chamber Commerce of U.S. (president 1925-27), Chicago Association Commerce (pres. 1916-18), Nat. Metal Trades Assn. (ex-pres.); was mem. President Wilson's 1st Industrial Conf.; apptd. by President Coolidge U.S. del. Internat. Econ. Conf., Geneva, 1927; vice treas. Rep. Nat. Com. of Hoover Campaign. Mem. Sigma Chi. Republican. Methodist. Clubs: Chicago, Commercial, Knollwood (Chicago); Cornell (New York); Metropolitan (Washington, D.C.). Home: Lake Forest, Ill. Office: 221 N. La Salle St., Chicago, Ill. Died Feb. 8, 1946.

O'LEARY, Thomas M., bishop; b. Dover, N.H., Aug. 16, 1875; s. Michael and Margaret (Howland) O'L.; grad. pub. schs., Dover, 1887; student Mungret Coll., Limerick, Ireland, 3 yrs.; grad. Grand Seminary, Montreal, Can., 1897. Ordained priest R.C. Ch., at Montreal, 1897; asst. pastor St. Ann's Ch., Manchester, N.H., 1898-99, St. John's Ch., Concord, 1899-1904; served as administrator of the parish for 4 mos. after death of Vicar Gen. John E. Barry, and assisted in adminstrn. for 3 yrs.; served as chancellor and sec. to Bishop J. B. Delancy; made vicar gen. and permanent rector of St. John's, Concord, N.H.; consecrated bishop of Springfield, Sept. 8, 1921. Home: 68 Elliot St., Springfield, Mass. Died Oct. 10, 1949.

OLIVER, Edna May, actress; b. Boston, Mass., Nov. 9, 1883; d. Charles Edward and Ida May (Cox) Oliver; left sch. at 14 and went to work; married, 1928; divorced, 1933. Worked as dressmaker's and milliner's asst., singer in light opera co., 1900; pianist in ladies' orchestra, 1904; actress with various stock cos., 1910-14; has appeared in numerous plays on legitimate stage, N.Y. City and elsewhere; moving-picture comedian since 1930. Democrat. Unitarian. Club: Bel-Air of Southern Calif. Home: "Brentwood," Los Angeles, Calif.* Died Nov. 9, 1942.

OLIVER, John Rathbone, psychiatrist, medical historian; b. Albany, N.Y., Jan. 4, 1872; s. Gen. Robert Shaw and Marion Lucy (Rathbone) O.; A.B., Harvard U., 1894; grad. Gen. Theol. Sem., 1900; M.D., U. of Innsbruck, Austria, 1910; Ph.D., Johns Hopkins, 1927; unmarried. Master at St. Paul's Sch., Concord, N.H., 1894-97; priest, P.E. Ch., 1900; curate St. Mark's Ch., Phila., Pa., 1900-03 (resigned; restored to orders 1927); surgeon, Austrian Army, 1914-15; psychiatrist, Johns Hopkins Hosp., 1915-17; chief med. officer to Supreme Bench of Baltimore, 1917-30; prof. history of medicine, U. of Med., 1927-30; asso. in history of medicine, Johns Hopkins U., since 1930; pvt. practice as psychiatrist; warden Alumni Memorial Hall, Johns Hopkins. Mem. Med. O.R.C. Mem. A.M.A., Am. Psychiatric Assn., Royal Soc. Medicine (Brit.), Phi Beta Kappa. Republican. Episcopalian (mem. clerical staff Mount Calvary Ch.). Clubs: University, Press, Harvard, Charcoal. Author: The

Good Shepherd, 1915; The Six-Pointed Cross in the Dust, 1917; Fear, 1927; Victim and Victor, 1928; Foursquare, 1929; Rock and Sand, 1930; Article Thirty-two 1931; Psychiatry and Mental Health, 1932; The Good Shepherd (reprinted and revised), 1932; Tomorrow's Faith, 1932; Priest or Pagan, 1933; The Ordinary Difficulties of Everyday People, 1935; Greater Love, 1936; Spontaneous Combustion, 1937. Contbr. to Jour. Criminal Law, Internat. Clinics, Johns Hopkins Hosp. Bull., etc. Home: 3333 N. Charles St. Office: Welch Medical Library, 1900 E. Monument St., Baltimore, Md. Died Jan. 21, 1943.

OLIVER, Thomas Edward, coll. prof.; b. Salem, Mass., Dec. 16, 1871; s. Samuel Cook and Mary Elizabeth (Andrews) O.; A.B., Harvard, 1893; Harvard Med. Sch., 1893-94; U. of Leipzig, 1894-95; U. of Heidelberg, 1895-99, A.M., Ph.D., 1899; also studied École des Hautes Études and the Sorbonne, Paris; m. Elisabeth Reinhardt, June 9, 1904; children—Elisabeth Andrews (Mrs. Webster C. Martin), Martha Reinhardt (Mrs. Harold W. Ragland), John Lee, Sarah Chever (Mrs. George E. Morgan). Instructor French, U. of Mich., 1899-1900; instructor, asst. prof. Romance languages, College for Women (Western Reserve Univ.), Cleveland, 1900-03; professor Romance langs., U. of Ill., Sept. 1903-40, prof. of French emeritus, since Sept. 1940, also at various times chmn. Dept. of Romance Langs. Unitarian. Mem. Modern Lang. Assn. America, Nat. Fedn. of Modern Lang. Teachers, Am. Assn. of Teachers of French, Corda Fratres, Assn. of Cosmopolitan Clubs, University of Illinois Chapter, The Players (University of Illinois), Phi Beta Kappa, Sigma Phi Epsilon, Tau Kappa Alpha, Phi Kappa Epsilon, Pi Delta Phi, Pi Gamma Mu. Mem. Commission for Relief in Belgium, 1915-16. Médaille du Roi Albert, Médaille Commémorative du comité National (Belgian); also Belgian League of Honor. Author: Jacques Milet's Drama, La Destruction de Troie la Grant, 1899; The Mérope of George Jeffreys as a Source of Voltaire's Mérope, 1927; The Modern Language Teacher's Handbook, 1935. Editor: Michel-Jean Sedaine's Le Philosophe sans le savoir (variorum critical edit.), 1913; Molière's Le Bourgeois Gentilhomme, 1914; Sedaine's Le Philosophe sans le savoir, 1914; Suggestions and References for Modern Language Teachers, 1914, 17; Voltaire's Mérope, 1925; Molière's Le Misanthrope, 1927. Address: 1004 W. California Av., Urbana, Ill. Died Sept. 14, 1946.

OLMSTEAD, Albert Ten Eyck (ŏm'stĕd), Orientalist; b. Troy, N.Y., Mar. 23, 1880; s. Charles and Ella (Blanchard) O.; A.B., Cornell U., 1902, A.M., 1903, Ph.D., 1906; fellow Am. Sch. Oriental Studies at Jerusalem, 1904-05, Am. Sch. Classical Studies at Athens, 1906-07; m. Cleta Ermine Payne, June 25, 1913; children—Cleta Margaret, Ella Mary, Ruth Carol. Dir. Cornell University expdn. to Asia Minor and the Assyro-Babylonian Orient, 1907-08; instr. in Greek and Latin, Princeton Preparatory Sch., 1908-09; instr. ancient history, 1909-11, asst. prof., 1911-14, asso. prof., 1914-17, U. of Mo.; teacher summer school, Columbia, 1914, 1927-29, 32, 38, 41, Cornell, 1917, 22, U. of Chicago (Assyrian and Oriental history), 1920; prof. history and curator, Oriental Museum, U. of Ill., 1917-29; Oriental Inst. prof. Oriental history, U. of Chicago, since 1929; Haskell lecturer Grad. Sch. of Theology, Oberlin. Annual professor Am. Sch. of Oriental Research, Baghdad, Iraq, 1936-37. Member Am. Hist. Assn., Am. Oriental Soc. (dir.; v.p. 1921-22, 1928-32; pres. 1922-23; also sec.-treas. Western branch, 1917-21, president 1921-22 and 1940-41), Soc. Bibl. Lit., Soc. Bibl. Research (vice-president 1924-25; president 1941-42), Washington Conf. on Regional Phenomena, Com. on Mediterranean Antiquities, Near East Com. of Am. Council of Learned Socs., Phi Beta Kappa (pres. Gamma of Ill., 1927-28; president Beta of Ill., 1942-43); secretary of advisory committee on cultural areas of Social Science Research Council, 1927-28; corp. rep. American Schs. of Oriental Research; dir. Am. Inst. for Iranian Art and Archaeology. Clubs: Quadrangle of U. of Chicago (sec. 1938-40); Andiron (New York). Author: Western Asia in the Days of Sargon of Assyria, 1908; Travels and Studies in the Nearer East (Cornell Expdn.), 1911; Assyrian Historiography, 1916; History of Assyria, 1923; Anthropology and History, in Ogburn and Goldenweiser's The Social Sciences, 1927; History of Palestine and Syria, 1931; Jesus in the Light of History, 1942; also chapter edits. Ancient Near East, Manual Historical Literature. Home: 5758 Blackstone Av. Address: Oriental Inst., Univ. of Chicago, Chicago, Ill. Died Apr. 11, 1945.

OLMSTED, Everett Ward, univ. prof.; b. Galesburg, Ill., May 12, 1869; s. Silas and Emily (Ward) O.; Ph.B., Cornell, 1891, Ph.D., 1897; post-grad. studies The Sorbonne, Coll. de France, École des Chartes, Paris, and Cornell, 1893-98; Litt.D., Knox Coll., Galesburg, Ill., 1918; m. Bula Hubbell, June 19, 1895; children—Ward Hubbell, Richard Hubbell, John Meigs Hubbell. Master of French, Cascadilla Sch., Ithaca, N.Y., 1891-93; instr. French, Cornell U., 1893-98, asst. prof. Romance langs., 1898-1909, prof., 1909-14; prof. Romance langs. and head of the dept., U. of Minn., 1914-37, prof. emeritus of Romance langs. since 1937. Decorated Comendador de la Real Orden de Isabel la Católica (Spain), 1922; Chevalier de la Légion d'Honneur (France), 1937. Mem. Modern Lang. Assn. America (v.p. 1909-10), Am. Assn. Univ. Profs., Assn. Modern Lang. Teachers Central West and South (pres. 1919-20), Am. Assn. Teachers of Spanish (v.p. 1924-25), Alliance Française of Minneapolis (pres. 1919-21), Beta Theta Pi, Pi Gamma Mu; hon. corr. mem. l'Institut Littéraire et Artistique de France (with Gold Medal of same). Clubs: Skylight, University (Minneapolis); University (St. Paul); Campus Club (U. of Minn.); Dinner Club (pres. 1925-26). Author: The Sonnet in French Literature and the Development of the French Sonnet Form (dissertation), 1897; A Spanish Grammar (with Arthur Gordon), 1911; Abridged Spanish Grammar (with same), 1914; Elementary French Grammar, 1915; First Course in French, 1917; First Course in Spanish, 1920; French Composition and Conversation (with F. B. Barton), 1926; Beginners' French Grammar (with E. H. Sirich), 1926; Practical French Grammar (with E. H. Sirich), 1933; First Spanish Grammar (with R. L. Grismer), 1933. Contributor to mags. Editor: A Selection from the Comedies of Marivaux, 1901; Le Malade Imaginaire, by Molière, 1904; Legends, Tales and Poems by Gustavo A. Bécquer, 1907; Elementary French Reader (with F. B. Barton), 1920; First Spanish Reader (with E. H. Sirich), 1924. Home: 808 Mt. Curve Av., Minneapolis, Minn.; (winter) 28 Avenida de Chapultepec, Cuernavaca, Mexico. Died Nov. 14, 1943.

OLNEY, Louis Atwell (ŏl'nē), chemistry; b. Providence, R.I., Apr. 21, 1874; s. Albert H. and Frances E. (Olney) O.; high sch. and business coll., Providence; B.S., Lehigh U., 1896, M.S., 1908, Sc.D., 1926; m. Bertha Haynes Holden, June 24, 1903; children—Margaret Lucia (Mrs. Edward Alan Larter), Edna Elizabeth (Mrs. Dexter Nichols Shaw), Richard Holden. Instr. in chemistry, Brown U., 1896-97; prof. chemistry and dyeing, and director department chemistry and textile coloring, Lowell (Mass.) Textile Institute, 1897-1944 professor emeritus since 1944. Chemist Lowell Machine Shop, 1902-03, Lowell Gas Light Company, 1904-05, Lowell Board of Health, 1904; pres. of Stirling Mills, 1912-42, treas., 1936-42; pres., director, Wannalancit Textile Co.; pres., dir., Lowell Lingerie Co.; trustee Lowell Instn. for Savings (president, chairman bd. of investment); dir. Lowell Morris Plan Co.; dir. Howes Publishing Co., N.Y. City. Asst. editor Chem. Abstracts since 1907; editor Am. Dyestuff Reporter since 1920. Mem. Draft Board No. 87, Lowell, Mass. Treas. Northfield Conf. of Religious Edn.; v.p. Lowell Ministry at Large; dir. Lowell Y.M.C.A. since 1914, pres., 1916-21, trustee since 1940. Dir. Isle of Shoals Congregational Corp. since 1944. Fellow A.A.A.S., Am. Inst. Chemists; mem. Am. Chem. Soc. (ex-chmn. N.E. Sect.), Am. Inst. Chem. Engrs., Am. Assn. Textile Chemists and Colorists (pres. 1921-27, now emeritus; chmn. research com. since 1921, dir. of research 1940-46, U.S. Inst. for Textile Research (v.p., mem. research com.: acting pres. 1941, dir. since 1930). Dir. Textile Research Institute since 1944. National Association Wool Mfrs., Soc. Philatelic Americans, Boston Philatelic Society, Lowell Philatelic Society, Lowell Histology Society, British Society Dyers and Colourists, British Society Chemical Industry, Sigma Xi (Lehigh chapter). Republican. Congregationalist. Mason (K.T., 32°). Clubs: Temple, Lowell Congregational (ex-pres.), Lehigh (ex-pres.); Engineers (Boston); Chemists (New York); Yorick (Lowell, Mass.), Vesper Country. Olney Medal est. 1943 by Am. Assn. of Textile Chemists awarded for achievement in textile chemistry; first medal awarded (1944) to L. A. Olney, for whom it was named. Author: Textile Chemistry and Dyeing, 1903; Chemical Technology of Fibers, 1921, 47; Elementary Organic Chemistry, 1941; Roger's Industrial Chemistry (with others), 1942; also chapters and sects. in Colloidal Chemistry, Chemistry in Industry, Municipal Chemistry, Textile Research, Acetate Silk and its Dyes, Review American Chemical Research, Casein. Asso. editor Century Dictionary, 1904-05. Home: 118 Riverside St., Lowell, Mass.; (summer) Lake Penacook, Concord, N.H. Died Feb. 11, 1949.

OLSEN, John Charles, chemist; b. Galesburg, Ill., July 22, 1869; s. Michael and Cecelia (Johnson) O.; A.B., Knox Coll., Galesburg, 1890, A.M., 1893; U. of Chicago, summers, 1897, 98; Ph.D., Johns Hopkins, 1900; Sc.D., Knox, 1925; m. Ella Walker, Aug. 31, 1898; children—Julian W., Eugene U., Elizabeth. Prin. schs., Ipava, Ill., 1891-94; teacher physics and chemistry, Austin (Ill.) High Sch., 1895-98; prof. analytical chemistry, Poly. Inst. of Brooklyn, 1900-14, Pratt Inst., Brooklyn, 1900-06, Adelphi Coll., 1913-14; prof. chemistry and head dept., Cooper Union, N.Y., 1914-19; prof. chem. engring., Poly. Inst. of Brooklyn, 1918-44, head department, 1918-37; professor emeritus of chem. engring. since 1944. Lecturer analytical chemistry and foods, Brooklyn Institute Arts and Sciences and for Bd. Edn. City of New York since 1900; editor Van Nostrand's Chemical Annual since 1907, and Trans. Am. Inst. Chem. Engrs., 1909-26; sec. Am. Inst. Chem. Engrs., 1908-26, dir. 1926-27, v.p., 1928-29, pres., 1931; mem. Am. Chem. Soc., Brooklyn Chamber of Commerce. Republican. Methodist. Mason. Author: Quantitative Chemical Analysis, 1904; Pure Foods, 1911; Qualitative Chemical Analysis, 1916; Unit Processes and Principles of Chemical Engineering, 1932. Clubs: Chemists (New York). Home: 316 Argyle Rd., Brooklyn 18, N.Y. Died June 8, 1948.

OLSEN, Julius, univ. dean; b. Chicago, Ill., May 5, 1873; s. Ole and Regina (Paulsen) O.; B. Accounts, Bethany Bus. Coll., Lindsborg, Kan., 1893; B.S., Bethany Coll., 1898, D.Sc., 1922; Ph.D., Yale, 1902; grad. study, U. of Berlin, 1905, Cambridge U., 1906, also summer schs., U. of Kan., U. of Colo., U. of Wis.; m. Clara Nelson, Dec. 25, 1902; children—Regina May (Mrs. Meredith Townsend Lewis), Claudine Juliette, Julius Nelson (dec.), Ollie Lena, Julian Clarence. Prof. mathematics, Simmons Coll. (now Univ.), 1902-10, acting dean and head of depts. of chemistry and physics, 1910-15, dean and head of same depts., 1915-26, dean and head of dept. of physics since 1926. Fellow A.A.A.S., Tex. Acad. Science; mem. Am. Physical Assn., Tex. Archeol. and Paleontol. Soc. (v.p.); Scholarship Socs. of the South (ex-pres.), Nat. Econ. League, Alpha Chi (nat. council). Republican. Baptist. Club: Lions. Home: 1204 Vogal Av., Abilene, Tex. Died Sep. 15, 1942.

OLSON, Edwin August, lawyer; b. Cambridge, Ill., Feb. 16, 1868; s. Charles and Christine (Hanson) O.; ed. pub. schs.; m. Mae Fitzgerald, Nov. 17, 1897; children—Edwin A. (dec.), Raymond F., Gerald C. Admitted to Ill. bar, 1892, and practiced in Chicago; U.S. dist. atty., Northern Dist. of Ill., 1923-27; chmn. bd. Mutual Trust Life Ins. Co. Republican. Mason (32°, Shriner). Home: 1448 Lake Shore Dr. Office: Field Bldg., Chicago, Ill. Died June 27, 1947.

OLSON, George Edgar, univ. dean; b. Ames, Ia., July 19, 1891; s. George Charles and Jennie Elizabeth (Van Delinder) O.; A.B., U. of S.D., 1914; student U. of Chicago, 1915, 1917; m. Ida Robinson, June 16, 1920; children—George Edgar, Robert Stanley. High sch. teacher, Flandreau, S.D., 1914-15, Devils Lake, N.D., 1915-16, U. of N.D. High Sch., 1916-17; prof. business adminstrn. U. of S.C., 1919-20, dean Sch. of Commerce since 1920. Served as private and 2d lt., U.S. Army, 1917-20. Exec. sec. A.A.A., S.C., 1934-36. C.P.A., S.C., 1920. Mem. S.C. Assn. of C.P.A.'s, Pi Kappa Alpha, Delta Sigma Pi, Omicron Delta Kappa. Mason (Shriner). Club: Rotary (Columbia, S.C.). Home: 3113 Amherst Av., Columbia, S.C. Died June 22, 1946.

OMAN, Charles Malden (ō'măn), naval officer; b. Columbia County, Pa., Oct. 23, 1878; s. Henry Freas and Mary Jane (Shannon) O.; M.D., U. of Pa., 1901; m. Heloise Graham Brinckerhoff, Jan. 3, 1916. Commissioned lt. (j.g.), Med. Corps, U.S. Navy, 1902, and advanced through all grades to rear adm., 1936; served at Asiatic Station (Philippines, U.S.S. Monadnock and Frolic), 1902-05; Naval Hosp., Norfolk, Va., 1905-07; U.S.S. Ohio, 1906-07; U.S.S. Illinois, 1907-09; assisted at rescue work Messina earthquake, 1909; Naval Hosp., N.Y. City, 1909-12, 1915-18; on flagship Wyoming, 1912-15; commanded hosp. ship Comfort and later Navy Base Hosp., Brest, France, during World War; fleet surgeon on staff Adm. Henry B. Wilson, Atlantic Fleet, 1919-20; comd. Naval Med. Sch., Washington, 1920-21; Naval Hosp., Washington, 1921-24; med. officer, American Legation, Peking, China, 1924-27; pres. Bd. of Med. Examiners, Washington, 1927-28; comd. Naval Dispensary, Washington, 1928-31; Naval Hosp., Annapolis, 1931-35; Naval Hosp., N.Y. City, 1935-37; dist. med. officer 3d Naval Dist., 1937-39; inspector Med. Dept. Activities of Atlantic Coast, 1939-41; comdg. Nat. Naval Med. Center, Bethesda, Md., 1941-42; comdg. U.S. Naval Convalescent Hospital, Harriman, N.Y., since 1942. Awarded Navy Cross with citation for distinguished service in line of profession as Officer in Command of Navy Base Hosp. at Brest, France, 1918; Philippine Campaign medal, 1902; Cuban Pacification medal, 1907; Vera Cruz medal, 1914; Great War medal with overseas clasp; Marine Expeditionary Force medal, Peking, China, 1925; Italian Red Cross medal (for work in Messina earthquake), 1909; Defense Medal, World War II Medal. Served as delegate of American Red Cross at the international congress of experts to consider the revision of the Hague Conv. of 1907, Geneva Switzerland, 1937; mem. Nat. Bd. of Med. Examiners since 1921. Mem. Am. Coll. of Surgeons (mem. bd. of govs.); fellow A.M.A.; Sigma Xi. Republican. Episcopalian. Mason (32°). Clubs: Chevy Chase, Army and Navy (Washington); N.Y. Yacht (N.Y. City). Author: Minor Surgery, Doctors Aweigh. Address: Beacon, N.Y. Died Nov. 1, 1948.

OMWAKE, Howard Rufus (ŏm'wāk), coll. pres.; b. Greencastle, Pa., May 1, 1878; s. Henry and Eveline (Beaver) O.; grad. Mercersburg (Pa.) Acad., 1897; A.B., Princeton, 1901, A.M., 1904; U. of Pa., 1914-16; Pd.D., Temple U., 1930; Litt.D., Gettysburg Coll., 1930; m. Frances Lauretta Geiger, June 20, 1906; children—Henri Geiger, Anna Evelyn, Mary Katharine, Eleanor Long. Instr., Syrian Protestant Coll., Beirut, 1901-04; head dept. of Latin, Mercersburg Acad., 1904-08; sr. master, The Harrisburg Acad., 1909-19; dean Franklin and Marshall Coll., Lancaster, Pa., 1919-31; pres. Catawba Coll., Salisbury, N.C., since 1931; pres. N.C. College Conf., 1936; mem. Bd. of Regents Mercersburg Acad. Mem. Assn. Am. Univ. Profs., A.A.A.S., N.C. State Edn. Assn., Phi Delta Kappa, Phi Beta Kappa, Phi Kappa Sigma. Mem. Evang. and Reformed Ch. (gen. council). Democrat. Home: Salisbury, N.C. Died July 20, 1942.

O'NEAL, William Russell, banking, ins.; b. Belpre, Washington County, O., June 4, 1864; s. Edwin Russell and Nancy Jane (Scott) O'N.; grad. high sch., Belpre; studied under pvt. tutors and in law office of Judge David R. Rood; LL.D., Rollins Coll., Winter Park, Fla., 1927; m. Mabelle Copeland (died Feb. 1910); children—Helen Kate, Mabelle; m. 2d, Jessie Mallory, Oct. 14, 1914 (died 1923). Began at 20 as spl. agt. Eagle Fire Ins. Co.; now pres. Curtis & O'Neal Co., fire ins.; pres. First Federal Loan and Savings Assn., O'Neal Investment Co., O'Neal-Branch Co.; dir. and chmn. finance com. Am. United Life Ins. Co. Republican candidate in Fla. for U.S. Senate, gov., and Congress, also del. Rep. Nat. Convs. Trustee, sec. and chmn. finance com. Rollins Coll. Presbyterian. Mason (32°, K.T.), Odd Fellow, Elk, K.P. Home: 614 S. Lake St. Office: 37 E. Pine St., Orlando, Fla. Died June 23, 1946.

O'NEILL, Charles, coal operator; b. near Clearfield, Pa., June 25, 1887; s. Hugh and Hannah (Ward) O.; LL.D. (hon.), St. Francis Coll., Loretto, Pa., 1932; m. Louise Smith, June 25, 1912; children—Mary Dolores (Mrs. William R. Resk), Agnes Josephine (Mrs. James C. Raymond), Charles Patrick, Suzanne, Hugh. Coal miner, 1898; asst. sec. United Mine Workers of America, Dist. 2, 1908-16, vice pres. 1916-18; sec. Central Pa. Coal Producers Assn., 1918-30; vice pres. sales and traffic, Peale, Peacock and Kerr, Inc., N.Y. City, 1930-34, pres. since 1934; pres. United Eastern Coal Sales Corp. since 1936. Chmn. Bituminous Coal Producers adv. bd., Dist. 1, since 1934; tech. adviser to pres. Coal Commn., 1919-20; mem. Solid Fuels Adv. War Council since 1942. Mem. Am. Acad. Professional Science, Soc. Friendly Sons of St. Patrick (N.Y. City). Club: West Chester Country (West Chester, N.Y.). Home: 69 Griffen Av., Scarsdale, N.Y. Office: 420 Lexington Av., New York 17, N.Y. Died Feb. 27, 1949; buried in Fishkill (N.Y.) Rural Cemetery.

O'NEILL, Edward L., ex-congressman; b. Newark, N.J., July 10, 1903; s. Joseph Luke and Margaret Cecilia (Quinn) O'N.; ed. St. James Grammar Sch.; mem. 75th Congress (1937-39), 11th N.J. Dist. Served in U.S. Navy, 1919-23. Democrat. Roman Catholic. Home: Newark, N.J.* Died Dec. 12, 1948.

O'NEILL, James Lewis, banker; b. Pittsburgh, Pa., Oct. 8, 1881; s. James and Martha (Torrance) O.; ed. in pub. schs. of Pittsburgh; m. Dorothy Craig, Jan. 7, 1916; children—James Craig, Martha Torrance, Jeremy Wilson. Began as messenger for Bradstreet Co., 1895-96; with Carnegie Steel Co., Pittsburgh, 1896-1918, becoming credit mgr.; apptd. v.p. Guaranty Trust Co. of New York, May 1, 1918, now operating v.p.; served as control officer NRA, Dec. 1934-June 1935; apptd. adminstr. NRA, Washington, D.C., June 1935; resigned Aug. 1, 1935, after arranging liquidation of that organization; v.p. and director Fidelitas Realty Co., New York; dir. Guaranty Safe Deposit Co., W. T. Grant Co. Apptd. dep. dir. Office of Production Management, 1941. Republican. Presbyterian. Mason (Shriner). Club: Duquesne (Pittsburgh). Home: Short Hills, N.J. Office: 140 Broadway, New York. Died Aug. 21, 1945; buried in Restland Memorial Park, Hanover, N.J.

OPPENHEIM E(dward) Phillips, author; b. 1866; ed. grammar sch.; m. Elsie Hopkins; 1 dau. Author Fortunate Wayfarer, 1928; Light Beyond, 1928; Matorni's Vineyard, 1928; Glenlitten Murder, 1929; Mr. Billingham, The Marquis and Madelon, 1929; Nicholas Goade, 1929; Game of Liberty, 1930; Lion and the Lamb, 1930; Million Pound Deposit, 1930; Slane's Long Shots, 1930; What Happened to Forester, 1930; Clowns and Criminals, 1931; Daughter of the Marionis, 1931; Inspector Dickens Retires, 1931; Simple Peter Cradd, 1931; Up the Ladder of Gold, 1931; Man from Sing Sing, 1932; Shudders and Thrills, 1932; Crooks in the Sunshine, 1933; Jeremiah and the Princess, 1933; Murder at Monte Carlo, 1933; Gallows of Chance, 1934; Man Without Nerves, 1934; Strange Boarders of Palace Crescent, 1934; General Besserley's Puzzle Box, 1935; Spy Paramount, 1935; Advice Limited, 1936; Floating Peril, 1936; Spies and Intrigues, 1936; Ask Miss Mott, 1937; Envoy Extraordinary, 1937; Dumb Gods Speak, 1937; Mayor on Horseback, 1937; Curious Happenings to the Rooke Legatees, 1938; Advice Limited, 1938; Colussus of Arcadia, 1938; Spymaster, 1938; And Still I Cheat the Gallows, 1939; Exit a Dictator, 1939; Pulpit in the Grill Room, 1939; Sir Adam Disappeared, 1939; Grassleyes Mystery, 1940; Last Train Out, 1940; Milan Grill Room, 1941; Shy Plutocrat, 1941; Great Impersonations, 1942; The Pool of Memory, 1942; The Man Who Changed His Plea, 1942. Address La Vauquiedor, Guernsey, C.I., England.* Died Feb. 5, 1946.

ORCUTT, William Warren, oil exec.; b. Dodge County, Minn., Feb. 14, 1869; s. John Hall and Adeline Marion (Warren) O.; grad. Santa Paula (Calif.) Acad., 1891; B.A. in C.E. and geology, Stanford U., 1895; m. Mary Logan, June 9, 1897; children—Gertrude Logan (Mrs. Jeremiah D. Maguire), John Logan. Civil and hydraulic engr. and dep. U.S. surveyor, Santa Paula, 1895-98; with Union Oil Co. of Calif. since 1898, gen. supt. northern div., 1898-99, chief engr. and mgr. geol. and land depts., 1899-1922, v.p. since 1922, and in charge geol. and land depts., 1922-33, in charge of field developments, production, geol. and land depts., 1933-39; retired Jan. 1, 1939; pres. Canoga Citrus Assn., Internat. Development Co., La Merced Heights Land & Water Co.; v.p. Standard Plaster Co., Midway Royal Petroleum Co.; dir. Union Oil Co. of Calif., Semi-Tropic Fruit Exchange. Mem. Am. Soc. C.E. (life), Pacific Geog. Soc., Seismol. Soc. Am., Southern Calif. Acad. Sciences, S.R., Americans Died Apr. 27, 1942.

O'REILLY, Andrew John Goldsmith, elec. and civ. engr.; b. Montgomery County, Mo., Jan. 13, 1863; s. Thomas (M.D.) and Helen Barbour (Dunlop) O'R.; B.E., Washington U., St. Louis, 1888; m. Mary E. Howard, Sept. 3, 1883 (dec.); children—Thomas (dec.), Helen (Mrs. Thomas Caldwell), Elizabeth (Mrs. Charles H. Lewis), Jeannette (Mrs. August J. Johnson), Margarette (dec.); m. 2d, Clara Witte, Feb. 23, 1924 (died Aug. 8, 1934). Began as pattern maker and draftsman, St. Louis, 1878; electrician and operator in Fire Alarm Office, 1884-86; engr. Municipal Electric Light & Power Co., 1889-90; supervisor of city lighting, 1890-1903; pres. Bd. of Pub. Improvements, 1905-09; consultant Laclede Gas Light Co., Union Electric Light & Power Co.; supt. plant construction Miss. River Power Distributing Co. since 1913; safety engr. Nat. Bd. Fire Prevention; mem. Pub. Service Commn. of Mo., 1921-25; chief elec. engr. Dept. Pub. Safety, 1925-32; consultant on public safety. Served as asst. supervisor of gauges, U.S. Ordnance Dept., 1917-19. Mem. A.A.A.S., Am. Inst. E.E., St. Louis Engrs. Club, St. Louis Acad. Science, Am. Geog. Soc., Mo. Acad. Science. Republican. Mason (33°; pres. Masonic Relief Bd.). Address: 2207 S. Grand Blvd., St. Louis, Mo. Died Jan. 27, 1943.

O'ROURKE, Charles Edward (ō-rôrk'), professor and consulting eng.; b. New York, N.Y., June 4, 1896; s. John Aloysius and Lillie Helen (Bailey) O'R.; C.E., Cornell U., 1917; m. Hilda Julia Mullen, Oct. 19, 1917; children—Patricia Ann, Robert Edward. Asst. to city engr., Ithaca, N.Y., 1916; with Wright-Martin Aircraft Co., New Brunswick, N.J., 1919; engr. Tenn. Inspection Bur., 1919; instr. structural engring., Cornell Univ., 1919-23, asst. prof., 1923-34, prof. since 1934; prof. concrete design, Carnegie Inst. Tech., 1921; prof. structural engring., Imperial Peiyang Univ., Tientsin, China (on leave from Cornell), 1926-27; vis. prof. structural engring., U. of Hawaii, 1941; designer Concrete Steel Co., N.Y. City, summers 1921-28; private cons. practice structural engring. 1924-45; consultant Internat. Corr. Schs. Scranton, Pa., 1933-35, cons. editor, same, since 1934; engr. Finger Lakes State Parks Commn., 1936-37; cons. engr., Cooperative Grange League Fed. Exchange, Inc., Ithaca, N.Y., since 1937; engineering consultant American LaFrance-Foamite Corporation, Elmira, New York, since 1943. Served as 2d lieutenant A.S., U.S. Army, Aug. 1917-Dec. 1918, World War. Pres. bd. trustees Union Free Sch., Ithaca; mem. exec. bd. local council, Boy Scouts of America. Mem. Am. Concrete Inst., Cornell Soc. Engrs., Gargoyle, Pyramid (Cornell), Tau Beta Pi, Chi Epsilon, Sigma Phi Sigma. Republican. Episcopalian. Author: Design of Concrete Structures, 1923; Stresses in Simple Structures, 1926; Design of Steel Structures, 1930; Elementary Structural Engineering, 1940 (all with L. C. Urquhart); Handbook of Formulas and Tables for Engineers (with C. A. Peirce and W. B. Carver), 1929. Editor-in-chief: General Engineering Handbook, 1932. Author of following textbooks for Internat. Corr. Schs.: Design of Flat Slab Floors, 1935; Elements of Masonry Design, 1936; Design of Culverts, 1938; Foundations and Piling, 1941. Cons editor Internat. Textbook Co., Civil Engring. Series. Contbr. tech articles to mags. Home: 424 Hanshaw Rd., Ithaca, N.Y. Died Jan. 10, 1947.

O'ROURKE, John T(homas), dir. of grad. and post-grad. studies; b. Saco, Me., Aug. 18, 1888; s. Francis and Bridget (Kearns) O'R.; D.D.S., Louisville (Ky.) Coll. Dentistry, 1917; B.S., Louisville University, 1932; Sc.D. (hon.) University of Louisville, 1944; m. Helen M. Cleaves, Mar. 15, 1918. Instr. dentistry, Louisville Coll of Dentistry, 1917, asst. prof., 1919-23, asso. prof., 1923-25, dean Sch. Dentistry, U. of Louisville, 1926-44. Chmn. com. on dentistry, procurement and assignment services, Fed. Security Agency, since 1941, consultant med. adv. bd., Office Civilian Defense; dir. grad. studies, Tufts Coll. Dental School, since 1944; Member com. Army and Navy Specialized Training Programs since 1942. Mem. Am. Dental Assn. (research com. since 1933; council on dental edn., since 1936; com. on dental preparedness, 1940-42; council on dental edn. since 1937; editorial bd.), Ky. State Dental Assn., Am. Coll. of Dentists (com. on journalism, 1932-36), N.Y. Acad. of Dentistry, Internat. Assn. for Dental Research, Pan-American Dental Assn., Louisville Dist. Dental Soc. (pres. 1931; chmn. Health om., 1932-36), Am. Assn. of Dental Schs. (sec. curriculum com. since 1930; exec. com., 1931-33), Am. Council on Edn. (com. on professional edn.), Louisville Philol. Soc., Omicron Kappa Upsilon, Psi Omega, Phi Kappa Phi, Sigma Xi. Pres. Am. Assn. Dental Schs., 1936. Club: Arts. Collaborator: Course of Study in Dentistry, 1934; Dental Journalism in the U.S., 1934; Dental Education in the United States, 1941. Editor: Journal of Dental Education, 1936-40. Home: New Castle, N.H. Office: 416 Huntington Av., Boston, Mass. Died June 3, 1948.

O'ROURKE, Patrick Ira (ō-rawk'), physician, surgeon; s. Patrick and Rose Ann (Callan) O'R.; student Brown U., 1904-05; M.D., Baltimore Med. Coll., 1909; m. Elizabeth Loretta Durrigan, Apr. 12, 1914; children—John Irving Cletus, Leslie Elmer Linus, Joseph Patrick, Justin Francis, Martha Marie. Asst. physician Mt. Hope Retreat, Md., 1909-10; house physician and surgeon St. Vincents Hosp., Bridgeport, Conn., 1910-11; chief physician Providence (R.I.) Coll., 1919-33; physician in chief St. Joseph's and St. Vincent De Paul Infant Asylum, Providence; mem. staff Roger Williams Gen. Hosp.; physician to Guzman Hall, Providence Coll., St. Pius Convent, Bell St. Chapel; consulting physician in psychiatry to Mount Hope Retreat, Md.; mem. of staffs of St. Joseph's Hosp., Providence College Med. Staff, all of Providence, R.I., pres. and mem. corp. St. Joseph's Hosp.; chief of med. service, sr. surgeon, St. Joseph's Hospital Military Unit; physician to Mount St. Rita's Sisters of Mercy Convent, Cumberland, R.I.; consultant physician, division of jails and reformatories, R.I. Dept. of Pub. Welfare; practice, Providence, R.I., since 1912; mem. med bd. of State of R.I. Retirement Board; mem. med. bd. of Retirement Board of Employees of State of R.I. and Providence Plantations. Served as member Selective Service Bd., R.I., World War; awarded testimonial by gov. of R.I. for service, Sept. 2, 1919; internist Med. Advisory Bd. No. 1, State of R.I., since 1940. Lt. colonel (R), U.S.P.H.S., since Aug. 16, 1943. Made an alumnus of U. of Md., 1924. Mem. A.M.A., R.I. Med. Soc., Providence Med. Soc. (exec. bd.), Holy Name Soc., Physicians Guild of Providence College, Delta Mu; honorary member Omicron Mu. Roman Catholic. K.C. (4°), Elk, Ancient Order Hibernians, Ind. Order Foresters, Modern Woodmen. Clubs: Friendly Sons of St. Patrick (Providence); Nooseneck Hill Rod and Gun (South County, R.I.). Contbr. articles on pneumonia, etc., to med. jours.; also lecturer. Toured Great Britain, visiting hosps. and clinics summers until 1939. Home: Breffny Villa, Riverview, R.I. Office: 60 Academy Av., Providence, R.I. Died April 3, 1948.

OROZCO, Jose Clemente (ŏ-rōz'cō), Mexican painter; b. Zapotlán, Jalisco, 1883; ed. Nat. Agricultural School (degree of agricultural engineer); U. of Mexico.; Academy of Fine Arts, Mexico. Found mem. El Colegio Nacional, Mexico; hon. mem. Am. Soc. Mural Painters, Sociedad de Arquitectos Mexicanos; hon. asso. Nat. Inst. Arts and Letters; corr. mem. Academia Nacional de Bellas Artes, Buenos Aires. Works: "Surrender of Spaniards at San Juan de Ulúa"; murals, Nat. Preparatory School, and Casa de Azulejos, Mexico City, 1922; frescos, New School of Social Research, Pomona Coll., New Sch. for Social Research, N.Y., Dartmouth Coll., others in Mexico. Exhibitions: Paris, New York, Philadelphia, Indiana. Address: Ignacio Mariscal 32 Mexico, D.F. Died Sept. 7, 1949.

ORROK, George Alexander (ôr'rŏk), consulting engr.; b. Dorchester, Mass., July 3, 1867; s. James L. P. and Laura (Davenport) O.; ed. Mass. Inst. Tech., 1885-88; M.E. honora causa, Stevens Inst. of Tech., 1929; m. Jessie Waldo, Dec. 24, 1898; m. 2d, Elene E. Geer, Oct. 20, 1923. With late Dr. F. S. Pearson, engr., 1891-98; with New York Edison Co., 1898-1928, cons. engr. since 1928; mem. Orrok & Myers Associates; lecturer on steam engring., Sheffield Scientific Sch., Yale, 1921-39, on power plant engring., Harvard, 1927-39; cons. engr. Board Water Supply, New York City, and Bureau of Yards and Docks, Navy Department. Honorary member American Society M.E.; mem. Am. Soc. C.E., Am. Inst. Mining Engrs., Inst. of Consulting Engrs., Franklin Inst., Instn. Mech. Engrs. (London). Republican. Unitarian. Club: Engineers (New York). Author: (with Professor R. H. Fernald) Engineering of Power Plants. Contbr. on tech. subjects to periodicals, Proc. Am. Soc. Mech. Engrs., etc. Home: Riverside, Conn. Office: 21 E. 40th St., New York, N.Y. Died Apr. 6, 1944.

ORTON, Samuel Torrey, neuropsychiatrist; b. Columbus, O., Oct. 15, 1879; s. Edward and Anna Davenport (Torrey) Orton; A.B., Ohio State University, 1901; M.D., University of Pennsylvania, 1905, D.Sc., 1945; A.M., Harvard Univ., 1906; m. Mary Pelton Follett, Oct. 15, 1908 (died Sept. 7, 1926); children—Samuel Torrey, Sarah Patterson, Mary Follett; m. 2d, June Frances Lyday, July 16, 1928. Pathologist and clin. dir. Worcester (Mass.) State Hosp., 1910-14; instr. neuropathology, Harvard, 1913; scientific dir. Pa. Hosp., Phila., 1914-19; prof. psychiatry, State U. of Ia., 1919-27, also dir. State Psychopathic Hosp. Neuropathologist, N.Y. Neurol. Inst., 1929-36; prof. neurology and neuropathology, Coll. Physicians and Surgeons (Columbia), 1930-36; Consultant in lang. disabilities, Inst. of Pa. Hosp., Phila., 1943; lecturer in neurology, Clark U., 1913-15. Mem. A.A.A.S., Am. Psychiatric Assn., A.M.A., Am. Assn. Research in Nervous and Mental Diseases, Am. Neurol Assn., N.Y. State Med. Soc., New York Academy of Medicine. Home: 12 E. 86th St., New York 28, N.Y. Died Nov. 17, 1948.

OSBORN, Albert Sherman (ŏz'bērn), author; b. Sharon, Mich., Mar. 26, 1858; s. William B. and Jane (Cole) O.; ed. pub. schs.; D.Sc., Colby Coll., 1938; m. Beth Dunbar, 1888. Examiner of questioned documents since 1887. Pres. Am. Soc. of Questioned Document Examiners since 1942. Mem. Phi Delta Theta. Republican. Unitarian. Mason. Author: Questioned Documents, 1910, 2d edit., 1929; The Problem of Proof, 1922; The Mind of the Juror, 1937, Questioned Document Problems, 1944. Home: 215 Midland Av., Montclair, N.J. Office: 233 Broadway, New York, N.Y. Died Dec. 14, 1946.

OSBORN, Chase Salmon, ex-governor, author; born in Huntington County, Indiana, January 22, 1860; s. George A. (M.D.) and Margaret (Fannon) O. (M.D.); B.S., Purdue University as of 1880; M.D., Detroit College of Medicine, 1909; LL.D., University of Michigan, 1911, Olivet College, 1911, Alma (Michigan) College, 1912, Northwestern U., 1922, Atlanta Law School, 1935; Sc.D. in Natural Science, Wayne U., 1944; m. Lillian G. Jones, May 7, 1881 (died Feb. 4, 1948); children—Ethel Louise, George Augustus, Lillian (dec.), Chase Salmon, Emily Fisher, Oren Chandler (dec.), Miriam Gertrude (dec.), Stella Brunt (adopted; adoption of her as daughter annulled, Apr. 1949); m. 2d, Stellanova Brunt Osborn, Apr. 9, 1949. Began newspaper work on Lafayette (Ind.) Home Journal; went to Chicago on Chicago Tribune and in 1880 to Milwaukee, reportorial and editorial work; purchased 1883, and pub. Florence (Wis.) Mining News; editor Miner and Manufacturer, Milwaukee, 1887; purchased, 1887, Sault Ste. Marie (Mich.) News and pub. it until 1901, when sold it and purchased the Saginaw (Mich.) Courier-Herald, which sold, 1912. Postmaster Sault Ste. Marie, Mich., 1889-93; state game and fish warden, Mich., 1895-99; commr. of railroads for Mich., 1899-1903; regent Univ. of Mich., 1908-11; gov. of Mich., 1911-12; candidate for U.S. Senate, 1918, 28; endorsed by Mich. for Rep. nomination as v.p. of U.S., 1928. Mem. Mich. Unemployment Commn., 1932; hon. chmn. Mich. Rep. State Central Committee, 1934; mem. Com. of 1912 Progressives for Landon, and Rep. presidential elector-at-large for Mich., 1936; v.p. National Com. of Independent Voters for Roosevelt, 1940. Mem. advisory com. Detroit and Mich. Expn., 1935, Mich. Works Progress Adminstrn., 1941. Hon. patron Ga. Bicentennial Commn.; patron founder, mem. advisory council, Herty Forest Inst., Ga.; mem. Future Farmers of America (hon.; Worth County (Ga.) chapter); mem. Gabriel Richard Day Com., Mich., 1937; hon. chmn. Mackinac Straits Bridge Assn.; chmn. State Com. for Mackinac Straits Bridge, 1938; vice chmn. Michigan Good Roads Fedn. Com. for Constl. Amendment No. 3, 1938; vice chmn. Mich. State Chamber of Commerce; nat. councillor Chamber of Commerce of U.S.; trustee and hon. life mem. Detroit Philos. Soc.; trustee, Detroit Hist. Soc.; mem. Advisory Bd. of Trustees Alexander Blain Hosp., Detroit; hon. life mem. Cranbrook Inst. Science. Fellow A.A.A.S.; mem. Lake Superior Mining Inst., Am. Ornithologists Union, Am. Inst. Mining and Metall. Engrs., Seismol. Soc. America, Ga. Mineral. Soc. (hon.), Am. Soc. Mammalogists, Sulgrave Instn., Nat. Audubon Soc., Am. Bison Soc., Am. Huguenot Soc., Mich. Acad. Science, Arts and Letters, Chippewa County (Mich.) Hist. Soc. (hon.), Wilson Ornithol. Club, Am. Pioneer Trails Assn. (charter), Tippecanoe County (Ind.) Hist. Assn., Atlanta (Ga.) Hist. Soc., Macon (Ga.) Hist. Soc., State Hist. Soc. of Mich., Essex County (Ontario) Humane Soc., Mark Twain Soc. America, Am. Geog. Soc., Am. Museum Natural History, Am. Forestry Assn., Mich. Authors Assn., Authors League America, Archeol. Inst. America, Nat. Rifle Assn. America, Lock City Chapter Izaak Walton League America (hon. life), Bibb County (Ga.) Fish and Game Club (hon. life), Northern Mich. Sportsmen's Assn., Sault Koorhaan Fly Club (hon.), Worth County (Ga.) Sportsman's Club, Outdoor Writers Assn. Am. (life), Ore. Trail Memorial Assn. (life), Spanish War Vets. (hon. medal "for extraordinarily distinguished service"), Red Arrow Div. A.E.F. (hon.), Co. B, 107th Engrs. Mich. Nat. Guard (first hon.), Nat. Council of Nat. Economic League, Roosevelt Memorial Association, American Red Cross (honorary chairman Chippewa County, Mich., Chapter), Boy Scouts of America (honorary president Chippewa Area Council; donor of 810 acre Boy Scout reservation for 15 Ga. counties), Sigma Chi (nat. grand orator 1933, 35, 37; grand trustee 1937-39; Significant Sig gold medal 1935), Sigma Rho, Sigma Delta Chi (hon. pres. 1912-19), Pi Gamma Mu (hon.), S.A.R.; hon. mem. Madagascar Acad. of Science (only Am. mem.), Mich. Amateur Press Assn., Georgia Press Assn., Geog. Soc. of Chicago, William T. Hornaday Foundation, National Parks Association, Mississippi Valley Historical Association, Great Lakes Historical Society (trustee), Hon. Sachem of Michigamua (Univ. of Michigan), Norse Civic Assn. Detroit (hon.), Leiv Eriksen Memorial Assn., Detroit. Discoverer of source of firefly's light; also discovered Moose Mountain iron range (Can.) and Ndanga iron range (S.E. Africa). An Accolade for Chase S. Osborn (605 pages) published and presented to him by City of Sault Ste. Marie, 1940; Jan. 22, 1941, proclaimed Chase Salmon Osborn Day in Mich. by Gov. Subject of (book) Eighty and On (by S. B. Osborn), 1941. Republican. Presbyterian. Mason (33°), Elk, Odd Fellow, K.P.; mem. Grange. Clubs: Detroit, University, Detroit Athletic, Prismatic, Gristmill, Purdue, Algonquin (active, life), Three Score and Ten (Detroit); Indiana Soc., Camp Fire of Chicago, University, Cliff Dwellers (Chicago); Press (life; Milwaukee); Nat. Repub., Nat. Arts (1st patron; hon. v.p.), Players, Camp Fire America (New York); Burns, Purdue (Atlanta); Sault Country, Sault Sportsman's (Sault Ste. Marie, Mich.); Kiwanis of Sault Ste. Marie (hon. pres.), Albany, Ga., Sylvester, Ga., and Waycross, Ga.; Lions (hon. life mem.) of Sault Ste. Marie; Heart o' Nature (hon.); Espanore Island (Lake Huron). Author: The Andean Land (2 vols.), 1909; The Iron Hunter, 1919; The Law of Divine Concord, 1921; Madagascar, the Land of the Man-Eating Tree, 1924; Short History of Michigan, 1926; The Earth Upsets, 1927; Following the Ancient Gold Trail of Hiram of Tyre, 1932; Northwoods Sketches, 1934; The Conquest of a Continent (with S. B. Osborn), 1939; Schoolcraft-Longfellow-Hiawatha (with same), 1942; Hiawatha with Its Original Indian Legends (with same), 1944; Errors in Official U.S. Area Figures (with same), 1945; Northwoods Sketches (with same), 1949. Contributing editor for the Detroit Free Press, Official Encyclopedia of Michigan, Michigan volume of Literary Digest's "The American States." Donor of many thousands of acres of Michigan land to various univs. Persuaded U.S. Govt. to add 40,000 square miles to official area of Mich., 21,000 to other Great Lakes states. Home: Sault Ste. Marie, Mich.; (winter) Poulan, Ga. Died Apr. 11, 1949; buried on Duck Island in St. Mary River, Mich.

OSBORN, Frederick Arthur, prof. physics; b. Tecumseh, Mich., Mar. 3, 1871; s. Benjamin A. and Sarah (Whittemore) O.; Ph.B., U. of Mich., 1896, Ph.D., 1907; m. Mary L. Osborn, Aug. 16, 1898; 1 dau., Margaret Anna. Asst. in physics, high sch., Saginaw, Mich., 1890-91; lab. instr. physics, high sch., Ann Arbor, 1893-96; prof. physics, Olivet (Mich.) Coll., 1896-1902; prof. physics and dir. physics labs. U. of Wash., since 1902. Mem. Am. Phys. Soc., Am. Assn. Univ. Profs., A.A.A.S., Illuminating Engring. Soc., Central Assn. Physics and Math. Teachers, Acoustical Soc. of America. Republican. Conglist. Mason. Author: Physics Manual, 1906; College Physics, 1920-24; Physics of the Home, 1925. Home: 17763 15th N.E., Seattle, Wash. Died Dec. 28, 1942.

OSBORN, Monroe, judge; b. Brownwood, Tex., July 15, 1887; s. Elijah J. and Nancy Belle (Jennings) O.; ed. U. of Okla., 1900-05; A.B., U. of Kan., 1907; m. Rowena L. Moseley, May 25, 1912; 1 dau., Nancy Trent. Admitted to Okla. bar, 1908; began practice at Pauls Valley, 1908; mem. firm Blanton, Osborn and Curtis, 1920-33; judge Supreme Court of Okla. since 1933, now chief justice. Mem. Am. Bar Assn. Democrat. Mason. Clubs: University (Oklahoma City); Rotary (Pauls Valley). Home: 801 East Drive. Address: State Capitol, Oklahoma City, Okla. Died June 20, 1947.

OSBORN, Sidney Preston, gov. Ariz.; b. Phoenix, Ariz., May 17, 1884; s. Neri Ficklin and Marilla (Murray) O.; grad. Phoenix Union High Sch., 1903; m. Marjorie Grant, Sept. 1912 (died Dec. 1918); 1 dau., Marjorie Grant; m. 2d, Gladys Smiley, June 1, 1926. Page boy in Territorial Legislature, 1899; sec. to Col. J. F. Wilson, Arizona del. to Congress, 1903-05; youngest rep. to the Constl. Convention, 1910; first sec. of State of Arizona, 1912-19, three terms. Editor and owner Dunbar's Weekly, 1925-41; collector of internal revenue, 1933-34. Inaugurated Gov. of Arizona, Jan. 6, 1941, now serving fourth term. Home: 1615 N. 9th Av., Phoenix, Ariz. Died May 24, 1948.

OSBORNE, Loyall Allen, mech. engr.; b. Newark, N.J., June 22, 1870; s. Frederick Allen and Eliza J. (Rathbone) O.; M.E., Cornell U., 1891; m. Emma Louise Hines, Nov. 27, 1895; children—Loyall A., Nancy B., John S., Louise. Engr., 1891-95, asst. supt., 1895-97, asst. to v.p., 1897-99, mgr. of works, 1899-1902, 4th v.p. in charge of mfg. and engring., 1902-04, 3d v.p., same duties, 1904-06, v.p. in charge of commercial and engring. dept., 1906-17, chmn. Gen. Commercial Com., Westinghouse Electric & Mfg. Co., 1917-29; v.p. New Eng. Westinghouse Co., 1915-19; mem. Nat. War Labor Bd., 1917-19; pres. Westinghouse Electric Internat. Co., 1920-34; now retired. Pres. Stockbridge Library Assn.; mem. Stockbridge Planning Bd.; chmn. Stockbridge Traffic Com. Fellow Am. Inst. Elec. Engrs.; mem. Franklin Inst., Am. Soc. M.E., Nat Industrial Conf Bd. (councillor; ex-chmn.), Kappa Alpha. Republican. Club: University (New York). Home: Stockbridge, Mass. Died Aug. 18, 1944.

OSBORNE, William Hamilton, lawyer, author; b. Newark, N.J., Jan. 7, 1873; s. Joseph P. and Kate (Hamilton) O.; grad. Newark High Sch., 1890; LL.B., New York Law Sch., 1892; m. Lydia Gelston Spring, June 1, 1898; children—William H., Frederick S. Admitted to N.Y. and N.J. bars, 1894, Washington, 1918, practicing N.Y. and N.J.; counsel for Authors League of America and Am. Dramatists. Republican. Author: The Red Mouse, 1909; The Running Fight, 1910; Catspaw, 1911; Blue Buckle, 1914; Boomerang, 1915; Neal of the Navy (moving picture serial), 1915; How to Make Your Will, 1917; also contbr. short stories to mags. Home: 213 Highland Av., Newark, N.J. Office: 744 Broad St., Newark, N.J.; also 6 E. 39th St., New York. Died Dec. 25, 1942; buried Rosedale Cemetery, Orange, N.J.

OSBOURNE, Lloyd, author; b. San Francisco, Cal., Apr. 7, 1868; s. Samuel Osbourne and Fanny Van de Grift (who afterwards married Robert Louis Stevenson); ed. pvt. schs. and U. of Edinburgh; m. Katharine Durham, 1896. Was U.S. vice consul gen. at Samoa, service ending 1897. Author: (with R. L. Stevenson) The Wrong Box, 1889; The Wrecker, 1892; The Ebb Tide, 1894. Author: (alone) The Queen vs. Billy, 1900; Love, the Fiddler; The Motormaniacs, 1905; Wild Justice, 1906; Three Speeds Forward, 1906; Baby Bullet, 1905; The Tin Diskers, 1906; Schmidt; The Adventurer, 1907; Infatuation, 1909; Person of Some Importance, 1911; Harm's Way; The Kingdoms of the World; The Exile (drama, with Austin Strong), starred by Martin Harvey, also The Little Father of the Wilderness. Address: The Lambs, 130 W. 44th St., New York. Died May 22, 1947.

OSGOOD, Wilfred Hudson, naturalist; b. Rochester, N.H., Dec. 8, 1875; s. Marion Hudson and Harriet Amanda O.; A.B., Stanford U., 1899; Ph.D., U. of Chicago, 1918; unmarried. Biologist in U.S. Dept. Agr., 1897-1909; in charge U.S. biol. investigation in Alaska, 1899-1909; asst. curator of mammalogy and ornithology, Field Museum of Natural History, Chicago, 1909-21, curator of zoölogy, 1921-40, retired. Conducted biol. explorations in Alaska, Canada, many parts U.S., Venezuela, Peru, Chile, Argentine, Brazil, Ethiopia, Indo-China; studied in European museums, 1906, 10, 30; spl. U.S. investigator fur-seal question, 1914; leader of Field Museum Abyssinian Expedition, 1926-27, and of Magellanic Expedition, 1939-40. Fellow A.A.A.S., American Ornithologists Union; founder and 1st pres. Cooper Ornithol. Club of Calif.; sec. Biol. Soc. Washington, 1900-09; corr. mem. London Zoöl. Soc., British Ornithol. Union; mem. Am. Soc. Mammalogists (pres. 1924-26), Chicago Zoöl. Soc. (trustee); associate mem. Boone and Crockett Club; Geog. Society, Chicago. Member div. biology, Nat. Research Council, 1919-20. Author of Revision of Pocket Mice, 1900; revision of Mice of Genus Peromyscus, 1909; Biological Investigations Alaska and Yukon, 1909; Fur Seals of Pribilof Islands, 1915 (joint author); Monographic Study of Cænolestes, 1921; Mammals of Asiatic Expeditions, 1932; Artist and Naturalist in Ethiopia, 1936 (joint author); Mammals of Chile, 1943; and about 180 shorter papers on classification, anatomy, and habits of mammals and birds. Contbr. zoöl. definitions to Webster's New Internat. Dictionary. Clubs: University, Quadrangle (Chicago); Explorers (New York). Home: 1155 E. 57th St., Chicago, Ill. Died June 20, 1947.

OSGOOD, William Fogg, mathematician; b. Boston, Mass., Mar. 10, 1864; s. William and Mary Rogers (Gannett) O.; A.B., Harvard, 1886, A.M., 1887; U. of Göttingen, 1887-89; Ph.D., U. of Erlangen, 1890; LL.D., Clark U., 1909; m. Therese Ruprecht, July 17, 1890; children—William Ruprecht, Frieda Bertha (Mrs. Walter Silz; now dec.), Rudolf Ruprecht; m. 2d, Mrs. Céleste Phelps Morse, Aug. 19, 1932. Instr. Harvard, 1890-93, asst. prof. mathematics, 1893-1903, prof., 1903-33, prof. emeritus; prof. mathematics, Nat. U. Peking, China, 1934-36. Mem. Internat. Commn. on the Teaching of Mathematics; editor Annals of Mathematics, 1899-1902, Transactions Am. Math. Soc., 1909-10. Mem. Nat. Acad. of Sciences, Am. Philos. Soc., Am. Math. Soc. (pres., 1904-05), Deutsche Mathematiker-Vereinigung, Leopoldinisch-Carolinisch Deutsche Akademie der Naturforscher, Circolo Matematico de Palermo; corr. mem. Math. Soc. of Charkow, Göttinger Gesellschaft der Wissenschaften; hon. mem. Calcutta Math. Soc.; mem. Phi Beta Kappa. Author: Introduction to Infinite Series, 3d edit., 1906; Lehrbuch der Funktionentheorie, 1905-07; First Course in Differential and Integral Calculus, 1907; Madison Colloquium Lectures, 1914; Analytic Geometry (with W. C. Graustein), 1921; Advanced Calculus, 1925; Functions of Real Variables, 1936; Functions of a Complex Variable, 1936; Mechanics, 1937; also monographs in math. jours. Home: 10 Dorset Rd., Belmont, Mass. Died July 22, 1943.

OSTER, Henry Richard, naval officer; b. Utica, N.Y., May 23, 1895; s. Henry and Carrie (Metzler) O.; B.S., U.S. Naval Acad., 1917; M.S., Mass. Inst. Tech., 1921; naval aviator, Flight Training, Naval Air Sta., Pensacola, Fla., 1932; m. Elda Kay, Dec. 25, 1934. Commd. ensign, U.S. Navy, 1917, advanced through the grades to rear adm., 1946. Specialist in aeronautical engring. since 1922; chief engr. and prodn. supt. Naval Aircraft Factory, Phila., Pa.; dir. design div., Bur. Aeronautics, Navy Dept., asst. chief, 1946-48; gen. rep. Western Dist., Bur. Aeronautics, since 1948; material officer on Adm. Halsey's staff, 1940-43; Bureau of Aeronautics, Western Dist., Los Angeles. Decorated Legion of Merit; Commendation ribbon; Campaign medals: World Wars I and II, Asiatic-Pacific Area, American Area. Home: 858 Devon Av., Los Angeles. Office: 1206 Santee St., Los Angeles 15. Died Aug. 1, 1949; buried in Arlington Nat. Cemetery.

OSTROLENK, Bernhard (ŏs'trō-lĕnk), editor and economist; b. Warsaw, Poland, May 14, 1887; s. Abraham A. and Rachel (Cherniakow) O.; B.Sc., Mass. State Coll., 1911; A.B., Boston U., 1911; studied U. of Minn., summers 1912-15; A.M., U. of Pa., 1919, Ph.D., 1922; hon. academic award, Mass. State Coll., 1936; m. Esther Weinstein, Oct. 10, 1918. Dir. agr., Canby (Minn.) State High Sch., 1913-16, and organizer of several community and co-operative assns.; dir. Nat. Farm Sch., at Farm Sch., Pa., 1916-27; lecturer on agrl. finance, U. of Pa., 1923-26; mem. editorial board The Annalist, 1929-31; dir. Madison House, 1930-31; instructor, assistant and associate professor of economics College City New York, since 1930; economist The Business Week, 1933-34. Sponsor and editor Works Projects Administration project on bibliography of cooperation. Fellow Am. Geog. Soc.; member American Economic Association, Am. Country Life Assn., Am. Farm Economics Assn., Inst. of Cooperation. Author: Social Aspects of the Food Surplus; Harvey Baum—A Study of the Agricultural Revolution (with E. S. Mead); Economics of Branch Banking; The Surplus Farmer; How Banks Buy Bonds (with A. M. Massie); Voluntary Allotment (with E. S. Mead); Electricity—for Use or for Profit; Economic Geography of the United States. Contbr. to Current History, Annalist, Atlantic Monthly, Annals of Acad. Polit. and Social Science, New York Times, etc. Home: Solebury, Pa. Office: 17 Lexington Av., New York, N.Y. Died Nov. 26, 1944.

O'SULLIVAN, Frank, publisher; pres. Country Life Press Corp. Address: Franklin Av., Garden City, Long Island, N.Y. Deceased.

OTERO, Miguel Antonio, ex-governor; b. St. Louis, Oct. 17, 1859; s. Don Miguel Antonio and Mary Josephine (Blackwood) O.; ed. St. Louis U. and Notre Dame U., Ind.; m. Caroline V. Emmett, Dec. 19, 1888; children—Miguel A., 3d (dec.), Miguel A., Jr., Elizabeth Emmett (dec.); m. 2d, Mrs. Maud Pain Frost, Oct. 1, 1913. Cashier San Miguel Nat. Bank, Las Vegas, 1880-85; city treas., Las Vegas, 1883-84; clerk San Miguel County, 1889-90; clerk U.S. Dist. Court, 4th Jud. District, N.M., 1890-93; gov. of N.M., 1897-1906; treas. of N.M., 1909-11; pres. Bd. of Penitentiary Commrs. and Parole Bd., 1913-17; U.S. marshal for Dist. of Canal Zone, Isthmus of Panama, 1917-21; pres. bd. regents, N.M. Normal Univ., 1923-25, 1933-34; chmn. State Adv. Bd., Fed. Emergency Adminstrn. of Pub. Works, 1933. Del. Rep. Nat. convs., 1892, 1900, 04, 08 (chmn. N.M. delegation 1900, 04); chmn. N.M. delegation Progressive Nat. Conv., 1912; mem. Progressive Nat. Com.; del. Progressive Nat. Conv., 1916; mem. Dem. Nat. Conv. (chmn. Canal Zone delegation), 1920, 24; mem. Dem. Nat. Com., 1920-24. Mason (32°, K.T., Shriner), K.P., Elk. Clubs: Santa Fe (N.M.), Panama Golf, Union (Panama). Officer or dir. in several large business enterprises. Author: Conquistadores of Spain and Buccaneers of England, France and Holland, 1925; My Life on the Frontier (1864-1882), 1925; The Real Billy the Kid with New Light on the Lincoln County War, 1935; My Memoirs, 1882 to 1897, 1935; My Nine Years as Governor of the Territory of New Mexico, 1897-1906, 1936. Home: 354 Palace Av., Santa Fe, N.M. Died Aug. 7, 1944.

OTIS, Charles, newspaper pub.; b. Yarmouthport, Mass., Aug. 19, 1872; s. George and Adelaide Frances Justine (Freeman) O.; ed. pub. schs., Yarmouth, Bryant & Stratton Commercial Coll., and Hickox Shorthand Sch., Boston, Mass.; m. Annabel Bodwell Vining, Oct. 10, 1898 (died Dec. 5, 1931); children—Marjorie (dec.), Edward Vining, Ellen (Mrs. Werner Carl Bruchlos), Charles Barron, Annabel (Mrs. Sherman H. Forbes), Viola Victoria Vining (Mrs. Frederick S. Steinmann); m. 2d, Dorothy Bacon Milliken, Jan. 3, 1938. Began with the Boston News Bureau, of which was asst. mgr., 1892-1904; became connected with The Wall Street Journal, 1904-12, and later pres. Dow, Jones & Co., its pubs., later also pres. Doremus & Co., advertising agency; owner and pub. Forest & Stream, 1911-15; pres. and pub. The Bond Buyer since 1913; also pres. and pub. Am. Banker since 1918; pres. West 86th Street Studios; vice-pres. and dir. First Nat. Bank of Yarmouth, Yarmouth Port, Mass. Trustee Gordon Coll. of Theology and Missions, Harlem Eye and Ear Hosp. Pres. Yarmouth Village Improvement Soc. Republican. Pres. bd. of trustees First Baptist Ch., N.Y. City. Club: Cummaquid Golf (Yarmouthport). Home: 257 W. 86th St., New York; (summer) Yarmouthport, Mass. Office: 67 Pearl St., New York, N.Y. Died Sep. 30, 1944.

OTIS, Merrill E., judge; b. Nodaway County, Mo., July 7, 1884; s. Newton and Eunice (Collins) O.; prep. edn., high schs., Hopkins and Maryville, Mo.; A.B., U. of Mo., 1906, hon. fellow in political science, 1906-07, A.M., 1910, LL.B., 1910, LL.D., 1941; LL.D, Park College, Parkville, Mo., 1935; m. Sophie Hersch, Oct. 8, 1916; 1 dau., Dorothy. Admitted to Mo. bar, 1910, Ia. bar, 1911, U.S. Supreme Court bar, 1923; began practice at St. Joseph, 1911; Rep. nominee for Congress, 1914; 1st asst. city counselor, St. Joseph, 1915-16; 1st asst. pros. atty., 1917-18; 1st asst. atty. gen. of Mo., 1921-23; chmn. Public Service Commn. of Mo., 1923-24; asst. to solicitor gen. of U.S., 1924-25; U.S. dist. judge, Western Dist. of Mo., by apptmt. of President Coolidge, since Apr. 25, 1925; pres. and prof. constitutional law, Kansas City School of Law, 1933-38. Mem. bd. of trustees Univ. of Kansas City. Mem. Am. Bar Assn. (mem. of council, sect. legal edn.; mem. of council, sect. judicial administration, chmn. 1941), Mo., Kansas City and St. Joseph bar assns., Am. Judicature Soc. (v.p.), Sons of Revolution (pres. K.C. chapter; v.p. Mo. Soc. 1943), Phi Beta Kappa, Phi Delta Phi, Delta Sigma Rho, Order of Coif. Unitarian. Mason, grand orator Mo. Grand Lodge, 1926-27; 33°. Author: In the Day's Work of a Federal Judge; The Judge to the Jury (1937 Morrison Foundation lecture to Calif. State Bar); A Proposed Tribunal: Is It Constitutional?; The Indeterminate Sentence; Selecting Federal Court Jurors; also addresses to numerous bar assns. Contbr. to legal periodicals. Home: 6417 Jefferson St. Address: U.S. Courthouse, Kansas City, Mo. Died Dec. 23, 1944.

OTT, William Pinkerton, prof. mathematics; b. Steele's Tavern, Va., Dec. 12, 1876; s. Franklin Augustus and Wilmonia (Pinkerton) O.; prep. edn., Ann Smith Acad., Lexington, Va., 1893-96; A.B., Washington and Lee U., 1900, M.A., 1901; Ph.D., U. of Chicago, 1917; unmarried. Instr. mathematics, University Sch., Nashville, Tenn., 1901-09; instr., asst. prof., asso. prof. mathematics, Vanderbilt, 1909-24; prof. and head dept. mathematics, U. of Ala., since 1924. Mem. O.T.C., Ft. Sheridan, Ill., 1918. Mem. Am. Math. Soc., Math. Assn. America, Ala. Acad. Science, A.A.A.S., Phi Beta Kappa, Sigma Xi, Gamma Alpha, Kappa Sigma. Democrat. Presbyn. Home: University, Ala. Now deceased.

OTTE, Hugo Emil (ŏt'tē), banker; b. Chicago, Ill., May 30, 1872; s. Emil and Catherine (Behrman) O.; ed. pub. schs., Chicago; m. Annetta Christian, June 7, 1894; children—Helen (dec.), Howard Allen, Milton Harvey. Began with Union Nat. Bank, Chicago, 1887; continuing until its consolidation with the First Nat. Bank in 1900; in employ of First Nat. Bank until 1904, when organized and became cashier of Union Stock Yards State Bank; later organized and was elected pres. Lake View Trust & Savings Bank; cashier Nat. City Bank, 1907-09, v.p., 1909-24, pres., 1924; upon consolidation of Nat. City Bank with Nat. Bank of the Republic, 1924, was elected pres. of latter, and upon consolidation with Standard Trust & Savings Bank, 1928, was vice chmn. of bd. Nat. Bank of Republic until consolidated, 1931, with Central Trust Co. as Central Republic Bank & Trust Co., and was vice chmn. bd. and dir. until resigned, Feb. 1933, to become pres. Moline Nat. Bank. Mason. Clubs: Bankers (Chicago); Outing (Davenport, Ia.). Home: Le Claire Hotel. Office: Moline National Bank, Moline, Ill. Died Mar. 9, 1942.

OTTLEY, John King (ŏt'lē), banker; b. Columbus, Miss., June 15, 1868; s. John King and Ellen Gertrude (Williams) O.; B.S., LL.D., Southwestern; D.C.S., Oglethorpe U., Atlanta; m. Passie Fenton McCabe, Mar. 21, 1890 (died 1940); children—Passie May (Mrs. George W. McCarty), John K.; m. 2d, Marian Elizabeth Woodward, Oct. 2, 1941. An organizer Fourth Nat. Bank, Atlanta, 1890, pres., 1919-29, when merged with Atlanta-Lowry Nat. Bank as First Nat. Bank, of which is chmn. bd.; dir. Southern Ry. Co., Southern Bell Telephone and Telegraph Co., Mutual Life Ins. Co. of N.Y.; dir. Atlanta Federal Reserve Bank 2 terms, mem. advisory council 1 term. Mem. Am. Bankers Assn. Chmn. bd. of trustees, Y.M.C.A., Atlanta. Democrat. Presbyterian (Elder). Mason (Shriner). Clubs: Capital City, Atlanta Athletic, Piedmont Driving. Home: 3415 Peachtree Rd. Office: First National Bank, Atlanta, Ga. Died Oct. 31, 1945.

OTTO, Benjamin, clergyman; b. New Haven, Conn., Nov. 7, 1862; s. Reinhart and Elizabeth (Kreg) O.; U. of Rochester, 1887; grad. Rochester Theol. Sem., 1890; D.D., U. of Rochester, 1922; m. Katherine Fellman, July 30, 1890; children—Harwood, Ilda (dec.), Gordon. Ordained Baptist ministry, 1890; pastor 2d Ch., Milwaukee, Wis., 1890-94, First Ch., Coldwater, Mich., 1894-97, North Ch., Jersey City, N.J., 1897-1906, First Ch., Kansas City, Mo., 1906-11, First Ch., Peoria, Ill., 1911-15, Morgan Park Ch., Chicago, 1915-20; supt. Bapt. Exec. Council of Chicago, 1920-30. Moderator, East N.J. Assn., 1899, 1900, East N.J. Permanent Council, 1904, 05; mem. exec. com. Northern Bapt. Conv., 1910-14; moderator, Peoria, Ill., Assn., 1914; pres. Ill. Ministers Union, 1919; mem. bd. mgrs. Chicago Bapt. Exec. Council, 1915-20, supt. Council, 1920-30; retired; acting pastor First Ch., Decature, Ill., 1930-31, First Ch., La Grange, 1931-33; spl. rep. Bd. of Missionary Cooperation, 1933; actg. pastor First Ch., Waycross, Ga., 1934, Central Ch., Springfield, Ill., 1935, Avondale Ch., Jacksonville, Fla., 1936, First Bapt. Ch., Wheaton, Ill., 1937, First Bapt. Ch., De Land, Fla., 1938; Southside Ch., Jacksonville, Fla., 1938-39; acting pastor First Bapt. Ch., Tallahassee, Fla., 1940; First Bapt. Ch., De Land, Fla., 1941. Mem. Delta Upsilon. Clubs: Theological, Hamilton, Coldwater Country. Author: Outlines of Life of Christ, 1894; His Death, 1919. Home: 11112 S. Hoyne Av., Chicago, Ill. Died Feb. 16, 1945.

OTTOFY, Ladislaus Michael (ŏt'tō-fī), physician, surgeon; b. Budapest, Hungary, Mar. 11 1865; s. Leopold and Louise (Lauffer) O.; brought to U.S., 1874; ed. pub. schs., St. Louis; M.D., Homeo. Med. Coll. of Mo., St. Louis, 1888; m. Frances Heald (g.d. Maj. Nathan Heald who was in command at Ft. Dearborn at the time of massacre, 1812), Dec. 5, 1894; 5 children. Practiced at St. Louis since 1888, originator serum treatment for cancer. Mem. Internat. Cancer Research Soc. (hon. pres.), St. Louis Soc. Med. Research (hon. pres.), Independent Am. Assn. Progressive Medicine (ex-pres.), Mo. Inst. Homeopathy (treas.), Allied Med. Assns. America (founder), Am. Assn. Orificial Surgeons, Mid-West Homeo. Alumni Assn. (sec.). Democrat. Presbyterian. Mason. Author: Thirty Day Cure for Cancer. Home and Office: 5228 Vernon Av., St. Louis, Mo. Died Oct. 15, 1942.

OUSLEY, Clarence, born in Lowndes County, Ga., December 29, 1863; s. William Henry and Henrietta (Scruggs) O.; A.B., Agrl. and Mech. Coll., Auburn, Ala., 1881; hon. A.M., Simmons Coll., Abilene, Tex., 1906; m. Mary Young, Nov. 8, 1888; children—Mrs. Angie Rosser, Mrs. Clare DuBose. Editor Farm and Ranch, Dallas, Tex., 1886; editorial writer and mng. editor, successively, Galveston News, Galveston Tribune and Houston Post, 1889-1903; founded Ft. Worth Record, Oct. 1903, and was its editor until 1913; made tour of Europe in a study of rural cooperation as a mem. of the Am. Commn., 1913; dir. of extension Agrl. and Mech. Coll. of Tex., 1914-17; asst. sec. of agr., U.S. Aug. 17, 1917-19; chmn. Globe Labs., Fort Worth, Tex., since Sept. 1, 1921. Del. at large Dem. Nat. Conv., 1904. Baptist. Mem. Phi Delta Theta. Address: Globe Laboratories, Fort Worth, Tex. Died Aug. 5, 1948.

OVERHOLSER, Earle Long, horticulturist; b. Kansas City, Mo., Dec. 19, 1888; s. Milton Plean and Fannie Elizabeth (Long) O.; grad. N.M. Mil. Inst., Roswell, N.M., 1909; B.S., U. of Mo., 1913, M.A., 1914; Ph.D., Cornell U., 1926; m. Grace Elizabeth McClary, Oct. 18, 1917; children—Earle Long, Grace Anne. Student asst. in botany U. of Mo., 1911-13, research fellow in botany, 1913-14; instr. pomology Cornell U., 1914-17, asst. prof., 1917-18, exchange prof. at U. of Calif., 1918-19; asst. prof. pomology U. of Calif., 1919-25, sabbatical leave prof. at Cornell U., 1925-26, asst. prof. pomology U. of Calif., 1926-29, asso. prof., 1929-30; prof. horticulture, head dept., and chmn. div. of horticulture State Coll. Wash., and Wash. Agrl. Expt. Sta., 1930-45; head dept. horticulture Va. Poly. Inst., Blacksburg, Va., since 1945. Del. of U. of Calif. and Pacific States Cold Storage Assn. to 4th Internat. Refrigeration Congress, London, Eng., 1924; conducted investigation marine refrigeration fruits enroute to Far East countries, 1929. Pres. Northwest Fertilizer Conf. Horticulturists, 1931-45. Mem. U. of Wash. Arboretum Council, 1940-45; mem. bd. dirs. Va. State Hort. Soc. since 1946; collaborator from Va. Agrl. Expt. Sta., Eastern Region Research Lab., 1947. Fellow A.A.A.S.; mem. Am. Soc. Hort. Science, Am. Soc. Plant Physiology, Am. Bot. Soc., Am. Pomol. Soc., Nat. Assn. Refrigerated Warehouses (hon.), Sigma Xi, Gamma Sigma Delta, Alpha Gamma Rho, Phi Sigma, Epsilon Sigma Phi. Editor V.P.I. sect. in Virginia Fruit. Contbr. to State Expt. Sta. agrl. publs. and other sci. pubs. Home: 801 Draper Rd., Blacksburg, Va. Died April 18, 1949; buried in Orient Cemetery, Harrisonville, Mo.

OVERTON, John Holmes, U.S. senator; b. Marksville, La., Sept. 17, 1875, s. Judge Thomas and Laura (Waddill) O.; A.B., La. State U., 1895; LL.B., Tulane U., 1897; LL.D., Duquesne U., 1939; m. Ruth Dismukes, Dec. 12, 1905; children—Katharine, Ruth, John Holmes (deceased), Mary Elizabeth. Admitted to La. bar, 1898, practiced since at Alexandria; mem. 72d Congress (1931-33), 8th La. Dist.; mem. U.S. Senate, since 1933. Former mem. bd. supervisors La. State U., Louisiana Southwestern U. Mem. Am. Bar Assn., S.A.R.; Soc. of the Cincinnati, Phi Kappa Phi, Sigma Nu. Democrat. Mason (K.T.), Elk. Home: Alexandria, La. Died May 14, 1948; buried in Mt. Olivet Cemetery, Alexandria, La.

OWEN, Charles Sumner, ex-mayor; b. Rochester, N.Y., Jan. 7, 1869; s. Wilbur Fisk and Mary Ellen (O'Connor) O.; ed. pub. schs., Rochester; m. Delphine Augusta Cragg, Apr. 18, 1893 (died Jan. 31, 1929); 1 dau., Dorothy Cragg (Mrs. Glenn Cook Morrow); m. 2d, Augusta Wagoner Castleman, Dec. 28, 1933. Began as errand boy, Sargent & Greenleaf, Inc., Rochester, 1883; salesman, advancing to v.p. Moore & Beir, mfrs. men's clothing, 1886-1908; commr. of pub. safety, Rochester, 1908-14; sheriff of Monroe County, N.Y., 1915-17; pres. and gen. mgr. Chapin-Owen Co., automotive equipment, 1918-29; became councilman at large, Rochester, 1931; mayor of Rochester, 1932-34. Republican. Presbyterian. Mason (Shriner), Elk, Red Man. Clubs: Automobile (pres. 1919), Rochester Ad (pres. 1921-22), Rochester. Home: 455 Mt. Vernon Av., Rochester, N.Y. Died Feb. 1, 1946.

OWEN, D. T., archbishop of Toronto; b. Twickenham, England, July 29, 1878; s. Trevor Randulph and Florence Owen; L.Th., Trinity College, University of Toronto, 1907, D.D., 1916; D.C.L., College of Lennoxville, P.Q.; D.D., Wycliffe Coll., Toronto, 1931, King's Coll., Halifax, N.S., 1937; S.T.D., Columbia, 1942; LL.D., Occidental Coll.; m. Nora Grier Jellett, Apr. 20, 1904; children—Gwynedd Derwyn (Mrs. Charles Monroe), Robert Derwyn, Derwyn Randulph Grier, Margaret Derwyn (Mrs. R.H.R. Gray), David Derwyn (killed in action). Archbishop of Toronto; primate of The Church of England in Canada. Mason (33°). Home: 186 Warren Rd. Office: 135 Adelaide St., E., Toronto, Ontario, Canada. Died Apr. 9, 1947; buried at York Mills, Ont.

OWEN, John Wilson, clergyman, editor; b. Littlestown, Pa., Sept. 3, 1871; s. Rev. Wilson and Margaret Ann (Thompson) O.; B.S., Lebanon Valley Coll., Annville, Pa., 1891, A.B., 1903, A.M., 1904, D.D., 1913; B.D., Union Bibl. Sem., Dayton, O., 1903; m. Minerva Wantz, Apr. 26, 1899; children—John Milton, Charlotte Margaret (Mrs. Robert H. Erisman). Ordained ministry United Brethren in Christ, 1898; pastor Frederick, Md., Walkersville, Md., Duncannon, Marion, Chambersburg and Gettysburg, Pa., High St. Ch., Dayton, O., Mechanicsburg, Pa., Franklin St. Ch., Baltimore, and Fifth Ch., York, Pa., until 1913; asso. editor Sunday Sch. Literature (10 periodicals, weekly, monthly, quarterly), U.B. Ch., 1913-25, editor in chief, 1925-41, editor emeritus since 1941. One of 2 editors of Book of Discipline, U.B. Ch., 1917, 21, 25, 29, 33, 37, 41, 45. Author and compiler, The Pastor's Companion. Author: A Brief History of the Church of the United Brethren in Christ. Statis. sec. 7 yrs., recording sec. 2 yrs., Pa. Conf. U.B. in Christ; mem. Gen. Conf., 1913. Former trustee Lebanon Valley Coll. Treas. Bonebrake Alumnal Assn., 1925-46. Home: 53 Fountain Av., Dayton, Ohio. Died Jan. 27, 1949.

OWEN, Robert Latham, ex-senator; b. Lynchburg, Va., Feb. 3, 1856; s. Robert Latham and Narcissa (Chisholm) O.; A.M., Washington and Lee Univ., 1877, LL.D., 1908; m. Daisey D. Hester, Dec. 31, 1889. Began practice of law, 1880; U.S. Indian agent for the Five Civilized Tribes, 1885-89; organizer First Nat. Bank of Muskogee and was its pres., 1890-1900; interested in banking, real estate, and pub. affairs. Mem. Dem. Nat. Com., 1892-96; U.S. senator from Okla., 3 terms, 1907-25; drafter Federal Reserve Act and Farm Loan Act in U.S. Senate; now engaged in practice of law. Pres. emeritus Nat. Popular Govt. League. Episcopalian. Life mem. Elks. Mason (32°). Office: 2400 16th St., Washington, D.C. Died July 19, 1947.

OWEN, William Frazer, ry. official; b. Mobile, Ala., Mar. 31, 1856; s. John Garland and Susan (Frazer) O.; ed. pub. schs.; m. Jennie Octavia Read, May 15, 1878 (died Nov. 26, 1910); m. 2d, Mary Cornelia Taylor, Sept. 15, 1921. Clerk, ticket agt. and asst. to freight agt., New Orleans, Mobile & Tex. R.R., at Mobile, 1871-77; clerk, freight agt., New Orleans, and passenger conductor, 1877-80; with Morgan's La. & Tex. R.R., as pass. conductor, master of trains, chief dispatcher, master of transportation and supt., 1880-1905; pres. New Orleans, Crowley & Western R.R., 1906-07; asst. to pres. Mobile, Jackson & Kansas City R.R., July-Aug. 1907; gen. mgr. same rd., 1907-09; gen. mgr., New Orleans, Mobile & Chicago R.R. Co., 1909-10, v.p. and gen. mgr., 1910-12, pres. and gen. mgr., 1912-13, and receiver, 1913-16; pres. Gulf, Mobile & Northern R.R. Co., 1917-18; gen. mgr. same, and Meridian & Memphis R.R., under U.S. R.R. Administration, 1918-20; retired. Home: 1257 Selma St., Mobile, Ala. Died Nov. 18, 1943.

OWENS, James Francis, pub. utilities; b. near Aurora, Ill., Apr. 1, 1878; s. Hugh and Sarah (Crane) O.; ed. Kan. State Teachers Coll., Emporia, and University of Kansas; m. Bessie Cloyd Turner, June 19, 1907 (died December 16, 1938); children—Hugh Franklin, James Francis, Betty June; m. 2d, Mrs. Esther Maynard, May 19, 1941. President, director Oklahoma Gas and Electric Company, Oklahoma City. Mem. Am. Assn. Engrs., Edison Electric Inst. (mem. operating com.), Nat. Electric Light Assn. (past pres.), U.S. Chamber Commerce (dir., v.p. and mem. exec. com.), Chamber Commerce State of Okla. (dir.). Democrat. K.C., Knight of St. Gregory. Clubs: Oklahoma University, Rotary (ex-pres.), Oklahoma City Golf and Country. Home: 6512 Hillcrest Av., Nichols Hills. Address: Oklahoma Gas & Electric Co., Oklahoma City, Okla. Died Feb. 20, 1942.

OWENS, Thomas L(eonard), congressman; b. Chicago, Ill., Dec. 21, 1897; s. John P. and Hannah (Burke) O.; LL.B., Loyola Univ., Chicago, Ill., 1926, LL.M., 1927; m. Emma Florence Ekberg, June 26, 1929; children—Charles John, Colleen Joan, Carol Jane. Wrapping clerk Sears Roebuck & Co., Chicago, 1911; machinist, accountant Crane Co., Chicago, 1911-19; salesman Western Plumbing Supply Co. (now Tyne Co.), Chicago, 1919-27; admitted to Ill. Bar, June 1927; practiced law in firm of Owens and Owens, Chicago, 1927-47; mem. 80th Congress (1947-49), 7th Dist. Ill. Mem. Am. Bar Assn., Ill. State Bar Assn., Chicago Bar Assn. Am. Legion, Lincoln Turner Orgn., Delta Theta Phi. Club: Executive's of Chicago. Home: 5731 N. Sacramento Av., Chicago 45, Ill. Office: 160 N. LaSalle St., Chicago 1, Ill. Died June 7, 1948.

OZLIN, Thomas William (ŏz'lin), lawyer; b. Lunenburg County, Va., July 12, 1884; s. William Thomas and Emma Virginia (Andrews) O.; prep. edn., La Crosse (Va.) Acad.; A.B., U. of Richmond, 1909, LL.B., 1909; m. Letty L. Hobgood, June 17, 1914 (died Mar. 31, 1924); m. 2d, Virginia Masten, Dec. 21, 1927. In practice at Kenbridge, Va., 1910-33; atty. Virginian Ry. Co.; Va. State Bankers Assn., The Bank of Lunenburg; dir. Farm Credit Adminstrn., Baltimore, since 1933. Mayor of Kenbridge, 1912-16; mem. Va. Ho. of Dels., 1916-30, speaker of House, 1926-30; vice chmn. Va. State Dem. Com., 1929-33; active in adoption of new constn., 1926-30; mem. State Corp. Commn. of Va. since 1933 (chmn. 1935, 38, 41, 44). Enlisted overseas service with Am. Red Cross, 1918. Mem. Am., Va. State bar assns., Phi Beta Kappa, O.D.K. Baptist, Mason, Shriner, Elk. Club: Kenbridge Golf. Active in bldg. state system of highways on "pay-as-you-go" plan. Home: Beaverdam, Va. Office: State Office Bldg., Richmond, Va. Died July 14, 1944.

P

PACE, Homer St. Clair, educator; b. Rehoboth, O., Apr. 13, 1879; s. John F. and Elizabeth Ellen (Hamilton) P.; C.P.A., Univ. State of N.Y.; m. Mabel E. Vanderhoof, 1898; children—Helen (Mrs. George Bowen), Robert S., Charles R. Pres. Pace Inst.; formerly editor and propr. The American Accountant; formerly prof. Columbia U.; served as acting dept. commr. Bur. Internal Rev., Treasury Dept.; reorganized and directed income tax unit, 1918-19. Mem. Am. Inst. Accountants, N.Y. Soc. Certified Public Accountants (former president). Republican. Mason. Author: Pace Secretarial Accounting and Financial Procedure; Theory and Practice of Accounts, 1917; Procedure and Practice of Auditing; Comprehensive Propositions in Accounting, 1939; Comprehensive Accounting and Financial Procedure; Personality Improvement. Home: 40 Monroe Pl., Brooklyn. Office: 225 Broadway, New York, N.Y. Died May 22, 1942.

PACKARD, Bertram E., educator; b. Augusta, Me., March 1, 1876; son Edward T. and Lois A. (Lapham) P.; graduated Litchfield (Me.) Academy, 1896; A.B., Bates Coll., Lewiston, Me., 1900, Ed.D., 1931; LL.B., University of Maine, 1910, honorary LL.D., from same, 1942; married Helen E. Bisbee, July 20, 1910; children—Martha Bisbee, Lucia Martin. Prin. Litchfield Acad., 1900-03, Leavitt Inst., Turner, Me., 1903-07, high sch., Hallowell, Me., 1907-08; supt. schs., Camden and Thomaston, Me., 1909-18, Sanford, Me., 1918-22; dep. state commr. of edn., Me., 1922-29, state commr. of edn., 1929-41; retired. Trustee U. of Maine, Maine Inst. for the Blind, 1929-41; trustee Bates College. Member Maine Historical Soc. Republican. Congregationalist. Mason. Clubs: Rotary, College. Author: A Bit of Old England in New England, 1925; John Gardiner—Barrister, 1926. Home: 127 Sewall St., Augusta, Me. Died Dec. 10, 1945.

PACKARD, Frank Lucius, author; b. of Am. parents, Montreal, Que., Can., Feb. 2, 1877; s. Lucius Henry and Frances (Joslin) P.; B.A.Sc., McGill U., 1897; post-grad. course L'Institut Montefiore, U. of Liège, Belgium, 1898; m. Marguerite Pearl Macintyre, Aug. 31, 1910; children—Lucius Henry, Robert Joslin, Horace Frank, Marguerite Pearl. Engaged in engring. work in U.S. for a number of yrs.; began writing for magazines, 1906. Mem. Phi Sigma Kappa. Mason (K.T.). Clubs: University, Royal Montreal Golf. Author: On the Iron at Big Cloud, 1911; Greater Love Hath No Man, 1913; The Miracle Man, 1914; The Beloved Traitor, 1916; The Adventures of Jimmie Dale, 1917; The Sin That Was His, 1917; The Wire Devils, 1918; The Further Adventures of Jimmie Dale, 1919; The Night Operator, 1919; From Now On, 1920; The White Moll, 1920; Pawned, 1921; Doors of the Night, 1922; Jimmie Dale and the Phantom Clue, 1922; The Four Stragglers, 1923; The Locked Book, 1924; Running Special, 1925; Broken Waters, 1925; The Red Ledger, 1926; Two Stolen Idols, 1927; The Devil's Mantle, 1927; Shanghai Jim, 1928; Tiger Claws, 1928; The Big Shot, 1929; Jimmie Dale and the Blue Envelope Murder, 1930; The Gold Skull Murders, 1931; The Hidden Door, 1932; The Purple Ball, 1933; Jimmie Dale and the Missing Hour, 1935; The Dragon's Jaws, 1937; More Knaves Than One, 1938. Home: Lachine, Que., Can. Died Feb. 17, 1942.

PACKARD, George, lawyer; b. Providence R.I., May 27, 1868; s. William L. and Mary Easton (Peckham) P.; A.B., Brown, 1889; LL.B., Northwestern, 1891; m. Caroline Howe, Jan. 23, 1893; children—Dorothy (Mrs. F. Farrington Holt), Frank H., Mary (Mrs. Fred W. Copeland). Admitted to bar, 1891, and entered office of Peckham & Brown; now mem. Packard, Barnes, Schumacher & Gilmore. Member Am., Ill. State and Chicago bar assns., Chicago Ethical Soc. (ex-pres.), Law Club. Democrat. Clubs: Chicago Literary, University. Home: 436 Barry Av., Chicago; (summer) Mackinac Island, Mich. Office: 38 S. Dearborn St., Chicago. Died Oct. 1, 1949.

PACKARD, Winthrop, naturalist; b. Boston, Mass., Mar. 7, 1862; s. Hiram Shepard and Maria (Blake) P.; Mass. Inst. Tech., class of 1885; m. Alice Harrington Petrie, 1905; children—John Winthrop, Theodore, David. Chemist with Henry A. Gould & Co., Boston, 1885; with A. W. Folsom & Co., Boston, 1889; editor Canton (Mass.) Journal, 1894; associated with National Magazine, Boston, 1896; editorial staff, Youth's Companion, 1899; mem. Corwin exploring expdn. to Alaska, Siberia and the Arctic, 1900, as corr. for Boston Transcript, New York Evening Post and St. Paul Dispatch. Then special article writer on Boston Transcript, and in general journalism; editor The New England Magazine, 1905-08. Served 3 yrs. in Mass. Naval Brigade; landsman, ordinary seaman and able seaman U.S. Navy, in Spanish-Am. War, 1898; 1st lt. Co. D, 13th Regt., Mass. State Guard, 1917. Field sec., Nat. Assn. Audubon Socs., 1914-18; field sec., then sec.-treas. and exec. officer Mass. Audubon Soc., 1913-36, an incorporator, 1915, established and financed society's nat. known Moose Hill Bird Sanctuary at Sharon, Mass., and established its ednl. and protective work there. Founder and editor Bull. of Mass. Audubon Soc., 1914-36. Established "Everything for Wild Birds," a nat. service in bird study and protection, 1936. Author: The Young Ice Whalers, 1908; Wild Pastures, 1909; Wildwood Ways, 1909; Woodland Paths, 1910; Wood Wanderings, 1910; Florida Trails, 1910; Literary Pilgrimages of a Naturalist, 1911; White Mountain Trails, 1912; Old Plymouth Trails, 1920; He Dropped Into Poetry, 1940. Home: Canton, Mass. Died Apr. 1, 1943.

PADDOCK, Charles William, editor; b. Gainesville, Tex., Aug. 11, 1900; s. Charles Hurd and Lulu (Robinson) P.; B.A., Southern Calif. U. at Los Angeles, 1922; Ph.D., U. of Paris, 1923; m. Neva Prisk, Dec. 11, 1930; children—Prisk, Paddy. Began as newspaper man, 1914; successively reporter, sports writer, short story writer, syndicate feature writer, editorial writer, columnist, business mgr. of newspapers, lecturer and editor; writer of column, "Thoughts of the Day," a daily feature, and editorial column, "Editorial Views of the Star-News," for the Star-News, Pasadena; v.p. and gen. mgr. Star-News Pub. Co., Star-News Building Co.; v.p. and sec. Press Co. and Press-Telegram Pub. and Bldg. Cos. of Long Beach. Mem. bd. dirs. Am. Red Cross, Boy Scouts, Community Chest, Long Beach Chamber of Commerce, Pasadena Preferred, Inc. Served as 2d lieutenant Field Artillery, 1918-19. Awarded Order of Danilo. Member Kappa Alpha (Southern), Delta Sigma Rho, Skull and Dagger. Republican. Mem. Christian Ch. Mason (32°). Clubs: Annandale, University, Athenaeum, Overland (Pasadena); Virginia, Pacific Coast (Long Beach); Los Angeles Athletic; Paris University. Author: The Fastest Human, 1932; Track and Field, 1933. Contbr. to Collier's, Saturday Evening Post, etc. Winner of 100 meter Olympic championship, 1920; Am. champion, 1920-29; Inter-Allied champion 100 and 200 meters, 1919. Home: 985 Linda Vista Av. Office: Star-News, Pasadena, Calif. Died July 22, 1943.

PADDOCK, Hiram Lester, mfr.; b. Wolcott, N.Y. June 8, 1860; s. William Warren and Mary Albertine (Lester) P.; ed. pub. schs. of Wolcott and Cazenovia (N.Y.) Sem.; m. May L. Weeks, June 17, 1886 (died 1925); 1 dau., Imogene (Mrs. Frank C. Ash). V.p. Lakeside Paper Co., Skaneateles, N.Y., 1885-95; treas. Oswego Falls Pulp & Paper Co., Fulton, N.Y., 1895-1906, pres., 1906-22; pres. Oswego Falls Corp., 1922-45, also chairman of bd. since 1922; chmn. bd. Sealright Corp.; chmn. bd. and dir. Citizens Nat. Bank & Trust Co., Fulton; pres. Oswego County Independent Telephone Co., 1906-18; vice pres. Albert Lindley Lee Memorial Hosp., 1908-39. Mem. English Speaking Union. Republican. Methodist (trustee First M.E. Church). Clubs: Fulton, Lake Placid. Address: Fulton, N.Y. Died June 22, 1948.

PADELFORD, Frank William, clergyman; b. Haverhill, Mass., Apr. 6, 1872; s. Adoniram Judson and Julia Smith (Morgan) P.; A.B., Colby Coll., Me., 1894, A.M., 1897, D.D., 1911; grad. Rochester Theol. Sem., 1897; LL.D., Denison U., Granville, O., MacMaster U., Hamilton, Ont., Can.; m. Grace C. Ilsley, Aug. 3, 1897 (deceased); 1 son, Norman Judson; m. 2d, Gertrude Lois Ilsley, Feb. 15, 1922. Ordained Bapt. ministry, 1897; pastor Portland St. Ch., Haverhill, Mass., 1897-1903, Washington St. Ch., Lynn, Mass., 1903-08; gen. sec. Mass. Bapt. Missionary Soc., Boston, Apr. 1908-13; exec. sec. Bd. of Edn., Northern Bapt. Conv., 1912-41. Mem. citizens com. of 4 which secured commn. form of govt. for Lynn. Mem. Ednl. Commn. to China, 1921-22, to Japan (chmn. Am. sect.), 1931-32, to India, 1932-33. Mem. Delta Kappa Epsilon, Phi Beta Kappa, Pi Gamma Mu. Republican. Author: The Commonwealths and the Kingdom. Co-Author: Christian Education in China; Christian Education in Japan. Clubs: University, Theological (Boston). Home: Robbinston, Me. Died Feb. 18, 1944.

PADELFORD, Frederick Morgan, coll. prof.; b. Haverhill, Mass., Feb. 27, 1875; s. Adoniram Judson and Julia Smith (Morgan) P.; A.B., Colby Coll., 1896, A.M., 1899, LL.D., 1934; Ph.D., Yale, 1899; LL.D., Mills Coll., Oakland, Calif., 1936; research work, British Museum and Oxford, 1905-06; research visiting scholar Huntington Library, 1935-36; m. Jessie Elizabeth Pepper, July 6, 1899; children—Morgan Grassie, Eunice Brewster (Mrs. James W. Clise, Jr.), Philip Sidney, Charles Gordon. Fellow Yale, 1898-99; prof. English, U. of Ida., 1899-1901; prof. English since 1901, dean Grad. Sch. since 1920, asst. dean of Faculties, 1927-31, asst. v.p., 1931-32, U. of Wash. Trustee Seattle Pub. Library, 1906-13, Seattle Art Museum since 1934; pres. Seattle Art Inst., 1907-10. Mem. Nat. Inst. Social Sciences, Am. Assn. Univ. Profs., Modern Lang. Assn. (v.p. 1941), Shakespeare Assn. America (v.p.), Delta Kappa Epsilon, Phi Beta Kappa (Senator). Clubs: Andiron (N.Y.), Monday (Seattle). Author: Old English Musical Terms, 1900; Early Sixteenth Century Lyrics, 1906; The Political and Ecclesiastical Allegory of the Faerie Queen, 1911; Samuel Osborne, Janitor, 1913; George Dana Boardman Pepper, A Biographical Sketch, 1914. Editor: The Poems of Henry Howard, Earl of Surrey, 1920, 28. Translator: Essays on the Study and Use of Poetry, by Plutarch and Basil, 1902; Select Translations from Scaliger's Poetics, 1905. Editor: Comedy of Errors; Tudor Shakespeare, 1913; The Ring and the Book, 1917; (with W. Howe and H. M. Ayres) Modern Student's Book of English Literature, 1924; (with Edwin Greenlaw, C. G. Osgood, and Ray Heffner) The Works of Edmund Spenser (variorum edit., 10 vols.); The Axiochus of Plato (transl. by Spenser), 1934. Contbr. to Cambridge History of English Literature and to European and Am. mags. Home: 4710 20th Av. N.E., Seattle, Wash. Died Dec. 3, 1942.

PADGETT, Earl C., plastic surgeon; b. Greenleaf, Kan., July 8, 1893; s. John Manson and Martha (McGinnis) P.; B.S., U. of Kan., 1916; M.D., Washington U., 1918; m. Winona Youmans, June 1, 1922; children—Joyce, Patricia, Earl, Calvin. Served as 1st lt. U.S. Army Med. Service, Base Hosp. 21, Rouen, France, 1918-19; successively interne, asst. resident and resident in surgery, Washington U., St. Louis, 1919-22; asst. to Dr. V. P. Blair, St. Louis, 1922-24; in practice of plastic surgery, Kansas City, Mo., since 1926; successively instr., asst. prof., asso. and prof. clin. surg. U. of Kan. Sch. of Medicine, 1925-43; clin. prof. oral surgery, U. of Kan. City Sch. of Dentistry, since 1926. On staff Mercy Hosp., Kansas City Gen. Hosp., Providence Hosp., exec. staff, St. Luke's Hosp. Conceived idea of a dermatome for cutting skin grafts in 1938, developing and designing same with mech. aid of George J. Hood. Received Distinguished Citizenship award for invention of dermatome, Am. Legion, 1940. Mem. founders' group Am. Bd. Surgery, Am. Bd. Plastic Surgery; fellow Am. Coll. Surgeons; mem. Am. Surg. Assn., A.M.A., Western Surg. Assn., Am. Assn. for Surgery of Trauma, Alpha Tau Omega, Nu Sigma Nu, Sigma Xi, Alpha Omega Alpha. Contbr. articles, especially on skin grafting, to med. jours. Home: 1425 Brookwood Rd. Office: 1316 Professional Bldg., Kansas City, Mo. Died Dec. 2, 1946.

PADWAY, Joseph A(rthur), lawyer; b. Leeds, Yorkshire, Eng., July 25, 1891; s. Morris and Rose Padway; prep. education grade and high school in Eng.; LL.B., Marquette U., 1912; m. Lydia Rose Paetow, Mar. 9, 1912; 1 dau., Ruth Doris. Admitted to Wis. bar, 1912, and practiced in Milwaukee; general counsel Wisconsin State Federation of Labor since 1915, and author of much labor legislation in Wis.; apptd. by gov. of Wis. as judge of Civil Court of Milwaukee County, 1925 (elected for full term, 1926, resigned, 1927); gen. counsel A. F. of L. since 1938; gen. counsel of a number of internat. unions affiliated with A. F. of L.; prof. of labor law, Columbus U., Washington, D.C. State senator, Wis., 1925; regent of the state teachers colleges of Wis., 1933-38. Mem. Progressive Party of Wis. Club: Milwaukee Athletic. Contbr. to law revs. and author of labor treatises. Home: La Jolla, Calif. Office: Bowen Bldg., Washington, D.C. Died Oct. 8, 1947.

PAGE, Curtis Hidden, writer, educator; b. Greenwood, Mo., Apr. 4, 1870; s. Benjamin Greely and Martha Frances (Hidden) P.; A.B., Harvard, 1890, A.M., 1891, Ph.D., 1894; U. of Paris, 1894-95; U. of Florence, 6 months, 1900; hon. A.M., Dartmouth, 1911; unmarried. Instr. French and lecturer on English literature, Western Reserve, 1891-92; instr. French, Harvard, 1893-94; lecturer and tutor, 1895-1906, adj. prof., 1906-08, prof. Romance langs.

and lits., 1908-09, Columbia; prof. English lit., Northwestern U., 1909-11; prof. English language and lit., Dartmouth Coll., since 1911. Asso. editor Poet Lore, 1905, The Pathfinder, 1906; univ. extension lecturer on English literature from 1891. Mem. N.H. State Legislature, 1933-34; State senator, 1939-40, and 1941-42; moderator, Town of Gilmanton, 1930-46; mem. Coastl. Conv., State of N.H., 1938-41; mem. State Library Commn., State of N.H., since 1941. Member Modern Language Assn. of America, Dante Soc., Dunlap Soc., Phi Beta Kappa, Delta Upsilon; fellow Am. Acad. of Arts and Sciences; pres Poetry Soc. America; v.p. Poetry Soc. of Great Britain. Trustee and treas. Gilmanton (N.H.) Acad. Clubs: Century, Authors, Andiron (New York); Authors' (London). Translator: A Voyage to the Moon, by Cyrano de Bergerac, 1899; Songs and Sonnets of Ronsard, 1903; new edit., re-written, 1924; The Best Plays of Molière (2 vols.), 1907; Tartuffe, in The Harvard Classics, 1909; the same, in Chief European Dramatists, 1915; The Man Who Married a Dumb Wife, by Anatole France, 1915; Tartuffe, prod. by Donald Robertson in Chicago, 1909, in Pittsburgh, 1915; The Learned Ladies, by The Drama Players, New York and Chicago, 1911-12; The Man Who Married a Dumb Wife, by Granville Barker, New York, Boston, etc., 1915-16, and London, 1917. Contbr. of poems, essays, stories in leading mags. Editor: British Poets of the Nineteenth Century, 1904, new enlarged edition, 1930; Rabelais (in series of French Classics for English Readers), 1905; The Chief American Poets, 1905. Author: A History of Japanese Poetry (with 230 translations), 1923. Pvt. Mil. Stores School, June 1917; commd. capt. and called to active service, Dec. 20, 1917; maj. U.S. Army, Oct. 25, 1918; comd. 2d Regt. Ordnance Corps and later Penniman (Va.) Gen. Ordnance Depot; commd. maj. U.S.R., Jan. 20, 1920. Home: Gilmanton, N.H. Died Dec. 12, 1946.

PAGE, George Bispham, architect. Mem. Am. Inst. Architects since 1899, fellow since 1931. Address: 315 S. 15th St., Philadelphia, Pa. Deceased.

PAGE, Herman, bishop; b. Boston, Mass., May 23, 1866; s. Eben Blake and Harriet Josephine (Woodward) P.; A.B., Harvard, 1888; B.D., Episcopal Theol. Sch., Cambridge, Mass., 1891; (D.D., U. of Pittsburgh, 1906); m. Mary M. Riddle, June 25, 1891; 1 son, Herman Riddle. Deacon, 1891, priest, 1891, P.E. Ch.; in charge mission chs. at Wallace and Coeur d'Alene, Ida., 1891-1900; rector St. John's Ch., Fall River, Mass., 1900, St. Paul's, Chicago, Oct. 1900-14; consecrated bishop of Spokane, Wash., Jan. 28, 1915; became bishop of Mich., Nov. 1923; became provisional bishop of Northern Mich., Nov. 1939; resigned as bishop of Mich., Dec. 31, 1939. Address: 1817 Cambridge Rd., Ann Arbor, Mich. Died Apr. 21, 1942.

PAGE, Ralph Walter, journalist; b. St. Louis, Mo., Oct. 2, 1881; s. Walter Hines and Willia Alice (Wilson) P.; A.B., Harvard, 1903, LL.B., 1906; m. Leila Heywood Tuckerman, Oct. 2, 1911; children—Leila Cary (died Feb. 12, 1933), Anderson. Began as clerk in law office, 1906; partner law firm Franklin & Page, 1908-10; planter, North Carolina, 1910-33, banker, North Carolina, 1920-33; mem. staff Philadelphia (Pa.) Evening Bulletin since 1933, writer of daily Washington column since 1943. Attended 1st Plattsburg O.T.C., 1915. Clubs: Century Association, Harvard (New York); Art Alliance, Franklin Inn (Philadelphia); Cosmos (Washington). Author: Dramatic Moments in American Diplomacy, 1916. Home: 1 Scott Circle. Office: 1276 National Press Bldg., Washington, D.C. Deceased.

PAGE, Robert Powel, Jr., automobile mfr.; b. Boyce, Va., Jan. 30, 1879; s. Robert Powel and Agnes (Burwell) P.; m. Helen Hamilton, June 1908; children—Robert Powel III, Hamilton, Peter Mayo (dec.). Successively salesman, Boston mgr., New Eng. dist. mgr., gen. sales mgr., The Autocar Co., Ardmore, Pa., now pres. Home: 250 Golf View Rd. Office: The Autocar Co., Ardmore, Pa. Died June 18, 1949; buried at Millwood, Va.

PAGE, Roger McKeene, journalist; b. Opelika, Ala., May 8, 1876; s. William Byrd and Annie M. (Greene) P.; ed. public schools Opelika; m. Louise Olivia Seals, June 15, 1904; children—Roger McKeene, Annie Louise (Mrs. William A. Bugg), Nettie Byrd (Mrs. Norman C. Wilson), W. Marion. Began as newspaper carrier on Columbus Ledger, 1890, becoming circulation mgr. for 10 years, and later city news editor and telegraph editor 7 years, asso. editor and editor 1910-30; editor in chief Ledger-Enquirer and sec. Ledger-Enquirer Co. since 1930. Mem. Chamber of Commerce, Ga. Press Assn., Southern Newspaper Pubs. Assn. Democrat. Methodist. K.P. Clubs: Kiwanis, Executives. Home: 1414 Forest Av. Office: 12th and Front Sts., Columbus, Ga. Died Nov. 19, 1942.

PAGE, William Tyler, retired clk. House of Rep.; b. Frederick, Md., Oct. 19, 1868; s. Walker Yates and Nannie (Tyler) P.; ed. acad. and pub. schs.; m. Mary Anna Weigandt, July 25, 1895 (dec.); children—Nannie Tyler (wife of H. W. Pierce, U.S. Navy), John Caspar, Eleanor L'Hommedieu (Mrs. Gordon F. Fox), Mary Addison (wife of J. H. Cronin, U.S. Navy), Catherine L'Hommedieu (dec.), William Tyler. Apptd. page in clk.'s office, U.S. Ho. of Rep., 1881, and in continuous service of the House, elected clk., May 19, 1919, and reëlected in each succeeding Congress until 1931. Clk. to the minority, U.S. Ho. of Rep., since 1931. Exec. sec. U.S. Commn. for Celebration of the 200th Anniversary of Birth of George Washington. Rep. nominee for Congress, 2d Md. Dist., 1902. Pres. Rep. State Voters' Assn. Episcopalian. Author: Page's Congressional Hand-Book, 1913. Wrote "The American's Creed," 1917. Address: 220 Wooten Av., Chevy Chase, Md.* Died Oct. 20, 1942.

PAHLOW, Edwin William (pä'lō), college prof.; b. Milwaukee, Wis., Jan. 11, 1878; s. Lewis F. and Anna (Becher) P.; B.L., U. of Wis., 1899; A.M., Harvard, 1901, Ph.D., 1912; m. Gertrude Curtis Brown, June 14, 1905 (she died Jan. 29, 1937); children—Hugh, Gertrude. Instr. in history, U. of Wis., 1905-06; preceptor, Princeton, 1907-10; head of history dept. Lawrenceville (N.J.) Sch., 1912-21, Ethical Culture Sch., New York, 1922-25; prof. teaching of history, Ohio State U., since 1925. Dean U.S. Army Ednl. Corps, Gt. Britain, 1918-19. Mem. Am. Hist. Assn., Phi Delta Kappa, Beta Theta Pi. Episcopalian. Home: 2026 Iuka Av., Columbus, O. Died June 19, 1942.

PAINE, Gregory Lansing, univ. prof.; b. Garrattsville, N.Y., Nov. 15, 1877; s. Lansing Barker and Julia (Gergory) P.; student State Teachers Coll., Albany, N.Y., 1900-02; Ph.B., Univ. of Chicago, 1914, A.M., 1920, Ph.D., 1924; m. Alice Thompson, Sept. 8, 1914. Teacher Shattuck Sch., Faribault, Minn., 1906-13; Normal Sch., Mayville, N.D., 1914-20; prof. English, Fargo (N.D.) Coll., 1920-21; asst. prof. English, Univ. of N.C., 1924-28, asso. prof., 1928-32, prof. since 1932; teacher summer session, Univ. of Ia., 1927, Univ. of Mich., 1932, Univ. of Wis., 1939; Mem. Modern Lang. Assn., Bibliographical Soc. of Am., Phi Kappa Sigma. Protestant Episcopalian. Editor: Annual Bibliography of Am. literature in Publications Modern Lang. Assn., 1927-41; Cooper's Deerslayer, 1927; Southern Prose Writers, 1947. Contbr. articles and reviews in Am. Lit., Studies in Philology, South Atlantic Bull., etc. Splist. Am. lit. with emphasis on James Fenimore Cooper, lit. of the South, bibliographies. Home: 120 S. Boundary St., Chapel Hill, N.C. Died Feb. 17, 1950.

PAINE, James Lawrence, merchant; b. Algona, Ia., Dec. 14, 1865; s. James Lawrence and Susan Pierce (Horton) P.; student Grinnell Coll., 1887-88; m. Agnes Cowley, June 23, 1897; children—Lawrence Cowley, Margaret Paine (Mrs. William Hutchinson Cowles, Jr.). Began as teacher, 1886; store clk., Algona, 1889; moved to Spokane, 1890; v.p. Spokane Dry Goods Co., 1895-1923, pres., 1924-33, chmn. bd. since 1934; pres. Seattle Dry Goods Co. since 1924; v.p. Dry Goods Realty Co.; dir. Old Nat. Bank & Union Trust Co., First Nat. Bank Spokane. Pres. Spokane Chamber of Commerce, 1917; dir. Community Welfare Federation, Nat. Retail Dry Goods Assn. Mem. Spokane War Appeals Review Com.; mem. advisory bd. Salvation Army; mem. Deaconess Hosp. Assn. Mason. Republican. Conglist. Clubs: Rotary, City, University, Country, Manito Golf (Spokane). Home: East 5, 8th Av. Office: 710 Riverside Av., Spokane, Wash. Died Sept. 8, 1943.

PAINE, John Gregg, orgn. executive; b. Columbia, Pa., July 11, 1889; s. Frank Gregg and Harriet (Skeen) P.; A.B., (Conn.) Wesleyan Univ., 1909; LL.B., George Washington Univ., 1913; m. Rhea Lewis, Feb. 9, 1914; 1 son, Robert Gregg. Lecturer, 1913-14; copyright counsel Victor Talking Machine Co., Camden, N.J., 1915-27, Warner Bros. Pictures, New York, 1928-29; chmn. bd. Music Pub. Protective Assn., 1929-37; gen. mgr. Am. Soc. Composers, Authors and Pub., New York, N.Y., since 1937. Pres. Confederation Internationale des Sociétés d'Autores et Compositeurs 1946; vice pres. Federación Interamericana Sociadades de Authores y Compositores, 1946. Trustee Wesleyan Univ. Made Officer French Acad., 1939, Chevalier Legion of Honor, 1946; recipient citation from Nat. Assn. Am. Composers and Condrs., 1943; citation for work in interamerican relations Dept. of State, 1945. Mem. Chi Psi, Phi Delta Phi. Republican. Methodist. Club: Lotos, New York (dir.). Home: Chestnut Hill, Wilton, Conn. Office: 30 Rockefeller Plaza, N.Y. City 20. Died Apr. 23, 1947; buried Columbus, Ohio.

PAINE, Nathaniel Emmons, M.D.; b. New Hartford, Oneida County, N.Y., July 14, 1853; s. Horace Marshfield (M.D.) and Charlotte (Mann) P.; A.B., Hamilton Coll., 1874, A.M., 1877; M.D., Albany Med. Coll., 1875; post-grad. med. study at Vienna, 1876-77; m. Harriet Banks Gould, June 5, 1879 (died July 8, 1905); children—William Gould (dec.), Alice (Mrs. Alice Paine Paul), Nathaniel Emmons, Mary (Mrs. Sydney Dakin Chamberlain); m. 2d, Martha Lee Gilmor, Feb. 14, 1907 (died July 21, 1925). Asst. physician Middletown (N.Y.) State Hosp. for Insane, 1877-80; prof. psychiatry, Boston U. Sch. Medicine, 1887-1925, now prof. emeritus; cons. physician in psychiatry, Mass. Memorial Hosps., also Newton Hosp.; propr. and med. dir. Newton Nervine, 1892-1910, and of Newton Sanitorium, W. Newton, Mass., 1894-1915; v.p. West Newton Savings Bank since 1929. Invented, 1878, Paine Nasal Feeding Tube, used in Am. and fgn. hosps., where forced feeding is necessary. Trustee, 1898-1926, cons. phys. in mental diseases, Mass. Homœo. Hosp. Connected with Westborough (Mass.) State Hospital 63 years, as construction adviser of trustees, 1884, agent of bd., 1935-36, first med. supt., 1886-92; mem. and sec. cons. bd. physicians and surgeons, 1895-1915, trustee and chmn. bd., 1915-42; mem. cons. bd. phys. and surg. since 1942. Awarded Certificate of Merit in Genealogy by Council of Inst. of Am. Genealogy, 1939. Mem. A.M.A., Am. Psychiatric Assn., Massachusetts Medical Society, Alpha Delta Phi; fellow American College Physicians. Congregationalist. Author: Book of Portraits of 280 Members of the American Medico-Psychological Association, 1916; Thomas Payne of Salem and His Descendants, 1928. Retired from active med. practice. Home: 1640 Washing St., West Newton, Mass. Died Nov. 30, 1948.

PAINE, Robert Treat II, lawyer, corp. officer; b. New Bedford, Mass., Dec. 3, 1861; s. William Cushing and Hannah Hathaway (Perry) P.; A.B., Harvard, 1882; m. Ruth Cabot, May 28, 1890. Trustee Museum of Fine Arts, Boston. Clubs: Somerset, Essex County, Country, Eastern Yacht, Harvard (Boston). Home: 305 Heath St., Brookline. Office: 10 Post Office Sq., Boston, Mass. Died Nov. 12, 1943.

PAINTER, Charles Fairbank, surgeon; b. Grand Haven, Mich., May 19, 1869; s. Charles C. and Martha (Gibson) P.; A.B., Johns Hopkins U., 1891; M.D., Harvard Med. Sch., 1895; served as house officer Children's Hosp., and Mass. Gen. Hosp.; m. Alice Angier, June 6, 1900; children—Charles F. (dec.), Whitfield, Eleanor. Practiced orthopedic surgery at Boston since 1895; orthopedic surgeon, and orthopedic surgeon-in-chief, Carney Hosp., until 1913; cons. orthopedic surgeon since June 1913; dean Tufts Med. Sch., 1912-21, prof. history of medicine, 1925; cons. surgeon Brockton (Mass.) Hosp., Sturdy Memorial Hosp., Attleboro, Mass., Beth Israel Hosp., Boston. Pres. Am. Orthopedic Assn., 1915-16. Fellow Am. Coll. Surgeons; mem. Mass. Med. Soc. Editor: Yearbook of Orthopedic Surgery. Home: Brookline, Mass. Died 1947.

PALFREY, John Gorham (pawl'frē), lawyer; b. Belmont, Mass., Oct. 2, 1875; s. John Carver and Adelaide Eliza (Payson) P.; grad. Browne & Nichols Sch., 1892; A.B., Harvard, 1896, LL.B., 1899; m. Methyl Oakes, Oct. 3, 1905; children—Margaret Germaine (Mrs. Charles Woodrow), Elizabeth Howland (wife of Dr. Harold W. Fullerton), Mianne (Mrs. Franklin Dexter), Sarah Hammond (Mrs. Elwood T. Cooke), Joanna Oakes (Mrs. Rodney W. Brown, Jr.), John Gorham, Jr. Admitted to Mass. bar, 1899; sec. to Justice Horace Gray of U.S. Supreme Ct., 1899-1900; associated with Brandeis, Dunbar & Nutter, 1900-04; mem. Boyden, Palfrey, Bradlee & Twombly, 1904-16; partner Warner, Stackpole, Stetson & Bradlee and predecessors, since 1916; counsel for New England Fuel Adminstr., 1917-18; asst. dir. Marine & Dock Industrial Relations Div., U.S. Shipping Bd., 1918-19; dir. Fiduciary Trust Co.; executor estate of Justice Oliver Wendell Holmes, 1935. Mem. Am., Mass. and Boston bar assns. Clubs: Somerset (Boston); The Country (Brookline); Harvard (New York). Sponsored and wrote intro. to Holmes-Pollock Letters, pub. 1941. Home: 108 Ivy St., Brookline, Mass. Office: 84 State St., Boston, Mass. Died July 25, 1945.

PALLETTE, Edward Marshall (păl-lĕt'), physician; b. Wichita, Kansas, January 13, 1874; s. Samuel Drew and Caroline Elizabeth (Cartwright) P.; Ph.B., Northwestern U., 1894, Ph.M., 1895; Oliver Marcy scholar of Northwestern U. at Marine Biol. Lab., Woods Hole, Mass., 1894; M.D., Coll. of Medicine U. of Southern Calif., 1898; grad. work, New York Polyclinic, 1901, univs. of London, Vienna and Berlin, 1902, 09, 24; m. Mary Elizabeth Brown, Sept. 16, 1903; children—Edward Choate, Warren Sumner, Drew Brown, Elizabeth Delight. Asst. instr. zoölogy, Northwestern U., 1894-95; instr. in biology, Los Angeles High Sch., 1896-98; instr. in histology and embryology, Coll. of Medicine, U. of Southern Calif., 1896-98; practiced at Los Angeles since 1898, giving spl. attention to gynecology; asst. health officer, Los Angeles, 1898-99; mem. Los Angeles City Bd. of Health, 1905-06; prof. physiology, Coll. of Dentistry, Univ. of Southern Calif., 1900-12; lecturer in obstetrics and gynecology, Training Sch. for Nurses, St. Vincent's Hosp.; examiner Calif. State Lunacy Commn., 1905-15; mem. staffs St. Vincent's (ex-pres.), Hollywood, French and Calif. Luth. hosps.; v.p. Los Angeles County Med. Holding Corp.; v.p. California State Board of Pub. Health, 1932-40; mem. Retirement Bd., Los Angeles City Schools, 1938-39; mem. (treas.) bd. dirs. Hosp. Service of Southern Calif. (Blue Cross) since 1938. Capt. Med. Corps, U.S. Army, World War I; served as surgeon Letterman Gen. Hosp., Presidio, San Francisco, and at Camp Crane, Allentown, Pa. Southern Calif. State chmn. procurement and assignment service for physicians War Manpower Commn. since 1942. Ex-pres. Los Angeles County Bd. of Edn. Mem. Med. Sch. Advisory Com. of U. of Southern Calif. Trustee Med. Soc. State of Calif.; fellow Am. Coll. Surgeons, A.M.A. (mem. Ho. of Dels., 1932-42; trustee since 1942); member California State Medical Assn. (pres. 1936-37); Los Angeles County Medical Assn. (ex-pres.), Los Angeles Surgical Society, Los Angeles Obstet. and Gynecol. Soc. (ex-pres.), Los Angeles Academy of Medicine, Southern California Medical Alumni (ex-pres.), S.R. (ex-pres. Calif. State Soc.), Hollywood Acad. of Medicine (hon.), Internat. Med. Club (hon.), Inst. of Am. Genealogy, A.A.A.S., Delta Tau Delta, Theta Nu Epsilon, Nu Sigma Nu (hon. nat. councilor), Psi Omega, Pi Gamma Mu. Republican. Mason (K.T., Shriner). Home: 5224 W. 2d St. Office: 1930 Wilshire Blvd., Los Angeles 5, Calif. Died Nov. 16, 1944.

PALLOTTI, Francis A., lawyer; b. Hartford, Conn., Aug. 21, 1886; s. Nicholas and Maria Antonia (Demma) P.; B.A., Holy Cross Coll., 1908; LL.B., cum laude, Yale, 1911; m. Mary Agnes Verdi, Apr. 12,

1915; children—Nicholas, Rosemary. Admitted to Conn. bar, 1911, and began practice in Hartford; judge Hartford Police Court, 1917-21; sec of state, Conn., 1923-29; atty. general, Conn., since 1938; elected pres. Nat. Assn. of Attorneys Gen. Rep. candidate for congressman, 1936. Dir. Dime Savings Bank, Hartford. Mem. Bd. Street Commrs., Hartford, 1911-17, v.p. 3 years. Dir. St. Francis Hosp.; chmn. Disabled Vets. Camp Fund. Mem. Am. and Conn. State bar assns., Nat. Assn. Attys. Gen. (v.p. 1943), Sons of Italy, Chi Tau Kappa. Republican. K.C., Elk. Club: Wampanoag Country (West Hartford). Home: 44 Kenyon St. Address: Hartford, Conn.* Died Dec. 21, 1946.

PALMA y VELASQUEZ, Rafael, educator; b. Tondo, Manila, Philippine Islands, October 24, 1874; s. Hermogenes and Hilaria (Velasquez) Palma; A.B., Ateneo de Manila, 1891; studied law, U. of Santo Tomas (non-grad.); LL.D., U. of Manila, 1924; m. Carolina Ocampo, Feb. 2, 1902; children—Virginia (Mrs. Arsenio Bonifacio), Hector, Alicia, Fe. Officer of internal revenue P.I., under Spanish regime, 1896-98; editor La Independencia, 1898-99, El Nuevo Dia, 1900, El Renacimiento, 1902-04; admitted to Philippine bar, 1901; prof. of law, Escuela de Derecho, 1901-05; rep. from Province of Cavite to first Philippine Assembly, 1907; mem. Philippine Commn., 1908-16, Philippine Senate, 1916-21; sec. Dept. of Interior, 1917-20; pres. Univ. of the Philippines, 1923-34. Mem. Am. Bar Assn., Philippine Bar Assn., Philippine C. of C. Clubs: Filipino, Philippine Columbian Assn. Mason (33°). Home: 553 Leroy, Paco, Manila, P.I. Died May 24, 1939.

PALMER, Albert Kenny Craven (päm'ẽr), retired army officer; b. Washington, D.C., June 5, 1887; s. Anlick and Alice (Craven) P.; ed. pub. and pvt. schs. of U.S. and Europe; grad. U.S. Mounted Service Sch., 1914, Field Arty. Sch., 1916; m. Josephine Hodges Lee, Sept. 25, 1917 (died 1935); children—Alice Craven, Joan, Kenny Craven; m. 2d, Ethel M. de Ortiz, Sept. 1935. Commd. 2d lt. Field Arty., U.S. Army, 1908, and advanced to lt. col. Nat. Army, June 18, 1918; maj. Q.M.C., 1920; retired, Nov. 13, 1920; lt. col. U.S. Army, June 21, 1930; mem. commn. in charge sale of U.S. Govt. horses in France, 1919. Engaged in investment banking, Denver, Colo., 1922-26, ins. business, N.Y. City, 1927-30; dir. Chile-Am. Assn. since 1930; foreign corr. of "El Mercurio," Santiago, Chile. Decorated Order of Al Merito (Chile), Grade Oficial; 1933, Grade Gran Oficial, 1935. Mem. Assn. of Foreign Corrs. in U.S., S.A.R.; Mil. Order World War. Republican. Episcopalian. Clubs: Knickerbocker (New York); Army and Navy (Washington). Author: Chiam News Service. Home: 55 E. 86th St. Office: 31 Nassau St., New York, N.Y. Died Aug. 28, 1942.

PALMER, Albert Robert, lawyer; b. East Orange, N.J., Apr. 15, 1880; s. Albert William and Susan Logan (Hansell) P.; A.B., Yale, 1901; grad. student N.Y. Law Sch., 1901-03; m. Florence M. Decker, Oct. 5, 1904 (now deceased); children—Robert Caton, Jean; m. 2d, Anna M. Vass, Sept. 26, 1936. Admitted to N.Y. bar, 1903, since partner firm of Palmer & Series; director United Wall Paper, Inc.; president Madison Trust Co.; director Starrett Corp., Starrett Bros. & Eken, Inc., Charles Pfizer & Company, Washburn Wire Company, Flake Products Co. Councilman, Madison, N.J., 4 yrs., pres. Borough Council, 2 yrs. Trustee Kent Place Sch., Summit, N.J. Mem. Am. Bar Assn., Assn. Bar City of N.Y. Republican. Mason, K.T. Clubs: Yale, Bankers (N.Y. City); Graduate (New Haven); Wannamoisett (Providence); Baltusrol Golf (Summit, N.J.); Racquet (Chicago). Home: Midwood Rd., Madison, N.J. Office: 46 Cedar St., New York, N.Y. Died Apr. 1, 1947.

PALMER, Andrew Henry, meteorologist, climatologist; b. Dubuque, Ia., May 1, 1886; s. John and Mary (Gorius) P.; A.B. ("with distinction"), U. of Minn., 1908; univ. scholar, Harvard, 1908-09, A.M., 1909; Ph.D., U. of Santa Clara, Calif., 1923; unmarried. Research asst., Blue Hill Meteorol. Obs. of Harvard U., 1908-12; instr. geography, Mass. State Normal Sch., Salem, 1912; magnetic observer, Carnegie Instn. of Washington, 1913; asst. observer, 1914-15, observer, 1915-18, and meteorologist, 1918-24, U.S. Weather Bureau, San Francisco; supt. Crop and Weather Dept., Automobile Insurance Co., San Francisco, since 1924. Fellow Am. Geog. Soc., Am. Meteorol. Soc.; mem. A.A.A.S., Seismol. Soc. Am., Calif. Acad. Sciences, Phi Beta Kappa. Co-author (with the late A. Lawrence Rotch): Charts of the Atmosphere for Aeronauts and Aviators, 1911. Editor of Notes on Meteorology and Climatology, in "Science," 1910-12; has written many papers on meteorol. and climatol. subjects. Home: 37 Columbus Av. Office: 37 Columbus Av., San Francisco. Died Dec. 20, 1942.

PALMER, Bradley Webster, lawyer; b. Wilkes-Barre, Pa., June 28, 1866; s. Henry Wilbur and Ellen (Webster) P.; A.B., Harvard, 1888, A.M., 1889; student Harvard U. Law Sch., 1888-89; unmarried. Began practice with Storey & Thorndike, Boston, 1891; admitted to firm, 1893, now Palmer, Dodge, Barstow, Wilkins & Davis; counsel of United Fruit Co.; counsel to Capital Issues Com., Washington, 1918; asst. counsel to U.S. alien property custodian, 1918; mem. staff Am. Commn. to Negotiate Peace, Paris, 1919. Private Co. D, 9th Regt., Pa. N.G., 1888-89; pvt. Battery A, Mass. Vol. Militia, 1895-99. Home: 318 Beacon St. Office: 53 State St., Boston, Mass.* Died Nov. 9, 1946.

PALMER, Charles M., newspaper pub. and appraiser; b. La Crosse, Wis., Oct. 3, 1856; student La Crosse Valley Acad.; m. Mary E. Sill, 1881. Started in 1875 with La Crosse (Wis.) Republican-Leader; later went to Minneapolis; owned the Northwestern Miller; at one time part owner all newspapers in that city; became asso. William Randolph Hearst as business mgr., San Francisco Examiner, 1890; later in Europe; purchased N.Y. Journal for Hearst, and Boston Record and Advertiser; now pres. St. Joseph (Mo.) Gazette and St. Joseph (Mo.) News-Press; intermediary in sales of nearly 200 newspapers in the U.S. and during 70 years in active newspaper work, has held important positions, owned or had investments in more than 50 newspapers in U.S.; formerly asso. in ownership in newspapers in New Orleans, La.; now sr. partner newspaper brokerage firm Palmer & Palmer, N.Y. City. Pres. Saranac Lake Hosp. Clinic. Republican. Episcopalian. Mason. Elk. At present oldest mem. of Asso. Press and Am. Newspaper Publishers Assn. Home: 135 Park Av., Saranac Lake, N.Y. Office: 1328 Broadway, New York, N.Y. Died Dec. 10, 1949.

PALMER, Dean, newspaper pub. and broker; b. Minneapolis, Minn., Nov. 30, 1889; s. Charles M. and Mary (Sill) P.; student Montclair (N.J.) Mil. Acad., 1898-1903, St. Joseph (Mo.) High Sch., 1903-05; also studied in schs. in Europe; unmarried. Newspaper reporter New Orleans, 1907; reporting and advertising St. Joseph (Mo.) News Press, 1908-11; partner Palmer & Richards, N.Y. City, rotogravure printing, 1911-14; editor and pub. Motor Bus, 1915-17; partner with C. M. Palmer, newspaper broker and appraiser of newspaper properties, since 1912, present brokerage firm of Palmer & Palmer; owner Marlboro (Mass.) Enterprise, Hudson Daily Sun, and 5 town weeklies, 1925-29; majority owner North Shore-Long Island Daily Journal, 1928-40; v.p. News Corp. (pub. News-Press and Gazette), St. Joseph, Mo. Served on French and Italian fronts with Am. Red Cross, Y.M.C.A. and ambulance service, 1917-19; newspaper corr. in Far East, 1919-20. Republican. Episcopalian. Clubs: Benton, St. Joseph Country (St. Joseph); Lambs, Lotos, Union League (N.Y. City); National Press Club (Washington). Home: Saranac Lake, N.Y. Office: 350 Madison Av., New York, N.Y. Died Sep. 18, 1942.

PALMER, Edgar, chmn. bd. The New Jersey Zinc Co.; b. N.Y. City, Nov. 12, 1880; s. Stephen Squires and Susan Flanders (Price) P.; B.S., Princeton, 1903, E.E., 1905; hon. E.D., Stevens Institute of Technology, 1938; m. Zilph Hayes, Nov. 22, 1910. President The New Jersey Zinc Co., 1912-27, now chmn. bd.; also chmn. bd. Bertha Mineral Co., Mineral Point Zinc Co., Empire Zinc Co. of Colo.; Empire Zinc Co. of Mo., The New Jersey Zinc Co. of Pa., Palmer Land Co., Palmer Water Co., Master Painter's Supply Co., N.J. Zinc Sales Co., Chestnut Ridge Ry. Co., The Franklin Water Co.; The Franklin Gen. Stores, Inc.; pres. and dir. Smith Valley Realty Corp., Princeton Municipal Improvement, Inc., Palmerton Hospital, Franklin Hosp.; v.p. and dir. Ahnapee & Western Ry. Co., Green Bay & Western R.R. Co., Kewanee, Green Bay & Western R.R. Co.; dir. Cayuga & Susquehanna R.R. Co., Fidelity-Phoenix Fire Ins. Co., Bankers & Shippers Insurance Co., Detroit, Hillsdale & Southwestern R.R. Co., Ft. Wayne & Jackson R.R. Co., New York & Queens Electric Light & Power Co., The Palmerton Co., Palmerton Disposal Co., Palmerton Lighting Co., Palmerton Telephone Co., 111 Main St. Corp., Marine Basin Co., Inc., Am. Eagle Fire Ins. Co., Nassau Bldg. & Loan Assn. (Princeton, N.J.), Saucon Valley Iron & R.R. Co., Ward Baking Co.; limited partner Henderson, Harrison & Co.; trustee Central Hanover Bank & Trust Co., Consol. Edison Co. of N.Y., Inc., Princeton U., Stevens Inst. Tech. Mem. Am. Inst. Mining and Metall. Engrs., Princeton Engring. Assn. Republican. Episcopalian. Clubs: Metropolitan (Washington); University, Union League, Blind Brook, Apawamis, New York Yacht, Eastern Yacht, American Yacht, Manursing Island, Nassau, Princeton, Down Town Association; Country Club (Havana); American (London). Home: 1 Bayard Lane, Princeton, N.J. Office: 20 Exchange Pl., New York, N.Y. Died Jan. 8, 1943.

PALMER, Howard, author, explorer; b. Norwich, Conn., Nov. 28, 1883; s. George S. and Ida Amelia (Cooke) P.; B.A., Yale, 1905; LL.B., Harvard, 1908; unmarried. Admitted to Mass. bar, 1908; sec. dir. Palmer Bros. Co., mfrs. bed comfortables, New London, 1918-28. A pioneer explorer, Selkirk Mts., B.C., 1907-15, ascending 50 new or little-visited peaks; made 1st conquest of Mt. Sir Sandford, 1912; Canadian Govt., confirmed his names for fifty new mountains, glaciers, etc., and named in his honor a peak, glacier and river; visited remote sections Canadian Rockies, 1916-27, ascending a score of new peaks; assisted in organizing Mt. Logan expdn. to Alaska, 1925; lecturer in mountaineering; made studies and measurements of movements of glaciers pub. by Royal Geog. Soc. (London) and Smithsonian Instn. Trustee Pub. Library, New London. Mem. exec. com. for celebration of Sesquicentennial of Battle of Groton Heights, 1931. Fellow Royal Geog. Soc.; mem. New London County Hist. Soc. (v.p.), Am. Inst. of Mining Engrs.; corr. mem. Geographic Soc. Phila. Republican. Clubs: Am. Alpine (pres. term 1926-29), British Alpine, Explorers', Harvard Travelers, Appalachian Mountain; Fresh Air, Century (N.Y. City); etc. Author: Mountaineering and Exploration in the Selkirks, 1914; A Pioneer of the Canadian Alps, 1931. Joint Author: A Climber's Guide to the Rocky Mountains of Canada, 1921, 40. Editor: Life on a Whaler, for New London County Hist. Soc., 1929; also editor of American Alpine Journal, 1930-33. Contbr. to Harvard Handbook of Travel, 1917, 35, Ency. Britannica, 1929, and periodicals on history and exploration of Canadian Cordillera. Home: Paweatuck, Conn. (P.O. Westerly, R.I.). Died Oct. 24, 1944.

PALMER, Leroy Sheldon, univ. prof.; b. Rushville, Ill., Mar. 23, 1887; s. Samuel C. and Annie Jane (Goodman) P.; B.S. in Chem. Engring., U. of Mo., 1909, A.M., 1911, Ph.D., 1913; m. Nina Gay Wilcox, Sept. 14, 1911; children—Bess Wilcox (Mrs. Andrew Justus), Leroy Sheldon, James Samuel. Chemist, dairy division U.S. Dept. Agr., 1909-11; chemist charge coop. lab. of dairy div., U.S. Dept. Agr., at U. of Mo., 1911-13; asst. prof. dairy chemistry, U. of Mo., 1913-19; asso. prof. agrl. biochemistry, U. of Minn., 1919-22, prof. since 1922, chief, div. of agrl. bio-chemistry, U. of Minn., since 1942; also dairy chemist Minn. Agrl. Expt. Station. Fellow A.A.A.S.; mem. Am. Chem. Soc (councillor 1925, 31, 37), Am Soc. Biol. Chemists, Soc. Exptl. Biology and Medicine, Am Dairy Science Assn., Am. Inst. of Nutrition, Am. Genetic Assn., Inst. Food Technologists, Am. Acad. Polit. and Social Science; Minn. United Nations Com., Phi Lambda Upsilon, Sigma Xi, Alpha Chi Sigma, Gamma Sigma Delta, Tau Beta Pi, Alpha Zeta, Phi Mu Alpha; v.p. World's Dairy Congress, 1923. Borden medal and award, Am. Chem. Soc., 1939. Republican. Conglist. Clubs: Eckles (permanent sec.), Campus. Author: Carotinoids and Related Pigments, 1922; Laboratory Experiments in Dairy Chemistry, 1926; also more than 175 papers and bulls. giving results of researches. Joint author: Fundamentals of Dairy Science, 1928, 1935; Outlines of Biochemistry (Gortner), 1929, 1938; asso. editor Journal of Dairy Science. Revised Eckles' Dairy Cattle and Milk Production (with E. L. Anthony), 1939. Home: 2262 Carter Av., St. Paul, Minn. Died Mar. 8, 1944.

PALMER, Potter, capitalist; b. Chicago, Ill., Oct. 8, 1875; s. late Potter and Bertha (Honoré) P.; A.B., Harvard, 1898; m. Pauline Kohlsaat, July 1908; children—Potter III, Bertha, Gordon, Pauline. Trustee Bertha Honoré Palmer Estate; dir. First Nat. Bank of Chicago. Pres. Art Inst. Chicago. Clubs: Chicago, Saddle and Cycle, Shoreacres (Chicago); Bar Harbor. Home: Schoonerhead Rd., Bar Harbor, Me. Died Sep. 3, 1943.

PALMER, Ray, consulting engr.; b. Sparta, Wis., Mar. 29, 1878; s. George Hegeman and Mary Delemar (Canfield) P.; B.S., U. of Wis., 1901; m. Daisy Wentworth, Dec. 11, 1901; children—Chester Llewellyn, Delemar Elizabeth, Ray. Began as asst. supt. J. G. White & Co., New York, 1901; with same firm, London, 1901-04; elec. engr., Union Traction Co., Chicago, 1904-05; cons. engr., Chicago and Milwaukee, 1905-12; commr. gas and electricity, Chicago, 1912-15; pres. and gen. mgr. New York & Queens Electric Light & Power Co., 1915-25; cons. engr., New York and Chicago, since 1925. Corpl. Wis. N.G., Porto Rico Campaign, Spanish-Am. War; Queensboro (N.Y. City) war industries commr., World War. Fellow Am. Inst. E.E.; mem. Illuminating Engring. Soc., New York Elec. Soc., Kappa Sigma. Republican. Clubs: Engineers (New York); Wyantenuck Country (Great Barrington, Mass.). Home: Great Barrington, Mass.; and Daytona Beach, Fla.* Died Sep. 10, 1947.

PANNELL, Henry Clifton (păn-nĕl), educator; b. Elmore County, Ala., July 24, 1897; s. William Henry and Emma Jeanette (Hodnett) P.; student Jacksonville (Ala.) State Normal Sch., 1915-18; B.S., U. of Ala., 1922; A.M., Teachers Coll., Columbia, 1925, Ph.D., 1933; m. Anne Thomas Gary, Sept. 2, 1936; children—Henry Gary, Clifton Wyndham. Teacher elementary schools, Elmore and Macon counties, Ala., 1918-20; prin. Jr. High Sch., Montgomery County, 1922-24; prin. Normal High Sch., Jacksonville, Ala., 1925-27; supervisor teacher training, U. of Ala., 1928-35, asso. prof. of edn., 1935-39, prof. of edn., 1939-43; supt. city schools, Tuscaloosa, Ala., 1943-46; elected State Supt. Edn., Ala., May 1, 1946. Member Coast Arty. Corps, O.T.C., 1918. Awarded General Education Bd. scholarship, Columbia, 1927-28. Mem. Ala. Edn. Assn. (pres. 1941), Newcomen Soc., Phi Beta Kappa, Phi Delta Kappa, Kappa Delta Pi. Democrat. Baptist. Mason. Odd Fellow. Club: National Exchange (Tuscaloosa). Author: The Preparation and Work of Alabama High School Teachers, 1933. Co-author: The World at Work. Contbr. to edn. jours. Home: 25 Patton Pl., Tuscaloosa, Ala. Died May 26, 1946.

PAQUIN, Samuel Savil (pă'kwĭn), newspaperman; b. Tripoli, Ia., Aug. 29, 1868; s. Cyril O. and Anne E. (Fitts) P.; A.B., U. of Minn., 1894; m. Helen A. Peck, Dec. 30, 1896 (died 1914); m. 2d, Josephine Frances O'Hara, Aug. 29, 1915; children—Josephine Elizabeth, Marjorie Genevieve, Samuel Savil. Editorial staff Minneapolis Tribune, 1894-96, Chicago Tribune, 1896-1900, Chicago Am., 1900-07, New York Evening Jour., 1907-09; asst. gen. mgr., Internat. News Service, 1909-16; bus. mgr. Internat. Feature Service, Inc., 1916; service mgr. King Features Syndicate, Inc., 1921-30, daily editor, 1931-38, research dir., 1938-41, editor since 1941. Councilman, Teaneck Tp., since 1930. Mem. Minn. Alumni Assn. of N.Y. (pres. 1922-24, v.p. 1925-26, treas. 1927-43), Psi Upsilon. Roman Catholic. Author: Garden Fairies, 1908. Home: Teaneck, N.J. Office: 235 E. 45th St., New York. Died Apr. 15, 1943; buried in St. Josephs Cemetery, Hackensack, N.J.

PARDEE, James Thomas; b. Cleveland, O., Sept. 18, 1867; s. James and Helen M. (Race) P.; B.S. in C.E., Case Sch. Applied Science, 1888, D.C.S., 1940;

m. Elsa Margaret Louise Uhinck, Feb. 21, 1914. Draftsman, later structural engr., Variety Iron Works Co., Cleveland, until 1893; apptd. engr. in charge bridges and viaducts, City of Cleveland, 1893, later also in charge river and harbor improvements; asst. to chief engr. Dept. of Pub. Works, Cleveland, 1901-03 (resigned). Designed and built piers, wharves, viaducts, bridges, including three electrically operated pivot swing bridges, at Cleveland, one of which—a double swing bridge—was the first of the kind in U.S. Sec.-treas. The Dow Process Co., 1895-97, became dir. of its successor, The Dow Chem. Co., 1897, v.p., 1901, sec., 1916, chmn. of bd. 1935-1941; v.p. and dir. Chemical State Savings Bank, Midland, Mich. Mem. corp. and trustee Case School Applied Science; trustee Midland Community Center. Mem. Am. Soc. Civil Engrs., Phi Kappa Psi. Republican. Episcopalian. Clubs: Union, Cleveland Automobile (Cleveland); Midland Country, Rotary Internat. Home: Midland, Mich. Died Jan. 3, 1944.

PARK, Charles Francis, prof. mechanism; b. Boston, Mass., Apr. 11, 1869; s. William Robert and Ann E. (Eldredge) P.; B.S. in Mech. Engring., Mass. Inst. Tech., 1892; m. Maud W. White, Oct. 31, 1894. Instr. mechanism, 1894-1900, asst. prof., 1900-06, asso. prof., 1906-12, prof., 1912-35, prof. emeritus since 1935, Mass. Inst. Tech., also dir. mechanical laboratories. Planned and organized, 1903, now emeritus; dir. Lowell Inst. Sch., Massachusetts Inst. Tech. Fellow Am. Acad. Arts and Sciences, A.A.A.S.; mem. Am. Assn. Univ. Prof., Am. Soc. Mech. Engrs., Soc. Promotion Engring. Edn., Alpha Tau Omega. Lt. col. Ord. O.R.C. Republican. Club: Harvard Segregansett Country (Taunton). Home: 21 Prospect St., Taunton, Mass. Died Sep. 26, 1944.

PARK, Guy Brasfield, ex-gov.; b. Platte City, Mo., June 10, 1872; s. Thomas Woodson and Margaret E. (Baxter) P.; prep. edn., Gaylord Inst., Platte City; LL.B., U. of Mo., 1896; m. Eleanora Gabbert, Nov. 16, 1909; 1 dau., Henrietta (Mrs. J. Marvin Krause). Began practice at Platte City, 1896; served as city atty., Platte City, and pros. atty. Platte County; judge Circuit Court, 5th Mo. Circuit, 1923-33; gov. of Mo., term 1933-37. Mem. State Constl. Convs. Mo., 1922 and of 1943-44. Mem. Beta Theta Pi. Democrat. Mem. Disciples of Christ Ch. Mason (K.T., Shriner). Home: Platte City, Mo. Address: Federal Reserve Bank Bldg., Kansas City, Mo. Deceased.

PARK, Orville Augustus, lawyer; b. Greenville, Ga., Mar. 11, 1872; s. John Wesley and Sarah Caroline (Bull) P.; LL.B., Vanderbilt, 1892, U. of Ga., 1893; LL.D., Emory U., 1931; m. Elmyr Taylor, Mar. 29, 1900; children—Frances (Mrs. Ray Carter), Orville Augustus, Elmyr (Mrs. Brainard Currie). Admitted to Georgia bar, 1893, and practiced since at Macon; professor of law, Mercer U., since 1907; gen. counsel Ga. Bankers Assn. since 1906. Mem. Ga. Ho. of Rep., 1931-32, 1933-34. Chmn. Macon Hosp. Commn., 1914-19; Ga. state chmn. Legal Advisory Bds., World War. Trustee Wesleyan Coll., Macon; curator Ga. Hist. Soc., 1930-36. Mem. Am. Bar Assn., Ga. Bar Assn. (sec. 1898-1917; pres. 1918), Am. Law Inst., Beta Theta Pi, Phi Beta Kappa, Pi Gamma Mu. Democrat. Methodist (supt. S.S. since 1898, chmn. bd. stewards 25 yrs., Mulberry Street M.E. Ch.; del. gen. conf. 1930, 34; member Judicial Council, 1934-39. Author: Index to Bar Association Publications, 1903; Georgia Bankers Code, 1906; Park's Annotated Code of Georgia, 1914; Park's Banking Law of Georgia, 1920; Georgia in the Eighteenth Century, 1921; Georgia Code, 1933; Georgia Code Annotated, 1936. Home: Park Haven, Route 2, Gray, Ga. Office: Persons Bldg., Macon. Ga. Died Jan. 27, 1943.

PARK, Robert Emory, coll. prof.; b. Tuskegee, Ala., Dec. 11, 1868; s. James Fletcher and Emma Augusta (Bailey) P.; student U.S. Mil. Acad., 1888-89; A.B., U. of Ala., 1892, A.M., 1893; U. of Chicago, 1899-1900; U. of Oxford, Eng., and travel, 1903-04; Litt.D., U. of Ala., 1905; m. Mary Belle Whelchel, July 15, 1896; children—Edward Douglas, James Holt, Catherine, Mary Holt. Supt. city schs., Gainesville, 1893-96; prin. pvt. sch., LaGrange, Ga., 1896-99; head of dept. rhetoric and English lit., U. of Georgia, 1900-41. Democrat. Methodist. Mem. Delta Kappa Epsilon, Phi Beta Kappa. Home: Athens, Ga. Died June 28, 1942.

PARK, Robert Ezra, sociologist; b. Luzerne County, Pa., Feb. 14, 1864; s. Hiram Asa and Theodosia (Warner) P.; Ph.B., U. of Mich., 1887; M.A., Harvard, 1899; Ph.D., Heidelberg, 1904; Dr. Humane Lit., U. of Mich., 1937; m. Clara Cahill, June 11, 1894; children—Edward Cahill, Theodosia Warner, Margaret Lucy, Robert Hiram. Newspaper work, 1887-98; studied and traveled in Europe, 1899-1903; asst. in philosophy, Harvard, 1904-05; ednl. work (most of time) among negroes, 1905-14; lecturer on sociology since 1914, prof., 1923-33, U. of Chicago (emeritus); visiting prof. Fisk U., since 1936; traveled and lectured in Orient, 1929-30; research prof. sociology, U. of Hawaii, 1931-32. Pres. Nat. Community Center Assn., 1922-24; pres. Am. Sociol. Soc., 1925-26; dir. Race Relations Survey of the Pacific Coast, 1923-25; mem. of Social Research Council, 1927; del. to 4th Pacific Science Congress, Java, 1929; U. of Chicago del. to Inst. Pacific Relations, 1927-31. Mem. Am. Acad. Polit. and Social Science, Internat. Inst. of African Language and Culture, Population Assn. of America, Inst. of Pacific Relations (Am. council), Ecol. Soc. America, Southern Sociol. Soc., American Sociological Society, A.A.A.S. Sociological Research Soc., Nat. Econ. and Social Planning Assn., Assn. for Study of Negro Life and History, Am. Polit. Science Assn., Phi Beta Kappa. Democrat. Mem. Disciples of Christ. Clubs: Quadrangle, City. Author: Introduction to the Science of Sociology (with E. W. Burgess), 1921; Old World Traits Transplanted (with Herbert A. Miller), 1921; The Immigrant Press and Its Control, 1922; The City—Suggestions for the Study of Human Nature in the Urban Environment, 1925. Editor: An Outline of the Principles of Sociology, 1939. Lecturer at Yenching U., China, fall of 1932; traveled and studied race relations problems, India, Africa, and Brazil, 1933. Home: (winter) 1809 Morena St., Nashville, Tenn.; (summer) Roaring Brook, Harbor Springs, Mich. Died Feb. 5, 1944.

PARKER, Addison Bennett, newspaper pub.; b. Fulton, N.Y., Aug. 26, 1869; s. David Dennison and Addie P.; ed. pub. and pvt. schs.; m. Grace Carpenter, Oct. 23, 1892; 1 son, Fred M. Pub. Odd Fellows Mag. since 1893; pub. Watertown Standard since 1921; pres. Parker Press. Dep. sec. state of N.Y., 1915-21; chmn. Bd. of Supervisors, Jefferson County, N.Y. Mason, Odd Fellow. Home: 262 Flower Av. Office: 252 State St., Watertown, N.Y. Died Mar. 28, 1944.

PARKER, Amasa Junius, lawyer; b. Delhi, N.Y., May 6, 1843; s. Judge Amasa Junius and Harriet Langdon (Roberts) P.; A.B., Union Coll., 1863, A.M., 1866, LL.D., 1904; LL.B., Albany Law Sch., 1864; m. Cornelia Kane Strong, 1868 (died 1883). Admitted to bar, and law partner with father, 1865-90; mem. N.Y. Assembly, 1882, Senate, 1886-87, 1892-93, 1894-95. A.-d.-c. and maj. 3d Div., N.G.S. N.Y., 1866; lt.-col., 1875; col. 10th Regt. Inf., 1877; gen. of its 3d Brigade, 1886-91. Chief organizer and pres. Nat. Guard Assn., 1878-80; during service in assembly compiled mil. code of State of N.Y.; drafted, 1894, and secured passage in Senate and Assembly, or a joint resolution calling upon Congress to provide the Nat. Guard of states with modern magazine rifles and ammunition, but the officers in charge of the resolution failed in their duty, and as a result thousands of Nat. Guard troops entered the Spanish-American War in 1898 with old weapons and black powder while Spanish troops were armed with modern weapons and smokeless powder. Rank of major general on retired list conferred by special act of legislature of N.Y., 1933. Trustee Albany Law School, and president board nearly 25 years; alumni trustee Union Coll. and gov. Union U. many yrs.; trustee Albany Med. Coll.; 16 yrs. trustee Union Trust Co. of New York; 16 yrs. mgr. and pres. bd. mgrs. Hudson River State Hosp. for Insane, Poughkeepsie, N.Y. Democrat. Episcopalian. Mem. Kappa Alpha. Clubs: Ft. Orange, University, Country. Home: 143 Washington Av., Albany, N.Y. Died May 2, 1938.

PARKER, Charles Wolcott, judge; b. Newark, N.J., Oct. 22, 1862; s. Hon. Cortlandt and Elisabeth Wolcott (Stites) P.; A.B., Princeton, 1882, A.M., 1885, LL.D., 1919; LL.B., Columbia, 1885; m. Emily Fuller, Nov. 22, 1893; children—Charles W. (dec.), Dudley F., Philip M., Elinor M., Robert M. (dec.). Practiced at Newark, 1885-90, later at Bayonne City and Jersey City; judge 2d Dist. Court, Jersey City, 1898-1903; judge New Jersey Circuit Court, 1903-07; justice Supreme Court of N.J., 1907-47; retired since Sept. 15, 1947. Supervising editor New Jersey Digest, 1907. Private, corporal and sergt. Essex Troop, of Newark, 1890-99; 1st lt. and capt. 4th N.J. Regt., 1899-1902; lt. col. and a.-a.-g. of N.J., 1902-07; a.-d.-c. on staff of Gov. Franklin Murphy. Pres. emeritus N.J. Hist. Soc.; ex-gov. Soc. Colonial Wars; mem. S.R., Founders and Patriots, N.J. State Bar Assn. Republican. Episcopalian (chancellor Diocese of Newark). Clubs: University (N.Y. City); Essex (Newark); Morris County Golf. Home: 63 Macculloch Av. Address: 19 South St., Morristown, N.J. Died Jan. 23, 1948.

PARKER, Chauncey Goodrich, lawyer; b. Newark, N.J., Sept. 19, 1864; s. Cortlandt and Elisabeth Wolcott (Stites) P.; A.B., Harvard, 1885, A.M., 1888; LL.B., Columbia, 1887; m. Dora M. Wright, Nov. 11, 1896; children—Chauncey G., Edith (Mrs. Albert J. Redway, Jr.), (twins) Edward Cortlandt and Dora Mason (Mrs. Howard P. Homans), Elisabeth (Mrs George L. Howe). Practiced at Newark since 1888; atty. for Newark Bd. of Health, 1890-94; counsel for N.J. in boundary controversy with Del. and commr. to settle that dispute. Receiver Internat. Mercantile Marine, and Rock Island Co., 1915; with U.S. Shipping Bd., 1921-33, gen. counsel, handling and overseeing all litigations, 1922-33; now practicing law, Washington, Newark, N.J. Mem. bars of N.J., N.Y., D.C. and U.S. Supreme Court. Spl. legal expert with War Risk Insurance Bur., Washington, July, Aug. 1918. Mem. N.G.N.J., 10 yrs. Republican. Mem. Essex County Lawyers' Club (ex-pres.), Assn. Bar City of N.Y., N.J. Hist. Soc., Newark Art Museum Assn.; pres. N.J. State Bar Assn., 1921-22. Attended Gen. Conf. of Nations on Communications and Transit, at Geneva, Switzerland, as adviser to Am. minister at Berne who represented the U.S. at the Conf., Aug. 20-Sept. 2, 1927. Clubs: Essex (Newark); Harvard (New York); Metropolitan, Chevy Chase (Washington). Home: 2523 Massachusetts Av. Office: Southern Bldg., Washington, D.C. Died July 11, 1943.

PARKER, DeWitt Henry, prof. philosophy; b. New York, N.Y., Apr. 17, 1885; s. DeWitt Henry and Jennie Ada (Stevens) P.; student Boston Latin Sch., 1898-1902; A.B., Harvard University, 1906, Ph.D., 1908; m. Lelia N. Webster, 1909 (divorced 1920); 1 son, DeWitt Webster (died in action, Belchite, Spain, Mar. 10, 1938); m. 2d, Martha McCorkle Vaughan, June 14, 1924; children—Gooch Vaughan, Jennie Katharine Stevens. Instr. philosophy, U. of Mich., 1908-09, U. of Calif., 1909-10; instr. philosophy, 1910-13, asst. prof., 1913-21, asso. prof., 1921-25, prof. since 1925, chmn. dept. since 1929, University of Michigan; lecturer University of California, 1924-25, Met. Mus., N.Y., Jan. 1926, U. of Wis. summer 1927, U. of Chicago, summer 1928, Harvard, summers, 1932, 35; visiting prof., Columbia Univ., winter 1946-47. Henry Russell lecturer, 1947. Mem. Am. Philos. Assn. (pres. Western branch, 1929-30), Phi Beta Kappa. Clubs: Research. Quadrangle (Ann Arbor), Catholepestemia. Author; The Self and Nature, 1917; The Principles of Æsthetics, 1920, 2d edit. 1946; The Analysis of Art, 1926; Human Values, 1931; Experience and Substance, 1941. Home: 2025 Hill St., Ann Arbor, Mich. Died June 21, 1949.

PARKER, Frank, army officer; b. Georgetown County, S.C., Sept. 21, 1872; s. Arthur Middleton and Emma Izard (Middleton) P.; grad. U.S. Mil. Acad., 1894; grad. Cav. Sch., Saumur, France, 1904; LL.D., U. of South Carolina, 1927, Mich. State Coll. Agr. and Applied Science, 1933; m. Katherine Hamilton Lahm, November 20, 1906; children—Katherine Lahm, Ann Middleton. 2d lieut 5th Cav., U.S. Army, 1894; promoted through grades to major general, 1929; brig. general (temp.) (World War), 1918-19. At Tampa, Fla., during Spanish-Am. War, 1898; in Puerto Rico, 1898-1900; instr. U.S. Mil. Acad., 1900-03; student at French cav. sch., 1903-04; mil. attaché, Caracas, Venezuela, 1904-05, Buenos Aires, Argentina, 1905-06, in Cuba, 1906-08; instr. and organizer of cav., Cuba, 1909-12; at École Supérieure de Guerre, France, 1912; mem. Cav. Bd., 1913-14; again at École Supérieure de Guerre, 1914-15; observer with French armies in field, 1916-17, chief of Am. Mil. Mission at French Gen. Hdqrs., Apr.-Dec. 1917; comdr. 18th Inf. and 1st Inf. Brigade (both of 1st Div.); apptd. comdr. 1st Div., A.E.F., Oct. 17, 1918, and recommended for promotion to maj. gen. by Gen. Pershing, but Armistice stopped all promotions of gen. officers; grad. École Supérieure de Guerre, France, 1920; asst. prof. and student in École Supérieure de Guerre and Centre des Hautes Études, 1920-21; grad. and instr. Command and Staff Sch., Leavenworth, 1923; grad. and instr. Army War Coll., 1923-24; comd. 2d Brigade, 1st Div., 1925-27; asst. chief of staff U.S. Army, 1927-29; comdr. 6th Corps Area, 1929-32, 2d Army, 1932-33, Philippine Dept., 1933-35, 1st Div., Feb.-Mar. 1936; 8th Corps Area and 3d Army, Mar.-Sept. 1936; retired, September 30, 1936. Executive director Illinois War Council, 1942-45. Awarded D.S.M.; 2 silver star citations U.S.); Comdr. Legion of Honor (France); Comdr. Order of the Crown (Belgium); War Cross with 3 palms (France); Order of Military Merit (Cuba); Grand Cross Order of Crown (Italy); Comdr. Order of Polonia Restituta; Order of St. Olaf, Norway (first class). Comdr. Dept. of Philippine Islands, Am. Legion, 1934-35; mem. nat. exec. com., Am. Legion, 1939-44; mem. Am. Legion 5 yr. Commn. on Postwar America, 1943-48. Mem. Nat. exec. com. and Nat. defense com., Am. Legion, 1939-41; mission to Gt. Britain (Am. Legion), 1941. Memorialized by National Convention, American Legion, Sept. 20, 1944. Awarded Certificate for Meritorious Service by U.S. Office Civilian Defense, 1945. Home: Union League Club, 65 W. Jackson Blvd. Office: 188 W. Randolph St., Chicago, Ill. Died Mar. 13, 1947.

PARKER, Frederic Charles Wesby, (sec. emeritus) Kiwanis Internat.); b. Worcester, Mass., May 8, 1872; s. Charles H. and Lizzie E. (Wesby) P.; grad. Colgate Acad., 1896; student Coll. of City of N.Y., Colgate U.; A.B., Brown, 1900; grad. work, U. of Chicago, 4 yrs.; m. Grace E. Reed, Sept. 12, 1901; children—Wesby Reed, Kent Hamilton, Muriel, Elizabeth. Ordained Bapt. ministry, 1900; asso. pastor First Ch., Chicago, 1900-04, Tremont Temple, Boston, Mass., 1904-08; state sec. Oregon Bapt. State Convention, 1908-12; vocational sec. Central Y.M.C.A., Chicago, 1912-17, exec. sec., 1917-21; sec. Kiwanis Internat. 1921-41, former editor The Kiwanis Mag. Voluntary sec. Industrial Relations Assn., Chicago, 1916-41. Mem. Delta Kappa Epsilon, Phi Beta Kappa. Republican. Home: (winter) 3013 52d St. S., Gulfport, Fla.; (summer) Pioneer Cottage, Monument Beach, Cape Cod, Mass. Died Dec. 28, 1945.

PARKER, Glenn Lane, hydraulic engr.; b. Butte, Mont.; s. Claude F. and Margaret (Lane) P.; B.S., C.E. University of Kansas, 1906; post-grad. work, 1908; m. Grace I. Guy, December 16, 1914; Chainman and topographer Western Pacific R.R., Calif., 1904-05; concrete insp., instrument man. and asst. div. engr. C.B.&Q. R.R., Lincoln, Neb., 1906-07; deck officer, U.S. Coast and Geodetic Survey, Washington, 1908; jr. engr., U.S. Geol. Survey, Washington, D.C., Nome and Fairbanks, Alaska, 1909-11; jr. and asst. engr., U.S. Geol. Survey, Portland, Ore., 1911-13, dist. engr. Tacoma, Wash., 1913-39, chief hydraulic engr., Washington, since 1939. Mem. Am. Soc. Civil Engrs. (past dir.), Am. Geophysical Union, Washington Acad. of Science, A.A.A.S., Washington Irrigation Inst. (life), Tau Beta Pi, Phi Kappa Psi. Republican. Presbyn. Club: Cosmos (Washington, D.C.). Joint author: Placer Mining in the Yukon-Tanana Region, Alaska, 1911; Water Powers of the Cascade Range, parts 2-3-4, 1913-15-22; Surface Water Supply of Seward Peninsula, Alaska, 1913; Summary of Hydrometric Data in Washington, 1923; Summary of Records of Surface Waters of Washington, 1940. Home: 2706 44th St. N.W. Address: U.S. Geol. Survey, 2223 Federal Works Bldg., Washington. Died Feb. 12, 1946; buried in Rock Creek Cemetery, Washington.

PARKER, George B., newspaper editor; b. Ithaca, Mich., Sept. 10, 1886; s. Dean S. and Harriet (Johnson) P.; A.B., U. of Okla., 1908; m. Adelaide Loomis, June 12, 1912; children—George B., Mary. Successively reporter, city editor, mng. editor and editor Oklahoma News, 1909-20; editor Cleveland (O.) Press, 1920-22; editor in chief of southwestern group of Scripps-Howard Newspapers, 1922-24, gen. editorial exec. Scripps-Howard Newspapers, 1924-27, editor in chief since 1927 (19 newspapers in cities of U.S.). Awarded Pulitzer prize for editorial writing, 1936. Mem. Kappa Alpha, Phi Beta Kappa, Sigma Delta Chi. Clubs: Lotos, Kappa Alpha (Southern), Dutch Treat (New York); Overseas Writers, National Press (Washington, D.C.). Home: 1840 24th St. N.W. Office: 1013 13th St. N.W., Washington, D.C. Died Oct. 10, 1949.

PARKER, Homer Cling, ins. commr.; b. Baxley, Ga., Sept. 25, 1885; s. William Cling and Sarah Belle (Mattox) P.; B.L., Mercer U., 1908; m. Annie Laurie Mallary, Nov. 9, 1910 (died Nov. 15, 1916); children—Martha Lewis, Helen Isabel, William Mallary; m. 2d, Lenore L. Leedom, Oct. 15, 1922 (divorced); m. 3d, Wilhelmina Lowe, Jan. 26, 1942. Practiced law, Statesboro, 1908-27; solicitor, City Court, Statesboro, 1914-17; mayor of Statesboro, 1924-27; elected mem. 72d Congress, Sept. 1931, to fill vacancy, and reelected to 73d Congress (1933-35), 1st Ga. Dist.; comptroller-general of Ga., June 1936-Jan. 1937; comptroller gen. and insurance commr. State of Ga., term 1941-42, re-elected for term, 1943-46. Cadet Officers Training Camp, Ft. McPherson, Ga., May-Aug. 1917; served as capt. inf., maj., judge advocate A.U.S., 1917-20; capt. regular army, 1920-22; maj., judge advocate Reserve Corps, 1922-28; adj. gen. Ga. Nat. Guard, 1927-31 (retired). Mem. Phi Delta Theta. Democrat. Baptist. Mason, Eagle, Elk. W.O.W. Home: 1097 Briarcliff Pl., N.E. Office: State Capitol, Atlanta, Ga. Died June 22, 1946.

PARKER, Horatio Newton, bacteriologist; b. Cambridge, Mass., Feb. 3, 1871; s. Horatio G. and Harriet (Newton) P.; student Mass. Inst. Tech., 1890-95; m. Margaret L. Irwin (A.B., U. of Kan.), Feb. 25, 1922; children—Jeannette Harriet, Horatio Newton, Margaret Irwin. Asst. biologist Boston Water Works, 1896-99; asst. and chief biologist, Metropolitan Water Works, 1900-01; health officer, Montclair, N.J., 1901-04; asst. hydrographer and asst. engr. U.S. Geol. Survey, 1904-10; dairy bacteriologist, U. of Ill., and asst. at Expt. Sta., 1910-17; lecturer on municipal sanitation, Ind. U., 1917; bacteriologist and program editor Delineator 7th baby campaign, 1917-18; city bacteriologist and chemist, Jacksonville, Fla., 1918-45; dir. food and lab. div., Health Dept., 1923-45. Fellow American Pub. Health Assn., A.A.A.S., Fla. Acad. Sciences; mem. Soc. Am. Bacteriologists, Am. Chem. Soc., Am. Dairy Science Assn., Internat. Assn. Milk Sanitarians (pres. 1932-33), Association Food and Drug Officials of U. S., Association Food and Drug Officials of S.E. States (pres. 1924), New England Water Works Assn., Fla. Pub. Health Assn. (pres. 1931-32), etc. Episcopalian. Mason (K.T.). Clubs: Torch, Civitan (pres. 1939-40). Author: City Milk Supply, 1917; also many repts. and tech. articles. Home: 3603 Hedrick St., Jacksonville 5. Office: Engineer Bldg., Jacksonville, Fla. Died Dec. 22, 1946.

PARKER, James Edmund, army officer; b. Anniston, Ala., Aug. 9, 1896; s. William Edmund and Margaret (Dothard) P.; student Ala. Presbyn. Coll., 1912-15, Ala. Poly. Inst., 1915-16, Marion Mil. Inst., 1916-17; B.S., U.S. Mil. Acad., 1919; grad. F.A. Sch., 1920, Air Corps Training Sch., 1921, Air Corps Engring. Sch., 1933, Air Corps Tactical Sch., 1936; m. Florence Olsen, Dec. 11, 1920; children—Shirley, James Edmund. Commd. 2d lt., Nov. 1918, 2d lt., F.A., June 12, 1919, and advanced through the grades to maj. gen., Nov. 7, 1944; now comdg. gen. 4th Air Force, San Francisco, Calif. Mason. Clubs: Olympic, Bohemian, Presidio Golf. Address: 341 Infantry Terrace, Presidio of S.F., San Francisco, Calif. Died Mar. 19, 1946.

PARKER, John Henry, army officer; b. nr. Tipton, Mo., Sept. 19, 1866; s. Thomas H. and Nancy (Maxey) P.; grad. U.S. Mil. Acad., 1892; admitted to Mo. bar, 1896; m. Ida Burr, Sept. 22, 1892; children—Mrs. Naidene Calvert, Henry Burr; m. 2d, Bertha E. (Blair) Bortell, July 13, 1935. Second lt. 13th Inf., U.S. Army, 1892; promoted through grades to col., July 1, 1920; retired Feb. 28, 1924; promoted to brig. gen. (retired), 1941. Comd. Gatling Gun Battery, Santiago, Cuba, 1898; hon. mem. Roosevelt's Rough Riders' Assn., 1898; in Philippines, 1899-1901, and was asst. to chief judge advocate; devised in 1903, and organized at Ft. Leavenworth, Kan., the first Model Machine Gun Detachment, U.S. Army, made permanent by Gen. Order 16, War Dept., Jan. 22, 1904. Adviser to gov. of Matanzas Province, Cuba, during second Cuban intervention, and in charge of municipal improvements of province; 1908 on spl. duty organizing first Model of Unit of Machine Guns (a company) for duty with a regt. of inf., and writing necessary texts for future development of machine gun service for infantry; judge advocate, punitive expdn. to Mex., 1916; went to France as machine gun expert on Gen. Pershing's Staff, May 1917; mem. gen. staff com. on orgn. A.E.F.; organized 1st Div. and 1st Corps automatic weapons schools at Gondrecourt, army automatic weapons schools at Langres; col. 102d Inf. (Charter Oak Regt.) at Chavignon, at Chemin des Dames, at Seicheprey, at Bois de Jury, and at Château-Thierry; col. 362d Inf. (Pine Tree Regt.) at Bois de Cheppy, at Epinonville, at Gesnes; organized and comd. Am. garrison in Paris, Jan.-June 1919. Put over vocational training with aid of Red Cross, Y.M.C.A., K. of C., and Salvation Army, for the first time in Am. Army. Thrice wounded in France. Gold medallist, Mil. Service Instn., 1911; awarded D.S.M.; citations in orders of 26th (Yankee) Div. for "gallantry in action" in 12 combats; Croix de Guerre with palm; Officer Legion of Honor; Distinguished Service Cross with two oak leaves; third oak leaf awarded, 1923; Commandeur Ordre de l'Étoile Noire; recommended for brig. gen. for services in battle. Author: Gatlings at Santiago, 1898; Tactical Uses and Organization of Machine Guns in the Field, 1898; Trained Citizen Soldiery, 1915. Also author of slogan "The Army Trains Young Men for Peace," 1920. Judge advocate Dept. of Com., Disabled Vets. of World War, 1936-37. Home: Garde Hotel, New Haven, Conn. Died Oct. 13, 1942.

PARKER, Junius, lawyer; b. Smithfield, N.C., Sept. 24, 1867; s. Edward S. and Ellen C. (Northam) P.; student academic and law depts., U. of N.C., 1885-8) (non-grad.); m. Mary W. Locke, Apr. 5, 1899; children—Edward L., Frances. Practiced at Durham, N.C., 1890-94, Knoxville, Tenn., 1894-99; moved to New York as asst. gen. counsel Am. Tobacco Co. and its allied companies, 1899; became gen. counsel same, 1912, chmn. bd., 1925; resigned 1929. Mem. Am. Bar Assn., N.Y. State Bar Assn., Assn. Bar City of New York (chmn. exec. com., 1922-23), N.Y. Southern Soc. (pres., 1922-23). Home: 300 Park Av. Office: 41 E. 42d St., New York, N.Y. Died June 11, 1944.

PARKER, Ralph Robinson, pub. health entomologist; b. Malden, Mass., Feb. 23, 1888; s. Frank Howard and Marion Ellen (King) P.; B.S., Massachusetts State Coll., 1912, M.Sc., 1914, Ph.D., 1915, LL.D., 1943; D.Sc., Montana St. U., 1937; married Adah L. Nicolet, 1916 (died 1931); children—Jane Louise, Robert Adams; m. 2d, Vivian Kaa, June 22, 1932. Asst. entomologist Mont. State Bd. of Entomology, 1915-21; spl. expert, U.S. Pub. Health Service, 1921-47, dir. since 1947; dir. Rocky Mountain Lab., U.S. Pub. Health Service, Hamilton, Mont., since 1928. Pres. Internat. Northwestern Conf. on Diseases of Nature Communicable to Man, 1947-48. Mem. Alpha Sigma Phi, Phi Kappa Phi, Phi Sigma. Author of over 100 papers on Rocky Mountain spotted fever and other diseases. Home: Hamilton, Mont. Died Sep. 4, 1949.

PARKER, Robert Shumate, pres. Fed. Reserve Bank of Atlanta, Ga.; Dalton, Ga., Aug. 23, 1884; s. Robert Everett and Catherine Bitting (Shumate) P.; B.A., Emory U., 1905; B.L., U. of Ga., 1907; m. Helen Jennings Cay, June 5, 1911. Admitted to Georgia bar, 1907; engaged in gen. practice of law with various firms, 1907-35; gen. counsel Fed. Reserve Bank of Atlanta, Ga., Dist. 6, 1931-36, 1st v.p. and gen. counsel, 1936-39, pres. since 1939. Mem. Phi Beta Kappa, Chi Phi. Democrat. Episcopalian. Clubs: Capital City, Rotary (Atlanta). Home: 34 Palisades Rd. Office: 104 Marietta St., Atlanta, Ga. Died Mar. 28, 1941.

PARKER, Theodore Bissell, civil engr.; b. Roxbury, Mass., Aug. 20, 1889; s. Franklin Wells and Sarah (Bissell) P.; B.S. in C.E., Mass. Inst. Tech., 1911, grad. study, 1912; grad. U.S. Army Engr. Sch., 1922, U.S. Command and Gen. Staff Sch., 1933; m. Estelle Peabody, May 10, 1913; children—Franklin Peabody, Nancy. Asst. instr. in civil engring., Mass. Inst. Tech., 1911-12; engr. with H. C. Keith, N.Y. City, 1912; engr. Utah Power & Light Co., Salt Lake City, 1912-17; with Elec. Bond & Share Co., N.Y. City, 1919-20; engr. with Stone & Webster, Inc., 1922-33; state engr. and acting state dir. Pub. Works Administrn. for Mass., 1933-35; chief constrn. engr. Tenn. Valley Authority, 1935-38, chief engr., 1938-43; prof. civil engring., Mass. Inst. Tech. and head dept. civil and sanitary engring. since 1943. Served as 1st lt. and capt. U.S. Army Engrs., 1917-19; capt. Corps of Engrs., 1920-22. Mem: American Soc. Civil Engrs., Soc. Am. Mil. Engrs., Boston Soc. Civil Engrs., Sigma Chi. Home: 115 Woodlawn Av., Wellesley Hills, Mass. Office: Mass. Institute of Technology, Cambridge, Mass. Died Apr. 27, 1944.

PARKER, Torrance; b. Richmond, Va., Apr. 22, 1872; s. David Bigelow and Victoria Anna (Howe) P.; A.B., Harvard, 1895; student law dept. same univ., 1894-95; m. Jessie Southard, Oct. 22, 1896; children—Mrs. Katherine Reswick, Torrance (dec.). Admitted to Mass. bar, 1896, and since practiced at Boston. Pres. The First Ch. of Christ Scientist, Boston, 1924-25; retired Aug. 1, 1943. Mem. Loyal Legion. Republican. Home: Belmont, Mass. Died Oct. 15, 1945.

PARKER, William Edward, civil engr.; b. Newton, Mass., Mar. 21, 1876; s. William Chipman and Emily A. (Goodwin) P.; B.S. in C.E., Mass. Inst. of Tech., 1899; m. Annie Marie Knowles, June 5, 1905; 1 dau., Emily Louise. With Boston & Albany R.R., 1899; asst. engr. Newport News (Va.) Shipbuilding & Dry Dock Co., 1900-01; successively aid, asst. hydrographic and geodetic engr., U.S. Coast and Geodetic Survey, since 1901; transferred to Naval R.F., Sept. 24, 1917, with rank of lt. comdr. for duration of war; in charge compass office, Naval Obs., to Mar. 1919; chief of div. of hydrography and topography, U.S. Coast and Geod. Survey, 1919-31; retired from active duty with relative rank of capt., U.S.N., Nov. 1934. Mem. Am. Soc. C.E., Am. Geophys. Union, Washington Acad. Sciences, Assn. Mil. Engrs., Am. Legion. Club: Federal (Washington). Home: Fort Lauderdale, Fla. Died Sept. 30, 1942.

PARKER, William M., judge; b. Oil City, Pa., Dec. 19, 1870; s. George W. and Rebecca (McCready) P.; A.B., Princeton, 1891; LL.D., Grove City Coll.; m. Helen Innis, Apr. 21, 1898; children—Helen Elizabeth (dec.), Marian (Mrs. John H. Johnson), Warren I., Rebecca M. (Mrs. Harry E. Cummins), William M. Admitted to Pennsylvania bar, 1895, and in general practice, 1895-1926; judge Common Pleas Court, Venango County, 1926-32; judge Superior Court of Pa., 1932-40; justice Supreme Court of Pa. since 1940. Republican. Presbyterian. Home: 305 W. 4th St., Oil City, Pa. Died Aug. 15, 1943.

PARKHURST, Lewis, businessman; b. Dunstable, Mass., July 26, 1856; s. Thomas H. and Sarah (Wright) P.; A.B., Dartmouth, 1878, A.M., 1908, LL.D., 1928; m. Emma Wilder, Nov. 18, 1880 (died Mar. 29, 1945); children—Wilder L. (dec.), Richard. Prin. gram. sch., Fitchburg, Athol and Winchester high sch.; 1st pres. Middlesex Co. Nat. Bank; trustee Winchester Savings Bank; treas. of Ginn & Co., pubs. (retired 1933). Mem. Mass. Ho. of Rep., 1908; state senator, 1921-22; del. Rep. Nat. Conv., Chicago, 1920; pres. Republican Club of Mass., 1915-16. Trustee Dartmouth Coll., 1908-40. Republican. Unitarian. Clubs: Union, Republican of Mass. Home: Winchester, Mass. Died Mar. 28, 1949.

PARKINSON, Donald Berthold, architect; b. Los Angeles, Calif., Aug. 10, 1895; s. John and Meta (Breckenfeld) P.; B.S., Mass. Inst. of Tech., 1920; special student Am. Acad. at Rome (Italy), 1921; m. Frances Grace Wells, Sept. 12, 1921; 1 son, Donald Wells. Began as an architect, 1920; now mem. John Parkinson & Donald B. Parkinson, architects, designed war plants for Lockheed Aircraft Corp., Vega Aircraft Corp. and Lockheed Navy Service Center; dir. Bowlus Sailplanes, Inc.; sec. and dir. Paul Mantz Air Services Ltd. Served in air service, U.S. Army, 1917-18; major, corps of engineers, U.S. Army, 1942-43, major, air corps, Nov. 1943-Dec. 1944, retired. Member Los Angeles Earthquake Advisory Commission 1933; mem. Los Angeles Municipal Art Commission 2 years. Received 5 honor awards of Am. Inst. of Architects, 2 certificates of merit; hon. mention in 5th Pan-Am. Congress of Architects, Montevideo, 1940; highest award Architectural Forum jury, 1940. Mem. Delta Kappa Epsilon. Democrat. Episcopalian. Clubs: Kennebunk (Me.) Beach Chowder and Marching; California; Los Angeles Country; Santa Monica (Calif) Beach. Home: 1605 San Vicente Blvd., Santa Monica, Calif. Died 1946.

PARKS, Addison Karrick, dentist; b. Perryville, Ky., June 7, 1875; s. William Huston and Rebecca Elizabeth (Karrick) P.; grad. Ewing (Ky.) Inst., 1894; D.D.S., Vanderbilt, 1898; grad. study, N.Y. City, 1916-17; m. Julia Edna Dugan, June 7, 1900; children—Woodford Huston, Julia Irvine. Began practice at Bloomfield, Ky., 1899-1905; removed to Montevallo, Ala., 1905, to Montgomery, Ala., 1917; specialist in denture prosthesis since 1917; chief of prosthetic div. of Coll. of Dentistry, U. of Tenn., since 1934. Pres. Ala. Bd. Dental Examiners, 1914. A.-d.-c., col., staff of gov. of Ky., 1935. Fellow Am. Coll. Dentists; mem. Nat. Soc. Denture Prosthetists (pres. 1929-30), Ala. Dental Assn. (pres. 1913), Delta Sigma Delta (grand master Ala. Auxiliary, 1924), Omicron Kappa Upsilon. Democrat. Presbyterian. Mason (Shriner), Odd Fellow. Club: Kiwanis. Collaborator Nichol's Prosthetic Dentistry; contbr. to Dental Digest. Home: 14 S. McLean; (summer) Montgomery, Ala. Office: Exchange Bldg., Memphis, Tenn. Died Jan. 5, 1943.

PARKS, Samuel Conant, banker; b. near Auburn, Ill., May 15, 1859; s. Thomas Scearle and Nancy C. Poley (Pauly) P.; A.B., U. of Mich., 1885; Ph.D., U. of Halle, Germany, 1888; m. Clara Hills, Apr 24, 1889; 1 son, Harold H. Settled at Lander, Wyo., 1888; v.p. 1st Nat. Bank, Lander, 1892, pres. since 1910; dir. Shoshone Nat. Bank (Cody, Wyo.), Jackson Park Town Site Co. Served as federal coal adminstr., Fremont County, Wyo., 1918-19. Trustee U. of Wyo., 1898-1903, Fremont County Library, 1907-19; mem. State Bd. of Edn., Wyo., 1917-33; dir. Bishop Randall Hosp., Landler, 1912-20. Mem. Am. Bankers Assn. (exec. council, 1926-29), Phi Kappa Psi, Phi Beta Kappa. Republican. Mason (K.T., 32°). Kiwanian. Home: Lander, Wyo. Died Dec. 25, 1944; buried at Auburn, Ill.

PARMENTER, Bertice Marvin (pär'mĕn-tẽr), ex-asst. atty. gen. U.S.; b. Bethel, Vt., Jan. 23, 1867; s. Marvin and Alzina Elizabeth (Clapp) P.; ed. pub. schs.; m. Emma Ellsworth, June 9, 1888; children—Gladys J. (Mrs. Wm. H. MacIlwain), Arch M. Admitted to Okla. bar, 1901, and began practice at Lawton; asst. atty. gen. of U.S., 1925-29; mem. law firm Parmenter & Kulp. Republican. Christian Scientist. Rotarian. Home: 524 Eubanks St. Office: First Nat. Bldg., Oklahoma City, Okla. Died Feb. 16, 1945.

PARRIOTT, James Deforis (păr'rĭ-ŏt), lawyer; b. New Martinsville, W.Va., June 16, 1880; s. George W. and Jane (Clark) P.; student W.Va. U., 1903-09; m. Elizabeth Sadler, Apr. 14, 1910; children—Foster Clark (U.S. Army), Susan A. Vitt, Joseph Marshall (U.S. Army), James Deforis (U.S. Army Air Corps). County supt. schs., Marshall County, W.Va., 1903-07; began law practice at Moundsville, W.Va., 1909; pros. atty. Marshall County, 1913-21; govt. appeal agt., Draft Bd., World War; removed to Denver, Colo., 1926; atty. for City and County of

Denver, 1931-35; Rep. nominee for gov. Colo., 1932; Rep. nominee for Congress, 1940. Pres. Colo. chapter 1, Am. War Dads, Inc., 1943. Mem. Am., Colo. State and Denver bar assns., S.R. (past pres. Colo. Soc.), Sigma Nu. Methodist. Mason. Clubs: Lakewood Country, Kiwanis (dist. gov. 1935); Lincoln Republican (pres. 1937-39). Pres., President's Round Table, 1939. Home: 4045 E. 18th Av. Office: Equitable Bldg., Denver, Colo. Died Nov. 24, 1948.

PARSONS, Charles Francis, lawyer; b. Mankato, Minn., Jan. 18, 1872; s. S. DeWitt and Frances (White) P.; LL.B., U. of Mich., 1893; unmarried. Practiced in San Diego, Calif., 1893-95, Los Angeles, 1895-98; admitted to practice before Supreme Court of Hawaii, 1898; mem. Smith & Parsons, Hilo, 1900-04; judge Circuit Court, 4th Circuit, H.T., 1904-16; U.S. atty. Dist. of Hawaii, Feb. 2, 1925-Feb. 25, 1926; judge 2d Div. 1st Circuit Court, Honolulu, Feb. 25-Oct. 25, 1926; asso. justice Supreme Court of Hawaii, 1926-35. Asso. mem. Legal Advisory Bd., 4th Jud. Circuit, Hawaii, 1917-18; chmn. of and counsel civilian relief and home service dept., Island of Hawaii br. Am. Red Cross, 1919; etc. Republican. Charter mem. U. of Mich. Chapter of Delta Chi. Mem. Am. Bar Assn., Hawaiian Soc. S.A.R., Hawaiian Hist. Soc., Am. Judicature Soc., Bar Assn. of Hawaii. Address: P.O. Box 378, Honolulu, Hawaii. Died Nov. 20, 1944.

PARSONS, Edward Smith, coll. pres.; b. Brooklyn, N.Y., Aug. 9, 1863; s. Charles Henry and Esther Rosetta (Smith) P.; grad. Brooklyn Collegiate and Poly. Inst., 1879; A.B., Amherst, 1883, A.M., 1886, L.H.D., 1903; Columbia U., 1883-84; B.D., Yale, 1887; LL.D., Ohio Wesleyan U., 1929, Marietta (Ohio) Coll., 1935; m. Mary Augusta Ingersoll, Dec. 4, 1889; children—Esther, Charles Edwards (dec.), Elizabeth Ingersoll, Josephine (dec.), Edward Smith, Talcott. Ordained Congl. ministry, 1888; pastor First Ch., Greeley, Colo., 1888-92; prof. English, 1892-1917, v.p., 1898-1916, dean, 1901-17, Colo. Coll., also co-founder and first pres. Rocky Mt. Athletic Conf.; asso. sec. War Personnel Bd., Nat. War Work Council of Y.M.C.A., New York, 1917-19; pres. Marietta (O.) Coll., 1919-36, now pres. emeritus. Mem. Assn. of Ohio Coll. Pres. and Deans (pres. 1922-23), Ohio Coll. Assn. (pres. 1923-24), Chi Psi, Phi Beta Kappa. Clubs: Century (New York); Authors (London). Author: The Social Message of Jesus, 1911. Editor: Milton's Minor Poems, 1900; The Earliest Life of Milton, 1902. Home: Jaffrey, N.H. Died Apr. 22, 1943.

PARSONS, Elsie Clews (Mrs. Herbert Parsons), anthropologist; b. 1875; d. Henry and Lucy Madison (Worthington) Clews; A.B., Barnard Coll. (Columbia), 1896, A.M., 1897, Ph.D., 1899; m. Herbert Parsons, Sept. 1, 1900. Pres. Am. Anthropol. Assn., 1940-41. Author: Educational Legislation and Administration of the Colonial Government (U.S.A.), 1899; The Family, 1906; The Old-fashioned Woman, 1913; Fear and Conventionality, 1914; Social Freedom, 1915; Social Rule, 1916; Notes on Zuni, 1917; Folk Tales of Andros Island, Bahamas, 1918; Winter and Summer Dance Series in Zuni, 1922; Laguna Genealogies, 1923; Folk Lore of the Sea Islands, S.C., 1923; Folk Lore from the Cape Verde Islands, 1924; Scalp Ceremonial of Zuni, 1924; Pueblo of Jemez, 1925; Pueblo Indian Journal, 1925; Tewa Tales, 1926; Kiowa Tales, 1929; Social Organization of the Tewa of New Mexico, 1929; Hopi and Zuni Ceremonialism, 1933; Folk Lore of the Antilles, French and English, 1933, 1936; Taos Pueblo, 1936; Mitla (Oaxaca, Mexico), 1936; Pueblo Indian Religion, 1939; Taos Tales, 1940; Notes on the Caddo, 1941. Editor: Notes on Cochiti (Dumarest), 1920; American Indian Life, 1922; Stephen's Hopi Journal, 1936. Died Dec. 19, 1941.

PARSONS, Philip Archibald, sociologist; b. Hamilton, Ill., Jan. 9, 1879; s. Henry Beeman and Martha Ann (Wagonner) P.; A.B., Christian U., Canton, Mo., 1904; student Union Theol. Sem., 1904-06; fellow New York Sch. of Philanthropy, 1908-09; Ph.D., Columbia, 1909; LL.D., Culver-Stockton Coll., Canton, Mo., 1927; m. Helen Therece Stahlberger, July 3, 1909; children—Katrine Wagonner and Helene; m. 2d, Lucile G. Bean, July 31, 1926. Ordained Presbyn. ministry, 1904; prof. sociology, Syracuse U., 1909-20 and head of dept., 1912-20; dir. University Settlement 1912-18; on leave of absence, 1918-19, with Commn. on Training Camp Activities; prof. applied sociology and dir. Portland Sch. of Social Work, U. of Ore., 1920-26, dean, 1926-29, dean Sch. of Applied Social Science, 1929-32, head dept. of sociology, Coll. of Social Science, also dir. Bureau Social Research and Service and editor Commonwealth Review. Ore. rep. Nat. Economic League; pres. Ore. Social Workers Assn., 1921 (exec. council, 1922-25); pres. Pub. Welfare Bur., 1922; pres. Americanization Council, 1925; v.p. Nat. Conf. of Social Work, 1925-26; dir. Travelers Aid Soc.; chmn. Ore. Child Welfare Commn., 1928-31, and mem. of the welfare com., 1931-36; pres. Portland Council Social Agencies, 1925, v.p., 1926; sec. Oregon Crime Commn.; chmn. Ore. Planning Council, 1934; mem. N.W. Regional Planning Commn., 1934, Ore. Planning Bd., 1935-39; chmn. Advisory Research Council, 1935; asso. mem. N.W. Regional Planning Commn. since 1935. Mem. Am. Sociol. Soc., Am. Inst. Criminal Law and Criminology, Nat. Council Am. Assn. Social Workers, Nat. Probation Assn., Nat. Liberal League, Am. Assn. Training Schs. for Professional Social Work, Am. Eugenics Soc., Nat. Council, Inst. Pacific Relations, Sigma Nu, Beta Epsilon, Alpha Kappa Delta, Phi Kappa Phi. Mason. Author: Responsibility for Crime, 1909; An Introduction to Modern Social Problems, 1924; Crime and the Criminal, 1926; Nature and Prospects of Civilization, 1936. Home: Eugene, Ore. Died Mar. 14, 1943.

PARSONS, Starr, lawyer; b. Lynnfield Center, Mass., Sept. 4, 1869; s. Eben and Mary Alvina (Dodge) P.; prep. edn. Boston (Mass.) Latin Sch.; A.B., Harvard, 1891; m. Minnie C. Bickford, June 26, 1894; 1 son, Eben. Admitted to Mass. bar, 1893, and practiced since at Lynn; mem. law firm Parsons & Wadleigh. City solicitor, Lynn, 1897-1907, Commr. of relief, Pythian Relief Fund. Mem. Am. Bar Assn., Mass. State Bar Assn., Essex County Bar Assn. (pres. 1916-20), Unitarian Layman's League, Phi Beta Kappa. Republican. K.P. Club: Colonial Golf and Country. Home: 17 Conant Rd., Marblehead, Mass. Office: 14 Central Av., Lynn, Mass. Died June 15, 1948.

PARSONS, William, clergyman, editor; b. Luton, Bedfordshire, Eng., Feb. 11, 1867; s. Alfred William and Sarah (Costin) P.; brought to U.S., 1870; A.B., Baker U., Baldwin, Kan., 1891, A.M., 1894; B.D., McCormick Theol. Sem., Chicago, Ill., 1894; D.D., Geneva Coll., Beaver Falls, Pa., 1906; m. Elizabeth Stevenson, July 3, 1894; children—Cecelia (dec.), Catherine (Mrs. C. D. Junkin), Margaret (Mrs. E. G. Butler). Ordained Presbyn. ministry, 1893; pastor successively Peoria and Sparta (Ill.), Beaver Falls (Pa.), Eugene (Ore.), Claremont, Jersey City (N.J.) until 1923; asso. editor The Christian Statesman, 1907-12; prof. Bible, Albany (Ore.) Coll., 1915-16; editor The Christian Statesman, 1926-29, now asso. editor. Sec. Nat. Reform Assn., 1905-12; asso. sec. Presbyn. Bd. of Temperance, 1918-19. Republican. Active promoter of prohibition. Home: Route 2, Windsor, Vt. Died Feb. 12, 1942.

PARTON, Lemuel Frederick, writer; b. Platteville, Colo.; s. George and Elizabeth (McCutcheon) P.; B.S., U. of Colo., 1903; m. Mary Field, June 19, 1913; 1 dau., Margaret Anne. Reporter Chicago City Press Assn., 1903, Chicago Tribune, 1904-07; writing and prospecting Nev. goldfields, 1907-08; writing and exploring S. America, 1908-10; city editor Los Angeles Herald, 1910-11; asso. editor San Francisco Bulletin, 1917-19; corr. in Europe, 1923, sub-Arctic, 1924; author of nationally syndicated newspaper column, "Who's News Today," N.Y. Sun, since 1931. Mem. Alpha Tau Omega. Mem. Soc. of Friends. Clubs: Dutch Treat (N.Y. City); National Press (Washington, D.C.). Contbr. articles to magazines; lecturer. Home: Palisades, N.Y. Office: 247 W. 43rd St., New York, N.Y. Died Jan. 30, 1943.

PARTRIDGE, Donald Barrows, ex-congressman; b. Norway, Me., June 7, 1891; s. Winfield Scott and Frances Rosamond (Barrows) P.; grad. high sch., Norway, 1910; B.S., Bates Coll., Lewiston, Me., 1914; m. Geneva Whitman Sturtevant, Dec. 30, 1914; children—Donald Barrows, Charles Sturtevant, Jerry Carleton. Prin. high sch., Canton, Me., 1914-17; admitted to Me. bar, 1924, to practice before Supreme Court of U. S. 1933; clerk, Supreme Judicial Court, Oxford County, Me., 1919-31; town clerk, Norway, 1925-31; mem. 72d Congress (1931-33) 2d Me. Dist.; now in practice of law; mem. Me. Industrial Accident Commn. since 1937. Mem. Sch. Bd., Norway, 1925-31. Chmn. Oxford County Rep. Com. 6 yrs. Mem. Me. State and Oxford County bar assns. Mason, K.P.; mem. O.E.S. Congregationalist. Clubs: Bates College, Kiwanis. Home: Norway, Me. Died June 5, 1946.

PARTRIDGE, Frank Charles, lawyer, ex-senator; b. East Middlebury, Vt., May 7, 1861; s. Charles F. and Sarah A. (Rice) P.; A.B., Amherst Coll., 1882; LL.B., Columbia U., 1884; LL.D., Middlebury Coll., 1909; m. Sarah L. Sanborn, May 7, 1907; children—Frances, Charles Frank, Sanborn, Ruth, David. Solicitor Dept. of State, Washington, 1890-93, U.S. minister to Venezuela, 1893-94; consul-gen. at Tangier, 1897-98; mem. Vt. Senate, 1898-1900; chmn. com. to propose amendments to Vt. Constn., 1909; mem. Vt. Com. of Public Safety, 1917-19; rewrote Consular Regulations, 1896; apptd. umpire British-Venezuela Claims Commn. and Netherlands-Venezuela Claims Commn., 1903, but unable to serve; del. of U.S. to 5th Pan-Am. Conf., Santiago, Chile, 1923; apptd. U.S. senator to fill vacancy, 1930, term expired 1931. Mem. exec. council Am. Soc. Internat. Law, 1906-23, and N.E. council, 1925-27; chmn. Vt. Bankers State Committee, 1932-33. Dir. Proctor Trust Co., 1891-1937, pres., 1908-19; pres. Vt. Marble Co., 1911-35, now chmn.; pres. Clarendon & Pittsford R.R. Co., 1911-37; pres. Crystal River and San Juan R.R. Co., 1928-35; director Rutland R.R. Co., 1925-41; president Vermont Flood Credit Corporation, 1927-35; dir. Nat. Life Ins. Co. Trustee Middlebury Coll. Mem. Phi Beta Kappa, Delta Upsilon, Phi Delta Phi. Club: Tobique Salmon (N.B.). Home: Proctor, Vt. Died Mar. 2, 1943.

PASCHAL, Franklin Cressey (păs'k'l), psychologist b. Chillicothe, Ill., Feb. 6, 1890; s. Frank Alexander and Hattie E. (Hendry) P.; A.B., De Pauw, 1911; A.M., U. of Pa., 1916, Ph.D., 1918; m. Gail M. Grant, July 23, 1924; children—Franklin C., Muriel, Eugene C. Prin. high school, Sibley, Ia., 1911-12; psychologist Ind. Reformatory, Jeffersonville, 1912-16, dir. research, 1914-16; Harrison fellow in psychology, U. of Pa., 1916-17, teaching asst., 1917-18; psychologist Med. Research Lab. of Air Service, Mineola, L.I., 1918-19; asst. prof., later prof. psychology, U. of Ariz., 1919-27, also dean of men, 1922-25 and registrar, 1925-27; asso. dean Coll. of Arts and Science and prof. of psychology, 1927-29, dean, 1929-35, Vanderbilt U., dean, Jr. Coll., 1935-44; prof. of psychology, Wittenberg Coll. since 1945. Chmn. Southern Dean's Conf., 1931; pres. Tenn. Coll. Assn., 1935. Mem. Am. Psychol. Assn., Phi Beta Kappa, Sigma Nu, Phi Kappa Phi. Presbyn. Mason. Home: 507 N. Woodlawn Ave., Springfield, Ohio. Office: Wittenberg College, Springfield, Ohio. Died Sep. 12, 1947.

PASMA, Henry Kay (păz'mȧ), clergyman, author; b. Oosterbierum, Friesland, Netherlands; s. Claus Peter and Clarissa (Nauta) P.; student Rutgers Coll., New Brunswick, N.J.; A.B, Hope Coll., Holland, Mich., 1910, A.M, 1913; grad. Western Theol. Sem., Holland, Mich., 1913; Ph.D., George Washington U., 1929; m. Olive Lucy Barnaby, May 21, 1913; children—Miriam Clarissa, Theodore Kay, Timothy Worden, Harriet Blanche (dec.). Came to U.S., 1899, naturalized citizen, 1913. Ordained ministry Reformed Ch. in America, 1913; pastor Oostburg, Wis., and Lynden, Wash., until 1922, Southern Presbyn. Church, Charleston, Miss., 1922-27, Presbyn. Ch., Rockville, Md., since 1927. Mem. bd. dirs. Wis. Memorial Acad., Cedar Grove, Wis., 1915-17; mem. Council of Hope Coll., 1921-22; stated clk. Classis of Cascades, Ref. Ch. of America, 1920-22; moderator Presbytery of Potomac, 1936. Fellow Am. Geog. Soc.; mem. Pi Gamma Mu. Mason. Club: Rockville Rotary (pres. 1937-38). Author: Things a Nation Lives By, 1925; God's Picked Young Men, 1926; Close-Hauled, 1930; The Enchanted Sword, 1932; also articles in mags. and religious periodicals. Home: 112 Forest Av., Rockville, Md. Deceased.

PASMORE, Henry Bickford (păz'môr), musician; b. Wis., June 27, 1858; s. John Lane and Mary Anne (Bickford) P.; studied with William Shakespeare and Richard Cummins, London, and with Jadassohn and Renicke, at Leipzig Conservatory of Music; m. May S. Stanton, 1886; children—Mary, Suzanne, Dorothy, Harriet (Radiana Pazmor), Edith Sappington, John L.—the first 4 professional musicians and the other two physicians. Formerly teacher of singing at Stern Conservatory, Scharwenka Conservatory (Berlin), Stanford U., Mills Coll., Coll. of the Pacific, etc. Mem. Calif. State Music Teachers' Assn., Pacific Coast-Acad. of Teachers of Singing (dir.). Clubs: Faculty (U. of Calif.); Musicians, Sequoia (San Francisco). Composer of numerous songs, choruses and orchestra pieces; Mass in 3 flats; "Ave Maria," solo, voice and organ, composed in 1882, no repetition of words; Lakora (opera; book by Ruth Comfort Mitchell); Communion Service in E; The Madonna and Child (poem by Dr. Derrick N. Lehmer); "Gloria California" (ode; poem by Charles Keeler; soli, chorus, orchestra). Address: 56 Lloyd St., San Francisco, Calif.* Died Feb. 22, 1944.

PASSANO, Edward B. (păs ăn'ō), printer, publisher; b. Baltimore, Md., Aug. 11, 1872; s. Louis Durbin and Alice (Magruder) P.; grad. Lehigh U., 1894; m. Eleanor Phillips Isaac, Oct. 25, 1900; children—William Moore, Edward Magruder. With William & Wilkins Co., Baltimore, Md., since 1898, pres., 1902-42, chmn. bd. since 1942; pres. Waverly Press since 1925. Spl. expert U.S. Shipping Bd., 1918. Established Passano Foundation, Inc., 1943 to aid med. research. Fellow A.A.A.S.; hon. life mem. Am. Soc. M.E.; mem. Soc. Colonial Wars in Md. (gov. 1939-40), S.R., Am. Clan Gregor, Delta Phi. Clubs: University, Engineers, Merchants, Elkridge Country (Baltimore). Trained as engr., economic circumstances led to connection with printing bus., and since scientific management became a recognized branch of mech. engring. has applied the principle to printing industry (since 1913); established first publishing orgn. in U.S. catering exclusively to pubs. for research science. Home: The Beeches, York Rd. and Susquehanna Av., Towson, Md. Office: Mt. Royal and Guilford Av., Baltimore, Md. Died June 13, 1946.

PATCH, Alexander McCarrell, Jr., army officer; b. Fort Huachucua, Ariz., Nov. 23, 1889; s. Alexander McCarrell and Annie (Moore) P.; student Lehigh U., 1908-09; grad. West Point Mil. Acad., 1913; student British G.H.Q. Machine Gun Sch., Sept.-Dec. 1917, Gen. Staff Coll., 1924-25, War Coll., 1930-31; m. Julia A. Littell, Nov. 20, 1916; children—Alexander McCarrell, III, (killed, France, October 22, 1944), Julia Ann. Commissioned 2d lieutenant, U.S. Army, 1913; promoted through grades to lt.-col., 1935; temporary rank of brig. gen., 1941; major gen., Mar. 1942; became comdr. U.S. Forces on Guadalcanal, Dec. 1943; returned to U.S. comdg. Desert Training Center; then comdr. IV Army Corps, Calif.; comdr. 7th Army, Allied invasion ground forces, Southern France, Aug. 1944. Comdr. 7th Army, Mar. 1, 1944, lt. gen. Aug. 7, 1944; brig. gen. (permanent), Oct. 1945. Mem. Psi Upsilon. Club: Army-Navy Country (Washington). Address: care War Dept., Washington, D.C. Died Nov. 21, 1945.

PATERSON, James Venn, shipbuilder; b. Glasgow, Scotland, June 17, 1867; s. Robert (M.D., F.R.C.S.) and Marion (Gunn) P.; spl. course in philosophy, mathematics and naval architecture, U. of Glasgow, 1888; m. Marie Josephine, d. David Provost Vandeventer, Apr. 28, 1898. Chief draftsman, Naval Works, Southampton, Eng., 1890-92; came to U.S., 1892; naval architect Internat. Nav. Co. and Internat. Mercantile Marine Co. at Phila. and N.Y. City, 1892-1905; v.p. and gen. mgr. The Moran Co., Seattle, Wash., 1906-08; pres. and gen. mgr. same, 1908-12; pres. and gen. mgr. Seattle Constrn. & Dry Dock Co., 1912-16; built submarines in Vancouver, B.C., for Electric Boat Co., 1917. Asso. mem. Naval Cons. Bd., U.S.; now cons. and designing practice. Mem.

Soc. Naval Architects and Marine Engrs., Am. Soc. M.E., Instn. Naval Architects (London), Inst. Engrs. and Shipbuilders in Scotland. Unitarian. Home: 1025 Boylston Av. N., Seattle 2, Wash. Died May 19, 1947

PATIÑO, Simon I. (pä-tē'nyō), Bolivian industrialist, "tin king"; b. Cochabamba, Bolivia, June 1, 1862; ed. pub. and pvt. schs., Bolivia; married; 2 sons, 3 daughters. Signed contract with owner of La Salvadora mine, Uncia Mountain, Bolivia, to buy, monthly, tin concentrates containing approximately two tons of fine tin, 1894; acquired half interest in property, 1895; had complete control, 1897, expanding until became owner of largest tin deposits in the world. Organized under the laws of Del., the Patiño Mines and Enterprises Consol. (Inc.), the largest tin producers in the world, 1924 (the tin ores are smelted in England for the use of the United Nations). Patiño Mines and other companies operating in Bolivia under its administration account for 50 per cent of Bolivia's tin output. Pres., Patiño Mines and Enterprises Consol. (Inc.), Bolivian Tin and Tungsten Mines Corp., Consol. Tin Smelters, Gen. Tin Investments. Established Banco Mercantil, and has given great impulse to cattle raising and breeding in Bolivia; also established Patiño Univ. Foundation; provides free grade school education for thousands of workmen's children. Bolivia's minister to Spain, 1920-26, to France, 1926-41. Awarded Grand Cross of Order of El Condor, Grand Cross order of Military Merit (Bolivia); Grand Cross of Order of Holy Sepulchre, Grand Cross of Order of Isabel la Católica (by the Spanish king). Died Apr. 20, 1947.

PATON, James Morton (păt'ŏn), archaelogist; b. New York, N.Y., May 12, 1863; s. Thomas C. M. and Elizabeth L. (Allen) P.; A.B., New York U., 1883; A.B., Harvard, 1884; grad. student, classical philology, Harvard, 1884-87; student U. of Bonn, 1891-92, 1893-94, Ph.D., 1894, Am. Sch. Classical Studies, Athens, Greece, 1892-93; unmarried. Prof. Latin, Middlebury (Vt.) Coll., 1887-91; instr., 1895-98, asso. prof. Greek, 1898-1905, Wesleyan U.; mng. editor, 1906-08, editor-in-chief from 1917-20, Am. Jour. Archæology. Mem. mng. com. Am. Sch. Classical Studies at Athens. Mem. Archæol. Inst. America, Am. Philol. Assn., Soc. Promotion of Hellenic Studies (Eng.), Delta Phi, Phi Beta Kappa; corr. mem. Numismatic and Antiq. Soc. (Phila.). Address: Hotel Vendome, 160 Commonwealth Av., Boston 16, Mass. Died Nov. 23, 1944.

PATON, Stewart, physician; b. New York, N.Y., 1865; s. William and Anne Stavely (Agnew) P., A.B., Princeton, 1886, A.M., 1889; M.D., Coll. Phys. and Surg. (Columbia), 1889; post-grad. study Germany and Italy; m. F. Margaret Halsey, 1892; children—F. Evelyn, William, R. Townley. Formerly asso. in psychiatry, Johns Hopkins, and dir. of lab., Sheppard and Enoch Pratt Hosp., Baltimore; lecturer in neurobiology, Princeton U., in psychiatry, Columbia; consultant in mental hygiene and lecturer in psychiatry, Yale, 1926-28. Trustee Carnegie Instn., Washington, D.C. Fellow A.A.A.S.; mem. Am. Philos. Soc., Am. Neurol. Assn., N.Y. Acad. Medicine, Eugenics Research Assn. (pres. 1919). Club: Century (New York). Author: Text-Book of Psychiatry for Use of Students and Practitioners of Medicine; Education in Peace and War, 1919; Human Behavior, 1921; Signs of Sanity and the Principles of Mental Hygiene, 1922; Prohibiting Minds, 1932. Died Jan. 7, 1942.

PATRICK, Edwin Davless, army officer; b. Tell City, Ind., Jan. 11, 1894; s. John Thomas and Anna Elizabeth (Menninger) P.; student Ind. U., 1912-15; U. of Mich., 1915-16; m. Nellie May Bowen, May 15, 1925; children—Edwin Daviess, Thomas Bowen, (stepson) Ulric Boquet. Commd. 2d lt., U.S. Army, Mar. 1917, and advanced through the grades to brig. gen., May 1943. Served on Mexican border, 1917-18; A.E.F., World War I, 1918-19, Luxemburg Army of Occupation, after Dec. 1918; China, 1926-29; served on staff, commdr. S. Pacific, Dec. 1942-June 1943; chief of staff, 6th Army, South Pacific Area and southwest Pacfic area, since Déc. 1943. Mem. Phi Delta Theta. Mason. Home: Tell City, Ind. Address: A.P.O. 442, care Postmaster, San Francisco, Calif. Died Mar. 15, 1945.

PATRICK, George Thomas White, univ. prof.; b. North Boscawen, N.H., Aug. 19, 1857; s. John and Harriet (White) P.; A.B., State U. of Ia., 1878; B.D., Yale, 1885; Ph.D., Johns Hopkins, 1888; student philosophy, Leipzig U., 1894; m. Maud Lyall, Nov. 28, 1889; children—Walden White, David Lyall. Prof. philosophy, State U. of Ia., 1887-1928, prof. emeritus since 1928. Mem. American Philos. Assn., A.A.A.S., Phi Beta Kappa. Author: The Fragments of the Work of Heraclitus of Ephesus, 1889; The Psychology of Relaxation, 1916; The Psychology of Social Reconstruction, 1920; Introduction to Philosophy, 1924, revised edit., 1935; The World and Its Meaning (trade edition of Introduction to Philosophy), 1925; What Is the Mind?, 1929. Translator Külpe's Philosophy of the Present in Germany (with Maud L. Patrick), 1913. Contbr. Idealistic Confessions of a Behaviorist in symposium, Has Science Discovered God?, 1931. Contbr. to Scientific Monthly since 1890. Contributor to psychol. and philos. jours. Home: 1440 California Av. Palo Alto, Calif. Died May 21, 1949.

PATTANGALL, William Robinson (păt'ăn-gawl), lawyer and banker; b. Pembroke, Me., June 29, 1865; s. Ezra Lincoln and Arethusa B. (Longfellow) P.; B.S., U. of Maine, 1884, M.S., 1897, LL.D., 1927; LL.D., Bowdoin Coll., 1930; admitted to Me. bar, 1893; m. Jean M. Johnson, June 6, 1884 (died 1888); 1 dau., Mrs. Katharine Brown; m. 2d, Gertrude McKenzie, Sept. 27, 1892; children—Mrs. Edith P. Gilman, Mrs. Grace P. Fassett, Mrs. Josephine P. Nicolet. Editor, 1903-09. Mem. Me. Ho. of Rep., 1897, 1901, 09, 11; candidate for Congress, 4th Me. Dist., 1904, 3d Dist., 1913, 14; mem. Dem. State Com., 1905, 06, 07, chmn., 1916, 19; apptd. atty. gen. of Me., Apr. 12, 1911; elected to same office for term, 1915-16; elected mayor of Waterville, 1911, re-elected, 1912, 13; del. Dem. Nat. Conv., 1920, 24, Rep. Nat. Com., 1936 (com. on resolutions each time); candidate for gov. of Me., 1922 and 1924; apptd. asso. justice Supreme Jud. Ct. of Me., June 26, 1926, chief justice, 1930-35; now in practice of law, partner Pattangall, Goodspeed & Williamson; pres. Depositors' Trust Co., Augusta, Me., since 1933. Trustee U. of Maine, 1912-16; gov. Soc. of Mayflower Descendants in Me., 1932-33. Mem. Beta Theta Pi, Phi Beta Kappa. Unitarian. Mason (K.T.), K.P., Elk. Home: Bradbury Rd. Office: Depositors Trust Co. Bldg., Augusta, Me. Died Oct. 21, 1942.

PATTEE, Ernest Noble (păt'tē'), chemist; b. Ottawa, Can., July 21, 1864; s. James Albert and Harriet (Inglee) P.; brought to U.S., 1870; B.S., U. of Rochester, 1886, M.S., 1888; D.Sc., Syracuse U., 1922; m. Mary Norton Peck, Apr. 30, 1891. Prof. chemistry, also organizer and head of dept., Syracuse University, 1890-1942, prof. emeritus since February 1942; consulting chemist; specialist in sanitary and agricultural chemistry; city chemist, Syracuse, 1920-31. Member Am. Chem. Soc., Delta Upsilon, Phi Beta Kappa, Sigma Xi. Republican. Methodist. Home: 408 Euclid Av., Syracuse 10, N.Y. Died Jan. 17, 1946.

PATTEN, Gilbert (pen name Burt L. Standish), author; b. Corinna, Me., Oct. 25, 1866; s. William Clark and Cordelia (Simpson) P.; ed. Corinna Union Acad., 1880-84; m. Alice Gardner, Oct. 25, 1886 (divorced 1898); 1 son, Harvan Barr; m. 2d, Mary Nunn, 1900 (divorced 1916); m. 3d, Carol Kramer, June 27, 1918 (died 1939). Marketed first work of fiction at 17 and regularly thereafter; had brief experience on weekly newspaper and with own paper; regular contbr. to juvenile weeklies and monthly mags.; was staff fiction writer for Am. Press Assn.; created character Frank Merriwell and wrote weekly stories about him through 18 yrs., beginning 1896, now printed in 208 books, of which 125 million have been sold; has contributed under contract to 3 newspaper syndicates; wrote scripts for radio program, Frank Merriwell's Adventures, 1934; wrote lyric of patriotic march song, "On Freedom's Shore," sponsored by Council Against Intolerance in America, and pub. 1939. Mem. Business Men's Assn. (Camden). Advertising Club of New York. Author: Merriwell Series (208 books); Rockspur Series (3 books); Cliff Stirling Series (5 books); College Life Series (6 books); Big League Series (14 books); Rex Kingdon Series (5 books); Oakdale Series (6 books); Mr. Frank Merriwell, 1941, etc. Home: Terracino Way, Vista, Calif. Died Jan. 16, 1945; buried in Boston, Mass.

PATTEN, Zeboim Charles, mfr., banker; b. Delavan, Tazewell County, Ill., Oct. 16, 1874; s. George W. and Charlotte (Holmes) P.; grad. high sch., Chattanooga; m. Helen Lyerly, Nov. 25, 1902 (died 1927); 1 dau., Dorothy. In business in Chattanooga since 1893; chmn. exec. com. Am. Trust & Banking Co.; chmn. Chattanooga Med. Co.; v.p. O.B. Andrews Co.; dir. Ala. Great Southern Ry.; pres. Episcopal Endowment Corp. of Tenn. Chmn. War Savings Com. of Hamilton County, Tenn., World War; chmn. campaign com. which raised $850,000 for U. of Chattanooga, 1922. Trustee U. of Chattanooga. Mem. Chattanooga Mfrs. Assn. (ex-pres.). Republican. Episcopalian. Elk. Clubs: Rotary (pres. 1920-21), Mountain City, Chattanooga Golf; Fairyland (Lookout Mountain); Bankers (New York). Home: 801 Oak St., Chattanooga, Tenn. Died June 7, 1948.

PATTERSON, Alexander Evans, life ins.; b. Washington, D.C., June 23, 1887; s. William Hart and Georgie Anna (Evans) P.; ed. pub. school in Middle West; LL.D., Coe Coll., 1938; married Eleanor Morgan, Oct. 5, 1920; children—Alexander Evans, Jr., Portia. Salesman, later mgr. Equitable Life Assurance Soc., Pittsburgh, New York, Chicago, 1908-28; genl. agent, later v.p., Penn Mutual Life Ins. Co., Chicago, Phila., 1928-41; v.p., later exec. v.p., Mutual Life Ins. Co. of N.Y., 1941, pres. until Sept., 1948. Served 27 months in U.S. Army, World War I, final rank, maj. F.A. Pres. Nat. Assn. Life Underwriters, 1936; chmn. Life Agency Officers' Assn., 1939-40. Trustee Mutual Life Ins. Co. of N.Y., Roosevelt Hosp., Sigma Alpha Epsilon. Dir. N.Y. chapter Am. Red Cross. Republican. Episcopalian. Clubs: Links, River (New York); Chicago Club (Chicago). Home: 455 E. 57th St., New York; also Pineville, Pa. Office: 34 Nassau St., New York, N.Y. Died Sept. 10, 1948; buried at Mifflintown, Pa.

PATTERSON, Catherine Norris, artist; b. Phila.; d. S. Henry and Mary (Yates) Norris; ed. Miss Agnes Irwin's School, Philadelphia and Pennsylvania Academy Fine Arts, Philadelphia; m. Charles Leland Harrison, Apr. 29, 1886; children—Henry Norris Harrison, John Harrison; m. 2d, Frank Thorne Patterson, Dec. 29, 1917. Miniature painter. Has exhibited at Pa. Acad. Fine Arts, Plastic Club. Mem. Fellowship Pa. Acad. of Fine Arts, Agnes Irwin Alumnæ, Landmarks Soc. (v.p.), Soc. of Little Gardens; former pres. Asso. Com. of Women of Pa. Museum of Art. Trustee and mem. bd. Phila. Museum of Art. Clubs: Acorn, Civic, Print Club. Home: The Barclay, 18th and Rittenhouse Square, East, Philadelphia, Pa. Died Mar. 23, 1943.

PATTERSON, Eleanor Medill, editor and publisher; b. Chicago, Ill., Nov. 7, 1884; granddaughter of Joseph Medill, founder Chicago Tribune; d. Robert W. Patterson, editor, pub. Chicago Tribune, and Elinor (Medill) Patterson; sister of Joseph Medill Patterson, editor and pub. N.Y. Daily News; ed. Miss Hersey's Sch., Boston, Mass.; m. Count Joseph Gizycki, Apr. 14, 1904 (dec.); 1 dau., Countess Felicia; m. 2d, Elmer Schlesinger, Apr. 11, 1925 (dec.). Editor, publisher and sole owner of Washington (D. C.) Times-Herald; dir. Chicago Tribune Co., New York Daily News Co. and all affiliated companies. Clubs: Chevy Chase, Soroptimist, 1925 F St., Women's Nat. Press, Am. Newspaper Women's, Grasslands Country, Sulgrave (Washington). Author: (under pen name Eleanor M. Gizycka) Glass Houses, 1926; Fall Flight, 1928. Home: 15 Dupont Circle. Address: 1317 H St. N.W., Washington, D.C. Died July 24, 1948; buried in Graceland Cemetery, Chicago.

PATTERSON, Frank Allen, prof. English; b. Allen's Hill, Ontario County, N.Y., Aug. 14, 1878; s. Wilson Howell and Gertrude (Allen) P.; Genesee Wesleyan Sem., Lima, N.Y., 1897-1900; A.B., Syracuse, 1904; A.M., Columbia, 1907, Ph.D., 1911; Litt.D., Syracuse, 1938; m. Bertha Cleveland, Sept. 10, 1910; children—William Allen, Myron Cleveland. Instr. in English, Syracuse, summer 1904, Blees Mil. Acad., Macon, Mo., 1904-06; asso. in English, U. of Ill., 1911-12; instr. in English, Columbia, 1912-14, asst. prof., 1914-19, asso. prof., 1919-31, prof., 1931-43, also asst. to dir. Univ. Extension, 1912-25, asst. to dir. Summer Session, 1913-18. Founder The Facsimile Text Soc., 1929. Mem. Modern Lang. Assn. of America, Bibliog. Soc. of England, Tudor Soc. of England. Club: Men's Faculty. Author: The Middle English Penitential Lyric, 1911. Editor: The Student's Milton, 1930; Complete Works of John Milton (18 vols.), 1931; Index to Complete Work of John Milton, 2 vols., 1940. Contbr. articles, essays and reviews. Home: 120 E. Harwood Terrace, Palisades Park, N.J. Died Aug. 4, 1944.

PATTERSON, Gerard Francis, clergyman; b. Peterboro County, Ont., Can., May 28, 1867; s. William Galbraith and Ray (Wigmore) P.; U. of Toronto, 1886-88; B.D., Nashotah Theol. Sem., 1891; D.D., Kenyon Coll., Gambier, Ohio, 1936; m. 2d, Blanche Ashley Randall, Oct. 1, 1925; children by first marriage—Jerome Fee, Wilda G. (dec.), Helen Ashley (Mrs. Don D. McLennan). Came to U.S., 1888, naturalized, 1894. Deacon, 1891, priest, 1892, P.E. Ch.; missionary, Okla. Ty., 1891-93; rector St. John's Episcopal Ch., Clinton, Ia., 1893-95, Calvary Ch., Sedalia, Mo., 1895-99, Ch. of the Incarnation, Cleveland, O., 1899-1921; archdeacon and exec. sec. Diocese of Ohio, 1921-39; secretary Synod of Province Mid-west P.E. Church since 1922; president Cleveland Church Federation, 1922-23; dep. gen. Conv., 1925, 28, 31, 34, 37. Retired. Republican. Mason. Home: 3450 Ingleside Rd., Shaker Heights, Cleveland, O. Died Mar. 4, 1944.

PATTERSON, Harry Jacob, chemist; b. Yellow Springs, Pa., Dec. 17, 1866; s. William Calvin and Adaline (Mattern) P.; B.S., Pa. State Coll., 1886; post-grad. work in chemistry, same; D.Sc., Md. State Coll., 1912; m. Elizabeth Hayward Hutchinson, Oct. 25, 1895; children—Blanche Seely (Mrs. Francis T. Mack), William Calvin. Asst. chemist, Pa. State Agrl. Expt. Station, 1886-88; chemist and vice-dir., Md. Agrl. Expt. Station, 1888-98, dir. and chemist, 1898; also pres. Md. Agr. Coll., May 1913-17; dean Coll. of Agr., U. of Md., 1925; emeritus since 1937. Specialist in food, fertilizer and dairy chemistry and corn fodder products; author bulletins and articles on these subjects. Fellow A.A.A.S.; mem. Assn. Official Agrl. Chemists, Am. Chem. Soc., Soc. Chem. Industry, London. Master Md. State Grange, 1905-13; sec. Md. State Bd. of Agr., 1907-17. Home: College Park, Prince Georges County, Md. Died Sept. 11, 1948; buried St. Johns' Cemetery, Beltsville, Md.

PATTERSON, Joseph M(edill), journalist; b. Chicago, Jan. 6, 1879; s. Robert Wilson and Elinor (Medill) P.; student Groton School, 1890-96; B.A., Yale, U., 1901; m. Alice Higinbotham, Nov. 19, 1902 (divorced); children—Elinor Medill, Alicia, Josephine Medill, James; m. 2d, Mary King, July 1938. With Chicago Tribune, 1901-05; with R. R. McCormick, co-editor and pub. same, 1914-25; founded Daily News, New York, 1919, editor and publisher, 1914-46. Member Illinois Ho. of Rep., 1903; commr. of public works, Chicago, 1905-06. War corr. in China, 1900, Germany and Belgium, 1914; in France, 1915. Noncommd. officer Ill. F.A. in Tex., 1916; capt. Battery B, 149th F.A., 42d (Rainbow) Div., in actions, Lorraine sector 3 months, defense of Champagne under Gouraud, 2d battle of Marne, St. Mihiel, Argonne. Author: A Little Brother of the Rich, Dope; The Fourth Estate (with J. Keeley and Harriet Ford); By-Products; Rebellion. Clubs: Yale, The Cloud (New York); Tavern, University (Chicago). Office: 220 E. 42d St., New York. Died May 26, 1946; buried in Arlington National Cemetery.

PATTERSON, Marion D., judge; b. Williamsburg, Pa., Oct. 20, 1876; s. George Marion and Mary Rebecca (Roller) P.; student Stewart's Acad., Hollidaysburg, Pa., 1895-99; student Dickinson Law Sch., Carlisle, Pa., 1903, hon. LL.D., 1940; m. Gertrude Gable Stewart, June 23, 1925; 1 son, Marion Dean,

Jr.; step-children—John Hollister Stewart, 1st lt., United States Army Air Corps (killed in New Guinea, Jan. 1944), Frances Stewart (Mrs. George T. Logan). Public school teacher, 1895-1901; admitted to Pennsylvania bar, March 1904; district attorney of Blair County for four successive terms, 1912-28; elected president judge, Court of Common Pleas, 24th Judicial Dist. of Pa., term, 1928-38, reelected term, 1938-48; elected asso. justice Supreme Court of Pa. for 21 years, term beginning 1940. Mem. Blair County, Pa. and Am. bar assns., Delta Chi. Mason. Club: Union League (Phila.). Home: Sylvan Hills. Office: 415 Allegheny St., Hollidaysburg, Pa. Died Jan. 6, 1950.

PATTERSON, Rufus Lenoir, 2d, tobacco products machinery; b. Salem, N.C., June 11, 1872; s. Rufus Lenoir and Mary Elizabeth (Fries) P.; attended U. of N.C., 1889-90, LL.D., 1935; m. Margaret Morehead, Nov. 21, 1895; children—Morehead, Mrs. Casimir de Rham. Perfected machine automatically to weigh, pack, stamp and label smoking tobacco, and in 1898 was placed in charge of all machinery of Am. Tobacco Co., advancing to v.p.; organized, 1900, Am. Machine & Foundry Co., pres., 1900-41, chmn. bd. since 1941; organized, 1901, Internat. Cigar Machinery Co., pres., 1901-41; dir. Am. Machine & Foundry Co., Industrial Machinery Co., Ltd. Trustee Roosevelt Hosp., New York. Served as chmn. Fourth Liberty Loan Machinery, Machine Tools and Supplies Com. Mem. Pilgrim Soc., Southern Soc., North Carolina Soc. Member Legion of Honor (France). Clubs: Links, Racquet and Tennis, Metropolitan (New York); Links Golf and all Southampton clubs, where he has his home "Lenoir". New York House: 15 E. 65th St. Office: 511 5th Av., New York, N.Y. Died Apr. 11, 1943.

PATTON, George Smith, Jr., army officer; b. San Gabriel, Calif., Nov. 11, 1885; s. George Smith and Ruth (Wilson) P.; student Classical Sch. for Boys, Pasadena, Calif., 1897-1903, Va. Mil. Inst., 1903-04; B.S., U.S. Mil. Acad., 1909; grad. Cavalry Sch., 1913; grad. Advanced Equitation Class, Cav. Sch., 1914; honor grad. Command and Gen. Staff Sch., 1923; grad. War Coll., 1932; m. Beatrice Ayer, May 26, 1910; children—Beatrice (wife of Col. John K. Waters, U.S. Army), Ruth-Ellen (wife of Lt. Col. James W. Totten, U.S. Army), George, IV. Began as 2d lt., 15th Cav., U.S. Army, 1909, and advanced through the grades to general, 1945; instr. in weapons, Cav. Sch., 1914-16; aide-de-camp to Gen. Pershing, Mexico, 1916-17; sailed to England as same, May 1917; first man detailed in Tank Corps, U.S. Army, Nov. 1917; organized and comd. Tank Sch. and 1st (later 304th) Brig., 1917-19; wounded, Sept. 1918; comd. 304th Tank Brig., Camp Meade, Md., 1919-21; comd. 1st Squadron, 3d Cav., Ft. Meyer, Va., 1921-22; on gen. staff, 1923-27; in Office Chief of Cav., 1928-31; exec. officer 3d Cav., 1932-35; on Gen. Staff, 1935-37; comd. 9th Cav., 1938, 5th Cav., 1938, 3d Cav., 1938-40, 2d Armored Brig., July-Nov. 1940; became comdg. officer 2d Armored Div., Fort Benning, Ga., Nov. 1940; comd. U. S. Forces on West Coast, Morocco, N. Africa, Nov. 1942; Comdr. Central Sector, Am. Forces in Tunisia, Mar. 1943; comd. 7th Army in Sicily, July 1943); organized and comd. desert training center, March 1944; comdr. 3d Army, in France, Belgium, Luxembourg, Germany, Aug. 1944; comdr. 15th Army, France, Oct. 1945. Decorated with D.S.C., Distinguished Service medal, Silver Star, Purple Heart; Congressional Medal of Honor for Life Saving (2d class), Mexican Service medal, World War medal with 4 battle clasps, D.S.C. (with Oak Leaf Cluster), D.S.M. (2 Oak Leaf Clusters), Silver Star (Oak Leaf Cluster), Legion of Merit, Bronze Star, Life Saving Medal, Companion of the Bath, Knight Commander of British Empire, French Legion of Honor (Grand Officier), Croix de Guerre (with palm), Medal of Verdun, Grand Cross of Ouissam Alaouite. Clubs: Army and Navy, Capital Yacht (Washington, D.C.); Eastern Yacht (Marblehead, Mass.); Manchester (Mass.) Yacht; Cruising of America. Died Dec. 21, 1945.

PATTON, Katharine, artist, teacher; b. Phila., Pa.; d. Walter M. and Mary E. (Dunn) Patton; grad. Drexel Inst., Phila.; studied Art Students' League New York; Pa. Acad. Fine Arts; London Sch. of Art under Frank Brangwyn, A.R.A.; also in Italy, France, etc. Had two "one man" exhbns. in Phila.; exhibited at Nat. Acad. Design, New York, Corcoran Gallery of Art, Washington, D.C., Art Inst., Chicago, Albright Gallery, Buffalo, Boston Art Club, Pa. Acad. Fine Arts, Art Club of Phila.; etc. Awarded silver medal, for water color, Knoxville, Tenn., 1913; landscape medal, Nat. Assn. Women Painters and Sculptors, New York, 1918; Mary Smith prize (oil painting), Pa. Acad. Fine Arts, 1921, etc. Water colors exhibited in many cities under direction of Am. Fed. Arts and Oil Paintings on traveling exhbns. of the Fellowship of Pa. Acad. Fine Arts, in the South and West. Represented in permanent collections of Pa. Acad. Fine Arts, Fellowship collection of same, Municipal collection, Trenton, N.J., gallery of Pa. State Coll., John H. Vanderpoel Art Gallery (Chicago), etc. Mem. Nat. Assn. Women Painters and Sculptors for 15 yrs.; now mem. Fellowship Pa. Acad. Fine Arts, Drexel Inst. Alumni Assn., City Parks Assn., Phila. Water Color Club, Art Alliance, Playground and Recreation assn.; asso. mem. Am. Museum of Natural History; was mem. Plastic Club over 20 years. Republican. Died Sept. 25, 1941.

PATTON, Robert Williams, religious education; b. nr. Lindsay, Albemarle County, Va., Feb. 18, 1869; s. John Mercer and Sarah Lindsay (Taylor) P.; ed. Randolph-Macon Coll., Ashland, Va., 1884-88; studied law, U. of Va., 1891-92; grad., Va. Theol. Sem., 1895; D.D., U. of the South, 1922; m. Janie Slaughter Stringfellow, Jan. 1, 1900; children—Alice Lee, Sarah Lindsay. Deacon, 1895, priest, 1896, P.E. Ch.; rector Christ Ch., Roanoke, Va., 1896-1900, St. Stephens Ch., Wilkinsburg, Pa., 1802-1906; provincial sec. Domestic and Foreign Missionary Soc. since June 1, 1906; also exec. sec. Am. Ch. Inst. for Negroes, 1914-43; originator and dir. nation-wide campaign, 1919, which resulted in doubling the missionary income of the church and in reorganizing the ch. under the administration known as The National Council. Served as chaplain 2nd Va. Regt., Spanish-Am. War, May-Dec. 1898. Mem. Beta Theta Pi. Democrat. Author of brochure entitled "The Budget, the Debt of the Dioceses," 1925, presenting a historic and philosophic parallel between the government of the Episcopal Church and that of the United States. Contbr. various articles to mags. Home: Lindsay, Va. Address: 281 Fourth Av., New York, N.Y. Died Sep. 10, 1944.

PAUL, Harry Gilbert, univ. prof.; b. New Orleans, La., Oct. 24, 1874; s. George Charles and Mary (Murphey) P.; A.B., U. of Mich., 1897; A.M., U. of Chicago, 1901; Ph.D., Columbia, 1910; m. Mary I. Norris, May 27, 1908. Prin. high sch., Escanaba, Mich., 1897-1900; asst. in English, U. of Chicago, 1900-01; instr. English, U. of Ill., 1901-05, asst. prof., 1905-16, asso. prof., 1916-19, prof. since 1919. Mem. Nat. Council of Teachers of English (pres. 1920-21), Central Ill. Teachers Assn. (pres. 1934-35), Modern Lang. Assn. America, Phi Delta Kappa, Kappa Delta Pi, Acacia. Mason. Club: University (Urbana, Ill.). Compiler: English Poems (with E. C. Baldwin), 1908; Atlantic Prose and Poetry, 1919; Story, Essay, and Verse, 1921 (with C. S. Thomas). Author: John Dennis: His Life and Criticism, 1911; Better Everyday English, 1924; (with W. D. Miller) Practical English Books (4 books), 1927-28; (with W. D. Miller), Essentials of English (2 books), 1929; Language Goals (6 books), 1933; Games and Other Devices for Improving Pupils' English (with W. W. Charters), 1934; Units in English (4 books), 1934-37; Units in English for the Seventh and Eighth Grades, 1940; Improving My English (with J. B. Sullivan and T. J. Lance), 4 books, 1941; In America (with P. E. Knight), 1942; Teaching of Composition, 1943. Editor, English Bulletin, 1911-1936. Home: 713 W. Oregon St., Urbana, Ill. Died Sep. 27, 1945.

PAUL, Maury Henry Biddle, society editor, writer; b. Phila., Pa., Apr. 14, 1890; s. William Henry and Eleanor Virginia (Biddle) P.; grad. Episcopal Acad., Phila., 1910; student U. of Pa., 1910; unmarried. Began newspaper work on Phila. Times, 1914; society editor New York Press, 1914-16, New York Post, 1916-18, Evening Mail, New York, 1918-23, New York American, 1919-37; society editor (under name of Cholly Knickerbocker), New York Journal-American since 1937, also writes a daily syndicated society column. Republican. Episcopalian. Club: New York Athletic. Author of "Feuds Over Fifth Avenue," "The International Set," "The Vital Vanderbilts," pub. serially in Cosmopolitan. Home: 136 E. 64th St., New York, N.Y.; also "Tall Trees," Wilton, Conn.; and 1870 S.W. 21st Terrace, Miami, Fla. Office: 220 South St., New York, N.Y. Died July 17, 1942.

PAULLIN, Charles Oscar, author; b. Jamestown, O.; s. Enos and Malinda (Moorman) P.; student Antioch College, 1890-93; grad. student Johns Hopkins University, 1894-95, 1901 (fellow); B.S.S., Catholic U. of America, 1897; Ph.D., U. of Chicago, 1904; unmarried. Instr. mathematics, Kee Mar Coll., Hagerstown, Md., 1893-94; nautical expert U.S. Hydrog. Office, Navy Dept., Washington, 1896-1900; research asst. of Carnegie Instn., Washington, in London, 1910-11; lecturer on diplomatic history, Johns Hopkins, 1911, on naval history, George Washington U., 1911-13; research staff Carnegie Instn. Washington, 1912-36. Mem. Am. Hist. Assn., Am. Polit. Science Assn., Naval History Soc., U.S. Naval Inst., Va. Hist. Soc., N.Y. Hist. Soc., Naval Hist. Foundation (trustee and treas.), Columbia Hist. Soc. (mgr.), Wilderness Soc. Club: Cosmos. Author: The Navy of the American Revolution, 1906; Commodore John Rodgers, 1773-1838, 1910; Diplomatic Negotiations of American Naval Officers, 1912; Guide to Materials for United States History since 1783, in London Archives (with F. L. Paxson), 1914; Atlas of the Historical Geography of the United States, 1932; (monographs) American Naval Administration, 1775-1911, 1905-14; Voyages of American Naval Vessels to the Orient, 1800-1910, 1910-12. Editor: Out-Letters of the Continental Marine Committee and Board of Admiralty, Aug. 1776-Sept. 1780, 2 vols., 1914-15; Documents Relating to the Battle of Lake Erie, 1918; European Treaties Bearing on the History of the United States and Its Dependencies, 1716-1815. Awarded (with John K. Wright) Loubat prize, Columbia Univ., 1933. Staff contbr. Dictionary of American Biography since 1941. Address: Cosmos Club, Washington, D.C Died Sep. 1, 1944.

PAXSON, Frederic Logan, historian; b. Phila., Pa., Feb. 23, 1877; s. Joseph A. (M.D.) and Ada (Fell) P.; B.S., U. of Pa., 1898, Harrison scholar, 1898-99, Harrison fellow, 1902-03, Ph.D., 1903; A.M., Harvard U., 1902; Litt.D., Lawrence Coll., 1932, U. of Wis., 1935, U. of Pa., 1940; LL.D., Mills College, Calif., 1933; m. Helen Hale, d. Joseph T. Jackson, Dec. 26, 1906; children—Jane T., Emma F., Patricia. Instr. history in secondary schs., 1899-1901; asst. prof., 1903-04, prof. history, 1904-06, of Colo.; asst. prof. Am. history, 1906-07, jr. prof., 1907-10, U. of Mich.; prof. Am. history, U. of Wis., 1910-32; Margaret Byrne prof. history, U. of Calif., since 1932. Prof. Am. history, (summers), U. of Chicago, 1909, U. of Calif., 1913, U. of Mich., 1915, U. of Pa., 1917, U. of Calif. (Los Angeles), 1929, U. of Wis., 1935-47, Columbia, 1941, Harvard, 1948; research asso. Carnegie Instn., in British archives, summer 1910; mem. Com. on Management Dictionary of Am. Biography, 1924-36; mem. bd. editors Pacific Hist. Review, 1933-39; mem. advisory com. Franklin D. Roosevelt Library, 1939. Major United State Army in charge economic mobilization section of historical branch war plans division General Staff, 1918-19. Member American Hist. Assn. (councillor 1921-25; 2d v.p. 1937; pres. 1938), State Hist. Soc. Wis. (curator 1911-32, v.p. 1919-32), Mass. Hist. Soc. (corr.), Miss. Valley Hist. Assn. (pres. 1917), Pacific Coast Br., Am. Hist. Assn. (pres. 1942-43); Phi Beta Kappa. Mem. Soc. of Friends (Quakers). Author: The Independence of the South American Republics, 1903, 1916; The Last American Frontier, 1910; The Civil War, 1911; The New Nation, 1915; Guide to Materials for United States History since 1783, in London Archives (with C. O. Paullin), 1914; Recent History of the United States, 1921, revised edit., 1928 and 1937; History of the American Frontier, 1924 (awarded Pulitzer prize for 1924); The United States in Recent Times, 1926; When the West Is Gone (Colver Lectures, Brown U.), 1929; American Democracy and the World War: Pre-War Years, 1913-1917, 1936; America at War, 1917-1918, 1939; The Great Demobilization and Other Essays, 1941. Editor Com. Pub. Information Handbook, War Cyclopedia, 1917; also (War Dept. monographs) Economic Mobilization for the War of 1917, 1918; Handbook of Economic Agencies of the War of 1917, 1919. Address: 30 Wheeler Hall, Berkeley 4, Calif. Died Oct. 24. 1948.

PAYNE, Charles Edward, prof. of history; b. Hamilton, Can., Nov. 11, 1879; s. Charles Hiatt and Sarah Ann (Jenkins) P.; came to U.S., 1885, naturalized, 1888; student Ind. State Normal Sch., Terre Haute, 1899-1902; A.B., Ind. State U., 1904, A.M., 1905; grad. student Harvard, 1905-06; m. Ina Chatterton, July 11, 1925. Supt. of schs., Pennville, Ind., 1906-07; with Grinnell (Ia.) Coll. since 1907, as instr. of history, 1907-09, asst. prof., 1909-12, asso. prof., 1912-18, prof. since 1918, head of dept., 1925-44; Grinnell College trustees' honor professor, 1947-48; visiting lecturer, Scripps Coll., 1935-36, Dean Grinnell Inst. Internat. Relations, 1935-39. Won prize in The Nation essay contest, 1928. Mem. Phi Beta Kappa, Am. Hist. Assn., Inst. Pacific Affairs, Ia. Hist. Soc., Sigma Delta Chi. Author: Imperial England (with Cecil F. Lavell), 1918; Josiah B. Grinnell, 1938. Contbr. to Autobiography of Jesse Macy, 1933; also to Dictionary Am. Biography, and jours. Home: 1205 Park St., Grinnell, Ia. Died Nov. 30, 1947.

PAYNE, Elisabeth Stancy, author; b. Brooklyn, N.Y.; d. John F. and Josephine (Greenwood) Magovern; ed. Packer Inst., Brooklyn; m. Edward M. Payne, June 12, 1894; 1 son, Richard M. Protestant. Club: Pen and Brush. Author: (novels) All the Way by Water, 1922; Fathoms Deep, 1923; Lights Along the Ledges, 1924; Singing Waters, 1925; Hearthstones, 1927; Painters of Dreams, 1928; Hedges, 1929; Easy Street, 1930; These Changing Years, 1931; The Quiet Place, 1932; Thou, My Beloved, 1933; Out of the Dusk, 1934; Shadow on the Brook, 1935; Something to Remember, 1936; The Tide Always Rises, 1937; The Steadfast Light, 1939; The Perfect Lamb, 1941. Home: Lakeville, Conn.; East Orange, N.J. Died Jan. 10, 1944.

PAYNE, George Henry, author; b. N.Y. City, Aug. 13, 1876; s. George Cooley and Katherine (Milligan) P.; student Coll. City of New York, 1891-93; spl. course, Coll. of Pharmacy; student N.Y. Law U.; m. Mrs. Emma James Sturdevant, Mar. 9, 1918. Propr., Long Branch Summer Season, 1893, The Gothamite, 1895-96; asso. editor, Criterion Magazine, 1896-99; exchange editor and editorial writer, Commercial Advertiser, 1895-96; musical and dramatic critic, New York Evening Telegram, 1903-07; polit. writer, Evening Post, 1909-12. Lecturer on history and development of Am. journalism, Cooper Union, 1915. Pres. Direct Nominations Club, 1901; mem. New York County Rep. Com., 1906-07; candidate for Assembly, 1908, mgr. lit. bureau for Henry L. Stimson, Rep. candidate for gov., 1910; one of the N.Y. campaign mgrs. for presdl. campaign of Theodore Roosevelt, 1912; mgr. campaign for George McAneny, pres. Bd. of Aldermen, 1913; tax commr. N.Y. City, 1916-33; mem. Federal Communications Commn. since 1934; N.Y. City rep. State Council Defense since 1917; organizer Com. of Am. Business Men, 1919; del. Rep. Nat. Conv. (floor mgr. for Gen. Wood), Chicago, 1920. Candidate for U.S. senator, Rep. primaries, against James W. Wadsworth, receiving 46,039 votes, 1920. Sec. Soc. for Preservation of Am. Rights in the Panama Canal, 1914; sec. Choate Memorial Com.; pres. City Traffic and Health Assn., Eastern and Middle West Travelers; mem. Mil. Order America, Union Soc. Decorated Order of Danilo I (Montenegro), 1921. Clubs: Metropolitan (Washington); Nat. Republican, Players (N.Y.); Cercle Interallié (Paris, France). Author: A Great Part and Other Stories of the Stage, 1901; The Birth of the New Party, 1912; History of the Child in Human Progress, 1915; History of Journalism in America, 1919; England—Her Treatment of America, 1931; The Fourth Estate and Radio, 1936; also (one-act musical comedy) In Silver Idaho, 1911; (one-act play) The Lightning Stroke, 1915. Home: 54 W. 40th St., New York, N.Y., and Islip, L.I., N.Y. Office: New Post Office Bldg., Washington, D.C. Died Mar. 3, 1945.

PAYNE, Jason Elihu, lawyer; b. Clay County, S.D., Jan. 22, 1874; s. Byron Spencer and Charlotte Elizabeth (Woodworth) P.; A.B., U. of S.D., 1894, M.A., 1895; law dept. U. of Minn., 1897-98; m. Iwae Sheppard, July 20, 1905; children—Elinore, Ruth. Began practice at Vermilion, S.D., 1898; now mem. firm Payne & Olson. City atty., Vermilion, 1902-04, 1910-16; mem. State Senate, S.D., 1903-04, 1905-06. Mem. faculty law dept., U. of S.D., since 1902, prof. law since 1905. Mem. Am. and S.D. bar assns., Am. Soc. Internat. Law, Phi Beta Kappa, Phi Delta Theta, Delta Theta Phi. Republican. Editor South Dakota Alumnus, U. of S.D., since 1905. Home: Vermilion, S.D. Died Sep. 11, 1941.

PAYNE, John A., mining exec.; b. Nashville, Tenn., Feb. 15, 1900; s. John Nicholas and Esther (Brooks) P.; A.B., Harvard, 1921; M.B.A., Harvard Business Sch., 1925; m. Elizabeth Downes, Feb. 15, 1933; children—Elizabeth Kennedy, William Downes. In investment banking, Kuhn, Loeb & Co., N.Y. City, 1926-32; partner N.Y. Stock Exchange firm of Parrish & Co., N.Y. City, 1932-40; pres. Consol. Coppermines Corp., N.Y. City, since 1940; chmn. bd. Titan Metal Mfg. Co., Bellefonte, Pa.; dir. Liberty Aircraft Products Corp., Farmingdale, L.I., The Highway Trailer Co., Egerton, Wis., Roberts Numbering Machine Co., Brooklyn, N.Y., The Autocar Co., Ardmore, Pa., also chmn. finance com. Mem. Assn. Am. Inst. Mining Engrs. Republican. Presbyterian. Clubs: Harvard of New York, Piping Rock, Turf and Field, Seawauhaka Yacht (Oyster Bay, L.I.); Mining. Home: Woodbury, L.I., N.Y. Office: 120 Broadway, New York, N.Y. Died April 18, 1947.

PAYNE, Leonidas Warren, Jr., prof. English; b. Auburn, Ala., July 12, 1873; s. Leonidas Warren and Mary Jane (Foster) P.; B.Sc., Ala. Poly. Inst., 1892, M.Sc., 1893; Ph.D., U. of Pa., 1904; m. Mary Susan Bledsoe, Oct. 27, 1897; children—Bledsoe, Leonidas Warren, Sarah Farnham, John Howard. Teacher of English, Southwestern Ala. Agrl. Sch., Evergreen, Ala., 1894-1901, Jacksonville (Ala.) State Normal Sch., 1901-02; Harrison fellow in English, U. of Pa., 1902-04; asso. editor revision of Worcester's Dictionary, 1904-06; asst. prof. English, La. State U., 1906; with U. of Tex. since 1906, prof. English since 1919. Co-founder and 1st pres. Tex. Folklore Soc., 1910. Mem. Modern Lang. Assn. America, Am. Dialect Soc., Am. and Tex. Folklore socs., Am. Assn. Coll. Profs., Pi Kappa Alpha. Baptist. Clubs: University, Town and Gown. Author: History of American Literature, 1919; A Survey of Texas Literature, 1928. Also compiler: Word List of Eastern Alabama, 1910; Learn to Spell, 1916. Editor: Hector of Germanie (by W. Smith), 1906; Southern Literary Readings, 1913; American Literary Readings, 1917; Selections from American Literature, 1919; Fifty Famous Southern Poems, 1920; Selections from English Literature (with N. Hill), 1922; Selections from Later American Writers, 1927; Literature for the Junior High School (with T. H. Briggs and C. M. Curry), 3 vols., 1929; Using Our Language (with A. Blount and C. S. Northup), 5 vols., grades 3 to 7, 1935; Enjoying Literature (with M. A. Neville and N. E. Chapman), 4 vols., grades 9 to 12, 1936; Enjoying Literature (with M. A. Neville) 3 vols., grades 6, 7, 8; 1942. Contbr. The South in the Making of the Nation, and various mags. Home: 2104 Pearl St., Austin, Tex. Died June 16, 1945.

PAYSON, Eliot Robertson, college prof.; b. New Hartford, N.Y., Feb. 24, 1846; s. Eliot Hale and Mary (Robertson) P.; A.B., Hamilton Coll., N.Y., 1869, A.M., 1872; univs. of Berlin and Leipzig, 1877-80; Ph.D., Rugers, 1893; m. Lillian Corbin, 1882. Teacher of mathematics, Homer, N.Y., 1870-73; teacher of classics, Utica (N.Y.) Free Acad., 1874-77; prin. high sch., Binghamton, N.Y., 1880-91; headmaster of Rutgers Prep. Sch., 1891-08; prof. history of edn. and of German, Rutgers Coll., since Sept., 1908. Episcopalian. Mem. Delta Upsilon, Phi Beta Kappa. Address: New Brunswick, N.J. Died Nov. 2, 1945.

PEABODY, Arthur, architect; b. Eau Claire, Wis., Nov. 16, 1858; s. Selim Hobart and Mary Elizabeth (Pangborn) P.; B.S. in architecture, U. of Ill., 1882; Litt.D., U. of Wis., 1930; m. Agnes Langdon Cochrane, 1885; children—Mrs. Marion Grace West, Arthur Cochrane, Mrs. Charlotte Elizabeth Kelsey. Archtl. work for Chicago Expn., 1891-94; practiced at Chicago, 1894-1905; architect, U. of Wis., 1905-15, designing 60 bldgs. for that instrn.; state architect of Wis., 1915 until retired. Sec. Bd. Examiners of Architects and Engineers, Wis. Fellow A.I.A.; mem. Wis. Assn. Engrs., Tau Beta Pi. Republican. Episcopalian. Home: 2114 Chadbourne St., Madison, Wis. Died Sept. 6, 1942.

PEABODY, Endicott, head master; b. Salem, Mass., May 30, 1857; s. S. Endicott and Marianne (Lee) P.; grad. Cheltenham Coll., Eng., 1876; LL.B., Trinity Coll. (U. of Cambridge), 1880, LL.M., 1884; B.D., Episcopal Theol. Sem., Cambridge, Mass.; hon. A.M., Yale Univ., 1902, LL.D., 1938; S.T.D., Harvard, 1904, LL.D., 1939, L.H.D., New York U., 1922; L.H.D., U. of the State of New York, 1935; D.D., Trinity College, Hartford, Connecticut, 1940; m. Fannie Peabody, June 18, 1885; children—Malcolm Endicott, Helen (Mrs. R. M. Sedgwick), Rose (Mrs. W. B. Parsons, Jr.), Elizabeth Rogers, Margery, Dorothy (Mrs. F. T. Davison). Deacon, 1884, priest, 1885, P.E. Ch.; head master, Groton Sch., 1884-1940, now emeritus. Address: Groton, Mass. Died Nov. 17, 1944.

PEABODY, Harry Ernest, clergyman; b. Princeton, Me., Apr. 13, 1865; s. Leonard and Mary Hill (Todd) P.; prep. edn., Phillips Exeter (N.H.) Acad.; A.B., Harvard, 1887; B.D., Yale, 1891; D.D., Grinnell (Ia.) Coll., 1915; m. Emily Stickney Clough, Aug. 16, 1894; children—Stephen Clough, Leonard Clough, Phillips Clough (dec.), Miriam. Minister Congl. Ch., Trinidad, Colo., 1891-96; asso. minister Ch. of the Redeemer, New Haven, Conn., 1896-99; minister Windsor Av. Congl. Ch., Hartford, Conn., 1899-1910, South Congl. Ch., Chicago, 1910-17, First Congl. Ch., Appleton, Wis., 1917-35, Rosendale, Wis., since 1935. Chmn. Wisconsin Interdenomination Industrial Relations Com.; dir. Appleton Pub. Library, Northland Coll., Ashland, Wis. Mem. League of Ind. Polit. Action, Signet Soc. (Harvard). Home: Rosendale, Wis. Died Jan. 16, 1940.

PEABODY, Stuyvesant, coal; b. Chicago, Ill., Aug. 7, 1888; s. Francis Stuyvesant and May (Henderson) P.; Yale, 1907-11; m. Anita Healy, Feb. 21, 1914; children—Stuyvesant, Patrick Healy. Pres. Peabody Coal Company; president Black Mountain Coal Corp., Crerar Clinch Coal Co., Cook County Coal & Ice Co., Am. Eagle Colliery, Bellwood Coal Co.; dir. Lyon & Healy, Inc., Chicago, and Eastern Air Lines, Inc., N.Y. City; v.p. and dir. Am. Turf Assn. Served in World War as 1st lt. Sanitary Corps, later capt. Chem. Warfare Service. Trustee Ill. Inst. Tech. Mem. Delta Kappa Epsilon. Catholic. Mem. K.C. (past grand knight; past dist. deputy). Pres. and dir. Lincoln Fields Jockey Club. Fellow Photographic Society of America; fellow Royal Photographic Society. Clubs: Chicago, University, Racquet (Chicago); Grolier (N.Y. City); Pendennis (Louisville, Ky.). Home: 1525 N. State Parkway. Office: 231 S. La Salle St., Chicago, Ill. Died June 7, 1946.

PEARCE, Haywood Jefferson, coll. pres.; b. Columbus, Ga., Aug. 26, 1871; s. Thomas Jefferson and Virginia (Biggers) P.; A.B., Emory Coll., Ga., 1891; A.M., U. of Chicago, 1901; Ph.D., U. of Würzburg, 1902; m. Lucile Townsend, Jan. 26, 1903. Pres. Brenau Coll. (sch. for girls) since 1893 (vacation 1900-03, for post-grad. work). Democrat. Methodist. Mem. Southern Soc. for Philosophy and Psychology (pres. 1912-13), Am. Psychol. Assn., Chi Phi. Mason. Author: Philosophical Meditations, 1917; Talks to College Girls; King Cotton (allegorical pageant), 1920. Club: Rotary. Presented deed of grounds and bldgs. of Brenau Coll. (valued at over $500,000) to a self-perpetuating bd. of trustees, 1928. Home: Gainesville. Ga. Died May 1, 1943.

PEARCE, McLeod Milligan, coll. pres.; b. Bellevue, Pa., July 16, 1874; s. William and Margaret (McKinney) P.; student Geneva Coll., Beaver Falls, Pa., 1891-96, Ref. Presbyn. Theol. Sem., Pittsburgh, Pa., 1896-99; D.D., Geneva, 1915; m. Carolyn McKaig, 1900. Ordained ministry Ref. Presbyn. Ch., 1900; pastor First Ch., St. Louis, Mo., 1900-11, East End Ch., Pittsburgh, 1911-13, First Ch., Phila., 1913-19; asst. editor Am. S.S. Union, 1919-23; pres. Geneva Coll. since Sept. 1923. Editor Olive Trees (mag.), 1916-23. Home: Beaver Falls, Pa. Died Nov. 22, 1948.

PEARCE, William, bishop; b. Hayle, Cornwall, Eng., Oct. 15, 1862; s. John Richard and Ann Bawden Hosking (Thomas) P.; ed. in Eng.; m. Alma E. Knoll, May 14, 1889 (died Oct. 3, 1908); 1 son, Bernard Asbury; m. 2d, Sarah Allen Dickson, July 21, 1915 (died Sept. 14, 1917); 1 dau., Emily Dickson; m. 3d, Mabel E. Kline, June 8, 1922; 1 dau., Gwendolen Elizabeth. Came to U.S., 1884; ordained Free Meth. Ch., 1888; pastor Corralitos, Calif., 1889-90, Ione, 1891, San Jose, 1892-93, Alameda, 1893-95, Ione, 1896; dist. elder Ione and San Jose dists., 1897-1900, Portland and Salem dists., 1901-03; pastor Jamestown, N.Y., 1904; dist. elder Genesee Dist., 1905-07; bishop Free Meth. Ch. since 1908. Mem. Gen. Conf., 3 times, now pres. bd. adminstrn.; del. World's Missionary Conv., Edinburgh, Scotland, 1910; missionary tour to Japan, 1927. Author: Our Incarnate Lord. Home: 67 Cambridge St., Rochester, N.Y. Died Sep. 2, 1947.

PEARSON, Gustaf Adolph, silviculturist, forestry; b. Holdredge, Neb., Nov. 14, 1880; s. Anders Peter and Anna Christina (Arvidson) P.; A.B., U. of Neb., 1906, B.S., 1906, A.M., 1907; m. May Perkins, June 14, 1910; children—Arthur Adolph, Margaret Angeline. In charge Ft. Valley Forest Expt. Sta., U.S. Forest Service, Flagstaff, 1909-29; dir. Southwestern Forest and Range Expt. Sta., 1930-35, senior silviculturist in charge Fort Valley Exptl. Forest, 1935-44; collaborator U.S. Forest Service, 1945. Pioneer research in reforestation, forest meteorology, forest ecology and silviculture; developed new method of improving forest stands. Trustee Northern Ariz. Soc. of Science and Art. Fellow A.A.A.S., Soc. Am. Foresters; mem. Ecol. Soc. Am., Sigma Xi (honorary scientific). Presbyterian. Mason. Author: Natural Reproduction of Western Yellow Pine, 1923; Forest Types in the Southwest as Determined by Climate and Soil, 1931; Timber Growing and Logging Practice (with R. E. Marsh), 1935; Forest Land Use, 1940. Author of govt. bulletins and contbr. to tech. jours. Received 1944 award of Soc. Am. Foresters for best article on forestry. Home: 1828 E. 5th St. Office: P.O. Box 951, Tucson, Ariz. Died Jan. 31, 1949.

PEARSON, T(homas) Gilbert, ornithologist, wildlife conservationist; b. Tuscola, Ill., Nov. 10, 1873; s. Thomas Barnard and Mary (Elliott) P.; B.S., Guilford (N.C.) Coll., 1897; B.S., U. of N.C., 1899, LL.D., 1924; spl. study Harvard; m. Elsie Weatherly, June 17, 1902; children—Elizabeth (Mrs. C. T. Jackson), T. Gilbert, William. Prof. biology, Guilford Coll., 1899-1901, State Normal and Industrial Coll. for Women, 1901-04; state game commr. of N.C., under title of sec. state Audubon Soc., 1903-10; sec. and exec. officer Nat. Audubon Soc. 1910-20, pres., 1920-35, now pres. emeritus. Founder, 1922, and pres., 1922-38, Internat. Com. for Bird Preservation (organized in 30 countries), now chmn. Pan-Am. Sect. of Com.; founder and chmn. Nat. Com. on Wildlife Legislation; mem. Conseil Internat. de la Chasse, advisory bd. Migratory Bird Treaty Act; mem. Pres. Hoover's Yellowstone Park Boundary Commn.; official collaborator Nat. Park and Federal Fish and Wildlife Services; nat. dir. Izaak Walton League of America. Decorated Nat. Order of Oaken Crown, Luxembourg, 1925; Société Nationale d'Acclimatation medal (France), 1937; John Burroughs Memorial Assn. medal, 1939. Clubs: Camp Fire (hon.), Boone and Crockett Club (New York City); Explorers Club of America. Author: Stories of Bird Life, 1901; The Bird Study Book, 1917; Adventures in Bird Protection—An Autobiography, 1937. Editor-in-chief: Birds of America, 3 vols., 1917; Tales from Birdland, 1918. Sr. author: Birds of North Carolina, 1919; Co-editor: The Book of Birds, 1937. Contbr. to scientific and popular mags. on ornithol. and wildlife conservation subjects. Lectured in Europe, North, Central and South America and West Indies. Home: 2257 Loring Pl. Office: 1006 5th Av., New York, N.Y. Died Sep. 3, 1943.

PEASE, Theodore Calvin, teacher, editor; b. Cassopolis, Mich., Nov. 25, 1887; s. Thomas Huntington and Caroline Phipps (Anderson) P.; grad. Lewis Inst., Chicago, 1904; Ph.B., U. of Chicago, 1907, Ph.D., 1914; m. Marguerite Edith Jenison, Aug. 15, 1927. Asso. in history, U. of Ill., 1914-17, 1919-20, asst. prof., 1920-23, associate prof., 1923-26, professor since 1926, head department of history since 1942. Agent of com. for ednl. survey of U. of Ill., 1926-27. Editor Ill. Hist. Collections of Ill. State Hist. Library, 1920-39; dir. Ill. Hist. Survey since 1939. Corr. mem. Chicago Hist. Soc.; chairman hist. manuscripts commn., Am. Hist. Assn., 1925-31. Second lt. inf. U.S.R., Nov. 27, 1917; 1st lt. 126th Inf., Sept. 5, 1918; served with A.E.F., Jan. 8, 1918-May 16, 1919; participated in battles with 32d Div., Alsace Marne-Aisne, Oise-Aisne, Meuse-Argonne offensives, and in Army of Occupation, Germany; hon. discharged, May 24, 1919. Mem. Ill. State Hist. Soc. (pres., 1946-47); founder mem. Soc. of Am. Archivists since 1936 (editor, 1937-46). Conglist. Clubs: University (Urbana, Ill.); Army and Navy (Chicago). Author: (or compiler) County Archives of Illinois, 1915; The Leveller Movement, 1917; Centennial History of Illinois, Vol. II, 1918; Illinois Election Returns, 1818-1848, 1923; Laws of the Northwest Territory, 1925; The Story of Illinois, 1925, revised edition, 1949; The United States, 1927; Diary of O. H. Browning I (with J. G. Randall), 1927; Selected Readings in American History (with A. S. Roberts), 1928; George Rogers Clark and the Revolution in Illinois, 1929; The French Foundations (with R. C. Werner), 1934; Anglo-French Boundary Disputes in the West, 1749-1763, 1936; Illinois on the Eve of the Seven Years' War, 1747-1755 (with Ernestine Jenison), 1939; also various articles in reviews. Editor The American Archivist since 1938. Home: 708 Indiana Av., Urbana, Ill. Died Aug. 11, 1948.

PECK, Darius Edward, corp. counsel; b. Hudson, N.Y., May 5, 1877; s. Willard and Mary Langford (Curran) P.; A.B., Yale, 1898; m. Mrs. Juliette M. Brown, June 19, 1922; children—Marjorie Brown (Mrs. Philip H. Thayer, Jr.), Willard Langford Peck, Molly Curran Peck. Admitted to New York bar, 1901; practiced in Hudson and N.Y. City, 1901-12; asso. in law dept. Gen. Electric Co., 1913-29, v.p. and gen. counsel since 1929. Clubs: University, Yale (New York); Mohawk, Mohawk Golf (Schenectady). Home: 1374 Lowell Rd. Office: 1 River Rd., Schenectady, N.Y. Died Dec. 16, 1944.

PECK, Frederick Stanhope; b. Providence, R.I., Dec. 16, 1868; s. Leander Remington and Sarah Gould (Cannon) P.; ed. pub. schs., Providence; LL.D., Villanova; M.B.A., Bryant Coll.; m. Mary Rothwell Burlingame, June 6, 1894. With Asa Peck & Co., 1885; treas. Asa Peck & Co., Inc., since 1909; president National Exchange Realty Company, Belton Corp.; vice pres. Industrial Trust Co., Felters Co., Metal Textile Corp.; director R.I. Ins. Co., United Electric Railways Co., Providence Gas Co., Terminal Warehouse Co. of R.I. Pres. Homeopathic Hosp. of R.I. Mem. R.I. Soc., S.A.R., Soc. Colonial Wars, Mayflower Descendants in R.I., R.I. Hist. Soc., Soc. Descendants of Pilgrim John Howland, Soc. Founders and Patriots of America, New Eng. Geneal. Hist. Soc., Newport Art Assn. Mason (33°). Clubs: Providence Art, Republican of R.I. Home: Belton Court, Barrington, R.I. Office: 17 Exchange St., Providence, R.I. Died Jan. 20, 1947.

PECK, William Buckley, surgeon; b. Freeport, Ill., Oct. 11, 1872; s. William Ford and Natalie (Price) P.; student, Willamette U., Portland, Ore., 1888-93; M.D., Rush Med. Coll., Chicago, 1897; post-grad. work, Univs. of Vienna and Berlin, 1907-08; m. Alvina Weber, Sept. 26, 1912. Intern, London (Eng.) Hosp., Whitechapel, 1909; in practice surgery at Freeport, Ill., since 1897; mng. dir. Inter-State Postgraduate Med. Assn. of North America since 1916, in charge of post-graduate div. arranging scientific and clin. post-graduate studies in cooperation with the leading univs. of U.S., Canada, Europe and South America since 1923, now also editor of proceedings of same; district surgeon Chicago & Northwestern R.R. Co. Fellow A.M.A., Am. Coll. Surgeons; mem. Ill. State and Stephenson County med. socs., Am. Assn. Ry. Surgeons, Assn. Pour le Developpement des Relations Medicales (Paris, France). Republican. Presbyterian. Mason. Clubs: Country, Rotary. Home: 1556 W. Lincoln Blvd. Office: State Bank Bldg., Freeport, Ill. Died Aug. 20, 1941.

PEEK, George Nelson; b. Polo, Ill., Nov. 19, 1873; s. Henry Clay and Adeline (Chase) P.; grad. Oregon (Ill.) High School, 1891; student Northwestern U., 1891-92; m. Georgia Lindsey, Dec. 22, 1903. With Deere & Webber Co., Minneapolis, Minn., 1893-1901; v.p. and mgr. John Deere Plow Co., Omaha, 1901-11; v.p. Deere & Co., Moline, Ill., 1911-19; commr. of finished products, War Industries Bd., 1918; chmn. Industrial Bd., U.S. Dept. of Commerce, 1919; pres. and gen. mgr. Moline Plow Co., Moline, Ill., 1919-23; administrator of A.A.A., May-Dec., 1933; special adviser to the pres. on foreign trade and pres. of Export-Import Bank of Washington and of 2d Export-Import Bank of Washington, Mar. 1934-Dec. 1935; dir. Maizewood Insulation Co. Pres. Am. Council of Agr. and chmn. exec. com. of 22 North Central States Agrl. Conf., 1925-28; chmn. Alfred E. Smith Independent Orgns. Com. presidential campaign, 1928. Decorated D.S.M.; Chevalier Legion of Honor (French); Comdr. Order of the Crown (Belgium); Knight of the Crown of Italy. Clubs: Rock Island Arsenal Golf; Omaha (Omaha); Chicago University (Chicago); National Press (Washington, D.C.); Rancho Santa Fe (California) Golf. Member Elks. Author of numerous pamphlets and articles on national agricultural policy and on foreign trade. Co-author: Equality for Agriculture; Why Quit Our Own. Home: Moline, Ill. Died Dec. 17, 1943.

PEELE, Robert (pēl), mining engr.; b. N.Y. City, July 15, 1858; s. Robert and Anne (Westervelt) P.; E.M., Sch. of Mines (Columbia), 1883; unmarried. In the field as mining engr., 1883-92; mem. firm of Olcott, Fearn & Peele, mining engrs., 1896-1901, Olcott, Corning & Peele, 1901-07; adj. prof. mining, Columbia, 1892-1904, prof. 1904-25, prof. emeritus. Presbyterian. Mem. Am. Inst. Mining and Metall. Engrs. (hon. 1937), Instn. Mining and Metallurgy of London (hon. 1921), Mining and Metall. Soc. Am. (gold medal for contbns. to lit. of mining engring., 1923), Tau Beta Pi. Clubs: Century, Columbia U. Author: Compressed Air Plant, 1908, 5th edit., 1930; Mining Engineer s Handbook, 1918, 3d edit., 1941. Translator (from German of J. Riemer) Shaftsinking Under Difficult Conditions, 1907. Contbr. on mining subjects. Traveled professionally in Peru, Bolivia, Chile, Colombia and Dutch Guiana, 1888-92; made trip around the world, 1903-04, to S. Africa and S. America, 1910. Home: 490 West End Av., New York, N.Y. Died Dec. 8, 1942.

PEELLE, Stanton Canfield, lawyer; b. Indianapolis, Ind., July 5, 1880; s. Stanton J. (late chief justice U.S. Ct. of Claims) and Mary Arabella (Canfield) P.; grad. Columbian Prep. Sch., D.C., 1895; A.B., Columbian U. (D.C.), 1899, LL.B., 1902; m. Julia F. Ravenel, Oct. 25, 1905; children—Stanton Canfield, Ellen duB. R. (Mrs. James Parker Nolan), Elizabeth R. (Mrs. Armistead L. Boothe), Mary Canfield (dec.), William Ravenel. Admitted to D.C. bar, 1902, and since practiced in Washington, D.C.; prof. Constitutional law, Washington Coll. of Law, 1904-06; 1st asst. U.S. atty., D.C., 1910-11; spl. asst. U.S. atty., 1911-12; partner firm Hoehling, Peelle & Ogilby and successors, 1913-33; now partner Peelle, Lesh, Drain & Barnard; dir. Mayflower Hotel Corp., LaSalle Apts., Inc., Capital Contsrn. Co. Mem. 3 Street Ry. Co. wage arbitrations. Mem. Am. Bar Assn., D.C. Bar Assn. (ex-pres.), Mil. Order Loyal Legion, S.R., Soc. Colonial Wars, Friends of Law Library of Congress (charter mem.), Theta Delta Chi. Republican. Clubs: Lawyers (ex-pres.), Metropolitan, Chevy Chase (gov.), University. Home: 5900 Connecticut Av., Chevy Chase, Md. Office: 1422 F St. N.W., Washington, D.C. Died Sep. 12, 1941.

PEET, Max Minor, surgeon; b. Iosco, Mich., Oct. 20, 1885; s. LaFayette and Eunice Ann (Minor) P.; A.B., U. of Mich., 1908, A.M., 1910, M.D., 1910; hon. M. Ed., Mich. State Normal Coll., Ypsilanti, Mich., 1934; m. Grace Stewart Tait, Oct. 5, 1915; children—Max Minor, Stewart Tait, Martha Eunice Ann. Intern, R.I. Hosp., Providence, 1910-12; Robert Robinson Porter fellow in research medicine, U. of Pa., 1912-13; asst. instr. surgery, U. of Pa., 1913-15; asst. chief surgeon, Phila. Gen. Hosp., 1914-16; instr. in surgery, U. of Mich., 1916-17, asst. prof., 1918-27, asso. prof. of neuro-surgery, 1927-30, prof. of surgery since 1930; chief of neurosurgical div., Univ. Hosp., University of Michigan, since 1918. Member general advisory committee, virus research, medical publications and chmn. ed. comm. Nat. Foundation for Infantile Paralysis. Mem. Internat. Neurol. Congress, Berne, 1931, London, 1935; Internat. Surg. Congress, Brussels, 1938. Fellow A.M.A., Am. Coll. of Surgeons; mem. Soc. of Neurol. Surgeons, Am. Surg. Assn., Am. Bd. of Surgery, Am. Neurological Assn., vice chmn. Am. Board Neurological Surg.; mem. Central Surgical Assn., Internat. Soc. of Surgery, Mich. State Med. Soc., Washtenaw Co. Med. Soc., Harvey Cushing Soc.; honorary mem. Sociedad Argentina de Cirujanos, Los Angeles Surgical Society, Detroit Academy of Surgery; member Alpha Omega Alpha, Sigma Xi, Alpha Kappa Kappa. Mason. Clubs: Cooper Ornithol., Wilson Ornithol., American Ornithologists Union, Barton Hills Country. Ornithologist, U. of Mich. Museums expdns., 1904, 05, 32. Contbr. numerous articles on neurosurgical problems to med. jours, and chapters on neuro-surgery in various surgical works. Home: 2030 Hill St. Office: University Hospital, 1313 E. Ann St., Ann Arbor, Mich. Died Mar. 25, 1949; buried Forest Hill Cemetery, Ann Arbor, Mich.

PEIRCE, William Henry, retired engr.; b. Baltimore, Aug. 22, 1865; s. William Henry and Georgia V. (Browne) P.; M.E. Stevens Inst. Tech., 1884, D.Engring., 1935; m. Esther Royston Belt, Aug. 23, 1933. Apprentice with Pa. R.R., Wilmington, Del., 1884-87; draftsman, etc., Aurora, Ill., 1887-88; asst. master mechanic, C.,B.&Q. Ry., Galesburg, 1888-89; supt. constrn. United Edison Co., New York, 1889-90; apptd. spl. investigator electrolytic copper refining Baltimore Copper Smelting & Rolling Co., 1890; asst. mgr., mgr., v.p. and pres. B.C.S.&R. Co., 1891-1933; ex-pres. Peirce-Smith Converter Co.; ex-v.p. Am. Smelting & Refining Co.; past dir. and 1st v.p. Revere Copper and Brass Inc. Mem. Am. Soc. M.E.; Am. Inst. Mining Engrs., Am. Electrochem. Soc., Sigma Chi. Republican. Episcopalian. Clubs: Merchants, Baltimore Country, Elkridge (Baltimore); Bankers (New York). Inventor of methods of smelting and refining of copper, particularly in basic converting of copper matte to blister copper and electrolytic refining of resulting blister copper. James Douglas medalist, Am. Inst. of Mining and Metal. Eugrs., 1931. Home: 100 W. University Parkway, Baltimore, Md.; and Western Run Farm, Cockeysville, Maryland. Died May 25, 1944.

PELL, Edward Leigh, author, lecturer; b. Raleigh, N.C., Sept. 7, 1861; s. Rev. William E. and Virginia C. (Ramsay) P.; student U. of N.C., 1878-80; D.D., Emory Coll., Ga., 1897; m. Lucy Hardison, Dec. 21, 1887; children—Lucy H., Mary Leigh, Edward Leigh (dec.), Robert H. (dec.), Allison H.; m. 2d, Florence I. West, Sept. 6, 1928. Entered M.E. Ch., S., ministry, 1881, retiring, 1891, on account of ill health. Lecturer on religious subjects. Author: Art of Enjoying the Bible, 1898; Life of Dwight L. Moody, 1900; Bright Side of Humanity, 1900; Commentary on Sunday School Lessons, 1890-1942; Superintendent's Book of Prayer, 1905; The Life Worth While, 1906; Little Guide Posts in the Way to Life, 1907; Prayers, 1911; Secrets of Sunday School Teaching, 1912; Story of Joseph as Told by Himself, 1912; Story of David, 1912; Story of Jesus for Little People, 1912; Our Troublesome Religious Questions, 1916; Four Feet on a Fender, 1917; What Did Jesus Really Teach About War?, 1917; Your Fallen Soldier Boy Still Lives, 1918; Adventures in Faith in Foreign Lands, 1918; How Can I Lead My Pupils to Christ?, 1919; Bringing Up John, 1920; Story of Paul, 1920; What Did Jesus Really Teach About Prayer?, 1921; Why I Believe in Jesus, 1926; Story of John the Beloved Disciple, 1929; also the Pell Series of Happier Living Booklets and several small vols. of Bibl. and missionary studies. Home: (winter) 1233 Oak St. N.E., St. Petersburg, Fla.; (summer) Montreat, N.C. Died June 11, 1943.

PELL, Williamson, banker; b. Goshen, N.Y., July 5, 1881; s. Arthur and Eve (Williamson) P.; A.B., Princeton, 1902; B.L., N.Y. Law Sch., 1904; m. Vida Kneeland, Dec. 4, 1906; children—Williamson, Angelene P. (Mrs. Norman H. Donald, Jr.). Admitted to N.Y. bar, 1904, practicing in N.Y. City, 1904-12; pres. U.S. Trust Co. of N.Y., 1938-47, chmn. bd. trustees since 1947; trustee Greenwich Savings Bank (N.Y. City), Atlantic Mutual Ins. Co., Atlantic Mutual Indemnity Co., Centennial Inc. Co.; dir. Great Northern Paper Co., Manhattan Fire & Marine Ins. Co., Coal Run Land Co.; chmn. local bd. Commercial Union Assurance Co. Ltd.; mem local bd., British Gen. Ins. Company. Trustee Society of N.Y. Hosp. Republican. Episcopalian. Clubs: Ivy; University, Down Town Assn. (N.Y. City); Apawamis (Rye, N.Y.). Home: 70 Dogwood Lane, Rye, N.Y. Office: 45 Wall St., N.Y. City. Died Aug. 22, 1949.

PELLEY, John Jeremiah, railway official; b. Anna, Ill., May 1, 1878; s. Joseph and Mary (Anders) P.; grad. high sch., Anna; spl. work, U. of Ill.; m. Alma Ethel Thompson, Aug. 22, 1908; 1 dau., Mary Jane (Mrs. W. D. Van Schalkwyk). Began as station clerk Illinois Central Railroad, at Anna, Illinois, 1899, and continued with same rd. consecutively as clk., at Carbondale, 1900-01, track apprentice, 1901, asst. foreman extra gang, 1902, foreman and gen. foreman, 1903, supervisor Peoria dist., 1904, Memphis div., 1905, asst. roadmaster, Clarksdale, Memphis div., 1906-07, roadmaster, at McComb, Miss., 1908-10, New Orleans, 1910, Fulton, Ky., 1911, supt. at Fulton, 1911-15, Memphis, 1915-17, gen. supt. Southern Lines, 1917-19, Northern Lines, 1919-20, chmn. com. on car service, Chicago, 1920-23, gen. mgr., I.C. R.R., 1923-24, v.p. in charge of operation, 1924-26; pres. Central of Ga. Ry., and Ocean Steamship Co. of Savannah, 1926-29; pres. N.Y.,N.H.&H. R.R. Co., 1929-34, Assn. Am. R.R.'s since 1934; dir. Western Union Telegraph Co., Equitable Life Assurance Soc. of U.S., Washington Properties, Inc. Clubs: Metropolitan, Burning Tree, Chevy Chase (Washington, D.C.). Address: Association of American Railroads, Transportation Bldg., Washington 6, D.C. Died Nov. 12, 1946.

PELOUZE, William Nelson (pē-lōōz'), mfr.; b. Washington, D.C., Sept. 12, 1865; s. Gen. L. H. (U.S. Army) and Ellen L. (Doolittle) P.; grad. Mich. Mil. Acad., 1882; m. Helen G. Thompson, Feb. 1, 1888; 1 dau., Medora. Came to Chicago, 1882; with Walter A. Wood, reaping machines, 1882-84; with the Tobey Furniture Co., 1884-92; pres. Pelouze Scale & Mfg. Co. (now the Pelouze Mfg. Co.) since 1884. Commd. capt. and adj. 2d Inf., Ill. Nat. Guard, 1883; capt. Co. H, 1885; maj. 2d Inf., 1890; asst. adj. gen., 1st Brigade Ill. Nat. Guard, 1894; col. 1st Inf. Ill. Reserves. Past chmn. Ill. Deep Waterway Commn.; mem. exec. com. Gt. Lakes-St. Lawrence Tidewater Assn.; pres. Assn. of Arts and Industries; ex-pres. Ill. Mfrs. Assn. Mem. Mil. Order Loyal Legion. Clubs: Chicago, Chicago Athletic, Lake Geneva Yacht (past commodore), Lake Geneva Country. Home: 2150 N. Lincoln Park W. Office: 232 E. Ohio St., Chicago, Ill. Died June 19, 1943.

PELZER, Louis, prof. history; b. Griswold, Ia., Feb. 4, 1879; s. Henry and Sophia (Wohlenhaus) P.; M.Di., Ia. State Teachers Coll., Cedar Falls, 1901; Ph.B., Ia. State U., 1906, Ph.D., 1909; m. Mildred Lenore Weenink, Jan. 1, 1917; children—Lorne Parker, Henry Louis. Began as teacher of country school, 1896; successively high school teacher, Griswold, Ia.; prin., Marne, Ia.; teacher high school, Colfax, Ia.; prin., Shelby, Ia.; research asst. Hist. Soc. of Ia.; prof., Mont. State Normal; asst. prof. of history, U. of Ia., 1911-17, asso. prof., 1917-25, prof. since 1925; lecturer summers, Winona (Minn.) State Teachers Coll., 1909, Ia. State Teachers Coll., 1912, 15, U. of Neb., 1929, U. of Mo., 1933, Cornell U., 1938, U. of Wyo., 1941. Sec. Western Conf. ("Big Ten"), 1927-29; mem. Ia. Territorial Centennial Com., 1938, com. on Am. History in Schs. and Colleges, 1943. Member Mississippi Valley Hist. Assn. (pres. 1936), Am. Hist. Assn., Am. Assn. Univ. Profs. Democrat. Clubs: Triangle, Research (Iowa City); Caxton (Chicago). Author Augustus Caesar Dodge (biography), 1907; Henry Dodge (biography), 1911; Marches of the Dragoons in the Mississippi Valley, 1917; The Cattlemen's Frontier, 1936. Editor of Miss. Valley Hist. Review since 1941. Editor: The Prairie Logbooks, 1943; also several books of U. of Ia. Social Science Series, etc. Home: 127 Ferson Av., Iowa City, Ia. Died June 28, 1946.

PEMBERTON, Brock, theatrical producer; b. Leavenworth, Kan., Dec. 14, 1885; s. Albert and Ella (Murdock) P.; grad. high sch., Emporia, Kan., 1902; student Coll. of Emporia, 1902-05; A.B., U. of Kan., 1908; m. Margaret McCoy, Dec. 30, 1915. Reporter Emporia Gazette, 1908-10; dramatic editor N.Y. Evening Mail, 1910-11; asst. dramatic editor N.Y. World and Times, 1911-17; theatrical work with Arthur Hopkins, 1917-20; independent producer since 1920. Pres. League of N.Y. Theatres, v.p. Theatre Authority; vice chmn., treas. Stage Relief Fund; mem. bd. of govs. Am. Theatre Council; bd. of directors American Theatre Wing. Member Phi Delta Theta. Protestant. Producer of Enter Madame; Zona Gale's Miss Lulu Bett and Mister Pitt; Sidney Howard's Swords; Pirandello's Six Characters in Search of an Author and the Living Mask; Maxwell Anderson's White Desert; Preston Sturges' Strictly Dishonorable; Frank Wead's Ceiling Zero; Lawrence Riley's Personal Appearance; Warden Lewis E. Lawes's and Jonathan Finn's Chalked Out; Clare Boothe's Kiss the Boys Goodbye; Margery Sharp's Lady in Waiting; Parker Fennelly's Cuckoos on the Hearth; Josephine Bentham and Herschel William's Janie; Mary Chase's Harvey. Home: 455 E. 51st St. Office: 244 W. 44th St., New York, N.Y. Died Mar. 11, 1950.

PEMBERTON, Ralph, M.D.; b. Phila., Pa., Sept. 14, 1877; s. Henry and Agnes (Williams) P.; B.S., U. of Pa., 1898, M.S., 1899, M.D., 1903, Woodward fellow in physiol. chemistry, Pepper Lab., 1908-10; grad. study Berlin, 1911, U. of Strassburg, 1912; m. Virginia Breckenridge Miller, May 23, 1911. Began practice, Phila., 1905; instr. in medicine, U. of Pa., 1907-10, asso. prof. medicine, Grad. Sch., 1928-31, prof. since 1931; asst. visiting physician, U. of Pa. Hosp., 1908-10; asst. visiting neurologist, Phila. Gen. Hosp., 1905-08; visiting physician and dir. dept. clin. chemistry, Presbyterian Hosp., 1913-33; visiting physician to Abington Memorial Hosp.; consulting physician to Chester County Hosp. Nat. consultant in rheumatism and arthritis under Program of War-Time Grad. Med. Meetings since 1943; chmn. com. on rheumatic diseases of Advisory Health Bd., Dept. of Health, Phila., since 1944. Served as major Medical Corps, U.S. Army, in charge intensive study and treatment of arthritis. Awarded meritorious service medal, Commonwealth of Pa., 1939. Dr. Ralph Pemberton, Prof. of Medicine, Grad. School, Univ. of Pa., was awarded the gold key of the American Congress of Physical Medicine at its 24th annual meeting New York City, Sept. 4 to 7, 1946. Dr. Pemberton was given the reward in recognition of his research on Arthritis and in the advance of Physical Medicine. Mem. standing com. on preventive medicine, Dept. of Health, Phila., 1921-22; chmn. American Committee for Control of Rheumatism, 1927-35; president American Rheumatism Association, 1938-39; president Ligue Internationale contre le Rhumatisme; president, Pan-American League for the Study and Control of Rheumatic Diseases since 1944. Fellow American College Physicians, Coll. Physicians Phila.; mem. A.M.A. (member standing council on physical therapy, 1928-42), Academy of Physical Medicine, American Soc. for Clin. Investigation, American Institute Nutrition, Phila. County Med. Soc. (med. advisory com. on pub. welfare, 1939), Acad. Natural Sciences, Franklin Inst., Internat. Soc. of Med. Hydrology, Mil. Order of the Loyal Legion of U.S., Sigma Xi, Delta Psi; hon. fellow Royal Soc. of Medicine, London; hon. mem., Societatea Anatomo Clinica, Bucharest, Liga Argentina contre el Reumatismo; hon. mem. Liga Uruguaya contre el Reumatismo; hon. member Liga Brasileira contra o Reumatismo. Unitarian.

Clubs: Philadelphia, Racquet, University Barge. Author: Arthritis and Rheumatoid Conditions, 1929, translated into French, 1933, second edition, 1935; (with R. B. Osgood) Medical and Orthopedic Management of Chronic Arthritis, 1934. Contbr. to Nelson Loose Leaf System of Medicine, 1922, Bedside Diagnosis (by American authors), 1927, Text book of Medicine (by same), 1928, internat. Ency. of Medicine since 1931, Tice System of Medicine since 1934; also articles to professional journals. Editor of vol. on Medicine in Principles and Practice of Physical Therapy, 1932. Home: Paoli, Pa. Office: 2031 Locust St., Philadelphia, Pa. Died June 17, 1949.

PENCE, William David, civil engr.; b. at Columbus, Ind., Nov. 26, 1865; s. David and Nancy (Hart) P.; student U. of Ill., 1883-86, C.E., 1895; m. Charlotte Gaston, Dec. 31, 1888 (died May 6, 1938); children—Ada (Mrs. S. H. Slichter), Helen Charlotte (Mrs. A. J. B. Wace), Esther Nancy (Mrs. A. F. Britton). Asst. and resident engr., A.T.&S.F. Ry., 1886-92; instr., asst. prof. and asso. prof. civ. engring., U. of Ill., 1892-99; prof. civ. engring., Purdue U., 1899-1906; prof. ry. engring., U. of Wis., 1906-15; editor publs. Am. Ry. Engring. Assn., 1903-15; mem. U.S. Commn. Investigation Drainage Kankakee Marsh Region, 1904-06; chief engr. Wis. Ry. Commn., and Wis. Tax Commn., 1906-13; mem. engring. bd. Interstate Commerce Commn., in charge of Central Dist., federal valuation of rys., May 1913-Nov. 1921; consulting practice. Awarded Octave Chanute medal, Western Soc. Engrs. (thermal expansion of concrete), 1901. Pres. Ind. Engring Soc., 1903-05; mem. Am. Soc. C.E., Am. Ry. Engring. Assn. (editor publications, 1903-15; dir. 1915-18), Western Soc. Engrs., Soc. Promotion Engring. Edn., Alpha Tau Omega, Sigma Xi, Tau Beta Pi. Author: Stand Pipe Accidents and Failures in the United States, 1895; Surveying Manual (with Milo S. Ketchum), 1900, 1904, 1915, 1932; also technical papers dealing with structural analysis, public regulation, railways, terminal air rights, etc. Home: 1201 Michigan Av., Evanston, Ill. Office: 120 S. La Salle St., Chicago, Ill. Died June 16, 1946.

PENDELTON, Charles Sutphin, educator; b. Findlay, O., Feb. 27, 1879; s. George Franklin and Mary Belle (Sutphin) P.; B.A., Oberlin, 1901, M.A., 1903; grad. study in English philology and edn., Univ. of Minn., 1908-10, Harvard, 1913-15, Univ. of Chicago, 1919-21, Ph.D., 1921; m. Lillian H., d. Henry James Bruce, missionary to India, Apr. 28, 1916. Asst. and instr. in English, Oberlin, 1901-04; instr. East High Sch., Minneapolis, 1904-10; acting prof. English, Carleton Coll., Northfield, Minn., 1910-13; teacher, Noble & Greenough Sch., 1914-15, Harvard, 1914-15; asst. prof. English U. of Wis., 1915-19, U. of Chicago, summers 1919-21; prof. of English, George Peabody Coll., Nashville, Tenn., 1922-46, emeritus since Sept. 1946; prof. English and chmn. div. langs., Austin Peay State Coll., Clarksville, Tenn., since Sept. 1946. Pres. Nashville Com. of 100 for Law Enforcement. Mem. Modern Language Assn. America. Regional chmn. Am. Dialect Society, Nat. Society for Study of Edn., Tennessee Folklore Soc., Am. Dialect Society, Am. University Professors, College English Assn., Nashville English Club, Tenn. Philol. Association, Tennessee Motor Assn. (chairman legislative com.), Pi Gamma Mu (gov. Southeastern region), Phi Delta Kappa. Congregationalist. Editor: Peabody Jour. of Education, 1923-29. Author: The Social Objectives of School English, 1924; also numerous articles in ednl. jours. Home: 3423 Love Circle, Nashville 5, Tenn. Died Oct. 21, 1948; buried Mount Oilvet Cemetery, Nashville, Tenn.

PENROSE, Stephen Beasley Linnard, prof. philosophy; b. Philadelphia, Pennsylvania, Dec. 20, 1864; s. Clement Biddle and Mary (Linnard) P.; A.B., Williams, 1885, D.D., 1905, LL.D., 1919; B.D., Yale, 1890; D.D., Ripon, 1902; Litt.D. Whitman, 1944; m. Mary Deming, dau. Judge Nathaniel Shipman, June 17, 1896; children—Mary Deming (Mrs. P. W. Copeland), Frances Shipman (Mrs. H. B. Owen), Clement Biddle, Nathaniel Shipman, Virginia (Mrs. B. E. Cagley), Stephen Beasley Linnard. Taught in Hill Sch., Pottstown, Pa., 1885-86, Williams Coll., 1886-87; ordained Congl. ministry, 1890; home missionary, Dayton, Wash., 1890-94; pres. and prof. philosophy, Whitman Coll., 1894-1934, pres. emeritus since 1934; editor Whitman Coll. Quarterly, 1896-1926. Hon. corporate member A.B.C.F.M. Mem. Academia Nacional de Ciencias Antonio Alzate (Mexico), Phi Beta Kappa, Delta Kappa Epsilon. Republican. Conglist. Author: Hist. pageant, How the West Was Won, and Whitman, an Unfinished Story; Philosophy for Lowbrows by One of Them, The Way of Experience (in preparation), also pub. essays, lectures and addresses. Address: 7 Colllege Av., Walla Walla, Wash. Died April 29, 1947.

PEPPER, William, physician, educator; b. Philadelphia, Pa., May 14, 1874; s. William and Frances Sergeant (Perry) P.; A.B., U. of Pa., 1894, M.D., 1897, Sc.D., 1932; LL.D., Temple University, 1942; m. Mary Godfrey, Dec. 31, 1904 (died Oct. 2, 1918); m. 2d, Phoebe S. (Voorhees) Drayton, Apr. 3, 1922 (dec.). With med. dept., U. of Pa., 1899; dean Sch. of Medicine, 1912-45. Lieut. col., M.C., U.S. Army, World War; comdg. officer Base Hospital 74. Fellow College Physicians of Phila., Assn. Am. Med. Colleges (pres. 1920-21); mem. A.M.A., Am. Philos. Soc., trustee Univ. of Pa., trustee Philadelphia Free Library. Zeta Psi. Republican. Episcopalian. Home: Ithan, Delaware Co., Pa. Died Dec. 3, 1947.

PERCY, James Fulton, surgeon; b. Bloomfield, N.J., Mar. 26, 1864; s. James and Sarah Ann (Fulton) P.; M.D., Bellevue Hosp. Med. Coll. (now Med. Dept. New York U.), 1886; postgrad. student on experimental problems in abdominal surgery, Chicago Vet. Coll., 1895; postgrad. student pathology and surgery, in Germany, Switzerland, Belgium, 1897-98; visited clinics in England, France, Germany, Austria, 1914; hon. A.M., Knox Coll., Galesburg, Ill., 1914; m. Mrs. Edna B. Post, 1925. Med. practice, Mazeppa, Minn., 1886-88, Galesburg, Ill., 1888-1917; developed surgical instruments, 1904, known as Percy actual cauteries for treatment of accessible cancers; practice limited treatment of cancer since 1917; surgical practice, San Diego, Calif., 1920-22, in Los Angeles, since 1922; attending sr. surgeon, cancer service, and founder member (1922) Malignancy Board and Tumor Clinic, Los Angeles County Hospital (vice chairman and chairman 8 years); clinical professor of surgery (neoplasms), College of Medical Evangelists Medical School (emeritus); attending surgeon French Hospital, 12 years; consulting surgeon, Orthopedic Hospital and School for Crippled Children (all in Los Angeles). Member 1st draft board, Knox County, Ill., 1916; student training courses for officers, Fort Riley, Kan., 1917; chief of surgical staff, U.S. Army Base Hosp., Camp Kearny, Calif., 1917-19; retired with rank of major; apptd. lt. col., Med. Reserves, U.S. Army, 1925, reapptd. for term, 1940-45, called first meeting, Galesburg, Ill., out of which grew Galesburg Cottage Hosp., 1888. Was honor guest at Clinical Congress of Surgeons, North America, at meeting held in London, 1914. Fellow Am. Coll. Surgeons (founder mem.); mem. A.M.A., Calif. Med. Assn., Los Angeles Med. Assn. (v.p. 1931), Los Angeles Surg. Soc. (pres. 1929), Los Angeles Cancer Soc. (pres. 1939), American Board of Surgery (founder member), Western Surgical Association (president 1918), Illinois State Medical Soc. (pres. 1907; sec. Jud. Council 17 years), Southern Calif. Med. Assn. (hon. 1914), Am. Soc. for Control of Cancer, Am. Assn. Obstet., Gynecol. and Abdominal Surgeons, Hollywood Acad. of Med. (hon. 1926), Reserve Officers Assn., U.S. Army, U.S. Mil. Surgeons Assn. Mason (32°). Bahai religion. Contbr. about 40 articles to med. jours., principally on actual cautery in treatment of cancer. Home: 1030 S. Alvarado St., Los Angeles 6. Died Apr. 26, 1946; buried in Forest Lawn Memorial Park, Glendale, Calif.

PERKINS, Charles Albert, physicist; b. Ware, Mass,. Oct. 31, 1858; s. Rev. Ariel Ebenezer Parish and Susan Osborn (Poor) P.; A.B., Willimas Coll., 1879; Ph.D., Johns Hopkins, 1884; m. Angie Villette Warren, Sept. 19, 1883 (died 1921); children—Marcia Villette, Margaret Duggan, Alice Warren, Warren A. Prof. mathematics, Lawrence, 1880-81; fellow in physics, 1883-84, asst. in physics, 1884-87, Johns Hopkins; prof. physics, Bryn Mawr Coll., 1887-91; prof. science, Hampden-Sidney Coll., 1891-92; prof. physics and elec. engring., 1892-1906, elec. engring., 1906-41, prof. elec. engring. emeritus since 1941; dir. Engineering Experimental Station, University of Tennessee, 1921-41, consultant since 1941. Fellow American Inst. Electric Engineers; mem. Nat. Conf. Electricians, 1884. Author: Outlines of Electricity and Magnetism, 1896. Contbr. to scientific jours. Address: 1715 W. Clinch Av., Knoxville, Tenn. Died Nov. 26, 1945.

PERKINS, Charles Elliott, corp. official; b. Burlington, Ia., Feb. 21, 1881; s. Charles Elliott and Edith (Forbes) P.; A.B., Harvard, 1904; m. Leita Amory, June 14, 1904; 1 son, Charles Elliott; m. 2d, Isabel McGunnegle Sheridan, Sept. 26, 1925; one son, Kennedy McGunnegle. Elected dir. C.,B.&Q. R.R. Co., 1914, pres., July 18, 1918, later v.p. to 1921 (resigned 1928); pres. Lincoln Land Co.; co-receiver, with W. Cameron Forbes, of Uruguay Ry. Co. and Brazil Land, Cattle & Packing Co., 1914-21; pres. Internat. Products Co., May 1917-July 1918; elected dir. S.P. Co., 1928, mem. exec. com., 1939. Mem. bd. overseers Harvard University. Mason (K.T.). Clubs: Chicago (Chicago); The Brook (New York); Somerset (Boston). Author: The Pinto Horse, 1927; The Phantom Bull, 1932. Home: Santa Barbara, Calif. Died June 19, 1943.

PERKINS, Clarence, univ. prof.; b. Syracuse, N.Y., Aug. 17, 1878; s. Jacob Neal and Ellen Maria (Harrington) P.; A.B., Syracuse U., 1901; A.M., Harvard, 1904, Ph.D., 1908; studied in London and Paris, 1906-07; travelled, studied and did research in hist. archives in London and Paris, summers, 1900, 07, 11, 14, 21, 29 and 39; m. Adelaide Rebecca Evans, 1913 (died Dec. 1918); 1 dau., Dorothy Ellen (Mrs. M. J. Wihnyk); m. 2d, Mildred Washburne Copeland, June 10, 1921; 1 son, Neal Copeland. Instr. history, high school, Bloomfield, N.J., 1901-03, U. of Mo., 1907-09; asst. prof. European history, Ohio State U., 1909-14, prof., 1914-20; prof. European history and head of department, U. of N.D., since 1920; acting prof. history, U. of Tex., 1929, U. of Vt., 1936-37; prof. European history, summers, U. of Calif., 1913, U. of Tenn., 1915, U. of Mo., 1912 and 19, U. of Colo., 1920, 22 and 24, U. of Tex., 1920, U. of Minn., 1923, U. of Ia., 1925, Western Reserve U., 1929, U. of Southern Calif., 1934 and 36, U. of Tex., 1945. Mem. Am. Hist. Assn., Fgn. Policy Association, Delta Upsilon and Phi Beta Kappa. Republican. Episcopalian. Mason (32°, Shriner). Author: An Outline of Recent European History, 1912, 5th edit., 1927; An Outline Analysis of History of England, 1912; History of European Peoples, 1927, revised edit., 1930; Introduction to World History, 1929; A Directed Study Notebook for World History, 1929; An Outline Analysis of History of Modern Europe (1915-29), 1929; Man's Advancing Civilization, 1934; revised edit., 1939; Workbook for Man's Advancing Civilization, 1934; Ancient History, 1936; Development of European Civilization (with R. I. Lovell and C. H. Matterson), 1940. Contbr. on hist. subjects. Home: 411 Belmont Road, Grand Forks, N.D. Died Oct. 13, 1946.

PERKINS, Frederic Williams, clergyman; b. Boston, Mass., June 16, 1870; s. Francis Blake and Mary Elizabeth (Williams) P.; grad. Roxbury Latin Sch., 1887; A.B., Tufts Coll., 1891, A.M., 1894; B.D., Tufts Div. Sch., 1894, D.D., 1908; m. Mary Sherman Thayer, June 21, 1894. Ordained Universalist ministry, 1894; pastor Ch. of The Redeemer, Hartford, Conn., 1894-1901, 1st Ch., Haverhill, Mass., 1901-05, 1st Ch., Lynn, 1905-27, Universalist Nat. Memorial Ch., 1927-39. Lecturer in theology, Tufts Div. Sch., 1912, 1913-14. Pres. Lynn Associated Charities, 1913-27; mem. board. Pub. Welfare D.C., 1934, 39; chmn. Central Fellowship Com. of Universalist Gen. Conv. Mem. Theta Delta Chi, Phi Beta Kappa. Republican. Address: 16 Beacon St., Boston, Mass. Died July 8, 1943.

PERKINS, Maxwell Evarts, editor, pub.; b. New York, N.Y., Sept. 20, 1884; s. Edward Clifford and Elizabeth Hoar (Evarts) P.; prep. edn., St. Paul's Sch., Concord, N.H., 1898-1903; A.B., Harvard, 1907; m. Louise Saunders, Dec. 31, 1910; children—Bertha Saunders (Mrs. John G. Frothingham), Elizabeth Evarts (Mrs. Douglas Gorsline), Louise Elvire (Mrs. Robert G. King), Nancy Galt, Jane Morton. Reporter staff of New York Times, 1907-10; with Charles Scribner's Sons since 1910, book advt. mgr., 1911-14, editor since 1914, dir. since 1915, sec., 1917-32, also v.p. Clubs: Harvard, Coffee House, Century Assn. (New York); Country (New Canaan, Conn.). Home: 56 Park St., New Canaan, Conn. Office: 597 Fifth Av., New York, N.Y. Died June 17, 1947.

PERKINS, William Robertson, lawyer; b. Elmington, Va., Nov. 3, 1875; s. Thomas Benjamin Moore and Judith Clough (Robertson) P.; LL.B., Washington and Lee U., 1897, LL.D., 1929; m. Mary Sarah Bell, Nov. 5, 1902; children—William Robertson, Thomas Lee, Mary Clough. Admitted to Va. bar, 1897, and began practice at Lynchburg; moved to Newport News, Va., 1901, N.Y. City, 1906; counsel for Am. Tobacco Co., 1906-11, P. Lorillard Co., 1911-13, J. B. and B. N. Duke interests since 1913; v.p. Duke Power Co.; dir. and counsel Am. Cyanamid Co.; counsel P. Lorillard Co. Trustee and vice chmn. The Duke Endowment; trustee Duke U. Mem. Am. and N.Y. State bar assns., Am. Acad. Polit. and Social Science, Va. Soc. of New York, Southern Soc., N.C. Soc. Republican. Methodist. Mason. Clubs: New York, Commonwealth, Uptown, Quill (New York); Upper Montclair Country. Home: 125 Lorraine Av., Upper Montclair, N.J.* Died June 15, 1945.

PERLZWEIG, William A. (pĕrl'svĭg), biochemist; b. Ostrog, Russia, Apr. 23, 1891; s. Isaac Boris and Miriam (Schreyer) P.; B.S., Columbia, 1913, M.A., 1914, Ph.D., 1915; m. Olga Marx, Apr. 26, 1919; 1 dau., Judith Margaret. Came to U.S., 1906, naturalized, 1909. Asst. biochemistry Columbia, 1913-16; asst. chemist Rockefeller Inst., New York, 1916-17; research biochemist U.S. Pub. Health Service, 1919-21; instr. and asso. in medicine. Med. Clinic Johns Hopkins U., 1921-30; prof. biochemistry Duke Med. Sch., biochemist, Duke Hosp. since 1930; consultant to surgeon gen., U.S. P.H.S. since 1946. Served as 1st lt., Sanitary Corps., U.S. Army, 1917-19. Fellow A.A.A.S.; mem. Am. Soc. Biol. Chemists, Inst. of Nutrition, Am. Chem. Soc., Soc. Exptl. Biol. and Medicine, Am. Assn. Univ. Profs., Phi Beta Kappa, Sigma Xi. Home: 3918 Dover Rd. Office: Duke Hospital, Durham, N.C. Died Dec. 10, 1949.

PERMAR, Robert (pĕr-mär'), writer; b. Steubenville, O., Sept. 15, 1895; s. Edwin Love and Seddie (MacFarland) P.; ed. high sch. 2 yrs. and under pvt. tutors. Formerly a free lance book and music reviewer; editor Wheeling Intelligencer for eight years; editor in chief of "West Virginians" (biog.), 1928; supervisor, 1930, Federal Census for 5 counties of W.Va.; dep. U.S. clerk, 1932-45; instr. Y.M.C.A. Junior Coll. Made national survey of industrial education in public schools. Republican. Episcopalian. Mason (32°, Shriner). Author: Training in the Trades, 1923; The Juggler, 1926; Shadows That Were Cast, 1936; and The Fourth Magi, 1937; also many syndicated newspaper and magazine article. Dir. of Research for Office of Civilian Defense in W.Va. Home: 102 14th St., Wheeling, W.Va. Died Nov. 29, 1948.

PEROT, T. Morris, Jr. (pĕ-rŏt'), malt mfr.; b. Phila., Pa., May 6, 1872; s. T. Morris and Rebecca C. (Siter) P.; grad. DeLancy Sch., Phila., 1891, Pricket's Business Coll., Phila., 1893; m. Mary Gummey, May 18, 1905; children—T. Morris III, Henry F., Mary Elizabeth. In malt mfg. business since 1893; president since 1903, Perot Malting Company, Phila. (oldest business house in the U.S., established in 1687, representing 8th generation). President The Seaside House for Invalid Women; treas. Friends Charity Fuel Association. Mem. Pa. Hist. Soc., Pa. Soc. S.R., Colonial Soc. of Pa. Republican. Quaker. Club: Union League. Home: 132 Bethlehem Pike, Chestnut Hill, Philadelphia. Office: 123 S. Broad St., Philadelphia 9, Pa. Died Nov. 29, 1945.

PERRIN, Fleming Allen Clay, prof. psychology; b. La Harpe, Ill., Apr. 29, 1884; s. William and Mary (Todd) P.; Ph.B., U. of Chicago, 1910, Ph.D.,

1913; m. Rhea Burgess, Sept. 22, 1921. Instr. psychology, U. of Pittsburgh, 1912-14, asst. prof., 1914-17; asst. prof. psychology, U. of Texas, 1917-25, prof. since 1925. Mem. Am. Psychol. Assn., A.A.A.S., Am. Assn. Univ. Profs.; Sigma Xi, Kappa Sigma. Co-author: (with David Ballin Klein) Psychology—Its Methods and Principles, 1926. Contbr. to Psychol. Abstracts, etc. Home: 2801 Rio Grande St. Address: University of Texas, Austin, Tex.* Died Dec. 1, 1944.

PERRIN, Lee J. (pâr'ĭn), lawyer; b. Cleveland, O., Dec. 27, 1884; s. Bernadotte and Luella P.; B.A., Yale, 1906, LL.B. Harvard, 1910; m. Hilda Woods Bull, Nov. 7, 1914; children—Suzanne, Anthony Lester. Mem. firm. Appleton, Rice & Perrin, N.Y. City, since 1916; dir. Ciba Pharm. Products Inc., Summit, N.J., Ciba Co. Inc., N.Y., Cincinnati Chem. Works, Inc., Norwood, O., Ciba Co. Ltd., Montreal. Clubs: Downtown Assn., Racquet (New York), Piping Rock (Long Island). Home: 45 E. 66th St. Office: 63 Wall St., New York, N.Y. Died 1946.

PERRY, Antoinette, actress, director, producer; b. Denver, Colo., June 27, 1888; d. William Russell and Minnie Betsy (Hall) Perry; m. Frank Wheatcroft Frueauff, Nov. 30, 1909 (died July 31, 1922); children—Margaret Hall (actress as Margaret Perry), Virginia Day (dec.), Elaine Storrs. Made debut as Dorothy in "Mrs. Temple's Telegram," Powers Theatre, Chicago, 1905; played the daughter in "The Music Master" with David Warfield, 1906-07, 1908-09, and Hallie in "The Grand Army Man," 1907-08; played Rachel Arrowsmith in "Mr. Pitt" with Walter Houston, 1924, Lil Corey in "Minick," 1924, Ma Huckle in "Dunce Boy," 1925, Belinda Treherne in "Engaged," 1925, Judy Ross in "Caught," 1925, Sophia Elphinstone Weir in "The Masque of Venice," 1926, Margaret in "The Ladder," 1926, Clytemnestra in "Electra," 1927; produced and directed with Brook Pemberton "Goin' Home," 1928, "Hot Bed," 1928, "Strictly Dishonorable," 1929, "Seven Year Love," 1929, "Gone Hollywood," 1930; directed "Three Times the Hour," 1931, "Divorce Me Dear," 1931, "Christopher Comes Across," 1932, "Personal Appearance," 1934, "Ceiling Zero," 1935, "Now You've Done It," 1937, "Chalked Out," 1937, "Red Harvest," 1937, "Kiss the Boys Goodbye," 1938; "Lady in Waiting," 1940, "Out from Under," 1940, "Glamour Preferred," 1940; "Cuckoos on the Hearth," 1941; "Janie," 1942; "Pillar to Post," 1943, "Harvey" 1944. Chairman Com. of Apprentice Theatre, Am. Theatre Council, and conducted auditions for theater aspirants, 1937-39. President Experimental Theatre, Incorporated (created by Actors Equity Assn.); trustee Actors' Fund of America; sec. Am. Theatre Wing of British War Relief Soc., 1940-41; chmn. bd. dirs. Am. Theatre Wing War Service, Inc., 1941-44. Mem. League of New York Theatres, Dramatists Guild, Actors Equity Association, Theatre Authority, Am. Theatre Council, Stage Relief Fund, D.A.R., Mayflower Descendants, Sons and Daughters of the Pilgrims. Clubs: Cosmopolitan, Junior League, National Arts, Twelfth Night (New York); Cherry Hills, Denver Country (Denver). Home: 510 Park Av. Address: 244 W. 44th St., New York, N.Y. Died June 28, 1946.

PERRY, Antonio, lawyer; b. Honolulu, Oahu, T.H., Jan. 5, 1871; s. Jason and Anna (dos Anjos) P.; ed. St. Alban's and Oahu colls., Honolulu; m. Eugenia May Vanderburgh, Jan. 9, 1912; children—Jacqueline Eugenia, Gail Antonia. Admitted to bar, 1893; dist. magistrate, Honolulu, 1894-96; 2d judge Circuit Court, 1st Jud. Circuit of H.I., 1896-97, 1st judge, 1897-1900; asso. justice Supreme Court of H. Ty., 1900-04, 1909-14 and 1922-26, chief justice, 1926-34; practicing law since 1934. Address Wailupe, Honolulu, T.H. Died July 13, 1944.

PERRY, Arthur F., banker; b. Carleton, Yarmouth County, N.S., Can., May 13, 1866; s. Nathan and Caroline (Dennis) P.; ed. Yarmouth (N.S.) Acad.; m. Isabelle C. Strawn, Oct. 7, 1890; children—Arthur F., Henry Clinton Strawn. Came to U.S., 1884, naturalized citizen, 1887. Began in banking as sec.-treas. Southern Savings & Trust Co., Jacksonville, Fla., 1894; pres. Fla. Nat. Bank, Jacksonville, 1913-29; now vice chmn. bd. Barnett Nat. Bank, Jacksonville. Mem. City Council, Jacksonville, 4 yrs., Bd. of Bond Trustees, 7 yrs. Fla. state treas. United War Work Campaign, World War. Trustee Jacksonville Free Pub. Library. Democrat. Conglist. Home: 1505 Riverside Av. Office: Barnett Nat. Bank, Jacksonville, Fla. Died Dec. 21, 1941.

PERRY, Charles Milton, prof. philosophy; b. North Batavia, Mich., Nov. 10, 1876; s. Joseph B. and Elizabeth (Johnson) P.; A.B., Albion (Mich.) Coll., 1900; Ph.D., U. of Mich., 1911; Morris fellow for philos. study in Europe, 1912-13; m. Winifred Johnston, Apr. 14, 1927. Served as teacher, prin. and supt. schs. in Mich., 1900-05; instr. philosophy, U. of Mich., 1911-12; pastor Unitarian Ch., Iowa City, Ia., 1914-19; social worker, Minneapolis, 1919-20; exec. sec. Social Welfare Assn., Grand Rapids, Mich., 1920-23; prof. and head dept. of philosophy, U. of Okla. since 1923. Manager Southwestern Conf. on Higher Edn., 1935; mem. Southwestern Philosophical Conf. (pres. 1939-40). Mem. Am. Philos. Assn., A.A.A.S., Am. Assn. Univ. Profs., Okla. Acad. Science (pres. 1937-38). Am. Civil Liberties Union (state chmn.). Democrat. Club: Faculty (pres. 1933-34). Author: Ironic Humanist, 1924; Henry Philip Tappan—Philosopher and University President, 1933; also chapters in William Torrey Harris Memorial Volume and Studies in Honor of William Torrey Harris, 1935; Introduction to Higher Education and Society, 1936; Toward a Dimensional Realism, 1939; The Multi-dimensional Society, 1940; Democracy in Change: A New Dimension, 1941. Editor: The St. Louis Movement in Philosophy, 1930. Contbr. articles to philosophical, historical and educational publs. Home: 516 Chautauqua Av., Norman, Okla. Died June 11, 1942.

PERRY, Clarence Arthur; b. Truxton, Cortland County, N.Y., Mar. 4, 1872; s. Duane Oliver and Hattie E. (Hart) P.; student Stanford 2 yrs.; B.S., Cornell U., 1899; studied Teachers Coll. (Columbia), summer, 1904; m. Julia St. John Wygant (M.D.), Apr. 27, 1901; 1 dau., Sara Janet. Prin. high sch., Ponce, Porto Rico, 1904-05; spl. agt. U.S. Immigration Commn., 1908-09; lecturer, New York U., summer, 1912; became connected with Russell Sage Foundation, 1909, asso. dir. dept. of recreation, 1913; retired, 1937. Student Business Men's Mil. Training Camp, Plattsburg, Aug. 1915, 16; commd. capt. Q.-M. R.C., U.S. Army, Aug. 9, 1917; maj. Q.-M.C., Oct. 26, 1918; in France with 77th Div., Apr. 1918-Apr. 1919; apptd. div. q.-m., Apr. 15, 1919; hon. disch. Oct. 14, 1919; commd. maj. Finance, O.R.C., Dec. 16, 1919; lt. col., Dec. 8, 1924. Mem. Sigma Alpha Epsilon, Sigma Xi. Conglist. Author: Wider Use of the School Plant, 1910; Educational Extension, 1916; Community Center Activities, 1916; Attitude of High School Students Toward Motion Pictures, 1923; The Work of the Little Theatres, 1933; The Rebuilding of Blighted Areas, 1933; Housing for the Machine Age, 1939; also pamphlets and bulletins on ednl. topics. Co-author: Neighborhood and Community Planning, 1929. Contbr. to Cyclo. of Edn., The Modern High Sch., Educational Hygiene, Principles of Secondary Education. Home: 80 Beechknoll Rd., Forest Hills, L.I., N.Y. Died Sep. 5, 1944.

PERRY, Ernest James, banker; b. Fond du Lac, Wis., May 11, 1873; s. James B. and Clara N. (Carey) P.; grad. St. John's Mil. Acad., Delafield, Wis., 1890; student St. Albans Sch., Knoxville, Ill., 1 yr; m. Jeanetta I. Andrae, Nov. 8, 1906; children—Andre, Patricia. Began with First Nat. Bank, Fond du Lac, July 1, 1891, pres., 1916; pres. First-Fond du Lac Nat. Bank (consolidation of First Nat. Bank and Fond du Lac Nat. Bank), 1918-48, chmn. bd., since Jan. 1948; dir. and mem. exec. com. Wis. Bankshares Corp., Milwaukee. Pres. Assn. of Commerce, 1912, 1913. Trustee and treas. (P.E.) Diocese of Fond du Lac. Mem. Am. Bankers Assn. (exec. council 1919-22), Wis Bankers Assn. (pres. 1918). Republican. Episcopalian. Rotarian (pres. Fond du Lac Club, 1935-36). Home: 250 E. Division St., Fond du Lac, Wis. Died Dec. 20, 1949.

PERRY, George Hough; b. Medford, Mass.; s. Baxter E. and Charlotte (Hough) P.; B.L., Boston U., 1888; m. Stella George Stern, Sept. 19, 1906; 1 son, Ralph R. Consulting specialist on merchandising, advt. and sales orgn.; writer and lecturer on theory and technique of advertising and creation of export markets. Dir. Div. of Exploitation, Panama Pacific Internat. Expn., 1913-15; chmn. Pan-Am. Exporters Assn.; dir. gen. Am. Nat. Expositions; pres. Airtress Corp. of America. Unitarian. Home: 37 Willow St. Office: 313 Belmont Av., Brooklyn, N.Y. Died Aug. 14, 1945.

PERRY, Henry Eldredge, president Commercial Solvents Corp.; b. Crete, Neb., Oct. 8, 1889; s. David B. and Helen (Doane) P.; B.A., Yale, 1912; m. Evelyn Hollister, Mar. 9, 1918; children—Phebe B., Henry E., Howard H., Evelyn K., Polly M. With the N.Y. Central R.R., 1912-17, 1918-22; served in U.S. Army, 1917-18; with Commercial Solvents Corp., N.Y. City, since 1922, v.p. and dir., 1938-46, dir., exec. vice pres., 1946, now pres.; v.p. and dir. Thermatomic Carbon Co.; pres. and dir. Commercial Molasses Corp. Dir. C.&E.I. Ry., Carrier Corp. Republican. Conglist. Clubs: Abenaqui (Rye Beach, N.H.); Yale (N.Y. City); Country (Terre Haute, Ind.); Creve Coeur (Peoria, Ill.). Home: Little Boars Head, N.H. Office: 17 E. 42d St., New York, N.Y. Died Mar. 16, 1950.

PERRY, James DeWolf, bishop; b. Germantown, Pa., Oct. 3, 1871; s. James De Wolf and Elisabeth Russell (Tyson) P.; grad. Germantown Acad., 1887; A.B., U. of Pa., 1891, S.T.D., 1911, LL.D., 1931; A.B., Harvard, 1892; B.D., Cambridge Theol. Sch., 1895; D.D., Brown, 1912, Trinity, 1932, U. of South, 1933; S.T.D., Gen. Theol. Sem., 1931; S.T.D., Columbia, 1931; S.T.D., Russian Orthodox Theol. Sem., Paris, 1940; married Edith Dean Weir, Jan. 2, 1908. Deacon, 1895, priest, 1896, P.E. Ch.; asst. minister Christ Ch., Springfield, Mass., 1895-97; rector Christ Ch., Fitchburg, Mass., 1897-1904, St. Paul's Ch., New Haven, Conn., 1904-11; consecrated bishop of R.I., Jan. 6, 1911; presiding bishop P.E. Ch. in U.S. 1930-37, Overseer Harvard University, 1937-43. Legion d'Honneur (France). Chaplain, 6th Massachusetts Infantry, 1898-1904; senior Red Cross chaplain, World War, 1918, 19. Member Phi Kappa Sigma, Soc. of the Cincinnati, Pilgrims of America (v.p.). Clubs: Art, Authors, Century. Home: 10 Brown St. Office: 101 Benefit St., Providence. Died March 20, 1947; buried in Juniper Hill Cemetery, Bristol, R.I.

PERRY, Oscar Butler, mining engr.; b. Bloomington, Ind., Sept. 1876; s. Maj. H. F. P.; A.B., Ind. U., 1897, LL.D., 1931; E.M., Columbia U., 1900; m. Anlo Marquee Cramer, Apr. 1923; children—Anlo Louise, Yvonne Chauvigny. Manager Ind. Gold Dredging Co., 1900, 02, Western Engring. & Construction Co., San Francisco, 1902-04; engr., 1904-06, gen. mgr. placer mining properties since 1906, Guggenheim Exploration Co.; gen. mgr. Yukon Gold Co., operating gold mines in U.S. and Yukon Territory, and tin mines in Malay, 1920-26; mng. dir. Bolivian Internat. Mining Corp. since 1930. Entered U.S. Army, May 1917; discharged, Apr. 1919, with rank of col. of engrs.; comd. 27th Engrs., A.E.F.; asst. engr. light rys. and roads, and engr. in charge of bridge sect., 1st Army. Mem. Beta Theta Pi, Tau Beta Pi. Clubs: Family (San Francisco); Engineers', Columbia University, Bankers (New York). Author of Gold Dredging in the Yukon and other professional papers. Home: 444 El Arroyo Rd., Hillsborough, Calif. Address: 315 Montgomery St., San Francisco 4, Calif. Died July 24, 1945.

PERSHING, James Hammond (pûr'shĭng), lawyer; b. Mount Pleasant, Pa., Dec. 27, 1863; s. John and Elizabeth (Hammond) P.; A.B., Princeton, 1888; m. Martha Kimbal Reymer, Sept. 3, 1889 (died Nov. 18, 1924); children—Alice Reymer, John. Began practice, Pittsburgh, 1890; removed to Denver, Colo., 1892; now sr. mem. Pershing, Bosworth, Dick and Dawson. Prof. of medical jurisprudence, U. of Colo., 1910-27. Mem. first Charter Conv., Denver, 1903; mem. Colo. State Bur. of Child and Animal Protection, 1905-10; mem. Colo. Civ. Service Commn., 1907-09; mem. and pres. Bd. of Charities and Correction, City and County of Denver, 1912-14; trustee U. of Denver, 1920-26; pres. United Charities, Denver, 1902-12, pres. Denver Community Chest, 1925; mem. Denver Public Library Commission. Mem. Am., Colorado and Denver bar assns. Republican. Episcopalian; deputy to Gen. Conv., and chancellor Diocese of Colo., 1914-44; mem., from 6th Province of Nat. Council, 1919-26. Clubs: Denver, Mile High, Cactus, Rocky Mountain, Princeton. Home: 930 Humboldt St. Office: Equitable Bldg., Denver, Colo. Died April 3, 1948.

PERSHING, John Joseph, general of Armies of U.S., b. Linn Co., Mo., Sept. 13, 1860; s. John F and Ann E. (Thompson) P.; student Kirksville (Mo.) Normal Sch., 1880; grad. U.S. Mil. Acad., 1886; LL.B., U. of Neb., 1893; LL.D., U. of Neb., 1917, U. of St. Andrews, Scotland, 1919, U. of Cambridge, Eng., 1919, Yale, 1920; D.C.L., U. of Oxford, Eng., 1919; Dr. Mil. Science, Pa. Mil. Acad., 1921; etc.; m. Washington, Helen F., d. Senator Francis E. Warren, of Cheyenne, Wyo., Jan. 26, 1905; 4 children (wife and 3 daughters lost their lives in the burning of the Presidio, Aug. 27, 1915). Commd. 2d lt. 6th U.S. Cav., July 1, 1886; 1st lt. 10th Cav., Oct. 20, 1892; maj. chief ordnance officer vols., Aug. 18, 1898; hon. disch. from vols., May 12, 1899; maj. a.-a.-g., vols., June 6, 1899; capt. 1st U.S. Cav., Feb. 2, 1901; hon. disch. from vols., June 30, 1901; transferred to 15th U.S. Cav., Aug. 20, 1901; brig. gen., Sept. 20, 1906; maj. gen., Sept. 25, 1916; gen. U.S. Army (emergency), Oct. 6, 1917; confirmed by U.S. Senate "General of Armies of United States," Sept. 3, 1919; retired Sept. 13, 1924. Served in Apache Indian campaign, N.M. and Ariz., 1886, and in Sioux campaign, Dak., 1890-91; comd. Sioux Indian scouts until Aug. 1891; mil. instr. U. of Neb., 1891-95; instr. in tactics, U.S. Mil. Acad., 1897-98; served with 10th Cav. in Santiago campaign, Cuba, 1898; organized the Bur. of Insular Affairs and was its chief until Aug. 16, 1899; served in P.I., Nov. 1899-June 1903; first as adj.-gen. Dept. of Mindanao till August 8, 1901; in charge Moro affairs and comd. military operations in Central Mindanao against Moros, April 1902-June 1903; military attaché Tokio, Japan, 1905-06, and was with Kuroki's army in Manchuria, Mar.-Sept. 1905; served on Gen. Staff, 1903-06; duty P.I., 1906-08, 1909-14; was comdr. Dept. of Mindanao, and gov. Moro Province; comd. successful mil. operation against hostile Moros terminating with their defeat at the battle of Bagsak, June 12, 1913; comd. 8th Brig., Presidio, Calif.; temporarily in command of El Paso patrol dist., on Mexican border; in command of U.S. troops sent into Mexico in pursuit of Villa, Mar. 1916. Comdr.-in-chief A.E.F. in World War, 1917-19; apptd. Chief of Staff, U.S. Army, July 1, 1921. Awarded D.S.M. (U.S.); Grand Cross Order of the Bath (British); Grand Cross Legion of Honor (French); Croix de Guerre and Médaille Militaire (French); Grand Cordon Order of the Paulawnia (Japanese); Grand Cordon Order of Leopold and Croix de Guerre (Belgian); Great Cross Order of White Lion and Croix de Guerre (Tcheco-slovaque); Order Saint Savoir (Greek); Grand Cross Order of St. Maurizio e Lazzaro, and Military Order of Savoy (Italian); Grand Cordon of Prince Danilo I, and Obilitch Medal (Montenegrin); Medal of La Solaridad (Panama); Virtuti Militari and Polonia Restituta (Polish); Grand Cordon Order of the Precious Light of Chia Ho (Chinese); Grand Cordon Order of the Star of Kara-Georges (Serbian); Order of Mihai Bravul (Rumanian); and others. Chmn. Am. Battle Monuments Commn.; chmn. Goethals Memorial Commn. Mason (33°). Clubs: Metropolitan, Army and Navy (Washington). Author: My Experiences in the World War, 1931. Address: War Dept., Washington, D.C. Died July 15, 1948; interred at Arlington National Cemetery, Arlington, Va.

PERSONS, Frederick Torrel, clergyman, librarian; b. Sandisfield, Mass., Feb. 2, 1869; s. Byron John and Ellen K. (Spaulding) P.; B.A., Yale, 1894; M.A., Columbia, 1902; grad. Union Theol. Sem., 1902; student Harvard Sch. of Architecture, 7 summers; m. Florence Isabel Cummings, Sept. 19, 1906; children—Theodore M., Stow S., Frederick D. Teacher and prin. acads. until 1899; asso. pastor United Ch., New Haven, Conn., 1902-04; ordained ministry Congl. Ch., 1903; pastor Woodbridge, Conn., 1904-11, Mt. Carmel, 1911-15; librarian Bangor Theol. Sem., 1915-24; librarian Congregational Library, 1924-47; retired. Lecturer on European and Am. architecture at Rollins Coll., Winter Park, Fla., 1940. Mem. Unitarian Hist. Society; moderator, Mass. Conv. of Congl. Ministers (oldest ministerial body in New Eng., and including both Unitarian and Trinitarian Congl. ministers). Mem. Spl. Libraries Assn. of Boston (pres. 1929-30), Am. Soc. Ch. History. Club: Winthrop. Has lectured extensively on architectural subjects; lecturer for many years on church architecture, Bangor Theological Seminary. Contributed 81 articles to the Dictionary of Am. Biography. Home: 306 Vinton St., Melrose Highlands, Mass. Died Sept. 2, 1948.

PESCHGES, John Hubert, bishop; b. West Newton, Minn., May 11, 1881; s. Peter and Mary (Pasch) P.; ed. St. John's U., Collegeville, Minn., 1891-99, St. Paul's (Minn.) Sem., 1899-1905, Cath. U. of America, 1906-07. Ordained priest R.C. Ch., Apr. 15, 1905; pastor St. Mary's Ch., Geneva, Minn., 1905-06; mission work, 1906-10; pastor Mt. Carmel Ch., Easton, Minn., 1910-13; v.p. St. Mary's Coll., Winona, Minn., 1913-18, pres., 1918-33; pastor St. Augustine's Ch., Austin, Minn., 1933-38; bishop of Crookston, Minn., since 1938. Address: Crookston, Minn. Deceased.

PETER, Arthur, lawyer; b. Rockville, Md., Nov. 16, 1873; s. George and Eliza Lavinia (Gassaway) P.; prep. edn., Rittenhouse Acad., Washington, D.C., and Rockville (Md.) Acad.; LL.B., summa cum laude, Nat. U. Law Sch., 1894; m. Edith Marshall, July 30, 1918; children—Humphrey Marshall, Arthur. Admitted to D.C. bar, 1894, and began practice at Washington; lecturer in law, Nat. U., 1899; prof. law, George Washington U., 1900-23; mem. Birney & Peter, 1897, Hemphill & Peter, 1900; chmn. bd. and gen. counsel Washington Loan & Trust Co.; dir. Equitable Coöperative Building Assn. Del. to Dem. Nat. Conv., 1904, 12 (vice-chmn. Md. delegation, 1912), vice-chmn., trustee George Washington U.; trustee John Dickson Home. Mem. Am. Bar Assn., Md. Bar Assn., Bar Assn. D.C., Soc. of the Cincinnati, Phi Delta Phi. Presbyterian. Mason. Clubs: Metropolitan, Lawyers, Chevy Chase. Home: Bethesda, Md. Office: Washington Loan & Trust Bldg., Washington, D.C. Deceased.

PETER, Luther Crouse, ophthalmologist; b. St. Clairsville, Pa., Feb. 14, 1869; s. Rev. Jacob and Harriet Jane (Crouse) P.; student Susquehanna U., 1887-88; A.B., Gettysburg Coll., 1891, A.M., 1894; M.D., U. of Pa., 1894; Sc.D., Gettysburg Coll. and Susquehanna Univ.; LL.D. Gettysburg Coll.; m. Carrie Chrystine Moser, June 20, 1916. Practiced in Phila. since 1894; prof. diseases of the eye, Temple Univ., 1917-30; prof. emeritus, diseases of eye, Grad. Med. Sch., U. of Pa.; cons. ophthalmologist to Graduate Hosp., Rush Hosp. for Consumption and Allied Diseases and Friends' Hosp. for Medical and Nervous Diseases and Roxborough Memorial Hosp. Fellow Am. Coll. Surgeons, Am. Ophthal. Soc., Coll. Physicians of Phila., Oxford Congress of Ophthalmology (England); mem. Internat. Congress Ophthalmology (sec. and treas. 1922), Nat. Bd. of Ophthalmology (pres. 1929-37), A.M.A., Am. Acad. Ophthalmology and Oto-Laryngology (ex-pres.), Phi Gamma Delta, Phi Beta Kappa. Republican. Lutheran. Mason (K.T., Shriner). Club: Union League. Author: The Principles and Practice of Perimetry, 4th edit., 1938; The Extra-Ocular Muscles, 3d edit., 1941. Home: 121 E. Mt. Pleasant Av., Mt. Airy. Office: 1930 Chestnut St., Philadelphia, Pa. Died Nov. 12, 1942.

PETERKIN, William Gardner, lawyer; b. Culpeper, Va., Oct. 21, 1870; s. George William and Constance Gardner (Lee) P.; LL.B., U. of Va., 1894; m. Ora Moss Martin, Apr. 18, 1912; children—Julia Moss, Constance Lee. Admitted to W.Va. bar, 1894, and since practiced in Parkersburg; atty. Parkersburg Rig & Reel Co., Parkersburg; city atty., 1926-29; mem. City Council, 1902-04; State Senate, 1910-14. Served as major W.Va. Nat. Guard, 1898-1909. Chmn. Draft Board, Wood County, during World War. Del. Dem. Nat. Conv., 1924; chmn. Community Chest campaign, 1937; sec. Wood County Am. Red Cross; vice-pres. W.Va. State Soc. for Crippled Children; sec. and treas. Wood County Soc. for Crippled Children; treas. Henry Logan Children's Home; past pres. Kiwanis Club. Trustee Protestant Episcopal High Sch. in Va., Alexandria; del. from Diocese W.Va. to triennial General Convention of P. E. Ch., 6 times; mem. Nat. Council Episcopal Ch., 1926-40; chmn. Bd. of Finance, Diocese of W.Va., since 1931. Mem. W.Va. State Bar Assn. (sec. 1905-07), Delta Psi. Democrat. Home: 1110 Ann St. Office: 217 4th St., Parkersburg, W.Va. Died Aug. 9, 1941.

PETERMANN, Albert E., lawyer, corp. official; b. Calumet, Mich., March 3, 1877; s. Ferdinand D. and Caroline (Bast) P.; Ph.B., Cornell U., 1900; hon. LL.D., U. of Arizona, 1939; m. Anna M. Grierson, July 2, 1903. Pres. Calumet & Hecla Consol. Copper Co.; pres. and dir. various mining companies. Mem. exec. com. U.S. Copper Assn. and Copper Institute; chmn. Bd. of Control, Mich. Coll. Mining and Technology. Member American Legion. Mason (32°). Home: 121 Calumet Avenue, Calumet, Michigan. Died Oct. 15, 1944.

PETERS, Le Roy Samuel, physician; b. St. Joseph, Mich., Apr. 6, 1882; s. William Franklin and Eleanor (Yund) P.; student lit. dept. U. of Minn. 2 yrs., med. dept. 2 yrs.; M.D., U. of Ill., 1906; m. Isabella Fyfe, Feb. 8, 1908; 1 son, Fyfe. Asso. med. dir. Cottage Sanatorium, Silver City, N.M., 1909-13, Albuquerque Sanatorium, 1913-17; med. dir. St. Joseph Sanatorium, Albuquerque, 1917-25. Mem. A.M.A., Nat. Tuberculosis Assn. (dir. 1915-20 and since 1923), Am. Sanatorium Assn., Phi Delta Theta, Nu Sigma Nu. Fellow Am. Coll. Physicians, Am. Assn. for Thoracic Surgery; pres. Am. Sanatorium Assn., 1933-34, Southwestern Med. Soc., 1938. Died Dec. 17, 1941.

PETERS, William John, explorer; b. Oakland, Calif., Feb. 5, 1863; s. William B. and Margaret (Major) P.; ed. Oakland High Sch.; m. Beatrice Boyd, Sept. 2, 1908; 1 son, Geoffrey Lloyd. Engaged in various U.S. Govt. surveys, 1885-97; in charge explorations in Alaska made by U.S. Geol. Survey, 1898, 99, 1900, 01, 02, accounts of which appear in publs. of that bur.; apptd. official rep. Nat. Geog. Soc. on Ziegler Polar expdn. to Franz Joseph Land, 1903-05; in command Magnetic Survey ships Galilee and Carnegie, 1907-13, Hudson Bay Expdn., 1914. Mem. Philos. Soc. Washington, Am. Geophysical Union, Am. Sect. Internat. Scientific Radio Union. Clubs: Cosmos, Arts. Home: Chevy Chase, Md. Address: Dept. Terrestrial Magnetism, Washington, D.C. Died July 10, 1942.

PETERSEN, Carl Edward, naval architect, marine engr.; b. Brooklyn, N.Y., Jan. 21, 1897; s. Christian Edward (Thinggaard) and Magdalene (Hoy) P.; ed. Pratt Inst., Tri-State Coll. of Engring., Brooklyn Poly. Inst.; grad. U.S. Navy Steam Engring. Sch., Stevens Inst. Tech., 1918; m. 2d, Ann Suber, Oct. 28, 1937; children—Carl Thinggaard (by 1st marriage), Dianne Mary. With Morse Dry Dock & Repair Co., 1910-18, successively as marine machinist, draftsman, estimator and outside superintendent; engr. officer, transport duty, U.S. Navy, 1918; supt. engr. U.S. Army Transport Service, during period of conversion of merchant vessels to troop ships, 1919; estimator in charge cost of ship repairs at Port of New York, U.S. Shipping Bd., 1919-20; naval architect U.S. Mail Steamship Co., 1920; naval architect U.S. Lines in charge reconditioning the George Washington, America, President Harding, President Roosevelt, etc., 1921-27; asst. to v.p. Newport News Shipbuilding Dry Dock Co., 1928-37; asst. mgr. const. and repair dept. Matson Navigation Co., 1938-41; had charge gen. design steamships President Hoover and President Coolidge. Lt. comdr. U.S. Naval Res. Called to active duty as comdr. Vol. Naval Res., engr. spl. service duties, Dec. 17, 1941; coordinator ship repairs and asst. material officer, Honolulu, T.H., on spl. orders from sec. of navy, Dec. 21, 1941-Apr. 1942; exec. and repair officer, U.S. Naval Sect. Base, New Orleans (Algiers), La., to July 1943; stationed Tampa, Fla., sr. asst. supervisor of shipbuilding U.S.N., 1943-44. Mem. Am. Soc. Mech. Engrs., Am. Bur. of Shipping (also Pacific Coast Com.); life mem., hon. corr. mem. Institution of Naval Architects, London; life mem. N. E. Coast Institution of Engrs. and Shipbuilders (Newcastle-on-Tyne, Eng.); life mem., v.p. Inst. Marine Engrs. (London), life mem. Soc. Naval Architects and Marine Engrs. (council mem.); naval mem. Am. Soc. Naval Engrs.; tech. mem. Tech. Com. of Engring. Am. Bur. Shipping. Fellow Am. Geographic Soc. Licensed engr. State of N.Y., chief engr. ocean steam vessels (any tonnage). Address: care Supervisor of Shipbuilding, U.S. Navy, Tampa, Fla. Died in active service, July 23, 1944.

PETERSON, Charles Simeon; b. Daglösen, Sweden, Aug. 29, 1873; s. Rev. Peter and Sophia Christina P.; ed. high sch., Stockholm; came to U.S., 1887; m. Thyra Hjertquist, Apr. 30, 1901 (dec.). Learned printer's trade; organizer, 1899, Peterson Linotyping Co., pres., 1899-1924; also head of Regan Printing House, and the G. D. Steere Co., 1914-24; v.p. The Inland Press. Mem. Board of Edn., Chicago, 1913-18; mem. Bd. County Commrs., Chicago, 2 terms, 1922-30; city treas., Chicago, 1927-31; city comptroller for short time; v.p. World's Fair, Chicago, 1933-34. Trustee Am. Scandinavian Foundation; hon. life governing mem. Chicago Art Inst. Republican. Clubs: Tavern, Chicago Athletic, Swedish, Cliff Dwellers. Home: 77 E. Elm St.; (summer) Sheboygan, Wis. Office: 328 S. Jefferson St., Chicago, Ill. Died Sep. 7, 1943.

PETERSON, Herbert, editor; b. Bridgeport, Conn., Nov. 21, 1870; s. George W. and Anna A. (Richard) P.; grad. high sch., Bridgeport; m. Georgianna Minty, Aug. 24, 1897; children—Olive Grace (Mrs. Edmund P. Davis), Herbert Minty. Former pub. New Haven (Conn.) Journal-Courier and former owner and editor of Washington (New Jersey) Star; editor-in-chief Peerless Newspapers since 1933. Served as auditor, justice of peace, and mem. Bd. of Edn., Milford, Conn. Mem. S.A.R. Democrat. Methodist. Mason (32°, K.T.). Club: Knights Templar. Author: Double Ma Jong, 1922; The Emerald Tablet, 1926; Seeing England, 1930; Contract Travels, 1933; Select Quotations, 1934. Home: New Haven, Conn. Died Sept. 30, 1943.

PETERSON, James Earl, Sr., business exec.; b. Dayton, O., July 29, 1891; s. Amos Milton and Mary Elizabeth (Hite) P.; ed. pub. schs.; m. Dollie E. Bruning, Apr. 5, 1918; 1 son, James Earl. Entire career with Gen. Machinery Corp., Hamilton, O., and its subsidiary; vice pres., sec. and dir.; pres. and dir. The Hooven, Owens, Rentschler Co., Hamilton; v.p. and dir. Niles Tool Works Co., Hamilton; sec., treas. and dir. United Welding Co., Middletown, O. Served in A.U.S., World War I. Mem. Soc. Naval Architects and Marine Engrs., Am. Soc. Naval Engrs. Republican. Methodist. Am. Legion. Elk. Mason (Scottish Rite). Club: Hamilton. Home: 306 Dick Av. Office: 545 N. 3d St., Hamilton, O. Deceased.

PETERSON, John Bertram, bishop; b. Salem, Mass., July 15, 1871; s. William Augustine and Margaret (O'Donnell) P.; A.B. and Ph.D., St. Anselm's Coll., Manchester, N.H., 1895; student St. John's Sem., Boston; S.T.B., Catholic U., Paris, 1900; studied French, Sch. of History, Rome, 1900-01; LL.D., Boston Coll., 1932, Univ. of N.H., 1935. Ordained priest R.C. Ch., 1899; prof. ecclesiastical history, 1901-06, St. John's Sem., prof. moral theology, 1906-11, rector, 1911-26. Has served as diocesan consultor, synodical examiner, judge of matrimonial court and moderator ecclesiastical confs. in the Curia of Archdiocese of Boston. Made domestic prelate by Pope Pius X, May 27, 1914; made titular bishop of Hippo and auxiliary to archibishop of Boston, November 10, 1927; made bishop of Manchester, July 14, 1932. Asst. at Papal Throne, 1934. Address: 151 Walnut St., Manchester, N.H. Died Mar. 15, 1944.

PETRIE, George (pē'trē), coll. dean; b. Montgomery, Ala., Apr. 10, 1866; s. George Laurens and Mary Jane (Cooper) P.; A.M., U. of Va., 1887; Ph.D., Johns Hopkins, 1891; LL.D., U. of Ala.; m. Mary Barkwell Lane, Aug. 30, 1893 (died July 13, 1942); 1 dau., Mary Cooper (dec.). Adjunct prof. modern langs. and history, 1887-89; prof. history and Latin, 1891-1922, prof. history since 1922, dean acad. faculty, 1908-22, dean Grad. Sch., 1922-42; Ala. Poly. Inst.; retired Aug. 31, 1942. Member summer faculty, George Peabody College for Teachers, 1916-17, Univ. of Va., 1923; lecturer southern history, U. of Chicago, summer 1918; lecturer U.S. history, George Peabody Coll. for Teachers, summer 1921. Mem. Ala. Centenary Commn. Mem. Assn. Grad. Deans of Southern Colls. (pres. 1932), Am. Hist. Association Alabama Educational Association, Alabama History Teachers' Assn. (pres. 1915), Phi Delta Theta, Phi Kappa Phi, Pi Gamma Mu, Newcomen Society. Democrat. Presbyterian. Contributor articles Historic Towns of Southern States, in The South in the Building of the Nation, and Cyclopedia of Southern Literature, also to ednl. jours. Editor of 3 series of Ala. Poly. Inst. Studies in Southern History. Joint Author: Mace-Petrie American School History; Mace-Petrie Elementary History. Author: Comments on Current Events; History of Alabama; Church and State in Early Maryland; Problems of the Graduate Dean; Trials of a Graduate Dean. Broadcast weekly over station WAPI; subject "Topics of the Day," 1930-31. Home: Auburn, Ala. Died Sept. 6, 1947.

PETROFF, Strashimer Alburtus (pĕt'rŏf), dir. med. research; b. Varna, Bulgaria, Aug. 20, 1883; s. Attanas and Dobra Ivanova (Pinchot) P.; Ph.D., Columbia, 1923; hon. Sc.D., Colgate, 1932; m. Mary Fears Gilmer, Jan. 18, 1912; 1 son, Gilmer. Came to U.S., 1900, naturalized citizen, 1907. Asst. in lab., Trudeau (N.Y.) Sanitarium, 1909-21, dir. med. research, 1921-35; now bacteriologist Sea View Hosp., S.I., N.Y. Mem. Am. Soc. Bacteriologist, Soc. Immunologists, Soc. Exptl. Biology and Medicine, Am. Med. Editors and Authors Assn. Republican. Presbyterian. Author: Tuberculosis Bacteriology, Pathology and Laboratory Diagnosis (with E. R. Baldwin and L. U. Gardner), 1927. Contbr. many papers and articles on bacteriology and immunity to tuberculosis. Died Nov. 26, 1948.

PETTER, Rodolphe C. (pĕ-târ'), missionary; b. Vevey, Switzerland, Feb. 19, 1865; s. Louis and Elise (Dubuis de la Praz) P.; ed. pub. schs., Switzerland; missionary course, 7 yrs., Basel Theol. Sch.; B.D. and D.D., Bethel Coll., Newton, Kan. Came to U.S., 1890; m. Marie Gerber, May 14, 1890 (died July 30, 1910); children—Olga Marie (Mrs. P. F. Schroeder), Valdo Rodolphe; m. 2d, Bertha Elise Kinsinger (also missionary), Nov. 28, 1911. Missionary among Southern Cheyenne Indians, Cantonment, Okla., 1891-1916, Northern Cheyennes at Lame Deer, Mont., since 1916. Mem. Internat. Hist. Soc. (Paris). Author of English-Cheyenne Dictionary, Cheyenne Grammar, and of various transls. into the Cheyenne lang., including Bunyan's Pilgrim's Progress and large portions of the Scriptures, besides several edits. of Cheyenne gospel song books. Completed transl. and publ. of N.T. into Cheyenne, 1934, and given trip to Switzerland in 1935 by friends in recognition. Published "Reisesegen," 1936; Mission Memoirs, 1936. Home: Lame Deer, Mont. Died May 6, 1935; buried at Lame Deer, Mont.

PETTIJOHN, Charles Clyde (pĕt'ĭ-jŏn), lawyer; b. Indianapolis, Ind., May 5, 1881; s. Otto Beecher and Lillian (Sloan) P.; LL.B., Indiana Univ., 1903; m. Helen Irene Lynch, Nov. 23, 1917; children—Charles C. Jr., Bruce David. Admitted to Ind. bar, 1903, N.Y. bar, 1917; counsel Motion Picture Producers and Distributors of America. Democrat. Home: Rye, N.Y. Office: 28 W. 44th St., N.Y. City. Died May 19, 1948.

PETTY, Orville Anderson, clergyman; b. Cadiz, O., Feb. 20, 1874; s. Asbury F. and Sarah (Kyle) P.; A.B., Muskingum Coll., 1898; Pittsburgh Theol. Sem., 1901; A.M., Colorado Coll., 1905; grad. student U. of Chicago, 1907-10; Ph.D. in Philosophy and Edn., Yale, 1915, D.D., Yale, 1919; m. Evelyn Hammond, July 17, 1902; 1 dau., Mabel Kyle. Ordained 1901; pastor Greeley, Colo., 1901-06, First Ch., Aurora, Ill., 1906-11, Plymouth Ch., New Haven, 1911-29; pres. Arnold Coll., 1929-30; mem. India staff of Laymen's Foreign Missions Inquiry, 1930-31, adviser of Appraisal Commn., same, 1931-32, and editor of research materials, same, 1932-33; dir. research A Movement for World Christianity (formerly The Modern Missions Movement) since 1934. Lecturer, Dept. Race Relations, Grad. Sch., Yale, 1938-41. Chaplain 2d Conn. Inf., Mexican border, 1916; served overseas as chaplain 102d Inf., and sr.

chaplain and morale officer, 1917-19; served as maj., chaplain 169th Inf., 1921-23; lt. col. same regt., 1923-29, and col. same regt., 1929-38; retired brig. gen. Cited in General Orders, and by General Pershing; decorated Croix de Guerre and Chevalier de L'Ordre de l'Etoile Noire (French); Chevalier Ordre de la Couronne (Belgian). Served as pres. Grace Hosp., City Mission, Conn. Council Religious Edn., New Haven Council Chs.; trustee Arnold Coll.; trustee Organized Charities, New Haven. Mem. S.A.R., Mil. Order Foreign Wars (chaplain gen.). Republican. Mason. Club: Graduate. Author: Did the Term "The Gospel" Originate with Paul?, 1925; Kindling the Christmas Fire (verse), 1929; Common Sense and God, 1935. Editor of Supplementary Series to Re-Thinking Missions (7 vols.). Home: 275 W. Rock Av., New Haven, Conn. Died Aug. 12, 1942.

PEW, James Edgar, oil exec.; b. Mercer, Pa., 1870; s. Thomas and Mary (Barr) P.; ed. Business Coll.; m. Martha E. Layng, 1899; children—John G., George L., Martha Elizabeth. Began with Peoples Natural Gas Co., Pittsburgh, Pa., 1886-96; joined Sun Oil Co., Toledo, 1896-1901, Beaumont, Tex., 1901-12; independent operator Tulsa, Okla., 1913-14; v.p. Carter Oil Co., 1914-18; v.p. Sun Oil Co., Dallas, Tex., 1918-26; v.p. in charge of production and pipe line transportation, Sun Oil Co. since 1918; pres. Sun Pipe Line Co. since 1918. Pres. Am. Petroleum Inst.; 1924-25, now dir.; mem. Am. Inst. Mining & Metall. Engrs. Clubs: Union League, Racquet, Philadelphia Country, Merian Cricket. Home: Mt. Moro Road, Villa Nova, Pa. Office: 1608 Walnut St., Philadelphia 3, Pa. Died Nov. 22, 1946.

PEYRAUD, Frank Charles (pā-rō'), artist; b. Bulle, Canton Fribourg, Switzerland, June 1, 1858; s. Henri and Romaine (Piloud) P.; ed. Coll. of Fribourg, Switzerland; student École des Beaux Arts, Paris, and Art Inst. Chicago; m. Elizabeth Krysher, June 14, 1906. Awards: Fortnightly prize, 1899, Municipal Art League and Edward B. Butler prizes, 1912, hon. mention, 1912, Clyde M. Carr prize, 1913, William F. Grower prize, 1914, at Art Inst. Chicago; bronze medal, Panama P.I. Expn., 1915; Martin M. Cahn prize, 1921; gold medal, Chicago Painters and Sculptors Soc., 1935. Mem. Chicago Acad. Design, Chicago Soc. Artists, Chicago Water Color Soc. Club: Cliff Dwellers. Home: Highland Park, Ill. Died May 30, 1948.

PEYTON, Bertha Menzler (Mrs. A. Conway Peyton), artist; b. Chicago; d. Hermann and Mathilda (Klemt) Menzler; grad. high sch.; grad. Art Inst. Chicago, 1893; studied with Olivier Merson, Aman Jean and Raphael Collin, Paris; m. A. Conway Peyton, May 9, 1912 (died 1936). Made splty. of western subjects—Arizona Desert, Grand Canyon of Ariz., etc.; represented in Union League Club, Chicago; Klio, Niké and North End Woman's clubs, Chicago; Evanston (Ill.) Woman's Club; panel decoration entitled "Music," Fine Arts Building, Chicago; decorations "The Yacht Race," Addison Gilbert Hosp., Gloucester, Mass.; water color painting, Brooklyn Museum, 1923. Spl. prize, 1903, Young Fortnightly prize, 1909, and William Frederick Grower prize, 1910, all Art Inst. Chicago; Nat. Assn. of Women Painters and Sculptors prize for the best landscape, 1925; Gilbert Davis prize, North Shore Art Assn., 1930. Christian Scientist. Mem. Assn. Women Painters and Sculptors (v.p. 1918-19, corr. sec. 1919-20), Am. Water Color Soc., Water Color Club (New York), Allied Artists America, N.Y. Society of Painters, Grand Central Art Galleries (New York), North Shore Arts Assn. (bd. dirs., Gloucester, Mass.). First reader First Ch. of Christ Scientist, Gloucester. Home: 4 Sayward St., Gloucester, Mass. Died March 21, 1947.

PFANSTIEHL, Carl (făn'stēl), b. Columbia, Mo., Sept. 17, 1887; s. Albertus A. (Rev.) and Julia (Barnes) P.; spl. work Armour Inst. Tech., Chicago; m. Caryl Cody, June 24, 1915; children—Cody, Alfred, Rose-Caryl, Grace. Organized (1907) Pfanstiehl Electrical Lab. (now Fansteel Metall. Corp.), pres. and dir. research until 1919; pres. and dir. res. Pfanstiehl Radio Co., 1922-28; v.p. and dir. res. Pfanstiehl Chemical Co. (chem. and metal Divs.) since 1918; special research work for War and Medical Depts. of the Government during World War; spl. interest in research in applied physics, metallurgy, radio, and consultant in these fields; has been granted 135 patents in elec., chem. and metall. fields; work largely concerned with prodn. of metals such as metallic tungsten, molybdenum, tantalum, rhenium, osmium, ruthenium and their alloys, special anti-friction and hard tipping alloys, and with cold lighting, fluorescent powders, and rare biol. chemicals. Mem. Am. Chem. Soc., Electrochem. Soc., A.A.A.S., N.Y. Acad. of Science, Am. Phys. Soc., Optical Soc. of America, Am. Inst. Mining and Metall. Engrs., Am. Soc. for Metals. Club: University (Chicago). Recipient of Modern Pioneer Award, 1940. Author: Ignition, 1912; also articles on radio theories and biochemical subjects. Home: 614 Wood Path, Highland Park, Ill. Died Mar. 1, 1942.

PFATTEICHER, Ernst Philip, author, clergyman; b. Easton, Pa., July 28, 1874; s. Philip and Emma (Spaeth) P.; A.B., Lafayette Coll., Easton, 1895, later A.M., Ph.D., 1901, D.D., 1918; grad. Luth. Theol. Sem., Phila., 1898; student U. of Erlangen, U. of Pa.; D.D, Muhlenberg Coll., 1918, LL.D., 1931; m. Helen Jacoby, June 27, 1905; children—Ernst Philip, Helen Emma. Ordained Luth. ministry, 1898; asst. to Rev. Dr. Theodore E. Schmauk, of Lebanon, Pa., 1898-1902; pastor Trinity Ch., Norristown, 1902-07, Holy Communion Ch., Phila., 1907-18, Old Trinity Ch., Reading, 1918-26. Pres. Luth. Ministerium of Pa. and Adjacent States since 1926; mem. internat. continuation com. of Stockholm Conf. on Life and Work; mem. Nat. Luth. Council; dir. Luth. Theol. Sem., Phila. Mem. Acad. Polit. and Social Science, Delta Kappa Epsilon. Republican. Club: Union League. Author: The Apostles Creed in Sonnets, 1900; King David's Earth Born Son, 1907; Think on These Things, 1917; Sermons on the Gospels, Vol. I, 1918, Vol. II, 1923; The Sunday Problem, 1923; Christian Social Science, 1933; The Man from Oxford, 1934; For Pastors Only, 1935; Youth Letters (in collaboration with his daughter), 1938. Home: 415 S. 44th St. Office: 1228 Spruce St., Philadelphia, Pa. Died Jan. 9, 1943.

PFEIFFER, Annie Merner (fī'fēr), philanthropist; b. New Hamburg, Ont., Sept. 23, 1860; d. John and Anna Marie (Zingg) Merner; ed. public schools of Ontario, Can.; hon. LL.D., Albright Coll., Reading, Pa., 1937, MacMurray Coll., Jacksonville, Ill., 1939; hon. Dr. of Humanities, Cornell Coll. (Mt. Vernon, Ia.), 1938, Florida Southern Coll., Lakeland, Fla., 1941; honorary Dr. of Humane Letters, Kansas Wesleyan University (Salina, Kan.), Bennett College, Greensboro, N.C., 1941, Southwestern Coll., Winfield, Kan., 1942; Dr. of Letters of Humanity, Illinois Wesleyan University, 1942; m. Henry Pfeiffer, March 7, 1882. Philanthropist, chiefly among churches, homes for children and aged, ch. directed schs. and colls., U.S. and fgn. countries. Trustee Colegio Ward (Buenos Aires), Yenching Univ. (Peiping, China), Ewha Coll. (Seoul, Korea), Albright Coll., Bennett Coll., Cornell Coll., North Central Coll., Ohio Wesleyan Univ., Syracuse Univ., Baldwin-Wallace Coll., Pfeiffer Junior Coll. (all U.S.), Drew Seminary for Women, Carmel, N.Y.; mem. bd. New York Deaconess Assn. and Methodist Church Home. Republican. Methodist. Home: 180 Riverside Dr. Office: 113 W. 18th St., New York, N.Y. Died Jan. 8, 1946.

PFEIFFER, Jacob, retired; b. Wadsworth, O., Apr. 7, 1861; s. Jacob and Henrietta (Zorn) P.; ed. high sch., Wadsworth; m. Kathryn D. Beck, Dec. 31, 1919; m. 3d, Julia F. Gray, Apr. 1, 1939. Began as clk. in employ of E. Steinbacher, wholesale and retail dealer in drugs, 1877; with Benton, Myers & Co., wholesale druggists, Cleveland, O., 1883-84; with John Lamparter in retail drug business, 1889; entered real estate bus., lands adjoining Akron, O., 1892; with others began mfr. of druggists' sundries in rubber and later in 1906 organized the Miller Rubber Co., Akron, now consolidated with The Goodrich Rubber Co. of Akron. Mason (32°, Shriner). Club: Congress Lake. Home: 585 N.E. 58th St., Miami, Fla. Died Feb. 1946.

PFINGST, Adolph O. (fingst), oculist; b. St. Joseph, Mo., Sept. 9, 1869; s. H. Adolph and Clara (Weiss) P.; grad. Louisville (Ky.) Male High Sch., 1888; M.D., Louisville Med. Coll., 1891; m. Lula Solger, 1901; 1 dau., Katherine (dec.). Served as asst. to Prof. Greeff, U. of Berlin, 1893-94; asst. Knapps' Hosp., New York, 1894-96; practiced at Louisville since 1896; prof. ophthalmology, U. of Louisville, since 1905. Mem. Med. Corps, U.S. Army, 1917. Mem. Pfingst & Townes; mem. staff Norton Memorial Infirmary, St. Joseph Infirmary, Children's Free Hosp., Kosair Hosp. for Crippled Children, Kentucky Baptist Hospital, Jewish Hospital. Republican. Unitarian. Mason (Knight Templar, Shriner). Clubs: Rotary, Louisville Country, Sleepy Hollow Fishing, Audubon Country. Home: 1009 Cherokee Rd. Office: Heyburn Bldg., Louisville, Ky. Died Feb. 25, 1944.

PFISTER, Jean Jacques (fĭst'ēr), painter; b. Hasle, Switzerland, July 10, 1878; s. Jacob and Anna (Mosemann) P.; came to America, 1898, naturalized, 1927; student Hopkins Sch. of Fine Art, San Francisco, 1903-06, Art Students League, 1922-23, with Wayman Adams, 1923-24, Art Sch., Bremen, Germany, 1912, 13, also 1916-20; m. Elizabeth L. Holt, Dec. 1, 1922. Head of art dept., Rollins Coll., Winter Park, Fla., 1931-34; prof. art, Miss Harris' Coll. Prep. Sch., Miami. Best known work, "'We' at Daybreak," recording Col. Lindbergh's trans-Atlantic flight, and reproduced in various publs.; (portraits) Dr. Thomas R. Baker, Dr. Edwin P. Hooker, Oliver Cromwell Morse, Loring C. Chase, Rev. Robert Ray Kendall, Dr. C. M. Bingham, Miss Louise M. Abbott, Mrs. W. C. Comstock, in Rollins Coll. Library, Dean Charles Atwood Campbell, Knowles Memorial Chapel, Winter Park, Fla.; Dr. William Hornell, Ohio Wesleyan U., Delaware, Ohio; Anne Lynch Botta, Vt. Hist. Mus., Old Bennington, Vt.; Mrs. Jeannette Hinsdill Palmer, Butterworth Hosp., Grand Rapids, Mich.; Gov. Frank L. Emerson, Normal Sch., Lander, Wyoming; Mary Baker Eddy, N.Y. World's Fair, and Golden Gate Expn., San Francisco, 1939-40; also portraits of Mrs. Eddy for The Principia (St. Louis), Principia Coll. (Elsa, Ill.), Christian Science Benevolent Assn. (San Francisco), Administration Bldg. of Christian Science (Boston), Longyear Foundation (Brookline, Mass.); landscapes in Vt. Hist. Museum, Columbia University Chapel, Palm Beach Woman's Club (West Palm Beach, Fla.), Elk Temple (Passaic, New Jersey), also series of 8 pictures in Montanans, Inc., Helena, Montana; Setting of the Rising Sun, Okinawa, Coral Gables Youth Center. Received 1st prize for best portrait, also "outstanding work" award (landscape), Palm Beach Art League, 1938; best landscape and "outstanding work" (2 awards) Palm Beach Art League, 1940; 1st award, The Royal Poincianna, Poincianna Festival, Miami, Fla., 1942 and 1947; best Fla. landscape, St. John River, Fla., Fedn. Art, 1944; mem. Am. Water Color Soc., Laguna Beach Art Assn., Carmel Art Assn., Yonkers Art Assn., New Rochelle Art Assn., Palm Beach Art League and Tampa Art Students Club (Fla.), Swiss Club of N.Y., The Palm Beach Art League (Palm Beach). Clubs: Nat. Arts, Salmagundi (New York). Studio: 614 Aledo Av., Coral Gables, Fla. Died June 7, 1949; buried in Cascade (Mich.) Cemetery.

PFISTER, Joseph Clement, univ. instr.; b. Newark, N.J., Mar. 10, 1867; A.M., Columbia, 1889; m. Emma A. C. Heim, 1891. Asst. in mathematics and astronomy, Columbia, 1889-90, tutor in higher mathematics, 1890-91, tutor in mechanics since 1891. Mem. N.Y. Acad. of Scis., Am. Math. Soc., A.A.A.S. Address: 240 Sixth Av., Roseville, Newark, N.J. Died Aug. 22, 1948.

PFUND, A. Herman (foont), physicist; b. Madison, Wis., Dec. 28, 1879; s. Herman and Anna (Scheibel) P.; B.S., U. of Wis., 1901; Ph.D., Johns Hopkins U., 1906; m. Nelle Fuller, Aug. 30, 1910; 1 dau., Alice Elizabeth. Carnegie research asst., 1903-05, asst. in physics, 1906-07, Johnston scholar, 1907-09, asso. in physics, 1909-10, asso. prof., 1910-27, professor since 1927, Johns Hopkins University. Member Am. Physical Society, Optical Society of America (pres. 1943), Gamma Alpha, Phi Beta Kappa. Awarded Science Club medal, U. of Wis., 1901; Longstreth medal, Franklin Inst., Phila., 1922; Dudley medal, Am. Soc. for Testing Materials, 1931; Frederic E. Ives medal of the Optical Society of America, 1939. Home: 4404 Bedford Place, Baltimore, Md. Died Jan. 5, 1948.

PHELPS, Arthur Stevens (fĕlps), clergyman; b. New Haven, Conn., Jan. 23, 1863; s. S. Dryden (D.D.) and Sophia Emilia (Linsley) P.; A.B., Yale, 1886, B.D., 1889; M.A., 1906; D.D., Occidental Coll., Los Angeles, Calif., 1909; m. M. Blanche Stroud, June 17, 1890; children—Mrs. Céleste Osgood, Dryden Linsley. Ordained Bapt. ministry, 1890; pastor Immanuel Ch., Denver, Colo., 1890-91, Central Ch., Los Angeles, Calif., 1905-12, First Ch., Waterville, Me., 1914-1920; stated preacher First Ch., San Francisco, 1920-22; prof. history and influence of the English Bible and pub. speaking, Berkeley Bapt. Div. Sch., 1922-25; ret. Member Phi Beta Kappa. Republican. Mason (K.T.). World traveler and platform lecturer. Author: Speaking in Public, 1929; The Bible Looks You Over, 1933. Contbr. to periodicals. Home: 1800 Thousand Oaks Blvd., Berkeley, Calif. Died Oct. 19, 1948.

PHELPS, George Harrison, public relations, advt.; born Millers Falls, Mass., May 20, 1883; s. William J. and Almira J. (Benjamin) P.; prep. edn., Worcester Acad.; student Cornell U., 1903-04; m. Laura Stephens, Oct. 27, 1904; children—William Erland, Harrison Stephens. Began in automobile business, Worcester, 1904; asst. mgr. Buick Motor Co., Boston, 1906-09; mgr. Studebaker Corp., at Boston, 1909-11, N.Y. City, 1911-14; dir. advertising Dodge Bros. motor cars, 1914-21; organizer, 1921, and head George Harrison Phelps, Inc., advtg.; pres. Dorland Internat. (internat. advtg.), 1931-33; partner Fenner & Beane, internat. brokers, 1934-39; pres. George Harrison Phelps, Ltd., London; v.p. Maxon, Inc., N.Y., advertising, since 1942. Special envoy Yachtmen's Assn. America to England, 1928; spl. commr. to Europe of United States Dept. of Labor, 1930. Chmn. Am. com. Internat. Colonial and Overseas Exposition, Paris, 1931; Am. com. Paris Internat. Exposition, 1937; counsel on public relations to corporations, individuals, governments since 1921. Mem. Chambre de Commerce Française des Etats Unis (hon. mem.; dir.), Cornell Univ. Alumni Association, S.A.R., Pilgrims of the U.S., Delta Upsilon. Awarded Cross of Legion of Honor (France), 1930, Officer, 1933; Grand Officer Order of Black Star (France), 1931; medal, City of Calais, France, 1930. Conglist. Clubs: Detroit Players (ex-pres.), Detroit Yacht (ex-commodore); Cornell (N.Y.); Westport (Conn.) Country; Mohawk (Schenectady, N.Y.). Author: "Go!", 1919; Our Biggest Customer, 1929; Tomorrow's Advertisers, 1930. Contributor to mags. Home: Lakeland Farm, Wilton, Conn. Office: 570 Lexington Av., New York, N.Y. Died Sept. 15, 1945.

PHELPS, Guy Merritt, univ. prof.; b. Abilene, Kan., June 13, 1887; s. Albert Henry and Nettie Whitcomb (Garfield) P.; C.E., Rensselear Poly. Inst., Troy, N.Y., 1909; m. Mary Frances Morrison, June 23, 1910; children—William Albert, Merritt Morrison. Chainman, dept. of state engr., New York State, 1907; asst., dept. of surveying, Rensselear Poly. Inst., 1909-12, instr., 1912-16, instr. dept. engring. drawing, 1916-19, asst. prof., 1919-26, asso. prof., 1926-37, prof. and head of dept. since 1937; engaged in private and consulting practice since 1919; with N.Y. state engr. office and dept. of highways, summers 1907, 1908, 1912, 1914-16; with Hartford Electric Co., Hartford, Conn., summer 1917. Served with U.S. War Dept., Watervliet Arsenal (part time), 1917-18. Licensed professional engr. and land surveyor, 1924. Mem. Soc. for Promotion Engring. Edn. (mem. bd. govs. drawing div.), nat. and state socs. of Professional Engrs., Soc. of Engrs. of Eastern N.Y. (past pres. and mem. bd. govs.), Tau Beta Pi. Clubs: Troy Club (Troy, N.Y.); Industrial (Troy, N.Y.); Kattskill Bay Yacht (Cleverdale on Lake George, N.Y.). Home: Brunswick Rd., Troy, N.Y.; and Kattskill Bay, N.Y. Office: Rensselaer Polytechnic Institute, Troy, N.Y. Died Sep. 28, 1946.

PHELPS, Helen Watson, artist; b. Attleboro, Mass.; d. Thaddeus and Mary (Watson) P.; ed.

Académie Julien, Paris, also studied with Raphael Collin; unmarried. Has exhibited paintings in Paris Salon, New York Acad. Design, Society Am. Artists, Pa. Acad. of Fine Arts, Boston Art Club, Art Inst. Chicago, Corcoran Gallery, Washington, D.C. Portrait of Dr. Henry Van Dyke acquired by Nat. Art Inst., Washington, D.C. Hon. mention, Buffalo Expn., 1901; Woman's Art Club prize, 1907; Mary B. Elling Woman's Art Club prize, 1909; Watrous figure prize, Assn. Women Painters and Sculptors, 1914. Mem. Assn. Women Painters and Sculptors, Nat. Arts Club, Pen and Brush Club (New York), Soc. of Painters, Providence Art Club. Home: 1 W. 64th St., New York, N.Y. Died Feb. 6, 1944.

PHELPS, Henry Willis; b. Lewistown, Fulton County, Ill., July 28, 1863; s. Henry and Anna Lambert (Proctor) P.; prep. edn., Lake Forest Acad. and Carroll Acad., Waukesha, Wis.; student Williams Coll. 3 yrs., class of 1886; m. Elizabeth B. Turner, June 22, 1886 (died 1889); m. 2d, Anna E. Olson, Dec. 22, 1892; children—Elizabeth Turner (Mrs. Robert L. Eddy), Raymond Willis. Mem. Ranney & Phelps, can makers, Lewistown, 1887-93; gen. mgr. Union Can Co., Hoopeston, Ill., 1894-1901; sales mgr. Am. Can Co., Chicago, 1901-02, gen. mgr. Pacific dist. for same co., 1902-05, gen. mgr. of sales, New York, 1905-13, v.p., 1913-23, pres., 1923-36, chmn. bd. of dir., 1936-41, retired Apr. 1, 1941. Mem. Kappa Alpha. Republican. Presbyterian. Clubs: New York Athletic, Sleepy Hollow Country, Union League (N.Y. City); Chicago Athletic, Pacific Union, San Francisco Golf and Country. Home: Hotel Ambassador. Office: 230 Park Av., New York, N.Y. Died July 7, 1944.

PHELPS, James Ivey, judge; b. Newton, Tex., June 20, 1875; s. Elza V. M. and Mary A. (Simmons) P.; LL.B., U. of Tex., 1899; m. Lydia B. Malcom, Feb. 1, 1903 (died Aug. 9, 1938); children—Thelma, Malcom E. Admitted to Okla. bar, 1899, and began practice at El Reno; county judge Canadian County, Okla., 1901-07; dist. judge 13th Jud. Dist., Okla., 1919-25; justice Supreme Court of Okla., 1925-29; mem. Shirk, Danner & Phelps, 1929-35; again elected justice Supreme Court of Okla. for term of 6 yrs., beginning Jan. 1935, resigned Dec. 1, 1938; now engaged in practice of law. Mem. Am. and Okla. bar assns. Democrat. Mem. Christian (Disciples) Ch. Mason (33°, K.T., Shriner); Grand Patron, O.E.S. of Okla., 1926; Grand Master A.F.&A.M. of Okla., 1932; Potentate of India Temple Shrine, Oklahoma City, 1927. Home: 733 N.E. 18th St. Address: 306 N. Robinson St., Oklahoma City, Okla. Died Jan. 5, 1947.

PHELPS, John Jay, capitalist; b. Paris, France, Sept. 27, 1861; s. William Walter and Ellen (Sheffield) P.; brought to America in infancy; B.A., Yale, 1883; m. Rose Janet Hutchinson, Apr. 26, 1888; children—Dorothy (Mrs. Davenport West), Rose. Dir. Hackensack Trust Co., U.S. Trust Co. Acting lt. U.S. Navy, Spanish-Am. War and World War; comdr. Div. B, Squadron XI, World War. Republican. Episcopalian. Mem. Am. Museum Natural History, N.J. State Chamber Commerce, Am. Geog. Soc., N.E. Soc., Founders and Patriots of America, Am. Forestry Assn., U.S. Reserve Officers' Assn., Waterway League of America, Roosevelt Memorial Assn., Naval Order of U.S., Navy Relief Society, National Security League, National Marine League, National Child Welfare Assn., Nat. Assn. of Audubon Soc., Big Brother Movement, N.J. Audubon Soc., N.Y. Zoöl. Soc., N.J. Hist. Soc., Bergen County Hist. Soc., Am. Legion, S.A.R., Mil. Order Foreign Wars (N.Y. and N.J.), Navy League U.S., United Spanish War Vets., Psi Upsilon (Beta Chapter), Scroll and Keys (Yale). Clubs: Union League, University, Yale, Circumnavigators, Submarine Chaser of America, Motor Boat of America (New York); Graduate, Conn. Auto, N.J. Auto and Motor (New Haven); Pine Orchard Club (Conn.); Lantern League (Boston); Oritani Field, Cruising Club of America. Home: Red Towers, Route 1, Hackensack, N.J. Office: 5 Mercer St., Hackensack, N.J. Died July 3, 1948; buried at Simsbury, Conn.

PHELPS, Shelton Joseph, college pres.; b. Nevada, Vernon County, Mo., Oct. 7, 1884; s. Joseph Clark and Mary Catherine (Short) P.; grad. high sch., Nevada, 1902; B.S., Mo. State Teachers Coll., 1915; A.M., George Peabody Coll. for Teachers, 1916, Ph.D., 1919; studied in Great Britain and in France, 1928-29; LL.D., U. of S.C., 1936; LL.D., Tusculum Coll., 1938; m. Emma Estella Higgins, Aug. 27, 1907; children—Mary An (Mrs. Dwight Bridges), John Shelton (dec.), Paul Higgins (dec.), Mildred Catherine (Mrs. Ewing Lawrence, Jr.). Successively prin. high sch., Mountain Grove (Mo.), Neosho (Mo.), and supt. schs., Mountain Grove, until 1913; prof. mathematics, Mo. State Teachers Coll., Springfield, Mo., 1913-16; prof. edn., U. of Vt., 1916-18; prof. sch. adminstrn., George Peabody Coll. for Teachers, 1919-34, dir. instrn., 1927, dean of Grad. Sch., 1931-34; pres. Winthrop Coll., the S.C. State Coll. for Women, 1934-43; retired on account of ill health. Professional member State Board of Education, Tennessee, 1923-34. Member White House Conference Child Health and Protection, 1929-30, Nat. Secondary Survey Commn., 1929-30, Nat. Survey Teacher Training Commn., 1929-30, S.C. Rural Electrification Authority since 1935. Pres. Peabody Alumni Assn., 1927-28, Tenn. State Ednl. Assn., 1928-29. Lecturer before state teachers assns. Mem. N.E.A. (supts. sect.), Tenn. Coll. Assn. (pres. 1923-24), Tenn. Acad. Science, Am. Council on Edn., Southern Assn. Colls. and Secondary Schs. (sec.-treas. since 1936), Phi Delta Kappa (nat. pres. 1928). Democrat. Presbyn. Mason (K.T., Shriner). Club: Charlotte Executives. Author: The Administration of County High Schools in the South, 1920; New Hanover County, North Carolina, Survey, 1921; (with others) Paducah, Kentucky, Survey, 1918; Arkansas State Survey, 1923; Survey of Presbyterian College of Clinton, S.C.; Survey of the City Schools of Jackson, Tennessee; College and University Education, 1931. Co-author: Anderson and Phelps Arithmetic for Every-Day Life. Contbr. ednl. articles. Asso. editor Jour. Ednl. Research, 1930, Jour. of Higher Edn., 1930. Home: Ponte Vedra Beach, Fla. Died April 8, 1948.

PHELPS, William Lyon, univ. prof., author; b. New Haven, Conn., Jan. 2, 1865; s. Rev. S. Dryden and Sophia Emilia (Linsley) P.; A.B., Yale, 1887, Ph.D., 1891; A.M., Harvard, 1891; Litt.D., Brown U., 1921, Colgate U., 1921, McMaster, 1927, Columbia U., 1933, Lafayette College, 1939, U. of Vermont, 1941; L.H.D., New York University, 1927, Muhlenberg Coll., 1931; LL.D., Kalamazoo College, 1927, Denison Univ., Ohio, 1931, Miami Univ., Oxford, O., 1933, Yale, 1934, Clark, 1939; D.D., Tusculum Coll., Tenn., 1928; S.T.D., Syracuse, 1930; D.C.L., Jefferson Med. Coll., 1940, Hahnemann Med. Coll., 1940, Pa. Mil. Coll., 1940; m. Annabel Hubbard, Dec. 21, 1892 (died 1939). Instr. English, Harvard, 1891-92; instr. English lit., Yale, 1892-96, asst. prof. English lit., 1896-1901, Lampson prof., 1901-33. Received gold medal, Holland Society (for eminence in literature); gold medal, Nat. Soc. New England Women; gold medal, Connecticut Foot Guard. Fellow American Academy Arts and Sciences, American Geog. Society; mem. Am. Acad. Arts and Letters, Am. Philos. Soc., Nat. Inst. Social Science (awarded gold medal). Clubs: Authors', Players (New York); Authors', Athenæum (London, Eng.). Author: The Beginnings of the English Romantic Movement, 1893; A Dash at the Pole, 1909; Essays on Modern Novelists, 1910; Essays on Russian Novelists, 1911; Teaching in School and College, 1912; Essays on Books, 1914; Browning, 1915; The Advance of the English Novel, 1916; The Advance of English Poetry, 1918; The Twentieth Century Theatre, 1918; Reading the Bible, 1919; Essays on Modern Dramatists, 1920; Human Nature in the Bible, 1922; Some Makers of American Literature, 1923; As I Like It, 1923; Human Nature and the Gospel, 1925; Adventures and Confessions, 1926; Happiness, 1926; Essays on Things, 1930; What I Like in Poetry, 1934; What I Like in Prose, 1934; Wm. Lyon Phelps Yearbook, 1935; Autobiography with Letters, 1939; Marriage, 1940; The Mothers' Anthology, 1940; The Children's Anthology, 1941. Dir. of the Hall of Fame. Home: 110 Whitney Av., New Haven, Conn. Died Aug. 21, 1943.

PHILIP, George, lawyer; b. Fort Augustus, Scotland, July 16, 1880; s. Robert and Catherine (Maclaren) P.; came to U.S., 1897, naturalized, 1906; LL.B., U. of Mich., 1906; m. Isle Waldron, May 30, 1911; children—George (comdr. U.S. Navy; killed at Okinawa, June 16, 1945), Jean Mitchell, Robert (aviator, major U.S. Marine Corps; killed in South Pacific, June 24, 1943). Admitted to South Dakota bar, 1906; in practice at Rapid City since 1917; member firm Philip & Leedom; United States district atty. for S.D. since 1934; dir. First Nat. Bank, Black Hills Power & Light Co., Alex Johnson Hotel Co., Rapid City. Mem. Am. and S.D. bar assns. Democrat. Mason (Past Grand Master 33°). Home: Rapid City, S.D. Address: Rapid City, S.D.; and Sioux Falls, S.D. Died March 13, 1948.

PHILIPPI, E. Martin, chmn. bd. Am. Thread Co., 260 W. Broadway, New York, N.Y.*Died July 2, 1946.

PHILIPSON, David, rabbi; b. Wabash, Ind., Aug. 9, 1862; s. Joseph and Louisa (Freudenthal) P.; A.B., U. of Cincinnati, 1883; grad. Hebrew Union Coll., Cincinnati, as rabbi, 1883, D.D., 1886; D.H.L., 1925; LL.D., U. of Cincinnati, 1914, Lincoln Memorial University, 1922, also from Jewish Institute of Religion; m. Ella Hollander, Sept. 9, 1886. Rabbi Har Sinai Congregation, Baltimore, 1884-88, B'ne Israel Congregation, Cincinnati, 1888-1938, rabbi emeritus since 1938; prof. homiletics, 1891-1905, lecturer on history of reform Judaism since 1905, Hebrew Union Coll.; mem. bd. editors of new Bible translation; cons. editor Jewish Encyclopedia; chmn. bd. Editors Union of Am. Hebrew Congregations and Hebrew Union Coll. Annual; pres. Nat. Conference on Jewish Activities at Universities. V.p. Am. Jewish Historical Soc.; mem. bd. governors Hebrew Union College, 1893-1947, honorary, 1947; member publ. committee Jewish Publ. Soc. America; mem. Synagogue Council America, Am. Jewish Com.; chmn. Commn. on Jewish Edn.; trustee Associated Charities, United Jewish Social Agencies, Young Men's Mercantile Library Assn.; mem. Jewish Community Council; pres. Central Conf. Am. Rabbis, 1907-09. Author: The Jew in English Fiction, 1890, 1002, 11, 19; Old European Jewries, 1894; The Oldest Jewish Congregation in the West, 1894, new edit., 1924; A Holiday Sheaf (sermons), 1898; The Reform Movement in Judaism, 1907, new edit., 1931; Max Lilienthal—American Rabbi, 1915; Centenary Papers and Others, 1919; History of the Hebrew Union College, 1925; My Life as an American Jew, 1941. Editor: The Selected Writings of Isaac M. Wise, 1900; Reminiscences by Isaac M. Wise, 1901; Letters of Rebecca Gratz, 1929. Contbr. to magazines. Home: 712 Gholson Av., Cincinnati, O. Died June 29, 1949; buried United Jewish Cemetery, Cincinnati.

PHILLIPS, Albanus, business exec.; b. Golden Hill, Md., Aug. 31, 1871; s. George W. and Mary Elizabeth (Leonard) P.; student pub. schs. of Md., 1877-83; m. Daisy Alma Lewis, Oct. 10, 1900; children—Alma (Mrs. Harry Wehr), Frances (Mrs. Edgar M. Skinner, Jr.), Albanus, Theodore. On sailing schooner, 1885, capt. coasting schooner, 1892; with wholesale oyster commn. mchts., Baltimore, 1893-99; engaged in business of packing vegetables, Cambridge, Md., as A. Phillips & Co., 1899-1902; an organizer and head of Phillips Packing Co., co-partnership, 1902-29, pres. and dir. since 1929, other plants, Newark, Townsend and Laurel, Del., and Denton, Cordova, Willoughby and Newbridge, Md.; pres., dir. Phillips Can Co., Phillips Hardware Co., Inc., Phillips Oil Co., Cambridge, Phillips Sales Co., Inc., Phillips Commission Co. of Md., Inc., Phillips Transport Co., Cambridge; dir. Del. R.R. Co., Baltimore & Eastern R.R. Apptd. mem. staff Gov. of Md. with rank of col., 1913. Mem. Md. State Roads Planning Commn. Mem. Md. Commn. to represent state at N.Y. World's Fair, 1939. Mem. bd. govs. Washington Coll., Chestertown, 1922-26. Past pres. Cambridge (Md) Hosp. Republican. Mason (Shriner), Elk. Clubs: Yacht (Cambridge); Maryland Yacht (Baltimore); Union League (Philadelphia). Home: 202 Mill St. Office: Race St., Cambridge, Md Died Jan. 17, 1949.

PHILLIPS, Alexander Roy, president Great Am. Ins. Co.; b. Waco, Tex., Feb. 8, 1880; s. George Pierce and Florence (Minney) P.; grad. Dallas (Tex.) Acad., 1897; m. Anna Garlington, Feb. 4, 1903; children—George Garlington, Alexander Roy (dec.), Anna Elizabeth (Mrs. Henry Hicks Hurt), Helen Moore, Martha Phillips (dec.). Clerk Tex. dept. of Hartford Fire Ins. Co., 1898-1902; spl. agt. Springfield Fire & Marine Ins. Co., 1902-06; spl. agt. Ins. Co. of N.A., 1906-12; spl. agt. Great Am. Ins. Co., 1912-16, asst. sec. at home office, 1916-23; v.p. and dir. Great Am. and Am. Alliance Ins. Cos., 1923-44, pres. since 1944; v.p. and dir. Rochester Am. Ins. Co., 1928-44, pres. since 1944; v.p. and dir. Mass. Fire & Marine Ins. Co., Am. Nat. Fire Ins. Co., N. C., Home Ins. Co., County Fire Ins. Co. of Phila., Detroit Fire & Marine Ins. Co., all since 1928; dir. Great Am. Indemnity Co., Underwriters Salvage Co. of N.Y. Mem. S.A.R., N.Y. Southern Soc. Presbyn. Club: Drug and Chemical (New York). Home: 62 Harrison Av., Montclair, N.J. Office: 1 Liberty St., New York, N.Y. Died Nov. 7, 1945.

PHILLIPS, Catherine Coffin (Mrs. Lee Allen Phillips), author; b. Oakland, Ill., Dec. 6, 1874; d. Tristram Sanborn and Susan Jane (Winkler) Coffin; A.B., Southwestern Coll., Winfield, Kan., 1893; A.M., De Pauw U., 1895, Litt.D., 1937; m. Lee Allen Phillips, Dec. 19, 1895; children—Lucile Gertrude (wife of Dr. Wayland A. Morrison), Katharine Louise (wife of Herbert Godfrey Day). Has spent much time in research and writing of Pacific slope history since 1910. Pres. Lee A. Phillips, Inc., since 1938; mem. bd. dirs. Western Personnel Service. Mem. bd. trustees Southern Calif. Symphony Assn., Southwest Archeol. Museum of Los Angeles; asso. Calif. Inst. Technology; mem. board Pasadena Civic Music Assn.; hon. alumna Scripps Coll., Claremont, Calif. Mem. Hist. Soc. Southern Calif. (mem. bd. dirs.), Daughters of American Revolution, Kappa Alpha Theta, Phi Beta Kappa. Republican. Conglist. Clubs: Women's University, Friday Morning, Women's Athletic (Los Angeles); Town (Pasadena). Author: Cornelius Cole—California Pioneer and United States Senator, 1929; Portsmouth Plaza—The Cradle of San Francisco, 1932; Jessie Benton Fremount—A Woman Who Made History, 1935; Through the Golden Gate, San Francisco, 1769-1937, 1938. Home: 611 Landor Lane, Pasadena, Calif. Died Dec. 9, 1942.

PHILLIPS, Ethel Calvert, author; b. Jersey City, N.J.; d. George Calvert and Olive Hanks (Hitchcock) P.; ed, Hasbrouck Inst. (Jersey City), Ethical Culture Sch. (N.Y. City) and Teachers Coll. (Columbia). Formerly teacher kindergarten, N.Y. City. Mem. Authors League of America. Democrat. Mem. Dutch Ref. Ch. Author: (juvenile stories) Wee Ann, 1919; Little Friend Lydia, 1920; Black-Eyed Susan, 1921; Christmas Light, 1922; A Story of Nancy Hanks, 1923; Humpty Dumpty House, 1924; Pretty Polly Perkins, 1925; Little Sally Waters, 1926; The Popover Family, 1927; The Santa Claus Brownies, 1928; The Lively Adventures of Johnny Ping Wing, 1929; Little Rag Doll, 1930; Gay Madelon, 1931; Pyxie, a Little Boy of the Pines, 1932; Ride-the-Wind, 1933; Jeanne-Marie and Her Golden Bird, 1934; Marty Comes to Town, 1935; The Saucy Betsy, 1936; Calico, 1937; Belinda and the Singing Clock, 1938; Peter Peppercorn, 1939; A Name for Obed, 1941; Brian's Victory, 1942. Home: 54 Wayne Pl., Nutley, N.J. Died Feb. 6, 1947.

PHILLIPS, Frank Reith, pres. Philadelphia Co.; b. Cleveland, O., Oct. 29, 1876; s. Stallham Wing and Marietta (Waite) P.; grad. Central High Sch., Cleveland, 1894; law study Adelbert Coll. (now Western Reserve U.) 3 yrs.; studied engring. Case Sch. of Applied Science; m. Stella Maud Newman, Dec. 4, 1905; children—Virginia Newman (Mrs. Charles C. Zimmerman), Martha Estelle (Mrs. Charles R. Ellicott, Jr.), Bertha Jane (Mrs. L. H. Phillips). With M. A. Hanna Co., Cleveland City Rys. Co. and Cleveland Shipbuilding Co., 1896-1903; master mechanic Cleveland City Rys. Co., 1903; mechanical engr. Cincinnati, Newport & Covington Light & Traction Co., 1904-07; design engr. Ohio Brass Co., 1907; chief engr. Mich. United Light & Traction Co., 1908-10; supt. of equipment, Pittsburgh Rys. Co., 1910-23, gen. mgr. for receivers, 1923, mech. and elec. engr., 1924-26; vice-pres. and gen. mgr. Duquesne Light Co., 1926-29, now pres.;

vice-pres. Equitable Gas Co., 1928; now pres.; sr. vice-pres. Philadelphia Co., 1929, pres. since 1931; also pres. Pittsburgh Rys. Co., Pittsburgh Motor Coach Co., Allegheny County Steam Heating Co., Equitable Sales Co.; dir. Farmers Deposit Nat. Bank, Reliance Life Ins. Co. Trustee U. of Pittsburgh; pres. Pittsburgh Assn. for Improvement of Poor. Mem. advisory board Chem. Warfare Service. Mem. Am. Inst. Elec. Engrs., Engrs. Soc. of Western Pa.; past pres. Am. Transit Assn. Presbyterian. Clubs: Duquesne, Fellows, Pittsburgh Athletic, Oakmont Country, St. David's Golf. Active in design of first efficient double-deck motor car, Pittsburgh, 1917; originator of low-floor street car, involving principle of small diameter wheels, since largely adopted by street ry. mfrs. and automobile designers. Home: 190 Orchard Drive, Mt. Lebanon, Pittsburgh. Office: 435 6th Av., Pittsburgh, Pa. Died Oct. 23, 1942.

PHILLIPS, James Andrew, labor official; b. Clay County, Ill., Sept. 10, 1873; s. John Jiles and Nancy (Bouseman) P.; student grade sch., Louisville, Ill., 1879-88; m. Inez Richey, Feb. 22, 1902 (died 1906); children—Frances (Mrs. Allie Crouch, Jr.); m. 2d, Cecil Black, Oct. 5, 1924. Began as brakeman Ohio & Miss. Ry., 1888; worked for number of rys. as conductor and brakeman; active as rep. of conductors since 1902; mem. Order of Ry. Conductors, served as local chmn. and gen. chmn. 1919, v.p., 1919-31, sr. v.p., 1931-34, pres. since 1934, Cedar Rapids, Ia. Chmn. Ry. Labor Execs. Assn. since 1939. Home: 1630 1st Av. Office: Order of Railway Conductors Bldg., Cedar Rapids, Ia.* Died Dec. 4, 1949.

PHILLIPS, J(ay) Campbell, portrait painter; b. New York, N.Y., Feb. 27, 1873; s. Isaac and Adeline (Cohen) P.; ed. Met. Museum of Art Schs., Art Students League and in studio of William Merritt Chase, New York; m. Martha H. L. Dorph, June 8, 1909. Began as illustrator for mags. at 15, later making a specialty of negro life. Exhibited oil painting in Nat. Acad., 1892, and has since often exhibited there; also in cities of U.S. Awarded Isidor portrait prize, Salmagundi Club, 1914; Corcoran Gallery purchase fund, 1914, "The First Born"; competition, portrait of Mayor William J. Gaynor, for city hall, New York, 1914; "Age of Wonder," in Albright Gallery, Buffalo; "Paradise Bay," Lake George, in Cleveland Museum of Art; portraits of William G. McAdoo and Carter Glass in U.S. Treas. Bldg., Washington; portrait Dr. Nicholas Murray Butler, in Lotos Club, New York; portrait Bernard M. Baruch; Dr. Stephen Smith, Met. Museum of Art, New York; Judge Samuel Kalisch and Judge Frank J. Swayze, State Capitol, Trenton, N.J.; Profs. Church and Chase, Cornell U.; Dr. Leigh Hunt and Dr. Stephen P. Duggan, Coll. City of New York; Dr. Ellery C. Huntington, Colgate U.; Mrs. James Roosevelt, the President's mother; also Lily Pons (also as "Daughter of the Regiment"), Mischa Elman, Ruggiero Ricci, Leopold Godowsky, Mary Astor, Dr. Frederick B. Robinson (pres. Coll. City of N.Y.) Edward Ridley Finch (Court of Appeals, Albany, N.Y.), James O'Malley (Appellate Div. Supreme Ct. N.Y. City), John J. Brady (Bronx County Ct. Ho., N.Y. City), Mitchell L., Erlanger (Supreme Court, N.Y. City), Gifford Beal and Frank Bicknell (owned by Nat. Acad. of Design, N.Y.), George J. Atwell (Nat. Dem. Club, N.Y. City), Solomon R. Guggenheim (owned by City Athletic Club, N.Y.); Wm. Ritschel, Carl Rungius, C. Glenn Newell (Nat. Acad. of Design), Edward Johnson (Met. Opera Co.), Dr. Simon Baruch (S.C. Medical Assn.); William H. Keller Pres. Superior Ct. Pa. Capitol Harrisburg also Lancaster Pa. Court House. Presidents of the Superior Court of Pa., Chas. E. Rice, Frank M. Trexler, State Capitol, Harrisburg, Pa. Wm. T. Collins, Supreme Court, N.Y.C. 1944. George W. Maxey, Chief Justice Supreme Ct. Pa. Phila Bar Assn. 1945; also 14 drawings of plantation life in N.Y. Pub. Library. Mem. S.A.R. Clubs: Lotos, Bohemian. Ex-champion Hollywood Golf Club, N.J. Author: Plantation Sketches, 1899. Rodin Studio 7A, 200 W. 57th St., New York. Died Sept. 24, 1948.

PHILLIPS, John C., ex-gov.; b. nr. Vermont, Ill., Nov. 13, 1870; s. William Henry and Elizabeth (Wood) P.; student Hedding Coll., Abingdon, Ill., 1889-93; studied law in law office and with Sprague Corr. Sch.; m. Minnie Rexroat, Oct. 24, 1895; children—Ralph Aubrey, Marian (Mrs. Joseph Shelby Robbins), Elizabeth (Mrs. Ray B. Quillin). Admitted to Ill. bar, 1896, and began practice at Vermont, Ill.; moved to Phoenix, Ariz., 1898; now mem. law firm Phillips, Holzworth & Phillips. Probate judge, Maricopa County, Ariz., 1902-12; judge Superior Court, Maricopa County, 1912; mem. Ariz. Ho. of Rep., 1916-22, Ariz. Senate, 1922-24; gov. of Ariz. for term 1929-31. Republican. Methodist. Home: Route 6, Box 627, Phoenix. Office: 317 Phoenix National Bank Bldg., Phoenix, Ariz. Died June 25, 1943.

PHILLIPS, John Sanburn, editor, publisher of books and mags.; b. Council Bluffs, Ia., July 2, 1861; s. Dr. E. L. and Mary (Sanburn) P.; A.B., Knox Coll., 1882, Litt.D., 1910; A.B., magna cum laude, Harvard, 1885; student University of Leipzig, 1885-86; married Jane B. Peterson, Oct. 2, 1890; children—Ruth Beale, Dorothy Sanburn (Mrs. Dorothy P. Huntington), Margaret Evertson, Elizabeth Peterson (Mrs. Bradford C. Colcord), John Peterson. Began mag. editing and publishing with S. S. McClure, Boston, 1882; partner in founding McClure's Mag., 1893, mgr. and treas. of this mag., 1893-1906; also mgr. book dept. McClure, Phillips & Co., Inc. (first Booth Tarkington and O. Henry books, best of Conan Doyle, Conrad, etc.), 1900-06; pres. Phillips Pub. Co., 1906-10; editor American Mag., 1906-15; editor Red Cross Mag., 1917-20; advisory editor American Mag., 1915-38. Clubs: Dutch Treat, Players (New York); Home: 48 South St., Goshen, N.Y.; (summer) Power Point, Duxbury, Mass. Died Feb. 28, 1949.

PHILLIPS, Lee Eldas, banker, oil producer; b. Conway, Ia., Aug. 18, 1876; s. Lewis Francis and Lucinda Josephine (Faucett) P.; LL.D., Washburn Coll., Topeka, Kan., Phillips U., Enid, Okla.; m. Lenora Carr, Nov. 26, 1902; children—Philip Rex, Lee Eldas, Martha Jane. Teacher country schs., 1896-97; insurance solicitor and coal salesman until 1902; organizer, and gen. mgr. coal co., 1902-04; moved to Indian Terr., 1904; in banking and oil business since 1904; formerly v.p., gen. mgr. Phillips Petroleum Co.; dir. Federal Reserve Bank of Kansas City; now retired. Chmn. Okla. and part Tex. dist. Am. Red Cross, and Liberty Loan drives, World War; mem. Okla. State Council of Defense; founder, with others, Internat. Police. Dir. U. of Kans. Endowment Assn., Okla. State Y.M.C.A.; pres. Bartlesville Y.M.C.A. Mem. Am. Bankers Assn., Okla. Bankers Assn. (ex-pres.). Republican. Mem. Christian (Disciples) Ch. Mason (K.T., Shriner), Elk. Clubs: Paris Country, Hillcrest Country (Bartlesville); Tulsa (Tulsa, Okla.); Kiwanis (hon. life), St. Andrews (Kansas City, Mo.); Ft. Worth (Ft. Worth, Tex.); Independence Country (Independence, Kan.); Anchor (Des Moines). Now breeds pure bred Black Poland China hogs and Hereford cattle for 4-H Club and Future Farmers of America members. Home: 1201 S. Cherokee Av. Office: Phillips Petroleum Co. Bldg., Bartlesville, Okla. Died Apr. 16, 1944.

PHILLIPS, Levi Benjamin, banker; b. Golden Hill, Dorchester County, Md., Nov. 21, 1868; s. George Washington and Mary Elizabeth (Leonard) P.; ed. country sch.; m. Florence T. Brannock, July 23, 1895; children—Florence Mary (Mrs. W. Fletcher Williamson), Viola Lee (Mrs. Carlton S. Brerewood), Levi B., Junior. Mariner, 1882-98, last 6 years as master of sea-going vessel; established firm of L. B. Phillips & Company, oyster packers, Cambridge, Maryland, 1898, Phillips Packing Co., 1902, Phillips Hardware Co., 1903, Phillips Can Co., 1914, retired from Phillips Packing Co., 1937; elected dir. Nat. Bank of Cambridge, 1905, pres., 1909-41; dir. Baltimore Br. Federal Reserve Bank, 1927-38; dir. Town Cemetery Company; member Eastern Shore Society, Soc. War of 1812. Republican. Methodist. Mason (Shriner), Elk. Clubs: Cambridge Yacht, Bishops Head Fish and Gun, Cambridge Country (retired pres.). Home: Cambridge, Md. Died April 7, 1945.

PHILLIPS, Robert, univ. prof.; b. Vulcan, Mich., Oct. 22, 1890; s. William and Molly (Fredericks) P.; A.B., Albion (Mich.) Coll., 1916; A.M., U. of Mich., 1917, Ph.D., 1929; m. Mary Bernice German, June 28, 1917; 1 dau., Marion Bernice. Instr. high sch., Battle Creek, Mich., 1917-19, Amherst Coll., 1919-20, U. of Me., summer 1920, U. of Mich., 1928-29; instr. in govt., Purdue U., 1920-22, asst. prof., 1922-25, asso. prof., 1925-28, prof. since 1929; platform and radio lecturer. Awarded Mich. State Coll. fellowship, 1916. Fellow American Geog. Society. Member American Political Science Association, Ind. Acad. of Social Science, Nat. Geog. Soc., Ind. State Hist. Assn., Scabbard and Blade, Pi Kappa Phi. Republican. Methodist. Mason. Clubs: Lafayette, Lions (internat. dir. Lions Internat., 1930-33). Author: The American Flag, 1931; American Government and Its Problems, 1937; Decisions of the Supreme Court (with C. L. Heyerdahl), 1938. Contbr. Dictionary of Am. History. Home: 1120 Ravinia Rd., West Lafayette, Ind. Died Sep. 28, 1944.

PHILLIPS, Watson Lyman, clergyman; b. W. Troy, N.Y., Jan. 28, 1850; s. Rev. Jonas and Maria E. (Nims) P.; A.B., Wesleyan U., Conn., 1872; student Boston Sch. of Theology, 1872-73; D.D., Wesleyan, 1898, and Dickinson Coll., 1898; m. Ella V. Stetson, June 22, 1873 (died July 16, 1939); children—Arthur V. (dec.), Frank L., Ruth P. Ordained M.E. ministry, 1875; pastor W. Duxbury, Mass., 1872-74; S. Yarmouth, 1874-77, First Ch., Fall River, 1877-79, New Bedford, 1879-81, Summerfield M.E. Ch., Brooklyn, 1881-84, St. John's Ch., Brooklyn, 1884-87, Summerfield, 1887-89, First Ch., Wilkes-Barre, Pa., 1889-90; became Congregationalist, 1890; pastor Ch. of the Redeemer, New Haven, Conn., 1890-1915; pastor emeritus since 1915; pastor Shelton (Conn.) Congl. Ch., 1916-23. Corporate mem. A.B.C.F.M., Conn. Bible Soc.; pres. Conn. Missionary Soc. Mem. Conn. Legislature, 1919-21, and chaplain of the House, 1927. Mem. Phi Beta Kappa, Alpha Delta Phi. Clubs: Graduate, Congregational. Home: New Haven, Conn. Died Dec. 30, 1944.

PHILLIPS, Ze Barney Thorne, clergyman; b. Springfield, O., May 1, 1875; s. Ze Barney and Sallie Essex (Sharp) P.; A.B., Wittenberg Coll., Springfield, O., 1895, A.M., 1896, D.D.; B.D. Gen. Theol. Sem., 1910; m. Mrs. Sallie Reeves Hews Winston, Sept. 1906; children—Sallie Hews, Faith. Deacon, 1899, priest, 1900, P.E. Ch.; with St. Mary's Ch., Hillsborough, O., 1899-1901; rector Ch. of Our Saviour, Cincinnati, 1901-02, Trinity Ch., Chicago, 1902-09; at Oxford, Eng., 1909-11; rector St. Peter's Ch., St. Louis, 1912-22, Ch. of the Saviour, Phila., 1922-24, Epiphany Ch., Washington, D.C., 1924-41; installed as dean, Washington Cathedral, Nov. 26, 1941. Apptd. chaplain of U.S. Senate, 1927. Republican. Home: Mt. Saint Alban, Washington, D.C. Died May 10, 1942; buried at Washington Cathedral, Washington.

PHILP, John W., ex-asst. postmaster gen.; b. Caldwell Tex., Oct. 7, 1874; s. William and Mary (Carroll) P.; student Southwestern U., Georgetown, Tex., 1887-90, Staunton (Va.) Mil. Acad., 1890-93, U. of Tex., 1893-95: m. Lillie May Smith, Nov. 10, 1898; children—William Hudson (lt. col. U.S.A.), Margarot (Mrs. Joe C. Thompson). Clk, traveling salesman, sales mgr. to 1905; with Pioneer Press, St. Paul, Minn., 1903-05; with advt. dept., Great Northern R.R., St. Paul, 1905-07; sales mgr. M. P. Exline, printers, Dallas, 1907-11; dir. and chmn. of bd. Huey & Philp Hardware Co.; postmaster of Dallas, 1922-29; 4th asst. postmaster gen. of U.S., July 9, 1929-Mar. 6, 1933. Rep. nominee for gov. of Tex., 1914. Dir. orgn., sec. and treas. Republican State Exec. Com. Elected State Chmn. of Republican Party in May, 1944. Mem. Dallas Petroleum Club, Kappa Alpha. Catholic. Knight Comdr., Order of St. Gregory the Great. K. of C. (4°), past master. Northern Dist. of Tex., Kiwanian (ex-pres.). Home: 4353 Fairfax Av. Office: 1900 Griffin St., Dallas, Tex. Died Jan. 5, 1948.

PICCIRILLI, Attilio (pē-chē-rēl′lē), sculptor; b Massa, Italy, May 16, 1868; s. Joseph and Barbera (Giorgi) P.; studied sculpture Accademia San Luca, Rome, Italy, 1881-88; m. Guilia Cavinato, Feb. 4, 1906. Came to U.S., Apr. 1888; asst. to various sculptors, New York, until 1898, meanwhile exhibiting annual exhbns. Soc. Am. Artists, Nat. Acad. Design, etc. Executed MacDonough monument, New Orleans, 1898; awarded contract (among 50 competitors) for Nat. Maine monument, 1901; designer Firemen's Monument, N.Y. City; war memorial for City of Albany, 1923; "Frageline," marble nude, Met. Museum of Art, Columbus monument, The Bronx, medallions for Morgan Library (New York); statue of Gov. Allen, State House, La.; Jefferson presidential medal, 1932; sculptures at Rockefeller Center, N.Y. City (door of Internat. Bldg., door of Italian Bldg., frieze over Life Bldg.), 1938; monument to Youth, Va. Mil. Inst., Marconi monument, Washington, D.C., 1940; Police monument, City of New York, 1941, and many others. Bronze medal, Buffalo Expn., 1901; silver medal, Charleston Expn., 1902; silver medal, St. Louis Expn., 1904; gold medal, San Francisco Expn., 1915; gold medal, Pa. Acad., 1909; Saltus medal of merit, N.A.D., 1929; Busch prize ($1,000), New York Central Galleries, 1930. Nat. Academician, 1935. Mem. Academia dei Virtuosi del Pantheon, Rome, Nat. Sculpture Society, Archtl. League America, Am. Italian Art Assn. (pres.). Pres. Leonardo da Vinci Art School. Studio: 467 E. 142d St., New York, N.Y.* Died Oct. 8, 1945.

PICKARD, Ward Wilson, lawyer, oil operator; b. Wilson, N.Y., Mar. 24, 1878; s. Ward Beecher and Myra (Gibbs) P.; A.B., Wesleyan U., Conn., 1899; LL.B., New York Law Sch., 1902; m. Alice Rossington, Sept. 14, 1910; children—William Rossington, Nicholas, Mary Linn. Admitted to N.Y. bar, 1902; in practice, 1902-15, and since 1925; pres. Eagle Saving & Loan Co., Brooklyn, N.Y., 1915-17; treas. Seabrook Co., Bridgeton, N.J., 1919-25; pres. Plains Oil Co., Wichita, Kan., since 1925; dep. administrator paper div. NRA, 1933-34; coördinator paper industries, 1935-36, mgr. eastern container group since 1936. Corpl. 1st Conn. Vol. Inf., Spanish-Am. War, 1898; chief of contract div. and chmn. claims bd. Q.M.C., 1917-19. Mem. Alpha Delta Phi. Clubs: Yountakah Country (Nutley, N.J.); Country (Pine Orchard, Conn.). Home: 131 Satterthwaite Av., Nutley, N.J. Office: 295 Madison Av., New York, N.Y. Died Aug. 23, 1943.

PICKENS, Andrew Calhoun, naval officer; b. Mobile, Ala.; s. Andrew Calhoun and Ella (Pollard) P.; grad. U.S. Naval Acad.; m. Harriette Fowle Taylor, Sept. 25, 1915. Comd. transport U.S. Navy, in first expdn. to France, World War, and then served with Brit. Grand Fleet in North Sea; commd. rear admiral U.S. Navy, 1937, now comdg. Cruisers, Atlantic Fleet. Democrat. Presbyterian. Clubs: Chevy Chase, Army and Navy (Washington, D.C.); New York Yacht; University, Racquet (Phila.). Address: Navy Dept., Washington, D.C. Died Nov. 29, 1944.

PIER, Garrett Chatfield, author, archaeologist; b. London, Eng., Oct. 30, 1875; s. Garrett Ryckman and Eleanor (Blackman) P.; student Columbia, 1896-98; studied in museums of Europe 2 yrs., in Egyptian and Arabic museums 2 years, Egyptology and Assyriology, U. of Chicago, 1906; m. Adelaide Wilson, June 25, 1902 (died Feb. 22, 1926); m. 2d, Riva Greenwood, Nov. 10, 1927. Asst. curator decorative arts, Met. Mus., New York, 1907-10; traveled in Japan, China and Orient, buying antiques for Met. Mus., 1911-14. Served as lt. Old Guard Vol. Regt., N.Y., Spanish-Am. War; commd. 1st lt. inf., 2d Plattsburg Camp, 1917; commd. capt. inf., Aug. 1918; in France, Oct. 1918-Apr. 1919; attached to Dept. of State, and with Peace Commn.; mem. state founders com. Woodrow Wilson Foundn., 1921. Mem. Alpha Delta Phi. Republican. Episcopalian. Clubs: Field, Greenwich Country (Greenwich, Conn.); Cliff Dwellers (Chicago); Salmagundi, Columbia, Coffee House (New York); Indian Harbor Yacht (Conn.). Author: Egyptian Antiquities in the Pier Collection, 1906; Inscriptions of the Nile Monuments, 1908; Pottery of the Near East, 1909; Catalogue of Pottery, Porcelain and Faience, 1911; Temple Treasures of Japan, 1914; Catalogue of the Draper Collection of Antique Gems, 1914; Hanit, the Enchantress, 1921; Hidden Valley,' 1925; Jeweled Tree (play), 1927; Kimon's Model, 1932. Died Dec. 30, 1943.

PIERCE, Claude Connor, sanitarian; b. Chattanooga, Tenn., June 15, 1878; s. David James and Annie (Flora) P.; Chattanooga High School, 1895; M.D., Chattanooga Med. Coll., 1898; m. Miss Reeves, May 17, 1905; children—John Reeves (killed in naval action Jan. 1943), George Ellis (U.S. Navy), Claude Connor, Jr. (U.S. Army). Served in Spanish-American War; appointed assistant surgeon U.S. P.H.S., June 20, 1900; passed assistant surgeon, July 26, 1905; surgeon, December 1912; senior surgeon, Act of Congress, March 4, 1915; assistant surgeon general, July 13, 1918. Quarantine officer, Panama, 1904-12; superintendent Colon Hospital, 1913; established disinfection plants along Texas-Mexico border to prevent introduction of typhus fever, 1916; in charge of extra cantonment sanitation, Little Rock, Ark., 1917; in charge div. of venereal diseases, U.S.P.H.S., Washington, 1918-22; director of District 3, Chicago, 1922-26; med. dir. in supervisory charge of U.S.P.H.S., activities in Europe, 1934-37; dir. Dist. 1, U.S.P.H.S., 1937-42; retired July 1942; now med. dir. Planned Parenthood Fedn. Member American Med. Assn., tel, Brooklyn, N.Y. Office: 501 Madison Av., New York, N.Y. Died Mar. 19, 1944.

PIERCE, Jason Noble, clergyman; b. Pittsburgh, Pa., Aug. 28, 1880; s. Albert Francis (D.D.) and Rebecca (Noble) P.; B.A., Amherst, 1902, D.D., 1922; B.D., Yale Div. Sch., 1906; m. Mary Gertrude Fairchild, March 9, 1904; children—Margaret Williams, Edward Fairchild. Ordained Congl. ministry, 1906; pastor Davenport Ch., New Haven, Conn., 1906-08, Puritan Ch., Brooklyn, 1908-10, 2d Ch., Oberlin, O., 1910-14, 2d Ch., Dorchester, Boston, Mass., 1914-20, First Ch., Washington, D.C., 1920-30, Collegeside Ch., Nashville, Tenn.; prof. practical theology, Atlanta Sem. Foundation and head dept. practical theology, Vanderbilt U. Sch. of Religion, 1930-32; pastor Christian Temple, Norfolk, Va., 1932-33, First Congregational Ch., San Francisco, since June 1, 1933. On staff of preachers at several colls. Sr. chaplain 2d Div. A.E.F., in France, Belgium and Germany, 1918-19; lt. col., chaplain O.R.C.; pres. Nat. Assn. Chaplains, U.S. Army, O.R.C. and N.G., 1926-28; pres. 2d Div. Assn., D.C., 1927-28. Trustee Amherst Coll., 1922-27; trustee Piedmont Coll., Ga.; pres. bd. trustees Country Life Acad., N.C.; pres. Congl. Home, D.C.; chmn. gen. com. Army and Navy Chaplains; dir. Boston City Missionary Soc., Mass. Home Missionary Soc., Congl. Ednl. and Pub. Soc.; trustee Uplands Sanatorium; ex-pres. Washington Federation Chs.; mem. exec. com. Nat. Council Congl. Chs.; trustee N. Calif. Congl. Conf., pres. San Francisco Fed. of Chs., 1936-37; pres. and moderator Bay Assn. Congl. Chs.; pres. bd. dirs. and mem. exec. com. Northern Calif. Congl. Conf., 1936-37; moderator State Conf. Congl. Churches; bd. of dirs. Prison Assn. of Calif.; vice-pres. and dir. Veterans Christian Service Commission since 1945; vice-pres. Chaplains Assn. San Quentin Prison since 1944; vice pres. and dir. N. Calif. and W. Nevada State Council of Churches since 1945; Christian Council on Palestine since 1945. Member Theta Sigma, Chi Phi, Delta Sigma Rho, Pi Gamma Mu, Am. Legion (post chaplain). Mason. Clubs: Monday (Boston); National Sojourners, Cosmos, Congregational, Torch (Washington, D.C.); Commonwealth, Presidio (San Francisco); Rotary (hon.). Author: The Masculine Power of Christ, 1912; The Mystery of His Own Person, 1913; Together in the Heavenly Home, 1916. Contbr. to Boston Monday Club Sermons since 1915. Address: 432 Mason St., San Francisco, Calif. Died March 16, 1948; buried in Golden Gate National Cemetery.

PIERCE, Norval Harvey, oto-laryngologist; b. Washington, May 13, 1863; s. Harvey Lindsley (M.D.) and Katherine Elizabeth (Purington) P.; M.D., Coll. P. and S., Chicago, 1885; post-grad. work, Royal U., Würzburg, Bavaria, and Imperial U., Vienna; m. Drucilla Wahl, 1895. Appointed prof. and head dept. laryngology, rhinology and otology, U. of Ill. Coll. of Medicine, 1915, now emeritus and head of dept.; formerly surgeon ear, nose and throat, Ill. Eye and Ear Infirmary and St. Luke's Hosp. Surgeon Ill. Naval Reserve, 1896-1900; passed asst. surgeon, rank of lt., sr. grade, U.S. Navy, Spanish-Am. War, 1898; apptd. 1st lt. Med. R.C., Feb. 1911; capt., Apr. 9, 1917; maj., M.C., Aug. 11, 1917; served as chief Camp Grant, and chief surg. diseases of oto-laryngology, Base Hosp. No. 115, Vichy, France. Fellow Am. Coll. Surgeons, Chicago Acad. Medicine, Inst. of Medicine (Chicago); mem. A.M.A., Ill. State and Chicago med. socs., Am. Laryngol., Rhinol. and Otol. Soc. (pres., 1903-04), Am. Laryngol. Assn. (pres., 1919), Am. Otol. Soc. (pres., 1917-18; chmn. research com. on oto-sclerosis), Chicago Medico-Legal Soc., Chicago Laryngol. and Otol. Soc. (pres. 1900), Nat. Inst. of Social Sciences, Chicago Hist. Soc., Chicago Soc. Med. History. Republican. Clubs: University, City, Army and Navy. Author numerous essays in otolaryngology. Address: Del Mar, Calif.* Died Oct. 26, 1946.

PIERCE, Ulysses Grant Baker (pĕrs), clergyman; b. Providence, R.I., July 17, 1865; s. Elisha Waterman and Mary Elizabeth (Barney) P.; ed. Hillsdale (Mich.) Coll., 1886-90; B.D., post-grad. studies, Harvard, 1890-91; D.D., George Washington U., 1909, Hillsdale Coll., 1909; Ph.D., George Washington U., 1915; m. Florence Lonsbury. Ordained Unitarian ministry, 1891; pastor Pomona, Calif., 1893-96, Ithaca, N.Y., 1897-1901, All Souls', Washington, since 1901; chaplain U.S. Senate, 1909-13. Pres. Bd. of Visitors, St. Elizabeth's Hosp.; sec. Columbia Instn. for the Deaf. Club: Cosmos. Author: The Soul of the Bible, 1907; The Creed of Epictetus, 1916. Address: 1748 Lamont St., Washington, D.C. Died Oct. 11, 1943.

PIERREPONT, Robert Low (pēr'pŏnt); b. Luzerne, N.Y., Aug. 12, 1876; s. Henry Evelyn and Ellen A. (Low) P.; A.B., Columbia, 1898; m. Kathryn Isabel Reed, Nov. 22, 1900. Dir. Home Life Ins. Co. of N.Y., Hanover Fire Ins. Co., Fulton Fire Ins. Co., Brooklyn Union Gas Co., Brooklyn Trust Co., South Brooklyn Savings Bank, Brooklyn City Safe Deposit Co., Green-Wood Cemetery, 580 Park Av., Inc. Republican. Episcopalian. Clubs: St. Anthony, Down Town (New York). Home: 580 Park Av. Office: 63 Wall St., New York, N.Y. Died Jan. 18, 1944.

PIERSON, Silas Gilbert, mining exec.; b. Otisville, N.Y., May 29, 1866; s. John and Elizabeth (Halsey) P.; m. Grace S. Tisdale, 1897; children—Orrin T., John H., Edward B., Frank C. With Colo. Fuel & Iron Corp. since 1892, v.p. and dir. since 1914. Mem. Y.M.C.A., Denver Country Club. Republican. Congregationalist. Home: 944 Pennsylvania St., Denver, Colo.* Died Oct. 16, 1946.

PIGFORD, Clarence E., lawyer, publisher; b. Lauderdale County, Miss., Nov. 11, 1873; s. James Farrier and Martha Jane (Delk) P.; A.B., Union U., Jackson, Tenn., 1893; hon. LL.D., 1943; B L., Cumberland U., Lebanon, Tenn., 1896; m. Sally Bransford Person, Nov. 27, 1907. Admitted to Tenn. bar, 1896, and since practiced in Jackson; city atty., 1889-1901; special judge, Tenn. Court of Appeals; president Sun Publishing Company (Jackson Sun), Jackson Transportation Corp.; v.p., Budde & Weiss Mfg. Co., Model Mill Co.; dir. and atty., First Nat. Bank, Jackson, Tenn. Trustee of George Peabody Coll. for Teachers, Nashville, Tenn.; dir. Southwestern College of the Mississippi Valley, Memphis, Tenn. Member Jackson Bar Association (past president), Tennessee Bar Assn., Am. Bar Assn., Tennessee Hist. Commn., State Planning Commn., Sigma Alpha Epsilon. Elk. Club: Jackson Golf and Country. Successfully attacked as discriminatory, constitutionality of Tenn. Statute before Supreme Court of U.S. resulting in one of the few reversals (12th) by that Court of Supreme Court of Tenn. Home: Chevy Chase, Trenton Road. Office: First Nat. Bank Bldg., Jackson, Tenn. Died Jan. 8, 1945.

PIGOTT, William Trigg, lawyer; b. Boonville, Mo., Nov. 3, 1861; s. John T. and Josephine (Trigg) P.; Kemper Mil. Sch., Boonville, Mo.; LL.B., U. of Mo., 1880; m. Virginia Curtis, Jan. 11, 1883; children—John T., Curtis, William T., Winifred. Practiced Va. City, Mont., 1880-83, 1886-90, Great Falls, Mont., 1890-97, Helena, Mont., from 1903. City atty., Virginia City, 1880-84; member State Bd. Edn., 1895-97; justice Supreme Court of Mont., 1897-1903; apptd. justice Supreme Court, 1918, to fill vacancy to Jan. 6, 1919; apptd. judge 1st Judicial Dist., 1934; resumed practice of law, Dec. 4, 1934. Pres. Montana Bar Assn., 1913-14; v.p. for Mont., Am. Bar Assn., 1916-19, 1922-23. Became mem. State Bd. of Law Examiners, 1922. Home: 721 Hauser St., Helena Mont. Died Mar. 1944.

PIHLBLAD, Ernst Frederick (pēl'blăd), coll. pres.; b. Kansas City, Mar. 18, 1873; s. John and Anna Louise (Nord) P.; A.B., Bethany Coll., Kan., 1891, A.M., 1895; grad. Augustana Theol. Sem., 1894; D.D., Augustana Coll., 1906; m. Marie Sjostrom, July 5, 1894; children—Carl David Terence, Helge Ernst. Ordained Luth. ministry, 1894; pastor Swedish Luth. chs., Paterson, N.J., and Passaic, N.J., 1894-95; prof. Latin, Bethany Coll., 1895-1904, v.p., 1900-04, pres., 1904-41. Mem. Kan. Text-Book Commn., 1912-14; mem. Kan. State Bd. of Edn., 1933-36, Kan. State Senate, 1936-40; chmn. Kan. State Civil Service Bd. Republican. Mem. Kan. advisory com. U.S. Food Adminstrn. Made Knight Order of Vasa, by Gustave V of Sweden, 1920; Comdr., 2d Class, Order of the White Rose of Finland, 1941. Home: Lindsborg, Kan. Died Dec. 9, 1943.

PIKE, Charles Burrall, capitalist; b. Chicago, Ill., June 29, 1871; s. Eugene S. and Mary (Rockwell) P.; A.B., Harvard, 1893, LL.B., 1896; m. Frances Alger, May 18, 1898. Admitted to Ill. bar, 1898, and began practice at Chicago; mem. firm Pike & Gade, 1899-1902; v.p. Western State Bank, 1901-02; pres. Hamilton Nat. Bank, Merchants Safe Deposit Co., 1903-10; mng. trustee Eugene S. Pike Estate Land Trust since 1917. Chief civilian aide to sec. of war, 1922-38; pres. Mil. Training Camps Assn., U.S. Army, 1922-38; mem. Chicago Hist. Soc. (1st v.p., 1924; pres. since 1927). Republican. Presbyterian. Clubs: Racquet (pres. 1924-29 and 1933-39), Chicago, Saddle Cycle, Old Elm, Shoreacres, Onwentsia. Home: 1100 Lake Shore Drive, Chicago; Lake Forest, Ill., and Bar Harbor, Me. Office: 6 N. Michigan Blvd., Chicago, Ill. Died Apr. 26, 1941.

PILCHER, James Taft (pĭl'chēr), surgeon; b. Brooklyn, N.Y., Mar. 31, 1880; s. Lewis Stephen and Martha S. (Phillips) P.; student New York U., 1898-1900; A.B., U. of Mich., 1902; M.D., Coll. Physicians and Surgeons, Columbia, 1904; studied univs. of Göttingen, Berlin and Vienna, 1907-08; m. Effie D. Curtis, June 30, 1909; children—Edith Mayo, Ruth Adelaide (dec.). Practiced in Brooklyn since 1904; founder and surgeon Pilcher Hosp.; cons. surgeon Eastern L.I. Hosp.; attending surgeon State Hosp. Commn. N.Y. Unity Hospital; visiting surgeon Peck Memorial; director urology, Downtown Hospital. Commd. maj. Med. Corps, 1st Cav., N.G.N.Y.; maj. comdg. Field Hosp. 108, World War, awarded D.S.O. and conspicuous service cross of N.Y. State, Am. Bd. of Surgery. Fellow Am. Coll. of Surgeons; mem. A.M.A., Med. Soc. State of N.Y., Kings County Med. Soc., Assn. Physicians L.I., Am. Gastro-Enterol. Assn., Mayo Clin. Soc., New York Surg. Soc., Brooklyn Surg. Soc., Pan-Am. Assn., Zeta Psi, Nu Sigma Nu, Theta Nu Epsilon. Republican. Episcopalian. Clubs: University, Brooklyn Cavalry, North Fork Country. Editor, Annals of Surgery. Home: 121 Gates Av., Brooklyn, N.Y. Died Apr. 4, 1947.

PINANSKI, Abraham Edward (pĭn-ăn'skĭ), judge; b. Boston, Mass., July 9, 1887; s. Nathan and Ida (Ginsburg) P.; A.B., Harvard, 1908, LL.B., 1910; m. Viola J. Rottenberg, Aug. 10, 1920; children—Jean Ida, Joan Rachel, Jane Irene, June Frances. Admitted to Mass. bar, 1910; with legal dept. Boston Elevated Ry. Co., 1910-12; mem. firm McConnell, Pinanski and Morris, 1912-30; justice Superior Court, Mass., since 1930. First lt. and capt. Ordnance Dept., U.S. Army, World War I. Member Sinking Fund Commn., Boston, 1926-31; served in State Dept. of Edn., Div. of Americanization, 1919-31; mem. bd. of mgrs. Boston Dispensary; mem. board Community Workshops, Inc.; pres. Jewish Child Welfare Assn., Hebrew Free Loan Soc. of Boston; mem. exec. com. and trustee Asso. Jewish Philanthropies; v.p., chmn. executive committee Beth Israel Hospital. Trustee Boston Public Library (pres.), Peter Bent Brigham Hosp., Temple Adath Israel. Dir. Community Fedn. of Boston. Mem. Am., Mass. and Boston bar assns., Harvard Law School Assn. (mem. Council), Am Judicature Soc. (dir.), Tau Epsilon Phi. Republican. Mason, Odd Fellow. Clubs: University, City, Harvard (Boston), Curtis. Home: 283 Buckminster Rd., Brookline, Mass. Address: Court House, Boston, Mass. Died Oct. 5, 1949.

PINCHOT, Amos Richards Eno (pĭn'shō), lawyer, publicist; b. Paris, France, Dec. 6, 1873 (parents traveling in France); s. James W. and Mary (Eno) P.; A B., Yale, 1897; studied law at Columbia and in New York Law Sch.; m. Gertrude Minturn, 1900; children —Gifford, Rosamond; m. 2d, Ruth Pickering, 1919; children—Mary, Antoinette Eno. Served in the 1st N.Y. Vol. Cav., Spanish-Am. War, Porto Rico. Deputy asst. dist. atty., New York, 1900-01. Club: Yale. Home: 1165 Park Av. Office: 101 Park Av., New York, N.Y. Died Feb. 18, 1944.

PINCHOT, Gifford, ex-gov., forester; b. Simsbury, Conn., Aug. 11, 1865; s. James W. and Mary (Eno) P.; A.B., Yale, 1889; studied forestry France, Germany, Switzerland and Austria; hon. A.M., Yale, 1901, Princeton, 1904; Sc.D., Mich. Agrl. Coll., 1907; LL.D., McGill, 1909, Pa. Mil. Coll., 1923, Yale, 1925, Temple, 1931; m. Cornelia Elizabeth Bryce, 1914; 1 son, Gifford Bryce. First Am. professional forester; began first systematic forest work in U.S. at Biltmore, N.C., Jan. 1892; mem. Nat. Forest Commn., 1896; forester and chief of div. afterward Bur. of Forestry, and now the Forest Service, U.S. Dept. Agr., 1898-1910; pres. Nat. Conservation Assn., 1910-25. Prof. forestry, Yale, 1903-36, professor emeritus since 1936. Commr. of forestry of Pa., 1920-22; gov. of Pa., 1923-27 and 1931-35. Inspected forests of P.I., 1902, and recommended forest policy for same; mem. com. on orgn. govt. scientific work, apptd. Mar. 13, 1903, commn. on pub. lands, apptd. Oct. 22, 1903, commn. on dept. methods, apptd. June 2, 1905, Inland Waterways Commn., apptd. Mar. 14, 1907, commn. on country life, apptd. Aug. 10, 1908; chmn. Nat. Conservation Commn., apptd. June 8, 1908; chmn. Joint Com. on Conservation, apptd. by the conf. of govs. and nat. orgns. at Washington, Dec. 1908. Member Society American Foresters, Royal English Arboricultural Soc., American Mus. Natural History, Washington Academy Sciences, Pennsylvania Academy of Sciences, American Academy Political and Social Science. Member of Commn. for Relief in Belgium, 1914-15. Mem. U.S. Food Administration, Aug. 1917-Nov. 1918. Negotiated settlement of anthracite coal strike in 1923. Clubs: Century, Explorers (New York); Cosmos of Washington (pres. 1908). Author: Biltmore Forest, 1893; The White Pine (with H. S. Graves), 1896; Timber Trees and Forests of North Carolina (with W. W. Ashe), 1897; The Adirondack Spruce, 1898; Report to the Secretary of the Interior on Examination of the Forest Reserves, 1898; A Study of Forest Fires and Wood Production in Southern New Jersey, 1899; A Primer of Forestry, Part I, Bull. 24, Div. of Forestry, 1899, Part 2, 1905; Recommendations on Policy, Organization and Procedure for the Bureau of Forestry of the Philippine Islands, 1903; The Fight for Conservation, 1909; The Country Church (with C. O. Gill), 1913; The Training of a Forester, 1914, 4th edit. (rewritten), 1937; Six Thousand Country Churches (with C. O. Gill), 1919; To the South Seas, 1930; Just Fishing Talk, 1936; Breaking New Ground, 1946. Home: Milford, Pike County, Pa. Died Oct. 4, 1946.

PINE, William Bliss, ex-senator; b. Bluffs, Ill., Dec. 30, 1877; s. Wm. G. and Margaret (Green) P.; m. Laura M. Hamilton, June 18, 1912; 1 son, William Hamilton. Settled in Okla., 1904; engaged in oil business in own name; pres. Burns Tool Co., Okmulgee Producers & Mfrs. Gas Co., Okmulgee Bldg. and Loan Assn., Central Nat. Bank; v.p. Southwestern Sheet Glass Co., Okmulgee; mem. U.S. Senate, term 1925-31 (elected by largest vote ever given in the state up to 1924). Republican. Methodist. Home: Okmulgee, Okla. Died Aug. 25, 1942.

PINNER, Max, physician; b. Berlin, Germany, Nov. 28, 1891; s. Emil and Ida (Rothe) P.; Abiturium, Ober-Real Sch., Constance, Germany, 1911; med. student U. of Berlin, 1911-15; M.D., U. of Tübingen, 1919; m. Berna Rudovic, Mar. 1, 1924. Came to U.S., 1921, naturalized, 1928. Became asst. Eppendorf Hosp., Hamburg, 1920; lab. asst. Municipal Tuberculosis Sanitarium, Chicago, Ill., 1924-26; instr.

pathology and bacteriology, U. of Ill., 1924-26; pathologist, Maybury Sanatorium and Herman Kiefer Hosp., Detroit, 1926-30; asso. dir. in charge labs. and research Desert Sanatorium, Tucson, Ariz., also cons. pathologist South Pacific Hosp., Tucson, 1931-35; pathologist tuberculosis hosps., N.Y. State Dept. Health, 1935-38; chief, div. pulmonary diseases, Montefiore Hosp., New York, 1938-45; clin. prof. medicine, Columbia, 1939-46; asst. editor Am. Rev. of Tuberculosis, 1937-40, editor since 1940. Fellow Am. Coll. Physicians; mem. Am. Assn. Thoracic Surgery, Am. Trudeau Soc., Soc. Exptl. Biology and Medicine, Am. Assn. Pathologists and Bacteriologists, Sigma Xi; hon. mem. Soc. Chiliena de Tisiologia and Sociedade Brasileira de Tuberculose. Author: Pulmonary Tuberculosis in the Adult, 1945. Contbr. to med. jours. of about 100 papers on tuberculosis and related subjects. Recipient of Trudeau Medal of Nat. Tuberculosis Assn., June, 1946. Home: 463 Vermont Av., Berkeley 7, Calif. Office: 364 14th St. Oakland 12, Calif. Died Jan. 7, 1948.

PINTEN, Joseph Gabriel, bishop; b. Rockland, Mich., Oct. 3, 1867; s. Joseph and Anna (Kloeckner) P. Ordained priest R.C. Ch., in Rome, Italy, Nov. 1, 1890; consecrated bishop of Superior, May 3, 1922; transferred to See of Grand Rapids, June 25, 1926. Home: 1225 Lake Drive, S.E., Grand Rapids, Mich.* Died Nov. 1945.

PINTNER, Rudolf (pĭnt'nẽr), psychologist; b. Lytham, Eng., Nov. 16, 1884; s. William and Irma P.; Royal High Sch.; M.A., Edinburgh U., 1906; Ph.D., U. of Leipzig, 1913; L.H.D., Gallaudet Coll., 1931; m. Margaret M. Anderson, Aug. 15, 1916; children—Irma Jane, Walter McKenzie. Came to U.S., 1912. Prof. psychology, Toledo U., 1912-13; instr. psychology, 1913-14, asst. prof., 1914-17, prof., 1917-21, Ohio State U.; prof. edn., Teachers Coll., Columbia, since 1921. Fellow A.A.A.S.; mem. Am. Psychol. Assn., Am. Assn. for Applied Psychology. Author: A Scale of Performance Tests, 1917; The Picture Completion Test, 1917; The Mental Survey, 1918; Intelligence Testing, 1923, 2d edit., 1931; Educational Psychology, 1929; The Psychology of the Physically Handicapped (with Eisenson and Stanton), 1941. Translator: An Introduction to Psychology (Wundt), 1912; Experimental Psychology and Pedagogy (Schulze), 1912; The Idea of the Industrial School (Kerschensteiner), 1913. Mem. editorial bd, Psychological Bulletin. Home; 60 Ridge Road Yonkers, N.Y. Died Nov. 7, 1942.

PINTO, Alva Sherman (pĭn'tō), surgeon; b. Chillicothe, O., May 29, 1872; s. Augustus Miles and Margaret (Reed) P.; grad. Omaha Commercial Coll., 1893; M.D., Creighton U., 1898; m. Mabel B. Spalding, Dec. 10, 1903; children—Sherman Spalding, Harvey Elmore. Enlisted as pvt. U.S. Vols., 1898, serving in Cuba and the Philippines, resigned as capt. Med. Dept., Feb. 1903; returned to Army as maj. Med. Dept., Aug. 7, 1918; served in France till July 1919; promoted lt. col.; comdg. officer Camp Hosp. No. 48, at Recey sur Orce; hon. discharged July 23, 1919; apptd. col. Med. Reserve Corps, U.S. Army, 1931. Health commr. of Omaha since 1921. Volunteered as one of first 3 to be bitten by infected mosquito, at Havana, Cuba, July 1900, proving the manner of infection of yellow fever. Mem. Am., Neb. State and Douglas County med. socs. Republican. Methodist. Mason. Elk. Clubs: Athletic, Prettiest Mile Country. Home: 6532 Florence Blvd. Office: First National Bank, Omaha, Neb.*
Died Dec. 7, 1944.

PITCAIRN, Norman Bruce, ry. official; b. Harrisburg, Pa., Nov. 8, 1881; s. Hugh and Annie M. (Sherfey) P.; C.E., Princeton, 1903; m. Mary Martin Leet, Oct. 15, 1913; children—Ruth Leet (Mrs. Thomas Franklin James, Jr.), Mary Leet, Norman Bruce. Began as rodman Pa. R.R. Co.. 1901, and advanced through various positions to gen. supt. Eastern Ohio Div., 1928; pres. Detroit, Toledo & Ironton R.R. Company, Jan. 16, 1931-Oct. 18, 1933; receiver and dir. Wabash Ry. Co., Oct. 19, 1933-Dec. 31, 1941; pres. and dir. Wabash R.R. Co., and subsidiary cos., Jan. 1, 1942-Apr. 17, 1947; chairman board since April 1947; receiver, pres., dir. Ann Arbor R.R. Co., Oct. 20, 1933-Dec. 31, 1942, pres. and dir., Jan. 1, 1943-May 22, 1947. Republican. Presbyterian. Mason. Clubs: Noonday, St. Louis Country (St. Louis); Chicago (Chicago); Union League (Phila.). Home: 6333 Ellenwood Av., Clayton 5, Mo. Office: 1618 Railway Exchange Bldg., St. Louis 1, Mo. Died Feb. 16, 1948.

PITMAN, Frank Wesley, prof. history; b. New Haven, Conn., Aug. 26, 1882; s. Edward Yard and Fannie Susan (May) P.; grad. Hillhouse High Sch., New Haven, 1901; Ph.B., Yale, 1904, M.A., 1906, Ph.D., 1914; research student in Great Britain, 1908-10, 1930-31, Jamaica, 1933; m. Delora Etta Armstrong, June 8, 1914; children—Frank Armstrong and Delora Armstrong (twins). Instr., later asst. prof. history, Yale, 1910-25; on leave, as acting prof. history, Pomona Coll., Claremont, Calif., 1924-25; prof. history and head dept. Pomona Coll., 1925-47; del. Anglo-Am. Hist. Conf., London 1931. Mem. American Historical Assn. (pres. Pacific coast br. 1930), New Haven Colony Hist. Soc., Phi Beta Kappa, Sigma Xi, Theta Xi. Conglist. Club: Graduate (New Haven). Author: Development of the British West Indies (1700-1763), 1917; Slavery on British West India Plantations in the 18th Century, 1926; also contbr. to New Internat. Ency., Dictionary of Am. Biography, and to revs. Home: 116 E. 12th St., Claremont, Calif.; (summer) Castine, Me. Died Apr. 11, 1949.

PITNEY, Shelton, lawyer; b. Morristown, N.J., Mar. 29, 1893; s. Mahlon and Florence T. (Shelton) P.; grad. Hill School, Pottstown, Pa., 1910; A.B., Princeton, 1914; LL.B., Harvard, 1917; m. Etta Carrington Brown, May 14, 1918; children—Shelton, Mary Foster, James Carrington. Admitted to N.Y. bar, 1920, N.J. bar, as atty., 1921, as counsellor, 1924; in practice since Mar. 1, 1919; mem. Pitney, Hardin & Ward since 1922; trustee Central R.R. Co. of N.J. since 1939; director Morristown Trust Co., director of New York, Long Branch R.R. Co., Served in U.S. Army, 1917-19; capt. 313th F.A., 80th Div., Sept. 1917-Feb. 1919; with A.E.F. in St. Mihiel and Argonne, wounded Oct. 2, 1918. Mem. Am. Bar Assn., N.J. Bar Assn., Essex County Bar Assn., Morris County Bar Assn. Republican. Presbyterian. Clubs: Essex, Down Town (Newark); Morris County Golf, Morristown (Morristown, N.J.); Edgartown Yacht (Edgartown, Mass.); Cap and Gown (Princeton). Railroad, Machinery Club (New York City). Home: Morristown, N.J. Office: 744 Broad St., Newark, N.J.
Died Jan. 13, 1946.

PLACE, Perley Oakland, prof. Latin; b. Oakland, Calif., Nov. 25, 1873; s. James A. and Mary Jane (Converse) P.; A.B., Dartmouth, 1893, A.M., 1896, Litt.D., 1934; A.B., Harvard, 1894; Litt.D., Colgate Univ., 1912; L.H.D., Syracuse Univ., 1945; m. Harriette E. Stanton, of Boston. Teacher Latin and Greek, Little Rock (Ark) Acad., 1894-97; classical master, high sch., Brookline, Mass., 1898-1900; in employ American Book Co., 1900-01; instr. Latin, Syracuse University, 1901-03, asst. prof., 1904, asso. prof., 1905, prof. since 1908. Mem. Am. Philol. Assn., Archeol. Inst. America, N.Y. State Classical Teachers Assn. (pres. 1912-13), Phi Beta Kappa, Theta Delta Chi, Phi Kappa Phi, Kappa Phi Kappa, Phi Delta Kappa, Mass. Soc. S.R. Republican. Methodist. Clubs: Harvard (Syracuse), University. Author: Beginning Latin; Second Year Latin; First Year Latin; Intermediate Latin Lessons; Second Latin Course; Manuals to Accompany First Year Latin and Second Latin Course; Our Legacy from Greece and Rome; Roman Vergil; A Roman Gentleman's Religion; Catullus, the Roman Burns; Horace, Roman Gentleman and Poet; Tacitus, Historian of the Early Roman Empire; Learnring in Living; Translations from Ovid; In the World of the Romans (Third and Fourth Year Latin). Contbr. on ednl. topics. Home: 1036 Lancaster Av., Syracuse, N.Y. Died Feb. 10, 1946.

PLACK, William L., architect; b. Altoona, Pa., June 18, 1854; s. Louis and Elizabeth (Wehn) P.; C.E., Lafayette Coll., 1876, D. Engring., 1926; studied design and sculpture, Md. Inst., Baltimore; married; worked for 3 yrs. as architectural draughtsman and traveled in Europe. Was chief draughtsman on the State Capitol bldg., Des Moines, Ia., 1882, then opened office; practiced in Altoona, Pa., 1887-90; moved to Phila., to design the new shops for Baldwin Locomotive Works; has designed many banks, schs., chs., theatres, business blocks, county ct. houses and pub. bldgs., Phila. and Pa. Fellow Am. Inst. Architects; mem. Nat. Fire Protection Assn., Franklin Inst., Am. Civic Assn., Phila. Chamber of Commerce, Wm. Penn Highway Assn. (gov.); U.S. del. Internat. Congress of Architects, Rome, Italy, 1911, London, 1924, Pan-Am. Congress of Architects, Santiago, Chile, 1923, Buenos Aires, Argentina, 1927, accredited del. of A.I.A. to World Engring. Congress, Tokio, 1929. Pres. Pa. State Assn. A.I.A., 1921-23; hon. corr. mem. Sociedad Central de Arquitectos, Uruguay, Argentina, Brazil and Chile; mem. Am. Interprofessional Inst. Clubs: Old Colony, Engineers', Art (Phila.). Home: Lenox Apts. Office: 1120 Locust St., Philadelphia, Pa.*
Died Aug. 27, 1944.

PLAGENS, Joseph Casimir (plā'gĕnz), bishop; b. Jan. 29, 1880; s. Andrew Joseph and Constance (Grygier) P.; attended St. Casimir parochial school; high school and college course at old Detroit (Jesuit) Coll. (now U. of Detroit); A.B., U. of Detroit, 1899, A.M., 1902, LL.D., 1923; S.T.B., St. Mary's Sem., 1903, D.D., 1923. Ordained priest R.C. Ch., 1903; pastor St. Michael, Port Austin, Mich., 1906-11, St. Florian, Detroit, 1912-19, Sweetest Heart of Mary, Detroit, 1919-35; auxiliary bishop of Detroit and vicar gen. of diocese of Detroit, 1924-35; apptd. and consecrated auxiliary bishop of Detroit, May 1924; apptd. bishop of Marquette, Nov. 1935; transferred to the See of Grand Rapids, Dec. 1940; bishop of Grand Rapids since Feb. 18, 1941. Mem. K.C. Club: Detroit Athletic. Home: 2006 Lake Drive, S.E., Grand Rapids, Mich. Died Mar. 31, 1943.

PLAISTED, Frederick William (plā'stĕd) ex-governor; b. Bangor, Me., July 26, 1865; s. Harris Merrill P. (maj.-gen. U.S.V., 1865) and Sarah Jane (Mason) P.; ed. pub. schs., Bangor, and St. Johnsbury (Vt.) Acad.; m. Frances Gullifer, Feb. 10, 1907. Editor and propr. The New Age, Augusta, 1889-1914. Del.-at-large Dem. Nat. convs., 1896, 1900, 12; nominee for Congress, 1897 (spl. election to fill vacancy), 1898; mem. Dem. Congl. Com., 1898-1900, mayor of Augusta, 1906, 07, 08, 10; sheriff Kennebec County, 1907-08; gov. Maine, term, 1911-13 (1st Dem. gov. of Me. since father, 1882); state park commr., term 1913-15; postmaster of Augusta, Jan. 27, 1914-23. Mem. School Com., Augusta, 10 yrs. (chmn.); trustee pub. library, Augusta Water Dist.; pres. Augusta Gen. Hosp., Masonic Bldg. Co. Chmn. Draft Exemption Bd., 1917. Corporator Augusta and Kennebec savings banks. Conglist. Mason (33°); past grand comdr., Grand Commandery Me. K.T.; past grand high priest, Grand Chapter of Me.; past exalted ruler B.P.O. Elks; past comdr. S. of V. Clubs: Abnaki (pres.), Augusta Country. Address: Augusta, Maine; (winter) Tujunga, Los Angeles County, Calif. Died Mar. 4, 1943.

PLATT, John, engineer; b. Gloucester, Eng., June 1, 1864; s. James and Elizabeth (Waddington) P.; engring. student Univ. Coll., London, 1886-87; m. Mary Bourne Bartlett, 1891; children—Hilda (Mrs. Wilfred H. Wolfs), John, Robert, Hugh. Came to U.S., 1888; introduced marine steam turbine into U.S. Navy and Merchant Marine. Mem. Am. Soc. M.E., Soc. Naval Architects and Marine Engrs., Instn. Civ. Engrs. (Eng.). Clubs: Engineers (New York); Army and Navy (Washington, D.C.); St. Stephen's (London). Collector early Chinese and Korean pottery. Home: 532 Woodland Av., Westfield, N.J.
Died Apr. 27, 1942.

PLATT, John O(sgood), insurance; b. Nyack, N.Y., June 21, 1874; s. Clayton Taylor and Martha DuBose (Lucas) P.; ed. Ury Private Sch. and St. Luke's Acad., Phila., 1883-91; m. Katharine Biddle Leonard, July 1917 (died 1918); 1 son, John Osgood; m. 2d, Mary Cox Page, 1922; children—Davis Page, William, Mary Cordes. Associated with Ins. Co. of N.A. since Oct. 1891, beginning as clerk and later becoming special agt., asst. sec., 1907-10, 2d v.p., 1910-16, 1st v.p., 1916-39, dir. since 1916, pres., 1939-41, vice chmn. bd. since Mar. 1941; pres. Alliance Ins. Co., Phila. Fire & Marine Ins. Co., Indemnity Ins. Co. of N.A. Mem. bd. mgrs. Children's Hosp., Phila.; pres. Williston Sch. Bd., Paoli, Pa. Mem. Del. Soc. of the Cincinnati. Republican. Episcopalian. Clubs: Philadelphia, University Barge (Phila.). Home: "Fairfields," Paoli, Pa. Office: 1600 Arch St., Philadelphia, Pa. Died July 11, 1947.

PLEHN, Carl Copping (plān), univ. prof.; b. Providence, R.I., June 20, 1867; s. Julius and Mary (Copping) P.; A.B., Brown U., 1889, LL.D., 1914; Ph.D., Univ. of Göttingen (Germany), 1891; m. Elizabeth Brainerd, May 16, 1894 (died April 13, 1929); children—Mary Elizabeth, Julius Brainerd; m. 2d, Emily Harris Noble, May 12, 1932. Prof. of history and polit. science, Middlebury Coll., 1892-93; asst. prof. polit. economy, U. of Calif., 1893-96, asso. prof. finance and statistics, 1896-1909, Flood prof. finance, 1909-37, prof. emeritus since July 1, 1937, dean College of Commerce, 1898-1910; faculty research lecturer, U. of Calif., 1924. Supervisor of Census 1st Dist. Calif., 1900; chief statistician with the Philippine Commn., 1900-01; mem. and sec. commn. on revision of the revenue laws of Calif., 1905-11; mem. Nat. Com. on Inheritance Taxation, 1925. Mem. Am. Econ. Assn. (pres. 1923), Nat. Tax Assn., American Statis. Assn. Author: Das Kreditwesen der Staaten und Städte der Nord-Amerikanischen Union in Seiner Historischen Entwickelung, 1891; Introduction to Public Finance, 1896, 5th edit., 1926; Revenue Systems of State and Local Governments, 1907; Government Finance, 1915. Contbr. to revs., etc., of articles on econ. subjects. Republican. Address: 2308 Warring St., Berkeley, Calif. Died July 21, 1945; buried at Providence, R.I.

PLESSNER, Theodore, pres. Northern Ins. Co. of N.Y., 83 Maiden Lane, New York, N.Y. Died Sep. 5, 1946.

PLUM, David Banks, newspaper pub.; b. Troy, N.Y., Oct. 7, 1869; s. Frederick A. and Mary S. (Fowler) P.; ed. pub. sch.; m. Harriet L. Barnes, Mar. 30, 1898. Began as clerk, Troy Record, 1897, treas., 1917-35, pres. since 1935, also pub.; pres. Averill Park Co.; dir. Mfr. Nat. Bank. First sergt. U.S. Vol. Inf., Spanish-Am. War; mem. Nat. Guard, N.Y., 10 yrs. Trustee Samaritan Hospital. Member Am. Geographical Society, N.Y. State Hist. Assn., Rensselaer County Hist. Soc., Soc. Colonial Wars, Order Founders and Patriots of America, S.R., Newcomen Soc. of England. Republican. Presbyterian. Mason. Clubs: Troy, Troy Country, North Woods; Union League (New York). Home: 25 Locust Av. Office: Broadway and 5th Av., Troy, N.Y. Died Aug. 31, 1948.

PLUNKETT, Edward Milton, business exec.; b. Vernon, Mich., 1886; s. Edward Milton and Elvira (Ervey) P.; A.B., U. of Mich., 1908, J.D., 1910; m. Mabel Townley, June 1914; children—Dorothy (Mrs. Donald S. Hutton), Edward Milton. Investment salesman, F. J. Lisman & Co., 1911; real estate rep., S. S. Kresge Co., 1913; vice-pres., S. S. Kresge Co., 1942; dir., 1945. Clubs: Economic (Detroit), Detroit Golf, Detroit Athletic, U. of Mich. (Detroit), Detroit Commandery K.T. Home: 216 Hawthorne Rd., Birmingham, Mich. Office: 2727 Second Av., Detroit 32, Mich. Died Mar. 13, 1948.

PODELL, David Louis (pō-dĕl'), lawyer; b. Nov. 21, 1884; s. Mordecai and Minna (London) P.; prep. edn., pub. schs., New York; A.B., Columbia, 1905; Columbia Law Sch., 1907; m. Sarah Falk, Dec. 6, 1925; children—Peggy, David L. Began practice, N.Y. City, 1907; lecturer on trial of cases, Coll. City of New York, 1917-18; spl. asst. U.S. atty. in charge of trial of Anti-trust cases, 1921-24; successfully conducted trial for Govt. of U.S. of Trenton Potteries case; defended constitutionality of Rent Laws before U.S. Supreme Court; lectured on Cross-Examination, Columbia U. Law Sch., 1932; at suggestion of President Roosevelt, served on Wagner Com. and assisted in formulation and preparation of Nat. Industrial Recovery Act, 1933; special asst. U.S. Atty. gen. in Anti-trust cases, 1938-41; trial counsel for plaintiff in Loft v. Pepsi-Cola and Guth suit; chief of complaints Small Business and Anti-trust Division Department Justice since 1942. gen. counsel Smaller

War Plants Corp., Washington, D.C. Trustee N.Y. Fedn. of Jewish Charities; trustee Educational Alliance; president Beth Israel Hospital, Council of Fraternal and Benevolent Organizations. Awarded Kings Crown by Columbia University. Member Am. and N.Y. State bar assns., N.Y. County Lawyers Assn. (chmn. commerce com.); dir. Trade and Commerce Bar Assn. (legislative com.). Democrat. Jewish religion. Clubs: Manhattan, Lawyers, Lambs, Bankers, City Athletic. Author of pamphlets, Trade Associations and the Law; Our Anti-trust Laws and the Economic Situation; Patent Pools and the Anti-trust Laws. Home: 1 E. 88th St. Office: 39 Broadway, New York, N.Y. and Smaller War Plants Corp., Washington, D.C. Died Feb. 1, 1947.

POE, Elisabeth Ellicott, artist, writer; b. Phila., Pa., July 27, 1886; d. George and Margaret Amy (Wallace) Poe; student Norfolk (Va.) Sch. for Girls, 1896-1900, Phillips Memorial Gallery Art Sch., Washington, D.C., 1933-42; pvt. instrn. in art; unmarried. Literary and music editor Washington (D.C.) Post, 1921-38; art editor Washington Times Herald since 1938; editor D.A.R. mag. since 1941; contbrg. editor Cathedral Age, Washington Cathedral since 1928; asso. editor Stylus mag., 1930-33. Exhibited frequently, held one-man shows, Corcoran Gallery of Art, Phillips Mem. Gallery, Washington, D.C., Syracuse (N.Y.) Mus. of Fine Arts. Served as commandant of Nat. Service Sch. for Women World War I; chmn. Woman's Naval Service, Inc., 1915. Mem. nat. com. Washington Cathedral. Republican. Episcopalian. Clubs: Water Color, Women's National Press, (past 1st vice pres.), Am. Newspaper Women's (past 1st vice pres.), Washington, D.C. Author: Half Forgotten Romances of American History, 1924; (with sister Vylla Poe Wilson) Edgar Allan Poe, High Priest of The Beautiful, 1932. Home: 3007 34th St. N.W., Washington. Office: Washington Times-Herald, Washington 6, D.C. Died Sept. 29, 1947; buried Glenwood Cemetery, Washington.

POINDEXTER, Miles, lawyer; b. Memphis, Tenn., Apr. 22, 1868; s. William B. and Josephine Alexander (Anderson) P.; ed. Fancy Hill Acad., Va., and Washington and Lee U.; LL.B., Washington and Lee, 1891; LL.D., George Washington U., 1919; moved to Walla Walla, Wash., 1891; m. Elizabeth Gale Page, June 16, 1892 (died Dec. 20, 1929); 1 son, Gale Aylett, comdr. U.S. Navy, retired. Elected pros. atty. Walla Walla County, 1892; moved to Spokane, Wash., 1897; asst. pros. atty., Spokane County, 1898-1904; judge Superior Court, 1904-08; mem. 61st Congress (1909-11), 3d Wash. Dist.; U.S. senator from Wash., 2 terms, 1911-23; acting chmn. Senate Com. on Naval Affairs, 1919-23; chmn. Rep. Senatorial Campaign Com., 1920-21; received 19 votes in Rep. Conv., 1920, for President of U.S.; A.E. and P. to Peru, 1923-28. Hon. mem. Geog. Soc. Lima, Am. Ethnol. Soc., A.A.A.S.; fellow Am. Geog. Soc., Royal Geog. Soc.; mem. Phi Beta Kappa. Mem. Order El Sol de'el Peru. Received special gold medal from City of Lima in recognition of travel in interior of Peru, 1923, '24. Author: Ayar-Incas; Peruvian Pharoahs; also articles in mags. and in Congressional Reports. Correspondence and papers deposited in Alderman Library, Univ. of Va. Home: Spokane, Wash. Address: Greenlee, Va. Died Sep. 21, 1946.

POLK, Frank Lyon, lawyer; b. New York City, Sept. 13, 1871; s. Dr. William M. and Ida A. (Lyon) P.; g.s. Leonidas P., "the fighting bishop"; grad. Groton Sch., 1890; B.A., Yale, 1894, hon. M.A., 1918; LL.B., Columbia, 1897; hon. D.C.L., U. of the South, Sewanee, 1928; LL.D., Rollins, 1930; LL.D., N.Y.U., 1935; m. Elizabeth Sturgis Potter, 1908; children—John M., Elizabeth S. (Mrs. Raymond Guest), Frank L., James P., Alice P. (Mrs. Winthrop Rutherfurd Jr. Began practice in N.Y. City, 1897; pres. Civil Service Commn. of N.Y., 1908-09; corp. counsel, 1914-15; counselor for Dept. of State, 1915-19; under sec. of State, 1919-20; acting sec. of State, Dec. 4, 1918-July 18, 1919; apptd. commr. plenipotentiary of the U.S. to negotiate peace, July 17, 1919; head of Am. delegation to Peace Conf. at Paris, July 28-Dec. 9, 1919. Dir. N.P. Ry Co.; trustee Bowery Savings Bank, U.S. Trust Co., Mutual Life Ins. Co. of N.Y. Pres. and trustee Pub. Library; trustee Cathedral of St. John. Mem. Troop A, N.Y. Nat Guard, Spanish-Am. War; served as capt. and asst. q.m. staff of Gen. Ernst, and in Porto Rico. Mem. N.Y. State and N.Y. County bar assns., Bar Assn. City of New York, Pilgrims Soc., New York Southern Soc., S.R. Episcopalian. Clubs: Knickerbocker, Racquet and Tennis, Down Town, Broad Street, Piping Rock, Century, Deepdale (New York); Metropolitan, University (Washington, D.C.). Office: 15 Broad St., New York, N.Y. Died Feb. 7, 1943.

POLLARD, Charles Louis (pŏl'ărd), botanist, entomologist; b. New York, N.Y., Mar. 29, 1872; s. Charles William and Sarah Ann (Lyman) P.; A.B., Columbia, 1893, A.M., 1894; unmarried. Asst. curator div. of botany, U.S. Dept. Agr., 1894-95, U.S. Nat. Museum, 1895-1903; consulting botanist G. & C. Merriam Co., Springfield, Mass., 1903-06; curator in chief and patron, Pub. Museum of Staten Island Assn. of Arts and Sciences, 1907-13; editor Plant World, 1897-1913. Founder and 1st pres. Washington Biologists Field Club; hon. mem. Phila. Bot. Soc. Spl. nat. field commr. Boy Scouts of America, 1917-20; scout executive, 1920; specialist in museum installation since 1926; librarian Martha Canfield Free Library, Arlington, Vt., since 1937. Contbr. many bot. terms to Supplement of Webster's Internat. Dictionary, also to Century Dictionary, 1898-1900; editor for botany and horticulture, Webster's New Internat. Dictionary. Has written many short articles. Address: Arlington, Vt. Died Aug. 16, 1945.

POLLARD, Henry Douglas, ry. official; b. Aylett, Va., Oct. 4, 1872; s. Edward Spotswood and Mary B. (Douglas) P.; prep. edn., Aberdeen (Va.) Acad.; student U. of Va., Drexel Inst., Phila., Pa.; m. Mabel Carpenter. Rodman with B.&O.R.R., 1892; asst. resident engr. Ohio Southern Ry., Feb.-June 1893; topog. survey, Baltimore, 1893-94; asst. engr. maintenance of way, B.&O. R.R., 1894-98; with Central of Ga. Ry., successively as transitman, asst. engr., resident engr., supervisor, trainmaster and roadmaster supt., 1898-1911; insp. gen. Sorrocabana Ry., Sao Paula, Brazil, later Auxiliare Ry., Santa Maria and Porte Allegre, Brazil, 1911-13; valuation engr. Central of Ga. Ry., 1913-15; pres. Wrightsville & Tennille R.R., 1915-18; asst. gen. mgr. Central of Ga. Ry., Feb.-June 1918, gen. mgr., 1918-20, gen. supt., 1920-24, gen. mgr., 1924-25, v.p. and gen. mgr., 1925-31, pres. and gen. mgr., 1931-32, receiver, 1932-40, trustee since Sept. 1940; pres. and dir. Ocean Steamship Co. of Savannah, Wrightsville & Tennille R.R., Wadley Southern Ry., Sylvania Central Ry., Louisville & Wadley R.R., Central of Ga. Motor Transport Co., Macon Terminal Co., Chatham Terminal Co., Albany Passenger Terminal Co.; dir. Central of Georgia Ry., Ocean Steamship Co. of Savh., Fruit Growers Express, Atlanta & West Point R.R., Western Ry. of Ala., Atlanta Terminal Co., Birmingham Terminal Co., Chattanooga Terminal Co., Citizens and Southern Nat. Bank, Ga. State Savings Assn. Pres. Bethesda-Union Society. Episcopalian. Clubs: Oglethorpe, Savannah Golf. Home: 2122 E. Henry St. Office: 233 W. Broad St., Savannah, Ga. Died Jan. 7, 1942.

POLLEY, Samuel Cleland, judge; b. Houston County, Minn., Jan. 13, 1864; s. John C. and Amanda A. (Korn) P.; student State Normal Sch., St. Cloud, Minn., 1886-88; LL.B., U. of Minn., 1890; m. Lenore V. McConnell, Nov. 15, 1899; children—Catherine Louise, Cleland Alexander, Chalmers. Admitted to S.D. bar, 1890, and practiced in Deadwood; state's atty., Lawrence County, 1901-02; sec. of state, S.D., 1909-12; judge Supreme Court of S.D. since 1913. Republican. Episcopalian. Deceased.

POLLOCK, Channing, author, dramatist, lecturer, publicist; b. Washington, Mar. 4, 1880; s. Alexander L. and Verona E. (Larkin) P.; grad. Bethel Mil. Acad., Warrenton, Va., 1897; studied Polytechnique, Prague, Austria; hon. Litt.D. Colgate U., 1938; LL.D., Northeastern University, Boston, 1942; m. Anna Marble, press agent, authoress, August 9, 1906; 1 dau., Helen. Dramatic critic Washington Post, 1898, Washington Times, 1899, 1900; gen. press representative for William A. Brady, New York, 1900-04; mgr. Woman's Exhbn., Madison Sq. Garden, summer of 1902; gen. press representative for Sam S. and Lee Shubert, 1904-06; retired to devote attention to dramatic writing. Regular dramatic critic of Ainslee's, The Smart Set and The Green Book successively, 1905-19. Founder and pub. The Show (mag.), 1904-06. Vice-pres. Am. Platform Guild. Author: (books) Behold the Man, 1900; Stage Stories, 1901; The Footlights—Fore and Aft, 1909; The Fool, 1925; The Enemy, 1926; Star Magic, 1933; Synthetic Gentleman, 1934; The Adventure of a Happy Man, 1939; Guide Posts in Chaos, 1942; Harvest of My Years (autobiography), 1943; The Home Front (lecture), 1943; (3 one-act plays) Winner Lose All, The Captains and the Kings, The Shot That Missed Lincoln, 1939; (plays) A Game of Hearts, 1900; The Pit (dramatization), 1900; Napoleon the Great, 1901; In the Bishop's Carriage (dramatization), 1902; The Little Gray Lady, 1903; Clothes (in collaboration with Avery Hopwood), 1906; The Secret Orchard (dramatization), 1907; The Traitor, 1908; Such a Little Queen, 1909; The Inner Shrine (dramatization), 1909; The Red Window (with Rennold Wolf), prod. by Raymond Hitchcock, 1911; Hell (with Rennold Wolf), prod. Folies Bergere, New York, 1911; My Best Girl (with Rennold Wolf), prod. by Clifton Crawford, 1912; The Beauty Shop and Her Little Highness (both with Rennold Wolf), prod. by Raymond Hitchcock and Werba and Luescher respectively, 1913; A Perfect Lady (with Rennold Wolf), prod. by Rose Stahl, 1914; Ziegfeld Follies of 1915 (with Rennold Wolf), 1915; The Grass Widow (with same), 1917; Roads of Destiny, prod. by A. H. Woods, 1918; The Crowded Hour (with Edgar Selwyn), prod. by Selwyn & Co., 1918; The Sign on the Door, prod. by A. H. Woods, 1919, and by Gladys Cooper, Playhouse, London, 1921; also at Theatre Renaissance, Paris, and in Vienna, Madrid, Amsterdam, etc.; Ziegfeld Follies of 1921; The Fool, prod. by Selwyn & Co., 1922, and by Frank Curzon in London, Sept. 18, 1924 (with Henry Ainley), also in Vienna (with Alexander Moissi); The Enemy, produced by Crosby Gaige (with Fay Bainter), Times Square Theatre, New York, 1925, and by Andre Charlot, in London, 1928; Mr. Moneypenny, prod. Liberty Theatre, New York, 1928; The House Beautiful, produced by Crosby Gaige, Apollo Theatre, New York, 1931; Stranglehold, produced 1932; Tangled Web, produced by Marcus Heiman, 1944. Lectures under the direction of Harold Peat. Contributor stories and articles to magazines, including essays regularly in Coronet Mag. Club: Players. Mem. Authors' League of America, Am. Society of Composers, Authors and Pubs., British Society Authors, Playwrights and Composers, French Soc. Dramatic Authors, Nat. Inst. of Social Sciences. Home: Shoreham, L.I., N.Y. Died Aug. 17, 1946.

POLLOCK, Edwin Taylor, naval officer; b. Mt. Gilead, O., Oct. 25, 1870; s. Joseph Harper and Olive Orlinda (Taylor) P.; 2 ancestors in the Mayflower and 7 in Am. Revolution; grad. credit U.S.N. Acad., 1891; hon. D.Sc., Wittenberg Coll., Springfield, O., 1926; m. Beatrice Law Hale, Dec. 5, 1893; 1 dau., Beatrice Hale (wife of Robert S. Chew, U.S.N.). Promoted ensign, U.S. Navy, July 1, 1893; lt. jr. grade, Mar. 3, 1899; lt., Sept. 9, 1899; lt. comdr., Sept. 30, 1905; comdr., Mar. 4, 1911; capt., Jan. 1, 1917. Served on New York, Spanish-Am. War, 1898; at Naval Sta., Cavite, P.I., 1905-06; aide to comdr.-in-chief Asiatic Fleet, 1906; navigator Alabama, 1906-07; instr. U.S. Naval Academy; exec. officer Massachusetts, 1910, Virginia, 1910-12; comd. Kearsarge, 1912-13; at Naval Obs., 1913-16; comd. Alabama, 1916, Hancock, 1916-17. Designated by President Wilson to represent U.S. in taking over the Danish West Indies, and acting gov. of Virgin Islands of the U.S., Mar. 31-Apr. 9, 1917; comd. 4th convoy group of first expdn. to France, June 1917, and comd. George Washington, 1917-18, carrying over 40,000 men to France, and comd. 8 convoy groups of over 140,000 men; mem. Naval Examining and Retiring Bds., 1918-20; Naval War Coll., 1920-21; comdg. Oklahoma and Battleship Div. 6, Pacific Fleet, 1921-22; gov. Am. Samoa, 1922-23; supt. U.S. Naval Obs., 1923-27; retired June 30, 1926, and placed on inactive list, Oct. 1, 1927. Campaign badges for West Indian, Spanish and Philippine campaigns, Cuban pacification, Mexican expdn., Dominican Occupation Victory (World War). Navy Cross; medal for expert rifleman; Order of El Sol, on Centenary of Peru, 1921. Mem. Order of Cincinnati of Mass., Soc. Colonial Wars, S.R., S.A.R. Republican. Presbyterian. Club: Army and Navy (Washington, D.C.). Head of depts. of mathematics and astronomy, Cranbrook School, Bloomfield Hills, Mich., 1928-30. Home: Jamestown, R.I. Address: 1661 Crescent Place N.W., Washington, D.C. Died June 4, 1943; buried in Arlington National Cemetery.

POLLOCK, Thomas Cithcart, clergyman; b. Ligonier, Westmoreland County, Pa., Sept. 5, 1873; s. Thomas C. and Martha (Barnett) P.; A.B., U. of Wooster (now coll.), O., 1894, A.M., 1897; grad. Pittsburgh Theol. Sem., 1897; m. Mary Clark Heade, Oct. 23, 1900; children—Thomas Clark, Margaret Heade, Martha Barnett, Jane McCracken. Ordained ministry U.P. Ch., 1897; pastor Cambridge, O., 1897-1901, 2d Ch., Monmouth, Ill., 1901-11, Oak Park Ch., Phila., 1911-46. Vice-pres. Board of Foreign Missions of the U.P. Ch. Moderator Gen. Assembly of United Presbyn. Ch., 1942-43. Home: 5034 Hazel Av., Philadelphia, Pa. Died Mar. 8, 1948.

POND, Philip, lawyer; b. New Haven, Conn., Aug. 8, 1866; s. Jonathan W. and Charlotte L. (White) P.; A.B., Yale Coll., 1888; LL.B., Yale Law Sch., 1890; m. Elizabeth B. Giles, Sept. 15, 1897. Admitted to Conn. bar, 1890, and since practiced in New Haven; mem. Pond, Morgan & Morse. Formerly dir. Grace Hosp. Mem. Internat. Law Assn., Am. Bar Grace Hosp. Mem. Internat. Law Assn., Am. Bar Assn., Conn. Bar Assn., New Haven Bar Assn. Republican. Episcopalian. Clubs: Graduate, New Haven Lawn, Mory's, Quinnipiack (New Haven). Home: Hotel Taft. Office: 39 Church St., New Haven, Conn. Deceased.

POOL, Eugene Hillhouse, surgeon; b. N.Y. City, June 3, 1874; s. John Hillhouse and Sophia (Boggs) P.; A.B., Harvard, 1895; M.D., College of Physicians and Surgeons (Columbia), 1899; m. Esther Phillips Hoppin, Apr. 29, 1904; children—James Lawrence, Beekman; m. 2d, Kitty Lanier Lawrance, June 10, 1932; m. 3d, Frances Saltonstall, Dec. 12, 1940. Assistant demonstrator anatomy, 1901-04, instr. surgery, 1904-12, asso., 1912-15, prof. clin. surgery, 1915-38, College Physicians and Surgeons; clinical professor surgery, Cornell University Medical College; senior attending surgeon New York Hospital; surgeon in chief emeritus Ruptured and Crippled Hosp.; cons. surgeon to Presbyn., French, Harlem and Woman's hosps., N.Y. Infirmary for Women & Children, North Country Community Hosp. (Glen Cove), Elizabeth A. Horton Memorial Hosp. (Middletown, N.Y.), Monmouth Memorial Hosp. (Long Branch, N.J.), United Hosp. (Portchester, N.Y.), N.Y. Eye & Ear Infirmary, Central Islip State Hospital, Berwind Free Outdoor Maternity Clinic. Fellow Am. Coll. Surgeons; mem. A.M.A., Med. Soc. State of N.Y., Am. Surg. Assn., New York Surg. Soc., Internat. Surg. Assn. Clubs: Harvard, Links (New York); Piping Rock (L.I.). Home: Locust Valley, L.I., N.Y. Died Apr. 9, 1949.

POOLE, Ernest, author; b. Chicago, Jan. 23, 1880; s. Abram and Mary (Howe) P.; A.B., Princeton, 1902; m. Margaret Winterbotham, Feb. 12, 1907; children—William Morris, Nicholas, Elizabeth Ann Lived in University Settlement, New York, 1902-05, and wrote articles and stories for mags., also corr. in U.S. and in Russia; correspondent in Germany and France, 1915, Russia, 1917, England, 1940-41. Club: Century Assn. (New York). Author: (play) None So Blind; (play) A Man's Friends; (novel) The Harbor, 1915; His Family, 1917; His Second Wife, 1918; The Dark People, 1918; The Village, 1919; Blind, 1920; Beggars' Gold, 1921; Millions, 1922; Danger, 1923; The Avalanche, 1924; The Little Dark Man, 1925; The Hunter's Moon, 1925; With Eastern Eyes, 1926; Silent Storms, 1927; Car of Croesus, 1930; The Destroyer, 1931; Nurses on Horseback, 1932; Great Winds, 1933; One of Us, 1934; The Bridge, 1940; Giants Gone, 1943; The Great White Hills, 1946. Home: Franconia, N.H. Died Jan. 10, 1950.

POOLE, Fanny Huntington Runnells, author; b. Orford, N.H.; d. Rev. Moses T. and Fanny Maria (Baker) Runnells; Tilton (N.H.) Sem., 1880-82;

studied and taught music, Boston and New York, 1883-90; m. Allan Paul Poole, 1890. Book reviewer for Home Journal (now Town and Country), 1894-98. Author: A Bank of Violets (verse), 1895; Three Songs of Love (music), 1906; Mugen, 1908. Contbr. to periodicals. Address: care Ethel Warde, 104 W. 58th St., New York. Died Feb. 1940.

POOLE, Franklin Osborne, librarian; b. Charlestown, Mass., Sept. 3, 1872; s. George Sanger and Sarah Poor (Osborne) P.; A.B., Harvard, 1895; m. Helen Bigelow Kendall, Sept. 25, 1901; children—Franklin O., Thornton Brodhead, Mary Rebecca, Charles Bigelow Kendall. Asst. in library of Boston Athenæum, 1896-1902; asst. librarian, 1902-05, librarian since 1905, Assn. Bar City of New York. Trustee Bd. of Edn., Mt. Vernon, N.Y., 1907-15. Republican. Charter mem. Am. Assn. Law Libraries (pres. 1912-13); mem. A.L.A., Delta Upsilon. Clubs: Harvard (New York); Corinthian Yacht (Marblehead, Mass.). Asst. editor 3d Supplement, 1892-96, Poole's Index to Periodical Literature, 1897; compiler, Index to Washington Collection Catalogue, in Library of Boston Athenæum, 1904. Home: Jefferson Valley, N.Y. Office: 42 W. 44th St., New York, N.Y. Died Feb. 6, 1943.

POPPENHUSEN, Conrad Herman (pŏp'ĕn-hōō-zĕn), lawyer; b. Long Island, N.Y., July 21, 1872; s. Herman C. and Caroline S. (Funke) P.; ed. Flushing (N.Y.) High Sch.; 8 yrs. in schs. and univs. in Europe, and later at Union College of law, 1891-92; and Northwestern Univ. Law School, LL.B., 1894; m. Harriet G. Gunn, June 25, 1895. Admitted to bar, 1893; mem. firm Gregory, Poppenhusen & McNab, Chicago, 1899-1914, Newman, Poppenhusen, Stern & Johnston, 1914-28, Poppenhusen, Johnston, Thompson & Cole, 1928-35, later Poppenhusen, Johnston, Thompson & Raymond. Formerly sec. and chief examiner Civ. Service Commn., Evanston, Ill.; alderman, Evanston, 1896-98; formerly mem. and pres. Evanston High Sch. Bd.; pres. Nat. Coll. of Edn. Mem. Chicago, Ill. State and Am. bar assns., Assn. Bar City of New York, Phi Delta Phi, Law Club (Chicago). Republican. Presbyterian. Clubs: Chicago, Union League, Glen View, Chicago Athletic, Press, Mid-Day (Chicago). Home: Evanston, Ill. Office: 11 S. La Salle St., Chicago, Ill. Died Mar. 20, 1949.

PORTAL, Baron Wyndham Raymond, industrialist; b. 1885; ed. Oxford Univ. Chmn. Great Western Ry. Co.; mng. dir. Portals, Ltd.; former chmn. Wiggins Teape, Ltd. and asso. cos.; dir. Comml. Union Assurance Co., Ltd., Compass Inc. Trust, Ltd., Great Western Ry. Co., Ltd. Chmn. Coal Prodn. Council since 1940. Address: Paddington Station, London, W. 2, England. Died May 6, 1949.

PORTER, Claude R., lawyer; b. Moulton, Ia., July 8, 1872; s. George D. and Hannah (Rodman) P.; ed. Centerville (Ia.) High Sch., Parsons Coll., Fairfield, Ia., 1 yr.; student St. Louis Law Sch., 1 year; m. Maude Boutin, Dec. 27, 1899; children—George, Julia, Martha, Mary. Admitted to Iowa bar, 1893, and began practice at Centerville; continued until 1918. Sergt.-maj. 50th Ia. Inf., Spanish-Am. War. Mem. Ia. Ho. of Rep., 1896-1900, Senate, 1900-04; Dem. candidate for sec. of state of Ia., 1898, for gov., 1906, 10, 18, for U.S. senator, 1908, 09, 11; U.S. atty. Southern Dist. of Ia., 1914-18 (resigned); spl. asst. atty. gen. of U.S., prosecution of I.W.W.'s during World War, including W. D. Haywood; asst. atty. gen. of U.S., in charge of criminal bus., 1918-July 16, 1919 (resigned); chief counsel Fed. Trade Commn., July 1919-Oct. 1, 1920, special counsel until 1924, resigned and resumed practice at Des Moines, Ia.; apptd. mem. Interstate Commerce Commn., to fill vacancy, Jan. 1928, and has since served as mem., chmn. commn. during 1932. Dem. candidate for U.S. senator, 1920, also 1926; del.-at-large and chmn. Ia. delegation to Dem. Nat. Conv., Denver, 1908, Baltimore, 1912, and New York, 1924. Former mem. Ia. State Board Edn. Presbyterian. Mason (Shriner). Club: Cosmos (Washington). Home: Des Moines, Ia. Address: Interstate Commerce Commn. Bldg., Washington, D.C. Died Aug. 17, 1946.

PORTER, David Dixon, officer U.S. Marine Corps; b. Washington, D.C., 1878; s. Col. Carlile Patterson Porter; g.s. famous admiral of same name; m. Winifred Metcalf Mattingly, June 24, 1908; 1 dau., Carlile Patterson. Commissioned officer U.S. Marine Corps, 1899, and advanced through the grades to maj. gen.; served through Spanish-Am. War, Boxer war in China and in Philippines; adj. and insp. U.S. Marine Corps, Washington, D.C., from 1929; now retired. Awarded Medal of Honor, 1933. Home: 2023 De Lancey Place, Philadelphia, Pa. Died Feb. 25, 1944.

PORTER, Frank Chamberlin, theologian; b. Beloit, Wis., Jan. 5, 1859; s. Prof. William and Ellen Gertrude (Chapin) P.; A.B., Beloit Coll., 1880, A.M., 1883, D.D., 1897; Chicago Theol. Sem., 1881-82; Hartford Theol. Sem., 1884-85; B.D., Yale, 1886, Ph.D., 1889, D.D., 1931; m. Delia W. Lyman, June 10, 1891; children—Lyman Edwards, William Quincy. Instr. Bibl. theology, Yale, 1889-91, Winkley prof., 1891-1927, prof. emeritus since 1927; lecturer on theology, Peking (China) U., 1924-25. Mem. Soc. Bibl. Lit. and Exegesis. Author: The Yecer Hara, in Biblical and Semitic Studies, 1901; Messages of the Apocalyptical Writers, 1905; The Pre-existence of the Soul in the Book of Wisdom and in the Rabbinical Writings, in O.T. and Semitic Studies, 1907; The Mind of Christ in Paul (Nathaniel W. Taylor lectures), 1929; Toward a Biblical Theology for the Present, in Contemporary American Theology, 2d series (contains list of publs.), 1933. Contbr. of articles in Hastings Bible Dictionary on Apocrypha, Judith, Proselyte, Book of Revelation, etc. Address: 266 Bradley St., New Haven, Conn. Died Jan. 24, 1946.

PORTER, Gilbert Edwin, lawyer; b. Eau Claire, Wis., Dec. 9, 1863; s. Gilbert Edwin and Kate (Tewkesbury) P.; m. Edith Lorimer; children—Gilbert Edwin (dec.), Burford Lorimer. Mem. Am. and Chicago bar assns. Clubs: Chicago, Saddle and Cycle, Old Elm. Home: 900 N. Michigan Av. Office: 72 W. Adams St., Chicago, Ill. Died Mar. 4, 1942.

PORTER, Henry Alford, clergyman; b. Fredericton, N.B., Nov. 15, 1871; s. Rev. Theodore Harding and Elizabeth (Estabrook) P.; U. of N.B.; B.A., McMaster U., Toronto, 1894; grad. Rochester Theol. Sem., 1899; D.D., Central Coll. of Iowa, 1905, McMaster U., 1915, Acadia U., 1929; m. Elizabeth Brethour, May 16, 1899. Ordained Bapt. ministry, 1895; pastor Bridgewater, N.S., 1895-96, Kentville, 1896-97, 1st Ch., Cedar Rapids, Ia., 1899-1904, 1st Ch., Oklahoma City, 1904-07, Walnut St. (1st) Ch., Louisville, Ky., 1907-13, Gaston Av. Ch., Dallas, Tex., 1913-16, 2d Ch., Atlanta, Ga., 1916-23, Third Church, St. Louis, Mo., 1923-29, First Ch., Charlottesville, Va., 1929-45. Pres. Met. Ch. Fed., St. Louis, 1926. Y.M.C.A. service 7 mos., World War. Frequent contbr. to secular and religious press; author of religious pamphlets. Club: Colonnade. Address: (winter) "Rock Hill," Charlottesville, Va.; (summer) "The Porter's Lodge," Oak Bluffs, Miss. Died Nov. 8, 1946.

PORTER, H(enry) Hobart, pub. utility official; b. New York, N.Y., Mar. 12, 1865; s. Henry Hobart and Annie Metcalf (Dwight) P.; M.E., Sch. of Mines (Columbia), 1886; hon. LL.D., Hobart Coll., 1930; D.Eng., Rennsselaer Poly., 1938; m. Katharine Delano Porter, June 18, 1891. Mining engring., Mexico and Ariz., until 1894; mem. firm Sanderson & Porter, 1894-1941; chmn. bd. Am. Water Works & Electric Co., West Penn Electric Co.; vice-pres. Esperanza Land Corp.; director McLellan Stores Co., Mercantile Ins. Co. of America (New York), Monongahela Power Co., Brooklyn-Manhattan Transit Corp., Hudson & Manhattan R.R. Co., W. Penn Power Co., Ann Arbor R.R. Co., Brooklyn & Queens Transit Corp., Chem. Bank & Trust Co., Tobacco Products Corp., United Stores Corp., North British & Mercantile Ins. Co., Mercantile Insurance of America, West Penn Railways Company. Trustee Columbia University. Member American Society Civil Engineers, American Inst. Mining and Metall. Engrs., Am. Soc. Mech. Engrs., Am. Soc. Elec. Engrs. Clubs: Century, University, City Midday, Union, Columbia University (New York); Rockaway Hunting; Bohemian (San Francisco); Lawrence Beach, The Pilgrims. Home: Lawrence, L.I. Office: 50 Broad St., New York, N.Y. Died Feb. 9, 1947.

PORTER, James Hyde, mfr.; b. Covington, Ga., Jan. 24, 1873; s. Oliver Saffold and Julia (McCrackin) P.; student Emory U., 1889; Goldsmith & Sullivan Business Coll., 1889; LL.D., Mercer U., 1937; m. Nancy Olive Swann, Dec. 18, 1902 (died Aug. 3, 1939). Clk. in cotton mill, 1890-1907; treas., later v.p., Bibb Mfg. Co., 1910-12, exec. v.p., 1914-35, vice chmn. bd. since 1935; dir. First Nat. Bank, Macon Federal Loan & Savings Assn. Trustee Wesleyan Coll., Bibb County Ednl. Bd. Democrat. Methodist. Mem. of Elks. Clubs: Rotary, Idle Hour Country. Home: P.O. Box 1061, Porterfield, Macon, Ga. Died June 13, 1949.

PORTER, Joseph Franklin, public utilities; b. near Woodbine, Iowa, June 27, 1863; s. Francis Joseph and Lucy Frances P.; B.C.E., Ia. State College, 1884; professional degree of Elec. Engring. from same, 1934; LL.D., Mo. Valley Coll., Marshall, 1933; m. Jennie R. Henderson, June 27, 1888; children—Clyde H., Dugald G. (dec.), Mildred (dec.), Marjory, Joseph F., Ralph E. (dec.). Began in electrical engineering, 1885; entered contracting work at St. Louis, 1887; sold out business to Edison United Mfg. Co., 1889, and was with that co. at N.Y. City 2 years. In street ry. supply and equipment business, 1891-92; pres. Alton Ry., Gas and Electric Co., 1893-1906, Tri-City Ry. and Light Co., Davenport, Ia., Rock Island and Moline, Ill., 1906-17; v.p. German Savings Bank, 1912-17; chmn. exec. com. United Light & Rys., 1912-15; pres. Cedar Rapids & Marion City Ry. Co., 1912-15; became pres. Kansas City Power & Light Co., 1917, now chairman. Pres. N.E. Nat. Bank & Trust Co., 1925-27, chmn. exec. com., 1928; dir. Safety Federal Savings & Loan Assn., Union Nat. Bank, Kansas City Fire & Marine Ins. Co., Nat. Fidelity Life Ins. Co., v.p. and dir. Mission Oil Co. (natural gas). Mem. Am. Inst. of Elec. Engrs., Am. Soc. M.E., Ia., Mo. and Kan. state hist. socs., Mo. Valley Hist. Soc., Tau Beta Pi. Republican. Presbyterian. Mason (Shriner). Clubs: University, Kansas City, Kansas City Athletic, Rotary, Kansas City Country, Mission Hills Country. Home: 825 W. 56th St. Office: 1330 Baltimore Av., Kansas City, Mo. Died Nov. 7, 1942.

PORTER, Louis Hopkins, lawyer; b. New York, N.Y., Mar. 16, 1874; s. Timothy Hopkins and Louise (Hoyt) P.; A.B., Yale, 1896; LL.B., New York Law Sch., 1898; m. Ellen Marion Hatch, Sept. 28, 1901; children—Louise Hoyt, Louis H. Joyce, Beatrice (dec.). Admitted to N.Y. bar, 1898; law clk., Wheeler Cortiss, 1898-1900; mem. firm Nicholas & Porter, 1900-02, Porter & Barnes, 1907-10, Porter & Taylor since 1920; dir. and gen. counsel Yale & Towne Mfg. Co., Alpha Portland Cement Co., Hans Rees' Sons, Inc.; dir. Atlantic, Gulf & Pacific Co. Mem. Am. and N.Y. State bar assns., New York County Lawyers Assn., Assn. Bar City New York, Phi Beta Kappa; asso. mem. Am. Ornithologists' Union. Clubs: Yale, Uptown (New York); Special Car, Woodway Country. Home: Stamford, Conn. Office: 60 E. 42d St., New York, N.Y. Died Jan. 10, 1940.

PORTER, Newton Hazelton, judge; b. Somerville, N.J., Apr. 13, 1877; s. Edward Baldwin and Emma Jane (Hazelton) P.; ed. evening sch., New York U., LL.B., 1902; m. Alice Bodine Chamberlain, June 15, 1904; children—Newton H., Jr., Elizabeth B. (Mrs. William H. Seyfert), Eleanor C. (Mrs. Alfred P. Degenhardt), Catherine A. (Mrs. W. Paul Bowden), Richard D. Advanced from office boy to chief deputy, Collector of Internal Revenue, Newark, 1889-1910; admitted to N.J. bar as atty., 1904, counsellor, 1907; practiced law, 1910-24; judge Court Common Pleas, Essex County, N.J., 1924-26; judge Circuit Court, 1926-38; justice Supreme Court of N.J. since 1938. Mem. Montclair Bd. of Edn., Jan.-Apr. 1924; pres. N.J. State Chamber of Commerce, 1921-23. Mem. Am., N.J. and Essex County bar assns. Republican. Episcopalian. Home: 337 Grove St. Address: 46 Church St., Montclair, N.J. Died May 16, 1945.

PORTER, Russell Williams, explorer; b. Springfield, Vt., Dec. 13, 1871; s. Frederick W. and Caroline (Sillsbie) P.; studied architecture, Mass. Inst. Tech.; M.S. (hon.), Norwich U., 1917; m. Alice Belle Marshall, 1907; children—Marshall (dec.), Caroline. Made 8 trips to Arctic regions with Peary, Fiala-Ziegler, Baldwin-Ziegler, as artist, astronomer, topographer, surveyor or collector for natural history; made 3 trips into interior of Alaska, British Columbia and Labrador. Instr. architecture, Mass. Inst. Tech., 1916-17; optical work, Bur. of Standards, Washington, D.C., 1917-18; now asso. in optics and instrumental design, Calif. Inst. Tech. Contbr. to astron. jours. Home: Pasadena, Calif. Died Feb. 22, 1949.

PORTER, William Townsend, physiologist; b. Plymouth, O., Sept. 24, 1862; s. Dr. Frank Gibson and Martha (Townsend) P.; M.D., St. Louis Med. Coll. (Washington U.), 1885, D.Sc., 1915; post-grad. studies univs. of Kiel, Breslau and Berlin, Germany; LL.D., U. of Md., 1908. Resident physician St. Louis City Hosp., 1886-87; for some time in charge of med. and surg. work in same; prof. physiology, St. Louis Med. Coll., 1887-93; asst. prof. physiology, Harvard, 1893-98, asso. prof., 1898-1906, prof. comparative physiology, 1906-28, now emeritus. Author: Introduction to Physiology, 1900; Shock at the Front, 1918; also various monographs and papers on physiol. subjects. Home: Dover, Mass.* Died Feb. 16, 1949.

PORTERFIELD, Lewis Broughton, naval officer; b. Greenville, Ala., Oct. 30, 1879; s. James Richard and Flora McFayden (Cowart) P.; B.S., U.S. Naval Acad., 1902; student U.S. Naval War Coll., 1924-25; m. Maud Paxton Starke, Aug. 5, 1908; children—Paul Lee, Alice Starke, James Temple Starke. Commd. ensign U.S. Navy, May 5, 1902, and advanced through grades to capt., Feb. 16, 1925; nom. rear adm., Dec. 12, 1935. Mem. Soc. of Cincinnati. Awarded D.S.M. (U.S.); Italian War Cross. Protestant. Clubs: Army and Navy (Washington, D.C.); Bohemian (San Francisco). Address: Navy Department, Washington, D.C. Died Apr. 5, 1942.

PORTNOFF, Alexander, sculptor and artist; b. Russia, Jan. 1, 1887; s. Esaia and Edith (Schapochnik) P.; came to U.S., 1908 and naturalized citizen, 1915; A.B. in Architecture, Odessa (Russia) Sch. Fine Arts, 1906; ed. Pa. Acad. Fine Arts, 1910; traveling scholarships in Europe, 1912-13; m. Marie Florence Brustin, 1920. Engaged in sculpture and painting since 1915. Represented in Allentown (Pa.) Museum, Milwaukee Art Inst., Brooklyn Museum of Art, Phila. Coll. of Pharmacy and Science, Philadelphia Museum of Art, American-Swedish Historical Museum, Hahnemann Medical Center, Univ. of Chicago, South Philadelphia High Sch., Atlanta (Ga.) Universities, Museum of Western Art, Moscow, U.S.S.R.; head of John Dewey at U. of Chicago; head of Carl Sandburg at Swedish Historical Mus., Phila.; Dr. Joseph Brinton, Phila. Mus. Art; Dr. W. E. B. Dubois, Atlanta U. Honor Award, Panama Pacific Internat. Exposition, San Francisco, 1915. Dir. Am.-Russian Inst. Editor of "Letters," American Russian Institute, Philadelphia. Member Nat. Sculpture Soc., Am. Fedn. of Arts. Studio: 908 Clinton St., Philadelphia 7; and High Point, Long Beach Island, N.J. Died Dec. 20, 1949. Buried in Philadelphia.

POST, Alice Thacher; b. Boston, Mass., June 8, 1853; d. Thomas and Katharine (Worcester) Thacher; g.d. of Rev. Thomas Worcester, (D.D.); ed. pvt. schs. of Newtonville, Mass., Brooklyn and New York; diploma Mrs. Sylvanus Reed's Sch., New York, 1871; m. Louis Freeland Post, Dec. 2, 1893 (died Jan. 10, 1928). Asst. on the New-Church Messenger, Orange, N.J., 1882-93; coadjutor editor of The New Earth, New York, 1889-93; coadjutor editor, 1898-1906, mng. editor, 1906-13, The Public, Chicago. Swedenborgian. Mem. Anti-Imperialist League (v.p.), Am. Proportional Representation League (v.p.), Women's Peace Party (v.p. 1915-17); del. Women's Internat. Congress, The Hague, 1915, Women's Internat. League of Peace and Freedom, Zürich, 1919, Washington, 1924; mem. U.S. sect. Pan-Am. Internat. Women's Com. Address: 2513 12th St. N.W., Washington 9, D.C. Died Feb. 2, 1947.

POST, Josephine Fowler, suffragist; b. Paducah, Ky., Nov. 25, 1870; d. Joseph Henry and Mattie

(Leech) Fowler; grad. Miss Florence Hines pvt. sch., Paducah, 1887; m. Edmund Morrow Post, Nov. 16, 1892 (died Sept. 17, 1900); 1 son, Joseph Fowler (dec.). Speaker on patriotic and woman suffrage topics. Lobbyist for Am. Woman Suffrage Assn. in behalf of Fed. Suffrage Amendment, 1917-19; mem. exec. bd. Am. Women Suffrage Assn., 1916-26; one of 4 dirs. for Ky. for League of Women Voters; a divisional dir. Y.W.C.A.; Ky. mem. women's div. of George Washington Sulgrave Manor Assn.; apptd. mem. Ky. State Commn. George Washington Bicentennial; Ky. chmn. for Woman's Centennial Congress, 1840-1940; a Ky. sponsor for Daughters of Am. Constn.; local chmn. Nat. Council of Women for W.C.T.U.; chmn. 1st Dist., Christian Citizenship, W.C.T.U.; mem. advisory bd. Salvation Army, Kentucky Defense Committee. Local chairman American Foundation; legislative chmn. Woman's Hosp. League; apptd. by Gov. to represent Ky. in The Centennial of Thomas Jefferson, July 1926, at Monticello and U. of Va.; mem. Ky. Museum Com., Ky. chapter "The English Speaking Union" (Louisville); Mayor's Reception Co., Paducah, during war duration. Paducah Museum Com. Ex-regent and vice regent Paducah Chapter D.A.R., U.D.C.; mem. Order of Book Fellows. Methodist (teacher of Bible class 20 years). Clubs: Delphic (pres.), Woman's (legislative chmn.), Paducah Country; Filson (Louisville); Woman's Nat. Democratic of Washington (charter mem.), Nat. Garden Club of America. Radio and pub. speaker. Received medal "The Pioneer Club Woman," Nat. Fedn. Women's Clubs, on Fedn.'s 50th anniversary, 1940; guest at presentation of Chi Omega Assn. medal to Mrs. Carrie Chapman Catt, White House, Washington, 1941. Home: 619 Kentucky Av., Paducah, Ky. Died Sept. 1, 1946; buried on Peace Av., Oak Grove Cemetery, Paducah, Ky.

POST, Régis Henri, ex-govenor; b. N.Y. City, Jan. 28, 1870; s. Albert Kintzing and Marie Caroline (de Trobriand) P.; A.B., Harvard, 1891; law student New York U., 1891; m. Carolyn Beatrice Post, Mar. 6, 1895. Mem. N.Y. Assembly, 1899-1900; auditor of Porto Rico, 1903, sec. of P.R., 1904-07, gov., 1907-09. Republican. Chmn. Prog. Party, Suffolk County, N.Y., 1912-14. Adj. Am. Ambulance Corps, Am. Hosp., Paris, 1914-15; sec. Am. Soc. Relief French War Orphans, 1915; capt. Am. Red Cross in Italy, 1917-18; chmn. N.Y. State Bur. Govt. Loan Orgn., 1919. Decorated Cavalier Ufficiale Corona d'Italia. Mem. Delta Phi. Club: Harvard. Home: Bayport, N.Y. Office: 16 Exchange Pl., New York. Died Oct. 5, 1944.

POTEAT, James Douglass, lawyer; b. Philadelphia, Pa., Apr. 14, 1903; s. Edwin McNeill and Harriet Hale (Gordon) P.; A.B., Furman U., Greenville, S.C., 1923; LL.B., 1926; J.S.D., Yale U., 1933; m. Mary W. Lawton, Feb. 21, 1924; children—Thomas Lawton, James Douglass, Jr. Admitted to S.C. bar, 1926, N.C. bar, 1937. Practice as asso. firm, Haynsworth & Haynsworth, Greenville, S.C., 1926-30; mem. Nettles & Poteat, Greenville, 1933-36; asso. prof. law, Furman U., 1929-30, prof., 1930-32; prof. law, Duke U., 1936-46 on leave, 1942-46; visiting prof., Univ. of N.C., summer, 1940. Univ. of California, 1941; assistant general counsel Board Economy Warfare Foreign Econ. Adminstrn., Washington, D.C.; dir. fgn. service personnel, Dep. Minister Econ. Warfare Div., U.S. embassy; spl. asst. to U. S. Ambassador, London, Eng., 1942-45. Deputy commr., Am. Red Cross, Pacific Ocean Areas, Hdqrs., Hawaii; executive vice chairman American Red Cross, 1945-46; executive vice pres. Am. Cancer Society, 1946. Mem. N.C. bar assn., Phi Delta Phi, Kappa Alpha. Democrat. Baptist. Author: Sturges' Cases and Material on the Law of Debtors' Estates (with Eugene V. Rostow), 3d edit., 1940. Home: 345 E. 68th St. Office: 444 E. 68th St., New York, N.Y. Died Mar. 17, 1950.

POTT, Francis Lister Hawks, coll. pres.; b. New York, N.Y., Feb. 22, 1864; s. James and Olivia (Hawks) P.; L.H.B., Columbia, 1883; B.D., Gen. Theol. Sem., 1886; D.D., Trinity Coll., 1900, U. of Edinburgh, 1910; S.T.D., Columbia, 1929; m. S. N. Wong, Aug. 23, 1888; children—James Hawks, William Sumner Appleton, Walter Graham Hawks, Olivia Hawks; m. 2d, E. G. Cooper, 1919. Deacon, 1886; priest, 1888, P.E. Ch.; pres. St. John's U., Shanghai, China, 1888-1941, now pres. emeritus. Elected missionary bishop of Wuhu, China, 1910, but declined. Decorated Order of Chiaho, 2d class (China). Translator: (into Chinese) Commentary on the Apostles' Creed, 1888; Science Primer, 1888; Physical Geography, 1890; Life of Christ, 1890; Parables of Christ, 1892; Extension of the Kingdom, 1894; Life of Alexander Hamilton, 1911. Author: The Outbreak in China, 1900; A Sketch of Chinese History, 1907; The Emergency in China, 1913; Short History of Shanghai, 1928. Address: St. John's University, Shanghai, China.* Died Mar. 7, 1947.

POTTER, John Milton, coll. president; b. Idaho Springs, Colo., Oct. 22, 1906; s. Milton Chase and Camilla (Barber) P.; A.B., Harvard, 1926, A.M., 1930, Ph.D., 1935; Ecole des Hautes Etudes, U. of Paris, 1926-27, 1932-33; L.H.D., Hamilton College, 1943; m. Faith Alden Eddy, June 16, 1928; children—Mary Alden, Nicholas Warren. Taught history and literature, Harvard, 1927-41; senior tutor Eliot House, 1933-41; special asst. Office of Coordinator of Information and Office of Strategic Services, Washington, D.C., 1941-42; pres. Hobart and William Smith Colleges, Colleges of the Seneca, Geneva, New York, since 1942. Mem. Am. Hist. Assn., Mediæval Acad., Nat. Edn. Assn., Assn. Colls. and Univs. of State of N.Y. (sec.-treas. 1944-47). Episcopalian. Clubs: Century, Harvard (N.Y. City); Rotary, University (Geneva, N.Y.). Home: 690 S. Main St. Office: Coxe Hall, Geneva, N.Y. Died Jan. 9, 1947; buried in Milwaukee, Wis.

POTTER, Mark Winslow, lawyer; b. Kaneville, Ill., Jan. 9, 1866; s. Dr. Merritt F. and Harriet E. P.; LL.B., New York U., 1888; m. Elizabeth Owens. Began practice at New York, 1888; formerly mem. firm Hornblower, Miller, Garrison & Potter; pres. Pa. Coal and Coke Corp.; mem. interstate Commerce Commn., June 1920-Feb. 1925; resumed practice. Receiver C.M.&St.P. Ry. until Mar. 1, 1928. Member N.Y. State Bar Assn., Assn. Bar City of N.Y. Clubs: Metropolitan, Midday (New York); Cosmos (Washington, D.C.). Home: 277 Park Av. Office: 70 E. 45th St., New York, N.Y. Died Aug. 12, 1942.

POTTER, Thomas Albert, chmn. Elgin Nat. Watch Co.; b. of American parentage, Dresden, Germany, June 16, 1883; s. Henry Clay and Emily (Spooner) P.; ed. Episcopal Acad., Phila., Closelet Sch., Lausanne, Switzerland, and Lawrenceville (N.J.) Sch. until 1902, Princeton, 1906; m. Eleanor Horn, Sept. 20, 1913; children—Thomas A., Gordon, Joan. Began as salesman Quaker Oats Co., N.Y. City, 1906, and continued in advertising and mfg. depts., then mill supt. at Hamburg, Germany, 1909-12, gen. mgr. at Saskatoon, Can., 1912-19, production and costs depts., Chicago, 1919-29, v.p in charge purchasing, 1929-31; pres. Elgin Nat. Watch Co., 1932-48; dir. Public Service Co. of Northern Ill., Chicago Nat. Bank, Mfrs. Assn., Continental Casualty Co., Bell & Howell Co. Episcopalian. Clubs: University, Onwentsia, Chicago. Home: Lake Forest, Ill. Office: Elgin National Watch Co., Elgin, Ill. Died Jan. 21, 1949.

POTTER, Wilfrid Carne, insurance exec.; b. Alexandria, Va., Feb. 10, 1861; s. George F. and Cecelia L. (Carne) P.; student St. John's Acad., Alexandria, 1870-72 and 1874-78; m. Kathryn Cullen, July 17, 1895; children—Ethel (Mrs. George Parkers), Olga (wife of Comdr. Liggett, U.S.N. retired), Loris; m. 2d, Minnie Gill, Apr. 6, 1908; children—Doreen (Mrs. Edward Staley, Jr.), Dorothy (Mrs. George L. Hack). Primary sch. teacher, 1878-82; local ins. agt., 1882-88; N.Y. state gen. agt., 1888-89, spl. traveling agt., 1890-1911; sec. Preferred Accident Ins. Co. of N.Y., 1912-27, pres. since 1928, chmn. bd. since 1929; chmn. bd. Indemnity Co. N.Y.; treas. and dir. Atwood Grape Fruit Co., N.Y. Fellow N.Y. Ins. Fraternity. Protestant. Mason (32°, Scottish Rite). Clubs: Downtown Athletic, Upper Deck (N.Y. City). Home: 20 Forest Rd., Madison, N.J. Office: 80 Maiden Lane, New York, N.Y. Died June 12, 1947.

POTTS, James Henry, editor; b. Woodhouse, Norfolk, Ont., June 12, 1848; s. Rev. Philip and Frances A. (Buck) P.; grad. Mayhew Business Coll., Albion, Mich., 1866; hon. A.M., Northwestern U., 1882; D.D., Albion Coll., 1885, LL.D., 1910; m. Alonsa C. Cole, Sept. 8, 1869 (died Feb. 8, 1922); children—James Riston, Oscar Ferdinand (dec.), Florence Alonsa, Alice Elna (Mrs. Prescott B. Ross), Arthur Ninde (dec.). Taught sch., 1866-69; entered M.E. ministry, 1869; asso. editor, 1877-85, editor, 1885-1917, Mich. Christian Advocate. Del. to Gen. Conf., 1888, 92, 96, 1900, 04; fraternal del. Gen. Conf. Methodist Ch. of Can., 1894, Ecumenical Meth. Conf., Toronto, 1911. Served in 6th Mich. Cav., 1865-66. Author: Pastor and People, 1879; Golden Dawn, 1880; Spiritual Life, 1884; Our Thrones and Crowns, 1885; Perrine's Principles of Church Government, 1887; Faith Made Easy, 1888; The Lord's Day Our Sabbath, 1890; Living Thoughts of John Wesley, 1891; Back to Oxford, 1903; The Upward Leading, 1905; Sunshine All the Year, 1907; Black and White, 1908; My Gift to Thee, 1910; Every Life a Delight, 1914; Songs of Character, 1923; Life, Faith and Home, 1923; All Things New, 1937. Home: Algonac, Mich. Died Mar. 11, 1942.

POUND, Earl Clifford, realtor; b. Wamego, Kan., July 14, 1876; s. Mandeville M. and Mary (Lyons) P.; grad. high sch., Neosha Falls, Kan., 1896; m. Erna M. Sacre, Oct. 21, 1909; children—Harold Sacre, Raymond Lyons, Marian. Engaged in farming and investigating farm practices, Kan., Minn., S.D., Ida., Wash. and Calif., 1896-1901; U.S. land atty., 1904-33; also engaged in farming and developing irrigated lands since 1904; mem. Pound & Plush, grading contractors, 1909-16; pres. Imperial Water Co. No. 8, 1913-14; v.p. Imperial Grain Growers, Inc., 1922-23; president Imperial Irrigation Dist., 1924-32. Mayor, City of Brawley, Calif., 1911-12. Member Calif.-Ariz., Colorado River Regulation Com., 1912-14; mem. Calif., Colorado River Commn., 1927-31 (chmn. preliminary commn. Jan.-July 1927); mem. exec. com. Boulder Dam Assn. Progressive Democrat; dir. Brawley Dem. Club, 1938-39; sec. Brawley Forum of Current Events, 1939-40. Mason (Shriner), Elk, Odd Fellow. Home: Brawley, Calif. Died May 28, 1945; buried in Forest Lawn Memorial Park, Glendale, Calif.

POWE, Thomas Erasmus (pō), nat. comdr. Sons of Confederate Vets.; b. Cheraw, S.C., Jan. 5, 1872; s. Capt. James Harrington (C.S. Army) and Josephine Elizabeth (Robbins) P.; ed. Harvard, 1890-94, astron. research, Astron. Observatory, 1890-95; m. Grace McCulloch, Nov. 10, 1910; children—Josephine Paxton (Mrs. Robert Haywood Jackson), Grace McCulloch (Mrs. Walker Evans Crosby), Margaret Lyhn. In lumber business in St. Louis and Memphis, Tenn., 1898-1909; organized Thomas E. Powe Lumber Co., St. Louis (mills at Texarkana, Tex., Americus, Ga.), 1909, and since pres.; pres. Powe Mill & Lumber Co., Texarkana, Tex. Mem. Sons of Confederate Vets. since 1899; comdr. Sterling Price Camp, St. Louis, 1905-09; adj. chief of staff Mo. Div., 1901-09; mem. staff of comdr. in chief, 1901-02, organizer gen. exec. council and mem., 1909-12, 1938-40; commissary in chief, 1936-37; comdr. Trans.-Miss. Dept., 1938-39; mem. staff of comdr. in chief, 1937-38, 1938-39; comdr. in chief since 1939. Chmn. Joint Americanism Com. of Mo. Mem. Sons of the Revolution (pres. 1935-36), Order of the Stars and Bars, Nat. Hardwood Lumber Assn., Nat. Lumber Exporters Assn., Philippine Mahogany Mfrs. Assn., Lumberman's Exchange of St. Louis (past pres.), St. Louis Chamber of Commerce (chmn. lumbermen's div.). Clubs: University, Noonday (St. Louis). Died Oct. 17, 1941.

POWELL, Caroline Amelia, engraver on wood; born Dublin, Ireland; pupil of W. J. Linton and Timothy Cole; studied drawing at the Cooper Union and the Nat. Acad. Design, New York; engraving under W.J. Linton and Timothy Cole. Engraved for the Century Magazine, 1880-95; only woman in America who practices wood engraving as an art in the style of the famous revival of about 1880. Exhibited at Berlin, Munich, Paris, etc.; medal, Chicago Expn., 1892; silver medal, Bufafalo Expn., 1901. Mem. Soc. Am. Wood Engravers. Home: 1762 N. St. N.W., Washington. Died Apr. 15, 1935.

POWELL, Carroll A., army officer; b. Ohio, Sept. 3, 1892; E.E., U. of Cincinnati, 1917; M.S., Yale, 1922; grad. Signal Sch., 1923, Army Indsl. Coll., 1935. Commd. 2d lt., U.S. Army, 1917, and advanced through the grades to brig. gen., 1944. Address: War Dept., Washington 25, D.C. Died June 20, 1948; buried in Arlington National Cemetery.

POWELL, Elmer Ellsworth, prof. philosophy; b. Clayton, Ill., Aug. 16, 1861; s. Curtis and Margaret (Welch) P.; A.B., U. of Mich., 1885; S.T.B., Boston U., 1890; studied univs. of Halle and Bonn, Germany, 1896-99, Ph.D., Bonn, 1899; m. Blanche Lottie Swasey, Nov. 8, 1893 (died Jan. 1931); 1 dau., Enrichetta Dorotea (wife of Prof. Carl Murchison); m. 2d, Mrs. Lady May Powell, Jan. 4, 1932. Began preaching during first year at Boston U. and organized West Roxbury Meth. Ch.; taught history of Christian Church and of Christian doctrine in a Methodist school of theology, Florence, Italy, later in Rome, 1890-96, also editor "Roman World"; prof. modern languages, Franklin and Marshall Coll., Lancaster, Pa., 1900-05; prof. philosophy, Miami U., 1905-22, now emeritus, acting prof. philosophy, 1929-30. Mayor of Oxford, O., 1924-25. Received diploma from the Alliance Française, Paris, 1900. Mem. Am. Philos. Soc., Am. Acad. of Science, Acad. of Polit. Science, Western Philos. Assn., Foreign Policy Association, Am. Polit. Science Assn., American Economic Association, Investors Fairplay League, Conf. of Methodist Laymen. Methodist. Mason (32°). Author: Spinoza's Gottesbegriff, 1899; Spinoza and Religion, 1906, 2d edit., 1941; also pamphlets New Testament Communism, So Called, Hasty Judgments; and monographs Hindrances to Straight Thinking about Social and Polit. Problems, The American Labor Racket, All Varieties of Communism and Socialism Compared with Am. Capitalism. Home: Oxford, O. Died July 7, 1947.

POWELL, Elmer Nathaniel, lawyer; b. Farmington, Del., Sept. 19, 1869; s. James B. R. and Mary Anna (Redden) P.; prep. edn., Wilmington (Del.) Conf. Acad. (Latin prize); student Johns Hopkins, 1887-88; LL.B., University of Kansas, 1895 (valedictorian), LL.M., University of Kansas City; m. Illga L. Herbel, Oct. 19, 1897; 1 dau., Dorothy Duer. Practiced at Kansas City, Mo., since 1895; head of firm Powell, Kirshner, House & Stroeker till 1923; former spl. master in chancery U.S. Dist. Court, Western Dist. of Mo. under spl. apptmts. since 1915; referee in bankruptcy, same district, 1923-27; former spl. judge State Circuit Court of Kansas City and Independence, Mo. A founder, 1895, and lecturer in the consolidated Kansas City School of Law with Univ. of Kansas City; now prof. law emeritus Univ. of Kan. City; was chmn., Ednl. Bd., southern dist. Kan. City, First World War. Apptd. mem. Non-Partisan Court Plan by pres. Mo. Bar Assn. Mem. Am. and Mo. State bar assns. (former Mo. council for same), Kan. City Bar Assn. (pres. 1915-16), Nebr. Professional Men's Club (Kan. City, Mo.), Beta Theta Pi (ex-pres.), Phi Delta Phi (ex-pres.). Congregationalist. Republican. Mason. Club: Mo. Republican (ex-pres.). Author: The Whip of Justice, 1923; The Real Mission of the Bankruptcy Court, 1924. Proposed Phi Delta Phi Inn (U. of Kansas City) was proposed to be named "Powell Chancery" in his honor. Home: Park Lane Hotel. Office: Grand Av. Temple Bldg., Kansas City, Mo. Died Aug. 25, 1946; buried in Mount Washington Cemetery, Kansas City, Mo.

POWELL, Fred Wilbur, economist; b. Three Rivers, Mass., July 21, 1881; s. Orion Alvarado and Sarah Matilda (Dunn) P.; grad. high sch., Palmer, Mass., 1899; A.B., Stanford, 1904, A.M., 1905; Ph.D., Columbia, 1918; m. Sophy Hill Hulsizer, Oct. 4, 1910 (died May 2, 1937); m. 2d, Mary Kenneth Maner, Aug. 19, 1939; 1 son, Rowland. With Haskins and Sells, certified pub. accountants, New York, 1905; successively in employ Bur. Municipal Research, New York and Phila. (dir. Phila. Bur. 1909-11), Peter White (Bridgeport, Conn., and St. Louis, Mo.), Haskins and Sells (Chicago), and again with Bur. Municipal Research (New York) until 1917 (editor, 1914-16); research asso. U. of Calif., 1917-18; trade commr. at London, Eng., 1919; chief of European Div., U.S. Bur. Foreign and Domestic Commerce, 1920; senior mem. of staff Inst. for Govt. Research (incorporated in Brookings Institution since 1928), Washington, D.C., 1920-43. Statistician U.S. Bd. of Arbitration, Conductors and Trainmen vs. Railroads, in Eastern territory, 1912; chief Div. of Tabulation and Statistics, U.S. War Trade Bd., 1918-19; mem. research staff, Fed. Coördinator of Transportation, 1933; research consultant Nat. Planning Bd., 1934. Club: Cosmos. Author: Railroad Promotion and Capitalization in the United States (with F. A. Cleveland), 1909; Railroad Finance (with same), 1912; Hall Jackson Kelley, Prophet of Oregon, 1917; The Recent Movement for State Budget Reform, 1917; British Industrial Reconstruction and Commercial Policies, 1920; The Railroads of Mexico, 1921; The Bureau of Mines, 1922; The Bureau of Animal Industry, 1927; The Bureau of Plant Industry, 1927; The Coast Guard (with D. H. Smith), 1929. Editor Hall J. Kelley on Oregon, 1932. Compiler: Control of Federal Expenditures, 1939. Home: 3705 McKinley St., Chevy Chase, D.C. Office: 722 Jackson Pl., Washington, D.C. Died June 12, 1943; buried in Rock Creek Cemetery, Washington.

POWELL, John Benjamin, newspaperman; b. Marion County, Mo., Apr. 18, 1886; s. Robert and Flora B. P.; grad. Gem City Business Coll., Quincy, Ill., also a student of the high school, same city; grad. School of Journalism, Univ. of Mo., 1910; m. Martha Hinton; children—Martha Bates, John William. Adv. mgr. Courier Post, Hannibal, Mo., 1910-13; instr. U. of Mo., 1913-17; mng. editor China Weekly Review, Shanghai, China, since 1917; editor China Press, Shanghai, 1923-25; spl. corr. Chicago Tribune, 1918-38; corr. Manchester Guardian, 1925-36; corr. at Conf. on Limitation of Armament and Pacific Problems, Washington, 1921-22; spl. rep. Am. commercial interests in China at Washington, 1920-22, and obtained Congressional enactment, China Trade Act. Reported Nationalist revolution, Central and South China, 1926-27, Sino-Russian conflict, North Manchuria, 1929, Sino-Japanese conflict, Manchuria, 1931-32; traveled in Soviet Union and Japan; wrote series for Chicago Tribune dealing with Russo-Japanese crisis and war preparation in Far East, 1934-35; corr. Daily Herald, London, 1937-41; mng. dir. China Press; covered outbreak Sino-Japanese War, Marco Polo Bridge, Peiping and Shanghai, 1937, later, in Nanking, Central and South China until outbreak of World War II; interned by Japanese, Shanghai, Dec. 20, 1941-May 23, 1942; released in serious physical condition; returned to U.S. on S.S. Gripsholm, Aug. 25, 1942; receiving med. treatment, Presbyn. Med. Center, N.Y. City, since 1942. Clubs: Overseas Press (New York); American, Columbia (Shanghai); Nat. Press (Washington). Author: Building Circulation for Country Newspapers; Who's Who in China, 1926; Efficiency in the Newspaper Plant; My Twenty-Five Years in China, 1945. Address: Grosvenor Hotel, New York, N.Y. Died Feb. 28, 1947.

POWELL, Lyman Pierson, author, editor; b. Farmington, Del., Sept. 21, 1866; s. James Ben Ralston and Mary Anna (Redden) P.; A.B., Johns Hopkins, 1890, grad. scholar, 1890-92; grad. student, U. of Wis., 1892-93; fellow, U. of Pa., 1893-95, univ. extension lecturer, 1893-95; grad. Phila. Div. Sch., 1897; D.D., Dickinson, and LL.D., U. Rochester, 1914; m. Gertrude Wilson, June 20, 1899; children—Talcott Williams, Francis Wilson. Deacon, 1897, priest, 1898, P.E. Ch.; minister, Ambler, Pa., 1897-98; rector St. John's, Lansdowne, Pa., 1898-1903, Northampton, Mass., 1904-12; prof. business ethics, New York U., 1912-13; pres. Hobart Coll. and William Smith Coll., 1913-18; vice-pres. Assn. Am. Colls., 1917-18; rector St. Margaret's Ch., N.Y. City, 1926-35. Lectured 1,500 times throughout U.S. and Can. since 1892. Mem. Phi Delta Theta, Phi Beta Kappa. Mason. Republican. Author: The History of Education in Delaware, 1893; Family Prayers, 1905; The Art of Natural Sleep, 1908; The Credentials of the Church, 1908; The Emmanuel Movement in a New England Town, 1909; Heavenly Heretics, 1910; Religion in Our Colleges and Universities, 1912; Lafayette, 1918; The World and Democracy, 1919; America and the League of Nations, 1919; The Teaching of Democracy, 1919; Popular Bibles in Cambridge Library of American Literature, 1921; So This Is School, 1922; Where the Good Schools Are (with wife), 1923; The Human Touch, 1925; Mary Baker Eddy, 1930; The Better Part, 1933; The House by the Side of the Road, 1933; The Second Seventy (with wife), 1937. Editor: American Historic Towns (4 vols.), 1898-1902; Current Religious Literature, 1902; Devotional Series (3 vols.), 1905-07; The Spirit of Democracy (with wife), 1918; The World Unrest and Its Relief (2 vols.) (with wife), 1919. Contbr. to mags. Editorial columnist Boonton Times-Bulletin and Mountain Lakes News since 1935. Home: Mountain Lakes, N.J.* Died Feb. 10, 1946.

POWELL, Richard Holmes, college prof.; b. Blakely, Ga., Mar. 3, 1875; s. Richard Holmes and Keturah Rebecca (Perry) P.; A.B., Mercer U., Macon, Ga., 1894; student U. of Chicago, 1896-97, 1900-02; M.A., U. of Colo., 1898; LL.D., U. of Ga., 1924; m. Frieda Berens, June 26, 1907; children—Alfred Edgar, Richard Berens, David Perry, Elizabeth. Prin. Tennille (Ga.) Inst., 1894-96; head dept. of English, N.M. Normal U., 1898-1903; asso. prof. English, Colo. State Teachers Coll., 1903-06; head English dept., Ga. Normal and Industrial Coll., Milledgeville, 1906-09; state supervisor of rural schs. for Ga., 1909-12; pres. Ga. State Woman's Coll., 1912-33; dean Coordinate Coll., U. of Ga., 1933-41; prof. English, University of Georgia, 1935-45; prof. emeritus English, since 1945. Member Kappa Alpha. Democrat. Presbyterian. Home: Athens, Ga. Died June 2, 1947.

POWELL, Thomas Carr, retired ry. official born Cincinnati, O.; s. William and Mary (Berrall) P.; ed. pvt. sch., Brooklyn, N.Y.; pub. schs., Dunellen, N.J., and Cincinnati, O.; Woodward High Sch., Cincinnati; m. Leigh Whittemore, June 16, 1910 (died Dec. 10, 1930); 1 dau., Mary Leigh (Mrs. Henry Fisk). Began as shipping clerk with the Monarch Oil Co.; entered railroad service with Queen & Crescent Route (now part of Southern Ry.) gen. freight office, 1915, continuing until June 1918, as asst. gen. freight agent, gen. freight agent, asst. freight traffic mgr., freight traffic mgr., v.p. in charge of all operations of So. Ry. (Lines West), C.,N.O.& T.P. Ry. Co., Ala. Great So. R.R. Co., and several subsidiary cos.; went to Washington, D.C. Nov. 1917, with War Industries Bd. as mem. Priorities Com.; made mgr., 1918, of Inland Traffic of the Bd. and spl. rep. of U.S.R.R. Adminstrn. with War Industries Bd., and served on committees having to do with transportation, including Port and Harbor Facilities Commn. of the U.S. Shipping Bd.; apptd. by Dir. Gen. Hines, Jan. 10, 1919, as dir. of Capital Expenditures of U.S.R.R. Adminstrn.; apptd. by President Wilson, Mar. 14, 1919, a mem. of Indl. Bd.; apptd. v.p. in charge of traffic and development of Erie R.R., headquarters N.Y. City, Feb. 15, 1920; pres. C.&E.I. Ry., Aug. 1, 1925, chmn. bd., Jan. 1, 1931; retired Aug. 1, 1931; pres. (1925-31) Chicago Hgts. Terminal Transfer Ry.; dir. Chicago & Western Indiana Belt Ry. of Chicago, Terminal Ry. Assn. of St. Louis, and Ry. Express Agency; dir. and mem. exec. com. Assn. of Ry. Execs.; now railroad cons.; rep. of U.S. rys. for Interstate Commerce Commn.; speaker on ry. questions. Formerly pres. C. of C., Young Men's Mercantile Library, Optimists Club (all of Cincinnati), and trustee Cincinnati Mechanics Inst. Clubs: Metropolitan, Chevy Chase (Washington); Boston (New Orleans). Home: (summer) Harbor Road, Gloucester, Mass.; (winter) 1721 State St., New Orleans. Died Sept. 9, 1945.

POWELL, William Dan, army officer; b. Kansas City, Mo., Nov. 11, 1873; s. Dan and Mary Idela (Porterfield) P.; B.S., U. of Mo., 1916; Inf. Sch., 1924-25, advanced course, Inf. Sch., 1931-32, Command and Gen. Staff School, 1939; m. Blanche Marin Sullivan, Feb. 12, 1923; children—Rosemary, Elizabeth Ann, William David. Commd. 2d. lt. inf., Reg. Army, 1917 and advanced through the grades to brig. gen.; served in France and Germany, 1917-22; prof. military science and tactics, U. of S.D., 1925-31; Philippine Islands, 1932-35; Gen. Staff duty, 3d Army Corps, 1940-41; foreign service since 1941. Decorated Liberty medal, Army of Occupation (Germany) medal, Emergency medal. Mem. Sigma Nu. Home: 7th and Casanova St., Carmel, Calif. Died Oct. 6, 1943.

POWERS, Delmar Thomas, univ. prof.; b. Greensburg, Ind., Feb. 19, 1865; s. David J. and Elizabeth (Adkins) P.; grad. Ind. State Normal Sch., 1892; A.B., Ind. U., 1897; A.M., Columbia, 1908; diploma Teachers Coll. (Columbia), 1908; studied U. of Berlin, 1912-13; m. Annette Keely, Dec. 25, 1900. Teacher, prin. and supt. schs. and instr. in normal sch.; asso. prof. and prof. edn. La. State U., dean Teachers Coll., since 1908. Mem. N.E.A., Nat. Assn. Coll. Teachers of Edn., La. State Council of Edn., Southern Soc. Philosophy and Psychology. Democrat. Baptist. Writer on ednl. topics. Home: Baton Rouge, La. Died June 29, 1948.

POWERS, Edwin B(ooth), zoologist; b. Ellis Co., Tex., Aug. 6, 1880; s. William Wilson and Evaline Crocia (Woods) P.; A.B., Trinity U., Waxahachie, Tex., 1906; M.S., U. of Chicago, 1913; Ph.D., U. of Ill., 1918; student, Cambridge U., Eng., 1922; m. Pauline Watkins, June 9, 1918; children—Edwine Watkins, Wilson Watkins, M.D. Instr. and prof. in biology, Trinity U., 1908-15; research asst. Puget Sound Biol. Sta., U. of Wash., summer, 1914, asst. in zoology, summer, 1918, prof. zoology, summers, 1919, 21, 22, 24, 27; asst. prof. zoology, Colo. Coll., 1918-19; traveled and studied Imperial Inst. (London), Danish Biol. Sta., Naples Biol. Sta., 1919-20; instr. in zoology, U. of Neb., 1920-22; asso. prof. anatomy and embryology, U. of Tenn. Med. Coll., Memphis, Tenn., 1922-23; prof. zoology and acting head of dept., U. of Tenn., Knoxville, Tenn., 1923-24, head of dept. zoology, 1924-41, head of dept. of zoology and entomology since 1941; at Marine Biol. Lab., Woods Hole, Mass., summer 1920; prof. limnology, Mt. Lake Biol. Sta., U. of Va., summer 1934; prof. physiology Franz Theodore Stone Lab., Put-in-Bay, Ohio State U., summers 1935 and 1936; stream pollution adv. to N.C. Pulp Co., 1940-41; at Solomon Island, Md. State Lab., 1945-46. Mem. A.A.A.S., Zool. Soc. America, Ecol. Soc. America (pres. 1933-34), Limnol. Soc. America, Am. Fish Soc., Entomol. Soc. America, Tenn. Acad. Science, Sigma Xi. Democrat. Presbyterian. Asso. editor of Ecology, 1925-32, Ecological Monographs, 1935-39. Contbr. of more than 65 sci. papers and monographs on salmon migration, toxicities, physiology of respiration of fishes, etc. Home: 133 E. Hillvale Drive. Office: University of Tennessee, Knoxville, Tenn. Died Aug. 25, 1949; buried Highland Memorial Cemetary, Knoxville, Tenn.

POWERS, Harry Joseph, theatrical mgr.; b. Nenagh, Tipperary County, Ireland, Sept. 15, 1859; s. Henry Joseph and Jane (Darcey) P.; brought to Chicago, with parents in childhood; ed. St. Patrick's Acad.; m. Marie F. Deegan, May 11, 1885. Began as usher, Hooley's Theatre, Chicago, 1877, became business mgr.; remodeled the theatre, 1898, changing name to Powers Theatre (building sold, 1923, and now occupied by annex to Hotel Sherman); pres. Amusement Co. of Ill., operating Illinois Theatre, Chicago. Catholic. Clubs: Union League, Exmoor Country. Home: 3800 Sheridan Rd. Office: Illinois Theatre, Chicago. Died Feb. 21, 1941.

POWLISON, Charles Ford (pou'lĭ-sŭn), sociologist; b. Pluckemin, N.J., Jan. 26, 1865; s. Joseph S. and Sarah (Van Arsdale) P.; grad. Internat. Y.M.C.A. Coll., Springfield, Mass., 1889; m. Harriet A. West, May 1, 1894 (died 1912); children—Arthur K., Mildred; m. 2d, Elise Oliphant Stearns, Aug. 25, 1920 (died Jan. 4, 1930). Was sec. to the Northwest Br. Y.M.C.A., Phila., 1889-92; instr. at Interrat. Y.M.C.A. Coll., 1893-96; sec. Y.M.C.A., Holyoke, Mass., 1896-99; dir. religious work, West Side Y.M.C.A., New York, 1899-1909; an organizer and gen. sec., New York Child Welfare Com., 1909-12; an organizer and gen. sec., Nat. Child Welfare Assn. since 1912. An originator and organize first child welfare exhibit, held New York, 1911. Mem. Am. Sociol. Soc., Nat. Conf. Social Work, Religious Edn. Assn., Nat. Kindergarten Assn. (dir.), Am. Patriotic League (gen. advisory bd.). Conglist. Home: Ridgefield, Conn. Office: 70 Fifth Av., New York, N.Y. Died July 1, 1942.

POWYS, Llewelyn, author; b. Dorchester, Eng., Aug. 13, 1884; s. Rev. Charles Francis and Mary Cowper (Johnson) P.; B.A., Corpus Christi Coll., Cambridge, 1906; m. Alyse Gregory, Sept. 30, 1924. Formerly rancher in Kenya Colony, Africa. Came to U.S. during 1920. Rationalist. Author: Confessions of Two Brothers (with John Cowper Powys), 1916; Ebony and Ivory, 1923; Thirteen Worthies, 1924; Black Laughter, 1925; Skin for Skin, 1925; The Verdict of Bridlegoose, 1926; Henry Hudson, 1927; The Cradle of God, 1929; Apples Be Ripe, 1930; Impassioned Clay, 1931; Earth Memories, 1933; Damnable Opinions, 1934; Dorset Essays, 1935. Address: Hillsdale, N.Y. Died Dec. 4, 1939.

PRAEGER, Otto, b. Victoria, Tex.; s. Herman and Louisa (Schultze) P.; attended U. of Tex., 1894-97; m. Annie C. Hardesty, Feb. 27, 1897; m. 2d, Carrie Will Coffman, Apr. 20, 1928. City clerk of San Antonio, Tex., 1900-04; postmaster Washington, D.C., 1914-15; asst. postmaster gen., Sept. 1, 1915-Mar. 31, 1921; adviser to Siamese govt. on communication and transportation, 1928-33; trustee and vice chmn. U.S. Shipping Board Merchant Fleet Corpn. since 1934. Established U.S. Govt. Air Mail, May 15, 1918, and Royal Siamese Air Mail, Mar. 1930. Democrat. Address: 1712 G St. N.W., Washington. Died Feb. 4, 1948.

PRATT, Daniel, mfr.; b. Prattville, Ala., Feb. 12, 1866; s. Merrill Edward and Julia Adelaide (Smith) P.; prep. edn., Prattville Acad.; B.A., U. of Ala., 1885, hon. LL.D.; m. Ellen Sims, Nov. 2, 1887; children—Merrill Edward, Leonard Sims (dec.), Ellen (Mrs. Oscar W. Underwood, Jr.), Julia (dec.), Jennie Allyn (Mrs. Robt. S. Wilkerson). Began active career in employ of Daniel Pratt Gin Co., Prattville, 1885; mgr. same from death of father, 1889, until 1899; an organizer, 1899, dir. Continental Gin Co., mfrs. cotton ginning machinery; an organizer Prattville Cotton Mills, 1887, and later treas. and pres.; pres. The Pratt Co. Trustee U. of Ala. for nearly 40 yrs. Mem. Phi Beta Kappa. Democrat. Methodist. Mason. Home: Prattville, Ala. Deceased.

PRATT, Don Forrester, army officer; b. Brookfield, Mo., July 12, 1892; student U. of Wis.; comd. 2d lt. Inf., Aug. 1917, and advanced through the grades to brig. gen., Aug. 1942; served as adjutant of the U.S. Army Troops, 15th Inf., Tientsin, China, 1932-36; returned to U.S., Aug. 1936; instr. Inf. Sch., Ft. Benning, Ga., 1937-41; chief of staff, 43rd Inf. Div., Camp Blanding, Fla., 1941-42; assigned to 101st Airborne Div., Aug. 1942.† Died June 6, 1944.

PRATT, Frederic Bayley, capitalist; b. Brooklyn, N.Y., Feb. 22, 1865; s. Charles and Mary Helen (Richardson) P.; A.B., Amherst, 1887, hon. A.M., 1904, and LL.D., 1917; m. Caroline A. Ladd, Oct. 17, 1889. Mem. firm Charles Pratt & Co., New York; pres. Morris Bldg. Co. Trustee and formerly pres. Pratt Inst. of Brooklyn. Clubs: University, Century. Home: 229 Clinton Av. Office: Pratt Inst., Brooklyn, N.Y. Died May 3, 1945.

PRATT, Harry Noyes, author, editor, lecturer; b. River Falls, Wis., July 14, 1879; s. George and Mary Madden (Noyes) P.; ed. pub. and normal schools; m. Antonita Cosby Gilkyson, Jan. 2, 1906. Editor and owner Lodi (Calif.) Post, 1913-14; Pacific coast rep. Old Colony Mag., 1921; asso. editor Western Jour. Edn., 1922; editor Overland Monthly and Out West Mag., 1923-25; curator Claremont Art Gallery, 1925-27. Chmn. history and landmarks com., Central Valley Council of State Chamber of Commerce, 1933-36. Dir. Louis Terah Haggin Memorial Galleries and Pioneer Museum, Stockton, 1931-36, dir. mgr. Crocker Art Gallery, Sacramento, since 1936. Mem. Am. Literary Assn. (pres. 1926-37), Calif. Writers' Club (pres. 1925-27), Poetry Soc. of America, Verse-Writers' Club of Southern Calif. (hon.), Calif. Soc. of Etchers (hon.); hon. mem. San Joaquin and Sierra camera clubs, Oregon Trail Assn. (life), Western Assn. Art Museum Dirs., Book Collectors Club; exec. sec. League of Western Writers, 1920-30. Author: Mother of Mine and Other Verse, 1918; Hill Trails and Open Sky, 1919; Etching in California, 1924; German Master Drawings of E. B. Crocker Collection, 1939. Address: E. B. Crocker Art Gallery, Sacramento, Calif. Died May 19, 1944.

PRATT, Henry Sherring, zoölogist; b. Toledo, O., Aug. 18, 1859; s. Charles and Catherine (Sherring) P.; A.B., U. of Mich., 1882; admitted to Ohio bar, 1885; Ph.D., Leipzig, 1892; univs. of Freiburg, Geneva, and Harvard, 1888-93; Innsbruck, 1902-03; Graz, 1910-11; m. Agnes Woodbury Gray, Sept. 1, 1894; 1 dau., Anna. Instr. biology, Haverford Coll., 1893-98, asso. prof. 1898-1901, prof., 1901-29, (emeritus). Instr. comparative anatomy, Cold Spring Harbor Biol. Lab., 1896-1926. Mem. Commn. for Relief in Belgium, 1916-17. Pres. Cambridge Entomol. Club, 1896; mem. Am. Soc. Naturalists, Am. Soc. Zoologists (sec. and treas. Eastern br., 1905-06); fellow A.A.A.S. Knight Order of the Crown (Belgium). Author: Invertebrate Zoölogy, 1902; Vertebrate Zoölogy, 1906, 2d edit., 1925, 3d edit., 1937; Manual of Common Invertebrates, 1916, revised edit., 1935; Manual of Vertebrates of the U.S., 1923, 2d edit., 1935; A Course in General Zoölogy, 1927; A Course in General Biology, 1927; General Biology—an Introductory Study, 1931; also various zoöl. papers. Home: Haverford, Pa. Died Oct. 6, 1946.

PRATT, Herbert Lee, corp. official; b. Brooklyn, N.Y., Nov. 21, 1871; s. Charles and Mary Helen (Richardson) P.; A.B., Amherst, 1895; m. Florence Gibb, Apr. 28, 1897. Dir. Charles Pratt & Co., Bankers Trust Co., American Can Co., Stone & Webster Inc., New York. Trustee Pratt Institute (Brooklyn). Clubs: University, Racquet and Tennis, Recess, The Links, Down Town, Riding, Piping Rock, Nassau Country. Home: 834 Fifth Av., New York, N.Y.* Died Feb. 3, 1945.

PRATT, James Bissett, coll. prof.; b. Elmira, N.Y., June 22, 1875; s. Daniel Ransom and Catharine (Murdoch) P.; A.B., Williams, 1898; A.M., Harvard, 1899; student Columbia Law Sch., 1899-1900, U. of Berlin, 1902-03; Ph.D., Harvard, 1905; LL.D., Amherst, 1930; L.H.D., Wesleyan, 1935; m. Caterina Mariotti, Aug. 5, 1911. Taught Latin in Berkeley Sch., New York, 1900; head of Latin dept., Elmira Free Acad., 1900-02; instr. philosophy, Williams Coll., 1905-06, asst. prof., 1906-13, prof. since 1913. In India, studying the native religions, 1913-14, Japan, China, and Siam, studying Buddhism, 1923-24; in Java, Indo-China and India, studying their religions, 1931-32. Pres. Am. Philos. Assn. (Eastern div.), 1935, Am. Theol. Soc., 1934-35; mem. Unitarian Commn. of Appraisal, 1934-36. Author: Psychology of Religious Belief, 1907; What Is Pragmatism?, 1909; India and Its Faiths, 1915; Democracy and Peace, 1916; The Religious Consciousness, 1920; Matter and Spirit, 1922; The Pilgrimage of Buddhism, 1928; Adventures in Philosophy, 1931; Personal Realism, 1937; Naturalism, 1939; Can We Keep the Faith?, 1941. Co-author of Essays in Critical Realism, 1920. Home: Williamstown, Mass. Died Jan. 15, 1944.

PRATT, Joseph Hersey, M.D.; b. Middleboro, Mass., Dec. 5, 1872; s. Martin Van Buren and Rebecca Adams (Dyer) P.; Ph.B., Yale, 1894; M.D., Johns Hopkins, 1898; A.M., Harvard, 1901; med. research work, univs. of Tübingen, 1902, Heidelberg, 1908; Sc.D., Colby Coll., 1941; m. Rosamond Means Thomson, Oct. 23, 1909; children—Sylvia Mayo (Mrs. John M. Kemper), Thomas Dennie, Rosamond (Mrs. Robert Walcott, Jr.), Joan. Asst. resident pathologist, 1898-99, then resident pathologist, 1899-1900, asst. visiting pathologist, 1900-02, Boston City Hosp.; asst. pathologist, Children's, and Carney hosps., and pathologist to Floating Hosp., 1900-02; instr. pathology, 1900-02, asst. in medicine, 1902-09, instr. medicine, 1909-17, Harvard Med. Sch.; prof. clinical medicine, Tufts Med. School, since 1929; fellow Rockefeller Inst., 1903-05; visiting physician to out-patient dept., Mass. Gen. Hosp., 1903-13, asst. visiting physician, 1913-17; physician in chief of Boston Dispensary, 1927-31, New England Medical Center since 1931, Joseph H. Pratt Diagnostic Hosp., Boston; cons. physician Brockton Hosp., Sharon (Conn.) Hosp., Eastern Maine Gen. Hosp. (Bangor). Mem. Assn. of Am. Physicians, Mass. Med. Soc., Am. Climatol. Clin. Assn. (pres. 1927-28), Soc. Exptl. Biology and Medicine, Soc. Advancement of Clinical Research (pres. 1910-11), Am. Physiol. Soc., Am. Pharm. Assn., Am. Soc. for Exptl. Pathology, Am. Assn. of Pathologists and Bacteriologists, Am. Acad. Arts and Sciences, Am. Coll. Physicians, Nat. Tuberculosis Assn. (dir. 1926-28). Mem. Alumni Council, Johns Hopkins U., 1908-16; advisory council, Phipps Inst., University of Pennsylvania; vice-pres. Bingham Associates Fund for Advancement of Rural Medicine. Author of numerous med. papers. Republican. Episcopalian. Clubs: Harvard, Boston. Author: (with Col. George E. Bushnell) The Physical Diagnosis of Diseases of the Chest, 1925. Commd. maj., Med. R.C., Sept. 20, 1917; chief med. service Base Hosp., and pres. tuberculosis board, Camp Devens, Mass., 1917. Home: 94 Upland Rd., Brookline, Mass. Office: 30 Bennet St., Boston, Mass. Died June 2, 1942.

PRATT, Joseph Hyde, geologist, engr.; b. Hartford, Conn., Feb. 3, 1870; s. James C. and Jennie A. (Peck) P.; Ph.B., Sheffield Scientific Sch. (Yale), 1893, Ph.D., 1896; hon. M.A., 1923; m. Mary Dicus Bayley, Apr. 5, 1899; 1 son, Joseph Hyde; m. 2d, Harriet White Peters, Aug. 29, 1930. Instr. mineralogy, Yale, 1895-97; summer, Harvard, 1895; lecturer mineralogy, U. of N.C., 1898-1901; state mineralogist of N.C., 1897-1906; state geologist, 1906-24; asst. field geologist, U.S. Geol. Survey, from 1899; prof. econ. geology, U. of N.C., 1904-25; chief Dept. Mines and Metallurgy, Jamestown Exposition, 1907. Member Internat. Jury of Awards, St. Louis Expn., 1904; spl. expert 12th U.S. Census on asbestos, etc.; dir. briquetting expts., U.S. Geol. Coal Testing Plant, St. Louis, 1904-05. Awarded diploma and gold medal, Pan-Am. Expn., 1901, for exhibit N.C. gems and gem minerals, etc.; diplomas, gold medal, and silver medals for same, Charleston Expn., 1902. Lt.-col. N.C. N.G. (engr. dept.). Pres. Am. Peat Soc., 1907-09, Southern Appalachian Good Roads Assn., 1909-15; sec. N.C. Drainage Assn., 1908-11 and 1912-23 (pres. 1911); sec. N.C. Fisheries Assn., 1911-19, N.C. Good Roads Assn., 1908-20, N.C. State Highway Commn., 1915-19, N.C. Lit. and Hist. Soc., N.C. Forestry Assn. (pres. 1925-27; chmn. exec. com., 1927-40), Am. Assn. State Highway Officials, 1914-20; pres. Nat. Assn. Shell Fish Commrs., 1912-13; dir. Am. Assn. Highway Improvement, Nat. Drainage Cong.; fellow Geol. Soc. America, Am. Chem. Soc., A.A.A.S., Nat. Geog. Soc., Mineralogical Soc. of America, Am. Geog. Soc.; mem. Am. Soc. Civil Engrs., Am. Inst. Mining Engrs., Mining and Metall. Soc. America, Sigma Xi, N.Y. Acad. Sciences, N.C. Acad. Science, Am. Forestry Assn. (dir. 1922-29 and since 1934), Nat. Parks Assn. (dir. since 1936), Wilderness Soc., Am. Road Builders Assn., Am. Fisheries Soc., Mil. Engineers Soc. (dir. since 1926); v.p. N.C. Agrl. Soc., 1921-28; pres. Western North Carolina, Inc., 1924-25; pres. Southern Forestry Congress, 1916-19 (chmn. exec. com., 1919-25; exec. sec., 1928-40); pres. Southern Appalachian Power Conf., 1922 (chmn. exec. com., 1923-40); pres. N.C. Conf. for Social Service, 1924, dir. since 1925; pres. N.C. Soc. for Preservation of Antiquities since 1940; hon. mem. Appalachian Engring. Soc.; apptd. by sec. of agr. mem. Appalachian Forest Research Council (chmn. exec. com. since 1925); chmn. Chapel Hill Chapter Am. Red Cross; pres. N.C. Symphony Soc. since 1932; pres. Battle Park Assn.; mem. advisory com. President Hoover's Timber Conservation Board; chmn. Central Welfare Com., Orange County; chmn. Chapel Hill Health and Welfare Com. since 1940; pres. Chapel Hill Pub. Recreation Commn. since 1940; chmn. Chapel Hill Negro Community Center Assn. since 1940; mem. Chapel Hill City Planning Board since 1941. Received annual award as Chapel Hill's most valuable citizen, 1940. Clubs: Cosmos (Washington, D.C.); Washington Philatelic Soc., Chapel Hill (North Carolina) Country. Contbr. many articles to scientific mags., domestic and foreign, on mineral., geol. and chem. subjects, since 1895. Publisher War Diary of Col. Joseph Hyde Pratt, 1928. Member State Council Defense. Major, Engr. R.C., 1917, and assigned to 105th Regt. Engrs.; lt. col., Nov. 11, 1917; col., Oct. 9, 1918; with regt. at Camp Sevier, Greenville, S.C.; ordered to France, May 1918; comdr. of regt. and div. engr., 30th Div., A.E.F., July 1918-May 1919; served 6 mos. at the front in Ypres sector, Flanders and Belgium, and in Somme offensive in breaking the Hindenburg line; former col. Engr. R.C., U.S. Army. Awarded D.S.M. State engr. C.W.A. for N.C., Nov. 1933-Feb. 1934; senior regional engr. C.W.A. and F.E.R.A., 1934-35; senior regional engr. Resettlement Adminstrn., 1935; research engr. Works Progress Adminstrn., 1936, 37; engr. consultant, U.S. Geol. Survey, 1938, senior engr., consultant, 1939, 40. Home: Chapel Hill, N.C. Died June 2, 1942.

PRATT, Joseph M., ex-congressman; b. Paterson, N.J., Sept. 4, 1891; s. William Brazell and Caroline Ann Pratt; ed. pub. schs., bus. colls., and Temple Univ.; m. Miriam D. Sherman, Jan. 30, 1942. Began as stenographer, then salesman, sales mgr., mfr. and distributor; owner of the J. M. Pratt & Co., and the Gochenaur Marine Co.; elected mem. 78th Congress, 2d Pa. Dist., Jan. 1943. Mem. Republican City Com., Rep. State Com.; mem. Maritime Society, Phila. Chamber of Commerce. Clubs: Penn Athletic, Poor Richard, Pen and Pencil. Mason (past. pres. Shrine Club of Phila.; rep. Grand Lodge of Free and Accepted Masons of Pa.). Home: 1901 Walnut St. Office: 525 Arch St., Philadelphia. Died July 19, 1946; buried in Arlington Cemetery, Drexel Hill, Pa.

PREBLE, Robert Bruce, physician; b. Chicago, Ill., Mar. 14, 1866; s. Eber C. and Mary Kate (Barnes) P.; A.B., U. of Mich., 1889, M.A., 1914; M.D., Northwestern U., 1891, D.Sc., 1931; interne Cook County Hosp., 1891-93; U. of Vienna, 1893-94; m. Alice M. Hosmer, June 12, 1889; children—Norman Hosmer, Barbara, Marcia. Prof. medicine, Northwestern U., since 1895; attending physician St. Luke's and Wesley hosps. Commd. maj. Med. R.C., Apr. 1917; med. chief hosp. center, Mars sur Alliers, France; discharged Jan. 31, 1919, with rank of lt. col. M.C., U.S. Army. Am. Citation and French Legion of Honor. Mem. Assn. Am. Physicians, A.M.A., Ill. State Med. Soc., Chicago Med. Soc. (pres. 1903-04), Phi Beta Kappa. Clubs: University, Racquet, Glenview Golf. Author: Pneumonia and Pneumococcus Infections, 1905. Home: 900 N. Michigan. Office: 30 N. Michigan, Chicago, Ill.* Died July 5, 1948.

PRELLWITZ, Edith Mitchill (prĕl'wĭts), painter; b. S. Orange, N.J., Jan. 28, 1865; d. Cornelius S. and Helen E. (Reed) Mitchill; studied at Art Students' League, New York, and for a short time at Paris.; m. Henry Prellwitz, Oct. 6, 1894; 1 son, Edwin Mitchill. Won 2d Hallgarten prize, Nat. Acad. Design, 1894, on picture of Hagar and Ishmael; Dodge prize, Nat. Acad. Design; received silver medal, Atlanta Expn.; won medal, Buffalo Expn., 1901; Shaw prize, Nat. Acad. Design, 1930. A.N.A. Home: 71 Cedar St., East Greenwich, R.I. Died Aug. 19, 1944.

PRENDERGAST, Charles (prĕn'dĕr-găst), artist; b. Boston, Mass. Began as carver in wood. Represented in Addison Gallery Am. Art; Phillips Acad., Andover, Mass.; Barnes Foundation, Merion, Pa.; Phillips Memorial, Washington, D.C.; Rhode Island Sch. of Design, Providence; Newark (N.J.) Mus.; Mus. Modern Art, Whitney Mus., Internat. House, N.Y. City; also many private collections. Asso. Nat. Acad. Design. Home: Westport, Conn. Died Aug. 20, 1948.

PRENTICE, Bernon Sheldon (prĕn'tĭs), investment banker; b. Brooklyn, N.Y., May 12, 1882; s. William Saterly Packer and Ella Crawford (Sheldon) P.; student St. Paul's Sch., Concord, N.H., 1897-1901; A.B., Harvard, 1905; m. Clare Ellsworth, 1908 (dec.); children—Clare Prentice (Mrs. C. Frederic Neilson, Jr.), Sheldon Ellsworth (killed in action in Pacific, Mar. 19, 1945); m. 2d, Josephine McFadden, 1924. Began with Harvey Fiske & Son, 1905; now partner Dominick and Dominick; director Fulton Trust Company, American Express Branch Chase National Bank, Fulton Safe Deposit Co. Treas. N.J. Rep. Com., 1926-31. Organized ambulance service Italian front, 1918. Former trustee and pres. Alumni Assn. St. Paul's Ch., Concord, N.H. Trustee Boys Club of N.Y., Monmouth Memorial Hosp. Decorated with Italian War Cross, Comdr. of Order of Crown of Italy; Medaille Commemorative Française (France). Mem. Fly Club, Hasty Pudding Club, Inst. of 1770 (Harvard). Republican. Episcopalian. Clubs: Union, Racquet, Harvard, Links, Recess, New York, National Golf Links, Seabright Lawn Tennis and Cricket, N.J., Jekyll Island (pres.). Home: Holmdel, N.J. Office: 14 Wall St., New York, N.Y. Died June 12, 1948.

PRESCOTT, Henry Washington, philologist; b. Boston, Mass., July 30, 1874; s. Washington L. and Rebecca A. (Boyce) P.; A.B., Harvard, 1895, A.M., 1896, Ph.D., 1901; m. Clara Walton, Apr. 27, 1905; children—Walton, Stephen, Richard. Instr. Latin, Trinity College, Hartford, Conn., 1898-99; instr. Greek and Latin, Harvard, 1899-1901; instr. Latin, U. of Calif., 1901-04, asst. prof. classical philology, 1904-09, asso. prof., 1909; asso. prof. classical philology, U. of Chicago, 1909, prof., 1911-40, prof. emeritus since 1940. Mem. Am. Philol. Assn., Am. Acad. Arts and Sciences, Delta Upsilon, Phi Beta Kappa. Club: Quadrangle. Address: 746 Cragmont Av., Berkeley, Calif. Died June 8, 1943.

PRESTON, Charles Miller, banker; b. Woodbury, Tenn., Aug. 8, 1874; s. Hugh Lawson and Thankful Caroline (Doak) P.; A.B., Bethany (W.Va.) Coll., 1897; unmarried. Began with Hamilton Nat. Bank, Chattanooga, Tenn., 1898; pres. Hamilton Nat. Bank, Knoxville, Tenn., since 1931; v.p. Hamilton Nat. Bank, Chattanooga, since 1905; dir. Hamilton Nat. Associates. Co-chmn. Reconstrn. Finance Corp. Commn. for Tenn. Presbyterian. Clubs: Cherokee Country (Knoxville); Chattanooga Golf and Country, Mountain City (Chattanooga). Home: 2722 Kingston Pike. Office: Hamilton Nat. Bank, Knoxville, Tenn. Died Sept. 5, 1947.

PRESTON, Frances Folsom (Cleveland); b. Buffalo, July 21, 1864; d. Oscar and Emma C. (Harmon) Folsom; (her father, a lawyer and former partner of Grover Cleveland, died in 1875); grad. Wells Coll., Aurora, Cayuga County, N.Y., 1885; m. President Cleveland in the White House, June 2, 1886; children—Ruth (died Jan. 7, 1904), Esther (Mrs. W. S. B. Bosanquet), Marion (Mrs. John H. Amen), Richard F., Francis G.; m. 2d, Thomas Jex Preston, Jr., at Princeton, Feb. 10, 1913. Home: Westland, Princeton, N. J. Died Oct. 29, 1947.

PRETTYMAN, Cornelius William (prĕt'ĭ-măn), college pres.; b. Leipsic, Del., July 21, 1872; s. Cornelius W. and Emma (Gooding) P.; A.B., Dickinson Coll., 1891; student Johns Hopkins, 1895-97; Ph.D., U. of Pa., 1899; m. Clara Bains, June 10, 1902; m. 2d, Charlotte Hopfe, Jan. 3, 1912. Engaged as instr., secondary schs., 1895-97; prof. of German, Dickinson Coll., 1899-44, president since December 1944. President board of trustees of Dickinson College. Dir. Camp Moosilauke, summer school for boys, Pike, N.H., 1920-30. Mem. Phi Beta Kappa, Beta Theta Pi, Omicron Delta Kappa, Republican. Methodist. Author: Higher Girls Schools of Prussia, 1910. Editor: Schiller's Dreissigjähriger, Krieg, Fulda's Der Talisman, Wildenbruch's Neid. Contbr. to ednl. iours. Home: Carlisle, Pa. Died Aug. 9, 1946.

PRETTYMAN, Forrest Johnston, clergyman; b. Brookville, Md., Apr. 7, 1860; s. Elijah B. (Ph.D.) and Lydia Forrest (Johnston) P.; student St. John's Coll. (now U. of Md.), 1876-79, Washington and Lee U., 1890-94; m. Elizabeth Rebecca Stonestreet, Oct. 17, 1888; children—Elijah Barrett, Edith S., Charles Wesley, Martha Barry. Ordained ministry M.E. Ch., S., 1888; served as pastor St. James Ch., Baltimore, Bridgewater Circuit, Va., St. Paul's Ch., Baltimore, Lexington, Va., Martinsburg, West Va., Staunton, Va., Mt. Vernon Place, Washington, D.C., Trinity Ch., Baltimore, Mt. Pleasant Ch. and Emory Ch., Washington, D.C.; served as presiding elder Washington Dist.; elected chaplain U.S. Senate for the first session of the 58th Congress, Nov. 1903 (resigned); again elected chaplain Senate, Mar. 13, 1913, and served 8 yrs. (resigned); in charge Church St. Ch., Knoxville, Tenn., to Mar. 1924, then pastor of Main Street M.E. Church, Gastonia, N.C., later of Wilson Memorial Ch., Baltimore; pastor, Fredericksburg, Va., 1930-37; retired, Oct. 1937. Member of Commn. on Universal Faith and Order, Commn. on War Work M.E. Ch., S., Ednl. Commn. M.E. Ch., S., Exec. Com. Francis Asbury Memorial Assn., Federal Council Churches of Christ; mem. Washington Com. of Federal Council on Army and Navy Chaplains. Mem. Ecumenical Conf. of Methodism, London, 1901,

Toronto, 1911; fraternal messenger to Gen. Conf. M.P. Ch., Baltimore, 1912, to Gen. Conf. Meth. Ch. of Can., Hamilton, Can., 1918. Trustee Emory U. (Atlanta, Ga.). Home: Rockville, Md. Died Oct. 12, 1945.

PREYER, Carl Adolph, musician, composer; b. Pforzheim, Germany, July 28, 1863; s. Jean and Marie (Heinz) P.; ed. Pforzheim, Germany; studied at Conservatory of Music, Stuttgart, and under Dr. Navratil, Vienna, and Profs. Urban and Barth, Berlin; m. Grace Havens, May 2, 1887; children—Frank A., Mrs. Mary McColloch, Grace; m. 2d, Frances Havens, Sept. 11, 1909; 1 dau., Emily Frances. Prof. piano, counterpoint and fugue, U. of Kan., since 1893, asso. dean School of Fine Arts since 1915. Composer: 3 sonatas for Piano (sonata in E flat major received highest rating for piano compositions with Nat. Fed. of Music Clubs, 1939); 2 Sonatas for Piano and Violin. Konzertstück for Piano and Orchestra; Theme and Variations; Scherzo in B flat minor; Preludes for Piano; Concert Etude; Improvisation; Sacred Music; The Lord's Prayer; Festival Te Deum. Strauss Concert Transcriptions for Piano; Thousand and One Nights Waltzes; Morning Journal Waltzes; Palisades (for piano); Concert Etude in F Sharp Minor (for piano). Also many Etudes and Piano Compositions. Home: 1125 Tennessee St., Lawrence, Kan. Died Nov. 10, 1947.

PRICE, Bertram John, lawyer; b. Landsford, Pa., Jan. 17, 1878; s. Thomas Morgan and Mary (Thomas) P.; A.B., Carleton Coll., 1897; m. Jessie Robinson, Feb. 21, 1905; children—Helen, John, Marian; m. 2d, Belle Moody, Feb. 10, 1923. Admitted to Ia. bar, 1899, and since practiced in Fort Dodge; county atty., Webster County, 1905-09, pres. Ia. Pub. Service Co. and Sioux City Gas and Electric Co., 1933-38, now v.p. and gen. counsel; dir. Tobin Packing Co., Ft. Dodge Nat. Bank, Ft. Dodge Gas and Electric Co. Pres. Ft. Dodge Chamber of Commerce, 1935, 36. Chmn. Cong. Dist. Rep. convs., 1910-14, Rep. county convs., 1912-14. Served as capt. inf., Ia. Nat. Guard, 1905-09. Mem. State and Webster County bar assns. Conglist. Mason (K.T.), Elk, K.P. Club: Country of Ft. Dodge (pres. 1933-35). Home: 1432 14th Av. N. Office: State Bank Bldg., Ft. Dodge, Ia. Died July 14, 1944.

PRICE, Carl Fowler, author; b. New Brunswick, N.J., May 16, 1881; s. Rev. Jacob Embury and Annie Bacon (Ware) P.; grad. Centenary Collegiate Inst., 1898; B.A., Wesleyan U., 1902, M.A., 1932; m. Leila A. Field, Apr. 24, 1905 (died Mar. 24, 1906); 1 dau., Nancy (dec.); m. 2d, Flora Draper Treat, June 19, 1913 (died Aug. 30, 1919); 1 son, Sherman. Ins. brokerage business, N.Y. City, since 1909. President The Hymn Society, 1922-26; trustee John Street Endowment Fund; mem. Meth. Ecumenical Conf., 1931, Meth. Gen. Conf., 1932. Mem. Psi Upsilon. Mason. Author: The Music and Hymnody of the Methodist Hymnal, 1911; A Year of Hymn Stories, 1914; Who's Who in American Methodism, 1916; One Hundred and One Hymn Stories, 1923; Curiosities of the Hymnal, 1926; More Hymn Stories, 1929; Wesleyan's First Century, 1932; The Mystical Seven, 1937; One Hundred and One Methodist Stories, 1938; Yankee Township, 1941. Editor: Wesleyan Song Book, 1901; A Year of Song (1910); Wesleyan Verse, 1914; Songs of Life, 1921; Hymns for Worship, 1927; Intercollegiate Song Book, 1931; Sing, Brothers, Sing, 1940; also 7 hymnals, etc. Composer of more than 200 hymn tunes and various cantatas. Home: 512 W. 156th St., New York 32, N.Y. Died Apr. 12, 1948.

PRICE, Enoch Jones, lawyer; b. Newark Twp., Licking County, O., Oct. 21, 1864; s. Thomas D. and Sarah Jane (Jones) P.; B.A., Denison U., Granville, O., 1888; LL.B., U. of Mich., 1891; m. Louise Allen, June 8, 1893; children—Lillis (Mrs. Emerson A. Armstrong), Allen Thomas, Owen Newton, John Marshall, Hugh Glynn, Jessica. Practiced law continuously in Chicago since 1891; mem. firm of Enoch J. Price & Owen N. Price since 1930; atty. for former village of Morgan Park, Ill., 9 yrs. Mem. High Sch. Bd. and Bd. of Edn., Morgan Park, 12 yrs.; trustee Morgan Park Mil. Acad. and pres. of bd. until 1942. Mem. Am., Ill. State and Chicago bar assns., Chicago Law Inst., Phi Gamma Delta, Phi Beta Kappa. Republican. Baptist. Home: 2124 W. 112th St. Office: 111 W. Washington St., Chicago. Died Feb. 25, 1945; Welsh Hills Cemetery, Granville Twp., Licking County, O.

PRICE, George Moses, physician; b. Poltava, Russia, May 21, 1864; ed. Real Gymnasium, Poltava; M.D., Univ. Med. Coll. (New York U.), 1895; m. Anna Kopkin, July 22, 1891. Sanitary insp., 10th Ward, 1885; insp., Tenement Commn., 1894; insp. Health Dept., New York, 1895-1904; dir. of investigation, New York Factory Commn., 1910-12; dir. Joint Bd. of Sanitary Control since 1912, also of Union Health Center. Mem. A.M.A. Author: A Handbook on Sanitation, 1901; Tenement Inspection, 1904; Hygiene and Public Health, 1910; Hygiene and Sanitation for Nurses; The Modern Factory. Office: 275 7th Av., New York, N.Y. Died July 30, 1942.

PRICE, Harrison Jackson, army officer; b. Belington, W.Va., Apr. 3, 1868; s. Albert and Sofia (Bonner) P.; A.B., Ohio Northern U., 1891; grad. Inf. and Cav. Sch., 1897, Sch. of the Line, 1920, Gen. Staff Sch., 1921; m. Lucille Longuemare, June 18, 1895; children—Helen (Mrs. W. F. Sutter), Hardin Bonner, Lucille (Mrs. P. S. Jessup). Commd. 2d lt. 24th Inf., Oct. 7, 1891; promoted through grades to lt. col., May 15, 1917; col. N.A., Aug. 5, 1917; brig. gen. (temp.), Oct. 1, 1918-June 30, 1919; col. regular army Apr. 2, 1920. In Cuba, June-Sept. 1898, and July-Oct. 1899; three tours to Philippines, 1900-03, 1906-07, 1915-17; comd. 350th Inf., 88th Div., Oct. 1917-Oct. 1918; comd. 154th Inf. Brigade, 77th Div., Oct. 1918-May 1919; participated in Alsace-Lorraine sector, and in Meuse-Argonne offensive, Oct. 28 to close of war; in drive from Grande Pré to Meuse River, east of Sedan, capturing 8 towns whose inhabitants had been cut off from the world for 4 yrs. Gen. staff corps and asst. chief of staff G-3, 2d Corps Area, Governors Island, N.Y., 1922-26; in charge Nat. Guard Affairs, 2d Corps Area, 1926-28; chief of staff, 80th Div., Richmond, Va., Sept. 1, 1928-Apr. 30, 1932; retired as brig. gen. Apr. 30, 1932. Decorated Purple Heart. Citation, "for exceptionally meritorious and conspicuous services," as comdr. 154th Inf. Brigade, A.E.F., in France. Mem. S.A.R. (pres. Va. Soc. 1941), Vets. of Foreign Wars, Soc. of Santiago de Cuba, Soc. of the Philippines. Clubs: Army and Navy (Manila); Army and Navy (Washington, D.C.). Home: 3605 Brook Rd., Richmond, Va. Died Sep. 16, 1945.

PRICE, James Hubert; gov. of Va. for term 1938-42. Address: Richmond, Va. Died Nov. 22, 1943.

PRICE, Julian, life insurance; b. Richmond, Va., Nov. 25, 1867; s. Joseph J. and Margaret (Hill) P.; ed. pub. schs.; m. Ethel Clay, Aug. 22, 1897; children—Kathleen Marshall (Mrs. Joseph M. Bryan), Ralph Clay. With Southern R.R., 1887-1903; with Am. Tobacco Co., 1903-05; began in ins. business as solicitor, 1905; pres. Jefferson Standard Life Ins. Co., Greensboro, N.C., since 1919; ex-pres. Federal Home Loan Bank (Winston-Salem); pres. Atlantic & Yadkin R.R.; dir. Mooresville Mills, Southeastern Cottons, Inc.; director Life Insurance Institute; mem. exec. com. American Life Conv. Mem. City Council, Greensboro, 1920-26, 1928-30; ex-chmn. N.C. State Salary and Wage Commn. Trustee Richardson Memorial Hosp., N.C. Agrl. and Tech. Coll.; mem. Nat. Harbors and Waterways Congress; mem. exec. com. Greensboro Council Jews and Christians; mem. exec. com., Elon Coll. (N.C.) Foundation. Member Life Insurance Association of America, Greensboro Chamber of Commerce (dir.), Southern Society of New York, Patriotic Sons of America (hon.), Nat. Econ. League (rep. in national council), Internat. Acquaintance League (hon.). Democrat. Mason (K.T., 33°, Shriner), Past Potentate Oasis Temple; Elk. Clubs: Greensboro, Merchants and Manufacturers, Sedgefield Country, Rotary, Greensboro Country. Home: 301 Fisher Park Circle. Office: Jefferson Standard Bldg., Greensboro, N.C. Died Oct. 25, 1946.

PRICE, Orlo Josiah, clergyman; b. Newark, O., May 11, 1870; s. Thomas D. and Sarah Jane (Jones) P.; B.A., Denison U., Granville, O., 1894; B.D., U. of Chicago Div. Sch., 1898; Ph.D., Leipzig, 1901; D.D., Hillsdale (Mich.) Coll., 1911, Denison, 1919; m. Eva Bronson Graves, Jan. 14, 1902; children—Albert Michael (dec.), Bronson, Mary G., Thomas Jones, Walter Bradford, Sarah Jane. Ordained Bapt. ministry, 1898; pastor Freeport, Ill., 1901-07, Lansing, Mich., 1907-19; with Y.M.C.A. hdqrs., World War, 1918-19; sec. of Mich. Fedn. of Chs., 1909-19; exec. sec. Rochester Fedn. of Chs., 1919-32. Mem. exec. com. Northern Bapt. Conv., 1915-18; sec. Nat. Assn. Ch. Fed. Secs., 1919-23; orgn. sec. N.Y. State Council Chs., 1922-23. Travel in U.S.S.R., Great Britain and Scandinavian countries (leave of absence), May 1930-Sept. 1931. Mem. Administrative Com. Federal Council Churches of Christ in America, 1925-32; chmn. Com. on Training of Inter-church Coöperation, 1929-32; mem. extension faculty U. of Rochester, 1928-30. Trustee Colgate-Rochester Div. Sch.; mem. bd. dirs. (National) Consumers' Mail-Order Coöperative since 1935. Mem. Phi Gamma Delta, Phi Beta Kappa. Clubs: University (Winter Park); Alpha Chi. Wrote: Martineau's Philosophy of Religion, 1901; One Hundred and Twenty Years of Protestantism in Rochester, 1933. Special contbr. Character and Citizenship (now The American Citizen), 1936-41. Contbr. on religious, social and philos. subjects. Home: Long Meadow, Pittsford, N.Y. Died Feb. 12, 1943.

PRICE, Walter Winston, broker; b. N.Y. City, May 23, 1866; s. William Henry and Eliza Tabb (Dyer) P.; LL.D., Colgate U., 1937; m. Ysobel Haskins, Apr. 24, 1901. Traveled in Europe, Africa, Australia and islands of Pacific until 1894; newspaper reporter, San Francisco, 1894-97; mem. firm Price, McCormick & Co., cotton brokers, New York, 1897-1900; mem. E. & C. Randolph, 1904-22; senior partner of Livingston & Co., 1922-34; now mem. Abbott, Proctor & Paine. Identified with pvt. wire business in U.S. and Can.; mem. New York Cotton Exchange, Chicago Bd. of Trade, New York Coffee Exchange, New York Produce Exchange, New York Chamber of Commerce. Mem. Troop A and Squadron A. Nat. Guard, N.Y.; served as pvt. Troop A, U.S. Cav. and transferred to Cuba as pvt. Troop L, Roosevelt's Rough Riders, 1898. Mason (32°, K.T.). Clubs: Racquet and Tennis, Union, The Brook, Century Assn. (New York); Chicago (Chicago); Algonquin (Boston); Nat. Golf Club of America, Southside Sportsmen's Club (L.I., N.Y.); St. James, Bath, Savage (London); Union Interalliée (Paris). Mem. S.A.R. Author: We Have Recovered Before. Home: 1 W. 72d St. Office: 120 Broadway, New York, N.Y. Died Nov. 18, 1943.

PRICHARD, Harold Adye (prĭch'ärd), clergyman, author; b. Clifton, Bristol, Eng., Dec. 14, 1882; s. Arthur William (M.D.) and Sarah (Adye) P.; B.A., Trinity Coll. (Oxford), 1906, M.A., 1907; post-grad. work, Johns Hopkins, 1907-08; student Gen. Theol. Sem., 1911-12; D.D., St. Stephen's Coll., Annandale, N.Y., 1926; m. Lucette Marguerite Hutton, Aug. 29, 1907; children—Margaret Celeste, Helen Lucette, Sybil Agnes, Norman Adye. Deacon, 1912, priest, 1913, P.E. Ch.; teacher Latin and Greek, Mackenzie Sch., 1908-10; asst., St. Peter's Ch., Morristown, N.J., 1912-14; rector St. Mark's Ch., Mt. Kisco, N.Y., since 1914. Apptd. hon. canon Cathedral of St. John the Divine, N.Y. City, 1920 (acting dean, 1924-25); exec. sec. missionary campaign, Diocese of N.Y., 1920-40; spl. preacher Westminster Abbey, Liverpool Cathedral, St. Paul's Ch. (Rome), etc.; lecturer in ethics, Spence Sch., New York, since 1930; chmn. Am. Ch. Congress, 1933-35, pres., 1937; mem. standing com. Diocese of N.Y., 1934-37. Naturalized citizen, 1922. Mem. Alpha Delta Phi. Republican. Club: University (New York). Author: Three Essays in Restatement, 1921; Christian Stewardship, 1922; The Sower, 1923; God's Communicating Door, 1929; A Country Parson Looks at Religion, 1931; The Minister, the Method, and the Message, 1932; What Did Jesus Think? (with Stanley Brown-Serman), 1935; If They Don't Come Back—Some Thoughts on Immortality, 1943; also articles and poems in periodicals. Editor: The Church and the Future, 1929; Charleston Papers, 1930; Cincinnati Papers, 1931; Hartford Papers, 1932; Chicago Papers, 1933. Home: Mt. Kisco, N.Y. Died May 7, 1944.

PRICHARD, Lev H., business exec.; b. Franklin County, Miss., July 19, 1883; s. Chas. A. and Cornelia (Byrd) P.; A.B., Miss. Coll., Clinton, 1906; student Milsaps Coll., Jackson, Miss., 1908; m. Louise Melton, June 26, 1906; 1 son, Lev H. Admitted to Miss. Bar, 1908, to Okla. Bar, 1909; practiced law, Meadville, Miss., 1908-09, Oklahoma City, 1909-15; in oil bus., Oklahoma City, Okla. 1915-22; organized Anderson Prichard Oil Corp., Oklahoma City, 1922, served as pres., later chmn. bd. until 1949; pres. Col Tex Refining Co., Colorado, Tex., (subsidiary of Standard Oil (Calif.) and own co.), 1926-49; pres. and dir. Anderson Prichard Pipe Line Corp. Home: Olmito, Tex. Office: Apco Tower, Oklahoma City, Okla. Died June 19, 1949; buried at Home Ranch, Olmito, Tex.

PRICHARD, Vernon E., army officer; b. Smithland, Ia., Jan. 25, 1892; s. Jacob A. and Emma Grace (Jones) P.; student Morningside Coll., Sioux City, Ia., 1908-11; B.S., U.S. Mil. Acad., 1915; m. Charlotte Gibbs Blesse, Sept. 6, 1916; 1 dau., Carlotta. Commd. 2d. lt., U.S. Army, 1915, and advanced through grades to maj. gen. (temp.), 1942; now with Gen. Staff, Dept. of the Army. Recipient Mex. Punitive Expdn. medal, D.S.M., Purple Heart (U.S.), Companion Order of Bath (Gt. Britain), Legion of Honor (France), Order of St. Maurice and St. Lazarus (Italy), War Cross (Brazil), War Cross (Czechoslovakia). Mason (32°). Home: Fort Myer, Va. Office: Pentagon Bldg., Washington 25. Died July 10, 1949.

PRIDDY, Lawrence, insurance; b. Keysville, Va., July 7, 1874; s. Robert T. and Lavinia (Watkins) P.; B.S., Va. Poly. Inst., 1897, hon. D.C.S., 1929. Promoted and directed activities toward the erection of a Y.M.C.A. Bldg., at Va. Poly. Inst., 1898-99; with N.Y. Life Ins. Co., since 1900, at Richmond, Va., 1900-01, agency dir. Md. and D.C., then New York, since 1905; one of the largest producers of life ins. business for past 25 yrs., sold a total of $1,157,000 in 1910, and his yearly average since that time has been approximately $1,500,000; appeared in interest of life ins. orgns. before Legislature of N.Y. and U.S. Congress. Past pres. $200,000 Club of N.Y. Life Ins. Co.; patron of Am. Museum Nat. History, Metropolitan Museum of Art. Mem. N.Y. Chamber of Commerce, Southern Soc. of New York, Gen. Alumni Assn. of Va. Poly. Inst. (past pres.), Life Underwriters Assn. of N.Y. (past pres.), Nat. Assn. Life Underwriters (past pres.). Club: Bankers. Home: (summer) Montclair, N.J.; (winter) Miami Beach, Fla. Office: 233 Broadway, New York, N.Y. Died Sep. 3, 1944.

PRIEST, George Madison, univ. prof.; b. Henderson, Ky., Jan. 25, 1873; s. George Madison and Philura (Lambert) P.; A.B., Coll. of N.J. (now Princeton U.), 1894, A.M., 1896; studied U. of Berlin, 1894-95, Freiburg, 1899, Leipzig, Marburg and Jena, 1901-02, Jena, 1906-07, Ph.D., 1907; unmarried. Began teaching at Princeton University, 1895, prof. Germanic languages, 1912-1941, professor emeritus since 1941. Presbyterian. Author: Ebernand von Erfurt, 1907; A Brief History of German Literature, 1909; Germany Since 1740, 1915. Translator: Goethe's Faust (parts I and II), 1932, rev. edit., 1941. Editor of Riehl's Spielmannskind, 1902; Sudermann's Fritzchen, 1929; Anthology of German Literature in the Eighteenth Century, 1934; Geissler's Der Liebe Augustin, 1938. Contbr. various Am. and German periodicals. Home: 10 Nassau St., Princeton, N.J. Died Feb. 17, 1947.

PRIESTLEY, Herbert Ingram, prof. history; b. Fairfield, Mich., Jan. 2, 1875; s. John Stanley and Sarah (Parker) P.; Ph.B., U. of Southern Calif., 1900, M.A., 1907; Ph.D., U. of Calif., 1917; m. Bessie Belle Snodgrass, July 18, 1901; children—Herbert Kenneth, Elizabeth Joy (Morby). Instr. U. Southern Calif., 1899-1900; teacher, Los Angeles Mil. Acad., 1900-01; teacher and supt. schs., Nueva Cáceres, Luzón, P.I., 1901-04; prin. grammar sch., Wilmington, Calif., 1904-07; teacher Spanish, Riverside (Calif.) High Sch., 1907-10; supt. schs., Corona, Calif., 1910-12; asst. curator Bancroft Library, U.

of Calif., 1912-20, librarian since 1920, dir. since 1940; asst. prof. Mexican history, U. of Calif., 1917-20, asso. prof., 1920-22, prof. since 1923. Mem. Am. Hist. Assn., Soc. Mexicana de Geog. y Estad., Acad. Cientifica "Antonio Alzate," Acad. de Historia Cubana; corr. mem. Hispanic Soc. of Amereia, Soc. Chihuahense de Estud. Hist. Hon. prof., Museo Nacional of Mexico. Mason. Author: José de Galvez, Visitor-General of New Spain, 1765-71, 1916; The Mexican Nation, a History, 1923; (with Moisés Saénz) Some Mexican Problems (Harris Foundation lectures, 1926); The Luna Papers, 1928; The Coming of the White Man, 1929; Tristán de Luna, Conquistador, 1936; France Overseas, A Study in Modern Imperialism 1938 (awarded Commonwealth Club medal 1938); France Overseas Through the Old Regime, 1939; also lectures on internat. relations; also various book reviews, and articles on California, Mexican and Spanish-Am. history and govt. and U.S. foreign affairs. Mem. bd. editors The Hispanic Am. Hist. Rev., The Pacific Hist. Rev., 1932-34, World Affairs, 1934, Am. Archivist since 1937. Awarded 2d Loubat prize, Columbia U., 1918, for 2d best work on history of N. America during the Colonial epoch. Has traveled in Philippines, China, Japan, Mexico, Canada, Spain, Cuba, England, and North Africa. Home: 1702 Arch St. Address: Bancroft Library, U. of Calif., Berkeley, Calif. Died Feb. 9, 1944.

PRINCE, John Dyneley, educator; b. N.Y. City, Apr. 17, 1868; s. John Dyneley and Anne Maria (Morris) P.; A.B., Columbia, 1888; U. of Berlin, 1889-90; Ph.D., Johns Hopkins, 1892; m. Adeline, d. Dr. Alfred L. Loomis, Oct. 5, 1889; 1 son, John Dyneley. Went to Babylonia with U. of Pa.'s expdn., 1888-89, as official rep. of Columbia U.; prof. Semitic langs., 1892-1902, dean of Grad. Sch., 1895-1902, New York U.; prof. Semitic langs., 1902-15, prof. Slavonic langs., 1915-21, Columbia; apptd. E.E. and M.P. to Denmark, 1921; E.E. and M.P. to Yugoslavia, 1926-33; prof. of Slavonic, Columbia U., 1933-35, prof. East European Langs., 1935-37, emeritus since 1937. Mem. Am. Oriental Soc., Am. Philos. Soc.; fellow New York Acad. Science. Mem. N.J. Assembly, 1906, 1908 (speaker, 1909), N.J. Senate, 1910-13 (leader, 1911); pres. N.J. Senate, 1912, and acting gov. of N.J., 1912; pres. N.J. Civ. Service Commn., 1917-21; mem. Am., Danish, Greenland Commn., 1940. Decorated with Order of St. Saba (Serbia), II Class, 1912; Grand Cordon Jugoslav Crown, 1933; Grand Cross of Dannebrog, 1933. Author: Mene, Mene, Tekel, Upharsin, 1893; A Critical Commentary on the Book of Daniel, Leipzig, 1899; Kulóskap the Master (Algonkin poems), with Charles Godfrey Leland, 1902; Materials for a Summerian Lexicon, 1908; Assyrian Primer, 1909; Russian Grammar, 1919; Practical Grammar of the Lettish Language (the first in English), 1925; Grammar of the Serbo-Croatian Language, 1929; Fragments from Babel, 1939. Contbr. to philol., anthrop. and scientific jours. on Assyrian subjects, on langs. of Am. Indians, on Scandinavian, and on Slavonic; writer for 11th edition of Encyclopedia Britannica and Hastings' Dictionary of Religions, etc. Home: Ringwood Manor, N.J.* Died Oct. 11, 1945.

PRINCE, Nathan Dyer, banker; b. Killingly, Conn., Dec. 1, 1878; s. Francis A. and Maria S. (Chaffee) P.; student high sch., Killingly, Conn.; m. Grace Evelyn Bitgood, 1905. Began banking business with Windham County Nat. Bank, Danielson, Conn., 1898; made v.p. Conn. Trust & Safe Deposit Co., Hartford, Conn., 1915; company merged, 1919, with Hartford Trust Co., pres. Hartford-Conn. Trust Co., 1924-32; pres., Windham County Nat. Bank, Killingly Trust Co.; trustee Hartford Soc. for Savings; dir. Terry Steam Turbine Co.; treas. Westfield Cemetery Assn. Trustee Mansfield (Conn.) State Training Sch. and Hosp.; trustee Boston U., Edw. W. Hazen Foundation; ex-treas. Am. Bankers Assn.; ex-pres. Conn. Bankers Assn. Mem. Conn. Hist. Soc., S.A.R. (life). Republican. Methodist (trustee Danielson Ch.). Mason (K.T.). Clubs: Hartford, Putnam Country. Home: 60 Elizabeth St., Hartford, Conn.; and 191 Main St., Danielson, Conn. Office: Windham County National Bank, Danielson, Conn. Died Sep. 3, 1942.

PRINCE, Sydney Rhodes, lawyer; b. Mt. Sterling, Ala., Sept. 11, 1876; s. Sydney T. and Helen (Rhodes) P.; A.B., U. of Ala., 1896; LL.B., Georgetown U., 1898; m. Hattie Beverly Smith, Nov. 23, 1904 (died Aug. 22, 1930); children—Sydney Rhodes, Gregory Smith; m. 2d, Tempie Harris, June 29, 1939. Admitted to Ala. bar, 1898, and began practice at Mobile; atty. M.&O. R.R., 1901-08, asst. gen. counsel, 1908-11, gen. counsel, 1911-18; gen. solicitor, Southern Ry. System, 1918-31; gen. counsel Southern Ry. System, 1932-Dec. 1946, Episcopalian. Mem. Am. Bar Assn., Phi Delta Theta, Phi Beta Kappa. Clubs: Chevy Chase, Lawyers, Alfalfa. Home: 5 Chevy Chase Circle, Chevy Chase, Md. Address: Southern Ry. Co., McPherson Sq., Washington. Died Mar. 20, 1948.

PRINCE, William Loftin, coll. dean; b. Sussex, Va., May 23, 1876; s. John David and Hannah Frances (Peters) P.; grad. Windsor Acad., 1894; B.A., Richmond Coll., 1898; M.A., Columbia, 1919; m. Grace Arlington Woodhouse, Dec. 7, 1904; 1 dau., Virginia Woodhouse (Mrs. William Bray Shinnick). Teacher, Windsor Acad., 1898; prin., Courtland, Va., grade sch., 1899, Emporia, Va., high sch., 1900; rep. Ginn & Co., pubs., 1902; prin., Richmond Acad., 1905; supt., Henrico County Schs., 1918; Va. state supervisor of high schs., 1919; dean of summer session and head dept. edn., U. of Richmond, 1920-46, dean of students, 1920-22, dean of Richmond College, 1922-32. Trustee Fork Union Military Academy. Mem. State Board of Accountancy, 1922-46. Mem. N.E.A., Va. Assn. Colleges, Va. Acad. Science, Va. Ednl. Assn., Kappa Sigma (nat. pres.), Omicron Delta Kappa (nat. pres.). Democrat. Baptist. Mason. Club: Westmoreland (Richmond, Va.). Home: 2423 Grove Av., Richmond 20, Va. Died Nov. 9, 1948.

PRINDLE, Edwin Jay, patent lawyer; b. Washington, Nov. 5, 1868; s. George Sidney and Ann (Sanderson) P.; M.E., Lehigh U., 1890; LL.B., Nat. Univ., Washington, 1892, LL.M., 1894, LL.D., 1930; Eng.D. from Lehigh U., 1934; married; children—Sidney Edwin (dec.), Margaret Sanderson (dec.) (Mrs. Daniel P. Foster), Lucy Gray, Winifred Maud; m. 2d, Maud (Towle) Gildersleeve, June 11, 1913; children—Gwendolyn (Mrs. Lathan C. Squire), Gordon Hamilton Gildersleeve. Asst. examiner, U.S. Patent Office, 1890-99; practiced patent law in Washington, 1899-1905, with father, 1899-1902, and in New York City since 1905; sr. mem. patent law firm of Prindle, Bean & Mann; patent counsel to many large corps.; lecturer on patent law, Lehigh U. Active since 1898 in promotion of appreciation of value of patent system on the part of public and Congress; led nat. orgns. of patent bar, mfrs. and engrs. in securing increases of Patent-Office salaries by passage of the Lampert Act, 1922, and of Act for Reclassifying Civil Salaries, 1923, and in campaigns of 1925 and 1926, in securing increase of salaries of fed. judiciary, serving as a vice chmn. Lawyers' Nat. Com. to Procure Adequate Compensation for latter; proposed and led in enactment of an amendment to the patent statue simplifying accountings and making recoveries possible in most cases in patent suits where defendants have made profits; started movement, in New England Soc. of Orange, New Jersey, resulting in mosquito extermination law of N.J. Proposed by N.Y. Patent Law Association to President Coolidge, 1928, for judge Court of Customs and Patents Appeals, but withdrew name for economic reasons. Mem. New York Patent Law Assn. (pres. 1927-28), Am. Bar Assn., N.Y. State Bar Assn., Assn. Bar City of New York, New York County Lawyers' Assn. (mem. com. on patents), Nat. Assn. Mfrs. (mem. patents com.; chmn. 1921-33), Nat. Research Council (mem. patents com.; chmn. 1919-33), Am. Engring. Council (chmn. patents com.), Am. Soc. Mech. Engrs., Am. Inst. Mining and Metall. Engrs., Am. Inst. E.E., Am. Chem. Soc., Am. Electrochem. Soc. (chmn. patents com.), S.A.R., Phi Gamma Delta, Tau Beta Pi. Republican. Mem. Riverside Christian Ch. Clubs: Lawyers, Phi Gamma Delta (New York); Gypsy Trail (Carmel, N.Y.). Author: Patents as a Factor in Manufacturing Business; The Farmer and the Patent System; The Marvelous Performance of the American Patent System; The Art of Inventing; The Doctrine of Equivalents as Applied to Claims of Patents; Evolution of a Typical Invention; Section on Patents and Patent Law, in Chemical Engineers' Hand Book; also numerous articles pertaining to inventions, the patent system and patent law. Under auspices of Am. Engring. Counsel, broadcast popular exposition of U.S. Patent System and its benefits to our country. Contbr. to Century Dictionary, 1899. Home: 461 Vose Av., South Orange, N.J. Office: 50 Wall St., New York. Died Dec 17, 1942.

PRINGLE, Henry Nelson; b. Ryegate, Vt., Oct. 21, 1864; s. Alexander Bullions and Julia Ann (Laughlin) P.; B.A., Dartmouth, 1890; B.D., Andover Theol. Sem., 1893; m. Emma Jane Prescott, Nov. 21, 1894; children—Alexander Moncrief, Margaret (dec.), William Prescott, Edward Edmond, Helen (dec.). Ordained Congl. ministry, 1893; pastor Anoka, Minn., 1893-97, Eastport, Me., 1898-1902; sec. Christian Civic League of Me., 1902-11; asst. supt. Internat. Reform Bur., Washington, D.C., 1911-23; supt. Soc. for Prevention of Crime, N.Y. City, 1923; nat. dir. Law Enforcement for International Reform Federation, Washington, D.C., 1924-39. Organized and endowed Social Reforms Foundation, a philanthropic, irrevocable trust for better government and citizenship, 1937. Donated Claystone Collection to New National Museum, Washington, D.C. Republican. Author various pamphlets on commercialized vices. Home: 208 Domer Av., Takoma Pk., Washington, D.C. Died Jan. 11, 1948; buried Waterville, Me.

PRINGLE, James Nelson, commr. of education; b. Ryegate, Vt., Dec. 2, 1874; s. Alexander Bullions and Julia Ann (Laughlin) P.; prep. edn., Phillips Andover (Mass.) Acad., 1892-94; B.A., Dartmouth, 1897; LL.D., University of New Hampshire, 1931; m. 2d, Lillian C. Parker, July 28, 1942; 1 son, Nelson Giles (by previous marriage). Principal high sch., Hillsboro, N.H., 1897-99, Sharon, Mass., 1899-1909; dist. supt. schs., Jaffrey, N.H., 1909-12; city supt. schs., Portsmouth, N.H., 1912-18; dep. state commr. of edn., 1918-30, commr. since 1930. Trustee Austin-Cate Acad., Strafford, N.H. Mem. Commn. N.H. Arts and Crafts. Mem. Phi Delta Theta. Republican. Conglist. Mason. Home: Concord, N.H. Died July 23, 1946.

PROSSER, Seward, banker; b. Buffalo, N.Y., May 1, 1871; s. Henry Wilbur and Anna (Fay) P.; ed. pub. schs. and Englewood (N.J.) Sch. for Boys; m. Constance Barber, Oct. 25, 1902; children—Barbara (Mrs. John A. Gifford), Anna Fay (Mrs. Leighton H. Stevens), Constance Mary (Mrs. Richard K. Mellon). Began career with Equitable Life Assurance Soc. of U.S., later mem. Prosser & Homans, representing same; v.p. Astor Trust Co., 1907-12; pres. Liberty Nat. Bank, 1912-14; pres. Bankers Trust Co., 1914-23, now dir., chmn. bd. and mem. exec. com.; dir. Bankers Safe Deposit Co., Internat. Nickel Co. of Can., Ltd., Kennecott Copper Corp., Graphite Metallizing Corp., Braden Copper Co., Utah Copper Co., etc. Republican. Episcopalian. Clubs: Union League, University. Home: Palisade Av. E., Englewood, N.J. Office: 16 Wall St., New York, N.Y. Died Oct. 1, 1942.

PROTTENGEIER, Conrad Gottfried (prŏt'ĕn-gīr), clergyman; b. Toledo, O., June 2, 1872; s. Christopher and Katharina (Volk) P.; A.B., Wartburg Coll., Waverly, Ia., 1890; Wartburg Sem., Dubuque, 1890-93, D.D., 1939; Chicago Luth. Sem., 1893-94; m. Emma Koeberle, July 1, 1896; children—Herbert Maurice, Lillian Marie, Margaret Emma (Mrs. William Tarr), Alfred Christopher, Kathryn Louise, Robert Martin. Ordained ministry Luth. Ch., 1894; pastor successively Peoria, Ill., Sterling, Ill., Somonauk, Ill., Dubuque, Ia., Saginaw, Mich., until 1917, Charles City, Ia., 1917-38; retired. Mem. joint commn. for orgn. of Am. Luth. Ch., of which was 2d v.p. and mem. exec. com., 1930-32, now mem. Commn. on Worship and Church Art of American Lutheran Church. Pres. Synod of Iowa and Other States. Translator: Luther's Catechism, 1906; Wartburg Lesson Helps, 2 vols., 1914; Topics for Young People's Societies, 1921 (all by Dr. M. Reu). Contbr. church jours. Home: 11775 Payton, Detroit 24, Mich. Died Mar. 15, 1949; buried at Forest Lawn Cemetery, Detroit.

PROVINE, John William, college pres.; b. Big Creek, Miss., June 19, 1866; s. Robert Neely and Nannie (Goyen) P.; B.S., U. of Miss., 1888, M.A., 1890; student Munich and Göttingen, A.M., Ph.D., Göttingen, 1893; m. Mary Sproles, Aug. 19, 1896; children—John William (dec.), Marion (Mrs. David Callahan), Henry Sproles. Pres. Mississippi Coll., Clinton, Miss., 1897-98, prof. chemistry, 1898-1911, again pres. since 1911. Commr. Miss. Insane Hospital. Mem. Am. Chem. Soc., Deutsche Chemische Gesellschaft, Southern Intercollege Athletic Assn. (pres. 1922-27), Assn. Miss. Colleges (pres. 1922-23), Miss. Teachers' Assn. (pres. 1922-29), Sigma Alpha Epsilon. Democrat. Baptist. K.P. Home: Clinton, Miss. Died Nov. 2, 1949.

PRYOR, Arthur (prī'ôr), band leader; b. St. Joseph, Mo., Sept. 22, 1870; s. Samuel D. P.; studied violin and cornet under father who was a band leader; m. Maud Russell, 1895; children—Arthur, Roger. Early became widely noted as a trombone soloist; joined Sousa's Band at World's Fair, Chicago, 1893, and made three world tours with Sousa, as premier trombone soloist, also asst. condr.; gave first concert as head of own band in N.Y. City, 1903, with which has since appeared in leading cities of the world. Mem. Am. Bandmasters Assn. Mason (33°, Shriner), Elk. Composer for band, also of three light operas—Uncle Tom's Cabin, Jingaboo, On the Eve of Her Wedding Night.* Died June 18, 1942.

PRYOR, James Chambers, rear adm.; b. Winchester, Tenn., Mar. 13, 1871; s. James Jones and Nannie Buchanan (Brazelton) P.; A.B., U. of Nashville; M.D., Vanderbilt, 1895; spl. med. courses in clinics, Vienna, Paris and London; M.A., Johns Hopkins, 1913; grad. U.S. Army War Coll., 1928; m. Georgia Leontine Mackay, June 16, 1906 (died 1914); 1 son, James Chambers; m. 2d, Frances Pierpont Sivitér, June 9, 1917; 1 dau., Frances Pierpont. Entered U.S. Navy as asst. surgeon with rank of ensign, 1897; advanced through grades to rear admiral, Oct. 1, 1934; retired April 1, 1935. Served on U.S.S. Albatross during Spanish-Am. War.; med. officer Agassiz Expdn. to South Pacific Ocean on same ship, 1898-99; served as med. attendant to Theodore Roosevelt at White House and Oyster Bay; brigade surgeon Naval forces ashore at Vera Cruz, Mexico, 1914; head dept. hygiene, U.S. Naval Med. Sch., Washington, D.C., 1917-20; prof. preventive medicine, George Washington U., 1917-19; lecturer on naval hygiene, Johns Hopkins, 1919; commanded U.S. Naval Hosps., Yokohama, Japan, Pensacola, Fla., Hampton Roads, Va., U.S. Naval Med. Sch., 1925-28; med. officer and head of dept. hygiene U.S. Naval Acad., 1928-31; comdg. Naval Med. Supply Depot, Brooklyn, N.Y. Spl. commendation of sec. of Navy "for extraordinary devotion in line of duty," at Battle of Ciudar Bolivar, Venezuela, 1903; service medals, Spanish-Am. War, Occupation of Vera Cruz, Mexico, and World War. Fellow Am. Coll. Surgeons; mem. A.M.A., Assn. of Mil. Surgeons of U.S. (ex-pres.), Med. Soc. of D.C.; sec. Sect. on Mil. Medicine 14th Internat. Congress on Hygiene and Demography; chmn. delegation sent by U.S. to 6th Internat. Congress on Mil. Medicine and Pharmacy, at The Hague, 1931, and delegate to 8th Congress, Brussels, 1935. Democrat. Methodist. Mason. Clubs: N.Y. Yacht, Quill (New York); Rembrandt (Brooklyn); Sherwood Forest (Md.); Army and Navy, Chevy Chase (Washington). Author: Naval Hygiene, 1918. Contbr. to Ency. Britannica, 14th edit., and to Johns Hopkins and U.S. Naval med. bulls. Home: 184 Columbia Heights, Brooklyn; (summer) Sherwood Forest, Md. Address: 184 Columbia Heights, Brooklyn, N.Y. Died Sept. 8, 1947; buried in Arlington National Cemetery.

PUGH, John Jones (pū), librarian; b. Columbus, O., Feb. 29, 1864; s. Richard and Elizabeth (Jones) P.; grad. Central High Sch., Columbus, 1881; grad. Central Ohio Normal Coll., 1883; m. Katharine Fornof, Aug. 22, 1888 (died 1900); children—Elizabeth Louise (Mrs. Herbert Janney Long), Katharine Loving, Mary Helen; m. 2d, Mary Famah Peters, May 25, 1925. Began as asst. librarian at Columbus City and Pub. Sch. Library, 1881; city librarian, Columbus, since 1896. Supervisor and organizer A.L.A. War Camp Libraries, World War. Mem. A.L.A., Ohio Library Assn. (pres.) N.E.A., Columbus Chamber Commerce (1st v.p.; dir.), Ohio Newsboys Assn., Inc. (pres.). Republican. Presbyterian. Mason (32°, K.T., Shriner), Odd Fellow; Dep. Supreme Dictator for Ohio of Loyal Order of Moose. Clubs: Rotary, Ohio State Univ. Faculty, Columbus Athletic. Wrote: A Classification System for Public Libraries; Historical Sketch of Ohio Libraries. Asso. editor Hooper's History of Columbus, Fess' History of Ohio and Moore's History of Franklin County, Ohio. Home: 2653 Glen Echo Drive. Office: Columbus Public Library, Columbus, O.* Died Aug. 9, 1946.

PULLER, Edwin Seward (pŏŏl'ēr), lawyer, author; b. St. Louis, Mo., Dec. 31, 1868; s. John J. and Eliza A. (Soley) P.; Ph.B., Marietta (Ohio) Coll., 1889; LL.B., Washington U., St. Louis, 1893; LL.M., Nat. U., Washington, 1920; LL.D., Chicago Law Sch., 1924; m. Mathilde Anderson, Oct. 5, 1903. Began practice, St. Louis, 1893; speaker on sociol. topics; lecturer on adolescent psychology and boy training. Investigated sociol. and ednl. problems in Europe, 1912-14. Chief foreign permits office, Dept. of State, 1918-20; lecturer on citizenship, Post-Grad. Sch. of Am. Univ., 1919-29; prof. comparative constl. law, Nat. Univ. Law Sch., Washington. Mem. Am. Bar Assn., Acad. Polit. Sciences, Am. Soc. Internat. Law; ex-pres. Scoutmasters' Assn. of St. Louis. Democrat. Methodist. Mason (K.T.), Elk. Clubs: Elks, Chevy Chase. Author: Your Boy and His Training, 1916; Biff McCarty, 1915; The Boy Scout Hero, 1917. Contbr. many articles to mags. on the boy problem. Home: 1742 18th St. N.W. Office: Woodward Bldg., Washington, D.C. Deceased.

PULLIAM, Roscoe, univ. pres.; b. Millstadt, Ill., Apr. 17, 1896; s. L. M. and Carolina (Peter) P.; B.Ed., Southern Ill. Normal U., Carbondale, 1923; A.M., U. of Ill., 1927; post grad. study, U. of Chicago, 1928-32; m. Mabel McGuire, Aug. 1, 1923; children—Robert, Patricia, Mary Joyce, Wallace. Began as teacher pub. schs., 1914; supt. schs., Bunker Hill, Ill., 1920-23, Staunton, 1923-26, Harrisburg, 1927-35; pres. Southern Ill. Normal U. since 1935; instr. in edn. Eastern Ill. State Teachers Coll., summers 1926-30, George Peabody Coll., Nashville, Tenn., 1931. Served in inf., Rainbow Div., A.E.F., World War. Mem. N.E.A., Southern Ill. Teachers Assn. (pres. 1931-32), Nat. Soc. for Study of Edn., Phi Delta Kappa, Kappa Delta Pi. Democrat. Presbyterian. Author: Extra Instructional Activities of the Teacher, 1931. Contbr. ednl. articles. Home: Carbondale, Ill. Died Mar. 27, 1944.

PULLMAN, John Stephenson, lawyer; b. New Haven, Conn., Feb. 25, 1871; s. Rev. Joseph and Mary Elizabeth (Cooke) P.; student Wilbraham (Mass.) Acad., 1885-88; A.B., Wesleyan U., Middletown, Conn., 1892; LL.B., Yale, 1896; m. Mary Nickerson Lakin, Nov. 25, 1905; children—Mary Elizabeth (wife of Dr. DeWitt Dominick), Alice Lakin (Mrs. George B. Longstreth III), Josephine Lakin (Mrs. Luther Tucker), John Stephenson. Admitted to Conn. bar, 1896, and since practiced in Bridgeport, sr. partner Pullman & Comley; judge of city court, 1905-07; city atty., 1909-11; v.p. Bridgeport People's Savings Bank; mem. bd. dirs. Morris Plan Bank, Middlesex Mut. Assurance Co.; sec. bd. of trustees of Wesleyan U. Chmn. U.S. Selective Service Bd., div. 2, World War, 1917-19. Mem. Am. and Conn. State bar assns., Assn. Bar City of New York, Alpha Delta Phi, Phi Beta Kappa. Republican. Methodist. Clubs: University, Brooklawn Country, Black Rock Yacht (Bridgeport); Pequot Yacht (Southport). Home: 50 Unquowa Hill. Office: 886 Main St., Bridgeport, Conn. Died Mar. 31, 1943.

PULSIFER, Harold Trowbridge (pŭl'sĭ-fēr), editor; b. Manchester, Conn., Nov. 18, 1886; s. Nathan Trowbridge and Almira Houghton (Valentine) P.; A.B., Harvard U., 1911 (winner Lloyd McKim Garrison prize, 1910; class poet, 1911); Litt. D., Bates Coll., 1935; m. Susan Farley Nichols, Oct. 11, 1924. Mem. editorial staff, The Outlook, 1913; pres. Outlook Co. and mng. editor Outlook, 1923-28, sec. and treas., 1928-29. Mem. bd. trustees Roosevelt Memorial Assn. Candidate for New York Assembly, 1st Assembly Dist., Orange County, 1912, 13; del. Prog. state and nat. conventions, 1912. Enlisted as pvt. Signal Corps, Jan. 30, 1917; promoted to master signal electrician, Feb. 7, 1918; hon. discharged, May 13, 1919; 1st lt. M.I.R.C., July 30, 1919. Mem. Poetry Soc. America (pres. 1931-32), N.E. Soc. Clubs: Harvard, Players, Authors (formerly on governing council), Century (New York); Megantic (pres. 1937-41), Three Lakes (Can.). Author: Mothers and Men (poems), 1916; Glory O' the Dawn, 1923; Harvest of Time (poems), 1932; First Symphony (poems), 1935; Elegy for a House (poems), 1935; Rowen (poems), 1937. Contbr. to many mags. Home: East Harpswell, Me. Died Apr. 8, 1948.

PULSIFER, Harry Bridgman, metallurgist; b. Lebanon, N.H., December 23, 1879; s. Charles Edward and Ellen Diantha (Bridgman) P.; B.S., Mass. Inst. Tech., 1903; post-grad. work, U. of Munich, 1906-07; Chem. E., Armour Inst. Tech., Chicago, 1915; M.S., U. of Chicago, 1918; m. Sarah Cecelie Cantlion, Sept. 9, 1909; children—Carmen, Phyllis, Verne, Harrison. Instr. chemistry, N.H. State Coll., 1903-04; chemist, Henry Souther Engring. Co., Hartford, Conn., 1904; assayer and mining engr., Sonora, Mex., 1905; supt. placer mine, Ore., 1907; wrote consular reports, "Zinc in Mexico," 1908; foreman, A.S.&R. Co., Murray, Utah, 1909-11, U.S. Co., Midvale, Utah, 1911; instr. metallurgy, 1911-15, asst. prof., 1915-17, Armour Inst. Tech., Chicago; prof. metallurgy, Mont. State Sch. of Mines, Butte, 1917-20; asst. prof. metallurgy, Lehigh U., 1920-24; metallurgist with Am. Steel & Wire Co., Cleveland, 1935-41; asst. to pres. Am. Metal Treating Co., Cleveland, since 1941. Mem. Am. Inst. Mining Engrs., Am. Soc. Metals, A.A.A.S., Inst. Metals (London). Contbr. on topics relating to mining, milling and metallurgy. Home: 9907 Lamont Av., Cleveland, O. Died Sep. 1, 1947.

PURCELL, William Henry, machinery mfr.; b. Crestline, O., Aug. 19, 1866; s. James and Ellen (Crowe) P.; ed. pub. schs., Alliance, O.; m. Gertrude Hartzell, Apr. 14, 1893; children—Hazel (Mrs. C. J. Rodman), Dorothy (Mrs. O. L. Lewis), Robert A. (dec.), Ruth E. (Mrs. H. A. Fennerty). Began work as machinist apprentice, Morgan Engring. Co., Alliance, 1882, later machinist, road rep., foreman, supt., gen. mgr., until 1901; organizer, 1901, since pres. Alliance Machine Co., mfrs. electric cranes and mill machinery; chairman board Alliance First National Bank; secretary Alliance Structural Company; director McCaskey Register Co., Transue & Williams Steel Forging Corp., Machined Steel Casting Co. Chmn. 3 Liberty Loan campaigns, Alliance, World War. Dir. Alliance Chamber Commerce. Republican. K.P. Clubs: Alliance Country; Congress Lake; Congressional, Army and Navy (Washington, D.C.). Home: 1315 S. Union Av. Office: Mahoning Av., Alliance, O. Died May 28, 1944.

PURDUM, Smith White, second asst. postmaster gen.; b. Montgomery County, Md.; Dec. 12, 1876; s. Thomas Fletchall and Emma (Lewis) P.; ed. pub. and pvt. schs. and prep. sch.; m. Laura Hastings Dolan, Sept. 17, 1902; children—Smith Hastings, Elizabeth Rosalie, Dorothy Lewis (Mrs. Raymond H. Hunt), Mildred Lee, Laura S., Ruth D. (Mrs. B. Brown). Ry. postal clk., 1898-1903; special agent and rural agent Postoffice Dept., 1903-06; apptd. post office inspector, 1906, inspector in charge, Washington Div., 1918-21; again postoffice inspector, 1921-33, deputy fourth asst. postmaster gen., 1933-34, fourth asst. postmaster gen. since June 1934. Democrat. Presbyterian. Odd Fellow. Home: Hyattsville, Md. Office: Post Office Dept., Washington, D.C.* Died Oct. 4, 1945.

PURDY, Corydon Tyler, civil engr.; b. Grand Rapids, Wis., May 17, 1859; s. Samuel J. and Emma J. (Tyler) P.; A.B., U. of Wis., 1885, C.E., 1886; m. Rose E. Morse, Mar. 19, 1892. Pres. and chmn. bd. Purdy & Henderson Co., engrs. and contractors, New York, many years, now retired. Chiefly known for activity in promoting development of modern building construction by use of steel and iron. Contributor to technical mags. Mem. Am. Soc. C.E., Western Soc. Engrs., Instn. C.E. Great Britain. Republican. Conglist. Clubs: Engineers' (New York); Commonwealth (Montclair, N.J.). Home: Melbourne, Fla. Died Dec. 26, 1944.

PURDY, Edward A., investment banking; b. Lansing, Ia., July 31, 1879; s. E. D. and Emma (Rockwell) P.; student Beloit (Wis.) Coll., 1901; grad. U. of Minn., 1903; m. Mary T. Milnor, Mar. 29, 1919; children—Rockwell, Rebecca, Prudence. Pub. Western Architect, 1903-14; postmaster Minneapolis, 1914-22; spl. asst. postmaster gen., 1920-21; v.p. Wells-Dickey Co., investment bankers, since 1922; assistant to president, Federal Cartridge Corporation, Minneapolis, since 1942. Dir. Regional Agricultural Credit Corp., Minneapolis; vice chmn., Fed. Home Loan Bank Board, Region 8, Des Moines. Minn. manager Woodrow Wilson campaign, 1912; del. Dem. Nat. Conv., 1916; formerly chmn. Hennepin County Dem. Com.; mem. Dem. Nat. Com., 1928. Mem. Mayor's Survey Commission; mem. bldg. com. and treas. Greater Univ. Corp. (financed and erected Minn. Stadium, Northrop Memorial, Minn. Union); bd. dirs., Investors Syndicate, Minneapolis, Minn.; chmn. Citizens Auditorium Com., 1924-27. Treas. and dir. Minn. Taxpayers Assn., Minneapolis Civic and Commerce Assn. Clubs: Minikahda, Minneapolis, Rotary. Home: 2400 Irving Av., S. Office: 2300 Foshay Tower, Minneapolis, Minn. Died Jan. 2, 1945.

PURUCKER, (Hobart Lorenz) Gottfried de (pōō-rōō'kēr), theosophical leader; b. Suffern, N.Y., Jan. 15, 1874; s. Gustaf Edmund and Juliana (Smyth) von P.; studied Collège de Genève, Switzerland; M.A., Theosophical U., Point Loma, Calif., 1919, D.Litt., 1921; unmarried. Returned to U.S. at age of 18 and worked on various ranches in Calif.; traveled in South America, 1897-98; returned to New York, 1899, and later to Geneva; asso. with Ralph Lane (later Sir Norman Angell) on editorial staff of Galignani's Messenger (then Daily Messenger), Paris; returned to U.S., 1903, and since mem. staff Theosophical Hdqrs., Point Loma; accompanied Katherine Tingley on her 2d world tour, 1903-04; prof. Sanskrit and Hebrew, Theosophical U., since 1919; succeeded Katherine Tingley as leader of Theosophical Soc., 1929; inaugurated world-wide Theosophical Fraternization Movement, 1930; made lecture-tours in U.S., Eng., Holland, Sweden, Finland, Germany and Switzerland, 1931; established temporary hdqrs. of Thesophical Soc., Kent, Eng., 1932-33; returned with staff to Point Loma, Calif., Oct. 1933. Editor-in-chief The Theosophical Forum. Author: Theosophy and Modern Science, 1929; H.P. Blavatsky, the Mystery (with Katherine Tingley), 1929; Golden Precepts of Esotericism, 1931; Fundamentals of the Esoteric Philosophy, 1932; Occult Glossary, Compendium of Oriental and Theosophical Terms, 1933; Questions We All Ask (2 vols.), 1930; The Esoteric Tradition, 1935. Translator (from the Sanskrit) of the Bhagavadgîtâ, 1930; The Story of Jesus, 1938; The Masters and the Path of Occultism, 1939; Man in Evolution, 1941. Has traveled and lectured extensively in many foreign countries. Address: Internat. Theosophical Headquarters, Point Loma, Calif. Died Sep. 27, 1942.

PUTNAM, Emily James, educator; b. Canandaigua, N.Y., Apr. 15, 1865; d. Judge James C. and Emily Ward (Adams) Smith; A.B., Bryn Mawr Coll., 1889; student Girton Coll., U. of Cambridge, Eng., 1889-90; teacher of Greek, Packer Collegiate Inst., Brooklyn, 1891-93; fellow in Greek, U. of Chicago, 1893-94; m. George Haven Putnam, Apr. 27, 1899. Dean Barnard Coll., 1894-1900, trustee 1901-05; lecturer on Greek lit. and history, same Coll., 1914-29; lecturer and mem. bd. dirs. at New School of Social Research, 1920-32. Member Classical Association Atlantic States. Author: The Lady, 1913; Candaules' Wife, 1926. Translator: Selections from Lucian, 1892; The Dread of Responsibility (E. Faguet), 1914; The Secret of the Marne (Marcel Berger), 1918; The Illusion (R. Escholier), 1921. Home: South Harwich, Mass. Died Sept. 7, 1944.

PUTNAM, George Palmer, publisher, author; b. Rye, N.Y., Sept. 7, 1887; s. John Bishop and Frances (Faulkner) P.; educated Harvard and U. of Calif.; m. Dorothy Binney, Oct. 26, 1911 (divorced 1928); children—David Binney, George Palmer III; m. 2d, Amelia Earhart, Feb. 7, 1931 (lost on Pacific flight, July 1937); m. 3d, Jean Consigney, May 21, 1939; (div. Feb. 15, 1944); m. 4th, Margaret Haviland, 1945. With ednl. dept. G. P. Putnam's Sons, pubs., New York, 1909; in newspaper and publicity work, Oregon, 1910; publisher and editor Bend (Oregon) Bulletin; mayor of Bend, Oregon, 2 terms, 1912-13; sec. to gov. of Ore., 1914-17. Lieut., F.A.R.C., U.S. Army, 1918. Pres. bd. of pubs. The American Legion Weekly, 1919; pres. The Knickerbocker Press, and treas. G. P. Putnam's Sons, New York, 1919-30; v.p. Brewer, Warren & Putnam, 1930-32; chmn. editorial board Paramount Productions, 1932-35. Director American Museum Natural History Greenland Expn., 1926. Putnam Baffin Island Expedition, 1927. Major, Army Air Forces, 1942-45; overseas service, India and China; intelligence officer, B-29 units. Member Psi Upsilon fraternity. Clubs: Coffee House, Explorers (New York). Author: The Southland of North America, 1913; In the Oregon Country; The Smiting of the Rock, 1918; Andree—The Record of a Tragic Adventure, 1930; Last Flight (with Amelia Earhart), 1938; Soaring Wings, 1939; Wide Margins, 1941; Duration, 1943; Death Valley, 1946; Mariner of the North, a Biography of Cap'n Bob Bartlett, 1947; Handbook of Death Valley, 1947; Hickory Shirt: A Tale of Death Valley in 1850. Home: Lone Pine, Calif. Died Jan. 4, 1950.

PUTNAM, John Risley, foreign service officer, retired; born in Long Branch, New Jersey, August 16, 1876; s. John Risley (justice Appellate Division New York Supreme Court) and Mary Steiner (Shoemaker) P.; educated private schools at Saratoga Springs, New York, and St. John's School, Sing Sing (now Ossining), New York; m. Charlotte Brownell Ives, March 13, 1899 (dec.); 1 dau., Doanda R. (wife of Capt. Charles Julian Wheeler, U.S.N.); m. 2d, Sidney Kendall Knapp, Jan. 21, 1939. Mem. of the Chinese Imperial Maritime Customs Service, 1896-1908; U.S. consul at Valencia, Spain, 1915-21; detailed to assist in commercial work at Havana, Cuba, 1921-23; detailed to Shanghai, China, 1923; to Nanking 2 mos. (1923); Foochow 6 mos. (Oct. 1923-March 1924); consul at Chefoo, 1924-26, at Amoy, 1926-31, Hongkong, 1931-32, Zurich, July-Nov. 1932, Leghorn, 1932-34, Genoa, 1934-37, Florence and San Marino, 1937-41; became consul gen., 1935; sec. Diplomatic Service, 1937; retired August 31, 1941. Mem. Am. Foreign Service Assn. Club: University (Winter Park, Fla.). Address: care State Dept., Washington, D.C. Died Apr. 7, 1949; buried at Falling Spring Presbyn. Ch. Cemetery, Chambersburg, Pa.

PUTNAM, Thomas Milton, college dean; b. Petaluma, Calif., May 22, 1875; s. Thomas Crow and Maria (Rutherford) P.; B.S., U. of Calif., 1897, M.S., 1899; Ph.D., U. of Chicago, 1901; m. Margaret E. Murray, June 2, 1904 (died 1911); 1 son, Murray; m. 2d, Mrs. Madeleine Blanchard Stone, July 8, 1916; children—Thomas Milton and Madeleine (step-dau.). Instr. in mathematics, U. of Tex., 1899-1900; same, U. of Calif., 1901-07, asst. prof. mathematics, 1907-15, asso. prof., 1915-19, prof. since 1919, dean of lower div., 1914-19, dean of undergrads., 1919-40; dean of Summer Session, U. of Calif. at Los Angeles, 1925-30; prof. mathematics, Mass. Inst. Tech., summer 1921. Trustee Calif. Sch. for Deaf and Blind, 1917-21. Mem. Am. Math. Soc., Math. Assn. America, A.A.A.S., Sigma Xi. Republican. Club: Faculty (Berkeley). Author: Mathematics of Finance, 1923. Home: 2740 Elmwood Av., Berkeley, Calif. Died Sep. 22, 1942.

PUTNAM, Warren Edward, physician; b. Putnam, Can., May 6, 1857; s. Thomas and Nancy (Harris) P.; M.D., Ohio State U., 1881; m. Anna Sherwood Hawks, Oct. 6, 1887. Practiced at Bennington, Vt. since 1892; former chmn. med. and surg. staffs Putnam Memorial Hosp., now cons. physician same; U.S. examining surgeon; ex-pres. Bennington Bd. Health; former pres. Corp. of Bennington, also of Bennington Gas Co.; corporator Bennington County Sav. Bank; pres. Cooper Industrial Sch. Surgeon Gen. of Vt., 1904-06; brig. gen. on mil. staff late Gov. Charles J. Bell; chmn. Div. Council Nat. Defense, Bennington Co., World War; ex-pres. Bennington Bd. of Trade.

Fellow A.M.A.; mem. Bennington County Medical Soc. (ex-pres.), Assn. Mil. Surgeons U.S., Soc. Colonial Wars, S.A.R. Republican. Club: Bennington (ex-pres.). Home: 203 Safford St., Bennington, Vt. Died Dec. 17, 1927.

PYEATT, John Samuel (pī'ăt), ry. official; b. Washington County, Ark., Sept. 29, 1874; s. John C. and Julia A. P.; ed. pub. schs.; m. Myra Syrena Loy, Mar. 20, 1912; children—Frances E., Martha E., John S. Station clk., C.,C.,C.&St.L. Ry., at Cairo, Ill., 1894; chief clk. to gen. supt. St.L.,I.M.&S. Ry., 1897-1901; chief clk. to mgr. M.P. and St.L.,I.M.&S. rys., 1901-04; supt. Buffalo div. P.M. R.R., at St. Thomas, Ont., 1904-05; supt. Detroit dist. same rd., 1905-11, Grand Rapids dist., Jan.-May 1911; supt. River and Cape div., St.L.&S.F. R.R., at Chaffee, Mo., 1911-12, and continued with same rd. as v.p. and gen. supt. lines in Tex. and of Ft. W.&R.G. Ry., at Ft. Worth, Tex., Feb.-June 1912, and as v.p. and gen. mgr. lines in Tex., comprising N.O., Tex. & Mex. R.R., Beaumont, Sour Lake & Western Ry., Orange & N.W. R.R., and St.L., Brownsville & Mex. Ry., 1912-16; pres. same lines, reorganized as Gulf Coast Lines, 1916-18; federal mgr. M.,K.&T. Ry. of Tex., G.C.&S.F. Ry., Ft. W. & Denver City Ry., H. &T.C. Ry. and others known as Group 6, 1918-19; federal mgr. St.L.&S.F. R.R., 1919-24; pres. Gulf Coast Lines, at Houston, Tex., 1924-36; pres. D.& R.G. Western R.R. since Dec. 20, 1924; chmn. bd. M.P. R.R. Co. since May 1938. Republican. Episcopalian. Clubs: Denver, Mile High, Denver Country. Home: 818 Vine St. Office: Continental Oil Bldg., Denver, Colo. Died Oct. 20, 1946.

PYLE, Ernest Taylor (pīl), newspaperman; b. Dana, Ind., Aug. 3, 1900; s. William Clyde and Maria (Taylor) P.; ed. grade and high sch.; student Indiana U., 1919-23; m. Geraldine Siebolds, July 7, 1925. Cub reporter LaPorte (Ind.) Herald, Jan.-May 1923; reporter, later desk man, Washington (D.C.) Daily News, 1923-26; desk man New York Evening World and New York Evening Post, 1926-27; aviation editor Scripps-Howard Newspapers, 1928-32; mng. editor Washington (D.C.) Daily News, 1932-35; roving columnist since 1935; war corr., 1942-45; daily column appears from all over world for Scripps-Howard Newspapers and others (about 200). Mem. Sigma Alpha Epsilon, Sigma Delta Chi. Author: Ernie Pyle in England, 1941; Here Is Your War, 1943; Brave Men, 1944; collection pre-war columns, Home Country (publ. posthumously), 1947. Received Pulitzer Prize for distinguished correspondence, 1944. Office: 1013 13th St. N.W., Washington. Killed by Japanese machine-gun fire, Ie Shima, Apr. 18, 1945; buried in Punchbowl Memorial Cemetery, Hawaii.

PYLE, William H., coll. prof.; b. Carmi, Ill., Feb. 27, 1875; s. John and Eliza (Stokes) P.; A.B., Ind. U., Bloomington, 1898; Ph.D., Cornell U., 1909; m. Bessie Irish, Apr. 6, 1901; children—Vernus, Bradford, William, Howard; m. 2d, Grace Rose, Dec. 24, 1920; children—Margaret, Alice. Teacher in rural sch., 1893, in high sch. and supt. pub. schools, Carlyle and Vandalia, Ill., 1898-1906; prof. ednl. psychology, U. of Mo., 1909-25; prof. ednl. psychology, Wayne U., 1925-45, dir. grad. sch., 1938-45; retired as dean, 1945. Member A.A.A.S., American Psychol. Assn. Author: Outlines of Educational Psychology, 1911; Psychology of Learning, 1921; Laboratory Manual in Psychology of Learning, 1923; nature and Development of Learning Capacity, 1925. Child Training, 1929; Psychology of Common Branches, 1930. Home: 2674 Collingwood, Detroit. Died March 3, 1946; buried at Stokes, Ill.

Q

QUARLES, Joseph Very III, lawyer; b. Kenosha, Wis., Sept. 8, 1874; s. Joseph Very II and Caroline A. (Saunders) Q.; Ph.B., U. of Mich., 1896; m. Ethel Julia Grant, Sept. 6, 1900; 1 son, Joseph Very IV. Admitted to Wis. bar, 1899; with Quarles, Spence & Quarles, Milwaukee, Wis., since 1899, partner since 1912; sr. partner since 1935; dir. Bonreco Corp., Bond Mfg. Co., The Oil Gear Co.; v.p., dir. Provident Realty Company. Served with 51st Training Battery, F.A., U.S. Army, 1918; in charge of food control in Milwaukee County, Wis., 1917-18. Pres. bd. of trustees, Village of Chenequa, Wis., 1928-36; dir. Milwaukee Country Day Sch. Mem. Inland Lake Yachting Assn. (dir.), Izaak Walton League (pres.), Am. Legion (mem. exec. com., Cudworth Post), Mil. Order Loyal Legion, Psi Upsilon (pres. assn. of Wis.). Republican. Conglist. Clubs: Milwaukee, University (pres.), City (Milwaukee); Chenequa Country, Pine Lake Yacht (Chenequa, Wis.). Home: 1224 N. Prospect Av.; (summer) Hartland, Wis. Office: 828 N. Broadway, Milwaukee 2, Wis. Died May 30, 1946.

QUAYLE, John Harrison, surgeon; b. Madison, O., June 25, 1874; s. Henry and Mary E. (Bower) Q.; grad. New Lyme Inst., 1892; M.D., Cleveland U. of Medicine and Surgery, 1895, New York Post-Grad. Coll., 1901, Cleveland Coll. Physicians and Surgeons, 1904; post-grad. work, Berlin, Vienna, London; m. Grace Dayton, Oct. 3, 1896; children—Mrs. Alice Lynnette Osborne, John H., Wm. Henry. Practiced at Cleveland since 1896. Devised plan for reclamation of men rejected for mil. service, which was adopted by Surgeon Gen. Gorgas, 1917, and which increased the accepted men from 17% to 90%. Mem. A.M.A., Ohio State Med. Assn., Cleveland Acad. Medicine, Cleveland Med. Library, Cleveland Chamber of Commerce (life). Clubs: Big Ten University (life), Cleveland Athletic, Cleveland Automobile, Shaker Heights Country, Willowick Country; Seaview Golf (Absecon, N.J.); Mentor Harbor Yacht (Mentor-on-the-Lake, O.); Surf, Committee of One Hundred, University, Miami -Quarterback (Miami, Fla.); Century (Coral Gables, Fla.). Home: Garden Lane Apts., 1100 Brickell Av., Miami, Fla.; (summer) Lake Shore Blvd., Willoughby, O. Office: Murray Hill Hotel, New York, N.Y. Died Apr. 25, 1945.

QUEZON y Molina, Manuel Luis (Manuel Quezon) (kä'sōn-ē-mō-lē'nä), president of Philippines; born Baler, Province Tayabas, P.I., Aug. 19, 1878; s. Lucio and Maria (Molina) Q.; B.A., Coll. of San Juan de Letran, Manila, 1893; studied law, U. of St. Thomas, Manila; m. Aurora Aragon, 1918; children—Maria Aurora, Maria Zeneida, Manuel L., Jr. Maj. in Philippine army, 1898-1900, serving on staffs of Gens. Aguinaldo and Mascardo. Admitted to bar, 1903; pros. atty., provinces of Mindoro and Tayabas, 1903-04; provincial gov. Tayabas, 1905-06; mem. Philippine Assembly, 1906-09; resident commr. to U.S., 1909-16, and campaigned for Philippine independence; sen. 5th Philippine Senatorial Dist. and first and only pres. Philippine Senate, 1916-35; pres. of Philippines since Sept. 17, 1935. Decorated Officer French Legion of Honor; mem. Order of Jade (China); Grand Cavalier of the Republic (Spain); Grand Cross of Order of Crown of Belgium. Founded Collectivist party, 1922, serving as pres. until 1928; head consolidated Nationalist party, 1928-33; pres. Nationalist Dem. party, 1934-35; pres. coalition of 2 major parties, 1935. Address: Shoreham Hotel, Washington, D.C. Died Aug. 1, 1944.

QUILLEN, Robert (kwĭl'ĕn), writer; b. Syracuse, Kan., Mar. 25, 1887; s. James Downey and Della (Joslin) Q.; ed. high sch.; m. Donnie Cox, Sept. 2, 1906; 1 dau., Louise (adopted); m. 2d, Marcelle Babb, Dec. 24, 1922. Contbr. spl. page and editorials to Saturday Evening Post, 1920-24, editorials, Baltimore Evening Sun, 1920-26, editorial, American Mag., 1928-29; contbr. syndicated editorial and column of paragraphs, also comic features, "Aunt Het," and "Willie Willis," in many papers, U.S. and Can.; editor and pub. Fountain Inn (S.C.) Tribune. Baptist. Mason. Rotarian. Author: One Man's Religion, 1923; The Path Wharton Found, 1924. Home: Fountain Inn, S.C. Died Dec. 19, 1948; interred Cannon Memorial Park Mausoleum.

QUILLER-COUCH, Arthur Thomas (kwĭl'ĕr-kōōch), author; b. Cornwall, Eng., Nov. 21, 1863; J.P., Cornwall U.; M.A., Oxford U. and Cambridge; LL.D., U. of Edinburgh; m. Louisa Amelia Hicks, 1889. Author: Dead Man's Rock; Troy Town; The Splendid Spur; Noughts and Crosses; The Blue Pavilions; I Saw Three Ships; The Warwickshire Avon; The Delectable Duchy; Green Bays; Verses and Parodies; Wandering Heath; The Golden Pomp; Ia; Adventures in Criticism; Poems and Ballads; The Ship of Stars; Old Fires and Profitable Ghosts; The Oxford Book of English Verse; The Laird's Luck; The Westcotes; The White Wolf; The Adventures of Harry Revel; Hetty Wesley; Two Sides of the Face; Fort Amity; Shining Ferry; Shakespeare's Christmas; From a Cornish Window; Sir John Constantine; Poison Island; Merry Garden; Major Vigoureux; True Tilda; Lady Good-for-Nothing; Corporal Sam and Other Stories; The Oxford Book of Ballads; Brother Copas; The Oxford Book of Victorian Verse; Hocken and Hunken; The Vigil of Venus and Other Poems; News from the Duchy; Nicky-Nan Reservist; On the Art of Writing; Memoir of Arthur John Butler; Mortallone and Aunt Trinidad; Foe-Farrell; Shakespeare's Workmanship; Studies in Literature (three series); On the Art of Reading; Charles Dickens and Other Victorians; The Poet as Citizen; Q's Mystery Stories. Editor: Oxford Book of Prose; co-editor: The New Shakespeare. Address: Jesus College, Cambridge, England. Died May 12, 1944.

QUILLIAN, Paul Whitfield (kwĭl'yŭn), clergyman; b. Conyers, Ga., Dec. 19, 1895; s. John Wiley (M.D., D.D.) and Lucy (Zachry) Q.; A.B., Emory U., 1914; B.D., Southern Meth. U., 1924, D.D., 1935; student U. of Chicago, summer 1923, Columbia, summer 1928; D.D., Hendrix Coll., 1929, LL.D., Fla. Southern Coll., 1938; m. Eula DuPree, July 4, 1916; 1 dau., Thelma (wife of Rev. Robert E. Goodrich, Jr.). Public school teacher, 1914-16; entered business, 1916; pres. Ark. Soft Drink Mfrs., 1920-21; ordained to ministry M.E. Ch. South, 1923; pastor Camden, Ark., 1924-27, Winfield Ch., Little Rock, Ark., 1928-32, St. Luke's Ch., Oklahoma City, 1933-36; pastor First Meth. Ch., Houston, Tex., since 1937. Mem. Gen. Conf. M.E. Ch. South, 1934, 38, gen. conf. Meth. Ch., 1940-48; mem. Commn. on Unification of Am. Methodism; mem. Bd. of Edn., Meth. Ch.; pres. Okla. Conf., same, 1935-36. Tex. Conf., same, since 1938, South Central Jurisdiction Bd. of Edn., 1940-44; chmn. com. on education, Uniting Conference American Methodism. Del. 7th Ecumenical Meth. Conf.; del. 1st Assembly World Council of Chs., Amsterdam, Holland, 1948. Thirkield lecturer, Gammon Theol. Seminary, 1945. Trustee Southwestern U., Georgetown, Tex., and Dillard U., New Orleans. Pres. Houston Assn. of Chs., 1941, Houston Ministerial Assn., 1939-40; mem. Nat. Christian Mission Team, 1941, 42, 44; mem. Phi Beta Kappa, Alpha Theta Phi, Theta Phi, Alpha Tau Omega. Democrat. Club: River Oaks Country (Houston). Contbr. to American Pulpit Series, 1945, 46, to Best Sermons of 1946, and to These Prophetic Voices. Home: 3469 Piping Rock Lane, Houston, Tex. Deceased.

QUINN, John Joseph, lawyer; b. Red Bank, N.J., May 15, 1892; s. John and Lenora (Reilly) Q., grad. New York Law Sch., 1914; m. Isabelle Olena, Mar. 18, 1920; children—Caro, Joanne. Admitted to N.J. bar, 1914, and began practice in 1915; mem. firm of Quinn & Doremus; asst. prosecutor, Monmouth County, 1917-25, prosecutor, 1925-30 and 1940-45; U.S. atty. for State of N.J., since 1935-40. Democrat. Catholic. Club: Elks. Home: 26 Caro Court. Office: 73 Broad St., Red Bank, N.J. Died May 5, 1947.

QUIRKE, Terence Thomas (kwĕrk), prof. geology; b. Brighton, Eng., July 23, 1886; s. William Michael and Ellen Maude (Grace) Q.; E.M., U. of N.D., 1912, M.Sc., 1913; Ph.D., U. of Chicago, 1915; m. Anne Laura McIlraith, Sept. 23, 1916; children—Frances Grace, Dorothy Geneva, Terence Thomas. Came to U.S., 1904. Field asst. State Geol. Survey of N.D. and Geol. Survey of Can. 4 summers each, and chief of survey party in Can., summers 1919-31; instr. in geology, U. of Minn., 1915-17, asst. prof., 1917-19; asso. prof. geology, 1919-25, U. of Ill., chmn. dept., 1919-28, prof. since 1925. Fellow Am. Mineral. Soc., Soc. of Economic Geologists, Geol. Soc. of America, Am. Inst. of Mining and Metall. Engineers; member Am. Acad. Advancement of Science, Sigma Xi, Sigma Nu. Del. Internat. Geol. Congress, Brussels, 1922, Madrid, 1926. Episcopalian. Author: Española District, Ontario, 1917; Michipicoten Iron Ranges (with others), 1926; Elements of Geology, 1925; Disappearance of the Huronian (with W. H. Collins), 1930; also numerous articles and repts. Consultant in ore deposits; specialized on deposits of Cuba and Pre-cambrian deposits of N.A.; research on optical mineralogy and problems of the Precambrian. Home: 705 W. Oregon St., Urbana, Ill. Died Aug. 9, 1947.

R

RABOCH, Wenzel Albert, organist, violinist; born Vienna, Austria, Apr. 23, 1854; s. Wenzel P. and Katherine (Shefchik) R.; came to America, 1863; B.S., Coll. City of New York, 1873, course civ. engring; M.A., Coll. of St. Francis Xavier, 1878; m. Katherine L. Rullmann, Apr. 30, 1896. Organist St. Michael's Ch., 1876-81, St. Chrysostom's Chapel, Trinity Parish, 1881-96, Our Lady of Mt. Carmel, Astoria, 1897-1906, Ch. of St. Mary the Virgin, West End Synagogue (Shaaray Tefila); conductor and choir trainer, St. Mary the Virgin Ch., to 1910; Anglican Catholic choir trainer and conductor, since 1906. Prof. music, St. Gabriel's Acad., Manhattan Coll., since 1900, Pawling (N.Y.) Sch., since 1908, St. Aloysius' Acad., Jersey City, N.J., since 1909. Condr. of boy choirs, quartettes, etc.; conducted 1st performance of The Bartered Bride (comic opera) in America, 1894. Anglican. Mem. Mus. Protective Union, Aschenbraedel Verein, Manuscript Soc. (composer). Composed music to The Eumenides, of Eschylus, in Greek style, performed in various cities of U.S. and in London, Eng.; also songs and instrumental numbers. Home: 72 W. 127th St., New York. Died July 18, 1942.

RACHMANINOFF, Sergei (Wassilievitch) (răx-mä'nē-nôf), pianist; b. Novgorod, Russia, Apr. 2, 1873; s. Basil and Liubov P. (Boutakoff) R.; studied at St. Petersburg and Moscow conservatories; gold medal, 1891; Mus. Dr., U. of Neb.; hon. academician St. Cecilia Soc., Rome; m. Natalie Satin, May 12, 1902; children—Irene (wife of Prince Peter Wolkonsky), Tatiana (Mrs. Boris Conus). Début in London, 1899; apptd. prof. piano, Maryinsky Sch. for Girls, Moscow, 1893; début in New York, 1909, followed by tour; has frequently appeared in musical centers. Composer 3 one-act operas, 4 piano concertos, also for orchestra, piano and voice. Home: 505 West End Av., New York, N.Y.* Died Mar. 28, 1943.

RAGSDALE, Bartow Davis, clergyman, educator; b. nr. Lithonia, DeKalb County, Ga., Feb. 7, 1861; s. John C. and Nancy (Lucas) R.; A.B., first honor, Mercer U., Macon, Ga., 1886, A.M., 1892, D.D., 1895; student Southern Bapt. Theol. Sem., Louisville, Ky., 2½ yrs., U. of Chicago, 2 summers; m. Lois Cloud, June 27, 1889; children—Cary (son), Eunice Elizabeth (Mrs. Alexander E. Wolfe). Ordained Southern Bapt. ministry, 1884; pastor successively at Albany, Quitman, Decatur and Conyers, Canton and Cairo, Ga., until 1914; bursar-treas. Mercer U., 1914-28; teacher Bible same univ., also in theol. dept., 1897-1905 and 1917-28; recording sec. Ga. Bapt. Conv. since 1895; has written, compiled and pub. 49 vols. of the Year Book of the Conv., served as historian since 1928, and as preacher ann. sermon, 1929. Mem. Phi Delta Theta. Democrat. Author: Story of Georgia Baptists, Vol. I, 1932, Vol. II, 1935, Vol. III, 1939; Memoir of Pinckney Daniel Pollock, 1942. Home: 553 Linden Av., Macon, Ga. Deceased.

RAIBLE, John R., business exec. Chmn. bd. dirs. Greif Bros. Cooperage Corp.; pres. and dir., Fanner Mfg. Co.; dir. Cleveland Welding Co., Cleveland Securities Co., A. C. Williams Co., Cleveland Worsted Mills Co., Cleveland Co-Operative Stove Co., Peuton Pub. Co. Home: 17866 Lake Road, Lakewood. Office: 2000 W. 25th St., Cleveland, Ohio. Died Mar. 3, 1948.

RAIFORD, Lemuel Charles (rā'fôrd), prof. organic chemistry; b. Southampton County, Va., Aug. 2, 1872; s. Junius Franklin and Juniata Frances (Bristow) R.; Ph.G., Md. Coll. Pharmacy, 1895; Ph.B., Brown U., 1900, M.A., 1904; Ph.D., U. of Chicago, 1909; m. Sara Alice Broomhead, Dec. 26, 1901 (died Apr. 4, 1939); 1 dau., Alice Mary (Mrs.

Mark C. Hagerman). Instr. in chemistry, Brown U., 1900-01, Clemson Coll., 1901-02; asso. prof. textile chemistry, Miss. Agrl. Coll., 1902-07; asso. in chemistry, U. of Chicago, 1907-09; research chemist, U. of Wyo., 1909-11; instr. in chemistry, U. of Chicago, 1911-15; prof. chemistry, Okla. Agrl. Coll., 1915-18; asso. prof. organic chemistry, State U. of Ia., 1918-27, prof. since 1927, visiting prof., Western Reserve Univ., summer, 1930, U. of Neb., summer, 1932. Fellow A.A.A.S., Am. Inst. Chemists; mem. Am. Assn. Univ. Profs., Am. Chem. Soc. (ex-sec. and chmn. Ia. sect.; chmn. organic chemistry div. 1937), Okla. Acad. Science (ex-pres.), Ia. Acad. Science, N.Y. Acad. of Science, Phi Beta Kappa, Sigma Xi, Alpha Chi Sigma, Phi Lambda Upsilon, Phi Delta Chi, Research Club (pres.). Presbyterian. Club: Triangle. Author: Laboratory Course in Color Chemistry, 1904. Mem. bd. of editors Jour. of Organic Chemistry since 1936. Contbr. to Am. Chem. Jour., Jour. Am. Chem. Soc. Home: 814 N. Linn St., Iowa City, Ia. Died Jan. 8, 1944.

RAINE, James Watt (rān), educator, clergyman; b. London, Eng., May 2, 1869; s. William and Janet Watt (Muir) R.; came to U.S., 1881; student Searcy Coll., Ark.; B.A., Oberlin College, 1893 (class orator), M.A., 1897; B.D., Union Theol. Seminary, 1897; D.D., Berea Coll., 1912; m. Harriet May, Aug. 14, 1894 (died 1895); 1 dau., Jessie Harriet (Mrs. U. V. Portmann); m. 2d, Clara Rebecca Martz, May 22, 1899; children—Forrester, Robert, William Thorwald, Kenneth Edgar, Dorothy (wife of R. P. Swire). Instructor at Kansas State Agrl. Coll., 1891-92, Oberlin Coll., 1894-96; ordained Congl. ministry, 1898; pastor successively Dayton, Litchfield, O., Cortland, and Riverhead, N.Y., until 1906; head Dept. English, Berea Coll., 1906-39, emeritus since 1939; dir. Coll. Theater. Dir. religious work Army Y.M.C.A., Camp Greenleaf, Ga., 1917-18, Camp Shelby, Miss., 1918-19. Author: Public Speaking (textbook), 1909; Mountain Ballads, 1920; The Land of Saddlebags, 1924; Bible Dramatics, 1927; Job, Prince of Uz (a play), 1938; Saddlebag Folk, the Way of Life in the Kentucky Mountains, 1941. Home: 46 Center St., Berea, Ky. Died Feb. 12, 1949.

RAIRDEN, Bradstreet Stinson, consul; b. New Orleans, Nov. 7, 1858; s. Bradstreet and Mary Brown (Tarbox) R.; grad. Bath High Sch., 1876; m. Elizabeth Berry Collins, Eng., Jan. 12, 1887; children—Frank Bradstreet, Percy Wallace, Mrs. Mamie Lowell Woodward, David Laurense, Albert Stuart. Followed the sea for 7 yrs., capt. for 3 yrs.; in ins. business, Java, 13 yrs.; consul at Batavia, Java, 1892-97 and Oct. 1900-Aug. 1917 at Riviere du Loup, P.Q., Can., 1917-20, Curacao, Aug. 11, 1920-July 1, 1924. Clubs: De Gezelligheid, Curacao (Curacao). Home: Santa Monica, Calif. Died Sept. 11, 1944.

RAITT, Effie Isabel (rāt), univ. prof.; b. Patterson, Ia., June 13, 1878; d. George Paterson and Jeannette (McFadden) Raitt; B.S., Columbia, 1903, A.M., 1919. Teacher in elementary sch., 1897-1901; dietitian, Mass. State Sanatorium, 1903-04, St. Luke's Hosp., New York, N.Y., 1904-05; house dir., Northwestern U., Evanston, Ill., 1905-11; dir. School of Home Economics, U. of Wash., since 1911. Chmn. nutrition com. King County, Wash., 1939-44; chmn. household management com. President's Conf. on Home Building and Home Ownership. Mem. Am. Assn. Univ. Profs., Am. Assn. Univ. Women, Am. Home Econ. Assn. (v.p. 1928-31, pres. 1934-36), Am. Dietetic Assn., (v.p. 1923-25), Nat. Conf. Family Relations, Sigma Xi, Iota Sigma Pi, Omicron Nu (v.p. 1933-35). Editor of household management com. report President's Conf. on Home Bldg. and Home Ownership, 1932; Economics of Household Production (Margaret Reid), 1934; Home Management (Irma Gross and Mary E. Lewis), 1938. Home: 2722 11th Av. N., Seattle 2, Wash. Died Dec. 4, 1945.

RALPH, Lester, artist; b. New York, July 29, 1876; s. Julian and Isabella (Mount) R.; ed. New York grammar schools and private schools; Brooklyn High School and Adelphi Acad., Brooklyn; student at Art Students' League, New York; also in London, Paris and Rome; m. Elsie Reasoner, May 15, 1904. Artist in Turko-Greek War, 1897; in South African War, 1900. Decorator and illustrator for mags. Address: 31 W. 33d St., New York. Died Apr. 5, 1927.

RALSTON, Anderson Wheeler, research dir.; b. Martins Ferry, O., Dec. 29, 1899; s. George Grant and Jessie Martha (Bachman) R.; B.S. cum laude, Kenyon Coll., Gambier, O., 1922, M.A., 1922; Ph. D., Ia. State Coll., 1927; m. Esther Carpenter, Aug. 29, 1923; 1 son, George Grant. Instr. chemistry, Ia. State Coll., 1923-27; research chemist Standard Oil Co. of N.J., 1929-31; research chemist, Armour & Co., Chicago, 1927-29, 1931-35, asst. dir. chem. research since 1935. Served in U.S. Army, 1918. Recipient Midwest Award, Am. Chem. Soc., 1946. Fellow A.A.A.S., Am. Inst. Chemistry; mem. Am. Chem. Soc. (dir. Chicago sect.), Am. Oil Chemists, Inst. Food Technologists, Soc. Chem. Industry, Sigma Pi, Phi Lambda Upsilon, Phi Kappa Phi, Sigma Xi. Republican. Episcopalian. Mason. Club: Beverly Hills Tennis (Chicago). Contbr. of articles to scientific journals. Holds many patents on fatty acids and their derivatives. Home: 8926 S. Hamilton Av. Office: Armour & Co., Chicago, Ill. Died Dec. 5, 1948.

RALSTON, Jackson Harvey (rawl'stŭn), lawyer; b. Sacramento, Calif., Feb. 6, 1857; s. Judge James H. and Harriet N. (Jackson) Ralston; educated, San Francisco High Sch., 1869-70; LL.B., Georgetown University, 1876; LL.D., National University, 1897; married Sara B. Rankin, June 1, 1887 (died Feb. 8, 1937); m. 2d, Opal V. Ralston, October 3, 1938. Engaged in law practice, Washington, D.C., 1878-1924. Delegate to France and Italy, Internat. Typographical Union of N.America, 1878; pres. Bd. Commrs. of Hyattsville, Md., when for first time the Single Tax system of taxation was applied for municipal purposes, 1892; counsel in Washington for Felipe Agoncillo, representing Filipino Republic, before war broke out, 1899; was Am. agent and mem. counsel in the case of the Pious Fund of the Californias against Mexico, the first dispute submitted to the Permanent Ct. of Arbitration at The Hague under The Hague Peace Convention of 1899; also named by U.S., 1903, as umpire for the Italian claims against Venezuela before the mixed tribunal at Caracas. Edited proc. of all mixed commns. at Caracas in vol. entitled Venezuelan Arbitrations of 1903; also report of French-Venezuelan Mixed Claims Commission under the Protocol of 1902. Lecturer at Stanford U., 1928-32. Democratic presdl. elector from Calif., 1932. Del. Dem. Nat. Conv., 1908. Dem. Congl. candidate 5th Md. Dist., 1916. Hon. v.p. Am. Soc. of Internat. Law. Clubs: Cosmos (Washington, D.C.); Commonwealth (San Francisco); Kiwanis (Palo Alto). Author: International Arbitral Law and Procedure, 1909; Democracy's International Law, 1922; Law and Procedure of International Tribunals, 1926, with Supplement, 1936; International Arbitration from Athens to Locarno, 1929; What's Wrong with Taxation?, 1931; A Quest for International Order, 1941; Confronting the Land Question, 1945. Author of taxation amendment of Md. Constitution, and co-author of referendum amendment adopted, 1915. Mason. Home: 1055 Cowper St., Palo Alto. Died Oct. 13, 1945; buried at Alta Mesa, Palo Alto, Calif.

RALSTON, Hon. James Layton, K.C., former minister national defence for Canada; b. Amherst, N.S., Sept. 27, 1881; s. Burnett William and Bessie (Layton) R.; ed. Amherst Acad. and Dalhousie Law Sch.; D.C.L. (hon.) Acadia U. (Wolfville, N.S.); LL.D. (hon.) U. of Dalhousie (Halifax, N.S.), Union Coll. (Schenectady, N.Y.), U. of Toronto (Toronto, Can.); married Nettie Winnifred McLeod, 1907; 1 son, Stuart Bowman Ralston. Read law in offices of Logan & Jenks, 1898-1903; admitted to Nova Scotia bar, 1903; partner Logan, Jenks & Ralston, 1903-09, Logan & Ralston, 1909-11, Ralston, Hanway & Ralston, Amherst, 1911-12, Maclean, Burchell & Ralston, Halifax, and later Burchell & Ralston, 1912-26; minister of National Defense, Ottawa, 1926-30; partner Mitchell, Ralston, Kearney & Duquet, Montreal, 1930-35, Ralston, Kearney & Duquet, 1935-39; Ralston, Kearney, Duquet & Mackay, since 1945. Dir. Eastern Tr. Co., Gillette Safety Razor Company of Canada, Ltd., Canadian Vickers, Limited, Montreal Dry Docks, Ltd., Montreal Locomotive Works, Ltd., Elected to Nova Scotia Legislature, Cumberland, 1911 and 1916; apptd. chmn. Royal Commission on Pensions and re-establishment by Federal Government, July 1922; accepted portfolio of National Defense, Mackenzie King Cabinet, October 8, 1926; elected to House of Commons, Shelburne-Yarmouth, 1926 and 1930; Canadian delegate to London Naval Conference, 1930; accepted portfolio of Finance in Mackenzie King Cabinet, September 6, 1939; elected to House of Commons (Prince, P.E.I.) by acclamation, January 2, 1940, re-elected March 1940; appointed minister nat. defence, July 5, 1940; resigned Nov. 1944. Commd. major, Can. Inf., Oct. 1916; commd. 85th Can. Inf. Batn., France, Apr. 1918-June 1919; gazetted lt. col., Aug. 21, 1918, col. Apr. 28, 1924. Decorated D.S.O., 1917, Bar to D.S.O., 1918, C.M.G. 1918; mentioned twice in dispatches. Gov. Acadia U. and McMaster U. Baptist. Clubs: Mount Royal, St. James; Forest and Stream, Montreal, Montreal Reform, Canadian Rotary (Montreal); Rideau (Ottawa); Halifax (Halifax, N.S.); Yarmouth Golf and Country; Summerside Rotary (Summerside, P.E.I.). Home: Gleneagles Apts. Office: 360 St. James St. West, Montreal 1, Que. Died May 22, 1948.

RAMAKER, Albert John (rā'mā-kĕr), prof. church history; b. Milwaukee, Wis., Oct. 3, 1860; s. John and Helen (Bongers) R.; grad. Rochester Theol. Sem., 1886; B.A., U. of Rochester, N.Y., 1895; D.D., Sioux Falls Coll., 1917; M.Th., Rochester Theol. Sem., 1927; m. Minna Winkler, Nov. 24, 1886; children—George W., Benjamin A. Ordained Bapt. ministry, 1886; pastor Cleveland, 1886-89; instr. German dept., Rochester Theol. Sem. (now Colgate-Rochester Div. Sch.), 1889-90, acting prof. ch. history and Greek lang., 1890-99, prof., 1899-1935, emeritus prof. since 1935. Dir. St. John's Charitable Assn. Mem. Acad. of Science, Rochester Hist. Soc. Republican. Mem. Phi Beta Kappa. Author: Ein Ueberblick über die Geschichte der deutschen Baptisten in America; Die Christliche Heiden-mission; Eine Kurze Geschichte der Baptisten; Our Missions in Germany and Central Europe; Das Täufertum im Reformationszeitalter; Die früheste Geschichte des Englischen Baptismus; Zur Feier des 75 Jährigen Bestehens der deutschen Abteilung des Seminars; Baptists in Russia; The German Baptists in the United States and Canada; Hymns and Hymnwriters Among the Anabaptists of the 16th Century. Home: Brighton, N.Y. Office: 246 Alexander St., Rochester, N.Y. Died Feb. 12, 1946.

RAMALEY, Francis (r'mā'lē), botanist; b. St. Paul, Minn., Nov. 16, 1870; s. David and Louisa Mary (DeGraw) R.; B.S., U. of Minn., 1895, Ph.D., 1899; m. Ethel Jackson, June 14, 1906; children—Edward Jackson, David, John DeGraw, Francis. Instr. botany, U. of Minn., 1894-98; asst. prof. biology, 1898-99, prof., 1899-1939, editor of University Studies since 1939, U. of Colo. Dir. Mountain Lab., Tolland, Colo., 1909-19; pres. Bd. Edn., Boulder, 1911-12. Republican. Fellow A.A.A.S. (pres. Southwestern div. 1930); mem. Am. Soc. Naturalists, Bot. Soc. America, Ecol. Soc. America (v.p. 1931, pres. 1940), Soc. Exptl. Biology and Medicine, Theta Delta Chi, Phi Beta Kappa, Sigma Xi. Author: Wild Flowers and Trees of Colorado, 1909; Prevention and Control of Disease, 1913; Outlines of Economic Botany, 1926; Colorado Plant Life, 1927; Plants Useful to Man, 1937; Plant Science Manual, 1937; Survey of Plant Kingdom, 1940; also articles in tech. jours. on botany and pub. health. Botanical editor of Ecology since 1940. Home: Boulder, Colo. Died June 10, 1942.

RAMSDELL, Charles William (rămz'dĕl), prof. Am. history; b. Salado, Tex., Apr. 4, 1877; s. Charles Henry and Augusta (Halley) R.; B.A., U. of Tex., 1903, M.A., 1904; Ph.D., Columbia, 1910; m. Susan Gertrude Griffith, Aug. 26, 1906; children—Mary Alice, Charles William. Instr. history, U. of Texas, 1906-12, adj. prof. Am. history, 1912-16, asso. prof., 1916-17, prof. since 1917. Asso. editor Southwestern Hist. Quarterly, 1910-38; editorial board Miss. Valley Hist. Review, 1930-33; mem. editorial bd. Jour. of Southern History, 1937-40; teacher summer schs., U. of Ill., 1923, 26, U. of Colo., 1924, Columbia, 1927, 40, Univ. of N.C., 1928, Western Reserve, 1930, Northwestern Univ., 1932, U. of W.Va., 1933, U. of Mo., 1935, Duke, 1938. Fellow Tex. State Hist. Assn. (sec.-treas. since 1907); mem. Miss. Valley Hist. Assn. (pres. 1928-29), Am. Hist. Assn. (exec. council 1931-34), N.C. Lit. and Hist. Assn., Southern Hist. Assn. (pres. 1936), Am. Assn. Univ. Profs., Philos. Soc. of Tex., Phi Beta Kappa. Democrat. Clubs: Town and Gown, University. Author: Reconstruction in Texas (thesis), 1910. Co-author of School History of Texas, 1912. Editor: History of Bell County, 1936; (with W. H. Stephenson), A History of the South, 10 vols., since 1938; Laws of the Last Session of the Confederate Congress, 1941. Contbr. to hist. jours. Home: 4403 Barrow St., Austin, Tex. Died July 3, 1942.

RAMSEY, George, patent lawyer; b. Preble County, O., Oct. 31, 1878; s. John M. and Susan (Reeves) R.; student Ohio Northern U., Ada, O., 1895-96; Asso. of Science, Bradley Poly. Inst., Peoria, Ill., 1915; LL.B., George Washington U., Washington, D.C., 1908; m. Edith A. Corey, Oct. 11, 1911. Asst. instr. mathematics, Bradley Poly. Inst., 1901-02; with U.S. Engr. Corps, on deep water survey, Chicago to St. Louis, 1902-05; examiner U.S. Patent Office, 1905-09; admitted to bar Supreme Court of D.C., and Court of Appeals for D.C., 1908, Supreme Court of U.S., 1913, N.Y. Supreme Court, 1919; also member bar many other U.S. courts; known in litigation relating to adding machines, typewriters, cash registers, metallurgy, glass machinery. Legal adviser Draft Board 66, New York; professor patent law, George Washington University, 1914-16. Dir. Valley Mold and Iron Corporation. Chmn. Sec. of Commerce's Committee on Patent Laws; mem. patent sect. Business Advisory Council; counsel for Department of Commerce before Temporary Nat. Econ. Committe; mem. Conn. Gen. Assembly, 1947-48, 1949-50 (judiciary com.). Pres. Eliza Fairchild Memorial Center. Chmn. Nat. Council of Am. Patent Law Association, 1940-41, chmn. Hampton Ration Board; member Am. Bar Association (council patent section 1936-37). Am. Patent Law Assn. (pres. 1940-41), N.Y. Patent Law Assn. (pres. 1935-36), Am. Judicature Society, Ohio Soc. of New York (v.p. 1942), Am. Soc. M.E., Acad. Polit. Science, Franklin Inst., Met. Museum of Art, Del. Conn. Rep. State Convention, 1944-46-48 (platform com., 1944-48). Am. Ordnance Assn. (pres.) Little River Grange. Phi Delta Phi, Phi Lambda Xi. Republican. Congregationalist. Mason (Aurora Grata Consistory; Clinton Commandery; Kismet Temple Shrine). Clubs: Downtown Athletic, Sound View Golf, Sphinx, Moslem Shrine. Author: Patents. Contbr. on patent law topics. Home: Hampton, Conn. Office: 11 Park Place, New York 7, N.Y. Died Feb. 11, 1950.

RAMSEY, George Samuel, lawyer; b. on farm near Viola, Warren County, Tenn., Aug. 18, 1874; s. George Washington and Elizabeth (King) R.; student Burritt Coll., Spencer, Tenn.; m. Earline Young, Nov. 28, 1898; 1 dau., Margaret (Mrs. William M. Smartt); m. 2d, Ethel P. Kerr, July 2, 1934. Admitted to Tenn. bar, 1896, and entered practice arguing cases before Supreme Court and Chancery Court of Appeals; moved to Muskogee, Indian Territory (now Okla.), 1905, and admitted to territorial bar and Okla. State bar; in practice at Tulsa since 1925, arguing many cases before U.S. Circuit Courts of Appeals and 15 before U.S. Supreme Court; mem. firm Ramsey, Martin & Logan since 1925. Rep. nominee for judge of Chancery Court of Appeals, Tenn., 1904; first Rep. justice of Supreme Court of Okla., 1920 (apptd. by Dem. gov.). Mem. Okla. State Bar Assn (pres. 1914-15). Elk. Independent Republican. Club: Tulsa. Author address to Tenn. Bar Assn. publ. in Am. Law Review. Home: 1131 E. 18th St. Office: 425 National Bank of Tulsa Bldg., Tulsa, Okla. Died Dec. 27, 1941.

RAMSEY, Horace Marion, clergyman; b. Salem, Ore., June 30, 1880; s. William Marion and Alzada (Harris) R.; B.A., Pacific U., Forest Grove, Ore., 1899; grad. Ch. Div. Sch., San Mateo, Calif., 1902; M.A., U. of Calif., 1902; studied Columbia, 1902-03, U. of Marburg, Germany, 1903-05; D.D., Seabury Div. Sch., 1920; m. Helen G. Ramsdell, June 9, 1908; children—Frederic Haynes, Stephen Marion. Temple

Emmanuel fellow, U. of Calif., 1901-02; Eigenbrodt fellow, Gen. Theol. Sem., 1902-05; deacon, 1902, priest, 1905, P.E. Ch.; asst. St. Stephen's Ch., New York, 1902-03; in charge English Chapel, Weimar, Germany, 1904, St. Paul's Ch., Rome, Italy, 1905; dean St. Stephen's Pro-Cathedral, Portland, Ore., 1905-16 and since May 1, 1923; prof. Greek and N.T. exegesis, Seabury Div. Sch., Faribault, Minn., 1916-23. Democrat. Home: 1928 S.W. Myrtle St., Portland. Ore. Died Oct. 6, 1942.

RAMSEY, Leonidas Willing, advt. counsel; b. Hazelhurst, Miss., May 22, 1891; s. Jacob Leonidas and Carrie (Willing) R.; Marion (Ala.) Inst., 1908-09; Millsaps Coll., 1909-11; B.S., in Landscape Gardening, U. of Ill., 1914; m. Norma Klindt, Nov. 3, 1917; children—Leonidas Willing, George Klindt, Julianne. Landscape architect, 1914-21; engaged in advt. work since 1921; pres. The L. W. Ramsey Co., advt. agts., since 1921. Served as ensign U.S.N.R.F., World War. Founder Nat. Yard and Garden Contest Association; director National Home Planting Bureau. Director The American Green Cross. President Davenport Municipal Art Gallery. Member University Landscape Architects Society, Kappa Sigma, Delta Sigma Chi, Scarab, Mawanda. Clubs: Davenport Outing, Davenport Country; Rock Island Arsenal Golf; Seven Twenty, Town (Davenport); Racquet, Tavern (Chicago). Author: Landscaping the Home Grounds, 1930; Garden Pools (with C. H. Lawrence), 1931; The Outdoor Living Room (with C. H. Lawrence), 1932; Time Out for Adventure, 1934. Contbr. to Am. Home, Ladies' Home Journal, Better Homes and Gardens, etc. Home: 834 Marquette St., Davenport, Ia. Office: Union Bldg., Davenport, Ia.; also 230 N. Michigan Av., Chicago, Ill. Died Jan. 2. 1947; buried, Davenport, Ia.

RAMSEYER, C(hristian) William (răm'sī-ẽr), ex-congressman; b. nr. Collinsville, Butler, O., Mar. 13, 1875; s. John and Anna (Ummel) R.; grad. Southern Ia. Normal Sch., 1897, Ia. State Teachers' Coll., 1902; LL.B., State U. of Ia., 1906; m. Ruby M. Phillips, 1915; children—Jane, Barbara. Teacher in pub. schs. 6 yrs.; admitted to Ia. bar, 1906, and practiced in Bloomfield. County atty. Davis County, Ia., 1911-15; mem. 64th to 72d Congresses (1915-33), 6th Ia. Dist.; commr. U.S. Court of Claims since 1933. Republican. Mem. Ia. State Bar Assn., Am. Bar Assn., Polit. Science Assn., Ia. State Hist. Soc. Home: Bloomfield, Ia. Address: U.S. Court of Claims, Washington, D.C. Died Nov. 1, 1943.

RANCK, Henry Haverstick, clergyman; b. nr. Lancaster, Pa., July 24, 1868; s. Jacob Eby and Martha Bausman (Haverstick) R.; A.B., Franklin and Marshall Coll., 1892 (D.D., 1916); studied Columbia U. and Union Theol. Sem., 1892-93; grad. Theol. Sem. Ref. Church in U.S., 1895; m. Mary Hill Byrne, April 22, 1897, died Sept. 16, 1934); children—James Byrne, Alice Bausman (Mrs. Alton E. Laughlin). Ordained to the ministry of the Reformed Church in U.S., 1896; pastor St. Paul's Ch., Mechanicsburg, Pa., 1896-99, St. John's Ch., Lebanon, Pa., 1899-1901, St. Andrew's Church, Reading, Pa., 1901-14, Grace Evangelical and Reformed Churches, Washington, D.C., 1914-39, now pastor emeritus. Member board of Education Eastern Synod, Reformed Church, 1909-1914, Potomac Synod, 1917-24; pres. Potomac Synod's Bd. Edn., 1920-23, mem. edn. commn., 1917-20; fraternal delegate to General Assembly United Presbyterian Church, 1916; trustee Huping Christian College, Yochow, China, 1922-30; dir. Hood Coll., 1924-28, Massanutten Acad., Woodstock, Va., 1919-30; mem. efficiency commission of General Synod, 1923-26; secretary executive committee Washinbton Federation of Chs., 1920-23, mem. exec. com., 1920-39; mem. exec. com. of "Religious Life in Nation's Capitol," 1935-39; mem. Washington com. Fed. Council of Chs., 1921-31; rep. Ref. Ch. on Federal Council's Com. of Army and Navy Chaplains, 1917-35; del. to Alliance of Ref. Chs., Cardiff, Wales, 1925; del. to Universal Christian Conf. on Life and Work, Stockholm, 1925 and to Oxford, 1937; del. to Faith and Order Conf., Edinburgh, 1937. Member Huguenot society of D.C. (honorary), Over 65 Club, Frederick, Maryland, Phi Beta Kappa. Mason. Author: History of St. John's Reformed Church, 1901; Historical Sketch of the Reformed Church and of Grace Reformed Congregation, D.C., 1923; Life of Rev. Benjamin Bausman, D.D., LL.D., 1912, 2d edit., 1935. Contbr. to Reformed Church Pulpit, to Pulpit Eloquence, and to religious press. Home: Route 1 Lancaster, Pa. Died Aug. 19, 1948.

RANCK, Than Vanneman, newspaperman; b. Philadelphia, Pa., Oct. 4, 1874; s. Isaac Winters and Harriet E. (Vanneman) R.; ed. Dickinson Coll., Carlisle, Pa.; m. May Maurer, Oct. 14, 1897; 1 dau., Doris (Mrs. Doris Ranck Rend). Began as reporter Shamokin Herald, 1896; reporter Phila. Inquirer, 1897-99; state editor and editor Sunday Magazine, Philadelphia North American, 1900-06; day city editor New York American, 1906-11; chief Washington corr. Hearst newspapers, 1911; mng. editor New York American, 1912-16; editor Chicago Herald-Examiner, 1916-18, New York American, 1918-20, reorganizer of foreign service, Hearst newspapers, 1919; organizer (for Hearst interests), Boston Daily Advertiser, 1921, and editor Daily and Sunday Advertiser until 1925; editor Chicago Herald-Examiner, 1926-28; editorial mgr. Hearst newspapers, 1928-37. (Mt. Ranck in Antarctic named for him by Sir Hubert Wilkins, 1928, because of his connection with organization of that expdn.). Methodist. Mason. Home: "Fairview," Easton, Talbot County, Md. Died July 30, 1947; buried in Woodlawn Cemetery, Port Deposit, Md.

RAND, Edward Kennard, educator; b. Boston, Mass., Dec. 20, 1871; s. Edward Augustus and Mary Frances (Abbott) R.; A.B., Harvard Univ., 1894, A.M., 1895; Ph.D., U. of Munich, 1900; Harvard Divinity Sch., 1894-95; Episcopal Theol. Sch., 1897-98; hon. Litt.D., Manchester U., 1926, Western Reserve U., 1931, Trinity College, Dublin, 1932, Harvard Univ., 1941; LL.D., Glasgow U., 1936; Pennsylvania Univ., 1942; m. Belle Brent Palmer, June 20, 1901. Instructor Latin, University of Chicago, 1895-98; instructor Latin, Harvard Univ., 1901-05, asst. professor, 1905-09, prof., 1909-42, emer. since 1942. Former trustee and life member Am. Acad. at Rome; annual prof. Am. Acad. at Rome, 1912-13, Sather prof. classical lit., U. of Calif., 1919-20; exchange professor at Sorbonne, Paris, 1933-34; sr. research fellow Dumbarton Oaks Research Library and Collection, Washington, D.C., 1943-44; resident scholar, 1944-45. Fellow American Acad. Arts and Sciences (emeritus), Mediæval Academy America (ex-pres.); mem. American Philosophical Society, American Philol. Society (ex-pres.), Archæol. Inst. America, Mass. Hist. Soc., Colonial Soc. of Mass., Dante Soc., Saturday Club of Boston; Cambridge Scientific Club, Harvard Faculty Club, Harvard Club of Boston, Harvard Signet Society; corr. fellow British Acad.; corr. mem. Bavarian Acad. of Sciences, Virgilian Soc. of Mantua, Kungl. Humanistika Vetenskapssamfundet, Lund, Société des Bollandistes, Institut de France, Acad. des Ins. et Belles Lettres. Republican. Episcopalian. Co-author: Dante's Alighierii Operum Latinorum Concordantiæ. Author: Ovid and His Influence; Founders of the Middle Ages; A Survey of the Manuscripts of Tours; The Earliest Book of Tours; In Quest of Virgil's Birthplace; A Walk to Horace's Farm; The Magical Art of Virgil; Les Esprits Souverains dans la Littérature Romaine; The Building of Eternal Rome; also numerous articles on classical and mediæval subjects. Joint editor and translator: Boethius' Opuscula Sacra and Consolatio Philosophiæ; co-editor, Harvard edit. of Servius. Address: 107 Lake View Av., Cambridge 38, Mass. Died Oct. 28, 1945.

RAND, Ellen Emmet (Mrs. William Blanchard Rand), artist; b. San Francisco, Calif., Mar. 4, 1876; studied in New York and Paris; married William Blanchard Rand. Portrait of Augustus Saint-Gaudens and Benjamin Altman, Metropolitan Museum, New York. Awarded silver medal, St. Louis Expn., 1904; bronze medal, Buenos Aires Expn., 1910; gold medal, Panama-Pacific Expn., San Francisco, 1915; Beck gold medal, Pa. Acad. Fine Arts, 1922; Gould prize, Nat. Assn. Women Painters and Sculptors, 1927. N.A., 1926. Died Dec. 18, 1941.

RAND, Frank Chambless, shoe mfr.; b. Marshall County, Miss., Feb. 25, 1876; s. Henry Oscar and Ada Elizabeth (Norfleet) R.; B.A., Vanderbilt, 1898; m. Nettie Lumpkin Hale, Oct. 5, 1904 (died 1942); children—Edgar E., Miriam L., Frank C., Henry H., Norfleet H., Laura H. Shoe salesman; Roberts, Johnson & Rand Co., St. Louis, 1898-1902, supt. factory, 1902-08, v.p., 1908-11; a v.p. Internat. Shoe Co. (combination various cos.), 1911-16, president, 1916-30, now chairman board; director Mercantile-Commerce Bank & Trust Company, St. Louis and S.F. R.R. (voting trustee), Union Electric Co., Southwestern Bell Telephone Co. Pres. bd. trustees Vanderbilt U.; chmn. bd. Webb School; chmn. bd. Barnes Hosp., St. Louis. Mem. Delta Kappa Epsilon. Democrat. Methodist. Clubs: Racquet, Noonday, St. Louis Country, Log Cabin. Home: 7100 Delmar Blvd. Office: 1509 Washington Av., St. Louis, Mo. Died Dec. 2, 1949.

RAND, Frederick Henry, fruit grower; b. Boston, July 19, 1846; s. Edward S. and Elizabeth A. (Arnold) R.; Norwich U., Vt., 1861-63, B.S., 1911, as of 1864; m. Julia Frances Hasbrouck, of Boston, Feb. 10, 1874. Engaged in mining in Cal.; in mercantile business, Boston, 1869-76; orange grower, Fla., 1876; incorporator South Fla. R.R., 1879, sec., gen. passenger and freight agent, 1879-86; pres. Sanford Water Works, 1886-1906; pres. Sanford Light & Fuel Co., 1886-1900; agent, atty. in fact and mgr. Fla. Land & Colonization Co., 1886-1916; pres. 1st Nat. Bank, Sanford, Fla. Commd. 1st lt. 1st Independent Battalion, 1st Mass. Cav., July 2, 1863; capt. 4th Mass. Cav., Jan. 19, 1864; hon. discharged Aug. 1864; 2d lt. 1st Battalion Cav., frontier service, Dec. 27, 1864; capt., Dec. 30, 1864; discharged Aug. 30, 1865. Trustee U. of the South, Sewanee, Tenn.; trustee Ch. Home and Hosp., Orlando, Fla. Mem. Loyal Legion, Theta Chi. Republican. Episcopalian (has served 4 times as deputy in Gen. Conv. P.E. Ch.). Mason (32°). Home: Sanford, Florida. Died July 12, 1933.

RAND, George Franklin, banker; b. North Tonawanda, N.Y., Dec. 9, 1891; s. George Franklin and Vina S. (Fisher) R.; B.S. and D.Sc., Univ. of Pa.; m. Isabel Hadley Williams, Mar. 28, 1922; children—George F., Isabel Hadley, Calvin Gordon. Asst. sec. Marine Trust Co., 1919, v.p., 1920, pres. since 1926; dir. Marine Trust Co., Am. Steamship Co., Remington Rand, Inc., Marine Midland Corp., Marine Midland Trust Co. (New York), Garlock Packing Co., Buffalo Ins. Co., Buffalo, Rochester & Pittsburgh R.R. Co., etc. With Y.M.C.A., in France, 1917-18, World War. Dir. Buffalo Foundation. Mem. Delta Upsilon. Officier de l'Instruction Publique and mem. Légion d'honneur, France. Republican. Presbyterian, Mason (33°). Clubs: Bankers (New York); Buffalo, Saturn, University, Buffalo Athletic, Saddle and Bridle, Buffalo Country. Home: 161 Nottingham Terrace. Office: 237 Main St., Buffalo, N.Y. Died Nov. 19, 1942.

RAND, John Langdon, judge; b. Portsmouth, N.H., Oct. 28, 1861; s. John Sullivan and Elvira Wallace (Odiorne) R.; A.B., Dartmouth, 1883; LL.D., Whitman Coll., Walla Walla, Wash., 1928; m. Edith G. Packwood, July 23, 1895. Admitted to Wash. bar, 1885, and began practice at Walla Walla; city atty. Baker, Ore., 1892-94; dist. atty. 6th Jud. Dist. of Ore., 1888-90 and 1894-96; mem. Ore. State Senate, 1903, 05; apptd. asso. justice Supreme Court of Ore., 1921, for term expiring 1922, elected 4 terms, 1922, 1928, 1934 and 1940, chief justice, 1927-28, 1933-34, 1939-40. Republican. Mason (K.T., 32°, Shriner). K.P., Elk. Home: 1391 Court, Salem, Ore. Died Nov. 19, 1942.

RANDALL, Albert Borland, master mariner, naval officer; b. Brookhaven, L.I., N.Y., Sept. 11, 1879; s. William Frederick and Sarah Elizabeth (Smith) R.; student Vermont Acad., Saxton's River, Vt., 1896-97; m. Dorothy Clara Boyer, June 6, 1908; children—Sylvia Elizabeth (wife of Dr. Harold S. Hain), Albert Borland, Jr., Dorothy Virginia (wife of Eugene Francis Mooney). Began as seaman in sailing vessels; promoted through grades and ranks, receiving his masters license, 1905, and receiving 1st command, January 17, 1907; commander various ships including the Republic, George Washington, Leviathan and Manhattan; commodore United States Lines, Jan. 1931-Oct. 1939; retired because of age limit, Oct. 2, 1939; apptd. rear adm., U.S. Naval Reserve, Jan. 17, 1942; recalled to active duty; assigned to War Shipping Administration Training Organization as comdt. stationed Washington, D.C., March 29, 1943. Member various Naval Reserve Organizations since May 12, 1902. Decorated Chevalier Legion of Honor (French); awarded Certificate of Appreciation, U.S. Navy Dept.; letter of commendation from President F. D. Roosevelt for outstanding service in Merchant Marine and Navy, upon retirement from Merchant Service. Mem. Marine Soc. of City of New York, S.A.R.; hon. mem. Propeller Club. Democrat. Mason (K.T.). Home: Whitestone, L.I., N.Y. Died Dec. 1, 1945.

RANDALL, Blanchard, merchant; b. Annapolis, Md., Nov. 12, 1856; s. Alexander and Elizabeth Philpot (Blanchard) R.; A.B., St. John's Coll., Annapolis, 1874 (hon. A.M., 1906); m. Susan Katharine Brune, 1884; children—Frederick Brune, Mrs. Susan Katharine Pincoffs, Emily Brune, Mrs. Elizabeth Blanchard Slack, Blanchard, Mrs. Evelyn Barton Hanrahan, Alexander. In mercantile business, Baltimore, since 1874; sr. mem. Gill & Fisher since 1907; dir. Safe Deposit & Trust Co., Maryland Life Ins. Co., The Savings Bank of Baltimore, Phila., Baltimore & Washington R.R. Co. Pres. Nat. Bd. of Trade, 1902 and 1903. Trustee Johns Hopkins U., Johns Hopkins Hosp. Republican. Mem. Md. Soc. of Cincinnati. Clubs: Grolier, Nat. Arts (New York); Maryland, University, South River, Catonsville Country. Home: 208 Kemble Road. Office: Chamber of Commerce, Baltimore, Md. Died Aug. 21, 1942.

RANDALL, Edward, physician; b. Walker County, Tex., Oct. 7, 1860; s. Samuel (M.D., surgeon in Confederate Army) and Texanna (Garrett) R.; A.B., Washington and Lee Univ., Va., 1879 (Phi Beta Kappa); M.D., U. of Pa., 1883; intern Phila. Gen. Hosp., 1883-84; post-grad. work, Berlin, Heidelberg and Vienna, 2 yrs.; m. Laura, d. Judge W. P. Ballinger, Apr. 30, 1889; 1 son, Edward. Practiced at Galveston since 1886; prof. materia medica and therapeutics and physical diagnosis, U. of Tex., Med. Dept., 1891-1929 (emeritus). Former mem. Board of Regents University of Texas; former chairman board John Sealy Hospital; president Rosenberg Library, Texas Philosophical Society; chairman Sealy-Smith Foundation. Mem. A.M.A., Tex. Med. Assn. (emeritus), Galveston County Med. Soc. (pres.), Beta Theta Pi, Alpha Mu Pi Omega, Alpha Omega Alpha. Democrat. Episcopalian. Home: 2004 Broadway. Office: Am. Nat. Ins. Co.'s Bldg., Galveston, Tex. Died Aug. 1944.

RANDALL, J(ohn) Herman, clergyman; b. St. Paul, Minn., Apr. 27, 1871; s. John H. and Sarah A. O. Randall; B.A., Colgate U., 1892; student U. of Chicago Div. Sch., 1893-96; m. Minerva I. Ballard, July 26, 1896; children—John Herman, Robert Hulbert. Licensed, 1888, ordained, 1895, Bapt. ministry; pastor Chenoa, Ill., 1893-95, Chicago Av. Ch., Minneapolis, 1895-97, Fountain St. Ch., Grand Rapids, Mich., 1897-1906, Mt. Morris Ch., N.Y. City, 1906-19; asso. minister Community Church, N.Y. City, Jan. 1920-27. Became dir. of World Unity Foundation and editor World Unity Mag., 1927, now retired. Mem. S.A.R., Phi Beta Kappa. Republican. Club: Dunwoodie Country. Author: A New Philosophy of Life, 1910; Culture of Personality, 1912; Humanity at the Crossroads, 1915; Life of Reality, 1916; The Philosophy of Power, 1917; The Essence of Democracy, 1918; With Soul on Fire, 1919; The Spirit of the New Philosophy, 1919; The New Light on Immortality, 1921; The Irrepressible Conflict in Religion, 1925; The Mastery of Life, 1925; Religion and the Modern World; A World Community. Home: 527 Riverside Drive, New York, N.Y. Died May 15, 1946.

RANDALL, Merle, chem. and chem. engring. cons.; b. Poplar Bluff, Mo., Jan. 29, 1888; s. Warren Smith and Anna Elizabeth (Marks) R.; A.B., University of Missouri, 1907, A.M., 1909; fellow Mass. Institute Technology, 1909-12, Ph.D., 1912; m. Lillian Frances Denham, June 14, 1916; children—Merle Denham, Robert Warren. Began as clk. in postoffice, Poplar Bluff, 1902-04; research asst. U. of Calif., 1912-13, research asso., 1914-17, asst. prof. chemistry, 1917-22, asso. prof., 1922-27, prof. 1927-44, prof. emeritus since 1944. Chmn. sub. com. on chemistry, Termite Investigations Com., 1929, mem. editorial bd., 1931; dir. research, Stuart Oxygen Co., 1944-48, Randall and Sons, since 1942. Fellow A.A.A.S.; member Society Promotion Engineering Education, American Inst. Chem. Engring., Am. Chem. Soc., Am. Soc. Testing Materials, Am. Soc. Refrig. Engrs., Am. Soc. Metals, Am. Welding Soc., Sigma Xi, Alpha Chi Sigma. Republican. Presbyterian. Mason. (K.T., Shriner). Club: Faculty. Author: Thermodynamics and the Free Energy of Chemical Substances, 1923; Termites and Termite Control, 1934; Elementary Physical Chemistry, 1942. Home: 2512 Etna St., Berkeley 4, Calif. Died Mar. 19, 1950.

RANDALL, Otis Everett, univ. prof.; b. N. Stonington, Conn., Feb. 28, 1860; s. Darius Hewitt and Abby Palmer (Frink) R.; A.B., Brown U., 1884, A.M., 1887, Ph.D., 1896; student at Technische Hochschule, Charlottenburg, Germany, and U. of Berlin, 1899-1900; m. Mabel Herbert Goffe, June 19, 1889; children—Wallace Everett, Mabel Maye (dec.). Served as teacher Providence High School, 1884-85; instr. mathematics and civil engineering, 1885-91, asst. prof., 1891-92, asso. prof. mech. drawing, 1892-96, prof., 1896-1905, prof. mechanics and mech. drawing, 1905-31, dean of the university, 1912-31, Brown University. Chmn. advisory bd. The Delphian Society. Mem. Sigma Chapter Psi Upsilon, Phi Beta Kappa, and Sigma Xi fraternities. Republican. Conglist. Author: Directions in Regard to the Construction of Plates in Mechanical Drawing, 1895; Directions in Regard to the Construction of Plates in Mechanical Drawing and in Descriptive Geometry, 1902; Shades and Shadows and Perspective, 1902; Elements of Descriptive Geometry; The Dean's Window, 1934. Retired, 1931. Home: 236 Butler Av., Providence, R.I. Died Aug. 11, 1946.

RANDOLPH, William Mann, M.D.; b. Albemarle County, Va., Jan. 14, 1870; s. William L. and Agnes (Dillon) R.; M.D., U. of Va., 1890; grad. study N.Y. Post Grad. Hosp., 1890-92, Vanderbilt Clinic, New York, 1890; m. Mary Walker, Oct. 20, 1894; children—Carolina R., Sarah Nicholas, Agnes Dillon, Thomas J., Mary Walker, Hollins N., Francis M. Practiced Charlottesville, Va., 1892-1913, and since 1930; prof. gynecology and surgery, U. of Va., 1905; surgeon Phelps-Dodge Corp., Douglas, Ariz., 1913-18, Central Copper Co., Mascot, Ariz., 1924-28; clinician and specialist in tuberculosis, Va. State Dept. of Health, since 1930, holding "traveling clinics" to reach effectively country dists. Capt. Troop K, Albemarle Light Horse, 1892-97; maj. Med. Service, 17th Inf., Va. Vols., 1898-1904, commd. capt. M.C., 1917; chief of med. service and comdg. officer hospital, Camp Harry J. Jones, Douglas, Ariz., 1918; maj. M.C., 1918, surgeon Ariz. dist. Mem. bd. visitors U. of Va., 1912; mem. sch. bd., Tombstone, Ariz., 1918, Dem. County Com., 1924. Democrat. Episcopalian. Address: State Dept. of Health, Richmond, Va.* Died Jan. 25, 1944.

RANGELER, William Francis (rānj'lēr), seminary prof.; b. Findlay, O., Aug. 8, 1869; s. Abraham and Clarinda Ann (Moore) R.; B.S., Ohio Northern U., Ada, O., 1892; A.M., Wittenberg Coll., Springfield, O., 1897; grad. Hamma Divinity Sch., 1898, D.D., 1917; m. India Herma Fellers, July 28, 1892; children—Ralph E., Luther W., Mary C., Hugh T. Teacher in public schools, 1885-93; Y.M.C.A. sec., 1893-95; ordained to Lutheran ministry, 1898; pastor, Wapakoneta, O., 1898-1900, Leipsic, O., 1900-03, Tippecanoe City, O., 1903-08, New Philadelphia, O., 1908-19; pres. East Ohio Synod Evang. Luth. Ch., 1912-14; pastor West Point, Neb., 1919-23; full time pres. Neb. Synod, 1923-26; mem. of faculty, Western Theol. Sem., since 1926, dean 1933-39; also prof. of N.T. history, Midland Coll. and mem. of its faculty since 1926; also head dept. of Christian edn. and religious councilor; prof. practical theology in Western Theol. Sem. Mem. commn. of adjudication United Luth. Ch. in America, 1926-38 (pres. 1936-38); mem. of Merger Convention Luth. Gen. Bodies, 1918; mem. bd. trustees Wittenberg Coll., 1911-19, Midland Coll., 1924-26. Emeritus professor of Practical Theology in Western Theological Seminary since 1943 and Honorary Chaplain of Midland College. Mem. Nat. Assn. of Bible Instructors; past pres. Fremont Kiwanis Club. Address: 125 Conger Av., Akron 3, O. Died June 29, 1949.

RANKIN, James Doig, theologian; b. Robinson, Ill.; s. Rev. Alexander R. and Vianna C. (De Groffe) R.; grad. Westminster Coll., New Wilmington, Pa., 1882, Pittsburgh Theol. Sem., 1885; D.D., Monmouth (Illinois) College, 1894, LL.D., 1929, Tarkio (Mo.) College, 1910; married Daisy Meloy, May 1894 (dec.); children—Mary Meloy Theobald (dec.), James Alex. Brownlee; m. 2d, Jessie McCormick, March 1940. Ordained U.P. ministry, 1885; pastor 1st Ch., Denver, Colo., 1885-1910, 1st Ch. Wilkinsburg, Pa., 1910-15; prof. theology and sociology, Pittsburgh Theol. Sem., 1914-30 (emeritus); pastor of First U.P. Church, Pasadena, 1929-37. Asso. editor Christian Statesman, Pittsburgh; since 1902, asso. editor United Presbyterian, Pittsburgh. Active in civic and reform work during 25 yrs. in Denver—chmn. Com. of Good Govt. 5 yrs., pres. Colo. Anti-Saloon League 12 years, chaplain, Colo. Senate, 1908-10. Moderator U.P. Synod of Neb., 1894; of Gen. Assembly U.P. Ch., 1910. Trustee Westminster Coll.; mem. bd. dirs. Pittsburgh Anti-Saloon League; pres. Bd. of Freedmen's Missions, U.P. Ch.; mem. Bd. Home Missions U.P. Ch. and of Evangelistic Com. U.P. Ch. Author: Nineteen Christian Centuries, 1901. Contbr. many articles to mags. Address: 715 S. El Molino Av., Pasadena, Calif. Died Sep. 22, 1949.

RANKIN, John Mercer, lawyer and atty. gen.; b. Fulton County, Ill., June 9, 1873; s. John and Anna (Dobson) R.; student Kent Coll. of Law, 1901-02; m. Marie Green Short, July 2, 1928; 1 dau., Mary Ann. Began as teacher, Ill., 1894; admitted to Ill. bar, 1904; began practice in Iowa, Sept. 1, 1917; mem. Ia. State Legislature, 1921-25; judge Ia. Dist. Court, 1925-39; asst. atty. gen. of Ia., 1939-40, atty. gen. since June 1940. Mem. Am., Iowa State and Lee County bar assns. Republican. Mason (Consistory). Club: Keokuk (Keokuk, Ia.). Home: Keokuk, Ia. Office: State House, Des Moines, Ia. Died June 21, 1947.

RANKIN, Walter Mead, biologist; b. Newark, N.J., Dec. 1, 1857; s. William and Ellen Hope (Stevens) R.; A.B., Williams, 1879; M.S., Princeton, 1884; Ph.D., U. of Munich, 1889; unmarried. Instr. biology, Princeton U., 1889-95, asst. prof., 1895-1901, prof., 1901-23, emeritus since 1923. Fellow A.A.A.S.; mem. Am. Soc. Naturalists. Presbyterian. Club: Nassau (Princeton). Home: 5 Evelyn Pl., Princeton, N.J. Died May 25, 1947; buried Mount Pleasant Cemetery, Newark, N.J.

RANKIN, William Durham, farmer, stockman; b. Onarga, Ill., Feb. 12, 1876; s. William A. and Mary (Durham) R.; ed. Grand Prairie Sem.; student Rush Med. Coll., Chicago, 1896-97; m. Nellie May Atwood, Feb. 21, 1914. Clerk Onarga Bank, 1899-1910; organized drainage dist., Iroquois County, Ill., 1910; pres. Iroquois Canning Co., 1912-16; succeeded father in live stock business at Tarkio, Mo., 1916; widely known for demonstration of sweet clover as a medium for increasing fertility of soil and for fattening cattle; also known for extensive use in tiling of a system of checks by which workmen may verify surveyor's figures and for erosion control in hilly country through certain types of dams. Republican. Mason. Home: 1800 S.W. 13th St., Miami, Fla. Died Mar. 5, 1943.

RANNEY, George Alfred (ră'nē), chmn. Peoples Gas Light & Coke Co.; b. Chicago, Ill., July 13, 1874; s. Henry Collings and Lucy Ann (Butler) R.; ed. gram. sch., Chicago; m. Cornelia Williams, Nov. 17, 1908; children—Dorothy Williams (Mrs. Gaylord Donnelly), George A., Cornelia (Mrs. Wyndham Hasler). With Bank of Montreal, Chicago, 1889-98; with McCormick Harvesting Machine Co., 1898-1902; with Internat. Harvester Co., 1902-33; elected sec. 1913, sec.-treas., 1916, v.p. and treas., 1922-32, v.p. in charge of sales, Jan. 1932-May 1, 1933; vice chmn. and dir. Commonwealth Edison Co., Peoples Gas Light & Coke Co. and Public Service Company of Northern Illinois—Chicago, 1933-35; chief executive officer (chmn.) Peoples Gas Light & Coke Co. since 1935, also dir.; director International Harvester Co. (mem. exec. com.), First Nat. Bank (member executive committee). Trustee Museum of Science and Industry (Chicago), University of Chicago. Republican. Episcopalian. Clubs: Chicago, Commercial, Casino, Onwentsia, Shore Acres, Old Elm. Home: 1260 Astor St. Office: 122 S. Michigan Av., Chicago 3, Ill. Died Aug. 15, 1947.

RANSOM, Frank Leslie, publisher; b. Albert Lea, Minn., Dec. 16, 1865; s. Zerah Augustus and Elvira Lavena (Hall) R.; A.B., Redfield (S.D.) Coll., 1893, A.M., 1915; LL.D., Yankton (S.D.) Coll., 1935; special studies in astronomy under Dr. Frank Leavenworth, U. of Minn.; m. Ida May Putney, Apr. 4, 1895; 1 son, Dillis Leslie. Teacher mathematics, Redfield Coll., 11½ yrs., also prin. Acad. and registrar of Coll.; county supt. schs., Spink County, 1905-08 inclusive; pres. Educator Supply Co. since 1908. Mem. Co. H, S.D. Nat. Guard, 14 yrs., retiring as 2d lt. Pres. Traffic Bur., 1938-44. Trustee Yankton Coll. since 1926. Mem. Order of Bookfellows, N.E.A. Republican. Conglist. K.P., Elk, Workman; mem. U.C.T. Kiwanian. Author: The Sunshine State—A History of South Dakota, 1912; Civil Government of the United States and South Dakota, 1912 (with Willis E. Johnson) Community Civics, 1922; Digest of Township Laws, 1922; The Young Citizen (civics of S.D. and the U.S.), 1937. Compiler: (with Ida P. Ransom) Favorite Poems for Children, 1922; Poems for the Course of Study, 1934; Science Paths, 1946. Editor The South Dakota Educator, 1914-25; The Rural School Board Magazine, 1938; President Young Men's Christian Assn., Mitchell, 1944-47. Home: 720 E. 5th Av. Office: 309 N. Lawler St., Mitchell, S.D. Died Nov. 11, 1947.

RANSOM, Ronald, vice chairman board of governors Federal Reserve System; b. Columbia, S.C., Jan. 21, 1882; s. Luther A. and Elizabeth Chaffin (Cocke) R.; LL.B., U. of Georgia, 1903; married Mary Brent, d. of Hon. Hoke Smith, of Atlanta, Dec. 19, 1908; 1 dau., Barbara (Mrs. Keith Jopson). Admitted to Ga. bar, 1903, and practiced at Atlanta until 1922; v.p. Fulton Nat. Bank of Atlanta, 1922-33, exec. v.p., 1933-36; mem. Bd. of Governors of Federal Reserve System since Feb. 1, 1936, vice chmn. since Aug. 6, 1936. Dir. in charge bur. of personnel for foreign service, southern div. Am. Red Cross, 1918; served as 1st lt. Chem. Warfare Service, U.S. Army, 1918. Pres. Atlanta Clearing House Assn., 1929; mem. Special Relief Com., Atlanta, 1932-33; chmn. Ga. Relief Commn., 1933. Mem. Am. Bankers Assn. (chmn. bank management commn., 1932-34, chmn. bankers NRA com., 1933-34, chmn. com. on federal legislation 1934-35, mem. com. on banking studies, mem. spl. com. on the Banking Act of 1935), Ga. Bankers Assn. (pres. 1931-32), Sigma Alpha Epsilon, Beta Gamma Sigma. Democrat. Episcopalian. Home: 2311 Connecticut Av. N.W., Washington 8. Office: Federal Reserve Bldg., Washington 25. Died Dec. 2, 1947.

RANSON, S(tephen) Walter, anatomist; b. Dodge Center, Minn., Aug. 28, 1880; s. Stephen William and Mary Elizabeth (Foster) R.; B.A., U. of Minn., 1902; M.S., U. of Chicago, 1903, Ph.D., 1905; M.D., Rush Med. Coll., 1907; m. Tessie Grier Rowland, Aug. 18, 1909; children—Stephen William, Margaret Jane, Mary Elizabeth. Fellow in neurology, U. of Chicago, 1904-06; intern Cook County Hosp., 1907-08; instr. anatomy, 1909-10, asst. prof., 1910-12, prof. and head of dept., 1912-24, Northwestern U. Med. Sch.; prof. neuroanatomy and head of Dept. of Neuroanatomy and Histology, Washington U. Med. Sch., 1924-27; prof. neurology and dir. Neurological Research Inst., Northwestern U. Med. Sch., since 1928. Fellow A.A.A.S.; mem. Am. Neurological Assn., Am. Assn. Anatomists (pres. 1938-40), Am. Physiol. Soc., Phi Beta Pi, Sigma Xi, Alpha Omega Alpha. Protestant. Author: The Anatomy of the Nervous System, 6th edition, 1939. Contbr. results of investigations on structure of the peripheral nervous system of mammals, etc. Mem. editorial bd. Archives of Neurology and Psychiatry. Address: 180 E. Delaware Pl., Chicago, Ill. Died Aug. 30, 1942.

RANTOUL, William Gibbons (răn-tōōl'), architect; b. Beverly Farms, Mass., Aug. 31, 1867; s. Robert Samuel and Harriet Charlotte (Neal) R.; A.B., Harvard, 1889; m. Eleanor Salisbury Driver, June 30, 1894 (deceased); 1 dau., Eleanor. In practice of architecture in Boston since 1897. Fellow of Am. Inst. of Architects (emeritus). Home: 19 Chestnut St., Salem, Mass. Died June 10, 1949.

RAPEE, Erno (rå-pē'), orchestra conductor; b. Hungary, June 4, 1891; ed. Budapest Conservatory; m. Mariska Peregy; children—George, Robert. Came to U.S., 1912. Began musical career as pianist in Hungary; was condr. Capitol Theatre orchestra 3 yrs., Roxy Theatre orchestra, 4 yrs.; later musical dir. Warner Bros.; has broadcast since 1920; condr. Gen. Motors Orchestra, 1935, 36, 37; dir. of music Radio City Music Hall Corp. since 1932; condr. Newark Symphony Orchestra of Essex County Symphony Soc., summers 1936, 37. Club: Lotos (New York). Compiled Encyclopedia of Music for Pictures, 1925. Home: 25 Central Park West. Office: Radio City Music Hall, Rockefeller Center, New York, N.Y. Died June 26, 1945.

RAPP, William Jourdan, editor, playwright; b. New York, N.Y., June 17, 1895; s. William Louis and Anna Elizabeth (Jourdan) R.; B.S., Cornell U., 1917; University of Paris, 1919-20; m. Virginia Venable, June 8, 1929; children—Anna Elizabeth, William Venable. Bacteriologist, New York City Department of Health, 1917; pub. health consultant, Europe and Near East, 1919-24; feature writer, New York Times, 1925; editor True Story Mag. since 1926; radio dramatist, Columbia and Nat. broadcasting systems, since 1928. Served as 2d lt. Med. Corps, U.S. Army, 1918. Lecturer, U. of Athens, 1922-23; sec. Internat. Malarial Commn. 1924. Mem. Dramatists Guild of Authors' League America. Episcopalian. Clubs: Authors, Overseas Press. Author: When I Was a Boy in Turkey, 1924; Osman Pasha, 1925; Poolroom, 1938; also (plays) Harlem, 1930; Whirlpool, 1930; Hilda Cassidy, 1931; Substitute for Murder, 1935; Holmses of Baker Street, 1936. Regular contbr. to leading nat. magazines. Home: 45 Gramercy Park. Office: Chatham Hotel, New York, N.Y. Died Aug. 12, 1942.

RARICK, Clarence Edmund (râr'ĭk), coll. pres.; b. Glen Elder, Kan., Mar. 17, 1879; A.B., Kan. Wesleyan U., 1904, Ed.D., 1928; post-grad. study, U. of Colo., 1915, U. of Kan., 1916 and 1929-30; m. May Jewell, June 1904; children—Margaret, Lois (Mrs. Edwin Cooke), Lawrence. Supt. pub. schs., Plainville, Kan., 1904-07, Rooks County, Kan., 1907-11, Stockton, 1911-12, Osborne, 1912-19; prof. rural edn. and dir. extension service, Kan. State Coll., Fort Hays, 1919-34, acting pres., 1933-34, pres. since 1934. Home: Hays, Kan. Died Aug. 1, 1941.

RASMUSEN, Edward A. (răs'mŭs-ŭn), vice-consul; born of Swedish parents, Apr. 5, 1882; reared in Sweden to 1882, when came to the United States; married Jenny Olson April 28, 1905; children—Evangeline Maude (Mrs. Robert Bruce Atwood), Elmer Edwin. Came to U.S., 1901, naturalized, 1910. Sch. teacher and missionary in Alaska, 1904-14; U.S. commr., 1914-18; pres. Bank of Alaska 1918-44, now chmn. bd.; pres. Bank of Wrangell, Wrangell, Alaska; v.p. Anchorage Light & Power Co.; Swedish vice consul Skagway, Alaska. Alaska mem. Rep. Nat. Com. Knighted by King of Sweden, 1937. Republican. Presbyterian. Mason (Shriner). Elk. Club: Arctic (Seattle). Address: Skagway, Alaska. Died Jan. 29, 1949.

RATHBONE, Albert, lawyer; b. Albany, N.Y., July 27, 1868; s. Clarence and Angelica Bogart (Talcott) R.; Williams, 1888, hon. M.A., 1913, hon. LL.D., 1939; LL.B., Albany Law Sch., 1889; m. Emma Marvin Olcott, April 14, 1891; children—Grace Olcott (Mrs. Leonard Dawson Adkins), Anna Talcott (Mrs. Robert Livingston Johnson). Admitted to N.Y. bar, 1890, and practiced at Albany; moved to N.Y. City, 1899; now mem. Larkin, Rathbone & Perry; asst. sec. U.S. Treasury; in charge fgn. loans, 1918-20; financial adviser to Am. Peace Commn. and unofficial rep. of U.S. on Reparations Commn., 1919-20. Mem. Am.; N.Y. State and N.Y. County bar assns., Bar Assn. City of N.Y. (ex-v.p.), Alpha Delta Phi, Loyal Legion, Saint Nicholas Soc. Democrat. Clubs: University, Union, Down Town, Williams, Alpha Delta Phi (New York). Home: 101

E. 72d St. Office: 70 Broadway, New York, N.Y. Died Aug. 21, 1943

RATHBONE, Alfred Day, IV, author; b. Grand Rapids, Mich., Jan. 19, 1897; s. Alfred Day, III, and Jessie Mary (Ball) R.; student U. of Mich., 1915-17, leaving to enter mil. service in May; m. Mary Frances Puffenbarger, Jan. 3, 1935. Began career doing gen. insurance, 1920-30; adv. mgr., The Air Pilot, 1933; sec., labor relations, The Natl. Code Authority for Trucking Industry, 1934-35; adv. mgr., Transport Topics (Am. Trucking Associations, Inc.), 1935-36; sales mgr., editor, Radio Reports, Inc., New York, 1937-40; departmental editor on arms and ammunition, Scientific Am., 1939-42; Game Breeder and Sportsman, 1940-42; accredited war corr., American Legion Magazine, since 1942; asso. editor, Scientific Am., 1940-43. Am. Ambulance Field Service with French Army at Verdun, 1917; U.S. Naval Reserve, 1918. Mem. Am. Legion, Sigma Phi Soc. Author: He's in the Paratroops Now, 1943; He's in the Sub-Busters Now, 1944; Shall We Scrap Our Merchant Marine?, 1944. Contbr. of articles to Natl. Sportsman, Hunting and Fishing, Outdoors, Outdoorsman, Country Life and The Sportsman, Rod and Gun in Canada, This Week, Who, Liberty, Chamber's Jour. (London), Am. Legion Mag., Reader's Digest. Address: 78 Ridgewood Terrace, Chappaqua, N.Y. Died Nov. 10, 1949.

RATHBONE, Henry Bailey, educator; b. Merrick, L.I., N.Y., July 3, 1871; s. John and Harriet (Crawford) R.; attended Colgate Acad. and Colgate U.; Litt.D., Colgate U., Hamilton, N.Y., 1931; m. Floy Langworthy, Dec. 25, 1897; children—Josephine Langworthy, Rosina Crawford, John Hollum. Professor of practice of journalism and chmn. dept. of journalism, N.Y. Univ., 1924-41; prof. emeritus of journalism since 1941; on staff Asso. Press, United Press, N.Y. American, N.Y. Evening Journal, Chicago American, Chicago Examiner, San Francisco Examiner, New York Press, New York Morning Sun, New York Evening Sun, 1895-1924. Exec. chmn. quota rationing N.Y. County, Office Price Adminstrn., 1942. Visiting professor Washington and Lee Univ., 1943; editor Hamilton Republican, 1943. U.S. del. 5th Triennial Congress of Internat. Soc. for Commercial Edn., London, 1932. Mem. Phi Kappa Psi, Theta Nu Epsilon, Kappa Tau Alpha, Beta Gamma Sigma. Baptist. Home: Hamilton, N.Y. Died June 13, 1945.

RATHBUN, Edward Harris; b. Woonsocket, R.I., Nov. 26, 1866; s. Hon. Oscar J. and Rachel (Harris) R.; ed. Brown U., 1885-89; m. Anna Reed Wilkinson, Oct. 9, 1895; children—Rachel H., Lawrance W., Anita R., Mabel. Pres. Stafford Worsted Mills; chmn. Dunn Worsted Mills; v.p. Woonsocket Instn. Savings; dir. New Eng. T. & T. Co., Safe Deposit Co., New York, New Haven & Hartford Railroad Co., Providence Terminal Co., Providence, Warren & Bristol R.R.; chmn. R.I. Boundary Commn. Republican. Episcopalian. Mason (K.T.). Clubs: Hope, Art, Agawan-Hunt. Home: 12 Olive St., Providence, R.I. Died Nov. 13, 1948.

RATHBUN, H. H., agrl. leader; born Las Vegas, N.M., May 12, 1891; s. Charles A. and Attie C. R.; grad. Culver Mil. Acad.; student Purdue U.; m. Estelle Masters, June 6, 1911; children—Josie (Mrs. Seth Cornish), Edith (Mrs. A. F. Roberts), Henry H., Estelle (Mrs. John Nelson). Purchased 192 acres near Oriskany Falls, N.Y., 1914, extended operations to 1,000 acres; pioneer mem. Dairymen's League Coop. Assn., Inc. (past dir. and pres. 1945-48); past pres. Nat. Council Farmer Coop.; past vice pres. Am. Inst. Coop.; past dir. Nat. Coop. Milk Producers Fedn.; past dir. George Junior Republic; N.Y. youth project, N.Y. State Park Com. Served as mem. N.Y. Food Com. during World War I, vice pres., bd. dirs. Utica Structural Steel Corp. Mem. exec. com. N.Y. State Rep. Orgn.. Nat. Rep. Club Republican. Episcopalian. Mason. Elk, Odd Fellow. Clubs: New York Athletic, Yahanundasis Golf, Winged Foot Country, Fort Schuler. Home: 23 Oxford Road, New Hartford, N.Y. Died Sept. 29, 1948.

RATLIFF, Alexander L., judge, lawyer; b. Ashcamp, Ky., Dec. 20, 1881; s. Marion and Polly (Francisco) R.; student Pikeville (Ky.) High Sch., 1902-05, Pikeville Coll., 1905-08; LL.B., U. of Louisville, 1910; unmarried. Began as teacher in pub. schs. of Ky., 1902; admitted to Ky. bar, 1910, and since practiced in Pikeville; city atty., 1917-25; judge of City Court, 1929-32; judge of the Ct. of Appeals of Ky. since 1932, re-elected 1940 for term ending 1949. Democrat. Mason. Clubs: Pike County Country, Franklin County Country. Home: Pikeville, Ky. Address: Frankfort, Ky.* Died Aug. 22, 1944.

RATSHESKY, Abraham C. (ră-chĕs'kĭ), banker; b. Boston, Mass., 1864; s. Asher and Bertha R.; pub. sch. edn., Boston; m. Edith Shuman, Feb. 19, 1894. Pres. U.S. Trust Co., 1895-1939, now chmn. bd.; dir. Am. Employers' Ins. Co., Employers Fire Ins. Co. and several large financial instns.; mem. Boston Common Council 3 yrs.; former mem. Clearing House Assn.; former U.S. minister to Czechoslovakia. Founder A. C. Ratschesky Foundation; formerly pres. Federated Jewish Charities; formerly v.p. Asso. Charities of Boston; ex-pres. Mass. Trust Co. Assn.; formerly mem. exec. com. Am. Jewish Com.; ex-chmn. Boston Metropolitan Chapter of Am. Red Cross; formerly trustee Asso. Jewish Philanthropies; mem. Nat. Council Am. Joint Distribution Com.; dir. Home for Jewish Children, Beth Irael Hosp.; commr. in charge Halifax relief expdn., 1917, and mem. other nat. relief coms., etc.; mem. council Boston Tuberculosis Assn., Mass. Civic League, Council Fgn. Policy Assn., former mem. Mass. Senate; former sec. Rep. State Com.; del. Rep. Nat. Conv. 6 times. Trustee Boston Metropolitan Dist., Temple Israel, Employers Group Assn. Mem. Nat. Conf. Social Work, asst. food adminstr. for Mass., and asst. exec. mgr. Mass. Pub. Safety Com. during war period. Former chmn. Mass. Dept. Pub. Welfare. Home: Beverly, Mass., and 65 Commonwealth Av., Boston. Office: 30 Court St., Boston, Mass. Died Mar. 15, 1943.

RAU, Albert George (rou), educator; b. Bethlehem, Pa., Aug. 7, 1868; s. Robert and Caroline A. (Bussè) R.; B.S., Lehigh U., 1888, M.S., 1900; Ph.D., Moravian Coll., 1910, LL.D., 1934; Litt.D., Muhlenberg, 1927; m. Gertrude L. Brunner, Feb. 6, 1894; children—Robert Otto (dec.), Henry Brunner. Supt. Moravian Prep. Sch., 1888-1909; dean Moravian Coll. and Theol. Sem. since 1909. Lecturer rural sociology Teachers' Coll., Columbia U., 1927. Mem. A.A.A.S., Am. Soc. Polit. and Social Science, Am. Math. Assn., Am. Math. Soc., Franklin Inst., Newcomen Soc., Phi Beta Kappa, Phi Gamma Delta, also many hist. and economic socs. Republican. Moravian Mason. Author: Formation of Modern Europe, 1898; also many monographs on Pa. colonial history. Contbr. to Am. Dictionary of Biography. Home: 38 W. Market St., Bethlehem, Pa. Died Feb. 23, 1942.

RAVEN, John Howard, theologian; b. Brooklyn, Oct. 3, 1870; s. Anton A. and Gertrude (Oatman) R.; A.B., Rutgers Coll., 1891, A.M., 1894; grad. New Brunswick Theological Seminary, 1894; Univ. of Berlin, 1902-03; D.D. Rutgers, 1899; Litt.D., Rutgers University, 1941; m. Elizabeth Grier Strong, May 29, 1894; 1 son, Anton Adolph. Ordained ministry Reformed Ch. in America, 1894; pastor at Metuchen, N.J., 1894-99; acting prof., New Brunswick Theol. Sem., 1898-99, prof. Old Testament langs. and exegesis, 1899-1939, emeritus since 1939, pres. faculty, 1922-23, pres. 1923-25. Lecturer on English Bible, Rutgers Coll., 1910-13; lecturer in Old Testament lit., Princeton Theol. Sem., 1926-31. Author: Old Testament Introduction, General and Special, 1906; Essentials of Hebrew Grammar, 1908; Biblical Hermeneutics, 1910; History of the Religion of Israel, 1933. Compiler of General Catalogue Rutgers College, 1766-1916; Biographical Record of New Brunswick Theological Sem., 1784-1934. Mem. com. on versions, Am. Bible Soc., 1922-40; trustee Rutgers since 1914 (sec. bd. 1922-40). Pres. Zeta Psi of North America, 1912; mem. Phi Beta Kappa. Clubs: University, Zeta Psi (New York). Mem. N.J. Hist. Soc., Soc. Bibl. Lit. and Exegesis. Home: 8 Bishop Pl., New Brunswick, N.J. Died Feb. 25, 1949.

RAVENEL, Mazyck Porcher, bacteriologist; born Pendleton, S.C.; s. Henry Edmund and Selina E.R.; grad. Univ. of the South; studied medicine, Med. Coll. State of S.C.; m. Jennie Carlile Boyd, Oct. 1898. Bacteriologist State Live Stock Sanitary Bd. of Pa., 1896-1904; asst. med. dir. Henry Phipps Inst. for Study, Treatment and Prevention of Tuberculosis; chief of laboratory, Henry Phipps Inst., 1904-07; prof. bacteriology, Univ. of Wis., since 1907. Mem. Nat. Assn. for Study and Prevention of Tuberculosis (1st v.p., 1907-08), Coll. Physicians, Phila., Am. Philos. Soc., Am. Pub. Health Assn., Am. Med. Assn., Am. Assn. Pathologists and Bacteriologists, Phila. Pathol. Soc., S.C. Huguenot Soc. Author numerous published papers on med and bacteriol. subjects, especially on tuberculosis and rabies. Residence: Madison, Wis. Died Jan. 14, 1946.

RAY, Anna Chapin, author; b. Westfield, Mass., Jan. 3, 1865; d. Edward Addison and Helen M. (Chapin) R.; A.B., Smith Coll., 1885, A.M., 1888; unmarried. Spent much time in Canada studying social and polit. conditions and writing of them since 1903. Republican. Episcopalian. Author: Half a Dozen Boys, 1890; Half a Dozen Girls, 1891; The Cadets of Fleming Hall, 1892; In Blue Creek Cañon, 1892; Margaret Davis, Tutor, 1893; Dick, 1896; the Teddy books, 6 vols., 1898-1904; Each Life Unfulfilled, 1899; Playground Toni, 1900; The Dominant Strain, 1903; Sheba, 1903; By the Good Sainte Anne, 1904; On the Firing Line (with Hamilton Brock Fuller), 1905; The Sidney books, 6 vols., 1905-10; Hearts and Creeds, 1906; Ackroyd of the Faculty, 1907; Quickened, 1908; The Bridge Builders, 1909; Over the Quicksands, 1910; A Woman with a Purpose, 1911; Buddie, 1911; The Brentons, 1912; Buddie at Gray Buttes Camp, 1912; On Board the Beatic, 1913; The Responsibilities of Buddie, 1913. Editor Letters of a Canadian Stretcher Bearer, 1917. Supervisor stenographic br. and head of print room, Dept. Soldiers' Civil Re-Establishment (formerly Mil. Hosps. Commn.), Ottawa, Can., 1916-20. In France, 1928-32, writing feature articles. Address: 169 Dwight St., New Haven, Conn. Died Dec. 13, 1945.

RAY, Milton S., industrialist, ornithologist, poet; b. San Francisco, Feb. 26, 1881; s. William S. Ray (mfr., ship-owner) and Julia Henrietta (Ruth) R.; ed. Crocker High Sch.; Univ. of Calif.; m. Rose Carolyn Etzel, Oct. 7, 1915; children—Cecily, Virginia, Rosalyn. Secretary, treas. and dir. W. S. Ray Mfg. Co., San Francisco, 1907, elected v.p., 1915; sec., treas. Ray Burner Co. of Calif., 1929, Ray Burner Co. of Delaware, 1930; pres., treas., dir. Ray Burner Co. of Del., San Francisco, and New York, 1933, and same, Ray Oil Burner Co. and subsidiaries since 1935; curator and director Pacific Museum of Ornithology since 1904; has made exploration trips to over 35 countries, obtaining specimens for the Museum. Owner, Ray Park Subdivision, Burlingame, Calif., and Raycliff Terrace Subdivision, San Francisco. Member San Francisco Contract Bd., War Dept., San Francisco Dist. Ordnance Office since 1934. Received Honor Flag from U.S. Government as dir. of an auxiliary War Plant, 1918. Academician Acad. of Coimbra, Portugal. Fellow Am. Geog. Soc.; asso. Am. Ornithologists Union; research asso. in ornithology, Calif. Acad. Sciences; mem. P.E.N., Am Ornithologists Union, Cooper Ornithol. Club, Nat. Geog. Soc. Brit. Oologists Club. Republican. Protestant. Club: Burlingame Country. Awarded prize for poem, "San Francisco," used for Sesquicentennial Celebration in San Francisco, 1926. Author: The Farallones, The Painted World and Other Poems (2 vols.), 1934; Poems (1 vol.), 1936; The Poet and The Messenger; Dune-Glade and Other Poems, 1945. also over 100 mag. articles. Home: 2901 Broadway; (summer) Snow Line Villa (Vade P.O.), Lake Tahoe, Calif. Office: 401-499 Bernal Av., San Francisco 12, Calif. Died May 5, 1946.

RAYMOND, Charles Beebe, mfr.; b. Akron, O., Feb. 12, 1866; s. William B. and Helen (Beebe) R.; B.S., Amherst Coll., 1888, M.A., 1918; M.A., Buchtel Coll., 1910; m. Mary Perkins, May 21, 1890; children—Mary Perkins Yule, George Perkins, Charles Goodrich. With B.F. Goodrich Co., Akron, since 1888, v. chmn. bd. since 1921, also vice pres.; dir. First Nat. Trust & Savings Bank (Santa Barbara, Calif); pres. and trustee Santa Barbara Foundation. President Akron Chamber of Commerce, 1908-10; pres. Y.W.C.A.; trustee Akron City Hosp. (pres. bd. 1912-22), Kenyon Coll., Santa Barbara (Calif.) Boys' Sch., Cottage Hosp. (Santa Barbara). Pres. Akron Chapter Am. Red Cross, World War; mem. Bd. of Edn., Akron. Mem. Beta Theta Pi. Republican. Sr. warden St. Paul's Episcopal Ch. Clubs: University, City, Portage Country (Akron): Montecito Valley Country, Santa Barbara Club. Home: Santa Barbara, Calif. Died July 29, 1945.

RAYMOND, Fred Morton, judge; b. Berlin (now Marne), Ottawa County, Mich., Mar. 22, 1876; s. Joseph and Elizabeth S. (McLennan) R.; prep. edn., high sch., Berlin and Grand Rapids; LL.B., U. of Mich., 1899; m. Mabel H. Kenworthy, Dec. 30, 1902; children—Elizabeth Estelle Kraber, Russell Kenworthy. Admitted to Mich. bar, 1899, and began practice with firm of Hatch & Wilson, Grand Rapids; mem. Jewell, Raymond & Face, 1923-25; U.S. dist. judge Western Dist. of Mich., by apptmt. of President Calvin Coolidge, since May 18, 1925; President Berlin Board of Education. Member American and Mich. State bar assns., Grand Rapids Bar Assn. (pres. 1923-24). Republican. Conglist. Mason (33°, Shriner). Clubs: Spring Lake Country, Union League of Chicago, Rotary, Torch. Home: 338 Morris Av. S.E. Address: Federal Bldg., Grand Rapids, Mich. Died Feb. 6, 1946; buried at Graceland Mausoleum, Grand Rapids, Mich.

RAYMOND, Howard Monre, retired coll. pres.; b. Grass Lake, Mich., Oct. 25, 1872; s. Morton and Geraldine (Crafts) R.; B.S., U. of Mich., 1893, grad. student physics and electricity, 1894; D.Sc., Colo. Sch. of Mines, 1922; m. Carrie Smith, June 21, 1898; 1 dau., Dorothy Geraldine (Mrs. L. Dean Alber). Successively instr., asso. prof. and prof. exptl. physics, Armour Sci. Acad., 1895-1910, prin., 1899-1903, dir. evening classes, 1903-21; dean engring., Armour Inst. Tech., Chicago, 1903-22; actg. pres, 1921-22, pres., 1922-32, pres. emeritus since 1932. Trustee Armour Inst. of Tech. Mem. Soc. Promotion Engring. Edn., Phi Delta Theta, Tau Beta Pi; fellow A.A.A.S. Editor-in-chief Cyclopedia of Modern Shop Practice, Cyclopedia of Engineering, Cyclopedia of Mechanical Engineering. Home: Grass Lake, Mich. Died Jan. 24, 1943.

RAYMOND, William Lee, author and lecturer; b. at Cambridge, Mass., Sept. 24, 1877; s. William Henry and Anna L. (Lovejoy) R.; A.B., Harvard, 1899; m. Phebe T. Candage, Aug. 31, 1905; 1 son, Richard Candage. Was connected with N. W. Harris & Co., bankers, Boston, 1901-12; mem. W. L. Raymond & Co., 1912-20. Member Battery A, Mass. Nat. Guard, 1902-05; served in Boston police strike of 1919. Democrat. Unitarian. Author: American and Foreign Investment Bonds, 1916; State and Municipal Bonds, 1923; An Occasional Diary by "X," 1924; National Government Loans, 1925; Poems of Love and Life, 1928; American and the World After the War (address), 1928; Our Heritage (radio address), 1929; Later Poems, 1937; The Repudiated Dept. of Mississippi (in Annual Report Council of Foreign Bondholders, London, 1931); The First Parish Wayland, Mass., 1640-1940, 1940. Has traveled extensively in Europe. Home: Wayland, Mass. Died Mar. 19, 1942.

REA, Paul Marshall (rā), museum consultant; b. Cotuit, Mass., Feb. 13, 1878; s. John T. and S. Helen R.; A.B., Williams Coll., Williamstown, Mass., 1899, A.M., 1901; student Marine Biol. Lab., Woods Hole, Mass., 1898-99, Columbia Grad. Sch., 1899-1900, 1902-03; m. Carolyn Morse, June 28, 1904 (died May 11, 1913); 1 son, John Morse; m. 2d, Marian Goddard Hussey, June 25, 1919; 1 dau., Dorothy Helen. Asst. in biology, Williams Coll., 1900-02; prof. biology, Coll. of Charleston, 1903-14; dir. Charleston Museum, 1903-20; instr. Marine Biol. Lab., 1906-11; prof. embryology and physiology, Med. Coll. of S.C., 1911-19, prof. embryology, 1919-20; dir. Cleveland Museum Natural History, 1920-28; exec. officer, Pa. Museum Art, 1929; consultant to advisory group on museum edn., Carnegie Corp., 1930-32; dir. Santa Barbara Museum Natural History, 1933-36. Vice dir. war savings for S.C., 1917-19. Fellow A.A.A.S., Ohio

Acad. Science (pres. 1925-26); member Am. Assn. Museums (sec. and editor Proceedings, 1907-17, pres. 1919-21). Formerly editor Bulletin Charleston Museum and Contributions from the Charleston Museum. Author: Directory of Am. Museums, 1910; The Museum and the Community, 1932. Also author annual reports on ednl. work Am. museums, in Ann. Rept. U.S. Commr. of Edn.; also papers on museum administration and ednl. work and on fungi of Southern Calif. Address: 436 E. Padre St., Santa Barbara, Calif. Died Jan. 15, 1948.

READ, Charles Francis (rēd), psychiatrist; b. Nevad, Ia., May 27, 1876; s. Henry Bierman and Julia Florence (Kellogg) R.; B.S., Beloit (Wis.) Coll., 1898; M.D., Rush Med. Coll. (U. of Chicago), 1901; m. Ethelwyn Eaton, Dec. 16, 1901 (deceased); children—Eaton Van Wart, John Barber. Gen. med. practice, Grand Rapids, Mich., and Geneva, Ill., 1901-09; staff physician Ill. State Hospital, Kankakee, Ill., 1909-11; asst. supt. East Moline, Kankakee, Chicago, Peoria state hospitals, 1911-15, supt. East Moline and Chicago state hosp., 1915-21; state alienist, Ill., 1921-25; practice neuro-psychiatry, Chicago, 1925-30; superintendent Elgin (Ill.) State Hosp. since 1930. Mem. A.M.A., American Psychiatric Assn., Chicago Neurological Soc. (ex-pres.), Ill. Psychiatric Society (ex-pres.), Beta Theta Pi, Phi Beta Kappa, Nu Sigma Nu. Episcopalian. Editor: Manual for State Hospital Attendants; Elgin Papers, vols. 1-5. Contbr. to med. jours. Home: 750 S. State St. Office: Elgin State Hospital, Elgin, Ill. Died Mar. 11, 1946.

READ, Harold D., public opinion analyst; b. Des Moines, Ia., Apr. 27, 1902; s. Arch E. and Laura Josephine (Trissel) R.; student Drake U., 1919-20, U of Iowa, 1920-23, Northwestern U., 1926-28; m. Marian Brown, Aug. 12, 1925. Advertising and editorial asst., Equitable Life Ins. Co. of Ia., 1923-26; asst. store mgr. and promotion mgr., Wieboldt Stores, Chicago, Ill., 1926-28, merchandising research dir., Montgomery Ward & Co., Chicago, 1928-30; asso. editor, Dartnell Business Publications, Chicago, 1930-33; partner and editor, Merchandising Data Bureau, Chicago, 1933-35; vice pres. Manufacturers Credit Service, Inc., Chicago, 1934-38; vice pres. Opinion Research Corp., Princeton, N.J., and New York, N.Y., since 1938; dir. U.S. Economics Corp. (New York), Rutland R.R. Co. (Vt.). Dir. Tome Sch. for Boys, 1940-42. Recipient Ins. Advt. Fedn. award for best life ins. advertising of year, 1926. Mem. Sigma Phi Epsilon, Sigma Delta Chi, Delta Sigma Rho, Phi Delta Phi, Chi Delta, Economic History Assn. Clubs: Union League (Chicago); Nassau (Princeton, N.J.); Western University (New York). Author: A Survey of Retailing Practices, 1931. Contbr. to gen. and bus. mags. Home: 15 Palmer Sq., Princeton, N.J. Office: Opinion Research Corp., 44 Nassau St., Princeton, N.J. and 10 Rockefeller Plaza, New York, N.Y. Died Oct. 9, 1945.

READ, Thomas T(hornton), mining engr.; b. Monmouth County, N.J., Feb. 10, 1880; s. Thomas H. and Hannah C. (Thornton) R.; E.M., Columbia, 1902, fellow, 1904-05, Ph.D., 1906; m. Mary C. Peck, July 26, 1910; children—Mary Celia, Thomas Albert, Myron. Asso. prof. mining, U. of Wyo., 1902-04; asst. in mineralogy, Columbia U., 1905-06; prof. mining and metallurgy, Colorado Coll., 1906-07; prof. metallurgy, Pei Yang U., Tientsin, 1907-10; associate editor Mining and Scientific Press, 1910-15; metall. engr. N.J. Zinc Co.; New York, 1916-18; metallurgist, Army Ordnance, 1918-19; chief of information service, U.S. Bur. of Mines, 1919-23, supervising mining engr., 1923-24, safety service, dir., 1924-26; asst. sec. Am. Inst. Mining and Metallurgical Engineers, 1926-29; Vinton prof. of mining engring., Columbia, since 1929. Editor of Mining and Metallurgy, 1926-32. Mem. A.A.A.S., Am. Inst. Mining Engrs., Council on Foreign Relations, Am. Acad. Polit. Science. Author: Our Mineral Civilization; Recent Copper Smelting; Ores and Industry of South America; Careers in the Mineral Industries; Mineral Industry Education in the U.S.; also numerous contbns. to scientific socs. and tech. jours. Home: 9 Windmill Lane, Scarsdale, N.Y. Address: Columbia University, New York. Died May 29, 1947; interred Ferncliff Mausoleum, Hartsdale, N.Y.

READY, Lester Seward (rĕd'ĭ), cons. engr.; b. Ventura, Calif., Dec. 9, 1888; s. William Edward and Martha Hind (Seward) R.; grad. Union High Sch., Ventura, 1907; B.S., U. of Calif., 1912; m. Eileen Ana Ong, Oct. 9, 1916; children—Lester Seward, Ralph William, Robert Allen, Richard Thomas. Asst. engr. Pacific Gas & Electric Co., Oakland, Calif., 1912-13; asst. gas and elec. engr. Calif. R.R. Commn., 1913-17, gas and elec. engr., 1918-23, chief engr., 1923-26; pres. Key System Transit Co., Oakland, Jan.-July 1927; cons. engr. since 1927; chief cons. engr. Nat. Power Survey, Electric Rate Survey, Federal Power Commn., 1934-36. Mem. bd. dirs. Oakland Forum, 1937-42: Registered civil engr. State of Calif.; registered professional engr., State of Ore. Fellow Am. Inst. E.E.; mem. Order of Golden Bear (U. of Calif.), Big "C" Soc., Sigma Xi, Eta Kappa Nu, Tau Beta Pi, Phi Beta Kappa. Republican. Presbyterian. Mason. Clubs: Engineers, Kiwanis (San Francisco); University (Los Angeles); Commonwealth Club of Calif. (bd. govs. 1932-35; chmn. exec. com.). Home: 1050 Mariposa St., Berkeley, Calif. Office: 116 New Montgomery St., San Francisco, Calif. Died April 9, 1947.

REAMES, Alfred Evan (rēmz), ex-senator; b. Jacksonville, Ore., Feb. 5, 1870; s. Thomas Givings and Lucinda (Williams) R.; student U. of Pacific, San Jose, Calif., 1888-89, U. of Ore., 1889-92; LL.B., Washington and Lee U., Lexington, Va., 1893; m. Lillian Lanning Opie, June 1923; 1 son, Edward Lanning. Admitted to Ore. bar, 1893, and practiced as mem. Skipworth & Reames, Eugene, 1893-94; practiced in Medford, Ore., 1895-96; mem. firm Colvig & Reames, Jacksonville, Ore., 1897-1900; dist. atty. Jackson, Josephine, Klamath and Lake cos., 1900-08; practiced in Medford, Ore., since 1908; mem. firm Reames & Reames, 1908-23; v.p. and dir. Deep Gravel Mining Co. Apptd. U.S. Senator from Ore. by Gov. Charles Martin, Feb. 1938, to fill unexpired term of Frederick Steiwer, resigned; now in practice of law, Medford, Ore. Chmn. exec. com. Dem. State Central Com. of Ore. since 1936. Mem. Am. Bar Assn., Ore. State Bar Assn., Southern Ore. Bar Assn., Am. Judicature Soc., Sigma Alpha Epsilon. Democrat. Mason, Elk. Club: University (Medford). Home: 816 W. 10th St., Medford, Ore. Died Mar. 4, 1943.

REANEY, George Humes (rān'ē), ins. exec.; b. New York, N.Y., Jan. 27, 1887; s. George Upton and Emma (Humes) R.; A.B., Columbia U., 1907; m. Gertrude C. Slattery, Oct. 23, 1912. In ins. brokerage, 1908-14; mgr., Aetna Life Ins. Co., Hartford, Conn., 1914-25; v.p. U.S. Guarantee Co., N.Y. City, 1925-29, pres. and dir. since 1929; dir. Guarantee Co. of N. Am. Capt. C.A.C., U.S. Army, 1917-19. Mem. Assn. of Casualty and Surety Execs. (exec. com.), Theta Delta Chi. Republican. Roman Catholic. Clubs: Columbia, Drug and Chemical, Down Town Assn. (New York, N.Y.); Siwanoy Country, Bronxville (N.Y.). Home: 25 Hillside Rd., Bronxville, N.Y. Office: 90 John St., New York. Died July 12, 1947.

REBEC, George (rē'bĕk), educator; b. Tuscola, Mich., Mar. 11, 1868; s. William and Tina (Herbeck) R.; A.B., U. of Mich., 1891, Ph.D., 1897; studied U. of Strassburg, 1893-94; studied art-history and esthetics in Italy, 1908-09; m. Mary Lowell, Jan. 19, 1910. Instr. in English, 1891-93, instr., asst. prof. and jr. prof. philosophy, 1895-1909, U. of Mich.; prof. philosophy and dean of Grad. School, U. of Ore., 1921-33; dean and dir. Grad. Div., Oregon State System of Higher Education, 1933-38; now Prince Lucien professor philosophy emeritus, dean emeritus and counsellor of Graduate Division of Oregon State System of Higher Education; also director educational and civic services of the university in City of Portland, 1912-18; dir. Portland Centre, U. of Ore., 1918-23. Lecturer under Dept. of Pub. Instrn., Hawaii, 1903; lecturer univ. extension, Phila., 1909-10; prof. edn., Reed Coll., 1920-21; prof. philosophy, U. of Calif., summer, 1926; prof. philosophy, Stanford, 1928; visiting prof. philosophy, Reed Coll., 1931-32. Mem. Ore. Child Welfare Commn. (chmn.), Ore. Anti-Tuberculosis Soc. (dir.), Ore. Social Hygiene Soc., Civil Liberties League. Mem. A.A.A.S., Am. Philos. Assn. (pres. Pacific div. 1924-25), Am. Acad. of Polit. Science, Nat. Economic League, Am. Assn. Univ. Profs., Phi Beta Kappa, Theta Delta Chi, Pi Delta Phi. Contbr. Internat. Jour. Ethics, Am. Philos. Review, etc.; also for 2 years to lit. edition Baltimore Sun. Spent 14 months, 1922-23, studying intellectual and social conditions in Europe. Clubs: University, Portland City. Home: 1650 E. 26th St., Eugene, Ore. Died May 27, 1944.

REBER, Louis Ehrhart (rē'bēr), engineer; b. Nittany, Pa., Feb. 27, 1858; s. Jacob and Elizabeth R.; B.S., Pa. State Coll., 1880, M.S., 1887; grad. student Mass. Inst. Tech., 1883; D.Sc., Pa. State Coll., 1908 m. Helen Jackson, June 1888; children—Louis E., Hugh Jackson. Prof. mech. engring., 1887-95, dean Sch. of Engring., 1895-1907, Pa. State Coll.; dean extension div., U. of Wis., 1907-26, now emeritus. Pa. commr. Paris Expn., 1889; Pa. asst. exec. commr. in charge mines, mining and machinery; mem. Jury of Awards, Chicago Expn., 1893; in charge dept. mines and metall., Pa. Commn., St. Louis Expn., 1904. Fellow Am. Soc. of Mech. Engrs.; mem. Franklin Inst., Phila. Soc. Promotion Engring. Edn., Nat. Soc. Promotion Industrial Edn., Nat. Univ. Extension Assn. (pres. 1914-15), Sigma Xi, Phi Kappa Phi. Asso. dir. public service reserve, labor dept., U.S. Army, Washington, Aug. 1917-Mar. 1918; dir. edn. and training, Emergency Fleet Corp., Mar.-Dec. 1918; dir. engring. and trade education, Army Ednl. Corps, A.E.F., France, Jan.-July 1919. Mem. Wis. State Bd. for Vocational Edn., 1911-17. Clubs: Madison, Maple Bluff (Madison); University (Madison and Milwaukee). Home: 242 Lakeland Drive, West Palm Beach, Fla. Address: care Fiduciary Trust Co., 1 Wall St., New York Died May 12, 1948.

REBERT, G(ordon) Nevin (rē'bērt), coll. prof.; b. Littlestown, Pa., May 7, 1889; s. Samuel Henry and Laura Belle (Hesson) R.; ed. Mercersburg Acad., 1905-06; A.B., Franklin and Marshall Coll., 1910; A.M., U. of Chicago, 1925, Ph.D., 1929; attended Eastern Theol. Sem., 1910-13, Johns Hopkins, 1918-21; m. Naomi S. Stonesifer, Aug. 10, 1911 (now deceased); children—Naomi Catherine (Mrs. Robert Kreh Kennedy), Margaret Elizabeth (Mrs. Howard MacGregor), Philip Nevin; m. 2d, Isabel Boone, June 10, 1943. Instr. Franklin and Marshall Acad., 1912-13; minister, Reformed Ch. in U.S., Orangeville, Ill., 1913-18; instr. and prin., Frederick (Md.) High Sch., 1918-21; prof. edn., dir. teacher training, Hood Coll. since 1921. Mem. N.E.A., Am. Assn. Sch. Administrs., Kappa Sigma, Phi Delta Kappa. Democrat. Mason. Home: 1005 Motter Av., Frederick, Md. Died May 3, 1948.

RECCORD, Augustus Phineas, author, clergyman; b. Acushnet, Mass., Feb. 14, 1870; s. Phineas White and Emma Henrietta (Dickens) R.; A.B., Brown U., 1892, D.D., 1922; S.T.B., Harvard, 1895; m. Mae A. Tripp, Oct. 30, 1895. Ordained Unitarian ministry, 1895; pastor 1st Unitarian Ch., Chelsea, Mass., 1895-97; pastor Third Congregational Soc. Church, Cambridge, Mass., 1897-1902, Channing Memorial Ch., Newport, R.I., 1902-05, Ch. of the Unity, Springfield, Mass., 1905-19, First Unitarian Ch., Detroit, Mich., 1919-32, Joint Unitarian-Universalist Ch., Detroit, 1933-34, Church of Our Father, Detroit, 1935-39. Mem. Unitarian Ministerial Union, Phi Beta Kappa, Phi Delta Theta. Republican. Clubs: University (Winter Park, Fla.); The City, Reality (Springfield, Mass.). Author: Who Are the Unitarians?, 1920. Home: The Sheraton, Springfield, Mass. Died Oct. 4, 1946.

RECORD, James Lucius; b. Franklin, Vt., Apr. 15, 1857; s. Harley C. and Hannah (Jones) R.; ed. St. Albans (Vt.) Acad. and business coll., La Crosse, Wis.; m. Fannie A. Cross, Jan. 30, 1886. Associated with L. C. Barnett, title of Barnett & Record, engrs. and contractors, Minneapolis, Minn., 1883, inc. 1891 as The Barnett & Record Co.; resigned, 1902, and organized Minneapolis Steel Machinery Co., of which was pres. until 1919, later chmn. bd.; now chmn. bd. Minneapolis Moline Power Implement Co. Home: 343 Oak Grove St., Minneapolis, Minn. Office: 30 9th Av. S., Hopkins, Minn. Died Mar. 2, 1944.

RECORD, Samuel J(ames), forestry dean; b. Crawfordsville, Ind., Mar. 10, 1881; s. James K. P. and Mary M. (Hutton) R.; grad. high sch., Crawfordsville, 1899; B.A., Wabash Coll., 1903, M.A., 1906, Sc.D., 1930; M.F., Yale, 1905; m. Mary E. Strauss, Apr. 1, 1906; children—Mason Thomas and Mary Elizabeth (twins), Alice Louise. Mem. U.S. Forest Service, 1904-10; first supervisor Nat. Forests of Ark.; with Yale U. since 1910, successively instr. in forestry, and asst. prof. forest products, then prof. of forest products, 1917-39, Pinchot prof. forestry and dean School of Forestry since 1939; in charge tropical forestry since 1923. Fellow A.A.A.S., Society American Foresters; mem. Internat. Assn. Wood Anatomists (council), Phi Beta Kappa, Sigma Xi, Phi Gamma Delta, Acacia. Republican. Mason. Club: Yale Graduate (New Haven). Author: Identification of the Economic Woods of the United States, 1912; Mechanical Properties of Wood, 1914; Timbers of Tropical America, 1924; Identification of the Timbers of Temperate North America, 1934; Forests of British Honduras, 1936; Timbers of the New World, 1943. Editor and mgr. Tropical Woods (quarterly) since 1925. Home: 208 W. Rock Av. Office: 205 Prospect St., New Haven, Conn. Died Feb. 3, 1945.

REDFIELD, Casper Lavater, patent atty., evolutionist; b. Closter, N.J., Nov. 22, 1853; s. James W. (M.D.) and Sarah H. (Bowen) R.; student Worcester (Mass.) Poly. Inst., 1873-74; m. Lillian A. Phillips, June 4, 1880; children—Howard A., Mabel G., Walter H., James C., Hazel L. and Harold P. Machinist, later draftsman, mech. engr., inventor. Consulting engr., Minneapolis, 1886-89; editor Wood and Iron, 1887-88; settled in Chicago, 1889; solicitor of patents and expert in patent causes since 1892. Designed many power plants and about 100 successful machines; partly originated, and developed new forms of machine design; designed 3 machines (bolt-cutting, engraving and brickmaking) receiving awards at Chicago Expn., 1893; received more than 50 patents for inventions. Original investigations in mathematics, mechanics and physics; first to solve problem of unbalanced rotating body on a yielding support; investigated effects of inertia in steam engines, ball-bearings, cam-operated machines; wrote first description of modern automatic telephone exchange, and successfully defended inventor's rights. Was first to make scientific investigation of inheritance of powers developed by exercise; devised math. formula to represent energy changes occurring from generation to generation in animals, and applied it to explain evolution of intelligence in man, etc. Author: Control of Heredity, 1903; Dynamic Evolution, 1914; (brochure) Great Men, 1915; Human Heredity, 1921. Contbr. about 400 articles to scientific jours. Home: 1842 N. Tripp Av. Office: Monadnock Block, Chicago, Ill. Died Dec. 15, 1943.

REDINGTON, Paul Goodwin, chief Bur. of Biol. Survey; b. Chicago, Jan. 25, 1878; s. Edward Dana and Mary Ann (Chamberlin) R.; A.B., Dartmouth, 1900; M.F., Yale, 1904; m. Ermina Elizabeth Weaver, Sept. 21, 1910; children—Edward Dana, Mary Ann, Paul Goodwin. Field work, U.S. Forest Service, 1904-Jan 1, 1918, July 1, 1918-26, district forester, 1926-27; chief of Bur. of Biol. Survey, U.S. Dept. Agr. since 1927. City mgr. Albuquerque, N.M., Jan.-July 1918. Mem. Soc. Am. Foresters (pres. 1929), Am. Ornithologists' Union, Am. Soc. Mammalogists, Calif. Acad. Sciences, Washington, (D.C.), Acad. Sciences S.A.R., Delta Kappa Epsilon, Sphinx; honorary member Phila. Acad. Natural Sciences; asso. mem. Boone and Crockett Club, New York. Republican. Conglist. Club: Washington Golf and Country. Contbr. to Jour. of Forestry, Am. Forests and Forest Life. Home: Falls Church, Va. Office: Biological Survey, U.S. Dept. Agriculture, Washington. Died Jan. 12, 1942.

REDMAN, Lawrence V.; b. Oil Springs, Ont., Can., Sept. 1, 1880; s. Richard and Mary Jane (Monteith) R.; A.B., U. of Toronto, 1908; fellow 1908-10, D.Sc., 1931; LL.D., U. of West Ontario, 1930; m. Ellen Blossom Corey, Dec. 22, 1909 (dec.); children—Alice Blossom, Lawrence Truman. Came to U.S., 1910. Asso. prof. industrial chemistry, U. of Kan., 1910-13; pres. Redmanol Chem. Products Co. since 1914; v.p. Bakelite Corp., 1922-40, also dir. research; now retired. Dir. Industrial Research Assn.; mem. Am. Inst. Chem. Engrs., Am. Inst. Chemists, A.A.A.S., Am. Chem. Soc. (ex-pres.); chmn. Chicago sect., 1918-19, N. J. sect., 1930-31), Soc. Chem. Industry (chmn. Am. and N.Y. sects., 1926-27), Farm Chemurgic Council (plastics com.), Sigma Xi, Alpha Chi Sigma. Awarded Grasselli medal, Soc. Chem. Industry, 1931. Methodist. Clubs: Chemists of New York (pres. 1929-30); National (Can.). Author: (with A.V.H. Mory) The Romance of Research (Century of Progress Series). Contbr. papers on tech. subjects. Address: Box 530, Burlington, Ontario, Can. Died Nov. 25, 1946.

REDWAY, Jacques Wardlaw, geographer; b. near Murfreesboro, Tenn., May, 1849; s. John W. and Lady Alexandrina (Wardlaw) R.; spl. studies at univs. of Calif. and at Munich; m. Lilian Burnham von Ebert, an American, residing in Dresden. Became instr. chemistry, U. of Calif., and prof. phys. geography and chemistry State Normal Sch. of Calif.; engaged in mining engring. and exploration in Calif. and Ariz., 1870-80; visited S. America, Europe and Asia for geog. study. Fellow Royal Geog. Soc.; hon. fellow Universidad Nacional La Plata. Author: Manual of Geography, 1887. Joint Author: New Basis of Geography, 1901; Commercial and Industrial Geography, 1923, revised edition of same, 1929; Making the Empire State; Inquiry Concerning the First Landfall of Columbus; The Treeless Plains of North America; Elementary Physical Geography, 1907; All Around Asia, 1909; Redway School History, 1910. Editor: Sir John Mandeville's Travels, 1899; Kinglake's Eothen, 1899; Observer's Handbook of Meteorology, 1920; Story of the Weather, 1931; The Case of Anne Hutchinson. Contbr. articles on atmospheric dust; editorial contributions to various newspapers. Home: 20 E. 4th St., Mt. Vernon, N.Y. Died Nov. 6, 1942.

REED, Alfred Zantzinger, educator; b. Colorado Springs, Colo., Jan. 31, 1875; s. Jacob (M.D.) and Charlotte Rochester (Cuming) R.; A.B., Harvard, 1897, A.M., 1898; Ph.D., Columbia, 1911; m. Stephanie Symonds Lancaster, June 30, 1921. Instructor Phila. Sch. Pedagogy, 1898-1902; pvt. tutor, N.Y. City, 1902-13; staff member ednl. inquiry, Carnegie Foundation for Advancement of Teaching, in charge studies of legal and professional education, 1913-40. Member American Numismatic Society. Author: The Territorial Basis of Government under the State Constitutions, 1911; Training for the Public Profession of the Law, 1921; Present-day Law Schools in the United States and Canada, 1928; Annual Review of Legal Education in the United States and Canada, 1927-34. Home: 827 N. Cascade Av., Colorado Springs, Colo. Died March 11, 1949.

REED, Amy Louise, prof. English; b. N.Y. City, Nov. 22, 1872; d. John Herbert and Anna (Bard) Reed; A.B., Vassar, 1892; studied Yale, 1908-10, Columbia, 1916-17, Ph.D., 1924. Teacher pvt. schs., N.Y. City, 1892-1904; with Vassar Coll. since 1904 (except 1908-10), successively instr. English until 1908, librarian, 1910-21, asso. prof. English, 1920-24, prof. 1924-43, emeritus since 1943. Mem. Phi Beta Kappa. Mem. American Labor Party. Presbyn. Author: The Background of Gray's Elegy, 1924. Editor: Letters from Brook Farm (by Marianne Dwight), 1928. Address: Vassar College, Poughkeepsie, N.Y. Died Jan. 24, 1949.

REED, Charles Dana, meteorologist; b. near Coon Rapids, Ia., Feb. 27, 1875; s. Dana and Alice Celesta (Webber) R.; B.Agr., Ia. State Coll., 1894, M.Sc. in Agr., 1896; m. Elmeta C. McGuire, Sept. 12, 1897 (died Mar. 3, 1941); children—Noama (dec.), Charles Dana, Charlotte Elmeta. Began as asst. in bacteriol. lab., Ia. State Coll., 1894; in charge Ia. State Coll. farm, 1895-96, of field experiments, Ia. Exptl. Sta., 1897; farmed, 1898; entered U.S. Weather Bur., at Vicksburg, Miss., 1899; served in Weather Bur., at Columbus, O., 1900, Omaha, Neb., 1900-05, in charge at Sioux City, Ia., 1905-10, 1st asst. at N.Y. City, 1910-16, in charge at Des Moines, Ia., 1918-44; exec. head weather and crop reporting and forecast service in Ia.; mem. faculty, School of Philosophy, U.S. Dept. Agr., Amarillo, Tex., Oct. 1940; nonresident lecturer in climatology, Ia. State Coll., 1944, research prof. since 1945. Served as coll. cadet capt. Member Weather Bureau Committee of Science Advisory Board, 1933; technical advisor of Iowa Planning Commn.; chmn. supervisory com. Federal Employees Credit Union. Fellow A.A.A.S.; mem. S.A.R. (Ia. pres. 1934-35; v.p. gen. Upper Miss. Valley states 1941-43, Am. Meteorol. Soc. (Minneapolis chmn. 1935; councilor 1936-41), Iowa Acad. Science. Republican. Mem. Church of Christ (treas. Ia. Student Centers Foundation). Mason (32°). Club: Des Moines Economic (1st pres.). Contbr. tech. articles. Office: U.S. Court House, Des Moines, Ia. Died Oct. 26, 1945.

REED, Clyde Martin, senator; b. Champaign County, Ill., Oct. 19, 1871; s. Martin V. and Mary A. R.; ed. pub. schs.; m. Minnie E. Hart, 1891; 7 children. Began as ry. mail clk., 1897, and advanced to supt. ry. mail service, various cities, till 1917; sec. to Gov. Henry J. Allen of Kan., 1919; judge Kan. Court of Industrial Relations, 1920; chmn. Kan. Pub. Utilities Commn., 1921-24; gov. of Kan., 1929-31; elected U.S. senator from Kan., Nov. 1938, for term, 1939-45; re-elected Nov. 1944 for term ending Jan. 1951. Pub. Daily Sun, Parsons. Republican. Methodist. Home: Parsons, Kan. Died Nov. 8, 1949.

REED, Frank Otis, b. Orange, Mass., July 20, 1876; s. William Gilman and Harriet (Otis) R.; A.B., Amherst, 1899; studied univs. of Paris, Madrid and Halle; M.A., Harvard, 1904, Ph.D., 1905; m. Helen Pollock, July, 1902. Began teaching at Amherst, 1899; later asst. prof. Romance langs., U. of Wis. Conglist. Mem. Delta Upsilon, Phi Beta Kappa. Address: 1910 Jeferson St., Madison, Wis. Died Dec. 6, 1928.

REED, Henry Morrison, manufacturer; b. Millvale Borough, Allegheny County, Pa., Sept. 16, 1880; s. John C. and Mary (Curts) R.; grad. Pittsburgh High Sch., 1897; m. Gwendolyn Daniels, Dec. 16, 1902; children—Henry Morrison, John Curts, Mary Gwendolyn (Mrs. James Nelson Stewart), William Theodore. With Standard Sanitary Mfg. Co., 1902-38, beginning as enamel mixer became asst. mgr. Pittsburgh Works, 1907, mgr. Louisville Works, 1910, asst. gen. mgr. factories, 1913, v.p. and gen. mgr. factories, 1925, 1st v.p. and chmn. exec. com., 1928, pres., 1930; now chmn. of bd. and pres. Am. Radiator and Standard Sanitary Corp. since 1938. Republican. Presbyn. Mason (32°, Shriner), Jesters. Clubs: Metropolitan, Engineers, Blind Brook (New York); Duquesne, Pittsburgh, Oakmont Country, Long Vue Country (Pittsburgh); Butler Country (Butler, Pa.). Home: 106 Dickson Av., Ben Avon, Pa. Office: 40 W. 40th St., New York, N. Y.; and Bessemer Bldg., Pittsburgh, Pa. Died Aug. 12, 1947.

REED, James A., ex-senator; b. Ohio, Nov. 9, 1861; s. John A. and Nancy R.; removed with parents to Linn County, Ia., 1864; ed. dist. schs., and spl. course Coe Coll., Ia.; studied law in offices of Hubbard, Clark & Dawley, Cedar Rapids, Ia.; admitted to bar, 1885; m. Lura M. Olmsted, August 1, 1887 (died Oct. 12, 1932); m. 2d, Mrs. Nell Q. Donnelly, Dec. 13, 1933. Practiced at Cedar Rapids, 1885-87; removed to Kansas City, Mo., 1887, actively identified with local and state Dem. politics since 1888; pros. atty., Jackson County, Mo., 1898-1900; tried 287 cases and secured convictions in 285 of them; "reform" Dem. mayor of Kansas City 2 terms, 1900-04. Del. at large Dem. Nat. Conv., Denver, 1908; U.S. senator, 3 terms, 1911-29; now practicing law, Kansas City. Served on commn. to supervise constrn. U.S. Supreme Ct. Bldg. Home: 5236 Cherry St. Office: 1215 R. A. Long Bldg., Kansas City, Mo. Died Sept. 8, 1944; buried Mt. Washington Cemetery, Kansas City, Mo.

REED, Robert Bowman, college pres.; b. Clearfield, Pa., May 26, 1881; s. Frank Bowman and Rebecca Weaver (Shaw) R.; B A., Princeton, 1903; M.A., Harvard University, 1910; m. Anne Irwin Blanchard, 1913 (died Nov. 17, 1942). Instructor in social sciences, American Univ. of Beirut, Syria, 1906-09, prof., 1910-17; ednl. dir. Red Cross Inst. for Blind (for soldiers blinded in World War), Baltimore, 1921-22; supt. Evergreen Inst. for Blind, 1923-24; dean St. Petersburg (Fla.) Jr. Coll., 1928-35, pres. since 1935. Asso. dir. Am. Red Cross Bur. Reconstruction and Relief, Paris, France, 1917-18. Mem. Fla. Acad. of Sciences, Pi Gamma Mu. Presbyterian. Club: University (pres.). Has traveled and studied problems of Europe and the Near East. Lecturer. Home: 819 25th Av. N., St. Petersburg, Fla. Died Nov. 14, 1944.

REED, Robert Rentoul, lawyer; b. Pittsburgh, Pa., June 24, 1876; s. Colin McFarquhar and Lida (Lord) R.; ed. Western U. of Pa. (now U. of Pittsburgh) and New York Law Sch. (LL.M., 1900); m. Christine Patten, Oct. 27, 1910; children—Robert Rentoul, Christine Patten (Mrs. George A. Cameron, Jr.), Eleanor Stockton (Mrs. Archibald Douglas, Jr.), William Wilberforce Lord, Ruth Wheelock (Mrs. Foster M. Fargo), John Davenport. Admitted to Pennsylvania bar, 1899, New York State bar, 1900; member firm Caldwell & Reed, 1908-15, Reed & McCook, 1915-19, Reed, Dougherty & Hoyt, 1919-27, Reed, Hoyt & Washburn since 1927; counsel Investment Bankers Association of America, 1913-21. Member American Bar Association, New York State Bar Association, Bar Assn. City of New York, Nat. Econ. League, Pa. Soc. Cleveland Democrat. Episcopalian. Club: Lawyers (New York). Contbr. to mags. and law reviews. Author of bill for federal corporate reform, 1912 (Atlantic Monthly, Jan. 1909, and Feb. 1914). Home: Robert's Lane, Yonkers, N.Y. Office: 52 Wall St., New York, N.Y. Died June 16, 1945.

REED, Willard, minister, educator; b. Mt. Vernon, N.Y., June 26, 1870; s. Jedidiah Harris and Mary Sophronia (Corner) R.; A.B., Harvard, 1891, A.M., 1896; studied Harvard Div. Sch., 1893-95, summer sessions, 1905, 1906, and yr. 1906-07; Harvard Grad. Sch., 1904-05; m. Ferdinanda Emilia Wesselhoeft, Mar. 28, 1896; children—Mary C., Nancy W., Willard. In business in Boston, 1886-87; prin. high sch., Sandwich, Mass., 1891-93; preaching since 1894; master Roxbury Latin Sch., 1895-98; minister Unitarian chs., Passaic and Rutherford, N.J., 1898-99; master Browne & Nichols Sch., Cambridge, 1899-1910, asso. prin. since 1910. Mem. Classical Assn. of N. E. (pres.), Private Sch. Assn. of Boston (pres.), Country Day School Conf. of U.S. (pres.), Inst. of Politics, Williamstown, Phi Beta Kappa, Delta Upsilon. Democrat. Home: 43 Linnaean St., Cambridge, Mass. Died Sept. 6, 1944.

REES, Thomas Henry, army officer; b. Houghton, Mich., Oct. 18, 1863; s. Seth and Eugenie (Livermore) R.; grad. U.S. Mil. Acad., July 1, 1886, Engring. Sch. of Application, 1889; Army War Coll., 1911; m. Miss Happersett, 1890; m. 2d, Mrs. Blanche (Baxter) Jones, Dec. 28, 1907. Apptd. add. 2d lt. engrs., July 1, 1886; 2d lt., Dec. 31, 1886; 1st lt., Apr. 1, 1890; capt., July 5, 1898; maj., July 11, 1904; lt. col., Feb. 27, 1911; col., July 1, 1916; nom. brig. gen. by Pres. Wilson, Jan. 4, 1918. Instr. civil and mil. engring., U.S. Mil. Acad., 1893-98; with battalion of engrs., 5th Army Corps, Santiago Campaign, 1898, comdg. same, Aug. 1898; comd. Co. C, Battalion of Engrs., Willets Pt., N.Y., 1898-99; in charge fortification work and river and harbor improvements, Fla. Dist., 1899-1901; duty Dept. of Engring., Inf. and Cav. Sch., and Army Staff Coll., Leavenworth, Kan., 1902-05; comdr. 3d Battalion Engrs., 1905-08; duty Army War Coll., 1910-11; dept. engr., and river and harbor works, Chicago, 1908-10, San Francisco, 1911-17; at Manila, P.I., and Honolulu, H.Ty., 1917; apptd. comdr. 152d Field Arty. Brigade, Camp Upton, L.I., N.Y., Feb. 6, 1918. Clubs: Bohemian, Family (San Francisco). Address: War Dept., Washington. Died Sept. 20, 1942.

REESE, Gilbert A., coal exec.; b. Centerville, O., July 28, 1885; s. David T. and Sarah (Davis) R.; ed. pub. schools, Columbus, O.; student Ohio State U., 1905-07; unmarried. Clerk Clinchfield Coal Corp., Atlanta, Ga., 1909; sales mgr. Clinchfield Fuel Co., Spartanburg, S.C., 1910-19, pres., 1919-40; chmn. bd. and pres. Clinchfield Coal Corp. since 1940. Home: 152 Advent St., Spartanburg, S.C. Office: Dante, Va.; Spartanburg, S.C. Died Oct. 28, 1943.

REESE, Lizette Woodworth, educator, author; born Baltimore County, Md., Jan. 9, 1856. Teacher English, Western High Sch., Baltimore. Author: (verse) A Branch of May; A Handful of Lavender, 1891; A Quiet Road, 1896. Address: Atlantic Av., Baltimore. Died Dec. 17, 1935.

REES, Maurice H(olmes), medical educator; b. Newton, Ia., Apr. 27, 1880; s. Spencer Harris and Margaret (Holmes) R.; A.B., Monmouth (Ill.) Coll., 1904; A.M., U. of Ill., 1905; Ph.D., U. of Chicago, 1917; student Rush Med. Coll., Chicago; M.D., Washington U., 1921; m. Elizabeth Prather, June 22, 1911; 1 son, Maurice Prather. Fellow in zoölogy, U. of Ill., 1904-05; prof. science, York (Neb.) Coll., 1905-06; prof. biology, Tarkio (Mo.) Coll., 1906-14; asst. prof. physiology, U. of Kan., 1914-16; asso. in physiology, U. of Chicago, 1916-17; prof. physiology, U. of S.Dak., 1917-21; prof. physiology and pharmacology, U. of Colo. since 1921, asst. dean Sch. of Medicine, 1924-25; now dean and supt. U. of Colo. Sch. of Medicine and Hosps. Fellow A.M.A., Am. College Hospital Adminstrs.; mem. American Physiol. Society, Denver Clinical and Pathological Society, Phi Beta Pi, Phi Eta, Alpha Omega Alpha, Sigma Xi. Republican. Conglist. Clubs: Denver City, Mile High, Cactus. Research in endocrine organs, pituitary extracts and their physiol. action. Home: 2810 E. 7th Av. Office: 4200 E. 9th Av., Denver, Colo. Died May 25, 1945.

REEVES, James Aloysius Wallace, college pres.; b. Latrobe, Pa., Feb. 8, 1892; s. Patrick Joseph and Mary Theresa (Noonan) R.; A.B., St. Vincent Coll., 1914, A.M., 1916; S.T.D., St. Vincent Sem., 1922; student Columbia Univ., University of Pittsburgh; LL.D., Duquesne U., 1933; Litt.D., St. Vincent's Coll., 1936. Ordained priest R.C. Church, 1918; instr. philosophy, Seton Hill Coll., Greensburg, Pa., 1921-23, asso. prof. philosophy and psychology, 1923-26, prof., 1926, acting pres., 1930-31, pres. and mem. bd. trustees since 1931; summer instr. Catholic U. of America, Washington, D.C., 1925; visiting lecturer psychology, Duquesne, 1930; sec. sch. bd., Diocese of Pittsburgh, since 1936. lecturer The Catholic Clergy Social Service Sch., Pittsburgh. Vice-pres. bd. dirs. Westmoreland County council Boy Scouts of America, 1939-44; mem. White House Conf. on Children in Democracy, 1940; coordinator of Nutritional Agencies in Westmoreland County for State Council of Defense, 1945. Mem. executive bd. Civic Music Assn. of Greensburg. Chevalier of the Crown of Italy, 1935. Mem. N.E.A. (dept. of superintendence), Nat. Cath. Ednl. Assn. (past pres. coll. sect.; gen. exec. bd. since 1932), Am. Council on Edn. (com. on standards), Am. Assn. Univ. Profs., Am. Psychol. Association (asso. mem.), American Acad. Polit. and Social Science, St. Vincent Coll. Alumni Assn. (pres. 1941-42), Medieval Acad. of Am., A.A.A.S., Assn. of Coll. Presidents of Pa., Delta Epsilon Sigma, Sigma Kappa Phi, Pi Kappa Delta. Republican. Club: University (Pittsburgh). Contbr. to ch. and ednl. mags. Speaker on Catholic Hour, Nat. Broadcasting Co., 1935. Address: Seton Hill College, Greensburg, Pa. Died March 7, 1947; buried in cemetery on Seton Hill College Campus, Greensburg, Pa.

REEVES, Jeremiah Bascom, author, educator; b. Siloam, N.C., Nov. 1, 1884; s. Micajah Coke and Mary Caroline (Mercer) R.; grad. Oak Ridge (N.C.) Sch., 1905; B.A., University of North Carolina, 1909; M.A., Yale, 1911; Ph.D., Cornell University, 1922; married Louise Calkins, September 15, 1942; one son, Jeremiah Early Krug. Professor of English, Westminster College, Fulton, Missouri, 1914-20, and since 1922; teaching fellow Cornell Univ., 1920-22. Mem. Central O.T.C., Camp Gordon, Ga., 1918. Mem. Modern Lang. Assn. America, Mo. Writers Guild, Inter-Collegiate Peace Assn. (state chmn.), Am. Legion (past comdr. Kingdom Post), Pi Kappa Delta, Phi Kappa Phi, Omicron Delta Kappa, Golden Fleece. Democrat. Author: The Hymn as Literature, 1924 (reissued as The Hymn in History and Literature, 1927); also mag. articles and verses. Address: 321 West 7th St., Fulton, Mo. Died Nov. 7, 1946.

REEVES, Jesse Siddall, univ. prof.; b. Richmond, Ind., Jan. 27, 1872; s. James Eyre and Hannah More

(Peters) R.; student Kenyon Coll., Ohio; B.S., Amherst Coll., 1891, hon. L.H.D., 1926; LL.D., Williams, 1933; Ph.D., Johns Hopkins U., 1894; m. Ellen Howell Griswold, Apr. 5, 1899; children—Arthur G., Ellen H. (Mrs. A. K. Gage, Jr.). Admitted to Ind. bar, 1897; practiced at Richmond, Ind., 1897-1907; instr. Am. history, Woman's Coll. of Baltimore, 1893-94; lecturer on diplomatic history, Johns Hopkins, 1905-06; asst. prof. polit. science, Dartmouth, 1907-10; prof. polit. science, U. of Mich., 1910-31, W. W. Cook prof. Am. institutions, same, 1931; tech. adviser to Am. delegation to The Hague Conf. for Codification of Internat. Law, 1930. Summer quarter, 1917, U. of Chicago, and convocation orator same, 1917; bd. of advisers, Inst. of Politics, Williamstown, Mass., since 1920, and Round Table leader, same, 1921-30; lecturer Acad. of Internat. Law, The Hague, 1924; Am. mem. Pan-Am. Commn. of Jurists, for the codification of international law, 1925-27; James Schouler lecturer in history and polit. science, Johns Hopkins, 1926. Capt., Air Service, 1917-18, dept. air service officer, S.E. Dept.; maj., judge advocate gen. R.C., judge advocate, 20th Div.; staff sch., Army War Coll., 1918; discharged, Dec. 23, 1918. Associé, Institut de Droit Int., 1932. Mem. Am. Inst. Internat. Law, Am. Soc. Internat. Law (v.p.), Am. Hist. Assn., Am. Polit. Science Assn. (pres. 1928), Am. Philos. Soc., Alpha Delta Phi. Clubs: University (Ann Arbor); Detroit (Detroit). Author: International Beginnings of Congo Free State, 1894; Napoleonic Exiles in America, 1905; American Diplomacy Under Tyler and Polk, 1907; La Communaute Internationale, 1925; essays and reviews in various publications. Asso. editor Am. Jour. of Internat. Law. Home: 1945 Cambridge Rd., Ann Arbor, Mich. Died July 7, 1942.

REEVES, Joseph Mason, admiral; b. in Illinois, Nov. 20, 1872; grad. U.S. Naval Acad., 1890; diploma Naval War Coll. Rear adm., June 2, 1927. Comdr. in chief U.S. Fleet, June 15, 1934-Dec. 1, 1936, retired, 1937; recalled to active duty, May 1940; U.S. rep. on Munitions Assignment Bd.; adm., June 16, 1942. Advanced "for eminent and conspicuous conduct" in battle, Spanish-Am. War; served as naval aviation observer. Awarded Navy Cross. Home: The Brighton Hotel, 2123 California St., Washington, D.C. Died Mar. 25, 1948.

REEVES, Perry Willard; b. Parke County, Ind., Aug. 28, 1878; s. John W. and Sarah Jane (Wells) R.; grad. Central Normal Coll., Danville, Ind., and business coll., Indianapolis; m. Blanche M. Cole, Mar. 27, 1900; 1 dau., Sarah Lucille. Teacher pub. schs., Parke County, Ind., 1897-1900; bookkeeper for retail store, 1900; in ry. work, 1900-24, advancing to train condr.; active in Order Ry. Condrs., 1905-24; mem. Ind. State Industrial Bd., in charge of employment service, 1925-27; labor mem. Federal Bd. for Vocational Edn., 1928-35. Republican. Methodist. Mason (Shriner). Home: R.F.D. 1, Rockville, Ind. Died Nov. 26, 1946.

REEVES, William Peters, coll. prof.; b. Richmond, Ind., June 7, 1865; s. James Eyre and Hannah More (Peters) R.; student Earlham Coll., Ind.; A.B., John Hopkins, 1889, Ph.D., 1893; m. Florence Merwin Beckwith, June 27, 1910; 1 dau., Hannah Merwin. Instr. English, Union Coll., 1895-97; prof. English, State U. of Ia., 1897-1900; prof. English and head of dept. and sec. of faculty, Kenyon Coll., since 1900. Mem. Linguistic Soc. America, Alpha Delta Phi. Home: Gambier, O. Died Jan. 30, 1945.

REGAN, Frank Stewart, lawyer, lecturer; b. Rockford, Ill., Oct. 3, 1862; s. Marshall H. and Adelaide R.; grad. Rockford High Sch., 1881; m. Helen M. Crumb, June 11, 1895; children—Adelaide (dec.), Frances L., Leland S. Made complete set abstract books of Winnebago County, Ill., 1888; admitted to bar, 1895. Elected alderman as Prohibitionist in strongest license ward in Rockford, while law student; elected to legislature of Ill. on straight Prohibition ticket, 1898, receiving largest vote of any candidate. Introduced court reporter bill, two-cent ry. fare bill, tax bill to assess equity to owner, and mortgage part to mortgagee; also bill to prohibit the use of the national emblem for any commercial purposes or as an advertising medium; first man in U.S. elected to legislative office on Prohibition ticket; had deciding vote in legislature 4 times. Lectures for lyceum bureaus as cartoonist, illustrating lectures by rapid crayon work. On Chautauqua platform over 22 yrs. and lyceum platform over 40 yrs.; candidate for v.p. U.S. on Prohibition ticket, 1932. Author: The Fool Taxpayer; What Is Wrong With Prohibition?; One Percent Tax Limit for Illinois; Things That Are Wrong Don't Pay; Taxes: Who Pays and Who Escapes. Editor: The Taxpayer. Home: 1201 N. Church St., Rockford, Ill. Died July 25, 1944.

REHDER, Alfred (rā'dĕr), botanist; b. Waldenburg, Sachs., Germany, Sept. 4, 1863; s. Paul Julius and Thekla (Schmidt) R.; ed. gymnasium and at univs. of Berlin and Göttingen; hon. A.M., Harvard, 1913; m. Anneliese Hedwig Schrefeld, Mar. 31, 1906; children—Harald Alfred, Gerhard Oskar and Sylvia Sophia (Mrs. Warren F. Witherell, II). Came to America, 1898; assistant, 1898-1918, curator Herbarium of Arnold Arboretum (Harvard), 1918; asso. prof. dendrology, Harvard, 1934-40, emeritus since 1940. Awarded gold medal by Mass. Horticultural Soc., 1937. Foreign member Linnean Soc. of London; hon. fellow Bot. Soc. of Edinburgh, Royal Hort. Soc. (London); fellow Am. Acad. of Arts and Sciences, A.A.A.S.; mem. Soc. Hort. Science, Deutsche Botanische Gesellschaft, Boston Natural History Soc., N.E. Bot. Club, Bot. Soc. America; hon. mem. Deutsche Dendrol. Gesellschaft, Dendrol. Soc. of Czechoslovakia, Rhododendron Soc., Pa. Hort. Soc.; corr. mem. Peking Soc. Nat. History, Bot. Soc. Japan. Author: Synopsis of the Genus Lonicera, 1903; Bradley Bibliography (5 vols.), 1911-18; Monograph of Azaleas (with E. H. Wilson), 1921; Manual of Cultivated Trees and Shrubs, 1927; 2d edit., 1940; Bibliography of Cultivated Trees and Shrubs, 1949. Editor: Journal of Arnold Arboretum, 1926-40. Collaborator of Standard Cyclopedia of Horticulture, and of Cultivated Evergreens by L. H. Bailey; of Plantae Wilsonianae, and of Trees and Shrubs by C. S. Sargent; of Species of Rhododendron. Has published many papers on woody plants in bot. and hort. jours. Home: 62 Orchard St., Jamaica Plain 30, Mass. Died July 21, 1949.

REICH, Max Isaac (rĭk), minister; b. Berlin, Germany, Mar. 17, 1867; s. Adolphus and Emma (Wolff) R.; ed. gymnasium, Berlin, Germany, and London, England; D.D., Wheaton Coll., Wheaton, Ill., 1936; m. Esther Mary Lorenzen, Sept. 5, 1888; children—Florence, Annie, William, Edward, Esther, Alice, John, Lawrence, Joseph. Came to U.S., 1915. British subject. Apprentice printing trade, London, 1880-86; served as minister Soc. of Friends; expositor of Bible; leader among Christian Jews U.S. and Germany; a founder, 1915, pres., 1921-27, 1935-38, Hebrew Christian Alliance America, hon. pres. 5 years; a founder Internat. Hebrew Christian Alliance, 1927; extension lecturer Moody Bible Inst., Chicago, now also mem. faculty. Wrote: Life and Letters of J. G. M'Vicar; Breathings After the Deeper Life; Deeper Still; The Deeper Life, Spiritual Aloneness; Studies in the Psalms of Israel; How Long?; Studies in Messianic Prophecy; The Mystery and Romance of Israel; Thoughts on the Resurrection; Sweet Singer of Israel (publ. posthumously); Jubilee and Other Poems. Home: George School, Pa. Died Aug. 11, 1945; buried in Friends Burial Ground, Bucks County, Pa.

REICHELDERFER, Luther (Halsey), ex-pres. Commrs. D.C.; b. Hallsville, O., Feb. 4, 1874; s. Alben and Sophia (Halsey) R.; grad. high sch., Washington, 1892; M.D., Columbian (now George Washington) U., 1899, LL.D., 1932; m. Mary Macauley, Nov. 18, 1903. Mem. faculty Business High Sch., Washington, 1895-99; supt. and chief resident physician Garfield Hosp., 1900-07; med. dir. George Washington U. Hosp., 1907-08; mem. faculty med. dept. George Washington U., 1900-24; mem. surg. staff Garfield, Children's and Tuberculosis hosps., until 1924; retired from med. practice, 1924; mem. cons. staff Garfield and Children's hosps.; pres. Bd. of Commrs., D.C., 1930-33; trustee George Washington U. since 1932. Served as 1st lt. and inspector rifle practice, advancing to lt. col. inf. and chief surgeon D.C. Nat. Guard, lt. col. Med. Corps, U.S. Army in France, World War; col. Med. R.C. Fellow Am. Coll. Surgeons; mem. A.M.A., Hippocrates-Galen Med. Soc., Clinico-Pathol. Soc., Anthropol. Soc. Washington, D.C., Med. Soc. (pres. 1923), Assn. Mil. Surgeons of U.S. Club: University. Home: 1661 Crescent Pl., Washington 9, D.C. Died June 19, 1945; buried in Arlington National Cemetery.

REID, Charles Simpson, judge; b. Blairsville, Ga., Sept. 25, 1897; s. Norville Young and Sarah Elizabeth (Daniel) R.; ed. Blairsville Collegiate Inst., 1910-13, Young Harris (Ga.) Coll., 1915-17, Atlanta (Ga.) Law Sch., 1918; LL.D., Atlanta Law Sch., 1940; m. Agnes Jones Baker, July 31, 1943. Asst. cashier First Nat. Bank, Lavonia, Ga., 1917; teller Lowry Nat. Bank, Atlanta, 1918; v.p. Citizens Bank, Gainesville, Ga., 1919-22; admitted to Ga. bar, 1922; mem. firm Davie & Reid, Gainesville, 1922-26, Jones, Davie & Reid, 1926-27, Jones & Reid, 1927-29, Little, Powell, Smith & Goldstein, 1929, Little, Powell, Reid & Goldstein, 1930-38; special counsel Ga. State Banking Dept., 1926-27; apptd. chief justice Ga. Supreme Court, 1938, resigned Aug. 7, 1943; dir. Fulton Nat. Bank, Atlanta. Chmn. State Dem. Exec. Com., 1937-38. Col., U.S. Army; chief, Property Control Branch, Office Military Govt., Germany; chmn. adv. bd., I. G. Farbenindustrie. Trustee and vice chairman endowment com. Young Harris Coll. Mem. Am., Ga. and Atlanta bar assns., Lawyers Club, Newcomen Soc., Delta Theta Phi. Mason (K.T., Shriner). Clubs. Capital City, Atlanta Athletic. Home: 4443 Wieuca Road, N.E., Atlanta, Ga. Died Nov. 7, 1947.

REID, Fergus, cotton mcht.; b. New York, N.Y., Feb. 26, 1862; s. Charles Henry and Mary Helen (Cochran) R.; student Hellmuth Coll., Ont., Can.; Pampatike, Hanover, Va.; m. Mary Wilson Chamberlaine, June 13, 1891; children—Baroness Helen de Lustrac, Fergus. Began in cotton business at Norfolk, 1884; mem. firm Price, Reid & Co., 1884-94, Reid & Co. since 1894; dir. Art Metal Construction Co., Industrial Finance Co., Industrial Acceptance Co., Chesapeake Ferry Co., Investment Corp. of Norfolk, Petroleum Corp. of Venezuela, Pantepec Consolidated of Venezuela; pres. bd. trustees Sweet Briar (Va.) College. Episcopalian. Clubs; Norfolk Country, Princess Anne Country, Cavalier Country (Norfolk); Metropolitan (New York); Tennessee (Memphis); York Country (York Harbor). Home: Norfolk, Va. Died Nov. 30, 1941.

REID, Frank R., ex-congressman; b. Aurora, Ill., Apr. 19, 1879; s. Thomas and Mary (Whiteside) R.; student U. of Chicago, 1899-1900, Chicago Coll. of Law, 1900-01; m. Emily Kelley, Mar. 18, 1905; children—Emily, Jean, Frank, Ruth, Marianna. Admitted to Ill. bar, 1901; county atty., Kane County, Ill.; state's atty., 1904-08; asst. U.S. atty. at Chicago, 1908-10; mem. Ill. Ho. of Rep., 1911-12; chmn. Rep. County Central Com., Kane County, 1914-15; mem. 68th to 73d Congresses (1923-35), 11th Dist.; resigned, Jan. 1934, to resume practice of law. Pres. Ill. State's Attys. Assn., 1908. Sec. League of Ill. Municipalities. Methodist. Mason. Woodsman. Counsel for Gen. William Mitchell in court martial proceedings. Home: Aurora, Ill. Died Jan. 25, 1945.

REID, Frederick Hormah, telephone official; b. Inverness, Scotland, Apr. 6, 1880; s. George and Catherine (Russell) R.; brought to U.S., 1890; ed. Fairmount Sch., Sherman Sch. and West Denver High Sch.; m. Lela Mae Kindig, July 3, 1907; children—Margaret Ruth, Leonard Russell, Roderick Hormah. Began with Colo. Telephone Co., 1902, and advanced to chief clerk to gen. mgr., 1907; with Mountain States Telephone & Telegraph Co. since 1911, chief clerk to gen. mgr., 1911-13, v.p., 1913-14, asst. gen. mgr., 1915-20, gen. mgr., 1920-22; operating v.p. Southern Bell Telephone & Telegraph Co. and Cumberland Telephone & Telegraph Co., Atlanta, Ga., 1922-24; pres. Mountain States Telephone & Telegraph Co. since June 11, 1924. Mem. bd. dirs. Presbyn. Hosp. of Colo. Republican. Presbyterian. Clubs: Denver, Denver Country, Cherry Hills Country. Home: 4500 E. 1st Av. Office: 931 Fourteenth St., Denver, Colo.* Died Oct. 1943.

REID, Harry Fielding, geologist; b. Baltimore, Md., May 18, 1859; s. Andrew and Fanny Brooke (Gwathmey) R.; A.B., Johns Hopkins, 1880; C.E., Pa. Mil. Acad., 1876; Ph.D., Johns Hopkins, 1885; studied in Germany and England, 1884-86; m. Edith Gittings, Nov. 22, 1883; children—Francis Fielding, Doris Fielding. Prof. mathematics, 1886-89, physics, 1889-94, Case School of Applied Science, Cleveland; lecturer Johns Hopkins, 1894-96; asso. prof. physical geology, U. of Chicago, 1895-96; asso. prof., Johns Hopkins U., 1896-1901, prof. geol. physics, 1901-11, prof. dynamical geology and geography, 1911-30, prof. emeritus since 1930. Chief of highway div., Md. Geol. Survey, 1898-1905; spl. expert in charge of earthquake records, U.S. Geol. Survey, 1902-14. Mem. Commn. Internationale des Glaciers; rep. of U.S. in the Internat. Seismol. Assn. since 1906; hon. mem. Société Helvétique des Sciences Naturelles; corr. mem. Phila. Acad. of Natural Sciences; fellow Geol. Soc. America, Am. Phys. Soc., Washington Acad. Sciences; mem. Nat. Acad. Sciences, Am. Philos. Soc., Seismol. Soc. America (pres. 1913), Am. Geophys. Union (chmn. 1924-26). Author: Parts vi, vii, viii of Highways of Maryland, 1899. Joint author: (with A. N. Johnson) Second Report on the Highways of Maryland, 1902; Vol. II of Report of Calif. State Earthquake Investigation Commn., 1910; also several reports and articles on glaciers, earthquakes, etc. Mem. com. Nat. Acad. Sciences apptd. at request of the President to report on the possibility of controlling the Panama slides, 1915. Home: 608 Cathedral St., Baltimore, Md.* Died June 18, 1944.

REID, Mont Rogers, surgeon; b. Oriskany, Va., Apr. 7, 1889; s. Benjamin Watson and Harriet Pendleton (Lemon) R.; student Daleville (Va.) Normal Sch., 1902-04; A.B., Roanoke Coll., Salem, Va., 1908; M.D., Johns Hopkins, 1912; m. Elizabeth Harmon Cassatt, Jan. 26, 1929; 1 son, Alfred Cassatt. Interne Johns Hopkins Hosp., Baltimore, Md., 1912-13, asst. resident pathologist, 1913-14, asst. resident surgeon, 1914-18, resident surgeon, 1918-21, asso. surgeon, 1921-22; instr. in pathology, Johns Hopkins, 1913-14, instr. in surgery, 1914-18, asso. in surgery, 1918-22; asso. prof. surgery, U. of Cincinnati, 1922-31, prof. since 1931; visiting prof. surgery, Peking (now Pieping, China) Union Med. Coll., 1925-26; dir. surg. service Cincinnati Gen. Hosp., Children's Hosp. Served as 1st lt. Med. Corps, U.S. Army, World War. Recipient of first presentation of Rudolph Matas vascular surgery award, 1934. Fellow Am. Coll. Surgeons; mem. A.M.A., Am. Surg. Assn. (v.p. 1934-35), Southern Surg. Soc., Internat. Surg. Assn., Soc. Clin. Surgery, A.A.A.S., Soc. of U. Surgeons, Central Surg. Assn., Nat. Advisory Cancer Council, Am. Soc. for the Control of Cancer (dir.), Phi Chi, Alpha Omega Alpha, Sigma Chi, Pi Kappa Epsilon; hon. mem. Detroit Acad. Surgery, Republican. Presbyterian. Clubs: Camargo, Optimists, Halsted, Cincinnati Country, Commercial, Commonwealth (Cincinnati); Queen City. Contbr. chapter on surgery of the arteries, Nelson's Loose Leaf System of Surgery, 1928; chapter on surgery of sympathetic nervous system, Dean Lewis' System of Surgery, 1929; also contbr. to Jour. Exptl. Medicine, Bulls. of Johns Hopkins Hosp., Trans. Southern Surg. Assn., Jour. A.M.A., Jour. of Medicine, etc. Home: 1908 Dexter Av. Office: Holmes Hospital, Cincinnati, O Died May 11, 1943.

REID, Ogden Mills, editor; b. New York, N.Y., May 16, 1882; s. Whitelaw and Elisabeth (Mills) R.; Browning Sch., New York; U. of Bonn, Germany; B.A., Yale, 1904, LL.B., 1907; m. Helen Miles Rogers, Mar. 14, 1911; children—Whitelaw, Elisabeth (dec.), Ogden Rogers. Worked in law office; admitted to N.Y. bar, 1908; began work on The Tribune (now Herald Tribune) as reporter, summer of 1908; in various depts. same paper, including copy desk, asst. to city editor, asst. night editor, mng. editor, spring of 1912, editor since 1913. Republican presidential elector, 1912. Episcopalian. Pres. Delta Kappa Epsilon, 1919; mem. Phi Delta Phi. Home: 15 E. 84th St., New York, N.Y. Died Jan. 3, 1947.

REID, William Clifford, lawyer; b. Etna Green, Ind., Dec. 16, 1868; s. John M. and Mary C. (Iden) R.; student Purdue U., Lafayette, Ind., 1 yr.; married; 1 son, Thomas M. Admitted to Ohio bar, 1894; moved to Roswell, N.M., and then to Albuquerque; asst. U.S. atty., Dist. of N.M., 1901-04; atty. gen.

N.M., 1906-07; solicitor for N.M. of A.,T.&S.F. Ry.; mem. law firm of Reid & Iden. Served as capt. Co. F, 1st Territorial U.S. Inf., Spanish-Am. War, 1898. Mem. Am. Bar Assn. Republican. Home: 1010 W. Tijeras Av. Office: First Nat. Bank, Albuquerque, N.M. Died Dec. 1, 1941.

REID, William Duncan, physician; b. Newton, Mass., Dec. 30, 1885; s. Robert Alexander and Carrie (Stickle) R.; A.B., Harvard, 1906, M.D., 1909; studied Berlin, Germany, 1911-12; m. Blanche Adeline McDonald, Sept. 23, 1913; children—William Duncan, Claire McDonald, James Alexander. Interne Boston City Hosp., 1909-11; served as chief of heart clinic, Boston Dispensary, and as jr. asst., phys., in charge of heart lab., Boston City Hosp. (resigned), 1923; asst. prof. in cardiology, Boston U. Sch. of Medicine and cardiologist Mass. Memorial Hosp. and heart consultant, Waltham Hosp. to 1939; retired from practice, 1940. Captain U.S. Army, 1917; with A.E.F. in France 17 months, 1917-18; lt. comdr., Medical Corps, U.S.N.R., Sept. 1944-Jan. 31, 1946; now on inactive duty; mem. U.S.N.R. Mem. A.M.A., Mass. Med. Soc., New Eng. Heart Assn., Am. Heart Assn., New Eng. Med. Soc., Alpha Omega Alpha; fellow Am. Coll. Physicians. Congregationalist. Club: Harvard. Author: The Heart in Modern Practice, 1923, 2d edit., 1928; Diseases of the Heart, 1933; Teaching Methods in Medicine, 1933; Manual of Cardiology, 1939. Home: North Parsonsfield, Me. Died Sep. 29, 1949.

REID, William James, Jr., clergyman; b. Pittsburgh, Pa., July 10, 1871; s. William James (D.D., LL.D.) and Mary (Bowen) R.; A.B., Princeton, 1893; grad. Pittsburgh Theol. Sem., 1896; D.D., Monmouth (Ill.) Coll., 1909; Litt.D., Westminster Coll., New Wilmington, Pa., 1940; m. Margaret Morton Thompson, July 28, 1896; children—Elizabeth Thompson (Mrs. Edward Cornell Emanuel), Mary Bowen (dec.), Margaret Anna (dec.), Janet Donaldson (Mrs. Albert Victor Crookston), Helen Louise (Mrs. Charles S. Ingham), Frances Bryce (Mrs. Joseph Tilton). Ordained ministry United Presbyn. Ch., 1896; pastor First Ch., Kittanning, Pa., 1896-1900; asso. pastor First Ch., Pittsburgh, 1900-02, pastor since 1902 (father and son have served this congregation since Apr. 7, 1862); editor Sabbath Sch. Dept. of The United Presbyterian, 1902-36; asso. editor The United Presbyterian, 1913-21, editor, 1921-41, now editor emeritus; dir. Murdock Kerr & Co., printers, 1902-25. Treas. Synod of Pittsburgh, 1902-33; mem. Bd. of Home Missions U.P. Ch., 1910-28; mem. Board of Administration, U.P. Church, since 1931; chmn. U.P. Com. on Presbyn. Unity; pres. bd. trustees Monongahela Presbytery since 1920. Republican. Home: 920 S. Aiken Av., Pittsburgh, Pa. Died Feb. 1943.

REIFFEL, Charles (rĭf'ĕl), landscape painter; b. Indianapolis, Ind., Apr. 9, 1862; s. Jacob and Nancy Ellen (Marshall) R.; ed. pub. schs., Kansas City, Mo., and Indianapolis; m. Elizabeth Frances Flanagan, Apr. 25, 1898. Represented in permanent collections of Corcoran Gallery of Art, Washington, D.C.; Fine Arts Gallery, San Diego, Calif.; Santa Cruz Art League, Municipal Collection, Phoenix, Ariz.; Wood Art Gallery, Montpelier, Vt.; Los Angeles Museum, 2 murals in Russ Auditorium, San Diego; 2 murals in Memorial Junior High Sch., San Diego; a group of paintings in San Diego public schools; John Herron Art Inst., Indianapolis; paintings in San Diego City and County Municipal Bldg.; 3 murals, Council Chamber, San Diego (with George Rhone). Awarded fellowship prize, Soc. of Artists, Buffalo, 1908; Norman Wait Harris silver medal, Art Inst. Chicago, 1917; 1st hon. mention, Soc. of Artists, Buffalo, 1920; hon. mention, Conn. Acad. Fine Arts, 1920, Carnegie Inst., 1922; Mrs. Daniel Rhodes Hanna, Jr. prize, Hoosier Salon, Chicago, 1925, Thomas Meck Butler prize, 1926, Tri Kappa Sorority prize, 1927; John C. Shaffer grand prize, 1928; William Preston Harrison prize, Los Angeles Museum, 1926; Art Guild prize, Fine Arts Gallery, San Diego, 1926, purchase prize, 1927; Hatfield gold medal, Calif. Art Club, Los Angeles Museum, 1928; 2d landscape prize, Phoenix, Ariz., 1928; Mrs. Keith-Spalding prize, Los Angeles Museum, 1929; grand prize, Calif. State Exhbn., Santa Cruz, 1929; Art Assn. prize, John Herron Art Inst., Indianapolis, 1929; Mary B. Falke prize, Richmond, Ind., 1930; 1st landscape prize, Sacramento, 1930, Phoenix, Ariz., 1930; gold medal, Painters of the West, Biltmore Salon, Los Angeles, 1930; 1st prize Pasadena Art Gallery, 1930; Thomas Meek Butler memorial prize, Hoosier Salon, Chicago, 1931; award of merit, Los Angeles Museum, 1932; John C. Shaffer, grand prize Hoosier Salon, Chicago, 1938; Bess Gilbert prize Art Guild Fine Arts Gallery, San Diego, 1939. Mem. Allied Artists America, Internat. Soc. Arts and Letters, Contemporary Group Painters and Sculptors (San Diego), Contemporary Artists, Ind. Fedn. of Artists, Conn. Acad. Fine Arts, North Shore Arts Assn., Buffalo Soc. Artists, Silvermine Guild (pres. 1923), San Diego Art Guild, Hoosier Salon, Laguna Beach Art Assn. Clubs: Salmagundi, Indiana (New York); Arts (Washington, D.C.); California Art (Los Angeles); San Diego Press. Address: Whispering Pines Dr., Box 224, Julian, Calif. Died Mar. 14, 1942.

REIGHARD, Jacob (Ellsworth) (rī'kärd), zoölogist; b. LaPorte, Ind., July 2, 1861; s. Dr. John Davison and Mary (Hulbert) R.; Ph.B., U. of Mich., 1882, hon. Sc.D., 1936; studied Harvard U., 1883-85, Univ. of Michigan Medical School, 1885-86, also Freiburg-in-Breisgau; married Katharine E. Farrand, July 1, 1887 (now deceased); children—Paul Roby (dec.), John Jacob, Catherine Farrand, Farrand Kitchel (dec.). Teacher of sciences, High Sch., LaPorte, Ind., 1882-83; pvt. tutor North Attleboro, Mass., 1883-85; instr. zoölogy, 1886-87 and 1888-89, acting asst. prof. zoölogy, 1887-88, asst. prof., 1889-91, prof. animal morphology, 1891-95, prof. zoölogy, 1895-1927, prof. emeritus in zoölogy since 1927, dir. zoölogy laboratory, 1895-1925, and dir. Biol. Sta., U. of Mich.; dir. Univ. Museum, 1895-1913. In charge of scientific work of Mich. Fish Commn., 1890-95; dir. biological survey of Great Lakes for U.S. Fish Commn., 1898-1901; formerly trustee Marine Biol. Lab., Woods Hole, Mass., and mem. bd. advisers Mich. State Geol. Survey. Fellow A.A.A.S.; mem. Am. Soc. Naturalists, Am. Soc. Zoölogists, Am. Fisheries Soc. (pres. 1916), Mich. Acad. Science. Clubs: University, Ann Arbor Golf and Outing, Pleasant Lakes, Research of Univ. of Mich., Delta Upsilon. Author: (with Dr. H. S. Jennings) Anatomy of the Cat, 1901, rev., 1937 also articles on lip reading for the adult deafened, and numerous scientific papers on fresh water biology, evolution, development, behavior and habits of fishes, sub-aquatic photography. Address: Natural Science Bldg., Ann Arbor, Mich. Died Feb. 13, 1942.

REILLY, John Liguori, clergyman; b. Albany, N.Y., May 25, 1853; s. John and Rose (O'Neill) R.; A.B., Niagara U., 1872, A.M., 1881, LL.D., 1906. Ordained priest R.C. Ch., at St. Joseph's Provincial Sem., Troy, N.Y., 1876; stationed, Adirondacks, 1876; asst. priest St. John the Evangelist Ch., Syracuse, N.Y., 1876-77; asst. priest Cathedral, Albany, N.Y., 1877; sec. and chancellor, Albany Diocese, 1881; pastor St. James's Ch., Cazenovia, N.Y., 1882-85; sec. and chancellor, Albany Diocese, 1885-86; pastor St. John the Evangelist Ch., Schenectady, 1886; rural dean; domestic prelate (Rt. Rev. Msgr.), 1904. Chaplain Schenectady Police and Fire Dept.; mem. Schenectady Park Bd.; mem. bd. mgrs. Schenectady Hosp. Assn.; mem. bd. visitors Albion State Training Sch. Rotarian. Home: 802 Union St., Schenectady, N.Y. Died Feb. 3, 1945.

REILLY, Michael Kiernan, ex-congressman; b. Empire, Fond du Lac County, Wis., July 15, 1869; s. Michael and Margaret (Phelan) R.; ed. country schs., normal school and U. of Wisconsin; married. Admitted to Wis. bar, 1895, and began practice at Milwaukee; mem. firm Reilly & Cosgrove; dist. atty. Fond du Lac County, Wis., 1899-1901; city atty. Fond du Lac, 1904-09; mem. 63d and 64th Congresses (1913-17), 6th Wis. dist.; del. to Dem. Nat. Conv., 1908, 24; Dem. nominee for U.S. senator, 1928; elected Nov. 4, 1930, to 71st Congress to fill unexpired term of Florian Lampert, deceased, and on same date elected for full term of 72d Congress (1931-33), and reelected 73d to 75th Congresses (1933-39), 6th Wisconsin District. Mem. Am. and Wis. State bar assns. Catholic. K.C., Elk, Moose; mem. Catholic Order of Foresters, Equitable Fraternal Union. Home: Fond du Lac, Wis.* Died Oct. 14, 1944.

REINHARDT, Aurelia Henry (Mrs. George Frederick Reinhardt) (rīn'härt), coll. pres.; b. San Francisco, Calif., Apr. 1, 1877; d. of William Warner and Mary Rogers (Merritt) Henry; B.L., U. of Calif., 1898; scholar in English, 1901-02, fellow in English, Yale, 1902-03, Ph.D., 1905; LL.D., U. of Calif., 1919, Mt. Holyoke Coll., 1937, Oberlin Coll., 1937; Litt.D., U. of Southern Calif., 1924; L.H.D., Colorado Coll., 1931, Williams Coll., 1937; m. Dr. George Frederick Reinhardt, Dec. 4, 1909 (died June 7, 1914); children—George Frederick, Paul Henry. Instr. Eng., U. of Ida., 1898-1901, Lewiston (Ida.) State Normal Sch., 1903-05, 1906-08; lecturer in English, U. of Calif., 1914-16; pres. Mills Coll., Oakland, Calif., 1916-43; now retired. Moderator, Unitarian Chs. of America, 1940-42; mem. bd. trustees, Calif., Coll. in China Foundation; mem. Alameda County Instns. Commn. since 1917; mem. Alameda County Charities Commn. since 1934; mem. East Bay Regional Park Bd. since 1934; mem. Nat. Com. on Mobilization for Human Needs, 1935-37. Mem. Dante Soc., Concordance Soc., Philol. Assn. Pacific Coast, Am. Assn. Univ. Women (pres. 1923-27; chmn. com. on internat. relations, 1927-33), Assn. Am. Colleges, Nat. Economic League (council), N.E.A., Inst. of Pacific Relations (bd. trustees of Am. Council), Pacific Geog. Soc., Gen. Fedn. Women's Clubs (chmn. dept. of edn., 1928-30), D.A.R., Colonial Dames, Phi Beta Kappa. Unitarian. Clubs: Book of Calif., San Francisco Mills, Sorosis, Town and Country, Century, Ebell. Editor: (with transl. and notes) The Monarchia of Dante Alighieri, 1904; (with glossary) Epicoene, or The Silent Woman, by Ben Jonson, 1906; Yale Studies in English XXXI; also contbr. of some transls. in Select Translations from Old English Poetry (Cook and Tinker, editors), 1903. Contbr. to jours. and mags. Address: 2215 Bywood Dr., Oakland, Calif. Died Jan. 28, 1948.

REINHARDT, Max (rīn'härt), producer of plays; b. Baden bei Wien, Austria, Sept. 9, 1873; s. Wilhelm Goldmann and Rosa (Wengraf) R.; studied for stage with Emil Buerde, Vienna; hon. Dr., Christian-Albrecht-Universitaet, Kiel, 1930, Goethe-Universitaet, Frankfurt am Main, 1930; D.C.L., Oxford U., Eng., 1933; m. Else Heims, of Berlin, July 22, 1910 (divorced 1932); children—Wolfgang, Gottfried; m. 2d, Helene Thimig, of Vienna, Austria, June 22, 1935. Left Germany, 1933; became a citizen of Czechoslovakia; later came to U.S. to live. Debut as performer, Salzburg, 1893; invited to Berlin by Otto Brahm; actor, later producer, plays at Deutsche Theater du Berlin, 1895-1932. Owner of theatre since 1905; founded Kammerspiele and Grosse Schauspielhaus (theatres), Berlin; produced German classic plays, the entire works of Shakespeare, also leading dramatic poets; one of first to collaborate with widely recognized painters and musicians; first to produce early works of Richard Strauss; productions taken on world tours; toured U.S. 5 times, with Am. actors 1912, 1934; produced The Miracle, A Midsummer Night's Dream; founded the Salzburg Festival; established the Reinhardt Seminars, Vienna, for training of young actors and producers. Died Oct. 31, 1943.

REINHEIMER, Bartel Hilen (rīn'hīm-ẽr), bishop; b. Sandusky, O., Apr. 6, 1889; s. Alfred and Beatrice (Savanack) R.; B.S., Kenyon Coll., Gambier, O., 1911, D.D., 1931; grad. Bexley Hall Divinity Sch., Gambier, 1914; LL.D., Hobart Coll., 1936; m. Helen Marie Smith, Aug. 31, 1914; children—Frederick Smith, John Bartel. Ordained deacon P.E. Ch., 1914, priest, 1915; minister in charge St. Mark's Ch., Shelby, O., 1914-16; curate Christ Ch., Dayton, O., 1916-18, rector, 1918-21; exec. secretary and archdeacon Southern Ohio Diocese, 1921-31; nat. sec. Field Dept., P.E. Church, 1931-36; bishop coadjutor Diocese of Rochester, N.Y., 1936-38, bishop since 1938. Trustee and hon. chancellor, Colleges of the Seneca. Pres. Province of N.Y. and N.J., Episcopal Ch., 1947-50. Trustee University of Rochester. Served as voluntary chaplain Wilbur Wright Field, Dayton, Ohio, 1918-19. Mem. Phi Beta Kappa, Delta Tau Delta. Mason (K.T., 33°). Clubs: Monroe Golf (Rochester); Genesee Valley; Rochester Country. Contbr. to religious jours. Home: 111 Douglas Road, Rochester 10. Office: 110 Merriman St., Rochester 7, N.Y. Died Nov. 12, 1949.

REINKE, Edwin Eustace (rĭn'kē), biologist; b. of Am. parents, Jamaica, W.I., June 27, 1887; s. Rev. Jonathan (D.D.) and Mary Virginia (Caffrey) R.; Moravian Preparatory Sch., Bethlehem, Pa.; B.A., Lehigh U., 1908, M.A., 1909; Ph.D., Princeton, 1913; m. Emily Feuring, Aug. 14, 1915; children—Mary Louise, Dorothy Virginia, Caroline Emily. Grad. asst. Lehigh U., 1908-09; fellow in biology, Princeton, 1909-13, Procter fellow, 1913-14; instr. in biology, Rice Inst., Houston, Tex., 1914-15; research asso. Dept. Marine Biology of Carnegie Instn., Washington, 1912-15; with Vanderbilt U. since 1915, successively asst. prof. biology until 1917, asso. prof., 1917-22, prof. since 1922, sec. of faculty, Coll. of Arts and Science, 1929-41, chmn. div. natural sciences and math. since 1941; dir. Highlands Museum and Biol. Lab., Inc., 1929-35 (resigned). Fellow A.A.A.S.; mem. Am. Soc. Zoölogists, Assn. of Southeastern Biologists (pres. 1938-39), Am. Assn. Anatomists, Ala. Acad. Science (hon.), Phi Beta Kappa, Sigma Xi. Democrat. Episcopalian. Home: 1702 Beechwood Av., Nashville, Tenn. Died Jan. 25, 1945.

REIS, Arthur M. (rēs), business exec.; b. New York, N.Y., Jan. 19, 1883; s. Robert and Sarah (Metzger) R.; A.B., Columbia, 1903; m. Claire Raphael, December 20, 1915; children—Hilda, Arthur. Junior. Began career as junior executive Robert Reis & Co., New York, N.Y., 1903, pres. since 1919; pres. Ford Mfg. Co., Waterford, N.Y., since 1931. Dir. Am. Arbitration Assn.; chmn. exec. com., N.Y. State Chamber of Commerce. Clubs: City of New York, Century Country, Advertising, Bankers. Home: 50 E. 68th St., New York 21. Office: 2 Park Av., New York 16. Died Dec. 23, 1947.

REISINGER, Harold Carusi (rī'sing-ẽr), Marine Corps officer; b. Washington, D.C., Oct. 10, 1876; entered Marine Corps, Feb. 1900; advanced through the grades to brig. gen., Mar. 1936; retired May 1938.†* Died Jan. 29, 1945.

REISNER, George Andrew, Egyptologist; b. Indianapolis, Nov. 5, 1867; s. George Andrew and Mary Elizabeth (Mason) R.; A.B., Harvard Univ., 1889, A.M., 1891, Ph.D., 1893, hon. Litt.D., 1939, grad. courses in Semitic langs.; m. Mary Putnam Bronson, Nov. 22, 1892. Asst. Egyptian dept., Royal Museum, Berlin, 1895-96; instr. Harvard, 1896-97; mem. Internat. Commn. on Catalogue Khedivial Museum, Cairo, 1897-99; Hearst lecturer in Egyptology and dir. Hearst Egyptian Expdn. from U. of Calif., 1899-1905; asst. prof. Semitic archeology, 1905-10, asst. prof. Egyptology, 1910-14, prof. since 1914 Harvard U. (leave of absence); dir. Egyptian expdn. of Harvard and Boston Museum Fine Arts since 1905; curator Egyptian dept. Boston Museum Fine Arts since 1910. Archeologist in charge of excavations of Egyptian Govt. in Nubia in preparation to flooding lower Nubia by raising the Assuan dam, 1907-09; dir. Harvard Palestinian Expdn., conducting excavations at Samaria, 1907-10; has excavated at Bersheh, Girga, Giza Pyramids, Samaria, in Lower Nubia, in Halfa, Dongola and Berber Provinces in the Sudan and tomb of Hetep-heres I, mother of Cheops. Delegate to Archeological Congress, Cairo, Egypt, 1909; fellow Am. Acad. Arts and Sciences; corr. mem. Sächsische Akademie der Wissenschaften (Phil. Hist. Klasse), 1929. Author: Sumerisch-Babylonische Hymnen, nach thontafeln Griechischer Zeit, 1896; Tempelurkunden aus Telloh, 1901; Hearst Medical Papyrus, 1905; The Early Dynastic Cemeteries of Naga-ed Der, Part 1, 1907; First Annual Report, Nubian Archeol. Survey, 1910; Models of Ships and Boats, 1913; Excavations at Kerma (2 vols.), 1923; Harvard Excavations at Samaria (2 vols.), 1924; Mycerinus, The Temples of the Third Pyramid at Giza, 1931; A Provincial Cemetery of the Pyramid Age, Naga-ed-Dêr III, 1932; The Development of the Egyptian Tomb, 1935. Address: Museum of Fine Arts, Boston, Mass. Died June 6, 1942.

REIST, Henry Gerber (rīst), engineer; b. Mount Joy, Pa., May 27, 1862; s. Henry B. and Catharine (Gerber) R.; ed. country, high and state normal schs.; M.E., Lehigh U., 1886, Eng.D., 1922; m.

Margaret E. Breed, Aug. 1907. Early life on farm; engr. for Harrisburg Car Co., 1886-88; accompanied Am. Engring. Soc. on trip to England and Paris Expn., 1899. Connected with the Thomson-Houston Elec. Co., 1889, and in 1894 took charge of designs of alternating current machinery for General Electric Co.; since then has designed much of the most important elec. machinery in this country and abroad; now retired. Fellow Am. Soc. Mech. Engrs., Am. Inst. E.E., A.A.A.S.; mem. Tau Beta Pi, Sigma Xi. Author: Peter Reist of Lancaster County, Pa., and Some of His Descendants, 1933. Contbr. to proc. engring. socs. and tech. press. Home: 1166 Avon Rd., Schenectady, N.Y. Died July 5, 1942; buried in Kraybill Mennonite Cemetery, Twp. East Donegal, Pa,

REMAK, Gustavus, Jr. (rē-māk), insurance exec.; b. Phila., Pa., Mar. 19, 1861; s. Gustavus and Sue M. (Scott) R.; grad. Episcopal Acad., Phila., 1878; A.B., U. of Pa., 1882; LL.B., 1884; m. Caroline H. Voorhees, June 10, 1896; children—Margaret Onderdonk (Mrs. Horatio H. Morris), Caroline Voorhees (Mrs. John B. Ramsay, Jr.). Admitted to Pa. bar, 1884, and practiced at Phila. until 1930; pres. The Insurance Co. of State of Pa., 1913-41, chmn. bd. since Jan. 20, 1941. Republican. Episcopalian. Clubs: Rittenhouse, Down Town. Home: Prospect Av., Chestnut Hill, Phila. Office: 308 Walnut St., Philadelphia, Pa. Died Nov. 10, 1944.

REMICK, James Waldron (rĕm'ĭk), judge; b. Hardwick, Vt., Oct. 30, 1860; s. Samuel K. and Sophia S. R.; ed. Colebrook (N.H.) Acad.; LL.B., U. of Mich., 1882; hon. A.M., Dartmouth; m. Mary S. Pendleton, Dec. 5, 1888; 1 dau., Gladys (Mrs. Jesse S. Wilson). Admitted to bar, 1882; U.S. dist. atty., N.H., 1889-93; asso. justice Supreme Court of N.H., 1901-04; war claims arbiter for U.S., 1930-31 Pres. Rep. State Conv., 1904; pres. Lincoln Rep Club, 1905-06; pres. N.H. Bar Assn., 1922-23; pres Kittery (Me.) Hist. Soc., 1935-37. Home: Concord N.H. Died Feb. 10, 1943.

REMINGTON, Harvey Foote, lawyer; b. Henrietta, N.Y., June 28, 1863; s. William Thomas and Sarah A. (Foote) Remington; Geneseo State Normal Sch.; LL.B., Albany Law School (Union University), 1887; LL.D., Keuka College, Keuka Park, New York, 1937; married Mary Agnes Brodie, May 28, 1889 (died June 19, 1945); children—William Brodie, Thomas Howard, Mrs. Agnes Harmon, Harvey Foote, John Warner, Mrs. Harriet Sulger, Francis Kirk. Began practice at Rochester, N.Y., 1887; now member of law firm of Remington, Gifford & Willey; dir. and counsel Bastian Bros. Co., First Nat. Bank of Caledonia, Clark-Stecko Co., and various other cos.; dir. and sec. Maplewood Cemetery Assn. Mem. Rochester Bd. of Edn., 1892; asst. corp. counsel, 1892-95; judge Municipal Court, 1896-97. Pres. bd. trustees Keuka Coll. Sec. Selective Service Draft Bd. 556, 1940-47. Mem. Am. and N.Y. State bar assns., Rochester Bar Assn. (pres. 1923), Empire State Soc. S.A.R. (pres. 1919-20; pres. National Society 1925-26), Rochester Hist. Soc. (pres. 1918-21), Soc. Colonial Wars (local sec.), Am. Flag Assn. Am. Scenic and Historic Preservation Soc. (trustee), Union Soc. Am. Wars. Pres. Rochester Pub. Library Bd.; mem. N.Y. State Library Assn., Am. Library Assn. Counsel and mem. exec. com. N.Y. Bapt. Missionary Conv.; pres. and trustee Bapt. Edn. Soc. State of N.Y.; trustee and mem. exec. com. Colgate-Rochester Div. Sch.; trustee Bapt. Home of Monroe Co.; trustee Rochester Museum of Arts and Sciences. Republican. Baptist. Mason (32°, Shriner), Odd Fellow. Clubs: Cosmos, Rochester Chamber of Commerce. Home: 1650 East Av., Rochester, N.Y.; (summer) Strathmore Lodge, Eagle Bay, N.Y. Office: Lincoln Alliance Bank Bldg., Rochester, N.Y. Deceased.

RENAUD, Ralph Edward, newspaperman; b. Washington, D.C., Feb. 27, 1881; s. Edward and Blanche Ella (Whelpley) R.; ed. Central High Sch., Washington, 1895-99; art end., Art Students League, 1897-99; student Stanford, 1899-1903; m. Helen Lamson, Jan. 14, 1911; children—Helen, Jeanne, Ruth Buckingham. Art reporter Washington Star, 1899; editor Stanford Chapparal, 1900-03, Stanford Quad, 1902; reporter San Francisco Examiner, 1903-07; dramatic critic San Francisco Bulletin, 1907-10; San Francisco Chronicle, 1910-12, N.Y. Globe, 1912; mgr. Chestnut Street Opera House, Phila., 1913-14; mem. staff N.Y. Tribune, 1916, later cable editor, news editor, night editor, until 1920; night mng. editor N.Y. Herald, 1921; asst. mng. editor N.Y. Tribune, 1922-25; mng. editor N.Y. Evening Post, 1925-28, N.Y. World, 1929-31; again with N.Y. Evening Post until 1933; mng. editor Washington Post; now mem. editorial council, N.Y. Times. Mem. Zeta Psi. Club: Dutch Treat. Author: (play) Betty Behave, 1916. Home: 9 Summit Av., Larchmont, N.Y. Died Aug. 10, 1948.

RENNIE, Joseph, clergyman; b. Richmond, Va., July 15, 1860; s. Joseph Richard and Ella Rosalin (Powell) R.; student Richmond Coll., 1880-82; B.A., Hampden-Sydney Coll. Va., 1885; B.D., Union Theol. Sem., Richmond, 1888; D.D., Central U. (now Center Coll.), Ky., 1902; m. Ellen Eugenia Goodall, Oct. 25, 1888; children—Mary Christian (Mrs. Robert Job Wyatt), Edith Cecil (wife of Rev. H. V. Carson), Eugenia Christian (Mrs. L. L. Rose), Joseph. Ordained ministry Presbyn. Ch. in U.S., 1888; pastor successively First Ch., Chase City, Va., First Ch., Oxford, N.C., Stuart Robinson Memorial Ch., Louisville, Ky., Madison Av. Ch., Covington, First Ch., Norfolk, Va., and First Ch., Greenwood, Miss., until 1923, First Ch., St. Joseph, Mo., 1923-31; supplied First Ch., Wilmington, N.C., Jan. 1-Apr. 1932; pastor First Ch., High Point, N.C., 1932-37, being called at age of 72; has been moderator of several presbyteries, also of Synod of Miss., many times commr. to Gen. Assembly of U.S.; often called upon for baccalaureate addresses. Active in Red Cross work, also in speaking for League to Enforce Peace and League of Nations, World War. Trustee Hampden-Sydney Coll., 1903-12, Southwestern Coll., Memphis, Tenn., 1917-23. Mem. Nat. Economic League, Phi Kappa Alpha. Democrat. Odd Fellow, Kiwanian. Home: 530 Blunt St., Raleigh, N.C. Died Sep. 30, 1943.

RENTSCHLER, Gordon S., banker and manufacturer; b. Hamilton O., Nov. 25, 1885; s. George A. and Phoebe (Schwab) R.; A.B., Princeton, 1907; m. Mrs. Mary Coolidge Atkins, July 23, 1927; children—Faith A. Witter, Phoebe, Mary Coolidge, Susan Helen. Formerly pres. Hooven, Owens, Rentschler Co. and associated foundry and machinery mfg. companies; an organizer and dir., 1915-32, Miami (Ohio) Conservancy Dist.; dir. Nat. City Bank of N.Y. since 1923, pres., 1929-40, chmn. since 1940; dir. and chmn. City Bank Farmers Trust Co. and Internat. Banking Corp.; dir. Anaconda Copper Mining Co., Consol. Edison Co. of N.Y., Corning Glass Works, Discount Corp. of N.Y., Federal Insurance Co., Home Insurance Co., National Cash Register Co., Union Pacific R.R. Co. Life trustee Massachusetts Institute of Technology; life trustee Princeton University. Trustee Carnegie Institution of Washington. Member Ohio Society of New York. Clubs: Cedar Creek, Piping Rock, Links, Princeton Club, Union League, University, Knickerbocker; Metropolitan (Washington). Home: Duck Pond Road, Locust Valley, L.I., N.Y. Office: 55 Wall St., New York. Died March 3, 1948; buried Greenwood Cemetery, Hamilton, O.

RENTSCHLER, Harvey Clayton, physics; b. Hamburg, Pa., Mar. 26, 1881; s. Joseph F. and Rebecca (Ritzman) R.; B.A., Princeton, 1903, M.A., 1904; Ph.D., Johns Hopkins, 1908, hon. D.Sc., Princeton University, 1941; LL.D., honorary, Ursinus College, 1942; m. Margaret Bender, 1904; 1 son, Lawrence Bender. Instr. physics, U. of Mo., 1908-10, asst. prof., 1910-13, asso. prof., 1913-17; dir. of research lamp div. Westinghouse Electric & Mfg. Co., 1917-47. Fellow A.A.A.S.; mem. Am. Optical Soc., Am. Physical Soc., Am. Inst. Elec. Engrs., New York Elec. Soc. (past pres.), Am. Inst. of Science (New York), Sigma Xi, Epsilon Chi, Sigma Pi Sigma. Presbyterian. Democrat. Mason. Contbr. to tech. publs. Home: 15 Monroe Av., East Orange, N.J. Died March 23, 1949.

REPASS, William Carlyle (rē-păs'), mng. editor; b. Lebanon, Va., Jan. 3, 1896; s. Joseph Wharton and Sarah (Barbe) R.; student Bethel Coll., Russellville, Ky., 1914-15, Princeton U., 1915-17; m. Zora Owings, May 20, 1924; children—Marjorie Ann, William Carlyle, Jr. Asst. city editor, San Antonio Light, 1919-21; night editor, Galveston News, 1921-22; state editor, Houston Chronicle, 1922-24; mng. editor, Fort Worth Press, 1924-25; news editor, Houston Chronicle, 1925-34, mng. editor since 1934. First lt., A.C., U.S. Army, 1918-19. Mem. Tex. Inst. of Letters, Sigma Alpha Epsilon. Democrat. Methodist. Club: Princeton Elm. Home: 2045 Brentwood Av. Office: Houston Chronicle Pub. Co., Houston, Tex. Died Mar. 11, 1945.

REPLOGLE, J(acob) Leonard (rĕp'lō-g'l), mfr.; b. Bedford County, Pa., May 6, 1876; s. Rhinehart Z. and Mary Ann (Furry) R.; ed. pub. schs., Johnstown, Pa.; m. Blanche Kenly McMillen, Jan. 10, 1905. Began as office boy, Cambria Steel Co., 1889; v.p. and gen. mgr. of sales, same company, 1912-15 (resigned); v.p. and gen. mgr. sales, Am. Vanadium Co., 1915-17, pres. 1917-19 (resigned); pres. Vanadium Corp. of America, 1919-23 (resigned); chmn. bd. Replogle Steel Co., 1919-24; pres. Wharton & Northern R.R. Co., 1919-29; special partner, Harris, Upham & Co., stock brokers, 1928-32 (resigned); chmn. bd. Warren Foundry & Pipe Corp.; dir. Wabash Ry. Co., Warren Foundry & Pipe Corp. and subsidiaries; dir. John Wanamaker, New York and Phila. Trustee Wanamaker Estate. Former Rep. Nat. committeeman from Fla. Dir. steel supply War Industries Bd. Council Nat. Defense, World War I. Decorated Distinguished Service Award; Chevalier Legion of Honor (France); Comdr. Order Crown of Italy; Comdr. Order of Crown (Belgium). Mem. Am. Iron and Steel Inst., Links, Racquet and Tennis, Bath and Tennis, Gulf Stream (Florida). Home: Palm Beach, Fla. Died Nov. 25, 1948; buried in Grand View Cemetery, Johnstown, Pa.

REPPY, Roy Valentine, lawyer; b. Rushford, Minn., Sept. 3, 1878; s. John Henry and Effie Inez (Valentine) R.; A.B., Stanford, 1902; LL.B., Harvard, 1905; m. Agnes Lawton Arneill, Sept. 16, 1909; children—Joan, William Arneill. Admitted to Calif. bar, 1905; with Stoney, Rouleau & Stoney, San Francisco, 1905-07; law practice, Los Angeles, 1908-14; asst. county counsel Los Angeles County, 1914-17; with O'Melveny, Milliken & Tuller, Los Angeles, 1917-19; gen. counsel Southern Calif. Edison Co. since 1919, v.p. since 1925. Mem. Am. Bar Assn. (mem. exec. council pub. utilities sect. 1928-32; v.p. for Calif. 1930), Los Angeles Bar Assn. (trustee 1939-41), Legal Aid Foundation of Los Angeles (pres. 1939-41), Los Angeles Tuberculosis and Health Assn. (pres. 1941), Barlow Sanatorium Assn. (trustee since 1940), Stanford Alumni Assn. (pres. 1930-31). Phi Beta Kappa, Beta Theta Pi, Phi Delta Phi, Order of Coif Republican. Mason (32°). Clubs: California, University (pres. 1918); Beach (Santa Monica). Home: 129 Stone Canyon Rd., Bel-Air. Office: Edison Bldg., Los Angeles. Calif. Died Dec. 10, 1943.

REU, Johann Michael (roi), prof. theology; b. Diebach, Bavaria, Germany, Nov. 16, 1869; s. Johann Friedrich and Margarete (Henkelmann) R.; grad. Sem. for Mission Workers, Neuendettelsau, 1889; (D.D., U. of Erlangen, 1910); m. Wilhelmine Schmitthenner, Nov. 16, 1892; children—Hedwig, Margarete, Albrecht, Elisabeth. Came to U.S., 1889, naturalized, 1900; asst. pastor Mendota, Ill., 1889; pastor Rock Falls, Ill., 1890-99; prof. theology, Wartburg Sem., Dubuque, Iowa, since 1899. Mem. of Am. Soc. for Church History, Verein für Reformationsgeschichte, Gesellschaft für Geschichte der Erzichung und des Unterrichts. Author: Alltestamentliche Perikopen, 1901; Quellen zur Geschichte des Kirchlichen Unterrichts, 9 vols., 1904-35; Wartburg Lesson Helps, 8 vols., 1911-16; Christliche Ethik, 1914; Thirty-five Years of Luther Research, 1917; Life of Dr. Martin Luther, 1917; Biblical History for Schools and Home, 1918; Catechetics, 1918; How to Tell Bible Stories, 2 vols., 1919-20; The Book of Life, Vol. I, 1921; Homiletics, 1922; also Explanation of Luther's Catechism; Topics for Young People's Societies; The Book of Books, 1926; For Beginners, 1927; Luther's Small Catechism (history of its origin, its distribution, and its use—a jubilee offering), 1929; The Augsburg Confession—A Collection of Sources with an Historical Introduction, 1931; Luther's German Bible, 1934; Lutheran Faith and Life, 1935; Sunday School Teachers Training Course, 1935; Christian Ethics, 1935; The Church and the Social Problem, 1936; How to Teach in Sunday School, 1937; How to Discuss the Stories, 4 vols., 1938-40; Unionism; What is Scripture; Luther and The Scriptures; Can We Still Hold to the Lutheran Doctrine of the Lord's Supper, 1940-41. Editor Kirchliche Zeitschrift since 1904. Home: Wartburg Place, Dubuque, Ia. Died Oct. 14, 1943.

REUTER, Edward Byron (roi'tẽr), sociology; b. Holden, Mo., July 19, 1882; s. Peter and Julia (Sullivan) R.; A.B., and B.S., U. of Mo., 1910, A.M., 1911; Ph.D., U. of Chicago, 1919; m. Mildred Goodspeed, June 30, 1914; 1 son, Donald Goodspeed. Instr. in sociology, U. of Ill., 1918-19; prof. sociology, Goucher Coll., 1919-20; prof. sociology and dir. Red Cross Sch. of Social Work, Tulane, 1920-21; asso. prof. sociology, State U. of Ia., 1921-24, prof. and chmn. dept., 1924-44, prof. sociology and research cons. since 1944; visiting research prof. Univ. of Hawaii, 1930-31; visiting prof. summers, U. of Colo., 1928, Cornell U., 1930, U. of Mich., 1939, Stanford U., 1941, also spring quarter U. of Chicago, 1935; special lecturer on population, U. of Minn., winter 1940; exchange prof., Univ. of Puerto Rico, 1941-42; Fisk University, 1944-45. Fellow A.A.A.S.; member American Sociol. Society (pres. 1933), Sociol. Research Assn. (sec. treas., 1936-38; pres. 1939). Club: Triangle. Author: The Mulatto in the United States, 1918; Population Problems, 1923, rev. edit., 1937; The American Race Problem, 1927, rev. edit., 1938; 3d edit., 1945; Race Mixture, 1930; The Family (with Jessie R. Runner), 1930; Introduction to Sociology (with C. W. Hart), 1933; Race and Culture Contacts, 1934; Sociology: A Student Manual, 1941. Consulting editor McGraw-Hill publs. in sociology. Home: 1607 Meharry Blvd., Nashville, Tenn. Died May 28, 1946.

REVERE, Clinton T., broker; b. San Francisco, Calif., 1873; ed. pub. schs.; married; 4 children. Admitted to bar and practiced law; in newspaper business, Washington, D.C., and N.Y. City, 1899-1903; began as broker, asso. with Daniel J. Sully in cotton market, 1903, now mem. Stock Exchange firm Laird, Bissell & Meeds. Mem. New York Coffee & Sugar Exchange, Commodity Exchange, N.Y. Cocoa Exchange. Clubs: Commodity of New York (pres.), Baltusrol Golf, Pine Valley Golf. Author: Representative industries (in collaboration with others), 1928; Hands as Bands (novel), 1932. Contbr. short stories and articles on econ. subjects to mags. Represented U.S. as guest speaker, Internat. Cotton Congress, Paris, 1931, Rome, 1935, Cairo, Egypt, 1938. Address on Individual Capitalism vs. Political Liberalism received internat. circulation and analyses of cotton problems attract world wide attention. Home: Westfield, N.J. Office: 120 Broadway, New York. Died May 8, 1949.

REYNDERS, John V. W. (rīn'dẽrz), steel maker; son of John and Louise (Sellers) R.; C.E., Rensselaer Poly. Inst., 1886, Dr. Engring., 1925; m. Clare Charlton, Oct. 4, 1894; children—John Van Wigheren (dec.), Charlton, Clare Charlton (Mrs. Byam K. Stevens). Began in mfr. of steel, at Pittsburgh, Pa., 1886; managing head Pa. Steel Co., 1892-1906; actively engaged for many yrs. in bridge building enterprises of this company, in the course of which built the steel ry. arch across the Niagara River; Gokteik Viaduct, 2,000 feet long, 320 feet high, Burma, India; Queensboro Bridge, N.Y.; Memphis Bridge, Miss. River; Williamsburg Bridge, N.Y.; rebuilt the steel-making facilitiies of Pa. Steel Co. and managed its affairs as v.p., 1906-16; had charge of construction Bear Mountain Bridge across Hudson River, north of Peekskill, N.Y.; receiver Central Iron & Steel Co., Harrisburg, Pa., 1912-17; pres. Am. Tube & Stamping Company. 1917-19; director Vt. Copper Company, Lone Star Steel Co., Russian Finance & Constrn. Corp., Brewing Corp. of America; tech. advisor and sponsor of initial manufacture of steel using native ores State of Texas, professional adviser steel works and banking institutions. Adviser to U.S. Govt. in formulation of code of fair practice for steel industry, 1933. Originated "Harrisburg Plan" of civic improvement, 1904, resulting in park system water filtration, sewage systems, and paving; pres. Town Council, Steelton, Pa., 1906-16, and completed many public improvements there; del. Rep. Nat. Conv., 1908. Trustee Bard Coll. (Columbia U.). Episcopalian. Mem. Am. Inst. Mining and Metall. Engrs. (past pres.), United Engring. Soc., Engineers Soc., Central Pa. (ex-pres.), American Inst. Mining and Metall. Engrs. (hon.). Alternate mem. representing Dept. of Commerce Temporary Nat. Econ. Com. during steel hearings, 1939-40. Clubs: University, City Midday, Bankers, Union, Greenwich Country. Home: Greenwich, Conn. Office: 120 Broadway, New York, N.Y. Died July 10, 1944.

REYNOLDS, Arthur, banker; b. Panora, Ia., Mar. 10, 1868; s. Elijah Jackson and Mary (Anderson) R.; Ia. (now Grinnell) Coll., 2 yrs.; m. Bertha Goodrich, Oct. 7, 1902; children—Arthur, Jeannette. Asst. cashier, and cashier, Guthrie County Nat. Bank, Panora, Ia., 1888-95; cashier, 1895-97, pres. Des Moines (Ia.) Nat. Bank, 1897-1915; 1st v.p. and dir. Continental & Commercial Nat. Bank, 1915; became pres. Continental & Commercial Trust & Savings Bank, 1918; pres. Continental & Commercial Securities Co., 1919, Continental & Commercial Nat. Bank, 1921, and upon merger of the two last named in 1927 under title of Continental Nat. Bank & Trust Co., was made pres.; chmn. bd. Continental Ill. Bank & Trust Co. (consolidation of Ill. Merchants Trust Co. and Continental Nat. Bank and Trust Co.) 1929-32, resigned; pres. Continental Ill. Co. and Continental Chicago Corpn. to 1932; vice chmn. bd. Bank of America Nat. Trust & Savings Assn. of San Francisco since Feb. 15, 1933; dir. Am. Alliance Ins. Co., Great American Indemnity Co., Great Am. Ins. Co., Rochester Am. Ins. Co., Associated Reinsurance Co. Mem. Am. Bankers Assn. (exec. council 1902; chmn. federal legislative com. 1905-11; mem. nat. currency com. 1906-11; treas. 1910; chmn. exec. council 1911; 1st v.p. 1912; pres. 1913-14). Republican. Writer on financial subjects. Home: 730 Chiltern Rd., San Mateo, Calif. Address: 1 Powell St., San Francisco. Died Jan. 1, 1943.

REYNOLDS, George William, printing and publishing; b. Indianola, Ia., Oct. 26, 1868; s. Anson O. and Mary Matson (Stone) R.; grad. Indianola High Sch., 1884; student Drake U., Des Moines, 1887-90; m. Mary Rockwell Dewey, Nov. 23, 1893; children—George Stoddard (M.D.), Katharine (Mrs. Benjamin Williams Brown). Insurance clerk Hawkeye Fire Ins. Co., Des Moines, 1891; began as salesman Osborne & Murphy Co., advertising calendars, Red Oak, Ia., 1892, and since continued with this company and successors, becoming treas. and v.p.; name changed to The Osborne Co., 1894; company moved to Newark, N.J., 1900; company merged with Chicago Colortype Co. and Am. Three Color Co. to form Am. Colortype Co. of N.J., 1902; successively sec., treas., v.p. to 1917, pres. and dir., 1917-29, chmn. of bd. since 1929; dir. Bloomfield (N.J.) Bank & Trust Co.; formerly mem. Bd. of Edn., Glen Ridge; trustee Mountainside Hosp., Montclair, N.J., 1924-30; trustee Montclair Art Museum, 1910-13; trustee Annuity Fund for Congl. Ministers, New York, 1925-32. Pres. Reynolds Family Assn. of America, 1932-33. Republican. Congregationalist. Home: 78 Ridgewood Av., Glen Ridge, N.J. Office: 9 Brighton Rd., Clifton, N.J.; and 200 Fifth Av., New York, N.Y. Died June 13, 1944.

REYNOLDS, Henry James; b. Meaford, Ont., Can., Apr. 26, 1852; s. James and Sarah (Wilkinson) R.; student Toronto U.; M.D., Bellevue Hosp. Med. Coll. (New York U.), 1875 (Mott prize); m. Caroline Whittlesey Reid, Oct. 4, 1911; m. 2d, Fredericka Haag Nolan, Mar. 28, 1940. Practiced in Mich., 1875-83, in Chicago since 1883; prof. dermatology U. of Ill. Coll. of Medicine, 1883-90, Harvey Med. Coll., 1900-05; editor Western Med. Reporter, 1886-93; pres. and prof., Chicago Sch. of Dermatology, 1887-91, U.S. Dental Coll., 1887-91; now pres. J. F. Bridges & Co., Inc., merchandise brokers. Served on Med. Advisory Board, World War, 1918. Mem. Ill. State and Chicago med. socs., A.M.A. (founder Sect. on Dermatology), Internat. Med. Congress. Mich. State Med. Assn., A.A.A.S., Ill. State Acad. Science. Founder of state regulation of med. practice and compulsory public sanitation in Mich., 1881; also founder Polyclinic Hosp., Chicago, 1887; founder suburb of Bellwood, 1889; founder Calumet Electric St. Ry. system, 1890; founder Reynolds Manor (home for retired and semi-retired), Ottawa, Ill. Democrat. Mason (K.T.). Clubs: Chicago Athletic Assn., Chicago Motor Club. Author: The World's Oldest Writings (a univ. reference work), 1938; writer of 37 pub. monographs, including, The Cell: Its Place in Organic Life; A New Concept of Instinct; The Guarantee of Evolution in Nature. Inventor of the Reynolds envelope sealer, 1909. Composer: Have You Ever Tried To Count To A Billion (Landon and Knox campaign song). Home: Reynold's Manor, North Bluff, Ottawa, Ill. Office: 224 S. Michigan Av., Chicago 4, Ill. Died April 13, 1949; buried, St. Mary's Cemetery, Evergreen Park, Ill.

REYNOLDS, James Burton, ex-sec. Rep. Nat. Com.; b. Saratoga, N.Y., Feb. 17, 1870; s. John H. and Sarah C. (Morgan) R.; A.B. (honors), Dartmouth Coll., 1890, A.M., 1895; m. Mrs. Charles Hearin, of Mobile, Ala., Dec., 1912. Reporter, 1890, State House reporter, 1891, Washington corr., 1892-94, Boston Advertiser and Record; editorial writer New York Press, 1895; sec. Rep. State Com., Mass., 1896-1905; asst. sec. of the treasury, 1905-09; chmn. of govt. commns. to France, Germany, Austria, and Great Britain, 1907 and 1908, to consider trade relations; mem. U.S. Tariff Bd., 1909-12; sec. Rep. Nat. Com., July 1912-Jan. 1920; resigned to take charge of Gov. Coolidge's campaign for presdl. nomination. Del. Rep. nat. convs., 1896, 1900, 04. Mem. Alpha Delta Phi. Clubs: Algonquin (Boston), Metropolitan, Chevy Chase, Cosmos (Washington), Lawyers, Union League (New York), Manufacturers (Philadelphia). Home: Boston. Died Feb. 7, 1948.

REYNOLDS, Paul Revere, literary agent; b. Boston, Mass., July 13, 1864; s. John Phillips and Jane Revere R.; A.B., Harvard, 1887, A.M., 1889; m. Amelia F. D. Stead, Sept. 26, 1899; children—Mary, Paul R., Wendell Phillips. Senior partner of Paul R. Reynolds & Son, established 1893 (first literary agency in America); first represented English publishers, now English and American authors. Clubs: Dutch Treat Club, Century Club. Home: Scarsdale, N.Y. Office: 599 Fifth Av., New York, N.Y.; 8272 Sunset Blvd., Hollywood, Calif.; 8 Halsey House, Red Lion Square, London, W.C.1., Eng. Died Aug. 19, 1944.

REYNOLDS, Thomas Harvey, lawyer; b. McArthur, O., July 31, 1866; s. Isaac and Sarah Frances (Roberts) R.; grad. (Latin course) Kan. State Normal Sch., Emporia, 1885 (life certificate to teach in Kan schs.); m. Ida Mary Barlow, Oct. 23, 1902 (died Jan. 18, 1906). Admitted to Kan. bar, 1889; practiced Great Bend, Kan., 1887-90; entered law office of Lathrop, Morrow & Fox, Kansas City, Mo., 1891; member Lathrop, Morrow, Fox & Moore, Jan. 1, 1899, firm name now Lathrop, Crane, Reynolds, Sawyer & Mersereau. Was v.p., lecturer on bankruptcy, Kansas City Sch. of Law. Rep. candidate for judge of Circuit Court, 1908. Was chmn. Local Bd. No. 8, Selective Service Bd. Conglist. Mem. Am. and Mo. State bar assns., Kansas City Bar Assn. (ex-pres.; del. to Internat. Bar Assn., Havana), Internat. Law Soc., S.R. (past pres. Kansas City Chapter; past pres. Mo. State Soc.). Mason (33°), A.A.S.R.; past venerable Master Lodge of Perfection and master Kadosh Consistory of Western Mo.; past grand comdr. Grand Commandery of Mo., past chmn. Jurisprudence Com. of Grand Commandery; past deputy Supreme Council of Scottish Rite for Mo.; mem. Jurisprudence Com.; Grand Encampment, K.T.; past grand master of Grand Council Royal and Select Masters; dep. grand master 22d Dist. A.F.&A.M. for 5 yrs.; past sovereign of Red Cross of Constantine, past illustrious potentate Ararat Temple, A.A.O. N.M.S., and rep. to Imperial Council, 1918-19; ex-pres. Kansas City Masonic Temple Assn.; dir. of Masonic Home of Mo. Mem. Royal Order of Scotland. Clubs: Commercial, University, Athletic (ex-pres.), Knife and Fork (ex-pres.), Blue Hills Golf (ex-pres.), Automobile Club of Mo. Home: 3523 Charlotte St. Office: Fidelity Bank Bldg., Kansas City, Mo. Died Sep. 18, 1943.

REYNOLDS, Walter Ford, mathematician; b. Baltimore, Md., May 25, 1880; s. Robert Fuller and Catherine (Myers) R.; Baltimore City Coll., 1899; A.B., Johns Hopkins, 1902; grad. work, same univ., 1902-05; m. Ada C. Williams, June 26, 1907; children—Catherine A. Mummert, Robert W., Walter F. Instr. Baltimore City Coll., 1905-06; computer U.S. Naval Obs., Washington, D.C., Jan.-Feb. 1907; with U.S. Coast and Geodetic Survey since 1907; computer U.S. and Can. boundary survey, 1908-11; chief mathematician, 1912-24; chief sect. triangulation, div. of geodesy, since 1924. Mem. Washington Philos. Soc., Math. Assn. of America, Am. Geophysical Union, Nat. Geog. Society, Washington Acad. Sciences, National Congress on Surveying and Mapping. Methodist. Author: Triangulation in Alabama and Mississippi, 1915; Triangulation in Maine, 1918; Relation between Plane Rectangular Co-ordinates and Geographic Positions, 1921; Manual of Triangulation Computation and Adjustment, 1927; First-Order Triangulation in Southeast Alaska, 1929; Triangulation in Missouri, 1934; Triangulation in Minnesota, 1935. Home: 848 W. 37th St., Baltimore, Md. Died May 1, 1942.

REYNOLDS, Wiley Richard, capitalist; b. Jackson, Mich., May 30, 1879; s. Wiley R. and Mary H. R.; prep. edn., Worcester (Mass.) Acad.; grad. Sigler Sch., Newburgh, N.Y., 1897, Eastman Business Coll., 1898; m. Nettie H. Hood, 1903; children—Wiley R., Annette Hood. With Peoples Nat. Bank, Jackson, 1898-1903, retiring as vice pres.; western mgr. for O'Connor & Kahler, investment bankers, New York, until 1912; organized McCuen-Reynolds & Co., name changed to W. R. Reynolds & Co., of which is pres.; pres. and dir. First Nat. Bank of Miami, First Nat. Bank, Palm Beach, Fla.; chmn. bd., dir. Am. Nat. Bank of Miami (Fla.), Little River Bank & Trust Co., Miami; Coral Gables (Fla.) First Nat. Bank, First Nat. Bank, Fort Lauderdale, Fla., First Nat. Bank, Lake Worth, Fla., First Trust Co., Miami; v.p. Genesee Corp.; dir. Fort Wayne & Jackson R.R. Mem. (vestryman) Bethesda-by-the-Sea Episcopal Ch., Palm Beach, Fla. Clubs: Bath and Tennis, Gulf Stream Golf, Seminole Golf, Everglades, Sailfish (Palm Beach); Metropolitan, Recess (New York); The Chicago (Chicago). Home: 172 South Ocean Boulevard, Palm Beach, Fla. Died Dec. 7, 1948.

RHEA, William Edward (rā), Land Bank commr.; b. Hale, Mo., Nov. 25, 1889; s. Dr. Calvin and Mae (Smith) R.; LL.B., Georgetown U., 1913, LL.M., 1914; m. Helen Dorothy Kelly, March 9, 1931; children—Dorothy Marlyn, William Edward. Admitted to Ark. bar, July 1915, and practiced in Ft. Smith, until 1919, in St. Louis, Mo., 1919-35; v.p. and gen. counsel St. Louis Joint Stock Land Bank, 1925-32; dep. Land Bank commr., Washington, D.C., 1935-40, commr. since 1940; dir. Regional Agr. Credit Corp., Washington, D.C., since Mar. 1943; dir. Fed. Farm Mortgage Corp. since Sept. 1940. Served in Inf., U.S. Army, 1918. St. Louis and Missouri Bar Assn. Member Delta Chi. Mason. Home: 300 E. 60th St. Office: 212 W. 14th St., Kansas City, Mo. Died May 30, 1946.

RHETT, A(ndrew) Burnet (rĕt), supt. schs.; b. Charleston, S.C., Nov. 22, 1877; s. Andrew Burnet and Henrietta (Aiken) R.; grad. high sch., Charleston, 1894; student Coll. of Charleston, 1894-96; B.A., U. of Va., 1899, M.A., 1899; studied same university, 1906-07, and at U. of Chicago and U. of Tenn.; LL.D., Coll. of Charleston, 1935; unmarried. Teacher high school, Charleston, 1899-1909; principal Mitchell Sch., Charleston, 1909-10; asst. supt. pub. schools of Charleston, 1910-11, supt. since 1911. Pres. Charleston Library since 1928. Mem. Chi Phi. Democrat. Episcopalian. Club: Carolina Yacht. Home: 48 Elizabeth St. Office: 11 S. Philip St., Charleston, S.C. Died Aug. 1946.

RHOADES, John Harsen, retired investment banker; b. New York, N.Y., Feb. 6, 1869; s. John Harsen and Annie Gardner (Wheelwright) R.; A.B., Harvard, 1892; m. Mrs. Bertha Ware Cady, Apr. 9, 1917; 1 dau., Joan Harsen. Began active career with Blake Bros. & Co., New York, 1892; mem. Rhoades & Richmond, bankers, 1898-1906, Rhoades & Co., 1907-38. Mem. Commn. to Revise New York State Banking Law, 1913. Unitarian. Clubs: University, Harvard. Author: Random Thoughts of a Man at Fifty, 1930; Church Without Walls, 1940; From the Crow's Nest, 1941; Jonathan's Apothegms, Vol. 1, 1941, Volume 2, 1942. Speaker and writer on banking subjects and financial reform; poet and rhythmist; expresses his thoughts in apothegms and in short poems; has had many poems published in newspapers and poetry mags. Interested in color photography; has a notable collection of Kodacolor films of the Hawaiian Islands, and New Hampshire. Home: 277 Park Av. Address: Harvard Club, 27 W. 44th St., New York, N.Y. Died Jan. 15, 1943.

RHOADS, McHenry, educator; b. near Browder, Muhlenberg County, Ky., July 27, 1858; s. Absalom Johnson and Tabitha Rice (Dennis) R.; A.B., West Ky. Coll., South Carrollton, Ky., 1880, A.M., 1884; Ph.M., Hartford (Ky.) Coll., 1887; LL.D., Georgetown (Ky.) Coll., 1924; m. Ree Crawford, Aug. 3, 1887; children—Crawford Carlisle, Wayland, Annie Laura (Mrs. E. P. Hatter), George William, Henry (dec.), Robert (dec.), Raymond, Harold. Was teacher of dist. school, 1878; prin. Prep. Sch., West Ky. Coll., 1880; prof. science, West Ky. Coll., 1881-84; prof. English lang. and lit., Hartford Coll., 1885-90; editor Hartford Herald, 1885-91; supt. schools, Frankfort, 1891-1900, Owensboro, 1900-11; prof. secondary edn., U. of Ky., 1911-23; part of time serving as state high sch. insp.; granted leave of absence to serve as state supt. pub. instrn., 1924-28; prof. of edn., U. of Ky., 1928-29, emeritus prof. of edn., since 1929. Organized city sch. system of Frankfort and reorganized city schs. of Owensboro; developed county high sch. system of Ky. to more than 400 county high schs.; reorganized state dept. of edn.; voted one of 5 leading educators in Ky. during the past 100 years; consultant on pronunciation for Webster's New International Dictionary, 2d edition; researches on legislation in Ky., relating to edn. completed in 1938; del. to World's Fed. of Ednl. Assns., Geneva, Switzerland, 1929. Mem. Nat. Assn. Coll. Teachers of Edn., N.E.A. (treas. 1903-04), Ky. Ednl. Assn., A.A.A.S., Pi Gamma Mu, Kappa Delta Pi, Phi Delta Kappa. Democrat. Baptist. K.P. Home: 1435 S. Limestone St., Lexington, Ky. Died Jan. 16, 1943.

RHODE, Paul Peter (rō'dē), bishop; b. Prussian Poland, Sept. 18, 1871; s. Augustine and Christine R.; father died, 1872; came to America with mother, 1879; studied St. Mary's Coll., St. Ignatius, Chicago; grad. St. Francis Sem. Ordained R.C. priest, 1894; asst. pastor St. Adelbert's; pastor St. Peter's, St. Paul's and St. Michael's chs., Chicago, 1896-1915; consecrated bishop of Barca, 1908; an auxiliary bishop of Archdiocese of Chicago, 1908-15; apptd. bishop of the Green Bay Diocese, Sept. 1915. Vicargen. Archdiocese of Chicago, 1909-15. Home: Green Bay, Wis. Died Mar. 1945.

RHODES, Frederic Harrison, life ins.; b. Moravia, Pa., July 14, 1878; s. Robert Morton and Mary (Witherspoon) R.; ed. pub. schs. and business coll.; m. Georgia O. Wilson, June 7, 1900; children—Paul W., Virginia, Barbara, Frederic, Charles Rhodes II. Began in business with Berkshire Life Ins. Co., Pittsburgh, 1892; pres. Berkshire Life Ins. Co. since 1925; trustee City Savings Bank. Dir. Pittsfield Boys' Club. Republican. Conglist. Mason (33°, Shriner). Clubs: Pittsfield Country; Advertising (New York). Home: 164 Bartlett Av. Office: 7 North St., Pittsfield, Mass. Died Oct. 31, 1942.

RHODES, John Franklin, lawyer; b. Vernon County, Mo., July 2, 1889; s. James Frederick and Charlotte (Zelhart) R.; A.B., U. of Mo., 1914; LL.B., Harvard, 1917; m. Helen Harned Williams, Dec. 1, 1917; children—Hulda Gordon, Richard Carlyle. Admitted to Kan. bar, 1919, and began practice at Hutchinson; mem. Beeching, Rhodes & Burnett, 1923-24; with Bowersock & Fizzell, Kansas

City, Mo., 1924-25; mem. Bowersock, Fizzell & Rhodes since 1926. Asst. atty. gen. of Kan., 1923-24; spl. counsel Kan. state supt. ins. in fire ins. rate litigation, 1924-30; spl. counsel Mo. state supt. ins., 1930-33. Served as pvt. U.S.M.C., U.S., P.I. and China, 1905-09; capt. inf., U.S. Reserve, 1917-19; instr. O.T.C., Plattsburg, N.Y., Aug.-Nov. 1917; with A.E.F., France, June 1918-May 1919. Trustee of Kansas City Art Inst., Mo. Hist. Soc.; dir. Kansas City Museum; pres. Kan. City Social Hygiene Soc., 1942-44. Chmn. industrial relations com. Kansas City Chamber of Commerce. Mem. adv. council U.S. Law Review. Mem. Am. Bar Assn. (house of dels., 1937-38 and since 1941; member American Bar Association war work committee 8th Circuit Court Appeals, since 1941), Missouri State Bar Association (president 1941), Lawyers Association Kansas City (ex-president), American Judicature Society, Academy of Political Science, Kappa Alpha (Southern), Theta Nu Epsilon, Acacia, Scabbard and Blade (nat. comdr. 1914-15, 1920-21), Phi Delta Phi (hon.), Mil. Order of World War (comdr.). Republican. Presbyterian. Mason (32°). Clubs: University, Harvard (ex-pres.), Kansas City, Kansas City Country, Mission Valley Hunt. Home: Huldix Farm, Lee's Summit, Mo. Office: Fidelity Bldg., Kansas City, Mo. Died Mar. 30, 1944.

RHODES, Robert Clinton, biology; b. Magnolia, Ark., Oct. 12, 1887; s. James Clinton and Virginia Isabella (Scott) R.; A.B., Henderson-Brown Coll., Arkadelphia, Ark., 1906; A.B., Vanderbilt, 1907, A.M., 1908; Ph.D., U. of Calif., 1917; grad. study, U. of Chicago and Marine Biol. Lab.; m. Lon Clark, Nov. 27, 1912; children—Marguerite, Robert Clark, James Scott, Martha. Instr. in biology, U. of Miss., 1908-10, asst. prof. biology, 1910-12; v.p. and prof. science, Henderson-Brown Coll., 1912-15; asst. in zoölogy, U. of Calif., 1915-17; prof. biology, Emory U., Atlanta, Ga., and chmn. dept., 1918-48. Ordained ministry Meth. Ch., 1905. Treas. bd. trustees, Emory Sch., 1922-27; chmn. adv. board Juvenile Ct. of De Kalb County, Ga., 1935. Fellow A.A.A.S.; mem. Am. Soc. Zoölogists, Ga. Acad. Sciences (pres. 1933-34), Am. Eugenics Soc., Ga. Ornithological Soc. (life mem.), Am. Soc. of Parasitologists, Am. Genetics Soc., Ga. and Atlanta Soc. Biologists, Southeastern Soc. of Biologists (pres. 1940-41), Southern Assn. for Advancement of Science, Sigma Xi, Phi Sigma, Pi Gamma Mu, Sigma Upsilon, Kappa Alpha, Omicron Delta Kappa, Alpha Epsilon Upsilon. Democrat. Author: Binary Fission in Collodictyon triciliatum Carter, 1918; Some Biological Factors Involved in Democracy, 1941. Home: 1126 Clifton Road N.E., Atlanta, Ga. Address: Emory University, Ga. Died Nov. 7, 1948.

RICE, Arthur Louis, publisher, mechanical engr.; b. Barre, Mass., May 14, 1870; s. Henry Edward and Elizabeth Fitch (Rawson) R.; B.S., Worcester (Mass.) Poly. Inst., 1891, E.E., 1893; M.M.E., Cornell U., 1896; m. Anne E. Cook, June 29, 1893; children—Kingsley Loring, Elisabeth Beals, Arthur Louis; m. 2d, Madge Waters, Jan. 21, 1928; 1 son, Reginald Waters. Was in charge of steam engring. lab., Worcester Poly. Inst., 1892-95; in charge dept. applied electricity, Pratt Inst., Brooklyn, 1896-1901; cons. engr. and asst. sec. Am. Soc. Mech. Engrs., New York, 1901-03; editor The Engineer, Cleveland and Chicago, 1903-08; mng. editor Practical Engineer, Chicago, 1908-11; consulting engr. on power plant constrn. and operation, and cons. engr. and mem. advisory bd. La Salle Extension U., 1909-10; treas. Tech. Pub. Co. since 1910; editor Power Plant Engineering since 1917. Trustee Wilmette Pub. Library; mem. Bd. Edn. Republican. Conglist. Mem. Am. Soc. M.E., Nat. Soc. Power Engrs., Western Soc. Engrs. Mason. Home: Wilmette, Ill. Office: 53 W. Jackson Blvd., Chicago. Died Nov. 10, 1946; buried in Memorial Park Cemetery, Evanston, Ill.

RICE, Cale Young, poet, dramatist; b. Dixon, Ky., Dec. 7, 1872; s. Laban M. and Martha (Lacy) R.; A.B., Cumberland U., 1893; A.B., Harvard, 1895, A.M., 1896; LL.D., U. of Ky., 1927; Litt.D., Rollins Coll., 1928; Litt.D., U. of Louisville, 1937; m. Alice Caldwell Hegan, Dec. 18, 1902. Author: (poems) From Dusk to Dusk, 1898; With Omar, 1900; Song-Surf, 1900; Nirvana Days, 1908; Many Gods, 1910; Far Quests, 1912; At the World's Heart, 1914; Earth and New Earth (containing Gerhard, of Ryle, a poetic drama), 1916; Trails Sunward, 1917; Wraiths and Realities, 1918; Songs to A.H.R., 1918; Shadowy Thresholds, 1919; Sea Poems, 1921; Mihrima (poetic drama) and Other Poems, 1922; A Pilgrim's Scrip, 1924; A Sea-Lover's Scrip, 1925; Bitter Brew, 1925; Selected Plays and Poems, 1926; Stygian Freight, 1927; Seed of the Moon, 1929; High Perils, 1933; (plays) Charles di Toca (poetic drama), 1903; David (poetic drama), 1904; (plays) Yolanda of Cypress, poetic drama, 1906, grand opera, 1929; A Night in Avignon (poetic drama), 1907; The Immortal Lure (4 one-act poetic dramas), 1911; Porzia (poetic drama), 1913; Collected Plays and Poems, 1915; (prose) Turn About Tales (with Alice Hegan Rice), 1920; Youth's Way (novel), 1923; Winners and Losers (short stories, with wife), 1925; Early Reaping (novel), 1929; The Swamp Bird (play), 1931; Love and Lord Byron (play), 1936; Passionate Follies (with wife), 1936; Poetry's Genii (criticism), 1937; Bridging the Years, autobiography, including Poetry's Genii, 1939. Mem. bd. govs. J. B. Speed Memorial Mus.; mem. Nat. Inst. Social Sciences, Poetry Soc. America, Soc. Am. Dramatists and Composers. Clubs: P.E.N.; Arts of Louisville (a founder and 1st pres.), Big Spring Golf. Home: 1444 St. James Court, Louisville, Ky. Died Jan. 23, 1943.

RICE, Devereux Dunlap, mfr. mica; b. Memphis, Tenn., Feb. 27, 1898; s. John Ewing and Willie McGavock (Dunlap) R.; B.S. (engring. chemistry), Ga. Sch. of Tech., Atlanta, 1921; m. Dorothy Bailey, Apr. 11, 1921; children—Martha, Charles Bailey. Began with La. Oil Refining Co., Shreveport, 1921; apptd. chemist Southern Mica Co., miners and grinders of mica, Franklin, N.C., and Johnson City, Tenn., 1923, continuing successively as sec.-treas., v.p. and gen. mgr.; pres. since 1940. Pres. Dry Ground Mica Assn., 1939-40; Johnson City Community Chest, 1944. Served as 2d lt. inf., U.S. Army, World War, 1918. Chmn. Divisional Code Authority of Mica Industry. Mem. Scabbard and Blade, Pi Kappa Phi (dist. archon, 1936-43, nat. historian, 1943-46, nat. pres. 1946-48). Democrat. Presbyterian. Mason (Shriner). Clubs: Rotary (pres. Franklin, N.C., Rotary, 1928-29; pres. Johnson City Rotary, 1945-46; dist. gov. 186th Dist., Rotary Internat., 1947-48), Johnson City Country (pres. 1941), Hurstleigh. Home: Johnson City, Tenn. Died Aug. 11, 1948.

RICE, George Brackett, M.D.; b. Westford, Mass., July 19, 1859; s. George Mathias and Persis Fayette (Weeks) R.; U. of Mich., 1880-81; M.D., Boston U., 1886; m. Jeanette M. Noyes, June 1886; m. 2d, Abbie Conley, Aug. 1916. Began practice at Lexington, Mass., 1886; removed to Boston, 1894; prof. diseases of nose and throat, Boston U. Sch. of Medicine, since 1900; consultant in surgery Mass. Memorial Hosp.; ex-mem. med. bd. Westboro State Hosp. Republican. Unitarian. Ex-pres. Am. Homœ. Otol., Laryngol. and Rhinol. Assn., 1903-04, Mass. Homœ. Med. Soc., 1910-11; fellow Am. College Surgeons. Mem. Med. Advisory Bd., 1918. Mem. Nat. Acad. of Ophthalmology and Oto-Laryngology, A.M.A., Mass. Med. Soc. Mason. Address: 99 Bay State Road, Boston, Mass. Deceased.

RICE, George Samuel, mining engr.; b. Claremont, N.H., Sept. 8, 1866; s. George Samuel and Abby Parker (Rice) R.; student Coll. City of New York, 2 yrs.; E.M., Sch. of Mines (Columbia), 1887; D.Sc., Lafayette, 1936; m. Julia Sessions, Dec. 23, 1891 (died Aug. 13, 1934); children—Abby (dec.), Katharine Peabody, Julian Brewster; m. 2d, Sarah M. Benson, Dec. 21, 1935. Was asst. engr., Colo.&Utah Railroad, 1887; mining engr. with Colo. Fuel Co., Denver, 1888-90; mining engr., Whitebreast Fuel Co., Ottumwa, Ia., 1890; chief mining engr., same co. and allied cos., Chicago, 1897, also gen. supt. Cardiff Coal Co., 1899, Shoal Creek Coal Co., 1902; consulting mining work for A.,T.&S.F. Ry., C.,M.& St.P. Ry., and other corps., 1900-08, also for Armour Fertilizer Works in phosphate fields, Tenn. and Fla., also reported on zinc and lead mines in Mo. and Wis., etc. Apptd. mining engr. in charge of field investigations, technologic br. of U.S. Geol. Survey, 1908; chief mining engr. U.S. Bureau of Mines from establishment, 1910, to his retirement, Sept. 1937; in charge government rescue and recovery work in mine fire and explosion disasters, 1908-26; sent on investigative trips to European mines and testing stations, 1908, to report on safety and conservation methods; in charge of unique series of investigations in govt. exptl. mine in which large coal dust explosions are produced; first in U.S. to advocate (1913) rock dusting for prevention such explosions; developed use in mines of gunite for fire protection and preventing weathering of roof; initiated, 1918, testing of liquid oxygen explosives; reported on oil sand and potash mining methods in Europe; investigated outbursts of gas, bumps, rockbursts in mines of U.S., Canada and Europe; chmn. Am. Inst. Mining and Metall. Engrs. Com. on ground movement and subsidence; reported on losses of coal in mining for U.S. Coal Commn., 1924; prepared regulations for coal mine leasing in Alaska, 1917, and Public Domain, 1920, covering conservation and safety; planned testing in exptl. mine of novel method of vehicular tunnel ventilation for Holland Tunnel, N.Y.-N.J., 1922. On committee to investigate post-war mining conditions in Europe, especially in devastated coal and iron regions of France; adviser on mining matters to Am. Economic Mission at Cologne Conf. with Germans, Mar. 1919. Episcopalian. Del. of Bur. Mines and Am. Inst. Mining & Metall. Engrs. to 6th Internat. Mining Exhbn. and Conf., London, 1923. Planned coöperation in research between British Mines Dept. and Bur. Mines. Chmn. Mine Safety Bd. since 1924. Hon. mem. British Instn. Mining Engrs., Am. Inst. Mining and Metall. Engrs., Mining Soc. Nova Scotia; member (hon.) Coal Mining Institute of America; fellow A.A.A.S.; mem. Washington Acad. Scis., Washington Geol. Soc., etc. Medalist British Instn. of Mining Engrs., 1929; awarded Columbia University medal, 1931. U.S. rep. to 7th Internat. Congress Mining, Metallurgy and Applied Geology, Paris, France, 1935. Club: Cosmos. Author of numerous papers for tech. socs. and jours. and bulls. of U.S. Bureau Mines. Home: Wellington Villa on Mt. Vernon Highway. Address: R.F.D. 1, Box 135, Alexandria, Va. Died Jan. 4, 1950.

RICE, John Pierrepont, prof. Romance langs.; b. N.Y. City, Mar. 22, 1879; s. John and Eliza (Blake) R.; study and travel in Europe 5 yrs. before entering coll.; A.B., Yale, 1900, A.M., 1901, Ph.D., 1909; post-grad. work at the Sorbonne, Paris, Biblioteca Laurenziana, Florence, etc.; m. Ethel M. Pool, July 8, 1914. Instr. French, Yale, 1903-09; instr. Romance langs., Williams, 1910-12; prof. French and head of dept., Acadia U., N.S., 1912-13; asst. prof. Romance langs., in charge of courses in Spanish and Italian, 1913-24, chmn. dept. of Romance langs., 1923-24, Williams Coll.; prof. and head dept. of Romance languages, U. of Buffalo, since 1924; visiting prof. College of Yale in China, 1919-20; George Westinghouse visiting prof. to Italy, 1929-30. Mem. Book and Bond (Yale), Modern Lang. Assn. America, Am. Assn. Univ. Profs., Dante League America (hon. v.p.), Cambridge Dante Soc., Mediæval Acad. America; corr. mem. Hispanic Soc. America. Contbr. to Hispanic Anthology (pub. by Hispanic Soc.), also to memorial volumes, reviews and mags. Died Dec. 24, 1941.

RICE, Merton Stacher, clergyman; b. Ottawa, Kan., Sept. 5, 1872; s. Rev. Cyrus R. and Lucy A. (McCormick) R.; B.S., Baker U., Kan., 1893, M.S., 1896, LL.D., 1920; student law dept. U. of Mich., 1893-94; D.D., Upper Ia. U., 1901; D.Litt., Albion (Mich.) Coll., 1926; LL.D., Ohio Northern U., 1932; m. Laura Buckner, Apr. 3, 1895. Ordained M.E. ministry, 1894; pastor Westphalia, Kan., 1894-95, Fontana, 1895-96, Ottawa, 1896-99, West Union, Ia., 1899-1903, Iowa City, 1903-04, Duluth, Minn., 1904-13, Metropolitan Ch., Detroit, since 1913. In Europe 6 mos., 1917-18, as spl. representative of Internat. Y.M.C.A. among soldiers. Del. Gen. Conf. M.E. Ch., five times; del. Uniting Conf. of Methodism, 1939. Mason (K.T.). Author: Dust and Destiny; The Expected Church; Preachographs; The Advantage of a Handicap; To Know Him; William Alfred Quayle; A Discontented Optimist; Diagnosing Today; Hearing the Unheard; The Man with the Hope. Home: 59 Alger Av., Detroit, Mich. Died Mar. 17, 1943.

RICE, Thomas Stevens, criminologist; born Baltimore, Feb. 21, 1878; s. Robert Wilbur and Margaret Lavinia (Mitchell) R.; grad. Baltimore City Coll., 1897; LL.B., U. of Md., 1899; m. Maude Anna Elderdice, Dec. 7, 1911. Admitted to Md. bar, 1899, and practiced in Baltimore; writer for Baltimore Sun, 1899-1902; legal expert, later sports writer Washington (D.C.) Times, 1903-10, same with Brooklyn Daily Eagle, 1911-29; asso. editor The Panel, criminal law mag., N.Y. City, 1930-35, The Police Journal, N.Y. City, since 1929; Sunday columnist on crime, Brooklyn Eagle, since 1932; Am. corr. Sporting Life, London, 1920-27; corr. for Sproting News, St. Louis, 1904-27; mem. N.Y. State Crime Commn., 1926-31, N.Y. City commn. on crime prevention, 1928-34; originator of "Rice Notations" on left handedness and circumcision, included in N.Y. State police and penal identification records, 1935. Mem. Am. Bar Assn. (mem. com. on criminal procedure, 1932-35; conf. of bar assn. dels. com. on co-operation between press and bar, 1932-35), Soc. Med. Jurisprudence, Am. Inst. Criminal Law and Criminology, Baseball Writers Assn. America, Kappa Sigma. Clubs: Newspaper (New York); National Press Club of Washington, D.C. (charter mem.); National Sporting (hon.); The Press (London, Eng.). Episcopalian. Mason. Editor: Criminal Receivers in the United States, 1928. Home: 42 Henry St. Address: Daily Eagle, Brooklyn. Died Feb. 14, 1942.

RICH, Charles Alonzo, architect; b. Beverly, Mass., Oct. 22, 1855; s. Rev. A. B. R.; grad. Chandler Sci. Sch. (Dartmouth), 1875; studied architecture in U.S., 1875-79, and in Europe, 1879-82; m. Miss Bradbury. Practiced in New York, 1882-1933; designer several bldgs. of Dartmouth Coll., many of the bldgs. of Smith, Amherst and Williams colls., all the bldgs. of Barnard Coll., Pratt Inst. and many opera houses, etc. Fellow Am. Inst. Architects; mem. Archtl. League, New York. Club: Century Assn. Home: Charlottesville, Va. Died Dec. 3, 1943.

RICH, Edgar Judson, lawyer; b. Milton, Mass., July 22, 1864; s. A. Judson and Harriet L. (Allan) R.; A.B., Harvard, 1887, A.M., 1891, LL.B., 1891; m. Mary Louise Aldrich, Nov. 23, 1893. Admitted to bar, 1891; became asst. atty., Boston & Me. R.R., 1895, atty., 1898, gen. solicitor, 1903-15; since in gen. practice, also gen. counsel Associated Industries of Mass. Has made splty. of interstate commerce law, and has been counsel for various rys.; lecturer on interstate commerce law, Harvard U., 1908-33. Republican. Mem. of the Union Club, Boston. Author of monographs on various subjects in polit. economy, etc. Home: 11 Pine St., Winchester, Mass. Office: 6 Beacon St., Boston, Mass. Died July 17, 1948.

RICH, Giles Willard, lawyer; b. Rochester, N.Y., Dec. 13, 1875; s. Willard Giles and Rebecca Cameron (Luitwieler) R.; ed. Purdue U., U. of Rochester, Mass. Inst. Tech.; m. Sarah T. Sutherland; children—Giles S., Eleanor H. (Mrs. H. H. Van Staagen). Admitted to N.Y. bar, 1899; Pa. bar, 1945; District of Columbia bar, 1947; member firm Williams, Rich & Morse, New York, 1928-41; specializes in patent law, trade marks and copyrights; partner in firm Church & Rich, Rochester, N.Y., 1905-19; patent counsel Western Electric Co., 1919-26; spl. asst. to atty. gen., 1934-37; became pres. Richtex Oil Corp., 1939; now mem. firm Munn, Liddy, Glaccum & Rich, Washington, D.C. Attended O.T.C., Plattsburg, New York, 1915; mem. Aircraft Prodn. Bd., equipment sect., during World War; lt. col. Air Corps Res. Head Army Air Corps Sect., Div. Contract Distribution, O.P.M., 1941. Mem. Am. Bar Assn., Assn. Bar City of N.Y., Am. Patent Law Assn., Air Reserve Assn. (exec. com. 2d Corps Area), Nat. Air Defense League (nat. v.p., dir. N.Y. Chapter), Soc. of Genesee (gov.), Mayflower Soc., S.R., Delta Psi. Democrat. Presbyn. Mason (32°, K.T., Shriner); past dist. dep. N.Y. State. Clubs: Advertising, Kiwanis (New York); Army and Navy (Washington, D.C.); Seigniory. Home: 1734 P St. N.W. Office:

1319 F St. N.W., Washington, D.C. Died Feb. 6, 1949.

RICH, S(amuel) Heath, editor; b. Rochester, N.Y., Nov. 24, 1856; s. Samuel Heath and Margaret (McLaughlin) R.; student Coffin Acad., Nantucket, Mass., 1870-74; m. Florence L. Doty, Mar. 2, 1880. Printer, 1875-78; asso. with Albert H. Fuller in establishment of Brockton (Mass.) Daily Enterprise, 1880; editor Brockton Enterprise since 1880; pres. Enterprise Pub. Co. Republican. Conglist. Club: Commercial (Brockton). Home: 12 Newton St. Office: 60 Main St., Brockton, Mass. Died June 8, 1947.

RICHARDS, Alfred Ernest, prof. English; b. Hartford, Conn., Mar. 11, 1874; s. Alfred Thomas and Laura (Johnson) R.; A.B., Yale, 1898, A.M., 1900; Ph.D., U. of Munich, 1904; m. Katharine Moore Barrows, Apr. 26, 1915; children—John Barrows (dec.), Katharine Edith, Priscilla Manning. Instr. modern langs., Lehigh U., 1904-05, in German, Princeton, 1905-11, in English, U. of Wash., 1911-12; courses in English, U. of Minn., summer 1912; prof. English, U. of N.H., since 1912, head of dept. until 1939, prof emeritus since 1943. Mem. Yale Library Assos., Am. Assn. Univ. Profs., College English Association, N.H. Assn. Teachers of English (pres. 1924-25), Lambda Chi Alpha, Phi Kappa Phi. Clubs: Quadrangle (Princeton), Elizabethan (Yale). Republican. Conglist. Author: Studies in English Faust Literature (Berlin), 1907; also articles in Modern Lang. Notes, The Nation, etc; (published) "Mister Boogaman," "Mon P'tit Brave Soldat." Composed music and words for official state 4-H Club song. Co-editor: University of New Hampshire Song Book, 1928. Contbr. to Am. Dictionary of Biography and Early Modern English Dictionary. Home: Durham, N.H. Died Sep. 25, 1946.

RICHARDS, Eben; b. St. Louis, Mo., Jan. 10, 1866; s. Eben and Caroline Beckwith (Maxwell) R.; A.B., Harvard, 1886; LL.B., Washington U., 1888; m. Perle Pierce, Apr. 15, 1896; children—Eben, Minnie Finlay (Mrs. Stuart B. Kaiser). Admitted to bar, 1888, and practiced at St. Louis; moved to New York, 1903; pres. Falcon Oil Corp.; dir. Brier Hill Collieries. Republican. Home: Tuxedo Park, N.Y.Died Oct. 9, 1942.

RICHARDS, George, officer U.S. Marine Corps; b. Ironton, O., Feb. 6, 1872; s. Samuel and Laura Ann (Westlake) R.; grad. U.S. Naval Acad., Academic Course, 1891, full course, 1893; grad. Sch. of Application, U.S. Marine Corps, 1894; m. Lydia Knechtel Putney, Sept. 28, 1936. Commd. 2d lt. U.S. Marine Corps, July 1, 1893; 1st lt., Feb. 11, 1898; maj. asst. paymaster, Mar. 11, 1899; paymaster U.S. Marine Corps with rank of brig. gen., Sept. 8, 1916. Served on Newark and Lancaster, S. Atlantic Sta., 1895-97; Newark, Spanish-Am. War, south coast of Cuba, May-Nov. 1898; participated in bombardment of Santiago de Cuba, July 2, 1898, and Battle of Manzanillo, Aug. 12, 1898; served in Philippine Islands, 1899-1900; in Boxer Rebellion, June-Sept. 1900; took part in Battle of Tientsin, July 14, 1900; participated in march to Peking and relief of the legations at Peking, Aug. 1900; served with Army of Cuban Pacification, Havana, Cuba, 1906-07; retired from service, Mar. 1, 1936. Was nominated bvt. lt. colonel "for distinguished conduct in the presence of the enemy," at the Battle of Tientsin; awarded Sampson medal, 1898; West Indian, Philippine, China and Cuban Pacification, Victory, Expeditionary, Nicaragua, and Brevet medals; D.S.M. for service in World War. Officer Legion of Honor (France); Merito Militar (Republica Dominicana); Order of Merit (Nicaraguan Rep.). Mem. D.C. Soc. S.R. (sec. 1914-16; pres. 1917-26). Episcopalian. Mason. Clubs: Army and Navy (ex-pres.), Chevy Chase. Address: Route 4, Staunton, Va.* Died Jan. 9, 1948.

RICHARDS, Janet E. Hosmer, lecturer; born in Granville, O.; d. William and Helen (Ralston) R.; ed. Eden Hall Acad. of Sacred Heart, Phila., and at home; was on lit. staff Washington Post; originated lecture classes on public questions, 1895; conducted regular courses many years in Washington, Baltimore, Phila., New York, Boston and other eastern cities; lectured also on travel, history and literature; gave regular courses before the League for Political Edn., New York, 16 yrs.; also before girls schs. and other organizations. Charter mem. D.A.R. No. 133, apptd. hon. chmn. of Golden Jubilee Com. and received special badge for distinction for that office; historian, past regent and sec. Mary Washington Chapter (D.C.); delegate and speaker annual congresses of the D.A.R.; del. Internat. Woman's Suffrage Alliance, Amsterdam, 1908, Stockholm, 1911, Rome, 1923; del. and speaker Quinquennial Internat. Council of Women, Rome, 1914, also first Women's Pan-Am. Congress, Washington, D.C., 1916, retired, 1937; mem. Nat. Geog. Soc., English-Speaking Union, D.A.R. (hon. member ex-Nat. Officers Club; member D.C. Officers Club). Clubs: Woman's City of D.C. (life), Soroptimist (hon. member). Contbr. to mags. and papers. Decorated for distinguished services Reconnaisance Française; Couronne d'Or of Leopold 2d (Belgium); medal for "Friends of Italian Culture" (Italy). Home: Wyoming Apts., Washington 9, D.C. Died Apr. 4, 1948.

RICHARDS, John Thomas, retired lawyer; b. Ironton, O., Oct. 13, 1851; s. Rev. John L. and Margaret (Jones) R.; reared on farm at Big Rock, Kane County, Ill.; Wheaton (Ill.) Coll., 1870-71; also under father and pvt. tutors; m. Lucy Keene, Mar. 21, 1888; children—Keene, Lucile (Mrs. H. G. Rife), Lillian. Admitted to Ill. bar, 1875, in gen. practice, Chicago; now retired. Was gen. counsel for Ill. U.S. Food Administrn., regional counsel for Federal Grain Corp., World War. Mem. Am. Bar Assn. (mem. exec. com. 1920-23), Ill. State Bar Assn., Chicago Bar Assn. (pres. 1912-13). Republican. Methodist. Mason (33°). Club: Union League. Author: Abraham Lincoln, the Lawyer-Statesman, 1916. Home: 7424 Oglesby Av., Chicago, Ill. Died July 19, 1942.

RICHARDS, Laura Elizabeth, author; b. Boston, Feb. 27, 1850; d. Samuel Gridley and Julia (Ward) Howe; m. Henry Richards, June 17, 1871; children—Alice Maude (dec.), Rosalind, Henry Howe, Julia Ward, Maud (dec.), John, Laura Elizabeth. Author: Sketches and Scraps, 1881; Five Mice, 1881; Joyous Story of Toto, 1885; Toto's Merry Winter, 1887; Queen Hildegarde, 1889; In My Nursery, 1890; Captain January, 1890; Hildegarde's Holiday, 1891; Hildegarde's Home, 1892; Melody, 1893; When I Was Your Age, 1893; Glimpses of the French Court, 1893; Marie, 1894; Hildegarde's Neighbors, 1895; Nautilus, 1895; Jim of Hellas, 1895; Narcissa, 1896; Isla Heron, 1896; Some Say, 1896; Hildegarde's Harvest, 1897; Three Margarets, 1897; Margaret Montfort, 1898; Love and Rocks, 1898; Rosin the Beau, 1898; Peggy, 1899; Rita, 1900; For Tommy, 1900; Snow White, 1900; Quicksilver Sue, 1901; Fernley House, 1901; Geoffrey Strong, 1901; Mrs. Tree, 1902; The Hurdy Gurdy, 1902; The Green Satin Gown, 1903; Five Minute Stories, 1895; More Five Minute Stories, 1903; The Golden Windows, 1903; The Merryweathers, 1904; The Armstrongs, 1905; Mrs. Tree's Will, 1905; The Piccolo, 1906; Letters and Journals of Samuel Gridley Howe, Vol. I, The Greek Revolution (edited), 1906; The Silver Crown, 1906; Grandmother, 1907; The Wooing of Calvin Parks, 1908; Letters and Journals of Samuel Gridley Howe, Vol. II, The Servant of Humanity, 1909; Florence Nightingale (Life of, For Young People), 1909; Up to Calvin's, 1910; A Happy Little Time, 1910; Two Noble Lives, 1911; Aboard the Mary Sands, 1911; Miss Jimmy, 1912; The Little Master, 1913; Three-Minute Stories, 1914; The Pig Brother Play Book, 1915; Life of Julia Ward Howe (with Maud Howe Elliott), 1916; Fairy Operettas, 1916; Life of Elizabeth Fry, 1916; Pippin, 1917; Life of Abigail Adams, 1917; "To Arms!" (war songs), 1917; A Daughter of Jehu, 1918; Life of Joan of Arc, 1919; Honor Bright, 1920; In Blessed Cyrus, 1921; The Squire, 1923; Oriental Operettas, 1924; Acting Charades, 1924; Honor's New Adventure, 1925; Star Bright, 1927; Laura Bridgman, 1928; Stepping Westward, 1931; Tirra Lirra, 1932; Samuel Gridley Howe, 1935; Merry-Go-Round, 1935; E.A.R., 1936; Harry in England, 1937; I Have a Song to Sing You, 1938; What Shall the Children Read?, 1939; The Hottentot and Other Ditties (author and composer), 1939. Home: Gardiner, Me. Died Jan. 14, 1943.

RICHARDS, Nathan Charles, lawyer; b. Jonesville, Mich., Aug. 28, 1864; s. Nathan Jay and Mary (Franklin) R.; student Hillsdale (Mich.) Coll., 1881-82; m. Maidie L. Rinker, Jan. 25, 1900. Admitted to Wash. bar, 1889, and began practice at Tacoma; moved to Yakima, 1909; mem. firm Richards, Gilbert & Conklin since 1920; pres. Yakima Valley Transportation Co. Del. to Rep. Nat. Conv., 1904, 20; mem. Rep. Nat. Com., 1924-28. Mem. Wash. State Bar Assn. (pres. 1917-18), Phi Delta Theta. Mason (32°, K.T., Red Cross of Constantine), Elk. Club: Rotary (pres.). Home: 115 N. Naches Av. Address: Miller Bldg., Yakima, Wash. Died May 4, 1943.

RICHARDS, Ralph Strother, sr. partner Kay Richards & Co.; b. Evanston, Ill., Mar. 4, 1881; s. William K. and Ida Katherine (Jones) R.; student pub. schs.; m. Carolyn McClurg Snowdon, Dec. 30, 1908; children—Snowdon, Mary E., Ralph S., Jr. Clerk Pa. R.R., June 1898-May 1904; in coal brokerage business, May 1904-Oct. 1914; mem. Pittsburgh Stock Exchange, Oct. 1914-May 1919; partner Holmes, Bulkley & Wardrop, May 1919-Apr. 1922; partner Kay Richards & Co. since Apr. 1922; dir. Penn Central Airlines. Pres. Asso. Stock Exchanges. Clubs: Duquesne, Edgeworth, Allegheny Country, Rolling Rock. Home: Woodland Road, Edgeworth, Pa. Office: Union Trust Bldg., Pittsburgh, Pa. Deceased.

RICHARDS, Robert Hallowell, metallurgist; b. Gardiner, Me., Aug. 26, 1844; s. Francis and Anne Hallowell (Gardiner) R.; B.S., Mass. Inst. Tech., 1868; LL.D., U. of Mo., 1908; m. Ellen Henrietta Swallow, June 6, 1875; m. 2d, Lillian Jameson, June 8, 1912. Asst. in chemistry, Mass. Inst. Tech., 1868-69, instr. assaying and qualitative analysis, 1869-70, asst. prof. analytical chemistry, 1870-71, prof. mineralogy and assaying and developed mining and metall. labs., 1871-72, prof. mining engring., 1873-84, head dept. mining, 1873-1914, prof. mining engring. and metallurgy, 1884-1914, emeritus prof. mining engring. since July 1, 1914, sec. faculty, 1878-83. Invented a jet aspirator for chem. and physical labs., 1873; a prism for stadia surveying in 1890; an ore separator for the Lake Superior copper mills, 1881, one for Va. iron ores in 1900, 3 for western U.S., 1906, 07, 08; designed and installed apparatus for Mass. Cremation Soc. Fellow Am. Acad. Arts and Sciences, A.A.A.S.; hon. mem. Am. Inst. Mining Engrs. (pres. 1886); mem. Mining and Metall. Soc. America, Am. Forestry Assn., Soc. of Arts, Am. Inst. Mining Engrs. Mem. Legion of Honor. Clubs: Economic Engineers', University, Technology. Holder of gold medal from Mining and Metall. Soc. America. Author: Ore Dressing, Vols. I and II, 1903, Vols. III and IV, 1909; Ore Dressing (text-book), 1909, revised (with Charles E. Locke), 1925. Home: 32 Eliot St., Jamaica Plain, Mass. Died Mar. 27, 1945.

RICHARDSON, Anna Steese, writer; b. Massillon, Stark Co., O., Apr. 5, 1865; d. Samuel and Sallie F. (Wood) Sausser; grad. Phila. Normal Sch. for Girls, 1885; m. William M. Richardson, Oct. 4, 1886; children—Lucy Milligan, George, Donald, Mary Nevins. Reporter Council Bluffs (Ia.) Nonpareil, 1894-98, Omaha Daily News, 1898-1900; with McClure Newspaper syndicate, 1900-03; staff New York World, 1903-05; now with Woman's Home Companion. Episcopalian. Author: For the Girl Who Earns Her Living, 1909; Better Babies and Their Care, 1914; Adventures in Thrift, 1916; Why Not Marry? 1917; Standard Etiquette, 1925; Etiquette at a Glance, 1927; The Bride's Book of Etiquette, 1929. Home: 145 E. 54th St. Address: care Crowell Publishing Co., 250 Park Av., New York. Died May 10, 1949.

RICHARDSON, Edward Peirson, surgeon; b. Boston, Mass., Apr. 7, 1881; s. Maurice Howe and Margaret White (Peirson) R.; A.B., Harvard, 1902, M.D., 1906; m. Clara Lee Shattuck, May 26, 1917 (died Dec. 6, 1921); children—Edward Peirson, Elliot Lee, George Shattuck. Surg. asst. to father, 1907-12; gen. practice, Boston, 1912-22; on staff Mass. Gen. Hosp., Boston, from 1911, now honorary mem. staff; with Harvard Med. Sch. from 1913, John Homans prof. surgery, now emeritus. Served with 1st Harvard Unit, 22, Gen. Hosp., B.E.F., 1915; capt., later maj. Med. Corps, U.S. Army, in France and Germany, 1918-19. Fellow Am. Coll. Surgeons; mem. A.M.A., Am. Surg. Assn., Southern Surg. Assn., Soc. Clin. Surgery. Republican. Clubs: Harvard, Somerset (Boston); Brookline Country. Co-author: (with J. H. Means) Diseases of the Thyroid, 1929. Contbr. various surg. articles. Home: 617 Boylston St., Brookline, Mass. Died Jan. 26, 1944.

RICHARDSON, Ernest Gladstone, bishop; b. St. Vincent, W.I., Feb. 24, 1874; s. Jonathan C. and Dorothea Ann (Davison) R.; B.A., Dickinson Coll., 1896; M.A., Yale, 1899; D.D., Wesleyan U., Conn., 1913; LL.D., Dickinson, 1920; m. Anna E. Isenberg, Apr. 21, 1897; children—Hallam Maxon, Marion (dec.), Winifred (dec.). Ordained Meth. ministry, 1896; pastor Wallingford, Conn., 1896-99, N.Y. City, 1899-1910, Bristol, Conn., 1910-13, N.Y. City, 1913-20; bishop Methodist Ch., 1920-44; now retired. Mem. Phi Beta Kappa, Phi Kappa Sigma. Home: 6733 Emlen St., Philadelphia 19, Pa. Died Sep. 5, 1947.

RICHARDSON, Friend William, former gov. of Calif.; b. in Mich.; s. William and Rhoda (Dye) R.; ed. pub. schs. and San Bernardino (Calif.) Coll.; m. Augusta Felder; children—Ruth, Paul W., John A. Newspaper publisher, at San Bernardino, 1896-1901, at Berkeley, 1901-19; state printer, 1912-15; elected state treas. 2 terms, 1915-23; gov. of Calif., term Jan. 1923-Jan. 1927; newspaper pub. Alameda Times Star, 1931-32; state bldg. and loan commr., 1932-33; state supt. of banks, 1934-39. Pres. Calif. Press Assn. 39 yrs. (exec. com.). Soc. of Friends. Republican. Mason (K.T., Shriner), Odd Fellow, Elk, Modern Woodman, Order Eastern Star, Moose, Sciot. Clubs: High Twelve (Berkeley); State Auto, Press (San Francisco); Athletic (Los Angeles); Pacific Coast (Long Beach); hon. mem. Rotary, Kiwanis. Home: 878 Arlington St., Berkeley, Calif. Office: 41 Sutter St., San Francisco, Calif. Died Sep. 5, 1943.

RICHARDSON, James Parmelee, coll. prof.; b. St. Johnsbury, Vt., May 29, 1878; s. Frank and Ella Florence (Parmelee) R.; A.B., Dartmouth, 1899; LL.B., Boston University, 1902; LL.D., Norwich University, 1943; married Anna Louise Pullen, June 24, 1908. Began practice at Boston, 1902; member Hale & Dickerman, 1910-17; Parker prof. law and polit. science, Dartmouth, since Sept. 1917; mem. Mass. Constl. Conv. from the city of Newton, 1917-18. Mem. exec. com. N. H. Com. Pub. Safety, 1918-19; mem. N.H. Spl. R.R. Commn., 1922-23; mem. N.H. Ho. of Rep., 1925-26, 1927-28; chmn. Commn. on Bank Taxation in N.H., 1926; mem. Commn. to Study Taxation in N.H., 1927-28; mem. N.H. Constitutional Conv., 1930; mem. N.H. Commn. on Uniform State Legislation, 1931-34; pres. N.H. conv. to consider repeal of 18th Amendment to Constitution of U.S., 1933; member N.H. Crime Commn., 1933-35; mem. of N.H. Local Selective Service Bd. No. 6, 1940-42. Trustee Kimball Union and St. Johnsbury Acads. Mem. com. on citizenship Am. Bar Assn., 1942-43; Mem. American Political Science Assn., Phi Beta Kappa (Dartmouth), Kappa Kappa Kappa (Dartmouth), Phi Delta Phi (Boston U.); pres. Am. Whist League, 1927. Author: History of Kappa Kappa Kappa, 1942. Home: Hanover, N.H. Died Mar. 24, 1947.

RICHARDSON, Norman Egbert, religious educator; b. Bethany, Ont., Can., Oct. 15, 1878; s. Alonzo and Sarepta Matilda (Gardner) R.; B.A., Lawrence Coll., Wis., 1902; S.T.B., Boston U. Sch. of Theology, 1906; Jacob Sleeper fellow of Boston U. at Berlin and Marburg, Germany, 1907-09; Ph.D., Boston U., 1911; m. Agnes Buckman Clough, June 12, 1906; children—Norman Egbert, Margaret, Channing Bulfinch. Pastor M.E. Ch., Mosinee, Wis., 1899-1901, Oconto, Wis., 1901-02, Woburn, Mass., 1903-06, Epworth Ch., Cambridge, Mass., 1910-11; prof. religious psychology and head of dept. religious edn., Boston U. Sch. of Theology, 1911-19; dean, Northfield Summer Sch. Religious Edn., 1919-24; prof. religious edn., Northwestern U., 1919-28; professor religious education McCormick Theological Seminary, Chicago, since 1928; dir. of summer session, 1928-42; dir. McCormick Extension Service, since 1945. Lecturer on religious education, Chicago Theological Seminary. Trustee International Society of Christian Endeavor. Mem. Internat. Council of Religious Edn. (mem exec. com.), Beta Theta Pi, Pi Gamma Mu, Phi Beta Kappa. Member Nat. Executive Committee Boy Scouts of America. Clubs: Cleric, Irving (Chicago). Author: Present Day Prayer Meeting Helps, 1910; The Religion of Modern Manhood, 1911; Boy Scout Movement Applied to the Church (with Ormond E. Loomis), 1915; Religious Education of Adolescents; The Church at Play; The Christ of the Class Room, 1931; Toward a More Efficient Church, 1940; The New Emphasis on Promotion in Protestant Churches, 1942; (brochures) Religious Education and Reconstruction; Moral Education as a Reconstruction Problem; Cardinal Principles of Christian Education; Kagawa's Magnificent Obsession; The Worship Committee in Action (with others). Editor of Abingdon Religious Education Texts, Community Training Schools Series. Translator: (with others) How to Teach Evangelical Christianity. Home: 840 Chalmers Pl., Chicago 14, Ill. Died Oct. 25, 1945.

RICHARDSON, Philip, architect. Mem. Am. Inst. Architects since 1913, fellow since 1931. Address: Room 211, 30 Ipswich St., Boston, Mass. Died April 9, 1948.

RICHARDSON, Roland George Dwight, mathematician; b. Dartmouth, N.S., May 14, 1878; s. George Josiah and Rebecca (Newcomb) R.; B.A., Acadia College, N.S., 1898, D.C.L., 1931; B.A., Yale 1903, M.A., 1904, Ph.D., 1906; Univ. of Göttingen, 1908-09; honorary LL.D. from Lehigh University, 1941; m. Louise J. MacHattie, June 4, 1908; 1 son, George Wendell. Teacher Margaretsville (N.S.) Sch., 1895-96, 1898-99; prin. Westport (N.S.) High Sch., 1899-1902; instr. in mathematics, Yale, 1904-07; asst. prof. mathematics, Brown U., 1907-12, asso. prof., 1912-15, prof. since 1915, head of department, 1915-42, dean of Graduate School since 1926, director of advanced instruction and research in mechanics, 1941-46. Fellow American Academy Arts and Sciences; member A.A.A.S., American Math. Soc. (v.p. 1920); sec. 1921-40; mem. bd. of trustees since 1923), Math. Assn. America (v.p. 1919), Deutsche Mathematiker Vereinigung, Phi Beta Kappa, Sigma Xi. Baptist. Contbr. to Trans. and Bull. Am. Math. Soc., Am. Jour. Mathematics, Mathematische Annalen, etc. Address: Brown University, Providence 12. Died July 17, 1949; buried in Camp Hill Cemetery, Halifax, N.S., Can.

RICHARDSON, William E., ex-congressman; b. Exeter Tp., Berks County, Pa., Sept. 3, 1886; s. Charles M. and Elizabeth (Snyder) R.; A.B., Princeton, 1910; LL.B., Columbia, 1913; m. Mary Eckert Potts, Feb. 24, 1926; 4 children. In practice of law at Reading, Pa., since 1914. Served with Ambulance Americaine, Belgium and France, 1915; with Squadron A, N.Y. Nat. Guard, Mexican Border, 1916; machine gunner, U.S. Army, World War, participating in major engagements. Mem. 73d and 74th Congresses (1933-37), 14th Pa. Dist. Mem. Com. Fgn. Affairs, Council of Interparliamentary Union. Democrat. Home: Wyomissing, Pa. Office: Berks County Trust Bldg., Reading, Pa. Died Nov. 3, 1948; buried in Schwartzwald Cemetery, Reading, Pa.

RICHEY, Thomas B., engring. cons.; b. Capon Rd., Va., Nov. 24, 1887; s. John Sinnard and Ellen Marshall (Locke) R.; student Augusta Mil. Acad., Ft. Defiance, Va., 1901-05, U.S. Naval Acad., 1905-09; M.S., Mass. Inst. Tech., 1914; m. Katherine M. Fowler, Nov. 6, 1914; children—Thomas Beall, Katherine Elizabeth. Passed midshipman, 1909, and advanced through the ranks to rear adm., 1942; indsl. dept., Boston Navy Yard, 1914-20, Naval Station, New Orleans (indsl. mgr.), 1920-21, San Diego, 1921-23, Norfolk Navy Yard (planning officer), 1923-27; production supt., Phila. Navy Yard, 1927-31, Mare Island Navy Yard, 1931-34, Brooklyn Navy Yard, 1934-41; mgr. Norfolk Navy Yard 1941 to 1943, attached to Joint Chiefs of Staff, Washington, D.C., 1943-45; retired from Navy Nov. 6, 1945. Consultant, Cargoaire Engring. Corp., N.Y. City, since 1945. Awarded Victory medal. Mem. Soc. Naval Architects and Marine Engrs., Soc. Naval Engrs., Naval Inst. Home: 405 W. 118th St., New York 27. Office: 15 Park Row, New York 7. Died March 30, 1949; buried Arlington National Cemetery, Washington.

RICHMAN, Arthur, playwright; b. New York, N.Y., Apr. 16, 1886; s. William and Jennie (Swan) Reichman; ed. under pvt. tutors; m. Madeleine Marshall, July 18, 1925 (divorced 1929); 1 son, John Marshall. Served as 2d lt. U.S. Army, 1918. Mem. Soc. Am. Dramatists and Composers (pres. 1925-27), Authors League America (pres. 1927-29), Screen Writers Guild. Chmn. amusement div. of Am. Com. for Christian German Refugees. Mem. bd. dirs. Am. Theatre Wing War Service, Inc. Author: Not so Long Ago, 1920; Ambush, 1921; The Serpent's Tooth, 1922; The Awful Truth, 1922; The Far Cry, 1924; Isabel (adapted), 1924; All Dressed Up, 1925; Antonia (adapted), 1925; A Proud Woman, 1927; Heavy Traffic, 1928; The Season Changes, 1936. Home: 419 E. 57th St., New York, N.Y. Died Sep. 10, 1944.

RICHMOND, James Howell, educator; b. Ewing, Va., Apr. 17, 1884; s. Nathaniel E. and Mary E. (Morison) Richmond; student Lincoln Memorial U., Harrogate, Tenn., 1898-1900; A.B., U. of Tenn., 1907; LL.D., Lincoln Memorial U., 1922, U. of Ky., 1933, U. of Louisville, 1937; m. Pearl J. Thompson, Dec. 15, 1917; children—Ruth Morison, Anne Howell. Teacher in various schs. (Tex., Tenn. and Ky.), 1907-12; prin. Richmond Sch., Louisville, Ky., 1914-28; high sch. supervisor, Ky. State Dept. Edn., 1928-32; supt. pub. instrn. of Ky., term 1932-36; pres. Murray (Ky.) State Teachers Coll. since 1935. Roosevelt campaign mgr. in Ky., 1932; Dem. nominee for Congress, 5th Ky. Dist., 1920. Mem. Ky. State Planning Bd.; nat. chmn. Com. on Emergency Aid to Schs., 1933-34; charter mem. Woodrow Wilson Foundation. Mem. N.E.A. (exec. com. of legislative commn.), Kentucky Education Assn. (president 1943-44), S.A.R., Pi Kappa Alpha, Phi Kappa Phi, Omicron Delta Kappa, Kappa Delta Pi, Tau Kappa Alpha, Phi Delta Kappa. Democrat. Mem. Disciples of Christ. Mason (chmn. ednl. trustees, Grand Lodge of Ky.). Club: Rotary (former dist. gov.). Lecturer. Address: Murray, Ky. Died July 24, 1945.

RICHTER, Paul E., airline exec.; b. Denver, Colo., Jan. 20, 1896; s. Paul E. and Margaret (Herpich) R.; student Colo. Agr. Coll.; m. Daisy Cooke, June 23, 1926; children—Paul E., Ruth Alice. V.p., gen. mgr. and dir. Aero Corp. of Calif., 1926-31; supt. Western Region Transcontinental & Western Air, Inc., 1931-34, dir. 1934-47, v.p. charge operations, 1934-38, exec. v.p., 1938-47; pres., chmn. bd. Taca Airways, Mobile, Ala., since 1947; exec. Coca Cola Bottling Co. of Calif., since 1949. Served as capt., U.S. Navy on active duty, 1943-45 Address: 1580 Hawthorne Terrace, Berkeley, Calif. Died May 15, 1949.

RICKARD, Richard Darke, railway official; born Eagle River, Mich., June 3, 1856; s. Richard Heath and Dorothy Ann (Darke) R.; Rensselaer Poly. Inst., 1875-78; m. Bessie J. Sims, 1886 (died 1904); children—Dorothy Sims (Mrs. John A. Rice), Richard D. (dec.), Mary Sims (Mrs. L. Rémy Hourdequin), Elizabeth Darke (Mrs. Francis L. Hamill), Donald Sims, Eric Martyn; m. 2d, Mrs. Eugénie Thomas Nunan, Aug. 1, 1917. Surveying and drafting, N.Y. & Oswego Midland R.R., 1878-91; sec. to gen. mgr. N.Y., O. & W. Ry., 1881-87, and has continued with same rd. as purchasing agt. and paymaster, 1887-89, sec. and treas., 1889-1930, v.p., 1919-30. Mem. bd. dirs. Kent Place Sch. for Girls, Summit, N.J., many yrs. Mem. R.R. Accounting Officers' Assn., Delta Kappa Epsilon. Episcopalian. Club: Delta Kappa Epsilon (New York). Home: Summit, N.J. Died Nov. 11, 1946.

RICKARDS, James S., educator; b. Terhune, Ind., July 26, 1883; s. William T. and Rebecca (Imler) R.; A.B., DePauw U., 1908; student Lyceum Arts Conservatory, Chicago, U. of Tenn., U. of Fla.; m. Grace Adelaide Havens, Dec. 23, 1914; children—Becky Lou, William, Dorothy Jane, Beth, James S. (dec.). Began as student teacher in Acad. of DePauw U., 1907-1908; prin. and supt. sch., Eaton, Ind., 1908-11, 1912; teacher Ark. State Normal Sch., 1911; prin. sch., Ft. Lauderdale, Fla., 1913-16; sec.-treas. Napoleon B. Broward Drainage Dist., Fla., 1917-29; also county supt. of schs., Broward County, Fla., 1919-29; former exec. sec. Fla. Edn. Assn., editor The Journal of Fla. Edn. Assn. since 1929. Life mem. N.E.A.; mem. Delta Upsilon, Kappa Delta Pi, Phi Kappa Phi. Democrat. Methodist. Home: 522 Williams St. Office: 6 Centennial Bldg., Tallahassee, Fla. Died Sept. 28, 1949.

RICKEY, James Walter, hydraulic engr.; b. Dayton, O., Nov. 10, 1871; s. James and Rosaltha Jane (Jones) R.; C.E., Rensselaer Poly. Inst., 1894; m. Lucy Amelia Mitchell, Jan. 24, 1899. Began as accountant, N.P. Ry., Minneapolis, 1894; prin. asst. engr. Lake Superior Power Corp., Sault Ste. Marie, Mich., 1896-97, St. Anthony Falls Water Power Co., and Minneapolis Mill Co., 1897-1907; chief hydraulic engr. Aluminum Co. of America, Pittsburgh, Pa., 1907-38, now cons. engr.; has designed and constructed large dams in the states of N.C., N.Y., Tenn., also Chute a Caron Dam, 200 ft. high, and 260,000 h.p. power-house, on Saguenay River, near Kenogami, Que. (the first stage of one of the largest hydro-electric developments in the world), 1927-30. Dir. Pittsburgh Branch, Pa. Assn. for Blind; mem. Engrs. Soc. of Western Pa. (dir.), Am. Soc. Civ. Engrs., Engring. Inst. of Can., Internat. Commn. on Large Dams (Am. Tech. Com.), Rensselaer Soc. of Engrs., Sigma Xi, Theta Nu Epsilon. Republican. Presbyterian. Contbr. tech. articles to mags. Home: 2101 Connecticut Av., Washington, D.C. Office: 801 Gulf Bldg., Pittsburgh, Pa. Died Apr. 19, 1943.

RICKS, Jesse Jay, chmn. bd. Union Carbide & Carbon Corp.; b. Taylorville, Ill., May 15, 1879; s. James Benjamin and Pammie Letitia (Geltmacher) R.; A.B., U. of Mich., 1901, LL.B., 1903; m. Sybil Hayward, Feb. 11, 1909; children—Jane Hayward (Mrs. Wilfred S. King), James Benjamin, John Thomas, Jesse Jay, Sybil Hayward (dec.). Admitted to Ill. bar, 1903, practiced at Chicago until 1917; pres. Union Carbide & Carbon Corp., 1925-41, chmn. bd. since 1941. Mem. Am. Bar Assn., Assn. Bar City New York, Sigma Chi. Clubs: University, New York Yacht (New York); Plandome Field; Manhasset Bay Yacht; North Hempstead Country; Nassau Country; University (Chicago). Home: Stonytown Rd., Plandome, N.Y. Office: 30 E. 42d St., New York, N.Y. Died Feb. 20, 1944.

RIDDELL, William Renwick, (rĭd'dĕl), Sr. Puisné Justice, Court of Appeal, Province of Ontario; b. Township of Hamilton, Upper Can., Apr. 6, 1852; s. Walter and Mary (Renwick) R.; student Cobourg Collegiate Inst., 1866-69; B.A., Victoria U., 1874, B.Sc., 1876, LL.B., 1878; L.H.D., Syracuse U.; LL.D., MacMaster, Toronto, Northwestern, Rochester, Lafayette, Wesleyan, Yale, Boston; J.U.D., Trinity; D.C.L., Colby; m. Anna Hester Kirsop Crossen, Mar. 5, 1884. Began as sch. teacher in back country, then in town sch.; successively mathematical master, Cobourg Collegiate Inst.; prof. mathematics, Ottawa Normal Sch. (governmental), lecturer on mathematical subjects; Dodge lectures, Yale; Blumenthal lectures, Columbia. Called to bar by Law Soc. of Upper Canada, with gold medal, 1883; King's Counsel, 1900; Justice of Court of King's Bench, 1906-20; Justice of Court of Appeal since 1920. Fellow Royal Hist. Soc. (London); Fellow Bot. Soc. of Edinburgh, Fellow Royal Soc. Can., Am. Bar Assn. (sr. hon. mem.); also hon. mem. 11 Am. state bar assns. Pres. Health League of Canada; hon. v.p. Victoria Alumni Assn. Hon. Col., Canadian Army, for services in World War I. Author: of books and editor of Canadian Encyclopedia Digest (Canadian Law), also of current The Canadian Abridgement, a Digest of Canadian decisions; contbr. articles on law, mathematics, history, medicine, etc. Home: 109 St. George St. Address: Osgoode Hall, Toronto, Can. Died Feb. 18, 1945.

RIDDICK, Wallace Carl (rĭd'ĭk), educator; b. Wake County, N.C., Aug. 5, 1864; s. Wiley Goodman and Anna Ivy (Jones) R.; ancestors among earliest settlers of Va. and N.C.; student Wake Forest Coll., 2 yrs.; A.B., U. of N.C., 1885; C.E., Lehigh U., 1890; LL.D., Wake Forest and Lehigh, 1917; D.Eng., N.C. State Coll., 1939; m. Lillian Daniel, Oct. 18, 1893; children—W. W., Lillian, Narcissa, Anna, Eugenia. Practiced as civ. engr., 1890-92; prof. civ. engring., N.C. Coll. Agrl. and Mech. Arts, 1892-1916, pres. 1916-23, resigned to become dean Sch. of Engring., 1923, dean emeritus and prof. of hydraulics since 1937 (name of coll. changed to N.C. State Coll. of Agr. and Engring. 1917). Had charge reconstruction water works of Raleigh, constrn. water works and sewers of Weldon, N.C., etc.; cons. expert to legal dept. Seaboard Air Line ry. until 1916; cons. hydraulic engr. since 1936; v.p. Neuse Mfg. Co.; mem. State Highway Commn., N.C., 1915-19; mem. State Bd. Vocational Edn., 1917-19; mem. Conservation Commn. N.C., 1918; mem. bd. visitors, U.S. Naval Acad., 1920-21. Lt. col. on staff of Governor Glenn, 1905-09. Mem. N.C. Acad. Science, N.C. Teachers' Assn., N.C. Soc. Engrs. (pres. 1919), Am. Soc. Civ. Engrs., Am. Assn. Engrs., Kappa Alpha, Phi Kappa Phi, Tau Beta Pi. Knight Order of St. Sava (Jugoslavia). Clubs: Capital, Rotary, Raleigh Country. Home: 225 Woodburn Rd., Raleigh, N.C.
Died June 9, 1942.

RIDDLE, John Wallace, diplomat; b. Phila., Pa., July 12, 1864; s. John Wallace and Rebecca Blair (McClure) R.; A.B., Harvard, 1887; student Columbia Law Sch., New York, 1888-91; École des Sciences Politiques, Paris, 1891-93; certificate of proficiency in Russian lang. from Collège de France, 1893; m. Theodate Pope, May 6, 1916. Sec. U.S. Legation to Turkey, 1893-1900; sec. U.S. Embassy to Russia, 1901-03; diplomatic agt. and consul-gen. to Egypt, 1903-05; E.E. and M.P. to Roumania and Servia, 1905-06; ambassador to Russia, 1906-09, to Argentina, 1921-May 28, 1925 (resigned). Served in Mil. Intelligence Div. of Gen. Staff, Army War Coll., Washington, 1917-18. Republican. Episcopalian. Clubs: Century, Union, Knickerbocker (New York); Rittenhouse, Philadelphia (Phila.); Minnesota (St. Paul); Cercle de l'Union (Paris); Brooks' (London). Died Dec. 8, 1941.

RIDDLE, Theodate Pope, architect; b. Salem, O.; d. Alfred Atmore and Ada (Brooks) Pope; ed. Miss Porter's Sch.; private architectural student 2½ years; m. John Wallace Riddle, May 6, 1916. Architect for Roosevelt House, N.Y. City, 1920, Westover Sch. for Girls, Middlebury, Conn., 1910, Hop Brook Sch., Naugatuck, Conn., founder and chmn. bd. dirs., prep. sch. for boys, Avon Old Farms, Avon, Conn. Awarded Leoni W. Robinson medal by New Haven Architectural Club, 1922; diploma and silver medal by 5th Pan-American Congress Architects, Montevideo, Uruguay, 1940. Licensed to practice architecture, N.Y. and Conn. Hon. mem. Central Society Architects, Buenos Aires; mem. American Institute Architects, Architectural League of N.Y., Archaeol. Inst. of America, Nat. Inst. Social Sciences, Mediaeval Acad. of Am., Colonial Dames, Soc. for Preservation of New Eng. Antiquities, Antiquarian and Landmarks Soc. of Conn. Clubs: Colony, Women's Cosmopolitan (New York); Town and County (Hartford, Conn.). Address: Farmington, Conn. Died Aug. 30, 1946.

RIDGWAY, Erman Jesse, publisher; b. nr. Otsego, Muskingum County, O., Aug. 6, 1867; s. Nathan B. and Catherine (Erman) R.; A.B., Yale, 1892; m. Anna Eleanora Robinson, June 28, 1899; children—Robin Elizabeth (Mrs. Ira A. Hinsdale), Eleanor (Mrs. E. Pulver Cook), Thayer. V.p. and gen. mgr. The Frank A. Munsey Co., 1894-1903; pres. The Ridgway Co., pubs. of Everybody's and Adventure mags., 1903-17; dir. The Butterick Co., pubs. of Delineator, Designer, and Woman's Mag., New York, 1910-17; associated with Frank A. Munsey, pub. New York Herald, New York Sun, Munsey's Mag., and other periodicals, 1917-24 (retired). Clubs: Ardsley, Country Club (New York), Tin Whistles (Pinehurst, N.C.). Home: The Wentworth, 59 W. 46th St., New York, N.Y. Died June 16, 1943.

RIDGWAY, William Hance, writer, mfr.; b. Bordentown, Burlington County, N.J., June 20, 1856; s. Craig and Susan (Hance) R.; B.Sc., Swarthmore Coll., 1875, C.E., 1878; m. Mary Graham Rambo, Feb. 28, 1884; 1 dau., Isabel Graham (Mrs. Harold

Dripps). Pres. Craig Ridgway & Son Co., mfrs. steam-hydraulic machinery; treas. Mutual Fire Ins. Co. of Chester County, Pa. Inventor Ridgeway steam-hydraulic system of cranes and elevators. Mem. Am. Acad. Natural Science; Franklin Inst., Philadelphia, N.J. Soc. of Pa. (pres.). Delivered addresses at mil. camps and navy yards, World War. Writer of column in S.S. Times (weekly) since 1907 and widely known for original style in advertising. Teacher Bible class 55 yrs., also head of mission Sunday School. Founder and pres. Coatesville Y.M.C.A.; mem. Nat. Council Y.M.C.A.; pres. of Pa. Y.M.C.A. Republican. Presbyterian. Club: Union League (Phila.). Author of the following brochures, booklets, etc.: How They Got There, 1912; Ridgway's Religion, 1909; The Way Up, 1925; The Christian Gentleman, 1932 (enlarged edit. 1937); Always Has Rained, Hasn't It?, 1932; In God We Trust; Tales of the Sawdust Trail, 1936; Draw Up a Chair, 1938. Has notable collection of things artistic from 5 and 10-cent stores. Owns what is said to be the only collection of artistic tape measures in the world. Home: Coatesville, Pa. Died Feb. 20, 1945.

RIEBER, Charles Henry (rē'bēr), coll. prof.; b. Placerville, Calif., Aug. 19, 1866; s. Louis and Christine (Lang) R.; A.B., U. of Calif., 1888; A.M., Harvard, 1899, Ph.D., 1900; LL.D., Mills College, California, 1929, also from University of California; m. Winifred Smith, June 15, 1890; children—Frank, Dorothy. Principal public schools, Placerville, Calif., 1888-90; instructor mathematics, Belmont (Calif.) Sch., 1890-98; asst. in philosophy, Harvard, 1898-1901; asst. prof. philosophy, Stanford U., 1901-03; asst. prof. logic, U. of Calif., 1903-05, asso. prof., 1905-10, prof., 1910-21, also dean summer session, 1907-15, prof. philosophy and dean Coll. of Letters and Science, 1921-36; emeritus prof. since 1936. Home: 13545 Lucca Drive, Pacific Palisades, Calif. Died Feb. 28, 1948

RIEDEL, Karl Heinrich (rē'dĕl), conductor; b. Vienna, Austria, Aug. 4, 1879; s. Heinrich and Henriette (Ladek) R.; grad. U. of Vienna, 1905, Dr. Philosophy and Music, 1922; m. Stefanie Ihle, June 22, 1922; 1 son, Hans Robert; m. 2d, Virginia Burbank, May 27, 1939. Came to United States, 1922, naturalized, 1928. A conductor Metropolitan Opera Co. since 1922. Address: Metropolitan Opera House, New York, N.Y. Died Feb. 2, 1946.

RIEHLE, Theodore Martin (rē'lē), insurance; b. New York, N.Y., Mar. 6, 1891; s. John Martin and Clara (Sulzer) R., ed. LL.B., LL.M., New York Univ., New York, American College of Life Underwriters; m. Katherine Bohn July 15, 1944; one son, Theodore Martin, Jr., from previous marriage. Pres. John M. Riehle & Co., Inc. (insurance); gen. agent, The Equitable Life Assurance Soc. of the United States; president North Shore Building Company, Long Island Sound Realty Co., Manhasset Park Co., twice president, Nat. Assn. of Life Underwriters, past chmn. and life mem., The Million Dollar Round Table. Mem. exec. com. and chmn. com. on ins., Chamber of Commerce, State of New York. Trustee, Lenox Hill Hospital; trustee, American College of Life Underwriters; pres. and dir. The Economic Club of N.Y.; mem. Kappa Sigma. Served in World War I. Lutheran. Clubs: Lawyers, Nat. Democratic, University, Metropolitan. Author: Riehle Business Insurance Sales Plan, 1929. Contbr. articles to various trade journals. Home: 340 Park Av. Office: 225 W. 34th St., New York 1, N.Y. Died Nov. 1, 1949.

RIETHMULLER, Richard Henri (rēt'mŭl-ēr), oral surgeon; b. Erzingen, Germany, Apr. 20, 1881; s. Carl L. and Minna (Oeffinger) R.; grad. Royal Carls-Gymnasium, Heilbronn, 1895; Royal Theol. sems., Maulbronn and Blaubeuren, 1899; U. of Grenoble, 1900; Royal Eberhard fellowship, U. of Tübingen, 1901; U. of Berlin, 1904; Harrison research fellow, U. of Pa., 1905-06, Ph.D., 1905; Medico-Chirurg. Coll., 1911, D.D.S., 1913; m. Eleanor Brunswick, Feb. 11, 1911; 1 dau., Thea Angelica; m. 2d, Lucy Doraine, Nov. 30, 1928. Instr. in German, 1905-07, lecturer in German lit., 1907-09, Univ. of Pa.; asso. editor Dental Cosmos, 1908-16; demonstrator, dental dept., Medico-Chirurg. Coll., Phila., 1913-16; instr. local anesthesia, Post-Grad. Sch. of Dentistry of Phila., 1914-16; attending oral surgeon, Lenox Hill Hosp., and oral surgeon, N.Y. Throat, Nose and Lung Hosp., 1916-17; instr. Post-Grad. Sch. Dentistry (Columbia), 1916-18; lecturer on oral hygiene, L.I. Hosp. Coll., 1916-18; prof. of anæsthesia, U. of Southern Calif. Coll. of Dentistry, since 1920; prof. stomatology, Coll. of Med. Evangelists, since 1923. Fellow A.M.A.; mem. Am. Dental Assn., Southern Calif. dental assns., Los Angeles County Dental Soc., Psi Omega; honorary mem. Eastern Dental Soc., Los Angeles County Dental Soc., Southwestern Dental Soc. Author: (articles) Walt Whitman and the Germans, 1904; Gleim's Imitations of the Middle High German Minnesong, 1905; The All-Porcelain Jacket Crown, 1905; Local Anesthesia in Dentistry, 1914; The Kinematograph, A Future Adjunct in Teaching Dentistry, 1914; Further Studies on Novocain-Suprarenin Anesthesia, 1915; Anoci-Association in Dentistry, 1915; Pyorrhea Alveolaris and Its Cure, 1915; Causes of Failures in Conduction Anesthesia, 1918; Oral Tumors, 1919; Anesthesia in Children's Work, 1924; The Reality of Focal Infections, 1925; Specific Treatment of Infectious Mouth Lesions, 1926; Removal of Impacted Third Molars as a Prophylactic Measure, 1926; Novocain-Cobefrin Solution in Local Anesthesia, 1936; George Washington and His Dentist, John Greenwood, 1937; The Dental Centenary Celebration, 1939; War Oral Surgery, 1940; Novocain-Pontocain-Cobefrin, 1941. Translator: Fischer's Dental Anesthesia, 1911. Contbr. to Am. Year Book. Home: 627 S. St. Andrews Pl. Office: 122 E. 16th St., Los Angeles, Calif. Deceased.

RIETZ, Henry Lewis (rĕtz), college prof.; b. Gilmore, O., Aug. 24, 1875; s. Jacob and Tabitha Jane (Gray) R.; B.Sc., Ohio State U., 1899; Ph.D., Cornell U., 1902. Asst. in mathematics, Cornell U., 1901-02; prof. mathematics and astronomy, Butler Coll., Ind., 1902-03; instr. mathematics, 1903-04, asst. prof., 1904-11, asso. prof., 1911-13, prof., Sept. 1913-18, U. of Ill., also statistician Agrl. Expt. Sta.; prof. and head dept. mathematics, U. of Ia., 1918-42, retired, 1942. Mem. Ill. Pension Laws Commn., 1916 and 1918, also cons. actuary of commn.; actuary Chicago Pension Commn., 1926; cons. actuary Nat. Com. on Econ. Security, 1934-35; mem. bd. trustees Teachers Insurance and Annuity Assn., 1934-37. Fellow Am. Inst. Actuaries (v.p. 1919), A.A.A.S. (v.p. 1929), Royal Statis. Soc.; mem. Am. Math. Soc. (v.p. 1928-29, also asso. editor Bull. 1920-38; asso. editor Transactions since 1937), Math. Assn. of America (pres. 1924), Am. Statis. Assn. (v.p. 1925), Ia. Acad. of Science (pres. 1931), Inst. of Math. Statistics (pres. 1935-37). Alpha Tau Omega, Sigma Xi, Phi Beta Kappa, Gamma Alpha. Methodist. Joint Author: College Algebra, 1909, rev., 1919, 29, 39; Exercises and Problems for College Algebra, 1911; School Algebra, 1915; Mathematics of Finance, 1921, rev. 1932; Introductory College Algebra, 1923, rev., 1933; Intermediate Algebra, 1940. Handbook of Mathematical Statistics, 1924; Mathematical Statistics (Carus monograph), 1927; Plane and Spherical Trigonometry, 1935; author of numerous papers on mathematics, actuarial theory, and statistics. Clubs: Triangle, Country (Iowa City). Home: 128 Fairchild St. Address: University of Iowa, Iowa City, Iowa. Died Dec. 7, 1943.

RIGBY, William Cattron, lawyer; b. Waterloo, Ia., May 11, 1871; s. William Titus and Eva (Cattron) R.; A.B., Cornell Coll., Mt. Vernon, Ia., 1892, Ph.B., 1892, A.M., 1897, LL.D., 1942; LL.B., Northwestern U., 1893; m. Grace Gilruth, Oct. 25, 1893 (died May 1, 1940); children—Cecil Collin (Mrs. Frederick L. Nussbaum), Eveyln Cattron (Mrs. Lewis B. Moore), Carol Gilruth (Mrs. Arthur Bronson Rigby); m. 2d, Mrs. Clare B. Hoffman, June 30, 1942. Admitted to bar, Ill., 1893, Calif., 1909, Canal Zone, 1924, Dist. of Columbia, 1927, N.Y., 1930; admitted to practice before U.S. Supreme Ct., 1917; practiced in Chicago, 1893-1918; commd. maj. judge advocate U.S. Army, 1918, advanced to lt. col., 1919; commd. lt. col. U.S. Army, 1920; col., 1931; detailed to examine adminstrn. of mil. law in allied armies and revise Articles of War and Manual for Courts Martial, 1919-20; chief Insular Affairs Sect. Judge Advocate Gen.'s Office, asst., and acting judge advocate general, 1931-34; retired, 1934; reentered private practice; recalled to active duty and detailed to examine and report on adminstrn. of mil. law and kindred matters in England, Oct. 1941-June 1942; counsel for Govt. of Puerto Rico, 1934-43; many cases before U.S. Supreme Court and other courts of appeal; lecturer Am. U. Grad. Sch., 1927-30. Mem. Inter-Am. Bar Assn. (chmn. organizing com. and provisional treas., 1940-41; chmn. exec. com. and treas. since 1941), Am. Bar Assn. (mem. gen. council, 1924-26; v.p. for Canal Zone, 1927; chmn. com. on Latin-Am. Law of Section of International and Comparative Law, 1937-40, of military and naval law, since 1942; member Dist. of Columbia, Chicago, and Federal bar assns., Assn. of the Bar of City of N.Y., Chicago Law Inst., Phi Beta Kappa, Delta Chi. Mason (K.T.). Clubs: University (Chicago); Army and Navy, Cosmos (Washington, D.C.); Lotos (N.Y.); Athenaeum (London, Eng.). Home: East Falls Church, Va. Office: Southern Bldg., Washington 5, D.C. Died Apr. 16, 1945.

RIGGS, Henry Earle, civil engr.; b. Lawrence, Kan., May 8, 1865; s. Judge Samuel Agnew and Catharine (Earle) R.; A.B., U. of Kan., 1886; C.E., U. of Mich., 1910; Dr. Engring., 1937; m. Emma King, d. late S. B. Hynes, Oct. 1, 1890; children—Ellen (Mrs. Stratford B. Douglas), Genevieve (Mrs. William B. Thom, dec.), Samuel H., Emma (Mrs. George L. Ohrstrom), Joseph A., Catherine (Mrs. James Mann Miller), Finley B. With engring. dept. Burlington and A.T.&S.F. rys., 1886-90; chief engr. Toledo, Ann Arbor & N. Mich. Ry., 1890-96; in pvt. practice as consulting and designing engr. as mem. Riggs & Sherman, 1896-1912; prof. and head dept. of civ. engring., U. of Mich., May 1, 1912-June 30, 1930, hon. prof. civ. engring. since 1930; retired; acted as cons. engr. in various cases for railroad commissions of several states and for cities in a number of states, 1916-21; cons. engr. on railroad grade separation for city of Detroit, 1915-20. Has devoted much time since 1920 to the subject of depreciation in connection with railroads, electric and gas utilities. In connection with valuation and recapture proceedings has represented a number of carriers, including Ill. Central System, N.Y. Central System, Union Pacific System, Frisco, Norfolk & Western, Virginian and Chesapeake & Ohio. Has also been retained in cases involving Detroit Edison Company, Alabama Power Company, Georgia Power Company, Carolina Power and Light Co., South Carolina Power Co. Mem. Bd. of Edn., Maumee, O, 1900-11, Ann Arbor, 1916-25. Mem. John Fritz Medal Board of Award, 1939-42, chmn., 1941. Mem. Am. Soc. C E. (dir. 1932-34, v.p. 1935-36, president 1938; made honorary member 1941), Engineering Institute of Canada, American Inst. Cons. Engrs., Am Ry. Engring. Assn., Engring. Soc. of Detroit, Am. Soc. for Engring. Edn.; hon. mem. Mich. Engring. Soc. (past pres.), Sigma Xi, Tau Beta Pi, Phi Kappa Phi, Phi Gamma Delta. Republican. Congregationalist. Club: Detroit (Detroit). Author: Depreciation, 1922; Principles of Railway Engineering (with W. G. Raymond and W. C. Sadler), 1937; Our Pioneer Ancestors, Vol. I, 1942, Vol. II, 1943; American Ancestors of Margaret Thom, 1945; The Troublesome Problem of Depreciation, 1947, also papers on different phases of regulation of public service property. Address: care Dept. Engring., Univ. of Mich., Ann Arbor, Mich. Died July 5, 1949.

RIGGS, Norman Colman, mathematician; b. Bowling Green, Mo., Nov. 1, 1870; s. James William and Lucretia Smith (Jones) R.; La Grange (Mo.) Coll., 1889-90; B.S. and M.S., U. of Mo., 1895; M.S., Harvard, 1898; m. Jean Augusta Shaefer, Aug. 15, 1905; children—Philip Shaefer, Paul Flood, William Horace. Inst. mathematics, Pa. State Coll., 1899-1902; asst. and asso. prof. mathematics, Armour Inst. Tech., Chicago, 1902-08; asst. prof. mathematics, Carnegie Inst. Tech., 1908-10, asst. prof. and prof. mechanics, 1910-40, prof. emeritus since 1940. Mem. Am. Math. Soc., Math. Assn. America. Am. Assn. Advancement of Science, Phi Beta Kappa, Tau Beta Pi. Author: Analytic Geometry, 1910. Reviser of Hancock's Applied Mechanics for Engineers, 1915; Applied Mechanics, 1930; Strength of Materials (with M. M. Frocht), 1938. Home: R.D. 9, So. Hills, Pittsburgh, Pa. Died July 18, 1943.

RIGGS, Thomas, internat. boundary commr.; b. Ilchester, Md., Oct. 17, 1873; s. Thomas and Catherine Winter (Gilbert) R; student Princeton 3 yrs., class of 1894; m. Renee Marie Coudert, Apr. 30, 1913; children—Elizabeth Catherine, Thomas. Lumber business, Wash., 1893-96; in Alaska, 1897-1901, Utah, 1902; with U.S. and Can. Boundary Survey, 1903-05, advancing to chief of party; topographer U.S. Geol. Survey; surveyor, later engr. to the Commn. Alaska Boundary Survey, 1906-13; apptd. member Alaskan Engring. Commn., 1914; in charge Fairbanks Div., location and construction Govt. railroads in Alaska; gov. Alaska, 1918-21; v.p. Macassa Mines Ltd; now commr. International Boundary Commission (Canada); mem. Alaska Internat. Highway Commission. Delegate to Democrat National Convention, 1920, 24. Member Am. Soc. C E., Am. Inst. Mining and Metall. Engrs., Am. Geophysical Union, Pioneers of Alaska, Colonial Order. Democrat. Clubs: Cosmos, Burning Tree (Washington); Mining, Racquet and Tennis (New York); Am. Alpine (hon. mem.). Home: Milbrook, N.Y.; and 1910 S St. N.W., Washington 9, D.C. Office: Commerce Bldg., Washington, D.C. Died Jan. 16, 1945.

RIHBANY, Abraham Mitrie, clergyman; b. El-Shiweir, Lebanon, Syria, Aug. 27, 1869; s. Mitrie and Marsha (Mutter) R.; ed. Am. Boarding Sch., Sûk El Gharb, Lebanon, 1886-88; student Ohio Wesleyan U., Delaware, O., 1895-96; D.D., Meadville (Pa.) Theological Sem., 1922; came to U.S., 1891; m. Alice May Siegle, Nov. 15, 1894; children—Marguerite R. (dec.), Edward H. Began preaching in Congl. Ch., Morenci, Mich., 1896; ordained Unitarian ministry, 1900; pastor 1st Ch., Toledo, 1902-11, Ch. of the Disciples (Unitarian) Boston, 1911-38, emeritus. Rep. Syrian socs. in America at Peace Conf., Paris, 1919. Republican. Club: Authors' (Boston). Author: A Far Journey, 1914; The Syrian Christ, 1916; Militant America and Jesus Christ, 1917; America, Save the Near East, 1918; The Hidden Treasure of Rasmola, 1920; Wise Men from the East and from the West, 1922; The Christ Story for Boys and Girls, 1923; Seven Days with God, 1926; The Five Titles of Jesus, 1940. Widely known as lecturer on contrasts and harmonies between Eastern and Western civilizations. Contbr. to mags. Home: Longwood Towers, Brookline, Mass. Died July 5, 1944.

RILEY, Cassius Marcellus, physician, chemist; b. Delaware Co., O., Apr. 16, 1844; s. Ezra and Louisa (Potter) R.; ed. Mt. Hesper Acad., Woodbury, O., and Ohio Wesleyan U.; M.D., Miami Med. Coll., 1870; m. Matilda Evans, Jan. 21, 1871. Practiced medicine Ohio and St. Louis, 1871-86; prof. chemistry and toxicology, Beaumont Hosp. Med. Coll., 1886-92, Barnes Med Coll. (now Barnes U.), 1892-1907; dean Barnes Coll. of Pharmacy, 1904-07; dir. Am. Research Lab. Mem. A.M.A., Am. Chem. Soc., S.R., Ohio Soc. of St. Louis. Author: Toxicology, 1901. Home: Alton, Ill. Office: 3664 Morgan St., St. Louis. Deceased.

RILEY, Leonard William, coll. pres.; b. Marietta, O., Feb. 6, 1872; s. John Newton and Harriet Margaret (Williams) R.; student Marietta Coll., 1890-92; B.A., Denison U., 1894, D D., 1909; grad. Rochester Theol. Sem., 1897; LL D., Linfield Coll., McMinnville, Ore., 1931; m. Julia Whipple Pearce, Sept. 1, 1897; children—John Kennth, Mrs. Janet Gladish, Mrs. Ruth Alden Carstens, Norman Pearce, Leonard William, Francis Chase. Ordained Baptist ministry, 1897; pastor, Lebanon, O., 1897-1901, First Church, McMinnville, Ore., 1901-03; state supt. of missions for Ore., 1903-06; pres. Linfield Coll., 1906-31, acting pres., Mar.-July 1931, pres. emeritus since 1931. Trustee Linfield Coll., 1903-31, Northern Bapt. Theol. Sem., Chicago, since 1921. Mem. bd. mgrs. Ore. Bapt. Conv., 1906-23; mem. exec. com. Northern Baptist Conv., 1918-21; mem. bd. mgrs. B.Y.P.U. of America, 1921-22; mem. and rec. sec. board education of Northern Bapt. Conv., 1910-40. Mem. Phi Gamma Delta, Phi Beta Kappa, Pi Gamma Mu, Pi Kappa Delta, Soc. Mayflower Descendants in Oregon, Alden Kindred of America. Mason. Address: Mc-

Minnville, Ore. Died Jan. 23, 1945; buried on Linfield College Campus, McMinnville, Ore.

RILEY, William Bell, clergyman; b. Greene County, Ind., Mar. 22, 1861; s. Branson Radish and Ruth Anna (Jackson) R.; Teacher's Course, Valparaiso (Ind.) Normal School; B.A., Hanover (Ind.) Coll., 1885, M.A., 1888; grad. Southern Bapt. Theol. Sem., 1888; LL.D., John Brown U., 1938; D.D., Union U., Jackson, Tenn., 1911; m. Lillian Howard, Dec. 31, 1890 (died Aug. 10, 1931); children—Arthur Howard, Mason Hewitt, Herbert Wilde, Eunice, William Bell, John Branson; m. 2d, Marie R. Acomb, Sept. 1, 1933. Ordained Bapt. ministry, Dallasburg, Ky., 1883; pastor at Warsaw and Carrollton, 1884-87, Tabernacle Ch., New Albany, Ind., 1887-88 First Ch., Lafayette, 1888-91, First Ch., Bloomington, Ill., 1891-93, Calvary Ch., Chicago, 1893-97, First Ch., Minneapolis, 1897-1942, now pastor emeritus; founder, 1902, and since pres. Northwestern Bible Training School, Minneapolis, Minnesota. Founder and pres. Northwestern Evangelical Seminary, 1935; founder Northwestern Coll. of Liberal Arts, 1944. Exec. secretary The World's Christian Fundamentals Assn., and editor of The Northwestern Pilot; president Minnesota Baptist State Conv., 1944-45. Author: The Greater Doctrines of Scripture, 1893; The Gospel in Jonah, 1895; The Seven Churches of Asia, 1895; Fads and Fanaticisms, 1895; Vagaries and Verities, 1903; Finality of the Higher Criticism, 1909; Messages for the Metropolis; The Perennial Revival; Evolution of the Kingdom, 1913; Crisis of the Church, 1914; Menace of Modernism, 1917; Daniel vs. Darwin, 1918; Ephesians the Threefold Epistle, 1919; Inspiration or Evolution?, 1923; Christ the Incomparable, 1924; The Blight of Unitarianism, 1926; Revival Sermons, 1929; Ten Burning Questions, 1932; The Philosophies of Father Coughlin, 1935; Youth's Victory Lies This Way; also, beginning in 1924, was author of a Series of 40 vols., completed in 1938, under title "The Bible of the Expositor and the Evangelist." Writer of many brochures and articles on religious subjects, including: The Coming and Kingdom of Christ, 1914; Light on Prophecy, 1918; God Hath Spoken, 1919; Sermons for the Times, 1924; The Minneapolis Pulpit, 1929; The Goal of Religion, 1935; Pastoral Problems; The Only Hope of Church or World, 1936; Saved or Lost, Is Jesus Coming Again?, My Bible—An Apologetic, Wives of the Bible, The Victorious Life, 1937; Seven New Testament Soul Winners, Wanted—A World Leader, 1939; Seven New Testament Converts, 1940; Christianity's Conflict with Its Counterfeit, 1940; Rethinking the Church, 1941; Problems of Youth, 1941; Sunset Sermons or After Eighty, 1943; The Preacher and His Preaching, 1947. Home: Twin Lakes Lodge, 3718 Golden Valley Rd. Address: 50 Willow St., Minneapolis. Died Dec. 5, 1947; buried Lakewood Cemetery, Minneapolis.

RINGLING, Robert Edward, operatic baritone, circus exec.; b. Baraboo, Wis., Aug. 16, 1897; s. Charles Edward and Edith (Conway) R.; grad. Evanston Acad. Fine Arts, 1914; Dr. Music, Rollins Coll., 1930; m. Virginia Elizabeth Sullivan, Dec. 8, 1920 (dec.); children—James Conway, Charles Josef; m. 2d, Irene Bauernfeind, October 23, 1940. Operatic début, Tampa, Fla., 1922; on tour of U.S., San Carlo Opera Co., 1922-23; with State Opera, Ulm, Germany, 1924-25, Nat. Opera, Munich, 1925-26, State Opera, Darmstadt, 1926-27; with Chicago Civic Opera Co., 1927-30; Chicago début as Tonio in "Pagliacci"; has repertoire of 104 roles, best known in Wagnerian parts; retired from opera, 1939; now president Ringling Bros.-Barnum and Bailey Combined Circus. Home: Sarasota, Fla.* Died Jan. 3, 1950.

RINGO, Hugh Fay (rĭn'gō), industrial physician; b. Bath County, Ky., July 2, 1884; s. Charles Estil and Emma (Gudgel) R.; student Transylvania U., Lexington, Ky., 1901-03; M.D., U. of Louisville, 1907; m. Agnes L. Johnson, Aug. 29, 1916; children—Phoebe Jane, Elizabeth Fay. Began as industrial physician at Montreal, Wis., 1909; gen. industrial practice with The Montreal Mining Co. at Montreal, 1909-32; engaged in study of clin. effects of dust inhalation by iron ore miners; now retired. Mem. com. on prevention of silicosis through med. control of Nat. Silicosis Conf. under direction of sec. of labor, 1936. Mem. Milwaukee County and Wis. State med. socs., Wis. and Am. Trudeau socs., Am. Coll. of Chest Physicians. Presbyn. Club: Univ. (Milwaukee, Wis.). Has presented exhibit of effects of dust inhalation by iron ore miners at Wis. State Med. Soc. meeting, 1936, and at Nat. Tuberculosis Assn. meeting, 1937. Home: 1717 E. Kane Pl., Milwaukee, Wis. Died Feb. 7, 1945.

RIOS, Juan Antonio, pres. Chile; b. Cañete, Prov. of Arauco, Chile, Nov. 10, 1888; s. Anselmo and Lucinda (Morales) Rios Gallegos; ed. public schools in Cañete, Lebú and Concepción; grad. in law and political science, U. of Chile, 1914; LL.D., Columbia U., 1945. m. Marta Ide Pereira; children—Carlos, Fernando Antonio, Juan Guillermo. Admitted to bar, 1914, and engaged in practice of law; held numerous positions in government; chargé d'affaires and consul for Chile in Panama and Canal Zone, 1921-23; became mem. Chamber of Deputies, 1923, senator, 1929; served in Congress until 1937; became pres. Mortgage Credit Bank (govt. bank), 1939; pres. of Chile since 1942. Roman Catholic. Address: Palacio Presidencial, Santiago, Chile. Died June 27 1946.

RIPLEY, Alfred Lawrence, banker; b. Hartford, Conn., Nov. 6, 1858; s. George and Mary E. (Aiken) R.; A.B., Yale U., 1878, A.M., 1888, LL.D., 1935; universities of Berlin and Bonn; LL.D., Dartmouth Coll., 1936; unmarried. V.p., Nat. Hide and Leather Bank, 1889-1901; v.p., 1901-08, pres., 1908-12, State Nat. Bank; 1st v.p., 1912-17, pres., 1917-29, now chmn. bd., Merchants Nat. Bank, Boston. Trustee Yale U., 1899-1933, Phillips Acad., Andover, since 1903. Mem. Phi Beta Kappa; asso. mem. Am. Acad. Arts and Sciences. Club: Union. Home: Andover, Mass. Office: 28 State St., Boston, Mass Died Oct. 13, 1943.

RIPLEY, Charles Trescott, mech. engr.; b. Oak Park, Ill., Apr. 20, 1886; s. Joseph Perce and Harriet (Konantz) R.; B.S. in E.E., U. of Ill., 1909, hon. M.E., 1912; m. Mabel Thomson, Apr. 20, 1918; children—Charles Purcell, Barbara Ann, Trescott. Began with A.,T.&S.F. Ry., Chicago, 1902, chief mech. engr., 1922-38; chief engr. Tech. Bd. Wrought Steel Wheel Industry, 1938-46; now cons. mech. engr. Fellow Am. Soc. M.E.; mem. Sigma Xi, Tau Beta Pi, Eta Kappa Nu, Beta Theta Pi. Republican. Presbyterian. Clubs: Union League, Edgewater. Inventor ry. devices and mfg. machinery. Home: South Laguna, Calif. Died Feb. 6, 1949.

RIPLEY, Giles Emmett, physicist; b. Adams County, Ind., June 18, 1874; s. John Frazer and Mary Elizabeth (Edwards) R.; B.S., Purdue U., 1899, M.S., 1902; studied U. of Chicago, summers 1907, 08; m. Harriet Louise Marsh, Oct. 18, 1900; children—Vincent Marsh, Kenneth Clay, Mary Pauline. Prof. science, Eastern Ind. Normal Sch., Muncie, Ind., 1899-1900; teacher physics and chemistry, high sch., Racine, Wis., 1900-02, Marquette, Mich., 1904-05; prof. phys. sciences, State Normal Sch., Valley City, N.D., 1905-08; prof. physics and head of dept., U. of Ark., 1908-40, dean of men since 1923, professor of physics, emeritus, since 1940. Pres. and mem. board directors, Vickers Cleaning and Laundry, Inc. Mem. A.A.A.S., Am. Inst. Elec. Engrs., Ark. Science Assn., Central Assn. Science and Mathematics Teachers. Progressive Rep. Methodist. Invented and patented with W. N. Gladson, improved motion picture apparatus; also inventor of new self-closing faucet without packing and springs and other devices, granted patent, 1937. Contbr. on tech. subjects. Home: 7 S. Duncan. Office: 323 W. Dickson, Fayetteville, Ark. Died Jan. 28, 1943.

RIPLEY, Hubert G., architect; mem. firm Ripley and Le Boutiller, Boston. Mem. Am. Inst. Architects since 1915, fellow since 1926. Address: 45 Bromfield St., Boston, Mass.* Died Dec. 15, 1942.

RIPLEY, Lucy Fairfield Perkins (Mrs. Paul Morton Ripley, sculptor, painter, medalist (descendant Colonial gov.); b. Winona, Minn.; d. Cyrus Maynard and Anna Payne (Fairfield) Perkins; ed. private schs., Art Students League, and in Paris; m. Paul Morton Ripley, Nov. 30, 1912. Exhibited at Paris Salon, 1935; Painters and Sculptors Gallery, N.Y. City; one man exhbn., St. Honoré, Paris; Georgette Passedoit Galleries, New York, 1936; Salon Les Tuilleries, Paris, 1934; Salon des Beaux Arts, 1935; awarded bronze medal, St. Louis Expn., Helen Barnet prize, Women Painters and Sculptors Assn., 1919. Unitarian. Address: 26 E. 63d St., N.Y. City. Died Sept. 3, 1949.

RIPLEY, Robert LeRoy, artist, author (Believe-It-Or Not); b. Santa Rosa, Calif., Dec. 25, 1893; s. Isaac Davis and Lily Belle (Yocka) R.; ed. high sch., Santa Rosa, Calif.; hon. A.M., Dartmouth Coll., 1939; Litt.D., Missouri Valley Coll., Marshall, Mo., 1939; Dr. of Oratory, Staley Coll. of the Spoken Word, Boston, Mass., 1940; unmarried. Began as sports cartoonist with San Francisco Bulletin, 1909; cartoonist with New York Evening Globe, 1913-27; creator of "Believe It or Not" cartoons, 1918, now syndicated to many newspapers of U.S., Europe, Asia and Australia; pres. Beieve It or Not, Inc. Featured in talking pictures and radio broadcasts. Fellow Royal Geog. Soc. (London), Am. Geog. Soc.; mem. Museum Natural History. Clubs: Adventurers, Explorers, Lotos, Circumnavigators, New York Athletic (New York); Royal Socs. (London). Author: Boxing Record, 1926; Handball Guide, 1927; Believe It or Not, vol. 1, 1929, vol. 2, 1931; Ripley's Big Book, 1935. Recipient of more than 1,000,000 letters a year. Has traveled in 200 countries of the world. Home: Taylor's Lane, Mamaroneck, N.Y. Hi-Mount, Palm Beach, Fla. Office: 235 E. 45th St., New York, N.Y. Died May 27, 1949.

RIPPEY, Harlan Watson, judge, lawyer; b. Griegsville, N.Y., Sept. 8, 1874; s. Joseph Nelson and Hester (Lynd) R.; A.B., U. of Rochester, 1898, A.M., 1899; m. Harriet C. Smith, June 30, 1908; children—Joseph Smith, Harriet Bertine, Catharine Adele. Admitted to N.Y. bar, 1901; in practice at Rochester since 1901; state tax appraiser, N.Y., 1913-15; inheritance tax atty. Tax Commn. of N.Y., 1922-27; justice Supreme Ct. of N.Y., 1927-28; liquidation atty. for State Supt. Banks and U.S. Comptroller, 1930-34; U.S. dist. judge, 1934-36; asso. judge N.Y. State Court of Appeals since Jan. 1, 1937; mem. State Commn. for Revision of Tax Laws, 1930-37; del. at large N.Y. State Constl. Conv., 1938; pres. and treas. Bircher Co., 1917-34; officer and dir. various corps., 1908-34. Chmn. Dem. Jud. Com., 7th Jud. Dist., N.Y., 1909-34; del. Dem. State Convs., 1922-34, Nat. Convs., 1924-32. Mem. bd. Geneseo State Teachers Coll. since 1934; Rochester Library Bd. 1934. Mem. Am., N.Y. State and Rochester bar assns., Am. Law Inst., Rochester Chamber of Commerce, Theta Delta Chi, Theta Nu Epsilon. Democrat. Presbyn. Elk, Moose. Clubs: Advertising (Rochester); Theta Delta Chi (New York); Fort Orange (Albany). Home: 165 Linden St. Address: Powers Bldg., Rochester, N.Y.* Died Mar. 11, 1946.

RISK, Charles Francis, lawyer, ex-congressman; b. Central Falls, R.I., Aug. 19, 1897; s. Thomas J. and Sarah (Cooney) R.; LL.B., Georgetown U., Washington, D.C., 1922; m. Ida F. Smith, Dec. 27, 1923; children—Elizabeth Ann, Charles Francis, Mabel Helen, James Thomas. Admitted to R.I. bar, 1923, and began practice in Central Falls; probate judge, 1929-31; judge of 11th Dist. Court of R.I., 1932-35; elected to 74th Congress to fill vacancy, Aug. 1935, term ending 1937; elected to 76th Congress (1939-41), 1st R.I. Dist. Served as pvt. U.S. Army, World War. Mem. Am. Legion (comdr. dept. of R.I. 1933), Gamma Eta Gamma. Republican. Catholic. K.C., Elk, Eagle. Home: 924 Smithfield Av., Saylesville, R.I. Office: 18 East Av., Pawtucket, R.I. Died 1943.

RISNER, Henry Clay, clergyman, author; b. Magoffin County, Ky., Nov. 11, 1869; s. Archibald and Narcissus (Prater) R.; student Georgetown (Ky.) Coll.; M.Th., Southern Bapt. Sem., Louisville, Ky., 1899; D.D., Women's Coll., Bryan, Tex., 1906; m. Hattie Carson, 1892. Ordained ministry Southern Bapt. Ch., 1887; teacher pub. schs. 3 yrs.; prin. high schs., Dunkirk, Ind., 1891-92; pastorates in Ky., Tex., Tenn., Md., N.J., Mass., Calif., etc., also supply various chs. including 5th Av. Ch., Huntington, W. Va. Mem. World's S.S. Conv., Jerusalem, 1904, and apptd. mem. of com. to write the "Jerusalem Pilgrim's Book," 1904; known as "The friend of the boys," in Am. Army camps, World War I, France and Germany; assigned to Army of Occupation at Coblentz 1 yr.; traveled extensively in Europe meeting the leaders in the interest of better relations between the U.S. and European countries; preaching tour in England, 1920; made prayer that unlocked the 13-day deadlock in Dem. Nat. Conv., New York, 1924. Author: Pinnacles of Personality, 1930, 32. Lecturer. Address: Huntington, W.Va. Died May 2, 1948.

RITCHIE, Andrew Jackson, educator; b. Rabun Gap, Ga., June 30, 1868; s. Riley Burton and Sarah Ann (Martin) R.; A.B., Harvard, 1899, A.M., 1901, hon. A.M. from the same university, 1924; LL.B., University of Georgia, 1897, A.B., 1899; Ped.D., 1926; m. Addie Corn, Aug. 19, 1900; 1 dau., Ruth. Worked way through college; prof. English, Baylor (Tex.) U., 1900-03; associated with wife in founding the Rabun Gap Sch., where old and young work their way through, on farm of 1800 acres. Mem. Ga. Legislature, 1945-46. Author of Rabun County History. Home: Clayton, Ga. Died Nov. 22, 1948.

RITCHIE, John A., motor coach executive; chmn. bd., dir., mem. exec. and finance coms., The Omnibus Corp., Chicago Motor Coach Co., New York City Omnibus Corp.; chmn. bd. Fifth Av. Coach Co., Eighth Av. Coach Corp.; dir. Motor Coach Supply Corp., Commercial Nat. Bank and Trust Co. Office: 605 W. 132d St., New York, N.Y. Died Mar. 16, 1950.

RITCHIE, John Woodside, teacher, author; b. near Sparta, Ill., Dec. 6, 1871; s. John Cameron and Sarah (McKelvey) R.; A.B., Maryville (Tenn.) Coll., 1898, Dr. Humane Letters, 1937; post-grad. work, 4 yrs., and fellow, U. of Chicago; m. Sarah Pearl Andrews, Jan. 15, 1902; children—Sara Margaret, Ruth Rathbone, Elizabeth Marshall, Mary Eleanor, John Andrews. Instr. in biology, Maryville Coll., 1899-1900; with Govt. schs. and Forestry Bur., Philippine Islands, 1902-04; prof. of biology, Coll. of William and Mary, Williamsburg, Va., 1905-19, dir. summer session, 1912-14; science editor World Book Co., Yonkers, N.Y., since 1915. Mem. A.A.A.S., Am. Pub. Health Assn., Phi Beta Kappa. Democrat. Presbyterian. Author: The Lives of Plants, 1904; Physiology and Hygiene, 1905; Human Physiology, 1908; Primer of Sanitation, 1909; Primer of Physiology, 1913; Public and Personal Health, 1916; Clearing the Way, 1917; Keeping the Laws, 1917. Joint Author: Philippine Chart Primer, 1906; First Year Book, 1906; Primer of Hygiene, 1910; Primer of Sanitation for the Tropics, 1910; Sanitation and Hygiene for the Tropics, 1916; Philippine Plant Life, 1929; Biology and Human Affairs, 1941. Editor of New-World Health Series, New-World Science Series, and other science and mathematics texts. Home: Flemington, N.J. Office: World Book Co., Yonkers, N.Y. Died May 29, 1943.

RITCHIE, Nelvia E. Webb, dir. Christian Science Ch.; b. Marion County, Ia.; d. William Henry and Martha Ann (Moore) Webb; ed. pub. and normal sch., Kan., and bus. coll., Kansas City, Mo.; C.S.B., Mass. Metaphysical Coll., 1928; m. Alva Bradley Ritchie, May 11, 1905. Field rep. of Christian Science Pub. Soc.; reader and practitioner, 1913-24; lecturer on Christian Science Bd. of Lectureship, 1925-34; dir. The Mother Ch., First Ch. of Christ, Scientist, Boston, since 1934; trustee Christian Science Benevolent Assn., Christian Science Pleasant View Home; also trustee under will of Mary Baker Eddy. Home: Chestnut Hill, Mass. Died May 7 1948.

RITCHIE, Robert Welles, journalist, author; b. Quincy, Ill., June 17, 1879; s. Robert and Hannah (Thomas) R.; grad. Oakland (Calif.) High Sch., 1898; B.S., U. of Calif., 1902; m. Jean Knight, Aug. 1, 1908. Began as newspaper reporter, San Francisco, 1902; editor Japan Advertiser, Yokohama, 1904-05;

on staff New York Sun, 1906-13, N.Y. Evening World, 1913-18; war corr. and London corr. Hearst papers, 1918-19; on editorial staff Country Gentleman, 1919-27; London corr. Hearst papers, 1928-31; spl. corr. N.Y. Sun in Mexico during Madero revolution, 1911, for Hearst papers at Treaty of Versailles, 1918; spl. assignments to Korea, Manchuria, San Francisco fire, to Labrador to meet Peary, etc. Mem. Sigma Alpha Epsilon. Democrat. Clubs: Family (San Francisco); Adventurers (New York). Author: Inside the Lines (with E. D. Biggers), 1915; Dust of the Desert, 1922; Drums of Doom, 1923; Stairway of the Sun, 1924; Deep Furrows, 1927; Hell-Roarin' Forty-Niners, 1928; Wheat, 1935. Home: Carmel, Calif. Died Aug. 2, 1942.

RITTENHOUSE, Daniel Franklin, clergyman; b. Ostrander, O., Mar. 14, 1882; s. George and Charlotte Louise (Parrott) R.; grad. Doane Acad., Granville, O., 1902; B.A., U. of the Pacific, San Jose, Calif., 1907; B.D., Pacific Coast Bapt. Theol. Sem., Berkeley, Calif., 1909; D.D., Denison U., Granville, O., 1929; m. Lilly C. Crees, Mar. 29, 1911; children—Lloyd-George, Lawren Baxter, Mary Louise, Daniel Franklin. Ordained Bapt. ministry, 1911; pastor First Bapt. Ch., Middletown, O., 1911-19, First Ch., Columbus, O., 1919-28, First Ch., Pasadena, Calif., 1928-37. Trustee U. of Redlands, Calif., since 1930, Berkeley Bapt. Div. Sch. since 1934. Established first radio broadcasting station (1922) owned and operated by a church. Trustee Ohio Bapt. Edn. Bd., and Ohio Bapt. Conv.; mem. exec. bd. Northern Bapt. Conv., 1932-36; pres. Southern Calif. Bapt. State Conv., 1933-34. Republican. Mason (32°). Home: 1000 N. Los Robles Av., Pasadena, Calif. Died July 17, 1943.

RITTENHOUSE, Jessie Belle, author, critic; b. Mt. Morris, N.Y.; d. John E. and Mary J. (MacArthur) Rittenhouse; grad. Genesee Wesleyan Sem., Lima, N.Y.; Litt.D., Rollins Coll., Winter Park, Fla., 1928; m. Clinton Scollard, author, 1924. Was teacher Latin and English in pvt. sch., Cairo, Ill., and Ackley Institute for Girls, Grand Haven, Mich., 1893-94. Began as contbr. to newspapers and press syndicates; in active newspaper work as corr. and reviewer until 1900. Lecturer on modern poetry in the extension courses of Columbia U.; with New York Times Review of Books and The Bookman. A founder Poetry Soc. America, also of Poetry Society of Florida (pres.). Editor: (with intro.) The Rubáiyát of Omar Khayyám (metrical transl. of Edward FitzGerald and E. H. Whinfield and the prose version of Justin H. McCarthy), 1900; The Lover's Rubáiyát (arranged from ten translations of Omar Khayyám), 1904; The Little Book of Modern American Verse, 1913; The Little Book of American Poets, 1915; Second Book of Modern Verse, 1919; The Little Book of Modern British Verse, 1924; (with memoir) Poems of Edith M. Thomas, 1926; Third Book of Modern Verse, 1927; The Bird Lovers' Anthology (with Clinton Scollard), 1930; Patrician Rhymes (with same), 1932; The Singing Heart (selected lyrics of Clinton Scollard), 1934. Author: The Younger American Poets (vol. of criticism), 1904; The Door of Dreams (verse), 1918; The Lifted Cup (verse), 1921; The Secret Bird (verse), 1930; My House of Life (autobiography), 1934; The Moving Tide: New and Selected Lyrics, 1939 (gold medal Nat. Poetry Center 1940). Awarded bronze medal by Poetry Soc. America for distinguished service to poetry, 1931. Lecturer on modern poetry, Rollins Coll. Home: Winter Park, Fla. Died Sept. 28, 1948.

RITTER, Verus Taggart, architect; b. Muncy, Pa., June 27, 1883; s. William L. and Amelia (Spangler) R.; ed. high sch. and pvt. sch., Bloomsburg, Pa.; archtl. training in brother's office; m. Edith E. Keller, Jan. 30, 1912 (died May 24, 1935); children—Verus Taggart, Eleanor Foster. Began practice at Williamsport, Pa., 1908, at Philadelphia, since 1917; sr. partner firm Ritter & Shay since 1920. Prin. works (alone): City Hall, First Nat. Bank Bldg., High Sch. and 3 jr. high schs.—all in Huntington, W.Va.; Virginian Hotel, Lynchburg, Va.; Arena for Commonwealth of Pa., Harrisburg; Office Bldg. for Commonwealth of Pa., Harrisburg; Vocational High Sch., Chester, Pa.; firm architects for Hotel Bethlehem, Lehigh Valley Nat. Bank Bldg., and Liberty High School, Bethlehem, Pa.; American Hotel, Allentown, Pa.; Masonic Temple, Chester, Pa.; 1500 Walnut St. Bldg., Market St. Nat. Bank, Drake Hotel, U.S. Custom House—all in Philadelphia, etc. Pres. Del. River Tunnel Corp. Firm awarded gold medal by Am. Inst. Architects for Packard Building, Phila. Republican. Presbyterian. Mason (32°, K.T.). Home: 356 N. Latches Lane, Merion, Pa. Office: 1500 Walnut Street Bldg., Philadelphia, Pa. Died Oct. 6, 1942.

RITTER, William Emerson, zoölogist; b. Hampden, Wis., Nov. 19, 1856; s. Horatio and Leonora (Eason) R.; grad. State Normal Sch., Oshkosh, Wis., 1884; B.S., U. of Calif., 1888; A.M., Harvard, 1891, Ph.D., 1893; student Stazione Zoölogica, Naples, Italy, and U. of Berlin, 1894-95; LL.D., U. of Calif., 1932; m. Mary E. Bennett, June 23, 1891. Was teacher in pub. schs., Wis. and Calif.; instr. biology, Univ. of Calif., 1891-93, asst. prof. biology, 1893-98, asso. prof. zoölogy, 1898-1902, apptd. prof., 1902, now emeritus. Ex-dir. Scripps Inst. for Biol. Research (now Scripps Instn. of Oceanography). Pres. Calif. Acad. Sciences, 1898-1900; fellow A.A.A.S. (v.p. sect. F, 1909-10, pres. Pacific div., 1920-21), Am. Acad. Arts and Sciences; mem. Am. Soc. Naturalists, Am. Soc. Zoölogists, Am. Ecol. Soc.; corr. Phila. Acad. Science; hon. pres. Science Service; honorary mem. Phi Beta Kappa (Berkeley chapter). Unitarian. Clubs: Commonwealth (San Francisco); Cosmos (Washington). Author: War, Science and Civilization; The Higher Usefulness of Science and Other Essays; The Probable Infinity of Nature and Life; The Unity of the Organism or the Organismal Conception of Life; and An Organismal Theory of Consciousness; The Scientific Method of Reaching Truth; The Natural History of Our Conduct (with Edna W. Bailey); The Organismal Conception (with same); Why Aristotle Invented the Word Entelecheia; Naturalism vs. Supernaturalism or Man as a Unified Whole and Part of Nature as a Unified Whole; The California Woodpecker and I (sub-title, A Study in Comparative Zoölogy); also of many contbns. to zoöl. and other journals. Home: Hotel Claremont. Address: University of California, Berkeley, Calif Died Jan. 10, 1944.

RITZ, Harold A., judge; b. Wheeling, W.Va., July 25, 1873; s. James M. and Catherine (McCarthy) R.; grad. Marshall Coll., State Normal Sch., Huntington, W.Va., 1889; m. Helen J. Jackson, Apr. 30, 1913. Admitted to W.Va. bar, 1894, and practiced at Bluefield; judge Circuit Court 8th W.Va. Jud. Dist., 1906; U.S. atty. Southern Dist. of W.Va., 1909-13; justice Supreme Court of Appeals of W.Va., term 1917-29; resigned, 1922, and resumed practice as mem. firm Brown, Jackson & Knight until 1925; gen. counsel United Fuel Gas Co., 1925-43; engaged in gen. practice of law since 1943. Republican. Mem. Am. Bar Assn., W.Va. Bar Assn. (pres. 1929-30); mem. Am. Museum of Natural History; fellow Am. Geog. Soc. Clubs: Bluefield Country, Edgewood Country; Lotus, Nat. Republican (New York). Address: 1608 Virginia St. E. Charleston, W.Va. Died April 10, 1948.

RIVERS, William Cannon, army officer; b. Pulaski, Tenn., Jan. 11, 1866; s. William and Julia (Flournoy) R.; grad. U.S. Mil. Acad., 1887; m. Mary Dancey Battle, Oct. 19, 1897; children—James Battle, William Flournoy. Commd. 2d lt. 1st Cav., U.S. Army, June 12, 1887; promoted through grades to col., July 1, 1916; brig. gen. (temp.), Oct. 1, 1918; apptd. by President Coolidge insp. gen. U.S. Army, rank of maj. gen., 1927, retired, Jan. 11, 1930. Served in troubles with Northern Cheyenne and Sioux Indians, 1890-91; in charge White Mountain Apache Indians, 1895-97; adj. U.S. Mil. Acad., 1899-1903; with regt. at Santiago, Cuba, June 25-June 30, 1898; duty Gen. Staff, 1903-04; asst. chief of constabulary, Philippines, rank of col., 1906-13; brig. gen. U.S. Army (temp.) and chief Philippines Constabulary, 1914; organized and trained the 76th Field Arty., 3d Arty. Brigade, 3d Regular Div., and commanded the regt. in Battle of the Marne at Chateau-Thierry, the advance to the North of the Ourcq to Aug. 2, 1918, and in battles of St. Mihiel and Meuse-Argonne; comd. 5th Brigade, F.A., 2d Army, between Pont-à-Mousson and Thiacourt, Oct. 14, until Armistice. Awarded D.S.M. (U.S.); Croix de Guerre (French); colors of 76th F.A. decorated with Croix de Guerre. Mem. Huguenot Soc. America, S.R. Soc. Army of Santiago de Cuba, Am. Acad. Polit. and Social Sciences. Episcopalian. Clubs: Army and Navy, Pilgrims, University (New York). Address: Warrington, N.C.* Died July 10, 1943.

ROBB, E(ccles) Donald, architect; b. Baltimore, Md., Jan. 10, 1880; s. Eliakim Tupper and Mary (Campbell) R.; ed. private and public schools, Chester, Pa.; grad. Dept. of Architecture, Drexel Inst., Phila., 1899; studied in Europe; m. Bertha Mooar, Oct. 24, 1906; children—Malcolm Campbell, Jean Howard, Doris (dec.), Miriam. With Theophilus P. Chandler, and Cope & Stewardson, Phila., Pa., 1899-1903, Cram, Goodhue & Ferguson, New York, 1903-11; mem. Brazer & Robb, New York, 1911-14; in office of Cram & Ferguson, Boston, 1914-18; mem. Frohman, Robb & Little, Boston, since 1920; firm architects for Nat. Episcopal Cathedral, Washington, D.C., Episcopal Cathedral, Baltimore, Md., and many other chs. Republican. Swedenborgian. Fellow Am. Inst. Architects, Boston Soc. of Architects. Has made a spl. study of the arts of the Middle Ages. Home: 30 Grove Hill Av., Newtonville, Mass. Office: 250 Stuart St., Boston, Mass. Died Jan. 8, 1942.

ROBBINS, Charles Burton, lawyer; b. Hastings, Ia., Nov. 6, 1877; s. Lewis and Harriett Elizabeth (Benson) R.; B.A., U. of Neb., 1898; studied Columbia U., College of Law; A.M., Columbia, 1903; m. Helen Larrabee, Sept. 9, 1903 (dec.); children—Anna Marcella (Mrs. Thomas C. Yarnall), Julia Larrabee (Mrs. Alvin W. Allen), Lewis Frederic. Served as pvt., 1st Neb. Inf., U.S.V., Apr. 28, 1898, first sergt. Co. B, May 10, 1898; 2d lt. Co. I, Apr. 27, 1899; served in the Spanish-Am. War at Manila until close of war; Philippine insurrection from outbreak, Feb. 3, 1899-June 1899; wounded in head at battle of Marilao, Mar. 27, 1899; took part in 27 engagements; awarded Silver Star and Purple Heart medals; mem. Co. C, 7th Regt., Nat. Guard, N.Y., 1901-03; capt. Ia. Nat. Guard, 1914-16; maj., adj. gen.'s dept., Ia., Nov. 2, 1916; maj., adj. 67th and later 69th Inf. Brigade., U.S. Army, Aug. 1917-May 1919; with A.E.F., 1918-19; maj. U.S.R., 1921; lt. col., 1923; col. since 1926; comdr. Ia. dept. Am. Legion, 1922-23. Civilian aide to sec. of War for Ia. C.M.T.C., 1924-27; asst. sec. of War, 1928-29. Admitted to Ia. bar, 1904; judge Superior Court, Cedar Rapids, 1909-19. Chmn. bd. Federal Home Loan Bank of Des Moines; dir. Merchants Nat. Bank, Cedar Rapids. Mem. exec. com. Am. Life Conv., 1925-33, pres., 1930-31, mgr. and gen. counsel since 1934. Republican. Universalist. Mem. Am. Bar Assn., Ia. State Bar Assn., Ia. State Hist. Soc., Delta Tau Delta. Mason (32°). Clubs: Cedar Rapids Country; Army and Navy, Nat. Press (Washington); Tavern, Union League (Chicago). Home: 3750 Lake Shore Drive. Office: 230 N. Michigan Av., Chicago, Ill. Died July 5, 1943.

ROBBINS, Edmund Yard, educator; b. Windsor, N.J., Oct. 3, 1867; s. George Randall and Anna Maria (Cubberly) R.; A.B., Princeton, 1889, A.M., 1890; studied U. of Leipzig, Germany, 1891-94; m. Emeline Place Hayward, Apr. 18, 1900. Instr. Greek, 1894, asst. prof., 1897, prof., 1902-36, Ewing prof. Greek lang. and lit., 1910-36, emeritus since 1936, Princeton. Annual prof. Am. Sch. of Classical Studies, Athens, Greece, 1921-22. Mem. Am. Philol. Assn., Phi Beta Kappa. Republican. Presbyterian. Translator: The Nature and Origin of the Noun Genders in the Indo-European Languages (by Karl Brugmann), 1897. Home: 144 Library Pl., Princeton, N.J. Died May 30, 1942.

ROBBINS, Edwin Clyde, economist; b. Rockford, Ia., June 19, 1883; s. Arthur and Eva (Moore) R.; Ph.B., State U. of Ia., 1910, M.A., 1912; Ph.D., Columbia Univ., 1915; m. Helen Hyde Mossman, Oct. 11, 1913 (died 1926); m. 2d, Evelyn H. Schenck, July 14, 1927 (died 1927); m. 3d, Marion Evelyn Brown, Jan. 19, 1929. Fellow in economics, Columbia, 1912-14; instr. economics and sociology, Mt. Holyoke Coll., 1914-15; asst. prof. economics and sociology, University of Oregon, 1915-17; assistant professor economics, University of Minnesota, 1917-19; asst. director Bureau Civilian Relief, Central Div., Am. Red Cross, in charge edn., 1918-19; prof. economics, 1919-20, dean Sch. of Business Administration, 1920-29, U. of Ore.; investigator for U.S. Coal Commn., 1923; lecturer on indsl. management, 1927-28, prof. indsl. management since 1928, Grad. Sch. of Business Administration, Harvard. Member American Economics Assn., Delta Sigma Rho, Beta Gamma Sigma. Conglist. Compiler: Selected Articles on a Central Bank of the United States, 1910; Selected Articles on the Commission Plan of Municipal Government, 1910; Selected Articles on the Open versus the Closed Shop, 1911; Selected Articles on Reciprocity, 1913; Socialism, 1915. Author: High School Debate Book, 1914; Railroad Conductors, 1914; Industrial Management, A Case Book (with F. E. Folts), 1932; Introduction to Industrial Management (with same), 1933. Home: 986 Memorial Drive, Cambridge, Mass. Died May 12, 1947.

ROBBINS, Harry Pelham; b. New York, N.Y., May 10, 1874; s. Henry Asher and Elizabeth Pelham (Bend) R.; A.B., Columbia, 1894; m. Emily Welles, Apr. 1908. Began as partner Vassar & Son, building constrn., 1897; was dir. Waltham Watch Co. (father a founder); dir. Empire Trust Co. since 1905. First lt. 12th Inf., N.Y. Nat. Guard, drilling draft recruits, World War; capt. regtl. adj. 369th Inf., 1921-22. Trustee Columbia U., Bard Coll., Am. Foundation Mental Hygiene, St. Andrew's Dune Ch. (Southampton, N.Y.); pres. Memorial Hosp. (N.Y. City). Pres. bd. of visitors Central Islip State Hosp.; mem. administrative com. Nat. Com. for Mental Hygiene. Mem. Am. Legion, S.R. Democrat. Episcopalian. Clubs: Knickerbocker, University, Columbia U. (New York); Meadow (Southampton). Home: 9 E. 79th St. Office: 500 5th Av., New York, N.Y.* Died Mar. 20, 1946.

ROBBINS, Leonard H., writer; b. Lincoln, Neb., Apr. 2, 1877; s. Leonard H. and Nannie (Cole) R.; ed. U. of Neb. and Princeton; m. Lena Anthony, Oct. 28, 1901; children—Ruth (Mrs. Rome A. Betts), Anthony. Began newspaper work at Lincoln, 1898; wrote the "In the Air" column in Newark (N.J.) Evening News, 1901-17, New York Times since 1923. Contbr. fiction to magazines. Mem. Kappa Sigma. Mason. Unitarian. Author: Jersey Jingles, 1908; Mountains and Men, 1931; Cure It with a Garden, 1933. Home: 210 Grove St., Montclair, N.J. Died June 24, 1947.

ROBERTS, Albert H., ex-governor; b. Overton County, Tenn., July 4, 1868; s. John A. and Sarah (Carlock) R.; A.B., Hiwassee Coll., Sweetwater, Tenn., 1889, A.M., 1892; m. Nora Deane Bowden, May 16, 1889. Teacher Alpine Inst., Nettle Carrier, Tenn., 5 yrs., and county supt. schs. 2 terms; practiced law in Overton County and adjoining counties, 1894-1910; chancellor 4th Jud. Div., Tenn., 1910-18; gov. of Tenn., 1919-21. Sr. mem. law firm Roberts & Roberts. Democrat. Mem. M.E. Ch., S. Mason, Odd Fellow. Office: Am. Trust Bldg., Nashville, Tenn.* Died June 25, 1946.

ROBERTS, Charles Wesley, surgeon; b. Nicholls, Ga., Dec. 13, 1883; s. John and Barbara Ellen (Denton) R.; grad. Southern Normal Inst., Douglas, Ga., 1902; M.D., U. of Md., 1906; m. Frances Blanche Purcell, June 5, 1909; 1 son, Charles Purcell. Resident surgeon, University Hosp., Baltimore, Md., 1906-08; engaged in gen. practice, Douglas, Ga., 1908-17; built and operated pvt. hosp., Douglas, 1909-16; in practice, Atlanta, Ga., since 1917; instr. surgery, Sch. of Medicine, Emory U., 1918-20, associate in surgery since 1920; attending surgeon Georgia Baptist, Crawford W. Long Memorial and Grady hosps. (Atlanta). Mem. advisory council Ga. State Bd. of Health. Med. adviser Industrial Commn. of Ga., 1921-38. Fellow Am. Coll. Surgeons, A.M.A. (mem. house of delegates 1925-28 and 1932-41; mem. council indsl. health 1937-41; elected mem. bd. trustees 1941), Southeastern Surg. Congress (pres. 1931), Am. Assn. Indsl. Phys. and Surg.; mem. Southern Med. Assn. (chmn. sect. indsl. medicine and surgery), 11th Dist. Med. Soc. of Ga. (pres. 1914), Chattahoochee Valley Med. Soc. (pres. 1930), Nu Sigma Nu. Mason (32°, Shriner), K.P. Club: Rush Medical (Baltimore). Recipient certificate of honor for excellence in examinations for degree in medicine, 1906. Home: 75 Ponce de Leon Av. N.E. Office: 26 Linden Av. N.E., Atlanta 3, Ga. Died July 29, 1947.

ROBERTS, Clarence, editor; b. Clarksville, Tenn., Oct. 18, 1890; s. Edwin Hightower and Julia Lowe (Harper) R.; B.S., Okla. Agrl. and Mech. Coll., 1915; m. Beulah Mae Mundy, June 30, 1917; children—Joseph Harper, Robert Mundy, Betty Lou, Donald Mundy. With The Farmer-Stockman since 1915, as asst. editor and associate editor to 1929, editor since 1929; dir. Federal Reserve Bank of Kansas City, Nat. Livestock Credit Corp.; partner Diamond Bar Ranch, Coal County, Okla. Dir. Okla. Crop Improvement Assn., Oklahoma City Chamber of Commerce. Served in R.O.T.C., Camp Pike, Ark., 1918. Democrat. Presbyterian. Club: Men's Dinner (Oklahoma City). Author: The Business of Farming, 1924. Contbr. to Daily Oklahoman. Guest member good will tour to South America, of Carnegie Endowment for Internat. Peace, 1941. Home: 801 N.E. 42d St. Office: Oklahoman Bldg., Oklahoma City, Okla. Died Dec. 4, 1942.

ROBERTS, George Evan, banker; b. Delaware County, Ia., Aug. 19, 1857; s. David and Mary (Harvey) R.; ed. common schs. of Ia.; learned the printer's trade; m. Georgena Kirkup, Nov. 10, 1885; children—George B., Amy L., Henry A. Proprietor Fort Dodge Messenger, 1878-1909; state printer of Iowa, 1883-89; dir. of Mint, 1898-1907, 1910-14; president Commercial Nat. Bank, Chicago, 1907-10; asst. to pres. Nat. City Bank of New York, 1914-19, vice pres., 1919-31, now econ. adviser. Mem. Gold Del. of Financial Com. of the League of Nations, 1930; 32. Author: Coin at School in Finance, 1895; Iowa and the Silver Question, 1896; Money, Wages and Prices, 1897; also numerous magazine articles and pamphlets upon economic subjects. Home: Larchmont, N.Y. Office: 55 Wall St., New York. Died June 7, 1948.

ROBERTS, Kate Louise, b. Lodi, N.J.; d. James and Jane (Chippendale) R.; grad. Normal Sch., Newark, N.J.; studied art and music in Berlin and Munich. Formerly with Pub. Library, N.Y. City; later reference librarian, Newark Pub. Library. Swedenborgian. Compiler: The Club Woman's Handybook of Programs and Club Management, 1914; Hoyt's New Cyclopedia of Practical Quotations, 1922, 27. Actively identified with ednl. and economic affairs. Home: 506 Meeker St., South Orange. N.J. Died Aug. 12, 1941.

ROBERTS, Kingsley, med. economist; b. New York, Dec. 29, 1893; s. George Watson and Emma (Robinson) R.; prep. edn. Fessendon Sch., West Newton, Mass., and Hill Sch., Pottstown, Pa.; Ph.B., Sheffield Scientific Sch. (Yale), 1914; M.D., Jefferson Med. Coll., Phila., 1920; m. Rowena Lawrence Staats, 1925; children—Eloise Staats (Mrs. Jere Baxter, 3d), Kingsley Roberts. Began as asst. surgeon Fifth Av. Hosp., 1921, later asso. surgeon; also asso. surgeon Post Grad. Hosp.; med. dir. Bureau of Cooperative Medicine, 1936-41; exec. dir. Med. Administration Service since 1941. Served in U.S.N.R.F., 1917-19. Fellow Am. Coll. Surgeons, N.Y. Acad. of Medicine; dir. Group Health Cooperative, Group Health Fedn. of Am.; mem. Am. Pub. Health Assn., Am. Hosp. Assn., Am. Pub. Welfare Assn., Acad of Polit. Science, Am. Acad. Polit. and Social Science, A.M.A., N.Y. State Med. Assn., N.Y. County Med. Assn. Contbr. on med. economics. Office: 1790 Broadway, New York 19, N.Y. Died Nov. 21, 1947.

ROBERTS, Percival, Jr.; b. Phila., Pa., July 15, 1857; s. Percival and Eleanor (Williamson) R.; A.B., Haverford Coll., 1876; post-grad. course, U. of Pa., 1877; m. Bessye Wolcott Frothingham, Nov. 11, 1885. Former dir. U.S. Steel Corp., Pa. R.R. Co. Mem. Am. Soc. C.E., Am. Soc. Mech. Engrs. Home: Narberth, Pa. Died Mar. 6, 1943.

ROBERTS, Thomas Sadler, physician, ornithologist; b. Phila., Pa., Feb. 16, 1858; s. John and Elizabeth Jane (Sadler) R.; moved to Minn., June 1867; U. of Minn., 1877-79; M.D., U. of Pa., 1885; D.Sc., U. of Minn., 1940; interne, Phila. Children's Hosp. and Phila. City Hosp.; m. Jane Cleveland, Oct. 19, 1887; children—Thomas Cleveland, Catherine Lyon, John Carroll; m. 2d, Mrs. Agnes Williams Harley, Oct. 9, 1937. Prof. pediatrics, 1901-06, clinical prof., 1906-13, emeritus prof. pediatrics since 1913, medical dept. U. of Minn.; prof. ornithology, Museum Natural History, U. of Minn. since 1915, also dir. Was 12 yrs. on staff St. Barnabas Hosp. and 6 yrs. chief of staff. Awarded Brewster gold medal for The Birds of Minnesota, by Am. Ornithologists Union, 1938. Fellow Am. Ornithologists' Union (past mem. council), A.A.A.S.; mem. Cooper Ornithol. Club, Wilson Ornithol. Club, Minn. Acad. Science (ex-pres.); corr. mem. Biol. Soc. Washington; mem. Minn. Acad. Medicine, County and State med. socs., A.M.A.; mem. Sigma Xi, Nu Sigma Nu, Alpha Omega Alpha. Clubs: Minneapolis, Automobile. Author: Birds of Minnesota (2 vols.); Bird Portraits in Color, 1936; Log-book of Minnesota Bird Life, 1938; Annals of Museum of Natural History (1872-1939), 1940. Home: 2303 Pleasant Av. Address: Minnesota Museum of Natural History, Univ. of Minn., Minneapolis, Minn. Died Apr. 19, 1946.

ROBERTS, Warren Russell, civil and mining engr.; b. Sadorus, Champaign Co., Ill., Oct. 20, 1863; s. Samuel Martin and Celestia Wood (Brayton) R.; B.S. in C.E., U. of Ill., 1888; m. Lucy C. Stewart, Oct. 7, 1891; children—Jerome G., Mary Brayton, Kathryn Stewart, Elizabeth Evans; m 2d, Jennie May Dean, 1907. Gen. engring. practice, 1888-92; engr. of bridges, Chicago, 1893-94; gen. engring., contracting, 1895-1903; pres. Roberts & Schaefer Co., engrs., contractors, 1904-39, chmn. bd. since 1939. Mem. Am. Soc. C.E., Am. Inst. Mining and Metall. Engrs., Am. Mining Congress, Western Soc. Engrs., Am. Forestry Assn., Am. Geog. Soc., Am. Legion (past post comdr.). Col. O.R.C., staff of Q.M. Gen. Democrat. Clubs: Chicago Illini; Army and Navy (Washington, D.C.). Home: Whitehall Hotel, 105 E. Delaware Pl. Office: 400 N. Michigan Av., Chicago. Died June 22, 1944.

ROBERTSON, Alexander George Morison, lawyer; b. Honolulu, T.H., Sept. 3, 1867; s. George M. and Sarah (Humphreys) R.; ed. pvt. sch., Honolulu, 1873-76, pub. sch., Oakland, Calif., 1877-79, pub. sch., Honolulu, 1880-82; accountant, Honolulu, 1883-90; LL.B., cum laude, Yale, 1893; m. Ululani McQuaid, May 29, 1907. Admitted to bar by Supreme Court of Hawaii, July 14, 1893, Supreme Court of U.S., Feb. 20, 1899, U.S. Circuit Court of Appeals, 9th Circuit, Oct. 31, 1902. Capt. Co. B, Honolulu Rifles, 1890; del. to Hawaiian Constl. Conv., 1894; on staff of gov. Republic of Hawaii, rank of capt., and judge-advocate Hawaiian Mil. Commn. for trial of state prisoners, 1895; deputy atty.-gen. Republic of Hawaii, 1895; mem. Hawaii Ho. of Rep., 1896, 1898, Ho. of Rep. Ty. of Hawaii, 1901; apptd. U.S. dist. judge, T.H., Jan. 25, 1910; apptd. chief justice Supreme Court, T.H., Mar. 7, 1911; resigned, Dec. 31, 1917, and resumed law practice; apptd. spl. asst. to Atty. Gen. as hearing officer for Hawaii, June 1941; mem. Equal Rights Commn. Del. Rep. Nat. Conv., Chicago, 1904, 08, 32, 36, Hawaii mem. Rep. Nat. Com., 1904-10. Pres. Bar Assn. of Hawaii, 1904-05. Episcopalian. Clubs: Pacific, Commercial. Home: 2429 Nuuanu Av., Honolulu, T.H. Died Aug. 21, 1947.

ROBERTSON, Ben, newspaperman; b. Clemson, S.C., June 22, 1903; s. Benjamin Franklin and Mary (Bowen) R.; B.S., Clemson Coll., 1923; B.J., U. of Mo., 1926; unmarried. On staff Honolulu Star-Bulletin, 1926-28; Adelaide (S. Australia) News, 1928; N.Y. Herald Tribune, 1929-34; corr. Asso. Press, Washington, D.C., and London, 1934-37; free lancing for Saturday Evening Post and other mags., 1937-40; London corr. for newspaper PM since 1940. Member Nat. Press Club (Washington, D.C.), Phi Delta Theta. Democrat. Baptist. Author: Travelers' Rest (novel), 1938; I Saw England, 1941. Contbr. Saturday Evening Post, Am. Mag., Asia, Travel, Scribner's. Home: Clemson, S.C. Office: Newspaper PM, New York, N.Y. Died Feb. 22, 1943.

ROBERTSON, Ella Broadus (Mrs. A. T. Robertson), author; b. Greenville, S.C., Apr. 19, 1872; d. John Albert and Charlotte Eleanor (Sinclair) Broadus; grad. Ky. Home School, Louisville, 1890; m. Archibald Thomas Robertson, D.D., Nov. 27, 1894 (died 1934); children—John Albert Broadus, Eleanor Martin (dec.), Charlotte Sinclair (dec.), Cary, Archibald Thomas. Baptist. Clubs: Query, Woman's of Louisville. Author: The Ministry of Women, 1922; Worship in the Home, 1922; The Fine Art of Motherhood, 1930; Half a Century (verse), 1938; These Things Remain, 1941; Along the Highway of Prayer, 1941; The Dark Valley, 1942. Editor: The Child's Bible, 1911. Address: 2945 Rainbow Drive, Cherokee Gardens, Louisville 6, Ky. Died Dec. 5, 1945.

ROBERTSON, H(arold) E(ugene), pathologist; b. Waseca, Minn., Oct. 8, 1878; s. James M. and Kate (Deuel) R.; A.B., Carleton Coll., Minn., 1899; M.D., U. of Pa., 1905; studied Columbia, 1900-01, U. of Berlin, 1914, U. of Freiburg, 1915; m. Edith Ellam, July 31, 1907. Instr. pathology, Albany Med. Coll., 1905-06; asst. pathologist Boston City Hosp., 1906-07; instr. pathology, Harvard, 1907 (resigned); instr. in pathology, U. of Minn., 1907, asst. prof. pathology and bacteriology, 1909, asso. prof., 1910, prof. pathology, 1914-21; also dir. dept. pathology, bacteriology and pub. health until 1921; prof. pathology, University of Minnesota Graduate School and head section pathologic anatomy, Mayo Clinic, 1921-43. Consultant, sect. pathologic anatomy, Mayo Clinic, since 1943 (Oct.) Commissioned maj. Med. O.R.C., June 20, 1917; sailed for France, July 26, 1917; served in laboratory div., A.E.F., 18 mos.; hon. discharged Jan. 28, 1919. Member American Association Pathologists and Bacteriologists, A.M.A., Am. Soc. of Clinical Pathologists, Assn. Military Surgeons of the U.S., Phi Beta Kappa, Sigma Xi, Alpha Omega Alpha, Nu Sigma Nu. Republican. Presbyterian. Club: University. Contributor of numerous articles on pathology of tetanus, pathology of poliomyelitis, etc. Col. Med. O.R.C. Home: Rochester, Minn. Died Mar. 8, 1946.

ROBERTSON, William Bryan, aviation exec.; b. Nashville, Tenn., Oct. 8, 1893; s. John Joseph and Myrtle (Harmon) R.; ed. pub. schs.; m. Marjorie Livingston, May 3, 1924; 1 son, James Livingston. Pres. Robertson Aircraft Corp., 1919-28; pres. and chmn. bd. Curtiss-Robertson Airplane Mfg. Co., 1928-30; v.p. Curtiss-Wright Airplane Co. and St. Louis Aviation Corp., 1930-33; now pres. Robertson Aircraft Corp. Was maj. Mo. N.G. A.S. and capt. Air Service, U.S. Army. Mem. Soc. Automotive Engrs., Quiet Birdmen of America, Inst. Aeronautical Sciences. Club: Bellerive Country. Was employer and backer of Charles A. Lindbergh. Home: Bridgeton, Mo. Office: Lambert Field, Robertson, Mo. Died Aug. 1, 1943.

ROBINS, Charles Russell, surgeon; b. Richmond, Va., Dec. 31, 1868; s. William Broaddus and Bessie (Mebane) R.; M.D., Med. Coll. of Va., 1894; studied Harvard University Medical School, summer 1895; married Evelyn Spotswood Berkeley, October 18, 1899; children—Francis Berkeley, Mrs. Dorothy Randolph Martin, Charles Russell, Jr. (M.D.), Mrs. Evelyn Berkeley Harrison, Mrs. Elizabeth Mebane Dowd, Alexander Spotswood (M.D.). Intern at U.S. Marine Hospital, Boston, 1893-95; assistant to Dr. George Ben Johnston, Richmond, 5 years; formerly member Drs. Robins and Geisinger; professor gynecology, Med. Coll. of Va., 1907-38, emeritus prof. since 1938; formerly chief surgeon of Virginia Hosp.; gynecologist Hosp. Div. Med. Coll. Va.; a founder and formerly mem. exec. com., sec., and treas. Memorial Hosp. Corporation; prin. work done at Stuart Circle Hosp., of which was an organizer and pres. many years; retired from practice, April 1, 1946; former dir. Broad St. Bank, State Planters Bank & Trust Co. Mem. Richmond Sch. Bd. 6 yrs. Served as 1st lt. and surgeon Richmond Light Inf. Blues, Va. State Militia, World War I; mem. Richmond Council of Defense; four-minute man. Chmn. Richmond Com. of Va. Hist. Commn.; mem. Southern Surg. Assn. (ex-v.p.), Tri State Med. Assn. of Va., N.C. and S.C., Founders Group Am. Bd. Surgery, Soc. of Colonial Wars (gov. for Va., 1940), S.R. (ex-pres. Va. Soc.), Society of the Cincinnati, Omega Upsilon Phi. Democrat. Baptist. Clubs: Old Westmoreland (mem. bd.), Commonwealth, Rotary (pres. 1928-29), Country of Virginia. Author: Notes on Obstetrics, 1895. Home: The Prestwould, 612 W. Franklin St., Richmond, Va. Died Oct. 16, 1948; buried Holly Wood Cemetery, Richmond, Va.

ROBINS, Edward, author; b. Pau, France, Mar. 2, 1862; s. Edward and Gertrude (Rodney-Fisher) R.; ed. Middletown, Conn., and mil. acad. Phila.; hon. A.M., U. of Pa., 1912; m. Emily Jewell Walton, Mar. 29, 1910. Began newspaper work, Kansas City, 1883; joined staff Philadelphia Public Ledger, 1884; asst. dramatic and music editor, 1888-94, dramatic and music editor, 1895-97, same paper; since then devoted to authorship. Pres. Hist. Soc. of Pa. and chmn. com. on library and collections; v.p. Geneol. Soc. Pa.; trustee Gilpin Library. Chmn. bd. Simon Gratz Collection MSS. Dir. Athenæum Phila., Welcome Soc. of Pa. Mem. Numismatic and Antiquarian Soc. of Pa., Phila. Soc. for Preservation of Landmarks; mem. adv. com. of Hist. and Patriotic Socs. for New York World's Fair, 1939. Author: Echoes of the Play House, 1895; Benjamin Franklin, 1898; The Palmy Days of Nance Oldfield, 1898; Twelve Great Actors, 1900; Twelve Great Actresses, 1900; Romances of Early America, 1902; Life of General Sherman, 1905. Juveniles: A Boy in Early Virginia; Chasing an Iron Horse; With Thomas in Tennessee; With Washington in Braddock's Campaign. Contbr. to newspapers and mags. on dramatic and hist. subjects. Address: Historical Society of Pa., 1300 Locust St., Philadelphia, Pa. Died May 21, 1943.

ROBINS, Henry Burke, theologian; b. Harlan, Ia., July 8, 1874; s. Charles McAlester and Rebecca Jane (Burke) R.; A.B., William Jewell Coll., Liberty, Mo., 1902, A.M., 1906; B.D., Rochester Theol. Sem., 1905; A.M., U. of Chicago, 1911, Ph.D., 1912; D.D., U. of Rochester, 1932; m. Mary Leone Crouch, June 6, 1905; 1 son, Henry Gordon. Ordained Bapt. ministry, 1898; pastor Oregon City, Ore., 1905-07; prof. systematic theology, Pacific Coast Bapt. Theol. Sem., 1907-10, 1912-13; prof. religious edn., and history and philosophy of religion, 1913-23, prof. history and philosophy of religion and missions, 1923-28, Rochester Theol. Sem.; prof. history and philosophy of religion, Colgate-Rochester Div. Sch., 1928-41, emeritus since 1941. Lecturer Divinity Sch., U. of Chicago, summer 1922; lecturer in religion, U. of Rochester, summer 1926, session 1926-27. Mem. bd. mgrs. Am. Baptist Foreign Mission Soc., 1919-39, pres. 1937-38; mem. bd. govs. West China Union Univ., 1923-39; trustee U. of Shanghai, 1921-39. Leave of absence, 1920-21, touring China, Japan and Philippines; touring India, 1928-29. Clubs: Alpha Chi, Theta Phi, Creighton Philos. Author: Aspects of Authority in the Christian Religion, 1911; The Basis of Assurance in Recent Protestant Theologies, 1912. Home: 840 Palm Dr., Orlando, Fla. Office: 1100 S. Goodman St., Rochester, N.Y. Died March 11, 1949.

ROBINS, Margaret Dreier (Mrs. Raymond Robins), social economist; b. Brooklyn; d. Theodor and Dorothea Dreier; ed. pvt. sch. and under tutors; L.H.D., Rollins Coll., Winter Park, Fla., 1931; m. Raymond Robins, June 21, 1905. A founder of Women's Municipal League, New York, chmn. legislative com., 1903-04; pres. N.Y. Assn. for Household Research, 1904-05; pres. N.Y. Women's Trade Union League, 1905, Chicago Women's Trade Union League, Jan. 1907-14, Nat. Women's Trade Union League, 1907-22; chmn. industrial com. of Ill. Fedn. of Women's Clubs, 1907-08; mem. exec. bd. Chicago Fedn. of Labor, 1908-17; mem. Com. on Industrial Edn., Am. Fedn. of Labor; mem. exec. com. Ill. sect. Am. Assn. for Labor Legislation. Mem. Am. Acad. Polit. and Social Science; served as mem. of Cook County Central Com. of the Progressive Party and mem. State Exec. Com. (Ill.). Apptd. by gov. mem. Unemployment Commn., 1915, and advisory com. Ill. State Free Employment Offices. Editor of Life and Labor. Dir. Training Sch. for Active Workers in the Labor Movement; mem. Leslie Suffrage Commn.; chmn. dept. of women and children in industry of Ill. Div. State and Nat. Councils Defense. Chmn. com. on women in industry League of Women Voters; mem. Rep. Nat. Exec. Com., woman's div., 1918-20; pres. First Internat. Congress of Working Women, Washington, Oct.-Nov. 1919, and elected pres. of permanent orgn., re-elected,

Geneva, Oct. 1921. Mem. com. to oppose Equal Rights Amendment, Nat. Women's Trade Union League of America, 1945. Convened 3d Internat. Congress of Working Women, in Schönbrunn Castle, Vienna, Austria, Aug. 1923; declined to stand for reëlection as pres. following European vote to convert the orgn. into a woman's dept. Internat. Fedn. of Trade Unions, hdqrs. Amsterdam; spl. del. apptd. by President Harding, to Pan Am. Congress of Women, Baltimore, 1922; hon. pres. Nat. Women's Trade Union League since 1922, also now chmn. Internat. Com. on America's Relations with the Orient, of Nat. Women's Trade Union League; elected mem. exec. bd. Nat. Woman's Trade Union League, fall of 1934, apptd. chmn. Regional Southern Com., same, 1937; vice convener of Standing Com. on Trades and Professions, of the Internat. Conf. of Women; mem. exec. com. Citizenship Conf., Washington, 1923, and of exec. com. to form a permanent nat. orgn. to continue work of Citizenship Conf., 1926; chmn. Am. Red Cross, Hernando County, Fla., Chapter since 1930, reëlected 1934; chmn. com. on edn. and the bookshop of Tamiami Trail, 1934-35; chmn. Women in Industry, Women's Div. Rep. Nat. Com., Herbert Hoover for President, 1928; mem. Women's Nat. Com. for Law Enforcement; mem. spl. com. demanding law enforcement in Presidential campaign of 1928; mem. Planning Com. by apptmt. of President Hoover, of White House Conf. on Child Health and Protection, 1929, also mem. of Continuing Com. of same; chmn. Com. on Unemployment, Hernando County Y.W.C.A.; trustee Fla. Bot. Garden and Arboretum Assn., Sebring, Fla.; pres. Hernando County (Fla.) Y.W.C.A.; mem. for Fla. of Nat. Advisory Com. for Women's Participation in the N.Y. World's Fair, 1938; mem. of exec. com. Conf. on Human Welfare, Birmingham, Ala., Nov., 1939; apptd. mem. Nat. Com. on The Mother's Declaration, 1939; Fla. State chmn. of finance, Women's Centennial Congress, 1940; mem. Fight for Freedom, Inc., Defense of America and All Aid to the Allies, Women's Com. for Action (all N.Y. City), 1940-41; mem. Hernando County Defense Com. Mem. N.Y. Bot. Society, Fla. Audubon Soc., Fla. State Bot. Soc., Bot. Soc. of S. Africa, Am. and Fla. rose socs., Fla. Social Service Conf., Fla. Hist. Soc. Mem. Nat. Com. World Fellowship of Faiths, also of Nat. Com. Religion and Welfare Recovery, Nat. Wild Life Fedn., Nat. Audubon Soc. Conglist. Clubs: Cosmopolitan; Woman's City (New York); Woman's City (Chicago). Vice-pres. First Nat. Bank, Brooksville, Fla. Home: Chinsegut Hill Sanctuary, Hernando County (P.O. Brooksville), Fla. Address: care National Women's Trade Union League, Machinists' Bldg., 9th St. and Mt. Vernon Pl., Washington, D.C. Died Feb. 21, 1945; buried under Altar Oak on grounds of Chinsegut Hill, Brooksville, Fla.

ROBINS, Reuben William, asso. justice, Supreme Court, Ark.; b. Conway, Ark., May 21, 1883; s. John William and Amelia (Freeman) R.; student Hendrix Coll., Conway, Ark., 1894-97, U. of Ark., Law Sch., 1903-04; m. Harriet Beatrice Powell, July 30, 1909; children—Beatrice, Virginia (Mrs. Roger Quarles Mills). Private practice, Conway, Ark., 1904-42; deputy prosecuting atty., 1906-07; asso. justice Supreme Court of Ark. since 1942. Home: 508 Locust Av., Conway, Ark. Office: State Capitol Bldg., Little Rock, Ark. Died June 30, 1949.

ROBINSON, Allan; b. Troy, N.Y., Mar. 31, 1868; s. Charles E. and Clara (Vaill) R.; A.B., Yale, 1891; LL.B., Columbia, 1894; m. Jean de Forest Knox Barbour; children—Edward, Jane Knox. Practiced law, 1894-1902; sec. to immigration commr. N.Y., 1902-05; pres. Allied Real Estate Interests, 1906-14; pres. City and Suburban Homes Co., 1915-22; pres. Commonwealth Bond Corp., 1922-28. Mem. N.Y. State Commn. to investigate Torrens system of title registration, 1908; mem. Municipal Commn. on Congestion of Population, 1909; chmn. N.Y. City Com. of Assn. to Prevent Corrupt Practices at Elections, 1909-11; chmn. N.Y. City Charter Conf., 1911; chmn. Citizens' Police Com. apptd. at Cooper Union Mass Meeting, 1912; chmn. spl. bldg. heights com. which established "set back" principle for N.Y. City bldgs., 1913; treas. Nat. Citizens' Com. on Russian Treaty Abrogation, 1911-12; chmn. Mayor's Com. on Building Inspection, 1914; chmn. Citizens' Com. on New York City's Financial Condition, 1915; chmn. Citizens' Com. for Support of Locked-Out Cloak and Suit Makers, 1916. Pres. Mendelssohn Glee Club, 1900-06 and 1927-36; pres. Schola Cantorum, 1912-13; pres. MacDowell Memorial Assn., Peterboro, N.H., 1911-13; dir. and mem. exec. com. Philharmonic Soc. of N.Y., 1912-13, etc.; retired 1928. Gen. mgr. in charge of munition and shipyard housing developments of the U.S. Housing Corp., 1918. Republican. Home: Washington, Conn. Died May 25, 1944.

ROBINSON, Annie Douglas Green ("Marion Douglas"), author; b. Plymouth, N.H., Jan. 12, 1842; d. William and Harriet (Kimball) Green; ed. mostly at private schools. All writings appeared under her pen name. Author: Peter and Polly, 1876; Picture Poems for Young Folks, 1882; In the Poverty Year, 1901; Days We Remember, 1903; etc. Address: Bristol, N. H. Died 1913.

ROBINSON, Benjamin Willard, educator; b. Phila., Pa., May 29, 1883; s. Willard Haskell and Ella (Moore) R.; A.B., U. of Chicago, 1901, Ph.D., 1904; Ph.D., Columbia, 1906; B.D., Union Theol. Sem., 1907; fellow Am. Sch., Jerusalem, 1907-08; studied U. of Berlin, 1908-09; m. 2d, Violet F. Adams, May 28, 1938; 1 dau., Margaret Fleming. Ordained, 1909; instr. N.T. literature and interpretation, Chicago Theol. Sem., 1909, asso. prof., 1910, prof. since 1914. Conglist. Clubs: Quadrangle, University, Irving. Author: Forcefulness in Jesus' Comparisons, 1904; Imagery in Deutero-Isaiah, 1906; The Life of Paul, 1918, enlarged edit., 1928; The Gospel of John, 1925; Commentary on First Peter, 1929; The Sayings of Jesus, 1930: Jesus in Action, 1942. Address: 5757 University Av., Chicago, Ill. Died May 22, 1942.

ROBINSON, Bill, dancer, actor; b. Richmond, Va., May 25, 1878; son Maxwell and Maria R.; educated pub. sch., Richmond; m. Elaine Plaines, Jan., 1944. Dancer; vaudeville actor; introduced stair dancing to vaudeville; instructor Master Dancers, New York; appeared in musical comedies, "Brown Buddies" and "Blackbirds of 1927"; in motion pictures, "Little Colonel," "In Old Kentucky," "Hooray for Love," "Big Broadcast of 1935," "One Mile from Heaven," "Rebecca of Sunnybrook Farm," 1937, "Just Around the Corner," "Up the River," 1938; played in "Hot Mikado," New York World's Fair, 1939. Won 1st prize for dancing at Nat. Dancing Contests, 1928, 29, 30, 31. Made "Mayor of Harlem" by League of Locality Mayors, 1934. Served in Spanish-Am. War and World War. Hon. mem. Dancing Masters Assn., Grand Street Boys of New York, N.J. State Police Dept. Democrat. Elk. Mem. Appommattox Club. Catholic. Home: 2588 7th Av., New York, N.Y.; also 1194 W. 36th Place, Los Angeles, Calif. Address: 1564 Broadway, New York, N.Y. Died Nov. 25, 1949.

ROBINSON, Chalfant, univ. prof.; b. Cincinnati, Mar. 14, 1871; s. William Adin and Elizabeth Jane (Page) R.; grad. U. of Cincinnati, 1893; student univs. of Berlin and Freiburg, 1900-01; Ph.D., Yale, 1902; m. Anne Shaw Hamilton, May 29, 1900; children—Agnes Elizabeth (dec.), Hamilton. Lecturer on history, Yale, 1902-03, Mt. Holyoke Coll., 1903-04; asso. prof. history, Smith Coll., 1905; asst. prof. history, Yale, 1910-14; visiting prof. mediæval history, 1914-15, curator mediæval manuscripts since 1920, Princeton U. Fellow Royal Hist. Soc.; hon. mem. Institut Historique et Heraldique (France); mem. Pipe Roll Soc. Republican. Clubs: Century, Yale (New York); Graduate (New Haven); Nassau (Princeton); Royal Soc. Club (London); Union Interalliée (Paris). Author: The History of Two Reciprocity Treaties, 1904; Continental Europe (1270-1598), 1916; The Great Roll of the Pipe, 1927; The Case of King Louis XI of France and Other Essays in Mediæval History, 1929; Memoranda Roll of the King's Remembrancer 1230-1, 1933. Also hist. monographs. Home: Princeton, N.J. Died Dec. 31, 1946.

ROBINSON, Dwight Nelson, univ. prof.; b. Winchester, Mass., Sept. 17, 1886; s. Edwin and Mary Bradford (Dodge) R.; A.B., Harvard, 1908, A.M., 1909, Ph.D., 1911. Instr. in Latin and Greek, Yale, 1911-16; asso. prof. Greek and Latin, Ohio Wesleyan U., 1916-18, prof. since 1918; asso. editor Classical Journal since 1935. Served in U.S.N.R.F., May-Dec. 1918. Mem. Latin Club of Columbus pres. 1931-32). Classical Assn. of Middle West and South (vice-pres. for Ohio 1932-40), Ohio Classical Conf. (pres. 1927-28), Am. Classical League, Am. Philol. Assn., Phi Kappa Epsilon, Omicron Delta Kappa, Phi Beta Kappa. Presbyterian. Clubs: Harvard (Boston); Harvard (Central Ohio), Singing Quill, Presbyn Poetry Soc. of Ohio. Author: Plays and Songs for Latin Clubs, 1921; Cleopatra and Other Latin Plays and Songs, 1924; Narcissus and Other Latin Plays, 1928; Vergilius and Other Latin Plays, 1937. Died Oct. 30, 1941.

ROBINSON, Edward Levi, banker; b. Lancaster County, nr. Kilmarnock, Va., May 3, 1864; s. Edwin Orem and Martha (Cox) R.; grad. Baltimore (Md.) City Coll., 1881; m. Hester Myra Dodson, Oct. 21, 1890 (died Nov. 1, 1930); m. 2d, Elizabeth Cheever Blaser, Apr. 28, 1933. Served en entry clerk in wholesale drug house, Baltimore, 1881-82; then connected with Drovers & Mechanics Nat. Bank, 1882-89; asst. paying teller, Eutaw Savings Bank, 1889-1905, v.p., 1905-19, pres. since 1927; v.p. Citizens Nat. Bank, Baltimore, 1918-27; dir. 1st Nat. Bank (Baltimore), Md. Casualty Co. Trustee Goucher Coll. (Baltimore) Y.M.C.A. Mem. Am. Bankers Assn. (pres. savings bank sect., 1910-11). Democrat. Baptist. Club: University. Home: 501 Overhill Rd., Roland Park. Office: Eutaw Savings Bank, Baltimore, Md. Died Jan. 15, 1943

ROBINSON, Edwin Meade ("Ted"), author; b. Lima (now Howe), Ind., Nov. 1, 1878; s. William Edwin and Alice Maude (Drake) R.; grad. Howe Sch., Lima, 1894; A.B., Wabash College, Crawfordsville, Ind., 1909, Litt.D., 1927; m. Martha Coon, Mar. 27, 1909. Instr. English high sch. Attica, Ind., 1901-02; staff corr. Indianapolis Sentinel, 1902; chief editorial writer same, 1903; editorial writer Indianapolis Jour., 1904; column conductor Cleveland Leader, 1905-10; column conductor and asso. editor Cleveland Plain Dealer since 1910, also lit. editor since 1922. Lecturer in philology, Cleveland Coll., 1926-42. Member Am. Press Humorists (pres. 1914), Am. Dialect Soc., Phi Kappa Psi. Clubs: City (pres. 1931-32), Playhouse Rowfant (pres. 1936-37), Rhymers' (Cleveland); Beachcombers' (Provincetown, Mass., hon. pres. since 1940). Author: The First Born, 1899; Mere Melodies, 1918; Piping and Panning, 1920; Enter Jerry, 1921; Life, Love and the Weather, 1945. Home: 1980 Ford Dr. Office: The Plain Dealer, Cleveland 14, O. Died Sep. 20, 1946.

ROBINSON, Ernest Franklin, surgeon; b. Lawrence, Kan., Feb. 13, 1872; s. David Hamilton and Henrietta (Beach) R.; B.A., U. of Kan., 1893; M.D., U. of Pa., 1896; m. Mary Kip, Feb. 6, 1904 (died 1923); children—Ernest Kip, Mary Clementine (Mrs. Fred Chase Koch), William Ingraham; m. 2d, Ruby Shellabarger, Apr. 9, 1927. Interne Philadelphia Emergency Hosp. and Boston Emergency Hosp., 1896-98; removed to Kansas City, Mo., 1901; surgeon, C.,B.&Q. R.R. and prof. surgery, Med. Dept. U. of Kan., 1901-09; chief surgeon Kansas City Terminal R.R., 1903-15; surgeon Kansas City Gen. Hosp., 1908-16; mem. and pres. Mo. State Bd. of Health, 1909-14; now surgeon St. Luke's Hosp., Research Hosps.; med. dir. Business Men's Assurance Co. Served in Spanish-Am. War, asst. surgeon U.S. Army, Philippine Islands, 1898-1900; maj. surgeon U.S. Army, World War. Fellow Am. Coll., Surgeons; mem. Mo. State Med. Assn., Jackson County Med. Soc., Acad. of Medicine, William Pepper Med. Soc., Phi Kappa Psi, Phi Alpha Sigma. Republican. Episcopalian. Clubs: University, Kansas City Country. Home: 5021 Sunset Drive. Address: Professional Bldg., Kansas City, Mo. Deceased.

ROBINSON, Frank Wisner, ry. official; b. Cherryville, Kan., May 22, 1874. With Union Pacific R.R. since 1889, v.p. since 1927. Address: Union Pacific Railroad, Omaha, Neb.* Died Dec. 10, 1948.

ROBINSON, George Thomas, coal operator; b. in Eng., Feb. 23, 1868; s. William and Mary Ann (Hadley) R.; came to U.S., 1882; ed. common schs., night schs. and corr. sch.; m. Laura Adelia Barry, Aug. 4, 1892; 1 son, Earle Barry. Began with Cambria Steel Co. (now Bethlehem Steel Co.), 1891, and was made supt. mines same co., 1901; entered business for self, 1912, after having organized the Valley Coal Co., Central Coal Co., Citizens Coal Co., Dixonville Coal Co., and other coal companies; now pres. Cambria-Stafford Coal Co., Robinson Motor Co., Dixonville Coal Co., Citizens Coal Co.; sec.-treas. Johnstown Retail Coal Producers' Assn.; v.p. and dir. Johnstown Finance & Loan Co. With U.S. Fuel Adminstrn., 1917-19. Mem. bd. dirs. Conemaugh Valley Memorial Hosp. (chmn. finance com.), Johnstown Y.M.C.A.; dir. Johnstown Salvation Army. Mem. Central Pa. Coal Producers' Assn., Johnstown Chamber Commerce (ex-pres.), Pa. Soc. of New York. Republican. Methodist. Mason, K.P. Clubs: Rotary (ex-president), Sunnehama Country. Home: 143 Greene St. Office: United States Bank Bldg., Johnstown, Pa.* Died Dec. 20, 1944.

ROBINSON, George William, retired telephone and telegraph official; b. Thomaston, Me., August 16, 1866; s. Edward Warren and Harriet Maria (Watts) R.; ed. pub. schs.; m. Lavicia T. Brandt, May 22, 1889; 1 son, Donald Brandt. Asst. sec. Union Investment Co., Kansas City, Mo., 1886-1891; banking and grain business, Kansas City, 1891-1901; treas. C. D. Gregg Tea & Coffee Co., St. Louis, Mo., 1901-04; became connected with Tri-State Telephone & Telegraph Co., St. Paul, 1904, pres., 1914-31 (retired); dir. Minn. Mutual Life Ins. Co., Northern Fed. Savings and Loan Assn. Republican. Conglist. Clubs: Minnesota, St. Paul Athletic, Town and Country, Somerset Country. Home: 2265 Summit Av. Office: Minnesota Bldg., St. Paul, Minn.* Died 1947.

ROBINSON, Harrison Sidney, lawyer; b. San Francisco, July 13, 1877; s. Sidney Milo and Sarah Elizabeth (Christy) R.; B.L., U. of Calif., 1900; student law same university; married; children—Marcia Elizabeth, Harrison Sidney, Jr. Admitted to California bar, 1902, and since practiced in Oakland; sr. partner Robinson, Price & Macdonald; chmn. bd. Wesco Waterpaints, Inc.; Franklin Land Co.; dir. and chmn. exec. com. Oakland Title Ins. & Guaranty Co., Marchant Calculating Machine Co.; dir. and treas. Coast Mfg. & Supply Co.; dir. Hale Brothers Stores, Inc., Weinstock-Lubin & Co., Inc., Calif. Pacific Title & Trust Co. Pres. Oakland Civil Service Bd., 1911-15; mem. or pres. Alameda County Instns. Commn., 1917-33; mem. Calif. State Chamber of Commerce (pres. 1944-46, dir. since 1927), Oakland Chamber of Commerce (pres. 1923), Oakland Major Highways and Traffic Committee (chairman 1927-30), Impartial Wage Bd. of San Francisco Bay Dist., 1928-29, San Francisco-Oakland Bay Bridge Financial Committee (chairman 1932-37). Member American and Alameda County bar. assns., State Bar of Calif., Phi Beta Kappa. Address: Financial Center Bldg., Oakland, Calif.; or 275 Bush St., San Francisco, Calif. Died Nov. 29, 1947.

ROBINSON, Harry Charles, paper; b. Royalton, O., Nov. 6, 1869; s. Charles and Maria (Bark) R.; B.S., Ohio Wesleyan U., 1891; m. Josephine Crawford, Nov. 1, 1900. Reporter Cleveland Press, 1892; admitted to Ohio bar, 1893, and practiced 2 yrs.; engaged in mfg. at Cleveland, 1895, 1904; with the Guardian Trust Co., 1904-33, the last 15 yrs. as exec. v.p.; dir. and v.p. Inland Investors, Inc.; dir. Farval Corp., Hampden Corporation, Cleveland Worm and Gear Company, Hinde and Dauch Paper Co., Industrial Sites Co. Member Board of Education Sinking Fund Commission of City of Cleveland; member President Hoover's Home Loan Conference Committee, 1932. Member Phi Delta Theta. Republican. Home: 13901 Shaker Blvd., Cleveland, Ohio. Deceased.

ROBINSON, James Dixon, banking; b. Monticello, Ga., Oct. 30, 1871; s. Augustus Marcellus and Jennie (Maddux) R.; ed. public schools, Atlanta, Ga., and mil. and private schools; m. Emily English, June 1, 1899. Began with A. M. Robinson Co., merchant and mfr., Atlanta, 1890, succeeding his father as pres., 1901-29; v.p. Fourth Nat. Bank, Atlanta, 1918-29; v.p. First Nat. Bank, Atlanta, 1929-37, pres. since 1937; dir. Ga. Power Co., Atlantic Co., Md. Casualty

Co. Methodist. Mason. Clubs: Capital City, Piedmont Driving, Atlantic Athletic; Jekyl Island, Jekyl Island Golf; Augusta National Golf. Home: 1328 Ponce de Leon Av. Office: First National Bank, Atlanta, Ga. Died Feb. 3, 1948.

ROBINSON, John W., bishop; b. Moulton, Ia., Jan. 6, 1866, s. Thomas J. and Julia (Swartz) R.; grad. Harlan (Ia.) High Sch., 1884; grad. Garrett Bibl. Inst., Evanston, Ill., 1892, B.D., 1897, D.D., 1912; m. Elizabeth Fisher, 1891 (dec.); children—Paul Fisher (dec.), Ruth (wife of Bishop J. W. Pickett), Miriam (Mrs. J. W. Hedenberg). Entered M.E. ministry, Des Moines Conf., 1890; transferred as missionary to N. India Conf., 1892; first stationed at Lucknow as pastor English-speaking work, continuing there twenty years, successively as agt. Meth. Pub. House, in the vernacular city and sch. work, and supt. Oudh dist.; also for 8 yrs. editor Kaukab-i-Hind, vernacular official organ of the mission; sec. exec. bd. M.E. Ch. in Southern Asia, 1904-12; elected missionary bishop M.E. Ch. for Southern Asia (including Beluchistan, India, Burma, Malaysia, Netherlands Indies, and P.I.), May 24, 1912; elected bishop M.E. Ch., 1920. Retired, 1936. Editor Indian Witness, 1937-38; in 1939 reappointed to episcopal work, and placed in charge of the Lucknow Area of the recently united Meth. Ch., resigned, 1941; elected agent Meth. Pub. House, Lucknow, 1941; retired, 1942; supt. of Delhi Dist. of Meth. Ch., 1945. Compiled Spiritual Songs, Indian Hymnal, Git hi Kitab; edited Book of Discipline of M.E. Ch. in Southern Asia. Address: 37 Cantonment Rd., Lucknow, India. Died May 30, 1947.

ROBINSON, Joseph, prof. English; b. Potsdam, N.Y., Sept. 3, 1874; s. Joseph and Mary Jane (Wooster) R.; A.B., U. of S.D., 1898, A.M., 1899, Harvard, 1905; m. Marietta Fine, July 12, 1917. Teacher high schs., S.D., 1899-1904; prof. English, Franklin (Ind.) Coll., 1905-07, Carson-Newman Coll.; Jefferson City, Tenn., 1907-18, Mercer U. since 1918; teacher summer sch., Appalachian State Teachers Coll., Boone, N.C., 1930-31. Writer Sunday column Macon Telegraph. Mem. Ga. Ednl. Assn., Phi Beta Kappa. Democrat. Baptist. Home: 503 Adams St., Macon, Ga. Died Jan. 1943.

ROBINSON, Julia Almira, librarian; b. Dubuque, Ia.; d. Wilbur Emory and Almira (Norris) Robinson; grad. Wis. Library Sch., 1909; unmarried. Asst. Carnegie Library, Dubuque, Ia., 1907-08; acting sec. N.Dak. Library Commn., Bismarck, N.D., 1909-10; acting sec. Ky. Library Commn., Frankfort, Ky., 1910-11; asst. same, July-Dec. 1911; supervising librarian State Instns. of Ia., under Bd. of Control, 1912-13; sec. Iowa Library Commn., 1913-38; retired, Sept. 1938. Custodian State Federation of Women's Clubs. Mem. Am. Library Assn., Iowa Library Assn., Ia. Social Workers, Wis. Library Sch. Alumni Assn., Votes for Women League, D.A.R. Clubs: Des Moines Woman's, Professional Woman's League, Des Moines Library, Iowa Press and Authors, Woman's City Club of Des Moines. Editor Ia. Library Quarterly. Address: 1004 Magnolia Av., Ontario, Calif. Died May 17, 1942.

ROBINSON, Leonard George, banker, lawyer; b. Russia, Mar. 11, 1875; came to U.S., 1890; A.B., Harvard U., 1902; LL.B., New York Law School, 1906; m. Betty F. Levey, Jan. 10, 1911 (divorced); 1 son, Leonard G. Was gen. mgr. of Jewish Agrl. Soc., New York (Baron de Hirsch Foundation), 1907-17; founder of pioneer agrl. credit unions in America; pioneer in farm credits movement. Cons. expert Joint Congressional Com. on Rural Credits which framed the Federal Farm Loan Act, of 1916; organized Federal Land Bank of 1st Dist. (Springfield, Mass.), 1917, pres., 1917-19; pres. Cosmopolitan Bank, New York, 1919-21. Gen. dir. of reconstruction in Europe for Am. Joint Distribution Com., operating in 10 countries—Austria, Czechoslovakia, Esthonia, Greece, Hungary, Latvia, Lithuania, Poland, Roumania, Turkey—with hdqrs. in Vienna, 1922-24; organized credit systems, including nearly 500 coöperative banks and other coöperative enterprises, and rebuilt over 8,000 war-destroyed homes in countries named; legal dept., Farm Credit Administration, Washington, D.C., 1933-41. Clubs: Harvard (New York). Author: Agricultural Activities of the Jews in America. Contbr. many articles to agrl., financial, economic, and other periodicals. Co-Author: Credit Union Primer. For many years consulting financial editor New York Times and Philadelphia Public Ledger. Address: Cosmos Club, Washington, D.C. Deceased.

ROBINSON, Maurice Henry, economist; b. in New Hampshire; s. Joseph Wadleigh and Frances Eliza (Weld) R.; B.L., Dartmouth, 1890, A.M., 1897; Ph.D., Yale, 1902; m. Elinor Corse, Sept. 10, 1890; 1 dau., Florence Elinor (Mrs. Frank W. Asper, dec.). Supt. city schs., N.Dak. and Minn., 1890-96; asst. in polit. science, Dartmouth, 1896-98; fellow in economics, 1898-99, instr. economics, 1899-1902, Yale; prof. economics, U. of Ill., 1902-33, emeritus; prof. economics, summers, Cornell, 1909, Columbia, 1914, U. of Calif., 1923, U. of Tex., 1926. Asso. editor Jour. of Accountancy, 1906-15. Spl. expert agt. of the Census Bur., 1903, in valuation of rys.; expert on corps. and ins., State of Ill. Efficiency and Economy Com., 1914-15. Mem. Am. Econ. Assn. (exec. com. 1919-22), American Association University Professors, Alpha Kappa Psi, Delta Kappa Epsilon, Phi Beta Kappa, Beta Gamma Sigma. Episcopalian. Clubs: University (ex-pres, Urbana); University (Winter Park, Florida). Author: A History of Taxation in New Hampshire, 1902; Business Organization, 1909; Organizing a Business, 1915; also articles pertaining to rys. and corps. and accounting. Coöperating author of American Securities Service Manuals and La Salle Extension Univ. books on business management. Address: Pine Orchard, Conn. Died Feb. 28, 1946.

ROBINSON, Millard Lyman, clergyman; b. Westfield, Mass., July 28, 1880; s. Lucius M. and Melinda J. (Bracken) R., student Westfield State Normal Sch., 1900, Monson Acad., 1901; A.B., Boston U., 1905, Ph.D., 1915; S.T.B., Boston U. Sch. of Theology, 1907; m. Marion L. Bean, Oct. 6, 1906 (died Jan. 26, 1911); 1 dau., Ruth Louise (Mrs. John C. Bancroft); m. 2d, Edna W. Stitt, Feb. 5, 1914. Entered ministry of the Meth. Episcopal Ch., 1906; pastor First Ch., Manchester, N.H., 1906-07; religious work dir. Y.M.C.A., Phila., 1908; asso. pastor Hanson Pl., New York, 1909-10; pastor 17th St. and 11th St. chs., until 1914; gen. sec. N.Y. City Soc. M.E. Ch., 1914-30; gen. sec. New York Bible Society since 1930; trustee New York Hist. Society. Member bd. dirs. N.Y. Fedn. Chs. Mem. S. R. (chaplain), Theta Delta Chi. Republican. Mason. Clubs: Union League, National Republican, Clergy, Quill. Wrote (brochures): The Case for Old New York, 1923; The Service of the New York City Society to New York Methodism, 1924. Home: 316 W. 79th St. Office: 5 E. 48th St., New York, N.Y. Died Apr. 23, 1947.

ROBINSON, Noel, pres. South Penn Oil Co.; b. Sewickley, Pa., Dec. 25, 1892; s. Alexander Cochran and Emma (Jones) W.; ed. Hill Sch., 1908-12; Litt. B., Princeton, 1916; m. Susan Marche, Aug. 12, 1938; children—William Benson, Polly Shipboy (Mrs. Robert Wilson Reniers). Clerk Nat. Bank of Commerce, N.Y. City, 1916-17; with Tide Water Oil Co., N.Y. City, 1917-28; vice-pres. in charge mfg. and dir., 1928-36; vice-pres. and dir. Tide Water Asso. Oil Co., 1936-40; vice-pres. South Penn Oil Co., 1940-42, pres. since 1942, dir. since 1940; pres. and dir. South Penn Nat. Gas Co.; dir. Peoples-Pittsburgh Trust Co., Pittsburgh, Pa. Home: Backbone Rd., Sewickley Heights, Pa. Address: Chamber of Commerce Bldg., Pittsburgh, Pa. Died July 16, 1944.

ROBINSON, R(oscoe) R., coll. pres.; b. Cambridge, O., June 19, 1885; s. William Brook and Mary Jane (Grear) R.; A.B., Lebanon U., 1911, Ph.B., 1911, M.A., U. of Okla., 1918; Ph.D., Peabody Coll., 1928; m. Tennie Ross, Dec. 27, 1927; children—Pauline (wife of Major Pratt Irby), Roscoe Ross, Lucy Jane. Teacher, rural, 1904-08; prin. Perry High, 1911-13, supt., 1913-17; in dept. edn. E. Central State Teachers Coll., Ada, Okla., 1918-21, head dept., and dir. training school, 1921-25, dean, 1926-28, acting pres., 1927-28; pres. Univ. Prep. Sch. and Jr. Coll, Tonkawa, Okla., 1928-39; pres. Central State Coll. since 1939. Mem. Phi Delta Kappa, Delta Kappa Phi. Methodist. Democrat. Clubs: Kiwanis, Lions. Mason (32°). Author: Two Centuries of Content in School Readers, 1928. Home: 400 E. Hurd, Edmond, Okla. Died Oct. 1, 1948.

ROBINSON, Samuel, surgeon; b. Augusta, Me., Feb. 23, 1877; s. Daniel C. and Mary Eliza (Lambard) R.; A.B., Harvard, 1898, M.D., 1902; m. Ellen D. Bellows, Apr. 1905 (divorced 1923); children—Anne Peabody, Thomas L., Katharine L.; m. 2d, Ida Gordon Fiske, Feb. 1924. Began practice at Boston, 1902; formerly mem. visiting staff Mass. Gen. Hosp.; mem. permanent staff Mayo Clinic, Rochester, Minn., 1914-18; chief of surg. service Letterman Gen. Hosp., San Francisco, 1917-18; now mem. surg. staff Santa Barbara Cottage Hosp., Gen. Hosp., St. Francis Hosp., all Santa Barbara, Calif. Fellow Am. Bd. Surgery, Am. Coll. Surgeons, A.M.A.; mem. Am. Assn. Thoracic Surgery (ex-pres.), Pacific Coast Surg. Assn. Republican. Episcopalian. Clubs: Santa Barbara, Montecito Valley. Home: Pepper Lane, Montecito, Santa Barbara. Office: 22 W. Micheltorena St., Santa Barbara, Calif. Died Sept. 17, 1947; buried Santa Barbara, Calif.

ROBINSON, Sanford, lawyer; b. North Adams, Mass., July 8, 1873; s. Arthur and Clara (Sanford) R.; prep. edn., Drury Acad., North Adams; A.B., Williams Coll., 1896; LL.B., Harvard, 1900; m. Ruth Edson, April 10, 1909 (she died June 22, 1935); children—Virginia (Mrs. Gordon W. Abbott), Priscilla (Mrs. Hervey Thompson), Jane (Mrs. Colby M. Chester, 3d), Ruth, Sanford. Admitted to Mass. bar, 1900, N.Y. bar, 1901, U.S. Supreme Court, 1907, D.C. bar, 1923; began law practice with Lincoln & Badger, Boston, 1900; with Cary & Whitridge, N.Y. City, 1901-05; mem. firm Cary & Robinson, N.Y. City, 1905-09, Robinson & Henson since 1932. Counsel for bond-holding creditors in suit of Va. vs. W.Va., 1906-19; counsel for Eastern Group Carriers in Federal valuation of rys. of U.S., 1914-30. Mem. Greenwich (Conn.) Chamber of Commerce, Am. Bar Assn., Delta Kappa Epsilon. Republican. Conglist. Clubs: Williams, Down Town, Bankers (New York); Ekwanok Country (Manchester, Vt.); Taconic Golf (Williamstown, Mass.). Author: John Bascom, Prophet, 1922. Home: Greenwich, Conn.; (summer) Cabins in the Hopper, Williamstown, Mass. Office: 120 Broadway, New York, N.Y. Died Sep. 18, 1942.

ROBINSON, Theodore Winthrop, mfr.; b. Boston, Mass., June 7, 1862; s. Theodore and Susannah Snelling (Powell) R.; S.B., Mass. Inst. Tech., 1884; m. Frances Steel, June 3, 1891; children—Edgar Steel (dec.), Mrs. Frances Boardman, Sanger Powell, Theodore Winthrop. V.p. Ill. Steel Co. until 1932; chmn. Ditto, Inc.; dir. City Nat. Bank & Trust Co., Ill. Bell Telephone Co. Mem. commn. to reorganize finances of Dominican Republic, 1929. Term mem. Corp. of Mass. Inst. Technology, 1909-14; trustee Northwestern U., also of Museum of Science and Industry, John Crerar Library, Passavant Memorial Hosp. Mem. Am. Iron and Steel Inst., Am. Inst. Mining and Metall. Engrs., Iron and Steel Inst., Great Britain. Clubs: Chicago, University, Mid-Day, Commercial, Shoreacres, Old Elm, Casino, Wild Wing Lodge, Coleman Lake. Home: Lake Forest, Ill. Office: 208 S. La Salle St., Chicago Ill. Died Dec. 30, 1948.

ROBINSON, Victor, medical historian, editor; b. The Ukraine, Russia, Aug. 16, 1886; s. William J. (M.D.) and Marie (Halper) R.; brought to America in infancy; student N.Y. Univ. Law Sch., 1906-08; Ph.G., N.Y. Coll. of Pharmacy, 1910; Ph.C., Columbia U., 1911; M.D., Chicago Coll. Medicine and Surgery (now Loyola U.), 1917. Since 1909 a contributor to med. history. Prof. history of medicine, Temple U. Sch. of Medicine, Phila., since 1929; lecturer on History of Nursing, Temple U. Sch. of Nursing, since 1937. Founding mem. History of Science Society, 1924; official del. Internat. Congress of the History of Medicine, Leyden-Amsterdam, Holland, 1927; council mem. Am. Assn. of the History of Medicine, 1939-41; president New York Society for Medical History, 1940-41. Fellow of the New York Academy of Medicine (chmn., Sect. on Hist. and Cultural Medicine, 1944-45); mem. Inst. Aeronautical Sciences. Editor of Historia Medicinæ (30 volumes), Medical Review of Reviews, Medical Life (only monthly jour. of med. history in English lang.), The Modern Home Physician, 1934-39. Am. edit. of Paolo Mantegazza, 1935-36, and Krafft-Ebing, 1939, Ency. Sexualis (with contributions by 100 scholars), 1936, The New People's Physician (8 vols.), 1941; Morals in Wartime, 1943. Author: William Godwin and Mary Wollstonecraft, 1907; Comrade Kropotkin (a biography of Prince Peter Kropotkin), 1908; An Essay on Hasheesh, 1912-30; Pathfinders in Medicine, 1912-29; Pioneers of Birth Control, 1919; Don Quixote of Psychiatry, 1919; Life of Jacob Henle, 1921; The Story of Medicine (several reprints), 1931; Syllabus of Medical History, 1933; The Way of Life of a Physician (Way of Life Series), 1941; Victory Over Pain: History of Anesthesia, 1946; White Caps: The Story of Nursing, 1946. Contributor to Archives of Dermatology and Syphilology, British Journal of Dermatology and Syphilis, Bulletin of the Inst. of History of Medicine of Johns Hopkins U., Ciba Symposia, Cyclopedia of Medicine, Dictionary of Am. History, Max Neuburger Festschrift, Medical Bulletin N.Y. Univ. College of Medicine, Scientific Monthly, The Laryngoscope. Founder of Froben Press for publ. of monographs on med. history. Five journeys to Europe, photographing objects of Medico-historica and archeological interest in Crete, Greece and Italy. Recipient of Festschrift on 60th birthday. Address: 4 St. Luke's Place, New York 14, N.Y.; and Temple University Sch. of Medicine, Philadelphia, Pa. Died Jan. 8, 1947.

ROBINSON, William S., artist; b. E. Gloucester, Mass., Sept. 15, 1861; s. Robert and Emeline S. R.; grad. Mass. Normal Art Sch., 1884; studied at Academy Julian, Paris, 1889-90; m. Lois E. Ball. Instr. in art, Md. Inst., Baltimore, 1885-89, Drexel Inst., 1891-93, Pa. Acad. Fine Arts, Phila., 1892-99, Teachers Coll. (Columbia U.), 1894-1904, Nat. Acad. Design, 1920-34; instr. Conn. Coll. for Women, New London, 1928-34. Represented in numerous important collections; honors at Paris, Buffalo, St. Louis and Panama expns. N.A., 1900; mem. Nat. Acad. Design, Am. Water Color Soc. (pres. 1914-20), New York Water Color Club. Clubs: Salmagundi, Lotos, National Arts. Home: (winter) 1722 W. Beach, Biloxi, Miss. Address: Old Lyme, Conn. Died Jan. 11, 1945.

ROBISON, William Ferretti, clergyman, educator; b. St. Louis, Mo., June 16, 1871; s. William Scott and Mary Frances (Firth) R.; A.B., St. Louis U., 1892, A.M., 1894, Ph.D., 1918; studied classics and lit., St. Stanislaus Sem., Florissant, Mo. Joined Soc. of Jesus (Jesuits), 1887; ordained R.C. ministry, 1902; teacher classics and lit., St. Ignatius Coll., Chicago, 1894-96, U. of Detroit, 1896-99, again at St. Ignatius, 1903-06; v.p. U. of Detroit, 1906-09; prof. ethics and natural law, 1909-12, fundamental theology, 1914-19, pres., Jan. 1, 1920-25, St. Louis U.; attached to Loyola U., Chicago, 1925; then pastor St. Francis Xavier (Coll.) Ch., St. Louis, Mo. Visited European univs., 1912-13. Author: Christ's Masterpiece, 1918; His Only Son, 1918; The Bedrock of Belief, 1918; The Undying Tragedy, 1919; The Sevenfold Gift, 1922; Milestones, 1923. Widely known as pulpit orator and lecturer. Address: Regis Coll., Denver, Colo. Died June 3, 1944.

ROBSION, John Marshall (rŏb'sĭ-ŏn), congressman; b. Bracken County, Ky., Jan. 2, 1878; s. John A. and Mary (Hyland) R.; B.S., Nat. Normal U., Lebanon, O.; LL.B., Centre Coll., Danville, Ky., 1898; m. Lida Stansberry, Jan. 25, 1902. Began practice at Barbourville, Ky., 1898; formerly mem. faculty, Union Coll., Barbourville. Member Republican National Convention, 1916, 1928, 1936, 1940, 1944; mem. 66th to 70th Congresses (1919-29), 11th Kentucky District, and reëlected to 71st Congress but resigned upon apptmt. to U.S. Senate Jan. 9, 1930, to succeed Frederick M. Sackett, for period expiring Mar. 3, 1931; elected to 74th to 80th Congresses (1935-49), 9th Ky. Dist. Mem. Christian (Disciples) Ch. Mason, Odd Fellow, K.P., etc. Home: Barbourville, Ky. Died Feb. 17, 1948.

ROBSON, Frank E. (rŏb'sŭn), lawyer; b. Lansing, Mich., July 20, 1859; s. John and Mary (Ingersoll) R.; B.S., Mich. Agrl. Coll., 1878; LL.B., U. of Mich.,

1883; J.D., Detroit College of Law, 1931; m. Caroline W. Claflin, June 10, 1885; 1 dau., Gertrude M. Admitted to Mich. bar, 1882, and began practice at Lansing; moved to Detroit, 1890; gen. atty. M.C. R.R., 1909-17, gen. counsel, 1917-31, advisory counsel since 1931, asst. v.p., 1930-32. Mem. Am. and Mich. State bar assns., Assn. Bar City of Detroit. Republican. Conglist. Club: Detroit (Detroit). Home: Wardell Sheraton Hotel, 15 Kirby Av. E. Office: Ford Bldg., Detroit, Mich. Died Feb. 28, 1948.

ROBSON, May, actress; b. in Australia; d. of Capt. Henry (British Navy) and Julia Robison; ed. Pension Semboiselle, Brussels; Pension Passy, Paris; came to America, 1879; m. Dr. Augustus H. Brown, May 29, 1889. First appearance on stage in Brooklyn, as Tilly in "The Hoop of Gold," 1884; later appeared in Madison Square Theatre as Susan in "Called Back"; engaged by Daniel Frohman, Madison Sq. and Lyceum Theatre, New York, 1886-93; engaged by Charles Frohman, 1893-1906; at Daly's in "The Billionaire," 1903; début as "star" in Lyceum Theatre, Scranton, Pa., as Aunt Mary Watkins in "The Rejuvenation of Aunt Mary," Oct. 3, 1907; first appearance in London at Terry's Theatre in same play, Aug. 22, 1910; appeared in "The Three Lights," "The Clever Woman," "The Making Over of Mrs. Matt," "A Star Is Born," "The Perfect Specimen," "Adventures of Tom Sawyer," "Bringing Up Baby," etc.; toured in "Tish," 1919-21; later star with various cos. and in talking pictures. Author: (with C. T. Dazey) A Night Out (play), 1911. Address: 229 S. Crescent Drive, Beverly Hills, Calif. Died Oct. 20, 1942.

ROCHESTER, Edward Sudler, publicist, author; b. Baltimore, Md., Aug. 13, 1885; s. Samuel Charles and Mollie (Sudler) R.; m. Annie Elizabeth Honeman, 1905; 1 dau., Vivian Louise. Mng. and city editor Washington Post, 1910-17; editor Official U.S. Bulletin (pub. daily by order of President of U.S.), May 1, 1917-19; pres. Nat. Publicity & Adv. Corp. (publications U.S. Daily News Service), 1920. Editor and mem. Washington staff Associated Press, Washington, D.C. Spl. asst. to atty. gens. of U.S., 1922-25; sec. Federal Oil Conservation Bd., apptd. by President of U.S., Apr. 1925, serving until 1933; Washington corr. various newspapers and dir. Nat. News Service since 1933. Episcopalian. Author and pub. various vols. dealing with governmental affairs; contbr. to mags. and other publs. Home: 3401 16th St. Office: 1710 G St. N.W., Washington, D.C. Died Mar. 10, 1946.

ROCK, George Henry, rear admiral; b. Hastings, Mich., Nov. 21, 1868; s. Adam and Sarah Anne (Crawley) R.; grad. U.S. Naval Acad., Annapolis, Md., 1889; B.S. in Naval Architecture, U. of Glasgow, Scotland, 1892; m. Edith Gertrude Neumann, January 5, 1893; children—Albert Neumann, Bertram Neumann. Constrn. officer U.S. Navy Yards, at N.Y. City, 1892-95, Portsmouth, N.H., 1902-06, Boston, 1909-11, New York, 1915-21; mem. Bd. of Inspection and Survey, 1911-15; superintending constructor, Baltimore, Md., 1895-98, Newport News, Va., 1898-1901, Bath, Me., 1901-02, Newport News, 1906-09; mgr. navy yard, Norfolk, Va., 1921-23; asst. chief of Bur. of Constrn. and Repair, 1923-29; promoted to rank of permanent rear admiral, Aug. 1, 1926; chief constructor 1929-32, retired from active service; head of Webb Inst. of Naval Architecture since Sept. 15, 1932. Mem. Soc. Naval Architects and Marine Engrs. (pres. 1934-37), Naval Inst. Awarded Navy Cross for services in World War I. Del. to Internat. Conf. on Safety of Life at Sea, London, 1929. Episcopalian. Clubs: Engineers (New York); Army and Navy (Washington, D.C. and N.Y.); Andiron Club of N.Y. City (dictator), 1937-41). Home: Webb and Sedgwick Av., New York. Died Apr. 20, 1946; buried in Arlington National Cemetery.

ROCKETT, James Francis, educator; b. Watertown, Mass., Dec. 29, 1884; s. Edward and Ellen (Dee) R.; A.B., Holy Cross Coll., Worcester, Mass., 1908, A.M., 1922; grad. Boston Normal Sch., 1909; grad. study in edn., Harvard, Boston Coll. and Boston U.; LL.D., Providence Coll., 1936; D.Sc. in edn., Bryant College, 1938; m. Mary Cecilia O'Brien, July 12, 1915; children—James Edward, Pauline Marie. Teacher and sub-master, Boston pub. schs., also teacher and prin. in evening schs., 1909-23; prin. Sr. High Sch., Woonsocket, R.I., 1924-25, supt. schs., 1925-35; dir. of edn., State of R.I., since Mar. 1, 1935-47; pres. St. Josephs Coll. for Women, Portland, Me., 1947-48; ex-pres. R.I. Inst. Instrn; mem. bd. trustees R.I. State Coll.; exec. officer R.I. Bd. of Vocational Edn.; trustee R.I. Sch. of Design; v.p. R.I. Humane Soc.; dir. Woonsocket Y.M.C.A., Am. Red Cross and Pub. Health Nursing Assn. Mem. N.E.A. (life), Dept. of Superintendence, R.I. Inst. of Instruction (sec. 1931-35), Henry Barnard Club of R.I. Catholic. K.C., Elk. Lecturer on ednl. and community subjects since 1920. Asso. ed. of Quarterly Journal of R.I. Inst. of Instrn. Home: Cumberland Hill, R.I. Office: 205 Benefit St., Providence 3, R.I. Died April 1, 1948.

ROCKWELL, Edward Henry, civ. engr.; b. Worcester, Mass., Apr. 20, 1869; s. Edward Munson and Martha Josephine (Smith) R.; B.S., Worcester Poly. Inst., 1890, C.E., 1920; hon. D.Eng. from same inst., 1933; m. Lena Hortense Warfield, Oct. 29, 1891; children—Grace Margaret (Mrs. Stanley R. Kingman), Dorothy (Mrs. Mark A. Burns), Doris, Donald Edward, Rosamond (Mrs. W. W. Cheney); m. 2d, Nellie May Owens, June 4, 1941; with George S. Morrison, cons. engr., Chicago, 1890-92; submaster high sch., Leominster, Mass., 1893-95; with Norcross Bros., bldg. steel work, Worcester, Mass., 1895-97; in charge installation of machinery, and supt. Holliston (Mass.) Yarn Co., 1897-99; draftsman Boston Bridge Works, 1899-1900, Boston Navy Yard, 1900-01; asst. engr. Boston Bridge Works, 1901-02; instr. in civ. engring., Tufts Coll., 1902-03, asst. prof., 1903-06, prof. structural engring., 1906-18, prof. civ. and structural engring., 1918-22; dean of engring. and prof. civ. engring., Rutgers U., 1922-28; Simon Cameron Long prof. civ. engring., Lafayette Coll., since 1928. With Boston Bridge Works, summer, 1906; asst. engr. Boston Transit Commn., summer, 1907; designing engr. Suffolk County Court House extension, Sept. 1907-June 1908, cons. engr. on constrn. same, June 1908-Jan. 1910; cons. engr. commn. on Galveston causeway reconstruction, Oct. 1916-Jan. 1917; engr. and architect in charge design, contract and constrn. of chem. lab., Tufts Coll., July 1921-Sept. 1922; cons. engr. Gen. Crushed Stone Co., Easton, Pa., City of Perth Amboy, N.J., Oliver Iron Mining Co., Duluth, Minn., etc. Mem. Am. Soc. Civil Engrs. (ex-pres. Lehigh Valley section), Soc. for Promotion Engring. Edn., Am. Assn. Univ. Profs., N.J. Soc. Professional Engrs. (ex-pres.), Phi Beta Kappa, Sigma Xi, Lambda Chi Alpha, Tau Beta Pi. Republican. Conglist. Club: Northampton County Country. Author: Vibrations Caused by Blasting and their Effect on Structures. Contbr. to Am. Highway Engrs. Handbook and bulls. Soc. for Promotion Engring. Edn. Home: 712 Cattell St., Easton, Pa. Died May 26, 1943.

RODDY, Harry Justin, b. Landisburg, Pa., May 25, 1856; s. William Henry and Susan Catherine (Waggoner) F.; B.S., First Pa. State Normal Sch., Millersville, 1881, M.S., 1891; Ph.D., Kansas City (Mo.) U., 1906; m. Anna Houck Graver, Dec. 21, 1891; children—Anna Mary (Mrs. Clair G. Kinter), Henry Justin. Teacher pub. schs., 1877-87; teacher, First Pa. State Normal Sch., 1887-1904, dir. geography and geology work, 1906-08, head of science work, 1908-26; curator of museum and prof. geology, Franklin and Marshall Coll., since 1926. Sec. Lancaster City Tree Commn. Dir. Nature Study Club, Lancaster. Author: Common School Geography (two books), 1913, 15; Industrial and Commercial Geography of Lancaster County, Pa., 1916; Origin of Concretions in Streams, 1917; The Reptiles of Lancaster County and the State of Pennsylvania, 1926; The Geology and Geography of Lancaster Co., Pa., 1920. Contbr. chapters on natural history to several books, also contbr. to newspapers; lecturer on natural history subjects. Home: Conestoga, Pa. Address: Franklin and Marshall Coll., Lancaster, Pa. Died Sept. 4, 1943.

RODGERS, William Ledyard, naval officer; born Washington, Feb. 4, 1860; s. John and Ann E. (Hodge) R.; grad. U.S. Naval Acad., 1878; unmarried. Ensign U.S.N., 1882; lt., 1894; lt.-comdr., 1901; comdr., 1905; capt., 1909; rear admiral, Aug. 29, 1916. Comdg. U.S.S. Georgia, 1909-11; pres. U.S. Naval War Coll., 1911-13; comdg. U.S.S. Delaware, 1913-15; mem. Gen. Bd. of the Navy, 1915-16; comdg. train, Atlantic Fleet, 1916-18, comdr.-in-chief Asiatic Fleet, 1918-19; mem. Gen. Bd. and chmn. exec. com., 1920-24, retired Feb. 4, 1924. Mem. adv. council, Conf. on Limitation of Armament, Washington, 1921; tech. adviser, Commn. of Jurists on Laws of War, The Hague, 1923. Clubs: Metropolitan (Washington); University, New York Yacht (New York). Author: Greek and Roman Naval Warfare; Naval Warfare Under Oars, 4th to 16th Centuries. Address: 1738 R St. N.W., Washington. Died May 7, 1944.

RODMAN, Walter Sheldon, elec. engring.; b. Wakefield, R.I., Sept. 1, 1883; s. Charles Lewis and Imogene Ethel (Sheldon) R.; B.S., R.I. State Coll., Kingston, 1904, M.S., 1907; Saltonstall fellow, Mass. Inst. Tech., 1909-10, M.S., 1909; m. Sarah Wilcox Palmer, Sept. 6, 1904. Instr. in physics, mathematics and elec. engring., R.I. State Coll., 1904-08; adj. prof. elec. engring., U. of Va., 1910-13, asso. prof., 1913-17, prof. since 1917 and apptd. acting dean of engineering, May 1931, dean since 1933, sec. engring. faculty, 1910-33. Asso. mem. Naval Cons. Bd. (dir. for Va., World War); asso. dir. in charge road work, Motor Truck Drivers' Training Detachment, U. of Va., 1918. Fellow A.A.A.S., Am. Inst. E.E. (v.p. Dist. 4, 1929-31); mem. Illuminating Engring. Soc., Soc. for Promotion Engring. Edn. (2d v.p. 1926-27), Am. Association Univ. Profs. asso. mem. Tau Beta Pi; hon. mem. Phi Beta Kappa (sec. 1922-40), Phi Sigma Kappa, Theta Tau, Phi Kappa Phi, Sigma Xi, Pi Gamma Mu; rep. of Am. Inst. E.E. on engineering research com. of Engineering Foundation, 1930-35, and in Assembly of Am. Engineering Council, 1931 and 1932. Republican. Episcopalian. Club: Colonnade. Contbr. to Engring. Edn., U. of Va., Jour. of Engring., Trans. Illuminating Engring. Soc. Home: Lyndhall Apartments, University, Va. Address: Thornton Hall, University of Va., Charlottesville, Va. Died Dec. 31, 1946.

RODMAN, William Blount, lawyer; b. Tarboro, N.C., Feb. 19, 1862; s. William Blount and Camilla H. (Croom) R.; ed. U. of N.C. through sophomore yr.; m. Addie Fulford, Oct. 7, 1888 (dec.); children—William Blount, Nathaniel F., Mrs. Cammie C. Robinson, Mrs. Hannah F. Curtis. Studied law and practiced at Washington, N.C., 1884-1904, at Charlotte, N.C., since 1904. Division attorney Southern Ry. Co., Sept. 1, 1904-July 1, 1911; gen. solicitor, Norfolk Southern R.R., 1911-20, gen. counsel, 1920-42; dir. Norfolk Southern R.R. Co., John L. Roper Lumber Co., Nat. Bank of Commerce; retired from all activities, Jan. 29, 1942. Mayor of Washington, N.C., 3 terms from 1897; elected code commr. to revise statute laws of N.C., 1903; served in N.G. of N.C., pvt. to col., 1881-94. Clubs: Princess Ann, Virginia. Episcopalian. Democrat. Home: 436 Mowbray Arch, Norfolk, Va. Deceased.

ROE, Arthur, lawyer; b. Shafter, Fayette County, Ill., July 18, 1878; s. Ezekiel and Nancy Jane (Browning) R.; LL.B., U. of Ill., 1901; m. Clarabell Grigg, June 5, 1905 (died Apr. 28, 1911); m. 2d, Elsie McGrue, June 18, 1917. Admitted to Ill. bar, 1901; atty. for City of Vandalia, 1904-08; master in chancery, Fayette County, 1911-13; U.S. atty. Eastern Ill. Dist. since 1935; served in Ill. Gen. Assembly, 1912-34, minority leader 2 sessions, speaker of the House 58th session; mem. Lincoln Memorial Commn. Democrat. Presbyterian. Mason, Elk. Home: Vandalia, Ill. Died Apr. 15, 1942.

ROEDDER, Edwin Carl Lothar Clemens, philologist; b. Niederwasser, Baden, Black Forest, Ger., Apr. 8, 1873; s. Johann and Karoline (Hitzfeld) R.; Gymnasium of Tauberbischofsheim, 1886-89; Gymnasium of Bruchsal, 1889-1891; U. of Heidelberg, 1891-92; A.B., U. of Mich., 1893, A.M., 1894, Ph.D., 1898; m. Cordelia Emma Selma Pacius, Aug. 2, 1899. Asst. in German, Univ. of Mich., 1895-96; instr. modern langs., Jarvis Hall Mil. Acad., Montclair, Colo., 1896-97; instr. German, Univ. of Mich., 1897-1900; instr. German, U. of Wis., 1900-03, asst. prof. German philology, 1903-10, asso. prof., since 1910. Mem. Modern Lang. Assn. Am., Wis. Acad. Sciences, Arts and Letters, Phi Beta Kappa. Asso. editor Monatshefte fuer deutsche Sprache und Paedagogik (Milwaukee). Editor: Augier et Sandeau, Le Gendre de M. Poirier, 1903; Schiller, Wilhelm Tell, 1906; Freytag, Das Nest der Zaunkoenige, 1912; Deutsche Gedichte und Lieder (with C. M. Purin), 1912; Schwarzwaldeut, 1913. Address: 38 Breeze Terrace, Madison, Wis. Died Oct. 21, 1945.

ROEHM, Alfred Isaac (rēm), coll. prof.; b. Sturgis, Mich., Jan. 29, 1880; s. Christian and Rosena (Hoelle) R.; grad. Ind. State Normal Sch., 1901; A.B., Ind. U., 1905, A.M., 1906; student U. of Leipzig, 1906-09; Ph.D., U. of Chicago, 1910; m. Daisy Ina Harner, Oct. 15, 1912; children—Frederick Ellis, Paul Alfred, Dan Christian. Teacher, pub. schs., Ind., 1897-1904; prof. modern langs., Wis. State Normal Sch., Oshkosh, Wis., 1910-17; dir. of edn. and teacher of French, Ft. Oglethorpe, Ga., 1917-19; prof. teaching modern langs., George Peabody Coll. for Teachers, Nashville, Tenn., since 1919. Decorated by French Govt. with Palmes Academique, Officier de l'Academie. Mem. Modern Lang. Assn. America, Linguistic Soc. America, Nat. Bur. Ednl. Corr. (organizer), Kappa Delta Pi. Presbyterian. Author: Practical Beginning German, 1915; Laboratory Method in French, 1925; Laboratory Manual for French Grammar, 1927. Co-Author: Spoken English, 1925; Laboratory Method in Spanish, 1926. Compiler or editor of Simple French from Great Writers, 1928; school edition of Le Voyage de M. Perrichon, 1929; Practice Leaves in Elementary French, 1931; First Year Text Book in French (La Famille Dupont), 1931; Introduction to French Civilization and Culture, 1938; General Romanic Language (Visual Dialogue), 1942; Speech Readiness in English, 1943; Audio-Visual Exercises in English Language and Grammar, 1944; Audio-Visual Chart Exercises in Good English Usage for the Grades, 1946. Home: Kinross and E. Morton Av., Nashville, Tenn. Died Aug. 25, 1949.

ROERICH, Nicholas K(onstantin) (rû'rĭk), artist; b. St. Petersburg, Russia, Sept. 27, 1874; s. Konstantin and Marie V. (Kalashnikoff) R.; grad. Law Sch., U. of St. Petersburg; studied drawing and paining under Michail O. Mikeshine, grad. Acad. Fine Arts, St. Petersburg, under Kuindjy, studied Paris under Cormon; m. Helena Ivanov Shaposhnikov, of St. Petersburg, grand-dau. Field-Marshal Golenistcheff Kutuzoff, 1901; children—George, Sviatoslav. Dir. Sch. for Encouragement of Fine Arts in Russia, 1906-16; sec. Soc. for Encouragement of Fine Arts in Russia, and asst. editor "Art," 1898-1900; served as pres. Museum Russian Arts, as 1st pres. "Mir Iskusstva" and as a leader in Moscow Art Theatre and Diagilev Ballet; came to U.S., 1920, under auspices of Art Inst. Chicago; hon. pres. of Cor Ardens, soc. of art workers of all nationalities, 1921; founder and hon. pres. Master Inst. United Arts, N.Y. City, 1921, Corona Mundi (internat. art center), 1922 Roerich Museum Press, 1925, Urusvati, Himalayan Research Inst. of Roerich Museum at Naggar, India, 1929; hon. pres. Roerich Museum. Made pilgrimage through Russia, 1901-04, producing 75 studies (exhibited at La. Purchase Expn., St. Louis, 1904); spent 5 yrs. in Central Asia as head expdn., making 500 paintings; has painted over 3,000 pictures; represented in Roerich Museum (1,006 paintings), the Louvre, Luxembourg, Victoria and Albert Museum, National Museum of Stockholm (Sweden), etc. Comdr., 1st Class, Royal Swedish Order of North Star; Grand Cross, Legion of Honor (France); Order of Saint Sava, 1st Class (Jugoslavia); Comdr. Order of Imperial Russians of St. Stanislas, St. Anne and St. Vladimir; awarded medal by City of Bruges, Belgium, for plan of Roerich Pact and Banner of Peace. Mem. Jugoslavian Acad. of Arts and Sciences; v.p. Archeol. Inst. America; hon. mem. Bose Inst., Calcutta; mem. Academy of Rheims. Author: Complete Work, 1914; Adamant, 1924; The Messenger, 1925; Paths of Blessing, 1925; Himalaya, 1926; Joys of Sikkim, 1928; Heart of Asia, 1930; Flame in Chalice, 1930; Shambahala, 1930; Realm of Light, 1931; Maitreya, 1932; Fiery Stronghold, 1933; Sacred Vigil, 1934; Gates into the Future, 1936; The Immutable, 1936. Excavated prehistoric burials, Pondicherry, French India, 1930. Executed a number of works for Chicago Opera

Co.; for Russian Ballet, scenery in "Prince Igor"; for Stanislavsky. setting of "Peer Gynt": wrote libretto, designed scenery and costumes for "Sacre du Printemps" for which Stravinsky composed music. Ten Roerich Halls established in Paris, Belgrade, Riga, Benares, Bruges, Allahabad, Zagreb, Buenos Aires, Kyoto and Praha. Headed expdn. for U.S. Dept. of Agr., 1934, through China and Mongolia in search of drought resisting grasses for America. Creator of Roerich Pact and Banner of Peace signed by 22 Pan-Am. countries at White House, Washington, 1935. Mem. Societaire Salon d'Automme, Paris; hon. pres. Flamma. Inc., Association for Advancement of Culture. 1937. Home: Naggar, Kulu, Punjab, British India. Died Dec. 12, 1947.

ROGERS, Alfred Thomas, lawyer; b. St. Joseph, Mo., May 18, 1873; s. John and Martha (McBride) R.; student acad. depts., U. of S.D. and U. of Wis.; LL.B., U. of Wis., 1895; m. Edna R. Chynoweth, June 30, 1910; m. 2d, Emily Bordeaux Elmer, Aug. 13, 1935. In practice at Madison since 1895. Del. Rep. Nat. Conv., 1908; Wis. mem. Rep. Nat. Com., 1908-24. Mem. Delta Tau Delta, Phi Delta Phi. Home: 4138 Mandan Crescent. Office: 1 W. Main St., Madison, Wis. Died March 27, 1948.

ROGERS, Charles Edwin, prof. civil engring.; b. Saratoga County, N.Y., June 5, 1874; s. Charles and Catherine (Schoonmaker) R.; C.E., Rensselaer Poly. Inst., 1896; M.C.E., Harvard, 1915; m. Sarah Elizabeth Chase, Sept. 7, 1898. Began teaching at Lehigh U., 1901; prof. civ. engring., Trinity Coll., Hartford, since 1905. Mem. Soc. for Promotion Engring. Edn., Am. Assn. Univ. Profs., Rensselaer Soc. Engrs., Harvard Engring. Soc., Conn. Society Civ. Engrs., Am. Astron. Soc., Sigma Xi, Pi Gamma Mu; Mem. Dutch Ref. Ch. Home: 33 Concord St., W. Hartford, Conn. Died June 30, 1942.

ROGERS, Edward Sidney, lawyer; b. Castine, Me., Apr. 15, 1875; s. James Harriman and Susan Hayden (Fisher) R.; ed. Mich. Mil. Acad.; LL.B., U. of Mich., 1895, hon. LL.M., 1910, LL.D., 1930; Pharm. D., U. of Southern Calif., 1938; m. Eva Thompson, Sept. 23, 1901; children—James Harriman, Edward Alden. Admitted to Ill. bar, 1895, and since practiced at Chicago and New York, specializing in the law of unfair competition, trade-marks and copyright. Lecturer on law of trademarks and unfair competition, Univ. of Michigan; chmn. of bd., Sterling Drug, Inc., N.Y. City. Am. del. to Inter-Am. Conf. to Negotiate Conv. Trade Marks and Commercial Names, 1929, Am. rep. Inter-Am. Commn. on Industrial Property; chmn. Trade Mark Commn. of Internat. Law Assn., London. Home: North Street, Greenwich, Conn. Offices: 122 S. Michigan Av., Chicago, Ill.; 41 E. 42d St., and 170 Varick St., New York, N.Y. Died May 22, 1949.

ROGERS, Ernest Elias; b. Waterford, Conn., Dec. 6, 1866; s. Elias Perkins and Lucy Almira (Smith) R.; desc. James Rogers, New London, Conn., born 1615; grad. Bulkeley High Sch., New London, 1884; m. Fanny Gorton, Oct. 28, 1896; 1 son, Ernest Gorton. Began with Brainerd & Armstrong, silk mfrs., 1884; with Arnold Rudd, wholesale flour and grain, 1905; pres. Arnold Rudd Co., Mystic Grain & Oil Co., etc.; pres. Winthrop Trust Co., 1922; mayor of New London, 1915-18; treas. State of Conn., 1925-29; lt. gov. State of Conn., term 1929, 30 inclusive. Mem. Coast Arty., 1902-09, retiring as capt. Mem. Selective Service Bd., 1917-19; mem. present Selective Service Bd. since 1940. Former pres. Conn. State Chamber Commerce; hon. pres. New London County Historical Soc. (pres. 25 yrs.); past pres. Am. Bapt. Home Mission Soc., New York; trustee Eastern Bapt. Theol. Sem., Phila.; mem. Nat. Soc. S.A.R. (former pres. gen.), Conn. Hist. Soc. (v.p.). Republican. Baptist. Mason. Author: Sesquicentennial of the Battle of Groton Heights and the Burning of New London, 1931; Connecticut's Naval Office at New London During the War of the American Revolution, 1933; New London's Participation in Connecticut's Tercentenary, 1935; Cedar Grove Cemetery, Vol. 1, 1941. Home: 605 Pequot Av. Office: Winthrop Trust Co., New London, Conn. Died Jan. 28, 1945.

ROGERS, Fred S., business exec.; b. Middletown, N.Y., Jan. 7, 1871; s. William Henry and Amelia (Chattle) R.; grad. Wallkill Acad., Middletown, N.Y.; m. Carolyn Howland, Nov. 15, 1899; (divorced 1942); 1 dau., Cynthai Howland; m. 2d, Eva L. Conklin, June 20, 1942. With McMonagle and Rogers since 1889, purchased half interest, 1898; vice pres. United Drug Co., Boston, 1913-14; dir. United Rexall Drug Co., 1900-49, dir. United Mutual Ins. Co., 1930-49; pres. Savings & Loan Assn. of Middletown since 1900 Pres. Nat. Assn. Flavor Extract Mfrs., 1924. Trustee, Albany Coll., 1929-32. Mem. Nat. Economy League Managing Com., Fed. of Orange County Taxpayers, (past pres.), Middletown C. of C. (past pres.), Mason. Home: 71 Highland Av. Office: 24 Union St., Middletown, N.Y Died Mar. 18, 1949.

ROGERS, George F., ex-congressman; b. Harwood, Ont., Can., Mar. 19, 1887; s. John and Emma (Kimmerley) R.; ed. public schools; m. Emily Scott, Apr. 18, 1912; children—George John, Ralph James. Naturalized Am. citizen since 1914. Began as printer, 1903; entered food business, 1911; mem. bd. dirs. Am. Brewing Co., Rochester (N.Y.) Grocery Co.; supervisor Monroe County, N.Y., 1934-35; state senator, New York, 1937-38; mem. 79th Congress (1945-47), 40th New York Dist. Commr. Genesee (N.Y.) State Park. Pres. Monroe County Food Merchants Assn. Odd Fellow, Elk, Kiwanian. Home: 19 Perrinton St. Office: 1458 Dewey Av., Rochester, N.Y. Died Nov. 20, 1948.

ROGERS, Hopewell Lindenberger, manufacturer; b. Chicago, Ill., Dec. 19, 1876; s. Joseph Martin and Katherine Mary (Gamble) R.; Ph.B., Sheffield Scientific Sch. (Yale), 1897; LL.B., John Marshall Law Sch., Chicago, 1906; m. Agnes Bourne Street, Jan. 3, 1917 (dec.); m. 2d, Dorothy Low Felton (Mrs. Charles Counselman), Mar. 7, 1924. Began as bookkeeper, advt. dept. Chicago Daily News, 1897, continued successively as business mgr., vice-pres., asst. to pub., and sec. and treas., 1897-1927; in exec. offices of Hearst Newspapers, 1932-35; chairman board directors Belden Manufacturing Co. since 1939. Dir. Am. Newspaper Publishers Assn., 1912-22 (pres. 1916-18); Industry mem. Regional War Labor Bd. (Chicago dist.), 1943. Mem. Commercial Club, Chicago Acad. Sciences (former trustee). Clubs: Chicago, Saddle and Cycle, Casino, Wayfarers (Chicago); Yale Club (New York), Filson Club (life) (Louisville, Ky.); Wharf Rats (Nantucket, Mass.). Home: 900 N. Michigan Av., Chicago 11. Office: 4647 W. Van Buren St., Chicago 44, Ill. Died Feb. 27, 1948.

ROGERS, James Gamble, architect; b. Bryants Station, Ky., Mar. 3, 1867; s. Joseph M. and Katharine (Gamble) R.; A.B., Yale U., 1889, M.A., 1922; LL.D., Northwestern Univ., 1927; Sc.B., Columbia, 1928; m. Anne Day, 1901. Practiced at N.Y. City since 1905; designed Sterling Memorial Library, Sterling Law Sch., Sterling Sch. of Grad. Studies, Jonathan Edwards Coll., Pierson Coll., Davenport Coll., Trumbull Coll., Berkeley Coll., Timothy Dwight Coll. and Harkness Memorial Quadrangle, at Yale; New Haven P.O.; Sophie Newcomb Coll., New Orleans; Shelby County Court House, Memphis, Tenn.; Brooks Memorial, Memphis; Columbia-Presbyn. Med. Center, N.Y. City; Colgate-Rochester Div. Group, Rochester, N.Y.; Northwestern U. Professional Group of Buildings, Chicago; Deering Library and Sorority Quadrangles, Northwestern U., Evanston, Ill.; New Columbia Library; Memorial Hospital, New York; Connecticut College Chapel; architectural adviser, Yale, 10 years. Member A.I.A. Clubs: University, Yale, Century, Pilgrims (New York); Onwentsia (Chicago). Home: 164 E. 70th St. Office: 70 East 45th St., New York, 17, N.Y. Died Oct. 1. 1947.

ROGERS, John Edward, osteopathic physician; b. Scales Mound, Ill., Oct. 3, 1884; s. Dr. Richard and Louisa (Kerslake) R.; A.B., Lenox Coll., Hopkinton, Ia., 1907; A.M., Northwestern U., Evanston, Ill., 1911; D.O., Des Moines (Ia.) Still Coll., 1924; hon. Ph.D., Lenox, 1917; LL.D., Phila. Coll. of Osteopathy, 1938; m. Lenore Howe, July 12, 1910; children—Richard Campbell, Jean Elizabeth; m. 2d, Marjorie Stanley, Oct. 18, 1930. Practiced osteopathy in Oshkosh, Wis., since 1924; pres. and chmn. council A. T. Still Research Inst.; counselor Northwestern U.; ednl. dir. Mass. Coll. of Osteopathy (Boston) since July 1943; sec. treas. Nat. Bd. Examiners for Osteopathic Physicians and Surgeons. Mem. Am. Osteopathic Assn. (vice-pres. 1935; president 1936; chmn. comm. on Ednl. Standards), Phi Sigma Gamma (national pres., 1927-32), Sigma Sigma Phi (former nat. pres.). Republican. Conglist. Mason (32°, Shriner, K.T.), Elk. Clubs: Kiwanis (ex-pres.), Oshkosh Power Boat (past commodore); Lake Shore Athletic (Chicago). Contbr. professional articles. Home: 23 Mt. Vernon St. Office: 16 Mt. Vernon St., Oshkosh, Wis. Died Feb. 25, 1950.

ROGERS, Walter Alexander, civil engr., contractor; b. Milwaukee, Wis., Jan. 19, 1868; s. Alexander H. and Martha M. (Ross) R.; C.E., U. of Wis., 1888; m. Julia Cushing, July 1, 1891; children—Lester, Margaret, Ross, Carl, Walter, John. In engring. dept. Wis. Central R.R. and N.P. RR., 1889-92, C.,M.& St.P. Ry., 1892-1901; pres. Bates & Rogers Constrn. Co., contractors, 1901-38, chmn. since 1938. Mem. Am. Soc. C.E., Western Soc. Engrs., Assn. Gen. Contractors of America. Republican. Clubs: Union League, Engineers, Chicago Golf. Home: Glen Ellyn, Ill. Office: 111 W. Washington St., Chicago, Ill. Died Jan. 3, 1944.

ROGERS, William Arthur, retired iron mfr.; b. Berkshire, N.Y., Sept. 8, 1851; s. Dr. M. and Mary (Leonard) R.; Ph.B., Sheffield Scientific Department (Yale), 1874; m. Eleanor R. Silliman, May 14, 1884 (dec.); children—William Silliman, Mabel Elizabeth (dec.), Douglas Trumbull (dec.), Alice (Mrs. Richard Dwight Hillis), Alden. Began as clerk L. R. Hull & Co., Cincinnati, 1874, jr. partner 3 yrs. later; title of firm changed to E. L. Harper & Co., later firm of Rogers & Trivett; est. firm of Rogers, Brown & Co., which long held a leading place in pig iron trade. Est. at N. Tonawanda, Tonawanda Iron and Steel Co., May 1890, took charge bus. and Buffalo br. of Rogers, Brown & Co.; retired, Jan. 1926; at various times was pres. Rogers-Brown Iron Co. (Buffalo), Punxsutawney (Pa.) Iron Co., Niagara Iron Mining Co., and Munro Iron Mining Co. (Mich.), also v.p. Iroquois Iron Co. (Chicago), Cleveland (O.) Furnace Co., Rogers, Brown Ore Co. (Minn.), Cascade Coal & Coke Co. (Pa.), Buffalo Steamship Co.; former dir. Marine Trust Co. (Buffalo), Am. Iron and Steel Inst. (New York), Ontario Power Co. (Can.), also Buffalo Fine Arts Acad.; now dir. Erie County Savings Bank, Am. Steamship Co. (Buffalo). Served as chmn. 1st United Charities Drive, Buffalo; chmn. United War Work Campaign, 1917. Trustee Univ. of Buffalo, Y.M.C.A. Presbyterian. Clubs: Century (New York); Buffalo, Saturn Athletic, Country (Buffalo). Home: 309 W. North St. Office: Erie County Bank Bldg., Buffalo, N.Y. Died Apr. 7, 1946.

ROGERS, William Nathaniel, lawyer; b. Sanbornville, N.H., Jan. 10, 1892; s. Herbert E. and Lilian A. (Sanborn) R.; student Dartmouth Coll., 1911-14; LL.B., U. of Me., 1916; children—Pauline Edwards, Una Cleveland, Will, John Sanborn. Began practice at Sanbornville, 1916; mem. Demond, Sulloway, Piper & Jones, Concord, N.H., 1923-43; mem. N.H. Ho. of Rep., 1917, 19, 21 (judiciary com.); mem. 68th and 72d to 74th Congresses (1923-25 and 1931-37), 1st N.H. Dist. Mem. N.H. Bar Assn., Carroll County Bar Assn. (pres. 1921-22), Am. Bar Assn., Phi Kappa Psi, Phi Alpha Delta. Democrat. Episcopalian. Mason (K.T., Shriner), K.P., Elk. Club: Wonolancet (Concord). Home: Sanbornville. Office: Sanbornville, N.H. Died Sept. 25, 1945.

ROGERS, Wynne Grey, judge; b. New Orleans, La., Dec. 26, 1874; s. Owen Wynne and Mary Elizabeth (Winkelmann) R.; LL.B., Tulane U., 1895; unmarried. Admitted to La. bar, 1896, and practiced at New Orleans; mem. firm Titche & Rogers, 1905-20; judge Civil Dist. Court, Parish of Orleans, 1920-24; asso. justice Supreme Court of La. since 1924; prof. of La. civil procedure, Tulane U., since Sept. 1920. Four-minute man, also mem. Legal Advisory Bd., World War. Member Am. and La. State bar assns., Tulane U. Alumni Assn., Delta Sigma Phi, Phi Alpha Delta. Democrat. Episcopalian. Mason (33°); Past Grand Master A.F. and A.M. of La.; Past Potentate Jerusalem Temple, A.A.O.N.M.S.; K.T. Clubs: Chess, Checkers and Whist, Church, Young Men's Gymnastic. Home: 4431 Canal St. Address: Supreme Court, New Orleans, La. Deceased.

ROLFE, Alfred Grosvenor (rŏlf), headmaster; b. Boston, Aug. 4, 1860; s. Henry Chamberlain and Abby Frances (Winchester) R.; grad. Ayer (Mass.) High Sch., 1876, Chauncy Hall Sch., Boston, 1878; A.B., Amherst, 1882, A.M., 1885, Litt.D., 1913; traveled and studied abroad, 1889-90; unmarried. Teacher, Black Hall Sch., Lyme, Conn., 1882-84, Cushing Acad., Ashburnham, Mass., 1884-85, Williston Sem., Easthampton, 1885-86, Graylock Inst., Williamstown, 1886-89, with The Hill Sch., Pottstown, Pa., since 1890, headmaster, 1913-14, sr. master since 1914. Mem. Delta Kappa Epsilon. Club: Amherst (New York). Author: Song of Saints and Sinners; A Little Book of Charades. Address: The Hill Sch., Pottstown, Pa. Died June 7, 1942.

ROLFE, George William, chemist; b. Cambridge, Mass., Feb. 10, 1864; s. William James and Eliza Jane (Carew) R.; A.B., Harvard, 1885, A.M., 1886; spl. grad. course, Mass. Inst. Tech., 1895; m. Mabel Stuart, Feb. 28, 1888 (died 1913); 1 dau., Dorothy Stuart; m. 2d, Mary Eager Gifford, Sept. 1914. Chemist, Charles Pope Glucose Co., Geneva, Ill., 1886-89, 1892-93; sub-master, Brookline High Sch., 1889-90; chemist, Parque Alto, Cuba, 1891, Central Soledad, Cuba, 1892; chemist sewer purification expert, George E. Waring, Newport, R.I., 1894; instr. analyt. chemistry and sugar analysis, Mass. Inst. Tech., 1895-1915; instr. chemistry, Franklin Union, Boston, 1913-19. Chemist and factory supt., Central Aguirre, Puerto Rico, Boston and Puerto Rico, 1900-02 and 1907-09, The Cuba Co., Jatibonico, Cuba, 1913-14, Constancia, Puerto Rico, 1906, Cortada, Puerto Rico, 1907, Central Manopla, Cuba, 1921-22, expert in U.S. and Canadian cts. on starch products. Mem. Am. Chem. Soc., Nat. Geog. Soc. Clubs: Pi Eta, Delta Upsilon (Harvard), Authors. Author: The Polariscope, 1905; also numerous scientific papers. Translator (with Wm. T. Hall): Claasen's Beet Sugar Manufacture, 1906. Contbr. to Rogers Industrial Chemistry, 1st to 5th edits. Unitarian. Home: Eastville, Oak Bluffs, Mass. Died June 21, 1942.

ROLFE, John Carew, univ. prof.; b. Lawrence, Mass., Oct. 15, 1859; s. William James and Eliza Jane (Carew) R.; A.B., Harvard, 1881; A.M., Cornell U., 1884, Ph.D., 1885; Litt.D., U. of Pa., 1925, Oberlin Coll., 1933; studied Am. Sch., Athens, 1888-89; m. Alice Griswold Bailey, Aug. 29, 1900; 1 dau., Esther (Mrs. Henry D. Gasson). Instr. Latin, Cornell, 1882-85; instr. Greek and Latin, Harvard, 1889-90; asst. prof. and prof. Latin, Univ. of Mich., 1890-1902; prof. Latin lang. and lit., Univ. of Pa., 1902-32, emeritus prof. since 1932, special lecturer in Latin, 1932-37; sec. Phila. Br. English-Speaking Union, 1937-38. Annual prof. Am. Sch. Classical Studies in Rome, 1907-08, prof. in charge, 1923-24; life mem. Am. Acad. in Rome. Mem. Am. Philos. Soc., Phi Beta Kappa, Phi Kappa Phi. Author: Cicero and His Influence, 1923. Editor of various textbooks, and with Prof. Charles E. Bennett, Allyn & Bacon's College Latin Series. Translator Suetonius, Sallust, Gellius, Nepos, Ammianus (Loeb Class. Lib.), Gentili, De Iure Belli (Classics Internat. Law). Contbr. on philol. and archeol. topics. Home: The Fairfax, 43d and Locust Sts., Philadelphia, Pa. Died Mar. 26, 1943.

ROLFE, Stanley Herbert, retired educator; born Nanticoke, Pa, Apr. 2, 1887; s. William and Margaret (Foster) R.; A.B., Bucknell U., 1909, LL.D., 1941; A.M., New York Univ., 1928, Ed.D., 1937; m. Blanche Margaret Whitebred, 1912; children—Doris Margaret (Mrs. Allen Herbert Jackson), Hilda A. (Mrs. Robert Martin Kugler), E. Jeanne (Mrs. Harry William Wenner); m. 2d, Emily V. Halberstadt, 1931. Teacher of grades and high sch., Nanticoke, Pa., 1910-12; teacher and vice prin., pub. schs., Newark, 1912-20, prin. elementary sch., 1920-29, asst. supt. of schs., 1929-36, dept. supt., 1936-37, supt., 1937-43, retired because of health. Mem.

N.J. Council of Edn., Phi Delta Kappa. Presbyterian. Clubs: Schoolmen's, N.J. Schoolmasters' (past pres) Home: 524 N. Palmway, Lake Worth, Fla. Died July 20, 1949; buried Hollywood Cemetary, Union, N.J.

ROLFS, Peter Henry, plant pathologist; b. Le Claire, Ia., Apr. 17, 1865; s. Maas Peter and Maria Christina (Neimeier) R.; B.S., Iowa State Coll., Ames, 1889, M.S., 1891, asst. in botany, 1891; D.Sc., U. of Fla., 1920; m. Effie Stone, Aug. 25, 1892 (died Mar. 31, 1929); children—Mrs. Effie Hargrave, Clarissa. Entomologist and botanist, 1891-92, botanist and horticulturist, 1892-98, Fla. Expt. Sta.; prof. botany and horticulture, Fla. Agrl. Coll., 1895-99; botanist and bacteriologist, Clemson Coll. (S.C.) and Agrl. Expt. Sta., 1899-1901; plant pathologist, Subtropical Lab., U.S. Dept. Agr., Miami, Fla., 1901-06; dir. Fla. Agrl. Expt. Sta., 1906-21; dir. extension div., 1913-21; dean Coll. of Agr., U. of Fla., 1915-21; commd. to locate, organize and conduct agrl. coll. for State of Minas Geraes, Brazil, 1921-29; consultor Technico de Agricultura do Estado de Minas Geraes, 1929-33; state supt. of Farmers' Inst., 1907-19; agrl. dir. Fla. State Fair, 1917. Chmn. State Food Commn. and State Council of Defense, 1917-18. Fellow A.A.A.S.; mem. Bot. Soc. America (hon. life mem. since 1938), Assn. Am. Agrl. Colls. and Expt. Stations, Fla. State Hort. Soc. (pres., 1907, 08), Internat. Assn. Botanists, St. Louis Acad. Science, Sociedade Mineira de Agricultura, Sociedade Nacional (Brazil) de Agricultura, Club de Engenharia (Nacional). Democrat. Methodist. Author: Vegetable Growing in the South for Northern Markets, 1896; Subtropical Vegetable Gardening, 1915; also numerous pamphlets on plant diseases, hort. and agrl. subjects. Address: 1422 W. Arlington St., Gainesville, Fla. Died Feb. 23, 1944.

ROLLAND, Romaine (rô-läɴ), author; b. Clamecy, France, Jan. 29, 1866; ed. Clamecy schs., École Normale Supérieure (Paris) and École Française de Rome (Italy); received Litt.D. Author: Le Théâtre du Peuple, 1901; François Millet, 1902; Beethoven, 1903; Michel-Ange, 1906; Cycle de la Revolution (series of seven plays), 1909; Jean-Christophe (three series), 1904-12; Colas Breugnon, 1919; Clerambault, 1921; L'Ame Enchantée (The Soul Enchanted; trilogy), 1922-27; Mahatma Gandhi, 1924; Goethe and Beethoven (Eng. trans.), 1931. Address: Vezelay (Yonne), France.* Died Dec. 30, 1944.

ROMAN, Frederick William, lecturer, author; b. Sidney, O.; s. Jacob and Caroline (Willhouse) R.; B.S., Nat. Normal Univ., Lebanon, O., 1897, A.B., 1899; A.B., Yale, 1902, A.M., 1905; Ph.D., magna cum laude, U. of Berlin, 1910; Docteur ès Lettres, très honorable, Sorbonne, U. of Paris, 1923. Instr. in sociology and economics, Smith Coll., 1911-12; prof. economics and sociology, Univ. of S.D., 1912-14; prof. economics and edn., New York U., 1923-26; dir. Associated Forums, Ltd., Los Angeles, Calif., since 1926; founder and dir. The Roman Forum, a California Corp., since 1935; regent of the Univ. of Calif. since 1940. Mem. British Soc. Authors; asso. mem. Institut International de Sociologie. Author: Die Deutschen Gewerblichen and Kaufmännischen Fortbildungs-und-Fachschulen, 1910; The Industrial and Commercial Schools of U.S. and Germany, 1914; La Place de la Sociologie dans l'Education, 1923; The New Education in Europe, 1923. Address: 2101 South Gramercy Place, Los Angeles 7, Calif. Died Apr. 9, 1948; buried in Forest Lawn Memorial Park, Glendale, Calif.

ROMMEL, George McCullough (rŏm′ĕl), agrl. consultant; b. Mt. Pleasant, Ia., Feb. 26, 1876; s. Alexander and Rachel Penn (McCullough) R.; B.S., Ia. Wesleyan Coll., 1897; B.S. Agr., Iowa State Coll., 1899; m. Sallie Russell Reeves, Sept. 19, 1906; children—Anna Margaret (Mrs. W. S. Tallman), Sarah Elizabeth (Mrs. J. M. Boze, Jr.), George McCullough (dec.), Alexander Ross. Asst. in animal husbandry, Iowa State Coll., 1899-1901; mgr. Ore. R.R. & Nav. Experimental Farm, Walla Walla, Wash., Mar.-June, 1901; expert in animal husbandry, U.S. Dept. Agr., 1901-05; animal husbandman, U.S. Dept. Agr., Jan. 1905-21, and chief of animal husbandry div., 1910-21; editor in chief, Am. Internat. Pubs., Inc., 1921-22; Morse Agrl. Service, 1923-28. Lecturer, Columbia U., 1923-26; technical consultant U.S. Dept. of Agr., 1927-28, U.S. Bur. Standards, 1928; became ind. commr. of Industrial Com. of Savannah, 1928; with Tennessee Valley Authority, Aug. 1, 1933-July 31, 1945; retired at own request, Aug. 1, 1945. Member United States Agricultural Commission to Europe, 1918; chairman Department of Agriculture committee on live stock drouth relief, 1919; U.S. del. 1st Pan-Am. Scientific Congress, Santiago, Chile; mem. executive com. 2d Congress, Washington, 1915; U.S. del. Inter-American Conf., Washington, 1930. Fellow A.A.A.S. Author: Farm Products in Industry, 1928. Contbr. to mags. Has written various bulletins and monographs on animal husbandry. Address: P. O. Box 1085, Bradenton, Fla. Died Nov. 26, 1945.

RONGY, Abraham Jacob (rŏn′jĭ), gynecologist, obstetrician; b. Russia, Sept. 27, 1878; s. Pincus and Lena (Bakst) R.; M.D., Long Island Coll. Hosp., 1899; m. Fanny F. Fields, Jan. 1, 1914. One of the founders of Jewish Maternity Hospital; attending gynecologist Lebanon Hosp. and Hosp. for Joint Diseases; consulting gynecologist Rockaway Beach Hospital and Royal Hospital; consulting gynecologist and obstetician, Bronx Maternity and Women's Hospital. Chmn., Greater New York Committee on Periodic Health Examination, 1928-33; chmn., Nat. Council, Zionist Orgn. of America, 1935-36; v.p., Am. Jewish Congress, 1925-26; del. World Relief Conf., Karlstad, 1924; mem. editorial bd. Preventive Medicine, 1929-40. Mem. bd. of dirs. Conf. on Jewish Relations; mem. American Jewish Com.; mem. of Nat. Council and dir., mem. exec. com. of Am. Joint Distribution Committee; chairman American Section Jewish Health Committee; honorary president Zionist Organization, 7th District; trustee at large Fedn. of Jewish Philanthropies. Honorable fellow, American Association of Obstetricians and Gynecologists, and Abdominal Surgeons. Fellow America College of Surgeons, N.Y. Academy of Medicine; mem. A.M.A., Medical Society State of New York, Medical Society County of New York, A.A.A.S., American Genetic Assn., Acad. of Polit. Science, Am. Med. Editors and Authors Assn., Phi Delta Epsilon, Judeans. Author: Abortion—Legal or Illegal?, 1933; Childbirth Yesterday and Today, 1937; Safely Through Childbirth, 1937; The Contribution of the German Jew to Medicine, 1933; Half a Century of Jewish Medical Activities in New York City, 1937; Collation Chats; The Palatal Arch and the Pelvis, 1940; Unusual Consultations, 1941; Radium Therapy in Benign Uterine Bleeding, 1942; Jews in American Medicine, 1949; also numerous articles on gynecology. Home: 40 Central Park South, New York 24. Address: 2 W. 71st St., New York, N.Y. Died Oct. 10, 1949.

RONNEBECK, Arnold (rŏn′nĕ-bĕk), sculptor; b. Nassau, Germany, May 8, 1885; s. Richard and Anna (Horn) R.; grad. Dorotheen Real-Gymnasium, Berlin, 1905; studied architecture at Royal Art Sch., Berlin, 1905-07; student of sculpture in Munich, 1907-08; pupil of Maillol and Bourdelle in Paris, 1908-14; m. Louise Harrington Emerson, Mar. 20, 1926; children—Arnold Emerson, Anna Marie Ursula. Came to U.S., 1923, naturalized, 1933. Prof. of sculpture, U. of Denver, 1929-35; dir. Denver Art Museum, 1926-31. Represented in permanent collections of museums in Europe and this country. Awarded gold medal, Kansas City Art Inst., 1929, silver medal, 1928; fine arts medal, Denver City Club, 1928. Club: Cactus. Contbr. articles on art to mags. and newspapers. Home and Studio: 435 Clermont St., Denver, Colo. Died Nov. 14, 1947.

ROOK, Charles Alexander (ro͝ok), journalist; b. Pittsburgh, Pa., Aug. 11, 1861; s. Alexander W. and Harriet L. (Beck) R.; ed. Ayers Latin Sch. and Western U. of Pa. (now U. of Pittsburgh); m. Anna B. Wilson, Sept. 9, 1884. Became connected with Pittsburgh Dispatch, 1880; sec., 1888-96, treas., 1896-1902, pres. and editor-in-chief same, 1902-23; dir. Dept. Pub. Safety, Pittsburgh, 1923-26. Served as dir. and mem. exec. com. Associated Press. On staff Gov. Stuart, with rank of lt. col., 1907; apptd. on staff of Gov. Brumbaugh, 1915; mem. bd. inspectors Western Penitentiary, Pa.; mem. State Prison Labor Commn., 1915; del.-at-large Rep. Nat. Conv., 1908. Apptd. by Pres. Taft E.E. and M.P. at One Hundredth Anniversary of Independence of U.S. of Mex., 1910; del. Nat. Rivers and Harbors Congress, 1907-23; del. Conf. on Conservation, The White House, 1908; rep. 31st Dist. of Pa. as elector of President and v.p., 1916; del. Rep. Nat. Conv., 1920. Episcopalian. Home: (winter) La Cañada, Calif. Office: The Dispatch Bldg., Pittsburgh, Pa. Died Oct. 20, 1946.

ROONEY, Marie Collins (Mrs. John Jerome Rooney) (ro͞o′nê), lecturer; b. Minn.; d. Michael Dunstan and Katharine (Kennelly) Collins; ed. U. of Minn., Ralston College (Washington, D.C.) and Columbia; m. John Jerome Rooney, 1903 (died 1934); children—John Jerome (lt. comdr. U.S.N.R.), Dunstan Collins, Roderick Shanahan (Comdr. U.S.S. Corvina, Missing off Johnson Island, Marshall's 1943), Moira Jerome. Formerly teacher Ralston College, Washington, D.C., (prin. 7 years), and Harvard Summer Schl.; lecturer Board of Education, New York City; founder and dir. N.Y. Inst. of Tutoring. Mem. local sch. bd., N.Y. City, 1919-33; has lectured throughout U.S. and in principal European countries; interpreter of Shakespeare, Ibsen, Vondel; writer of Am. Indian legends, folk-lore tales; compiler (with Edwin Markham) The Collected Poems of John Jerome Rooney. Chmn. of Woman's Nat. Soldier Bonus Com. (3,000,000 signatures presented to U.S. Senate); chmn. Washington Heights Assn. and Playground Conf.; mem. Minn. Club in the East (former pres.), Poetry Soc. of America, Am. Irish Hist. Soc. N.Y. Folklore Soc., Art Center of Washington Heights. Catholic. Home: 619 W. 145th St., New York, N.Y. Died Dec. 22, 1949.

ROOSEVELT, Edith Kermit Carow; b. Norwich, Conn., Aug. 16, 1861; d. Charles and Gertrude Elizabeth (Tyler) Carow; ed. Miss Comstock's School; m. Theodore Roosevelt, 26th President of U.S., in London, Eng., Dec. 2, 1886; children—Theodore J., Kermit (dec.), Ethel Carow (Mrs. Richard Derby), Archibald Bullock, Quentin (dec.). Home: Oyster Bay, N.Y. Died Sept. 30, 1948.

ROOSEVELT, Franklin D(elano) (rō′zĕ-vĕlt), thirty-first President of the United States; b. Hyde Park, N.Y., Jan. 30, 1882; s. James and Sara (Delano) R.; A.B., Harvard, 1904; Columbia U. Law Sch., 1904-07; LL.D., Rutgers, 1933, Washington Coll., 1933, Yale, 1934, William and Mary Coll., 1934, U. of Notre Dame, 1935; Litt.D., Rollins Coll., 1936; Dr. Civil Law, Oxford U., Eng., 1941; m. Anna Eleanor Roosevelt, Mar. 17, 1905; children—Anna Eleanor (Mrs. John Boettiger), James, Elliott, Franklin D., John A. Admitted to New York bar, 1907; practiced with Carter, Ledyard & Milburn, New York, 1907-10; mem. firm of Roosevelt & O'Connor, 1924-33. Mem. N.Y. Senate, 1910-Mar. 17, 1913 (resigned); asst. sec. of the Navy, 1913-20; elected gov. of New York for 2 terms, 1929-33; Dem. nominee for vice-pres. of U.S., 1920. Dem. nominee for President of U.S., 1932, elected for term, 1933-37; Dem. nominee for second term, 1936, re-elected for term 1937-41; Dem. nominee for third term, 1940, re-elected for term 1941-45. Dem. nominee for fourth term, 1944; re-elected for term, 1945-49. Mem. Hudson-Fulton Celebration Commn., 1909, Plattsburgh Centennial, 1913; member National Commission Panama P.I. Expedition, 1915, overseer Harvard U., 1918-24. Pres. American National Red Cross, Georgia Warm Spring Foundation. In charge of inspection United States Naval forces in European waters, July-Sept. 1918, and of demobilization in Europe, Jan.-Feb. 1919. Mem. Naval History Soc., N.Y. Hist. Soc., Holland Soc., Alpha Delta Phi, Phi Beta Kappa. Mason. Episcopalian; sr. warden St. James Ch., Hyde Park. Author: Whither Bound, 1926; The Happy Warrior—Alfred E. Smith, 1928; Government—Not Politics, 1932; Looking Forward, 1933; On Our Way, 1934. Home: Hyde Park, Dutchess County, N.Y. Address: The White House, Washington, D.C. Died April 12, 1945; interned at Hyde Park, N.Y.

ROOSEVELT, Kermit; b. Oyster Bay, N.Y., Oct. 10, 1889; s. Theodore (26th President of U.S.) and Edith Kermit (Carow) R.; A.B., Harvard, 1912; m. Belle Wyatt Willard, June 11, 1914. With father on hunting trip in Africa, 1909-10, also exploration trip on "River of Doubt," in Brazil, 1914; engaged in engring. and banking in S. America, 1911-16; pres. Roosevelt Steamship Co.; v.p. U.S. Lines Co. Commd. capt. in British Army, July 1917, and served with Motor Machine Guns, in Mesopotamia; trans. to 7th F.A., 1st Div., U.S. Army, June 1918; hon. discharged, Mar. 1919. Commd. major Middlesex Regt., Brit. Army, Oct. 10, 1939; col. in Finnish Army to raise vols. in England for Finnish campaign, Jan.-Feb. 1940; with Brit. Army in Norwegian campaign, Mar.-June 1940; to Egypt, Aug. 1940; invalided to England, Dec. 1940, to U.S. June 1941. Awarded Military Cross (British); Montenegrin War Cross. Republican. Member Dutch Reformed Church. Clubs: Knickerbocker, Racquet, River (founder), India House, Boone and Crocket (former pres.). Author: War in the Garden of Eden, 1919; The Happy Hunting Grounds, 1920; Quentin Roosevelt—A Sketch with Letters; (with brother Theodore) East of the Sun and West of the Moon, 1926; Cleared for Strange Ports, 1927; American Backlogs, 1928; Trailing the Giant Panda (with brother Theodore), 1929. Home: Oyster Bay, N.Y. Office: One Broadway, New York, N.Y. Died on active service in U. S. Army on June 4th, 1943; buried in Military Cemetery, Fort Richardson, Alaska.

ROOSEVELT, Philip J(ames), corp. exec.; b. New York, N.Y., May 15, 1892; s. W(illiam) Emlen and Christine Griffin (Kean) R.; prep. edn., St. Mark's Sch., Southboro, Mass.; A.B., Harvard, 1913; married, May 9, 1925; children—Philippa, Philip James, John Ellis II. Reporter, 1913-15; investment dealer, 1919-33; partner Roosevelt & Son; officer or dir. many other corps. Served as lt., capt. and maj. Air Service, U.S. Army, 1918; awarded Croix de Guerre with palm (France). Trustee Village of Cove Neck, N.Y. Pres. North Am. Yacht Racing Union. Clubs: Cruising Club of America, Knickerbocker, Downtown, Lunch, New York Yacht, Seawanhaka-Corinthian Yacht (commodore), Cold Spring Harbor Beach, Beaver Dam Winter Sports. Died Nov. 8, 1941.

ROOSEVELT, Theodore, Jr., soldier, publisher, author; b. Oyster Bay, New York, September 13, 1887; s. Theodore (26th President of the United States) and Edith Kermit (Carow) Roosevelt; B.A., Harvard University, 1908, hon. M.A., 1919; m. Eleanor Butler Alexander, June 20, 1910; children—Grace Green, Theodore, Cornelius Van Shaack, Quentin. Member New York State Assembly, 1919-20; assistant sec. of the navy, Mar. 4, 1921-Oct. 5, 1924 (resigned); chmn. com. of naval experts at Limitation of Armament Conf., 1922; Rep. candidate for gov. of N.Y., 1924; temp. chmn. N.Y. State Rep. Conv., 1927; leader of James Simpson-Roosevelts-Field Museum Expdn. to Asia, 1925; of Kelley-Roosevelts-Field Museum Expdn., Asia, 1928-29; gov. of Puerto Rico, 1929-32; gov. gen. of Philippine Islands, 1932-33; chmn. bd. American Express Co., 1934-35, vice-president Doubleday Doran & Co. since 1935. Commd. major 26th Inf., U.S. Army, 1917; lt. col., Sept. 2, 1918; arrived in France, June 1917; with 1st Div., 1st Army, A.E.F.; participated in battles at Cantigny, Soissons, Argonne-Meuse offensive, St. Mihiel offensive; twice wounded. Returned to active duty, U.S. Army, as colonel commanding 26th Infantry, 1st Div., Apr. 1941; advanced to brig. gen., Dec. 1941. Decorated D.S.C. and D.S.M., Order of Purple Heart, Silver Star with Oak Leaf Cluster (United States); Legion of Honor and Croix de Guerre with three palms (France); Grand Cordon of Prince Danilo I and War Cross (Montenegro); Grand Croix de la Couronne and Croix de Guerre with palms (Belgium); Grand Blue Cordon of Order of the Jade (China) (World War I); two Oak Leaf Clusters for Silver Star, Legion of Merit, French Croix de Guerre, Legion of Honor (World War II); (posthumously awarded) Medal of Honor (U.S.A.); Croix de Guerre (French). President National Health Council, 1935; national chairman United Council for Civilian Relief in China, 1938-40; chmn. Am. Bur. for Med. Aid to China, 1940. V.p. Boy Scouts of Am. An organizer American Legion, 1919. Member American Geog. Soci; mem. bd. trustees Field Museum Natural History; fellow Royal Geog. Soc. (London). Republican. Clubs: Harvard, River, Nat. Republicans of New York (pres. 1934-36), Explorers. Author: Average Americans, 1919; (with brother Kermit) East of the Sun and West of the Moon, 1926; Rank and File, 1928; All in the Family, 1929; (with brother Kermit) Trailing the Giant Panda, 1929; Taps (with Grantland Rice), 1932; Three Kingdoms of Indo-China (with Harold J. Coolidge, Jr.), 1933; Colonial Policies of the United States, 1937; The Desk Drawer Anthology (with Alice Roosevelt Longworth), 1937. Home: Oyster Bay, L.I., N.Y. Office: 14 W. 49th St., New York, N.Y. Died July 12, 1944; buried in Am. Military Cemetery, St. Laurent, Fr.

ROOT, Chapman Jay (root), mfr.; b. Wayne County, Pa., Nov. 22, 1867; s. Jay Chapman and Mary Jane (Wood) R.; ed. pub. schs., Ravenna, O.; m. Ellen A. Ruffle, July 12, 1891. Vice-pres. and treas. Ravenna Glass Co., 1890-91; mgr. Cream City Glass Co., Milwaukee, Wis., 1894-99; sec. North Baltimore Bottle Glass Co., 1899-1901; organizer, 1901, since pres. Root Glass Co., Terre Haute, Ind.; pres. Orlando Investment Co.; pres. Florida Coca-Cola Bottling Co.; dir. The Coca-Cola Co., Owens-Illinois Glass Co., Continental Gin Co., N.Y. Coca-Cola Bottling Co., Phila. Coca-Cola Bottling Co., St. Louis Coca-Cola Bottling Co., Kansas City Coca-Cola Bottling Co. Dir. Rose Polytechnic Inst. Mason (trustee Zorah Shrine Temple, at Terre Haute, Ind.), Elk. Clubs: Country (Terre Haute); Indianapolis Athletic; Chicago Athletic; Congressional Country (Washington); Capital City (Atlanta); Bath, Indian Creek, Cocolobo Cay (Miami Beach); Biscayne Bay Yacht (Miami). Home: 924 Lafayette Av., Terre Haute, Ind. Office: 14th and Market Sts., Jacksonville, Fla. Died Nov. 20, 1945.

ROOT, E(dward) Tallmadge, clergyman; b. Springfield, O., March 19, 1865; s. Edward Warren and Mary (Tallmadge) R.; grad. N.Y. Classical Inst., 1883; A.B., Yale Coll., 1887; B.D., Yale, 1890; m. Georgiana Merrill, Feb. 21, 1893; children—Edward Merrill, Winthrop Hegeman. Ordained to the ministry of the Presbyterian Ch., 1890; asst., University Place Presbyterian Ch., N.Y. City, 1890-91; pastor, Second Congl. Ch., Baltimore, Md., 1891-96; Elmwood Temple Congl. Ch., Providence, R.I., 1896-1904, sec. R.I. Fedn. Chs., 1903-12, Mass. Fedn. Chs., 1904-30; pastor Congl. Ch., Westmore, Vt. (to test work in a rural community), 1933-35. Trustee R.I. and Mass. Anti-Saloon Leagues. Prohibition cand. for governor, 1940, for U.S. Senator, 1944. Mem. Brotherhood of Kingdom, 20th Century Assn. (Boston), N.E. Town and Country Ch. Commn. Author: Profit of the Many, 1898; The Red Swan (verse drama), 1932; Bible Economy of Plenty, 1938. Address: 55 Putnam St., Somerville, Mass. Died Oct. 7, 1948.

ROOT, Oren; b. Columbia, Mo., June 20, 1873; s. Oren and Ida C. (Gordon) R.; nephew late Senator Elihu R.; Hamilton Coll., class of 1894; M.A.; married; 2 children. Became identified with pub. utility corps. in New York, 1895; active operating head of all st. surface rys. in New York, 1902-12; asst. gen. mgr., 1902-03, gen. mgr., 1903-06, 1st v.p., gen. mgr., 1906-08, gen. mgr. for receivers, 1908-12, then dir. and mem. exec. com., New York City Ry. Co.; v.p., 1900-02, pres., 1902-05, Central Crosstown R.R. Co.; pres. Republic Ry. & Light Co., and chmn. bd. Central States Electric Corp., 1912-17; dir., 1917, pres., 1919-31, Hudson & Manhattan R.R. Co.; dir. M.P. R.R. Co., 1922-23, and mem. exec. com., 1923; dir. T.&P. Ry. Co., 1923. Mem. Sigma Phi, Phi Beta Kappa. Clubs: University, Links, Racquet and Tennis, Piping Rock, Nat. Golf Links America, City Midday. Home: 737 Park Av., New York, N.Y. Died Aug. 29, 1948; buried in Hamilton College Cemetery, Clinton, N.Y.

ROOT, William T(homas), psychologist; b. Concordia, Kan., June 2, 1882; s. William T. and Katherine (York) R.; grad. Los Angeles State Normal, 1905; A.B., Stanford, 1912, A.M., 1913, Ph.D., 1921; m. Ida May Nyce, June 27, 1914; 1 son, William Calvin. Instr. in psychology, Los Angeles State Normal, 1913-19; prof. psychology, U. of Pittsburgh, 1921-29, also head of dept. since 1929 and dean of the Graduate School since 1935. Trustee Western Penitentiary for Pa. Mem. Am. Psychol. Assn., Am. Statis. Assn., A.A.A.S., Phi Delta Kappa, Sigma Xi. Author: A Socio-Psychological Study of Fifty-three Supernormal Children, 1921; A Psychological and Educational Survey of 1916 Prisoners in the Western Penitentiary for Pa., 1927; Psychology for Life Insurance Underwriters, 1929. Contbr. articles to psychol. periodicals. Home: Valencia, Pa. Died Jan. 25, 1945; buried in Mount Royal Mausoleum, Glenshaw, Pa.

ROOT, Winfred Trexler, prof. history; b. Mt. Joy, Lancaster County, Pa., Mar. 9, 1879; s. Benjamin Mylin and Martha Elizabeth (Trexler) R.; A.B., Princeton, 1902; Ph.D., U. of Pa., 1908; m. Anna Harper, June 3, 1908; 1 dau., Anne Davidson (Mrs. Gordon W. Prange). Instr. Peekskill (N.Y.) Mil. Acad., 1903-05; instr. history, U. of Wis., 1908-11, asst. prof., 1911-15, asso. prof., 1915-19, prof., 1919-25, prof. history, head dept. history, U. of Ia. since 1925; prof. history, summers, U. of Chicago, 1917, U. of Mich., 1919, Harvard, 1923, Stanford U., 1931. Fellow Royal Hist. Soc.; mem. Am. Hist. Assn., Miss. Valley Hist. Assn. Club: Triangle. Author: Relations of Pennsylvania with the British Government, 1696-1765, 1912; Syllabus Am. Colonial History, 1912; also reviews and papers on Am. History. Home: 214 E. Church St., Iowa City, Ia. Died Dec. 9, 1947; buried Oakland Cemetery, Iowa City, Iowa.

ROOTS, Logan Herbert, bishop; b. near Tamaroa, Perry County, Ill., July 27, 1870; s. Philander Keep and Frances Maria (Blakeslee) R.; A.B., Harvard, 1891; student Harvard Grad. Sch., and grad sec. Harvard Christian Assn., 1891-92; traveling sec. intercollegiate dept. Internat. Com., Y.M.C.A., 1892-93; B.D., Episcopal Theol. Sch., Cambridge, Mass., 1896; D.D., U. of the South, 1906, Episcopal Theol. Sch., Cambridge, Mass., 1922, Harvard Univ., 1925; m. Hankow, China, Eliza Lydia McCook, Apr. 17, 1902; children John McCook, Logan Holt, Sheldon, Frances Blakeslee, Elizabeth Butler. Deacon, 1896, priest, 1898, P.E. Ch.; went to China, 1896, and studied the language at Wuchang for 2 yrs.; moved to Hankow, where was engaged in gen. missionary work until spring of 1904; consecrated, at Boston, Nov. 14, 1904, 2d bishop of Hankow, China. Chmn. China Continua- Died Sep. 23, 1945.

ROPER, Daniel Calhoun, lawyer; b. Marlboro County, S.C., April 1, 1867; s. John Wesley and Henrietta V. (McLaurin) R.; A.B., Duke Univ., N.C., 1888; LL.B., National Univ., Washington, 1901; LL.D., Tusculum College, 1927, National Univ., 1933; M.B.A., Bryant & Stratton Coll., Providence, R.I., 1933; L.H.D., Rollins College, 1934; m. Lou McKenzie, Dec. 25, 1889; children—May (Mrs. D. R. Coker), James H., Daniel C., Grace H. (Mrs. Frank Bohn), John W., Harry McK., Richard Fred. Mem. S.C. Ho. of Rep., 1892-94; clk. U.S. Senate Com. on Inter-State Commerce, 1894-97; expert spl. agt. U.S. Census Bur., 1900-10; clk. Ways and Means Com., Ho. of Rep., 1911-13; first asst. postmaster-gen., Mar. 14, 1913-Aug. 1, 1916; chmn. Orgn. Bur., Woodrow Wilson campaign, 1916; vice-chmn. U.S. Tariff Commn., Mar. 22-Sept. 25, 1917; commr. of Internal Revenue, 1917-20; sec. of Commerce, 1933-38; minister to Canada, May 9-Aug. 20, 1939. Mem. board of dirs. Atlantic Coast Line Railway. Developed in U.S. Census Bur. a plan for collecting cotton statistics by a count at frequent intervals during harvesting seasons of bales turned out at the ginneries. Mem. Am. Bar Assn.; mem. Gen. Conf. M.E. Ch., S., 1930; mem. 6th Ecumenical Conf., 1931. Mem. Bd. of Edn., D.C., 1932. Trustee Duke University. Mem. Sigma Alpha Epsilon, Phi Beta Kappa. Democrat. Methodist. Mason (32°, Shriner). Clubs: Chevy Chase (Md.); Nat. Press, University (Washington). Author: The United States Post Office, 1917; Fifty Years in Public Life, 1941. Home: 2700 Tilden St. Office: Tower Bldg., Washington, D.C. Died Apr. 11, 1943.

RORER, Virgil Eugene (rōr'ẽr), clergyman; b. Oak Lane, Phila., Pa., Mar. 18, 1867; s. David and Mary Felton (Bickley) R.; direct desc. of George Rorer who with 5 other learned men and several rabbis assisted Martin Luther in translating the Old Testament into German; A.B., Central High Sch., Phila., 1886, A.M., 1891; LL.B., Yale, 1889; student Boston U. Sch. of Theology, Boston Sch. of Expression; D.D., Dickinson Coll., 1919; m. Nellie Minora Blakely, Feb. 11, 1892 (died Dec. 27, 1924); children—Dwight Eugene, Nelson Virgil, Adele Madelene. Taught sch. 2 yrs.; admitted to bar, 1889; entered M.E. ministry, Phila. Conf., 1890; pastor successively at Jenkintown and North Wales, Pa., St. Luke's Ch., 19th St., Wissahickon, 7th St., Grace and Arch St. chs., Phila., until 1920, Meridian St. Ch., Indianapolis, 1920-30, St. Paul's Ch., Wilmington, Del., 1930-33; retired to devote himself to writing, lecturing, travel, and preaching on special occasions. Built St. Luke's and Wissahickon chs. Traveled in Can., 1927, Europe, 1928, 31, 32, Central America, 1929. Republican. Clubs: Literary (Indianapolis); Yale. Address: Flori-De-Leon Apartments, Inc., 130-132 Fourth Av., North, St. Petersburg, Fla. Died June 15, 1944.

ROSE, George B., lawyer; b. Batesville, Ark., July 10, 1860; s. U. M. and Margaret T. (Gibbs) R.; moved to Little Rock, Ark., with parents in 1865, and has resided there ever since; m. Marion Kimball, May 2, 1882; children—Clarence Edward, Miriam (dec.). Admitted to bar, 1879, and since in practice at Little Rock; mem. Rose, Loughborough, Dobyns & House. Has traveled much in the study of Renaissance art. Author: Renaissance Masters—Art of Raphael, Michelangelo, Leonardo da Vinci, Titian, Correggio, Botticelli, Rubens and Claude Lorraine, 1898, 1900, 1908; The World's Leading Painters, 1911; also numerous articles in revs. on lit. and art. Mem. Am. Bar Assn., Ark. State Bar Assn. (pres. 1902-03), Little Rock Bar Assn. (pres. 1923-24), Internat. Law Assn., Am. Law Inst., Judicature Soc., Conf. on Uniform State Laws. Clubs: Little Rock Country, Spring Lake Club. Home: 516 W. 16th St. Office: 314 W. Markham St., Little Rock, Ark. Died June 10, 1943.

ROSE, Herschel Hampton, judge; b. near Mannington, W.Va., Apr. 20, 1877; s. Thomas Martyn and Mary Ann (Barton) R.; graduate Fairmont State Normal School, 1897; LL.B., W.Va. U., 1906; m. Dessie Mae Miller, Oct. 25, 1911; children—Herschel Hampton, Jr., Helen Miller. Taught school, 1897-1900; bank teller, asst. cashier, 1900-03; admitted to W.Va. bar, 1906; practiced, Wetzel County, 1908-17, Fairmont, 1917-40; judge Supreme Court of Appeals, W.Va. since 1941. Dir. and pres. Fairmont Gen. Hosp.; pres. Bd. Edn., Marion County, 1933-39; exec. sec. to fuel adminstr. of W.Va., 1917-18. Mem. Marion County Bar Assn., W.Va. State Bar Assn., Am. Bar Assn., Phi Kappa Psi. Democrat. Methodist. Mason (K.T., Scottish Rite, 33°, Shrine, grand master Masons of W.Va. 1937-38), Elk. Club: Rotary (Fairmont). Home: 1511 Lee St. Address: State Capitol, Charleston, W.Va.* Died June 17, 1945.

ROSE, Hugh Edward, Hon., chief justice of the High Court, Ontario; b. Toronto, Can., Sept. 16, 1869; s. Hon. John Edward and Kate (MacDonald) R.; student Toronto Collegiate Inst. to 1886; B.A., U. of Toronto, 1891, LL.B., 1892; unmarried. Admitted as solicitor and called to bar Ontario, 1894; practiced law in Toronto; apptd. King's Counsel, 1908; apptd. justice of Supreme Court of Ontario, High Court Div., 1916; chief justice High Court since 1930. Mem. bd. govs. U. of Toronto. Clubs: Toronto, Toronto Golf. Mem. Ch. of England. Home: 86 Roxborough St., East. Address: Osgoode Hall, Toronto, Ontario, Can. Died Oct. 13, 1945.

ROSE, Maurice, army officer; b. Middletown, Conn., Nov. 26, 1899; s. Samuel and Katherine (Brown) R.; grad. Inf. Sch., Columbus, Ga., 1926, Cavalry Sch., Ft. Riley, Kan., 1931, Command and Gen. Staff Sch., Ft. Leavenworth, Kan., 1937, Army Industrial Coll., Washington, D.C., 1940; m. Virginia Barringer, Sept. 12, 1934; 1 son, Maurice Roderick. Commd. 2d lt. Inf., Aug. 1917, capt. 1920; major Cav., Aug. 1930, and advanced through the grades to brig. gen., June 1943; served with A.E.F., 1918, World War I; on Gen. Staff duty with troops, chief of staff, 2d Armored Div., Jan. 1942-June 1943; overseas assignment since Dec. 1942. Awarded Silver Star with 2 oak leaf clusters, Purple Heart. Home: 20 S. Ogden St., Denver, Colo. Killed in action, Mar. 1945.

ROSE, William Brandon, judge; b. Grove City, Pa., Jan. 25, 1862; s. James McKinley (double cousin William McKinley, Sr.) and Maria Catherine (Brandon) R.; ed. pub. schs.; LL.D., Grove City Coll.; m. Genevieve Eaton, Nov. 18, 1893 (died July 6, 1914); 1 dau., Genevieve (Mrs. David Earl Faust); m. 2d, Lillian Trester, June 21, 1919. Admitted to Pa. bar, 1888; asst. state librarian of Neb. and reporter of decisions of Supreme Court of Neb., 1889-1901; asst. atty. gen. of Neb., 1901-08; judge Supreme Court of Neb., Dec. 1, 1908-Jan. 6, 1943. Chmn. Rep. State Central Com. of Neb., 1906; mem. Am. Bar. Assn. Presbyterian. Edited Neb. Supreme Court Reports, vols. XXXV-LIX. Home: 1712 E. St., Lincoln, Neb. Died Jan. 16, 1946.

ROSEBAULT, Charles Jerome (rōz'bawlt), writer; b. Hartford, Conn., Aug. 16, 1864; s. David and Cecilia (Fleischman) R.; ed. high sch., Hartford; m. Laura Danziger (pianist), Apr. 12, 1897. Reporter New York Sun, 1884-92, Chicago corr., 1892, asst. city editor, 1892-96, business manager, 1902-07; sec. Retail Dry Goods Assn., 1896-1902; mng. editor newspaper and mag. service of the Vigilantes (war work orgn. of authors), 1918. Mem. Acad. Polit. Science, Authors League of America, Rockport (Mass.) Art Assn. Clubs: Players, Silurians, Dutch Treat (New York); Savage (London). Author: Saladin, Prince of Chivalry, 1930; When Dana Was the Sun, 1931. Contbr. articles and sketches to newspapers and mags. Home: 1 W. 67th St., New York, N.Y. Died Mar. 18, 1944.

ROSEBUSH, Judson George, paper mfr.; b. Alfred, N.Y., Nov. 9, 1878; s. George Wesley and Sara Maria (Burdick) R.; A.B., Alfred Coll., 1900, A.M., 1901, LL.D., 1930; scholar in politics, U. of Pa., 1900-01; fellow economics, Cornell, 1901-02, U. of Wis., 1902-03; U. of Berlin fall 1910; m. Barbara J. McNaughton, June 2, 1908; children—Judson George, John McNaughton, Barbara Jane. Succeeded father-in-law, John McNaughton, in business, 1910, and with others founded Inland Empire Paper Co., of Millwood, Wash.; chmn. bd. Craig Mountain Lumber Co.; dir. Nekoosa-Edwards Paper Co.; pub. interest dir. and mem. exec. com. Federal Home Loan Bank of Chicago, 1937. Pres. Wis. Loyalty League, World War, also mem. local exemption bd. Trustee Alfred Univ. Mem. Wis. Hist. Soc. Mem. Gen. Conf. M.E. Ch., Des Moines, Ia., 1920; mem. Internat. Com. and pres. Internat. Conv. Y.M.C.A., Atlantic City, N.J., Nov. 1922. Republican. Author: The Ethics of Capitalism, 1922; Rethinking the Y.M.C.A., 1933. Home: Appleton, Wis. Died July 31, 1948.

ROSECRANS, Egbert (rōz'krănz), judge; b. Hoboken, N.J., Oct. 7, 1891; s. Dr. James Hankinson and Maja (Lowell) R.; ed. Hoboken public schools, Blair Acad., Blairstown, N.J., Wesleyan U., Conn., and New York Law Sch.; m. Edith Wilson, June 4, 1914 (died July 27, 1926); 1 dau., Constance; m. 2d, Aileen Rittenhouse, Feb. 15, 1931 (divorced July 24, 1936); 1 dau., Rhonda Rittenhouse; m. 3d, Marian E. Willcox, Oct. 10, 1941; 1 dau., Lesley. Admitted to bars of N.J., 1913, Calif., 1923, Nevada, 1923, U.S. Supreme Ct., 1923; began practice in Blairstown, N.J.; county counsel Warren County, N.J. 1917, 1921-23; municipal accountant for N.J., 1918-21; counsel and special counsel for various municipal and county govts.; counsel for N.J. commr. of banking and ins., 1931-36; pres. judge Court of Common Pleas, Warren County, N.J., 1938-1943; special master in chancery and N.J. Supreme Court commissioner; asso. counsel in defense of Hauptman in Lindbergh Kidnaping trial, 1935, and leading counsel upon the appeals; mem. law faculty, John Marshall Coll., N.J., 1938. Chairman Selective Service Advisory Bd., Warren County, N.J., since 1940. Chmn. Commn. of State Judges designated by Chancellor which prepared the 1941 Revision of the Rules of the Probate Courts of Trustee N.J. Inst. for Practicing Lawyers since 1941; mem. Judicial Council, N.J., since 1941. Member Am. Bar Assn., N.J. State Bar Assn. (director), Warren County Bar Assn. (pres. 1935, trustee), Nev. and Calif. State bars, Soc. Sons of Revolution. Democrat. Presbyterian. Home: Blairstown, N.J.; and N.J., 1938-41; mem. N.J.-U.S. Constitution Commn. Plymouth, Vt. Died Jan. 20, 1948.

ROSEN, Baron, diplomatist. Formerly Russian minister at Tokio, Japan; was consul-gen. at New York and chargé d'affaires at Washington during Cleveland's first term; apptd. ambassador to U.S., 1905; joint plenipotentiary with Count Witte during peace negotiations, Portsmouth, N.H., 1905. Address: Russian Embassy, Washington. Died Dec. 31, 1921.

ROSENAU, Milton Joseph (rōz"n-now), sanitarian; b. Phila., Pa., Jan. 1, 1869; s. Nathan and Matilda (Blitz) R.; pub. and high schs., Phila.; M.D., U. of Pa., 1889; post-grad. studies in Hygienische Institut, Berlin, 1892-93; L'Institut Pasteur, Paris, 1900; Pathologisches Institut, Vienna, Austria, 1900; hon. A.M., Harvard U., 1914; m. Myra F. Frank, July 16, 1900 (dec.); children— William Frank (dec.), Milton J., Bertha (Mrs. Max L. Ilfeld); m. 2d, Maud H. Tenner, Jan. 13, 1934; 1 stepson, Leonard P. Tenner. Surgeon U.S. Pub. Health and Marine Hosp. Service, 1890-1909, dir. Hygienic Lab. same, 1899-1909, resigned; prof. preventive medicine and hygiene, Harvard Med. Sch., 1909-35, prof. emeritus since 1935; prof. epidemiology, Harvard School Public Health, 1922-35; dir. Div. Pub. Health, U. of N.C., since 1936; dean, Sch. of Pub. Health, U. of N.C., 1940-41; dir., same, 1941-43; dean, same since 1943; mem. of the adv. bd., National Health Council, U.S. Public Health Service, since 1929; mem. science adv. board National Research Council since 1934. Dir. School of Public Health of Harvard Univ. and Mass. Inst. Tech., 1913-22; mem. Mass. Bd. of Health, 1912-14; dir. Antitoxin and Vaccine Laboratory and chief division of biologic laboratories, same, 1914-21. Quarantine officer, San Francisco, 1895-98; del. of U.S. to 10th Internat. Conf. Hygiene and Demography, and 13th Internat. Congress Medicine and Surgery, Paris, 1900; mem. Internat. Com. Revision of Nomenclature of the Causes of Deaths, Paris, 1900; sanitary expert to 2d Pan-Am. Conf., Mexico, 1901; special lecturer on tropical diseases, Georgetown U. Awarded gold medal of Am. medicine for service to humanity, 1912-13; awarded the Sedgwick memorial medal for achievements in pub. health, 1934; awarded Gold Medal of Annual Forum on Allergy for outstanding contribution to allergy, 1945; mem. Association of Am. Physicians, A.M.A., Soc. of Am. Bacteriologists (pres. 1934) Am. Assn. Pathologists and Bacteriologists and others. Organized quarantine at Santiago and other Cuban ports, 1898-99. Author: Disinfection and Disinfectants, 1902; Experimental Studies in Yellow Fever and Malaria, 1904; The Immunity Unit for Diphtheria Antitoxin, 1905; A Method of Inoculating Animals with Precise Amounts, 1905; The Cause of Sudden Death Following the Injection of Horse Serum, 1906; Experimental Gastric Ulcer, 1906; The Origin and Spread of Typhoid Fever, 1907; The Standardization of Tetanus Antitoxin, 1908; The Milk Question, 1912; Preventive Medicine and Hygiene, 6th edition, 1935; also writer of many papers and articles on anaphylaxis, foot and mouth disease, pasteurization, milk and its relation to the public health, viability of the tubercle bacillus, infantile paralysis, organic matter in the expired breath, influenza, etc., and reports on sanitary and bacteriol. subjects. Mem. med. advisory bd. Am. Red Cross. Med. insp. (comdr.), U.S. bd. Am. Red Cross. Med. insp. (comdr.), U.S. N.R.F., 1917-19; capt. (ret.); asst. surgeon-gen., U.S. P.H. Service (ret.). Home: Laurel Hill Road, Chapel Hill, N.C. Died Apr. 9, 1946.

ROSENBERG, Arthur, prof. history; b. Berlin, Germany, Dec. 19, 1889; s. Georg Henry and Helene (Engel) R.; Ph.D., U. of Berlin, 1911; m. Ella Woehlmann, Oct. 28, 1919; children— Liselott, Wolfgang, Peter Michael. Came to U.S., 1937. Lecturer of history, U. of Berlin, 1914-30, prof. history, 1930-33; visiting prof., U. of Liverpool, England, 1934-37; lecturer Brooklyn Coll., Brooklyn, N.Y., since 1938. Mem. German Reichstag, 1924-28. Author (pub. in English, German, French, Italian, Spanish, Norwegian, Swedish and Hebrew): The State of Ancient Italy, 1913; Introduction and Sources of Roman History, 1921; Birth of the German Republic, 1931; History of Bolshevism, 1934; History of the German Republic, 1936; Democracy and Socialism, 1939. Home: 1316 E. 26th St., Brooklyn, N.Y. Died Feb. 8, 1943.

ROSENFELD, Paul, author; b. N.Y. City, May 4, 1890; s. Julius S. and Clara (Liebmann) R.; grad. Riverview Mil. Acad., 1908; B.A., Yale, 1912; Litt. B., Columbia U. Sch. of Journalism, 1913; unmarried. Reporter New York Press, 1913; musical critic The Dial, 1920-27; co-editor The American Caravan—a Yearbook of Am. Literature, since 1927. Pvt., U.S.A., Camp Humphries, Va., 1918. Jewish religion. Club: Yale (New York). Author: Musical Portraits (20 modern composers), 1920; Musical Chronicle (1917-23), 1923; Port of New York (14 American Moderns), 1924; Men Seen (24 Modern Authors), 1925; The Boy in the Sun (novel), 1928; By Way of Art (essays), 1928; An Hour with American Music, 1929; Discoveries of a Music Critic, 1936. Home: 270 W. 11th St., New York. Died July 21, 1946.

ROSENGARTEN, Adolph George; b. Phila, Pa., Feb. 22, 1870; s. Harry Bennett and Clara Johanna (Knorr) R.; ed. Faires Classical Inst. and William Penn Charter Sch.; B.S., U. of Pa., 1892; m. Christine Penrose, April 30, 1901; children—Adolph G., Jr., (U.S. Army), Emily Penrose (Mrs. Samuel Goodman). Entered employ Rosengarten & Sons, 1892, partner, 1898-1901, bus. incorporated, 1901, sec.-treas., 1901-05, bus. merged with Powers & Weightman and name changed to Powers-Weightman-Rosengarten Co., 1905, treas., 1905-17, v.p. and treas., 1917-21, pres., 1921-27, merged with Merck & Co., Rahway, N.J., 1927, dir. Merck & Co. since 1927. Dir. Phila. Nat. Bank, Pa. Salt Mfg. Co.; trustee Penn Mutual Life Ins., Mutual Assurance Co. for Insuring Houses from Loss by Fire, past dir. Phila. Trust Co., 1916-40. Served in First Troop Phila. City Cavalry, 1893-1903; in P. R. expdtn. Spanish-Am. War; chief miscellaneous chem, sect. chem. div. War Industries Bd., 1918. Dir. Zoölogical Soc. Phila., trustee U. of Pa., Lankenau Hosp. Mem. Am. Philos. Soc., Am. Inst. Chem. Engrs., Am. Chem. Soc., Wistar Assn., Phi Kappa Sigma. Republican. Episcopalian. Hereditary companion Mil. Order Loyal Legion U.S. Club; Philadelphia, Rittenhouse, Rabbit. Author of article: Romance in Research (Gen. Mag. U. of Pa.) Oct. 1937. Home: St. Davids, Del. Co., Pa. Office: 1520 Locust St., Philadelphia. Died April 22, 1946; buried in Old St. David's Church, Devon, Pa.

ROSENHEIM, Alfred Faist (rō-zĕn-hīm'), architect; b. St. Louis, Mo., June 10, 1859; s. Morris and Matilda (Ottenheimer) R.; ed. Hassel's Inst., Frankfort-on-the-Main, Germany, 1872-74; Washington U., St. Louis, 1874-79; Mass. Inst. Tech., 1879-81; m. Frances Graham Wheelock, Sept. 30, 1884 (died Apr. 23, 1931); m. 2d, Ruth R. Salmons, June 10, 1935. In offices of various architects, 1881-84; asso. with Maj. Francis D. Lee, widely known architect of St. Louis, Mo., until his death, 1885, succeeding to his business; practiced on own account in St. Louis and other cities, 1886-1903; removed to Los Angeles, 1903; associated with firm Austin & Ashley, 1926-35. Architect for the H. W. Hellman Bldg., Hamburger Dept. Store, 2d Ch. of Christ, Scientist, Security Bank, Merchants Nat. Bank, Los Angeles Brewery, pub. schs. and many pvt. residences, notably those of E. L. Doheny, Judson C. Rives, Robert Marsh, E. W. Britt, A. J. McQuatters, C. Leonardt, John Howze, James B. True; retired after 55 years of practice, Oct. 1, 1941. Fellow Am. Inst. of Architects since 1889 (former dir.); mem. Southern Calif. Chapter A.I.A. (3 times pres.), Archtl. League Pacific Coast (twice pres.), Fine Arts League Los Angeles (ex-pres., and sec.), Municipal Art Commn. (past pres., sec., and mem. since 1928), Museum of History, Science and Art (mem. bd. govs. 10 yrs.), etc. Home: 5408 Victoria Av., Los Angeles, Calif. Died Sep. 9, 1943.

ROSENTHAL, Lessing (rō'zĕn-tăl), lawyer; b. Chicago, Ill., Nov. 23, 1868; s. Julius (for many years a leading member of Chicago bar) and Jette (Wolf) R.; A.B., Johns Hopkins, 1888; LL.B., Northwestern, 1891, LL.D., 1931; Chicago Coll. of Law (post-grad. course), 1892; admitted to Ill. bar, 1891; m. Mrs. Lillie Frank Myres, Dec. 10, 1901; 1 dau., Juliette (dec.). Member firm of Julius & Lessing Rosenthal from 1894 until father's death, May 14, 1905; organized, May 1, 1906, with Charles H. Hamill, firm of Rosenthal & Hamill; title changed to Rosenthal, Hamill & Wormser, Jan. 1, 1917, Rosenthal, Hamill, Eldridge & King, Feb. 1,1937, Rosenthal, Eldridge, King & Robin, March 1942. Director Hart, Schaffner & Marx since 1928 (member of executive com. 1930-35 and since 1945). President of Civil Service Reform Association of Chicago, 1906-08, Municipal Voters' League, 1910-15, Law Club of Chicago, 1911-12; chmn. com. on municipal elections, etc., of Chicago Charter Conv., 1905-09; chmn. citizens' com. re South Park Commrs.-Ill. Central R.R. contract, 1912, through whose efforts lake front settlement was materially modified and arranged, and the railroad's suburban service electrified. Member exec. com. Chicago Council on Foreign Relations, 1925-36, English-Speaking Union of Chicago, 1932-37. Trustee Brookings Instn., Washington, D.C., since 1931; trustee Johns Hopkins U. since Feb. 1938. Member visiting com. Harvard Law School, 1931-41. Mem. Am. and Ill. State bar assns., Chicago Bar Assn. (v.p. 1903-04), Bar Assn. City of New York, Am. Law Inst., Am. Judicature Soc. (dir. 1920-32), American Institute of Graphic Arts (honorary vice-president 1938-41), Bibliographical Soc. of America, Northwestern Assn. of Johns Hopkins Alumni (pres. 1921-24), Book and Play Club (pres. 1925-28); chmn. Chicago Com. Am. Soc. for Control of Cancer since 1926; governing life mem. Art Inst. Chicago. Ind. Republican. Clubs: Union League, City, Caxton, Chicago Literary (pres. 1930-31), Executives', Tavern, Standard, Mid-Day (Chicago); Grolier, Harvard (N.Y.); Book Club of California (San Francisco); Soc. of Typographic Arts (Chicago). Home: Hotel Sherry, 1725 E. 53d St. Office: 105 W. Monroe St., Chicago, Ill. Died Dec. 13, 1949.

ROSENTHAL, Louis S., banker; b. St. Louis, Mo., Nov. 9, 1890; s. Louis S. and Margaret (Burke) R.; ed. Cornell U. (class of 1912); m. Sara Beauvais, Dec. 14, 1917; children—Sally Ann Beauvais, Louis S. Asst. resident engr., Alaskan Engring. Commn., 1914-16; 1st lt. Coast Arty., U.S. Army, 1917-19; asst. mgr. Mercantile Bank of the Americas, 1919-20; asst. mgr., then gen. mgr., Nat. Bank of Nicaragua, Managua, Nicaragua, also gen. mgr. Cia. Mercantil de Ultramar, Managua; 2d v.p. Chase Nat. Bank of the City of New York, 1931-33, v.p. since 1934. Mem. Republic of Nicaragua Bd. to supervise expenditures from $1,500,000 loan for payment troops, settlement war claims, Nicaragua, 1928; mem. Social Service Commn. to Venezuela apptd. by Pres. Lopez Contreras, Venezuela, 1939; dir. Am. Chamber of Commerce of Cuba since 1931; dir. Haytian Corp. of America, New York. Major U.S. Marine Corps Reserve since 1934. Clubs: India House (New York); Larchmont Shore Club (Larchmont, N.Y.); Havana Country, Jaimanitas Yacht, Havana Yacht, American (Havana). Home: Country Club Park, Marianao, Cuba. Office: Aguiar 310, Hávana, Cuba. Died Jan. 20, 1943.

ROSEWATER, Charles Colman; b. Omaha, Neb., May 24, 1874; s. Edward and Leah (Colman) Rosewater; A.B., Cornell, 1894; M.A., Columbia, 1895; m. Julia Alice Warner, June 15, 1898; children—Charlotte, Warner. With circulation dept., later business mgr. Omaha Bee, 1895-99; organizer, 1900, and publisher Twentieth Century Farmer; gen. mgr. and v.p. Bee Pub. Co., Omaha, 1905-17; gen. mgr. Los Angeles Express, 1917, Los Angeles Times, 1918; pres. Kansas City Journal Co., 1912-21; v.p. and pub. Seattle Post-Intelligencer, 1922-24; v.p. Success Magazine, New York, 1924-27; now v.p. The New Age, Illustrated. President Farm Press Club of America, 1908-11; organizer, National Corn Exposition, 1909, and chmn. Expn. Co.; pres. Western Land Products Expn., 1911; sec. Omaha Tornado Relief Com. and chmn. com. in charge of relief, 1913. Treas. Am. Agrl. Publishers Assn., 1915. Mason (32°). Office: The New Age, Illustrated, Graybar Bldg., New York. Died Oct. 3, 1946.

ROSS, Carmon, educator; b. New York, N.Y., Feb. 28, 1884; s. Michael and Angela (Guzza) R.; Ph.B., Lafayette Coll., 1905; A.M., U. of Pa., 1916, Ph.D., 1922; m. Emma W. Kratz, Dec. 30, 1914 (died 1937); children—Angela, Barbara, Catherine; married 2d, Mary E. Read on October 18, 1941. Employed as superintendent schs., Doylestown, Pa., 1906-34; dir. summer demonstration school, Pa. State Coll., 1922-33; pres. Edinboro State Teachers Coll., 1931-40; Dept. Pub. Instruction, 1941; supt. of schools, Lansdowne, Pa., 1941-45; executive director Public Edn. Assn. of Pa., since 1946. Served as member N.J. Sch. Survey Commn., Pinchot Sch. Finance Commn. Mem. Ten Yr. Plan Pa. Edn. Commn. Mem. N.E.A., Pa. State Edn. Assn. (pres. 1934; mem. legislative com.). Phi Delta Kappa, Kappa Phi Kappa. Republican. Presbyterian. Mason (32°). Clubs: Kiwanis (lieut. gov. 1928-34), Rotary (1942), Contemporary (Phila.). Author: "Status of County Institutes in Pa.," etc. Home: Lansdowne, Pa. Died Oct. 12, 1946.

ROSS, Charles Ben, ex-gov.; b. Parma, Ida.; s. John M. and Jeannette (Hadley) R.; ed. business colls., Boise and Portland, Ore.; m. Edna R. Reavis; children (adopted)—Dewey H., Earl, Helen. Farmer and stockraiser for many years. Chmn. Bd. of County Commrs., Canyon County, Ida., 1915-21; pres. and sec. Ida. Farm Bur., 1921-23, v.p. Riverside Irrigation Dist., 1906-15; mayor of Pocatello, Ida., 1922-30; gov. of Ida., 1930-37. Democrat. Conglist. Elk, Eagle, Rotarian, Kiwanian. Home: 1615 Warm Springs Av., Boise, Idaho.* Died Mar. 31, 1946.

ROSS, Clarence Frisbee, educator; b. Sheakleyville, Pa., Apr. 7, 1870; s. John Seymour and Nancy Maria (Frisbee) R.; A.B., Allegheny Coll., Meadville, Pa., 1891, A.M., 1893, LL.D., 1932; Litt.D., Dickinson Coll., Carlisle, Pa., 1921; fellow U. of Chicago; studied U. of Berlin, Am. Sch. of Classical Studies, Rome; m. Etta Amelia Lenhart, Aug. 28, 1899; children—Lanora Lenhart (dec.), Julian Lenhart. Prof. Greek, Mo. Wesleyan Coll., 1891-92; prin. Allegheny Coll. Prep. Sch., 1892-1902; prof. Latin, Allegheny Coll., 1902-35, sec. faculty, 1901-07, 1910-18, registrar, 1893-95, 1907-08, 1918-40, dean of men, 1919-30, acting pres., 1924-26, 1930-31, v.p., 1931-38, dean of College, 1938-40, dean emeritus since 1940; visiting prof. Greek, U. of Chicago, summer 1904, 06; dir. New 1st Nat. Bank, Meadville, Pa., Crawford County Mutual Ins. Co. Exec. sec. Crawford County, Pub. Safety Com. of Pa., 1917-19; mem. Selective Service Bd. Republican. Methodist; mem. univ. senate, M.E. Ch., 1931-32. Mason (33°). Mem. Am. Philol. Assn., Archeol. Inst. America (Pittsburgh br.). Phi Delta Theta, Phi Beta Kappa, Kappa Phi Kappa, Pi Delta Epsilon. Home: 355 Ben Avon St., Meadville, Pa. Died Oct. 18, 1942.

ROSS, Clay Campbell, prof. ednl. psychology; b. Church Hill, Tenn., June 12, 1892; s. John Rogers and Mary (Darter) R.; A.B., Carson-Newman Coll., Jefferson City, Tenn., 1914; A.B., U. of Tenn., 1916; A.M., Teachers Coll., Columbia U. 1920; Ph.D., Teachers Coll., Columbia U., 1925; m. Vera Kite, Dec. 30, 1926; children—Clay Campbell, John Newton. Prin., Edgefield (S.C.) High Sch., 1914-15, Hancock County, (Tenn.) High Sch., 1916-17; Psychologist, U.S. War Dept., 1920-21; prof. edn. Furman U., 1921-22; asso. prof. psychology, Ia. State Coll., 1923-26; visiting instr. Ohio State U., summers 1923-24; prof. ednl. psychology, Coll. of Edn., U. of Ky., 1926-47; instr. Shrivenham Am. Univ., England, July-Dec. 1945. Consultant on Measurement, Lexington Signal Depot, 1944-45; mem. editorial board ham Am. U., England, 1945-46; mem. editorial bd. Journal of Educational Research. Mem. Am. Psychol. Assn., Southern Assn. Philosophy and Psychology, Am. Ednl. Research Assn., Am. Assn. Univ. Profs., Phi Delta Kappa, Kappa Delta Pi. Ind. Republican. Baptist. Club: Kiwanis (Lexington, Ky.). Author: Measurement in Today's Schools, 1941; revised (with workbook) 1947; Factors Associated with State's Educational Level, 1945. Contbr. tech. articles to ednl. pubs. Home: 131 Arcadia Park, Lexington 10, Ky. Died Mar. 8, 1947; buried Lexington Cemetery, Lexington, Ky.

ROSS, David E.; b. Brookston, Ind., Aug. 25, 1871; E.E., Purdue U., 1893. Inventor of Ross gears; v.p. and gen. mgr. for many yrs. of Ross Gear & Tool Co., La Fayette, Ind.; was actively identified with many industrial projects; retired, 1927, to devote attention to promotion of Purdue U.; now chmn. bd. Ross Gear & Tool Co., Rostone Corp. One of donors Ross-Ade Stadium to the univ., also donor, to the univ. of various tracts of land as well as money, patents and inventions. Pres. bd. trustees Purdue U. Fellow Am. Soc. Mech. Engrs.; hon. mem. Sigma Xi, Sigma Pi Sigma. Home: La Fayette, Ind. Died June 28, 1943.

ROSS, Harry Seymour, educator; b. E. Haddam, Conn., Apr. 5, 1868; s. David and Helen (Calhoun) R.; ed. Oberlin (O.) Acad.; spl. coll. work, Oberlin Coll.; grad. B.L.I., Emerson Coll. of Oratory, Boston, 1897; hon. A.M., Owensboro (Ky.) Coll., 1914; Litt.D., Piedmont College, Demorest, Ga., 1945; m. Ella M. McDuffee, June 24, 1903; 1 dau., Helen Willard. Instr. Worcester Acad., 1897-1900, master in English, 1900-08, principal's asst., 1905-07, acting prin., 1907-08; dean Emerson Coll. of Oratory, 1908-33, pres., 1933-45, pres. emeritus since 1945, also trustee. Life mem. Mass. Schoolmasters Club (dir.), Pi Gamma Mu. Conglist. Home: 2A Walnut Av., Cambridge, Mass. Office: Beacon and Berkeley Sts., Boston, Mass. Died June 5, 1948.

ROSS, Henry Davis, judge; b. Berryville, Ark., Sept. 12, 1861; s. William Henry and Emily (Terrell) R.; Clark's Acad., Berryville, Ark.; LL.B., Iowa State Univ., 1883; LL.D., U. of Ariz., 1938; D.C.L., University of Southern California, 1941; m. Margaret Wheeler, Apr. 24, 1890; children—Henry Davis, John Wheeler. Removed to Ariz., 1886; dist. atty. Yavapai County, Ariz., 1888-90, Coconino County, 1890-92; mem. Ariz. Ter. Ho. of Rep., 1892-94; registrar U.S. Land Office, Prescott, 1894-98; dist. atty., Yavapai County, 1898-1911 (resigned); justice Supreme Court of Ariz. since 1911, present term ends 1947 (chief justice during 4 periods). Democrat. Presbyterian. Mem. Am. Acad. Polit. and Social Science. Home: 371 E. Monte Vista Rd., Phoenix, Ariz. Died Feb. 9, 1945.

ROSS, John Elliot, clergyman; b. Baltimore, Md., Mar. 14, 1884; s. John R. and Cecilia M. (Elliot) R.; A.B., Loyola Coll., Baltimore, Md., 1902; M.A., George Washington U., 1908; entered Paulist house of studies at Catholic U., 1909; Ph.D., Catholic U., 1912; D.D., Papal U., Rome, 1913. Ordained priest R.C. Ch., 1912; stationed at St. Mary's Ch., Chicago, 1913-14; chaplain and approved lecturer to Catholic students, U. of Tex., 1914-23; pastor St. Austin's Ch., Austin, Tex., 1916-23; lecturer in social ethics Our Lady of the Lake Coll., San Antonio, Tex., 1921-23; prof. moral theology, St. Paul's Coll., Catholic Univ. of America, 1923-24; chaplain to Catholic students, Columbia U. and lecturer in religious edn., Teachers College, 1925-29; prof. and asso. dir. Sch. of Religion, State U. of Ia., 1929-30; lecturer in religion, Newman Foundation, U. of Ill., 1930-31. Awarded Gottheil medal for distinguished service to cause of Jewry, 1933. Mem. The Ark and The Dove Soc. Author: Consumers and Wage Earners, 1912; The Right to Work, 1917; Christian Ethics, 1918; Sanctity and Social Service, 1921; Five Minute Sermons, 1925, 2d series, 1928, 3d series, 1934, 4th series 1937; Truths to Live By, 1929; Faith That Conquers Fear; John Henry Newman, 1933; Not in Bread Alone (sermons), 1940; Cooperative Plenty, 1941. Wrote sect. on "Catholicism" in Religions of Democracy, 1941. Translator: Innocence and Ignorance, 1917; Indulgences as a Social Factor in the Middle Ages, 1922; Ethics from the Standpoint of Scholastic Philosophy, 1938; Cooperative Plenty, 1941; Treasures in Heaven (sermons), 1943. Address: 415 W. 59th St., New York, N.Y. Died Sep. 18, 1946.

ROSS, John Mason, lawyer; b. Alfordsville, Ind., May 6, 1874; s. Edwin and Mary Chambers (McCoy) R.; B.A., Stanford, 1897; m. Mabel Edward Landers, Feb. 27, 1904; children—Hugh Landers, Lydia Goodwin, Everett Mason; m. 2d, Eva (Wolcott) Wallace, Dec. 16, 1922. Admitted to Calif. bar, 1898, and began practice at San Francisco; moved office to Prescott, Ariz., 1902, to Bisbee, 1910, to Phoenix, 1929; mem. firm Ellinwood & Ross; firm gen. attys. for Phelps Dodge Corp. in the Southwest. Mem. Ariz.-Colo. River Commn., 1929-30 and 1933-35; del. Rep Nat. Conv., Chicago, 1932. Mem. Am. Bar Assn. Presbyterian. Club: Arizona (Phoenix). Address: Title & Trust Bldg., Phoenix, Ariz. Died Aug. 1, 1944.

ROSS, Peter V., lecturer and author; b. Howell, Mich., May 9, 1870; s. Thomas and Jane (Van Winkle) R.; B.S., Michigan State College, 1895; student Univ. of Nebraska, 1898-99; married Emily B. Webster, July 1947. Teacher public schools, 1888-91 and 1895-98; in practice of law, 1899-1911; Christian Science reader and practitioner, 1912-15; chmn. Christian Science Com. on Publication, 1916-21; Christian Science editor and lecturer, 1922-42; writer and author since 1942. Democrat. Club: Commonwealth of Calif. Author: Probate Law and Practice, 1908; Inheritance Texation, 1912; A Digest of the Bible, 1938; The Bible in Brief, 1942; If a Man Die He Shall Live Again, 1945; Letters of a Traveler, 1945; Lectures on Christian Science, 1946; Leaves of Healing, 1946. Address: 166 Geary St., San Francisco, Calif. Died Sept. 22, 1947.

ROSS, Wilbert Davidson, educator; b. on farm, near Washington, Pa., Aug. 9, 1870; s. Joseph Wise and Anna Mary (Henderson) R.; A.B., U. of Kan., 1893, A.M., 1894; m. Eleanor Gephart, Sept. 4, 1901; children—Marian Elizabeth (Mrs. Edmund K. Hall), Constance Eleanor (Mrs. Arthur Edwards). Teacher and prin. high schs., 7 yrs.; co. supt., Jefferson County, Kan., 1901-05; supt. city schs., 1905-09; mem. State Ednl. Commn., 1909; state high sch. insp., 1909-12; state supt. pub. instrn., Kan., Nov. 19, 1912-Jan. 13, 1919; mem. Ednl. Corps, A.E.F., and supt. edn. St. Aignan area, France, also extension lecturer, Beaune Univ., 1919; mem. training staff, Federal Bd. for Vocational Edn., 1919-20; prof. Am. history and govt. and dir. sch. service, Kan. State Teachers' Coll., Emporia, 1920-24, head dept. hist. and govt. since 1925. Contbr. to Educational Review, Journal of Education, and other periodicals. Mem. Phi Beta Kappa. Republican. Conglist. Mason (32°, K.T.). Clubs: Kansas Schoolmasters' (past-pres.), Current (past-pres.). Home: Emporia, Kan. Died Aug. 16, 1944.

ROSS, William Horace, chemist; b. N.S., Can., Dec. 27, 1875; s. Daniel and Mary (Murray) R.; B.Sc., Dalhousie U., Halifax, N.S., 1903, M.Sc., 1904, 1851 sci. research scholar, 1905-07; Johns Hopkins, 1904-05; Ph.D., U. of Chicago, 1907; m. Catherine Allen, June 10, 1908; children—Allen Murray, William Horace. Asst. chemist, Agrl. Expt. Sta., U. of Ariz., 1907-12; scientist Bur. of Soils, 1912-27; sr. chemist, Bur. of Chemistry and Soils, 1927-40; senior chemist Bureau of Plant Industry, 1940-44; principal chemist 1944-45. Capt., C.W.S., United States Army, 1918-19. Abstracter Chemical Abstracts since 1907. Mem. Am. Chem. Soc., A.A.A.S., Am. Soc. Agronomy, Am. Inst. Chemists, Assn. of Official Agricultural Chemists (pres. 1945-46), Sigma Xi. Presbyterian. Co-author: Fixed Nitrogen; Principles and Practice of Agricultural Analysis. Contbr. to chem. and other scientific jours. Home: 2811 Woodley Rd., Washington, D.C. Died May 16, 1947.

ROSSEY, Chris C. (rŏ'sē), coll. pres.; b. Montrose, W.Va., July 19, 1889; s. George H. and Isabel (Byrd) R.; B.Pd., Bethany (W.Va.) Coll., 1913, Litt.B., 1914; M.A., Teachers Coll., Columbia U., 1923; Ed.D., New York U., 1941; m. Lela Longman, July 31, 1925; children—Paul William, Christine Isabel. Rural sch. teacher, 1906-09; grad. sch. prin., 1912-13; high sch. prin., Wheeling, W.Va., 1913-18; teacher, Bethany Coll., summer, 1915; pres. Concord State Teachers Coll., Athens, W.Va., 1918-24; prin. elementary school and experimental school, Jersey City, 1931-37; dean of instruction, State Teachers College, Jersey City, 1937-40, president since 1940; board directors Christ Hospital, Jersey City; member Consistory of Old Bergen Church; member American Assn. Teachers' Coll. Pres., Am. Assn. Sch. Adminstrs., Am. Council on Edn., N.J. Schoolmasters' Assn., N.Y. Schoolmasters' Club, Kappa Delta Pi. Mason (Scottish Rite). Clubs: Kiwanis, Chamber of Commerce (Jersey City, N.J.). Home: 244 Fowler Av., Jersey City, N.J. Died June 21, 1946.

ROSSI, Angelo Joseph (rŏs'sĭ), ex-mayor; b. Volcano, Calif., Jan. 22, 1878; s. Angelo and Maddalena (Gueirolo) R.; student grammar and night schs.; LL.D. (hon.), U. of San Francisco, 1935; m. Grace Allen, 1902; children—Clarence A., Eleanor (Mrs. Henry Morris), Rosamund (Mrs. John Cleese). Began as errand boy, 1887; now sr. partner Angelo J. Rossi Co., Inc., San Francisco, Calif., Playground commr., San Francisco, 1914-21; supervisor City and County of San Francisco, 1921-25, 1929-31; mayor of City and County of San Francisco, 1931-44. Awarded Presidential Medal of Honor (Nicaragua); Grande officiale della Corona d'Italia; Officer Legion d'Honneur (France). Pres. Dante Hosp., San Francisco. Founder and former pres. San Francisco Downtown Assn. Republican. Catholic. Elk, K. of C., Native Son of the Golden West, Moose, Son of Italy. Clubs: Olympic, Elks (San Francisco). Home: 2466 Union St. Office: City Hall, San Francisco, Calif. Died Apr. 5, 1948.

ROSSI, Louis Mansfield, corp. exec.; b. Flushing, L.I., N.Y., Aug. 3, 1877; s. James Camille and Caroline Alice (Frame) R.; E.M., Columbia Sch. of Mines, 1899; m. Agnes Langan, June 8, 1907 (died Apr. 2, 1939); children—Margaret Archer (Mrs. Thomas Owen Meacham), Thomas Langan. Engr. Perth Amboy Terra Cotta Co., 1900-01, Nat. Fireproofing Co., 1901-03; works mgr. Perth Amboy Chem. Works, 1903-08; research Roessler & Hasslacher Chem. Co., 1908-10; works mgr. Gen. Bakelite Co., 1910-19, gen. mgr., 1919-22; with Bakelite Corp. since 1923, as dir. mfg., 1923, v.p. and dir. mfg. since 1924; director of Bakelite Gesellschaft (Berlin), Bakelite, Ltd. (London). Mem. Bd. of Edn., Perth Amboy, 1910-15, City Planning Commn., 1920-24. Mem. Am. Inst. Chem. Engrs., Am. Soc. Testing Materials, Soc. Chem. Industry (England), Plastic Materials Mfrs. Assn., Synthetic Resin Mfrs. Assn. Republican. Catholic. Club: Forsgate Country (Jamesburg, N.J.). Home: 135 Rector St., Perth Amboy, N.J. Office: 30 E. 42d St., New York, N.Y. Died May 25, 1944.

ROSSITER, Ehrick Kensett (rŏs'ĭ-tēr), architect; b. Paris, France, Sept. 14, 1854; s. Thomas P. and Anna (Parmly) R.; ed. Cornell; m. Mary Heath, June 14, 1877; children—Frank Heath, Kensett, Mrs. Edith Bevan, Ehrick Winthrop. Mem. Architectural League, U.S. Pub. Architects League, A.I.A., Am. Fine Arts Soc. (trustee). Clubs: Century, Cornell, MacDowell. Former treas., mgr., dir. Central Park Studios. Died Oct. 15, 1941.

ROTH, Frederick George Richard, sculptor; b. Brooklyn, N.Y., Apr. 28, 1872; s. Johannes and Jane Gray (Bean) R.; ed. pub. and pvt. schs., Bremen, Germany, until 1888, Acad. Fine Arts, Vienna, 1892, Acad. Fine Arts, Berlin, 1894; m. Madeleine E. G. Forster, Apr. 29, 1905; children—Jack Richard, Roger Frederic. Professionally engaged as sculptor since 1890; exhibited in New York, Phila., St. Louis, Chicago, Portland, Düsseldorf, Nat. Academician, 1906, mem. Nat. Sculpture Soc. (pres. 1919-21), Archtl. League, Nat. Inst. Arts and Letters, New Soc. of Artists, Soc. of Animal Painters and Sculptors. Silver medals, St. Louis, 1904, Buenos Aires, 1910; gold medal, Panama P.I. Expn., 1915; Helen Speyer memorial prize, 1924; Nat. Arts Club prize, 1924; William Goodman prize, Grand Central Galleries, New York, 1928; National Arts Club prize, 1931; Cary Ramsey memorial prize, 1931; Helen Speyer memorial prize, 1942. Instructor modeling, women's class, N.A.D., 1915-18; member committee on monuments, New Jersey State Architects, 1919. Pres. Nat. Sculpture Soc., 1919-20; mem. Grand Central Art Galleries. Chief sculptor Park Dept. of N.Y. City under Pub. Works Adminstrn., 1934-36. Address: Sherwood Pl., Englewood, N.J. Died May 21, 1944.

ROTHERMEL, Amos Cornelius, normal sch. prin.; b. Moselem, Pa., Jan. 6, 1864; s. Lewis W. and Lydia R.; grad. Keystone State Normal Sch., Kutztown, Pa., 1886; A.B., Franklin and Marshall Coll., 1891, A.M., 1894, Litt.D., 1910; Pd.D., Dickinson Coll., 1906; m. Ada L. Spatz, June 30, 1894. Pub. sch. teacher, 1881-85; prin. Polytechnic Acad., Gilbert, Pa., 1886-87; prof. phys. sciences, 1891-99, prin., 1899-1934, Keystone State Normal Sch. (now Kutztown State Teachers Coll.); retired. Republican. Mem. Reformed Ch. Address: Kutztown, Pa. Died Oct. 5, 1946.

ROTHSCHILD, Maurice, business exec.; chmn. bd. and dir., Albert Pick Co.; dir. John Simmons. Pres. The Off-the-Street Club, Chicago. Home: 2350 Lincoln Park West. Office: 2159 W. Pershing Rd., Chicago. Died July 23, 1949.

ROTHWELL, Bernard Joseph, mfr.; b. Dublin, Ireland, Aug. 1, 1859; s. Thomas Henry and Rosanna (Fagan) R.; came to America, 1869; ed. pub. schs., and under pvt. tutors; m. Emily Jane Taylor, July 9, 1889 (died, June 15, 1903); 1 son, Paul Taylor; m. 2d, Henrietta Ismon Goodrich, Nov. 28, 1911 (died Feb. 8, 1943). Chmn. bd. Boston Elevated Ry. Co., 1930-34; dir. 1941-47; chmn. Bay State Milling Co.; dir. Mass. Bonding & Ins. Co., 1907-47; trustee Union Savings Bank, 1915-47, Mass. Savings Bank Life Ins. Guaranty Fund, 1920-46; chmn. Fed. Home Loan Bank of Boston, 1933-47. Trustee Long Island (City of Boston) Almshouse, 1904-06. Pres. Boston Chamber Commerce, 1908-10; dir. and mem. exec. com. Chamber Commerce, U.S.A., 1919-21; chmn. Mass. Bur. of Immigration, 1913-14 and 1917-19. Jury commr., U.S. Dist. Ct. 1912-47; mem. N.E. Govs'. R.R. Com., 1929-31; chmn. Gov's., Com. on Street and Highway Safety, 1930-35. Independent Democrat. Club: Down Town. Home: 34 W. Cedar St., Boston, Mass., and Island Creek, Duxbury, Mass. Office: Grain and Flour Exchange, Boston, Mass. Died Nov. 27, 1948.

ROUDEBUSH, Alfred Holt (rou'dē-bo͝osh), lawyer; b. New Orleans, La., Apr. 12, 1873; s. Rev. George Shotwell (D.D.) and Margaret Hughes (Moore) R.; A.B., U. of Miss., 1894; LL.B., Washington U., 1900; m. Susan D'Arcy, Nov. 30, 1907; children—George Shotwell, Jane D'Arcy (Mrs. John Linscott Horner). Admitted to Mo. bar, 1901, and began practice at St. Louis, asst. city counselor St. Louis, 1907-10; asso. city counselor, 1910-11; v.p. and counsel Miss. Valley Trust Co. Mem. St. Louis Bd. of Edn., 1915-17. Mem. Am. and St. Louis bar assns., Am. Bankers Assn. (mem. exec. com. of trust div.), Blackstone Soc. (ex-pres.), Miss. Soc. of St. Louis, Delta Psi, Phi Delta Phi. Democrat. Presbyterian. Home: 6218 Washington Av. Office: 506 Olive St., St. Louis, Mo.* Died Mar. 29, 1946.

ROULAND, Orlando (rou'lănd), artist; m. Minnie T. Dwight. Has painted portraits of Theodore Roosevelt, Thomas A. Edison, John Burroughs, E. H. Sothern, Mme. Melba, and many others. Mem. Nat. Acad. Design; mem. nat. council Am. Artists Professional League; former pres. Allied Artists of America. Clubs: Lotos, Salmagundi. Address: 130 W. 57th St., New York 19, N.Y. and (summer) Lookout Court, Marblehead, Mass. Died June 26, 1945.

ROUNDS, Ralph Stowell, lawyer; b. Cleveland, Sept. 3, 1864; s. Charles Collins and Kate Nixon (Stowell) R.; A.B., Amherst, 1887; LL.B., Columbia U. Law Sch., 1892; J.D., New York U., 1904; m. Mary Helen Ricks, May 29, 1905; children—Stowell, Elizabeth. Admitted to N.Y. bar, 1892; prize lecturer Columbia U. Law Sch., 1892-95; prof. law, New York U. Law Sch., 1895-99. Mem. bd. dirs. Fgn. Policy Assn., 1921-48, chmn., 1939-43. Trustee Antioch Coll., Yellow Springs, O., 1927-35, 1936-42, hon. trustee, 1946-48. Mem. Am. Bar Assn., Assn. Bar City of New York. Club: University. Home: Cannondale, Conn. Died Oct. 22, 1948.

ROUNTREE, George, lawyer; b. Kinston, N.C., July 7, 1855; s. Robert Hart and Cynthia Biddle (Loftin) R.; Bethany (W.Va.) Coll., through jr. yr.; A.B., Harvard, 1877; m. Meta Alexander Davis, Oct. 27, 1881. Began practice at Kinston, N.C., 1885; mem. firm Rountree & Rountree, Wilmington, North Carolina. Mem. N.C. Ho. of Rep., 1899-1901; judge Superior Courts of N.C., 1913-16 (resigned). Mem. N.C. Bar Assn. (pres. 1906), Am. Bar Assn. Ind. Democrat. Episcopalian; lay deputy Triennial Conv., 1925, 28 and 31. Clubs: Cape Fear, Carolina Yacht. Home: 1 N. 18th St. Office: Murchison Bldg., Wilmington, N.C. Died Feb. 19, 1942.

ROWAN, Andrew Summers (rou'ăn), army officer, author; b. Gap Mills, Va., Apr. 23, 1857; s. John

M. and Virginia Wirt (Summers) R.; grad. U.S. Mil. Acad., 1881; m. Ida Symms, Apr. 12, 1887; m. 2d, Mrs. Josephine Morris de Greayer, 1904. Commd. 2d lt. infantry, U.S. Army, June 11, 1881; promoted through grades to maj. Oct. 11, 1905; served on staff of Gen. Nelson A. Miles, Cuban and Porto Rico campaigns, as lt. col. 6th U.S. Vols.; retired, Dec. 1, 1909. Member Intercontinental Ry. Survey, in charge hypsometric work of Central Am. party; spl. duty information Bureau, in charge map sect., adj.-gen. office; mil. attaché, Chile; sent to communicate with Gen. Garcia after declaration of Spanish-Am. War; landed from open boat near Turquino Peak, Apr. 24, 1898; successfully executed mission, bringing full information as to insurgent army; was 1st U.S. Army officer to enter Cuba after the declaration of war, and for this service was the subject of Elbert Hubbard's essay, "A Message to Garcia," which holds the world's record for circulation and translation into foreign tongues. Awarded D.S.C. "for extraordinary heroism in connection with the operations in Cuba in May 1898, securing secret information relative to existing conditions in that region of such great value that it had an important bearing on the quick ending of the struggle and the complete success of the U.S. Army." On duty Visayas Group, P.I., 1899-1902; prof. mil. science and tactics, Kan. State Agrl. Coll., 1902-03; on duty Fort Riley, Kan., 1902; at West Point, in Kentucky, and at Fort Riley, 1903, and at American Lake, Washington, 1904; on duty Island of Mindanao, 1905-07, in the Lake Lanao region; in command of the Malaig River expdn., 1906. Awarded S.S.C. "for gallantry in action displayed while placing and operating a field gun during the attack on Sudlón Mountain, Cebú, Philippine Islands, Jan. 8, 1900"; mem. Legion of Valor (U.S.); decorated Order Carlos Manuel de Céspedes (Cuba), 1938; awarded Distinguished Service medal by W.Va. Legislature, 1940. Author: The Island of Cuba, 1898; How I Carried the Message to Garcia, 1923. Clubs: Army and Navy (Washington, New York and Manila); Strollers (New York); Commonwealth (San Francisco). Address: 1036 Vallejo St., San Francisco, Calif.; (summer) Mill Valley, Marin Co., Calif. Died Jan. 10, 1943.

ROWAN, Charles Joseph (rō'ān), surgeon; b. Chicago, Ill., Nov. 28, 1874; s. Peter J. and Mary I. (Murray) R.; A.B., St. Ignatius Coll., Chicago, 1895; M.D., Rush Med. Coll., Chicago, 1898; post-grad. work, U. of Vienna, 1902; m. Maud B. Miller, Apr. 29, 1907 (deceased); m. 2d, Sophia Potgieter, Oct. 6, 1941. Began practice in Chicago, 1898; acting asst. surgeon U.S. Army, in China and P.I., 1900-01; asst. prof. surgery, Rush Med. Coll., 1906-14; attending surgeon, Cook County Hosp., 1904-14; asso. attending surgeon, Presbyn. Hosp., 1907-14; prof. surgery and head of dept., State U. of Ia., 1914-31; prof. surgery, University of Southern Calif., 1931-39; professor emeritus of surgery since 1939; senior attending surgeon Los Angeles County General Hosp. since 1931. Fellow Am. Coll. Surgeons; mem. A.M.A., Am. Surg. Assn., Western Surg. Assn., Chicago Surg. Soc. Catholic. Home: 226 Cliff Drive, Laguna Beach, Calif. Died May 7, 1948.

ROWE, Frederick William, ex-congressman; born Wappingers Falls, N.Y., Mar. 19, 1863; s. Daniel C. and Susan A. (Townsend) R.; A.B., Colgate, 1887, A.M., 1890, LL.D., 1918; m. Miss S. Loraine Meeker, Oct. 17, 1894. Admitted to N.Y. bar, 1889; practiced in Brooklyn and Manhattan, N.Y. City, until 1904, since in real estate business. Mem. 64th to 66th Congresses (1915-21), 6th N.Y. Dist. Conglist. Mem. C. of C. of N.Y., Brooklyn C. of C. (dir.); trustee Colgate Univ., Hamilton, N.Y., Adelphi Coll., Brooklyn, N.Y. Republican. Clubs: Brooklyn, Municipal, Union League. Address: 26 Court St., Brooklyn, N.Y. Died June 20, 1946.

ROWE, Leo S. (rou), publicist; b. McGregor, Ia., Sept. 17, 1871; s. Louis R. and Katherine (Raff) R.; A.B., Central High Sch., Philadelphia, 1887; Ph.B., U. of Pa., 1890, LL.B., 1895; Ph.D., U. of Halle, 1892; hon. LL.D., Nat. U. of La Plata, Argentine, 1906, U. of San Marcos, Lima, Peru, U. of Chile, Santiago, Chile, 1907; U. of Pa., 1931, Georgetown U., 1933. Admitted to bar; instr. in municipal government, U. of Pa., 1895-96, asst. prof. polit. science, 1896-1904; head prof. polit. science, 1904-17. On leave of absence, 1900-01, as mem. Commn. to Revise and Compile the Laws of Puerto Rico; and 1901-02 as chmn. Insular Code Commn., reporting codes which were, with some modifications, adopted as the law under which island is now governed. U.S. del. to 3d Internat. Conf. of Am. States, Rio Janeiro, 1906; chmn. delegation of U.S. to 1st Pan-Am. Scientific Congress, Santiago, Chile, 1908-09; mem. U.S.-Panama Mixed Claims Commn., 1913; sec. gen. Pan-Am. Financial Conf., Washington, 1915; sec. gen. Inter-Am. High Commn., 1915-17; U.S. del. 2d Pan-Am. Scientific Congress, 1915-16; sec. American-Mexican Mixed Commn., 1916-17; asst. sec. of the Treasury, 1917-19; chief Latin Am. Div., State Dept., Nov. 1919-Sept. 1920; dir. gen. Pan-Am. Union since Sept. 1920. Hon. prof. polit. science, Nat. U. of Mex. Hon. mem. Nat. Hist. Soc. of Argentine, Mex. Geog. Soc.; pres. Am. Acad. Polit. and Social Science, 1902-30; mem. Am. Philos. Soc., Am. Internat. Law Assn., Am. Polit. Science Assn., Hispanic Society New York, Pan.-Am. Soc. of U.S. (hon. pres.); corr. mem. Société d'Anthropologie. Mem. com. on organization First Internat. Congress on Mental Hygiene. Author: Report of the United States Commission to Revise the Laws of Puerto Rico (with Judge Daly and Hon. Juan Hernandez-Lopez), 2 vols., 1901; Report of the Insular Code Commission (with Hon. J. M. Keedy), 8 vols., 1902 (San Juan, P.R.); The United States and Porto Rico, 1904; Problems of City Government, 1908; Problemas americanos, conferencias, 1915; Early Effects of European War upon the Finance, Commerce and Industry of Chile, 1918; The Early Effects of the War Upon the Finance, Commerce and Industry of Peru, 1920; The Federal Systems of the Argentine Republic, 1921; also many reports, monographs and articles in econ. journals, revs. and Annals Am. Acad. Polit. and Social Science. In charge Latin Am. Round Table, Inst. of Politics, Williamstown, Mass., 1921-26; U.S. del. Fifth Internat. Conf. of Am. States, Santiago, 1923; chmn. delegation of U. S. to the Pan-Am. Scientific Congress, Lima, Peru, Dec. 1924-Jan. 1925. Mem. U.S. delegation to 6th Internat. Conf. Am. States, Jan.-Feb. 1928; rep. of Pan-Am. Union at 7th Internat. Conf. Am. States, 1933; rep. of U.S. on Permanent Commn. of Internat. Assn. of Road Congresses; attended the Inter-Am. Conf. for the Maintenance of Peace as guest of the Argentine Govt., Buenos Aires, Dec. 1936; guest of Peruvian Govt., 8th Internat. Conf. on Am. States, Lima, 1938, as rep. to the Pan-American Union; attended 1st meeting of ministers of Foreign Affairs of Am. Republics, Panama, 1939; 8th Am. Sci. Congress, Washington, 1940; 2d meeting of Ministers of Fgn. Affairs, Havana, Cuba. 1940; 3d meeting Ministers of Fgn. Affairs, Rio de Janeiro, Brazil, 1942. Awarded Order of Liberator, Venezuela, 1921; The Grand Order of Sun, Peru, 1921; Order of Carlos Manuel de Céspedes, Cuba, 1932; Order of Merit, Chile, 1933; Grand Official Order of Boyaca, Colombia, 1933; Grand Official Order of the Condor de los Andes, Bolivia, 1934; Order of Merit, Ecuador, 1934; Order of Juan Pablo Duarte, Dominican Republic, 1936; Order of Merit with the grade of comdr., Haiti, 1937; comd. Order of Vasco Nunez de Balboa, 1939; U. of Pa. Alumni Award of Merit, 1940; gold medal award of achievement of the Poor Richard Club of Phila., 1940, the Heraldic Order of Christopher Columbus, Dominican Republic, 1940; gold insignia of the Pan-Am. Society, 1940; Medal of Honor 1st Class Red Cross of Chile, 1941; Grand Officer of the Order of the Southern Cross, Brazil, 1942. Mem. Am. Bar Assn., Am. Nat. Com. on Internat. Intellectual Coöperation; fellow Am. Acad. Arts and Sciences. Address: Pan-American Union, Washington. Died Dec. 5, 1946; ashes in Pan American Union Bldg.

ROWE, Peter Trimble, bishop; b. Meadowville, Can., Nov. 20, 1856; s. Peter and Mary R.; grad. Trinity Coll., Toronto, 1880, A.M., 1882; D.D., Hobart Coll., and Toronto, U., 1895; m. Dora H. Carry, June 5, 1882 (died May 22, 1914); 2 sons; m. 2d, Rose Fullerton, Oct. 21, 1915; 3 sons. Deacon, Nov. 3, 1878, priest, Nov. 14, 1880, Protestant Episcopal Church; missionary Garden Rover, Ont., 1878-82; rector St. James', Sault Ste. Marie, Mich., 1882-95; commr. pub. schs., Chippewa County, Mich., 1891-95; elected 1st missionary bishop of Alaska, Oct. 17, consecrated, Nov. 30, 1895. Office: Mutual Life Bldg., Seattle, Wash. Died June 1, 1942.

ROWELL, Chester Harvey (rou'ĕl), editor; b. Bloomington, Ill., Nov. 1, 1867; s. Jonathan Harvey and Maria Sanford (Woods) R.; Ph.B., U. of Mich., 1888; grad. student same, 1888-89, also of univs. of Halle, Berlin, Paris and Rome; LL.D., Coll. of the Pacific, 1927, U. of Mich., 1928; Litt.D., U. of So. Calif., 1928; m. Myrtle Marie Lingle, Aug. 1, 1897; children—Cora Winifred (Mrs. J. A. Givens), Barbara Lois (Mrs. W. D. Laughlin), Jonathan Harvey. Clerk com. on elections, U.S. Ho. of Rep., 1889-91; teacher acads. Kan., Wis. and Calif.; instr. in German, U. of Ill., 1897-98; editor and pub. Fresno Republican, 1898-1920; lecturer on journalism, U. of Calif., summer 1911; lecturer polit. sci., same, and Stanford, 1927-34; lectures on ednl., civic and polit. subjects; editor of San Francisco Chronicle, 1932-39, now editorial columnist. Pres. and gen. mgr. Fresno Republican Pub. Co., 1912-20. Trustee of World Peace Foundation, 1932-39. An organizer and pres. Lincoln-Roosevelt Rep. League, 1907-11; mem. Rep. State Com., 1906-11; chmn. Rep. State Conv., 1910; del. Rep. Nat. Conv., and Prog. Nat. Conv., 1912; mem. Prog. Nat. Com., 1912-16; del. Prog. Nat. Conv., 1916; mem. Rep. Nat. Campaign Com., 1916; chmn. Rep. State Com., 1916-18; chmn. Social Ins. Commn.; mem. Calif. State Council Defense, 1917-18; bd. state commrs. Panama P.I. Expn., 1913-15; regent U. of Calif.; v.p. Nat. Municipal League. Mem. U.S. Shipping Bd., 1920-21; mem. Calif. R.R. Commn., 1921-23; del. Internat. Congress of Penal Law, Brussels, 1924; del. Internat. Labor Conf., Geneva, 1939; dir. Science Service, 1924-26. Mem. Inst. Pacific Relations Conferences, 1925, 27, 29, 31, 36; mem. Nat. Crime Commn., 1926-30; mem. Calif. Tax Commn., 1927; mem Calif. Constl. Commn., 1929-31; pres. Calif. League of Nations Assn., 1927-39; del. Rep. Nat. Conv., 1928, 36; mem. Nat. Rep. Program Com., 1938, 39; pres. Calif. Conf. on Social Work, 1928-29; mem. presdl. emergency bds. on railroad strikes, 1928, 29, 31; mem. Am. Youth Commn. since 1935; dir. Internat. House, U. of Calif.; mem. Social Science Research Council of Pacific Coast. Awarded Theodore Roosevelt medal "for distinguished public service as a private citizen," 1940. Mem. A.A.A.S., Phi Beta Kappa, Delta Tau Delta, Golden Bear (hon. soc. U. of Calif.). Clubs: University, Country (Fresno); University, Commonwealth, Bohemian (San Francisco); Faculty Club (Berkeley); Century Assn. (New York). Author of Digest of Contested Election Cases House of Representatives of U.S.. First to Fifty-sixth Congress, 1901; also many mag. articles, etc. Engaged largely in foreign travel, lecturing and newspaper syndicate writing since 1923. Home: 149 Tamalpais Rd., Berkeley, Calif. Office: San Francisco Chronicle, San Francisco, Calif. Died April 12, 1948.

ROWELL, Ross Erastus, Marine Corps officer; b. Ruthven, Ia., Sept. 22, 1884; s. Elmore Curtis and Jessie Maria (Rogers) R.; student Ia. State Coll., 1901-03, U. of Ida., 1904-05; grad. naval aviator, Naval Flying Sch., 1923, mil. aviator, Air Corps Advanced Training Sch., 1924, air observer, Air Corps Tech. Sch., 1929; m. Marguerita Isabel Sangren, Mar. 6, 1912. Commd. 2d lt., U.S. Marine Corps, 1906, and advanced through the grades to brig. gen., 1939, maj. gen., 1942; served in Cuba, Haiti, Santo Domingo, Nicaragua, Philippine Islands, Great Britain, the Middle East, France and at sea; qualified as naval aviator, 1923; trained with Army Air Corps, 3 years; naval attaché, Am. Embassy, Havana, 1939-40; commanding general, Marine Aircraft Wings, Pacific Fleet from July 1942-Sept. 1944, chief of United States Naval Aviation to Peru since Nov. 1944. Decorated Navy Distinguished Service medal, Legion of Merit, Distinguished Flying Cross, Nicaraguan Cross of Distinction, Nicaraguan Medal of Merit; Cuban Naval Medal of Merit; 7 campaign medals. Member Phi Delta Theta. Clubs: Army and Navy, Army and Navy Country (Washington, D.C.); Cuyamaca (San Diego). Contbr. prof. articles on aviation to jours. Home: Am. Embassy, Lima, Peru. Died Sep. 6, 1947.

ROWELL, Wilbur Everett, lawyer, corp. official; b. Amesbury, Mass., Aug. 28, 1862; s. Charles E. and Judith M. (Gile) R.; grad., Wilbraham (Mass.) Acad., 1881; A.B., Wesleyan U., 1885, A.M., 1888; student Harvard Law Sch., 1887-88; m. Mary A. Rand, September 22, 1891 (she died May 4, 1905); m. 2d, Lillian Bridges, March 18, 1908 (she died August 13, 1941). Admitted to Massachusetts bar, 1888, began practice at Lawrence; member Rowell, Clay & Tomlinson; trustee and former pres. Broadway Savings Bank (Lawrence); dir. Beach Soap Co.; special justice District Court of Lawrence, 1898-1937. Chairman Selective Draft Board, Lawrence, World War I. Mem. Sch. Com., Lawrence, 1909-15; trustee White Fund; pres. Lawrence Home for Aged People; mem. adv. bd. Lawrence Gen. Hosp.; trustee Lawrence Pub. Library; trustee and mem. Finance Com. Mass. Congl. Conf. and Missionary Society. Mem. Mass. Congl. Fund, Phi Beta Kappa, Psi Upsilon. Republican. Conglist. Home: 96 Saunders St. Office: 301 Essex St., Lawrence, Mass. Died Mar. 4, 1946.

ROXAS, Manuel (raw'häsh), pres. of Philippines; b. Capiz, Capiz, The Philippines, Jan. 1, 1892; s. Gerardo and Rosario (Acuna) Roxas; LL.D. (honoris causa), Univ. of Manila, Philippines, 1913; m. Trinidad de Leon, 1921; children—Ruby, Gerardo. Admitted to bar of Philippines with highest rating, 1913; law clerk to Chief Justice Arellano, Manila, 1913-17; municipal councilor, Capiz, Capiz, 1918; provincial gov., Capiz, 1920; rep. 1st dist. of Capiz, 1924-36, speaker of House of Rep., 1924-35; sec. of Finance, 1938-41; elected to senate 1941, pres. 1945; pres. of the Philippines since 1946. Mem. Constitutional Conv., 1934; head of Philippine independence missions in Washington, 1923, 29, 31-33, with others secured the Hare-Hawes Cutting Law; mem. joint preparatory com. on Philippine Affairs, 1935; chmn. Nat. Econ. Council, Tax Commn., Rural Progress Adminstrn., bd. of dirs. of Nat. Development Co., Com. on Ednl. Policy to reorganize the Univ. of Philippines; mem. Nat. Rice and Corn Corp., 1939-41, Mindanao Land Settlement Project, 1939-41, the Nat. Relief Bd., 1939-41, Bd. of Regents of Univ. of Philippines, 1936-41. Entered Philippine Army as colonel Dec. 1941; brig. gen. as aide to Gen. MacArthur, 1942. Mem. Nationalista Liberal Party. Roman Catholic. Club: Wack Wack Golf and Country. Home: Malacanan Palace, Manila, Philippines. Died Apr. 15, 1948; buried in North Cemetery, Manila, P.I.

ROY, Arthur J(ay), astronomer; b. Clyde, New York, Nov. 7, 1869; s. Lyman and Ann Eliza (Bishop) R.; descendant on mother's side of Richard Warren and John Howland of the Mayflower; C.E., Union College, Schenectady, N.Y., 1893, A.M. from same school, 1897; m. 2d, Carolyn E. Eyre, Oct. 16, 1912; children—(by first marriage) Earl Bishop (dec.), Olive Elizabeth (Roy) Armstrong. First asst. Dudley Obs. (astronomy dept. Union U.) since 1893; chief astronomer Dept. of Meridian Astronomy of Carnegie Institution, Washington, D.C., 1907-36, research asso., 1936-39. Has specialized in meridian astronomy for many years; associated with Dr. Lewis Boss (in charge of Dudley Obs.) on positions and motions of the stars, until his death, 1912; in charge of tech. operations at San Luis, Argentina, 1909-11, making over 80,000 observations; discovered that the personal equation of the observer and the atmospheric refraction are different north and south. Supervised formation of the General Catalog. An organizer Albany Civic League, 1905; dir. Albany City Mission. Mem. Am. Astron. Soc., A.A.A.S., Albany Philos. Soc., Sigma Xi. Democrat. Baptist. Club: Aurania. Author: Albany Zone Catalogs for 1900 (with Lewis Boss), 1918; San Luis Catalog of Stars for 1910, 1918; Albany Catalog of Stars for 1910, 1932; Madison Catalog of Stars for 1910, 1939. Contbr. to Astron. Jour. Home: 369 Morris St., Albany, N.Y. Died Sept. 11, 1948.

ROY, P(ercy) A(lbert), born in New Orleans, Louisiana, Jan. 8, 1889; s. William Alexander and

Anna Xavier (Strong) R.; A.B., Immaculate Conception Coll. (now Loyola U.), New Orleans, 1907; A.B., Woodstock (Md.) Coll., 1914, Ph.D., 1925; A.M., St. Louis (Mo.) U., 1922. Teacher English, Latin and Greek, Jesuit High Sch., New Orleans, 1915-17, St. Charles Coll., Grand Coteau, La., 1917-20, also asst. dean, 1918-20; prin. Jesuit High Sch., New Orleans, 1925-34; asst. dean Coll. of Arts and Sciences and faculty chmn. of athletics, Loyola U., New Orleans, 1934-37, dean, 1937-39, mem. bd. of dirs. 1938-45, pres. 1939-45. Ordained Catholic priest, 1922. Prof. math. and mil. law, Citizen's Mil. Training Corps, St. Charles Coll., 1918. Mem. Council, also Com. on Nat. Defense of New Orleans Assn. of Commerce, 1942-45; pres. Marquette Assn. for Higher Edn. 1939-45; vice president Assn. Am. Colls., 1945; mem. Commn. on Liberal Arts Colls. of Jesuit Ednl. Assn. 1941-46; mem. gen. exec. bd. Nat. Cath. Ednl. Assn., 1935-38, sec. secondary sch. dept., 1931-33, v.p., 1933-35, pres., 1935-37, v.p. coll. and univ. dept., 1941-44, pres. 1944-46; asst. pastor, Gesu Ch., Miami, Fla., 1945-47; asst. pastor St. Anne's Ch., West Palm Beach, Fla., since 1947; organizer and 1st chmn. southern regional unit of secondary schs. of the assn.; mem. secondary sch. commn. Southern Assn. of Colls. and Secondary Schs., 1928-34, mem. exec. com. Commn. on Curricular Problems and Research, 1935-41, pres. of the assn. and mem. exec. com., 1939-40; vice chmn. southeastern unit Nat. Conf. Church-related Colls., 1941-45; mem. of executive com. and chmn. of sub-com. on edn. of La. Economic Development Commn., 1943-45; chmn. dept. of presidents La. Coll. Conf., 1941; mem. Board of Visitors to U.S. Naval Academy for 1945, Le Cercle Française, Blue Key, Delta Epsilon Sigma, Beta Theta. Address: 215 Second St., West Palm Beach, Fla. Died July 1, 1949.

ROYAL, Forrest, naval officer; b. New York, N.Y., Feb. 10, 1893; s. Forrest Betton and Mary Cornelia (Holmes) R.; B.S., U.S. Naval Acad., 1915; post grad. work in ordnance, Post Grad. Sch., Annapolis, Md., 1921-22; S.M., Mass. Inst. Tech., 1924; grad. senior class, Naval War Coll., 1939; m. Katharine Knight, Dec. 28, 1922; children—Elizabeth Harwood (wife of Lt. James Wood Burch, U.S.N.R.), Katharine Knight. Commd. ensign, U.S. Navy, 1915, promoted through grades to rear adm., 1944; mem. U.S. Naval Mission to Brazil, 1939-41; comdg. officer U.S.S. Milwaukee, 1941-42; U.S. sec. Combined Chiefs of Staff, 1942-44; comdr. Amphibious Group Six since June 1944; comd. attack group in amphibious assault on Leyte, P.I., Oct. 1944, on Lingayen, Luzon, P.I., Jan. 1945, Mindanao invasion, March 1945; also Bruni Bay and Borneo. Decorated Cruzeiro do Sul, Medal of Services of War (Brazil); Distinguished Service Medal (star in lieu of second medal presented posthumously); Order Comdr. of British Empire. Mem. Am. Soc. Naval Engrs., Naval Inst., Mil. Order World War, Newcomen Soc. Clubs: Union League (New York); Army and Navy (Washington); Army-Navy Country (Arlington, Va.). Home: 2208 Knoll Road South, Arlington Ridge, Arlington, Va. Address: Navy Dept., Washington 25, D.C. Died June 18, 1945; buried in Arlington National Cemetery.

ROYLE, Edwin Milton, dramatist, actor; b. Lexington, Mo., Mar. 2, 1862; s. Jonathan C. and Eliza (Kirtley) R.; A.B., Princeton, 1883; post-grad. course U. of Edinburgh, Scotland; student Columbia Law Sch.; m. Selena Fetter, Oct. 16, 1892; children—Josephine Fetter, Selena Kirtley. Since production of first play, "Friends," 1892, has starred with wife in own plays. Mem. Authors League of America, Phi Delta Phi. Clubs: Players, Lambs. Author: The Silent Call, 1912; Peace and Quiet, 1916. Plays (produced): Friends; Captain Impudence; The Squaw Man; The Struggle Everlasting; These Are My People; The Silent Call; The Unwritten Law; The Winning of Barbara Worth (dramatization); Peace and Quiet; The Longest Way 'Round; Launcelot and Elaine (poetic tragedy), prod. Greenwich Village Theatre, New York; The Conqueror, 1923; My Wife's Husbands, prod. Madison Square Theatre, afterwards a musical play, Marrying Mary; Her Way Out, prod. 1925; Edwin Booth As I Knew Him, 1933; also vaudeville farces; also play (unproduced) Man and Beast and brochure The Why Of It All. Co-author: Moonshine (musical play); Barberry Bush (dramatization). Home: 780 West End Av., New York, N.Y. Died Feb. 16, 1942.

ROYSE, Samuel Durham (rois), lawyer; b. Terre Haute, Ind., Aug. 8, 1878; s. Samuel and Harriett (Durham) R.; student Mich. Mil. Acad., Orchard Lake, Mich., 1894-96, Ind. U., 1896-97; A.B., Amherst Coll., 1900; LL.B., Columbia, 1903; unmarried. Admitted to Ind. bar, 1903, and since practiced in Terre Haute; sr. partner firm of Cooper, Royse, Gambill & Crawford and its predecessors; mem. Ind. State Senate, 1909-13; county atty. Vigo County, 1911-17; v.p. Ind. Gas and Chem. Corp., J. W. Davis Co.; v.p. and chmn. bd. Terre Haute Boiler Works Co.; director Merchants National Bank of Terre Haute. Served as captain infantry, U.S. Army, 1917-18; maj. 39th Machine Gun Batt., 1918-19, World War. Dir. Union Hosp., Terre Haute, Rose Poly. Inst.; trustee Ind. World Memorial since 1920. Mem. Am., Ind. State and Vigo County bar assns., Delta Kappa Epsilon, Phi Delta Phi. Democrat. Methodist. Mason, Elk. Clubs: Terre Haute Country; Indianapolis Athletic; University (Washington, D.C., and Indianapolis); Bankers of America. Home: 431 S. 5th St. Office: Merchants Nat. Bank Bldg., Terre Haute, Ind. Died Apr. 8, 1945.

RUCH, Giles Murrel (rōō), educator; b. Guthrie Center, Ia., July 7, 1892; s. William Wallace and Libbie (Young) R.; A.B., U. of Ore., 1914; Ph.D., Stanford, 1922; m. Verness Fraser, Sept. 10, 1924; 1 dau., Arlysle Carolyn. Instr. high sch., Ashland, Ore., 1914-17; instr. in edn., Univ. High Sch., Eugene, Ore., 1917-18; asst. prof. edn., U. of Ore., 1919-20; instr. in edn., Stanford, 1921-22; asst. prof. edn. and psychology, State U. of Ia., 1922-23, asso. prof., 1923-26; asso. prof. edn., U. of Chicago, summer 1926; prof. edn., U. of Calif., 1926-35. Visiting lecturer, Harvard, 1934; editorial dept. Scott, Foresman and Co., 1934-38; consultant Office of Edn., U.S., 1938-39, chief Research and Statistical Service since 1939. Fellow A.A.A.S.; mem. Am. Psychol. Assn., Am. Ednl. Research Assn., Am. Statis. Assn., Nat. Soc. Study of Edn., Sigma Xi, Phi Delta Kappa. Democrat. Author: Improvement of the Written Examination, 1925; Influence of the Factor of Intelligence on the Form of the Learning Curve, 1925; Arithmetic Work-Books (with F. B. Knight and J. W. Studebaker), 1925, 26; Objective Examination Methods in the Social Studies, 1926; Tests and Measurements in High School Instruction (with G. D. Stoddard), 1927; Objective or New-Type Examination, 1928; Specimen Objective Examinations (with G. A. Rice), 1930; (with others) Study Arithmetics (Grades 3-8); 1936, Mathematics and Life (Grades 7-9), 1938, Standard Service Algebra, 1937, and other textbooks in mathematics. Co-author: Readings in Educational Psychology, 1937; Minimum Essentials of the Personal Inventory in Guidance, 1939; Occupational Information and Guidance; Organization and Administration. Contbr. to Jour. Ednl. Psychology, Jour. Ednl. Research, Jour. Applied Psychology, etc. Originator many standardized ednl. tests. Address: 4225 43d St. N.W., Washington, D.C. Died Nov. 15, 1943.

RUCKER, Atterson Walden, congressman; b. Harrodsburg, Ky., Apr. 3, 1847; s. James Willis and Elizabeth (Jones) R.; ed. common schs., Ky. and Mo.; served 4 yrs. in C.S.A.; m. Celeste E. Caruth, 1873 (dec.). Admitted to bar, 1869; practiced in Mo., Kans., and Colo.; was judge County Ct., Lake County, Colo.; mem. 61st and 62d Congresses (1909-13), 1st Colo. Dist.; Democrat. Now retired. Address: Mt. Morrison, Colo. Died July 19, 1927.

RUCKER, Casper Bell, army officer; b. Mo., Sept. 9, 1886; student U. of Mo.; commd. 2d lt. Inf., Sept. 1911, and advanced to brig. gen., June 1943; asst. inspector gen., Philippine Dept., Manila, P.I., July 1938-40; chief of staff, 5th Div., Fort Benjamin Harrison, Ind., and Fort Custer, Mich., 1940-41; dep. chief of staff, Eighth Corps Area (now Eighth Service Command), Fort Sam Houston, Tex., 1941-42; chief of staff, Eighth Service Command, Army Service Forces, Dallas, Tex., since Jan. 1942.†* Died Mar. 30, 1948.

RUCKSTULL, F(red) Wellington (rŭk'stŭl), sculptor; b. Breitenbach, Alsace, May 22, 1853; s. John and Jeanette R.; pub. schs., St. Louis; studied art in Paris, 12 yrs.; m. Adelaide Pohlman, 1900; 1 son, Myron J. Hon. mention, Paris Salon, 1888; grand medal, Chicago Expn., 1893; mem. Jury Fine Arts, Atlanta Expn.; chief of sculpture, St. Louis Expn. Prin. works in sculpture: "Evening," life-size female, marble, Met. Museum, New York; "Mercury Amusing Himself," bronze heroic group, Portland Pl., St. Louis; "Victory," bronze, heroic size, on Soldiers' and Sailors' Monument, Jamaica, L.I.; "Solon," heroic bronze, Library of Congress, Washington; Franklin, Goethe and Macaulay, colossal granite heads, façade, Library of Congress; equestrian statue Brig.-Gen. John F. Hartranft, Capitol Hill, Harrisburg, Pa.; bronze "Color Bearer," Pa. soldier monument, Petersburg (Va.) battlefield; "Wisdom" and "Force," colossal marble, N.Y. Appellate Ct., New York; heroic bronze, "Gloria Victis," Baltimore Confed. monument, replica erected at Salisbury, N.C.; Confederate monument, "The Defense of the Flag," Little Rock, Ark.; equestrian statue of Gen. Wade Hampton, Columbia, S.C.; marble statue of John C. Calhoun for capitol, Washington; Woman's monument, Columbia, S.C.; monument to Dr. Charles D. McIver, Raleigh, N.C.; marble statue of U.M. Rose, of Ark., Capitol, Washington; monument to "The Three Partisan Generals," Columbia, S.C.; "Phœnicia," marble façade, N.Y. Customs House; McIver monument, Raleigh, N.C., replica at Greensboro, N.C.; "Minerva," bronze, Battle of L.I. monument, Brooklyn; "America Remembers," heroic bronze statue, Civil War monument, Stafford Springs, Conn.; heroic marble statue of Wade Hampton, Statuary Hall, Washington, D.C. Mem. Nat. Inst. Arts and Letters; 1st sec. Nat. Sculpture Soc.; 2d v.p. Municipal Art. Soc., Archtl. League New York; mem. Nat. Arts Club. Editor The Art World, New York. Author: The Great Works of Art and What Makes Them Great, 1925. Address: care Nat. Inst. of Arts and Letters, New York, N.Y. Died May 26, 1942.

RUEDIGER, William Carl (rōō'dĭ-gẽr), univ. prof.; b. Fountain City, Wis., Mar. 29, 1874; s. Ernst and Auguste (Heise) R.; Ph.B., U. of Wis., 1899, Ph.M., 1903; Ph.D., Columbia, 1907; Doctor's Diploma, Teachers Coll. (Columbia), 1907; m. Mary Hazel Pietsch, Sept. 4, 1906 (died Dec. 22, 1919); children—Monta Hazel, Karl; m. 2d, Imogene Ickis, Aug. 19, 1922. Began as teacher in graded schools of Alma, Wis., 1893-94, high schs., Eau Claire, Wis., and Winona, Minn., 1899-1902; asst. in pedagogy, U. of Wis., 1902-03; prof. methods, Mont. State Normal Coll., 1903-05; fellow in edn., Teachers Coll. (Columbia), 1905-06; asst. in psychology, Columbia, 1906-07, asst. prof. ednl. psychology, 1907-11, prof. since 1911, dean Teachers Coll., 1912-36, provost, 1936-39, prof. emeritus since 1939; dir. Summer School, George Washington U., 1915-25; acting prof. edn., Howard U., 1910-13, Cornell, 1931-32; lecturer Summer Sch., U. of Va., 1908, 09, U. of W.Va., 1912, 13, Dartmouth Coll., 1914, Cornell, 1921, 26, 28, 31, U. of S. Calif., 1925, 27, 30, 33, Pa. State Coll., 1938; instr. Am. Seminar, Wolfeboro, N.H., 1940. Mem. A.A.A.S., Phi Beta Kappa, Phi Delta Kappa. Conglist. Club: Federal Schoolmen's. Author: The Field of Distinct Vision, 1907; The Principles of Education, 1910; Agencies for the Improvement of Teachers in Service, 1911; Vitalized Teaching, 1923; Teaching Procedures, 1932. Home: 2836 28th St., Washington 8, D.C. Died July 4, 1947.

RUFF, Robert Hamric, clergyman, educator; b. Chester, Miss., July 27, 1887; s. George Thomas and Mary (Hamric) R.; B.A., M.A., Millsaps Coll., Jackson, Miss., 1910; B.D., Emory U., Atlanta, Ga., 1915; grad. study Vanderbilt, U. of Chicago, Columbia U.; D.D., Kentucky Wesleyan College, 1928; LL.D., Ohio Northern University, 1929, Millsaps College, 1941; m. Annie Mae Gallbreth, July 15, 1925 (died May 6, 1931). Principal high school, Rolling Forks, Miss., 1910-11, Moorhead, Miss., 1911-13; ordained ministry M.E. Ch., S., 1915; pastor Moorhead, Miss., 1915-17; sec. rural work, Bd. Missions, M.E. Ch., S., 1921-26; sec. adult edn., Gen. S.S. Bd., M.E. Ch., S., 1926-27; pres. Morris Harvey Coll., Barboursville, W.Va., 1927-29; pres. Central Coll., Fayette, Mo., since 1930. Served as 1st lt., chaplain, U.S. Army, 1917-19. Mem. Mo. Conf., Meth. Ch.; pres. Ednl. Assn. Meth. Ch. Mem. Kappa Sigma, Sigma Upsilon, Omicron Delta Kappa. Democrat. Mason. Club: Kiwanis. Contbr. to religious and ednl. press. Home: Fayette, Mo. Died May 5, 1942.

RUFFIN, Sterling, M.D.; b. Graham, N.C., July 20, 1866; s. John Kirkland and Sarah Elizabeth (Tayloe) R.; U. of N.C., 1882-84; M.D., hon. mention, Columbian (now George Washington) U., 1890, D.Sc., 1932; London Sch. of Tropical Medicine, 1900; unmarried. Began practice at Washington, 1893; prof. medicine, George Washington U., 1902-24, now emeritus; physician-in-chief George Washington U. Hosp., 1902-24; consulting phys. George Washington and Garfield Memorial hosps., Washington, D.C. Mem. A.M.A., Clinico-Pathol. Soc. of D.C., Am. Climatol. and Clin. Assn., Med. Soc. of D.C. (pres. 1935-36), Washington Acad. Medicine, Alpha Tau Omega, Phi Chi. Democrat. Episcopalian. Address: 1150 Connecticut Av., Washington, D.C. Died June 1, 1949.

RUFUS, Will Carl, astronomer; b. of Am. parents, at Chatham, Can., July 1, 1876; s. William James and Eliza Ann (Comer) R.; A.B., Albion (Mich.) Coll., 1902, A.M., 1908; Ph.D., U. of Mich., 1915; m. Maude Squire, Sept. 29, 1902; children—Merlin Quinton (dec.), Clinton Howard, Herman Douglas. Asst. mathematics, Albion Coll., 1901-02; teacher high sch., Flint, 1902-04, Lansing, 1904-05; pastor M.E. Ch., Dryden, Mich., 1905-06, Owosso, 1906-07; instr. in mathematics and astronomy, Union Coll., Pyeng Yang, Korea, 1907-11; supt. edn., M.E. Mission, Seoul, Korea, 1911-13; fellow U. of Mich., 1913-15; prof. mathematics and astronomy, Chosen Christian Coll., Seoul, 1915-17; instr. in astronomy, U. of Mich., 1917-20, asst. prof., 1920-1934, asso. prof., 1934-41, professor since 1941; acting director Observatory, 1930-31; acting chmn. dept. astronomy, 1930-31, 1938-39, and since 1942; sec. of com. in charge Barbor Scholarships for Oriental Women, since 1920; prof. math. and astronomy, U. World Cruise, 1926-27. Del. of History of Sci. Soc. to Rittenhouse Bicentenary, 1932. Fellow A.A.A.S. (v.p. sect. L, 1926-27), Am. Geog. Soc., Soc. for Research on Meteorites; mem. Am. Astron. Soc., History of Science Soc. of America (mem. council), Rittenhouse Astron. Soc., Mich. Acad. Science, Am. Council Inst. of Pacific Relations, Korea Br. Royal Asiatic Soc., Sigma Nu. Hon. member Detroit Astronomical Society, Astronomical Society of the Philippines, Samfundet for Astronomisk Historieforskning I Lund. Republican. Clubs: Junior Research (pres. 1925-26), Research, University. Research in stellar spectroscopy, atmospheric motion in Cepheid variables; established place of class R stars in evolutionary sequence; contbr. on astron. and Asiatic subjects. Home: 1334 Arlington Blvd., Ann Arbor, Mich. Died Sep. 21, 1946.

RUGG, Robert Billings, banker; b. Boston, Mass., Sept. 17, 1886; s. Frederic W. and Luella (Billings) R.; ed. Dartmouth, 1908; m. Margaret Hurley, 1923; 1 son, Frederic W., II. Mgr. Shawmut Corp., Boston, and then exec. v.p. and subsequently pres. The Nat. Rockland Bank of Boston; dir. Mass. Bonding & Ins. Co., Joseph Warren Co-operative Bank, Boston; trustee Instn. for Savings in Roxbury and its Vicinity, Boston. Clubs: University, Brae Burn Country. Home: 112 Bullough Park, Newtonville, Mass. Office: 30 Congress St., Boston, Mass.* Died May 28, 1946.

RUGGLES, E. Wood, dermatologist; b. Oneida, N.Y., Feb. 22, 1861; s. Samuel Newton and Mercy A. (Wood) R.; prep. edn., Onondaga Acad., Syracuse, N.Y.; A.B., Hamilton Coll., Clinton, N.Y., 1885, A.M., 1888; M.D., Coll. Phys. and Surg. (Columbia), 1888; post-grad. work in Europe, 1888-90; m. Grace Adelaide Gordon, Apr. 14, 1892; 1 dau., Dorothy. Practiced in N.Y. City, 1890-92, then returned to Europe and studied until 1898; has specialized in dermatology at Rochester, N.Y., since 1898; dermatologist Infants' Summer Hosp. Member A.M.A., Am. Dermatol. Assn., Am. Assn. Genito-Urinary Surgeons,

Am. Urol. Assn., N.Y. State Med. Soc., Monroe County Med. Soc. (pres. 1916-17), Rochester Acad. Medicine, Rochester Pathol. Soc. (pres. 1906-07), Phi Beta Kappa, Theta Delta Chi. Mem. Med. Advisory Bd. (as to dermatology and urology), connected with Draft Bd., 1917-18, World War. Republican. Presbyterian. Mason. Club: Oak Hill Country. Contributor many articles on dermatology to med. press, especially with reference to treatment. Home: 348 University Av., Rochester, N.Y.* Died Nov. 7, 1942.

RUNYON, (Alfred) Damon (rŭn'yŭn), writer; b. Manhattan, Kan., Oct. 4, 1884; s. Alfred Lee and Elizabeth (Damon) R.; ed. pub. schs., Pueblo, Colo.; m. Ellen Egan, May 1911 (dec.); children—Mary Elaine, Damon; m. 2d, Patrice del Grande, July 7, 1932. Successively reporter Pueblo Chieftain, Colorado Springs (Colo.) Gazette, Denver News, Denver Post, San Francisco Post, 1900-10; sports writer New York American, 1911; war corr. Hearst Newspapers, Mexico, 1912, Pershing Punitive Expn., 1916, World War, 1917-18; columnist and feature writer, King Features, Internat. News Service since 1918; producer at RKO and 20th Century-Fox, Hollywood, 1942-43. Pvt. Minn. Vol. Inf., Spanish-Am. War and Philippine Insurrection, 1898-1900. Mem. Vets. Foreign Wars. Author: Tents of Trouble (verse), 1911; Rhymes of the Firing Line, 1912; Guys and Dolls (short stories), 1932; Blue Plate Special (stories), 1934; Money From Home (stories), 1935; Best of Runyon (stories); (play) A Slight Case of Murder (with Howard Lindsay), 1935; My Wife Ethel (stories), 1939; Take It Easy (stories), 1939; My Old Man (essays), 1939. Contbr. fiction to Cosmopolitan, Collier's, etc. Home: Las Melaleuccas, Hibiscus Island, Fla. Office: King Features, New York, N.Y. Died Dec. 10, 1946.

RUPERTUS, William Henry (rōō pĕr'tŭs), Marine Corps officer; b. Washington, D.C., Nov. 14, 1889; s. Charles and Augustina (Meile) R.; ed. U.S. Coast Guard Acad., 1910-13; Army Command and Gen. Staff Sch., 1925-26; m. Alice Hill, Mar. 4, 1933; 1 son, Patrick Hill. Commd. 2d lt. Marines, 1913; promoted through grades to maj. gen., 1943; commanded operations against Japanese in Tulagi area, Br. Solomon Islands, 1942. Decorated D.S.M. of Haiti. U.S. Navy Cross. Home: 3732 Van Ness St., N.W., Washington, D.C. Died Mar. 25, 1945.

RUPPERT, George E., pres. Jacob Ruppert, beverages, New York City. Office: 1639 Third Av., New York, N.Y. Died Nov. 5, 1948.

RUSH, Benjamin, underwriter; b. Chestnut Hill, Pa., Nov. 28, 1869; s. Richard Henry and Susan (Yerby) R.; ed. Episcopal Acad., Phila.; m. Mary Wheeler Lockwood, June 5, 1895. In ins. business since 1885; chmn. bd. Ins. Co. of N. A., Indemnity Ins. Co. of N.A., Alliance Ins. Co. of Phila., Phila. Fire & Marine Ins. Co.; dir Fidelity-Phila. Trust Co.; trustee Penn Mut. Life Ins. Co. of Phila., Mut. Assurance Co. of Phila. Mem. Average Adjusters' assns. of U.S. and Eng., Hist. Soc. Pa., Pa. Acad. Fine Arts, Newcomen Soc. of England (vice-chmn. Phila. com.). Republican. Episcopalian. Clubs: Philadelphia, Rittenhouse. Wrote: A Treatise on Marine Cargo Insurance; A Treatise on Marine Hull Insurance; The Road to Fulfillment. Home: R.F.D. No. 1, West Chester, Pa. Office: 1600 Arch St., Philadelphia, Pa. Died Apr. 25, 1948.

RUSH, John Andrew, lawyer; b. Richland County, Ill., Mar. 9, 1865; s. Jacob and Eliza Ann (Stout) R.; A.B., U. of Kan., 1890, A.M., 1893, LL.B., 1893; m. Elsie E. Dodd, Feb. 12, 1895; children—John Louis, Robert. Teacher country sch., Kan., 1885-86; pres. Kansas State Oratorical Assn., 1889; city editor Lawrence (Kan.) Journal, and reporter Kansas City (Mo.) Journal, 1890-91; editor of the University Courier, 1892-93; admitted to bar, Kan. and Colo., 1893; began practice at Denver; county chmn. Nat. Silver Party, 1896; sec. judiciary com. Colo. Ho. of Rep., 1897; mem. Denver Charter Conv., 1898; mem. Colo. State Senate, 1901-04 (chmn. judiciary com.); author Article XX, Colo. Constn., creating City and County of Denver, with one set of officials and with absolute "home rule"; county atty. Arapahoe County, Colo., 1902-03; mem. and v.p. Denver Charter Con., 1903; organizer Municipal Ownership League and Citizens Party (carried municipal election 1912); dist. atty., Denver, 1913-16; moved to Los Angeles, 1921; pres. Bond & Securities Co.; mem. and v. chmn. Citizens Com. on Governmental Reorganization, apptd. by mayor of Los Angeles, 1935. Mem. State Bar of Calif., Phi Kappa Psi. Club: Los Angeles Country. Author: The City-County Consolidated, 1941. Home: 121 S. Hudson Av., Los Angeles, Calif. Died Nov. 1, 1943.

RUSHTON, Herbert J., atty. gen. for Mich.; b. 1878; grad. U. of Mich.; admitted to Mich. bar, 1908; practiced in Escanaba. Address: State Capitol, Lansing, Mich.* Died Dec. 11, 1947.

RUSSELL, Arthur Perkins, railway exec.; b. Leominster, Mass., June 16, 1871; s. Rev. Thomas Clarkson and Helena (Taylor) R.; ed. pub. schs.; m. Mae A. Kimball, Sept. 29, 1904; children (adopted)—Kenneth B., Leon B., Clayton B. Began as clk. N.Y.&N.E. R.R., 1888, sec. to v.p. and gen. mgr. until 1898; chief clk. of law dept. for Mass., N.Y., N.H.&H. R.R., 1898-1907; admitted to Mass. bar, 1907, and apptd. asst. atty. same railroad, at Boston, served as Mass. legislative counsel, of the road, 1910-13, in charge valuation dept., at New Haven, Conn., 1914-18, federal counsel, in charge valuations and relations with the govt., Feb.-July 1918, asst. gen. counsel and corporate commr. real estate, 1918-20, v.p. in charge real estate, valuation and ins. depts., 1920-30, in charge pub. relations since 1923, exec. v.p., 1929-35, v.p. since 1935; founder-pres. New England Transportation Co., 1925-30; chairman trustees Boston Terminal Co.; pres. Old Colony R.R. Co., Union Freight R.R. Co., Boston R.R. Holding Co., Providence Produce Warehouse Co.; v.p. New England Steamship Co.; dir. Providence,Warren& Bristol R.R. Co., Providence Securities Co. Member Mass. House of Rep., 1899-1902. Chmn. War Bur. Town of Woodbridge (Conn.), World War. Moderator town of Hingham, 1934-39. Republican. Mason. Club: Algonquin (Boston). Home: Hingham, Mass. Office: New York, New Haven & Hartford R.R., Boston, Mass.* Died Oct. 16, 1946.

RUSSELL, Clinton Warden, army officer; b. Hico, Tex., May 6, 1891; s. William E. and Mollie (Anderson) R.; student Tex. A. and M. Coll., 1907-08; B.S., U.S. Mil. Acad., 1913; grad. Command and Gen. Staff Sch., 1925, Army War Coll., 1930, Naval War Coll., 1931; m. Dorothy Kendall, Jan. 11, 1917; children—William Kendall, Peter Talbot, Kendall. Commd. 2d lt., U.S. Army, 1913, and advanced through grades to brig. gen., 1940; served in Inf., U.S. and P.I., 1913-16; took flying training, 1916; served in punitive expdn. to Mexico, 1916; comdr. 7th Aero Squadron, Canal Zone, 1917; served in various capacities at flying fields during World War; instr. R.O.T.C., Tex. A. and M. Coll., 1920-24; instr. Command and Gen. Staff Sch., 1924-29; in War Dept. Gen. Staff, 1931-35; chief of staff, Air Force Combat Command, since 1938. Awarded Victory medal, 1918; Punitive Expdn. medal, 1917; Mil. medal "La Estrella de Abdon Calderon" (Ecuador), 1935. Home: Hico, Tex. Address: care Adjutant General, U.S. Army, Washington, D.C. Died Mar. 24, 1943.

RUSSELL, Daniel, clergyman; b. Manchester, Ia., Mar. 23, 1873; s. Daniel and Mary (Wing) R.; B.S., Lenox Coll., Hopkinton, Iowa, 1894, B.A., 1895; A.M., Princeton, 1898; grad. Princeton Theol. Sem., 1898; D.D., Lenox Coll., 1905, N.Y. U., 1918; m. Caroline Kelso, Sept. 13, 1899 (dec.); children—Mary Helen, Josephine (Mrs. Campbell Robertson), Carolyn (Mrs. Ralph G. Miller, Jr.). Ordained to the ministry of the Presbyn. Ch., 1898; pastor Hancock, N.Y., 1898-99, Harlem Ch., New York, 1899-1904, Bellefield Ch., Pittsburgh, Pa., 1904-09, Irvington-on-Hudson, N.Y., 1910-15, Rutgers Ch., N.Y. City, Sept. 1915-Oct. 1943, now emeritus. Instrumental in rebuilding and transforming this ch. into community enterprise with completely equipped plant and adequate endowment, 1924-25. Moderator Presbytery of New York, 1902-03, 1933-36; formerly mem. General Educational Board Presbyterian Church. Member Chi Alpha. Clubs: Quill (president 1935-36). Mason. Author: The Substance of Happiness, 1914; The Cleansing of Life, 1931; Preaching the Apocalypse, 1935; O Steadfast Face, 1936; Meditations for Men, 1945. Home: 360 Riverside Drive, New York 25, N.Y. Died Feb. 10, 1947.

RUSSELL, George Louis, Jr., pres. John B. Stetson Co.; b. Lewistown, Pa., May 6, 1896; s. George Louis and Annie L. (Brisbin) R.; grad. Lawrenceville Sch., 1913; A.B., Princeton U., 1917; m. Dorothy Reach Christ, Feb. 9, 1917; children—George Louis, 3d. With John B Stetson Co since 1917, beginning as clerk, asst. treas., 1919-32, treas., 1932-38, v.p. and treas. 1938-39, pres. and dir. since 1939; chmn. of bd., John B Stetson Co. (Canada), Ltd., John B. Stetson Bldg. & Loan Assn., Stetson Hosp. of Phila.; dir. Fidelity-Phila. Trust Co. Director Fidelity Mutual Life Insurance Co., Phila.; dir. and ex-president Hat Institute, Incorporated, New York City. Clubs: Princeton, Union League, Philadelphia Country (Phila.); Princeton Quadrangle (Princeton, New Jersey). Home: The Cambridge at Alden Park. Office: John B. Stetson Co., Philadelphia, Pa. Died Mar. 4, 1947.

RUSSELL, Henry, managing dir.; b. London, Eng., Nov. 14, 1874; s. Henry (composer) and Hannah R.; ed. in London; married. Prof. singing at London, and Rome until 1904; dir. season of opera, Covent Garden Theatre, London, 1904; came to America, 1905; now mng. dir. Boston Opera House, and Boston Opera Co. Address: Boston Opera House, Boston. Died Oct. 11, 1936.

RUSSELL, Henry Benajah, journalist; b. Russell, Mass., Mar. 9, 1859; s. Edwin A. and Sarah L. (Tinker) R.; A.B., Amherst, 1881; L.H.D., Am. Internat. Coll., 1941; m. Louisa A. Clark, Sept. 25, 1885 (died June 10, 1904); 1 son, Fordham Clark; m. 2d, Helen V. Mason, Jan. 1, 1910. Reporter Springfield Republican, 1881-82; editor Meriden (Conn.) Press-Recorder, 1882-84; spl. writer, New York Sun, 1884-88; editorial writer Providence Journal, 1888-90; editor Hartford (Conn.) Post, 1891-98; editor Springfield (Mass.) Homestead, 1902-17; associate editor Springfield (Mass.) Union, 1917-26, editor 1926-41, retired. Author: Life of William McKinley, 1896; International Monetary Conferences, 1898; Our War with Spain, 1899; Man Proposes, a New England Story, 1939. Home: Suffield, Conn. Died Nov. 25, 1945.

RUSSELL, Howard Hyde, founder the Anti-Saloon League; b. Stillwater, Minn., Oct. 21, 1855; s. Joseph A. and Sarah Emogene (Parker) R.; student Griswold Coll., Ia., 1870-72; LL.B., Indianola (Ia.) Coll., 1878; B.D., Oberlin Theol. Sem., 1888, hon. A.M., 1895, D.D., 1921; D.D., Ohio Wesleyan, 1896; LL.D., Otterbein, 1922, L.H.D., 1935; m. Lillian Davis, Aug. 17, 1880 (died 1939); children—Julia, Capt. Ernest Clement (died 1939). Commanding officers' clerk, Rock Island Arsenal, 1872-73; cowboy, 1874; editor and business manager Adams County (Ia.) Gazette, 1875; admitted to bar Ia., 1878, Ohio, 1894, N.Y., 1905, Supreme Court of U.S., 1919; practiced law at Corning, 1878-83; county supt. schs., Adams County, Ia., 1881-82; ordained Congl. ministry, 1885; pastor N. Amherst and Berea, O., while student, 1883-88; organized in a tent, erected church building, and was first pastor of the Tabernacle Congregational Church, Kansas City, 1888-91; pastor Armour Mission, Chicago, 1891-93; at request of Oberlin Temperance Alliance organized, 1888, temporary state local option league and secured enactment of Beatty twp. local option law; this success led to initiation of Anti-Saloon League movement in Ohio, 1893, and was first state supt., 1893-97; one of organizers and first gen. supt. of the (Nat.) Anti-Saloon League of America, 1895-1903, during which time started the league in 36 states, traveling annually more than 50,000 miles; supt. New York Anti-Saloon League, 1901-09, and chmn. exec. com. Anti-Saloon League America, 1903-09; recalled 1909 to Nat. Anti-Saloon League as asso. gen. supt., chmn. financial management com. and as gen. sec. of its moral suasion dept., the Lincoln-Lee Legion, also founded by him, which has an enrollment of over 5,000,000; from July 4, 1915, to Sept. 5, 1915, with male quartette, conducted the first transcontinental "water wagon" tour from New York to San Francisco, in automobiles, over the Lincoln Highway. One of organizers, first Am. Pres. World League Against Alcoholism, 1919; U.S. del. World Congress Against Alcoholism, Washington, D.C., 1920; visited Europe twice in 1921, assisting anti-liquor orgns. in British Isles, France, Norway and Sweden; del. to Lausanne Congress Against Alcoholism. Mem. Nat. Council Congl. Chs., 1918-20; mem. Federal Council of Chs. of Christ in America, 1920-32. Life mem. Nat. W.C.T.U.; mem. Sons of Am. Revolution. Author: A Lawyer's Examination of the Bible, 1893, 7th edition, 1935 (approved as keybook of Bible Bond, Inc., started in Ohio by Christian lawyers to promote the reading of the Bible); also many pamphlets and articles on methods to promote total abstinence and abolish the liquor traffic. Declared officially by nat. officers at conv., Chicago, Nov. 5, 1925, "Founder of Anti-Saloon League." In 1937-41, in Lincoln-Lee Legion Dept., organized dramatic court trials of case of "Church vs. Booze," with judges and juries in several cities, including Phila. and Boston. Home: Westerville, O. Died June 30, 1946.

RUSSELL, James Earl, coll. prof., dean emeritus; b. Hamden, Delaware County, N.Y., July 1, 1864; s. Charles and Sarah (McFarlane) R.; A.B., Cornell, 1887; univs. of Jena, Leipzig, Berlin, 1893-95; Ph.D., Leipzig, 1894; LL.D., Dickinson, 1903, U. Colo., 1905, McGill, 1909, Iowa, 1923; Litt.D., Columbia, 1927, U. State of N.Y., 1927; m. Agnes Fletcher, June 19, 1889 (died 1927); children—William F., Charles, James Earl, John M.; m. 2d, Alice F. Wyckoff, Jan. 24, 1929. Teacher in secondary schs., 1887-90; prin. Cascadilla Sch., Ithaca, N.Y., 1890-93; European commr. Regents of the U. of the State of N.Y., 1893-95; European agt. Bur. of Edn., Washington, D.C., 1893-95; prof. philosophy and pedagogy, U. of Colo., 1895-97; prof. of edn., Teachers Coll. (Columbia), 1897-1927, prof. edn. on Richard March Hoe Foundation, 1927-31; dean Teachers College, 1897-1927, dean emeritus since 1927; Barnard prof. of edn., Columbia, 1904-27. Mem. N.J. State Board of Health, 1932-40, N.J. Milk Control Bd., 1933. Pres. Am. Assn. for Adult Edn., 1926-30 (chmn. since 1930); mem. Am. Psychol. Assn., Nat. Council Edn., Nat. Council on Radio in Edn., Nat. Occupational Conf. Author: The Extension of University Teaching in England and America, 1895; German Higher Schools; The History, Organization and Methods of Secondary Education in Germany, 1899; Trend in American Education, 1922; Founding Teachers College, 1937. Editor Am. Teachers Series. Contbr. to ednl. jours. Home: 1824 Riverside Dr., Trenton, N.J. Died Nov. 4, 1945.

RUSSELL, John Henry, major gen. U.S. Marines; b. Mare Island, Calif., Nov. 14, 1872; s. John Henry and Cornelia Pierrepont (Treadway) R.; grad. U.S. Naval Acad., class of 1892; m. Mabel Howard, June 12, 1901; 1 dau., Roberta Brooke (Mrs. Charles H. Marshall). Served through grades to maj. gen. U.S. M.C., Sept. 13, 1933; mem. staff U.S. War Coll., 1908-10; served in Spanish-Am. War, World War and several Marine Corps expeditionary campaigns; American high commissioner with the rank of ambassador Port-au-Prince, Haiti, by appointment of President Harding, 1922-30; appointed assistant to maj. gen. comdt., Feb. 1933, then comdt. Marine Corps; retired, Dec. 1, 1936; now in newspaper work. Awarded U.S. Navy Cross, D.S.M., Haitian Medaille Militaire and campaign medal, West Indies medal, Spanish Campaign medal, Expeditionary medal with Numeral 4, Mexican Service medal, Victory medal with West Indies clasp. Mem. (by desc.) Calif. Pioneers. Episcopalian. Club: Army and Navy (Washington, D.C.). Home: Coronado, Calif. Died Mar. 6, 1947.

RUSSELL, Lee Maurice, ex-governor; b. nr. Oxford, Miss., Nov. 16, 1875; s. William Eaton and Louisa Jane (Mackey) R.; B.S., Toccopola College, 1897; Ph.B., U. of Miss., 1901, LL.B., 1903; m. Ethelmary Day, June 28, 1905. Began practice at Oxford, Miss., 1901; real estate business, Gulfport, Miss. Mem. Miss. Ho. of Rep., 1908-12, Senate, 1912-16; lt. gov. of Miss., 1916-20; gov. of Miss., 1920-24. Democrat. Methodist. Mason, K.P., Woodman. Home: Gulfport, Miss. Died May 16, 1943.

RUSSELL, Paul Snowden, banker; b. Oak Park, Ill., May 10, 1893; s. John Kent and Adelyn Frances

(Mayo) R.; A.B., University of Chicago, 1916; married Carroll A. Mason, April 7, 1922; children—Carroll Russell Sherer, Paul Snowden, Jr., Adelyn Mayo, Ann Mason, Harold Swift. With Harris Trust & Savings Bank, Chicago, since 1916, v.p., 1930-46, pres. since 1946, dir. since 1942; dir. Hoover & Mason Phosphate Co. Served as capt., Inf., U.S.A., 5th Div., World War, 1917-1918. Trustee U. of Chicago, Chicago Orphan Asylum; governor of International House. Member advisory committee Chicago Loan Agency of Reconstruction Finance Corp. Mem. adv. bd., Research and Development Br. Office Q.M. Gen., Washington, D.C. Mem. adv. council, Chicago Community Trust; mem. Assn. Reserve City Bankers. Trustee Chicago Memorial Hosp.; v.p. and dir. C. of C. Assn., 1944-45; mem. Assn. of Reserve City Bankers, Newcomen Soc., Delta Kappa Epsilon. Republican. Clubs: University, Chicago, Attic, Economic, Commercial, Glen View (Golf, Ill.); Old Elm (Fort Sheridan, Ill.). Chikaming Country Club (Lakeside, Mich.). Home: 4901 Greenwood Av., Chicago 15. Died Jan. 8, 1950.

RUSSELL, Walter Earle, educator; b. Fayette, Me., Aug. 6, 1869; s. Charles (M.D.) and Asenath R.; prep. edn., Maine Wesleyan Sem.; A.B., Wesleyan U., Conn.; Ed.D., R.I. College of Edn.; m. Winifred P. Stone, Jan. 25, 1896; children—Earle Stone, Willis Cleaves, Helen Gertrude, Robert Edward, Celia Asenath. Teacher Normal Sch., New Britain, Conn., 1893-94, State Normal Sch., Gorham, Me., 1894-1905; prin. Gorham State Normal Sch., 1905-40, prin. emeritus since 1940. Mem. Maine legislature, 1945-48. Republican. Methodist. Club: Lions. Home: Gorham, Me. Died July 6, 1948.

RUSTGARD, John, lawyer; b. Beidstaden, Norway, Oct. 21, 1863; s. Andreas Hoe and Anne (Maere) R.; LL.B., U. of Minn., 1890; m. Alice Jane Adeane, Apr. 25, 1903 (died May 30, 1923); m. 2d, Josephine Halvorsen, June 24, 1926. Came to U.S., 1881, naturalized, 1890. Admitted to Minn. bar, 1890; in practice at Minneapolis, Tower and Duluth, Minn., 1890-1899, at Nome, Alaska, 1900-09, Juneau since 1909; asso. city atty. of Duluth, 1897-98; mayor of Nome, 1903-04; U.S. dist. atty. 1st Div. of Alaska, 1910-14; atty. gen. of Alaska, 1921-33. Author: The Problem of Poverty, 1935, rev., 1936; Bottom Side Up and Other Essays, 1936; Sharing the Wealth, 1937; International Vagaries, 1939; Our Sacred Cow and the New World Order, 1941; The Bankruptcy of Liberalism, 1942. Home: Babson Park, Fla. Died Feb. 12, 1950.

RUTH, George Herman (Babe Ruth), professional baseball player; b. Baltimore, Feb. 6, 1894 (sometimes given as 1895); m. Helen Woodford, 1914 (dec.); 1 dau., Dorothy; m. 2d, Claire Hodgson, Apr. 1929; 1 dau. (adopted stepdaughter), Julia. Signed as pitcher-outfielder Baltimore Orioles (Baltimore-Providence Club of Internat. League), 1913; with Boston Red Sox (Am. League) as pitcher, 1914-20; with N.Y. Yankees as outfielder, 1920-34; became v.p., asst. mgr. and part-time player Boston Braves (Nat. League), 1935; coach Brooklyn Dodgers (Nat. League), 1938. Voted most valuable player in Am. League, 1923; mem. Am. League All Star Team, 1933; played in 10 World Series, a total of 41 games; in total series games made most runs, 37; most home runs, 15; most strikeouts, 30; pitched most innings in Series game, Boston against Brooklyn, Oct. 9, 1916; as pitcher had most consecutive scoreless innings in total Series, 29 2/3 (13 1/3, Oct. 9, 1916; 9, Sept. 5, 1918; 7 1/3, Sept. 9, 1918); held lowest earned run average in season, for left-handed pitcher, Boston (Am. League), 1.75, 1916; highest batting average in Am. League, .692 for 21 yrs.; held numerous other records, including: most runs in season, Am. League, 177 in 152 games, 1921; most home runs in major leagues, 714 (708 Am. League, 6 Nat. League), 1914-35; most home runs in season, 60 in 151 games, 1927; most yrs. leading Am. League in home runs, 12 (1918-25 and 1926-31); most runs batted in, Am. League, 2197 (1914-34); most yrs. leading Am. League in runs batted in, 6 (1919-23, 1926, 1928); world record for strikeouts, 1330 in 22 yrs. Broadcast radio program, 1943-44; appeared in films, including Pride of the Yankees (RKO), 1942; consultant to William Bendix in his role as Babe Ruth, in film, The Babe Ruth Story, 1948. Died Aug. 16, 1948.

RUTLAND, James Richard (rŭt'lănd), prof. English; b. Fredonia, Ala., Nov. 8, 1879; s. John Blake and Eugenia (Askew) R.; B.S., Ala. Poly. Inst., 1900, M.S., 1901; B.A., Harvard, 1904; grad. study, U. of Chicago, summers 1907, 09, 10, 23, and session, 1923-24; m. Hulda Mary Horton, June 22, 1910 (died Aug. 6, 1928); children—James Richard, Robert Horton, Hulda. Grad. asst., Ala. Poly. Inst., 1900-01; teacher, pub. schs., Wylam, Ala., 1901-02; teacher Memphis (Tenn.) Mil. Inst., 1902-03; instr. in English, Ala. Poly. Inst., 1904-08, asst. prof., 1908-11, asso. prof., 1911-12, prof. since 1912 and head of dept. since 1927, librarian, 1905-19, dir. Summer Session, 1913, 14, 15; insp. county high schs., State of Ala., 1908-10, 1914-15; in charge English dept., Oglethorpe U., summers 1921, 22; lecturer Northwestern Univ., 1923-24. Mem. Ala. Library Assn. (pres. 1920-24), Ala. Assn. English Teachers (pres. 1923-30), Alabama Education Association, Kappa Sigma. Democrat. Methodist. Club: Rotary. Editor: Irving's Tales of a Traveler, 1911; Old Testament Stories, 1912; Stevenson's Treasure Island, 1929. Compiler: Notes on Contemporary British and American Writers, 1920; State Censorship of Motion Pictures, 1923. Editor Auburn Alumnus, 1912-20. Home: Auburn, Ala. Died Jan. 13, 1948.

RUTLEDGE, George Perry, clergyman; b. Blacksburg, Va., May 16, 1869; s. Anderson and Ellen Jane (Kirk) R.; B.A., Milligan (Tenn.) Coll., 1891, A.M., 1895; LL.D., Atlantic Christian Coll., Wilson, N.C., 1001, Bethany (W.Va.) Coll., 1917; m. Carrie Wellford McCurdey, Dec. 22, 1896 (dec.); children—Frances Ellen (Mrs. Brent S. Finch, dec.), Pauline (Mrs. Warren W. McIntire), Carol (Mrs. W. K. Tevis). Ordained ministry Disciples of Christ, 1890; pastor First Ch., Norfolk, Va., 1891-96, 3d Ch., Phila., 1897-1912, Broad St. Ch., Columbus, O., 1913-16; editor in chief Christian Standard, 1916-22; founder Pacific Bible Sem., Los Angeles (now at Long Beach), Calif., 1928; now pastor Central Church of Christ, Mt. Vernon, Ill. Mem. Richmond (Va.) Bicentennial Adv. Com., 1937. Mem. North Am. Com. of One Thousand, China's Children Fund, Inc. Mason (32°, Shriner). Author: The Pledge in Sermon, 1895; Center Shots, 1914; Pushing the World Along, 1916; The Miracle of the Ages, 1926; Systematic Stewardship, 1937; Our Pleas for Christian Unity, 1942. Home: 220 N. 10th St., Mt. Vernon, Ill. Died June 20, 1947.

RUTLEDGE, Wiley Blount, judge; b. Cloverport, Ky., July 20, 1894; s. Wiley Blount and Mary Lou (Wigginton) R.; A.B., U. of Wis., 1914; LL.B., U. of Colorado, 1922; m. Annabel Person, Aug. 28, 1917; children—Mary Lou, Jean Ann, Neal. Teacher in high schs., Ind., N.M. and Colo., 1915-22; admitted to Colo. bar, 1922; in practice at Boulder, 1922-24; asso. prof. law, U. of Colo., 1924-26, visiting prof., summers, 1927-32, 1934-36, 42; prof. of law, Washington U., 1926-35, actg. dean, 1930-31, dean Sch. of Law, 1931-35; prof. of law and dean, College of Law, State U. of Ia., 1935-39; asso. justice U.S. Ct. of Appeals for D.C., 1939-43; asso. justice Supreme Court of U.S. since 1943. Member for Missouri of Nat. Conf. of Commrs. on Uniform State Laws, 1931-35, for Ia., 1937-43; mem. bd. trustees, Washington Coll. of Law, Washington, D.C., 1941-43. Mem. Am., Ia., Mo., St. Louis and Johnson County (Ia.) bar assns., Alpha Sigma Phi, Phi Alpha Delta, Delta Sigma Rho, also various edni. and learned socs. Democrat. Mason. Clubs: Rotary, Torch; A Declaration of Legal Faith, 1947. Legal residence: Iowa City, Ia. Address: Supreme Court of the United States, Washington 13. Died Sept. 10, 1949.

RYALS, Thomas Edward (rī'ălz), lawyer; b. Bartow County, Ga., July 3, 1863; s. Rev. James Gazaway and Mary Elizabeth (Janes) R.; student pvt. schs.; A.B., Mercer U., Macon, Ga., 1885, LL.D., 1928; student law and metaphysics, U. of Va., 1886-87; m. Daisy Clisby, Mar. 28, 1900 (died Jan. 13, 1911); m. 2d, Lily Wade Little, June 10, 1922. Admitted to Ga. bar, 1888, and since practiced at Macon; mem. firm Ryals & Stone, 1888-98, Steed & Ryals, 1898-1908, Ryals & Anderson since 1908; mem. City Council, 1894-96; mem. Gen. Assembly, Ga., 1907-08. Trustee and chmn. exec. com. Mercer U. Mem. Am. Bar Assn., Ga. Bar Assn., Kappa Alpha. Democrat. Baptist. Home: 201 Clisby St. Office: First Nat. Bank Bldg., Macon, Ga. Died June 3, 1943.

RYAN, C(lement) D(aniel), ex-pres. Montgomery Ward & Co.; b. Buffalo, N.Y., Dec. 19, 1895; s. George W. and Nellie T. (O'Callahan) R.; studied at coll., 3 yrs.; m. Claire M. Oliver, July 19, 1917; 1 dau., Eileen. Successively with J. N. Adam & Co., Buffalo, J. L. Hudson & Co., Detroit, Wm. Hengerer & Co., Buffalo, The Fair, Chicago, and Hahn Dept. Stores (now Allied Stores), N.Y. City; became gen. mdse. mgr. Montgomery Ward & Co., Chicago, 1939, v.p. and dir., 1940, pres. 1943-45; resigned as pres., Aug. 1945; owner and operator Whitney Dept. Store, San Diego, Calif.; dir. Spiegel, Inc., Chicago. Republican. Clubs: Chicago, Racquet (Chicago); Westchester Hills Country (New York); San Diego Yacht, Cuyamaca, Cloud; La Jolla Beach and Tennis. Home: 1120 Muirlands Dr., La Jolla, Calif. Office: 946 Sixth Av., San Diego 1, Calif. Died Oct. 24, 1947.

RYAN, George Joseph; b. Long Island City, N.Y., July 7, 1872; s. George and Julia R.; ed. pub. schs. of L.I. City, St. Gabriel's Acad. and St. Francis Xavier Coll.; LL.D., Fordham U., 1925; Dottore in Belle Lettere, honoris causa, Bologna, Italy, 1934; LL.D., St. Francis College, 1937; m. Annie M. Fitzpatrick, Nov. 4, 1903. President Long Island City Savings Bank. Member State Constitutional Convention, N.Y., 1915. Fuel administrator Borough of Queens, World War. Past pres. Chamber of Commerce, Borough of Queens. Trustees St. John's Hosp., Roman Catholic Orphan Asylum; president George Washington Foundation for Citizenship and Edn. since 1931; nat. chmn. Patriots Pledge of Faith Com.; dir. Thomas Jefferson Memorial Foundation; former regent of U. of State of New York; former pres. Board of Edn., City of New York; mem. Hon. Advisory Council Am. Dickens League; mem. U.S. Commn. for erection of memorial to Thomas Jefferson; hon. pres. Am. Com. F.I.D.E.S.; hon. Comité des amis Saint-Leu Saint Gilles; fellow Am. Geog. Soc.; mem. Pi Gamma Mu. Papal marquis; Chevalier Order Crown of Belgium; Officer Order of the Crown of Italy; Officer Legion of Honor (France); Knight of Honour, Order of St. John the Baptist; Grand Cross, rank of Bailli of Honour, Order of St. Lazare of Jerusalem; awarded Cross of the Order of Loretto; Cross Dedicacao, Portugal; gold medal for the diffusion of Italian language and culture. Democrat. Catholic. Club: Catholic, Nat. Democratic. Home: 143-29 38th Av., Flushing, L.I., N.Y. Died Oct. 4, 1949.

RYAN, James Hugh, bishop, educator; b. Indianapolis, Ind., Dec. 15, 1886; s. John Marshall and Brigid (Rogers) R.; student Duquesne U., Pittsburgh, Pa., Mt. St. Mary's Sem. of the West, Cincinnati, Am. Coll., Rome; S.T.B., Coll. of Propaganda, Rome, 1906, S.T.D., 1909; Ph.D., Roman Acad., 1908; LL.D., Marquette U., 1929, Manhattan Coll., 1931; hon. Litt.D., Nat. U. of Ireland, 1929. Ordained priest, R.C. Ch., 1909; created domestic prelate with title of monsignor, 1927, prothonotary apostolic, 1929; titular bishop of Modra, 1933, bishop of Omaha, Neb., since Aug. 1935; archbishop of Omaha Archdiocese. Professor psychology, St. Mary of the Woods College, Indiana, 1911-21; instr. in philosophy; Catholic U. of America, 1922-26, asso. prof., 1926-28, Elizabeth Breckenridge Caldwell prof. philosophy, 1929, rector emeritus of univ. Del. to 6th Internat. Congress of Philosophy. Trustee Catholic U. of America. Fellow Mediæval Acad. America, Am. Acad. Arts and Sciences, American Geographical Soc.; mem. Am. Philosophical Assn., Am. Historical Assn., Am. Catholic Historical Association, American Catholic Philosophical Association, British Institute Philos. Studies, Société Thomiste, Phi Beta Kappa; asso. Société Philosophique de Louvain. Decorated Knight Comdr. Crown of Italy, 1930; Grand Cordon, Order of St. Sava (Yugoslavia), 1932; Chevalier Legion of Honor (France), 1934; Knight of Malta, 1935; Grand Officer Crown of Italy, 1935; Commander Order of Polonia Restituta, 1936. Club: University. Author: Directory of Catholic College and Schools, 1921; An Introduction to Philosophy, 1924; The Encyclicals of Pius XI, 1927; The Peace Points of Pope Pius XII, 1942. Address: 2507 Cass St., Omaha, Neb. Died Nov. 23, 1948.

RYAN, John Augustine, theologian; b. Dakota County, Minn., May 25, 1869; s. William and Mary (Luby) R.; grad. St. Thomas Sem., St. Paul, 1892; student theol. dept., same, 1892-94; St. Paul Sem., 1894-98; ordained R.C. priest, 1898; post-grad. student Catholic U., Washington, 1898-1902, D.D., 1906. Prof. moral theology and economics, St. Paul (Minn.) Sem., 1902-15; prof. moral theology and industrial ethics, Catholic U., 1915-37, sociology, 1937-39; now retired from Catholic Univ.; also prof. polit. science, Trinity Coll., since 1915, and prof. social ethics, Nat. Cath. Sch. of Social Service, since 1921. Dir. social action dept. of the Nat. Cath. Welfare Conf. Author: A Living Wage, 1906; Francisco Ferrer, 1910; Alleged Socialism of the Church Fathers, 1913; (with Morris Hillquit) Socialism—Promise or Menace, 1914; Distributive Justice, 1916; The Church and Socialism and Other Essays, 1919; Social Reconstruction, 1920; The Church and Labor, 1920; The State and the Church, 1922; Declining Liberty, and Other Papers, 1927; The Catholic Church and the Citizen, 1928; Questions of the Day, 1931; A Better Economic Order, 1935; Seven Troubled Years, 1937; Catholic Principles of Politics, 1940; Social Doctrine in Action: a Personal History, 1941. Elevated to rank of domestic prelate by Pope Pius XI, Aug. 12, 1933. Address: 1312 Massachusetts Av., N.W., Washington, D.C. Died Sep. 16, 1945.

RYAN, Michael J., lawyer; b. Philadelphia, Pa., June 13, 1862; s. James and Margaret (Howden) R.; ed. La Salle Coll., Phila.; m. Eleanor Kemper, June 9, 1886. Began practice at Phila., 1884; city solicitor (corp. counsel), Phila., 1911-16; pub. service commr. of Pa. by apptmt. of gov. of Pa., Jan. 1916-Feb. 1919; pres. Girard Avenue Title & Trust Co., 1907-1931. Trustee Temple U., Phila. Dental Coll., and Samaritan Hosp., 1908-28. Mem. com. of three, representing Friends of Ireland in U.S., at World Peace Conf., Paris, 1919. Mem. Am. Bar Assn., Pa. Bar Assn., Phila. Bar Assn. Roman Catholic. Club: Clover. Office: Land Title Bldg., Philadelphia, Pa. Died Sep. 7, 1943.

RYDER, Arthur Hilton (rī'dẽr), organist; b. Plymouth, Mass., Apr. 30, 1875; s. Samuel Thomas and Eva Ling (Pooley) R.; music study with his mother, with Rev. F. H. Rowse and Loraine Holloway (organ), music theory and composition at Harvard; m. Frances Warren Moore, May 4, 1898; m. 2d, Emilie Hermine Lovell, June 29, 1940. Organist St. Stephen's Ch., Boston, 1894-99; with Grace Ch., Providence, R.I., as organist, 1901-04, organist and choirmaster, 1904-10; later organist and choirmaster Christ Ch., Quincy, Mass., Harvard Ch., Brookline, 1916-24, St. Paul's Ch., Dedham, since 1924; has given recitals at Brown U., Wellesley Coll., and at other instns.; instr. in organ, Wellesley Coll., 1926-28; instr. in radial harmony, Mass. Univ. Extension Courses, 1935-37; teacher of music, Boston; formerly dir. People's Choral Assn., Providence, and director chapel music, Brown University, and of Milton (Mass.) Chorus. Colleague of American Guild of Organists. Composer of songs, anthems and instrumental pieces, also active as editor, reviser and arranger of music. Lecturer on musical subjects. Author and teacher of the system "Radial Harmony." Formerly mem. editorial staff Oliver Ditson Co.; also associated with various other music publishers. Home and Studio: 144 Ridge Av., Newton Centre, Mass. Died July 18, 1944.

RYDER, Chauncey Foster, artist; b. Danbury, Conn., 1868; pupil, Art Inst. Chicago, and Raphael Colin and Jean Paul Laurens, Paris, France. Hon. mention, Société des Artistes Français, Paris, 1907; silver medal San Francisco Expn., 1915. Mem. N.A., 1920, Am. Water Color Soc., Soc. of Am. Etchers, Chicago Soc. of Etchers. Address: 171 W. 12th St., New York, N.Y. Died May 18, 1949.

RYDER, George Hope, M.D.; b. Plainfield, N.J., Oct. 24, 1872; s. Charles Edwin and Katherine (Culver) R.; A.B., Yale, 1894; M.D., Coll. of Phys. and Surg. (Columbia), 1899; unmarried. Surg. interne St. Vincent's Hosp., New York, 1899-1901; med. interne New York Foundling Hosp., 1901-02; gynecol. interne Roosevelt Hosp., New York, 1902-03; resident obstetrician Sloane Hosp. for Women, Columbia U., 1904-07, clin. prof. obstetrics since 1927, cons. obstetrician since 1920; cons. obstetrician 5th Av. Hosp., New York; attending obstetrician and 1st v.p. Doctors' Hosp., New York. Fellow Am. Coll. Surgeons; mem. A.M.A., Am. Bd. of Obstetrics and Gynecology, Harvey Soc., Quiz Med. Soc., Medico-Surg. Soc., Med. Soc. State of N.Y., N.Y. Acad. Medicine, N.Y. Obstet. Soc. Republican. Episcopalian. Clubs: University, Yale, West Side Tennis, Omega of Columbia (New York); Elihu (Yale); Babylon Yacht (life). Author: (with late Edwin Bradford Cragin) Practice of Obstetrics, 1916. Contbr. to med. jours. Address: 47 E. 63d St., New York, N.Y. Died Aug. 27, 1946.

RYERSON, Joseph Turner, iron and steel; b. Chicago, Nov. 21, 1880; s. Edward Larned and Mary Pringle (Mitchell) R.; Ph.B., Sheffield Scientific Sch. (Yale), 1901; m. Annie Lawrie McBirney, Dec. 29, 1909; children—Joseph T., Mary McBirney (Mrs. Donald A. K. Brown), Annie Lawrie (Mrs. Charles N. Breed Jr.), Ellen Larned. Began in employ Am. Sheet Steel Co. (now Am. Sheet & Tin Plate Co. of U.S. Steel Corp.), at Vandergrift, Pa.; with Joseph T. Ryerson & Son, iron and steel, Chicago, since 1902, v.p. and treas., 1916-23, pres. and treas., 1923-29, now mem. bd. dirs.; dir. Inland Steel Co., Belden Mfg. Co. Trustee Art Institute, Museum of Science and Industry (founded by Julius Rosenwald), Chicago Hist. Soc., St. Luke's Hosp. Republican. Episcopalian; senior warden of St. James Church. Clubs: Chicago, Commercial, Casino, Attic, Racquet, Tavern, Wayfarers, Saddle and Cycle (Chicago); Yale Racquet and Tennis, Squadron A (New York). Home: 1406 Astor St. Office: 135 S. La Salle St., Chicago, Ill. Died Dec. 7, 1947.

RYS, C(arl) F(riedrich) W(ilhelm) (rēs), metall. engr.; b. Essen, Germany, Mar. 23, 1877; s. Francis and Louise (Hausmann) R.; grad. high sch., Essen; studied mech. engring., tech. schs., Hagen, Germany, 2 yrs.; grad. Sch. of Mines, Freiberg, 1902, grad. study England, 6 mos.; Dr. Engineering, U. of Freiberg, 1930; m. Helen M. Witt, June 24, 1908; children—Louise, Frederick. Came to U.S., 1903, naturalized, 1911. Began with Krupp Works, Essen; with LaBelle Iron Works, Steubenville, O., 1903-04; in metall. dept., Homestead Steel Works (Carnegie Steel Co.), 1904-08; in inspection dept., Pittsburgh office, Carnegie Steel Co., 1908-10, asst. metall. engr., 1910-11, metall. engr., in charge metall. dept., since 1911, apptd. asst. to pres., May 7, 1928, also continuing as metall. engr.; apptd. chief metall. engr. of Carnegie-Ill. Steel Corp., Oct. 1, 1935, chief consulting metallurgist, June 1, 1942. Member American Iron and Steel Inst., Engrs. Soc. Western Pa., Am. Soc. for Metals, Soc. Automotive Engrs., Am. Inst. Mining and Metall. Engrs., Am. Ry. Engring. Assn., Am. Soc. for Testing Materials, Brit. Iron and Steel Inst., Army Ordnance Assn. Republican. Protestant. Mason (Shriner). Clubs: Duquesne, Railway, Pittsburgh Athletic Assn. (Pittsburgh). Home: 5463 Aylesboro Av. Office: Carnegie Bldg., Pittsburgh, Pa. Died Oct. 11, 1946.

S

SABATINI, Rafael (sä-bä-tē'nē), author; b. Jesi, Central Italy, Apr. 29, 1875; s. Vincenzo and Anna (Trafford) S.; student Ecole Cantanole de Zoug, Switzerland, Lycee Oporto, Portugal, and U. of Coimbra, Portugal; m. Christine Oxon, Mar. 5, 1935. Served in Mil. Intelligence Dept., British War Office, 1917-18. Author: The Tavern Knight, 1904; Bardelys the Magnificent, 1906; The Shame of Motley, 1908; The Life of Cesare Borgia, 1912; The Sea Hawk, 1915; Scaramouche, 1921; Captain Blood, 1922; The Strolling Saint, 1924; Trampling the Lilies, 1926; The Hounds of God, 1928; Banner of the Bull, 1930; King's Minion, 1930; The Black Swan, 1932; The Romantic Prince, 1932; Stalking Horse, 1933; Heroic Lives, 1934; Venetian Masque, 1934; Chivalry, 1935; The Fortunes of Captain Blood, 1936; The Lost King, 1937; The Sword of Islam, 1939; Master-at-Arms, 1940; Columbus, 1942; The Birth of Mischief, 1945 (Lit. Guild selection). Home: Clock Mill, Clifford, Herefordshire, Eng. Address: care Houghton Mifflin Co., 2 Park St., Boston. Died Feb. 13, 1950.

SABIN, Ellen Clara, educator; b. Sun Prairie, Dane County, Wis., Nov. 29, 1850; d. Samuel Henry and Adelia M. (Bordine) Sabin; student U. of Wis., 1865-68, hon. A.M., 1895; Litt.D., Beloit, 1912; LL.D., Grinnell, 1915; unmarried. Teacher at Madison, Wis., 1869-72, Portland, Ore., 1873-85; in Europe, 1885-86; supt. city schs., Portland, Ore., 1887-90; pres. Downer Coll., Fox Lake, Wis., 1891-95; pres. Milwaukee-Downer Coll., 1895-1921, pres. emerita since June 1921. Juror of ednl. exhibit, Chicago Expn., 1893; mem. Nat. Council Edn., 1886-92; mem. Wis. State Bd. of Edn., 1919-23: Mem. Am. Assn. Univ. Women, Milwaukee Coll. Endowment Assn., League of Women Voters, Phi Beta Kappa. Conglist. Republican. Club: Wisconsin Woman's. Home: 3865 Nakoma Rd., Madison 5, Wis. Died Feb. 1, 1949.

SABIN, Frances Ellis, educator; b. Naperville, Ill., Sept. 6, 1870; d. Albert and Sarah (Ellis) S.; Ph.B., U. Mich., 1895, A.M., 1896; student in Germany 1 summer; student Am. Sch. of Classical Studies, Rome, 1900-01; U. of Chicago 3 yrs.; unmarried. Teacher of Latin, Ft. Wayne, Ind., Oak Park, Ill., and Northern Ill. State Normal Sch., De Kalb, until 1914; asst. prof. Latin, in charge demonstration Latin classes in Univ. High Sch. and courses for training of Latin teachers, U. of Wis., 1914-22, and in summer sessions, U. of Calif., U. of Pa., and Columbia; organizer 1922, and dir. Service Bur. for Classical Teachers (established by Am. Classical League), at Teachers Coll. and New York U.; asso. prof. Latin and edn., New York U., 1930-36, asso. prof. emeritus since 1936. Mem. N.E.A., Am. Classical League, Classical Assn. of Middle West and South, Classical Assn. of Atlantic States, Am. Assn. of Univ. Women, Pen and Brush Club, Phi Beta Kappa, Pi Beta Phi. Author: Relation of Latin to Practical Life, 1913; Classical Associations of Places in Italy, 1921; Classical Myths That Live Today, 1927, revised edit. 1940; Classical Allusions in the New York Times, 1936; also many bulls. and supplements sent out by the Service Bur. for Classical Teachers. Home: 26 E. 10th St., New York. Died Jan. 10, 1943.

SABINE, Wallace Clement, physicist; b. Richwood, O., June 13, 1868; s. Hylas and Anna (Ware) S.; A.B., Ohio State U., 1886; A.M., Harvard, 1888; m. Jane Downs Kelly, Aug. 22, 1900. Asst. physics, 1889-90, instr., 1890-95, asst. prof., 1895-1905, prof. since 1905, and dean of Scientific Sch., Harvard. Fellow Am. Acad. Arts and Sciences, A.A.A.S.; mem. Am. Physical Soc. Author: Laboratory Course in Physical Measurements; Architectural Acoustics, 1900. Home: 348 Marlborough St., Boston. Died Jan. 10, 1919.

SACHS, Bernard (säks), neurologist; b. Baltimore, Md., Jan. 2, 1858; s. Joseph and Sophia (Baer) S.; A.B., Harvard, 1878; M.D., U. of Strassburg, 1882; m. Bettina R. Stein, Dec. 18, 1887; children—Alice (Mrs. J. M. Plaut), Helen (Mrs. Nathan Straus); married 2d, Rosetta Kaskel, 1940. Formerly alienist and neurologist, Bellevue Hospital; neurologist, Mt. Sinai Hospital; consulting physician Manhattan State Hospital, Montefiore Home; director emeritus Division Child Neurology, Neurol. Institute; dir. Child Neurology Research (Friedsam Foundation); prof. clin. neurology, Coll. of Physicians and Surgeons. Pres. of First Internat. Neurol. Congress; ex-pres. N.Y. Acad. Medicine; mem. Assn. Am. Physicians; hon. mem. Royal Soc. of Medicine, Sect. of Neurology (London); corr. mem. Paris and Moscow neurol. socs., etc. Author: Mental and Nervous Diseases of Children, 1895; Nervous Disorders from Birth Through Adolescence (with Dr. L. Hausman), 1926; Keeping Your Child Normal, 1936; also many med. monographs. Address: 2 W. 59th St., New York, N.Y. Died Oct. 26, 1943.

SACHS, Joseph, engr., inventor; b. N.Y. City, Aug. 17, 1870; s. Louis Von and Bertha (Sanger) S.; student Coll. City of N.Y. (non grad.); spl. tutoring and study; m. Caroline Norman, June 5, 1895; children—Kelvin N., Margaret N. (Mrs. J. J. Bissell). Began with Sprague Elec. Motor Co. prior to 1890, later with Edison Machine Works (now Gen. Electric Co.), Schenectady, N.Y.; developed trolleyless elec. ry., nonarcing enclosed fuse, elec. ry. appliances, 1892-94; cons. patent expert, also engaged in constrn. and operation engring., work and pioneer magnetic ore separating plant, 1892-98; developed electric fire alarm signalling system, elec. fire engine system, canal boat haulage, cable and elec. ry. signals, elec. type-setting machinery, electric metal heating and melting, 1893-98, elec. drive and control for motor vehicles, electrically controlled carburetor, elec. primer and other automobile accessories, 1900-15; cons. and chief engr. Johns-Pratt Co. (later elec. div. Colts Patent Fire Arms Mfg. Co.), mfrs. elec. devices, Hartford, Conn.; pres. and mgr. The Sachs Co., and v.p. and mgr. Sachs Laboratories, Inc.; identified with development, mfr. and sale of Sachs inventions, including elec. protective devices, enclosed fuses, cutouts, switches, sockets, circuit breakers, enclosed safety switches, meter service switches, meter testing devices, standardized service installations, etc., 1898-1937; research and invention, also engring. and development consultant for several mfg. cos. since 1939; awarded over 250 U.S. patents. Awarded John Scott Legacy Medal by Franklin Institute for pioneer invention electric fuse protective devices, 1903. Fellow Am. Inst. E.E.; mem. Am. Soc. M.E., Nat. Elec. Mfrs. Assn. Republican. Episcopalian. Mason (32°). Clubs: Engineers, Hartford, Get-Together, Hartford Golf, Wampanoag Country, Automobile, Church Club (of Conn.). Author: (with T. C. Martin) Electrical Boats and Navigation, 1894. Contbr. articles to technical publs.; lecturer before technical socs. Home: 1900 Albany Av., West Hartford 5. Office: 1900 Albany Av., West Hartford 5, Conn. Died Nov. 15, 1946.

SACKETT, Robert Lemuel, cons. engr.; b. Mt. Clemens, Mich., Dec. 2, 1867; s. Lemuel Miller and Emily Lucinda (Cole) S.; B.S. in C.E., U. of Mich., 1891, C.E., 1896, Dr.Engring., 1937; m. Mary Lyon Coggeshall, July 22, 1896; children—Ralph L., Mrs. Frances L. Kramer (dec.). Prof. applied mathematics, Earlham Coll., 1891-1907; prof. sanitary and hydraulic engring., Purdue U., 1907-15; dean Sch. of Engring., Pa. State Coll., Sept. 1, 1915-June 30, 1937; dean emeritus; also dir. Engring. Expt. Sta., and of engring. extension, Fellow A.A.A.S. (v.p. 1928 and 1940), Am. Soc.. mech. engrs.; mem. Am. Soc. Civil Engrs., Soc. for Promotion Engineering, Education, (president 1927-28), Engineer's Council for Professional Development, 1944-45; member Sigma Xi, Tau Beta Pi, Phi Kappa Phi, Phi Gamma Delta. Republican. Mem. Friends Ch. Consulting engr. to Ind. State Bd. of Health, 1910-15, and to other state comns. Author: The Engineer, His Work and His Education; also numerous technical articles. Home: 303 Lexington Av. Office: Secretary Am. Soc. Mech. Engrs., 29 W. 39th St., New York, N.Y. Died Oct. 6, 1946.

SADLER, E(verit) J(ay), oil producer; b. Brockport, N.Y., May 1, 1879; s. Holmes E. and Mary (C.) S.; grad U.S. Naval Acad., Annapolis, Md., 1899; m. Lorena Bilisoly, Aug. 2, 1902; children—Elizabeth, Isabel. Midshipman and ensign U.S. Navy, 1899, and served in Navy until 1902; roustabout and operator Kan. oil fields, 1902-06; draftsman, civ. engr., Prairie Oil & Gas Co., 1906-09; mng. dir. Romano-Americano, Bucharest, Rumania, 1909-16; served as lt. comdr. U.S.N.R.F., 1917; pres. Transcontinental Oil Co., Mexico, 1918-19; dir. Standard Oil Co. (N.J.), 1920-42, vice-pres., 1930-42. Clubs: University, Army and Navy. Home: Scarsdale, N.Y. Office: 30 Rockefeller Plaza, New York, N.Y. Died Oct. 28, 1947.

SADLER, Herbert Charles, naval architect; b. London, Eng., Aug. 27, 1872; s. Frederick Charles and Christina de Wilde (Cater) S.; Dulwich Coll., England, 1890; B.Sc., Glasgow U., 1893, D.Sc., 1902, LL.D., 1927; m. Margaret, d. Professor R. M. Wenley, Apr. 25, 1919; children—Robert Charles Wenley, Christine Wenly, Margaret de Wilde (Mrs. George Henry Gardner, Jr.), Winifred Alice. Engaged in practical shipbuilding on Clyde, 1890-96; asst. prof. naval architecture, Glasgow University 1896-1900; junior professor naval architecture and marine engring., 1900-04, prof., 1904-28, dean Coll. of Engring., U. of Mich., 1928-37, Alexander Ziwet prof. engring., 1937-39; dean emeritus, 1939-40; retired. Appraiser vessel properties, Mich. State Ry. Appraisal, 1901; naval architect to Miss. bd. U.S. Army engrs., 1912-13; naval architect and consulting engr. U.S. Shipping Bd., 1918-19. Mem. Inst. Naval Architects, London, Inst. Engrs. and Shipbuilders, Scotland, Am. Soc. Naval Architects and Marine Engrs. (v.p.), Sigma Xi (pres., Mich. Chapter, 1908-10), Soc. Automotive Engrs., Soc. Promotion Engring. Edn. Clubs: Engineers (New York); University, Barton Hills (Ann Arbor). Author numerous papers on science and art of shipbuilding. Mem. U.S. Load Line Com., 1917; mem. tech. com. Am. Bur. Shipping; mem. Marine Standards Com. Home: 1510 Hill St., Ann Arbor, Mich. Died Dec. 15, 1948.

SAFFOLD, William Berney (săf'föld), univ. prof.; b. Selma, Ala., July 11, 1867; s. Benjamin Franklin and Mary Ellen (Brown) S.; A.B., U. of Ala., 1887, LL.B., 1888, A.M., 1889; Ph.D., Johns Hopkins U., 1898; LL.D., U. of Alabama, 1927; m. Margaret Parsons, Nov. 6, 1902. Tutor, U. of Ala., 1887-88; prof. Latin and Greek, Marion Mil. Inst., 1888-91, Searcy Coll., Ark., 1891-92, Little Rock (Ark.) Acad., 1892-94; became prof. Greek and Latin, U. of Ala., 1897, acting pres., Sept.-Dec. 1911, now prof. Latin and history, same univ. Mem. Phi Beta Kappa. Author: The Construction with "Iubeo," 1902. Address: Tuscaloosa, Ala. Died Dec. 21, 1941.

SAFFORD, Harry Robinson, ry. official; b. Madison, Ind., Feb. 7, 1875; s. James Broderick and Josephine (Branham) S.; B.C.E., Purdue U., 1895, C.E., 1918, Dr. Engring., 1920; m. Nell Gertrude Whittemore, Dec. 12, 1900; 1 son, Harry Robinson. Began with engring. dept., I.C. R.R., 1895, advancing to chief engr. maintenance of way, 1909; chief engr. Grand Trunk Ry., 1911-18; asst. regional dir. U.S. R.R. Adminstrn., 1918-20; asst. to pres. C.,B.&Q. Ry., 1920-21, v.p., Dec. 1921-Feb. 1925; asst. to pres., Colo. & Southern, Ft. Worth & Denver City and Wichita Valley rys., Dec. 1921-Feb. 1925; v.p. Missouri Pacific; exec. v.p. Gulf Coast Lines, Internat.-Great Northern rys. since Feb. 1925. Mem. Am. Soc. C.E., Am. Railway Engineering Assn. (ex-president); Engineering Institute of Can. (ex-counsellor); Houston Chamber Commerce (ex-pres., dir.), Sigma Alpha Epsilon. Presbyn. Mason (32°, Shriner). Clubs: Houston, Houston Country (Houston); Boston (New Orleans). Home: Lamar Hotel. Office: Union Station, Houston, Tex. Died Apr. 10, 1943.

SAGE, Dean, lawyer; b. Brooklyn, N.Y., Dec. 13, 1875; s. Dean and Sarah A. (Manning) S.; grad. Albany (N.Y.) Acad., 1893; A.B., Yale, 1897, hon. A.M., 1928; LL.B., Harvard, 1900; LL.D., Columbia, 1928; m. Anna Parker, June 9, 1900; children—Cornelia (Mrs. Staunton Williams), Sarah (Mrs. Sage Stewart), Dean. Admitted to N.Y. bar, 1900, and began practice in New York; mem. Sage, Gray, Todd & Sims since 1905; dep. asst. dist. atty. New York County, 1902; trustee N.Y. Trust Co.; dir. Commonwealth Ins. Co., Sage Land & Improvement Co. Served in New York office of Army Transport Service and later New York office of real estate div. of Gen. Staff during World War. Dir. Commonwealth Fund, Josiah N. Macy, Jr. Foundation; mgr. and pres. Presbyn. Hosp., New York; trustee and chmn. bd. Atlanta Univ., Atlanta, Ga.; mem. exec. com. Prison Assn. of N.Y. Mem. Bar Assn. City of New York, New York County Lawyers Assn., N.Y. State Bar Assn., Am. Bar Assn. Republican. Episcopalian. Clubs: Yale, Racquet and Tennis, Links (New York). Home: Bernardsville, N.J. Office: 49 Wall St., New York, N.Y. Died July 1, 1943.

SAGER, Edward Anton (sā'gēr), judge; b. Bremer County, Ia., Oct. 17, 1872; s. John and Theresa (Sipple) S.; LL.B., State U. of Ia., 1894; m. Nellie R.

Mooney, Nov. 9, 1899; 1 dau., Margaret Mary. Admitted to Ia. bar, 1894; mem. firm Sager & Sweet, Waverly, Ia., and Sager, Sweet & Sager, Waterloo, Ia.; asso. justice Ia. Supreme Court since 1936. Mem. Am. and Ia. bar assns. Catholic. K.C., Catholic Order Foresters. Home: 314 First St. S.E., Waverly, Ia. Address: State House, Des Moines, Ia.
Died Feb. 7, 1943.

SAIT, Edward McChesney (sāt), polit. science; b. Montreal, Can., Aug. 24, 1881; s. Edward and Caroline (Macdonald) S.; Upper Canada Coll., 1895-99; B.A., Toronto U., 1902, M.A., 1903; Ph.D., Columbia, 1911; m. Una Mirrielees Bernard, June 2, 1910; children—Edward McChesney, Henry Bernard. Lecturer in history, Toronto U., 1903-06; fellow Columbia, 1906-08; lecturer in pub. law and asst. prof., same univ., 1909-20; prof. polit. science, U. of Calif., 1920-26; lecturer Scripps Coll., Claremont, Calif., 1927-28; professor govt., Pomona College, since 1928. Mem. N.J. State Militia Res., World War. Mem. Am. Polit. Sci. Assn., Am. Soc. Internat. Law, Am. Hist. Assn., Skull and Keys, Phi Beta Kappa. Mem. Social Science Research Conf. of Pacific Coast. Episcopalian. Author: Clerical Control in Quebec, 1911; Government and Politics of France, 1920; British Politics in Transition (with D. P. Barrows), 1925; American Parties and Elections, 1927, rev. edits., 1939, 42; Democracy (lectures), 1929; Political Institutions, A Preface, 1938. Editor: Houghton Mifflin Government Series. Home: 238 E. 7th St., Claremont, Calif. Died Oct. 25, 1943.

SALT, Albert Lincoln; b. Brooklyn, N.Y., Oct. 4, 1865; s. Luke Ryder and Elizabeth Leonard (Booz) S.; ed. pub. schs., Brooklyn; m. Mary Thompson Bergen, Apr. 15, 1891; 1 son, Lloyd Bergen. Began as office boy with Western Electric Co., 1881, advancing through various positions to v.p.; elected pres. Graybar Electric Co., successor to supply dept. of Western Electric Co., 1925; dir. Commercial Trust Co. of N.J., Eastern Offices, Inc.; mem. advisory com. Chase Nat. Bank. Mem. Telephone Pioneers of America (past pres.). Protestant. Office: Graybar Bldg., New York, N.Y. Died Sep. 29, 1945.

SALTEN, Felix, German author; b. Budapest, Hungary, Nov. 6, 1869; s. Philipp and Marie (Singer) S.; brought to Vienna when an infant; ed. Gymnasium, Vienna; m. Ottilie Metzl, Apr. 13, 1902. Novelist, essayist, playwright; formerly theatrical critic Neue Freie Presse, Vienna; now living in Switzerland. Books have been translated into many langs., including Chinese. Made hon. citizen of Vienna; hon. pres. Austrian P.E.N. Club. Author: (all translated from German) The Hound of Florence, 1930; Fifteen Rabbits, 1930; Sampson and Delilah, 1931; City Jungle, 1932; Bambi, 1932; Florian, The Emperor's Stallion, 1934; Perri, 1938; Bambi's Children, 1939; Renni, the Rescuer, 1940; Good Comrades, 1942. Home: Wilfriedstrasse 4, Zurich, Switzerland. Died Oct. 8, 1945.

SALTER, Sumner, composer, director; b. Burlington, Ia., June 24, 1856; s. Rev. William and Mary Ann (Mackintire) S.; A.B., Amherst, 1877; studied music in Boston with Eugene Thayer, J. K. Paine, J. C. D. Parker and George L. Osgood; m. Mary E. Turner, May 26, 1881; children—Edward Winthrop, Harold (deceased), Edith Marie, William Frost. Began as teacher, Petersilea Academy of Music, Boston, 1878; director Arion Club (male voices); organist 1st Unitarian Church, Lynn, Eliot Congl. Ch., Roxbury, Euclid Av. Bapt. Ch., Cleveland, O., 1879-81; St. Paul's P.E. Ch., Syracuse, N.Y., and condr. Cecilia Soc., 1881-86; organist 1st Meth. Ch., Atlanta, Ga., and condr. Atlanta Music Assn., 1886-89; organist 1st Presbyn. Church, New York, 1889-92, West End Collegiate Ch., 1892-1900, Sage Chapel, Cornell U., 1900-02, Broadway Tabernacle, New York, 1902-05; dir. of music Williams Coll., 1905-23; condr. Mendelssohn Choir, Williamstown. Organist Pan-American, St. Louis and San Francisco expns. Mem. Co. E, 20th Regt., Mass. State Guard. A founder Am. Guild Organists (warden, 1899-1900); past mem. M.T.N.A., Internat. Music Soc., N.Y. State Music Teachers' Assn., (pres. 1897-98), St. Wilfred Club (N.Y.); mem. Alpha Delta Phi, Pi Gamma Mu. Republican. Conglist. Author: Early Organs in America, 1890; Ornaments in Bach's Organ Works, 1930; Appoggiaturas in the Solos of Handel's Messiah, 1931; Early Encouragements to American Composers, 1932; The M.T.N.A. in its Early Relation to the American Composer, 1932; What Makes a Good Touch, 1934; etc. Composer of songs, part songs and anthems for men's, women's and mixed voices, ch. and organ music, arrangements, transcriptions, etc.; conducted performance of Handel's "Messiah" Apr. 1887, Atlanta, Ga. Editor The Pianist and Organist, New York, 1895-98. Contbr. to many musical periodicals. Home: 72 Barrow St., New York, N.Y. Died Mar. 5, 1944.

SALTZMAN, Charles McKinley, army officer; b. Panora, Ia., Oct. 18, 1871; s. F. J. and Lovina Elizabeth (Lahman) S.; grad. U.S. Mil. Acad., 1896; honor grad. Signal Sch., 1906; grad. Army War Coll., 1921; m. Mary Peyton Eskridge, May 9, 1899; 1 son, Charles Eskridge. Apptd. add. 2d lt. 5th Cav., June 12, 1896; promoted through grades to col., May 15, 1917; brig. gen. N.A., July 24, 1917. A.d.c. to Brig. Gen. H. C. Merriam, 1900-01; engagements at Guasimas and San Juan, Santiago Campaign, 1898, also in Philippine Insurrection and Moro campaigns; signal officer, Eastern Dept., 1913-15; signal officer, U.S. troops, Panama, C.Z., 1915-16; apptd. exec. officer, Office of Chief Signal Officer, Sept. 1, 1916; chief signal officer, rank of maj. gen., Jan. 9, 1924; retired Jan. 8, 1928; apptd. mem. Federal Radio Commn., 1929, chmn., 1930-32 (resigned); appointed vice-pres. U.S. Shipping Board Merchant Fleet Corp., 1933. Delegate from U.S. to Internat. Radio Conf., London, 1912, to Internat. Telegraph Conference, Paris, 1925, Internat. Radio Telegraph Conf., Washington, D.C., 1927; chmn. U.S. delegation to Internat. Radio Tech. Consulting Com., The Hague, 1929. Given two citations "for gallantry in action," Spanish-Am. War; awarded D.S.M., "for exceptionally meritorious and conspicuous services," World War; Silver Star medal with Oak Leaf Cluster, 1934. Address: Burnt Mills Hills, Silver Spring, Md.
Died Nov. 25, 1942.

SALVAGE, Sir Samuel Agar (săl'vāj), industrialist; b. London, Eng., Nov. 20, 1876; s. John Samuel and Margaret (Smith) S.; student Queens Coll., Taunton, Somersetshire, Eng.; m. Mary Katharine Richmond, June 8, 1908; children—Katharine Hoppin (Mrs. Frank L. Polk, Jr.), Margaret Smith (Mrs. James Potter Polk), Magdelaine Richmond (Mrs. Silas Reed Anthony). Came to U.S., 1893. Worked in Cincinnati, 1893-96; with imported cotton yarn firm, N.Y. City, 1896; obtained agency for British firms and started business in own name; obtained agency for Samuel Courtauld & Co. (now Courtaulds, Ltd.), London, mfrs. rayon yarn, 1907; they formed Am. Viscose Co., 1910; reorganized as The Viscose Co., 1915; v.p. same, 1916-23, pres. 1923-32, chmn. bd., 1932-39; now consultant and dir. Am. Viscose Corp.; dir. Park and 46th St. Corp., Eastern Offices, Inc., Continental Realty Investing Co. Served as branch chmn., Am. Red Cross, World War; hon. chmn. Brit. War Relief Soc. Chmn. com. which selected name "rayon" for artificial silk, 1924. Mem. Am. Assn. Textile Technologists. Episcopalian. Clubs: Union, New York, River (New York City); Piping Rock (Locust Valley, N.Y.). Home: Glen Head, L.I., N.Y. Office: 350 5th Av., New York, N.Y. Died July 10, 1946.

SAMAROFF, Olga (Mrs. Leopold Stokowski) (să-mä'rŏf), pianist; b. San Antonio, Tex., Aug. 8, 1882; d. Carlos and Jane Hickenlooper; studied Paris Conservatory, 1894-97, with Ernst Jedlitzke, Berlin, 1901-03; hon. Dr. of Music, U. of Pa., 1931; m. Leopold Stokowski, conductor, Apr. 24, 1911; 1 dau., Sonya Maria Noël. Début with New York Symphony Orchestra, Jan. 18, 1905; has frequently toured U.S. and Europe and has played with practically all large orchestras; now mem. piano faculty, Juilliard Grad. Sch. of Music, N.Y. Head piano faculty Phila. Conservatory; founder of Schubert Memorial, Inc. (1928); founder and dir. The Listeners Music Courses, Inc., of New York and Phila. Author: The Layman's Music Book, 1935; The Magic World of Music, A Music Manual, 1937; An American Musician's Story, 1939. Lecturer on musical subjects. Home: 24 W. 55th St., New York. Died May 17, 1948.

SAMFORD, Thomas Drake, lawyer; b. Auburn, Ala., Nov. 2, 1868; s. Hon. William James (Gov. Ala., died in office, 1901) and Caroline Elizabeth (Drake) S.; B.Sc., Ala. Poly. Inst., Auburn, 1888, LL.D., 1938; m. Louise Andrew Westcott, July 5, 1899; children—William James, Thomas Drake, Millard Westcott. Admitted to Ala. bar, 1891, and practiced in Opelika; pres. Bank of Opelika, 1911-12. Mem. Dem. State Exec. Com., Ala., 1896-98; pvt. sec. to Gov. William J. Samford, 1900-1901; U.S. atty. Middle District of Ala., 1913-24, and from May 1934 to Dec. 1, 1942; retired after 20 years in service. Capt. Co. H. Ala. Nat. Guard, 1890-95. Trustee Ala. Poly. Inst. since 1910. Del. Gen. Conf. M.E. Ch., S., 5 times to 1930; del. Ecumenical Conf., Toronto, 1911; mem. commn. to Unify Meth. Chs. in America, 1912-18. Pres. U.S. Attys. Assn., 1940-41. Mason, K.P. (Grand Chancellor, Ala., 1909-10). Home: Opelika, Ala. Died Feb. 26, 1947.

SAMMONS, William Henry, publisher; b. Hokah, Minn., Feb. 16, 1861; s. Marcus C. and Susan (Spence) S.; ed. Bailey's Coll., Keokuk, Ia.; m. Clara L. Perkins, Oct. 2, 1895; children—Louise J. (Mrs. H. G. Freese), Elizabeth. Began as bookkeeper with lumber co., St. James, Minn., 1880; with Perkins Bros. Co., pubs. Sioux City (Ia.) Journal, since 1882, pres. since 1914; pres. Journal-Tribune Publishing Co. since 1941; dir. Terminal Grain Elevator Co., Northwestern Dock & Transfer Co., Sioux City and New Orleans Barge Lines, Inc. Home: 1507 Jackson Blvd. Office: The Journal, Sioux City, Ia. Died Jan. 7, 1944.

SAMPEY, John Richard, theologian; b. Fort Deposit, Ala., Sept. 27, 1863; s. Rev. James L. and Louisa Z. (Cochran) S.; A.B., Howard College, Ala., 1882; grad. Southern Bapt. Theol. Sem., 1885; D.D., Washington and Lee, 1887; LL.D., Howard, 1901, Baylor, 1920; m. Annie, d. Rev. J. J. D. Renfroe, Sept. 16, 1886; children— Anita (dec.), Eleanora Scott, John R., Elsie Louise; m. 2d, Ellen, d. Felix M. Wood, May 16, 1926. Ordained Bapt. ministry, Sept. 27, 1885; instr., 1885-87, asst. prof., 1887-90, asso. prof., 1890-92, librarian, 1889-1929, Prof. Old Testament interpretation, 1892-1943, president, 1929-42, pres. emeritus since 1942, Southern Baptist Theological Seminary. Member International S.S. Lesson Committee, 1895-1942 (chairman 1921-22; chairman sub-committee on improved uniform lessons, 1915-42). Tour through Egypt and Palestine, 1897; in Europe, 1907; missionary journey through Brazil, summers of 1925, 1926 and 1928, through China, 1936; contbr. to revs. of Old Testament Scriptures, 1898; mem. revision com. of Am. Standard Bible, and chmn. Old Testament section, 1930-38; pres. Southern Baptist Convention, 1935-38. Author: The First Thirty Years of the Southern Bapt. Theol. Sem., 1890; Syllabus for Old Testament Study, 1925; The Heart of the Old Testament, 1922; The Ethical Teaching of Jesus, 1909; The International Lesson System, 1911; Ten Vital Messages, 1946; Memoirs of John R. Sampey, 1946; etc. Home: 1313 Willow St. Address: 2825 Lexington Rd., Louisville. Died Aug. 18, 1946; buried Cave Hill Cemetery, Louisville, Ky

SAMPLE, William Dodge, naval officer; b. Buffalo, N.Y., Mar. 9, 1898; s. Brig. Gen. (ret. U.S.A.) William Roderick and Elizabeth (McCullough) S.; grammer sch., Spokane and Seattle, Wash., Chicago, Ill., St. Louis, Mo., Alaska and Philippine Islands, 1904-11; Lowel High Sch., San Franciseo, 1912-14; New Mexico Mil. Inst., Roswell, N.M., 1914-15; B.S., U.S. Naval Acad., 1918; m. Mary Lee Lamar, Apr. 18, 1928; 1 dau., Carolyn. Midshipman, U.S. Navy, 1915; commd. ensign, 1918, and advanced through the grades to rear admiral, 1943; naval aviator, 1923; exec. officer, Naval Air Station, Pensacola, 1941-42; comdg. officer, 10th fleet, 1943-44; comdg. officer, U.S.S. Intrepid, 1944; comdg. officer, U.S.S. Hornet, 1944; comdr. carrier div. 27, 1944-45; comdr. carrier div. 22, 1945. Awarded Legion of Merit with two Gold Stars; Commendation Ribbon, Purple Heart. Club: Army and Navy Country (Washington). Address: 204 W. Gonzalez St., Pensacola, Fla.
Died Oct. 3, 1946.

SAMPSON, Emma Speed, author; b. Louisville, Ky., Dec. 1, 1868; d. George Keats and Jane Butler (Ewing) Speed; grad. Hampton Coll., Louisville, Ky.; student Art Students League, N.Y. and Julian Acad. and Lasar's, Paris, 1888-92; m. Henry Aylett Sampson, 1896 (died Mar. 11, 1920); children—Emma Keats (Mrs. James Thornton Franck), Judith Aylett (Mrs. Robert Wood Vincent, Jr.). Member Va. State Board of Motion Picture Censors, 1922-33; was feature writer on the Richmond Times Dispatch. Unitarian. Clubs: Va. Writers, Woman's, Altrusa, Woman's Party of Richmond, Va. (v.p.). Author: Billy and the Major, 1917; Mammy's White Folks, 1919; Miss Minerva's Baby, 1920; also (under name of Nell Speed), Tucker Twins, series, yearly since 1914; Carter Girls, series, since 1916; The Shorn Lamb, 1922; Miss Minerva on the Old Plantation, 1923; The Comings of Cousin Ann, 1923; Masquerading Mary, 1924; Miss Minerva Broadcasts Billy, 1925; Miss Minerva's Scallywags, 1927; Miss Minerva's Neighbors, 1929; The Spite Fence, 1929; Miss Minerva Goin' Places, 1931; Miss Minerva's Cook Book, 1931; Miss Minerva's Mystery, 1933; Miss Minerva's Problem; Miss Minerva's Vacation, 1939. Broadcasting over Radio Sta. WRVA, Richmond. Home: 2228 Hanover Av., Richmond, Va.
Died May 7, 1947.

SAMPSON, Henry Ellis, lawyer; b. Audubon County, Ia., Mar. 6, 1879; s. Cyrus Henry and Martha (Ellis) S.; A.B., Cornell Coll., Mt. Vernon, Ia., 1903; student State U. of Ia., 1902-03; B.Ph., U. of Chicago, 1904, J.D., 1905; m. Mary Luella Stubbs, Oct. 18, 1905. Admitted to Ia. bar, 1905; U.S. Supreme Court bar, 1916; practiced in Des Moines as senior mem. firm Sampson & Dillon, specializing in corp., ins., constitutional law, malpractice and taxation litigation, since 1905; asst. atty. gen. of Ia., 1910-17; spl. counsel Ia. Ins. Dept., 1911-16, Ia. State Highway Com. and Ia. Industrial Commr., 1914-16, Ia. State Corp. Dept., 1912-17; spl. counsel Pub. Examiners Div. and in charge of cases for removal from office of pub. officials; counsel for State defending patent suits based on Luten's patents; prof. of malpractice and med. jurisprudence in Still Osteopathic Coll.; gen. counsel Ia. Mfrs. Assn. since 1917. Mem. Des Moines Plan of City Govt. Com., 1907; member State Advisory Council of Ia. Unemployment Compensation Commn. Trustee and mem. exec. com. Simpson Coll. Mem. Ia. State Bar Assn., Polk County Bar Association, Delta Chi; only lay member Atlas Club, national fraternity of osteopathic physicians. Republican. Methodist (member of board First Church, Des Moines, superintendent Adult Sunday School). Mason (K.T., 32°, Shriner). Clubs: University, Cornell (v.p.), University of Chicago (Des Moines). Author of monographs: One Year Under the Des Moines Plan; Workman's Compensation Laws; Temperance Laws of Iowa; Highway Laws of Iowa; Obligations of the Osteopathic Profession; Social Security Legislation—Who Pays for It; Major Tax Commission (2 vols.), 1929; also articles on malpractice and med. jurisprudence. Home: 671 33d St. Office: 1132 Des Moines Bldg., Des Moines, Ia.
Died Jan. 5, 1944.

SAMPSON, John Albertson, gynecologist; b. 1873; A.B., Williams Coll., 1895, A.M., 1899; M.D., Johns Hopkins, 1899; D.Sc., Union College, 1940, Rensselaer Poly. Inst., 1942. Practiced at Albany, N.Y., since 1905; also prof. emeritus gynecology, Albany Med. Coll.; sr. gynecologist to Albany Hosp. Fellow Am. Coll. Surg., Am. Gynecol. Soc.; mem. A.M.A., Med. Soc. State of N.Y. Address: 180 Washington Av., Albany, N.Y. Died Dec. 23, 1946.

SAMUEL, Bunford, librarian; b. Phila., Pa., Sept. 16, 1857; s. John and Rebecca (Levy) S.; ed. classical sch. Dr. John W. Fairies; m. Ella Salomon, Mar. 2, 1882; children—Alma R. (dec.), Emma L. Dorothea (Mrs. C. Livingstone Pelton); m. 2d, Edith Lamberton, Feb. 24, 1925. Asst. librarian Library Co. of Phila., in charge of the Ridgway Branch, 1878-1932. Projected, about 1880, general index of printed portraits, and compiled in pursuance thereof an index of portraits, now covering about 150,000 subjects, and of engravers thereof, extensively used, though as yet largely in M.S. Contbr. to The Bookman, Pa. Mag. of History, Scribner's, the Supplement to 9th edit. Ency. Britannica, etc. Club: Author's (London). Author: Secession and Constitutional Liberty. Home: 2129 DeLancey St., Phila., Pa. Died May 19, 1949.

SAMUELS, Maurice Victor, playwright; b. San Francisco, Calif., Oct. 3, 1873; s. David and Matilda (Freund) S.; A.B., U. of Calif., 1894; m. Mrs. Kathryn de Montford, née Kathryn Wood, 1914. Practiced law in San Francisco, 1895-1902; since in literary work largely in New York. Mem. Dramatists' Guild of Authors' League, Authors' League of America, Sigma Nu. Clubs: Lambs, The Masquers. Author: The Florentines; The Conflict; The Wanderer; Zadig and Flame of Love (collaboration); Drift; The Maid of Orleans; A Pageant of the Strong and Other Plays. Home: 1261 N. Flores St., Hollywood, Calif. Died Apr. 1, 1945.

SANBORN, Elwin Roswell, photographer wild-life; b. Dunkirk, Chautauqua County, N.Y.; s. Charles Henry and Ellen (Seymour) S.; ed. pub. sch., Bradford, and Art Student's League, N.Y. City; m. Katherine Anne Seyfang (died Jan. 1, 1946). Became illustrator magazines, 1896; became official photographer New York Zoöl. Park, 1899; now retired; N.Y. aquarium, 1902, and editor the Bulletin (bi-monthly) and scientific publs., N.Y. Zoöl. Soc., since 1903. Engaged in scientific study of the photography of marine and land wild-life, gen. zoölogy and biology. Life mem. N.Y. Zoöl. Soc.; mem Photographers' Assn. America. Home: Norwalk, Fairfield County, Conn.; also care Bank of the Manhattan Co., Tremont Branch, New York. Died Dec. 19, 1947.

SANDERS, Jared Young, Jr., ex-congressman; b. Franklin, La., Apr. 20, 1892; s. Jared Young and Ada (Shaw) S.; A.B., La. State U., 1912; LL.B., Tulane U., New Orleans, 1914; grad. study Washington and Lee U., Lexington, Va., 1912-13; m. Mary Briggs, Oct. 5, 1921; 1 dau., Mary Elizabeth. Admitted to La. Bar, 1914; practiced in Baton Rouge; formerly sr. partner Sanders & Miller; now sr. mem. Sanders, Miller & Herget. Elected to 73d Congress from 6th La. Dist., May 1, 1934, to fill vacancy caused by death of B. E. Kemp, and reëlected to 74th Congress (1935-37); elected to 77th Congress, Nov. 5, 1940, from 6th Congressional Dist. of La. Served in A.E.F., U.S. Army, 1917-19. Democrat. Mason. Home: Baton Rouge, La. Died Mar. 23, 1944.

SANDERS, Thomas Jefferson, educator; b. near Burbank, O., Jan. 18, 1855; s. Isaac and Mary (Stratton) S.; A..B, Otterbein U., 1878, A.M., 1881, LL.D., 1912; Ph.D., U. of Wooster, 1888; m. E. Gertrude Slater, June 2, 1878; 1 son, Ernest Avery. Supt. pub. schs., Ohio and Ind., 1878-91; pres., 1891-1901, Hulitt prof. philosophy, 1901-31, Otterbein College. Charter mem. Central Ohio Sch. Masters' Club. Author: Philosophy of the Christian Religion, 1888; Transcendentalism, 1889; God—The Ultimate a Priori Condition, 1890; The Unconscious in Education, 1892; The Place and Purpose of the College, 1895; The Nature and the End of Education, 1896; Relations of Soul and Body, 1905; The Place and Purpose of Art in the Realm of Thought and Knowledge, 1909. The Place of Music in a Liberal Education, 1930; The Value of Philosophy for the College Student, 1931; Some Fundamentals in Philosophy—The Infinitude of Space and Time and The Absoluteness of Causality, 1935. Contbr. articles disproving evolution, 1925-26. Home: Westerville, O. Died Dec. 26, 1946.

SANDERSON, (Ezra) Dwight, sociologist, entomologist; b. Clio, Mich., Sept. 25, 1878; s. John P. and Alice G. (Wright) S.; B.S., Mich. Agrl. Coll., 1897; B.S. Agr., Coll. of Agr. Cornell U., 1898; Ph.D., U. of Chicago, 1921; m. Anna Cecilia Blandford, Sept. 19, 1899; 1 dau., Alice Cecilia. Asst. state entomologist of Md., 1898-99; asst. Div. Entomology, U.S. Dept. Agr., summer 1899; entomologist Del. Agrl. Expt. Sta. and asso. prof. zoölogy, Del. Coll., 1899-1902; State entomologist of Tex. and prof. entomology, Tex. Agrl. and Mech. Coll., 1902-04; prof. zoölogy, N.H. Coll., and entomologist, N.H. Agrl. Expt. Sta., 1904-07; dir. N.H. Agrl. Expt. Sta., 1907-10; dean, Coll. of Agr., W.Va. U., 1910-15; and dir. W.Va. Agrl. Expt. Sta., 1912-15; fellow in sociology, U. of Chicago, 1916-17; prof. rural sociology, Cornell University, 1918-43, professor emeritus since 1943. Fellow A.A.A.S.; member American Sociological Society, Sigma Xi, Phi Kappa Phi; past pres. Association Economic Entomologists, Rural Sociol. Society, Am. Country Life Assn. Author: Insects Injurious to Staple Crops, 1902; Insect Pests of Farm, Garden and Orchard, 1911; Elementary Entomology (with C. F. Jackson), 1911; School Entomology (with L. M. Peairs), 1916; The Farmer and His Community, 1922; The Rural Community, 1932. Rural Community Organization (with R. A. Polson), 1939; Leadership for Rural Life, 1940; Rural Sociology and Rural Social Organization, 1942; reports and bulls. of Del., Tex., N.H., W.Va. and Cornell agrl. expt. stas., and U.S. Bur. of Entomology. Editor Proc. 1st Nat. Country Life Conference; Farm Income and Farm Life, 1927. Home: Ithaca, N.Y. Died Sep. 27, 1944.

SANDS, Herbert Stead, elec. engr.; b. Stamford, Conn., July 27, 1874; s. James Stopford and Elizabeth Victoria (French) S.; prep. edn., St. Austin Sch., Staten Island, N.Y.; completed course of the Edison General Electric Co., 1893; E.E. from U. of Colorado, 1926; m. Elizabeth Westcott Clarke, Sept. 10, 1919. Supt. Baltic (Conn.) Power Co., 1893-98, Colorado Springs and Cripple Creek Dist. Ry., 1898-99, La Bella Mill, Water & Power Co., Goldfield, Colo., 1899-1901, Seaton Mountain Electric Light & Power Co., Idaho Springs, Colo., 1901-05; mgr. indsl. div. Westinghouse Electric & Mfg. Co., Denver, Colo., 1905-27; private practice since April 1, 1927. Mem. bd. of dirs. Home Loan Bank, Topeka, Kan. Pres. Colo. Engring. Council, 1925-27; mem. Am. Inst. E.E. (v.p. from dist. 6, 1923-27), Colo. Scientific Soc. (pres. 1923-25); mem. State Bd. Engr. Examiners of Colo. since 1919, pres. since 1922; dir. Denver C. of C., 1928-30, pres., 1929-31; mem. Denver Bd. Water Commissioners since 1933, pres. 1943. Mem. Tau Beta Pi (University of Colo.), Eta Kappa Nu (asso.). Episcopalian (mem. Vestry St. John's Cathedral). Mason (33°; grand comdr. K.T. 1931). Clubs: Cactus, Rotary, Denver Athletic. Home: 2515 Ash St. Office: First National Bank Bldg., Denver, Colo. Died Dec. 13, 1944.

SANDS, William Franklin, author; b. Washington D.C., July 29, 1874; s. James Hoban and Mary Elizabeth (Meade) S.; ed. Feldkirch, Austria, r.o. B.A., LL.B., Georgetown Univ., 1896; m. Edith Gertrude Keating, Aug. 17, 1909; children—James, William Franklin, Robert John, John Keating. Apptd. 2d sec. Am. Legation at Tokyo, Japan, 1896; 1st sec. at Seoul, Korea, 1898, chargé d'affaires ad interim, 1899; adviser to Emperor of Korea, 1900-04; sec. legation and chargé d'affaires ad interim, Panama, 1905-07, Guatemala, 1907-08; sec. embassy, Mexico, and chargé d'affaires ad interim, 1908-09; E.E. and M.P. to Guatamala, 1909-10; resigned. With Speyer & Co., New York, 1911, Central Aguirre Sugar Co., Boston, 1912-14, George H. McFadden & Bros., Phila. and London, 1914-15; mem. Commn. on Relief of Prisoners of War in Russia, under State Dept., 1916-17; with Am. Internat. Corp., New York, 1917-22; formerly held chairs of diplomacy and Am. history in Sch. of Fgn. Service, Washington. Author: Undiplomatic Memories, 1930; Our Jungle Diplomacy, 1944. Mem. Mex. Geog. Soc. Decorated Chevalier Legion of Honor, France; Companion Loyal Legion. Catholic. Home: 2034 Hillyer Pl. N.W., Washington, D.C. Died June 18, 1946.

SANER, John Crawford (sā'nēr), lawyer; b. Washington, Ark., May 1, 1874; s. J. Frank and Sue (Crawford) S.; student Vanderbilt, 1893-95; LL.B., U. of Tex., 1897, LL.M., 1898; m. Mrs. M. R. Schluter, Nov. 7, 1906; children—John Crawford, Robt. William. Admitted to Tex. bar, 1898, and began practice at Dallas; mem. firm. Saner, Saner & Jack; pres. Schluter Whiteman Lumber Co., 1906-20, Saner Whiteman Co. since 1906, W. G. Ragley Lumber Co. since 1913; pres. United Securities Co., Washington Oil Corp., Texas Investment Co., Beauregard Oil Co., Provident Loan Soc.; v.p. Quincy (Calif.) Lumber Co., Quincy R.R. Co. Mem. Alpha Tau Omega. Democrat. Elk. Clubs: City, Athletic, Lakewood Country. Home: Melrose Hotel. Office: Republic Bank Bldg., Dallas, Tex. Died July 9, 1948.

SANFORD, Alfred Fanton, pres. realty co.; b. Knoxville, Tenn., Feb. 21, 1875; s. Edward Jackson and Emma Francillon (Chavannes) S.; student U. of Tenn., 1891-93; m. Eleanor Spence, Nov. 1903; m. 2d, Mrs. Minnie Howard Lockett, June 1, 1945. Pub. Knoxville Journal and Tribune, 1898-1928; pres. Sanford Realty Co., Empire Bldg. Corp., Leasing Co. No. 1; dir. Sanford Investment Co. Mem. Sigma Alpha Epsilon. Republican. Episcopalian. Club: Cherokee Country. Home: 2890 Kingston Pike. Address: Fidelity-Bankers Trust Bldg., Knoxville, Tenn. Died May 22, 1946.

SANFORD, Allan Douglas, lawyer; b. Covington, Tenn., July 3, 1869; s. William and Elizabeth (Douglas) S.; student Southwestern Presbyn. U., Clarksville, Tenn., 1886-89; LL.B., Law Dept., U. of Tex., 1892; m. Mary Stella Shepard, Jan. 30, 1900; m. 2d, Mrs. Frances Boddie, Nov. 11, 1903. Began practice at Waco, Texas, 1892; city atty. of Waco, 1899-1903; and 1936-39; mayor of Waco, 1903-04; spl. asso. justice appellate courts of Tex. at various times; now rent dir., atty., Waco Area for rent control, O.P.A. Author (with W. M. Sleeper) of a history of the Waco, Texas, Bar. Democrat. Presbyterian. Mem. Am. Bar Assn., Tex. State Bar Assn., (pres. 1914-15), Tex. State Hist. Soc., Alpha Tau Omega. Home: 2000 Austin Av. Office: 410 Professional Bldg., Waco, Tex. Died Jan. 22, 1950.

SANFORD, Chester Milton, author, lecturer; b. Shehawken, Pa., June 10, 1872; s. James C. and Aspia (Haynes) S.; A.B., Cornell U., 1905; m. Ella Stillson, 1895; children—Robert S., Frances A., C. Wilson. Prin. schs., Ore Hill, Conn., 1906-07; prin. Evansville (Wis.) Sem., 1907-08; headmaster Rock River Mil. Acad., Dixon, Ill., 1908-10; supt. schs., Sparta, Wis., 1910-16; prof. geography and geology, Platteville (Wis.) State Normal Sch., 1916-21; head Dept. of Expression, Ill. State Normal U., Normal, Ill., 1921-26. Platform lecturer. Mem. Internat. Lyceum and Chautauqua Assn. Republican. Methodist. Author: Geography of North America and Its Possessions, 1915; Modern Americans, 1918; Modern Europeans, 1919; Other Soldiers, 1920 (all with G. A. Owen); Community and Its Young People, 1923; How to Choose Your Vocation, 1926; Developing Teacher Personality That Wins, 1938. Home: 611 W. Green St., Urbana, Ill. Address: care Redpath Bureau, Kimball Hall Bldg., Chicago, Ill. Died Aug. 19, 1944.

SANFORD, Fernando, physicist; b. Taylor, Ill., Feb. 12, 1854; s. Faxton and Mariah (Bly) S.; B.S., Carthage (Ill.) Coll., 1879, M.S., 1882, Sc.D., 1920; studied with Helmholtz in Berlin, 1886-88; m. Alice E. Crawford, Aug. 12, 1880; children—Burnett, Alice. Prof. physical science, Mt. Morris Coll., 1879-82; county supt. schs., Ogle County, Ill., 1882-86; instr. in physics and chemistry, Englewood High Sch., Chicago, 1888-90; prof. physical science, Lake Forest U., 1890-91; prof. physics, Leland Stanford Jr. University, 1891-1919, since prof. emeritus. Fellow A.A.A.S., Am. Phys. Soc. Author: Elements of Physics, 1902; A Physical Theory of Electrification Charges of Atoms and Ions, 1919; A Diurnal Variation in the Electrical Potential of the Earth, 1920; Terrestrial Electricity, 1931; also numerous monographs pertaining to original investigations in physics. Engaged in investigations in the terrestrial electric observatory which he established at Palo Alto, 1920. Address: Palo Alto, Calif. Died May 21, 1948.

SANFORD, Francis B(aird), lawyer; b. Warwick, N.Y., Oct. 30, 1871; s. George W. and Frances (Baird) S.; A.B., Rutgers Coll., 1893, A.M., 1896; grad. New York Law Sch., 1896; LL.B., Regents State of N.Y., 1896; LL.D., Hope College, Holland, Mich., 1935; m. Sara McC. Welling, Nov. 30, 1898; children—Mary B. (Mrs. Archibald Taylor), Helen (Mrs. John Charles Straton). Admitted to N.Y. bar, 1897, and began practice at N.Y. City; formerly dir. and gen. counsel American News Company and subsidiaries, now emeritus. Trustee emeritus Rutgers Coll.; trustee Hope Coll.; dir. New Brunswick Theol. Sem.; formerly pres. Bd. of Edn. Ref. Ch. in America, now emeritus; pres. N.Y. Bible Society. Mem. N.Y. State Bar Assn., New York County Lawyers Assn., New York Law Inst., Phi Beta Kappa, Delta Kappa Epsilon. Republican. Clubs: University, City, Railroad Machinery. Author: Letters of a Rambler, 1921. Home: Hotel Carlyle, 35 E. 76th St., New York 21, N.Y.; also "Shadow Lawn," Warwick, N.Y. Office: 165 Broadway, N.Y. City. Deceased.

SANFORD, Graham, editor; b. Daviess County, Ind., Oct. 22, 1876; s. William Clark and Maria (Graham) S.; student Washington (Ind.) High Sch., 1881-92; m. Gertrude Aikman, July 25, 1904 (died Dec. 29, 1919); children—Gertrude, John, William Clark. Began as office boy and reporter on Washington (Ind.) Herald, 1892; editor Washington (Ind.) Herald, 1897-1904; mng. editor Reno (Nev.) Evening Gazette, 1904-07; owner Reno Printing Co., 1907-15; editor Reno Evening Gazette, 1915-39, editorial dir., 1939-40; pres. Reno Evening Gazette, 1920-39; pres. Gazette Bldg. Corp., 1920-39; dir. Nev. Fire Ins. Co., 1914-18. Chmn. finance com. Rep. State Central Com., 1926-30; mem. Nev.-Calif. joint water com., 1930-34. Mem. Nev. Council of Defense, 1917-19; also mem. Nev. War Industries Bd. during World War. Republican. Mem. Reno Chamber of Commerce. Home: 559 Ralston St. Office: Gazette Bldg., Reno, Nev. Died Jan. 21, 1942.

SANFORD, Louis Childs, bishop; b. Bristol, R.I., July 27, 1867; s. Henry and Mary Childs (Esleeck) S.; A.B., Brown U., 1888; S.T.B., Episcopal Theol. School, Cambridge, Mass., 1892; D.D. from Brown Univ., 1913; LL.D. from College of the Pacific, 1933; m. Annie Pepper, Oct. 5, 1892 (died July 8, 1895); m. 2d, Ellison Vernon, Feb. 3, 1898; children—Edward Nicholson, Mary Esleeck, Royal Kendrick. Deacon, 1892, priest, 1893, P.E. Ch.; missionary in charge St. Luke's Mission, Selma, Calif., and St. Michael's Mission, Fowler, Calif., 1892-98; rector St. Paul's Ch., Salinas, Calif., 1898-1900, Ch. St. John the Evangelist, San Francisco, 1900-07; sec. 8th missionary dept., 1908-10; consecrated missionary bishop of San Joaquin Dist., Calif., Jan. 25, 1911; retired Jan. 7, 1944. Mem. Zeta Phi. Address: Route 1, Box 1196, Los Gatos, Calif. Died Aug. 10, 1948.

SANFORD, Orin Grover, educator; b. Newark, Mo., Aug. 29, 1877; s. Richard Butler and Lida Jane (Downing) S.; B.S., N.E. Mo. State Teachers Coll., Kirksville, Mo., 1913; A.M., U. of Missouri, 1930; grad. study, U. of Colorado, 1915, Teachers Coll. (Columbia), 1935 and summer, 1937; m. Nancy Della McEntire, Aug. 22, 1900; 1 son, Richard Paul. Rural teacher in Mo., 1898-1904; supt. schs., Armstrong, Mo., 1909-12, Palmyra, 1912-19, Trenton, 1919-27, also dir. Junior Coll.; dir. teacher training, Mo. State Dept. Edn., 1927-29; asst. state supt. schs. in Mo. for Gen. Edn. Bd., N.Y., 1929-33; dean U. of Kansas City (Mo.), 1933-38, dean of men, 1938-40, chmn. department of education, 1939-47, professor emeritus since 1947. Member of the Marion County (Mo.) Exemption Bd., World War. State rep. in N. Central Assn. and mem. State Accrediting Com., 1927-33; trustee and treas. Cottey Coll., Nevada, Mo. (operated by P.E.O.); dir. Chamber Commerce, Trenton, Mo. Mem. N.E.A., Mo. State Edn. Assn., State High Sch. Athletic Assn. (pres. 1925-30), Phi Delta Kappa, Hi Twelve Club (pres. 1940). Democrat. Presbyterian. Mason (K.T.), Elk (exalted ruler). Club: Rotary of Trenton, Mo. (pres. 1926), South Kansas City Business, (pres. 1942-43). Home: 5500 Harrison St. Office: 5100 Rockhill Rd., Kansas City, Mo. Died March 4, 1948.

SANFORD, Steadman Vincent, educator; b. Covington, Ga., Aug. 24, 1871; s. Charles Vincent and Lizzie (Steadman) S.; A.B., Mercer U., 1890, LL.D., 1932; student U. of Berlin, 1912-13; Oxford U., Eng., summer, 1913; Litt.D., U. of Ga., 1914; m. Grace McClathey, June 16, 1895; children—Shelton Palmer, Grace Devereaux (dec.), Charles Steadman, Homer Reynolds. Pres. Marietta Male Acad., 1890-92; prin. Marietta High Sch., 1892-97; supt. schs., Marietta, 1897-1903; successively instr., adj. prof. and jr. prof. rhetoric and Eng. lit., 1903-13, prof. English lang.

since 1913, head and founder Henry W. Grady School of Journalism since 1921, U. of Ga., dean of the U., 1927-32, pres., 1932-35; chancellor University System of Ga. since 1935. Pres. Southern Conf., 1921-30. Capt. Co. F, 3d Regt. Inf., U.S. Vols., Spanish-Am. War, 1898; lt.-col. a.-d.-c. staffs of Govs. Brown, Slaton and Harris. Mem. Assn. of Am. Schs. of Journalism, S.A.R., United Spanish War Veterans (dept. comdr. Ga., 1942-43), Georgia Edn. Assn. (pres. 1936); mem. Am. Acad. Polit. and Soc. Sci. Kappa Alpha, Phi Kappa Phi, Phi Beta Kappa, Omicron Delta Kappa, Sigma Delta Chi, Blue Key. Democrat. Baptist. Mason, Odd Fellow, Knight of Pythias. Part Author: Literature and Composition, 1914; Composition and Grammar, 1914; English Grammar for High Schools, 1914. Home: Athens, Ga. Address: State Capitol Bldg., Atlanta, Ga. Died Sept. 15, 1945.

SANSUM, William David, M.D.; b. Baraboo, Wis., Sept. 25, 1880; s. David and Elizabeth (Risby) S.; student Wis. State Normal Sch., Stevens Point, 1901-03; B.S., U. of Wis., 1912, M.S., 1913; M.D., Rush Med. Coll., 1915, cum laude, 1916; m. Mabel Barbara Drew, July 31, 1906; 1 son, Donald R. Teacher of physics, pub. schs., Wis., 1899-1911; Otho S. A. Sprague fellow, Rush Med. Coll., 1913-20, instr. in medicine, 1918-20; dir. Potter Metabolic Clinic, Cottage Hosp., since 1920. Mem. med. advisory bd., Chicago, 1917-18. Fellow and life mem. Am. Coll. Physicians; specialist in internal medicine, Am. Bd. of Internal Medicine; mem. A.M.A., Calif. State and Santa Barbara County med. assns. Conglist. Mason (32°. K.T., Shriner). Club: University. Author: The Normal Diet, 1925; The Treatment of Diabetes Mellitus with Higher Carbohydrate Diets, 1929; The Normal Diet and Healthful Living, 1936; A Manual for Diabetic Patients, 1939. Research work on diabetes, high blood pressure, underweight and overweight. Home: 2800 Tallant Rd. Office: 317 W. Pueblo St., Santa Barbara, Calif. Died Jan. 5, 1948.

SANTELMANN, William Henry, musician; born Offensen, Hanover, Ger., Sept. 24, 1863; s. Heinrich W. and Henrietta (Sohnemann) S.; grad. Conservatory of Leipzig, Germany, in practical and theoretical music; Mus.D., George Washington Univ., 1908; m. Washington, Clara Becke, Nov. 10, 1888. Enlisted as mem. U.S. Marine Band, Sept. 24, 1887; resigned and became leader orchestra, Columbia Theatre, Washington, Sept. 4, 1895; apptd. capt. U.S.M.C. by spl. act of Congress, Mar. 3, 1898; leader of band, U.S. Marine Corps, until May 1, 1927 (retired). Home: 44 Grafton St., Chevy Chase, Md. Died Dec. 18, 1932.

SAPHORE, Edwin Warren (săf'ō-rē), bishop; b. Rahway, N.J.; grad. S. Jersey Inst., Bridgeton, N.J.; B.A., Pa. State Coll.; Madison Theol. Sem.; D.D., U. of South; m. Frances E. Cumber. Deacon, 1897, priest, 1898, P.E. Ch.; rector Jordan, N.Y., 1898-99, Ch. of St. John the Divine, Syracuse, 1899-1901, St. Paul's Ch., Watertown, 1901-06, also prof. St. Andrew's Div. Sch., Syracuse, 1900-03; rector All Saints Ch., Syracuse, 1906-08; arch-deacon, Ark., 1909-17; suffragan bishop of Ark., 1917-35; bishop of the Diocese of Ark., May 1935-Jan. 1, 1938 (retired). Address: 613 Clarendon St., Syracuse, N.Y.* Died May 22, 1944.

SAPP, Arthur Henry, lawyer; b. Ravenna, O., Jan. 13, 1883; s. Charles Henry and Sarah (Hall) S.; A.B., Ohio Wesleyan U., 1907; student U. of Chicago; grad. Ind. Law Sch., Indianapolis, 1912; m. Clara Yingling, Oct. 14, 1909; 1 dau., Helen Louise. Admitted to Ind. bar, 1912, and began practice at Huntington; mem. firm Sapp & Sees since 1926; pros. atty., 56th Judicial Dist., Ind., 1914-20; pres. Rural Bankers Legion Life Ins. Co. of Ind. Mem. Ind. Highway Commn., 1931-33; chmn. Ind. State Sch. Aid Commn., 1931, Conciliation Commn., Huntington County, since 1933; chmn. Ind. Peace Com.; mem. Ind. Publicity Com., 1940. Dir. James Whitcomb Riley Memorial Hosp. for Crippled Children; trustee De Pauw U., Warren Home for the Aged. Mem. nat. council Young Men's Christian Assn. Dist. Gov. Ind. Rotary Clubs, 1923-24; 1st v.p. Rotary Internat., 1925-26, pres., 1927-28. Mem. Am., Ind. State and Huntington bar assns., Phi Delta Theta. Mem. Gen. Conf. M.E. Ch., 1924; pres. North Indiana Conf. Laymen's Assn., M.E. Ch.; dir. Laymen's Commn. M.E. Ch.; pres. Men's Commn. of M.E. Ch., 1932-34; chmn. governor's Commn. to choose site for Southern Indiana Tuberculosis Hosp., 1938. Indiana representative Salvation Army. Republican. Mason (32°, Shriner), Elk. Clubs: Rotary (Huntington); Columbia (Indianapolis); Ft. Wayne Country, Lafontaine Country, Executives (Ft. Wayne). Home: 834 N. Jefferson St. Office: 346 N. Jefferson St., Huntington, Ind. Died Aug. 9, 1946.

SAPPINGTON, Clarence Olds, cons. industrial hygienist; b. Kansas City, Mo., Sept. 29, 1889; s. Lewis James and Cecelia May (Thompson) S.; A.B., Whitman Coll., 1911; M.D., Stanford, 1918; Dr.P.H., Harvard, 1924; m. Bertha Radovich, Feb. 3, 1920; 1 son, John Harvard (killed in action, Germany, Dec. 17, 1944). Assistant resident physician, Sacramento County Hosp., Calif., 1918-19, San Quentin Prison, Calif., 1919; alternating chief of Women's clinic Stanford U. Med. Sch., San Francisco, 1919-20; chief surgeon Pacific Coast Shipbuilding Co., Bay Point, Calif., 1919; asst. surgeon U.S.P.H.S., since 1920 (inactive list); fellow and teaching fellow in industrial hygiene, Harvard Sch. of Pub. Health, Boston, 1922-24; spl. lecturer in indsl. hygiene, Stanford U., 1924-28; med. dir. Montgomery Ward & Co., Oakland, Calif., 1924-28, also served as spl. lecturer Stanford U., U. of Calif. and spl. editor on industrial medicine for "California and Western Medicine"; dir. Div. of Industrial Health of Nat. Safety Council (advisory service to industry on problems of health and safety), 1928-32; consultant, Indsl. Vision Inst., Purdue Univ. Pres. Central States Society Industrial Medicine and Surgery, 1942-43. Fellow Am. Med. Assn., Am. Public Health Assn., A.A.A.S., Am. Assn. Industrial Phys. and Surg.; fellow Am. Acad. Occupational Medicine; diplomate Am. Bd. Preventive Medicine and Public Health; mem. Am. Industrial Hygiene Assn., Indsl. Hygiene Foundation of Am.; chairman sect. on Preventive and Indsl. Medicine and Public Health, A.M.A., 1946-47; pres. Harvard Pub. Health Alumni Assn., 1945-47. Member Am. Chem. Soc., Nat. Safety Council, Indsl. Management Soc., Ill. Mfrs. Assn., Ill., State and Chicago Med. Socs., Ill. State Acad. Science, Delta Omega, Alpha Kappa Kappa, Pi Gamma Mu. Del. Internat. Hygiene Congresses, Dresden, 1930; mem. 6th Internat. Congress Industrial Accidents and Diseases, Geneva, 1931 and 7th Congress, Brussels, 1935. Republican. Congregationalist. Mason. Clubs: South Shore Country, Executives (Chicago). Contbr. on industrial hygiene, industrial medicine and occupational diseases. An authority on medico-legal aspects of occupational diseases and indsl. health adminstrn. First American to receive degree of Dr.P.H. in the field of industrial hygiene. Mem. bd. editors Sight Saving Review. Editor of "Industrial Medicine." Author: Medicolegal Phases of Occupational Diseases, 1939, (received the first Wm. S. Knudsen award for the most outstanding contribution to industrial medicine, 1938-39); Industrial Health—Asset or Liability, 1939; Essentials of Industrial Health, 1943. Recently lecturer on indsl. health, univ. nursing schs., Loyola U. and U. of Chicago, U. of Ill., Med. Sch., and Purdue U. Engring. Schs. Home: 1949 E. 73d Pl. Office: 330 S. Wells St., Chicago 6. Died Nov. 6, 1949.

SARG, Tony (Anthony Frederick) (särg), b. Guatemala, C.A., Apr. 24, 1882; s. Francis Charles and Mary Elizabeth (Parker) S.; ed. German Mil. Sch., Lichterfelde, Germany; m. Bertha Eleanor McGowan, 1910; 1 dau., Mary Eleanor Norcliffe. Officer in German Army until 1905; began as illustrator, London, Eng., 1905; came to U.S., 1915, naturalized citizen, 1921; illustrator of humorous stories for Saturday Evening Post, Red Book, Collier's, Cosmopolitan, etc.; creator of "Tony Sarg's Marionettes," 1915; prop. of Tony Sarg Co. (marionette shows), Tony Sarg Stnudios, Tony Sarg Workshops (makers of window displays), creator of monster balloon parades all over the country. Clubs: Salmagundi, Advertising, Coffee House, Nantucket Yacht. Author: (and illustrator) Tony Sarg's Book for Children, 1924; Tony Sarg's Animal Book, 1925; Tony Sarg's Alphabet, 1926; Tony Sarg's Wonder Zoo, 1927; Tony Sarg's New York, 1927; Tony Sarg's Trick Book, 1928; Book of Marionette Plays, 1927; Tony Sarg's Wonder Zoo, 1939; Tony Sarg's Wonder Book, 1941. Lecturer. Designer of textiles, pottery, wall papers, rugs, furniture, etc., for children. Home: 112 W. 11th St., New York, and 47 N. Liberty St., Nantucket, Mass. Studio: 46 E. 9th St., New York, N.Y. Died Mar. 7, 1942.

SARTAIN, Paul Judd (sär-tān), physician; b. Phila., Pa., Nov. 26, 1861; s. Samuel and Harriet Amelia (Judd) S.; A.B., U. of Pa., 1883, A.M. and M.D., 1886; post-grad. studies in Vienna, Berlin, Paris, etc., 1886-88, hosps. of London, 1888-89; unmarried. Practiced at Phila. since 1889. Fellow Coll. of Physicians (Phila.), Am. Acad. Ophthalmology and Oto-Laryngology; mem. A.M.A., Med. Soc. State of Pa., Phila. County Med. Soc., Pathol. Soc., Franklin Inst., Hist. Soc. of Pa., Zoöl. Soc. of Phila., Geog. Soc. Phila. (sec. since 1894), Med. Club of Phila. (v.p. 1925), Oxford Ophthal. Congress, Colonial Society of Pa., Société Française d'Ophthalmologie, Delta Phi. Republican. Unitarian. Clubs: Union League, St. Elmo; Royal Socs. (London). Home: 2006 Walnut St., Philadelphia, Pa. Died Apr. 9, 1944.

SARTORI, Joseph Francis (sär-tō'rē), banker; b. Cedar Falls, Ia., Dec. 25, 1858; s. Joseph and Theresa (Wangler) S.; B.A., Cornell Coll., Mt. Vernon, Ia., 1879; LL.B., U. of Mich., 1881; studied U. of Freiburg, Germany; m. Margaret Rishel, July 3, 1885. Practiced law, Le Mars, 1882-87; cashier First Nat. Bank, Monrovia, Calif., 1887-88; an organizer, and cashier Security Savings Bank (now Security-First Nat. Bank), Los Angeles, pres., 1895-1934, and now chmn. of bd. of dirs. Republican. Clubs: California (ex-pres.), Jonathan, Los Angeles Country (pres.), Los Angeles Athletic, University. Home: 725 W. 28th St. Office: Security-First National Bank, Los Angeles, Calif. Died Oct. 6, 1946.

SATTERFIELD, Dave Edward, Jr., attorney; b. Richmond, Va., Sept. 11, 1894; s. Dave Edward and Martha Elizabeth (Garthright) S.; ed. John Marshall High. Sch.; LL.B., U. of Richmond, 1916; m. Blanche Kidd, Oct. 2, 1919; children—Dave Edward III, Richard Benjamin. Practiced law, Richmond, 1916-17, 1919-21; state's atty. for City of Richmond, 1921-33; mem. law firm, Tucker, Bronson, Satterfield & Mays, 1933-45; mem. 76th to 79th Congresses (1937-47), 3d Va. Dist.; mem. Judiciary Com. Ho. of Rep.; resigned from Congress Feb. 1945; now exec. dir. and gen. counsel, Life Ins. Assn. of Am., N.Y. City. Enlisted, U.S.N., transferred to U. S. N. R. Flying Corps, M.I.T. Ground Sch., 1917-19; lt. comdr. Naval Res.; naval observer under Adm. Robt. L. Ghormley, London, 1941. Mem. Va. and Am. bar assns., Phi Beta Kappa, Phi Gamma Delta, Omicron Delta Kappa, Delta Theta Phi. Country of Virginia, Commonwealth, Richmond First (Richmond); Kiwanis; Lawyers (New York). Democrat. Baptist. Office: 165 Broadway. Home: Gramercy Park Hotel, New York, N.Y. Died Dec. 27, 1946.

SATTERFIELD, Robert Samuel, clergyman; b. Surry County, N.C., Feb. 27, 1873; s. John Dillard and Jennie Ingram (Atkinson) S.; student Univ. of N.C., 1894-97, Vanderbilt U., 1902-04; grad. theol. dept., Vanderbilt, 1904; A.B., Scarritt Coll. for Christian Workers, 1925; m. Willie Mai Smith of Nashville, Tenn., Sept. 12, 1905; children—Robert Samuel, Annie Beth. Ordained ministry M. E. Ch., S., 1905; pastor Lawton, Okla., 1905-07, Oklahoma City, 1907-09, Cordell, Okla., 1909-11, Oklahoma City, 1911-12, Pauls Valley, Okla., 1912-16, Lawton 1916-18; prof. Bibl. history and Old Testament Epworth U., Oklahoma City, 1907-09; sec. W. Okla. Annual Conf. M.E. Church, S, 1910-25 sec. East Oklahoma Conf., 1926-38; press secretary six Gen. Confs.; assistant editor Christian Advocate, Nashville, Tenn., 1918-22, asso. editor, 1922-24; pastor 1st M.E. Ch., S., Muskogee, Okla., 1925, 26, and 1930-32, El Reno, Oklahoma, 1932-35; associate editor Southwestern Advocate, Dallas, Tex., 1935-1938; pastor Barnard Memorial Ch., Holdenville, Okla., 1935-36; presiding elder, Vinita, Okla., 1936-38. Del. Gen. Confs. 1922, 26, 38, president Southern Meth. Press Assn., 1922-25; missionary secretary East Oklahoma Conference, M.E. Church, South, 1926-30; reserve delegate to General Conference, M.E. Church, South, Jackson, Miss., 1934. Dist. supt. Vinita Dist., East Okla Conf., Meth. Ch., 1939-42, retired, Nov. 1, 1942; first reserve del. Gen. Conf., Meth. Ch., Atlantic City, 1940; del. Jurisdictional Conference, Methodist Church, Oklahoma City, 1940. Mem. Pi Gamma Mu. Del. to Uniting Conf. of Methodist Churches, Kansas City, 1939. Club: Rotary. Home: 1933 S. Indianapolis St., Tulsa 4. Died Nov. 6, 1945; buried in Rose Hill Mausoleum, Tulsa, Okla.

SATTERLEE, Herbert Livingston, lawyer; b. New York, N.Y., Oct. 31, 1863; s. George B. and Sarah S.; B.S., Ph.B., Columbia, 1883, A.M., 1884, Ph.D., LL.B., cum laude, 1885; m. Louisa Pierpont, d. J(ohn) Pierpont Morgan, Nov. 15, 1900. Pvt. sec. Senator William M. Evarts, 1885-87; navigator 1st Naval Battalion, N.Y., 1891-95; col. and a.-d.-c. to Gov. L.P. Morton, 1895-96; capt. (naval militia) and a.-d.-c. to Gov. Frank S. Black, 1897-98; lt. U.S. Navy (war with Spain) and chief of staff to Capt. John R. Bartlett, U.S. Navy; counsel M.K.&T. Ry. Co., 1898-1902; asst. sec. of the Navy, Dec. 1, 1908-Mar. 6, 1909; chmn. N.Y. State Commn. for the Blind, 1914-16; now mem. firm of Satterlee, Warfield & Stephens, N.Y. Capt. Naval Militia Reserve List. Trustee Columbia U., 1917-23; pres. Wilmer Foundation, pres. Naval Militia Vet. Assn., 1891-1922; mem. Nat. Inst. Social Sciences, Soc. Colonial Wars, S.R., Soc. War 1812, Soc. Foreign Wars, Vet. Arty. Corps; a founder Navy League U.S.; comdr. gen. Naval Order U.S., 1925-28; mem. Mil. and Naval Order Spanish-Am. War, Am. Bar Assn., N.Y. State Bar Assn., Assn. Bar City N.Y., Am. Mus. Natural History, N.Y. Hist. Soc., Met. Mus. Art, American Geographic Society, St. Nicholas Society (president 1936-38), Medal of Merit, 1946, Seamen's Church Institute of New York City (vice pres.), Life Saving Benevolent Assn. (president 1930-40), State Charities Aid Assn., Grant Monument Assn. (pres.); hon. mem. Naval Acad. Grads. Assn. of New York, Marine Museum City of N.Y. (pres. 1934-44). Clubs: Century, Uniersity, Church, Union League (pres. 1938-39), Military and Naval, Columbia University, St. Anthony (New York); Army and Navy (Washington); Bohemian (San Francisco. Home: 1 Beekman Pl. Office: 49 Wall St., New York 5, N.Y. Died July 14, 1947.

SAUL, Charles Dudley, physician; b. Phila., Pa., Jan. 25, 1880; s. Charles G. and Lidie (Bower) S.; student Temple U., 1897-98; M.D., Hahnemann Med. Coll. and Hosp., Phila., 1901; m. Fay Bruch, June 17, 1915; children—Charles Dudley, Jr., Maurice Biddle. Began as asst. med. dept., Hahnemann Hosp., later demonstrator, asso. prof. medicine, 1931-36, lecturer, medicine, 1928-31; pres. State Homeopathic Hosp. of Pa., 1934-35; chief, dept. of medicine, St. Luke's and Children's Med. Center, 1935-41, med. dir. since 1940. Pres. League for Socialized Med. of Pa. Served as capt., U.S. Army, Base Hosp. 48, A.E.F. Mem. Homeopathic Med. Soc. Episcopalian. Contbr. monographs to med. publs. Home: 1512 Spruce St. Office: 1530 Locust St., Philadelphia, Pa.* Died Jan. 8, 1947.

SAUNDERS, Joseph H. (sôn'dẽrs), city supt. of schools; b. Portsmouth, Va., June 21, 1876; s. Robert Johnson and Mary Elizabeth (Avery) S.; A.B., William and Mary Coll., 1917, hon. Pd.D., 1941; A.M., Univ. of Chicago, 1924; m. Lola Beale, Sept. 3, 1907; children—Frances Beale (Mrs. Harold V. Chisolm), Elizabeth Avery (Mrs. Franklin Pierce Greenman), Joseph H., Robert Milton, Jane Beale (Mrs. George Keith McMurran). High school teacher, Bland County School, 1896-97, Churchland, 1897-98; assistant principal, Portsmouth High School, 1899-1900, principal, 1903-07; principal Park View Sch., 1900-03; asst. edn. dir. Jamestown Exposition, 1907-08; state sch. examiner and insp., Va., 1907-08; prin. Omohundro Sch., Norfolk, 1908-11, Bellevue Sch., Richmond, 1911-12, Fox and Richmond City Normal Schs., 1912-15, Binford Junior High Sch., Richmond,

1915-21; city supt. of schools, Newport News, since 1921; dir. State Summer Normal Sch., Covington, 1908-18. Organized Dept. of Records and Returns, Fed. Bd. Vocational Edn., Rehabilitation Div., 1919-20; mem. Va. State Bd. Edn. since 1930, pres. since 1941. Dir. Newport News Public Library. Mem. N.E.A. (chmn. bd. trustees, mem. exec. com. and bd. dir. since 1931), Va. Edn. Assn. (chmn. bd. trustees since 1935), Nat. Edn. Assn., Am. Assn., Sch. Adminstrs., Nat. Soc. for Study of Edn., Soc. for Advancement of Edn., A.A.A.S., Phi Beta Kappa, Phi Delta Kappa, Kappa Phi Kappa. Mason (past master, past comdr. K.T., past potentate). Club: Rotary (past pres.). Home: 5906 Huntington Av. Office: 222 31st St., Newport News, Va. Died Nov. 25, 1945.

SAUNDERS, Joseph Taylor, v.p. Southern Pacific Lines; b. Ft. Worth, Texas, May 25, 1885. Has held various official positions in Freight Traffic Dept. of Southern Pacific Lines during past 20 years; now v.p. System Freight Traffic; dir. Northwestern Pacific R.R., San Francisco, Calif. Clubs: Family, Olympic, Bohemian, Transportation, Golf and Country (San Francisco); California (Los Angeles). Home: Stanford Ct. Apts. Office: 65 Market St., San Francisco, Calif. Died Nov. 11, 1942.

SAUNDERS, Marshall (Margaret Marshall Saunders), author; b. Milton, N.S., Apr. 13, 1861; d. Rev. Edward Manning and Maria K. (Freeman) S.; ed. pvt. schs., Nova Scotia, Scotland, France; M.A. (hon.), Acadia U., Nova Scotia. Contbr. to mags.; unmarried. Author: Beautiful Joe, 1894 (awarded $200 prize of Am. Humane Edn. Soc.); Daisy, 1894; The House of Armour, 1897; For the Other Boy's Sake, and Other Stories, 1896; Charles and His Lamb, 1896; The King of the Park, 1897; Rose à Charlitte, (novel), 1898; Deficient Saints, a Tale of Maine, 1899; Her Sailor, 1899; For His Country, 1900; Tilda Jane, 1901; Beautiful Joe's Paradise, 1902; The Story of the Graveleys, 1903; Nita, 1904; Princess Sukey, 1905; Alpatok, the Story of an Eskimo Dog, 1906; My Pets, 1908; Tilda Jane's Orphans, 1909; The Girl from Vermont, 1910; Pussy Blackface, 1912; The Wandering Dog, 1914; Golden Dicky, 1919; Bonnie Prince Fetlar, 1920; Jimmie Gold Coast, 1923; Esther de Warren, 1927; also essay, Cause and Prevention of Crime (awarded $300 prize of Am. Humane Edn. Soc.), in "Our Dumb Animals," Jan. 1906. Awarded medal, Société Protectrice Des Animaux, Paris; Comdr. Order of British Empire, 1934; hon. corr. sec. Inst. Artistique et Litteraire of France. Apptd. mem. Internat. Joint Park Commn., U.S. and Can., 1935. Address: 62 Glengowan Road, Toronto, Can. Died Feb. 15, 1947.

SAUNDERS, Paul Hill, banker; b. Hernando, Miss., Aug. 4, 1870; s. Lucien L. (M.D.) and Anne (Lyons) S.; B.A., U. of Miss., 1890 (1st honors), Ph.D., 1894; studied U. of Chicago, Halle-Wittenberg U., Germany; m. Mabel Shands, July, 1895; children—Garvin S., Maridel. Pres. Commercial Bank & Trust Co., Laurel, Miss., 1905-11; pres. Mortgage Securities Co., New Orleans, 1911-15; pres. Commercial Trust & Savings Bank, 1917, later Canal-Commercial Nat. Bank, of which was pres. until 1920; mem. firm Isadore Newman & Son, 1922, reorganized as Newman, Saunders & Co., Inc., of which was v.p. until 1929; organized P. H. Saunders Co., 1929, pres. same; dir., chmn. bd. Kansas City Pub. Service Co.; pres. Hugo Stinnes Corp., Hugo Stinnes Industries, Inc.; dir. Kansas City Southern R.R., United Fruit Co., Nat. Power & Light Co., Maison Blanche Co., B. Lowenstein & Bros., Loveman, Joseph & Loeb, Peabody Hotel Co., Memphis Street Ry. Co. Trustee Tulane U. Dir. War Savings for State of La.; dir. Fed. Reserve Bank of Atlanta, 1914-18; dir. N.O. branch Fed. Res. Bank of Atlanta, 1916-32; chmn. bd. N.O. branch, 1920-32. Mem. Delta Kappa Epsilon, Phi Beta Kappa. Democrat. Methodist. Clubs: Boston, New Orleans Country, Pelham Country, Cloud, Kansas City Club. Home: 500 Walnut St. Office: Maison Blanche Bldg., New Orleans, La. Died April 12, 1947.

SAVAGE, (Charles) Courtenay, writer; b. New York, N.Y., July 29, 1890; s. Charles Edward and Frances Mary Courtenay (Hennessy) S.; ed. pub. and private schs. and under tutors; spl. student, Columbia, 1911-12; m. Valerie Osborn Dade, June 28, 1924 (divorced 1937). Began writing fiction, 1909; was associated with late Janette Gilder on "The Reader" 2 yrs.; sec. Forum Pub. Co. and asso. editor The Forum, 2½ yrears; dir. dept. of dramatics and continuity, Columbia Broadcasting System, 1933-36; author and dir. of daytime radio serials for nat. advertisers. Dir. pub. relations, United Service Orgns.-Nat. Cath. Community Service, Washington, D.C., 1942-43; information specialist, chief technical information, Armed Forces Radio Services, Information and Education Division, Army Service Forces, 1943. Mem. Catholic Theater Conference, vice-president Cathedral Guild of Catholic Actors of Chicago. Roman Catholic. Mem. Dramatists Guild, Authors League of America (v p. Radio Writers Guild), Soc. of Authors, Playwrights and Composers (London). Club: Athletic (New York). Author (plays): (with E. B. Dewing) Don't Bother Mother, prod. 1925; They All Want Something, prod. 1926; The Buzzard, prod. 1928; (with Wallace Peck) The Queen of Kingdom Corners, 1929; I'm Wise, prod. in England, 1929; Virtue's Bed, prod. 1930; (with Vivian Cosby and Shirley Warde) The Queen at Home, prod. 1930; The Flying Vagabond, pub. 1931; Nellie Was a Lady, prod. 1933; The Little Dog Laughed (adapted from Leonard Merrick's Elevation of Lulu), prod. 1933; Loose Moments (with Bertram Hobbs), prod. 1935; Forever and Forever, 1937; Safe Crossing, 1940; Home is the Hero, 1945. Frequent contbr. of short stories and articles to mags. Home: 1255 N. State St., Chicago, Ill. Died Aug. 23, 1946.

SAVAGE, Elmer Seth, prof. animal husbandry; b. Lancaster, N.H., June 15, 1884; s. John and Catherine M. (Daley) S.; B.S.A., N.H. Coll., Durham, 1905; M.S.A., Cornell, 1909, Ph.D., 1911; hon. D.Sc., U. of New Hampshire, 1933; m. Clara Blandford, Sept. 9, 1908; children—Ruth Cecelia, Clara Catherine Margaret; m. 2d, Genevieve Boyle, June 29, 1916; children—Mary Gene, Joan. Asst. in animal husbandry, 1907-08, instr., 1908-10, asst. prof., 1910-13, prof. since 1913, Cornell U. Fellow A.A.A.S.; mem. Am. Soc. Animal Production, Sigma Xi, Gamma Alpha, Kappa Sigma, Alpha Zeta. Republican. K.C. Author: Feeds and Feeding Manual, 1913; Feeding Dairy Cattle, 1917; (with L. A. Maynard) Better Dairy Farming, 1923. Home: 106 Harvard Pl., Ithaca, N.Y. Died Nov. 22, 1943.

SAVAGE, Marion Alexander, designing engr.; b. Walterboro, S.C., Sept. 3, 1885; s. Charles Alexander and Ina (Dunwody) S.; B.S., Clemson Coll., 1906, hon. E.E., 1927; m. Jessie Rivers, June 20, 1911; children—Jessie Rivers, Evelyn Henderson. With Gen. Electric Co. since 1909, in alternating current engring. sect., 1909-23, in charge turbine generator dept., 1923-31, designing engr. turbine generator dept., Schenectady, N.Y., since 1931; has worked on transformer tests, built tech. foundation in marine equipment, induction motors, generators, turbines, etc. Received Coffin award, 1932; Lamme medal, 1938. Mem. Am. Inst. E.E. Contbr. numerous scientific articles to Am. Inst. E.E. publs.; presented paper on "Economic Development in Turbine Generators in the U.S." before Second World Conf. of Am. Inst. E.E., Berlin, Germany, 1930. As result of numerous inventions he has made possible use of high speed steam driven generators of large capacity. Home: 17 Sunnyside Rd., Scotia 2, N.Y. Office: General Electric Co., Schenectady, N.Y. Died Apr. 9, 1946.

SAVAGE, Maxwell, minister; b. Boston, Mass., June 13, 1876; s. Minot Judson and Ella (Dodge) S.; grad. Noble and Greenough Sch., 1895; A.B., Harvard, 1899; grad. Meadville Theol. Sch., 1903, D.D., 1924; m. Marguerite Downing, Jan. 18, 1911; children—Maxwell, David Downing, Philip Minot. Ordained Unitarian ministry, 1903; pastor Redlands, Calif., 1903-10 (built new ch.), Louisville, Ky., 1910-16, Lynn, Mass., 1916-19, Worcester, 1919-46, pastor emeritus since June 1946. Trustee Proctor Acad., Worcester Art Museum. Mem. Unitarian Laymen's League, Newcomen Soc. Mason. Clubs: University, Prouts'-Neck Country, Worcester. Home: Encino, Calif.; and Prouts' Neck, Me. Died Nov. 4, 1948.

SAVAGE, Toy Dixon, lawyer; b. Como, Hertford County, N.C., Sept. 13, 1878; s. Robert R. and Rowena (Vann) S.; A.B., Wake Forest (N.C.) Coll., 1899; B.L., U. of Va., 1902; m. Hildreth Gatewood, Nov. 24, 1915; children—Hildreth G. (dec.), Toy Dixon. Admitted to Va. bar, 1902, and since in practice at Norfolk; mem. Peatross & Savage, 1907-18; partner Savage & Lawrence, Norfolk, since 1918; v.p., dir. and gen. counsel Investment Corp. of Norfolk; gen. counsel and dir. Camp Mfg. Co., Chesapeake-Camp Corp., Colonial Oil Co., Inc., Charles W. Priddy & Co., Inc. Dir. Norfolk Gen. Hosp.; mem. Va. Baptist Bd. of Missions and Edn. Mem. Norfolk and Portsmouth Bar Assn. (pres. 1940), Am. and Va. State bar assns., Phi Kappa Sigma. Democrat. Baptist. Clubs: Virginia, Pewter Platter, Norfolk Saddle (Norfolk); Princess Anne Country, Surf Beach, Cavalier Beach (Virginia Beach, Va.). Home: 1429 W. Princess Anne Rd. Office: 203 Granby St., Norfolk, Va. Died Oct. 25, 1941.

SAVERY, William (sā'vēr-y), univ. prof.; b. Attleboro, Mass., Sept. 26, 1875; s. Job Briggs and Dora Briggs S.; A.B., Brown U., 1896; A.M., Harvard, 1897, Ph.D., 1899; student, U. of Berlin, 1897-98; Walker fellow, Harvard, 1897-98, Morgan fellow, 1898-99; m. Isabella Barnett, June 23, 1903, (dec. 1918); children—William, Jr., Barnett, James Palmer, Isabella; m. 2d, Helen Halley Brewster, May 29, 1926. Asst. in ethics, Harvard, 1896-97; asst. in hist. of philosophy, Harvard and Radcliffe, 1899-1900; prof. philosophy, Fairmount Coll. (now U. of Wichita), 1900-02; prof. philosophy and chmn. dept., U. of Wash. since 1902; lecturer in philosophy, U. of Calif., Berkeley, 1933; vis. prof., Columbia U., 1935-36. Mem. Am. Philos. Assn. (pres., Pacific div., 1931), Assn. Univ. Profs., A.A.A.S., Phi Beta Kappa, Phi Kappa Sigma. Contbr. Possibility, U. of Calif., 1934; The Philosophy of John Dewey, 1939, and philos. journals. Home: 4711 15th Av. N.E. Office: U. of Washington, Seattle 5, Wash. Died Dec. 8, 1945.

SAWYER, Hiram Arthur, lawyer; b. Hartford, Wis., Sept. 4, 1875; s. Hiram Wilson and Josephine B. (Coxe) S.; B.L., U. of Wis., 1896 (Phi Beta Kappa), LL.B., 1899; m. Eleanor J. Dillman, Feb. 28, 1924. Dist. atty., Washington County, Wis., 1907-15; U.S. dist. atty., Eastern Dist. of Wis., by appmt. of Pres. Wilson, July 13, 1915-Mar. 1923; resumed practice. Democrat. Mem. Phi Delta Phi, Phi Beta Kappa. Mason (32°, Shriner). Clubs: Milwaukee Athletic, North Hills Country. Home: 2017 N. Terrace Av. Office: Century Bldg., Milwaukee, Wis. Died Nov. 17, 1946.

SAWYER, John Pascal, physician; b. Kent, O., Apr. 10, 1862; s. Pascal Hall (M.D.) and Caroline Louisa (Barber) Sawyer; A.B., Adelbert College, 1883; honorary H.H.D., 1941; M.D., Western Reserve University, 1886; married Mary Candee Baldwin, Feb. 13, 1893; children—Charles Baldwin, David Pascal. Practiced at Cleveland since 1886; emeritus prof. clin. medicine and therapeutics, Western Reserve Univ. Fellow Am. Coll. Physicians; mem. A.M.A., Ohio State Med. Assn., Am. Gastroenterol. Assn., Cleveland Acad. Medicine, Cleveland Med. Library Assn. (trustee), Am. Climatol. and Clin. Assn., Delta Upsilon, Nu Sigma Nu; fellow Am. Coll. Physicians. Conglist. Clubs: Union (Cleveland); Riomar Country (Vero Beach, Fla.). Home: 2745 Edgehill Rd., Cleveland, O.; (winter) Riomar, Vero Beach, Fla. Died June 17, 1945.

SAWYER, Paul Backus, business exec.; b. Lafayette, Ind., May 8, 1879; s. Arthur Lovell and Harriet (Backus) S.; B.S. in E.E., Purdue U., 1900, E.E., 1902; m. Cecilia Sherman, Sept. 28, 1904 (divorced 1932); children—John Sherman, Paul B., Jr. Pres. National Power & Light Co. Member Sigma Alpha Epsilon. Republican. Presbyterian. Clubs: Union League, Bankers, Lawyers (New York); Saucon Valley Country, Pine Valley Golf. Home: Pocono Lake Preserve, Pocono Lake, Pa. Office: 2 Rector St., New York, N.Y. Died Apr. 8, 1946.

SAWYER, Philip, architect; b. New London, Conn., 1868; s. George A. (U.S.N.) S.; studied civ. engring. With U.S. Geol. Survey, Div. of N.M., 1888; in charge of irrigation survey Yellowstone drainage, 1889; studied architecture at Columbia U., Sch. of Beaux Arts, office of McKim, Mead & White, New York; m. Mildred, d. Moncure D. Conway, 1895; children—Mildred Conway, Eleanor Conway. Mem. firm of York & Sawyer, firm architects of Pershing Square Building, New York; Federal Bldgs., Honolulu; Children's Village, Dobbs Ferry; N.Y. Acad. of Medicine, Guaranty Trust Co. Bldg., Manhattan Eye, Ear and Throat, Ruptured and Crippled, Fifth Avenue and Orthopædic hosps., New York; Chester County Hosp., West Chester, Pa.; Fed. Reserve Bank of New York, Bowery Savings Bank, Greenwich Savings Bank, Central Savings Bank, New York; Brooklyn Trust Co., Brooklyn; R.I. Hosp. Trust Co., Providence, R.I.; First Nat. Bank of Boston; Riggs Nat. Bank, Am. Security & Trust Co. bldgs., Washington, D.C.; Royal Bank of Canada, Montreal; bldgs. at U. of Mich., Vassar, Smith, Middlebury and Rutgers colls., Dept. of Commerce Bldg., Washington, D.C.; Allegheny General Hospital, Pittsburgh; Goldwater Memorial Hosp., Welfare Island; Clason Point Housing, N.Y. City; Naval Hosp., St. Albans, L.I.; cons. architects to Treasury Dept., 1909-13, to Bd. of Water Supply of New York City, 1907-19, 1931 and since 1936 to St. Luke's Hospital, Tokyo; Tripler Gen. Hosp., Honolulu (under constrn.); war work at West Point, N.Y., St. Clare's Hosp., Schenectady, N.Y. (under constrn.), Vets. Adminstrn. Hosp., Washington, D.C. (in association). Mem. Beaux Arts Society, Am. Society C.E., Society of the Cincinnati. Clubs: Century (New York); Metropolitan (Washington, D.C.). Home: 132 E. 72d St. Office: 101 Park Av., New York 17, N.Y. Died May 21, 1949; buried Stonington, Conn.

SAYLES, Robert Wilcox, geologist; b. Pawtucket, R.I., Jan. 29, 1878; s. Frederick Clark and Deborah Cook (Wilcox) S.; A.B., Harvard, 1901; m. Adelaide K. Burton, June 1, 1904; children—Deborah W., Robert W. Began geol. work in Montana, 1899; curator Harvard Geol. Museum, 1907-28; research asso. Division of Geology, Harvard, since 1928. President Baltic Mills Co., Baltic Ct. Fellow Geol. Soc. Am., A.A.A.S., Am. Acad. Arts and Sciences, Am. Geog. Soc.; mem. Seismol. Soc. America, Am. Meteorol. Soc., Boston Soc. Natural History, Geol. Soc. Boston (pres. 1928-29), Washington Acad. Sciences, Conf. Geophys. Union. Trustee of the Boston, Mass., Children's Museum. Author of monographs and papers on glacial geology and seismology. Research work on origin of Bermuda Islands, on seasonal banding in rocks and on glacial geology of Southern Maine and Cape Cod. Home: 263 Hammond St., Chestnut Hill, Mass. Died Oct. 23, 1942; buried in Swan Point Cemetery, Providence, R.I

SAYWARD, William James, architect; b. Woodstock, Vt., Sept. 23, 1875; s. Charles Woodbury and Melissa (Follansbee) S.; B.S., U. of Vt., 1897; B.S. in Architecture, Mass. Inst. Tech., 1901; m. Clara Louise Purple, 1904; children—Mary Follansbee, Madeline. Began practice at N.Y. City, 1901; practiced in Seattle, 1908-13; moved to Atlanta, Ga., 1913; mem. Edwards & Sayward since 1914, firm name Sayward & Logan since 1939, firm architects for bldgs. at U. of Fla., Fla. State Coll. for Women, Winthrop Coll., Columbia Sem., Agnes Scott Coll., also Sr. High Sch. for Girls (Atlanta), York (S.C.) County Court House, Bank of Tifton (Ga.). Mem. Bd. of Edn., Decatur, Ga., University Housing Project, Atlanta. Fellow Am. Inst. Architects (v.p.); mem. Affiliated Tech. Socs. of Atlanta (ex-chmn.). Mason (Shriner). Clubs: City, Civitan, Atlanta Athletic. Office: Palmer Bldg., Atlanta, Ga. Died Dec. 21, 1945.

SCALA, Francis M(aria), musician; b. Naples, Italy, about Nov. 1819; student divinity and music, Univ. and Convent of Naples, until 1940; m. Olivia Arth, 1862. Came to U.S., 1840, became citizen about 1841. Enlisted as musician on U.S.S. Brandywine, 1840; leader U.S. Marine Corps Band (then known as Fife and Drum Corps), Aug. 1842-June 7, 1848; formed own band; served as leader U.S. Marine Corps Band, Oct. 30, 1848-Dec. 13, 1871 (officially by Act of Congress, made U.S. Marine Band, July 1861); retired. Tutor of John Phillip Sousa (enlisted as music boy in U.S. Marine Band). Served as comdg. officer U.S. Marine Barracks during Civil War. Received numerous hon. degrees and decorations. Composer: Buchanan's Inaugural March, 1857; Lincoln's Inaugural March, 1861; Grant's Inaugural March, 1869; Bridal Schottische; The Lady Polka; The Mocking Bird, 1857; The Dirge (composed and played at Tomb of Washington in honor of visit of Prince of Wales visit there); Forevermore (vocal duet, unpublished). Home: 918 S. Carolina Av. S.E. Office: U.S. Marine Barracks, 8th and I Sts. S.E., Washington. Died April 1903; buried in Congressional Cemetery, Washington.

SCALES, Alfred Moore, lawyer; b. Greensboro, N.C., Aug. 20, 1870; s. Col. Junius Irving and Effie (Henderson) S.; ed. U. of N.C.; m. Bessie Taylor; children—Elizabeth W., Alfred M. (dec.), Douglas Taylor, Wallace N., Frances T.; m. 2d, Mary L. Pell.; children—Mary L., Archibald H., Junius. Admitted to N. C. bar, 1892; practices Greensboro; v.p. and gen. counsel Pilot Life Ins. Co., George Washington Fire Ins. Co., Greensboro Fire Ins. Co., Pilot Fire Ins. Co.; gen. counsel, dir. Am. Exchange Nat. Bank, etc. Mem. N.C. Senate, 1897, 1905, 17, 19; pres. Commn. to Amend Constitution of N.C., 1913. Trustee, chmn. finance com. and mem. exec. com., U. of N.C., trustee Flora McDonald Coll. Union Theol. Sem., Richmond, A. and T. Coll.; Greensboro, N.C. Moderator Presbyn. Synod N.C.; pres. N.C. Children's Home Soc. Democrat. Mem. Beta Theta Pi. Mem. N.C. Ship and Water Transportation Commn., 1923; chmn. Com. of One Hundred on Prison Reform; pres. N.C. Conf. Social Welfare. Pres. Hamilton Lakes, Inc.; mayor town of Hamilton Lakes, N.C. Home: Greensboro, N.C. Died Jan. 13, 1940.

SCARBOROUGH, Lee Rutland, clergyman; b. Colfax, La., July 4, 1870; s. George W. and Martha Elizabeth (Rutland) S.; A.B., Baylor U., Waco, Tex., 1892; A.B., Yale, 1896 (Phi Beta Kappa); D.D., Baylor U., 1908; LL.D., Union U., 1927; student Southern Bapt. Theol. Sem., Louisville, Ky., 1899-1900; m. Mary P. Warren, Feb. 4, 1900; children—Warren, Euna Lee, Lawrence, Neppie, Ada Beth, Byron. Ordained ministry, Missionary Bapt. Ch., 1896; pastor Cameron, Tex., 1896-99, First Ch., Abilene, 1901-08; teacher, Southwestern Bapt. Theol. Sem., since 1908, pres. since 1915. Raised funds to erect 2 large bldgs. for Simmons Coll., Abilene, and 3 bldgs. for Southwestern Sem.; mem. exec. bd. Missions and Edn., Bapt. Conv.; gen. dir. of "75 million campaign" for Southern Baptists, 1919; pres. Southern Baptist Conv., 1938-40. Mem. bd. dirs. Baptist Standard. K.P. Author: Recruits for World Conquests, 1914; With Christ After the Lost, 1919; Marvels of Divine Leadership, 1920; The Tears of Jesus; Prepare to Meet God, 1922; Endued to Win, 1923; Christ's Militant Kingdom, 1924; Holy Places and Precious Promises, 1924; How Jesus Won Men, 1926; Ten Spiritual Ships, 1927; Products of Pentecost, 1934; My Conception of Gospel Ministry; A Blaze of Evangelism Across the Equator, 1937; A Modern School of the Prophets, 1939. Address: R. 3, Edinburg, Tex.* Died Apr. 10, 1945.

SCATTERGOOD, Ezra Frederick, elec. and hydr. engr.; b. Burlington County, N.J., Apr. 9, 1871; s. Ezra and Lucy Ann (Engle) S.; B.S., Rutgers, 1893, M.S., 1896, Sc.D., 1931; fellow Cornell University, 1898-99, M.M.E., 1899; LL.D., University of California, 1944; m. Lulie Chilton, April 17, 1901; 1 dau., Elisabeth Harding. Instr. in mathematics and elec. science, Rutgers Coll., 1894-98; prof. physics and elec. engring., later elec. and experimental engring., Ga. Sch. Tech., 1899-1901; spl. engr. Huntington Light, Power and Elec. Ry. Cos., Los Angeles, Calif., 1902-06; cons. elec. and hydr. engr., Los Angeles, 1906-09; chief Electrical Engr., General Mgr. Bureau of Power & Light, Dept. of Water and Power, Los Angeles, 1909-40; adv. engr. to dept. water and power, City of Los Angeles, 1938-47; pres. Am. Public Power Assn. 1947-48; non-resident lecturer, electrical engineering, Stanford, since 1926. Apptd. mem. Pub. Works Adv. Com. for Calif. under NRA, 1933; advisory engr. Nat. Power Policy com., 1939-40; mem. Colo. River Bd. of Calif.; chairman of the Committee on Electric Power of Calif. State War Council, 1942-43. Fellow American Institute Electric Engineers; mem. Seismological Society of America, Los Angeles Art Assn., Southern Calif. Symphony Assn., Pacific Geographic Soc., Sigma Xi, Phi Beta Kappa, Tau Beta Pi. Quaker. Clubs: California, Los Angeles Athletic, Engineers. Contbr. papers to tech. jours. and engring. socs. Home: 524 Muirfield Rd., Los Angeles 5. Office: 207 S. Broadway, Los Angeles 54, Calif. Died Nov. 15, 1947; buried in Forest Lawn Memorial Park, Glendale, Calif.

SCHAEFER, Albert A., professor; b. Middletown, Conn., Feb. 25, 1884; s. Jacob and Elizabeth Margaret (Olt) S.; A.B., Harvard, 1906, LL.B., 1909; m. Ethel K. Potter, Feb. 1, 1935. Admitted to Mass. bar. 1909; pvt. practice, Boston, Mass., 1909-35; special asst. dist. atty., northern dist. Mass., 1910-12; dir. of enforcement, New England Fuel Adminstrn., 1917-19; counsel, numerous railroad and steamship lines receiverships, 1914-35; lecturer law and govt., Mass. Inst. Tech., 1930-35, prof. since 1935. Arbitrator, American Arbitration Assn. Member American Management Assn. (hon.), mem. Boston Bar Assn., Mass. Bar Assn., Am. Bar Assn. Episcopalian. Republican. Mason (grand master, Mass., 1941-43; dir. of Grand Lodge since 1942; hon. past grand master, Grand Lodge, Ill.; holder of distinguished service medals, Me., N.H., R.I., Conn.; recd. Henry Price and Paul Revere Medals, Mass.; hon. 33). Royal Order Jesters; Chf. Adept Mass. Coll. Rosicruciana. Clubs: Harvard; Rotary (Cambridge, Mass.). Home: 280 Beacon St., Boston, Mass. Office: Massachusetts Institute of Technology, Cambridge, Mass. Deceased.

SCHAFF, Charles E., ry. official; b. Licking County, O., Feb. 4, 1856; married; children—Howard Ellsworth, Frederic Alan. Held various ry. positions prior to 1893; asst. to pres., 1893-94, asst. gen. mgr., 1894-95, gen. mgr., 1895-1906, v.p. 1906-12, New York Central Lines west of Buffalo; pres. M., K.&.T. Ry. and W. Falls & Northwestern Ry., Apr. 15, 1912-Sept. 26, 1915, receiver same, 1915-23, pres. 1923-26; served as v.p. St. Louis Transfer Ry., Mo. & Ill. Bridge Co., Wiggins Ferry Co., and as dir. Miss. Valley Trust Co., until 1926; pres. M., K. & T. Lines, 1922-26. Home: Hotel Chase. Address: 1779 Railway Exchange, St. Louis. Died Nov. 5, 1945.

SCHAFF, Frederic Alan (shăf), corp. official; b. Nelsonville, O., May 24, 1884; s. Charles Ellsworth and Leila Belle (White) S.; student Culver Mil. Acad., 1900-03; B.S., Purdue U., 1907; m. Mary Lee Brittain, July 23, 1911; children—Jane Lee (Mrs. Albert B. Boardman, 2d), Mary Alan (Mrs. E. Austin Byrne). Pres. and dir. Superheater Co. since 1930; pres. and dir. Am. Throttle Co., Inc., Combustion Pub. Co., Inc.; dir. Furnace Engring. Co., Inc., Furnace Engring. Co. of Del., Lima Locomotive Works, Inc.; chmn. of bd. and dir. Superheater Co., Ltd., Canada, Combustion Engring. Co., Inc., Combustion Engring. Co., Ltd. (Canada), Air Preheater Corp., The Lummus Co.; pres., dir. and chmn. of bd. Hedges-Walsh-Weidner Co., Heine Boiler Co., Raymond Brothers Impact Pulverizer Co. Mem. Sigma Chi. Home: 27 Masterton Rd., Bronxville, N.Y. Office: 60 E. 42d St., New York, N.Y.
Died Feb. 7, 1950; buried in Kensico Cemetery, Valhalla, N.Y.

SCHAFFNER, Robert C. (shăf'nẽr), chmn. bd. A. G. Becker & Co., Inc.; b. Chicago, Ill., July 6, 1876; s. Herman and Rachel M. (Becker) S.; ed. Chicago pub. schs.; m. Frances Stettauer, Oct. 18, 1905. Chmn. A. G. Becker & Co., Inc., Chicago, Ill.; pres. Consol. Dearborn Corp.; dir. Goodyear Tire & Rubber Co., Hammermill Paper Co., Penick & Ford, Ltd., Valley Mould & Iron Corp. Clubs: Tavern, Lake Shore Country, Standard; Mid-Day (New York); Bond Men's of Chicago. Home: 100 Ravine Drive, Highland Park, Ill. Office: 120 S. La Salle St., Chicago 3, Ill. Died Nov. 13, 1946.

SCHALL, John Hubley (shawl), surgeon; b. Phila., Pa., July 23, 1871; s. John Hubley and Mary Wallace (Main) S.; M.D., Hahnemann Med. Coll., 1893; student Carnegie U.; post grad. work Vienna, Heidelberg, Paris and London; m. Nina Dennis, Feb. 18, 1907; 1 son, John Hubley. Physician since 1893, became asst. demonstrator of anatomy, Hahnemann Med. Coll., 1894; house surgeon Cumberland St. Hosp., Brooklyn, 1894-95, Hahnemann Hospital, New York, 1896-97; Hahnemann Hospital, Phila., 1898; visiting surgeon Cumberland St. Hosp., Prospect Heights Hosp., Brooklyn. Fellow Am. Coll. Surgeons, Internat. Coll. of Surgeons; member A.M.A., Kings County Med. Soc., Soc. Colonial Wars. Dir. Lake Wesauking Assn., Bradford County, Pa. Republican. Contbr. to med. jours. Address: 119 St. Marks Av., Brooklyn, N.Y.* Died July 10, 1947.

SCHANFARBER, Tobias (shăn'făr-bẽr), rabbi; b. Cleveland, O., Dec. 20, 1862; s. Aaron and Sarah (Newman) S.; B.A., U. of Cincinnati, 1885; grad. as rabbi, Hebrew Union Coll., Cincinnati, 1886, hon. Dr. Hebrew Laws, 1933; student Johns Hopkins, under Paul Haupt, 1894-99; m. Carrie Phillipson, Oct. 15, 1890. Ordained to ministry, 1886; rabbi, Toledo, O., 1886-87, Ft. Wayne, Ind., 1887-88, Baltimore, Md., 1888-98, Mobile, Ala., 1899-1901, Kehilath Anshe Mayriv, Chicago, 1901-25 (rabbi emeritus). Editor Jewish Comment, and Jewish Chronicle; editor Reform Advocate (Chicago), 1901-02, and Chicago Israelite a number of yrs. Elected hon. pres. for life of Chicago Rabbinical Assn., 1933; corr. sec. Central Conf. Am. Rabbis, 1906-08; mem. Chicago Hebrew Inst., Ill. Vigilance Assn. (v.p.), Nat. Probation League, Nat. Civic Federation. Address: 5044 Drexel Blvd., Chicago, Ill. Died Mar. 4, 1942.

SCHAUB, Howard Churchill, newspaper pub.; b. Charleston, Ill., June 21, 1863; s. William H. and Georgianna (Bishop) S.; spl. student Ill. Coll., Jacksonville, 1887-88; Litt.D., (hon.) James Millikin Univ., June 5, 1945; m. Winifred Weiennett, June 21, 1899; children—Frederick W., Georgianna B. (wife of Rev. Wilder W. Towle), Robert C., Charles M. (dec.), Elizabeth H. (wife of Charles K. Teare). Began as reporter Decatur (Ill.) Review, 1888; pres. Review Pub. Co., 1894-1931; pres. Decatur Newspapers, Inc., since 1931. Food administrator 10th Ill. Dist., World War. Member Board of Decatur Park District 1924-45; made hon. life member. Democrat. Conglist. Club: Decatur. Home: 748 W. North St. Office: 361 N. Main St., Decatur, Ill. Died Dec. 2, 1947.

SCHAUB, Mother Jerome, superior of Ursuline Convent, Paola, Kan.; b. Pittsburgh, Pa., Aug. 24, 1856; d. Andrew and Magdalen (Heil) Schaub; ed. Ursuline Coll., Louisville, Ky., 1874. Music teacher, Louisville, Ky., and Cumberland, Md., 18 years; founded Ursuline Acad., Paola, Kan., 1895, and since continued as head; also head of junior coll. since 1924; superior of convent and directs 9 other schools in Kan. and Okla., taught by her Sisters. Address: Ursuline Convent, Paola, Kan. Died Dec. 18, 1942; buried in Convent Cemetery, Ursuline Coll. of Paola.

SCHEER, Edward Waldemar (shẽr), ry. pres.; b. Zaleski, O., Apr. 28, 1875; s. Charles and Maria Ursala (Rockenbach) S.; ed. pub. schs.; m. Alice Maude Wilkinson, Apr. 28, 1903 (now deceased); children—Georgia Rebecca, Margaret Stewart (Mrs. John F. Harper), Edward Waldemar; married 2d, Freda Harper, November 7, 1943. Was associated with the Baltimore & Ohio Railroad Company, 1890-1932, successively as office boy, messenger, clk., stenographer, chief clk. to div. supt., sec. to v.p. and gen. mgr. B.&O.S.-W. R.R., chief clk. to gen. mgr. of same, asst. sec. and chief clk. to gen. mgr., same to gen. supt., asst. to gen. supt., asst. sec. of line, supt. Ill. and Ind. divs. same, gen. supt. in charge successively of S.W., N.W. and Md. dists., gen. mgr. B.&O. Eastern Lines; v.p. Reading Co., 1932-35, C. R.R. of N.J., 1933-35; pres. Reading Co. and C. R.R. of N.J. since 1935, and chief exec. officer C. R.R. of N.J., 1940-43; president, Pa.-Reading Seashore Lines, ret., 1944; dir. and mem. exec. com. Lehigh & Hudson River Railway Co., and Pa. Co. for Ins. on Lives and Granting Annuities; dir. County Fire Ins. Co. of Philadelphia, John B. Stetson Company. Served in U.S. Army, Spanish-American War. Republican. Methodist. Mason (32°, K.T., Shriner). Clubs: Union League of Phila., Huntingdon Valley Country and Marine. Address: Royal Oak, Md. Died June 16, 1949.

SCHELL, Frank Cresson, artist, editor; b. Philadelphia, May 3, 1857; s. Frank H. and Martha A. (Carr) S.; studied Pa. Acad. Fine Arts; m. Clara V. Saylor, Feb. 18, 1880. Illustrated for mags. and periodicals until 1898; artist and corr. Leslie's Weekly, Spanish-Am. War; art editor Leslie's Weekly, 1898-1903; art editor North American, Phila., 1905, retired Jan. 1925. Exhibited in New York, Chicago, Phila., Buffalo, etc. Mem. Phila. Sketch Club, Musical Arts Club of Phila., Fellowship of Pa. Acad. Fine Arts, Art Alliance of Phila., Fairmont Park Art Assn., City Parks Assn. Home: 14 Simpson Rd., Ardmore, Pa. Died Feb. 23, 1942.

SCHELLING, Felix Emanuel (shĕl'ĭng), educator; b. New Albany, Ind., Sept. 3, 1858; s. Felix and Rose (White) S.; A.B., U. of Pa., 1881, LL.B., 1883, A.M., 1884; Litt.D., U. of Pa., 1903, Princeton, 1934; LL.D., U. of Pa., 1909, Haverford, 1920; m. Caroline Derbyshire, Mar. 7, 1886 (died 1935); children—Dorothea D. (wife of Prof. Joseph Seronde), Felix D.; m. 2d, Gertrude Bueb, 1909. John Welsh Centennial prof. English lit., U. of Pa., 1893-1929, Felix E. Schelling prof. since 1929. Mem. Nat. Inst. Arts and Letters, Am. Philos. Soc., Modern Lang. Assn. America. Author: Literary and Verse Criticism of the Reign of Elizabeth, 1891; Life and Works of George Gascoigne, 1893; A Book of Elizabethan Lyrics, 1896; A Book of Seventeenth Century Lyrics, 1899; The English Chronicle Play, 1902; The Queen's Progress and Other Elizabethan Sketches, 1904; History of Elizabethan Drama, 1908; English Literature During the Lifetime of Shakespeare, 1910; The Restoration Drama, Cambridge History of Literature, 1912; The English Lyric, 1913; A History of English Drama, 1914; Thor and Other War Verses, 1918; Appraisements and Asperities as to Some Contemporary Writers, 1922; Foreign Influences in Elizabethan Plays, 1923; Elizabethan Playwrights, 1925; Shakespeare and "Demi-Science," 1927; Pedagogically Speaking, 1929; Shakespeare Biography, 1927. Editor: Ben Jonson's Discoveries, 1892; Elizabethan Lyrics, 1895; Seventeenth Century Lyrics, 1899; Eastward Ho, and The Alchemist, 1903; The Merchant of Venice, 1903; Macbeth, 1910; Beaumont and Fletcher, 1912; Typical Elizabethan Plays, 1926. Home: Mount Vernon, N.Y. Died Dec. 15, 1945.

SCHENCK, Michael, judge; b. Lincolnton, Lincoln County, N.C., Dec. 11, 1876; s. Judge David and Sallie Wilfong (Ramseur) S.; student U. of N.C., 1893-95; student law dept., 1902-03, LL.D., 1936; m. Rose Few, Nov. 15, 1909; children—Michael, Rosemary Ramseur, Emily Floreid. Admitted to N.C. bar, 1903, and began practice at Greensboro; moved to Hendersonville, N.C., 1905; mayor of Hendersonville, 1907-09; solicitor 18th Jud. Dist., N.C., 1913-18 (resigned to enter army); maj. Judge Advocate Gen.'s Dept., U.S. Army, 1918-19; reelected solicitor but did not accept; judge Superior Court, 18th Jud. Dist. of N.C., 1924-34; asso. justice Supreme Court N.C., 1934-48. Mem. N.C. Constitutional Commn. to redraft Constn. of N.C., 1931. Mem. N.C. bar. assn. (ex-v.p.), Am. Legion. Democrat. Episcopalian; former mem. Bishop's Council Diocese of Western N.C. Mason. Home: Hendersonville, N.C. Address: Raleigh, N.C. Died Nov. 5, 1948.

SCHERER, James Augustin Brown (shẽr'ẽr), educator; b. Salisbury, N.C., May 22, 1870; s. Rev. Simeon and Harriet Isabella (Brown) S.; A.B., (with first honors), Roanoke Coll., Va., 1890, A.M., 1895; Ph.D., Pa. Coll., 1897; LL.D., S.C. Univ., 1905; m. at Kobe, Japan, Bessie Brown, July 5, 1894; children—Isabel Brown, Paul Armand. Instr. in English, Imperial Govt. Sch., Saga, Japan, 1892-97; prof. of history, Luth. Sem., Charleston, S.C., 1898-1904; pres. Newberry (S.C.) Coll., 1904-08. Calif. Inst. of Tech., Pasadena, 1908-20; dir. of Southwest Museum, Los Angeles, 1926-31. Visited chief technical schools of world, 1909, and reorganized "Throop Poly. Inst." into coll. of tech. (trustees placed plaque in Administration Bldg. honoring him for services as first pres., 1941). Secured amendment to Calif. constitution, exempting colleges from taxation, 1913; apptd. del. from Calif. to Anglo-Am. Expn., London, 1914; mem. Calif. Council of Defense, June 1917; mem. Council of Nat. Defense, 1917, and chief of travel service, state councils section; special rep. U.S. Shipping Bd., 1917. Revisited Orient, 1923-24, 1931-36. Lecturer, Garton Foundation, Oxford and Cambridge univs., 1914, on "Economic Causes in Am. Civil War." Mem. Calif. Hist. Soc., Nat. Council of Pacific Relations (New York City), Asiatic Society Japan (life member), Phi Gamma Delta, Phi Beta Kappa. Decorated by Emperor of Japan, 1937, "for valuable services in cause of international peace and friendship," with Order of Sacred Treasure (decoration returned to Japan). Clubs: Scribes, Sunset, University of Los Angeles (honorary); University of Pasadena (hon.); Commonwealth (San Francisco); Pan-Pacific Club, Tuna of Catalina Island (hon.). Author: Four Princes, 1902; Japan To-day, 1904; Young Japan, 1905; The Holy Grail, 1906; What Is Japanese Morality?, 1906; The Japanese Crisis, 1916; Cotton as a World Power, a Study in the Economic Interpretation of History, 1916; The Nation at War, 1918; The Tree of Light, 1921; The First Forty-Niner, 1925; The Romance of Japan, 1926 (pub. in Japan, 1932); Japan—Whither?, 1932; Manchukuo—A Bird's Eye View, 1933; Japan's Advance, 1934; America—Pageants and Personalities, 1934; Pilot and Shogun, a Story of Old Japan, 1935; Three Meiji Leaders, 1936; Japan Defies the World, 1938; "The Lion of the Vigilantes," 1939; Thirty-first Star, 1942; "Bombed Tokio 40 Times" over sta. KGEI, 1942. Address: 820 3d St., Apt. 4, Santa Monica, Calif. Died Feb. 15, 1944.

SCHERMERHORN, James (skẽr'mẽr-hôrn), editor; b. Hudson, Mich., Mar. 13, 1865; s. William Ten Broeck and Jane Adelaide (Terry) S.; ed. pub. schs. and printing office; learned printing and newspaper trade under father in the office of the Hudson Gazette; prepared for U.S. Mil. Acad. at Oberlin Coll., 1884; cadet U.S. Mil. Acad., 1885, 1886, resigning to take charge of Hudson Gazette; elected orator and historian, Class of 1889; m. Adaline M. Jenkins, July 13, 1891 (died May 16, 1915); children—Gretchen (Mrs. Harry E. Kinney), James, Katrina (Mrs. George C. Forman), Helen Christine (Mrs. Otto P. Dallavo). Pub. Hudson Gazette, 1886-95; reporter, then Washington corr., Detroit News, 1895-96; editorial writer, then political editor, Detroit Free Press, 1896-1900; established Detroit Times (first called Detroit Today), 1900, and was pres. and gen. manager 21 yrs. Addressed conventions and clubs in U.S. and Europe as to the advanced editorial and advertising policies of The Times and on current issues; holds that publishers should not accept public office or have business or social ties that interfere with editorial independence. Now engaged in traveling, writing and after dinner and radio speaking. Ex-pres. Mich. Press Assn.; hon. mem. Nat. Exchange, Mich. Assn. of Chicago; mem. Assn. of Graduates of U.S. Mil. Acad., West Point. Democrat. Conglist. Author: Advertising, the Light that Saves and Serves, 1914; Testing the Beatitudes—An Adventure in Twentieth Century Journalism, 1915; Schermerhorn's Stories, 1928; Schermerhorn's Speeches, 1930; also various brochures, magazine articles, etc. Died Dec. 2. 1941

SCHERMERHORN, William David, clergyman, educator; b. Lincoln, Kan., Oct. 23, 1871; s. Frank Alonzo and Mary (Myers) S.; A.B., Kan. Wesleyan Univ., 1899; S.T.B., Garrett Bibl. Inst., 1904; M.A., U. of Chicago, 1914; D.D., Kan. Wesleyan, 1909, Garrett, 1917; LL.D., Dakota Wesleyan, 1924; m. May D. Hoffman, May 29, 1900; children—Richard Alonzo, Charles Vincent (deceased), Miriam Julia (deceased). Ordained M.E. ministry, 1899; pastor Lincoln, Kan., 1899-1901, Chicago, 1901-04, Wilson, Kan., 1904-05; missionary in India, 1905-10; prof. English Bible, Kan. Wesleyan U., 1911-12; asst. prof. N.T., interpretation, Garrett Bibl. Inst., 1912-17; pres. Dakota Wesleyan, S.D., 1917-22; head dept. church history and missions Garrett Bibl. Inst., 1922-39; retired Sept. 1939; lecturer on missions, Northwestern Univ., 1922-27; visiting prof. history of the early church, U. of Chicago, summer 1927. Sent to Orient on study trip by Am. Soc. of Ch. History, Sept. 1931-Mar. 1932. Mem. Soc. Bibl. Research, Am. Ch. History Assn. Mason. Author: Beginnings of the Christian Church, 1929; The Christian Mission in the Modern World, 1933. Home: 2128 Maple Av., Evanston, Ill. Died Apr. 19, 1942.

SCHEVILL, Rudolph (shĕ-vĭl'), prof. Spanish; b. Cincinnati, June 18, 1874; s. Ferdinand August and Johanna (Hartmann) S.; B.A., Yale, 1896; Ph.D., U. of Munich, 1898; Sorbonne, Paris, Collège de France, and Universidad Central, Madrid; m. Margaret Erwin, May 22, 1912; children—Erwin (dec.), Karl Erwin, James S. Erwin; m. 2d, Isabel Magaña, June 4, 1939. Instr. in French and German, Bucknell U., Lewisburg, Pa., 1899-1900; instr. in German, Sheffield Scientific Sch., Yale, 1900-01; instr. in French and Spanish and asst. prof. Spanish, Yale, 1901-10; prof. Spanish, U. of Calif., since 1910. Mem. Hispanic Soc. America (New York), Phi Beta Kappa (Yale); corr. mem. Spanish Acad., Acad. Hist., Acad. Polit. and Moral Sciences, Acad. Buenas Letras, Barcelona; mem. Hispano-Am. Acad. of Cádiz; fellow Am. Acad. Arts and Sciences, Modern Language Assn. America (president 1943). Clubs: Athenian (Oakland, Calif.); Faculty (Berkeley). Contbr. of articles on Spanish lit. Co-editor new edit. Complete Works of Cervantes, 18 vols., Madrid, 1914-42; The Dramatic Art of Lope de Vega, 1918; Life of Cervantes, 1919; The Dramatic Works of Luis Vélez de Guevara, 1937. Awarded Medal of Arts and Literature of the Hispanic Soc. America (N.Y.), 1942. Address: 1824 Arch St., Berkeley 4, Calif. Deceased.

SCHICK, Herman John, clergyman; b. Milltown, N.J., Aug. 30, 1878; s. Gottlob Benjamin and Caroline (Knausenberger) S.; studied Elmhurst (Ill.) Coll., 1893-97, Eden Theol. Sem., St. Louis, 1897-1900, McCormick Theol. Sem., 1903, U. of Chicago, 1921, 22, A.M., 1922; B.D., McCormick, 1923; S.T.D., Temple U., Phila., 1925; m. Louise M. Wagner, June 2, 1903; children—Vernon Wagner, Armin Frederick, Dorothy Louise. Ordained ministry Evangelical Synod of North America, 1900; pastor Sandwich, Ill., 1900-02, Bensenville, Ill., 1903-09, Evansville, Ind., 1909-19; pres. Elmhurst Coll., 1919-24; pastor Immanuel Evang. and Reformed Ch., Chicago, 1924-44. Co-editor of Evang. Book of Worship; Pastor's Pocket Manual; also of Little Prayers for Little Children, The Way of Life, In Loving Memory, Afterwards, Jesus of the Twentieth Century. Home: 8424 Ingleside Av., Chicago, Ill. Died Dec. 8, 1949.

SCHINZ, Albert, univ. prof.; b. Neuchâtel, Switzerland, Mar. 9, 1870; s. Charles Emile and Ida (Diethelm) S.; A.B., U. of Neuchâtel, 1888, A.M., 1889; U. of Berlin, 1892-93; Ph.D., Tübingen, 1894; U. of Paris, 1894-96; officier d'Académie, 1906; L.H.D., 1928; Litt.D., 1940. Instr. philosophy, U. of Neuchâtel, 1896-97; came to America, traveled and attended Clark U., 1897-98; instr. French, U. of Minn., 1898-99; prof. of French lit., Bryn Mawr Coll., 1899-1913; prof. French lit., Smith Coll., 1913-28; prof. French, U. of Pa., 1928-41, prof. emeritus since 1941. Visiting prof., Johns Hopkins U., 1928-29, Columbia U., 1939-40, Ind. Univ., U. of Tex., 1941-42. Author: Anti-Pragmatism, or Intellectual Aristocracy Versus Social Democracy, 1909; J. J. Rousseau, a Forerunner of Pragmatism, 1909; Accent dans l'écriture française, 1912; La question du Contrat Social, 1913; J. J. Rousseau et Michel Rey, 1916; French Literature of the Great War, 1919; Pensée religieuse de Rousseau et ses récents interprètes, 1927; Jean-Jacques Rousseau, interprétation nouvelle, 1929; Etat présent des études Rousseauistes, 1941. Editor: XVII Century French Texts; XVIII Century French Texts; XIX Century French Texts; Nouvelle Anthologie française; Jean J. Rousseau, Vie et Oeuvres; Victor Hugo, Selected Poems; also editor selections from Maupassant, Mérimée, Gautier, Laboulaye, etc. Contbr. to scientific revs. and to mags. and papers, Europe and America. Mem. Modern Lang. Assn. America, Soc. Hist. Lit. de France, Soc. J. J. Rousseau, Phi Beta Kappa, Gamma Mu, Pi Delta Phi; mem. Legion of Honor (France). Address: care French Dept., University of Pennsylvania, Philadelphia, Pa. Died Dec. 19, 1943.

SCHLESINGER, Frank (slĕs'ĭn-jẽr), astronomer; b. New York, May 11, 1871; s. William Joseph and Mary (Wagner) S.; B.S., Coll. City of New York, 1890; M.A., Columbia, 1897, Ph.D., 1898; Sc.D., U. of Pittsburgh, 1920; Sc.D., Cambridge, 1925. In charge Internat. Latitude Obs., Ukiah, Calif., 1899-1903; astronomer Yerkes Obs., under auspices of Carnegie Instn., 1903-05; dir. Allegheny Obs. (U. of Pittsburgh), 1905-20; dir. Yale Univ. Obs., 1920-41; dir. emeritus since July 1, 1941. Fellow A.A.A.S. (past chmn. Sect. A), Am. Acad. Arts and Sciences; mem. Nat. Acad. Sciences, Am. Philos. Soc., Am. Astron. Soc. (past pres.), Internat. Astron. Union (past pres.), Phi Beta Kappa, Sigma Xi; hon. asso. Royal Astron. Soc. Can.; fgn. asso. Royal Astron. Soc. of London; hon. mem. Mexican Astron. Soc., Italian Soc. of Spectroscopists; corr. mem. French Acad. Sciences, French Bureau de Longitudes, Swedish Acad. Scis. Awarded Valz medal, French Acad. Sciences, 1926; gold medal, Royal Astron. Soc., 1927; Bruce gold medal, Astron. Soc. of Pacific, 1929; Officer Legion of Honor (France), 1935; Townshend medal, College of City of N.Y., 1935. Collaborating editor Astrophys. Journal. Author of 200 monographs in scientific journals on reduction of photographic plates, stellar parallaxes, variations of latitude, spectroscopic binaries. Home: Lyme, Conn. Died July 10, 1943.

SCHLESINGER, Louis, real estate, insurance; b. Newark, N.J., Dec. 16, 1865; s. Alexander and Fanny (Fleischer) S.; ed. pub. schs. of Newark; m. Sophie Levy, Oct. 8, 1890 (died May 19, 1937); children—Alexander L. (dec.), Joel L. Began as office boy, Brown & Volk, real estate, Newark, 1880; in real estate and insurance business since 1890; pres. Louis Schlesinger, Inc., since 1911; pres. Schlesinger-Heller Agency; director United States Trust Company; secretary-treasurer Union Bldg. Company, 1904-28. Nat. chmn. state bd. dirs. Nat. Farm Sch., Bucks County, Pa. Organizer Newark Real Estate Bd.; past pres. N.J. Assn. Real Estate Bds.; mem. N.Y. Real Estate Bd.; mem. exec. bd. Union of Am. Hebrew Congregations since 1913; mem. admission com. Jewish Children's Home, Newark; mem. Congregation B'nai Jeshurun (Reformed Hebrew). Mason (Shriner). Clubs: Mountain Ridge Country of West Caldwell, N.J. (charter mem.); Newark Athletic, Downtown (Newark); Advertising (New York). Has made collection of theatre programs since 1879. Home: 45 Beverly Rd., West Orange, N.J. Office: 31 Clinton St., Newark, N.J. Died Sep. 15, 1942.

SCHLEY, Kenneth Baker; b. New York, Nov. 19, 1881; s. Grant B. and Elizabeth (Baker) S.; Ph.B., Yale, 1902; m. Ellen H. Rogers, June 11, 1912; children—Anne Caroline, Kenneth Baker. Mem. firm of Moore & Schley, bankers, New York; v.p., dir. Electric Storage Battery Co.; mem. exec. com. and dir. Telautograph Co.; dir. Underwood-Elliott-Fisher Co., Howe Sound Co., Permutit Co., etc. Republican. Unitarian. Clubs: Knickerbocker, The Links, Yale, New York Athletic, Racquet and Tennis. Home: Far Hills, N.J. Office: 100 Broadway, New York, N.Y. Died June 12, 1944.

SCHLING, Max, horticulturist; b. Austria, Mar. 1, 1874; educated public and private schools and horticultural night school and college, Vienna; m. Louise Schling, June 5, 1904; children—Elizabeth, Max. Came to U.S., 1899, naturalized citizen, 1906. Began as retail florist, N.Y. City, 1901; now pres. Max Schling, Inc.; pres. Max Schling Seedsman, Inc. Chmn. Horticultural Assn., N.Y. Botanical Garden. Mem. Soc. Am. Florists and Ornamental Horticulturists, Rose Soc. Am., Am. Dahlia Soc., Orchid Soc. America, Canadian Gardeners Assn., Metropolitan Retail Florists, Hort. Soc. N.Y., Hort. Soc. Mass., Merchants Assn. New York, Fifth Ave. Assn. New York, Florists Telegraph Delivery Assn., Pi Alpha Xi (hon. mem. Alpha Chapter, Cornell U.); fellow Am. Hort. Legion of Honor (chmn.). Founder Max Schling's Students' Loan Fund, Cornell, 1926. Republican. Mason. Club: Westchester Country (Rye, N.Y.), Rotary. Home: 14 E. 75th St. Office: Savoy-Plaza, New York, N.Y. Died Feb. 12, 1943.

SCHLUTZ, Frederic William (shlo͞otz), pediatrist; b. Greene, Ia., Nov. 10, 1880; s. Rev. Henry and Augusta (Lemann) S.; A.B., Wartburg Coll., Clinton, Ia., 1898; M.D., U. of Maryland, 1902; M.S., U. of Minn., 1936; studied in Berlin, Strassburg, London, Kiel, Paris and at Harvard; m. Emma M. Handke, June 14, 1905; 1 dau., Margaret (wife of Dr. Harry A. Tinker). Instr. in biochemistry, U. of Minn., 1910-12; teacher of pediatrics, U. of Minn., 1912-24, prof. and head of dept., 1924-30; prof. pediatrics and head of dept., U. of Chicago, since Apr. 1, 1930. Asst. to med. chief Base Hosp. 12th Div., Camp Devens, 1918. Mem. A.M.A., Am. Pediatric Soc., Am. Acad. of Pediatrics, Am. Biochem. Soc., Soc. for Exptl. Biology and Medicine, Pan Am. Union (exec. com.), Soc. for Pediatric Research (hon.); hon. mem. Argentine, Uruguay, Colombia, Cuban and Mexican pediatric societies. Clubs: University, Quadrangle (Chicago). Home: 5838 Stony Island Av., Chicago, Ill. Died Mar. 8, 1944.

SCHMEDEMAN, Albert George (shmē'dē-măn), ex-gov.; b. Madison, Wis., Nov. 25, 1864; s. Henry and Wilhelmine (Camien) S.; ed. pub. schs. and commercial coll.; m. Kate M. Regan, June 1, 1892; children—Katharine, Albert George. Mem. Common Council, Madison, 1903-07; E.E. and M.P. to Norway, 1913-21; del. to represent U.S. at Internat. Conf. on Spitzbergen, 1914; mayor of Madison, 1925-32; Dem. candidate for gov. of Wis., 1928; gov. of Wis., 1933-35; state dir. Federal Housing Adminstrn., Wis., 1935-42, now retired. Episcopalian. Mason. Club: Madison (Madison, Wis.). Home: 504 Wisconsin Av., Madison, Wis. Died Nov. 26. 1946.

SCHMIDT, Carl Louis August, coll. prof.; b. Brown County, S.D., Mar. 7, 1885; s. Gustav and Fridericke (Unverzagt) S.; B.S., U. of Calif., 1908, M.S., 1910, Ph.D., 1916; m. Esther May Skolfield, Apr. 11, 1914; children—Stanwood Skolfield, Alfred Carl, Esther Fredericka. Chemist gas company, San Francisco, 1908-09; expert chemist Referee Board, U.S. Dept. Agr., 1909-12; bacteriologist and chemist City of Berkeley, 1912-14; research asst. in physiology, U. of Calif., 1915-17, asst. prof. biochemistry, 1918-20, asso. prof., 1921-23, prof. since 1924, dean Coll. of Pharmacy, 1937-44; acting dean of the Med. School, 1939; cons. tech. advisor Western Regional Research Lab. since 1941; cons. bio-chemist Southern Pacific Gen. Hosp.; mem. commn. A, com. on aviation medicine, com. on chemistry of proteins, Nat. Research Council. Awarded Carl Schurz fellowship, 1932. Mem. Am. Chem. Soc., Am. Soc. Biol. Chemists, Soc. Exptl. Biology and Medicine, Calif. Acad. of Medicine, Western Society of Naturalists, Kerr Medical Club, Pacific Coast R.R. Surgeons, Sigma Xi. Club: Faculty (U. of Calif.). Author: Fundamentals of Biochemistry (with F. W. Allen), 1938; The Chemistry of the Amino Acids and Proteins, 1938, 44. Mem. editorial com. Annual Review of Biochemistry since 1932; pres. Annual Reviews Inc. Mem. U.S. Pharmacopoeia revision com., 1940-50. Home: 2612 Piedmont Av. (4). Office: 1557 Life Sciences Bldg., Univ. of Calif., Berkeley, Calif. Died Feb. 23, 1946.

SCHMIDT, Edward Charles, mech. engr.; b. Jersey City, N.J., May 14, 1874; s. John Frederick and Katharine (Bisbord) S.; M.E., Stevens Inst. Tech., Hoboken, N.J., 1895; m. Violet Delille Jayne, June 15, 1904; 1 dau., Katharine. In employ of Kalbfleisch Chem. Co., New York and Buffalo, 1895-96; with C. W. Hunt Co., New York, 6 mos., 1896; in steam dept., as asst. to mech. engr., Edison Electric Illuminating Co., Brooklyn, 1897; with Am. Stoker Co., New York, 6 mos., 1898; instr. in machine design, later instr. and asst. prof. ry. engring. and experimental engring., U. of Ill., 1898-1903 (made many tests with 2 ry. dynamometer cars owned by U. of Ill., I.C. R.R. and C.,C.,C.&St.L. Ry.); asst. engr. Am. Hoist & Derrick Co., St. Paul, Minn., 1903-04; engr. of tests, Kerr Turbine Co., Wellsville, N.Y., 1904-06; asso. prof. and prof. ry. engring., U. of Ill., July 1, 1906-Apr. 12, 1919. Commd. maj., Ordnance Dept. U.S. Army, Aug. 11, 1917; served in N.Y. Dist. Ordnance Office, and on detached service in U.S. Fuel Adminstrn. and U.S. R.R. Adminstrn.; discharged, July 16, 1919. Mech. engr. North American Co., New York, 1919-21; prof. ry. engring. and head of dept., U. of Ill., 1921-40, prof. ry. engring. emeritus since

Sept. 1, 1940. Mem. Am. Soc. M.E., mech. div. of Am. Ry. Assn., Western Ry. Club, Ry. Fuel and Traveling Engrs. Assn., Soc. Promotion Engring. Edn., Tau Beta Pi, Sigma Xi, etc. Club: University. Author of numerous articles, reports, etc., in the tech. press and trans. tech. socs. Home: 1 University Pl., Apt. 19C, New York, N.Y. Died Mar. 21, 1942.

SCHMIDT, Francis Albert, football coach; b. Downs, Kan., Dec. 3, 1885; s. Francis Walter and Emma Katherine (Mohrbacher) S.; LL.B., U. of Neb., 1907; m. Evelyn Keesce, June 9, 1926. Admitted to Neb. bar, 1907; practiced in Neb. and Kan., 1907-10; coach of athletic sports in Arkansas City, Kan., to 1915; dir. of athletics and athletics coach, Kendall Coll., 1915-19, U. of Tulsa, 1920-21, U. of Ark., 1922-28; head football and basketball coach, Texas Christian U., 1929-33; head football coach, Ohio State U., 1934-40; head football coach, U. of Idaho, since 1941. Served capt. 347th Inf., 87th Div., U.S. Army, 1917-19; with A.E.F., 12 months; head bayonet instr. for 87th Div.; also capt. 50th Inf. Regular Army. Formerly mem. Nat. Basketball Com. of U.S. and Canada. Mem. Am. Football Coaches Assn., Am. Legion, Sigma Alpha Epsilon, Phi Delta Phi, Theta Nu Epsilon. Mason (K.T., 32°, Shriner), Elk. Mem. Rotary Internat. Home: 605 Moore Av., Moscow, Idaho. Died Sep. 19, 1944.

SCHMIDT, Friedrich Georg Gottlob, univ. prof.; b. Untermagerbein, Bavaria, Nov. 17, 1868; s. Rev. Ernst and Sophia (Horn) S.; U. of Erlangen, Bavaria, 1888-90; came to U.S., Sept. 1890; student in philology, 1893-96, univ. scholar, 1894-95, fellow, 1895-96, Ph.D., 1896, Johns Hopkins; m. Elizabeth Heymer, July 9, 1904 (dec.). Acting prof. German, Cornell Coll., 1896-97; taught several yrs. in different parts of U.S.; traveled extensively; head and prof. German lang. and lit., U. of Ore., 1897-1939 (retired). Mem. Modern Lang. Assn. America, Assn. of Am. Univ. Profs., Verein für bayerische Volkskunde und Mundartforschung. Author: Die Rieser Mundart, Munich, 1897; Berühmte Deutsche neuerer Zeit, 1928. Editor (with introduction and notes) Von Wildenbruch's Das edle Blut, 1898; Von Wildenbruch's Der Letzte, 1899; Sudermann's Johannes, 1900; Le Verre d'Eau, par Scribe; Dahn's Sigwalt und Sigridh, 1900; Münchhausen's Reisen und Abenteuer, 1906; Sudermann's Heimat, 1909, 1938; Meyr's Ludwig und Annemarie, 1913. Transl. of Goethe's Faust into English prose (Leipzig), 1935; Tieck's Der blonde Eckbert und Die schöne Magelone, 1940. Contbr. to scientific jours. in Europe and America. Home: Eugene, Ore. Died Apr. 24, 1945.

SCHNEIDER, Adolph Benedict (shnī'dēr), physician; b. Dunkirk, N.Y., Dec. 31, 1866; s. Benedict and Anna Marie (Abrecht) S.; ed. pub. schs.; M.D., Cleveland Med. Coll., 1894; post-grad. work, New York, Berlin and Vienna; m. Ila Belle Roberts, Dec. 12, 1906; children—Mary, Adolph Benedict. Practiced, Cleveland, 1894; demonstrator anatomy, 1894-98, prof. anatomy, Cleveland Med. Coll., 1898-1904, prof. clin. medicine, 1904-15; now dir. of med., Cleveland Homeopathic and Huron Road Hosps. Conglist. Mem. Am. Inst. Homeopathy, Ohio State Homeo. Soc., A.M.A. Home: 1940 E. 89th St. Office: 9400 Euclid Av., Cleveland, Ohio. Died Sep. 3, 1946.

SCHNEIDER, Frederick William, clergyman; b. Boonville, Warwick County, Ind., Dec. 28, 1862; s. Charles and Philippine (Hepp) S.; B.A., German Wallace Coll., Berea, O., 1886, M.A., 1888; B.D., Drew Theol. Sem., 1899; D.D., Baldwin U., 1906; LL.D., Morningside College, 1936; m. Mary Anna Severinghaus, 1890; children—Herbert Wallace, Ruben Percival; m. 2d, Emma Josephine Freyhofer, Aug. 15, 1899. Teacher German Wallace Coll., 1886-94; pastor M.E. Ch., Delaware, O., 1894-95, Pittsburgh, Pa., 1895-96; mem. faculty German Wallace Coll., 1897-1909; pastor Brooklyn, N.Y., 1909-14; with Bd. of Sunday Schools, M.E. Ch., 1914-18; editorial work, Cincinnati, 1918-20; v.p. and prof. Bible and religion, Morningside Coll., Sioux City, Iowa, 1920-36, retired. Member Soc. Bibl. Lit. and Exegesis, Pi Gamma Mu. Republican. Author: System der christlichen Lehre, 1908. Translator: The Christian Life (Paulus), 1892; The Bible the Word of God (Bettex), 1904. Home: 444 Evergreen Av., East Lansing, Mich. Died Dec. 18, 1941.

SCHOELLKOPF, Alfred Hugo (shĕl'kŏpf), b. Buffalo, N.Y., July 12, 1893; s. C. P. Hugo and Emily (Annette) S.; grad. Lafayette High Sch., Buffalo, 1909; grad. Phillips Acad., Andover, Mass., 1911; student Mass. Inst. Tech., 1915; m. Virginia Pardridge, Feb. 24, 1916; children—Annette, Joan. Vice-pres. The Niagra Falls Power Co., 1920-26, gen. mgr., 1925-26; v.p. Buffalo Niagara & Eastern Power Corp., 1925-29, pres., 1929-33, now dir. and v.p.; chmn. bd. N.Y. Power & Light Corp.; pres. Niagara-Sprayer & Chem. Co., Niagara Hudson Power Corp.; dir. Hudson Valley Fuel Corp., Lockport & Newfane Power & Water Supply Co., Niagara Junction Ry. Co. Mem. Chamber of Commerce of State of N.Y. Chmn. bd. N.Y. State Bd. of Social Welfare; pres. Welfare Council of New York; alumni mem. Mass. Inst. Tech. Corp.; mem. Acad. Polit. Science, Adirondack League Club, Delta Kappa Epsilon. Mason. Clubs: River Club, Century Association, Recess, Leash (New York); Saturn (Buffalo); Ft. Orange (Albany); Country (Norfolk, Conn.). Home: 136 E. 79th St. Office: 15 Broad St., New York, N.Y. Died Sep. 9, 1942.

SCHOELLKOPF, Jacob F., mfr. aniline colors; b. Buffalo, N.Y., Feb. 27, 1858; s. Jacob F. and Christiana (Duerr) S.; prep. edn., St. Joseph's Coll., Buffalo; student poly. schs., Stuttgart and Munich, Germany, 1873-79; m. Wilma Spring, Mar. 31, 1882. Began in aniline business at Buffalo, 1880; inc., 1900, as Schoellkopf Aniline & Chem. Works, merged with Nat. Aniline & Chem. Co., Inc., 1917; retired from this company, Mar. 1918. Pioneer in aniline color industry in the U.S. Became connected, 1900, with Hydraulic Power Co., Niagara Falls, merged with Niagara Falls Power Co., 1917; chmn. bd. Schoellkopf, Hutton & Pomeroy, Buffalo. Trustee Univ. of Buffalo, Buffalo Foundation, Buffalo. Republican. Clubs: Buffalo, Buffalo Athletic, Wanakak Country. Home: Lake View, Erie County, N.Y. Office: 70 Niagara St., Buffalo, N.Y. Died Sep. 9, 1942.

SCHOELLKOPF, Paul Arthur (shawl'kôf), pres. Niagara Falls Power Co.; b. Niagara Falls, N.Y., Mar. 7, 1884; s. Arthur and Jessie (Gluck) S.; B.A., Cornell U., 1906; m. Mattie Irwin Penn, Aug. 16, 1911; children—Jasmine, Paul A. Engaged with father in power development at Niagara Falls; president Niagara Falls Power Co. since 1919, director; chairman board and director Power City Trust Co., Buffalo Niagara & Eastern Power Corp.; president and dir. Gluck Realty Co., Lewiston Heights Co., Pine Av. Corp.; dir. Canadian Niagara Power Co., Ltd., Lower Niagara River Power & Water Supply Co., Lockport and Newfane Power & Water Supply Co., Niagara Junction Ry. Co., and numerous other cos. Mem. N.Y. State War Council. Dir. Falls Memorial Hosp., Y.M.C.A., Buffalo Museum Natural Science. Trustee Cornell Univ. Vice chmn. Niagara Frontier State Park Commn.; vice-pres. Niagara Frontier Authority. Mem. Niagara Falls Chamber of Commerce, Zeta Psi. Clubs: Niagara, Cornell, Bath, Niagara Falls Country; Buffalo, Country (Buffalo); Broad Street, Cornell (N.Y.). Home: Lewiston Hts., Niagara Falls. Office: Niagara Falls Power Co., Niagara Falls, N.Y. Died Sep. 30, 1947.

SCHOFIELD, Frank Herman, naval officer; b. Jerusalem, N.Y., Jan. 4, 1869; grad. U.S. Naval Acad., 1890; m. Clara Isabel Cox, July 1, 1893; 1 son, Franklin Perry (U.S. Naval Reserve). Commissioned ensign, July 1, 1892; advanced through grades to rear admiral, Feb. 4, 1924. Exec. officer, Hawk, Spanish-Am. War, 1898; duty with Bur. of Ordnance, Navy Dept., 1905-07; comd. Supply, 1907-09, Concord, 1909; exec. officer New Hampshire, 1909-11; at Naval War Coll., 1911-13; exec. officer Arkansas, 1913-14; comd. Isla de Luzon, 1914; exec. officer Delaware, 1914-15; comd. Chester, 1915-16; assigned duty Office Chief of Naval Operations, May 10, 1916; staff of comdr. U.S. Naval forces in Europe, Dec. 1917-Dec. 1918; U.S. naval advisory staff to Peace Commn., Paris, Dec. 1918-May 1919; made comdr. U.S.S. Texas, July 1919; mem. Gen. Bd., Navy Dept., 1921-23; comdr. Destroyer Squadrons, Battle Fleet, 1924-26; head of War Plans Div., Office of Chief of Naval Operations, 1926-29; mem. Naval Advisory Staff, Geneva Conf., 1927; apptd. comdr. Battleship Div., June 1929; comdr. Battle Fleet, 1930; comdr. in chief U.S. Fleet, 1931; retired, Feb. 1, 1933. Address: Navy Dept., Washington, D.C. Died Feb. 20, 1942.

SCHOFIELD, Mary Lyon Cheney; b. New Britain, Conn., Dec. 24, 1868; d. Edwin Bradbury (M.D.) and Charlotte (Ward) Lyon; student Wellesley Coll., 1888-90; hon. M.A., U. of N.H., 1929; m. Charles Paine Cheney, Apr. 27, 1893 (died Feb. 3, 1897); m. 2d, William Henry Schofield, Sept. 4, 1907 (died June 24, 1920). Chmn. for N.H. of Woman's Dept. of Nat. Civic Federation, 1916-19; chmn. N.H. Woman's Liberty Loan Com.; nat. pres. Women's Land Army of America, 1917-19; mem. Woman's Com. Council Nat. Defense, 1917-19; established 1st nursery sch. in northern New England, 1925. Trustee N.H. Sch. for Feeble-Minded, 1919-24; 1st chmn. N.H. Republican Women's Com., 1919; del.-at-large Rep. Nat. Conv., 1924; 1st woman pres. N.H. Electoral Coll., 1924; F.I.D.A.C. nat. chmn. Am. Legion Auxiliary, 1927; hon. pres. for N.H. of Am. Assn. Univ. Women, 1930; pres. N.H. Soc. of Colonial Dames of America, 1932-35; N.H. chmn. Women's Com., Washington Nat. Cathedral, 1930-37; N.H. chmn. Women's Participation, New York World's Fair, 1939; nat. v.p. Soc. Colonial Dames of America, 1939-41; regional chmn. United Service Orgn. for Nat. Defense, 1941. Episcopalian; mem. 3d Order of St. Anne. Donor Commons of Brantwood Camp for Boys, 1905; All Saints Ch. and Parish House and Rectory, Peterborough, 1917-25. Clubs: Colony (New York); Chilton, Boston; Sulgrave (Washington). Home: "Beside Still Waters," Peterborough, N.H., and Le Manoir, Dorval, P.Q., Can. Died Jan. 10, 1943.

SCHOLZ, Emil Maurice (shōlz), editor, pub.; b. Chicago, Ill., Dec. 25, 1881; s. Carl and Ottilie (Seibt) S.; student Lewis Inst., Chicago, 1899-1902, U. of Pa., 1907-10; m. Marion Evelyn Reis, Sept. 9, 1933 (divorced 1937); m. 2d, Nan Traveline, Oct. 27, 1938. Asst. mgr. Philadelphia Press, 1905-10, Chicago Herald, 1910; gen. mgr. Pittsburgh Post, 1911-13; pub. and part owner, New York Evening Post, 1913-19; Am. editor Trans-Pacific Mag., 1919-21, and rep. Shunpao (Shanghai Chinese Daily News), 1920-24, and other foreign publs.; pres. World Wide Adv. Corp.; mng. dir. World Wide News Assn. Capt. O.R.C., Motor Transport Div., 1918-35; chief of administrative div., transportation service, General Headquarters. War Plans Div. Member Committee on Public Information for N.Y. War Fund, 1943-44 and Red Cross War Fund for Greater N.Y., 1943-45. Fellow Am. Geog. Soc., Royal Economic Soc.; Soc of the Silurians; Soc. of Am. Wars. Democrat. Luth. Mason. Clubs: New York Athletic (New York); Univ. of Pa. (Phila); Nat. Press (Washington). Hon. trustee Boys' Club, New York, 1918-33. Home: 100 W. 55th St. Office: 11 W. 42nd St., New York. Died Jan. 31, 1948.

SCHOONMAKER, Frederic Palen (shōōn'mā-kēr), judge; b. Limestone, Cattaraugus County, N.Y., Mar. 11, 1870; s. Elijah R. and Eliza (Palen) S.; student, Alfred U.; A.B., Cornell U., 1891; LL.D., Alfred, 1917; studied law under Judge James Schoonmaker, of St. Paul, Minn., and Col. W. W. Brown, of Bradford, Pa.; m. Jessie L. Brown, June 23, 1892 (died 1921); children—Susie Rae (Mrs. Walter G. Blaisdell), Fay Lillian (Mrs. Laurent Erny), Max Van Palen; m. 2d, Virginia Elliott Taylor, Dec. 23, 1937. Mem. Brown & Schoonmaker, of Bradford, Pa., 1894-1913, then Brown, Schoonmaker & Nash; became judge of U.S. Dist. Court, Western Dist. of Pa., Jan. 2, 1923. Joined Pa. Nat. Guard, 1912; capt. 16th Regt., Mexican border service, 1916-17; entered U.S. service, 1917, with regt. as 112th Inf., 28th Div., A.E.F., also served as asst. chief of staff G-2, 28th Div. and 92d Div., A.E.F.; detached duty with Army Gen. Staff, Langres, France, also with 2d Can. Div., B.E.F.; hon. discharged Feb. 1919, as lt. col. inf. Mem. Psi Upsilon, Phi Beta Kappa. Mason, Odd Fellow, Elk. Republican. Baptist. Clubs: Bradford, University, Athletic (Pittsburgh, Pa.); Psi Upsilon (New York). Home: Bradford, Pa. Died Sep. 6, 1945.

SCHRADER, Frank Charles (shrā'dēr), geologist; b. Sterling, Ill., Oct. 6, 1860; s. Christian C. and Angeline Marie (Piepo) S.; B.S., M.S., U. of Kan., 1891; A.B., Harvard, 1893, A.M., 1894; m. Kathrine Batwell, Nov. 19, 1919. Teacher of geology, Harvard, 1895-96; geologist U.S. Geol. Survey, 1896-1932; retired at age 72 on account age limit; since 1932 has done 5 years of scientific work; completed gratis the U.S. Geol. Survey report on mining dists. in the Carson Sink Region, Nev.; specialized in mining geology; has traveled widely on professional work in nearly all parts of Alaska and the U.S. Fellow Geol. Soc. Am.; mem. Am. Inst. Mining and Metall. Engrs., Nat. Geog. Soc., Am. Forestry Assn., Washington Acad. Sciences, A.A.A.S., Mining and Metall. Soc. America (mem. sub-com. on antimony), Soc. Econ. Geologists, Geol. and Mineral. societies, Washington Petrologists Club, Pick and Hammer Club, Mineral. Soc. of America. Clubs: Cosmos, Midriver. Contbr. to Reports U.S. Geol. Survey on ore deposits of Western States and Alaska; also articles to geog. mags. Has been chief examiner of mining properties and chief witness in important mining cases in the federal courts in many cities of U.S. Home: 20 Old Chester Rd., Bethesda, Md. Died Feb. 1944.

SCHRADER, Frederick Franklin, journalist, dramatist; b. Hamburg, Germany, Oct. 27, 1857; s. George Frederick and Sophia Maria (Hennecke) S. (Am. citizens); came to U.S. with parents, July 28, 1869; ed. in Hamburg and U.S.; m. Anna McNulty, June 6, 1879 (died Feb. 16, 1894; m. 2d, Marie R. Bailey, Nov. 6, 1895. Mng. editor Denver Republican, 1879-81, St. Joseph Herald, 1882-84; mgr. Tootle's Opera House, St. Joseph, Mo., 1884-85, Pope's Theater, St. Louis, 1885-86; sec. St. Joseph Bd. of Trade, 1886-91; Washington corr. St. Louis Globe-Democrat, 1891; polit. writer Washington Post, 1894-96; asst. and acting sec. Rep. Congl. Com. (nat.), 1896-1900, compiler and editor Rep. Campaign Text Book for 1898; dramatic critic Washington Post, 1901-06; on literary staff David Belasco, New York, 1906-08; dramatic critic N.Y. Globe, 1908-09; editor N.Y. Dramatic Mirror, Aug. 12, 1912-Sept. 9, 1916. Co-founder and editor The Fatherland, 1914-17; was editor of Issues and Events until 1918, later editor of Issues of Today and The Progressive. Ex-mem. Sch. Bd. 9th Dist., New York. Author: Jose, 1890; German-American Handbook, 1915-16 (2 edits.); "1683-1920," 1920 (10,000 copies sold); The Germans in the Making of America, 1923; When Hell Broke Loose in the U.S., 1931. Plays: At the French Ball (played 5 years by Fanny Rice); The Man from Texas; A Modern Lady Godiva (played by Amelia Bingham); Hawkeye; Corsica, 1-act lyric drama, music by Irenée Bergé, prod. 1910; Love Laughs at Locksmiths, 1-act comic opera, music by Joesph Breil, 1910. Translator: Max Nordau's Pairs Sketches (Freie Liebe); Baron Trenck, music by Felix Albini, prod. London, 1911, and New York, 1912. Also wrote Our Debt to France, Frederick the Great's Influence on the America Revolution; The Enemy Within, 1940. Holder medal, German Red Cross and of Hamburg Univ.; awarded bronze plaque, United German Socs. of Greater New York, 1938. Supplied the Friars' Club with its name. Home: 540 W. 112th St., New York, N.Y. Died Mar. 7, 1943.

SCHREMBS, Joseph (shrĕms), archbishop; b. Ratisbon, Bavaria, Germany, Mar. 12, 1866; s. George and Mary (Gess) S.; came to U.S., 1877; St. Vincent's College, Pa.; philosophy and theology, Grand Sem., Montreal, to 1889; B.T., Laval U., Montreal, 1888; D.D., Rome, 1911, U. of Freiburg, 1923. Ordained R.C. priest, June 29, 1889; asst. pastor and pastor, W. Bay City, Mich., 1889-1900; pastor St. Mary's Ch., Grand Rapids, Mich., 1900-11, and apptd. irremovable rector same and vicar-gen. diocese of Grand Rapids, 1902; created a domestic prelate of Pope Pius X, 1906; named auxiliary bishop of Grand Rapids, Jan. 5, 1911; consecrated bishop, Feb. 22, 1911; apptd. 1st bishop of diocese of Toledo, O., Aug. 11, 1911, installed Oct. 4, 1911; made asst. at the pontifical throne, June 29, 1914; appointed bishop of Cleveland, June 16, 1921, installed Sept. 8, 1921; apptd. archbishop, Mar. 25, 1939. Mem. bd. trustees, Cath. Univ. of America, Washington,

D.C.; pres. and protector Priests' Eucharistic League of U.S.; promoter or eucharistic congresses in U.S. Home: 18401 Shaker Blvd., Shaker Heights, Cleveland, Ohio.* Died Nov. 1, 1945.

SCHUCHERT, Charles, paleontologist; b. Cincinnati, July 3, 1858; s. Philip and Agatha (Müller) S.; common sch. edn.; A.M. (hon.), Yale, 1904; LL.D., New York U., 1914; unmarried. Began as collector of fossils and made study of paleontology; asst. in paleontology to Mr. E. O. Ulrich, Newport, Ky., 1885-88, to Prof. James Hall, Albany, N.Y., 1888-91; geol. survey of Minn., 1891-92; preparator of fossils with Dr. Charles E. Beecher, Yale Univ., 1892-93; asst. paleontologist, U.S. Geol. Survey, 1893-94; asst. curator sect. paleontology, U.S. Nat. Mus., 1894-1904; prof. paleontology, Yale, prof. hist. geology, Sheffield Scientific Sch. and curator geol. collections, Peabody Mus., Yale, 1904-23 (emeritus). Mem. Nat. Acad. Sciences, Geol. Soc. Am. (pres. 1922), A.A.A.S. (v.p. sect. E, 1927). Author: Textbook of Historical Geological Paleogeography of North America; The Earth and Its Rhythms. Address: Peabody Museum, New Haven, Conn. Died Nov. 20, 1942.

SCHUETZ, Leonard William (shōōts), congressman; b. Posen, Poland, Nov. 16, 1887; s. Vincent W. and Florence (Witucki) S.; brought to the United States, 1891; educated public schools, Lane Technical High Sch. and Bryant & Stratton Business Coll., Chicago; m. Martha Schelm, Sept. 28, 1910; 1 dau., Florence. Began as stenographer with Wilber Mercantile Agency, 1898; with the Nonotuck Silk Co., 1902-06; in exec. positions with Swift & Co., 1906-23; organizer, 1923, since pres. and treas. Schuetz Construction Co. Mem. 72d to 78th Congresses (1931-45), 7th Illinois District Democrat. Home: 4445 W. Wrightwood Av., Chicago; (summer) Nippersink Lodge, Genoa City, Wis. Office: 3620 N. Kilbourn Av., Chicago, Ill. Died Feb. 13, 1944.

SCHULER, Anthony J. (shōōl'ĕr), bishop; b. St. Mary's, Elk County, Pa., Sept. 20, 1869; s. Joseph and Albertine (Algeier) S.; ed. St. Stanislaus Sem., Florissant, Mo., 1886-90, science and philosophy, St. Louis U., 1890-93, theol. studies, Woodstock (Md.) Coll., 1898-1902; (D.D.). Joined Soc. of Jesus (Jesuits), 1886; ordained priest R.C. Ch., 1901; prof. various branches, Sacred Heart Coll., Denver, Colo., 1893-98 and 1902-03; pres. Sacred Heart (now Regis) Coll., Denver, 1903-06; spl. work, St. Stanislaus Sem., 1906, 07; parish work, El Paso, Tex., 1907-10; asst. to Rev. Edward Barry, Denver, 1910-13; pastor Sacred Heart Ch., Denver, 1913-15; consecrated 1st bishop of El Paso, Oct. 28, 1915. Built St. Patrick's Cathedral, St. Patrick's Sch. and Community Center, chs., chapels, hosps. and sanatoria in El Paso and in various parts of diocese. Now retired. Home: Regis College, Denver, Colo. Died June 5, 1944.

SCHULTE, David A., tobacconist; b. Thomasville, Ga., Mar. 7, 1873; s. Louis and Bertha (Davis) S.; ed. country public school, Riverhead, L.I.; m. Hattie H. Harris, 1905; children—Arthur D., John S., David A.; m. 2d, Carrie E. Koehler, Sept. 22, 1928. Clerk, World Bldg. store, 1890-1900; gen. mgr. D. A. Schulte, Inc., 1900-03, pres. since 1903; pres. Dunhill Internat., Inc.; chmn. bd. Park and Tilford. Mem. Temple Emanu El, New York City. Home: Holmdel, N.J. Office: D. A. Schulte, Inc., 384 Broadway, New York. Died July 29, 1949.

SCHULTZ, Alfred Reginald, geologist; b. Tomah, Wis., Mar. 26, 1876; s. John Fredrick and Ida M. (Kirst) S.; B.S., U. of Wis., 1900; teacher mathematics and physics, high sch., Wausau, Wis., 1900-02; fellow U. of Chicago, 1904-05, Ph.D., 1905; m. Helene E. Burkhardt, Oct. 26, 1910; children—Irene Esther, Maxine Dorothy, John Burkhardt (dec.). Resident hydrologist, Wis., 1903; geologist in charge Leith exploration party, Ont., Can., 1904; became connected with U.S. Geol. Survey, 1905, has served as field asst., hydrologic aid, geologic aid, asst. geologist and geologist; mem. Coal Bd. (classification and valuation pub. coal lands), 1910; geologist Barber Asphalt Co. and Bermuda Oil Co., Venezuela and Trinidad, South America, 1910-11; chmn. Phosphate Board and Metall. Bd. Land Classification, U.S. Geol. Survey, 1912-16, geologist in charge mineral div. land classification, U.S. Geol. Survey, 1916-18; geologist, oil div. U.S. Fuel Adminstrn., 1918; mgr. Burkhardt Milling & Electric Power Co., 1918-42; pres. Willow River Power Co., 1922-42; pres. Afton Power Co., 1921-42; pres. Hudson Hotel Co., 1929-42; dir. First Nat. Bank; cons. geologist. Mem. Geol. Soc. America, A.A.A.S., Am. Foresty Assn., Sigma Xi, etc. Republican. Lutheran. Clubs: St. Paul (Minn.) Athletic; Commercial (Hudson, Wis.). Writer numerous papers and govt. bulls. on stratigraphic and economic geology, gold, soda, oil, coal, leucite, potash, phosphate, water supplies, etc. Home: 800 Vine St., Hudson, Wis. Died Sep. 30, 1943.

SCHULTZ, James Willard, author; b. Boonville, N.Y., Aug. 26, 1859; s. Philander B. and Frances A. (Joslin) S.; ed. under pvt. tutor and 4 yrs. at Peekskill Mil. Acad.; m. Mut-si-ah-wō-tan-ahki ("Fine Shield Woman"), 1879 (died 1903); 1 son, Hart Merriam ("Lone Wolf"); m. 2d, Celia B. Hawkins, 1907, m. 3d, Jessie Louise Donaldson, 1931. Mem. of the S.A.R. Club: University. Author: My Life as an Indian, 1907; With the Indians in the Rockies, 1910; Sinopah, the Indian Boy, 1911; Quest of the Fish-Dog Skin, 1912; Apauk, Caller of Buffalo, 1913; The Gold Cache, 1914; On the War Path, 1915; Lone Bull's Mistake, 1916; Blackfeet Tales of Glacier National Park, 1917; Bird Woman, 1918; Running Eagle, Virgin Warrior, 1919; Rising Wolf, The White Blackfeet, 1919; Dreadful River Cave, 1920; In the Great Apaihe Forest, 1920; War Trail Fort, 1921; Seizer of Eagles, 1922; The Danger Trail, 1923; Friends of My Life as an Indian, 1923; (with Vance Thompson) The White Chief (scenario), 1923; Plumed Snake Medicine, 1924; Questers of the Desert, 1925; Sun Woman, 1926; A Son of the Navajos, 1926; Signposts of Adventure, 1926; William Jackson, Indian Scout, 1927; Red Crow's Brother, 1927; In Enemy Country, 1928; The Sun God's Children—The Blackfeet Indian Tribes, 1929; Skull Head, the Terrible, 1929; The White Beaver, 1930; Alder Gulch Gold, 1931; Friends and Foes in the Rockies, 1933; Gold Dust, 1934; Theft of the White Buffalo Robe, 1936; Stained Gold, 1937; Short Bow's Big Medicine, 1940. Died June 11, 1947.

SCHULTZ, John Richie, coll. pres.; b. Canton, Mo., Dec. 12, 1884; s. John Christian and Laura (Piner) S.; A.B., Culver-Stockton College, Canton, 1905; M.A., Yale U., 1909, Ph.D., 1917; LL.D., Allegheny Coll., Mt. Union Coll., U. of Pittsburgh and Culver Stockton Coll.; studied Univ. of Chicago, summer 1906, 42. British Museum, summers 1914, 23, Huntington Library, 1933; m. Dora Nelson, Aug. 8, 1917; children—James Richie, Nelson (dec.), Laurana. Prin. high sch., Canton, 1905-08; head of English dept., E. St. Louis High Sch., 1909-11; instr. English, Yale, 1912-17; prof. of English lit., Allegheny Coll., Meadville, Pa., 1917-42, dean of men, 1930-42; acting pres., 1942, pres. since 1943. Mem. Meadville Civil Service Commn. Mem. C. of C., Am. Dialect Soc., Alpha Sigma Phi, Acacia, Phi Beta Kappa, Pi Delta Epsilon. Mason (32°). Republican. Methodist. Clubs: Round Table, Rotary, Duquesne (Pittsburgh), University (New York). Editor: (with J. M. Berdan and H. E. Joyce) Modern Essays, 1915. Unpublished Letters of Bayard Taylor, 1937. Contbr. to professional jours. Home: 380 N. Main St., Meadville, Pa. Died Aug. 11, 1947.

SCHULZ, Leo, musician; b. Posen, Poland, Mar. 28, 1865; s. Clemens S.; Real Gymnasium, 1872-80; studied Royal Acad. High Sch. of Music, Berlin; m. Ida Bartsch, Apr. 12, 1885 (died 1935); m. 2d, Johanna Beetz, March 30, 1937. Traveled through Germany as a "child wonder," giving concerts, 1870-73; resumed concert work, 1876; became soloist and 1st cellist, Philharmonic Orchestra, Berlin, 1885; soloist and cellist, Gewandhaus Orchestra, Leipzig, 1886-89; soloist Boston Symphony Orchestra and prof. N.E. Conservatory, 1889-98; soloist and 1st cellist New York Philharmonic Soc., 1890-1906; prof. and conductor Nat. Conservatory Orchestra; soloist and 1st cellist of the New York Symphony Orchestra; soloist Philharmonic Soc., New York; now retired; pres. N.Y. Tonkuenstler Soc. Prof. music, Yale. Composer of many cello compositions, songs, string quartettes, overtures for orchestra, cantata for chorus and orchestra, performed in pub., but not published; 2 books, Cello Album, and 2 books, Cello Classics, published in Leipzig; also 2 books, Cello Compositions; for cello and piano—3 Polish character pieces, Butterflies, Concert Study; Theme and Variations for 4 cellos; Amerindian Fantasy Variations for cello and orchestra. Retired, 1929, and pensioned by the New York Philharmonic Symphony Soc. after 30 years' service. Author: Memories—Sixty Years in the Realm of Music. Home: Los Angeles. Died Aug. 12, 1944.

SCHULZE, Paul (shōōl'tsĕ), mfr.; b. Osterode, foot of Harz Mountains, Germany, June 13, 1864; s. Gustav and Henrietta (Roeper) S.; ed. high sch., Osterode; came to America, 1883; m. Ida Johl, May 24, 1892; children—Walter H. (killed in World War), Paul, Helen Louise (Mrs. Edgar F. Burch, Jr.), Victor Hugo. Clerk in store, Big Stone City, S.D., 1883-87; with wholesale hardware house, Minneapolis, 1887; bookkeeper wholesale flour house, St. Paul, 1887-91; rep. of Washburn-Crosby Co., Minneapolis, in Chicago, 1891-1902; organized Schulze Baking Co., 1893, and pres. same 28 yrs., company becoming one of largest of the kind in U.S.; sold out, 1921; acquired business of F. Westerman Co., operating as the Quaker Biscuit Works and the McMahon Biscuit Co., cracker and biscuit business, and inc. same, 1924, as Paul Schulze Biscuit Co.; the Paul Schulze Biscuit Co. and the Burch Biscuit Co., Des Moines, combined, 1939, and built a new plant in Chicago, now running under the name of Schulze & Burch Biscuit Co., of which he is chmn. bd. of dirs. Trustee Concordia Teachers Coll., River Forest, Ill. Mem. Chicago Natural Museum History, Municipal Art League of Chicago (pres.), Art Inst. Chicago (gov. mem.), Chicago Galleries Assn. (treas.), Ill. Mfrs. Assn. (advisory board), Ill. and Chicago hist. socs. Republican. Lutheran. Clubs: Union League, Cliff Dwellers, Arts, Palette and Chisel, German, Skokie Country, Army Athletic Assn. (West Point, N.Y.), U.S. Naval Inst. (Annapolis, Md.). Received hon. degree of Dr. Fine Arts, Boguslawski Coll. of Music, Chicago, 1940; hon. degree Doctor of Laws, Concordia Theological Sem., St. Louis, 1945. Home: 2305 Commonwealth Av. Office: 1133 W. 35th St., Chicago 9. Died Aug. 14, 1948.

SCHUMACHER, Thomas Milton, ry. official; b. Williamsport, Pa., Feb. 16, 1862; married; children—Mary (Mrs. Jose M. Ferrer, Jr.), Alice (Mrs. John M. Sturges). Began as telegraph operator, Atlantic & Gt. Western (now Erie) R.R.; bill clk. C.B.&Q. Ry.; chief clk in gen. agent's office, U.P. R.R., St. Louis; chief clk. gen. freight office, same rd., Omaha, 1894, and gen. agt. same, San Francisco, 1894-98; v.p. and gen. mgr. Continental Fruit Express, Chicago, 1898-1900; gen. agt. U.P. R.R., San Francisco, 1900-01; traffic mgr. Oregon Short Line, Salt Lake City, 1901-05, United Fruit Co., New York, 1905-06; gen. traffic mgr., Chicago, of railroads and industrial cos. in control of Phelps Dodge Corp., 1906-09; asst. dir. of traffic, U.P. and S.P. ry. systems, Chicago, 1910; traffic mgr. Am. Smelting & Refining Co. and allied cos., New York, 1910-12; v.p. El Paso & Southwestern Ry. System (now Southern Pacific) in charge all depts. New York, 1912-17, and pres. same, May 1917-Jan. 1, 1925. Was chmn. bd. and chmn. exec. com. R.I. Ry. Co., Oct. 29, 1913-Oct. 1915; exec. v p., S.P. Co., New York and Chicago, Jan. 1925-July, 1926; chmn. exec. com., dir., W.P.R.R., July 1926-May 21, 1945, trustee same, Nov. 1935-May 21, 1945; pres. W.P.R.R. Corp., July 1926-Feb. 1942; was chmn. bd. of exec. com., D.&R.G.W. R.R. Co., Rio Grande Junction, D.&S.L.W. R.R, New York, July 1926-May 1945; now dir. D.&R.G.W. R.R. Co., Rio Grande Junction Ry., Denver & Salt Lake Western R.R. Co., Denver & Salt Lake Ry., Magma Ariz. R.R., W.P. R.R. Corp. Clubs: Links, Traffic (New York); Nat. Golf Links of America (Southampton, N.Y.); Chicago Traffic (Chicago); Pacific Union (San Francisco); Travelers (Paris). Home: 2 East 88th St., New York 28. Died Feb. 26, 1948.

SCHUMPETER, Joseph Alois (shōōm'pē-tĕr), prof. economics; b. Triesch, Moravia (now Czechoslovakia), Feb. 8, 1883; s. Joseph Alois and Joan Marguerite (Gruener) S.; B.A., High Sch. (Theresianum), Vienna, Austria, 1901; Dr. in Law, U. of Vienna, 1906; Ph.D., Columbia U., 1913; Ph.D., Sofia, Bulgaria, 1939; m. Elizabeth Boody, Aug. 16, 1937. Came to U.S., 1932. Began practice of law, 1907; became lecturer U. of Vienna and prof. economics at U. of Gernowitz, 1909; prof. economics at U. of Graz, 1911-14; Austrian exchange prof. Columbia U., 1913; Austrian Minister of Finance, 1919-20; prof. economics, U. of Bonn, Germany, 1925-32, Harvard since 1932. Mem. Am. Econ. Assn., A.A.A.S., Am. Statis. Assn., Royal Econ. Soc., Econometric Soc. (pres. 1939-41). Author: Theory of Economic Development, 1911 (Eng. trans. 1934); Business Cycles, A Theoretical, Statistical and Historical Analysis of the Capitalist Process, 1939; Capitalism, Socialism and Democracy, 1942. Lutheran. Club: Harvard (Boston and New York). Home: Taconic, Conn. Died Jan. 8, 1950.

SCHUPP, Robert William (shŭp), lawyer; b. Chicago, Ill., Jan. 4, 1890; s. Philip and Caroline (Regensberger) S.; grad. Crane Tech. High Sch., 1908; LL.B., Northwestern U., 1911; m. Edwina Crittenden; 1 dau., Ada. Practiced at Chicago since 1911; with Adams, Follansbee, Hawley & Shorey, 1911-20, mem. of firm, 1920, of successor, Follansbee, Shorey & Schupp in 1925. Mem. Am., Ill. State and Chicago bar assns., Law Club, Legal Club, Order of Coif. Club: University. Home: 94 Essex Road, Winnetka, Ill. Office: 135 S. La Salle St., Chicago, Ill. Died Dec. 19, 1946.

SCHURMAN, Jacob Gould (shûr'măn), educator diplomat; b. Freetown, P.E.I., May 22, 1854; s. Robert and Lydia S.; won Canadian Gilchrist scholarship, 1875, in connection with U. of London; A.B., U. of London, 1877, A.M., 1878; studied at Paris and U. of Edinburgh, 1877-78; Sc.D., Edinburgh, 1878; studied univs. of Heidelberg, Berlin and Göttingen and in Italy (Hibbert traveling fellowship), 1878-80; LL.D., Columbia, 1892, Yale, 1901, Edinburgh, 1902, Williams, 1908, Dartmouth, Harvard, 1909, Brown, 1914, Pa., 1917, Mo., 1921; Ph.D., Heidelberg, 1927, Marburg, 1927; m. Oct. 1, 1884, Barbara Forrest, d. George Munro (died Nov. 21, 1930); children—Catherine Munro (Mrs. Raymond Ware, dec.), Robert, George Munro, Helen (Mrs. John Magruder), Jacob Gould, Barbara Rose (Mrs. Vladimir Petro-Pavlovsky), Dorothy Anna Maria (Mrs. James M. McHugh). Prof. logic and English literature, Acadia and Dalhousie colls., 1880-86; Sage prof. of philosophy, 1886-92, and pres., 1892-1920, Cornell U. Pres. first U.S. Philippine Commn., and spent most of 1899 in P.I.; U.S. minister to Greece and Montenegro, 1912-13. Stafford Little lecturer, Princeton, 1914. First v.p. N.Y. State Constitutional Convention, 1915; mem. N.Y. State Food Commn., 1917-18. E.E. and M.P. to China, from June 1921-May 1925; A.E. and M.P. to Germany, June 1925-Jan. 1930; hon. lecturer on internat. relations, Inst. Technology, Pasadena, Calif., 1931-32. Traveler and student in Europe, Asia and Africa, 1932-39. Clubs: University, Century, National Republican (New York); Cosmos (Washington); Town and Gown (Ithaca). Mem. Prussian Acad. Sciences, 1929, German Acad. (Munich), 1929. Author: Kantian Ethics and the Ethics of Evolution, 1881; The Ethical Import of Darwinism, 1888; Agnosticism and Religion, 1886; A Generation of Cornell, 1898; Report (to Congress) of the Philippine Commission (joint author), 4 vols., 1900; Philippine Affairs—A Retrospect and Outlook, 1902; The Balkan Wars, 1912-13; Why America Is in the War, 1917. Address: Bedford Hills, N.Y. Died Aug. 12, 1942.

SCHWAB, Francis Xavier, ex-mayor; b. Buffalo, Aug. 14, 1874; s. Frank and Anna (Bauer) S.; ed. St. Ann's Sch., Buffalo; m. Teresa Lauser, Sept. 24, 1901; children—Theresa Marie, Frank Xavier, Josephine Odelia, Anna Frances, Martin Joseph, Anthony Paul, Mary Magdalene. Pres. Mohawk Products Co. to 1922 (resigned). Mayor of Buffalo, term 1922-26; reelected, term 1926-29. Republican. Catholic. Mem. Elk. Moose, Eagle, Oriole, Knight of St. John.

Home: 645 Humboldt Parkway, Buffalo, N.Y. Died Apr. 23, 1946.

SCHWAB, John George (shwawb), clergyman; b. near Walnut, Bureau County, Ill., Feb. 11, 1865; s. George P. and Catherine (Keiber) S.; student Northwestern Coll., Naperville, Ill., 1882-84; m. May E. Kandall, May 29, 1889 (dec.); children—Ralph Kandall, George Stephen, Paul Josiah, Charles Willard; m. 2d, Ada Weibel, Mar. 16, 1899; 1 dau., Ruth May. Ordained ministry Evang. Assn., 1888; pastor St. Francis, Kan., 1887-89, Culbertson, Neb., 1889-92, Nelson, 1892-95; presiding elder Lincoln Dist., 1895-1900; pastor Wood River, Neb., 1900-01, Forreston, Ill., 1901-04; presiding elder Naperville (Ill.) Dist., 1904-08, Freeport Dist., 1908-12; pastor Mendota, Ill., 1912-14; presiding elder Chicago Dist., 1914-18; pastor Ebenezer Ch., Highland Park, Ill., 1918-20, First Ch., Streator, Ill., May 1920-24; presiding elder Freeport dist., 1924-27; supt. Evang. Deaconess Hosp., 1927; pastor Lockwood Av. Ch., Chicago, 1928-31; dist. supt. Chicago Dist., 1931-35. Mem. Gen. Conf. 8 times. Historian Ill. Conf. Evang. Ch. since 1927. Mem. Nat. Social Science Soc., Pi Gamma Mu. Author: History of the Illinois Conference, 1937. Home: 6323 N. Campbell Av., Chicago, Ill. Died Oct. 6, 1943.

SCHWAB, Martin Constan, cons. engr.; b. Baltimore, Md., 1880; s. Maurice and Laure (Constan) S.; (forebears settled Maryland 1780); preparatory education, Polytechnic Inst., Baltimore; grad. engring. course, John Hopkins, 1896; hon. Bach. Engring., extra-ordinem, same univ., 1926; m. Elizabeth Weisel, April 1904; children—Mrs. Katharine Boutet Scallan, Mrs. John E. B. Shaw. Assisted in electrification of B.&O. R.R., 1896; later apptd. cons. engr. for Md. Electric Co.; active in reconstruction of Baltimore after the fire; served as cons. engr. Soldiers' Home, Washington, D.C., and in design and construction of bldgs. in Washington, Phila. and New York, under firm name of Adams & Schwab; settled in Chicago and est. engring. business as Martin C. Schwab; served as cons. engr. for Sears, Roebuck & Co. since 1905 (installed first high speed vertical and horizontal assembly line; also first air-conditioned administration bldg. in U.S. with sealed windows, 1905); cons. engr. for electrification of drainage canal under Mayor Dunne's adminstrn.; cons. engr. Ill. State Bd. of Administration, 1913; identified with construction of the Bell Bldg., Mallers Bldg., Michigan Square Bldg., Adler Planetarium, Harris Trust & Savings Bank Bldg., Corn Exchange Nat. Bank, Hotel Sherman, Morrison Hotel, Mandel Bros., Rothschilds and the Lytton stores, 30 N. Michigan Av. Bldg., 333 N. Michigan Av. Bldg., WLS Broadcasting Station, Yellow Cab Bus properties; (all of Chicago), Gen. Am. Tank Car Corp., East Chicago, Ind., Union Station, Kansas City, Mo., Bamberger Dept. Store, Newark, N.J., Julia Lathrop Government Housing Project, Chicago. Patentee of various devices applied in large bldg. structures throughout the country. Has constructed bldgs. in approximately 150 cities in 43 states. Chmn. bd. Hosp. Liquids Corp., Chicago. Member of Friends of China, Rennaisance Club, Field Museum (governing life mem.), Chicago Art Institute, Oriental Inst. (U. of Chicago). Clubs: Engineering, Tavern, Lake Shore Country, Chicago Fishing (Chicago). Collector of etchings, early Chinese, Persian and Egyptian ceramics. Home: Ambassador East Hotel. Office: 333 N. Michigan Av., Chicago, Ill. Died Jan. 2, 1947.

SCHWAB, Sidney Isaac, neuro-psychiatrist; b. Memphis, Tenn., Nov. 22, 1871; s. Isaac and Ella (Marks) S.; Harvard, 1890-92; M.D., Harvard Med. Sch., 1896; univs. of Berlin, Paris and Vienna, 1896-99; m. Helen Stix, 1903; children—Robert S., Frances Troy, Mack W. Practiced neurology at St. Louis, Mo., since 1899; became prof. clin. neurology, Washington U., 1917, now prof. emeritus; consulting neurologist Barnes Hospital; neurologist Jewish Hospital, St. Louis Children's and Maternity Hosps.; served as mil. neurologist to Base Hospital 21 and med. dir. Base Hospital 117, A.E.F., June 1917-Jan. 1919, rank of captain, maj. Formerly councillor Med. Council of U.S. Vets. Bureau, Washington, D.C. Mem. Am. Neurol. Assn. (pres. 1920-21), A.M.A., etc. Mem. commn. of Assn. for Research in Nervous and Mental Disease. Clubs: University; Harvard (New York). Author: The Adolescent—His Conflicts and Escapes, 1929; also articles on neurology and psychiatry. Mem. sub-com. war neurosis Nat. Research Council. Home: Old James Town Road, Florissant, Mo. Office: Beaumont Medical Bldg., St. Louis, Mo. Died Nov. 12, 1947.

SCHWACKE, John Henry, educator; b. Phila., Sept. 13, 1879; s. James Deemer and Emma (Hillen) S.; grad. Central Manual Training Sch., Phila., 1896; A.B., Central High Sch., Phila., 1897; studied law in offices of Hon. Sheldon Potter and Joseph De Forest Junkin, both of Phila.; law course, Temple Coll. (now Univ.), Phila.; A.M. (hon.), Oskaloosa (Ia.) Coll., 1915; unmarried. Admitted to Pa. bar, 1901; began teaching old Cheltenham Mil. Acad., 1903; headmaster Yeates Sch., Lancaster, Pa. (oldest ch. boarding sch. for boys in U.S.), since 1911. Deacon, 1918, ordained priest, June 22, 1919, by Bishop Darlington of the P.E. Ch. and Archbishop Alexander Rodosdolow, of the Greek Orthodox Ch. (first time since 15th century that the eastern and western chs. have joined in conferring Holy orders). Mem. Assn. Masters of Ch. Schs. of N.E., Am. Hist. Assn., Assn. History Teachers, Alumni Assn. Central Manual Training Sch., Central High Sch., Temple Coll. Law Assn., Sigma Kappa. Episcopalian. Elk. Club: Lawyers (Phila.). Address: Yeates School, Lancaster. Pa. Died Feb. 21, 1942.

SCHWARTZ, Andrew Thomas, artist; b. Louisville, Ky., Jan. 1867; s. Joseph and Margaret (Kuhn) S.; ed. art schs., Cincinnati and N.Y. City; Lazarus scholarship, Rome, Italy, 1900; unmarried. Represented in Cincinnati Art Museum. Murals: Kansas City (Mo.) Life Ins. Co. Bldg.; Christ the Good Shepherd, Bapt. Ch., South Londonderry, Vt.; ballroom ceiling, residence of Mrs. E. D. Brandagee, Brookline, Mass.; 9 murals, Atkins Memorial Museum, Kansas City; 3 murals in County Ct. House, N.Y. City; "The Thread of Life" (in West Side Y.M.C.A., New York City), etc. Mem. Archtl. League New York, Am. Water Color Soc., Allied Artists of America, Am. Acad. Alumni. Club: Salmagundi of New York. Home: 246 Fulton St., Brooklyn, N.Y. Died Sep. 15, 1942.

SCHWARTZ, Harwood Muzzy, college prof.; b. Adams Center, N.Y., Aug. 16, 1881; s. Harry Scott and Jessie Marie (Muzzy) S.; B.S., Hamilton Coll., Clinton, N.Y., 1907, M.S., 1910; Ph.D., Teachers Coll., Columbia, 1927; m. Kathrina Burr Burlingame, Jan. 9, 1909; children—Katherine Burlingame (Mrs. Benedict Rich), Hilda Muzzy (Mrs. Mack D. Parks), Harwood Muzzy. Teacher mathematics, High Sch., Little Falls, N.Y., 1908; prin. Norwich, N.Y., 1909-10, Utica, N.Y., 1910-11; supt. of schs., Ilion, N.Y., 1911-23; head dept. of edn., St. Lawrence U., since 1926, also dir. extension dept. since 1932, dir. Summer Sessions, 1941 and 1942; prin. Jr.-Sr. High Sch., Hastings-on-Hudson, 1943-44; retired 1944. Served as sergt. U.S. Vol. Inf., Philippine Insurrection, 1899-1901. Life mem. N.E.A.; mem. Delta Kappa Epsilon, Phi Delta Kappa, Kappa Delta Pi, Lions Club (pres. 1935-37, deputy dist. gov., 1937-38). Mason. Episcopalian. Contbr. to sch. surveys, etc. Home: 465 Broadway, Hastings-on-Hudson, N.Y. Died Sept. 9, 1945.

SCHWARZE, William Nathaniel (shwär'tsē), clergyman, educator; b. Chaska, Minn., Jan. 2, 1875; s. Ernst N. and Wilhelmine (Moench) S.; B.A., Moravian Coll., Bethlehem, Pa., 1894, M.A., 1904, Ph.D., 1910; B.D., Moravian Theol. Sem., 1896, D.D., 1928; m. Ethel Greider, July 19, 1905; children—Margaret, Leonore (Mrs. A. W. Hesse, Jr.) and Herbert Edwin. Ordained to the ministry of the Moravian Church, 1896; pastor Bruederfeld and Bruederheim, Alberta, Can., 1896-1900; dir. Buxton Grove Theol. Sem. for native ministers, St. John's, Antigua, B.W.I., 1900-03; prof. of philosophy and church history, Moravian Coll., since 1903; pres. Moravian Coll. and Theol. Sem., 1928-43; president emeritus since 1943; archivist Moravian Church, Northern Province of North America, since 1905. President board trustees Bethlehem Public Library; member School Board, Bethlehem, 1911-21; trustee Linden Hall Sem., Lititz, Pa., St. Luke's Hosp., Bethlehem, Pa. Mem. Am. Ch. History Soc. (ex-pres.), Moravian Hist. Soc. (pres.), Am. Philos. Soc., Newcomen Soc., Phi Beta Kappa (hon.). Republican. Club: Rotary (hon.). Author: History of the Moravian College and Theological Seminary, 1910; John Huss, the Martyr of Bohemia, 1915. Translator: History of the North American Indians (by David Zeisberger), 1910; also many other manuscripts. Contbr. to "The Outline of Christianity," also of numerous articles in mags. Home: 1118 Main St., Bethlehem, Pa. Died March 14, 1948.

SCHWEIGARDT, Frederick William (shwī'gärt), sculptor; b. Wuerttemberg, Germany, May 3, 1885; s. Matthäus and Marie (Molt) S.; studied in Switzerland, France, Austria, Italy and England; grad. Acad. of Fine Arts, Munich, 1925; pupil of Perrotte and Rodin; m. Baroness Thora von Brockdorff, Oct. 15, 1925; m. 2d, Enny Wedepohl, Dec. 26, 1936. Came to U.S., 1930, naturalized, 1937. Mem. staff Deutsches Mus., Munich, 1925-30, Mus. of Science and Industry, Rockefeller Center, 1930-32; official sculptor Calif.-Pacific Internat. Expn., 1935-36. Works: Taj Mahal, Mausoleum of Theodorich the Great, Minaret of Buchara, Deutsches Mus., Munich; works of art for historical development, Museum of Science and Industry, Rockefeller Center, New York; heroic bronze bust of Pres. Roosevelt, White House, and of Dr. Albert Einstein, at the Univ. of Calif., Berkeley; fountain group, "The Four Cornerstones of Am. Democracy," Balboa Park; fountain group, "Youth Triumphant," U. of Southern Calif.; heroic figures and animals, Calif. State Bldg., San Diego; Col. David Charles Collier Memorial, Balboa Park; heroic statue "Democratic Education—The Light of Civilization," Calif. State Dept. of Edn., Golden Gate Internat. Expn.; bust of George Arthur Merrill, Patrick Noble Auditorium, San Francisco; bust of Rufus Bernhard von KleinSmid, U. of Southern Calif.; bust of Isadore Zellerbach, Crown Zellerbach, Inc., San Francisco; busts of Consul of Netherlands J. J. van Eizenga and Mrs. van Eizenga, San Diego, Calif.; monument to Joseph B. Strauss, plaza Golden Gate Bridge. Heroic bust of Gen. Douglas MacArthur for Victory Exhbn. at Calif. Palace of the Legion of Honor, San Francisco, 1945; bust of Gilbert Aubrey Davidson, San Diego, Calif., 1947, and other work in pub. and private collections in Europe and America. Awarded 1st prize and diploma, Baden, Germany, 1903; 1st prize and medal, Concours d'après Nature, Paris, 1913; hon. award Acad. of Fine Arts, Munich, 1923; certificate of merit and gold medal, Calif.-Pacific Internat. Expn., 1935-36, of appreciation from State of Calif. at Golden Gate Internat. Exposition, 1940. Awarded National Logan Medal at the annual exhbn. at Calif. Palace of the Legion of Honor, San Francisco, for heroic bust of Will Rogers, 1940. Mem. Fine Arts Soc. of San Diego, Art Assn. of Los Angeles Am. Artists Professional League; mem. bd. Society of Western Artists, San Francisco. Mem. bd. San Diego Hall of Edn. Lecturer on art. Home: 4010 Fulton St., San Francisco 18. Died Sept. 21, 1948.

SCHWELLENBACH, Lewis Baxter (shwĕl'ĕn-bäk), sec. of labor; b. Superior, Wis., Sept. 20, 1894; s. Francis W. and Martha (Baxter) S.; LL.B., U. of Wash., 1917; m. Anne Duffy, Dec. 30, 1935. Asst. instructor, Univ. of Washington, 1916-17; admitted to Wash. bar, 1919, and began practice at Seattle; asso. with firm Roberts & Skeel, 1919-21; asso. Schwellenbach, Merrick and Macfarlane, 1925-31; practiced alone, 1931-35; U.S. senator, 1935-Dec. 16, 1940; resigned to become U.S. dist. judge, Eastern Dist. of Wash., 1945. Apptd. Sec. of labor by Pres. Truman, May, 1945. Pvt. 12th Inf. during World War I. Chmn. Dem. State Conv., 1924, King Co. Dem. Com., 1928-30; candidate for gov. Dem. primaries, 1932; del. Interparliamentary Union, The Hague, 1938. Pres., Alumni Assn., U. of Wash., 1928-29; pres. bd. of regents U. of Wash., 1933. Mem. adv. bd. Wash. State Coll., Salvation Army (Spokane). Dean, Gonzaga U. Law Sch., Spokane, since 1944. Mem. Am. Legion (dept. comdr., 1922-23); mem. Am. council Inst. of Pacific Relations, Am. Soc. Internat. Law, Am. Acad. Polit. and Social Science, Am. Bar Assn., Spokane. Democrat. Episcopalian. Elk, Eagle. Died June 10, 1948.

SCHWYZER, Arnold (shvēt'sēr), surgeon; b. Zurich, Switzerland, May 23, 1864; s. Col. A. and Katherine (Iten) S.; M.D., U. of Zurich, 1888; m. Marguerite Mueller, Sept. 14, 1906; children—Marguerite, Arnold Gustav, Hans Carl. Came to U.S., 1891; settled in St. Paul, Minn., 1891; surgeon St. Joseph's Hosp. since 1900; formerly clin. prof. surg. pathology and clin. prof. surgery, Hamline U.; professorial lecturer emeritus, U. of Minn. Fellow Am. Coll. Surgeons; mem. A.M.A., Am. Surg. Soc., Minn. State Med. Assn., Minn. Pathol. Soc., Western Surg. Assn., Minn. Acad. Medicine, Swiss Surg. Soc. Swiss Protestant. Clubs: Minnesota, Automobile. Home: 8 Crocus Hill. Office: 123 W. 7th St., St. Paul, Minn. Died Feb. 19, 1944.

SCONCE, Harvey James (skŏns), farmer; b. Indianola, Ill., Mar. 7, 1875; s. James Silas and Emma (Sodowsky) S.; ed. Coll. of Agr., U. of Ill.; m. Eva L. Fisher, June 2, 1897. Part owner and operator Fairview Farm, Sidell, Ill.; dir. Armour & Co., 1923-33, Resources Corp. Internat. (Chicago and Mexico), 1931-33. Mem. Gov. Lowden's Agrl. Advisory Com., 1917-21; Gov. Emmerson's Agrl. Adv. Com., 1930-31; dir. in charge of research Resources Corp. Internat. (Chicago and Mexico) since 1931; chief of agrl. div. A Century of Progress Expn., Chicago, 1933; dir. Star Popcorn Products, Inc., concessionaire to the N.Y. World's Fair, 1939; dir. Tall Pine Lumber Corp. (Buffalo and Mexico), 1939. Mem. Ill. Agrl. Assn. (pres. 1919), Am. Farm Bur. Fedn. (exec. com. 1920), U.S. Chamber of Commerce (transp. and finance coms., 1921-23), Internat. Chamber of Commerce (finance com.), Wheat Council of U.S. (v.p.), Farm Chemurgic Council, Dearborn, Mich. (chmn. Cellulose Com. for Perennial Crops; regional dir. Chicago and Mid-West area) since 1937. American rep. to Internat. Inst. Agr., Rome, Italy, 1920. Mem. Am. Genetic Soc., Internat. Congress Eugenics, Ill. Seed Corn Breeders' Assn., Am. Com. Internat. Inst. Agr., Kappa Sigma, Alpha Gamma Rho. Republican. Methodist. Mason (32°, Shriner). Clubs: University (Chicago and Urbana, Ill.); Adventurers, Ill. Athletic (Chicago). Author: The Romance of Everifarm, 1922; To Market, 1928. Home: Sidell, Ill. Died Dec. 4, 1943.

SCORE, John Nelson Russell, univ. pres.; b. White Church, Mo., Apr. 21, 1896; s. Rev. John and Katie Marie (Ebrecht) S.; A.B., Scarritt-Morrisville Coll., Morrisville, Mo., 1914; B.D., Emory U., 1916; Th.D., Pacific School of Religion, 1925; D.D., Centenary College, Shreveport, La., 1931; LL.D., Central College, 1943; LL.D., Southern Methodist University, 1945; student New College and University of Edinburgh, Edinburgh, Scotland, 1919; married Margaret Ruth Smith, Jan. 12, 1921; 1 son, John Nelson Russell. Entered ministry M.E. Ch., S., 1913, ordained, 1917; pastor, Parkin, Ark., 1916-17, Wynne, Ark., 1919-22, Epworth University Ch., Berkeley, Calif., 1922-26, St. Paul's Ch., Houston, Tex., 1926-34, First Ch., Ft. Worth, 1934-42; pres. Southwestern U., Georgetown, Tex., since June 1, 1942. Built Epworth Univ. Ch. (cost, $200,000), St. Paul's Ch. (cost, $810,000). Chaplain U.S. Army, 1918-19. Conf. sec. of edn., Pacific Conf., 1923-26; mem. Gen. Epworth League Bd., 1926-30, Gen. Bd. Christian Edn. 1930-39; pres. bd. Christian Edn. of Central Tex. Conf., 1938-42; chmn. Central Texas Conf., Minimum Support Commn., since 1940; mem. Gen. Conf. M.E. Ch., S., 1934 and 1938, Uniting Conf., the Meth. Ch., 1939, visiting preacher at annual conf., Czechoslovakia, Poland and Belgium, 1936; preacher under Exchg. Com., Gt. Brtain, 1936. Del. first Gen. Conf., Methodist Ch., 1940; del. Gen. Conf. 1944; mem. South Central Jurisdictional Conf., 1940, 1944. Mem. Commn. on Ritual and Orders, Bd. of Edn. of the Methodist Ch. (pres.), South Central Jurisdiction Bd. of Edn. since 1944, South Central Jurisdiction Coordinating Com., 1940-44, mem. South Central Jurisdictional Council, mem. Meth. Ecumenical Council Nat. Preaching Mission, 1941; mem. bd. trustees Methodist Hosp., Ft. Worth, Methodist Home, Waco,

Southwestern U. Georgetown, Tex., Sam. Houston College. Ex-pres. Houston Ministerial Alliance, pres. Ft. Worth Ministerial Alliance, 1939-40; mem. Southwestern Science Soc., Scholia, Am. Acad. Polit. and Social Science, Am. Assn. School Administrs., Am. Legion, Pi Gamma Mu, Theta Pi, Alpha Chi. Mason. Clubs: Lions. Home: 1305 E. 12th St., Georgetown, Tex. Died Sep. 26, 1949.

SCOTT, Albert Lyon, mill engr.; b. Cleveland O., June 21, 1878; s. John Hart and Florence Madeline (Davis) S.; A.B., Brown U., 1900; m. Alice May Chamberlin, June 12, 1906; children—Alice Chamberlin, David Hart, Albert Lyon, Richard Chamberlin, Robert Litchfield. Began with Lockwood, Greene & Co., 1900, dir., 1903, treas., 1905, v.p., 1920, pres., 1926; became pres. Lockwood Greene Engrs., Inc., July 1, 1928. Mem. Com. on Supplies of Council of Nat. Defense, May 1-Dec. 17, 1917; chief of Supply. and Equipment Div., Q.M.C., U.S. Army, 1917-18. Fellow Brown U.; trustee University of Chicago, Riverside Ch., N.Y. City, Spelman College, Morehouse College, Atlanta University; trustee Textile Museum. Member American Society of Civil Engineers, N.Y. State Soc. of Professional Engrs., Inc.; Soc. Am. Mil. Engrs.; mem. Am. Hist. Assn., Delta Upsilon. Republican. Baptist. Clubs: Merchants, University (New York); University (Boston). Mem. Laymen's Inquiry Commn., which wrote "Re-thinking Missions"; with Raymond B. Fosdick wrote "Toward Liquor Control," 1933. Home: Chappaqua, N.Y. Office: 10 Rockefeller Plaza, New York, N.Y. Died Mar. 2, 1946.

SCOTT, Angelo Cyrus, educator; b. near Franklin, Johnson County, Ind., Sept. 25, 1857; s. John Walter and Maria Protsman; A.B., Kansas U., 1877; A.M., 1880; LL.B., LL.M., George Washington Univ. Law Sch., 1885; hon. Litt.D., Emporia College (Kan.); m. Lola May Smeltzer, May 31, 1894. Began as lawyer, Iola, Kan., 1885; in Oklahoma City in the land rush, 1889; founded (with W. W. Scott) The Okla. City Times; apptd. by Pres. Harrison, 1890, to townsite bd. to determine controversies; U.S. commr., 1891-92; Okla. exec. commr. to World's Columbian Expn., 1893; territorial senator, 1895-97; pres. Okla. A. and M. Coll. (Stillwater), 1899-1908; served since then on faculty Epworth U., Okla. U., and Okla. City U. (prof. emeritus English lit.). Mem. State Bd. of Edn., 1912-14. One of the founders of 1st. Presbyn. Ch. Okla. City, 1889; a founder and first president Y.M.C.A., 1889; founder Oklahoma Institute of Arts and Sciences, 1916 (dir. 5 years); founder Men's Dinner Club and president, 1909-1944, now hon. pres.; selected as Oklahoma City's "most useful citizen," 1937; chosen for citation for distinguished service, 1946, by Kansas U. Alumni Assn. Mem. Beta Theta Pi, Phi Beta Kappa. Republican. Clubs: The Oklahoma, Men's Dinner, Young Men's Dinner, Sequoyah. Author: Scott's Practical English, 1908; The Story of Oklahoma City, 1939; also many pamphlets, brochures, etc. Home: 310 N.W. 16th St. Office: Oklahoma Club, Grand and Robinson Av., Oklahoma City. Died Feb. 6, 1949; buried in Highland Cemetery, Iola, Kan.

SCOTT, Carlyle MacRoberts, music educator; b. Lawrence, Mass., Dec. 1, 1873; s. Adam and Elsie (MacRoberts) S.; ed. high schs., Lawrence and Amesbury, Mass., and Lyndon (Vt.) Inst.; student Leipzig Conservatory and U. of Leipzig, 1895-1900; Mus.D., St. Olaf Coll., Northfield, Minn., 1934; m. Verna J. Golden, Oct. 25, 1902; children—Horace Golden, Elspeth, Jane. Prof. music and head of dept., U. of Minn., 1904-42, prof. emeritus since June 30, 1942 Republican. Presbyterian. Club: Evergreen. Home: 2305 Aldrich Av. S., Minneapolis, Minn. Died Aug. 2, 1945.

SCOTT, Carrie Emma, librarian; b. Mooresville, Ind., Aug. 22, 1874; d. Robert R. and Lavicy (Harvey) Scott; A.B., Ind. U., 1898; student N.Y. State Library Sch., 1905-06, Carnegie Library Sch., Pittsburgh, Pa., 1906-07; spl. training in library work for children. Teacher high sch., Rockville, Ind., 1899-1900, Mooresville, 1900-03; with Ind. State Library, 1903-04, Children's dept. Carnegie Library, Pittsburgh, 1906-07; asst. state organizer Pub. Library Commn. of Ind., 1907-17; supervisor children's work, Indianapolis Pub. Library since 1917, also dir. training class; instr. Library Sch., U. of Iowa, summer 1938, U. of Minn., summers 1939, 40, 41. Mem. Am. Library Assn., Ind. Library Assn. (pres. 1924-25), Ind. Library Trustees Assn., Woman's Press Club of Ind. Methodist. Author: Manual for Institution Libraries, 1916. Compiler: Popular books for boys and girls, 1911; Children's Books for Christmas Presents, 1912; (with Harriet E. Hassler) Graded List of Stories to Tell or Read Aloud, 4th edit., 1923. Editor: (with Edna Johnson) Anthology of Children's Literature, 1935. Home: Mooresville, Ind. Address: Public Library, Indianapolis, Ind. Died July 27, 1943.

SCOTT, Charles Felton, engineer; b. Athens County, Ohio, Sept. 19, 1864; s. William Henry and Sarah (Felton) S.; A.B., Ohio State U., 1885; post-grad. course 1½ yrs., Johns Hopkins; A.M., Yale, 1911; Sc.D., U. of Pittsburgh; D.Eng., Stevens Inst. Tech., 1912, Brooklyn Poly. Inst., 1935; D.Sc., Ohio State U., 1937; LL.D., Rose Poly. Inst., 1939; m. Emily Clark, Oct. 15, 1895. With Westinghouse Electric & Mfg. Co., Pittsburgh, 1888-1911, prof. elec. engring., Yale, 1911-33 (emeritus). Pres. Nat. Council State Bds. Engring. Examiners, 1938-39. Pres. Engrs. Soc. Western Pa., 1902, Am. Inst. Elec. Engrs., 1902-03; chmn. bldg. com. Engring. Socs. Bldg. (gift of Andrew Carnegie), New York; mem. Soc. Promotion Engring. Edn. (pres. 1921-23; chmn. bd. investigation and coördination, 1922-33); mem. administrative bd. Am. Engring. Council, 1921-33; chmn. Engrs. Council for Professional Development, 1935-38, chmn. Com. on Professional Recognition since 1938; chmn. Conn. Bd. of Registration for Professional Engrs. and Land Surveyors since 1935. Awarded Edison medal by Am. Inst. Elec. Engrs.; Lamme medal by Soc. Promotion Engring. Edn. Mem. Am. Soc. Mech. Engrs., Am. Inst. Consulting Engrs., Sigma Xi, Tau Beta Pi, Phi Beta Kappa; hon. mem. Conn. Soc. Civil Engrs. Home: 19 Trumbull St., New Haven, Conn. Died Dec. 17, 1944.

SCOTT, Frank Augustus; b. Cleveland, March 22, 1873; s. Robert Crozier and Sarah Ann (Warr) S.; ed. grammar schs., Cleveland, and under tutelage of John H. Dynes, of Western Reserve Univ.; LL.D., Western Reserve U., 1926; m. Bertha B. Dynes, 1896 (died 1909); children—Katherine B. (Mrs. M. Roy Ridley), Chester B. (died 1937), Eleanor L. (Mrs. W. G. Nealley); m. 2d, Faith A. Fraser, 1911 (died 1936); children—F. Elizabeth, Malcolm F.; m. 3d, Dulcie Shifflett Scott, 1938. Asst. sec. and sec. Cleveland Chamber of Commerce, 1895-1905; sec. and treas. Superior Savings & Trust Co., 1905-08; successively sec. and treas., v.p., pres. and chmn. bd. The Warner & Swasey Co., mfrs. precision instruments, 1909-27; receiver Municipal Traction Co., Cleveland, 1908-09, The Standard Parts Co., 1920-22; dir. Cleveland Trust Co., Ohio Bell Telephone Co. Trustee Univ. Hosps. of Cleveland, Western Reserve U. Chmn. Gen. Munitions Bd., and War Industries Bd., Washington, 1917; awarded D.S.M. "for meritorious services," 1919; col., Ordnance O.R.C.; chief of Cleveland Ordnance District, 1924-28; appointed hon. adviser to Army Industrial College, U.S. Army, 1925; awarded gold medal, Army Ordnance Assn., U.S. Army, for notable contributions to development of army ordnance, 1932. Mem. Western Reserve Hist. Soc. (trustee), Army Ordnance Assn. (dir.), Reserve Officers' Assn. Republican. Episcopalian. Clubs: Union, Kirtland (Cleveland); Green Mountain Club (Rutland, Vt.). Home: "Chesterfield," Mentor, O. Office: Union Commerce Bldg., Cleveland. Died April 15, 1949.

SCOTT, Franklin William, editor; b. Centralia, Ill., Nov. 12, 1877; s. William Walter and Mary Ellen (Maddux) S.; A.B., U. of Ill., 1901, A.M., 1903, Ph.D., 1912; Harvard Grad. Sch., 1903-04; independent research and study, New York, 1909-10; m. Ethel Clara Forbes, June 18, 1908; children—Mary Forbes (Mrs. T. M. Cox), Hugh Forbes, Thomas William. Instr. in English, U. of Ill., 1901-03, 1905-06, associate, 1906-12, asst. prof., 1912-21, asso. prof., 1921-23, prof., 1923-25 head of dept., 1924-25, in charge courses in journalism, 1905-18, and 1921-25; editor-in-chief with D. C. Heath & Co., 1925-46, dir. since 1927, secretary, 1934-46; retired May 1946. Trustee Christian Register, 1935-39. Member American Hist. Assn., Modern Lang. Assn. of America, Alpha Tau Omega, Sigma Delta Chi, Phi Beta Kappa; sec. U. of Ill. Alumni Assn., 1906-19; exec. sec. Alpha Tau Omega, 1918-25; pres. Unitarian Laymen's League, 1935-39. Founder, 1906, and editor, 1906-18, Alumni Quarterly of U. of Ill.; editor Alpha Tau Omega Palm, since 1918. Democrat. Unitarian. Author: Alumni Record of the University of Illinois, 1906, 18; Newspapers and Periodicals of Illinois, 1910; College Readings in English Prose (with J. Zeitlin), 1914, 4th edit., 1936; Directory of Alpha Tau Omega, 1921; Composition for College Students (with J. M. Thomas and F. A. Manchester), 1923, 5th edit., 1947; New Handbook of Composition (with E. C. Woolley), 1927; Essays Formal and Informal (with J. Zeitlin), 1927; College Handbook of Composition (with E. C. Woolley), 1928, 4th edit., 1943; High School Handbook of Composition (with E. C. Woolley and J. C. Tressler), 1929. Home: 701 W. Iowa St., Urbana, Ill.; (summer) 3X Bar Ranch, Birney, Mont. Died Jan. 10, 1950.

SCOTT, George Cromwell, judge; b. Monroe County, N.Y., Aug. 8, 1864; moved to Ia., 1880; ed. high sch.; m. Laura Trimble, June 14, 1888. Admitted to Ia. bar, 1887; practiced at Le Mars, 1888-1901, since at Sioux City; elected to 62d Congress, 1912, to succeed late E. H. Hubbard, and reelected to 63d and 65th Congresses (1913-15, 1917-19), 11th Ia. Dist.; judge U.S. Dist. Ct., Northern Dist. of Ia., 1922-43; retired Nov. 1, 1943. Republican. Home: Sioux City, Ia. Died Oct. 6, 1948.

SCOTT, George Winfield, lawyer; b. Adams, N.Y., Aug. 25, 1875; s. W. G. and Georgia (Tripp) S.; student Hobart Coll., 1892-93; A.B., Stanford, 1896, Cornell, 1896-98; fellow U. of Chicago, 1899-1900, Columbia, 1900-01, U. of Pa., LL.B., 1902, Ph.D., 1903; m. Clara Hotopp, 1910; children—Clara, George Winfield. Admitted bar, Pa., 1902, D.C., 1905, N.Y., 1907, Calif., 1917; instr. internat. law, U. of Pa., 1901-03; in Europe for Library of Congress to report on law and documentary lit. to be acquired, 1904; prof. law, George Washington U., 1905-06; law librarian of Congress and Supreme Ct., 1903-07; mem. President Roosevelt's Commn. on Efficiency in Deptl. Methods, 1905-08; prof. internat. law, ad interim, U. of Pa., 1906-07; prof. internat. law and diplomacy, Columbia, 1907-10; research asst. Carnegie Instn., 1911-14; engaged in research on internat. law diplomatic claims for indemnity, 1911-16; dir. of study of Mexican institutions conducted by Edward L. Doheny Research Foundation, associated with U. of Calif.; mem. firm Scott & Eberhard, attys., Los Angeles. Organized and directed legislative drafting work first established in Library of Congress, Washington, and later at Columbia U., N.Y.; mem. Internat. Debts Roundtable Inst. of Politics, 1927. Mem. Phi Beta Kappa (pres. Alumni Assn. of Southern Calif.), Sigma Chi, Phi Delta Phi. Club: Wilshire Country (Los Angeles). Author: Index Analysis of Federal Statutes (with Middleton Beaman), 1908; also articles and reviews on legal and hist. subjects. Law editor Standard Dictionary. Address: 822 S. Alvarado St. Office: 739 S. Spring St., Los Angeles, Calif. Died June 5, 1944.

SCOTT, Hamilton Gray, pub. utility exec.; b. Paterson, N.J., Dec. 29, 1883; s. William Gavin and Rosa (Gray) S.; prep. edn., pub. schs.; studied elec. engring. under pvt. tutor; m. Jane Barnette, Mar. 15, 1913. Began in elec. dept. Rogers Locomotive Works, Paterson, 1905; elec. salesman, Fletcher Stanley Co., 1908; with Shelby lamp div. of Nat. Electric Lamp Assn., 1909-12; in charge power contracts, Atlanta, Ga., for Central Ga. Power Co., 1912; gen. mgr. in charge constrn. and operation, Va. Power Co., 1912-15, v.p., 1915-18; pres. Charleston Industrial Corp., 1918-23, chmn. bd., 1923-25; v.p. Columbia Gas & Electric Co. and subsidiaries, 1923-25; organizer, 1927, Fidelity Pub. Service Co., succeeded by Union Utilities, Inc.; organized Memphis Natural Gas Co.; also dir. various corps. Mem. Am. Inst. Elec. Engrs. Republican. Episcopalian. Mason. Clubs: Bankers Club of America, Union League (New York); Blind Brook Golf (Portchester, N.Y.). Home: 299 Park Av. Office: 120 Broadway, New York, N.Y. Died Nov. 1, 1943.

SCOTT, Henri (Guest), basso; b. Coatesville, Pa., Apr. 8, 1876; s. John Wallace and Mary (Roney) S.; ed. pub. schs., Phila.; Mus. D., Valparaiso U., 1925; m. Alice Macmichael Jefferson, Dec. 30, 1902; children—Randolph J., Henriette G., Eunice T., Janet C., J. P. Jefferson. Intended by father for bus. career, but became concert singer, appearing in many cities in oratorio; sang in concert tour with Caruso, 1908; engaged by Oscar Hammerstein for 5 yrs., 1909. Leading basso. Manhattan Opera Co., New York, season 1909-10, Adriano Theatre, Rome, Italy, 1910-11, Chicago Grand Opera Co., 1911-14, Met. Opera Co., New York, 1915-19. Made operatic début as Ramfis, in "Aïda." Protestant. Mason. Clubs: Art Alliance, Pa. Barge (Phila.); Bohemian (San Francisco). Home: 136 Broadway, Hagerstown, Md. Died Apr. 2, 1942.

SCOTT, Henry D(ickerson), steel mfr.; b. Bridgeport., O., Feb. 26, 1893; s. Isaac MacBurney and Flora Belle (Dickerson) S.; student Hotchkiss Sch., Lakeville, Conn., 1907-10, Yale, 1910-14; m. Lillian Elizabeth Malone, 1919. Bookkeeper Buckeye Rolling Mill Co., Steubenville, O., 1914-15; accountant Wheeling Steel & Iron Co., 1915-17; supt. Wheeling Steel Corp., 1919-26, asst. v.p., 1926-30, v.p. in charge operations, 1937-43; chmn. Scott Lbr. Co., Bridgeport, O., since 1943, Steel Service Inc., The Parkersburg (W.Va.) Steel Co.; president Sharon (Pa.) Tube Co. since 1930. Entered O.T.C., 1917; commd. capt. field arty. U.S. Army, 1918, with A.E.F., 1917-18. Decorated with Croix de Guerre (France). Mem. Am. Legion, Am. Iron and Steel Inst., Am. Petroleum Inst., Phi Beta Kappa, Psi Upsilon. Republican. Presbyterian. Clubs: Ft. Henry, Wheeling Country (Wheeling); Country (Youngstown); Yale (New York). Author: Iron and Steel in Wheeling, 1928. Home: 36 Orchard Rd. Office: Wheeling Steel Corp., Wheeling, W.Va. Died Apr. 21, 1947.

SCOTT, Henry Edwards, editor; b. Wiscasset, Me., Oct. 17, 1859; s. Jonathan Edwards and Eliza Ann (Clark) S.; A.B., Harvard, 1881 (Phi Beta Kappa); post-grad. work, U. of Berlin, 1881-83, U. of Leipzig, 1883-84, École des Chartes, Paris, 1888, Harvard Grad. Sch., 1889-90; m. Harriet Adelia Chapman, Feb. 14, 1888; children—George Chapman, Elizabeth Fletcher (Mrs. Samuel E. Alley, dec.), Henry Edwards, Harriet Adelia (Mrs. Chaplin Tyler). Instr. history, Harvard, 1884-85; prof. Latin, Middlebury (Vt.) Coll., and master St. Paul's Sch., Concord, N.H.; master Medford (Mass.) High Sch., and head of dept. of history, 1903-11; editor of publs. of New Eng. Historic Geneal. Soc., Oct. 1912-Oct. 1937, editor emeritus since 1937. Mem. Am. Hist. Assn., A.A.A.S., Astron. Soc. of the Pacific, New Eng. Historic Geneal. Soc. (life), Mass. Soc. Colonial Wars (hon.), Wiscasset (Me.) Fire Soc.; corr. mem. Me. Hist. Soc. Episcopalian. Club: Boston City. Home: 71 Otis St., Medford, Mass. Office: 9 Ashburton Pl., Boston, Mass. Died Jan. 23, 1944.

SCOTT, Henry Wilson, judge; b. Sangamon County, Ill., Jan. 26, 1866; s. Caleb Longest and Charlotte (Templeton) S.; ed. pvt. tutors and acad.; admitted to bar at age of 18 and engaged in practice at Lyons, Kans., 1881 87; m. Mrs. Marion L. Patton, June 6, 1908. Register U.S. Land Office, Larned, Kan., 1888-91; Dem. candidate for judge, 16th Jud. Dist., Kan., 1889; U.S. dist. judge for Oklahoma Ty., 1893-96; in practice at New York since 1896; resigned to engage in practice in New York. Author: Probate Law and Practice, 1887; Distinguished American Lawyers, 1891; The Evolution of Law, 1908 (4th edit.), 1909; The Courts of the State of New York, 1909; Commentaries of the Evolution of Law; 2 vols., 1909; The Laws of Nations, 3 vols., 1909; The Corporate Institution, 1910. Office: 111 Broadway, New York. Died July 8, 1935.

SCOTT, Isaac MacBurney, mfr.; b. Tuscarawas County, O., Feb. 19, 1866; s. Dr. Wm. Briar and Mary (Boyd) S.; ed. pub. schs., Morristown, O.; m.

Fora B. Dickerson, Jan. 1, 1890; children—Hugh Briar, Henry Dickerson, Arthur MacBurney. Began with Ætna Iron & Nail Co., Bridgeport, O., 1883; sec. Beaver Tin Plate Co., Lisbon, O., 1894-98; sec. Ætna Standard Iron & Steel Co., Bridgeport, O., 1898-1900; auditor Am. Sheet Steel Co., N.Y. City, 1900-03, sec. La Belle Iron Works, Steubenville, O., 1903-04, pres., 1904-13; organized, 1913, Wheeling Sheet & Tin Plate Co., and built tin plate plant at Yorkville, O. (1st plant in world to successfully produce black-plate for tinning by cold-reducing process), merging with Wheeling Steel & Iron Co., 1914, and pres. latter, 1914-20; company merged, 1920, with La Belle Iron Works and Whitaker-Glessner Co., forming Wheeling Steel Corp., of which was pres. until Oct. 31, 1930; chmn. bd. Sharon Tube Co., Scott Lumber Co., Nat. Bank of W.Va.; pres. Buckeye Rolling Mill Co. Republican. Presbyterian. Clubs: Fort Henry (Wheeling); Duquesne (Pittsburgh); Ohio Soc. (N.Y.). Home: Stamm's Lane. Office: Wheeling Bank & Trust Bldg., Wheeling, W.Va. Died Apr. 27, 1942.

SCOTT, James Brown, lawyer, educator; b. Kincardine, Bruce County, Ontario, June 3, 1866; s. John and Jeanette (Brown) S.; A.B., Central High School, Philadelphia, Pa., 1885; A.B., Harvard U., 1890, A.M., 1891; Parker fellow, Harvard U., specializing in internat. law, 1891-94; studied Berlin, Heidelberg and Paris; J.U.D., Heidelberg, 1894; m. Adele C. Reed, 1901 (died Oct. 15, 1939). Formerly engaged in academic work. Solicitor Dept. of State, 1906-10; trustee Carnegie Endowment for Internat. Peace since 1910, sec. of orgn. and dir. Division of International Law, 1910-40, sec. emeritus since 1940; tech. del. to 2d Hague Peace Conf., 1907; spl. adviser Dept. of State, chmn. Joint State and Navy Neutrality Bd., 1914-17; tech. del. to Paris Peace Conf., 1919; tech. adviser to Arms Conf., 1921-22. Pres. Am. Inst. International Law since 1915; president Inst. International Law, 1925-27, 1928-29; sec. Am. Soc. Internat. Law, 1906-24, pres., 1929-39, hon. pres. since 1939; editor in chief Am. Jour. Internat. Law, 1907-24; chmn. U.S. Pan-Am. Com. of Jurists to prepare codes of private and pub. internat. law, Rio de Janeiro, 1927; del. to 6th Pan-Am. Conf., Havana, 1928; chmn. Am. del. to Congress of Rectors, Deans and Educators, Havana, 1930; del. to 4th Pan-Am. Commercial Conf., Washington, 1931. Pvt. and corporal Co. C, 7th Calif. Inf., Spanish-Am. War, 1898; maj. and judge advocate U.S. Army, 1917-19. Commr. of U.S. on the commn. created under the Bryan Treaty for the Advancement of Peace between the U.S. and Norway, 1928; prs. Permanent Commn. Conciliation, Belgium and Switzerland, 1928; designated by Guatemala as mem. Central Am. Internat. Tribunal, 1928; apptd. pres. Danish-Polish Conciliation Commn., 1929; mem. Polish-Brazilian Conciliation Commn., 1935, Commn. of Investigation and Conciliation between Cuba and Peru, 1936, Dano-Venezuelan Permanent Commn. of Conciliation, 1937, Permanent Commission of Conciliation between Belgium and Switzerland, 1937; appointed chairman Permanent Commn. of Conciliation between Chile and Poland, 1937. Mem. Am. Philos. Soc. Author: The Hagues Peace Conferences of 1899 and 1907 (2 vols.), 1909; An International Court of Justic, 1916; Peace Through Justice, 1917; Survey of International Relations Between the United States and Germany (Aug. 1, 1914-Apr. 6, 1917), 1918; James Madison's Notes on Debates in the Federal Convention of 1787 and Their Relation to a More Perfect Society of Nations, 1918; The United States of America, 1920; Robert Bacon, Life and Letters, 1923; Le Français—Langue Diplomatique Moderne, 1924; Sovereign States and Suits, 1925; Cuba, La America Latina, Los Estados Unidos, 1926; The United States and France: Some Opinions on International Gratitude, 1926; Le Progrès du Droit des Gens, 1930, 31, 34; De Grasse à Yorktown, 1931; The Spanish Origin of International Law—Part I; Francisco de Vitoria and His Law of Nations, 1934; The Catholic Conception of International Law, 1934; The Spanish Conception of International Law and of Sanctions, 1934; Conferencias—en homenaje a la Universidad Mayor de San Marcos, Lima, Peru, 1938; Law, the State and the International Community, 2 vols., 1939. Clubs: Century (New York); Army and Navy, Metropolitan, Cosmos (Washington). Home: Wardour, Anne Arundel County, Md. Office: 700 Jackson Pl., Washington, D.C. Died June 25, 1943.

SCOTT, John Adams, college prof.; b. Fletcher, Ill., Sept. 15, 1867; s. James Sterling and Henrietta (Sutton) S.; grad. classical dept. Ill. State Normal Sch., 1887; A.B., Northwestern U., 1891; Ph.D., Johns Hopkins, 1897; studied at Göttingen and Munich, Germany; LL.D., Illinois Coll., Jacksonville, 1916; m. Matilda J. Spring, Sept. 1, 1892; children—Dorothy L., Frederic S. (dec.). Instr., asst. and asso. prof. Greek, Northwestern U., 1897-1901, prof., 1901-04, head prof., 1904-23, John C. Shaffer prof. of Greek, 1923-38, emeritus, Sather prof. classical lit., Univ. of Calif., 1920-21. Councillor Am. Sch. at Athens. Mem. Am. Philol. Assn. (ex-pres.), Classical Assn. Middle West and South (ex-pres.), Archeol. Inst. America, Phi Beta Kappa. Author: The Unity of Homer, 1921; Homer, Our Debt to Greece and Rome Series, 1925; Socrates and Christ, 1929; Luke, the Greek Physician, 1930; We Would Know Jesus, 1937; also numerous pamphlets, articles and reviews. Formerly asso. editor Classical Jour. Clubs: Gull Lake Country (ex-pres.), Shuffle Board, (Dunedin, Fla.); University. Home: North Shore Hotel, Evanston. Ill. Died Oct. 27. 1947.

SCOTT, John R. K., congressman; b. Bloomsburg, Pa., July 6, 1873; A.B., Central High Sch., Phila., 1893; student U. of Pa., Law Sch. and under W.W. Smithers and James N. Shakespeare. Admitted to Pa. bar, 1895; mem. Pa. Ho. of Rep., 1899, 08, 10, 13; mem. 64th and 65th Congresses (1915-19), Pa. at-large. Republican. Office: Lincoln Bldg., Philadelphia. Died Dec. 9, 1945.

SCOTT, Jonathan French, author; b. Newark, N.J., Dec. 10, 1882; s. Austin and Anna Prentiss (Stearns) S.; A.B., Rutgers Coll., New Brunswick, N.J., 1902, A.M., 1905; Ph.D., U. of Wis., 1913; m. Marguerite Egbert, Nov. 22, 1910; children—Margaret Phillips, Genevieve Louise. Instr. in history, U. of Mich., 1913-18; actg. asst. prof. history, U. of Rochester, 1918-21, asst. prof., 1921-24; travel and research in Europe, 1924-26; lecturer on history, New York U., Washington Sq. Coll., 1927-29, asst. prof. history since 1929. Mem. Am. Hist. Assn., Delta Phi, Phi Beta Kappa. Mem. Dutch Ref. Ch. Author: Historical Essays on Apprenticeship and Vocational Education, 1914; Patriots in the Making—What America Can Learn from France and Germany, 1916; The Menace of Nationalism in Education, 1926; Five Weeks—The Surge of Public Opinion on the Eve of the Great War, 1927; The Twilight of the Kings, 1938; Editor: (with A. Baltzly) Readings in European History since 1814, 1930; (with A. Hyma and A. H. Noyes) Readings in Medieval History, 1933; (with F. H. McCloskey and J. S. Terry) What College Offers, 1941. Home: 167 Glenwood Av., Yonkers, N.Y. Died May 30, 1942.

SCOTT, Miriam Finn (Mrs. Leroy Scott), child diagnostician; b. Russia, Aug. 9, 1882; d. Moses and Gittel (Seletchnick) Finn; came to U.S., 1893; A.B., Hunter's Coll., N.Y. City, 1903; spl. work, Barnard Coll., Columbia; A.M., N.Y. State U., 1936; m. Leroy Scott, June 24, 1904; children—Helen Finn (Mrs. George H. Waltz, Jr.), Hilda (Mrs. Herbert Lass), David. In charge of 1,000 children on first roof playground in New York City, 1898; became actively identified with various institutions, in educating young children through play and intimate personal contact; dir. of children's work, Univ. Settlement, N.Y. City, 1899-1903; dir. of girls' work, Speyer Sch. (Columbia U.), 1903-06; founder The Children's Garden; now specializes in development of the individual child through the extensive coöperation of home and school; dir. Sch. for Parents since 1937; lecturer; delivered 6 lectures at univ. of Leningrad and Moscow, Russia, summer, 1928. Mem. Am. Social Hygiene Assn., Nat. Bd. of Review, Motion Pictures, Inc., Common Council for American Unity, Authors League America, American Russian Inst., Pi Gamma Mu Frat. Clubs: Pen and Brush, Woman's City. Author: How to Know Your Child, 1915; Meeting Your Child's Problem, 1922. Contbr. to mags. Radio speaker on parent edn. over stations WEAF, WOR, WHN, WNYC, 1934-37. Address: 200 E. 16th St., New York, N.Y. Died Jan. 6, 1944.

SCOTT, Richard Hugh, automobile mfr.; b. Renfrew County, Ont., Can., July 23, 1869; s. Thomas and Mary Jane (Scott) S.; ed. country sch.; m. Gertrude E. Teel, Aug. 24, 1898; 1 son, Maurice M. Came to U.S., 1886, naturalized citizen. Began as an apprentice machinist with The Paige Tube Co., Warren, O., 1886; with Reo Motor Car Co. since 1904, pres. and gen. mgr. since 1917; pres. Atlas Drop Forge Co., Novo Engine Co.; dir. Michigan Screw Co. Republican. Methodist. Home: 109 W. Main St. Office: Reo Motor Car Co., Lansing, Mich. Died March 11, 1944.

SCOTT, William Amasa, univ. prof.; b. Clarkson, Monroe County, N.Y., Apr. 17, 1862; s. Thomas and Huldy Ann (Richards) S.; A.B., U. of Rochester, 1886, A.M., 1887, LL.D., 1911, U.S.D., 1922; Ph.D., Johns Hopkins U., 1892; m. Lizette F. Rockwell, June 1889 (died Feb. 1896); m. 2d, Nellie Irene Nash, June 13, 1899; 1 son, Stuart Nash. Prof. history and polit. science, U. of S.D., 1887-90; grad. student and instr. history, Johns Hopkins, 1890-92; asst. prof. polit. economy, U. of Wis., 1892-93, asso. prof., 1893-97, prof., 1897-1931, dir. Sch. of Commerce, 1900-27. Mem. Am. Econ. Assn., Am. Statis. Assn., Am. Acad. Polit. and Social Science, Wis. State Hist. Soc., Wis. Acad. Sciences, Arts and Letters, Alpha Delta Phi, Phi Beta Kappa. Author: Repudiation of State Debts, 1893; Money and Banking, 1903, revised, 1910, 16, 26; Money and Banking, 1913; Austrian School and Recent Developments, ch. VII revised edit. Ingram's History of Political Economy, 1915; Development of Economics, 1933. Translator: Bohm-Bawerk's Recent Literature on Interest, 1903. Contbr. to econ. jours. Home: Winter Park, Fla. Died Nov. 6, 1944.

SCOTT, William Berryman, geologist; b. Cincinnati, Feb. 12, 1858; s. Rev. William M. and Mary E. (Hodge) S., g.g.d. of Benjamin Franklin; A.B., Princeton, 1877; Ph.D., Heidelberg, 1880; LL.D., U. of Pa., 1906; Sc.D., Harvard, 1909, Oxford U., 1912, Princeton, 1930; m. Alice A. Post, Dec. 15, 1883. Asst. in geology, Princeton U., 1883, prof. geology and paleontology, 1884-1930, now emeritus prof. Mem. Nat. Acad. Sciences, Am. Philos. Soc. (pres. 1918-25), Geol. Soc. America (pres. 1924-25). Awarded E. K. Kane medal, Geog. Soc. Phila.; Wollaston medal, Geol. Soc., London, 1910; F. V. Hayden medal, Acad. Nat. Sci., Phila., 1926; Elizabeth Clark Thompson gold medal, Nat. Acad. Sciences, 1931; R. A. Penrose gold medal, Geol. Soc. Am., 1939; Daniel Girand Elliot gold medal, Nat. Acad. Sciences, 1941. Author: An Introduction to Geology, 1897, 3d edit., 1932; A History of Land Mammals in the Western Hemisphere, 1913, 2d Edit., 1937; The Mammalian Fauna of the White River Oligocene, 1935-41; Mammalian Fauna of the Duchesne River, 1945; The Theory of Evolution, 1917; Physiography, 1922; also about 60 monographs upon geol. and palæontol. subjects. Editor and joint author of Reports Princeton University expdns. to Patagonia (9 vols.). Home: 7 Cleveland Lane, Princeton, N.J. Died Mar. 29, 1947.

SCRUGHAM, James Graves (skrŭg'ăm), U.S. senator; b. Lexington, Ky., Jan. 19, 1880; s. James Grinstead and Theodotia (Allen) S.; B.M.E., State U. of Ky., 1900, M.E., 1906; m. Julia McCann, Aug. 4, 1904; children—James G., Martha. Successively with Creaghead Engring. Co. (Cincinnati), Met. West Side Elevated Ry. Co. (Chicago), Abner Doble Co. (San Francisco), 1899-1903; prof. of mech. engring., Engineering College, University of Nevada, 1903-14, dean, 1914-17; state engineer of Nevada, 1917-23. Pub. service commr., State of Nev., 1919-23; gov. of Nev., term 1923-27; spl. adviser to the sec. of the Interior, on Colorado River development projects, 1927; mem. 73d to 77th Congresses (1933-43), at large, Nev.; chmn. subcom. on Naval Appropriations, Ho. of Reps.; elected U.S. senator from Nev., Nov. 1942. Associate member of U.S. Naval Consulting Bd., 1916. Commd. maj., O.R.C., 1917; lt. col. U.S. Army, 1918; lt. col. 517th Regt. Coast Arty., U.S. Army Res. Commr. exhibits for Nev., San Francisco Expn., 1915; Nevada agt. and signatory Colorado River Compact, 1922; Nat. v. comdr. Am. Legion, 1920-21 (State comdr., 1919-20). Mem. Tau Beta Pi, Sigma Chi, Phi Kappa Phi. Democrat. Mason, Elk. Former pub. Nevada State Journal, Reno. Address: Reno, Nev. Died June 2, 1945.

SCRUGHAM, William Warburton, lawyer; b. Yonkers, N.Y., Feb. 18, 1860; s. William Warburton and Mary (Kellinger) S.; A.B., 1st honors, Columbia, 1880; LL.B., 1882; m. Margaret Bradford Otis, Oct. 26, 1891. Admitted to N.Y. bar, 1882, and began practice at N.Y. City; practiced at Yonkers since 1887; mem. firm Scrugham & Arbuckle since 1920; pres. Yonkers Gas Light Co., 1895-1900; pres. Westchester Lighting Co., 1900-05; pres. First Nat. Bank of Yonkers, 1910-11, 1920-21, chmn. bd., 1922-29; same, Central Nat. Bank of Yonkers since 1929; v.p. Yonkers Savings Bank, 1925-35; dir. Central Safe Deposit Co. of Yonkers; trustee and counsel Yonkers Bldg. & Loan Assn; trustee, Oakland Cemetery. Acting city judge, Yonkers, 1889-90 and 1893-94; mem. Bd. of Edn., Yonkers, 1888-91; mem. legal advisory board of the Selective Draft, Westchester County, World War. Recipient of medal for conspicuous alumni service. Pres. Yonkers Public Library, 1924-35; trustee Supreme Court Library, Westchester County, 1918-38; trustee House of Rest, Yonkers. Mem. Am. and Westchester County bar assns., N.Y. State Bar Assn. (mem. exec. com. and com. on law reform), Assn. Bar City, New York, Yonkers Lawyers Assn. (pres. 1926-29), Phi Beta Kappa. Republican. Episcopalian. Clubs: Columbia University, Century Assn. (New York). Home: 15 Greystone Terrace. Office: 45 S. Broadway, Yonkers, N.Y. Died July 19, 1944.

SCUDDER, Charles Locke (skŭd'ẽr), surgeon; b. Kent, Conn., 1860; s. Evarts and Sarah (Lamson) S.; A.B., Yale, 1882, Ph.B., 1883; M.D., Harvard U., 1888; m. Abigail T. Seelye, Sept. 5, 1895. Cons. surgeon to Mass. Gen. Hosp. Fellow Am. Coll. Surgeons, Am. Surg. Assn.; mem. Soc. Clin. Surgery, A.M.A., Am. Coll. Surgeons, Mass. Med. Soc., Boston Surg. Soc.; hon. mem. Am. Acad. of Orthopaedic Surgeons, Am. Assn. for Surgery of Trauma. Club: Harvard. Author: Treatment of Fractures (11 edits.), 1900-39; Tumors of the Jaw, 1912. Address: 20 Chapel St., Brookline, Mass. Died Aug. 19, 1949.

SCUDDER, Doremus, clergyman; b. New York, N.Y., Dec. 15, 1858; s. Rev. Henry Martyn and Fanny (Lewis) S.; grad. Adelphi Acad., Brooklyn, 1875; A.B., Yale, 1880; Union Theol. Sem., 1880-82; Coll. Phys. and Surg. (Columbia U.), 1881-82; M.D., Chicago Med. Coll. (Northwestern U.), 1884; D.D., Whitman Coll., Wash., 1898; m. Eliza Canfield Kendall, June 21, 1888 (died June 26, 1914); children—Stephen (dec.), Dorothy (dec.); m. 2d, Mabel E. Bosher, Jan. 25, 1916; 1 dau., Katharine. Commd. missionary of A.B.C.F.M. to Japan, 1884; ordained Kobe, Japan, June 17, 1885; stationed at Niigata, Japan, 1885; returned to U.S., 1889; pastor Workers' (now Doremus Congl.) Ch., Chicago, 1890-92, East Ch., Brooklyn, 1892-95, First Ch., Woburn, Mass., 1895-1901; missionary of the Hawaiian Bd. as supt. of Japanese work, 1902-04; sec. and gen. supt. of all Congl. missions, H.I., 1904-07; minister Central Union Ch., Honolulu, 1907-16; v.p. bd. mgrs. Mid-Pacific Inst., 1909-15, pres., 1915-16; mem. Federal Council Commn. Am. Relations with Japan. Editor-in-chief The Friend, 1904-16, Far East editor, 1917; pastor Tokyo Union Ch., 1916-19. Maj., Am. Red Cross, 1918; Am. Red Cross dir. civilian relief, Eastern Siberia, 1918, Western Siberia, 1919. Exec. sec. Hawaii Centennial, 1919-20. Exec. sec. Greater Boston Federation of Churches, 1920-22; minister-at-large since 1922. Newspaper corr. Mem. exec. com. Southern Calif. Civil Liberty Union since 1923; mem. editorial bd. Open Forum since 1924. Author: Our Children for Christ, 1899; The Passion for Reality, 1910. Home: 133 W. 9th St., Claremont, Calif. Died July 23, 1942.

SEABROOK, William Buehler, writer; b. Westminster, Md., Feb. 22, 1886; s. William Levin and Myra Phelps (Buehler) S.; grad. Mercersburg (Pa.) Acad., 1901; student Roanoke Coll., Salem, Va., 1902; Ph.B., Newberry (S.C.) Coll., 1905, A.M., 1906; grad. study in philosophy, U. of Geneva, Switzerland, 1908; m. Katherine Pauline Edmondson, Nov. 1912 (div. 1934); m. 2d, Marjorie Worthington, Feb.

1935 (div. 1941); m. 3d Constance Kuhr, 1942; one son, born Feb. 21, 1943. Reporter and city editor Augusta Chronicle, 1906; tramping through Europe and free lance writer, 1907-08; reporter Atlanta Journal, 1909-10; partner Lewis-Seabrook Advertising Agency, Atlanta, 1911-15; reporter N.Y. Times, 1917; feature writer, newspaper syndicates, 1917-24; engaged in travel, exploration and writing since 1924. Has lived as member Bedouin trible, with Druses in Arabian mountains, in whirling dervish monastery at Tripoli, with Zezidee devil worshippers in Kurdistan; spent 1 yr. with voodoo worshippers in mountains of Haiti and 1 yr. in West Africa; crossed and explored Sahara, by airplane. Served as private with French Army; gassed at Verdun. Mem. Phi Gamma Delta. Author: Adventures in Arabia, 1927; The Magic Island, 1929; Jungle Ways, 1931; Air Adventure, 1933; The White Monk of Timbuctoo, 1934; Asylum, 1935; These Foreigners, 1938; Witchcraft, 1940; Modern Wizard of the Laboratory (a biography of Robt. W. Wood), 1941; No Hiding Place (autobiography), 1942. Contbr. to Collier's, McCall's Magazine, Cosmopolitan, Forum, Atlantic Monthly, Vanity Fair, American Magazine, Town and Country, Reader's Digest, English Review, Nash's Magazine, Revue de Paris, Mercure de France, Candide, Nouvelle Literaire, Gringeire, l'Intransigeant. Home: Rhinebeck, N.Y. Address: care J. B. Lippincott Co., 521 Fifth Av., New York, N.Y. Died Sept. 20, 1945.

SEABURY, Francis William, lawyer; b. Norfolk, Va., May 10, 1868; s. William Henry and Martha Maria (Hicks) S.; prep. edn., Norfolk Acad.; grad. U. of Va., 1888; m. Margaret Cater, Sept. 25, 1901; children—Margaret (Mrs. E. A. Rendall), Mary Gray (Mrs. H. G. Stilwell, Jr.), Edward (dec.), Martha (Mrs. Robt. G. Norfleet, II.). Admitted to Tex. bar, 1891, began practice, Brownsville; city atty. Brownsville, Tex., 1893; mem. Tex. Ho. of Rep., 1894-98, 1900-06 (speaker 1904-06); county atty. Starr County, Tex., 1907; mem. Bd. Legal Examiners, Tex., 1911-15; chmn. Dem. County Executive Com., Cameron County, Texas, 1920-24. Mem. Am. Bar Assn. Episcopalian. Home: 147 W. Levee St. Office: Seabury, George & Taylor Bldg., Brownsville, Tex. Died Feb. 6, 1946.

SEABURY, George Tilley, sec. Am. Soc. of Civil Engrs.; b. Newport, R.I., Apr. 12, 1880; s. T. Mumford and Mary S. (Tilley) S.; S.B. in Civil Engring., Mass. Inst. Tech., 1902; m. Margaret Howard Knight, Sept. 6, 1904; children—Howard Knight (dec.), T. Mumford III (dec.), Mary Knight (Mrs. Mary Seabury Ray). Field engr. for contractors and construction engr. on subways, Riverside Drive, Grand Central Terminal, etc., N.Y. City, 1902-06; engr. with Bd. of Water Supply, N.Y. City, on Catskill Aqueduct, 1906-15; div. engr. Water Supply Bd., Providence, R.I., on new water supply development, 1915-18; maj. Q.M.C., U.S. Army, and supervising constrn. q.m., Apr. 1918-June 1919; pres., gen. mgr. George T. Seabury, Inc., gen. constrn., 1919-23; sec. Am. Soc. C.E. since Jan. 1, 1925. Mem. Am. Soc. C.E., Engring. Inst. of Can., Delta Upsilon, Chi Epsilon (nat. hon.). Episcopalian. Office: 33 W. 39th St., New York, N.Y. Died May 25, 1945.

SEABURY, William Marston, lawyer; b. N.Y. City, Mar. 18, 1878; s. William Jones (D.D.) and Alice Van Wyck (Beare) S.; gt. gt. g. s. Rev. Samuel Seabury, 1st bishop in America; ed. pvt. schs. and under tutors; LL.B., cum laude, N.Y. Law Sch., 1898; m. Katharine Emerson Hovey, Nov. 10, 1900; children—Lispenard (Mrs. Edward Savage Crocker), Etheldreda Winthrop (Mrs. Fergus Reid, Jr.), Muriel Gurdon (Mrs. William White Howells). Admitted to N.Y. bar, 1899, later to bars of Ariz., Calif., Mass., and to federal courts; moved to Phoenix, Ariz., 1910, on account of ill health; resumed practice in N.Y. City, 1915. Awarded decoration known as University Palms and nominated Officier d' Académie (France) in recognition of writings on subject of motion pictures in their relation to pub. welfare and their internat. and economic aspects; Knight Commander, Order of Polonia Restituta (Poland); Comdr. Order of St. Sava (Yugoslavia); Chevalier Legion of Honor (France); commander Portuguese Order of Public Instruction. Episcopalian. Club: Century (New York). Author: The Public and the Motion Picture Industry; Motion Picture Problems—The Cinema and the League of Nations. Home: 535 Park Av., New York 21, N.Y. Died Nov. 8, 1949.

SEACREST, Joseph Claggett (sē'krĕst), newspaper pub.; b. Franklin County, Pa., Dec. 7, 1864; s. Jacob Benedict and Emma (Winger) S.; ed. country sch.; m. Jessie Snively, Nov. 24, 1892; children—Fred, Joe W., Jessie (Mrs. Alan McIntosh; deceased). With Greencastle (Pa.) Press, beginning as apprentice, 1878-1887; with Neb. State Journal, Lincoln, Neb., since 1887; pres. State Journal Co. Republican. Conglist. Mason. Rotarian. Home: 33d and Sumner Sts. Address: State Journal Co.'s Bldg., Lincoln, Neb. Died Apr. 21, 1942.

SEAGER, Charles Allen, Anglican archbishop; b. Goderich, Ont., Can., July 9, 1872; s. Charles and Margaret E. (Padfield) S.; A.M., Univ. of Trinity Coll., Toronto, 1895, D.D. (hon.), 1915; LL.D. (hon.), Univ. of Toronto, 1921; LL.D. (hon.) Univ. of Western Ont., 1936; m. Mary Lilian Paterson, Oct. 17, 1905; children—Margaret L. (Mrs. James L. Auld), Hilda M. (Mrs. Paul Rechnitzer), Marion G. (Mrs. J. Billingsley), Charles. Ordained to ministry of Anglican Ch., 1896, archbishop of Ont., Nov. 24, 1943; rector St. Cyprians Ch., Toronto, Ont., 1891-1911, All Saints Ch., Vernon, B.C., 1911-12; prin. St. Marks Theol. Hall, Vancouver, B.C., 1912-17; rector St. Matthews Ch., Toronto, 1917-21; provost and vice chancellor Univ. of Trinity Coll., Toronto, 1921-26; canon and chancellor St. Alban's Cathedral, Toronto, 1919-26; bishop of Ont., 1926-32, bishop of Huron, 1932-43; archbishop and metropolitan of Ont. since 1943. Pres. Huron Coll. Council, London, Ont., since 1932. Mason (32°, master, 1927, grand chaplain, 1928; pres. exec. com. Red Cross of Constantine), Royal Order of Scotland. Home: 150 James St. Office: Synod Offices, London, Ont., Can. Died Sept. 9, 1948.

SEAGLE, Oscar, baritone singer, teacher; b. Chattanooga, Tenn., Oct. 31, 1877; s. James and Mary (McNabb) S.; studied voice with Jean de Reszke, Paris, France, 12 yrs. (also assistant and associate until 1925); m. Nell de Wees, Sept. 17, 1901; children—Jean Dewees, Betty Eleanor. Début in Paris, 1902; sang in opera houses throughout Europe; settled in New York, 1914; established, 1922, the de Reszke-Seagle Sch. for Singers at Schroon Lake, N.Y., and Nice, France. Presbyterian. Home: 160 W. 73d St., New York. Died Dec. 20, 1945.

SEARBY, Edmund Wilson (sēr'bĭ), army officer; b. Berkeley, Calif., Mar. 7, 1896; s. Frederick Wright and Ellen (Porter) S.; U. of Calif., 1914-16; B.S., U.S. Mil. Acad., 1918; grad. Field Arty. Sch., 1928; Command and Gen. Staff Sch., 1940; Cav. Sch., 1929; attended Ecole d'Application d'Artillerie, 1920-21; m. Muriel MacLeod, Aug. 26, 1930; children—Lucy Carter, Frederick Wright, Daniel MacLeod. Commd. 2d lt. F.A., 1918; promoted through grades to brig. gen., 1943; comdg. gen. 80th Div. Arty. Awarded Victory medal. Mem. Delta Chi. Home: Sebastopol, Calif. Died Sep. 14, 1944.

SEARS, Charles Hatch, church official; b. Preble, N.Y., Nov. 21, 1870; s. Henry and Mary (Hatch) S.; grad. Colgate Acad., 1894; B.A., Colgate U., 1898, D.D., 1918; M.A., Columbia U., 1900; B.D., Union Theol. Sem., 1901; m. Jeannette F. Allen, Sept. 7, 1899 (died Apr. 9, 1930); children—Miriam Jeannette, Raymond (adopted); m. 2d, Miss Minnie Vera Sandberg, July 1933. Ordained ministry Baptist Ch., 1901; asst. pastor Judson Memorial Ch., New York, 1901-04; founder and co-pastor Creston Av. Ch., 1903-07; exec. officer New York Baptist City Soc. since 1904, now gen. sec.; gen. sec. Bapt. Ch. Extension Soc. since 1918; treas. Am. Bible Union; mem. bd. dirs., New York Federation Churchs since 1908; mem. Japan Church Survey Layman's Foreign Mission Inquiry, 1930-31; mem. research committee Welfare Council; mem. executive committee Federal Council of Chs.; rec. sec. Federal Council Churches since 1938. Trustee Colgate U., Colgate-Rochester Div. Sch. Mem. Am. Sociol. Soc., Phi Beta Kappa, Delta Upsilon. Republican. Clubs: Clergy, Quill, Union League (New York). Author: The Redemption of the City, 1911; Life of Edward Judson, 1917; The Crowded Ways, 1929; City Man, 1936; also numerous articles in religious papers. Editor: New American Series (6 vols.), 1922; Baptist City Planning, 1926; Church City Planning, 1928. Home: 35 Edgecliff Terrace, Yonkers, N.Y. Office: 152 Madison Av., New York, N.Y. Died May 3, 1943.

SEARS, Edmund Hamilton, educator; b. Wayland, Mass., Apr. 20, 1852; s. Edmund Hamilton and Ellen (Bacon) S.; grad. Boston Latin Sch., 1870; A.B., Harvard, 1874; A.M., spl. work in classics, Washington U., St. Louis, 1897; Litt.D., 1925; m. Hellen Clark Swazey, June 19, 1895. Teacher Hampton (Va.) Normal and Agrl. Sch., 1874-75; instr. Latin and Greek, U. of Calif., 1875-83; established and conducted pvt. sch. for girls at Boston, 1885-91; prin. Mary Inst. (inc. under charter of Washington U.), 1891-1925. Swedenborgian. Author: Political Growth in the Nineteenth Century, 1900; The Son of the Prefect, 1915; Zatthu, A Tale of Ancient Galilee, 1925; A Worker in Wood, 1929; Meeting Currents, 1930. Contbr. New Jerusalem Magazine. Clubs: Round Table, Classical, Authors (St. Louis); Algonquin, Authors (Boston); California (Los Angeles); Authors' (London). Mem. Phi Beta Kappa. Address: California Club, Los Angeles, Calif. Died July 29, 1942.

SEARS, Herbert Mason, trustee; b. Boston, Mass., Nov. 12, 1867; s. Frederick Richard and Albertina Homer (Shelton) S.; A.B., Harvard, 1889; m. Caroline Bartlett, June 2, 1891 (died 1908); children—Elizabeth (Mrs. Bayard Warren), and Phyllis (Mrs. Bayard Tuckerman, Jr.). Clk. Lee Higginson & Co., bankers, Boston, 1890-95; mem. firm Curtis & Motley, 1895-1900; pres. Fifty Associates (real estate); 1st v.p. Suffolk Savings Bank; dir. New Eng. Trust Co., Boston & Albany R.R. Served with Am. Red Cross, attached to French Army in Belgium, 1917-18. Mem. bd. Free Hosp. for Women. Decorated Croix de Guerre and Reconnaissance (French). Republican. Clubs: Tennis and Racquet (Boston); Somerset; Eastern Yacht (Marblehead); New York Yacht (New York). Home: 287 Commonwealth Av. Office: 53 State St., Boston, Mass. Died Feb. 19, 1942.

SEARS, Joseph Hamblen, author, pub.; b. Boston, Mass., Apr. 10, 1865; s. J. Henry and Emily (Nickerson) S.; A.B., Harvard, 1889; Berlin and Paris, 2 yrs.; m. Anna Wentworth Caldwell, 1891. With Harper & Bros., 10 yrs.; pres. D. Appleton Co., pub., New York, 1904-18; pres. J. H. Sears & Co., publishers, 1922-34. Clubs: Garrick (London); Cercle Union Artistique (Paris); Century, Harvard, Union, Piping Rock (New York). Author: The Governments of the World Today, 1893; Fur and Feather Tales, 1897; None But the Brave, 1902; A Box of Matches, 1904; The Career of Leonard Wood, 1916; The Ormsteads. Home: Oyster Bay, L.I., N.Y. Died Feb. 15, 1946.

SEARS, Nathan Pratt, physician; b. Syracuse, N.Y., Feb. 8, 1886; s. Frederick William and Jessie (Pratt) S.; Ph.B., Syracuse U., 1908; M.D., Johns Hopkins U., 1912; m. Emily Constantia Rivers, Jan. 4, 1915 (div. July 1944); children—Kathryn Virginia, (Mrs. Paul Frederick MacLeod), Helen Rivers (Mrs. Willard Alexander Healy); married 2d, Minnie Hughes Burrill, May 23, 1945. In practice, Syracuse, N.Y., since 1915; mem. faculty, Syracuse U. Coll. of Med. since 1915, prof. gynecology since 1940; gynecologist in chief Syracuse Memorial Hosp. since 1932; pathologist Hazard Memorial Lab. since 1917; attending gynecologist Univ. Hosp. since 1929; cons. gynecologist Syracuse Free Dispensary since 1915, City and Psychopathic Hosps. since 1937. Diplomate Am. Bd. Obstetrics and Gynecology; fellow Am. Coll. Surgeons; mem. Am. Gynecol. Soc., Am. Assn. Obstet., Gynecol. and Abdominal Surgeons, A.M.A., Med. Soc. of State of N.Y., Onondaga Med. Soc. (former pres.), Syracuse Acad. Med., A.A.A.S., Sigma Xi. Phi Delta Theta. Republican. Clubs: Innominate, Confreres; University (Syracuse). Home: Morrisville, N.Y., R.D. No. 2. Office: Med. Arts Bldg., 713 E. Genesee St., Syracuse, N.Y. Died Feb. 25, 1946.

SEARS, William Joseph, ex-congressman; b. Smithville, Ga., Dec. 4, 1874; A.B., Fla. State Coll., Lake City, 1895; B.L., Mercer U., Macon, Ga., 1896 (hon. A.B., U. of Fla., 1911); m. Daisy Watson, 1901. Admitted to practice in Ga. and Fla., 1896, Supreme Court of U.S., 1912. Mayor of Kissimmee, Fla., 1899-1900; mem. City Council, 1907-11; county supt. pub. instrn., 1905-15; mem. 64th to 70th Congresses (1915-29), 4th Fla. Dist., and 73d and 74th Congresses (1933-37), Fla. at large. Mem. U.S. Tariff Commn., Washington, 1937; now mem. bd. Vet. Appeals. Democrat. Home: 700 Atlantic Nat. Bank Bldg., Jacksonville, Fla. Office: Veterans Adminstrn., Washington, D.C. Died Mar. 20, 1944.

SEASHORE, Carl Emil, coll. dean; b. Mörlunda, Sweden, Jan. 28, 1866; s. Carl Gustaf and Emily Charlotta (Borg) S.; A.B., Gustavus Adolphus Coll., 1891, D.Litt., 1937; Ph.D., Yale, 1895; Sc.D., 1935; LL.D., Wittenberg Coll., 1927; Sc.D., U. of Pittsburgh, 1931; LL.D., U. of Southern Calif., 1935; L.H.D., Augustana Coll., 1939; Mus.D., Chicago Musical Coll., 1939; m. Mary Roberta Holmes, June 7, 1900; children—Robert Holmes, Carl Gustav, Marion Dubois, Sigfrid. Asst. in Psychol. Lab., Yale, 1895-97; asst. prof. philosophy, State U. of Ia., 1897-1902, prof. psychology since 1902, head dept. psychology, 1905-37, dean Grad. Coll., 1908-36, dean emeritus since 1936, dean pro tempore, 1942-46. Mem. Nat. Acad. Sciences, Acoustical Soc. Am., American Psychol. Assn. (president 1911), Sigma Alpha Epsilon, Gamma Alpha, Phi Delta Kappa (laureate in edn. of Kappa Delta Pi); chairman division anthropology and psychology, National Research Council, 1921-22; chairman division anthropology and psychology, National Acad. Science, 1933-39; fellow A.A.A.S., Soc. Exptl. Psychologists, (hon. fellow) British Psychological Assn. Author: Elementary Experiments in Psychology, 1908; Psychology in Daily Life, 1913; The Psychology of Musical Talent, 1919; Introduction to Psychology, 1922; Learning and Living in College, 1927; Trends in Graduate Study, 1931; Psychol. of Music, 1938; A Preview to College and Life, 1938; The Junior College Movement, 1941; Why We Love Music, 1941; Pioneering in Psychology, 1942; Psychology and Life in Autobiography, 1949; also papers on work and fatigue, mental work, illusions, psychology of music, gifted students, etc. Editor: Univ. of Iowa Studies in Psychology, vols. 2-12; Studies in the Psychology of Music. Originator, Seashore Measures of Musical Talents, 1919, revised, 1939; In Search of Beauty in Music, 1947. Address: Iowa City, Ia. Died Oct. 16, 1949.

SEAVEY, Clyde Leroy, mem. Fed. Power Commn.; b. Dixon, Ill., Aug. 10, 1874; s. Fletcher and Eveline (Eastwood) S.; ed. Ill. Normal Sch. and Dixon Bus. Coll., 1892-96; m. Lucile Follett, May 11, 1903; children—Clyde Follett, Wilma, Lucile. In assay office and in charge gen. supply store of mining company, Tucson, Ariz., 1896-98; newspaper bus. and editorial depts., Pasadena, Calif., 1898-1903; asst. sec. State Bd. of Examiners of Calif., auditing, accounting, etc., 1903-11; mem. State Bd. of Control state instns., accounting, etc., Calif., 1911-15; chmn. State Tax Commn., 1915-17; again mem. State Bd. of Control 1917-21; mem. State Civil Service Commn., 1921-23, also city mgr., Sacramento; mem. Railroad Commn., Calif., 2 terms, 1923-34, advancing to pres.; apptd. mem. Fed. Power Commn., Washington, D.C., Aug. 13, 1934, reapptd. for term 1935-40, elected vice chmn., 1937, chmn., 1939. Republican. Clubs: Commonwealth of Calif., Sierra (San Francisco). Legal Residence: Berkeley, Calif. Home: 3700 Massachusetts Av. Office: 1800 Pennsylvania Av. N.W., Washington, D.C. Died Aug. 5, 1943.

SEAY, Edward Tucker (sē), lawyer; b. Hartsville, Tenn., Oct. 15, 1868; s. George Edward and Mary Jane (Lauderdale) S.; LL.B., Vanderbilt, 1891; m. Polly Barr, Mar. 29, 1893; children—Mary Laura (Mrs. J. C. Edwards), Katherine L., Edward T. (dec.). Admitted to Tenn. bar, 1891, and began practice at Gallatin; moved to Nashville, 1907; mem. firm Seay, Stockell & Edwards; dist. atty., L.&N. R.R.; prof. law, Vanderbilt U., 1908-31; dir. Nat. Life and Accident Ins. Co. Mem. Tenn. State Senate, 1899, 1901, 03; lt. gov. of Tenn., 1903-05; spl. justice Supreme Court and Court of Appeals, Tenn. Mem. bd.

trustees Vanderbilt U. Mem. Am. and Tenn. State bar assns., Nashville Chamber Commerce, Kappa Alpha. Democrat. Mem. Christian (Disciples) Ch. Mason (32°, Shriner), K.P. Clubs: Kiwanis, Round Table, Belle Meade Country. Home: 3702 Richland Av. Office: American Nat. Bank Bldg., Nashville, Tenn. Died Aug. 19, 1941.

SECRIST, Horace (sē'krist), economist, statistician; b. Farmington, Utah, Oct. 9, 1881; s. Jacob M. and Polly Estella (Smith) S.; A.B., U. of Wis., 1907, A.M., 1909, Ph.D., 1911; m. May Alexander, Sept. 14, 1904; children—Horace Alexander, Lee Horton. Instr. economics, U. of Wis., 1910-11; statistician, Wis. Industrial Commn., 1911-12; asst. prof. economics, Northwestern U., 1912-16, same, economics and statistics, 1916-18, prof. since 1918, dir. Bur. Bus. Research, 1919-33; expert spl. agt., U.S. Census Bur., 1909; U.S. Commn. on Industrial Relations, 1914; statistician tonnage sect., div. of planning and statistics, U.S. Shipping Bd., 1918; supervising statistician, U.S. R.R. Labor Bd., 1920-21; dir. of research, Claremont (Calif.) Colleges, 1928-30. Fellow Am. Statistical Assn.; mem. Am. Econ. Assn., Assn. Univ. Profs., Phi Beta Kappa, Alpha Kappa Psi; corr. mem. Manchester (England) Statis. Soc. Clubs: University (Evanston, Ill.); Executives, University (Chicago). Author: An Economic Analysis of the Constitutional Limitations on Public Indebtedness in the U.S., 1914; An Introduction to Statistical Methods, 1917, 25; Statistics in Business, 1920; Costs, Merchandising Practices, Advertising and Sales in the Retail Distribution of Clothing (6 vols.), 1921; Selling Expenses and Their Control, 1922; The Widening Retail Market, 1926; Banking Standards Under the Federal Reserve System, 1928; Margins, Expenses and Profits in Retail Hardware Stores (Part I), 1928; Banking Ratios, 1930; The Triumph of Mediocrity in Business, 1933; National Bank Failures and Non-Failures—An Autopsy and Diagnosis, 1938. Home: 811 Gaffield Pl., Evanston, Ill. Office: 339 E. Chicago Av., Chicago, Ill. Died Mar. 5, 1943.

SEDGWICK, Allan E. (sĕj'wĭk), geologist, civil engr.; b. York, Neb., May 6, 1881; s. David Ernest and Jennie (Treat) S.; student U. of Neb., 1899-1902; Sch. of Mines, Columbia, 1902-05; B.S., in C.E., U. of Southern Calif., 1918, M.S., 1919; m. Jeannette Post, Sept. 5, 1906; children—Wallace Ernest, David Allan, Robert Post. Engr. Greenback (Ore.) Gold Mining Co., 1905-06; engr., constrn. hydro-electric plant and aerial tram, Tezuitlan Copper Co., La Aurora, Mexico, 1907-08; gen. mgr. Am. Engring. & Constrn. Co., Mexico City, Mex., 1908-10; gen. mgr. Me. & Neb. Mining & Smelting Co., Balsas, Guerro. Mex., 1910-12; designing engr., with Noonan & Richards, architects, Los Angeles, 1912-15; cons. engr., geology, mining, oil, water supply, elect. distribution, flood control, etc., Los Angeles, since 1915; asst. prof. geology, U. of Southern Calif., 1918-21, asso. prof., 1921-24, prof. and head dept., 1924-27, head dept. petroleum engring., 1927-29; cons. geologist, Dept. Water and Power, Los Angeles, City of Santa Barbara, Montecito County Water Dist.; chief engr. Seventh St. Light & Power Co. since 1918; consulting geologist Golden Gate Bridge & Highway Dist., San Francisco, since 1930. Instr. in hydrology, U.S. Coast Arty., 1918. Mem. Los Angeles County Commn. to investigate St. Francis Dam failure, 1928; mem. Los Angeles County Flood Control Commn., to investigate San Gabriel Dam site, 1929, to investigate Tejuna Dam site, 1930; chmn. Bd. of Consulting Engrs., and mem. Bd. of Edn., Los Angeles, 1933-35 (pres. 1934-35); cons. geologist Los Angeles County Flood Control Dist., 1934-35; cons. geologist Los Angeles Bur. of Water and Power, Mono Project, since 1931, Imperial Irrigation Dist. since 1940. Mem. Am. Soc. C.E., Seismol. Soc. America, Phi Kappa Psi. Republican. Presbyn. Died Nov. 16, 1941.

SEEGER, Charles Louis (sē'gēr), musician; born Mexico City, Mex., Dec. 14, 1886; s. Charles Louis and Elsie Simmons (Adams) S.; A.B., Harvard, 1908; m. Constance de Clyver Edson, Dec. 22, 1911; children—Charles Louis, John, Peter; m. 2d, Ruth Crawford, Nov. 14, 1931; children—Michael, Margaret, Barbara Mona, Penelope. Volontär condr. at Cologne Opera, 1910-11; prof. music, U. of Calif., 1912-19; lecturer, Inst. of Musical Art, 1921-33, and New Sch. for Social Research, N.Y. City, 1931-35; technical adviser, spl. skills div. Resettlement Adminstrn., Washington, D.C., 1935-38; asst. to dir. Fed. Music Project, Works Progress Adminstrn., 1938-40; chief, music div., Pan-Am. Union, Washington, D.C., since 1941. Mem. Am. Musicol. Soc. (pres. since 1945); Am. Folklore Soc., Southeastern Folklore Soc., Music Educators, Nat. Conf. Music Teachers Nat. Assn. Composer miscellaneous compositions. Author: (with E. G. Stricklen), Harmonic Structure and Elementary Composition, 1916; article on Music and Musicology in Encyclopedia of the Social Sciences. Contbr. to musical jours. Address: 7 West Kirke St., Chevy Chase 15, Md. Died Nov. 6, 1943.

SEELY, Fred Loring, businessman; b. Orange, N.J., Dec. 22, 1871; s. Col. Uriah and Nancy (Hopping) S.; pub. schs.; m. Evelyn Grove, Oct. 10, 1900; children—Alice Gertrude (Mrs. John DeW. Eller), Mary Louise (Mrs. John M. Beard), John Day, James Grove, Fred Loring. Founder, and publisher of the Atlanta Georgian until paper was sold to W. R. Hearst, 1912; builder and pres. Grove Park Inn, Asheville, N.C.; pres. Biltmore Industries, Grove Park Motor Car Co.; sec. and treas. Paris Medicine Co., St. Louis, Mo.; dir. Wachovia Bank & Trust Co., Am. ENKA Corp. Home: Overlook Castle, Asheville, N.C. Died Mar. 14, 1942.

SEES, John Vincent, insurance exec.; b. Huntington, Ind., Jan. 11, 1875; s. Patrick A. and Mary Jane (Cummins) S.; Ind. State Teachers Coll., 1895-99; LL.B., Ind. Law Sch., Indianapolis, 1904; m. Olive M. Royston, Dec. 20, 1905; children—May Louise (Mrs. Kenneth E. Hamilton), Mary Elizabeth, John Vincent. Admitted to Ind. bar, 1904, and since practiced at Huntington; partner Sapp & Sees; gen. counsel Am. Ins. Union, 1909-21, Acacia Mut. Life Insurance Co., 1921-25; dir. Globe Life Insurance Co. since 1927; pres. Rural Bankers Life Ins. Co., 1931-38; sec. The Standard Life Assn., 1936-45, and pres. of the company since Feb. 5, 1945. Pres. Bd. Sch. Trustees, Huntington, 1932-35; pres. Bd. of Tax Adjustments, Huntington Co., 1927-37; trustee Defiance (O.) Coll.; dir. Chicago Theo. Sem.; Director Kan. State C. of C., 1940-43; Mem. Kan. State Bar Assn. Fraternal Soc. Law Assn. Republican. Conglist.; pres. Eel River Congl. Assn., 1930-40; pres. Ind. State Congl. Conf., 1934-35; 1st asst. moderator Gen. Council Congl. and Christian Chs. since 1934, moderator, 1936 and 1942; pres. Gen. Conv. of Christian Ch. since 1936. Mason (32°), Elk. Clubs: Kiwanis, University. Author: The Open Contract (booklet). Home: 812 Louisiana, Lawrence, Kan. Office: 346 N. Jefferson St., Huntington, Ind.; and Standard Life Assn. Bldg., Lawrence, Kan. Died Aug. 31, 1946; buried, Huntington, Ind.

SEEVER, William John, archeologist; b. St. Louis, Mo., July 20, 1860; s. William and Christiana (Erler) S.; common sch. edn. Illustrator and engraver, but best known by his archeol. researches; conducted archeol. explorations in Mo., Ill., Ark., Tenn. and Ky., 1880-1917, 1925; collected and exhibited for the State, the Mo. archeol. exhibit at Chicago Expn., 1893; rec. and curator Mo. Hist. Soc., 1893-1900; now engaged in archeol. research in Miss. Valley, especially the central portion; asst. in exploration of Cahokia mounds, Madison and St. Clair counties, Ill., for U. of Ill.; has large collections. Sec. St. Louis World Fair, 1896-1900. Home: Webster Groves, Mo. Deceased.

SEIBERLING, Charles Willard (sī'bēr-lĭng), manufacturer; b. Western Star, O., Jan. 26, 1861; s. John Frederick and Catherine (Miller) S.; student Oberlin Coll., 1878-80; m. Blanche Carnahan, Nov. 18, 1895 (died July 5, 1932); children—Charles Willard (dec.), T. Karnaghan, Lucius Miles, Catherine Miller (Mrs. Bartlett H. Stewart, Jr.). Began in mfg. business, 1881; supt. J. F. Seiberling & Co., 1883-95; sec. Akron India Rubber Co., 1895-98; v.p. Goodyear Tire & Rubber Co., 1898-1921; v.p. and treas. Seiberling Rubber Co. since 1921; also pres. Thomas Phillips Co., Seiberling Latex Products Co.; dir. Citizens Savings & Loan Co., Macedonia-Northfield Banking Co. Treas. Edwin C. Shaw Sanatorium. Mem. bd. of trustees Akron Children's Hosp., Barberton Citizen's Hosp., Akron Y.W.C.A., Barberton Y.M.C.A., Akron (Ohio) Art Inst.; mem. Akron Girl Scout Council. Republican. Clubs: City, University (Akron). Home: Route 1, Macedonia, O. Office: Seiberling Rubber Co., Akron, O. Died Sep. 20, 1946.

SEIBERLING, Francis, ex-congressman; b. Des Moines, Ia., Sept. 20, 1870; s. Nathan Septimus and Joseva Ann (Myers) S.; student Wittenberg Coll., Springfield, O., 2 yrs.; A.B., Wooster (O.) Coll., 1892; m. Josephine Laffer, June 16, 1897; children—Eleanor S. (Mrs. Raymond Gregory Shirk), Josephine S. (Mrs. Donald M. Mell). Began practice of law at Akron, 1894; mem. firm Slabaugh, Seiberling, Huber & Gruntler; dir. The Goodyear Tire & Rubber Co., Wellman Engineering Co.; mem. 71st and 72d Congresses (1929-33), 14th Ohio Dist. Dir. Peoples Hosp., Y.M.C.A. (Akron); trustee Wittenberg Coll., Springfield, O. Mem. Phi Kappa Psi. Republican. Lutheran. Mason (32°, Shriner). Clubs: Masonic, City. Home: 229 Hampshire Road. Office: Second Nat. Bank Bldg., Akron, O.* Died Feb. 1, 1945.

SEIBOLD, Louis (sī'bōld), writer; b. Washington, D.C.; s. Louis P. and Josephine Burrows (Dawson) S.; ed. pub. schs.; m. Jennie L. Hopkins (dec). Reported Ute Indian War (Colo. and Utah); war staff New York World Cuba-Am. War; first corr. at explosion of Mt. Pelee, Martininque, in which 30,000 lives were snuffed out; made public (New York World) secret report New York insurance scandals resulting in extensive reforms; obtained confession of woman claiming to be widow of J. Gould, the financier, resulting in deportation; made public in a series of articles totalling 150,000 words confidential evidence collected by British and Am. secret services of German plottings terminating in the dismissal of the German Ambassador Count Bernstorff; exposed activities of promoters of Non-Partisan League some of whom convicted of conspiracy; brought from Europe first information dispatching British expeditionary force to Antwerp rejected by London censors; corr. Paris Peace Conf.; exposed lobby activities resulting in resignation of two members in Congress; successfully challenged power of Congress Investigating Com. in same matter to disclose sources of information; exposed custom frauds resulting in conviction of two steamship officials and restitution of several hundred thousand dollars; reported conviction and death sentence imposed upon Czolgosz, assassin of President McKinley; wrote first interview in White House with President of U.S. (Wilson); awarded diploma and Pulitzer prize of $1,000 by Columbia U. for best example of reporting in 1920; tour and series of articles in South America for N.Y. World; also in Japan, China and Corea for N.Y. Herald; series of articles for N.Y. Evening Post on collapse of St. Paul system resulting in govt. investigation. Mem. Acad. of Political Science. Clubs: Manhattan (New York); National Press (Washington). Author: The Workings of Prohibition; History of Non-Partisan League; Japan and Its Expansion. Contributor to magazines and other periodicals. Home: The Manhattan Club, New York, N.Y. Died May 10, 1945.

SEIDEL, Emil, mayor; b. Ashland, Pa., Dec. 13, 1864; s. Otto F. T. and Henriette S.; common sch. edn. till 13; learned wood carving in Germany, 1885-93; m. Lucy Geissel, May 8, 1894. Asst. in German exhibit, Chicago Expn., 1893, one of the organizers of Wood Carvers' Union, and founder of the Socialist party organization at Milwaukee; Socialist party candidate for gov. of Wis., 1902; alderman 20th Ward, Milwaukee, 1904-08; declined renomination. 1908; elected alderman-at-large, 1909, mayor, 1910, for term 1910-12; candidate of Socialist Party for Vice-President of U.S., 1912; again nominated for mayor, Mar., 1914. Address: Milwaukee. Died June 24, 1947.

SEIFERT, Mathias Joseph, physician, surgeon; b. Chicago, Ill., Mar. 2, 1866; s. Anthony V. and Margaret (Kannen) S.; Catholic Normal Sch., St. Francis, Wis., 1885, Bryant & Stratton Business Coll., 1886, Normal Dept. of Chicago Musical Coll., 1887; M.D., University of Illinois, 1901; clinics in 12 countries of Europe and U.S.; m. Mary C. Karst, Feb. 8, 1888; children—Earl (dec.), Myra, Marie. Teacher, choir director, church organist, Chicago, 1885-1896; organizer and pres., Western Musical Acad., 1888-96; intern and extern Marion Sims Hosp., 1899-1905; instr. gynecology, Chicago Polyclinic, 1900-05; asst. prof. physiology, U. of Ill. Coll. of Med., 1900-05; instr. senior medicine, 1901-05; dispensary staff, Alexian Bros. Hosp., 1901-06; adj. prof. operative surgery, U. of Ill. Med. Dept., 1904-09; prof. phys. diagnosis and anesthesiology, U. of Ill. Dental Dept., 1904-09; prof., head dept. surgery, Chicago Med. Sch., 1910-16; surgical staff St. Mary of Nazareth Hosp. since 1904, cons. surgeon since 1915; editorial staff Internat. Abstract of Surgery, Gynecology and Obstetrics since 1913; senior surgeon and pres. exec. staff Columbus Hosp. since 1915. Mem. Ill. governing com., Gorgas Memorial Inst. Fellow Am. Coll. Surgeons; mem. Chicago Med. Soc., Ill. State Med. Soc., Alpha Kappa Kappa, Miss. Valley Med. Editors Assn. (Ill. exec.). Catholic. Clubs: Native Chicagoan, Nippersink Country. Author: Eccyesis, with Prolonged Lactation; Case Report, 1920; Synthesis of Medical Terminology, 1925; Gynecology for Nurses, 1925; Cardio-Vascular Health Maxims, 1927; Olympian Rules, 1928. Contbr. to (books) Obstetrics, Gynecology and Abdominal Surgery, 1920; International Clinics, 1920; also numerous articles to med. jours. Made motion picture, "A High Posterior Gastro-Enterostomy," which he has exhibited since 1929. Radio speaker under auspices of Gorgas Memorial Inst. and Edn. Com. of the Ill. State Med. Society since 1926. Home: 585 Hawthorne Pl. Office: 30 Michigan Av., Chicago, Ill. Died Jan. 31, 1947; buried St. Boniface Cemetery, Chicago.

SEITZ, George Albert, naval officer; b. Mar. 13, 1897; entered U.S. Navy, 1916, and advanced through the grades to commodore, 1944. Address: care Chief of Naval Personnel, Navy Department, Washington 25, D.C. Died Nov. 1947.

SELFRIDGE, H(arry) Gordon (sĕl'frĭj), merchant; b. Ripon, Wis.; s. Robert O. and Lois Frances (Baxter) S.; pub. sch. edn.; m. Rose Buckingham, Nov. 11, 1890 (died May 1918); children—Rosalie (wife of Prince Wiasemsky), Violette (wife of Vicomte Jacques de Sibour), Harry Gordon, Beatrice (wife of Comte de Sibour). Entered employ of Field, Leiter & Co., Chicago, 1879, advancing through various positions until he became a partner of firm of Marshall Field Co., and manager of the retail store; sold out his interest and retired, 1904; with others bought out the firm of Schlesinger & Mayer, changing the name to H. G. Selfridge & Co.; sold out to Carson, Pirie, Scott & Co., Aug. 1904; went to London, 1906, and organized Selfridge & Co., Ltd., wholesale and retail mchts., and built one of the largest stores in Europe, opened spring of 1909. Became British subject by naturalization June 1, 1937. Author: The Romance of Commerce. Club: Pilgrims. Home: Ross Court, Putney Heath S.W. 15. Office: 400 Oxford St., London, W. 1, England.* Died May 8, 1947.

SELIG, William Nicholas, motion pictures; b. Chicago, Ill., Mar. 14, 1864; s. Francis Joseph and Antonia (Lunsky) S.; ed. pub. schs., Chicago; m. Mary H. Pinkham, Sept. 7, 1900. Early became interested in photography; actor and theatrical mgr., 1888-99; inventor of many appliances used in motion picture photography; in motion picture business since 1896; pres. Selig Polyscope Co., Chicago, also of Los Angeles, Calif., and London, Eng. First producer to make long hist. photodrama "Coming of Columbus," and first to introduce wild animals in dramatic action in photoplays. Finance expdns. of Prof. Frederick Starr to interior of Africa, Korea, Japan and Philippines; expdns. of Dr. E. B. McDowell to China, Africa and India; expdn. of Emmett O'Neill to the Amazon River, 1912. Presented medal, 1912, by Pope Pius X for "Coming of Columbus." Episcopalian. Mason. Clubs: Republican (New York); Chicago Athletic. Home: 112 N. Wilton Pl. Office: 6606 Sunset Blvd., Los Angeles, Calif. Died July 15, 1948.

SELLECK, Willard Chamberlain (sĕl'ĕk), clergyman; b. Ogdensburg, N.Y., Dec. 29, 1856; s. William Henry and Catherine (Phelps) S.; ed. State Normal Sch., Potsdam, N.Y.; grad. Theol. Sch. St. Lawrence U., 1881, D.D., 1903; m. Louise Blackmon, Oct. 27, 1881; children—Marjorie Louise (dec.), Willard Martineau; m. 2d, Mrs. Florence E. Hinde, July 31, 1932. Ordained Universalist ministry, 1881; pastor, First Ch., Clifton Springs, N.Y., 1881-83, First Ch., Norwood, Mass., 1883-84, First Ch., Franklin Mass., 1884-90; founded 1891, and pastor, First Ch., Denver, Colo., 1891-95; pastor, Ch. of the Mediator, Providence, R.I., 1895-1910, also First Ch., Valley Falls, R.I., 1901-08; pastor Ch. of the Reconciliation, Utica, N.Y., 1915-19; All Souls', Riverside, Calif., 1919-38, now pastor emeritus. Vice-pres. Riverside Council of Social Agencies. Grand chaplain Masonic Order State of N.Y., 1919; founder and conductor Reconciliation Forum, Utica, 1917-19. Trustee Dean Acad., 1907-35. Pres. Calif. Universalist Conv., 12 yrs. Clubs: The Twenty. Author: The Spiritual Outlook, 1902; The New Appreciation of the Bible, 1907; Main Questions in Religion, 1916; The Significance of Jesus Christ, 1929; Personal Words, 1937. Contbr. to econ. and Universalist jours. Address: 3460 Orange St., Riverside, Calif. Died July 4, 1941.

SELLECK, William Alson, banker; b. Owatonna, Minn., May 30, 1857; s. Alson and Mary (Kent) S.; A.B., and B.Litt., Carleton Coll., Northfield, Minn., 1882; m. Nellie Horton, Nov. 26, 1888; children—John Kent, Marjorie Cornelie (Mrs. George E. Clark), Anna Horton (dec.). Admitted to Neb. bar, 1885, and began practice at Lincoln; partner Western Supply Co., wholesale plumbing and heating supplies, since 1900; formerly pres. Lincoln Nat. Bank & Trust Co.; v.p. Fremont (Neb.) Joint Stock Land Bank; dir. Lincoln Joint Stock Land Bank, Lincoln Federal Savings & Loan Association, Midwest Life Ins. Co. Mem. Neb. State Senate, 1911-13; mem. Neb. Constl. Conv., 1920. Trustee Doane Coll., Crete, Neb. Dir. Lincoln Chamber of Commerce (pres. 1909-11). Republican. Conglist. Mason. Club: Lincoln University. Home: 1936 F St. Office: 1339 O St., Lincoln, Neb. Died June 5, 1949.

SELLERS, David Foote, naval officer; b. Fort Austin, Austin, Tex., Feb. 4, 1874; s. Maj. Edwin Elias and Olive Lay (Foote) S.; B.S., U.S. Naval Acad., 1894; grad. U.S. Naval War Coll., 1917; LL.D., St. John's Coll., Annapolis, Md.; D.Sc., U. of Southern Calif.; m. Anita Clay Evans, Nov. 1, 1905. Commd. ensign U.S. Navy, July 1, 1896; advanced through grades to rear admiral, June 2, 1927; advanced to admiral on retired list, June 16, 1942. Served on Alliance and Philadelphia, Spanish-Am. War, taking part in Samoan campaign, 1899; served on New York, Philippine campaign, 1901-02; comdr. battleship Wisconsin, also transport Agamemnon (had engagement with German submarine), World War. Naval aide at White House, 1903-04; on duty Bureau Navigation, Navy Dept., 1907-09; aide to sec. of navy, 1921-22; comdg. officer Naval Tr. Sta., San Diego, Calif., 1923-26; became comdr. Special Service Squadron, of 5 cruisers, 1927; judge advocate gen. of the Navy, 1929-31; comdr. in chief of the United States Fleet, 1933-34; supt. Naval Acad., Annapolis, until retired, Mar. 1, 1938. Decorated D.S.M. for "exceptionally meritorious services in Nicaragua"; Navy Cross, with citation "for exceptionally meritorious service in a duty of great responsibility"; Victory medal with star, Spanish Campaign, Philippine Campaign, Mexican Service medals (all U.S.); medal El Merito (Nicaragua); Order of Abdon Calderon (Ecuador). Episcopalian. Clubs: Army and Navy, Army, Navy and Marine Corps Country, Chevy Chase (Washington); University, New York Yacht (New York); University (Buffalo). Author: Unofficial Navy Code, 1909. Home: 2216 Wyoming Av., Washington. Address: Navy Dept., Washington. Died Jan. 27, 1949; buried in Arlington National Cemetery.

SELVIDGE, Robert Washington (sĕl'vij), educator; b. Mount View, Mo., Aug. 11, 1872; s. James S. and Susannah J. (Kirby) S.; B.Pd., State Normal Sch., Warrensburg, Mo., 1900; grad. Bradley Poly. Inst., Peoria, Ill., 1907; B.S. and M.A., Columbia, 1908; m. Ivy Frances Harner, Oct. 11, 1908; children—Harner, Helen Elizabeth. Teacher rural and village schs. until 1895; county supt. schs., Johnson County, Mo., 1895-97; teacher Joplin (Mo.) High Sch., 1900-03; prof. manual arts, La. Industrial Inst., Ruston, La., 1903-07; asso. prof. industrial arts, U. of Mo., 1908-13; prof. industrial edn., George Peabody Coll. for Teachers, 1913-19; prof. industrial edn., U. of Mo., since 1919, chmn. of dept. mech. engring. since 1925. Chmn. Mo. State Planning Bd., 1933-35. Dist. vocational edn. dir., Com. on Edn. and Spl. Training, War Dept., 1918; consulting expert, war plans div., Gen. Staff, 1919-20; supervisor of instrn., E. and R. special school, War Dept., 1920; editor trade manuals, War Dept. Mem. N.E.A., Coll. Teachers of Edn., Am. Soc. Mil. Engrs., Am. Soc. of Mech. Engrs., Western Drawing and Manual Training Assn. (pres. 1914), Phi Delta Kappa; fellow A.A.A.S. Served as 1st sergt. Co. L, 4th Mo. Regt., U.S. Vol. Inf., Spanish-Am. War. Unitarian. Mason (32°, K.T.). Author: How to Teach a Trade, 1923; Individual Instruction Sheets—How to Write and How to Use Them, 1926. Joint author: Teaching the Manual Arts, 1910; Manual for Sheet-Metal Workers, 1925; Blacksmithing, 1925; Principles of Trade and Industrial Teaching, 1930. Editor The Selvidge Series of Instruction Manuals. Address: Univ. of Missouri, Columbia, Mo. Died Nov. 16, 1941.

SELWYN, Edgar (sĕl'wĭn), theatrical producer, dramatic author; b. Cincinnati, O., Oct. 20, 1875; m. 2d, Ruth Virginia Wilcox, actress, Jan. 7, 1926. Made first appearance on stage at Garrick Theatre, New York, with William Gillette in "Secret Service," Oct. 1896; subsequently appeared with E. H. Sothern as Dugard in "The King's Musketeers," 1898; appeared at Herald Square Theatre, New York, as Tony in "Arizona," 1900; début on the London stage, at the Adelphi Theatre, same play, in 1902; later played in "A Gentleman of France," "Ulysses," "The Pretty Sister of Jose," "Sunday," "A Doll's House," "The Mills of the Gods"; starred in "Strongheart," "Pierre of The Plains" (his own dramatization of Sir Gilbert Parker's novel, "Pierre and His People"), and "The Arab"; retired from stage 1912; now pres. of Selwyn & Company. Clubs: The Lambs, Soundview Country, Lakeville Golf and Country. Author: (plays) The Country Boy; I'll Be Hanged If I Do (with William Collier); Pierre of the Plains; The Arab; The Wall Street Girl (with Margaret Mayo); Rolling Stones; Nearly Married; The Naughty Wife (with Fred Jackson); The Crowded Hour (with Channing Pollock); The Mirage; Anything Might Happen; Dancing Mothers (with Edmun Goudling); Judy; Pierre of the Plains, etc. Died Feb. 13, 1944.

SENIOR, John Lawson, lawyer, mfr.; b. Montgomery, Orange County, N.Y.; s. George Edward and Hannah Wellar (Sears) S.; Univ. Prep. Sch., Ithaca, N.Y.; LL.B., Cornell U., 1901; m. Maud Louise Cowham, June 7, 1913; children—Mary C., John L. First grad. mgr. of athletics, Cornell U., 1901-06; practice of law, firm of Blair & Senior, N.Y. City, 1906-12, Hurley, Mason & Senior, Tulsa, Okla., 1912-14; pres. Signal Mountain Portland Cement Co. (Chattanooga, Tenn.), Fla. Portland Cement Co. (Tampa, Fla.), Cowham Engring. Co. (Chicago), Trinity Portland Cement Co. (Dallas, Fort Worth and Houston, Tex.); chmn. bd. Consolidated Cement Corp. Trustee Cornell U., 1918-28, com. on gen. administration, 1923-28. Member Association of Bar of City of New York, Psi Upsilon (exec. council 1908-09); life mem. Ill. Chapter S.R. Republican. Presbyterian. Mason (K.T., Shriner), Elk. Clubs: Racquet (Chicago); Brook Hollow (Dallas); Mountain City (Chattanooga, Tenn.); Cornell Club (New York); Pittsfield (Mass.) Country. Home: Lenox, Mass. Office: 111 W. Monroe St., Chicago, Ill. Died Apr. 29, 1946.

SENN, Thomas J., naval officer; b. S.C., Dec. 21, 1871; grad. U.S. Naval Acad., 1891. Commd. ensign U.S. Navy, 1891; promoted through grades to rear admiral, June 1924, now retired. Address: 1021 Adella Av., Coronado, Calif.* Died Feb. 11, 1947.

SENSENEY, George Eyster (sĕns'nē), etcher; b. Wheeling, W.Va., Oct. 11, 1874; s. Charles Henry and Anna May (Eyster) S.; prep. edn., Linsley Inst., Wheeling; art edn., Corcoran Sch. of Art, Washington, D.C., and Julian Acad., Paris; pupil of Jean Paul Laurens and Benjamin Constant; m. Dorothy Lucile Stewart, Oct. 25, 1912; children—Virginia, George Leonard, William Stewart. Served as teacher of etching, Art Students League, N.Y. City; organizer New Sch. of Art, Chicago, 1916-17; asst. prof. design, Smith Coll., 1917-21; art dir. Am. Writing Paper Co., 1919-21; pres. Marvellum Co., mfrs. decorative papers, Holyoke, Mass., since 1921. Etcher. Represented in Library of Congress, Washington, D.C., Public Library, N.Y. City, South Kensington Museum, London, Eng. Dir. Holyoke League Arts and Crafts. Mem. Société des Graveurs Originale en Couleurs (Paris). Awarded silver medal, Panama-Pacific Expn., 1915. Inventor of process for printing textiles known as "Sentone Process." Democrat. Free Thinker. Club: Salmagundi (New York). Home: Ipswich, Mass. Office: Marvellum Co., Holyoke, Mass. Died Nov. 19, 1943.

SENTER, Ralph Townsend, rapid transit; b. Columbus, O., Feb. 27, 1876; s. Orestes A. B. and Mary (Townsend) S.; ed. Mich. Mil. Acad. and U. of Mich., Armour Inst. Tech. Mason (K.T., 32°). Office: 1405 Locust St., Philadelphia, Pa. Died Jan. 24, 1948.

SERVEN, Abram Ralph, lawyer; b. Waterloo, N.Y., July 23, 1862; s. Abram and Maria (Henry) S.; A.B., Hamilton Coll., 1887, A.M., 1890; m. Harriet M. Thompson, Dec. 26, 1889 (died May 19, 1941); children—Mrs. Ida Thompson Barlow, Lydia Maria (Mrs. C. E. Vrooman). Admitted to bar at Buffalo, N.Y., Jan. 1891; practiced at Waterloo, 1891-93; chief of orgn. division office comptroller of currency, U.S. Treasury Dept., 1893-96; chief examiner U.S. Civ. Service Commn., 1896-1903; since practicing law; mem. firm of Serven & Patten. Mem. Psi Upsilon. Mason. Club: National Press. Editor and Compiler: National Bank Act and Digest of National Bank Decisions, 1895; U.S. Navigation Law, 1896. Wrote The Constitution and the Pocket Veto, for New York Law Jour., 1929. Home: 3133 Connecticut Av. N.W. Office: 1422 F. St. N.W., Washington, D.C. Died July 12, 1942.

SESSIONS, Charles H., newspaper editor; b. Woodstock, O., Feb. 1, 1868; s. Minard L. and Mary A. (Reynolds) S.; hon. A.B., Baker U., Baldwin, Kan.; m. Mary E. Barker, Dec. 28, 1892; 1 son, Charles Barker. Began as reporter Kansas City Times, 1888; reporter Kansas City Journal, at Kansas City, Topeka, Washington, D.C., 1892-1910; also sec. to Gov. Hoch, Kan., 1905-06; sec. of state, Kan., 1911-15; sec. to Gov. Capper, Kan., 1915-17; member Kan. State Utilities Commn., 1917-19; mng. editor Topeka Daily Capital, 1919-22, and since 1925; postmaster of Topeka, 1922-25; dir. Jayhawk Hotel Co., Capper Pub., Inc. Chmn. Citizens Ednl. Council of Kan.; mem. Kan. Chamber of Commerce. Republican. Universalist. Mason. Author of Kan. auto license law and Kan.-corp. license law. Home: 311 W. 11th St. Office: Capper Bldg., Topeka, Kan. Died Dec. 25, 1942.

SESSIONS, Kenosha, medical and social work; b. Anna, Ill., Mar. 23, 1862; d. Richard W. and Mary A. (House) S.; prep. edn., high sch.; M.D., Woman's Med. Sch. of Northwestern U., 1893; post-grad. work, Chicago Med. Coll., M.A., Forest Park Univ. Teacher pub. schs. and Union Acad., Anna, Ill., and at Kirkwood (Mo.) Sem., and Bryant & Stratton Business Coll.; in charge Daily News Sanitarium for Sick Babies, Chicago, 1894; pvt. practice, Calif. and Ind., 1894-97; asst. physician in charge dept. for women, Evansville State Hosp. for Insane, 1897-1909; pvt. practice, Anna, 1909-11; became supt. Indiana Girls Sch., Indianapolis, 1911. Mem. Voluntary Med. Corps during World War I. Received award of merit for worthy achievement, Northwestern U. Alumni Assn., 1940. Mem. Governor's Com. on Law Observance and Enforcement, Ind.; pres. Indiana Conf. of Social Workers, 1917. Member Am. and Indianapolis med. assns., Nat. Conf. of Social Workers, Child Welfare League of America, Nat. Conf. of Juvenile Agencies. State Conf. on Social Work, Internat. Mental Hygiene Congress, Am. Assn. Univ. Women. Democrat. Presbyterian. Clubs: Indianapolis Propylæum, Fortnightly. Address: 102 E. Spring St., Anna, Ill. Deceased.

SETCHELL, William Albert, botanist; b. Norwich, Conn., Apr. 15, 1864; s. George Case and Mary Ann (Davis) S.; A.B., Yale, 1887; A.M., Harvard, 1888, Ph.D., 1890; m. Clara Ball (Pearson) Caldwell, Dec. 15, 1920. Morgan fellow, Harvard, 1887-88, asst. in biology, 1888-91, instr. biology, Yale, 1891-95; prof. botany, U. of Calif., 1895-1934, now emeritus; instr. botany, Marine Biol. Lab., Woods Hole, Mass., 1890-95. Fellow Am. Acad. Arts and Sciences, A.A.A.S., Calif. Acad. Sciences, Torrey Bot. Club; mem. Nat. Acad. Sciences, Am. Philos. Soc., Washington Acad. Sciences, Bot. Soc. America, Am. Assn. Univ. profs., Calif. Bot. Club, Soc. Biogéraphie, Soc. Linn. de Lyons; asso. mem. New York Academy Science; honorary mem. Botanical Soc. Japan; fgn. mem. Linnæan Soc., London, Kunglig Vetenskaps och Vitterhets Samhället i Göteborg. Clubs: Bohemian (San Francisco); Athenian-Nile (Oakland, Calif.); Faculty (Berkeley). Author: Laboratory Practice for Beginners in Botany, 1897. Contbr. to bot. jours. Home: 2441 Haste St., Berkeley, Calif. Died April 5, 1943.

SETON, Ernest Thompson (sē'tŭn) (surname changed from Thompson to Seton), animal painter, author, lecturer; b. S. Shields, Eng., Aug. 14, 1860; s. Joseph L. and Alice (Snowden) Thompson; lived in backwoods of Can., 1866-70; on Western plains, 1882-87; ed. Toronto Collegiate Inst. and Royal Acad., London; m. Grace Gallatin, June 1, 1896; 1 dau., Ann (Mrs. Hamilton Chase); m. 2d, Julia M. Moss Butree, Jan. 22, 1935. Served as official naturalist govt., Manitoba; studied art in Paris, 1890-96; one of chief illustrators of Century Dictionary; has delivered over 3,000 lectures. Silver medalist, Société d'Acclimatation, France, 1918; awarded John Burroughs medal, 1926, Daniel Girard Elliot medal, 1928. Mem. Nat. Inst. Arts and Letters; pres. Seton Inst.; chief Woodcraft League of America; chief scout Boy Scouts of America, 1910-15; founder Woodcraft Indians, 1902. Author: (and illustrator) Mammals of Manitoba, 1886; Birds of Manitoba, 1891; Art Anatomy of Animals, 1896; Wild Animals I Have Known, 1898; The Trail of the Sandhill Stag, 1899; The Biography of a Grizzly, 1900; Wild Animal Play for Children, 1900; Lobo, Rag and Vixen, 1900; Lives of the Hunted, 1901; Pictures of Wild Animals, 1901; Krag and Johnny Bear, 1902; American Woodcraft for Boys, 1902; Two Little Savages, 1903; Monarch, the Big Bear, 1904; Woodmyth and Fable, 1905; Animal Heroes, 1905; The Birchbark Roll, 1906; Natural History of the Ten Commandments, 1907; Biography of a Silver Fox, 1909; Life-histories of Northern Animals, 1909; Scouting for Boys, 1910; Rolf in the Woods, 1911; The Arctic Prairies, 1911; Forester's Manual, 1911; Woodcraft and Indian Lore, 1912; Wild Animals at Home, 1913; Manual of Woodcraft Indians, 1915; Preacher of Cedar Mountain, 1916; Wild Animals' Ways, 1916; Woodcraft Boys, Woodcraft Girls, 1916; Sign Talk, 1918; Woodland Tales, 1921; Bannertail, 1922; Lives of Game Animals, 1925-28; Cute Coyote and Other Animal Stories, 1930; Lobo, Bingo and the Racing Mustang (pub. in Russia), 1930; Billy the Dog, 1930; Famous Animal Stories, 1932; Gospel of the Redman, 1936; Biography of an Arctic Fox, 1937; Mainly About Wolves, 1937; Great Historic Animals, 1937; Buffalo Wind, 1938; Trail of an Artist-Naturalist, 1940; Trail and Campfire Stories, 1944; Santana, Hero Dog of France, 1945. Home: Santa Fe, N.M. Died Oct. 23, 1946; buried in Seton Village, Santa Fe, N.M.

SETTI, Giulio, conductor; b. Treviglio, Lombardia, Italy, Oct. 3, 1869; s. Giovanni and Teodora (Degani) S.; ed. in Italy; m. Irene Tavallini. Conductor and chorus dir. in theatres, Milan, Rome, Trieste, Madrid, Paris, Buenos Aires, etc.; came to U.S., 1908; connected with the Metropolitan Opera Co. since 1908. Home: 305 W. 46th St. Address: Metropolitan Opera House, New York. Died Oct. 2, 1938.

SEUBERT, Edward George (sōō'bĕrt), business executive; b. Syracuse, N.Y., June 20, 1876; s. Nicholas and Johanna (Neumeister) S.; ed. high sch., Syracuse; unmarried. With Standard Oil Co. (Ind), since 1891, clerk, 1891-1911, auditor 1911-19, asst. sec. and asst. treas., Mar.-Nov. 1919, dir. sec. and treas., 1919-20, vice pres., 1920-27, pres., 1927-45, chmn. exec. com. bd. dirs., 1945-46; retired June 20, 1946. Clubs: Chicago, South Shore Country, Economic (Chicago). Home: 6925 Constance Av. Office: 910 S. Michigan Av., Chicago 80. Died Nov. 17, 1949.

SEVERANCE, Henry Ormal (sĕv-ēr-ăns), librarian; b. St. Johns, Mich., Feb. 19, 1867; s. Charles Lamb and Louisa (Forbush) S.; B.Pd., Mich. Normal Coll., 1894, hon. M.Pd., 1912; Mich. Agrl. Coll., summers, 1892, 93; A.B., U. of Mich., 1897, A.M., 1899; Litt.D., Central Coll., Fayette, Mo., 1929; m. Anna M. Lane, Jan. 18, 1898; children—Philip Lane, Esther Grace. Supt. schs., Lakeview, Mich., 1891-93; asst. in Gen. Library, U. of Mich., 1899-1906; librarian, U. of Mo., 1907-37, librarian emeritus since 1937; hon. consultant Library of Congress since 1937. European rep. A.L.A. and librarian of Am. Library, Paris, 1920. Mgr. comp. libraries, A.L.A. Library War Service, 1919. Mem. A.L.A., Am. Bibliog. Soc., Am. Library Inst., Mich. State Hist. Soc., Mich. Authors Assn., Eugene Field Soc. (hon.), Inter-Am. Library and Bibliog. Soc., D.C. Library Assn. Clubs: University, Kiwanis. Republican. Author: A Guide to the Current Periodicals and Serials of U.S. and Canada, 1907, 5th edit., 1931; Facilities and Resources of the University of Missouri Library for Research Work, 1926; A Library Primer for High Schools, 2d edit., 1927; The Severance Genealogy, 1927; History of the Library University of Missouri, 1928; Michigan Trail Makers, 1930; The Story of a Village Community, 1931; Missouri in the Library War Service, 1931. William Benjamin Smith, 1936; Palmer Hartsough, Michigan, Song Writer, 1937; Richard Henry Jesse, President University of Missouri, 1891-1908, 1937; Resources of the University of Missouri Library for Graduate Work, 1937; Handbook of the Learned and Scientific Societies and Institutions of Latin-America, 1940. Address: Library of Congress, Washington, D.C. Died Oct. 10, 1942.

SEVIER, Henry Hulme (Hal Sevier), ambassador; b. Columbia, Tenn., Mar. 16, 1878; s. Theodore Francis and Mary (Douglas) S.; self-educated; m. Clara Driscoll, July 31, 1906. Began career as the editor of a country newspaper, 1895; mem. Tex. House of Representatives 2 terms, 1902-06; founder, owner and editor Austin (Tex.) American until 1917; apptd. to visit S. America to conduct ednl. and informative campaign to combat propaganda against U. S. at time of World War I; apptd. A.E. and P. to Chile, 1933; vice pres. Corpus Christi (Tex.) Bank & Trust Co.; mem. bd. of dirs. Corpus Christi Nat. Bank. First pres. Austin Pub. Library Assn. Democrat. Episcopalian. Mason; mem. Woodmen of the World. Former contbr. articles on econ. and polit. subjects. Home: Corpus Christi, Tex. Died March 10, 1940.

SEWALL, James Wingate (sē'wăl), consulting forester; b. Old Town, Me., Feb. 12, 1884; s. James Wingate and Harriet Sterling (Moor) S.; A.B., Bowdoin Coll., 1906; m. Louise Belinda Gray, May 12, 1908—children—George Tingey, Mary Braley (Mrs. Richard C. Alden), Margaret Grazebrook, Joseph, Elizabeth Gray. Forester with David Pingree, Bangor, Me., and Salem, Mass., 1906-09; mem. firm Appleton & Sewall, cons. foresters, Bangor, Old Town and N.Y. City, 1910-12; practicing in own name since death of partner, 1912; has valued and mapped over 35 million acres of land in the United States, Canada and Newfoundland; acting forester in charge civilian conservation work for state camps, Me., 1933-36. Postmaster of Old Town, 1915-21, also various other pub. offices; Dem. candidate for Congress, 1922. Mem. Soc. Am. Foresters, Psi Upsilon, Phi Beta Kappa. Episcopalian. Mason, Elk. Club: Rotary. Home: Old Town, Me. Died July 20, 1946.

SEXTON, Walton Roswell, naval officer; b. Monmouth, Ill., Sept. 13, 1876; s. William Harvey and Marian (Burlingim) S.; grad. U.S. Naval Acad., 1897, U.S. Naval War Coll., 1915; unmarried. Ensign U.S. Navy, July 1, 1899; advanced through grades to rear adm., Mar. 31, 1930. Comdr. Destroyer Squadrons, Scouting Force, 1929-31; asst. chief of naval operations, 1931-33; vice adm., comdr. battleships, U.S. Fleet, 1933-34; mem. Gen. Bd., 1934-37; comdr. destroyers Battle Force, 1937-39; chmn. Gen. Bd., 1939. Awarded medals Spanish-Am. War, Philippine Insurrection, Occupation Vera Cruz, World War; decorated Navy Cross. Baptist. Clubs: Army and Navy, Army and Navy Country (Washington); Chevy Chase; New York Yacht. Home: Monmouth, Ill. Address: Navy Dept., Washington, D.C. Died Sep. 9, 1943.

SEYMOUR, Flora Warren (Mrs. George Steele Seymour), writer; b. Cleveland, O., d. Charles Payne and Eleanor De Forest (Potter) Smith; A.B., George Washington U., 1906; LL.B., Washington Coll. of Law, 1915; LL.M., Kent Coll. of Law, Chicago, 1916; married George Steele Seymour, July 3, 1915 (died Sept. 7, 1945). Admitted to District of Columbia bar, 1915, to Illinois bar, 1916, to bar Supreme Ct. of U.S., 1919; became mem. U.S. Bd. of Indian Commrs., 1922; editor Quest Mag., 1908-12; asso. editor Woman Lawyer's Jour., 1918. Pres. Bur. of Volunteer Social Service, 1916-17. Mem. Women's Com. Ill. State Council of Defense, 1917-18; del. of Nat. Council of Women, 1917 and 1919. Mem. Am. Bar Assn., D.A.R., Soc. of Midland Authors, Order of Bookfellows (co-organizer, clerk since 1919), Ore. Hist. Soc., Colo. Hist. Soc., Chicago Hist. Society. Author: William De Morgan, 1922; The Indians Today, 1925; Boy's Life of Fremont, 1928; Boy's Life of Kit Carson, 1929; Story of the Red Man, 1929; Lords of the Valley, 1930; Sam Houston-Patriot, 1930; Women of Trail and Wigwam, 1931; Daniel Boone—Pioneer, 1931; Meriwether Lewis, Trail Blazer, 1937; LaSalle; Explorer of Our Midland Empire, 1939; We Called Them Indians, 1940; Indian Agents of the Old Frontier, 1941; Handbook of Indian Wardship, 1943; chapter Indian-White Relations, in book, The Indian In American Life, 1944; Bird Girl, Sacogawea, 1945; Pocahontas, Brave Girl, 1946. Contbr. to The Step Ladder, Saturday Evening Post and other mags. Home: 4917 Blackstone Av., Chicago 15, Ill. Died Dec. 9, 1948.

SEYMOUR, George Dudley (sē'mēr), lawyer; b. Bristol, Conn., Oct. 6, 1859; s. Henry Albert and Electa (Churchill) S.; LL.B., Columbian (now George Washington) U., 1880, LL.M., 1881, L.H.D., 1921; hon. M.A., Yale, 1913; unmarried. Has practiced at New Haven, Conn., since 1883; mem. Seymour, Earle & Nichols; specializes in patent cases. Interested in advancing municipal and harbor improvements, and in the fine arts; was mem. New Haven Commn. on City Plan (sec., 1913-24), Commn. on Zoning, com. on restoration of the Glebe House (Woodbury), com. for building new public library for New Haven, Conn. Mem. S.A.R., Conn. Soc. Colonial Wars, Conn. Soc. of the Cincinnati (hon.), Conn. Hist. Soc. (v.p.), Am. Antiquarian Soc., New Haven County Bar Assn., Yale Alumni Assn.; hon. mem. Beaumont Med. Soc.; corr. mem. A.I.A. Trustee Thomas Lee House, East Lyme, Wadsworth Atheneum, Hartford; mme. State Commn. on Sculpture, 25 years, resigned 1938; dir. Donald G. Mitchell Memorial Library, Westville; v.p. Am. Fedn. of Arts, Soc. for Preservation of N.E. Antiquities; asso. fellow Berkeley Coll. of Yale; chmn. New Haven Municipal Art Commn.; chmn. sub-com. on medals of Tercentenary Commn. State of Conn. Mem. State Commn. for Development of New Haven Harbor. Republican. Conglist. Clubs: Century, Ends of the Earth (New York); Graduate, Elizabethan, Walpole Soc. Author: The Familiar Hale; The Old Time Game of Wicket; Hale's Last Words Derived from Addison's Cato; Jeremiah Leaming, LL D., a Tory Parson; Hale and Wyllys—A Digressive History; A Partial History of the Seymour Family; A Documentary Life of Nathan Hale, New Haven, 1942. Contbr. on municipal improvements, architecture, sculpture, etc. Purchased, 1914, birthplace of Nathan Hale to preserve it as a permanent memorial. Country Home: "The Birth-Place," South Coventry, Tolland County, Conn. Home: 223 Bradley St. Office: 157 Church St., New Haven, Conn. Died June 21, 1945.

SEYMOUR, George Steele, auditor; b. Jersey City, N.J. Jan. 20, 1878; s. William Henry and Louise Gautier (Steele) S.; ed. high schs., New York and Chicago; LL.B., Chicago-Kent Coll. of Law, 1916, LL.M., 1917; C.P.A. (Ill.), 1922; m. Flora Warren Smith, July 3, 1915. Was a page in U.S. Senate, 1890-94; clerk N.Y.C.&H.R. R.R. Co., New York City, 1894-1900; auditor Beech Creek Coal & Coke Co., N.Y. City, 1900-07; examiner accounts, Interstate Commerce Commn., Washington, D.C., 1907-10; auditor Alberta & Great Waterways Ry Co., Edmonton, Can., 1910; accountant, 3d asst. auditor, The Pullman Co., Chicago, 1910-13; auditor miscellaneous accounts same, 1913-32, asst. gen. auditor since 1932. Served in Co. G, 7th Regt., N.Y.N.G., 1904-07. Admitted to bar, Illinois, 1916. Mem. Order of Bookfellows (founder with wife), Chicago Literary Club. Unitarian. Author: Adventures with Books and Autographs, 1921; Advice to Poets, 1923; Chronicles of Bagdad, 1923; Wide Spreading Piony, 1931; Cargoes of Ivory, 1937 Hilltop in Michigan, 1940. Co-author: (with 3 others) Estrays, 1919. Contbg. editor The Step Ladder (pub. by The Bookfellows). Home: 4917 Blackstone Av. Office: 79 E. Adams St., Chicago Ill. Died Sept. 7, 1945.

SEYMOUR, James Alward, mfr.; b. Auburn, N.Y., Oct. 11, 1864; s. James, Jr., and Mary Osborne (Lodewick) S.; Ph.B., Sheffield Scientific Sch. (Yale), 1885, M.E., 1890; m. Marion Melita Smith, Apr. 11, 1894; children—Jane Chedell (Mrs. Paul W. Hills), Mary Melita (Mrs. Pennington Sefton), James Sayre. Associated with John E. McIntosh, 1886, founding McIntosh, Seymour & Co., mfrs. of steam engines, Auburn, N.Y., and employing 700 persons; firm incorporated, 1911, as McIntosh & Seymour Co., of which was pres.; business sold, 1913, to McIntosh & Seymour Corp., mfrs. of diesel engines, of which became pres. and later chmn. bd. and cons. engr. until 1922, retired (dir. until 1936). Mem. Seymour (Public) Library Assn., Auburn City Hosp. Assn. Hon. mem. Am. Soe. M.E.; asso. mem. Am. Soc. Naval Engrs. Republican. Clubs: University, Yale (New York); Graduate (New Haven); Owasco Country Club (Auburn). Address: 64 South St., Auburn, N.Y. Died June 28, 1943.

SHACKELFORD, Edward Madison, educator; b. Pintlala, Ala., Feb. 1, 1863; s. Madison and Sophronia (Ledbetter) S.; A.B., U. of Ala., 1885, A.M., 1888 (LL.D., 1913); m. Rosa Lee Brantley, Feb. 1, 1886; m. 2d, Mrs. Julia J. Darby, June 8, 1928. Prof. English and civics, 1887-99, pres., 1899-1937; pres. emeritus since 1937, State Teachers Coll. of Ala. Mem. Ala. Text-Book Commn., 1913-18. Capt. state militia, 1885-89. Mem. Ala. Edn. Assn. (pres. 1924-25), Phi Beta Kappa, Kappa Delta Pi. Author of "The First Fifty Years of the State Teachers College at Troy"; "George Shackelford and Annette Jeter and Their Descendants." Home: Troy, Ala. Died Oct. 28, 1943.

SHACKELFORD, Virginius Randolph, lawyer; b. Orange, Va., Apr. 15, 1885; s. Judge George Scott and Virginia Minor (Randolph) S.; prep. edn., Woodberry Forest (Va.) Sch., 1899-1903; A.B., B.L., U. of Va., 1907; m. Peachy Gascoigne Lyne, Nov. 10, 1910; children—Lyne Moncure, Virginius Randolph, George Green. Admitted to Va. bar, 1907; partner with Judge George S. Shackelford, 1907-18; sr. partner with A. Stuart Robertson since 1919; asst. div. counsel Southern Ry. Co.; counsel, dir. and member exec. com. Nat. Bank of Orange; pres. Univ. of Va. Alumni Assn., 1940-42. Mem. Va. State Bd. of Edn.; pres. Va. State Normal Sch. Bd.; formerly mem. bd. of visitors U. of Va.; mem. U. of Va. Alumni Bd. of Mgrs. Trustee and mem. exec. com. Woodberry Forest Sch. Mem. Va. State Bar Assn. (pres. 1931; chmn. 8 Dist. Com.), Am. Bar Assn., Raven Soc. (Scholastic soc. U. of Va.), Phi Beta Kappa, Delta Psi. Mason. Clubs: Woodberry Forest Golf (president); Rotary (Orange). Address: Orange, Va. Died Jan. 19, 1949.

SHAFER, George F. (shā'fēr), ex-gov.; b. Mandan, N.D., Nov. 23, 1888; s. Charles E. and Eva D. S.; student Univ. of N.D., 1908-12; m. Frances Kellogg, Sept. 1, 1915; children—George, Richard, Charles, Virginia. Admitted to N.D. bar, 1912, and began practice at Schafer; state's atty. McKenzie County, 1915-19; asst. atty. gen. of N.D., 1921-22, atty. gen., 1923-29; gov. of N.D., 2 terms, 1929-33. Republican. Mason. Odd Fellow. Kiwanian. Home: Bismarck, N.D. Died Aug. 13, 1948.

SHAFER, George H., educator; b. Saylorsburg, Pa., Mar. 8, 1879; s. Roman and Sarah (Hufsmith) S.; student Allegheny Coll., 1898-1900; A.B., U. of Chattanooga, 1906; A.M., Clark U., 1911; studied U. of Pa., New York U., Columbia; m. Grace H. Hall, 1902; 1 son, Harley Hall. Supt. schs., Del Norte, Colo., 1902-05; instr. in edn., Edinboro (Pa.) State Normal Sch., 1908-10; head of ednl. dept., Fairmont (W.Va.) State Normal Sch., 1911-15; dir. Bridgeport (Conn.) City Training Sch., 1915-18; prin. Willimantic (Conn.) State Normal Sch., 1918-37; pres. Willimantic State Teachers Coll., 1937-47; retired since Jan. 1, 1947. Mem. Kappa Delta Pi. Conglist. Home: Williamantic, Conn. Deceased.

SHAFFER, Edward H., newspaper editor; b. St. John, Kan., Feb. 23, 1898; s. George Riley and Stella (Beard) S.; B S., Northwestern U., 1923; m. Elizabeth Dickens, Oct. 5, 1923; children—Edward Dickens, Stella Mary, George Robert. Reporter Lima (O.) News, 1923; reporter Albuquerque Herald, 1923; reporter, later mng. editor Albuquerque Tribune (Scripps-Howard newspaper), 1923-27, editor since 1927. Served as pvt., inf., U.S. Army, World War; 1 yr. overseas; wounded twice in action. Mem. Sigma Delta Chi. Contbr. articles, book reviews and fiction to mags. Home: 130 N. Girard Av. Office: Albuquerque Tribune, Albuquerque, N.M. Died Apr. 3, 1944.

SHAFFER, John Charles, newspaper publisher; b. Baltimore, Md., June 5, 1853; s. James and Ann (Crout) S.; ed. pub. schs. of Baltimore; m. Virginia Conser, Dec. 23, 1878. Head of J. C. Shaffer & Co., grain merchants, Chicago, 1904-20; head of J. C. Shaffer Grain Co., 1920-34; pres. Richmond (Ind.) St. Ry. Co., 1888-93; organized syndicate and purchased all the st. rys. of Indianapolis, and was pres., 1889-93; pres. Asbury Park St. Ry. Co., 1892; built Chicago & Englewood Electric Ry., 1893; pres. and pub. Chicago Evening Post, 1901-31; pres. and publisher Indianapolis Star, Muncie Star; owner and pub. Louisville Herald 14 yrs., also Rocky Mountain News and Denver Times. Methodist. Clubs: American (London); Denver (Denver); Chicago, Union League, Press (pres. 1910), Glen View, Congressional Golf. Office: 111 W. Jackson Blvd., Chicago, Ill. Died Oct. 5, 1943.

SHAFFNER, Henry Fries (shăf'nēr), banker; b. Winston-Salem, N.C., Sept. 19, 1867; s. John Francis and Caroline Louisa (Fries) S.; Ph.B., U. of N.C., 1887; m. Agnes G. Siewers, Nov. 21, 1901; children—Henry Siewers (dec.), Eleanor C. (Mrs. R. E. Guthrie), Anna P. (Mrs. R. S. Slye), Emil N., Louis de S. Began as pharmacist, 1887; sec.-treas. Wachovia Loan & Trust Co. (later Wachovia Bank & Trust Co.), 1893-1911; v.p. Wachovia Bank and Trust Co. in Winston-Salem, 1911-31, chmn. bd. dirs., 1931-1941; pres. Winston-Salem Bldg. and Loan Assn.; pres. Briggs-Shaffner Co., Oakdale Cotton Mills. Mem. financial bd. Southern Province, Moravian Ch. Mem. Sigma Alpha Epsilon. Democrat. Clubs: Twin City, Forsyth Country (Winston-Salem). Died Dec. 3, 1941.

SHALER, Clarence Addison (shā'lēr), sculptor, philanthropist; b. Mackford, Green Lake County, Wis., May 29, 1860; s. Ansel and Sally (Stuart) S.; student Ripon (Wis.) Coll., 1873-79, hon. M.A., 1936; m. Blanch Bancroft, 1895 (now deceased); 1 dau., Marian (Mrs. Arthur Hanisch). Began as mfr. of umbrellas and other patented inventions, Waupun, Wis., 1893; founded C. A. Shaler Co., for mfg. of automobile tire vulcanizers (his own invention), Waupun, 1903; retired from business, 1928; now devotes his time to sculpturing. Founded Shaler Scholarship to finance college courses for grads. of Waupun High School, 1920. Donated his statues, "Genesis" (1936) and "Abraham Lincoln" (1939) to Ripon Coll. (also large gifts to the endowment). Principal works: Dawn of Day, Pioneers, Group of Deer, Waupun; The Unfolding Flower, Diogenes, By the Roadway of Life, Nydie, Youth, My Mexico, The Choir Boy, Inspiration, Whither, Pasadena, Calif.; Genesis, Abraham Lincoln, Ripon Coll.; Morning of Life, Mackford, Wis.; Tomorrow Is Today's Dream, Miami, Fla.; The Vision, Forest Lawn Memorial Park; The Citadel, U.

of Southern Calif.; He Who Plants Believes in God. Died Dec. 16, 1941.

SHALLCROSS, Cecil Fleetwood, ins. pres.; b. Cheshire, Eng., Nov. 28, 1872; s. Thomas Richard and Elizabeth (Gillespie) S.; ed. English pvt. schs.; m. Laura Milliken Post, Apr. 25, 1905; children—John, Elizabeth. With Commercial Union Assurance Co., Ltd., Liverpool, Eng., 1891-93; became connected with Royal Ins. Co., Ltd., Liverpool, 1893, mgr. at Calcutta, India, 1897-99, mgr. and gen. atty. at New York, 1900-19; U.S. mgr. North British & Mercantile Insurance Co., Ltd. and Ocean Marine Ins. Co., Ltd.; pres. The Pennsylvania Fire Insurance Co., Mercantile Ins. Co. of America, Commonwealth Ins. Co. of New York, Homeland Ins. Co. of America since Apr. 14, 1919. Naturalized citizen of U.S., 1908. Episcopalian. Clubs: Down Town, Union, Piping Rock, Garden City Golf, St. George's Society, The Pilgrims. Home: 131 E. 66th St. Office: 150 William St., New York, N.Y. Died Apr. 9, 1947.

SHANK, Corwin Sheridan, lawyer; b. Wooster, Wayne County, O., Sept. 14, 1866; s. George Washington and Mary Catherine (McEwen) S.; student McMinnville (Ore.) Coll., 1884-85; LL.D., 1910; student Bishop Scott's Mil. Acad., Portland, Ore., 1885-86; LL.B., Yale, 1891; m. Jennie Mabel Baker, Dec. 22, 1892; children—Corwin Philip, Mrs. Katherine Lee, Mrs. Virginia Anderson. Practiced at Seattle, Wash., since 1891; sr. mem. firm of Shank, Rode, Cook & Watkins; chairman board of directors Northwest Casualty Company, Northwestern Mutual Fire Association; atty. Commonwealth of Australia, 1917-24. "Father" of Wash. State Reformatory, Monroe, Wash., and pres. bd. mgrs. until 1914. Mem. Am. Bar Assn.; mem. Institute Pacific Relations, Hangchow, China, 1931; spl. messenger of good will to Japan, 1924. Republican. Pres. Northern Bapt. Conv. of America, 1923-24; spl. presiding officer Bapt. World Alliance, Stockholm, 1923, Berlin, 1934; trustee Linfield Coll.; hon. v.p. Colgate-Rochester Divinity Sch. Mason (32°). Clubs: Rainier, Broadmoor Golf. Home: 1017 Minor Av. Office: Joseph Vance Bldg., Seattle, Wash. Died Nov. 9, 1947.

SHANKLAND, Sherwood Dodge; b. Willoughby, O., Apr. 6, 1874; s. Sherwood Whitmore and Martha Josephine (Kelsey) S.; A.B., Western Reserve U., 1894; A.M., Teachers Coll. (Columbia), 1918; m. Ethel Ada Haskell, July 12, 1904; children—Frances (Mrs. Frances S. Ball), Virginia Haskell. Science teacher and high sch. prin., 1894-96; supt. schs., Willoughby, 1896-1909; supt., later gen. mgr. Andrews Inst. for Girls, Willoughby, 1909-22; sec. Dept. of Superintendence, N.E.A., 1922-37; exec. sec. Am. Assn. Sch. Adminstrs., N.E.A., since 1937; sec. Am. Council on Edn., 1927-29; mem. Ednl. Policies Commn. since 1936; mem. Nat. School Work Council, 1940-42. Mem. Ohio Ho. of Rep., 1906-11; trustee Ohio State Normal Coll., Kent, 1915-23. Pres. 1912, exec. sec. 1915-22, Northeastern Ohio Teachers Assn.; fellow A.A.A.S.; mem. Delta Tau Delta, Phi Delta Kappa. Republican. Methodist. Mason (K.T., 32°), K.P. Clubs: Federal Schoolmen's Abracadabra, Cleveland Advertising. Received Am. Edn. Award from Associated Exhibitors of N.E.A., 1946. Home: 2830 Rittenhouse St. N.W. Office: 1201 16th St. N.W., Washington, D.C. Died May 27, 1947; buried, Willoughby, O.

SHANNON, Joseph B., congressman; b. St. Louis, Mo., Mar. 17, 1867; s. Francis P. and Mary (McKenna) S.; ed. pub. schs., St. Louis and Kansas City, Mo.; m. Cecelia Hutawa, Nov. 22, 1892; children—Joseph B. (dec.), Helen (Mrs. John F. Deveney), Frank P. Began practice of law, Kansas City, 1905; mem. 72d Congress (1931-33), 5th Mo. Dist.; and re-elected to 73d Congress (1933-35), Mo. at large and to 74th to 77th Congresses (1935-43), 5th Dist., Mo. Del. to Dem. Nat. Conv., 6 times since 1908; chmn. Mo. Dem. State Com., 1910; mem. Constl. Conv., Mo., 1922-23. Served as chmn. com. investigating Govt. competition with private business, 72d Congress. Home: Hyde Park Hotel. Office: Scarritt Bldg., Kansas City, Mo. Died Mar. 28, 1943.

SHAPLEIGH, Alfred Lee (shăp'lē), mcht.; b. St. Louis, Mo., Feb. 16, 1862; s. Augustus Frederick and Elizabeth Anne (Umstead) S.; ed. in acad. dept., and 2 yrs. in undergrad. dept., Washington U.; m. Mina Wessel, Nov. 21, 1888. Clerk Merchants Nat. Bank, and for Thomson & Taylor, wholesale coffee and spices, to 1882; cashier Mound City Paint & Color Co., 1882-85; became sec. A. F. Shapleigh Hardware Co., 1885, and has been treas. of its successor, the Shapleigh Hardware Co. since July 1901, and chmn. of bd. since Jan. 1, 1912; pres. Shapleigh Investment Co., Washington Land & Mining Co.; chmn. exec. com. Miss. Valley Trust Co.; v.p. Am. Credit Indemnity Co. of New York; dir. P.,C.,C.&St.L. R.R.; dir. St. Louis Public Service Co., South West Bell Telephone Company, American Auto Insurance Company, Scruggs-Vandervoort-Barney, Incorporation, Mermod, Jaccard & King Jewelry Company. Pres. St. Louis Light Arty. Armory Asso.; pres. David Ranken, Jr. Sch. of Industrial Trades; trustee Mercantile Library Assn.; v.p. Washington Univ.; dir. Lindenwood Coll.; was dir. and mem. exec. com. La. Purchase Expn. Co. Ex-mem. Rep. State Committee; ex-mem. Rep. Nat. Finance Com. Mem. Chamber of Commerce of St. Louis (ex-pres.). Mem. Soc. of the Cincinnati, S.R., Soc. Colonial Wars (gov. of Mo. Soc.), Mo. Hist. Soc. Presbyterian. Clubs: St. Louis Country; Bogey Golf, Noonday, Harbor Point Country, Little Harbor. Home: 6 Portland Pl. Office: Corner 9th and Spruce Sts., St. Louis 2, Mo. Died Dec. 24, 1945.

SHAPLEIGH, Bertram (Lincoln), composer; b. Boston, Mass., Jan. 15, 1871; s. Thomas Wentworth and Emma Frances (Hovey) S.; desc. Alexander Shapleigh, Kittery, Me., 1635; ed. under pvt. tutors and spl. courses a various colls.; early musical ed. in Boston, continued in France and Germany; grad. N.E. Conservatory of Music, 1891; M.D., Vt. Med. Coll., 1893; studied musical composition under Whiting, Chadwick, McDowell; piano under Faelton and Bendix; married, 1898 (divorced); m. 2d, 1928 (divorced); Wrote for mags. and newspapers; author of three vols. of poems; Collection of Early Poems, 1891; Harmony of the Spheres, 1893; The Quest of the Beautiful, 1894. Gave lecture recitals on musical history, Oriental music and Wagner's music dramas; went to Europe in 1898 and lived in Germany, France, Belgium, Spain and Italy; settled in England in 1902 and built "Weird Wood" in Kentish hills, which burned down with library of 7000 vols.; returned to U.S., 1917; lectured widely; art advisor to Breitkopf & Hartel, pubs. Composer: Dance of the Dervishes (chorus and orchestra; Wolverhampton Festival), 1905; The Raven (chorus and orchestra; Middlesborough and Bishop Auckland Festivals), 1907; Ramayana Suite (orchestra, Eastbourne Festival), 1908; Gur Amir (symphonic orchestral suite; St. James Hall, London), 1908; Romance of the Year (London), 1907; Three Songs of England (Liverpool Symphony Orchestra), 1909; Mirage (tone poem, Philharmonic Orchestra, Sheffield, Eng.), 1910; Tale of the Dismal Swamp, and Vedic Hymn (London Choral Soc.), 1910; Firtree and Brook (8-part chorus, London), 1912; also various other works including 2 symphonies, string quartette, piano trio, 3 sonatas for cello, 2 sonatas for violin; about 30 pieces for violin or cello, a number of operas and over 200 songs; numerous works still unpublished at time of death. Author: (novel) The Story of Mervin Danvers. Musical compositions are now property of Bertram Shapleigh Foundn., 2220 20th St. N.W., Washington. Died July 2, 1940.

SHARP, Edgar A., ex-congressman; b. Patchogue, L.I., N.Y., June 3, 1876; s. Michael and Margaret (Fisher) S.; ed. public schools and high sch., Patchogue, N.Y.; m. Seraphine Ginocchio, Mar. 7, 1916. Began as postal clerk, 1894; overseas supt. Knights of Columbus, 1918-21; engaged in real estate and insurance business, Patchogue, N.Y., 1921-36 and since 1944; supervisor Brookhaven Township, Suffolk County, N.Y., 1936-44; mem. 79th Congress (1945-47), 1st N.Y. Dist. Served with Knights of Columbus in England, and as building contractor in France, during World War I. Mem. Patchogue Chamber of Commerce. Republican. Elk. Home: 39 Church St. Office: 7 S. Ocean Av., Patchogue, N.Y. Died Nov. 27, 1948.

SHARP, Frank Chapman, prof. philosophy; b. Union City, N.J., July 30, 1866; s. Alexander Hall and Eliza Jeanette (Chute) S.; A.B., Amherst, 1887; U. of Berlin, 1888-92, Ph.D., 1892; m. Bertha Staples Pitman, June 30, 1896; children—Malcolm Pitman, Eliot Hall, Richard Lauriston. Private tutor, 1887-88; teacher of German, Condon Sch. for Boys, New York, 1892-93, also head worker in Univ. Settlement, New York; instr. in philosophy, U. of Wis., 1893-96, asst. prof., 1896-1904, asso. prof., 1904-05, prof., 1905-36, prof. emeritus since 1936. Member Am. Philos. Assn., Western Philos. Assn. (pres. 1907), Chi Phi, Phi Beta Kappa. Club: University. Author: The Æsthetic Element in Morality, 1893; Shakespeare's Portrayal of the Moral Life, 1902; The Influence of Custom on the Moral Judgment, 1908; A Course in Moral Instruction for the High School, 2d edit., 1913; Education for Character, 1917; Ethics, 1928; Business Ethics, 1937. Contbr. to philol. and ednl. jours. Home: 922 Van Buren St., Madison, Wis. Died May 4, 1943.

SHARP, Joseph C., admiralty lawyer; b. Glasgow, Scotland, Jan. 23, 1898; s. Max and Ette (Weiner) S.; A.B., U. of Calif., 1918, J.D., 1921; m. Miriam Asher, June 26, 1925; children—Joseph C., Daniel Asher. Came to U.S. 1899, naturalized 1918. Admitted to Calif. bar, 1921, and since practiced in San Francisco; with Edward F. Treadwell as counsel for Miller & Lux and affiliated banks, cattle ranches and water companies, 1921-25; mem. admiralty law firm, Derby, Sharp, Quinby & Tweedt, since 1926. Served with U.S. Army, 1918-19; mem. local draft bd., San Francisco, 1940-44, chmn. Selective Service Appeal Bd. Asso. editor Calif. Law Rev., 1919-21, writer and lecturer on water and irrigation law; lecturer, Hastings Law School (Univ. of Calif.), since 1941. Rep. state bar before Calif. Supreme Ct. in Herrscher disbarment proceeding; pres. J. M. Moore, Inc., and Am. Property Co., Ltd.; past pres. San Francisco chapter Nat. Lawyers Guild. Dir. Hancock Bros., R. H. Anderson, Inc.; trustee J. M. Moore Charitable Trust; pres. San Francisco Order of Cincinnatus, 1938-39; gov. Commonwealth Club, 1935-38, chmn. internat. relations sect., 1910 11; pres. Pacific Philatelic Soc., 1938-39, San Francisco Stamp Soc., 1940. Mem. Am., Calif. State, San Francisco Bar Assns., Masters, Mates and Pilots Assn. (hon.), Marine Engrs. Beneficial Assn. (hon.), Am. Legion (comdr. Blackstone Post, 1935-36), Forty and Eight, Phi Beta Kappa. Mason. Clubs: Collectors (New York); Sierra (San Francisco). Office: 1000 Merchants Exchange Bldg., San Francisco 4, Calif. Died Apr. 7, 1946.

SHARP, William F., army officer; b. Yankton, S.D., Sept. 22, 1885; grad. Sch. of the Line, Ft. Leavenworth, 1922, Command and Gen. Staff Sch., Ft. Leavenworth, 1925, Chem. Warfare Sch., Edgewood Arsenal, Md., 1926. Enlisted as private Co. G, 2d Batt. Engrs., U.S. Army, Aug. 29, 1904; commd. 2d lt. Regular Army, 1907, and advanced through the grades to maj. gen. (temp.), October 1945. Served with 14th Inf., Vancouver Barracks, Wash., 1st F.A., Ft. Sill, 2d F.A., Ft. Russel, Wyo., 1907-10; in Philippines, 1910-13; then with Nat. Guard, Denver; inspector Nat. Guard, Kansas City, Mo., Yankton, S.D., Topeka, Kans., 1917; instr. Ft. Leavenworth, 1917; sailed as lt. col. with 11th F.A., with A.E.F., July 4, 1918; comdg. officer 11th F.A., later 78th F.A., France, 1918; took part in Meuse-Argonne offensive; returned to U.S. in command 318th F.A.; prof. mil. science, Ore. Agrl. Coll., Corvallis, 1919-21; instr. F.A. Sch., Ft. Sill, 1922-23; with 6th F.A., Ft. Hoyle, 1926-28; at Holabird Q.M. Depot, Md., then Aberdeen (Md.) Proving Ground, 1918; plans and training officer, 3d Corps Area, 1928-32, dir. extension courses, 1932-35; with 10th F.A., Ft. Lewis, 1935-36; dist. recruiting officer, Seattle, 1936-37; supply officer 4th Army, San Francisco, 1937-40; in charge civilian component affairs, 9th Corps Area, San Francisco, 1940-41; assigned duty with F.A., Philippine Dept., Mar. 17, 1941; Comdr. U.S. Forces on Mindanao, P.I., and surrendered to Japanese Army, May 1942; prisoner of war with Gen. Wainwright, released Aug. 1945. Awarded D.S.M., Nov. 1942. Home: Monkton, Md. Died March 30, 1947; buried National Cemetery, Fort Leavenworth, Kan.

SHARPE, Francis Robert, mathematician; b. Warrington, Eng., Jan. 23, 1870; s. Alfred and Mary (Webb) S.; A.B., Cambridge U., 1892; Manchester U., 1900-01; Ph.D., Cornell U., 1907; m. Jeannette Welch, Sept. 1900; children—Elfreda J., Frances M., Edith J. Lecturer in mathematics, Queen's U., Kingston, Can., 1901-04; instr. mathematics, 1905-10, asst. prof., 1910-19, prof., 1919-38, emeritus prof. since 1938, Cornell U. Naturalized citizen of U.S., 1910. Mem. Am. Math. Soc., Sigma Xi. Republican. Presbyterian. Contbr. hydrodynamics and algebraic geometry. Home: Central Av., Ocean City, N.J. Died May 18, 1948.

SHARPE, Henry Granville, army officer; b. Kingston, N.Y., Apr. 30, 1858; s. Gen. George Henry and Caroline (Hasbrouck) S.; grad. U.S. Mil. Acad., 1880; hon. M.Sc., Rutgers, 1917; m. Kate H. Morgan, June 2, 1887. Apptd. 2d lt., 4th inf., June 12, 1880; resigned June 1, 1882; reapptd. in army as capt. staff commissary of subsistence, Sept. 12, 1883; promoted through grades to brig. gen. commissary gen. U.S. Army, Oct. 12, 1905; brig. gen. Q.M. Corps, Aug. 24, 1912; maj. gen., Sept. 16, 1916; q.m. gen. U.S. Army, 1916; maj. gen. line of the army, July 12, 1918; retired, May 1, 1920. Commissary in relief of flood sufferers at Cairo, Ill., and Memphis, Tenn., 1897; chief commissary Camp George H. Thomas, Chickamauga Park, Ga., Apr.-July 1898, 1st Army Corps, July-Oct. 1898, Dept. Porto Rico, Oct. Dec. 1898; purchasing and depot commissary, San Juan, P.R., Oct. Nov. 1898; chief commissary Div. of Philippines, 1902-04. Comdg. Southeastern Dept., June 13, 1918-May 28, 1919; in France, June 4-Sept. 1919. Author: The Art of Subsisting Armies in War; The Art of Supplying Armies in the Field as Exemplified During the Civil War (gold medal prize essay Mil. Service Instn. for 1895); The Provisioning of the Modern Army in the Field; The Quartermaster Corps in the Year, 1917, in the World War, 1921. Address: Navy Club, Washington, D.C. Died July 13, 1947.

SHARPE, John C., clergyman, educator; b. Shippensburg, Pa., July 4, 1853; s. Elder W. and Elizabeth (Kelso) S.; grad. Cumberland Valley State Normal Sch., Shippensburg, 1874; A.B., U. of Wooster, 1883, A.M., 1887, D.D., 1898; D.D., Lafayette Coll., 1899; LL.D., 1915; m. Mary E. Reynolds, Dec. 24, 1885. Teacher pub. schs., Cumberland County, Pa., 1871, 72, Glen Mills, Delaware County, Pa., 1874, Indiana (Pa.) State Normal Sch., 1876-78, Calif. State Normal Sch., 1878-79, U. of Wooster, 1883-84, Shady Side Acad., Pittsburgh, 1885-98; prin. Blair Acad., Blairstown, N.J., since 1898, headmaster emeritus since Aug. 1, 1927. Mem. Phi Beta Kappa. Republican. Minister Presbyn. Ch.; moderator N.J. Synod, 1913-14. Pres. Assn. Colls. and Prep. Schs. Middle States and Md., 1916-20, Headmasters' Club N.J., Pa., Del., and Md., 1916-20; mem. Headmasters Assn. Address: Blairstown, N.J. Died Mar. 18, 1942.

SHASTID, Thomas Hall (shăs'tĭd), novelist, ophthalmologist; b. Pittsfield, Ill., July 19, 1866; s. Thomas Wesley and Louisa Minerva (Hall) S.; student Eureka (Ill.) Coll., 1883-86; student Med. Dept., Columbia, 1886-87; M.D., with special diploma of honors, U. of Vt., Coll. of Medicine, 1888; post-grad. study, U. of Vienna, 1888-89; A.B., cum laude, Harvard, 1893; A.M., U. of Mich., 1901, LL.B., 1902; diploma Am. Bd. of Ophthalmology, 1917; hon. Sc.D., U. of Wis., 1922; m. Fannie Fidelia English, May 16, 1897 (died Feb. 29, 1940); children—Louisa Minerva (dec.), Helen Margaret Lehman (adopted, now Mrs. Donald R. Husband). Began practice of medicine, Pittsfield, 1889; prof. history of medicine, Am. Med. Coll., St. Louis, 1907-12, later hon. prof.; resided at Duluth, Minn., since 1928; cons. ophthalmologist St. Mary's and Miller Memorial hosps., Duluth, St. Mary's Hosp., Superior, Wis.; visiting ophthalmologist St. Luke's Hosp., Duluth, Minn.; oculist Lyceum Clinic, Duluth, 1920-25, Acad. of Clin. Medicine, Duluth, 1925-30. Fellow Am. Med. Assn., Am. Acad. of Medicine, Am. Medico-Legal and Toxicol. Soc., Am. Acad. of Ophthalmology and Oto-Laryngology, Am. Coll. Surgeons, Am. Coll. Physicians; asso. mem. Am. Museum Nat. Hist.; mem. A.A.A.S., World Calendar Assn., Nat. Soc. for Prevention of Blindness, History of Science Soc., Internat. Acad. Hist. of Science, Am. Assn. of History of Medicine,

St. Louis County and Minn. State med. socs., Internat. Congress of Ophthalmology, Washington, 1922, Eastern Coll. Men's Assn. (Duluth and Superior), Authors League America; hon. mem. Interurban Acad. of Medicine (Duluth-Superior), Minn. Acad. Ophthalmology and Oto-Laryngology; Eugene Field Soc.; hon. mem. Internat. Mark Twain Soc.; hon. life mem. Société Académique d'Histoire Internationale (with gold medal), Académie Latine des Sciences, Arts et Belles-Lettres (with gold cross); life mem. Pi Gamma Mu; founder, pres. Give the People Their Own War Power, Inc., The War Check Vote, Inc. Republican. Presbyterian. Mason. Clubs: Harvard (Milwaukee and Minneapolis); Exchange, International War Vote (pres.). Author: Newspaper Ballads, 1880; Poems, 1881; A Country Doctor, 1898; May the Patient in a Personal Injury Suit be Compelled to Exhibit his Injuries?, 1903; A Case of Gratitude—Spontaneous Recovery, 1905; How to Suppress a Malpractice Suit and Other Medical Miscellanies, 1906; Practicing in Pike, 1907-08; Southern Ill. Character, 1908; The Forensic Relations of Ophthalmic Surgery, 1911; Medical Jurisprudence in America, 1912; Ophthalmic Jurisprudence, 1916; Simon of Cyrene (novel), 1923; Who Shall Command Thy Heart? (novel), 1924; The Duke of Duluth (novel), 1926; Our Own and Our Cousins' Eyes (evolution of eyes), 1926; The Only Way (peace), 1926; The People Must Make Their Own Plowshares (peace), 1926; Outline History of Ophthalmology, 1927; Give the People Their Own War Power (peace), 1927; Just One Check on War, 1928; How to Stop Internation War, 1928; How to Stop War Time Profiteering, 1931; Ophthalmology, Sex Factors In, 1935; The Eye and Sex, 1936; Peace Measures in the Light of History, 1936; Twelve Who Tried War, 1936; Light, the Raw Material of Vision, 1936; How to Stop War-Time Profiteering, 1937; Tramping to Failure (autobiog.), 1937; My Second Life (2d autobiog.; Spanish transl. by Dr. Arturo Lopez), 1944. Translator: Helmholtz's Description of an Ophthalmoscope, 1916; works from German, French, Latin, Greek. Collaborator with Dr. Howard A. Kelly on Cyclopedia of Am. Med. Biography, 1912, and Am. Med. Biographies, 1920; with Dr. James Moores Ball on Modern Ophthalmology, 3d, 4th, 5th, 6th edits.; with Dr. Conrad Berens, The Eye and Its Diseases, 1936; with Dr. Casey A. Wood on numerous volumes. Former editorial secretary Ophthalmic Record; former asso. editor Mich. Law Review; collaborator Am. Jour. of Ophthalmology and "Revista Cubana de Oftalmologia"; collaborator with Dr. Victor Robinson on Encyclopedia Sexualis, 1935; mem. editorial staff Eugenics; contbr. to scientific and other jours., also more than 3,000 articles to Am. Ency. of Ophthalmology. Inventor of numerous eye, ear, nose and throat instruments, and optical procedures; author of Shastid proposed peace amendments to the constitutions of various lands (popular referendums on extra-territorial wars and on governmental foreign gifts and loans). Public lecturer on animals' eyes, light, blindness, permanent internat. peace, etc. Home: 629 E. First St. Office: Sellwood Bldg., Duluth, Minn. Died Feb. 15, 1947.

SHAW, Albert, editor; b. Shandon, Butler County, O., July 23, 1857; s. Dr. Griffin and Susan (Fisher) S.; A.B., Ia. (now Grinnell) Coll., 1879, A.M., 1882; Ph.D., Johns Hopkins, 1884; studied in Europe, 1888-89; LL.D., U. of Wis., 1904, U. of Mo., 1908, Marietta Coll., 1910, U. of Cincinnati, 1913, Western Reserve U., 1917, Grinnell Coll., 1918, U. of Puerto Rico, 1921; Litt.D., New York U., 1924, Rollins Coll., 1927, Hampden-Sydney Coll., 1928, Miami U., 1929; m. Elisabeth L. Bacon, 1893 (died 1931); children—Albert, Roger; m. 2d, Virginia McCall, May 1933. Editor Minneapolis Tribune, 1883-88, 1889-90; apptd. prof. polit. institutions and internat. law, Cornell U., 1890, declined; established Am. Review of Reviews, 1891, editor, 1891-1937; then editor of The Digest (Review of Reviews and Literary Digest having been merged), now retired. Has lectured in many univs. and colls.; awarded John Marshall prize by Johns Hopkins, 1895, for books on municipal government. Mem. Gen. Edn. Bd., 1902-29; trustee Grinnell Coll. (Iowa), Berry Schools (Ga.), Southern Ednl. Foundation, Anatolia Coll. (Thessaloniki, Greece), Roosevelt Memorial Assn.; member Council on Foreign Relations. Elector Hall of Fame. Fellow Am. Statistical Assn., Am. Geog. Soc.; mem. Am. Antiquarian Soc., Am. Economic Assn., Am. Hist. Assn.; pres. Am. Polit. Science Assn., 1906; trustee Acad. Polit. Science. Pres. Jury of Awards, Jamestown Expn., 1907. Mem. bd. of arbitration in controversy between Eastern railroads and the locomotive engrs., 1912. Life senator, United Chapters of Phi Beta Kappa; mem. Beta Theta Pi. Clubs: Cosmos (Washington, D.C.); Century, Sleepy Hollow, St. Andrew's, Town Hall; Winter Park Country (Florida), Schroon Lake Country (Adirondacks). Author: Icaria—A Chapter in the History of Communism, 1884; Local Government in Illinois, 1883; Coöperation in the Northwest, 1888; Municipal Government in Great Britain, 1894; Municipal Government in Continental Europe, 1895; The Business Career, 1905; Political Problems of American Development, 1907; The Outlook for the Average Man, 1907; A Cartoon History of Roosevelt's Career, 1910; Abraham Lincoln (2 vols.), 1929; International Bearings of American Policy, 1943; Woodrow Wilson, Memories and Reflections; Life in Ohio: History of a Pioneer Family; Thomas Jefferson, and other Virginia addresses. Home: Hastings-on-Hudson, N.Y.; (winter) Winter Park, Fla. Died June 25, 1947; buried Sleepy Hollow Cemetery, Tarrytown, N.Y.

SHAW, Avery Albert, educator; b. South Berwick, N.S., Oct. 2, 1870; s. Isaac and Salome (Freeman) S.; B.A., Acadia Coll., Wolfville, N.S., 1892, M.A., 1894, D.D., 1915, D.C.L., 1927; grad. Rochester Theol. Sem., 1896; LL.D., McMaster U., 1927, Bucknell Coll., 1927; m. Clara S. King, June 8, 1897. Ordained Bapt. ministry, 1896; pastor Windsor, N.S., 1896-1900, Brookline, Mass., 1900-07; 1st Ch., Winnipeg, Can., 1907-11, East End Ch. Cleveland, O., 1911-14, Emmanuel Ch. Brooklyn, N.Y., 1914-27; pres. Northern Baptist Convention, 1934-35; pres. Denison U., 1927-40, pres. emeritus since 1940. Naturalized citizen, 1920. Mem. Ministers and Missionaries Benefit Bd. Club: University (Claremont, Calif). Home: Claremont, Calif. Died March 18, 1949.

SHAW, Charles Gray, univ. prof.; b. Elizabeth, N.J., June 23, 1871; s. Horace Gray and Emma Catherine (Gouge) S.; 9th in descent from John Alden; B.L., Cornell U., 1894; Ph.D., New York U., 1897; B.D., Drew Theol. Sem., 1897; studied philosophy at Jena and Berlin, 1897-99; m. E. Belle Clarke, Sept. 21, 1897; children—Winifred Clarke, Lydia Gray. Asst. prof. philosophy, New York U., 1899-1904, prof. ethics, 1904-20, professor philosophy 1920-41. Sec. Nat. Housing Com. for Congested Areas, 1927-28. Mem. Am. Philos. Soc., British Inst. of Philos. Studies, Soc. Mayflower Descendants, Soc. Colonial Wars, S.R., Andiron Club, Phi Gamma Delta, Sphinx Head (Cornell). Author: Christianity and Modern Culture, 1906; The Precinct of Religion, 1908; "Schools of Philosophy," in Vol. X of Science-History of the Universe, 1909; The Value and Dignity of Human Life, 1911; The Ego and Its Place in the World, 1913; The Ground and Goal of Human Life, 1919; Short Talks on Psychology, 1920; Outline of Philosophy, 1930; The Road to Culture, 1931; The Surge and Thunder—Trends of Civilization and Culture, 1932; Logic in Theory and Practice, 1935; The Road to Happiness, 1937. Editor: The 101 World's Classics, 1937; Basic Thoughts of Philosophy and Religion, 1938. Contbr. to Ency. of Religion and Ethics, Ency. Britannica, and various mags., etc. Pedestrian; on Sept. 13, 1916, walked from Phila. to New York in 23 hours and 40 min. Lecturer on psychology, art and education. Club: Faculty (New York U.). Home: Spring Lake, N.J. Died July 28, 1949.

SHAW, Edwin Coupland; b. Buffalo, N.Y., Feb. 1, 1863; s. Edwin Augustus and Clara (Coupland) S.; Ph.B., Sheffield Scientific School (Yale Univ.), 1886; LL.D., U. of Akron, 1933; m. Jennie L. Bond, Jan. 12, 1898. Formerly v.p., dir. and gen. mgr. of works, B. F. Goodrich Co. (Akron, O.); formerly chmn. Ohio State Bd. of Administration, Ohio State Prison Commn., Ohio State Bd. Pardons and Parole, advisory bd. Ohio State Dept. of Welfare, Summit County Sanatorium Building Commn.; dir. Akron Art Inst. (past pres.); trustee Ohio Inst. Public Efficiency; pres. emeritus bd. trustees Edwin Shaw Sanatorium; chmn. Summit County Gen. Hosp. Building Commn. Fellow Nat. Acad. Design; mem. Am. Soc. Mech. Engrs., Nat. Tuberculosis Assn., Acad. Polit. Science, Am. Acad. Polit. and Social Science, Yale Engring. Assn., Nat. Sculpture Soc., Nat. Tuberculosis Assn., Chi Phi; life member Navy League of United States, Archeol. Inst. of America. Mason (32°), Elk (hon.). Clubs: Social Workers of Akron (hon.), University, Masonic, City, Liedertafel (hon.), Torch (hon.), Rotary (hon.), Fifty Year, Garden (hon.), Yale (Akron). Died Nov. 26, 1941.

SHAW, Frederick William, prof. bacteriology; b. Halifax, Eng., Dec. 14, 1882; s. Rowland and Ellen (Stansfield) S.; M.D., U. of Kan., 1906; B.Sc., U. of Mo., 1921, M.Sc., 1921; m. Elizabeth Martin, Nov. 10, 1909; 1 dau., Elizabeth. Came to U.S., 1887, naturalized, 1897. Intern Bethany Hosp., Kansas City, Kan., 1906-07; govt. service as physician, 1907-16; physician Mo. State Sanatorium, 1916-17; asso. prof. hygiene, U. of Mo. Sch. of Mines, 1919-22, prof., 1922-24; asso. prof. bacteriology, Med. Coll. of Va., 1924-29, prof. bacteriology and parasitology since 1929. Maj. Med. Corps, U.S. Army, 1917-18. Richmond Acad. Medicine, Va. Med. Soc., A.M.A., Socio Fundador, Sanatorio Belem, Porto Alegre, Brazil. Phi Beta Pi, Sigma Zeta. Clubs: Deep Run Hunt (Richmond, Va.); Army and Navy (Washington, D.C.) Collaborator: Approved Laboratory Technic. Contbr. to Physicians Library, Practice of Allergy, also to med. jours. Home: 2312 Stuart Av., Richmond, Va.; (summer) Rolla, Mo. Died May 29, 1945.

SHAW, Howard Burton, elec. engr.; b. Winslow, Me., Aug. 5, 1869; s. Henry Harrison and Mary E. (Hawes) S.; A.B., Univ. of N.C., 1890, B.C.E., 1891; A.M., Harvard, 1894; m. Gertrude Matthews, June 10, 1900 (dec.); children—Howard Burton, George Matthews; m. 2d, Eleanora Pratt, Sept. 6, 1930. Instructor in mathematics, 1889-90, math. surveying and drawing, 1891-93, U. of N.C.; asst. elec. laboratory, Lawrence Scientific Sch. (Harvard), 1894-96; asst. prof. elec. engring., 1896-99, prof., 1899-1913, dean Sch. Engring., 1907-13, dir. engring., Expt. Sta., 1909-13, U. of Mo. Commr. Mo. Pub. Service Commn., 1913-17; ednl. dir. Doherty Training Schs., New York, Denver, Toledo, Bartlesville, 1917-22; dir. Engring. Expt. Sta., N.C. State Coll., 1923-32, prof. indsl. engring. since 1932. Mem. Soc. Promotion Engring. Edn., N.C. Soc. of Engrs., Phi Beta Kappa, Sigma Xi, Zeta Psi, Tau Beta Pi, Phi Kappa Phi; asso. mem. Am. Institute E.E., Society for the Advancement of Management. Mem. highway economics dept. of the Highway Research Board. Democrat. Episcopalian. Author: Dynamo Laboratory Manual, Vol. 1, 1906, Vol. 2, 1910. Home: 1507 Ambleside Drive, Raleigh, N.C. Died Dec. 15, 1943.

SHAW, James Byrnie, coll. prof.; b. Remington, Ind., Mar. 20, 1866; s. James Birney and Martha Jane Morgan (Beal) S.; B.S., Purdue U., 1889, M.S., 1890, D.Sc., 1893; m. Martha Elizabeth Whittlesey, Dec. 31, 1891 (died Mar. 5, 1897); m. 2d, Charlotte May Joy, July 30, 1901; 1 son, Richard Joy. Prof. mathematics, Central U., Pella, Ia., 1890, professor mathematics and physics, Ill. Coll., Jacksonville, 1890-98; prof. mathematics, Mich. Mil. Acad., Orchard Lake, 1898-99; prof. mathematics and astronomy, Kenyon Coll., Gambier, O., 1899-1903; prof. mathematics, James Millikin U., Decatur, Ill., 1903-10; Univ. Chicago, summer 1909; assist. professor mathematics, Univ. of Illinois, 1910, associate prof., 1915, prof., 1918-33 (now emeritus). Episcopalian. Member Sociètè Mathématique (France), Sigma Delta Pi, Pi Mu Epsilon, Sigma Chi, Phi Beta Kappa, Sigma Xi. Author: Synopsis of Linear Associative Algebra, 1907; Lectures on the Philosophy of Mathematics, 1918; Vector Calculus, 1922; Freshman Algebra, 1929. Address: Tsai-Eeka Ranch, Cochise Stronghold, Cochise, Ariz. Died Mar. 2, 1948; buried Cochise, Ariz.

SHAW, Oliver Abbott, educator; b. Carrollton, Miss., Sept. 24, 1870; s. Hobart Doane and Addie (Hemphill) S.; fifth in descent from Carter Braxton, signer of the Declaration of Independence; Ph.B., U. of Miss., 1895, A.M., 1899; grad. work, U. of Chicago, Harvard and U. of Tenn.; m. Alma Billingsley, June 8, 1917; children—Oliver Abbott, Winfred Aldridge, Anna Brooke, Frances Page, Mary Katheryn, Maynard Devotie. Prin. Winona (Miss.) High Sch., 1898-1901; supt. schs., Winona, 1901-20; dean Sch. of Edn., U. of Miss., and dir. placement bur., 1920-35, now professor secondary education and dean emeritus, and acting dean since 1942. Member State Textbook Commission, 1905-10 and 1915-20. State Board of Examiners, 1917-24, Miss. School Survey Commn., 1925. Mem. N.E.A. (consultant ednl. policies commn.), Miss. Education Assn. (pres. 1915), founder Ex-Presidents Club, Miss. Junior College Commission (charter member 1922), Classical Association Middle West and South (charter mem. exec. com., 1905-10), State Assn. Mississippi Colls. (founder and pres. 1926), Assn. Colls. and Secondary Schs. of Southern States (commn. on accredited schs., 1920-39); apptd. chmn. State Merit System Council, 1941. Democrat. Presbyterian (elder). Mason (Shriner), Odd Fellow, K.P. Club: U. of Miss. Faculty (pres. 1924-25). Originator, 1929, at U. of Miss., of a model teacher training program with demonstration high school. Declined presidency of Miss. State Coll., 1920. Library of the Univ. High School named "Oliver Abbott Shaw Library" by Univ. trustees in recognition of his services to U. of Mississippi; oil portrait (gift of Winona High School Alumni) placed in Library, bronze tablet placed in Library by State Board of Trustees. Author of "Mississippi Code of Ethics for Teachers," 1917; "The Administrative School System of Mississippi," 1922; "A Brief Survey of the Rise and Development of Secondary Education in Mississippi." President Mississippi Education Assn., 1884-1942. Home: Oxford, Mississippi (P.O. University, Miss.). Died April 4, 1945.

SHAW, Phillips Bassett, pub. utility exec.; b. New York, N.Y., Jan. 14, 1895; s. John Balcom and Allena (Bassett) S.; A.B., Williams Coll., 1916; student Columbia U. Law Sch., 1917; grad. Sch. of Mil. Aeronautics, Atlanta, Ga., 1918; m. Olive Greene, June 15, 1921; children—Murray H., William C.; married 2d, Jane Bales, August 20, 1946. Began in public utility field, Summit, New Jersey, 1920; operating v.p, Nat. Electric Power Co. and affiliated cos., 1923-25, v.p. and dir., 1925-27; pres. North Amer. Gas & Electric Co., 1929-36; pres. Ariz. Edison Co., Inc., since 1937; mng. dir. Ohio Service Holding Corp., and subsidiaries, 1936-43. Served as 2d lt. arty., later Air Service, U.S. Army, Aug. 1917-Jan. 1919. Mem. Phi Delta Theta. Democrat. Presbyterian. Clubs: Bankers (N.Y.); Williams, Phoenix Country. Home: 2939 E. Manor Drive. Office: Title and Trust Bldg., Phoenix, Ariz. Died Nov. 10, 1947.

SHAW, Ralph Martin, lawyer; b. Paris, Ky., Feb. 18, 1869; s. Hiram and Harriet (Martin) S.; A.B., Transylvania U., 1888; A.B., Yale, 1890; law dept. U. of Mich., 1892; m. Mary Stephens, Aug. 29, 1896 (dec.); 1 son, Ralph Martin, Jr.; m. 2d, Louise Sheppard Tyler, Sept. 29, 1914. Practiced at Chicago since 1892; mem. Winston, Strawn & Shaw; chairman board directors and gen. counsel C.G.W. Ry.; director and counsel Union Stock Yard & Transit Co., U.S. Pipe and Foundry Co., Stewart-Warner Corp., Chicago Junction Ry. Co., Dy-Dee Wash, Live Stock Nat. Bank; counsel Joyce & Co., Pullman Co., etc.; dir. Chicago Junction Railroad Co. Member American, Illinois State and Chicago bar assns., Law Club of Chicago. Republican. Episcopalian. Clubs: Chicago, Mid-Day, Law, Casino (Chicago); Old Elm (Ft. Sheridan, Ill.); Yale (N.Y.). Home: 1427 N. State Parkway. Office: 1400 First Nat. Bank Bldg., Chicago 3, Ill. Died May 3, 1947.

SHAW, Robert Alfred, business exec.; b. New York, N.Y., July 10, 1865; s. Robert and Harriette (Ebrey) S.; ed. pub. schs.; unmarried. Treas. W. J. Matheson & Co., Ltd., 1898-1912; v.p. Cassella Color Co., 1902-18; v.p. Nat. Aniline & Chem. Co., 1918-19; pres. North Dorset Land Co. Pub. dir. for State of N.Y. in Brooklyn-Manhattan Transit Corp., during its lifetime. President Swedenborg Publishing Assn., New Church Board of Publication; trustee Brooklyn Poly. Inst., Brooklyn Inst. Arts and Sciences;

treas. Am. Folk Art Soc.; pres. Brooklyn Hill Assn.; dir. Park Assn., of N.Y. Mem. Pan-Am. Soc. Past mem. bd. dirs., New York Philharmonic Society. Democrat. Swedenborgian. Clubs: Rembrandt, Bankers (N.Y.); Equinok (Manchester, Vt.); American (London). Home: 145 Lafayette Av., Brooklyn; (summer) North Dorset, Vt. Office: 252 Fulton St., Brooklyn Heights, New York, N.Y. Died Sept. 8, 1948.

SHAW, William Bristol, editor; b. Ripon, Wis., Aug. 4, 1863; s. Dr. George R. and Mary White (Goodell) S.; Ripon Coll., 1881-84; A.B., Oberlin Coll., 1885, A.M., 1892; Johns Hopkins, 1888-90; m. Mary Helen Marsh, Sept. 7, 1892; children—Marian, Isabel. Held clerkship in U.S. civ. service, Washington, 1887-88; sub-librarian N.Y. State Library, Albany, 1891-93; mem. staff American Monthly Review of Reviews, 1894-1928, editor "World of Books" dept., 1929-31. Contbr. to Dictionary of American Biography, Internat. Ency. Supplement. Home: Scarboro, Me. Died Apr. 11, 1943.

SHAW, William Edward, coll. pres.; b. Preston, Minn., July 2, 1869; s. William C. and Sarah (Smith) S.; A.B., Moore's Hill (Ind.) Coll., 1889, D.D., 1910; B.D., Garrett Bibl. Inst., Evanston, Ill., 1896, S.T.D., 1926; LL.D., Union College, Barbourville, Ky., 1936; Illinois Wesleyan U., Bloomington, 1937; MacMurray College, Jacksonville, 1941; m. Mary Ellen Morgan, Sept. 22, 1908; 1 dau., Eloise Morgan (Mrs. George H. Orser). Teacher Union Coll., Barbourville, Ky., 1889-93, pastor M.E. Ch., Chebanse, Ill., 1895-1901, Saunemin, Ill., 1901-06, Onarga, Ill., 1906-10, First M.E. Ch., Peoria, Ill., 1910-32; dist. supt. Peoria Dist. of M.E. Ch., 1932-36; corr. sec. Bd. Fgn. Missions, M.E. Ch., 1936-40; pres. Illinois Wesleyan Univ., Bloomington, 1940. Mem. Board Foreign Missions, M.E. Ch., 1924-40; mem. Gen. Conf. M.E. Ch., 1916, 20, 24, 28, 32, 36, Ecumenical Meth. Ch., London, 1921; mem. Commn. on Union of M.E. Chs. in Korea, 1930; mem. Uniting Conf. of Methodist Ch., 1939, General Conf., 1940; member Fed. Council of Churches. Trustee M.E. Hosp. of Cen. Ill., Peoria (ex-pres. bd.). Mason (32°). Rotarian. Contbr. articles to religious publs. Home: 1307 N. Park St. Address: Illinois Wesleyan University, Bloomington, Ill. Died Feb. 22, 1947; buried in Park Hill Cemetery, Bloomington, Ill.

SHAYLER, Ernest Vincent, bishop; b. North Moreton, Eng., Oct. 11, 1867; s. Charles and Charlotte (Sherman) S.; m. Mignon L. Knight (died 1932). Deacon, 1893, priest, 1897, P.E. Church; asst. Trinity Ch., Columbus, O., 1893-94; rector Calvary Ch., Sandusky, O., 1894-1900, Grace Ch., Oak Park, Ill., 1900-09, St. Mark's Ch., Seattle, Wash., 1909-19; elected bishop of P.E. Ch., May 1919; now retired. Dep. to Gen. Conv., 1907, 10, 13, 16. Independent. Wrote: The Making of a Churchman, 1908; The Making and Life of the Church, 1912. Home: 172 S. McCodden Place, Los Angeles, Calif. Died June 25, 1947.

SHEAFER, Arthur Whitcomb (shā'fẽr), mining engr.; b. Pottsville, Pa., Sept. 16, 1856; s. Peter Wenrich and Harriet Newell (Whitcomb) S.; B.S., U. of Pa., 1877, post-grad. work, 1 yr.; m. Mary Cope Russel, Apr. 20, 1904. Asst. geologist, 2d geol. survey of Pa., 1878-81; in gen. practice as mining engr. Mem. Am. Inst. Mining Engrs., A.A.A.S., N. of England Inst. of Mining Engrs., Engrs. Club of Phila., Am. Acad. Polit. and Social Science, Acad. Natural Sciences of Phila. Clubs: University (Philadelphia); Univ. of Pa. Club (New York). Home: Pottsville, Pa. Died Sept. 1, 1943.

SHEAFFER, Walter A. (shāf'fẽr), mfr.; b. Bloomfield, Ia., July 27, 1867; s. Jacob Royer and Anna Eliza (Walton) S.; ed. Bloomfield public schs.; m. Nellie Davis, Feb. 8, 1888 (dec.); children—Clementine (Mrs. Harry E. Waldron), Craig Royer; m. 2d, Mrs. Jean Lawrence, Nov. 19, 1927. Began as jeweler, Bloomfield, 1882; propr. Sheaffer Jewelry and Music Co., Bloomfield, 1888-1906, Sheaffer Jewelry Co., Fort Madison, Ia., 1906-18; organized W. A. Sheaffer Pen Co., Fort Madison, 1912, pres., 1912-38, chmn. of bd. since 1938. Protestant. Mason (32°, Shriner), Elk. Clubs: Fort Madison Country; Los Angeles Country. Address: Fort Madison, Ia. Died June 19, 1946.

SHEAR, Theodore Leslie, archeologist; b. New London, N.H., Aug. 11, 1880; s. Theodore R. and Mary Louise (Quackenbos) S.; A.B., New York U., 1900, A.M., 1903; Ph.D., Johns Hopkins, 1904; studied Am. Sch. at Athens, 1904-05, U. of Bonn, 1905-06; L.H.D., Trinity Coll., Hartford, Conn., 1934; m. Nora C. Jenkins, June 29, 1907 (died Feb. 16, 1927); 1 dau., Chloe Louise; m. 2d, Josephine Platner, Feb. 12, 1931; 1 son, Theodore Leslie, Jr. Instr. Greek and Latin, Barnard Coll., N.Y. City, 1906-10; asso. in Greek, Columbia, 1911-23; lecturer on art and archeology, Princeton U., 1921-27, prof. classical archeology since 1928; also curator of classical art in Museum of Hist. Art. Trustee Am. Sch. of Classical Studies, Athens, 1936-42; dir. excavation of Athenian Agora, 1930-42. Served as 1st lt. Air Service, U.S. Army, 1917-18. Mem. Archeo. Inst. America, Am. Philol. Assn., Am. Oriental Soc., Am. Numismatic Soc., Royal Soc. of Arts (London), Hellenic Soc. (London), Assn. des Etudes Grecques (Paris), Am. Geog. Soc., Psi Upsilon, Phi Beta Kappa; hon. mem. Greek Archeol. Soc. (Athens); fellow Am. Acad. Arts and Sciences, Am. Philos. Soc. Republican. Episcopalian. Clubs: Century Assn. (New York); Nassau (Princeton). Conducted archeol. excavns. at Cnidus, 1911, Sardis, 1922, Corinth, 1925-31, Athens, 1931-40. Author: Influence of Plato on St. Basil, 1907; Sardis—Architectural Terracottas, 1925; Corinth—The Roman Villa, 1930; also numerous articles in archeol. periodicals. Home: Princeton, N.J. Died July 3, 1945.

SHEATSLEY, Clarence Valentine (shēts'lē), clergyman; b. Paris, O., Nov. 25, 1873; s. William and Maria C. (Mong) S.; A.B., Capital U., Columbus, O., 1895; B.D., 1898, D.D., 1928; student U. of Erlangen, Germany, 1898-99, U. of Halle, Germany, 1899-1900; m. Addie Sponseller, Sept. 25, 1900 (dec.); children—Milton Daniel, Clarence Valentine, Elizabeth L., Alice Marie; m. 2d, Rosa E. Stukey, May 28, 1929. Ordained to ministry Lutheran Ch., 1900; pastor, Brentwood, Pa., 1900-13; Pittsburgh, 1913-17, Bexley, O., 1917-29; prof. Bible, Capital U., 1917-27, student pastor, 1917-29; exec. sec. Fgn. Bd., Luth. Ch., since 1930. Pres. Hist. Soc. Am. Luth. Ch., 1918-38, Luth. Fgn. Missionary Conf. of America, 1936-38; commr. to India, 1920-21, to Germany, 1929. Author: History of Joint Synod of Ohio, 1918; History of India Mission Field, 1921; History of First Lutheran Seminary of the West, 1930; Good News, 1931; On Both Sides of the Equator, 1937; Our Church at Work. Contbr. to Luth. jours. Home: 105 Oakland Park Av. Office: 57 E. Main St., Columbus, O. Died Jan. 19, 1943.

SHEDD, Solon, geologist; b. Illinois, May 25, 1860; s. Frank and Emily L. (Olin) S.; grad. Ore. State Normal Sch., Monmouth, Ore., 1889; A.B., Stanford U., 1896, A.M., 1907, Ph.D., 1910; m. Jeannette Wimberly, June 4, 1907. Teacher natural sciences, Ore. State Normal Sch., Monmouth, Ore., 1890-94; prof. geology and mineralogy, Wash. State Coll., 1896-1925; asst. state geologist, Wash. Geol. Survey, 1909-13, state geologist, 1921-25; curator Branner Memorial Geol. Library, Stanford U., since 1925. Acting asso. prof. geology, Stanford U., summer and autumn quarters, 1921, and actg. prof. same, summer quarter, 1922. Fellow Geol. Soc. America; mem. Am. Inst. Mining and Metall. Engrs., Seismol. Soc. America, A.A.A.S., Am. Ceramic Soc. Author of reports on iron ores, building and ornamental stones, clays, cement materials, etc., of Wash., bibliography of the geology and mineral resources of Calif. Home: Stanford University, Calif. Died Mar. 4, 1941.

SHEEHAN, Robert Francis, Jr. (shē-hăn'), physician; b. Buffalo, N.Y., Dec. 5, 1879; s. Robert F. and Pauline (Hitschler) S.; grad. St. Joseph's Collegiate Inst., 1900; M.D., U. of Buffalo, 1904; M.Sc., Manhattan Coll., New York, 1906; grad. U.S. Naval Med. Sch., Washington, D.C., 1910; m. Irene Scholl, Sept. 27, 1921; 1 son, Robert Francis III. Began practice at Buffalo, 1904; psychiatrist U.S. Naval Med. Sch. and Naval Med. Officer Govt. Hosp. for the Insane, Washington, D.C., 1914-16; psychiatrist, 3d Naval Dist., 1918-21; prof. of psychiatry, Fordham Univ., 1937-39; attending neurologist St. Mary's Hosp., Brooklyn, 1935-44; cons. neuropsychiatrist Kings Park State Hospital, U.S. Naval Hospital, Harlem Valley State Hospital; chief neurologist, St. Vincent's Hosp. 1924-46, Community Hosp., N.Y.; consulting neurologist Misericordia Hospital and St. Clare's Hospital, New York City; dir. child guidance clinic, St. Vincent's Hosp., 1934-42; cons. psychiatrist to St. Vincent's Retreat; cons. neurologist Benedictine Hosp.; pres bd. of visitors of Harlem Valley State Hosp., 1928-35. Lieutenant commander Med. Corps, U.S. Navy, 1910-22, serving in Mexican Expdn. and World War. Fellow A.A.A.S., Am. Psychiatric Assn., A.M.A.; mem. Med. Soc. State of N.Y., New York County Med. Soc., Dutchess County Psychiatric Soc., Assn. Mil. Surgeons of U.S., Eugenics Research Assn., N.Y. Soc. Clin. Psychiatry, Soc. Medical Jurisprudence, Nu Sigma Nu. Catholic. Clubs: Catholic (New York); University (Buffalo); Army and Navy (Washington, D.C.); Larchmont Yacht. Contbr. on military psychiatry. Home: 48 Hampton Rd., Scarsdale, N.Y. Died April 16, 1947.

SHEEHAN, Winfield R., motion picture producer; b. Buffalo, N.Y., Sept. 24, 1883; s. Jeremiah F. and Angeline M. (Hens) S.; ed. St. Canisius Coll., Buffalo, 1897-1901 (studies interrupted by Spanish-Am. War); m. Maria Jeritza, Aug. 12, 1935. Reporter Buffalo Courier, 1901, New York World and New York Evening World, 1902-09; sec. to fire commr., N.Y. City, 1910, to police commr., 1911-14; organized studios of Fox Film Corp., Hollywood, Calif., 1914; organized Am., European and other foreign distribution branches and newsreel for same, 1914-21, v.p. and gen. mgr. of the corp. and studios, Hollywood, Calif., resigned 1935; produced "In Old Arizona," the first feature picture with sound on films; actively identified with development of sound recording on films; also produced "What Price Glory," "Seventh Heaven," "Four Sons," "State Fair," "Cavalcade," "Captain Eddio," 1014, and about 130 talking and musical motion pictures. Democrat. Catholic. Home: Hidden Valley, Camarillo, Calif. Died July 25, 1945.

SHEERIN, Charles Wilford (shēr'in), clergyman; b. Pittsburgh, Pa., Aug. 2, 1897; s. James and Mary (Picking) S.; A.B., Columbia, 1921; B.D., Theol. Sem., Alexandria, Va., 1924; D.D., U. of the South, 1936; m. Maria Ward Skelton Williams, Jan. 24, 1925; children—Charles Wilford, Maria Ward, Elizabeth Lewis. Ordained ministry P.E. Ch., 1924; asst. minister St. Thomas's Ch., New York, N.Y., 1924; rector Trinity Ch., Fredericksburg, Va., 1925-28, St. Paul's Ch., Waco, Tex., 1928-29, Grace and Holy Trinity Ch., Richmond, Va., 1929-35, St. Paul's and asso. churches, Chattanooga, 1935-38, Church of the Epiphany, Washington, since 1942. Dir. The Southern Churchman Co. (editor, 1932-38). Trustee St. Paul's Normal and Industrial Sch., Lawrenceville, Va.; regent U. of the South. Mem. Forward Movement Commn. P.E. Ch.; v.p. Nat. Council P.E. Ch., 1938-42; deputy to Gen. Conv. P.E. Ch., 1937-46; pres. Nat. Council Ch. Mission of Help since 1944. Contbr. various religious publs. Address: 2312 Tracy Pl., N.W., Washington 8. Died April 5, 1948.

SHELDON, Addison Erwin, author; b. Sheldon, Minn., Apr. 15, 1861; s. Rolland Fuller and Mary Adel (Hassett) S.; Doane Coll., Neb., 1881-82; A.B., U. of Neb., 1902, A.M., 1904; Ph.D., Columbia, 1919; m. Jennie A. Denton, Oct. 18, 1884 (died July 20, 1897); children—Lynn (dec.), Esther (dec.), Philip Lisle, Ruth; m. 2d, Margaret E. Thompson, Sept. 19, 1907. Editor and pub. Burnett (Neb.) Blade, 1884-86, Chadron Advocate and Chadron Signal, 1888-97; mem. Neb. Ho. of Rep., 1897; dir. Neb. Legislative Reference Bur., May 1, 1906-21; active in law forbidding further sale of school land, 1897; advocated Unicameral Legislature for Neb., 1914 (adopted 1934). Supt., sec. Neb. State Hist. Soc., since 1917. War corr., Europe, 1918-19. Lecturer on Neb. history and instns., U. of Neb.; mem. Neb. Conservation and Pub. Welfare Commn.; sec. Neb. Workman's Compensation Commn., 1912-13; pres. Neb. Writers Guild, 1937; Conglist. Awarded Kiwanis medal for distinguished service, 1934. Mem. Am. Hist. Assn., Am. Polit. Science Assn., Am. Economic Assn., Am. Sociol. Assn., A.A.A.S., Neb. Academy Sciences, Neb. Ethnology and Folk-Lore Soc., Neb. Soc., S.A.R. Clubs: Commercial, Kiwanis, University of Neb., Laymen's. Author: Semi-Centennial History of Nebraska, 1904; Nebraska Constitutional Conventions (2 vols.), 1905-07; Poems and Sketches of Nebraska, 1907; History and Stories of Nebraska, 1913; Report on Nebraska Archives, 1910; Land Systems and Land Policies of Nebraska, 1919; Nebraska Civil Government, 1925-'39; History of the Land and People of Nebraska (3 vols.), 1930; Nebraska Old and New, 1937; Nebraska: A Guide to the Cornhusker State, 1939; Corporation Contributions to Nebraska State Gen. Fund, 1941. Editor of Nebraska History Magazine, 1917-41. Home: 1319 S. 23rd St. Address: State Historical Society, Capitol, Lincoln, Neb. Died Nov. 24, 1943.

SHELDON, Charles Monroe, clergyman; b. Wellsville, N.Y., Feb. 26, 1857; s. Stewart and Sarah (Ward) S.; A.B., Brown U., 1883; grad. Andover Theol. Sem., 1886; (D.D., Temple Coll., 1898, Washburn Coll., 1900, Brown, 1923); m. Mary Abby Merriam, May 20, 1891; 1 son, Merriam. Ordained Congl. ministry, 1886; pastor Waterbury, Vt., 1886-88, Central Congl. Ch., Topeka, Kan., 1889-1912, minister-at-large same, 1912-15, and again active pastor same, 1915-19; editor-in-chief Christian Herald, New York, 1920-25, contbg. editor since 1925. Edited the Topeka Capital one week 1900, as a distinctively Christian daily. Author: Richard Bruce, 1891; Robert Hardy's Seven Days, 1892; The Twentieth Door, 1893; The Crucifixion of Philip Strong, 1893; John King's Question Class, 1894; His Brother's Keeper, 1895; In His Steps, 1896; Malcolm Kirk, 1897; Lend a Hand, 1897; The Redemption of Freetown, 1898; The Miracle at Markham, 1898; One of the Two, 1898; For Christ and the Church, 1899; Edward Blake, 1899; Born to Serve, 1900; Who Killed Joe's Baby?, 1901; The Wheels of the Machine, 1901; The Reformer, 1902; The Narrow Gate, 1902; the Heart of the World, 1905; Paul Douglas; The Good Fight; A Sheldon Year Book, 1909; Howard Chase, 1917; A Little Book for Every Day, 1917; All the World, 1918; Heart Stories, 1920; In His Steps Today, 1921; The Richest Man in Kansas, 1921; Dramatic Version of In His Steps, 1923; The Everyday Bible, 1924; The Happiest Day of My Life, 1925; Two Old Friends, 1925; Charles M. Sheldon—His Life and Story, 1925. Editor: One Hundred and One Poems of the Day, 1896; The High Calling, 1911; The War Ship Builders, 1912; Jesus Is Here, 1913; Everyday Bible, 1923; The Thirteenth Resolution, 1928; Let's Talk It Over, 1929; The Treasure Book, 1930; He Is Here, 1931; The Marks of a Christian, 1935; A Vote on War, 1935; All Over Forty, 1935; The Ministers' Strike, 1941; The Scrap Book, 1942. Home: 1621 College Av., Topeka, Kan. Died Feb. 24, 1946.

SHELDON, Edward Brewster, playwright; b. Chicago, Ill., Feb. 4, 1886; s. Theodore and Mary (Strong) S.; A.B., Harvard, 1907, A.M., 1908; unmarried. Clubs: Harvard, Players, University (New York City); Garrick (London). Author: (plays) Salvation Nell, 1908; The Nigger, 1909; The Boss, 1911; The Princess Zim-Zim, 1911; Egypt, 1912; The High Road, 1912; Romance, 1913; Song of Songs, 1914; Garden of Paradise, 1915; The Lonely Heart, 1920; (with Dorothy Donnelly) The Proud Princess, 1924; (with Sidney Howard) Bewitched, 1924; (with Charles MacArthur) Lulu Belle, 1926; (with Margaret Ayer Barnes) Jenny, 1929; (with same) Dishonored Lady, 1930. Address: 35 E. 84th St., New York. Died Apr. 1, 1946; buried Oak Hill Cemetery, Lake Geneva, Wis.

SHELDON, Henry Davidson, univ. prof.; b. Salt Lake City, Utah, Oct. 3, 1874; s. Henry Martin and Mary (Davidson) S.; A.B., Stanford, 1896, A.M., 1897; Ph.D., Clark U., 1900; m. Florence Vivian Perry, Aug. 20, 1902; children—Henry, Marian. Prof. State Normal School Systems in the United States; History of the University of Oregon. Contbr. to psychol. and pedagog. jours. Home: 1343 University philosophy and edn., U. of Ore., 1900-11; prof. history of edn., U. of Pittsburgh, 1911-14; prof. edn. and history and dean Sch. Edn., U. of Ore., 1914-32, chmn. adminstrn. com. in charge same univ., 1924-26; research prof. history of edn., since 1932. Pres. Ore. Teachers' Assn., 1918; pres. Inland Empire Teachers' Assn., 1926. Author: Student Life and Customs, 1901; St., Eugene, Ore. Died May 14, 1948.

SHELLEY, Harry Rowe, organist, composer; b. Conn., June 8, 1858; organist of Center Church, New Haven, at 14; studied music at Yale under Prof. Stoeckel, at Brooklyn under Dudley Buck and 3 yrs. under Dr. Anton Dvořák, later studied in London and Paris. Organist in Brooklyn till 1899; organist Fifth Av. Bapt. Ch., New York, since 1899. Mem. Nat. Inst. Arts and Letters. Most widely known as composer of ch. music: Hark, Hark, My Soul; cantatas: Vexilla Regis; Inheritance Divine; Our Lord Victorious; etc. Romeo and Juliet (pub. in Berlin). Address: 26 E. 62d St., New York, N.Y.* Died Sep. 12, 1947.

SHELLEY, Oliver Hazard Perry, editor, publisher; b. Albany, Clinton County, Ky., Mar. 4, 1875; s. Lewis L. and Melissa Helen (Snow) S.; ed. pub. schs.; m. Mary Iva Nicholson, June 4, 1899; children—Ermine B., Velma Lee Shelley; m. 2d, Mildred S. Dickinson, July 21, 1921; 1 dau., Mary Kathleen. State mgr. for Mont. of Modern Brotherhood of America, 1903-13; editor and mgr. Mont. Progressive, 1914-17; gen. agent Calif. State Life Ins. Co., 1914-18; supervisor agents Western Union Life Ins. Co., 1918; now editor and owner Carbon County News, Red Lodge, Mont.; established Red Lodge Daily News, Oct. 13, 1931, also owner and editor of same; owner and publisher Picket-Journal, Red Lodge. Formerly mem. City Council, Helena, also Red Lodge; was active in Prog. Party as sec. State Central Com. and mem. Prog. Nat. Com.; mgr. Hiram Johnson primary campaign for Mont., 1920; managed Harding campaign in Mont., 1920; publicity dir. and mgr. Gov. Ford's campaign, 1940; mem. Rep. Nat. Committee, 1920-24; federal prohibition director for Mont., Sept. 1, 1921-Aug. 10, 1922. Unitarian. Formerly state secretary Eagles. Clubs: Red Lodge Commercial; former secretary Beartooth Boosters. Sponsored and secured appropriation of $3,000,000 from the federal govt. in 1930 to build a road through national forests from Red Lodge to Cook City, Mont., making a new entrance to Yellowstone Nat. Park. Home: Red Lodge, Mont. Died Apr. 11, 1943.

SHEPARD, Finley Johnson, railway official; b. Saybrook, Conn., Oct. 8, 1867; s. Rev. Peter Lake and Mary Anna (Burr) S.; ed. Seabury Institute, Saybrook, Conn.; m. Helen Miller Gould, Jan. 22, 1913. With N.P. Ry., St. Paul, Minn., 1889-1901; with A.,T.&S.F. Railway, 1901-05; 3 yrs. as gen. supt. Santa Fe Coast Lines, Los Angeles, Calif.; in commercial business, Chicago, 1905-11; became connected with exec. offices of the Mo. Pacific Ry., St. Louis, 1911, trans. to New York, 1911; dir. Merchants Fire Assurance Corp., Tex. & Pacific Ry., Mo. Pacific Ry., New Orleans, Tex. & Mexico Ry., D.&R.G. Western R.R. Co., Western Pacific R.R. Co., Ampere Bank & Trust Co. Clubs: Union League, Metropolitan, Bankers, Links, Railroad Recess (New York); Sleepy Hollow Country (N.Y.); Chicago; Yeamens Hall, Charleston. Home: 579 Fifth Av. Office: 120 Broadway, New York, N.Y. Died Aug. 22, 1942.

SHEPARD, Harriett Elma, club woman; b. Ft. Hunter, N.Y., Jan. 16, 1853; d. Stephen Van Rensselaer and Nancy (Clark) Ohlen; A.B., Vassar, 1874; m. Edward Martin Shepard, June 28, 1881. Prof. Nat. Science, Milwaukee Coll., 1875-78; head of woman's dept., Drury Coll., Mo., 1878-81. Contbr. to ednl. and lit. jours. Dir. Ozark Br. Assn. Collegiate Alumnæ, 1908-25, assn. Collegiate Alumnæ school patroness for Mo. of N.E.A., 1908-13; pres. Mo. Fed. Women's Clubs, 1909-13 (v.p. at large, 1907-09); Mo. del. Am. Civic Assn., 1910; mem. Am. Lyceum Club. Saturday Club (local). Mem. bd. mgrs. Springfield (Mo.) Pub. Library 1911-39. Mem. exec. com. Mo. Conservation Assn.; vice chmn. woman's com. Mo. div., Council of Nat. Defense; chmn. Red Cross Nursing Service Com., Greene County, 1917-18. Mem. Am. Assn. Univ. Women (pres. Ozark br. 1921-23; v.p. Mo. div. 1922-23), mem. bd. mgrs. Mary E. Wilson Home for Aged Women. Life mem. asso. Alumnæ of Vassar Coll.; hon. life mem. University Club (men's), Springfield, Mo. Conglist. Democrat. Home: 1403 Benton Av., Springfield, Mo. Died Nov. 3, 1946.

SHEPARD, Horace B., lumber mcht.; b. Dorchester, Mass., 1885; s. Otis and Emily E. S.; m. Florence O. Gaut, Feb. 14, 1882; children—Ralph A., Otis N., Herman G. (dec.), I. Minot (dec.), Eliot B., H. Wentworth. Pres. Shepard & Morse Lumber Co., Shepard Steamship Co., Shepard Lumber Co.; Mem. Boston Chamber Commerce. Unitarian. Clubs: First Parish (Brookline). Home: Brookline, Mass. Office: 31 Milk St., Pilgrim Bank Bldg., Boston 3, Mass. Died Sep. 6, 1944.

SHEPARD, James Edward, coll. pres.; b. Raleigh, N.C., Nov. 3, 1875; s. Augustus (D.D.) and Hattie E. (Whitted) S.; ed. Shaw U., Raleigh, 1883-90, Ph.G., Dept. of Pharmacy, 1894, LL.D., 1945; pvt. course in theology; D.D., Muskingum Coll., Ohio, 1912; A.M., Selma U., Ala., 1913; Litt.D., Howard U., 1925; m. Annie Day Robinson, Nov. 7, 1895; children—Marjorie A., Annie Day. Comparer of deeds, recorder's office, Washington, D.C., 1898; deputy collector U.S. internal revenue, Raleigh, N.C., 1899-1905; field supt. Internat. Sunday Sch. Assn. (work among Negroes), 1905-09; pres. Nat. Training Sch. (for colored race), Durham, N.C., 1910-23, Durham State Normal Sch., 1923-25; pres. N.C. Coll. for Negroes since 1925. Dir. Mechanics & Farmers Bank. Trustee of Lincoln Hospital. Grand master of F. and A.A. Masons. Delegate and only Negro speaker World's Sunday Sch. Conv., Rome, 1907. Club: Civic. Has traveled extensively in Europe, Africa and Asia; lecturer. Home: Durham, N.C. Died Oct. 6, 1947.

SHEPARD, John, Jr., capitalist; b. Boston, Mass., Jan. 2, 1857; s. John Shepard and Susan Annie (Bagley) S.; educated pub. schools; married Maude Miller, January 10, 1911; sons (by former wife, deceased) John Shepard III, Robert Ferguson Shepard. Chairman of board and owner The Shepard Stores, Providence, R.I., since 1880. Owner several corporations; mayor, Palm Beach, Fla., 1930-35. Home: (winter) Palm Beach, Fla.; (summer) Lenox, Mass. Died Dec., 1948.

SHEPARD, William Pierce, coll. prof.; b. Utica, N.Y., June 9, 1870; s. Leroy Ferry and Marian (Barber) S.; A.B., Hamilton Coll., 1892, A.M., 1893; Ph.D., U. of Heidelberg, Germany, 1896; Litt.D., Hamilton, 1940; m. Agnes Stewart, June 20, 1901 (died June 8, 1939). Asst. in biology, 1892-93, asso. prof. Romance langs., 1896-1900, prof., 1900-40, Hamilton College. Mem. Modern Lang. Assn. America, Am. Folk-Lore Soc., Am. Philol. Assn., Am. Dialect Soc., Société des anciens textes français, Delta Upsilon, Phi Beta Kappa. Mem. War Industries Board, Washington, 1918. Clubs: Fort Schuyler (Utica); Mastigouche Fish and Game. Wrote: Contributions to the History of the Unaccented Vowels in Old French, 1897; Les Poésies de Jausbert de Puycibot, 1924; The Oxford Provençal Chansonnier, 1927; La Passion provençale du manuscrit Didot, 1927. Contbr. to philol. jours. Home: 104 Prindle Av., Johnstown, N.Y. Died Nov. 15, 1948.

SHEPARDSON, Ruth Pearson Chandler (Mrs. Douglas Auld), educator; b. Scranton, Pa., 1897; d. Charles Henry and Ellen Catherine (Williams) Chandler; Ph.B., Pembroke Coll., Brown U., 1920; m. Douglas Auld, 1945. Head English dept. St. Margaret's Sch., Waterbury, Conn., 1920-48, asst. prin., 1947-48, headmistress since 1948. Mem. Conn. Heads of English, Nat. Council Teachers of English, Secondary Edn. Bd.; reader in English for Coll. Entrance Exam. Bd.; recording sec. Sch. and Coll. Conf. on English. Home: P.O. Box 308, Wallingford, Conn. Died Nov. 18, 1949.

SHEPHERD, Ernest Stanley, chemist; b. Remington, Ind., Mar. 30, 1879; s. William and Harriette Ellen (Lockwood) S.; student Ind. U., 1897-1900; A.B., Cornell, 1902; private asst. to Prof. Bancroft, at Cornell, June-Sept. 1902; asst. in electrochemistry, Cornell, Sept.-Nov. 1902; resigned to take up research on Carnegie grant, under Prof. Bancroft, 1902-04; physical chemist, Geophys. Lab., Washington in charge research on lime-aluminasilica series of minerals, 1904-46, ret.; chemistry of volcanic phenomena. Member Am. Chem. Soc., Sigma Xi, etc. Club: Cosmos. Writer of numerous papers on alloys, minerals and chemistry of volcanic phenomena pub. in Journal of Physical Chemistry, Journal of Science, etc. Address: 426 Willard Av., Chevy Chase 15, Md. Died Sept. 29, 1949.

SHEPHERD, Russell E., mgr. irrigation projects; b. Sackett Harbor, N.Y., Dec. 15, 1860; s. Thomas B. and Augusta O. (Easton) S.; law dept. U. of Mich., 1882-83; m. Nellie Kelton, Oct. 1884; children—Mrs. Ruth E. Hayward, Mrs. Helen A. Tiffany, Mrs. Irene K. Parry. Practiced law at Austin, Minn.; moved to Mont., 1906, to Ida., 1914, and engaged extensively in irrigation enterprises; chmn. bd. Ida. Farms Co. since 1914; mem. National Farm Chemurgic Council; pres. Am. Falls Reservoir Dist. Chmn. Ida. State Com. on Relation of Electricity to Agriculture; dir. Ida. State Chamber Commerce. Republican, Episcopalian. Mason. Home: Jerome, Ida. Died July 3, 1944.

SHEPPARD, John Rutherford, business exec., b. Rising Sun, Md., June 18, 1873; s. Horatio John and Sarah Elizabeth (Brown) S.; ed. pub. schs. of Rising Sun, Md.; m. Ruth Potts, Oct. 31, 1900; 1 son, John Rutherford. Kent Iron and Hardware Co., Wilmington, Del., 1889-90; stenographer Wilmington Dental Mfg. Co., 1890-95; with Consolidated Dental Mfg. Co., New York City, 1895-99; sec. and treas. Dentists' Supply Co., N.Y. City, 1899-1932, pres. and dir., 1932-44, chmn. since 1944. Mason. Clubs: Wykagyl Country (New Rochelle, N.Y.); Yacht (Larchmont, N.Y.). Home: 1021 Park Av. Office: 220 W. 42d St., New York, N.Y. Died Oct. 17, 1945.

SHEPPARD, John Shoemaker, lawyer; b. Penn Yan, N.Y., July 20, 1871; s. John Shoemaker and Julia Morton (Dodson) S.; A.B., Williams Coll., 1891; LL.B., Harvard Law Sch., 1895; m. Jeanie Rumsey, Sept. 30, 1899; 1 dau., Janet (Mrs. Alfred Easton Poor). Formed law firm of Sheppard & Ingalls, 1897; mem. firm Rumsey, Sheppard & Ingalls, 1901-24, Sheppard, Jones & Seipp, 1924-37, Sheppard & Seipp since 1937; dir. and mem. exec. com. Middle States Petroleum Corp.; dir. Nation-wide Securities Co. Served as pvt., advancing to sergt., Squadron A, 1895-1900. Mem. Assn. of Bar of City of N.Y., Chi Psi. Republican. Clubs: Century, University, Down Town, Harvard. Author: Rumsey's Practice (rev. edit.), 1902-04. Home: 1220 Park Av. Office: 27 Cedar St., New York, N.Y. Died May 14, 1948.

SHEPPARD, Morris, U.S. senator; b. Wheatville, Morris County, Tex., May 28, 1875; s. John Levi and Alice (Eddins) S.; A.B., U. of Tex., 1895, LL.B., 1897; LL.M., Yale U., 1898; LL.D., Southern Methodist U.; m. Lucile Sanderson, Dec. 1, 1909; children—Janet, Susan, Lucile. Practiced law, Pittsburg, Tex., 1898-99, moved to Texarkana, 1899. Elected to 57th Congress, Nov. 15, 1902, for unexpired term (1902-03) of his father, deceased; reëlected 58th to 62d Congresses (1903-13), 1st Tex. Dist.; elected U.S. senator, Jan. 29, 1913, for unexpired term (ending Mar. 3, 1913) of Joseph W. Bailey, resigned; also elected on same day for term, 1913-19; reëlected for 4 terms, 1919-43. Treas. Woodmen of the World Life Ins. Assn. since 1899. Mem. Phi Beta Kappa. Democrat. Home: Texarkana, Tex. Died Apr. 9, 1941.

SHEPPARD, Samuel Edward, research chemist; b. Hither Green, Kent, Eng., July 29, 1882; s. Samuel and Emily Mary (Taplin) S.; B.Sc., 1st class honors in chemistry, University Coll., London, 1903, D.Sc., 1906; 1851 Exhbn. scholar, same univ., 1907; studied Marburg U., Sorbonne, Paris, and Cambridge, Eng.; m. Eveline Lucy Ground, Nov. 27, 1912; 1 son, Samuel Roger. Photographic research practice, Eng., 1910-11; chemist with Eastman Kodak Co., Rochester, N.Y., since 1912; asst. supt., in charge depts. of inorganic and physical chemistry of Research Lab., 1920, and asst. dir. of research since 1923. Carried out chem. development of colloidal fuels with Submarine Defense, 1917-19. Awarded Progress medal, Royal Photographic Soc., 1928; Adelsköld medal, Photog. Soc. of Stockholm, 1929; William H. Nichols medal, Am. Chem. Soc., 1930. Honorary fellow Photographic Society of America. Fellow Soc. Motion Picture Engrs., Chem. Soc., London; hon. fellow Royal Photographic Soc.; mem. Am. Chem. Soc., Am. Electrochem. Soc., American Standards Assn. (committee on photographic standards). Member Anglican Church. Author: Photochemistry, 1914; Gelatin in Photography, Vol. I, 1923. Part Author: Investigations on the Theory of the Photographic Process, 1907; Silver Bromide Grain of Photographic Emulsions, 1921; Photography as a Scientific Implement, 1923. Contbr. numerous papers on chem. topics. Developed process of electrodeposition of rubber. Hurter and Driffield Memorial lecturer, Royal Photographic Soc., 1928. Home: 183 Monteroy Road, Brighton, Rochester, N.Y. Died Sept. 29, 1948.

SHEPPEY, Marshall, merchant; b. Ogdensburg, N.Y., Nov. 16, 1869; s. Alonzo N. and Clara Jane (Benedict) S.; grad. high sch., Wilmington, Del.; m. Cousie C. Berdan, Oct. 25, 1893 (died Mar. 23, 1919); m. 2d, Maria G. Berdan, June 9, 1936. Clerk Commercial Nat. Bank, Cleveland, O., 6 years; with Cleveland Cliffs Iron Co., Ishpeming, Mich., 1 year; pres. The Berdan Co., general merchants (founded 1836), since 1897; dir. Marlin Rockwell Corp. Vet. 1st Cleveland Troop, O. Nat. Guard; ex-v.p. Toledo Sinking Fund Commrs.; mem. Toledo City Bd. of Arbitration; mem. Ohio Bd. of Adminstrn.; chmn. Lucas County (O.) Prog. Campaign Com., 1912; mem. Rep. State Central Com., 1919-29. Presbyterian. Home: Sheerness House, Ottawa Hills, Toledo, Ohio.* Died Feb. 3, 1945.

SHERBON, Florence Brown (Mrs. John Bayard Sherbon) (shĕr'bŭn), child care; b. Washington County, Ia., Feb. 11, 1869; d. James and Viola (Gardner) Brown; Ph.B., U. of Ia., 1892, A.M., M.D., 1904; m. John Bayard Sherbon, M.D., June 2, 1904 (divorced); children—Elizabeth Maude and Alice Isabelle (twins). Teacher high sch., Des Moines, Ia., 1893; nurse attendant, Ia. State Hosp., Independence, Ia., 1895; supt. State Hosp. Training Sch., 1895-99; supt. University Hosp., Iowa City, 1900, Victoria Sanatorium, Colfax, Ia., 1904-15; field agt. Federal Children's Bur., 1916; with Extension Inst., Ind. U., 1917; in charge physical edn., U. of Kan., 1918-19; chief Div. of Child Hygiene, Kan. State Bd. of Health, 1919-20; prof. child care, U. of Kan., since 1921, also dir. child research. Gave social hygiene lectures, Defense Council, World War. Mem. Am. Home Economics Assn., Am. Eugenic Soc., Nat. Med. Women's Assn., A.A.A.S., Kan. Mental Hygiene Assn., Kan. Conf. Social Work, Kan. Council of Women, Kan. State Tuberculosis Assn., Omicron Nu, Alpha Epsilon Iota, etc. Unitarian. Author: Health of the Family and Home Care of Sick, 1917; Maternity and Infant Care in a Rural County in Wisconsin, 1919; The Mother's Manual, 1920; The Child, His Origin, Development and Care, 1934; The Family in Health and in Illness, 1937. Mem. editorial bd. Medical Women's Journal. Home: Crescent Rd., Lawrence, Kan. Died Feb. 16, 1944.

SHERMAN, Althea Rosina, ornithologist; b. Farmersburg Twp., Clayton County, Ia., Oct. 10, 1853; d. Mark Bachelor and Sibyl Melissa (Clark) Sherman; student Upper Ia. U., Fayette, Ia., 1865-66; A.B., Oberlin, 1875, A.M., 1882; studied Art Inst. Chicago, Art Students' League, New York. Teacher pub. schs., 1875-78; instr. drawing and painting, Carleton Coll., Northfield, Minn., 1882-87; supervisor drawing, city schs., Tacoma, Wash., 1892-95. Conglist. Mem. A.A.A.S., Am. Ornithologists Union, Nat. Assn. Audubon Socs., Cooper and Wilson ornithol. clubs, Am. Museum Natural History, Am. Soc. Mammalogists, Am. Genetic Assn., Biol. Soc. Washington, Ia. Acad. Science, State Hist. Soc. Ia., Miss. Valley Hist. Assn., Soc. of Mayflower Descendents. Has published many articles in ornithol. mags. on life histories of birds. Home: National, via McGregor, Ia. Died Apr. 16, 1943.

SHERMAN, Charles Pomeroy, lawyer; b. Brooklyn, Dec. 6, 1847; s. Byron and Mary (Pomeroy) S.; ed. Phillips Acad., Andover, Mass.; studied law in offices; m. Phila., Apr. 9, 1891, Laura Middleton Alexander. Admitted to Phila. bar, 1881. Mem. Pa. Soc. S.R., Founders and Patriots of Am., Hist. Soc. of Pa., Site and Relic Soc., Pa. State Bar Assn., Law Assn. of Phila. Republican. Clubs: Arts, Pegasus. Author: A Bachelor's Wedding Trip, 1889. Residence: 5402 Wayne Av., Germantown, Phila. Office: 1011 Chestnut St., Philadelphia. Died Jan. 21, 1944.

SHERMAN, Clifton Lucien, newspaper editor; b. East Dover, Vt., Sept. 1, 1866; s. Sidney Harvey and Mary Elizabeth (Farnsworth) S.; A.B., Amherst, 1888; m. Edith Holton, Apr. 25, 1889; children—Ellen Hoit (Mrs. Sanford B. Perkins), Dorothy Mary (Mrs. Thorsten E. Lommen). Began as reporter Springfield (Mass.) Union, 1888; state editor Hartford (Conn.) Courant, 1890-93, mng. editor, 1893-1900; with New York Sun, 1900-04; mng. editor Hartford Courant, 1904-19; mng. editor Hartford Times, 1919-21, editor, 1921-29. Mem. S.A.R. Home: 24 Meadowbrook Rd., West Hartford. Office: 36 Pearl St., Hartford, Conn. Died Feb. 6, 1946.

SHERMAN, Franklin, zoölogist, entomologist; b. Ash Grove, Va., November 2, 1877; s. Franklin and Caroline (Alvord) S.; ed. Maryland College of Agriculture (now University of Maryland), 1893-97, and Cornell U., 1899-1900 (B.S. in Agr., 1900); hon. M.S., Md. Agrl. Coll., 1912; m. Grace Berry, May 12, 1903; children—Franklin, Josephine (dec.), Dallas Berry, Joseph Edgar, Grace Caroline. Entomologist N.C. State Dept. Agr., 1900-05, 1906-25; prof. zoölogy and entomology, Ont. (Can.) Agrl. Coll., 1905-06; head dept. zoölogy and entomology, Clemson Agrl. Coll. of S.C., entomologist S.C. Expt. Sta. and state entomologist since 1925. Fellow A.A.A.S.; mem. Am. Assn. Econ. Entomologists (ex-pres.), N.C. Acad. Science (ex-pres.), S.C. Acad Science (ex-pres.), Sigma Xi, Gamma Alpha. Democrat. Methodist. Mason. Club: Tri-state Country (Walhalla, S.C.). Author of bulletins of depts. of agr. and expt. stations. Contbr. to jours. Home: Clemson, S.C. Died June 23, 1947.

SHERMAN, Homer Henkel, clergyman; b. Mt. Crawford, Va., July 27, 1870; s. John Wise and Nancy (Henkel) S.; A.B., Randolph-Macon Coll., 1892, A.M., Ph.B., 1893, D.D., 1914; spl. student Johns Hopkins, 1902; m. Laura Catherine Bowman, Mar. 24, 1896 (died Apr. 24, 1904); children—Florence Lucile (Mrs. William Hawley Sewell), Elizabeth Bowman; m. 2d, Ellen Harper Holmes, June 19, 1907. Prof. French and mathematics, Randolph-Macon Acad., Front Royal, 1893-97; ordained ministry M.E. Ch., S., 1895; pastor Shenandoah, Va., 1897-99, Luray, Va., 1899-1902, Baltimore, 1902-06, Roanoke, 1906-09, Harrisonburg, 1909-12, Staunton, 1913-16; field sec. Randolph-Macon Acad., 1916-18; conf. sec. Centenary Movement, 1918-20; sec. Christian Edn. Movement, 1920-23; mem. Gen. Conf. Bd. of Edn., M.E. Ch., S., Nashville, 1914-30, asso. sec., 1923-28, sec., 1928-30. Pres. Baltimore Conf. Bd. of Edn., 1903-23; sec. Commn. on Unification with M.E. Ch., 1922-26; mem. Gen. Conf. M.E. Ch., S., 8 times, 1914-38; exec. sec. Bd. of Christian Edn., Baltimore Conference, 1930-39; director Virginia Conference Ministerial Training Board, 1939-1943; member executive committee Federal Council Churches of Christ in America, 1932-34; pres.-elect Kentucky Wesleyan Coll., 1928. Trustee Randolph-Macon Coll., 1914; mem. Joint Commn. on Meth. Ch. Union, 1938-39, and of Uniting Meth. Conf., Kansas City, Mo., 1939. Democrat. Home: Front Royal, Va. Died Dec. 3, 1948; buried Prospect Hill Cemetery, Front Royal, Va.

SHERMAN, Maurice Sinclair, editor; b. Hanover, N.H., Apr. 19, 1873; s. Frank Asbury and Lucy R. (Hurlbutt) S.; B.S., Dartmouth, 1894; hon. M.A., Connecticut, Wesleyan Univ., 1936; married Florine A. Sunderland, Apr. 12, 1905; 1 dau., Janet Lucile (Mrs. Boardman F. Lockwood). Formerly editor The Springfield Union; editor and publisher, The Courant, Hartford, Conn. Trustee Carnegie Endowment for Internat. Peace; Bromley lecturer on journalism at Yale, 1934. Mem. Beta Theta Pi, Hartford C. of C., Am. Soc. Newspaper Editors, Newcomen Society, S.A.R. Republican. Conglist. Clubs: Dartmouth Lunch, Reality, University, Hartford, 20th Century, Twilight, Barkhamsted, Coventry Game, Monday Evening. Home: 19 Bainbridge Rd., West Hartford 7. Office: 64 State St., Hartford 1, Conn. Died June 27, 1947.

SHERMAN, Ray Eugene, realtor; b. Humboldt County, Ia., Oct. 16, 1885; s. Edward and Sarah (White) S.; student U. of Ia. Coll. of Law, 1904-05; m. Tillie Eleanor Dykeo, Dec. 2, 1914 (died May 30, 1926); 1 son, Ray Eugene; m. 2d, Mary Catherine Stedmond, June 11, 1931; children—Katherine Sarah, Edward. Newspaper reporter, Fort Dodge, Ia., and San Antonio, Tex., 1905-11; realtor, 1913, and since mem. Leavell and Sherman, real estate, El Paso, Tex. Alderman, City of El Paso, 1927-31, mayor, 1931-37; mem. bd. dirs. El Paso Branch, Federal Reserve Bank of Dallas since 1937. President El Paso Adclub, 1915, El Paso Real Estate Board, 1916; v.p. Tex. Assn. Real Estate Bds., 1924. League of Tex. Municipalities, 1932; mem. City Planning Commn. of El Paso, 1922-26; dir. Associated Charities of El Paso, 1932. Regional mgr. War Finance Com. of Tex., since 1943. Mem. Nat. Econ. League, Am. Acad. Polit. and Social Science. Democrat. Home: 909 E. Rio Grande St. Office: 210 N. Stanton St., El Paso, Tex. Died Apr. 30, 1947.

SHERO, William Francis (shē-rō'), clergyman; b Fredonia, N.Y., June 24, 1863; s. Lewis and Clarissa (Francis) S.; grad. State Normal Sch., Fredonia, 1882; A.B., U. of Rochester, 1887; Gen. Theol. Sem., 1887-88; M.A., Hobart, 1890; Ph.D., Franklin and Marshall Coll., Pa., 1906; m. Lucy Rogers, June 11, 1890; children—Lucius Rogers, Livia Francis. Prin. Smethport Sch., 1888-90; deacon, 1889, priest, 1891, P.E. Ch.; rector Angelica, N.Y., 1891-93; chaplain de Veaux Coll., Niagara Falls, N.Y., 1893-97, head master Yeates Sch., Lancaster, Pa., 1897-99; rector St. John's Ch., Lancaster, 1898-1908; warden Racine (Wis.) Coll., 1908-16; rector Christ Ch., Greensburg, Pa., since 1916. Sec. Standing Com. of Diocese, 1918-34; pres. same since 1934. Mem. Delta Psi, Phi Beta Kappa. Author: Instruction in Christian Religion, 1903, 1913; Implications of the Religious Experience, 1907; Instructions in Holy Scripture, 1910. Home: 444 N. Main St., Greensburg, Pa. Died May 12, 1943.

SHIBER, Etta (shī'bēr), b. N.Y. City, Jan. 20, 1878; student Normal Coll. (now Hunter Coll.), N.Y. City, Ethical Culture Kindergarten Training Dept.; m. William Noyes Shiber, Apr. 2, 1901 (died Apr. 1936). Kindergarten teacher 2½ years; after death of her husband, lived in Paris; imprisoned for harboring British soldiers at time of Nazi occupation but finally exchanged and returned to U.S. Author: Paris —Underground, 1943. Address: care Press Alliance, Inc., 235 E. 45th St., New York 17, N.Y. Died Dec. 23, 1948.

SHIELDS, A. C., ry. executive; b. Eldon, Ia.; s. Robert and Anna (Bullock) S.; ed. Ia. State Coll., Ames; unmarried. Began in engring dept., C.,R.I.&P. Ry., 1898; vice-pres. and gen. mgr. D.&R.G.W. R.R., 1923-37; now pres. Pittsburg & Shawmut R.R. Co. Mem. Am. Soc. C.E., Am. Ry. Engrs. Assn. Club: Denver. Home: Kittanning, Pa. Died Jan. 18, 1943.

SHIELDS, Edmund Claude, lawyer; b. Howell, Mich., Dec. 30, 1871; s. Dennis and Lydia (Lonergan) S.; B.L., U. of Mich., 1894, LL.B., 1896; m. Mary Foley, Dec. 28, 1900. Admitted to Mich. bar, 1896; pros. atty., Livingston County, 1901-04; chmn. commn. to compile Mich. state statutes, 1915; mem. Shields, Ballard, Jennings & Tabor; pres. Central Trust Co., Lansing, Mich., Mich. Surety Co.; v.p. W. S. Butterfield Theatres, Inc., Bijou Theatrical Enterprise Co.; dir. Motor Wheel Corp., Grand Trunk Western R.R., Melling Forging Co., Duplex Truck Co. Served as 2d lt., 35th Regt., Spanish-American War. Mem. Dem. Nat. Com. Regent U. of Mich. Mem. Am., Mich. and Ingham County bar assns., Phi Delta Phi. Democrat. Catholic. Clubs: City, Country; Chemung Hills (Howell). Home: Hotel Olds. Office: 1400 Olds Tower, Lansing, Mich. Died Jan. 6, 1947.

SHIELDS, George Robert, lawyer; b. Pigeon Forge, Tenn., Oct. 21, 1879; s. William Jesse and Sarah Ellen (Carter) S.; B.S., Murphy Collegiate Inst., Sevierville, Tenn., 1898; student Peabody Coll. for Teachers, 1899-1900; LL.M., Nat. U. Law Sch., 1912; m. Agnes Richardson Hill, Nov. 14, 1902; children—Frederick Wyatt, Mary Elizabeth, Roger Denton (killed in Germany, Feb. 7, 1945). Teacher public schools of Tennessee, 1897-1901; admitted to bar, D.C., 1911; legal aide, Office of Comptroller U.S. Treasury, 1912-16; with King & King, attys., Washington, D.C., 1917-19, mem. of firm (sr. member), 1920-47; retired. Specialist in matters involving suit or claim against the Federal Government. Served as capt., U.S. Army, aide to Brig. Gen. Herbert M. Lord, 1918-19. Mem. Am. and D.C. bar assns., Soc. Am. Mil. Engrs. Republican. Clubs: University, Columbia Country, National Press. Contbr. to Income Tax Mag., The Constructor, Engineering News-Record, etc. Home: The Baronet, 1737 H St., Washington 6, D.C. Died Nov. 20, 1947.

SHIELDS, John Franklin, lawyer; b. Chester, Pa., June 25, 1869; s. William and Sarah Elizabeth S.; B.Sc., Pa. State Coll., 1892; U. of Pa., 1892-93; LL.B., U. of Pa., 1902; m. Lorene B. Mattern, Feb. 28, 1912. Mem. Am. and Pa. bar assns., Hist. Soc. Pa., Pa. Acad. Fine Arts, Phi Kappa Phi, Beta Theta Pi. Chmn. exec. com., pres. bd. trustees, Pa. State College. Clubs: Union League, University, Phila. Cricket. Home: Alden Park Manor, Germantown, Phila. Office: Girard Trust Bldg., Philadelphia, Pa. Died Oct. 1, 1947.

SHIELS, George Franklin, surgeon; b. San Francisco, Calif., Apr. 15, 1863; s. William and Sarah Esdale (Lynham) S.; M.D., M.B., M.S., Edinburgh U., 1878-86; fellow Royal Coll. Surgeons, Edinburgh, 1880-86; post-grad. studies, Berlin, Paris, Vienna, and London; m. Emily Mead, 1902 (died 1913). Began practice at San Francisco, 1888; lecturer on med. jurisprudence, U. of Calif., 1890-92, prof. surgery, 1892-98; prof. clin. surgery, post-grad. dept., 1894-98; asst. lecturer on surgery, New York Polyclinic, 1904-06; prof. surgery, Fordham U., 1905-07; dir. Shiels Estate Co., San Francisco. Maj. and brigade surgeon, Spanish-Am. War, 1898; on staffs of Gens. Otis, King, Wheaton, Grant and MacArthur; hon. mustered out 1900; maj. M.C., World War, 1917-19; now col. M.R.C. Fellow Am. Coll. of Surgeons. Calif. Acad. of Medicine; member A.M.A., Calif. State and San Francisco County med. socs., Mil. Order Fgn. Wars, Naval and Mil. Order Spanish-Am. War, Assn. Army of U.S., Mu Sigma Mu. Awarded Congressional Medal of Honor "for most distinguished gallantry in action"; Spanish-Am. War, Philippine Insurrection, and Victory medals; 3 citations "for distinguished gallantry." World War (U.S.); Croix de Guerre with 2 Palms, Chevalier Légion d'honneur (French); 3 Silver Star citations. Republican. Protestant. Clubs: Pacific Union (San Francisco); Army and Navy (New York). Contbr. papers on professional subjects. Home: 337 Hopkins Av., Redwood City, Calif. Died Oct. 26, 1943

SHIMP, Herbert Gilby, insurance; b. Holmberg, Washington County, Kansas, July 17, 1887; s. Henry C. and Frances Victoria (Gordy) S.; ed. pub. schs. and business coll.; m. Hazel Bernice Dale, Jan. 18, 1908; 1 son, Dale Henry. Organizer 1918, and ex-pres. Internat. Ins. Service Co.; also ex-pres. Old Line Service, Inc.; pres. Am. Conservation Co. since 1930. Editor The American Conservationist. Originated the plan and directed readjustment of rates by which over one billion dollars of outstanding ins. of over 40 fraternal beneficiary socs. and legal reserve cos. was placed on a sound basis; originated the insured bank savings plan now in thousands of banks. Republican. Mem. all Masonic orders. Editor of History of Life Insurance in Its Formative Years. Home: 1111 Sheridan Rd., Wilmette, Ill. Office: 35 E. Wacker Drive, Chicago, Ill. Died Apr. 4, 1943.

SHINN, Henry Arthur, univ. dean; b. Cherryvale, Kan., Dec. 1, 1890; s. Henry David and Emma Elizabeth (Voorhees) S.; A.B., U. of Kan., 1916; student Sch. of Law, 1920-22; Yale U. Sch. of Law, summer 1924; J.D., Leland Stanford U. Sch. of Law, 1926; m. Frances Susan Ingalls, June 2, 1917; 1 dau., Elizabeth. Prin., Jewell and Caney, Kan., High Sch., 1916-18; instr., asst. prof., asso. prof., English, U. of Kan., 1918-23; lecturer and supt., Redpath-Horner Chautauquas, summers 1918-22; prof. Eng., Kan. State Coll., 1923-24; acting asso. prof. Eng., Stanford U., 1926-27; admitted Calif. bar, 1927, in practice Calif., 1927-28; trust dept., Bank of Italy, San Francisco, 1928-29; prof. law, Mercer U., 1929-34, U. of Ga. since 1934; dean of Univ. and prof. law, U. of Ga. since 1940, acting dean Sch. of Law since 1941. Four-minute speaker World War; mem. Selective Service Bd., 1940; mem. Regional War Labor Bd., 1943; mem. Regional Fed. Bd. of Legal Examiners, 1943. Mem. Calif. Bar Assn., Am. Bar Assn., Internat. Rotary, Nat. Econ. League, Phi Alpha Delta, Delta Sigma Rho, Phi Kappa Phi. Democrat. Presbyterian. Contbr. articles to numerous literary mags. and law jours. including Forum, Current History, Yale Law Journal, North American Review. Home: 495 Rutherford St., Athens, Ga. Died Feb. 20, 1948; buried in Alta Mesa Memorial Park, Palo Alto, Calif.

SHIPLEY, Frederick William, univ. prof.; b. Cheltenham, Ont, Can., Jan. 15, 1871; s. William and Harriet (Hagemann) S.; A.B., U. of Toronto, 1892; student Am. Sch. Classical Studies in Rome, and in Vatican Library, 1895-97; Ph.D., U. of Chicago, 1901; Litt.D., U. of Toronto, 1925; LL.D., Colorado Coll., 1925; m. Antoinette Cary, Mar. 28, 1899; children—Frederick Cary, Walter Cleveland. Classical master, Collegiate Inst., Collingwood, Ont., 1893, Lindsay, 1894; asst. in Latin, U. of Chicago, 1897-98; head Latin dept., Lewis Inst., Chicago, 1898-1901; prof. Latin, Washington U., 1901-41, professor emeritus, 1941; dir. div. univ. extension, 1914-31, dir. summer sessions, 1923-25, dean of Univ. Coll., 1931-32, dean of College of Liberal Arts, 1932-37, dean Sch. of Graduate Studies, 1937-41, dean emeritus, 1941; annual professor School Classical Studies, American Acad. in Rome, 1928-29. Member Archæol. Inst. of America (pres. 1913-17, hon. pres. since 1917), Am. Sch. of Classical Studies at Athens (mng. com. 1913-17), Egyptian Research Account (vice pres. Am. Branch), Am. Sch. for Oriental Research in Jerusalem (dir. 1913-17), Am. Philol. Assn. (chmn. committee on monographs, 1929-33), Classical Assn. of Middle West and South (pres. 1934-35), Sch. of Am. Archæology, Santa Fe (dir. 1913-17); mem. advisory com. of Am. School of Classical Studies, Am. Acad in Rome, 1913-17; pres. Assn. Urban Univs., 1931-32; v.p. Nat. Univ. Extension Assn., 1923-24; 2d vice chmn. Am. Council on Education, 1931-33. Mem. Chi Psi, Phi Beta Kappa. Chmn. bd. of publn. Art and Archæology, editor 1917-18; hon. editor Am. Jour. of Archæology, 1913-17; editor Bull. of Archæol. Inst. America, 1912, gen. editor Washington University Studies since 1937. Clubs: University, Contemporary (exec. com.), Town and Gown (sec.). Mem. Chamber Commerce of St. Louis (chmn. ednl. com., 1919-23); pres. St. Louis Classical Club, 1919-23, and since 1927. Vice-pres. Bd. of Education, University City, Mo., 1914-21 (pres. 1921). Baptist. Author: Sources of Corruption in Latin Manuscripts, 1904; Velleius Paterculus (Loeb Classical Library); Res Gestæ Divi Augusti, 1924; Chronology of Building Operations in Rome from Death of Cæsar to Death of Augustus, 1931; Agrippa's Building Activities in Rome, 1933; Studies in Honor of Frederick W. Shipley, by his Colleagues, Washington Studies, St. Louis, 1942. Contbr. to classical philol. and archæol. journals. Home: 149 N. Hanley Rd., Clayton, Mo. Address: Washington University, St. Louis, Mo. Died Feb. 11, 1945.

SHIPLEY, George, educator; b. at Baltimore, Md., Mar. 13, 1867; s. Rev. J. Lester and Elizabeth Augusta (Gere) S.; A.B., Randolph-Macon Coll., 1887, A.M., 1888; Ph.D., Johns Hopkins, 1897; m. Dorothy, d. William B. and Anne (Tyson) Willson, Nov. 20, 1913. Editor Baltimore American, 1897-1916; asso. headmaster Boys' Latin School, Baltimore, 1914-16, and headmaster, 1917-34. Mem. Phi Beta Kappa, Beta Theta Pi, Modern Lang. Assn. America. Clubs: University, Baltimore Country, Chesapeake Bay Yacht.

Author: The Genitive Case in Anglo-Saxon, 1903. Address: "Fairhaven," Easton, Md. Died May 5, 1944.

SHIPLEY, Richard Larkin, clergyman, editor; b. Harman, Md., June 10, 1879; s. Theodore Alexander and Cecelia (Shipley) S.; grad. Westminster (Md.) Theol. Sem., 1903; D.D., Western Md. Coll., 1921; m. Cora Belle Roberts, June 20, 1907; children—Mary Louise, Roberta Cecilia. Ordained to ministry Meth. Protestant Ch., 1905; pastor various churches in Maryland, First Methodist Protestant Church, Newark, New Jersey, 1926-32; pastor West Baltimore Methodist Ch., Baltimore, 1941; editor Meth. Protestant Recorder, 1932-40; sec. Assn. of Meth. Hist. Societies. Trustee Western Md. Coll. Mem. Am. Fedn. Arts, Interchurch Club of Baltimore; member Fed. Council of Chs. Democrat. Mason, Jr. O.U.A.M. Mem. bd. of special writers for the Christian Advocate. Lecturer Westminster Theol. Sem. Editor: How Methodism Came (by Mrs. Arthur B. Bibbins), 1944; Finding God Through Christ (C. E. Forlines). Home: 4135 Forest Park Av., Baltimore 7, Md. Died Nov. 25, 1947; buried in Woodlawn Cemetery, Baltimore.

SHIPLEY, Walter Penn, lawyer; b. Phila., June 20, 1860; s. Thomas and Eliza M. (Drinker) S.; student Haverford Coll., class of '81; LL.B., U. of Pa., 1883; m. Anne Emlen, Oct. 17, 1889. Admitted to bar, 1883, and since in practice at Phila.; sr. mem. Shipley & Vaux since 1887. Half owner of Girard Shoe Mfg. Co. since 1915. Dir. and treas. Trustees of Germantown Preparative Meeting of Friends since 1900, Home for Aged and Infirm Colored Persons, since 1893. Clubs: Manhattan Chess (New York), Franklin Chess (pres. since 1904), University. Home: 477 Locust Av., Germantown. Office: Morris Bldg., Philadelphia. Died Feb. 17, 1942.

SHIPPEE, Lester Burrell (shĭp'ē), prof. history; b. East Greenwich, R.I., Jan. 28, 1879; s. George Smith and Susan Maria (Greene) S.; A.B., Brown U., 1903, A.M., 1904, Ph.D., 1916; m. Edna Isabel Warner, Aug. 2, 1905; children—Elizabeth Greene, Burrell Warner, Margaret Siddell. Teacher secondary schs. until 1910; prof. history and polit. science, Pacific U., Forest Grove, Ore., 1910-13; asst. prof. history, Washington State Coll., 1913-16; lecturer in history, Brown U., 1916-17; lecturer in history, 1917-18; asst. prof., U. of Minn., 1918-20, asso. prof., 1920-25, prof. since 1925, chmn. 1931. Member Am. Hist. Assn., Miss. Valley Hist. Assn. (pres. 1934-35), Minnesota Historical Society (president), Phi Beta Kappa, Delta Upsilon. Club: Campus. Author: Recent American History, 1924, 1930; Canadian-American Relations, 1849-1874, 1939; also articles in Am. Secretaries of State, Am. Hist. Rev., Miss. Valley Hist. Rev., Polit. Science Rev., Dictionary of Am. Biography, Dictionary of Am. History. Editor: Bishop Whipple's Southern Diary, 1937. Address: University of Minnesota, Minneapolis, Minn. Died Feb. 9, 1944.

SHIRAS, George 3d (shī'răs), lawyer and biologist; b. Allegheny, Pa., Jan. 1, 1859; s. George Jr. and Lillie E. (Kennedy) S.; A.B., Cornell, 1881; LL.B., Yale Univ., 1883; Sc.D., Trinity Coll., 1918; m. Frances P. White, Oct. 31, 1885 (died Sept. 16, 1938); children—Ellen Kennedy (Mrs. Frank J. Russell), George Peter (dec.). Admitted to bar State of Pa., 1883; asso. in practice with his father until appmt. of latter to U.S. Supreme bench, 1892; mem. Shiras & Dickey, Pittsburgh, until 1904. Mem. Pa. Ho. of Rep., 1889-90; elected to the 58th Congress (1903-05), as an avowed Republican, on an independent ticket; writer since 1905, upon biol. subjects and legal questions connected with federal jurisprudence; pres. Kawbawgam Hotel Co. (Mich.). Noted as amateur photographer of wild animals; student of natural history; invented methods for taking pictures of wild animals at night by flashlight; promoter of legislation for protection of wild animals and birds. Author of bills putting under federal control migratory birds and migratory fish, the former becoming a law Mar. 4, 1913. Awarded gold medal at Paris Expn., 1900, and grand prize at St. Louis World Fair, 1904, for photographs of wild animals. V.p. Am. Game Protective Assn. since 1912; mem. advisory bd. Migratory Bird Treaty Regulations, Department of Agriculture, since 1914; trustee Nat. Geog. Society since 1908. Clubs: Boone and Crockett, Explorers' (New York); Chevy Chase (Md.); Cosmos (Washington); Rotary of Marquette, Mich. (hon.). Presented a club house to Marquette Fedn. of Women's Clubs, and a municipal swimming pool and extensive lake shore frontage (now Shiras Park), City of Marquette. Donor with Mrs. Shiras of trust fund called the Shiras Inst., incorporated 1938, for recreational and cultural benefits of Marquette and vicinity. Author: Hunting Wild Life with Camera and Flashlight, 2 vols., 1935, 2d edit., 1936. Home: 460 E. Ridge St., Marquette, Mich. Died Mar. 24, 1942.

SHOEMAKER, Charles Chalmers, author; b. W. Newton, Pa., Mar. 2, 1860; s. John and Isabelle S.; grad. high sch., Pittsburgh; m. Louise F. Super, Nov. 7, 1893. Mgr. and treas. Penn. Pub. Co., Phila. Mem. Am. Publishers' Assn., Am. Booksellers' Assn., Booksellers' League (New York), Browning Soc. Clubs: Athletic, Franklin Inn, Writeabout (Phila.). Author: Young Folks Dialogues, 1885; Choice Humor, 1886; Holiday Entertainments, 1886; Choice Dialect, 1887; Humorous Dialogues, 1888; One Hundred Choice Selections, 1899. Residence: St. Davids, Pa. Office: 923 Arch St., Philadelphia. Died May 22, 1937.

SHOEMAKER, Harlan, surgeon; b. 1875; A.B., Stanford, 1899; M.D., U. of Pa. Sch. of Medicine, 1902. Practices at Los Angeles; sr. surgeon Los Angeles County Hosp.; surgeon St. Vincent's Hosp. Fellow A.M.A., Am. Coll. Surgeons. Office: 1930 Wilshire Blvd., Los Angeles, Calif. Died Dec. 1943.

SHOHAT, James Alexander (shō'hät), prof. mathematics; b. Brest Litovsk, Russia, Nov. 18, 1886; s. Abraham Joseph and Esther (Goldberg) S.; grad. U. of Petrograd, 1910, fellow, 1912-16, Magister of Pure Mathematics (Ph.D.), 1922; m. Nadiashda Galli, Jan. 17, 1922. Came to U.S., 1923, naturalized, 1929. Instr. mathematics, Polytechnic Institute, Petrograd, 1913-17; instr. same, Mining Inst. of Petrograd, 1916-17; prof. mathematics, Ural U., Ekatherineburg, Russia, 1917-21, Pedagogical Inst. of Petrograd, 1921-23; asst. in mathematics, U. of Chicago, 1923-24; asst. prof. mathematics, U. of Mich., 1924-29; research in mathematics, Institut Henri Poincaré, Paris, 1930; asst. prof. mathematics, U. of Pa., 1931-35, associate professor, 1935-42, professor since 1942. Fellow Institute of Math. Statistics, A.A.A.S.; member American Math. Soc., Math. Assn. America, Sigma Xi. Mem. Orthodox Greek Ch. Home: 600 S. Eagle Rd., Upper Darby P.O., Pa. Died Oct. 8, 1944; buried in Arlington National Cemetery.

SHORT, Walter Campbell, army officer; b. Fillmore, Ill., Mar. 30, 1880; s. Hiram Spait and Sarah Minerva (Stokes) S.; A.B., U. of Ill., 1901; m. Isabel Dean, Nov. 4, 1914; 1 son, Walter Dean. Commd. 2d lt. U.S. Army, 1902, and advanced through grades to maj. gen., 1936; served in France with 1st Div. on Gen. Staff at G.H.Q. and as asst. chief of staff, 3d Army, during World War; comd. 2d Brigade, Fort Ontario, N.Y., 1937-38; comd. 1st Div., Fort Hamilton, N.Y., 1938-40; comd. 4th Army Corps, March-June 1940, 1st Army Corps, Oct.-Dec. 1940; promoted to lt. gen. Feb. 1941, comdg. Hawaiian Department, Feb. to Dec. 1941. Assigned to head traffic dept., Ford Motor Co., Dallas, Tex., Sept. 1942. Decorated D.S.M. (U.S.); Officer Legion of Honor (France). Mem. Phi Beta Kappa. Republican. Clubs: Army and Navy, Army and Navy Country (Washington, D.C.). Author: Employment of Machine Guns, 1922. Home: 3141 Southwestern Blvd., Dallas 5, Tex. Died Sept. 3, 1949; buried in Arlington National Cemetery.

SHORTS, Bruce Carman, lawyer; b. Bellville, Ont., Can., Jan. 15, 1878; s. Robert and Eliza Jane (Armstrong) S.; LL.B., U. of Mich., 1901; m. Carrie Atkinson, Nov. 28, 1908; children—Bruce, Calhoun. Came to U.S., 1885, naturalized, 1899. Admitted to Wash. bar, January 13, 1905; vice-president National Bank of Commerce of Seattle, Marine Bancorporation; secretary and director Marine National Co.; director Centennial Flour Mills. Mem. Phi Delta Phi. Republican. Mason (Shriner). Clubs: Rainier, Arctic, Seattle Golf. Home: 923 16th Av. N. Office: Stuart Bldg., Seattle, Wash. Died Mar. 28, 1945.

SHOUP, Arthur Glendinning (shōōp), lawyer; b. Challis, Ida., Nov. 27, 1880; s. James McCain and Amelia Betsy (Ellis) S.; student U. of Wash., 1899-1901; m. 2d, Madge Kemp, Aug. 28, 1915. Dep. U.S. marshal, Alaska, 1902-10; admitted to Alaska bar, 1913; mem. Alaska Legislature, 1913-15; mayor of Sitka, 3 terms; U.S. atty., 1st Div., Alaska, by apptmt. of President Harding, Aug. 1921, and reapptmt. of President Coolidge, 1926; retired Mar. 16, 1927; moved to San Jose, Calif., and associated with Louis O'Neal in practice of law; apptd. U.S. commr., Northern Dist. of Calif., 1933 (reappointed, 1937). Dist. food administrator, World War, also active in various war bds. Del. Rep. Nat. Conv., Cleveland, 1924. Supt. Alaska Pioneers Home, 1913-19. Mem. Am. Bar Assn., Calif. Bar Assn., Santa Clara County Bar Assn. (elected pres. Oct. 1935), Alaska Hist. Assn., Pioneers of Alaska. Episcopalian. Elk. Home: 1505 McKendrie St. Address: First Nat. Bank Bldg., San Jose, Calif. Died Apr. 1942.

SHOUP, Paul (shoup), ry. official; b. San Bernardino, Calif., Jan. 8, 1874; s. Timothy and Sarah S. (Sumner) S.; ed. high sch., San Bernardino; m. Rose Wilson, Dec. 1, 1900; children—Carl, Jack, Louise. Began with A.,T.&S.F. Ry.; later with Southern Pacific Co., advancing to asst. gen. freight agt., apptd. asst. gen. manager in charge of electric lines, 1910; made pres. Pacific Electric Ry. Co., 1912, and apptd. v.p. when U.S. Govt. took over operation of the steam rys. of S.P. Co. during World War; exec. v.p. S.P. Co., 1925-28, pres. 1929-32, vice-chmn., 1932-38, retired; pres. Merchants and Manufacturers Assn., Inc., dir. Tidewater Asso. Oil Co.; trustee, Sanford Univ. Clubs: Bankers (New York, N.Y.); Bohemian, Pacific Union (San Francisco, Calif.); Jonathan, California (Los Angeles). Industry mem. Regional War Labor Bd. Home: Los Altos, Calif. Office: 725 S. Spring St., Los Angeles, Calif. Died July 30, 1946.

SHOWMAN, Harry Munson, educator; b. Denver, Colo., Apr. 17, 1889; s. Harry Duval and Alice Virginia (Munson) S.; E.M., Colo. Sch. of Mines, 1910; Shattuck scholar, Harvard, 1918-19; M.A., Harvard U., 1919; studied U. of Chicago, 1925; m. Verdie Gertrude Crews, Apr. 20, 1911; 1 son, Harry Crews. Teacher of civil engring., Colo. Sch. of Mines, 1910-18; mechanics, Case Sch. of Applied Science, 1919-20; instr. mathematics, U. of Calif. at Los Angeles, 1920-28, registrar and lecturer since 1928. Mem. Math. Assn. America, Am. Assn. Collegiate Registrars, Pacific Coast Assn. of College Registrars, Tau Beta Pi. Republican. Presbyterian. Mason. Home: 10770 Weyburn Av., Los Angeles, Calif. Died June 24, 1943.

SHREVE, Richmond Harold, architect; b. Cornwallis, Can., June 25, 1877; s. Richmond (D.D.) and Mary C. P. (Hocken) S.; B.Arch., Cornell U., 1902; m. Ruth Bentley, Oct. 15, 1906; children—Richmond Bentley, Robert Wilton, Thomas Charles. Came to U.S., 1885, naturalized, 1906. Mem. faculty Cornell U., 1902-06; began with Carrere & Hastings, architects, N.Y. City, 1906, mem. Carrere & Hastings, Shreve & Lamb, 1920-24, Shreve and Lamb, 1924-29, Shreve, Lamb & Harmon since 1929. Prin. works of partnerships: Standard Oil, Macmillan, Fisk, Gen. Motors, Empire State, Insurance Co. of North America buildings; new building for Bankers Trust Co., N.Y. City, Acacia Mut. Life Insurance Co. Bldg., Washington, D.C., R. J. Reynolds Tobacco Co. Office Bldg., Winston-Salem, N.C., Hudson House, Ardsley-on-Hudson, New York; 5 dormitories, auditorium, library and faculty housing, Connecticut Coll. for Women, new building, Hunter Coll., New York; chem. engineering bldg., Cornell University; dormitories and academic buildings, Kent (Conn.) School; Newfoundland Defense Base for U.S. Army; U.S. Naval Training Station, Sampson, N.Y., etc. Chief architect Williamsburg and Vladeck housing projects, New York; dir. Slum Clearance Com. of N.Y.; chmn. bd. of design and chief architect Parkchester, Metropolitan Life Ins. Housing Project; gen. chmn. Construction League of U.S., 1936-37. Mem. Real Estate Bd. New York (mem. bd. govs., 1930-32, 1935-37, and 1940-42); mem. New York Bldg. Congress (pres. 1927, 28, 29); mem. bd. of design N.Y. World's Fair 1939; mem. of advisory bd. of architects Goucher Coll.; mem. advisory council, coll. of Architecture, Cornell U. Fellow Am. Inst. Architects (chmn. com. on housing 1935-36; dir. 1935-40; pres. 1941-43); mem. Architectural League New York, Sigma Xi; hon. corr. mem. Royal Inst. of British Architects. Republican. Episcopalian. Clubs: Cornell (pres. 1924-27), Union League; Ardsley Country (former mem. bd. govs., v.p.); Cosmos (Washington, D.C.); Union (Cleveland, O.). Partnership has received medals in recognition of professional work from New York chapter A.I.A., Architectural League of New York and Fifth Avenue Association, also Grand Prix, Paris Expn. Home: 50 Euclid Av., Hastings-on-Hudson, N.Y. Office: 11 E. 44th St., New York, N.Y. Died Sep. 10, 1946.

SHRIVER, George McLean, ry. official; b. Hightstown, N.J., 1868; s. Rev. Samuel S. and Caroline (McCluskey) S.; ed. pub. schs., Baltimore, Md.; m. Elizabeth M. Chism, June 1891 (dec.). Clerk in accounting dept. B.&O. R.R. Co., 1886; private secretary to pres. same rd., 1888-1901, asst. to pres., 1901-11, 2d v.p., Jan. 12, 1911, sr. v.p. since Mar. 1, 1920. Clubs: Maryland, Chesapeake, Merchants (Baltimore); Metropolitan, Bankers, Recess (New York); University (Phila.). Home: "Alsenborn," Pikesville, Md. Office: Baltimore & Ohio Railroad Co., Baltimore, Md. Died May 11, 1942.

SHULL J(ames) Marion, artist-botanist; b. Clark County, O., Jan. 23, 1872; s. Harrison and Catharine (Ryman) S.; ed. pub. schs., business coll., and through brief attendance at Valparaiso U. and Art Students' League, New York; m. Addie Virginia Moore, Dec. 20, 1906 (died April 2, 1937); children—Virginia Moore, Francis Marion; m. Mary Ethel Lerch, of Penn Yan, N.Y., April, 1947. Student and instr. Antioch Coll., Yellow Springs, O., 1896-98; supervisor music and drawing, Boise, Ida., 1898-99; teacher pub. schools, Ohio, and commercial artist, Memphis, Tenn., 1899-1906; in U.S. Post Office Dept., 1906-07; dendrological artist U.S. Forest Service, Washington, D.C., 1907-09; bot. artist Bur. Plant Industry, 1909-25, asso. botanist, 1925-42, now retired. Has made over 1700 water color drawings and many in black and white for Dept. of Agr.; widely known as breeder of new varieties of iris and hemerocallis. Mem. A.A.A.S., Am. Hort. Soc., Bot. Soc. Washington, Am. Iris Soc. (silver medal), Nat. Carillon Assn. Distinguished Service medal of The Am. Iris Soc., 1944. Club: Arts. Author: Rainbow Fragments—A Garden Book of the Iris, 1931. Contbr. articles and illustrations to mags. Home: 207 Raymond St., Chevy Chase 15, Md. Died Sept. 1, 1948.

SHULL, Joseph H., congressman, lawyer; b. Martin's Creek, Pa., Aug. 17, 1848; s. Hon. Elias and Margaret S.; ed. Blair Presbyterial Acad., Blairstown, N.J., Lafayette Coll.; m. M. Virginia Flory, May 1, 1874. Teacher pub. schs., Easton, Pa.; grad. Univ. of New York, 1873, med. dept., 1878; admitted to bar, 1878; mem. Pa. State senate, 1886-91; mem. Congress, 1903-05. Democrat. Address: Stroudsburg, Pa.

SHURTER, Edwin DuBois (shûr'tẽr), educator, author; b. Samsonville, N.Y., Oct. 24, 1863; s. Martin and Mary C. (DuBois) S.; Ph.B., Cornell U., 1892; m. Alice Burtt, Aug. 16, 1893. Instr. elocution and English, Stanford U., 1893-94; instr. oratory, Cornell, 1894-99; practiced law in Ithaca, N.Y., 1896-99; prof. pub. speaking, U. of Tex., 1899-1923. Founder of Tex. Interscholastic League (state chmn. 1910-22). Mem. New York Bar, Tex. Bar. Mem. Am. Bar Assn., Am. Assn. of Univ. Profs, Phi Gamma Delta, Delta Chi, Delta Sigma Rho. Republican. Presbyterian. Mason. Clubs: Rotary, Civitan. Author: Extempore Speaking, 1908; Science and Art of Debate, 1908; The Rhetoric of Oratory, 1909; One Hundred Questions Debated, 1913; Oral English, 1918; New American Readers, 1919; Public Speaking, 1927; Practical Speech-Making, 1929; Citizenship Readers, 1930; New Citizenship Readers, 1939; Effective Debating. Compiler of Masterpieces of Modern Oratory, 1907; Speeches of Henry W. Grady, 1908; Oratory of the South, 1910; American Oratory of Today, 1911; Poems for Oral Expression, 1925; Masterpieces of Modern

Verse, 1926; Winning Declamations, 1929, Representative College Orations; etc. Address: Sweetacre, Brooktondale, N.Y. Died Oct. 13, 1946; buried Brooktondale, N.Y.

SHUTE, A(braham) Lincoln (shōōt), clergyman, educationist; b. Braman's Corners, Schenectady County, N.Y., Feb. 15, 1865; s. Lewis Parkes and Lucinda (Foote) S.; B.A., Cornell Coll., Mt. Vernon, Ia., 1887, M.A., 1890; B.D., Drew Theol. Sem., 1890; studied Ill. Wesleyan, U. of Chicago; D.D., Fargo, 1913; Am. School of Oriental Research, Jerusalem, summer session, 1925; Th.D. summa cum laude, Southern Bapt. Theol. Sem., Louisville, Ky., 1927; m. Nellie Haney, 1887; children—Lewis Haney (now deceased), Vivian Lizzie (Mrs. George Barney Thompson; now deceased), Zelma Luella, Harold James (now deceased), Olin Yates, Clarence William; m. 2d, Laura Belle Ward, 1914. Began in M.E. ministry, 1885; pastor in Ill., N.J., Wis. and N.D. over 30 yrs.; chaplain N.D. Ho. of Rep., 1911; centenary stewardship lecturer, financial agt., evangelist, 1919-20; Near East lecturer and organizer in N.D., 1920-21; pastor Thoburn Ch., Calcutta, 1921-22; prof. English Bible and systematic theology, Bareilly Sem., India, 1922-23; founder, organizer, first prin. India Meth. Theol. Coll., Jabalpur, C.P., India (now Leonard Theol. Coll.), 1923-25; world tour of missionary and archeological investigation, incl. Ur, Babylon, Kish, Birs Nimrud, Palestine, Egypt, 1921-25; Bibl. research and burn Ch., Calcutta, 1921-22; prin. and prof. English Bible and systematic theology, India Meth. Theol. Coll., Bareilly, India, 1922-23, and Jabalpur, C.P., India, 1923-25, now known as Leonard Theological College; world tour of missionary and archeological investigation, including Ur, Babylon, Kish, Birs Nimrud, Palestine and Egypt, 1921-25; Bibl. research and lit. work, S. Bapt. Theol. Sem., Louisville, Ky., 1926-27; head of dept. of Bible and theology, Taylor U., 1929-34. Mem. exec. bd. World's Purity Fed., 1913-21; supt. N.D. Purity Fedn., 1915-20. Apptd. by gov. of Bengal mem. bd. govs. Bruce Instn., 1921. Mem. Palestine Oriental Soc., Nat. Assn. of Biblical Instructors, Pi Gamma Mu. Prohibitionist. Author: The Fatherhood of God, 1904; What Shall I Do with My Life?, 1922; Old Testament History, Literature and Theology, 1922; The Battle of Beth-horon in Bibliotheca Sacra, Oct. 1927; Old Testament History and Literature in the Light of Archæological Research, from the Creation to the Birth of Christ. Bible lectures: The Antiquity and Character of Primitive Man; Creation Stories of Non-Biblical Religions and Literatures, and Their Relation to the Genesis Creation Story; Science, Evolution and the First Chapter of Genesis; Origin and Spread of Civilization; Who Wrote the Pentateuch? Who Wrote Isaiah, Chapters 40-66? Jewish Apocryphal, Pseudepigraphic and Apocalyptic Literature Between the Testaments; Jewish and Pagan Preparation of the World for the Supreme Crisis of Human History, the Birth of Christ; also illustrated lectures on the Bible and on travel; wrote reply to Interpretation of Isaiah 18 as Isaiah's Vision of the U.S.—"The U.S. in Prophecy"—in Christian Faith and Life, April 1935, "Esau I Hated," in Review and Expositor, July 1936; also contbd. to jours. Fosdick's "Beyond Modernism," a Reply; Who Were the Hyksos?, Apr. 1937; booklets on Revolutionary Changes in Pension Legislation of M.E. Church, 1936-40; also booklets Revolutionary Episcopal Decisions, and Revolutionary Episcopal Decisions Violative of Church Supreme Court Decisions Affecting Pension Laws of the M.E. Church, 1937-38; and articles; The Book of Revelation in Review and Expositor, Apr. 1941; Jehovah, July 1942; Theology, 1942. Lecturer on archeology, Bible, travels, missions, etc. Home: Penney Farms, Fla. Died Oct. 25, 1947; buried Green Cove Springs, Fla.

SHUTE, Henry Augustus, author; b. Exeter, N.H., Nov. 17, 1856; s. George S. and Joanna (Simpkins) S.; A.B., Harvard, 1879; m. Amelia F. Weeks, Oct. 18, 1885 (died Jan. 26, 1895); children—Richard E., Nathalie; m. 2d, Ella Kent, Aug. 12, 1897. Admitted to bar, 1882; judge police court, Exeter, 1883-1926; in practice as mem. Henry A. and Richard E. Shute until 1927. Republican. Treas. Farmers' Ins. Co. Author: Real Diary of a Real Boy; Sequel, 1904; Letters to Beany and Love Letters of Plupy Shute, 1905; Real Boys, 1905; A Few Neighbors, 1906; A Profane and Somewhat Unreliable History of Exeter, 1907; The Country Band, 1908; Farming It, 1909; Plupy, 1910; A Country Lawyer, 1911; Plupy, 1912; Misadventures of Three Good Boys, 1914; The Youth Plupy, 1917; The Lad with the Downy Chin, 1917; Brite and Fair, 1918; The Real Diary of the Worst Farmer, 1919; Plupy and Old J. Albert, 1924; Plupy, Beany and Pewt, Contractors, 1926; Chadwick and Shute, Gob Printers, 1927; Plupy, The Wirst Yet, 1929. Contbr. weekly column in Exeter News Letter, also articles to mags. Home: Exeter, N.H. Died Jan. 25, 1943.

SHUTTS, Frank Barker (shŭts), lawyer; b. Dearborn County, Ind., Sept. 11, 1870; s. Abram P. and Amanda (Barker) S.; grad. high sch., Aurora, Ind., 1887; LL.B., DePauw U., 1892; m. Agnes John, June 8, 1910; children—Marion Julia (Mrs. Shutts Stevens), Elinor (Mrs. Bernard R. Baker II). Began practice of law at Aurora, Illinois, 1891; moved to Miami, Florida, 1910; organizer and now senior member Shutts, Bowen, Simmons, Prevatt & Julian; founder, and formerly president and publisher Miami Herald; former dir. First Nat. Bank of Miami; former director Miami Beach First Nat. Bank; dir. Miami Bridge Co.; pres. South Atlantic Telephone & Telegraph Co., 1917-25 (when it was acquired by the Southern Bell Tel. & Tel. Co.); gen. counsel Dade County Defense Council. Lt. col. on staff of Gov. Cary A. Hardee, of Florida, 1921-25. Local chmn. Advisory Board of Salvation Army. Chmn. bd. trustees Jackson Memorial Hosp. Mem. Am. and Fla. State bar assns., Com. of 100 (Miami Beach), Phi Gamma Delta, etc. Democrat. Methodist. Mason, Elk. Clubs: Surf, Bath, Indian Creek Country (Miami Beach). Home: 1438 S. Bay Shore Drive. Office: First National Bank Bldg., Miami, Fla. Died Jan. 7, 1947.

SIBLEY, Bolling (sĭb'lē), life insurance; b. Augusta, Georgia, Aug. 20, 1873; s. Robert Pendleton and Susie Wheless (Bolling) S.; grad. Richmond Acad., Augusta, 1889; m. Erle Beasley, Sept. 17, 1903; children—Dorothy Leigh (Mrs. Arthur Mosely Hopkins, Jr.), Erle Bolling (dec.). Began as clerk, manufacturing company, 1889; banking, 1892-1904; life insurance since 1904; general agent Penn Mutual Life Insurance Company, 1908-41, associate general agent since 1941. Vice-president National Assn. Life Underwriters, 1912, sec., 1913; organizer and 1st pres. Memphis Life Underwriters Assn., 1910. Del. Dem. Nat. Conv., San Francisco, 1920. Mem. com. of 100 of M.E. Ch., S., to celebrate centenary of mission enterprise and raise $35,000,000, 1918; member Memphis C. of C. (director 1940-41). President Memphis Y.M.C.A., 1915, dir., 1908-28; mem. Memphis Chamber Commerce; pres. Tennessee State Life Underwriters Assn., 1932, Memphis Life Managers Assn., 1937; member advisory board Salvation Army, Memphis; mem. bd. dirs. Memphis Sunshine Home for Aged Men; mem. bd. dirs. Hosp. for Crippled Adults, Memphis. Democrat. Mem. bd. stewards and trustee St. John's Meth. Ch., Memphis. Mason (32°, K.T., Shriner). Clubs: Memphis Sales Managers (charter mem. bd. 1938-39). Memphis Rotary (charter mem.; v.p. 1942-43). Apptd. mem. Alien Enemy Hearing Bd., West Tenn. Dist., 1942. Home: 1512 Vinton Av. Office: Sterick Bldg., Memphis, Tenn. Died April 24, 1949.

SICKELS, Ivin, coll. prof.; b. Nyack, N.Y., Aug. 13, 1853; s. John N. and Harriet Louise (Gesner) S.; B.S., Coll. City of N.Y., 1874, M.S., 1878; M.D., Univ. Med. Coll. (New York U.), 1883; unmarried. Instr. and later asst. prof. chemistry and physics, Univ. Med. Coll., 1883-98; asst. prof. chemistry and physics, Cornell U. Med. Coll., 1898-1909; asst. prof. and asso. prof. natural history, Coll. City of N.Y., 1897-1910, prof., 1910-17, prof. geology, since 1917. Fellow N.Y. Acad. Scis.; mem. Am. Chem. Soc., A.A.A.S., Phi Beta Kappa, etc. Author: Wood-Working, 1890. Home: W. Nyack, N.Y. Died Aug. 5, 1943.

SIDDALL, Hugh Wagstaff (sĭd'dăl), chmn. Transcontinental and Western passenger assns.; b. Evanston, Ill., April 1, 1885; s. Theodore Percival and Bella Jane (Glassey) S.; ed. pub. schs.; married; children—Hugh Badger, William Shreve, James Sheridan. Office boy in passenger dept. C.M.,St.P.&P. R.R., 1898; continued with Company in var. capac. 20 yrs.; with U.S. R.R. Adminstrn., 1918-20; sec. Trans-Continental Passenger Assn., 1920-28, chairman, 1929-31; chmn. Transcontinental and Western passenger assns. since 1932; also chmn. Western Mil. Bur., the Folder Distributing Agency, Rail Travel Promotion Agency, Railroad Clearing House for Unclaimed Baggage, Rail Travel Credit Agency; Interterritorial Military Com. Mem. Newcomen Soc., Army Transportation Assn. Republican. Episcopalian. Clubs: Rotary, Chicago Traffic, Union League, Evanston Golf. Home: Morrison Hotel. Office: 516 W. Jackson Blvd., Chicago, Ill. Died June 28, 1948.

SIEGEL, Isaac, ex-congressman; b. New York, N.Y., 1880; s. Kive and Leah Siegel; LL.B., New York U. Law Sch., 1901; m. Annie Natelson, 1907; children—Seymour N. (U.S.N.), Mrs. Gertrude J. Cohen, Marc Monroe (U.S.A.). Admitted to N.Y. bar, 1902, U.S. Supreme Ct., 1916; spl. atty. gen. for prosecution of election frauds, 1909, 1910; sr. mem. Siegel & Corn, 1914-39; mem. 64th to 67th Congresses (1915-23), 20th N.Y. Dist.; chmn. Congl. Com. which investigated Japanese immigration on Pacific Coast and gen. conditions at Angel Island and Ellis Island, 1921. Chmn. overseas commn. which visited France and Italy; apptd. city magistrate by Mayor LaGuardia for term, 1939-49; apptd. justice of the Domestic Relations Court of City of New York, for term, 1940-50. Del. to Rep. Nat. Conv., 1916, 20, 36; Rep. candidate for presdl. elector, 1932, for City Council, 1937; pres. 18th Assembly Dist. Republican Club, 1920-39; member Army and Navy Com. of Jewish Welfare Bd. Pres. Institutional Synagogue. Mem. Am. Bar Assn., N.Y. County Lawyers Assn., Grand Street Boys Assn. Home: 221 W. 82d St. Address: 135 E. 22d St., New York 10, N.Y. Died June 29, 1947.

SIEMS, Allan Gleason (sīms), gen. contracting; b. St. Paul, Minn., July 29, 1888; s. Peter and Josephine Almira (Gleason) S.; grad. Harstrom Prep. Sch., Norwalk, Conn., 1908; law student, Yale U., 1908-10; unmarried. Construction work, N. P. Ry. Co., 1910-11; incorporator, and officer Siems-Carey Co. and Siems-Carey Co., Ltd., constrn. work on Grand Trunk Pacific Ry. and Canadian Northern Ry. in British Columbia, 1911-14; an organizer E. A. Wickham Co., building aviation and balloon fields for U. S. Govt., 1917-18; incorporator, and chmn. bd. Siems-Stembel Co., ry. car repair and constrn., 1919-25; officer Siems, Helmers & Schaffner Co., Inc., gen. contractors, 1926; with brother acquired and reorganized Sims, Inc., 1926, and Trussbilt, Inc., 1927; now chmn. bd. Siems Bros., Inc., Siems Bros.-Helmers, Inc., Siems-Helmers, Inc., Siems-Spokane Co. (with Johnson, Drake & Piper, Inc. and Puget Sound Bridge & Dredging Co. now engaged in constructing the Alaska Naval Air Bases at Sitka, Kodiak and Unalaska), Pensacola Bridge Corp., Midway Agency, Inc. (gen. ins.). Trustee and first v.p. St. Paul Inst.; mem. bd. govs. Charles T. Miller Hosp., St. Paul. Life mem. Izaak Walton League; mem. Minn. Acad. Science, St. Paul Zoöl. Soc. (dir.). Clubs: Minnesota, University, Somerset (St. Paul); Surf, Bath, Indian Creek (Miami Beach, Fla.); St. Croix Falls (Wis.) Golf; Cat Key of Cat Cay (B.W.I.). Home: Miami Beach, Fla. Office: 2575 Como Av. W., St. Paul, Minn. Died May 2, 1943.

SIGERFOOS, Charles Peter (sī'gẽr-fōōs), zoölogist; b. nr. Arcanum, O., May 4, 1865; s. George W. and Nancy (Shanck) S.; B.S., Ohio State U., 1889; Ph.D., Johns Hopkins, 1897; unmarried. Asst. in Ohio State U., 1889-91; instr. U. of Va., 1891-92, Johns Hopkins, 1895-97; asst. prof. animal biology, 1897-1900, prof. zoölogy, 1900-30, U. of Minn., now emeritus; was instr. embryology, Cold Spring Lab., summers, 1897-1902. Fellow A.A.A.S.; mem. Am. Soc. Naturalists, Am. Soc. Zoölogists, Phi Beta Kappa, Sigma Xi, Beta Theta Pi. Republican. Conglist. Clubs: Campus, Gown-in-Town. Address: Arcanum, Ohio. Died Nov. 26, 1944.

SILBERMAN, Alfred M., business exec.; b. New York City, 1890. Pres. and dir. Consolidated Cigar Corp. Home: 1161 Prospect Av., West Hartford, Conn. Office: 444 Madison Av., New York 22, N.Y. Died Dec. 21, 1948.

SILBERSTEIN, Ludwik (sĭl'bẽr-stīn), scientist; b. Warsaw, Poland, May 17, 1872; s. Samuel and Emily (Steinkalk) S.; grad. Gymnasium, Cracow, 1890; studied at Cracow, Heidelberg and Berlin U., Ph.D. in math. physics, Berlin, 1894; m. Rose Eisenman, June 29, 1905; children—George Paul, Hedwiga Renata, Hannah Emily. Asst. in physics, Lemberg, 1895-97; lecturer in math. physics, U. of Bologna, Italy, 1899-1904, U. of Rome since 1904; math. physicist at research lab., Eastman Kodak Co., 1920-29; cons. math. physicist since 1930. Lecturer on relativity and gravitation, Cornell, 1920, Toronto U. and Chicago U., 1921. Naturalized U.S. citizen since 1935. Mem. Am. Astron. Soc. Author: Vectorial Mechanics, 1913, 26; The Theory of Relativity, 1914, 24; Simplified Method of Tracing Rays Through Lenses, etc., 1918; Projective Vector Algebra, 1919; Elements of Electromagnetic Theory of Light, 1918; Elements of Vector Algebra, 1919; Theory of General Relativity and Gravitation, 1922; The Size of the Universe, 1930; Causality, 1933; also numerous papers on physics. Home: 129 Seneca Parkway, Rochester, N.Y. Died Jan. 17, 1948.

SILVA, William Posey, landscape painter; b. Savannah, Ga., Oct. 23, 1859; s. James Sylvester and Margaret Susan (Askew) S.; grad. Chatham Acad., Savannah, 1875; m. Caroline Walker Beecher, Jan. 1, 1885 (died Feb. 2, 1940); 1 son, Abbott Beecher; m. 2d, Mrs. Ruth Hanford Matthews Lewis, Dec. 1, 1940. In chinaware business with father, 1876-87, and as Silva & Abbott, Chattanooga, Tenn., until 1906; studied art, Julian Acad., Paris, under Laurens and Henri Royer, 1907-09, landscape under Chauncy Ryder, Etaples, France. Returned to Chattanooga, 1909; in Washington, D.C., 1910-13, Carmel-by-the-Sea, Calif., since 1913. Exhibited at the Salon des Artistes Français, Paris, 1908, 22, 23, 26, Autumn Salon, 1908; Corcoran Gallery, Nat. Acad. Design, Pa. Acad. Fine Arts, Art Inst. (Chicago), Buffalo Fine Arts Acad. Albright Gallery, Peabody Inst. (Baltimore), Southern States Art League and elsewhere in U.S. Held one-man shows, Paris, 1909, 22, 26, London, 1922, in cities of U.S., 1911-37 (one show was circulated by Am. Fedn. of Arts, 1926-27-28). Awarded silver medal Appalachian Expn., Knoxville, Tenn., 1910; highest award, Miss. and Gulf Coast Expn., 1911; silver medal Panama-Calif. Expn., San Diego, 1915; gold medal, Miss. Art Assn., 1916; silver medal, Panama-Calif. Internat. Expn., 1916; landscape prize, California State Fair, 1920; hon. mention, Paris Salon, 1922; Southern States Art League prize, Atlanta, 1925; popular prize, New Orleans Art Assn., 1926; grand prize, Ga.-Ala. Exhibit, 1926, purchased by French Govt., Paris, 1926; popular prize, Southern States Art League, 1927; $2,000 Davis prize, San Antonio Art League, 1928; popular prize, State-Wide Exhbn., Santa Cruz, Calif., 1929; first prize, Springville (Utah) Nat. Exhbn., 1929; honorable mention, Davis National, San Antonio, 1929; first prize, Miss. State Fair, Jackson, 1929; public approval prize, Southern States Art League, 1930; Haverty landscape prize from same, 1931; Reaugh Art Club prize, 1932; 1st prize (oil), Art Assn. of New Orleans, 1932; gold ribbon, Miss. Art Assn., 1932; 2d marine prize, Calif. State Fair, 1935; Gov. Olson bronze medal, Golden Gate Internat. Expn., 1939, silver ribbon, 1940; popular purchase prize Granger Exhibit of Contemporary Am. Artists (Dodge City, Ia.), 1940. Represented in permanent collections Gibbs Art Gallery, Charleston, S.C.; Milwaukee Art Inst.; Museums of Fine Arts, Montgomery, Ala., and Houston, Tex.; Luxembourg Gallery, Paris, France; Delgado Museum, New Orleans; Columbia (S.C.) Coll.; Emporia (Kan.) State Teachers Coll.; Vanderbilt U., Nashville Art Association, Centennial Club (Nashville); De Cordoba Collection, Lincoln, Massachusetts; Keeler Collection, Los Angeles; Blanden Memorial Museum, Ft. Dodge, Ia.; U. of Va. Alumni Hall; public libraries at Birmingham, Ala., Carmel, Calif., Chattanooga, Tenn., Fort Worth, Tex., Marquette, Mich., Palo Alto, Calif., Edgefield, S.C.; high schools at Austin, Tex., Fort Worth, Tex., King City, Calif., Monterey, Calif., Salinas, Calif.,

Salt Lake City and Springville, Utah, Savannah, Ga.; First Presbyterian Church, Monterey, California; also many art associations, art clubs, etc.; photographs of paintings in Congressional Library, Washington, D.C.; color slides of 2 paintings in Met. Museum (N.Y.), and in Congressional Library, 1942. Mem. Society Washington Artists, Southern States Art League (1st v.p. 1927), Miss. Art Assn., Am. Art Assn. (Paris), New Orleans Art Assn., Am. Artists' Professional League, Calif. Art Club, Chattanooga Art Assn. (hon.), Carmel Art Assn. Mem. U.S. Revolver Assn. and of Carmel Pistol Club; winner Honor Medal (Class G) U.S.R.A., 1934; mem. team of Carmel Pistol Club which won 1st prize, Sr. League, U.S.R.A. (Class B), 1935. Address: Box 1956, Carmel, Calif. Died Feb. 10, 1948; buried Laurel Grove Cemetery, Savannah, Ga.

SILVERS, Earl Reed, author; b. Jersey City, N.J., Feb. 22, 1891; s. Earl Brittin and Evelyn (Reed) S.; A.B., Rutgers College, 1913, hon. A.M., 1923; Rutgers University Award, 1936; Litt.D., 1942; m. Edythe I. Terrill, Dec. 14, 1916; children—Earl Reed, Edith Evelyn, Terrill (dec.). Alumni sec., 1913-16, asst. to pres., 1916-25, dir. of public information, 1925-33, dir. of alumni, and public relations, 1933-44; associate professor English, 1929-44; Rutgers Univ. Editor Rutgers Alumni Quarterly, 1914-21, Rutgers Alumni Monthly, 1921-29, and since 1938, Univ. Extension Record, 1926-33, Alumni Council Bulletin, 1933-36; exec. sec. Rutgers U. Fund Council, 1935-37; on leave of absence, 1937-38; dir. Rutgers U. Press, 1938-44; dean of men since 1944. Mem. Am. Coll. Publicity Assn. (pres. 1929-30), Phi Beta Kappa, Delta Phi, Theta Nu Epsilon, Tau Kappa Alpha. Presbyterian. Clubs: Rutgers (New Brunswick); Delta Phi (New York); Colonia (N.J.) Country. Author: Dick Arnold of Raritan College, 1920; Dick Arnold Plays the Game, 1921; Dick Arnold of the Varsity, 1921; Ned Beals, Freshman, 1922; At Hillsdale High, 1922; Ned Beals Works His Way, 1923; Jackson of Hillsdale High, 1923; The Hillsdale High Champions, 1924; Barry, the Undaunted, 1924; Barry and Budd, 1925; The Spirit of Menlo, 1926; The Menlo Mystery, 1926; Carol of Highland Camp, 1927; Team First, 1929; The Redheaded Halfback, 1929; Carol of Cranford High, 1930; The Scarlet of Avalon, 1930; The Glory of Glenwood, 1931; Code of Honor, 1932; The Editor Accepts—How to Write Short Stories That Magazines Buy, 1943; If This Be Forgetting, 1944; Son of Tomorrow. 1947. Home: New Brunswick, N.J. Died Mar. 26, 1948.

SIMMONS, Elizabeth Margret, writer, speaker; b. Hardeman, Mo., Jan. 18, 1891; d. Thomas Jefferson and Alice Lavinia (Smith) Davis; student Mo. Valley Coll., 1903-08; m. George Bartlett Simmons, Mar. 29, 1909; children—Valerie Ruth (Mrs. Percy Franklin Vesser), Vivien Virginia (Mrs. Hartzell I. Bozarth), Genevieve Elizabeth (Mrs. Charles Emerson Clark), Alice Temple, Georgena Gay. Writer since 1920; has been contbr. to Leghorn World, editor Western Poultry Jour., editorial writer and copy editor Plymouth Rock Monthly; editorial writer Rhode Island Red Jour. and Wyandotte Herald; editor poultry information columns Corn Belt Farm Dailies (which include Chicago Daily Drovers Journal, St. Louis Daily Livestock Reporter, Kansas City Daily Drovers Telegram, Omaha Daily Journal-Stockman) since 1922. Lecturer Farm Inst., Mo. State Bd. of Agr.; speaker "Grass Roots" Rep. Conv., Springfield, Ill., June 1935. Received award from Mo. Writers Guild for most outstanding writing on any Mo. author, 1935. Hon. mem. Tex. Women's Press Assn. Presbyterian. Contbr. feature articles to Saturday Evening Post, Country Gentleman, Cosmopolitan, Pictorial Review, Good Housekeeping, Farm Journal, Hearst Sunday Papers. Speaker annual Lincoln dinner, New York, 1936. Home: Marshall, Mo. Office: 836 Exchange Av., Chicago 9, Ill. Died June 11, 1947; buried Historical Cemetery, Arrow Rock, Mo.

SIMMONS, Thomas Jackson, coll. pres.; b. Wake Forest, N.C., Apr. 18, 1864; s. William Gaston and Mary Elizabeth (Foote) S.; A.M., Wake Forest Coll., 1883; LL.D., 1905; m. Lessie Muse Southgate, Nov. 11, 1891 (died May 19, 1914). Teacher pub. schs., Fayetteville, N.C., 1 yr. Durham, 6 yrs.; prin. high sch., Athens, Ga., 1890-91; supt. pub. schs., Dawson, Ga., 1891-93; pres. Union Female Coll., Eufaula, Ala., 1893-98; pres. Shorter Coll., Rome, Ga., 1898-1910, pres. and trustee Brenau Coll., 1910-28, pres. emeritus, trustee and prof. philosophy since 1928. Mem. Phi Beta Kappa. Democrat. Baptist. World traveler, art connoisseur and collector; founder Simmons Art Museum of Wake Forest Coll. Home: 304 N. Boulevard, Gainesville, Ga. Died Mar. 17, 1942.

SIMMONS, Warren Seabury, surgeon; b. Providence, R.I., Feb. 27, 1867; s.* Warren Seabury and Mary Jane S.; Ph.B., Brown U., 1889; M.D., Coll. Physicians and Surgeons, New York, 1892; m. Angela Field, Oct. 19, 1899; m. 2d, Carolyn Osborne, Oct. 10, 1904; m. 3d, Leila Welker, Aug. 14, 1928. Physician and surgeon, Brooklyn, N.Y., since 1892; intern and asst. surgeon St. Johns Hosp., Brooklyn, 1892-1903, attending surgeon, 1903-11; attending surgeon Bushwick Hosp., Brooklyn, 1914-18, Swedish Hosp., Brooklyn, since 1909; pres. Warsimco Realties, Inc. Fellow Am. Coll. Surgeons, Psi Upsilon. Republican. Mason. Address: 2653 E. 26th St., Brooklyn, N.Y.* Died May 22, 1944.

SIMMONS, Will (William Francis Bernard), artist; b. Elchè, Spain, June 4, 1884; s. Edward (Emerson) and Vesta (Shallenberger) S.; preparatory education, Cheam School, England, and St. Paul's Sch., Concord, N.H.; student Harvard, 1901-02; art edn., Julian Academy, Paris, 1904-07; married Teresa (Ludovica) Cerutti, May 26, 1910 (deceased); married 2d, Gertrude Steele, 1947. Painter, etcher, sculptor and writer of wild life, now portraiture. Works on permanent exhibition at Library of Congress, Corcoran Gallery, U.S. Nat. Collection (Washington, D.C.), New York Pub. Library, Bibliotheque Nationale, Paris, etc. Censorship service of U.S., New York, 1917-19. Mem. Soc. Am. Etchers (sec. 1922-24), Chicago Soc. Etchers, Print Makers of Calif., Prairie Print Makers (hon.). Awarded "best print" prize, Brooklyn Museum, 1928. Democrat. Contbr. to Mentor, Christian Science Monitor, Arts and Decoration, Am. Forests and Forest Life, etc. Home: 4706 Roland Av., Baltimore, Md. Deceased.

SIMMS, P(aris) Marion, clergyman, lecturer; b. Lawrenceburg, Tenn., May 2, 1869; s. Andrew Francis and Martha Ann (Bryan) S.; A.B., Cumberland Univ., 1899, B.D., same, 1902, Ph.D., 1907; m. Edna Earl Johnson, June 8, 1893; children—Burney Gilmore, P. Marion. Ordained ministry Cumberland Presbyn. Ch., 1893 (transferred to Presbyterian Ch., U.S.A., at time of union, 1907); registrar Cumberland Univ., 1902-06, also acting pres.; pastor 1st Cumberland Presbyn. Church, St. Joseph, Mo., 1906-07, 1st Presbyn. Church, Vinton, Ia., 1907-16; with Ia. Congl. Hosp., 1916-17; army Y.M.C.A. work, World War I; field sec. Am. Tract Soc. in Iowa, 1918-20; field agent for Near East Relief in Iowa, 1920-24. Commr. to Gen. Assembly Cumberland Presbyn. Ch. 4 yrs. in succession, Chatauqua lecturer, 1909-26. The only man who ever went on the chautauqua platform with a lecture, "The Calf Path," devoted wholly to a plea for the union of Protestantism. Owns probably the largest private collection of versions of the Bible, or its parts, in English in America, now loaned to the McCormick Theol. Sem., Chicago, Ill. Pastor Presbyterian chs. in Neb., 1924-39; pastor in Kansas, 1939-42. Dir. finance, Neb. Christian Endeavor Union, 1927-32; retired, Sept. 1943. Mem. Pi Kappa Alpha. Mason. Author: What Must the Church Do to Be Saved?, 1913; The Bible from the Beginning, 1929; The Bible in America—Versions That Have Played Their Part in the Making of the Republic, 1936. Home: Big Spring, Tex. Died 1946.

SIMMS, Ruth Hanna (Mrs. Albert G. Simms); b. Cleveland, O., Mar. 27, 1880; d. late Senator Marcus A. and Charlotte A. (Rhodes) Hanna; ed. pvt. schs., Dobbs Ferry, N.Y. and Farmington, Conn.; m. Medill McCormick, June 10, 1903 (died Feb. 25, 1925) m. 2d, Albert G. Simms, Mar. 9, 1932. Interested in political, industrial and civic problems; active mem. Women's Trade Union League, Business and Professional Women's Clubs, Rep. Women's Orgn.; joined Prog. Party and took active part at hdqrs. in nat. campaign, 1912; represented Ill. Consumers' League, as a mem. of its state bd., before Ill. legislature, 1915, working for a child labor bill; mem. Am. Assn. for Labor Legislation, Women's Clubs for Civic Improvement in Chicago. Mem. Nat. Am. Livestock Assn., Holstein-Friesian Assn.; active in developing pure-bred Holsteins. Rep. nat. committeewoman from Ill., 1924-28; mem. 71st Congress (1929-31), Ill. at-large; Rep. nominee for U.S. Senate, 1930. Pres. Rockford (Ill.) Consolidated Newspapers. Trustee Fountain Valley Sch. (boys'), Colorado Springs, Colo. Mgr. Trinclura Ranch (cattle and sheep) in Colo. Home: Los Poblanos Ranch, Albuquerque, N. Mex. Died Dec. 31, 1944.

SIMON, Edward Paul, architect and engineer; born in Philadelphia, Pennsylvania, June 1, 1878; son of Fred Paul and Mary Ann (Miles) S.; grad. Central High School, Philadelphia, 1896, Drexel Inst., 1900; m. Edith M. Darby, Nov. 5, 1904; children—Marion Darby, Elizabeth Esten. Draftsman, Dull & Coates, architects and engrs., 1900-03; mem. firm Caldwell & Simon, 1903-06, Edward P. Simon, 1907-08, Simon & Bassett, 1908-19; pres. and treas. Simon & Simon, 1919-26, Office of Edward P. Simon since 1926. Principal works include: Manufacturers Club, Fidelity-Philadelphia Trust Bldg., Strawbridge & Clothier Store, Drexel Inst. Tech., Van Rensselaer Dormitory for Women, Curtis Hall of Engring. (all Phila.); Meade Memorial, Washington, D.C.; First Camden (N.J.) Nat. Bank & Trust Co. Bldg.; office bldg. of Baldwin Locomotive Works, Eddystone, Pa. Trustee Drexel Inst. (chmn. com. on bldgs. and grounds). Mem. Am. Inst. Architects, Archtl. League of N.Y., Am. Soc. Professional Engrs., Pa. and N.J. Soc. of Architects. Republican. Presbyterian. Mason. Clubs: T Square, Midday. Home: 1530 Locust St. Office: Fidelity-Philadelphia Trust Bldg., Philadelphia, Pa. Died May 19, 1949.

SIMONDS, William Edward, coll. prof.; b. Peabody, Mass., Sept. 10, 1860; s. Edward and Mary A. (Chase) S.; A.B., Brown U., 1883, Litt.D., 1911; univs. Berlin and Strassburg, 1885-88, Ph. D., Univ. of Strassburg, 1888; L.H.D., Knox, 1919; m. Katherine Courtright, June 22, 1898; children—Marjorie (Mrs. William J. Andrews), Katherine (Mrs. Royal H. Wensberg), Eleanor. Teacher high sch., 1883-85; instr. German, Cornell, 1888-89; prof. English lit., 1889-1930, and dean, 1912-30, Knox Coll. Mem. Modern Lang. Assn. America. Author: Sir Thomas Wyatt and His Poems, 1889; Introduction to the Study of English Fiction, 1894; A Student's History of English Literature, 1902; A Student's History of American Literature, 1909. Editor: DeQuincey's Revolt of the Tartars, 1898; Scott's Ivanhoe, 1901; Gaskell's Cranford, 1906; Scott's Quentin Durward, 1909; Washington's Farewell Address and Webster's Bunker Hill Oration, 1911. Home: 205 Elmwood Av., Ithaca, N.Y. Died June 24, 1947.

SIMONE, G. F. Edgardo, sculptor; b. Brindisi, Italy, June 20, 1890; s. Salvatore and Maria Antonia (Vitali) S.; student Univ. and Inst. of Fine Arts, Rome, Italy, 1911-13, Inst. of Classics in Leece, 1907; m. Radie Brilain, 1941; children—Vera, Silvan. Came to U.S., 1927, naturalized, 1933. Executed 33 monuments in 26 cities of world since 1919; war monuments in Ferrara, Monopoli, Brindisi, Sarno, Verona, Pianura, Avezzano, Majori, St. Bartolemeo in Bosco, Cerreto, Sannita, Marrara, St. Marzano sul Sarno Minore, St. Pietro a Majella, Viggiano, St. Vito dei Normanni, Tampa, Fla.; civic monuments: Naples, The Sacred Heart of Jesus, Dr. Antonio Coppola; in Ravenna, Engr. Alfonso Barbe; Monopoli, Dr. Giovanni Barnaba; Sarno, St. Francis of Assisi; Nocera, Superiore, St. Francis of Assisi; Benevento, Consul Dr. Clino Ricci; Verona, statue of Madonna in cathedral. Funeral monuments: Monumental Mausoleum to Heroes of the War in Brindisi; sculpturing Monumental mausoleum of the Heroes of the War in Bari; mausoleum of the Count Balsamo family in Brindisi; mausoleum of the Cattino family, Torino, of the Cascio family, Naples; monumental mausoleum in Caracas, Venezuela, Sao Paulo, Brazil, Fena (for the Duchessa Massari). Works exhibited: Anderson Galleries of New York; Boston; Nat. Gallery, Washington, D.C.; Pittsburgh; Detroit; Chicago (Internat. House, Univ. of Chicago, Italian Pavilion and Horticultural Exhbn. World's Fair); San Diego (Calif.) Mus. Served as volunteer with Italian Army, World War I. Decorated 3 times by King Victor Emmanuel III, and by S.M. Queen Margherita. Awarded Concourse Nationale 12 times; 3d prize internat. competition for monument to Czar Alexander II, 1912; 2d prize erection of monument to Independence of Brazil at Sao Paulo, 1920; 1st prize erection war memorial in Ferrara, 1922, 1st prize in internat. competition for war memorial, Tampa, Fla., 1927. Recipient Cross of War, Italy, 3 times. Hon. prof. of sculpture, Royal Acad. of Arts, Naples and Leece. Cavaliere and Commendatore of the Crown of Italy. Prominent persons sculptured include Justice Frank Murphy, Thomas Edison, ex-pres. Taft, Justice Oliver Wendell Holmes, Ethel Barrymore Colt. Clubs: California Arts, Painters and Sculptors, Sanity in Art, Allied Art Council. Lecturer. Engaged in research on the life and art of Giorgione. Home: 1945 N. Curson, Hollywood 46, Calif. Died Dec. 19, 1948; buried in Forest Lawn Memorial Park, Glendale, Calif.

SIMONS, Kenneth W., newspaper editor; b. Lima, O., Feb. 15, 1898; s. Charles A. and Myrtle M. (Wetherill) S.; student Wittenberg Coll., Springfield, O., 1923; m. Marie E. Malloy, Nov. 19, 1926; children—Kenneth W., Marie Joanne, Robert James, Paul Bernard. N.D. corr. Asso. Press, 1925-30; editor Bismarck (N.D.) Tribune since 1930, sec. Bismarck Tribune Co. since 1936, vice pres. since 1941. Awarded Pulitzer prize for pub. service, 1937. Mem. N.D. Water Conservation Commn. since 1937 (vice chmn. since 1941). Mem. Am. Legion (comdr. Bismarck post, 1935). Roman Catholic. K.C. Elk. Home: 811 Mandan St. Office: Bismarck Tribune, Bismarck, N.D. Died April 20, 1948.

SIMONS, May Wood, economist, writer; b. Baraboo, Wis.; d. Philip Aurey and Anna (Crook) Wood; Ph.B., with honors, U. of Chicago, 1905; A.M., Northwestern U., 1909 (Harris prize in economics), Ph.D., 1930; studied in France and Belgium; m. Algie M. Simons, 1897; children—Lawrence Wood, Miriam Eleanor. Teacher in high school 10 yrs.; instr. in economics, Ruskin Coll., 1906, 07; asso. editor Chicago Daily Socialist, 1907-10; lecturer for Intercollegiate Socialist Soc., Nat. Lyceum Bur. of Socialist Party. Del. Nat. Conv. Socialist Party, 1908, 10; del. Internat. Socialist Congress, Copenhagen, Denmark, 1910; mem. Nat. Com. Socialist Party; mem. Nat. Socialist Woman's Com.; chmn. Nat. Socialist Edn. Com. Was teacher, Riverside High Sch., Milwaukee; now instr. Dept. of Economics, Northwestern U. Chmn. Americanization com. Milwaukee County Council of Defense; chmn. citizenship training, Ill. League of Women Voters, 1922-30. Mem. Am. Polit. Science Assn., Am. Assn. Univ. Profs., Am. Assn. Univ. Women, Royal Economical Soc., Am. Economics Assn., Pi Beta Phi and Alpha Pi Zeta; fellow A.A.A.S. Episcopalian. Club: Evanston Woman's. Author: Woman and the Social Problem, 1899; Wisconsin Citizens' Handbook, 1920; Outline of Civics. Everyday Problems in Economics, 1945. Contbr. to tech. jours. Asso. editor Coming Nation. Home: New Martinsville, W.Va. Died Dec. 3, 1948.

SIMPICH, Frederick (sĭm'pĭch), editor; b. Urbana, Ill., Nov. 21, 1878; s. Charles Frederick and Sarah Elizabeth (Brash) S.; m. Margaret Elliot Edwards, Aug. 7, 1909; children— Frederick Edwards, George Cary, William Morris. Newspaper writer in Shanghai, China, Manila, San Francisco, and other cities until 1909; contbr. to mags. including Century, Sat. Eve. Post, Nation's Business, Adventure, Argosy, etc. Apptd. to U.S. Foreign Service, 1909, and served in Germany, Turkey and Mexico; received thanks of British, German and Chinese govts. for services in behalf of their nationals during the Carranza revolution; duty with Div. of Mil. Intelligence, U.S. Army, 1918, Am. Commn. to Germany, 1919; assigned consul gen. at Guatemala, 1920; assigned as asst. foreign trade adviser, Dept. of State, 1920; assigned to Div. of Western European Affairs, April

1921; retired, Apr. 1, 1923, to resume literary work; investigated econ. and trade conditions in Porto Rico, Panama and Mexico, 1924-25, contributing articles to various Am. mags. Visited southwest and Mexico and wrote articles for The Century and The Independent, 1927; covered the Mississippi Flood for Nat. Geog. Mag., Apr.-June 1927, also 1937; now asst. editor same magazine. Leader of Aerial Expdn. of Nat. Geog. Society, 1930, surveying proposed air mail lines over West Indies, Caribbean Sea and around east coast of S.A.; made special study of gold and silver problems for Nat. Geog. Mag., 1933; visited Far East and reported on situation there, 1940. Wrote "As London Toils and Spins," 1936, "Speaking of Kansas," 1937. Visited Egypt, Palestine and Irak and wrote "Change Comes to Bible Lands," 1938; also led Nat. Geog. Society's Rio Grande Expdn., 1938. Studied economic and social changes in Hong Kong, Singapore and Manila in 1939. Writer of various mil. articles since 1940; accompanied R.C.A.F. on bomber patrols, 1942; made survey of Mo. river watershed, 1945, as guest of U.S. Army Engrs., and wrote, Taming the Outlaw Missouri River; author of These Missourians, Arkansas Rolls Up Its Sleeves, More Water for California, 1946. Clubs: Nat. Press, Cosmos, Overseas, Writers, Chevy Chase. Home: 3309 Macomb St. Address: National Geographic Mag., Washington, D.C. Died Jan. 25, 1950.

SIMPSON, Frank Edward, dermatologist; b. Saco, Me., Sept. 7, 1869; s. Charles P. and Adelaide (Reade) S.; A.B., Bowdoin, 1890; M.D., Northwestern U. Med. Sch., 1896; post-grad. work, Paris, Berlin and Vienna; m. Beulah Lichty, Nov. 22, 1898 (dec.); m. 2d, Beryl Lucile Kanagy, 1922; children—Frank Edward, Hugh Mills, William Langdon. Intern Cook County Hosp.; practiced at Chicago since 1897; prof. skin and venereal diseases, Chicago Policlinic, 1912-22; clin. prof. dermatology, Northwestern U. Med. Sch., and attending dermatologist Cook County, Wesley and Policlinic hosps. Former pres. Am. Radium Soc.; mem. A.M.A., Chicago Med. Soc., Chicago Dermatol. Soc., Phi Beta Kappa, Psi Upsilon, Nu Sigma Nu. Republican. Methodist. Club: University. Author: Radium Therapy, 1922; Radium in Cancer and Other Diseases, 1926. Contbr. to Oxford Surgery, Lahrbuch der Strahlentherapie, and spl. articles on radium therapy and dermatology to foreign and Am. scientific books and jours. Home: 445 Barry Av., Chicago 14. Office: 50 E. Madison St., Chicago, Ill. Died Dec. 13, 1948; buried Graceland Cemetery, Chicago.

SIMPSON, James Clarke, merchant; b. Punxsutawney, Pa., Apr. 13, 1864; s. William Evan and Sarah Ann (Means) S.; ed. common schs., acad. and business coll.; m. Harriette H. Post, Feb. 17, 1897; children—Sidney Post, Cornelia Ann (Mrs. Wallace Thompson), William Evan, Harriet (Mrs. Willson Bovard), Mary Coe (Mrs. Allen Lind), Helen Jean (Mrs. James B. Pinkerton). School teacher; steamboated on Mississippi River for five seasons; began in lumber business, Rock Island, Ill., 1889; settled at Galesburg, 1894; chmn. bd. Simpson Powelson Lumber Co.; pres. J. C. Simpson Lumber Co. Chmn. finance com. Knox Coll., 6 yrs.; pres. Galesburg Hosp, 3 terms. Del. to Rep. county and state convs.; alternate del. Rep. Nat. Conv., 1912; mem. exec. com. Liberty Loan drives. Protestant. Clubs: Galesburg, Soangetaha. Home: 516 N. Prairie St., Galesburg, Ill. Died June 27, 1948.

SIMPSON, John Nathan, physician; b. Mason, W.Va., Mar. 19, 1869; s. George Perry and Phoebe (Kennedy) S.; grad. Peabody Coll. for Teachers, Nashville, Tenn., 1891; A.B., U. of Nashville, 1893; M.D., Johns Hopkins, 1902; studied univs. of Paris, Vienna and Berlin, 1905; m. Grace Emily Donley, Dec. 20, 1906 (died, August, 1929); children—John Nathan, Patricia Donley. Organized, 1902, School of Medicine, West Virginia University, and dean until 1935, also professor physiology, 1902-20, professor medicine since 1920, dean emeritus since 1935. Director Hygiene Laboratory, Dept. of Health, W.Va., 1913-17; surgeon Cadet Corps, W.Va. U., 1902-27; major Med. R.C., U.S. Army. Fellow Am. Acad. Medicine, Am. Coll. Physicians (gov. for W.Va.); mem. W.Va. State Med. Assn. (pres. 1923), A.M.A., A.A.A.S., Phi Beta Pi, Theta Nu Epsilon. Democrat. Presbyterian. Home: Morgantown, W.Va. Died Nov. 23, 1947.

SIMPSON, Joseph Warren, chmn. bd. Milwaukee-Western Fuel Co.; b. E. Dubuque, Ill., Jan. 15, 1872; s. William Henry and Sarah Margaret (Cheetham) S.; ed. high sch. and Spencerian Business Coll., Milwaukee, Wis.; m. Charlotte Bartlett Flanders, Feb. 15, 1900; children—Joseph Warren, Mary Flanders. With Northwestern Fuel Co., Milwaukee, 1890-99; propr. Jos. W. Simpson Coal Co., 1899-1909 (sold to Milwaukee-Western Fuel Co.); salesman, Milwaukee-Western Fuel Co., 1909-12, asst. to pres., 1912-19, v.p. in charge sales, 1919-23, became pres. 1923, now chmn. bd.; trustee Northwestern Mutual Life Ins. Co. Presbyterian. Clubs: Milwaukee, Milwaukee Country. Home: 4145 N. Downer Av. Office: 2150 N. Prospect Av., Milwaukee, Wis. Deceased.

SIMPSON, Sidney Post, lawyer; b. Galesburg, Ill., Aug. 4, 1898; s. James Clarke and Harriette Helene (Post) S.; A.B., Knox Coll., 1917; LL.B., Harvard, 1922. Practiced law in Washington, D.C., 1922-25, New York City, 1925-31, and since 1944; partner Hines, Rearick, Dorr, Travis & Marshall, 1930-31; consultant on cost of crime National Commission on Law Observance and Enforcement, 1929-31; professor law, Harvard University, 1931-46 (on leave since 1940); professor School of Law, New York University, since 1946. Special asst. to asst. secretary of war, 1940; principal business specialist Office of Price Adminstr., 1941; dir. Survey Legal Edn., State Bar Calif., 1948-49; gen. counsel Melpar, Inc. (electronics), since 1947. Served as private, Ordnance Department, later 2d lt., F.A., World War I; mem. O.R.C. since 1919, becoming major, F.A., 1936; active duty as major and lt. col., F.A., World War II. Fellow Am. Acad. Arts and Sciences; mem. Am. Bar Assn. (chmn. com. on continuing edn. of bar, 1946-47), Phi Beta Kappa. Republican. Club: Harvard (N.Y.). Author: Report on the Cost of Crime (with G. H. Dorr), 1931; Cases on Equity (with Z. Chafee, Jr.), 1934, N.Y. edit. (with Z. Chafee, Jr. and J. P. Maloney), 1939; Cases on Judicial Remedies (with A. W. Scott), 1938; Law and Society (with Julius Stone), 1948; articles in legal periodicals. Mem. editorial bd. Modern Law Review, London, England. Address: 26 W. 9 St., New York 11. Died Oct. 6, 1949.

SIMPSON, Virgil Earl, physician; b. Jefferson County, Ky., May 11, 1875; s. Grandison Scott and Jennie (James) S.; student Danville Normal Sch., 1896-98; A.B. and M.D., U. of Louisville; married. Teacher high sch., 1895-97; instr. pharmacology and therapeutics, U. of Louisville Med. Sch., 1903-05, asso. prof., 1906-08, prof., 1908-24, prof. clin. medicine since 1920; mem. staff Louisville City Hosp., Baptist Hosp., St. Joseph's Infirmary, Norton Memorial Infirmary; consultant Kosair Crippled Children's Hospital. Member revision committee of United States Pharmacopeia, XI-XII; member house of delegates American Medical Association, 1930-43. Capt. Med. Corps, Ky. Nat. Guard, 1911-17; maj. Med. Corps, U.S. Army, 1918-19; comdg. officer Camp Hosp. No. 8, Montigny le Roi, France, 1918-19. Fellow Am. Coll. Physicians; mem. Am. Heart Assn., Am. Gastro-Enterol. Assn., Southern Med. Assn., Ky. State Med. Assn., Am. Med Assn. Fellow Am. Coll. Chest Physicians. Democrat. Scottish Rite. Mason. Club: Louisville Country. Home: Heathen Hall, Shelbyville, Ky. Office: Brown Bldg., Louisville, Ky. Died May 3, 1943.

SIMPSON, William B., business exec.; b. Ayr, Scotland, Jan. 23, 1876; s. William and Isabella (Brechin) S.; ed. pub. schs. and business coll.; m. Marie L. Cavanna, Dec. 11, 1916. Chmn. bd. A. M. Castle & Co., Chicago, Ill., since 1930. Mason. Club: Chicago Athletic Assn. Home: 209 Lake Shore Drive, Chicago. Office: 1132 West Blackhawk St., Chicago 22, Ill. Died Jan. 13, 1948.

SIMRALL, Josephine Price (sĭm'răl), coll. prof.; b. Covington, Ky., July 19, 1869; d. Charles Barrington and Isabella Downing (Price) Simrall; B.S., Wellesley, 1893; post-graduate work, U. of Cincinnati, Johns Hopkins and Columbia. Head dept. of psychology, Sweet Briar (Va.) Coll., 1916-19; dean of women and asst. prof. English, U. of Ky., 1919-21; dean of women and lecturer, U. of Cincinnati, 1921-36; retired June 1936. An organizer and ex-pres. Woman's City Club, Cincinnati; twice pres. College Club; etc. Independent. Episcopalian. Mem. Phi Sigma (Wellesley). Home: 2356 Park Av., Cincinnati 6, Ohio. Died July 3, 1949.

SIMS, Charles Abercrombie, civil engr., ry. contractor; b. Memphis, Tenn., June 5, 1866; s. Clifford Stanley and Mary Josephine (Abercrombie) S.; m. Julia Watkins, Apr. 21, 1897 (died Jan. 10, 1940). Filled various positions on Pennsylvania R.R. engring. Corps, 1882-86; asst. engr. in charge constrn. W.Va. Central R.R., 1886-87; asst. engr. in charge constrn. surveys, etc., Pa. R.R. Co., 1887-90. Was resident engr. in charge bldg. Pa. R.R. Co's stone arch bridge over Conemaugh River that stood flood of 1889 at Johnstown, Pa.; was contractor Pa. R.R. 4-track stone arch bridge over Delaware River at Trenton, N.J. Mem. Soc. of the Cincinnati, Loyal Legion. Episcopalian. Address: 10 S. 18th St., Philadelphia, Pa. Died May 15, 1942.

SIMS, Edwin W., lawyer; b. Hamilton, Ont., Can., June 4, 1870; s. Walter and Elizabeth (Knowles) S.; acad. edn., Bay City, Mich.; LL.B., U. of Mich., 1894; m. Charlotte Smith, Feb. 9, 1898; children—Mrs. Charlotte Elizabeth Krupp, Mrs. Helen V. McLaughlin, Frank S., Mrs. Susan Knowles Coffin, Edwin W., Mrs. Priscilla S. Evans. Admitted to bar, 1894; county atty., Cook County, 1900-03; special attorney Bureau of Corporations, Washington, 1903-05; solicitor Dept. of Commerce and Labor, 1905-06. Sent by President Roosevelt to investigate fur seal fisheries, Alaska, 1906; as U.S. atty., Chicago, 1906-11, tried the $29,000,000 Standard Oil Case. Mem. advisory bd. Fur Seal Service, 1909; pres. Chicago Crime Commn., 1919-22. Mem. Am., Ill. and Chicago bar assns., Mich. Soc. of Chicago. Republican. Clubs: Chicago, Union League, Law, Forty (Chicago). Home: Sims Ranch House, Au Gres, Mich.; also 112 Bellevue Pl., Chicago, Ill. Died June 16, 1948; buried in Sims Private Cemetery, Sims Ranch, Au Gres, Mich.

SINCLAIR, Earle Westwood, oil producer; b. Wheeling, W.Va., May 5, 1874; s. John and Phoebe (Simmons) S.; ed. Indiana Normal Sch., Valparaiso, Ind.; m. Blanche Stich, May 20, 1902; children—Kathleen (Mrs. L. F. Bishop, Jr.), John Wm. Began with Independence Gas Co., 1904; an organizer, 1908, and cashier State Bank of Commerce, Independence, Kan., v.p., 1908-10; v.p. Exchange Nat. Bank, Tulsa, Okla., 1910-13, pres., 1913-21; pres. Sinclair Consolidated Oil Corp. and Sinclair Refining Co. since 1921; chmn. finance com. Consol. Oil Corp., 1932-43; chmn. exec. com. Sinclair Oil Corp. since 1943. Republican. Presbyterian. Clubs: Lotos, Metropolitan, Rockefeller Center Luncheon (New York); Maidstone, Devon Yacht (Easthampton, L.I.). Home: 300 Park Av. Office: 630 5th Av., New York, N.Y. Died Sep. 22, 1944.

SINCLAIR, James Herbert, ex-congressman; b. St. Marys, Can., Oct. 9, 1871; s. Daniel and Mary Jane (Bothwell) S.; brought to U.S. at age of 6; grad. Mayville (N.D.) Normal Sch.; student summer, U. of Minn., and Sprague Corr. Sch. of Law 2 yrs.; m. Laura Retzlaff, Feb. 1, 1898 (died Aug. 11, 1915); children—James Henry, Eleanor May, Muriel Jean, Daniel Montgomery; m. 2d, Florence E. Kittel, Feb. 9, 1937. Superintendent schools, Cooperstown, N.D., 1896-98; registrar of deeds, Cooperstown, 1899-1905; engaged in farming and real estate business since 1908; pres. and treas. J. H. Sinclair Co. Mem. N.D. Ho. of Rep., 1915-19; mem. 66th to 72d Congresses (1919-33), 3d N.D. Dist., and 73d Congress (1933-35), N.D. at large; mem. Spl. Mexican Claims Commn., 1935-38. Republican. Presbyterian. Mason, Elk. Home: Kenmare, N.D. Died Sept. 5, 1943.

SINGER, Harold Ralph; b. Larned, Kan., Oct. 24, 1891; s. John H. and Jennie (Beardsley) S.; ed. pub. schs. Calif. and Ariz.; m. Ruby Nancy McGill, Nov. 2, 1910. Exec. sec. Okla. Christian Endeavor Union, Okla. City, 1921-28; mid-western sec. Internat. Soc. Christian Endeavor, 1928-31; became nat. dir. Allied Youth, 1931, now mem. exec. com.; exec. adviser Okla. Christian Endeavor Union; trustee Internat. Soc. Christian Endeavor. Presbyterian. Author: Alcohol and My Generation (with Bert Davis and Nettie Allen Thomas), 1933. Home: 1675 Earll Drive. Office: Title and Trust Bldg., Phoenix, Ariz. Died July 23, 1942.

SINGER, Israel Joshua, author; b. Bilgoraj, Poland, Nov. 30, 1893; s. Pinchos and Sheba (Silberman) S.; student Rabbinical Yeshivah Sch., Warsaw, 1906-13; m. Genie Kupferstock, May 12, 1923; 1 son, Joseph. Came to U.S., 1934; naturalized, 1939. Writer newspapers and periodicals, Kiev, Russia, 1918-22; foreign corr. Jewish Daily Forward, New York, in Warsaw; writer novels and articles for Jewish Daily Forward. Mem. I. L. Peretz Jewish Writers Union. Author: (translated in English, Swedish, Norwegian, Danish, Dutch, Polish and Hebrew); The Sinner (Yoshe Kalb), 1933; The Brothers Ashkenazi, 1936; The River Breaks Up, 1938; East of Eden, 1939; Blood Harvest, 1936; Frühling (Spring), 1938; Perl, 1923; Alstadt, 1926. Home: 4204 Atlantic Av., Sea Gate, Brooklyn, N.Y. Died Feb. 10, 1944.

SINGLETON, Asa Leon, army officer, educator; b. Taylor County, Ga., Aug. 31, 1876; s. Franklin Parnell and Mildred Leonard (Hayes) S.; grad. Reynolds (Ga.) High Sch.; student Emory U.; grad. Command and Gen. Staff Sch., 1908, Army Signal Sch., 1910, Army War Coll., 1921; m. Elizabeth Forrest Day, June 26, 1903. Enlisted as private in U.S. Army during Spanish Am. War; commd. 2d lt. of infantry, 1901, and advanced through the grades to brig. gen., 1936; served in Philippines during Spanish-Am. War; went with A.E.F., Dec. 1917, as lt. col. and chief of staff, 41st Div., later col. G.S.C. with 8th and 4th Divs.; Gen. Staff, War Dept., after World War, also mem. Army and Navy Joint Planning Com.; Office of Chief of Inf., Washington, D.C., in charge of training and personnel, 1930-35; comd. 29th Inf., 1935-36; comdt. Inf. Sch., Ft. Benning, Ga., 1936-40; retired from active service Aug. 31, 1940; supt. Manlius (N.Y.) Sch. since Oct. 1, 1940. Decorated D.S.M. (U.S.); Legion of Honor (France). Mem. Sigma Nu. Methodist. Mason. Address, Manlius, N.Y. Died June 7, 1943; buried in Arlington National Cemetery.

SINGLETON, Albert Olin, univ. prof.; b. Ellis County, Tex., July 16, 1882; s. Joe William and Lydia (Moore) S.; B.S., U. of Tex., 1905, M.D., 1910; m. Will Dean Bivens, Dec. 19, 1912; children—Albert Olin (M.D.), Edward Bivens. High sch. teacher, 1905; instr. in surgery, U. of Tex., 1911-14, adj. prof., 1914-20, asso. prof., 1920-27, prof. since 1927; chief surgeon John Sealy Hosp., Galveston, Tex. Fellow Am. Coll. Surgeons (mem. bd. govs., 1937-39; v.p. 1939-40); mem. Tex. Surg. Soc. (pres. 1930-31), Am. Assn. for Surgery of Trauma, Am. Surg. Assn. (v.p. 1944), Southern Surg. Assn. (v.p. 1928-29; pres. 1938-39), Am. Assn. Thoracic Surgery, Internat. Surg. Soc., Kappa Sigma, Phi Alpha Sigma, Alpha Omega Alpha. Democrat. Methodist. Mason (Scottish Rite). On editorial bd. of S.G. & O., also editorial bd. of surgery. Sr. surgeon, U.S.P.H.S. Reserve. Club: Galveston Country. Contbr. numerous papers to surg. meetings and med. and surg. jours. Author of: Chapter on "Diseases of the Lymphatics" for Lewis's Surgery. Home: 1602 Av. J. Office: Medical Branch, University of Texas, Galveston, Tex. Died June 12, 1947.

SINNOTT, Arthur J. (sĭn'nŭt), newspaper man; b. Newark, N.J., Apr. 4, 1886; s. John F. and Ellen T. (Scott) S.; ed. Cathedral School, Newark, Newark Tech. Sch.; New York U. Law Sch., 1910; m. Anne Dervin, Jan. 18, 1913. Reporter, Newark News, 1905-09, city editor, 1910-12; rep. same in Europe, 1918, Washington corr., 1912-25; became mng. editor Newark News, Nov. 1, 1925, editor in chief Jan. 1, 1933. Clubs: Gridiron, Nat. Press, Overseas Writers, Baltusrol Golf (Short Hills); Essex (Newark). Office: care Newark News, 215 Market St., Newark, N.J. Died Aug. 8, 1944.

SISE, Lincoln Fleetford (sīs), physician; b. Medford, Mass., July 1, 1874; s. Albert Fleetford and

Edith (Ware) S.; A.B., Harvard Coll., 1897, M.D., Med. Sch., 1901; m. Eleanor Gertrude Stanwood, Oct. 20, 1904; children—Albert Fleetford, Herbert Stanwood. Began as physician, Medford, Mass., 1901; visiting anesthetist, Boston City Hosp., 1915-27; anesthetist, Lahey Clinic, Boston, 1923-40, New Eng. Bapt. Hosp., 1923-40; mem. of corp. Lawrence Memorial Hosp. of Medford, 1923-41; cons. anesthetist, New Eng. Deaconess Hosp., 1923-40; retired from active practice, 1939. Served in Med. Corps, U.S.N.R.F., 1918-19; disch. as lt. Mem. Boston Soc. of Anesthetists (sec. 1920-21; pres. 1929-32), Eastern Soc. of Anesthetists (pres. 1931), Internat. Anesthesia Research Soc., New England Soc. of Anesthesiology, Asso. Anesthetists of U.S. and Can., Am. Soc. of Anesthetists. Republican. Author 70 to 80 articles in med. jours. Home: 697 Boylston St., Brookline, Mass. Died Apr. 28, 1942.

SISSON, Charles Newton (sis'ŭn), prof. history; b. Jacksonville, Ala., Oct. 1, 1892; s. William Anderson and Nancy Anne (Hamilton) S.; grad. Jacksonville Normal Coll., 1914; A.B., highest honors, Roanoke Coll., Salem, Va., 1916; A.M., Princeton, 1917; diploma, Sorbonne, Paris, 1919; Ph.D., U. of N.C., 1933; student summer sch. Harvard Univ., 1940-41; m. Louise Hendrick, Aug. 4, 1920. Prof. history and French, Marion (Ala.) Inst., 1919-21, prof. history, politics and French, 1922-24, supt., 1924-27; also head of depts. of history and French, Northwestern Mil. Acad., Lake Geneva, Wis., 1921-22; prof. history, polit. science and French, Lee Sch. for Boys, Blue Ridge, N.C., Sept.-Nov. 1929, headmaster, Nov. 1929-33; head dept. of history Coker Coll., since 1933; hist. research staff, U. of Chicago, summer 1934. Capt. inf., U.S. Army, World War; wounded at Rambroucourt, July 30, 1918; participated in St. Mihiel and Meuse-Argonne offensives. Awarded D.S.C. "for bravery in action"; received 3 gen. citations; decorated Croix de Guerre with Palm (France); Merito di Guerra (Italy). Mem. Am. Acad. Polit. Sci., Am. Hist. Assn., S.C. Hist. Assn., Southern Hist. Assn., Am. Legion (commander Marion post 1924-25). Democrat. Methodist. Author: History of the World War, 1921; Outline of American History, 1925; Creation, Organization and Mobilization of the Army of the French Revolution, 1933. Contbr. to Dictionary of Am. History. Home: Hartsville, S.C. Died Dec. 2, 1947.

SISSON, Charles Peck, lawyer; b. Providence, R.I., Feb. 9, 1890; s. Charles and Elizabeth D. (Eyre) S.; A.B., Brown U., 1911; LL.B., Harvard, 1914; m. Margaret A. Gifford, June 17, 1916; children—Mary Eyre, Hope. Admitted to R.I. bar, 1914; asst. city atty., Providence, 1916-19; asst. atty. gen. of R.I., 1919-22, atty. gen., R.I., term 1925-29, reëlected for term, 1929-30, res. June 10, 1929; asst. atty. gen. U.S., 1929-32; gen. counsel Fed. Home Loan Bank Bd., 1932; mem. Sisson, Fletcher, Worrell and Hodge. Chmn. Rep. City Com., Providence, 1923-24; chmn. Rep. State Central Com., R.I., 1933. Delegate Republican National Conventions, 1928, 1936. Vice president, Mt. Hope Bridge Corp.; dir. Personal Finance Companies, Columbus National Bank. Lt. col., Air Corps Allied Mil. Govt. in Italy and Germany World War II. Trustee Brown University, Lincoln School, Moses Brown School. Chairman City of Providence Charter Commn., 1939. Mem. American Bar Assn., R.I. Bar Assn., Alpha Delta Phi, Phi Beta Kappa. Clubs: Turks Head, Art, Agawam Hunt. Home: 117 Everett Av. Office: Turks Head Bldg., Providence, R.I. Died Aug. 2, 1947.

SISSON, Edgar Grant, editor, author; b. Alto, Wis., Dec. 23, 1875; s. Earl Truman and Lucy (Learned) S.; Northwestern U., 1894-97; m. Dixie, d. Ralph A. and Frances M. Ladd, Apr. 27, 1898; children—Mildred (Mrs. Charles Daly King), Edgar. Coll. corr. and staff reporter Chicago Chronicle, 1895-98; reporter, 1898-99, dramatic editor, 1899-1901, Chicago Tribune; asst. city editor Chicago American, 1902, city editor, 1903; asst. city editor Chicago Tribune, 1903-09, city editor, 1909-11; mng. editor Collier's Weekly, 1911-14; editor Cosmopolitan Mag., 1914-17; asso. chmn. Com. on Pub. Information, Washington, D.C., May 13, 1917-Apr. 1, 1919, and gen. dir. of fgn. sect.; organized the publication and distribution of President Wilson's speeches throughout Russia, winter of 1917-18; made to President Wilson the personal report pub. by the govt., Sept. 1918, under the title "The German-Bolshevik Conspiracy"; organized the committee's service at the Paris Peace Conf., 1918-19. Mem. Delta Upsilon. Decorated Cavalier Order of the Crown (Italy), 1919. Clubs: The Players, Dutch Treat (New York). Author: 100 Red Days, a Personal Chronicle of the Bolshevik Revolution, 1917-18, 1931. With Office of War Information 1942-45; editorial staff, Magazine Corp. of America, 1946. Home: 210 E. 73d St. Office: 25 W. 45th St., New York 19, N.Y. Died March 12, 1948.

SISSON, Fred James, ex-congressman; b. Wellsbridge, N.Y., Mar. 31, 1879; s. Elbert Alanson and Emily Josephine (Yorke) S.; A.B., Hamilton Coll., 1904; m. Grace McCormick, July 13, 1912; children—Marion E., Anne M., Elbert R., Margaret C., John M. Prin. Vernon (N.Y.) High Sch., 1904-07 and 1908-10; admitted to N.Y. bar, 1911, and since in practice at Utica; now mem. Sisson & Hartness. Sheriff's atty., 1913; corp. counsel, Utica, 1914. Dem. nominee for Congress, 1922 and 1928; mem. 73d and 74th Congresses (1933-37), 33d N.Y. Dist.; asst. to atty. gen., 1937-39; pvt. practice law since 1939, Wash., D.C. Mem. N.Y. State and Oneida Co. bar assns., Emerson Lit. Soc. Hamilton Coll. Mason. Clubs: Democratic (Utica); Masonic (Whitesboro, N.Y.); Nat. Democratic (New York). Mem. of Banking and Currency Com., House of Reps., 1933-37; author of numerous provisions of the Nat. Housing Act; active in securing passage of Federal Deposit and Insurance law, 1933, 1934, and amendments R.F.C. Act, including provision relative to direct loans to industry; author of law of repeal of so-called "Red Rider" which interfered with the curriculum of the schools of the Dist. of Columbia and required teachers' oath; active in legislation to keep the U.S. out of war. Home: 1882 Columbia Road N.W. Office: Woodward Bldg., Washington, D.C. Died Oct. 22, 1949.

SITTERLY, Charles Fremont, theologian; b. Liverpool, N.Y., June 4, 1861; s. Peter and Lucy Bancroft (Walker) S.; A.B., Syracuse U., 1883; A.M., 1885, Ph.D., 1886, S.T.D., 1900; B.D., Drew Theol. Sem., 1886; studied Oxford, Bonn, Heidelberg, Leipzig, Berlin, 1890-92; m. Julia Cobb Buttz, Dec. 22, 1891; children—Anson Buttz (dec.), Bancroft Walker, Alice Hoagland, Emily Buttz, Hildegarde Anne, Katharine, Julia Charlotte, Lois Elizabeth. Ordained M.E. ministry, 1887; pastor Chester, N.J., 1886-87, Cranford, 1888-89, Madison, 1889-90; adj. prof. Greek and prof. English Bible, 1892-94, prof. Bibl. lit. and English Bible, 1895-1935, Drew U. Theol. Sch. Mem. Phi Beta Kappa, Am. Philol. Assn., Soc. Bibl. Lit. and Exegesis. Author: Praxis in Manuscripts of Greek New Testament, 1898; History of English Bible (with S. G. Ayres), 1899; Canon, Text and Manuscripts of the New Testament, 1914; Jerusalem to Rome—The Acts of the Apostles, 1915; Henry Anson Buttz—His Book (Life and Writings), 2 vols., 1922; The Building of Drew University, 1937. Contbr. to religious periodicals. Address: 30 Green Av., Madison, N.J. Died Nov. 8, 1945.

SIVRIGHT, Cal (siv'rit), pres. Oliver Farm Equipment Co.; b. Hutchinson, Minn., Mar. 12, 1886; s. William W. and Harriet (James) S.; student U. Minn. Coll. Law, 1911; m. Gertrude Chloe Stearns, July 12, 1913; children—James McKee, Edgar Stearns. Credit mgr. Minneapolis Steel Machinery Co., 1916-24, treas., 1924-25; v.p. Minn. State Fair; mgr. tractor plant Oliver Farm Equipment Co., Chicago, 1930-31, asst. to pres., 1932, gen. sales mgr., 1932-35, exec. v.p., 1936-37, pres. since 1937, dir. since 1936; dir. Am. Nat. Bank, Chicago, 1943. Mem. Farm Equipment Inst. (exec. com.). Home: 1606 Hinman Av., Evanston, Ill. Office: 400 W. Madison St., Chicago, Ill.* Died Oct. 10, 1945.

SKAGGS, William Henry, author, publicist; b. Talladega, Ala., Sept. 16, 1861; s. James M. and Lavinia A. (Smith) S.; ed. pvtly.; m. Ella Earle Yancey, 1885 (died 1902); children—Wm. Yancey (dec.), Mary Lanier (dec.); m. 2d, Julia Frances Ollis, 1908. Elected mayor of Talladega at 23 and served 3 terms; speaker and writer against corrupt practices; prospected and discovered North River coal field in Ala. Author: Public Schs. in the South, 1910; Vice Regent of God and His Chosen People, 1914; German Conspiracies in America, 1916; The Outlaws of Christendom, 1918; The Southern Oligarchy, 1924. Address: 607 W. 191st St., New York. Died Jan. 19, 1947; buried in Graceland Cemetery, Chicago.

SKARSTEDT, Ernst Teofil, writer; b. Solberga, Sweden, Apr. 14, 1857; s. Carl Wilhelm and Hedvig Elina (Wieselgren) S.; grad. Cathedral Sch. of Lund, Sweden, 1877; Tech. High Sch., Stockholm, Sweden, 1877-78; agrl. course U. of Cal., winter, 1902-03; m. Ellen Maria Hogberg, Nov. 22, 1893. Came to Am., 1878; pub. and editor Kansas Stats-Tidning, Lindsborg, Kan., 1879-80; editor Svenska Amerikanaren, Chicago, 1880-84; editorial writer on Svenska Tribunen, Chicago, 1884-85; editor Vestkusten, San Francisco, 1891-96; extensive contbr. to Swedish-Am. papers; farmer. Republican. Mem. Nat. Geog. Soc.; hon. mem. Swedish Singing Soc., San Francisco. Author of many books in Swedish language, also translator, prose and poetry. Address: Friday Harbor, Wash. Died March 13, 1929.

SKEVINGTON, Samuel John, clergyman; b. Lille, France, of English father and Scotch mother, July 11, 1871; s. William and Marion (Dippie) S.; student Collegiate Institute, Calais; graduate Crozer Theological Seminary, Chester, Pa., 1897; D.D., Shurtleff College 1918; married Lucy Benjamin, June 29, 1897 (died January 25, 1944); children—Gladys Marion and Florence Morrill (both missionaries in China, but now teaching in N.Y. high schools). Ordained Bapt. ministry, 1897; pastor successively Clinton, N.J., Nyack, N.Y., Clinton Av. Ch., Newark, N.J., Belden Av. Ch., Chicago, until 1920, First Ch., Hollywood, Los Angeles, Calif., 1920-28, Temple Baptist Ch., Albany, N.Y., since March 1928. First v.p. Gen. Bd. Missionary Coöperation of Northern Bapt. Conv. and chmn. State Bd. Missionary Coöperation, Southern Calif. Bapt. Conv.; moderator Chicago Bapt. Assn., 1920, Hudson River Bapt. Assn., North, 1932-33. Camp pastor, Camp Logan, Houston, Tex., World War; ex-pres. Los Angeles Bapt. Ministers' Conf.; pres. Albany Ministers (Union) Assn., 1934-35; trustee of Crozer Theol. Seminary since 1937; mem. bd. mgrs. N.Y. State Bapt. Conv., 1942-45. Republican. Mason. Visited West China, 1927, as fraternal messenger of Northern Baptists to foreign missionaries and Chinese chs. Author: The Prince of Peace (booklet), 1906; Abraham Lincoln (oration), 1909; The Distinctive Principle of the Baptists, 1917; Benjamin Franklin (booklet). Spl. lecturer on China and the Oriental life and history. Home: 11 S. Lake Av., Albany, N.Y. Died Apr. 25, 1944.

SKIDMORE, Hubert Standish, author; b. Webster Springs, W.Va., Apr. 11, 1911; s. Neil Patrick and Daisy (Mollohan) Skidmore; student University of Michigan, 1930-35; married Maritta M. Wolff, Nov. 25, 1943. Received Avery Hopwood award ($1500), 1935. Commissioned 2d lt. Army of U.S., Signal Corps, Oct. 10, 1942. Author: I Will Lift Up Mine Eyes, 1936; Heaven Came So Near, 1938; River Rising!, 1939; Hill Doctor, 1940; Hawk's Nest, 1941; Hill Lawyer, 1942; also articles. Lecturer on folklore, customs and history of Blue Ridges. Home: 1317½ Lake St., Elmira, N.Y. Died Feb. 2, 1946.

SKILES, William Vernon, educator; b. Troygrove, Ill., Apr. 23, 1879; s. James Spiers and Elizabeth Louisa (Steve) S.; grad. State Normal U., Normal, Ill., 1901; S.B., Univ. of Chicago, 1906; A.M., Harvard Univ., 1911; Sc.D., U. of Georgia, 1926; m. Ethel Agnes McWhirter, Nov. 28, 1901; 1 son, William Vernon. Supt. schs., Melvin, Ill., 1901-02, Loda, 1902-04; with Ga. Sch. of Tech. since 1906, asst. prof. math. until 1910, asso. prof., 1911-20, prof. since 1920, mem. dean, 1925-45, dean emeritus since 1945. Fellow A.A.A.S.; mem. Soc. for Promotion Engring. Edn., Ga. Acad. Sci., Phi Beta Kappa, Phi Kappa Phi, Beta Theta Pi. Democrat. Presbyterian. Home: 1057 Springdale Rd. Address: Georgia School of Technology, Atlanta 6a. Died Sept. 10, 1947; buried West View Cemetery, Atlanta, Ga.

SKINNER, Charles Wilbur, irrigation specialist; b. Troy, O., July 12, 1864; s. Elias and Martha Jane (Orbison) S.; ed. country schs.; m. Elena M. Dougherty, June 18, 1895; children—Ella (Mrs. Philip Clark Hanford), Charles Robert, Edna Kate, Henry Vance. Began as market gardener, 1874; constructed rude system of overhead field irrigation lines in order to save crops during period of drought, 1896; worked on improvements and perfected systems first placed on sale, 1904; founder of Skinner Irrigation Co., Troy, O., 1904; established firm of C. W. Skinner & Co., Newfield, N.J., 1912. Republican. Presbyterian. Home: Newfield, N.J. Deceased.

SKINNER, Clarence Russell, clergyman, educator; b. Brooklyn, N.Y., Mar. 23, 1881; s. Charles Montgomery and Ada (Blanchard) S.; B.A., St. Lawrence Univ., Canton, N.Y., 1904, M.A., 1910; D.D. from Meadville (Pa.) Theol. School, 1926; D.D., from St. Lawrence Univ., 1933; studied Harvard, Columbia, and Sch. for Social Workers; m. Clara L. Ayres, Oct. 16, 1906. Ordained Universalist ministry, 1904; asst. pastor in N.Y. City, 1904-06; pastor Mt. Vernon, N.Y., 1906-11, Lowell, Mass., 1911-14; prof. applied Christianity, Tufts College, since 1914, also dean since Feb. 1933. Engaged in social work, University Settlement, New York, 1908-09; social service sec., Universalist Denomination, 1910-19; pres. State Conv. Mass. Universalists, 1918-20; chmn. Commn. on Social Welfare Universalist Ch., 1935-44; chmn. League for Democratic Control. Trustee St. Lawrence University, Canton, N.Y. Leader, Community Ch., Boston, 1920-36; editorial staff, Unity. Mem. Am. Sociol. Soc., Am. Association of University Professors, American Civil Liberties Union (dir.), Beta Theta Pi, Phi Beta Kappa. Author: Social Implications of Universalism; A Free Pulpit in Action, 1931; Liberalism Faces the Future, 1937; Human Nature and the Nature of Evil, 1939. Co-author: Life of John Murray, Founder of Universalism, "A Religion for Greatness." Lecturer on social economic, internat. topics. Home: 5 Concord Av., Cambridge 38, Mass. Died Aug. 27, 1949.

SKINNER, John Harrison, animal husbandman; b. Romney, Ind., Mar. 10, 1874; s. William and Mary (Alexander) S.; B.S., in Agr., Purdue, 1897; D.Agr. (hon.), Mich. State Coll., Lansing, 1935; m. Mary Edna Throckmorton, Sept. 3, 1903; children—John H., Mary Elizabeth, William E., Robert E. Instr. animal husbandry, U. of Ill., 1901-02; chief of dept. animal husbandry, Purdue Univ., 1902-28, became dean Sch. of Agr., 1907, dir. agrl. expt. sta. and extension dept., 1928-39 (retired; now dean and dir. emeritus). Mem. Animal Nutrition Soc., Am. Genetic Assn., Soc. Promotion Agrl. Science, Ind. Livestock Breeders' Assn., Ind. Corn Growers' Assn., Sigma Xi, Alpha Zeta. Republican. Presbyterian. Mason. Address: West Lafayette, Ind. Died Apr. 28, 1942.

SKINNER, Joseph Allen, silk mfr.; b. Williamsburg, Mass., May 20, 1862; s. William and Sarah E. (Allen) S.; Ph.B., Yale, 1883; L.H.D., Mt. Holyoke, 1925; m. Martha C. Hubbard, June 29, 1887. Treas. William Skinner & Sons, silk mfrs., Holyoke, Mass.; chmn. bd. Hadley Falls Trust Co., Holyoke; dir. N.E. Telephone & Telegraph Co. Republican. Conglist. Address: Holyoke, Mass.* Died Sep. 6, 1946.

SKINNER, Laurence Hervey, univ. prof.; b. Arcola, Ill., Dec. 12, 1897; s. Samuel Robert and Eleanor Delia (Hervey) S.; A.B., U. of Fla., 1919; certificate, U. of Grenoble, France, 1922; diploma, U. of Caen, France, 1923; A.M., Ohio State U., 1927; Ph.D., Columbia U., 1933; m. Virginia Kerr, Jan. 30, 1926. Instr. Barnes Sch., Montgomery, Ala., 1921-22; exchange fellow, Ecole Normale d'Instituteurs, Valence, France, 1922-23; asso. headmaster, Castle Heights Mil. Acad., Lebanon, Tenn., 1923-25; asst. prof. Romanic langs., Miami U., 1925-34, asso. prof., 1934-40, prof. since 1940. Served as 2d lt., Inf., U.S. Army, 1918. Mem. Modern Lang. Assn. America, Nat. Fedn. Modern Lang. Teachers, Am. Assn. Teachers of French (ex-sec. Ohio Chapter), Kappa Alpha, Beta Pi Theta. Democrat. Baptist. Author: Collin d' Harleville, Dramatist, 1933. Editor: Notre-Dame de Paris (Hugo), 1930; Quinze Conteurs, 1940. Joint editor: Le Comte de Monte-Cristo (Dumas), 1928;

La Tulipe Noire (Dumas), 1929; Gil Blas (Le Sage), 1938; Vingt Contes Divers, 1938. Contbr. articles and professional reviews to Romanic Review, Modern Lang. Jour., Books Abroad, etc. Home: 204 N. Bishop St., Oxford, O. Deceased.

SKINNER, William, silk mfr.; b. Northampton, Mass., June 12, 1857; s. William and Sarah Elizabeth (Allen) S.; ed. Williston Sem., Mass., and Yale Coll.; unmarried. Mem. firm William Skinner & Sons, Holyoke, Mass.; dir. Irving Trust Co., Mass. Mut. Life Ins. Co., Equitable Life Assurance Soc.; trustee Am. Surety Co. Conglist. Clubs: Manhattan, Union League. Home: 910 Fifth Av., New York, N.Y. Office: 45 E. 17th St., New York, N.Y. Died Oct. 17, 1947.

SLACK, Charles William, lawyer; b. Milroy, Mifflin County, Pa., Dec. 12, 1858; s. Uriah and Catharine (Straley) S.; Ph.B., U. of Calif., 1879, LL.D., 1929; LL.B., Hastings Coll. of Law, 1882; m. Katherine Woolsey, 1886; children—Edith, Mrs. Ruth S. Zook. Admitted to Calif. bar, 1882, and began practice at San Francisco; prof. law, Hastings Coll. of Law, 1885-1901, dean of faculty, 1899-1901; judge Superior Court, San Francisco, 1890-98; resigned and resumed practice, 1898; asso. in practice with Edgar T. Zook since 1920. Regent U. of Calif., 1894-1911; declined reappointment by Gov., Hiram W. Johnson of Calif., dir. Hastings Coll. of Law since 1903, v.p. since 1918. Mem. Am., Calif. and San Francisco bar assns., Order of Golden Bear (Univ. of Calif.), Calif. Hist. Soc., Calif. Acad. Sciences, Phi Beta Kappa, Phi Delta Phi. Clubs: Pacific Union (pres. 1923-25), Bohemian, Commonwealth. Home: 2224 Sacramento St. Office: Alaska Commercial Bldg., San Francisco, Calif. Died Dec. 20, 1945.

SLADE, Charles Blount, physician; b. Columbus, Ga., May 15, 1874; s. James J. and Leila (Bonner) S.; ed. U. of Ga., 1891-92; M.D., Bellevue Hosp. Med. Coll., 1896; m. Constance A. Thill, Sept. 12, 1901. Interne Bellevue Hosp., 1896-98; traveled in Mexico and Europe, 1898-1900; gen. practice in New York since 1900, except 18 mos., 1902-04, in Mexico organizing med. service of Mut. Life Ins. Co. of New York; chief of clinic and instr. in physical diagnosis, Univ. and Bellevue Hosp. Med. Coll., 1905-14; physician N.Y. City Dept. of Health, 1906-33; cons. physician to Municipal Sanatorium, N.Y. Pres. Soc. Alumni of Bellevue Hosp., 1920; mem. N.Y. State Med. Soc., etc. Officer Reserve Corps, U.S. Army, 1917-18. Author: Physical Examination and Diagnostic Anatomy, 1910; The Establishment and Conduct of a Tuberculosis Sanatorium, 1917; also numerous monographs on medicine and pub. health. Home-Office: Greenwood Park, Greenwood Lake, N.Y. Died Aug. 23, 1942.

SLADEN, Fred Winchester, army officer; b. Mass., Nov. 24, 1867; s. late Maj. Joseph A. (U.S. Army) and Martha (Winchester) S.; grad. U.S. Mil. Acad., 1890; m. Elizabeth Lefferts, Oct. 8, 1903; children—Elizabeth Morris, Fred Winchester. Commd. 2d lt. 14th inf., June 12, 1890; promoted through grades to major gen., Jan. 19, 1924. Duty in Ore., Wash. and Ida., to 1897; aide to Maj. Gen. E. S. Otis, on Pacific Coast and while mil. gov. of Philippines, 1897-1900; duty U.S. Mil. Acad., 1900-04; relief work, San Francisco, after earthquake and fire, Apr.-June 1906; sec. Gen. Staff Corps, 1907-11; comdt. of cadets, U.S. Mil. Acad., 1911-14; in China, 1914-16; on Mexican border, 1916-17; comdt. 1st and 2d O.T.C., Presidio, San Francisco, May-Oct. 1917; sec. War Dept. Gen. Staff, 1917-18; comd. 5th Inf. Brig., 3d Regular Div., France and Germany, Apr. 1918-Aug. 1919, during Aisne defensive, Château Thierry defensive sector, Champagne-Marne defensive, Aisne-Marne offensive, St. Mihiel and Meuse-Argonne offensives, and march into and occupation of Germany; comd. 1st Brig. Am. Forces in Germany, Sept. 1919-July 1921; comd. Ft. Sheridan, Oct. 1921-Apr. 1922; supt. and comdt. U.S. Mil. Acad., July 1922-Mar. 23, 1926; comdg. Philippine Dept., Manila, 1926-28, 3d Corps Area, Baltimore, Md., 1928-31; retired, Nov. 30, 1931. Clubs: University (N.Y.); Army and Navy, Chevy Chase (Washington). Home: New London, New Hampshire. Died July 10, 1945.

SLATEN, A(rthur) Wakefield, clergyman, educator; b. Labette County, Kan., Aug. 8, 1880; s. Hugh Jefferson and Jerusha (Durham) S.; A.B., William Jewell Coll., Liberty, Mo., 1908; B.D., Rochester Theol. Sem., 1912; studied New Testament at univs. of Glasgow, Marburg and Leipzig; Ph.D., U. of Chicago, 1916; m. Mary Fitzhugh, June 8, 1904; children—Edward Fitzhugh, Champe Douglas. Prof. and head dept. of religion and ethics, Y.M.C.A. Coll., Chicago, 1918-22; organizer edni. dept. Y.M.C.A., Salonika, Greece, 1921; prof. Bibl. lit. and religious edn., William Jewell Coll., 1922; pastor Third Unitarian Ch., Chicago, 1923; chaplain Mills Coll., Oakland, Calif., 1924-25; Davis prof. New Testament, Pacific Unitarian Sch. for the Ministry, Berkeley, Calif., 1924-25; minister West Side Unitarian Church, New York, 1925-29; literary editor and columnist Honolulu (Hawaii) Star-Bulletin and author daily column, "Aloha Tower" to 1942; director Century Research Institute and associate editor Skyways (aviation mag.), 1942-43; doing independent literary work since 1943. President Pacific Coast Conf. Unitarian Churches, 1924-25; pres. Pacific Unitarian Hdqrs., 1925. Mem. Soc. Bibl. Lit. and Exegesis, Am. Classical League, Science League of America, Nat. Fellowship of Religious Liberals, Am. Rationalist Assn., Rationalist Press Assn., Kappa Delta Pi. Democrat. Mason. Author: Qualitative Nouns in the Pauline Epistles and Their Translation in the Revised Version, 1916; What Jesus Taught, 1922; Words of Aspiration, 1927; also numerous mag. articles and published addresses. Address: 2930 Montana Av., Santa Monica, Calif. Died July 29, 1944.

SLATTERY, Harry, lawyer; b. Greenville, S.C., June 13, 1887; s. John and Mary (Grace) S.; ed. Mt. St. Mary's Coll. (Md.), Georgetown U. and George Washington U.; LL.D., University of South Carolina (1944); unmarried. Secretary to Gifford Pinchot, 1909-12; sec. National Conservation Assn., 1912-17; counsel same, 1919-23; spl. asst. to Franklin K. Lane, sec. of Interior, 1917-18; special asst. to William Wilson, Sec. Labor, 1918-19; exec. and counsel Nat. Boulder Dam-Assn., 1925-29; counsel Nat. Conservation Com., 1929-32; Washington rep. N.Y. Power Authority, 1931-33; practice of law, Washington, D.C., concurrently, 1923-33; personal asst. to Harold L. Ickes, sec. of interior, 1933-38; asst. to adminstr. Fed. Emergency Administrn. of Pub. Works, 1933-38; undersec. of interior, 1938-39, adminstr. Rural Electrification Adminstrn., 1939-1944; mem. Nat. Power Policy Com.; mem. Energy Resources and Land Coms. of Nat. Resources Planning Bd.; consultant to power sub-com. of adv. commn. Council of Nat. Defense, 1940-42; mem. Inter-bureau Coordinating Committee. Mem. Fed. States Relations Com. Took active part in passage of Federal coal and oil leasing measure, Federal water power legislation, Alaska coal and home rule acts, forestry legislation investigation of naval oil reserve, rural electrification legislation, etc. Mem. Soc. Am. Foresters, Delta Theta Phi. Clubs: Nat. Press, Missouri Athletic. Author: Rural America Lights Up; Roosevelt to Roosevelt. Contbr. on conservation. Home: The Sedgwick, 1722 15th St. Office: National Press Bldg., Washington, D.C. Died Sep. 1, 1949.

SLATTERY, James M., lawyer; b. Chicago, Ill., July 29, 1878; s. John and Catherine (Healy) S.; student St. Ignatius Coll., 1893-94; LL.B., Ill. Coll. of Law, 1908; m. Alice Beever, 1902 (now dec.); children—James H., Alice M. (Mrs. Stephen R. Pietrowicz, Jr.), Dorothy, Albert B., Edith M. Philip J., William J., Ethel, Grace, Ruth, Ann; m. 2d, Ruth Anderson, Aug. 3, 1933. Began as sec. bldg. dept. City of Chicago, 1905; admitted to Ill. bar, 1908, since in practice in Chicago; instr. contract law, Ill. Coll. of Law, Chicago, 1909-12; private practice of law, 1908-10, and 1912-32; supt. of pub. service, Cook County, 1910-12; atty. for Lincoln Park Commn., 1933-34; gen. atty. for Chicago Park Dist., 1934-36; chmn. Ill. Commerce Commn., 1936-39; apptd. to U.S. Senate to succeed late James H. Lewis, 1939, serving to Dec. 1940. Mem. Legal Adv. Bd. of Exemption Bd. during World War; 4-minute speaker in Liberty Loan drives, 1917-18. Sec. Webster Coll. of Law, 1912-14. Mem. Am., Ill. State and Chicago bar assns. Democrat. Catholic. K.C. Clubs: Chicago Athletic, Iroquois, Lake Shore. Home: 3500 Lake Shore Drive. Office: 111 W. Washington St., Chicago, Ill. Died Aug. 28, 1948.

SLATTERY, Margaret, author, lecturer; d. Philip J. and Margaret E. (Eliot) Slattery; educated pub. schs., Fitchburg, Mass., and State Teachers College, Framingham, Mass.; D.Litt., Elon College (North Carolina), 1942; Teacher, Grammar School, Fitchburg, later mem. faculty State Teachers Coll., Fitchburg, advancing to prin. of training dept., until 1910; lecturer and writer since 1910; asso. editor Congl. publs. Apptd. mem. Mass. State Bd. of Edn., 1912. resigned. Spent 7 mos. in Europe, World War, and later made study of youth problems around the World; speaker before internat. confs. on religion. Author: The Girl and Her Religion, 1913; A Girl's Book of Prayers, 1914; He Took It Upon Himself, 1914, 30; The American Girl and Her Community, 1918; The Second Line of Defense, 1918; Highway to Leadership, 1920; Just Over the Hill, 1920; New Paths Through Old Palestine, 1921; You Can Learn to Teach, 1925; Two Words, 1927; Important to Me, 1929; Thy Kingdom Come—But Not Now, 1938; One in Seven, 1939; A Primer for Teachers, 1942. Address: 14 Beacon St., Boston 8, Mass. Died April, 1947.

SLEE, John B., architect; b. Harford County, Md., June 16, 1875; s. Cicero and Annie Martin (Latty) S.; student, Maryland Inst., 1891-93. Private practice, Brooklyn, N.Y., 1901-03; formed partnership with Robert H. Bryson, 1903, continued this partnership until 1938; private practice since 1938. Awarded certificate from Nat. Council of Registered Architects. Fellow Am. Inst. Architects; mem. N.Y. State Assn. of Architects, New York Southern Soc. Club: Brooklyn. Home: 102 Pierrepont St. Office: 16 Court St., Brooklyn, N.Y. Died Jan. 14, 1947.

SLEEPER, Henry Dike, educator; b. Patten, Me., Oct. 9, 1865; s. Rev. William T. and Emily (Taylor) S.; grad. Worcester Acad., 1885; Harvard U., 1885-87, 1912; grad. Hartford Theol. Sem., 1891; student of music, Worcester, Hartford, Chicago, Phila., London; m. Mary Peet, Aug. 28, 1894; children—Mary Olive, Henry Dike (dec.), Harriet, William Denison (dec.). Ordained Congl. ministry, 1891; instr. music, Beloit Coll., 1891-94; prof. music, Georgetown Coll., Ky., 1894-95; instr. music, U. of Wis., 1895-98; instr. music, Smith Coll., 1898-1903, asso. prof., 1903, prof., 1904-24. Prof. Dartmouth Coll. Summer Sch., 1913, 14. Organist First Congl. Ch., Madison, Wis., 1895-98, Union Ch., Worcester, Mass., 1899-1902, Fourth Congl. Ch., Hartford, Conn., 1902-04, 1st Congl. Ch., St. Petersburg, Fla., 1925-26. Examiner in music, Hartford Pub. High Sch., 1919-25; part owner Camp Marbury (camp for girls on Lake Champlain) since 1921. Editor coll. edit. Hymns of Worship and Service, 1909. Asso. editor Common Order Choir Book, 1903. Composer and arranger of numerous pieces of ch., organ and orchestra music, part songs, etc. Writer upon mus. edn., ch. music, etc. Henry Dike Sleeper professorship of music, established at Smith Coll. by class of 1908. Feb. 1924. Fellow Am. Guild Organists; mem. Music Teachers Nat. Assn., Am. Musicol. Soc. Clubs: The Bohemians (New York); Vergennes Country; Clearwater (Fla.) Art; University (Winter Park, pres. 1943-44). Mem. Beethoven Assn., and MacDowell Club of N.Y. until orgns. dissolved. Home: Camp Marbury, Vergennes, Vt.; (winter) Winter Park, Fla. Died Jan. 28, 1948.

SLEMONS, J(osiah) Morris (slĕm'ŭnz), obstetrician, gynecologist; b. Salisbury, Md., Nov. 9, 1876; s. Francis Marion and Martha Ann (Morris) S.; A.B., Johns Hopkins, 1897, M.D., 1901; grad. student U. of Berlin, 1907; A.M., Yale, 1915; m. Anne M. Goodsill, Aug. 2, 1905. Instr. in obstetrics, Johns Hopkins U., 1901-09, asso. prof., 1909-13; prof. obstetrics and gynecology, U. of Calif., 1913-15; prof. obstetrics and gynecology, Yale Med. Sch., 1915-20; removed to Los Angeles, Calif.; attending obstetrician and gynecologist, Good Samaritan Hosp. Dir. Obstet. Survey of France, Am. Red Cross, 1917; maj., M.C., U.S. Army, 1918-19. Fellow Am. Coll. Surgeons; mem. Pacific Coast Soc. Obstetrics and Gynecology, Phi Gamma Delta; Nu Sigma Nu, Phi Beta Kappa, Sigma Xi. Author: The Prospective Mother; The Nutrition of the Fetus; John Whitridge Williams, Academic Aspects and Bibliography, Progress in Obstetrics (1890-1940); A Cross-light on Doctor Holmes and His Investigation of Childbirth Fever; also numerous med. monographs. Home: 309 S. Westmorland Av., Los Angeles 5, Calif. Died April 30, 1948.

SLEMP, C(ampbell) Bascom, lawyer; b. Turkey Cove, Lee County, Va., Sept. 4, 1870; s. Campbell and Nannie B. (Cawood) S.; grad. Va. Mil. Inst., Lexington, 1891; studied law, U. of Va.; unmarried. Adj. prof. mathematics, Va. Mil. Inst., 1900-01, then practiced law at Big Stone Gap, Va.; also pres. Slemp Coal Co., and various corps. Chmn. Rep. State Com., Va., since 1905; elected to 60th Congress, Dec. 17, 1907, to fill unexpired term of father, deceased; reelected 61st to 67th Congresses (1909-23), 9th Va. Dist.; sec. to President Coolidge, Sept. 4, 1923-Mar. 4, 1925; commr. gen. French Colonial Expn., Paris. Mem. Bd. Visitors, U.S. Naval Acad.; one of founders Inst. of Pub. Affairs at U. of Va. Comdr. Legion of Honor (France). Mem. Am. Soc. French Legion of Honor, Nat. Rep. Club, N.Y. Southern Soc. Clubs: Lonesome Pine, Burning Tree, Metropolitan, Press. Author: The Mind of the President; Selected Addresses; Addresses of Famous Southwest Virginians. Home: Big Stone Gap, Va. Died Aug. 7, 1943.

SLEYSTER, Rock (slī'stēr), psychiatrist; b. Waupun, Wis., June 14, 1879; s. William and Addie (Butts) S.; M.D., U. of Ill., 1902; hon. LL.D., Marquette Univ., Milwaukee, 1941; m. Clara Sarah Swift, Apr. 15, 1903. Private practice as physician, Appleton, Wis., 1902-09; med. dir. Central State Hosp., Waupun, Wis., 1909-19; med. dir. Milwaukee Sanitarium, Wauwatosa, Wis., since 1919. Trustee Northwestern Mutual Life Ins. Co., Marquette U. Med. Sch., Wis. Anti-Tuberculosis Assn. Served as maj. Med. Corps, U.S. Army, during World War. Awarded gold service medal by Wisconsin Med. Soc. and American Medical Association. Fellow Am. Coll. Physicians (former mem. bd. govs.), Am. Med. Assn. (chmn. bd. trustees 1926-37; pres. 1939); mem. Wis. Med. Soc. (past pres.), Am. Psychiatric Assn., Chicago Neurol. Soc., Chicago Inst. of Medicine, Milwaukee Acad. Medicine, Am. Assn. for Research in Nervous and Mental Diseases, Alpha Mu Pi Omega; hon. mem. Chicago Med. Soc. Republican. Episcopalian. Clubs: University, Milwaukee Country (Milwaukee). Editor of Wis. Med. Jour., 1917-22. Contbr. to med. jours. Home: 1220 Dewey Av., Wauwatosa, Wis. Office: Milwaukee Sanitarium, Wauwatosa, Wis.; Marshall Field Annex, Chicago, Ill. Died Mar. 7, 1942.

SLEZAK, Leo, operatic tenor; b. Schonberg, Austria, Aug. 18, 1875. Engaged for several yrs. at Royal Opera House; sang at Covent Garden, London. 1900, Vienna, 1900-08; studied under Jean de Reszke, Paris, 1908; New York début at Met. Opera House, in "Otello," Nov. 18, 1909; has appeared in song recitals in leading cities of U.S. Address: AEolian Hall, New York. Died June 1946.

SLICHTER, Charles Sumner (slĭk'tēr), univ. dean; b. St. Paul, Minn., Apr. 16, 1864; s. Jacob B. and Catherine (Huber) S.; B.S., Northwestern U., 1885, M.S., 1887, Sc.D., 1916; m. Mary L. Byrne, Dec. 23, 1890; children—Sumner Huber, Louis Byrne, Allen McKinnon, Donald Charles. Instr., U. of Wis, 1886, asst. prof. mathematics, 1889, prof. applied mathematics since 1892, also dean of the Grad. Sch., emeritus, 1934. Cons. engr. U.S. Geol. Survey; engr. in charge of investigation of movements of underground waters, U.S. Reclamation Service. Mem. Wis. Acad. Sciences, Arts and Letters (pres. 1900-03), Am. Math. Soc., Math. Assn. America, Am. Geophys. Union, Sigma Xi, Phi Beta Kappa, Gamma Alpha. Author: Theoretical Investigations on Underground Waters, 1898; Motions of Underground Waters, 1902; Field Measurements of the Motions of Groundwaters, 1904; Science in a Tavern, 1938; also gen. math. textbooks and many U.S. Geol. Survey reports on underground waters published by U. S. Geol. Survey. Episcopalian. Contbr. to tech. jours. Address: R.F.D. 1, Madison 4, Wis. Died Oct. 4, 1946.

SLINKER, Clay Dean, educator; b. Logan County, Ill., Sept. 10, 1864; s. John B. and Sarah Decker

(Westfall) S.; ed. pub. schs., commercial coll., spl. course Drake U., U. of Colo.; m. Tillie Ganz, Dec. 30, 1897; children—Philip Dean, Dorothy Anna. Teacher West High School, Des Moines, 1888-1912; dir. business edn. Des Moines Pub. Schs., 1912-37 (retired); teacher Grad. Sch. of Edn., Harvard, summer, 1925; teacher, Sch. of Education, U. of Mich., summers, 1926-27; teacher Univ. of Wis., summer, 1928, Wash. State College, summer, 1932; organizer and dir. Junior Chamber of Commerce, Des Moines, Ia., also organizer of its bur. of edn. (first of kind in U.S.). Mem. of board and vice-pres. of Thrift, Inc. Mem. Nat. Commercial Teachers' Fedn. (pres. 1916), Am. Vocational Assn. (v.p. 1926-29), N.E.A. (chmn. commercial sect. 1921-22); chmn. bureau edn. Des Moines Chamber of Commerce, 1924; dir. Des Moines Chamber of Commerce, 1924. Chmn. boys' work com. Des Moines Rotary Club, 1922-24, dir., 1936-37; vice-pres. Tall Corn council Boy Scouts of America (chmn. reading com.); awarded Silver Beaver, Boy Scouts of America; chmn. com. on business courses of study, Iowa State Dept. of Edn. U.S. del. to Internat. Congress on Commercial Education, Amsterdam, 1929. Republican. Methodist. Mason (33°, K.T., Shriner). Clubs: Walt Whitman, Rotary, Schoolmasters, Employment Managers. Author: Yours Truly (a dictation manual), 1901; Typewriting Diagnostic Chart, 1928; Course of Study in Gen. Business Training, 1933. Joint Author: General Business Training, 1927; General Business, 1936; Self-dictated Shorthand Practice. Contbr. to professional jours. on business edn. Home: 2915 School St., Des Moines, Ia. Died Dec. 14, 1943.

SLOAN, Charles H., ex-congressman; b. Monticello, Ia., May 2, 1863; s. James W. and Elizabeth (Magee) S. (Scotch-Irish parents); B.Sc., Ia. State Agrl. Coll., 1884, Master of Agriculture, 1935; m. Emma M. Porter, Oct. 1, 1889; children—Ethel, Frank Blaine (dec.), Charles Porter, William McKinley. Supt. schs., Fairmont, Neb., 1884-87; admitted to bar, 1887; practiced at Fairmont, 1887-91, Geneva since 1891; mem. firm Sloans, Keenan & Corbitt; chmn. bd. Geneva State Bank. County atty., Fillmore County, Neb., 2 terms, 1891-95; mem. Neb. Senate, 1894-96; mem. 62d to 65th Congresses (1911-19), and 71st Congress (1929-31), 4th Neb. Dist. (was mem. Ways and Means Com. abt. 4 yrs.). Author and advocate of legislation for eradication of tuberculosis in cows and of hog cholera. Mem. Am. and Neb. State bar assns. Republican. Methodist. Mason (K.T., Scottish Rite). Author of Biography of Frank W. Sloan. Address: Geneva, Neb. Died June 2, 1946.

SLOAN, Edgar J., ins. official; b. Hartford, Conn., Nov. 4, 1870; s. Adrian P. and Mary J. (Boyd) S.; ed. pub. schs.; m. Abbie Avery, Oct. 4, 1893; children—Ruth (Mrs. Frederic L. Way), Edgar T. Examiner for Phoenix Ins. Co., 1888-97; spl. and state agt. Home Ins. Co., 1897-1903; successively spl. agt., gen. agt., asst.-sec., sec., v.p., and dir. Aetna Ins. Co., since 1903; also v.p. and dir. World Fire & Marine Ins. Co., Century Indemnity Co., Cushman Chuck Co.; v.p. Standard Ins. Co. of N.Y., Standard Surety & Casualty Co. of N.Y., Factory Insurance Assn. Building Corp., Mechanics Bank; dir. Phoenix State Bank & Trust Co.; trustee Mechanics Savings Bank. Mem. bd. dirs. Conn. Chamber Commerce. Fellow Ins. Inst. of America. Mem. Royal Arcanum. Clubs: Hartford, Get Together, Hartford Golf. Home: 154 Oxford St. Office: 670 Main St., Hartford, Conn. Died Sep. 27, 1942.

SLOCUM, Frederick (slō'kŭm), astronomer; b. Fairhaven, Mass., Feb. 6, 1873; s. Frederick and Lydia Ann (Jones) S.; A.B., Brown U., 1895, A.M., 1896, Ph.D., 1898, Sc.D., 1938; m. Carrie E. Tripp, June 29, 1899 (died 1942). Began as instructor in mathematics, 1895-1900, assistant professor astronomy, 1900-09, and acting director Ladd Observatory, 1904-05, Brown University; at Royal Astrophysical Observatory, Potsdam, Germany, 1908-09; lecturer on mathematics, New York U., summer of 1908; research asst., summer of 1907; instr. in astrophysics, 1909-11, asst. prof. astronomy, 1911-14, Yerkes Obs., U. of Chicago; prof. astronomy and dir. Van Vleck Obs., Wesleyan U., Conn., 1914-18 and since 1920; prof. nautical science, Brown U., 1918-20. Instr. navigation for U.S. Shipping Bd., 1917-18. Research asso. Carnegie Inst., Washington, 1920; prof. astronomy, Columbia U., summer 1923. Conglist. (Unitarian). Fellow Royal Astron. Soc., A.A.A.S. (ex-v.p. sect. D.); mem. Am. Acad. Arts and Sciences, Astronomische Gesellschaft, Société Astronomique de France, Am. Astron. Soc. (ex-v.p.), Internat. Astron. Union, Nat. Research Council (1934-37), Phi Beta Kappa, Sigma Xi, Phi Delta Theta. Author: Stellar Parallaxes From Photographs Made With the 20-inch Refractor of Van Vleck Observatory (with C. L. Stearns and B. W. Sitterly), 1938. Contbr. to Astrophysical Journal and other publs., chiefly as to observations on the sun and to determination of stellar distances. Home: 74 Wyllys Av., Middletown, Conn. Died Dec. 4, 1944.

SLOAN, Laurence Henry, economist and editor; b. Spencer, Ind., Apr. 29, 1889; s. Albert F. and Martha Henry (Wiles) S.; A.B., De Pauw U., Greencastle, Ind., 1912; student Columbia U. Sch. of Journalism, 1912-13; m. Florence Margarett Black, Oct. 14, 1915; 1 dau., Martha Lucy. Reporter and sub-editor N.Y. American, 1913-16; reporter and night city editor, N.Y. Tribune, 1916-18; advertising manager and assistant economist, Nat. City Bank of N.Y., 1918-21; v.p., director Standard Statistics Co., Standard & Poor's Corp., New York, since 1921. Trustee Quill Endowment Fund. Member American Statistical Assn., Acad. Polit. Science, Phi Delta Theta, Sigma Delta Chi (co-founder). Republican. Presbyterian. Author: Security Speculation—The Dazzling Adventure, 1926; Corporation Profits, 1929; Everyman and His Common Stocks, 1931; Two Cycles of Corporation Profits, 1936; Postwar Savings and Investments, 1945. Collaborator on numerous other volumes. Home: 2 Bonsilene Av., Woodmont, Conn. Office: 345 Hudson St., N.Y. City. Died May 6, 1949.

SLOAN, Matthew Scott, corp. official; b. Mobile, Ala., Sept. 5, 1881; s. Matthew Scott and Mary Elizabeth (Scott) S.; B.S., Ala. Poly. Inst., Auburn, 1901, M.S., 1902, E.E., 1911, Dr. Eng., 1929; lectures in engring., Union Coll., Schenectady, N.Y.; m. Lottie Everard Lane, Feb. 23, 1911; 1 dau., Lidie Lane (Mrs. Andrew M. McBurney, Jr.). With Gen. Electric Co., Schenectady, N.Y., 1902-06; with Birmingham (Ala.) Ry., Light & Power Co., 1906-14, chief engr. to asst. to pres. with supervision over all depts.; v.p. and gen. mgr. New Orleans Ry. & Light Co., 1914-17; asst. to v.p. and gen. mgr. New York Edison Co., 1917-19, pres., 1928-32; also pres. United Electric Light & Power Co., New York & Queens Electric Light & Power Co. and Yonkers Electric Light & Power Co., 1928-32, Brooklyn Edison Co., Inc., 1919-32, Amsterdam Electric Light, Heat & Power Co., 1920-32, Edison Construction Co., Inc., 1923-32; treas. Electrical Testing Labs., 1919-32; chmn. bd. and president Missouri-Kansas-Texas R.R. Co.; pres. and dir. Wichita Falls Ry., San Antonio Belt & Terminal Ry., M.K.T. R.R. Co. of Texas, Beaver, Meade & Englewood Railroad Company, Texas Central Railroad, Wichita Falls & N.-W. Ry., Wichita Falls & Wellington Ry., M.K. &T. Transportation Company (St. Louis); director Galveston, Houston & Henderson Rail Road Company, Missouri & Illinois Bridge & Belt R.R. Co., Terminal R.R. Assn. of St. Louis, Pacific Southern Investors, Inc., Chrysler Corp., Continental Can Co., Globe & Rutgers Fire Insurance Company, Overseas Securities Company, Inc., American Home Fire Assurance Company; trustee Bowery Savings Bank, American Surety Co. of New York. Clubs: University, City, Recess, Kappa Alpha Southern Club (New York); Lake Placid (N.Y.); Burning Tree Golf (Bethesda, Md.); Noonday (St. Louis, Mo.). Home: 2 Montague Terrace, Brooklyn, N.Y. Office: 25 Broad St., New York. Died June 14, 1945; buried at Auburn, Ala.

SLOPER, Leslie Akers (slō-per), newspaperman; b. East Pepperell, Mass., May 31, 1883; son of Rev. Phineas Cone and Carrie Eliza (Marsh) S.; B.A., Harvard, 1906; married Margaret Thayer, Apr. 3, 1915; children—Elizabeth, John Thayer, Anne. Editorial staffs newspapers and mags. in Boston, Montreal, Toronto and Washington, D.C.; spl. writer Bur. of Information, U.S. Dept. of Labor, 1918; with Christian Science Monitor since 1919, music editor since 1922, literary editor, 1924-1944, dramatic and art editor since 1929. Contbr. to mags. Home: 46 Garrison Rd., Brookline 46, Mass. Address: One, Norway St., Boston 15, Mass. Died Nov. 13, 1949.

SLOSSON, Leonard B(utler) (slŏs'ŭn), lawyer; b. Sabetha, Kan., Apr. 13, 1875; s. Willis Merton and Marian Ella (Butler) S.; grad. Mich. Mil. Acad., Orchard Lake, 1893; private study and instrn. Lansing, Mich.; m. Elvinia J. Jackson, Jan. 15, 1907. In practice of law at Los Angeles, Calif., since 1904; mem. Farrand & Slosson, 1921-40. Mem. Am. Bar Assn., State Bar of Calif. (pres. 1930-31). Republican. Mason. Clubs: University, California, Beach, Los Angeles Country. Home: 426 S. Arden Blvd. Office: 215 W. 6th St., Los Angeles, Calif. Died June 4, 1946.

SMALL, Ernest Gregor, naval officer; b. Feb. 15, 1888; entered U.S. Navy, 1907, and advanced through the grades to rear adm., 1942. Decorated Distinguished Service Medal, Navy Cross, Legion of Merit (2). Address: Navy Dept., Washington 25. Died Dec. 26, 1944; buried in Arlington National Cemetery.

SMALL, Harold Patten, lawyer; b. New London, Conn., Mar. 31, 1888; s. Robert Henry and Katie (Patten) S.; student Amherst Coll., 1907-09; LL.B., Yale Law Sch., 1912; m. Elizabeth Gordon, Sept. 8, 1923; children—Gordon Patten, Nancy Elizabeth, Robert Keeney. Admitted to Conn. bar, 1913, Mass. bar, 1914; mem. firm Wooden & Small, later Wooden, Small & Mallory; now mem. Small & Brooks. Served as ensign, U.S.N.R.F., 1917-19. Mem. City Council, Springfield, Mass., 1917, asst. city solicitor, 1919-20; mem. Sch. Bd., Town of Longmeadow, Mass., since 1936. Mem. Am. and Mass. bar assns., Bar Assn. of Hampden County. Republican. Conglist. Mason. Clubs: Colony, The Club, Century (Springfield); Tunxis (Tolland, Mass.); Longmeadow (Mass.) Country. Home: 129 Farmington Av., Longmeadow, Mass. Office: 1387 Main St., Springfield, Mass. Died Jan. 1, 1943.

SMALL, John Humphrey, ex-congressman; b. Washington, N.C.; s. John Humphrey and Sally A. (Sanderson) S.; ed. Trinity Coll. (now Duke U.), N.C.; m. Isabella C. Wharton, June, 1890; children—Mary Belle (wife of H. C. Neblett, M.D.), Katherine (wife of Dr. J. S. Gaul), John Humphrey. Taught sch., 1876-80; admitted to the bar, 1881; reading clerk, N.C. Senate, 1881; supt. public instr., Beaufort County, 1881; solicitor Inferior Ct., Beaufort County, 1882-85; propr. and editor Washington (N. C.) Gazette, 1883-86; atty. bd. of commrs., Beaufort County, 1888-96; mem. city council, 1887-90, and 1 yr. mayor Washington, N.C.; Dem. presdl. elector, 1896; mem. 56th to 66th Congresses (1899-1921), 1st N.C. Dist.; was mem. legal staff Securities and Exchange Commn., Washington, resigned June 30, 1937; practiced law with son as Small & Small, Charlotte, N. Carolina, 1937-39. Chairman Dem. Exec. Com., Beaufort County, 1889-98. Advocated and secured inland waterway from Norfolk, Va., to Beaufort Inlet, N.C., and is interested in constrn. and extension of other inland waterways; pres. Nat. Rivers and Harbors Congress; chmn. Com. on Rivers and Harbors, 65th Congress; v.p. Atlantic Deeper Waterways Assn. Clubs: Cosmos (Washington, D.C.); Town Hall (New York). Home: 428 W. Main St. Office: Washington, N.C. Died July 13, 1946.

SMALL, Vivian Blanche, coll. pres.; b. Gardiner, Me., Sept. 17, 1875; d. Leander Marshall and Annie Blanche (Payne) S.; B.A., Mt. Holyoke Coll., 1896, Litt.D., 1912; M.A., U. of Chicago, 1905; LL.D., Western Reserve U., 1913. Asst. in high sch., Gorham, Me., 1896-98, Howe Sch., Billerica, Mass., 1898-1901; asst. in Latin, 1901-02, instr., 1902-08, asso. prof. Latin, 1908-09, head of Mead Hall, 1907-09, Mt. Holyoke Coll.; pres. Lake Erie Coll., since July 1, 1909. Conglist. Home: Painesville, O. Died May 15, 1946.

SMALL, Willard Stanton, teacher; b. N. Truro, Mass., Aug. 24, 1870; s. Thomas Kenney and Maria Jerusha (Baldwin) S.; A.B., Tufts Coll., 1894, A.M., 1897; Tufts Theol. Sch., 1894-96; Clark U., 1897-1900, Ph.D., 1900; m. Harriet Alice Turner, Dec. 27, 1899; children—Willard Stanton, John Robinson. Prof. English, Lombard Coll., 1896-97; prof. psychology, Mich. State Normal Coll., 1901-02; prof. psychology and dir. of training, State Normal Sch., Los Angeles, Calif., 1902-04; supt. city schs., San Diego, Calif., 1904-05; prin. Eastern High Sch., Washington, 1906-18; spl. agt., 1915-18, specialist in sch. hygiene, 1918-20 and 1921-22, U.S. Bur. of Edn., Washington; dir. ednl. research, Interdepartmental Social Hygiene Bd., 1920-21; dean Coll. of Edn., U. of Md., 1923-40, dean emeritus since 1940. Lecturer edn., George Washington U., 1907-22; expert adviser financial statistics of schs., 13th Census; lecture sch. administration, Johns Hopkins Summer Sch., 1912-14 and 1916, 17. Mem. N.E.A., Delta Upsilon, Phi Beta Kappa, Phi Kappa Phi, Omicron Delta Kappa. Universalist. Contbr. to ednl. mags. Author numerous govt. reports. Home: 31 White St., South Weymouth, Mass. Died Jan. 31, 1943; buried at North Truro, Mass.

SMALLWOOD, William Martin, coll. prof.; b. Warsaw, N.Y., Apr. 30, 1873; s. William Waltrous and Eloise (Martin) S.; A.B., Syracuse U., 1896, A.M., 1897; Ph.D., Harvard Univ., 1902; honorary Sc.D., Syracuse University, 1943; m. Mabel Sarah Coon, Sept. 6, 1899. Instr. biology, Syracuse U., 1896-98; prof. biology and geology, Allegheny (Pa.) College, 1898-1902; asst. prof. zoölogy, Syracuse Univ., 1903-07, prof. comparative anatomy, 1907, and head department zoölogy, 1921-43, professor emeritus comparative anatomy since 1943. Fellow A.A.A.S., mem. N.Y. State Science Teachers' Assn. (pres., 1909), Am. Zoöl. Soc., Phi Beta Kappa, Sigma Xi, Phi Kappa Psi. Republican. Methodist. Author: Syllabus of Lectures on Animal Biology, 1908; Textbook on Biology, 1913, 6th edit., 1930; Practical Biology, 1916; Biology for High Schools, 1920; Man—the Animal, 1921, 27; The New Biology, 1924; New General Biology, 1929; New Biology, 1934; Natural History and the American Mind (with Mabel C. Smallwood), 1941. Contbr. to scientific jours. Awarded the Arents Medal, June 1939. Home: 525 Euclid Av., Syracuse 10, N.Y. Died Nov. 20, 1949.

SMART, E(dmund) Hodgson, artist; b. Alnwick, Eng., Mar. 12, 1873; s. George Stott and Jane Anne (Watson) S.; ed. Antwerp Acad., Acad. Julian, Paris, and under Sir Hubert von Herkomer; m. Catherine Gordon Mackay, Feb. 1896. Exhibited Royal Acad., London; Paris Salon; etc.; has traveled widely and painted portraits in various countries; came to U.S., 1916. Prin. works: Portraits of King Edward and Queen Alexandra; Mrs. Annie Besant; President Warren Harding (in Nat. Gallery, Washington, D.C.); Marshal Foch (in Cleveland Mus. Art); Gen. John J. Pershing; Admiral William S. Sims; Sir Robert L. Borden; Newton D. Baker; Dr. Francis L. Patton, emeritus pres. Princeton; Sir Arthur Currie, pres. McGill U.; etc. Address: 9192 Beverly Blvd., Beverly Hills, Calif.; also Princess Hotel, Bermuda.* Died Nov. 16, 1942.

SMEALLIE, John Morris, navy officer; b. Sept. 5, 1886; promoted through grades to rear adm., June 23, 1938.† Died Nov. 24, 1947.

SMILEY, Charles Newton, prof. Latin; b. Hamilton, Mo., Jan. 4, 1873; s. Charles N. and Ellen Louisa (Flagg) S.; A.B., Drury Coll., Mo., 1897, L.H.D., 1922; A.M., Harvard, 1903; Ph.D., U. of Wis., 1905; studied U. of Berlin, 1909-10; m. Bertha Kathleen Shutts, Aug. 23, 1916. Instr. Greek and Latin, Drury Acad., 1897-1902; teaching fellow in Greek, U. of Wis., 1903-04; instr. Latin, U. of Wis., 1904-05; Benedict prof. Latin, Grinnell Coll., 1905-26; prof. Latin, Carleton Coll., 1926-40; lecturer summers, Harvard, Columbia, 1926-37, univs. of Wis., Ill. and Ia.; chmn. dept. classics, summer session, U. of Wis., 1923. Mem. editorial bd. Richards Cyclopædia. Mem. Classical Assn. Middle West and South (pres. 1917), Am. Philol. Assn., Am. Assn. Univ. Profs., Phi Beta Kappa. Wrote: Latinitas and Hellenismos; The Stoic Theory of Literary Style. Contbr. to philol., archeol. and lit. mags. Knighted by the Italian Government for services as regional dir. Y.M.C.A. with Italian Army, 1918-19. Home: Northfield, Minn. Died Feb. 8, 1943.

SMILEY, John Stanley, judge Supreme Court of Nova Scotia; b. Milltown, New Brunswick, Jan. 20, 1885; s. John and Flora Elizabeth (McKenzie) S.; B.A., Mount Allison Univ., Sackville, N.B., 1907, M.A., 1909; LL.B., Dalhousie Law Sch., Halifax, N.S., 1912; m. Celia Ganong Kierstead, Aug. 24, 1909: children—Muriel Kierstead, John McKenzie (deceased). Began as school teacher, Aug. 1902; called to Nova Scotia bar, May 7, 1912; apptd. King's counsel by Provincial Govt., 1922; practiced law, Amherst, N.S., 1912-38; apptd. judge of the Supreme Court of Nova Scotia, Sept. 1938. Mem. N.S. Assembly (Liberal) for Cumberland County, 1933-37; former pres. Amherst Bd. of Trade; former Mem. Bd. of Regents, Mt. Allison Univ. Mem. Canadian Bar Assn. Clubs: Halifax Rotary, Halifax Canadian; former pres. Amherst Canadian Club. Mason. Mem. United Ch. of Can. (elder). Home: 247 Jubilee Rd. Address: Judge's Chambers, Law Courts, Halifax, Nova Scotia, Can. Died Aug. 21, 1945.

SMILEY, William Henry, supt. emeritus pub. schs.; b. Malden, Mass., Apr. 28, 1854; s. Henry Lyman and Mina Abigail (Grover) S.; A.B., Harvard, 1877; A.M. (hon.), U. of Denver, 1906; Litt.D., Colo. Coll., 1913; LL.D., U. of Colorado, 1913, U. of Denver, 1914; m. Mary S. Chandler, June 26, 1884. Prin. New Salem Acad., Sept. 1877; instr. Latin and Greek, St. John's (boys') Sch., Boston, 1880; prin. Jarvis Hall, boys' sch., Denver, 1883-86; instr. Latin and Greek, Denver High Sch., dist. No. 1, 1886-92, prin., 1892-1912; supt. pub. schs., City and County of Denver, 1912-15; supervisor, high school education, same, 1915-16, asst. supt. of schools, 1917-23, supt. emeritus since 1924. Mem. Conf. on Secondary Instrn. in Greek, U. of Mich., Dec. 1892; mem. N.E.A. (pres. dept. secondary edn., 1895; sec. com. on coll. entrance requirements, rep. pub., 1899; v.p. dept. higher edn., 1902, dept. secondary edn., 1904); mem. com. Nat. Council Edn., of N.E.A., 1909; pres. Ednl. Council of Colo.; mem. Art Commn. City and County of Denver, 1906-12; pres. Colo. State Teachers' Assn., 1907; mem. Nat. Inst. Social Sciences, Denver Art Museum Assn. Trustee Colo. Sch. of Mines, 1922-27, pres. of bd. since 1925. Clubs: University, Mile High, Kiwanis, Cactus, City, Colo. Schoolmasters. Home: 1115 Race St., Denver. Died March 24, 1934.

SMITH, Abiel Leonard, army officer; b. Fayette, Howard County, Mo., July 14, 1857; s. Joseph D. and Martha (Leonard) S.; grad. U.S. Mil. Acad., 1878; Army War Coll., 1914; m. Florence Compton, June 19, 1890; children—Abiel Leonard, Dorothy, Charles Compton, Margaret. Commd. 2d lt. 19th Inf., June 28, 1878; brig. general, Sept. 22, 1916; retired Jan. 3, 1918. Participated in campaigns against Indians, 1878-86; Spanish-Am. War, 1898; also in World War. Brevetted capt., Feb. 27, 1890, "for gallant and meritorious service" in Geronimo Campaign, 1886. Episcopalian. Home: Carmel, N.Y.* Died Apr. 24, 1946.

SMITH, Addison R(omain), ry. official; b. Louisville, Ky., Mar. 30, 1872; s. Horace F. and Jane (Davis) S.; ed. pub. schs.; m. Nellie S. Escott, Apr. 15, 1895; children—Horace F., Addison E., Frances E. Filled various clerical positions, L.&N. R.R., 1890-97; chief clk. to mgr. Asheville line, 1897-98; sec. Southeastern Miss. Valley Assn., 1898-99; chief clk. Western Traffic offices Southern Ry., 1899-1903; gen. freight agt. Atlanta & West Point R.R. and Western Ry. of Ala., 1904-05; 3d v.p. L.&N. R.R. Co., 1905-18; asst. regional dir. Southern Region, U.S.R R. Administration, 1918-20; v.p. L.&N. R R. Co. since Mar. 1, 1920 Club: Pendennis. Home: Commodore Apts. Address: Louisville & Nashville R.R. Co., Louisville, Ky.* Died Nov. 5, 1946.

SMITH, Albert William, engineer, educator; b. Westmoreland, Oneida County, N.Y., Aug. 30, 1856; s. William and Caroline Georgiana (Strong) S.; B. M.E., Cornell, 1878, M.M.E., 1886; m. Ruby Green Bell, Aug. 16, 1905; children—Alpheus, Dorothy (Mrs. Harold Raynolds), Ruth Althea (Mrs. Robert P. Ludlum). Asst. prof. mech. engring., Sibley Coll., Cornell U., 1887-91; prof. machine design, U. of Wis., 1891-92; prof. mech. engring., Stanford U., 1892-1904; dir. Sibley Coll., Cornell U., 1904-15, dean, 1915-21, and acting pres. Cornell U., 1920-21 (retired). Mem. Am. Soc. M.E. Author: Elementary Machine Design, 1895; Materials of Machines, 1902, 14; John Edson Sweet, A Biography, 1923; A Biography of Walter Craig Kerr, 1927; A Biography of Ezra Cornell, 1934; Poems, 1934; A Spring Time Odyssey on the Shores of Southern Seas, 1939; Facing Life, 1939. Editor: The Bells of Cornell, 1930; Poems of Cornell, 1941. Home: 13 East Av., Ithaca, N.Y. Died Aug. 10, 1942.

SMITH, Alfred Emanuel, ex-governor; b. New York, N.Y., Dec. 30, 1873; s. Alfred Emanuel and Catherine (Mulvihill) S.; ed. parochial sch.; LL.D., Columbia, Harvard, Fordham University, University of State of New York, Manhattan College, and Dublin University; D.Litt., from Catholic U. of America; m. Catherine A. Dunn, 1900; children—Alfred E., Emily (Mrs. J. A. Warner), Catherine (Mrs. Francis Quillinan), Arthur, Walter. Clerk in office commr. of jurors, N.Y. City, 1895-1903; mem. N.Y. Assembly, 1903-15; became Dem. leader in Assembly, 1911, speaker of Assembly, 1913; del. State Constl. Conv., 1915; sheriff of New York County, 1915-17; pres. Bd. of Aldermen of Greater New York, 1917; gov. of N.Y., 4 terms, 1919-20, and 1923-28; Dem. candidate for President of U.S., 1928; pres. Empire State, Inc.; chmn. bd. Lawyers Trust Co.; dir. N.Y. Life Ins. Co., Knott Hotels Corp.; apptd. a trustee in reorganization of Postal Telegraph and Cable Co. Editor in chief New Outlook (mag.), 1932-34. Sachem of Soc. of Tammany. Catholic; trustee Catholic U. of America since 1933; one of founders of Am. Liberty League. Awarded Laetare medal, U. of Notre Dame, 1929. Clubs: Nat. Democratic, Press (N.Y.); Ft. Orange (Albany); Wolferts Roost Country. Office: Empire State Bldg., New York, N.Y. Died Oct. 4, 1944.

SMITH, Alvin Augustine, clergyman; b. Galena, Ill., Feb. 16, 1884; s. Helmer T. and Martha (Becker) S.; ed. high sch., Chicago, and Wheaton (Ill.) Acad., until 1901; A.B., Wheaton Coll., 1906, D.D., 1928; grad. McCormick Theol. Sem., Chicago, 1909; m. Mildred A. Ferris, May 4, 1909; 1 dau., Mildred Louise. Ordained Presbyn. ministry, 1909; pastor Greenfield, Ia., 1909-17, Grand Island, Neb., 1917-22, Kansas City, Mo., 1922-30, Rogers Park Church, Chicago, since Mar. 1930. Moderator Chicago Presbytery, Presbyn. Ch. in the U.S.A. Mem. bd. dirs. Chicago Christian Industrial League. Mem. bd. dirs. Presbyn. Theol. Sem., Chicago. Home: 1140 Morse Av., Chicago, Ill. Died Aug. 22, 1943.

SMITH, Arthur L. J., publisher, insurance journalist; b. Charleston, S.C., May 31, 1860; s. William Wragg and M. T. S.; g.s. William Loughton S. (representative S.C. in first 5 Congresses, 1879-99); ed. high sch., Astoria, N.Y. Began newspaper work as court reporter in New York; entered office of The Spectator Company, publishers, September 1877; had charge statistical work on paper, later part time, on editorial work, 1877-86; purchased proprietary interest, 1888, becoming business manager and editor The Spectator; president The Spectator Company, 1908, retired, 1929; trustee Dime Savings Bank of Brooklyn; dir. Manhattan Bridge Three Cent Line, Hampton Point Estates Corp. Mem. Chamber Commerce State N.Y. Republican. Clubs: Montauk, Quogue Field Club. Home: Montauk Club, Brooklyn. Office: 102 Maiden Lane, New York. Died Dec. 16, 1946; buried Greenwood Cemetery, Brooklyn, N.Y.

SMITH, Arthur St. Clair, rear admiral; b. Cedar Rapids, Ia., Dec. 31, 1873; s. Arthur St. Clair and Harriet Rogerson (Baker) S.; grad. U.S. Naval Acad., 1899; m. Anne Salley, June 8, 1907; children—Anne St. Clair, Donald Bruce. Commd. ensign U.S. Navy, June 1897, and advanced through grades to capt., June 1921; rear admiral, May 1930. Served in Spanish-Am. War, Philippine Insurrection; comdr. Lafayette Radio Station, Bordeaux, France, 1918-19; commander of Battleship Idaho, 1925-27; chief of staff to comdr. battleships, 1928-29; chief staff to comdr. in chief of Battle Fleet, 1929-30; apptd. comdr. Spl. Service Squadron, Canal Zone, 1930, later apptd. comdt. Norfolk Navy Yard, Portsmouth, Va. Comdr. Battleship Div. 3, Comdt. 12th Naval Dist.; retired Jan. 1, 1938. Awarded 6 campaign badges and medals (U.S.); Officer of Legion of Honor (France). Presbyterian. Clubs: Army and Navy (Washington); University (New York). Home: 6 Southgate Av., Annapolis, Md. Address: Navy Dept., Washington, D.C. Died Mar. 26, 1942.

SMITH, Burton, lawyer; b. Chapel Hill, N C., Sept. 18, 1864; s. Hosea Hildreth (LL.D.) and Mary Brent (Hoke) S.; Master of Instrn., Sam Houston Normal Sch., Huntsville, Tex., 1880; Ph.B., U. of Ga., 1882; m. Frances, d. Gen. J. B. Gordon, June 19, 1888. In law practice at Atlanta, 1883-1917; mem. Bourke Cockran, as trial counsel; in gen. practice in N.Y. for 6 yrs., serving part of time as special deputy attorney general; mem. legal staff of Home Owners' Loan Corp., in charge of preparing legal opinions from May 1934 to Mar. 1938; counsel for New York, Georgia and 20 other states in Washington on federal tax matters. Was formerly captain and adjutant 5th Regiment Infantry, National Guard of Ga., and was on duty in Pittsburgh and Atlanta riots. Pres. Ga. Bar Assn., 1902-03; v.p. Am. Bar Assn., 1900; first pres. and organizer of Atlanta A.C. Democrat. Episcopalian, vestryman of St. Luke's Cathedral, Atlanta. Contbr. to legal publs.; frequently addresses legal bodies. Address: 5000 14th St. N.W., Washington, D.C. Died Oct. 4, 1944.

SMITH, Charles Perley, judge, Tax Court of U.S.; b. Windham, N.H., Dec. 12, 1878; s. Charles and Sarah Jane (Goodwin) S.; A.B., Brown U., 1902; m. Clara Blanche Taplin, May 3, 1905; 1 dau., Marjorie Eloise. Statis. asst. U.S. Bur. of Census, 1905-14; admitted to D.C. bar, 1911, and began practice at Washington; asst. to commr. Internal Revenue, 1921-23; mem. U.S. Tax Simplification Bd., 1921-24; member United States Board of Tax Appeals (now Tax Ct. of the United States) 1924-34, reappointed, 1934, for term ending 1946; mem. of Excess Profits Tax Council, Bureau of Internal Revenue, Washington, D.C. since 1946. Republican. Episcopalian. Mason. Home: 3817 Kanawha St. N.W. Office: Internal Revenue Bldg., Washington, D.C. Died July 6, 1948.

SMITH, Chester C(linton), public utilities; b. Kansas City, Mo., June 12, 1888; s. Henry and Varina (Courtney) S.; ed. high school, Kansas City, Mo., and Kansas City Sch. of Law (now part of Univ. of Kansas City); m. Eva Madeline Snow, December 25, 1920; 1 dau., Virginia Anne. With Public Utilities Commn., Kansas City, Mo., 1910-12; accountant with Bion J. Arnold, 1912-14; asst. to pres. Kansas City Rys. Co., 1914-18; with Kansas City Power & Light Co. since 1919, as sec. 1920-24, v.p. and sec., 1924-38, president since 1938, also director; director United Light & Rys. Co., Continental Gas & Electric Corp., Business Men's Assurance Co. Dir. Kansas City War Chest Fund, Kansas City chapter of Am. Red Cross; trustee Kansas City Conservatory of Music; honorary director Rockhurst College; Trustee Kansas City Art Institute. Member Kansas City (Missouri) Chamber of Commerce (former vice-pres.; mem. industrial and trade development com.), also mem. Chambers of Commerce of Kansas City, Kan., and North Kansas City. Trustee Midwest Research Institute. Member Real Estate Board of Kansas City, Mo., Mo. Assn. Pub. Utilities (exec. com.), Missouri Valley Electric Association (exec. com.), Electric Assn. of Kansas City, Nat. Assn. Mfrs., Citizen Hist. Assn., Patriots and Pioneers Memorial Assn., Sons of the American Revolution, Assn. of Edison Illuminating Companies, Edison Elec. Inst., American, Missouri and Kansas City bar assns., Army Ordnance Assn., Nat. Industrial Conf. Bd., Navy League of U.S., Am. Legion. Member Country Club Christian Church. Clubs: Engineers, Kansas City, Kansas City Athletic, Saddle and Sirloin, Mission Hills Country, Native Sons of Kansas City, Quarter Century Club of Kansas City Power & Light Co. Home: 1259 Stratford Road. Office: 1330 Baltimore Av., Kansas City, Mo. Died Jan. 24, 1947.

SMITH, Clifford P(abody), editor; b. Geneva, Ind., Mar. 4, 1869; s. Joseph Benson and Amelia (Pabody) S.; LL. B., State U. of Ia., 1891; m. Myrtle Holm, Jan. 31, 1900; 1 dau., Mrs. Winter Dean. Admitted to Ia. bar, 1891; Mass. bar, 1908; judge Dist. Court, Ia., 1900-08; 1st reader First Ch. of Christ, Scientist, Boston, 1908-11, pres. 1911-12 and 1937-38; mem. Board of Lectureship, 1911-14; mgr. Com. on Publication, 1914-29; editor Christian Science periodicals, 1930-32; editor Bureau of History since 1932. Home: 196 Kent Rd., Waban 68, Mass. Office: 107 Falmouth St., Boston, Mass. Died Aug. 9, 1945.

SMITH, Dan Morgan, lecturer, soldier, lawyer; b. Orange, Va., Oct. 2, 1873; s. Dan Morgan (M.D.) and DeLacy (Cave) S.; cadet Fla. State Coll. (now U. of Fla.), and under pvt. teacher 6 yrs.; m. Frances McKinney, Dec. 27, 1897. Admitted to bar, Fla., 1892, Ga., 1897, Ill., 1899, U.S. Supreme Court, 1908; Dem. nominee for Congress, 3d Ill. Dist., 1902; spl. asst. corp. counsel, City of Chicago, 1905-06; judge adv. State of Ill., 1914-16; spl. asst. U.S. atty., 1915-16. Engaged in "gun running" for Cubans; lt. Fla. Nat. Guard, 1891-98; 1st lt. 3d U.S.V. during Spanish-Am. War; lt., capt., maj., Ill. Nat. Guard, 1900-17; served on Mexican border as capt. Co. D, 7th Ill. Nat. Guard, 1916-17; enlisted as pvt., United States Army, 1917; commd. maj. inf., September 15, 1917; assigned to 357th Inf. and sent to France; major commanding "Battalion of Death" (1st Battalion) 358 Infantry, 90th Division; participated in St. Mihiel drive, Fey en Haye, Hill 350.4, Vilsey, Les Quatres Chemins, Les Huit Chemins, Prany, Meuse-Argonne, Verdun sector Argonne Forest; twice wounded; promoted lt. col. "for gallantry in action"; commd. col. of inf., R.C., Army of U.S. Grad. Am. Field Officers' Sch., Langres, France. Mem. S.R., Veterans of Foreign Wars, Am. Legion, Army Assn. of United States. Author of short stories and treatises—"America," "The Constitution," "Who's Running This Country?" etc. Lecturer on "Better Americanism," "Courage or Cowardice," etc. Home: Nuestro Ranchito. Covina Highlands, Covina, Calif. Died Dec. 8, 1947.

SMITH, David Eugene, mathematician; b. Cortland, N.Y., Jan. 21, 1860; s. Hon. Abram P. and Mary E. (Bronson) S.; Ph.D., Syracuse U., 1881, Ph.M., 1884, Ph.D., 1887, LL.D., 1905; Master of Pedagogics, Mich. State Normal Coll., 1898; student in Europe at various times, also 1907-08; D Sc., Columbia University, 1929; L.H.D., Yeshiva Coll., 1936; m. Fanny Taylor, Jan. 19, 1887; m. 2d, Eva May Luse, November 5, 1940. Practiced law at Cortland, 1881-84; taught mathematics, State Normal Sch., Cortland, 1884-91; prof. mathematics, Mich. State Normal Coll., 1891-98; prin. N.Y. State Normal Sch., Brockport, 1898-1901; prof. mathematics, Teachers Coll. (Columbia), 1901-26 (emeritus). Librarian, 1902-20, v.p., 1922, and asso. editor Bull. of Am. Math. Soc., 1902-20; math. editor New Internat. Ency., 1902-16, Monroe's Cyclo. of Education, 1911-13, New Practical Reference Library, 1912, Ency. Britannica, 1927, Nat. Ency., 1933; asso. editor Am. Mathematical Monthly since 1916, Scripta Mathematica since 1932. Vice-pres. Internat. Commn. on the Teaching of Mathematics, 1908-20, pres., 1928-32, hon. pres. since 1932. Fellow Mediæval Acad. America, A.A.A.S.; mem. Math. Assn. America (pres. 1920-21), History and Science Soc. (pres. 1927), Am. Math. Soc., Deutsche Math. Verein, Phi Beta Kappa, Psi Upsilon, Pi Nu Epsilon, etc.; hon. mem. Calcutta Math. Soc. Trustee Lingnan U., China. Decorated Gold Star, Order of Elmi, by Persian Govt., 1933. Author: History of Modern Mathematics, 1896; Teaching of Elementary Mathematics, 1900; Rara Arithmetica, 1907; Teaching of Arithmetic, 1909, 13; Teaching of Geometry, 1911; Hindu-Arabic Numerals (with L. C. Karpinski), 1911; History of Japanese Mathematics, 1912; Union List of Mathematical Periodicals (with C. E. Seely), 1918; Number Stories of Long Ago, 1919; The Sumario Compendioso of Juan Diez, 1920; Our Indebtedness to Greece and Rome in Mathematics, 1922; Essentials of Geometry, 1923; Historical-Mathematical Paris, 1924; Mathematics Gothica, 1925; History of

Mathematics (2 vols.), 1924, 25; Progress of Arithmetic in 25 years, 1924; Progress of Algebra in 25 years, 1925; Computing Jetons, 1924; Teaching of Junior High School Mathematics (with W. D. Reeve), 1927; Le Comput Manuel de Magister Anianus, 1928; Source Book in Mathematics, 1929; History of American Mathematics Before 1900 (with J. Ginsburg), 1934; The Rubáiyát of Omar Khayyam (metrical version), 1933; Poetry of Mathematics and Other Essays, 1934; Numbers and Numerals (with J. Ginsburg), 1937; The Wonderful Wonders of 1, 2, 3, 1937; also over 40 math. textbooks and many articles in various journals. Translator: Descartes's La Géométrie, 1925. Editor: A Portfolio of Portraits of Eminent Mathematicians, Part I, 1905, Part II, 1906, high school edit., 1907; DeMorgan's Budget of Paradoxes (2 vols.), 1915; Portraits of Eminent Mathematicians, Portfolio I, 1936, Portfolio II, 1937; Firdausi Celebration, 1936. Extensive traveler; book collector. Address: 501 W. 120th St., New York, N.Y. Died July 29, 1944.

SMITH, David Stanley, coll. prof.; b. Toledo, O., July 6, 1877; s. William H. H. and Julia Welles (Griswold) S.; B.A., Yale, 1900, Mus.B., 1903, M.A., 1916; studied under Horatio Parker, and later for 2 yrs. abroad; hon. Mus.D., Northwestern U., 1918, Cincinnati Conservatory Music, 1927; m. Cora Deming Welch, 1913; 1 son, Christopher Stanley. Instr. theory of music, 1903-09, Yale asst. prof., 1909-16, prof., 1916-25, dean Sch. of Music, 1920-40, Battell prof. of Music since 1925, Yale; asso. fellow, Berkeley Coll., Yale, since 1936. Conductor New Haven Symphony Orchestra since 1919. Fellow Am. Guild of Organists; mem. Nat. Inst. Arts and Letters, Am. Acad. Arts and Sciences, Alpha Delta Phi, Elizabethan Club, etc. Clubs: Century (New York); Graduate, Elihu, New Haven Lawn. Composer of symphonic chamber and ch. music, Quartet in E minor, op. 19; Symphony No. 1, in F minor, op. 28; "Prince Hal" overture, op. 31; "Rhapsody of St. Bernard," for chorus and orchestra, op. 38, perf. at Chicago North Shore Festival, 1918; Symphony No. 2, in D major, op. 42; "Impressions," orchestral suite, op. 40; Quartet in C, op. 46; Fête Galante, op. 48; Sonata for violin and piano, op. 51; Cathedral Prelude, for organ and orchestra, op. 54; Quintet in E flat, op. 56; Epic Poem, for orchestra, op. 55; Quartet in E flat, op. 57; Vision of Isaiah, for chorus and orchestra, op. 58; Sonata, for violoncello and piano, op. 59; Symphony in C Minor, op. 60; Piano Sonata in A Flat, op. 61; Quartet in D, op. 62; String Sextet, op. 63; a Satire, for orchestra, op. 66, No. 1; Tomorrow, overture, op. 66, No. 2; Concerto, for violin and orchestra, op. 69; Quartet No. 6, op. 71; Rondo Appassionato, for violin and orchestra, op. 73; Quartet No. 8, op. 77; Symphony No. 4, op. 78; Quartet No. 9, op. 80; Requiem, for Violin and Orchestra, opus 81; Dramatic Fantasy for Piano, op. 82; "Credo," Poem for Orchestra, op. 83; Sonata for Clarinet and Piano, op. 84; Concerto No. 2 for Violin and Orchestra, op. 86; Compositions for Piano, op. 87; Four Pieces for String Orchestra, op. 89; Quartet No. 10, op. 90; "The Apostle," for orchestra, op. 92; also much music in smaller forms. Guest conductor various orchestras. Home: Fairgrounds Rd., Woodbridge, Conn. Address: Yale School of Music, New Haven, Conn. Died Dec. 17, 1949.

SMITH, Edward Grandison, lawyer; b. Horse Run, Harrison County, W.Va., Apr. 8, 1868; s. Thomas Marion and Amy Minerva (Hoff) S.; LL.B., W.Va. Univ., 1889, LL.D., 1932; LL.B., Washington and Lee, 1892; LL.D., Salem (W.Va.) Coll., 1911; m. Jessie Blackshere, Oct. 18, 1899; children—John Blackshere, Jill. In practice of law at Clarksburg, W.Va., 1892-1937. Dem. nominee for judge Supreme Court of Appeals, 1912; del. to Dem. Nat. Conv., 1920; spl. atty. U.S. Dept. Justice, 1935-36; trial examiner Nat. Labor Relations Board in the U.S. Stamping Co., Washington Mfg. Co. and Weirton Steel Company cases, 1937; on regular trial examining staff, National Labor Relations Board, 1937-43; atty. in legal research, trial examining division since 1942; member of College of Electors of Hall of Fame, New York University, 1935 and 1940. Member bd. govs. W.Va. U., 1927-38, pres. bd., 1927-38. Mem. W.Va. Bar Assn. (chmn. com. on legal history until 1938), Am. Law Inst., S.R., S.A.R. (pres. W.Va. Soc., 1938-40), W.Va. U. Alumni Assn. (ex-pres.), Phi Delta Theta, Phi Delta Phi, Phi Beta Kappa, Order of Coif, Scabbard and Blade. Mason, Elk (life mem.). Has written The Plutocrat, 1892; Our Judiciary, 1912; Needs of the University, 1913; Power Dams in Public Waters, 1914; Liberation, 1919; Price Regulation by Legislative Power, 1921; A Stonewall Phase, 1925; Judicial Law, 1928; The Amendment Tax Limitation of W.Va. of 1932: Incidentally Non Justiciable Constitutional Questions Involved, 1933; Our Changing Constitution, 1934; Six Reasons for Supporting the President, 1936; Federal Measure of the Constitutionality of a Statute, 1936-37; The President's Supreme Court Proposal, 1937; Fundamentals, 1938; The Sit Down, 1939; The True Measure for Proposed Amendments to the National Labor Relations Act, 1939; Intermediate Reports to Nat. Labor Relations Bd., Cases Heard up to Dec. 1, 1942, 1942; The Closed Shop and The National Labor Relations Act, 1943. Home: East Cottage, Dixie Farm, West Milford, W.Va. Deceased.

SMITH, Edward North, judge; b. Little Falls, N.Y., Nov. 30, 1868; s. Hannibal and Amelia C. (Marsh) S.; B.A., Hamilton Coll., 1890, M.A., 1893, LL.D., 1927; LL.B., Buffalo Law School, 1892; m. Alice Lamon Powers, Jan. 2, 1894 (died May 29, 1906); 1 son, Chard Powers; m. 2d, Marion E. Ward, Apr. 16, 1923. Admitted to N.Y. bar, 1892, and began practice at Watertown; mem. Smith & Smith until 1899, Smith & Reeves, 1899-1906, Smith & Phelps, 1906-23; served as city atty., Watertown; chmn. Rep. County Com., Jefferson County, 1895-96; del. N.Y. Constl. Com., 1915; mem. Bd. of Edn., Watertown, 8 yrs., pres. 4 yrs.; apptd. justice Supreme Court of N.Y., 5th Jud. Dist., Dec. 30, 1922, to fill vacancy; nominated and elected on both Rep. and Dem. tickets, same office, 1924, reëlected, 1937, retired by age limitation, Dec. 31, 1938; official referee of Supreme Court since 1939. Largely responsible for preparation of Constl. Amendment, 1913, and Ch. 662 Laws, 1915, authorizing regulation of flow of the rivers of N.Y. State. Mem. Jefferson County Hist. Soc., Phi Beta Kappa, Psi Upsilon. Presbyterian. Mason, Odd Fellow. Clubs: Black River Valley, Lincoln League. Home: Watertown, N.Y. Died Mar. 25, 1943.

SMITH, Egbert Watson, clergyman; b. Greensboro, N.C., Jan. 15, 1862; s. Rev. J. Henry and Mary Kelly (Watson) S.; A.B., Davidson Coll., N.C., 1882; grad. Union Theol. Sem., Va., 1886; (D.D., Davidson, 1894); m. Mary Wallace, Apr. 15, 1891; children—Margaret Heiskell, Egbert Watson, Jessie Wallace, Marion Wallace. Ordained Presbyn. ministry, 1886; became supt. of evangelistic work, N.C. Synod, 1891; pastor First Ch., Greensboro, N.C., 1893-1905, Second Ch., Louisville, Ky., 1906-11; sec. of foreign missions of Presbyterian Ch. in U.S., Nashville, since July 1, 1911. Author: The Creed of Presbyterians, 1901, rev. and enlarged edit., 1941; Present Day Japan, 1920; Manual for Missionaries on Furlough, 1921; Manual for New Missionaries, 1921; The Desire of All Nations, 1928; Christ and Latin America, 1935. Address: 113 16th Av. S., Nashville, Tenn. Died Aug. 25, 1944.

SMITH, E(lias) A(nthon) Cappelen, metall. engr.; b. Trondhjem, Norway, Nov. 6, 1873; s. Elias Anthon and Anna T. (Rovig) S.; grad. Tech. Coll., Trondhjem, Norway, 1893; m. Mary Ellen Condon (died 1927); m. 2d, Carmen Arlegui. Asst. chemist Armour & Co., Chicago, 1893-95; chemist Chicago Copper Refining Co., 1895-96; supt. of electrolytic copper refinery, Anaconda Copper Mining Co., Mont., 1896-1900; metall. engr. in charge metall. operations, Baltimore Copper Smelting & Rolling Co., 1901-10; cons. metall. engr. Am. Smelting & Refining Co., New York, 1910-12; cons. metall. engr. Guggenheim Bros. of New York, Chile Exploration Co., Braden Copper Co., 1912-25; mem. Guggenheim Bros., since 1925; v.p. and dir. Peirce-Smith Converter Co. (holder of patent on his method of copper converting) since 1908; pres. and dir. Minerec Corp.; dir. Chilean Nitrate Sales Corp., Anglo-Chilean Nitrate Corp., Lautaro Nitrate Co., Ltd., Cia. Salitrera Anglo Chilena, Pacific Tin Corp. Trustee Am. Scandinavian Foundation, New York. Awarded gold medal of Mining and Metall. Soc. of America for distinguished service in art of hydrometallurgy, 1920; decorated Knight Comdr., 1st class, Order of St. Olaf by King of Norway, 1925; Commendador, Order Al Merito, 1943 (highest civilian decoration of government of Chile). Member Mining and Metallurgical Society America, Am. Inst. Mining and Metallurgical Engineers, Royal Norwegian Scientific Society. Clubs: Piping Rock, Bankers; Embassy (London); Nordmands-Forbundet, Norske Selskab (Norway). Inventor of extraction method in use at Chuquicamata plant of Chile Exploration Co., Chile; originator of Guggenheim method of extracting nitrate from caliche. Office: 120 Broadway, New York, N.Y. Died June 25, 1949.

SMITH, Elliott, astronomer; b. Blue Earth County, Minn., Jan. 19, 1875; s. Frank Y. and Harriet Amanda (Cornish) S.; A.B., U. of Minn., 1903; student U. of Calif., 1905-06; Ph.D., U. of Cincinnati, 1910; m. Louise Josephine Strautman, Nov. 28, 1908; children—Harriet Louise (Mrs. Paul Herget), Stephen E. Asst. in astronomy, U. of Minn., Licks Obs., 1903-05; fellow, U. of Calif., 1905-06; asst. in obs., Univ. of Cincinnati, 1907-10; asst. prof. astronomy, U. of Cincinnati, 1910-20, associate, 1920-36, prof. since 1936, prof. and dir. of obs. since 1940. Served as pvt. Co. D, 12th Minn. Vol. Inf., U.S. Army, Spanish-Am. War. Mem. A.A.A.S., Am. Astron. Soc., Astron. Soc. of the Pacific, Ohio Soc., Sons of the Am. Revolution, Phi Beta Kappa, Sigma Xi. Presbyterian. Clubs: Schoolmasters, Torch (Cincinnati). Author: Catalog of Proper Motion Stars (with others), 1916, 1930; A Catalog of 4,683 Stars Observed by Elliott Smith, 1922; The Luminosity of Meteors and Comets, 1940. Home: 3264 Observatory Av., Cincinnati, O. Died Sep. 29, 1943.

SMITH, Ellison DuRant, senator; b. Lynchburg, S.C., Aug. 1, 1864; s. Rev. William H. and Mary Isabella (McLeod) S.; student U. of S.C.; A.B., Wofford Coll., S.C., 1889; m. Mattie Moorer, May 26, 1892 (dec.), m. 2d, Annie Farley, 1906. Is a farmer; organizer, 1901, The Farmers' Protective Assn.; was one of prime movers at Boll Weevil Conv., Shreveport, La., 1905, which ultimately resulted in organization of Southern Cotton Assn. in New Orleans same yr.; field agent and gen. organizer of this assn., 1905-08, and gained nat. recognition in this capacity. Mem. S.C. Ho. of Rep. from Sumter County, 1896-1900; U.S. senator, 6 terms, 1909-45. Democrat. Methodist. Address: Lynchburg, S.C. Died Nov. 17, 1944.

SMITH, Elmer Dennison, florist; b. Detroit, Nov. 20, 1854; s. Nathan and Helen Antonette (Green) S.; ed. pub. schs. and 1 yr. at Evans Business Coll., Adrian, Mich.; Master of Horticulture (hon.), Mich. State Coll., 1927; m. Carrie Lee Bailey, Nov. 30, 1886. Began as florist, Adrian, 1876; originated 493 varieties of chrysanthemums. Mem. S.A.R.; Phi Alpha Xi (hon.). Republican. Author: Smith's Chrysanthemum Manual. Home: 957 W. Maumee St., Adrian, Mich. Died Nov. 11, 1939.

SMITH, Ernest G(ray), newspaper pub.; b. Martins Ferry, O., Oct. 26, 1873; s. Hiram Wolfe and Evangaline (Lash) S.; Ph.B., Lafayette Coll., Easton, Pa., 1894, honorary Litt.D., 1943; M.S., 1897; LL.B., Yale University, 1896; married Marjorie Harvey, October 14, 1913; children—Harrison Harvey, Lois Gray, Andries DeWitt. Began as pub. Wilkes-Barre Times Leader, 1905; pres. Wilkes-Barre Pub. Co., T. L. Printery, Inc., Wilkes-Barre Airport Co., Lafayette Press, Inc., Easton, Pa.; dir. Second Nat. Bank, Wilkes-Barre Hotels Corp., Lehigh Valley Railroad, Wyoming Valley Building and Loan Association; vice chmn. Luzerne County Civilian Defense Council; chmn. Luzerne County Blood Plasma and Victory Garden Coms.; mem. Fed. Reserve Bank Bond Sale Com. Served as private and 2d lieutenant infantry U.S. Army, Cuba and Philippines, 1898-1902; major and lieutenant colonel, infantry World War I. President Wilkes-Barre Playground and Recreation Association; v.p. Pa. Parks Assn.; president board trustees F. M. Kirby Am. Legion Foundation; trustee Luzerne County Industrial School; life trustee Lafayette College. Awarded Certificate for long and meritorious service in newspaper work, P.N.P.A. Convention, Waldorf Astoria, New York City, 1943. Co-author Harvey-Smith History of Wilkes-Barre. Decorated D.S.M. (U.S.), 1919; Officer Black Star (France), 1919. Author: History of Northeastern Pennsylvania. Home: 4 Riverside Drive. Address: Times-Leader Bldg., Wilkes-Barre, Pa. Died Dec. 27, 1945.

SMITH, Ethan Henry, surgeon; b. Berrien County, Mich., Mar. 14, 1864; s. James and Malvina (Babcock) S.; student U. of Mich. Med. Dept., 1883-84; M.D., Bellevue Hosp. Med. Coll., New York U., 1889; m. Mrs. Mary J. Cook Saxe, Jan. 25, 1894. Prof. orthopedic surgery and clin. surgery, Coll. of Phys. and Surgs., San Francisco since 1904, trustee and dean of faculty, 1908-13; surgeon to San Francisco Hosp.; orthopedic surgeon Northwestern Pacific Ry. Mem. A.M.A., Med. Soc. State of Calif., San Francisco County Med. Soc., Western Orthopedic Club. Protestant. Home: 640 29th St. Office: Flood Bldg., San Francisco. Died Jan. 30, 1937.

SMITH, Frank Austin, clergyman; b. Lynn, Mass., June 25, 1866; s. Herbert Austin and Helen Maria (Burrill) S.; grad. Adelphi Acad., 1885; A.B., Brown U., 1889, D.D., 1917; grad. Crozer Theol. Sem., 1892; m. Blanche A Voorhees, Sept. 23, 1902; 1 son, Herbert Stanley (dec.). Ordained Bapt. ministry, 1892; pastor 1st Ch., Somerville, 1892-1902, 1st Ch., Haddonfield, 1902-12, Central Ch., Elizabeth, 1912-24; mem. bd. mgrs. Am. Bapt. Home Mission Soc., 1919-24, sec. of missions, 1924-36; Bd. of Edn. of Northern Bapt. Conv., 1936-42; sec. of edn., N.J. Bapt. Conv., 1898-1924, life mem. bd. mgrs. since 1941; mem. exec. com. Internat. S.S. Assn., 1901-08; mem. Bapt. Deputation to Far East, 1907. Mem. John Milton Foundation, 1932-36. Trustee Crozer Theol. Sem., Peddie Inst., etc. Mem. Nat. Soc. S.A.R. (chaplain gen.), Phi Delta Theta. Home: 219 Stiles St., Elizabeth 3, N.J. Died Mar. 26, 1948.

SMITH, Frank Webster, educator, publicist; b. Lincoln, Mass., June 27, 1854; s. Francis and Abigail Prescott (Baker) S.; grad. Phillips Acad., Andover, 1873; A.B., Harvard, 1877, grad. study classical philology and economics, 1881-83, A.M., 1882, psychology, summer, 1894; Teachers Coll. (Columbia), 1899-1900; grad. student and teacher, U. of Neb., 1901-04, Ph.D., 1904; studied in England, summer, 1902; m. Annie Noyes Sinclair, Dec. 1894 (died 1897); m. 2d, Helen Louise Moore, Oct. 23, 1900; children—Francis Prescott, Charles Webster. Teacher Atlanta U., 1877-81, Boston Evening Sch., 1882-83, State Normal Sch., Westfield, Mass., 1883-96; supt. pub. schs., Grand Junction, Colo., 1896-99; sec. Teachers Coll. (Columbia), 1900; prin. Gordon Acad. and Training Sch., Salt Lake City, and supt. Congl. Schs. of Utah, 1900-01, also city examiner Salt Lake City, 1900; adj. prof. edn. U. of Neb., 1903-05; prin. City Normal Sch., Paterson, N.J., 1905-23, and city examiner, Paterson, 1905-20; 1st prin. State Normal Sch., Paterson (city normal sch. adopted by state), 1923-25; pres. emeritus State Normal Sch. (later State Teachers Coll.), Paterson, N.J., since 1925; state examiner, N.J., 1923-25. Has served as pres. ednl. organizations; exec. sec. and treas., Municipal Normal School and Teachers Coll. Assn., 13 yrs. to 1936, now pres. emeritus; dir. Colo. state ednl. exhibit, Trans-Mississippi Expn., 1898. Mem. N.E.A., Paterson Teachers Assn., Phi Beta Kappa (Harvard), Pythagorean Club (ex-pres.). Republican. Presbyterian; commr. Gen. Assembly, 1927. Author: The High School—a Study of Origins and Tendencies, 1916; Jesus—Teacher, Principles of Teaching for Secular and Bible School Teachers, 1916; Heresies of the New Deal, 1940; contbr. on edn. and economics. Address: 29 Lenox Av., Ridgewood, N.J., and Box 442, Winter Haven, Fla. Died Feb. 11, 1943.

SMITH, Frank Whitney, public utility official; b. Alden, N.Y., June 22, 1867; s. George Henry and Mary Matilda (Drake) S.; ed. pub. schs.; (hon.) D.Eng., Stevens Inst. Tech., June 1937; m. Nellie Grant Harris, June 1, 1892. Trustee, Consolidated Edison Co. of New York; dir. Brooklyn Edison Co., Inc., Consol. Telegraph & Electrical Subway Co.,

Municipal Lighting Co., Inc., New York & Queens Electric Light & Power Co., New York Steam Corp., Tarrytown Terminal Corp., Westchester Lighting Co., Yonkers Electric Light & Power Co. Hon. mem. bd. Elec. & Gas Assn. of N.Y.; hon. mem. N.Y. Electrical Soc., Am. Inst. of Elec. Engrs., N.Y. Elec. Soc. Trustee, Northwestern Mutual Life Ins. Co., Waldorf Astoria Corp. Republican. Episcopalian. Club: Manhattan. Home: 277 Park Av., New York; and Tomkins Corners, Putnam County, N.Y. Office: 4 Irving Pl., New York, N.Y. Died July 22, 1946.

SMITH, Fred M., physician; b. Yale, Ill., May 31, 1888; s. John Alfred and Sarah Ellen (Newlin) S.; student Eastern Ill. State Normal Sch., 1905-09; B.S., U. of Chicago, 1914; M.D., Rush Med. Coll., 1914; post-grad. work, Vienna, 1927; m. Helen Louise Bushee, May 9, 1917; children—Fred Richard, Barbara, James Herrick. Asst. in medicine, Rush Med. Coll., 1916-18, asso., 1918-20, instr., 1920-24, asst. prof. clin. medicine, 1924; prof. theory and practice of medicine and head of dept., State U. of Ia., 1924, prof. internal medicine since 1924. First lt. Med. Corps, 1918-19. Fellow Am. Coll. Physicians; mem. A.M.A., Assn. of Am. Physicians, Am. Soc. for Clin. Investigation, Am. Physiol. Soc., Soc. Exptl. Biology and Medicine, Chicago Inst. of Medicine, Chicago Society Internal Medicine, Association of American Pilgrims (recorder), Phi Delta Theta, Phi Rho Sigma, Sigma Xi. Democrat. Episcopalian. Wrote "The Coronary Arteries" in Cyclopedia of Medicine, 1932; "Diseases of the Heart" in Text Book of Medicine by Musser, 1932; extensive contbr. to med. jours. Editor in chief of American Heart Jour. Home: Ridge Road. Address: University Hospital, Iowa City, Ia. Died Feb. 23, 1946.

SMITH, Frederick Madison, pres. Reorganized Ch. of Jesus Christ of Latter Day Saints; b. Plano, Ill., Jan. 21, 1874; s. Joseph and Bertha (Madison) S.; student State U. of Ia., 1894-95; B.S., Graceland Coll., Ia., 1898, D.D., 1923; U. of Mo., 1908-09; A.M., U. of Kan., 1911; Ph.D., Clark U., 1916; m. Ruth L.; d. Elijah and Alice E. Cobb, of Lamoni, Ia., Aug. 3, 1897. First counselor, 1902-15, and pres. since 1915, Reorganized Ch. of Jesus Christ of Latter Day Saints, 1902. Prof. of mathematics, Graceland Coll., 1899-1900; editor Lamoni Chronicle, 1900-02; asst. and asso. editor Saints' Herald, 1900-04; editor Journal of History, 1908-12; apptd. col. on Missouri Governor's Staff. President board Independence Santarium and Hosp.; v.p. Jackson County Tuberculosis Soc.; v.p. Kansas City Tuberculosis Soc.; bd. dirs. and v.p., Mo. T.B. Assn. Mem. Am. Geog. Soc., State Hist. Soc. Mo., Mo. Valley Hist. Soc, Quincy (Ill.) Hist. Soc., Ill. State Hist. Soc., Independence Chamber Commerce. Mem. S.A.R. Soc. Colonial Wars. Editor Saints' Herald since 1917. Republican. Mason (potentate Ararat Shrine Temple 1941). Clubs: University, Nat. Press (Washington). Home: Holke and DeKalb Roads, Route 3, Box 514, Independence. Office: The Auditorium, Independence, Mo. Died Mar. 20, 1946.

SMITH, George Harris, lawyer; b. Salt Lake City, Utah, Nov. 29, 1873; s. George and Eliza Martha (Williams) S.; grad. Salt Lake City High Sch., 1896; LL.B., U. of Mich., 1899; m. Euphemia Luhn, July 5, 1905; 1 dau., Euphemia. Began as law clk. Ore. S.L. R.R., 1899; apptd. prin. asst. to gen. atty. same rd., 1900, gen. solicitor since 1915; also gen. atty. for Utah of U.P. R.R. and L.A.&S.L. R.R. Co.; gen. solicitor U.P. R.R. Co. since 1936. Retired from Ry. work Dec. 1, 1943, acc. of age rules, then became chmn. of Salt Lake County Chapter, Am. Red Cross, which is voluntary work. Member Am. and Utah State bar assns., Am. Judicature Soc. (dir.), Am. Law Inst., Delta Chi. Clubs: University, Alta, Country. Home: 55 Laurel Av. Office: Union Pacific Bldg., Salt Lake City, Utah. Died Feb. 24, 1947.

SMITH, George Otis, geologist; b. Hodgdon, Me., Feb. 22, 1871; s. Joseph O. and Emma (Mayo) S.; A.B., Colby Coll., 1893, A.M., 1896, LL.D., 1920; Ph.D., Johns Hopkins, 1896; Sc.D., Case Sch. Applied Sci., 1914, Colo. Sch. Mines, 1928; m. Grace M. Coburn, Nov. 18, 1896 (died Mar. 3, 1931); children—Charles Coburn (dec.), Joseph Coburn, Mrs. Helen Coburn Fawcett, Elizabeth Coburn (dec.), Louise Coburn. Engaged in geol. work in Mich., Utah, Washington, and in N.E., 1893-1906; asst. geologist and geologist, 1896-1907, dir. U.S. Geol. Survey, 1907-30, except 1922-23 while mem. U.S. Coal Commn.; chmn. Federal Power Commn., Dec. 1930-Nov. 1933; dir. Central Me. Power Co. Chmn. board of trustees, Colby Coll.; pres. board of trustees Redington Memorial Hosp. and Bloomfield Acad. Fellow Geol. Soc. America, A.A.A.S.; mem. Coal Mining Inst. America (hon.), Am. Inst. Mining and Metall. Engrs. (ex-pres.), Am. Forestry Assn., Wash. Acad. Sciences, Mining and Metall. Soc. America, Am. Assn. Petroleum Geologists, Nat. Geog. Soc. (trustee), Delta Kappa Epsilon, Phi Beta Kappa, etc. Author of reports on areal, economic, petrographic and physiographic geology in pubs. U.S. Geol. Survey, also papers and addresses on economics of mineral and power resources and administration of scientific work by govt.; editor and co-author of Strategy of Minerals, 1919. Baptist. Republican. Clubs: Cosmos, Press. Home: 2 Coburn Av., Skowhegan, Me. Died Jan. 10, 1944.

SMITH, Gordon Arthur, author; b. Rochester, N.Y., Nov. 18, 1886; s. Arthur Cosslett and Elisabeth Storer (Atkinson) S.; A.B., Harvard, cum laude, 1908; studied architecture École des Beaux Arts, Paris, 1909-14 (no degree); unmarried. Trained to fly seaplane, winter 1916-17, and later at Port Washington; enlisted in U.S.N.R. Flying Corps, Oct. 1917; served in France, Oct. 1917-Mar. 1919, chiefly in liaison with French Naval aviation; hon. discharged as lt. (j.g.). Republican. Episcopalian. Clubs: Harvard, Union, Players. Author: Mascarose, 1913; The Crown of Life, 1915; The Pagan, 1920; There Goes the Groom, 1922. Contbr. short stories to mags. Address: 10 W. 74th St., New York. Died May 7, 1944.

SMITH, Hal Horace, lawyer; b. Ionia, Mich., May 1, 1873; s. Vernon H. and Rachel (Worthington) S.; A.B., U. of Mich., 1895; m. Bell Yates, June 21, 1898; children—Yates Gorham, Hal Horace. Admitted to Mich. bar, 1896; practiced in Ionia until 1905 and in Detroit since; partner Beaumont, Smith & Harris since 1908; dir. various cos. Dir. Detroit Museum of Art Founders Society Sec. and Mich. mem. Pan-Am. World's Fair Commn., 1901, and La. Purchase Expn., 1904. Mem. Am., Mich. State and Detroit bar assns., Alpha Delta Phi. Republican Clubs: Detroit, University, Grosse Pointe, Country; Metropolitan (Washington, D.C.). Home: 15530 Windmill Point Drive, Grosse Pointe Park. Office: Ford Bldg., Detroit, Mich. Died Dec. 21, 1944.

SMITH, Harold Dewey, former dir. Fed. budget; b. Haven, Kan., June 6, 1898; s. James William and Miranda (Ebling) S.; B.S. in engring., U. of Kan., 1922; A.M. in Pub. Adminstrn., U. of Mich., 1925; LL.D. (hon., American U., 1942, Grinnell Coll., 1943; m. Lillian Mayer, Apr. 18, 1926; children—Lawrence Byron, Mary Ann, Sally Jane, Virginia Lee. Mem. staff Detroit Bureau of Govt. Research, 1924-25; staff of League of Kansas Municipalities, 1925-28; dir. Mich. Municipal League, 1928-37; dir. Bureau of Govt., U. of Mich., 1934-37; budget dir. State of Mich., 1937-39; dir. Fed. budget, Apr. 1939-46; v.p. Internat. Bank for Reconstruction and Develop. since June 1946. Former mem. Mich. State Planning Bd., adv. bd., State of Mich. Accident Fund; mem. urbanism com. and research consultant, Nat. Resources com. on pub. adminstr., Social Sci. Research Council; former chmn. Gov's. Welfare Study Com. (Mich.). Past pres. Am. Municipal Assn., 1933-34; pres. Am. Soc. for Public Adminstrn., 1941; mem. Am. Polit. Sci. Assn., Nat. Muncipal League, Am. Acad. Polit. and Social Sci. Served as seaman, U.S. Navy, during World War I. Registered professional engineer. Mem. Mich. Engrs. Soc., Alpha Kappa Lambda. Author (book) The Management of Your Government; of articles in field of govt. and research; editor Mich. Municipal Review, 1928-37; ed. numerous bulletins of Mich. Municipal League, 1928-37, U. of Mich. Bureau of Govt., 1934-37. Home: 3125 N. Abingdon St., Arlington, Va. Office: Bureau of the Budget, Exec. Office of the President, Washington. Died Jan. 23, 1947; buried in Arlington National Cemetery.

SMITH, Harriet Lummis (Mrs. William M. Smith), writer; b. Auburndale, Mass.; d. Henry and Jennie (Brewster) Lummis; A.B., Lawrence Coll., Appleton, Wis.; m. William M. Smith, Oct. 11, 1905. Began writing for newspapers and mags. as a girl; has contributed to McClure's, Munsey's, Harper's Bazaar, Youth's Companion, Delineator, etc. Presbyterian. Clubs: Woman's Literary (Baltimore); Philomusian (Phila.). Writer of continuation of "Pollyanna" series of books begun by Eleanor Porter. Author: Girls of Friendly Terrace, 1912; Peggy Raymond's Vacation, 1913; Other People's Business, 1916; Peggy Raymond's School Days, 1916; Friendly Terrace Quartette, 1920; Agatha's Aunt, 1920; Peggy Raymond's Way, 1922; Pollyanna of the Orange Blossoms, 1924; Pollyanna's Jewels, 1925; Uncertain Glory, 1926; Pollyanna's Debt of Honor, 1927; Pat and Pal, 1928; Pollyanna's Western Adventure, 1929; (one-act play) There's Many a Slip, 1938. Home: 942 S. 49th St., Philadelphia, Pa.* Died May 9, 1947.

SMITH, Harry Worcester, sportsman, financier, inventor; b. Worcester, Mass., Nov. 5, 1865; s. Charles Worcester and Josephine (Lord) S.; ed. Worcester Poly. Inst., Mass. Inst. Tech., Chemnitz (Germany) Weaving Sch., Glasgow Sch. of Design, Bradford (Eng.) Tech. Sch.; m. Mildred Crompton, Oct. 19, 1892. Inventor of more than 40 patents pertaining to automatic weaving and design; consolidated the Crompton-Thayer and Crompton-Knowles cos., 1907, the combination making the largest loom works in the world; effected sale of the Queen Dyeing Co., of Providence, R.I., to the U.S. Finishing Co., of N.Y. City, for $2,000,000, in 1909; sold Thomas G. Plant shoe factory, at Jamaica Plains, Mass., and all his patents on shoe machinery, to U.S. Shoe Machinery Co. of America for $6,000,000, in 1910; consolidated the F. E. Reed and Prentice Bros., machine tool mfrs., the Reed Foundry, Reed-Curtis Screw Co. and the Crompton Associates plants into the Reed-Prentice Co., 1912. Mem. Worcester Park Commn. 7 yrs. Founder Masters of Foxhounds Assn. America, 1907; master of the Grafton Hounds; ex-master of Piedmont and Loudoun hunts, Virginia, and Westmeath, Ireland. Republican. Brought champion greyhounds of Eng. to America, 1885; won Fox Terrier Club grand challenge cup twice; won $10,000 champion Steeplechase of America, riding own horse, The Cad, Calvert Steeplechase, Baltimore, 1900, 1st and 2d $8,000 Grand National Steeplechase, Sheepshead Bay, etc.; won the Grafton-Middlesex American-English Internat. Foxhound match for $2,000 stake and plate, in Virginia, 1905; won, owner up, the Aiken and Camden, South Carolina, Hunter Trials, 1929, 30, 31. Established present Am. Foxhound standard. Judge of horse and hound shows, matches and tests in U.S. and Can.; founded the Frank Forester Soc. of America; collected funds and dedicated the memorial to Henry William Herbert ("Frank Forester"), at Warwick, Orange County, N.Y. Wrote: A Sporting Tour Through Ireland, England, Wales and France; The True American Foxhound; Fox Hunting in America; The Cubbing Season; Amateur Sunday Games; The Pulse of the People; also introductory chapters and published the Warwick Valley edit. of The Warwick Woodlands, 1921; wrote the foreword to the limited edit. of Trouting Along the Catasauqua, by Frank Forester, privately printed for The Angler's Club of New York, 1927; the foreword to the Hitchcock edit. of the works of Somerville and Ross; the foreword to Cooking in Old Creole Days, by Celestine Eustis, 1928; Steeplechasing in America, for the 14th edit. of the Ency. Britannica; Steeplechasing in America for "Racing at Home and Abroad," London, 1929; Life and Sport in Aiken and Those Who Made It, 1935; A Sporting Family of the Old South, 1937. Reviewer of books on racing and hunting. Mem. Engineers Club (New York). Home: Worcester, Mass. Died Apr. 5, 1945.

SMITH, Herbert A(ugustine); b. Southampton, Mass., Dec. 6, 1866; s. Rev. Burritt Augustus and Ellen Maria (Rowley) S.; A.B., Yale, 1889; Ph.D., 1897; student Sorbonne, France, 1899-1900; m. Loretta Josephine Mead, Apr. 15, 1895 (died Jan. 15, 1925); children—Gifford Pinchot (dec.), Theodore Studwell, Earl, Sarah Frances (Mrs. William Peter Marseilles, Jr.); m. 2d, Mrs. John Moncure Conway (née Lilian Taliaferro), Dec. 12, 1928. Asst. in English, Yale, 1891-92, instr., 1892-98; editorial writer N.Y. Evening Post and World's Work, 1900-01; editor Div., later Bur. of Forestry and now the U.S. Forest Service, 1901-20, asst. forester in charge public relations, 1920-25, spl. assignments, 1926-34; editor in chief Journal of Forestry, 1935-37; historical studies Forest Service, 1937, collaborator, 1938. Chmn. com. on editorial work of Pres. Theodore Roosevelt's Com. on Departmental Business Methods. Fellow Soc. of Am. Foresters, A.A.A.S.; mem. Agricultural History Society (member editorial board Agricultural History, quarterly publication), Phi Beta Kappa, Alpha Delta Phi, Skull and Bones (Yale). Clubs: Cosmos (Washington, D.C.); Yale (N.Y. City); Graduates (New Haven, Conn.); Waccabuc Country Club (Waccabuc, N.Y.). Author of govt. publs. and articles on forestry. Address: The Ontario, Washington 9, D.C. Died July 21, 1944.

SMITH, Hiram Moore, lawyer; b. Richmond, Va., Nov. 23, 1884; s. Henry Marston and Lucy Conway (Gordon) S.; student Richmond Coll., 1904; LL.B., U. of Va., 1907; m. Caroline Gordon Rennolds, Nov. 2, 1910; children—Hiram Moore, Jr., Caroline Smith O'Ferrall, Eleanor Smith Dudley, Lucy Gordon Sutton; m. 2d, Willis Wilson Lathrop, Aug. 20, 1931. Admitted to Va. bar, 1907, practicing at Richmond. Formerly mem. City Dem. Com.; del. Dem. State Conv., 1916, 20; del. Dem. Nat. Conv., 1920; asst. U.S. atty., Eastern Dist. of Va., 1913-19; U.S. atty., Jan. 1919-Oct. 15, 1920. Apptd. chief of staff of Gov. E. Lee Trinkle, Feb. 1, 1922. Mem. Virginia State Bar Assn., Bar Assn. City of Richmond, New York Southern Soc., Mil. Order Fgn. Wars, S.R., Mass. Soc. of Cincinnati (hereditary mem.), Kappa Sigma, Phi Delta Phi. Presbyn. Club: Virginia Boat. Home: 814 Westover Rd. Office: Mutual Bldg., Richmond, Va.* Died July 17, 1946.

SMITH, Horatio Elwin, prof. Romance langs.; b. Cambridge, Mass., May 8, 1886; s. Elwin Hartley and Eliza Burroughs (Taylor) S.; A.B., Amherst, 1908; Ph.D., Johns Hopkins, 1912; Doctor, honoris causa, University of Grenoble, 1939; m. Ernestine Failing, July 3, 1911; children—Eliza Alvord, Mary Hillard. Instr. in French, Yale, 1911-17, asst. prof. French, same univ., 1917-18; prof. French, Amherst, 1919-25; prof. Romance langs. and head of dept., Brown U., 1925-36; prof. of French and chmn. French sect. of Dept. of Romance langs., Columbia U., since 1936; general editor French series, Scribner's; research work in modern French lit. Chmn. com. on modern langs., Coll. Entrance Exam. Bd., 1930, 31, dir. of reading, 1937-41. Dir., regional dir., etc., in Foyer du Soldat, Franch Army, 1918-19. Mem. bd. dirs. Federation of French Alliances, 1938-41. Mem. Modern Lang. Assn. Am. (exec. council 1938-42), Am. Assn. of University Professors (exec. council, 1940-43), Providence Athenæum (dir. 1932, 33), Phi Beta Kappa, Theta Delta Chi; fellow Am. Acad. Arts and Sciences, 1932. Decorated War Service Medal and Médaille de la Reconnaissance Française, also Officier d'Académie (1931), and Chevalier de la Légion d'Honneur (1934) —all of France. Author: The Literary Criticism of Pierre Bayle, 1912; Advanced French Composition, 1916; Masters of French Literature, 1937. Editor: Balzac's Le Père Goriot, 1928. Editor in chief, Romantic Review, since 1937. Gen. editor, Columbia Dictionary Modern European Literature. Contbr. to Modern Lang. Notes, Modern Philology, etc. Address: Columbia University, New York, N.Y.* Died Sep. 0, 1946.

SMITH, Hugh Carnes, army officer; b. Trenton, Mo., Apr. 17, 1873; s. George Washington and Rose Margaret (Carnes) S.; LL.B., U. of Michigan, 1894; LL.M., American U., Washington, D.C., 1924; m. Leona Conover, Sept. 26, 1899; children—Conover Carnes (officer U.S. Army), Hule Austin (officer U.S. Army). Admitted to Mo. bar, 1894, Supreme Court of U.S., 1919, dist. court of D.C., 1937, U.S. Court of Appeals for D.C., 1939; in gen. practice of law, Trenton, Mo., 1894-1905; prosecuting atty., Grundy County, Mo., 1899-1903; general practice of law, St. Joseph, Mo., 1905-10; 1st asst. U.S. atty. Western Dist. Missouri, 1910-13; in gen. practice of law,

Kansas City, Mo., 1913-18, also lecturer on medical jurisprudence, Kansas City Dental Coll.; in mil. service, 1918-37; gen. practice of law, Washington, D.C., also asst. gen. counsel in U.S. for Puerto Rico, 1937-40; mil. service since 1940; dir. Richards & Conover Hardware Co., Kansas City, Mo., and Oklahoma City, Okla. Served as major, Judge Adv. Gen.'s Dept., U.S. Army, 1918; asst. judge adv., G.Q.H., A.E.F., 1918-19, disch., 1920; commd. lt. col., 1920; gen. counsel and later mem. War Dept. Bd. of Contract Adjustment, 1920-21; served as mem. mil. justice sect. Judge Adv. Gen.'s Dept., later chief of sect., mem. review bd., 1920-24, corps area judge adv., III Corps Area, Baltimore, Md., 1924-25, dept. judge advocate, Philippine Dept., 1925-27; chief civil affairs sect. and chief contract and reservations sect., Judge Adv. Gen.'s Office, 1927-31, head of commn. to Europe to investigate foreign patent claims, 1929; promoted to colonel, May 1, 1931; corps area judge advocate, IX Corps Area, San Francisco, California, 1931-34; the assistant judge advocate general and intermittently acting judge advocate general, 1934-37; retired, 1937; recalled to active duty, 1940; chief legal sect. purchase and contracts branch office, asst. secretary of war (later office under sec. of war), chmn. advisory com. on claims Mar.-Aug. 1942; pres. War Dept. Bd. of Contract Appeals since Aug. 1942. Awarded Legion of Merit, Sept. 1945. Mem. Am., Mo., Fed. and D.C. bar assns., Am. Judicature Soc., Am. Soc. Internat. Law, Sigma Chi. An organizer Inter-Am. Bar Assn. Club: Army and Navy (Washington). Home: 4343 Cathedral Av. N.W., Washington 16, D.C. Colonel Hugh Carnes Smith died March 30, 1946.

SMITH, Hugh F., Jr., broker; b. Nashville, Tenn., June 12, 1892; s. Hugh F. and Mary C. (Tanksley) S.; student Hume Fogg High Sch., Nashville, 1907-08, Wallace U., Nashville, 1908-09; m. Amelia Metz, June 10, 1914; children—Hugh F., 3d, William Randolph. Buyer of fruits and vegetables in carload lots, 1909-10; newspaper work, Nashville Democrat, 1911; salesman Nat. Biscuit Co., 1912-15; head salesman H. J. Heinz Co., 1915-22; pres. Hugh F. Smith, Jr., Brokerage Co., fruits and vegetables, since 1922. Mem. Code Authority of Wholesale Fresh Fruit and Vegetable Distributive Industry. Member National League of Distributors. Colonel on the staff of Gov. Henry Horton of Tenn. and on staff of Gov. Ruby Laffoon of Ky. Dir. finance bd. Junior League Crippled Children's Hosp.; trustee Battle Ground Academy, Franklin, Tenn. Awarded, by mayor and commrs. of Nashville, sterling silver cup as outstanding citizen in civic work, 1930. Democrat. Episcopalian. Mason (33°, Shriner; Knight Comdr. Ct. of Honors in Scottish Rite Bodies of Southern Jurisdiction; Illustrious Potentate Al Menah Temple, Nashville, 1930); past dir. of Jester's Court No. 92; Elk. Clubs: Scottish Rite (past pres.), Shrine, Automobile, Sulphur Dell Civic, Cercle Magique, Rotary, Belle Meade Country. Home: Jackson Blvd., Belle Meade, Nashville. Office: 815 4th Av. N., Nashville, Tenn.* Died Nov. 7, 1946.

SMITH, Isaac B., pub. utilities; chmn. bd. and pres. Ia. Electric Co.; pres. Ia. Electric Light & Power Co., Central States Electric Co., Northwestern Light & Power Co., Wyoming Ry. Co., Buffalo Wyoming Coal Co., and officer or dir. various other corps. Home: 500 Country Club Drive. Office: Security Bldg., Cedar Rapids, Ia. Deceased.

SMITH, James Gerald, economist; b. Denver, Colo., Feb. 13, 1897; s. John G. and Sigrid (Miller) S.; A.B., Princeton, 1920, A.M., 1922, Ph.D., 1926; m. Dorothy H. Zapf, June 29, 1922; children—Barbara Jean, Leila Ann. Instr. in economics Princeton U., 1922-27, asst. prof., 1928-32, asso. prof., 1932-38, prof. since 1938; instr. Am. Inst. Banking, Trenton, 1928-30; investigator Princeton Survey of Adminstrn. and Expenditures of State Govt. of N.J., 1932-33. Mem. Am. Econ. Assn., Am. Statis. Assn., Am. Assn. of Univ. Profs. Author: Development of Trust Companies in the United States, 1928; Facing the Facts (with others), 1932; The New York Money Market (with B. H. Beckhart), 1932; Economic Planning and the Tariff, 1934; Elementary Statistics, 1934; Introduction to Economic Analysis (with A. M. McIsaac), 1936; Essential Economic Principles (with A. M. McIsaac), 1941; Money Credit and Finance (with G. F. Luthringer and D. C. Cline), 1937; Elementary Statistics and Applications (with A. J. Duncan), 1944; Sampling Statistics and Applications (with A. J. Duncan), 1946. Editor: Facing the Facts, 1932; Economics and Social Institutions, 1938. Contbr. articles to financial and econ. jours. Presbyterian. Home: 20 Murray Pl., Princeton, N.J. Address: Princeton University, Princeton, N.J. Died Nov. 28, 1946; buried, Princeton, N.J.

SMITH, James Walter, editor; b. E. Boston, Mass., Oct. 27, 1868; s. James and Hannah Jane S.; A.B., Harvard, 1894; m. Martha Elizabeth Fletcher, Mar. 27, 1895. Went to Eng., Sept., 1894; contbr. to Am. and English papers and mags.; editor Am. edit. Strand Magazine, 1896-1908; chief editor of the House of Cassell, London, since May, 1908, and exercises gen. control over all the Cassell publs. Founded, for Sir George Newnes, "The King," and was its editor, 1900-02. Clubs: Savage, Whitefriars, Yorick, Wigwam. Home: 23 Acacia Rd., St. John's Wood, N.W. Address: Cassell & Co., Ltd., LaBelle Sauvage, E.C., London, England. Died Nov. 17, 1948.

SMITH, J(ames) Willison, banker; b. Philadelphia, Pa., Mar. 30, 1879; s. James and Margaret (McCorkell) S.; ed. pub. schs., Phila.; (hon.) LL.D., Washington and Jefferson College; m. Sarah Winslow Drummond, June 16, 1903; children—J. Willison, Renée L., Robert Drummond, John Winslow, David Pierson. Began with The Land Title & Trust Co.; pres. The Real Estate-Land Title & Trust Co., since Nov. 1, 1927 (now The Land Title Bank & Trust Co.), chmn. bd. Jan. 9, 1940; dir. Franklin Fire Ins. Co., Giant Portland Cement Co., Am. Surety Co. of N.Y., Philadelphia & Reading Coal & Iron Co., Philadelphia Traction Co., John Wanamaker Stores, Philadelphia and New York. Commr. Delaware River Joint Commn.; trustee Estate of Rodman Wanamaker (dec.). Asst. mgr., later mgr. div. housing and transportation, Emergency Fleet Corp., U.S. Shipping Bd., World War. Trustee Maryville (Tenn.) Coll. Mem. Beta Gamma Sigma (hon.). Republican. Presbyterian. Mason. Clubs: Union League, Manufacturers, Penn Athletic, Aronimink Golf. Home: 511 S. 48th St. Offices: 100 S. Broad St., Philadelphia, Pa. Died Mar. 10, 1942.

SMITH, Jim Clifford, lawyer; b. Jasper, Ala., Dec. 10, 1894; s. James Allen and Martha Elizabeth (Blackwell) S.; ed. Walker County (Ala.) High Sch., 1908-12; Wheeler Business Coll., Birmingham, Ala., 1912-13; m. Mary Ferguson, Sept. 15, 1927; 1 dau., Mary Jane. Began as clk. to U.S. dist. atty., Birmingham, Ala., 1915-18; dep. clk. U.S. Dist. Ct., 1919-21; admitted to Ala. bar, 1921; asst. U.S. dist. atty. Northern Dist. Ala., 1921-25; mem. London, Yancey, Smith & Windham, 1926-33; U.S. dist. atty. for Northern Dist., Ala., since July 1, 1933; former sr. mem. Smith, Windham, Jackson & Rives, and of Smith, Jackson & Rives (both firms dissolved); now practicing alone. Student F.A. Officers Sch. Camp Taylor, Ky., 1918-19. Mem. Am. and Ala. State bar associations, Birmingham Bar Association (ex-pres). Judge advocate, Civitan Internat., 1939-40. Democrat. Methodist. Mason (K.P.; Past Master Birmingham Temple A.F.&A.M.). Club: The Country (Birmingham). Home: 1122 Columbiana Rd. Office: Federal Bldg., Birmingham, Ala. Died July 16, 1947.

SMITH, John P., army officer; b. Jan. 28, 1883; E.E., Pa. State Coll. 1907; distinguished grad. Coast Arty. School 1914; grad. Command and Gen. Staff School 1925, Army War Coll. 1926, Naval War Coll. 1932; m. Cornelia Parmelee, Long Island, 1912. Commd. 2d lt. Coast Arty. Corps, Sept. 25, 1908; promoted through grades to Maj. Gen. April 1941. Service in the U.S., Hawaii, Philippines, and France (W.W.I.). Active in battles Ainse-Marne, St. Mihiel and Meuse-Argonne offensives. Mem. Gen. Staff Corps 1920-24, 1932-36, 1939-40. Commanded Fourth Corps Area Oct. 1940 to March 1942, Chief of Administrative Services War Dept., mem. Permanent Joint Board on Defense, Canada-United States, and Joint Mexican-United States Defense Commn. Army mem. Planning Group, O.S.S. Awarded Distinguished Service Medal, Purple Heart and Victory Medal (W.W.I.) with four stars and bars.† Died Nov. 4, 1948.

SMITH, John Thomas, lawyer; b. New Haven, Conn., Jan. 17, 1879; A.B., Creighton U., Omaha, Neb., 1899; LL.B., Yale, 1901; m. Mary A. Smith, June 22, 1910; children—Mrs. Maureen S. Shanley, Gregory B., Gerard C. Practiced at N.Y. City since 1901; gen. counsel, dir. and v.p. Gen. Motors Corp.; pres. Argonaut Mining Co., Ltd.; pres. and dir. G. M. Shares, Inc.; dir. Underwood Elliott Fisher Co., Ecuadorian Corp., Ltd., Ethyl Corporation. Clubs: Yale, The Links (New York); Garden City (L.I.) Golf; Nat. Golf (Southampton, L.I.); Shinnecock Hills Golf, Meadow. Home: 19 E. 72d St. Office: 1775 Broadway, New York, N.Y.* Died Sep. 28, 1947.

SMITH, J(oseph) Brodie, v.p. Public Service Co. of New Hampshire; born at Richville, N.Y., April 6, 1861; s. William Priest and Sarah (Hungerford) S.; ed. Union Free Sch. of Richville and courses in high mathematics; m. Charlotte Dodd Stewartson (M.D.), July 14, 1909. Started with his brother in drug business in Manchester, 1880, later became a registered pharmacist in N.H. and N.Y.; retired from drug business, 1886; became supt. Fire Alarm Telegraph Service, Manchester, 1885. On organization of the Ben Franklin Electric Light Co., 1886, was appointed its first supt.; this company later consol. with Manchester Electric Light Co. of which he was supt. and dir. until the company was succeeded by the Manchester Traction, Light & Power Co. when he was made gen. mgr.; v.p. and gen. mgr., 1905-41 (co. merged with Pub. Service Co. of N.H., 1926), v.p. since Apr. 25, 1941; gen. mgr. Manchester St. Ry. (now part of Pub. Service Co. of N.H.), 1899-1937; trustee of the Manchester Savings Bank since 1901, pres. since 1925. Pres. Weare Improvement & Reservoir Assn.; sec.-treas. Assn. of Pub. Utilities of N.H.; appted, director and associate mem. U.S. Naval Consulting Board, 1916, representing the Am. Institute of Elec. Engrs. Chairman board trustees Masonic Home. Member Board of Water Commissioners, Manchester, since 1919, and pres. since 1926. Pres. N.H. Soc. for Crippled Children; mem. Am. Inst. Elec. Engrs., Manchester Inst. of Arts and Sciences (councillor and one of founders), Manchester Hist. Assn. (v.p.), N.H. Assn. for Prevention of Tuberculosis (first pres., 2 yrs.), Manchester Chamber of Commerce; life mem. N.H. Pharm. Assn.; life mem. Am. Pharm. Assn. Odd Fellow; mem. all Masonic York Rite bodies and Scottish Rite 33° since 1905. Clubs: Rotary (treas. and dir.), Manchester Country, Manchester Radio (1st pres.), N.E. Transit (life). Address: Manchester, N.H.* Died May 8, 1947.

SMITH, Joseph Francis, clergyman; b. Cleveland, O., Feb. 7, 1865; s. Thomas and Johanna (Asple) S.; student Am. Assumption Coll., Ont., Can., 1884; studied philosophy, St. Mary's Sem., Cleveland, 1884-86, divinity, 1886-89; LL.D., St. Louis U., 1922. Ordained priest R.C. Ch., 1889; pastor Ashtabula, O., 1894-1901, St. Philomena's Ch., Cleveland, 1901-28; pastor St. John's Cathedral, Cleveland, since 1928; apptd. diocesan consultor, 1921, chmn. bd., 1921; created monsignor and mem. Papal Household by Pope Pius XI, 1921; appointed vicar general Cleveland Diocese, 1922, prothonotary apostolic, 1927. Celebrated golden jubilee to the priesthood, June 15, 1939. Republican. Home: 1007 Superior Av., Cleveland, O. Died May 24, 1942.

SMITH, June C., judge; b. Irvington, Ill., Mar. 24, 1876; s. Isaac C. and Alma (Maxey) S.; LL.B., Southern Normal U., Huntingdon, Tenn., 1899; m. Metta Bates, Sept. 30, 1900; children—Ruth (Mrs. Robert J. Dobler), Maurine (Mrs. Bethuel Gross). Admitted to Ill. bar, 1904; engaged in practice of law, Centralia, since 1904, partner law firm Noleman & Smith, 1908-28, Smith & Murray since 1935; state's atty., Marion County, 1904-08; asst. atty. gen., 1909-13; judge Supreme Court of Ill., 2d Dist., since 1941. Served as maj. inf., U.S. Army, 1917-18. Republican. Methodist. Mason (32°), Odd Fellow, Elk. Home: 520 E. Broadway. Office: Old Nat. Bank Bldg., Centralia, Ill. Died Feb. 7, 1947; buried Hillcrest Memorial Park, Centralia, Ill.

SMITH, Kenneth Gladstone, chmn. bd. dirs. The Pepsodent Co.; b. Feb. 14, 1892; s. Douglas Smith (founder of The Pepsodent Co.); m. Cora S. Clements. Chmn. bd. dirs. The Pepsodent Co. Home: Winnetka, Ill.; (winter) Palm Beach, Fla. Office: 919 N. Michigan Av., Chicago, Ill. Died Dec. 4, 1945.

SMITH, Leonard Minuse, dir. cinematography; b. Brooklyn, N.Y., Apr. 25, 1894; s. Josiah Tuttle and Mae Elizabeth (Minuse) S.; ed. public school and high school, Brooklyn, and Rutgers Coll.; m. Gertrude Gauthier, June 29, 1921. Dir. of cinematography, Metro-Goldwyn-Mayer Studios, Culver City, Calif.; pictures include: Broadway Melody, Broadway Rhythm, Billy the Kid, Lassie Comes Home. National Velvet, Courage of Lassie. Served with Signal Corps Photographic Unit, World War I. Pres. Am. Soc. of Cinematographers; mem. Am. Legion. Congregationalist. Home: 268 N. Rexford Dr., Beverley Hills, Calif. Office: M.G.M. Studios, Culver City, Calif.; also 1782 N. Orange Dr., Hollywood 28, Calif. Deceased.

SMITH, Lewis Worthington, author, coll. prof.; b. Malta, Ill., Nov. 22, 1866; s. Dwight A. and Sarah Elizabeth (Lewis) S.; studied Beloit (Wis.) Coll.; Ph.B., Fairfield Coll., Neb. 1889; studied U. of Neb.; A.M., Cotner U., Neb., 1901; m. Jessica Welborn, Aug. 24, 1897; 1 dau., Marjorie Elizabeth Welborn. High school and college teacher in Nebraska after graduation; professor English, Tabor Coll., Ia, 1899-1902; prof. English, Drake U., since 1902, dean Grad. Div. Drake U. since 1936, prof. English and dean emeritus since 1940. Reviewer, The Dial, 1899-1902. Mem. board Edmundson Foundation (for erection of an Art Mus. in Des Moines). Republican. Conglist. Mem. Eugene Field Soc., Sigma Delta Chi, Sigma Tau Delta. Clubs: Iowa Authors' (pres. 1915-16, 1922-24), Prairie (pres. 1916-17, 1927-28). Editor: Tennyson's The Princess, 1899; Irving's Sketch Book, 1909; Scott's Lay of the Last Minstrel, and Lady of the Lake, 1910; Macaulay's Lays of Ancient Rome, 1911; Short Stories for English Classes, 1928; Women's Poetry Today, 1929. Author: A Modern Composition and Rhetoric, 1901; God's Sunlight, 1901; The Writing of the Short Story, 1902; In the Furrow, 1906; (drama) The Art of Life, presented by Donald Robertson, 1909-10; A Candle and the Stars (serial), 1911; The English Tongue (poems), 1916; The Mechanism of English Style, 1916; Ships in Port (poems), 1916; In Sunday's Tent (poem), 1916; Sun-burst Across the World (patriotic song), 1917; The Sky-Line in English Literature, 1920; Current Reviews, 1927; Writing for Freshmen, 1930; Grammar for Speech, 1931; Exercises in Language Habits (with H. F. Watson), 1933; Types and Times in English Literature (4 books; with others), 1940. Compiler: Ventures in Contemporary Reading (with V. H. Ogburn and H. F. Watson), 1932. Mem. Am. bd. Yenching Univ., Peiping, China. Editor: Fiction and the Screen (with Mrs. Marguerite Ortman, 1935. Crises (poetry sequence) 1946; numerous contbns. to papers and magazines. Home: 4023 Cottage Grove Av., Des Moines, Ia. Died Dec. 27, 1947; buried Resthaven Park Cemetery, West Des Moines, Ia.

SMITH, Lloyd Raymond, mfr.; b. Chicago, Ill., Aug. 21, 1883; s. Arthur Oliver and Edith (Nichols) S.; prep. edn., West Division High Sch., Milwaukee; student U. of Wis., LL.D., 1930; m. Agnes Gram, Jan. 30, 1915; children—Robert, Lewis (dec.), June Ellyn, Lloyd Bruce, Suzanne, Dana Lou, Arthur Oliver. Began with The A. O. Smith Corp., mfrs. of automobile frames, etc., 1905, became pres. 1913, now chmn. bd., gen. mgr. and dir. Mem. advisory com. Milwaukee County Community Fund, Milwaukee Children's Hosp. Mem. Sigma Chi. Republican. Clubs: Milwaukee, Milwaukee Country. Developer of automatic plant for mass production of automobile frames, (10,000 frames per day with force of 120 men); automatic steel pipe plant, having capacity of 32 miles of steel pipe per day; also the Smith-welding process. Home: 2220 N. Terrace Av. Office: The A. O. Smith Corp., Milwaukee, Wis.* Died Dec. 23, 1944.

SMITH, Logan Pearsall, author; b. Millville, N.J., Oct. 18, 1865; s. Robert Pearsall and Hannah (Whitall) S.; student Harverford (Pa.) Coll., 1881-84, Harvard Coll., 1884-85, Belliot Coll., Oxford, 1887-90; B.A., Oxford U., 1903, M.A., 1906; unmarried. Author: The Youth of Parnass, 1895; Life and Letters of Sir Henry Wotton, 1907; Trivia, 1918; More Trivia, 1921; Words and Idioms, 1925; Unforgotten Years, 1939; Milton and His Modern Critics, 1941. Home: 11 St. Leonard's Terrace, London, S.W. 3, England. Died Mar. 2, 1946.

SMITH, Lowell H., army officer; b. Santa Barbara, Calif., Oct. 8, 1892; s. Jasper G. and Nora M. (Holland) S.; ed. high sch., San Fernando, Calif., and San Fernando Academy; m. Madelaine Symington, June 12, 1926. With the Aviation Service of Mexican Army, 1915; mechanical engineer, silver mines of Nevada, 1916-17; enlisted as private Aviation Service, N.A., Apr. 1917; commd. 1st lt., Dec. 1917; capt., Oct. 1918; participated in endurance test, New York to San Francisco, 1919; commd. capt. U.S. Army (regular army), July 1, 1920; comdr. round the world airplane flight, 1924, a distance approximately of 26,103 miles in 365 hours 11 minutes flying time, and a total period of 175 days between departure from Seattle, Wash., Apr. 6, and return to Seattle, Sept. 28. Held 16 world flying records for speed, duration and distance. Awarded D.S.M. (U.S.), "for distinguished service" in World War; Mackay medal, 1919 and 1924, as the outstanding mil. flyer during those yrs.; D.S.M. for world flight, 1924; Distinguished Flying Cross for first refueling of airplanes in flight, 1924; Helen Culver gold medal, "for distinction in broadening the boundaries of world knowledge," 1925. Officer Legion of Honor (France). Advanced 1,000 files in promotion list of U.S. Army, Feb. 25, 1925; became Air Corps rep. at Curtiss Consolidated Corp. and Keystone Aircraft Corp., 1929; advanced to col., Feb. 1942. Protestant.†* Deceased.

SMITH, Lybrand Palmer, naval officer, prof.; b. Decatur, Ill., Jan. 24, 1891; s. Charles Ellsworth and Jennie Agnes (Palmer) S.; ed. Acad. of James Milliken U., 1905-07; B.S., U.S. Naval Acad., 1911; student U. of Santo Domingo, 1919-20; Sc.D., Am. Univ., 1935; m. Katherine Snowden Atwater, April 20, 1912; children—Damaris (wife of Col. A. J. Shower), Towneley (Mrs. Warren M. Rohsenow), Rosalind (wife of Comdr. Robert L. Neyman), Lybrand Palmer. Past midshipman, U.S. Navy, 1911, advanced through grades to capt.; at sea, 1911-19; during mil. occupation of Santo Domingo, held cabinet posts, minister of finance and commerce, sec. state for fgn. affairs, minister of improvements and communications, 1919-21; engring. duty (including command of 2 destroyers), 1923-43; asst. coordinator research and development, Office sec. of Navy, July 15, 1941-45; mem. Nat. Defense Research Com., July 1941-45; Navy Dept. mem. uranium com., 1941-45; mem. war metallurgy com., 1941-45; sr. naval liason officer on Com. Selection and Training of Service Personnel and Com. Applied Math. Statistics, 1942-45; ret. because of phys. disability, 1945; now prof. naval engring. Grad. Sch. Mass. Inst. Tech. Served in Mexican, Haitian, Dominican campaigns, World Wars I and II. Decorated Mexican Campaign Medal, Victory Medal with Silver Star, Haitian Campaign, 2d Marine Expdn. medal, Am. Defense medal, Legion of Merit, Am. Theater Victory Medal, World War II. Registered professional engr., Md. Fellow A.A.A.S.; mem. Am. Soc. Naval Engrs. (mem. council 1936-40), Soc. Naval Architects and Marine Engrs., Soc. Colonial Wars, Chi Psi Omega. Clubs: Army and Navy (Washington, D.C., bd. govs. 1936); Algonquin (Boston). Contbr. tech. papers to professional jours. Address: Massachusetts Institute of Technology, Cambridge, Mass. Died Nov. 25, 1948.

SMITH, Mabell Shippie Clarke, author; b. Boston, Mass., Nov. 14, 1864; d. Edward Augustus May and Frances Dexter (Young) Clarke; A.B., Boston U., 1887; A.M., U. of N.C., 1905; m. F. Alaric Pelton, Oct. 17, 1891 (dec.); m. 2d, James Ravenel Smith, Oct. 22, 1907 (dec.). Mem. sch. com., Dedham, Mass., 1893; sec. Mass. Soc. for Univ. Edn. of Women, 1892; pres. Boston Branch of the Assn. of Collegiate Alumnæ, 1892; 3d v.p. Southern Assn. of Coll. Women, 1904. Acting dean of women, U. of Tenn., 1904; on editorial staff the Chautauquan, 1909, asst. editor same, 1910-14; magazine publicity, Near East Relief, 1922-28. Lecturer, Brooklyn Inst. Arts and Sciences, N.Y. City Bd. of Edn., and before clubs. Govt. service 13 months during World War period. Mem. Soc. Mayflower Descendants, N.C. Soc. Colonial Dames, Authors' League of America, Phi Beta Kappa, Kappa Kappa Gamma. Club: Pen and Brush. Author: A Tar-Heel Baron, 1903; The Spirit of French Letters, 1912; Twenty Centuries of Paris, 1913; Ethel Morton Books, 6 vols., 1915; The Maid of Orleans, 1919; Appendix to Duruy's History of France, 1920; Heroes of the Black Continent, 1921; Appendix to Duruy's History of the World, 1925, 29; Story of Napoleon, 1928. Editor: Studies in Dickens, 1910; Dickens Day by Day, 1911; Class of 1887, 1937. Home: 81 Irving Pl., New York, N.Y. Died May 23, 1942.

SMITH, Marion, lawyer; b. Atlanta, Ga., Nov. 16, 1884; s. Hoke and Marion (Cobb) S.; A.B., U. of Ga., 1903; LL.D., Oglethorpe Univ., 1937; m. Sarah Brock Rawson, Nov. 12, 1913; children—Lucia (Mrs. John L. Tison, Jr., Marion (Mrs. Chauncey Battey), Sarah (Mrs. R. M. Jordan), Lt. Comdr. Hoke Smith, U.S.N.R. Admitted to Ga. bar, 1904, and began practice at Atlanta; mem. Smith, Kilpatrick, Cody, Rogers & McClatchey; dir. Fulton Nat. Bank, Piedmont Hotel Co., Colonial Stores, Inc. Formerly capt. F.A., U.S. Reserve. Chmn. Atlanta Regional Labor Board, 1933-35; mem. President's Bd. of Inquiry for the Cotton Textile Industry to handle nat. textile strike, 1934; mem. Regional War Labor Bd. (part time public member Fourth Regional War Labor Bd.). Alumni trustee Univ. of Ga., 1927-31; chairman bd. regents Univ. System of Ga., 1934-36, 1937-40 and since Jan. 1943. Member American Law Institution, Am. Judicature Soc. (dir.), Am. Bar Assn., Ga. State Bar Assn. (pres. 1932-33), Atlanta Bar Assn. (pres. 1924-25), Phi Beta Kappa, Phi Delta Phi, Sigma Alpha Epsilon. Democrat. Episcopalian. Mason. Clubs: Capital City, Piedmont Driving, Capital City Gun. Contbr. to Jour. Am. Bar Assn., Columbia Law Review, and other legal publs. Home: 80 11th St. N.E. Office: Hurt Bldg., Atlanta, Ga. Died Sept. 9, 1947.

SMITH, Mark A., chief economist, U.S. Tariff Commn.; b. Reading, Vt., Sept. 10, 1886; s. Frank Anson and Martha Alice (Warren) S.; A.B., Dartmouth Coll., 1909, M.A., Univ. of Wis., 1913, Ph.D., Harvard, 1917; m. Alice Marion Hanson, Dec. 3, 1912. Asso. prof. econ. Univ. of Kan., 1917-18, spec. expert, U.S. Tariff Comm., Washington, D.C., 1918-22; research asso. Inst. Econ., 1922-25; economist U.S. Tariff Comm., 1925-34, asst. dir. research, 1934-37, chmn. Planning and Reviewing Com., 1937-42, chief economist, since 1942; professional lecturer George Washington Univ., 1929-32. Mem. Am. Econ. Assn., Am. Statis. Assn., Phi Beta Kappa, Chi Phi, Delta Sigma Rho, Delta Phi Epsilon. Mason. Club: Cosmos (Washington, D.C.). Home: 3711 35th St., N.W. Office: 7th and E Sts., N.W., Washington, D.C.* Deceased.

SMITH, Orma Jacob, coll. dean; b. New Jasper, O., May 3, 1879; s. William Albert and Keziah Elizabeth (Thomas) S.; B.S., in horticulture and forestry, Ohio State U., 1907; M.S., in agr., Ia. State Coll., 1909; student U. of Colo., summers 1916, 24; m. Ora May Vandervort, June 12, 1907; children—Helen (Mrs. Alexander Hanchett Smith), Wendell Vandervort, Harriet Elizabeth (dec. July 31, 1945). Teacher rural schs., 1897-1902; instr. horticulture, Ia. State Coll., 1907-09; prof. biology, Coll. of Ida., since 1910, dean, 1931-June 1941, head dept. of biology since 1941, acting pres., 1936-37, 1938-39. Mem. A.A.A.S., Ida. Edn. Assn., Northwest Scientific Assn. Republican. Methodist. Mason. Home: 1822 Dearborn St., Caldwell, Ida. Died March 11, 1948.

SMITH, Reed, educator; b. Washington, N.C., Jan. 16, 1881; s. Samuel Macon and Ella Friend (Daniel) S.; A.B., Davidson Coll., 1901; A.M., U. of S.C., 1902; A.M., Harvard, 1904, Ph.D., 1909; Litt.D., Davidson (N.C.) Coll., 1935; m. Margaret Dick, Nov. 11, 1920; children—Margaret, Reed; m. 2d, Elizabeth Griffin Henderson, Aug. 26, 1939. Prof. of English, Ala. Presbyn. Coll., 1905-07; ins. in English, U. of Cincinnati, 1909-10; prof. of English, U. of S.C., since 1910, also dean Grad. Sch. since 1929 and founder of extension dept. of univ. First editor Univ. Weekly News. Pres. S.C. Tuberculosis Assn. and organizer of Christmas seal sale in S.C.; was exec. sec. S.C. State Council of Defense; mem. State Memorial Commn. Mem. Mod. Lang. Assn. America, Am. Dialect Soc., Am. Folk-Lore Soc., S.C. Folk-Lore Soc. (pres.), Kappa Sigma, Phi Beta Kappa, Omicron Delta Kappa. Democrat. Presbyn. Editor: Good Reading for High Schools; Open Road to Reading (series). Author: South Carolina Ballads, 1928; The Teaching of Literature, 1935; Learning to Write, 1936; American Anthology of Old-World Ballads, 1937; Learning to Write in College, 1939; also author of brochures, etc. Contbr. to journals. Home: 330 Harden St., Columbia, S.C. Died July 24, 1943.

SMITH, Richard Hewlett, banker; b. Richmond, Va., July 27, 1859; s. Samuel Brown and Margaret (Strother) S.; ed. Strother's Univ. Sch., Richmond, and under Thomas H. Norwood; m. Mary Donthat Barton, Oct. 18, 1882. With Planters Nat. Bank, Richmond (now State-Planters Bank & Trust Co.), since 1885, beginning as clk. and successively cashier, 1892, vice pres., 1911, pres., 1915, chmn. bd. since Aug. 18, 1920. Pres. Family Service Soc., Richmond, since 1925. Chmn. Liberty Loan Com. for State of Va. for three loans, World War I. Democrat. Episcopalian. Clubs: Westmoreland, Virginia Boat. Home: 4050 Forest Hill Av. Office: State-Planters Bank & Trust Co., Richmond, Va. Died Dec. 15, 1945.

SMITH, Robert Brandon, newspaper corr.; b. Canal Dover, O., Jan. 19, 1891; s. Philip Sheridan and Katherine (Shultz) S.; ed. pub. schs.; m. Louise Ballenger, Mar. 24, 1917; children—Robert Brandon, Richard Ballenger, Sherwood. Newspaper work, Massillon, Canton, Cleveland, O., and Washington, D.C., 1907-14; reporter for United Press, Washington, 1914-15, Internat. News Service, 1915-18; with Washington bureau Chicago Tribune, 1918-24; Washington corr. Phila. Pub. Ledger, 1924-34; asst. to adminstr. and dir. of pub. relations, Federal Housing Adminstrn., since July 1934. Clubs: Nat. Press, Gridiron. Home: 8 Albemarle St., Westmoreland Hills, Washington, D.C. Office: Federal Housing Adminstrn., 1001 Vermont Av. N.W., Washington, D.C. Deceased.

SMITH, Thomas R., editor; b. Phillipsburg, N.J., Dec. 13, 1880; s. William and Anne F. S.; ed. partly in London and N.Y.; m. Lucy Blemly, Apr. 2, 1905; 1 dau., Doris L. Lit. adviser to various pub. houses; mgr. Moffat, Yard & Co., pubs., 1911-14; mng. editor The Century Magazine, 1914-20; dir. Horace Liveright, Inc., since 1921. Author: The Woman Question, 1919. Compiler: Swinburne's Poems—an Anthology, 1917. Baudelaire's Poems—an Anthology, 1918. Contbr. to revs. and periodicals. Office: 386 4th Av., New York, N.Y. Died Apr. 11, 1942.

SMITH, Ulysses Simpson, clergyman; b. Davis County, Ia., Feb. 2, 1869; s. Samuel and Mary K. (Smith) S.; Ph.B., Ia. Wesleyan Coll., Mt. Pleasant, 1900, D.D., 1912; m. Eva May Patterson, Aug. 17, 1892 (died Nov. 16, 1930); children—Hazel, Pauline; m. 2d, Mary Hunter, June 27, 1932. Entered Meth. Episcopal ministry, 1892; pastor Montrose, Ia., 1892-95, Batavia, 1895-97, West Burlington, 1897-98, Eddyville, 1898-99, Pulaski, 1900-02, What Cheer, 1902-03, Montezuma, 1903-07, Washington, 1907-14, 1st Ch., Muscatine, 1914-19; trustee Iowa Wesleyan Coll., 1912-19, pres., 1919-27; pastor First M.E. Ch., Fairfield, Ia., 1927-36; pastor Perry, Ia., 1936-40, New London, 1940-42; retired, 1942. Del. Gen. Conf. M.E. Ch., 1912, 20, 24, 36; mem. Uniting Conf. of Methodism, Kansas City, 1939. Traveled abroad visiting Europe, Egypt, Palestine and Syria, 1910. Mason. Clubs: Rotary, Lions. Home: Agency, Ia. Died June 21, 1946.

SMITH, Walter Byron, banker; b. Chicago, Ill., Dec. 29, 1878; s. Byron Laflin and Carrie Cornelia (Stone) S.; A.B., Yale, 1899; m. Florence McCullough, June 6, 1905 (dec.); 1 dau., Winifred Byron McCormack; m. 2d, Grace Mary Ryan, Sept. 5, 1936. Began with John H. Wrenn & Co., Chicago, 1900, partner, 1905-10; dir. Northern Trust Co. (founded by father); chmn. of the bd. Ill. Tool Works. Pres. James C. King Home for Old Men; trustee Art Inst. Chicago, St. Luke's Hosp., John Crerar Library, Glenwood Manual Training Sch. Republican. Presbyn. Clubs: Commercial, Mid-Day, Chicago, Union League, University, Yale, The Attic, Chicago Athletic, Shoreacres, Onwentsia, Old Elm, Racquet. Home: 1175 N. Lake Rd., Lake Forest, Ill. Office: 50 S. La Salle St., Chicago. Died Apr. 2, 1945; buried in Rosehill Cemetery, Chicago.

SMITH, Walter Tenney, importer; b. Pepperell, Mass., Apr. 2, 1870; s. Noah Payson and Caroline Parsons (Baker) S.; grad. high sch., Pepperell; student Harvard Univ., 2 yrs.; m. Minnie Lee Turrentine, June 23, 1898; children—Kenneth Baker, Dudley Tenney. Formerly asst. engr. Metropolitan Elevated Ry., Chicago, in charge constrn. downtown loop; in bldg. constrn. work, 1897-1913; v.p. George A. Fuller Co., builders, 1913-1933; now pres. Thompson & Smith, Inc., importers; v.p. George A. Fuller Co. of Can., Ltd. Served as capt. engrs., N.Y.N.G., 1917-19. Mem. Board of Adjustment, City of Montclair. Mem. Newark C. of C., S.A.R. Conglist. Mason. Clubs: Rotary, Montclair Athletic (ex-pres.), Montclair Golf, The Knoll. Address: 51 3d Av., Newark, N.J. Died Nov. 11, 1940.

SMITH, Walter Winfred, banker; b. St. Louis, Mo., Jan. 19, 1877; s. James A., Jr., and Elizabeth J. (Milford) S.; prep. edn., high sch., St. Louis; grad. Benton Coll. Law, St. Louis; m. Elsie Thompson, Aug. 16, 1904; children—Alan Thompson, Stuart Hoxton. Began in banking business with Miss. Valley Trust Co., St. Louis, 1900; clearing house bank examiner, 1908-11; nat. bank examiner, 1911-14; class C dir. Federal Reserve Bank of St. Louis, 1914-15; v.p. 3d Nat. Bank of St. Louis, 1915-19; v.p. 1st Nat. Bank of St. Louis, 1919-27, pres. 1928-48, chairman since 1948; director Mo. Pacific R.R., Am. Automobile Ins. Co., Securities Investment Co., United Wood Heel Co., Monsanto Chem. Co., Southwestern Bell Telephone Co., General Am. Life Ins. Co., Am. Central Ins. Co. Chmn. Liberty Loan Campaign, World War. Republican. Episcopalian. Clubs: Noonday, Mo. Athletic Assn., Log Cabin, Racquet, St. Louis, Country. Home: 9948 Litzinger Rd. St. Louis 17, Mo. Office: 1st Nat. Bank, St. Louis 2, Mo. Died April 26, 1949.

SMITH, William Eason, railroad exec.; b. Georgetown, Ga., Sept. 13, 1868; s. James Allen and Sarah Elizabeth (Harrell) S.; ed. Southern Normal Bus. Coll., Bowling Green, Ky., Laurel Sem., London, Ky.; m. Sarah Catherine Rogers, Sept. 11, 1889; children—Roger Downes (dec.), Harrell Walton, Cecil Howard, Mary Elizabeth (Mrs. William C. Robbins), Grace (Mrs. Harry S. Coffman). Track supervisor L.&N. R.R., 1890-95, roadmaster, 1895-1905, asst. supt., 1905-12, supt. constrn., 1912-14, div. supt., Evansville, Ind., and Birmingham, Ala., 1914-23, asst. gen. mgr., 1924-31, gen. mgr., 1931-37, v.p. and gen. mgr. June 1, 1937-Nov. 1, 1946; retired; dir. Cincinnati Union Terminal Co.; v.p. Gulf Transit Co.; v.p., dir. Louisville & Nashville Terminal Co., Memphis Union Sta. Co., Newport & Cincinnati Bridge Co. Mason (Shriner). Home: 2220 Alta Av. Address: 9th and Broadway, Louisville, Ky. Died Jan. 17, 1948; buried Elmwood Cemetery, Birmingham, Ala.

SMITH, William Clarke, teacher; b. Manchester, N.H., Feb. 22, 1857; s. Isaac William and Amanda White (Brown) S.; student Dartmouth, 1880; M.A., U. of Berlin, 1895; unmarried. Teacher, U. of Wyo., 1887; master and part owner St. Luke's Sch., Wayne, Pa. Republican. Episcopalian. Mem. N.E. Soc., Phila., Alpha Delta Phi. Clubs: Alpha Delta Phi (New York); Church (Phila.). Author: About Us and the Deacon, 1911; Roger, 1911; The Vigil, 1912; The Manger, 1913; Songs from the Foot-hills, 1915. Home: Wayne, Pa. Died Jan. 5, 1942.

SMITH, William Cunningham, educator; b. Greensboro, N.C., Apr. 19, 1871; s. Samuel Cunningham and Ella (Cunningham) S.; Ph.B., U. of N.C., 1896, grad. study, 1898-1900, Litt.D., 1920; grad. study Harvard and U. of Wis.; m. Gertrude Allen, Aug. 12, 1897; children—Gertrude Allen, Linda Rogers, Margaret Ella, Elizabeth Cunningham, William Cunningham. Instr. in history, U. of N.C., 1896-97, instr. in English, 1897-1900; prof. history, N.C. Coll. for Women (now Women's Coll. of Univ. of North Carolina), 1900-03, prof. English, 1903-38, prof. emeritus since 1938, head of dept., 1904-38, also dean Coll. Liberal Arts, 1920-38, extension lecturer. Mem. N.C. Literary and Hist. Assn., N.C. Folk-Lore Soc., Greensboro Merchants Assn., Phi Beta Kappa, Kappa Alpha, Pi Gamma Mu. Democrat. Presbyterian. Mem. Jr. Order United Am. Mechanics. Rotarian. Author: Charles D. McIver (biography), 1907. American Authors, 1913. Home: 1500 Spring Garden St., Greensboro, N.C. Died Dec. 17, 1943.

SMITH, William Edward; b. Buffalo, N.Y., Mar. 12, 1873; s. Harry and Sarah A. S.; student Fredonia (N.Y.) State Normal Sch.; m. Eunice Greenwood Weaver, Apr. 8, 1918. Clerk and salesman, 1895-97; with Standard Oil Co. of N.J., 1897-1901; gen. salesman for Standard Oil Co. of Ky., 1901-06, sales mgr. Standard Oil Co., of New York, 1906-21, vice pres., 1921-27, pres. 1927-45; retired Mar. 15, 1945, with fifty yrs. service. Mason. Clubs: Pendennis, Louisville Country (Louisville). Home: Prospect, Ky. Died Oct. 21, 1946.

SMITH, William Griswold, prof. engring.; b. Toledo, O., July 18, 1869; s. William Henry Harrison and Julia Welles (Griswold) S.; Yale, 1887-89; M.E., Cornell U., 1892; m. Marion Evans Twiss, June 23, 1904; children—Madeleine Marion, Janet Griswold. Bicycle mfr., Toledo, O., 1894-99; instr. mech. engring., U. of N.D., 1902-04; asso. prof. mech. engring., Armour Inst. Tech., 1905-20; prof. engring., Northwestern U., 1920-39; prof. emeritus Northwestern Tech. Inst. since 1939; spl. lecturer, Defense Training Inst. New York, 1941-43; spl. lecturer descriptive geometry and industrial management, U. of Calif., 1923-24. Mem. Delta Kappa Epsilon, Sigma Xi. Republican. Methodist. Club: University. Author: Practical Descriptive Geometry, 1912; Engineering Kinematics, 1923; Motor Tour of British Isles, 1930; Engineering Drafting, 1934. Home: 161 Beechwood, Packanack Lake, N.J. Died Dec. 25, 1943.

SMITH, W(illiam) Hinckle, capitalist; b. Phila., Pa., June 16, 1861; s. J. Frailey and Harriet L. (Hinckle) S.; B.S., U. of Pa., 1882; m. Jacqueline Harrison, Nov. 28, 1883; 1 son, Col. Hoxie Harrison. Dir. Girard Trust Co., Penn Mutual Life Ins. Co., Kennecott Copper Co., Mack Trucks Inc., Nevada Northern R.R. Co., Midland Valley R.R. Co., Curtiss-Wright Corp.; Wright Aeronautical Corp., Muskogee Corp., Am. Briquet Co., Adams Express Co., Braden Copper Co., Tubize Chatillon Corp. Trustee Univ. Museum of Phila. (v.p.), Pa. Hort. Soc., Bryn Mawr (Pa.) Hosp. Clubs: Rittenhouse, Philadelphia (Phila.); Midday (New York); Yacht Club du France. Home: Bryn Mawr, Pa. Office: Girard Trust Co. Bldg., Philadelphia, Pa. Died Jan. 28, 1943.

SMITH, William Hopton, physician; b. Goldsboro, N.C., May 29, 1882; s. Wiley Hopton and Mary Elizabeth (McArthur) S.; ed. N.C. Agrl. and Mech. Coll., Raleigh, N.C., 1899-1900; student U. of N.C., 1900-04; M.D., U. of Pa., 1906; m. Mary Elizabeth Pool, Jan. 3, 1905; children—William H. (dec.), Mary Elizabeth, Wiley. Resident physician Phila. Polyclinic Hosp., 1907-08; began practice at Bailey, N.C., 1908; moved to Goldsboro, 1916; mem. Dist. Med. Advisory Bd., 1917-18; county physician, Wayne County, 1917-20; dir. Smith Hardware Co. Mem. and ex-pres. N.C. State Bd. Med. Examiners. President N.C. Tuberculosis Association, 1942-43. Diplomate of Am. Bd. of Internal Medicine. Fellow Am. Coll. of Physicians; mem. Am. and Southern med. socs., N.C. State Med. Assn., N.C. State Tuberculosis Assn. (dir.), Zeta Psi, Nu Sigma Nu. Democrat. Presbyterian. Mason. Home: 309 S. William St. Office: Bank of Wayne Bldg., Goldsboro, N.C. Died Sep. 29, 1945.

SMITH, William Owen, lawyer; b. Koloa, Kauai, N. I., Aug. 4, 1848; s. Dr. J. W. and M. K. S.; ed. common sch., Honolulu; studied law with Alfred S. Hartwell, Honolulu; m. Mary A. Hobron, Mar. 23, 1876. Sheriff Kauai and Maui, 1870-74; admitted to bar, 1876; mem. Hawaiian legislature, 1878-98, 1907; atty.-gen. Hawaii, 1893-99. Republican. Clubs: Pacific, University, Social Science (Honolulu); Metropolitan (Washington). Address: Honolulu, T.H. Died Apr. 13, 1929.

SMITH, William Thomas, industrial finance and management; b. Chicago, Ill., Feb. 5, 1884; s. Samuel and Mary Jane (Thomas) S.; ed. grammar sch.; m. Gertrude Hammond, May 10, 1905; children—Gertrude Hammond, May Janet, William Thomas. Studied and practiced architecture under Bruce Price, N.Y. City, 1898-1905; v.p. of constrn., Thompson Starrett Co., 1909-13; pres. Industrial Service Corp., 1913-17; operating v.p. Merchant Shipbuilding Corp., 1917-21; partner and vice-pres. W. A. Harriman & Co., industrial finance and management, 1921-30; chmn. bd. Wm. Cramp & Sons Ship & Engine Bldg. Co.; also officer or dir. Am. Ship & Commerce Corp., Bear Mountain Hudson River Bridge Co., Russian Finance & Construction Co., Georgian Manganese Co., Ltd.; Modern-Housing of Washington Inc., N. Washington; Housing Corp., Mt. Airy Corp., Sligo Park Properties, Inc., M.D.D.C. Corp., Norcastle Corp., Sterling Iron & Ry. Co. Republican. Mason. Club: Whitehall. Home: 61 Duffield Drive, South Orange, N.J. Office: 39 Broadway, New York, N.Y.* Deceased.

SMITH, William Walter, clergyman; b. N.Y. City, May 27, 1868; s. William Gordon and Henriette Louise (Krüger) S.; A.B., Princeton, 1889, A.M., 1892; grad Gen. Theol. Sem., 1892; M.D., Coll. Physicians and Surgeons (Columbia), 1895; Regent's diploma and N.Y. City license, 1895; New York Dental Coll., 1895-97; post-grad. work in New York Lying-in Hosp., Manhattan Eye and Ear Hosp., DeMilt Dispensary; Teachers Coll. (Columbia), 1900-04; m. Maud Parsons Canfield, June 28, 1909. Deacon, 1892, priest, 1893, P.E. Ch.; lay reader, "Heavenly Rest," New York, 1886-92, curate, 1892-1900; founder, and missionary, Christ Ch., Bronxville, 1900-02; on staff City Mission Soc., 1901-07; chaplain House of Refuge, 1901-07; curate St. Andrew's Ch., New York, since 1909. Mem. New York Churchmen's Assn., Alumni Assn. Gen. Theol. Sem. Democrat. Author: Sunday School Teaching, 1903; The Doctrines of the Church, 1903; The History and Use of the Prayer Book, 1903; The Making of the Bible, 1903; The Ageless Hymns of the Church, 1904; From the Exile to the Advent, 1904; Religious Education, 1909; The Sunday School of Today, 1911; The Elements of Child Study and Religious Pedagogy, 1912; The Student's Historical Geography of the Holy Land, 1912; Five Minute Addresses to Young People, 1915; Life of Christ in the Prayer Book Gospels, 1919. Home: 33 E. 22d St. Address: 416 Lafayette St., New York, N.Y. Died Mar. 2, 1942.

SMITH, William Wilberforce, educator; b. Ontonagon, Mich., Apr. 22, 1858; s. Rev. James Irwin and Martha (Bracken) S.; A.B., Lafayette Coll., 1880, A.M., 1883; Princeton Theol. Sem., 1881-83; LL.D., Lafayette, 1905; m. Anna Wills Page, Aug. 2, 1905. Prin. Englewood (N.J.) Sch. for Boys, 1885-95; engaged in business, New York, 1896-1900, San Francisco, 1901-03; head master Berkeley Sch., New York, 1905; pres. Coe Coll., 1905-08; dir. Sch. of Commerce and Finance, James Millikin U., since Jan., 1909. Address: Decatur, Ill. Died Feb. 25, 1943.

SMITHERS, William West (smĭth'ẽrz), lawyer; b. Phila., Pa., May 5, 1864; s. William Henry and Mary J. (Reed) S.; LL.B., U. of Pa., 1887; m. Virginia Lyons, June 4, 1889 (died Jan. 14, 1924); m. 2d, Anne C. McDonnell, May 18, 1929. Practiced, Philadelphia, since 1887, spl. attention late years to corp., ins., negligence, probate and internat. law. Member Am. Bar Assn. (chmn. Comp. Law Bur. and mem. since its orgn., 1908), Am. Inst. Criminal Law and Criminology (chmn. com. on transls., pub. Criminal Science Series), Bar Assn. Philadelphia (treas. and mem. bd. govs., 1902-23), Am. Soc. Internat. Law, Hist. Soc. of Pa., Internat. Law Assn., Am. Foreign Law Assn. (pres.), Société de Leg. Comparée, Institut de Droit Comparé; del. of Am. Bar Assn. to conf. Inter-Am. Bar Assn., Havana, Mar. 1941. Republican. Methodist. Clubs: University, Racquet. Author: Relation of Attorney and Client, 1887; Coaching Trip Through Delaware, 1892; Life of the Milford Bard, 1894; Executive Clemency in Pennsylvania, 1909; also many legal mag. articles, including "Code Napoleon"; "Imperial German Civil Code"; "Russian Civil Law"; "The Pardoning Power." Translator: Which Was the Greater Love? (from French of Henry Bordeaux), 1930. Speaks French and Spanish. Mason (K.T.). Home: Spring Lake, N.J. Office: Otis Bldg., Philadelphia, Pa.* Died Mar. 19, 1947.

SMYTH, Ellison Adger (smĭth), mfr.; b. Charleston, S.C., Oct. 26, 1847; s. Rev. Thomas and Margaret M. (Adger) S.; ed. S.C. Mil. Acad.; served in C.S.A.; m. Julia Gambrill; children—J. Adger (dec.), Mrs. A. F. McKissick, Mrs. L. D. Blake, Mrs. J. A. Hudgens, Jenny (dec.). Former pres. Belton (S.C.) Cotton Mills, Bank of Belton, Pelzer (S.C.) Mfg. Co., Chicora Bank (Pelzer, S.C.); pres. Greenville (S.C.) News Co., Balfour (N.C.) Mills; also dir. and officer other corps. Mem. U.S. Industrial Commn., Washington. Ex-pres. Am. Cotton Mfrs. Assn., Cotton Mfrs. Assn. of S.C. Home: Flat Rock, N.C. Died Aug. 3, 1942.

SMYTH, Henry Lloyd, univ. prof.; b. near St. Mary's, Ontario, Jan. 11, 1862; s. Rev. Thomas Henry and Charlotte (Hughes) S.; A.B., Harvard, 1883, C.E., 1885; m. Margarita Pumpelly, Nov. 8, 1894; children—Mrs. Charlotte P. Russell (dec.), Mrs. Pauline P. Fraser-Campbell, Henry Lloyd, Barbara E. Instr. geol. surveying, 1893-95, asst. prof. of mining, 1895-1900, prof. mining and metallurgy, Harvard, 1900-24, dir. mining and metall. labs., emeritus since 1924. Fellow Am. Acad. Arts and Sciences, Geol. Soc. Am.; mem. Am. Inst. Mining Engrs., Mining and Metall. Soc. Am. Clubs: Century, Harvard (New York); St. Botolph, Oakley, Harvard (Boston). Author various monographs, and contbr. to procs. of scientific socs. and jours. Home: Belmont St., Watertown, Mass. Died Apr. 2, 1944.

SMYTH, Herbert C(rommelin), lawyer; born in New York, N.Y., December 19, 1870; s. Joseph Kennedy and Gabriella (Ogden) S.; LL.B., New York Law Sch., 1892; m. Maimieé S. Murray, Apr. 8, 1896; children—H. Crommelin, Murray Ogden, Thelma S. Admitted to N.Y. bar, 1892 and since in practice in N.Y. City; mem. firm Nadal, Smyth & Berrier, 1894-1902, Wellman & Smyth, 1902-33, later Smyth & Smyth, now Wellman, Smyth, Lowenstein & Fennelley; associated as trial counsel with most of New York's prominent law firms 35 years; trial counsel in Gloria Vanderbilt-Whitney custody case; trial counsel in petroleum cracking process cases; atty. in important anti-trust cases. Spl. asst. to atty.-gen. of U.S., 1912-17. Served at Plattsburg Training Camp, 1916. Mem. Am. and N.Y. State bar assns., Assn. Bar of City of N.Y. Democrat. Clubs: Metropolitan, Manhattan. Writer of lectures on "Trial Tactics" and "Interesting Trials." Office: 25 Broad St., New York, N.Y. Died Jan. 15, 1944.

SNAPE, John, clergyman; b. Odessa, Del., Dec. 13, 1870; s. John and Esther J. (Dyer) S.; St. Luke's Acad., Phila.; grad. Crozer Theol. Sem., Chester, Pa., 1897; D.D., Redlands (Calif.) U., 1918; m. Grace S. Bradbury (dec.); children—Alice F., Ruth Anna J. (dec.); m. 2d, Marion M. Lansing. Ordained Bapt. ministry, 1894; pastor 3d Ch., Camden, N.J., 1893-96, Emanuel Ch., Camden, 1896-99, Delaware Av. Ch., Wilmington, 1899-1903, 1st Ch., Newcastle, Pa., 1903-08, Tabernacle Ch., Utica, N.Y., 1908-14, 1st Ch., Spokane, Wash., 1914-16, Hollywood Ch., Los Angeles, Calif., 1916-20 (built ch.), Oakland, 1920-26, Euclid Av. Ch., Cleveland, O., 1926-28, Temple Ch., Los Angeles, 1928-33; retired, 1933. Mem. exec. com. Northern Bapt. Conv., 1920-26; pres. Northern Calif. Bapt. Conv., 1921-23; pres. Am. Bapt. Publn. Soc., 1926-27; trustee Redlands U., Berkeley Baptist Divinity School; mem. bd. Am. Bapt. Foreign Missionary Soc. (pres. 1932-33). Republican. Mason; chaplain Grand Lodge Masons of Calif. Clubs: Lions, Optimist, Breakfast, Country. Author: The Ideal Christian, 1900; Dedication of Children, 1909; Soul Trapping, 1927; Remember Jesus Christ, 1930; also numerous hymns and poems. Platform lecturer. Address: 210 S. Larchmont Blvd., Los Angeles, Calif. Died Sep. 5, 1941.

SNEED, William Lent, orthopedic surgeon; b. Nashville, Tenn., Mar. 21, 1881; s. William Lent and Mary Lucy (Waller) S.; student Nashville Bible Coll., 1904-06; M.D., Vanderbilt Med. Sch., 1910; m. Marion E. Stokes, June 19, 1920; children—William Lent, Constance Blake, Pamela Ann Waller. Instr. in anatomy, Vanderbilt U., 1910-11; became attending surgeon orthopedic dept., Hosp. for Ruptured and Crippled, New York, 1912; now cons. surgeon Hosp. for Ruptured and Crippled and Meadow Brook Hosp. (Hempstead, L.I.); instr. in applied anatomy, Cornell U. Med. Coll., since 1917; cons. orthopedic surgeon Nassau County, French and North Shore Community hosps. Lt. Med. Corps, World War. Fellow Am. Coll. Surgeons; mem. A.M.A.; Acad. of Medicine, N.Y. Southern Soc., Tenn. Soc. of N.Y. Democrat. Clubs: Cornell, Racquet and Tennis (New York); Golf. Author: Orthopedics in Childhood, 1931. Home: 570 Park Av. Office: 654 Madison Av., New York, N.Y. Died Dec. 7, 1941.

SNELL, Earl (Wilcox), gov. of Ore.; b. Olex, Ore., July 11, 1895; s. William Henry and Mattie (Balding) S.; student Ore. Inst. Tech., 1920-22; m. Edith Welshons, July 10, 1920; 1 son, William Earl. Co-owner automobile agency and garage, Arlington, 1915-46; mem. House of Reps. of Ore., 1927, 29, 31, 33 (speaker of house, 1933); elected sec. of state, 1934, 1938; elected governor of Oregon, 1942; reelected 1946. Served in World War I. National president American Association Motor Vehicle Administrators, 1941-42; national secretary, National Secs. of State, 1941-42; mem. bd. trustees, Pacific U. Chmn. Western Govs. Conf., 1947. Mem. Scabbard and Blade, Beta Theta Pi. Protestant. Republican. Home: 160 E. Lincoln, Salem, Ore. Address: State Capitol, Salem, Ore. Died Oct. 28, 1947.

SNELL, Henry Bayley, artist; b. Richmond, Eng., Sept. 29, 1858; s. Edward and Elizabeth S.; studied Art Students' League, New York; m. Florence Francis, 1888. Gold medal, Phila. Art Club; 1st prize, Tenn. Centennial, Nashville, 1897; hon. mention, Paris Expn., 1900; asst. dir. of Fine Arts, U.S. Commn., Paris Expn., 1900; Officier de l'Académie et de l'Instruction Publique; silver medal, Buffalo Expn., 1901, St. Louis Expn., 1904; silver and gold medals, Panama P.I. Expn., 1915. N.A., 1906; hon. life pres. New York Water Color Club; mem. Am. Water Color Soc. Home: New Hope, Pa. Died Jan. 17, 1943.

SNIDER, Luther Crocker (snī'dẽr), geologist; b. Mt. Summit, Ind., Sept. 13, 1882; s. John and Lou (Leath) S.; student Rose Poly. Inst., 1903-04, U. of Okla., 1910-11; A.B., Ind. U., 1908, A.M., 1909; Ph.D., U. of Chicago, 1915; m. Ruth Gladys Marshall, Mar. 31, 1907; children—Hester Bernice, John Luther. Teacher common and high schs., 1901-03 and 1904-06; chemist, field geologist and asst. dir. Okla. Geol. Survey, 1909-15; field geologist Pierce Oil Corp., Tulsa, Okla., 1915-16, Cosden Oil & Gas Co., 1916-17; asst. chief and chief geologist Empire Gas & Fuel Co., Bartlesville, Okla., 1917-25; cons. geologist Henry L. Doherty & Co., 1925-35; same, Cities Service Co., 1935-40; prof. of geology, U. of Texas, since 1941. Fellow A.A.A.S., Geol. Soc. America, Soc. Econ. Geology; mem. Am. Assn of Petroleum Geologists (editor 1933-37; pres. 1940), Sigma Xi, Phi Beta Kappa (alumnus). Republican. Methodist. Mason. Author: Petroleum and Natural Gas in Oklahoma, 1913; Oil and Gas in the Mid-Continent Fields, 1920; Earth History, 1932; also various bulls. of Okla. Geol. Survey, 1910-16. Contbr. to scientific mags. Home: 1300 Northwood Rd., Austin 21, Tex. Died May 24, 1947; buried Mount Summit, Ind.

SNODGRASS, John Harold, former consul-gen.; b. Marietta, O.; s. William A. and Elizabeth (Dye) S.; A.B., Marietta Coll., 1891; student Cincinnati Law Sch.; m. Helen Bancker Hardy, Nov. 28, 1901. Newspaper work, 1893-1904; Am. consul at Pretoria, 1905-08, Kobe, Japan, 1908-09; consul gen. at Moscow, Russia, May 31, 1909-Jan. 1, 1917. In charge of German and Austrian interests and relief of civil and mil. prisoners by direction of sec. of state, Aug. 1, 1914-Sept. 1, 1916, in Central, Western and Southern European Russia, Siberia and Central Asia. Acting q.m. and commissary 2d W.Va. Vol. Inf. during Spanish-Am. War. Mem. Acad. Polit. Science, Council of Fgn. Relations, Alpha Sigma Phi (ex-grand sr. pres. Nat. Chapter), etc. Clubs: Nat. Republican, Merrick Country; Ohio Soc., etc. Author: Handbook on Russia. Home: Westbury, L.I. Office: 54 W. 40th St., New York. Died Dec. 1943.

SNOOK, H(omer) Clyde (snŏŏk), electrophysicist; b. Antwerp, O., Mar. 25, 1878; s. Wilson Hunt and Nancy Jane (Graves), S.; A.B., Ohio Wesleyan U., 1900, M.S., 1910, Sc.D. from same university, 1926; A.M., Allegheny Coll., Meadville, Pa., 1902; post-grad. work, U. of Pa., 1904-08; m. May Eusebia McKee, June 24, 1903. Prof. physics and chemistry, High Sch., Ohio Soldiers and Sailors Orphans' Home, Xenia, O., 1900-01; asst. prof. chemistry, Allegheny Coll., 1901-02; wireless telegraph expert, with Queen & Co., Phila., Pa., 1902-03; pres. Roentgen Mfg. Co., Phila., 1903-13, Snook-Roentgen Mfg. Co., Phila., 1913-16; v.p. Victor Electric Corp., Chicago, 1916-18; elec. engr. with Western Elec. Co., 1918-25; elec. engr. with Bell Telephone Labs., 1925-27; cons. engr. since 1927. Fellow Am. Inst. E.E., Am. Physical Soc.; mem. Am. Roentgen Ray Soc., Phila., Roentgen Society, Phi Beta Kappa, Phi Delta Theta. Awarded Edward Longstreth medal, Franklin Inst., 1919; gold medal, Radiol. Soc. of North America, 1923; hon. fellowship and gold medal, Am. Coll. Radiology, 1928. Chmn. noise elimination com. Nat. Safety Council, 1930. Presbyterian. Mason. Inventor X-ray transformer; numerous patented developments in X-rays, radio, the communication art, metallurgy and optics. Home: 45 Woodland Av., Summit, N.J. Died Sep. 22, 1942.

SNOW, Franklin Augustus, civil engr., retired; b. Providence, R.I., Feb. 10, 1856; s. Stephen W. and Harriet R. (Fisher) S.; ed. pub. schs., Providence, R.I.; m. Grace Darling, Feb. 23, 1887; children—Irene, Beatrice. Began as civil engr. at Providence, R.I., 1873; followed civil engring. for 9 yrs. in Brazil, Central Am. and Colo.; studied rys. of Peru and Chile, 1885; made surveys for the first steam railroad in Salvador, C.A., and helped to build same; chief engr. for the Dutch contractors for excavating the Culebra Cut, Panama Canal, also for Am. Contracting & Dredging Co., at Colon, Panama Canal, 1885, 86, during the time of Ferdinand de Lesseps; returned to U.S., 1886, and engaged in gen. contracting, building waterworks and sewerage systems; contractor since 1901 for underground conduit systems for Edison Electric Illuminating Co., of Boston, Fall River Electric Light Co., Cambridge Electric Light Co., and New Bedford Electric Light Co. Fellow Royal Geog. Soc., London; mem. Am. Soc. C.E., Boston Soc. C.E., Soc. Mayflower Descendants, Boston C. of C. Clubs: Engineers, University, Algonquin, Boston Art, Brae Burn Country, Boston Athletic. Home: 199 Dean Rd., Brookline, Mass. Died March 19, 1942.

SNOW, Sydney Bruce, clergyman, educator; b. Winchester, Mass., Mar. 19, 1878; s. William Alanson and Helen Florence (Winde) S.; A.B., Harvard, 1900; S.T.B., Harvard Divinity Sch., 1906; D.D., Meadville Theol. Sch., 1923; Ph.D., Royal Hungarian Francis Joseph U. (Szeged), 1938; m. Margrette Kennedy, Dec. 25, 1901; children—William Lowell (dec.), Donald Kennedy, Alice (Mrs. John B. Frosst), Helen (Mrs. Roger T. Maher). Ordained minister Unitarian Ch., 1906; pastor Palo Alto, Calif., 1906-09, Concord, N.H., 1909-12; asso. minister King's Chapel, Boston, Mass., 1912-20; pastor Montreal, Can., 1920-28; pres. Meadville Theol. Sch., Chicago, also dean of faculty and prof. practical theology since 1928. Served with Army Ednl. Corps, A.E.F., 1918-19. Chmn. commn. of American Unitarian Assn. to investigate Unitarian Ch. in Transylvania under Roumanian rule, 1920. Hon. mem. Brit. Assembly of Unitarian Chs., Chief Consistory of Unitarian Ch. of Transylvania. Chaplain Mass. Commandery, Mil. Order Loyal Legion since 1941. Mason. Clubs: Century (New York); Union (Boston); University, Quadrangle (Chicago). Home: 5700 Woodlawn Av., Chicago, Ill. Died Apr. 7, 1944.

SNOW, William Josiah, army officer; b. in New York, Dec. 16, 1868; s. William Dunham and Mary Elizabeth (Newell) S.; grad. U.S. Mil. Acad., 1890, Arty. Sch., 1898; Army War Coll., 1908; LL.D., Yale, 1919; m. Isabel Locke, Apr. 19, 1892; 1 son, William Arthur (deceased). Commd. 2d lieut. 1st Arty., June 12, 1890; promoted through grades to maj. gen., June 28, 1918; served as brig. gen. N.A., 1917-18. Duty at forts Hamilton, Slocum and Monroe until 1898; regimental q.-m. 7th Arty., 1898-99; with regt. in Philippine Islands, 1900-01; organized, and comd. 20th Battery, Field Arty., at Ft. Riley, Kan., and Ft. Robinson, Neb., to Dec. 1905; sec. Sch. of Application for Cav. and Field Arty., 1906-07; duty with War Dept., 1910-14; on Mexican border, 1917; in P.I. and Hawaii, 1915-17; reorganizing Sch. of Fire for F.A., Ft. Sill, Okla., 1917; apptd. comdr. 156th Field Arty. Brig., Camp Jackson, Columbia, S.C., Sept. 1917; chief of F.A., U.S. Army, Feb. 10, 1918-Dec. 19, 1927 (retired). Awarded D.S.M.; Comdr. Legion of Honor; Companion of the Bath. Home: 2220 20th St. N.W., Washington, D.C.; (summer) Blue Ridge Summit, Pa. Died Feb. 27, 1946.

SNYDER, Baird, III, civ. engr.; b. Lansford, Pa.; s. Baird and Jennie Craig (Romig) S.; student Cornell U., Yale; grad. Mass. Inst. Tech., 1924; m. Beatrice B. Short, Nov. 14, 1936; children—Baird, IV, Collins. Engr. ry. and anthracite mining, 1918-25; asst. supt., Lawrence Colliery, Madera Hill Coal Co., Frackville, Pa., 1925; pres. and gen. mgr., Snyder Engring. Co., 1926-35; chief engr., U.S. Farm Security Adminstrn., 1937-39; dep. adminstr., Wage and Hour Div., U.S. Dept. Labor, 1939-42; became asst. (dep.) adminstr., Federal Works Agency, 1942. Mem. Sigma Phi. Episcopalian. Home: 8 Blackstone Rd., Westmoreland Hills, Md. Office: 6137 Federal Works Agency Bldg., Washington, D.C. Died May 18, 1946.

SNYDER, Carl, statistician, author; b. Cedar Falls, Ia., 1869; m. Madeline Murphy. Pres. Am. Statis. Assn., 1928; mem. Am. Acad. Arts and Sciences. Author: New Conceptions in Science, 1904; The World Machine, 1907; American Railways as Investments, 1907; Business Cycles and Business Measurements, 1927; Capitalism the Creator: The Economic Foundations of Modern Industrial Society, 1940; also many papers in jours. on economics and banking. Office: care Federal Reserve Bank, 33 Liberty St., New York, N.Y. Died Feb. 15, 1946.

SNYDER, Henry Nelson, coll. pres.; b. Macon, Ga., Jan. 14, 1865; s. Henry Nelson and Ann (Hill) S.; A.B., Vanderbilt U., 1887, A.M., 1890; grad. work, at Vanderbilt, Göttingen, British Museum, 1887-90 and 1898-99; hon. D.Litt., S.C. U., 1902, LL.D., 1905; LL.D., Duke U., 1935; LL.D., Furman U., 1937; m. Lula Eubank, July 9, 1889; children—Hugh, Ellen, Lula Nelson. Asst. in Latin, Vanderbilt U., 1887-90; prof. English lit. since 1890, pres., 1902-42, Wofford Coll. Author: Sidney Lanier—A Study in Interpretation, 1906; The Persistence of Spiritual Ideals in English letters, 1927; An Educational Odyssey, 1947; also articles on literature and educational subjects. Compiler: Old Testament Narratives, 1928. Mem. Assn. S.C. Colleges (pres.). Mem. Unification Commn. M.E. Ch., S., and Gen. Bd. Christian Edn. same. Mem. Joint Hymnal Com. Meth. Chs. Retired 1942. Home: Spartanburg, S.C. Died Sept. 18, 1949.

SNYDER, J(ohn) Buell, congressman; b. Somerset County, Pa., July 30, 1879; grad. Lock Haven (Pa.) Teachers Coll.; student summer sessions Harvard and Columbia. Prin. various schs., 1901-12; western Pa. dist. mgr. The Macmillan Co., 1912-32. Mem. 73d to 79th Congresses (1933-46), 23d Dist. Pa. Legislative rep. for Pa. School Dirs. during sessions of State Legislature, 1921-23; mem. Nat. Commn. of 100 for Study and Survey of Rural Schs. in U.S., 1922-24; mem. Bd. of Edn. of Perry Township and sec. County Sch. Dirs'. Assn., 1922-32. Founder and organizer Pa. Inter High Sch. Forensic and Music Assn.; mem. Postwar Mil. Policy Com., 1944-45. Coauthor of Guffey-Snyder Bituminous Coal Act passed by 73d Congress. Chmn. House Com. on Army appropriations since 1937. Home: Perryopolis, Pa. Died Feb. 24, 1946.

SNYDER, Leroy Edwin, newspaper exec.; b. Ligonier, Ind., Feb. 9, 1879; s. Ammon and Amelia Maria (Beber) S.; student de Pauw U., 1897-99; m. Antoinette Euphemia Wilkin, Apr. 2, 1904. Circulation mgr., later reporter, South Bend (Ind.) Times, 1899-1903; reporter and editor various Indianapolis papers, 1903-07; exec. officer Indianapolis Bd. of Park Commrs. 1907-10; sec. Indianapolis Trade Assn., 1910-13; mem. staff N.Y. Bur. of Municipal Research, 1913-15; dir. Rochester (N.Y.) Bur. of Municipal Research, 1915-19; exec. sec. Rochester Clothiers Exchange, 1919-23; asst. to pres. of Gannett Newspapers since 1923; v.p. Gannett Co., Inc. Dem. candidate for mayor of Rochester, 1925; nonpartisan candidate councilman-at-large, 1931, vice chmn. Genesee State Park Commn.; dir. Rochester Civic Music Assn.; trustee of the Family Soc. of Rochester. Mem. bd. of mgrs. Memorial Art Gallery. Mem. Rochester Chamber of Commerce, N.Y. State Soc. of Newspaper Editors, Phi Kappa Psi. Democrat. Unitarian. Clubs: University, Ad, City, Torch, Twenty, Blind Alley, Print (Rochester). Author: A Layman's Religion, 1938. Home: 221 Cobbs Hill Drive. Office: Times-Union Bldg., Rochester, N.Y. Died Feb. 16, 1944.

SNYDER, Oscar John, osteopathic physician; b. St. Louis, Mo., Nov. 17, 1866; s. Joseph Nicholas and Catherine (Legner) S.; ed. State Normal Sch., Winona, Minn., 1884-90; B.S., Columbian (now George Washington) U., 1894, M.S., 1896; D.O., Northern Inst. of Osteopathy, Minneapolis, Minn., 1899; D.Sc., Phila. Coll. of Osteopathy, 1929; m. Aline Cantwell, June 22, 1904; children—Joseph Cantwell, Honora, James Ayers. Lt. Engr. Corps, Washington, D.C., 1900-03. Began practice, 1899; pres. Phila. Coll. of Osteopathy, 1899-1907; pres. Pa. State Bd. Osteopathic Examiners, 1909-30. Pres. Pa. Osteopathic Assn., 1900-09; pres. Associated Coll. of Osteopathy, 1905; pres. Osteopathic Clin. Research, 1914-16; pres. Am. Osteopathic Assn., 1916-17; mem. Pa. Osteopathic Assn., Phila. Osteopathic Assn., Am. Chem. Assn., Iota Tau Sigma, Phi Sigma Gamma. Awarded Distinguished Service Certificate, Am. Osteopathic Assn., 1929. Republican. Presbyterian. Author published addresses, also articles in osteopathic mags. Home: Narberth, Pa. Office: Witherspoon Bldg., Philadelphia, Pa.* Died June 10, 1947.

SNYDER, Virgil, coll. prof.; b. Dixon, Ia., Nov. 9, 1869; s. Ephraim and Elisa Jane (Randall) S.; B.Sc., Iowa State Coll., 1889; Cornell U., 1890-92; Ph.D., U. of Göttingen, 1894, studied same, 1899, 1903, Italy 3 yrs.; Heckscher fellow, Italy, 1921-22 and 1928-29; hon. doctorate, U. of Padua, 1922; m. Margarete Giesinger, Dec. 28, 1894; children—Herbert, Norman. Instr. mathematics, Cornell U., 1895-1903, asst. prof., 1903-10, prof., 1910-38, now emeritus. Visiting prof. mathematics, Brown Univ., 1942-43, Rollins College, Winter Park, Florida, 1943-44. Mem. National Research Council, 1926-29. Republican. Conglist. Mem. Am. Mathematical Society (editor Bulletin, 1903-21; mem. committee on publication, 1907-21; review editor since 1938; president, 1927-28), Deutscher Mathematiker-Verein, Circolo Matematico di Palermo, Sigma Xi, Gamma Alpha; fellow Am. Acad. Arts and Sciences, 1919. Club: Tennis Club. Author: Differential Calculus (with James McMahon, q.v.), 1898; Differential and Integral Calculus, 1902; Elementary Text-book on the Calculus, 1912; Analytic Geometry of Space, 1913; Topics in Algebraic Geometry, 1928, Supplement, 1935. Editor: Plane Geometry, 1910; Solid Geometry, 1912; also semi-centennial publs. of Am. Math. Soc., 1938. Home: 214 University Av., Ithaca, N.Y. Died Jan. 4, 1950.

SOBOL, Louis (sō'b'l), columnist; b. New Haven, Conn., Aug. 10, 1896; s. Jacob and Sonya (Secoll) S.; ed. Crosby Sch., 1910-14; m. Lee Helen Cantor, Apr. 26, 1919; 1 dau., Natalie Muriel. Started as reporter on Waterbury (Conn.) Republican, 1913; since then on various newspapers in Conn.-N.Y. Currently Manhattan columnist N.Y. Journal-American and King Features Syndicate. Served in U.S. Army 1917-19. Mem. Authors and Writers, Authors Guild of America. Author: High Hatters (play), 1928; Six Lost Women, 1936; Some Days Were Happy, 1947. Contbr. articles and fiction to leading national magazines. Office: 220 South St., New York, N.Y. Died Jan. 19, 1948.

SOILAND, Albert, physician; b. Stavanger, Norway, May 5, 1873; s. Edward and Axelina Christine (Halvorsen) S.; brought to U.S., 1883; student U. of Ill., 1895-97; M.D., U. of Southern Calif., 1900; D.M.R.E., U. of Cambridge, Eng., 1926; m. Dagfinn Berner Svendsen, Sept. 17, 1902. Practiced in Los Angeles since 1900; dir. of group specializing in the study and treatment of neoplastic disease, Los Angeles Tumor Institute; chief roentgenologist A.T.& S.F. Ry.; cons. radiologist S.P. Co., Pacific Electric Ry. Co.; dir. and mem. senior staff Calif. Hospital. Est. Albert Soiland Cancer Foundn. for cancer research and fellowships in cancer study, Apr. 1946. Asst. surgeon Med. R.C., World War; now on active duty as capt., Medical Corps, U.S. Naval Reserve. Fellow Am. Coll. Phys., Am. Coll. Radiology, Los Angeles Clin. and Pathol. Soc.; hon. fellow Northern Soc. for Med. Radiology (Europe); hon. prof. U. of Guadalajara, Mexico; mem. A.M.A. and constituent societies, Military Surgeons World War I, American Radium Soc., Am. Roentgen Ray Soc., Radiol. Soc. of N.A. Republican. Lutheran. Clubs: California, Army and Navy, Athletic Club group; Newport Harbor Yacht Club, Los Angeles Yacht, Santa Barbara Yacht (hon.), Transpacific Yacht (hon. commodore), Corinthian Yacht (hon.), Royal Norwegian Yacht, Pacific Coast Yachting Assn., Southern Calif. Yachting Assn. Home: 1407 S. Hope St., Los Angeles, Calif. Died May 15, 1946; ashes in Stavenger, Norway.

SOLBERG, Charles Orrin (sŏl'bērg), clergyman, educator; b. Rushford, Minn., Dec. 24, 1869; s. Halvor Knudson and Annie Jane (Natesta) S.; B.A., Beloit (Wis.) Coll., 1893, M.A., 1901; B.D., Chicago Luth. Theol. Sem., 1896; D.D., 1917; m. Anna Louise Jacobson, Sept. 2, 1896. Teacher, Pleasant View Luth. Coll., Ottawa, Ill., 1896-1901; ordained Luth. ministry, 1901; pastor Rockford, Ill., 1901-03, Covenant Ch., Chicago, 1903-07; head dept. of English, St. Olaf Coll., Northfield, Minn., 1907-15, dept. of religion, 1915-20; pres. Augustana Coll. and Normal Sch., Sioux Falls, S.D., 1920-28; dean Chicago Luth. Bible School, 1928-32; head dept. of religion, Gustavus Adolphus Coll., St. Peter, Minn., 1932-38. Pres. Luther League of Ill., 1900-04; pres. Luth. Student Conf. America, 1915-18, English Assn. of Norwegian Luth. Church America, 1917-38. Mem. Wis. State Hist. Soc. Republican. Author: The Spirit of American Lutheranism and Other Essays, 1917; Blind Tim and Other Christmas Stories, 1926; Oliver Nidson, 1927. Translator: Altar Book (of the Norwegian Luth. Ch.), 1915; From Fjord to Prairie (from the Norse of Simon Johnson), 1916; Challenge of a Constructive Faith, 1934. Lecturer on religious and patriotic subjects. Home: Leslie, Mich. Died Dec. 28, 1944.

SOLBERG, Thorvald, writer on copyright; b. Manitowoc, Wis., Apr. 22, 1852; s. Charles and Mary (Larson) S.; ed. pub. schs.; m., Mary Adelaide Nourse, Aug. 1, 1880 (died Mar. 7, 1920).. On staff of the Library of Congress, 1876-89; manager library dept., Boston Book Co., 1889-97, spending greater part of time abroad until July 1897; register of copyrights, Washington, D.C., 1897-1930; active in securing internat. copyright; mem. Am. (Authors) Copyright League, Internat. Lit. and Artistic Assn. of Paris, A.L.A., Am. Library Inst. Attended Internat. Copyright Congress, Barcelona, 1893, Antwerp, 1894, Paris, 1900, Berlin, 1908, Luxembourg, 1910, Paris, 1925, Rome, 1928, last 5 as official del. of U.S. Club: Cosmos. Author: Bibliography of Literary Property, 1886; Annual Reports Copyright Business, 1897-98, 1928-29; Copyright Enactments, 1783-1906 (2d edit.), 1906; Copyright in England, 1902; Copyright in Canada and Newfoundland, 1903; Report on Copyright Legislation, 1904; Foreign Copyright Laws, 1904; Copyright Protection and Statutory Formalities, 1904; Copyright in Congress—Bibliography and Chronological Record, 1905; International Copyright Union—Report on the Berlin Conference of 1908; Report on Copyright Relations with South American Republics, 1915; The United States and International Copyright, 1929; Bibliography of the Balearic Islands, 1929; The Development of International Copyright Relations between the U.S. and Foreign Countries, 1933; The Present International Copyright Situation, 1934; Copyright Miscellany (limited edition), 1939; Revision of Copyright Laws, 1936; International Convention of the Copyright Union, 1937; The Long Struggle for Honorable International Copyright Relations, 1937; A Great Church: The Cathedral at Palma, 1944. Has compiled several bibliographies; contbr. to various Am. and foreign jours. Home: Brickyard Rd., Bethesda 14, Md. Address: Cosmos Club, Washington. Died July 15, 1949.

SOLIDAY, Joseph Henry (sŏl'ĭ-dā), banker; pres. Franklin Savings Bank, Boston; dir. State Street Trust Co., Norfolk and Dedham Mut. Fire Ins. Co., Boston Elevated Ry. Co.; officer or dir. other corps. Home: 141 Highland St., Dedham, Mass. Office: 6 Park Sq., Boston, Mass. Died Dec. 17, 1947.

SOLIS-COHEN, Solomon, physician; b. Phila., Sept. 1, 1857; s. Myer David and Judith Simiah (da Silva Solis) C.; A.B., Central High Sch., 1872, A.M., 1877; M.D., Jefferson Med. Coll., 1883, hon. Sc.D., 1933; hon. D.H.L., Jewish Theol. Sem. of America, 1928; hon. Sc.D., Phila. Coll. of Pharmacy and Science, 1939; m. Emily Grace, d. David Hays da Silva Solis, 1885; children—D. Hays, Emily, Leon, Francis N. Lecturer clin. medicine, 1888-1902, prof. clin. medicine, 1902-27, emeritus since 1927, Jefferson Medical College; professor clinical medicine and therapeutics, Philadelphia Polyclinic and College for Graduates in Medicine, 1887-1902, since emeritus. Lecturer in therapeutics, Dartmouth, 1890-92; physician to Philadelphia General, Jefferson and Jewish hosps., 1887-1927, now consulting phys. to these hospitals. Mem. publ. committee of Jewish Publication Society of America. Trustee U.S. Pharmacopœia, 1920-40. Fellow College Physicians, Philadelphia, American Coll. Phys., A.A.A.S., A.M.A. (ex-chmn. therapeutics sect.); pres. Phila. Co. Med. Soc., 1898-99; recorder Assn. Am. Physicians, 1899-1913; hon. mem. Med. and Chirurg. Faculty of Md. and other med. socs. Del. 3d Zionist Congress, Basle, 1899; mem. Council Jewish Agency for Palestine, 1920-40. Mem. Board of Edn. of Philadelphia, 1925-44. Author: Therapeutics of Tuberculosis, 1891; Essentials of Medical Diagnosis (with A. A. Eshner), 1892-1900; Pharmacotherapeutics (with T. S. Githens), 1928; When Love Passed by and Other Verses, including Translations from Hebrew Poets of the Middle Ages, 1929. Editor and contbg. author: A System of Physiologic Therapeutics (11 vols.), 1901-05. Translator: Selections from (Hebrew) Poems of Moses ibn Ezra, 1933. A selection of writings and addresses, with bibliography appended, was pub. in 1940, under the title, Judaism and Science and Other Addresses. Contbg. editor and contbr. various med., Jewish and general cyclopedias and periodicals. Home: Cheltenham and Mountain Avs., Philadelphia 26, Pa. Died July 12, 1948.

SOMERS, Andrew L. (sŭm'ẽrz), ex-congressman; b. Brooklyn, N.Y.; s. Arthur S. and Virginia (Lawrence) S.; educated Manhattan Coll., N.Y. City, and New York U.; m. Ruth Edna McCormick; children—Arthur S., Andrea Meave, Edward McCormick, Edna Valerie, Andrew, Jr. Mem. 69th to 78th Congresses (1925-45), 6th N.Y. Dist. Member Brooklyn Chamber of Commerce. Mem. Am. Legion, Knights of Columbus. Democrat. Home: 1328 President St., Brooklyn, N.Y.* Died Apr. 6, 1949.

SOMERVILLE, James Fownes, British royal naval officer; b. Weybridge, Eng., July 17, 1882; s. Arthur Fownes and Ellen (Sharland) S.; ed. Fairfield Sch., Malvern, Eng.; naval training, H.M.S. Brittania, 1897-98; m. Mary Kerr Main, Jan. 7, 1913; children—John Fownes; Rachel Fownes. Entered British Royal Navy, 1897, advancing through the grades to admiral of the fleet, 1945; served at Dardanelles (World War I), 1915-16; dir. signal dept., Admiralty, 1925-27; flag capt. to Vice Adm. John D. Kelly, 1927-29; naval instr., Imperial Defence Coll., 1929-31; in H.M.S. Norfolk, 1931-32; commodore of Royal Naval Barracks, Portsmouth, 1932-34; dir. personal services, Admiralty, 1934-36; comdg. destroyer flotillas, Mediterranean Fleet, 1936-38; comdr. in chief, East Indies, 1938-39; spl. service, Admiralty, 1939; comdr. in chief Eastern Fleet, 1942-44; served as head of British Admiralty delegation, Washington, D.C., 1944-45. Lord Lieut. County of Somerset. Decorated Knight Grand Cross of the Bath, Knight Grand Cross Order of British Empire, Distinguished Service Order. Clubs: Junior United Service, Royal Cruising (London). Home: Dinder House, Dinder, Wells, Somerset, Eng. Died March 19, 1949.

SOMMER, Luther Allen, pres. The Sommer & Adams Co.; b. Springfield, Ill., Nov. 3, 1878; s. William C. and Mary A. (Pierik) S.; ed. Armour Inst. Tech., Chicago, 1896-1900; m. Zoe M. Cobb, 1901; 1 dau., Mildred D. Employed in mfr. printing machinery, 1894, in mfg. scientific instruments, 1899; constrn. experimental apparatus, Armour Inst., 1900-04; instr. Armour Inst. Tech., 1904-07; engaged in mfg. automobile engines; pres. The Sommer & Adams Co., mfrs. special machinery, tools, fixtures, etc. Past pres. Nat. Tool and Die Mfrs. Assn.; former pres. Cleveland Tool, Die and Machine Shops Assn. Mem. Cleveland Chamber of Commerce, also Ohio Chamber of Commerce. Mem. Am. Tool Engineers Soc. Mason. Club: Mid-Day. Home: 3009 Lincoln Blvd. Office: 18511 Euclid Av., Cleveland, O. Died Mar. 2, 1946.

SOPER, George Albert, consulting engr.; b. New York, N.Y., Feb. 3, 1870; s. George A. and Georgianna Lydia (Bucknam) S.; B.S., Renssalaer Poly. Inst., Troy, N.Y., 1895; A.M., Columbia, 1898, Ph.D., 1899; m. M. Virginia McLeod, July 18, 1895; m. 2d, Eloise Liddon, Dothan, July 12, 1923. Began as civ. engr. with Boston Water Works; later engr. Cumberland Mfg. Co., builders of filtration works in many cities; engr. in charge sanitary work, rehabilitation of Galveston, Tex., after storm of 1900; sanitary engr. N.Y. City Health Dept., 1902; expert N.Y. State Health Dept. in charge of suppression of typhoid epidemic at Ithaca, N.Y., 1904, and subsequently for many other cities; discoverer of typhoid carrier, "Typhoid Mary," 1904; expert of Rapid Transit Commn., N.Y. City, in charge of investigation of subway air conditions, making over 5,000 analyses, etc., 1906, and recommending plan of ventilation subsequently adopted; mem. Met. Sewerage Commn. of N.Y. City, 1906-14 and pres. and dir. of its scientific work, 1908-14, resulting in comprehensive plan and policy of sewage disposal for N.Y. City; chmn. Internat. Bd. Engrs. on water supply and sewage disposal of Chicago, 1914-15; mng. dir. Am. Soc. for Control of Cancer, 1923-28; consulting engr. since 1928; consultant U.S. Housing Authority, 1939-1944. Del. 1st Internat. Conf. on Pub. Cleansing, London, 1931, 2d Conf., Frankfort-on-Main, 1935. Maj. Sanitary Corps, Medical Dept., U.S. Army, 1918-19. Fellow A.A.A.S.; mem. Am. Soc. C.E., Am. Pub. Health Assn., Delta Phi, Sigma Xi; hon. fellow Royal Sanitary Inst. Gt. Britain. Episcopalian. Club: Century. Author: The Air and Ventilation of Subways, 1908; Modern Methods of Street Cleaning, 1909; also numerous published scientific articles and published addresses. Home: Hampton Bays, Long Island, N.Y. Office: 154 Nassau St., New York, N.Y. Died June 17, 1948.

SORRELLS, John Harvey (sŏr'ĕlz), newspaperman; b. Pine Bluff, Ark., Mar. 31, 1896; s. Walter Bartlett and Mary Iva (Fletcher) S.; student Washington and Lee U., 1917; m. Ruth Arnett, Aug. 5, 1921; children—John Harvey, Peggy Ann, William Gordon, Robert Talliferro. Began as reporter Daily Graphic, Pine Bluff, Ark., 1919, editor, 1922; news editor Daily Oklahoman, 1923-26; mng. editor Cleveland Press, 1926, Memphis Press-Scimitar, 1926-27; editor Fort Worth Press, 1927-30; exec. editor Scripps-Howard Newspapers since 1930; pres. and pub. Memphis Commercial Appeal since 1936; dep. dir. of censorship, Jan. 1, 1942-Jan. 1, 1943. Served as 1st lt., U.S. Army, World War I. Author: The Working Press, 1930. Home: 52 W. 9th St. Office: 230 Park Av., New York, N.Y. Died Feb. 25, 1948; buried Graceland Cemetery, Pine Bluff, Ark.

SOUDER, Edwin Mills (soud'ẽr), newspaper editor; b. Carthage, Ind., Nov. 23, 1872; s. William Mills and Amanda Maria (Walker) S.; student Wabash Coll., 1890-92; m. Linnea Augusta Cooper, Oct. 25, 1898. With Kokomo (Ind.) Tribune since July 1, 1897, beginning as reporter, editor since Jan. 1, 1919. Republican. Presbyterian. Mason, Elk. Clubs: Kokomo Town, Rotary. Author of "Tale of a Real Town," "Biography of Elmer Apperson." Lectures, "Bygones," "Peter Hersleb." Home: 715 W. Walnut St. Office: Tribune, Kokomo, Ind. Died July 24, 1947; buried Crown Point Cemetery, Kokomo, Ind.

SOUTHGATE, George Thompson, cons. engr.; b. Nashville, Tenn., June 26, 1886; s. William Wall and Martha Carrie (Thompson) S.; student Vanderbilt U., 1904-05, U. of Mo., 1905-06; B.S. in E.E., Mass. Inst. of Tech., 1910; m. May Collins, 1917. Field elec. engr. Ford, Bacon & Davis, New York, 1910-13; sponsor engr. Electric Bond & Share Co., New York, 1913-18; research engr. Am. Cyanamid Co., developing elec. phosphoric smelting, 1918-22; cons. engr. Swann Chem. Co., Grasselli Chem. Co., Electro-Metall. Co., developing elec. furnace processes, 1922-29; research engr. Union Carbide & Carbon Research Labs., Inc., 1929-34; cons. engr., New York, 1934-43; chief engr. Vanadium Corp. of America since 1943. Fellow Royal Soc. of Arts; mem. Am. Inst. Elec. Engrs., Electrochemical Society, American Society for Metals. Democrat. Episcopalian. Inventor combustion-electric process of smelting and vibratorily commutated electric power conversion. Home: 1303 Shady Av., Pittsburgh 17, Pa. Office: Vanadium Corp. of America, Bridgeville, Pa. Died Nov. 8, 1946.

SOUTHGATE, Richard, govt. official; b. Worcester, Mass., May 5, 1893; s. Louis W. and Clara (Brigham) S.; grad. Milton Acad., 1911; A.B., Harvard, 1915; student Harvard Law Sch., 1915-16; m. Lila Lancashire, June 1, 1927; children—Patricia, Richard Wright, Sarita. Served in Am. Embassies, Paris, 1917-18, Rome, 1919-21, Legation in Guatemala, 1921-22, Embassies, Constantinople, 1922-23, Havana, 1925-26; in banking business Chicago and New York, 1927-29; with State Dept., Washington, D.C., as chief of protocol and chief Div. of Internat. Confs., 1929-39; regional dir. for Europe, Pan American Airways, Feb. 1939-July 1940; Washington rep. Lockheed Aircraft Corporation, 1940-42; special assistant, Office of Strategic Services, Washington, D.C., since Feb. 1, 1942. Member American delegations to Limitation of Armaments Conferences, Washington, D.C., 1921, London Naval Conf., 1935, Radio Conf., Madrid, 1932, Maintenance of Peace Conf., Buenos Aires, 1936, Aviation Conf., Lima, 1937. Clubs: Metropolitan, Burning Tree, Chevy Chase (Washington, D.C.). Home: 2406 Kalorama Rd., Washington, D.C. Died June 10, 1946.

SOUTHWORTH, Franklin Chester (south'wûrth), theologian; b. N. Collins, N.Y., Oct. 15, 1863; s. Nathaniel Chester and Chloe (Rathbun) S.; A.B., Harvard, 1887, A.M., 1892, S.T.B., 1892; D.D., Buchtel, 1911; LL.D., Allegheny, 1915; m. Alice A. Berry, Sept. 6, 1893. Teacher Fish's Sch. for Boys, Worcester, Mass., 1887-88; sub-master Adams Acad., Quincy, Mass., 1888-89; ordained Unitarian ministry, 1892; pastor Duluth, Minn., 1892-97, Third Unitarian Ch., Chicago, 1897-99, sec. Western Unitarian Conf., 1899-1902; pres., Meadville Theol. Sch. (moved to Chicago, 1926), dean of the faculty and prof. practical theology, 1902-29; pres. emeritus, 1929; pres. All-India Theistic Conf., Calcutta, 1928. Lecturer Manchester Coll., Oxford, 1909, U. of Madras, India, 1929. Pres. Little Compton Hist. Assn., 1935. Home: Marshside, Little Compton, R.I. Died May 21, 1944.

SOWELL, Ashley B. (sō'ĕl), fgn. service officer; b. Columbia, Tenn., Aug. 12, 1893; s. Felix C. and Mary (Evans) S.; ed. Columbia, Tenn.; studied journalism and economics, N.Y. City, Washington, D.C., Nashville; hon. degree, Columbia Mil. Acad.; m. Winnie Davis Estes, Aug. 4, 1917; 1 dau., Jane Howard (Mrs. Robert Lloyd Douglas). In newspaper business through all depts. successively to editor, gen. mgr., publisher, 1910-34; business specialist and spl. asst. to sec., U.S. Dept. of Commerce, Washington, D.C., 1934-39; commercial attaché to Panama since 1939; v.p. Maury Democrat Co., 1941-42; former dir. Middle Tenn. Bank; sec. Bd. of Trade; sec. City Bd. of Edn., ex-pres. Tenn. Press Assn. Clubs: Kiwanis, Century, Elks (Columbia, Tenn.); Union (Panama). Home: Columbia, Tenn. Address: Dept. of State, Washington, D.C. Died July 10, 1945.

SOWELL, Ingram Cecil, naval officer; b. Lawrenceburg, Tenn., Aug. 3, 1889; s. Henry Bascomb and Eustatia (Goodloe) S.; Columbia Military Acad., 196-08; B.S., U.S. Naval Acad., 1912; grad. U.S. Naval War Coll., 1935; m. Frances Jack, Apr. 17, 1917; children—Mary Ellen (Mrs. Henry Wells Lawrence), Frances Jack (Mrs. Walter Lee Wood), Ingram Cecil, Jr. Passed midshipman, 1912 and advanced through the grades to rear admiral, Sept. 1942; served in armored cruisers, 1912-16; student, Submarine School, New London, Connecticut, 1917, Submarine K-2, 1917; commanded U.S.S. L-2, 1918, U.S.S. S-3, 1919, U.S.S. 49, 1921-24; Navy Department, 1920-21; instructor Naval Academy, 1925-37; commanded U.S.S. Henshaw and U.S.S. Wasmuth, 1927-30; recruit training officer, Great Lakes Training Station, 1930-32; comd. Submarine Div. Four, 1932-34; student, Senior War Coll., 1934-35; Navy Dept., 1935-36; exec. officer, U.S.S. New Orleans, 1936-38; training station, San Diego, 1938-39; comd. U.S.S. Concord, 1940-42; comdt. U.S. Naval Training Station, Farragut, Ida., 1942-43; comdt. Activity No. 1, Navy No. 138, overseas, since Apr., 1943. Awarded Navy Cross, Nicaragua, Mexican Campaign medals (World War I); Victory medal, World War II. Mem. Vets. of Foreign Wars. Home: Lawrenceburg, Tenn. Address: Bureau of Navy Personnel, Navy Dept., Washington. Died Dec. 21, 1947.

SOWERS, Don Conger (sō'ẽrz), economist; b. Spring Hill, Kan., Feb. 17, 1883; s. James W. and Electa (Telford) S.; A.B., Baker U., Baldwin, Kan., 1904; Ph.D., Columbia, 1915; m. Helen Smith, June 29, 1914; children—Don Conger, Robert Moulton, Helen Catherine. Observer for Dept. of Terrestrial Magnetism of Carnegie Instn. of Washington, D.C., 1904-10, making trips through West Indies, South America, the Pacific, China and India; dir. Municipal Research Bur., extension div. and prof. municipalities and pub. accounting, U. of Ore., 1914-16; asst. dir. Bur. of Research, Dayton, O., 1916-17; dir. Bur. Municipal Research, Akron, O., 1917-22; prof. finance, dir. Bur. of Business and Govt. Research, Extension Div., U. of Colo., since 1922; sec. Ohio Bd. of Adminstrn., 1921; asst. budget commr. State of Colo., 1923; installed city mgrs. and improved systems in several Am. cities. Mem. Govtl. Research Conf., Am. Municipal Assn., Colo. Municipal League (sec.-treas. since 1923), Nat. Municipal League, Am. Assn. Univ. Profs., Colo.-Wyo. Acad. Science, Boulder Chamber Commerce, Kappa Sigma. Elected fellow Royal Geog. Soc. of Eng. for observations in China. Conglist. Clubs: Rotary, Country, Schoolmasters. Author: Financial History of N.Y. State (1789-1912), 1914; Financing Public Education in Colorado (2 vols.), 1924; Tax Problem in Colorado, 1928; Old Age Pensions in Colorado, 1938. Editor of Colorado Municipalities Magazine. Contbr. to professional publs. Home: 1500 Baseline, Boulder, Colo. Died July 19, 1942.

SPAFFORD, Edward Elwell; b. Springfield, Vt., Mar. 12, 1878; s. Hiram Duncan and Georgiana (Fowler) S.; grad. U.S. Naval Acad., 1901; student law, Columbia Univ., 1915-16; m. Lucille Stevens, May 23, 1912 (died 1914); 1 dau., Lucille. Resigned from U.S. Navy as lt. comdr., 1914; returned to Navy and served in the Mediterranean, World War. Served as chmn. naval affairs of Am. Legion 3 yrs., as comdr. Dept. of N.Y., 1923-24; elected nat. comdr., term 1927-28. Awarded D.S.M. (U.S.); Comdr. Legion of Honor (France); Comdr. Order of Crown of Italy; Comdr. Order of Phoenix (Greece). Republican. Episcopalian. Mason. Clubs: University, New York Yacht, Sleepy Hollow Country, Army and Navy (Washington); Chevy Chase (Chevy Chase, Md.). Died Nov. 13, 1941.

SPAFFORD, George Catlin, banker; b. Rockford, Ill., May 7, 1864; s. Amos Catlin and Elizabeth Burns (White) S.; ed. Rensselaer Poly. Inst., Troy, N.Y.; unmarried. Began as clerk with Third Nat. Bank, Rockford, 1884, pres. since 1906. Republican. Clubs: University (Rockford); Union League (Chicago). Home: 501 N. Prospect St. Office: 401 E. State St., Rockford, Ill. Died Oct. 11, 1943.

SPARKS, Thomas J., lawyer; b. Muhlenberg County, Ky., Nov. 4, 1868; s. Charles M. and Sally (Miller) S.; ed. pub. schs.; m. Montie Oates, Feb. 27, 1894; children—Mabel (Mrs. Guy D. Martin), Bradley, Dewey, Thomas Elbert. Admitted to Ky. bar, 1900, and began practice at Greenville; county judge, Muhlenberg Co., 1897-1905; apptd., 1909, commonwealth's atty. by Gov. Wilson to fill out unexpired term of Hon. R. Y. Thomas, congressman-elect; county atty., Muhlenberg Co., 1917-21; U.S. atty. Western Dist. Ky. 2 terms, 1927-35; in practice at Greenville since 1935. Republican. Baptist. Home: Greenville, Ky. Died Oct. 27, 1946; buried in Evergreen Cemetery, Greenville, Ky.

SPARKS, Will M(orris), judge; b. Charlottesville, Ind., Apr. 28, 1872; s. James Bascomb (M.D.) and Harriet Jane (Johnson) S.; A.B., DePauw U., Greencastle, Ind., 1896, LL.D.; student Ind. Law Sch.; m. Della Young, Nov. 23, 1897; children—Dorothy Young (Mrs. Foster), William George. Admitted to Ind. bar; mem. Ind. Ho. of Rep., 1901-03; judge, Circuit Court, 16th jud. circuit, Ind., 1904-10, 1914-29; judge, U.S. Circuit Court of Appeals, 7th circuit, since 1929. Republican. Methodist. Mason (K.T.). Clubs: Columbia (Indianapolis); Union League. Home: Rushville, Ind. Died Jan. 7, 1950.

SPAULDING, Helim G., editor, pub.; b. Manchester, Mich., July 24, 1869; s. George Ralston and Harriet (Hoag) S.; ed. high sch.; m. Gertrude H. Sturtevant, Oct. 29, 1888 (died 1932); 1 dau., Grace; m. 2d, Frances M. Thurman, Apr. 17, 1933 (died February 4, 1936); m. 3d, Mrs. Emma Mesow Fitch, Feb. 11, 1937. Began in newspaper work on The Evening Call of Battle Creek, Mich., 1888, later publisher of Perry (Mich.) Sun, and with Daily Jour. and Morning Tribune, Knoxville, Tenn., until 1892; successively on editorial staff Newark (N.J.) Times, Oneonta (N.Y.) Star, Burlington (Vt.) News, St. Albans (Vt.) Messenger; moved to Tex., 1903; with Beaumont Enterprise until 1907; civic and comml. organizer, 1907-16; pub. Daily Ardmoreite, Ardmore, Okla., 1916-19; pub. Morning News, Shawnee, Okla., 1919-29; editor and pub. Daily Times Star, Alameda, May 1932-Sept. 1939. Awarded Lord & Thomas cup, 1937, for greatest community service; also plaque of Sigma Delta Chi of Stanford U. for courage in journalism. Pres. Okla. Press Assn., 1926-27; pres. Associated Press Papers of Okla., 1927-29. Mem. Calif. Press Assn.; pres. Alameda Chamber of Commerce, 1937-39; pres. Alameda Forum, 1939; mem. Alameda County Planning Commn. Elected to Sigma Delta Chi, Okla. U., 1924. Mason (Oakland Consistory; Scottish Rite). Clubs: Rotary (Alameda); Press (San Francisco). Home: 1127 Sherman St., Alameda, Calif. Died Feb. 23, 1943.

SPAULDING, Oliver Lyman, army officer; b. St. Johns, Mich., June 27, 1875; s. Oliver Lyman and Mary Cecilia (Swegles) S.; A.B., U. of Mich., 1895, LL.B., 1896; LL.D., 1938; A.M., Harvard U., 1932; grad. Arty. Sch., Ft. Monroe, Va., 1903, Army Staff Coll. Ft. Leavenworth, 1905; graduate Army War Coll., Washington, 1911, 1925; m. Alice Chandler, Dec. 29, 1902; 1 son, Edward Chandler. Commd. 2d lt., arty., U.S. Army, 1898; promoted through grades to col., field arty., 1920; retired as brig. gen., 1939; recalled to active duty, 1941; served in N.W. Alaska, 1898-99, China Relief Expdn., 1900, Philippine Insurrection, 1900-01, Panama, 1908, Mexican Border, 1913-15, P.I., 1915-17; brig. gen. with A.E.F. in France, Luxemburg and Germany, 1918-19; served in Hawaii, 1926-29. Instr. Army Service Schs., Ft. Leavenworth, 1905-10; asst. comdt. Field Arty. Sch., Ft. Sill, Okla., 1917-18; prof. mil. science, Harvard U., 1931-35; lecturer in mil. history, Lowell Institute, Boston, 1939, and George Washington University, 1939-41; chief historical section, General Staff, A.E.F., 1919, Army War Coll., 1919-24, 1935-39 and since 1941. Decorated: Distinguished Service Medal, Legion of Merit (U.S.); Commander Order of the Black Star (French). Mem. Phi Beta Kappa, Beta Theta Pi, Phi Delta Phi. Episcopalian. Mason. Clubs: Army and Navy (Washington and Manila); Cosmos (Washington). Author: Notes on Field Artillery, 4th edit., 1918; Warfare (with Hoffman Nickerson and John Womack Wright), 1925, 2d edit., 1937; The United States Army in War and Peace, 1937; Pen and Sword in Greece and Rome, 1937; The Second Division, A.E.F., in France, 1917-19 (with John Womack Wright), 1937; Ahriman, A Study in Air Bombardment, 1939. Writer of articles on mil. and hist. subjects. Home: 1870 Wyoming Av. Address: War Dept., Washington, D.C. Died Mar. 27, 1947.

SPAULDING, Rolland Harty, ex-gov.; b. Townsend Harbor, Mass., Mar. 15, 1873; s. Jonas and Emeline (Cummings) S.; ed. Phillips Acad., Andover, Mass.; M.A., Dartmouth, 1915; LL.D., U. of N.H., 1916; m. Vera Going, Dec. 18, 1918; children—Virginia Pauline, Betty Louise. Began, 1895, in mfg. business founded by father, and now pres. Spaulding Fibre Co., mfrs. vulcanized fibre, laminated bakelite and fibre products, etc., at Townsend Harbor, Mass., Rochester, North Rochester and Milton, N.H., and Tonawanda, N.Y.; pres. Three Line Counter Co.; pres. Rochester (N.H.) Trust Co.; treas. Spaulding & Frost Co.; v.p. First Nat. Bank (Rochester, N.H.); dir. Spauldings Limited (London, Eng.), Internat. Leather Co., Atlas Leather Co., United Life & Accident Ins. Co. (Concord, N.H.), Keyes Fibre Co. (Waterville, Me.), N.E. Pub. Service Co., Pub. Service Co. of N.H., St. Maurice Paper Co. (Canada); trustee Northern New England Company, Gafney Home for the Aged. Delegate Republican National Convention, 1912; governor of N.H., 1915-16. Vice-chairman Public Safety Committee; member Reorganization Committee B.&M. R.R., 1925; gen. chmn. N.E. Governors R.R. Com. Club: Rochester Country. Home: Rochester, N.H. Died Mar. 14, 1942.

SPEAKS, John Charles, ex-congressman; b. Canal Winchester, O., Feb. 11, 1859; s. Charles W. and Sarah (Hesser) S.; ed. pub. schs.; m. Edna Lawyer, 1889; children—Charles, Stanford, John, Margaret. Milling and lumber business. Fish, game and conservation officer of Ohio, 1907-18; mem. 67th to 71st Congresses (1921-31), 12th Ohio Dist. Mem. of the Ohio N.G. 40 yrs., advancing from pvt. through grades to brig. gen.; maj. 4th Ohio Vol. Inf., Spanish-Am. War, participating in Porto Rican Campaign; comdr. 2d Brig., Ohio N.G., on Mexican border, 1916; comdr. 73d Brigade 37th Div., from call of troops, World War, until Mar. 1, 1918. Mason (32°, K.T., Shriner), K.P. Republican. Methodist; del. to Gen. Conf., 1936. Rotarian. Home: 309 King Av., Columbus, O. Died Nov. 6, 1945.

SPEAKS, Oley, composer, baritone; b. Canal Winchester, O., June 28, 1876; s. Charles W. and Sarah A. (Hesser) S.; ed. in music in N.Y. City; unmarried. Soloist St. Thomas P.E. Ch., 5 yrs., Ch. of the Divine Paternity, 4 yrs. Mem. Ohio Soc. of New York, Am. Soc. Composers, Authors and Publishers (dir.). Clubs: Mendelssohn, Musicians, Lambs, Town Hall (New York); Athletic (Columbus, O.). Composer of more than 250 songs, among them: Morning; To You; Sylvia; On the Road to Mandalay; The Bells of Youth; The Secret; When the Boys Come Home; The Prayer Perfect; The Message; In May Time; Fuzzy Wuzzy; The Lord Is My Light. Mem. Beethoven Soc. Home: 5 Riverside Drive, New York. Died Aug. 27, 1948.

SPEAR, John William, editor; b. Fredericktown, O., Sept. 10, 1859; s. John and Emily (Singrey) S.; ed. pub. schs. and under pvt. tutors; m. Mrs. Julia Frances Hartman, May 10, 1890. Began as teacher pub. schs., Ohio; reporter, St. Joseph (Mo.) Gazette, 1890; mng. editor Pueblo (Colo.) Star, 1891; news editor Ariz. Republican, 1892-94; editor Ariz. Star, Tucson, 1895-96; mng. editor Ariz. Republican, 1897-1910; in editorial charge Bisbee Rev. and Ariz. Star, 1911; editor Ariz. Republican since 1912. Presbyterian. Home: Phoenix, Ariz. Died Feb. 8, 1943.

SPEAR, Nathaniel, business exec.; b. Plymouth, O., Nov. 5, 1867; s. Sol and Augusta (Billstein) S.; student Hughes High School, Cincinnati; m. Adeline Levy, Oct. 21, 1895. Pres. and dir. Spear & Co., Pittsburgh and N.Y. City; dir. Liberty-Sixth, Inc., Pittsburgh, and Nadeline, Inc., N.Y. City. Sec. and assoc. chmn. building com., Rodef Shalom Congregation; pres. chmn. bldg. com. and trustee Irene Kaufman Settlement; pres., chmn. building com. and trustee, Montifiore Hosp. Assn. Trustee, Y.W. and Y.M.H.A. Clubs: Concordia, Westmoreland Country, Broadhead Forest and Stream, Bungalow Island Fishing. Home: 5321 Northumberland Av. Office: Wood St. at 6th Av., Pittsburgh, Pa.* Died June 19, 1947.

SPEARING, J. Zach (spēr'ing), lawyer; b. Alto, Tex., Apr. 23, 1864; s. John F. and Margaretta (Sanders) S.; LL.B., Tulane U., 1886; m. Lulie M. Cooke, Nov. 20, 1889; children—Cora (Mrs. Frank E. Demarest), Margaretta. Admitted to La. bar, 1886, and began practice at New Orleans; served as mem. Orleans Parish Sch. Bd. (pres. 1919); mem. State Bd. of Edn., 1912; elected, Apr. 22, 1924, to fill vacancy in Congress caused by death of H. Garland Dupré, and reëlected 69th to 71st Congresses (1925-31), 2d La. Dist.; now mem. firm Spearing, Cahn, Cahn & Duval. Mem. Nat. Sojourners; hon. mem. Phi Alpha Delta. Democrat. Episcopalian. Mason (Shriner); K.P., Elk, Druid. Clubs: Paul Morphy Chess, Tally Ho. Home: 1419 Amelia St. Office: Whitney Bldg., New Orleans, La. Died Nov. 2, 1942.

SPEARL, George, architect; b. Brooklyn, N.Y., Aug. 24, 1882; s. Ernest Sofian and Mary (Whitaker) S.; B.S., U. of Pa., 1903 (won Arthur Spayde Brook gold medal with honors in design), won John Stewardson Travelling Scholarship, 1904; 4 years travel and study abroad, including study at Am. Acad. in Rome, 1905-06; m. Helen Lesley Matcham, June 12, 1911. With Cope & Stewardson, architects, Phila., 1907-12, James P. Jamieson, 1912-18; jr. partner Jamieson & Spearl, architects, St. Louis, Mo., 1920-32, sr. partner since 1932; consulting architect, U.S. Army Corps of Engrs. on Upper Miss. Valley Div. for archtl. design of dams between St. Louis and St. Paul; cons. architect Special Div. U.S. Army Corps of Engrs. for 3rd Locks Project, Panama Canal; architect for Washington Univ., St. Louis, Univ. of Missouri, Stephens Coll., Columbia, Mo., and other colleges; numerous laboratories, hospitals and industrial buildings. Vice pres. and former chmn. bd., St. Louis Symphony Orchestra; dir. McMillan Hosp., Oscar Johnson Inst.; fellow Am. Inst. of Architects; past pres. Mo. State Assn. of Architects, past pres. St. Louis chapter, Am. Inst. of Architects, Sigma Xi. Clubs: St. Louis Country, Noonday, Round Table, University (St. Louis), The Newcomen Soc. of England. Home: 21 Dartford Av., Clayton, Mo. Office: 1690 Arcade Bldg., St. Louis, Mo. Died Feb. 18, 1948; buried Bellefontaine Cemetery, St. Louis.

SPEER, J(ames) Ramsey, retired mfr.; b. Pittsburgh, Pa., July 23, 1870; s. John Z. and Katharine (McKnight) S.; B.S., Mass. Inst. Tech., 1893; m. Jeannette Lowrie Childs, 1898; children—Gertrude Childs, James Ramsey. Began with Shoenberger Steel Co., 1893, gen. mgr., 1898, v.p. and gen. mgr. for Am. Steel & Wire Co., purchasers of same, 1899-1900; v.p. S. Jarvis Adams Co., Midland, Pa., 1899-1911, pres., 1911-19, chmn. board, 1921; and organizer and pres. until 1904, Brownsville Glass Co., an organizer, 1905, v.p. until 1911, Midland Steel Co.; pres. Mackintosh-Hemphill Co., mfrs. rolling mill machinery, Pittsburgh, 1924-29; pres. Easton Publishing Co.-The Easton Star-Democrat; director Easton (Md.) National Bank. Director, officer for alien property custodian, World War I, of Bayer Company, Hayden Chemical Works, Berlin Aniline Works, Kalli Color and Chemical Company. A founder and former trustee Arnold School. Democrat. Episcopalian. Clubs: Tred Avon Yacht; Talbot Country, Chesapeake Bay Yacht. Author: Chronology of Iron and Steel, 1920. Inventor of Adamite, a high carbon nickel-chrome steel alloy, also of molybdenum nickel chrome steel alloy, and of improvements in mechanical glass, etc. Joint inventor of electric ingot stripper. Home: "Wilderness," Trappe, Talbot County, Md. Office: care W. C. Rice, William Penn Hotel, Pittsburgh, Pa. Died Oct. 1, 1941.

SPEER, Robert Elliott, missionary sec.; b. Huntingdon, Pa., Sept. 10, 1867; s. Hon. Robert Milton and Martha Ellen (McMurtrie) S.; A.B., Princeton, 1889; student Princeton Theol. Sem., 1890-91; hon. A.M., Yale, 1900; D.D., U. of Edinburgh, 1910; LL.D., Rutgers, 1920, Otterbein, 1926, Washington and Jefferson, 1938; Litt.D., Juniata Coll., 1922 Princeton, 1939; m. Emma Doll Bailey, Apr. 20, 1893; children—Elliott (dec.), Margaret B., Eleanor McM. (dec.), Constance S., William. Sec. Presbyn. Bd. Foreign Missions, 1891-1937. Made visitation of Christian missions in Persia, India, China, Korea, Japan, in 1896-97, S. America in 1909, 25, Japan, China, Philippines and Siam, 1915, India and Irak and Persia, 1921-22, Japan and China, 1926. Mem. advisory com. on religious and moral activities of the Army and Navy, during war period; chmn. Gen. Wartime Com. of Chs.; ex-pres. Federal Council of Churches of Christ in America; moderator Presbyn. Ch. in U.S.A., 1927; chmn. Com. on Coöperation in Latin America, 1910-36. Author: The Man Christ Jesus, 1896; The Man Paul, 1900; Missions and Politics in Asia, 1898; A Memorial of a True Life, 1896; Remember Jesus Christ, 1899; Studies in the Book of Acts; Studies in the Gospel of Luke; Christ and Life, 1901; The Principles of Jesus, 1902; Missionary Principles and Practice, 1902; Presbyterian Foreign Missions, 1901; A Memorial of Horace Tracy Pitkin, 1903; Missions and Modern History, 1904; The Marks of a Man, 1907; Christianity and the Nations, 1910; The Light of the World, 1911; South American Problems, 1912; Studies in Missionary Leadership, 1914; One Girl's Influence, 1914; Studies in the Gospel of John, 1915; The Stuff of Manhood, 1917; The Gospel and the New World, 1919; The New Opportunity of the Church, 1919; Race and Race Relations, 1924; The Unfinished Task, 1926; The Church and Missions, 1926; Seeking the Mind of Christ, 1926; Sir James Ewing, 1928; Some Living Issues, 1930; Owen Crimmins, 1931; The Finality of Jesus Christ, 1933; Christian Realities, 1935; Memoir of George Bowen, 1938; Memoir of John J. Eagan, 1939; When Christianity Was New, 1939; Five Minutes a Day, 1943; Jesus and Our Human Problems, 1946. Home: Lakeville, Conn. Died Nov. 23, 1947.

SPEIDEL, Edward, obstetrician and gynecol. surgeon; b. Philadelphia, Pa., Nov. 12, 1859; s. Charles Edward and Marie Luise (Uber) S.; Ph.G., Cincinnati Coll. of Pharmacy, 1880; M.D., U. of Louisville, 1895; m. Emma Keisker, July 6, 1886; children—Emma Luise (Mrs. Harry Hoffeld), Frederick George, Marie Alicia (Mrs. Thomas Allen Moore), Frank Keisker. Pharmacist, 1876-95; in practice of medicine since 1895; was prof. obstetrics and head of dept., U. of Louisville, now emeritus prof. obstetrics after forty years of teaching. Fellow Am. Coll. Surgeons; mem. Am. Assn. Obstetricians, Gynecologists and Abdominal Surgeons, Ky. Med. Assn., Jefferson County Med. Assn. (pres. 1911), Louisville Obstet. Soc. (pres. 1928), Southern Med. Assn. (chmn. obstet. sect. 1925). Mason. Republican. Unitarian. Home: 2014 Cherokee Parkway. Office: Francis Bldg., Louisville, Kentucky. Died Apr. 13, 1948.

SPENCE, Frederick, clergyman; b. Leeds, England, Nov. 22, 1872; s. Thomas and Eliza (Warrington) S.; ed. in England; candidate for Meth. ministry in England; D.D., Albion (Mich.) Coll., 1922; m. Maude E. Hayler, July 3, 1894; children—Dorothy (Mrs. Carleton Reads), Elizabeth Warrington (Mrs. Frank G. Rutherford). Began preaching in England, 1888; came to U.S., 1893; joined Detroit Conf. M.E. Ch., 1894; pastor successively, Saginaw, Bridgeport, Burt, Reese, Sebewaing, Munising, Escanaba and Saginaw (all Mich.), to 1918; pastor First Ch., Jackson, Mich., since 1918, beginning with small membership, now 2160 members and bldg. and grounds that cost $700,000. Mem. Bd. of Temperance and Public Morals of M.E. Ch.; del. to Gen. Conf., 1928; del. Ecumenical Conf., Atlanta, Ga., 1931. Mason (32°). Author of various booklets and pamphlets on religious subjects. Joint author: The Light Shines Through, 1930. Contbr. to church papers and mags. Home: 432 Michigan Av. W. Jackson, Mich. Died May 5, 1943.

SPENCER, Edward Buckham Taylor, college prof.; b. Delmar, Ia., Apr. 26, 1863; s. Benjamin and Mary (Ware) S.; A.B., DePauw U., 1888, A.M., 1891; post-grad. work, Johns Hopkins, 1892-94, Harvard, 1901-02, Columbia, 1902-03; m. Lulu Belle Ward, Aug. 9, 1894 (died June 4, 1896); m. 2d, Helen Imogen Hathaway, July 31, 1906; children—John Hathaway, Edward Hathaway, Mary Hathaway (Mrs. Howard M. Warrington), Imogen Hathaway. Prof. ancient langs., Moores Hill (Ind.) Coll., 1888-92; prof. Latin, U. of Denver, 1894-1905; dir. Collegio Metodista, Rome, Italy, 1905-11; prof. classics, Grinnell (Ia.) Coll., 1911-16, Carter-Adams prof. Greek, 1916-41, prof. emeritus since 1941. Mem. Am. Inst. Archeology (life), Delta Kappa Epsilon, Phi Beta Kappa. Mason. Conglist. Club: Fortnightly. Wrote: Adnominatio in the Plays of Plautus, 1906. Address: 21 W. Underwood St., Chevy Chase 15, Md. Died Oct. 28, 1945.

SPENCER, Hazelton, univ. prof.; b. Methuen, Mass., July 7, 1893; s. George Hazelton and Rosetta Mary (Munroe) S.; Norwich U., 1910-11; A.B., Boston U., 1915; A.M., Harvard, 1920, Ph.D., 1923; m. Gladys Louise Woodward, 1917 (divorced); children—Cynthia (Mrs. Tyler Marcy), John Hazelton, Jane (Mrs. Frank S. Fussner), Lydia; m. 2d, Louise Smurthwaite Cline, 1933. English teacher, secondary schools, 1915-19; asst. in English, Harvard, 1921-23; asst. prof. English, U. of Minn., 1923-24; asso. prof., prof., and head dept. of English, State Coll. of Wash., 1924-28; asso. prof. English, Johns Hopkins, 1928-37, prof. since 1937; visiting instr., summers, University of Iowa, 1926, Harvard, 1930, 32, Duke Univ., 1937, 39, 40, 42. Bread Loaf School of English, 1938, Northwestern University, 1941. Member Modern Lang. Assn. America, Modern Humanities Research Assn., Am. Assn. Univ. Profs., Lambda, Theta Delta Chi, Phi Beta Kappa. Democrat. Clubs: Johns Hopkins, Tudor and Stuart. Author: Shakespeare Improved, 1927; The Art and Life of William Shakespeare, 1940. Editor: Selected Poems of Vachel Lindsay, 1931, Shakespeare's King Richard III, 1933; Elizabethan Plays, 1933. Contbr. to Am. and foreign philol. and lit. jours. Co-editor of Modern Language Notes since 1930. Address: Johns Hopkins University, Baltimore, Md. Died July 28, 1944.

SPENCER, Kenneth, exec. dir. Globe Indemnity Co.; b. Marshall, Mo., May 26, 1888; s. Thomas Edwin and Mary Lavinia (Strother) S.; student of engring., U. of Mo., 1904-08; m. Mignon Martina Grasse, Oct. 24, 1910; children—Mary Lavinia, Elizabeth Jane. Newspaper reporter Globe-Democrat, St. Louis, 1908-10, St. Louis Star, 1910-11; special agent Ocean Accident & Guarantee Corp., Ltd., Ill., 1911-12; asst. Western mgr. Globe Indemnity Co., Chicago, 1912-16, asst. Pacific Coast mgr., San Francisco, 1916-20; Pacific Coast mgr, Norwich Union and Phoenix Ind. Cos., San Francisco, 1920-25; asst. sec. Globe Indemnity Co., New York, 1925-27, v.p., 1927-39, pres. and dir. since 1939. Mem. Sigma Alpha Epsilon. Methodist. Mason (K.T.). Home: 52 Llewellyn Rd., Montclair, N.J. Office: 150 William St., New York, N.Y. Died July 25, 1946.

SPENCER, Robert Lyle, dean; b. St. Johnsbury, Vt., Mar. 7, 1887; s. Carl McClelland and Mary (Burbank) S.; B.S. in M.E., Ia. State Coll., Ames, Ia., 1912; m. Gertrude Levering, July 8, 1914; children—Marion Stephens (Dr. Marion S. Dressler), Kathleen (Mrs. Fritz S. Rostler), Roberta Levering (Mrs. Earl B. Schoen). Instr. mech. engring., Lehigh U., 1912-14, asst. prof., 1914-18; combustion engr. Bethlehem (Pa.) Steel Co., 1918-20; supt. of steam Standard Oil Co. of Ind., Casper, Wyo., 1920-23; chief engr. Heine Boiler Co., St. Louis, Mo., 1925-27; proposition engr., Combustion Engring. Corp., New York, 1927-28; dean of engring., U. of Del., Newark, Del., 1928-45. Dir. Del. Safety Council. Fellow A.A.A.S.; mem. Am. Soc. M.E., Soc. for Promotion Engring. Edn., Newcomen Soc. (Eng.), Phi Kappa Phi, Tau Beta Pi. Republican. Conglist. Address: 46 E. Delaware Av., Newark, Del. Died Oct. 10, 1945.

SPENCER, Theodore, univ. prof., author, poet; b. Villa Nova, Pa., July 4, 1902; s. Theodore and Helena Carroll (Frazier) S.; A.B., Princeton, 1923; B.A., Cambridge U., 1925; Ph.D., Harvard, 1928; m. Anna M. Murray, 1927 (div. 1946); 1 son, John; married 2d, Eloise (Bergland) Worcester, 1948. Instr. and tutor in English, Harvard, 1927-33, asst. prof., 1933-39; apptd. lecturer in English literature, Cambridge U., 1939, but because of war remained at Harvard as visiting lecturer from Cambridge U., 1939-40; resigned Cambridge lectureship, becoming asso. prof. English, Harvard, 1940-46. Boylston Prof. Rhetoric, Oratory, Harvard, since 1946. Lowell lecturer, 1942. Phi Beta Kappa poet, Coll. of William and Mary, 1942, Tufts Coll., 1943, Harvard, 1943. Trustee, Boston Athenaeum, New England Conservatory of Music, Wellesley Coll. Fellow in American letters, Library of Congress. Mem. Modern Language Association of America, Charter Club (Princeton). Phi Beta Kappa. Democrat. Clubs: Tavern (Boston); Harvard (New York City). Editor: A Garland for John Donne, 1931; Stephen Hero, by James Joyce, 1944. Author: Death and Elizabethan Tragedy, 1936; Studies in Metaphysical Poetry (with Mark Van Doren), 1939; The Paradox in the Circle (verse), 1941; Shakespeare and the Nature of Man, 1942; The World in Your Hand (verse, 1943, An Act of Life (verse), 1944; Poems 1940-47; 1947; An Acre in the Seed, 1949. Contbr. of articles and verse to various mags. Office: 147 Widener Library, Cambridge 38, Mass. Died Jan. 18, 1949.

SPENCER, Vernon, musician; b. Belmont, County Durham, Eng., Oct. 10, 1875; s. Alfred and Isabella (Innes) S.; grad. Royal Conservatory of Music, Leipzig, Germany, 1897; m. Elsa Haase, Aug. 21, 1899; children—Percival I.V., Elsa M.I., Carl A.M.; m. 2d, Ruth Huntsberger, Aug. 22, 1917; 1 son, James Newton. Teacher of piano, Leipzig, 1897-1903, and Berlin, 1908-11; came to U.S., 1903; head of piano dept. and dir. Neb. Wesleyan U. Conservatory of Music, Lincoln, Neb., 1903-08; settled in Los Angeles, Calif., 1911; asst. prof. music, U. of Calif. at Los Angeles, 1921-24; concert pianist and teacher. Editor The Music Student (monthly mag.), 1915-16. Pres. Los Angeles Music Teachers' Assn., 1913-15; pres. Bohemians, 1922-23. Clubs: Los Angeles Athletic, Pacific Coast Club. Composer of songs, piano pieces, and ednl. works, etc.; lecturer and writer on music. Home: 4452 Dundee Drive, Los Angeles, Calif. Died Jan. 9, 1949; buried Inglewood Park Cemetery, Inglewood, Calif.

SPERRY, Marcy Leavenworth, pres. Washington Gas Light Co.; b. Annapolis, Md., Oct. 5, 1877; s. Charles Stillman (rear adm. U.S. Navy) and Edith (Marcy) S.; student Pratt Inst., 1895-96, Mass. Inst. Tech., 1896-1900; m. Anne Hunter, Feb. 22, 1911 (dec.); children—Marcy Leavenworth, William Hunter, Margaret, Edith, Anne. Mech., 1900; storekeeper Savannah (Ga.) Electric Co., 1902-03; asst. treas., then mgr. Ponce Electric Co., 1903-06; gen. supt. Minneapolis Gen. Electric Co., 1906-07; mgr. Savannah Electric Co., 1907-13; with Stone & Webster Service Corp., Boston, 1913-31; v.p. and gen. mgr. Fall River Gas Works Co., 1931-32; pres. Washington Gas Light Co. and subsidiaries since 1932. Mem. Delta Psi. Episcopalian. Clubs: Metropolitan, Alfalfa (Washington); Chevy Chase. Home: 1806 24th St., N.W. Address: 1100 H St. N.W., Washington 1, D.C. Died Mar. 30, 1949.

SPIEGEL, Modie Joseph (spē′g'l), mail order; s. Joseph and Matilda (Lebenstein) S. Entered father's home furnishing bus., Spiegel's House Furnishing Co., treas. and dir. until 1931; now chmn. bd. Spiegel, Inc., mail order. Apptd. mem. Ill. Ednl. Commn. by Gov. Horner; former mem. Chicago Bd. Edn. Clubs: Standard, Post and Paddock, Northmoor Country, Lake Shore Country, Illinois Athletic. Home: 140 Melrose Ave, Kenilworth, Ill. Address: 1061 W. 35th St., Chicago, Ill.* Died Jan. 8, 1943.

SPILLANE, Richard, author; b. N.Y. City, Apr. 23, 1864; s. Morgan and Elizabeth (Orpheus) S.; ed. pub. sch. N.Y. City, 2 yrs.; m. Mrs. Rowena Williams Spillane, 1896; stepchildren—M. M., J. R., Mrs. Rowena Stone. On editorial staff New York Herald, 4 yrs., New York Press 10 yrs., New York Evening Mail 2 yrs.; asso. editor Commerce and Finance 7 yrs.; business editor Public Ledger 3½ yrs.; served as financial editor New York American; v.p. Theo. H. Price Pub. Co. Trustee Nat. Farm Sch. Democrat. Mem. Franklin Soc. Catholic. Author: Oil and Sea Power, 1917; Life of Cyrus H. K. Curtis, 1921. Home: Hotel Holley, Washington Sq. W., New York. Died June 29, 1936.

SPINK, Mary Angela, physician; b. Washington, Ind., Nov. 18, 1863; d. Urban and Rosanna (Morgan) S.; ed. St. Simon's Acad., Washington; M.D., Med. Coll. of Ind., 1887; post grad. course in mental and nervous diseases, New York Post Grad. Sch. Pathologist at Central Ind. Hosp. for Insane, 1886-87; with Dr. William Baldwin Fletcher, est. the Dr. W. B. Fletcher's Sanatorium, Indianapolis, 1888; became supt. after Dr. Fletcher's death, 1907, now pres. Mem. Ind. State Bd. Charities for 30 years. Mem. A.M.A., State and Co. med. socs. Home: 1140 E. Market St., Indianapolis. Died Dec. 2, 1939.

SPINKS, Lewis, corp. exec.; b. Leesburg, Va., Nov. 10, 1879; s. Alexander and Ada (Nixon) S.; ed. pub. schs. of Leesburg, night courses, New York U., Am. Bankers Inst. and other finance schs.; m. Ila Steger, May 28, 1899 (died 1908); 1 son, Russell Dudley; m. 2d, Louise Mason, June 8, 1911; 1 dau., Orra. Began as cost accountant Crescent Shipyard, 1898; timekeeper Naughton & Co., contractors, 1900-02; cost accountant Internat. Powder Co., 1902-03; treas. Standard Motor Constrn. Co. of N.J., 1903-08, v.p. and treas. 1908-30; v.p. and mgr. Raritan River Sand Co. 1930-41; v.p. Nixon Nitration Works since Jan. 1, 1942. Mem. State Fish and Game Commn. since 1922 (treas. 8 yrs., v.p. since 1937). Mem. S.A.R. (Md. Soc.). Democrat. Home: 501 Raritan Av., Highland Park, N.J. Office: Nixon, N.J. Died Feb. 1946.

SPINNEY, George Wilbur, banking; b. Yarmouth, N.S., Can., Apr. 3, 1889; s. George N. and Josephine (Doty) S.; ed. pub. sch. and acad., Yarmouth, N.S.; D.C.L. (hon.), Acadia U., Wolfville, N.S., Can., 1942; m. Martha Maud Ramsay, Aug. 1916; children—Wilbur Ramsay (lt., Royal Can. Naval Vol. Res dec.), Ruth Josephine Lindsay, Martha Louise. Clerk. Bank of Montreal, 1906-15, successively at Yarmouth, Edmundston, Quebec, Hamilton, Montreal, sec. to gen. mgr., head office, 1915-22, asst. to gen. mgr., 1922-28, asst. gen. mgr., 1928-36, gen. mgr., 1936-42, pres. and chief exec. officer since 1942; chmn. Canadian advisory bd. Royal Exchange Assurance; vice pres., mem. exec. com. Royal Trust Co.; dir., mem. exec. com. Consol. Mining and Smelting Co. of Can.; Ltd., Canadian Pacific Ry. Co.; dir. Canadian Industries, Ltd., Montreal, London & Gen. Investors, Ltd., Internat. Nickel Co. of Can., Ltd., The Steel Co. of Can., Ltd., Sun Life Assurance Co. of Can. Companion of Order of St. Michael and St. George. Chmn. Can. First Victory Loan, 1941, Nat. War Finance Com., 1941-43; hon. chmn. Nat. War Finance Com. since 1943. Gov. McGill Univ.; pres. Royal Victoria Hosp. (Montreal). Clubs: Mount Royal (Montreal); Rideau (Ottawa). Home: 1 Braeside Pl., Wesmtount, Quebec, Can. Office: 119 St. James St. W., Montreal, Que., Can. Died Feb. 1, 1948; buried Mount Royal Cemetery, Montreal, Que., Can.

SPOHN, George Welda (spōn), prof. English; b. Krumsville, Pa., Aug. 19, 1879; s. Franklin and Katie Amanda (Weida) S.; B.E., State Normal Sch., Kutztown, Pa., 1896; student Muhlenberg Coll., Allentown, Pa., 1902-03; A.B., Princeton, 1906, Charles Scribner fellow in English 2 yrs., A.M., 1907, Ph.D., 1915; visiting scholar, Harvard, 1922-23; m. Mary Lucy Tyler, July 21, 1911; children—Mary Tyler, Cynthia Tyler (dec.). Teacher country sch. 5 yrs.; teacher German, Western Md. Coll., Westminster, 1908-09, and part-time teacher of German, Princeton, 1909-10; prof. German, St. Olaf Coll., Northfield, Minn., 1910-14, head of English dept. since 1915; teacher of English, State U. of Ia., 3 summers, U. of N.D., 1 summer. Chmn. Am. Red Cross Chapter, World War, also mem. Home Guard, four-minute man and dir. Victory Loan. Mem. bd. Carnegie Library, Northfield. Mem. Modern Lang. Assn. America, Lions Internat., Phi Beta Kappa. Democrat. Lutheran. Club: Northfield Lions (ex-pres.). Author: Milestones and Other Poems; The Second Fall. Writer of verse; frequent lecturer before high schs. and colleges; staff lecturer Radio Sta. WCAL. Co-editor: A College Book of American Literature. Home: 206 E. 2d St., Northfield, Minn. Died Aug. 31, 1943; buried in West Claremont Cemetery, Claremont, N. H.

SPRAGUE, Albert Arnold (sprāg), wholesale grocer; b. Chicago, Ill., May 13, 1874, s. Otho Sylvester Arnold and Lucia Elvira (Atwood) S.; A.B., Harvard U., 1898; LL.D., Northwestern U., 1938; m. Frances Fidelia Dibble, June 22, 1901; children—Albert Arnold, Laura, Otho S. A. Chairman bd. of directors, Consolidated Grocers Corp.; director Continental Ill. Nat. Bank & Trust Co., Internat. Harvester Co., Clearing Industrial Dist., B.&O. R.R. Co., Wilson & Co., Marshall Field & Co., B. F. Goodrich Co.; trustee Chicago Rapid Transit Company. Trustee Chicago Natural History Museum, John Crerar Library, Children's Memorial Hosp., Chicago Symphony Orchestra, Shedd Aquarium, Mus. of Sci. and Industry, Sprague Meml. Institute. Student, O.T.C., Ft. Sheridan, Ill.; command. maj. inf., Nov. 27, 1917; assigned to 341st Regt. Inf., 86th Div., and detailed to hdqrs.; sailed for France, July 1918; lt. col. Nov. 9, 1918; returned to U.S., Mar. 1919; hon. discharged, Mar. 28, 1919; col. O.R.C. Commr. of pub. works, Chicago, 1923-27 and 1931-33. Dem. candidate for U.S. Senate, 1924. Episcopalian. Clubs: City, Chicago, Mid-Day, Commercial, Saddle and Cycle, Old Elm Club (Chicago); Harvard, Racquet (New York); Harvard (Boston). Home: 1130 Lake Shore Drive. Office: 72 W. Adams St., Chicago. Died Apr. 6, 1946.

SPRAGUE, Benjamin Oxnard, pres. Savannah Sugar Refining Corp.; b. Reedville, Mass., June 13, 1878; s. Richard T. and Fanny A. (Oxnard) S.; student St. Ignatius School, San Francisco High School, Bates Prep. School, Boones Prep. School, all of San Francisco, and Stanford U.; m. Mee Elizabeth Potts, Dec. 31, 1903. Chemist Western Sugar Co., San Francisco, 1897-99; engr. and asst. supt. Am. Beet Sugar Co., Oxnard, Calif., 1899-1904; supt. Am. Beet Sugar Co., Chino, Calif., 1905-10; engr. and gen. mgr. The Adeline Sugar Factory Co., Ltd., Adeline, La., 1911-15; with the Savannah Sugar Refining Corp. since 1916, successively as engr. and designer, gen. supt., and now pres. and dir.; dir. The Citizens & Southern National Bank. Mem. American Society Mechanical Engrs., Soc. of Am. Mil. Engrs. Clubs: The Oglethorpe, Savannah Golf, Woodsville Gun, Forest City Gun. Home: 105 E. 37th St. Office: Savannah Sugar Refining Co., Savannah, Ga. Died Jan. 31, 1944.

SPRAGUE, Ezra Kimball, med. director U.S.P.H.S., sanitarian; b. Milo, Me., May 26, 1866; s. Dr. Seth Billington and Maria Edgeworth (Kimball) S.; A.B., Bates College, Me., 1887; M.D., Coll. Phys. and Surg., Boston, 1890; post-grad. work, Post-Grad. Med. Sch., New York, 1891-92, Harvard Med. Sch., 1897; m. Clara Rebecca Blaisdell, Aug. 22, 1893; children—Kimball Deering, Olive. Commd. asst. surgeon U.S.P.H.S., 1893; promoted to higher grades and retired as colonel in 1931; served in U.S. and at Antwerp (Belgium) and Calcutta; prof. tropical medicine, Detroit Med. Coll., 1901-02; made a study of bubonic plague, Calcutta, 1903-04; chief medical officer, Ellis Island, 1925-28; dir. No. Atlantic Dist. U.S.P.H.S., 1928-32. In charge extra cantonment zone sanitation, Camp Dodge, Des Moines, and Camp Devens, Ayer, Mass., during World War. Mem. A.M.A. Republican. Episcopalian. Mason. Brought about installation of filtration plant at Washington, D.C., as result of reports on drinking water, 1898. Author of articles and addresses on bacteriology, pub. health and sanitation. Club: Army and Navy (New York). Home: 462 Rugby Rd., Flatbush, Brooklyn, N.Y. Died Feb. 2, 1943.

SPRAGUE, Jesse Rainsford (sprag), writer; b. Middlebury, N.Y., Mar. 23, 1871; s. George Finley and Susan (Tomlinson) Sprague; educated at Le Roy Academic Institute; married Edna M. Dolloff, Mar. 15, 1899 (died February 4, 1941). In mercantile business, Newport News, Va., 1900-09, San Antonio, Tex., 1909-21; moved to New York, 1921. Democrat.

Has written for magazines since 1915; contbr. travel articles, stories and essays to Harper's, Scribner's, Am. Mercury, Saturday Evening Post, etc. Author: The Making of a Merchant, 1928; The Middleman, 1929; An American Banker, 1929; On the Road, 1930; James Read, 1930; The Chain Store Man, 1931; King Cotton Carries On, 1932; The Lumberman, 1933; High Pressure, 1938; The Romance of Credit, 1943; Career Suggestions for G.I. Joe, 1946. Home: 21 E. 9th St., New York. Died Sept. 4, 1946.

SPRAGUE, Thomas Henry, clergyman, lecturer, writer; b. Wine Harbour, Nova Scotia; s. John and Ruth Ann Sprague; Ph.B., Bucknell U., Lewisburg, Pa., 1897, M.A., 1906; Crozer Theol. Sem., Chester, Pa., 1900; D.D., Stetson U., DeLand, Fla., 1912; m. Jessie Barton Lovell. Ordained Baptist ministry; pastorates at Haddon Heights, N.J.; Chester Avenue Ch., Phila.; Fulton Av. Ch., Baltimore; Temple Ch., Phila.; First Ch., Troy, N.Y.; Emanuel Ch., Ridgewood, N.J.; First Ch., Hollywood, Fla. Representative Am. Baptist Home Mission Soc., Cuba. Mem. Phi Gamma Delta. Mason. Pres. Conn. Tourist Club, Fort Lauderdale, Fla. Author: Think On These Things; The Mountain Road (verse); History of First Baptist Church, Troy, N.Y.; Deeds not Things and other stories; My Christianity; also many magazine articles. Home: (winter) Hollywood, Florida; (summer) Deep River, Conn. Died March 20, 1949; buried West Laurel Hill Cemetery, Philadelphia.

SPRENG, Samuel Peter, bishop; b. Wayne County, O., Feb. 11, 1853; s. Christian and Julia (Grimm) S.; student Northwestern Coll., Naperville, Ill., 1872-75; D.D., Evang. Theol. Sem., 1901; m. Margaret A. Beck, Sept. 18, 1878; children—Edmund George Christian, Lillian Ethel, Ralph Waldo Emerson, George Beck. Ordained ministry Evang. Assn., 1875; pastor Bellevue, O., 1875-76, Cleveland, 1876-79, Napoleon, O., 1879-81, Columbus, 1881-82, Circleville, 1882-83; presiding elder, Columbus Dist., 1883-86; editor Evangelical Messenger, Cleveland, 1887-1907; became bishop Evang. Ch., Oct. 1907, now emeritus. Dir. Evang. Deaconess Hosp. and Sch. for Nurses. Vice-pres. Nat. Anti-Saloon League. Author: Life of Bishop John Seybert, 1884; Rays of Light on the Highway to Success, 1885; History of the Evang. Assn., 1894; The Sinner and His Savior, 1900; The Most Wonderful Book in the World, 1903; History of the Evang. Ch., 1924; What Evangelicals Believe, 1929. Traveled and preached in Europe, and made extended tour of missions in China and Japan, 1908-09. Celebrated golden jubilee, at Bellevue, O., Sept. 20, 1925, completing 50 yrs. of uninterrupted service in the ministry of the Evang. Ch. Made bishop emeritus by Gen. Conf. Evang. Ch., 1930. Has attended 16 Gen. Confs. of Evang. Ch. Home: Naperville, Ill.* Died Apr. 19, 1946.

SPRINGER, Alfred, chemist; b. Cincinnati, O., Feb. 12, 1854; s. Lemuel and Antonie (Fries) S.; pub. and high schs., Cincinnati; A.M., Ph.D., U. of Heidelberg, Germany, 1872; Dr. Natural Science, Ruperto Carola U., Heidelberg, Germany, 1931; m. Eda Elsas, Dec. 30, 1879; children—Elsa (Mrs. Christian Meyer), Alfred. Sole owner Alex. Fries & Bro., mfg. chemists, Cincinnati, 1873, until retired, 1936. Fellow A.A.A.S. (gen. sec., 1884; v.p., 1892); mem. Am. Chem. Soc.; corr. mem. Brit. Assn. for Advancement of Science. Awarded John Scott Legacy premium and medal, Franklin Inst., 1891. Has written many papers on chem. and phys. subjects. Co-inventor of the torsion balance, also patentee of same and of aluminum soundboards for mus. instruments. Home: Belvedere Apts., Avondale, Cincinnati. Office: 312 E. 2d St., Cincinnati, O.* Died Feb. 24, 1946.

SPRINGER, John Franklin, writer; b. Hagerstown, Md., Sept. 18, 1866; s. John and Annie Jerry (Dowler) S.; ed. Baltimore City Coll. (non-grad.); student Johns Hopkins, 1891-92; self-instructed, especially in mathematics; m. Amelia Lavinia Horpel, 1890 (died 1902); children—Allan Paul, Clarence Stephen, Joseph Arthur, Gladys Marguerite (dec.); m. 2d, Carlie McClure, 1909; 1 son, Maurice Gilbert. Teacher, Milton Acad., 1890-93; prin. and owner same, 1893-1902; prin. and mgr. Erie (Pa.) Acad., 1901-06; writer on engring., scientific and technical topics; researcher and writer criticism of the four Gospels. Author: Oxy-Acetylene Torch Practice, 1912. Part Author: Autogenous Welding, 1914. Author of extensive critical examination of Synoptic Problem, Bibliotheca Sacra, 1923-27. Home: 238 W. 106th St., New York, N.Y. Died Jan. 6, 1943.

SPRINGER, Raymond Smiley, congressman; b. Rush County, Ind., Apr. 26, 1882; s. Lorenzo D. and Josephine (Smiley) S.; student Earlham College, 1901-02, Butler U., 1903-04; LL.B., Indiana Law School, 1904; m. Nancy Emmons, Sept. 18, 1904. Admitted to Ind. bar, 1904; county atty., 1908-14; judge 37th and 73d Circuits, 1916-22; in practice of law, Connersville, since 1922. Rep. candidate for gov. of Ind., 1932 and 1936; mem. 76th to 80th Congresses (1939-49), 10th Ind. Dist. Commd. capt. inf., U.S. Army, World War; now lt. col. Inf. U.S. Res. Corps. Mem. Am. Legion (past state comdr.). Mason, Elk, Eagle, K.P. Club: Columbia (Indianapolis). Home: Connersville, Ind. Died Aug. 28, 1947.

SPRINGS, Mrs. Leroy (Lena Jones Springs); b. Pulaski, Tenn.; d. Thomas Meriwether and Lena May (Bulford) Jones; ed. private schs., Dallas, Tex.; Martin Coll., Pulaski; B.A., Sullins Coll., Bristol, Tenn.; post-grad. work, Virginia Coll., Roanoke, Va.; D.Litt., Presbyn. Coll. of S.C., 1924; m. Leroy Springs, Nov. 29, 1913. Head of English dept., Queen's Coll., Charlotte, N.C., 1911-13. Treas. S.C. Equal Suffrage League, 1916; pres. Lancaster Equal Suffrage League, 1916-18; v.p. S.C. Equal Suffrage League, 1917, dist. dir., 1917-20; organizer and chmn. Lancaster Red Cross, 1917-18; establshed 2 emergency hosp. during influenza epidemic, 1917; dist. v.p. S.C. Federation Women's Clubs, 1917-18; dist. chmn. Liberty Loan S.C., also chmn. S.C. Women's organs. 3d Liberty Loan, 1917-18; pres. S.C. Fedn. Women's Clubs, 1918-19; mem. S.C. Commn. World War Memorial, 1919; chmn. S.C. Fed. Endowment Fund, 1920-25; dist. dir. S.C. League Women Voters, 1920-25; Dem. Nat. Committeewoman, term, 1922-28; del. at large Dem. Nat. Conv., New York, 1924 (nominated there for v.p. of U.S.); state chmn. of S.C. of Com. for Law Enforcement, 1924-25; mem. bd. "Women's Citizen." 1924-25. Mem. Nat. Soc. D.A.R., Internat. Council of Women (life). Presbyterian. Clubs: Regency (New York); Congressional Country, Dem. Nat. Woman's (Washington). Speaker on ednl., patriotic, polit. topics. Home: Hotel Plaza, New York, N.Y. Died May 18, 1942.

SPRONG, Severn D., elec. engr.; b. East Greenbush, Rensselaer County, N.Y., Oct. 27, 1873; s. Willard D. and Pauline A. (Melius) S.; ed. pub. and private schs. and under tutelage; m. Margaret A. McMullen, Oct. 21, 1897; 1 dau., Katharine W. Supt. elec. dept., Consolidated Gas Co. of N.J., Long Branch, N.J., 1898-1901; chief engr. Central Electric Co., Metuchen, N.J., 1901-02; asst. chief elec. engr., N.Y. Edison Co., 1902-07; asst. elec. engr. United Electric Light & Power Co., New York, 1907-10; chief elec. engr., J. G. White Co., New York, 1910-12; elec. engr., Brooklyn Edison Co., 1912-22; v.p. Orange County Pub. Service Corp., 1922; pres. Engring. Products Corp. since 1924. Republican. Conglist. Fellow Am. Inst. E.E. (v.p. 1912-13); mem. Am. Soc. M.E., N.Y. Elec. Soc., A.A.A.S. Clubs: Engineers' (New York), Lawyers, Montauk Home: Monroe, N.Y. Office: 39 Cortlandt St., New York, N.Y.* Died June 27, 1946.

SPROTT, Jarl S., business exec.; b. Auburn, Ind., Aug. 21, 1881; s. Thomas H. and Abbie (Potter) S. Gen. mgr. Globe-Wernicke Co. Cincinnati, since 1932 pres. and dir. since 1934. Clubs: Hyde Park Country, Queen City, Rotary. Home: Keller and Miami Rd. Office: Cincinnati. Died Feb. 11, 1949.

SPYKMAN, Nicholas John (spĕk'mån), univ. prof.; b. Amsterdam, Holland, Oct. 13, 1893; s. Klaas and Elizabeth (van Vorstenberg) S.; A.B., U. of Calif., 1921, A.M., 1922, Ph.D., 1923; m. Elizabeth Choate, Aug. 20, 1931; children—Angelica, Patricia. Came to U.S., 1920, naturalized, 1928. Journalist, Near East, 1913-16; Middle East, 1916-19; Australasia, Far East, 1919-20; instr. polit. science and sociology U. of Calif., 1923-25; asst. prof. internat. relations, Yale, 1925-28, prof. since 1928, chmn. Dept. of Internat. Relations, 1935-40 and dir. Yale Inst. of Internat. Studies, 1935-40. Mem. Am. Acad. Polit. Science, Am. Acad. Polit. and Social Science, Am. Geog. Soc., Am. Polit. Science Assn., Am. Soc. Internat. Law. Council on Foreign Relations, Inst. of Pacific Relations. Clubs: Century, Yale (N.Y. City). Author: Hindia Zelfbestuur, 1919; The Social Theory of Georg Simmel, 1925; American Strategy in World Politics, 1942. Home: Rimmon Rd., Woodbridge, Conn. Died June 26, 1943.

SQUIER, J(ohn) Bentley (skwīr), surgeon; b. New York, N.Y., Nov. 6, 1873; s. J. Bentley and Adelaide (Lum) S.; M.D., Columbia, 1894; LL.D., U. of Pittsburgh, 1925; m. Ursula Bradt, Aug. 21, 1902; children—John Bentley, Ursula. Interne St. Luke's Hosp., N.Y. City, 1894-97; attending surgeon Dept. of Charities, N.Y. City, 12 yrs.; prof. genito-urinary surgery, New York Post-Grad. Med. Sch., 1909-24, also dir.; prof. urology, Columbia, 1917-39, emeritus; attending genito-urinary surgeon, Presbyn. and New York Post-Grad. hosps.; cons. surgeon to St. Luke's Hosp. and Roosevelt Hosp.; dir. Squier Urol. Clinic; originator Columbia War Hosp.; mem. Gen. Medical Bd. of Council Nat. Defense; served as major M.R.C. during World War. Fellow Am. Coll. Surgeons (a founder and gov. and regent; pres. 1932-33), L'Assn. Internationale d'Urologie; mem. Am. Urol. Assn. (pres. 1913), Am. Assn. Genito-Urinary Surgeons (pres. 1919-20), Med. Soc. County of N.Y. (pres. 1917), New York Physicians' Mutual Aid Assn. (treas. 1915), Psi Upsilon. Clubs: University, Union. Author of numerous monographs on subjects relating to surgery of the bladder and kidneys. Home: 995 Fifth Av., New York. Died March 1, 1948.

SQUIRE, Amos Osborne, physician, lecturer; b. Cold Spring, N.Y., May 28, 1876; s. Lewis Nelson and Mary Louise (Rose) S.; M.D., Coll. Physicians and Surgeons, Columbia, 1899; m. Matilda E. Nation, Apr. 29, 1903; 1 dau., Evelyn Osborne. In practice at Ossining, N.Y., since 1899; coroner Westchester County, 1906-12; health officer Ossining, chief phys. Sing Sing Prison, 1910-25; owner private sanitarium, 1910-20; med. examiner, Westchester County since 1925; also med. dir. Alcock Mfg. Co. Surgeon N.Y. State Naval Militia, 1912-19, res. list since 1919. Fellow Am. Psychiatric Soc.; mem. N.Y. State Med. Soc., Westchester Med. Soc., Med. Surg. Soc. N.Y., Clin. Soc. of Psychiatry, Am. Prison Physicians Assn. (past pres.). Dir. N.Y. State Soc. for Crippled Children; dir. Ossining Trust Co. Republican. Methodist. Mason (K.T., Shriner). Clubs: Rotary Internat. (dir.); National Republican, Columbia (New York); City (Yonkers); Masonic, Shattemuc Yacht and Canoe (Ossining). Author: Sing Sing Doctor (pub. also in Eng.). Lecturer on criminology since 1914. Home: 36 S. Highland Av., Ossining, N.Y. Died Feb. 11, 1949.

SQUIRES, Charles William, clergyman; b. Harbor Grace, Newfoundland, Jan. 23, 1877; s. Rev. John and Amelia Davis (Hippisley) S.; B.A., Mt. Allison U., Sackville, N.B., 1900, M.A., 1902, B.D., 1905; M.A., Harvard Div. Sch., 1903; B.D., Wesleyan Theol. Coll., Montreal, 1918, Princeton Theol. Sem., 1919, Presbyn. Theol. Coll., Montreal, 1921; S.T.D., Wesleyan Theol. Coll., 1920; D.D., Presbyn. Coll., Montreal, 1923; m. Ethel May Hoyle, July 6, 1905; children—Virginia Lora Sybil, Cedric Wilmot Harvard, Arleen, Evelyn Gloria. Ordained Meth. ministry, 1900, changed to Presbyn., 1918; began preaching in Newfoundland, 1893, continued there until 1902; pastor Andover, N.B., 1905-07, St. John, 1907-10, Campbellton, 1912-16, Newcastle, 1916-18, Presbyn. Ch., Lehighton, Pa., 1919-23, Lynn, Mass., 1923-34, First Baptist Ch., Limerick, Me., since Oct. 1934. Moderator Boston Presbytery, 1925-26; chmn. Lynn Inter-Ch. Union, 1926; chmn. Lynn Chapter League of Nations Assn.; commr. to Presbyn. Gen. Assembly, Pittsburgh, 1931; chmn. Presbyn. Ministers Assn., Boston, 1931. Naturalized citizen of U.S., 1925. Mason, Odd Fellow. Author: Münsterberg and Militarism Checked, 1915; Is God a Personality?, 1923; The Sky-Pilot Crashes, 1937. Contbr. to Boston Ideas, Boston Herald, etc. Home: Campello, Me. Died Aug. 9, 1948.

SQUIRES, William Henry Tappey (skwīrz), clergyman, author; b. Petersburg, Va., Apr. 14, 1875; s. Brigadier-General Chas. Winder and Emily Elizabeth (Tappey) S.; A.B., Hampden-Sydney Coll., 1895; D.D., 1916; M.A., King Coll. Bristol, Tenn., 1897, Litt.D., 1930; B.D., Union Theol. Sem., 1901; studied Columbia U., summer, 1922; m. Anna Sarah Hull, Apr. 26, 1905; children—David Denton, Emily Elizabeth (Mrs. John Hanning), William Henry Tappey, Graham Bane. Ordained Presbyn. ministry, Oct. 20, 1901; founded and organized Overlook Ch., Richmond, 1900, Ch., Damascus, Va., 1904, Lafayette Ch., Norfolk, 1911, New Jamestown Ch., Norfolk, 1916, Lynnhaven Ch., 1917, Glenwood Park Ch., Norfolk, 1931; pastor Central Ch., Bristol, Va., 1901-09, Knox Ch., Norfolk, 1909-29, Ingleside and Glenwood Park churches, 1930-41. Apptd. asst. historian in chief National Societies Sons of Confederate Veterans, 1933; member Historical Commission, Norfolk Virginia, World War II, 1943-45, 1946-47. Awarded Washington Bi-Centennial medal, Soc. of the Cincinnati, 1932; Algernon Sidney Sullivan medallion, Southern Soc. of New York, 1933. Trustee Hampden-Sydney Coll. (pres. bd. 1923-25), King Coll. (Bristol, Tenn., 1901-03), Stonewall Jackson Coll., (Abingdon, Va., 1901-09), Bonney Home for Girls, Norfolk, since 1942. Mem. Va. Hist. Soc., Theophilus Soc. (clerical), Sons of Confederate Vets. (chaplain Pickett-Buchanan Camp 1933; state historian 1935), S.A.R. (state historian 1929-41; nat. historian-general, 1939-40); charter mem. Norfolk Memorial Assn. (grand marshal Memorial Celebration 1939, orator, 1941), Norfolk Hist. Society. Vice chmn. Bicentennial Committee for Celebration of the establishment of Norfolk by Chamber of Commerce, 1936. Democrat. K.P., Knight of the Golden Eagle. Appointed chaplain, rank of lt. col. Army of Northern Va., United Confederate Vets., 1937. Mem. of General Assembly of Presbyterian Church in U.S. (Southern), 1907, 14, 27, 38; charter mem. Order of Stars and Bars (Confederate), 1937, registrar-general, 1938, chaplain, 1940-43; charter member Order of Cape Henry, 1940, trustee, 1940-43. Charter member and vice-president Norfolk New Citizens Association, 1941. Author: Guide Book to Norfolk, Virginia, 1916; William Maxwell, a Virginian of the Ante-Bellum Days, 1918; Rise of the Presbyterian Church in Tidewater, Virginia, 1920, rev. and enlarged, 1940; Acadie Days—A Sketch of New Scotland, 1921; Peregrine Papers, 1923; Virginia, a State Song, 1923 (music by S. K. Emurian); Life of Samuel Davies (serial in Presbyterian of the South), 1925; Who Am I? (a geneal. record), 1926; John Holt Rice (in Virginia Portraiture), 1929; The Days of Yester-Year in Colony and Commonwealth, 1928; Through Centuries Three—A Short History of Virginia, 1929; The Land of Decision—the Splendor of Virginia's Story, 1931; Those Years Forgotten, the Story of Reconstruction in Va. (serial) 1933; Norfolk in By-Gone Days (serial in Ledger-Dispatch), 1935-43; Through the Years in Norfolk, 1937; The Presbyterian Church in the Colony of Virginia, 1938; Unleashed at Long Last, The Story of Reconstruction in Virginia, 1939; Petersburg, Va.—an Anthology (State Library of Va.), 1941; The Rose Family of Colonial Virginia and Medieval Scotland, 1942. Associate editor Know Norfolk (magazine), 1937-43. Contributor to magazines. Appointed by governor to rep. Virginia, King's Mountain Centennial, 1930, Am. Library Assn., 1936 and 1937. Awarded Cosmopolitan medal as "first citizen of Norfolk," 1939. Home: Massawomack, Riverview, Norfolk, Va. Died Apr. 20, 1948.

ST. SURE, Adolphus Frederic, judge; born at Sheboygan, Wis., March 9, 1869; s. Frank A. and Ellen (Donoghue) St. S.; ed. pub. schs.; m. Ida Laura Pettes, Oct. 31, 1897; children—William Pettes, J. Paul. Admitted to Calif. bar, 1895, and began practice at Alameda; served as city recorder and city atty., Alameda; judge Superior Court of Alameda County; ass. justice Dist. Court of Appeal, 1st Dist. of Calif., 1923-25; judge U.S. Dist. Court, Northern Dist. of Calif., since Mar. 2, 1925. Mem. Phi Delta Phi. Republican. Home: Oakland, Calif. Address: U.S. Post Office Bldg., San Francisco, Cal. Died Feb. 5, 1949.

STABLER, Herman (stāb'lẽr), civil engr.; b. Brighton, Md., Feb. 3, 1879; s. George Lea and Annie Dickinson (Cotton) S.; B.S., Earlham Coll., 1899; spl. course in engring., Columbian (now George Washington) U., Washington, 1902-03; m. Bertha R. Buhler, Nov. 1, 1905. Instr. mathematics and engring., Nat. Corr. Inst., Washington, 1899-1903; hydraulic and sanitary engr. with the U.S. Geol. Survey and U.S. Reclamation Service, 1903-22; chief of land classification br. U.S. Geol. Survey, 1922-25 and of conservation br. since 1925. Mem. Am. Soc. C.E. (dir., 1935-37), Am. Inst. Mining and Metall. Engrs., Washington Soc. of Engineers, Geol. Society of Washington, Washington Acad. Sciences, Am. Geog. Soc. Mem. Friends Ch. Mason. Clubs: Cosmos, Columbia Country. Author of numerous bulls. and papers relating to disposal of wastes of mfg. establishments and recovery of products therefrom; pollution of streams; composition of stream waters; development of ground waters; rate of erosion; silt accumulations; water power; industrial uses of water, etc. Home: 2700 Connecticut Av. Address: Cosmos Club, Washington, D.C. Died Nov. 24, 1942.

STACE, Arthur William (stās), editor, writer; b. Marshall, Mich., Apr. 26, 1875; s. Francis A. and Margaret Mary (McMahon) S.; Litt.B., Notre Dame U., 1896, grad. student, 1897; m. Lillian M. O'Connor, June 1, 1899; children—Donald, Francis (reserve officer U.S.A.F.), Margaret Anne, Vincent Arthur (officer U.S. Army Air Forces). Reporter Grand Rapids (Mich.) Democrat, 1897; telegraph editor, Grand Rapids Press, 1897, city editor, editorial writer, special writer, 1900-13, managing ed., 1913-23; special writer and research worker Mich. subjects for Booth Newspapers, Inc. (8 Mich. papers), 1923-27; director Mich. Utilities Inf. Bur., 1927-34; editor Ann Arbor News, dir. Ann Arbor Bur. Booth Newspapers, writer for Booth Newspapers since 1935. Dir. Southeastern Mich. Tourist Assn., Washtenaw Br. of Mich. Auto. Assn. Hon. alumnus Mich. U., 1936. Mem. Am. Soc. Newspaper Editors, Mich. Acad. Science, Mich. Authors Assn., Mich. Forestry Assn., Nat. Com. for Mental Hygiene. Ind. Republican. Roman Catholic. Clubs: Rotary, Ann Arbor, University, University of Michigan, Barton Hills Country, Ann Arbor Golf and Outing (Ann Arbor); National Press (Washington, D.C.). Author of serial "Dreamland Adventures," syndicated by Phila. Ledger, 1917-25; many studies on resources, problems and possibilities of Mich., pub. in Booth Newspaper. Home: 1046 Baldwin Av. Office: Ann Arbor News, Ann Arbor, Mich. Died Jan. 10, 1950.

STACEY, Anna Lee, artist; b. Glasgow, Mo.; d. John and Eliza (Fisher) Dey; student at Prichett Inst. (now Prichett Coll.); studied at Art Inst. of Chicago; m. John F. Stacey, Oct. 15, 1891. Awards: Young Fortnightly prize, Chicago Artists' Exhbn., 1902; Martin B. Cahn prize, Exhbn. by Am. Artists, 1902; Marshall Field prize, 1907; Clyde M. Carr prize, Chicago Artists' Exhbn., 1912; Artist Guild prize, 1937; Logan bronze medal, 1921; hon. mention Calif. Artists and Pasadena Soc. Artists, 1938. Picture, "Vista from the Ponce de Leon," purchased by City Commn. for City of Chicago, 1914. Mem. Soc. Chicago Painters and Sculptors, Calif. Soc. Artists, Pasadena Soc. Artists. Clubs: The Cordon, Arts. Home: 499 Prospect Terrace, Pasadena, Calif. Died March 4, 1943.

STACKHOUSE, Perry James, clergyman; b. St. John, N.B., Can., Feb. 4, 1875; s. James Albert and Abbie (Ring) S.; grad. Union Bapt. Sem., N.B., 1893; A.B., Acadia Coll., 1899; B.D., Div. School Univ. of Chicago, 1904; D.D., Colgate U., Hamilton, N.Y., 1919, Acadia, 1927; m. Minnie Florence Branscombe, Dec. 24, 1901; children—Stirling Perry (M.D.), Florence Mona (Mrs. Burnice Lefler). Was ordained to ministry of Baptist Church, 1899; pastor Tabernacle Bapt. Ch., St. John, N.B., 1899-1901 and 1904-07, Austin Av. Bapt. Ch., Chicago, 1901-04, First Bapt. Ch., Campbellton, N.B., 1907-10, First Bapt. Ch., Amherst, N.S., 1910-14, Tabernacle Bapt. Ch., Utica, N.Y., 1914-21, 1st Ch., Chicago, 1921-41, pastor emeritus, 1942. President Baptist Ministers Conference, Chicago, 1923, 36, Hyde Park and Kenwood Council of Churches, Northwestern Baptist Education Society; member Pi Gamma Mu. Club: Theophilus. Author: The Baptist Position and the Question of Honesty, 1908; The Social Ideals of the Lord's Prayer, 1916; The Sword of Christ, and the World War, 1917; Bible Dramas in the Pulpit, 1926; also The Drama in the Church in Religion Today (Chicago Tribune religious editorials), 1926; Chicago and the Baptists—A Century of Progress, 1933; Protestantism in Chicago Prior to 1850, 1933. Lamplight Illustrations for Pulpit, Platform and Forum, 1939. Home: 2220 Third Av. N., St. Petersburg, Fla. Died Dec. 22, 1944.

STADTFELD, Joseph (stät'fĕld), judge; b. New York, N.Y., Aug. 12, 1861; s. Moritz and Sophie (Spier) S.; grad. Central High Sch., Pittsburgh, 1878; m. Carrie Edmundson Herron, Jan. 31, 1895; children—Rodgers Morrow, Joseph Randolph (dec.), Harold Randolph. Admitted to Pa. bar, 1886, and began practice, Pittsburgh; apptd. solicitor City of Pittsburgh, 1914, but declined; apptd. judge Common Pleas Court of Allegheny County, June 24, 1930; apptd. judge Superior Court of Pa., Nov. 7, 1931, elected for term, 1932-42; dir. Kaufmann Dept. Stores. Mem. Am. Bar Assn. (exec. council for Pa., 1931), Pa. State Bar Assn. (v.p. 1929), Allegheny County Bar Assn. (pres. 1928-29). Mem. B'nai B'rith. Republican. Hebrew religion. Mason. Club: Concordia. Home: 5575 Wilkins Av. Chambers: City-County Bldg., Pittsburgh, Pa. Died Dec. 12, 1943.

STAFFORD, Thomas Polhill, clergyman, educator; b. Robertville, S.C., Feb. 17, 1866; s. William John and Mary Ellen (Jaudon) S.; A.B., William Jewell Coll., Liberty, Mo., 1890, A.M., 1892, Th.M., Southern Bapt. Theol. Sem., 1893, Th.D., 1894, Ph.D., 1930; studied Univ. of Halle, 1903-04; m. Anna Gardner Tutt, 1895 (died 1912), children—Nell Thornton (Mrs. Fairchild Gill), Dorothy (Mrs. E. S. Thomas), Paul Tutt; m. 2d, Grace Harriet Utley, June 29, 1914. Ordained Bapt. ministry, 1890; pastor Liberty, 1894-1900; prof. theology and philosophy, William Jewell Coll., 1900-10; pastor Canon City, Colo., 1910-12; prof. Christian doctrines, Kansas City Bapt. Theol. Sem., 1912-37, dean of grad. work, 1930-37, resigned; pastor Leeds Bapt. Ch., Kansas City, 1916-22, Beaumont Bapt. Ch., 1923-29, Marlborough Bapt. Ch., 1929-31. Mem. Am. Research Soc. Author: The Origin of Christian Science, 1912; A Study of the Holy Spirit, 1920; A Study of the Kingdom, 1925; A Study of Christian Doctrines, 1936. Contbr. on religious subjects. Lecturer. Home: 815 E. 30th St., Kansas City, Mo. Died Jan. 23, 1942.

STAGE, Charles Willard, lawyer; b. Painesville, O., Nov. 26, 1868; s. Stephen Keyes and Sarah McCartney (Knight) S.; A.B., Western Reserve U., 1892, A.M., 1895, LL.B., 1895; m. Miriam Gertrude Kerruish, Aug. 29, 1903; children—Charles Willard, William Sheldon Kerruish, Miriam, Edward Whitney. Admitted to O. bar, 1895, and began practice at Cleveland; sec. Municipal Traction Co., 1906-08, City Sinking Fund Commn., 1910-12; gen. counsel O. P. & M. J. Van Sweringen, 1916-22; v.p., sec. and gen. counsel Cleveland Union Terminals Co., 1922-38, retired Dec. 1, 1938; mem. bd. of dirs. Morris Plan Bank (Cleveland), Elwell Parker Electric Co. Mem. Ohio Ho. of Rep., 1902-03; county solicitor Cuyahoga County, 1903-08; dir. pub. safety, Cleveland, 1912-14; dir. pub. utilities, Cleveland, 1914-16. Mem. Alpha Delta Phi. Democrat. Episcopalian. Club: Country Club. Home: Shaker House, 12931 Shaker Blvd. Office: Terminal Tower, Cleveland, O. Died May 17, 1947.

STAHL, K(arl) F(riedrich), chemist; b. Zwiefalten, Wurttemberg, Germany, Mar. 14, 1855; s. Johann Jacob and Luise (Kurz) S.; student Inst. of Tech., Stuttgart, 1872-75; U. of Tübingen, 1875-76, D.Sc., 1876, renewed 1926; m. Emma Onyx Johnson, Aug. 8, 1881 (died Nov. 1924); 1 dau., Minneola Luise. Came to U.S., 1876, naturalized, 1888. Chemist Charles Lennig & Co., Phila., 1876-80, Northwestern Fertilizer Co., Chicago, 1880-82; supt. Nat. Fertilizer Co., Nashville, Tenn., 1882-84, Johnstown (Pa.) Chem. Works, 1884-90, James Irwin & Co., Pittsburgh, 1890-99; supt. Pittsburgh works, Gen. Chem. Co., 1899-1913; research chemist Gen. Chem. Co. and cons. chemist since 1914. Fellow A.A.A.S.; mem. Am. Chem. Soc. (chmn. Pittsburg sect., 1916, emeritus 1933), Engr. Soc. of Western Pa. (dir. 1895; chmn. chem. sect. 1902), Nat. Assn. German-Am. Technologists (pres. 4 terms, hon. mem. 1937), Verein Deutscher Chemiker, Soc. Chem. Industry (England). Republican. Lutheran. Home: 839 Chislett St., Pittsburgh 6, Pa. Died Aug. 26, 1946.

STAHL, John Meloy (stäl), writer lecturer; b. Mendon, Ill., Aug. 24, 1860; s. Elias and Ann Elizabeth (Nutzelle) S.; grad. Quincy (Ill.) High Sch., 1881; m. Mary Chouteau Platt, June 25, 1900; children—Mary Edith, Chouteau Platt. Contbr. first article for farm paper at 14; an editor Ohio Farmer at 18; editor, 1881-1916, propr., 1883-1916, Ill. Farmer and Farmer's Call; pres. Farmers' Nat. Life Ins. Co., 1913-24. Lecturer at farmers' meetings, Chautauqua assemblies, etc.; leader in the "good roads" movement; asst. sec. Farmers Nat. Congress, 1891-93, sec. 1893-1905, pres. 1905-08, legislative agt., 1908-14; mem. Conf. on Trusts of Chicago Civic Fedn., 1899; opposed free silver, 1896; an organizer Nat. Civic Fedn., 1900, and mem. exec. com. until 1917; sec. Nat. Conv. for Uniform State Legislation, 1913. First to propose free mail delivery to farmers, 1879; a com. of ten prominent farmers, who made a thorough investigation, reported that rural mail delivery was owing to him more than to all others combined; declined apptmt. as sec. of Agr. under President Harrison and a place in Cabinet under President Wilson; an early advocate of direct election of U.S. senators; on request of Postmaster Gen. Meyer, led in the successful movement for a modern parcel post. Mem. Am. Acad. Polit. and Social Science, Ill. Hist. Soc., Am. Flag Assn. (life), S.A.R., S.R., Ill. Soc. War of 1812 (ex-pres.), Writers Guild (past master), Drama League America (life mem., pres. 1920-21), Soc. Midland Authors (founder and pres. 1919-22), Allied Arts Assn. (founder and pres. 1923-27; declined reëlection as pres. 1927), Dickens Fellowship of Chicago, Friends of Am. Writers, Poetry Lovers of America. Republican. Clubs: Nat. Arts (New York); Authors (London). Mason (32°, K.T.). Traveled abroad, 1888, 95, 99, to study agrl. and econ. conditions. Specially known as writer on economic-agrl. subjects and lecturer on authors he has known personally, and lit. subjects. Author: The Real Farmer, 1908; Just Stories, 1916; The Battle of Plattsburg, 1918; Invasion of the City of Washington, 1918; Battle of New Orleans, 1930; Growing with the West (autobiography), 1930. Home: Chicago, Ill.; (summer) "Grovemont," Swannanoa, N.C.* Died Oct. 17, 1944.

STALDER, Walter, cons. petroleum geologist; b. Oakland, Calif., Apr. 6, 1881; s. Joseph and Mary Amy (Birner) S.; B.S., U. of Calif., 1904, M.S., 1907; unmarried. Chemist, San Francisco Chem. Co., 1904-07; petroleum geologist since 1907; with M.L. Requa and Nev. Petroleum Co., 1909-11; land valuation, Union Oil Co. of Calif., 1911, when and where fundamentals of present decline curve method of estimating oil reserves originated; Nevada Petroleum Co., 1911-13; chief geologist on valuation, Independent Oil Producers, 1914-15; cons. practice since 1916. Mem. Am. Assn. Petroleum Geologists, Am. Inst. Mining and Metallurgical Engineers (chairman San Francisco section 1945), Am. Chem. Soc., A.A.A.S., Seismol. Soc. America, Calif. Acad. Sciences. Episcopalian. Mason (Shriner). Clubs: Engineers, Commonwealth Club of Calif. (chmn. mineral resources sect. 1922-29). Recommended and brought in Marysville Buttes Gas Field (1st real commercial discovery in Northern Calif.). Contbr. on early Calif. oilfield history and its geology. Home: 1812 12th Av., Oakland, Calif. Office: Crocker Bldg., San Francisco. Died March 15, 1949.

STANCLIFT, Henry Clay, coll. prof.; b. Spencer, N.Y., Jan. 11, 1864; s. Isaac Stone and Jane Anna (Cowell) S.; Ph.B., Cornell U., 1889; univs. of Berlin and Leipzig, 1889-92, Ph.D., Leipzig, 1892; in Oxford, London, and other places, using libraries, hearing lectures, and studying polit. and social conditions, 1897-99. Teacher high sch., 1883-85; acting prof. in History Dept., Northwestern U., 1892-97; prof. history and politics, 1899-1923, prof. history, 1923-34, Cornell Coll., Mount Vernon, Ia., now prof. emeritus. Mem. Am. Hist. Assn., Phi Beta Kappa, etc. Home: Mount Vernon, Ia. Died Nov. 21, 1948.

STANDER, Henricus Johannes, obstetrician, gynecologist; b. Georgetown, Cape Colony, S. Africa, June 21, 1894; s. Frans Sebastian and Catherine (Visser) S.; student S. African Coll., Capetown, 1911-13, Harvard, 1913-14; M.S., University of Arizona, 1916; M.D., Yale, 1921; hon. M.D., Trinity, Dublin, 1947; married Florence Mary Leigh Creelman, Sept. 12, 1927; children—Robert Angus, Catherine Leigh, Henry John, Margaret Florence. Chemist, 1916-22; practice of medicine since 1922; asso. in obstetrics, Johns Hopkins, 1922-27, asso. prof., 1927-29; prof. obstetrics and gynecology, Cornell U., since 1929; obstetrician and gynecologist in chief, New York Hosp.; dir. New York Lying-In Hosp. Fellow Am. Coll. Surgeons, Am. Gynecol. Soc.; mem. N.Y. Obstet. Soc., Acad. Science and Medicine, Havana, Cuba, Phi Kappa Phi, Sigma Xi, Nu Sigma Nu. Awarded Medal of Orden de Finlay of Havana, 1937. Republican. Mem. Dutch Ref. Ch. Clubs: Yale, Scarsdale Golf. Author: The Flotation Process, 1916; Toxemias of Pregnancy, 1929; Williams Obstetrics, 1936, 41. A Textbook of Obstetrics, 1945. Contbr. to medical magazines. Home: 65 Brite Av., Scarsdale, N.Y. Office: 525 E. 68th St., New York. Died May 2, 1948.

STANDEVEN, Herbert Leslie (stănd'ē-vĕn), lawyer; b. Boone, Ia., Nov. 20, 1878; s. Joseph H. and Susan L. (Norton) S.; student U. of Omaha, 1897-99; LL.B., U. of Mich., 1900; m. Iva Eugene Norton, Mar. 31, 1902; children—Norton, Ruth, Ione, Ora. Admitted to Okla. bar, 1900, and practiced at Omaha, Neb. and Hobart, Okla.; county atty., Kiowa County, Okla., 1907-11; county judge, Tulsa County, Okla., 1917-18; v.p. and trust officer Exchange Bank & Trust Co., Tulsa, 1918-32; member City Water Commn., Tulsa, during building of Spavinaw Water Project, 1921-25; mem. Okla. State Bank Commn., 1929-32, First reader First Ch. of Christ, Scientist, Tulsa, 1917-20; mem. Christian Science Com. on Publn., State of Okla., intermittently, 1921-40; trustee Christian Science Pub. Soc., Boston, since 1940. V.p. and chmn. exec. com. Trust Div. of Am. Bankers Assn., 1931-32. Democrat. Mason (32°, K.T.). Club: University (Boston). Home: 465 Park Drive. Office: 1 Norway St., Boston, Mass. Died Aug. 28, 1942.

STANFIELD, Robert Nelson, ex-senator; b. Umatilla, Ore., July 9, 1877; s. Robert Nelson and Harriet (Townsend) S.; ed. State Normal Sch., Ore. Engaged in live stock and banking business. Mem. Ore. Ho. of Rep. 3 terms (speaker 1 term.); mem. U.S. Senate, term 1921-27. Republican. Episcopalian. Mason. Elk. Home: Portland, Ore. Died Apr. 13, 1945.

STANLEY, Frederic Bartlett, lawyer; b. Lawrence, Kan., Apr. 25, 1874; s. Edmund and Martha Elmyra (Davis) S.; student U. of Kan., 1891-94; A.B., Earlham Coll., Richmond, Ind., 1895; LL.B., Law Dept., U. of Mich., 1897; m. Martha Ethelyn Stanley, Oct. 31, 1899. Began practice at Kansas City, Mo., Nov. 1, 1898; located in Wichita, Kan., Nov. 1, 1899, and asso. in practice with brother, as Stanley & Stanley; mem. Stanley, Stanley & Hegler, 1913-27; city counsellor, Wichita, 1905-07; spl. counsel for city in Supreme Ct. of Kan., 1908. Active in Rep. Party since 1898; chmn. Rep. State Conv., Kan., 1912; mem. Rep. Nat. Com., 1912-20. Mem. Delta Chi (U. of Mich.). Mason (32°). Clubs: Wichita; Writers, Los Angeles Country. Home: 1025 Chevy Chase Drive, Beverly Hills, Calif. Died May 17, 1943.

STANLEY, James G., lawyer; b. Gary, S.D., Mar. 4, 1881; s. William Hughes and Rebecca (Aiken) S.; student Black Hills Coll., Hot Springs, S.D., 1898; B.S., U. of Minn., 1902; LL.B., Columbian Univ., 1904; m. 2d, Doris A. Currington, Oct. 28, 1933; 1 dau., Meredith. With firm Kellar & Stanley, attys. Homestead-Mining Co., Lead, S.D., 1904-18; Hagens & Stanley, Casper, Wyo., 1918-20; gen. counsel, Continental Oil Co., Denver, Colo., and affiliated companies, 1920-28; private law practice specializing in oil law, Washington, D.C., and Okla., 1928-38; adminstr. Metropolitan Brewers Inst., New York, N.Y., since 1938. Delegate to Rep. Nat. Conv., 1916; mem. S.D., State Rep. Exec. Com., 1909-18. Mem. Delta Tau Delta, Phi Beta Phi. Mason. Elks. Home: 1133 5th Av. Office: 21 East 40th St., New York. Died Sept. 2, 1947.

STANLEY, Walter Lawrence, ry. official; b. Wytheville, May 24, 1871; s. Bolling Fleming and Martha Harris (Birchfield) S.; prep. edn., Wytheville Male Academy; B.A., Emory and Henry College, 1890; graduate study, University of Virginia, 1890-91; m. McClure Rayburn Allison, Apr. 5, 1893; children—Laura Lee, Bolling Craig, Martha Guthrie (Mrs. T. R. Waggoner). Law partner of Judge W. H. Bolling (father of Mrs. Woodrow Wilson), 1893-98; claim agt. N.&W.Ry. Co., 1898-1901; claim agt., later claims atty. S.A.L. Ry., 1901-07, gen. claim agt., 1907-16, asst. to pres., 1916-17; asst. to federal mgr. same ry., U.S.R.R. Administration, also mem. staff of regional dir. for Southern Region, 1918-19; gen. atty. S.A.L. Ry. Co., 1920-22, v.p. since 1922, also chief pub. relations officer for receivers since 1930; v.p. Brooksville & Inverness Ry., Charlotte Harbor & Northern R.R. Co., Charlotte, Monroe & Columbia R.R. Co., Chesterfield & Lancaster R.R. Co., Fla. Western & Northern R.R. Co., Jacksonville, Gainesville & Gulf Ry., Macon, Dublin & Savannah R.R. Co., Prince George & Chesterfield Ry., Seaboard-All Fla. Ry., Tampa Northern R.R. Co., Tavares & Gulf R.R. Co.; chief pub. relations officer for receivers of Chesterfield & Lancaster R.R., Raleigh & Charleston R.R. -Mayor of Wytheville, 1892-97. Mem. Kappa Sigma. Democrat. Methodist. Clubs: Traffic, Capital City, Piedmont Driving. Home: 930 Lullwater Rd. N.E. Office: 22 Marietta St. Bldg., Atlanta, Ga. Died July 3, 1943.

STANLEY, William, lawyer; b. Laurel, Md., Mar. 17, 1891; s. Charles Harvey and Margaret (Snowden) S.; A.B., St. John's Coll., Annapolis, Md., 1911; LL.B., U. of Md., 1913; m. Mary Gilbert, Oct. 1, 1914; children—Mary Jane, Elizabeth Snowden (dec.), William, Snowden. Admitted to Md. bar, 1913, practicing in Baltimore; partner Stanley & Boss, 1913-28; Hershey, Donaldson, Williams & Stanley, 1928-33; apptd. spl. asst. to atty. gen. of U.S., Washington, D.C., Apr. 1933; asst. to the atty. gen. of U.S., 1933-35; formed partnership with Homer Cummings, former atty. gen. U.S., under name of Cummings & Stanley, Feb. 15, 1939. Apptd. mem. Md. Commn. on Higher Edn., 1928; chmn. com. of arrangements atty. gen.'s Conf. on Crime, Dec. 1934; mem. Atty. Gen.'s Advisory Com. to plan establishment of nat. scientific and ednl. center at Washington to train adminstrs. of criminal law, also com. to formulate new rules for pleading, practice and procedure in civil actions in federal dist. courts. Mem. Pi Sigma Kappa. Democrat. Episcopalian. Clubs: Metropolitan, Burning Tree, Chevy Chase (Washington); Maryland (Baltimore, Md.). Home: 2701 Chesapeake St. N.W., Washington, D.C. Office: Normandy Bldg., Washington, D.C. Died July 26, 1946.

STANLEY-BROWN, Joseph, banker; b. Washington, Aug. 19, 1858; s. John Leopold and Elizabeth M. Stanley-Brown; grad. Yale, 1888, Ph.B., as of class of 1888, 1895; m. Mary Garfield, June 14, 1888. Stenographer to late Maj. John Wesley Powell, on geol. survey of Rocky Mountains, 1877-79; pvt. sec. to President Garfield, 1880-81; mem. U.S. Geol. Survey, 1882-85, asst. geologist, 1888-89; expert Bering Sea Arbitration, 1891-93; supt. N. Am. Comml. Co., Alaska, 1894-99; asst. sec. U.P. and S.P. ry. systems, New York, 1899-1902; asst. to the pres. L.I. R.R. Co., 1902-04; mgr. railroad dept. Fisk & Robinson, bankers, New York, 1905. Fellow A.A.A.S., Am. Geol. Soc. (editor Bull. since 1892), etc. Home: Cold Spring Harbor, L.I. Office: 26 Exchange Pl., New York. Died Nov. 2, 1941.

STANNARD, E. Tappan, corporation executive; b. Chittenango, New York; graduate Phillips Andover Academy; Ph.B., Yale University; D.E., Michigan School of Mines; married Jeannette Condon, June 11, 1918; 1 daughter, Ann (deceased). Pres. dir. Kennecott Copper Corp., Braden Copper Co.; dir. Johns-Manville Corp., J. P. Morgan & Co., Inc. Home: 1 Beekman Place. Office: 120 Broadway, New York 5, N.Y. Died Sep. 9, 1949.

STANTON, Charles Spelman, editor, pub.; b. Middleburg, N.Y., Mar. 13, 1868; s. George S. and Julia (Hallenbeck) S.; ed. Albany (N.Y.) High Sch.; A.B., Union Coll., Schenectady, N.Y., 1888, hon. M.A., 1916; m. Maia Pratt, June 5, 1888; m. 2d, Helen Dickins, Feb. 18, 1931. Reporter, later asst. mng. editor of N.Y. World, 1885-1893; editor Albany Evening Union, 1893; night editor Chicago Tribune, later editorial writer under Joseph Medill, 1894-1906; mng. editor San Francisco Examiner, 1906-14; editor Chicago Examiner, 1914-18; pub. San Francisco Examiner, 1918-24; pub., editor in chief and part owner San Francisco Bulletin, 1924-27; then mng. editor Chicago Herald-Examiner, then editor San Francisco Examiner. Mem. bd. dirs. San Francisco Expn., 1915. Pub. relations counsel Calif. Commn., Golden Gate Internat. Expn., 1939. Mem. Kappa Alpha. Clubs: Bohemian, San Francisco Golf and Country. Home: Hotel Broadmoor. Office: San Francisco Examiner, San Francisco, Calif.* Died July 31, 194[illegible].

STAPLES, John Norman, business exec.; b. Greensboro, N.C., Oct. 9, 1881; s. John N. and Mary D. (Appleton) S.; ed. pub. schs. and private instrn.; m. Margaret Isabelle Peacock, May 10, 1915. V.p. Havana-American Co., 1904-06, Havana Tobacco Co., 1906-10, Henry Clay & Bock Co., Ltd., 1906-10; v.p. and gen. mgr. United Drug Co., 1914-21; v.p. Liggetts Internat., Inc., 1919-23; chmn. bd. Caribbean Sugar Co., 1919-21; reorganizing dir. various chain store cos., 1923-29; treas. E. R. Squibb & Sons, N.Y. City, 1930-42, v.p., dir. and treas. 1942-43, sr. v.p., dir. 1943-46, v.p., dir. Squibb Properties Corp.; pres., dir. Jones Estate Corp.; senior v.p. and dir. E. R. Squibb & Sons Internat. Corp., E. R. Squibb Inter-American Corp.; dir. E. R. Squibb & Sons Ltd. (Can.), Lentheric, Inc., Lentheric Internat., Inc. Clubs: Metropolitan, Union, Knickerbocker (New York); Lawrence Beach (Long Island). Home: 2 E. 56th St. Office: 745 Fifth Av., New York. Died May 8, 1947.

STAPLES, Philip Clayton, dir. Bell Telephone Co. of Pa.; b. Revere, Mass., Oct. 24, 1882; s. John and Josephine (Goodwin) S.; A.B., Harvard, 1904; LL.D., U. of Pa., 1940; m. Mary K. Hartman, Oct. 30, 1912; children—Philip Clayton, Jr., John Hartman. Telephone salesman, 1904-10; publicity manager Bell Telephone Company of Pa., 1910-18, div. mgr., 1918-19, asst. to pres., 1919-20, v.p., 1920-23, pres., 1933-47; dir. Pa. Co., Phila. Saving Fund Soc., Insurance Co. of N.A.; mem. bd. trustees Penn Mutual Life Insurance Co. Vice-pres. Phila. Orchestra Assn.; director Community Chest.; mem. bd. trustees, Philadelphia Award; vice-pres. Hosp. Service of Phila.; trustee Drexel Inst. Tech.; dir. Haverford Sch.; mem. bd. U. of Pa. Hosp., Bd. of Mgrs. Franklin Inst.; former chmn. Phila. County Relief Bd.; chmn. Phila. Traffic Commission; v.p. Harvard Alumni Assn., Harvard Fund Council; pres. Telephone Pioneers of America. Republican. Episcopalian. Clubs: Harvard (N.Y. City); Harvard, Philadelphia, Poor Richard, Rittenhouse, Racquet, Engineers (Phila.); Merion Cricket (Haverford, Pa.); Merion Golf, Woodmont. Home: Ardmore, Pa. Died June 28, 1949.

STARBUCK, Edwin Diller, univ. prof.; b. Bridgeport, Ind., Feb. 20, 1866; s. Samuel and Luzena (Jessup) S.; A.B., Indiana U., 1890; A.M., Harvard, 1895; Ph.D., Clark U., 1897; U. of Zürich, 1904-05; m. Anna M. Diller, Aug. 5, 1896 (now dec.); children—Alonzo D. (dec.), Arthur Diller (dec.), Anna Margaret, Edwin (dec.), Helen, Winifred, Dorthea Ansley, Edmund Osborn. Prof. mathematics, Vincennes University, 1891-93; asst. prof. education, Stanford University, 1897-1904; prof. education, Earlham Coll., 1904-06; prof. philosophy, State University of Ia., 1906-30, also head of dept., 1927-30; director Inst. of Character Research, 1923-30; prof. philosophy and director character research, University of Southern California, 1930-39, professor of psychology, 1939-43, emeritus since 1943. Lecturer Inst. for Comparative Study of Human Culture, Oslo, Norway, 1925. Chmn. winning com. in $20,000 prize contest for best methods in character training in pub. schs. Consulting psychologist, Beacon Press, 1912-14. Chmn. Am. delegation to Internat. Conf. on How to Meet Religious Needs of Young Men of the World, Geneva, 1929. Fellow A.A.A.S.; mem. Am. Philos. Soc., Am. Psychol. Assn., N.E.A., Pacific Geog. Soc., Nat. Soc. Scientific Study of Edn., Internat. Gesellschaft für Religionspsychologie, Phi Delta Kappa, Phi Epsilon Theta, Phi Beta Kappa. Club: University. Author: Psychology of Religion, 1899; Moral Education in the Public Schools, 1904; Guide to Literature for Character Training, Vol. I, Fairy Tale, Myth and Legend, 1927, Vol. II, Fiction, 1929; The Wonder Road (3 vols.), 1929; Living Through Biography (Vols. I, II and III), 1936; Look to This Day, 1944. Contbr. Hastings Ency. of Religion and Ethics. Address: University of Southern Calif., Los Angeles. Died Nov. 18, 1947.

STARK, Henry Ignatius, priest; b. San Francisco, Calif.; s. John and Kathleen O'Moore; student St. Ignatius Coll., 1892-96. Sacred Heart Coll., 1896-98; A.B. and A.M., St. Mary's Coll., Oakland, Calif.; S.T.B., Catholic U., Washington, 1903. Ordained priest, 1903; founded Catholic Chinese Mission, San Francisco; was Paulist Missionary, Pacific Coast, Hawaii and Mid-West U.S.; has been pastor St. Lawrence Ch., Minneapolis, Ch. of St. Paul the Apostle, Los Angeles, Ch. of St. Paul the Apostle, N.Y. City; later asst. Procurator-Gen., Santa Susanna, Rome, Italy, elected Superior-Gen., 9th in succession to Father Isaac Hecker, 1940. Address: 415 W. 59th St., New York, N.Y.* Died Dec. 13, 1946.

STARRETT, Milton Gerry (stăr'ĕt), engineer; b. Francestown, N.H., Jan. 24, 1861; s. James H. and Theresa (Morgan) S.; prep. edn. Francestown Acad.; C.E., Tufts Coll., 1886, Sc.D., 1905; m. Ruth Eastman Morrill, Dec. 28, 1893. Instr. mathematics, Tufts Coll., 1886-89; asst. engr. West End St. Ry. Co., Boston, 1889-91; chief engr. Brooklyn City R.R. Co., 1891-96; asst. chief engr., 1896-99, chief engr., 1899-1906, Met. St. Ry. Co. and its successors; consulting engr. until 1935; now retired. Mem. Am. Soc. C.E., A.A.A.S., New Eng. Assn. of New York. Home: New Canaan, Conn. Died Sep. 18, 1942.

STATHERS, Birk Smith (stă'thĕrz), lawyer; b. Middlebourne, Tyler County, W.Va., July 13, 1884; s. Walter E. and Mary (Smith) S.; A.B., W.Va. U., 1906, LL.B., 1907; m. Margaret Anne Richards, July 3, 1923; children—Mary Jeannette, Margaret Annette, Birk Smith, Jr. Admitted to W.Va. bar, 1907; asso. in practice of law with Hon. W. W. Brannon, Weston, W.Va., 1907-23; mem. and chmn. W.Va. Pub. Service Commn., 1923-25; returned to practice of law, 1937, and since sr. mem. firm Stathers, Stathers & Cantrall, Clarksburg, W.Va. Commd. capt. inf., Nov. 27, 1917; capt. Co. D, 332d Inf., 83d Div., May 1918-May 1919; with A.E.F., June 1918-Apr. 1919; hon. discharged May 19, 1919. Mem. Am., W.Va. State and Harrison County bar assns., Phi Beta Kappa, Sigma Chi. Episcopalian. Mason. Home: 600 Stanley Av. Office: Goff Bldg., Clarksburg, W.Va. Died Dec. 28, 1945.

STAUB, Walter Adolph; b. Phila., Pa., Feb. 27, 1881; s. Adolph and Wilhelmine (Voegelin) S.; grad. Girard Coll., 1897; C.P.A., New York, Pennsylvania, New Jersey, Michigan, Ohio, California and D.C.; married Ida Charlotte Fleury, Apr. 12, 1904; children—Walter Richard, Ernest Fleury, Edmund Arthur, Helen Elizabeth, Elmer Norman, Robert Joseph, Grace Ida. With firm of Lybrand, Ross Bros. & Montgomery since 1901, mem. of firm since 1911. Mem. Bd. of Edn., Milburn, N.J., 1924-36. Dickinson lecturer at Harvard Univ. Graduate Sch. of Business Administration, 1941. Pres. Overlook Hosp., Summit, N.J. Mem. Am. Inst. Accountants, N.Y. State Soc. C.P.A. (ex-pres.), Pa. Inst. C.P.A., N.J. State Society of C.P.A., National Association of Cost Accountants. Republican. Baptist. Clubs: Lawyers', Accountants, Quill (New York); Baltusrol Golf, and Short Hills (Short Hills, New Jersey). Author: Income Tax Guide, 1913; Consolidated Returns (in Federal Income Tax), 1921; Auditing Principles (with Robert H. Montgomery), 1923; Wills, Executors and Trustees (with W. J. Grange and E. G. Blackford), 1933; Auditing Developments during the Present Century, 1942. Winner prize for best paper on "Mode of Conducting an Audit," Congress of Accounting, St. Louis Expn., 1904. Home: Woodcrest Av. and Farley Rd., Short Hills, N.J. Office: 90 Broad St., New York 4, N.Y. Died Nov. 4, 1945.

STAUFFER, Grant (stŏf'fĕr), coal; b. Hope, Kan., Dec. 1, 1888; s. Solomon Engle and Elizabeth (Conrad) S.; grad. Hope High Sch., 1907; student Coll. of Emporia, Kan., 1907-08; m. Gladys Ketchersid, Dec. 26, 1912; children—Sarah Jane, Dorothy Ann. Successively coal salesman, coal jobber and operator and producing and marketing of coal since 1912; pres. Sinclair Coal Co., Hume-Sinclair Coal Mining Co., Huntsville-Sinclair Mining Co., Sentry Coal Mining Co.; v.p. Seneca Coal & Coke Co., Marigold Coal Mining Co.; dir. Stauffer Publs., Commerce Trust Co., Kansas City, Mo., Business Men's Assurance Company, Kansas City, Mo.; director American Mining Congress; director and chairman of the Executive Committee of the Kansas City Southern R.R. Co.; dir. of the Louisiana and Arkansas Railroad. Trustee Kansas City Conservatory of Music; member bd. govs. Kansas City Art Institute. Mem. Nat. Coal Assn. (dir. mem. exec. bd.). Republican. Mason (32°). Clubs: Kansas City, Mission Hills Country (Kansas City); Chicago (Chicago). Home: 5049 Wornall Rd. Office: 114 W. 11th St., Kansas City, Mo. Died Mar. 31, 1949.

STAUNTON, William Field (stawn'tŭn), mining engr.; b. Toledo, O., Dec. 23, 1860; s. William Field and Mary De Wolf (Gray) S.; prep. edn., Charlier Inst., N.Y. City; E.M., Columbia, 1882; m. Mary Fulton Neal, Mar. 23, 1892; children—William Field, Neal (dec.), Maria Gage. Supt. Tombstone (Ariz.) Mill & Mining Co., 1884-94; mgr. Congress (Ariz.) Gold Co., 1894-1910; vice-pres. and gen. mgr. Tombstone Consol. Mines Co., 1901-10, Imperial Copper Co., Southern Ariz. Smelting Co., Ariz. Southern R.R. Co., 1904-10; cons. mining engr., chiefly in oil and copper, Los Angeles, Calif., since 1910. Formerly mem. Ariz. Mining Code Commn. Mem. Am. Inst. Mining and Metall. Engrs., Mining and Metall. Soc. America, S.R., Tau Beta Pi. Republican. Episcopalian. Clubs: California, Engineers. Home: 512 S. Harvard Blvd. Office: I. W. Hellman Bldg., Los Angeles, Calif.* Died Feb. 12, 1947.

STAYTON, William H., ocean transportation; b. Smyrna, Del., Mar. 28, 1861; s. Charles Emerson and Susan (Moffatt) S.; grad. U.S. Naval Acad., 1881; LL.B., Columbia (now George Washington) U., 1889, LL.M., 1890; m. Annie Henderson, June 2, 1887; children—Charles H., Mrs. Catharine Hulett, William H., Thomas Truxtun. Resigned from navy, 1883; with U.S.M.C., 1883-91; with Naval Militia, N.Y., 1893-98; again in navy during Spanish-Am. War, commdg. various vessels. Practiced as admiralty lawyer, gradually shifting into management steamship cos.; now pres. Balto. Steamship Co., Baltimore Trading Co.; mem. board of dirs. Baltimore Ship Supply Company. Mem. Soc. Naval Architects and Marine Engrs., Governing Council of Naval Acad. Graduates (pres.), U.S. Naval Acad. Alumni Assn. (pres. emeritus). Founder and chmn. bd. Assn. Against Prohibition Amendment; chmn. bd. Repeal Associates; dir. and mem. exec. com. and administrative com. Am. Liberty League; chmn. bd. Assn. for Interstate Tax Agreements; chmn. bd. Dual Domicile Information, Inc. Episcopalian. Clubs: Metropolitan (Washington, D.C.); University, Merchants', Elkridge Country, Maryland (Baltimore); Army and Navy of America, Naval Acad. Officers, Annapolis Yacht, New York Yacht. Home: Smyrna, Del. Office: National Press Bldg., Washington, D.C. Died July 12, 1942.

STEAD, Robert, architect; b. N.Y. City, Jan. 27, 1856; s. Edward Briggs and Matilda Lavinia (Hagthrop) S.; ed. Coll. City of N.Y., 1872-76; studied architecture in Atelier DeMonclos, Paris, France; m. 3d, Helen Louise Coates, June 8, 1921; children (by first marriage)—W. Force, Robert, Mary, Manning F., Edward. Practiced, Washington, since Mar. 1, 1884. Architect: Metzerott (office) Bldg.; Lovejoy Sch.; Bowen Sch.; Mt. Vernon Seminary; Epiphany Mission House; Epiphany Chapel; office bldg. at 1307 and 1309 G St. N.W.; residences of E. K. Johnson, Mrs. J. F. Barbour, W. R. Riley, etc. Rep. candidate for Md.

State Senate, 1899. Episcopalian. Fellow Am. Inst. Architects; mem. Archæol. Inst. America. Mason. Clubs: Cosmos, Chevy Chase (Washington); Art Alliance, Plays and Players (Phila.). Home: 1817 De Lancey Pl., Philadelphia, Pa. Died Dec. 19, 1943.

STEADMAN, John Marcellus, Jr., prof. of English; b. Greenwood, S.C., June 20, 1909; s. John Marcellus and Elizabeth Briggs (Kennerly) S.; A.B., Wofford Coll., Spartanburg, S.C., 1909, A.M., 1912, Litt.D., 1941; student U. of N.C., 1913-14; Ph.D., U. of Chicago, 1916; m. Medora Rice Rembert, Dec. 28, 1916 (died Dec. 19, 1938); children—John Marcellus III, Alice Duncan. Instr. in Latin, Wofford Fitting Sch., 1909-12, joint headmaster, 1912-13; teaching fellow, U. of N.C., 1913-14, instr. in English, 1916-19; asso. prof. English, Emory U., 1919-20, prof., 1920, now retired. Mem. Am. Assn. U. Profs., South Atlantic Modern Lang. Assn., Modern Lang. Assn. Am., Nat. Council Teachers' Eng., Omicron Delta Kappa, Phi Beta Kappa, Phi Delta Theta. Methodist. Author: Sentences and Thinking (with Norman Foerster), 1919, 23; Spelling for Everyday Use (with K. C. Garrison and H. H. Bixler), 1930; Writing and Thinking (with Norman Foerster), 1931, 41; Exercises in Writing and Thinking (with H. P. Miller and P. S. Grant), 1933; Vocabulary Building, 1937; Spelling in Everyday Life (with H. H. Bixler), 1940. Contbr. to professional jours. Home: 30 Haygood Drive, Emory University, Ga. Died Dec. 20, 1945.

STEADWELL, B. Samuel, editor, reformer; b. nr. Albany, N.Y., Dec. 18, 1871; s. William E. and Melissa L. (Blynn) S.; ed. Wis. State Normal Sch., Whitewater, Wis.; U. of Wis., 1893-95; m. Clara V. Oswald, Nov. 20, 1895; 1 son, Forrest Carleton (dec.). Founder, 1898, and since editor and pub. The Light (mag.); founder, 1898, since president, Northwestern Purity Assn. Pres. World's Purity Fed. from its foundation, 1905, and chmn. Nat. Com. out of which it grew, 1900-05; organizer and pres. 12 internat. Purity congresses since 1901. Contbr. articles on white slave traffic, commercialized vice, sex hygiene, etc.; also lecturer. Pres. Parents' Internat. League, 1922; chmn. Com. on Social Morality, 2d and 3d World's Christian Citizenship confs., 1913, 1919; v. pres. America for God Crusade, N.Y. City. Home: 303 Division St., La Crosse; (winter) Portland, Tex. Office: "The Light," La Crosse, Wis. Died Apr. 5, 1947.

STEAGALL, Henry Bascom (stĕg'äl), congressman; b. Clopton, Dale County, Ala., May 19, 1873; s. William Collinsworth and Mary Jane (Peacock) S.; ed. Southeast Ala. Agrl. Sch., Abbeville, Ala., 1890-92; LL.B., U. of Ala., 1893; m. Sallie Mae Thompson, Dec. 27, 1900. Admitted to Ala. bar, 1893; county solicitor Dale County, 1902-08; mem. Ala. Ho. of Rep., 1906-07; pros. atty. for 3d Dist., 1907-14; mem. Dem. State Exec. Com., 1906-10; del. Dem. Nat. Conv., Baltimore, 1912; mem. 64th to 77th Congresses (1915-43), 3d Ala. Dist. Mem. Ala. State Bar Assn., Sigma Nu. Mem. M.E. Ch., S. Mason. Home: Ozark, Ala. Died Nov. 22, 1943.

STEARNS, Alfred Ernest, academy prin.; b. Orange, N.J., June 6, 1871; s. William French and Mary Emeline (Kittredge) S.; grad. Phillips Acad., Andover, Mass., 1890; A.B., Amherst, 1894, L.H.D. from same, 1915; A.M., Yale, 1905; Litt.D., Dartmouth, 1912; L.H.D., Williams, 1921; LL.D., Harvard, 1928; m. Kate Belle Deane, Aug. 29, 1900; children—Alfred D. (dec.), Charles Deane, Marjorie; m. 2d, Grace P. S. Clemons, Sept. 23, 1933. Teacher, The Hill Sch., Pottstown, Pa., 1894-97; registrar, 1900-02, vice prin., 1902-03, headmaster, 1903-33, Phillips Acad. (now emeritus). Mem. Committee of 1,000; chm. Overseas Sch. Com. Clerk Andover Savings Bank Trustees. Trustee Lawrence Acad., New England Home for Deaf Mutes, John G. Whittier Homestead Assn., Essex Inst.; regent Mercersburg (Pa.) Acad.; chmn. Amherst Coll.; mem. advisory council Yenching Univ., Peiping, China, Western Reserve Acad. Home: 12 Locke St., Andover, Mass. Died Nov. 15, 1949.

STEARNES, Reaumur Coleman (stûrnz), educator; b. Dublin, Pulaski County, Va., Apr. 8, 1866; s. John Lewis (M.D.) and Phoebe Ann (McDermed) S.; Greek medal U. of Richmond (Va.), 1884, philosophy medal same, 1887, A.M. and valedictorian of class, 1887; A.M., Columbia Univ., 1925; Ph.D., New York Univ., 1936; m. Mary Elizabeth Arnold, Dec. 27, 1888; children—Bessie Arnold (Mrs. H. H. Donnally), John Lewis (dec.), Reaumur Coleman, Jr. Instructor mathematics and science, Allegheny Institute, Roanoke, Va., 1888-91; division superintendent public schools, Roanoke County, Va., 1892-1906; practiced law at Salem, 1896-1906; sec. State Bd. of Edn., Richmond, Va., 1906-13; supt. pub. instrn., Va., 1913-18; community organizer, War Camp Community Service, Atlanta, 1918, dist. rep. same for Ga., 1918-19, spl. rep. same, 1919-20; community organizer and spl. rep. community service, 1920-22. Student Columbia University, lit. work and lecturing, 1922-25; master mathematics, Stony Brook School, New York, 1925-29; instr. mathematics, New York University, 1925-39; instr. in mathematics Hofstra Coll., 1938-39; lecturer on business adminstrn. and secretarial studies, Merchants and Bankers Business and Secretarial School, New York, 1929-38; head of sch. presenting mathematics for recreational and other special purposes since 1939. Assisted in establishing Virginia State Teachers' Association, 1901, and its pres. 1901-06; one of organizers of Coöperative Edn. Assn. of Va., 1904, and chmn. exec. com., 1913-18; aided in forming Va. Ednl. Conf. to unite all existing ednl. committees and associations in Va., 1906. Mem. S.A.R., Phi Delta Theta, Phi Delta Kappa, Pi Mu Epsilon. Democrat. Presbyterian. Mason; Grand Regent Royal Arcanum, Va., 1912-13. Home: 7 Surrey Lane, Hempstead, N.Y. Died 1945.

STEARNS, Charles Falconer, judge; b. Smithfield, R.I., July 27, 1866; s. Henry A. and Kate (Falconer) S.; A.B., Amherst, 1889; LL.B., Harvard, 1893; LL.D., Amherst, 1929, R.I. State Coll., 1930; m. Amelia F. Lieber, June 30, 1904. Began practice at Providence, R.I., 1893; asst. atty. gen. of R.I., 1897-1902, atty. gen., 1902-05; asso. justice Superior Court of R.I., 1905-17; asso. justice Supreme Court of R.I., 1917-29, chief justice, 1929-35; now retired. Republican. Clubs: University, Providence Art. Home: 168 Bowen St., Providence, R.I. Died Sep. 3, 1946.

STEARNS, Harold Edmund, author, newspaper man; b. Barre, Mass., May 7, 1891; s. Frank and Sarah Ella (Doyle) S.; A.B., Harvard, 1913; 1 son by first marriage, Philip Stearns Macdougal (adopted by Dr. Daniel T. McDougal); m. 2d, Elizabeth Chalifoux Chapin, Aug. 1937. Began as newspaper writer, 1912, and served successively on New York Evening Sun, New York Dramatic Mirror, New York Press; then editor Dial, Chicago, later New York; served on staff of New Republic and Freeman, staff of Paris edition of New York Herald and corr. Baltimore Sun and Town and Country (New York), staff of Paris edition London Daily Mail. Democrat. Author: Liberalism in America, 1919; America and the Young Intellectual, 1921; Rediscovering America, 1934; The Street I Know, 1935; America—A Re-Appraisal, 1937. Editor: Civilization in the United States, 1922; America Now, 1938. Contbr. to jours. Home: Locust Valley, L.I., N.Y.* Died Aug. 13, 1943.

STEARNS, Joyce Clennam, dean of faculties; b. Meadville, Mo., June 23, 1893; s. W. E. and Elizabeth (Hallenberg) S.; A.B., Kingfisher (Okla.) Coll., 1917; M.S., Univ. of Chicago, 1925, Ph.D., 1929; LL.D., Westminster Coll. (Pa.), 1946; m. Gertrude E. Fisk, Aug. 1, 1921; children—Brenton Fisk, Margaret Ann. Prin. Clinton (Okla.) High Sch., 1919-21; instr. in physics and math., Kingfisher Coll., 1921-22, Denver pub. schs., 1922-23; instr. in physics, Albion (Mich.) Coll., 1923-25; asso. prof. of physics, Univ. of Denver, 1929-30, prof., 1930-42, head of dept., 1941-42, dir. High Altitude Cosmic Ray Lab., 1938-42; personnel dir. metall. lab., Univ. of Chicago, 1942-43, dir. div. of physics, 1943-44, dir. of lab., 1944-45; dean of faculties, Washington Univ., St. Louis, Mo., since July 1945. Served with U.S. Navy, World War I. Served in metall. lab. (atomic bomb), World War II. Fellow Am. Physical Soc., A.A.A.S.; mem. Am. Assn. Physics Teachers, Sigma Xi, Gamma Alpha, Omicron Delta Kappa, Sigma Pi Sigma (nat. pres. 1941-46), Phi Beta Kappa. Conglist. Author: (with D. K. Froman) Cosmic-Ray Showers and Bursts, Rev. of Modern Physics, July 1938. Principal research field X-Rays, Cosmic Rays. Home: 144 S. Rock Hill Rd., Webster Groves 19, Mo. Office: Washington Univ., St. Louis 5. Died June 11, 1948.

STEBBINS, Arthur D., business exec., pres. and dir. Merchants & Miners Transportation Co.; vice pres. Century Coal Co. of West Va.; dir. Mercantile Trust Co., Central Savings Bank, Transportation Mutual Ins. Co. Home: Towson, Md. Office: Pier 3, Pratt St., Baltimore, Md.* Died Jan. 18, 1950.

STEBBINS, George Coles, hymn writer; b. East Carlton, N.Y., Feb. 26, 1846; s. William V. and Teressa (Waring) S.; ed. acad. at Albion, N.Y., 1864-66; studied music Rochester, Chicago, and Boston; m. Elma Miller, 1868; 1 son, G(eorge) Waring. Musical career began Chicago, 1869; dir. music First Bapt. Ch., 1874, Clarendon St. Ch. and Tremont Temple, Boston, 1874-76; entered evangelistic work under director D. L. Moody, 1876. Author: The Northfield Hymnal, 1904. Joint author: (with Ira D. Sankey and James McGranahan) Gospel Hymns, Nos. 3, 4, 5, 6, 1877-91; Sacred Songs, Nos. 1, 2; Gospel Choir, Church Hymns and Gospel Songs, Male Chorus, Nos. 1, 2 and Male Quartet, 1896-1902; editor Greatest Hymns, 1924; New Church Hymnal, 1925. Address: 19 Verona Pl., Brooklyn, N.Y. Died Oct. 6, 1945.

STEDMAN, John Moore, biologist; b. Brockport, N.Y., Nov. 2, 1864; s. George Lemon and Mary (Moore) S.; B.S., Cornell, 1888; m. Edith Van Aiken, July 1, 1888; children—Barbara Mary, Lulu Rachel. Instr. entomology and invertebrate zoölogy, and 1st asst. entomologist, expt. sta., Cornell, 1888-90; biologist U.S. Dept. Agr., Washington, 1890-91; prof. biology, Trinity Coll., Durham, N.C., 1891-93; prof. biology and biologist, expt. sta., State Agrl. and Mech. Coll., Auburn, Ala., 1893-95; prof. entomology, U. of Mo., and entomologist expt. sta., 1895-1909; specialist in agrl. edn. extension, U.S. Dept. Agr., 1909-34. Mem. Am. Assn. Econ. Entomologists, Entomol. Soc., Washington, Entomol. Soc. of America, A.A.A.S., Sigma Xi. Has published many papers on biol. and entomol. subjects. Home: 48 Mountainview St., Springfield, Mass. Died Nov. 6, 1949.

STEED, J. Lyman; b. Wentzville, St. Charles County, Mo., Mar. 3, 1880; s. Henry Harvey and Helen Elizabeth (Lyman) S.; B.L., Westminster Coll., Fulton, Mo., 1900; B.Pd., Warrensburg (Mo.) State Normal Sch., 1904; Normal fellow Gallaudet Coll., Washington, D.C., 1905-06, M.A., 1906; m. Miss E. C. Leonard, Dec. 28, 1918; children—Wallace Leonard, Caroline Elizabeth, Virginia Leonard, Herbert Lyman. Prin. pub. schs., Jefferson City, Mo., 1903-05; prin. Md. Sch. for Colored Blind and Deaf, Baltimore, 1906-09; prin. Kendall Sch. for the Deaf, Kendall Green, Washington, 1909-18; prin. Pa. Instn. for Deaf, Phila., Sept. 1918-24, asst. supt., 1924-26; supt. Ore. State Sch. for the Deaf since Jan. 1, 1926. Harvard R.O.T.C., 1918. Mem. Am. Assn. to Promote the Teaching of Speech to the Deaf, Am. Conv. Instructors of the Deaf, Federal Schoolmen's Club, Kappa Alpha. Presbyterian. Mason (32°), K.T. Clubs: Rotary Internat., Orpheus. Address: Oregon State School for the Deaf, Salem, Ore. Deceased 1941.

STEED, Robert Dennis, lawyer; b. Hamlin, W.Va., Nov. 13, 1880; s. William Henry and Margaret Jane (Snyder) S.; student Marshall Coll., Huntington, W.Va., 1898-1902, W.Va., Univ., 1905-06; studied law pvtly. and at W.Va. Univ.; m. Vivian R. Workman, June 18, 1912; children—Mary Margaret, William Hugh. Prin. Point Pleasant (W.Va.) High Sch., 1902-03; supt. Guyandotte (W.Va.) city schs., 1903-05; admitted to W.Va. bar, 1906, and since practiced at Hamlin and in Charleston; also admitted to practice before Supreme Court of U.S.; now mem. firm Lee, Blessing & Steed; pros. atty. Lincoln County, W.Va., 1908-12; mayor City of Hamlin, 1910-12; mem. W.Va. State Senate, 1912-16; atty. for W.Va. Pub. Service Commn., 1916-20; asst. atty. gen. of W.Va., 1920-35. Republican. Methodist. K.P. Home: 3 Grosscup Rd. Office: Union Bldg., Charleston, W.Va.* Died Aug. 15, 1944.

STEEL, Alfred G. B., banker; b. Phila., Pa., Apr. 24, 1886; s. Francis Penn and Elizabeth Emerick (Errickson) S.; student Friends Select Sch., Phila., 1893-99; De Lancey Sch., 1899-1900; William Penn Charter Sch., 1900-04; U. of Pa., 1904; m. Elizabeth Amanda Howe, Feb. 1, 1910; children—Francis Penn (commander U.S.N.), Herbert Howe (deceased), Alfred, Amanda Fell. Began as employe, Graham & Co., investment bankers, Phila., Dec. 1904; partner, Graham, Parsons & Co., 1914-26; v.p. in charge trust dept. of Tradesmen's Nat. Bank and Trust Co., Phila., Sept. 1929-Dec. 1944; pres. and dir. Aldrich Pump Co., Allentown Rolling Mills, E.T. & W.N.C. Transportation Co., East Tenn. & Western N.C.R.R., Tennolina Co. Pres. North Pa. R.R.; dir. Tradesmens Nat. Bank & Trust Co., Chelten Title Co., pres. and dir., Black Creek Improvement Co., pres. and director, Jefferson Coal Co.; director Rockhill Coal Company, East Broad Top R.R. & Coal Co., Delaware Bound Brook R.R., Little Schuylkill R.R., Navigation & Coal Co. Pres. Pa. Acad. Fine Arts; pres. bd. trustees, Moore Inst. Art, Science and Industry; v. p., dir. American Acad. of Music. Mem. Art Jury of Phila.; trustee Fairmount Park Art Assn. Mem. Zeta Psi. Clubs: Rittenhouse, Racquet, Sunnybrook Golf (Phila.); Century Assn. (New York). Home: 9230 Germantown Av., Chestnut Hill, Phila. 18. Address: 1420 Walnut St., Philadelphia, Pa. Died June 7, 1949.

STEELE, David McConnell, clergyman; b. Pittsburgh, Pa., June 11, 1873; s. John Cameron and Margaret (McConnell) S.; B.A., Wooster, 1895; M.A., Columbia, 1899, D.D., 1916; B.D., Union Theol. Sem., 1899; m. Martha Virginia Mills, May 23, 1930. Deacon, 1899, priest, 1900, P.E. Church; asst. Holy Trinity Ch., Brooklyn, N.Y., 1898-1901, St. Bartholomew Ch., New York, 1901-04; rector St. Luke and Epiphany Ch., Phila., 1904-34, rector emeritus since 1934. Author: Going Abroad Overland, 1916; Vacation Journeys, East and West, 1917; Addresses and Sermons to Students, 1918; Papers and Essays for Churchmen, 1919; After Dinner Speeches, 1920. Address: Newton Square, Pa. Died Feb. 23, 1945.

STEELE, Frederic Dorr, illustrator; b. Marquette, Mich., Aug. 6, 1873; s. William H. and Zulma DeL. (Dorr) S.; studied Nat. Acad. Design and Art Students' League, New York; m. Mary Shaw Thyng, 1898. Contbr. to leading Am. periodicals since 1897, making specialty of drawings for "direct process" reproduction; bronze medal, St. Louis Expn., 1904. Mem. Soc. Illustrators. Club: Players. Address: The Players, New York. Died July 6, 1944.

STEELE, John (Scott), journalist; b. Belfast, Ireland, Dec. 15, 1870; s. Frederick Macauley and Annie (Scott) S.; m. Clare Krimont, 1894 (died 1929); children—John Scott, Thomas Scott; m. 2d, Winifred A. Herbert, 1934. Came to U.S., 1885, naturalized, 1893. Began as reporter N.Y. Herald, 1889, later with N.Y. World, N.Y. Times and night editor N.Y. Commercial; London corr. Chicago Tribune, 1919-35; now European rep. Mutual Broadcasting System, Inc. Mason. Clubs: Silurians (New York); American, Savage (London). Home: Underdowns, 134 Chaldon Way, Coulsdon, Surrey, England.* Died Jan. 8, 1947.

STEELE, Leon Charles, vice pres. Cudahy Packing Co.; b. Huntsville, Ala., Jan. 8, 1889; s. Andrew and Mary (Redus) S.; grad. U. of Ala., 1909; m. Suzanne Carbeth, Dec. 26, 1913; children—Elizabeth Susan, Edward. With Cudahy Packing Co., Chicago, since 1909, v.p. since 1938; pres. Am. Salt Co., Kansas City, Mo.; v.p. Red Wing Co., Fredonia, N.Y. Clubs: Casino, Racquet. Republican. Presbyterian. Home: 1300 N. State St. Office: 221 N. La Salle St., Chicago, Ill. Died Feb. 10, 1945.

STEELE, Thomas M., lawyer, banker; b. Geneva, N.Y., Dec. 4, 1878; s. Charles A. and Gertrude E. (Hawkes) S.; A.B., Trinity Coll., Conn., 1902; LL.B., Harvard, 1905; LL.D., Hobart, 1934; m. Edla Lansing Stout, Sept. 10, 1907. Practiced in N.Y. City, 1905-06; claims atty., N.Y.,N.H.&H. R.R. Co., New Haven,

1906-07; became connected with Watrous & Day, New Haven, 1907 admitted to firm, 1912; chairman of the board First National Bank & Trust Co. of New Haven; dir. Geometric Tool Co., New Haven Savings Bank; mem. federal advisory council for First Federal Reserve Dist., 1932-40. Mem. Am. and Conn. State bar assns., Am. Soc. Internat. Law, Alpha Delta Phi, Phi Beta Kappa. Republican. Episcopalian. Clubs: Graduate, Quinnipiack, New Haven Country. Home: 135 Cliff St. Office: First Nat. Bank & Trust Co., New Haven, Conn. Died July 29, 1944.

STEELE, William La Barthe, architect; b. Springfield, Ill., May 2, 1875; s. Robert Clingan and Mary Eleanor (La Barthe) S.; grad. high sch., Springfield, 1892; B.S. in Architecture, U. of Ill., 1896; m. Mariana Green, Apr. 30, 1901; children—Mariana, Melissa (Sister M. Philip, O.P.), William La Barthe, Harriet Gertrude (dec.), Jane Raymond (Mrs. G. F. Dashiell), Sarah Green (Mrs. Thomas S. Noble, Jr.), Philip Joseph. Draftsman in architectural offices of Louis H. Sullivan, Chicago, 1897-1900, Thos. Rodd, Pittsburgh, Pennsylvania, 1900-01, Alden & Harlow, Pittsburgh, 1901-02, Sidney F. Heckert, Pittsana Green, Apr. 30, 1901; children—Mariana, Melissa, William La Barthe, Harriet Gertrude (dec.), Jane Raymond, Sarah Green, Philip Joseph. Draftsman in archtl. offices of Louis H. Sullivan, Chicago, 1897-1900, Thos. Rodd, Pittsburgh, Pa., 1900-01, Alden & Harlow, Pittsburgh, 1901-02, Sidney F. Heckert, Pittsburgh, 1902-04, W. W. Beach, Sioux City, Ia., 1904-05; mem. firm Beach & Steele, 1905-07; practiced alone, Sioux City, Ia., 1907-26; mem. firm Steele & Hilgers, 1926, 28; mem. firm Kimball, Steele & Sandham, Omaha, 1928-46; mem. firm Steele, Sandham & Steele, since 1946. Principal works: Woodbury County Court House, Sioux City, Ia.; with William Gray Purcell and George G. Elmslie Associated: First Congl. Ch., Davidson Office Building, Saint Vincent's Hospital (all of Sioux City, Ia.); Sacred Heart Hospital, Le Mars, Ia.; Kappa Sigma fraternity house, Iowa City; with Kimball, Steele & Sandham, Omaha: Fed. Office Bldg. (G. B. Prinz, asso.), St. Cecilia's Cathedral, Jefferson Pub. Sch., all Omaha; First Ch. of Christ Scientist (Adminstrn. Bldg.), Minneapolis; 14 exchange bldgs. for N. W. Bell Telephone Co. in Nebraska and S.D.; Roosevelt Memorial, Missoula, Mont., architect-engr. with Kimball, Steele & Sandham and Chas. W. Steinbough, U.S. Housing Project, Alliance, Neb.; 3 buildings for Neb. State Bd. of Control, Hastings and Lincoln; fire station, Omaha. Past member Mayor's Committee of Housing, past treasurer Omaha Community Playhouse; dist. officer for Neb.-Kan. Historic Am. Buildings Survey. State archtl. adviser Home Owners Loan Corp.; chief architect Fontenelle Homes Housing Project. Former mem. Library Board, Planning Commn., Sioux City, Ia.; member Nebraska State Bd. Examiners Professional Engrs. and Architects. Fellow Am. Inst. Architects (ex-vice pres.); former mem. Am. Inter-professional Inst. (Omaha Chapter); mem. Omaha Chamber Commerce, Fontenelle Forest Bd., Sigma Chi. K.C. Contbr. to Jour. Am. Inst. Architects, House Beautiful, Architect, Ecclesiastical Rev. Home: 126 E. Division St., Neillsville, Wis. Died Mar. 4, 1949.

STEELL, Willis, playwright; b. Detroit; s. William and Jessica (Tait) S.; A.B. from Albion (Mich.) Coll., 1885; m. Emily Higman, Nov. 27, 1898. Episcopalian. Author: Isidra, 1888; Mortal Lips; Mountain of Gold; Death of the Discoverer; In Seville; Vaudevilles, 1908; The Fifth Commandment, 1907; (plays) The Kindergarten (1900), A Juliet of the People (1901), Battle of the Strong (1901), Consuelo (1902), Firm of Cunningham (1905), Morning After the Play (1906), Brother Dave (1907), Girl of the Golden Horn (mus. comedy, with Reginald de Koven), 1909; The Prospector, prod., Pittsburgh, 1912; Lionnette, prod., Princess Theatre, New York, 1914; The Gift of the Madonna, prod. at Inceville, Calif., by New York Picture Co., 1914; also (books) The Prospector, 1912; We're Ready!, 1915; Art and the New Religions, 1916; Parerga, 1919; The Long Walk of Samba Diouf, 1923; Forgotten People, 1926; Benjamin Franklin of Paris, 1928. Address: 3 Square Robiac, (7e) Paris, France. Died Jan. 31, 1941.

STEEP, Thomas, newspaper corr.; b. Cincinnati, O., Apr. 3, 1880; s. George W. and Lillie (White) S.; ed. Nat. Normal Sch., Lebanon, O.; m. Miriam Alter, 1918. Began newspaper work in Cincinnati; traveled afoot through Southern States writing sketches on rural life; sent by Scripps-McRae League to join Cuban insurrectos, 1896; witnessed surrender of Santiago, 1898; corr. in St. Petersburg, 1905; with Daily Mail, London, Eng., 1906-07; corr. Associated Press in Mexico, 1911-14; corr. in Scandinavian countries, 1914-15; corr. for New York Tribune at Washington Conf., 1921-22, at Peking, 1922-23; corr. New York Herald Tribune with Carmi Thompson mission to P.I., 1926; in charge Far Eastern service, same paper, Peking, 1926-27; mgr. N.Y. bureau Pan Pacific Press; pub. relations counsel for Hawaii, New Zealand and Australia. Contbr. to Asia, Current History, Readers' Digest, Am. Mercury, on Asiatic problems. Clubs: Overseas Press (New York); Nat. Press (Washington, D.C.). Author: Chinese Fantastics, 1925. Home: Greenwich, Conn. Office: National Press Bldg., Washington, D. C. Died Sep. 3, 1944.

STEFANINI, Francois Ange Antoine (stĕ-fä-nē-nē), U.N. official; b. Marseille, France, Sept. 7, 1909; s. Dominique and Marie (Catanei) S.; student Lycee of Marseille, 1919-24, Faculte of Aix, 1925-27; LL.B., Faculte of Paris, 1928; m. Odile Fournier, Aug. 12, 1941. Colonial officer, 1931-40; legal adviser French Provisional Govt., London, 1942-44; govt. official Ministry of Home Affairs, Paris, 1944-45; prefet of Vaucluse, France, 1945-46; dir. tech. services, United Nations, New York, since June 1946. Served as lt.-comdr., French Navy, 1940-42. Office: United Nations, Lake Success, L.I., N.Y. Died March 29, 1948.

STEGEMAN, Gebhard (stĕ'gĕ-män), physical chemistry; b. Holland, Mich., June 14, 1890; s. John and Hannah (Kamps) S.; A.B., Hope Coll., Holland, Mich., 1913; A.M., Ohio State U., 1915, Ph.D., 1917; m. Mildred Smith, June 11, 1932. Instr. in chemistry, U. of Wash., 1917-18; asst. prof. of chemistry, U. of Pittsburgh, 1919-24, prof. since 1924; official investigator for the N.D.R.C., 1942-45. Served as chemist with Chemical Warfare Service, U.S. Army, 1918-19. Mem. Am. Chem. Soc., Alpha Chi Sigma, Sigma Xi. Republican. Mem. Dutch Reformed Ch. Club: Shannopin Country (Pittsburgh). Contbr. to Am. Chem. Soc. Jour., Jour. Phys. Chem. Home: 6 Oxford Rd., Ben Avon Heights, Pittsburgh 2. Died Sept. 5, 1949.

STEIGER, George (stī'gĕr), chemist; b. Columbia, Pa., May 27, 1869; s. Benjamin F. and Martha L. (Young) S.; B.S., Columbian (now George Washington) U., 1890, M.S., 1892; unmarried. Chemist, U.S. Geol. Survey 1892, chief chemist, 1916-30, chemist, 1930-39, retired; now continuing work through facilities of the Geol. Survey. Mem. Am. Chem. Soc., Am. Inst. Mining Engrs., Geol. Soc. Washington, Mineral Soc., Wash. Acad. Scs.; S.A.R.; fellow A.A.A.S. Club: Cosmos. Has published various papers, mostly on original research on the constitution of certain silicates and methods of chem. analysis. Home: The Portner, Washington, D.C.* Died Apr. 18, 1944.

STEIGUER, Louis Rudolph de, naval officer. See Louis Rudolph de Steiguer

STEIN, Gertrude (stīn), writer; b. Allegheny, Pa., Feb. 3, 1874; d. Daniel and Amelia (Keyser) Stein; student Radcliffe, 1893-97, Johns Hopkins Med. Sch., 1897-1902. Author: Three Lives, 1908; Tender Buttons, 1915; Geography and Plays, 1923; Making of Americans, 1925; Useful Knowledge, 1928; Acquaintance with Description, 1929; Ten Portraits, 1930; Lucy Church Amiably, 1930; Before the Flowers of Friendship Faded Friendship Faded, 1931; How to Write, 1931; Operas and Plays, 1932; Matisse, Picasso and Gertrude Stein, 1932; The Autobiography of Alice B. Toklas, 1933; Four Saints in Three Acts, 1934; Portraits and Prayers, 1934; Lectures in America, 1935; Narration, 1936; Geographical History of America, 1936; Everybody's Autobiography, 1937; Picasso, 1938; The World Is Round, 1939; Paris, France, 1940; Ida, 1941; Three Lives, 1942; Wars I Have Seen, 1945; Brewsie and Willie, 1946; Selected Writings, 1946; Four in America, 1947; Blood on the Dining Room Floor, 1948; Last Operas and Plays, 1949. Contbr. prose and verse to mags. Address: 5 rue Christine, Paris. Died July 27, 1946; buried in Pere la Chaise Cemetery, Paris, France.

STEINER, Leo K., banker; b. Bohemia, Austria, Feb. 18, 1870; s. Isaac and Lottie (Hecht) S.; came to U.S., 1885; ed. pub. schs. and Eastman Business Coll., Poughkeepsie, N.Y.; m. Dian Holzer, Nov. 27, 1900; children—Leo Keith, Bernard S. Entered mercantile business at Hamburg, Ala., 1885; in banking business at Birmingham, Ala., since 1888, now pres. Steiner Bros. (Inc.); pres. Cullman Property Co.; dir. Old Republic Credit Life Ins. Co. of Chicago. Treas. Ala. Motorists Assn., Ala. Assn. for the Blind. Democrat. Clubs: Birmingham Automobile, Hillcrest Golf and Country. Home: 2900 Argyle Rd. Office: 2101 1st Av., Birmingham, Ala.* Died Oct. 22, 1944.

STEINER, Walter Ralph, physician; b. Frederick City, Md., Nov. 18, 1870; s. Lewis Henry (M.D.) and Sarah Spencer (Smyth) S.; A.B., Yale, 1892, A.M., 1895; grad. student Johns Hopkins, 1892-94, M.D., 1898; L.H.D., Trinity, 1931. House med. officer, Johns Hopkins Hosp., 1898-99; practiced in Hartford, Conn., since 1900; pathologist and bacteriologist, Hartford Hosp., 1901-12, asst. visiting physician, 1905-07, visiting physician, 1908-34, cons. pathologist and bacteriologist since 1912, cons. physician since 1934, chmn. med. and surg. staff, 1925-33; cons. physician Hartford Orphan Asylum, Bristol, New Britain, Meriden, Torrington and Middlesex (Middletown, Conn.) hosps.; hon. physician Manchester Memorial Hosp. Sec. Congress of Am. Physicians and Surgeons, 1911-32. Fellow A.A.A.S., Am. Coll. Physicians, A.M.A.; mem. Assn. Am. Physicians, Med. Library Assn. (pres. 1931-33), Conn. State Med. Soc. (sec. 1905-12; chmn. council 1929-33; pres. 1934-35), Hartford County Med. Assn., Hartford Med. Soc. (librarian, 1903-41; pres. 1920), Am. Assn. Pathologists and Bacteriologists, Am. Clin. and Climatol. Assn. (pres. 1934-35), N.Y. Acad. Medicine, Am. Assn. for Study of History of Medicine (pres. 1937-39), S.A.R., Soc. Colonial Wars, Md. Hist. Soc., Conn. Hist. Soc., Va. Hist. Soc., Zeta Psi, Elihu Club. Republican. Conglist. Clubs: Hartford, University, Hartford Golf, Twentieth Century, Graduate (New Haven); Century (New York). Contbr. articles on internal medicine, pathology and med. history. Home: 646 Asylum Av., Hartford, Conn. Died Nov. 4, 1942.

STEINER, Williams Kossuth, organist; b. Pittsburgh, Pa., June 9, 1874; s. Kossuth L. and Marie (Williams) S.; pupil of S. Bissell, F. Zitterbart, Theodor Salmon, Walter E. Hall, and Heinrich Germer (Dresden), 1894-99; m. Edna A. Steiner, July 2, 1902; children—Margaret Brown (Mrs. Charles Graham Kiskaddon), Jane Louise, Edwina Lewis, Stuart Grey, Howard Markley. Organist Grace Ref. Ch. and Trinity Luth. Ch., 1891, North Av. Meth. Ch., 1893-94, Calvary M.E. Ch., 1899-1904, all of Pittsburgh; designed organ, 1907, for Rodelph Shalom Temple, Pittsburgh, and organist same, 1904-25. Teacher of piano, organ and theory. Has given 50 recitals at Carnegie Inst.; played at Buffalo and St. Louis expns., also with various symphony orchestras. Composer anthems and organ and piano music. Dir. the Germer Piano School, Pittsburgh; musical dir. Western Pa. Sch. for the Blind since Sept. 1927. Asso. Am. Guild Organists, by exam., 1899, local examiner since 1908. Mem. Musicians Club of Pittsburgh, Pa. Soc. S.A.R. Home: 4400 Center Av. Studio: 201 Bellefield Av., Pittsburgh, Pa. Died Sep. 10, 1945.

STEINHARDT, Laurence A. (stīn'härt), lawyer, economist and diplomat; b. N.Y. City, Oct. 6, 1892; s. Adolph M. and Addie (Untermyer) S.; A.B., Columbia, 1913, M.A., 1915, LL.B., 1915; m. Dulcie Yates Hofmann, Jan. 15, 1923; 1 dau., Dulcie Ann. Accountant, 1915-16; admitted to N.Y. bar, 1916; mem. Guggenheimer, Untermyer & Marshall, 1920-33; E.E. and M.P. from U.S. to Sweden, 1933-37; ambassador from United States to Peru, 1937-39, to U.S.S.R., 1939-41; ambassador to Turkey, January 1942-45; ambassador to Czechoslovakia, June 1945-48; U.S. ambassador to Canada since August, 1948. Counsel to Waslaw Nijinsky, 1916, to Archduchess Marie Theresa in recovery of Napoleon necklace. Associate counsel, United States War Department, 1919. Private, later sergt., 60th Field Artillery. Provost Marshal Gen.'s staff, 1918. Del. 8th Pan-Am. Conf., Lima, 1938. Awarded United States Medal of Merit, July, 1946. Member executive finance com. Dem. Nat. Com.; mem. President Roosevelt's preconvention campaign com., 1933. Awarded U.S. Medal of Mérit, 1947. Mem. Am. Bar Assn., N.Y. County Lawyers Assn., Bar Assn. City of N.Y. (council on fgn. relations, 1947), Pi Lambda Phi (nat. pres.), permanent treas. class of 1913 Columbia U. and 1915 Columbia U. Law Sch. Clubs: National Democrat, Bankers, Columbia Univ. (New York); Atlantic Beach (N.Y.). Author various books and articles on med. jurisprudence, trade unions, economics and finance. Office: 30 Pine St., New York, N.Y. Address: Am. Embassy, Ottawa, Ont., Can. Died Mar. 28, 1950.

STEJNEGER, Leonhard (stīn'ĕ-gĕr), naturalist; b. Bergen, Norway, Oct. 30, 1851; s. P. Stamer and Ingeborg C. (Hess) S.; grad. R. Frederic's U., Christiania, 1875 (Cand. jur.); Dr. Philosophy, hon. causa, same univ., 1930; m. Marie Reiners, Mar. 22, 1892; 1 dau., Inga. Came to U.S., 1881; on a natural history expdn. to Bering Island and Kamchatka, 1882-83, collecting for U.S. Nat. Museum, asst. curator of birds, 1884-89, curator reptiles since 1889, head curator of biology since June 1, 1911. Revisited Commander Islands, 1895, for Fish Commn. to study fur-seal question, 1896-97, as mem. U.S. Fur Seal Commn., and again in 1922 for Dept. of Commerce. Del. from Smithsonian Instn. to Zoöl. Congress 7 times, 1901-35, to Internat. Ornithologists Congress, 1905; studied museum administration and finances in Europe, 1901, 04, 05, 13. Life mem. Bergen Museum; mem. Nat. Acad. Sciences, Acads. Sciences, Christiania and Washington; fellow Am. Ornithologists Union, A.A.A.S.; fgn. mem. Zoöl. Soc., London, Ornithol. Soc. Bavaria, Acad. Natural Sciences Phila.; mem. Biological Soc. Washington (pres. 1907, 08), Am. Soc. Ichthyol. and Herpetol. (ex-pres.), Com. on Nomenclature and of Permanent Com. of Internat. Zoöl. Congress, Assn. Am. Geographers, Sigma Xi; hon. mem. Calif. Acad. Sciences, British Ornithol. Union, Am. Soc. of Mammalogists, German Ornithol. Soc. Decorated Knight 1st class Royal Norwegian Order of St. Olav, 1906, Comdr., 1939. Walker Grand Prize, Boston Soc. Nat. Hist. Author: Norsk Ornitologisk Ekskursjonsfauna, 1873; Norsk Mastozoologisk Ekskursjonsfauna, 1874; Results of Ornithological Explorations in the Commander Islands and in Kamchatka, 1885; Standard Natural History, Vol. IV, Birds (greater part), 1885; Report of the Rookeries of the Commander Islands, Season of 1897, 1897; The Asiatic Fur-Seal Islands and Fur-Seal Industry, 1898; The Relations of Norway and Sweden, 1900; The Herpetology of Porto Rico, 1904; The Herpetology of Japan and Adjacent Territory, 1907; The Origin of the So-called Atlantic Animals and Plants of Western Norway, 1907; Georg Wilhelm Steller, pioneer of Alaskan Natural History, 1936, also many monographs and contbns. on zoöl. subjects. Club: Cosmos. Address: Smithsonian Instn., Washington, D.C. Died Feb. 28, 1943.

STELLA, Joseph, artist; b. Muro Lucano, South Italy, June 13, 1880; s. Michael and Vincenza (Cerone) S.; B.S. and M.A., Liceo Umberto 1, Naples, Italy, 1895; student New York Sch. of Art; student old and modern art, Italy and France, 1910-11; unmarried. Came to U.S. from Italy, 1896; engaged in med. work 2 yrs.; drew for The Outlook and Century; oil painting "Old Man"; made 100 drawings of miners and steel mill workers in crayon and pastel, 1908; exhibited in Pittsburgh, Chicago and New York; made huge canvas "Coney Island, Battle of Lights, Mardi Gras" exhibited at first show of Modern Am. Art, Montross Gallery, N.Y. City, 1914; also exhibited at Bourgeois Gallery, Valentine Gallery; 1-man shows in Paris, Rome and at Asso. Am. Artists. Prin. works: Brooklyn Bridge, Tree of My Life, New York, Birth of Venus, Ondina, Nocturen, Factory, Song of Barbados, Song of the Nightingale, Dance of Spring, Last Toast of Polichinelle, Lotus.* Died Nov. 5, 1946.

STELLWAGEN, Seiforde Michael (stĕl′wäg-ĕn), lawyer; b. St. Ignace, Mich., Dec. 2, 1890; s. Michael Frederick and Lillie Anderson (Pierson) S.; A.B., U. of Minn., 1915; LL.B., 1915; grad. student in law, Harvard, 1915-16; m. Elinor Walker Lynch, Aug. 20, 1918; 1 dau., Barbara Pierson. Admitted to Minn. bar, 1915, and practiced in Minneapolis; atty. for Alien Property Custodian, Washington, D.C., 1917-18, 1919-20; sec. Ry. Loan Advisory Com. to Federal Res. Bd., 1920-21; asso. with former atty. gen. of U.S., A. Mitchell Palmer, and others in practice of law since 1921; firm name Palmer, Stellwagen & Neale since 1939; prof. law, Knights of Columbus Law Sch., Washington, D.C., 1924-25, Columbus U., Washington, D.C., since 1938; counsel Tacna-Arica Plebiscitary Commn., Arica, Chile, 1926. Served as private and 2d lt. field arty., U.S. Army, 1918-19. Trustee Legal Aid Bur. Dist. of Columbia. Mem. Am. Dist. of Columbia, and Federal bar assns., Am. Legion, Alpha Delta Phi, Phi Delta Phi. Democrat. Methodist. Club: Cosmos (Washington, D.C.). Home: 5124 Loughboro Road N.W., Washington 16. Office: 815 15th St. N.W., Washington 5, D.C. Died Nov. 25, 1946.

STEMPF, Victor Herman, public accountant; b. Minneapolis, Minn., Apr. 28, 1893; s. Richard and Jessie (Cirkler) S.; B.C.S., St. Louis (Mo.) U., 1915; m. Dorothy Meissner, Apr. 12, 1917; children—Charles R. (officer U.S.N.R.), Dorothy Elise. Certified public accountant with Touche, Niven & Co., New York, N.Y., since 1915, became mgr. St. Louis office, 1918, admitted to partnership, 1921, resident partner, N.Y. City, since 1926. C.P.A. in Mo., N.Y., Mich., Ill., Calif., Ohio, Minn. and Conn. treas., University City, Mo., 1921-25. Police commr., Mamaroneck, N.Y., 1936-45. Mem. Com. Postwar Tax Policy, under grant from Falk Foundation. Mem. Nat. Assn. Cost Accountants (pres. 1940-41; founder mem. and v.p. St. Louis chapter 1921). N.Y. State Soc. C.P.A.'s (bd. dirs. 1926-40; pres. 1939-40), Am. Inst. of Accountants (chmn. com. on fed. income taxation 1937-40; pres. 1943-44), Am. Accounting Assn. (past v.p.). Vice pres. Mo. State Soc. C.P.A.'s, 1925. Clubs: Downtown Assn., Union League (New York). Cons. editor: Cost Accountants Handbook and Accountants Handbook, 1944. Contbr. to professional jours. Has served as speaker or special lecturer for forums at numerous universities and schools of commerce in U.S. Home: 38 Vine Road Larchmont, N.Y. Office: 80 Maiden Lane, N.Y., N.Y. Died Apr. 1946.

STEPHAN, George (stē′vĕn), lawyer; b. Cleveland, O., Mar. 30, 1862; s. John C. and Elizabeth (Watson) S.; ed. pub. schs.; m. Helen A. Carr, June 28, 1891. Removed to Colo., 1881; admitted to Colo. bar, 1900; served as city atty., Delta, county atty. Delta County, and dep. dist. atty. same county; then pres. Delta Town & Improvement Co.; dir. Farmers and Merchants Bank of Delta, Delta Nat. Bank. Mem. Colo. Senate from Delta and Mesa counties, 1910-16; lt. gov. of Colo., 1919-21, acting gov. part of that time; registrar State Land Bd., Colo., 1921-23; U.S. atty., Dist. of Colo., 1924-29; private practice in Denver, 1929-33. Was referee in bankruptcy 7th Judicial Dist. Food administrator, Delta, World War; mem. Planning Commn. of Denver. Vice-pres. La Jolla Chamber of Commerce, 1935-36; dir. San Diego Chamber of Commerce; dir. San Diego Community Chest; mem. San Diego Planning Commn.; mem. exec. bd. San Diego Council Boy Scouts of America. Mem. adv. com. U. of Colo., 1917-23; mem. Asso. Alumni, U. of Colo. Mem. Colo. State and Denver bar assns., S.A.R. (pres. state soc., 1932-33). Republican. Mason (K.T., 32°, Shriner). Club: La Jolla Kiwanis (pres. 1936), Cuyamamca. Home: La Jolla, Calif. Died Sep. 9, 1944.

STEPHENS, George, investments; b. Guilford County, N.C., April 8, 1873; s. Addison H. and Lydia (Lambeth) S.; Ph.B., U. of N.C., 1896; m. Sophie Convere Myers, Dec. 9, 1902; children—George Myers, Sophie Myers. Pres. Am. Trust Co., Charlotte, 1902-18, v.p., 1918-22; pres. Asheville Citizen, Inc., co-pub. Asheville Citizen, 1919-30; dir. The Stephens Co. since 1912 (pres. 1912-22). Sec. and treas. Charlotte Park and Tree Commn. 10 yrs.; chmn. Asheville City Planning Commn., 1921-33; trustee Univ. of N.C. since 1901; mem. Univ. of N.C. Building Com.; pres. Beverly Hills Co., Asheville, 1938-42; museum com. Great Smoky Mountains Nat. Park; mem. nat. advisory com., New York World's Fair, 1939, 40. Mem. S.A.R., Sons of Confederate Vets., N.C. State Lit. and Hist. Assn., Sigma Nu, Order of Gimghouls (U. of N.C.); mem. council Nat. Econ. League. Democrat. Episcopalian. Clubs: Pen and Plate, Carolina Motor (dir.; v.p.); Biltmore Forest Country. Home: 12 Evergreen Lane. Office: 50 Walnut St., Asheville, N.C. Died Apr. 1, 1946.

STEPHENS, Harry T. (stē′vĕns), **architect, engr.; b. Paterson, N.J. Fellow A.I.A.; past pres. N.J. chapter A.I.A., N.J. Soc. of Architects, The Architects League of Northern N.J. Address: 152 Market St., Paterson 1, N.J. Died March 14, 1946.**

STEPHENS, Hubert Durrett, lawyer, senator; b. New Albany, Union County, Miss., July 2, 1875; s. Judge Z. M. and Lethe A. (Coker) S.; ed. pub. schs.; LL.B., U. of Miss., 1895; m. Delia Glenn, Oct. 18, 1899. Began law practice at New Albany, 1895; dist. atty., 1907-10; mem. 62d to 66th Congresses (1911-21), 2d Miss. Dist.; mem. U.S. Senate, 2 terms, 1923-35; mem. bd. dirs. Reconstruction Finance Corp., 1935-36; now retired. Democrat. Home: New Albany, Miss.* Died Mar. 14, 1946.

STEPHENS, John Vant, clergyman; b. Blackwells, near St. Louis, Mo., Sept. 16, 1857; s. Willis Andrew and Mary Emily (Boyer) S.; student, Wabash Coll., Ind., class of 1884; A.B., Lincoln (Ill.) Coll., 1884; Union Theol. Sem., 1884-85; B.D., Cumberland Theol. Sem., Lebanon, Tenn., 1886; D.D., Trinity U., Tex., 1900, m. Willie H. Buchanan, Jan. 31, 1888; 1 son, John Vant. Ordained Cumberland Presbyn. ministry, 1880; pastor Knoxville, Tenn., 1886-87, Chattanooga, 1888; corr. sec. Bd. Missions Cumberland Presbyn. Ch., St. Louis, 1889-91; pastor, Bowling Green, Ky., 1891-94; prof. hist. theology, Cumberland Theol. Sem., 1894-1910; prof. practical theology, 1910-13, prof. ch. history, 1913-32, chmn. faculty, 1925-26, Lane Theol. Sem., Cincinnati. Editor Missionary Record, St. Louis, 1889-91; editor, Bible Study (magazine), Nashville, 1894-98. Member World's Parliament of Religions, Chicago, 1893; mem. Alliance Ref. Chs. Holding Presbyn. System, 1896-1921; mem. com. to prepare an intermediate catechism for Presbyterian Ch. Mason (K.T.), Odd Fellow. Author: Infant Church Membership, 1897; The Causes Leading to the Organization of the Cumberland Presbyterian Church, 1898; Cumberland Presbyterian Digest, 1899; Elect Infants or Infant Salvation in the Westminster Symbols, 1900; Presbyterian Government, 1907; The Presbyterian Churches, 1910; The Providential Purpose of Our Nation, 1918; The Story of the Founding of Lane Theol. Sem., 1929; The Story of the Founding of the Theological School in the Cumberland Presbyterian Church, 1933; The Lebanon Theological Seminary, 1934; The Christianization of Great Britain, 1937; Fourscore, Life Story of John Vant Stephens, 1938; "An Affirmation" with Supplemental Events, Antecedent and Subsequent, 1939; The Cumberland University Theological School, 1939; The Genesis of the Cumberland Presbyterian Church, 1941; The New Lights (The Christian Church), 1942; The Organic Union of the Cumberland Presbyterian Church in the United States of America, 1943; also various pamphlets, etc. Home: 4 Beecher Apts., Sta. D (Cincinnati), O. Address: Lane Seminary Bldg., Station D., Cincinnati, O. Died Mar. 3, 1946.

STEPHENS, Percy Rector, conductor, voice teacher; b. Chicago, Sept. 24, 1876; s. Henry and Rhoda Celestine (Comstock) S.; ed. U. of Notre Dame, Ind.; studied violin and composition with Prof. Jacques Paul, elocution and dramatic art with Dr. Francis Lyman at Notre Dame, stage direction and played in stock repertoire with Hart Conway, voice lessons with Luman A. Phelps and various others in New York; opera and mise-en-scene with Victor Capoul (Paris); m. Edna Rosiland Park (composer), 1903 (died 1904); m. 2d, Jeannette Vreeland, Sept. 14, 1921. Began as a teacher in New York, 1897; has contributed much toward advancement of higher standard in women's choral singing; teacher of Reinald Werrenrath, Paul Althouse, Jeannette Vreeland, Olga Averino, Lois Bennett, Dan Gridley, Douglas Stanbury, etc. Prominent in investigations and research Am. Acad. Teachers of Singing, through Carnegie Foundn., and in association with Prof. G. Oscar Russell of Ohio State U. Pres. New York Singing Teachers Assn.; mem. Am. Acad. of Teachers of Singing. Clubs: Musicians, Bohemians. Composer and arranger of choral works in collaboration with Deems Taylor. Home-Studio: 27 W. 67th St., New York. Died June 16, 1942.

STEPHENS, Robert Allan, lawyer; b. Potomac, Ill., June 9, 1878; s. Rev. Robert and Mary Ellen (Smith) S.; student Northwestern Univ., 1896-98; LL.B., George Washington U., 1901, LL.M., 1902; m. Helen Prentiss Bennett, Sept. 1, 1903; children—Robert Allan, Mary Ellen (Mrs. George J. Metcalf), Charles Bennett, William Cleaves, Page Prentiss. Admitted to Ill. bar, 1902; mem. Swallow, Stephens and Swallow, Danville, Ill., 1903-04, Stephens and Barnhart, 1904-06; practiced alone, 1906-21; mem. Brown, Hay and Stephens, Springfield, Ill., since 1921; sec. Ill. Pub. Utilities Commn., 1918-21. President Abraham Lincoln Council Boy Scouts of America, 1935-36, nat. rep., 1936. Mem. Am. Bar Assn. (mem. house of delegates 1937-39; state del. 1940; v.p. 7th Circuit 1933-34; council legal edn., 1929-39; council mem. bar orgn. activities 1934, chmn. 1938-39), Ill. State Bar Assn. (sec. since 1916), Am. Law Inst., Am. Judicature Soc., Chicago Bar Assn., Sangamon County Bar Assn., Ill. Ch. Council (pres. 1937, 38), Springfield Art Assn. (pres. 1931-34), Kappa Sigma. Republican. Methodist (pres. Springfield Methodist Union 1935-40). Mason (32°), K.P. (grand chancellor, Ill., 1920-21), Odd Fellow. Clubs: University (Chicago); Rotary (Danville); Mid Day of Springfield (pres. 1941). Editor Illinois Bar Jour., 1913-35; contbr. to legal jours. Lecturer Northwestern U., U. of Mich., and U. of Chicago law schs. Home: 1700 Park Av. Office: First National Bank Bldg., Springfield, Ill. Died July 26, 1942.

STEPHENS, William Dennison, ex-governor; b. Eaton, Preble County, O., Dec. 26, 1859; s. Martin F. and Alvira (Leibee) S.; grad. Eaton High Sch.; taught school and read law; LL.D., U. of Southern Calif., 1921; m. Flora Rawson, June 17, 1891 (died Apr. 21, 1931); 1 dau., Barbara (Mrs. John N. Osburn). Mem. engring. corps on railway construction in Ohio, Ind., Ia. and Louisiana, 1880-87; removed to Los Angeles, 1887; mgr. and traveling salesman, 1888-1902; mem. firm Carr & Stephens, grocers, 1902-09. Mem. Los Angeles Bd. Edn., 1906-07; mayor of Los Angeles, 1909; pres. board water commrs. and mem. advisory com. for bldg. Los Angeles aqueduct, 1910; mem. 62d Congress (1911-13), 7th Calif. Dist., and 63d and 64th Congresses (1913-17), 10th Dist.; resigned from 64th Congress, 1916, and was apptd. lt. gov. of Calif.; became gov. of Calif., Mar. 15, 1917, upon resignation of Gov. Johnson (elected to U.S. Senate), for term expiring Jan. 1, 1919; elected gov. for term, 1919-23. Republican. Admitted to bar, 1919. Mem. Los Angeles Chamber Com. (dir. 1902-11, pres. 1907). Maj. and commissary 1st Brigade Calif. N.G., 1903-13. Mason (33°, grand comdr. K.T. of Calif., 1908; charter mem. Red Cross of Constantine and Shrine Potentate, 1904). Home: 3191 W. 7th St., Los Angeles, Calif. Died Apr. 25, 1944.

STEPHENSON, James, actor; b. Selby, Yorkshire, England, Apr. 14, 1898; s. John Gathorne Stansfield and Emma (Longbottom) S.; ed. privately; m. Lorna Hewitt Kilby Dinn, July 30, 1937; 1 son, Peter Stansfield. Came to U.S., 1937. Cotton merchant, Manchester, England, 1920-32; actor Liverpool Repertory Theatre, England, 1932-36, on London stage and in films, 1936-37; actor for Warner Bros., since 1937. Served as capt., East Lancashire Regt., British Army, World War. Episcopalian. Mason. Club: Radio (London). Address: 400 N. Camden Drive, Beverly Hills, Calif. Died 1941.

STEPHENSON, Joseph Maxwell, editor and pub.; b. Rochester, Ind., June 22, 1892; s. Rome Charles and Ella Jane (Maxwell) S.; prep. edn., Winona Acad. (Winona Lake, Ind.) and Staunton (Va.) Mil. Acad.; student U. of Notre Dame, 1910-11, Ind. U., 1911-13; m. Marjorie Sweet, Apr. 5, 1927; children—Jo Ann, Thomas Louis. Asst. cashier Internat. Trust & Savings Bank, Gary, Ind., 1913-15, cashier, 1915-17; business mgr. South Bend News-Times, 1917-20, pub., 1920-32, editor and publisher, 1933-38; treas. Conservative Life Ins. Co. of America, 1919-25, pres., 1925-45; retired, Aug. 1, 1945. Member Delta Tau Delta. Catholic. Clubs: Indiana (South Bend); Indiana Society (Chicago); Kentucky Colonel Assn. (Louisville). Home: 1329 E. Washington Blvd. Address: Conservative Life Ins. Bldg., South Bend, Ind. Deceased.

STEPHENSON, Sam, lawyer, banker; b. Carroll County, Ind., Aug. 9, 1868; s. John and Nancy Jane (Alexander) S.; A.B., Miami U., Oxford, O., 1891; m. Anne Nelson, July 12, 1906; children—John De Camp, Sam. Admitted to Mont. bar, 1892, and since practiced at Great Falls; mem. firm Cooper, Stephenson & Glover; became pres. First Nat. Bank, 1915, now chmn. bd.; officer or dir. various other corps. Mem. Phi Delta Theta. Republican. Club: Meadow Lark Country. Home: 727 4th Av. N. Office: First Nat. Bank, Great Falls, Mont. Died Jan. 26, 1942.

STEPTOE, Philip Pendleton (stĕp′tō), lawyer; b. Brandy Station, Va., Feb. 6, 1877; s. Charles Yancey and Frances (Wallace) S.; B.L., U. of Va., 1902; m. Mary Lou Wetherell, Nov. 15, 1911; children—Philip Pendleton, Thomas Wetherell, Robert Mason, Nancy Moss. Admitted to the bar, 1902, and since in practice at Clarksburg, W.Va.; mem. of firm Steptoe & Johnson, Clarksburg and Charleston, W.Va., since 1912. Home: Shepherdstown, W.Va. Office: Clarksburg, W.Va. Died Oct. 16, 1944.

STERLING, Ross Shaw, ex-governor, oil operator; b. Anahuac, Tex., Feb. 11, 1875; s. Benjamin Franklin and Mary Jane (Bryan) S.; ed. pub. schs. to 12; m. Maud Abbie Gage, Oct. 10, 1898; children—Walter Gage, Mildred, Ruth, Ross S. (dec.), Norma. On farm till 21, then entered business for self; operating in oil since 1903; chmn. bd. Sterling Oil & Refining Corp.; pres., chmn. bd. Humble Oil & Refining Co., 1917-25; gov. of State of Texas, term 1931-32. Chmn. bd. Hermann Hosp. Estate; mem. bd. trustees Texas Christian U. Democrat. Prohibitionist. Mem. Christian Ch. Mason, K.P. Clubs: Houston, Houston Country, Riveroaks Country, Congressional Country of Washington, D.C. (life). Home: 21 West Lane. Office: Sterling Bldg., Houston 2, Tex. Died March 25, 1949.

STERN, Nathan, rabbi; b. New York, N.Y., Feb. 12, 1878; s. Julius and Jeannette (Young) S.; B.A., Columbia, 1898, M.A., 1899, Ph.D., 1901; studied St. John's Coll., Cambridge, Eng.; studied Jewish Theol. Sem. of America; rabbi, Hebrew Union Coll., Cincinnati, 1904. Rabbi at Marion and Wabash, Ind., 1904-05, Trenton, N.J., 1905-10, Providence, R.I., 1910-15; asst. rabbi, West End Synagogue, N.Y. City, 1915-16, asso. rabbi, 1916-23, rabbi since 1923. Chaplain N.J. State Prison; lecturer Brown U. Mem. New York Bd. Jewish Ministers (pres. 1920-21); mem. Central Conf. Am. Rabbis; mem. Commn. on Edn. of Am. Hebrew Congregations; pres. Assn. of Reform Rabbis of N.Y. and Vicinity; mem. exec. bd. N.Y. Jewish Big Brothers; commr. Pub. Library, Trenton, N.J. Founder-chmn. Jewish Inst. for Youth Leadership. Mem. exec. bd. of Nat. Peace Conf., exec. bd. of Soc. for Jewish Deaf; mem. bd. of govs. Hebrew Union Coll., Cincinnati, O.; mem. Acad. for Jewish Research; pres. Hebrew Union Coll. Alumni Assn. since 1938. Clubs: University (Providence); Clergy, City Athletic, Judeans. Author: The Jewish Historico-Critical School of the Nineteenth Century, 1901. Contbr. to Jewish Ency., to year books of Central Conf. Am. Rabbis, etc. Address: West End Synagogue, 160 W. 82d St., New York, N.Y. Died Jan. 24, 1945.

STERNBERG, Charles Hazelius, naturalist; b. Middleburg, N.Y., June 15, 1850; s. Levi (D.D.) and Margaret Levering (Miller) S.; ed. Hartwick Sem. (N.Y.), Ia. Lutheran Coll. (Albion), Kan. State Agrl. Coll.; hon. A.M., Midland Coll., Atchison, Kan., 1911; m. Anna Musgrove Reyholds, July 7,

1880; children—George Fryer, Charles Mottram, Maud (dec.), Levi. In charge of parties collecting fossils for late Professor E. D. Cope, 1876-79 and 1894, 96, 97; in charge for late Prof. Agassiz, 1881, 1882; for late Prof. O. C. Marsh of Yale, 1884, and of expdns. for Munich (Bavaria) Paleontol. Mus., 1892, 95, 1901, 02, 05, etc. Was in charge collecting party for Geol. Survey of Can., and vertebrate paleontol. lab. at Victoria Memorial Mus., Ottawa, Can., and head collector and preparator of vertebrate fossils, Victoria Memorial Museum, Geol. Survey of Can. until 1916, resigned; conducting own lab., Lawrence, Kan., since 1917. Discovered 2 nearly complete skel tons 32 ft. long, Red Deer River, Alberta, 1916; also large skeleton Dimetrodon Permian of Tex., 1916, in Nat. Mus.; conducted expdn. to the Permian of Tex. and Kan. Chalk, 1918, to the Kansas Chalk and to Texas, in 1919; found four skeletons of Mosasaurs, 2 Pterodactyls, 3 of the great fish, a fine skeleton of Equus Scotti; explored the San Juan Basin, N.M., 1921-23; discovered new genera of ceratopsians and duckbilled dinosaurs and many turtles. Fellow A.A. A.S.; mem. Kan. Acad. Science (life), Soc. Am. Vertebrate Paleontologists. Republican. Lutheran. Author: The Life of a Fossil Hunter, 1909; Hunting Dinosaurs on Red River, 1916. Home: 603 Claxton Blvd., Toronto, Canada. Died July 20, 1943.

STERNER, Albert, artist; b. London, England, Mar. 8, 1863; s. Julius L. and Sarah Sterner (both parents Americans) S.; ed. King Edwards School, Birmingham, England; came to U.S., 1879; studied Julian's Académie and École des Beaux Arts, Paris, France; m. 2d, Flora Temple Lash, Oct. 4, 1924; children (by 1st marriage)—Harold Olivia. Painter, etcher and lithographer, Chicago, 1879-84; opened studio, New York, 1885. Hon. mention for oil painting, "The Bachelor," at Paris Salon, Champs Elysées; bronze medal, Paris Expn., 1900; silver medals, Buffalo Expn., 1901; gold medal for painting, "Portrait of My Son," Munich, 1905; Clara Obrig prize, Nat. Acad. Design, 1935, for painting, "Artist's Table"; Carnegie prize Nat. Academy, for painting "Furbelows," 1941. Rep. in Met. Museum and Public Library (New York), Brooklyn Museum, Carnegie Inst., Toronto Museum, Yale Univ. Library, South Kensington, Victoria, and Albert Museums (London), Royal Collection of King of Italy, Royal Print Collections of Munich and Dresden, Library of Congress Print Collection. One of founders of Painter-Gravers of America (pres. 1918), and of Soc. of Illustrators; secretary New Soc. Artists, 1925-26. Instr. School of Nat. Acad., Art Students League, Sch. of Design for Women. Nat. Academician. Mem. Soc. Am. Etchers, Nat. Inst. Arts and Letters. Lecturer and writer on art subjects. Address: Brick House, Richmond, Mass.; P.O., Pittsfield, R.F.D. No. 1, Mass.* Died Dec. 16, 1946.

STERRETT, Frances Roberta, author; b. Red Wing, Minn.; d. Francis R. and Sarah M. (Hahn) Sterrett; grad. St. Paul (Minn.) High Sch.; Phila. Sch. of Design. In newspaper work 10 yrs.; contbr. short stories to leading mags. Club: Woman's (Minneapolis). Mem. D.A.R. Author: The Jam Girl, 1914; Up the Road with Sallie, 1915; Mary Rose of Mifflin, 1916; William and Williamina, 1917; Jimmie the Sixth, 1918; Rebecca's Promise, 1919; Nancy Goes to Town, 1920; These Young Rebels, 1921; An Amazing Inheritance, 1922; Little Florine, 1925; Sophie, 1927 (awarded $5,000 prize by the People's Popular Monthly for the best serial); The Golden Stream, 1931; Years of Achievement, 1932; (juveniles) Rusty of the Tall Pines, 1928; Rusty of the High Towers, 1929; Rusty of the Mountain Peaks, 1930; Rusty of the Meadow Lands, 1931. Home: 2309 Girard Av. S., Minneapolis, Minn. Died Nov. 11, 1947.

STETTINIUS, Edward R., Jr., former Secretary of State; b. Chicago, Oct. 22, 1900; s. Edward R. and Judith (Carrington) S.; student Pomfret (Conn.) Sch., U. of Va., 1919-24; hon. degrees: LL.D., Union, Colgate, Lafayette, Elmira Colls.; LL.D., American, Rutgers, New York Universities; Dr. Engring., Stevens Inst. of Tech; LL.D., University of Calif., U. of Chattanooga, Columbia University; Dr. of Civil Laws, Oxford; L.H.D., Roanoke Coll; m. Virginia Gordon Wallace, May 15, 1926; children—Edward R., Wallace, Joseph. Began with Hyatt Roller Bearing Works, Harrison, New Jersey, becoming employment manager 1924; assistant to John L. Pratt, vice president General Motors Corp., 1926-30; asst. to Alfred P. Sloan, Jr., pres. Gen. Motors, 1930; v.p. Gen. Motors, in charge indusl. and public relations, 1931; vice chmn. finance com., U.S. Steel Corp., dir. and chmn. finance com., 1936; chmn. bd. dirs., mem. finance com. 1938; resigned all positions and directorships with U.S. Steel Corp. to accept Presidential appt. to membership, Advisory Com. to Council Nat. Defense, 1940; chmn. priorities bd. and dir. priorities div., Office of Prodn. Management, Jan.-Sept. 1941; Lend-Lease administrator, U.S.A., and special assistant to President, 1941-43; Under-Secretary of State, September 1943-Nov. 1944, Secretary of State, November 1944-June 1945; personal representative of the President, since June 1945; apptd. U.S. rep. to United Nations Gen. Assembly, Dec. 1945. In charge Nat. Share the Work Movement, 2d Fed. Reserve Dist., 1932; liaison officer between Nat. Indusl. Recovery Adminstrn. and Indusl. Adv. Bd., 1933; chmn. 1939 Roll Call, N.Y. chapter Am. Red Cross; chmn. War Resources Bd.; adv. bd., Petroleum Adminstrn. for War; chmn. Dumbarton Oaks Conversations on Internat. Security, Aug. 1944; chmn. Am. delegation to Inter-Am. Conf. on Problems of War and Peace, Mexico City, Mar. 1945; mem. Pres. Roosevelt's party at meeting of Big Three, Yalta, Jan. 1945; chmn. Am. delegation to United Nations Conf. on Internat. Orgn., San Francisco, April-June, 1945; gen. assembly U.N. (London), 1946; Security Council, U.N. (N.Y. City), 1946; res. as U.S. representative to U.N., June, 1946. Awarded Medal for Merit, 1946; Nat. Acad. Soc. Sci. Gold Medal; Nat. Conf. Christians and Jews Hero of Peace award; comdr. Legion of Honor (France). Dir. General Aviation Corp. (v.p., 1934), Western Air Express Corp., Eastern Air Lines, Inc., Metropolitan Life Ins. Co.; (1930-34); General Electric Co., Internat. General Electric Co., Fed. Reserve Bank of Richmond; dir., mem. exec. comm. North Am. Aviation, Inc., Transcontinental and Western Air, Inc. (1930-34); chmn. bd. Liberia Co.; dir. World Commerce Corp. Mem. bd. dirs. Thomas Jefferson Memorial Foundation; rector, U. of Va., 1946-47; chmn. nat. bd. English Speaking Union, 1947; trustee Va. Episcopal Theol. Sem. Honorary mem. Am. Foreign Service Assn., The Pilgrims (London), India House. Episcopalian. Clubs: Union, Century (New York). Author: Roosevelt and the Russians, 1949. Address: The Horseshoe, Rapidan, Culpepper Co., Va. Died Oct. 31, 1949.

STEVENS, Beatrice, painter, illustrator; b. New York, N.Y., Sept. 4, 1876; d. John Baker and Lucy (Baldwin) S.; ed. private schs., tutors and art schs., N.Y. City. Painter of landscapes and murals; has exhibited in N.Y. City and Boston; book illustrations for Little, Brown & Co., Duffield & Co., Atlantic Monthly Co., Houghton Mifflin Co., Doubleday Page & Co., Brentano, Volland Co., The Brimmer Co., etc.; mag. illustrations for Century, Scribner's, Woman's Home Companion, Country Life in America, House Beautiful, St. Nicholas, etc. Home: Pomfret, Conn. Died Oct. 20, 1947.

STEVENS, David, editor, author; b. Fitchburg, Mass., Aug. 12, 1860; s. Samuel and Sarah (Fay) S.; ed. pub. schs. and under pvt. teachers; student law dept. Boston U., 1880-81; m. Jennie W. Waite, 1885 (died 1910); m. 2d, Cordelia Brooks Fenno Browne, May 12, 1921 (she died Apr. 22, 1934). Practiced law in Boston, 1881-89, in Tacoma, Washington, 1889-98; returned to Boston, 1898, and devoted time to writings, chiefly librettos for musical pieces; joined editorial staff of C. C. Birchard & Co., pubs. ednl. works, 1914, now editorial mgr. Formerly mem. 2d Mass. Regt. and 1st Corps Cadets; mem. 1st Motor Corps, Mass. State Guard, during World War. Clubs: Boston Art, Algonquin; Badminton (London). Author: Lays of a Lazy Dog, 1903; Lyrics of Eliza, 1905; Ballads of Be-Ba-Boes, 1910; The Dim Forest, Cruise of the Beebird. Wrote librettos for The Green Bird; The Sphinx; Tomioko; The Madcap Duchess; Azora (grand opera); and numerous short pieces and verses for mags. Home: 293 Commonwealth Av. Office: 221 Columbus Av., Boston, Mass.* Died June 29, 1946.

STEVENS, Edward Fletcher, architect; b. Dunstable, Mass., Oct. 22, 1860; s. Kimball A. and Mary Elizabeth (Woodbury) S.; student spl. archtl. design with class of 1883, Mass. Inst. Tech.; m. Helen Ward Leach, June 28, 1905; 1 dau., Edna May (Mrs. Simon B. Landis). Studied architecture, offices of Allen & Kenway, Boston, and McKim, Mead & White, New York; mem. Kendall & Stevens, Boston, later Kendall, Taylor & Stevens; pvt. practice, 1907-12; mem. Stevens & Lee, 1912-33; now mem. Stevens, Curtin, Mason & Riley, Boston. Planned over 100 instns., including Buffalo Gen. Hosp., Royal Victoria Hosp., Providence Lying-in Hosp., Ohio Valley Gen. Hosp., Springfield Hosp., Mixto Hosp. and Maternidad Hosp., Lima, Peru, etc. Civil hosp. specialist U.S. Engring. Dept., designing overseas hosps. 1st World War; was mem. special commn. apptd. to revise plans of army hosps. Fellow A.I.A.; mem. Boston Soc. Architects. Republican. Episcopalian. Mason. Club: University. Author: The American Hospital of the Twentieth Century, 1918, revised edits., 1921, 27. Retired from active practice, 1943. Home: 10 Hawthorne Rd., Wellesley Hills, Mass. Office: 45 Newbury St., Boston, Mass.* Died Feb. 28, 1946.

STEVENS, Frederic Bliss, banker; b. Albany, N.Y., June 9, 1871; s. Albert Parsons and Emma Henrietta (McMullen) S.; ed. pub. schs. and Albany Acad. for Boys; m. Janet Lindsay, Jan. 21, 1919; children—Janet Lindsay, Lindsay. With National Savings Bank, Albany, New York, 1888, pres. since 1925. Sergt. Nat. Guard N.Y., 5 yrs. Mem. Savings Banks Assn. State of New York (vice-president). Presbyterian. Mason. Clubs: University, Albany Country, Fort Orange. Author: History of Savings Bank Assn. of the State of New York, 1913. Home: 559 Providence St. Office: 90 State St., Albany, N.Y. Died June 22, 1947.

STEVENS, Nathaniel, woolen mfr.; b. North Andover, Mass., Sept. 11, 1857; s. Moses T. and Charlotte E. (Osgood) S.; ed. Phillips Acad., Andover, Mass.; m. Elizabeth P. White, Mar. 25, 1885 (died Jan. 18, 1940). Began in woolen mfg. business, 1876; partner M. T. Stevens & Sons, 1886-1900; pres. M. T. Stevens & Sons Co. since 1900; chmn. of the bd. dirs. of J. P. Stevens & Co., Inc.; dir. Andover Nat. Bank. Mem. Nat. Assn. Wool Mfrs. Unitarian. Home: North Andover, Mass. Office: 201 Devonshire St., Boston, Mass.* Died June 15, 1946.

STEVENS, Neil Everett, plant pathologist; b. Portland, Me., Apr. 6, 1887; s. Thomas Jefferson and Hattie (Mantle) S.; B.A., Bates Coll., 1908; Ph.D., Yale, 1911; m. Maude Bradford, Aug. 31, 1914; children—Russell Bradford, Carl Mantle II, Mary Christine. Inst. botany, Kan. State Coll., 1911-12; pathologist Bur. Plant Industry, U.S. Dept. Agr., 1912-28, sr. pathologist 1928-36; adjunct prof. at George Washington U., 1931-36; prof. of botany, U. of Ill., 1936-47, professor of plant pathology since 1947; senior specialist, Wisconsin Dept. of Agr., summers 1937-44; sec. and dir. Arlington and Fairfax Building and Loan Assn., 1933-35. Delegate Internat. Botanical Congress, 1930 and 1935. Mem. Am. Phytopathol. Soc. (v.p. 1933; pres. 1934), Bot. Soc. of Washington (sec. 1927; pres. 1931), A.A.A.S. (council 1947-50; v.p. and chmn. Sect. G, 1939), Mycol. Soc. of America (council 1932; v.p. 1944), Botanical Soc. of Am. (v.p. 1940, pres., 1946), Nat. Research Council (mem. exec. com. dir. of biology and agriculture, 1944), Sigma Xi, Phi Beta Kappa. Club: University (Urbana). Advisory editor of The Botanical Rev. since 1935. Writer of government bulletins and tech. papers on diseases of plants and the history of botany. Address: University of Illinois, Urbana, Ill. Died June 26, 1949; buried Clements Cemetery, Urbana, Ill.

STEVENS, Raymond Bartlett, ex-congressman; b. Binghamton, N.Y., June 18, 1874; s. Pliny Bartlett and Lillian (Thompson) S.; student Harvard, 2 yrs., class of 1897; Harvard Law Sch., 3 yrs., class of 1899; married; 1 son, David S. Admitted to N.H. bar, 1899; mem. N.H. Ho. of Rep., 1909, 11, 13, 23; member Constutitional Conventions, N.H., 1912, 38; mem. 63d Congress (1913-15), 2d N.H. Dist.; spl. counsel Federal Trade Commn., Washington, 1915-17; vice-chmn. U.S. Shipping Board, 1917-June 1920. Am. rep. Allied Maritime Transport Council, 1917-18. Adviser on fgn. affairs to Siamese Govt., 1926-35; mem. Fed. Trade Commn., 1933; mem. U.S. Tariff Commn. since 1935, chmn. since 1937. Democrat. Home: Landaff, N.H. Address: U.S. Tariff Commission, Washington, D.C. Died May 18, 1942.

STEVENS, Rollin Howard, physician; b. Blenheim, Ont., Can., Jan. 7, 1868; s. Nathan Howard and Ada Jane (Burk) S.; Toronto U., 1 yr.; M.D., Homœ. Coll., U. of Mich., 1889; Coll. Physicians and Surgeons, Ont., Can., 1889; house surgeon, Grace Hosp., Detroit, 1889-91; spl. course Stanford, 1892; m. Mary Ella Thompson (A.B., M.D.), Mar. 16, 1892; children—Margaret (dec.), Frances Eleanor (Mrs. M. C. Davis). In gen. practice, Detroit, 1892-1903; went to Copenhagen, Denmark, 1903, to study the Finsen light and its use in lupus and other skin diseases, under Prof. Finsen; then went to Berlin, Vienna and Hamburg and studied diseases of the skin and the Roentgen ray; practice limited to dermatology and radiology since 1904; visited Paris for study, 1909; successively pathologist, surgeon and gynecologist, 1892-1904, dermatologist and Roentgenologist, since 1904, Grace Hosp.; lecturer on dermatology, Homœ. Coll. of U. of Mich., 1904-09; asst. clin. prof. Roentgenology, Detroit Coll. of Medicine, 1910-14, and asso. clin. prof. dermatology since 1925; extramural lecturer in post-grad. medicine, University of Mich., 1929; dir. and sec. Radiol. Research Inst.; founder Detroit Inst. of Cancer Research, Inc., pres. 1943-46 (Rollin Howard Stevens Research Laboratory, Memorial in his honor). Dir. Board of Commerce, Detroit, 1913; founder, 1900, and ex-president Detroit Mycological Club, later Detroit Inst. Science; founder and pres. Mich. Soc. for Social Hygiene; sec.-treas. Boys' Home and D'Arcambal Assn. Fellow A.M.A., Am. Coll. Physicians, Am. Coll. Radiology (pres. 1931), Radiol. Society N. America (pres. 1923); mem. Am. Roentgen Ray Soc., Wayne County Med. Soc., Mich. State Med. Soc., Am. Radium Soc. (pres. 1933-34), Am. Bd. Radiology, Detroit Roentgen Ray and Radium Soc. (pres. 1926-27), Detroit Dermatol. Soc. (pres. 1926-27), British Inst. Radiology, Mich. Assn. of Roentgenologists, Am. Malacological Society, Am. Assn. for Study of Neoplastic Diseases (v.p., 1939, Laymen's League (Unitarian), Foreign Policy Assn.; hon. mem. Chicago Roentgen Ray Soc. Mason. Clubs: Rotary, Detroit Yacht, Michigan Union of Ann Arbor (life), Torch. Extensive contributor on med. topics. Home: 47 Pingree Av. Office: David Whitney Bldg., Detroit 26, Mich. Died May 17, 1946.

STEVENS, Roy George, surgeon; b. 1880; M.D., U. of Ill. Coll. of Medicine, 1905. Practiced at Sioux Falls, S.D., since 1909; pres. Sioux Falls Medical and Surgical Clinic; mem. surg. staff McKennan and Sioux Valley hosps. Fellow A.M.A., Am. Coll. Surgeons. Address: 301 S. Minnesota Av., Sioux Falls, S. Dak. Deceased.

STEVENS, Thomas McCorvey, lawyer; b. Claiborne, Ala., July 31, 1866; s. Thomas Jefferson and Lydia Adelaide (McCorvey) S.; A.B., U. of Ala., 1888, LL.B., 1890, LL.D., 1927; m. Lillian S. Burke, June 29, 1936. Began practice at Brewton, Ala., 1890; County solicitor, Escambia County, 1890-92; circuit solicitor, 2d Jud. Circuit, 1892-03; removed to Mobile, Ala., 1896; mem. State Senate from Mobile County, 1911-15. Trustee U. of Ala., 1901-23; retired mem. firm Stevens, McCorvey, McLeod, Goode and Turner; since Jan. 1, 1937, v.p. and gen. counsel of Waterman S.S. Corp. and Pan Atlantic S.S. Corp. Home: 950 Government St. Office: Merchants Nat. Bank Bldg., Mobile, Ala. Died Jan. 29, 1946.

STEVENS, Thomas Wood, author; b. Daysville, Ill., Jan. 26, 1880; s. William Gurney and Charlotte (Wood) S.; grad. Armour Scientific Acad., 1897; took 3 yrs'. course in mech. engring., Armour Inst. Tech., Chicago; m. Helen F. Bradshaw, 1904. Founded the Blue Sky Press, Chicago; became lit. critic to The Inland Printer, 1902; took charge dept.

of illustration, Art Inst. of Chicago, 1903; lecturer art history, U. of Wis., 1912-13; head of sch. of drama, Carnegie Inst. of Tech., 1913. Mem. Phi Kappa Sigma, Chicago Soc. Etchers, 1913 (pres.), American Pageant Assn. (pres. 1915-19). Club: Players. Author: The Lesser Tragedy (prize story in Metropolitan Mag. literary competition), 1904; The Etching of Cities, 1913; Lettering, 1916. Co-author: (with Alden C. Noble) The Morning Road, 1902. Dramatic Works: The Chaplet of Pan (with Wallace Rice), prod. by Donald Robertson, 1908; A Pageant of the Italian Renaissance, prod. and published, Chicago Art Inst., 1909; An Historical Pageant of Illinois, prod. and published, Northwestern U., 1909; Pageant of the Old Northwest, Milwaukee, 1911; Independence Day Pageant (with K. S. Goodman), Chicago, 1911; Masques of East and West (with same), Chicago, 1915; The Pageant of St. Louis, 1914; The Pageant of Newark, 1916; The Drawing of the Sword (Red Cross pageant), 1917; pageant-play, Joan of Arc, prod. with John Craig, with Am. troops at Domremy, France, Sept. 1918; Pageant of Victory and Peace, 1919; other city pageants and masques. Contbr. to mags. and reviews. Home: 5542 Pocussett St., Pittsburgh. Died Jan. 29, 1942.

STEVENS, W(illiam) Bertrand, bishop; b. Lewiston, Me., Nov. 19, 1884; s. Albion Morse and Ada (McKenzie) S.; B.A., Bates Coll., as of 1906, D.D., 1922; M.A., Columbia, 1911; Ph.D., New York University, 1916; B.D., Episcopal Theol. Sch., 1910; LL.D., University of Southern Calif., 1921; LL.D., University of California, 1946; also studied at Harvard and Union Theol. Seminary; m. Violet Heathcote Bond, Oct. 10, 1911; children—Ellen Hewson (Mrs. G. P. Prince), Ann Heathcote (Mrs. Edw. McNair), Edith McKenzie (Mrs. Reaford Haney), Emily McIlvaine (Mrs. Kempton B. Hall). Deacon, 1910, priest, 1911, P.E. Ch.; curate Holy Trinity Ch., New York, 1910-12; rector St. Ann's Ch., New York, 1912-17, St. Mark's Ch., San Antonio, Tex., 1917-20; consecrated bishop coadjutor of Los Angeles, 1920, bishop of Los Angeles, 1928. Dir. Los Angeles War Chest, Los Angeles chapter Am. Red Cross. Mem. Nat. Council Episcopal Church. Hon. fellow Sch. of Philosophy, Univ. of Southern California. Asst. field dir. Am. Red Cross, at Ft. Sam Houston, Tex., 1918; major (chaplain) O.R.C.; capt. (chaplain) Calif. Naval Militia. Pres. bd. dirs. Good Samaritan Hospital and other institutions. Trustee Occidental College, Bishop's School for Girls, Scripps College, Harvard School, School for Christian Service, California College in China. Mem. of council, Mills College. Mem. S.R. Mem. Am. Inst. of Archaeology, mem. of council, American and British Commonwealth Assn., pres. Los Angeles Art Assn., Soc. Colonial Wars, Phi Beta Kappa, Phi Gamma Delta, Phi Mu Alpha, Theta Phi. Republican. Mason (33°, K.T.). Order of the Red Cross of Constantine. Clubs: University, Los Angeles Country, Los Angeles Athletic, Jonathan, Sunset, Twenty, Kiwanis (Los Angeles); hon. chmn. Los Angeles Chapter English-Speaking Union. Author: A Bishop Beloved, 1936; The Reconciling Christ (collaborator), 1938; Getting Together, 1938; Reality in Fellowship, 1939; Editor's Quest, 1940; Victorious Mountaineer, 1943; Towards the Increase of the Ministry, 1944. Home: 929 Buena Vista St., South Pasadena, Calif. Address: 615 S. Figueroa St., Los Angeles 14, Calif. Died Aug. 22, 1947.

STEVENS, William Dodge, illustrator; b. Tidioute, Pa., Sept. 13, 1870; s. William Stone and Ellen (Dodge) S.; ed. pub. and private schs.; student Art Inst. Chicago, under Oliver Dennett Grover and John H. Vanderpoel, and in Paris; later Mr. Grover's asst. while he was engaged on decorations; unmarried. Has illustrated for most of leading mags. and weekly papers. Mem. Artists Guild. Club: Players. Studio: 51 West 10th St., New York, N.Y. Died July 23, 1942.

STEVENSON, Alexander Russell, Jr., engring.; b. Schenectady, N.Y., May 28, 1893; s. Rev. A. Russell and Mary M. (Kennedy) S.; C.E., Princeton, 1914; M.S., Union Coll., Schenectady, N.Y., 1915, Ph.D., 1917; m. Helene Elink-Schuurman, May 5, 1934; children—Mary Kennedy, Alexander Russell III, Agathe Elink-Schuurman. With Gen. Electric Co., Schenectady, N.Y., 1917 and since 1919, in research laboratory, 1917, in power and mining engring. dept., specializing in application of synchronous elec. machinery connected to reciprocating apparatus, 1919-23, mem. staff of vice pres. in charge of engring. 1923; assisted Dr. Robert E. Doherty in starting advanced course in engring. in Gen. Electric Co., 1923, in complete charge of this ednl. program since 1930. Served in World War I, 1917-18; officer in charge testing, Langley Field, U.S.; in charge radio and elec. sect. Air Service, France; in charge flying and testing, Army Exptl. Field, France. Mem. spl. subcom. on jet propulsion Nat. Advisory Com. for Aeronautics, 1941-44; mem. Civilian Advisory Council, Mil. Training Div., Ordnance Dept., since 1942; advisory mem. N.Y. State Aviation Council, Inc. Pres. bd. trustees Brown Sch., Schenectady, N.Y. Past pres. Am. Soc. Refrigerating Engrs., Private Flyer's Assn. Fellow Am. Inst. E.E., Am. Soc. M.E. (vice president); mem. Engineer's Council for Professional Development, Soc. Promotion Engring. Edn. (chmn. com. on relations with industry), Phi Beta Kappa, Sigma Xi. Republican. Presbyterian. Contbr. of numerous scientific articles to technical publs. Home: 6 Union St. Office: General Electric Co., I River Rd., Schenectady 5, N.Y. Died Aug. 28, 1946.

STEVENSON, Charles Hugh; b. Snow Hill, Md., Dec. 6, 1869; s. Hugh Saunders and Jane Catharine (Bailey) S.; student Lehigh U., 1886-88; Columbian (now George Washington) U., 1894-99, LL.M., 1897, D.C.L., 1899; m. Elizabeth, d. Richard Helson, Apr. 21, 1909; children—(Charles) Hugh, Richard H., Mary. Asst. U.S. Fish Commn., 1891-1909; admitted to bar, 1896; special agent Bur. of Census, 1909; investment banker in Detroit since 1910; pres. Davenport Realty Co., Stevenson Realties Co., Orion Development Co., Stevenson-Woodward Co., Pleasant Lake Land Company; vice-pres. Woodmere Cemetery Assn.; an organizer and pres. several yrs. Great Lakes Tours Association. Mem. of NRA Code Com., 1933. An organizer and dir. Detroit Zoöl. Soc.; an organizer and ex-pres. Mich. Hotel Assn.; mem. exec. council and chmn. copyrighted music com., Am. Hotel Assn.; pres. Detroit Hotel Assn., 1921-23; mem. Am. Bar Assn. Club: Detroit. Smithsonian prize at Fourth Internat. Fishery Congress, 1908; various awards by U.S. Govt. for investigations; decorated by Belgium and France, 1926. Author: International Regulation of Fisheries on the High Seas; The Book of the Pearl (with Dr. George Frederick Kunz), 1908; Preservation of Fishery Products; Foreign Fishery Trade; The Shad Fisheries; Fishery Legislation; Oyster Industries; Fishery Products in Arts and Industries; and numerous other reports and articles related to fisheries. Home: Detroit Club. Office: 800 Prentis St., Detroit, Mich. Died July 30, 1943.

STEWART, Donald Farquharson, editor; b. Fletcher, Ont., Can., Mar. 4, 1882; s. John Grasie and Elizabeth (Maitland) S.; ed. high schs. at Chatham, Ont., and Detroit, Mich.; m. Mary Etta McIntyre, June 23, 1902; children—Dorothy Margaret (Mrs. Albert Deane), Robert Donald (dec.). Came to U.S., 1898, naturalized, 1912. Artist and writer for American Boy Mag., 1900-03, Detroit Free Press, 1903-06, New York Globe, 1906-07, Detroit News, 1907-09; founder and mgr. Stewart & Stewart Engraving & Electrotyping Co., 1909-12; editor and pub. Days Work, 1912-18; with Boni & Liveright, New York, 1918-23, Am. Viewpoint Soc., 1923-24; editor and pub. official L.O.O.M. publs. since 1924. Wilson award for pub. speaking, Ont., 1896. Republican. Presbyterian. Moose. Home: 1366 N. Dearborn St. Office: 737 N. Michigan Av., Chicago, Ill. Deceased.

STEVENSON, Edward Luther, coll. prof.; b. Rozetta, Henderson County, Ill., Oct. 18, 1858; s. Thomas Porter and Cassandra Booker (Ewing) S.; A.B., Franklin (Ind.) Coll., 1881, A.M., 1884, LL.D., 1913; student history and polit. economy, Johns Hopkins, 1887-88; student, Jena, Halle, Heidelberg, 1888-91; Ph.D., U. of Heidelberg, 1890; Litt.D., Rutgers, 1922; m. Grace Rue Runyon, June 20, 1895; children—Katharine Lawrence (Mrs. Harvey W. Bell), Edward Luther. Principal Franklin (Ind.) High Sch., 1881-82, Rising Sun (Ind.) High Sch., 1882-83; supt. schs. in Ill., 1883-87; prof. history, Rutgers Coll., 1891-1911; sec. Hispanic Soc. America, 1910-15 (acting dir. 1915). Non-resident lecturer Johns Hopkins, 1904, 09; lecturer on hist. geography, Columbia, 1906-07, U. of Calif., 1917, King's Coll., London, 1928; also before scientific and ednl. instns. on cartographical subjects, history and hist. geography. Mem., editor Hispanic Soc. of America. Mem. Mediæval Acad. America, Phi Beta Kappa (mem. council N.Y. alumni), Phi Delta Theta, Internat. Geographic Congress, 1904, 25, 28 (gave prin. address, 1925, and 2 important ones, 1928), Am. Antiquarian Soc., Assn. Am. Geographers, History of Science Soc., Am. Hist. Assn., Royal Acad. Arts and Sciences, Spain, 1927; corr. mem. of Cuban Acad. of History; fellow A.A.A.S.; hon. mem. Royal Geog. Soc. of Madrid. Mem. N.J. Jamestown Expn. Commn. Decorated Comendador Royal Order of Isabella the Catholic, Spain, 1913; Order of Bolivar, Venezuela, 1915; Grand Officer Order of the Nile, Egypt, 1925; Rutgers Univ. award, 1938. Presbyterian. Republican. Author: Maps Illustrating Early Discovery and Exploration in America, 1502-1530 (large folio atlas), 1903-06; Charter of Queens College (now Rutgers Univ.) of 1772, 1907; Hondius World Map of 1611, 1907; The Marine World Chart of Nicolo de Canerio, 1908; Early Spanish Cartography of the New World, 1909; Atlas of Portolan Charts, 1911; Portolan Charts, Their Origin and Characteristics, 1911; The Genoese World Map, 1457, 1912; Christopher Columbus and His Enterprise, 1913; Willem Janszoon Blaeu, his life and work, with facsimile of his large World Map of 1605, 1914; Portolan atlas, signed "Joan Martines en Messina añy, 1582," 1915; Portolan atlas, "Conte de Ottomano Freducci, 1537," 1915; Facsimiles of Portolan Charts (large folio atlas and text), 1917; Terrestrial and Celestial Globes (2 vols.), 1921; Sebastian Cabot and His Spanish Services, with facsimile of his map (1544), 1928; The Derotero of Alonso de Chavis (2 vols.), 1929; English transl. of Claudius Ptolemy's Geography with his maps, 1931; Geography of Claudius Ptolemy (photographed and hand colored reproduction of one of the finest mss.), 1930; also numerous other publs. Home: 17 Lake Av., Yonkers, N.Y. Died July 16, 1944.

STEWART, Fred Carlton, plant pathologist; b. French Creek, N.Y., Feb. 13, 1868; s. Almeron L. and Charlotte E. (Hubbard) S.; B.Sc., Ia. State Coll., 1892, M.Sc., 1894; grad. work, Harvard, Cornell U., U. of Munich; m. Alene Chestek, Nov. 20, 1895; children—Harland Hubbard, Ralph Walton, Hermine, Charlotte Amelia, Mayalene. Mycologist, N.Y. Agrl. Expt. Sta., 1894-98, botanist, 1898-1919, chief in research (botany), 1920-36; also prof. botany, N.Y. State Coll. of Agr., Cornell, 1920-36, emeritus prof. since 1936. Emeritus life mem. A.A.A.S. Author of numerous expt. sta. bulls. on plant diseases. Home: Geneva, N.Y. Died Apr. 24, 1946.

STEVENSON, Edward Irenaeus (Prime), author, critical editor; b. in U.S., 1868; early edn. in America. Began writing for press when in sch.; was admitted to bar (N.J.), but did not practice. Mem. lit. staff The Independent, Harper's Weekly, etc., many yrs.; became widely known as musical, dramatic and lit. critic; also as lecturer; specializing fgn. literatures (including Europe and Orient), belles-lettres. Active co-editor A Library of the World's Best Literature. Ret. from all profl. engagements. Author of many novels and short stories, including: A Matter of Temperament; White Cockades; Left to Themselves; Mrs. Dee's Encore; The Square of Sevens; Her Enemy, Some Friends, and Other Personages, etc. Also much lit. and musical criticism, travel-papers, hist. studies, prose and verse contbns. to mags., etc. Author (under pseudonym) of important studies in a branch of psychiatrics of sex, etc. Addresses: Fifth Av. Bank, N.Y. City, and care Morgan, Grenfell & Co., London, E.C., Eng. Died July 23, 1942.

STEVENSON, Frederick Alfred, pres. and dir. Am. Car & Foundry Co.; b. Detroit, Mich.; s. John S. and Mary (Reeves) S.; m. Henriette M. Evelynd; 1 dau., Countess Andréa Marco Guiseppi Soranzo di Baruaba. President and dir. Am. Car & Foundry Co., N.Y. City; dir. Am. Car & Foundry Export Co., Carter Carburetor Co. Mem. Newcomen Soc., Am. Soc. of Mech. Engrs. Clubs: Sleepy Hollow Country, New York Athletic, New York Railroad, Railroad-Machinery, Metropolitan, Recess. Home: Hotel Pierre. Office: 30 Church St., New York, N.Y. Died July 29, 1948.

STEVENSON, John Alford, life ins. official; b. Cobden, Ill., Mar. 1, 1886; s. John Miles and Elizabeth Candace (Wilkins) S.; grad. Southern Ill. Normal U., 1905; A.B., Ewing (Ill.) Coll., 1908; A.M., U. of Wis., 1912; Ph.D., U. of Ill., 1918; L.H.D., (hon.) Hahnemann Med. Coll. and Hosp., Phila. 1943; m. Josephine Reese, Sept. 19, 1914; 1 son, John Reese. Asst. prin. high sch., Nashville, Ill., 1905-06, prin., 1906-07; prin. high sch., Olney, Ill., 1907-09; supt. schs., Olney, 1909-11; lecturer in edn., U. of Wis., 1911-12; mgr. dept. music, drawing and manual arts, Scott, Foresman & Co., pubs., Chicago, 1912-16; lecturer in edn. and sec. appointments com., dept. of edn., U. of Ill., 1916-18, asst. prof. secondary edn. and dir. summer session, 1918-19; prof. edn. and dir. Sch. of Life Ins. Salesmanship, Carnegie Inst. Tech., Pittsburgh, 1919-20; 3d v.p. Equitable Life Assurance Soc. of U.S., 1920-21, 2d v.p., 1921-28; mgr. John A. Stevenson Agency, Penn Mutual Life Ins. Co., 1928-36; v.p. Penn Mutual Life Ins. Co., 1931-33, exec. v.p., 1936-39, trustee since 1938, pres. since 1939. Mem. bd. mgrs. Girard Trust Co. (Phila.); mem. bd. dirs. Fire Assn. of Phila., Franklin Fire Ins. Co., Bell Telephone Co. of Pa. (exec. com.), Inst. of Life Ins. (chmn. bd. 1944); mem. bd. dirs. and chmn. exec. com. Ins. Fedn. of Pa. (pres. 1937-38); mem. exec. com., trustee and sec. Am. Coll. of Life Underwriters; pres. Marketing Execs. Soc., 1928-38; mem. Phila. and Pa. State C. of C.; mem. N.Y. State C. of C. (mem. ins. com. U.S. C. of C.), vice chmn. Pa. Bd. of Pub. Assistance; dir. Y.M.C.A. (Philadelphia), Community Fund, Library Co. of Philadelphia, Am. Management Assn. (1939-42); mem. nat. panel of arbiters, Am. Arbitration Assn.; mem. Council, Nat. Civil Service Reform League; mem. adv. bd., Met. Opera Com. for Phila., Salvation Army (Phila.), chmn. 1936-38; mem. Citizens Enrollment Com., 4th Naval Dist., U.S. Navy; exec. com. Naval Training Assn. of U.S.; dir. and former nat. v.p. Navy League of U.S. Mem. Navy Manpower Survey Bd., Phila. Medal of Merit, 1944; Navy's Distinguished Civilian Service Award, 1944. Chmn. for Pa. War Savings Com., 1941-43; chmn. consultant bd., War Finance Com. of Phila.; dir. Eastern Pa., British War Relief Soc., Inc.; v.p. and mem. exec. com. United Nations Council of Phila., 1943-44; pres. and chmn. adv. council Phila. Regional Inter-Am. Center, 1943-44; mem. bd. trustees Council for Inter-Am. Co-op., Inc. Trustee, U. of Pa.; pres. Friends of U. of Pa. Library, 1938-44; trustee Berea Coll., 1932-43, Temple U., U. of Chicago, St. George's School. Dir. (mem. finance com.) Southern Ill. Normal U. Foundation; mem. finance com. U. of Illinois Alumni Assn.; mem. corp. Babson Inst., mem. adv. bd. Admiral Farragut Acad.; mem. com. on pharmaceutical survey of Am. Council on Education; mem. Nat. Council, Junior Achievement; mem. bd. mgrs. Ministers and Missionaries Benefit Bd. of Northern Bapt. Conv. (chmn. exec. com., 1931-34); mem. Sales Mgrs. Assn. of Phila. (pres. 1934-36), N.E.A., Nat. Assn. Life Underwriters, Assn. of Life Agency Officers (vice chmn., 1932-33, chmn. 1933-34), American Assn. University Teachers of Ins. (charter mem.), Nat. Inst. Social Sci., Am. Acad. Polit. and Social Science, St. Andrews Soc. (Phila.), Newcomen Soc. of Eng., Sigma Nu, Kappa Delta Pi, Phi Delta Kappa, Phi Eta, Pi Gamma Mu. Republican. Baptist. Clubs: Union League, Rittenhouse, Franklin Inn (Phila.); Merion (Pa.) Cricket (mem. bd. govs. 1940-45); Canadian (New York); Indian Creek Country, Bath (Miami Beach, Fla.). Author: The Project Method of Teaching, 1921; Meeting Objections, 1921; Selling Life Insurance, 1922; Farm Projects (with Carl Colvin), 1922; Constructive Salesmanship, 1923; Problems and Projects in Salesmanship, 1923; Education and Philanthropy, 1927. Co-editor: Harper's Life Insurance Library. Contbr. to mags. Home: "Chimneys," Bryn Mawr, Pa. Office: 530 Walnut St., Philadelphia 5, Pa. Died Aug. 31, 1949.

STEVENSON, William Francis; b. Loray, Iredell County, N.C., Nov. 23, 1861; s. William Sydney and Elizabeth (McFarlan) S.; A.B., Davidson Coll., 1885, LL.D., 1921; read law under Gen. W. L. T. Prince and R. T. Caston; m. Mary Elizabeth, d. Gen. W. L. T. Prince, Nov. 13, 1888 (died 1924); m. 2d, Mrs. Clara Malloy Finney, Apr. 6, 1926 (died March 24, 1931); m. 3d, Ruth Culbertson, June 24, 1936. Was admitted to the bar of South Carolina, 1887, and began practice at Chesterfield, S.C. General counsel for State Dispensary Commission, directing the litigation through the Supreme Court of the U.S., in winding up the S.C. State Dispensary. Member Dem. Exec. Com. of Chesterfield County, 1888-1914 (chmn., 1896-1902) mem. Dem. State Exec. Com., S.C., since 1901; mayor of Cheraw, 1895, 96; mem. S.C. Ho. of Rep., 1896-1903 (speaker of House last 2 yrs.) and 1910-14; mem. 65th to 72d Congresses (1917-33), 5th S.C. Dist.; mem. Federal Home Loan Bank Bd., 1933-38, chmn., Mar. 6-Nov. 12, 1933. Presbyterian. Home: Cheraw, S.C. Address: 1629 Columbia Road, N.W., Washington, D.C. Died Feb. 12, 1942.

STEWARD, LeRoy T. (stū'ērd); b. Dayton, O., Mar. 24, 1860; s. Thomas L. and Frances (Garber) S.; ed. pub. schs.; m. Florence Donovan, Apr. 14, 1895 (died Nov. 1921); m. 2d, Helen Gertrude Scott, Apr. 13, 1935. Supt. Chicago Post Office and general supt. city mail delivery, 1897-1909; gen. supt. police, Chicago, 1909-11; returned to former position in post office (retired 1925). Served in Ohio Nat. Guard, 1877-79, and as an officer 1st and 2d regts. Ill. Nat. Guard, advancing to rank of col.; brigadier general Ill. Reserve, 1917-20. Organized 1st ship's crew, Ill. Naval Militia, and 1st squadron of cav., Ill. Nat. Guard; served on Cook County Mil. Affairs Com. during war period, and was active in the organization of reserve troops, etc. Chmn. com. on pub. information, Chicago Expn., 1893; active in securing filling of "lake front," at Chicago, also in securing park lagoons and street renumbering. Scout commr. Boy Scouts of America, Chicago, Ill., 1918-27, now Chief Scout, Chicago; has been actively identified for many years with public welfare, organization and boys' work. Mem. Ohio Soc. (pres. 1919-20). Republican. Presbyterian. Mason (32°, Shriner). Clubs: Hamilton, Union League. Home: Watervliet, Mich. (R.F.D. No. 1). Died Apr. 26, 1944.

STEWART, Alpheus Lloyd (stū'ērt), supt. The Tamalpais School; b. Stockton, Calif., Nov. 20, 1890; s. James Alpheus and Sarah (Higgins) S.; A.B., U. of Calif., 1915; grad. study same, 1916-17; m. Dorris Meacham, Nov. 2, 1931; children—Sally, James, Sandra, Susan. Served in U.S. Army, Sept. 1917-June 1919; overseas with 91st Div., July 1918-May 1919. Supt. and owner San Rafael Mil. Acad., 1925-45; now supt. Tamalpais Sch. (San Rafael). Pres. Alpine Mining Co. Mem. Am. Legion, Phi Gamma Delta, Theta Chi (high sch. fraternity). Clubs: Marin Yacht (San Rafael); Meadow. Mason, Elk. Rotarian. Home: San Rafael, Calif. Died Nov. 19, 1948.

STEWART, Cecil Parker, insurance; b. Lachine, Quebec, Can., Sept. 9, 1881; s. Henry and Ann (Adams-Hamm) S.; ed. private schs.; m. Reine Marie Tracy, Dec. 8, 1908 (divorced 1924); children—Jacqueline (Mrs. Giovanni Cardelli), James; m. 2d, Dorothy Kimball Wallace, September 24, 1932. In ins. business with father, 1898-1904; mem. Henry Stewart & Son, 1904-11; mem. Frank B. Hall & Co. since 1911, pres. since 1916, also dir.; pres. and dir. Am. Merchant Marine Steamship Corp., C. P. Stewart & Co., Inc.; chmn. and dir. C. P. Stewart & Co., Ltd. (London); pres. of Securities Corp. General; chmn. U.S. Marine and Fgn. Agencies, Ltd., Warren Brothers Company; director All America Corporation, American Cable & Radio Corporation, Atlantic Coast Fisheries Co., Commercial Mackay Corp., Electric Ferries, Inc., Pell, Ltd., Smith, Kirkpatrick & Co., Inc., U.S. Life Insurance Co., Gen. Pub. Service Corp., Internat. Utilities Corp., La Metropolitana Compania Nacional de Seguros, S.A., Havana, Cuba, Louisville Fire & Marine Ins. Co., R.I. Ins. Co., South Am. Trading Corp., Southern Transportation Co., Dominion Gas & Electric Company, General Water, Gas, and Electric Company, Fidel. Assn. N.Y. Member committee for holders of Central States Electric Corp. Debentures. Mayor of the Incorporated Village of Centre Island, L.I.; dir. Downtown Hosp. (New York). Mem. Assn. Average Adjusters of U.S.; mem. Chamber of Commerce of the State of New York, Maritime Assn. of the Port of New York, New York Board of Trade, Inc. Mem. Pilgrims of the U.S., Soc. of the Cincinnati, S.A.R. Clubs: India House, Recess, N.Y. Athletic, Metropolitan, St. Nicholas, New York Yacht, Seawanhaka Corinthian Yacht (New York); Cedar Creek (Locust Valley, N.Y.); Nassau Country (Glen Cove, L.I.); Bohemian (San Francisco); Cat Cay (Bahamas); American (London); Royal Belgian Yacht (Antwerp). Home: (summer) Centre Island, L.I., N.Y.; (winter) 770 Park Av., New York. Office: 67 Wall St., New York. Died May 29, 1945; buried in Adams family plot (Samuel Adams family), Portsmouth, N.H.

STEWART, Colin C(ampbell), prof. physiology; b. Owen Sound, Ont., Can., Aug. 15, 1873; s. Rev. Colin Campbell and Elizabeth (McOuat) S.; A.B., U. of Toronto, 1894; scholarship in physiology, Clark U., 1894-95, fellow in physiology, 1895-97; Ph.D., 1897; m. Zoe E. Smiley, July 26, 1898; children—Dorothy Robson, Colin Campbell III. Summer sch. instr., Clark U., 1895, 97; asst. in physiology, Harvard Med. Sch., 1897-98; tutor in physiology, Coll. Phys. and Surgeons (Columbia), 1898-1900; demonstrator, U. of Pa., 1900-03, asst. prof. physiology, 1903-04, instr. summer sch., 1902; asso. prof. physiology, Dartmouth Med. Sch., 1904-07, prof. since 1907, also sec., 1913-24, acting dean, 1925-27; Brown prof. physiology, Dartmouth Coll., since 1908. Fellow A.A.A.S.; mem. Am. Physiol. Soc., A.M.A., N.H. Med. Soc. (hon.), N.H. Surg. Club (hon.), N.H. Acad. Science, Am. Museum of Natural History, Mt. Washington Observatory, Am. Soc. of Zoölogists, Am. Forestry Assn., Phi Alpha Sigma, Sigma Xi, Gamma Alpha. Home: Hanover, N.H. Died Jan. 22, 1944.

STEWART, J. D., dir. Citizens Union Nat. Bank, Louisville, Ky., Fidelity & Columbia Trust Co., Louisville Pub. Warehouse Co.; v.p. and dir. Federal Chem. Co. Home: Douglass Blvd. and Cherokee Park, Louisville, Ky.* Died July 3, 1943.

STEWART, James Christian, engring. contractor; b. Kingston, Ont., Can., Sept. 16, 1865; s. James and Martha (Lyall) S.; brought to U.S. in childhood; ed. pub. and high schs.; student prep. sch. of Washington U., St. Louis; m. Amelia Cora Breden, Sept. 27, 1885 (died Oct. 3, 1934); children—Alexandra (Mrs. William Woods Plankington), Fanniebelle (Mrs. C. P. Ellis, Jr.), James Breden (dec.). Began in employ of Todd & Stanley, St. Louis, 1885; entered contracting business as v.p. with father and brother, as James Stewart & Co., Inc., 1892-1920, pres. with hdqrs. in N.Y. City, since 1920; rebuilt Galveston (Tex.) waterfront after storm of 1899; built British Westinghouse Works at Manchester, Savoy Hotel in London; reconstructed Mersey Tunnel, Liverpool, and a large part of the London underground ry. systems; designed first woven cable submarine mats at mouths of Thames and Humber rivers; built N.Y. Central office bldg., 60 Wall Tower (3d tallest bldg. in world), Interstate Commerce and Dept. of Labor bldgs., Washington, D.C., State Capitol bldgs. at Salt Lake, Utah; also (during World War) a shipyard and many govt. bldgs. in the U.S. and France; dredged 65 miles of N.Y. Barge Canal; etc. Chairman of board James Stewart & Co. of N.J., James Stewart & Co., Inc., of N.Y., Canadian Stewart Co., Ltd.; dir. Stewart Realty Co., Stewart Land Co. of Pittsburgh, Continental Baking Corp. Mem. The Pilgrims. Decorated Grand Comdr. Officers of the Crown (Italy), 1925. Democrat. Presbyn. Clubs: N.Y. Yacht, N.Y. Athletic, Appawamis Country. Home: 79 E. 79th St. Office: 200 Park Av., New York, N.Y. Died Jan. 17, 1942.

STEWART, Jane Agnes, editor, author; b. Boston, Mass.; d. Alexander Paton and Mary Davidson (Denyven) Stewart; ed. pub. and pvt. schs., Boston, Glasgow, Scotland, and Toledo, O. Editor The Oak and Ivy Leaf, Chicago, 1891-96; asso. editor The Union Signal, Chicago, 1892-97; editorial writer Boston Beacon, 1898-1902, Boston Transcript, since 1898; press corr. in Europe, 1895, 1900; editor Am. Sunday Sch. Union since 1909. Chmn. nat. press com. Nat. Congress of Mothers, 1902-10; chmn. nat. press com. Am. School Peace League since 1908; treas. Pa. State Woman's Press Assn., 1906-08; dir. Pa. Arbitration and Peace Soc., 1908-21; mem. Am. Acad. Polit. and Social Science, Pa. Soc. New Eng. Women, Woman's Ednl. Club, Toledo Woman's Club; gen. sec. Central High Alumni Assn. since 1925. Author: The Frances Willard Book, 1906; The Christmas Book, 1908; Perpetual Calendar, 1920; Suffrage Women, 1920; Temperance Women, 1920; I Have Recalled (autobiography), 1938; The Girl from Ohio (autobiography), 1938; The Frances Willard Birthday Book, 1939; At the Homes of Great Women, 1941. Contbr. to newspapers and periodicals. Address: 1603 22d St., Toledo, O. Died Feb. 2, 1944.

STEWART, Joseph William Alexander, seminary dean; b. Waterloo, Ont., Can., Jan. 17, 1852; s. Alexander and Esther Stratton (Wilson) S.; B.A., U. of Toronto, 1876 (gold medalist in metaphysics and ethics); grad. Toronto Bapt. Coll., 1879; D.D., U. of Rochester, 1893; LL.D., McMaster U., 1907; m. Mary McGinn, July 13, 1875. Ordained Bapt. ministry, 1876; pastor St. Catharines, Ont., 1877-81, Hamilton, Ont., 1881-87, First Ch., Rochester, N.Y., 1887-1903; dean and prof. Rochester Theol. Sem., since 1903. Mem. Alpha Chi. Author many printed sermons, addresses and papers. Home: 46 Prince St., Rochester, N.Y. Died June 26, 1947.

STEWART, Oscar Milton, univ. prof.; b. Neosho, Mo., Nov. 3, 1869; s. Oliver Mills and Eleanor (Bell) S.; Ph.B., DePauw Univ., 1892, D.Sc., 1928; Ph.D., Cornell Univ., 1897; m. M. Estelle Williams, June 23, 1899 (dec.); 1 son, Lawrence Williams (dec.). Prof. physics and chemistry, Baker U., 1892-94; fellow, 1895-96, asst. in physics, 1896-98, instr. physics, 1898-1901, Cornell Univ.; asst. prof., U. of Missouri, 1901-05, prof., 1905-40, emeritus prof. physics since 1940. Fellow A.A.A.S., Am. Physical Soc.; mem. Soc. Promotion Engring. Edn., Am. Assn. Physics Teachers, Am. Assn. Univ. Prof., Phi Kappa Psi, Phi Beta Kappa, Sigma Xi, Tau Beta Pi. Author of numerous research articles in Physical Rev. since 1897, also a text book of coll. physics and joint author of a textbook of physics for secondary schs. Home: 211 Westmount Av., Columbia, Mo.* Died May 17, 1944.

STEWART, Robert Wright, corp. executive, lawyer; b. Cedar Rapids, Ia., Mar. 11, 1866; s. William and Eliza Mills (Lucore) S.; B.S., Coe Coll., Ia., 1886; LL.B., Yale, 1888; LL.D., Blackburn Coll., 1922, Coe Coll., 1927; m. Maude Bradley Elliott, July 14, 1906; children—Donald William, John Elliott; (by first marriage) Robert Giffen, James Wright. State's atty., Hughes County, S.D., 1893-95; Supreme Court reporter, 1893-98; mem. S.D. Senate, 1899-1903; gen. atty., 1907-15, general counsel, May 1, 1915-Oct. 1918, and chmn. bd. dirs. Standard Oil Co. of Ind., Chicago, 1918-29; dir. Hanover Fire Ins. Co., Fulton Fire Ins. Co. (New York), National City Bank (New York), 1921-31, Continental Ill. Nat. Bank & Trust Co. (Chicago), 1918-34. Maj. 3d U.S. Vol. Cav. ("Rough Riders"), May-Oct. 1898; col. 4th Regt., S.D. Nat. Guard, 1899-1907. Member American Bar Association, Illinois Bar Association, South Dakota Bar Association. Republican. Presbyterian. Clubs: Chicago, University, Racquet, Commercial, Saddle and Cycle (Chicago); University (Washington, D.C.). Home: 181 Lake Shore Drive, Chicago, Ill. Died Feb. 24, 1947.

STEWART, Russell C., lawyer; b. Easton, Pa., Sept. 2, 1859; s. Charles and Anna E. (Chidsey) S.; A.B., Lafayette Coll., 1878, A.M., 1881; studied Columbia Law Sch.; LL.D., Muhlenberg Coll., 1917, Lafayette, 1919; m. Mattie M. Seitz, Jan. 25, 1885. Admitted to bar, 1881; dist. atty., Northampton County, Pa., 1886-89; Rep. candidate for Congress, 1900; del. Rep. Nat. Conv., 1900; judge 3d Jud. Dist. of Pa., since Dec. 31, 1906. Del. Universal Congress Lawyers and Jurists, St. Louis, 1904; v.p. Pa. State Bar Assn., 1905-06; mem. Am. Bar Assn. Clubs: Pomfret, Northampton Country. Address: Easton, Pa. Died Feb. 5, 1942.

STEWART, Thomas Milton, oculist, neurologist; b. Cincinnati, May 13, 1866; s. Henry Crossley and Irene (Roll) S.; ed. Chickering Inst., 1882-85; M.D., Pulte Med. Coll., Cincinnati, 1887; New York Ophthalmic Hosp., 1887-88, degree "Oculi at Auris Chirurgus," 1888; U. of Berlin, 1888; m. Alice Buck, Feb. 12, 1889. In practice as oculist and aurist at Cincinnati, 1889. Fellow Am. Coll. Surgeons; mem. A.M.A., Am. Acad. Ophthalmology and Otolaryngology, Am. Indian Assn. Clubs: Cincinnati Literary; Authors' (London). Author: Ancient Symbolic Teachings; Temple Symbolism of Egypt; Temple Teachings of India; The Symbolism of the Gods of the Egyptians; The Inner Meaning of Indian Myths, etc. Lecturer on comparative mythology. Home: 814 Blair Av., Avondale, Cincinnati. Office: Union Central Bldg., Cincinnati, O. Died Dec. 10, 1945.

STEWART, William Kilborne, coll. prof.; b. Hamilton, Ont., Can., Jan. 2, 1875; s. William Boyd and Augusta (Kilborne) S.; A.B., U. of Toronto, 1897; A.M., Harvard, 1898; studied at univs. of Leipzig, Berlin and Paris; m. Ethel Scott, June 18, 1903. Asst. in German, Harvard, 1898-99; instr. German, 1899-1907, asst. prof., 1907-14, prof. comparative lit. since 1914, Dartmouth Coll. Mem. Modern Lang. Assn. America, Soc. Advancement of Scandinavian Studies, Delta Upsilon, Phi Beta Kappa. Club: Graduate. Home: Hanover, N.H. Died May 6, 1944.

STEYNE, Alan Nathaniel (stīn), foreign service officer; b. New York City, Nov. 19, 1898; s. Abram and Nina (Herzog) S.; student Phillips Andover; Ph.B., Yale, 1921; unmarried. Advertising and asst. sales mgr., 1922-27; metal export business, China, 1928-29; vice consul, Montreal, Can., 1930-31; vice consul, Hamburg, 1931-35; consul, Hamburg, 1935-36. Dept. of State, Div. Trade Agreements, 1936-37; 2d sec. (consul), Am. embassy, London, 1937-43 1st. sec., 1943. Assigned to Dept. of State, Sept. 1943. Special asst. to Dir. Gen. UNRRA, first session of the United Nations Relief and Rehabilitation Administrn, 1943; Division of Commercial Policy, Dept. of State, Sept. 1943-Mar. 1944; sec. exec. com. on Economic Fgn. Policy, Mar.-Apr. 1944. Asst. chief of planning staff, Office of Foreign Service, May-Dec. 1944; special asst. to dir., Office of Foreign Service, Jan.-Mar. 1945; exec. asst. to dir. Office of Foreign Service, Apr. 1945. Am. mem. Inter-Allied Com. on Postwar Requirements, 1941-43; Am. del. Internat. Sugar Council, 1941, Consumers Panel, Internat. Tin Com., 1941; chmn. Joint Survey Group for Improvement Fgn. Service Reporting, 1944-45. Served as corpl., 16th Field Arty., 4th Div., 2d lt. aerial observer, 90th Aero Squadron, 3d Army Corps, A.E.F., 1918-19, World War I. Clubs: Metropolitan, Cosmos (Washington); Yale (New York); Reform, St. James, Bath (London); Guana Island (Virgin Islands, B.W.I.). Address: Metropolitan Club, Washington, D.C. Died May 22, 1946.

STIBITZ, George (stib'its), clergyman, educator; b. Schuylkill County, Pa., Mar. 10, 1856; s. John and Catherine (Herrmann) S.; A.B., Ursinus Coll., Collegeville, Pa., 1881, A.M., 1887, D.D., 1905; student Ursinus Sch. Theology, 1883; Ph.D., Yale, 1887; m. Alice R. Schlessman, Mar. 1884 (died 1901); m. 2d, Mildred A. Murphy, Mar. 1903; children—George Robert, Mildred Theresa, Edward Earle, Eleanor. Ordained ministry Ref. Ch. in U.S., 1883; pastor Shenandoah, Pa., 1883-85, Leighton, Pa., 1885-87; prof. Latin and O.T. studies, Ursinus Coll., 1889-96; pastor Presbyn. Ch., Glenolden, Pa., 1896-98, Zion Ref. Ch., York, Pa., 1898-1907; prof. O.T. lang., lit. and theology, Central Theol. Sem. of Ref. Ch., 1907-26, and of N.T. lang., lit. and theology, 1926-34, retired. Author: Analysis of the Books of the Bible, 1892; Biblical Catechism, 1905; Historic-Literary Outlines of the Old Testament, 1914; The Message of Isaiah, 1914; Messianic Prophecy, 1923. Home: 37 Seminary Av., Dayton, O. Died Mar. 11, 1944.

STIDGER, William Leroy (stid'jēr), clergyman; b. Moundsville, W.Va., Mar. 16, 1885; s. Leroy Lester and Etta B. (Robinson) S.; student Allegheny Coll.

3 yrs.; Ph. B., Brown, 1912; theology, Boston U., 1 yr.; D.D. Allegheny Coll., Meadville, Pa., 1923; Litt.D., Kansas Wesleyan Univ., 1928; D.H.L., Salem College, 1935; m. Iva Berkey, June 7, 1910; 1 dau., Mrs. Elisabeth Robinson Hyland. Ordained ministry, M.E. Church, 1914; pastor Calvary M.E. Ch., San Francisco, 1913-16, First Ch., San José, 1916-19; publicity trip through Far East for Methodist Centenary, 1919-20; pastor St. Mark's Ch., Detroit, Sept. 1920-25, Linwood Blvd. Ch., Kansas City, Mo., 1925-29; head of dept. preaching, Boston U. School of Theology; preacher at Church of All Nations, Boston, Mass. Served in France as truck driver for Y.M.C.A., 1918. Member Phi Delta Theta, Theta Phi, Delta Sigma Rho, Pi Gamma Mu. Mason (32°), Odd Fellow. Democrat. Clubs: Puddingstone, University (Boston). Author: Giant Hours with Poet Preachers, 1918; Soldier Silhouettes, 1919; Star Dust from the Dugouts, 1919; Outdoor Men and Minds, 1920; Standing Room Only, 1921; Flash Lights of the Seven Seas, 1921; Flames of Faith, 1922; There Are Sermons in Books, 1922; Henry Ford—The Man and His Motives, 1923; The Epic of Earth, 1923; That God's House May Be Filled, 1923; The Symphonic Sermon, 1923; Finding God in Books, 1924; A Book of Sunsets, 1925; Pulpit Prayers and Paragraphs, 1926; Building Up the Mid-Week Service, 1926; Building Sermons with Symphonic Themes, 1926; God Is at the Organ, 1927; The High Faith of Fiction and Drama, 1927; Personal Power, 1928; Preaching Out of the Overflow, 1929; Planning Your Preaching, 1932; Edwin Markham—a Biography, 1932; I Saw God Wash the World (poems), 1934. Editor: If I Had Only One Sermon to Preach on Immortality, 1929; The Pew Preachers, 1930; Men of the Great Redemption, 1931; Those Amazing Roosevelts, 1938; How to Get the Most Out of Life, 1939. Contbr. to Best Sermons of 1925, If I Had Only One Sermon to Preach, Great Southern Preaching, Contemporary Preaching, and others; The Human Side of Greatness, 1940; There Are Sermons in Stories, 1941; Keeping the Soul of the World Alive, 1943; Greatness Passing By, 1943; (poems) Rainbow Born Is Beauty, 1941; More Sermons in Stories, 1944; Sermon Nuggets in Stories, 1945. Member editorial staff and conductor of the column, "Conrad the Cobbler," The Christian Herald. Broadcasts Great American personalities, Station WHDH, Boston, Mass.; Church of the Air, Columbia Network; Happy Days, Columbia Network for Democratic National Committee; Are You Getting the Most Out of Life, Yankee Network; on national broadcast, NBC, 1939-41; broadcast for Chicago Daily News, WENR, broadcasts Boston University Vespers program, Book Talks, sta. WHDH, Blue network for N.E.; also Church of the Wildwood, NBC, station WJZ. Thanks to America (1943-44), Broadcast Yankee Network. Winner of Radio Certificate of Merit, also first honors, for "producing a radio program of excellence and real public service" from Nat. Fedn. of Press Women, Inc. Introduced first course in radio preaching, Boston U. Sch. of Theology, 1938. Conducts syndicated newspaper column Getting the Most Out of Life. Conducts Daily Meditations, Christian Herald; author: Immortals of the Christian Ministry, 1947. Pres. Allegheny Coll. Boston Alumni Assn. Lecturer under Coll. Ins. Management, Rochester, N.Y. Broadcast 150 stations with Milton Cross on Crusade for Christ, 1947. Home: 19 Oakwood Terrace, Newton Center, Mass. Office: 72 Mt. Vernon St., Boston, Mass. Died Aug. 7, 1949.

STIEGLITZ, Alfred (stēg'lĭts), photographer, editor; b. Hoboken, N.J., Jan. 1, 1864; s. Edward and Hedwig (Werner) S.; ed. private and pub. schs. and City Coll., New York, 1879-81; studied mech. engring., 1881-84, photo-chemistry and photography, 1884-88, Berlin Polytechnic; chemistry, U. of Berlin, 1889-90; m. Emmeline Obermeyer, Nov. 16, 1893; 1 dau., Katherine Stearns; m. 2d, Georgia O'Keeffe, Dec. 11, 1924. Returned to New York, 1890; in photo-engraving business 3 yrs., experimenting in 3-color work, etc.; retired in 1895; editor Am. Amateur Photographer, 1892-96; founded, 1897, mgr. and editor, 1897-1903, Camera Notes (photog. jour.); editor and pub. Camera Work (photog. quarterly) since Jan. 1, 1903. Hon. fellow Royal Photog. Soc., London, Vienna Camera Club (Austria); hon. mem. L'Effort (Brussels, Belgium), Photog. Club (Vienna, Austria), Photog. Soc., Hamburg, Germany, Am. Photog. Soc., Phila. Photog. Soc., Chicago Soc.; hon. v.p. Soc. of American Painters and Sculptors; dir. and founder Photo-Secession (nat. orgn. of pictorial photographers); founder of Little Galleries of the Photo-Secession (eventually known as "291"); famed for introducing modern Am. and European Art, 1905-17; founder, 1925, dir. Intimate Gallery; founder, 1929, Am. Place. With his series of "Equivalents" has demonstrated photography as an objectified philosophy. Has won over 150 medals for photography, Paris, London, Vienna, Berlin, Calcutta, New York, etc.; received, as dir. of the Photo-Secession, at Turin International Art Exhibition, the King of Italy's special prize for collection of Am. work exhibited. Has written photographic and scientific articles to tech. and art jours. the world over. Co-editor of "291" (monthly, devoted to development of art, literature and music). Awarded Progress medal, 1924, of Royal Photographic Soc. of London. Home: Lake George, N.Y. Died July 13, 1946.

STIFLER, James Madison, clergyman; b. Alton, Ill., Feb. 10, 1875; s. James Madison and Jennie Mary (Carr) S.; B.A., U. of Pa., 1896; grad. Crozer Theol. Sem., 1899; D.D., Denison, 1913, Brown Univ., 1925; m. Lucy H. Burnley, Dec. 6, 1900 (dec.); children—James Madison, Francis McIlhenny; m. 2d, Mary Cloyd Burnley, July 28, 1909; children—Lucy, Cloyd. Ordained Bapt. ministry, 1899; pastor First Ch., Roselle, N.J., 1899-1909, First Ch., Evanston, Ill., 1909-31, Roser Memorial Ch., Anna Maria, Fla., since 1942; mem. Bd. Edn. Northern Bapt. Conv., 1912-35; camp dir. religious work Y.M.C.A., Camp Dodge, Ia., 1917-18. Pres. Central Assn. Evanston Charities, 1925-31; mem. bd. trustees U. of Chicago, chairman development com., 1931-34, secretary of the U., 1934-40; retired. Mem. Psi Upsilon, Phi Beta Kappa. Republican. Clubs: University, Quadrangle, Westmoreland Country. Author: The Fighting Saint, 1909; The Christ of Christianity, 1915; The Religion of Benjamin Franklin, 1925. Editor: "My Dear Girl," Correspondence of Benjamin Franklin with Polly Stevenson, Catherine and Georgiana Shipley, 1927. Home: 315 16th St., Bradenton, Fla. Died April 6, 1949; buried Upland, Pa.

STILLMAN, James Alexander, banker; b. N.Y. City; s. James and Elizabeth (Rumrill) S.; A.B., Harvard, 1896; m. Anne U. Potter. Pres. Nat. City Bank; chmn. bd. Nat. City Co.; v.p. Fifth Av. Safe Deposit Co.; dir. Am. Alliance Ins. Co., Am. Internat. Corp., C.&N.W. Ry. Co., D.,L.&W. Coal Co., Great Am. Ins. Co., Mont. Farms Corp., Queen Ins. Co. America, Second Nat. Bank, etc. Clubs: Knickerbocker, University, Brook, Automobile, Racquet and Tennis, Down Town, Golf Links, Garden City Golf, Sleepy Hollow Country, New York Yacht (New York); Tennis and Racquet (Boston). Office: 55 Wall St., New York. Died Jan. 12, 1944.

STILLMAN, Paul Roscoe, dentist; b. Greenwich, N.Y., June 4, 1871; s. Stephen L. and Ruth (McGown) S.; D.D.S., Baltimore Coll. Dental Surgery, 1899; m. Irene Simpson, Dec. 27, 1897; children—Ruth Evelyn (Mrs. Richard Trudeau Salmon), Irene, Stephen L., Paul R.; m. 2d, Mrs. Josephine Smith Maloney, 1929. Began practice at Greenwich, 1899; instr. in advanced dentistry, Columbia, 1916-20; clin. prof. periodontia, New York U., since 1924; postgrad. lecturer on periodontia, Harvard, 1928. Mem. Med. Exemption Bd., New York, World War; capt. 1st Field Hosp., N.Y. Nat. Guard; 1st lt. N.Y. Nat. Guard. Mem. advisory bd. N.Y. City Dept. of Health. Fellow Am. Coll. Dentists, N.Y. Acad. Dentisty; Am. Acad. Periodontia (ex-pres.); mem. Am. Dental Assn. (pres. periodontia sect., 1920), First Dist. Dental Soc. N.Y. City (v.p.), Internat. Assn. Dental Research, A.A.A.S., Psi Omega, Omicron Kappa Epsilon; official arbitrator, Arbitration Soc. America; pres. Section Periodontia, 7th Internat. Dental Congress, Phila. Democrat. Catholic. Author: (with John Oppie McCall) Textbook of Clinical Periodontia, 1923, 2d edit., 1936; also article on Periodontia in Ency. Britannica, 1928. Asso. editor Jour. of Am. Coll. Dentists. Home: Longwood, Fla. Died Dec. 15, 1945.

STILWELL, Joseph W., army officer; b. Florida, Mar. 19, 1883; B.S., U.S. Mil. Acad., 1904; grad. Advance Course, Inf. Sch., 1924, Command and Gen. Staff Sch., 1926; married; 3 daus., 2 sons. Comd. 2d lt., June 15, 1904; promoted through grades to maj. gen., Oct. 1, 1940; lt. gen., Feb. 1942, gen., Aug. 1, 1944; with 12th Inf., P.I., 1904-06 and 1911-12; instr. U.S. Mil. Acad., 1906-10, 1913-17; with A.E.F. General Hdqrs. and as asst. chief of staff, 4th Corps to May 1919; studied Chinese language, U. of Calif., 1 year, and in Peking, China, 3 years, 1920-23; served in Tientsin, China, 1926-29; instr. Inf. Sch., Fort Benning, 1929-33; mil. attache, Peiping, China, 1935-39; com. 3d Inf. Brigade, Fort Sam Houston, 1939, 7th Div., Fort Ord, Calif., 1940-41, 3d Army Corps, Presidio of Monterey, Calif., 1941-42; apptd. comdr. 5th and 6th Chinese Armies in Burma by Chiang Kai-Shek, Mar. 1942; comdg. gen. U.S. Forces in China-Burma-India, 1942-44; relieved, Nov. 1944; apptd. comdr. U.S. ground forces, Jan. 1945. Apptd. comdr. 10th army, Pacific Theater, June, 1945. Awarded D.S.C.; D.S.M. with Oak Leaf Cluster; Legion of Merit; Philippine Campaign; Victory Medal, 2 Stars; China Service Ribbon, Navy Decoration; American Defense Service; Asiatic-Pacific, 3 stars; French Chevalier de Legion d'Honneur; La Solidaridad (2nd Class), Panama. Home Carmel, Calif. Died Oct. 12, 1946.

STIMSON, Frederic Jesup ("J. S. of Dale"), lawyer, author; b. Dedham, Mass., July 20, 1855; s. Edward and Sarah Tufts (Richardson) S.; A.B., Harvard, 1876, LL.B., 1878, LL.D., 1922; m. Elizabeth Bradlee Abbot, June 2, 1881; m. 2d, Mabel Ashhurst, Nov. 12, 1902. Asst. atty.-gen., Mass., 1884-85; gen. counsel U.S. Industrial Commn., 1898-1902, Mass. Commn. on Corp. Laws, 1902-03; Dem. candidate for Congress, 12th Mass. Dist., 1902; prof. comparative legislation, Harvard, 1903-14. Mass. commr. for uniformity of legislation. Ambassador extraordinary and plenipotentiary to Argentine Republic, 1914-21; special ambassador to Brazil, 1919. Chmn. Democratic Mass. State Conv., 1904, 08; del. and alternate-at-large, nat. convs. Mem. Nat. Inst. Arts and Letters, Mass. Hist. Soc.; fellow Am. Acad. Arts and Sciences; mem. German and French socs. of Comparative Legislation, Academia Americana de Historia. Clubs: Somerset, Tavern (Boston), Harvard (New York). Besides writing law books he has written several novels (the earlier ones under the pen-name "J. S. of Dale"), essays, etc. Author: Rollo's Journey to Cambridge, 1879; Guerndale, 1882; The Crime of Henry Vane, 1884; American Statute Law (2 volumes), 1886; The Sentimental Calendar, 1886; First Harvests, 1887; Stimson's Law Glossary, 1890; In the Three Zones, 1892; Government by Injunction; Labor in Its Relation to Law, 1894; Mrs. Knollys and Other Stories, 1894; Handbook to the Labor Law of the U.S., 1895; Uniform State Legislation; Pirate Gold, 1896; King Noanett, 1896; Jethro Bacon of Sandwich, 1901; In Cure of Her Soul, 1906; The American Constitution (Lowell Inst. lectures), 1906; The Law of the Constitutions, State and Federal, 1907; Popular Law-making, 1910; The Light of Provence (poem-play); My Story (an imagined autobiography of Benedict Arnold), 1917; Ariel (Rodó), with essay, 1922; American Constitution as It Protects Private Rights, 1923; The Western Way—American Democracy, 1929; My United States, 1931; The New Deal Under the Constitution, 1936; Critique of Pure Science, 1938. Home: Dedham, Mass. Address: State Street Trust Co., Boston, Mass. Died Nov. 19, 1943.

STIMSON, Julia Catherine, nurse; b. Worcester, Mass., May 26, 1881; d. Henry A. (D.D.) and Alice Wheaton (Bartlett) Stimson; prep. edn., Brearley Sch., N.Y. City; A.B., Vassar Coll., 1901; A.M., Washington U., 1917; hon. Sc.D., Mt. Holyoke Coll., S. Hadley, Mass., 1921; unmarried. Grad. as nurse, New York Hosp., 1908; supt. nurses, Harlem Hosp., N.Y. City, 1908-10; adminstr. of hosp. social service, Washington U., 1911-12; dir. Sch. of Nursing, St. Louis, 1913-17; chief nurse Base Hosp. No. 21, A.E.F., 1917-18; dir. nursing service, A.E.F., 1918-19; supt. Army Nurse Corps, U.S. Army, since 1919; rank of maj. since Nat. Defense Act, June 4, 1920. Retired from active service, May 30, 1937; recalled to active duty in Army Nurse Corps, 1943-44; advanced to col. U.S. Army Nurse Corps, ret., June 1948. Member Am. Nurses Assn. (pres. 1938-44). Decorations: D.S.M. (U.S.); Royal Red Cross, 1st Class (Great Britain); Medaille de la Reconnaissance (France); Florence Nightingale medal, Internat. Red Cross Com. Democrat. Congregationalist. Club: Army-Navy Country (Washington, D.C.). Author: Nurses' Handbook of Drugs and Solutions, 1910; Finding Themselves (war letters), 1918. Home: Horse-chestnut Road, Briarcliff Manor, N.Y.; (summer) Rockland, Me. Died Sept. 30, 1948.

STINCHFIELD, Frederick Harold, lawyer; b. Danforth, Me., May 8, 1881; s. Amaziah and Rose Brown (Foss) S.; A.B., Bates Coll., 1900, LL.D., 1937; LL.B., Harvard, 1905; LL.D., Bowdoin Coll., 1937, LL.D., American U., 1938; m. Elizabeth Shrader, Oct. 31, 1928. Admitted to N.Y. bar, 1906, and began practice at N.Y. City; moved to Minneapolis, 1908; mem. Jamison, Stinchfield & Mackall, 1918-29, Stinchfield, Mackall, Crounse, McNally & Moore, 1929-40, Stinchfield, Mackall, Crounse & Moore since 1940; dir. and counsel Twin City Federal Savings & Loan Assn.; director Public Markets Inc., United Fur Ranches. Major, judge advocate general's dept., U.S. Army, 1918. Mem. Draft Board, Minneapolis, World War I. Member American Bar Association, president 1936-37), Minn. State Bar Assn. (ex-pres.), Hennepin County Bar Assn. (ex-pres.), Am. Law Institute (charter member), Nat. Econ. League, Am. Liberty League (advisory council), Am. Judicature Soc. Republican. Baptist. Mason (Shriner). Clubs: Minneapolis, Minikahda (ex-pres.), Minneapolis Athletic. Home: 1819 Mt. Curve Av. Office: 1100 First Nat. Soo Line Bldg., Minneapolis, Minn. Died Jan.15, 1950; buried Lakewood Cemetery, Minneapolis

STIRLING, Yates, Jr., naval officer, author; b. Vallejo, Calif., Apr. 30, 1872; s. Rear Admiral Yates and Ellen Salisbury (Haley) S.; grad. U.S. Naval Acad., 1892; Naval War Coll., 1912; m. Adelaide Egbert, Dec. 12, 1903; children—Yates, Ellen E., Adelaide Y., Harry E., Kathrin G. Midshipman, 1892-94; promoted through grades to capt., Aug. 1917. Participated in expedition for recovery of Spanish contact mines in Guantanamo Harbor, 1898; served in Philippines during insurrection there, comdg. gunboat Paragua; made world's cruise in battleship Connecticut, 1907-08; comd. destroyer Paulding, 1910-11; staff, Naval War Coll., 1912-13, exec. officer battleship Rhode Island, 1913-14; comd. submarine flotilla, Atlantic fleet, 1913; comd. monitor Ozark, 1914, cruiser Columbia, 1918, and submarine flotilla and base at New London, Conn., 1916; at outbreak of war fitted out and comd. navy transport President Lincoln, 1917; comd. auxiliary cruiser Von Steuben (ex-German Crown Prince Wilhelm), 1917-18; chief of staff Naval Dist., New York, 1918-19; comd. battleship Connecticut, 1919; duty Navy Yard, Phila., 1920. Comdg. battleship New Mexico, 1922-24; at Navy Yard, Washington, D.C., 1925; promoted to rear admiral 1926; apptd. chief of staff, U.S. Fleet, 1927; then comdr. Yangtze Patrol, China; later comdt. 14th Naval Dist., hdqrs. Pearl Harbor, T.H.; comdt. 3d Naval Dist., New York; retired, Apr. 30, 1936. Service Medals: Spanish War, Santiago Campaign; Philippine Insurrection; Mexico, 1914; World War, Legion of Honor (France), Navy Cross; Comdr. Order of Bolivar (Venezuela). Presbyn. Clubs: Army and Navy (Washington); New York Yacht. Author: U.S. Midshipman Series (5 vols.); Fundamentals of Naval Service; Sea Duty; How to Be a Naval Officer; Why Seapower Will Win the War. Address: 375 Park Av., New York, N.Y.* Died Jan. 27, 1948.

STITT, Edward Rhodes, rear adm. med. Corps, U.S. Navy; b. Charlotte, N.C., July 22, 1867; s. William Edward and Mary (Rhodes) S.; A.B., U. of S.C., 1885; M.D., U. of Pa., 1889; studied London Sch. of Tropical Medicine, 1905; LL.D., Univ. of S. Carolina, 1917, U. of Mich., 1921; Sc.D., Jefferson Med. Coll., 1920; Ph.M., Phila. Coll. of Pharmacy and Science, 1921; Sc.D., U. of Pa., 1924; m. Emma Woodruff Scott, July 19, 1892; children—Edward Wynkoop, Mary Raguet, Emma Scott; m. 2d, Laura Armistead Carter, June 22, 1935; m. 3d, Helen Bennett Newton, May 3, 1937. Apptd. asst. surgeon U.S. Navy, Mar. 27, 1889; passed asst. surgeon, Mar.

27, 1892; surgeon, June 7, 1900; med. dir. with rank of rear adm., Oct. 15, 1917. Has specialized in tropical diseases; teacher in U.S. Naval Med. Sch. and in service in Philippines; prof. tropical medicine, Georgetown U., and George Washington U.; lecturer on tropical medicine, Jefferson Med. Coll., Phila.; comdg. officer U.S. Naval Med. Sch., 1916-20; apptd. surgeon general, Nov. 30, 1920, re-appointed Nov. 30, 1924, retired Aug. 1, 1931. Mem. Nat. Bd. of Medical Examiners, 1915-29, pres., 1926-28. Consultant on tropical medicine to Sec. of War since 1941. Hon. Fellow Am. Coll. Surg.; mem. Am. Med. Assn., Assn. of American Physicians, American Coll. Physicians, Southern Med. Assn., Am. Soc. Tropical Medicine (pres., 1912), American Assn. Military Surgeons (pres. 1925-26), Royal Soc. Medicine, Sigma Alpha Epsilon, Phi Beta Kappa, Sigma Xi. Episcopalian. Clubs: Army and Navy, Cosmos (Washington); Rittenhouse, University (Phila.); New York Yacht. Author: Practical Bacteriology—Haematology and Animal Parasitology, 9th edit., 1938; Diagnostics and Treatment of Tropical Diseases, 5th edition, 1929 Home: 1625 R St. N.W., Washington 9, D.C. Died Nov. 13, 1948.

STIVEN, Frederic Benjamin (stī'vĕn), educator; b. Ionia, Mich., July 17, 1882; s. Frederick Alexander and Mary Hortense (Covert) S.; Mus.B., Oberlin (O.) Coll. Conservatory of Music, 1907; Mus. Doc., Chicago (Ill.) Mus. Coll., 1937; pupil Guilmant and Widor, Paris, 1909-11; student, Europe, 1936; m. Alice Forrest Beckwith, Jan. 1, 1908; children—Elizabeth Covert (Mrs. Leonard Grable), Capt. Robert Beckwith, Mary Jean (Mrs. Spencer Erwin Cram), Katherine Burr (Mrs. Robbins Strong), Louise (Mrs. Arthur Clifton Caps). Instr. organ, 1907-09; asst. prof. organ, Oberlin (O.) Coll., 1911-18, prof., 1918-21; prof. music and dir. Sch. of Music, U. of Ill., since 1921. Mem. Am. Guild Organists, Assn. Music Execs. in State Univs. (past pres.), Music Teachers Nat. Assn. (past pres.), Nat. Assn. of Schools of Music (past v.p.), Pi Kappa Lambda (past pres.), Phi Mu Alpha, Alpha Sigma Phi. Republican. Protestant. Clubs: University (Urbana); Cliff Dwellers (Chicago). U.S. rep. to Internat. Music Congress, Prague, Czechoslovakia, 1936. Author: The Organ Lofts of Paris, 1924. Contbr. professional articles to various periodicals. Home: 804 W. Oregon, Urbana, Ill. Died Jan. 21, 1947.

STOCK, Frederick A., musical condr.; b. Julich, Germany, Nov. 11, 1872; s. Frederick Carl and Maria S.; mus. edn. at Cologne U.; Mus.D., Northwestern U., 1915, U. of Mich., 1924, U. of Chicago, 1925, Cornell Coll., Mount Vernon, Ia., 1927; m. Elsa Muskulus, May 22, 1896; 1 dau., Vera F. (Mrs. Alfred M. Wolfe). Came to Chicago, 1895, to join the Chicago Orchestra as viola player; was asst. dir. several yrs., and after death of Theodore Thomas, 1905, became the dir. Theodore Thomas Orchestra (now Chicago Symphony Orchestra) and so continues. Naturalized citizen of U.S., 1919. Decorated Chevalier Legion of Honor (France), 1925. Compositions include a symphony in C minor, a set of variations on an original theme, a tone poem for large orchestra, concerto for violin and orchestra, 2 overtures, Festival March and Hymn to Liberty, March and Hymn to Democracy, an elegy, several smaller orchestral works, Psalmodic Rhapsody for orchestra, chorus and soloist, also a number of string quartettes and songs. Conducted several performances of Wagnerian opera for Civic Opera Co. of Chicago, 1923; gen. music dir. Century of Progress Expn., Chicago, 1933. Home: 1325 Astor St. Office: Orchestra Bldg., Chicago, Ill. Died Oct. 20, 1942.

STOCKBERGER, Warner W., botanist; b. Licking County, O., July 10, 1872; s. George Francis and Roena (Warner) S.; Ohio State U., summer courses in biology, 1900, 01; B.S., Denison Univ., 1902; Ph.D., George Washington Univ., 1907; D.Sc., Denison Univ., 1937; m. Maude N. Streeter, July 6, 1896; 1 dau., Lucile (Mrs. Earl W. Boyer). Teacher common schs., O., 3 yrs.; supt. schs., Hanover, O., 1895-97; student asst., Denison U., 1897-1900, instr. botany, 1901-03; entered service of U.S. Dept. Agr., July 1, 1903. Expert in histology, 1903-08, pharmacognocist, 1908-10, plant physiologist, 1910-13, in charge of drug, poisonous and oil plant investigations, July 1, 1913-40, personnel classification officer, 1923-25, dir. of personnel and business adminstrn., 1925-34, of personnel, 1934-38; special adviser to sec. of agriculture since 1938. Fellow A.A.A.S.; mem. Am. Pharm. Assn., Am. Soc. Pub. Adminstrn., Am. Polit. Science Assn., Civil Service Assembly of U.S. and Canada, Soc. for Personnel Adminstrn. (pres. 1937), Nat. Geneal. Society, Bot. Society Washington (pres. 1912-13), Am. Pharmaceutical Conv. (asst. sec., 1920-30), Am. Oil Chem. Society (hon.), Phi Beta Kappa, Sigma Xi, Editor Bulletin of Scientific Lab., Denison Univ., 1901-03; pres. Granville (Ohio) Bd. of Edn., 1901-03; service for Joint Congressional Commn. for Reclassification of Salaries, 1919-20. Presbyterian. Club: Cosmos. Author of various papers on medicinal plants and reports and articles in publs. of Dept. of Agr.; contbr. to scientific jours. and to The Book of Rural Life. Home: 529 Cedar St. N.W. Address: Dept. of Agr., Washington, D.C. Died May 27, 1944.

STOCKSTROM, Louis, chmn. bd. Am. Stove Co. Home: 3263 Hawthorne Blvd. Office: 825 Chouto Av., St. Louis, Mo. Died July, 1945.

STOCKTON, Edward A., Jr., army officer; b. Phila., Pa., Apr. 22, 1886; s. Edward A. and Sara E. (Mann) S.; A.B., Central High Sch., Phila., Pa., 1904; B.S., U.S. Mil. Acad., 1908; grad. Coast Arty. Sch., Fort Monroe, Va., 1927, Command and Gen. Staff Sch., 1928, Army War Coll., 1931; m. Theodosia Roberts, Mar. 25, 1908; 1 dau., Marion Roberts (Mrs. Donald C. Graves). Commd. 2d lt., Coast Atty. Corps, U.S. Army, 1908; advanced through the grades to brig. gen., 1941; later comdg. gen. Harbor Defenses of San Francisco; comdg. Antiaircraft Replacement Training Center, Fort Eustis, Va. Decorated Legion of Merit, French Croix de Guerre with gilt and silver stars. Member Sons of Am. Revolution. Club: Army & Navy (Washington, D.C.). Address: War Dept., Washington 25, D.C. Died July 13, 1948.

STOCKWELL, Frank Clifford, prof. elec. engring.; b. Warwick, Mass., Apr. 22, 1883; s. Frank Perley and Leonora Hannah (Chapin) S.; A.B., Bates Coll., Lewiston, Me., 1905; B.S., Mass. Inst. Tech., 1907; m. Sara Symonds, June 30, 1911; 1 dau., Mary Leonora. Instr. in physics, Stevens Inst. Tech., Hoboken, N.J., 1907-10, and in elec. engring., 1910-17; chief instr., lab. practice courses, New York Edison Co., 1913-25, ednl. dir., 1925-32; asst. prof. elec. engring., Stevens Inst. Tech., 1917-21, asso. prof., 1921-25, prof. and head dept. since 1925, Anson Wood Burchard prof. elec. engring. since 1930, dean, Grad. Sch., 1939-44. Mem. Am. Inst. E.E., Inst. Radio Engrs., Soc. for Promotion Engring. Edn., Phi Beta Kappa, Tau Beta Pi. Republican. Universalist. Author: Laboratory Practice Manual, 1915. Home: Castle Point, Hoboken, N.J. Died Dec. 29, 1946.

STODDARD, Henry Luther, journalist; b. New York, N.Y., Oct. 7, 1861; s. William B. and Ann (O'Brien) S.; ed. Coll. City of New York; m. New York, Emma I. Garretson, Dec. 23, 1886. After serving as Washington and field corr. for various newspapers became editor N.Y. Daily Illustrated Graphic, 1888; editor The Evening Mail, 1897, and purchased controlling interest, Nov. 1900; solid interest, Jan. 1924. Author: As I Knew Them From Grant to Coolidge; It Costs to Be President; Horace Greeley, Printer, Editor, Crusader. Clubs: Union League, New England Society, St. Nicholas. Home: 66 Park Av., New York, N.Y. Died Dec. 27, 1947.

STOESSEL, Albert (stĕs'ĕl), conductor; b. St. Louis, Mo., Oct. 11, 1894; s. Albert J. and Alfreda (Wiedmann) S.; ed. pub. schs., St. Louis; studied music, Berlin Hochschule; hon. M.A., New York, U., 1924; m. Julia Pickard, June 27, 1917; children—Albert Frederick (dec.), Edward Pickard, Frederick. Violin virtuoso since 1913; début Berlin, later Paris and New York; mem. faculty Inst. Musical Art, New York, 1919; musical dir. Symphony at Chautauqua Instn., summers since 1920; condr. N.Y. Oratorio Soc. since 1921; head of music dept. New York U., 1923-30; condr. Worcester (Mass.) Festival, 1925, Westchester (N.Y.) Festival, 1927-33; dir. opera and orchestra depts., Juilliard Grad. Sch. Served as 2d lt. 301st Inf., U.S. Army, 1917-19; dir. A.E.F. Bandmasters' Sch., Chaumont, France. Mem. Am. Soc. Composers, Authors Pubs., Nat. Inst. Arts and Letters, U.S. sect. Internat. Soc. for Contemporary Music. Officier d'Académie, France. Clubs: Town Hall, Century, Bohemians. Author: Technique of the Baton, 1919. Composer: Sonata in G (violin and piano); suite for 2 violins and piano; suite Antique for orchestra; Hispania (suite for piano); Garrick Opera in 3 acts; Concerto Grosso for Strings; also songs, choruses, orchestral and violin pieces, pedagogical works. Home: 14 E. 90th St. Office: 113 W. 57th St., New York, N.Y. Died May 12, 1943.

STOKDYK, Ellis Adolph (stŏk'dīk), agrl. economist; b. Sheboygan County, Wis., Apr. 11, 1897; s. Peter and Nellie (Verhulst) S.; B.S., U. of Wis., 1920; M.S., Kan. State Coll., 1924; Ph.D., U. of Wis., 1930; m. Virginia Lundy Gibson, June 29, 1921; children—Barbara Ann, Virginia Florence, John Ellis. Asst. state club leader, U. of Wis., 1920-21; extension plant pathologist, Kan. State Coll., 1921-24, extension agrl. economist, 1924-28; fellow in agrl. economics, U. of Wis., 1928-29; asso. prof. agrl. economics, U. of Calif., 1929-33; pres. Berkeley Bank for Cooperatives, 1933-38; dep. gov. Farm Credit Adminstrn., Washington, D.C., 1938-39; pres. Berkeley Bank for Cooperatives, Berkeley California, 1939; member Calif. Agricultural Prorate Commn., 1934-38; mem. bd. of dirs. Commodity Credit Corp., 1938-39. Served in U.S. Navy, 1918-19. Mem. Am. Farm Econ. Assn., Theta Delta Chi, Gamma Sigma Delta. Methodist. Mason. Club: Berkeley Rotary (pres. 1943-44). Author: The Farm Board (with West), 1930; The Law of Cooperative Marketing (with Evans), 1937; also numerous agrl. bulletins. Contbr. to jours. Home: 702 Hilldale Av., Berkeley, Calif. Office: Farm Credit Administration, Berkeley, Calif. Died Jan. 22, 1946.

STOKES, Edward Casper, ex-governor; b. Phila., Pa., Dec. 22, 1860; s. Edward H. and Matilda G. (Kemble) S.; A.B., Brown Univ., 1883; LL.D., Temple Univ., 1909, same from Rutgers and Dickinson; unmarried. Engaged in banking since 1883; chmn. bd. First-Mechanics' Nat. Bank, Trenton. Supt. pub. schs., Millville, N.J., 1889-98; mem. N.J. Assembly, 1891-92, Senate, 1892-1901 (pres. 1895); v.chmn. State Rep. Com., 1900; clerk Court of Chancery, 1901-05; gov. of N.J., 1905-08. First pres. N.J. Bankers Assn. Office: First-Mechanics' Nat. Bank, Trenton, N.J. Died Nov. 4, 1942.

STOKES, Horace Winston, publisher; b. New York, N.Y., Mar. 2, 1886; s. Frederick Abbot and Ellen Rebecca (Colby) S.; prep. edn. Phillips Acad., Andover, Mass., 1904-05; A.B., Yale, 1909; m. Mary Sanford Wheeler, May 22, 1920; children—Ellen, Mary Wheeler. Began as newspaper reporter on N.Y. Sun, also on N.Y. Herald-Tribune, 1910; editorial work with American Magazine, 1914-17; advertising with Frank Seaman, Inc., Crowell Pub. Co., 1920-26; with Frederick A. Stokes Co., Inc., 1926-41, pres., 1939-41. Served as private Squadron A, 1st Cav., N.G.N.Y., on Mexican border, 1916-17; 1st lt. 165th Inf., 306th Inf., U.S. Army, with A.E.F., 1917-19. Mem. Alpha Delta Phi, Wolf's Head (Yale). Club: The Players (N.Y. City). Author: Frog Face (a novel), 1946. Contbr. to mags. in the U.S. and Eng. Address: care W. C. Heaton Co., 25 W. 45th St., New York, N.Y. Died Jan. 18, 1950.

STOKES, I(saac) N(ewton) Phelps, architect; b. New York, N.Y., Apr. 11, 1867; s. late Anson Phelps and Helen Louisa (Phelps) S.; ed. St. Paul's Sch., Concord, N.H., and Berkeley Sch., N.Y. City; A.B., Harvard, 1891; studied banking with J. Kennedy Tod & Co., bankers, 1891-92; studied architecture (especially housing), Columbia U., 1893-94; École des Beaux Arts, Paris, 1894-97; L.H.D., New York U., 1932; Litt.D., Columbia U., 1937; m. Edith Minturn, Aug. 21, 1895 (died June 12, 1937); 1 dau., Mrs. Edwin K. Merrill. Formerly mem. Howells & Stokes, New York and Seattle, 1897-1917; firm designed St. Paul's Chapel, Columbia U.; Woodbridge Hall, Yale; Dudley Memorial Gateway, and Music Sch., Harvard; Baltimore Stock Exch. Bldg.; University Site development, Seattle; Am. Geog. Soc. Bldg., New York; Royal Insurance office bldgs., New York and San Francisco; Woodbridge Bldg. and Title Guarantee and Trust Co. Bldg., New York; Turks Head Bldg., Providence; First Congl. Ch., Danbury, Conn.; University Settlement and other pioneer settlements, New York. Associated as officer or dir. with several organizations in development, management and sale of N.Y. City real estate for 50 years. Apptd. by Gov. Theodore Roosevelt member New York State Tenement House Commission, 1900; architectural mem. committee of three which drafted N.Y. State Tenement House Law of 1901; architectural mem. Art Commn. City of N.Y., 1911-13, also, ex-officio, representing N.Y. Pub. Library, 1916-18, 1921-38, pres., 1929-38; mem. staff, 1918, and mgr. prelim. investigations div. of U.S. Labor Dept., Bur. Industrial Housing and Transportation, later U.S. Housing Corp.; etc. Formerly mem. Troop A, Nat. Guard N.Y. Dir. Phelps-Stokes (ednl. and housing) Fund, 1911-39, pres., 1911-24; trustee New York Pub. Library, 1916-38; hon. v.p. Community Service Soc. of New York; hon. v.p. Fine Arts Fedn. of New York, 1939-40 (medallist, 1939); hon. v.p. Municipal Art Society of New York since 1937. Fellow New York State Hist. Assn.; hon. member N.Y. Hist. Soc. (medallist 1925); corr. mem. N.Y. Geneal. and Biog. Soc.; recipient of Mayor's certificate for public service, 1939. Democrat. Episcopalian. Clubs: Grolier (hon.), University (New York); Delta Phi, D.K.E., A.D. (Harvard). Author: The Iconography of Manhattan Island, 6 vols., 1915-28; also chapter on low cost housing in N.Y. City (printed as appendix to Slums and Housing, by James Ford), 1936; Annual Reports of Art Commission, 1928-29, 1930-37; New York, Past and Present—Its History and Landmarks, 1939. Co-author of History and Catalogue of the Works of the Society of Iconophiles of City of N.Y., 1930; American Historical Prints, Early Views of American Cities, etc., 1932, 1933. Home: 28 E. 70th St., New York, and Greenwich, Conn. Office: 33 Madison Av., New York, N.Y. Died Dec. 19, 1944.

STOKES, John Stogdell, mfr.; b. Moorestown, N.J., Feb. 26, 1870; s. Nathaniel Newlin and Martha Eastburn (Stokes) S.; student Haverford (Pa.) Coll., 1886-89; m. May Margaret Egan, May 31, 1919; children—John Stogdell, Martha Eastburn (Mrs. John Sergeant Price, III). Began as clerk, Queen & Co., Philadelphia, 1889; vice president and gen. mgr. Am. Metal Edge Box Co., Phila., 1889-1900; pres. Stokes & Smith Co., Phila., mfrs. of machinery since 1900; pres. Durite Plastics, Inc.; v.p. Yarnall-Waring Co., mfrs. of engring. specialties; dir. Provident Trust Co., Pa. Salt Mfg. Co. Pres. Phila. Museum of Art; dir. Bryn Mawr Coll.; mem. bd. dirs. Phila. Orchestra; trustee Haverford Coll., Acad. of Natural Sciences of Phila.; pres. Art Jury of City of Phila.; dir. Fairmont Park Art Assn. Mem. Colonial Soc. of Pa., and Soc. of Colonial Wars. Decorated Chevalier Legion d'Honneur (France), 1937. Clubs: Philadelphia, Rittenhouse, Union League, Hunting Valley Country. Medalist Franklin Inst. of Phila. Home: Spring Valley Farm, Huntington Valley, Pa. Office: Summerdale, Philadelphia, Pa. Died Sept. 26, 1947.

STOLL, Richard Charles, judge; b. Lexington, Ky., Mar. 21, 1876; s. Richard Pindell and Elvina (Stoll) S.; student Allegan Acad., Lexington, 1887-91; A.B., State Coll. of Ky., Lexington, 1895; LL.B., Yale, 1897; LL.D., U. of Ky., 1913; m. Angelene Chesnut, Sept. 24, 1919; 1 son, Richard Pindell. Admitted to Ky. bar, 1897, and began practice at Lexington; mem. firm Darnall & Stoll, 1902-04, Stoll & Bush, 1904-15; v.p. and gen. counsel Lexington Water Co., 1907-21; gen. counsel Ky. Traction & Terminal Co. and Lexington Utilities Co., 1911-21; v.p. Lexington Gas Co., 1911-21; dir. First Nat. Bank & Trust Co., Ky. Securities Corp. Judge Circuit Court, 22d Jud. Dist. of Ky., 1921-31; mem. Stoll, Muir, Townsend & Park; gen. counsel and dir. Southeastern Greyhound Lines, Ala. Bus Co., Ky. Traction & Terminal Co., Lexington Utilities Co. Spl. judge Jessamine Circuit Court, 1934; chief justice Special Court of Appeals of Ky., 1940. Chmn., Civil Service Commn., Lexington, Ky.; mem. Special Com. on Practice and Procedure, Court of Appeals of Ky., since 1938; mem. Ky. Council on Higher Edn.; dir. of the Federal Home Loan Bank of Cincinnati, representing the public, 1932-34; member

Citizens Advisory Com. apptd. by gov. to recommend a reörganization of Ky. state govt.; chmn. Com. Pub. Safety and Ky. Council Defense; head of Am. Protective League, Ky., World War I. Del. to Rep. Nat. Conv., 1912, 16, 20; chmn. Rep. State Conv., 1924; chmn. com. on resolutions, Ky. State Conv., 1931; chmn Ky. State Bd. Election Commrs., 1914-15, mem. Judicial Council of Ky., 1928-31; mem. 6th Circuit Com. to advise with judges Circuit Ct. of Appeals as to new rules of federal practice; pres. Circuit Judges of Ky., 1928-31. Trustee U. of Ky. since 1898, chmn. its exec. com. and vice chmn. trustees; chmn. bd. Ky. Agrl. Expt. Sta. Mem. Am. Bar Assn. (mem. com. on judicial procedure, 1937-38), Am. Law Inst., Assn. Bar City N.Y., Ky. State Bar Assn. (pres. 1923), Am. Judicature Soc. (dir. for Ky., 1937-38), Nat. Econ. League (mem. nat. council), Nat. Inst. Social Sciences, Am. Soc. Polit. Science, Am. Museum of Natural History (asso.), Sons of Revolution (pres. Kentucky soc.), Kneeland Assn. (dir.), Kentucky Trotting Horse Breeders Association (president, 1910-14), Newcomen Society of England. Order of Coif, Phi Beta Kappa Associates (founding mem.), Phi Beta Kappa, Kappa Alpha, Omicron Delta Kappa, Book and Gavel, Southern Soc. of New York. Presbyn. Clubs: Lexington, Ashland, Lexington Country (Lexington); Pendennis, Filson (Louisville); University, Queen City (Cincinnati); Yale, Republican (New York); Union League, Electric (Chicago). Home: 444 W. 3d St. Office: Bank of Commerce Bldg., Lexington, Ky. Died June 26, 1949.

STOLEE, Michael J. (stō'lē), theologian; b. Haugesund, Norway, Sept. 24, 1871; s. Jacob and Knutianna (Rover) S.; came to U.S., 1886; student Augustana Coll., Canton, S.D., 1890-94; B.A., St. Olaf Coll., Northfield, Minn., 1897; grad. Theol. Sem. of United Luth. Ch., Minneapolis, 1900; studied the Sorbonne, Paris, France, 1911, U. of Christiania, 1912; D.D., Augustana Coll. and Sem., Ill., 1923; Th.M. from Drew Univ., 1928, Th.D., 1929; m. Martha Josephine Knutsen, June 27, 1900. Ordained Luth. ministry, 1900; missionary to Island of Madagascar, 1901-09, and gen. supt. of missions there, 1903-09; pres. Nat. Young People's League of Norwegian Luth. Ch. of America, 1913-15; prof. practical theology, 1912-20, prof. dogmatics and missions since 1920, Luther Theol. Sem., St. Anthony Park, Minn.; also pastor Wartburg Luth. Ch., St. Paul, Minn. Commr. on reconstruction work in Europe, in France and Poland, by apptmt. of Nat. Luth. Commn., Mar.-Sept. 1919, Pastor Gethsemane Lutheran Church Minneapolis, since 1941. Sec. Bd. of Foreign Missions Norwegian Luth. Co. Republican. Author: The Genesis of Religion, 1930. Home: 1036 Van Slyke St., St. Paul 3, Minn. Died Nov. 24, 1946.

STOLPER, Gustav (stŏl'pēr), economist; b. Vienna, Austria, July 25, 1888; Dr. Law and Economics, U. of Vienna, 1911. Became pub. and editor Oesterreichischer Volkswirt (Austrian Economist) and prof. of polit. economy, Vienna Acad. of Commerce, 1912; head of research and statistical div., Imperial Gen. Commissariat for War Economy during World War I; editor in chief Berliner Boersen-Courier, 1925; editor and pub. Deutscher Volkswirt (German Economist), Berlin and Berlin corr. of London Economist, 1926-33; mem. German Reichstag for Hamburg and mem. budget com. and banking com., 1929-32 (to the coming to power of Hitler); came to U.S., 1933, became naturalized citizen; now consultant economist; chmn. Conf. Am. Business Economists, 1947; mem. com. for econ. policy, U.S. Chamber Commerce; econ. expert on Herbert Hoover's presdl. mission to Ger., Feb. 1947. Author: (recent books) German Economy, 1870-1940; This Age of Fable, 1941; German Realities, 1948. Contbr. to mags. Home: 75 Greenhaven Road, Rye, N.Y. Office: 52 Wall St., New York 5, N.Y. Died Dec. 27, 1947

STOLTZ, Robert Bear (stōlts), prof. dairy technology; b. Bradford, O., Mar. 6, 1890; s. James Franklin and Ida (Bear) S.; B.S., Ohio State U., 1912; student U. of Wis., summers 1915, 16; m. Marie Cassel, June 12, 1912; children—Philip Cassel, Bonnie Marie, Susan Ann, Roberta Mary. Instr. in dairying, Ohio State U., 1912-14, asst. prof., 1914-23, prof., 1923-29, chmn. and prof. dairy technology since 1929; studied dairy conditions in New Zealand and Australia, 1937. Sec.-treas. Ohio Swiss Cheese Assn. 1918-45; sec. Nat. Cheese Assn., 1920-23, treas. 1923-25; sec. Columbus Milk Dist. Assn., 1933-45. Mem. Am. Dairy Science Assn. (pres. 1934, sec.-treas. since 1936), Acacia, Delta Theta Sigma, Gamma Sigma Delta. Republican. Mem. Community Church. Mason (33°, Scottish Rite). Officer in Gen. Grand Council of R. & S.M. of U.S. America. Home: 1971 Concord Rd., Columbus 12, O. Died Oct. 2, 1948; buried at Columbus, O.

STOLZ, Karl Ruf (stōlts), educator; b. Traverse City, Mich., Jan. 9, 1884; s. John Conrad and Anna Barbara (Ruf) S.; B.A., Baldwin-Wallace Coll., Berea, O., 1907, D.D., 1928; B.D., Garrett Bibl. Inst., 1909, D.D., 1927; M.A., Northwestern U., 1909; Ph.D., State U. of Ia., 1911; m. Fern Marie Buchanan, July 17, 1912; children—Arthur Buchanan, Karl Robert. Prof. religious edn., Wesley Coll., 1912-24; head of dept. of Bibl. lit. and religious edn., Y.M.C.A. Coll., Chicago, 1924-27; prof. English Bible and dean Sch. of Religious Edn., Hartford Sem. Foundation, since 1927; visiting prof. religious psychology, Presbyn. Theol. Sem., 1932, Garrett Bibl. Inst., 1934. Mem. Religious Edn. Assn., Am. Assn. Univ. Profs. Republican. Conglist. Author: Psychology of Prayer, 1923; Evolution and Genesis, 1927; Pastoral Psychology, 1932; Psychology of Religious Living, 1937; Tricks Our Minds Play On Us, 1939; Making the Most of the Rest of Life, 1941; (with others) Jesus and a Boy's Philosophy of Life, 1926; Studies in Religious Education, 1931; Religion and the Church Tomorrow, 1936; also articles on Bibl. interpretation and religious edn. Address: Hartford School of Religious Education, Hartford, Conn. Died Mar. 29, 1943.

STOMBERG, Andrew Adin, educator; b. Carver, Minn., Mar. 29, 1871; s. Andrew and Majastina (Andersdotter) S.; A.B., Gustavus Adolphus Coll., 1895; A.M., U. of Minn., 1896; studied U. of Leipzig, Germany, 1897-98; Austin scholar, Harvard U., 1904-05; Scandinavian scholar, Univ. of Upsala, Sweden, 1916; Litt.D., Gustavus Adolphus Coll., 1933; m. Caroline J. Holcomb, 1899; children—Carl Winfred, Dwight William. Prof. history Gustavus Adolphus College, 1898-1907; prof. Scandinavian, U. of Minn., 1907-29, now professor of Scandinavian emeritus, same univ.; lecturer at U. of Upsala, Sweden, 1927-28, under auspices Olaus Petri Foundation, and as visiting prof., Carnegie Foundation for International Peace; taught Scandinavian, Extension Division, University of California, 1939-40. Director American Institute of Swedish Arts, Literature and Science, director of its cultural activities and editor of Bulletin; mem. A.A.A.S., Society for Advancement of Scandinavian Study, Swedish Cultural Society America, Lambda Alpha Psi. Knight Order of the North Star, conferred by Gustaf V of Sweden, 1925. Editor: College and University edition of Tegner's Frithof's Saga, 1914; The Swedish Race element in America, 1928; A History of Sweden, 1931. Home: 2224 Seabury Av., Minneapolis, Minn.* Died Nov. 16, 1943.

STONE, Arthur Fairbanks, journalist; b. St. Johnsbury, Vt., Feb. 18, 1863; s. Charles Marshall and Sarah (Fairbanks) S.; grad. St. Johnsbury Acad., 1881; A.B., Amherst, 1885; m. Helen S. Lincoln, Jan. 1, 1890; children—Edith Lincoln (Mrs. Frank H. Taft; now dec.), Eleanor Fairbanks, Robert Lincoln, Laura Helen. Began as reporter Northampton Herald, 1885; reporter Fall River (Mass.) News, 1888-90; editor St. Johnsbury Caledonian, 1890-1914, St. Johnsbury Daily Caledonian, 1921-23; spl. newspaper writer since 1923. Postmaster, St. Johnsbury, 1909-12; mem. Vt. Ho. of Rep., 1929, State Senate, 1931. Trustee Sunset Home for Women. Mem. Phi Beta Kappa, Beta Theta Pi. Republican. Conglist. Mason, Elk, Rotarian. Author: St. Johnsbury Illustrated, 1892; The Vermont of Today, 1929; Life of Henry Clay Ide, 1935; History North Congregational Church, St. Johnsbury, 1942. Home: St. Johnsbury, Vt. Died Sep. 2, 1941.

STONE, Charles Arthur, prof. education; b. Chicago, Ill., Aug. 17, 1893; s. Abraham and Anna Gertrude (Guerber) S.; student Crane Jr. Coll., Chicago, 1912-14; B.S., U. of Ill., 1917; A.M., U. of Chicago, 1925; LL.D., Niagara U., 1930; m. Sylvia H. Goldberger, May 22, 1915; children—Audrey Gertrude, Betty Rivian (twins). Ceramic engr., Basic Products Co., Kenova, W.Va., 1917-18; teacher and prin. high sch., Kenova, 1918-19; teacher and asst. prin. high sch., Des Plaines, Ill., 1919-21; instr. in lab. schs., U. of Chicago, 1922-37, prof. edn., De Paul U., since 1924, dir. Air Corps Inst., DePaul U.; mathematics editor of F. W. Davis Pub. Co. since 1931. Mem. N.E.A., Nat. Council Mathematics Teachers, Central Assn. Science and Mathematics Teachers (v.p. 1932; pres. 1933), Am. Assn. of Univ. Profs., Am. Assn. Sch. Adminstrs., Phi Delta Kappa. Mason. Club: Quadrangle. Author: Trigonometry (with E.R. Breslich), 1928; The Slide Rule (with same), 1929; The Teaching Unit (with D. Waples), 1930; Work Units in Algebra (with J. S. Georges), 1931; New Mathematics Work-Book (with J. S. Georges), 1933; New Mathematics Work-Book, II (with J. S. Georges), 1936; Work Units in Educational Statistics (with J. S. Georges), 1942. Mathematics editor School Science and Mathematics (mag.). Home: 4300 Lake Shore Drive., Chicago, Ill. Died Aug. 14, 1944.

STONE, Clyde Ernest, judge; b. Mason County, Ill., s. Claudius L. and Mary (sometimes called Martha) Gertrude (Marot) S.; LL.B., U. of Illinois, 1903; m. Jessie Browning, Nov. 14, 1900; children—Claudia Ellen Cassell, Inez Browning, Mabel Lee Shaw. Mem. Stone & Fuller, Peoria, 1903-06, Graff & Stone, 1906-10; 1st asst. state's atty., Peoria County, Ill., 1906-09; county judge Peoria County, 1910-15; circuit judge 10th Jud. Circuit, 1915-18; justice Supreme Court of Ill. since 1918, 5 times chief justice of Court. Mem. Order of the Coif. Phi Kappa Sigma, Phi Delta Phi. Republican. Presbyterian. Mason (33°, K.T., Shriner), Imperial Grand Sovereign Red Cross of Constantine, Odd Fellow. Clubs: Creve Coeur, Country. Home: Pere Marquette Hotel. Office: First National Bank Bldg., Peoria, Ill. Died Jan. 14, 1948.

STONE, Harlan Fiske, jurist; b. Chesterfield, N.H., Oct. 11, 1872; s. Frederick Lauson and Ann Sophia (Butler) S.; B.S., Amherst College, 1894, M.A., 1897; LL.B., Columbia U. Sch. of Law, 1898; LL.D., Amherst, 1913, Yale, 1924, Columbia, 1925, Williams, 1925, George Washington, 1927, Harvard, 1931, Dartmouth, 1934, Univ. of Mich., 1934, Univ. of Pa., 1934, Univ. of Chicago, 1938, Oberlin Coll., 1939, Kenyon Coll., 1940, Princeton, 1942, Tufts Coll., 1942, Colgate Univ., 1942, Yeshiva Coll., Bowdoin Coll., 1944; D.C.L., Syracuse, 1928; m. Agnes Harvey, Sept. 7, 1899; children—Marshall H., Lauson H. Admitted to N.Y. bar, 1898; lecturer on law, 1899-1902, prof., 1902-05, dean Columbia University, Sch. of Law, 1910-23; was mem. law firm of Sullivan & Cromwell; apptd. atty. gen. of U.S., by President Coolidge, Apr. 7, 1924; asso. justice Supreme Court of U.S., by apptmt. of President Coolidge, Mar. 2, 1925- June 1941, chief justice since 1941. Vice president Am. Red Cross; v.p. Washington Monument Soc.; hon. pres. Nat. Assn. of Legal Aid Orgns., 1941; trustee, Amherst College; chmn. bd. trustees National Gallery of Art, Washington, D.C.; chancellor Smithsonian Instn. Pres. Assn. Am. Law Schs., 1919. Fellow Am. Acad. Arts and Sciences; mem. Am. Law Inst., Am. Bar. Assn. (council legal edn.), N.Y. State Bar Assn., Assn. Bar of City of N.Y., Internat. Acad. Comparative Law, Soc. of Comparative Legislation (London), Am. Philos. Soc., Am. Judicature Soc., Phi Beta Kappa, Alpha Delta Phi, Phi Delta Phi; hon. mem. Soc. of Pub. Teachers of Law (Great Britain); hon. bencher Lincoln's Inn (London). Republican. Clubs: Century, Lawyers, University (New York); University (Washington); Athenaeum (London). Home: 2340 Wyoming Av., Washington, D.C. Died Apr. 22, 1946.

STONE, Horace M., lawyer; b. Marcellus, N.Y., Jan. 6, 1890; s. Rollin M. and Mary A. (Baker) S.; LL.B., Syracuse U., 1912; m. Norma L. Walsh, June 14, 1916; children—Horace M., Norma S., Marguerite A., Nan Roberta. Admitted to N.Y. bar, 1913; mem. Stone, Marvin & Hand; dir. State Tower Bldg., First Nat. Bank of Marcellus; mem. bd. dirs. Lincoln Nat. Bank & Trust Co., Syracuse. Mem. N.Y. Legislature, 1923-36. Mem. Beta Theta Pi. Republican. Presbyterian. Mason. Clubs: Onondaga Country, Tuscarora Country; Citizens' (Syracuse); Citizens' (Marcellus). Home: Marcellus, N.Y. Office: State Tower Bldg., Syracuse, N.Y. Died Mar. 7, 1944.

STONE, John Stone, electrical engr.; b. Dover, Va., Sept. 24, 1869; s. Gen. Charles Pomeroy and Jeannie (Stone) S.; ed. Columbia Grammar Sch., New York, 1884-86; Sch. of Mines (Columbia), 1886-88; Johns Hopkins, 1888-90; m. Sibyl Wilbur, Nov. 28, 1918. Experimentalist in laboratory, Am. Bell Telephone Co., 1890-99; gen. consulting elec. engr., 1899-1920; spl. lecturer on elec. oscillations, Mass. Inst. Tech., for a number of years; dir., v.p., and chief engr. from incorporation, 1902-08, pres. and chief engr. June 10, 1908-10, Stone Telegraph & Telephone Co. (mfg. and leasing wireless telegraph apparatus). Has been granted over 135 U.S. patents for inventions relating to improvements in telephony and telegraphy. Read papers before Internat. Elec. Congress, St. Louis, in 1904, and Canadian Soc. Civ. Engrs., Montreal, 1905, before Soc. Wireless Tel. Engrs., 1908, 09, 10, before Wireless Inst., 1909, before Inst. of Radio Engrs., 1914-15; contbr. numerous papers on elec. subjects to scientific and technical press. Fellow Am. Acad. Arts and Sciences, A.A.A.S., Inst. of Radio Engrs. (v.p. 1913-14, pres. 1914-15, dir. 1912-18); organizer, vice chmn. Radio Engrs.' Com. on National Defense; del. Internat. Elec. Congress, 1904, 2d Pan-Am. Scientific Congress, 1917; mem. advisory com. Am. Defense Society; pres. Soc. of Wireless Telegraph Engineers, 1906-09; member Franklin Institute, Alpha Delta Phi; asso. mem. Am. Inst. E.E. Awarded Edward Longstreth Medal for paper on "The Practical Aspects of the Propagation of High Frequency Waves Along Wires," by the Franklin Inst., 1913; medal of honor of Inst. of Radio Engrs. "for distinguished service in radio communication," 1923. Asso. Engr. at large dept. of development and research of Am. Tel. & Tel. Co., 1920-35. Clubs: Army and Navy (Washington); Radio Club America (hon.). Address: 1636 Torrence St., San Diego, Calif. Died May 20, 1943.

STONE, Joseph Cecil, lawyer; b. Big Rock, Stewart County, Tenn., Nov. 8, 1870; s. William Jesse and Mary Ellen (Beresford) S.; A.B., Howard Payne Coll., Brownwood, Tex., 1897, LL.D., 1927; A.B., U. of Chicago, 1899; m. Louise Beatrice Webb, June 7, 1904; 1 dau., Mary Louise (Mrs. Gordon Watts). Admitted to Tex. bar, 1901, and began practice at Okmulgee, Ind. Ty., 1902; moved to Muskogee, 1903; city atty., Muskogee, 1908-10; mem. com. which wrote city charter for managerial form of govt. for Muskogee; mem. firm Owen & Stone, 1908-17, Stone, Moon & Stewart, 1917-37, Stone & Moon since 1937; gen. practice. Mem. Okla. State Bar Assn. (pres. 1924-25). Episcopalian. Mason. Home: 401 S. 12th St. Office: Barnes Bldg., Muskogee, Okla. Died Aug. 23, 1948.

STONE, Julius Frederick, mfr.; b. nr. Devil's Lake, Lenawee County, Mich., June 1, 1855; s. Franz Theodore and Emilie Julia Johanna (Sydow) Stein (anglicized to Stone on coming to U.S., 1848); ed. country sch. about 6 yrs.; hon. D.Sc., Ohio State Univ., 1888 married Edna Alice Andress, May 24, 1900; children—Julius Frederick, George Andress, Theodora Martha, Franz Theodore, Natalia Sydow. Began as telegraph operator, 1871, continuing in various ry. positions until 1885; engaged in coal mining, Ohio; W.Va., Ill. and Ia., until 1903; actively identified with mfg. and banking since 1903; now chmn. bd. Seagrave Corp., mfrs. motor driven fire apparatus; dir. Columbus-McKinnon Chain Co., pres. Ohio State Univ. Research Foundation. Fellow Am. Geog. Soc., Royal Astron. Soc. (Eng.); mem. Am. Astron. Soc., Am Soc. Mech. Engrs., etc. Rep. Clubs: Engineers (Dayton, O.); Explorers (New York). Author: Canyon Country, 1932. Presented Gibraltar Island, in Lake Erie, to Ohio State U., as an aquatic lab. Explored the Grand Canyon of the Colorado. Home: 1065 Westwood Av., Columbus, O. Office: Columbus, O. Died July 25, 1947.

STONE, Lauson, steel corp. exec.; b. Amherst, Mass., 1883; ed. Purdue Univ., 1905. Chmn. of bd., pres., mem. exec. com. and dir. Follansbee Steel Corp.; pres. and dir. Sheet Metal Specialty Co.; dir. Beaver Trust Co. Home: 734 Fourth St., Beaver. Office: Third and Liberty Avs., Pittsburgh, Pa. Died Oct. 8, 1948.

STONE, Royal Augustus, judge; b. LeSueur, Minn., June 26, 1875; s. Herman Ward and Polly (Wells) S.; student Carleton Coll., 1892-94, U. of Minn., 1895; LL.B., Washington U., 1897; m. Edith Olive Whiting, Aug. 14, 1901. Admitted to Minn. bar, 1897, and began practice at Morris; asst. atty. gen. of Minn., 1905-07; mem. O'Brien, Stone, Horn & Stringer, St. Paul, 1907-23, except during war; apptd. by gov. asso. justice Supreme Court of Minn., 1923, and elected to same office, 1924, 1930 and 1936, 3d term ending 1942. Served as pvt. and sergt. 15th Minn. Vol. Inf., 1898, Spanish-Am. War; also as capt. and maj. 349th Inf., 88th Div., and 14th Inf., 19th Division, United States Army, World War. Chairman Minnesota Judicial Council. Member American, Minn. State and Ramsey County bar assns., Am. Law Inst. Conglist. Mason. Clubs: Minnesota, St. Paul Athletic. Home: 903 Goodrich Av. Address: State Capitol, St. Paul, Minn. Died Sep. 13, 1942.

STONE, Willard John, physician; b. Gloversville, N.Y., May 31, 1877; s. John Butler and Marietta (Brown) S.; Union Coll., Schenectady, N.Y., 1895-96; B.S., U. of Mich., 1899; M.D., Med. Dept., U. of Mich., 1901; studied U. of Vienna, 1902-03; m. Charlotte Hall Walker, Nov. 25, 1911; children—Willard J., Louise Hall. Practiced, Toledo, O., 1904-19, Pasadena, since 1919; attending physician Huntington Memorial Hosp., Pasadena; clinical prof. of Medicine, U. of Southern California, Los Angeles. Formerly maj. Med. Corps, U.S. Army; chief of med. service U.S. Army Base Hosp., Ft. Riley, Kan., 1917-19. Member A.M.A., Los Angeles Academy of Medicine, Am. Soc. for Clinical Investigation, Am. Climatol. Assn., Alpha Delta Phi, Nu Sigma Nu; F.A.C.P. Mem. Liberal Ch. Contbr. numerous articles on medical topics. Home: 1475 E. California St. Office: Professional Bldg., Pasadena, Calif. Died Oct. 30, 1943.

STONER, Dayton (stōn'ẽr), zoölogist; b. North Liberty, Ia., Nov. 26, 1883; s. Marcus and Nancy (Koser) S.; A.B., U. of Iowa, 1907, M.S., 1909, Ph.D., 1919; m. Lillian Rebecca Christianson, Aug. 3, 1912. Began as asst. in museum U. of Iowa, 1908-12, instr. in zoölogy, 1912-16, asso. in zoölogy, 1916-22, asst. prof., 1922-28; instr. ornithology and entomology U. Mich. Biol. Sta., summers, 1919-20; temp. field asst. U.S. Bur. Entomology, winters 1928-31; field ornithologist Roosevelt Wild Life Forest Exptl. Sta., summers 1928-32; state zoölogist N.Y. State Museum Albany since 1932. Conducted ornithol., entomol. and mammalol. field work in Ia., Colo., Mich., Fiji Islands, New Zealand, West Indies, Fla., New York and Vancouver Island. Fellow A.A.A.S., Ia. Acad. Science; mem. Am. Ornithol. Union, Am. Soc. Mammalogists, Wilson Ornithol. Club, Eastern Bird Band Assn., Wildlife Soc., Ia. Ornithol. Union, Sigma Xi. Author: Rodents of Iowa, 1918; Scutelleroidea of Iowa, 1920; Ornithology of Oneida Lake Region, 1932; Studies on The Bank Swallow, 1936; Wildlife Casualties on the Highways, 1936; Ten Years' Returns from Banded Bank Swallows, 1937; Temperature, Growth and Other Studies on the Eastern Phoebe, 1939; also other papers on birds, mammals, insects. Home: 399 State St. Address: N.Y. State Museum, Albany, N.Y. Died May 8, 1944.

STOREY, Thomas Andrew, coll. prof.; b. Burden, Kan., Jan. 29, 1875; s. Riley Clark and Rose Margaret (Schafer) S.; A.B., Leland Stanford Jr. Univ., 1896, A.M., 1900, Ph.D., 1902; Hopkins Marine Lab., Pacific Grove, Calif., summers, 1896, 97; grad. work, U. of Mich., 1900; M.D., Harvard, 1905; diploma, Boston Long Island Hosp., 1905; resident medical service, Boston Children's Hosp., 1906; m. Parnie Olive Hamilton, June 26, 1899; children—Margaret Hamilton, Parnie Hamilton, Marion Hamilton. Asst. prof. hygiene, Stanford U., 1902-06; asso. prof. phys. instrn. and training, 1906-10, prof. phys. instrn. and hygiene, 1910-13, prof. hygiene, 1913-26, Coll. City of New York; prof. and dir. hygiene and physical edn., Stanford Univ., 1926-29, gen. dir. Sch. of Hygiene and Phys. Edn., Stanford, 1929-40; spl. consultant Am. Social Hygiene Assn. since 1940. Sec.-gen. 4th Internat. Congress on Sch. Hygiene and editor its Proceedings 1913; chmn. Nat. Conf. on College Hygiene, 1931; fellow of A.A.A.S., Am. Acad. of Physical Edn., Am. Pub. Health Assn., Am. Phys. Edn. Assn.; mem. Am. Physiol. Soc., Soc. Exptl. Biology and Medicine, San Francisco Acad. of Medicine, Soc. Dirs. Phys. Edn. in Colls. (pres. 1908-09), Am. Student Health Assn. (pres. 1925-27), A.M.A., Phi Kappa Psi, Sigma Xi. Mem. hygiene reference bd. Life Extension Inst., etc. Author of N.Y. State program and syllabus on phys. training; state insp. phys. training with Mil. Training Commn., Albany, 1917-21. Exec. sec. U.S. Inter-departmental Social Hygiene Bd., Washington, D.C., 1918-21. Organized dept. hygiene, Coll. City of New York; exec. sec. President's Com. of Fifty on coll. hygiene. Clubs: Harvard (New York, N.Y.); Bohemian, Commonwealth (San Francisco, Calif.); Cosmos (Washington, D.C.). Awarded Luther Halsey Guilick medal "for distinguished service in physical edn. and allied fields," 1926; award of honor in recognition of distinguished service in cause of physical education, American Physical Education Association. Writer on hygiene and physical education. Home: 739 Santa Ynez Rd., Box 1606, Stanford University, Calif. Died Oct. 28, 1943.

STORKE, Arthur Ditchfield, business exec.; b. Auburn, N.Y., 1894. Pres. and dir. Climax Molybdenum Co.; dir. Roan Antelope Copper Mines, Ltd., London, Eng., American Metal Co., Mufulira Copper Mines, Ltd., Rhodesian Selection Trust, Ltd. Address: 500 Fifth Av., New York, N.Y. Died Sept. 9, 1949.

STORM, Hans Otto, radio engr., author; b. Bloomington, Calif., July 26, 1895; s. Joachim Otto and Marie (Rehwoldt) S.; A.B. in Engring., Leland Stanford Jr. U., 1920; m. Grace Cleone Camp, May 21, 1921. Radio engr. in radio telegraphy with Federal Telegraph Co., Palo Alto, Calif., 1920-21; with San Francisco Water Dept., 1922-24; radio telegraphy Mackay Radio, 1925-30, All-American Cables, Nicaragua and Peru, 1931-32, Mackay Radio, 1932-34; design and installation of radio equipment Globe Wireless, Ltd., San Francisco, since 1935. Asso. mem. Inst. Radio Engrs. Author: Full Measure, 1929; Pitty the Tyrant, 1937 (gold medal Commonwealth Club of Calif.); Made in U.S.A., 1939; Count Ten, 1940. Short story, "The Two Deaths of Kaspar Rausch," appeared in O'Brien's Best Stories, 1940. Home: 1539 Greenwich St. Office: 311 California St., San Francisco, Calif. Died Dec. 11, 1942.

STORRS, Lewis Austin, lawyer; b. Hartford, Conn., Aug. 28, 1866; s. Zalmon A. and Mary (Rowell) S.; B.A., Yale, 1889; studied law at Columbia; M.A., Trinity, 1904; m. Bessie Whitmore, Feb. 19, 1895; children—John Whitmore, Mrs. Ruth Castator, Mrs. Una Riddle, Mrs. Marabeth Finn, Lewis Austin, Robert. Admitted to bar, 1891; practiced at New York, 1891-98, Hartford, since 1898. Clubs: Yale (New York); University (Hartford). Author: Koheleth, 1897; Tragedy of Saul, 1904. Home: 360 Farmington Av. Office: 36 Pearl St., Hartford, Conn. Died July 4, 1945.

STORY, Russell McCulloch, coll. pres.; b. Washburn, Ill., Apr. 9, 1883; s. William Murray and Zillah Belle (McCulloch) S.; A.B., Monmouth (Ill.) Coll., 1904; A.M., Harvard, 1908, Ph.D., 1917; m. Gertrude Anderson, Sept. 1909; 1 dau., Kathrine McCulloch. Engaged in journalism, 1904-07; teacher at Clark Coll., 1909-10; prof. history, Monmouth Coll., 1910-14; instr., asst. prof. and asso. prof. polit. science, U. of Ill., 1914-24; prof. polit. science, Syracuse U., 1924-25; prof. polit. science, Pomona Coll., 1925-37; pres. and prof. polit. science, Claremont Colleges, since 1937. Vice pres. Claremont Bldg. and Loan Assn.; mem. Com. on Governmental Simplification, Los Angeles County, 1933-35; sec. Ill. Municipal League, 1919-24. Served as war work secretary Y.M.C.A. in Russia and Siberia, 1917-18. Decorated Cross of War (Czechoslovakia), 1919. Trustee Southwest Museum, Los Angeles. Mem. Regional Com., Social Science Research Council; mem. Am. Polit. Science Assn., Acad. Polit. Science, Am. Acad. Polit. and Social Science, Pacific-Southwest Acad., Nat. Municipal League, Social Science Research Conf. of Pacific Coast, Western Governmental Research Assn., Am. Council of Inst. of Pacific Relations, Sigma Phi Epsilon, Phi Beta Kappa, Sigma Delta Chi. Conglist. Clubs: University (Los Angeles); University, Indian Hill Golf (Claremont); Los Serranos Golf and Country (Chino, Calif.). Author: The American Municipal Executive, 1917. Editor of Polit. Science Monograph Series, Pomona Coll., 1929-39; founder and editor, 1921-23, Ill. Municipal Rev. Contbr. to jours. Home: 831 Dartmouth Av., Claremont, Calif. Died Mar. 26, 1942.

STOTESBURY, Louis William (stōts' bĕr-ĭ), lawyer; b. Beacon, N.Y., Oct. 21, 1870; s. William, Jr., and Charlotte F. (Meyer) S.; B.S., Rutgers Coll., 1890, M.S., 1893; LL.B., New York U., 1892; m. Helen Mathers Tompkins, Oct. 7, 1897; 1 dau., Helen Mathers. Practiced N.Y. City, since 1892; counsel to N.Y. State Transit Commn., 1924. Served in 7th Inf. Nat. Guard N.Y., 1892-1912; a.d.c. staffs of Govs. Hughes and White; insp. gen. N.Y. Div. Nat. Guard, 1912-14; adj. gen. State of N.Y., 1915-17; commd. maj. Insp. General's Dept., U.S. Army, 1918, duty with Gen. Staff U.S. Army, 1918; lt. col. Insp. General's Sect. U.S.R., 1919, col., 1923. Trustee Rutgers Coll.; pres. bd. Collegiate School; bd. of management Y.M.C.A. Mem. S.A.R., Sons of Vets., Loyal Legion, Mil. Service Instn. of U.S., Naval Order of U.S., 7th Regt. Vet. Assn. (pres.), Delta Upsilon, Colonial Wars, Nicholas Soc., Officers of Foreign Wars, Military and Naval Officers World's War, Humane Soc. of New York (pres.). Trustee Excelsior Savings Bank. Republican. Mem. Dutch Ref. Ch. Clubs: Union League, Republican, University, Southern Dutchess Country, City, New York Athletic. Home: 154 W. 74th St. Office: 505 5th Av., New York, N.Y. Died June 25, 1948.

STOUDT, John Baer (stout), historian-librarian; b. Topton, Pa., Oct. 17, 1878; s. John Reppert and Amanda Carl (Baer) S.; student Keystone State Normal Sch., Pa., 1898-1901; A.B., Franklin and Marshall Coll., Lancaster, Pa., 1905; student Eastern Theol. Sem., 1905-08, U. of Chicago, 1906; D.D., Univ. of Montpelier, France, 1924; married Elisabeth Agnes DeLong, October 15, 1908; 1 son, John Joseph (chaplain in U.S. Army). Teacher, 1896-1902; ordained ministry Reformed Church, 1908; pastor, Emmaus, Pa., and Northampton, Pa., 1908-22; mem. administrative committee Federal Council of Chs. of Christ in America, 1922-25; asso. to pres. Cedar Coll., Allentown, Pa., 1925-26; dir. public and private hist. activities since 1926. Hon. chaplain Belgian Army. Chmn. hist. com. Reformed Ch. in U.S.; mem. Hist. Commn. of Pa., 1927-31; dir. Allentown (Pa.) Masonic Library. Organized Huguenot Soc. of Pa., 1917 (chmn. exec. com.), Pa. German Folklore Soc., 1935 (historian, exec. com.); mem. Nat. Fed. of Huguenot Soc. of America (chmn. exec. com.), John Calvin Soc. of Geneva, Waldensian Soc. of Italy, French Protestant Hist. Soc., Huguenot Soc. of London, Huguenot Soc. of Berlin. Awarded Order of the Crown (Belgium), 1924; Legion of Honor (France), 1924. Republican. Mason. Author: Folklore of Pennsylvania Germans, 1916; Shenandoah Pottery (with A. H. Rice), 1929; Liberty Bells of Pennsylvania, 1930; Nicolas Martiau (colonial ancestor of George Washington), 1932. Editor numerous hist. publs. Home: 1054 Tilghman St., Allentown, Pa. Died Apr. 8, 1944.

STOUGHTON, Charles William (stô'tŭn), architect; b. N.Y. City; s. Charles and Sarah Jane (Warren) S.; C.E., Columbia, 1889. Began as architect, 1894; mem. Stoughton & Stoughton since 1894; designed Canton Christian Coll. (China), Polytechnic Inst. (Puerto Rico), police sta. and Jacob Reiss Free Bathing Pavilion (New York), stone highway bridges for city and state of N.Y. and John D. Rockefeller, Jr., Soldiers Monument (Riverside Park, N.Y. City). Mem. emeritus Am. Inst. Architects; mem. Fine Arts Fedn. (mem. council since 1915, dir. 1918-23), Municipal Art Soc. of N.Y. (dir. since 1912, pres. 1914-16), Westchester Hist. Soc.; Bronx Soc. Arts and Sciences (v.p.). Republican. Conglist. Home: 169 Elm Av., Mt. Vernon, N.Y. Office: 156 E. 42d St., New York, N.Y. Died Jan. 8, 1945.

STOUT, John Elbert, teacher; b. Lisbon, Ia., Dec. 15, 1867; s. Benjamin Freeman and Eliza Jane (Gray) S.; A.B., Cornell Coll., Ia., 1904; Ph.M., U. of Chicago, 1908, Ph.D., magna cum laude, 1918; m. Alma N. Taylor, 1892 (died 1904); m. 2d, Grace Farwell, June 29, 1911 (died Nov. 1, 1932). Prof. edn., Cornell Coll., 1906-20; prof. of adminstrn. in religious edn., Northwestern U., 1920, dean Sch. of Edn., 1926-34. Prof. edn., U. of Chicago and U. of Ill., summers. Dir. Jr. Red Cross, Central Div., 1918-19. Mem. Ia. Better Schs. Commn., 1912-14; pres. Ia. State Teachers' Assn., 1914; mem. Commn. on Units and Curricula, N. Central Assn. Colls. and Secondary Schs., 1916; chmn. Com. on Reorganization Secondary Sch. Curricula, 1919-24. Republican. Methodist. Mason. K.P. Club: University (Evanston). Author: The High Sch., 1914; Development of the High School Curriculum, 1920; Organization and Administration of Religious Education, 1921. Home: Georgian Hotel, Evanston, Ill. Died Dec. 20, 1942.

STOUT, Joseph Duerson, neuropsychiatrist; b. Washington, D.C., Nov. 20, 1886; s. Henry Isaiah and Nellie Wallace (Duerson) S.; A.B., George Washington U., 1910, M.D., 1913, A.M., 1914, Ph.D., 1915; grad. Army Med. Sch., 1918; m. Agnes Josephine Mills, July 14, 1921; children—Betty Jane, Joseph Duerson, Henry Wallace, Robert West. Prof. of physiology, dept. of dentistry, and prof. pharmacology and asso. prof. of physiology, dept. of medicine, George Washington U., 1913-17, prof. nervous diseases, 1920-27; prt. practice as neuropsychiatrist, Washington, since 1920. Asst. surgeon U.S. Pub. Health Service, 1916-17; 1st lt. Med. Corps, U.S. Army, 1917; lt. col. Med. R.C., 1932-34, M.I. Res. since 1934; on extended active duty with U.S. Army, at Army Med. Center, Washington, Mar. 1941; lt. col. M.C., Sept. 30, 1942, col. Med. Corps, U.S. Army, Dec. 9, 1942; comdg. officer, 136th Sta. Hosp., Oct. 10, 1942. Mem. Washington Soc. Nervous and Mental Diseases, Phi Chi. Republican. Baptists. Mason (32°, K.T., Shriner). Home: 3530 Porter St. N.W., Washington, D.C.* Died Nov. 6, 1944.

STRADER, Bernard Earl, business exec.; b. Hammond, La., Oct. 10, 1892; s. Edward Charles and Catherine (Walz) S.; ed. in high sch.; m. Laure Marie Cazenavette, Oct. 23, 1933. Operated automobile agency, Hammond, La., 1913-16; salesman, Peters Cartridge Co., 1916-23, southern sales mgr., 1924-31, gen. sales mgr., Cincinnati, O., 1931-34; dir. of sales, Remington Arms Co., Inc., Bridgeport, Conn., 1935-43, vice pres. and dir. of sales since 1944; president Am. Hardware Mfrs. Assn., N.Y. City, 1948; pres. Old Guard (Southern Hardware Salesmen's Assn.) 1947; exec. com. Am. Wildlife Inst. Republican. Clubs: Brooklawn Country, Commodore, Black Rock Yacht, (all in Bridgeport). Home: Old Battery Rd. Office: Remington Arms Co., Inc., Bridgeport, Conn. Died Jan. 3, 1949; buried in Metairie Cemetery, New Orleans.

STRAEHLEY, Erwin, Sr. (strā'lē), physician; b. Cincinnati, O., Sept. 25, 1868; s. John and Regina (Oesper) S.; M.D., Med. Coll. of Ohio, 1889; studied univs. of Würzburg, Strassburg and Kiehl, Germany, and Vienna, Austria, 1889-91; m. Carrie Lydia Miller, Sept. 21, 1892; children—Erwin (M.D.), Clifford J. (M.D.). Practiced at Cincinnati since 1892; specializes in internal medicine and pediatrics; asst. health officer, Cincinnati, 1892-94; mem. staffs Christ and Deaconess hosps.; mem. firm Drs. Straehley & Straehley. Vol. reserve med. officer, World War. Mem. bd. dirs., U. of Cincinnati, 1915-32. Fellow Am. Med. Assn.; mem. Ohio State Med. Assn., Acad. Medicine (Cincinnati). Republican. Presbyterian. Mason. Presented with the gold medal commemorating 50 years in Masonry, 1945. Club: Blaine. Presented "Golden Key," 1930, for service on staff of Christ Hosp.; "Golden Key," 1938, for services on Staff of Deaconess Hosp. Home: 2828 Vernon Pl. Office: Provident Bank Bldg., Cincinnati 2, O. Died Nov. 6, 1947.

STRAHAN, Charles Morton, civil engr.; b. Goochland County, Va., May 9, 1864; s. Charles and Jane Cave (Morton) S.; C.M.E., U. of Georgia, 1883, hon. D.Sc., 1915; studied Cornell U., summer, 1894; studied architecture, Columbia, and abroad; m. Margaret Amelia Basinger, Oct. 31, 1894; 1 dau., Mary. Tutor, instr. and adj. prof. chemistry, U. of Ga., 1883-90, prof. civil engring., 1890-1934, prof. emeritus, actg. prof. mathematics, since 1934; also cons. engr. Mem. Water Works Commn., Athens, Ga., 1892-94; county surveyor Clarke County, Ga., 1890-1908, county engr., since 1908; mem. Court House Commn., Athens; mem. City Bd. of Health; chmn. Ga. State Highway Bd., 1919-21, dir. of research, same, 1921-28; mem. Bd. of Rd. Commrs., Clarke County, Ga., 1930; mem. com. on design of roads of Nat. Research Council. Democrat. Episcopalian. Charter mem. Ga. Acad. Science, 1921; mem. Am. Soc. C.E., Am. Assn. State Highway Officials, Kappa Alpha. Author of Research on Top Soil, Sand-Clay, and Semi-Gravel Roads, 1921, reissued in fuller form by U.S. Bur. Pub. Roads, in Sept. number of "Good Roads," 1929. Home: Athens, Ga. Died Dec. 28, 1947.

STRAHORN, Robert Edmund (strā'hôrn), ry. builder and exec.; b. Center County, Pa., May 15, 1852; s. Thomas F. and Rebecca (Emmert) S.; ed. pub. schs., Stephenson County, Ill., and in printing offices; m. Carrie Adell Green, Sept. 19, 1877 (dec.); m. 2d, Ruby Garland, Oct. 5, 1927 (dec.). Newspaper work, 1866-77; corr. Chicago Tribune and other papers during Sioux campaigns, 1876-77; organized, and conducted publicity dept. U.P.R.R., 1877-83; ry., irrigation, power and colonization enterprises, Ida., Ore., Wash., 1883-90; bond business, Boston, 1890-98; builder and operator pub. service corps. in Ida., Ore., Wash., at Spokane, 1898-1905; builder and pres. N. Coast R.R., 1905-12; also v.p. and gen. mgr. Ore.-Wash. R.R. & Navigation Co.; builder, and pres. Portland, Eugene & Eastern Ry. Co., 1912-15, and later builder and pres. Ore., Calif. & Eastern Ry. Co., and Surprise Valley Ry. Co.; pres. Western Cities Co., Garland Co., West States Mines, Inc. Author of Wyoming Black Hills and Big Horn Regions; To the Rockies and Beyond; The Enchanted Land; Where Rolls the Oregon; Ninety Years of Boyhood; and other works on Far West resources, attractions and adventures. Trustee and largely builder of Coll. of Ida. (LL.D.). Home: (temp.) Stewart Hotel, San Francisco. Office: Eastman Bldg., Boise, Ida.* Died Mar. 31, 1944.

STRANAHAN, Edgar Howard (străn'á-hăn), clergyman; b. New Paris, O., Apr. 10, 1875; s. John and Othelia (Kemp) S.; B.Litt., Earlham Coll., Richmond, Ind., 1898, A.M., 1906; Master Religious Edn., Boston U., 1922, Doctor Religious Edn., 1927; m. Irene Dickinson, Apr. 12, 1900; children—Esther, Ruth (dec.). Pastor Friends chs. in Ind., Ohio, Kan. and Ia. until 1917; prof. Bible, Wilmington (O.) Coll., 1903-04, 1906-07; prof. ch. history, Friends U., Wichita, Kan., 1907-11; sec. Ch. Federation, Wichita, 1911-14; prof. religious education, Penn College, Oskaloosa, Ia., 1917-33; lecturer on psychology, Grant County, Ind., Nurses Training School, 1934-35; prof. religious edn. Friends U., Wichita, Kan., 1936-40; dean, William Penn Coll., Oskaloosa, Ia., 1940-43. Pres. Kansas State Sunday Sch. Assn., 1914, Ia. State Sunday Sch. Assn., 1918-24; mem. exec. com., Internat. Council Religious Edn.; chmn. bd. on Christian edn., Five Years Meeting of Friends, 1922-37, chmn. exec. com., 1935-37, reading clerk, 1940; pres. Iowa Council of Christian Edn., 1924-33, and since 1941; clerk Iowa Yearly Meeting of Friends, 1929-33 and since 1941; pastor of the First Friends Church, Marion, Indiana, 1933-36. President Kansas Council of Christian Education, 1938-40; pastor Minneapolis Friends Church, since 1943. Member Pi Gamma Mu Fraternity. Republican. Clubs: Rotary (president 1929-30), Lions International, 1933-36. Author: Lessons in Friends History, 1924; Outline Studies of the Old Testament, 1925; Outline of Friends History, 1930. Editor Friends Graded Sunday Sch. Lessons, 1931; Friends and Baptism, 1938. Contbr. to The Am. Friend. Address: 111 W. 45th St., Minneapolis 9, Minn. Died Oct. 22, 1944.

STRAUCH, John B. (strouk), corp. exec.; b. Marine, Ill., Nov. 29, 1869; s. John B. and Catherine (Schneider) S.; ed. pub. sch., Marine, and business coll., St. Louis; m. Ottilie C. Schmidt, June 14, 1894; children—John Andrew (dec.), Alice Frances. director Midwestern Fire & Marine Insurance Co., General American Life Insurance Company (St. Louis), First National Bank, St. Louis Union Trust Co., Securities Investment Co., Am. Central Insurance Co., Anheuser-Busch, Inc. Dir. Washington University, St. Louis, Mo. Republican. Clubs: Noonday, Mo. Athletic Assn., Racquet, Log Cabin Club, Bogey Club. Home: Village of Huntleigh, St. Louis County, Mo. Office, 4930 Manchester Av., St. Louis, Mo. Died June 22, 1945.

STRAUP, Daniel Newton (stroup), lawyer; b. Juniata County, Pa., Sept. 29, 1862; s. Daniel B. and Susanah (Barner) S.; B.S., Valparaiso U., also B.L., and LL.D.; m. Della Lindley, Apr. 1889; children—Cordelia (Mrs. Arthur J. Mays), Rosalind (Mrs. Royal Dustan), Danella (Mrs. Wm. J. Cope). Admitted to Ind. bar, 1888; moved to Salt Lake City, Utah, 1890; justice Supreme Court of Utah, 1905-17, and 1925-35; since in law practice. Lecturer on law, U. of Utah. Republican. Unitarian. Odd fellow, Elk, K.P. Home: 225 S. 12th E. St. Office: Boston Bldg., Salt Lake City, Utah. Died Nov. 1, 1945.

STRAUS, Percy Selden, mcht.; b. New York, N.Y., June 27, 1876; s. Isidor and Ida (Blun) S.; prep. edn., Sach's Collegiate Inst., N.Y. City; A.B., Harvard, 1897; m. Edith Abraham, Nov. 27, 1902; children—Ralph I., Percy S., Donald B. Began with R. H. Macy & Co., Inc., dept. store, N.Y. City, 1897, now chmn. bd.; dir. L. Bamberger & Co., Newark, N.Y. Life Ins. Co. Chmn. industrial training service, Dept. of Labor, also indsl. adviser to N.Y. City Draft Board, 1917-18. Mem. Council of N.Y. Univ.; trustee N.Y. Pub. Library; chmn. bd. Fedn. for Support of Jewish Philanthropic Socs. of N.Y. City; chmn. com. on architecture and physical planning, also dir. and mem. exec. com. N.Y. World's Fair, 1939; identified with many civic, edni. and charitable orgns. Clubs: Harvard; Westchester (N.Y.) Country. Home: 875 Park Av. Office: 151 W. 34th St., New York, N.Y. Died Apr. 6, 1944.

STRAUSS, Joseph, naval officer; b. Mt. Morris, New York, November 16, 1861; graduate United States Naval Academy, 1885. Ensign, June, 1887; junior lieut., June 1896; promoted through grades to rear admiral, February 1, 1918; admiral on the retired list, June 21, 1930. Cruised in various parts of the world, 1885-87; engaged in hydrog. surveys on east and west coast of U.S. and in Alaska, 1887-90; cruising, 1890-93; in Bur. of Ordnance, Navy Dept., 1893-96; invented superposed turret system of mounting guns on battleships, 1895; cruised in S. America, 1896-1900, and engaged in blockade of Cuban Coast; in charge of U.S. Naval Proving Ground, 1900-03; insp. ordnance Naval Proving Ground, 1906-08; comdr. cruiser Montgomery in experimental work on torpedoes, 1909-10; asst. aid for material, Navy Dept., 1910-12; comd. Battleship Ohio, 1912-13; chief Bur. Ordnance, with rank of rear-admiral, Oct. 1913-Dec. 1916; apptd. comdr. Battleship Nevada, Dec. 1916; apptd. comdr. mine force Atlantic Fleet, Mar. 1918; laid mine barrage across North Sea, Norway to Scotland, planting over 56,000 Am. mines; comd. expdn. that cleared North Sea of Mines, completing the work, Sept. 30, 1919; mem. Gen. Bd., 1920; comdr.-in-chief Asiatic Fleet, Feb. 1921-Sept. 1922; was mem. Gen. Bd. Sampson medal for Spanish-Am. War; U.S. Navy D.S.M.; Knight Comdr. St. Michael and St. George; Comdr. Legion of Honor of France; Comdr. Order of Sacred Treasure of Japan. Comdr. Order of Wen Hu, first class of China. Mem. Commn. to finally determine cause of destruction of Maine after she had been uncovered in Havana Harbor. Retired by operation of law, Nov. 16, 1925; recalled to active service as mem. bd. on Safety and Salvage of Submarines, June 1928-Mar. 1929, and again in 1937 as mem. of board to pass upon the design for new battleships. Has written various articles on ordnance and ballistics. Home: 2208 Mass. Ave. N.W., Washington. Died Dec. 30, 1948; buried in Arlington National Cemetery.

STRAUSS, Richard, composer; b. Munich, June 11, 1864; m. Pauline de Ahna, 1894. Dir. Vienna State Opera, 1919-24. Decorated Chevalier and Officer Legion of Honor. Composer: Tod und Verklärung; Don Juan; Macbeth; Till Eulenspiegel; Don Quixote; Ein Heldenleben; Elektra; The Rose Cavalier; operatic version of Le Bourgeois Gentilhomme; The Woman Without a Shadow; Intermezzo; Domestica; Arabella; Die Schweigsame Frau; Friedenstag; Daphne; also many others. Address: Strauss Villa, Garmisch Partenkirchen, Bavaria. Died Sept. 8, 1949.

STRAWN, Julia Clark, surgeon; b. Ottawa, Ill.; d. Abner and Eliza (Hardy) Strawn; M.D., Hahnemann Med. Col., Chicago, 1897, Coll. Physicians and Surgeons (U. of Ill.), 1903; post-grad. work in Vienna, Berlin, Munich, and clinic in med. centers of U.S., including Johns Hopkins, Phila., New York, Boston, Rochester, Minn., and in Europe, Japan, India, etc. Practiced in Chicago since 1897; prof. gynecology, Hahnemann Med. Coll., 16 yrs. Mem. bd. trustees Chicago Memorial Hosp., 12 yrs. Fellow Am. Coll. Surgeons; mem. A.M.A., Ill. State and Chicago med. socs., Nat. and Internat. Med. Women's Assn., Ill. Homeo. Med. Assn., Chicago Homeo. Med. Soc., Woman's Med. Club, North Side Med. Soc. Clubs: Arts, Chicago Woman's. Address: 223 E. Delaware St., Chicago, Ill. Died May 31, 1942.

STRAWN, Silas Hardy, lawyer; b. near Ottawa, Ill., Dec. 15, 1866; s. Abner and Eliza (Hardy) S.; LL.D., Northwestern U., U. of Mich., Knox, Lake Forest and Middlebury colls.; m. Margaret Stewart, June 22, 1897; children—Margaret (Mrs. James A. Cathcart), Katherine (Mrs. Wesley M. Dixon). Admitted to bar, Ottawa, 1889, practicing there to 1891, since in Chicago; mem. Winston, Payne, Strawn & Shaw to Jan. 1, 1918, since sr. mem. Winston, Strawn & Shaw; gen. solicitor Alton R.R.; dir. and mem. exec. com. First Nat. Bank, Chicago; dir. Montgomery Ward & Co.; firm gen. counsel Union Stock Yard & Transit Co.; attys. for Monon R.R., Nickel Plate R.R. Del. of U.S. to special conf. at Peking, on Chinese customs tariff, American mem. and chmn. Chinese Extra-territoriality Commn. Mem. Am. Bar Assn. (pres. 1927-28), Ill. State Bar Assn. (pres. 1921-22), Chicago Bar Association, (president 1913-14). Chicago Law Club, Commercial Club (ex-president). Life trustee Northwestern University; trustee Carnegie Endowment for International Peace, Chicago National History Museum; hon. v.p. U. S. Chamber Commerce, 1928, pres., 1931-32. Clubs: Chicago, Economic, Chicago Athletic (hon.), Mid-Day (ex-pres.), Old Elm, Casino (Chicago), Ex-pres. U.S. Golf Assn. Home: 209 Lake Shore Drive. Office: 38 S. Dearborn St., Chicago, Ill. Died Feb. 4, 1946.

STREAN, Maria Judson (străn), artist; b. Washington, Pa.; d. Robert Fulton and Ann Maria Judson (Greenleaf) Strean; ed. country schs. and Washington (Pa.) Sem. Represented by miniatures "Coral," Metropolitan Museum of Art, and in permanent collection of Corcoran Gallery, Washington, D.C.; "Dorothy," Pa. Museum of Fine Arts; "Child at Play," Brooklyn (N.Y.) Museum. Awarded Pa. Soc. of Miniature Painters medal of honor, 1921; Los Angeles Museum prize, 1932; Nat. Assn. of Women Painters and Sculptors portrait prize, 1931, miniature prize, 1939. Mem. Am. Soc. of Miniature Painters. Allied Artists of America, Nat. Assn. of Women Artists (formerly Nat. Assn. Women Painters and Sculptors), Pa. Soc. of Miniature Painters, Am. Water Color Soc. Presbyterian. Address: 800 South Aiken Ave. Pittsburgh 6. Died July 14, 1949; buried Washington, Pa.

STREAT, Hearn W., vice chmn. bd., chmn. exec. com. and dir. Blair & Co., Inc.; dir. Houston Gulf Gas Co. Home: 1165 Park Av. Office: 44 Wall St., New York, N.Y.* Died Feb. 19, 1946.

STREET, J. Fletcher, architect; b. Beverly, N.J., June 11, 1880; s. John Fletcher and Emily Virginia (Phillips) S.; student Farnum Prep. Sch., Beverly; m. Ethel Frances Parker, Apr. 28, 1910; children—Edward Parker, Phillips Borden. Draftsman, 1898-1907; in business for self since 1907; designer chs., schs., mfg. bldgs., residences, also landscape architecture. Mem. Am. Inst. Architects, Acad. Natural Sciences of Phila., Phila. Geog. Soc. (past pres.). Democrat. Clubs: University, Franklin Inn, Botanical (Phila.), Del. Valley Ornithol. Club. Author: Brief Bird Biographies. Contbr. to scientific jours. Home: Beverly, N.J. Office: 1120 Locust St., Philadelphia, Pa.* Died Sep. 18, 1944.

STREET, Julian, author; b. Chicago, Ill., Apr. 12, 1879; s. Arthur Wray and Mary Ross (Low) S.; ed. Chicago pub. schs. and Ridley Coll. Prep., St. Catharines, Ont., Can.; m. Ada Hilt, Jan. 13, 1900 (died July 1926); children—Julian Leonard, Rosemary Hale; m. 2d, Marguerite Skibeness, May 12, 1930. Reporter Mail and Express, New York, 1899, in charge dramatic dept., 1900-01. Mem. Nat. Inst. of Arts and Letters, Authors' League of America, S.R. Clubs: Colonial (Princeton); Century, Dutch Treat (New York). Author: My Enemy the Motor, 1908; The Need of Change, 1909; Paris a la Carte, 1911; Ship-Bored, 1911; The Goldfish (children's story), 1912; Welcome to Our City, 1913; Abroad at Home, 1914; The Most Interesting American, 1915; American Adventures, 1917; After Thirty, 1919; Sunbeams, Inc., 1920; Mysterious Japan, 1921; Rita Coventry, 1922; Cross-Sections, 1923; Mr. Bisbee's Princess, 1925; Tides (in collaboration with Ada Street), 1926; Where Paris Dines, 1929; Wines, 1933 (rev. edit., 1948). Men, Machines and Morals, 1942; also comedy, The Country Cousin (with Booth Tarkington). Winner, 1925, O. Henry Memorial prize for short story. Awarded Cross of Chevalier, Legion of Honor (France) 1935, for works on wines and gastronomy. Contbr. to mags. Home: Lakeville, Conn. Died Feb. 19, 1947.

STREET, Oliver Day, lawyer; b. Warrenton, Ala., Dec. 6, 1866; s. Thomas Atkins and Julia Ann (Beard) S.; A.B., U. of Ala., 1887, LL.B., 1888; m. Mary Emma, d. Dr. Lorenzi D. Lusk, of Guntersville, Ala., Feb. 17, 1892 (died Oct. 21, 1923); children—Margarette, Mary Julia, Oliver Day, Thomas Atkins (dec.), John Edwin Campbell; m. 2d, Mrs. Mary Curd Allen, September 17, 1927; 1 son, Charles Alfred Street. Admitted to Alabama bar, 1888; active in state and local politics since 1892; nominee for United States Congress, 7th Alabama District, 1898, 1902; U.S. Dist. Atty., Northern Dist. of Ala., May 1907-Feb. 1914; special asst. to the atty. general of U.S., 1914-20. Chmn. Rep. Exec. Com. 7th Congressional Dist. of Ala., 1904-08; del. Rep. Nat. Conv., 1912, 16, 20, 32, 36; mem. Rep. Nat. Com., 1916-36; mem. Rep. Nat. Platform Committee, 1938-40. Nominated by the Rep. party of Ala., for gov., 1914 (declined). Rep. nominee for Congress, 7th Ala. Dist., 1918; Republican nominee for gov., 1922. Mem. Ala. Hist. Soc.; trustee Dept. Archives and History of Ala., 1901-20; sec., treas. Tenn. Valley Hist. Soc. Foreign corr. Grand Lodge of Masons of Alabama, 1915-22, Junior Grand Warden of Masons, 1919-21, Senior Grand Warden, 1921-23, Dep. Grand Master, 1923-25, Grand Master, 1925-27. Author: The Symbolism of the Three Degrees of Masonry, 1922; World Masonry, 1922; History of Freemasonry in Alabama, 1940; also numerous monographs and articles, chiefly on Ala. history. Editor 14th edition Alabama Masonic Manual, 1940. Home: Guntersville, Ala. Died Aug. 3, 1944.

STREETER, George Linius (strēt'ẽr), anatomist; b. Johnstown, N.Y., Jan. 12, 1873; s. George Austin and Hannah Green (Anthony) S.; A.B., Union Coll., New York, 1895, D.Sc., 1930; A.M., M.D., Columbia Univ., 1899; D.Sc., Trinity College, Dublin, 1928; LL.D., U. of Michigan, 1935; m. Julia Allen Smith, Apr. 9, 1910; children—Sarah Frances, George Allen, Mary Raymond. Asst. and instr. anatomy, Johns Hopkins 1902-06; asst. prof. anatomy, Wistar Inst. Anatomy, Phila., 1906-07; prof. anatomy and dir. anat. lab., U. of Mich., 1907-14; research asso. Carnegie Instn. of Washington, 1914-18, dir. dept. of embryology, 1918-40, chmn. division animal biology, 1935-40, research asso. since 1940. Trustee Samuel Ready School, Baltimore. Fellow Royal Society (Edinburgh). Mem. American Philos. Soc. of Philadelphia, American Soc. Naturalists, National Acad. Sciences, Am. Assn. Anatomists, Am. Soc. Zoologists, Inst. Internat. d'Embryologie; fgn. mem. Zoöl. Soc. London; hon. mem. Anat. Soc. Gr. Britain and Ireland.

Home: 3707 St. Paul St., Baltimore 18, Md. Died July 27, 1948.

STRICKLAND, Robert Marion, banker; b. Tallapoosa, Ga., March 1, 1895; s. Robert Marion and Leola Ruth (Atkinson) S.; student Emory U., 1910-12; LL.B., Atlanta Law Sch., 1914; m. Jessie Dickey, Oct. 15, 1919; children—Mary Jessie, Robert Marion III. Practiced law as associate with Brandon & Hynds, Atlanta, 1913-17; with Fourth Nat. Bank (now First Nat. Bank), 1919-33, v.p., 1922-33; dir., exec. v.p. Trust Co. of Ga. and Trust Co. of Ga. Associates, 1933-36, pres. since 1936; dir. Coca Cola International Corp., Wilmington, Del.; Federal Reserve Bank of Atlanta (Ga.), Tubize Rayon Corp., New York, N.Y.; Dyersburg (Tenn.) Cotton Products Co., N.C. & St. L. Ry., Nashville. Mem. Am. Bankers' Assn., Treasury War Borrowing Com., vice chmn. Southern Research Inst., Birmingham, Ala. Pres. Atlanta Clearing House Assn., 1927, also pres. same, 1944. Pres. Georgia Bankers Assn., 1927-28, Reserve City Bankers Assn., 1937-38; mem. exec. council nat. bank division, American Bankers Association, 1927, vice president, 1931-32. Trustee John Bulow Campbell Foundation, Atlanta, Ga. Mem. Omicron Delta Kappa, Kappa Alpha. Methodist. Clubs: Capital City, Piedmont Driving, Rotary, Oglethorpe; Augusta Nat. Golf (Augusta, Ga.). Home: 525 W. Wesley Rd., N.W. Office: Trust Co. of Ga., Atlanta 2, Ga. Died Aug. 8, 1946.

STRIKE, C(lifford) J(ohn), pub. utilities; b. New Hampton, Ia., Apr. 11, 1895; s. F. B. and Delphine (Sheldon) S.; student pub. schs.; m. Olga Solberg, Mar. 21, 1916; children—Edith Olga, Beverly Jeanne. Pres., chmn. bd. Ida. Power Co., Boise, since 1938. Mem. Ida. State C. of C., Edison Electric Inst. Club: Rotary (Boise). Home: 1414 Warm Springs Av. Office: Ida. Power Co., Boise, Ida. Deceased.

STRINGER, Lawrence Beaumont, ex-congressman; b. Atlantic City, N.J., Feb. 24, 1866; s. Firth and Maria (Shaw) S.; A.B., Lincoln U., 1887; grad. Chicago Coll. of Law, 1896; LL.B., Lake Forest U., 1897; LL.D., James Millikin U., 1921; m. Helen Pegram, Dec. 18, 1890. Practiced, Lincoln, Ill., since 1897; lyceum lecturer since 1906. Mem. Ill. Ho. of Rep., 1890-94, State Senate, 1900-04 (minority leader); Dem. nominee for gov. of Ill., 1904; chief justice Ill. State Ct. of Claims, 1905-13; Dem. primary nominee for U.S. senator, 1908; mem. 63d Congress (1913-15), Ill. at large; judge of Logan County, Ill., since 1918; candidate for U.S. senator, 1915; candidate for justice Supreme Court of Ill., 1924. Trustee Millikin U.; mem. bd. mgrs. Lincoln College. Mem. Ill. State Bar Assn., Abraham Lincoln Assn., Ill. Acad. Science. Author: History of Logan County, Illinois, 1910; Civil Government in Illinois, 1925; also monographs. Home: Lincoln, Ill. Died Dec. 5, 1942.

STRODACH, Paul Zeller (strō-dŏk'), clergyman, editor; b. Norristown, Pa., Mar. 27, 1876; s. Henri Jean Baptiste and Mary Louise (Zeller) S.; A.B., Muhlenberg Coll., Allentown, Pa., 1896, A.M., 1899; B.D., 1918, D.D., 1922, Litt.D., 1944; graduate Philadelphia Theological Seminary, 1899; graduate work, Princeton; married Bertha Laubach Kleppinger, April 6, 1904; 1 son, George Kleppinger. Ordained ministry Evangelical Lutheran Church, 1899; successively pastor Ch. of the Saviour (Trenton, N.J.); asso. pastor St. John's Ch. (Easton, Pa.); pastor First Ch. (Washington, Pa.), Trinity Ch. (Canton, O.), Grace Ch. (Roxboro, Phila.), and Ch. of the Trinity, Norristown; lit. editor United Luth. Ch. Pub. House. Mem. Common Service Book Com. of United Luth. Ch., mem. Joint Commn. on Common Hymnal, Joint Commn. on Common Liturgy, also officer or member other church organizations. Ecclesiastical illuminator and liturgiologist. Member Alpha Tau Omega. Republican. Author: The Church Year, 1924; Oremus, 1925; A Manual on Worship, 1929, revised and enlarged, 1946; In the Presence, 1931; His Glorious Hour, 1932; The Road He Trod, 1932; Luther's Liturgical Writings, 1932; Before the Cross, 1933; Lift Up Your Heart, 1934; The Collect for the Day, 1939; Were You There, 1942; also monographs and essays on liturg. and hymnol. subjects and on church art and music. Translator: The Jesuits, 1927. Editor: The Parable of the Empty Soul, 1940; Calling All Christians, 1942; God, the Eternal Paradox, 1943; But Christ Did Rise, 1944; Victim or Victor, 1945; Divine Invasion, 1946; Book of Family Worship; The Children's Hymnal and Service Book. Co-editor of Luther's Works, Parish School Hymnal, Army and Navy Service Book, Hymns and Prayers, etc. Home: 264 W. Walnut Lane, Germantown, Philadelphia 44, Pa. Office: 1228 Spruce St., Philadelphia 7, Pa. Died May 30, 1947.

STRONG, Charles Howard, lawyer; b. Jerseyville, Ill., Oct. 6, 1865; s. John Caldwell and Mary Cornelia (Dutcher) S.; student Harvard U., 1887; LL.B., 1890, hon. A.M., 1922; m. Angelia L. Longfellow, June 28, 1893 (died Aug. 26, 1934); m. 2d, Anne T. Barstow, June 25, 1937. In practice of law in N.Y. City since 1890; mem. Peckham, Warner & Strong, 1895-1907; practiced alone, 1907-10; mem. Strong & Mellen, 1910-25, Strong, Mellen & Fuller, 1925-27; alone since 1927. Active in municipal affairs; pres. Good Govt. Club "A," about 1895 (one of a series of neighborhood clubs formed by City Club of New York); pres. Council of Confederated Good Govt. Clubs, 1896; pres. Citizens' Union Club 29th Assembly District (formerly Club "A"), and later mem. of a com. of which Charles S. Fairchild was chmn., and which placed the Citizens' Union on a permanent basis; later became chmn. N.Y. County Committee of Citizens' Union; mem. N.Y. Charter Revision Commn. under appmt. of Gov. Hughes, 1907-09; counsel to State Tax Commn. to revise all tax laws of State of N.Y., 1913; pres. bd. mgrs. N.Y. State Training Sch. for Girls, Hudson, by appmt. of Govs. Odell, Higgins, and Dix, 1902-12, pres. bd. trustees Roger Ascham Sch., White Plains, N.Y.; commr. to investigate and suggest revision charities law in New York, 1915, by appmt. Gov. Whitman. Counsel to Senator James D. Phelan, spl. commr. of State Dept. to investigate charges against James M. Sullivan, U.S. minister to Santo Domingo, 1915; counsel for Scopes on appeal to Tenn. Supreme Court in famous evolution case. Republican. Unitarian; pres. Unitarian Club, 1910-11; pres. bd. trustees and senior deacon All Souls' Ch., 1921; pres. Unitarian Laymen's League, 1919-26; mem. bd. dirs. and exec. com. of Greater New York Fedn. of Churches, 1939-42; secretary Assn. Bar City of New York 1917-46; vice-president Am. Bar Assn., 1933; chmn. joint committee of New York City Bar Assns., 1940-41; member council Harvard Law School Assn.; a founder Am. Law Institute; dir. Museum of Science and Industry; pres. Century Opera Company, 1914; exec. com. Citizens' Com. of 1000 for Law Enforcement; chmn. bd. trustees Meadville Theol. Sch. (Chicago); pres. New York Infirmary for Women and Children, 1928-30. Mem. N.Y. State World's Fair Commn. Member N.Y. State Commission to commemorate 250th Anniversary founding N.Y. State Supreme Court, 1941. Clubs: Century, City (pres 1909-14) Harvard. Home: 737 Park Av., New York, N.Y. Died July 29, 1949; buried Sleepy Hollow Cemetery, Tarrytown, N.Y.

STRONG, George Veazey, army officer; b. Chicago, Mar. 14, 1880; s. John Winder and Elizabeth (Veazey) S.; student Mich. Mil. Acad., 1898-1900; B.S., U.S. Mil. Acad., 1904; LL.B., Northwestern U., 1916, LL.D., 1943; grad. Army War Coll., 1924, Command and Gen. Staff Sch., 1931; m. Gerda E. Loenholm, June 2, 1909; children—George Loenholm, Elizabeth Veazey (dec.), William Ronald, Commd. 2d lt. cav., U.S. Army, June 15, 1904, and advanced through the grades to maj. gen. Apr. 1941; retired Feb. 1944; became asst. chief of staff, Oct. 1938; comdg. gen. 8th Army Corps, May, 1941; apptd. head Military Intelligence, June, 1942; Joint chiefs of staff, Apr. 1944-45. Decorated D.S.M. with Oak Leaf Cluster, Legion of Merit, Purple Heart (U.S.), Legion of Honor (France). Adviser to Traffic in Arms Conf., Geneva, Switzerland, 1925; tech. adviser Preparatory Commn., 1927-30; mil. adviser, Disarmament Conf., 1930-34. Adviser, Dumbarton Oaks Conf., 1944, Pan-Am. Conf., Mexico City, 1945. Episcopalian. Mason. Clubs: Army and Navy (Washington, D.C.); Army-Navy Country (Arlington, Va.). Author: Japanese-English Military Dictionary, 1911; Common Chinese-Japanese Characters, 1911. Address: New War Dept. Bldg., Washington. Died Jan. 10, 1946; buried at West Point, N.Y.

STRONG, Richard Pearson, tropical medicine; b. Fortress Monroe, Va., Mar. 18, 1872; s. Col. Richard P. and Marion B. (Smith) S.; Ph.B., Yale, 1893; M.D., Johns Hopkins, 1897; ed. U. of Berlin, and Institut für Infektionskrankheiten, Berlin, 1903; hon. Sc.D., Yale, 1914, Harvard, 1916; m. Grace Nichols, July 23, 1936 (died April, 1944). Resident house physician Johns Hopkins Hospital, 1897-98; 1st lt. and assistant surgeon United States Army, 1898-1902; appointed, 1899, by sec. of war as president board for the investigation of tropical diseases in P.I., and served until 1901; established and directed work of Army Pathol. Lab.; dir. Govt. Biol. Lab., Manila, 1901-13 (resigned); resigned from army Dec. 5, 1902; sent by govt. to Berlin, 1903, for scientific investigation; prof. tropical medicine, Coll. Medicine and Surgery, Univ. of P.I., 1907-13 (resigned); prof. tropical medicine, Harvard, 1913-38, prof. emeritus since 1938, Lowell lecturer, 1916; consultant on tropical medicine, Secretary of War, 1941. Col. M.C., U.S. Army, 1942-46, dir. tropical medicine, Army Med. Sch., 1942-45. Mem. council Massachusetts Department of Health, 1921-42. Trustee Carnegie Institution. Was chief med. dept. P.I. Gen. Hosp., 1910-13, also editor medical sect., Philippine Journal of Science. Del. Internat. Congress of Hygiene and Demography, 1907; hon. v.p. Sect. Pathology and Bacteriology, Internat. Congress of Tuberculosis, Washington, D.C., 1908; Am. del. Internat. Plague Conf., Peking, 1911; med. dir. of Internat. and Am. Red Cross Sanitary Commn., Serbia, 1915. Hon. fellow Royal Soc. Tropical Medicine and Hygiene, London; fellow Am. Acad. Arts and Sciences, A.A.A.S. (v.p. sect. N, 1923-24); asso. mem. Société de Pathologie Exotique, Paris; mem. Assn. Am. Physicians (pres. 1925-26), A.M.A., Soc. Exptl. Biology, Acad. of Tropical Medicine (pres. 1936), Am. Soc. of Tropical Medicine (pres. 1914), Am. Assn. of Pathologists and Bacteriologists, Mass. Med. Soc., Boston Soc. Natural History, Am. Soc. Exptl. Pathology, Am. Soc. Parasitologists (pres. 1927), Aurelian (Yale U.), Soc. de Biologie (Paris), Soc. Belge de Med. Tropicale (honorary), Soc. Medico Chirurgica (Bologna). Mem. med. advisory board Council Nat. Defense; mem. foreign service com. Nat. Research Council, which visited France and England, Apr. 1917, to study orgn. and development of scientific activities in connection with warfare. Commd. maj. Med. R.C., May 9, 1917; duty with British and French armies, May 23-Aug. 4, 1917; assigned Hdqrs. A.E.F.; later promoted to lt. col. and col.; mem. Hdqrs. Investigating Com. and Inter-Allied Sanitary Commn., in charge Div. Infect. Diseases, A.E.F., during war; dir. Dept. Med. Research, Am. Red Cross, Dec. 2, 1918-Apr. 1919; organizer and del. from U.S. to Inter-Allied Med. Conf., Cannes, France, 1919; gen. med. dir. League of Red Cross Societies, 1919-20; v.p. sect. of tropical medicine and hygiene, Royal Inst. Pub. Health Congress, Bordeaux, June 1924. Decorated D.S.M.; Companion of the Bath (British); Officier Légion d'Honneur (French); Striped Tiger (Chinese); Grand Officer Cross of St. Sava (Serbian); awarded Theobald-Smith medal of Am. Acad. of Tropical Medicine, 1939; medal of Am. Foundation for Tropical Medicine, 1944; Legion of Merit, 1946. Clubs: Somerset, Tavern, Westwood Polo, Travelers, Yale, Harvard, Brookline Country, Army and Navy, Metropolitan (Washington); Harvard, River (New York); Chevy Chase, Authors, Boodles (London); Casino, Spouting Rock Beach, Clambake Reading Room (Newport). Author: (textbook) Diagnosis, Prevention and Treatment of Tropical Diseases (7th edit., 1944); reports on tropical diseases and expdns. to South Am. and Africa. Home: 107 Chestnut St., Boston, Mass.; and "Riddle Rocks," Newport, R.I. Died July 4, 1948.

STRONG, Wendell Melville, actuary; b. Indianapolis, Ind., Feb. 6, 1871; s. Melville and Persis F. (Griffith) S.; B.A., Yale, 1893; M.A., Cornell U., 1894; fellow in mathematics, Yale, 1894-95, Ph.D., 1898; LL.B., New York U., 1903; m. Susan Hoyt Evans, 1909; 1 dau., Helen Griffith. Instr. in mathematics, Yale, 1895-1900; entered actuary's dept. Mut. Life Ins. Co. of New York, 1900, becoming successively asst. actuary, asso. actuary, vice-pres. and actuary; now retired. Fellow Actuarial Soc. America, Casualty Actuarial Soc., Am. Inst. Actuaries; mem. Am. Math. Soc., London Math. Soc., Phi Beta Kappa, Sigma Xi, Phi Delta Phi, Elihu Club. Vice-pres. for U.S. and Can. of Internat. Congress Actuaries, 1930. Clubs: University, Bankers, Glen Ridge Country. Author: (with Andrew W. Phillips) Trigonometry, 1899; Logarithmic and Trigonometric Tables, 1899. Editor Trans. of Actuarial Soc. America, 1909-16; (sec. 1916-22; v.p. 1922-24, and 1926-28; mem. council 1928-30 and since 1932; pres. 1930-32). Contbr. to math. and actuarial publs. Home: Glen Ridge, N.J. Died Mar. 30, 1942.

STROUP, Thomas Andrew, mining engr.; b. Lewistown, Mo., Dec. 2, 1885; s. John Knox and Eliza (Weaver) S.; B.S., Sch. of Mines (U. of Mo.), 1912; spl. work, Armour Inst. Tech., and McGill U., Montreal, Can.; unmarried. Mech. engr. with Jeffrey Mfg. Co., Columbus, O., 1912-15; mining engr., Tenn. Copper Co., 1915-16, Utah Copper Co., 1916-18; mining engr. and supt. of mines, Utah Fuel Co., 1918-25; now cons. engineer W.Va. Coal & Coke Corp., Ohio River Co. Engaged in exploration and production of rare minerals, Utah and Nev., World War. Mem. Am. Inst. Mining and Metall. Engrs., Rocky Mountain Coal Mining Inst., Tau Beta Pi. Democrat. Unitarian. Mason. Club: University. Contbr. on coal mining and labor problems. Home: 710 N. 4th St., Quincy, Ill. Died Aug. 27, 1943.

STRUBLE, Mildred (Mrs. Charles E. Carpenter) (strū'b'l); university professor, author; born at Menominee, Mich., June 19, 1894; daughter Edward Sidney and Clara Louise (Alvord) Struble; grad. Lewiston (Ida.) State Normal Sch., 1912; A.B., University of Washington, 1917, A.M., 1920, Ph.D., 1924; study in Europe, 1930, 1938-39; m. Charles E. Carpenter, Sept. 4, 1940. Teacher pub. schs., 1912-13, 1914-16; instr. Ellensburg (Wash.) High Sch. and State Teachers' Coll., 1917-19; asso. in English, U. of Wash., 1919-23; with U. of Southern Calif. since 1923, prof. comparative lit. and chmn. of dept. since 1927; guest prof. English, N.Y. Univ., summer, 1927. Chmn. War Camp Community Service, Central Wash., 1917-19. Mem. Am. Assn. Univ. Profs., Modern Lang. Assn. America, Philol. Assn. Pacific Coast, Am. Assn. Univ. Women (lecturer since 1932), Pi Kappa Phi, Pi Lambda Theta, Mu Phi Epsilon, Sigma Kappa. Episcopalian. Author: A Johnson Handbook, 1933. Editor of A Critical Edition of Ford's Perkin Warbeck, 1924. Co-editor of Essays for the New America, 1930. Contbr. articles and verse to lit. mags. Home: 100 S. Van Ness Av., Los Angeles, Calif. Office: University of Southern California, Los Angeles. Died Jan. 14, 1949.

STRUCK, F(erdinand) Theodore, indsl. educator; b. Hamburg, Germany, Mar. 18, 1886; s. Ludwig Christian Nicholous and Bertha (Runge) S.; brought by parents to U.S., 1893; grad. high sch., Hood River, Ore., 1907; B.S., in C.E., U. of Ore., 1911; A.M., Teachers Coll. (Columbia), 1914; Ph.D., Columbia, 1920; m. Alice Clark, Nov. 25, 1915; children—Robert Theodore, John Warren, Barbara Alice. Journeyman trade experience in carpentry and drafting. Teacher shop work and drawing, high sch., Tacoma, 1911-13; dir. West Orange (N.J.) Industrial Sch., 1914-15; head teacher, Essex County (N.J.) Vocational Sch., 1915-18; asso. prof., later prof. agrl. edn., Pa. State Coll., 1918-20; asst. dir., later dir. vocational bur., State Dept. Pub. Instrn., Pa., 1920-26; prof. industrial edn. and head of dept., Pa. State Coll., since 1926; instr. summer sessions, Del. State Coll., N.C. State Coll., Colo. State Coll., Pa. State Coll., Ia. State Coll., Harvard University. Consultant in vocational education, U.S. Office of Education, Washington, D.C., Jan. 1-July 1, 1941. Trustee Nat. Assn. of Industrial Teacher-Trainers, 1938-39, pres., 1940-41. Mem. Nat. Edn. Assn., Am. Vocational Assn., Am. Assn. Univ. Profs., Nat. Soc. Coll. Teachers of Edn., Pa. State Education Assn., Pa. Vocational Education Assn. (sec.-treas. since 1938), Phi Delta Kappa, Kappa Phi Kappa, Kappa Delta Pi.

Iota Lambda Sigma (pres. Grand Chapter 1931; nat. advisory council since 1931). Methodist. Mason. Club: Pa. School Men's. Author: Construction and Repair Work for the Farm, 1923; Methods in Industrial Education, 1929; Foundations of Industrial Education, 1930; Creative Teaching, 1938; also writer of tech. reports for Pa. State Coll. and Pa. State Dept. Pub. Instrn. Mem. editorial advisory bd. School Shop mag.; contbr. to ednl. jours. Home: 527 W. Fairmount Av., State College, Pa. Died Nov. 22, 1943.

STRUNSKY, Simeon (strŭn'skē), editor; b. at Vitebsk, Russia, July 23, 1879; s. Isadore and Pearl (Weinstein) S.; A.B., Columbia, 1900; m. Rebecca Slobodkin, 1905 (dec.); m. 2d, Manya Gordon, Sept. 11, 1910 (dec.); children—Robert, Frances. Department editor New Internat. Encyclopedia, 1900-06; editorial writer New York Evening Post, 1906-20, editor, 1920-24; mem. editorial staff New York Times, since 1924. Member National Institute of Arts and Letters, Phi Beta Kappa. Author: The Patient Observer, 1911; Post-Impressions, 1914; Belshazzar Court, 1914; Professor Latimer's Progress, 1918; Little Journeys to Paris, 1918; Sinbad and His Friends, 1921; King Akhnaton, 1928; The Rediscovery of Jones, 1931; The Living Tradition, 1939; No Mean City, 1944; Two Came to Town, 1947. Contbr. to mags. Club: Century. Home: 1215 5th Av., New York 29. Address: The Times, New York, N.Y. Died Feb. 5, 1948.

STRUNK, William, univ. prof.; b. Cincinnati, O., July 1, 1869; s. William and Ella (Garretson) S.; A.B., U. of Cincinnati, 1890; Ph.D., Cornell U., 1896; studied U. of Paris, 1898-99; m. Olivia Emilie Locke, June 30, 1900; children—Oliver, Edwin Hart, Dr. Catherine Amatruda. Instructor in mathematics, Rose Polytechnical Institute, Terre Haute, Indiana, 1890-91; instructor in English, Cornell University, 1891-98, fellow, 1898-99, assistant professor English, 1899-1909, professor, 1909-37, now emeritus. Member Phi Beta Kappa. Democrat. Editor: Macaulay's and Carlyle's Essays on Boswell's Johnson, 1895; Dryden's Essays on the Drama, 1898; Cooper's Last of the Mohicans, 1900; Cynewulf's Juliana, 1904; Dryden's All for Love, and The Spanish Friar, 1911; Romeo and Juliet, 1911; Julius Caesar, 1915. Joint Editor: Studies in Language and Literature, in Honor of James Morgan Hart. Author: The Elements of Style, 1918; English Metres, 1923. Officier d'Académie, France. Acting prof. English, summer session, Ohio State U., 1920; lit. consultant for motion picture Romeo and Juliet, 1935. Home: 301 W. State St., Ithaca, N.Y.* Died Sep. 26, 1946.

STUART, Charles Edward (stū'ărt), consulting engr.; b. Alexandria, Va., Aug. 29, 1881; s. Judge Charles Edward and Ruth (Yeaton) S.; E.E., Va. Mil. Inst., 1901; engring. course, Westinghouse Electric & Mfg. Co.; m. Dorothy Sanders, Apr. 16, 1911; children—Dorothy Du Val, Elizabeth Charles, Patricia. Principal Ashland, Va., High School, 1901-02. With Westinghouse Electric & Mfg. Co., Pittsburgh, Pa., 1902-11; sr. partner and pres. Stuart, James & Cooke, New York, since 1911; cons. engr. to Govt. of Russia in relation to the projection of new mines and rehabilitation of old in coal, iron and copper; report to Russian Govt., 1931, on the subject of rationalization, 1926-32; exec. vice-pres. of Export-Import Bank, Washington, D.C., 1934-36; has carried out many assignments in U.S., Great Britain and European Continent. Served as chief of Power Conservation, Bureau, U.S. Fuel Adminstrn., World War; also mem. of Nat. Production Com. for fuel administration and asso. mem. Power Com. and of War Industries Bd. Following conferences with leading govt. officials and industrial authorities, made several reports on internat. trade and export credits for State and Commerce Depts., 1935; visited Europe summer of 1936 as mem. of Com. of Inquiry into Cooperative Enterprise sent abroad by the President. Dir. Am.-Russian Chamber of Commerce; governing mem. Nat. Fgn. Trade Council. Mem. Am. Inst. E.E., Am. Institute Mining and Metall. Engrs. Clubs: New York Athletic, Virginians, Southern Society of New York; Whitehall, New York; Oakland Golf, Long Island, Duquesne, Pittsburgh. Contbr. tech. and economic articles to U.S. and foreign mags. Office: 52 William St., New York, N.Y.; and Hibbs Bldg., Washington, D.C. Died June 20, 1943.

STUART, Elbridge Amos, chmn. bd. Carnation Co.; b. Guilford County, N.C., Sept. 10, 1856; s. Amos and Matilda (Hadley) S.; ed. pub. schs.; m. Mary J Horner, Nov. 13, 1884. Pres. Carnation Co. (formerly Carnation Milk Products Co.), 1899-1932, chmn. bd. since Feb. 1932; pres. Carnation Milk Farms, Carnation Farm Products Co.; pres. emeritus Pacific Internat. Live Stock Expn. (Portland, O.); mem. bd. dirs. Metropolitan Co. (Seattle). Exhibitor at live stock shows; developed "world's three greatest milk cows"—Segis Pietertje Prospect—with a record of 37,381 pounds of milk and 1,448 pounds of butter in 365 consecutive days, Carnation Ormsby Butter King with records of 38,606 6 pounds of milk and 1,752.5 pounds of butter in 365 consecutive days; Carnation Ormsby Madcap Fayne with records of 41,943.4 pounds of milk and 1,740.5 pounds of butter in 365 consecutive days; started stable of gaited saddle horses and hackney harness horses and ponies, in 1922. Mem. Holstein Friesian Assn., Am. Hackney Horse Soc.; formerly pres. Seattle Internat. Horse Show Assn. Republican. Conglist. Mason (Shriner). Clubs: Rainier, Seattle Golf (Seattle). Home: 161 N. June St., Los Angeles, Calif.; (summer) 720 14th Av. N., Seattle, Wash. Office: Stuart Bldg., Seattle, Wash. Died Jan. 14, 1944; buried in Forest Lawn Memorial Park, Glendale, Calif.

STUART, George, retired banker; b. Cranston, R.I., Sept. 29, 1843; s. Hon. David and Margaret M. (Aldrich) S., both of Providence, R.I.; g.s. Sir David and Lady Margaret Stuart-Stuart, of Edinburgh, Scotland; ed. Eton and Oxford, England; m. Elizabeth Aborn (d. Maj. James Aborn Barnes, g.d. Gen. George Leonard Barnes, of Providence, R.I.); children—Harold Leonard (pres. of Halsey, Stuart & Co., bankers), Charles Jenckes Barnes (v.p. Halsey, Stuart & Co.), Harriet Frances Barnes, Elizabeth Barnes. In banking business, with N. W. Halsey & Co., firm later becoming Halsey, Stuart & Co.; now retired. In volunteer service as scholar from Boston, Mass., Civil War, Oct. 8, 1862-Sept. 1, 1863. Republican. Episcopalian. Home: 999 Lake Shore Drive, Chicago. Died Nov 19, 1943; buried at Swan Point, Providence, R.I.

STUB, Jacob Aall Ottesen, clergyman; b. Utica, Dane County, Wis., Aug. 6, 1877; s. Hans Gerhard and Didrikke Aall (Ottesen) S.; A.B., Luther Coll., Decorah, Ia., 1898 (D.D., Wittenberg Coll., Springfield, Ohio, 1919); m. Aleda Hooverson, Aug. 26, 1902; children—Didrikke Aall Ottesen, Bertha, Reese, Ann Elizabeth, Jacob A. O. Ordained Luth. ministry, 1901; pastor Viroqua, Wis., 1901-02, Stoughton, Wis., 1902-17, Central English Ch., Minneapolis, Minn., since June 1919. Apptd. field representative Nat. Luth. Commn. for Soldiers and Sailors, Oct. 1917; exec. sec. same, Mar. 1918-June 1919. Pres. bd. dirs. Albion (Wis.) Acad., 1917, 19; pres. Luth. Brotherhood of America 3 terms to 1925; pres. Am. Luth. Conf., 1925-31. Mem. Minn. State Crime Commn., 1925-26, Minn. State Liquor Commn., 1933-34. Decorated Knight Order of St. Olaf by King Haakon of Norway, 1940. Author: Verbal Inspiration, 1912; Vestments and Liturgies. Home: 2449 Third Av. S., Minneapolis, Minn. Deceased.

STUBBS, Ralph Sprengle, corp. exec.; b. Ashland, O., Feb. 3, 1882; s. Joseph Edward and Ella (Sprengle) S.; B.S., U. of Nev., 1901; m. Leonora H. Keck, Dec. 11, 1912; m. 2d, Virginia C. Bowker, Sept. 25, 1941. Worked as clerk, San Francisco, Chicago, San Jose, California, 1901-04; with Southern Pacific R.R., Tucson, Arizona, and New York City, 1905-15; traffic mgr. Am. Sugar Refining Co., N.Y., 1916, gen. mgr., 1917-19, v.p. since 1920, dir. since 1929; pres. Franklin Sugar Refining Co. since 1929, also dir. subsidiary corps.; dir. Spreckels Sugar Co., Am. Sugar Refining Co.; chmn. bd. Motor Haulage Co. since 1947. Dir. Post-Graduate Hosp. Repub. Episcopalian. Clubs: University, Traffic (N.Y.); The Pilgrims, Blind Brook Club. Home: 399 Park Av. Office: 120 Wall St., New York, N.Y. Died Apr. 27, 1948.

STUDLEY, Elmer E., ex-congressman; b. on farm, Cattaraugus County, N.Y., Sept. 24, 1869; s. Jonathan Andrew and Lestina (Hadley) S.; lineal desc. of Henry Dunster, 1st pres. of Harvard Coll.; A.B., Cornell, 1892, LL.B., 1894; m. Louise Knapp Foster, Nov. 21, 1906 (died Jan. 6, 1924). Began as newspaper reporter, 1894; admitted to N.Y. bar, 1895; in practice Buffalo, N.Y., 1896-98, Raton, N.M., 1900-17, Long Island City, N.Y., since 1917. Mem. N.M. Territorial Legislature, 1907, Territorial Statutory Revision Commn., 1908; dist. atty. N.M., 1909-10; mem. N.M. State Bd. of Water Commrs., 1913-15; dep. atty. gen. State of N.Y., 1924; U.S. commr., Eastern Dist. of N.Y., 1925-26; mem. 73d Congress (1933-35), N.Y. at large; mem. Board of Veterans' Appeals since 1935. First lt. inf., Spanish-American War, 1898-99, in Cuba. Mem. Vets. of Foreign Wars, S.A.R., Phi Delta Phi. Democrat. Mason (32°), Elk. Clubs: Cornell, Army and Navy. Home: Flushing, L.I. Office: 444 Jackson Av., Long Island City, N.Y. Died Sep. 6, 1942.

STURGIS, William Codman, botanist; b. Boston, Mass., Nov. 15, 1862; s. Russell and Susan Codman (Welles) S.; A.B., Harvard, 1884, A.M., 1887, Ph.D., 1889; m. Carolyn Hall, Apr. 4, 1889. Asst. in Cryptogamic Lab., Harvard, 1888-89; vegetable pathologist Conn. Agrl. Expt. Sta., 1891-1901; lecturer Yale Sch. of Forestry, 1899-1901, Colo. Coll., 1904-17; ednl. sec. Bd. of Missions P.E. Ch., New York, 1917 to 1927; lecturer, Coll. of Preachers, Washington, D.C., 1928-31; warden St. Martin's House, Bernardsville, N.J., 1934-37. Fellow A.A.A.S.; mem. Am. Forestry Assn., N.E. Bot. Club, Boston Soc. Natural History, Alpha Delta Phi, Delta Kappa Epsilon. Home: Annisquam, Mass. Died Sep. 30, 1942.

STURTEVANT, Sarah Martha, prof. education; b. Sonora, Calif., Feb. 22, 1881; d. Andrew Judson and Martha Ella (Doe) Sturtevant; A.B., U. of Calif., 1904; A.M., Teachers Coll., Columbia, 1920; hon. Pd.D., Russell Sage Coll., Troy, N.Y., 1939; unmarried. Teacher Ft. Bragg (Calif.) Union High Sch., 1904-12, Anna Head Sch., Berkeley, 1912-15, in pub. schs., Oakland, 1915-18; asst. in dept. of secondary edn., Teachers Coll., 1919-20; dean of girls, Univ. High Sch., Oakland, 1920-22; asso. in U. of Calif., 1920-23; asso. prof. edn. Teachers Coll., 1923-34, prof. since 1934. Mem. com. of 15 of Calif. High Sch. Teachers Assn. on Secondary Edn., 1922-23; mem. Nat. Com. to Survey Secondary Edn., 1930; pres. N.Y. State Assn. of Deans, 1927-33. Mem. Associated Bds. for Christian Colls. in China (Cheeloo Univ.), Am. Council of Guidance and Personnel Assns. (chmn. 1935-36). Mem. N.E.A., Prytanean Honor Soc., Nat. Assn. of Deans of Women, Am. Assn. Univ. Women (bd. dirs. N.Y. branch 1932-34), Foreign Policy Assn., Nat. Council for Prevention of War, Acad. of Polit. Science, Chi Omega, Kappa Delta Pi, Phi Delta Gamma. Republican. Baptist. Clubs: Women's Faculty; Sierra of Calif. Author: Personnel Study of Deans of Women in Teachers Colleges and Normal Schools (with R. M. Strang), 1928; Personnel Study of Deans of Girls in High Schools (with R. M. Strang), 1930. Editor: Deans at Work (with H. Hayes), 1930; Trends in Personnel Work, as Represented in the Positions of Dean of Women and Dean of Girls in Colleges and Universities, Normal Schools, Teachers Colleges and High Schools (with Ruth Strang and Margaret McKim), 1940. Contbr. to mags. Home: 501 W. 120th St., New York, N.Y. Died Dec. 18, 1942.

STYER, Henry Delp (stīr), army officer (retired); b. Sellersville, Pa., Sept. 21, 1862; s. William Barrett and Katherine (Delp) S.; student Franklin and Marshall Coll., Lancaster, Pa., 1877-79; grad. U.S. Mil. Acad., 1884, Army War Coll., 1914; m. Bessie Wilkes, g d. Admiral Charles Wilkes, June 3, 1891. Commd. 2d lt. 21st Inf., June 15, 1884; 1st lt. 22d Inf., May 19, 1891; transferred to 13th Inf., July 20, 1891; capt. inf., Oct. 4, 1898; assigned to 13th Inf., Jan. 1, 1899; trans. to 11th Inf, Mar. 8, 1907; maj. 29th Inf., May 6, 1907; lt. col. 17th Inf., Nov. 12, 1912; col., July 1, 1916; brig. gen. N.A., Aug. 5, 1917. Served in Wyo., Utah, Ind. Ty. and at Ft. Niagara, N.Y., 14 yrs.; as capt. in Philippine Islands, 1899-1902, mentioned in orders for capture of Vicente Prado, notorious guerilla leader; prof. mil. science and tactics, Utah Agrl. Coll., 1892-96, 1903-06; comd. Ft. Niagara, 1909-12; duty with 2d Div., in Tex., 1913; on Mexican border at Eagle Pass, 1914, at Yuma, 1917; apptd. comdr. 181st Inf. Brigade, Camp Lewis, Tacoma, Wash., Sept. 4, 1917; first comdr. A.E.F., Siberia, Aug. 1918; comdr. Am. Zone of Advance on Amur River, to Apr. 1919; retired at his own request, Apr. 10, 1919; on active duty, Detroit, Nov. 1919 to Aug. 1922. Decorated Order of Rising Sun (Yoshihito); War Cross (Czechoslovakia). Elected nat. comdr. Nat. Assn. Vets. of A.E.F. in Siberia (1918-20), 1941. Mem. mil. affairs com., San Diego Chamber of Commerce. Mem. German Reformed ch. Mason. Address: 400 2d St., Coronado, Calif. Died May 11, 1944.

SULLIVAN, Arthur George, surgeon; b. Eau Claire, Wis., Feb. 27, 1885; s. Florance David and Anna E. (McCarthy) S.; student U. of Wis., 1903-05; M.D., Coll. of Phys. and Surg. (Columbia), 1909; m. Florence D. Stott, Sept. 9, 1908; children—Arthur George, Frances Beal. Began practice in surgery at Madison, Wis., 1909; propr. (with Dr. E. S. Sullivan) of Sullivan Clinic; chief surgeon and cons. surgeon for numerous insurance and industrial cos.; attending surgeon St. Mary's Hosp., Madison Gen. Hosp., St. Mary's Ringling Hosp. (Baraboo, Wis.). Served in Med. R.C. and on Madison Draft Bd., World War; mem. U.S. Pension Bd., 1916-27. Fellow Am. Coll. Surgeons, A.M.A.; mem. Interstate Post Grad. Med. Assn. (trustee; dir. exhibits), Wis. Med. Soc., Civic Soc., Phi Delta Theta. Republican. Roman Catholic. Rotarian. Contbr. med. articles. Home: 930 E. Gorham St. Office: Gay Bldg., Madison, Wis. Died Aug. 20, 1941.

SULLIVAN, Christopher D., congressman; b. N.Y. City, 1870; ed. St. Mary's Acad. In real estate business; mem. N.Y. Senate, 1908-16; mem. 65th to 76th Congresses (1917-41), 13th N.Y. Dist. Democrat. Home: 62 Forsyth St., New York. Died Aug. 3, 1942.

SULLIVAN, George F., judge; b. Shakopee, Minn., Jan. 30, 1886; s. James and Bridget C. (O'Regan) S.; LL.B., U. of Minn., 1908; m. Mary E. Morrison, May 1, 1926; 1 son, George Mark. Admitted to Minn. bar, 1908, and practiced in Jordan; county atty. Scott County, Minn., 1913-23; U.S. Dist. Atty., Dist. of Minn., 1933-37; U.S. dist. judge since 1937. Del. Dem. Nat. Conv., St. Louis, 1916, Chicago, 1932. Mem. Minn. Bar Assn., Sigma Nu. Democrat. Catholic. Club: St. Paul Athletic. Home: 1911 Summit Av. Address: Federal Court Bldg., St. Paul, Minn. Died Apr. 14, 1944.

SULLIVAN, Jerry B(artholomew), lawyer; b. Mt. Pleasant, Ia., Jan. 1; 1859; s. Stephen and Mary (Bresnahan) S.; ed. pub. schs. and privately by Hon. James W. McDill of Iowa; m. Martha Groves, Dec. 1886. Admitted to Ia. bar, 1881; practiced in Creston, Ia., 1882-1904, Des Moines, 1904-13; was mem. Sullivan & Sullivan. City atty., Creston, 1887-89; mem. Bd. of Edn., Creston, 6 years; Dem. candidate for gov. of Ia., 1903; mem. Bd. Edn., Des Moines, 1907-12 (pres. 1 yr.); U.S. gen. appraiser (now U.S. Customs Court), by appmt. of President Wilson, since May 5, 1913, and pres. Bd. of Gen. Appraisers, 1914-25; retired from U.S. Customs Court, Sept. 30, 1939. Catholic. Mem. Am. Bar Assn., Ia. State Bar Assn. Home: 601 W. 110th St. Office: 201 Varick St., New York, N.Y. Died Apr. 17, 1948.

SULLIVAN, Patrick U., ex-congressman; b. Pittsburgh, Pa., Oct. 12, 1877; s. Cumming and Catherine (O'Connor) S.; ed. pub. and parochial schs., Pittsburgh; m. Caroline Wallisch, Nov. 1901; children—Margaret, Catherine, Loretta. Alderman, Pittsburgh, 1910-29; police magistrate, Pittsburgh, 1914-21; mem. bd. assessment and revision of taxes, Allegheny County, Pa., 1921-28; mem. 71st and 72d Congresses (1929-33), 34th Pa. Dist. Republican. Knight of Columbus, Elk. Home: 176½ Hallock St., Pittsburgh. Died Dec. 31, 1946.

SULTAN, Daniel Isom, army officer; b. Oxford, Miss., Dec. 9, 1885; s. Daniel Isom and Emma Linda (Wohlleben) S.; student U. of Miss., 1901-03; B.S., U.S. Mil. Acad., 1907; grad. Army Engring. Sch., 1909, Command and Gen. Staff Sch., 1923, Army War Coll., 1926; m. Florence Braden, Jan. 29, 1916; children—Sheila, Linda Faser. Commd. 2d lt., June

14, 1907; advanced through grades to brig. gen., Dec. 1, 1938; instr. civil and mil. engring., United States Military Acad., 1912-16; commander Engineer troops and engaged in construction of roads and fortifications in P.I., 1916-17; col. Gen. Staff, World War; dist. engr., Savannah, Ga., 1923-25; mem. Bd. Engrs. for Rivers and Harbors, 1926-29; in command of U.S. Army troops in Nicaragua and mem. Interoceanic Canal Bd., 1929-31; district engineer, Chicago, 1932-34; engr. commissioner, D.C., 1934-38; comdg. 2d Engr. Regiment, Ft. Logan, Colorado, 1938; commanding general 22d Inf. Brigade, Schofield Barracks, T.H., 1939-41; comdg. gen. Hawaiian Div., Mar.-Apr. 1941; comdg. gen. 38th Div., Camp Shelby, Miss., May 1, 1941-Apr. 6, 1942; comdg. VIII Army Corps, Apr. 1942-43; apptd. dep. comdr. in chief China-Burma-India Theater, Jan. 1943-44; comdr. U.S. Forces in India-Burma Theater since Nov. 1944; maj. gen., inspector gen., July 1945. Decorated D.S.M. with Oak Leaf Cluster (U.S.), Presidential Medal of Merit and Congressional Medal of Distinction (Nicaragua). Mem. Am. Soc. Mil. Engrs., Sigma Chi. Presbyterian. Clubs: Army and Navy, Army and Navy Country (Washington). Writer of articles. Address: War Dept., Washington, D.C.* Died Jan. 14, 1947.

SULZER, Albert Frederick, vice chairman of bd. Eastman Kodak Co.; b. Chicago, Ill., Dec. 22, 1878; s. Frederick and Anna M. C. (Beuther) S.; student Purdue U.; B.S., Mass. Inst. of Tech., 1901; m. Glyder Roberts, Oct. 15, 1908. With Eastman Kodak Co., Rochester, N.Y., since Aug. 1, 1901, entering its employ as asst. chemist, becoming supt. of chem. plant, June 1, 1905, gen. supt. of film mfg., Nov. 14, 1913, asst. mgr. Kodak Park works, Aug. 6, 1920, gen. mgr. of same, Jan. 28, 1929, dir. Eastman Kodak Co., Feb. 10, 1932, v.p., Sept. 12, 1934, asst. gen. mgr., Jan. 8, 1936, gen. mgr., May 7, 1941, vice chmn. of bd. since Nov. 10, 1943. Dir. Lincoln-Alliance Bank & Trust Co.; dir. and sec. Rochester Athenæum and Mechanics Inst.; dir. and v.p. Eastman Savings and Loan Assn.; trustee, Chamber of Commerce; v.p. Rochester Community Chest, Inc. Clubs: Country of Rochester, Genesee Valley. Home: 96 Pelham Rd., Brighton, N.Y. Office: 343 State St., Rochester, N.Y. Died Aug. 6, 1944.

SUMMERFIELD, Solon E., hosiery mfr.; b. Lawrence, Kan., Apr. 19, 1877; s. Marcus and Sara (Erb) S.; A.B., Univ. of Kan., 1899, LL.B., 1901; married. Began as hosiery mfr., N.Y. City, 1906; became chmn. bd. Gotham Silk Hosiery Co., retired 1940. Member of Phi Delta Phi, Phi Kappa Psi, Theta Nu Epsilon. Clubs: North Hills Golf, Westchester Country. Founder of Summerfield Scholarships, U. of Kan., for needy students. Home: 107 Station Road, Great Neck, N.Y. Office: 30 Rockefeller Plaza, New York, N.Y.* Died Sep. 2, 1947.

SUMMERLIN, George Thomas, diplomatic service; b. Rayville, La., Nov. 11, 1872; s. John S. and Mary (Davis) S.; student La. State U. and A. and M. Coll.; grad. U.S. Mil. Acad., 1896. Served in Puerto Rico, 1898, later in Philippines; resigned from Army as capt. of cav., May 17, 1903; apptd. clk. Dept. of State July 1, 1909; 2d sec. Embassy, at Tokyo, Japan, 1910; 2d sec. Legation, Peking, 1911-14; sec. Legation, Santiago, Chile, 1914-17; sec. Embassy, Class I, Feb. 5, 1915; assigned to Mexico, Feb. 2, 1917; apptd. counselor of Embassy, Jan. 7, 1918; chargé d'affaires, ad interim, at Mexico City, 1919-24; counselor of Embassy, to Rome until Mar. 1925; E.E. and M.P. of U.S. to Honduras, 1925-29, to Venezuela, 1929-34, to Panama, 1934-37; chief of protocol, Dept. of State, since July 29, 1937; also special asst. to sec. of state, January 1944 with the rank of Minister. Member Kappa Alpha. Presbyterian. Clubs: Metropolitan, Army and Navy, Chevy Chase, Alibi (Washington); India House (New York). Home: Rayville, La. Address: 1718 H St. N.W., Washington. Died July 1, 1947; buried in Arlington National Cemetery.

SUMNER, Edward Alleyne, mfr.; b. Jackson, Mich., Oct. 26, 1874; s. Edward Alleyne and Florence (Bingham) S.; grad. Detroit Univ. Sch., 1904; student Mass. Inst. Tech., Class of 1897; 3 yrs.; m. Ernestine Davenport Tappey, Oct. 28, 1905. Began as foundry molder, 1896; engr. Cie. Nationale des Radiateurs, Dole, Jura, France, 1899; sec., mfg. com., Am. Radiator Co., Chicago, Ill., 1900, sec. operating bd., Detroit, Mich., 1901-07, mgr. Detroit plant, 1907-10; mem. bd. dirs. Am. Radiator Co., 1930-38; retired since 1938. Captain, Reserve Corps, U.S. Army, 1916. Decorated Chevalier Legion of Honor. Pres. Childrens Aid Soc. Detroit, 1908; pres. Detroit Bd. of Commerce, 1909. Chmn. Mil. Training Camps Assn. for Mich., 1916. First vice pres. Am. C. of C., France, 1935; 1st vice pres. Am. Club of Paris, 1935; chmn. and pres. Am. Library in Paris, Inc., 1939-45; senior warden American Pro Cathedral of Holy Trinity, Paris, 1938-47. Represented Am. industry on League of Nations Econ. Consultative Com., 1929. Chmn. Eastern Indusl. Sect. of Republican Nat. Com., 1936. Clubs: Knickerbocker (New York); Apawamis (Rye, N.Y.); Detroit, Country (Detroit); Travellers, Cercle Interallie, Golf de St. Cloud (Paris). Home: The Plaza, Fifth Av. and 59th St., New York 19, N.Y. Died May 2, 1948.

SUMNER, Francis Bertody, zoölogist; b. Pomfret, Conn., Aug. 1, 1874; s. Arthur and Mary Augusta (Upton) S.; B.S., U. of Minn., 1894; Ph.D., Columbia, 1901; m. Margaret Elizabeth Clark, Sept. 10, 1903; children—Florence Anne, Elizabeth Caroline, Herbert Clark. Tutor and instr. natural history, Coll. City of New York, 1899-1906; dir. biol. lab., U.S. Bur. Fisheries, Woods Hole, Mass., 1903-11; naturalist, U.S. Bur. Fisheries steamer "Albatross," 1911-13; asst. prof. biology, Scripps Inst. for Biol. Research (later Inst. of Oceanography), U. of Calif., 1913-19, asso. prof., 1919-26, prof. since 1926, acting dir., 1923-24; research asso. Carnegie Instn., Washington, D.C., 1927-30. Fellow A.A.A.S. (chmn. sect. F, 1938), Calif. Acad. of Sciences, San Diego Natural History Soc.; mem. Am. Soc. Zoölogists, Am. Soc. Naturalists, Western Soc. Naturalists (pres. 1921-22), Am. Soc. Mammalogists, Ecol. Soc. America, Am. Genetic Assn., Am. Soc. Ichthyologists and Herpetologists, Nat. Acad. of Sciences, (corr.) Phila. Acad. of Sciences, Am. Philos. Soc., Soc. for Exptl. Biology and Medicine, Phi Beta Kappa, Sigma Xi. Author papers on embryology and physiology of fishes, marine ecology, geographic variation, heredity and evolution. Address: Scripps Institution, La Jolla, Calif. Died Sep. 6, 1945.

SUNDERLAND, Wilfred Wilt, business exec.; b. Dayton, Ohio, 1873; s. William H. and Martha (Crawford) S.; student Dayton High Sch.; m. Anne Ampt, 1908; 1 son, Francis A. Treas. Kinnard Mfg. Co., 1891-1901; with Chicago Coated Board Co., 1901-02; branch manager American Straw Board Company, 1903-06; assistant sales manager United Box Board & Paper Co., 1907; receiver Friend Paper Co., 1908-12; pres. Miami Paper Co., 1913-27; became pres. Western Tablet & Stationery Corp., Dayton, O., 1927, chmn. bd. Dir. Hat Corp. of Am., New York, since 1943. Home: 77 Deepwood Rd., Roslyn Heights, N.Y. Died May 6, 1948.

SUNDHEIM, Anders M. (sŭnd'hīm), publisher; b. Valdres, Norway, Oct. 25, 1861; s. Mons A. and Marie (Kirkeberg) S.; ed. in Norway and in high sch., Elk Horn, Ia.; m. Maren Oilo, of Oilo, Valdres, Aug. 8, 1896; children—Marie Inez, Marcus Gerhard, Borghild Katherine. Came to U.S., 1878, naturalized, 1898. Publisher and editor "Bien," San Francisco, 1889-90; with Augsburg Pub. House, Minneapolis, since 1890, supt. until 1904, asst. mgr., 1904-17, general manager, 1917-29, literary consultant, 1929-38. Dir. and exec. mem. of bd. Fairview Hosp.; dir. Book Mission. For many yrs. exec. dir. Norwegian Soc. of America; officer or mem. Norwegian Danish Press Assn., Valdres Samband, Council of Bygdelags. Decorated Knight of the Order of St. Olaf, by King of Norway, 1923. Republican. Author: Valdreser i America, 1922; Nordlandet; Jul i Vesterheimen (annual), 1911-38; Fort Good Hope, 1942; Skiftende Horisonter, 1943, Under Norden's Kimmel, 1945. Editor Samband (quarterly mag.). Home: 1212 Powderhorn Terrace. Office: 425 S. 4th St., Minneapolis, Minn. Died Dec. 21, 1945.

SUNNY, Bernard Edward, former telephone official; b. Brooklyn, N.Y., May 22, 1856; pub. sch. edn.; Dr. Engring., Armour Inst. Tech., 1908; m. Ellen Clifton Rhue, 1878 (dec.); children—Helen T. (Mrs. George B. McKibbin), Arthur E. (dec.); m. 2d, Emma Holland Derby, Jan. 17, 1925. Telegraph operator, night mgr. and mgr. Chicago office A.&P. Telegraph Co., 1875-79; supt. Chicago Telephone Co., 1879-88; pres. Chicago Arc Light & Power Co., 1888-91; western mgr. Thomson-Houston Electric Co. and western mgr., also v.p. of its successor, the Gen. Electric Co., 1889-1908; pres. Chicago Telephone Co. (now Ill. Bell Telephone Co.), 1908-22, chmn. bd., 1922-30; pres. Wis. Telephone Co., 1911-22, chmn. bd., 1922-30; was also pres. Central Union, Mich. State and Cleveland telephone cos., 1911-20; dir. and mem. exec. com. Ill. Bell Telephone Co., Gen. Electric Co., First Nat. Bank; dir. Public Service Co. of Northern Ill., Pub. Service Subsidiary Corp., Wilson & Co., Edison Electric Appliance Co., Gen. Electric X-Ray Corp., Internat. Gen. Electric Co., Chicago City Ry. Co.; chmn. protective com. bond holders Chicago City & Connecting Rys.; ex-vice-pres. bd. South Park Commrs., Chicago, 1923-28. Dir. Columbian Expn. and pres. of Intramural Railroad at the World's Fair; del. Rep. Nat. Conv., Phila., 1900; pres. Civic Fedn. Chicago, 1901-04; pres. trustees Ill. Eastern Hosp. for Insane, 1904-08; pres. Police Pension Fund 4 yrs.; mem. visitation com., Juvenile Court, 3 yrs.; commr. to select site for State Home for Delinquent and Dependent Boys; trustee Ill. Manual Training Sch. for Boys, and served 1 yr. as trustee of Sch. for Delinquent Girls, Geneva, Ill. Trustee Central Ch. (pres. bd.), Chicago Sunday Evening Club, Carson Long Inst., New Bloomfield, Pa., Armour Inst. Tech.; dir. Chicago Boys Club, Boys Clubs of America. Fellow Am. Inst. Elec. Engrs.; mem. Western Soc. Engrs., Art Inst. Chicago, Field Museum Natural History, Chicago Hist. Soc., Am. Red Cross (exec. com.). Clubs: Commercial (pres. 1914-15, 1922-23), Chicago, Union League, Midday, Flossmoor Country. Home: 4913 Kimbark Av. Office: 38 S. Dearborn St., Chicago, Ill. Died Oct. 5, 1943.

SURLES, Alexander D(ay) (sûrlz), army officer; b. Milwaukee, Wis., Aug. 14, 1886; s. William Henry and Caroline (Pascoe) S.; student U. of Mich., 1906-07; B.S., U.S. Mil. Acad., 1911; grad. Cav. Sch. Advanced Course, 1924, Command and Gen. Staff Sch., 1925, Army War Coll., 1935; m. Anne Lee Gaines, Feb. 27, 1915; children—Alexander Day (U.S. Army), William G. Commd. 2d lt. U.S. Army, 1911, and advanced through the grades to maj. gen. (temp.), Feb. 16, 1942; with 15th Cavalry, U.S., 1911-15, Philippines, 1915-17, A.E.F. (France) Mar. 1918-Aug. 1919; instr. United States Mil. Acad., 1919-23; with 7th Cav., Ft. Bliss, Tex., 1925-27; asst. chief of staff Mil. Intelligence, 1st Cav. Div., Ft. Bliss, 1927-30; chief pub. relations branch, Mil. Intelligence Div., War Dept., 1935-39; with 7th Cav. Brigade (mechanized), later comd. 1st Armored Regt. (light tanks), Armored Force, Ft. Knox, 1939-40; with 1st Armored Div., Ft. Knox, 1940-41; dir. bur. public relations, War Dept., Aug. 1941-45; dir. of information, War Dept., Sept. 1945; mem. Chief of Staff's Adv. Group, Dec. 1945-47. Decorated Distinguished Service Medal, and decorations from France, England, Brazil and Ecuador. Mem. Chi Psi. Clubs: Army and Navy (Washington, D.C.); Chevy Chase Country (Md.). Address: 2022 Columbia Rd., Washington. Died Dec. 6, 1947; buried in Arlington National Cemetery.

SUSSMAN, Otto, chmn. Am. Metal Co.; b. Bavaria, Jan. 31, 1879; s. Lazarus and Matilda (Baer) S.; grad. Mining Engr., Royal Acad. Mines, Clausthal im Harz; Ph.D., U. of Wuerzburg, Bavaria; spl. study U. of Munich and U. of Leipzig; m. Edna Alberta Bailey (divorced); 1 dau., Margaret Lois. Engaged in engring. work, Germany, until 1904; came to U.S., 1904, naturalized, 1915; with The Am. Metal Co., Ltd., since 1904, now chairman; vice president U.S. Metals Refining Co., Blackwell Zinc Co., director Consolidated Coppermines Corp., Cotopaxi Exploration Co., O'Kiep Copper Co. Ltd., Climax Molybdenum Co., American Zinc & Chemical Company, The Anglo Metal Co., Ltd., Rhodesian Selection Trust, Ltd., Roan Antelope Copper Mines. Comdr. Order of Couronne, Belgium. Mem. Am. Inst. Mining and Metall. Engrs., Mining and Metall. Soc. (past pres.). Clubs: City Mid-Day, Bankers, Metropolitan Opera (New York); Alta (Salt Lake City); American (London). Home: 300 West End Av. Office: 61 Broadway, New York 6, N.Y. Died Feb. 3, 1947.

SUTER, John Wallace (sōōt'ẽr), clergyman; b. Boston, Mass., Dec. 1, 1859; s. Hales Wallace and Harriet Emily (Bingham) S.; A.B., Harvard, 1881; B.D., Episcopal Theol. Sch., Mass., 1885, S.T.D., 1920; m. Helen Jenkins, Jan. 12, 1888; children—Philip Hales, John Wallace. Deacon, 1885, priest, 1886, P.E. Ch.; rector Ch. of the Epiphany, Winchester, 1885-1912; during this period rector also, at different times, of Ch. of Our Redeemer, Lexington, Mass., Trinity Ch., Woburn, Mass., St. James Ch., West Somerville, Mass.; now rector honorarius Ch. of the Epiphany. Mem. Commn. on Revision and Enrichment of the Prayer Book since 1913; was sec. of Liturgical Commn.; custodian of Standard Book of Common Prayer. Registrar of Diocese of Mass. Mason; chaplain of Lodge of St. Andrew. Clubs: Union (Boston, Mass.). Author: The People's Book of Worship (with Rev. C. M. Addison), 1919; Life and Letters of William Read Huntington, 1925. Compiler: (with Rev. C. M. Addison) Book of Offices and Prayers, 1896; Offices for Special Occasions, 1904. Compiler: Devotional Offices for General Use, 1928. Home: 100 Beacon St., Boston, Mass. Died Apr. 11, 1942.

SUTHERLAND, Annie (Mrs. Richard F. Carroll), actress; b. Washington; m. Richard F. Carroll. Joined the Chicago Church Choir "Pinafore" Co. and made her début at Haverly's (late Columbia) Theatre, Chicago; later was with Lydia Thompson, Henry E. Dixey, Eben Plympton, Nat C. Goodwin and Mrs. Potter and Kyrle Bellew; has taken leading roles in numerous comedies and dramas. Died June 22, 1943.

SUTHERLAND, George, coll. pres.; b. St. George, N.B., Canada, Aug. 3, 1848; s. Andrew and Catherine (McVicar) S.; A.B., U. of Chicago, 1874, also A.M.; B.D., Bapt. Union Theol. Sem. (U. of Chicago), 1877; D.D., Ottawa (Kan.) U., 1898; m. Lizzie T. Pickett, Sept. 27, 1877; children—Arthur Howard, Nellie May, Edwin Hardin, Bertha R. (dec.), Lillian Jane, William Stanley (dec.), George Fred (dec.). Ordained Bapt. ministry, 1876; pastor Deer Creek, Ill., 1875-77, Minonk, Ill., 1877-79, Independence, Ia., 1879-81; prof. Greek, Gibbon (Neb.) Sem., 1881-84; prof. Greek, Ottawa (Kan.) U., 1884-89, history and economics, 1889-93, acting pres., 1886-90; pres. and prof. economics, Grand Island (Neb.) Coll, 1893-1911, pres. emeritus since 1911 (and of Sioux Falls Coll. since 1931 merger, prof. psychology and education, 1915-19, prof. Bibl. lit., 1924-28, acting pres. since 1929. Editor of Western Baptist, 1884-85; corr. N.Y. Examiner, 1882-94; chmn. Neb. Prohibition Conv., 1906; mem. exec. com. Anti-Saloon League, State Temperance Union, State Com. for Neb. of Prohibition Party. Mem. Am. Econ. Assn., Gen. Com. Bapt. Congress, Kan. State Lit. Soc., Am. Bapt. Hist. Soc. (v.p. 1931), Delta Kappa Epsilon. Lecturer on ednl. subjects. Home: Grand Island, Neb. Died Dec. 11, 1943.

SUTHERLAND, George, jurist; b. Buckinghamshire, Eng., Mar. 25, 1862; s. Alexander G. and Frances (Slater) S.; Brigham Young U., 1881; law student, U. of Mich., 1882-83; LL.D., Columbia, 1913, U. of Mich., 1917, George Washington, 1921, Brigham Young U., 1941; m. Rosamond Lee, June 18, 1883; children—Mrs. Emma Sutherland Hempstead, Philip Lee (dec.), Mrs. Edith Sutherland Bloedorn. Admitted to bar, Mich., 1883; began practice at Salt Lake City, Utah. Mem. 1st Utah Senate, 1896, and has held other positions; del. Rep. Nat. convs., 1900, 04, 08, 12, 16; mem. 57th Congress (1901-03), Utah (declined renomination); U.S. senator, terms 1905-11, 1911-17; apptd. by President Harding, Sept. 5, 1922, asso. justice Supreme Court of U.S., and immediately confirmed by the Senate; retired, Jan. 5, 1938. Pres. Am. Bar Assn., 1916-17. Author: Constitutional Power and World Affairs, 1919. Home: 2029 Connecticut Av., Washington, D.C. Died July 18, 1942.

SUTHERLAND, Howard, ex-senator; b. near Kirkwood, Mo., Sept. 8, 1865; s. John Webster and Julia P. (Reavis) S.; A.B., Westminster Coll., Fulton, Mo., 1889; studied law at Columbian (now George Washington) U., hon. LL.D.; m. Effie Harris, May 28, 1889. Editor Republican (daily and weekly), Fulton, Mo., 1889-90; served from clk. to chief of population div., 11th Census, 1890-93; removed to Elkins, W.Va., 1893; with Davis-Elkins coal and r.r. interests 10 yrs., becoming gen. land agt.; later coal and timber land business on own account. Mem. W.Va. State Senate, 1908-12; mem. 63d and 64th Congresses (1913-17), W.Va. at large; elected U.S. senator for term 1917-23; del. at large to Rep. Nat. Conv., 1924, 28, 32, 36; alien property custodian, 1925-33. Republican. Presbyterian. Mem. Beta Theta Pi. Mason (32°). Home: Elkins, W.Va.; 406 Wyoming Apts., Washington, D.C.* 1950.

SUTHERLAND, John Bain, prof. physical edn.; b. Coupar, Angus, Scotland, Mar. 21, 1889; s. Archibald and Mary (Burns) S.; D.D.S., U. of Pittsburgh (Pa.), 1918; unmarried. Came to U.S., 1904, naturalized, 1914. Football coach, Lafayette Coll., Easton, Pa., 1919-23, U. of Pittsburgh, 1924-39; also teacher of dentistry, 1919-33, prof. phys. edn., since 1932. Appointed football coach Brooklyn Professional Football Team, 1940. Served in Med. Res. Corps, U.S. Army, 1917-18, World War I. Fellow Am. Coll. Dentists; mem. Am. Dental Soc., Druids, Scabbard and Blade. Sigma Chi, Psi Omega, Omicron Delta Kappa. Presbyterian. Mason (32°, Shriner). Clubs: Rotary, Variety, Pittsburgh Athletic Association, Pittsburgh Breakfast (pres. 1938). Home: Pittsburgh Athletic Assn. Address: University of Pittsburgh, Pittsburgh. Died Apr. 11, 1948.

SUTPHEN, William Gilbert Van Tassel, author; b. Phila., May 11, 1861; s. Rev. Morris Crater and Eleanor (Brush) S.; A.B., Princeton U., 1882; hon. A.M., 1926. Author: The Golficide, 1898; The Golfer's Alphabet, 1899; The Cardinal's Rose, 1900; The Golfer's Calendar, 1901; The Nineteenth Hole, 1901; The Gates of Chance, 1904; The Doomsman, 1906; In Jeopardy, 1922; The Sermon on the Cross, 1927; King's Champion, 1927; I, Nathaniel, Knew Jesus, 1941. Ordered deacon, P.E. Ch., 1921, ordained priest, 1923. Clubs: Morristown, Morris County Golf. Home: Morristown, N.J. Died Sep. 20, 1945.

SUTRO, Alfred (sōō'trō), lawyer; b. Victoria, B.C., Oct. 15, 1869; s. Emil and Adelheid (Zadig) S.; brought to U.S., 1875; grad. Urban Sch., San Francisco, 1887; A.B., Harvard, 1891; LL.B., Hastings Law Coll., San Francisco, 1894; m. Rose Newmark, Sept. 11, 1902; children—Adelaide (Mrs. Robert Paul Bullard, now dec.), John Alfred, Margot (dec.). Law clerk in offices of Pillsbury, Blanding & Hayne, San Francisco, 1891; admitted to Calif. bar, 1894, and since practiced in San Francisco; partner Pillsbury, Madison & Sutro since 1904; counsel for various corps.; dir. Pacific Lighting Corp., Pacific Telephone and Telegraph Co. Republican. Clubs: Book Club of Calif. (pres.), Roxburghe, First Edition (London, Eng.). Home: 3660 Jackson St. Office: Standard Oil Bldg., San Francisco, Calif. Died Mar. 9, 1945.

SUTTON, John Brannen, lawyer; b. Lakeland, Fla., Mar. 15, 1891; s. Charles Needham and Rachel (Keen) S.; LL.B., U. of Fla., 1914; m. Belva Floyd, Oct. 17, 1917; children—Belva Floyd, John Brannen, Mary Rachel. Admitted to Fla. bar, 1914, since practiced in Tampa; gen. solicitor Atlantic Coast Line R.R. Co. for Fla., Ga. and Ala.; mem. Sutton, Reeves & Allen; v.p. and dir. Tampa Southern R.R. Co.; dir. Atlanta & East Coast Terminal Co., Exchange Nat. Bank of Tampa. Trustee U. of Tampa; former mem. Fla. State Board of Control; mem. State Board of Law Examiners, 1926-27. Mem. Am. Bar Assn., Fla. State Bar Assn. (pres. 1927-28), Hillsborough County Bar Assn. (ex-pres.), U. of Fla. Alumni Council, Alpha Tau Omega. Democrat. Methodist. Clubs: Palma Ceia Golf, Tampa Yacht and Country, Ye Mystic Krewe of Gasparilla. Home: 1209 Bayshore Blvd. Office: Stovall Professional Bldg., Tampa, Fla. Died Nov. 24, 1944.

SUTTON, Loyd Hall, lawyer; b. Marlboro, Mass., Feb. 15, 1885; s. Henry Willie and Carrie Frances (Hall) S.; B.S., Mass. Inst. of Tech., 1908; LL.B., George Washington Univ., 1913; m. Sarah Irma Brashears, Aug. 20, 1910; children—Virginia H. (Mrs. Jean Carl Harrington), Dorothy P. (Mrs. Frederick Mettam Shaffer), Patricia (Mrs. Stephen Edmund Clabaugh). Asst. instr., Mass. Inst. Tech., 1908-09; asst. examiner U.S. Patent Office, Washington, D.C., 1909-16; admitted to bar of Dist. of Columbia, 1912; mem. of law firm Cameron, Kerkam & Sutton, Washington, D.C., since 1916; instr. George Washington Univ., 1914-17, asso. prof., 1917-35, adjunct prof. of law, 1935-48; J. M. Flowers lecturer, Duke University, 1947-48. Patent adviser to Nat. Research Defense Com., 1941-46. Recipient George Washington Law Sch. Alumni Citation for contbns. to legal profession, 1941, and Gen. Alumni Citation for contbns. to teaching profession, 1942. Chmn. sect. of Commerce's Patent Office adv. com., 1933-35. Mem. Am. Patent Law Assn. (pres., 1946-47, member board management since 1947), American Bar Association (chairman section of patent, trademark and copyright law, 1940-41, mem. council, 1941-45, mem. house of dels., 1940-41, 43, 44), D.C. Bar Assn., S.A.R., Order of Colf. Baptist. Mason. Club: Cosmos. Deptl. adv. editor George Washington Law Review since 1932. Home: 5601 Western Av., Washington 15. Office: 700 Tenth St. N.W., Washington 1. Died July 23, 1949.

SUTTON, Wilbur Ervin, writer, editor; b. Muncie, Ind., Sept. 30, 1878; s. Samuel Roberts and Amelia (Coffeen) S.; grad. high sch., Muncie, 1897; m. Allie Elizabeth Snell, Apr. 14, 1904; 1 son, Donald Thomas. Began as city editor Muncie Times, 1898; editor Muncie Press since 1917; formerly writer of syndicated columns of humor, verse and editorials appearing in some 100 newspapers under titles, "The Way I Feel About It," "Today's Editorials," etc. V.p., Ind. Taxpayers' Assn.; dir. Del. County Tuberculosis Assn., Muncie Boys' Club; mem. Muncie Chamber Commerce; v.p. Eddie Thomas Memorial Mission; dir. Del. County Hist. Soc. Del. Rep. Nat. Conv., 1940. Republican. Kiwanian. Co-editor and co-author of The Book of Indiana (biographical history of the state), 1929; asso. editor-author Indiana Today (biographical history), 1942. Contbr. to Nat. Republic Magazine, etc. Home: 108 McCulloch Blvd. Address: Muncie Press, Muncie, Ind. Died Sept. 15, 1949.

SWAINE, Robert Taylor, lawyer; b. Tingley, Ia., Apr. 29, 1886; s. Charles and Alice (Taylor) S.; Ph.B., State U. of Iowa, 1905; LL.B., Harvard, 1910; m. 2d, Elizabeth W. Stauffer, July 1929; 1 dau. (by first marriage), Vivian Margaret (Mrs. Marshall M. Holcombe). Admitted to N.Y. bar, 1911, to U.S. Supreme Court, 1927; mem. firm, Cravath, Swaine & Moore and its predecessors since 1917; dir. and mem. exec. com. Westinghouse Electric Corp.; dir. and mem. trust com. Chemical Bank & Trust Co. Dir. and mem. exec. com. Philharmonic-Symphony Soc. of N.Y., Legal Aid Soc., Travelers Aid Soc. of N.Y.; dir. and chmn. exec. com., Visiting Nurse Service, N.Y. Mem. Am. and N.Y. State bar assn., New York County Lawyers Assn., Bar City of N.Y., Harvard Law Sch. Assn., Phi Beta Kappa (asso.), Delta Sigma Rho. Clubs: University Harvard, Broad Street, Century Association. Author: The Cravath Firm and Its Predecessors, Vol. 1, 1946; Vol. 2, 1948. Contbr. to legal publications articles on corporate finance. Home: 150 Central Park S., New York 19; and Wilton, Conn. Office: 15 Broad St., New York 5. Died Sept. 25, 1949.

SWAN, Joseph Rockwell, retired executive; b. Utica, N.Y., Oct. 21, 1878; s. Joseph Rockwell and Emma (Mann) S.; A.B., Yale, 1902; m. Nathalie Henderson, Dec. 20, 1911; children—Nathalie (Mrs. Philip Rahv), Emma, Lois (Mrs. Joseph DeF. Junkin). Treas. Union Trust Co., Albany, N.Y., 1907-10; partner Kean Taylor & Co., New York, N.Y., 1910-19; v.p. Guaranty Trust Co., New York, N.Y., 1919-28, pres. and dir. Guaranty Co. of N.Y., 1928-34; partner E. B. Smith & Co., New York, 1934-37, Smith Barney & Co., New York, 1938-44; president and director American Hard Wall Plaster Company. Served as major, Am. Red Cross, France, World War I. Pres. and mem. bd. mgrs. New York Bot. Garden. Clubs: Century Association, Links (New York, N.Y.). Home: Salisbury, Conn. Office: 14 Wall St., New York, N.Y. Died Sept. 13, 1948.

SWANEY, William Bentley (swā̆n'ē), lawyer; b. Castalian Springs, Sumner County, Tenn., Feb. 13, 1858; s. Dr. A. J. and Nancy E. S.; A.B., U. of Tenn., 1878; studied Harvard law course, under Hon. James M. Head, at Gallatin, Tenn., 30 mos.; LL.B., Cumberland U., 1881; admitted to bar, 1881; m. Mary Cooke, Jan. 8, 1885; children—Burch Cooke (dec.), Penelope McDermott (dec.), Frances L., Mary Elizabeth (Mrs. B. B. Bouknight), Elma Roberta (Mrs. Harry G. Nelson). Mem. law firm of Cooke, Swaney & Cooke, Chattanooga. Was spl. judge Supreme Court of Tenn. Instr. law of contracts and pvt. corps. and constl. law, Chattanooga Coll. Law, since 1899, dean since 1920. Instr. in citizenship, Mil. Training Camp, Ft. Oglethorpe, Ga., since 1929. Member Bar Assn. Tenn. (ex-pres.), Alumni Assn. U. of Tenn. (pres.), Chattanooga Chamber Commerce (ex-pres.), Am. Bar Assn. (chmn. com. on law enforcement, 1921, 22). Author: Safeguards of Liberty (intro. by William G. McAdoo), 1920 (adopted as text-book by many ednl. instns.); also wrote: Statutory Charters for Private Corporations in Tennessee; Revenue Laws of Tennessee; and numerous articles of legal topics. Active in promotion of citizenship movement in conjunction with Am. and Tenn. bar assns. and high schs., colls. and univs. Home: 401 High St. Office: James Bldg., Chattanooga, Tenn.* Died July 28, 1946.

SWANSON, John A., lawyer; b. Chicago, Ill., Apr. 14, 1874; s. John and Anna G. (Johnson) S.; ed. pub. schs.; Chicago Coll. of Law, 1893-95; m. Cecile A. Leason, June 17, 1896; children—Charlotte Anna, Ruth Henrietta. Admitted to Ill. bar, 1895, and practiced at Chicago; mem. Ill. Ho. of Rep., 1910-12, Senate, 1914-16; judge of the Municipal Court of Chicago, 1916-21; judge of Circuit Court of Cook County, 1921-29; state's atty. Cook County, Ill., 1929-32; now mem. firm Swanson, Dodge & Dornbaugh. Mem. Am., Ill. State and Chicago bar assns., Nat. Prosecuting Attys. Assn. (first pres.). Mason, K.P., Odd Fellow, Moose. Office: 111 W. Washington St., Chicago, Ill. Deceased.

SWART, Robert Emerson, corporation exec.; b. Detroit, Mich., Feb. 21, 1901; s. Robert Beaumont and Aurilla (Pearsall) S.; B.S. in M.E., U. of Mich., 1922; student Coll. of Law, New York U., 1922-25; m. Marion Louise Robinson, Mar. 19, 1927. Assistant district sales manager Hudson Motor Car Company, 1922; with P. W. Chapman & Co., Inc., investment bankers, New York, 1923, v.p., 1925-31; pres. Community Water Service Co., 1929-31, and dir. subsidiaries; formerly dir. Union Utilities, Tex. Cities Gas Co., Am. States Utilities Corp., Morgan Engring. Co.; pres. R. E. Swart & Co., Inc., R. E. Swart Engring Co., 1931-42; pres. and dir. Huyler's since 1942; pres. and dir. Metro Chocolate Co. Inc; chmn. bd. Southeastern Corp., Hogerstrom Ice Co., Southeastern Gas Co., Royal Palm Ice Co.; dir. Louis Sherry, Inc., Munson Line Inc., Thompson Gas Co., Hamilton Gas Co., Miami-Flagler Corp. Appointed member N.Y. City Com. on Industrial Disputes. Trustee, The Am. Univ. (Wash., D.C.); Drew University, N.Y. State Inst. of Applied Arts and Sciences, bd. of visitors N.Y.U. Law Sch.; pres. Am. Arbitration Assn.; dir. Soc. of Prevention of Crime, Goodwill Industries of N.Y., Protestant Council; treas. N.Y. Rep. County Com. Mem. bd. mgrs. N.Y. Soc. Meth. Chs.; dir. Broadway Meth. Temple. Mem. Holland Soc. of N.Y., S.A.R., St. Nicholas Soc., Chi Psi, Tau Beta Pi, Phi Delta Phi. Mason. Methodist (steward Christ Ch.). Clubs: Young Men's Republican, Union League, Pilgrim's (New York); Hudson River Country. Home: 440 Park Av., New York, N.Y. Office: 30-30 Northern Blvd., Long Island City, N.Y. Died May 7, 1947.

SWART, Walter Goodwin, mining engr.; b. Fredonia, N.Y., Feb. 19, 1868; s. Eddy F. and Sarah H. (Bradish) S.; ed. Auburn (N.Y.) High Sch., Cornell U. and U. of Denver (non-grad.); E.M., Colorado Sch. of Mines, 1917; m. Clara C. Chollar, Sept. 5, 1894; children—Richard Houghton, Ellen Orinda (wife of Dr. H. R. Smithies), John Alvah. With Ark. Valley Smelter, Leadville, Colo., 1890-92, and various mining companies; operated laboratory on own account in Denver, 1895-99; with Blake Mining & Milling Co., developing ore separating apparatus, 1899-1907; mgr. separating dept., Am. Zinc, Lead & Smelting Co., Denver; now v.p. and gen. mgr. Mesabi Iron Co., Babbitt, Minn.; consulting engineer Ill. Zinc Co., Hayden, Stone & Co. and others. Mem. Am. Inst. Mining Engrs., Mining and Metall. Soc. America, Am. Iron and Steel Inst., Duluth Engrs. Club (first pres.), Engrs. Club of Northern Minn., Teknik Club of Denver, San Francisco Engring. Club, etc. Mason (32°). Republican. Home: 1712 High St., Alameda, Calif.* Died Apr. 17, 1946.

SWARTWOUT, Egerton (swârt'out), architect; b. Ft. Wayne, Ind., Mar. 3, 1870; s. Satterlee and Charlotte Elizabeth (Egerton) S.; B.A., Yale, 1891; m. Isabelle Geraldine Devonport, 1904; 1 son, Robert Egerton. Practiced in N.Y. City since 1900; architect of Mo. State Capitol and Dept. of Highways Bldg. (Jefferson City, Mo.), U.S. Post Office and Court House (Denver, Colo.), George Washington Memorial Bldg. (Washington), Mary Baker Eddy Memorial (Cambridge, Mass.), Elks Nat. Memorial Bldg. (Chicago), U.S. Nat. St. Mihiel Monument, Montsec, France, and Memorial Chapel, Brookwood, Eng., for Am. Battle Monuments Commn., Yale Museum Fine Arts, Municipal Auditorium (Macon, Ga.), Home Club (New York), Town Hall (Milford, Conn.), New Haven City Hall, Baily Memorial Fountain (Brooklyn), French Group, States Sector, N.Y. World's Fair 1939. Mem. bd. visitors Sch. of Architecture, Columbia; apptd. by Pres. Hoover to Nat. Commn. of Fine Arts; mem. Coop. Architects Plan of N.Y. and Environs. Fellow A.I.A. (past pres. N.Y. Chapter, A.I.A.; gold medal, 1920); elected Nat. Academician, 1934; past dir. of Fine Arts Fed., New York; mem. Inst. Arts and Letters, hon. mem. Société Nationale des Beaux Arts, Paris, France. Clubs: Century, University (New York). Author: The Classical Orders of Architecture, 1918; The Use of the Order in Modern Architecture, 1920; also many monographs on architectural subjects contbr. to architectural mags. Office: 139 E. 53d St., New York, N.Y. Died Feb. 18, 1943.

SWARTZ, Charles Kephart, geologist; b. Baltimore, Jan. 3, 1861; s. Joel and Adelia (Rosecrans) S.; A.B., Johns Hopkins, 1888, Ph.D., 1904; U. of Heidelberg, 1889; fellow, Clark U., Mass., 1889-90; B.D., Oberlin Theol. Sem., 1892; m. Elizabeth A. Howard, Dec. 12, 1892; children—Joel Howard, William Hamilton, Frank McKim, Howard Currier, Charles Dana. Instr. geology, Johns Hopkins U., 1904-05, asso., 1905-06, asso. prof. geology and paleontology, 1907-10, collegiate prof. geology, 1910-31, emeritus prof. since 1931. Fellow Geol. Soc. of Am., A.A.A.S. Pres. Paleontological Soc., 1935; v.p. Geol. Soc. of America, 1936. Home: 2601 Lyndhurst Av., Baltimore 16, Md. Died Nov. 28, 1949.

SWARTZ, Harry Raymond, mfr. printing presses, machinery and saws; b. Lehighton, Pa., Dec. 23, 1874; s. George and Katherine (Bailey) S.; ed. pub. schs., Hazleton, Pa., and business coll., Scranton, Pa.; m. Edna Lee, Oct. 17, 1899. Sec. and treas. Sprague Electric Co., 1900-05; pres. Interstate Telephone Co., 1905-10; receiver and reorganizer various corps., 1910-16; pres. Intertype Corp., 1917-26; pres. R. Hoe & Co., mfrs. printing presses, machinery and saws, 1926-35. Decorated silver and gold crosses Order Social and Civil Service and Chevalier Legion of Honor (both of France). Republican. Presbyterian. Mason (32°, Shriner). Clubs: Union League, Bankers Club of America, Sleepy Hollow Country. Home: 20 E. 76th St., New York. Died June 9, 1945.

SWEET, Ellingham Tracy, newspaper editor; b. LeRaysville, Pa., Apr. 27, 1853; s. Ambrose Spencer and Cynthia (Nichols) S.; student common schs., Montrose, Pa.; m. Fannie Foster, May 28, 1879.

Learned printer's trade at Montrose, Pa., became pub. Montrose (Pa.) Chronicle, 1885; pub. Scranton (Pa.) Cricket (weekly), 1889-90; editor The Scrantonian, Scranton, Pa., since 1889, The Scranton (Pa.) Tribune since 1938. Mem. Scranton Chamber of Commerce, New England Soc. of Northeastern Pa., Am. Press Humorists Assn. Home: 1124 Diamond Av. Office: 232 N. Washington Av., Scranton, Pa. Deceased.

SWEET, William Ellery, ex-governor; b. Chicago, Ill., Jan. 27, 1869; s. Channing and Emeroy L. (Stevens) S.; A.B., Swarthmore, 1890 (Phi Beta Kappa), LL.D., 1936; m. Joyeuse L. Fullerton, 1892; children—Lennig, Channing Fullerton, Joyeuse Elise, William Ellery. Established, 1894, firm of William E. Sweet & Co., investment bankers, Denver, Colo., title later becoming Sweet, Causey, Foster & Co.; retired 1920; gov. of Colo., 1923-24; Dem. candidate for U.S. senator, 1926. Moderator Gen. Council Congl. Christian Ch., 1940-42. Mem. Nat. Council Y.M.C.A. Mem. S.R. of Colo. (pres.), Phi Kappa Psi. Democrat. Conglist. Clubs: Denver, Denver Country. Home: 1075 Humboldt St. Office: U.S. National Bank Bldg., Denver, Colo. Died May 9, 1942.

SWEETSER, John Anderson, pres. Bigelow-Sanford Carpet Co.; b. Boston, Mass., 1889; s. Frank E. and Susan J. (Anderson) S.; A.B., Harvard, 1911; m. Violet Shepley, Mar. 17, 1917. Pres. Bigelow-Sanford Carpet Co. since 1927. Home: Brookline, Mass. Office: 140 Madison Av., New York, N.Y. Died Aug. 18, 1944.

SWENSON, Eric P., banker; student Trinity Coll., Conn.; m. Amelia B. Bertelot. Sr. mem. firm S. M. Swenson & Sons; became chmn. bd. Nat. City Bank, now dir.; also officer or dir. various other cos. Clubs: Metropolitan, St. Anthony, New York Athletic, Sleepy Hollow Country, Racquet and Tennis, The Links, Links Golf, Nat. Golf, Lido Country, Westchester-Biltmore. Home: 13 E. 71st St. Office: 52 Wall St., New York, N.Y.* Died Aug. 14, 1945.

SWENSON, Laurits Selmer, diplomat; b. New Sweden, Minn., June 12, 1865; s. Swen and Kristi Swenson; A.B., A.M., Luther Coll., Ia., 1886; Johns Hopkins, 1886-87; m. Ingeborg Odegaard, 1887; children—Mabel Constance (dec.), Viola Beatrice (Mrs. Tim Nörgaard). Prin. Luther Acad., Albert Lea, Minn., 1888-97; E.E. and M.P. to Denmark, 1897-1905; apptd. E.E. and M.P. to Switzerland, Dec. 1909, to Norway, 1911; Am. del. Spitzbergen Conf., Christiania, Norway, 1913. Mem. bd. regents U. of Minn., 1895-97; del. Rep. Nat. Conv., 1896. V.p. Union State Bank, Minneapolis, 1905-10, Mercantile State Bank, 1915-21; apptd. E.E. and M.P. to Norway, Oct. 1921, E.E. and M.P. to The Netherlands, 1931-34. Republican. Lutheran. Died Nov. 3, 1947.

SWIFT, Charles Henry, chmn. bd. Swift & Co.; b. Lancaster, Mass., Dec. 27, 1872; s. Gustavus Franklin and Ann Maria (Higgins) S.; ed. pub. schs., Chicago, and business schs. Boston and Chicago; m. Claire Dux, Aug. 1926. Chmn. bd. of dirs. Swift & Co.; director and honorary president Compania Swift Internacional; Trustee Orchestral Association, Chicago. Commd. maj. U.S. Res., Jan. 1918, lt. col., Sept. 1918, and in active service Ordnance Dept., Washington and overseas. Clubs: Chicago, Chicago Athletic Association, South Shore Country (Chicago); Chevy Chase (Washington). Home: 209 Lake Shore Drive. Office: Union Stock Yards, Chicago. Died Sept. 30, 1948.

SWIFT, Douglas, lawyer; b. Cuba, N.Y., Apr. 26, 1882; s. George H. and Lucy (Eaton) S.; A.B., Cornell U., 1904; m. Monique Johnson, Nov. 5, 1910; children—Eleanor, Barbara. Admitted to N.Y. bar, 1907, and began practice in N.Y. City; v.p. and gen. counsel D.,L.&W. R.R. Co.; dir. First Nat. Bank of Jersey City. Mem. Zeta Psi. Republican. Home: 24 Clinton Av., Maplewood, N.J. Office: 140 Cedar St., New York, N. Y. Died Feb. 16, 1946.

SWIFT, Fletcher Harper, prof. education; b. New York City, May 20, 1876; s. Rev. Judson and Julia Elizabeth (Peters) S.; A.B., Dartmouth, 1898; B.D., Union Theol. Sem., 1903; A.M., Columbia Univ., 1904, Ph.D., 1905; hon. Ped.D., Dartmouth Coll., 1933; m. Mary E. Edge, Apr. 18, 1915; children—Mary Ruth, Julia Elizabeth. Teaching fellow, Teachers Coll. (Columbia), 1904-05; asst. prof. edn., U. of Washington, 1905-07; asst. prof. edn., 1907-09, prof., 1909-25, U. of Minn.; prof. edn., U. of Calif., since 1925. Visiting prof. in ednl. administration, Teachers Coll. (Columbia) U., 1924-25; lecturer in ednl. administration, U. of Pa., 1924-25; served as lecturer, summer sessions, Harvard U., Teachers Coll., U. of Calif., U. of Utah, Dartmouth Coll., U. of Wyo.; apptd. by U.S. C. of C. to prepare report on Federal Aid to Public Schools for U.S. Chamber of Commerce, 1922; dir. surveys of public school finance in Ark., 1922, Minn., 1922, Okla., 1923, Utah, 1925; dir. of Survey of Denver Opportunity Sch., 1931, by appointment of Am. Association for Adult Edn.; studied European sch. systems, 1911-12, 1928-29, 1938-39; consultant in sch. finance, U.S. Office of Edn., serving as mem. nat. advisory com. on edn., 1929-31, and nat. survey of sch. finance, 1931-33; mem. Nat. Com. on Food for Small Democracies, 1941. Mem. Liaison Com. for Internat. Edn, rep. Assn. Am. Colls., United Nations Conf., San Francisco, 1945. Apptd. by U.S. Commr. of Edn. to draft plan for national survey of school finance, 1929. Chevalier Legion of Honor (French), 1936; received award from Am. Ednl. Research Assn., 1941. Hon. life mem. Calif. Kindergarten Primary Assn.; mem. Nat. Soc. College Teachers Edn., Ednl. Research Assn., N.E.A. (mem. advisory com. on internat. relations since 1938), Am. Assn. Univ. Professors, Eugene Field Society (honorary life), S.A.R., Phi Beta Kappa, Alpha Delta Phi, Phi Delta Kappa, Acacia. Democrat. Congregationalist. Clubs: Teachers College, Faculty Club (Berkeley). Author: The Most Beautiful Thing in the World, 1905; Joseph—A Drama for Children, 1907; Public Permanent Common School Funds in the United States (1795-1905), 1911; (monograph) Social Aspects of German Student Life, 1916; Education in Ancient Israel (to 70 A.D.), 1919; Studies in Public School Finance—Vol. I, The West, 1922, Vol. II, The East, 1923, Vol. III, The Middle West, 1925, Vol. IV, The South, 1925; Emma Marwedel, 1818-1893, 1931; Federal and State Policies in Public School Finance, 1931; European Policies in Financing Public Educational Institutions: France, Czechoslovakia, Austria, Germany, England and Wales, 1933-39; also author many brochures and bulls. on kindred subjects. Joint Author: Twenty-five Years of American Education, 1924; Problems in Educational Administration, 1925; The Construction of Orientation Courses for College Freshmen, 1928; State School Taxes and State School Funds, 1929; The Changing Educational World, 1931; Introduction to the Study of Education, 1932; What Is This Opportunity School?, 1932. Contbr. to Monroe's Cyclo. of Edn., Compton's Ency., Dictionary of Am. Biography, Contemporary Review, London Times, etc. Home: 2943 Russell St., Berkeley 5, Calif. Died May 28, 1947.

SWIFT, Gustavus Franklin, vice chmn. bd. Swift & Co.; b. Chicago, Ill., Mar. 1, 1881; s. Gustavus Franklin and Ann Maria (Higgins) S.; ed. pub. schs., Chicago; m. Marie Fitzgerald, June 10, 1907; children—Geraldine (Mrs. Albert Thomas Taylor), Marie, Gustavus F., III, Jane Gertrude. Pres. and dir. Swift & Co. until 1937, now vice chmn. bd. Clubs: Commercial, Casino, Chicago, Shoreacres Golf. Home: 1551 Astor St. Office: Union Stock Yards, Chicago, Ill. Died Oct. 28, 1943.

SWIFT, Ivan, author, artist; b. Wayne County, Mich., June 24, 1873; s. John and Jennie (Birge) S.; grad. Harbor Springs (Mich.) High Sch., 1892, Petoskey Normal Acad., 1895; studied Art Inst. Chicago, 3 yrs.; unmarried. Mem. 1st Ill. Cav., Spanish-Am. War; R.O.T.C., Ft. Sheridan, Ill., 1917. Landscape painter; has exhibited in New York and Pa. Acad. Fine Arts; represented in Detroit Pub. Library, Detroit Inst. of Arts, Mich. State Library (Lansing), John H. Vanderpoel Gallery (Chicago), Harbor Springs C. A. Library, Delgado Mus. (New Orleans). Mem. Mich. Audubon Soc., Poetry Soc. America, Soc. Mich. Authors (exec. council); hon. mem. Eugene Field Soc. Author: Fagots of Cedar; Blue Crane (poems); 7 pages in New Michigan Verse, 1940; 6 pages in Songs of Horses and Bird Lovers' Anthology. Address: Harbor Springs, Mich. Died Oct. 5, 1945.

SWIFT, James Marcus, lawyer; b. Ithaca, Mich., Nov. 3, 1873; s. Marcus G. B. and Mary D. (Milne) S.; Mich. State Normal Sch.; A.B., U. of Mich., 1895, hon. LL.M., 1925; Harvard Law Sch., 1895-97; m. Olive U. Sterling, Feb. 26, 1907 (died Jan. 29, 1936). Began practice at Fall River, Mass., now at Boston. Asst. dist. atty., Southern Dist. of Mass., 1899-1902; dist. atty., 1902-10; atty.-gen. of Mass., 1911-13. Republican. Conglist. Mem. Am. Bar Assn., Mass. Bar Assn., Delta Tau Delta. Mason (32°); Chief Grand Tribune K. of P. of Mass. Clubs: University, Harvard (Boston); Quequechan (Fall River). Home: 8 Morton Terrace, Milton, Mass. Office: 50 Congress St., Boston, Mass. Died July 12, 1946.

SWIFT, Jireh, Jr., banker; A.B., Harvard, 1879; m. Elizabeth B. Hawes (died July 1, 1931); children—Jireh, 3d, Elizabeth H. Watson. With Henry Forster & Co., at Pernambuco, Brazil, until 1901; in cotton brokerage business with Stephen M. Weld & Co., later Cooper & Bensh, Boston, 1901-16; now pres. New Bedford Five Cents Savings Bank. Clubs: Harvard (Boston); Wamsutta (New Bedford). Home: 102 Elm St. S., Dartmouth, Mass. Office: 791 Purchase St., New Bedford, Mass. Died Dec. 25, 1941.

SWIFT, Josiah Otis, journalist; b. Farmington, Me., Mar. 1, 1871; s. Elkanah Sprague and Emma Louise (Butler) S.; ed. pub. schs. of Maine; m. Daisy Belle Peabody, June 14, 1893; children—Otis Peabody, Norman Guernsy. Staff writer and city editor Lewiston (Me.) Journal, 1885-1900; spl. writer New York Evening World, 1900-02; asso. editor Boston (Mass.) Journal, 1903; spl. writer and nature editor New York Morning World, 1904-31; nature editor New York World-Telegram since 1931, author and editor daily column, News Outside the Door, New York World (later New York World-Telegram) since 1922. A founder Yosian Brotherhood, nature and pedestrian soc., 1922, since served as leader. Episcopalian. Home: The Treetops, 81 Summit Dr., Hastings on Hudson, N.Y. Office: 125 Barclay St., New York 15. Died May 14, 1948.

SWIFT, Willard Everett, envelope mfr.; b. Worcester, Mass., Oct. 16, 1879; s. Henry Daniel and Emma Colburn (Fuller) S.; grad. Haverford (Pa.) Coll., 1903; m. Alice Metcalfe, June 15, 1904; children—Chrystella Alice, Willard Everett, Arthur Henry. Began in mill dept. U.S. Envelope Co., 1903, now pres. and chmn. exec. com.; mem. bd. of dirs. Worcester Mfrs. Mutual Ins. Co. Mem. exec. com. Associated Industries of Mass. Trustee Moses Brown Sch., Providence, R.I., Independent Industrial Schs., Worcester, Hahnemann Hosp., Worcester. Republican. Mem. Soc. of Friends. Member Newcomen Soc. of England (American Branch). Clubs: Worcester, Economic, Worcester Country. Originator of many labor saving devices and machines used in envelope mfr. Home: 5 Massachusetts Av. Office: 75 Grove St., Worcester, Mass. Died Jan. 14, 1947.

SWIGGETT, Douglas Worthington (swig'ĕt), editor; b. Morrow, O., Sept. 11, 1882; s. Rev. Edward T. and Eleanor Strode (Mansfield) S.; A.B., Harvard, 1906; unmarried. Teacher Marietta O., U. of Mo. and at Cicero, Ill., until 1908; with Longmans, Green & Co., publishers, 1909-11; editorial writer The Journal, Milwaukee, Wis., 1912-17 and 1919-47. Enlisted in U.S. Army, Aug. 27, 1917; commd. 2d lt., F.A., Nov. 27, 1917; served with 53d Arty., C.A.C., Meuse-Argonne offensive and St. Mihiel and Verdun sectors; discharged, Apr. 1, 1919; capt., O.R.C., 1924-29. Mem. Am. Soc. Newspaper Editors. Presbyterian. Clubs: University, City. Editor: Selections from Malory's Morte d'Arthur, 1909. Received hon. mention for distinguished editorial, Pulitzer award, 1938. Home: University Club. Address: 924 E. Wells St., Milwaukee 2, Wis. Died Feb. 12 1950; buried Spring Grove Cemetery, Cincinnati.

SWINGLE, D. B., dean of science, Mont. State Coll. Address: Bozeman, Mont. Died Jan. 18, 1944.

SWINNEY, Edward Fletcher (swĭn'ē), banker; b. Campbell County, Va., Aug. 1, 1857; s. John H. and Celina F. (Jasper) S.; Va. Poly. Inst., Blacksburg, Va., 1873-75; m. Ida Lee, Nov. 14, 1882. Went from Va. to Fayette, Mo., 1875; in Hendrix Bank there until 1882; cashier Farmers & Mfrs. Bank, Rich Hill, Mo., 1882-83; then cashier Colorado (Tex.) Nat. Bank, 1883-87; cashier, 1887-1900, became pres., 1900, chmn. bd., 1927, First Nat. Bank of Kansas City, Mo.; dir. K.C. Southern Ry. Co. Pres. Am. Bankers Assn., 1904-05. Episcopalian. Clubs: Country, Kansas City. Office: First Nat. Bank, Kansas City, Mo.* Died Oct. 24, 1946.

SYDNOR, Giles Granville, clergyman; b. Halifax County, Va., Dec. 10, 1864; s. Giles and Rebecca Pleasant (Royster) S.; A.B., Hampden-Sydney Coll., 1887; B.D., Union Theol. Sem., Va., 1893; D.D., Presbyn. Coll. of S.C.; m. Evelyn Aiken Sackett, June 24, 1897; children—Charles Sackett, Giles Granville, Henry Mosley, Louise Leyburn, James Rawlings. Ordained ministry Presbyn. Ch. in U.S., 1893; pastor successively Academy, Ottewood and Leesville chs., Va., Greene Street Ch., Augusta, Ga., First Ch., Rome, Ga., until 1919, Charles Town, W.Va., 1919-41, pastor emeritus since Jan. 1, 1941. Moderator of the Synod of Ga., 1910; moderator Synod of Va., 1940; instr. ch. music, Union Theol. Sem., Richmond, Va., 1920-25, spl. lecturer on Great Hymns of the Ch., 1926. While pastor at Rome conducted funeral services of Mrs. Woodrow Wilson, formerly a member of the ch.; mem. of com. which prepared and published The Presbyterian Hymnal, 1927. Mem. Sigma Chi. Democrat. Kiwanian. Home: Charles Town, W.Va. Died Sep. 26, 1941.

SYKES, Charles Henry (sīks), cartoonist; b. Athens, Ala., Nov. 12, 1882; s. William Henry and Jane Palmyra (Hayes) S.; ed. high sch.; studied art at Drexel Inst., Phila.; m. Charlotte Kennedy Hannum, Sept. 11, 1907; children—William Henry (dec.), Charles Henry, John Marshall. Illustrator, 1904-06; art dept. of Phila. North American, 1906; cartoonist Williamsport (Pa.) News, 1906-08, Nashville (Tenn.) Banner, 1909-11, Phila. Public Ledger, 1911-14, Evening Public Ledger since 1914; political cartoonist, "Life" (New York), 1922-28. Mason. Clubs: Players, Bala Golf, Phila. Art. Home: Bala-Cynwyd, Pa. Address: Evening Public Ledger, Philadelphia, Pa. Died Dec. 19, 1942.

SYKES, Eugene Octave (sīks), judge; b. Aberdeen, Miss., July 16, 1876, s. Judge Eugene Octave and India (Rogers) S.; student St. John's College, Md., U.S. Naval Acad.; LL.B., U. of Miss., 1897; m. Malvina Scott, Nov. 17, 1903; children—Major Charles Scott, Octavia S. Stevenson, Malvina Yerger Scott. Practiced at Aberdeen; Dem. presdl. elector-at-large from Miss., 1904; apptd. justice Supreme Court of Miss. by Gov. Bilbo, 1916, and elected to same office Nov. 1916, for term ending 1924; voluntarily retired from bench, 1924, and resumed practice; apptd. federal radio commr. by President Coolidge, Mar. 1927, reapptd. by President Hoover, Feb. 24, 1930, by President Roosevelt, Mar. 20, 1933; apptd. mem. Federal Communications Commn., 1934, resigned, Apr. 6, 1939; now member of the law firm of Spearman, Sykes & Roberson, Washington, D.C. Episcopalian. Mem. Delta Kappa Epsilon, Sons of Confederate Vets. Mason. Elk. Home: 3202 Cleveland Av. N.W. Address: Munsey Bldg., Washington, D.C. Died June 21, 1945; buried in Odd Fellows Rest Cemetery, Aberdeen, Miss.

SYKES, Richard Eddy, clergyman, educator; b. Canton, N.Y., Jan. 3, 1861; s. Edwin Jones and Louise (Brewer) S.; B.S., St. Lawrence U., 1883, M.S., 1887, D.D., 1906; grad. Theol. Sem., same Instn., 1885; m. Mabel Houghton, Oct. 18, 1887; children—Dorothy Louise (Mrs. Felix Morse Frederiksen), Elizabeth Blanche (Mrs. Ralph H. Michaels). Ordained Universalist ministry, 1885; pastor 34 yrs., successively at Little Falls, N.Y., Denver, Colo., and Malden, Mass., building 3 chs.; pres. St. Lawrence U., 1919-35, president emeritus since 1935; carried out campaign successfully for $1,000,000 endowment, 1922-25. Mem. Beta Theta Pi, Phi Beta Kappa. Mason. Clubs:

University, Universalist Men's (Malden, Mass). Home: Canton, N.Y. Died Oct. 1, 1942.

SYME, Conrad Hunt (sīm), lawyer; b. Lewisburg, W.Va., Jan. 13, 1868; s. Samuel Augustus Maverick and Mary Maxwell (Hunt) S.; student Georgetown Law Sch., 1887-89; LL.M., Nat. U. Law Sch., 1901, LL.D., 1920; m. Vovio B. Forsyth, Harrodsburg, Ky., Nov. 11, 1896; children—Leander Dunbar (capt. U.S. Army), Samuel Augustus. Admitted to D.C. bar, 1894, bar of U.S. Supreme Court, 1900; in practice at Washington since 1894; now senior member Syme & Syme; became prof. Nat. U. Law Sch., 1901, now emeritus. Counsel for Armour and Swift Companies in litigation over Consent Decree, 1921; counsel in Amos will case, 1901, in contest over will of Mrs. Ellen M. Coulton, 1908; counsel for stock and bond holders, F. H. Smith Co. and Wardman Properties cases, 1930; corp. counsel D.C., 1914-20; gen. counsel Pub. Utilities Commn. of D.C., 1914-20. Democrat. Christian Scientist. Mason. Clubs: Lawyers, Nat. Press, Congressional Country. Home: 3458 Macomb St. N.W. Office: Southern Bldg., Washington, D.C. Died 1943.

SYMINGTON, Donald (sĭ'mĭng-tŭn), corp. official; b. Baltimore, Md., Oct. 28, 1881; s. W. Stuart and Lelia Wales (Powers) S.; prep. edn., McCabe's Univ. Sch., Richmond, Va., and high sch., Bellevue, Va.; student Amherst Coll., 1904; m. Elsie Hillen Jenkins, Apr. 19, 1909; 1 dau., Martha Skipwith. Pres. McConway & Torley Corp.; dir. United States Lines Co., Canton Co., Canton R.R. Served as chief munitions officer 1st Army, A.E.F., World War; capt. O.R.C. Address: Darlington, Md.* Died May 22, 1941.

SZOLD, Henrietta (zōld); b. Baltimore, Md., Dec. 21, 1860; d. Benjamin and Sophia (Schaar) S.; grad. high sch., Baltimore, 1877. Teacher in pvt. sch., Baltimore, 1878-92; editorial sec. publ. com. Jewish Publ. Soc. America, 1892-1916; associated with Zionist undertakings in U.S. and Palestine since 1916. Editor Am. Jewish Year Book (Jewish Publ. Soc.), 1904-08. Founder and pres. (Hadassah), Women's Zionist Orgn. in U.S., 1912-26; mem. Palestine Zionist Exec., with portfolio health and education, 1927-30; mem. exec. Vaad Leumi (Jewish Gen. Council), 1931-33, dir. dept. social service, 1932-42. Dir. Dept. Youth Immigration of Central Bureau for Settlement of German Jews, 1935-43; head youth immigration bur. Jewish Agency for Palestine since 1943. Translator: Jewish Ethics (by Lazarus); Legends of the Jews (by Ginsburg); Hebrew Renaissance (by N. Slouschz), 1909. Home: Pension Romn, 11 Ramban St., Jerusalem, Palestine. Office: care Jewish Agency, Jerusalem, Palestine; also care Hadassah, 1819 Broadway, New York, N.Y.

T

TABER, Erroll James Livingstone (tā'bẽr), judge; b. Austin, Nev., Nov. 29, 1877; s. Joseph Milo and Celia Agnes (McKimmons) T.; student Lincoln grade sch. and Lowell High Sch., San Francisco, 1892-96, Santa Clara (Calif.) Coll., 1896-98, St. Paul (Minn.) Sem., 1898-1900; LL.B., Columbia, 1904; m. Frances Mildred Smiley, Dec. 27, 1904; children—William Farrington, Wallace Erroll, Frances Dorothy (dec.). Admitted to Nev. bar, 1904, and practiced in Elko; dist. atty. Elko County, 1909-11; dist. judge 4th Jud. Dist. of Nev., 1911-23; justice Supreme Court of Nev. since 1935, chief justice, 1939-40, 1945-46. Mem. Am. Bar Assn., State Bar of Nev., Am. Judicature Soc., Western Probation and Parole Conf. (pres.). Republican. Home: Elko, Nev. Address: Carson City, Nev. Died Feb. 6, 1947.

TACK, Augustus Vincent, artist; b. Pittsburgh, Pa., Nov. 9, 1870; s. Theodore Edward and Mary A. (Cosgrave) T.; B.A., St. Francis Xavier Coll., New York, 1890; B.F.A., Yale, 1912; Doctor Fine Arts (hon.) George Washington University, 1946; m. Violet Fuller, 1900; children—Agnes Gordon, Robert Fuller. Portrait and mural painter; represented in Met. Museum Art, New York; Cleveland Art Museum; Phillips Memorial Gallery, Washington, D.C.; Newark Art Museum, Snead Memorial Museum, Louisville, Ky., National gallery, Washington, D.C., Fogg Museum, Cambridge, Mass., Greimen Winthrop Collection, Lawrence Art Museum, Williamstown, Mass., Washington County Art Museum, Hagerstown, Md. Painted mural decorations for legislative chamber new Parliament Bldg., Manitoba, Canada; governor's suite, Nebraska State Capitol; Church of St. Paul, New York; Church of St. James, South Deerfield, Mass.; Ch. of St. Agnes, Dalton, Mass.; Charles J. Dunlap Memorial, New Rochelle, N.Y., Schelmerdive Memorial, Phila. Pa. Club; Century (New York). Home: Deerfield, Mass. Studio: 15 Vanderbilt Av., New York, N.Y. and 1028 Connecticut Av., Washington, D.C. Died July 21, 1949.

TAFF, Joseph Alexander, geologist; b. Ten Mile, Tenn., Nov. 20, 1862; s. Albert G. and Tirzah A. T.; student U. of Ark., 1886-88; B.S., U. of Tex., 1894; m. Mary M. Leverett, Dec. 24, 1891; children—Elizabeth Simonds, Charles Leverett, Mary Willis, Joseph Whitham, Rosa LeRoche. Mem. Ark. and Tex. geol. surveys, 1888-94; geologist on U.S. Geol. Survey, 1894-1909; geologists S.P. Co., 1909-25, cons. geologist, 1925-32; chief geologist, Associated Oil Co., 1921-29; cons. geologist, 1929-37; retired, 1937. Mem. Geol. Soc. America (hon.), Geol. Soc. Washington, A.A.A.S., Am. Inst. Mining Engrs., Seismol. Soc. America, Nat. Geog. Soc., Calif. Acad. Science, Am. Assn. of Petroleum Geologists (hon.), Sigma Xi. Author of papers, folios and bulletins in publs. of Tex., and U.S. geol. surveys and in jours. of tech. socs. on gen. and econ. geology of coal, oil, asphalt and cement resources in 11 states. Home: 628 Cowper St., Palo Alto, Calif. Deceased.

TAFT, Henry Waters, lawyer; b. Cincinnati, Ohio, May 27, 1859; s. Alphonso (secretary of war and later attorney gen. in Grant's administration, minister to Austria, 1882-84, to Russia, 1884-85) and Louisa Maria (Torrey) T.; brother of former Pres. and Chief Justice William Howard and of late Horace Dutton and half brother of late Charles Phelps T.; A.B., Yale Univ., 1880, hon. A.M., 1905; studied Cincinnati Law Sch., Columbia Law Sch.; m. Julia W. Smith, Mar. 28, 1883 (died Dec. 9, 1942); children—Walbridge S., Marion J. (dec.), William Howard II, Louise W. (Mrs. George H. Snowdon, dec.). Admitted to bar, 1882; since in practice of law at N.Y. City; mem. Cadwalader, Wickersham & Taft, formerly Strong & Cadwalader; spl. asst. to atty. gen. of U.S. in investigation and prosecution of tobacco trust (resigned Jan., 1907); trustee Mut. Life Ins. Co.; trustee Central Savings Bank, New York, 1932-36. Mem. Bd. of Edn. City of New York, 1896-1900; mem. Charter Revision Commn. to revise charter of Greater New York, 1901; trustee Coll. City of New York, 1903-05, New York Pub. Library, 1908-19; pres. of University Settlement Soc., N.Y. City, 1917-20; mem. Commn. on Reorganization N.Y. State Govt., 1925-26; apptd., 1931, member of advisory com. to investigate public schools of New York City; apptd. by Governor Lehman, 1933, mem. of Com. on Cost of Public Education. Candidate, 1898, for justice of N.Y. Supreme Court on Republican ticket and defeated; tendered by Gov. Theodore Roosevelt in 1900, appointment as justice Supreme Court of N.Y., but declined. Chmn. Permanent Legal Advisory Board for Greater New York under selective service regulations, 1917-19; del. Rep. Nat. Conv., 1920-24; chmn. Coalition Campaign Com., mayoralty election, 1921; vice chmn. Spl. Calendar Com., apptd. 1926 by the Appellate Div. of Supreme Court, First Dept., N.Y. City (resigned, 1932). Decorated Order of the Double Rays of the Rising Sun, by Emperor of Japan, 1929. Mem. Assn. Bar City of New York (v.p. 1911-12; chmn. war com. 1917-20; pres. 1923-25), N.Y. County Lawyers Assn. (v.p. 1914-18, 1923-30, pres. 1930-32), N.Y. State Bar Assn. (pres. 1919-20), Am. Bar Assn. (chmn. com. on jurisprudence and law reform 1925-28), American Law Institute., International Law Association, Maritime Law Association, League for Polit. Edn. (now The Town Hall, Inc.; pres., 1919-35), Salvation Army Adv. Bd. for N.Y. City (chmn., 1920-40), N.Y. Law Inst. (v.p.), Skull and Bones, Psi Upsilon, Ohio Soc. (pres., 1908-10), New Eng. Soc., Pilgrims Soc., Sons of Revolution of N.Y. (v.p. 1937-38), Am. Friends of Lafayette, Park Avenue Assn. Clubs: University, Century, Down Town, City Midday (pres. 1916-20). Author: Occasional Papers and Addresses of an American Lawyer, 1920; Japan and the Far East Conference, 1921; Law Reform—Papers and Addresses by a Practicing Lawyer, 1926; An Essay on Conversation, 1927; Kindred Arts—Conversation and Public Speaking, 1929; Japan and America—A Journey and a Political Survey, 1932; Witnesses in Court, 1934; Opinions—Literary and Otherwise, 1934; A Century and a Half at the New York Bar, 1938; Legal Miscellanies—Six Decades of Changes and Progress, 1941. Home: 300 Park Av. New York 22, N.Y. Office: 14 Wall St., New York 5, N.Y. Died Aug. 11, 1945.

TAFT, Horace Dutton, head master; b. Cincinnati, O., Dec. 28, 1861; s. Alphonso (Atty. Gen. 1876-77), and Louisa Maria (Torrey) T.; brother of President William Howard and Henry Waters and half brother of Charles Phelps T.; B.A., Yale, 1883, M.A., 1893; L.H.D., Williams College, 1920; LL.D., Union College, 1924; LL.D., Dartmouth Coll., 1935, Amherst Coll. and Yale U., 1936; studied at Cincinnati Law School, 1884-85, admitted to bar, 1885; m. Winifred S. Thompson, June 29, 1892 (died Dec. 1909). Tutor of Latin, Yale, 1887-90; founded, 1890, and head master The Taft Sch. until 1936, since emeritus. Address: Watertown, Conn. Died Jan. 28, 1943.

TAGGARD, Genevieve (Mrs. Kenneth Durant) (tăg'ẽrd), poet; b. Waitsburg, Wash., Nov. 28, 1894; d. James Nelson and Alta Gale (Arnold) Taggard; student Oahu Coll., Honolulu, T.H.; A.B., U. of Calif., 1919; m. Robert Wolf, Mar. 21, 1921; 1 dau., Marcia; m. 2d, Kenneth Durant, 1935. One of founders, 1920, an editor until 1926, The Measure, a Journal of Verse; instr. in English lit., Mt. Holyoke Coll., 1929-31; teacher, Bennington (Vt.) Coll., 1932-35, Sarah Lawrence Coll., Bronxville, N.Y., 1935-46. Mem. bd. editors, Young People's Record Club. Author: For Eager Lovers, 1922; Hawaiian Hilltop, 1923; Words for the Chisel, 1926; Traveling Standing Still, 1928; Life and Mind of Emily Dickinson (biography), 1930; Remembering Vaughan in New England, 1933; Not Mine to Finish, 1934; Calling Western Union, 1936; Collected Poems (1918-38), 1938; Long View, 1942; Falcon, 1942; A Part of Vermont, 1945; Slow Music, 1946; Origin Hawaii, 1947. Editor: May Days, (anthology of verse from Masses-Liberator) 1925; The Unspoken and Other Poems by Anne Bremer, 1927; Circumference—Varieties of Metaphysical Verse, 1459-1928 (an anthology), 1929. Joint editor of Continent's End, an anthology of contemporary California poets, 1925; Ten Introductions (with Dudley Fitts), 1934. Contbr. to mags. Apptd. to fellowship Guggenheim Memorial Foundation for creative writing abroad, 1931-32; author of words for Prologue, by William Schuman for chorus of 200 voices with orchestra, first performed Carnegie Hall N.Y. City, 1939; also text of Secular Cantata, No. 1, This Is Our Time (music by William Schuman), Holiday Song (first performed Town Hall by Collegiate Chorale), Lark, four part chorus (music by Aaron Copland), and other texts. Home address: East Jamaica, Vt. Died Nov. 8, 1948

TAGGART, Frank Fulton (tăg'ärt); b. Massillon, O., Aug. 22, 1873; s. Isaac Milton and Luna Amaryllis (Fulton) T.; student Massillon (O.) High Sch.; m. Lula Reed, Apr. 28, 1898. Owner and operator of coal mines since 1897; pres. and treas. Pleasant Valley Mining Co., Spruce River Coal Co.; propr. Taggart Coal Co; first v.p. Ohio-Merchants Trust Co. Ohio mem. Rep. Nat. Com., 1936-40, also mem. exec. com., 1937-40. Dir. and treas. McKinley Nat. Memorial Assn. Mem. Ohio Soc. of N.Y. Episcopalian. Clubs: Union (Cleveland); Canton (Canton, O.); Massillon (Massillon, O.); Brookside Country. Home: 610 Lincoln Way, E. Office: Ohio-Merchants Bank Bldg., Massillon, O. Died July 24, 1945.

TAGGART, Thomas Douglas, ex-mem. Democratic Nat. Com.; b. Indianapolis, July 16, 1886; s. Thomas and Eva (Bryant) T.; Ph.B., Yale, 1909; m. Adele Pringle, June 6, 1922 (now deceased); 1 dau., Eva. Pres. French Lick Springs (Ind.) Hotel Co.; dir. Am. Nat. Bank (Indianapolis); ex-mem. Dem. Nat. Com. Maj. staff former Gov. James P. Goodrich. Mem. George Rogers Clark Memorial Assn., Indiana Lincoln Union, Honorable Order of Ky. Cols., Chi Phi. Mason, Elk. Clubs: University, Athletic, Dramatic, Ind. Democratic (Indianapolis). Home: French Lick, Ind. Died Jan. 7, 1949.

TAITT, Francis Marion (tāt), clergyman; b. Burlington, N.J., Jan. 3, 1862; s. James Monroe and Elizabeth Ward (Conway) T.; A.B., Central High Sch., Phila., Pa., 1880, A.M., 1885; grad. Phila. Div. School, 1883; S.T.D., U. of Pa., 1920, Phila. Div. School, 1930; LL.D., Temple U., 1932; Litt.D., Hahnemann Coll., 1937; unmarried. Deacon, 1883, priest, 1886, P.E. Ch.; asst. St. Peter's Ch., Phila., 1883-87; rector Trinity Ch., Southwark, 1887-93, St. Paul's Ch., Chester, Pa., 1893-1929; mem. faculty, Ch. Training and Deaconess House, 1906-29; bishop coadjutor of Pa., 1929-31, bishop of Pa. since 1931. Dean of Convocation of Chester, 1903-29; dep. to Gen. Conv., 1922-28. Trustee Pa. Mil. Coll. (pres. bd.), Crozer Hosp.; dir. Chester Hosp.; mem. bd. overseers Phila. Div. Sch. Mason (grand chaplain Grand Holy Royal Arch chapter of Pa.). Home: 300 Broad St., Chester, Pa. Office: 202 S. 19th St., Philadelphia, Pa. Died July 17, 1943.

TAKACH, Basil, bishop of Pittsburgh (Greek Rite). Address: 425 East 11th Av., Munhall, Pa. Died May 13, 1948.

TALBOT, Adolphus Robert (tawl'bŭt), lawyer; b. near Alexis, Warren County, Ill., Apr. 11, 1859; s. William and Amy (Godfrey) T.; Ph.B., Hedding Coll., Abingdon, Ill., 1881, LL.D., 1894; LL.B., Union Coll. of Law, Chicago, 1883; m. Addie Harris, May 15, 1884; children—Marie Frances (Mrs. Charles Stuart), Robert Harris, Eleanor Virginia (Mrs. Richard L. Kimball). Began practice of law, Lincoln, Neb., 1883; dir. Woodmen Accident Assn.; mem. Neb. Senate, 1897-1900 (pres. 1899, 1900). Republican. Methodist. Nat. pres. Modern Woodmen of America, 1903-38, pres. emeritus since Jan. 1, 1938; mem. all Masonic lodges and many fraternal beneficiary socs.; pres. bd. trustees, Bryan Memorial Hosp. of M.E. Ch., Lincoln Neb. Clubs: Commercial Country, Lincoln Automobile, Neb. State Automobile. Home: 2001 B St. Office: Stuart Bldg., Lincoln, Neb. Died Jan. 28, 1941.

TALBOT, Arthur Newell, engineer; b. Cortland, Ill., Oct. 21, 1857; s. Charles A. and Harriet (Newell) T.; B.S., U. of Ill., 1881, C.E., 1885, LL.D., 1931; Sc.D., U. of Pa., 1915; D.Eng., U. of Mich., 1916; m. Virginia Mann Hammet, June 7, 1886 (died Dec. 4, 1919); children—Kenneth Hammet, Mrs. Mildred Virginia Gilkey, Mrs. Rachel Harriet Westergaard, Mrs. Dorothy Newell Goodell. Engring. work on rys., roads, bridges, bldgs. and municipal pub. wks. since 1881; asst. prof. engring. and mathematics, U. of Ill., 1885-90, prof. municipal and sanitary engring. and in charge theoretical and applied mechanics, 1890-1926, now prof. emeritus; made many investigations on properties of steel, brick, concrete, reinforced concrete, etc., and on bldgs. in connection with U. of Ill. Engring. Exptl. Sta. and as consultant, also investigations of water purification, sewage treatment and hydraulic questions; dir. investigation conducted by Am. Soc. C.E. and Am. Ry. Engring. Assn. to determine stresses in railroad track since 1914. Mem. Am. Soc. C.E. (pres. 1918; hon. mem. 1925), Soc. for Promotion Engring. Edn. (pres. 1910-11), Am. Soc. Testing Materials (pres. 1913-14; hon. mem. 1923), Am. Water Works Assn. (hon. mem. 1930), Western Soc. Engrs. (Washington award, 1924; hon. mem. 1927), Am. Public Works Assn., Am. Ry. Engring. Assn. (dir. 1915-18, 1928-31; hon. mem. 1933), Am. Soc. Mech. Engrs., New Eng. Water Works Assn., A.A.A.S. (v.p. 1928), Am. Concrete Inst. (Turner medal, 1928; hon. mem. 1932), Instn. Civ. Engrs. (London); hon. mem. Instn. Structural Engrs. (London); mem. bd. visitors U.S. Naval Acad., 1918-21; etc. Awarded Henderson medal, Franklin Institute, 1931; Lamme medal, Soc. for Promotion Engring. Edn., 1932; John Fritz medal of the Founder Societies, 1937. Clubs:

University, Engineers (Chicago). Author: The Railway Transition Spiral, 1901, 27; also many tech. articles and Experiment Sta. bulls. on engring. researches. Home: 1113 W. California Av. Address: 122 Talbot Laboratory, Urbana, Ill. Died Apr. 3, 1942.

TALBOT, Marion, univ. dean; b. Thun, Switzerland (Am. parents), July 31, 1858; d. Israel Tisdale (M.D.) and Emily (Fairbanks) Talbot; A.B., Boston U., 1880, A.M., 1882; S.B., Mass. Inst. Tech., 1888; LL.D., Cornell Coll., 1904, Boston U., 1924, Tulane U., 1935. Lecturer Lasell Sem., 1888-90; instr. domestic science Wellesley Coll., 1890-92; asst. prof. sanitary science, U. of Chicago, 1892-95, dean of women, 1892-1925, asso. prof. sanitary science, 1895-1904, asso. prof. household administration, 1904-05, prof. household administration, 1905-25, dean of Jr. Coll. of Science (women), 1905-09; acting pres. Constantinople Coll. for Women, 1927-28, 1931-32. Trustee Boston U.; mem. bd. of visitors of Wellesley Coll.; mem. advisory com. Guggenheim Foundation. Fellow American Geog. Soc., fellow A.A.A.S.; charter fellow Am. Pub. Health Assn.; mem. Am. Hist. Assn., Women's Internat. League, Assn. Deans of Women (hon.), Am. Home Econ. Assn. (hon.), Assn. Collegiate Alumnae (now Am. Assn. U. Women—hon. mem., a founder, later pres., sec. 13 yrs.), hon. mem. North Central Assn. of Colls., Bostonian Soc. Nat. Inst. Social Sciences, Ill. Home Econ. Assn. (hon.), Am. Assn. Univ. Profs., Mass. Soc. Univ. Edn for Women (sec. and pres.), Phi Beta Kappa. Clubs: Fortnightly (hon.), Chicago Woman's, and College (Chicago), Saturday Morning and College, both of Boston (hon.), Boston U. Women Graduates (hon.) Author: Home Sanitation (with E. H. Richards), 1887; Education of Women, 1910; The Modern Household (with S. P. Breckinridge), 1912; House Sanitation, 1912; History of the American Association Univ. Women (with Lois K. M. Rosenberry), 1930; More than Lore, 1936. Home: 5758 Kenwood Av. Address: University of Chicago, Chicago 37, Illinois. Died Oct. 20, 1948.

TALBOT, Walter LeMar, life ins.; b. Phila., Pa., Aug. 23, 1870; ed. pub. schs.; m. Estelle Mair; 1 son, Walter LeMar. Began as office boy with Fidelity Mutual Life Ins. Co., 1882, pres. since Feb. 24, 1914; dir. Corn Exchange Nat. Bank, John B. Stetson Co. Episcopalian. Mason (32°). Clubs: Union League; Skytop (pres.). Home: Germantown, Pa. Office: The Parkway at Fairmount Av., Philadelphia, Pa. Died Feb. 20, 1943.

TALBOTT, E(verett) Guy (tawl'bŏt), social service; b. Tuscola, Ill., Oct. 26, 1883; s. Albert Gallatin and Martha Ellen (Maris) T.; grad. Southwest Mo. State Teachers Coll., 1903; A.B., U. of Southern Calif., 1912, B.D., 1919, D.D., 1936; m. Ida Taylor, Aug. 9, 1905; children—Floyd, Elwood, Ruth, Marie. Pastor M.E. Ch., Estrella, Calif., 1905-08, Lamanda Park M.E. Ch., Pasadena, Calif., 1909-12; Calif. sec. M.E. Fedn. for Social Service, 1913; exec. sec. Calif. State Ch. Fedn., 1915-18; field sec. Nat. Com. on Chs. and Moral Aims of the War, 1917-18; field sec. Inter-Ch. World Movement, 1919-20; Pacific Coast dir. Near East Relief, 1921-28; asso. nat. sec. Golden Rule Foundation, 1929-31; regional dir. Nat. Council for Prevention of War, 1931-38; field sec. World Alliance for Internat. Friendship through the Churches since 1938; director San Francisco International Center since 1942; managing editor The Argonaut since 1942; chairman Pacific Coast Com. for World Economic Cooperation since 1937; Pacific Coast dir. League of Nations Assn., Com. to Defend America by Aiding the Allies, Council Against Intolerance in America, and Am. Union for Concerted Peace Efforts, since 1939; asst. dir. Peace Projects at Golden Gate Internat. Exposition, 1939; mem. commn. to Near East and Russia, summer 1921; headed Goodwill Mission to Far East, summer 1935. Mem. Inst. of Pacific Relations, Pacific Geog. Soc., Am. Acad. Polit. and Social Sciences. Western Poetry League, Pan-Pacific Union, U.S. Naval Inst., Phi Beta Kappa. Republican. Club: Commonwealth of California (chairman section on international relations). Contributing editor Christian Work, 1915-27; Author of (brochures) The Church and the Labor problem, 1913; The Price of Peace, 1935; Peace in the Pacific, 1936; Essential Conditions of Peace, 1937; Building a New World, 1943; also A Better World (poem), 1937; contbr. to periodicals. Home: 1225 Taylor St. Office: 68 Post St., San Francisco, Calif. Died Feb. 5, 1945.

TALCOTT, J(ames) Frederick (tăl'cŏt), merchant; b. New York City, Sept. 14, 1866; s. James and Henrietta Elizabeth (Francis) T.; B.A., Princeton, 1888, M.A., 1890; Oxford Univ., 1890-91; U. of Berlin, 1891; Union Theol. Sem., 1892; m. Miss Frank Vanderbilt Crawford, 1890 (died 1915); children—James, Hooker, Julia Lake (Mrs. Thomas M. McMillan, Jr.), Martha Everitt (Mrs. Marshall P. Blankarn); m. 2d, Louise Simmons, Feb. 17, 1917. Pres. James Talcott, Inc., New York; dir. Am. Hosiery Co., Lawyers Mortgage Corp. Pres. James Talcott Fund, Inc. Trustee McAuley Water Street Mission, Lincoln U., Fort Valley Normal and Industrial Sch., Manhattan Sch. of Music; dir. Children's Welfare Fedn., Bowery Branch Y.M.C.A., Union Settlement Assn., New York Bible Soc., Am. Tract Soc., St. Bartholomew's Community House, Boy Rangers America (nat. chmn.), Monmouth County Y.M.C.A., Fedn. of Protestant Welfare Agencies, Inc. (sec.), Friends of Boys, Inc. (pres.), N.Y. Soc. for Suppression of Vice; mem. Princeton-Yenching Foundation, Friends of Princeton Library. Mem. Chamber Commerce State N.Y., New York Bd. of Trade, N.Y. Geneal. and Biog. Soc., Rumson Borough Improvement Assn., Am. Metr. Museum of Art, English-Speaking Union, Monmouth County Hist. Assn., New Eng. Soc., Union Theol. Sem. Alumni. Republican. Episcopalian. Clubs: Republican, Pilgrims, Union League, Princeton, National Arts (pres.), Church, Clergy, Nassau Country, Empire State, Princeton University Cottage, Monmouth County Hunt, Adirondack League, Rumson Country, Seabright Lawn Tennis and Cricket, Seabright Beach, Metropolitan. Home: Sea Bright, N.J.; and 16 East 66th St., New York. Office: 225 Fourth Av., New York, N.Y. Died Feb. 6, 1944.

TALIAFERRO, James Piper, ex-senator; b. Orange Court House, Va., Sept. 30, 1847; ed. in Va., leaving sch. of William Dinwiddie, Greenwood, to volunteer in C.S.A., continued until close of war. Removed to Jacksonville, Fla.; engaged in logging and saw mill enterprise; now identified with banking interests. U.S. senator, 1899-1905, 1905-11. Chmn. Dem. State Exec. Com. 3 yrs. Address: Jacksonville, Fla. Died Oct. 6, 1934.

TALL, Lida Lee, educator, pres. teachers college; b. Dorchester County, Md., Nov. 17, 1873; d. Washington and Sarah Elizabeth (Humphreys) T.; grad. Western High School, Baltimore; student normal extension courses, Johns Hopkins; studied Univ. of Chicago, summer of 1904; Columbia, summer, 1907; B.S. and bachelor's diploma in education, Teachers College, Columbia, 1914; Litt.D., U. of Maryland, 1926. Served as teacher and critic teacher in Baltimore city schs., instr. in edn., literature and history, Teachers' Training Sch., Baltimore, 1904-08; supervisor of grammar grades, Baltimore County, Md., 1908-17; asst. supt. of schs., Baltimore County, Md., 1917-18; prin. elementary dept. Lincoln Sch., Teachers Coll., 1918-20; pres. Md. State Normal Sch. (name of school changed to Teachers College, 1935), Towson, 1920-38; retired, Sept. 1938. Instr. in edn., Johns Hopkins, summer, 1912. Teachers Coll. (Columbia), summers, 1907, 20. Asso. editor Atlantic Ednl. Jour., 1907-11 Alumna trustee Teachers Coll., 1915-17. Sec. dept. superintendence N.E.A., 1916-17; citation conferred by Gov. of Maryland for work on women's committee on education in World War; mem. Nat. Advisory Com. of Education; apptd. by President Herbert Hoover. Pres. of the Maryland Children's Aid Society since 1938; mem. Md. State Teachers' Assn. (pres. 1935), Am. Hist. Assn., Am. Assn. U. Women, English Speaking Union. Clubs: College, Quota (Balti.); Woman's City Club, Women's Eastern Shore Society. Author: Bibliography of History for Schools and Libraries (with Charles M. Andrews and J. Montgomery Gambrill), 1910. Compiler Baltimore County Course of Study (with Albert S. Cook and Isobel Davidson), 1915; How the Old World Found the New (with Eunice Fuller Barnard), 1929. Address: Eden Hall Apts, Baltimore, Md. Died Feb. 21, 1942.

TALLERDAY, Howard G., business exec.; pres. Western Pipe & Steel Co. of Calif.; v.p. Yosemite Portland Cement Corp. Home: Stanford Ct. Apts., California and Powell Sts. Office: 444 Market St., San Francisco, Calif. Died Jan. 1946.

TALLEY, Dyer Findley, surgeon; b. Woodlawn, Ala., Dec. 5, 1865; s. Nicholas Davis and Mary (Hawkins) T.; B.A., U. of Ala., 1887, hon. M.A., 1892; post-grad. work, New York Polyclinic, and post-grad. hosps., London, 1899, and surg. clinics in the large cities on continent of Europe, 1914; m. Elizabeth Fitzhugh Byrd, Oct. 17, 1917. Ambulance surgeon Charity Hosp., New Orleans, 2 yrs.; practiced at Birmingham, Ala., since 1892; attending surgeon Norwood Hospital; surgeon Norwood Clinic. Fellow American College Surgeons, Southern Surgical Society; mem. Founders Group American Bd. Surgery; mem. American Med. Association, Med. Assn. State of Ala., Birmingham Surg. Soc., Jefferson County Med. Soc., Southern Med. Assn., Phi Delta Theta. Democrat. Mason (32°). Clubs: Country, Pen and Key. Home: 1220 N. 12th Ct. Office: 2501 N. 16th Av., Birmingham, Ala. Died Jan. 8, 1947.

TALLEY, Lynn Porter, banker; b. Belton, Tex., Oct. 30, 1881; s. Ratliff Palmer and Lavinia Caroline (Porter) T.; grad. high sch., Temple, Tex., 1898; student Galveston Business U.; m. Martha Browning Downs, Dec. 4, 1907; children—Kathleen Downs (Mrs. Charles M. Spence), Martha Downs, Carolynn Downs, Beatrice Anne. Began as stenographer with Weld & Neville, Temple, and G.C.&S.F. R.R., 1900-01; traffic clk., Weld & Neville, Waco, Tex., 1901-02; with City Nat. Bank, Dallas, as exchange teller, dept. head, asst. cashier, and cashier, 1903-11; cashier Lumberman's Nat. Bank (now 2d Nat. Bank), Houston, 1911-15; cashier, later dep. gov., Fed. Res. Bank of Dallas, 1915-21; v.p. Southwest Nat. Bank of Dallas (now consol. with Republic Nat. Bank & Trust Co.), 1921-23; again with Federal Reserve Bank of Dallas as dir., chmn. bd. and federal reserve agt., 1923-25, gov. and chmn. exec. com., 1925-31; chmn. bd. Bank of America Nat. Trust and Savings Assn., San Francisco, 1931-32; apptd. asst. to dirs. Reconstruction Finance Corp., Washington, D.C., 1932; apptd. pres. and chmn. exec. com. Commodity Credit Corp., 1933, 39; treas., trustee and mem. exec. com. Export-Import Banks of Washington, 1933; retired, 1940. Mem. Am. Economic Assn. Republican. Address: 2540 Massachusetts Av. N.W., Washington, D.C.; and 3808 Miramar Av., Dallas, Tex.

Died Oct. 8, 1942.

TALMADGE, Eugene (tăl'măj), ex-governor; b. Forsyth, Ga., Sept. 23, 1884; s. Thomas Romalgus and Carrie (Roberts) T.; LL.B., U. of Ga., 1907; m. Mattie Thurmond, Sept. 12, 1909; children—John A. Peterson (step-son), Vera (Mrs. Charles T. Smiley), Herman Eugene, Margaret. Admitted to Ga. bar, 1908, in practice at McRae, 1908-26; actively engaged in farming since 1912; solicitor city court, McRae, 1918-20; atty. Telfair County, 1920-23; commr. of agr., Ga., 1927-33; governor of Ga., 1933-37 and 1940-43; in practice of law, 1937-40 and since 1943. Mem. Sigma Nu, Phi Kappa Phi. Democrat. Baptist. Mason, Odd Fellow, Woodman of World. Home: McRae, Ga. Address: William-Oliver Bldg., Atlanta, Ga. Died Dec. 21, 1946.

TAMARKIN, Jacob David (tà-mär'kin), prof. mathematics; b. Chernigoff, Russia, July 11, 1888; s. David and Sophy (Krassilschikoff) T.; grad. Gymnasium of Emperor Alexander I, St. Petersburg (Leningrad), Russia, 1906; diploma, U. of St. Petersburg, 1910, Master of Applied Mathematics, 1917; m. Helen Weichardt, St. Petersburg, Nov. 23, 1919 (died 1934); 1 son, Paul. Came to U.S., 1925. Instr. mathematics, U. of St. Petersburg and Sch. of Railroads, 1910-17, prof. mathematics, 1917-25; instr. in mathematics, Electro-Tech. Sch., 1913-17, prof. mathematics, 1917-25; asst. prof. mathematics, Dartmouth, 1925-27; asst. prof. mathematics, Brown U., 1927-28, prof. since 1928. Editor: colloquium publs. Am. Math. Soc. Fellow Am. Acad. Arts and Sciences; mem. Am. Math. Soc., Polish Math. Soc., Warsaw Scientific Soc., French Math. Soc. Mem. Greek Orthodox Ch. Home: 59 Keene St., Providence, R.I. Died Nov. 18, 1945.

TAMMEN, Agnes Reid (Mrs. Heye Harry Tammen) (tăm'ĕn); b. Petersburg, Va.; d. William and Jessie Murray (Kelly) Reid; ed. East Denver High Sch.; m. Harry Tammen, Mar. 24, 1892 (died 1924). Part owner and active in management of Denver Post; a liberal patron of the Children's Hospital; noted for her many outstanding philanthropies. Mem. bd. Children's Hosp. Republican. Divine Scientist. Clubs: Cherry Country, Mt. Vernon Country. Home: 1061 Humboldt St. Address: Denver Post, Denver, Colo. Died July 2, 1942.

TANNENBAUM, Samuel Aaron, physician, writer; b. Hungary, May 1, 1874; s. Morris and Hannah (Stahlberger) T.; student Coll. City of New York, 1891-94; M.D., Coll. Physicians and Surgeons, Columbia, 1898; m. Jeannette S. Rosett, Nov. 26, 1901; children—Arthur (dec.), Herman; married 2d, Dorothy Rosenzweig, 1942. Came to United States in 1886, naturalized, 1895. Practiced in N.Y. City since 1898; specializes in psychotherapy. Mem. New York County Med. Soc. Club: Shakespeare. Author: The Psychology of Accidents, 1924; Problems in Shakespeare's Penmanship, 1927; The Booke of Sir Thomas Moore, 1927; The Assassination of Christopher Marlowe, 1928; Shakespeare Forgeries in the Revels Account, 1928; Shakespeare and Sir Thomas Moore, 1929; The Handwriting of the Renaissance, 1930; Shakespearean Scraps and other Elizabethan Fragments, 1933; The Patient's Dilemma, 1935; Christopher Marlowe—A Concise Bibliography, 1937; also (brochures) Was William Shakespeare a Gentleman?, and Shakespeare's Coat of Arms; More About the Forged Revels Accounts, 1932; Ben Jonson—A Concise Bibliography, 1938. Editor: The Drinking Academy (by Thomas Randolph), 1930. Bibliographies of Beaumont and Fletcher, Chapman, and Massinger, 1938, T. Heywood and T. Dekker, 1939, Robert Green, 1939, Thomas Lodge, John Lyly, John Marston, and George Peele, 1940, Thomas Kyd and John Webster, 1941, Macbeth, Shakespeare's Sonnets, Merchant of Venice, King Lear, Othello, Montaigne, Middleton, T. Nash, F. Ford, Drayton, Sidney, Gascoigne, S. Daniel, Troilus and Cressida, Marie Stuart, Cyril Tourneur, James Shirley, George Herbert, R. Ascham, J. Heywood, supplements to C. Marlowe and B. Jonson. Translator: The Depths of the Soul (by W. Stekel), 1921; Essays (by same), 1922. Editor of the Shakespeare Association Bulletin. Contbr. to mags. Home: 601 W. 113th St., New York, N.Y. Died Oct. 31, 1948.

TARBELL, Arthur Wilson, editor; b. Jamaica Plain, Mass., Sept. 22, 1872; s. Eben Richards and Ellen (Jackson) T.; ed. Harvard, class of 1895; m. Edith Stone Kendall, Oct. 1, 1902. Asst. editor, 1896, editor, 1897-99, National Magazine; editor the Brown Book, 1900-05; asso. editor of Human Life, Boston, 1905-08; registrar, Carnegie Tech. Schs., Pittsburgh, since 1908. Home: 1113 Sherwood Pl., Pittsburgh. Died Nov. 25, 1946.

TARBELL, Ida Minerva (tär'bĕl), author; b. Erie County, Pa., Nov. 5, 1857; d. Franklin S. and Esther Ann (McCullough) Tarbell; A.B., Allegheny Coll., Meadville, Pa., 1880, A.M., 1883, L.H.D., 1909, LL.D., 1915; L.H.D., Knox Coll., 1909. Associate editor of The Chautauquan, 1883-91; student in Paris at The Sorbonne and Collège de France, 1891-94; editor on staff, and asso. editor McClure's Magazine, 1894-1906; asso. editor American Magazine, 1906-15. Mem. Am. Hist. Assn., English Soc. of Women Journalists, Am. Woman's Assn. Clubs: National Arts, Cosmopolitan, Pen and Brush. Mem. woman's com. Council of National Defense; mem. President Wilson's Industrial Conf. 1919, and Pres. Harding's Unemployment Conf.; mem. Nat. Women's Com. Mobilization for Human Needs, 1933-38. Author: Short Life of Napoleon Bonaparte, 1895; Life of Madame Roland, 1896; Early Life of Abraham Lincoln (with J. McCan Davis), 1896; Life of Abraham Lincoln (2 vols.), 1900; History of the Standard Oil Co. (2 vols.), 1904; He Knew Lincoln, 1907; Father Abraham, 1909; The Tariff in Our Times, 1911; The Business of Being a Woman, 1912; The Ways of Women, 1915;

New Ideals in Business, 1916; The Rising of the Tide, 1919; In Lincoln's Chair, 1920; Boy Scouts' Life of Lincoln, 1921; He Knew Lincoln, and Other Billy Brown Stories; In the Footsteps of Lincoln, 1924; Life of Judge Gary, 1925; A Reporter for Lincoln, 1927; Owen D. Young—a New Type of Industrial Leader, 1932; The Nationalizing of Business, 1878-98, 1936; All in the Day's Work (autobiography), 1939. Lecturer. Home: Route 1, Bethel, Conn. Died Jan. 6, 1944.

TARBELL, Martha, author; d. Horace Sumner and Martha A. (Treat) Tarbell; A.B., DePauw U., 1884, A.M., 1887; A.M., Brown, 1894, Ph.D., 1897; Litt.D., DePauw U., 1933. Mem. Kappa Kappa Gamma, Phi Beta Kappa, American Assn. Univ. Women, Pi Gamma Mu, D.A.R. Clubs: East Orange Garden; Woman's, Woman's College (Orange). Author: Tarbell's Teachers' Guide to the Internat. Bible Lessons for Christian Teaching, annually since 1906; Geography of Palestine in the Time of Christ, 1907; In the Master's Country, 1910; (with Horace Sumner Tarbell) a series of sch. geographies, 1896, 99, text-books in language, 1891-1903. Address: East Orange, N.J. Died Oct. 27, 1948.

TARKINGTON, (Newton) Booth, author; b. Indianapolis, July 29, 1869; s. Hon. John Stevenson and Elizabeth (Booth) T.; ed. Phillips Exeter Acad., Purdue U. and Princeton U.; hon. A.M., Princeton, 1899, and Litt.D., 1918; also Litt.D., De Pauw U., 1923; Litt.D., Columbia University, 1924; L.H.D., Purdue University, 1939; m. Laurel Louisa Fletcher, June 18, 1902; m. 2d, Susannah Robinson, 1912. Mem. Ind. House of Representatives, 1902-03. Twice awarded Pulitzer prize for literature. Awarded gold medal, Nat. Inst. Arts and Sciences, 1933; Theodore Roosevelt Memorial medal, 1942. Member American Academy of Arts and Letters. Clubs: Ivy, Nassau (Princeton); Players, Century (New York); University (Indianapolis). Author: The Gentleman from Indiana, 1899; Monsieur Beaucaire, 1900; The Two Vanrevels, 1902; Cherry, 1903; In the Arena, 1905; The Conquest of Canaan, 1905; The Beautiful Lady, 1905; His Own People, 1907; Guest of Quesnay, 1908; Beasley's Christmas Party, 1909; Beauty and the Jacobin, 1911; The Flirt, 1913; Penrod, 1914; The Turmoil, 1915; Penrod and Sam, 1916; Seventeen, 1917; The Magnificent Ambersons, 1918; Harlequin and Columbine, 1918; Ramsey Milholland, 1919; Alice Adams, 1921; Gentle Julia, 1922; The Fascinating Stranger and other stories, 1923; The Midlander, 1924; Women, 1925; Looking Forward and Others, 1926; Growth, 1927; The Plutocrat, 1927; The World Does Move, 1928; Claire Ambler, 1928; Young Mrs. Greeley, 1929; Mirthful Haven, 1930; Penrod Jashber, 1931; Wanton Mally, 1932; Mary's Neck, 1932; The Complete Penrod, 1932; Presenting Lily Mars, 1933; Little Orvie, 1934; Mr. White, The Red Barn, Hell and Bridewater, 1935; The Lorenzo Bunch, 1936; Rumbin Galleries, 1937; Some Old Portraits, 1939; The Heritage of Hatcher Ide, 1940; The Fighting Littles, 1941; Kate Fennigate, 1943. Wrote plays: Monsieur Beaucaire, 1901; The Gentleman from Indiana, 1905; with Harry Leon Wilson) The Man from Home, 1906; Cameo Kirby, 1907; Your Humble Servant, 1908; Springtime, 1908; Getting a Polish, 1909; Mister Antonio, 1916; (with Julian Street) The Country Cousin, 1917; (with Harry Leon Wilson) The Gibson Upright, and Up From Nowhere, 1919; Clarence, 1919; Poldekin, 1920; The Wren, 1921; The Intimate Strangers, 1921; Rose Brier, 1922; Tweedles, Magnolia, 1923; Colonel Satan, 1930. Home: 4270 N. Meridian St., Indianapolis, Ind. Died May 19, 1946.

TARLER, G(eorge) Cornell, diplomatic service; b. N.Y. City, Oct. 4, 1876; s. George A. and Sarah (Cornell) T.; B.S., Coll. City of New York, 1895, M.S., 1898; A.M., Columbia, 1897, LL.B., 1899, completed courses and passed Ph.D. examinations; m. Mary Angela Brett, Feb. 19, 1927. Practiced law, New York, 1899-1908; 2d sec. Am. Legation at Havana, Cuba, 1908-09; sec. legation and consul gen. to Siam, 1909-11; spl. rep. of President Taft at coronation ceremonies of King Vajiravudh of Siam, Nov. 1910; sec. of legation to Uruguay and Paraguay, Aug. 1911; 2d sec. of Embassy at Constantinople, 1911, first sec., 1916, in charge of diplomatic interests and nationals of Allied Powers in Turkey, 1914-17, and chargé d'affaires at time of rupture of diplomatic relations, Apr. 20, 1917; spl. adviser to Pan Am. Commercial Conf., 1917; 1st sec. of Embassy at Rio de Janeiro, 1917-19; in charge spl. mission of President-elect Pessoa of Brazil in U.S., June-July 1919; in charge of Royal Abyssinian Mission in the U.S., July-Aug. 1919; detailed to accompany King Albert of the Belgians and in charge of Royal Mission in the U.S., Oct. 1919; attached to Mission Prince of Wales, Nov. 1919; del. to 2d Pan Am. Financial Congress, Jan. 1920; duty Dept. of State, 1919-20; with Am. Mission, Vienna, 1920; duty Dept. of State, 1921-22; retired Jan., 1922; practiced law, internat. relations, 1922-39; protocol adviser U.S. Commn. N.Y. World's Fair, May, 1939; sr. cons. on trade, polit., legal and diplomatic matters, N.Y. Office of Federal Postal Censorship since 1942. Decorated Legion of Honor and Order of Merit (France); Comdr. Order of Leopold and Order of Crown (Belgium); Comdr. Order of Crown (Italy). Clubs: Columbia U., Pilgrims, Huntington Bay, Huntington Yacht (New York); Am. Soc. French Legion of Honor; Belgian League of Honor. Address: 930 5th Av., New York, N.Y. Died Dec. 26, 1945.

TARR, Frederick Hamilton, lawyer; b. Rockport, Mass., Oct. 8, 1868; s. George Washington and Eliza (Hamilton) T.; grad. high sch., Gloucester, Mass., 1886; A.B., Amherst Coll., 1891; LL.B., Harvard, 1896; m. Angie Choate Parker, June 19, 1901; children—Frederick H., Louise. Admitted to Mass. bar, 1896, and began practice at Gloucester; pres. Rockport Nat. Bank; dir. Gloucester Nat. Bank, Gorton Pew Fisheries Co., Perkins & Corliss Co.; trustee Cape Ann Savings Bank. Spl. counsel for U.S. before Am. and Brit. Tribunal. U.S. dist. atty., Mass., 1926-33; mem. exec. council of Mass. Trustee Addison Gilbert Hosp., Gloucester. Episcopalian. Mason, Odd Fellow. Clubs: University; Mass. Republican; Essex Republican; Rockport Country. Home: Rockport, Mass. Office: Gloucester, Mass.* Died May 14 1944.

TATLOCK, Henry, clergyman; b. Dublin, Ireland, May 27, 1848; brought to America in infancy; B.A., Williams Coll., Mass., 1871, M.A., 1874, D.D., 1911; student Gen. Theol. Sem., New York, 1884-85; S.T.D., Hobart, 1907; m. Margaret Tatlock, Aug. 15, 1872; children—Margaret Lloyd, Elizabeth Abbot (dec.), Lloyd (dec.), Louise H. (dec.), Orrett. Prin. high sch., Grafton, Mass., 1871-73; prin. and propr. Park Inst., Rye, N.Y., 1873-84; teacher and student, New York, 1884-88; deacon, 1888, priest, 1889, P.E. Ch.; asst. minister Ch. of Holy Trinity, New York, 1888-89; rector St. Andrew's Church, Ann Arbor, Mich., 1889-1921, became rector emeritus, 1921. Examining chaplain, Diocese of Mich., 1891-1919; dean Southern Convocation of the Diocese, 1894-97; del. Gen. Conv., P.E. Ch., 7 times to 1922; chmn. Diocesan Com. on Canons, 1900-23; mem. Standing Com. of diocese, 1904-23, pres. from 1917; del. Pan-American Congress, London, 1908; chmn. Diocesan Commn. on Social Service, 1910-15. Mem. Phi Beta Kappa. Mason. Contbr. numerous papers on theol. and religious subjects. Club: University. Home: Ann Arbor, Mich. Died Oct. 30, 1942.

TATLOCK, John S. P., prof. English; b. Stamford, Conn., Feb. 24, 1876; s. William and Florence (Perry) T.; A.B., Harvard, 1896, A.M., 1897, Ph.D., 1903; Litt.D., U. of Mich., 1938; LL.D., Kenyon, 1939; m. Marjorie Fenton, June 17, 1908 (died 1937); children—Percival (dec.), Hugh, Jean Frances (dec.). Instructor English, Univ. of Mich., 1897-1901, 1903-05, professor (various grades), 1905-15; professor English, Stanford U., 1915-25; prof. English, Harvard, 1925-29; prof. English, U. of Calif., 1929-46, prof. emeritus since 1946. Episcopalian. Mem. Mediæval Acad. Am. (fellow, councilor, 1926-28; v.p., 1932-35; pres. 1942-45), Modern Lang. Assn. America (v.p., 1914; councillor, 1932-36; pres., 1938), Am. Philol. Assn., Philol. Assn. Pacific Coast (v.p., 1918-19, pres., 1919-20), Am. Assn. Univ. Profs. (council, 1919-22; v.p., 1927), Am. Philos. Soc., Phi Beta Kappa; fellow Am. Acad. of Arts and Sciences. Research associate Carnegie Institute of Washington, 1916-23; dist. dir. in ednl. work of War Dept., 1918. Author: Development and Chronology of Chaucer's Works, 1907; Harleian MS. 7334, and Revision of Canterbury Tales, 1909; The Scene of Franklin's Tale Visited, 1915. Editor: Shakespeare's "Troilus and Cressida," 1912; The Modern Reader's Chaucer (with Percy MacKaye), 1912; Representative English Plays (with R. G. Martin), 1916, rev. edit., 1938; Concordance to Chaucer (with A. G. Kennedy), 1927; The Legendary History of Britain: Geoffrey of Monmouth to Lawman, 1949; numerous articles in philology, hist., ednl. and lit. jours. Address: 1560 Euclid Av., Berkeley, Calif. Died June 24, 1948.

TATMAN, Charles Taylor, lawyer; b. Worcester, Mass., Dec. 16, 1871; s. Reuben James and Susan M. (Taylor) T.; student Worcester Poly. Inst., 1889-91; LL.B., Harvard U., 1894; m. Anna C., d. Anders and Christina F. Svedberg, Aug. 28, 1901. Practiced at Worcester since 1894. Chmn. Republican City Com., 1898; rep. Gen. Court of Mass., 1899-1900; alderman City of Worcester, 1906; dir. Worcester Free Pub. Library, 1907-13 (pres. 1912); mem. exec. com. Rep. State Com., 1914-16; del.-at-large Mass. Constl. Convention, 1917-18. Decorated Officier d'Académie (France). Mem. American Bar Assn., Mass. Bar Assn. (v.p., 1942-45), Worcester County Bar Association (pres. 1920), American Antiquarian Society, Worcester Chamber of Commerce (pres. 1909-11), Alliance Française (pres. 1934-35), S.A.R., Am. Numismatic Soc., one of founders American Numismatic Assn. (1891), Worcester Hist. Society (pres. 1913), Sigma Alpha Epsilon, Rotary Club of Worcester (pres. 1927-28), The Bohemians. Mem. M.V.M. 3 yrs. Clubs: Tatnuck Country, Worcester Economic (pres. 1940-41). Unitarian. Writer on numismatics. Served as Govt. appeal agt. in the Selective Service during war period. Home: 242 Salisbury St. Office: 900 Slater Bldg., Worcester 8, Mass. Died Dec. 23, 1945.

TAUBER, Richard (tou'bĕr), opera singer, composer, conductor; b. in Austria. Debut in Germany; has made tours through most of Europe, America and Australia. Became British subject, 1940. Address: Grosvenor House, London W. 1, England; also care Metropolitan Musical Bureau, 113 W. 57th St., New York 19, N.Y. Died Jan. 8, 1948; buried in Brompton Cemetery, London, Eng.

TAUBMAN, George Primrose (toub'măn), clergyman; b. Isle of Man, June 30, 1869; brought to U.S., 1871; s. Thomas T. and Margaret Ann (Qualtro) T.; student Transylvania (Ky.) Coll., 1891-94; D.D., Eugene Bible U., Ore., 1923; m. Anne Peyton Greene, Jan. 9, 1896; children—George P., Mrs. Margaret Kirkpatrick, Mary Hughes (Mrs. Charles Way). Ordained to the ministry of Christian (Disciples) Church, 1894; pastor Newport, Ky., 1895-97, Mays Lick, Ky., 1897-99, First Church, Portsmouth, O., 1899-1906, Hyde Park Ch., Kansas City, Mo., 1907-12, First Ch., Tulsa, Okla., 1913-14, First Ch., Long Beach, Calif., 1915-39; retired Sept. 1940. Has received over 7,100 members into ch. at Long Beach, and built ch. at cost of $600,000; teacher of Men's Bible Class of over 2,000, and running as high as 5,000. Mem. Pi Gamma Mu. Prohibitionist. Mason (K.T., Shriner), Modern Woodman. Kiwanian. Home: 3551 Brayton Av., Long Beach, Calif.* Died Mar. 12, 1947.

TAUSSIG, Albert Ernst (tou'sĭg), physician; b. St. Louis, May 6, 1871; s. Joseph S. and Mary L. (Cuno) T.; A.B., Harvard, 1891; M.D., Washington U. Med. Sch., St. Louis, 1894; m. Harriet Palmer Learned, 1903; children—Joseph Bondi, Barrett Learned, Lucelia Wakefield, Mary Cuno, Leonore Parker. Asso. prof. medicine, Washington U. Med Sch., 1913-31; prof. of clinical medicine since 1931; physician to Barnes and Jewish hospitals. Mem. Assn. Am. Physicians, A.M.A., Mo. State Med. Assn. Democrat. Unitarian. Club: University. Home: 5038 Washington Av. Office: 4500 Olive St., St. Louis, Mo. Died Jan. 16, 1944.

TAUSSIG, Charles William, mfr., author; b. N.Y. City, August 9, 1896; s. Noah William and Constance (Goldsmith) T.; ed. Stuyvesant High Sch., N.Y. City; m. Ruth Adler, Aug. 9, 1917; children—Ruth Jean Pearsall, Patricia Ann. Chmn. bd. and pres. Am. Molasses Co.; chmn. bd. The Nulomoline Co., Sucrest Corp.; chmn. and pres. Boston Molasses Co.; pres. Am. Molasses Co. of La., Applied Sugar Laboratories, Inc., Am. Molasses Tank Storage Corp.; director American Molasses Co. of Maine, and Am. Molasses Company of North Carolina, Inc., and Nulomoline, Ltd. (Montreal, Canada). Appointed by President Roosevelt, technical adviser during Washington confs. with fgn. powers, 1933; one of 6 original mems. of Roosevelt "Brain Trust"; tech. adviser to World Economic Conf., 1933; chmn. Nat. advisory com., Nat. Youth Adminstrn., 1935-43; mem. President's Advisory Council for Virgin Islands, 1934; mem. com. on Dependent Areas, Dept. of State. Chmn. U.S. Commn. to Study Social and Economic Conditions in the British West Indies, 1940; apptd. U.S. chmn. Anglo-Am. Caribbean Commn. (Dept. of State), 1942; apptd. by President Roosevelt adviser to U.S. delegation, United Nations Conference on Internat. Organization, San Francisco, 1945. Adv. to Sec. of State on Caribbean Affairs, 1945. Chmn., U.S. Sect., Caribbean Commn., 1946; spl. adv., Sec. of State, 1947. Member board trustees, Town Hall, Incorporated. Served as radio electrician, United States Navy, World War I. Member Pan-American Soc., Inst. Radio Engrs. Awarded National Order Merit, Carlos Manuel de Cespedes (Cuba). Clubs: Radio of America, Advertising, Bay Shore Yacht, Town Hall, India House; South Bay Golf (Bay Shore, L.I.). Author: Book of Radio, 1922; Book of Hobbies (with T. A. Meyer), 1924; Rum, Romance and Rebellion, 1928; American Etchers—Philip Kappel, Vol. IV, 1929; Some Notes on Sugar and Molasses, 1940; also various mag. articles. Home: 30 E. 71st St. Office: 120 Wall St., New York, N.Y. Also Dept. of State, Washington, D.C. Died May 9, 1948.

TAUSSIG, Frederick Joseph, gynecologist; b. Brooklyn, N.Y., Oct. 26, 1872; s. Joseph S. and Mary L. (Cuno) T.; A.B., Harvard, 1893; M.D., Washington U., 1898; m. Florence Gottschalk, May 4, 1907; children—Mary Bolland (Mrs. L. Benoist Tompkins), Frederick. Served as interne and assistant supt. St. Louis Female Hospital, 1898-1901; intern Imperial and Royal Elizabeth Hosp., Vienna, Austria, 1902-03; practiced in St. Louis since 1902; clin. prof. of gynecology and prof. of clin. obstetrics, Washington U. Med. Sch. since 1911; gynecologist Barnard Free Skin and Cancer, Jewish and St. Louis City hosps.; obstetrician St. Louis Maternity Hosp. Fellow Am. Coll. Surgeons; mem. Am. Gyneol. Soc. pres. 1936-37), Am. Assn. for Cancer Research, Am. Soc. for Control of Cancer (dir, 1938), A.M.A., St. Louis Med. Soc., Central Assn. Obstetricians and Gynecologists (pres. 1932-33), St. Louis Surg. Club. Member of Ethical Society. Clubs: Harvard, University Club. Author: Diseases of the Vulva, 1923; Abortion, Spontaneous and Induced, Medical and Social Aspects, 1935. Contbr. Nelson's Loose-Leaf Surgery, Lewis' Practice of Surgery, Curtis' Obstetrics and Gynecology, 1929-33, Christopher Surgery, Davis' Obstetrics and Gynecology, Brenneman's Pediatrics, Pack's Treatment for Cancer and Allied Diseases. Home: 50 Westmoreland Pl. Office: 3720 Washington Av., St. Louis, Mo. Died Aug. 21, 1943.

TAUSSIG, James Edward, ry. pres.; b. St. Louis, Mo., May 4, 1865; s. Edward and Ottilie (Fisher) T.; ed. London, Eng., Darmstadt, Germany, and Brussels, Belgium; m. Harriet Holmes, Jan. 20, 1892; 1 son, Edward Holmes. Apprentice in mech. dept. Terminal R.R., St. Louis, 1884; later agt., dispatcher, chief dispatcher and trainmaster Mo.P. Ry.; supt. Wheeling Term. Ry., 1895-1900, W.&L.E. Ry., 1900-04, Wabash Ry., 1904-10, S.P. Ry., 1910-11; gen. supt. T.&P. Ry., 1911-15; v.p. and federal mgr. Wabash Ry. Co., 1915-21, pres. 1921-32 (retired); was also pres. or officer various other cos. Republican. Episcopalian. Mason (K.T., Shriner). Clubs: Noonday, Racquet, Traffic, Bogey Golf, Bellerive Country (St. Louis); Traffic (Chicago); Los Angeles Athletic; Riviera Country (Los Angeles). Home: 275 Union Blvd., St. Louis. Died Oct. 3, 1949.

TAUSSIG, Joseph Knefler (taw'sĭg), naval officer; b. of Am. parentage, Dresden, Germany, Aug. 30,

1877; s. Edward David and Ellen (Knefler) T.; grad. Western High Sch., Washington, D.C., 1895; B.S., U.S. Naval Acad., 1899; grad. Naval War Coll., 1920; m. Lulie Augusta Johnston, Oct. 18, 1911; children—Emily Johnston (Mrs. Henry Wadsworth Whitney), Margaret Stewart (Mrs. George Philip), Joseph Knefler. Commd. ensign in U.S. Navy, Jan. 29, 1901; promoted through grades to rear admiral, July 1, 1931; assistant chief of naval operations, 1933-36; commandant, 5th Naval District and Naval Operating Base, Norfolk, Va., 1938-41; retired as vice admiral Sept. 1, 1941. Participated in Spanish-American War, Philippine Insurrection, Boxer Campaign, Cuban Pacification, World War I, Nicaraguan Campaign of 1927. Recalled to active duty, June 1943; Office of Secretary of Navy, Navy Department, 1945. Chairman Hampton Roads Sanitation Commission. Was awarded Distinguished Service Medal (United States); Sampson medal (Spanish-American War); Life Saving Medal of Honor; Order of Saint Michael and Saint George (England); Order of Merit First Class (Chile); Naval Institute gold medal, 1939; advanced "for eminent and conspicuous conduct in battle," Boxer Campaign, 1900. Unitarian. Clubs: Army and Navy (Washington); Rotary International; New York Yacht; University (Phila.); Wardroom (Boston). Home: Washington, D.C., and Jamestown, R.I. Died Oct. 29, 1947.

TAVENNER, Clyde Howard, ex-congressman; born Cordova, Ill., Feb. 4, 1882; s. John E. and Lucinda (Vanderburgh) T.; ed. country schs.; m. Isabel E. Martin, July 11, 1912; children—Isabel Lucinda, Elsa Mildred, Clyde H. Writer for city daily newspapers; began to write daily signed article, 1908, for 10 years syndicated a daily Washington letter to 100 daily papers, weekly letter to 2,600 weekly papers; wrote series of letters on tariff systems of England, France, Germany, and Italy. Dir. publicity for Dem. Nat. Congressional Com., Campaigns of 1910, 12; mem. 63d and 64th Congresses (1913-17), 14th Ill. Dist. Democrat. Visited Sibera, Japan, and Philippines, 1919, and wrote series of articles favoring Philippine independence. Founded The Philippine Republic, monthly mag., 1923. Address: care Bill Clerk, House of Reps., New House Office Bldg., Washington. Died Feb. 7, 1942.

TAVES, Brydon, newspaper corr.; b. New York, N.Y., Nov. 9, 1914; s. Archibald William and Isabel (Brydon) T.; student St. Christopher's Sch., Eastbourne, Eng., 1921-27, Radley Coll., Eng., 1927-30; m. Diana Parnham, May 31, 1943. Began as apprentice reporter N.Y. Herald Tribune, 1931; with United Press since 1932, at Rio de Janeiro, Brazil, 1932, mem. fgn. cable staff, New York, 1937-38, on staff, Rio de Janeiro, 1939, London, 1939-41, West Africa, Capetown, Johannesburg, Durban, 1941-42, mgr. for Australia since Mar. 1942. Office: United Press Assns., 220 E. 42d St., New York, N.Y. Killed in action as a reporter, 1943.

TAWNEY, Guy Alan, psychologist, philosopher; b. Tippecanoe City, O., Mar. 11, 1870; s. Daniel Abraham and Adelle (Paige) T.; student McAlester College, Minnesota, 1887-88, Wabash College, Indiana, 1888-89, 1890-91; A.B., Princeton, 1893, M.A., 1894; Ph.D., Leipzig, 1896; m. Marietta Busey, April 1909; children—George Busey (deceased—member A.U.S.), Elizabeth Paige, Catherine Jane. Demonstrator in psychology, Princeton, 1896; Squier professor mental science and philosophy, Beloit (Wis.) College, 1897-1907; lecturer in philosophy, Columbia U., 1906-07; asst. prof. philosophy, U. of Ill., 1907-08; prof. philosophy, U. of Cincinnati, 1908-27, Obed J. Wilson prof. of ethics, 1927-30; prof. philosophy, U. of Ill., 1930-39, retired Sept. 1, 1939. Chmn. bd. Busey First Nat. Bank since 1933. Mem. bd. McCormick Theol. Sem., Chicago. Mem. Am. Philos. Assn., Phi Beta Kappa; fellow A.A.A.S., British Inst. Philos. Studies. Contbr. on psychol. and philos. subjects. Home: 502 W. Main St., Urbana, Ill. Died Jan. 5, 1947.

TAWRESEY, John Godwin (taw'rê-sê), naval officer; b. Odessa, New Castle County, Del., Jan. 23, 1862; s. Joseph Squires and Mary Jane (Rust) T.; grad. U.S. Naval Acad., 1885; student Royal Naval Coll., Greenwich, Eng., 1888-90; m. Edith Jane Haken, Apr. 3, 1892; children—Alfred Purl Haken, John Squires, Harold R., Edith Virginia (Mrs. Alexander Whitney), Mary Constance (Mrs. John Stuart Milne II), Barrett Godwin. Began as cadet engr., 1881; naval cadet, 1883-87; commd. ensign, 1887; became asst. naval constructor, 1889; commd. comdr., Construction Corps, U.S. Navy, 1901, capt., 1917, rear admiral, 1925; retired since 1926. Del. Internat. Conf. of Safety of Life at Sea, London, Eng., 1929, Internat. Conf. on Load Lines, London, 1930. Mem. Soc. Naval Architects and Marine Engrs., Instn. of Naval Architects (London), Am. Soc. of Naval Engrs., U.S. Naval Inst., Franklin Inst. Baptist. Clubs: Army and Navy (Washington); Engineers (Phila.). Address: 514 Cheltena Av., Jenkintown, Pa. Died Feb. 17, 1943.

TAYLOR, Alfred Simpson, surgeon; b. Manchester, Conn., Dec. 17, 1868; s. John and Sarah (Parker) T.; Ph.B., Brown U., 1891, A.M., 1892; M.D., Coll. Phys. and Surg. (Columbia), 1895; m. Lucy E. Weeks, Sept. 18, 1907; 1 dau., Helen Gelsey. Began practice at N.Y. City, 1895; prof. clin. surgery, Cornell U. Med. Coll., 1910-30; cons. neurol. surgeon Neurol. Institute, St. Luke's Gen. Memorial, and Tarrytown hosps.; retired. Mem. Am. Surg. Assn., Soc. for Neurol. Surgeons, Am. Neurol. Assn., N.Y. Surg. Soc., N.Y. Neurol. Soc., New York Acad. Medicine, Delta Upsilon, Phi Beta Kappa. Clubs: Brown University Century. Address: care N.Y. Trust Co., Rockefeller Plaza, New York, N.Y. Died Jan. 16, 1942.

TAYLOR, Aubrey E., publicist; b. Washington, D.C., July 19, 1899; s. John E. and Sarah Elizabeth (West) T.; ed. Business High School, Washington, D.C.; m. Jane E. Boudwin, Sept. 29, 1927; children—Ellen Blanch, Jane Elizabeth. Reporter with Washington Times, 1916-17; with Washington Post, 1917, as reporter, until 1925, city editor, 1925-30, assistant managing editor, 1930, managing editor, 1931, 32; Washington representative Nat. Economy League, 1933; asst. dir. pub. relations, Pub. Works Adminstrn., 1933; asst. dir. information, U.S. Dept. of the Interior, 1937-39; dir. of information, Public Works Adminstrn., 1939-40; specialist, Federal Works Agency, 1941, asst. dir. of information, 1942-44, dir. of information, 1944-45. Club: National Press (bd. govs. 1931-33). Home: 6309 Oakridge Av., Chevy Chase, Md. Died Apr. 22, 1947.

TAYLOR, Benjamin Irving, congressman; b. New York, Dec. 21, 1877; s. Maurice H. and Ella M. (Archer) T.; grad. New Rochelle (N.Y.) High Sch.; LL.B., Columbia Law Sch., 1899; m. Harriet Bulkley, Apr. 27, 1907. Began practice, Port Chester, N.Y., 1899; mem. firm. of Taylor & Coward; mem. 63d Congress (1913-15), 25th N.Y. Dist. Democrat. Episcopalian. Mason. Address: Harrison, Westchester County, N.Y. Died Sept. 1946.

TAYLOR, Charles Vincent, univ. dean; b. Whitesville, Mo., Feb. 8, 1895; s. Isaac Newton and Christina (Bashor) T.; A.B., Mt. Morris (Ill.) Coll., 1911; M.A., U. of Calif., 1915, Ph.D., 1917; m. Lola Lucile Felder, May 6, 1921; children—Jeanne Lucile, Elouise Christine, Lola Lenore, Isaac Newton. Prin., high sch., Valley City, N.D., 1911-14; teaching fellow, U. of Calif., 1914-17, instr. zoölogy, 1917-18; Johnston scholar, Johns Hopkins U., 1918-20; asst. prof. zoölogy, U. of Calif., 1920-23, U. of Mich., 1923-24, U. of Calif., 1924-25; research asso. Carnegie Inst., Tortugas Lab., 1924, 26; acting asst. prof., Hopkins Marine Sta., summers, 1922, 23, asso. dir. since 1925; asso. prof. biology, Stanford U., 1925-26, prof., 1926-30; prof. zoölogy, U. of Chicago, 1930-31; Herztein prof. biology, head dept. zoölogy, Stanford Univ., 1931-34; Herztein prof. biology since 1931, dean, Sch. of Biol. Sciences, since 1934. Mem. Nat. Acad. of Sciences, A.A.A.S., Am. Soc. Zoölogists, Soc. Exptl. Biology and Medicine, Nat. Geog. Soc., Am. Naturalists Soc., Western Soc. Naturalists (former pres.), Pacific Oceanographic Soc., Sigma Xi. Edited Contributions to Marine Biology, 1930; The Cell and Protoplasm, 1940. Research contributions (a) on living cells: function of fibrillar systems, role of micronucleus, development of egg fragments, etc.; (b) on protoplasm: sol-gel reversibility; cataphoresis of ultramicroscopic inclusions, etc. Home: 562 Gerona Rd., Stanford U., Calif.* Died Feb. 22, 1946.

TAYLOR, Charles William, state supt. schs.; b. Red Oak, Ia., June 3, 1874; s. James Henry and Tamar Anne (Ratliff) T.; A.B., U. of Neb., 1898; grad. study same and Columbia; m. Sarah Elizabeth Wert Smith, July 3, 1899; children—Seth Charles Henry, John William, Beth Elaine, Marie Provo (dec.), Hutch Nordel (dec.), James (dec.). Teacher, W. Riverside Rural Sch., Montgomery County, Ia., 1893-94; supt. schs., Ohiowa, Neb., 1898-1901, Geneva, Neb., 1901-07; sec., treas. and mgr. S. R. Smith Furniture Co., Lead, 1907-08; supt. city schs., McCook, Neb., 1908-11; prof. sch. adminstrn., dir. teacher training and prin. Teachers Coll. High Sch., U. of Neb., 1911-27; state supt. pub. instrn., Neb., since 1927. Mem. Ia. Nat. Guard, 1893-96, 2d lt., 1902-03; mem. U. of Neb. cadets, 1894-98; served as capt., inf., later machine gun officer, U.S. Army, 1917-18; capt., inf., O.R.C. Chmn. advisory bd. Salvation Army, Lincoln. Mem. Neb. State Library Commn.; sec. Neb. State Bd. Vocational Edn.; former sec. Neb. State Illiteracy Commn.; now chmn. State Bd. Advisory Com. on Illiteracy; mem. Bd. of Edn. of State Normal Schs.; under constl. amendment, 1940, a member of Board of Educational Lands and Funds; mem. Bishop Clarkson Memorial Hosp. Assn. Life mem. N.E.A. (state chmn. rural life com.); mem. Am. Assn. Univ. Profs., Neb. Ednl. Assn., Neb. State Teachers Assn. (ex-v.p.), Nat. Inst. on Mercenary Crime (dir.), Lincoln Chamber Commerce, Neb. School Master's Club, Sons of the Am. Revolution (state pres.), Sons of Vets. Civil War, Am. Legion (state comdr. 1924), Res. Officers Assn., Phi Delta Kappa, Acacia. Republican. Episcopalian. Mason; mem. O.E.S., Royal Neighbors America. Clubs: Lincoln Auto, Knife and Fork, Lincoln University. Home: 2127 Harwood St. Office: State Capitol Bldg., Lincoln, Neb. Died Jan. 21, 1943.

TAYLOR, E. Leland, mayor; b. Knoxville, Tenn.; s. Eugene Augustin and Margaret (Jordan) T.; B.A., U. of Va., 1909; m. Edith Somers, Sept. 19, 1914; children—Carolyn Somers (Mrs. James D. Marret), Margaret (Mrs. James T. Skelly, Jr.), Marion Elliott (Mrs. Albert E. Hulbert, Jr.), Edith Somers. Sec. Wright and Taylor, Inc., distillers, Louisville, 1920-21; pres. Wright and Taylor, Inc., real estate, Louisville, since 1921. Mayor of Louisville, 1945. Served as 1st lt., F.A., U.S. Army, 1918. Mem. Louisville Bd. Edn., 1922-32. Mem. Kappa Alpha. Clubs: Country, Pendennis (Louisville). Home: Millvale Rd. Office: 1016 Francis Bldg., Louisville, Ky. Deceased.

TAYLOR, Earl Burt, coll. prof.; b. Middletown, N.Y., Feb. 22, 1889; s. Alfred Burt and Alice (Earl) T.; A.B., U. of Rochester, 1912, A.M., 1913; Ed.M., Harvard, 1929; grad. work Columbia, 1917; m. Judith Ogden, July 15, 1915; children—Anne, Alice, Jane, Judith. Instr. in English, Kiskiminetas Springs (Pa.) Sch., 1913-15; prin. Albion (N.Y.) High Sch., 1915-17; supt. Le Roy (N.Y.) pub. schs., 1917-28; prof. of edn. and chmn. of dept., U. of Rochester, since 1928, also dir. of extension since 1928. Dean, The Univ. School of Liberal and Applied Studies since 1944. Mem. Am. Assn. of Univ. Profs., Phi Beta Kappa, Theta Delta Chi, Phi Delta Kappa. Home: 105 Beckwith Terrace, Rochester, N.Y. Died Nov. 18, 1946.

TAYLOR, Edwy Lycurgus, pub. utilities; b. Albany, N.Y., Sept. 8, 1879; s. Edwy Lycurgus and Elizabeth Ellison (Taylor) T.; Ph.B., Yale, 1901, C.E., 1904; m. Helen Very Curtis, Dec. 9, 1911; children—John, William Curtis, Helen Angeline. Asst. instr. Yale, 1901-03, instr., 1904-06; asst. prof., U. of Kan., 1903-04; with engring. dept. N.Y., N.H.,&H. R.R., 1906; with N.Y.C. R.R., 1906-12, maintenance of way dept., 1906-08, asst. engr. electric div., 1908-11, asst. engr. in office of designing engr., 1911-12; with N.Y.,N.H.&H. R.R., 1912-18, 1919-30, asst. engr. 1912-14, contract agt., 1914-18, 1919-25, asst. to v.p., 1925-29, asst. to exec. v.p., 1929-30; asst. to treas. Conn. Savings Bank, New Haven, Jan.-May 1931; mem. Conn. Pub. Utilities Commn., 1931-41, chmn., 1934, 35 and 38; corporator Conn. Savings Bank. Trustees for Receiving Donations for Support of the Bishop of Conn.; col. on Governor's staff, 1931-38. Served as 1st lt. engrs., U.S. Army, with A.E.F, 1918-19; capt. Engrs. Res. Corps, 1920-24, maj., 1924-39, lt. col. since 1939. Mem. Soc. Am. Mil. Engrs., Am. Soc. Civil Engrs., Conn. Sect. Am. Soc. Civil Engrs., Conn. Soc. Civil Engrs. (hon.), Am. Legion, Mil. Order of the World War, Res. Officers Assn., Nat. Assn. of R.R. and Utilities Commrs., Am. Ry. Engring. Assn., Am. Water Works Assn., Am. Gas Assn., New England Regional Planning Commn. (advisory com.), New Haven Colony Hist. Soc., Sigma Xi, Berzelius Soc. (Yale). Democrat. Episcopalian (warden). Clubs: New Haven Lawn, Graduate (New Haven); Yale (N.Y. City); Hartford (Hartford); Army and Navy (Washington, D.C.); Camden Yacht, Megunticook Golf (Camden. Me.). Home: 165 Everit St., New Haven, Conn. Deceased.

TAYLOR, F. W. Howard, physician, lawyer; author; b. Chicago, Ill., Mar. 14, 1891; s. Frank Wing and Minnie (Cray) T.; student University of Calif., 1910-13; M.D., University of Southern California, 1917; law study, University of Southern California, 1927-31, LL.B.; m. Helen Irene Clark, Sept. 18, 1916; 1 son, Howard Clark; m. 2d, A. Verna Nelson, August 12, 1925; children—Robert Nelson, Verna Belle. Began practice at Los Angeles, 1917; roentgenologist, Clara Barton, French, Angelus, Roosevelt hosps., Pottenger Sanatorium, U.S. Vets. Bur., 1919-29; instr. in x-ray and electrotherapy, U. of Southern Calif., 1919-20; became dir. Coop. Diagnostic Labs., Los Angeles, 1928; vice-pres. Taylor Holding & Investment Corp. Instr. in mil. x-ray and chief roentgenologist, Med. Corps, U.S. Army, later lt. comdr., Navy Res., World War. Mem. A.M.A. (adviser to council on hosps. and edn.), Med. Soc. State of Calif., Los Angeles County Med. Society, Am. Radiological Soc., Phi Kappa Sigma, Phi Rho Sigma. Republican. Episcopalian. Clubs: California Yacht, Deauville Beach, Swimming, Fox Hills Country. Author: Lawyers Text and Atlas of the Human Body. Contbr. to med. and legal journals. First research in use of x-ray in whooping cough. Admitted to practice of law; now medico-legal consultant and medical X-ray consultant. Home: 10393 Ilona Av. Office: 1709 W. 8th St., Los Angeles, Calif. Died July 2, 1943.

TAYLOR, Frederic William, agriculturist; b. Weeping Water, Neb., Apr. 13, 1860; s. William and Sophronia (Isbell) T.; educated high sch. and by private instruction; m. Stella Arnold, 1885 (died July 9, 1891); children—Jettie Arnold (Mrs. J. H. Gray), Herbert Solomon, Mary Stella (wife of Capt. R. M. Lhamon, U.S. Navy); m. 2d, Marion Treat, 1898; children—William Treat, George Frederic. Received training in horticulture under his father, a nurseryman; later employed in leading nurseries. Prof. horticulture, U. of Neb., 1891-93; sec. U.S. Agrl. Expt. Sta., Lincoln, Neb., 1894-95; sec. Neb. State Hort. Soc., 1892-95; supt. Neb. fruit exhibit, Chicago Expn., 1893; supt. agr. and horticulture, Omaha Expn., 1898; supt. horticulture and dir. of concessions, Buffalo Expn., 1901; chief, depts. agr. and horticulture St. Louis Expn., 1904; dir. of agr., P.I., 1911-14; dir. general of agr. of El Salvador, C.A., 1923-27; v.p. Am. Rubber Producers, Inc., since 1927. Fellow Royal Geog. Soc., etc.; mem. A.A.A.S., S.A.R. Clubs: Circumnavigators (New York); University (Los Angeles). Officer Legion of Honor, France; Knight of the Order of Jesus Christ, Portugal; Order of the Rising Sun, Japan; Order of the Crown, Italy. Wrote monographs: The Apples, 1894; Small Fruits, 1895, and other reports Neb. State Hort. Soc.; also contbns. to mags. Has traveled widely, including two trips around the world. In 1897 introduced from Russia a number of cereals, of which the variety of oats, Kherson, has been widely distributed and is grown extensively in the West. Made ascent of Mt. Popocatepetl, 17,780 ft., 1894. Republican. Conglist. During war was agrl. adviser to Draft Bd. for Southern dist. Ariz. Home: 3939 W. 7th St., Los Angeles, Calif. Died Jan. 12, 1944.

TAYLOR, George Braxton, clergyman; b. Staunton, Va., Apr. 25, 1860; s. Rev. George Boardman and Susan Spotswood (Braxton) T.; direct descendant of Carter Braxton, one of signers of the Declaration of Independence; B.A., Richmond Coll., Va., 1881; U.

of Va.; grad. Southern Bapt. Theol. Sem., Louisville, Ky., 1886; attended lectures Univ. of Rome (Italy); D.D., Mercer U., Ga., 1894; m. Jessie Cabell, Dec. 19, 1888 (died Aug. 31, 1893); 1 son, George Cabell (dec.). Ordained Bapt. ministry, 1886; pastor Fairmont, Mt. Shiloh, Mt. Plain, Va., 1886-87, Chapel Hill, N.C., 1887-89; asso. pastor 1st Ch., Baltimore, 1889-91; pastor 1st Ch., Macon, Ga., 1891-94, Liberty and Hebron, Appomattox County, Va., 1894-1903, Enon and Troutville, 1903-40; prof. English Bible, Hollins Coll., 1903-28, resident chaplain, 1903-33, emeritus since 1933. Preached his first sermon in Rome, Italy, 1882, in Italian. Del. to Baptist World Alliance, London, 1905, Berlin, Germany, 1934; trustee U. of Richmond (v.p. of board; mem. centennial com.), Southern Bapt. Theol. Sem., Bapt. Orphanage, Salem, Va.; v.p. Bapt. Young Peoples Union of America, 1894-95; moderator Appomattox Assn., 1898-99; pres. Va. Bapt. Hist. Soc. since 1934. Mem. Judson Centennial Com. of Southern Baptist Conv., 1911-16; moderator of Valley Baptist Assn., 1926, 27. Mem. Soc. Descendants Signers Declaration of Independence, Phi Delta Theta and Phi Beta Kappa. Democrat. Author: Life and Letters of Rev. George Boardman Taylor, D.D., 1908; Virginia Baptist Ministers, 3d Series, 1912, 4th Series, 1913, 5th Series, 1915, 6th Series, 1935; Southern Baptists in Sunny Italy, 1929; The First Hundred Years (with Drs. R. E. Gaines and R. H. Pitt), 1932. Contbr. articles and stories and author of sermons and addresses. Founder Sunbeam Missionary Socs. (for children) of Southern Bapt. Conv. Publicity man (Valley Assn.) of $75,000,000 Bapt. campaign. Apptd., 1931, chmn. local com. George Washington Bicentennial, 1932. Address: Roanoke, Va. Died Mar. 9, 1942.

TAYLOR, Graham Romeyn; b. Hopewell, Dutchess County, N.Y., Mar. 17, 1880; s. Graham and Leah (Demarest) T.; student Lewis Inst., Chicago, 1896-1900; A.B., Harvard, 1903; m. Florence, d. S. Frederick Taylor, Sept. 7, 1918; children—Graham Romeyn, Jean Demarest. Resident of Chicago Commons (social settlement), 1896-1900 and 1904-12; mem. of editorial staff of Survey Magazine, 1904-16; spl. asst. to the Am. ambassador to Russia, 1916-19. Traveled in Siberia, Korea, China and India, 1919. Exec. sec. Chicago Commn. on Race Relations, apptd. by Gov. Lowden, 1920-21; exec. sec. Am. Assn. of Social Workers, 1921-22; mem. commn. of Nat. Information Bur. to study and report upon famine relief in Russia, 1922; connected with activities of the Commonwealth Fund since 1922, dir. its div. of publications since 1927. Member Council on Foreign Relations; Nat. Conf. Social Work. Conglist. Clubs: Century, Harvard (New York); Nat. Press (Washington. Author: Satellite Cities—A Study of Industrial Suburbs, 1915; also numerous mag. articles. Home: 397 Bleecker St., New York; (summer) Ossining, N.Y. Office: 41 E. 57th St., New York, N.Y. Died Aug. 30, 1942.

TAYLOR, Herbert Addison, lawyer; b. Beverly, N.J., Oct. 6, 1876; s. Addison W. and Emma L. (Herbert) T.; A.B., Cornell U., 1897; LL.B., U. of Buffalo, 1898; m. Harriet Ward Foote, Sept. 23, 1902; children—Harriet Ward Foote (Mrs. Federico F. Mauck), Adeline Herbert (Mrs. Howard Vermilya), Herbert Addison. Admitted to N.Y. bar, 1899; asso. in legal dept. Erie R.R. Co., 1899-1918, and since 1920, gen. solicitor, 1920-31, gen. counsel, 1931-37, vice-pres. and gen. counsel 1937-46, retired; held same offices with N.Y., Susquehanna & Western R.R. Co., and other Erie Railroad subsidiaries; apptd. counsel for trustees of Erie R.R. Co., Nypano R.R. Co., and N.J.&N.Y. R.R. Co. in reorganization, 1938; dir. Erie R.R. Co. and subsidiaries since 1932. With U.S. R.R. Adminstrn., 1918-20, gen. asst. to dir. gen., 1919-20. Mem. Am. and N.Y. State bar assns., Delta Phi. Republican. Unitarian. Club: Century Assn. (New York). Home: Little Compton, R.I. Died June 28, 1948; buried Little Compton, R.I.

TAYLOR, Howard Canning, gynecologist; b. Green's Farms, Conn., March 17, 1868; s. Arthur Canning and Mary Ellen (Wakeman) T.; Ph.B., Sheffield Scientific Sch. (Yale), 1888; M.D., Coll. Physicians and Surgeons (Columbia), 1891; m. Alice Cornforth Gibbs, July 14, 1898; children—Howard C., Edward J. (killed in action, Okinawa, May 1, 1945), Burton W. Intern, Roosevelt Hospital, 1891-94; instructor gynecology, 1893-1912, prof. clin. gynecology since 1913, Coll. Physicians and Surgeons; consulting gynecologist, Roosevelt Hosp., Tarrytown, Greenwich, Stamford, Sharon and Horton Memorial hosps. Mem. Am. Medical Assn., Med. Soc. of State of N.Y., Am. Gynecol. Soc., N.Y. Obstet. Soc., N.Y. Acad. Medicine. Republican. Presbyterian. Clubs: University, Century. Home: 876 Park Av., N.Y. City. Died March 27, 1949.

TAYLOR, Joseph Jackson, newspaper writer; b. Wilson, N.C., July 13, 1869; s. Joseph Marcellus and Mary (Windrom) T.; hon. D.Litt., Baylor U., 1920; m. Maggie Lamb, Jan. 27, 1897; children—Noden Windrom, Joseph M. Editor Clarksville (Tex.) Times, 1892-1904; on staff of Dallas News since 1904, editor-in-chief since Jan. 1937. Democrat. Baptist. Clubs: Dallas Athletic, Town and Gown, Bonehead. Home: 3625 Rawlins St., Dallas, Tex. Died May 24, 1943.

TAYLOR, Laurette, actress; b. New York City, April 1, 1887; m. Charles A. Taylor; m. 2d, J. Hartley Manners, dramatist, 1912 (he died in 1929). First appeared on the stage as a child, in vaudeville, at Gloucester, Massachusetts; played at Boston Athenæum, 1903; starred in "His Child Wife," and in "From Rags to Riches," with Joseph Santley; made debut in New Star Theatre, New York, Nov. 2, 1903, in "From Rags to Riches"; played at Seattle, Wash., and traveled with stock co. in the west; appeared in "The Devil," "The Ringmaster," "The Bird of Paradise," "The Girl in Waiting," "Peg o' My Heart," etc.; played in England 1914, again in 1920; has met with marked approval as Juliet, Portia, and Katherine, in scenes from Shakespeare, appeared in revival of "Peg o' My Heart" at Cort Theatre, New York, 1921, later in "The Harp of Life," "Out There," "Happiness" (by J. Hartley Manners), "The Furies" (by Zoe Aikens), then in "Alice Sit by the Fire" and "The Old Lady Shows Her Medals" (by Sir James M. Barrie); The Glass Menagerie.* Died Dec. 7, 1946.

TAYLOR, Lloyd William, prof. physics; b. Pittsfield, Me., Jan. 4, 1893; s. Levi William and Carrie Elnora (Brown) T.; B.S., Grinnell (Ia.) Coll., 1914; Ph.D., U. of Chicago, 1922; m. Esther Elenora Bliss, Dec. 11, 1917; children—Ruth Mildred, Edwin Floriman. Prin. high sch., Grandview, Ia., 1914-15; instr. in physics and mathematics, Grinnell Coll., 1915-17; asst. in physics, U. of Chicago, 1919-22, instr. in physics, 1922-24; prof. physics and head of dept., Oberlin (O.) Coll., since 1924. Served as 2d, later 1st lt. C.A.C., U.S. Army, 1917-19. Mem. A.A.A.S., Am. Physical Soc., Ohio Acad. Science, Am. Assn. Physics Teachers (pres. 1943-44), Am. Inst. Physics (mem. governing bd., 1944-48), Optical Soc. of America, Gamma Alpha, Phi Beta Kappa, Sigma Xi. Congregationalist. Author: College Manual of Optics, 1924; General Physics for the Laboratory (with W. W. Watson and C. E. Howe), 1926, revised, 1943; A Numerical Drill Book on Physics, 1926; Physics: the Pioneer Science, 1941; Fundamental Physics, 1943. Contbr. tech. articles in professional mags. Address: Oberlin College, Oberlin, O. Died Aug. 8, 1948; buried Grinnell, Ia.

TAYLOR, Thomas, judge; b. in England, Nov. 18, 1860; s. Thomas and Jane (Holloway) T.; came to U.S., 1866; B.S., Knox Coll., 1881, LL.D., 1930; LL.B., Harvard, 1885; studied civil law at univs. of Berlin and Vienna; m. Florence Clarkson, 1891; children—Thorne Clarkson (deceased), Wilberforce (deceased). Began practice at Boston; came to Chicago, 1887; master in chancery Circuit Court, 1893-1915; elected judge Circuit Court, 1915; justice Appellate Court, 1916-28, chief justice Circuit Court, 1928-33 (retired). Mem. Am., Ill. State and Chicago bar assns., Chicago Hist. Soc. Republican. Clubs: University (v.p. 1918), Harvard of Chicago (pres. 1903), Chicago, Onwentsia (v.p. 10 yrs.), Old Elm, Law (ex-pres.). Home: Carmel, Calif. Died Feb. 19, 1942.

TAYLOR, Victor V., army officer; b. Stockton, Calif., July 24, 1893; s. Robert William and Harriet Frances (Vaughan) T.; B.S., U.S. Mil. Acad., 1915; grad. Command and Gen. Staff Sch., Leavenworth, Kan., 1923, Army War Coll., 1939; m. Dorothy Edith Hossie, Apr. 12, 1924; children—Henry L., Victor Vaughan, Jr., Robert Scott. Commd. 2d lt., 1915, and advanced through the grades to brig. gen. Decorated Mexican Service, and Victory (1 star) medals; European Theater ribbon. Clubs: Army-Navy. Home: 4818 Woodway Lane N.W., Washington. Died Sept. 22, 1944; buried in Arlington National Cemetery.

TAYLOR, William Albert, surgeon; b. Port Perry, Ont., Can., July 21, 1881; s. Henry and Sarah (Steele) T.; M.B., U. of Toronto, Can., 1907; grad. study, U. of Vienna, Austria, 1913-14, 1923-24; m. Frances Hubbell, Dec. 23, 1914. Came to U.S., 1907, naturalized, 1916. Practiced medicine in Ellensburg since 1908; organized Taylor-Richardson Clinic, 1923; chief surgeon Ellensburg Gen. Hosp.; surgeon C.,M.,St.P.&P. R.R. Co. Fellow Am. Coll. Surgeons, A.M.A.; mem. Am. Assn. Traumatic Surgeons, Am. Bd. of Surgery, Western Surg. Soc., Pacific Coast Surg. Assn., N. Pacific Surg. Assn., Puget Sound Surg. Soc. Republican. Mason (Shriner). Clubs: Rainier, Seattle Athletic, Seattle Golf and Country, Rotary, Ellensburg Golf, Yakima Golf and Country. Contbr. research papers in med. jours. Home: 306 C St. Office: 200 E. 6th St., Elensburg, Wash. Died June 17, 1947; buried Ellensburgh, Wash.

TAYLOR, William Alton, pomologist; b. Chelsea, Mich., June 23, 1863; s. Rev. James Franklin and Mary Ann Lewis (Porter) T.; B.S., Mich. State Coll., 1888, D.Sc., 1913; m. Helen C. Patterson, Dec. 15, 1891 (died Aug. 29, 1921); children—Porter Ross, Ritchie Patterson; m. 2d, Marie Patton Cisco, June 6, 1923; 1 son, William Cisco. Mgr. fruit farm and nursery, Douglas, Mich., 1888-1891; asst. pomologist, U.S. Dept. of Agr., 1891-1901; pomologist in charge of field investigations, 1901-10 (agricultural exploration Canal Zone, 1909), and assistant chief Bur. Plant Industry, U.S. Dept. Agr., 1910-13; chief of Bureau Plant Industry, 1913-33, collaborator since 1934. Expert in horticulture U.S. Commn. to Paris Expn., 1900 (mem. Internat. jury on fruit trees and fruit); mem. Internat. Jury Dept. of Horticulture, St. Louis Expn., 1904. Mem. Agrl. Commn. to Europe, 1918. Chevalier du Mérite Agricole, 1900; silver medal, Societe Nationale d'Horticulture de France, 1900, silver medal, Societe des Agriculteurs de France, 1918; gold medal, Mass. Hort. Soc., 1939. Fellow A.A.A.S.; mem. Am. Pomol. Soc. (sec. 1897-1903, v.p. 1934-35), Bot. Soc. Washington (pres. 1910), Am. Soc. for Hort. Science (pres. 1908-09), Agrl. Hist. Soc., Biol. Soc. Washington. Presbyterian. Club: Federal. Author numerous papers and addresses before hort. and pomol. socs., bulletins and papers U.S. Dept. Agr. Home: Lake Ridge Farm, R.D. 2, Fennville, Mich.; (winter) 30 Berkley Place, Columbus 1, O. Died Feb. 8, 1949.

TAYLOR, William James, educator; b. Dublin, Ind., Aug. 8, 1867; s. Aurelius Pryor and Mary (Vore) T.; B.A., U. of Neb., 1891, M.A., 1897; univ. fellow in philosophy, Yale, 1898-1901, Ph.D., 1901; m. Blanche Glasgow, July 15, 1896. Prin. high sch., S. Omaha, 1891-98; head of dept. of classical langs., Pittsburgh (Pa.) Acad., 1901-02; teacher modern langs., New Haven (Conn.) High Sch., 1902-05; lecturer on history and philosophy of edn., Yale, 1902-05; instr. history of edn., logic and psychology, 1905-10, head dept. psychology and principles of edn., 1910-33, Maxwell Teachers' Training Coll. Lecturer psychology, Brooklyn Institute Arts and Sciences, 1912; lecturer ednl. psychology and principles of education, Long Island U., 1938-44. Mem. Nebraska Alpha Chapter of Phi Delta Theta. Republican. Episcopalian. Author: An Elementary Logic, 1909; A Syllabus of the History of Education, 1909. Wrote article on "Consciousness and Attention," in Encyclopedia Americana; contbr. to pedagog. jours. Home: 738 St. Marks Av., Brooklyn, N.Y.; (summer) Greensboro, Vt. Died March 14, 1949.

TAYLOR, William Mode, manufacturer, engr.; b. Indianapolis, June 29, 1865; s. Franklin and Phebe (Mode) T.; student Purdue U., 1881-82; B.S. in Mech. Engring., Mass. Inst. Tech., 1886; m. Mary Shepard Allen, Feb. 16, 1893; children—Dudley F., Frederic W., Eleanor. Entered employ of Chandler & Taylor Co., mfrs. engines, boilers and machinery, Indianapolis, 1886, pres., 1897-1926; partner Malum-inum Co., mfrs. of foundry fluxes, 1931-44. Mem. Indianapolis Sch. Bd., 1902-17 (pres. 1914); chmn. bldg. com. Indianapolis City Library, 1916-17; mem. Library and Historical Bd., State of Ind., 1925-33 (pres. 1926-27); mem. Ind. State Library Building Commn., 1929-31 (chmn. legislative com. to secure funds, 1929). Mem. Am. Soc. Mech. Engrs., Ind. Hist. Soc., Ind. Engring. Council, Sigma Chi. Club: Dramatic. Home: 124 W. 41st St., Indianapolis 8, Ind. Died Apr. 24, 1947.

TAYLOR, William Septimus, educator; b. Beaver Dam, Ky., Jan. 20, 1885; s. Herschel Berry and Ellen Orah (Render) T.; diploma, Western Teachers Coll., Bowling Green, Ky., 1910; B.S.A., U. of Ky., 1912; M.S., U. of Wis., 1913; Ph.D., Columbia University, 1924; University of London, 1937-38; married Helen Josephine Dodge, Feb. 3, 1923; 1 dau., Nancy Ellen. Asso. prof. agrl. edn. and supervisor high schs., U. of Tex., 1913-18; agt. for agrl. edn. of Federal Bd. for Vocational Edn., 1918-19; prof. rural edn. and head dept. rural life, Pa. State Coll., 1919-20; asst. dir. Teachers' Bur., Dept. Pub. Instrn., Harrisburg, Pa., 1920-22; dean Coll. of Edn., U. of Ky., since 1923. Mem. A.A.A.S., Nat. Soc. for Study of Edn., N.E.A. (chmn. com. on reorganization, 1936-37; chmn. com. on academic freedom, 1939-43; state dir. 1933-41; mem. exec. com., 1946-47), Kentucky Edn. Assn. (pres. 1928-29), American Vocational Assn., Nat. Assn. of Colleges and Depts. of Education (pres. 1926-27, sec.-treas. 1941-47), Southern Assn. Colls. (chmn. com. on Curricular Problems and Research and sec. schs., 1946-47), Alpha Zeta, Phi Delta Kappa, Kappa Delta Pi, Acacia. Baptist. Mason. Kiwanian (pres. Lexington Club 1927). Author: Development of Professional Education of Teachers in Pennsylvania, 1924. Co-author: (with J. G. Fowlkes, Thomas E. Goff, and W. W. Wright) Practical Arithmetic Work Books (with Jesse E. Adams) an Introduction to Education and the Teaching Process; Education in England. Editor of Ky. Sch. Journal, 1927-34. Home: 112 Cherokee Park, Lexington 1, Ky. Died Aug. 26, 1949.

TAYLOR, Willis Ratcliffe, army officer; b. Parkersburg, W.Va., Feb. 24, 1897; s. Nathaniel Ratcliffe and Josephine (Golden) T.; student, U. of Calif., 1917; m. Anne Addison, Dec. 18, 1920; children—Addison, Jo Anne. Commd. 2d lt., 1918, and advanced through the grades to brig. gen., 1942; Photographic Sch., 1921; serial survey program, Manila, P.I., 1921-23; mapping of northwest territory in Wash. and Ore., 1923-28; Scott Field, Ill., comd. photographic section, 1928-31; comdr. Observation Squadron, Mitchel Field, 1931-34; comdg. officer, Bombardment Squadron, Panama, 1934-37; served on boundary settlement comm. to Guatemala, Honduras and Salvador; comd. 27th Pursuit Squadron, Selfridge Field, Mich., 1937-39; with R.A.F., in England and Scotland, 1939-40; exec. officer, 2d Interceptor Comd., Seattle, Wash., 1941-42; organized Fighter Comd. Sch., Orlando, Fla., 1942; comd. I Fighter command, Mitchel Field, since 1942. Address: Mitchel Field, Hempstead, L.I., N.Y. Died June 14, 1945.

TEALL, Edward Nelson (tēl), editor, author; b. Brooklyn, N.Y., Mar. 23, 1880; s. F. Horace and Elizabeth (Lowry) T.; A.B., Princeton, 1902, A.M., 1905; married Jean Christie Gillies, February 18, 1905 (died August 29, 1933); children—Edward N. (captain U.S. Navy), Robert G. (died September, 1934), William H., Archie E. (commander U.S. Navy); married 2d, Helen Hatfield, March 5, 1934. On editorial staff New York Sun, 1903-17; in editorial dept. Princeton Univ. Press, 1917-19; sec. Marshall Jones Co., pubs., Boston, Mass., 1919-20; head of press dept. Chautauqua Instn., 1920-21; chief editorial writer Worcester (Mass.) Gazette, 1921-24, Camden (N.J.) Courier, 1925-28; mem. editorial staff G. & C. Merriam Co., dictionary pubs., 1928-29; editorial writing, Phila. Record, 1929-31, Pittsburgh Post-Gazette, 1932-36; specialist in compounding for Standard Dictionaries, 1936-37; editor Webster's New

Am. Dictionary and Webster's New Handy Pocket Dictionary, 1938-39; with Encyclopedia Americana, N.Y. City, 1940-42; editor Modern Business Eney., 1942; member of editorial staff, Macmillan Company, Publishers, New York, since Mar. 1944. Wrote "Watch Tower" comment department, St. Nicholas Magazine, 1917-27; conductor of Proofroom Dept. (department in Inland Printer) and contributor of monthly article to Inland Printer since 1923. Author Verse History of the College of New Jersey, 1915; Books and Folks, 1921; Meet Mr. Hyphen, 1967; Putting Words to Work, 1940. Home: Byers Lane, Matawan, N.J. Died Feb. 17, 1947.

TEEVAN, John Charles, prof. of business law; b. Liverpool, England, Nov. 1, 1880; came to U.S., 1903, naturalized, 1913; s. James and Mary Jane (Foster) T.; LL.B., Northwestern Univ. Sch. of Law, 1917; LL.M., 1924; m. Gertrude Johanna Battjes, July 18, 1910; children—John Montague, James Foster. Admitted to Ill. bar, 1917; gen. practice of law in Chicago, 1917-31; lecturer on bus. law, Northwestern Univ. Sch. of Commerce, 1917-23, asst. prof., 1923-31, prof. 1931-46, dept. chmn. 1937-46; prof. of bus. law, emeritus since 1946; temporarily teacher and acting chmn. dept., 1946-47. Mem. Am. Bus. Law Assn. (pres. 1938), Delta Sigma Rho, Delta Sigma Pi. Club: University of Evanston. Author: C.P.A. Law Questions and Answers, 3 vols., pub. 1925, 35, 42; (with L. Y. Smith) Business Law, Vols. I, II, 1945. Home: 724 Simpson St., Evanston, Ill. Died March 7, 1948.

TEGGART, Frederick John (tĕg'ărt), univ. prof.; b. Belfast, Ireland, May 9, 1870; student Methodist Coll., Belfast; Trinity Coll., Dublin; came to America, 1889; B.A., Stanford University, 1894; LL.D., University of California, 1943; m. Adeline Margaret Barnes, May 24, 1894; children—Barnes (dec.), Richard Victor. Asst. and acting librarian, Stanford, 1893-98; librarian Mechanics Mercantile Library, San Francisco, 1898-1907; asso. prof. Pacific Coast history, 1911-16, of history, 1916-19, of social institutions, 1919-25, prof. social instns., 1925-40, prof. emeritus since 1940, U. of Calif. Mem. American Academy of Arts and Sciences, American Sociol. Soc., Am. Assn. Univ. Profs., Phi Beta Kappa. Club: Faculty (Berkeley). Author: Prolegomena to History, 1916; The Processes of History, 1918; Theory of History, 1925; Rome and China, a Study of Correlations in Historical Events, 1939; Theory and Processes of History, 1941. Compiler: Catalogue of the Hopkins Railway Library, Leland Stanford Jr. University, 1895; General Index to the Library Journal, 1898. Editor: Publs. of Acad. of Pacific Coast History, 1909-1919; Around Horn to Sandwich Islands and Calif., 1845-1850 (diary of Chester S. Lyman), 1924. Home: 2532 Durant Av., Berkeley, Calif. Died Oct. 12, 1946.

TELLO, Julio C. (tāl'yō), Peruvian archæologist; b. Huarochiri, 1880; Bachelor of Medicine, U. of San Marcos, Lima, 1908, M.D., 1909, M.S., 1918; M.A., Harvard, 1911; Dr. Sciences, U. of Berlin, 1918. Peruvian del. to Congress of Americanists of London, 1912; dir. archæol. bur. of Nat. Hist. Mus., 1913-14; Peruvian del. to Pan-Am. Sci. Congress of Wash., 1915; prof. anthropology and archeology, U. of San Marcos, 1923-33; dir. archeol. studies, Dept. of Ica, 1925-30; prof. anthropology, Catholic U. of Lima, 1931-33. Mem. Academic de la Historia of Colombia, Royal Anthropological Inst. of London, Société des Américanistes (Paris), Academia de Medicinia (Perú). Author of Antigo Perú, 1929; Introducción a la historia antigua del Peru, 1921. Office: Museo de Arqueología, Universidad de San Marcos, Casilla 343, Lima, Perú.* Died June 4, 1947.

TEMPEST, Marie Susan, opera singer; b. London, July 15, 1866; d. Edwin and Sarah Etherington; musical edn., Convent des Ursulines, Thildonck, Belgium, and Royal Acad. Music, London; m. Cosmo Charles Gordon-Lennox (Cosmo Stuart), son of late Lord Alexander Gordon-Lennox, 1898. First sang in concert, but soon went into light opera in leading rôles; came to U.S. as prima donna in New York Casino Co.; appeared in comic opera in prin. Am. cities and in England. Created Nell Gwyn in "English Nell," 1900; "Becky Sharp," 1901; appeared in "The Marriage of Kitty," 1903; played in "The Freedom of Suzanne," London, 1905-06, etc. Received numerous medals for Italian and declamatory English singing. Died Oct. 15, 1942.

TEMPLE, Seth Justin, architect; b. Winona, Minn., Aug. 15, 1867; s. Holmes and Mary Eliza (Ford) T.; Ph.B. in Architecture, Columbia, 1892; studied, traveled in Europe, 1894-96; m. Alice Maud Gamble, June 12, 1896 (dec.); children—Holmes (dec.), Gilbert, Arthur, Malcolm, Alice Muriel. Instr. architecture, Met. Mus., New York, 1892-94; instr. architecture 1896-97, asst. prof., 1897-1904, U. of Ill.; in practice, as mem. Temple, Burrows & McLane, 1904-10, Temple & Burrows, 1910-25, Seth J. Temple, 1925-40, now Seth J. Temple-Arthur Temple. V.p. bd. trustees Davenport Pub. Museum, trustee Davenport Municipal Art Gallery. Mem. Davenport C. of C. Republican. Episcopalian. Fellow A.I.A.; pres. Ia. Chapter A.I.A., 1909-10; hon. mem. Tau Beta Pi. Clubs: Outing, Davenport. Home: 25 McClellan Blvd. Office: Putnam Bldg., Davenport, Ia. Died June 4, 1949.

TEMPLIN, Olin, coll. prof.; b. Camden, Ind., Dec. 6, 1861; s. L. J. and Mary (Lerner) T.; A.B., U. of Kan., 1886, A.M., 1889; U. of Göttingen, 1888; U. of Berlin, 1889; m. Lena A. Van Voorhis, Aug. 6, 1886; children—Alice (Mrs. H. W. Rankin), Marjorie (Mrs. W. H. Wellhouse). Asst. prof. mathematics, U. of Kan., 1884-90, asso. prof. philosophy, 1890-93, became prof. and head of dept., 1893, dean Coll. Liberal Arts and Sciences, 1903-21, became prof. of logic, ethics and esthetics, 1921. Dir. school and coll. activities, U.S. Food Administration, Washington, 1917-19. Author: A Guide to Thinking (with Anna McCracken), 1927. Home: Lawrence, Kan. Died Mar. 4, 1943.

TENER, John Kinley (tĕn'ĕr), ex-gov.; b. in County Tyrone, Ireland, July 25, 1863; s. George Evans and Susan (Wallis) T.; came to America at age of 9; ed. pub. and high schs., Pittsburgh, Pa.; m. Harriet J. Day, Oct. 1889 (died, 1935); m. 2d, Leone Evans, 1936 (died, 1937). Clerk for Oliver Bros. & Phillips, Pittsburgh, 1881-85; played professional baseball, 1886; officer Chartier's Valley Gas Co., 1887; played baseball, Nat. League, 1888-90; located in Charleroi, Pa., 1891; pres. First Nat. Bank, Charleroi. Mem. 61st Congress (1909-11), 24th Pa. Dist.; gov. of Pa., term 1911-15. Republican. Pres. Nat. Baseball League, resigned 1918. Club: Duquesne (Pittsburgh). Home: 5864 Marlborough Av., Pittsburgh, Pa.* Died May 19, 1946.

TEN EYCK, Peter Gansevoort, ex-congressman; b. Bethlehem, N.Y., Nov. 7, 1873; s. Abraham Cuyler and Margaret Matilda (Haswell) T.; ed. Albany Acad., Rensselaer Polytechnic Inst., Troy, N.Y., 1892-96; m. Bertha F. Dederick, Apr. 15, 1903; 1 son, Peter Gansevoort Dederick. With N.Y.C.&H.R. R.R., 1896-1903, becoming signal engr., organized signal dept. and designed signal standards; signal engr., treas., 1903, later v.p. and gen. mgr., Federal Ry. Signal Co.; inventor many signal devices, some of which are now in general use; consulting engr. Chmn. committee to revise by-laws of C.,R.I.&P. and Pa. R.R. cos., 1915; chmn. Highways Transport Com. of N.Y., to establish rural motor express service; chmn. N.Y. State Advisory Bd. under Federal Emergency Adminstrn. of Public Works; former commr. N.Y. State Dept. of Agr. and Markets; former dir. Manhattan Ry. Co.; dir. Nat. Commercial Bank & Trust Co. Mem. Local Draft Board for Div. No. 4, City of Albany, N.Y., World War I. Del. to Dem. Nat. Conv., 1912, 20; mem. 63d and 67th Congresses (1913-15 and 1921-23), 28th N.Y. Dist. Mem. Old Guard, 3d Sig. Corps, 3d Brig. Nat. Guard N.Y.; designated as expert in Council National Defense, 1917. Chmn. Deeper Hudson Gen. Com.; dir. Nat. Rivers and Harbors Congress; dir. at large, Atl. Deeper Waterways Assn.; mem. Hudson Valley Federated Chamber Commerce (dir. at large), Albany Chamber Commerce (ex-pres.), N.Y. State Assn. Real Estate Bds., N.Y. State Farm Bur. Fed. (ex-pres.), N.Y. State Agrl. Soc. (ex-v.p.), Albany County Agrl. Soc. and Expn. (ex-pres.), Albany County Farm Bur. (ex-pres.); mem. bd. visitors, New York State School of Agr., Cobleskill; trustee Albany Pub. Library; ex-trustee Cornell U., Exptl. Sta., Geneva; vice chmn. Empire State Business Alliance; ex-pres., Memorial Hosp.; mem. Great Lakes, Hudson Waterways Assn.; ex-chmn. Albany Port Dist. Commission. Ex-pres. N.Y. State Automobile Assn., mem. N.Y. State Guernsey Breeders' Assn. (ex-pres.), Albany Inst. of History and Art (trustee), Saratoga Battlefield Assn., Inc. (charter mem.), Albany Soc. of New York, Albany Soc. of Engrs., Soc. Engrs. of Eastern N.Y. (hon. mem.), N.Y. State Hist. Assn., Dutch Settlers Soc. of Albany, Capital Dist. Guernsey Breeders Assn., Am. Guernsey Cattle Club, New York State Hort. Soc., Phillip Livingston Chap. S.R. (ex-regent), Holland Soc., Rensselaer Poly. Inst. Alumni Assn., Albany Acad. Alumni Assn., Am. Ry. Engring. Assn., Ry. Signal Assn., Am. Assn. Maintenance of Ways, Am. Soc. C.E., Grange, Delta Phi. Mem. First Church in Albany of the Reformed Church in America. Clubs: Albany (ex-pres.), Albany Automobile (ex-pres. and dir.), Ft. Orange (ex-pres.), University, Burns, Elks, Albany Country, Kiwanis (hon.); Nat. Democratic (New York). Mason. Home: 479 State St. Office: 74 Chapel St., Albany, N.Y. Died Sep. 2, 1944.

TENNEY, Albert Ball, public utilities; b. Everett, Mass., Jan. 8, 1873; s. Henry Augustus and Mary Elizabeth T.; B.S., Mass. Inst. Tech., 1894; m. Mary Augusta Comey, May 29, 1902. In employ of Locke & Green Co., mill engrs., later with Charles A. Campbell Co., wholesale coal, Boston Rubber Co., N. V. Perry Mfg. Co., machine tools, until 1900; identified with public utilities, 1900-33, retired; pres. and dir. Brockton Gas Light Co., Standard Crayon Mfg. Co.; dir. Concord Electric Co., Rockland Light & Power Co., Springfield Gas Light Co., Springfield Navigation Co., etc. Mem. Bd. Appeals, Selective Service, World War. Mem. Am. Soc. Mech. Engrs., Delta Upsilon. Republican. Unitarian. Clubs: Algonquin, University, Cliff Lake (dir.), Mass. Auto, Lexington Golf, Kingswood Golf Club, St. Bernard Fish and Game. Home: 1 Adams St., Lexington, Mass. Office: 3 Joy St., Boston. Died Dec. 5, 1948.

TENNEY, Charles Irving, corp. official; b. Plymouth, Ia., Oct. 10, 1864; s. Charles Williams and Mary Aurelia (LaDue) T.; ed. pub. schs.; m. Ida Eliza Cole, Mar. 22, 1888; children—Clayton Wilbert (dec.), Mary Alice, Minta Irene (Mrs. Arthur Wellesley Secord), Glenn Irving (dec.), Charles Emory. Experimented in design and constrn. of gasoline gas generating plants, 1894-1902; pres. Standard Gas Constrn. Co., Chicago, 1902-06; organized Am. Gas Constrn. Co. (with associates), and pres. of same since 1906; developed patents and processes for coal and water gas mfr.; pres. C. I. Tenney Engring. Co., Continental Pub. Utilities Co., Mont. Utilities Co., Hutchinson Gas Co., Wilmar Gas Co., Merrill (Wis.) Gas Company. Mem. bd. regents Greenville (Ill.) Coll., 1915-35. Mem. Am. Gas Assn., Midwest Gas Assn. Republican. Free Methodist. Home: 2600 Pleasant Av. Office: Frontenac Bldg., Minneapolis, Minn. Died June 6, 1945.

TERHUNE, Albert Payson (tûr-hūn'), author; b. Newark, N.J., Dec. 21, 1872; s. Rev. Edward Payson and Mary Virginia (Hawes) ("Marion Harland") T.; A.B., Columbia, 1893; m. Anice Morris Stockton; 1 dau., Mrs. Lorraine Stevens. Traveled on horseback through Syria and Egypt, 1893-94, investigating leper settlements, living among Bedouins of desert, etc. On staff N.Y. Evening World, 1894-1916. Park commr. State of N.J. since 1925. Clubs: Players, Adventurers. Dutch Treat, Century. Author: Syria from the Saddle, 1896; Columbia Stories, 1897; (with Marion Harland) Dr. Dale—A Story Without a Moral, 1900 (first instance of mother and son co-authors of novel); libretto of Nero, a comic opera (in collaboration with William C. de Mille), 1904; Caleb Conover, Railroader, 1907; The World's Great Events, 1908; The Fighter (novel), 1909; The New Mayor (novel), 1910; The Woman (novel), 1912; the New York World's various series of hist. articles, 1906-20; Raegan Stories (Smart Set Mag.), 1913-14; Dad, 1914; Dollars and Cents, 1915; The Locust Years, 1915; Fortune, 1918; Wonder Women of History, 1918; Lad: A Dog, 1919; Bruce, 1920; The Pest, 1920; Buff: A Collie, 1921; The Man in the Dark, 1921; Black Gold, 1921; Further Adventures of Lad, 1922; His Dog, 1922; Black Cæsar's Clan, 1923; The Amateur Inn, 1923; Lochinvar Luck, 1923; Wolf, 1924; Treve, 1924; The Tiger's Claw, 1924; Now That I'm Fifty, 1925; The Runaway Bag, 1925; The Heart of a Dog, 1926; Treasure, 1926; Gray Dawn, 1927; Bumps, 1927; The Luck of the Laird, 1927; Lad of Sunnybank, 1928; Proving Nothing, 1929, To the Best of My Memory (autobiography), 1930; A Dog Named Chips, 1931; The Son of God, 1932; The Way of a Dog, 1934; The Book of Sunnybank, 1935; Unseen (novel), 1936; A Book of Famous Dogs, 1937; Loot! (novel), 1940; also more than 30 motion picture plays; short stories, verse in mags. Expert on physical culture topics; breeder of prize-winning collies. Received Medal of Excellence from Columbia U., 1933. Address: 67 Riverside Drive, New York, N.Y.; and "Sunnybank," Pompton Lakes, N.J. Died Feb. 18, 1942.

TERRAL, Tom J. (tĕr'ăl), ex-governor; b. Union Parish, La., Dec. 21, 1884; s. George W. and Celia T.; ed. Ky. State U.; LL.B., U. of Ark.; m. Eula Terral, Feb. 25, 1914. Formerly teacher pub. schs., Ark.; admitted to Ark. bar; asst. secretary Ark. Senate, 1911, sec., 1913, 15; asst. dep. state supt. pub. instrn., 1912-16, resigning during each session of the Senate; sec. of State of Ark. 2 terms, 1917-21; gov., 1925-27. In successful practice of law in Little Rock since 1927. Democrat. Address: Wallace Bldg., Little Rock, Ark.* Died Mar. 9, 1946.

TERRELL, George B., congressman; b. Alto, Tex., Dec. 5, 1862; s. Sam Houston and Juliar (Butler) T.; student Sam Houston Teachers Coll., Huntsville, Tex., and Baylor U.; m. Allie Turney. Taught schs. in Tex. and served in Tex. State Legislature; commr. of agr., Tex., 1921-31; mem. 73d Congress (1933-35), Tex. at large. Engaged in farming for many years. Home: Alto, Tex. Died Apr. 18, 1947.

TERRIBERRY, George Hitchings (tĕr'ĭ-bĕr'ĭ), lawyer; b. Galveston, Tex., Feb. 10, 1875; s. John Stires and Frances (Johnson) T.; A.B., Tulane U., 1898, LL.B., 1900; m. Miriam Alroy Patrick, July 26, 1905. Admitted to La. bar, 1900, since practicing in New Orleans; mem. firm of Terriberry, Young, Rault & Carroll; dir. Times-Picayune Publishing Co., New Orleans. Served as private U.S. Volunteers, Spanish-Am. War. Pres. New Orleans Symphony Orchestra; pres. La. Vocational Guidance Assn. Mem. Maritime Law Assn., Assn. of Bar City of N.Y., Am. Bar Assn. (ex-v.p.), La. Bar Assn. (ex-pres.), New Orleans Bar Assn. Clubs: New Orleans Athletic, Boston (New Orleans). Home: 1407 First St. Office: Whitney Bldg., New Orleans, La. Died Oct. 19, 1948.

TERRIBERRY, William S(toutenborough) (tĕr'ĭ-bĕr-ĭ), U.S. Pub. Health Service; b. Paterson, N.J., July 3, 1871; s. George W. and Martha Griffith (Stoutenborough) T.; grad. St. Paul's Sch., Garden City, N.Y., 1889; A.B., Yale, 1893; M.D., Columbia, 1896; m. Emilie Varet Reinhart, Oct. 17, 1907. Interne Bellevue Hosp., 1896-98: asst visiting surg., 1902-13. Asst. surg. (1st lt.) N.J. Vols., 1898; contract surg. U.S. Army, 1896-99; lt. col. Med. Corps, N.Y. Nat. Guard, 1916; lt. col. Med. Corps, U.S. Army, 1918; assigned as comdg. officer Embarkation Hosp., Newport News, Va.; advanced to col., Aug. 1918, hon. discharged, Nov. 1919; commd. asst. surgeon U.S.P.H.S., Dec. 1919, sr. surgeon, Jan. 1920, asst. surgeon gen., July 1920, med. dir. 1930; retired, Nov. 1937. Awarded Conspicuous Service Cross, 1922. Mem. Zeta Psi. Clubs: Yale (N.Y. City); Army and Navy (Washington, D.C.). Home: Old Lyme, Conn. Died Oct. 13, 1948.

TERRILL, Mortimer Clark, exec. v.p. Phoenix Mutual Life Ins. Co.; b. Newtown, Conn., Nov. 4, 1888; s. Mortimer B. and Ellen (Clark) T.; student Ansonia (Conn.) High Sch., 1901-05; A.B., Yale U., 1909; m. Ellen Mommers, June 21, 1913 (dec.); children—Robert Clark, Richard Mommers. Asso. with Phoenix Mutual Life Ins. Co., Hartford, Conn., continuously since 1909, v.p. and dir. since 1935; dir. Hartford Nat. Bank & Trust Co. Trustee, Soc.

for Savings, Hartford. Dir. Conn. Inst. for the Blind, Hartford; director Institute of Living, Hartford. Republican. Episcopalian. Mason. Clubs: Yale (N.Y. City); Hartford, University (Hartford); Country (Manchester). Home: Manchester, Conn. Office: Phoenix Mutual Life Insurance Company, Hartford, Conn. Died Mar. 25, 1944.

TERRY, John Taylor, lawyer; b. Tarrytown, N.Y., Aug. 17, 1857; s. John Taylor and Elizabeth R. (Peet) T.; B.A., Yale, 1879; Sch. of Mines, Columbia; LL.B., Columbia Law Sch., 1881; studied U. of Bonn, Germany, 1881-84; m. Bertha Halsted, June 24, 1885; children—Mary Halsted, John T. Practiced, New York, 1881—; trustee Bowery Savings Bank. Republican. Presbyn. Mem. Soc. Mayflower Descendants, New York Soc. S.R., Soc. Colonial Wars. Clubs: University, Yale. Home: 340 E. 72d St. Office: 31 Nassau St., New York, N.Y. Died May 30, 1942.

TESLA, Nikola (tĕs′lȧ), electrician; b. Smiljan, Lika (border of Austria-Hungary), July 9, 1856; s. of Greek clergyman and orator, and of Georgina Mandic, who was an inventor, as was her father; ed. 1 yr. at elementary sch., 4 yrs. at Lower Realschule, Gospic, Lika, and 3 yrs. at Higher Realschule, Carlstadt, Croatia, graduating 1873; student 4 yrs. at Polytechnic Sch., Gratz, in mathematics, physics and mechanics; afterward 2 yrs. in philos. studies at U. of Prague, Bohemia; hon. M.A., Yale, 1894; LL.D., Columbia, 1894; D.Sc., Vienna Polytechnic. Began practical career at Budapest, Hungary, 1881, where made his first electrical invention—a telephone repeater—and conceived idea of his rotating magnetic field; later engaged in various branches of engring. and manufacture. Since 1884 resident of U.S., becoming naturalized citizen. Inventor and discoverer: System of arc lighting, 1886; Tesla motor and system of alternating current power transmission, 1888; system of elec. conversion and distribution by oscillatory discharges, 1889; generators of high frequency currents, and effects of these, 1890 Tesla coil, or transformer, 1891; system of wireless transmission of intelligence, 1893; mech. oscillators and generators of elec. oscillations, 1894-95; researches and discoveries in radiations, material streams and emanations, 1896-98; high-potential magnifying transmitter, 1897; system of transmission of power without wires, 1897-1905; Tesla's steam and gasturbine and pump; etc. Chiefly engaged, since 1903, in development of system of telegraphy and telephony, and designing plant for transmission of power without wires, to be erected at Niagara. Address: The New Yorker Hotel, New York, N.Y.* Died Jan. 7, 1943.

TETE, Auguste J., (tĕt); b. New Orleans, La., May 12, 1882; s. Auguste and Virginia (Mercier) T.; B.Engring., Tulane Univ., 1906, M.A., 1923; m. Laure Beauregard Chiapella, June 20, 1907; 1 dau., Virginia (Mrs. Walter Pond). Engr., elec. and mech., 1906-09; high sch. teacher, 1909-18 and 1921-23; instr. mathematics, Tulane Summer Sch., 1910-21, Tulane Univ., 1921; asst. supt. New Orleans Public Schs., 1923, asst. supt. in charge of business, 1910, supt. since 1942; supt. Orleans Parish Sch. Bd. Chief instr. Camp Martin, La. 1918, instr. army officers, Tulane Univ., 1919. Mem. bd. mgrs. Isaac Delgado Central Trades Sch.; trustee Teachers Retirement Fund. Club: Rotary. Home: 731 Pine St. Office: 703 Carondelet St., New Orleans, La. Died June 22, 1944.

TEWKSBURY, Elwood Gardner, missionary; born West Newbury, Mass., Mar. 6, 1865; s. James G. and Sarah J. (Whittier) T.; A.B. cum laude, Harvard, 1887; grad. Hartford Theol. Sem., 1890; m. Grace Holbrook, May 28, 1889; children—Malcolm Gardner, Donald George, Helen Roberta. Ordained Congl. ministry, 1890; missionary A.B.C.F.M., 1890-1907; prof. physics and chemistry, North China Union Coll., 1890-1906; lecturer on Far East for N.Y. City Bd. of Edn., Brooklyn Inst., etc., 1898-99 and 1906-09; Thompson lecturer on missions, Hartford Theol. Sem., 1907; sec. Y.P. Missionary Movement and N.Y. Laymen's Missionary Movement, 1908-09; founder 1st China "Northfield," 1903; became gen. sec. China S.S. Union, 1910. Mem. Delta Upsilon. Address: 5 Quinsan Gardens, Shanghai, China. Died Nov. 5, 1945.

TEWSON, W(illiam) Orton (tū′sŭn); editor, columnist; b. Penge, Surrey, Eng., Mar. 21, 1877; s. William and Lydia (Orton) T.; ed. grammar sch. and under pvt. tutors; m. Winifred Hunter (pianist), Jan. 28, 1910. Began with N.Y. City News Assn., 1904; joined staff N.Y. Times, 1907, later going to London office of same paper as spl. corr.; editorial charge of Hearst newspapers and news agencies in Europe, 1912-16; resigned to engage in war work, first with British Ministry of Food and later as official British rep. in Paris of Inter-Allied Wireless, under Ministry of Information, until close of war; literary editor Phila. Public Ledger, 1921-26, also editor Literary Review, New York Evening Post, 1924-26; writer weekly literary column "An Attic Salt Shaker," since Sept. 1921, widely syndicated. Mem. N.Y. staff Brit. Library of Information, 1941-42; revised and brought up-to-date Encyclopedia Britannica article "Newspapers" (1945). Author: Types of London Life. Clubs: Savage (London); Overseas Press (N.Y. City). Home: 162 W. 56th St., New York 19, N.Y. Died Mar. 14, 1947.

THACKER, J(ames) Ernest, clergyman; b. Columbia, Mo., Dec. 14, 1869; s. John Hayes and Mary E. (Thom) T.; A.B., Davidson Coll., N.C., 1890, D.D., 1910; grad. Union Theol. Sem., Richmond, Va., 1893; m. Addie May Dixon (lecturer), Mar. 14, 1894; children—Mrs. May Frame, Mrs. Pierre Schmitz. Ordained Presbyn. ministry, 1893; pastor Oxford, N.C., 1893-96, Louisville, Ky., 1896-97, Second Ch., Alexandria, Va., 1897-1900, Second Ch., Norfolk, Va., 1900-09; organized evangelistic dept. Presbyn. Ch. in U.S., 1909, and Assembly evangelist since that time; moderator Presbyn. Synod of Va., 1932. Mem. Sigma Alpha Epsilon. Platform lecturer and evangelist. Home: 627 Raleigh Av., Norfolk, Va. Died 1945.

THARALDSEN, Conrad Engerud (tär′äld-sĕn), prof. anatomy; b. Battle Lake, Minn., May 20, 1884; s. Iver and Caroline Emelie (Engerud) T.; B.S., St. Olaf Coll., Northfield, Minn., 1907; post-grad. work, Harvard, Columbia, U. of Wis. and Marine Biol. Lab., Woods Hole, Mass.; M.A., Columbia, 1918, Ph.D., 1925; m. 2d, Ethel M. Smith, 1927; children—Margaret Emelie, Constance Ethel. Instr. biology, Blaine High Sch., Superior, Wis., 1907-09; head of biology dept., State Normal Sch., Mayville, N.D., 1909-17; prof. zoölogy, Northwestern U., 1919-27; prof. anatomy and head of dept., New York Homeo. Med. Coll. (now New York Med. Coll.) since 1927, chmn. Grad. Edn. Div. Inventor micro-vivisection apparatus and other biol. research appliances. Mem. bd. mgrs. of Collegiate Div. of Y.M.C.A. Fellow A.A.A.S., N. Y. Acad. Science; mem. Am. Assn. Univ. Profs., Soc. Exptl. Biology and Medicine, History of Science Soc., Sigma Xi.; hon. mem. New York Acad. Pathol. Science (pres. 1937-40), Am. Assn. Anatomists. Investigator and contbr. on zoöl. topics. Home: 51 Biltmore Av., Crestwood, N.Y. Office: 1 E. 105th St., New York, N.Y. Died May 20, 1944.

THIEME, Theodore F. (thēm), mfr.; b. Fort Wayne, Ind., Feb. 7, 1857; s. Frederick J. and Clara (Weitzman) T.; Concordia Coll., Ft. Wayne, 1871-73; Columbia U., 1874-76; Ph.G., 1876; m. Bessie Loring, Jan. 18, 1894. In drug business 12 yrs.; organizer and pres., 1891, Wayne Knitting Mills mfrs. hosiery (now retired); pres. Morris Plan Co., 1909, Thieme Bros. Co. (Ft. Wayne, Ind.), Thieme Hosiery Co. (Los Angeles, Calif., 1923), and dir. various banks and corps. State chmn. Business System of City Govt. Com. of Ind., chmn. exec. com. Citizens' League of Ind., 1911-17, Founder Fort Wayne Art School and Museum. Mem. Am. Acad. Polit. and Social Science, Acad. Polit. Science, Nat. Assn. Mfrs., C. of C. U.S.A., Ind Soc. of Chicago. Republican. Mason (Shriner). Clubs: Commercial, Fort Wayne Country (Ft. Wayne); Wilshire Country, Jonathan, Del Mar Beach (Los Angeles, Calif.). Author (brochures); Municipal Sidelights, 1910; A Modern System of City Government, 1911; Business System of City Government Charter, 1912; What Ails Us?, 1913; A New State Constitution for Indiana, 1914; Liquor and Public Utilities in Indiana Politics, 1914; Home Rule for Cities, 1915; Municipal Ownership, the Salvation of Our Cities, 1916(book) A Business System of City Government, 1934. Home: Thieme Gardens, Covington Road, Ft. Wayne. Ind. Died Aug. 11, 1949.

THELIN, Ernst, prof. psychology; b. Sheffield, Pa., Sept. 23, 1888; s. Per William and Minnie Sofia (Halfstrom) T.; A.B., Marietta (O.) Coll., 1914; student Yale Sch. of Religion, 1914-15, Pacific Sch. of Religion, 1915-16; M.A., U. of Mont., 1917; studied U. of Birmingham, England, 1919; Ph D., U. of Chicago, 1926;.m. Martha Marie Vogt, Sept. 2, 1927. Began as pub. sch. teacher, 1917; prin. Twodot (Mont.) Pub. Sch., 1917, Dixon (Mont.) Pub. Sch, 1919-20; supt. Cutbank (Mont.) Pub. Sch., 1920-22; asst. prof. edn. W.Va. Wesleyan Coll., 1922-23; prof. edn. Hanover Coll., Hanover, Ind., 1923-24; asst. prof. psychology, U. of Cincinnati, 1926-27; asso. prof. psychology, Fla. State Coll., 1927-28; asso. prof. psychology, Syracuse U., 1928-35, prof. since 1935, head dept. since 1931, dir. psychol. lab. since 1928. Served with First U.S. Engrs., France, 1917-19. Fellow A.A.A S.; mem. Am. Assn. Univ. Profs., Am. Psychol. Assn. (associate), Sigma Xi, Psi Chi. Republican. Methodist. Mason. Club: Faculty of Syracuse U. Contbr. to psychol. jours. Home: 1022 Lancaster Av., Syracuse, N.Y. Died Nov. 9, 1945.

THICKENS, John Herman, business executive; b. Appleton, Wis., May 18, 1884; s. John William and Harriet (Erb) T.; B.S., U. of Wis., 1908, Chem.E., 1911; m. Lulu Delle Wellman, Sept. 16, 1908; children—Richard, Beatrice; m. 2d, Joyce Renira McKessar, Nov. 4, 1937. Research asst., C. F. Burgess, Madison, Wis., 1906-09; appraisal engr. Wis. R.R. commn., Madison, 1909-10; chem. engr. U.S. Forest Service, Wausau, Wis., 1911-13; supt. Brunet Falls Mfg. Co., Cornell, Wis., 1913; dir. labs. Beaver Board Co., Buffalo, N.Y., 1914; mgr. pulp and paper div., Bathurst Paper Co., New Brunswick, 1915-19; v.p. and gen. mgr. Mead Fibre Co., Kingsport, Tenn., 1919-28; mgr. Masonite Corp., Laurel, Miss., 1928-35, v.p. mfg. since 1935; v.p. Comml. Nat. Bank, Laurel, since 1936. Dir. New Orleans & North Eastern Ry., 1940. Mem. Am. Inst. Chem. Eng., Tech. Assn. Pulp and Paper Industry, Am. Chem. Soc., A.A.A.S.; mem. Theta Delta Chi, Phi Lambda Upsilon, Tau Beta Pi. Democrat. Home: Homewood, Laurel, Miss. Office: Masonite Corp., Laurel, Miss. Died Jan. 28, 1946.

THISTLETHWAITE, Mark, newspaper corr.; b. Richmond, Ind., Mar. 17, 1879; s. John P. and Mary Jane (Fleming) T.; grad. high sch., Richmond, Ind., 1898; Litt.B., Swarthmore Coll., 1901; m. Mable Whisner, Mar. 18, 1914. Began as reporter The Press, Philadelphia; successively with Star, Sentinel and News (all of Indianapolis), until 1909; private sec. to Thomas R. Marshall (gov. of Ind., 1909-13; vice-president of U.S., 1913-21), 1909-21; Washington corr. Indianapolis News, Fort Wayne Journal Gazette and Terre Haute Tribune (all of Indiana). Member Kappa Sigma. Democrat. Clubs: National Press (sec. 1930), Gridiron. Home: 200 Holly Av., Takoma Park, Md. Office: Albee Bldg., Washington, D.C. Died Jan. 14, 1947.

THOMAS, A(lbert) E(llsworth), dramatist; b. Chester, Mass., Sept. 16, 1872; s. Oscar Dwight and Nellie Louise (Ring) T.; A.B., Brown U., 1894, A.M., 1895; m. Ethel L. Dodd, 1918. Engaged in newspaper work, successively on staffs N.Y. Tribune, N.Y. Evening Post, N.Y. Times, N.Y. Sun, 1895-1909. Mem. Nat. Inst. of Arts and Letters, Delta Phi, Phi Beta Kappa. Clubs: Players, Century, Coffee House (New York City). Author: Cynthia's Rebellion (novel), 1903; The Double Cross (novel), 1924; (plays) Her Husband's Wife, prod., 1910; What the Doctor Ordered, 1911; The Divorce Fund, 1911; Little Boy Blue, 1911; The Rainbow, 1912; The Big Idea, 1914; Come Out of the Kitchen, 1916; The Matinee Hero, 1919; The Champion, 1920; Just Suppose, 1920; Only 38, 1921; Our Nell, 1922; The French Doll, 1922; The Jolly Roger, 1923; Embers, and Close Quarters, 1925; Vermont, 1928; Her Friend the King, 1929; White Magic, 1926; No More Ladies, 1936; Merely Murder, 1937. Chmn. Pulitzer Prize Drama Jury, 1926, 27, 28. Dir. Dramatists Guild of America. Motion picture scenarist. Address: 16 Gramercy Park, New York, N.Y. Died June 18, 1947.

THOMAS, Cecil Vincent, coll. pres.; b. Lima, O., Sept. 17, 1892; s. Melvin Orin and Lillie May (McPheron) T.; B.S. in Edn., Ohio State U., 1916; M.A., Western Reserve University, 1927; LL.D., Baldwin-Wallace University, Berea, O., 1937; LL.D., Ohio State University, 1947; m. Sylvia May Moore, Dec. 23, 1916; children—Theodore Vincent, Marjorie Beth, Aliee Ann. Prin. high sch., Belle Center, O., 1913-16; teacher English, Y.M.C.A. Sch., Cleveland, 1916-17; dir. evening div., Y.M.C.A. Night Sch., 1917-19; dir. Y.M.C.A. Schs., 1919-30; pres. Fenn Coll., Cleveland since 1930; gen. sec. Y.M.C.A., Cleveland, since 1938; mem. World's Comm. Y.M.C.A. Mem. Cleveland Chamber of Commerce (chmn. ednl. com.); v.p. Cleveland Church Federation. Bd. trustees St. Luke's Hosp., Cleveland (mem. exec. com.). Mem. Phi Delta Kappa. Methodist. Mason. Clubs: Mid-Day, Union (Cleveland). Home: 1482 Arthur Av., Lakewood, O. Office: 2200 Prospect Av., Cleveland, O. Died Nov. 28, 1947.

THOMAS, Charles Randolph, Jr., editor, engineer; b. Beaufort, N.C., Mar. 29, 1888; s. Charles Randolph and Laura Pasteur (Davis) T.; B.S., in C.E., U. of N.C., 1912; spl. student U. of Wis., Columbia, Pa. State Coll., and Northwestern U.; m. Clara Norwood MacNeill, 1915 (died 1919); children—Charles Randolph, III, Francis Pasteur; m. 2d, Elzada Mackie, June 29, 1927. Engring. work with U.S. Bur. Pub. Roads and state highway depts.; mem. engring. research staff, Pa. State Coll.; asso. prof. civil engring., N.C. State Coll.; in charge sect. of review of results, U.S. Forest Products Lab.; successively asso. editor Engineering and Contracting, editorial dir. Successful Methods, editor, mgr. Professional Engineer, editor, pub. Reclamation and Farm Engineering until 1926; mng. editor and editor Highway Engr. and Contractor since 1926. Mem. Am. Soc. C.E., Kappa Sigma. Episcopalian. Club: University (Evanston, Ill.). Author: (technical bulletins) Highway Culverts and Bridges in North Carolina (with T. F. Hickerson), 1913; Tests of Vertical Pressure Through Earth (with R. B. Fehr), 1914; Highway Maintenance in North Carolina (with D. H. Winslow), 1917; also articles in Nation's Business, Saturday Evening Post, Engineering News-Record, etc. Compiler: Publicity Methods for Engineers, 1922. Home: Kedzie St., Evanston, Ill. Office: 53 W. Jackson Blvd., Chicago. Died March 8, 1931.

THOMAS, Charles Swain, educator, author, lecturer; b. Pendleton, Ind., Dec. 29, 1868; s. John Lewis and Caroline (Swain) T.; A.B., Ind. U., 1894, A.M., 1895; A.B., Harvard, 1897; Litt.D., R.I. Coll. of Edn., 1933; post-grad. study, U. of Chicago, 1902; m. Charlotte Thornton, July 23, 1896; 1 son, Thornton Swain (dec.). Teacher pub. schs., Pendleton, 1887-89; prin. high sch., Bedford, 1891-92, supt. schs., 1892-93; instr. English, Ind. U., 1894-97; prof. English, Centre Coll., Danville, Ky., 1897-1901; head of English dept., Shortridge High Sch., Indianapolis, 1901-08, Newton (Mass.) High Sch., 1908-18; dir. English, Junior and Senior High Schs., Cleveland, 1918-20; on editorial staff Atlantic Monthly Press, 1920-25; lecturer on teaching of English, Harvard, 1920-30, asso. prof. edn., 1930-36, emeritus since 1936; visiting prof. edn., Wellesley Coll., 1936-39; visiting prof. Cornell U., summers 1937, 38. Mem. Nat. Council Teachers of English (pres. 1934-35), New Eng. Assn. Teachers of English, Harvard Teachers Assn. (sec. 1927-41), Alumni Assn. of Harvard Grad. Sch. of Edn. (sec. 1936-40), Phi Beta Kappa, Phi Delta Kappa, Beta Theta Pi. Republican. Mem. Soc. of Friends (Quakers). Clubs: English Lunch (pres.), Tuesday (pres.). Author: Composition and Rhetoric (with others), 1908; How to Teach The English Classics, 1910; Teaching of English in the Secondary School, 1916, rev. edit., 1927; When I Write a Theme (with J. C. Bowman), 1930; Examining the Examination in English (with others), 1931. Editor: Tom Brown's School Days, 1909; Cooper's The Spy, 1911. Compiler and editor: Selections from Byron, 1910; Milton's Minor Poems, 1911; Bret Harte's

Stories and Poems, 1912; Selected Lyrics (2 vols.), 1913; Atlantic Narratives, Series I and II, 1918; Atlantic Prose and Poetry (with H. G. Paul), 1920; Story, Essay and Verse (with same), 1921; Atlantic Book of Junior Plays, 1924; Modern Atlantic Stories, 1932; Thought and Expression (with others), 2 vols., 1938; English For Junior Americans (with others), 2 vols., 1941. Editor of The English Leaflet, 1909-40, and of Harvard Teachers Record, 1931-36; The Saunterer Column in Harvard Educational Review since 1936. Author: Your English and Your Personality, Your Command of Oral English, Your Command of Written English, Your Reading and Its Values, Your Language and Your Thinking, Your Manuscript and Your Publisher, 1941. Contbr. articles and editorials to various pubis. Home: 283 Highland Av., W. Newton, Mass. Died Jan. 26, 1943.

THOMAS, David Yancey, coll. prof.; b. Fulton County, Ky., Jan. 19, 1872; s. James Fuller and Eliza Ann (Ratliff) T.; student Marvin Training Sch., Clinton, Ky., 1888-90; A.B., Emory Coll., Oxford, Ga., 1894; A.M., Vanderbilt U., 1898; studied U. of Chicago, summers, 1899, 1900; Ph.D., Columbia, 1903; m. Sarah Elizabeth Janney, June 21, 1905; children—Mary Elizabeth, Albert Janney. Prof. Latin and Greek, Hendrix Coll., Conway, Ark., 1898-1901; univ. fellow in history, Columbia, 1901-02; prof. history and polit. science, Hendrix Coll., 1902-05; prof. same, U. of Fla., 1905-07; asso. prof. history and polit. science, U. of Ark., 1907-12, prof. since 1912, also head of dept.; mem. summer faculty, Peabody College for Teachers, 1917, U. of Tex., 1924, 30, 40, also fall 1941. Mem. Southwestern Polit. Science Assn. (ex-pres.), Am. Hist. Assn., Univ. Race Commns., Ark. Edni. Assn., Delta Tau Delta, Phi Beta Kappa. Democrat. Methodist. Mason. Mem. University Club. Author: History of Military Government in Newly Acquired Territory of the United States, 1904; (with J. H. Reynolds) History of University of Arkansas, 1910; 100 Years of the Monroe Doctrine, 1923; Arkansas in War and Reconstruction (1861-1874), 1926; Arkansas and Its People, a History (1541-1930), 1930; also numerous mag. articles. Contbr. to "The South in the Building of the Nation," Cyclo. of Am. Government, Ency. Americana, Ency. Britannica. Editor, Ark. Hist. Quarterly. Home: 912 Fairview, Fayetteville, Ark. Died Apr. 18, 1943.

THOMAS, Guy Alfred, flour milling, grain; b. Kesseville, N.Y., Oct. 28, 1879; s. Gorton Tallman and Frances Augusta (Nimocks) T.; ed. pub. schs., Fargo, N.D., and Minneapolis, Minn.; m. Lulu Frisk, Feb. 18, 1903; 1 son, Guy Alfred. Began as stenographer, Washburn Crosby Co., flour mills, Minneapolis, 1892, sales director same, 1910-24; organizer, 1918, pres. Millers & Traders Bank, Minneapolis, 1915-22; organizer Nat. Tea Co. of Del. (operating in Northwest), 1917, v.p., 1918-29; pres. John W. Thomas Co., Minneapolis, 1922-25; pres. Guy A. Thomas Investment Co., New York, 1924-28; dir. C.G.W. Ry., 1934-39; pres. Nateco Realty Co., Nat. Tea Co. Trust, 1929-39; chmn. bd. Commander-Larabee Milling Co., Minneapolis, 1931-43; now pres., gen. mgr. and dir. Colo. Mill & Elevator Co., Denver; pres. Snelling Field, Inc.; dir. Archer-Daniels-Midland Co., 1931-43; dir. Chicago, St. Paul, Minneapolis & Omaha Ry., Chicago & Northwestern R.R., Nat. Tea. Co., Allied Mills, Inc., Century Distilling Company. Joint organizer Minneapolis Civics and Commerce Association. Mem. Ill. Soc. of Order of Founders and Patriots of America, Huguenot Soc. of New England, Minn. State Soc. of S.A.R., Soc. of Am. Wars (Commandery of State of N.J.), New York Chapter of Colonial Order of the Acorn, Soc. War of 1812 (D.C.), Soc. Colonial Wars (Minn.), New York Commandery of Mil. Order Loyal Legion, New England Historic-Geneal. Soc., Inst. Am. Genealogy, Pioneers of America, Soc. Plymouth Colony Descendants. Episcopalian. Elk. Clubs: Denver, Denver Country, Denver Athletic; Minneapolis, Minikahda (Minneapolis); Everglades, Bath and Tennis (Palm Beach, Fla.). Home: 1600 Mount Curve Av., Minneapolis. Office: care Colorado Mills & Elevator Co., Denver, Colo. Died Mar. 9, 1946.

THOMAS, John Peyre, Jr., lawyer; b. Columbia, S.C., Dec. 9, 1857; s. John Peyre and Mary Caroline (Gibbes) T.; matriculated in U. of S.C. at age of 15; B.S., Carolina Mil. Inst., Charlotte, N.C., 1876; A.M., U. of S.C., 1919, LL.D., 1922; m. Mary Sumter Waties, Jan. 29, 1879 (died May 10, 1918); children—John Waties, Mary Sumter (Mrs. A. M. Lumpkin), Caroline Gibbes (dec.). Admitted to S.C. bar, 1879; practiced in Columbia, 1880-1916; prof. of law, 1906-20, dean, 1910-20, U. of S.C. Law Sch. School commr., Columbia, 1883-95; mem. legislature, 1892-98, 1901-04; chairman Board of Education, Richland Co., 1916-20, Standard B. & L. Association, Equitable Trust Co. of Columbia. President Richland Anti-Tuberculosis Association. Member Huguenot Soc. of S.C., Chi Psi. Col. staff of Gov. Ellerbe, 1898-1900. Mem. Gen. Conv., P.E. Ch., 1901-25; sec. and treas. bd. trustees P.E. Ch. in S.C. Democrat. Author: Digest of Reports of Supreme Court of South Carolina, 1837; History of Formation of Political Subdivisions in S.C.; also sketches of James L. Petigru, Charles Pinckney and The Barbadians in Early South Carolina, James Moore, Thomas Walter, the botanist. Home: 1731 College St. Office: Palmetto Bldg., Columbia, S.C. Died June 13, 1946.

THOMAS, John W., senator; b. Phillips County, Kan., Jan. 4, 1874; s. Daniel W. and Mary Elizabeth (Sparks) T.; grad. high sch., Phillipsburg, Kan., 1891; student Central Normal College; m. Florence Johnson, Oct. 25, 1906; 1 dau., Mary Elizabeth. County supt. schs., Phillips County, Kan., 1898-1903; register, land office, Colby, Kan., 1906-09; organizer First National Bank, Gooding, Ida.; formerly president of the First Security Bank, Shoshone, Ida., First Security Bank, Jerome, Ida.; engaged in sheep raising; formerly director of the First Security Corporation, Ogden, Utah. Was mayor of Gooding; chmn. Ida. Rep. State Com., 1922-24; mem. Rep. Nat. Com. since 1925. Apptd. mem. U.S. Senate, June 30, 1928, for unexpired term of Senator F. R. Gooding, dec.; elected to same office, Nov. 1928, for unexpired term ending March 3, 1933, again elected to fill unexpired term of William E. Borah, ending 1943; re-elected for term, 1943-49. Mason. Home: Gooding, Ida. Died Nov. 10, 1945.

THOMAS, Joseph Peter, business executive; b. Kenosha, Wis., 1893; s. Joseph Thomas and Emma Thomas; ed. high sch. and coll.; m. Marguerite Harbaugh, 1924; children—Marilyn Jane, Joan Marguerite. With firm of Gugler Lithog. Co., Milwaukee, 1915-26; sec.-treas. Theo. A. Schmidt Lithog. Co., Chicago, 1926-37; with U.S. Printing & Lithographing Co., Norwood, since 1937; mgr. Western Div. until Oct. 1938, pres. since that date. Clubs: Queen City, Cincinnati, Kenwood Country. Home: 729 Wakefield Dr., Cincinnati, O. Office: U.S. Printing & Lithographing Co., Norwood, O. Died Dec. 9, 1948.

THOMAS, Lucien Irving, Standard Oil Co. official; b. Richmond, Va., Dec. 4, 1876; s. William Lucien and Elizabeth Frances T.; ed. pub. schs.; m. Beryl Helen Penderel Mackenzie, Feb. 14, 1906; children—William Mackenzie (dec.), Mrs. W. B. Phillips, Donald Irving (lt. U.S. Navy), Francis J. Grant (dec.), Mrs. Jas. N. Bell, Jr., Lola Evanthea, Lucien Irving, Helen Penderel, Richard Nicolls. Mgr. of coast ports of China for Standard Oil Co. of N.Y., 1904-13, and gen. mgr. for the Near East, 1913-15; became dir. Standard Oil Co. of N.Y., 1917, now retired. Served as Am. del. in Europe, Inter-Allied Petroleum Conf., Allied Maritime Transport Council, and as spl. commr. U.S. Shipping Bd., World War. Episcopalian. Clubs: India House, Pilgrims (New York); Country (Va.); Thatched House, Pilgrims, Coombe Hill Golf (London). Home: Hillcrest, Richmond, Va.; and Virginia Beach, Va. Died Jan. 24, 1942.

THOMAS, M. Louise, educator; b. Columbia, Mo.; d. Judge Thomas A. and Martha Louisa (Lenoir) Russell; ed. St. Louis High Sch.; U. of Mo.; m. Joseph D. Thomas, of Paris, Tex., Oct. 23, 1889. Mem. Christian (Disciples) Ch. Organizer and pres. Lotus Club, Paris, Tex.; organizer Texas Fedn. Women's Clubs, 1897, and 1st corr. sec.; pres. Tex. Nat. Household Economics Assn., 1898-1900; organizer and pres. Lenox Hall, Sept. 1907. Mem. D.A.R., St. Louis Soc. of Authors, Kappa Kappa Gamma. Club: Town. Address: Lenox Hall, Kirkwood, St. Louis County, Mo. Died Apr. 19, 1947.

THOMAS, Walter Horstmann, architect; b. Phila., Pa., Dec. 29, 1876; s. Richard Newton and Clara L. (Horstmann) T.; B.S., in Architecture, U. of Pa., 1899; student École des Beaux Arts, Paris, 3 yrs.; m. Natalie Taylor, Oct. 1905; children—Claire, Florence; m. 2d, Ruth Sterling Boomer, Dec. 5, 1919; 1 son, Brooks. Began practice at Phila., 1906; sr. mem. Thomas & Martin; dir. city architecture, Phila., 1930-31; advisory architect, M.E. Ch. in U.S.A., 1925-33. Architect many chs., Y.M.C.A. buildings, hotels. Pres. of the Church Architectural Guild of America. Chmn. exec. com. City Planning Commn., Phila.; tech. dir. Phila. Housing Authority. In charge erection, maintenance and decoration of Y.M.C.A. huts, France, 1918-19. Fellow Am. Inst. Architects (v.p. Phila. chapter 1925-27; pres. 1928-30); mem. Zeta Psi. Episcopalian. Home: 47 E. Wynnewood Av., Merion, Pa. Office: 1100 Architects Bldg., Philadelphia 3, Pa. Died May 4, 1948.

THOMAS, William Holcombe, judge; b. near Oakbowery, Chambers County, Ala., July 10, 1867; s. William Erasmus Crawford and Emma Jane (Avary) T.; A.B., Emory Univ., Ga., 1887, hon. A.B., 1925, LL.D., 1936; m. Lulu Marian McCurdy, June 4, 1891; 1 dau., Mrs. George Willie Varner. Practiced law, 1888-1902; asso. judge, City Court of Montgomery, Ala., Feb. 7, 1902-09; elected judge, same, by Ala. Senate, 1909; retired, 1910, to resume law practice; justice Supreme Court of Ala., Jan. 9, 1915, present term expiring 1950. Mem. of com. 1903, which secured passage of Child Labor Bill by Ala. legislature; mem. Child Labor Com., 1907. Mem. Ala. Hist. Soc., Am. and Ala. State bar assns.; del. Universal Congress Lawyers and Jurists, St. Louis, 1904; mem. Internat. Congress Arts and Sciences, 1904; mem. Conf. for Edn. in the South; chmn. exec. com. Ala. Reform Sch. for Negro Boys, Mt. Meigs. Mem. Phi Beta Kappa. Democrat. Clubs: Thirteen, Country. Author: Birth and Growth of the Constitution of Ala., 1900; has also written many monographs, etc. His decisions as justice of the Supreme Court of Ala. reported in Vols. 193-236, Alabama Reports; 67 to 2d Series 33, et seq., Southern Reporter. Home: 526 S. Perry St. Office: Capitol, Montgomery, Ala. Died Dec. 22, 1945; buried in Greenwood Cemetery, Montgomery, Ala.

THOMAS, William Isaac, sociologist; b. Russell County, Va., Aug. 13, 1863; s. Thaddeus Peter and Sarah (Price) T.; A.B., U. of Tenn., 1884; student Berlin and Göttingen, 1888-89; Ph.D., U. of Chicago, 1896; m. Harriet Park, June 6, 1888; m. 2d, Dorothy Swaine Thomas, Feb. 7, 1935. Instr. English and modern languages, U. of Tenn., 1884-88; prof. English, Oberlin Coll., 1889-94, prof. sociology, 1894-95; instr. sociology, U. of Chicago, 1895-96, asst. prof., 1896-1900, assoc. prof., 1900-10, prof., 1910-18; lecturer New School for Social Research, 1923-28, Harvard, 1936-37; in charge Helen Culver fund for race psychology, 1908-18, research on Jewish Culture and behavior since 1918. Member Am. Sociol. Soc. (pres. 1927), Am. Acad. of Arts and Sciences. Clubs: Stockholm Golf, Claremont Country. Author: Sex and Society, 1907; Source Book for Social Origins, 1909; Standpoint and Questionnaire for Race Psychology, 1912; Suggestions of Modern Science Concerning Education, 1914; The Polish Peasant in Europe and America (with F. Znaniecki), 1918-21; The Unadjusted Girl, 1923; The Unconscious (with others), 1927; The Child in America (with D. S. Thomas), 1928; Primitive Behavior, 1936. Address: 2710 Garber St., Berkeley 5, Calif. Died Dec. 5, 1947.

THOMASON, John William, Jr., (thŏm'ă-sŭn), author, Marine Corps officer; b. Huntsville, Walker County, Tex., Feb. 28, 1893; s. John William (M.D.) and Sue (Goree) T.; student Southwestern U., Tex., 1909-10, Sam Houston Normal Inst., Huntsville, Tex., 1910-11, U. of Tex., 1912-13, Art Students League, New York, 1913-15 Army War Coll. 1937 Navy War Coll., 1938; Litt.D., Southwestern U., 1938; hon. Litt.D., Southwestern U.; m. Leda Bass, Aug. 24, 1917; 1 son, John William III. Commd. 2d lt. U.S. Marine Corps, Apr. 1917, colonel, 1942; served in 4th Brigade, 2d Div., A.E.F., also in West Indies, Central America, China and at sea. Mem. Kappa Sigma; hon. mem. Phi Beta Kappa. Mason. Clubs: Army and Navy, Army, Navy and Marine Corps Country, Peking, Chevy Chase, Metropolitan. Author: Fix Bayonets, 1926; Red Pants, 1927; Marines and Others, 1929; Jeb Stuart, 1930; Salt Winds and Gobi Dust, 1934; Gone to Texas, 1937; Lone Star Preacher, 1941; also articles in mags., short stories, etc. Address: Hdqrs. U.S. Marine Corps, Washington, D.C.* Died Mar. 12, 1944.

THOMASON, Samuel Emory, newspaper publisher, lawyer; b. Chicago, Ill., Jan. 24, 1883; s. Frank Davis and Diana M. (Bean) T.; A.B., U. of Mich., 1904; LL.B., Northwestern U., 1906; m. Alexina E. Young, Sept. 10, 1907; 1 dau., Elizabeth (Mrs. James A. Griffin, Jr.). Admitted to Ill. bar, 1906; mem. of firm of Stuart G. Shepard & Robert R. McCormick, 1909-11, firm of Shepard, McCormick, Thomason, Kirkland & Patterson, 1911-18; v.p. and business mgr. Chicago Tribune, 1918-27; now pub. Tampa (Fla.) Tribune and Chicago Daily Times. Pres. Am. Newspaper Publishers Assn., 1924-26. Mem. Am., Ill. State and Chicago bar assns., Theta Delta Chi. Clubs: University, Commonwealth, Legal, Tavern, Beverly, Ridge Country; Tampa Yacht, Palma Ceia (Tampa). Home: 10432 Longwood Drive, Chicago. Offices: 211 W. Wacker Drive, Chicago, Ill.; and Tribune Bldg., Tampa, Fla. Died Mar. 20, 1944.

THOMEN, August A. (thō'men), physician, author; b. New York, N.Y., Jan. 16, 1892; s. Louis and Lena (Astor) Thommen (name changed to Thomen); student Sch. of Applied Science, New York U., 1914; M.D., Univ. and Bellevue Hosp. Med. Coll., 1918; grad. student N.Y. Post Grad. Med. Sch. and Hosp., 1919, Cornell U., 1921; m. May Miriam Bellin, Oct. 14, 1920. Attending physician allergy clin., Cornell U., N.Y. Hosp., 1920-27; dir. allergy clinic, College of Medicine, New York U., 1927-35; lecturer in medicine, Coll. of Medicine, New York U., 1925-35; lecturer on popular medicine and conductor courses in applied psychology and public speaking. Fellow N.Y. Acad. of Medicine; mem. Soc. for Study of Asthma and Allied Conditions, A.A.A.S., A.M.A., Am. Assn. for Adult Edn. Democrat. Co-author: Asthma and Hay Fever in Theory and Practice, 1931. Author: Hay Fever: A Study in Applied Botany, 1933; Don't Believe It! Says the Doctor, 1935; Doctors Don't Believe It—Why Should You?, 1941. Contbr. to med. jours. and popular mags. Home: 260 Riverside Drive. Office: 667 Madison Av. New York, N.Y. Died Sep. 11, 1943.

THOMPSON, Calvin Miles; b. Muskingum County, O., Nov. 19, 1866; s. Charles and Sarah (Thompson) T.; prep. edn., Louisville Boys' High Sch. and under pvt. tutors; Th.B., Southern Bapt. Theol. Sem., 1898, Th.M., 1899; D.D., Georgetown (Ky.) Coll., 1906; m. Clara Belle Morrison, Dec. 27, 1888 (died Jan. 9, 1936); children—Clara Belle (widow of Dr. Wm. Chambers Powell, Jr.), Helen, Calvin M., Will C. Jno. M., Walter Scott. Began preaching, 1883; ordained ministry Southern Bap. Ch., 1888; pastor successively at Clayton, N.Y., Clarksburg, W.Va., Louisville, Newport, Ky., Denver, Colo., and Paducah, Ky., until 1907; editor Western Recorder and pres. Baptist Book Concern, at Louisville, 1907-09; pastor Hopkinsville, Ky., later Winchester, until 1921; became corr. sec. and treas. Bapt. State Bd. of Missions, Ky., 1921, also corr. sec. and treas. Bapt. Edn. Soc. of Ky.; trustee Theodore Harris Estate; chmn. board trustees Bethel Woman's Coll., Hopkinsville, Ky., 1909-17, pres., 1918; pres. Associated Charities, Hopkinsville, 1911-18. Moderator Gen. Assn. Ky. Baptists, 1911-13; mem. Conv. Commn. and Coöperation Program Commn. Southern Bapt. Conv. since 1921; etc.; now retired. Democrat. Mason (K.T.). Clubs; Athenæum, Lions. Home: 1401 S. 3d St., Louisville, Ky.* Died July 10, 1944.

THOMPSON, Carl Dean; b. Berlin (now Marne), Mich., Mar. 24, 1870; s. Abram and Rachel (Eddy) T.; A.B., Gates Coll., Neligh, Neb., 1895; B.D., Chicago Theol. Sem., 1898; M.A., U. of Chicago, 1900; LL.D., Doane Coll., 1930; m. Kate Mygatt,

Aug. 3, 1898; children—Harold Dean, Stanley Wendell. Minister Congl. Ch. until 1901; mem. Wis. Ho. of Rep., 1907-09; city clerk Milwaukee, 1910-11; mem. Am. Nat. Com., 3d World Power Conf.; consultant, Bonneville Power adminstrn., U.S. Dept. Interior, 1938-47; dir. Public Ownership League of Am.; econ., lecturer, pub. utility expert. Mem. Am. Acad. Polit. and Social Science, Am. Polit. Science Assn., Pi Gamma Mu. Democrat. Congregationalist. Author: Municipal Ownership, 1917; Public Ownership, 1924; Public Superpower, 1925; Confessions of the Power Trust—a Review of the Findings of the Federal Trade Commission, 1932; also (brochures) Public Ownership of Railways, and Municipal Electric Light and Power Plants in the United States and Canada; chapters on Municipal Railways in United States and Canada; The Biggest Dam on Earth (Grand Coulee); Studies in Public Power. Editor Public Ownership of Public Utilities (bimonthly). Home and Office: 4131 N. Keeler Av., Chicago 41. Died July 3, 1949; buried Lincoln, Neb.

THOMPSON, Carmi Alderman, ex-treasurer of the U.S.; b. Wayne County, W.Va., Sept. 4, 1870; s. Granville and Mary E. T.; Ph.B., Ohio State U., Columbus, 1892, LL.B., 1895; m. Leila E. Ellars, May 3, 1899. Admitted to bar, 1895, and practiced at Ironton, Ohio; was city solicitor, Ironton, 1896-1903; mem. Ohio Ho. of Rep., 1904-07 (speaker of House, 1906-07); sec. of state, Ohio, 1907-11; asst. sec. of the Interior, U.S., Mar. 6, 1911-July 1, 1912; sec. to Pres. Taft, July-Nov. 1912; treas. of U.S., Nov. 20, 1912-Apr. 1, 1913; gen. mgr. Great Northern Iron Ore Properties (a James J. Hill interest); pres. Cottonwood Coal Co., S. Butte Mining Co., St. Paul, 1913-17; pres. The Tod-Stambaugh Co., iron ore, Cleveland, 1917-24; chmn. bd. of Midland Steamship Co. since 1924; organized law firm of Thompson & Smith, 1925. Mem. advisory com. to the Am. delegation at the Conf. for Limitation of Armament, Washington, 1921; apptd. by President Coolidge, 1926, spl. commr. to make a survey of economic and internal conditions in Philippines. Republican. Mason, K.P. Clubs: Columbus (O.); University, Nat. Press (Washington); Minnesota (St. Paul); Union (Cleveland). Home: 22801 Lake Shore Drive. Office: Terminal Tower, Cleveland, O. Died June 22, 1942.

THOMPSON, Charles Miner, author; b. Montpelier, Vt., Mar. 24, 1864; s. George R. and Serafina (Taplin) T.; A.B., Harvard, 1886; m. Isabella Wayman Carr, Apr. 28, 1898; m. Leonora Bailey Coit, Aug. 12, 1939. Lit. editor Boston Advertiser, 1887-90; asso. editor, 1890-1911, editor-in-chief Youth's Companion, 1911-25; connected with the Harvard U. Press, Cambridge, until 1936. Hon. mem. Harvard Chapter of Phi Beta Kappa. Author: The Nimble Dollar (a book for boys), 1896; The Calico Cat, 1908; An Army Mule (humorous fiction), 1910. Translator: Wild Heart (from the French of Isabelle Sandy), 1926; Demosthenes (from the French of Georges Clemenceau), 1926; In the Evening of My Thought (from the French of Georges Clemenceau), 1929; America, the Menace (from the French of Georges Duhamel), 1931; Independent Vermont: A History of the State down to its admission into the Union in 1791, 1941. Died Dec. 19, 1941.

THOMPSON, Charles Willis, author; b. at Kalamazoo, Mich., Mar. 15, 1871; s. Charles Albert, Jr., and Emily (Logie) T.; LL.B., New York Univ., 1892. Reporter New York World, 1895, Tribune, 1896, Times, 1897-99; asst. Washington corr., New York Times, 1899-1905; Washington corr., Times, 1905-07, World, 1907-08; asst. Sunday editor, Times, 1908-11; editor New York Times Review of Books, 1912; traveling polit. corr. New York Times, 1912-14, editorial writer, Times, 1914-21, Phila. Press, 1917-18, Public Ledger, Phila., 1921-22, The Commonweal, 1930-31; polit. mag. writer since 1922. Author: Party Leaders of the Time, 1906; The New Voter, 1918; Presidents I've Known, 1929; The Fiery Epoch, 1931. Address: 603 E. 236th St., New York, N.Y. Died Sep. 8, 1946.

THOMPSON, Clarence Elmer, banker; b. Brooklyn, N.Y., Jan. 29, 1888; s. William D. and Hannah D. (Haight) T.; grad. The King Sch., Stamford, Conn., 1906; m. Lucy E. Billeter, Oct. 18, 1910; children—Douglas J. (lt. U.S.N.R.), Ralph S. (lt. U.S.N.R.). Began as messenger First Nat. Bank, Stamford, 1906; successively bookkeeper, teller, asst. treas., treas., and vice pres., The Stamford Trust Co., pres. since 1932; asst. treas. and dir., Stamford Water Co.; mem. Stamford div. com., Conn. Power Co.; dir. Norma-Hoffman Bearings Corp.; dir. and treas. Bouton & Reynolds, Inc. Trustee Family and Children's Center, Y.M.C.A. Mem. City Council of Stamford, 1922-24; mem. Bd. of Pub. Safety, Stamford, 1930-36. Mem. Conn. State Guard. President Stamford Hosp. Republican. Presbyterian. Mason, Odd Fellow, Elk. Club: Woodway Country. Home: 40 Hillside Av. Office: 300 Main St., Stamford, Conn. Died Oct. 5, 1946.

THOMPSON, David E., ex-ambassador; b. Bethel, Mich., Feb. 28, 1854; s. John H. and Rhoda (Bennett) T.; ed. in pub. schs. in Mich. until 13; LL.D., Milton (Wis.) Coll., 1910; m. Jeannette Miller, Jan. 18, 1892; 1 son, David E.; m. 2d, Gladys Dana Garber, June 9, 1921 (died 1928); m. 3d, Helen K. Fitzhugh, Aug. 23, 1930. Truckman and brakeman on ry. in 1872, supt. in 1881. E.E. and M.P. of U.S. to Brazil, 1902-05; ambassador, same, Jan. 10, 1905-Jan. 1906; ambassador to Mexico, Jan. 1906-Dec. 1909. Pres. Pan-Am. Ry., New York office, since Nov. 1, 1909. Republican. Home: Del Mar, Calif. Died Aug. 25, 1942.

THOMPSON, Elbert-Nevius Sebring, educator; b. Orange, N.J., Dec. 15, 1877; s. Wilmot Haines and Laura (Garrigues) T.; B.A., Yale, 1900, Ph.D., 1903; unmarried. Teacher English lit., Lehigh U., 1903-06, Yale, 1906-09, asso. prof. English, 1909-20, prof. since 1921, State U. of Iowa. Mem. Modern Lang. Assn. of America. Unitarian. Club: Graduate (New Haven, Conn.). Author: Controversy Between the Puritans and the Stage, 1903; English Moral Plays, 1909; Essays on Milton, 1914; Literary Bypaths of the Renaissance, English Essay of the Seveneteenth Century. Compiler: Topical Bibliography of Milton, 1916. Contbr. articles in Modern Lang. Notes, Publs. Modern Lang. Assn. America, Studies in Philology, etc. Republican. Home: Iowa City, Ia. Died Sept. 13, 1948.

THOMPSON, Ernest, clergyman; b. Bartow County, Ga., Nov. 10, 1867; s. Gilbert Taylor and Josephine Amanda (King) T.; A.B., Drury Coll., Springfield, Mo., 1888, A.M., 1891, D.D., 1902; grad. McCormick Theol. Sem., 1891; studied New Ch. Coll. (U. of Edinburgh), 1896-97; m. Jimmie Sawyer Graves, Oct. 15, 1891; children—Allison Garnett, Ernest Trice, Hugh Graves, Graves Haydon. Ordained Presbyn. ministry, 1891; pastor First Ch., Texarkana, Tex., 1891-95; asst. Stockbridge Free Ch., Edinburgh, 1895-96; pastor Stuart Robinson Memorial Ch., Louisville, Ky., 1897-1902; pastor First Church, Charleston, W.Va., 1902-38, now emeritus. Mem. executive com. of religious edn., Presbyn. Ch. in U.S.; chmn. home mission com. Kanawha Presbytery; moderator Gen. Assembly Presbyn. Ch. in U.S., 1933-34. Trustee Hampden-Sydney Coll., Union Theol. Sem. (Va.), Mountain Retreat Assn. (Montreat, N.C.). Democrat. Mason (32°, Shriner). Clubs: Rotary (ex-pres.), Kanawha County. Author: Veto Power; The Presbyterian Church in the U.S. Contbr. articles and verse to ch. papers. Home: 2006 Kanawha St., Charleston, W.Va. Died Dec. 12, 1945.

THOMPSON, Ernest Seton, see Seton, Ernest Thompson.

THOMPSON, Frank E., lawyer; b. Duluth, Minn., Aug. 16, 1875; s. William Andrew and Caroline (Anderson) T.; ed. high sch.; student Chicago Coll. of Law, 1895-98; m. Ella Lewis, Dec. 1903 (now dec.); 1 son, Frank E.; m. 2d, Alice Roth, June 20, 1912; children—Barbara, Dixie (Mrs. Samuel Carnes Collier), William Roth. Practiced at Honolulu, T.H., since 1900; served as 1st referee in bankruptcy, U.S. Dist. Court of Hawaii; admitted to practice Supreme Court of U.S., 1908; specializes in admiralty law and represents various cos.; was atty. for Queen Liliuokalani in claim against U.S. for seizure of her personal crown lands; personal atty. for Princess Abigail Kawananakoa; atty. Matson Navigation Co.; pres. Lines, Isthinian S.S. Co., Royal Hawaiian Hotel, Civic Auditorium, Finance Corp., Consolidated Motors; dir. Hawaiian Contracting Co., Ltd., The von Hamm-Young Co., Ltd., Mfrs. Shoe Co., Ltd. Served in Spanish-Am. War; capt. U.S. Res., 1914-17; served with Draft Bd., Hawaii, World War. Mem. bd. Community Chest Fund, Honolulu, two terms. Mem. Am. Bar Assn., Bar Assn. Ty. of Hawaii (twice pres.); mem. Honolulu Commn. on Uniform laws. Republican. Mason. Clubs: Pacific, University, Waialae, Schofield Barracks Golf, Waialae Golf (Honolulu). Home: 1559 Thurston Av. Office: 5th Floor, Inter-Island Bldg., Honolulu, T.H. Deceased.

THOMPSON, Gustave Whyte, chemist; b. Brooklyn, N.Y., July 27, 1865; s. John and Lucy (Whyte) T.; Dr. Sc., Armour Inst. of Technology, 1927; m. Alice C. Wilmarth, Apr. 1897. Chief chemist Nat. Lead Co., 1892-1938, dir., 1916-40; dir. of Titanium Pigment Company. Fellow A.A.A.S.; mem. Am. Chem. Soc., Soc. Chem. Industry, Am. Inst. Chem. Engrs. (ex-pres.), Am. Soc. for Testing Materials (v.p. 1926, pres. 1928), Internat. Assn. for Testing Materials. Clubs: Chemists. Home: 39 Plaza St., Brooklyn, N.Y. Died Apr. 22, 1942.

THOMPSON, Hollis Ring, aviation exec.; b. San Dimas, Calif., Aug. 6, 1898; s. Herbert Wellington and Flora (Ring) T.; student U. of Redlands, 1916-18; A.B., U. of Calif., 1921; m. Margaret Currence, Aug. 31, 1929. Industrial sec. Y.M.C.A., Berkeley, Calif., 1921-24; officer First Nat. Bank, Berkeley, 1924-27; mng. dir. Berkeley Chamber of Commerce, 1927-30; city mgr., Berkeley, 1930-40; now v.p. Am. Airlines, Inc. Director First Dist. Agrl. Assn. (mem. district board agriculture); mem. board trustees Univ. of Redlands. Mem. Officers Training Corps, Ft. McArthur, Waco, Tex., during World War. Mem. Internat. City Mgrs. Assn. (pres. 1935, mem. bd. dirs.), League of Calif. Municipalities (pres. 1936, mem. bd. dirs.), Am. Legion, Pi Kappa Delta, Pi Sigma Alpha. Republican. Baptist. Mason. Clubs: Lions, American, Mexico City Country, Club de Banqueros (all Mexico City). Office: American Airlines De Mexico, Ejido No. 7, Mexico, D.F. Died July 7, 1944.

THOMPSON, Hugh Lindsay, cons. engr.; b. Thistle, Md., Dec. 8, 1863; s. Robert Hughes and Margaret Helen (Bone) T.; student Knapp's Acad., Baltimore, 1877-80; m. Caroline Goss, Oct. 17, 1900; children—Caroline Goss, Helen Lindsay (widow of Rev. Arthur F. McKenny). Began as mech. draftsman's apprentice Robt. Poole & Son Co., 1880, draftsman, engr. and designer of engines, boilers, machinery, etc., 1880-93; asst. supt., Waterbury Farrel Foundry & Machine Co., 1893-96; cons. engr., Waterbury, since 1897; cons. and administrative engr., Scovill Mfg. Co., Waterbury, 1900-46; invented improvements in design and arrangement of rolling mills and in annealing furnaces; designed and installed various brass and copper rolling mills in New Eng. and the Middle West; director Citizens and Mfrs. National Bank, Waterbury. Member executive committee Waterbury Com. on Additional Water Supply. Mem. Mattatuck Hist. Soc. Council, Am. Soc. M.E. Republican. Conglist. Clubs: Waterbury, Country (Waterbury). Home: 129 Pine St., Waterbury, Conn. Died Feb. 14, 1949.

THOMPSON, John, clergyman; b. Nenthead, Eng.; s. Jonathan and Hannah (Erwine) T.; ed. London Poly., Wesleyan Meth. Theol. Sch., Oxford U. and Garrett Bibl. Inst., Evanston, Ill.; D.D., Garrett, 1921; m. Jane Cousin, June 8, 1888; children—Sarah Hannah (Mrs. W. A. Gamon), Howard Newton; m. 2d, Ruth Clegg, Oct. 16, 1907. Came to U.S., 1892, naturalized, 1897. Ordained M.E. ministry, 1897; supt. Chicago Home Missionary and Ch. Extension Soc., 1914-35; pastor First M.E. Ch. (Chicago Temple) 1920-41, retired. Trustee Garrett Bibl. Inst., Wesley Hosp. Republican. Author: Soul of Chicago, 1920. Home: 824 Euclid Av., Oak Park, Ill. Died Sep. 19, 1944.

THOMPSON, John Gilbert, educator; b. New Bedford, Mass., June 23, 1862; s. Thomas and Margaret (Fitzgerald) T.; A.B., Dartmouth, 1886, A.M., 1889; m. Helen Susan Titus, Dec. 27, 1886. Teacher grammar and high schs. until 1886; prin. Winchester (N.H.) High Sch., Sandwich (Mass.) Grammar Sch., Southboro (Mass.) High Sch.; supt. schs., Northboro (Mass.) Dist., Leominster, Mass.; prin. Fitchburg (Mass.) Normal Sch. since 1895. Trustee Wallace Library, Fitchburg. Club: Fay. Author: New Century Readers, 1895; Word from Word Readers, 1915; The Thompson Readers, 1917. Joint author (with Inez Bigwood, 2 vols. of World War stories); Lest We Forget; Winning a Cause. Dir. Fitchburg Open Forum. Home: Fitchburg, Mass. Died Oct. 31, 1940.

THOMPSON, J(oseph) Whitaker, judge; born Stroudsburg, Pa., Aug. 19, 1861; s. Charles Impey and Gertrude Kimber (Whitaker) T.; prep. edn., Rugby Acad.; student U. of Pa., 1883, LL.B., 1887; m. Anna Pennypacker Williamson, Dec. 4, 1889; children—Elisabeth Williamson, Charles Impey, Martha Josephine. Asst. U.S. atty., Eastern Dist. of Pa., 1900-04; U.S. atty., same dist., 1904-12; judge U.S. Dist. Court, same dist., 1912-31; judge U.S. Circuit Court of Appeals, 3d Circuit, 1931-38; retired, May 1, 1938. Trustee State Hosp. for Insane, Eastern Pa., 1914-23, 1927-35, State Inst. for Feeble Minded and Epileptic (pres. bd.), 1913-23. Mem. Delta Psi. Club: Union League. Home: 2323 De Lancey St., Philadelphia, Pa. Died Jan. 7, 1946.

THOMPSON, Mills, artist, decorator; b. Washington, Feb. 2, 1875; s. John Barker and Ida (McClery) T.; ed. pub. schs., Corcoran Art Sch. and Art Students League, Washington and New York; m. Frances Moore, May 22, 1913. Worked on decoration of Library of Congress, 1896; art editor Saturday Evening Post, 1900. Decorated Siam building at St. Louis Expn. Knight Most Honorable Order of Crown of Siam. Mem. S.A.R., Soc. Washington Artists. Club: Cosmos. Address: Saranac Lake, N.Y. Died Oct. 18, 1944.

THOMPSON, Milo Milton, exec. Associated Press; b. Joliet, Ill., Nov. 25, 1894; s. James Milton and Anamarie (Clouse) T.; ed. schs. of Ontario, Canada, Prep. Sch. of Beloit, Wis., Harvard U.; m. Florence Weston, Sept. 18, 1916; children—Ellsworth Sinclair, Lois Knight; 2d m. Patience L. Brouilette. Began as reporter Joliet Herald, 1909; city editor, 1912-15; Washington corr., Christian Science Monitor, 1917, chief of Southern Bureau, 1917-18; political writer Atlanta (Ga.) Constitution, 1918; polit. and editorial writer Idaho Statesman, Boise, Ida., 1919-20, mng. editor, 1920-22, editor-in-chief, 1922-28; with Associated Press since 1928, as Bur. chief, Des Moines, Ia., 1928-29, news editor in charge Southwestern Div., Kansas City, Mo., 1929-34, exec. asst. to gen. mgr., New York, 1935-36, chief of Bur., Washington, D.C., 1937-38, gen. exec. for Europe, London, England, 1939-40; managing dir. Associated Press of Great Britain, Ltd., 1940-43; pres. La Prensa Asociada, Inc., 1941-43 (dir. 1941); dir. Associated Press of Great Britain, Ltd., 1939-41. Served as regimental supply sergt. U.S. Engrs. and 2nd lt. U.S. Signal Corps, World War. Mem. advisory com., Rep. Campaign, Ida. Republican. Methodist. Mason. Clubs: Harvard, Kansas City Athletic, Rotary, National Press (Washington), London Press (England), Asociation Cristiana de Jovenes (Buenos Aires), Army-Navy (New Orleans), Sands Point Golf (Long Island). Several articles of foreign corr., London Blitz (1940). Home: 1314 E. Washington St., Joliet, Ill. Office: 50 Rockefeller Plaza, New York, N.Y. Died Mar. 26, 1945.

THOMPSON, Oscar, music critic, writer; b. Crawfordsville, Ind., Oct. 10, 1887; s. Will H. and Ida (Lee) T.; student U. of Washington, 1907-08; m. Janviere Maybin, Apr. 14, 1914; children—Hugh, Keith, Letitia (wife of Lt. John F. Cassil, U.S. Army), Janet (Mrs. Roger Scudder). Reporter, Seattle (Wash.) Times, 1903, Seattle News, 1906; reporter, later asst. editor, Seattle Star, 1907-09; telegraph editor, Tacoma (Wash.) News, 1909-13; mng. editor, Tacoma Ledger, 1913-17; music critic,

Musical America, 1919-25, New York Evening Post, 1926-34; editor Musical America, 1936-43; music critic New York Sun since 1937. Served as capt., Mil. Intelligence, U.S. Army, during World War I. Editor: International Cyclopedia of Music and Musicians, 1938; Plots of the Operas: Great Modern Composers, 1939. Author: Practical Musical Criticism, 1934; How to Understand Music, 1935; The American Singer, 1937; Debussy, Man and Artist, 1937. Home: 200 W. 58th St., New York 19. Office: New York Sun, 280 Broadway, New York 4, N.Y. Died July 2, 1945.

THOMPSON, Paul, banker; b. Phila., Pa.; grad. Episcopal Acad.; C.E., U. of Pa., 1885. Pres. Corn Exchange Nat. Bank and Trust Co., Phila. Clubs: Rittenhouse, Racquet, Merion Cricket, Manufacturers and Bankers; Ordinary Point (Md.) Yacht. Home: Haverford, Pa. Office: 1512 Chestnut St., Philadelphia, Pa. Died Dec. 12, 1942.

THOMPSON, Sanford Eleazer, engineer; b. Ogdensburg, N.Y., Feb. 13, 1867; s. Eleazer and Harriet Newell (Sanford) T.; Adelphi Acad., Brooklyn, and Danbury (Conn.) and Medway (Mass.) high schs.; S.B. in Civ. Engring., Mass Inst. Tech., 1889; m. Stella Antoinette Converse, 1900 (dec.); children—Katharine Converse (dec.), Marion Sanford (Mrs. Ward Beckwith), David Sanford Taylor (dec.), Dr. Dorothy Dewhurst; married 2d, Frances Lord Marsh, Mar. 1947. Engaged in civil and management engring. since 1889; now pres. The Thompson & Lichtner Co., Inc., engrs. in management, industrial research and constrn.; president The Thompson Co., Inc., of New York. Lt. col., Ordnance Dept., U.S. Army, chief of progress sect.. Office Chief of Ordnance, 1917-19. Apptd. by Herbert Hoover, mem. com. on elimination of waste in industry of Federated Am. Engring. Soc., 1921; apptd. by President Harding, mem econ advisory bd. to the Unemployment Conf., 1921; chmn. bd. of arbitration Rochester (N.Y.) shoe industry, 1921; apptd. by Sec. Hoover to study methods of stabilizing production and distribution (pub. as chapter of "Business Cycles and Unemployment"), 1922; apptd. by U.S. Coal Commn. as engr. to investigate underground management in bituminous coal mines, 1923; apptd. by Boston Chamber of Commerce to make report on boot and shoe industry in New Eng., 1924, also report on metal trades industry of New Eng., 1925; supervised New Eng. Council surveys of shoes, knit goods and textiles, 1926; prepared outline for distribution survey for Twentieth Century Fund, Inc., 1930; mem. waste com. of Nat. Construction Conf., 1931; represented various U.S. technical societies at 38th Oxford Management Conf., England, 1938; expert consultant to sec. of war, 1941-42. Trustee Chaplain David Sanford Fund. Fellow Am. Inst. of Management, Am. Soc. M.E., life mem. Am. Soc. C.E., Soc. for the Advancement of Management, Am. Management Assn.; mem. American Soc. Testing Materials, Boston Soc. C.E., Taylor Soc. (ex-pres.); honorary member American Concrete Inst., Institut Naukowej Orfanizacji (Warsaw, Poland). Clubs: Brae Burn Country, Appalachian Mountain. Author: Treatise on Concrete, Plain and Reinforced (with Frederick W. Taylor), 1905; Concrete Costs (with same), 1912; Reinforced Concrete Bridges (with Frederick W. Taylor and Edward Smulski), 1939. Writer of papers on scientific management and constrn. for tech. socs. Home: Newton Highlands, Mass. Office: Park Square Bldg.. Boston, Mass.; and 8 Alton Pl., Brookline, Mass. Died Feb. 1, 1949.

THOMPSON, Thomas Edward, educator, author, lecturer; b. New Bedford, Mass., May 6, 1864; s. Thomas and Margaret (Fitzgerald) T.; grad. Waukegan (Ill.) High Sch., 1883; courses Clark U., Worcester, Mass., U. of Calif. and Normal Sch., Fitchburg, Mass.; grad. Hyannis (Mass.) Normal Sch., 1911, and Occidental Coll., 1919; m. Mary Lucia Hagar, Dec. 1891; 1 dau., Dorothy. Teacher in Vt., N.H. and Mass., 1885-95; supt. schs., Leominster, Mass., 1895-1914, Monrovia, Calif., 1914-19; with U. of Calif. at Los Angeles, 1922-36. Author: A Nature Calendar, 1898; Self-Verifying Seat Work, 1904; Minimum Essentials, a New System of Education (series of 40 publs.), 1918; Non-Dictation Spelling, 1915; Standardized Tests in the Fundamentals, 1916; Standardized Practice Tests, Automatically Corrected, 1916. Joint Author: Fables and Rhymes, 1894; Fairy Tale and Fable, 1895; For Childhood Days, 1899; Story, Myth and Fable, 1903; Practice Tests in Arithmetic, 1926; Automatic Correction; Essentials of English Instantaneous Correction, 1928; Silent Reading Sentence Completion—Primer Grade, 1931; Silent Reading Sentence Completion—First Reader Grade, 1931. Address: 10552 Blythe Av., Los Angeles, Calif.* Deceased.

THOMPSON, William Hale, ex-mayor; b. Boston, May 14, 1869; s. William Hale and Medora (Gale) T.; LL.D., Wilberforce Univ., 1927; m. Mary Walker Wyse, Dec. 5, 1901. Spent five seasons on ranches of Standard Cattle Co., in Colo., Mont. and Wyo.; mgr. cattle ranch in Neb. 3 yrs.; managed real estate interests left by father and other real estate interests. Mem. Chicago Real Estate Bd. Alderman from 2d Ward, Chicago, 1900-02; county commr., Cook County, 1902-04; mayor Chicago 3 terms, 1915-23 and 1927-31. Mem. Rep. Nat. Com., 1916-20. Clubs: Chicago Yacht, Hamilton, Chicago Athletic, South Shore Country, Illinois Athletic (ex-pres.), Columbia Yacht. Home: 1420 Lake Shore Drive. Office: 33 N. La Salle St., Chicago. Died March 18, 1944.

THOMPSON, William Herbert, lawyer; b. Winchester, Ind., May 25, 1878; s. William Albert and Elizabeth (Lamb) Thompson; Ph.B., DePauw U., Greencastle, Ind., 1899, hon. LL.D., 1937; student Leland Stanford Jr. U. Law Sch. (now Stanford U.), 1900-02; m. Florence Gregory, Apr. 4, 1907. Admitted to Ind. bar, 1902, and began practice at Muncie; moved to Indianapolis, Ind., 1908; mem. firm Miller, Dailey & Thompson, 1916-28, Thompson, Rabb & Stevenson, 1928-37, Thompson & Rabb, 1937-40, Thompson, O'Neal & Smith since 1940. Asst. atty. gen., Ind., 1908-10. Served as capt., Am. Red Cross, France, 11 mos., World War. Mem. Phi Beta Kappa, Phi Kappa Psi, Phi Delta Phi. Republican. Clubs: Dramatic, Columbia. Home: 1321 N. Meridian St. Office: Consolidated Bldg., Indianapolis, Ind. Died Dec. 1, 1945.

THOMPSON, William Joseph, clergyman; b. Woolford's Creek, Dorchester County, Md., Sept. 22, 1864; s. Rev. James and Julia Ann (Woolford) T; B.S., U. of Pa., 1884; B.D., Drew Theol. Sem., Madison, N.J., 1892; A.M., Harvard, 1901; Ph.D., New York U., 1910; D.D., Dickinson, 1906; LL.D., Hamline, 1913; m. Mary S. McLean, June 14, 1898. Ordained M.E. ministry, 1892; pastor 4th St. Ch., Washington, D.C., 1892-93, Kensington, Md., 1893-94, Grace Ch., Worcester, Mass., 1894-99, Newtonville, Mass., 1899-1904, Simpson Ch., Brooklyn, N.Y., 1904-10; prof. religious psychology and pedagogy, Drew Theol. Sem., 1911-34. Mem. Gen. Conf. M.E. Ch., 1924; mem. Sunday Sch. Bd. M.E. Ch.; trustee Western Maryland Coll., Yenching U., Peiping, Meth. Hosp., Brooklyn; asso. supt. Brooklyn and L.I. Ch. Soc. Mem. Alpha Kappa, Brooklyn Clerical Union, Southern Soc., Sons of the Revolution, Phi Beta Kappa, Soc. Colonial Wars; pres. Alumni of Grad. Sch. N.Y. Univ. Mason. Club: Univ. of Pa. (New York). Medallion alumnus of New York U. Contbr. to religious press. Home: 610 Park Av., New York, N.Y. Died Nov. 24, 1944.

THOMPSON, William Ormonde, lawyer; b. in Eng.; s. Edwin T.; m. Eleanor Frances Gregsten. Formerly mem. firm Altgeld, Darrow & Thompson; was mem. bd. of arbitration, Hart, Schaffner & Marx, mfrs., Chicago, also for cloak industry, New York, 1914-15; was counsel for late U.S. Commn. on Industrial Relations, Washington; labor mediator for U.S. Govt. for First Dist. Cantonments; apptd. mem. Nat. Recovery Review Bd., 1934; mem. Lord Morley Commn. on Saar Valley, 1934. Was sec.-treas. and pres. Am. Cotton Oil Co., New York. Mem. Nat. Inst. Social Sciences. Club: Nassau Country (Glen Cove, L.I.). Address: Hinsdale, Ill. Died Dec. 8, 1942.

THOMS, Craig Sharpe (thŏmz), clergyman, educator; b. Elgin, Ill., Dec. 20, 1860; s. Robert and Jane (Patrick) T.; student old U. of Chicago, 2 yrs.; B.A., Northwestern U., 1888, M.A., 1891; B.D., U. of Chicago, 1891; Ph.D., Shurtleff Coll., Ill., 1901; m. Effie Belle Walker, July 7, 1892. Ordained Bapt. ministry, 1891; pastor 1st Ch., Morris, Ill., 1891-95, Forest Av. Ch., Des Moines, Ia., 1895-1900, 1st Ch., Vermilion, S.D., 1900-14, 1st Ch., Moline, Ill., 1914-15; prof. sociology, U. of S.D., 1915-31, prof. Biblical lit., 1931-40; retired. Pres. S.D. State Conf. of Social Work, 1925. Mem. Phi Kappa Psi, Phi Beta Kappa. Author: The Bible Message for Modern Manhood, 1912; The Workingman's Christ, 1914; The Essentials of Christianity, 1919; (with W. H. Over) Birds of South Dakota, 1921; Social Imperatives, 1923; Facing Old Testament Facts, 1931. Home: Vermilion. S.D. Died Sep. 27, 1945.

THOMS, William Edward, lawyer; b. Plymouth, Conn., Dec. 22, 1870; s. William P. and Fanny (Ould) T.; B.A., Yale, 1894 (salutatorian); studied law pvtly.; m. Harriet Joy Dutton, June 29, 1898; children—Elinor Joy, John Dutton, Frederic, Mrs. Fanny Burke. Began as high sch. teacher, Waterbury, 1894; admitted to Conn. bar, 1896, and since practiced in Waterbury; mayor of Waterbury, 1906-10; mem. Conn. Gen. Assembly, 1911-13 (Dem. leader, 1913); judge City Court, Waterbury, 1913-15. Del. to Dem. Nat. Conv., 1912-24, 28, 32 (chmn. Conn. delegation, 1928; mem. resolutions com. 1932). Mem. Am., Conn. State and New Haven County bar assns. Methodist. Mason (32°, Shriner), Odd Fellow (past grand master), K.P. (past grand chancellor). Mem. Elks, Foresters of America. Clubs: Waterbury, Yale (New York). Home: 60 Fiske St. Office: 111 W. Main St., Waterbury, Conn.* Died Aug. 9, 1939.

THOMSEN, Rasmus, clergyman; b. Denmark, Jan. 23, 1875; s. Thomas and Maren (Christiansen) Neilsen; grad. Cumberland U. Theol. Sem., 1900; D.D., Coll. of the Ozarks, 1909, Trinity U., 1915, LL.D., 1937; m. Bessie M. Bliss, June 26, 1901; children—Carl W. (dec.), Daniel Bliss, Martha Neilsine (dec.), Dorothy Ann (Mrs. T. Arthur Quine). Ordained ministry Presbyterian Church, 1900; pastor Central Presbyterian Church (Memphis), 1900-01, Central Presbyterian Church (Fayetteville, Ark.), 1901-07, First Presbyn. Ch. (Independence, Kan.), 1907-10, First Presbyn. Ch. (Amarillo, Tex.), 1910-45, retired, 1945; elected pastor emeritus for life, 1945; member Board Nat. Missions of Presbyn. Ch. U.S.A., 1914-40; mem. Permanent Judicial Commn. Presbyn. Ch., 1930-31, mem. Gen. Council, 1940-46; moderator Synod of Ark., 1910, Synod of Tex., 1916. Exec. sec. for recruiting service, Tex. Y.M.C.A., 1918-19. Pres. Llano Cemetery Assn.; trustee Amarillo Presbytery, Presbyn. Home for Children; chmn. bd. trustees Trinity Univ.; mem. bd. dirs. Amarillo Housing Authority; pres. Ministerial Alliance, Amarillo, 1944. Presented with gift by citizens of Amarillo and Panhandle on 25th anniversary of pastorate; also funds for tour to Egypt and Holy Land and Europe, 1928. Presented with home by First Presbyn. Ch. upon retirement after 35 years service as pastor. Mason (32°). Clubs: Rotary, Knife and Fork (dir.). Lecturer. Home: 1513 Bonham St., Amarillo, Tex. Died May 22, 1948; buried Llano Cemetery, Amarillo, Tex.

THOMSON, Arthur Conover, bishop; b. Fredericksburg, Va., Apr. 16, 1871; s. Elliot Heber and Jeanette Risdelle (Conover) T.; student U. of Pa., 1887-90; grad. Theol. Sem., Va., 1893, D.D., 1915; m. Mary Grayson Fitzhugh, 1893. Deacon, 1893, priest, 1895, P.E. Ch.; rector South Farnham Parish, Tappahannock, Va., 1893, Ch. of the Resurrection, Cincinnati, O., 1895; Trinity Ch., Portsmouth, Va., 1899-1917; consecrated suffragan bishop Diocese of Southern Va., Sept. 27, 1917; bishop coadjutor, Diocese of Southern Va., May 26, 1919; bishop of Southern Va., Jan. 17, 1930-Oct. 9, 1937, resigned. Mem. Delta Upsilon. Democrat. Home: Portsmouth, Va.* Died Dec. 16, 1946.

THOMSON, Charles Marsh, lawyer; b. Chicago, Ill., Feb. 13, 1877; s. James and Julia (Marsh) T.; A.B., Washington and Jefferson Coll., 1899; A.M., 1902, LL.D., 1933; LL.B., Northwestern, 1902; m. Besse Holbrook, Oct. 24, 1905; children—Dorothy, John Holbrook. Began practice, Chicago, 1902; mem. City Council, Chicago, 3 terms, 1908-13 (resigned 1913); mem. 63d Congress (1913-15), 10th Ill. Dist.; judge Circuit Court of Cook County, Ill., 1915-17; judge Ill. Appellate Court, 1st District, Chicago, 1917-27; trustee C.&E.I. R.R., 1933-39; trustee C.&N.W. Ry. Co. since May 22, 1939. Republican. Presbyn. Home: Winnetka, Ill. Office: 400 W. Madison St., Chicago, Ill. Died Dec. 30, 1943.

THOMSON, Logan G., pres. Champion Paper & Fibre Co.; b. Cincinnati, O., Dec. 2, 1884; s. Peter G. and Laura (Gamble) T.; student Asheville School (N.C.) and Williams Coll.; m. Sylvia V. Johnston, Jan. 7, 1914. Started with Champion Paper & Fibre Co., formerly Champion Coated Paper Co., as mill worker and rose through various depts. to prodn. mgr., later sec. and treas., vice-president, 1931-35, president since 1935; pres. and dir. The Stacey Engring. Co. Clubs: Queen City, Cincinnati Country, Camargo, Chicago Yacht, Belvedere, Charlevoix. Home: Oakwood and Belmont Avs., College Hill, Cincinnati, O. Office: North B St., Hamilton, O. Died Aug. 9, 1946.

THOMSON, O(smund) R(hoads) Howard, librarian; b. London, Eng., Dec. 5, 1873; s. John (Litt.D.) and Mary Ann (Faulkner) T.; father organized Free Library of Phila.; brought to U.S., 1881; ed. under father; professional training under Thomas L. Montgomery and John Ashhurst; Litt.D., Dickinson Coll., Carlisle, Pa., 1935; naturalized citizen of U.S.; m. Theodora Adelheid (Theivagt) Nice, Apr. 18, 1901. Librarian West Phila. br. Free Library of Phila., 1899-1901, Wagner Inst. br. Free Library of Phila., 1901-06; organizer, 1906, and since librarian and sec. J. V. Brown Library, Williamsport, Pa. Chmn. for Pa. for A.L.A. in United Drive; chmn. for 12 counties, A.L.A. drive; chmn. Williamsport Red Cross Book and Mag. Service (World War I); chmn. Victory Book Drives, Lycoming Co. (World War II). Member American Library Association, Pennsylvania Library Association (ex-president), Pa. Folk Lore Soc. Episcopalian. Clubs: Williamsport Chess, Kit-Kat (pres.), Williamsport Country. Author: Contribution to Classification of Prose Fiction, 1904; History of the Bucktails (with W. H. Rauch), 1906; A Normal Library Budget, 1913; Resurgam—Poems and Lyrics, 1915; Christmas, 1916; Modern Comedy and Other Poems, 1918; John Franklin Meginess, 1919; Joseph H. McMinn, 1920; Reasonable Budgets for Public Libraries (A.L.A.), 1925. Editor Lycoming Hist. Soc. publs. Lecturer on English and American poetry; contbr. poems and critical articles to mags. Address: J.V. Brown Library, Williamsport, Pa. Died Dec. 23, 1943.

THOMSON, William H.; pres. Anglo-California Nat. Bank of San Francisco. Home: 2500 Steiner St. Office: 1 Sansome St., San Francisco, Calif. Died May 2, 1946.

THORINGTON, James (thôr'ing-tŭn), surgeon; b. Davenport, Ia., June 6, 1858; s. James and Mary (Parker) T.; ed. Davenport until 1874; studied Princeton, 1875-76; M.D., Jefferson Med. Coll., Phila., 1881; hon. A.M., Ursinus, 1894; m. Florence May Jennings, Sept. 15, 1885; children—James Monroe, Richard Wainwright. Surgeon of Panama R.R. Co., Colon (Aspinwall), Isthmus of Panama, 1882-89; now emeritus prof. diseases of the eye, Phila. Polyclinic and Graduates in Medicine. Mem. Am. Ophthal. Soc., A.M.A. Author: Retinoscopy, 6th edit.; Refraction and How to Refract, 7th edit., 1930; The Ophthalmoscope and How to Use It, 1906; Prisms, Their Use and Equivalents, 1913; Refraction of the Eye, 1916, 30; Methods of Refraction, translated into Chinese. Has written much in med. jours. Address: 2031 Chestnut St., Philadelphia, Pa. Died Oct. 27, 1944.

THORNBURG, Charles Lewis (thôrn'bûrg), mathematician; b. Barboursville, W.Va., Apr. 17, 1859; s. James Lewis and Virginia Frances (Handley) T.; grad. Marshall Coll., Huntington, W.Va., 1876; B.S., Vanderbilt, 1881, B.E., 1882 C.E., 1882, C.E., 1883, Ph.D., 1884; LL.D., Lehigh, 1925; m. Mary Eulalia Creen Nov. 4, 1886; children—Eulalie, Charles Garland, Chesley Covington, Lewis, Marion, Richard Beaumont, Lucille Leighton, Frances Green. Fellow in mathematics, 1881-82, grad. in mathematics, 1882-84, instr. engring. dept., 1884-86, Vanderbilt; adj.

prof. in engring. dept. and astronomy, 1886-95, prof. mathematics and astronomy, 1895-1925, sec. of faculty, 1900-23, Lehigh U., now prof. emeritus. Fellow A.A.A.S.; mem. Am. Math. Soc., Soc. Promotion Engring. Edn., Beta Theta Pi, Phi Beta Kappa, Tau Beta Pi. Democrat. Methodist. Author: Calculus Notes, 1906; (brochure) Elementary Differential Equations, 1914. Home: 238 E Market St., Bethlehem, Pa.* Died Oct. 14, 1911.

THORNDIKE, Edward Lee, psychologist; b. Williamsburg, Mass., Aug. 31, 1874; s. Edward R. and Abby B. (Ladd) T.; A.B., Wesleyan U., Conn., 1895; A.B., Harvard, 1896, A.M., 1897, LL.D., 1933; Ph.D., Columbia U., 1898, Sc.D., 1929; Sc.D., Wesleyan and LL.D., Iowa, 1923; Sc.D., U. of Chicago, 1932; LL.D., Edinburgh, 1936; Sc.D., Athens, 1937; m. Elizabeth Moulton, Aug. 29, 1900; children—Elizabeth Frances, Virginia (dec.), Edward Moulton, Robert Ladd, Alan Moulton. Instr. edn. and teaching, Western Reserve U., 1898-99; instr. genetic psychology, Teachers Coll., Columbia, 1899-1901, adj. prof. ednl. psychology, 1901-04, prof., 1904-40, emeritus prof. since 1941; Wm. James lecturer, Harvard University, 1942-43. Fellow A.A.A.S. (president, 1934), N.Y. Acad. Sciences; mem. Nat. Acad. Science, Am. Philos. Soc., Am. Psychol. Assn., Am. Acad. of Arts and Sciences; hon. mem. Brit. Psychol. Assn. Clubs: Century (New York); Cosmos (Washington). Author: Educational Psychology, 1903; Mental and Social Measurements, 1904; Elements of Psychology, 1905; Principles of Teaching, 1905; Animal Intelligence, 1911; The Original Nature of Man, 1913; The Psychology of Learning, 1914; Psychology of Arithmetic, 1922; Psychology of Algebra, 1923; The Measurement of Intelligence, 1926; Fundamentals of Learning, 1932; Your City, 1939; Human Nature and the other books, monographs and articles on psychological Social Order, 1940; Man and His Works, 1943; also various and educational subjects. Home: Montrose, N.Y. Died Aug. 9, 1949.

THORNE, Charles Hallett, retired mcht.; b. Chicago, Ill., Dec. 3, 1868; s. George R. and Ellen (Cobb) T.; ed. Hyde Park High Sch., Chicago, and U. of Mich.; m. Belle Wilber, Dec. 31, 1891; children—Hallett, Elizabeth (Mrs. Robert Andrews), Leslie (Mrs. Palmer D. Kountze). Entered employ of Montgomery Ward, as stock clerk, 1889, becoming treasurer, 1893, president, 1914, later, chairman board (now retired). Life trustee Northwestern University; trustee Occidental Coll. Clubs: Chicago, Chicago Athletic, Chicago Yacht, Annandale Golf. Home: 114 Los Altos Drive, Pasadena, Calif. Office: 30 N. Michigan Av., Chicago, Ill. Died Oct. 10, 1948.

THORNE, Oakleigh, capitalist; b. New Hamburg, N.Y., July 31, 1866; s. Edwin Thomas and Charlotte (Pearsall) T.; ed. Poughkeepsie, N.Y.; m. Helen T. Stafford, Feb. 26, 1889. Dir. Corp. Trust Co., Bank of Millbrook, N.Y. Mem. Nat. Acad. Design. Home: Millbrook, N.Y. Died May 23, 1948.

THORNTON, E(dward) Quin, physician; b. Merion, Ala., 1866; s. of Prof. Edward Quin and Sallie (Cocke) T.; M.D., Jefferson Med. Coll., Phila., 1890; m. Elizabeth Smith; 1 dau. Practiced in Phila. since 1890; prof. of therapeutics, Jefferson Med. Coll., emeritus since 1934; asso. visiting physicians, Pa. Hosp. Mem. A.M.A., Med. Soc. State of Pa., Pathol. Soc. Phila.; fellow Coll. of Physicians, Phila. Author: A Manual of Materia Medica; Dose Book and Manual of Prescription Writing; Medical Formulary, 1930. Editor: Tarrard on Treatment; Bruce on Treatment. Address: 1331 Pine St., Philadelphia, Pa.* Died Jan. 16, 1945.

THORP, Charles Monroe, lawyer; b. Hawley, Pa., Mar. 16, 1863; s. Lewis Hale and Anna Atkinson (Wise) T.; Ph.B., Cornell, 1884; m. Jessie Boulton, May 22, 1888 (died 1930); children—Margaret (Mrs. W. D. Stewart), George Boulton, Evelyn (Mrs. John R. Minter, dec.), Charles Monroe, Jessie (Mrs. E. W. Fiske, Jr.), Eleanore (Mrs. William F. Whitla); m. 2d, Goldie Donnell, Nov. 22, 1933. Admitted to Pa. bar, 1886, and practiced at Pittsburgh since; mem. Thorp, Bostwick, Reed & Armstrong; dir. Nat. Steel Corp., Edgewater Steel Co., Blaw-Knox Co., Copperweld Steel Co. Trustee C. C. Mellor Memorial Library, Edgewood (Pittsburgh). Mem. Am., Pa. State and Allegheny County bar assns., Phi Beta Kappa, Theta Delta Chi. Presbyterian. Clubs: Duquesne, University, Edgewood, Longue Vue, Pittsburgh Athletic; Surf, Indian Creek Country (Miami Beach). Home: 326 Maple Av., Edgewood, Pittsburgh, Pa.; and 42 La Gorce Circle, Miami Beach, Fla. Office: Grant Bldg., Pittsburgh, Pa. Died Dec. 14, 1942.

THRASHER, Paul McNeel, pres. Porter Mil. Acad.; b. Royal Oak, Md., July 9, 1886; s. John Calvin and Nannie Eliza (McNeel) T.; student Shepherd Coll. State Normal Sch., Shepherdstown, W.Va., 1900-03; B.A., Randolph-Macon Coll., Ashland, Va., 1906; grad. study, Lehigh U., Bethlehem, Pa., 1908-10; m. Nelle C. Sipe, Aug. 18, 1914; 1 son, Paul McNeel. Instr. McFerrin Sch., Martin, Tenn., 1906-08; instr. Porter Mil. Acad., Charleston, S.C., 1910-14; prin. McFerrin Sch., 1914-18; comdt. Porter Mil. Acad., 1918-27, Riverside Mil. Acad., Gainesville, Ga., 1927-28; pres. Porter Mil. Acad. since 1928. Democrat. Episcopalian. Contbr. to ednl. mags. Home: Military Academy, Charleston, S.C. Died Aug. 31, 1947.

THROOP, Frank Dwight (thrōōp), publisher; b. Mt. Pleasant, Ia., Sept. 23, 1878; s. George Eugene and Ida (Gimble) T.; grad. high sch., Mt. Pleasant, 1895, B.S., Ia. Wesleyan Coll., 1899, D.Litt., 1938; m. Mabel Leverich, June 21, 1905; children—Marjorie R. (Mrs. O. V. Calhoun), Mary Katharine (Mrs. W. P. McDonald). Began as reporter Muscatine (Ia.) Journal, 1900, later city editor, managing editor, and publisher, 1907-15; pub. Davenport Democrat, 1915-30; now pub. Lincoln (Neb.) Star; v.p. Lee Syndicate, consisting of 11 newspapers in Middle West. Trustee Iowa Wesleyan Coll. Mem. Associated Press, Am. Newspaper Publishers' Assn., Inland Daily Press Assn., Nat. Editorial Assn., Phi Delta Theta. Democrat. Episcopalian. Elk. Clubs: Commercial, University, Rotary, Country. Home: 2510 S. 24th St. Office: Star Bldg., Lincoln, Neb. Died Mar. 4, 1943.

THROOP, George Reeves (trōōp), ret. educator; b. Boydsville, Tenn., Jan. 24, 1882; s. George Reeves and Althea (Edwards) T.; A.B., De Pauw, 1901, A.M., 1903, LL.D., 1929; Ph.D., Cornell, 1905; studied U. of Chicago, 1907; studied and traveled abroad, 1910, 27; LL.D., U. of Mo., 1930; m. Esther Lincoln Fellows, Dec. 30, 1910; children—Alice Fellows, George Reeves, Esther Lincoln. Prof. Greek, Ill. Coll., Jacksonville, 1905-07; instr. Latin and Greek, 1907-09, asst. prof., 1909-14, asso. prof., 1914-17; Collier prof. Greek, 1917-18, Washington U.; asst. librarian, St. Louis Pub. Library, 1918-21; Collier prof. Greek and asst. to chancellor, Washington U., 1921-27, acting chancellor, 1927-28, chancellor 1928-44; prof. Latin, U. of Colo., summer 1909, Pa. State Coll., summers 1914, 16. Mem. Am. Philol. Assn., Archeol. Inst. America, Phi Beta Kappa, Phi Delta Theta. Democrat. Clubs: University, Round Table. Home: 121 N. Hanley Road, Clayton, Mo. Died Nov. 11, 1949.

THRUSTON, R(ogers) C(lark) Ballard (thrŭs′tŭn), b. Louisville, Ky., Nov. 6, 1858; s. Andrew Jackson and Frances Ann (Thruston) Ballard; Ph.B., Sheffield Scientific School, Yale Univ., 1880; M.A., University of Louisville, 1937; LL.D., University of Ky., 1942; at mother's request, 1884, added mother's family name, Thruston, to that which he had previously borne; bachelor. Metall. and asst. geol., Ky. Geol. Survey, 1882-87; resigned to engage in pvt. enterprises, and has devoted attention mainly to scientific, historic and patriotic work. Chmn. Louisville Chapter of Am. Red Cross, 1917-18; asst. mgr. lake div. Am. Red Cross, for Ky., 1918-20. Episcopalian. Mem. Sons of Am. Revolution (pres.-gen., 1913, 1914); mem. S.C.W. (gov. Ky. Soc., 1909-11, 1922), Va. Soc. of the Cincinnati, Yale Alumni Assn. of Ky. (pres. 1911-15, 19), Engrs. and Architects Club, Louisville, A.A.A.S., The Filson Club (pres. since 1923), Am. Miss. Valley, Ky., Ill., Va. and Md. hist. socs., etc. Clubs: Pendennis (Louisville); Cosmos (Washington). Address: The Filson Club, Louisville, Ky.* Died Dec. 30, 1946.

THURNAUER, Gustav (tûrn′ou-ĕr), chemist; b. San Francisco, Calif., Jan. 30, 1867; s. William and Minna (Bruell) T.; ed. Realschule, Bayreuth, Germany, 1877-83; Industrieschule, Nuremberg, 1884-86; A.M., Ph.D., U. of Berlin, 1890; m. Therese Mayer-Weismann, May 21, 1907. Asst. chemist Gewerbemuseum, Nuremberg, 1890-92; chemist Fairfield (Conn.) Chem. Works, 1893; chemist Chicago & Aurora Smelting & Refining Works, 1894-99; sec. and treas. Aurora Metal Co., mfrs. bearing metals, metallic packing for locomotives and aluminum-bronze diecastings, 1899-1912, vice-president and treasurer, 1912-1934, president, 1934-40, chairman board since 1941. Mem. Aurora Public Library, 1905-43; treas. Anti-Tuberculosis Soc., 1911-39; dir. Pub. Health Assn. since 1919; first pres. Aurora Social Service Fedn. (now Aurora Community Chest), 1922, 23, dir. budget com. 1923-43 (past chmn.). Mem. Am. Chem. Soc. (v p. Chicago sect., 1901, 09; councilor, 1908), Aurora Chamber Commerce. Elk. Clubs: Chemists, Ill. Athletic (Chicago). Contbr. articles pertaining to metals and alloys, etc. Home: 563 Downer Pl. Address: Aurora Metal Co., Aurora, Ill. Died 1947.

THURSBY, Emma Cecelia, singer, teacher concert, oratorio and operatic singing; b. Brooklyn, Feb. 21, 1854; d. John Barnes and Jane Ann (Bennet) Thursby; ed. Moravian Sem., Bethlehem, Pa.; studied music under Julius Meyer, Achille Errani, Madame Rudersdorff, and under Maurice Strakosch; unmarried. Sang for a year in Plymouth Ch., Brooklyn; traveled with Gilmore; later sang at Broadway Tabernacle; toured U.S. and Canada with Maurice Strakosch; in 1878 went to England; toured that country and provinces; appeared in Paris and prin. cities of Europe. Last public tour in U.S. as soloist with Thomas Orchestra; gave concerts in Japan and China, 1903. Mem. Assn. Artists and Musicians of Paris. Address: 34 Gramercy Park, New York. Died July 4, 1934.

THURSTON, Edward Sampson (thûrs′tŭn), prof. law; b. New York, N.Y., Aug. 8, 1876; s. William R., Jr., and Maria (Sampson) T.; A.B., Harvard, 1898, A.M., 1900, LL.B., 1901; hon. M.A., Yale, 1919; m. Florence Chapman Holbrooke, Apr. 21, 1908; children—Ethel Holbrooke, William Richardson. Practiced law in N.Y. City, 1901-06; instr. law, Ind. U., 1906; asst. prof. and prof. law, George Washington U., 1906-10; prof. law, U. of Ill., 1910-11, U. of Minn., 1911-19, Yale, 1919-29, Harvard, 1929-42; prof. emeritus, 1942. Vis. lecturer Sch. of Jurisprudence, U. of Calif., 1942-43; prof. law, Hastings College of Law, U. of Calif., since 1943. Maj. and lt. col., Judge Advocates Dept., Washington, D.C., World War I, later judge advocate A.E.F. in North Russia. Mem. Am. Acad. of Arts and Sciences, Am. Law Inst., Am. Bar Assn. Author: Cases in Quasi-Contract, 1916; Cases on Restitution, 1940; Cases on Torts (with Warren A. Seavey), 1942. Address: Hastings College of Law, 515 Van Ness Av., San Francisco 2, Calif. Died Feb. 10, 1948.

THURSTON, Henry Winfred, social worker; b. Barre, Vt., Feb. 28, 1861; s. Wilson and Frances Lois (Kinney) T.; A.B., Dartmouth, 1886; Ph.D., Columbia, 1918; m. Charlotte E. Skinner, Nov. 27, 1890 (dec.); children—Henry Winfred, Marjorie (dec.), Charlotte Howe, Robert Ray. Supt. schs., Elk Point, Dak., 1886-87; teacher of science, Hyde Park High Sch., Chicago, 1887-88; prin. Lyons Twp. High Sch., LaGrange, Ill., 1888-93; teacher Englewood High Sch., Chicago, 1893-94; teacher civics and economics, Hyde Park High Sch., 1894-99; prin. branch, same sch., Jan.-May, 1900; head dept. of sociology, Chicago Normal Sch., 1900-05; chief probation officer, Cook County Juvenile Court, Chicago, 1905-09; state supt. Ill. Children's Home and Aid Soc., Apr. 1, 1909-12; head Children's Dept., New York Sch. of Social Work, 1912-31. Chmn. sub-com. on probation N.Y. C.O.S. Criminal Courts Com., 1914-34. Contrbg. editor on children The Survey, 1914-17. Chmn. div. on children Nat. Conf. Social Work, 1917-20; exec. com. Child Welfare League America (chmn. 1923-26); chmn. advisory com. Dept. of Boarding Homes, N.Y. Children's Aid Soc., 1923-34; sec. Class of 1886, Dartmouth Coll., 1936-43. Mem. Theta Delta Chi. Presbyn. Author: In Memoriam—W. H. Ray, 1891: Economics and Industrial History, 1899; Spare Time and Delinquency, 1918; The Dependent Child, 1930; Concerning Juvenile Delinquency, 1942. Home: 215 Walnut St., Montclair, N.J.* Died Sep. 19, 1946.

TIBBALS, C(harles) Austin, Jr. (tĭb′ăls), educator; b. N.Y. City, July 23, 1881; s. Rev. Charles Austin and Mary Louise (Watkins) T.; student Columbia, 1899-1902; A.B., U. of Wis., 1904, A.M., 1906, Ph.D., 1908; m. Miriam Keith Reed, Dec. 10, 1908 (died Sept. 1925); children—Mary Reed, John Reed. Asst. and instr. chemistry, U. of Wis., 1902-08; later asst. prof., asso. prof. and prof. chemistry and dean of Armour Inst. Technology; dean, Armour Coll. Engring., Ill. Inst. Technology, 1937-43; dean of students, Ill. Inst. Tech., 1943-46; now dean emeritus, Ill. Inst. of Technology (retired Sept. 1946). Served as captain Ordnance Department, United States Army, 1918; engaged in research on high explosives and projectile loading; now capt. Ordnance Res. Fellow A.A.A.S.; mem. Soc. Promotion Engring. Edn., Western Soc. Engrs., Am. Coll. Personnel Assn., Nat. Assn. Deans and Advisers of Men, Am. Chem. Soc., Army Ordnance Assn., Tau Beta Pi, Sigma Xi, Phi Gamma Delta. Episcopalian. Clubs: University (Chicago); University of Wisconsin, Ill. Club of Columbia Alumni. Home: 511 Hawthorn Lane, Winnetka, Ill. Died Dec. 29, 1948.

TIDWELL, Josiah Blake, clergyman, educator; b. Cleveland, Ala., Oct. 8, 1870; s. Rev. Francis and Ann (Chambers) T.; A.B., Howard Coll., Birmingham, Ala., 1898, D.D., 1914; A.M., Baylor U., Waco, Tex., 1903; corr. work, U. of Chicago; LL.D., Union U., Jackson, Tenn., 1921; m. Kansas I. Reid, 1887 (died 1907); children— Eris (dec.), Reginal Arthur (dec.), Sallie Ann, Kalvart Kay, Francis (dec.), Broadus; m. 2d, Minnie Lee Hayes, Sept. 7, 1910 (died 1925); m. 3d, Mrs. Alma Wilson Lile, 1926. Successively teacher, pres. and business mgr. Decatur (Tex.) Bapt. Coll., 1898-1909; endowment sec. Baylor U., 1909-10, raising about $100,000; prof. Bibl. lit. same univ., since 1910; chmn. Baylor U. Com. on Research Work; mem. Baylor U. Student Loan Fund Com. Has served as mem. Bapt. Edn. Bd. of Tex., Exec. Bd. of Bapt. Conv. of Tex., Edn. Commn. of Southern Bapt. Conv., pres. Bapt. Gen. Conv. Tex. Trustee Southwestern Bapt. Theol. Sem., Ft. Worth, Tex. Mem. Am. Assn. Univ. Profs., Religious Edn. Assn., Assn. Bapt. Bible Teachers of the South, Tex. Hist. Soc. Democrat. Author: The Bible, Book by Book, 1914 (revised, 1922); An Outline for the Study of the Life of Christ, 1915; The Bible, Period by Period, 1916 (revised, 1923); The Sunday School Teacher Magnified, 1918; The Gospels and The Life of Christ, 1921; Genesis—A Study in the Plan of Redemption, 1924; Introducing the Old Testament, 1925; Christian Teachings, 1929; Thinking Straight About the Bible, 1935; Concerning Preachers, 1937; John and His Five Books, 1937; also wrote Christian Teachings About Social Problems, Bible Lands and Places, Christ in the Pentateuch, 1940, Syllabus of Three Months Lectures on "Preachers and Preaching"; Things You Should Know about the Bible, 1942. Contbr. to religious papers; has written Standard for 26 years. Speaker in churches and before religious assemblies. Traveled and studied in Europe, Syria, Palestine and Egypt, 1923. Has conducted many evangelistic meetings, and baptized more than 4,500 persons. Mem. exec. com. Southern Assn. Baptist Colls. and Secondary Schs.; mem. edn. commn. Southern Coöperative League; mem. Southwestern Assn. for Biblical Study and Research, etc. Home: 1309 S. 8th St., Waco, Tex. Died Mar. 17, 1946.

TIERNEY, John Thomas, corp. official; b. Woodland, Wis., Dec. 21, 1882; B.S., University of Wisconsin, 1903; m. Ellen Lewis Bradford; 1 son, John Thomas. President, trustee and member executive committee Koppers United Co., since 1933; chmn. of board, mem. exec. com. and trustee Eastern Gas & Fuel Associates; dir. Westinghouse Air Brake Co., Union Switch & Signal Co, Virginian Ry. Co., Flannery Bolt Co. Home: Schenley Apts. Office: Koppers Bldg., Pittsburgh, Pa. Died Oct. 25, 1944.

TIETJENS, Eunice (tē′jĕns) (Mrs. Cloyd Head), writer, lecturer; b. Chicago, Ill., July 29, 1884; d.

William A. and Idea (Strong) Hammond; student U. of Geneva, and Sorbonne, Paris; grad. Froebel Kindergarten Inst., Dresden, Germany; m. Paul Tietjens, 1904 (divorced 1914); 1 dau., Janet; m. 2d, Cloyd Head, Feb. 1920; 1 son, Marshall. On staff Poetry, Chicago, since 1913; war corr., Chicago Daily News, in France, 1917-18; lecturer poetry, U. of Miami, 1933-35. Dir. Pan-Am. League, Soc. Midland Authors. Author: Profiles from China (poems), 1917; Body and Raiment (poems), 1919; Jake (novel), 1921; Japan (textbook), 1924; Profiles from Home (poems), 1925; Arabesque (with husband; play), 1925; Boy of the Desert (juvenile fiction), 1928; Poetry of the Orient (anthology), 1928; Leaves in Windy Weather (poems), 1929; The Romance of Antar (fiction), 1929; The Jaw-Breakers Alphabet (with daughter; juvenile), 1930; China (textbook), 1930, Boys of the South Seas (juvenile fiction), 1931; The World at My Shoulder (autobiography), 1938. Address: 4176 Ingraham Highway, Coconut Grove, Fla. Died Sep. 6, 1944.

TIFFANY, Charles Lewis (tĭf'ă̆n-ĭ), merchant; b. New York City, Jan. 7, 1878; s. Louis Comfort and May (Goddard) T.; A.B., Yale, 1900; m. Katrina Brandes Ely, June 24, 1901 (died Mar. 11, 1927); m. 2d, Emilia A. Howell, May 6, 1931. Club: The Links. Home: 53 E. 66th St. Office: 727 Fifth Av., New York, N.Y. Died April 3, 1947.

TIFFANY, Herbert Thorndike, law author and compiler; b. New York, N.Y., Nov. 17, 1861; s. George Peabody and Anne Dickey (Thorndike) T.; A.B., Johns Hopkins U., 1883; LL.B., U. of Md., 1885; m. Harriet F. Poultney, Apr. 21, 1908 (died 1933). State reporter Md. Court of Appeals since 1920. Mem. Am. Law Inst. Unitarian. Club: University (Baltimore). Author: Law of Real Property, 1903, enlarged edit. 1920; Law of Landlord and Tenant, 1910; Outlines of Real Property (with Herbert M. Brune, Jr.), 1929. Editor of Md. Reports, vols. 135-171. Home: 701 Cathedral St., Baltimore, Md.* Died Aug. 14, 1944.

TIGERT, John James (tī'gẽrt), univ. pres.; b. Nashville, Tenn., Feb. 11, 1882; s. John James (bishop M.E. Ch., S.) and Amelia (McTyeire) T.; B.A., Vanderbilt U., 1904, B.A., Honor Sch. of Jurisprudence, Oxford U., Eng., 1907 (1st Rhodes scholar from Tenn.), M.A., 1915; studied Grad. Sch. U. of Minn., 1916; L.L.D., U. of Ky., 1921; Ed.D., Rhode Island, 1923; LL.D., Bates Coll., 1924, U. of N.M., 1924, Dickinson, 1928; D.C.L., Hillsdale, 1928; L.H.D., Muhlenberg, 1928; D.Litt., Fla. Southern College, 1933; LL.D., Rollins College and Stetson University, 1935, Louisiana State University, 1943; m. Edith Jackson, d. of M. C. Bristol, Aug. 25, 1909; children—John James 5th, Mary Jane (Mrs. William Blaine Thompson). Professor of philosophy and psychology, Central College, Fayette, Mo., 1907-09; pres. Ky. Wesleyan Coll., Winchester, 1909-11; prof. philosophy and psychology, U. of Ky., 1911-17, prof. psychology, 1917-21; U.S. commr. of edn., 1921-28; pres. U. of Fla. since 1928. Pres. Assn. of Colls. and Univs. of Ky., 1911; del. 4th Ecumenical Meth. Conf., Toronto, 1911. With Y.M.C.A., A.E.F., June 1918-July 1919; mem. Army Ednl. Corps, Apr.-July 1919; extension lecturer, A.E.F., U. of Beaune, France; lt. col. Spl. Res., U.S. Army. Chmn. edn. sect., 1st Pan-Pacific Conf. on Edn., Rehabilitation, Reclamation and Recreation, Honolulu, 1927; chmn. Federal Council on Citizenship Training, 1925-28, also of Com. on Selection of Rhodes Scholars; vice chmn. Federal Bd. for Vocational Edn., 1924-28; mem. Nat. Com. on Research in Secondary Edn., 2d Pan-Am. Scientific Congress, Federal Bd. of Maternity and Infant Hygiene (1921-28), 6th Industrial Congress for Art Edn., Drawing and Art Industry (v.p.), Am. Council on Edn., Boy Scouts of America (nat. council), President's Outdoor Recreation Conf. (1924), Federal Com. on Overseas Possessions, White House Conference on Child Health and Protection (1930), Nat. edn. com. Thomas Jefferson Memorial Foundation, Nat. Advisory Com. on Illiteracy, Nat. Council of Edn., Assn. of Am. Colleges, Am. Sportsmanship Brotherhood (dir.), Americanism Commn. of Am. Legion, N.E.A. (life dir.), Assn. Land-Grant Colls. and Univs. (exec. com.), Nat. Assn. of State Univs. (mem. exec. com., 1936-42); pres. 1939-40; chmn. Joint Com. on Accrediting representing Assn. Land-Grant Colls. and Univs., Nat. Assn. of State Univs., Assn. of Urban Univs. and Assn. of Am. Univs. Chmn. Conf. State Instns. in South, 1942-43; mem. Advisory Council Inst. of Pacific Relations; mem. Sponsoring Com. of Nat. Conf. for Mental Hygiene; mem. Com. on Inter-Am. Intellectual Cooperation, Department of State; member Southern Council on International Relations (director); member Advisory Council, Inst. of Indsl. Progress; mem. adv. com. Army Specialized Training Program, War Dept.; mem. bd. visitors U. S. Naval Acad., 1944; mem. bd. dirs. Nat. War Fund; chmn. Fla. War Fund; member Fla. School Code Com., Fla. State Chamber of Commerce (dir.), Gainesville (Fla.) Chamber Commerce, Southeastern (Athletic) Conf. (pres. 1935, 36, 46, 47), Southern University Conference (exec. com.; president 1940-41), Phi Beta Kappa (member Senate and Foundation), Phi Delta Theta (past pres.), Alpha Delta Sigma (v.p.), Kappa Delta Pi, Phi Kappa Phi, Kappa Phi Kappa, Phi Alpha Delta, Omicron Delta Kappa, Tau Kappa Alpha (nat. council), Pi Gamma Mu, Blue Key, etc. Trustee Vanderbilt Univ.; dir. Ringling Museum. Awards: George Washington Bicentenary medal; King Christian X (Denmark) Medal of Liberation. Mason. Moose. Clubs: Congressional Country (Washington, D.C.), University, Rotary, Golf and Country (Gainesville), Propeller. Author: Philosophy of the World War (monograph), also many addresses and pub. articles on edn. Co-author: The Child—His Nature and His Needs; The Book of Rural Life; High School Anthology—American Literature, English Literature, and Literary Types. Home: 1200 E Blvd., Gainesville, Fla. Deceased.

TIGHE, Lawrence Giblin, business exec.; b. Saratoga Springs, N.Y., Oct. 10, 1886; s. Thomas C. and Mary (Giblin) T.; ed. pub. schs.; m. Elizabeth Nichols, Oct. 29, 1913; children—Mary Jane, Daniel Lawrence. Salesman Gen. Electric Co., 1909-12; asst. mgr. AuSable Electric Co., Jackson, Mich., 1913-16; gen. supt. prodn. and distbn. Northern Ohio Power & Light Co., 1917-24, asst. gen. mgr., 1924-30; v.p. and Akron div. mgr. and dir. Ohio Edison Co. since 1930. Chairman executive committee Summit County Civilian Defense Council. Past president Akron Chamber of Commerce, Akron Better Business Bureau; director Akron Y.M.C.A. Trustee Catholic Service League. Elk, K.C. Clubs: Akron City (dir.), Portage Country, Akron Kiwanis (pres.). Home: Fairlawn, O. Office: Edison Bldg., Akron, O.* Deceased.

TILDSLEY, John Lee (tĭlds'lē), educator; b. Pittsburgh, Pa., Mar. 13, 1867; s. John and Elizabeth (Withington) T.; B.A., Princeton, 1893, M.A., 1894; studied univs. of Halle and Berlin, 1896-98, Ph.D., Halle, 1898; economics, Columbia, 1902; m. Bertha Alice Watters, June 24, 1896; children—Jane (dec.), John Lee (dec.), Margaret, Kathleen (dec.). Boudinot fellow in history, Princeton, 1893-94; teacher Greek and history, Lawrenceville (N.J.) Sch., 1894-96; teacher history, Morris High Sch., N.Y. City, 1898-1902; head of dept. of economics, High School of Commerce, 1902-08; principal De Witt Clinton High Sch., 1908-14; prin. High Sch. of Commerce, 1914-16; asso. supt. schs., Oct. 1916-July 1920, asst. supt., 1920-37, asso. supt., 1937, retired, Sept. 1, 1937, City of New York; lecturer New School of Social Research; Inglis lecturer, 1936. Mem. Headmasters Assn., Phi Beta Kappa. Democrat. Episcopalian. Speaker and writer on teaching and problems of sch. administration. Editor: Better Teaching in the High Schools, Teaching Science as a Way of Life, Ten Years Progress in the High Schools of New York, Developing the Inquiring Mind. Author: The Mounting Waste of the American Secondary School. Club: Nipnichsen. Home: 2741 Edgehill Av., Spuyten Duyvil, New York, N.Y. Died Nov. 21, 1948.

TILLEY, Morris Palmer, prof. English; b. Norfolk, Va., Feb. 7, 1876; s. Thomas Clark and Lois Frances (Miller) T.; grad. Norfolk Acad., 1894; A.B., U. of Va., 1897, M.A., 1899; Ph.D., U. of Leipzig, Germany, 1902; m. Mabel Louise Cook, June 14, 1906; children—Lois Frances, George Cook, Katherine Carhart (dec.), Thomas Clark. Teacher of English, Norfolk Acad., 1897-98; asst. in English, U. of Va., 1898-99; instr. in German, Syracuse U., 1902-03, instr. in English, 1903-05, asso. prof. English, 1905-06; asst. prof. English, U. of Mich., 1906-12, jr. prof., 1912-15, asso. prof., 1915-18, prof. since 1918. Dir. Cranbrook Sch. for Boys, Bloomfield Hills, Mich. Mem. Modern Lang. Assn. America, Mich. Acad. Sciences, Phi Beta Kappa, Phi Gamma Delta. Episcopalian. Author: Elizabethan Proverb Lore, 1926. Contbr. to tech. jours. Asst. editor of Early Modern English Dictionary. Home: 1015 Ferdon Rd., Ann Arbor, Mich. Died June 24, 1947.

TILLMAN, Abram Martin, lawyer; b. near Shelbyville, Tenn., Sept. 8, 1863; s. Lewis and Mary Catherine (Davidson) T.; LL.B., LL.M., Columbian (now George Washington) U. Law Sch., Washington, D.C., 1886; m. Sarah Clayton Ford, Nov. 28, 1894 (died Sept. 16, 1923); children—Louise Clayton (Mrs. Lee Clyde Gammill) Kathleen (Mrs. Ralph C. Hughes). Admitted to bar, 1886. In 1896 Rep. candidate for presdl. elector 6th Cong. Dist. Tenn., also sec. Rep. State Exec. Com. of Tenn.; U.S. atty. Middle Dist. of Tenn., 1898-1914; Rep. nominee for Congress, 6th Dist., 1902; endorsed by many members bench and bar for U.S. Dist. judge, Middle Dist. of Tenn., 1923; now atty. with U.S. Bd. of Tax Appeals. Mem. Bd. of Edn., Nashville, 1897-1900. Admitted to practice in Supreme Court of U.S., Court of Customs and Patent Appeals, Court of Claims of U.S., U.S. Court of Appeals for D.C., Dist. Court of the U.S. for D.C., U.S. Treasury Dept., Interstate Commerce Commn. Mem. Am. D.C., Federal and Tenn. bar assns., Am. Soc. Internat. Law. Mem. Southern Soc. of Washington, D.C., Tenn. Soc., D.C. Soc. Sons of Am. Revolution, Acad. Polit. Science, Nat. Geog. Soc., George Washington Univ. Gen. Alumni Assn. (life). Home: 1901 Wyoming Av. N.W. Office: Internal Bldg., Washington, D.C. Deceased.

TILLMAN, Samuel Escue, army officer; b. near Shelbyville, Tenn., Oct. 2, 1847; s. Lewis and Mary Catherine (Davidson) T.; grad. U.S. Mil. Acad., 1869; hon. M.A., Yale, 1906; m. Clara Williams, Apr. 20, 1887; 1 dau., Mrs. Katharine Tillman Martin. Second lt. 4th Arty., June 15, 1869; on frontier duty in Kan., 1869-70; asst. prof., 1870-73, and 1879-80, prof. chemistry, mineralogy and geology, with rank of col., 1880-1911, U.S. Mil. Acad.; retired by operation of law, Oct. 2, 1911; recalled to active service, June 6, 1917, and assigned to duty as supt. U.S. Mil. Acad. until June 12, 1919; brig. gen. U.S. Army retired, Mar. 4, 1919. D.S.M., June 11, 1919 "for especially meritorious and conspicuous services as supt. U.S. Mil. Acad. during the period of the emergency." Asst. astronomer U.S. Transit of Venus Expdn., Tasmania, 1874-75; instr. in mechanics, U.S. Mil. Acad., 1875-76; asst. engr. on the U.S. (Wheeler) explorations west of the 100th meridian, 1873-74 and 1876-79. Author: Essential Principles of Chemistry, 1884; Elementary Lessons in Heat, 1889; Elementary Mineralogy, 1894; Descriptive General Chemistry, 1899; Important Minerals and Rocks, 1900. Address: Century Assn., 7 W. 43d St., New York, N.Y. Died June 24, 1942.

TILLSON, John Charles Fremont, army officer; b. N.Y., May 26, 1856; grad. U.S. Mil. Acad., 1878; Army War Coll., 1910. Commd. add. 2d lt. 5th Inf., June 14, 1878; 2d lt., June 21, 1878; 1st lt., Mar. 24, 1883; capt. 14th Inf., Mar. 18, 1897; maj. 4th Inf., Mar. 12, 1902; lt. col. 18th Inf., Dec. 7, 1908; col. of inf., Nov. 27, 1911; assigned to 8th Inf., Mar. 28, 1912; trans. to 15th Inf., July 1, 1913. Prof. mil. science and tactics, North Ga. Agrl. Coll., Dahlonega, Ga., 1897-98; comd. Co. F, 14th Inf., China Relief Expdn., 1900; participated in capture of Peking and attack on Forbidden City; provost marshal, Am. Dist., Chinese City, until withdrawal of forces, May 1901; in charge Officers' Sch., Ft. Thomas, Ky., 1905-06; in Philippine Islands, 1908; duty Ft. Jay, N.Y., 1917. Address: War Dept., Washington. Died Dec. 15, 1941.

TILLY, David L., pres. New York Dock Co.; b. Brooklyn, N.Y., Dec. 14, 1887; s. William and Carrie (Norton) T.; student New York U.; m. Gertrude J. Tolkamp, Dec. 11, 1913; 1 son, Willard C. (dec.). With Erie R.R. Co., 1910-16; with N.Y. Dock Co. since 1916, now pres.; pres. N.Y. Dock Trade Facilities Corp., N.Y. Dock Ry.; dir. Intertype Corp.; trustee Brooklyn Savings Bank. Mem. Brooklyn Chamber of Commerce (chmn. exec. com. and dir.), N.Y. State Chamber of Commerce, N.Y. State Warehousemens Assn. (dir.), Commerce and Industry Assn. of New York (dir.); dir. Am. Short Line R.R. Assn.; Sec., dir. Maritime Assn. of New York. Trustee Polytechnic Inst. of Brooklyn, Brooklyn Hosp. Trustee Industrial Home for the Blind. Dir. Brooklyn Chapter, Am. Nat. Red Cross. Presbyterian. Mason (K.T., 32°, Shriner). Clubs: Whitehall, New York Produce Exchange Luncheon (New York); Rembrandt, Municipal (Brooklyn). Home: 235 Dover St., Brooklyn 29, N.Y. Office: 44 Whitehall St., New York 4, N.Y. Died Oct. 19, 1949.

TILSON, William J(osiah), judge; b. Clear Branch, Tenn., Aug. 13, 1871; s. William E. and Katharine M. (Sams) T.; A.B., Yale, 1894, LL.B., 1896, LL.M., 1897; m. Julia C. Romare, June 9, 1904; 1 son, Paul Romare. Admitted to Ga. bar, 1898, and practiced at Atlanta until 1926; judge, U.S. Dist. Court, Middle Ga. dist., 1926-28; judge, U.S. Customs Court, N.Y. City, since Mar. 17, 1928, presiding judge, June 1932-Dec. 1934. Republican. Episcopalian. Clubs: (hon. mem) Atlanta Athletic, Piedmont Driving (Atlanta); Kiwanis (Macon, Ga.). Home: 47 Woodland Av., Summit, N.J. Office: U.S. Customs Court, 102 Varick St., New York, N.Y. Died May 26, 1949.

TILTON, Frederic Arthur, ex-3d asst. postmaster gen.; b. Cleveland, O., July 10, 1876; s. Alfred and Mary Ann (Rieley) T.; student Western Reserve U., 1896-99; m. Rena Wilhelmina Wright, Nov. 26, 1919; 1 dau., Constance Elizabeth (adopted). Certified public accountant, Mich., 1910, N.Y., 1933, Fla., 1937; partner Haskins & Sells, 1921-29, and since 1933; 3d asst. postmaster gen. of U.S., 1929-33, in charge of fiscal affairs of dept. Chmn. State Bd. of Accountancy, Mich., 1913-25. Mem. Am. Inst. Pub. Accountants, Mich. Assn. Certified Pub. Accountants, Fla. Inst. Certified Public Accountants, Jacksonville Bd. of Commerce. Republican. Mason (32°, K.T.). Clubs: Congressional Country (Washington, D.C.); Timuquana Country (Jacksonville, Fla.). Home: 1633 Van Buren Av. N.W., Washington, D.C.; and Mandarin, Fla. Office: care Haskins & Sells, 67 Broad St., New York, N.Y.; and Barnett Nat. Bank Bldg., Jacksonville, Fla. Died Mar. 2, 1942.

TILY, Herbert James (tī'lē), merchant; b. Farnham, Eng., Feb. 3, 1866; s. James and S. Letitia (Coleman) T.; brought to U.S. in infancy; ed. pub. schs., business coll. and under pvt. tutors; hon. Mus.D., Villa Nova, 1913; LL.D., Lafayette Coll., 1932; A.M., Hahnemann Med. Coll., 1932; Mus.D., U. of Pa., 1937; L.H.D., Pa. Mil. Coll., 1939; m. Lucy P. Allen, Jan. 21, 1889; children—Harry Coleman, Lewis Herbert, Ethel Henrietta, Dorothy Osborne. Connected with Strawbridge & Clothier, Phila., since 1879, gen. mgr., 1905-1944, admitted to firm, 1918, v.p., 1922, pres. 1927-46, elected vice-chairman of the Board, 1947. Chairman National War Service Com. Dry Goods and Dept. Stores, World War. Mem. Com. on Business Ethics, NRA. Pres. Nat. Retail Dry Goods Assn., 1925-26; colleague Am. Guild Organists. Republican. Episcopalian. Mason (K.T., 32°). Clubs: Union League, Racquet, Musical Art (pres. 1922-23), Pen and Pencil. Home: Cynwyd, Pa. Office: 801 Market St., Phila., Pa. Died Dec. 28, 1948.

TIMBERMAN, Andrew, oculist, aurist; b. Hamilton, O., May 10, 1864; s. Andrew and Elizabeth (Flickinger) T.; student Otterbein Coll., Westerville, O., 1881-84, B.A., 1903; student U. of Mich., 1890-91; M.D., Miami Med. Coll., Cincinnati, O., 1894 (valedictorian); intern Cincinnati Gen. Hosp., 1894-95; studied univs. of Halle, Vienna and London, 1895-96; spl. study of cataract in India, 1910; m. Lelia Stanbery, June 19, 1895; children—Katharine (Mrs.

Francis J. Wright), Jean (Mrs. Harold D. Carter), Lelia (Mrs. Gerald Battelle Fenton), Elizabeth Anne (wife of Colonel Clayton E. Mullins, U.S. Army). Practiced, Columbus, O., since 1896; prof. ophthalmol., Ohio Med. U., 1899-1907, Starling-Ohio Med. Coll., 1907-13, Coll. of Medicine, Ohio State U., 1913-26; ophthal. surgeon Grant Hosp.; oculist for Medical Advisory Board, Columbus District, U.S. Army, 1917-19. Trustee Otterbein Coll., Columbus Y.M.C.A. Fellow Am. Coll. Surgeons; mem. A.M.A., Ohio State Med. Soc., Am. Acad. Ophthalmology and Oto-Laryngology, Columbus Acad. Medicine (pres. 1900). Republican. Presbyterian. Mason. Clubs: University, Crichton, Torch, Optimist. Contbr. numerous articles on med. and surg. topics. Retired July 1, 1942. Home: 91 Hamilton Park, Columbus, O. Died Oct. 15, 1946; buried in Venice Cemetery, Ross-Butler County, O.

TINKER, Clarence L., army officer; b. Nov. 21, 1887. Commd. 2d lt. inf., June 12, 1924; promoted through grades to lt. col.; temp. rank of brig. gen., Oct. 1940; apptd. comdr. Air Force in Hawaii, Dec. 1941. Address: War Dept., Washington, D.C.* Died June 7, 1942.

TINSMAN, Homer E(llsworth), lawyer; b. Romeo, Mich.; s. William H. and Mary J. (Hosner) Tinsman; A.B., Univ. of Mich., 1883; m. Christina P. Dale, Oct. 24, 1894. Admitted to Ill. bar, 1885; began practice, 1886; mem. firm of Burke, Hollett & Tinsman, 1887-93, then successively mem. Hollett & Tinsman, Hollett, Tinsman & Sauter, Tinsman, Rankin & Neltnor, and since 1913, of Tinsman & Blocki. Asst. county atty., 1889, 90; alderman 32d Ward, 1908, 09. Chmn. Draft Registration Bd. during World War. Mem. Am., Ill. State and Chicago bar assns., Chicago Law Inst., Art Inst. Chicago, Evanston Hist. Soc. Republican. Congregationalist. Mason (32°, Shriner), Odd Fellow. Clubs: Union League, Hamilton, Collegiate. Home: 418 Hamilton St., Evanston, Ill. Office: First Nat. Bank Bldg., Chicago. Died March 11, 1937.

TITTLE, Ernest Fremont (tĭt'l), clergyman; b. Springfield, O., Oct. 21, 1885; s. Clayton Darius and Elizabeth (Henry) T.; A.B., Ohio Wesleyan U., 1906; B.D., Drew Theol. Sem., 1908; D.D., Ohio Wesleyan U., Garrett Biblical Inst. and Yale; LL.D., Wittenberg Coll.; m. Glenna Myers, June 11, 1908; children—John Myers, Elizabeth Ann, William Myers. Ordained Meth. ministry, 1910; pastor Christiansburg, O., 1908-10, Riverdale, Dayton, O., 1910-13, University Ch., Delaware, O., 1913-16, Broad St. Ch., Columbus, O., 1916-18, 1st Ch., Evanston, Ill., since Dec. 1918. Lecturer, Lyman Beecher Foundation, Yale U., 1932, Ayer Foundation, Colgate-Rochester Div. Sch., 1935; also Earl lectures Pacific Sch. of Religion, 1934, Gates Memorial lectures, Grinnell Coll., 1934, and Wilkin lectures U. of Ill., 1931, Mendenhall lectures DePauw U., 1921, Russell lectures Auburn Theol. Sem., 1934, Merrick lectures, Ohio Wesleyan U., 1940. Univ. preacher, Univ. of Chicago, Cornell Univ. With Army Y.M.C.A. in U.S., 2 mos., in France, 6 mos.; participated in St. Mihiel offensive. Trustee Northwestern U. Mem. World Peace Commn., Meth. Ch.; mem. Fed. Council Commn. to Study the Basis of a Just and Durable Peace, Fed. Council Commn. on the War in the Light of Christian Faith, and the Dept. of International Justice and Goodwill. Mem. Oxford Conf., 1937, Del. Conf., 1942, Cleveland Conf., 1945. Mem. Phi Kappa Psi, Phi Beta Kappa. Mason. Author: What Must the Church Do to Be Saved?, 1921; The Religion of the Spirit, 1928; The Foolishness of Preaching, 1930; We Need Religion, 1931; Jesus After Nineteen Centuries, 1932; A World that Cannot Be Shaken, 1933; A Way to Life, 1935; Christians in an Unchristian Society, 1939; The Lord's Prayer, 1942. Home: 1810 Hinman Av., Evanston, Ill. Died Aug. 3, 1949.

TITUS, Ellwood Valentine, farming; b. nr. Glen Cove, L.I., Jan. 11, 1853; s. James and Caroline (Valentine) T.; ed. pub. and pvt. schs.; m. M. Louise Cox, Apr. 15, 1875; 1 dau., Caroline (widow of Percy Eastment). Engaged in farming in Nassau County, N.Y., until 1900; actively identified with promotion of improvements in farming for many years; a founder, and for 16 years chmn. bd. Nassau County Farm Bur., hon. dir. for life since Jan. 1934; a leader in orgn. of N.Y. State Farm Bur. Fedn. and its transportation dir. for 12 yrs. (also v.p. and mem. exec. com.; hon. dir. for life); noted for success in promoting the spirit of coöperation between farmers and railroad officers. Dir. of Merchants Mutual Casualty Co. of Buffalo, 12 yrs. Officer or dir. many charitable and civic orgns. Awarded gold medal by Am. Farm Bur. Federation, 1931 "for distinguished service in organized agriculture." Republican. Mem. Soc. of Friends. Home: 57 Duck Pond Rd., Glen Cove, L.I., N.Y. Died Jan. 23, 1941.

TOBIN, Daniel Aloysius (tō'bĭn); b. New York, N.Y., Nov. 23, 1883; s. William D. and Mary (Mullen) T.; ed. pub. sch. and St. Stephens Sch.; Coll. City of New York, 1900-04; m. Martha D. Dolgner, Oct. 26, 1904. Connected with brokerage business since 1905; investment counsel. Supreme dir. Knights of Columbus since 1924. Pres. K. of C. Hospital Association of New York State; treasurer National Catholic Community Service, Brooklyn and Long Island; national director Boy Scouts of America since 1925. Awarded Silver Buffalo "for distinguished service to boyhood," 1935. Elk. Clubs: Catholic (New York); Crescent Athletic (Brooklyn). Home: 305 Linden Blvd., Brooklyn, N.Y. Office: 405 Lexington Av., New York, N.Y. Died May 28, 1942.

TOCH, Maximilian (tŏk), chemist; b. New York, N.Y., July 17, 1864; s. Moses and Caroline (Levy) T.; spl. course in chemistry, New York U., 1882, LL.B., 1886; post grad. special course, Columbia U., 1896; Chem. E., Cooper Union; D.Sc., Peking Univ., 1924; m. Hermine E. Levy, Oct. 14, 1891; children—Elaine Constance, Alma, Maxine. Lecturer on organic chemistry, Columbia, 1905-06; municipal lecturer on paint, Coll. City of New York, 1909; adj. prof. industrial chemistry, Cooper Union, 1919-24; hon. prof. chem. engring. and industrial chemistry, U. of Peking and Nat. Inst. Technology, China, 1924; prof. chemistry of artistic painting, Nat. Acad. Design, New York, 1924-36; pres. and chief chemist Toch Bros., Inc.; chmn. bd. Standard Varnish Works, mfrs. paints, varnishes, enamels and chemicals. Fellow A.A.A.S., Micros. Soc. of New York, Royal Photographic Soc., Chem. Soc. of London, Am. Inst. Chemists (pres.); mem. Am. Chem. Soc., Soc. Chem. Industry, Am. Inst. Chemical Engineers, Hon. member American Institute of Chemists. Society of American Magicians. In charge of camouflage, United States, World War I, and originator of Toch system of camouflage. Clubs: Chemists' (ex-pres.), Camera (New York); Cosmos (Washington). Author: Materials for Permanent Painting, 1911; How to Paint Permanent Pictures, 1921; Chemistry and Technology of Paints, 3d edit., 1925; Protection and Decoration of Concrete, 1930; Paint, Painting and Restoration, 1931, 2d edition, 1945. Home: 50 Central Park West, New York, N.Y. Office: 2600 Richmond Terrace, Staten Island, N.Y. Died May 26, 1946.

TODD, Albert W., president United Shoe Machinery Corp.; b. Boston, Mass., May 16, 1884; s. Charles R. and Annie E. (Beale) T.; m. Gertrude E. M. Todd, Oct 17, 1917; 1 son, Norman M. With United Shoe Machinery Corp. since Aug. 25, 1901, became gen. mgr., 1927, dir., 1930, v.p., 1934, mem. exec. com., 1937, and pres. since June 1939; also pres. Campbell Bosworth Machinery Co., W. W. Cross & Co., Littleway Process Co.; dir. Brit. United Shoe Machinery Co., B. B. Chemical Co., S. A. Felton & Son Co., Krippendorf Kalculator Co., Security Eyelet Co., Turner Tanning Machinery Co., United Last Co., Davis Paper Co. Clubs: Algonquin, Cohasset Golf, Sand Bridge; Union (Boston). Home: Cohasset, Mass. Office: 140 Federal St., Boston, Mass. Died May 26, 1949.

TODD, Ambrose Giddings, lawyer; b. Brooklyn, N.Y., Apr. 24, 1863; s. Edward and Lydia Alden (Giddings) T.; A.B., Princeton, 1884, M.A., 1887; LL.B., Columbia, 1887; m. Eveline T., d. of Forrest H. Parker, June 3, 1908. Admitted N.Y. bar, 1887; became mem. Reeves & Todd, 1890, and since of its various successors; mem. Reeves, Todd, Ely & Beaty until retirement; dir. Am. Metal Co., Ltd., U.S. Metals Refining Co., N.Y. and Honduras Rosario Mining Co.; mem. adv. bd. Produce Exchange Branch of Chase Nat. Bank. 1st lt. Co. G, 7th Regt., N.Y.; awarded Cross of Honor of 7th Regt. and N.Y. State. Formerly pres., now life mem. grad. council, Princeton U.; trustee N.Y. State Colonization Soc., Princeton Yenching Foundation. Mem. Am. Bar Assn., N.Y. County Lawyers Assn. Democrat. Episcopalian. Clubs: University, Princeton, Bankers (New York); Adirondack League. Home: 29 E. 64th St., New York, N.Y.* Died Aug. 10, 1947.

TODD, Arthur James, sociologist; b. Petaluma, Calif., May 6, 1878; s. Hugh Galbraith and Clara (Tuller) T.; B.L., U. of Calif., 1904; studied univs. Aix-Marseilles, Paris and Munich, 1909-10; Ph.D., Yale, 1911; m. Martha Nancy Gaddis, Sept. 14, 1904. Dir. boys' work, Coll. Settlement, West Berkeley, Calif., 1903, South Park Settlement, San Francisco, 1903-06; chief probation officer, San Francisco, 1905-08; instr. sociology, Univ. of Ill., 1911-13, asso., 1913-14; prof. and head dept. sociology, Univ. of Pittsburgh, 1914-15; prof. sociology and dir. training course for social and civic work, 1915-21 (on leave 1919-21), U. of Minn.; dir. industrial relations, B. Kuppenheimer & Co., Chicago, 1919-25; and visiting prof. of sociology, Northwestern University, 1919-21, prof., 1921-43, also chairman of department of sociology, emeritus since 1943. Special examiner National War Labor Board, 1942-44. Mgr. Washington office, Christian Science Committee on Publication, since 1944. President Central Council of Social Agencies, Minneapolis, Minn., 1916-19, Am. Assn. Amateur Art Clubs, 1925-27, Nat. Assn. Schs. Social Adminstrs., 1943-45; mem. Chicago Recreation Commn., Am. Sociol. Society, Am. Assn. Social Workers, Am. Inst. Criminal Law and Criminology, International Kriminalistische Verein, Delta Upsilon, Phi Beta Kappa, Kappa Delta Pi, Associé de l'Institut International de Sociologie. Clubs: Cosmos, Arts (Washington); Business Men's Art (Chicago); Univ. (Evanston). Author: The Primitive Family as an Educational Agency, 1913; Theories of Social Progress, 1918; The Scientific Spirit and Social Work, 1919; Three Wise Men of the East, 1927; The Secularization of Domestic Relations, 1928; Industry and Society, 1933. Co-author: Democracy and Reconstruction, 1919; College Teaching, 1920. Editor: Recreation Survey of Chicago, 5 volumes, 1937-40; Life and Letters of Martha Gaddis Todd, 1940. Home: 1623 Lanier Place, N.W. Office: 1127 Munsey Bldg., Washington, D.C. Died Nov. 28, 1948.

TODD, G(eorge) Carroll, lawyer; b. Smithfield, Va., Feb. 1, 1879; s. John W. and Everallin (Carroll) T.; B.S., Columbian (now George Washington) Univ., 1899, A.M., 1903, LL.B., from same, 1902, LL.M., 1903, LL.D., 1919; m. Pocahontas Bolling Smith, Sept. 20, 1905 (died 1935); children—Mary Meredith (Mrs. Christopher Stuart), Frances Carroll; m. 2d, Pauline Bourke Maish, Nov. 25, 1939. With U.S. Dept. Justice, Washington, engaged in proceedings under the Anti-Trust Act, 1902-05; moved to New York, 1905; later spl. asst. to atty.-gen. of U.S. in proceedings under Sherman Act and Interstate Commerce Act against anthracite railroads, also in proceedings leading to final decree in Union Pacific-Southern Pacific merger case; apptd. by Pres. and confirmed by Senate as the asst. to atty. gen. of U.S., 1913-19; in charge of enforcement of Sherman Anti-Trust Act and other interstate commerce laws; resigned, Apr. 1, 1919, and returned to gen. practice; dir. and mem. exec. com. Equitable Life Assurance Soc. of U.S. Democrat. Episcopalian. Mem. Bar of D.C., New York, and of Supreme Court of U.S. Clubs: Metropolitan, Chevy Chase; University (New York). Home: 2029 Connecticut Av. N.W., Washington, D.C.; and Cobham, Va. Office: 1001 15th St. N.W., Washington, D.C. Died Dec. 12, 1947.

TODD, Hiram Eugene, lawyer; b. Kankakee, Ill., Sept. 10, 1874; s. Walter Wilson and Asenath (Gerard) T.; student U. of Ill., 1893-94; LL.B., Kent Coll. of Law, Chicago, 1897; m. Bertha M. Ferris, Sept. 10, 1900; children—Sarah Gerard (Mrs. William E. Connell), Harriet Asenath, James Rowcliffe. Admitted to Ill. bar, 1897, and since practiced in Peoria; pres. and treas. Hart-Carter Co., Hart Grain Weigher Co., v.p. and dir. Central Nat. Bank and Trust Co. of Peoria, Allaire, Woodward & Co.; dir. Central City Loan & Home Assn. Mem. Peoria City Council 2 yrs.; mem. Bd. of Supervisors Peoria County 3 yrs.; mem. Constl. Conv. of Ill., 1920. Mem. Kappa Sigma. Republican. Presbyterian. Mason. Clubs: Creve Coeur Country; Union League (Chicago). Home: Hotel Pere Marquette. Office: Central Nat. Bank Bldg., Peoria, Ill. Died Oct. 1, 1946.

TODD, John Reynard, engring. exec.; b. Johnstown, Wis., Oct. 27, 1867; s. Rev. James D. and Susan S. (Webster) T.; A.B., Princeton, 1889, A.M., 1891; student New York Law Sch., 1892-93; LL.D., Davidson (N.C.) Coll., 1923; m. Alice Peck Bray, July 16, 1895; children—Frances Bray (Mrs. Newell C. Bolton), Webster Bray. Admitted to bar, 1894, and practiced at New York. Republican. Presbyterian. Clubs: Union League, Baltusrol Golf. Home: (summer) East Hampton, L.I., N.Y. Office: 420 Lexington Av., New York. Died May 12, 1945.

TOLAN, John Harvey (tō'lăn), congressman, lawyer; b. St. Peter, Minn., Jan. 15, 1877; s. George and Elizabeth (Hunter) T.; LL.B., U. of Kan., 1902; m. Alma D. Deschamps, Sept. 4, 1907; children—Denise, John H., Adrienne, George E., Alma Jean. County atty., Deer Lodge County, Mont., 1902-06; practiced law in Oakland, Calif., since 1915; mem. 74th to 79th Congresses 1935-47), 7th Calif. Dist. Democrat. Catholic. K.C. Eagle, Moose. Home: 1749 Pleasant Valley Av., Oakland; also Dorchester House, Washington, D.C. Office: Broadway Bldg., Oakland, Calif.* Died June 30, 1947.

TOLAND, Edmund M. (tō'lănd), lawyer; b. Boston, Mass., Nov. 15, 1898; s. John Francis and Mary Ann (Fallon) T.; LL.B., Georgetown U., 1924; m. Lenora S. Sheehan, Jan. 16, 1930; children—Margaret Mary, Laura Marie, Edmund M., John Francis S., Francis. Admitted to U.S. Dist. Court bar, 1924; in pvt. practice, Washington, D.C., since 1927; with Bur. of Investigation, Dept. of Justice, 1924-Apr. 1925; spl. asst. to atty. gen. of U.S., 1925-27; asso. counsel Bankruptcy Investigation, N.Y. City, 1929; gen. counsel to Spl. Congl. Com. to Investigate Nat. Labor Relations Bd., since 1929; apptd. gen. counsel for the House Naval Affairs Com., Apr. 16, 1941. Mem. Am. and D.C. bar assns., Friendly Sons of St. Patrick. Catholic. Club: Press (Washington). Home: 3749 Jocelyn St. Office: 940 Investment Bldg., Washington, D.C. Died June 4, 1942.

TOLBERT, Ward Van der Hoof (tŏl'bērt), lawyer; b. Weston, N.Y., Apr. 28, 1877; s. Isaac L. and Emma C. (Van der Hoof) T.; student Cook Acad., Mountour Falls, N.Y., 1897; A.B., U. of Rochester, 1902; LL.B., Columbia, 1905; m. Edith L. Williams, Jan. 16, 1906; 1 dau., Kathryn (Mrs. Robert J. Smith). Admitted to N.Y. bar, 1905; pres. N B Investment Corp., Delas Investment Corp.; v.p. and dir. Frances Investment Corp.; dir. H. Clay Glover Co., McRae Bldg. Co., Woolrae Realty Corp., 47 E. 88th St. Corp., 585 West End Av. Corp. N.Y. State senator, 1920-22; Rep. candidate for Supreme Court, 1st Judicial Dist., N.Y., 1924; Rep. presidential elector, 1936; mem. Rep. State Com., 1935-38. Mem. Am., N.Y., N.Y. County and Westchester County bar assns. Republican. Presbyterian. Mason. Clubs: National Republican, Downtown Athletic, Drug and Chemical (New York); Pelham (N.Y.) Country; Kishawana Country (Brewster, N.Y.). Home: 16 Bonmar Road, Pelham Manor, N.Y. Office: 55 Liberty St., New York, N.Y. Died Apr. 11, 1946.

TOLLESON, William N. (tŏl'ĕ-sŭn), pres. Civitan Internat.; b. Kirby, Ark., Sept. 22, 1886; s. Robert A. and Marie (McElroy) T.; grad. Amity Military Acad., 1902; student Henderson-Brown Coll., Arkadelphia, Ark.; m. Nell Cordelia Thompson, Sept. 10, 1908; children—Bobbie Joy, William N. Jr. Admitted to Okla. bar, 1908; began in mortgage and loan dept. of bank; with Gen. Am. Life Insurance Co., St. Louis, Mo., in various capacities since 1914, now investment supervisor of Southwest territory. Mem. Civitan Internat. since 1936, dist. gov., 1936-43, pres., 1943-44. Republican. Methodist. Mason (Shriner). Active in civic affairs in many capacities

Home: 4564 Bordeaux. Address: 1019 Republic Bank Bldg., Dallas, Texas. Died Apr. 1, 1946.

TOLMAN, Cyrus Fisher, Jr., geologist; b. Chicago, June 2, 1873; s. Rev. Cyrus F. and Mary (Bronson) T.; B.S., U. of Chicago, 1896; grad. student and fellow in geology, same, 1896-99; m. Hannah Martha Van Steen, Aug. 22, 1900. Spl. asst. geologist, U.S. Geol. Survey, 1896; cons. geologist and mining engr. since 1899; prof. geology, U. of Ariz., 1905-06, prof. geology and mining, 1906-12; territorial geologist of Ariz., 1910-12; asso. prof. econ. geology, Stanford U., 1912-19, and prof. since 1919. Mem. 1st Ill. Vols., Spanish-Am. War, 1898, service in Cuba. Fellow Geol. Soc. Am.; mem. Am. Inst. Mining Engrs., Seismol. Soc. Am. (v.p.). Author: The Graphic Solution of Fault Problems, 1911. Contbr. on geol. processes of semi-arid regions, geology of Ariz. and Calif., ore deposits, ground water, oil (especially origin of oil), the geology of dam foundations and reservoir sites, etc. Home: Stanford University, Calif. Died Oct. 13, 1942.

TOLMAN, Edgar Bronson (tŏl'măn), lawyer; b. Nowgong, British India, Sept. 5, 1859; s. Rev. Cyrus Fisher (D.D.) and Mary Ruth (Bronson) T.; A.B., U. of Chicago, 1880, A.M., 1883; LL.B., Union Coll. Law, 1882; LL.D., Northwestern U., 1927; m. Nellie M. Browne, 1883 (died 1888); children—Ruth M., Helen I.; m. 2d, Blanche N. Stevens, 1889 (died 1903); children—Mary L. (Mrs. Eric W. Stubbs), Edgar B., Blanche S. (Mrs. Albert C. Fiedler). Practiced in Chicago since 1882; mem. Tolman, Megan & Bryant. Corp. counsel, Chicago, 1903-06; spl. asst. to U.S. atty. gen., 1934-38. Mem. adv. com. to U.S. Supreme Court to draft and submit federal rules of civil procedure since 1934. Major 1st Ill. Volunteer Inf., Spanish-Am. War; participated in Santiago campaign; maj. of Inf. U.S. Army, assigned to supervise adminstrn. of the draft in Ill., 1917-18; awarded D.S.M. and promoted to rank of lt. col. J.A.G. Awarded Am. Bar Assn. medal, July 12, 1939. Editor-in-chief Am. Bar Assn. Jour., 1920-47, editor-in-chief emeritus since 1946. Mem. Illinois State Bar Assn. (pres. 1917-18), Chicago Bar Assn. (pres. 1911-12), Law Club of Chicago (pres. 1910-11), Am. Law Inst. (council, 1924-47), Ill. Soc. S.A.R. (ex-pres.), Ill. Commandery Soc. Foreign Wars of U.S. (ex-pres.), Ill. branch Soc. Army of Santiago de Cuba, Am. Legion, Delta Kappa Epsilon. Democrat. Clubs: Chicago Athletic, Flossmoor Country, Iroquois, Quadrangle. Home: 5554 Woodlawn Av. Office: 30 N. La Salle St., Chicago, Ill. Died Nov. 20, 1947.

TOLMAN, Judson Allen (tŏl'măn), educator; b. Sandwich, Ill., July 23, 1879; s. Judson Allen and Mary Earhart (Weeks) T.; student Northwestern U., 1897-98; A.B., U. of Chicago, 1901, A.M., 1903, Ph.D., 1911; m. Eva Rawlings, Sept. 29, 1903; children—William Allen, Helen Louise. Prof. Latin, Des Moines Coll., 1901-02; teacher Latin, high sch., El Paso, Tex., 1904-08; head of dept. Greek and Latin, Hardin-Simmons U., Abilene, Tex., 1908-17; pres. Howard Payne Coll., Brownwood, Tex., 1917-19; pres. Okla. Bapt. U., 1919-22; head of dept. ancient langs., A. and M. Coll., Stillwater, Okla., 1922-23; head dept. of edn. and dir. Summer Sch., Georgetown Coll., 1923-26, also dean of freshmen, 1924-26; prof. history of edn., U. of Ky., summer 1925; pres. Alderson Junior Coll., 1926-29; resigned to become head of dept. of classical langs., Georgetown Coll., 1929. Mem. Kappa Delta Pi, Pi Gamma Mu; mem. Kiwanis (lt. gov., 4th Division, Ky.-Tenn. Dist., 1941; past president). President, Kentucky Classical Association, 1944. Baptist. Mason (K.T.). Author: Essentials of Latin for College Students, 1933; also (brochure) Study of Sepulchral Inscriptions in Buecheler's Carmina Epigraphica Latina. Home: 121 Jackson St., Georgetown, Ky. Died Jan. 30, 1949.

TOLMAN, Richard Chace (tŏl'măn), physicist; b. West Newton, Mass., Mar. 4, 1881; s. James Pike and Mary (Chace) T.; S.B., Mass. Institute of Technology, 1903, Ph.D., 1910; Sc.D., Princeton University, 1942; studied at Charlottenburg and Crefeld, Germany, 1903-04; m. Ruth Sherman, Aug. 5, 1924. Instr. in theoretical chemistry, 1907-09, research asso. in physical chemistry, 1909-10, M.I.T.; instr. physical chemistry, U. of Mich., 1910-11; asst. prof. same, U. of Cincinnati, 1911-12, U. of Calif., 1912-16; prof. physical chemistry, U. of Ill., 1916-18; chief dispersoid sect. Chem. Warfare Service, rank maj., 1918; asso. dir., 1919-20, and dir., 1920-22; Fixed Nitrogen Research Lab., War Dept.; prof. physical chemistry and mathematical physics and dean of the Grad. Sch., Calif. Inst. Tech., since 1922. Vice chmn. Nat. Defense Research Com., 1940. Sci. adv. to U.S. rep., U.N. Atomic Energy Comn., 1946. Fellow Am. Acad. Arts and Sciences, A.A.A.S.; mem. Am. Chem. Soc., Nat. Acad. Sciences, Am. Philos. Soc., Am. Physical Soc., Washington Acad. Sciences. Author: The Theory of the Relativity of Motion, 1917; Statistical Mechanics with Applications to Physics and Chemistry, 1927; Relativity, Thermodynamics and Cosmology, 1934; The Principles of Statistical Mechanics, 1938; Investigations on theory of colloids, theory of relativity, theory of similitude, mass of the electron, nature of the fundamental quantities of physics, partition of energy, behavior of smokes, electric discharge in gases, reactions of nitrogen compounds, rate of chem. reaction, specific heat and entropy of gases, quantum theory, statistical mechanics, relativistic thermodynamics, cosmology, etc. Address: Calif. Institute of Technology, Pasadena, Calif. Died Sep. 5, 1948.

TOMLINSON, Charles Fawcett (tŏm'lĭn-sŭn), furniture mfr.; b. Archdale, Randolph County, N.C., Dec. 24, 1871; s. Allen Josiah and Anna (Fawcett) T.; B.S., Guilford Coll., 1893; Ph.B., U. of N.C., 1895; m. May A. Lovelance, Nov. 25, 1914; children—Charles F., Sarah Lacy, Anna Fawcett. Mfr. of furniture since 1904; treas. Tomlinson of High Point, Inc.; pres. High Point, Thomasville & Denton R.R.; dir. High Point Hotel Co.; supt. pub. schs., Winston-Salem, N.C., 1899-1904. Chmn. Board School Commissioners, High Point; chmn. exec. com. and dir. Southern Furniture Expn. Bldg., High Point. Ex-pres. Nat. Council Furniture Assns.; ex-nat. pres. Travelers' Protective Assn.; ex-pres. Southern Furniture Mfrs. Assn.; pres. High Point Mfrs. Assn. Mem. Phi Beta Kappa, Phi Gamma Delta. Ind. Democrat. Quaker. Club: Emerywood Country. Home: 529 Parkway, High Point, N.C. Died Jan. 28, 1943.

TONE, Frank Jerome, chmn. Carborundum Co.; b. Bergen, N.Y., Oct. 16, 1868; s. Thomas J. and Catherine (Spafford) T.; M.E., Cornell U., 1891; Dr. of Science, Univ. of Pittsburgh, 1935; m. Gertrude Franchot, June 28, 1900; children—Frank Jerome, Franchot. Engr. with Thomson-Houston Electric Co., Lynn, Mass., 1891-93, Pittsburgh Traction Co., 1893-95; works mgr. Carborundum Co., Niagara Falls, 1895-1919, pres., 1919-42, now chmn.; pres. Republic Carbon Co.; director, Canadian Carborundum Co., Ltd.; dir. Power City Bank. Originated first commercial process for production of silicon metal, silicon carbide heating elements, and Electric Furnace Mullite. Awarded medals: Paris Expn., 1900; Pan Am. Expn., Buffalo, 1901; St. Louis Expn., 1904; Jacob F. Schoellkopf medal by Am. Chem. Soc., 1931; Edward Goodrich Acheson medal, by Electrochem. Soc., 1935; Perkin medal, Soc. Chemical Industry and Am. Chem. Soc., 1938. Mem. Am. Electrochem. Soc. (ex-pres.), Am. Inst. Chem. Engrs., Am. Chem. Soc., Am. Inst. Mining Engrs., Soc. Chem. Industry (London), Soc. Colonial Wars, Sons of the Am. Revolution, Phi Kappa Psi, Sigma Xi. Republican. Presbyterian. Clubs: Niagara, Rotary, Niagara Falls Country; Chemists' (New York). Home: 131 Buffalo Av. Address: The Carborundum Co., Niagara Falls, N.Y. Died July 26, 1944.

TOOHEY, John Peter (too'ē), writer; b. Binghamton, N.Y.; s. Patrick Joseph and Mary Anne (Nolan) T.; ed. pub. and high schs., Binghamton; m. Viola Virginia Latham, Oct. 14, 1911; 1 son, John Latham. Began as reporter, Scranton (Pa.) Tribune; later spl. writer Washington Post, and on editorial staff New York Evening World; gen. rep. Sam H. Harris Theatrical Enterprises, 1930-42; now free lance publicity agent; contbr. articles to New York newspapers and to Ladies' Home Jour., and short stories to Saturday Evening Post, Collier's, and other mags. Author: Fresh Every Hour, 1922; Growing Pains, 1929; Young Mr. Dudley (play, with Le Roy Clemens); Swifty (play, with Walter C. Percival); In Freedom's Name (play, with Thomas Beer); Jonesy (play, with Anne Morrison). Clubs: Players, Dutch Treat. Home: 43 Fifth Av., New York, N.Y.* Died Nov. 7, 1946.

TOOTLE, Milton, Jr., (too't'l), banker; b. St. Joseph, Mo., Mar. 18, 1872; s. Milton and Katherine (O'Neill) T.; ed. Saint Paul's Sch., Concord, N.H.; m. Lillian Duckworth, Nov. 9, 1892; children—George Duckworth, Milton, William Dameron. Pres. Tootle Lacy Nat. Bank, and officer or dir. various financial, mercantile and other corps. Republican. Presbyterian. Clubs: Chicago (Chicago); St. Joseph Country (St. Joseph); mem. at large Garden Club of America. Home: 301 S. 11th St. Office: 210 N. 6th St., St. Joseph, Mo. Died Dec. 26, 1946.

TORREY, Elliot (Bouton), artist; b. East Hardwick, Vt., Jan. 7, 1867; s. Joseph and Maria Thorpe (Noble) T.; B.A., Bowdoin Coll., 1887, M.A., 1890; studied in Paris and Florence, Italy; unmarried. Maintained studio in Boston several yrs.; in Europe, 1908-11; resided in N.Y. City, 1911-23, since in Calif. Exhibited in Paris Salon, Nat. Acad. Design, Nat. Arts Club, Salmagundi Club (New York), Corcoran Gallery (Washington), Carnegie Internat. Exhbn. (Pittsburgh), Art Inst. Chicago, etc. Represented in permanent collections of Art Inst. Chicago, Cleveland Museum of Art, Boston Art Club, Akron Art Inst., San Diego Fine Arts Museum. Mem. Alpha Delta Phi, Phi Beta Kappa. Home-Studio: 4716 Panorama Drive, San Diego 3, Calif. Died March 9, 1949.

TORREY, George Burroughs, portrait painter; b. New York, N.Y., 1863; s. Joseph and Harriet Louise (Burroughs) T.; ed. New York and Paris, France; m. Almirita Howes, Nov. 10, 1891; m. 2d, Lillie Hart Gay, d. of Judge Hart, Nov. 1925. Exhibited at Paris Salon, 1900, and afterwards. Painted portraits of all presidents of U.S., starting with Grover Cleveland, King Edward of England, etc. Decorated by King of Greece with Grecian Order of the Savior, 1904. Home: 3148 Kalihi Valley Road. Studio 414 Kuamoo St., Honolulu, T.H. Died Apr. 14, 1942; buried in Bridgeport, Conn.

TOTTEN, Joe Byron, playwright, stage dir.; b. Brooklyn, N.Y., June 1, 1875; s. James and Margaret (MacCusker) T.; ed. St. Francis Xavier Coll., New York, and St. Francis of Assisi Coll., Brooklyn; m. Leslie Bingham, Sept. 8, 1902. Started theatrical career under Charles Frohman; dir. for the Shuberts, Comstock & Gest, and gen. stage dir. for A. H. Woods, David Belasco and the Theatre League; producer, star and writer for Essanay Film Co., also the Vitagraph Co. Mem. Authors' League Am., Soc. Am. Dramatists, Actors' Equity Assn., Nat. Vaudeville Artists. Mason. Elk. Author: The Cowboy and the Squaw, 1907. Also plays: Alibi Bill; Red Head; The World and a Woman; The Cowboy and the Squaw; Young Buffalo; The Girl Worth While; The Call; Set a Thief; The First Lady in the Land; A Precious Cavalier; The Real Thing; Far Out West; The Forger; Getting Away with It; Mexico; Bought Cheap; Proof Positive; The Half-breed; Boys Will Be Boys; The Hall Room Boys; Hands Up; Us 4; 3 M's; In Soft; Going Through; Help! Help! Love's Call; So That's That; The Up and Up; In Confidence; Spook House; Hell's Kitchen; Taken For a Ride; and others. Dramatized The House of Bondage (by Reginald Wright Kauffman); Arms and the Woman (by Harold MacGrath); Riders of the Purple Sage (by Zane Grey); John Barleycorn (by Jack London); The Valiants of Virginia (by Hallie Erminie Rives); The Strange Death of President Harding. Died Apr. 1946.

TOTTEN, Ralph James (tŏt'ĕn), diplomatist; b. Nashville, Tenn., Oct. 1, 1877; ed. Montgomery Acad. and business coll., Nashville. In ry. and commercial business to 1907; apptd. consul at Puerto Plata, Dominican Republican, June 10, 1908; consul at Maracaibo, Venezuela, 1910-11, at Trieste, Austria, 1911-13, at Montevideo, Uruguay, 1913-14; became consul gen. at large, Inspection Dist. Western Europe, 1914; detailed in Dept. of State, Mar. 6-Dec. 18, 1917; sent to Mexican border to investigate passport control of aliens entering U.S., Dec. 1917; consul gen. at Barcelona, Spain, 1922-24; on detail at Dept. of State as mem. exec. com. Foreign Service Personnel Bd., 1925-26; headed spl. mission to Ethiopia, 1926; consul gen. at Cape Town, 1926-30, minister resident, 1930; E.E. and M.P. to Union of South Africa, 1930-37; retired with 30 years service, Aug. 31, 1937; now painting and etching and writing memoirs. Author: Rhymes and Things, 1938. Address: 2800 Ontario Road, Washington 9, D.C. Died May 9, 1949.

TOURET, Frank Hale (too-rĕt'), bishop; b. Salem, Mass., Mar. 25, 1875; s. Benjamin Augustus and Lucy Hatch (Marks) T.; A.B., Harvard, 1897, A.M., 1901; B.D., Episcopal Theol. Sch., Cambridge, 1903; D.D., Whitman Coll., Walla Walla, Wash., 1921; m. Irene Chittenden Farquhar, May 19, 1906; 1 son, William Chapin. Deacon and priest P.E. Ch., 1903; curate St. John's, Providence, R.I., 1903-04, Christ Ch., Detroit, Mich., 1904-06; treas. Colorado Coll., Colorado Springs, 1907-08; rector St. Luke's, Ft. Collins, Colo., 1908-10, Grace Ch., Colorado Springs, 1910-17; elected bishop Missionary Dist. of Western Colo., Oct. 25, 1916; consecrated, Feb. 2, 1917; elected bishop of Idaho, Oct. 10, 1919; resigned Oct. 9, 1924; rector Ch. of the Good Shepherd, Waban, Mass., 1926-29; resigned 1929. Home: Tryon, N.C. Died Aug. 2, 1945.

TOURTELLOT, George P(latt) (toor'tĕ-lŏt), army officer; b. Dows, Ia., Nov. 5, 1895; s. George Mason and Mary Eleanor (Platt) T.; ed. Carroll Coll., 1915-17; Army Flying Sch., 1917-18; Air Corps Engring. Sch., 1928-29; Air Corps Tactical Sch., 1936-37; Command and Gen. Staff Sch., 1939-40; m. Peggy Leota Strane, April 23, 1921; 1 son, George Platt. Commd. 2d lt. Air Service, 1918; promoted through grades to brig. gen., 1943; on duty in France and Germany with combat pursuit units, 1918-19; comdg. officer 75th Service Squadron, Wheeler Field, Hawaii, 1930-33 and aeronautical insp. for Commerce Dept.; aviation instr., Mich. Nat. Guard, 1938-39; comdg. officer 35th Pursuit Group, Hamilton Field, Calif., 1940-41; exec. officer 2d Interceptor Command, Seattle, 1942; comdg. officer 111th Fighter Command, Drew Field, Fla., 1942; comdg. general 24th Composite Wing, 1942-44; comdg. general 72d Fighter Wing, Peterson Field, Colo., 1944; assigned to Hdqrs. A.A.F., Washington, D.C., 1945; comdr. McDill Field, Fla. until Oct. 15, 1946; comdr. Selfridge Field, Mich., Oct. 16-Oct. 26, 1946. Rated combat pilot and combat observer. Mem. Quiet Birdmen, Daedalians. Address: 3102 Oaklyn Drive, Parkland Estates, Tampa, Fla. Died Oct. 26, 1946; buried in Arlington National Cemetery.

TOWART, William G., clergyman; b. Glasgow, Scotland, Jan. 1, 1880; s. William G. and Mary (Morrison) T.; came to U.S., 1899 and naturalized citizen, 1913; student Colgate Acad., 1901-05; A.B., Colgate U., 1909; grad. Union Theological Sem., 1913; A.M., Columbia, 1913; (hon.) D.D., Colgate, 1929; m. Mabel Starkey, Aug. 28, 1912; children—Joel Franklin, William George, Jr., James Robertson, Miriam Alice. Ordained to ministry Bapt. Ch.; asso. sec. New York City Bapt. Mission Soc. and dir. Vacation Schs. for this Soc. and the Fedn. of Chs., New York, N.Y., 1909-13; pastor Grace Bapt. Ch., New York, N.Y., 1912-15; pastor First Bapt. Ch., Bennington, Vt., since 1915; First Baptist Cr., Plymouth, Mass., 1948-49; retired 1949. Served with Seventh Regt., New York, N.Y., 1909-15; mem. Home Guard, Bennington, Vt., during World War. Pres. bd. trustees Vt. Bapt. State Conv. since 1930; pres. Vt. Bapt. Ministers' Assn., 1927-28, Vt. Council Religious Edn., 1930-33; Vt. Bapt. Council of Churches, 1944-46; dean Vt. Sch. Religious Edn., 1921-32; dir. Vacation Sch. Northern Bapt. Conv., 1918; dean N.E. Bapt. Sch. Methods, Ocean Park, Me., since 1932; elected president Vermont Bible Society, 1941. Member Theta Phi, Delta Kappa Epsilon, Phi Beta Kappa (hon.). Republican. Baptist. Mason (K.T., Past Comdr.). Author: Dan of Nazareth, 1918; Playing the Game, 1919; also courses for vacation Bible schs. Home: South Stream Rd., Bennington, Vt.

Died Dec. 6, 1949; buried Park Lawn Cemetery, Bennington, Vt.

TOWER, James Eaton, editor; b. Groton, Mass., Mar. 17, 1863; s. James Edwin and Harriet (Eaton) T.; A.B., Amherst Coll., 1885; m. Harriet Tannatt, June 18, 1890. Reporter Worcester (Mass.) Gazette, 1885; editor Springfield Homestead, 1895-98; lit. editor Phelps Publishing Co. and Orange Judd Co., 1898-1900; editor Good Housekeeping Magazine, 1900-1913, The Designer, New York, 1915-18; mng. editor The Delineator, 1919-21, Pictorial Review, 1922-23. Congregationalist. Mem. Beta Theta Pi. Home: Hotel La Salle, 30 E. 60th St., New York 22. Office: care Fifth Av. Bank, New York, N.Y. Died Jan. 1, 1947.

TOWER, Olin Freeman, chemist; b. Brooklyn, Mar. 19, 1872; s. Freeman Pratt and Julia Ann (Cleveland) T.; A.B., Wesleyan U., Conn., 1892, A.M., 1893; Ph.D., U. of Leipzig, 1895; m. Elizabeth Williams, June 1899. Asst. in chemistry, Wesleyan U.; 1893-94; 1896-98, instr. chemistry, Adelbert Coll. of Western Reserve U., 1898-1901, asst. prof., 1901-07, Hurlbut prof. chemistry, 1907-42, prof. emeritus since 1942. Fellow A.A.A.S.; mem. London Chem. Soc., Am. Chem. Soc., Phi Beta Kappa, Sigma Xi, Phi Nu Theta (Wesleyan). Author: The Conductivity of Liquids, 1905; Qualitative Analysis, 1909. Contbr. to various chem. jours. Home: Sylvan Drive, Mt. Dora, Fla. Died Dec. 21, 1945.

TOWL, Forrest Milton (tōl), civil engr., corp. pres.; b. Parma, Cuyahoga County, O., Jan. 14, 1863; s. Theodore M. and Sarah L. (Ackley) T.; C.E., Cornell U., 1886, M.C.E., 1935; m. Mary Elizabeth Dean, Dec. 18, 1888; children—Theodore Clinton, Sarah Dean, Forrest Milton (dec.). Engaged in surveys of pipe lines, summers, 1879-86; asst., later chief engr. Nat. Transit Co., 1886-1902; mgr. pipe line dept. Pacific Coast Oil Co. (now Standard Oil Co. of Calif.), 1902-03, designed and built first long hot oil pipe line from Bakersfield to San Francisco Bay; gen. supt. trunk pipe lines controlled by Standard Oil Co., 1903-06; consulting engr. Standard Oil Co., 1906-11; pres., 1911-32, chmn. bd. since Jan. 1, 1932, Southern Pipe Line Co., Eureka Pipe Line Co., South West Pa. Pipe Lines, Cumberland Pipe Line Co.; engaged in research work, at Cornell U., in pipe line flow of fluids since Sept. 1934; has had charge of building over 7,000 miles of pipe line. Mem. fuel and fuel handling sub-com. U.S. Navy; consulted with U.S. Navy and British Admiralty on pipe line across Scotland to supply allied navies with fuel oil and recruited U.S. Navy unit which built this 36 mile 8-in. pipe line in 60 days, 1918. Hon. lecturer on mech. engring., Columbia U., 1911. Mem. Am. Soc. C.E., Am. Soc. M.E., Am. Inst. Mining and Metall. Engrs., Cornell Engring. Assn., Chi Psi, Chi Epsilon; fellow A.A.A.S. Republican. Mem. Dutch Ref. Ch. Wrote: The Pipe Line Flow Factor, 1934; The Pipe Line Flow Constant 0.0283 (in press). Home: Dering Harbor, N.Y., and 45 Montgomery Pl., Brooklyn, N.Y. Office: 30 Rockefeller Plaza, New York, N.Y. Died Jan. 3, 1946.

TOWNE, Charles Hanson (toun), editor, author; b. Louisville, Ky., Feb. 2, 1877; s. Prof. Paul A. and Mary Stuart (Campbell) T.; ed. common schs., New York, and 1 yr. at Coll. City of New York, and privately; unmarried. Author: The Quiet Singer and Other Poems; Manhattan, a Poem; Youth, and Other Poems; Beyond the Stars, and Other Poems; Today and Tomorrow, and Other Poems; The Tumble Man (with Hy. Mayer); Jolly Jaunts with Jim; Autumn Loiters; Shaking Hands with England; A World of Windows, 1919; The Rise and Fall of Prohibition, 1920; The Bad Man, 1921; Loafing Down Long Island; The Chain, 1922; Ambling Through Acadia, 1923; The Gay Ones, 1924; Tinsel (novel), 1925; Selected Poems, 1925; This New York of Mine, 1931; Good Old Yesterday, 1935; An April Song, New Poems, 1937; The Shop of Dreams, 1939; Jogging Around New England, 1939; Pretty Girls Get There, 1940; Gentlemen Behave, 1941; A Testament of Love. Wrote, 1919, English lyrics for Offenbach's opera, "La Belle Helene," produced at Boston. Editor: For France, 1917; The Balfour Visit, 1917; Roosevelt as the Poets Saw Him, 1923; 2 song cycles in collaboration with H. Clough-Leighter—"A Love Garden," and "An April Heart"; and 4 in collaboration with Amy Woodforde-Finden—"A Lover in Damascus," "Five Little Japanese Songs," "A Dream of Egypt," and "The Magic Casement"; one with Bruno Huhn, "Love's Triumph"; with Deems Taylor, "The City of Joy." Formerly editor of The Designer and of The Smart Set; mng. editor of McClure's Mag., 1915-20; editor Harper's Bazar, 1926-31; conducted daily lit. column, New York American, 1931-37; contbr. to mags. Author: So Far, So Good (autobiography), 1945. In 1940-41 he went on the stage, appearing as the clergyman in "Life with Father," touring the United States. Home: 165 E. 60th St., New York, N.Y. Died Feb. 28, 1949; buried Earlville, N.Y.

TOWNE, John Henry, chmn. bd. The Yale & Towne Mfg. Co.; b. Phila., Pa., Jan. 2, 1869; s. Henry R. and Cora E. (White) T.; ed. Mass. Inst. of Tech., 1890; m. Eleonora Swenson, Apr. 18, 1900; 1 dau., Eleanor. Chmn. bd. The Yale & Towne Mfg. Co.; dir. The Fifth Av. Assn., Inc. Mem. Community Service Soc. V.p. and dir. N.Y. Eye and Ear Infirmary. Clubs: University, St. Anthony. Home: 101 E. 72nd St. Office: 405 Lexington Av., New York, N.Y. Died Sep. 29, 1942.

TOWNER, Rutherford Hamilton, author; b. Kenwood, Madison County, N.Y., May 12, 1870; mostly self-ed.; grad. New York Law Sch. (night course), 1897. Began as clk. with Am. Surety Co., New York, 1896; admitted to N.Y. bar, 1897, and served as atty. for Am. Surety Co. until 1909; founder, 1909, Towner Rating Bur. which makes premium rates for practically all the fidelity and surety cos. of U.S. Mem. Am. Econ. Assn., N.Y. Bar Assn. Author: The Philosophy of Civilization, 1920; The Third Kingdom, 1940. Home: 237 Clay St., Reno, Nev. Died Jan. 23, 1950.

TOWNLEY, Sidney Dean, astronomer; b. Waukesha, Wis., Apr. 10, 1867; s. Robert and Mary (Wilkinson) T.; B.S., U. of Wis., 1890, M.S., 1892; Sc.D., U. of Mich., 1897; studied universities Calif., Berlin and Munich; m. Frances Wright, July 1, 1895; children—Lucile, Isabel, Ruth (dec.), Frances Jane. Instr. astronomy, U. of Mich., 1893-98, U. of Calif., 1898-1903; astronomer in charge Internat. Latitude Obs., Ukiah, Calif., 1903-07; lecturer in astronomy, U. of Calif., 1904-07; asst. prof. applied mathematics, Stanford U., 1907-09, asso. prof., 1909-18, prof., 1918-29, prof. astronomy and geodesy since 1929; visiting lecturer in astronomy, Harvard, 1925-26. Mem. Calif. Acad. Sciences, A.A.A.S., Am. Astron. Soc., Astron. Soc. Pacific, Seismol. Soc. America (sec.-treas. 1910-30; pres. 1935), Sigma Xi, Phi Beta Kappa. Author: Descriptive Catalog of Earthquakes of the Pacific Coast of the United States, 1769-1928 (with Maxwell W. Allen), 1939; Diary of a Student of the University of Wisconsin, 1886-1892, 1940; also about 100 articles in astron. and seismol. jours.; editor of Bull. of Seismol. Soc. America, 1911-35; former editor publs. of Astron. Soc. Pacific. Address: Stanford University, Calif.* Died Mar. 16, 1946.

TOWNS, Charles B.; b. La Grange, Ga., Jan. 12, 1862; s. J. Oliver and Sarah E. (Barnes) T.; m. Mary M. Barbour. Founder, 1903, and head Charles B. Towns Hosp., for alcohol and drug addictions, N.Y. City; visited China in 1908 and established hosps. for drug addictions in Peking and other cities. Author of the act known as the Boylan Law, passed by N.Y. legislature, 1913. Mem. So. Soc. Clubs: New York Athletic, Englewood Country. Author: Alcohol and Tobacco, and the Remedy, 1915; Habits that Handicap, 1920; The Menace of Opium; Reclaiming the Drinker, 1931; Drug and Alcoholic Sickness, 1934; also various brochures. Address: 293 Central Park W., New York. Died Feb. 20, 1947.

TOWNSEND, Charles Haskins, zoölogist; b. Parnassus, Pa., Sept. 29, 1859; s. Rev. D. W. and Elizabeth (Kier) T.; ed. pub. schs.; hon. Sc.D., Washington and Jefferson Coll., 1909. Asst. U.S. Fish Commn. in salmon propagation in Calif., 1883; naturalist U.S.S. Corwin, Arctic Expdn., 1885; resident naturalist, U.S.S. Albatross, deep-sea investigations in Atlantic and Pacific, 1886-96; actg. dir. Am. Museum Natural History, 1910; dir. investigations U.S.S. Albatross, Gulf of Calif., 1911; mem. Bering Sea Fur Seal Commn., 1896; chief of fisheries div. U.S. Fish Commn., 1897-1902; fishery expert, Russo-Am. arbitration at The Hague, 1902; dir. New York Aquarium, 1902-37. Mem. Am. Fisheries Soc. (pres. 1912-13); fellow New York Acad. Sciences, N.Y. Zoöl. Soc.; mem. council Oceanographic Inst., Paris, since 1923. Club: Century. Author 100 documents on the fisheries, fur seal industries, deep-sea exploration and gen. zoölogy. Address: 3985 Douglas Road, Coconut Grove, Fla. Died Jan. 28, 1944.

TOWNSEND, Charles H(enry) T(yler), biologist, physicist; b. Oberlin, O., Dec. 5, 1863; s. Nathan Haskin and Helen Jeannette (Tyler) T.; Columbian (now George Washington) U. Sch. of Medicine, 1887-91; B.S., George Washington U., 1908, Ph.D., 1914; m. Caroline W. Hess, Sept. 10, 1889 (died 1901); children—Karl Hess, Leland (dec.), Helen Tyler (dec.); m. 2d, Margaret C. Dyer, June 1, 1908; children—Charles Henry Tyler, Edward Dyer, Nathaniel Ostend, Mary Louise. Asst. entomologist, U.S. Dept. Agr., 1888-91; prof. entomology, zoölogy, and physiology, N.M. Agrl. Coll., and entomologist, Expt. Sta., 1891-93; curator Museum, Inst. Jamaica, 1893-94; field agt. div. entomology, U.S. Dept. Agr., 1894-98; again with N.M. Agrl. Coll. Expt. Sta., 1898-99; prof. biol., etc., Batangas Provincial Sch., P.I., 1904-06; expert, Gipsy Moth Lab., Bur. Entomology, U.S. Dept. Agr., 1907-09; govt. entomologist and dir. entom. stations, Peru, 1909-14; entom. asst., Bur. Entomology, U.S. Dept. Agr., 1914-19; hon. custodian muscoid diptera, U.S. Nat. Museum, 1914-25; chief entomologist, State of São Paulo, Brazil, 1919-22; ant expert in Brazil for Am. Cyanamid Co., 1923; dir. Cotton Plagues Lab., Piura, Peru, 1923-24; cotton plagues expert, Chamber Commerce and Agr., Iquitos, Peru, 1925; chief Inst. Parasitologia Agricola, Lima, Peru, 1926; chief entomologist Estacion Experimental Agricola S.N.A., Lima, 1927-29; head firm Charles Townsend & Filhos, São Paulo, since 1929; cons. entomologist Cia. Ford Industrial do Brasil, Rio Tapajós, Pará, since 1932. Author: Manual of Myiology (12 parts); also about 1000 titles on muscoid flies, cotton plagues, med. entomology, biogeography, ecology and physics. Pioneer work on American cotton weevils; discovered mode of transmission of disease, verruga, in Peruvian Andes; first analysed insect environments; demonstrated Cephenemyia as the swiftest organism; established about 1000 valid muscoid genera; explained gravity; recorded exact atomic weights; determined exact velocity of light; defined cosmic units of length, time and mass; explained moon's origin and earth's axial inclination; set Pleistocene duration and man in America at two million years. Home: Fazenda Casagrande Velha, Itaquaquecetuba, São Paulo, Brazil S.A. Died Mar. 17, 1944.

TOWNSEND, Edward Waterman, author, ex-congressman; b. Cleveland, Feb. 10, 1855; s. Horace Gilbert and Ann Eliza (Thornton) T.; ed. pub. and pvt. schs.; m. Annie Lake, Apr. 16, 1884. Dem. candidate for 61st Congress, 1908; elected to 62d Congress (1911-13), 7th N.J. Dist., and 63d Congress (1913-15), 10th N.J. Dist. Author: Chimmie Fadden and Major Max, 1895; A Daughter of the Tenements, 1896; Near a Whole Cityful, 1897; Days Like These, 1901; Lees and Leaven, 1903; A Summer in New York, 1903; Reuben Larkmead, 1905; Our Constitution—Why and How It Was Made, Who Made It, and What It Is, 1906; Beaver Creek Farm, 1907; The Climbing Courvatells, 1909; Co-author: (plays) Marquis of Michigan; Head of the House. Mem. Nat. Inst. Arts and Letters, Dramatists' Guild. Home: 129 Grove St., Montclair, N.J. Died March 16, 1942.

TOWNSEND, Ernest Nathaniel, artist; b. New York, June 26, 1893; s. Ellsworth Strong and Phyllis (Thompson) T.; student Mechanics Inst., 1911, Nat. Acad. of Design, 1913, Art Students League, 1915; unmarried. Paints landscapes and murals; does design and book illustration; teacher; works in major art exhibits, galleries and private collections. Awarded Isidor prize, 1938; Anonymous prize, Allied Artists, 1940; Layman's award, Salmagundi Club, 1941. Associate N.A.D. Mem. Am. Artists Professional League, Allied Artists America, Artists Fellowship, Am. Water Color Soc. Episcopalian. Republican. Clubs: Salmagundi, Murals, N.Y. Historical Soc. Illustrated Walton's Compleat Angler, 1936, Good Bye, Mr. Chips, 1938; Eneas Africanus (Edwards), 1940; The American Scene (Barnes), 1940. Studio: 45 E. 59th St., New York, N.Y. Died Oct. 16, 1945.

TOWNSEND, Frederick, banker; b. Albany, N.Y., Oct. 28, 1871; s. Frederick and Sarah (Rathbone) T.; grad. Albany Acad., 1889; A.B., Harvard, 1893, LL.B., 1897; m. Harriet Davis Fellowes, Apr. 17, 1911; children—Sarah R., Frederick. Admitted to N.Y. bar, 1897, and practiced at Albany until 1920; mem. firm Tracey, Cooper & Townsend, 1899-1920; pres. Albany Savings Bank, 1920-41, chmn. bd. since 1941. Chmn. Albany County Draft Bd., 1917-18. Clubs: Fort Orange (Albany); University (New York); etc. Home: Loudonville, N.Y. Office: 20 N. Pearl St., Albany, N.Y.* Died Dec. 4, 1949.

TOWNSEND, Harvey Gates, prof. philosophy; b. David City, Neb., Jan. 27, 1885; s. Horatio Gates and Annie Lois (Young) T.; A.B., Neb. Wesleyan U., 1908; Ph.D., Cornell, 1913; m. Adele Annette McGillivrae, Sept. 24, 1906; children—James Edwin, Andrew Gates. Actg. prof. philosophy and edn., Central Coll. (Mo.), 1910-11, prof., 1911-14; instr. in edn., Smith Coll., 1914-15, asst. prof. of edn., 1915-17, asso. prof., 1917-23, prof., 1923-25, prof. philosophy, 1925-26; prof. philosophy, U. of Ore., since 1926. Mem. A.A.A.S., Am. Philos. Assn. (sec. 1927-30, 1933-36, pres. 1936). Conglist. Club: Faculty (U. of Ore.). Author: The Principle of Individuality in the Philosophy of Thomas Hill Green, 1914; Philosophical Ideas in the United States, 1934; The Philosophy of Jonathan Edwards as found in his private notebooks, 1947. Home: Crow Road, Eugene, Ore. Died Dec. 19, 1948.

TOWNSEND, Sylvester D., banker; b. Odessa, Del., July 25, 1870; s. George L. and Cornelia (Scott) T.; educated public schools; m. Helen Price Cheairs, Oct. 16, 1902; children—Helen C., Sylvester D. Teller Delaware National Bank, 1895-1902; treas. Chambersburg Trust Co., 1902-03; with Wilmington Trust Co. since 1903, treas., later v.p., pres. since 1934 (now chairman board); director Penroad Corp., Farmers Mutual Fire Ins. Co. Dir. and treas. Wilmington Chamber of Commerce; v.p. Tri-State Regional Planning Fedn.; dir. New Castle Regional Planning Bd.; dir. Wilmington Park Bd.; dir. Penn. Hall Sch. Republican. Episcopalian. Clubs: Wilmington, Wilmington Country, Wilmington Whist. Home: 1304 Broome St. Office: Wilmington Trust Co., Wilmington, Del. Died May 13,* 1947.

TOWNSEND, S(mith) DeLancey, clergyman; b. N. Attleboro, Mass., Mar. 27, 1860; s. Rev. Julius Sylvester and Martha Louise (Rice) T.; A.B., Hobart Coll., 1880, A.M., 1883, D.D., 1901; Ph.D., St. Stephen's Coll., 1894; LL.D., St. John's Coll., Annapolis, Md., 1903; m. Kathryn Cranston Smith, Oct. 2, 1884; children—Mary Allen, Kathryn Van Vleck (Lady Upcott, wife of Sir Gilbert Upcott, London); m. 2d, Mrs. Elinor W. Squier, June 5, 1928. Became deacon, 1883, priest, 1884, P.E. Ch.; rector St. Luke's, Whitewater, Wis., 1884-87; asso. rector, 1887-97, rector, 1897-1928, All Angels' Ch., N.Y. City; now rector emeritus. Club: Century. Address: All Angels Church, 251 W. 80th St., New York. Died Sept. 16, 1944.

TOZZER, Arthur Clarence, constrn. engr.; b. Lynn, Mass., July 18, 1879; s. Samuel Clarence and Caroline Blanchard (Marston) T.; B.S., Dartmouth, 1902, C.E., 1903; m. Dorothy LaCroix, June 1, 1916; children—Edith, Caroline, Dorothy; m. 2d, Isabel Kellers, Sept. 28, 1937; stepson, James McW. Kellers. Assistant engr. with Henry F. Bryant, Brookline, Mass., 1903; with Foundation Co., N.Y. City, East River Tunnel, Pa. R.R. Tunnel, S. Pearson & Son, 1904-05; supt. Turner Constrn. Co., 1905-13, gen. supt., 1913-18, exec. mgr. (in charge constrn. $28,000,000 U.S. Army Supply Base, Brooklyn), 1918-19, v.p. since 1919, dir. dir. since 1925; ex-pres., dir. Asso. Gen. Contractors of America, Inc.; dir. Turner Rostock Corp., Overseer Thayer Sch. of Civ. Engring. (Dartmouth). Mem. Am. Soc. C.E., Am. Concrete Inst., Archtl. League N.Y. City, Chi Phi. Republican. Club: Dartmouth (New York). Contbr. to tech. press. Home: 47 Brookline

Rd., Scarsdale, N.Y. Office: 420 Lexington Av., New York, N.Y. Died Sep. 9, 1942.

TRABUE, Charles Clay (trā-bū), lawyer; b. Nashville, Tenn., Mar. 9, 1872; s. George W. and Ellen (Dunn) T.; prep. edn. Montgomery Bell Acad. and Wallace Univ. Sch., Nashville; A.B., Vanderbilt, 1892, LL.B., 1894; m. Julia Malone, Nov. 4, 1909; children—Charles Clay, Thomas Malone. Admitted to Tenn. bar, 1894, and practiced since at Nashville. Mem. Am. Bar Assn., Tenn. Bar Assn. (pres. 1931-32), Phi Beta Kappa, Beta Theta Pi. Democrat. Presbyn. Home: Harding Rd. Office: American Trust Bldg., Nashville, Tenn. Died Sep. 12, 1942.

TRACY, Ernest B., dir., U.S. & Fgn. Securities Corp., U.S. & Internat. Securities Corp.; pres. La. Land & Expln. Co.; dir. Amerada Petroleum Corp., United Gas Corp., Great Am. Ins. Co. Office: 120 Broadway, New York 5, N.Y. Died June 25, 1948.

TRACY, Howard Van Sinderen, stocks and bonds; b. Louisville, Ky., Oct. 8, 1887; s. Howard and Bessie (Lindsley) T.; ed. pvt. schs.; Harvard Univ., 1906-08; m. Ruth Wilbur Alexander, Apr. 19, 1916 (divorced 1925); 1 dau., Anne Alexander (Mrs. William Rossmore). Partner firm of A. E. Butler & Co., stocks and bonds, Chicago, until 1914; exec. and dir. John Burnham & Co., 1916-24; pres. Rogers & Tracy, Inc., 1924-37; pres. Hoyburn Co., 1916-20; pres. R.&T. Syndicate, 1931-34; pres. Md.-Ill. Co.; former dir. Holland-St. Louis Sugar Co. of Mich., Tracy & Avery Co. of Ohio. Active in civic affairs, serving on many coms. of the Chicago Assn. of Commerce; one of founders and dir. (1924-25) Chicago Advertising Council (forerunner of Better Business Bureau); founded, 1919, and became first pres. (now sec. and dir.) Investors Protective Bur., organized to aid Chicago newspapers in censoring their financial columns, assist the State in administering its "Blue Sky" law and to cause the arrest of bucket shop operators and fake promoters; the Bur., attracted national attention by its success and its activities were copied in other cities; consulted by gov. in drafting of the Ill. "Blue Sky" law, 1919, and wrote several sections including that covering "Class C" securities, the idea of which he originated. Pres. Citizens' Assn. of Chicago, 1937, 1938, v.p., 1936; dir. Chicago Crime Commn., 1931-46; dir. Chicago Area Project, 1937-46; dir. Central Howard Assn., 1937-42; mem. Chicago Acad. Criminology since 1936; co-chmn. (with Prof. W.E. Puttkammer) of Ill. Citizens' Com. on Parole. Interested in development of nat. system of waterways; frequently apptd. by gov. as Ill. delegate to nat. and internat. waterways congresses. Writer of articles used in Rep. presidential campaigns. With War Prodn. Bd., 1943-44. Republican. Episcopalian. Clubs: University, Literary; Harvard (New York); Pendennis (Louisville, Ky.), Durham Woods Riding; Nat. Fox Hunters Assn. America, Va. Fox Hunters Assn. Address: University Club, Chicago, Ill. Died Dec. 23, 1945.

TRACY, James Grant, lawyer; b. Syracuse, N.Y., Dec. 24, 1873; s. Osgood Vose and Ellen (Sedgwick) T.; Ph.B., Cornell U., 1898, LL B., 1900; m. Florida Bayard Seay, Oct. 2, 1901; children—Osgood Vose, John Bayard, Ellen Sedgwick, Charles Sedgwick. Admitted to N.Y. bar, 1900, and practiced in Syracuse; asst. corp. counsel, Syracuse, 1904-10; mem. Tracy, Chapman & Tracy; pres. Sedgwick Farm Land Co., pres. Sedgwick Farm Club, Whalen Oil Co.; dir. Merchants Nat. Bank, O. V. Tracy Co. Mem. Onondaga Bar Assn. (dir.), Hist. Assn. of Onondaga, Chi Phi, Quill and Dagger Soc. (Cornell). Republican. Unitarian. Clubs: Century, University, Cornell, Republican Escort; Cornell (New York); etc. Home: 107 Sedgwick Drive. Office: State Tower Bldg., Syracuse, N.Y. Died Sep. 17, 1943.

TRACY, Martha, pub. health; b. Plainfield, N.J., Apr. 10, 1876; d. Jeremiah Evarts and Martha Sherman (Green) Tracy; B.A., Bryn Mawr Coll., 1898; M.D., Woman's Med. Coll. of Pa., 1904; studied Sheffield Scientific Sch. (Yale) and U. of Pa.; Dr. P.H., U. of Pa., 1917; unmarried. With research dept. of exptl. pathology, Cornell U. Med. Sch., N.Y. City, 1904-07; asst. to Meningitis Commn., New York Bd. of Health, 1905; worker under Huntington Fund for Cancer Research, N.Y. City, 1907-19; prof. physiol. chemistry, Woman's Med. Coll. of Pa., 1912-20, and dean, 1918-24, dean and prof. preventive medicine, 1924-31, dean, 1931-40; retired June 1940. Asst. dir. of public health, Phila., Pa., 1940. Mem. Phila. Board of Health, 1936-40. Fellow Am. Coll. Physicians, Coll. of Physicians of Phila., A.M.A.; mem. Phila. County Med. Soc., Am. Assn. Univ. Women, Sigma Xi, Phi Beta Kappa (hon.), Alpha Omega Alpha. Presbyterian. Clubs: Women's City, Business and Professional Woman's. Home: 516 W. Coulter St. Address: 503 City Hall Annex, Philadelphia, Pa. Died Mar. 22, 1942.

TRACY, Merle Elliott, publisher; b. Southwest Harbor, Me., May 7, 1879; s. Henry and Flavilla (Benson) T.; ed. Perkins Instn. for the Blind, Boston, 1891-97; m. Harriet Ella Benson, Feb. 24, 1907; children—Elizabeth Wells (wife of Rev. William Bruce Sharp), Henry Lewis. Editorial writer Houston (Tex.) Chronicle, 1913-24; editorial columnist Scripps-Howard Newspapers, 1924-34; editor and pub. Current History (purchased from New York Times), 1936-39. Chmn. Houston City Planning Commn., 1924-26. Episcopalian. Author: Our Country, Our People and Theirs, 1938; New World Challenge to Democracy, 1940. Home: Garden City, L.I., N.Y. Died Mar. 4, 1945.

TRACY, Russel Lord, banker; b. Mansfield, O., Dec. 10, 1860; s. Frederick Earl and Anna (Lord) T.; student Oberlin Coll., 1877-80; Carleton Coll., Northfield, Minn., 1880-82 (pres. of class); m. Katie Elizabeth Shook, June 30, 1927; children—(1st marriage) Edward Lord (deceased), Russel Lord, Jr. (deceased). Organized Tracy Loan & Trust Co., Salt Lake City, 1884, pres., 1884-1933, chmn. bd. dirs., since 1933. Known as "Father of the Salt Lake newsboys" who for 40 years brought their school reports to him each month and received cash awards according to standing in school, also furnished Thanksgiving dinner to newsboys for 40 years. In 1882 accompanied Gen. Phil Sheridan on trip of inspection through Wyoming and Yellowstone Park where he erected the Tracy Club House, on Snake River, presenting it to the Tracy Loan & Trust Co. Active in Boy Scout work for whom he built $10,000 wigwam, also presented to the boys and girls of Salt Lake City the Tracy Aviary worth $25,000. Received Silver Beaver award, Boy Scouts. Hon. mem. Sons of the Utah Pioneers, Rotary Internat. Mem. Sons Am. Revolution (past pres.), Chamber of Commerce. Clubs: Alta, Elk's University, Salt Lake Country. Mason. (32°, Shriner). Republican. Congregationalist. Author: Some Experiences of Russel Lord Tracy, 1860-1941. Home: 1285 Second Av. Address: 151 S. Main St., Salt Lake City, Utah. Died May 17, 1945.

TRAER, Charles Solberg (trā'ĕr), corp. official; b. Chicago, Ill., Nov. 24, 1890; s. Glenn Wood and Ida (Solberg) T.; Ph.B., Yale, 1910; m. Josephine Louise Thomas, July 2, 1931; m. 2d, Marjorie Arnold, Aug. 23, 1940; children—Mary Rose (by former marriage), Patricia Arnold (step-dau.). Began as mining engr. Traer Coal Co., 1910-12; mining engr. Ill. Coal Operators Mut. Employers Liability Ins. Co., 1912-15; treas. and gen. mgr. MacMurray Steel Hoop Co., 1915-17; with Acme Steel Co., Chicago, Ill., since 1919, as mgr. Riverdale Works, 1919-36, also treas., 1922-35, second v.p., 1935-36, v.p. and mgr. Production, 1936-41, pres. since 1941; dir. Truax-Traer Coal Co. During World War I, served as lt. and capt., 10th U.S. Inf. Mem. Am. Iron and Steel Inst., Chi Phi. Clubs: South Shore Country, Swan Lake Gun, Chicago Athletic, La Crosse River Reserve Fishing, Fin 'n' Feather. Home: 5555 Everett Av. Office: Riverdale Station, Chicago 27, Ill. Died Oct. 24, 1949.

TRAFFORD, Bernard Walton, banker; b. Dartmouth, Mass., July 2, 1871; s. William Bradford and Rachel Mott (Davis) T.; grad. Phillips Exeter Acad., Exeter, N.H., 1889; A.B., Harvard, 1893; m. Leonora Brooks Borden, June 5, 1901; children—Leonora (Mrs. George Owen, Jr.), Rachel (Mrs. Herbert S. Carter, Jr.), Bernard W., Annette (Mrs. H. Harrison Hadley, Jr.), Ada Brooks (Mrs. Charles E. Mason, Jr.). Began with Am. Telephone & Telegraph Co.; later mem. engring. staff Bell Telephone Co., became sr. operating v.p., Middle West; v.p. First Nat. Bank of Boston, 1912-28, pres., Mar. 1928-Dec. 1929, vice-chmn. bd., 1929-35, chmn. since 1935; pres. Sterling Ring Traveller Co.; dir. N.E. Telephone & Telegraph Co., Westport Mfg. Co.; mem. corp. Suffolk Savings Bank. In charge membership campaign, N.E., Am. Red Cross, 1917, war fund campaign, 1918. Trustee Phillips Exeter Acad.; regent Avon Sch., Farmington, Conn. Clubs: Harvard, Union, Milton, Hoosic-Whisick (Boston); Country (Brookline). Died Jan. 2, 1941.

TRAFTON, Gilbert Haven, teacher; b. South Elliot, Me., Jan. 9, 1874; s. Asbury Caldwell and Abbie Frost (Taylor) T.; Ph.B., Wesleyan U., Conn., 1898, M.S., 1901; A.M., Teachers' Coll. (Columbia), 1911; m. Mary Adams, Aug. 16, 1898; children—Ruth May, Leroy Haven; m. 2d, Grace M. Romans, Apr. 1930. Science teacher at Beaver (Pa.) Coll., 1898-99, East Greenwich (R.I.) Acad., 1899-1900, State Normal Sch.; Randolph, Vt., 1900-03, Passaic (N.J.) High Sch., 1903-11; prof. nature study, State Teachers' Coll., Mankato, Minn., since 1911. Teacher nature study, U. of Minn., summers, 1917, 18, U. of Chicago, summer 1919. Mem. Am. Nature Study Soc., Minn. Ednl. Assn., N.E.A. (pres. science sect. 1921-22). Unitarian. Author: Field and Laboratory Exercises in Physical Geography, 1905; Methods of Attracting Birds, 1906; Bird Friends, 1916; The Teaching of Science in the Elementary School, 1918; Science of Home and Community, 1919, revised edit., 1926; Biology of Home and Community, 1923; Nature Study and Science for Intermediate Grades, 1927; Star Guide, 1928. Co-author: (with Victor C. Smith) Science in Daily Life, 1936; Workbook in General Science, 1938; Exploring Science, 1942; Enjoying Science, 1942; Using Science, 1942. Home: Mankato, Minn. Died Oct. 31, 1943.

TRAIN, Arthur, novelist, playwright; b. Boston, Mass., Sept. 6, 1875; s. Charles Russell and Sarah M. (Cheney) T.; A B, Harvard University, 1896, LL.B., 1899; married Ethel, d. Benjamin P. Kissam, Apr. 20, 1897 (died May 15, 1923); children—Mrs. Boris Samsonoff, Mrs. Lucy Worcester, Arthur K., Mrs. Helen Hilles; m. 2d, Mrs. Helen Coster (Gerard), Jan. 6, 1926; 1 son, John. Assistant district attorney of New York County, 1901-08, and 1914-15; special deputy attorney general State of New York, 1910, to investigate and prosecute political offenders in Queens County; also prosecuted Henry Siegel, banker, 1914, at Geneseo, New York; member firm Perkins & Train, New York City, 1916-23. Pres. National Institute of Arts and Letters. Clubs: Century, University, Harvard. Author: McAllister and His Double, 1905; The Prisoner at the Bar, 1906; True Stories of Crime, 1908; The Butler's Story, 1909; Mortmain, 1909; Confessions of Artemus Quibble, 1909; Courts, Criminals and the Camorra, 1911; The Goldfish, 1914; The Man Who Rocked the Earth, 1915; The Earthquake, 1918; Tutt and Mr. Tutt, 1920; By Advice of Counsel, 1921; The Hermit of Turkey Hollow, 1921; As It Was in the Beginning, 1921; His Children's Children, 1923; The Needle's Eye, 1924; The Lost Gospel, 1925; Page Mr. Tutt, 1926; The Blind Goddess, 1926; High Winds, 1927; When Tutt Meets Tutt, 1927; Ambition, 1928; Illusion, 1929; Paper Profits, 1930; The Adventures of Ephraim Tutt, 1930; Puritan's Progress, 1931; The Strange Attacks on Herbert Hoover, 1932; Tutt for Tutt, 1934; Manhattan Murder, 1936; Mr. Tutt's Case Book, 1937; Old Man Tutt, 1938; My Day in Court, 1939; From the District Attorney's Office, 1939; Tassels on Her Boots, 1940; Mr. Tutt Comes Home, 1941; Yankee Lawyer, The Autobiography of Ephraim Tutt, 1943. Home: "Sol's Cliff," Bar Harbor, Me. Temporary winter address: 113 E. 73d St., New York, N.Y. Died Dec. 22, 1945.

TRALLE, Henry Edward, religious educator; b. Independence, Missouri, May 19, 1867; s. Henry and Catherine Elizabeth (Cooke) T.; B.A., William Jewell Coll., Mo., 1894; M.A., Columbian (now George Washington) U., 1898; Th.D., Southern Bapt. Theol. Sem., 1901; studied U. of Chicago, 1918; m. Bertha Baldwin, Dec. 22, 1892 (died July 14, 1931); m. 2d, Helen Pearson Walter, July 24, 1935. Ordained Bapt. ministry, 1890; pastor Immanuel Bapt. Ch., Louisville, Ky., 1901-04; supt. Bapt. S.S. work in Mo., 1904-06; editor Central Baptist, 1906-09; pastor Carthage, Mo., 1909-11; head dept. religious edn., Hardin Coll., Mexico, Mo., 1911-15; pres. Kansas City Sch. Religious Pedagogy, 1915-20; editor training publs. Am. Baptist Publ. Soc., 1920-22; lecturer and adviser to churches since 1922. Mem. Religious Edn. Assn. Author: The Sunday School Teachers' School, 1908; Teacher Training Essentials, 1911; Sunday School Experience, 1912; Story-Telling Lessons, 1921; Planning Church Buildings, 1921; Dynamics of Teaching, 1924; Psychology of Leadership, 1925; Building for Religious Education, 1926. Advocate of complete rooms for depts. and classes in ch. bldgs. Consultant for chs. in connection with building projects. Home: Cavalier Hotel. Address: 715 8th St. N.W., Washington, D.C. Died June 9, 1942.

TRAVER, John Gideon, seminary prof.; b. Rhinebeck, N.Y., Dec. 24, 1863; s. Gideon A. and Mary C. (Teal) T.; prep. edn. Hartwick Sem., Otsego County, N.Y.; A.B., Pa. Coll., Gettysburg, 1886 (Greek oration), A.M., 1889; theol. course, Hartwick Sem., 1891; D.D., Susquehanna U., 1901; m. Ettie F. Tompkins, Aug. 22, 1888; 1 son, Amos J. Began as asst. teacher, Hartwick Sem., 1886; advanced to professorship, 1888, prin., 1893-1920, prof. Latin, 1920-33, now emeritus; editor Hartwick Monthly, 1910-20. V.p. Milford Nat. Bank. Formerly sec., pres. and treas. Hartwick Synod Luth. Church; treas. Synod of N.Y. Republican. Address: Hartwick Seminary, Otsego County, N.Y. Died Aug. 20, 1941.

TRAVERS, Edward Schofield (trăv'ĕrz), clergyman; b. Meriden, Conn., Oct. 10, 1874; s. John and Eleanor (Howarth) T.; B.A., Trinity Coll., Conn., 1898, M.A., 1901, S.T.D., 1918; grad. Berkeley Div. Sch. Middletown, Conn., 1901; D.D., U. of Pittsburgh, 1918; m. Louise Ellen Allderdice, Nov. 18, 1913; children—Jane, Eleanor, Edward Schoefield. Deacon, June 5, 1901, priest, June 1, 1902, P.E. Church; asst. minister Grace Chapel, New York, 1901-02, Christ Ch., Poughkeepsie, N.Y., 1902-04, on the Greene Foundation, Trinity Ch., Boston, 1904-06; chaplain, U.S. Mil. Acad., Dec. 1, 1905-13; rector Trinity Ch., Pittsburgh, 1913-22, St. Peter's Ch., St. Louis, 1922-31, Ch. of the Messiah, Rhinebeck, N.Y., since Oct. 1931. Private 1st Connecticut Vol. Inf., Spanish-Am. War. Pres. Metropolitan Ch. Fed., St. Louis, 1925. Republican. Mem. Psi Upsilon, Army and Navy Union, United Spanish War Veterans. Mason. Clubs: Army and Navy (New York); West Point Army Mess; Duquesne, Allegheny Country (Pittsburgh); Bellerive Country (St. Louis). Dep. to Gen. Conv., 1919, 28. Home: Rhinebeck, N.Y. Died Apr. 14, 1942.

TRAVIS, Charles Mabbett (trā'vis), lawyer; b. Brooklyn, N.Y., Dec. 6, 1885; s. Eugene Mabbett and Fannie Bell (Peck) T.; A.B., Wesleyan U., Conn., 1906; LL.B., Columbia, 1909; m. Agnes Mitchell, Feb. 11, 1914 (died Jan. 31, 1937); 1 son, Craig; m. 2d, Irma I. Bartlett, Mar. 6, 1940. Associated in practice of law with Byrne & Cutcheon, N.Y. City, 1909-15; partner Travis, Spence & Hopkins, 1915-26, Travis, Paxson, Wallace & Philbin, 1926-32, Travis, Brownback & Paxson, 1933-40. Mem. Am. and N.Y. State bar assns., Bar Assn. City of New York, Delta Kappa Epsilon, Phi Beta Kappa. Republican. Methodist. Clubs: University, Downtown Athletic (New York). Home: 1711 Glendon Av., Westwood Hills, Los Angeles, Calif. Died Aug. 3, 1948.

TRAVIS, Philip H., lawyer; b. Hartford, Mich., Jan. 3, 1865; s. John W. and Philany (Engle) T.; B.L., U. of Mich. Law Sch., 1890; m. Virginia Johnson, Feb. 6, 1934. Admitted to Mich. bar, 1890; mem. firm Travis, Merrick, Barnum & Riddering, Grand Rapids, Mich., since 1892. Republican. Clubs: University, Torch, Kent Country (Grand Rapids). Home: 244 Morris Av. Office: Michigan Trust Bldg., Grand Rapids, Mich. Died Nov. 4, 1942.

TREADWAY, Allen Towner, (ex-congressman; born Stockbridge, Mass., Sept. 16, 1867; s. William Denton and Harriet (Heaton) T.; A.B., Amherst, 1886, LL.D., 1934; m. Sylvia Shares, October 25, 1893 (died May 22, 1943). Trustee Lee (Mass.) Savings

Bank. Director New England Fire Insurance Co., Berkshire Life Insurance Co. Member Mass. House of Rep., 1904 (com. on ways and means), Senate, 1908-11 (pres. 1909, 10, 11); mem. 63d to 78th Congresses (1913-45), 1st Mass. Dist.; mem. Ways and Means Com., Joint Congressional Com. on Internal Revenue Taxation, Library. Republican. Del.-at-large, Rep. Nat. Conv., 1936. Episcopalian. Mem. Alpha Delta Phi. Mason (active 33°). Home: Stockbridge, Mass.* Died Feb. 16, 1917.

TREADWELL, Aaron Louis (trĕd′wĕl), biologist; b. Redding, Conn., Dec. 23, 1866; s. Aaron and Lois (Mead) T.; B.S., Wesleyan U., Middletown, Conn., 1888, M.S., 1890, hon. D.Sc., 1938; fellow, 1897-98, Ph. D., 1899, U. of Chicago; m. Sarah Hill, June 15, 1892 (died May 25, 1938); children—Lois (Mrs. Beardsley Ruml), Merlin (dec.), Alvin Hill (dec.), Arthur Burr, Louis Mead (dec.). Asst. in natural history, Wesleyan U., 1888-91; prof. biology and geology, Miami U., Oxford, O., 1891-1900; prof. biology, Vassar Coll., 1900-14, prof. of zoölogy, 1914-37, emeritus since 1937. Instr. Marine Biol. Lab., Woods Hole, Mass., 1898-1906, 13, Cold Spring Harbor, L.I., 1907; hon. curator annulates, American Museum of Natural History, N.Y., 1909-18, research associate in same since 1918; mem. research staff, N.Y. Zoöl. Soc., 1930, 31. Fellow A.A.A.S.; mem. Am. Soc. Zoölogists (v.p. 1921), Am. Soc. Naturalists (sec. 1912), Phi Beta Kappa, Chi Psi. Writer of biology and zoölogy articles in New Internat. Ency. Year Book, since 1907, and various papers in zoöl. jours. With Carnegie Instn. expdns. through West Indies, Fiji and Samoa. Address: Vassar Coll., Poughkeepsie, N.Y.; (summer) Redding, Conn., P.O. R.D. 2, Danbury, Conn.* Died June 24, 1947.

TRECKER, Joseph Leonard, mfr.; b. Milwaukee, Wis., Feb. 20, 1902; s. Theodore and Emma (Pufahl) T.; student Ia. State Coll. Ames, Ia., 1921-24; m. Florence Volz, June 5, 1926; children—Robert Joseph, Joan Mary, Theodore Simon. With Kearney & Trecker Corp., Milwaukee, Wis., since 1925; began as engr., became dir. 1928, treas., 1934, vice pres., 1936, exec. vice pres. and dir. since 1942; vice pres. and dir. Kearney & Trecker Products Corp.; dir. The Controls Labs., Inc.; pres. Amtea Corp.; consultant to sec. of war, 1941; organized and became chief of sub-contract branch O.P.M., also served as dep. dir. contract distribution div. O.P.M., 1941. Mem. machine tool industry advisory com. W.P.B. Mem. Nat. Machine Tool Builders Assn. (dir. 1942-45, pres. 1944-45), Am. Soc. Mech. Engrs. Am. Soc. Tool Engrs., Sigma Alpha Epsilon. Clubs: Wisconsin, Athletic, Blue Mound Golf and Country (Milwaukee). Home: 630 Honey Creek Pkwy., Milwaukee 13. Office: 6784 W. National Av., Milwaukee 14, Wis. Died Oct. 7, 1947.

TREES, Joe Clifton, oil and gas operator; b. Westmoreland County, Pa., Nov. 10, 1869; s. Isaac T. and Lucy Ann (Johnston) T.; grad. Ind. Normal Sch., 1892, U. of Pittsburgh, 1895; m. Claudine Virginia Willison, Dec. 20, 1894; m. 2d, Edith Lehm, Jan. 10, 1929. Began in oil and gas business, western Pa., 1890; v.p. Benedum Trees Oil Co. Trustee U. of Pittsburgh. Republican. Presbyterian. Mason (32°, K.T., Shriner). Clubs: Duquesne, Pittsburgh Athletic, Oakmont Country. Home: Gibsonia, Pa. Office: Benedum Trees Bldg., Pittsburgh, Pa. Died May 19, 1943.

TRELEASE, William, botanist; b. Mt. Vernon, N.Y., Feb. 22, 1857; s. Samuel R. and Mary (Gandall) T.; B S., Cornell, 1880; Sc D., Harvard, 1884; LL.D., U. of Wis., 1902, U. of Mo., 1903, Washington U., 1907; m. Julia M. Johnson, July 19, 1882; children—Frank Johnson, Marjorie (dec.), Sam Farlow, Sidney Briggs, William. In charge Summer Sch., Botany, Harvard, 1883-84; lecturer botany, Johns Hopkins, 1884; instr. botany, U. of Wis., 1881-83, prof., 1883-85; prof. botany, Washington U., 1885-1913; dir. Mo. Bot. Garden, 1889-1912; prof. botany, U. of Ill., 1913-26, emeritus since 1926. Mem. Ill. State Board Natural Resources and Conservation since 1917. Chmn. Am. board editors Botanisches Centralblatt, 1900-21. Fellow Am. Acad. Arts and Sciences (1892), A A.A S.; mem. Nat. Acad. Sciences (1902), Am. Philos. Soc. (1903), etc., diréctеur (pres) Académie Internationale de Géographie Botanique, 1896; 1st pres. Bot. Soc. America, 1894-95 and 1918; pres. Am. Soc. Naturalists, 1903, Cambridge Entomol. Club, 1889, Engelmann Bot. • Club, 1898-99 (hon. pres. since 1909); sec. Wis. Hort. Soc., 1882-85, Acad. Science St. Louis, 1896 (president 1909-11). Club: Round Table (St. Louis). Mem. of Delta Upsilon, Sigma Xi, Phi Beta Kappa, Pi Gamma Mu. Edited (with Asa Gray) Botanical Works of the late George Engelmann. Translated Poulsen's Botanical Micro-Chemistry and Salomonsen's Bacteriological Technology. Author: Agave in the West Indies, 1913; The Genus Phoradendron, 1916; Plant Materials of Decorative Gardening, 1917, 21, 26, 30; Winter Botany, 1918, 25, 30; The American Oaks, 1925; also many papers and reports on botany and entomology. Commemorated in many plant names and in Mount Trelease (12,500 ft. high), at head of Clear Creek, Colo., at first ascent to Loveland Pass. Home: 804 S. Lincoln Av., Urbana, Ill. Died Jan. 1, 1945.

TREMAIN, Eloise Ruthven, educator; b. New York, N.Y.; d. Louis Halleck and Sarah Charlotte (Connolley) Tremain; B.A., Bryn Mawr, 1904; studied U. of Pa.; hon. M.A., Lake Forest Coll., 1927. Teacher mathematics and history, Davison Dodge Sch., Louisville, Ky., 1904-07; teacher Latin and history, Oldfields Sch., Glencoe, Md., 1907-09; teacher history and mathematics, Phila. High Sch. for Girls, 1909-17; prin. Rowland Hall, Salt Lake City, Utah., 1917-18, Ferry Hall, Lake Forest, Ill., since 1918. Mem. N.E.A., Nat. Assn. Principals of Schs. for Girls (pres. 1922-24), Am. Assn. Univ. Women (pres. Chicago br. 1924-28). Children's Scholarship League of Chicago (dir.), Prog. Edn. Assn., Bryn Mawr Alumnae Assn. Episcopalian. Clubs: Chicago College. Home: Ferry Hall, Lake Forest, Ill. Died Nov. 15, 1946.

TREMAINE, Burton Gad (trê-mān), hon. vice-pres. Gen. Electric Co.; b. Marine City, Mich., Oct. 14, 1863; s. Warren and Ellen Matilda• (Freeman) T.; married; children—Gretchen (dec.), Mrs. Bertine Tremaine Treat, B. Carl, Burton G., Jr., Warren D., H. Alan (dec.). With Gen. Electric Co. 32 yrs., co-founder Gen. Electric Co.'s Nela Park, dir. 1923-45, hon. vice-pres.; organized Fostoria Lamp Co., 1898, later merged with Sunbeam Incandesc. Lamp Co., gen. sales mgr., 1901-11, co-mgr. when merged with Edison Lamp Works of Gen. Electric Co. Director Cities Service Co. since Jan. 17, 1912. Clubs: Union, Country (Cleveland, O.); Mohawk (Schenectady, N.Y.). Address: 17455 Shelbourne Rd., Cleveland Hts., Ohio. Died Feb. 16, 1948.

TRESIDDER, Donald Bertrand (trĕs′ĭ-dẽr), pres. Stanford U.; b. Tipton, Ind., Apr. 7, 1894; s. James T. and Sarah Emily (Daum) T.; student U. of Chicago, 1914; A.B., Stanford U., 1919, M.D., 1927; m. Mary Louise Curry, June 16, 1920. Asst. mgr. Curry Camping Co., Yosemite Nat. Park, Calif., 1921-25; pres. Yosemite Park and Curry Co., Yosemite Nat. Park, since 1925; pres. Stanford U. since Sept. 1943. Trustee Stanford U., 1939-43, pres. of bd. of trustees, 1942. Served with Med. Corps, U.S. Army, 1917; transferred to Signal Corps as aviation cadet, Jan. 1918, commd. 2d lt., June 1918; disch. Jan. 1919. Mem. Sigma Xi. Clubs: Bohemian, Commonwealth, University, Pacific Union (all San Francisco), University (New York); Cosmos (Washington). Address: Stanford University, Calif. Died Jan. 28, 1948.

TRESSLER, Irving Dart (trĕs′lẽr), author; b. Madison, Wis., Aug. 12, 1908; s. Albert Willis and Arlouine (Dart) T.; A.B., U. of Wis.; m. Anne Kendall, July 1, 1931. With Washington Bureau of Minneapolis Journal, 1933-34; asso. editor Life Mag., 1934-36; author of Scribner's Mag. Quiz, 1936-39; author of Look Mag. Quiz, 1939-40; author Parents' Mag. Adult Quiz, 1940-41. Mem. Alpha Delta Phi. Baptist. Author: How to Lose Friends and Alienate People, 1937; The Tressler Quiz, 1938; With Malice Towards All, 1939; Horse and Buggy Daze, 1940; Readers Digest Very Little, 1941. Contbr. to Esquire, Commentator, Fortune, Mademoiselle, Coronet. Address: 2909 Columbia Rd., Shorewood Hills, Madison, Wis.* Died Feb. 16, 1944.

TREVORROW, Robert Johns (trē-vŏr′ō), clergyman; b. St. Ives, Eng., May 21, 1877; s. Anthony and Dorcas Quick (Johns) T.; A.B., Coll. of Pacific, San Jose, Calif., 1898, A M., 1901, D D., 1913; B D., Drew Theol. Sem., Madison, N.J., 1903; Union Theol. Sem., New York, 1911-12; m. Editha Carpenter, Oct. 25, 1905; 1 son, Robert Johns. Ordained M.E. ministry, 1898; pastor Stockton, Calif., 1898-1900, St. Paul's Ch., New York, 1900-05, Elmhurst, L.I., Carmel, Modena, Central Valley and Woodlawn Heights, 1905-13; pres. Drew Sem. for Young Women, Carmel, N.Y., 1913-17; pres. Centenary Collegiate Inst., Hackettstown, N.J., since Apr. 1917. Pres. Ednl. Assn. of M.E. Ch., 1928-29, Am. Assn. of Junior Colleges, 1935-36, Junior Council of Middle States Assn. of Colls. and Secondary Schs., 1935-37. Decorated Comdr. Order of the Crown of Roumania, 1932; Officer of the Order of the White Lion, Czechoslovakia, 1937. Clubs: Musconetcong Country, Canoe Brook Country, Sky Top, Interchurch Clergy. Address: Hackettstown, N.J. Died Jan. 31, 1943.

TREXLER, Frank M., judge; b. Allentown, Pa., Jan. 9, 1861; s. Edwin W. and Matilda Sauerbeck) T.; A.B., Muhlenberg Coll., Allentown, 1879, A.M., 1882, LL.D., 1910; m. Jennie R. Shelling, Nov. 7, 1889 (dec.); children—Edwin W., Mrs. Dorothy Williams, Mrs. Frances Schmidt, Mrs. Marion Baldrige, Robert W. Began practice at Allentown, 1882; city solicitor, 11 yrs.; president judge, Lehigh County, Pa., 1902-13; elected associate justice of Superior Court of Pa., Feb. 1914, pres. judge, 1930-35, retired, Jan. 1935. President Allentown Y.M.C.A., 1890-1940; mem. state com., Y.M.C.A. Mem. Pa. State Bar Assn., Am. Bar Assn., Hist. Soc. of Pa., Lehigh Co. Hist. Soc. (past pres.), Pa. German Soc., Huguenot Soc., Pa. German Folklore Soc. (past pres.), Pa. Fedn. of Hist. Socs. (past pres.), S.R. Republican. Presbyterian. Mason (33°), Odd Fellow. Home: 1115 Walnut St., Allentown, Pa. Died Feb. 22, 1947.

TREXLER, Samuel Geiss, clergyman; b. Bernville, Pa., October 19, 1877; s. Rev. Daniel D. and Agnes A. (Geiss) T.; A.B., Muhlenberg Coll., Allentown, Pa., 1896, D.D., 1919; grad. Luth. Theol. Sem., Phila., 1899; student at U. of Jena, 1913; S.T.D., Syracuse U., 1941, LL.D., Thiel. Coll., 1943. Ordained Lutheran ministry, 1899; pastor Messiah Church, Brooklyn, N.Y., 1899-1912 (which he organized); student pastor of New York and N.E. Synod, 1912-14; organized religious work among Luth. students at Columbia, Harvard, Yale and Cornell univs.; pastor Ch. of the Redeemer, Buffalo, 1914-20; pres. Synod of N.Y. and N.E., 1920-29; first pres. United Lutheran Synod of New York, 1929-34, 1939-44; commr. Lutheran World Fedn. for Russia, 1946; pres. Bd. of Fgn. Missions of United Lutheran Ch. of Am., 1940-44; del. to 3d Lutheran World Conv., Paris, 1935; toured South America to inspect missions and schools, 1941. Chaplain U.S. Army in France and Germany, 1917-19. Univ. preacher, Columbia and Cornell U.; trustee Hartwick Coll., Josiah Macy Junior Foundation, Endicott Coll. Mem. S.R., Pilgrims, Phi Gamma Delta. Clubs; Univ., Clergy (past pres.). Author: Crusaders of the Twentieth Century, 1926; Out of Thirty-five Years, 1936; John A. Morehead, 1938, A Pastor Wings over South America, 1941. Home: 1170 Fifth Av., New York 29, N.Y. Died May 30, 1949.

TRIMBLE, South, govt. official; b. Hazel Green, Ky., Apr. 13, 1864; s. Francis Asbury and Mary Elizabeth (South) T.; ed. pub. schs., Frankfort, Ky., and Excelsior Inst.; m. Carrie Belle Allan, Nov. 24, 1885; children—James Francis, Maria Fenwick (wife of Dr. Carlos Albert Fish), Stephen Asbury (dec.), Margaret Allan (Mrs. David Lynn), South Jr. Fannie May (Mrs. Austin Cooper Waller). Engaged in farming since 1883; elected mem. Kentucky Ho. of Reps., 1898 and 1900 (served as speaker last year of term); mem. 57th to 59th Congresses; clerk House of Reps., 62d to 65th and 72d to 79th Congresses. Democratic nominee for lt. gov. of Ky., 1907. Home: 10 Grafton St., Chevy Chase, Md. Office: U.S. House of Representatives, Washington, D.C. Died Nov. 23, 1946.

TRIMBLE, William Pitt, lawyer; b. Cynthiana, Ky., Feb. 2, 1863; s. William Wallace and Mary (Barlow) T.; prep. edn., Woodward High Sch., Cincinnati, O., and École Alsacienne, Paris, France; A.B., U. of Cincinnati, 1885; student Cincinnati Law Sch., 1886; m. Cannie Ford, Nov. 10, 1897; children—Ford, Mary (Mrs. Lancelot E. Gowen), William Pitt, Augusta Ware Webb (Mrs. Wm. Meade Fletcher, Jr.). Admitted to Washington bar, 1890, and began practice at Seattle. Rep. presdl. elector, Wash., 1908. Episcopalian. Clubs: University, College, Rainier, Engineers, Seattle Golf; Tacoma (Wash.) Golf and Country; Chevy Chase (Washington, D.C.); National Republican (New York). Home: 532 Belmont Av. N. Office: Dexter Horton Bldg., Seattle, Wash. Died Mar. 19, 1943.

TRIPLETT, John Edwin, clergyman; b. Cynthiana, Ky., Oct. 14, 1880; s. Rev. John Edwin and Anna Carrie (Johnston) T.; grad. Shepherd Coll. State Normal Sch., Shepherdstown, W.Va., 1896; A.B., Hampden-Sydney Coll., 1900; A.M., Princeton, 1903; B D., Princeton Theol. Sem., 1904; D.D., Richmond Coll., 1914; unmarried. Ordained Presbyn. ministry, 1904; pastor 2d Ch., N.Y. City, 1904-07, Bedford Park Ch., 1907-09, First Ch., Woodbury, N.J., 1909-20, Girard Av. Ch., Phila., since 1920; prof. Greek and N.T. lit., Temple U., since 1923. Mem. Phi Gamma Delta. Democrat. Mason, Odd Fellow. Lecturer on religious and lit. subjects. Home: 930 N. 15th St., Philadelphia, Pa. Died May 31, 1943.

TRITLE, John Stewart (trĭ′t′l); b. Virginia City, Nev., Mar. 22, 1872; s. Frederick Augustus and Jane Catherine (Hereford) T.; Hopkins Grammar Sch., New Haven, 1889-90, Sheffield Scientific Sch. (Yale), 1891-92; m. Eleanor L. Hoblitzelle, Mar. 7, 1905; children—John Stewart, Clarence Hoblitzelle. Became contracting engr., 1895; chief supt. of constrn. World's Fair, St. Louis, 1903-04; with Westinghouse Electric & Mfg. Co. since 1905, dist. mgr., Kansas City, Mo., 1905-16, St. Louis, 1916-22, mgr. merchandising dept., New York, 1922-25, gen. mgr. merchandising dept., Mansfield, O., 1925-29, v.p. in charge mfg., 1929-31, v.p. from 1931 until retired. Mem. Berzelius Soc. (Yale). Republican. Episcopalian. Home: 410 N. Newstead Av., St. Louis, Mo. Died Mar. 7, 1947.

TROUBETZKOY, Amélie Rives (troo-bĕts-koi), novelist; b. Richmond, Va., Aug. 23, 1863; d. Alfred Landon Rives; ed. by pvt. tutors; m. John Armstrong Chanler, 1888 (divorced); m. 2d, Prince Pierre Troubetzkoy (Russian), Feb. 18, 1896. Author: The Quick or the Dead, 1888; A Brother to Dragons, 1888; Virginia of Virginia; Herod and Mariamne; Witness of the Sun; According to St. John; Barbara Dering; Athelwold; Damsel Errant; Meriel; Tanis; Selené, 1905; Augustine the Man, 1906; The Golden Rose, 1908; Trix and Over-the-Moon, 1909; Pan's Mountain, 1910; Hidden House, 1911; The World's End, 1913; Shadows of Flames, 1915; The Fear Market (dramatic comedy, prod. Booth Theatre, New York, winter 1916); The Ghost Garden (novel), 1918; Allegiance (drama, prod. Maxine Elliot's Theatre, Aug. 1918); The Prince and the Pauper, dramatization by Amélie Rives, prod. Booth Theatre, New York, Nov. 1920; As The Wind Blew (poems), 1922; The Sea-Woman's Cloak and November Eve, 1923 (prod. Laboratory Theatre, Nov. 1925); The Queerness of Celia, 1926; Love-in-a-Mist (with Gilbert Emery) prod. Gaiety Theatre, New York, 1926; Firedamp (novel), 1930; The Young Elizabeth (drama, won prize of Little Theatre of St. Louis, Mo.), 1937. Contbr. to mags. Home: Castle Hill, Cobham, Albemarle County, Va. Died June 15, 1945.

TROY, John Weir, ex-gov. of Alaska; b. Dungeness, Wash., Oct. 31, 1868; s. Smith and Laura Bass (Weir) T.; ed. pub. and pvt. schs.; m. Minerva Lewis, 1892; children—Helen Marion (Mrs. Robert W. Bender), Dorothy Minerva (wife of George A. Lingo); m. 2d, Ethel Crocker Forgy, 1916. Reporter Port Townsend Argus, 1886-87; dep. auditor Clallam County, Wash., 1889-91; dep. county clk., 1891-92, county auditor, 1892-97; pub. and editor Weekly Democrat Leader, Port Angeles, 1891-97; editor Skagway (Alaska) Daily Alaskan, 1899-1907; publicity rep., Seattle, 1907-11; pub. and editor Alaska Yukon Mag., 1911-12; editor Daily Alaska Empire, Juneau, 1913, owner since 1914; collector of customs, Dist. of Alaska, 1919-22; governor Alaska, 1933-39. Alaskan del. to Dem. Nat. convs., 6 times; sec. Wash. Dem. State Com., 1912-13; chmn. Dem. Alaska Territorial Com., 1932-34. Mem. Sigma Delta Chi, Alaska Pioneers. Democrat. Elk, Moose. Clubs: Racquet (Washington, D.C.); Arctic (Seattle, Wash.). Address: Juneau, Alaska. Died May 2, 1942.

TRUESDALE, Philemon E. (trōōz'dăl), surgeon; b. 1874; M.D., Harvard, 1898. Practiced in Fall River, Mass., since 1900; limiting practice to surgery. Fellow Am. Coll. of Surgeons, A.M.A.; member Am. Surg. Assn., New Eng. Surg. Soc., Am. Assn. for Thoracic Surgery, Am. Bd. Surgery. Home: Tunipus Farm, Westport, Mass. Office: 151 Rock St., Fall River, Mass.* Died June 12, 1945.

TRUETT, George W. (trōō'ĕt), clergyman; b. Clay County, N.C., May 6, 1867; s. Charles L. and Mary R. (Kimsey) T.; A.B., Baylor U., 1897, D.D., 1899; LL.D., Baylor U., U. of Ala., Southern Meth. U.; m. Josephine Jenkins, June 28, 1894. Projected Hiawassee (Ga.) High Sch. and was its prin., 1887-89; financial sec. Baylor Univ., 1890-92 (elected to presidency but declined); ordained to Bapt. ministry, 1890; pastor at Waco, 1893-97, First Bapt. Ch., Dallas, since 1897. Ex-pres. Southern Bapt. Conv.; pres. Bapt. World Alliance 1934-39. Address: 5105 Live Oak St., Dallas, Tex.* Died July 7, 1944.

TRUMBULL, Annie Eliot, author; b. Hartford, Conn.; d. J. Hammond and Sarah A. (Robinson) Trumbull; grad. Hartford High Sch., 1876. Author: An Hour's Promise, 1889; White Birches, 1893; A Christmas Accident, and Other Stories, 1897; A Cape Cod Week, 1898; Rod's Salvation, 1898; Mistress Content Cradock, 1899; A Masque of Culture (play), 1893; A Wheel of Progress (play), 1897; Life's Common Way, 1903. Address: 734 Asylum Av., Hartford, Conn. Died Dec. 23, 1949.

TSCHUDY, Herbert Bolivar (chōō'dĭ), artist, museum curator; b. Plattsburg, O., December 28, 1874; s. Bolivar and Katherine (Miller) Judy; ed. U. of Ill., 1893-95, Art Students' League, N.Y. City, 1898-99; m. Gertrude E. Ridenour, Aug. 27, 1904 (died July 1931). Artist at Brooklyn Museum, 1900-23, curator paintings and sculpture, 1923-37; represented in Brooklyn Museum collection of water colors, also mural paintings; represented in Am. Museum Natural History, N.Y. Hist. Soc. (N.Y. City), Santa Fe (N.M.) Museum, N.Y. Aquarium, Nat. Museum (Warsaw, Poland), Nat. Museum (Sofia, Bulgaria), Public Library (Yellow Springs, O.), Antioch Coll., and pvt. collections. Mem. Laboratory of Anthropology, Inc., Santa Fe, N.M. Mem. Metropolitan Mus. of Art, Contemporary Arts, Phila. Water Color Club, Am. Water Color Soc., Brooklyn Soc. Artists (Brooklyn), Fifteen Gallery. Republican. Unitarian. Club: Salmagundi. Writer. Contbr. Brooklyn Museum Quarterly. Address: 21 E. 14th St., New York 3, N.Y. Died Apr. 16, 1946.

TUBBS, Arthur Lewis (Arthur Sylvester), playwright; b. Glens Falls, N.Y., July 2, 1867; s. George W. and Mary L. (Lewis) T.; ed. Glens Falls High Sch.; studied music in Glens Falls and Syracuse, N.Y., and Phila.; unmarried. Engaged in newspaper work since 1885; was dramatic and musical critic for Phila. Evening Bulletin 38 years, retiring, July 1935. Contbr. many poems and short stories to newspapers and magazines; writer of plays used by amateur theatrical cos. and also for professional stage. Plays: Cowslip Farm, The Fruit of His Folly; Followed by Fate; Valley Farm; Heart of a Hero; Willowdale; Penalty of Pride; The Country Minister; Miss Buzby's Boarders; Farm Folks; The Village Schoolma'am; For the Old Flag; Alias Miss Sherlock; Home Acres; Rose Lawn; etc. Address: 311 S. Hicks St., Philadelphia, Pa.* Died Jan. 27, 1946.

TUBBS, Eston Valentine, educator; b. Hillsboro, Ind., Feb. 14, 1883; s. Daniel A. and Harriet (Cheney) T.; A.B., Northwestern U., 1909; awarded fellowship U. of Ill., A.M., 1910; Ph.D., U. of Chicago, 1924; m. Vinnie I. McAllister, Feb. 24, 1904; children—Edwin D., Dorothy L., Genevieve B., Marian L., Deane R. Teacher country schs., Ill., 1902-04; supt. schs. Cheneyville, Ill., 1904-05; prin. Township High Sch., Lawrenceville, 1910-12; supt. Township High Sch., Centralia, 1912-17; prin. high sch., Tulsa, Okla., 1917-18; supt. New Trier Township High Sch., Winnetka, Ill., 1919-23; lecturer on edn., Northwestern U., 1921-22; lecturer on edn., Art Inst. Chicago, 1924-28; prof. and head dept. edn., Lewis Inst., Chicago, 1924-27; prin. Chase, Budlong, Brentano and Gale schs., Chicago, 1927-36; dir. Bur. of Curriculum, Chicago Pub Schs., 1928-32; Lecturer in Education, Loyola Univ., Chicago, 1930-31; prin. Morgan Park High Sch., Chicago, since 1936. Mem. N.E.A. (dept. secondary-school prins.), Ill. State Teachers Assn., Phi Delta Kappa, Delta Kappa Pi, Phi Beta Kappa, Alpha Delta Phi; organizer and mem. exec. com. Phi Beta Kappa Assn. of Chicago Area. Methodist. Author: Universal Teachers' Plan Book, 1929; (with W. E. McVey) Find Yourself, 1929; Living on the Farm and in a Village; Living in Towns and in Small Cities; Living in Large Cities, 1942; Illinois: The State and Its Government, 1944; also many articles in mags. Professorial lecturer in edn., De Paul Univ., Chicago, 1930-37. Founder of Am. Youth League. Home: 11031 S. Church St., Chicago, Ill. Died June 15, 1947.

TUBBY, William Bunker, architect; b. Des Moines, Ia., Sept. 21, 1858; s. Josiah Thomas and Phebe Anna (Bunker) T.; prep. edn., Friends Sch., Brooklyn, N.Y.; student Poly. Inst. of Brooklyn; m. Clara Jane Prentiss, June 24, 1885; children—George Prentiss, Ruth, William Bunker, Paul Bunker. Began as draftsman, with E. L. Roberts, architect, N.Y. City, 1875; in practice as architect, N.Y. City, since 1883. Prin. works: Pratt Inst. Library, Poly. Inst., Wallabout Market, Brooklyn Warehouse & Storage Co. Bldg., 5 Carnegie Library bldgs. (all in Brooklyn); Nassau County Court House, Mineola, N.Y.; People's Natural Gas Co. Bldg., Pittsburgh, Pa.; East O. Gas Co. Bldg., Cleveland; Norwalk (Conn.) Hosp. and Nurses Home; Westport (Conn.) Y.M.C.A.; Greenwich (Conn.) Library; Greenwich Municipal Hosp.; also many sch. bldgs. and residences. Mem. A.I.A., Archtl. League, Greenwich Chamber Commerce, Nantucket Soc. Quaker. Club: Rembrandt (New York). Home: North St., Greenwich, Conn. Office: 444 Madison Av., New York, N.Y. Died May 19, 1944.

TUCKER, Beverley Randolph, neuropsychiatrist; b. Richmond, Va., Apr. 26, 1874; s. John Randolph and Fannie Booth (Crump) T.; ed. Va. Mil. Inst., 1890-92; M.D., Med. Coll. of Va., Richmond, 1905; post-grad. work, Phila., New York, London and Vienna; m. Elsie Boyd, Apr. 3, 1907; children—Mary Hannah, Elsie Boyd, Weir Mitchell, Beverley R. Asst. to Dr. S. Weir Mitchell, Phila., 1906, 07; adj. prof. nervous and mental diseases, Med. Coll. of Va., 1907-12, prof. 1912-1938. President and physician in charge Tucker Hospital, Inc.; member State Board of Health, Va. (mem. exec. com., 1917-1920; member of board Nemours Foundation. Editor Old Dominion Journal Medicine and Surgery, 1908-14. Member Richmond Light Inf. Blues 2 yrs. Contract surgeon U.S. Army, 1918; mem. med. advisory bd., Selective Service; mem. Am. bd. Am. Hosp., Paris. Pres. Richmond Acad. Medicine, 1942-43. Diplomate Am. Bd. Psychiatry and Neurology. Fellow Am. Coll. Physicians, Am. Psychiatric Assn. Mem. Soc. of Cincinnati (pres. in State of Va., 1933-35), Am. Neurol. Assn., Med. Soc. of Va. (councilor), Tri-State Med. Assn. (pres. 1931-32), Mental Hygiene Soc. of Va. (pres.), Pi Mu, Phi Beta Kappa. Democrat. Episcopalian. Clubs: Commonwealth, Westmoreland (pres. 1924-25), Country; Writers Club of Va. Author: S. Weir Mitchell, 1914; Nervous Children, 1916; Verses of Virginia, 1923; The Lost Lenore (one-act play), 1929; The Gift of Genius, Adolescence; Narna Darrell (hist. novel), 1936; Various Verse, 1938; Tales of the Tuckers, 1942; also of sect. on cranial nerves, Tice's Practice of Medicine, 1920. Contbr. articles to med. publs., poems to newspapers and mags. Home: 2700 Monument Av. Office: 212 W. Franklin St., Richmond, Va. Died June 19, 1945.

TUCKER, Frank, publicist, editor; b. New York, N.Y., Oct. 21, 1861; s. George Henderson and Julia Augusta (Underhill) T.; B.S., Coll. City of New York, 1880; m. Felicia Mariana Leiss, Jan. 17, 1894. In business in New York, 1880-82; went to Jamestown, N.D., to start a wheat ranch, 1882; bought and was editor Jamestown Alert, daily and weekly newspaper; reporter and asst. city editor N.Y. Herald, 1887-89; founder, publisher and editor Jersey City News, 1889-98; exec. officer N.Y. Assn. for Improving the Condition of the Poor, 1898-1902; mgr. Charles M. Schwab's park playgrounds for children, S.I., 1902-04; v.p. Provident Loan Soc. of New York, 1904-28. Initiated injury into standard of living by com. N.Y. State Conf. of Charities and Correction; initiated inquiry into social and industrial conditions of Pittsburgh, known as the Pittsburgh Survey; prepared report on pub. baths that resulted in establishment by New York of system of interior baths; initiated inquiry into salary and chattel loans in New York. Trustee and incorporator Bur. of Municipal Research, New York; treas. N.Y. State Conf. Charities and Correction; mem. bd. mgrs. Mohansic State Hosp. for the Insane, and of Prison Assn. of N.Y.; treas. Survey Associates, Inc. (publs. of "The Survey"); treas. and mem. council of University Settlement Soc. of New York; mem. bd. govs. New Rochelle Hosp.; chmn. Charter Revision Commn. of New Rochelle; now retired from active work. Pres. Nat. Conf. Charities and Correction, 1912-13. Mem. Alpha Delta Phi (Manhattan Chapter). Home: 32 Carleon Av., Larchmont, N.Y. Died Apr. 30, 1946.

TUCKER, Harry, highway engr.; b. Amherst County, Va., Feb. 7, 1890; s. Cornelius Sale and Sallie (Stickley) T.; A.B., and B.S., Washington and Lee U., 1910, C.E., 1923; m. Mary Lillian Briggs, May 5, 1918 (died Aug. 24, 1930); children—Harry, Robert Briggs. Admitted to N.C. bar, 1914; instr. in civil engring., N.C. State Coll. of Agr. and Engring, 1910-16, prof. of highway engring. since 1920, dir. Engring. Expt. Sta. since 1932; cons. engr. and tech. expert in civil engring., highway transportation and safety. Served with 105th Engrs., U.S. Army, with A.E.F., advancing from pvt. to capt., 1917-19. Mem. N.C. Utilities Commn. Mem. Am. Society Civil Engrs., Inst. of Traffic Engrs., N.C. Bar Assn., Sigma Phi Epsilon, Theta Tau, Phi Kappa Phi. Ind. Democrat. Presbyterian. Author: The History of the 105th Engineer Regiment (with W. P. Sullivan), 1919; Highway Accidents in North Carolina and Guides to Safety, 1935; Manual in the Testing of Materials, 1935; Highway Economics (with M. C. Leager). Contbr. many articles on highway transportation, accidents, etc., to jours. Home: 20 Logan Court, Raleigh, N.C. Died Mar. 18, 1942.

TUCKER, Irvin B., lawyer; b. Winston-Salem, N.C., Sept. 17, 1878; s. Francis A. and Nannie E. (Charles) T.; N.C. State Coll. Agr. and Engring., Raleigh, N.C., 1897-1900; student law dept., U. of N.C., 1900; m. Bessie Richardson, 1910; children—Irvin B., Amanda, Charles R. (dec.). Admitted to N.C. bar, 1901, and began practice at Whiteville; supervisor of census, 6th dist. of N.C., 1910; chmn. Draft Bd., Columbus County, N.C., World War; U.S. dist. atty., Eastern Dist. of N.C., 1921-30; mem. U.S. Bd. of Parole, Washington, D.C., 1930-35. Served as U.S. commr., 1902-14; mayor of Whiteville, 1915-16. Trustee, mem. exec. com. N.C. State U. Del. Rep. Nat. Conv., 1916, 20, 32. Mem. Am. Bar Assn., N.C. Bar Assn. (v.p. 1935). Am. Prison Assn. Mem. and sec. N.C. Bd. of Appeals No. 3, Selective Service System, 1941-42, chmn., 1942. Pres. Whiteville Rotary Club, 1939. Baptist. Mason, K.P. Home: Whiteville, N.C. Died Dec. 23, 1943.

TUECHTER, August Herman (tĭk'tēr), mfr.; b. Cincinnati, O., Aug. 15, 1869; s. William Rudolph and Louise (Geier) T.; ed. high sch. and business coll.; unmarried. Office mgr. Bickford Drill Co., 1887-92; gen. mgr. and partner Bickford Drill & Tool Co., 1893-98; business mgr. and half owner Cincinnati Machine Tool Co., 1899-1908; pres. Cincinnati Bickford Tool Co. since 1909; v.p. Cincinnati Rubber Mfg. Co.; secretary The Factory Power Co.; director Lincoln National Bank. Trustee Ohio Mfrs. Association, 1932; councilor Nat. Metal Trades Assn., 1932; v.p. General Protestant Orphan Home, Cincinnati. Mem. Nat. Machine Tool Builders Assn. America (pres. 1920-23), Nat. Metal Trades Assn. (pres. Cincinnati Br. 1916, 17); Army Ordnance Assn. (pres. Cincinnati post, 1922-23); associate mem. Am. Society M.E. Republican. Mem. Evangelical Reformed Ch. Clubs: Engineers, Cincinnati Club (v.p. 1918), Rotary, Queen City (Cincinnati). Home: 2662 Madison Rd., Cincinnati 8. Office: Oakley, Cincinnati 9, O. Died May 17, 1947.

TUFTS, James Hayden, univ. prof.; b. Monson, Mass., July 9, 1862; s. Rev. James and Mary E. (Warren) T.; A.B., Amherst, 1884, A.M., 1890, LL.D., 1904; B.D., Yale, 1889; student Freiburg and Berlin, 1891-92; Ph.D., Freiburg, 1892; LL.D., U. of Calif. at Los Angeles, 1937; m. Cynthia Hobart Whitaker, Aug. 25, 1891 (died Jan. 11, 1920); children—Irene, James Warren; m. 2d, Matilde Castro, June 18, 1923. Instr. mathematics, Amherst, 1885-87; instr. philosophy, U. of Mich., 1889-91; asst. prof. philosophy, U. of Chicago, 1892-94, asso. prof., 1894-1900, prof., 1900-30, now emeritus, head of dept., 1905-30, dean Sr. Coll., 1899-1904 and 1907-08, dean of faculties, 1923-26, vice-pres., 1924-26. Lecturer in philosophy, U. of Calif. at Los Angeles, 1931-33. Mem. A.A.A.S., Am. Philos. Assn. (pres. 1914), Western Philos. Assn. (pres. 1906, 14); Pacific Philos. Assn. (pres. 1934). Author: (with J. Dewey) Ethics, 1908, 1932; Our Democracy, 1917; The Real Business of Living, 1918; Ethics of Coöperation, 1918, Education and Training for Social Work, 1923; America's Social Morality, 1933; also author various monographs on philos. subjects. Translator and Editor: Windelband's History of Philosophy, 1893, 1901. Contbr. to Baldwin's Dictionary of Philosophy and Psychology, 1901. Co-editor: Studies in Philosophy and Psychology, 1906; Letters, Lectures and Addresses of Charles Edward Garman, 1909. Editor The School Review, 1906-09, International Journal of Ethics, 1914-30. Clubs: Quadrangle, Faculty (Berkeley). Address: Care County National Bank, Santa Barbara, Calif. Died Aug. 5, 1942.

TULEY, Philip Speed (tū'lē), mfr.; b. Louisville, Ky., Jan. 26, 1868; s. Enos Seth and Mary Eliza (Speed) T.; grad. Louisville Male High Sch., 1887; m. Lida Swope, Oct. 9, 1901 (died Feb. 18, 1927); 1 son, Philip Speed (dec.); m. 2d, Mrs. Jesse Walbeck Jones, June 16, 1928. With Ky. Union Land Co., until 1890; elected sec., treas. Louisville Cotton Mills Co., 1890, later pres.; organizer and pres. Louisville Textile Co.; pres. Louisville Textiles, Inc. (consolidation of both cos.) until retired, 1936. Chmn. advisory bd. for Ky. of Liberty Mutual Ins. Co. of Boston. Former pres. and hon. life dir. Associated Industries of Ky.; pres. Ky. Mfrs. Assn., 9 yrs. Chmn. Jefferson County (Ky.) Fuel Com. during World War. Mem. Ky. State Hist. Soc. Republican. Episcopalian, mem. exec. council and bd. trustees, Diocese of Ky.; lay del. of Diocese to Gen. Conv. of 1934, 37, 40. Clubs: Pendennis, Filson (dir.). Home: 410 Mocking Bird Hill Road, Louisville, Ky. Died June 22, 1943.

TULLY, Jim (tŭl'ĭ), author; b. near St. Marys, O., June 3, 1891; s. James Dennis and Marie Bridget (Lawler) T.; ed. St. Joseph Orphan Asylum, Cincinnati, Ohio, 1895-1900; married Florence Bushnell, 1913; married 2d, Myrtle Zwetow, 1933. Successively farm laborer, link heater, tramp, circus roustabout, chainmaker, professional pugilist, reporter on Akron Press and Beacon Jour., tree surgeon, is now engaged exclusively in writing. Tramped across U.S. 3 times; first verse appeared in Cleveland Plain Dealer, 1911. Govt. chain insp., World War. Author: Emmett Lawler, 1922; Beggars of Life, 1924; Jarnegan, 1925; Life of Thomas H. Ince, 1926; Life of Charlie Chaplin, 1926; Twenty Below (with Robert Nichols), 1926; Black Boy (with Frank Dazey), 1926; Passing Strangers, 1926; Circus Parade, 1927; Denis Darel, 1928; Shanty Irish, 1928; Shadows of Men, 1929; God Loves the Irish, 1929; Beggars Abroad, 1930; Close Ups, 1930; Adventures in Interviewing, 1931; Blood on the Moon, 1931; Laughter in Hell, 1932; Men in the Rough, 1933; Ladies in the Parlor, 1934; The Bruiser, 1936; Half Sister of the Lord, 1937; A Hollywood Decameron, 1937; Tullygrams, 1939; Children of Thieves, 1939; A Stranger

Appears, 1939; Men I Remember, 1940; Ringside, 1940; Biddy Brogan's Boy (novel), 1941; A Dozen and One (book of character sketches), 1942; Rave Lafferty (novel), 1943. Dialogue writer for talking pictures, teller of tales for radio. Contbr. to Ency. Britannica. Home: 258 Carmelina Av., Brentwood, Los Angeles. Died June 22, 1947; buried in Forest Lawn Memorial Park, Glendale, Calif.

TULLY, Richard Walton, dramatist, producer; b. Nevada City, Calif., May 7, 1877; s. Richard Whiteside and Louisa Jane (Hinds) T.; B.Litt., U. of Calif., 1901; m. Eleanor Gates, 1901 (divorced 1914); m. 2d, Gladys Campbell Hanna, Aug. 28, 1915; 1 dau., Maya Constance. Began as playwright, 1900, later producer plays and motion pictures. Mem. Order of the Golden Bear (California), Alpha Delta Phi. Clubs: Alpha Delta Phi (New York); Bohemian (San Francisco). Author: (play) A Strenuous Life (jr. prize winning college farce, U. of Calif.), 1900; My Cinderella Girl (musical comedy); Rose of the Rancho (prod. with David Belasco), 1906; The Bird of Paradise, 1911; Omar, The Tent Maker, 1913; The Flame, 1916; Blossom Bride, 1928. Producer of The Masquerader; Keep Her Smiling; The Right to Strike; etc. Film productions: The Masquerader, 1922; Omar the Tentmaker, Trilby, and Flowing Gold, 1923. Home: Sierra Madre, Calif. Died Jan. 31, 1945.

TURK, Milton Haight, coll. dean; b. Norwalk, Conn., June 28, 1866; s. Jacob and Esther Cornwall (Street) T.; A.B., Columbia, 1886; student univs. of Strasburg, Berlin, and Leipsic, 1886-89; A.M., Ph.D., U. of Leipsic, 1889; Litt.D., Columbia, 1929; LL.D., Hobart Coll., 1938; m. Margaret Soutter Bell, July 30, 1895 (died Apr. 1938); children—Esther Cornwall, Margaret Soutter; m. 2d, Margaret Anthony Young, Sept. 12, 1940. Horace White prof. of English, Hobart Coll., 1890-1924, Beverly Chew prof. of English lang. and lit., 1924-38, sec. faculty, 1890-1907, registrar, 1903-07; 1st dean William Smith Coll., 1907-15; librarian, Hobart, 1915-25, acting dean, 1924-25, acting pres., 1929, dean, 1925-38; visiting prof. English, U. of Utah, 1933. Mem. Phi Beta Kappa, Modern Lang. Assn. America, Am. Dialect Soc. Episcopalian. Independent Democrat. Author: Syllabus of English Literature, 1893; Hobart—the Story of a Hundred Years, 1921; Anglo Saxon Reader, 1927, rev. edit., 1930. Editor: (with introduction and notes) The Legal Code of Alfred the Great, 1893; De Quincey's Flight of a Tartar Tribe, 1897; Selections from De Quincey, 1902; De Quincey's The English Mail-Coach and Joan of Arc, 1905. Contbr. to Dictionary of Am. Biography, Jour. of Higher Edn. Delivered Hobart Centennial Address, 1922. Home: 2545 Oak St., Jacksonville 4, Fla. Died May 28, 1949.

TURLEY, Jay (tûr'lē), engineer; b. Beaver City, Utah, Apr. 16, 1877; s. Omner and Louisa Ann (Woodhouse) T.; both born west of Rocky Mts.; ran away from home at 17 to attend sch.; matriculated in Ore. State Agrl. Coll., 1895; but did not grad.; spl. advanced studies in U. of Tex. and George Washington U.; m. Urna Bradford Hickox, Sept. 7, 1904 (divorced Apr. 28, 1921). Apptd. U.S. dep. surveyor for Ida., 1899, for N.M., 1900-06; formulating extensive irrigation projects in Rio San Juan, N.M., since 1901; made original draft of irrigation laws for State of N.M., 1903-05; cons. engr. for N.M. in suit against Tex. over boundary along Rio Grande, 1913-16, 1921, 25; admitted to practice law, N.M., 1916, D.C., and Supreme Court of U.S., 1921. Mem. Idaho Nat. Guard, 1894-98; capt. engrs., U.S. Army, 1917-19, serving with 316th Engrs., 91st Div., and with 116th Engrs., 41st Div., A.E.F., also spl. staff and liaison service; retired as capt. Engrs., May 20, 1929. Republican. Mason (32°). Opposed, 1925, bldg. of St. Francis Dam, near Los Angeles, Calif., which burst in 1928; reported, 1928, on "astral collision," at Crater Mound, Ariz., contending that it caused fissures forming Grand Canyon of the Colorado; reported, 1929, geological and other conditions for building high dam above Grand Canyon, instead of below at Boulder site; on spl. scientific research and writing up data since 1931; working on case of old Spanish grant community ditches of central N.M. in connection with suit before Supreme Court since 1934 and on development of water supply sources near Albuquerque, N.M. Home: near Albuquerque, N.M. Address: P.O. Box 161, Albuquerque, N.M. Died Sep. 17, 1942.

TURNBULL, Barton P.; pres., dir., Rockefeller Center, Inc.; dir., Pittsburgh Consolidation Coal Co., Chase Nat. Bank. Home: 87 Hillcrest Av., Summit, N.J. Office: 30 Rockefeller Plaza, New York, N.Y. Died May 11, 1948.

TURNBULL, Margaret, author; b. Glasgow, Scotland; d. Thomas Easton and Jean (Craig) Turnbull; brought to U.S. at age of 2; ed. pub. schs., Arlington, N.J., and by pvt. study. Mem. Soc. Am. Dramatists and Composers, New York, Authors League, New York, Phillips Mill Community Assn., British War Relief Soc., Women's Nat. Rep. Club, New York. Presbyterian. Author: W. A. G.'s Tale, 1913; Looking After Sandy, 1914; Handle with Care, 1916; The Close-Up, 1918; Madame Judas, 1925; Alabaster Lamps, 1925; The Left Lady, 1926; Rogues' March, 1928; The Handsome Man, 1928; A Monkey in Silk, 1931; The Return of Jenny Weaver, 1932; In the Bride's Mirror, 1934; The Coast Road Murder, 1934; also (plays), Genesee of the Hills (dramatization of Told in the Hills), prod. 1903; A Society Policeman, prod. Atlantic City, N.J., 1905; Classmates (with William C. de Mille), prod. New York, 1907; On the Square (with Hector H. Turnbull), prod. New York, 1913; The Deadlock, prod. Washington and New York, 1913; At the Mitre, prod. Fine Arts Theatre, Chicago, 1914; also author of many motion picture plays and scenarios; at least seven of Miss Turnbull's novels have a Bucks County, Pa., background. Home: New Hope, Pa.; and 35 5th Av., New York, N.Y. Died June 12, 1942.

TURNBULL, Martin Ryerson, clergyman, educator; b. Waterford, Loudon County, Va., July 2, 1886; s. Lennox B. and Amelia (Ryerson) T.; B.A., Washington and Lee U., 1906; student Bibl. Sem., New York; B.D., Union Theol. Sem., Richmond, Va., 1915, D.D., 1920; m. Mary Spottswood Carmichael, June 10, 1920; children—Lucy Carmichael, Lennox Birkhead. Ordained ministry Presbyn. Ch. in U.S., 1915; pastor Mossy Creek Ch., Va., 1916-17; acting prof. Bible, Union Theol. Sem. in Va., 1917-19; prof. English Bible, Presbyn. Gen. Assembly's Training Sch., Richmond, Va., since 1919; editor of dept. Sunday School Lessons and Studying the Bible by Books, The Christian Observer, of Southern Presbyn. Ch. Mem. Phi Gamma Delta. Democrat. Author: Studying the Book of Genesis, 1924; Studying the Book of Exodus, 1925; Studying the Book of Leviticus, 1926; Studying the Epistle to the Hebrews, 1927. Home: 3400 Brook Road, Richmond, Va. Died Jan. 31, 1949.

TURNER, Abe W., judge; b. Heber City, Utah, Apr. 26, 1893; s. William Lindsay and Jane (Hatch) T.; student U. of Utah, 1910-15; LL.B., Georgetown U., Washington, D.C., 1916; m. Merline Roylance, July 26, 1917; children—William Roylance, Dorothy Ann (Mrs. William Dee Orser). Admitted to Utah bar, 1916; engaged in stock farming and business, 1916-19; in private practice of law, Provo, Utah, 1919-30, city atty., 1930-33; dist. judge 4th Judicial Dist., Utah, 1933-44; apptd. justice pro tempore, Supreme Court of Utah, May 1, 1944. Democratic precinct chmn., Provo, Utah, 1920-24; mem. Dem. Central Com., 1932. Mem. Utah State Bar Assn., Delta Theta Phi. Home: 194 N. 4th East, Provo, Utah; also 19 A St., Salt Lake City 1. Office: State Capitol, Salt Lake City 1, Utah. Died May 25, 1947.

TURNER, Charles Root, prof. of dentistry; born Raleigh, N.C., Nov. 3, 1875; s. Vines Edmund and Love Gales (Root) T.; grad. Raleigh Male Acad., 1891; A.B., U. of N.C., 1895; D.D.S., U. of Pa., 1898, Sc.D., 1933; M.D., Med. Coll. of Va., 1899, Sc.D., 1935; m. Sara Cameron Clark, June 21, 1906; 1 dau., Sara Clark. Began practice at Richmond, 1900; prof. prosthetic dentistry, U. of Pa., since 1902; dean Sch. of Dentistry, same univ., 1917-41. Mem. American Dental Association, Phi Beta Kappa, Sigma Xi, Phi Kappa Sigma, Delta Sigma Delta, Pi Mu. Democrat. Episcopalian. Club: University. Author: American Text Book of Prosthetic Dentistry, 1932. Home: 755 Beacom Lane, Marion, Pa.* Died June 11, 1947.

TURNER, William Jay, lawyer; LL.B., U. of Pa., 1891. Practiced in Phila. since 1891; gen. counsel Lehigh Coal & Navigation Co., Lehigh & N.E. R.R. Co.; dir. Phila. Nat. Bank. Mem. Am. Bar Assn. Office: 123 S. Broad St., Philadelphia, Pa. Died Dec. 2, 1943.

TURPIN, C. Murray, ex-congressman; b. Kingston, Pa., Mar. 4, 1878; grad. high sch., Kingston, and Wyoming Sem.; D.D.S., U. of Pa., 1904; m. Anna M. Manley, 1907 (died 1929); 4 children. Carpenter, grocery clk. and steamboat capt. before entering dental practice at Kingston; mem. Bd. of Edn., 6 yrs., burgess of Kingston 4 yrs., prothonotary of Luzerne County, Pa., 4 yrs.; elected to 71st Congress, 1929, to fill vacancy; reëlected to 72d to 74th Congresses (1933-37), 12th Pa. Dist. Corpl. Co. F, 9th Pa. Vol. Inf., Spanish-Am. War, later capt. Pa. N.G. Mem. Veteran Firemen's Assn., Jr. Order United Am. Mechanics, United Spanish War Vets., Westside Vets. Assn., Psi Omega, etc., also hon. life mem. various orgns. Republican. Clubs: Wyoming Valley Automobile, etc. Home: Kingston, Pa. Died June 4, 1946.

TURPIN, Rees, lawyer; b. Carrollton, Mo., May 4, 1869; s. Henry Ballinger and Sarah Elizabeth (Rees) T.; grad. high sch., Carrollton, 1888; B.L., Washington and Lee U., Lexington, Va., 1892; m. Mary Roberts Quarles, Oct. 11, 1904. Admitted to Mo. bar, 1892, and since practiced in Kansas City; sr. partner Turpin, Behrendt & Searing; elected to sit as spl. judge in various divs. of Circuit Court, 1906-12. Trustee and former mem. bd. govs. Kansas City Art Inst. Mem. Am. and Mo. State bar assns., Kansas City Bar Assn. (ex-treas.; ex-pres.), Phi Kappa Psi. Democrat. Club: University (pres. 1903). Annotated the charter and ordinances of Kansas City, 1909. Home: 3552 Broadway. Office: N.Y. Life Bldg., Kansas City, Mo. Died Aug. 11, 1949.

TUTTLE, Arthur J. (tŭt''l), judge; b. Leslie, Mich., Nov. 8, 1868; s. Ogden Valorous and Julia Elizabeth (McArthur) T.; Ph.B., U. of Mich., 1892, LL.B., 1895, hon. LL.M., 1930; m. Jessie B. Stewart, Mar. 11, 1903 (died Aug. 24, 1912); children—Ruth Beatrice (Mrs. Howard Blair Freeman), Esther Louise (Mrs. Thomas J. Bailey). Admitted to Mich. bar, 1895; pros. atty., Ingham County, 1899-1902; mem. State Senate, 14th Dist., 1907-10; U.S. dist. atty., Eastern Dist. of Mich., 1911-12; U.S. dist. judge for Eastern Dist. of Mich., by appmt. of President Taft, since Aug. 12, 1912; pres. Peoples Bank, Leslie, Mich. Mem. Am., Mich., and Detroit bar assns., Council of Am. Law Inst., Mich. State Hort. Soc., S.A.R., Phi Beta Kappa, Phi Alpha Delta, Phi Phi, Pi Gamma Mu; past eminent supreme archon Sigma Alpha Epsilon. Republican. Mason (32°, K.T., Shriner), Odd Fellow, K.P., Elk, Eagle, Maccabee, Woodman, Loyal Guard, Moose, Order of Ahepa. Clubs: Univ. of Mich., Detroit, Detroit Boat, Detroit Athletic, Rotary, Automobile of Michigan, Detroit Golf, University. Office: Federal Bldg., Detroit, Mich. Died Dec. 2, 1944.

TUTTLE, Arthur Smith, cons. engr.; b. Burlington, Conn., Mar. 26, 1865; s. Theron and Jennie E. (Beach) T.; C.E., New York U., 1885; D.Eng., Rensselaer Poly Inst., 1942; m. Helen Aldridge Smith, June 1, 1892; children—Marguerite, Walter Aldridge, Laurence C. Assistant engineer, Brooklyn Water Works, 1884-1901; chief engineer investigation for proposed irrigation and water power development, Bishop Estate, Honolulu, 1901-02; prin. asst. and deputy chief engr. Bd. Estimate and Apportionment, City of N.Y., 1902-20, chief engineer, 1921-28, consulting engineer, 1928-33; consulting engr. Citizen Budget Commission, 1933; New York state engineer Federal Emergency Administration of Pub. Works, Aug. 1933-36, state dir., 1936-37; federal project engr. or acting project engr. Triboro Bridge, Lincoln Tunnel and Queens Midtown Tunnel, 1933-37; mem. N.Y. City Adminstrn. for Work and Home Relief, Apr.-Aug. 1933; private practice and cons. engr. for WPA, 1937-41; dir. N.Y. City, Fed. Public Works Reserve, 1941-42; mem. Tuttle, Seelye, Place & Raymond, cons. engrs., 1941-44; consulting engr. and chmn. Tuttle-Haller Cos. since 1944; (engineering, inspection, testing); inventor water meter for large mains. Twice cited for distinguished service by Mayor La Guardia, 1937-39. Honorary member American Society C.E. (formerly president, v.p., treasurer and director); former member and ex-chairman John Fritz Medal Board. of Award; mem. United Engring. Trustees (past v.p.), Am. Inst. Cons. Engrs. (past mem. council), Municipal Engrs. of N.Y. City (ex-pres.), Regional Plan Assn., Am. Shore and Beach Preservation Assn. (dir.), Sound View Assn. (dir.), N.Y. Univ. Alumni Fedn. (ex-pres.), New York Univ. Council, Phi Beta Kappa, Tau Beta Pi, Delta Phi; former mem. Engring. Foundation. Clubs: Engineers of New York (dir., ex-pres.); Cosmos (Washington); St. Georges Golf and Country; Municipal of Brooklyn (ex-pres.), Pleiades (ex-pres.), Brooklyn Engineers. Author of many articles for tech. press and engring. socs. Mem. advisory bd. of editorial staff, Sewage Works Engring. Home: 24 Monroe Pl., Brooklyn, N.Y. (winter) and Stony Brook, L.I., N.Y. Office: 801 Second Av., New York, N.Y. Died May 19, 1949.

TUTTLE, (Henry) Emerson, artist, coll. master; born in Lake Forest, Ill., Dec. 10, 1890; s. Henry Nelson and Fannie (Farwell) T.; A.B., Yale, 1914, A.M., 1930; grad. student Slade Sch., Univ. Coll. (England), 1924; m. Isabelle Hollister, June 17, 1916; children—Isabelle Hollister, Grace Emerson, Harriet Ann, Nancy Jackson. Master at Westminster Sch., Simsbury, Conn., 1916-18, Groton (Mass.) Sch., 1918-29; master of Davenport Coll., and curator of prints, Yale Univ., since 1930; acting dir. Yale Univ. Art Gallery, 1942-45; artist and etcher since 1919; master of Davenport College. Represented by prints in collections of British Museum, Metropolitan Mus. (N.Y.), Art Inst. (Chicago), Yale Univ. Gallery of Fine Arts; Library of Congress, Bibliotheque Nationale (Paris, France). Trustee, St. Timothy's Sch., Catonsville, Maryland. Mem. American Society of Etchers, Chicago Soc. of Etchers, Psi Upsilon, Scroll and Key (Yale). Presbyterian. Clubs: Graduate, Elizabethan (New Haven); Century (New York). Home: 271 Park St., New Haven, Conn. Died March 8, 1946; buried Old North Burying Ground, Nantucket, Mass.

TUTTLE, George Albert, physician; b. Hadley, Mass., Dec. 2, 1859; s. Wooster Henry and Margaret Elizabeth (Helmsing) T.; A.B., Amherst, 1883; M.D., Coll. Physicians and Surgeons, Columbia, 1886; unmarried. Surg. interne Roosevelt Hosp., New York, 1886-88; practiced at New York, 1888-1935; asst. prof. clin. medicine, Coll. Physicians and Surgeons, 1913-35; now retired. Mem. Delta Kappa Epsilon, Phi Beta Kappa. Republican. Protestant. Address: 222 College St., Middletown, Conn. Died May 10, 1942.

TUTTLE, Julius Herbert, librarian, editor; b. Littleton, Mass., Mar. 7, 1857; s. Edmund Sherman and Eliza Ann (Conant) T.; ed. Lawrence Acad., Groton, Mass., State Normal Sch., Bridgewater, Mass.; m. Jennie Crehore Carroll, Nov. 17, 1881 (died July 28, 1935). Teacher pub. schs., 1876, 77; asst. librarian Mass. Hist. Soc., 1878-1912, actg. librarian, 1912-19, librarian, Apr. 1919-34; librarian emeritus since Sept. 1934. Actg. editor Proceedings Mass. Hist. Soc., 1907-08, asst. editor, Jan. 1909-Sept. 1934. Mem. School Com., Dedham, 1890-1907 (chmn. 1899-1907); trustee Dedham Pub. Library, 1896-1910 (chmn. bd. 1906-1910). Republican. Unitarian. Mem. Am. Antiq. Soc., Colonial Soc. Mass., Mass. Hist. Soc., Dedham Hist. Soc. (pres. 1907-1940; now pres. emeritus), Bay State Hist. League (pres. 1919, 20), Phi Beta Kappa (hon. 1918). Editor Dedham Hist. Register, 1890-1903; Dedham Town Records, 1706-1736. Author: The Libraries of the Mathers, 1910; Massachusetts and her Royal Charter (granted Mar. 4, 1628-29), 1924-29; Point Connett in Ancient Mattapoisett, Massachusetts, 1941. Home: 838 High St., Dedham, Mass.* Died Feb. 10, 1945.

TWEED, George P(eter), iron mining; b. Warsaw, Goodhue County, Minn., Apr. 19, 1871; s. Evan J. and Anne P. (Hulback) T.; grad. high sch., Duluth, Minn., 1890; m. Alice Lyon, June 30, 1909; 1 dau. (adopted), Bernice Adele (Mrs. John W. Brickson).

Engaged in exploration and development of iron ore properties, 1900-22; then pres. various corps. in production of iron ore and coal; chmn. bd. First and American National Bank, Duluth; director Northwestern Bancorporation, Minneapolis, Marshall-Wells Company, Duluth, President Ordean Charity, Duluth. Member American Iron and Steel Inst., Am. Inst. Mining and Metall. Engrs., Am. Fedn. Arts, Painters and Sculptors Assn., Duluth Chamber Commerce. Republican. Episcopalian. Clubs: Kitchi Gammi (Duluth); Gogebic Country (Ironwood, Mich.); Chicago Club (Chicago); Bankers (New York). Home: 2531 E. 7th St. Office: First National Bank Bldg., Duluth, Minn. Died Apr. 30, 1946.

TWINING, Frank Barton (twīn'ĭng); b. Troy, N.Y., Sept. 3, 1856; s. Alfred C. and Mary Frances (Barton) T.; m. Nomina Bucklin, Dec. 12, 1889 (died Oct. 4, 1936); children—Eleanor Frances (Mrs. Gardner B. Perry, now deceased), Nomina Bird (Mrs. James W. Cox). Mem. firm George P. Ide & Co., 1880-1926, pres., 1920-26; chmn. bd. Mfrs. Nat. Bank of Troy; dir. Troy Savings Bank. Trustee Russell Sage Coll. Episcopalian. Club: Troy (Troy). Home: 865 Second Av., Troy, N.Y. Died May 19, 1945.

TWISS, George Ransom (twĭs), educator; b. Columbus, O., June 6, 1863; s. George Henry and Susan H. (Ransom) T.; B.Sc., Ohio State U., 1885; studied Harvard, U. of Chicago, Teachers Coll. (Columbia); Ph.D., Columbia, 1925; m. Helen Gladden, Mar. 1886 (died Apr. 1890); 1 dau., Alice (Mrs. Stanton Coit Kelton); m. 2d, Nellie D. Leaming, June 1898 (died Dec. 1902); m. 3d, Blanche M. Olin, June 28, 1915; 1 son, Page Charles. Teacher sciences at the Rayen High Sch., Youngstown, O., 1885-91, Central High Sch., Columbus, 1891-94; head science dept. of Central High Sch., Cleveland, 1894-1908; high school visitor, Ohio State U., 1908-14; state high school insp. (half time) and prof. principles and practice of edn., Ohio State U., 1914-21, full time prof., 1921-34, prof. emeritus since 1934; prof. sch. administration, summer sessions U. of Mo., 1916, 17, 18; in War Dept., dist. supervisor personnel methods, S.A.T.C., Oct. 15-Dec. 31, 1918. Ednl. survey, state industrial schs. of Ohio, 1919; mem. U.S. Bur. Edn. sch. survey commns., Memphis, 1919, Hawaii, 1919-20, Winchester, Mass., and Wilmington, Del., 1920; survey for Niles (O.) Bd. Edn., 1921; for Gen. Edn. Bd. in 13 colls. for negroes, 1922; for Chinese Nat. Assn. for Advancement of Edn. as dir. science edn. in China, 1922-24 (on leave of absence); for The Art Inst. of Chicago, 1929. Mem. bd. dirs. Lee County Welfare Fedn., Fort Myers Public Library, and Com. on Lit. and Reading, Sunnyland Council Boy Scouts of America. Past pres. science dept. N.E.A.; chmn. for physics, Nat. Commn. for Reorganization of Secondary Edn. Hon. adviser on science edn. Chinese Nat. Assn. for Advancement of Edn., 1925. Conglist. Clubs: Fort Myers Rotary, Men's, Edison Park Community Church. Author: Laboratory Exercises in Physics, 2d edit., 1916; Physics (Mann and Twiss), 2d edit., 1910; Principles of Science Teaching, 1917; Science and Education in China (Shanghai), 1925. Contbr. to Monroe's Principles of Secondary Education, 1915; also reports of ednl. surveys, and to ednl. periodicals. Address: 227 First St., Ft. Myers, Fla. Died Feb. 16, 1944.

TWITMYER, Edwin Burket (twĭt'mī-ẽr), prof. psychology; b. McElhattan, Pa., Sept. 14, 1873; s. George Wells and Johanna (Reese) T.; Ph.B., Lafayette Coll., Easton, Pa., 1896; Ph.D., U. of Pa., 1902; LL.D., Lafayette Coll., 1933; m. Mary E. Marvin, Dec. 26, 1907; children—Edward Marvin, Georgiana Jane. Instr. in psychology, U. of Pa., 1897-1907, asst. prof. psychology, 1907-14, prof. since 1914, also dir. Psychol. Lab. and Clinic and chief of Speech Clinic, U. of Pa. Trustee Pa. Sch. for the Deaf, Delaware County Hosp. Fellow A.A.A.S., Am. Soc. for Study Disorders of Speech, Am. Assn. Applied Psychologists; mem. Am. Psychol. Soc., Sigma Xi, Theta Delta Chi. Democrat. Presbyterian. Mason (32°). Clubs: University, Lenape. Co-author (with Nathanson); The Correction of Defective Speech, 1932. Contbr. to various mags. Home: Secane, Pa. Died Mar. 3, 1943.

TWOMBLY, Clifford Gray (twŏm'blĭ), clergyman; b. Stamford, Conn., May 7, 1869; s. Alexander Stevenson and Abigail Quincy (Bancroft) T.; student Boston Latin Sch., 1880-86; B.A., Yale, 1891; B.D., Episcopal Theol. Sch., Cambridge, Mass., 1894; student Andover Theol. Sem., 1891-93; D.D., Franklin and Marshall Coll., 1916; m. Edith Cazenove Balch, July 1, 1897; children—Gray Huntington, Alexander Stevenson. Deacon, 1894, priest, 1895, P.E. Ch.; asst. minister Grace Ch., New Bedford, Mass., 1894-97; rector St. Paul's Ch., Newton Highlands, Mass., 1897-1907; rector St. James' Ch., Lancaster, Pa., 1907-39; retired, May 1, 1939; canon St. Stephens' Cathedral, Harrisburg, Pa. Mem. exec. council of Harrisburg Diocese. Writer and lecturer on sociol. subjects, especially reform of the movies. Home: 14 Auburn St., Concord, N.H. Died Dec. 29, 1942.

TWOMEY, M. Joseph (too'mē), clergyman; b. Killarney, Ireland, Jan. 10, 1871; s. Timothy and Hannah (Conner) T.; B.Ph., Brown U., 1900, D.D., 1921; grad. Newton Theol. Instn., Newton Centre, Mass., 1903; LL.D., Temple U., Phila., 1934; m. Ella Caroline Stanton, Nov. 4, 1903. Came to U.S., 1890, naturalized, 1902. Ordained ministry Bapt. Ch., 1903; pastor Danielson, Conn., 1903-05, Portland, Me., 1905-14, Peddie Memorial Church, Newark, N.J., 1914-30, Baptist Temple, Phila., 1930-35, North Orange Baptist Ch., Orange, N.J., 1937-42; interim pastor First Baptist Ch., Oct. 1942-Feb. 1943, First Baptist Church, Williamsport, Pa., Sept. 1943-Apr. 1946, Yarmouth, Maine since September 1946. Mem. exec. com. Northern Bap. Conv., 1913-19, mem. Bd. Am. Baptist Foreign Mission Soc., 1922-37; pres. Bapt. Conv. of Pa., 1931-33; mem. bd. Me. Bapt. Conv. 1908-13, N.J. Bapt. Conv., 1916-30; pres. Me. Sunday Sch. Assn., 1913-14; pres. Am. Baptist and Foreign Bible Soc., 1940. Mem. bd. trustees, N.J. Bapt. Conv., 1937-42; trustee Hebron (Me.) Acad., Eastern Bapt. Theol. Sem. (Phila.). Republican. Mason (32°). Address: Waterboro, Me.; also 41 Rackleff, Portland, Me. Died Oct. 29, 1948; buried, Central Village, Conn.

TYE, Hiram H. (tī), lawyer; b. Whitley County, Ky., May 7, 1868; s. James Cooper and Elizabeth (Brummett) T.; B.S., Nat. Normal U., Lebanon, O., 1887, A.B., 1890, LL.B., Centre Coll., Danville, Ky., 1895; m. Lila Johnson, 1895 (dec.); m. 2d, Stella Grace Tucker, Apr. 1901 (dec.); 1 son, William Gosper (died Feb. 1937); m. 3d, Lillian South, July 8, 1926. Admitted to Kentucky bar, 1891; now mem. firm Tye & Siler, Williamsburg; local atty. for L.&N. R.R. Co., Southern Ry. Co. and various coal cos. over 40 yrs.; judge (by apptmt.) 34th Judicial Dist., Ky., for yr. 1917, during World War. Owner of private library of 5000 vols. Mem. Am. Bar Assn., Ky. State Bar Assn., Whitley County Bar Assn. (pres. since organized). Democrat. Baptist. Mason (K.T.). Clubs: Arts, Pendennis, Louisville Country (Louisville); Williamsburg Country. Author: Broomsedge Philosophy. Home: Williamsburg, Ky. Died July 3, 1948

TYLER, George Crouse, theatrical mgr.; b. Circleville, O., Apr. 13, 1867; s. George H. and Harriet (Parkhurst) T.; ed. pub. and pvt. schs., Chillicothe; unmarried. Theatrical producing mgr. since 1895; has produced more than 350 plays, about 90 per cent of them for the first time on any stage. Most of the prominent stars and actors of the period have been at times under his management. Home: 136 W. 77th St., New York, N.Y.* Died Mar. 14, 1946.

TYLER, Odette, actress; b. Savannah, Ga., Sept. 26, 1869; d. Gen. William W. and Susan (Hardee) Kirkland; ed. at convent, Georgetown, D.C., and Loretto Convent, Guelph, Ont.; m. Rezin Davis Shepherd (stage name R. D. MacLean), Apr. 1, 1897. Debut about 1887 at Madison Sq. Theatre, New York, under Daniel Frohman's management as "Odette Tyler"; later in Minnie Maddern's, Charles Frohman's and other companies; successful commedienne. Author: Boss—a Story of Virginia Life, 1896; also several mag. stories. Address: Dunmore Flats, 230 W 42d St., New York. Died Dec. 8, 1936.

TYNDALL, Henry Myron (tĭn'dăl), clergyman; b. Alton, N.Y., July 21, 1885; s. Myron Parks and Emeline (York) T.; prep. edn., Sodus (N.Y.) Acad.; grad. N.Y. State Normal Coll., 1883, Auburn (N.Y.) Theol. Sem., 1886, New York U., 1894; S.T.D., Am. Univ., Harriman, Tenn., 1901; m. Phoebe Ann Mitchell, Jan. 31, 1877 (now deceased); children—Mabel Emeline (Mrs. Frank H. Mills), Carlton Henry, Paul (dec.), Ruth Mitchell (Mrs. Harold J. Bortle); m. 2d, Mary Elizabeth Duncan, Dec. 25, 1929. Teacher, 1873-78; ordained ministry Presbyn. Ch., 1886; pastor Iron Mountain, Mich., 1886-91; asso. pastor with bro. Charles H., Broome St. Tabernacle, N.Y. City, 1891-92; founded People's Tabernacle, Inc. (inter-denominational), in a dist. of 60,000 people without church privileges (upper east side of N.Y. City), and pres., trustee, treas. and pastor of same since 1892; built Emeline York Tyndall Home for Business Women to give living at low cost, 1905; founded coöperative housing project for the poor, 1921, also founded a social and religious federation of Jews and Gentiles, 1935. Lecturer on cooperative housing. Mem. Am. Geogl. Soc., Nat. Assn. Real Estate Boards, Fundamentalist League, Presbyterian Union. Clubs: Clergy, Walkers of America. Co-editor: The Celtic Cruise of the 800, 1902. Compiler and author of Illustrative Anecdotes for Preachers and Sunday School Teachers, 1925. Editor of The Little Evangelist, 47 yrs. Contbr. to Standard Dictionary. Address: 56 E. 102d St., New York, N.Y.; (country) North Rose, N.Y. Died Jan. 18, 1943.

TYNDALL, Robert H. (tĭn'dăl), mayor; born at Indianapolis, Indiana, May 2, 1877; son of William E. and Alice (Boyd) T.; student pub. schs.; married Hazel Dean Spellman, June 24, 1908; children—Ann, Samuel Spellman, Ruth. Formerly vice-pres. Fletcher Am. Nat. Bank, Indianapolis, Ind., also vice-pres. treas. Carl G. Fisher Co. and Subsidiaries, Miami Beach, Florida and Montauk Point, Long Island. Served with 27th Indiana Vols., Spanish-Am. War; col. comdg. 150th F.A., 42d (Rainbow) Div., U.S. Army, World War; commd. major gen. on return from France, and assigned to comd. 38th Nat. Guard Div.; comd. 38th Div. and camp comdr., Camp Shelby, Miss., Jan.-May 1941; retired, May 2, 1941; mayor Indianapolis, Ind., since Jan. 1, 1943; dir. Marion County Civilian Defense Council; dir. Marion County Red Cross. Past pres. Ind. S.A.R.; mem. Am. Legion (nat. treas. 1919-27). Decorated D.S.M. (U.S.); Croix de Guerre with two Palms, Comdr. Legion of Honor (French). Republican. Mason (33°). Clubs: University, Columbia, Athletic, Woodstock, Traiders Point Hunt, Country (Indianapolis). Home: 2016 N. Meridian St. Office: City Hall, Indianapolis, Ind. Died July 9, 1947.

TYNG, Sewell Tappan (tĭng), lawyer, mining exec.; b. New York, N.Y., Apr. 30, 1895; s. Sewell Tappan and Edith (Gale) T.; prep. edn. Groton Sch., 1908-14; A.B., Williams College, 1917; LL.B., Harvard University, 1923; m. 3d, Virginia Bennett Crocker, July 14, 1943. Admitted to New York bar, 1924; associated with the firm of Larkin, Rathbone & Perry, 1923-30, mem. firm, 1930-32; on staff Special Prosecutor Thomas E. Dewey, 1935-36; mem. firm Searle, James & Tyng, 1936-38; asst. dist. atty. N.Y. County, 1938-39; pres. South Am. Mines Co. and subsidiaries since Sept. 1, 1939. Served in France in Ambulance Service, Am. Red Cross, and as 2d lt. A.E.F., May 1917-Sept. 1919; sec. to Herbert Hoover, 1919. Apptd. mem. Quetico-Superior Com. by President Roosevelt, 1934. Mem. Am. Bar Assn., Alpha Delta Phi. Republican. Episcopalian. Clubs: University, River, Down Town Assn., Harvard, Mining (all N.Y. City). Author: Campaign of the Marne, 1914, pub. 1935. Contbr. to military journals. Home: 525 Park Av. Office: 75 West St., New York, N.Y.* Died May 7, 1946.

TYRRELL, Henry Grattan (tyr'rĕl), cons. engr.; b. Weston, Ont., Can.; s. William and Elizabeth (Burr) T.; grad. school Practical Science, Toronto; C.E., University of Toronto, 1894; married Alicia Bryant, January 1, 1890 (died January 1906); children—George, Bryant, Alicia; m. 2d, Mary Maude Knox, Nov. 7, 1907; 1 son, H. Grattan Knox. On exploration surveys in western Canada discovering large coal deposits, and railroad construction, Quebec and Maine, 4 yrs.; design and constrn. bridges and bldgs., 1888-1904, including designs and plans for all bridges, viaducts on railway line Lake Superior to Hudson Bay; spl. engr. bridges and bldgs., Harriman Rys., 1906-08; cons. engineer since 1908; prop. Tyrrell Engring. Co.; gave services to U.S. Govt., World War, in designing, building and valuation of war plants. Has been connected with constrn. of many notable bridges and other structures in U.S. and foreign countries; reported on rebuilding the twice-destroyed line of ry. through Rainbow Canyon between Salt Lake City and Los Angeles; designed improved type of ry. crossing gates; also types of regulating gates for canals and waterways; plans for St. Clair Memorial Bridge, and high level crossings of rivers at Detroit, Montreal, Norfolk, Va., Sidney, Australia, etc.; spanning 20 miles of Chesapeake Bay, from Baltimore to Eastern Shore; crossing Irish Channel from Ireland to Scotland by means of bridge and tunnel; prepared standard designs and estimated costs for bridges of ordinary span, steel and concrete, and published original charts and formulæ for weight and cost, now in general use; since World War I and through World War II, to present date, has prepared engineering reports for construction (U.S. and foreign) together with writing and other engineering work, to the approximate value of $3,000,000,000. Awarded medal and diploma by Colonial and Indian Exhibition (London). Built hospital buildings in New Eng. for U.S. Govt. Mem. Soc. Promotion Engring. Edn., Am. Assn. Engrs., A.A.A.S. Clubs: Canadian (Washington); Engineers, Civitan. Author: Mill Building Construction, 1900; Concrete Bridges and Culverts, 1909; Mill Buildings, 1910; History of Bridge Engineering, 1911; Artistic Bridge Design; Engineering of Shops and Factories; Movable Bridges; Structural Engring. Manual, etc.; and several non-tech. writings, nearly all being pioneer works on the subjects. Assisted by his wife in publication of his books (see Women of America, London). Extensive contbr. to engring. and scientific jours. of Am. and Europe. Proprietor Grattan Tyrrell Co., Baltimore. Home: "Grattanwood," Catonsville, Md. Office: 100 Eutaw St., Baltimore, Md. Died Feb. 4, 1948; buried in Loudon Park Cemetery, Baltimore.

U

UBICO, Jorge (oo-bĕk'ō), former pres. of Guatemala; b. Guatemala City, Nov. 10, 1878; s. Arturo and Matilde (Castaneda) U.; student Polytechnic School, Guatemala City, and Mil. Acad. of Guatemala. Entered Army service as an officer, 1897, becoming gen. of a div.; participated in mil. campaign against El Salvador, 1906; political chief and comdr. armed forces in Alta Veparaz, 1907-11; chief of sanitation of Pacific Coast region fighting yellow fever, 1918; became mem. war commn. of Nat. Assembly, minister of industry, chief of gen. staff and comdr. city's armed forces, 1920; became minister of war, 1931; candidate for pres. of Guatemala, 1922, 26; pres. as mem. Liberal Prog. party, Feb. 1931-44; while the Constitution prohibits presidential succession, he ordered a plebiscite to extend his term for a second 6-year period. Address: 6 A Avenida Norta No. 4, Guatemala.* Died June 14, 1946.

UHLER, Joseph Michael (ū'lẽr), coll. pres.; b. Elizabethville, Pa., May 5, 1881; s. Michael and Sarah (Kramer) U.; student, Shippensburg (Pa.) Normal Sch., 1902-05, Franklin and Marshall Coll., 1906, Dickinson Coll. (Carlisle), 1909-11; A.B., U. of Pittsburgh, 1918, A.M., 1927, Ed.D., 1939; m. Naomi Sarah Dohner, Dec. 24, 1907; children—Lowell Dohner, Raymond Cramer, Ruth Naomi, Helen Louise. Rural school teacher, Dauphin County, Pa., 1899-1902; teacher and prin., Cresson (Pa.) High Sch., 1907-09; prin. and supt. schs., Conemaugh, 1911-25; teacher and head edn. dept., State Teachers Coll., Indiana, Pa., 1925-39, dir. student teaching and placement, 1939-42, acting pres., June-Oct. 1942, pres. since Oct. 1942. Dir. Indiana Hosp. Corp.; ex-pres., Cambria County Sabbath Sch. Assn.; dir. Indiana County Chapter, Am. Red Cross. Member

N.E.A., Pa. State Edn. Assn., Gen. Council Pa. Synod Presbyn. Ch., Phi Delta Kappa, Kappa Delta Pi. Presbyterian. Republican. Mason. Kiwanis (ex-pres.). Club: Shakespeare. Address: State Teachers Coll., Indiana, Pa. Died Aug. 17, 1947.

ULLMAN, Frederic, Jr., bus. exec.; b. Buffalo, N.Y., Apr. 19, 1903; s. Frederic and Beatrice (Hirsh) U.; Ph.B., Yale, 1925; m. Janine Voisin, Mar. 21, 1941; 1 son, Anthony Voisin; 1 dau. by previous marriage, Abby. Connected with motion picture theatres since 1926; mgr. chain of motion picture theatres, Buffalo, 1926-31; with Pathe News, Inc., since 1931, beginning as head of comml. dept., became vice pres. and gen. mgr., 1937, pres. since 1942; producer of film series "This Is America" for RKO Radio Pictures; pres. R.K.O. Television Corp., 1944-47; resigned; now producer RKO Radio Pictures. Mem. Acad. Motion Picture Arts and Sciences; Yale Club (New York). Home: 715 N. Maple Dr., Beverly Hills, Calif. Office: 780 Gower St., Los Angeles, Calif. Died Dec. 26, 1948.

ULMAN, Joseph N. (ŭl'mȧn), judge; b. Baltimore, Md., Aug. 9, 1878; s. Nathan and Dina (Oppenheim) U.; A.B., Johns Hopkins, 1898; A.M., Columbia, 1900; m. Ella Guggenheimer, June 23, 1903; children—Joseph N., Elinor. Admitted to Md. bar, 1901, and began practice at Baltimore; mem. Knapp, Ulman & Tucker, 1910-24; mem. faculty U. of Md. Law Sch., 1908-28; judge Supreme Bench of Baltimore since 1924. Pres. Md. Prisoners' Aid Assn., 1910-12, 1919-24, now dir.; treas. Montrose Sch. for Girls, 1920-24; pres. Hebrew Benevolent Soc., 1925-28; chmn. Com. on Prison Labor, apptd. by Nat. Industrial Recovery Bd., 1934; chmn. Prison Industries Reorganization Adminstrn., 1935-36, mem. of board since 1936; dir. and mem. exec. com. Community Fund of Baltimore, 1925-30; pres. Baltimore Urban League, 1931-34; v.p. Baltimore branch, Am. Jewish congress, 1937-41, now dir.; consultant Pub. Works Adminstrn. since 1938; dir. Nat. Probation Assn., Nat. Urban League, Legal Aid Bur. of Baltimore. Mem. Advisory Com. on Criminal Justice, Am. Law Inst., 1934, advisor criminal justice and youth since 1938; member board of mgrs. Cheltenham School for Boys, apptd. by governor of Md., 1940. Mem. Am. Bar Assn. (mem. com on edn. and practice of Criminal Law Sect, 1938-40), Md. State Bar Assn., Baltimore City Bar Assn. (grievance com., 1914-15 and 1920-22), Am. Law Inst. (elected 1936), Am. Sociol. Soc., Md. Com. on Prison Labor, Johns Hopkins Alumni Assn. (past pres.), Phi Beta Kappa, Phi Alpha, Omicron Delta Kappa (hon. 1935). Democrat. Clubs: University, Chesapeake. Author: A Judge Takes the Stand, 1933; also wrote intro. to Marshall & May's The Divorce Court—Maryland, 1932, and "The Trial Judge's Dilemma," in Glueck's Probation and Criminal Justice, 1933. Contbr. chapter, "Law as a Creative Force in Social Welfare" to Lowry's Readings in Social Case Work, 1939. Contbr. to Year Book of Nat. Probation Assn., 1932-33, 1936, 38, 41; also mag. articles. Asso. editor Jour. Criminal Law and Criminology. Home: 2615 Talbot Road. Office: Court House, Baltimore, Md. Died Apr. 18, 1943.

ULLMANN, Albert, author; b. N.Y. City, July 2, 1861; s. Edward and Philippine U.; B.S., Coll. City of New York, 1881; m. Tillie Sulzbacher, May 3, 1893. Mem. New York Stock Exchange firm since 1899. Trustee Am. Scenic and Historic Preservation Soc. Mem. Am. Hist. Assn., N.Y. Hist. Soc., City History Club. Phi Beta Kappa. Author: Frederick Struther's Romance, 1889; Chaperoned, 1894; A Landmark History of New York, 1901; New York's Historic Sites, 1902; History of Maiden Lane, 1911; (with Grace Charlotte Strachan) Tales of Old New York, 1914. Asso. editor Historical Guide to the City of New York, 1909. Historian of Maiden Lane Hist. Soc. Home: 101 W. 80th St., New York. Died Oct. 8, 1948.

ULRICH, Barry Stribling, lawyer; b. Chicago, July 6, 1888; s. Augustus Louis and Louisa (Stribling) U.; A.B., Harvard, 1910, LL.B., 1913; m. Evelyn Wells, June 22, 1918; children—Priscilla Louise, Barry Wells. Began practice at Honolulu, T.H., 1913; associated with Pillsbury, Madison & Sutro, San Francisco, 1914-16, alone, 1916-17; mem. Thompson, Cathcart & Ulrich, Honolulu, 1919-23, again in San Francisco, 1923-25; now in practice alone; spl. prosecutor for Ty. of Hawaii in case against Grace Fortescue, Massie, et al., 1932. Enlisted in 144th F.A. ("California Grizzlies") summer of 1917; lt. U.S.A., at Camp Zachary Taylor, Louisville, Ky., until close of war. Republican. Presbyterian. Mason (32°, Shriner). Club: Pacific. Home: 1951 Vancouver Highway. Office: Dillingham Bldg., Honolulu, T.H. Died Aug. 9, 1936.

ULRICH, Edward Oscar (ŭl'rĭk), paleontologist; b. Cincinnati, O., Feb. 1, 1857; s. Charles and Julia (Schnell) U ; studied German Wallace Coll , Berea, O.; hon. A.M., 1886, D.Sc., 1892; studied Ohio Med. Coll.; m. Albertine Zuest, June 29, 1886; m. 2d, Lydia Sennhauser, June 20, 1933. Curator geology, Cincinnati Soc. Natural History, 1877-81; paleontologist to geol. surveys of Ill., Minn. and Ohio, 1885-96; geologist U.S. Geol. Survey since 1897. Asso. in paleontology, U.S. Nat. Museum, 1914-32, retired; asso. editor Am. Geologist for 10 years. Author: American Paleozoic Bryozoa, 1884 (Cincinnati Soc. Natural History); American Paleozoic Sponges and Paleozoic Bryozoa (Vol. VIII, Ill. Geol. Survey), 1890; monographs in Vol. III, Geol. Survey of Minn., on the Lower Silurian Bryozoa, Lamellibranchiata, Ostracoda and Gastropoda of Minn. (2 parts), 1893-97; Geology of the Lead, Zinc and Fluor Spar District of Western Ky., 1901; Revision of Paleozoic Systems, 1911; The Ordovician-Silurian Boundary, 1914; Formations of the Chester Series, 1917; Correlation by Displacements of the Strandline, 1916; Major Causes of Land and Sea Oscillations, 1922; Silurian Formations of the Appalachian Region, 1923; Monograph of Silurian Ostracoda and New Classification of Paleozoic Ostracoda, 1923; Formations and Breaks between Paleozoic Systems in Wisconsin, 1924; Classification of the Conodonta, 1925; Relative Values of Criteria Used in Defining Paleozoic Systems, 1927; Monograph of the Telephidae, 1929; Monograph Dikellocephalidae, Parts 1 and 2, 1932. Contbns. to textbooks and journals on paleontol. and stratigraphic themes. Mem. Nat. Acad. Sciences, Washington Acad. Sciences; fellow Geol. Soc. America, Paleontol. Soc.; foreign mem. Geol. Society London; corr. member Geol. Society of Sweden, Senkenberg, Naturforsch. Gesells.; corr. Phila. Acad. Science, 1932. Awarded Mary Clark Thompson medal, 1930. Penrose medal, 1932. Home: 611 Butternut St., Takoma Park, D.C. Office: U.S. National Museum, Washington, D.C. Died Feb. 22, 1944.

UMBEL, Robert Emory, lawyer; b. Henry Clay Twp., Fayette County, Pa., July 11, 1863; s. Samuel C. and Martha L. (Brown) U.; prep. edn. Georges Creek Acad., Smithfield, Pa.; grad. Western Pa. Classical and Scientific Inst., Mt. Pleasant, Pa., 1885; m. Frances Grier White, Nov. 29, 1899; 1 dau., Margaret Grier (Mrs. Roger G. Newland; now dec.). Admitted to Pa. bar, 1887, and began practice at Uniontown; judge Courts of 14th Jud. Dist. of Pa., 1900-15; pres. Fayette Title & Trust Bldg.; v.p. and dir. White Swan Hotel Co. Am., Pa., Fayette County bar assns. Democrat. Presbyterian. Mason (33°, Shriner). Clubs: Triangle (pres.), Uniontown Country. Home: 50 W. Main St. Office: Fayette Title & Trust Bldg., Uniontown, Pa. Died Apr. 25, 1945; buried Hill Grove Cemetery, Connellsville, Pa.

UNDERHILL, Charles Lee, ex-congressman; born Richmond, Va., July 20, 1867; s. Jesse Johnson and Sallie (Clements) U.; ed. pub. schs.; m. Edith Lamprey, Feb. 25, 1892 (died June 9, 1931); children—Helen Louise (dec.), Phoebe Willis, Doris, Albion Perry, Jesse Johnson. Began as office boy, later coal teamster and learned blacksmith's trade; entered hardware business as Underhill Hardware Co., 1896, now retired. Mem. Mass. Ho. of Rep. 10 terms; mem. Mass. Constl. Conv.; mem. 67th to 72d Congresses (1921-33), 9th Mass. Dist.; chmn. Com. of Accounts. Republican. Conglist. Mason. Address: 7048 Harrow St., Forest Hills, N.Y. Died Jan. 28, 1946.

UNDERHILL, John Garrett, playwright, critic, producer; b. Brooklyn, N.Y., Jan. 10, 1876; s. Francis French and Frances Henrie (Bergen) U.; A.B., Poly. Inst. of Brooklyn, 1894; A.M., Columbia, 1896, Ph.D., 1899; m. Louisa Man Wingate, 1911 (died 1927); children—Susan Prudence (Mrs. Richard Crane), John Garrett. Asst. in comparative lit., Columbia, 1899-1901; actor, 1901; gen. rep. Soc. of Spanish Authors in U.S. and Can., 1911-20; editor Poet Lore, 1918; producer with Crosby Gaige of "Spanish Art Theatre" at Forrest Theatre, New York, 1927; has produced "Bonds of Interest" with the Theatre Guild, 1919, with Walter Hampden, 1929; "The Passion Flower," with Nance O'Neil, 1920; "Field of Ermine," 1922, 35; "Saturday Night" with Eva Le Gallienne, 1926; "The Cradle Song," London, 1926, New York, 1927, etc., also with Wendy Hiller, directed by Gielgud, London, 1944 Awarded Caballero de la Real Orden de Isabel la Católica, Mem. Hispanic Soc. Am., Instituto de las Españas. Club: The Players (New York). Author: Spanish Literature in the England of the Tudors, 1899. Translator: Plays by Jacinto Benavente, 4 series, 1917, 19, 23, 24; Plays of G. Martinez Sierra (with Helen and Harley Granville-Barker), 1923; The Cradle Song and Other Plays, 1929; Four Plays by Lope de Vega, 1936; The Great Theatre of the World, by Calderon, 1944. Contbr. to encyclopedias. Home: Twilight Park, Haines Falls, N.Y. Town address: The Players, 16 Gramercy Park, New York, N.Y. Died May 15, 1946.

UNDERWOOD, Bert Elias, publisher of photographs; b. Oxford, Ill., Apr. 29, 1862; s. Rev. Elias and Lavina (Elmer) U.; ed. Ottawa (Kan.) U.; m. Susan Stannard, Dec. 1, 1887; children—Elmer Roy, Esther Lael (Mrs. Charles Evans, Jr.), Robert Stannard. Began selling stereoscopic photographs in Kan., 1882, forming partnership (with brother) of Underwood & Underwood (later incorporated); activities extended to Pacific Coast states, 1884; office opened in Baltimore, 1886, later in Toronto, New York, Chicago, also in many countries of Europe and Asia; began selling pictures with news interest to periodicals, 1896, with photographs and articles descriptive of Greco-Turkish War for Illustrated London News and Harpers Weekly; was the only photographer to take picture of Edward VII and Queen Alexandria wearing coronation crowns and robes; made trips into many parts of the world to develop picture "tours," sets of photographs with descriptions in book form; pres. Underwood & Underwood (from time of incorpn.) until retirement in 1925, now dir.; dir. El Encanto Estates, Inc. Del. Nat. Progressive Conv., Chicago, 1912, 16; mem. of Mayor's Com. of Welcome to City of New York to returning soldiers, 1918-19. Served as maj. Signal Corps, U.S. Army, and comdg. officer of photographic div., during World War. Commr. Gen. Assembly, Presbyn. Ch. 1936. Mem. Am. Legion, S.A.R. (former nat. trustee; state chaplain), Hiram Internat. Ind. Republican. Presbyn. (mem. Nat. Missions Bd. Presbyn. Ch.). Mason. Clubs: Lake Placid (N.Y.); Canoebrook Country (Summit, N.J.). Author: A Stereograph Record of William McKinley, 1901. Home: El Encanto Estates, Tucson, Ariz. Died Dec. 23, 1943.

UNDERWOOD, Frederick Douglass, retired ry. pres.; b. Wauwatosa, Wis.; s. Enoch Downs and Harriet (Denny) U.; ed. Wayland Acad., Beaver Dam, Wis.; children—Enoch William, Russell Sage. Began ry. service as clerk and brakeman, continued in ry. and transportation interests in various capacities, first on the C.,M.&St.P. Ry., became supt.; gen. supt. Minneapolis & Pacific Ry.; later gen. mgr. Minneapolis, St. Paul & Sault Ste. Marie Ry.; gen. mgr. and v.p. B.&O. R.R., 1899-1901; pres. Erie R.R. and its allied companies, May 1901-Dec. 31, 1926. chmn. exec. com., 1920-26; dir. N.Y.S. & W.R.R. Clubs: Metropolitan (New York); Milwaukee (Milwaukee). Home: 151 Central Park W. Office: 50 Church St., New York. Died Feb. 18, 1942.

UNDERWOOD, George Arthur, coll. prof.; b. Joplin, Mo., Nov. 20, 1882; s. Stephen A. and Sarah Anna (Whitwell) U.; A.B., U. of Mo., 1905, A.M. and B.S. in Edn., 1906; A.M., Harvard, 1909, Ph.D., 1914; studied U. of Paris, 1911-12; m. Catherine De Puy Allison, June 24, 1916. Prof. of French and Latin, Missouri Valley Coll., Marshall, Mo., 1906-08; instr. Romance langs., U. of Mo., 1912-13; prof. Romance langs., Kenyon Coll., Gambier, O., 1913-14; instr. and asst. prof. French, Smith Coll., Northampton, Mass., 1914-18; prof. and head of dept. of Romance langs., Ia. State Teachers Coll., 1918-24; prof. Romance langs., Woman's Coll., U. of N.C., Greensboro, since 1924. Mem. of Modern Lang. Assn. America, Phi Beta Kappa, Delta Tau Delta. Episcopalian. Contbr. to periodicals. Home: 212 W. Avondale, Greensboro, N.C. Died Nov. 24, 1944.

UNDERWOOD, Ira Julian, lawyer; b. McLeansboro, Ill., July 28, 1891; s. David Jasper and Ruth (Campbell) U.; A.B., Ill. Coll., 1911; LL.B., Washington U., St. Louis, 1914; m. Marion Waller Taylor, Jan. 2, 1917; children—Marion McNair, Elinor Campbell, Julie Ann. Admitted to Okla. bar, 1914, and since in general civil law practice at Tulsa; general counsel Okla. Natural Gas Co.; dir. Fourth Nat. Bank of Tulsa; city counselor, Tulsa, 1922-25. Mem. Phi Delta Phi. Independent Democrat. Unitarian. Mason (Scottish Rite, Shriner). Clubs: Tulsa, Southern Hills Country (Tulsa). Home: 1340 E. 19th St. Office: 5th Floor, Oklahoma Bldg., Tulsa, Okla. Died July 10, 1947.

UNDSET, Sigrid (ŭn'sĕt), novelist; b. Kallundborg, Denmark, May 20, 1882; d. Ingvald Martin and Charlotte (Gyth) Undset; grad. Ragna Nielsens Skole, Oslo, Oslo Handelsgymnasium; Litt.D., Russell Sage Coll., 1941; m. A. C. Svarstad, June 23, 1912; children—Anders (dec.), Maren Charlotte (dec.), Hans Benedikt Undset. Stenographer and secretary in an Oslo office, 1898-1909; author since. Awarded Nobel prize in lit., 1929. Received Cross of Islands Falk (Iceland), St. Olavs Order (Norwegian), Pro Ecclesia and Pontifice (Roman Catholic). Chmn. Norwegian Authors Union since 1933. Mem. European P.E.N. in America. Roman Catholic. Author: Kristin Lavransdatter; Master of Hestviken; Return to the Future, 1942; Christmas and Twelfth Night; also other novels, essays, and translations from old Norse and English into Norwegian. Contbr. to mags. Address: Lillehammer, Norway. Died June 10, 1949.

UPDIKE, Daniel Berkeley (ŭp'dīk), printer, publisher; b. Providence, R.I., 1860; s. Hon. C. A. and Elisabeth Bigelow (Adams) U.; ed. private schs., Providence; hon. M.A., Brown Univ., 1910; hon. M.A. from Harvard, 1929; unmarried. Work done under name of D. B. Updike, The Merrymount Press, Boston, founded in 1893; has been one of chief factors in the improvement of typography in America. Lecturer on printing, Post-Graduate Business Sch., Harvard, 1910-17; visiting lecturer, Dept. of Printing and Graphic Arts, 1940, Calif. Inst. of Technology and Huntington Library, Pasadena, 1940. Mem. bd. mgrs. John Carter Brown Library, Providence; trustee Boston Athenæum. Mem. Antiquarian Soc. (Worcester), Mass. Hist. Soc., Am. Library Assn.; hon. Phi Beta Kappa (Harvard and Brown); hon. mem. and gold medalist Am. Inst. of Graphic Arts. Clubs: Somerset, Club of Odd Volumes (Boston); Elizabethan (New Haven); Grolier Club of New York (hon.). Author: (with Harold Brown) On the Dedications of American Churches, 1892; Printing Types—Their History, Forms and Use, 1922; In the Day's Work, 1924. Editor: More's Dissertation on English Typographical Founders and Foundries, 1924; Notes on the Merrymount Press, 1934; Richard Smith, First English Settler of The Narragansett Country, R.I., 1937; Some Aspects of Printing, Old and New, 1941. Died Dec. 28, 1941.

UPHAM, Alfred Horatio (ŭp'ȧm), univ. pres.; b. Eaton, O., Mar. 2, 1877; s. John and Laura (Gardner) U.; A.B., Miami Univ., Oxford, O., 1897, A.M., 1898, LL.D., 1927; A.M., Harvard, 1901; Ph.D., Columbia, 1908; LL.D., Wabash Coll., 1932; m. Mary Collins McClintock, June 28, 1905; 1 dau., Margaret Louise (Mrs. Howard A. Offers). Instr. Latin and Greek, Miami U., 1897-1900; prof. English, Agrl. Coll. of Utah, 1902-05, Miami U., 1906-10, asso. prof. English lit., Bryn Mawr Coll., Pa., 1910-13; prof. English, Miami U., 1913-20; pres. U. of Ida., 1920-28; pres. Miami Univ. since 1928; mem. summer faculty Columbia U., 1914, U. of Ill., 1916. Mem. Modern Lang. Assn. America, Nat. Assn. State Univs. (sec.-treas. 1927-35, pres. 1935-36), Delta Kappa Epsilon, Phi Beta Kappa, Tau Kappa Alpha, Omicron Delta Kappa, Phi Mu Alpha. Presbyterian. Author: The French Influence in English Literature from the Accession of Elizabeth to the Restoration, 1908; Old Miami, The Yale of the Early West, 1909; Typical Forms of English Literature, 1917; Rhyming Round the World, 1939. Contbr. to various periodicals. Address: Miami University, Oxford, O. Died Feb. 17, 1945.

UPJOHN, Hobart Brown (ŭp'jŏn), architect; b. Brooklyn, N.Y., May 2, 1876; s. Richard Michell and Emma Degen (Tyng) U.; Poly. Inst. of Brooklyn, 1890-95; M.E., Stevens Inst. of Tech., 1899; LL.D., Hobart Coll., Geneva, N.Y., 1933; m. Margaret Miller, Apr. 8, 1902; children—Everard Miller, Elizabeth Degen, Dorothy. In shops of Worthington Pump Co., 1899-1900; 3d asst. engr. S.S. New York, 1900; with New York Shipbuilding Co., 1900-01, Lackawanna & Wyo. Valley R.R., 1901; asst. prin. Sch. of Archtl. Engring., Internat. Corr. Schs., 1901-03; engr. Eidlitz & McKenzie, architects, N.Y. City, 1903-05; in practice as architect since 1905. Prin. works: First Presbyterian chs., Wilmington, Greensboro and Concord, N.C.; Sprunt Memorial Presbyn. Ch., Chapel Hill, N.C.; St. Luke's Ch., Montclair, N.J.; St. Catherine's Sch., Richmond, Va.; All Souls Unitarian Ch., N.Y. City; Hobart, William Smith and N.C. State colleges; etc. Awarded diploma of merit from Internat. Expn., Turin, Italy, for Village Chapel, Pinehurst, N.C., Chapel of the Cross, Chapel Hill, N.C., and N.C. State Coll. Library; winner of competition for commission, First Park Bapt. Ch., Plainfield, N.J. Mem. Commn. on Architecture and Allied Arts, P.E. Ch. America; mem. N.J. Naval Reserve, 1895-96; exec. asst. in housing dept. U.S. Shipping Board, 1918. Fellow Am. Inst. Architects (pres. N.Y. Chapter). Republican. Episcopalian. Mason. Clubs: Church Club; Century (New York City). Wrote textbooks for archtl. course of International Corr. Schs.; also monographs and articles on architecture. Home: 9 Church Lane, Scarsdale, N.Y. Office: 101 Park Av., New York 17, N.Y. Died Aug. 23, 1949.

UPSHUR, William Peterkin (ŭp'shûr), Marine Corps officer; b. Richmond, Va., Oct. 28, 1881; s. John Nottingham and Elizabeth Spencer (Peterkin) U.; grad. Va. Mil. Inst., 1902; law student U. of Va., 1902-03; grad. Command and Gen. Staff Sch., U.S. Army, 1925, Naval War Coll., 1932, Army War Coll., 1933; m. Lucy Taylor Munford, Dec. 20, 1904; 1 son, William Peterkin (died in infancy). Commd. 2d lt., U.S. Marine Corps, 1904, and advanced through the grades to maj. gen., Oct. 1, 1939; has served in nearly all Marine barracks within U.S. and with forces in Haiti, Cuba, Santo Domingo, China, France, Philippines, also on U.S.S., California, Maine, Kearsarge, Rainbow and Buffalo; Force Marine officer Battle Force, U.S. Fleet, 1929-31; service at Navy Department, Washington, D.C., in the office of the Major General, Commandant of the Marine Corps, and of the Chief of Naval Operations; dir. Marine Corps Reserve; became comdg. gen. Fleet Marine Force and Marine Corps Base, San Diego; now comdg. Marine Corps Dept. of the Pacific, San Francisco. Decorated Congl. Medal of Honor, 1915, Haitian Campaign, Cuban Campaign, Santo Domingo Campaign, Expeditionary medals, Victory medal with French clasp. Mem. Mil. Order Foreign Wars, Mil. Order of Carabao. Episcopalian. Clubs: Army and Navy, Army and Navy Country (Washington, D.C.); Aztec Club of 1847. Home: 1613 Grove Av., Richmond, Va. Address: care Headquarters U.S. Marine Corps, Washington, D.C. Died July 1943.

UPSON, Fred Wilbert, educator; b. Byron, Ill., Feb. 2, 1883; s. Richard Empey and Mary (Johnston) U.; B.S., U. of Neb., 1907, A.M., 1908; Ph.D., U. of Chicago, 1910; m. Georgia Field, June 16, 1915; 1 son, John Field. Instr. in chemistry, U. of Cincinnati, 1910-12; research instr. in chemistry, U. of Chicago, 1912-13; prof. agrl. chemistry, U. of Neb., 1913-18, prof. chemistry and chmn. dept. of chemistry, 1918-39, dean of Graduate School, 1929-39, dean and prof. emeritus since 1939. Fellow A.A.A.S.; mem. Am. Chem. Soc., Am. Assn. Univ. Profs., Sigma Xi. Republican. Protestant. Author of numerous articles in chemistry, chiefly in the fields of carbohydrate chemistry and of chem. mechanism. Home: 4642 Bancroft Av., Lincoln, Neb. Died Feb. 10, 1942.

UPSON, Lent Dayton; b. De Leon Springs, Fla., Nov. 5, 1886; s. Jesse Bronson and Mary (Sibley) U.; B.A., U. of Wis., 1908, M.A., 1909; Ph.D., U. of Ill., 1911; studied New York Training Sch. for Pub. Service; m. Marie E. Rehmert, May 29, 1917; children—Mary Ellen, Betty Jean. Dir. Dayton Bur. Municipal Research, 1912-15; sec. Dayton Citizens' Relief Com., 1913; asst. dir., New York Bur. Municipal Research, 1914; exec. sec. Nat. Cash Register Co., 1915-16; in joint charge surveys of state govts. of Ohio and Va.; also in charge, survey of Cincinnati and Hamilton County, Atlantic City, N.J., and local govt. in Mich.; dir. Detroit Bur. Governmental. Research, 1916-44; dir. Nat. Training Sch. for Pub. Service since 1944; chief statis., Div. of Taxation, United States Bureau of Census, 1934; dean School of Public Affairs and Social Work, Wayne U., Detroit, since 1935; lecturer in pub. adminstrn. and dir. of student training, U. of Mich., 1918-32, 1935-38; consultant municipal finance and services for Federal Emergency Relief Adminstrn. and Works Progress Adminstrn., 1934-37; chmn. and dir. Mich. Tax Study Commn., 1937-39; research dir. Mich. Com. on Inquiry into Local Govt., 1932-34. Mem. Governmental Research Assn. National Municipal League (v.p.), Mich. Civil Service Study Commn., 1935-37, Mich. State Planning Bd., 1935-36, Sons Revolution, Pi Gamma Mu, Psi Sigma Alpha, Acacia. Unitarian. Mason (K.T., Shriner). Club: Wayne U. Faculty. Author: Sources of Municipal Revenue in Illinois, 1912; A Syllabus of Municipal Administration, 1923; Practice of Municipal Administration, 1926; The Growth of a City Government, 1931; Crippled Children in Michigan (with O. V. Matson), 1931; Government of the Detroit Metropolitan Area (with J. M. Leonard), 1934; Urban Tax Delinquency (with L. D. Woodworth), 1935; An Outline of American Local Government (with others), 1937; We Bought an Abandoned Farm, 1941; Letters from a Dean on Administration, 1941; Organized Citizen Concern with Government, 1946. Editor and joint author: The Government of Cincinnati and Hamilton County, 1924; Government of the City of Atlantic City, N.J., 1930; Local Government in Michigan, 1933; Report of Mich. Tax Study Commn., 1939. Home: 3271 Taylor Av., Detroit 6, (summer) Cyrus Stage Rd., Rowe, Mass. Office: 5229 Cass Av.; and Wayne University, Detroit 1, Mich. Died May 10, 1949.

UPTHEGROVE, Fay R(oscoe), army officer, b. Port Allegany, Pa., Jan. 28, 1905; s. Frank Ellis and Cora Jane Upthegrove; B.S., U.S. Mil. Acad., 1927; grad. Air Corps Primary Flying Sch., 1928, Advanced Flying Sch., 1928, Tactical Sch., 1939; m. Marcella Gretchen Driscoll, Sept. 6, 1930; children—Sophie-Lou, Mary Jane. Commd. 2d lt., U.S. Army, 1927, advancing through the grades to brig. gen., 1944; served at domestic stations in U.S. and in Hawaii; rated command pilot, aerial navigator, sr. aircraft observer. Decorated Distinguished Service Medal, Silver Star, Distinguished Flying Cross with oak leaf cluster, Air Medal with 9 oak leaf clusters, Am. Defense and Am. Theater ribbons, African-European Theater Ribbon with 5 stars, Presidential Unit Citation. Home: 127 S. 12th St., Olean, N.Y. Died Oct. 22, 1946.

UPTON, George Burr, univ. prof.; b. Newark Valley, N.Y., Oct. 16, 1882; s. Charles Olmstead and Ella (Burr) U.; M.E., Cornell U., 1904, M.M.E., 1905; m. Lulu Marie Newlon, June 18, 1923. Instr. exptl. engring., Cornell U., 1905-09, asst. prof., 1910-18, prof., 1919-36, prof. of automotive engring. since 1936; analyst and cons. engr. Curtiss Airplane Co., U.S. Govt., Nat. Advisory Com. for Aeronautics, etc.; expert in patent infringement cases; patentee Upton-Lewis fatigue testing machine. Mem. Am. Soc. Testing Materials, Am. Soc. Mech. Engrs., Soc. Automotive Engrs., Am. Soc. for Metals, Sigma Xi, Tau Beta Pi, Phi Kappa Phi. Republican. Author: Materials of Construction, 1916. Contbr. chapters to Experimental Engineering Manual by Carpenter and Diederichs, 1911. Contbr. numerous articles to tech. jours. Home: 121 Cayuga Park Rd., Ithaca, N.Y. Died Oct. 29, 1942.

UPTON, Harriet Taylor (Mrs. George Upton); b. Ravenna, O.; d. Ezra B. and Harriet (Frazer) Taylor; ed. pub. schs. Warren, O.; m. George W. Upton, July 9, 1884. Active in woman suffrage movement from 1890; pres. Ohio Woman Suffrage Assn.; treas. Nat. Woman Suffrage Assn. 15 yrs.; patron Nat. Council Women; ex-pres. Warren Bd. of Edn.; vice chmn. Rep. Nat. Exec. Com. Episcopalian. Author: Our Early Presidents, Their Wives and Children, 1892; History of Turnbull County, Ohio; History of the Western Reserve. Apptd. by Gov. Cooper departmental rep. Dept. of Pub. Welfare. Home: Warren, O. Address: State Dept. of Public Works, Columbus, O. Died Nov. 2, 1945.

URNER, Hammond (ûr'nẽr), judge; b. Frederick, Md., Dec. 4, 1868; s. Milton G. and Laura A. (Hammond) U.; A.B., Dickinson Coll., Pa., 1890, A.M., 1893; LL.D., St. John's Coll., Annapolis, 1918; m. Mary L. Floyd, May 3, 1893; children—George Floyd (dec.), Joseph Walker, Francis Hammond, Martin Jonas. Admitted to bar, 1891, and practiced at Frederick; mem. Urner, Keedy & Urner, 1891-1901, Urner & Urner, 1901-09. City atty., Frederick, 1898-1901; Rep. candidate for atty.-gen. of Md., 1907; chief judge 6th Jud. Circuit of Md. and asso. judge Court of Appeals of Md., 1909-26, reëlected for 2d term of 15 yrs., 1926; retired from Bench, Dec. 4, 1938, at 70 years of age, under provision of Md. Constitution, and returned to practice of law. Republican. Methodist. Trustee Frederick City Hosp. Pres. Md. State Bar Assn., 1916. Home: 215 E. 2d St., Frederick, Md. Died Sep. 27, 1942.

USHER, Robert James, librarian; b. South Wayne, Wis., July 10, 1880; s. John Mitchell and Harriet (McGinley) U.; A.B., U. of Wis., 1907; m. Ethel Mae Wight, Sept. 2, 1922. Asst., U. of Wis. Library, 1906-08; asst. reference librarian, John Crerar Library, Chicago, 1909-14; supt. of circulation, U. of Calif. Library, 1914-17; reference librarian, John Crerar Library, 1917-27; became librarian, Howard Memorial Library, New Orleans, La., 1927; directing libraries of Tulane Univ., Newcomb Coll. and Howard Memorial Library, 1938-40; librarian Howard-Tilton Memorial Library since 1940. Mem. A.L.A., Bibliog. Soc. America, A.A.A.S., Louisiana Library Association, Southwestern Library Assn. (pres.), New Orleans Library Club, Louisiana Historical Society, Wis. Hist. Soc., New Orleans Acad. of Science (curator), Athénée Louisianais, Member's Council New Orleans Assn. Commerce. Club: Round Table (sec.). Contbr. to library and bibliog. jours. Home: 1531 Audubon St. Office: Howard-Tilton Memorial Library, Tulane University, New Orleans, La. Died Aug. 4, 1944.

UTERHART, Henry Ayres (ū tẽr-härt), lawyer; b. New York, N.Y., Jan. 5, 1875; s. Henry and Emma Jane (Ayres) U.; B.A., Columbia, 1894, M.A., LL.B., 1896; m. Josephine Stein, Apr. 27, 1903; 1 dau., Josephine H. Practiced at N.Y. City since 1896; counsel L.I. R.R. Co., many yrs.; counsel Commercial Cable Co.; counsel in many important cases. Served as capt. U.S. Army, A.E.F., 1918; mil. attaché to Italy, 1919. Mem. Assn. Bar City of New York, Am. and N.Y. State bar assns., N.Y. County Lawyers Assn., Nassau County Bar Assn. (pres.), Modern Lang. Assn. America, Am. Legion, Mil. Order World War, Theta Delta Chi. Republican. Episcopalian. Mason. Clubs: Lawyers, Republican, Columbia Univ., Piping Rock (New York); The Travellers, L'Etrier (Paris). Home: East Norwich, L.I. and 42 E. 51st St., New York. Office: 36 W. 44th St., New York. Died April 12, 1946; buried in Arlington National Cemetery.

UTLEY, George Burwell, librarian; b. Hartford, Conn., Dec. 3, 1876; s. George Tyler and Harriet Ella (Burwell) U.; Colgate U., 1 yr.; Ph.B., Brown U., 1899 (hon. A.M., 1923); m. Lou Mabel Gilbert, Sept. 4, 1901. Asst. librarian, Watkinson Library, Hartford, Conn., 1899-1901; librarian Md. Diocesan Library, Baltimore, 1901-05; librarian Pub. Library, Jacksonville, Fla., 1905-11; sec. and exec. officer Am. Library Assn. and its pub. bd., Chicago, 1911-20; librarian Newberry Library, Chicago, 1920-42, emeritus since Sept. 1, 1942. Executive secretary, 1917-19, Library War Service of A.L.A., which supplied reading matter to military and naval forces during the war and demobilization period of World War I. Decorated Order of the Crown of Italy, 1922. Mem. A.L.A. (mem. exec. bd., 1920-23; pub. bd., 1920-21; chmn. editorial com., 1924-31; chmn. finance com., 1920-22; pres. 1922-23), Am. Library Inst. (pres. 1937-39), Am. Hist. Assn., Ill. Library Assn. (pres. 1924-25), Chicago Hist. Soc., Conn. Hist. Soc., Geog. Soc. Chicago (pres. 1929-31), Bibliog. Soc. America, Am. Inst. Graphic Arts, Phi Beta Kappa, Delta Kappa Epsilon. Clubs: Grolier (New York); Chicago Library (pres. 1912-13), Chicago Literary (pres. 1935-36), Cliff Dwellers, University, Writers' Guild (pres. 1935-37), Caxton (mem. council, 1939-45) (Chicago). Author: The Life and Times of Thomas John Claggett, 1913; Fifty Years of the Am. Library Assn., 1926; also papers on libraries, library work and other subjects in various professional journals. Contbr. to Dictionary of Am. Biography. Address: Newberry Library, Chicago, Ill.; (summer) Pleasant Valley, Conn. Died Oct. 4, 1946.

UTLEY, Joseph Simeon, judge; b. Greenbrier, Ark., Oct. 18, 1876; s. Francis David and Melvina (Snow) U.; A.B., Hendrix Coll., Ark., 1906; m. Vivian Rockwood Williams, June 18, 1903. Teacher and supt. schs. in Ark. 4 yrs.; began law practice at Benton, Ark., 1908; pros. atty. 7th Jud. Dist. of Ark., 1911-14; mem. Ark. Senate, 1917-21; atty. gen. of Ark., 1921-25; chmn. Dem. State Central Co., 1927-28; has served as special counsel State of Ark., special probate judge and special circuit judge; circuit judge 6th Judicial District, Ark., since 1935. Former member examining bd. for admission to bar of State Supreme Court. Former state counsel for Ark. of Home Owner's Loan Corp.; former pres. Ark. Pros. Atty's. Assn.; chmn. for Ark. of Antietam Celebration Commn., U.S. Constl. Sesqui-Centennial Commn. Mem. bd. trustees Hendrik College, since 1941. Member Am., Ark. and Little Rock bar assns.; judge advocate in chief of national orgn. Sons Confed. Vets. (former comdr. Arkansas State Div.; past comdr. Trans-Mississippi Dept.); mem. Ark. Soc. S.A.R. (pres. 1936-38). Hendrix Coll. Alumni Assn. (pres. 1937-38). Del. to Gen. Conf. M.E. Ch., S., Atlanta, 1918. Mason (32°); past grand orator Grand Lodge of Ark. Masons; Odd Fellow, Elk. Club: Lions. Home: 2404 Schiller Av. Address: County Court House, Little Rock, Ark. Died Dec. 13, 1943.

UTLEY, Stuart Wells, mfr. steel castings; b. Pontiac, Mich., June 25, 1879; s. Wells Hiram and Emma Jane (Adams) U.; A.B., U. of Mich., 1902; m. Helen W. Kurtz, June 26, 1915. Began as clk. with Am. Radiator Co., Detroit, 1902; with Detroit Steel Casting Co. since 1906, advancing from cost clk. to purchasing agent, asst. sec., sec., v.p. and gen. mgr., and since Feb. 1, 1932, pres. and gen. mgr.; dir. Mich. Mutual Liability Co., Asso. General Fire Co., National Assn. of Manufacturers; trustee Bureau of Governmental Research. Member National Founders Assn. (ex-pres.), Am. Foundrymens Assn. (ex-pres.), Employers Assn. of Detroit (ex-president), Mich. Mfrs. Assn. (ex-pres.), Am. Soc. for Testing Materials, Am. Iron and Steel Inst., Detroit Bd. of Commerce (ex-pres.), Delta Upsilon. Republican. Congregationalist. Clubs: Detroit, Detroit Athletic, Detroit Boat Club, Detroit Golf Club (Detroit); The Old Club (St. Clair Flats, Mich.). Author of numerous published addresses: The New Deal, On the Road to Moscow, American Principles or Planned Economy, the Duty of the Church to the Social Order, The Future of the American Citizen, The American System—Shall We Destroy It, etc. Home: 1964 Edison Av., Detroit 6. Office: 4069 Michigan Av., Detroit 10, Mich. Died Feb. 13, 1946.

UTTERBACK, Hubert (ŭt'tẽr-băk), lawyer; b. near Hayesville, Ia., June 28, 1880; s. A. M. and Julia Esther (Hayes) U.; A.B., Drake U., Des Moines, 1903, LL.B., 1906, LL.M., 1908; m. Edith Gwynne, Oct. 4, 1904 (died May 3, 1930); children—Esther (Mrs. Morris O. Penquite), Gretchen (Mrs. Paul K.

Ashby); m. 2d, Cora Alice Prine, Dec. 25, 1934. Admitted to Ia. bar, 1906; practiced in Des Moines; instr. law dept., Drake U., 1908-35; lecturer on law, Still College, Des Moines, 1911-33; judge Police Court, Des Moines, 1912-14; judge 9th Ia. Judicial Dist., 1915-27; elected justice Supreme Court of Ia., 1932; mem. 74th Congress (1935-37), 6th Ia. Dist. (mem. judiciary com.; pres. New Members Club, 74th Congress). Long active in Red Cross work (chmn. Des Moines and Polk County Chapter, 1916-28; chmn. Ia. State Council Red Cross Chapters, 1919-34; chmn. Nat. Conv. Am. Nat. Red Cross); chmn. Court of Honor, Boy Scouts of America, Des Moines, since 1915; mem. for Ia. of Grand Council Order of De Molay for Boys; chmn. legislative com. Ia. State Conf. of Social Work, 1923-25. Mem. Iowa Board of Parole, 1938-39. Democratic Nat. Committeeman for State of Iowa, 1936-40. Mem. Phi Beta Kappa, Alpha Phi Omega, Delta Theta Phi, Acacia. Mem. Christian (Disciples) Ch. Mem. Lions (past dist. gov. of Ia. clubs). Home: 2935 Cottage Grove Av. Office: Southern Surety Bldg., Des Moines, Ia. Died May 12, 1942.

V

VAHEY, James Henry (vā'ē), lawyer; b. Watertown, Mass., June 29, 1900; s. James Henry and Margaret (White) V.; student Princeton U. and Boston U. Law Sch.; m. Edith Wyant, Feb. 11, 1928; children—Nancy, Judith. Admitted to Mass. bar, 1926, and since in practice in Boston. Served in U.S.N. R.F., 1917-19. Discharge review counsel for American Red Cross 1943-46. Asst. corp. counsel City of Boston, since 1946. Mem. Phi Delta Phi. Democrat. Catholic. Club: Cannon. Home: 490 Commonwealth Av. Office: 11 Beacon St., Boston, Mass. Died Nov. 3, 1949.

VAIL, Charles Davis, civil engr.; b. Lone Tree, Ill., Sept. 11, 1868; s. Richard R. and Catherine (Brokaw) V.; B.S., U. of Ill., 1891, C.E., 1936; m. Jessie Poden, Sept. 7, 1893; children—Richard R. (dec.), Allan P., Kenyon C., Charles C. (dec.), Vera M. (Mrs. Willis Winslow). Civil engr. for U.P. R.R., O.S.L. R.R., and others, 1891-93; water works and irrigation engring. in Mont., Idaho, Nev. and Colo., 1895-1917; engr. Pub. Utility Corp. of Colo., 1917-23; mgr. improvements and parks, city of Denver, 1923-30; state highway engr. of Colo. since 1930. Mem. Am. Soc. C.E., Colo. Soc. of Engrs., Am. Assn. of State Highway Officials (v.p.). Democrat. Mason (32°, Shriner), Elk. Clubs: Denver Athletic, Rotary, Democratic (pres.). Home: 547 S. Corona St. Office: State Office Bldg., Denver, Colo.* Died Jan. 9, 1945.

VAILLANT, George Clapp (väl'yänt), archeologist; b. Boston, Mass., Apr. 5, 1901; s. George Wightman and Alice Vanlora (Clapp) V.; student Phillips Acad., Andover, Mass., 1916-18; A.B., Harvard, 1922, A.M., 1925, Ph.D., 1927; m. Mary Suzannah Beck, Mar. 10, 1930; children—Joanna Beck, George Eman, Henry Winchester. Mem. archeol. expdn. to Me., 1919; field asst. archeol. expdns. in N.M. and Ariz., 1921, 22, 25, to Egypt, 1923-24, to Yucatan, 1926; in charge Valley of Mexico excavations of Am. Museum Natural History, N.Y. City, 1928-36; tutor in anthropology, Harvard, 1924-25; asst. curator Am. Museum Natural History, 1927-30, asso. curator of Mexican archeology, 1930-41, hon. curator 1941-44; dir. Univ. Museum, U. of Pa., since 1941; cultural attache, U.S. Foreign Service Auxiliary, Lima, Peru, 1943-44; appmt. asst. professor, Yale Univ., 1938-40; lecturer, New York Univ., 1938-39, Columbia Univ., 1930-40, 1941-42, Am.-Philosophical Soc., 1941-43; prof. anthropology, Univ. of Pa., since 1944, hon. prof. Museum of Mexico, since 1938. Served in U.S. Marine Corps, part of 1918. Mem. Am. Ethnol. Soc., Am. Anthrop. Assn., Soc. for Am. Archeology, Soc. de Americanistes de Paris, Soc. Antonio Alzate, Inst. for Andean Research. Mem. joint com. on Latin-Am. Studies, Pan-Am. Assn. (Phila.), Inter-Am. Soc. Anthropology and Geography. Mem. adv. com. on Art, State Dept.; trustee, Archaeological Inst. of Am.; co-trustee, grad. studies, Div. Fine Arts, Univ. of Pa. Clubs: Harvard, Century Assn. (New York); Franklin Inn, Rittenhouse (Phila.). Author: (all anthropological papers of Am. Museum Nat. History), Excavations at Zacatenco (vol. 32, no. 1), 1930: Excavations at Ticoman (vol. 2, no. 2), 1931; (with S. B. Vaillant) Excavations at Gualupita Val. 35, no. 1), 1934; Excavations at El Arbolillo (vol. 35, no. 2), 1935; Early Cultures of the Valley of Mexico (vol. 35, no. 3); (with R. E. Merwin) Ruins of Holmul, Guatemala, 1932; Indian Arts in North America, 1939; Aztecs of Mexico, 1941. Contbr. articles and reviews. Home: Old Orchard Farm, New Centerville, Devon, Pa. Address: University Museum, Univ. of Pa., Philadelphia, Pa. Died May 13, 1945.

VAILLANT, Louis David, mural painter; b. Cleveland, O., December 14, 1875; s. George Henry and Maria J. (Wightman) V.; ed. Art Students' League, New York, under H. Siddon Mowbray; in Paris under Luc Olivier Merson; in Florence and Rome; unmarried. Principal works: Stained glass windows in meeting house of Soc. of Ethical Culture, New York; medallions in ceiling of tea house, Rockefeller Gardens, Pocantico, N.Y.; decorations in Hotel Hermitage, New York. Second Hallgarten prize Nat. Acad. Design, 1910. Mem. Soc. Mural Painters. Club: Century Association. Home: Washington, Conn. Studio: 219 E. 61st St., New York, N.Y. Died Feb. 7, 1944.

VALENTINE, Lewis Joseph, police commr. New York, N.Y.; b. Brooklyn, N.Y., Mar. 19, 1882; s. John and Elizabeth (Daly) V.; student Manual Training High Sch., Brooklyn, 1896-98; m. Elizabeth J. Donohue, Oct. 12, 1904 (died Aug. 18, 1910); children—Elizabeth (Mrs. Charles A. Locke), Edward Lewis (dec.), Dorothy G. (Mrs. William J. McBride, Jr.), Ruth J. (Mrs. William H. Cahill); m. 2d, Teresa A. Donohue, July 6, 1914; 1 dau., Miriam. With delivery dept., Abraham & Strauss Dept. Store, 1898-1903; patrolman, Police Dept., N.Y. City, 1903-13, successively sergt., lt. and capt., 1913-26, dep. inspector and inspector, 1926-28, dep. chief inspector, 1928-34, chief inspector, 1934; apptd. police commr. N.Y. City, Sept. 25, 1934; retired, Sept. 1945; commentator on radio program, Gang Busters, since Sept. 1945. Catholic. K.C. Home: 1650 68th St., Brooklyn, N.Y. Office: 240 Centre St., New York, N.Y. Died Dec. 16, 1946.

VALENTINE, Willard Lee, editor; b. Chillicothe, O., 1904; s. Elmer Lee and Kate A. (Near) V.; A.B., Ohio Wesleyan U., 1925, M.A., 1926; Ph.D., Ohio State U., 1929; m. Grace Leora Jones, 1926 (dec.); children—Richard Marvin, Virginia Leora; m. 2d, Sally Cooper, 1941 (divorced); m. 3d, Norma Lawrence, 1945. Instr. psychology, Ohio Wesleyan, 1926-28; instr. psychology Ohio State U., 1928-29, asst. prof., 1929-31, asso. prof., 1931-40; head dept. psychology Northwestern U., 1940-45; editor Science since 1946; business mgr. publications Am. Psychol. Assn., 1938-46; mem. bd. dirs. Science Service since 1946. Mem. Am. Psychol. Assn. (treas. since 1937). Author: Readings in Experimental Psychology, 1931; Experimental Foundations of Psychology, 1938; contbr. tech. articles to psychol. jours. Home: 3317 Alabama Av., Alexandria, Va. Office: 1515 Massachusetts Av., N.W., Washington, D.C. Died Apr. 5, 1947.

VALLENTINE, Benjamin Bennaton ("Fitznoodle"), author, dramatist, journalist; b. London, Eng., Sept. 7, 1843; s. Benjamin Vallentine; ed. at King Edward VI's School, Birmingham, England; studied for English bar; unmarried. One of founders of Puck and its editor, 1877-84; editorial work on many papers; dramatic critic New York Herald. Compiler and author dramatic biographies, Johnson's Universal Ency.; one of judges of novels, short stories and epic poems for New York Herald's $25,000 competition, 1897; asso. and biog. editor E. C. Stedman's History of the New York Stock Exchange; sec. of com. of Am. Dramatists' Club apptd. to present to public project for Nat. Am. endowed theatre. Author: The Fitznoodle Papers; Fitznoodle in America; (plays) Fitznoodle; A Southern Romance; In Paradise; Fritz in New York; A Parisian Mystery; Madame Saccard (authorized adaptation of Emile Zola's drama of "Renée"); a version of Daudet's "Sapho," etc. Contbr. stories, etc., to mags. Financial editor New York Record, Real Estate Record and Builders' Guide. Clubs: Lotos, Press, Am. Dramatists (dir.). Residence: 10 W. 39th St. Office: 220 Broadway, New York. Died March 30, 1926.

VAN ALSTYNE, Eleanor Van Ness, M.D.; b. 1881; d. Charles Gilbert and Rachael Landon (Huyck) Van Alstyne; student Cornell U., 1909-16, Ph.D., 1916; M.D., Cornell U. Med. Coll., N.Y. City, 1917. Practiced at N.Y. City since 1917. Mem. A.M.A., New York County Med. Soc. Address: Woodstock, N.Y. Died Sep. 17, 1942.

VAN ALSTYNE, J. H., pres. Otis Elevator Co. Office: 260 11th Av., New York, N.Y.* Died Dec. 25, 1944.

VANAMEE, Grace Davis (vȧ-nä'mē), b. North Adams, Mass., Sept. 15, 1876; d. George and Electa (Magoon) Davis; grad. Drury High Sch., North Adams, 1894, Bliss Business Coll., 1895, Emerson Coll. Oratory, Boston, 1899; post-grad. study same coll., 1900; m. William Vanamee, 1909 (died 1914). Platform reader and lecturer, also teacher pvt. schs., 1901-07; lecturer city schs., New York, and Brooklyn Inst. Arts and Sciences, 1907-09; connected with Am. Acad. Arts and Letters since 1915, asst. to pres., 1921-41; resigned to do literary work; asst. sec. and asst. treas. Nat. Inst. Arts and Letters, 1925-40; served as acting dir. Hall of Fame, 1920. Chmn. Rep. Women's State Speaker's Bur. and mem. Women's Rep. State Com., 1920. Asst. to chmn. Am. Poets' Ambulance Com. and sec. Italian War Relief Com. of New York, World War. Awarded gold medal by Italian Red Cross, 1920. One of founders, 1921, mem. bd. govs. Women's Nat. Repub. Club, 1920-34, member of national council, 1934-42; editor The Guidon, 1927-30, a director of its school of politics, 1933-34; founder and president Uptown Medical Center Assn., 1926-30; member Women's Organization for National Prohibition Reform, 1926-34; mem. advisory council Rep. Ednl. League, Inc., of N.Y State, 1933-35; trustee Emerson Coll., term 1938-43; pres. and dir. Henry Hadley Foundation (founded 1938), 1938-41, 1943-48. Awarded Issachar Hoopes Eldridge citation for character and distinguished services, Emerson College of Oratory, 1934. Protestant. Clubs: Emerson College, Women's National Republican. Author of poems, "He Kept His Rendezvous with Death," "Roosevelt," "Farewell to Alexandra," "True Living," "The Price of Versailles," "To England," "Hail to Youth"; "Our Prayer," 1943; "A Miracle," 1944. "Aftermath of War," 1945. Contbr. to mags.; speaker on polit. and lit. subjects. Home: 520 85th Av. N., St. Petersburg, Fla. Died Dec. 10, 1946.

VAN ANDA, Carr V., editor; b. Georgetown, O., Dec. 2, 1864; s. Frederick C. and Mariah E. (Davis) Van A.; ed. Ohio U., Athens, O., 1880-82; m. Harriet L. Tupper, Dec. 16, 1885 (died Dec. 1887); m. 2d, Louise Shipman Drane, Apr. 11, 1898. Telegraph editor, Cleveland Herald, 1883-85, Cleveland Plain Dealer, 1885; night editor Baltimore Sun, 1886-88; with N.Y. Sun, 1888-1904, night editor, 1893-1904; mng. editor N.Y. Times, 1904-32. Home: 1470 Park Av., New York, N.Y. Died Jan. 29, 1945.

VAN BARNEVELD, Charles Edwin, mining engr.; b. Doetinchem, Netherlands, Nov. 26, 1874; s. Arnout S. D. and Louisa (deLacy) Van B.; ed. Holland, France, Eng. and Can.; M.Sc. and E.M., McGill Univ., Montreal, 1895; m. Mary Caroline Howard, Dec. 7, 1897; children—Frances Louise, John Howard, Elizabeth Grace, Mary Alice. Assayer in N.M., 1895; supt. Enterprise Mine, Ariz., 1896; engr. and chemist, Globe, Ariz., 1896-97; cons. engr., Mexico, 1897-99; asso. prof. mining, 1899-1900, head of mining dept., 1901-13, U. of Minn.; chief Dept. Mines and Metallurgy, Panama, P.I. Expn., 1913-15; prof. mining, U. of Calif., 1915-16; supt. Southwestern Expt. Sta., U.S. Bur. of Mines, Tucson, Ariz., 1917-21; supt. Miss. Valley Expt. Sta., U.S. Bur. of Mines, St. Louis, 1922-24; consulting practice. Has served as cons. mining engr. and reported on many mining projects since 1900. Mem. Am. Inst. Mining and Metall. Engrs. Author: Iron Mining in Minnesota, 1912; Leaching Nonsulphide Copper Ores with Sulphur Dioxide, 1923; Mechanical Underground Loading in Metal Mines, 1924. Home: Chatsworth, Calif. Died Sep. 1942.

VAN BEUREN, Frederick Theodore, Jr. (văn-bū'rĕn), surgeon; b. New York, N.Y., Feb. 10, 1876; s. Frederick T. and Elizabeth A. (Potter) Van B.; A.B., Yale, 1898; M.D., Coll. Phys. and Surg. (Columbia), 1902; m. Jessica T. Mohlman, May 26, 1906; children—Frederick T. III, Jessica, Michael M. II, John M. Asso. in anatomy, 1905-13, asso. in surgery, 1920, asst. professor, 1922, asso. prof. clin. surgery since 1929, asso. dean, 1921-34, Coll. of Physicians and Surgeons (Columbia); pres. Morristown (N.J.) Memorial Hosp. since 1933; asst. attending surgeon, Lincoln Hosp., 1910-13, Roosevelt Hosp., 1913-21; attending surgeon Volunteer Hosp., 1915-17, Sloan Hosp. for Women, 1920-38, asso. visiting surgeon Presbyn. Hosp. Mem. Squadron A., Nat. Guard N.Y., 1899-1910, resigned as capt.; 1st lt. M.R.C., U.S. Army, 1910-18; capt. and maj. M.C., U.S. Army, 1918-19; with A.E.F., July 1918-Feb. 1919; hon. disch. Feb. 2, 1919; maj. M.R.C., U.S. Army, 1920-35. Fellow Am. Coll. Surgeons, Am. Surg. Assn., Am. Foundation of Surgery; mem. A.M.A., New York Surg. Soc., Acad. Medicine, Alpha Delta Phi, Wolf's Head. Republican. Presbyterian. Clubs: Century (New York); Morris Country Golf; Yeamans Hall. Home: Morristown, N.J. Office: 65 5th Av., New York, N.Y. Died Mar. 13, 1943.

VAN BRUNT, Jeremiah Rutger (văn-brŭnt), corp. official; b. Brooklyn, N.Y., Dec. 3, 1867; s. Jeremiah and Mary Lott (Van Pelt) Van B.; ed. grammar sch.; m. Anna Gertrude Remsen, Oct. 22, 1890; children—Jeremiah Rutger (dec.), Elizabeth Remsen, Mary Lott (wife of Dr. George G. Cochran, Jr.), Catherine Schenck, Gertrude Covert (wife of Jon Stanton Jackson). Vice-president and director Chase Brass & Copper Company; treasurer Hallenbeck Hungerford Realty Corp. Mem. New York State Chamber Commerce, Brooklyn Chamber Commerce. Trustee Brooklyn Y.M.C.A. Mem. Dutch Ref. Church. Clubs: Union League, Merchants (New York). Home: Kitchawan, Westchester County, N.Y. Died Mar. 13, 1950.

VANCE, John Thomas, librarian; b. Lexington, Ky., Aug. 24, 1884; s. John Thomas and Emily Chew (Gibney) V.; A.B., Ky. U. (now Transylvania Coll.), 1905; LL.B., U. of Mich., 1909, hon. LL.M., 1933; spl. work in civil law, U. of Santo Domingo, Dominican Republic, 1920-21; S.J.D., Catholic University of America, 1937; Hon. LL.D., Transylvania Coll., 1940; m. Margaret Scott Breckinridge, Mar. 1, 1917; children—John Thomas, Henry Breckinridge, Louise Ludlow Dudley. Admitted to Ky. bar, 1909, and practiced at Lexington, 1909-13, as mem. Vance & Harbison; dep. gen. receiver Dominican customs Santo Domingo, 1913-19; mem. Lippitt & Vance, Santo Domingo, 1920-21, Washington, D.C., 1922-24; law librarian of Congress since 1924. Mem. Board of Curators, Transylvania Coll. A del. of A.L.A. to 1st World Library and Bibliog. Congress, Rome and Venice, 1929; member Second Pan Am. Congress of History and Geography (Washington, D.C.), 1935; del. to 2d Congress of Comparative Law, The Hague, 1937; del. to 1st Inter-American Bar Assn. Conf., Havana, 1941; pres. D.C. Library Assn., 1935-37; pres. Instituto de las Españas (Washington chapter), 1937-39. Mem. Am. Assn. Law Libraries (pres. 1933), Am. Law Inst., Am. Bar Assn. (chmn. sect. on internat. and comparative law, 1940-41), Am. Soc. Internat. Law, Am. Foreign Law Assn., Société de Législation Comparée, Riccobono Seminar of Roman Law, Am. Documentation Institute, Bibliog. Soc. Am., Kappa Alpha, Phi Delta Phi. Presbyterian. Clubs: Chevy Chase, Cosmos. Author: Background of Hispanic American Law, 1936. Contbr. to legal periodicals. Home: 16 W. Irving St., Chevy Chase, Md. Address: Law Library, Library of Congress, Washington, D.C. Died Apr. 11, 1943.

VANCE, J(ames) Milton, coll. prof.; b. Lexington, Ill., May 21, 1875; s. Rev. Samuel Elbridge and Kate (Frame) V.; A.B., Lake Forest (Ill.) Univ., 1896; Princeton Theol. Sem., 1899-1900; grad. McCormick

Theol. Sem., 1903, Blackstone N.T. fellowship, 1903-04, B.D., 1909; studied U. of Marburg, 1903, U. of Berlin, 1903-04, U. of Jena, 1904-06, Ph.D., Jena, 1906; student Teachers Coll., Columbia, 1917-18; m. Elizabeth May Wood, Nov. 29, 1906. Ordained to the ministry of the Presbyterian Church, 1903; Mercer prof. of religion, 1906-43, professor emeritus since 1943, acting dean, 1908-09, dean of men, 1921-30, College of Wooster. Lecturer, summer Y.W.C.A. conferences, Estes Park, Colo., 1913, Geneva Lake, Wis., 1915, Eaglesmere, Pa., 1920; acting pastor North Presbyn. Church, Cincinnati, Ohio, summer 1907, Stamford (Conn.), Presbyn. Church, summer 1929; member staff Madison Av. Presbyterian Church, N.Y. City, summer 1928; exchange preacher, England, 1934. Capt. Am. Red Cross Commn. to Palestine, Feb. 1918-June 1919. Republican. Member Phi Beta Kappa. Rotarian. Author: Beitraege zur Byzantinischen Kulturgeschichte, 1907; Eight Studies in Jeremiah, 1913; Six Studies in the Acts of the Apostles, 1931; The Life and Teaching of Jesus Christ, 1939. Editor: (with John Winter Thompson, Mus.D.) The Musical Compositions of Elizabeth Wood Vance, 1942. Visited Europe, summers 1912, 14, 22, 30, 34; during Sabbatical leave, 1932-33, made world tour, visiting mission stations in India, P.I., China, Korea and Japan; taught in Ewing Christian College, Allahabad, India, July 1932-Feb. 1933. Home: 930 N. Bever St., Wooster, O. Died July 5, 1948.

VANDEGRIFT, Rolland A; b. Washington, D.C., Nov. 19, 1893; s. Samuel A. and Margaret (McClay) V.; B.A., U. of Calif., Berkeley, 1917, M.A., 1921, candidate Ph.D., 1923; m. Margaret Teresa Bickford, Aug. 15, 1917 (divorced); children—Margaret Jean, Rolland A, Clarinda, Lucian Bickford; m. 2d, Ella B. Rawlings, Sept. 4, 1937. Resident fellow Native Sons of Golden West in Pacific Coast history, 1919-20; traveling fellow same, carrying on research in Archives of Spain, France and England, 1921-22; asst. in history, U. of Calif., Berkeley, 1920-21 and 1922-23; asst. prof. history and govt., U. of Southern Calif., 1923-24, asso. prof., 1924-25, prof., 1925-26; dir. of research Calif. Taxation Improvement Assn., Los Angeles, 1925; dir. of research Calif. Taxpayers Assn., 1926-29, sec.-mgr., 1929-30; head of Vandegrift Research Associates, doing governmental and economic research in Calif., Utah, Nev., and Ariz., 1928-30; engaged in research of tax situation and governmental orgn. of State of Utah for Metal Mining Industry of Utah, 1929-30; dir. of finance State of Calif. and chmn. State Bd. of Control, 1930-34; chmn. State Emergency Council, Calif.; first pres. Calif. State Employees Retirement Board; pub. Stockton (Calif.). Independent, 1933-34; mng. own interests and ranching in Ventura and Yolo counties, 1934-35; gen. agt. Occidental Life Ins. Co. of Calif. for Sacramento and Superior, Calif. (18 counties), 1935-36, br. mgr., 1936-39, associate gen. agent, same, Oakland, 1939-40, agent since Oct. 19, 1940; research and tax consultant for Utah Foundation since 1945; legislative auditor, State of Calif. (1st to hold this office), since Oct. 20, 1941. Mem. State Postwar Pub. Works Review Bd., Sept. 1944-47. Chartered Life Underwriter (charter mem. East Bay chapter of C.L.U. assn.). Served in Calif. Nat. Guard, 1913-16; Mexican border service, 1916; 2d lt., U.S. Army, 1918-19. Mem. Phi Delta Kappa, Sigma Delta Pi, Acacia. Republican. Mem. Christian (Disciples) Church. Mason (Shriner). Author of numerous papers and pamphlets on history, taxes, and other econ. subjects. Breeder of registered Hampshire and Southdown sheep. Home: 5V Ranch, Pleasant Grove, Sutter County, Calif. Office: 445 Capitol Bldg., Sacramento, Calif. Died Dec. 17, 1949.

van den BERG, Lawrence H(offman), normal sch. prin.; b. Grand Haven, Mich., Feb. 26, 1877; s. Albert G. and Jane (Hoffman) van den B.; B.A., U. of Mich., 1898; M.A., Columbia, 1913; hon. PdD., State Coll. for Teachers, Albany, N.Y., 1925; m. Clara A. Vyn, Mar. 31, 1903; children—C. Janet (Mrs. Hazen J. Hatch), Dora Vyn (Mrs. George W. Perrett), Lawrence H. Prin. high sch., Grand Haven, 1898-1904, Owosso, Mich., 1904-07; supt. schs., Grand Haven, 1907-12; dir. training, State Normal Sch., Mount Pleasant, Mich., 1912-16; State Normal Sch., Oswego, N.Y., 1916-21; supt. schs., Grand Haven, 1921-23; prin. State Normal Sch., New Paltz, N.Y., since 1923. Mem. N.E.A., Normal Sch. Faculty Assn. (pres.). Republican. Mem. Ref. Dutch Ch. Mason. Club: University (Albany). Home: New Paltz, N.Y. Died Sep. 27, 1943.

VANDERBILT, Cornelius, III, capitalist; b. New York, 1873; s. Cornelius and Alice Claypoole (Gwynne) V.; A.B., Yale, 1895, Ph.B., 1898, M.E., 1899; m. Grace, d. Richard T. Wilson, 1896; children—Cornelius, Jr., Grace. I.C. R.R. Co. Commd. col. 102d U.S. Engrs., 1917; brig. gen. N.A., July 6, 1918; now brig. gen. O.R.C. Home: 640 5th Av. Office: 32 Nassau St., New York, N.Y. Died Mar. 2, 1942.

VANDERBILT, William Kissam; b. New York, N.Y., Oct. 26, 1878; s. William Kissam and Alvia Murray (Smith) V.; Harvard U., 1897-99; m. Virginia Fair, Apr. 4, 1899 (divorced 1927); m. 2d, Mrs. Rosamund Lancaster Warburton, 1927. Began with N.Y. Central Lines, 1903, became asst. to the pres., 1910, v.p., 1912, pres. 1918 (for 1 yr.); now dir. and mem. exec. com. N.Y. Central R.R. Co. and subsidiary lines; dir. Western Union Tel. Co. Served in U.S. Navy, 1917-18. Clubs: Union, Knickerbocker, The Links, The Brook, Harvard, Seawanhaka-Corinthian Yacht, N.Y. Yacht, Huntington Country, Deepdale National Golf. Home: "Eagles Nest," Huntington, L.I., N.Y. Office: 230 Park Av., New York, N.Y. Died Jan. 8, 1944.

VANDERPOOL, Frederick William, composer; b. New York, N.Y., May 8, 1877; s. Frederick Brown and Matilda (Neitzer) V.; studied organ with R. Huntington Woodman, of New York, and voice with Louis Koemmenich, Dr. Carl Dufft and Dr. Frank Dossert; m. Emily Evelyn Beglin, May 8, 1924. Traveled with various musical and theatrical cos.; published first song about 1900. Served as yeoman, U.S. Navy, Spanish-Am. War, 1898. Republican. Mason, Elk. Clubs: Musical Optimist, Writers'. Composer: (songs) If; Values; I Did Not Know; Songs of Dawn and Twilight; The Autumn Moon; Ma Little Sun Flower; Ye Moanin' Mountains; The Want of You; Come Love Me. Mem. Am. Soc. Composers, Authors and Publishers. Home: 47 South St., Newark, N.J. Died Feb. 13, 1947.

VANDERPOOL, Wynant Davis, banker, lawyer; b. Newark, N.J., Aug. 15, 1875; s. Wynant and Alice Wayland (Davis) V.; ed. Princeton, 1894-98, Harvard Law Sch., 1898-1901; m. Cornelia Willis, Oct. 17, 1905; children—Eugene, Mary Willis (Mrs. William W. Cochran), Wynant Davis. Admitted to N.J. bar, 1903; v.p. Howard Savings Instn., Newark, 1917, pres. since 1924; pres., mem. bd. mgrs. Howard Savings Instn. of Newark; dir. Nat. Newark & Essex Banking Co., Am. Ins. Co., Mutual Benefit Life Ins. Co., Bankers Indemnity Ins. Co. (all of Newark), Nat. Biscuit Co. of New York, Morristown (N.J.) Trust Co., United N.J. R.R. and Canal Co., Trenton, N.J. Capt. motor transport, U.S. Army, 1918. Trustee Morristown Memorial Hosp., Morristown Library, St. Barnabas Hosp. Mem. Am. and Essex County bar assns., Am. Inst. Banking, Harvard Law Sch. Assn., Holland Soc. of N.Y., N.J. Hist. Soc., The Pilgrims, Newcomen Soc. of England, Bond Club of N.J., Chamber of Commerce. Episcopalian. Home: 86 Miller Rd., Morristown, N.J. Address: P.O. Box 177, Newark, N.J. Died Aug. 19, 1944.

VANDEVENTER, Braden, lawyer; b. Loudoun County, Va., May 5, 1878; s. Charles O. and Virginia (Kilgour) V.; student Washington and Lee U., 1895-96; LL.B., Georgetown U. Law Sch., 1899; m. Phelan Ruffin, Oct. 7, 1920; children—Braden, Mary Dunn. Admitted to Va. bar, 1900; and in pvt. practice at Newport News to 1903, Norfolk, 1903-11; partner Hughes & Vandeventer, 1911-18, Hughes, Vandeventer & Eggleston, 1918-36, Vandeventer & Black, Norfolk, Va., since 1936; served as chmn. Norfolk Legal Advisory Bd. No. 2, 1917-18. Entrant, Officers Arty. Training, Camp Zachary Taylor, 1918. Occupied chair of admiralty law Georgetown Univ., 1923-25; spl. counsel for the State in fire insurance rates investigation, 1928-29; vice-chmn. Norfolk City Sch. Bd., 1930-33; chmn. admiralty com. Am. Bar Assn., 1932-33; pres. Norfolk-Portsmouth Bar Assn., 1936; vice-chmn. Va. Conservation Commn., 1931-38; chmn. bill of rights com. Va. State Bar Assn., 1939; vice-pres. Norfolk Community Concert, 1941; vice-chmn. Hampton Roads Sanitation Commn., 1941; co-chmn. Norfolk Chapter Am. Red Cross; mem. and dir. Norfolk Assn. Commerce; dir. Maritime Exchange, Norfolk, and other corps. Mem. Assn. Bar of the City of N.Y., Maritime Law Assn. of U.S.; mem. Phi Kappa Psi. Democrat. Episcopalian. Clubs: Virginia, Princess Anne Country. Contbr. newspaper articles on govtl. questions. Home: 1303 Hampton Blvd. Office: 819 Citizens Bank Bldg., Norfolk, Va. Died Sep. 28, 1943.

VAN de WATER, Virginia Terhune, author; b. Newark, N.J.; d. Rev. Edward Payson and Mary Virginia Terhune ("Marion Harland"); ed. by governesses and at private schs., America, and in Rome, Italy, and Geneva, Switzerland; m. Frederic Franklyn Van de Water, Mar. 5, 1889 (dec.); children—Frederic Franklyn, Edward Terhune, Sterling. Clubs: Barnard, National Woman's Republican. Collaborated with mother in Everyday Etiquette, 1905. Author: From Kitchen to Garret, 1910; Little Talks with Mothers of Little People, 1911; Why I Left My Husband, 1912; The Shears of Delilah, 1914; The Heart of a Child, 1927; also novels and many serials. Contbr. to Cosmopolitan, Good Housekeeping, Scribner's, American, Liberty, This Week. Editorial writer New York American; N.E.A. Service and other syndicates; writer of serial fiction for Internat. Feature Syndicate; mem. faculty Paramount Picture Sch. of Famous-Players Lasky Co., 1925-26. Mem. Authors' League America. Home: (summer) "Kanesata," Pompton Lakes, N.J.; (winter) 68 W. 58th St., New York, N.Y. Died Oct. 17, 1945.

VAN DOORN, William (vān-dōrn′), general mgr. Holland Am. Line; b. Amsterdam, Holland, Feb. 13, 1872; s. Gerard Dirk and Adriana ('t Hoen) V.; ed. pub. and private schs.; m. Henriette Van Breemen, Nov. 30, 1900; children—Henriette, William (officer U.S.N.R.). With Holland Am. Line since 1892; mgr. Amsterdam office, 1904-06; asst. gen. mgr. New York office, 1906-12, becoming gen. mgr., 1912; now retired. Pres. the Queen Wilhelmina Fund, Inc., since 1940. Knight Comdr., Order of Orange Nassau, Netherlands, 1923. Clubs: Netherlands; Tiffin (New York). Home: 153 Park St., Montclair, N.J. Died June 27, 1944.

VAN LAHR, Leo J. (vān-lär′), banker; b. Cincinnati, O., s. John H. and Caroline (Beitmann) Van L.; grad. St. Xavier Coll., Cincinnati; m. Clara Herschede. Began in banking business, 1890; organizer Columbia Bank & Savings Co.; later v.p. Provident Savings Bank & Trust Co., now pres.; effected consolidation and merger with Provident Savings Bank & Trust Co. of Cincinnati (O.), East End Banking Co., Liberty Savings & Banking Co., Cincinnati Trust Co., Queen City Savings Bank & Trust Co., Madisonville Deposit Bank, Unity Savings Banking Co., Bank of Commerce & Trust Co. Trustee Fleischman Foundation. K.C., Elk. Clubs: Queen City, Cincinnati, Hyde Park Golf and Country. Home: 3793 Erie Av. Office: Provident Bank Bldg., Cincinnati, O.* Died Feb. 12 1946.

van LOON, Hendrik Willem (vān-lōn′), journalist; b. Rotterdam, Holland, Jan. 14, 1882; s. Hendrik Willem and Elisabeth Johanna (Hanken) van L.; A.B., Cornell U., 1905; studied, Harvard, 1903-04; Ph.D., U. of Munich, 1911; m. Eliza Bowditch, June 1906; m. 2d, Helen Criswell (Bryn Mawr 1904), Aug. 1920. Asso. Press corr. in Washington, and at Moscow, St. Petersburg, Warsaw, during revolution in Russia, 1906; lecturer on history and history of art at various univs. in U.S., 1911-14; Associated Press corr. in Belgium at outbreak of European War, 1914; corr. in Eng., France, Italy, Switzerland, Holland, Norway, Sweden and Denmark, May 1915-Feb. 1918. Lecturer modern European history, Cornell, 1915-16. Prof. of history, Antioch Coll., Ohio, 1922-23; asso. editor Baltimore Sun, 1923-24. Lectured in New Zealand, Australia, S. Africa, S. America, 1934. Member National Institute of Arts and Letters. Clubs: Cosmos (Washington); Harvard, Players (New York). Author: The Fall of the Dutch Republic, 1913; The Rise of the Dutch Kingdom, 1915; The Golden Book of the Dutch Navigators, 1916; A Short History of Discovery, 1918; Ancient Man, 1920; The Story of Mankind, 1921; The Story of the Bible, 1923; The Story of Wilbur the Hat, 1925; Tolerance, 1925; America, 1927; Life of Peter Stuyvesant, 1928; Man, the Miracle Maker, 1928; R.v.R., Life and Times of Rembrandt van Rijn, 1931; Van Loon's Geography, 1932; An Indiscreet Itinerary, 1933; An Elephant up a Tree, 1933; Ships, 1935; Around the World with the Alphabet, 1935; Air-Storming, 1935; The Songs We Sing, 1936; The Arts, 1937; Christmas Carols, 1937; Folk Songs of Many Lands, 1938; Our Battle, 1939; Life and Music of Carl Michael Bellman, 1939; The Pacific Ocean, 1939; Songs of America, 1939; Invasion, 1940; Life & Times of Johann Sebastian Bach, 1940; Van Loon's Lives, 1942; Thomas Jefferson, 1943; Simón Bolivar, 1943. Contbr. article on history to American Civilization, 1921. Awarded John Newbery medal for 1923; Officer of the Order of Orange Nassau, 1937; Order of Lion of Netherlands, 1942. Address: Old Greenwich, Conn. Died Mar. 11, 1944.

VAN MAANEN, Adriaan (vān-mä′nĕn), astronomer; b. Sneek, Holland, Mar. 31, 1884; s. Johan Willem Gerbrand and Catharina Adriana (Visser) Van M.; B.A., U. of Utrecht, 1906, M.A., 1909, Sc.D., 1911; U. of Groningen, 1909-10; came to U.S., 1911; unmarried. Volunteer asst., Yerkes Obs., Williams Bay, Wis., 1911-12; astronomer, Mt. Wilson Obs., since 1912. Has specialized in study of parallaxes and proper motions of stars and nebulæ; gen. magnetic field of the sun. Mem. Astron. Soc. America, Astron. Soc. Pacific, Internat. Astron. Union, Soc. Astron. de France, Astr. Gesellschaft, Royal Astr. Soc., Amsterdam Acad., Utrecht Soc., Sigma Xi, etc. Clubs: Valley Hunt (Pasadena, Calif.); Student Fund of Pasadena. Home: Terrace Villa No. 4, Pasadena 2, Calif. Died Jan. 26, 1946.

VANN, Richard Tilman, educator; b. Hertford County, N.C., Nov. 24, 1851; s. Albert G. and Harriet L. (Gatling) V.; A.B., head of class, Wake Forest Coll., N.C., 1873; Southern Bapt. Theol. Sem., Ky., 1873-74, 1875-76; m. Ella Rogers McVeigh, Oct. 21, 1885. At 12 yrs. of age lost both hands in cane mill; teacher Academy for Girls, Scotland Neck, N.C., 1877-79, Chowan Bapt. Female Institute (now Chowan Coll.), 1881-83; ordained Bapt. ministry, 1874; missionary pastor in N.C., 1879-81; pastor Murfreesboro, 1881-83, Wake Forest, 1883-89, Edenton, 1889-91, Scotland Neck, 1892-1900; pres. Bapt. Univ. for Women (now Meredith Coll.), Raleigh, N.C., 1900-15; corr. sec. Bd. Edn. of Bapt. State Conv., 1915-24, asso. sec. of edn., 1924-26, sec. of Benevolence, 1926-40. Trustee Wake Forest Coll. Democrat. Home: Raleigh, N.C.* Deceased.

VANNAH, Kate, verse writer, composer of music; b. Gardiner, Me., Oct. 27, 1855; d. Isaac G. and Eliza C. Vannah; ed. in grammar and high schools; St. Joseph's Acad., Emmitsburg, Md. Journalist and miscellaneous writer, now best known as writer of songs, notably "Good-bye, Sweet Day." Author: Verses, 1883; From Heart to Heart (poems), 1893. Address: Gardiner, Me. Died Oct. 11, 1943.

VAN NAMEE, George Rivet (vān-nā′mē), lawyer, b. Watertown, N.Y., Dec. 23, 1877; s. Eugene Clarence and Adele (Rivet) Van N.; LL.B., Cornell U., 1902; m. Rose Fallon, Feb. 26, 1927. Admitted to N.Y. bar, 1902, and began practice at Watertown. Clerk of N.Y. Assembly, 1911, 13; com. Legislative Bill Drafting Commn., N.Y., 1913-19; sec. to Gov. Alfred E. Smith, 1919-20, 1922-23; mem. Pub. Service Commn., N.Y., 1920-21 and 1924-43. Sec. Dem. State Com., N.Y., 1912-19; mgr. pre-conv. presidential campaign for Alfred E. Smith, 1928; mgr. campaign of Franklin D. Roosevelt for gov. of N.Y., 1928; mgr. campaign of Robert Wagner, 1932 and 1938. Mem. Psi Upsilon. Democrat. Catholic. Clubs: Manhattan, Cornell. Home: 4 W. 56th St. Office: 15 Broad St., New York 5. Died Dec. 6, 1949.

VAN NESS, Isaac J., clergyman; b. East Orange, N.J., July 15, 1860; s. Austin and Caroline R. (Jacobus) Van N.; grad. Southern Bapt. Theol. Sem., Louisville, Ky., 1890; D.D., Mercer U., Ga., 1897; LL.D., Baylor, 1920; m. Frances V. Tabb, June 24, 1891; children—Stephen Austen (dec.), Allan Edward, Noble, Lucy Tabb (Mrs. Julian L. Hagan),

Edwin Bell. Ordained Bapt. ministry, 1890; pastor Nashville, Tenn., 1890-96; editor Christian Index, Atlanta, Ga., 1896-1900; editorial secretary, 1900-17, and exec. sec. and treas., 1917-35, S.S. Board of Southern Bapt. Conv.; dir. Fourth First Bank & Trust Co. (Nashville), John Milton Foundation (New York). Pres. S.S. Editors' Assn. of U.S. and Can., 1906-07; chmn. editorial section, 1912-14, pres., 1916-17, S.S. Council of Evangelical Denominations; mem. Internat. S.S. Lesson Com. since 1915 (chmn. 1925-26), World's S.S. Exec. Com., 1916-18. Mem. bd. dirs. Southern Bapt. Theol. Sem. (Louisville), Bapt. Bible Inst. (New Orleans). Author: Training in Church Membership; Training in the Baptist Spirit. Home: 31st Av. N. (West End Park). Address: 3101 West End Circle, Nashville, Tenn. Died Feb. 13, 1947.

VANNEST, Charles Garrett, writer, educator; born at Clinton, Indiana, June 7, 1880; son of Taylor and Catherine (Henry) V.; Ph.B., University of Chicago, 1919; A.M., Indiana University, 1921; Ph.D., St. Louis University, 1928; married Maud Estelle Carmichael, May 13, 1903. Editor newspapers, Clinton, 1902-06; prin. sch., Spencer, Okla., 1907-09, Morrison, 1909-10; county supt. schs., Noble County, Okla., 1910-15; city supt. schs., Medford, Okla., 1915-17; inst. instr. and conductor; instr. history, Ind. U., 1919-21; prof. history, Evansville (Ind.) Coll., 1922-25; prof. history, Harris Teachers Coll., St. Louis, 1925-33, prin., 1933-40; ednl. lecturer and counselor since 1940; visiting prof. history, summers, Indiana University, Harris Teachers College, George Peabody Coll., U. of Chicago, U. of Oregon. Mem. Phi Beta Kappa, Phi Delta Kappa. Republican. Methodist. Mason, Odd Fellow. Co-author; Socialized History of the U.S., 1931; Missouri Anthology, 1932; Social Studies for Minnesota Schools, 1933. Author: Lincoln the Hoosier, 1928; United States History Workbook, 1930; Social Studies for the Lower Grades, 1930; Community Civics Workbook, 1931; Key to Correct Responses in Workbook in American History, 1931; Socialized History Workbook, 1932; Key to Workbook in United States History, 1934; (with J. T. Adams) The Record of America, 1935; Workbook for the Record of America, 1936; Guide and Answer Book to the Workbook for the Record of America, 1936. Contbr. hist. and ednl. articles to jours. Home: 546 Blackman St., Clinton, Ind. Died May 23, 1947.

VAN NUYS, Ezra Allen (vān-nēs'), clergyman; b. Franklin, Ind., July 21, 1877; s. Garrett List and Mary Alma (McCaslin) Van N.; B.A., Franklin (Ind.) Coll., 1900; M.A., Princeton, 1902; grad. Princeton Sem., 1903; D.D., Wabash College 1919; L.H.D., Franklin (Indiana) College, 1945; married Gladys Donnell Miller, Sept. 5, 1905; children—Hervey Alan, Mary Rebekah, Margaret Donnell, John Richard. Ordained Presbyn. ministry, 1903; pastor Goshen, Ind., 1903-19; asso. sec. men's work, Presbyn. Churches in U.S.A., 1919-21; asso. pastor Fourth Ch., Chicago, 1921-22; pastor Calvary Ch., San Francisco, since 1922. Pres. bd. trustees San Francisco Theol. Sem.; moderator of the Synod of Indiana, 1917, Synod of Calif., 1933. Mem. Sigma Alpha Epsilon. Republican. Rotarian. Home: 1 6th Av., San Francisco, Calif. Died Dec. 1, 1947.

VAN NUYS, Frederick (vān-nēs'), senator; b. Falmouth, Ind., Apr. 16, 1874; s. David H. and Katharine (Custer) Van N.; Ph.B., Earlham Coll., Indiana, 1898, LL.D., 1938; LL.B., Ind. Law Sch., 1900; m. Marie Krug, May 5, 1924; 1 son, William. Began practice at Shelbyville, Ind., 1900; pros. atty. Madison County, 1906-10; mem. Ind. Senate, 1913-16; chmn. Dem. State Com., 1917-18; U.S. atty., Dist. of Ind., 1920-22; mem. U.S. Senate since 1933; chmn. senate com. in the judiciary. Mem. Am., Ind., and Indianapolis bar assns., Am. Acad. Polit. and Social Science. Home: Indianapolis, Ind. Office: Senate Office Bldg., Washington, D.C. Died Jan. 25, 1944.

VAN ORNUM, John Lane (vān-ôr'nŭm), civil engineer; b. Hartford, Vt., May 14, 1864; s. Adoniram Judson and Sarah Josephine (Lane) Van O.; B.S. in C.E., U. of Wis., 1888, C.E., 1891; m. Carrie Beattie Scott, July 25, 1894; children—Thurwood, Judson (dec.). Municipal engring. work, Milwaukee, Wis., July-Nov. 1888; surveyor and inspector U.S. harbor works, Ga. and Fla. coasts, 1888-90; asst. engr. Milwaukee, Lake Shore & Western R.R., in Mich. and Wis., May-Oct. 1890; U.S. asst. engr. on river surveys, etc., in Ga. and Tenn., 1890-91; chief topographer Mexican Boundary Survey, 1891-94; instr. civ. engring., Washington U., 1894-97; traveled in Europe, 1897-98; capt. and maj. 3d U.S. Vol. Engrs., Spanish-Am. War, 1898-99, assisting in elimination of yellow fever at Cienfuegos, Cuba, etc.; prof. civ. engring., Washington U., 1899-1934, emeritus prof. since 1934. Fellow A.A.A.S.; mem. Am. Soc. Civil Engrs., Am. Soc. Testing Materials, Internat. Assn. Navigation Congresses (life mem.), Soc. for Promotion Engring. Edn., Engineers Club St. Louis (past pres.), Mil. Order Foreign Wars, Sigma Xi, Tau Beta Pi (hon. mem.), Beta Theta Pi, etc. Presbyterian. Author: The Regulation of Rivers, 1914; also many articles in tech. mags. as result of original research, etc. Home: 126 Linden Av., Clayton, Mo. Died Nov. 6, 1943.

VAN PRAAG, Henry L.; chmn. Julius Kayser & Co. Office: 500 Fifth Av., New York, N.Y. Died Oct. 11, 1946.

VAN VALKENBURGH, Arba Seymour, judge; b. Syracuse, N.Y., Aug. 22, 1862; s. Lawrence and Sarah A. (Seymour) Van V.; A.B., U. of Mich., 1884; LL.D., U. of Mo., 1935; U. of Mich., 1938; m. Grace Elizabeth Ingold, Sept. 25, 1889 (died Apr. 21, 1933). Admitted to Mo. bar, 1888; gen. practice in firm of Haff & Van Valkenburgh, Kansas City, until Oct. 1897; asst. U.S. atty. Western Dist. of Mo., 1898-1905; U.S. atty. same, 1905-10; U.S. dist. judge, Western Dist. Mo., June 26, 1910-Mar. 22, 1925; U.S. circuit judge since Mar. 23, 1925. Republican. Mem. Phi Beta Kappa. Club: University. Home: Woodlea Hotel. Address: U.S. Courts Bldg., Kansas City, Mo. Died Nov. 4, 1944.

VAN VALZAH, Robert (văn-văl'zä), prof. medicine; b. Spring Mills, Pa., Nov. 1, 1882; s. Frank H. and Jane R. Van V.; A.B., Princeton, 1904; M.D., U. of Pa., 1908; m. Aglae Keen, Aug. 24, 1912; children—Robert, Aglae Louise. Chief resident physician University Hosp., Phila., 1909; instr. clin. medicine, University of Wisconsin, 1910, asst. prof., 1911, asso. prof., 1913, prof. since 1918. Chmn. Med. Advisory Bd. No. 13, Selective Service, U.S. Army, 1917. Fellow Am. Coll. of Physicians; mem. A.M.A., Phi Alpha Sigma, Alpha Omega Alpha. Home: Goby, Va. Address: 1300 University Av., Madison, Wis. Died Nov. 23, 1946.

VAN VLECK, Edward Burr (văn-vlĕk'), mathematician; b. Middletown, Conn., June 7, 1863; s. John Monroe and Ellen Maria (Burr) Van V.; A.B., Wesleyan U., Conn., 1884, A.M., 1887; grad. student mathematics and physics, 1885-87, fellow, 1886-87, Johns Hopkins; student mathematics, U. of Göttingen, 1890-93, Ph.D., 1893; LL.D., Clark U., 1909, Wesleyan U., 1925; Dr. of Mathematics and Physics, U. of Groningen, 300th Anniversary, 1914; Sc.D., U. of Chicago, 1916; m. Hester Laurence Raymond, July 3, 1893; 1 son, John Hasbrouck. Instr. mathematics, Wesleyan U., 1887-90; instr. mathematics, U. of Wis., 1893-95; asso. prof. mathematics, Wesleyan U., 1895-98, prof., 1898-1906; prof. mathematics, U. of Wis., 1906-29, prof. emeritus since 1929. Mem. Nat. Research Council, 1921-24. Mem. Nat. Acad. Sciences, Am. Math. Soc. (v.p., 1909, pres., 1913-15), Deutsche Mathematiker-Vereinigung, Société Mathématique de France, Circolo Matematico di Palermo; fellow A.A.A.S. (v.p. Sect. A, 1912); mem. Phi Beta Kappa, Nat. Arts Club (New York). Asso. editor, 1902-05, editor 1905-10, Trans. Am. Math. Soc., and del. of soc. to Abel Centenary, Christiania, Norway, 1902. Sec. Local Draft Bd., Madison, Wis., 1917-18. Officier de l'Instruction Publique (France). Author: Theory of Divergent Series and Algebraic Continued Fractions, 1903; also monographs in math. jours. Home: 519 N. Pinckney St., Madison, Wis. Died June 2, 1943.

VAN WINKLE, Isaac Homer, lawyer; b. Halsey, Linn County, Ore., Dec. 3, 1870; s. Isaac Newton and Elizabeth Ann (Pearl) Van W.; B.A., Willamette U., Salem, Ore., 1898, LL.B., 1901; m. Lella V. Parrish, Sept. 3, 1902 (died 1918); 1 dau., Mrs. Rosalind Ann Melton. Admitted to Oregon bar, 1901, and began practice at Salem; admitted to U.S. Supreme Court bar, 1928; 1st asst. atty. gen. of Ore., 1904-20, except from 1913-15; apptd. atty. gen. of Ore., 1920, and elected to same office for term, 1921-24 inclusive, and reëlected for 5 terms, 1925-45. Instructor College of Law, Willamette Univ., 1905-13, dean, 1913-27, dean emeritus since 1927. Trustee Willamette U. Republican. Methodist. Woodman, Artisan, Kiwanian. Home: 145 N. 17th St. Address: Supreme Court Bldg., Salem, Ore. Died Dec. 14, 1943.

VAN WYK, William P. (văn-wik'), clergyman; b. Haarlemmermeer, The Netherlands, Dec. 3, 1874; s. Cornelius and Maria (Van Andel) Van W.; came to U.S., 1893; ed. prep. sch. of Calvin Coll. and Seminary, Grand Rapids, Mich., 1895-99; grad. Calvin Seminary, 1902; m. Jennie Heeringa, 1902; children—Maria (wife of E. Vander Berg, M.D.), Ida (wife of Rev. Ralph Heynen), Cornelia, (wife of Gelmer Van Noord, M.D.), Gerald Jacob. Became naturalized citizen of U.S., 1900; ordained to the ministry of Christian Ref. Ch., 1902; pastor successively New Holland, S.Dak., Sioux Center, Ia., Oakdale Park Ch., Grand Rapids, Orange City, Ia., and since 1925, Eastern Av. Ch., Grand Rapids. Trustee Calvin Coll. and Sem. since 1914 (now pres. bd.); pres. Christian Ref. Synod 4 terms to 1934; now retired. Author: (brochures) Manual for the Study of the Compendium of the Christian Religion (with Rev. W. Stuart), 1912; De Poortan Van Sion, 1913; Over the Top With God, 1918; also editor or joint editor other publs. Contbr. to Dutch Weekly and writer of outline on Confessions in "Federation Messenger." Home: 89 W. 32d St., Holland, Mich. Died June 29, 1943.

VARNEY, William Wesley, engr., lawyer; b. Boston, Mass., Sept. 17, 1864; s. William Henry (capt. U.S. Navy) and Mary E. (Hoffman) V.; mech. engring. course, Mass. Inst. Tech., 1883-86; LL.B., U. of Md., 1893; m. Edith McDonnal, Sept. 6, 1899; children—William Henry, John Hoffman. Draftsman, superintending constructor's office, U.S. Navy, Cramp's Shipyard, Phila., 1886-89; draftsman in charge superintending constructor's office, U.S. Navy, Baltimore, 1889-92; admitted to bar, federal and state, 1893; cons. engineer, Baltimore, 1893-99; city commissioner, Baltimore, 1899-1900; also city engr., pres. Bd. Pub. Works and mem. Water Bd.; cons. engr., Baltimore City, 1903-17, harbor engr., 1917-18; also in practice as patent lawyer since 1895. Mem. Am. Soc. M.E. (Am. Engring. Council 1925-27), Am. Soc. C.E., Soc. Naval Architects and Marine Engrs. Mem. Christian (Disciples) Ch. Odd Fellow; Grand Master I.O.O.F. of Md., 1910. Club: Maryland Yacht. Pioneer in television; filed application for 2 patents, Jan. 1892, on method of elec. transmission of optical impressions, and transmission of moving pictures in natural colors from life as well as from films. Home: 6017 Bellona Av., Baltimore, Md. Died July 30, 1943.

VARNUM, William Harrison, artist, educator; b. Cambridge, Mass., Jan. 27, 1878; s. William Harrison and Sarah Frances (Tibbetts) V.; grad. Rindge Tech. Sch., Cambridge, Mass., 1894; Julien Académie, Paris, France, 1901; Mass. State Normal Art Sch., 1903; pupil of Woodbury, DeCamp, etc.; married; 1 son, William H. Instr. in art, pub. schs. of Boston and Cambridge, 1898-1903; prof. fine and applied arts, James Millikin U., Decatur, Ill., 1903-12; asst. prof. drawing and design, U. of Wis., 1912-17, asso. prof., 1918-30, prof. art education and chmn. dept. since 1930. Exhibited paintings at Milwaukee and Madison, Wis., Boston, Mass., etc. Mem. College Art Assn., Western Arts Assn. (v.p. 1938), Midwestern Arts Conference (pres. 1941), Am. Vocational Association, N.E.A., Delta Phi Delta. Republican. Member State Council of Defense, 1942. Unitarian. Clubs: University, Wisconsin Painters and Sculptors. Author: Industrial Arts Design, 1916; Teaching of Manual Arts, 1917; Pewter Design and Construction, 1925. Creative Design in Furniture, 1937; Art Aptitude Tests, 1938; Validation, Reliability and Rating Mnaual, 1939; Scoring and Interpretation Manual, 1939, second printing, 1944. Editor International Text Book Co., 1941. Address: 207 Forest St., Madison, Wis. Died July 4, 1946.

VAUGHAN, Arthur Winn (vawn), coll. prof.; b. Colorado Springs, Colo., June 30, 1882; s. James Russell Adams and Martha (Winn) V.; student Westminster Coll., 1898-99, Vanderbilt U., 1900-01; B.S., Central Coll., 1902; A.M., Harvard, 1912; Ph.D., George Peabody Coll., 1928; m. Harriett Shores, June 8, 1910; children—Lenice Evelyn (Mrs. Leon LeMar Stephan), Gordon Roberts (dec.), Donald Shores. Teacher Marvin Jr. Coll., Fredericktown, Mo., 1902-03, Central Coll., Acad., 1903-05; ednl. dir. St. Louis Y.M.C.A., 1905-08; teacher in English and speech, Southeast Mo. State Teachers Coll., 1908-28; head dept. of English and chmn. div. of lang. and lit., Ala. Coll., since 1928. Chairman Dancy Foundation for Study of Lang. and Lit. in Southern States. Austin scholar in English, Harvard, 1911-12. Mem. Nat. Council Teachers of English, Modern Lang. Assn., Ala. Edn. Assn., N.E.A., Kappa Sigma, Kappa Delta Pi, Phi Delta Kappa. Democrat. Methodist. Author: Curricula for Teachers of English, 1928. Advisory editor of College English. Home: College View Apts., Montevallo, Ala. Died Sept. 26, 1948.

VAUGHAN, George, lawyer, tax consultant; born Fayetteville, Arkansas, May 20, 1873; son of George Allen and Frances Elizabeth (Williamson) Vaughan; A.B., University of Arkansas, 1896, LL.B., 1898, LL.D., 1926; married Frances Emily Edwards, April 17, 1901; children—Burton Edwards, Frances (wife of W. H. Groves, M.D.), George Allen, Virginia Eleanore, Paul (dec.). Admitted to Ark. bar, 1897, and began practice at Little Rock; moved to Fayetteville, Ark., 1929; prof. law, U. of Ark., 1929-40. Member Ark. State Senate, 1919-21; mem. com. on state and local taxation and expenditures, U.S. Chamber Commerce, 1927-29; mem. State Highway Audit Commn., 1931-32. Mem. American, Ark. State and Washington County bar assns., Southwestern Polit. and Social Science Assn. (ex-pres.), Am. Assn. Title Men (ex-pres.), Nat. Tax Assn. (ex-pres.), Kappa Sigma (editor 1897 catalogue), Phi Beta Kappa. Democrat. Methodist. Kiwanian (life). Author: Road Improvement in Arkansas, 1920; Report of Ark. Commn. on Business Laws and Taxation, 1929; Bench and Bar of Arkansas, 1930; The Arkansas Revenue System, 1932; Cases on Land Titles, 1938; Temples and Towers—A Survey of the World's Moral Outlook, 1941. Contbr. to Bulletin of Nat. Tax Assn., Cornell Law Quarterly and other periodicals. Address: Pyramid Bldg., Little Rock, Ark. Died Apr. 18, 1945.

VAUGHAN, George Tully, surgeon, soldier, teacher; b. Arrington, Va., June 27, 1859; s. Dr. James Walter Washington Lafayette and Frances Ellen (Shields) V.; M.D., U. of Va., 1879; M.D., Bellevue Hosp. Med. Coll. (N.Y.U.), 1880; post-grad. courses in N.Y. Polyclinic, Univ. of Berlin, and Jefferson Med. Coll., Phila.; LL.D., Georgetown U., 1919; m. May Townsend Venable, June 27, 1883; children—Vera V., William W. Asst. surgeon, Jan. 25, 1888, passed asst. surgeon, 1892, surgeon, 1900, asst. surgeon-gen., 1902-06, U.S. Pub. Health and Marine Hosp. Service; maj. and brigade surgeon, 7th Army Corps, during war with Spain; became prof. surgery, Georgetown U. Med. Sch., 1897; now emeritus professor of surgery; chief surgeon Georgetown University Hospital; surgeon Tuberculosis Hospital and consulting surgeon St. Elizabeth Hosp. and Washington Asylum Hosp., U.S. Vets. Bureau; was operating surgeon in the navy in Mexican imbroglio at Vera Cruz, 1914, and surgeon U.S.S. Leviathan in the World War, 1917-19; comdr. Med. Reserve Corps, U.S. Navy. Pres. Assn. Mil. Surgeons, 1907-08; fellow Internat. Surg. Assn.; mem. A.M.A., Am. Surg. Assn., Am. Coll. of Surgeons (a founder), Washington Acad. Sciences, Washington Surg. Soc. (pres.), Soc. Colonial Wars, Soc. of the Cincinnati, Order of Washington (comdr. gen.), Southern Surg. Assn., S.A.R., Naval and Mil. Order Spanish-Am. War, Mil. Order World War, Am. Legion, Pi Gamma Mu, Kappa Sigma, Phi Chi, Alpha Omega Alpha and Phi Beta Kappa. Clubs: Cosmos, Army and Navy (Washington). Author: Principles and Practice of Surgery, 1903; Papers on Surgery and Other Subjects, 1932. Frequent contbr. on med. and surg. subjects to tech. jours. Address: 1718 I St., Washington, D.C. Died April 26, 1948.

VAUGHAN, Herbert Hunter, educator, lecturer; b. Ann Arbor, Mich., Apr. 2, 1884; s. Victor and Dora (Taylor) V.; A.B., U. of Mich., 1903; Ph.D., Harvard, 1906; unmarried. Began instr. Romanic langs., U. of Kan., 1905; teacher, U. of Mich., Dartmouth, U. of Pa., 1912-19; 1st lt. Mil. Intelligence Div., Gen. Staff, U.S. Army, 1918-19; prof. modern langs., U. of Neb., 1919-22; asst. prof. Italian, Yale, 1922-23; prof. Italian, U. of Calif., since 1923. Mem. Modern Lang. Assn. America, Am. Legion, Am. Assn. Teachers of Italian (pres. 1936), Am. Assn. Univ. Profs. Writer of modern lang. textbooks, and studies on Italian dialects. Address: Wheeler Hall, Univ. of California, Berkeley, Calif. Died Jan. 4, 1948; buried Buchanan, Mich.

VAUGHAN, John George, physician; b. Titusville, Pa., May 31, 1878; s. John and Margaret Ann (Potts) V.; B.S., Northwestern U., 1903, M.D., 1907; house physician, Wesley Hosp., Chicago, 1907-09; student London School of Tropical Medicine, May-Aug. 1909; m. Daisy Mathis, Apr. 9, 1909 (died Feb. 20, 1917); children—John George, Marcelia Helen, Daisy Mathis; m. 2d, Golda Faye Sherwood, Sept. 17, 1921; 1 son, David Sherwood. Conducted med. work of Bd. of Fgn. Missions M.E. Church, at Nanchang, China, 1909-16, also med. adviser to City of Nanchang and Provincial Court of Kiangsi; on staff of chief surgeon C.,R.I.&P. Ry., 1917-18; asso. sec. for med. work, Bd. of Fgn. Missions M.E. Ch., 1919-24; med. adviser Internat. Com. of Y.M.C.A., Bd. of Missions and Ch. Extension, Meth. Ch. since 1924; Dept. of Missions of P.E. Church; Christian and Missionary Alliance; lecturer Drew Theological Sem., 1924-29; acting supt. Wuhu (China) Gen. Hosp., 1929-30; asst. physician New York Hosp., N.Y. City, 1933-39; dir. Am. Mission to Lepers since 1923. Trustee Internat. Med. Missionary Soc. since 1922; dir. Christian Council for Overseas Med. Work since 1938; Save the Children Federation since 1930; dir. Asso. Mission Med. Office since 1933. Mem. Am. Soc. Tropical Medicine, N.Y. Soc. Tropical Medicine, A.M.A., N.Y. State and Westchester County med. socs., China Med. Assn. Home: 8 Lee Av., White Plains, N.Y. Office: 150 5th Av., New York 11, N.Y. Died May 17, 1948.

VAUGHAN, J(ohn) Walter, surgeon; born Mt. Airy, Mo., Aug. 6, 1880; s. Victor and Dora (Taylor) V.; B.S., U. of Mich., 1902, M.D., 1904; m. Gertrude Leffingwell, Dec. 12, 1906. Practiced at Detroit, since 1905; prof. surgery, Detroit Coll. of Medicine and Surgery, 1907-17; attending surgeon Harper Hosp.; mem. Detroit Bd. of Health, 1914-17. Served in Med. Corps, U.S. Army, in France, Aug. 1917-Feb. 1919; with the French at Soissons, with the British at Cambrai, with Americans at Château Thierry, Juvigny and Verdun; hon. discharged as lt. col. Cited by Gen. Pershing "for exceptionally meritorious and conspicuous services" as cons. surgeon 32d Div. Fellow Am. Coll. Surgeons; mem. A.M.A., Mich. State Med. Soc., Detroit Surg. Soc., Detroit Acad. Medicine, Am. Surg. Assn. Episcopalian. Clubs: University, Detroit Athletic, Detroit Boat, Lochmoor Golf. Author: (with V. C. Vaughan and V. C. Vaughan, Jr.) Protein Split Products. Also several short articles upon professional topics. Address: Veterans Administration Hosp., Roanoke, Va. Died Jan. 21, 1949.

VAUGHAN, Warren Taylor, physician; b. Ann Arbor, Mich., Feb. 22, 1893; s. Victor Clarence and Dora Catherine (Taylor) V.; student Lancy, Switzerland, 1908-09; A.B., U. of Mich., 1913, M.D., 1916, hon. M.S., 1941; m. Emma Elizabeth Heath, June 21, 1917; children—Victor Clarence III, Warren Taylor, John Heath, David DuPuy. House officer, Peter Bent Brigham Hosp., Boston, Mass., 1916-17; asst. in preventive medicine and hygiene, Harvard Med. Sch., 1919-20; in practice internal medicine, specializing in allergy, Richmond, Va., since 1920; dir. Vaughan-Graham Clinic. Served as 1st lt., advancing through grades to lt. col. Med. Corps, U.S. Army, 1917-19; chief of med. service, Camp Hosp. 41, A.E.F. Mem. advisory com. to Committee on Costs of Medical Care; mem. com. on aerobiology and food habits of Natural Research Council; mem. Research Council on Problems of Alcohol (dir.); chmn. com. on medicaments and pharmaceuticals, American Academy of Allergy. Fellow A.A.A.S. (council since 1938); mem. Medical Society of Virginia (vice-pres. 1931-32), Southern Medical Assn., A.M.A., Am. Society Clin. Pathologists, Am. Assn. Study Allergy (sec.-treas. 1928-38, pres. 1939), Soc. for Study Asthma and Allied Conditions (pres. 1938-39), Am. Rheumatism Assn., Soc. of Investigative Dermatology, Internat. Soc. Gastroenterology, Inst. of Practice of Medicine, Barcelona, Spain (hon.), Soc. Study Allergy, Argentina (hon.), Va. Acad. Science (chmn. biol. sect., 1931), Huguenot Soc., Beta Theta Pi, Phi Rho Sigma, Sigma Xi, Alpha Omega Alpha. Formerly mem. Assn. Am. Phys., Am. Coll. Physicians. Episcopalian. Clubs: Commonwealth, Harvard Club of Va. (pres. 1940-41). Author: Influenza, An Epidemiologic Study, 1921; Allergy and Applied Immunology, 1931; Practice of Allergy, 1939; Primer of Allergy, 1939; Strange Malady, 1941. Editor in chief Journal Laboratory and Clinical Medicine; asso. editor Jour. of Allergy; mem. editorial bd. Am. Jour. Digestive Diseases, Am. Journal Clin. Pathology; formerly mem. editorial bd. Review of Gastro-enterology, Am. Jour. Syphilis and collaborating editor Folia Clinica Chimica et Microscopica (Bologna, Italy). Contributor of over 150 articles to current med. lit.; also contbr. to Ency. Americana and Oxford Medicine. Office: 201 W. Franklin St., Richmond, Va. Died Apr. 2, 1944.

VAN VLIET, Robert Campbell, army officer; b. in Kan., Aug. 22, 1857; grad. U.S. Mil. Acad., 1876. Commd. 2d lt. 10th Inf., Dec. 14, 1876; 1st lt., May 7, 1884; capt., Mar. 8, 1898; maj., Oct. 3, 1902; lt. col. 16th Inf., June 12, 1910; col. 25th Inf., Mar. 3, 1911; assigned to 4th Inf., Aug. 30, 1913; brig. gen. N.A., Aug. 5, 1917. Duty on Mexican border, 1916-17; apptd. comdr. 173 Inf. Brigade, Camp Pike, Little Rock, Ark., Sept. 1917. Address: War Dept., Washington. Died Oct. 27, 1943.

VAN VOORHIS, Henry Clay, ex-congressman; b. Licking Tp., Muskingum County, O., May 11, 1852; ed. Denison U.; m. Mary A. Brown, Dec. 15, 1875. Admitted to bar, 1874; practices at Zanesville, O. Del. Rep. Nat. Conv., Chicago, 1884, 1916; mem. 53d to 58th Congresses (1893-1905), 15th Ohio Dist. Republican. Pres. Old Citizens' Nat. Bank. Address: Zanesville, O. Died Dec. 12, 1927.

VEEDER, Curtis Hussey, inventor, mfr.; b. Allegheny, Pa., Jan. 31, 1862; s. Herman and Hannah (Adair) V.; grad. Lehigh Univ., 1886, M.E. and Dr. Engring., 1939; m. Louise G. Stutz, Sept. 19, 1908; children—Josephine Adair (Mrs. Donald H. Andrews), Dorothy Irwin (Mrs. Charles E. Tilton). Draftsman Pope Manufacturing Co., bicycle mfrs., July-Oct. 1886; chief draftsman, mech. dept., Calumet & Hecla Mining Co., Calumet, Mich., 1886-89; draftsman and engr., Thomson-Houston Elec. Co., Lynn, Mass., 1889-93; draftsman, Hartford Cycle Co., 1894-95; pres. Veeder Manufacturing Co., Hartford, Conn., 1895-1928; dir. Veeder-Root, Inc., Automatic Signal Corp. Prin. inventions and patents: bicycle saddles, 1880, 82; cyclometer for bicycles, 1894; automatic casting machine and spl. alloys, 1896, 98; liquid tachometer, 1901. Mem. Am. Soc. Mech. Engrs., A.A.A.S., Am. Geog. Soc., Army Ordnance Assn., Franklin Inst., Am. Astron. Soc., Am. Forestry Assn., Soc. Automotive Engrs., Holland Soc. New York, Sigma Xi. Republican. Clubs: University, Hartford, Appalachian Mountain, Auto (Hartford); University (New York); Laurentides Fish and Game (Quebec). Home: 1 Elizabeth St., Hartford, Conn. Died Dec. 27, 1943.

VEEDER, Henry, lawyer; b. Galva, Ill., May 13, 1867; s. Albert Henry and Helen L. (Duryee) V.; student prep. dept. U. of Chicago, 1880-86; B.A., Yale, 1890; LL.B., Northwestern U., 1892; m. Darlene Gibons, Dec. 29, 1892 (dec.); children—Albert Henry, Helen Frances (dec.). Admitted to Ill. bar, 1892, and began practice at Chicago; asso. in practice with Albert H. Veeder until his decease, 1914, since alone; gen. counsel Swift & Co., Libby, McNeill & Libby, St. Joseph (Mo.) Stock Yards Co.; dir. Drovers Nat. Bank, and Drovers Trust & Savings Bank (Chicago). Mem. Am., Ill. State and Chicago bar assns. Clubs: University, Chicago Athletic Assn., South Shore Country, Mid-Day. Home: 179 Lake Shore Drive. Office: 33 S. Clark St., Chicago, Ill. Died June 9, 1942.

VEEDER, Van Vechten, judge; b. Schenectady, N.Y., July 4, 1867; s. John Wynkoop and Margaret (Van Vechten) V.; ed. U. of Va. and Columbia U.; hon. M.A., Union Coll., 1904; m. Margaret Lounsbery DeWitt, June 30, 1909; children—John Van Vechten, Margaret DeWitt. Admitted to Ill. bar, 1890, N.Y. bar, 1900; judge U.S. Dist. Court, Eastern Dist. of N.Y., 1911-17; mem. Burlingham, Veeder, Masten & Fearey and Burlingham, Veeder, Clark & Hupper (counsel), N.Y. City, since 1918. Chmn. of Appeal Bd. of Motion Picture Arbitration Tribunals, constituted pursuant to consent decree of the U.S. Dist. Court for Southern Dist. of N.Y., Nov. 20, 1940. Mem. Harvard Research in Internat. Law, Internat. Maritime Com., Maritime Law Assn. of U.S. (pres. 1930-36), Am. Law Inst. (adviser on torts), Assn. of Bar City of New York, Am. Hist. Assn., N.Y. State Hist. Assn., Medieval Acad. America, St. Nicholas Soc., Holland Soc. Club: Century. Contbr. to law reviews. Home: 755 Park Av. Office: 27 William St., New York, N.Y. Died Dec. 4, 1942.

VEITCH, Fletcher Pearre (vēch), chemist; b. Baltimore, Md., May 22, 1868; s. Fletcher Roberts and Caroline Virginia (Pearre) V.; B.S., Md. Agrl. Coll., 1891, D.Sc., 1914; M.S., George Washington U., 1899; m. Laura T. Boyle, May 12, 1896. Asst., Md. Agrl. Expt. Sta., 1891-92; chemist with W. S. Powell & Co., Baltimore, 1892-93; asst. chemist, Md. Agrl. Coll., 1894-99; asst. soil physicist, Md. Agrl. Expt. Sta., 1899-1901; with Dept. Agr., Washington, since 1901; asst. chemist, Bur. of Soils, 1901-02; same, Bur. of Chemistry, 1902-04; chief of Leather and Paper Lab., 1904-14; chemist in charge same, 1914-27; chemist in charge division industrial farm products, Bureau Chemistry and Soils, 1927-35; chief naval stores division Food and Drug Adminstrn. and naval stores research division Bureau Chemistry and Soils, 1935-38. Fellow A.A.A.S.; mem. Am. Chem. Soc., Am. Leather Chemists' Assn. (ex-pres.), Society Leather Trades Chemists, Am. Soc. Testing Materials (chmn. naval stores com.), Assn. Agrl. Chemists (pres. 1922). Democrat. Author of 275 bulletins and articles on soils, fertilizers, tanning materials, leathers, turpentine, wood products, paper and paper making materials. Mem. com. on leather of Nat. Research Council, 1917-18, div. research extension, 1919-24; chmn. com. on paper specifications to joint com. on printing, 1913-36; mem. paper tech. com. Federal Specifications Bd., 1923-36; v. chmn. div. leather and gelatine, Am. Chem. Soc., 1923. Home: College Park, Md. Died Oct. 14, 1943.

VERITY, George Matthew, iron and steel mfr.; b. E. Liberty, O., Apr. 22, 1865; s. Jonathan and Mary Ann (Deaton) V.; grad. high sch. and commercial coll.; LL.D., Miami U., Oxford, O., 1925; hon. Dr. Engring., Stevens Inst. of Tech., 1938; m. Jennie M. Standish, Oct. 19, 1887. Manager W. C. Standish Wholesale Grocery Co., Cincinnati, 1886; made mgr. Sagendorf Iron Roofing & Corrugating Co., 1889, reorganized, 1891, as Am. Steel Roofing Co., of which was v.p. and mgr.; in 1899 worked out consolidation and reorganization, which resulted in founding of Am. Rolling Mill Co., of Middletown, O., of which was pres. until 1930, also mgr. 20 yrs., chmn. bd. since 1930; dir. Westinghouse Electric & Mfg. Co. (Pittsburgh). Councillor Nat. Industrial Conf. Bd., New York. Chmn. Minute Men of Middletown Chamber Commerce which handled all war fun campaigns, Red Cross drives, etc. Mem. Am. Iron and Steel Inst. (hon. v.p.), Ohio Soc. of New York. Republican. Mason. Clubs: Queen City (Cincinnati); City Midday (New York). Home: 230 S. Main St. Office: 703 Curtis St., Middletown, O. Died Nov. 6, 1941.

VERMEULE, Cornelius Clarkson, civil engr.; b. New Brunswick, N.J., Sept. 5, 1858; s. Adrian and Maria (Veghte) V.; B.Sc., Rutgers Coll., 1878, M.S., C.E., 1880; m. Carolyn Carpenter Reed, June 7, 1888; children—Cornelius Clarkson, Warren Carpenter. In charge topog. survey, State of N.J., 1878-88, and continued until 1918 as consulting engr. State Geol. Survey; in gen. practice at New York since 1888, as consulting or construction engr. for many cities and pvt. corps., in the United States and Cuba, also to Cuban government; organized York Cliffs (Me.) Improvement Co., 1892; obtained action by U.S. Govt., 1908, in rehabilitation of the sanitation of Cienfuegos, Cuba, at cost of $3,000,000, the work having been interrupted by political disturbances; engr. in charge of dismantling and reconstruction of Morris Canal for State of N.J. Mem. N.J. Hist. Society, N.J. Sanitary Assn., Am. Water Works Assn., Am. Soc. Civil Engrs., Holland Soc., New York Geneal. and Biographical Soc., New England Soc. of New York. Presbyterian. Has written various monographs upon topography, water supply, etc.; author of map of Manhattan Island as it existed in 1776, and of several hist. monographs. Home: E. Orange, N.J. Office: 38 Park Row, New York, N.Y. Died Feb. 1, 1950.

VERMILYE, William Moorhead (vĕr-mĭl'yē), banker; b. Orange, N.J., Apr. 6, 1880; s. Daniel Babbitt and Mary Cornelia (Holmes) V.; prep. edn. Staten Island (N.Y.) Acad.; student Mass. Inst. Tech., 1897-99; m. Ethel Howard Simpson, Oct. 11, 1905; children—Mary Nazro (Mrs. Phillip E. McKenney), William Howard, Ethel Cornelia (Mrs. William Russell Eaton), Ridgeley Clare (Mrs. William Allen Gilroy, Jr.). Treasurer Manhasset Manufacturing Co., Providence, R.I., 1921-22; exec. v.p. Nat. Aniline & Chem. Co., New York, 1923-30; v.p. Thomaston (Ga.) Cotton Mills, 1931-32; treas. Knox Hat Co. and chmn. bd. Hat Corp. of America, 1932-33; treas. Eitingon Schild Co., New York, 1933-35; pres. and chmn. Susquehanna Silk Mills, New York, 1936-37; v.p. Nat. City Bank of N.Y. since 1937; American Type Founders, Byrndun Corp., Virginia-Carolina Chem. Corporation. Endowed Vermilye medal (awarded biannually for contribution to industrial management by Franklin Inst.); mem. bd. of Mgrs. Franklin Inst. Mem. Newcomen Society of England (pres.), Holland Soc., St. Nicholas Soc., Huguenot Soc., Soc. Colonial Wars of N.J., Sons of the Revolution, Sons of the American Revolution, New Jersey Society of the Order of the Founders and Patriots of America, St. Andrews Society. Republican. Episcopalian. Clubs: Union League, Merchants, Recess (New York). Home: 930 Madison Av., Plainfield, N.J. Office: 55 Wall St., New York, N.Y. Died Aug. 30, 1944.

VERNIER, Chester Garfield (vĕr'nĭ-ĕr), prof. of law; b. Ansonia, Darke County, O., Jan. 19, 1881; s. Augustus Emanuel and Sarah Catherine (Black) V.; A.B., Butler Coll., Indianapolis, 1903; Ph.B., U. of Chicago, 1904; J.D., cum laude, U. of Chicago Law Sch., 1907; m. Lura Hazel Anderson, Aug. 17, 1909; children—Robert Louis, Helen May, Dorothy Jane. Instr. in law, Ind. U., 1907-08; prof. law, U. of Neb., 1908-09, Ind. U., 1909-11, U. of Ill., 1911-17, Stanford U. 1917-46; emeritus since 1946; now prof. law, Hastings Coll. Law, San Francisco. Mem. Am. Bar Assn., Am. Inst. Criminal Law and Criminology, Am. Polit. Science Assn., Order of the Coif, Phi Delta Phi. Independent Republican. Mem. Christian (Disciples) Ch. Author: Cases on Marriage and Divorce, 1913; American Family Laws, 6 vols., 1931-38. Asso. editor Journal of Criminal Law and Criminology, 1911-32. Contbr. to American Year Book and various law journals. Home: Stanford University, Calif. Died March 5, 1949. buried Alta Mesa, Palo Alto, Calif.

• **VERNON, Clarence Clark,** chemist, educator; b. Milo, Ia., Apr. 28, 1896; s. Marion T. and Martha Jane (Clark) V.; B.S., Ia. State at Ames, 1921, M.S., 1924, Ph.D., 1928; m. Anna Bernice Brooks, Sept. 20, 1922; 1 dau., Mary Bernice. Grad. asst., Ia. State Coll., 1921-22, instr., 1924-26, sr. instr., 1926-28; asst. prof. organic chemistry, Univ. of Louisville (Ky.), 1928-36, asso. prof. 1936-42, asso. prof. and acting head chemistry dept., 1942-46, prof. and head chemistry dept. since 1946. Served U.S. Navy, 1917-19; active duty U.S.S. Pa., 1918-19; civilian instr. in charge of chemistry, V-12 training program, U.S.N., Univ. of Louisville, 1942-45; served as regional mem. adv. com. Am. Chem. Soc., War Prodn. Bd., 1942-45. Mem. Am. Chem. Soc. (local chmn. 1936, mem. exec. com., etc.; asst. in compiling nat. organic chemistry exams. since 1940); Ky. Acad. Sci.

(chmn. chemistry sect., 1944-45), Phi Lambda Upsilon, Theta Chi Delta (grand regional vice pres.), Alpha Epsilon Delta (faculty adviser). Contbr. articles on organic chem. to nat. and fgn. chemistry jours. Home: 17 Avon Rd., Louisville, Ky. Died Sept. 20, 1948.

VESTLING, Axel Ebenezer, college prof.; b. Osage City, Kan., June 22, 1879; s. Rev. Claus Victor and Sofia Mathilda (Swensson) V.; B.A., Bethany Coll., Kan., 1900; B.A., Yale, 1903, M.A., 1905, Ph.D., 1907; studied univs. of Berlin and Marburg; m. Bertha Swensson, June 27, 1907; children—Bertha Louise and Carl Swensson (twins). Supt. schs., Marquette, Kan., 1900-02; instr. German, Dartmouth, 1903-04, Yale, 1904-12; prof. German, 1912-26, dean of men, 1921-25, dean, 1925-26, Carleton Coll., Northfield, Minn.; pres. Olivet (Mich.) College, 1926-30; again prof. German, Carleton College, since 1930. Ordained minister Congl. Ch., 1918; acting pastor First Congl. Ch., Northfield, 1919; lecturer in German, Yale, 1920-21. Mem. Phi Beta Kappa. Republican. Editor: Wildenbruch's Kindertränen, 1911. Home: Northfield, Minn. Died Apr. 29, 1944.

VEZIN, Charles (vē-zăn'), b. Phila., Apr. 9, 1858; s. Charles and Carolina (Kalisky) V.; ed. Dr. Faires' Sch., Phila.; Pa. Mil. Acad., Chester; schs. in Germany; m. Adah De Lamater, June 14, 1883; children—Louise (Mrs. Walter L. Niles), Charles, Cornelius De Lamater, Zillah (Mrs. Arthur B. Holmes). Mem. Hinchman, Vezin & Co., dry goods commn., 1895-1919, retired. Landscape painter and writer. Has exhibited Nat. Acad. Design, Soc. Am. Artists, Art Inst. Chicago, Carnegie Inst., Corcoran Gallery, Pa. Acad. Fine Arts, Worcester Mus., St. Louis Art Inst., Montclair Museum, High Museum, Atlanta, Museum of U. of Neb., etc. Hon. mention Soc. of Washington Artists, Conn. Acad. Fine Arts, Palm Beach Art Center, Allied Artists of America, Ogonquit Art Center. Awarded Vezin prize, Lyme Art Assn.; Josephine Hancock Logan special prize at Chicago, 1941. Pres. Art Students League, 1911-15; mem. Sch. Art League, Art Alliance, Am. Fine Arts Soc., Am. Fedn. of Arts, N.Y., New Haven Paint and Clay Club, Lyme Art Assn., New York Soc. Painters, Allied Artists America, Soc. for Sanity in Art. Unitarian. Clubs: Salmagundi (pres. 1914), National Arts, Century. Author of numerous brochures on art. Home: Lyme, Conn.; (winter) 1924 Ferdinand St., Coral Gables, Fla. Died Mar. 13, 1942.

VICHERT, John Frederick (vĭk'ĕrt), clergyman; b. Gobles, Ontario, Can., Aug. 10, 1874; s. Frederick William and Janet (Edmiston) V.; Woodstock Coll., Ont.; A.M., McMaster U., Toronto, 1898, B.D., 1904, D.D., 1919; fellow in ch. history, U. of Chicago, 1904, 05; D.D., Franklin Coll., Ind., 1912; m. Nettie Douglas Wallace, Sept. 20, 1899 (died Apr. 30, 1918); children—Frederick Wallace, Clarence Gordon; m. 2d, Margaret Wallace, Dec. 27, 1921. Ordained Bapt. ministry, 1899; pastor Calvary Ch., Victoria, B.C., 1899-1904, 1st Ch., Fort Wayne, Ind., 1906-12, 1st Ch., Providence, R.I., 1912-16; dean and prof. pastoral and systematic theology, Colgate Theol. Sem., 1915-23; prof. practical theology, Rochester Theol. Sem., 1923-28, Colgate-Rochester Div. Sch., 1928-40; now retired. Sec. Bapt. Edn. Soc., N.Y., 1915-23; pres. Bapt. Missionary Conv., N.Y., 1921-24. Republican. Mem. Lambda Chi Alpha. Home: 930 19th Av. N., St. Petersburg 6, Fla. Died Jan. 17, 1948.

VICKERY, Howard Leroy, naval officer, U.S. maritime commr.; b. Bellevue, O., Apr. 20, 1892; s. Willis and Ann (Schneider) V.; B.S., U.S. Naval Acad., 1915; M.S., Mass. Inst. Tech., 1921; grad. Army Indsl. Coll., 1934; m. Margurite Blanchard, Apr. 9, 1917; children—Hugh Blanchard, Barbara Willis. Commd. ensign, U.S.N., 1915; assigned to navy constrn. corps as lt., 1918; rear adm., Apr. 1942, vice admiral, Oct. 1944; assistant to supt. in charge submarine construction Bethlehem Shipbuilding Co., San Francisco, 1920; outside supt., new work supt. and docking supt., Boston Navy Yard, 1921-25; loaned to Govt. of Haiti as treaty engr. and dir. of shop, Supply and Transportation Div., 1925-28; head materials, equipment, and inspection div., Bur. of Construction and Repair, U.S. Navy, 1928-29; tech. adviser on shipping to gov.-gen. of P.I., 1929-33; head War Plan Sect., design branch, Bur. of Construction and Repair, 1934-37; asst. to chmn. of U.S. Maritime Commn., 1937-40; mem. since Sept. 1940; vice chmn., Feb. 1942-Dec. 1945; deputy administrator War Shipping Adminstrn. since June 1942; member production exec. committee War Production Board, and member War Manpower Commn.; chairman Postwar Planning Com., U.S. Maritime Commn. Awarded Morehead Medal, 1945. Decorated Victory medal (Cruiser); Lieut. of Grand Dragon of Anam (French Indo-China); Distinguished Service Certificate, Am. Legion; Distinguished Service Medal (United States Army). Member Council Society Naval Architects and Marine Engineers; member Naval Architecture and Classification Committee, Am. Bureau of Shipping. Chmn. bd. trustees Cleveland Law Sch. Republican. Conglist: Clubs: Chevy Chase Country, Army-Navy (Washington); Army-Navy Country (Arlington, Va.); Polo (Manila). Home: 4420 Dexter St. N.W. Office: U.S. Maritime Commission, Washington. Died Mar. 21, 1946; buried in Arlington National Cemetery.

VIESSELMAN, Percival William (vēs'ĕl-măn), prof. law; b. Fairmont, Minn., Dec. 28, 1890; s. William and Lottie (Diehl) V.; A.B., with distinction, U. of Minn., 1912, A.M., 1913, LL.B., 1915; m. Roxie B. Utley, Aug. 21, 1918; children—Joyce Jeanette (Mrs. John French McCarty), Mark Utley, Burt William, Roxie Claire (Mrs. Burton Cossey). Instr. polit. sci., Univ. of Minn., 1915-21; admitted to Minn. bar, 1915, N.D., 1929, Kan., 1936; practiced law in Minneapolis, 1917-28; prof. law, U. of N.D., 1928-33; atty. Northwestern Nat. Life Ins. Co., Minneapolis, 1933-35; prof. law, U. of Kan, since 1935, on sick leave since 1943. Mem. Am., Kan., State bar associations, Order of Coif, Phi Beta Kappa, Alpha Sigma Phi, Phi Alpha Delta. Republican. Presbyterian. Author: Dakota Practice, 1930; Kansas Annotations to A.L.I. Restatement of Agency, 1940; Cases and Materials on Trial Practice, 1940, Reviser: Phillips' Code Pleading (2d edit.), 1932; Abbott's Civil Jury Trials (5th edit.), 1935; Abbott on Facts (5th edit.), 1937; Abbott's Criminal Trial practice (4th edit.), 1939; Hughes Federal Practice, Pocket Parts, 1940, 1941, 1942, 1943; Pocket Supplement to Manual of Federal Procedure, 1943; Blashfield's Cyclopedia of Automobile Law and Practice, Pocket Parts, 1941; Winslow's Forms of Pleading and Practice, Pocket Parts, 1945; American Jurisprudence, Article on Venue; Revision of Keigwin's Cases on Code Pleading. Home: 1138 Mississippi St., Lawrence, Kan. Died Aug. 11, 1946; buried at Fairmont, Minn.

VILLENEUVE, J. M. Rodrigue (vēl'nûv), cardinal-archbishop; b. Montreal, Can., Nov. 2, 1883; s. Rodrigue and Marie-Louise (Lalonde) V.; ed. Mont-Saint-Louis, Montreal, P.Q.; Scolasticat, Pères Oblats, Ottawa, Ont.; Oblat de Marie Immaculée; D.Ph., U. of Ottawa, 1919, D.Th., 1922, Dr. Canon Law, 1930; D.Ph., Laval U., 1930; LL.D. McGill University, 1933, Toronto, 1934, University of Edmonton, 1936, University of Queens, 1944. Priest since 1907; prof. philosophy, U. of Ottawa, 1907-13, prof. theology, 1913-20; became bishop of Gravelbourg, Saskatchewan, Can., 1930; archbishop of Quebec since 1931, cardinal since 1933. Author: L'un des Votres, 1927; Le Mariage, 1936; Entretiens liturgiques, 1937; La Messe, 1938; Quelques Pierres de doctrine, 1938; Le Saint Baptême, 1940; Le Sacrement de la Confirmation, 1941; Le Extreme Onction, 1945; Le Sacrement de l'Ordre, 1945; Sacramentaux et Devotions, 1946. Contbr. numerous articles on religious philosophy to reviews and journals. Home: Archeveche de Quebec, Quebec, Can. Died Jan. 17, 1947; buried in cathedral, Quebec, Can.

VIEWEG, Frederic, pres. Am. Potash and Chemical Corp. Address: 609 S. Grand Av., Los Angeles 14. Died Mar. 3, 1947.

VIGNESS, Lauritz Andreas (vĭg'nĕs); b. Fillmore County, Minn., Jan. 14, 1864; s. Ole L. and Anna (Hallum) V.; student Marshall (Wis.) Acad., 1879-81, Augustana Coll., Canton, S.D., 1881-84; A.B., Dixon (Ill.) Coll. and Normal Sch., 1885; Augustana Sem., Beloit, Ia., 1885-86; D.D., Capital U., 1927; m. Margaret Krogness, June 9, 1887. Prof. Greek and Latin, Augustana Coll., 1886-90; same, Highland Park Coll., Des Moines, Ia., 1890-94; prin. Jewell (Ia.) Luth. Coll., 1894-95; pres. Pleasant View Luth. Coll., Ottawa, Ill., 1895-1914; ordained to ministry, St. Paul, Minn., June 17, 1894; pastor Des Moines, Ia., 1894-95, Ottawa, Ill., 1901-14; pres. St. Olaf Coll., Northfield, Minn., 1914-18; exec. sec. board of education, Norwegian Lutheran Ch. of America, 1918-31. Editor of Lutheraneren, 1925-39; now retired. Republican. Lutheran. Address: 3708 Upton Av. S., Minneapolis, Minn. Died Sept. 1, 1947.

VILES, Blaine Spooner (vī'lĕs), lumberman; b. Somerset County, Me., July 22, 1879; s. Edward Payson and Ada Augusta (Spooner) V.; A.B., Bowdoin Coll., 1903; M.F., Yale, 1904; A.M., U. of Me., 1935; m. Annie Ethel Johnson, June 30, 1901; children—Dorothy, William Payson. Pres. Augusta Lumber Co., treas. Kennebec Land Co., C. M. Rice Paper Co., Brown and White Paper Co. Has been mayor of City of Augusta and mem. State House of Reps., Me. Senate and Governor's Executive Council, Maine Fish and Game Commn., Me. Forest Commn. Mem. Delta Kappa Epsilon. Republican. Mason, Elk. Clubs: Cumberland, Tin Whistle (N.C.); Augusta Country. Home: 154 State St. Office: 284 Water St., Augusta, Maine. Died Sep. 9, 1943.

VILES, Jonas; b. Waltham, Mass., May 3, 1875; s. Charles Lowell and Almira (Hubbard) V.; A.B., Harvard, 1896, A.M., 1897, Ph.D., 1901; m. Ruth Bennett Hayes, June 10, 1903; children—Jonas (dec.), Charles Lowell, Philip Hubbard, Peter Hayes (dec.). Teacher, Dalzell Sch. for Boys, Worcester, Mass., 1896-98; asst. in history Harvard, 1898-1901; successively instr. in history, asst. prof., and prof. Am. history, University of Missouri, 1902-45, prof. emeritus since 1945. Mem. American Historical Association, Miss. Valley Hist. Assn. (pres. 1933-34), State Hist. Soc. of Mo. (trustee), Am. Assn. Univ. Profs., Phi Beta Kappa. Episcopalian. Club: Faculty (Columbia, Missouri). Author: Archives of Missouri, 1910; History of Missouri, 1912, 33; Outline of American History, 1915; The University of Missouri, a Centennial History, 1839-1939, 1939; also articles in revs. and periodicals. Home: Sunset Hill, Columbia, Mo. Died Feb. 6, 1948.

VILLARD, Oswald Garrison, journalist; b. Wiesbaden, Germany, Mar. 13, 1872; s. Henry and Fanny (Garrison) V.; g.s. William Lloyd Garrison, the Abolitionist; A.B., Harvard, 1893, A.M., 1896; Litt.D., Washington and Lee U., 1906; LL.D., Lafayette College, 1915, Howard Univ., 1933; LL.D., U. of Oregon, 1935; m. Athens, Ga., Julia Breckinridge Sandford, Feb. 18, 1903; children—Dorothea M., Henry Hilgard, Oswald Garrison. Asst. in U.S. history, Harvard, 1894-96; reporter Phila. Press, 1896-97; was editorial writer and pres. New York Evening Post, 1897-1918 (sold the property July 1918); editor and owner N.Y. Nation, 1918-32, pub. and contbg. editor, 1932-35; was also owner of The Nautical Gazette, New York, which sold in 1935. Author: John Brown—A Biography Fifty Years After, 1910; Germany Embattled, 1915; Newspapers and Newspaper Men, 1923; Prophets True and False, 1928; The German Phoenix, 1933; Fighting Years; Memoirs of a Liberal Editor, 1939; Our Military Chaos, 1939; Within Germany, 1940; The Disappearing Daily, 1944; Free Trade-Free World, 1947. Founder of "Yachting" mag., 1907. One of five to found Nat. Assn. for the Advancement of Colored People, 1910. Home: 79 E. 79th St., New York 21. Died Oct. 1, 1949.

VILLAROEL, Gualberto, pres. Bolivia; b. Cochabamba, Bolivia, 1907; honor student graduate of The Military School. Served as gen. staff officer in Chaco War, comdg. bn. in defense of Villa Montes; continued as gen. staff officer after the war; hon. student of his class, Superior War School. Pres. of Bolivia since Dec. 20, 1943. Died July 21, 1946.

VINCENT, Clarence Augustus, clergyman; b. Bainbridge, O., Dec. 17, 1859; s. Augustus Runnells and Lurancy Aurelia (Bonney) V.; A.B., Oberlin, 1884; B.D., Oberlin Theol. Sem., 1888; post-grad. study, Yale, 1888-89; D.D., Hillsdale (Mich.) Coll., 1898; m. Lucy Seymour Hall, Nov. 14, 1888; children—Hope Edith, Ruth, Helen Dorothy (Mrs. Franklin C. McLean), Clarence Hall, Donald Chamberlain, Howard Paton. Ordained Congl. ministry, 1888; pastor Sandusky, O., 1894-98, Central Ch., Galesburg, Ill., 1898-1907, Eliot Ch., Boston, 1907-14, Mt. Pleasant Ch., Washington, D.C., 1914-17, First Church, Winter Park, Fla., 1917-34, Miami Shores Community Church, 1934-41, pastor emeritus since 1941. Pres. Ohio Congl. Assn., 1896, Ill. Congl. Assn., 1900, Fla. Congl. Assn., 1921; mem. Com. on Missions, Congl. Chs. of U.S. 6 yrs., etc.; ex-pres. Parents Assn. of Pub. Schs. (Boston); pres. World's Scientific Assn.; also pres. Hungerford Industrial Sch. for Negroes, Eatonville, Fla. Mason. Kiwanian. Author: Acts of Modern Apostles, 1893; Providence in America, 1897; Night and the Stars, 1906. Asso. editor The Christian at Work many yrs. Contbr. poems. Home: 490 Chase Av., Winter Park, Fla.; also Henniker, N.H. Died Mar. 31, 1943.

VINSON, Robert Ernest, educator; b. White Oak, Fairfield County, S.C., Nov. 4, 1876; s. John and Mary Elizabeth (Brice) V.; A.B., Austin Coll., Sherman, Tex., 1896; B.D., Union Theol. Sem., Va., 1899; studied U. of Chicago, 1902; D.D., Austin, 1905; L.L.D., Southwestern Presbyn. U., 1910, Baylor U., 1918, Austin Coll., 1921, Oberlin, 1923, U. of Tex., 1923, Washington U., 1925, Trinity Coll., 1926; L.H.D., Denison U., 1927; m. Katherine Elizabeth Kerr, Jan. 3, 1901; children—Mary Elizabeth (Mrs. Alfred K. Kelley), Helen Rutherford (Mrs. Hiram O. Studley), Katherine Kerr (Mrs. Richard Kimball). Ordained to Presbyn. ministry, 1899; asso. pastor of 1st Presbyn. Ch., Charleston, W.Va., 1899-1902; prof. 1902-16, and pres. 1908-16, Austin (Tex.) Presbyn. Theol. Sem.; pres. U. of Tex., 1916-23; pres. Western Reserve U., 1923-34. Trustee Carnegie Foundation, 1920-34. Democrat. Mem. Alpha Tau Omega. Phi Beta Kappa. Address: 2839 Manchester Rd., Shaker Heights 22, O. Died Sept. 2, 1945.

VINSONHALER, Frank (vĭn'sŭn-hā-lĕr), ophthalmologist; b. Graham, Mo., Apr. 14, 1864; s. George and Sarah (Rea) V.; Northwestern Normal Sch., Oregon, Mo., M.D., Coll. Physicians and Surgeons, Columbia, 1885; student extraordinary U. of Vienna, 1892; Royal Ophthalmic Hosp., London, England; LL.D., U. of Ark., 1929; m. Wrennetta Beidelman, Feb. 9, 1898; children—Marion Wilmer, Frances Rea, George. In practice at Little Rock since 1893; prof. ophthalmology, U. of Ark., since 1893, also dean Med. Sch.; retired. Commd. maj., Med. R.C., 1917; lt. col., 1919; comd. Base Hosp. 109, Vichy, France. Colonel U.S.R. Fellow Am. Coll. Surgeons; pres. Ark. Med. Soc., 1900-01. Awarded medal Columbia Univ., 1935. Mem. Phi Beta Kappa. Home: 500 E. 9th St., Little Rock, Ark. Died Sep. 1, 1942.

VITTUM, Edmund March, clergyman; b. Sandwich, N.H., Oct. 24, 1855; s. Stephen and Ruth (Tappan) V.; A.B., Dartmouth, 1878, A.M., 1888; B.D., Yale, 1884; D.D., Ia. (now Grinnell) Coll., 1898; m. Annie Griswold, May 16, 1889 (died 1903). Prin. Orleans Liberal Inst., 1873-74; prof. mathematics, Robert Coll., Constantinople, 1878-81; ordained Congl. ministry, 1884; pastor Guilford, Conn., 1884-88, Cedar Rapids, Ia., 1888-91, Grinnell, Ia., 1891-1907; pres. Fargo (N.D.) Coll., 1907-09; prof. English lit., Ga. Normal Coll., Milledgeville, 1910-17; pastor Grinnell, Ia., 1917-19, Muscatine, Ia., 1919-25, retired. Republican. Author: Church Festivals in a Meetinghouse, 1888; Faith on the Frontier, 1890; Head of the Firm, 1891; A Modern Dreamer, 1919; The Vittum Folks, 1921. Mem. Phi Beta Kappa. Home: 1132 West St., Grinnell, Ia. (summer, N. Sandwich, N.H.). Died 1938.

VOEGELI, Henry Edward (vō'gĕl-ī); b. St. Louis, Mo., Oct. 12, 1876; s. Henry J. and Bertha (Brewer) V.; ed. pub. and private schs. and Colo. State Agrl. Coll.; Ft. Collins, Colo.; m. Frances Reynolds, Apr. 24, 1902. Sec. Chicago Banker Co., 1899-1900; asst. mgr. Chicago Symphony Orchestra, 1900-26, and of Orchestra Hall, Chicago, 1905-26, mgr. of both since 1927; asst. treas. Orchestral Assn. since 1908; mem. Wessels & Voegeli, concert management, 1909-26, now Henry E. Voegeli Management; sec. Northwestern Univ. Festival Assn., 1939. Mem. 1st Ill. Inf., Spanish-Am. War. Mem. Soc. Santiago de Cuba. Republican. Clubs: Lotos (New York); Arts Club, Bohemians, Cliff Dwellers. Home: 1360 E. 48th St. Office: 220 S. Michigan Av., Chicago, Ill. Died Dec. 28, 1943.

VOLIVA, Wilbur Glenn (vŏl'ī-vȧ), clergyman; b. near Newton, Ind., Mar. 10, 1870; s. James H. and Rebecca (Griffith) V.; B.A., Hiram Coll., Ohio, 1897; B.D., Union Christian Coll., Merom, Ind., 1897; m. Mollie Steele, Aug. 11, 1892. Ordained to ministry Christian Ch., 1889; pastor Linden, Ind., 1889-92, Urbana, Ill., 1892-93; studied theology, Stanfordville, N.Y., 1893-94; supplied pulpit Chestnut St. Christian Ch., Albany, 1893-94, York Harbor, Me., 1894-95; pastor Christian Ch., Washington C.H., O., 1897-99; became mem. Christian Catholic Ch., 1899; ordained elder, Apr. 1899; elder in charge N. Side Zion Tabernacle, Chicago, 1899-1900, Cincinnati, 1900-01; overseer Christian Catholic Ch. in Zion, Australia, 1901-06; returned to Zion City, Ill., 1906, and was asst. to John Alexander Dowie until his death, Mar. 1907; gen. overseer since 1907. Home: Zion, Ill. Died Oct. 11, 1942.

VOLKER, William (vŏl'kẽr), mfr., civic leader; b. Hanover, Germany, Apr. 1, 1859; s. Frederick and Dorothea (Busche) V.; came to America 1871; ed. pub. schs., Chicago; m. Rose Roebke, Sept. 7, 1911. Began active career at Kansas City, Mo., 1882; now retired. Known for philanthropic, civic and business activities. Evangelical Lutheran. Home: 3717 Bell St. Office: 3d and Main Sts., Kansas City, Mo. Died Nov. 7, 1947.

VOLSTEAD, Andrew J. (vŏl'stĕd), ex-congressman; b. Goodhue County, Minn., 1859; ed. St. Olaf's Coll. and Decorah Inst.; m. Nellie Gilruth, 1894; 1 dau., Laura. Admitted to bar, 1884, and began practice at Granite Falls, Minn., 1886. Pres. bd. edn., city atty. and mayor; county atty. Yellow Medicine Co., Minn., 14 yrs.; mem. 58th to 67th Congresses (1903-23), 7th Minn. Dist.; author of the "Volstead Act" for federal prohibition; also the Farmers' Co-operative Marketing Act; legal advisor to prohibition units, St. Paul, 1924-31; practiced law at Granite Falls, 1931-41; retired 1941. Republican. Home: Granite Falls, Minn. Died Jan. 20, 1947.

von HOFFMANN, Bernard, business executive; b. Milwaukee, Wis., Nov. 3, 1900; s. Albert and Anna (Albrecht) von H.; A.B., Univ. of Mo., 1921; m. Dorothy Elizabeth McClintock, Sept. 6, 1922; children—Bernard, Beverly (Mrs. Wm. H. Macon), Barbara. Pres. and mem. bd. dirs. Von Hoffmann Corp., St. Louis, Mo., since 1928; treas. and mem. bd. dirs. Von Hoffmann Press since 1931; pres. and mem. bd. dirs. Von Hoffmann Distributing Co. since 1933; treas. and mem. bd. dirs., Mid-State Printing Co. since 1942; chmn. bd. dirs. Meat Merchandising, Inc., since 1940. Partner Midland Stationery & Printing Co., Jefferson City, Mo., since 1944. Enlisted U.S. Army Air Corps, Apr., 1942; placed in inactive status Aug. 1945, rank of major. Mem. bd. dirs. Jefferson Coll., 1939-42. Dir. St. Louis Aviation Council. Mem. Scabbard and Blade. Elk. Clubs: Algonquin Golf (Webster Groves); Missouri Athletic (St. Louis). Licensed free balloon pilot, 1917; rep. U.S. in Internat. Balloon Races, Brussels, Belgium, 1921; airplane pilot, 1926. Filmed Life of the Djukas of Interior Surinam, Jan.-Apr., 1940. Home: 7730 Mohawk Dr., Clayton, Mo. Office: 105 S. 9th St., St. Louis 2, Mo. Died May 31, 1947; interred Valhalla Crematorium, St. Louis.

VON KLENZE, Camillo (vŏn-klĕn'zĕ), prof. German; b. Freiburg, Switzerland, Mar. 22, 1865; s. Eugene and Clara (Anders) Von K.; A.B., Harvard, 1886; Ph.D., U. of Marburg, Germany, 1890; Litt.D., U. of Wis., 1932; m. Henrietta Becker, June 18, 1906. Came to U.S., 1879. Instr. in Romance languages, Cornell U., 1890-91, instr. in Germanic langs., 1891-93; instr. in German lit., U. of Chicago, 1893-96, asst. prof., 1896-1902, asso. prof., 1901-06; head of dept. of German, Brown U., 1906-16, Coll. City New York, 1916-27; hon. prof. Am. Lit., U. of Munich, Germany, 1928-33; lecturer summers, Cornell U., 1902, 06, U. of Wis., 1908, Columbia, 1911, 12, 14, 16, 24, 36, Stanford, 1930, 34. Mem. Modern Lang. Assn. America, Germanistic Soc. America, Goethe Soc. America, Phi Beta Kappa, Delta Upsilon. Chmn. Com. on Cultural Relations Between America and Germany of Deutsche Akademie; Munich, 1928-37. Democrat. Unitarian. Author: Interpretation of Italy, 1907; From Goethe to Hauptmann, 1926; Charles Timothy Brooks, Translator from the German, and the Genteel Tradition, 1937. Contbr. numerous articles and reviews. Editor: Deutsche Gedichte, 1895, 1910; Hebbel's Agnes Bernauer, 1911, 22. Address: 72d St. and Broadway Branch Nat. City Bank, New York, N.Y. Died Mar. 17, 1943.

von PAGENHARDT, Maximilian Hugo (fŏn-pä'gĕn-härt), cons. engr.; b. Stuttgart, Germany, June 20, 1884; s. Baron Robert and Princess Alexandria (zu Ysenburg-Budingen-Wachtersbach) von P.; B.A., Royal Sch. of Cadets, Berlin, 1904; grad. as lt., Student Sch. of Ensigns, Potsdam, 1905; lt. inf., 120th Regt., "Kaiser Wilhelm II," Ulm; naval architect, Royal Polytechnicum, Charlottenburg, 1910; m. Marie Dupuy Adams, May 25, 1918; 1 son, Maximilian F. Robert. Came to U.S., 1910, naturalized, 1932. Naval architect for Miss. Valley Transportation Co., St. Louis, 1910-11, for Kansas City-Mo. River Transportation Co., 1912-17; naval architect and cons. engr., St. Louis, 1917-23, designing fleet for U.S. Dept. of War for Miss. River, for Magdalena River (Colombia, S.America), for Standard Oil Co., for Panuco River (Mexico), for Cities Service Co., etc.; founder, 1924, and now pres. of M. H. Pagenhardt & Co., engrs., designers and constructors of power plants, Washington, D.C.; registered professional engr. Commonwealth of Pa. Mem. Am. Soc. Mech. Engrs. Evang. Lutheran. Contbr. tech. articles on marine engring. to tech. jours. Home: 2415 Foxhall Rd., Washington. D.C. Died Oct. 25, 1943.

von PHUL, William (vŏn-pōōl), consulting engr.; b. New Orleans, La., July 20, 1871; s. William and Mary McDougall (Williams) P.; B.S., Tulane U., 1891, M.E., 1893, Dr.Engring., 1931; m. Marie Alzire Cade, Nov. 19, 1895; children—William, Mrs. A. A. Uebelacker, Mrs. W. T. Smith, Mrs. R. M. Ollinger, Mrs. Charles G. Ollinger, Jr. Engr. with Edison Electric Co., New Orleans, La., until 1902; with Sargent & Lundy, Chicago, Ill., 1902, and was in charge of construction of works, later of operation, Cincinnati Gas & Electric Co.; joined staff of Ford, Bacon & Davis, New York, 1905, in operation of pub. utilities in New Orleans, Memphis, Nashville, Birmingham, Little Rock and Houston; mem. same firm, 1912-45; with his partners designed and built the cotton warehouses for Bd. of Commrs. of Port of New Orleans; v.p. Am. Cities Co., 1911-13; v.p., gen. mgr. United Railroads of San Francisco, 1916, pres., 1919; pres., gen. mgr. Market St. Ry. Co., San Francisco, 1919-22; dir. United Rys. Inv. Co., Calif. Ry. & Power Co.; pres. and dir. Ford, Bacon & Davis, Inc., engrs., New York, 1922-42, chmn. exec. com. and dir. 1942-43; formerly dir. Ford, Bacon & Davis Construction Corp., Interstate Natural Gas Co., Inc., Easy Washing Machine Corp., L. C. Smith & Corona Typewriters, Inc., Lackawanna & Wyo. Val. R.R. Co., Lackawanna & Wyoming Valley Power Co., Laurel Line Transportation Co. Fellow A.A.A.S.; mem. Am. Soc. Municipal Engrs., Am. Soc. C.E., Am. Soc. M.E., La. Engring. Soc., Am. Acad. Polit. and Social Science, S.A.R., Sons of the Revolution, Kappa Alpha. Republican. Catholic. Clubs: Boston (New Orleans); City Midday (New York). 82 Willows Av., Larchmont, N.Y. Died Apr. 17, 1949.

von TEMPSKI, Armine (vŏn-tĕmp'skē), author; b. Maui, T.H., Apr. 1, 1899; d. Louis and Amy (Wodehouse) von T.; ed. by governesses and correspondence courses; m. Alfred L. Ball, July 14, 1932. Mem. P.E.N., Author's League of America. Author: Hula, 1927; Dust, 1928; Fire, 1929; Lava, 1930; All True (with chapters by Amelia Earhart, Mrs. Kermit Roosevelt and others), 1931; Hawaiian Harvest, 1933; Ripe Breadfruit, 1935; Pam's Paradise Ranch (juvenile for girls), 1940; Born in Paradise, 1940; Judy of the Islands, 1941; Aloha, 1945; Bright Spurs, 1945. Contbr. to mags. Address: 3905 Crest Dr., Manhattan Beach, Calif. Died Dec. 2, 1943; buried in Forest Lawn Memorial Park, Glendale, Calif.

VOORHEES, John Howard, lawyer; b. South Branch, N.J., Feb. 20, 1867; s. Samuel G. and Jane (Brokaw) V.; A.B., Rutgers Coll., 1888; A.M., 1891; m. Bessie A. Tabor, June 5, 1894; children—Mrs. Lorraine B. Loynachan, Mildred T. Admitted to S.D. bar, 1890. Mem. firm Bailey, Voorhees, Woods & Fuller, Sioux Falls, since 1891. Mem. Nat. Conf. Commrs. on Uniform State Laws since 1907 (exec. com. 1922-27; sec. 1928-36). Mem. Am. Bar Assn. (exec. com., 1912-15; treas. since 1927), S.D. Bar Assn. (sec. 1897-1926; pres. 1928-29). Mem. Phi Beta Kappa, Phi Delta Phi, Zeta Psi. Republican. Episcopalian. Mason (32°), Elk. Club: Minnehaha Country. Home: 924 W. 11th St. Office: Bailey-Glidden Bldg., Sioux Falls, S.D. Died Sep. 19, 1946.

VOORHEES, Louis A(ugustus), chemist; b. New Brunswick, N.J., Mar. 6, 1865; s. Charles Holbert (M.D.) and Charlotte (Bournonville) V.; A.B., Rutgers Coll., 1885, A.M., 1888; m. May Wilcox, Oct. 24, 1900. Began with N.J. State Agrl. Expt. Sta., 1885, and advanced to chief chemist, 1895; resigned and opened own lab., 1905; chemist to Dept. of Health, City of New Brunswick, since 1920. A pioneer in various agrl. investigations, 1885-1905. Charter mem. Inst. of Food Technologists; mem. A.A.A.S., Am. Chem. Soc., Am. Pub. Health Assn., Assn. Official Agrl. Chemists, Am. Dairy Science Assn., Internat. Assn. of Milk Sanitarians, N.J. Health Officers Assn., N.J. Health and Sanitary Assn., Inst. Food Technologists, New Brunswick Scientific Soc., S.A.R., Sons of Union Vets., Phi Beta Kappa. Democrat Mason, Elk. Home: 357 George St. Office: City Hall, New Brunswick, N.J. Died Aug. 14, 1945.

VOORHEES, Oscar McMurtrie, clergyman; b. nr. Somerville, N.J., Dec. 29, 1864; s. Samuel S. and Elizabeth (McMurtrie) V.; A.B., Rutgers Coll., 1888, A.M., 1891; grad. Theol. Seminary Reformed Church, New Brunswick, N.J., 1891; D.D., Miami University, Oxford, Ohio, 1911; LL.D., College of William and Mary, 1927; m. Alice R. MacNair, Oct. 29, 1891; children—Helen McMurtrie, Frances Van Kleek, Ralph Whitaker (dec.), Marian MacNair (dec.); m. 2d, Martha S. Elmendorf, June 25, 1902. Ordained Reformed (Dutch) ministry, 1891; pastor Three Bridges, N.J., 1891-1903, High Bridge, N.J., 1903-09, Mott Haven Church, New York, 1909-22. Secretary United Chapters of Phi Beta Kappa, 1901-31, treas., 1901-13, historian since 1931. Pres. Hunterdon County Hist. Soc., 1903-04; mem. Delta Upsilon. Author of Historical Sketch of Phi Beta Kappa Soc. and many hist. papers. Editor Phi Beta Kappa Key, 1910-31; editor Phi Beta Kappa General Catalog, 1923; Phi Beta Kappa senator, 1901-46; secretary Phi Beta Kappa Foundation, Inc.; 1924-31, trustee, 1924-45. Chmn. War Service Commn. Reformed Ch. in America, 1917. Y.M.C.A. service, France, 1918-19, representing Phi Beta Kappa Alumni in New York. Wrote: Ralph and Elizabeth Rodman Voorhees—a Tribute, 1927. Compiler: A Condensed Genealogy of the Van Voorhees Family, 1932; The Historical Handbook of the Van Voorhees Family in the Netherlands and America, 1935. The Van Voorhees Association at its Tenth Anniversary, 1942; The History of Phi Beta Kappa, 1946. Home: Basking Ridge, N.J. Office: 5 E. 44th St., New York 17, N. Y. Died Aug. 29, 1947.

VORENBERG, Felix, merchant, importer; b. Grebenstein, Ger., June 10, 1868; s. Bernard and Henrietta (Brandenstein) V.; grad. Frankfort-on-Main Gymnasium; m. Rose Frankenstein, Oct. 18, 1898. Came to U.S., 1888, naturalized citizen, 1895. Began in foreign dept. Horace Partridge Co.; founder, 1896, and since pres. and treas. F. Vorenberg Co., importers; v.p. and gen. mgr. Gilchrist Co. since 1913. Mem. Mass. Com. on Public Safety, 1917-21, Boston Sinking Fund Commn., 1917-23, Com. on Soldiers' Memorial, 1919-21. Mem. Retail Trade Bd. (pres. governing council since 1920), Mass. Credit Union Assn. (1st pres.), Harvard Mercantile Health Com., Community Health Assn., Boston Chamber Commerce (charity finance com.), Mass. State Com. on Higher Edn., Federated Jewish Charities (v.p.). Clubs: Exchange, Elysium, Republican, Jewett Repertory, Kernwood Country, Marlboro Country. Office: 417 Washington St., Boston. Died Aug. 10, 1943.

VORHIES, Charles Taylor (vŏr'hēz), prof. zoölogy; b. Lockridge, Ia., Sept. 7, 1879; s. Daniel and Rachel Elizabeth (Taylor) V.; B.S., Ia. Wesleyan Coll., Mt. Pleasant, 1902; Ph.D., U. of Wis., 1908; m. Marie Isabel Tuttle, Sept. 7, 1901 (died 1928); 1 son, Charles Tuttle; m. 2d, Georgia Ann Clark, July 29, 1929. Instr. biology, Ia. Wesleyan Coll., 1902-04; asst. in zoölogy, U. of Wis., 1904-08; prof. zoölogy and botany, U. of Utah, 1908-15, actg. dean Med. Sch., 1911-13; instr. in entomology, Cornell U., summer, 1915; asst. prof. biology, U. of Ariz., 1915-16, prof. zoölogy, 1916-18, prof. entomology, 1918-33, prof. zoölogy, and econ. zoölogist since 1933; actg. dean of agr., actg. pres. and administrative adviser at various times. Fellow A.A.A.S. (pres. S.W. div. 1933); asso. Am. Ornithologists Union; mem. Ecological Soc. America (pres. 1939), Am. Soc. Mammalogists. Cooper Ornith. Club, Wildlife Soc., Am. Soc. Ichthyologists and Herpetologists, Ariz. Wildlife Federation (sec'y-treas. 1939-), Sigma Xi, Phi Kappa Phi, Phi Delta Theta. Methodist. Author numerous bulls., also articles in scientific books and mags. Has done outstanding research work on rodents of the range and desert. Home: 1424 E. Fifth St., Tucson, Ariz. Died March 10, 1949.

VOS, Bert John (vŏs), univ. prof.; b. Katwyk aan Zee, The Netherlands, Oct. 27, 1867; s. Jan Hendrik and Aaltje (Beuker) V.; A.B., U. of Mich., 1888; scholar and fellow Johns Hopkins, 1888-91, Ph D., 1892; U. of Leipzig, 1891-92; m. René Moelker, June 27, 1894; children—Maude Alida (Mrs. S. W. Seaney), John Hendrik, Cornelia Gertrude (Mrs. C. L. Christenson), Bert John. Instr. German, U. of Chicago, 1892-93; asso. German, Johns Hopkins, 1893-98, asso. prof., 1898-1908; pro. German, Ind. U., 1908-37; prof. emeritus of German since 1937; research asso. Univ. of Calif. at Los Angeles since 1937. Council Am. Assn. Univ. Profs. Pres. Assn. Modern Lang. Teachers of Central West and South, 1917-18, 1924-25; chmn. Western Sect. Modern Lang. Assn. America, 1917-20; v.p. Modern Lang. Assn., 1926-27. Spl. asst. to Am. Legation at the Hague, and mem. mission to Berlin, 1918-19. Author: The Diction and Rime-Technic of Hartman von Aue, 1896; Materials for German Conversation, 1900; Essentials of German, 1903; Oral and Written German, 1932; A First German Reader, 1933; Concise German Grammar (with H. Leser), 1941. Translator: Chantepie de la Saussaye's Religion of the Teutons, 1902. Editor: Schiller's Wilhelm Tell, 1911; Grimm's Kinder- und Hausmärchen, 1903; Heine's Harzreise, 1907; German Lyrics and Ballads (with P. A. Barba), 1925. Contbr. to current German and Am. periodicals. Asso. editor Modern Lang. Notes (1913-15) and Modern Lang. Jour. Home: 911 N. 6th Av., Tucson, Ariz. Died Mar. 28, 1945.

VOSE, Edward Neville (vōs), b. Albany, Kan., Aug. 1, 1870; s. Prof. James Edward and Mary (Neville) V.; grad. Cushing Acad., Ashburnham, Mass., 1889; student Williams Coll., 1889-91; A.B., Harvard, 1894; m. Pauline Bezin, Aug. 24, 1899 (died 1920); m. 2d, Ida Wilson, Sept. 2, 1922; children—Hollis Wilson (Mrs. Norman P. Arnold), Jean Mary (Mrs. Hetrick A. Foss). Instr. Lawrence (Mass.) High School, 1895-96; New England salesman for Allyn & Bacon, publishers, 1896-97; editor Am. Exporter, 1897-1902; asso. editor Dun's Rev., 1902-03, editor Dun's Internat. Review, 1903-25; also editor of The World's Markets, 1917-23; pres. Fairfield County Realty Service, Stamford, Conn., 1927-30; head of Edward N. Vose, real estate, Niantic, Conn., 1933-34; editor Exporter's Digest, 1935-38; resumed real estate activities, 1938. Author: Commercial Monographs, 1913-14; The Spell of Flanders, 1915; Seventy-Five Years of The Mercantile Agency, 1916; The World's Markets, 1916. Contbr. on fgn. trade. Home: Saunders Point, Niantic, Conn. Died Aug. 31, 1949.

VOSS, Carl August (vŏs), clergyman; b. Wheeling, W.Va., Aug. 17, 1876; s. Rev. Edward and Anna (Diedrich) V.; g.g.s. Johann Heinrich Voss, German poet; prep. edn., high sch., Cincinnati, O.; student Elmhurst (Ill.) Coll.; grad. Meadville Theological Sch., 1896; post-grad. work, Lane Theol. Sem. and U. of Cincinnati; D.D., U. of Pittsburgh, 1909; m. Lucy Wilms, Apr. 19, 1898; children—Edward Wilms, Victor Emanuel, Carl Hermann, Dorothy C. Casselman. Ordained ministry Evang. Protestant Ch., 1896, pastor Immanuel Ch., Fairmount, Cincinnati, 1897-1905; pastor German Evang. Protestant (Smithfield) Ch., Pittsburgh, since 1905. Conglist. Ex-trustee Meadville Theol. Sch.; mem. Congl. Nat. Commn. on Missions; pres. German Protestant Orphanage, Allegheny County Mothers Pension League; dir. German Protestant Home for Aged; v.p. Allegheny County Milk and Ice Assn.; dir. Pub. Health Nurses Assn.; mem. advisory bd. Chicago Theol. School; pres. Evang. Protestant Church, 1913-20. Mem. Pi Gamma Mu. Mason (K.T., 32°, Shriner); grand chaplain, Pa. Clubs: Hungry, Agora, Rotary. Author: History of German Evangelical Protestant Smithfield Church of Pittsburgh (1782-1907), 1907, and (1782-1932), 1932; History of the German Protestant Orphanage, Pittsburgh, 1912; History of the German Protestant Home for Aged, Pittsburgh, 1913. Contbr. to theol. jours. Lecturer. Home: 221 Buchanan Place, Mt. Lebanon, Pittsburgh, Pa. Died Dec. 24, 1943.

VREELAND, Herbert Harold, corp. exec.; b. Glen, Montgomery County, N.Y., Oct. 28, 1856; s. Rev. Abraham H. and Jane (Van Ryper) V.; ed. common schs.; m. Carrie L. Reed. At age of thirteen began to earn his living by filling ice carts, then worked shoveling gravel on a night constrn. train on the L.I. R.R.; later trackwalker, switchman, fireman, freight brakeman, conductor; afterward on New York and Northern, of which he became gen. mgr.; from that went to New York as pres. and gen. mgr. Houston, West St. & Pavonia Ferry R.R. Co.; pres. and gen. mgr. Met. St. Ry. Co. many yrs. from 1893; took leading part in subsequent consolidations. Chmn. bd. Royal Typewriter Co.; dir. Clinchfield Coal Corp., Clinchfield R.R. Co. Decorated Officer of Crown, Belgium, 1932. Mem. exec. com. Belgian League of Honor; mem. Holland Soc., Pilgrims of U.S. Clubs: Railroad-Machinery, New York Railroad (bd. govs.), Engineers', Metropolitan; Ridgewood Country (Danbury, Conn.); Kishawana Golf (Brewster, N.Y.). Office: 2 Park Av., New York, N.Y.* Died Jan. 31, 1945.

VREELAND, Williamson Updike, coll. prof.; b. Rocky Hill, N.J., Aug. 30, 1870; s. Jacob M. and Louisa (Updike) V.; A.B., Princeton, 1892, Boudinot fellow in modern langs., 1892-93, A.M., 1896; the Sorbonne, Paris, 1892-93; Faculties of Letters, Florence, Italy, and Madrid, Spain, 1893-94; Doctorat es Lettrès, U. of Geneva, Switzerland, 1901; m. Alice May Brown, May 9, 1900; 1 dau., May. Instr. French, Princeton U., 1894-97, asst. prof., 1897-1903, Woodhull professor Romance languages and head modern lang. department, 1903-13; professor emeritus since July 1938. Mem. Société Jean-Jacques Rousseau of Geneva. Presbyterian. Mem. Phi Beta Kappa. Clubs: Princeton (New York and Phila.). Author: Selections from Gil Blas, 1900; Jean-Jacques Rousseau et les rapports littéraries entre Genève et l'Angleterre, 1901; French Syntax and Composition (with Prof. William Koren), 1907; Anthology of French Prose and Poetry (with Prof. Régis Michaud), 1910; Anthology of 17th Century French Literature (in collaboration), 1927; Anthology of 18th Century French Literature (in collaboration), 1930. Home: 180 Mercer St., Princeton, N.J. Died Nov. 6, 1942.

VROOMAN, Clare Martin (vrō'măn), lawyer; b. Monroeville, O., Mar. 7, 1892; s. Benjamin and Frances (Firby) V.; A.B., Oberlin (Ohio) Coll., 1915; LL.B., Western Res. U. Law Sch., 1918; m. Jessie Lois Baker, July 3, 1916; children—Clare Martin, Jr., Richard, Jean Eleanor. Admitted to Ohio bar, June 1918; supt. Coit-Alber Chautauqua, 1916-17; asso. with Henderson, Quail, Siddall & Morgan, 1918-19; partner, Clarke, Vrooman & Costello, 1919-22; partner, Davis, Young & Vrooman, 1922-29; pvt. law practice, 1930-33; partner, Garfield, Cross, Daoust, Baldwin & Vrooman, 1933-41; partner, Garfield, Baldwin & Vrooman, since 1941; pres. The Defiance Pressed Steel Co., Marion, O.; v.p. Realty Investment Co., Cleveland. Asst. sec. Civic League of Cleveland, 1917-18; exec. director Citizens Bureau Cleveland, 1918-19; pres. Lakewood Rep. Club, 1920-22; chmn. City Mgr. Plan, Lakewood, O., 1926; pres. Oberlin Coll. Alumni Assn., 1934-36; pres. Cleveland Council on Inter-Am. Relations, Cleveland. Trustee Citizens Bur. since 1919, Cleveland Ch. Fedn.; mem. bd. dirs. Council on World Affairs, Cleveland; mem. Com. on Foreign Relations, Cleveland; active in promotion of Basic English as internat. language since 1939. Mem. Cleveland, Ohio State, Am. and Calif. bar assns., Internat. Assn. of Ins. Counsel, Am. Judicature Soc., Cleveland and Marion, O., Chambers of Commerce, Phi Alpha Delta. Clubs: Union, Canterbury Golf, City (Cleveland); Marion Country (Marion, O.). Mason. Conglist. Co-author: (with Raymond Moley) Lessons in American Citizenship, 1919; Various Aspects of the Surety's Right of Indemnity, 1939. Contbr. articles to law and trade jours. Home: 22040 McCauley Rd., Shaker Heights, O. Address: 1401 Midland Bldg., Cleveland, O Died Feb. 21, 1944.

W

WADDELL, Charles Edward (wă-dĕl'), consulting engr.; b. Hillsboro, N.C., May 1, 1877; s. Francis Nash and Ann Ivy (Miller) W.; ed. Bingham Mil. Sch., N.C., and in shops of Gen. Electric Co.; Sc.D., N.C. State Coll. Agr. and Engring., 1925; m. Eleanor Sheppard Belknap, Apr. 19, 1904; children—Eleanor B. (Mrs. George M. Stephens), Charles E. Built various steam and hydraulic plants along the eastern seaboard; cons. engr. to George W. Vanderbilt, for "Biltmore" (designed and built majority of engring. works at Biltmore); designer, and builder of N.C. Elec. Power Co.'s system, 1903-23; cons. engr. United Electric Securities Co., Boston, 1912; consulting engr. on State water powers for the City of Medellin, Colombia, South America, 1927. Cons. engr. to power sect. Council of Nat. Defense, in surveying and analyzing the power resources of the Southern States for war emergency, 1917; engr. to Q.-M. Dept., U.S. Army, for constrn. of gen. hosps. No. 12 and No. 19, 1918; dir. of conservation for the State of N.C., U.S. Fuel Administration. Chmn. and mem. N.C. Board Engring. Examiners, 1921-26; mem. N.C. Ship and Water Transportation Commn., 1923-24; commr. Biltmore Forest, 1923-27; pres. Biltmore Hosp., 1920-23; cons. engr. City of Asheville, 1925-27; cons. engr. to N.C. Corp. Commn. in readjustment of utility rates, 1932-34. Cons. engr. Tenn. Valley Authority, 1936-38, and for City of Asheville, N.C., 1940; for Ecusta Paper Corp., Pisgah Forest, N.C., since 1941; for Am. Enka Corp., 1943-44. Fellow American Institute Electrical Engrs. (chmn. N.C. sect. 1936); mem. Am. Soc. C.E. (pres. N.C. sect. 1923-24; hon. mem. N.C. sect. 1943), Am. Soc. M.E., N.C. Soc. Engrs. (pres. 1928; hon. mem. 1942). Clubs: Asheville Civitan (president 1923), Pen and Plate (president 1916), Biltmore Forest Country (gov. 1922-30). Episcopalian. Home: Biltmore, N.C. Office: Asheville, N.C. Died Apr. 20, 1945.

WAESCHE, Russell Randolph (wā'chê), admiral U.S. Coast Guard; b. Thurmont, Md., Jan. 6, 1886; s. Leonard Randolph and Mary Martha (Foreman) W.; student Purdue U., 1903-04; grad. U.S. Coast Guard Acad., 1906; m. Dorothy Luke, 1911; children—Russell Randolph, Harry Lee, James Mountford; m. 2d, Agnes Rizzuto, 1933; 1 son, William Alexander. Commd. ensign, U.S. Coast Guard, 1906, and promoted through grades to admiral, 1945; apptd. rear adm. and comdt. U.S. Coast Guard, June 15, 1936, and reappointed, 1940; apptd. vice adm. for temporary service, March 10, 1942; reapptd. comdt., June 1944; member Newcomen Society, National Sojourners, Propeller Club of United States Society of Naval Architects and Marine Engrs., Soc. of Am. Mil. Engrs., Mil. Orders of World War, Am. Legion. Episcopalian. Mason. Clubs: University, Army and Navy (Washington). Home: 7005 Rolling Rd., Chevy Chase, Md. Address: U.S. Coast Guard Hdqrs., Washington, D.C. Died Oct. 17 1946; buried in Arlington National Cemetery.

WAGGENER, William Peyton (wăg'ĕn-ĕr), lawyer; b. Atchison, Kan., June 18, 1870; s. Balie Peyton and Emma Louise (Hetherington) W.; student St. Benedict's Coll., Atchison, 1881-82, Midland Coll., Atchison, 1882-83, Kemper Mil. Acad., Boonville, Mo., 1883-87; m. Martha Spurr, Nov. 23, 1892 (dec.); children—Louise (Mrs. Albert L. Bartlett, Jr.), Balie Peyton, Marcus Spurr; m. 2d, Gertrude H. Seaton, Dec. 28, 1931. Admitted to Kan. bar, 1890, and began practice at Atchison; mem. Waggener, May, Waggener & Hope; pres. Exchange Nat. Bank; gen. atty. Mo. P. Ry., Western Coal & Mining Co.; dir. Exchange State Bank. County atty., Atchison County, Kan., 1900-03; mem. city council Atchison; mem. board mgrs. World's Fair, St. Louis, Mo., 1903. Mem. S.A.R. Democrat. Episcopalian. Mason, K.P., Odd Fellow, Elk, Modern Woodman. Clubs: Bellevue Country (Atchison); Kansas City (Mo.). Home: 819 N. 4th St. Office: 603 Commercial St., Professional Bldg., Atchison, Kan. Died Oct. 11, 1943.

WAGGONER, David E. (wăg'ŭn-ĕr), insurance; b. Fannin County, Tex., June 28, 1867; s. Ferdinand D. and Mary A. (Blackwell) W.; educated public schools and business college; married Linna Easley, 1891; children—D. Easley, Mrs. Elizabeth Burgher, Mrs. Joel Nash. Actively identified with banking in Texas many years; founder and past president Security National Bank, Dallas, Texas; president United Fidelity Life Insurance Co.; director Dallas Federal Savings & Loan Association. City treasurer of Dallas 2 terms. Mem. Dallas Astron. Soc. Republican (nominee for state treas. 1932, for gov. 1934). Methodist. Clubs: Idlewild, Dallas Athletic, Dallas Country. Home: Melrose Hotel, Dallas. Office: Texas & Pacific Bldg., Dallas, Tex. Died Mar. 15, 1948.

WAGNER, Henry Franklin, lawyer; b. West Lancaster Twp., Keokuk County, Ia., Feb. 11, 1874; s. John Michael and Caroline (Meyer) W.; LL.B., State U. of Ia., 1898; m. Lillian Updegraff, Oct. 12, 1898; 1 dau., Gladys (Mrs. J. C. Eichhorn). In practice of law at Sigourney, Ia., 1898-1919; judge Dist. Court, 6th Ia. Dist., 1919-27; judge Supreme Court of Ia., 1927-33; now engaged in practice of law at Sigourney, Ia. Mem. Council of Defense, World War. Member Am., Ia. State and Keokuk County bar assns., Delta Theta Phi, Order of the Coif. Republican. Mason (Shriner), K.P., Odd Fellow (Grand Master of Ia. 1913-14). Home: Sigourney, Ia. Died Nov. 10, 1943.

WAGNER, Herbert Appleton, public utilities; b. Phila., Pa., Feb. 24, 1867; s. William and Clara W. (Appleton) W.; grad. Stevens Inst. Tech., 1887; (hon.) Dr. Engring., Johns Hopkins Univ., 1937; m. Rose Margaret Keller, Jan. 12, 1920; children—Herbert A., Mrs. John P. Zamboni. Constrn. engr. Westinghouse Electric Co., Pittsburgh, 1887; installed for same, St. Louis, the first large alternating central sta. in the West, 1888; gen. supt. Mo. Edison Co., St. Louis, 1888-1900; organizer, 1891, and first pres. Wagner Electric Mfg. Co., developing the first successful alternating current single phase motor, and other elec. devices; settled in Baltimore, 1911; v.p. and dir. Consol. Gas Electric Light & Power Co. and affiliated cos., 1910-15, pres. and dir. 1915-39, chmn. of bd., pres. and dir., 1939-42; chmn. bd. until May 1943, now retired; dir. The Lyric Co. Trustee Union Memorial Hospital, Stevens Inst. Tech., Children's Hospital School. Life member American Institute Electrical Engineers, Md. Acad. Sciences (hon. chmn. bd. of trustees). Mem. Newcomen Society of England. Episcopalian. Clubs: Maryland, Maryland Jockey. Home: Garrison, Md. Died Dec. 5, 1947.

WAGNER, Rob (Robert Leicester), artist, writer, motion picture dir., editor; b. Detroit, Mich., Aug. 2, 1872; s. Robert and Mary Leicester (Hornibrook) W.; student U. of Mich., 1891-94; studied art in Paris; m. Jessie Willis Brodhead (died 1906); children—Leicester, Thornton; m. 2d, Florence Welch, Jan. 18, 1914. Illustrator, Detroit Free Press, Criterion (New York), Ency. Britannica (London); portrait painter; writer for Saturday Evening Post, Collier's and other nat. mags.; motion picture dir. of Will Rogers. Author: Film Folk; Tessie Moves Along. Editor Rob Wagner's Script, Beverly Hills, Calif. Home: 608 N. Crescent Drive. Office: 9480 Dayton Way, Beverly Hills, Calif. Died July 20, 1942.

WAGONER, Winfred Ethestal, coll. adminstr.; b. Wallace, Ind., May 31, 1889; s. William Alfred and Ginevra Jane (Clouse) W.; A.B., Indiana U., 1912, grad. student 1913, 1915, 1920, 1921; m. Glossie Lavonne Goddard, May 10, 1914; children—George Alfred, Glossie Lavonne (Mrs. Orlen Ervin Baker, Jr.), Winfred. Teacher in public schools, Fountain County, Ind., 1907-11; prin. of sch., Mount Auburn, Ind., 1912-14; Milroy, Ind., 1914-19, Posey Township Schs., Rush County, Ind., 1919-21; county supt., Rush County, Ind., 1921-22; asst. state Sch. insp., Ind., 1922-24; asst. prof. hist., Ball State Teachers Coll., Muncie, Ind., 1924-25, sec.-registrar, 1925-36, controller, 1936-42, acting pres. and controller, 1943-45, controller since 1946. Director Ball Memorial Hosp. School of Nursing. Mem. bd. trustees Wesley Foundation, Indiana University, also Ball State Teachers Coll.; pres. Delaware County Community Fund. Mem. Ind. State Teachers Assn., N.E.A., Ind. Schoolmens Club, Central and Ind. assns. of univ. and coll. bus. officers, Ednl. Buyers Assn., Ind. Ednl. Buyers Assn., Pi Omega Pi, Phi Delta Kappa. Methodist. Mason. Club: Exchange (Muncie). Mem. financial adv. com. editing bulletins of financial adv. service, Am. Council on Education. Mem. editorial com. of Accounting for Teachers Colleges, published 1940. Home: 2119 W. Jackson St., Muncie, Ind. Died June 7, 1948.

WAINWRIGHT, Jonathan Mayhew, lawyer; b. New York, N.Y., Dec. 10, 1864; s. John Howard and Margaret Livingston (Stuyvesant) W.; A.B., Ph.B., Columbia U., 1884, LL.B., 1886; hon. A.M., 1908; m. Laura Wallace Buchanan, Nov. 23, 1892; 1 dau., Laura F. Admitted to bar, 1886, and practiced at N.Y. City; partner Barry, Wainwright, Thacher & Symmers since 1913. Mem. N.Y. Assembly, 1902-08, Senate, 1909-13; asst. sec. of war, 1921-23; mem. 68th to 71st Congresses, (1923-31), 25th N.Y. Dist. Commd. 2d lt., advancing to lt. col., 12th Regt., Nat. Guard N.Y., 1889-1906; capt. 12th N.Y. Vols., Spanish-Am. War; lt. col. insp. gen.'s dept., Nat. Guard, N.Y., Mexican border, 1916; lt. col. and div. insp., N.Y. Div., Feb. 1917; mustered into U.S. service as lt. col., div. insp. 27th Div., U.S. Army, July 15, 1917; served in France and Belgium, participating in all battles and engagements of 27th Div.; hon. discharged Mar. 31, 1919; col. O.R.C., Inf., 1921-29, auxiliary, 1929; col. inactive since Nov. 23, 1937. Decorations: D.S.M., A.E.F. (U.S.); Officier Legion d'Honneur (French); Croix de Guerre with Palm (Belgian); conspicuous Service Cross of State of N.Y., Silver Star medal for "exceptional courage under fire." Awarded Columbia University medal for service, 1934; president Intercollegiate Athletic Association, 1884. Chairman Westchester County Defense Council, 1941. Member board mgrs. St. Luke's Hosp., and Seamen's Ch. Inst., N.Y. City. Mem. bd. trustees Grant Monument Assn. of N.Y. City. V.p. Westchester County Historical Society. Member Assn. Bar City of New York, Westchester County Bar Assn. (pres. 1903-04), Westchester County Park Commn., 1930-37; Mil. and Naval Order Spanish-Am. War, Mil. Order World War, N.Y. Soc. Mil. and Naval Officers of World War, S.R., St. Nicholas Soc., Pilgrims of U.S., United Spanish War Vets., Am. Legion, Delta Psi, Phi Beta Kappa. Mason. Republican. Episcopalian (warden Christ's Ch., Rye, N.Y.). Clubs: Union, Republican (New York); Army and Navy (Washington); Apawamis, American Yacht. Home: Rye, N.Y. Office: 72 Wall St., New York, N.Y. Died June 3, 1945.

WAITE, Alice Vinton, prof. English; b. Battleboro, Vt., Jan. 16, 1864; d. Silas Merrick and Sophia Zilpha (Eager) Waite; B.A., Smith Coll., 1886, M.A., 1894; studied Yale. Teacher English, Mary Inst. (Washington U.), 1887-93; instr. English, 1896-1903, asso. prof., 1903-11, prof., 1911-36, Wellesley, also dean, 1913-36, now emeritus. Mem. Am. Assn. Univ. Women, Phi Beta Kappa. Editor: Ben Jonson's English Grammar, 1909. Compiler: Modern Masterpieces of Short Prose Fiction (with Edith Mendall Taylor), 1911. Home: 16 Appleby Rd., Wellesley, Mass. Died Apr. 6, 1943.

WAITE, Henry Matson, civil engr.; b. Toledo, O., May 15, 1869; s. Henry Selden and Ione (Brown) W.; grad. Toledo High Sch.; student Mass. Inst. of Tech.; LL.D., Univ. of Miami; Dr. of Engring., Univ. of Cincinnati; m. Mary Mason Brown, Apr. 15, 1914. With C.,C.,C.&St.L. Ry. as transitman, 1890-92, engr. maintenance of way, 1892-93; div. engr. C.,N.O.&T.P. Ry., 1893; bridge engr., roadmaster and supt. Cincinnati div., same rd., 1899-1905, supt. Chattanooga div., 1905-07; supt. Seaboard Air Line Ry., 1907-09; v.p. and chief engr. Clinchfield Coal Corp., Dante, Va., 1909-12; chief engr. City of Cincinnati, 1912-14; city mgr., Dayton, 1914-18; v.p. and chief engr., Lord Constrn. Co., N.Y., 1919-20; pres. Lord Dry Dock Corp., N.Y., 1920; in private practice at N.Y., 1920-27; chief engr. Cincinnati Union Terminal Co., 1927-1933; dep. adminstrn. of Public Works, July 1933-Sept., 1934; dir. Regional Dept. of Economic Security, Cincinnati, since Sept. 1934; private practice cons. engr. since 1937; chmn. Chicago Subway Commn., Public Works Adminstrn.; chmn. public works com. Nat. Resources Com. Col. of engrs. Transportation Corps, U.S.A., with A.E.F., 1918-19; served as chief engr. Trans. Corps, asst. dep. gen. of transportation, 2d Army, in Advance Zone, and as a.d.g. Trans., 3d Army in Germany; one of members of Am. Bridgehead Commn. at Coblenz before arrival of Am. Army; asst. to officer in charge civ. affairs at advanced G.H.Q. at Treves, Germany. Mem. Am. Soc. C.E., Am. Inst. Mining and Metall. Engrs., Am. Ry. Engring. Assn. Awarded D.S.M. (U.S.); Officer Légion d'Honneur (French). Club: Engineers. Home: 3515 Cornell Place, Cincinnati. Died Sept. 1, 1944.

WAITE, Merton Benway, plant pathologist; b. Oregon, Ill., Jan. 23, 1865; s. E. J. and Elizabeth (Benway) W.; B.S., U. of Ill., 1887; D.Agr., Univ. of Md., 1919. Asst. pathologist, U.S. Dept. Agr., 1888-1901, pathologist in charge of fruit disease investigations, 1901. Mem. Bot. Soc. America, Am. Phytopath. Soc., etc. Author: Pollination of Pear Flowers; Pear Blight and Its Remedy; and other bot. papers. Home: 1447 Euclid Av. N.W., Washington. Died June 5, 1945.

WAITS, Edward McShane, clergyman, educator; b. Cynthiana, Ky., Apr. 29, 1871; s. of Charles Martel and Mary Ellen (Moore) W.; student Ky. Wesleyan Coll., Millersburg, Ky.; A.B., Transylvania Univ., Lexington, Ky., 1896; grad. Coll. of Bible, same univ., 1896; traveled in Orient and studied in Europe; LL.D., Transylvania, 1923, Texas Christian U., 1923, Austin Coll., Sherman, Tex., 1924; m. Sarah Wooten, May 23, 1898 (died 1915). Ordained ministry Disciples of Christ, 1896; pastor Fulton, Ky., 1896-1901, El Paso, Tex., 1902-06, Magnolia Av. Ch., Ft. Worth, 1906-16; pres. Tex. Christian U., 1916-41, pres. emeritus and ambassador of good will since 1941; supt. state Bible Sch. work. Asso. editor Courier, Dallas, Tex. Democrat. Prohibitionist. Mason. Home: 2916 Princeton St., Ft. Worth, Tex. Died Dec. 26, 1949; buried Greenwood Cemetery, Fort Worth, Tex.

WAKEFIELD, Arthur Paul, physician; b. North Bloomfield, O., Oct. 5, 1878; s. Edmund Burritt and Martha (Sheldon) W.; Ph.B., Hiram (O.) Coll., 1900; M.D., Rush Med. Coll. (U. of Chicago), 1904; A.M., Bethany (W.Va.) Coll., 1907; Rockefeller Foundation fellow, Sch. Tropical Medicine, Harvard, 1917; resident Boston City Hosp., Westfield (Mass.) Sanatorium; m. Olive Catharine Lindsay, June 14, 1904; children—Vachel Lindsay, Mary Churchill (dec.), Catharine Frazee, Martha Isabel. Began practice at Springfield, 1904; med. missionary, China, 1905-27, at Nanking, 1905, in charge hosp., Luchowfu, 1912-19, in charge student health work, Boone U., Wuchang, 1919-27 (aided in saving univ. property when Wuchang was seized by soviet-nationalist army, 1927); chief of Chadwick Clinics (state child tuberculosis clinics), Mass., 1928-33; supt. Central Me. Sanatorium, Fairfield, Me., 1932-36; supervisor State Clinics for Crippled Children, Mass. Dept. of Pub. Health, since 1936. Decorated by Chinese Nat. Red Cross for flood relief work on Yangtze and reconstruction Yangtze dyke at Wuhu. Episcopalian. Mason. Home: 75 Richardson Road, Belmont, Mass. Address: Dept. of Pub. Health, State House, Boston, Mass. Died Feb. 6, 1942.

WAKEFIELD, Lyman E., banker; b. Long Lake, Hennepin County, Minn., July 7, 1880; s. Warren and Abby (Eldredge) W.; ed. high sch., Wayzata, Minn.; m. Elizabeth Anderson, Oct. 17, 1906; children—Lyman E., Samuel Chace. With First Nat. Bank, Austin, Minn., 1897-1902, Northwestern Nat. Bank, Minneapolis, Minn., 1902-11; treas., later v.p. Wells-Dickey Co., investment bankers, 1911-23; v.p. 1st Minneapolis Trust Co., 1923-26; pres. First Nat. Bank, Minneapolis & Eastern Railway; v.p. and mem. exec. com. First Bank Stock Corp; dir. Soo Line, Geo. A. Hormel Co., Northwestern Fire & Marine Ins. Co., First Nat. Bank (Minneapolis), Northwestern Nat. Life Ins. Company. Trustee Carleton Coll., Minneapolis Foundation; dir. Minneapolis Council Social Agencies, Y.M.C.A. Mem. Fed. Advisory Council since 1941. Pres. Assn. Reserve City Bankers, 1934-35. Trustee Carnegie Endowment for Internat. Peace. Presbyterian. Clubs: Minneapolis, Minikahda, Woodhill (Minneapolis); Minnesota (St. Paul); Chicago (Chicago). Home: 4700 Fremont Av. S. Office: First Nat. Bank, Minneapolis, Minn. Died July 24, 1945.

WAKEFIELD, Ray Cecil, lawyer; born at Fresno, California, August 12, 1895; son of Hugh Franklin and Clara Isabella (Harris) W.; A.B., Stanford University, 1916, J.D., 1918; married Laureda Thompson, Aug. 30, 1930; children (by previous marriage), Doris (Mrs. George Robert Jenkins), John. Admitted to California bar, 1918, and practiced in Fresno, 1918-37; was deputy district attorney, Fresno County, 1920-23; inheritance tax appraiser for State of Calif. in Fresno County, 1923-37; mem. Wakefield & Hansen, 1928-32, Wakefield & Staniford, 1935-37; mem. Calif. Railroad Commn., 1937-41 (pres. Aug. 1938-Jan. 1940); mem. Nat. Assn. R.R. and Utilities Commrs., pres. 1941; mem. Federal Communications Commn., 1941-47; now chmn. U.S. delegation to Provincial Frequency Board of the International Telecommunication Union. Secretary Republican Central Committee, Fresno County, 1920-21; chmn. 1922-23; mem. State Rep. Central Com., 1922-23; del. Rep. Nat. Conv., Chicago, 1932. Pres. Calif. State Soc. of Washington, D.C., 1943. Mem. Am. Bar Association, Calif. State Bar Association, Order of Coif, Delta Chi. Republican. Member First Christian Ch., Fresno. Mason. Clubs: Kiwanis Internat. (lt. gov. Calif.-Nev. Dist. 1932); Commonwealth (San Francisco). Home: Fresno, Calif. Died Sept. 29, 1949.

WAKELEE, Edmund Waring, pub. utility exec.; b. Kingston, N.Y., Nov. 21, 1869; s. Nicholas and Eliza C. (Ingersoll) W.; grad. Kingston Acad., 1887; LL.B., New York U., 1891; unmarried. Admitted to N.Y. bar, 1891, N.J. bar, 1896; president Public Service Corp. of N.J. and subsidiaries; chmn. bd. Palisades Trust & Guaranty Co., Englewood, N.J.; pres. 825 Fifth Av. Corp. (N.Y.); dir. Sedgwick Machine Works (N.Y. City), N.J. Mfrs. Casualty Ins. Co., N.J. Mfrs. Assn. Fire Ins. Co., N.J Mfrs. Assn. Hosps., Inc. Mem. New Jersey General Assembly, 1899-1900, State Senate, 1901-10 (served as floor leader, pres. of Senate and acting gov.). Pres. Palisades Interstate Park Commn., v.pres. and trustee Englewood Cemetery Assn. Member American, N.J. State and Bergen County bar associations, New York County Lawyers Assn., Edison Electric Inst. (trustee), Am. Gas Assn., Am. Transit Assn., N.J. Hist. Soc.; Bergen County Hist. Soc., Newcomen Society of Eng. (Am. branch), Nat. Assn. Motor Bus Operators (v.p. and director), U.S., N.J. State and Bergen County, chambers of commerce, Alumni Assn. N.Y. Univ. Law Sch., Delta Upsilon, Phi Delta Phi. Republican. Presbyterian. Mason (32°), Elk. Clubs: Lotos, Faculty (N.Y.U.), Nat. Republican (all New York); Essex (Newark); Englewood; Knickerbocker Country (Tenafly, N.J.); Arcola Country; Aldecress Country (Demarest). Home: Demarest, N.J.; also 825 5th Av., New York, N.Y. Office: 80 Park Pl., Newark, N.J. Died Apr. 26, 1945.

WALCOTT, Chester Howe, architect; b. Chicago, Ill., Feb. 2, 1883; s. Chester Pratt and Martha Cook (Howe) W.; B.S., Princeton, 1905; studied in Paris and Italy; m. Julie Commins, June 27, 1912; children—Helen (Mrs. Roderick McKenzie), Julie Cummins (Mrs. David R. Gallagher). Began practice of architecture, Chicago, firm Brown and Walcott, 1911, practiced under own name, 1916-19; mem. Clark & Walcott, 1919-24; in his own name since 1924; has specialized in residences, chs. and clubs. Principal works: St. Chrysostom's Ch. and parish bldgs.; Evanston Y.M.C.A. Bldg. Instr. Lake Forest Acad., 1942-46. Mem. Am. Institute Architects. Republican. Club: University Cottage Club of Princeton. Home: Lake Forest, Ill. Died Oct. 25, 1947.

WALCOTT, Harry Mills, artist; b. Torringford, Conn., July 16, 1870; s. Dana Mills and Elizabeth (Billings) W.; ed. Rutherford (N.J.) pub. sch., Nat. Acad. Design, New York, Académie Julien, Paris; m. Belle Havens, June 1, 1905. Awarded hon. mention, Paris Salon; Clark prize and 1st Hallgarten prize, Nat. Acad. Design; Shaw fund, Soc. Am. Artists; hon. mention Carnegie Inst., Pittsburgh; medals, Pan-Am. and St. Louis expns.; Wanamaker prizes, Am. Art Assn., Paris; Daniel G. Reid Purchase Fund, Richmond (Ind.) Art Assn.; silver medal, Panama P.I. Expn., 1915. Represented in the H. C. Frick, John Wanamaker, Samuel T. Shaw, and Salmagundi Club collections, New York; W. S. Stimmel collection, Pittsburgh; Richmond, Ind., and Erie, Pa., Art Assns., A.N.A.; mem. Am. Art Assn. (Paris). Republican. Home: 46 The Terrace, Rutherford, N.J. Died Nov. 4, 1944.

WALDEN, Percy Talbot, prof. chemistry; b. Brooklyn, N.Y., June 29, 1869; s. Daniel Treadwell and Caroline Amelia (Williams) W.; Ph.B., Sheffield Scientific Sch. (Yale), 1892; Ph.D., Yale, 1896; studied univs. of Leipzig and Munich; m. Sarah Scovill Whittelsey, June 22, 1905; children—Sarah Scovill, Joseph Whittelsey. Asst. in chemistry, 1892-94, instr., 1894-99, asst. prof., 1900-19, prof. 1919-37, Yale, also chmn. freshmen chemistry faculty, acting dean of freshmen, 1924-25, dean of freshmen, 1925-37, dean and prof. emeritus since 1937, was also chmn. bd. of admissions. Chief examiner in chemistry and chmn. chem. commn. for College Entrance Exam. Bd. since 1918. Mem. Am. Chem. Soc., A.A.A.S., Aurelian Soc., Sigma Psi, Chi Phi. Episcopalian. Club: Graduate. Contbr. to professional jours. Home: 210 St. Ronan St., New Haven, Conn. Died Apr. 14, 1943.

WALDO, George E., ex-congressman; b. Brooklyn, Jan. 11, 1851; s. George and Sarah Ellen (Jagger) W.; ed. Cornell U,; m. Flora Henderson, May 11, 1896 (died Feb. 18, 1939); children—John Henderson, Cornelius Thornton. Admitted to bar, 1876; mem. N.Y. Assembly, 1896; commr. of records, Kings County, N.Y., 1899-1904; del. Rep. Nat. Conv., 1900; mem. 59th and 60th Congresses (1905-09), 5th N.Y. Dist. Removed to Pasadena, Calif., 1913; mem. law firm Waldo & Waldo. Mem. Los Angeles County and Calif. State bar assns. Mason (32°). Home: 1346 Locust St. Office: 15 N. Raymond Av., Pasadena, Calif. Died June 11, 1943.

WALDO, Richard H., editor; b. New York, N.Y., Sept. 28, 1878; s. Howard Lovett and Clara Waldo (Sullivan) W.; ed. Friends Acad., Locust Valley, N.Y., Hawkins Collegiate Inst., New Brighton, N.Y.; married; children—Allan Stone, William Stone, Howard Lovett, Thayer Everett. Advertising rep. Harper & Brothers, 1902-05; adv. and business mgr. Good Housekeeping Mag., 1905-14; established and developed Good Housekeeping Inst. with licensing of mfrs.; sec. and associate gen. mgr. N.Y. Tribune, 1914-17. Created and caused to be adopted "Truth" emblem by Associated Advertising Clubs of the World (Advertising Fedn. of America), 1909-14. Chmn. publicity com. Chamber Commerce U.S.A., 1913-17; established and staffed The Nation's Business, Washington, D.C. Commd. capt. Inf. U.S.R., Plattsburg, N.Y., Nov. 8, 1917; duty A.E.F., Dec. 1917-Aug. 1919; organized War Risk Insurance in Gt. Britain and Ireland; as business mgr. organized "The Stars and Stripes," G.-2, Chaumont; comd. troops 111th Inf., 28th Div., field service; also sec. and organizing officer Inter-allied Games, Paris, 1919, G.-5, Chaumont. U.S. Army, 1919. Decorated Order of the Holy Redeemer (Greece), 1919. Pub. Hearst's Internat. Mag., New York, 1921-23; adv. counsel and management, John Wanamaker New York, 1923-28; pres. and editor McClure Newspaper Syndicate since 1928. Dir. Pollak Foundation for Econ. Research since 1929. Treas. Grand Jury Assn., N.Y. County, 1934-37; historian N.Y. Chapter Mil. Order World War, 1935-39, nat. historian, 1939-40; dir. Sales Execs. Club of N.Y. since 1939. Clubs: Atlantic Beach, Mil.-Naval, Metropolitan (New York). Home: 37 Washington Sq. W. Office: 75 West St., New York, N.Y. Died June 11, 1943.

WALDON, Sidney Dunn; b. London, Eng., Jan. 29, 1873; s. James Ley and Julia (Dunn) W.; ed. in London and South Kensington schs.; m. Lois Strong Burton, Oct. 20, 1898 (now dec.); 1 dau., Maunie (Mrs. M. W. Lacy); m. 2d, Helen Rentschler, June 27, 1928. Came to U.S., 1893, naturalized. With Cooper Engine Works, Mt. Vernon, O., 1893-96; in employ Ball Engine Co., Erie, Pa., 1896-1900; then with Foster Auto Co., Rochester, N.Y., 1900-02; was v.p. Packard Motor Car Co.; then with Cadillac Motor Car Co., Detroit; now with Gen. Machinery Corp., Hamilton, O. Formerly pres. Street Ry. Commn., Detroit, 1918-19; pres. Rapid Transit Commn., Detroit, since 1922; street ry. commr., 1930-34, pres., 1933-34; mem. State Highway Advisory Board since 1934; dir. Detroit Auto Club since 1916; pres. 1921-23; chmn. Attorneys-in-Fact Auto Inter-Insurance Exchange since 1922; mem. Huron-Clinton Met. Authority since 1941. Served in World War, 1916-18, including overseas, in aviation. Republican. Episcopalian. Mason. Clubs: Detroit, Detroit Athletic, Grosse Pointe Country, Bloomfield Hills Country. Home: "Pine Knob," Clarkston, Mich. Office: 4612 Woodward Av., Detroit 1, Mich. Died Jan. 20, 1945.

WALDORF, Ernest Lynn, bishop; b. South Valley, Otsego County, N.Y., May 14, 1876; s. David Hiram and Mercy Ann (Thrall) W.; A.B., Syracuse U., 1900; D.D., Syracuse, 1915; LL.D., Kan. Wesleyan and Albion (Mich.) Coll., 1920; also LL.D. from De Pauw U., 1934; m. Flora Janet Irish, Jan. 1902; children—Lynn Osbert, Ethel Margaret, Paul Douglas, John David, Robert James. Ordained M.E. ministry, 1900; pastor Shortsville, N.Y., 1900-02, Union Springs, 1902-03, Phelps, 1903-05, Clyde, 1905-07, Centenary Ch., Syracuse, 1907-11, Plymouth Ch., Buffalo, 1911-15, 1st. Ch., Cleveland, O., 1915-20; bishop M.E. Ch., 1920-24, in charge states of Kan., Okla., Tex., and La.; of Kansas City area, covering Kan., Okla., Tex., La., Ark. and Mo., 1924-32; assigned to Chicago Area (covers work of M.E. Chs. in Ill. together with bilingual confs. of Swedish and Norwegian-Danish work between Atlantic Ocean and Rocky Mountains), May 1932. Chaplain 74th Rgt., Nat. Guard N.Y., Buffalo, 1911-15. Trustee Garrett Biblical Inst., Ill. Wesleyan Coll., McKendree Coll. Mason, K.P. Club: Union League. Home: 941 Sheridan Rd., Wilmette. Address: 77 W. Washington St., Chicago, Ill. Died July 27, 1943.

WALDORF, Wilella Louise, dramatic critic; b. South Bend, Ind., Nov. 22, 1899; d. James Morris and Carrie (Throckmorton) Waldorf; A.B., Mount Holyoke Coll., 1922; unmarried. With Phila. Public Ledger Syndicate, 1923-25; film critic New York Post, 1926-30, dramatic editor, 1930-41. Address: 31 E. 12th St., New York. Died March 12, 1945; buried in Riverview Cemetery, South Bend, Ind.

WALDRON, Clare Bailey, horticulturist; b. Ravenna, O., Dec. 6, 1865; s. David S. and Louisa (Root) W.; B.S., Mich. Agrl. Coll., 1887, post-grad. study, 1887-89; D.Agr., North Dakota Agrl. Coll., 1939; m.

Lois Hooper, Dec. 24, 1891. Instr. botany, Michigan Agrl. Coll., 1888-89; prof. horticulture and forestry, N.D. Agrl. College, since 1890, dean of agr. since 1915. Mem., jury awards, St. Louis Expn., 1904; chairman jury awards, Portland (Oregon) Expn., 1905. Park commr., Fargo, N.D., since 1910; mem. N.D. Conservation Commn.; pres. Tri-State Grain and Stock Growers Assn.; chmn. agrl. com. State Council Defense. Fellow A.A.A.S.; mem. N.D. Acad. Science (pres. 1910). Development specialist in vocational edn., U.S. Army, 1920-21. Address: 1404 12th Av. N., Fargo, N.D.* Died Mar. 6, 1947.

WALDRON, Webb, editor, author; b. Vergennes, Mich., Sept. 8, 1882; s. William Augustus and Alice (Hubbs) W.; A.B., U. of Mich., 1905; m. Marion Keep Patton, March 29, 1915; 1 daughter, Patricia Ann. Ranching, teaching and wandering in western United States, 1905-11; advertising writer New York City, 1911-16, asso. editor Collier's Weekly, 1917-18; European editor, same, 1918-20; the first American magazine writer to enter Germany after the Armistice, and author of first magazine articles in America on the German revolution; staff writer Reader's Digest since 1938. Member Authors' League of America, Phi Beta Kappa Fraternity; honorary life member Mich. Authors Assn. Clubs: Dutch Treat, The Players (New York). Author: The Road to the World (novel), 1922; We Explore the Great Lakes, 1923; Shanklin, 1925; Blue Glamour, 1929; Fortunate Isle, 1934; Uncharted, 1936; Changing the Skyline (with Paul Starrett), 1938; Americans, 1941. Contbr. to Collier's, Woman's Home Companion, Harper's Bazaar, Pictorial Review. Am. Magazine, etc. Home: Westport, Conn. Address: care The Reader's Digest, Pleasantville, N.Y. Died Aug. 5, 1945.

WALDRON, William Henry, army officer, author; b. Huntington, W.Va., June 28, 1877; s. William and Helena Frances (Thomas) W.; distinguished grad. Inf. and Cav. Sch., 1905; grad. Army Staff Coll., 1906, Army War Coll., 1911; m. Allie McClure Powell, Nov. 14, 1901; 1 son, William Henry. Enlisted as sergt. Co. E, 2d W.Va. Inf., June 24, 1898; commd. 2d lt. 9th Inf., Apr. 10, 1899; lt. col. N.A., Aug. 17, 1917; col. N.A., Aug. 1, 1918; lt. col. U.S. Army, July 1, 1920; col., May 7, 1924. Sec. U.S. Inf. Assn. and editor its journal, 1919-24. Service in Spanish-Am. War, 1898, Philippine Insurrection, 1899-1900, Boxer Rebellion, 1900; wounded at Ho-siwo, China, Aug. 24, 1900; assigned duty Gen. Staff, Dec. 20, 1917; in France with A.E.F., May 23, 1918-May 17, 1919; chief of staff, 80th Div., N.A., Aug. 17, 1917-June 5, 1919; participated in battles Artios sector, British front, June 10-Aug. 22, 1918, Battle of St. Mihiel salient, Sept. 12-16, 1918, battles of the Meuse-Argonne, Sept. 26-Oct. 12, Nov. 1-11, 1918. Chief of staff 100th Div. Org. Res., 1924-27; comdg. 10th U.S. Inf., 1927-29; detailed Gen. Staff, July 1, 1929; chief of staff 5th Corps Area, July 1, 1929-Feb. 1, 1930; exec. officer Militia Bur., Washington, D.C., 1930-33; chief of staff 100th Div. Organized Reserves, 1933-37; also comd. the W.Va. Dist. of Civilian Conservation Corps, Apr. 1935-Nov. 1936; retired Jan. 31, 1938. Awarded D.S.M., 1922, "for distinguished service" in France; D.S.C., 1922, "for heroism" at battle of Tien Tsin, China, July 13, 1900; citation General Order 18, Headquarters 80th Div., also from comdr. in chief A.E.F.; decorated Officer Legion of Honor (France), 1919; awarded W.Va. Distinguished Service medal, 1940. Dir. Huntington, W.Va., Chamber of Commerce; pres. Community Chest. Author: Scouting and Patrolling, 1916; Tactical Walks, 1917; Company Administration, 1917; Army Physical Training, 1919; Platoon Training (2 vols.), 1919; Thirty Minute Talks (with Merch Brant Stewart), 1919; Terrain Exercises, 1922; The Old Sergeant's Conferences, 1930; Flags of America, 1935; America's Flags, 1938. Dir. of Civilian Defense, Huntington-Cabell County. Home: 530 13th Av., Huntington, W.Va. Died Oct. 1, 1947.

WALDROP, R. Walter, surgeon; b. Jefferson County, Alabama, Aug. 1, 1872; s. B. Bradford and Nellie (Huey) W.; M.D., U. of Louisville, also N.Y. Polyclinic and surgery under Dr. Harvey Cushing; m. Minnie Benton, June 25, 1902; children—Ralph Williams, Lewis Benton. In practice at Bessemer since 1897; owner, chief surgeon of Bessemer General Hospital. Fellow Am. Coll. Surgeons; mem. Am. Med. Assn., Southern Med. Assn., Med. Assn. State of Ala. Democrat. Baptist. Rotarian, Mason. Home: 1811 5th Av. Office: Realty Bldg., Bessemer, Ala. Died Oct. 11, 1948; buried Cedar Hill Cemetery, Bessemer, Ala.

WALKER, Abbie Phillips (Mrs. Fred Allan Walker), writer; b. Exeter, R.I., June 6, 1867; d. Thomas and Frances Davis (Congdon) Phillips; ed. pub. schs., Providence, R.I.; m. Fred Allan Walker, Nov. 19, 1901. Christian Scientist. Author: Told by The Sandman, 1916; Sandman Tales, 1917; The Sandman Hour, 1917; Sandman's Christmas Stories, 1918; Sandman's Twilight Stories, 1918; Sandman's Rainy Day Stories, 1919; Sandman's Drusilla Doll Stories, 1919; Sandman's Goodnight Stories, 1921; Sandman's Fairy Stories, 1922; Sandman's Might-Be-So Stories, 1922; Sandman's Stories of Twinkle Eyes, 1923; Sandman's Stories of Snowed-In Hut, 1923; Three Minute Stories, 1925; Once-Upon-a-Time Stories, 1925. Also more than 2,000 stories in newspapers, for children. Home: 2 E. 86th St., New York. Died Jan. 10, 1943.

WALKER, Alfred, dentist; b. New York, N.Y., May 22, 1876; s. Alfred and Jane (Finnegan) W.; D.D.S., New York Coll. of Dentistry, 1897; m. Elizabeth Muir, Jan. 24, 1912; children—Alfred, John Muir. Practiced in N.Y. City since 1897; formerly mem. Bd. of Dental Examiners, State of N.Y.; prof. emeritus of pulp canal therapy, New York Univ. Coll. of Dentistry. Served as pvt. 7th Regt., Nat. Guard N.Y., 1901-11; 1st lt. and capt. 107th Inf., Nat. Guard N.Y., 1918-23; lt. comdr. U.S. Naval Res. (hon. retired list). Hon. trustee Boys' Club. Pres. dental sect. Pan Am. Med. Assn. Recipient of N.Y. U. Alumni Federation Medallion, 1935. Pierre Fauchard Medal Award, 1940. Fellow Am. Coll. Dentists, N.Y. Acad. Dentistry, Internat. Coll. Dentists; mem. Am. Dental Assn. (life), Dental Soc. State N.Y. (pres. 1930-31, life mem.), 1st Dist. Dental Soc. (pres. life mem.), Florida State Dental Society, Miami Dental Society, F.A.A.A.S., New York Academy Sciences, Psi Omega, Omicron Kappa Upsilon. Democrat. Author of numerous papers and repts. on dental subjects. Co-author, vol. on Dental Practice Management; co-author, vol. on Oral Diagnosis and Treatment. Home: 2131 Biarritz Drive. Office: 420 Lincoln Rd., Miami Beach, Fla. Died Oct. 16, 1948.

WALKER, Arthur Tappan, prof. Latin; b. Jersey City, N.J., June 18, 1867; s. Alexander J. and Frances Antill (Lewis) W.; B.A., New York U., 1887; M.A., Vanderbilt U., 1892; Ph.D., U. of Chicago, 1898; m. Elizabeth Stone, June 14, 1899; children—Arthur Tappan, Margaret, Elizabeth Stone. Prof. Latin and Greek, Juniata Coll., Pa., 1888-90; teaching fellow in Latin, Vanderbilt U., 1890-92; prof. Latin and Greek, Emory and Henry Coll., Va., 1892-93; fellow in Latin, 1893-94, instr. in Latin, 1894-97, U. of Chicago; prof. Latin, U. of Kan., 1897-42, retired, 1942; dir. Summer Sch., same, 1906-13. Mem. Classical Assn. of Middle West and South (pres. 1908-09), Am. Philol. Assn., Am. Assn. Univ. Profs., Phi Beta Kappa, Psi Upsilon. Episcopalian. Editor: Cæsar's Gallic War, 1907 (revised, 1926); joint mng. editor of Classical Jour., 1909-23, joint editor-in-chief, 1923-32. Home: Lawrence, Kan. Died Sept. 3, 1948.

WALKER, Mrs. Barbour (Mary Adelaide), educator; b. Savannah, Ga., Aug. 2, 1866; d. Col. St. George and Josephine (Baynard) Rogers; B.A., Md. Coll. for Women, 1898; B.S., Teachers Coll. (Columbia), 1904, M.A., 1905; m. Barbour Walker, 1883 (died 1892); 1 dau., Mary Barbour (Mrs. Edward Lyndon). Prin. Coll. of Sisters of Bethany, Topeka, Kan., 1900-03; prin. Nat. Cathedral Sch. for Girls, Washington, D.C., 1906-13; called by Bishop C. H. Brent to establish a sch. for Am. girls at Baguio, P.I., 1913, with Am. Red Cross in France, Sept.-Dec. 1917; with Y.M.C.A., France and Germany, Dec. 1917-Sept. 1919; dean William Smith College, Geneva, N.Y., 1920-29 (emerita). Mem. Serbian Edn. Assn. Decorated by Serbian Govt. for work for Serbian students in Am. colls. Episcopalian. Home: 520 W. 114th St., New York, N.Y. Died Jan. 1950.

WALKER, Bradford Hastings, life ins. exec.; b. Newton Center, Mass., Nov. 11, 1884; s. Benjamin Powell and Olivia Hitchcock (Mackie) W.; ed. pub. schs., Concord, Mass.; children—Judith Ann., Bradford Hastings, Jr., David Harris. Advanced in all branches of field work and investment dept. to pres. Life Ins. Co. of Va.; also pres. John G. Walker Investment Corp.; dir. First & Merchants National Bank. Episcopalian. Clubs: Racquet and Tennis, River (New York); Commonwealth, Country, of Virginia (Richmond); Bath and Tennis, Everglades (Palm Beach); Havana Country, Yacht (Havana), Piping Rock, L.I.; Turf and Field, Lunch, City Mid Day, N.Y. City. Home: Windsor Farms, Richmond, Va. Office: Life Ins. Co. of Virginia, Richmond, Va. Died Nov. 29, 1949.

WALKER, Buz M., educator; b. Starkville, Miss., Aug. 20, 1863; s. William and Mary E. (Hines) W.; B.Sc., Miss. Agrl. and Mech. Coll., 1883, M.Sc., 1886; studied U. of Va., U. of Göttingen, U. of Berlin; Ph.D., U. of Chicago, 1906; m. Blanche White, Dec. 23, 1890. Instr. mathematics, Miss. Agrl. and Mech. Coll., 1883-84, asst. prof., 1884-88, prof., 1888-1925, dean Sch. of Engring., 1902-25, v.p., 1913-25, pres., 1925-30; pres. West Point (Miss.) Oil Mill, West Point Ice & Gin Co. Mem. Am. Math. Soc., Deutsche Mathematiker Vereinigung, Circolo Matematico di Palermo, Nat. Council Econ. League, Stable Money Assn., Internat. Assn. Patentees. Democrat. Baptist. Home: Starkville, Miss. Died Aug. 21, 1949.

WALKER, Dow Vernon, lawyer; b. Greensprings, O., Dec. 28, 1885; s. Lindsey E. and Lillie Belle (Harris) W.; grad. Ore. State Coll., 1906; LL.B., U. of Ore., 1912; m. Mabel Davis, Dec. 15, 1906; children—Marshall Vernon, Dow Edwin. Cashier Northern Pacific Terminal Co., Portland, Ore., 1906-08; mgr. Multnomah Amateur Athletic Club, Portland, Ore., 1908-19; admitted to Ore. bar, 1912 and since practiced in that state; county commr., Multnomah Co., Ore., 1921-24. Nat. comdr. Disabled Am. Veterans, 1945-46, mem. finance com. since 1942; trustee Disabled Am. Vets. Service Foundation since 1942. Served as div. staff officer, 39th Div., U.S. Army, 1917; with French gen. staff, 1918; mem. Gen. Pershing's hdqrs. staff, Adj. Gen.'s Office, Chaumont, France, 1918; assigned to G-3, in charge moving 41st Div., U.S. Army, to U.S., 1919. Mem. Am. Legion, Veterans Fgn. Wars, Mil. Order of World Wars, Phi Delta Phi. Elk. Club: Multnomah Amateur Athletic (hon. life mem.). Address: Box 276, Newport, Ore. Died July 25, 1947.

WALKER, Ernest George, newspaper man; b. Embden, Me., Sept. 1, 1869; s. Stillman Atwood and Martha Richardson (Wentworth) W.; Colby Coll., 1887-89; A.B., Harvard, 1892; m. Romaine Mannix, Oct. 26, 1898; 1 son, Mannix. Successively reporter, Sunday editor, news editor and leading polit. writer, Washington Post, 1893-1905; in charge Washington bur. of Boston Herald, 1905-15; Washington corr. Springfield Republican and Sacramento Bee, 1915-21. Sponsored numerous residence and apartment house enterprises in Washington, D.C., and in nearby parts of Virginia, 1917-26. Awarded Freemasonry medal, for 50 years of service, Grand Lodge of Maine, 1942. Compiled and published the Official Blue Book of Roosevelt-Garner Inaugural Observances in 1937. Author: Embden Town of Yore; Forty-Eight Gridiron Years; Walkers of Yesterday; South of "Lost Nation" (Tale of a Neighborhood); also other local Me. histories. Mem. D.C. Dem. Com. in Victory Fund Campaign of 1932; nat. finance dir. for Dem. Nat. Com. in charge of Deficit Fund Campaign in D.C.; pres. Nat. Dem. Council for D.C., 1936-37. Mem. Me. Hist. Soc., Zeta Psi. Clubs: Chevy Chase; Gridiron (historian, pres. 1914), Nat. Press. Home: 3035 Dumbarton Av., N.W., Washington, D.C. Died Feb. 6, 1944.

WALKER, Francis, economist; b. Washington, D.C., Dec. 27, 1870; s. Gen. Francis Amasa and Exene (Stoughton) W.; B.S., Mass. Inst. Tech., 1892; A.M., Columbia, 1893, Ph.D., 1895; studied univs. of Munich and Berlin; m. Helen O'Sullivan, June 25, 1908 (died 1938); children—Francis Stoughton, Helen, Evelyn. Spl. agt. Mass. Bd. to Investigate the Unemployed, 1894-95; instr. economics, Colo. Coll., 1895-97, prof., 1898-1900, prof. economics, Western Reserve U., 1900-02; economic study and pvt. research in Europe, 1902-03; spl. examiner, U.S. Bur. Corp., 1904-12; dep. commr. of corps., 1912-15; chief economist, Federal Trade Commn., 1915-Jan. 1, 1941; retired. Extensive researches European coal industry, 1903, oil industry, 1905, steel industry, 1908. As chief economist, Fed. Trade Commn. was in charge of govt. cost finding work during World War, 1917-19, of the corporate and financial phases of electric and gas utility industries, 1928-35, and of many other inquiries. Mem. Am. Statis. Assn., Am. Econ. Assn. Clubs: Cosmos, Chevy Chase. Author: Double Taxation in the United States, 1895; Monopolistic Combinations in the German Coal Industry, 1904; also numerous articles and papers on econ. subjects, especially trusts. Address: 3081 Cleveland Av., Washington, D.C. Died Jan. 15, 1950.

WALKER, Frank Ray, architect; b. Pittsfield, Mass., Sept. 29, 1877; s. Frank and Helen Theresa (Ranous) W.; grad. Mass. Inst. Tech., 1900; student in Italy and in atelier of M. Redon, Paris; m. Katharine Follett Stone, Oct. 23, 1915; children—Richard Stone (dec.), Joan. Began practice of architecture with firm of Guy Lowell, Boston, Mass., later becoming mgr. N.Y. office; with Alden & Harlow and with McClure & Spahr (both Pittsburgh); with J. Milton Dyer, Cleveland, O., 1905-11; partner Walker & Weeks since 1911. Mem. Cleveland C. of C. (past dir.; mem. city plan com.). Trustee Cleveland Natural Hist. Mus. Trustee Coll. of Architecture of Western Reserve U. (also mem. faculty). Mem. adv. staff Mass. Inst. Tech.; mem. adv. board Cleveland Sch. of Art. Cons. architect Army Med. Library, Washington, D.C. Fellow A.I.A. (life mem.; mem. and past pres. Cleveland chapter); mem. Cleveland (past trustee) and Indiana engring. socs., Cleveland Soc. Artists, Cleveland Museum of Art (life). Republican. Mem. St. Christopher's Episcopal Church, Gates Mills, O. (vestryman). Clubs: Union, Mid-Day; Chagrin Valley Hunt (Gates Mills); Mass. Inst. Tech. (New York); Royal Canadian Yacht (Toronto, Can.). Home: Gates Mills, O. Office: 1240 Huron Rd., Cleveland, O. Died July 9, 1949.

WALKER, Fred Allan, editor, pub.; b. S. Berwick, Me., Mar. 27, 1867; s. James and Marion (Farrington) W.; B.L., Dartmouth, 1888; hon. M.A., 1925; m. Abbie P. Jacobs, Nov. 19, 1901. Mng. editor Springfield (Mass.) Union, 1893-96, Boston Journal, 1896-1909, Baltimore News, 1909-11; pub. Washington Times, 1911-19; editorial asst. to Arthur Brisbane on Hearst publs., 1919-20; pub. Evening Telegram, New York, 1920-25; chmn. exec. bd. New York Sun, 1925-34, retired. Chmn. Publishers' Assn. of N.Y. City, 1923-33. Mem. Psi Upsilon, Sphinx. Christian Scientist. Mason. Home: "Fawnwood" Hadlyme, Conn. Died Mar. 25, 1947.

WALKER, George Winfield, banker; b. Albany, N.Y., Oct. 7, 1861; s. Robert and Mary Elizabeth (Moore) W.; ed. pub. schs.; m. Margaret Sophia Holmes, Nov. 1884; 1 dau., Mrs. Ethelwyn Jarnagin. In banking business, Los Angeles, since 1906; chmn. board Citizens Nat. Trust & Savings Bank; pres. Olig Crude Oil Co., Munroe Oil Co., Business Corners Co.; dir. Buena Vista Oil Co. Police commr. City of Los Angeles, 1906-10. Republican. Protestant. Clubs: California, Los Angeles Athletic, Los Angeles Country, Beach. Home: 109 Fremont Pl. Office: 736 South Hill St., Los Angeles, Calif.* Died May 16, 1943.

WALKER, Hugh Kelso, clergyman; b. Rogersville, Hawkins County, Tenn., Dec. 5, 1861; s. Joseph Rogers and Mary Ann (Lynn) W.; student Sweetwater (Tenn.) Coll.; grad. Auburn Theol. Sem., 1884; D.D., U. of Ga., 1899; LL.D., Occidental, 1912; m. Elizabeth Moyers Moore, June 5, 1884 (died Dec. 19, 1936); children—Wm. Moore, Hugh K., Allie Rhea, Elizabeth Stirling, Mary Lynn, Jane S., Ruth Rankin, Joseph Rogers, Margaret Eleanor; m. 2d, Mrs. Jane E. Fullwood, 1938 (died June 30, 1943). Ordained to the Presbyterian ministry, 1884; pastor Wilmington,

Delaware, 1884-85, Valatic, New York, 1885-87, Marietta, Georgia, 1887-91, 1st Church, Birmingham, Ala., 1891-94, Central Ch., Baltimore, Md., 1894-98, Immanuel Ch., Los Angeles, Calif., 1898-1912, First Church, Atlanta, Ga., 1912-14, First Church, Long Beach, Calif., 1914-17, First Church, Los Angeles, Nov. 1, 1917 to Nov. 1, 1937; now pastor emeritus Immanuel Presbyn. Ch., Los Angeles. President Anti-Saloon League of Southern Calif., 12 yrs. Trustee Occidental College, 40 years; pres. bd. of trustees, 14 years; dir. San Francisco Theol. Sem., 42 years.; trustee nat. bd. of Christian Endeavor Soc.; delegate from U.S.A. Presbyterian Church World's Missionary Conference, 1910; member General Assembly's dept. of Ch. Coöperation and Union; del. Nat. Organic Union and World Conf. on Faith and Order; moderator Presbyn. Church, U.S.A., 1928; mem. Gen. Council Presbyn. Ch., 1928-31; del. World's Sunday Sch. Conv., Jerusalem, 1904. Pres. Olmsted Memorial, Presbyn. Hosp. Mem. Hist. Soc. of Southern Calif., S.R. Mason (K.T.). Club: University. Home: 1131 W. Adams Blvd., Los Angeles. Died Sept. 19, 1949.

WALKER, J(ames) Herbert, business exec.; b. Detroit, Mich., Mar. 9, 1890; s. Herbert Campbell and Leila Ellen (Carter) W.; student Detroit Univ. Sch., 1902-07; B.M.E., Univ. of Mich., 1911, M.E., 1937; m. Gertrude Morley, Apr. 14, 1914; children—James Herbert, Morley. Entire career with The Detroit Edison Co. and predecessor cos., in charge of district heating, 1918-45 also various engring. and administrative assignments; asst. to gen. mgr., 1943-45, since 1945. Mem. Am. Soc. Mech. Engrs., Am. Soc. Heating and Ventilating Engrs., Instn. of Heating and Ventilating Engrs. (British), Nat. Dist. Heating Assn. (past pres., hon. mem.), Sigma Xi, Tau Beta Pi. Presbyterian. Clubs: Detroit, Detroit Athletic. Author: (with John W. James and the late John R. Allen) Heating and Air Conditioning (6 editions 1918-47). Contbr. Ency. Brit.; author numerous engring. papers and articles in tech. mags. Home: 432 Arlington Rd., Birmingham, Mich. Office: 2000 Second Av., Detroit 26, Mich. Died Dec. 1, 1947.

WALKER, James J., ex-mayor; b. Greenwich Village (N.Y. City), 1881; ed. Coll. of St. Francis Xavier; LL.B., New York Law Sch., 1912; m. Janet Allen, 1912 (divorced 1933); m. 2d, Betty Compton, 1933 (divorced 1941). Admitted to N.Y. bar, 1912, and practiced in N.Y. City; was mem. N.Y. Senate from 12th Dist. (majority leader); mayor of New York, 2 terms, 1925-33, resigned Sept. 1, 1932; indsl. arbiter N.Y. Cloak and Dress Industry, 1940-45. Democrat. Catholic. Died Nov. 18, 1946.

WALKER, John Baldwin, surgeon; b. Lodi, N.J., Jan. 16, 1860; s. Avery Skinner and Rosanna (Baldwin) W.; A.B., Harvard, 1884, M.D., 1888; post-grad. work in Vienna, Munich, Paris, London and Berlin, 1890-93; Sc.D., Amherst Coll.; m. Mai Elmendorf Hackstaff, June 22, 1910. House surgeon, Boston City Hosp., 1888-89; instr. in surgery, N.Y. Polyclinic Med. Sch. and Hosp., 1894-97; asst. surgeon, 1894-1902, asso. surgeon, 1902-09, instr. operative surgery, 1897-1910, prof. clin. surgery since 1910, Coll. Phys. and Surg. (Columbia); consulting surgeon Manhattan State and Bellevue hosps., Hosp. for the Ruptured and Crippled. V.p. Eugene A. Hoffman Estate. Mem. A.M.A., Am. Coll. Surgeons, Am. Surg. Assn., Med. Soc. State of N.Y., New York County Med. Soc., New York Surg. Soc., New York Acad. Medicine, Société Internationale de Chirurgie, New England Soc., S.R., Soc. Colonial Wars, Am. Bible Soc. Trustee Bard Coll., City Mission, Home for Old Men and Aged Couples. Republican. Episcopalian. Clubs: Century, University, Union, Harvard, Church, Army and Navy, Holland Lodge. Author: Vol. IX—Hernia—in Twentieth Century Practice of Medicine. Contbr. papers upon operative treatment of fractures in Trans. Am. Surg. Assn. and in various other surg. publs. Col. Med. R.C., 1917; commanding officer Base Hosp. 116, A.E.F. Awarded D.S.M. Home: 117 E. 72d St., New York, N.Y. Died Apr. 13, 1942.

WALKER, Joseph, lawyer, trustee; b. Worcester, Mass., July 13, 1865; s. Joseph Henry and Hannah Maria (Kelley) W.; A.B., Brown U., 1887; LL.B., Harvard, 1890, hon. A.M., 1890; m. Caroline, d. Walter Richmond, June 30, 1890; children—Joseph R., Richmond, George R., Mrs. Katharine Bradford, Mrs. Evelyn MacDuffie, II. Practiced, Boston, 1890-95; prin. business trustee of real estate. Mem. Sch. Com. Brookline, 1896-1902; chmn. Rep. Town Com., moderator town meeting, etc. Mem. Rep. State Com., 1901-03; mem. Mass. Ho. of Rep., 1904-11 (speaker 1909-11); Rep. candidate for gov., 1912. Changed from Rep. to Prog. party, 1913; Prog. candidate for gov., 1914. Mem. State Bd. of Charity, 1904. Unitarian. Clubs: Union (Boston), Country (Brookline). Mem. Mass. Constl. Conv., 1917, 18, 19. Author: Humanism As a Way of Life. Died Nov. 25, 1941.

WALKER, Lewis Carter; b. Stratford, Ont., Can., July 30, 1875; s. Charles and Abigail (Rice) W.; ed. Collegiate Inst. and Central Business Coll., Stratford; m. Geneva Little, Mar. 12, 1909; 1 dau., Elisabeth. Connected with Fraser & Chalmers, mfrs. of machinery, 1891-93; with Aermotor Co., Chicago, since 1893, pres. since 1919. Trustee Estate of La-Verne Noyes. Trustee Chicago Academy of Sciences; director Evanston Community Chest. Treasurer of Second Baptist Church, Chicago. Republican. Clubs: Union League, Westmoreland Country, University (Evanston). Home: 1630 Judson Av., Evanston, Ill. Office: 2500 W. Roosevelt Rd., Chicago. Died June 11, 1947.

WALKER, Meriwether Lewis, army officer; b. Lynchburg, Va., Sept. 30, 1869; s. Thomas Lindsay (M.D.) and Catherine Maria (Dabney) W.; grad. U.S. Mil. Acad, 1893; grad. U.S. Engr. Sch., 1896, Army War Coll., 1920; m. Edith, d. Gen. A. B. Carey, Sept. 28, 1904; 1 dau., Cary Dabney (Mrs. R. B. Luckey). Commissioned additional 2d lt. Corps of Engineers, June 12, 1893; promoted through regular grades to col., July 1, 1920; col. and brig. gen. N.A., World War. Dir. Army Field Engr. Sch., 1912-14; prof. practical mil. engring., U.S. Mil. Acad., 1914-16; chief engr. Punitive Expdn. into Mexico, 1916-17; went to France as chief engr. 41st Div., Nov. 1917; prin. asst. to chief engr. A.E.F., Jan.-July 1918; dir. Motor Transport Corps, A.E.F., Aug. 1918-Aug. 1919; instr. Army War Coll., 1919-20; comdr. U.S. Engr. Sch., 1920-21; engr. of maintenance, Panama Canal, 1921-24; apptd. gov. Panama Canal, Oct. 16, 1924; promoted to brigadier general, July 1, 1927; comdg. 18th Brig., U.S. Army, Boston, Oct. 16, 1928-Aug. 16, 1933; retired Sept. 30, 1933. Decorated D.S.M. (U.S.); Officer Legion of Honor (French). Episcopalian. Home: Vineyard Haven, Mass. Died July 29, 1947.

WALKER, Nat Gaillard, architect; b. Charleston, S.C., Mar. 21, 1886; s. Henry Mazyck and Elizabeth Jenkins (Prentiss) W.; grad. Crafts Sch., Charleston, 1900; Porter Military Acad., 1903; pvt. study, University Extension; 1 yr. in England, 1913; Engineer Officers Training Sch., Belvoir, Va., 1918; m. Pauline Bradley, July 15, 1919. Architect, Rock Hill, S.C., Charlotte, N.C., 1914-24, Ft. Myers, Fla., since 1924; highway commr., State of S.C., 1921-23; president, Bayside Developers; pres. Ceiba Corp., Fort Myers, Fla.; regional dir. Am. Inst. of Architects, 1921-25; pres. Chamber of Commerce. Served as 1st lt., Engineers, 1918. Fellow Am. Inst. Architects; mem. Fla. Assn. of Architects. Club: Fort Myers Golf. Home: 2065 Coconut Dr. Office: 1614 McGregor Boulevard, Ft. Myers, Fla. Died June 10, 1946.

WALKER, Nelson Macy, army officer; b. Pittsfield, Mass., Sept. 27, 1891; s. Elliot and Alice (Macy) W.; ed. Infantry Sch., Ft. Benning, Ga., 1923-24; Command and Gen. Staff Sch., Ft. Leavensworth, Kan., 1928-30; Army War Coll., Washington, D.C., 1932-33; m. Doris Katherine Wyke, June 21, 1921; children—Perrin, Nancy Ann (twins). Commd. 2d lt. Inf., 1917, and advanced through the grades to brig. gen., Sept. 1942; with 47th Inf. France, as regimental signal officer, 1918; aide de camp to Gen. Hines, Camp Jackson, S.C., 1920; assigned to 30th Inf. at Presidio, San Francisco, 1930-32; Operations and Training Div., G-3, 1933-37; Office of Chief of Inf., Washington, D.C., 1937; plans and training officer, 15th Inf., Tientsin, China, 1937-38; prof. mil. tactics and science, Manlius Sch., Manlius, N.Y., 1938-40; Operations and Training Div., G-3, War Dept. Gen. Staff, Washington, D.C., 1940-42; hdqrs., army ground forces, Washington, D.C., 1942; assigned to 84th Inf. Div., Aug. 1942. Awarded Purple Heart. Address: 275 South St., Pittsfield, Mass. Killed in action July 9, 1944.

WALKER, Thomas Joseph, judge; b. Plymouth, Pa., Mar. 25, 1877; s. David and Ellen (Comerford) W.; student classical course Georgetown U., law course U. of Va.; m. Maude Galen, June 7, 1905. Admitted to Mont. bar, 1902, and began practice at Butte; partner of Frank C. Walker under name of Walker & Walker; pros. atty. Silver Bow County, Butte, 1906-10; mem. House of Mont. State Legislature, 1905, Senate, 1922-34; associate judge U.S. Customs Court, N.Y. City, since 1940. Democrat. Roman Catholic. Home: 1088 Park Av. Office and Chambers: 201 Varick St., New York, N.Y. Died Jan. 18, 1945.

WALKER, Willis J., lumber mfr.; b. Minneapolis, Minn., Nov. 6, 1873; s. Thomas B. and Harriet Granger (Hulet) W.; student Hamline U., 1893, U. of Minn., 1893-96; m. Alma Bennett Brooks, Oct. 27, 1897; 1 son, Leon Brooks. In lumber mfg. business since 1896; now chmn. bd. Red River Lumber Co.; pres. Shasta & Eastern Ry. Republican. Protestant. Home: 840 Powell St. Office: Monadnock Bldg., San Francisco, Calif. Died Mar. 15, 1943.

WALL, Albert Chandler, lawyer; b. Kingston, N.J., Jan. 24, 1866; s. Edward and Sara (Berry) W.; grad. Stevens Sch., Hoboken, N.J., 1882; A.B., Princeton, 1886, A.M., 1889; studied Columbia Law Sch.; m. Maria Carey, Apr. 30, 1896; children—Mrs. Josephine W. Gibson, Albert Carey. Admitted N.J. bar, 1890, and began practice at Jersey City, N.J.; mem. Wall, Haight, Carey & Hartpence since 1920; dir. and gen. counsel Federal Ins. Co.; dir. Prudential Ins. Co. of America, Commercial Trust Co. of N.J. Mem. Am. Bar Assn., State Bar Assn., N.J. (ex-pres.). Episcopalian. Clubs: Essex County Country; University (New York). Home: Llewellyn Park, West Orange, N.J. Office: 15 Exchange Pl., Jersey City, N.J. Died May 3, 1945.

WALL, Alexander James, librarian; b. New York, N.Y., Oct. 25, 1884; ed. high sch. and spl. courses in French and Spanish; m. Lillian B. Hashagen, Nov. 28, 1906; 1 son, Alexander J. Began in library work, 1898; librarian, New York Hist. Soc., 1921-37, dir. since 1937, also sec. bd. trustees and editor Quarterly Bull., 1917-36. Mem. Am. Hist. Assn., A.L.A., Bibliog. Society of America (treas. since 1942), N.Y. Hist. Assn., Fla. Hist. Soc., N.Y. Library Club, Am. Antiquarian Soc., Soc. of Am. Archivists, Am. Assn. of Museums. Pres. Buck Hill Art Assn., 1933-39, Early Am. Industries Assn., 1941-42. Associate in history, Columbia, since 1942. Trustee Lynbrook Bd. of Edn., 1926-36; v.p. Associated Sch. Bds., State of N.Y., 1929-31. Member Society of Friends. Clubs: Salmagundi (corresponding secretary since 1942), Grolier. Wrote: List of New York Almanacs (1694-1850), 1921; Sketch of Samuel Loudon (1727-1813), 1922; Books on Architecture Printed in America (1775-1830), 1925; Wax Portraiture, a contribution towards the study of wax work done in America, 1925; The Story of the Convention Army (1777-1783), 1927; Sketch of the Life of Horatio Seymour (1810-1886), 1929; The Story of Time Stone Farm, 1936; American Genealogical Research, Its Beginning and Growth, 1912. Home: 35 W. 81st St., New York, N.Y.; also Buckhill Falls, Pa. Office: 170 Central Park W., New York 24, N.Y. Died Apr. 15, 1944.

WALL, Edward Everett, civil engr.; b. Cambridge, Saline County, Mo., Aug. 15, 1860; s. John and Mary Brown (Gault) W.; C.E., U. of Mo., 1884, LL.D., 1935; m. Jessie Towne, Feb. 20, 1901. Engaged in ry. surveys and constrn., in Kan., Mo. and Neb., 1885-88; U.S. asst. engr. on secondary triangulation of upper Mo. River, 1889; municipal engring. and contracting, St. Louis, 1890-95; engr. in charge of sewer constrn. and reconstruction, St. Louis, 1895-1903, continuing as prin. asst. engr., Water Dept., 1903-06, asst. water commr., 1906-11, water commr., rebuilding and modernizing Water Works, 1911-25; dir. pub. utilities, 1925-26 and 1933-41; cons. engr., 1926-33. Designed supplementary water works for St. Louis to cost $25,000,000; designed and began construction new lighting system to cost $8,000,000. Mem. Am. Soc. Civil Engrs. (dir. 1918-20; v.p. 1921-22; hon. mem. since Oct. 1938), Am. Water Works Assn. (hon. mem. since 1936), St. Louis Inst. Cons. Engrs. (v.p. 1927; pres. 1933), St. Louis Acad. of Science, Engineers Club (pres. 1909; hon. mem. since 1940), Beta Theta Pi, Tau Beta Pi. Awarded Thomas Fitch Rowland prize, 1908, by Am. Soc. C.E., for best paper of the year. Mason. Clubs: Noonday, Circle. Author: Engineers, Engineering and Some Vagaries, 1931; Literary Productions of Two Engineers, 1940. Address: 5361 Pershing Av., St. Louis, Mo. Died June 26, 1944.

WALL, Frank Jerome, ry. official; b. Hartford, Conn., May 8, 1886; s. Jeremiah and Mary Ellen (Harvey) W.; student Yale, 1903-04; m. Anna May Marley, Apr. 14, 1915. Began as clerk with N.Y., N.H.&H. R.R., 1905; agt. later supt. of same, 1912-20, asst. to v.p., 1920-30, gen. traffic mgr. and v.p. since 1930; v.p. and dir. New Eng. Steamship Co., New Eng. Transportation Co.; Fruit Growers Express Co. Mem. Soc. of Naval Architects and Marine Engrs. Clubs: Algonquin, Braeburn, The Country (Boston); Quinnipiack (New Haven); New Haven Country. Home: 250 Beacon St. Office: South Station, Boston, Mass. Died Nov. 18, 1947.

WALLACE, Benjamin Bruce, tariff expert; b. Wooster, O., Dec. 16, 1882; s. James (pres. Macalester Coll. 1894-1906) and Janet M. (Davis) W.; B.A., Macalester Coll., St. Paul, Minn., 1902; 1st Rhodes scholar from Minn. at Oxford U., 1904-07; Ph.D. in Polit. Science, U. of Wis., 1912; m. Katharine Seelye (instr. U. of Ill.), June 1922; married 2d, Leta Brown Wright, November, 1945. Teacher, Macalester Acad., 1902-04, Wooster Coll., 1907-08, Princeton, 1910-11, U. of Mich., 1911-12, Northwestern U., 1913-18, Georgetown Sch. of Foreign Service, 1925-29; spl. expert U.S. Tariff Commn., 1918, chief div. of internat. relations, 1921-28 and 1933-38; mem. Kemmerer Commn. and adviser to ministry of finance of Nat. Govt. of China, 1929-31; office of economic adviser, Dept. of State, 1931-32; adviser to U.S. Tariff Commn. on internat. trade policies, 1938. Mem. Am. Polit. Science Assn., Am. Econ. Assn., Acad. Polit. Science. Presbyterian. Club: Cosmos. Address: U.S. Tariff Commission, Washington 25, D.C. Died Jan. 5, 1947.

WALLACE, Charles Hodge, surgeon; b. Jackson County, Mo., June 24, 1858; s. Rev. Joseph William and Jessamine (Young) W.; A.B., Westminster Coll., Fulton, Mo., 1880, A.M., 1890 (Sc.D., 1900); M.D., Bellevue Hosp. Med. Coll. (N.Y.U.), 1883; m. Sarah Ketcham, Jan. 4, 1888; children—Mrs. Robert B. Orr, Hilen K. (M.D.), Charles H., Jr. (dec.). Interne Blackwell Island Hosp., 1883; asst. supt. State Hosp. No. 2 for Insane, St. Joseph, Mo., 1884-92; prof. clin. surgery, Ensworth Med. Coll., St. Joseph, Mo., 1897-1913; chief surgeon St. Joseph Light, Heat & Power Co.; chief surgeon for St.J.&G.I. Ry., 1903-19, div. surgeon, 1919-31; med. dir. St. Joseph Life Ins. Co., 1913-31; chief surgeon Union Depot Co., 1925-31; now retired. Mem. Mo. State Ho. of Rep., 1927-30. Pres. St. Joseph Park and Blvd. Commn. since 1936. Fellow Am. Coll. Surg.; mem. A.M.A., Mo. State Med. Assn. (pres. 1907-08), Western Surg. Assn. Republican. Presbyterian. Club: St. Joseph Country. Home: 605 N. 8th S. Office: 301 N. 8th St., St. Joseph, Mo. Died Aug. 27, 1946.

WALLACE, Charlton, orthopedic surgeon; b. Lexington, Ky., Oct. 18, 1872; s. John Barnes and Lucy Wilhoit (Sims) W.; grad. Transylvania U., 1894; M.D., Coll. Physicians and Surgeons (Columbia), 1898; m. 2d, Lillian Wright Dimond, Dec. 14, 1920. Prof. clin. surgery, dept. of orthopedics, Cornell U. Med. Coll., 1913-35; prof. orthopedic surgery, New York Polyclinic Med. Sch.; consulting orthopedic surgeon Hosp. for Ruptured and Crippled; surgeon in chief Reconstruction Hosp., 1918-23, St. Charles Hosp. for Crippled Children, 1908-20; now consultant St. Charles and St. Agnes hosps., Hosp. for Ruptured and Crippled; surgeon-in-chief, N.Y. State Reconstruction Home, West Haverstraw, N.Y., 1929-40; chmn. Med. Adv. Bd. No. 18, Selective Service, and surgeon (res.) U.S. Public Health Service; cons. orthopedic surgeon Stamford, Conn. Diplomate, Am. Acad. Orthopedic Surgeons; fellow Am. Coll. Surgeons; mem. Am. Orthopedic Assn., New York Acad. Medicine, N.Y. County Med. Soc., A.M.A., Nu Sigma Nu, Kappa Alpha (Southern). Democrat. Address: 140 E. 54th St., New York 22, N.Y. Died Aug. 16, 1946.

WALLACE, George Barclay, prof. pharmacology; b. Detroit, Mich., Sept. 21, 1874; s. Hugh W. and Catherine (Barclay) W.; U. of Ore., 1890-92; M.D., U. of Mich., 1897; hon. A.M., U. of Mich., 1935; hon. Sc.D., N.Y.U., 1941; m. Georgina Burns, 1912; children—Craig, Virginia. Prof. emeritus pharmacology, Univ. and Bellevue Hosp. Med. Coll. (N.Y.U.). Editor, Jour. Pharm. and Exptl. Therapy, 1943-46. Maj. M.C., 1917-19; served as director A.R.C. Hosp. 1, in France; col. Med. R.C. Mem. Soc. Exptl. Biology and Medicine (pres. 1921-23), Harvey Soc. (pres. 1915-17), Am. Physiol. Soc., Am. Soc. Biol. Chemistry, Am. Pharmacol. Soc. (pres. 1929-31), A.M.A., N.Y. Acad. Medicine (trustee, 1925-28), A.A.A.S., Am. Soc. Naturalists, Am. Soc. Anaestetists (hon.), Nu Sigma Nu, Sigma Xi. Decorated by Chinese govt. Republican. Presbyterian. Club: Century. Contbr. to med. and scientific jours. Home: 145 E. 54th St., New York, N.Y. Died Jan. 15, 1948.

WALLACE, Oates Charles Symonds, clergyman; b. Canaan, N.S., Nov. 28, 1856; s. William John and Rachel Louisa Harris (Witter) W.; A.B., Acadia U., N.S., 1883; A.M., 1889; A.M., McMaster Univ., Ont., 1894; D.D., Acadia, 1897; LL.D., Mercer University, Ga., 1897, Queen's, Can., 1903, McMaster, 1909; D.Litt., Acadia Univ., 1926; m. Leonette Moore Crosby, May 30, 1885 (died June 2, 1902); children—Rachel Leonette, Oates Crosby Saunders; m. 2d, Frances Moule Wells, June 30, 1904 (died May 20, 1917); m. 3d, Helen Moore, d. of Rev. John Wright Moore, of Folkestone, Eng., Mar. 2, 1919. Country schoolmaster at 15; home missionary preacher at 17; ordained Bapt. ministry, 1885; pastor First Ch., Lawrence, Mass., 1885-91, Bloor Street Ch., Toronto, Can., 1891-95; chancellor McMaster U., 1895-1905; pastor First Ch., Lowell, Mass., 1905-08, First Ch., Baltimore, 1908-13, Westmount Bapt. Ch., Montreal, Can., 1913-21, Eutaw Pl. Bapt. Ch., Baltimore, Md., 1921-35, pastor emeritus since Jan. 1, 1936. Author: Life of Jesus; What Baptists Believe; Looking Towards the Heights; Clover, Brier, and Tansy; As Thorns Thrust Forth; Pastor and People. Editor: From Montreal to Vimy Ridge and Beyond. Was editorial writer Am. Bapt. Publ. Soc. many yrs. Address: 2223 Sulgrave Av., Baltimore 9. Died Aug. 29, 1947; buried in Mount Pleasant Cemetery, Toronto, Ont., Can.

WALLENIUS, Carl Gideon (wäl-lĕn'yŭs), theologian; b. Stockholms län, Sweden, Dec. 28, 1865; s. Carl and Gustava Elizabeth (Bjorklund) W.; grad. Collegiate Sch., Visby, Gottland, 1886; student Upsala U., 1 yr.; D.D., Northwestern U., 1913; m. Hilda Louise Johnson, Oct. 25, 1894; children—Irene (Mrs. C. Olcen), Carl, Elsa, Eugene, Henry. Prof. theology and Swedish lang., Swedish Theol. Sem., Evanston, Ill., 1889-1906, pres., 1909-18; later pastor Bethany M.E. Ch., Chicago; pres. Wesley Acad. and Theol. Sem., Evanston, Ill., 1924-31; pastor of Emmanuel M.E. Ch., Evanston, since 1931. In pastoral work, 1906-09; asso. editor Sändebudet (official organ Swedish Meth. Ch.), 1901-03. An organizer, and pres. 1910-12, sec. 1912-14, Swedish Hist. Soc. America. Republican. Decorated Royal Order of North Star (Swedish), 1929. Author: Swedish Methodism in America (in the Swedish), 1895. Address: 1605 Ridge Av., Evanston, Ill. Died Jan. 14, 1947.

WALLER, Willard Walter, sociologist; b. Murphysboro, Ill., July 30, 1899; s. Elbert and Margaret Dora (Clendenin) W.; A.B., U. of Ill., 1920; M.A., U. of Chicago, 1925; Ph.D., U. of Pa., 1929; m. Josephine Wilkins, Aug. 13, 1929; children—Peter, Bruce, Suzanne. Reporter, Evansville (Ind.) Courier, 1920; teacher Latin and French, Morgan Park Mil. Acad., 1920-26; instr. sociology, U. of Pa., 1926-29; asst. prof. U. of Neb., 1929-31; prof., Pa. State Coll., 1931-37; asso. prof. Barnard Coll., Columbia U., since 1937. Served in U.S.N.R.F., 1918. Mem. Am. Sociol. Soc., Eastern Sociol. Soc. (pres. 1940). Author: The Old Love and the New, 1930; The Sociology of Teaching, 1932; The Family, 1938; War and the Family, 1940; War in the Twentieth Century, 1940; The Veteran Comes Back, 1944. Contbr. Am. Sociol. Rev., Am. Jour. of Sociology, Saturday Rev. of Lit., Readers' Digest, Ladies Home Journal. Home: 366 Owen Av., Fairlawn, N.J. Office: Columbia University, New York, N.Y. Died July 26, 1945.

WALLIN, Van Arthur, mfr. b. Saugatuck, Mich., Aug. 10, 1866; s. Franklin Bogue and Orcelia (Tanner) W.; grad. high sch., Saugatuck, 1881, high sch., Grand Rapids, Mich., 1883; m. Elizabeth Galt Whittelsey, June 21, 1893; children—Franklin Whittelsey, Orcelia Elizabeth (Mrs. Harry A. Torson). With Wallin Leather Co., Grand Rapids, 1883-1918, pres. 1905-18; pres. Tanners Council of America, hdqrs. Washington, D.C., 1917, 18, representing entire tanning industry of U.S., World War; dir. Am. Hair & Felt Co., Chicago, and allied organizations; Nat. Retarder Co. and Dry-Zero Corp.; owner of Wallinwood Farms, Jenison, Mich. Republican. Conglist. Mason (K.T., Shriner). Club: Union League (Chicago). Home: Jenison, Mich. Office: Merchandise Mart, Chicago, Ill. Died Aug. 24, 1942.

WALSH, Arthur, exec. v.p. Thomas A. Edison, Inc.; b. Newark, N.J., Feb. 26, 1896; s. Michael Joseph and Mary Ann (Shane) W.; ed. Newark pub. schs. and by private tutor; New York U. Sch. of Commerce; m. Agnes Mulvey, June 8, 1920; 1 dau., Barbara Louise (Mrs. Millard Carnrick, Jr.) Recording violinist for Thomas A. Edison, 1915; successively advertising mgr., v.p. and gen. mgr. phonograph div., Thomas A. Edison, Inc., 1924-31, vice-president on general staff and director since 1931; served as New Jersey director Federal Housing Adminstrn., 1934-35, dept. adminstr., Washington, D.C., later asst. adminstr., 1935-38; pres. and dir. Edison-Splitdorf Corp., Edison Wood Products, Inc., Thomas A. Edison of Can., Ltd., Ediphone Corp. Dir. Thomas A. Edison, Ltd., of London, 1938. Apptd. U.S. Senator, Nov. 26, 1943 to serve until Dec. 7, 1944. Charter trustee, Rutgers U., 1945. Commr. Port of N.Y. Authority, 1943. Mem. N.J. Workmen's Compensation Investigation Commn. Dir. Am.-Russian C. of C., 1943. Mem. N.J. Bd. of Regents, 1941-42. Served in U.S. Marine Corps during World War I; lt. U.S.N.R., 1929-32; col. N.J. Nat. Guard, 1941. Mem. Nat. Assn. Mfrs. (dir.; v.p., 1946), Alpha Kappa Psi, Beta Gamma Sigma. Democrat. Roman Catholic. Elk. Clubs: Baltusrol Golf (Springfield, N.J.); Essex (Newark, N.J.); Traffic, Metropolitan (New York, N.Y.). Contbr. to business papers. Home: 332 Redmond Rd. Office: West Orange, N.J. Died Dec. 13, 1947.

WALSH, Basil Sylvester, insurance; b. Phila., Pa., June 13, 1878; s. Daniel John and Mary E. (O'Connor) W.; ed. pub. schs., Phila.; m. Margaret A. Howlett, Mar. 1, 1905; children—Basil Francis (dec.), Ann (dec.), Daniel John, William David, Margaret May. Entered office Daniel J. Walsh's Sons, 1895, treas. since 1910; pres. Home Life Ins. Co. of America since 1912, Mutual Guarantee Building & Loan Assn., City Investment Co., Urbaine Corp.; v.p. and treas. Glen Willow Ice Mfg. Co. Mem. Cath. Philopatrian Lit. Inst. Republican. Catholic. Clubs: Seaview Golf (Absecon, N.J.); Phila. Country, Penn Athletic, Germantown Cricket, Bala Golf, Downtown, Friendly Sons of St. Patrick (Phila.). Home: City and Maple Aves., Bala Cynwyd, Pa. Office: 504 Walnut St., Philadelphia, Pa. Died Oct. 9, 1943.

WALSH, Catherine Shellew; b. Dungarvan, Waterford, Ireland, June 20, 1882; d. Declan Andrew and Catherine (Shelloe) Walsh; came to U.S., 1891; ed. grammar and high sch.; Quincy, Mass., Pace & Pace Inst., Boston and by pvt. tutors; unmarried. Accountant R. E. Foy & Co., Quincy, Mass., 1904-07; office mgr. A. E. Hurlburt, Boston, 1908-16; chief accountant Lucien Boomer Hotel Co., N.Y. City, 1917-19; resident auditor United Hotels Co., 1919-20; office mgr. Hotel Devon, N.Y. City, 1920-25; publ. accountant, Miami, Fla., 1925-29; owner and dir. Walsh Sch. of Business Science, Miami, since 1927. Dir. Opera Guild of Miami; vice-pres. Miami Civic Music Assn.; regional chairman Zonta Internat.; treas. board of trustees Dade County Fedn. of Women's Clubs. Mem. bd. dirs. Miami Y.W.C.A. (treas.), Travelers Aid Soc. (v.p.). Mem. Fla. Inst. Accountants, Bus. and Professional Women's Club. Pi Rho Zeta International (grand 1st v.p.). Catholic. Clubs: Zonta of Miami (founder-pres.). Home: 1005 Brickell Av. Office: Professional Bldg., Miami, Fla. Died Oct. 27, 1944.

WALSH, Charles Clinton, retired banker, author; b. Kirkwood, Warren County, Ill., May 29, 1867; s. James B. and Katherine (Long) W.; desc. of Revolutionary ancestry; grad. Monticello (Ill.) High Sch., 1886 (valedictorian); LL.B., with honors, U. of Mich., 1893; m. Emma Farnsworth, June 11, 1890; 1 dau., Gladys A. (wife of Maj. Mark R. Woodward). Teacher pub. schs., 1886-91; admitted to Tex. bar, 1893, and practiced as mem. firm Harwood & Walsh, at Gonzales, Tex., until 1904; banking business, 1904-38; associated with George W. Hay in organizing chain of banks in North Tex., consisting of Farmers Nat. Bank of Van Alstyne, Allen State Bank, Melissa State Bank, Tom Bean State Bank and First Nat. Bank of Franklin, serving as pres. Van Alstyne Bank; disposed of stock in these instns., 1907, and moved to San Angelo, organizing San Angelo Bank & Trust Co., pres. 7 yrs., pres. its successor, Central Nat. Bank of San Angelo, 1914-25; chmn. bd. and federal reserve agt. of Federal Reserve Bank of Dallas, 11th Dist., 1925-38; retired from banking and now devotes his time to completing manuscripts on folklore and pioneer history of the Southwest; currently engaged in writing the history of the formative years of Southern Meth. Univ. of Dallas, Tex. Active in promotion agrl., live stock and other interests; originator of plan to concentrate wool and mohair of West Tex. in warehouses and selling in pools; organizer Wool Growers' Central Storage Co., the pioneer wool coöp. orgn. in Tex., making San Angelo the largest inland wool and mohair market in the world; organized and was chmn. bd. Security Bldg. & Loan Assn. of San Angelo; a founder, 1915, of W. Texas Chamber Commerce (pres. 1923-24). Del. Gen. Conf. M.E. Church, S., Hot Springs, Ark., 1922, and mem. unification Commn., 1924, resulting in the union of M.E. Ch. in U.S.A. and M.E. Ch., S.; treas. W. Tex. Conf. 17 yrs., treas. Bd. of Missions and sec.-treas. Superannuate Endowment Fund; mem. of original commn. to locate and establish Southern Meth. U., Dallas (1910-12), and trustee of Univ., 1910-25. Mem. English-Speaking Union, Dallas Hist. Soc., Texas State Hist. Soc. (life). Democrat. Mason (32°, K.T., Shriner). Clubs: Dallas Writers, Critic. Author: The Student's Quiz Book, 1892-94; (verse) Early Days on the Western Range, 1917; The Nester and the Tenderfoot, 1918; America's Tribute to Great Britain, 1918; How Uncle Sam Got Ki Bill's Goat, 1919; Heavenly Mansions, 1920; The Old Quartette, 1923; The Passing of the Years, 1928; Memories of '93, 1928. Known as "Poet Laureate of the Southwest." Home: 3606 Crescent Av. Address: Southern Methodist Univ. Substation, Box 219, Dallas 5, Tex. Died Dec. 20, 1943.

WALSH, David Ignatius, U.S. senator; b. Leominster, Mass., Nov. 11 1872; s. James and Bridget (Donnelly) W.; A.B., Holy Cross Coll., Worcester, Mass., 1893; LL.B., Boston U. Law Sch., 1897; LL.D., Holy Cross College, Notre Dame University, Georgetown University, Fordham University, Boston Univ.; unmarried. Admitted to Massachusetts bar, 1897; chmn. Dem. Town Com., Clinton, 1898-1900; moderator town meetings, 1898, 99, 1900; mem. Mass. Ho. of Rep., 1900-01 (author of laws requiring the state to pay wages weekly to its officers, and regulating unemployment of laborers on public works); removed to Fitchburg, 1907; Dem. candidate for lt.-gov. of Mass., 1911 (defeated); lt.-gov., 1913; gov. of Mass., 1914, 15; mem. Mass. Constl. Conv., 1917; U.S. senator from Mass., 1919-25, and for unexpired term, 1926-29; reëlected for terms 1929-47. Del.-at-large Dem. Nat. Conv. 9 times to 1944. Home: Clinton, Mass. Office: Kimball Bldg., Boston, Mass. Died June 11, 1947.

WALSH, Edward J., univ. pres.; b. Brooklyn, N.Y., 1877; s. Edward and Bridget A. (Hamilton) W.; ed. St. John's Coll. (now Univ.), Brooklyn, and St. Vincent's Sem., Phila.; LL.D., Manhattan Coll.; Litt.D., St. Francis' Coll., 1935. Entered Congregation of Mission (Vincentian Fathers); ordained R.C. priest, 1901; teacher languages, St. Vincent's Sem., 1901-03; teacher English lit., ecclesiastical history and sacred eloquence, Niagara U., 1903-07; v.p. Niagara U., 1907-08, pres., 1908-12; superior and dir. missions and retreats, St. Vincent's Mission House, Springfield, Mass., 1912-26; v.p. St. John's U., 1926-35, pres., 1935-42; pres. emeritus since 1942. Lectured widely on edn., lit., pub. questions and religion, and contbr. many treatises on such subjects. Address: 75 Lewis Av., Brooklyn, N.Y. Died Mar. 22, 1947.

WALSH, James Joseph, physician; b. Archbald, Pa., Apr. 12, 1865; s. Martin J. and Bridget (Golden) W.; A.B., Fordham Coll., N.Y., 1884, A.M., 1885, Ph.D., 1889; M.D., U. of Pa., 1895; univs. of Paris, Vienna, Berlin, 1895-98; LL.D., Georgetown U., 1912; Litt.D., Catholic U. of America, 1915; Sc.D., Notre Dame, 1909; D.E., U. of San Francisco, 1930; m. Julia H. Freed, 1915; children—James J., Jr., Moira. In practice at New York since 1898; prof. physiol. psychology, Cathedral Coll., New York, since 1906; cons. physician Gabriels Sanatorium. Fellow N.Y. Acad. Med.; mem. A.M.A.; N.Y. State and N.Y. County med. socs., A.A.A.S.; life mem. N.Y. Hist. Soc., Nat. Arts Club. Catholic. Knight Comdr. Papal Order of St. Gregory; Knight of Malta. Democrat. Author: Makers of Modern Medicine, 1907; Catholic Churchmen in Science (3 volumes), 1917; The Popes and Science, 3d edition, 1916; The Thirteenth, Greatest of Centuries, 10th edit., 1937; Old Time Makers of Medicine, 1911; Education, How Old the New, 1910; Modern Progress and History, 1912; The Century of Columbus, 1914; History of Medicine in New York (5 vols.), 1919; Medieval Medicine, 1920; Health Through Will Power, 1920; Religion and Health, 1920, Success in a New Era, 1919; What Civilization Owes to Italy, 1923; Cures, 1923; Psychotherapy, 1912; World's Debt to the Catholic Church, 1924; Safeguarding Children's Nerves (with Dr. John Foote), 1924; Eating and Health, 1925; Spiritualism a Fake (contains also Spiritualism a Fact, by Hereward Carrington), 1925; Our American Cardinals, 1926; The World's Debt to the Irish, 1926; These Splendid Priests, 1926; These Splendid Sisters, 1926; Laughter and Health, 1927; The Church and Healing, 1928; History of Nursing, 1929; Priests and Long Life, 1927; Mother Alphonsa, 1930; Sex Instruction, 1931; A Golden Treasury of Medieval Literature, 1931; American Jesuits, 1934; Education of the Founding Fathers of the Republic, 1935; High Points of Medieval Culture, 1937. Co-author: Essays in Pastoral Medicine, Makers of Electricity. Trustee Catholic Summer Sch. of America. Address: 344 W. 72d St., New York, N.Y. Died Feb. 28, 1942.

WALSH, Joseph, judge; b. Boston (Brighton), Mass., Dec. 16, 1875; s. Michael H. and Abby A. (Norton) W.; ed. pub. schs., Falmouth, Mass., and Boston U. Law Sch.; m. Katherine E. Duff, Sept. 12, 1901; children—Joseph N., Donald V., Arthur C. Admitted to Mass. bar, 1906, and practiced in New Bedford. Mem. 64th to 67th Congresses (1915-23), 16th Mass. Dist.; resigned Aug. 1922, and apptd. justice Superior Court of Mass. Republican. Home: 266 Hawthorn St., New Bedford, Mass. Died Jan. 12, 1946.*

WALSH, John, lawyer; b. Two Rivers, Wis., Jan. 15, 1872; s. Felix and Bridget (Comer) W.; grad. high sch., Two Rivers; student U. of Wis., 1893-95; m. Ethel A. Staveley, Feb. 6, 1899 (died May 3, 1938); 1 dau., Elizabeth (wife of Augustus C. Long); m. 2d, Edna Preble Jones, June 28, 1939. Began practice at Kewanee, Wis., 1895; judge Municipal Court, Kewanee County, Wis., 1898-1901; moved to Washburn, Wis., 1901; special counsel Fed. Trade Commn., 1915-17; first chief counsel, same, 1917-19; special asst. atty. gen. U.S., 1920. Successfully tried suits that tested constitutionality of the Federal

Trade Commn. Mem. Dist. of Columbia Bar Assn. Formerly trustee Belleau Wood Memorial Assn.; formerly dir. Nat. Fedn. Big Brothers and Big Sisters. Del. Dem. Nat. Convs., 1908, 12, 20, 36, 40 (seconded nomination for President Woodrow Wilson, 1912, of Franklin D. Roosevelt, 1936, 40). Club: Chevy Chase. Catholic. Home: 2311 Connecticut Av. Office: 1317 F St. N.W., Washington, D.C. Died Aug. 25, 1941.

WALSH, William Francis, prof. law; b. Hancock, Mass., May 6, 1875; s. Michael and Ellen (Robinson) W.; A.B., Williams, 1898, LL.D., 1932; LL.B., New York U., 1900, J.D., 1905; m. Nina Ashurst, Dec. 26, 1907 (died 1919); children—William Ashurst, Thomas Ashurst, Nina Walsh Hartman, David; m. 2d, Margaret Sefton, Aug. 16, 1923; 1 son, John Sefton. Admitted to N.Y. bar, 1900, practiced until 1916; lecturer Law Sch., New York U., 1902-05, asst. prof., 1905, prof. law since 1906. Mem. Phi Gamma Delta, Phi Beta Kappa. Dem. Roman Catholic. Club: Longshore (Westport). Author: Treatise on the Law of Real Property, 1915; Outlines of the History of English and Am. Law, 1923; The Law of Property, 2d edit., 1927; Treatise on Equity, 1930; Future Estates in New York, 1931; History of Anglo-Am. Law (2d edit., 1932) A Treatise on Mortgages, 1934; Commentaries on Property (2 vols.) 1946; New York Law, 1946. Compiler: Select Cases in the Law of Real Property, 1906, 23, 31, 39; Cases on Equity, 1937; Cases on Mortgages, 1941. Home: Greens Farms Rd., Westport, Conn. Died Sep. 15, 1946.

WALSH, William Thomas, author; born Waterbury, Conn., Sept. 11, 1891; s. William Thomas and Elizabeth Josephine (Bligh) W.; A.B., Yale, 1913; Litt.D., Fordham University, 1933; m. Helen Gerard Sherwood, May 25, 1914; children—Elizabeth, Jane Mary (Mrs. Francis J. Close), Grace S. (Sister M. Concepta, S.M.), William T. (dec.), Helen T. (Mrs. W. H. Poisson), Peter. Newspaper reporter, 1911-17; prof. of English, Manhattanville Coll. of the Sacred Heart, N.Y., 1933-47. Awarded Laetare medal by U. of Notre Dame, 1941. Author: Isabella of Spain (biography), 1930; Out of the Whirlwind (novel), 1935; Shekels (play), 1937; Philip II (biography), 1937; Poems, 1939; Characters of the Inquisition (biography), 1940; St. Teresa of Avila (biography), 1943; Our Lady of Fátima, 1947; St. Peter The Apostle, 1948. Received Catholic Literary award, Gallery of Living Catholic Authors, 1944, for St. Teresa. Awarded Cross, Commander Order of Alfonso the Wise, by Spanish Ministry of Edn., 1944, and Grand Cross of Isabella the Catholic, 1947. Contbr. to mags. Home: 110 Beach Av., Larchmont, N.Y. Died Feb. 22, 1949.

WALTER, Frank Keller, librarian and bibliographer; born at Pt. Pleasant, Pennsylvania, July 23, 1874; son of Samuel A. and Elizabeth A. (Keller) Walter; graduate West Chester (Pa.) State Normal Sch., 1894; B.A., Haverford, 1899, M.A., 1900; student George Washington U., 1903-04; B.L.S., N.Y. State Library Sch., 1906, M.L.S., 1913; m. S. Ruth McMichael, June 25, 1907; 1 son, Richard Keller (dec.). Teacher until 1904; asst. in English and German, Haverford Coll., 1899-1900; reference asst. Brooklyn Public Library, 1906-07; director's asst., N.Y. State Library, 1907-08; v.-dir., N.Y. State Library School, 1908-19; librarian, Gen. Motors Corp., 1919-20; instr. library science, U. of Ill., 1921; asso. prof. library methods, U. of Mich., summer, 1921; univ. librarian, University of Minn., 1921-43, librarian and professor emeritus since Sept. 1943; engaged in bibliographical work since 1943; professor and head library methods department, 1922-28, director div. of library instruction, 1928-43; lecturer Univ. of Wis. Library Sch., 1922-31; lecturer Coll. of St. Catherine, St. Paul, Minn., 1930-32. Pres. N.Y. Library Assn., 1915-16, Assn. of Am. Library Schs., 1919; fellow Am. Library Inst. (sec.-treas. 1930-33); life mem. A.L.A. (council, 1912-17; editorial com., 1924-27; exec. bd., 1924-28), Assn. Coll. and Research Libraries (pres. 1939-40), Bibliog. Soc. America, Twin City Library Club, Minnesota Library Assn. (pres. 1922-23; hon. life member); mem. Library Assn. (Eng.), Assn. Am. Univ. Profs. (emeritus), Minn. Acad. of Science, Phi Beta Kappa, Pi Gamma Mu, Delta Phi Lambda (hon.); dir. Assn. Research Libraries, 1940-43. Clubs: Campus (inactive); Gown in Town (associate); Founders (Haverford Coll.); Ampersand. Author: Modern Drama and Opera (joint), Vol. 1, 1911, Vol. 2, 1915; Abbreviations and Technical Terms, 1912; Periodicals for the Small Library, 1913, 7th edit., 1938. Library Printing, 1913, 23; Bibliography (with H. B. Van Hoesen), 1928; The Library's Own Printing, 1934. Address: 1560 E. River Terrace, Minneapolis 14, Minn. Died Oct. 28, 1945.

WALTER, Herbert Eugene, biologist; b. Burke, Vt., Apr. 19, 1867; s. Augustus Porter and Betsey Ann (Brockway) W.; A.B., Bates Coll., 1892; A.M., Brown U., 1893; studied several summers, Woods Hole, Mass., 1892-1905, U. of Freiburg, Germany, 1894, 1903, Ph D., Harvard, 1906; Sc.D., Middlebury (Vt.) Coll., 1934; Sc.D., Bates Coll., 1939; m. Alice E. Hall, Aug. 25, 1896. Instr. biology, Chicago High Sch., 1894-1904; asst. prof. comparative anatomy, Brown U., 1906-13, asso. prof., 1913-23, prof., 1923-37, emeritus since 1937; instr. field zoölogy, Cold Spring Harbor, N.Y., 1906-17, asst. dir., 1917-26. Fellow A.A.A.S.; mem. Am. Soc. Naturalists, Am. Soc. Zoölogists, Am. Genetics Assn. Eugenics Research Assn., Am. Museum Natural History, Sigma Xi, Phi Beta Kappa, Am. Ornithologists Union. Republican. Unitarian. Author: The Birds of Androscoggin County, 1891; The Reactions of Planarians to Light., 1907; Genetics, 1913 (3d rev. 1938); The Human Skeleton, 1918; Biology of the Vertebrates, 1928 (revised 1939); One Innocent Abroad, 1913; also studies of Animal Life (with Worrallo Whitney and F. Colby Lucas), 1900; Wild Birds in City Parks (with wife), 1901 (many editions and revisions); Biology: The Story of Living Things (with George William Hunter and George William Hunter III), 1937. Home: 67 Oriole Av., Providence, R.I. Died Oct. 1, 1945.

WALTER, Luther Mason, lawyer; b. Blaine, Ky., Mar. 2, 1877; s. Monroe Madison and Ann (Patrick) W.; student State Coll. of Ky., 1893-95; Bachelor of English, Nat. Normal U., Lebanon, O., 1896; LL.B., Columbian (now George Washington) U., 1901, LL.M., 1902, D.C.L., 1903, M.Dip., 1904; hon. LL.D., Simpson Coll., 1939; m. Anna Bradbury, Dec. 12, 1901; children—Paul Bradbury, Helen Virginia (Mrs. Kenneth W. Munsert). Teacher pub. schs. of Ky., 1893-98; practiced law, Louisa, Ky., 1898-99; clerk U.S. Census Bureau, Washington, D.C., 1900-02; member U.S. Bd. of Pension Appeals, 1902-03; successively, atty. Inter-state Commerce Commn., spl. asst. U.S. atty. and spl. asst. atty. gen. of U.S, 1903-10; moved to Chicago, 1910; mem. firm of Walter, Burchmore & Belnap and its predecessors since 1910; trustee C.G.W. R.R., 1935-41. Asst. dir. pub. service and accounting, U.S. R.R. Administration, World War, 1918. Mem. Am., Ill. State and Chicago bar assns., Ky. Bar Assn. Republican. Methodist. Mason. Clubs: Union League, Traffic; Minocqua (Wis.) Country (pres.). Home: 6726 Euclid Av. Office: 2106 Field Bldg., Chicago, Ill. Died June 30, 1947.

WALTERS, Gus Washington, educator; b. Feb. 14, 1857; B.S., Ia. Wesleyan Coll., Mt. Pleasant, Ia., 1879, M.S., 1882. Prin. high sch., Ft. Madison, Ia., 1879-80, Whittier Coll., Salem, Ia., 1880-83; mem. faculty, Howes Acad., Mt. Pleasant, Ia., 1883-85; prof. mathematics, Ia. Wesleyan Coll., 1885-91, prof. philosophy, 1891-93, v.p., 1891-93; with Ia. State Teachers Coll. since 1895, head dept. of edn., 1916-30, became prof. edn., 1930, now retired. Dem. candidate for state supt. instrn., Ia., 1918. Methodist. Member Ia. Acad. Science, Beta Theta Pi. Mason (K.T.). Author: (outlines) Principles of Education, 1904; History of Education, 1905. Home: Cedar Falls, Ia. Died May 14, 1942.

WALTERS, Rolland J. D., educator; b. Weston, O., Oct. 1, 1878; s. Martin L. and Mary Ellen (Long) W.; A.B., Tri-State Coll., Angola, Ind., 1904; A.M., Columbia, 1914; Litt.D., U. of Denver, 1920; grad. student U. of Chicago; m. Olive A. Good, June 24, 1908; children—Newell Burl, Margaret Mary, Rolland Good. Teacher pub. schs., Wood County, O., 1898-1903; prin. high sch., Berne, Ind., 1904-05; supt. schs., Warren, Ind., 1906-11, Momence, Ill., 1911-14; dir. teachers' training, Teachers Coll., Warrensburg, Mo., 1915; supt. schs., Rocky Ford, Colo., 1915-24; prin. Training Sch. and prof. edn., U. of Denver, 1924-30; dean Coll. of Liberal Arts, same univ., 1930-41; dean emeritus and prof. of edn. emeritus since 1941. Mem. Am. Assn. Univ. Profs., Nat. Soc. Study of Edn., Colo. Edn. Assn. (past pres.), N.E.A. (life), Phi Delta Kappa, Kappa Delta Pi. Republican. Methodist. Mason. Clubs: Schoolmasters (hon.), Scholia, Buchtel. Home: 2045 S. Clarkson St., Denver, Colo.* Died Mar. 31, 1944.

WALTHER, Henry Wellman Emile, urologist; b. New Orleans, La., Sept. 7, 1888; s. Otto and Georgiana (Brown) W.; M.D., Tulane U. of La., Sch. of Medicine, 1910; m. Lilian Helen Cormier, Mar. 12, 1912 (now dec.); 1 dau., Lilian Helen (Mrs. Alfred F. Page, Jr.); m. 2d, Mrs. Elsie Cottrell Landram, Sept. 21, 1941. Interne, U.S. Marine Hospital, New Orleans, 1910; practiced New Orleans since 1910; former prof. urology, Tulane U., Loyola U. of the South, and La. State U.; chief urologist, Southern Bapt. Hosp.; former sr. visiting urologist Charity Hosp.; cons. urologist, U.S. Marine Hosp., 1918-22; urologist to Illinois Central Ry. Hosp., 1918-22; attending urologist, Hotel Dieu. V.p. 2d Pan-Am. Med. Congress. Asst. surgeon U.S. Pub. Health Service during World War I; consulting urologist Medical Advisory Board, Selective Service System, World War II. Member Board of New Orleans City Park Commrs. Pres. New Orleans Graduate Medical Assembly, 1945. Fellow Am. Coll. Surgeons. Am. Bd. Urology (Founders Group), fellow Am. Urol. Assn. (co-founder and pres. Southeastern Branch 1936), Southeastern Surg. Congress; mem. Am. Med. Assn. (in house of del. 1930-36; chmn. sect. on urology 1937), Am. Neisserian Soc., Southern Med. Assn. (chmn. sect. on urology 1923), La. State Med. Soc. (chmn. sect. on urology 1927), Orleans Parish Med. Soc. (treas. 1917-18), La. Urol. Soc. (co-founder and pres. 1941), New Orleans Social Hygiene Soc. (co-founder and pres. 1933-35); corr. member German Urol. Soc.; mem. Art Assn. of New Orleans (pres. 1930-34), Isaac Delgado Museum of Art (vice-pres.), Friends of the Howard-Tilton Memorial Library of Tulane U. (co-founder and pres. 1941), Japan Soc. of New Orleans (v.p. 1928-34), Bibliog. Soc. of America, Phi Beta Pi (supreme southern praetor 1909, editor of Quarterly 1910-12, supreme vice archon 1913), Pi Gamma Mu. Democrat. Methodist. Clubs: Armor and Arms (New York); New Orleans Country; Southern Yacht; Grolier (New York); Arts and Crafts (New Orleans). Member Lafcadio Hearn Society, Shakespeare Society, La., Soc. Print Connoisseurs, Hist. Soc. Library (Bibliotheca Waltheriana) presented to Tulane Univ. in 1942. Contbr. of many articles to the urol. lit. Inventor of numerous instruments used in urol. surgery. Home: 424 Pine St. Office: Whitney Bank Bldg., New Orleans 12, La. Died Jan. 6, 1945.

WALTON, James Henry, chemist; b. Deer Isle, Me., Feb. 26, 1878; s. James Hume and Florence Strode (Hewlett) W.; B.S., Mass. Inst. Tech., 1899; Austin traveling fellow from M.I.T., 1901-03; Ph.D., U. of Heidelberg, Germany, 1903; m. Dorothy Brockway Dana, Apr. 20, 1918; children—Marcia Dana, Judith Dana. Asst. in chemistry, U. of Ill., 1899-1900, Mass. Inst. Tech., 1900-01; instr. chemistry, 1903-06, asso., 1906-07, U. of Ill.; asst. prof. chemistry, 1907-12, asso. prof., 1912-19, prof. since 1919, U. of Wis. Commd. capt. Sanitary Corps, Sept. 20, 1917; maj. engrs., May 3, 1918; in charge training in gas defense in U.S., Sept. 1917-July 1918; 1st army gas officer, A.E.F., Aug. 1918-Jan. 1919; hon. disch., Jan. 25, 1919; lt. col. C.W. Res., May 8, 1926-May 8, 1931. Mem. Am. Chem. Soc. (ex-pres. Wis. sect.), Zeta Psi, Sigma Xi, Alpha Chi Sigma, Phi Lambda Upsilon, Scabbard and Blade. Unitarian. Club: University. Author: (with A. T. Lincoln) Elementary Quantitative Chemical Analysis, 1907; (with L. Kahlenberg) Qualitative Chemical Analysis, 1911; (with F. C. Krauskopf) A Laboratory Manual of General Chemistry, 1921; (with C. H. Sorum) Introduction to Qualitative Analysis, 1937; An Introduction to General Chemistry (with F. C. Krauskopf), 1943; numerous papers in scientific jours. Collaborated with Lt. Col. S. J. M. Auld, of Brit. Mil. Mission in preparation of 4 monographs on gas warfare, used in training troops in U.S. and in A.E.F. Home: 2122 Vilas Av., Madison, Wis. Died June 6, 1947.

WALTON, Norman Burdett, railroad exec.; b. Palmerston, Ont., Can., July 27, 1884; s. Henry and Elizabeth (Rowan) W.; ed. pub. schs., high sch. and bus. coll., Stratford, Ont.; m. Eva Tait, Dec. 5, 1911; children—Norman T., Catherine (Mrs. John D. Horn). Clerk and stenographer, Grand Trunk Ry., 1900-02, sec. to supt., 1902, telegraph operator and sec. to vice pres., Montreal, 1903-06, asst. trainmaster, Palmerston, Ont., 1906; sec. to vice pres. Great Northern Ry., St. Paul, Minn., 1907, inspector transportation, 1907; claims agent, personal injuries, Grand Trunk Ry., Toronto, 1908; sec. to gen. supt. Grand Trunk Pacific Ry., Winnipeg, 1908-10, trainmaster Wainwright, Alberta, Can., 1910, asst. and supt., Edmonton, 1911-20; asst. general supt., Prince Rupert, Can. Nat. Rys., 1920-24, gen. supt., Winnipeg, 1924-30, gen. supt. transportation, western region, 1930-36, chief of transportation, Montreal, 1936-38, vice pres. of operation, construction and maintenance, Montreal, 1938-43, exec. vice pres., Montreal, since 1943. Decorated Comdr. Order British Empire. Clubs: St. James (Montreal); Manitoba (Winnipeg); Canadian. Home: The Towers, Cote St. Luc Road. Office: 360 McGill St., Montreal, Que., Can. Died Jan. 21, 1950.

WANAMAKER, Allison Temple, physician; b. St. Martins, New Brunswick, Can., Mar. 3, 1881; s. James Frances and Cecelia Jane (Smith) W.; came to U.S., 1889, citizen, 1894; Ph.G., U. of Wash., 1901; M.D., Northwestern, 1907; m. Helen Allmond, Oct. 20, 1915; children—Alice Jane, Allison Temple. Pharmacist, 1901-03; intern Pittsburgh Hosp., 1907-08, Ill. Charitable Eye and Ear Infirmary, 1908-09; practiced in Chicago, 1909-10; moved to Seattle, Wash., 1910; cons. physician Harbor View Hosp. since 1931, Children's Orthopedic Hosp. since 1922; mem. staff Providence and Swedish hosps. since 1920. Fellow Am. Coll. Surgeons; mem. A.M.A., King County Med. Soc. (pres. 1926), Am. Laryngol., Rhinol. and Otol. Soc. (chmn. Western sect., 1931), Am. Laryngol. Soc., Pan-Am. Surg. Soc. Republican. Conglist. Mason (32°, Shriner). Clubs: University, Washington Athletic, Broadmoor Golf. Author of many papers on laryngol., rhinol. and otol. subjects; contbr. to med. publs. Home: 600 Harvard Av. N. Office: 1317 Marion St., Seattle, Wash. Died June 21, 1944; interred Acacia Mausoleum, Seattle, Wash.

WANDELL, Samuel Henry (wăn-děl'), lawyer; b. W. Monroe, Oswego County, N.Y., Apr. 19, 1860; s. William Haight and Ellen Louisa (Leonard) W.; m. Flora Gaige Hartson, Dec. 14, 1886 (died July 18, 1934); m. 2d, Mrs. Maud Oursler Hill, Apr. 23, 1940. Admitted to New York bar, October 6, 1882; asst. district attorney, Oswego County, 1882-83; practiced Syracuse (N.Y.), 1883-94; 1 yr. in Washington as counsel to corps.; in New York since 1895; became atty. Dept. of Finance, N.Y. City, 1925; asst. corp. counsel of New York City since 1929. Scribe of Tammany Soc. Mason, K.P. Presbyterian. Club: Authors. Author: The Law of Inns, Hotels and Boarding Houses, 1888; The Law Relating to Disposition of Descendants' Real Estate, 1889; The Law of the Theatre, 1891; Analytical Chart of the Law of Costs, 1891; You Should Not, 1895; The Law Relating to Public Contract Liens, 1932; Aaron Burr in Literature, 1936; Oliver Phelps, 1941; with late Justice David McAdam new edit. McAdam on Law of Landlord and Tenant, 1899 (with Meade Minnegerode) Aaron Burr (2 vols.), 1925; also writer legal and historical monographs. Home: Holley Chambers, 33 Washington Sq. W. Office: Municipal Bldg., New York, N.Y. Died Sep. 25, 1943.

WANDS, Ernest Henry; b. London, Eng.; s. Ebenezer Henry and Elizabeth (English) W.; brought to U.S. in infancy; ed. pub. schs. and by tutors at home and abroad; m. Louise Russell Welling, Jan. 26, 1911 (died Dec. 14, 1937). On editorial staff The Courier, Buffalo, 1891-96; editor and part owner The Gazette, Niagara Falls, N.Y., 1896-98; on editorial staff, The Tribune, New York, 1898-1901; foreign commr. World's Fair, St. Louis, 1901-04; commr. of U.S. to Internat. Expn., Quito, Ecuador, 1909; commr. gen. of U.S. to Internat. Agrl. Expn., Buenos Aires, 1910; financial adviser Govt. of Nicaragua, 1911-14; chmn. com. apptd. by sec. of Treasury, to return visits of delegates from West Coast countries of S.A. to Pan. Am. Financial Conf., 1916; banking and spl. financial work at home and abroad since 1916. Decorated Order of Bust of Bolivar (Venezuela), 1901. Co-founder and dir. Pan. Am. Soc. Fellow Royal Geog. Soc.; mem. geog. socs. Mexico and Peru, Newcomen Soc. of England. Republican. Episcopalian. Clubs: Metropolitan of New York, chmn. Library Com.; Metropolitan (Washington); Harvard Travelers (Boston); Union Interalliee (Paris); The Pilgrims (New York); University (Niagara Falls, N.Y.); Ends of the Earth. Home: 11 E. 68th St., New York 21, N.Y. Died May 28, 1947.

WANGENHEIM, Julius (wäng'ĕn-hīm); b. San Francisco, Calif., Apr. 21, 1866; s. Sol. and Fannie (Newman) W.; B.S., U. of Calif., 1887; m. Laura Klauber, Nov. 21, 1892; 1 dau., Alice (Mrs. George Heyneman). Bridge engr. Southern Pacific Ry., 1887-89; partner Simon Newman Co., Newman, Calif., 1889-95, Klauber-Wangenheim Co., San Diego, 1895-1903; pres. Bank of Commerce, San Diego, 1903-17; now chmn. bd. Klauber-Wangenheim Co., Southern Title and Trust Co., and chmn. finance com. First Nat. Bank. Chmn. at various times of Park Commn., City Planning Commn., Water Commn., Harbor Commission. Pres. Liberty Loan coms. for San Diego County during World War. Regent U. of Calif., 1927-28; trustee Scripps Coll., Claremont, 1925-37; pres. Alumni Assn. of U. of Calif., 1927-28. Mason. Clubs: University, Cuyamaca (San Diego); Country (Chula Vista). Home: 148 W. Juniper St. Office: Southern Title Bldg.. San Diego, Calif. Died Mar. 10, 1942.

WANNAMAKER, John Skottowe, banker, planter; b. Louisville (now St. Matthews), S.C., Sept. 25, 1869; s. Francis Marion and Eleanor Margaret (Bellinger) W.; educated in common schools and through home study; married Lillian Bruce Salley, June 24, 1896; children Lillian Mackey (dec.), Francis Marion (Mrs. Laurie E. Moore), Jennie Bruce (Mrs. John Blanton Belk), Ella Salley (Mrs. William Lambert DePass, Jr.), Frances Margaret (Mrs. W. Herbert Smith). Began as telegraph operator and railway agent at 15; long identified with mercantile and banking business and extensively engaged in farming. Made address before World's Cotton Conf., 1919, and addresses and hearings before U.S. Senate on agrl. and financial subjects (pub. in Senate documents); joint chmn. Com. of World's Requirements and Stabilizing Production and Prices, World's Cotton Conf., New Orleans, 1919, Manchester, Eng., 1921; named pres. Am. Cotton Growers at latter conf., 1921. Chmn. commn. for formation of Calhoun County, S.C., 1908-12. Mayor of St. Matthews, 1902-12. Mem. Am. Cotton Assn. (pres. since 1916); pres. S.C. Cotton Assn., 1915-19. Mem. bd. dirs. and exec. com. Chicora Coll. (Columbia, S.C.), Roosevelt Mil. Acad. (West Englewood, N.J.). Pres. S.C. Bankers Assn., 1918-19; pres. Farmers' and Taxpayers' League, 1929-30, exec. committeeman at large, 1930-40, mem. nat. com. on govt. and taxes, 1930; mem. Nat. Council of Nat. Econ. League. Adminstr. U.S. Emergency Relief Calhoun County, 1934-36. Mem. Nat. Emergency Council, 1939; co-chmn. Conf. on Internat. Interests of the South, 1940; County chmn. S.C. Council for Nat. Defense, 1941-43. Democrat. Presbyterian (elder). Mason, K.P. Author of several family genealogies. Contbr. to newspapers and mags. Home: St. Matthews, S.C. Died July 7, 1944.

WARD, Charles Howell, osteologist; b. Rochester, N.Y., Oct. 28, 1862; s. Henry Augustus and Phoebe Ann (Howell) W.; ed. Alfred U. and U. of Rochester; m. Anna T. Cheek, 1920 (dec.); 1 son, Roswell H.; m. 2d, Gertrude L. Green, Sept. 1925. In charge dept. human anatomy, Ward's Natural Science Establishment, Rochester, 1891-99; mgr. Anatomical Lab. of Chas. H. Ward, 1899-1926, pres. of same, inc., since 1926; has for many years devoted his time to the collecting and preparation anatomical specimens for ednl. purposes. Mem. A.A.A.S.; hon. mem. Rochester Dental Soc., 7th Dist. N.Y. Dental Soc.; fellow Rochester Acad. Science. Home: 598 Monroe Av. Office: 205 Main St. W., Rochester, N.Y. Died Jan. 18, 1943.

WARD, Christopher Longstreth, lawyer, author; b. Wilmington, Del., Oct. 6, 1868; s. Henry and Martha Potter (Bush) W.; A.B., Williams Coll., 1890; LL.B., Harvard U., 1893; Litt.D., U. of Del., 1934; m. Caroline Tatnall Bush, May 5, 1897; children—Christopher L., Esther (Mrs. Philip J. Kimball), Rodman, Alison (Mrs. C. Lalor Burdick). Admitted to Del. bar, 1893, and began practice at Wilmington; pres. Corp. Service Co. since 1920. Exec. chmn. Del. Tercentenary Commn.; mem. U.S. Del. Valley Tercentenary Commn. Decorated Comdr. Royal Order Vasa, 2d class, by King Gustaf V of Sweden, June 17, 1938. Mem. Hist. Soc. of Del. (pres.), Wilmington Fine Arts Soc., Soc. Colonial Wars (gov., Del.), Delta Kappa Epsilon. Clubs: University, Wilmington Country; University, Williams (New York). Author: The Triumph of the Nut, 1923; Gentleman Into Goose, 1924; Twisted Tales, 1924; Foolish Fiction, 1925; One Little Man, 1926; Starling, 1927; The Saga of Cap'n John Smith, 1928; The Dutch and Swedes on the Delaware, 1930; Strange Adventures of Jonathan Drew, 1932; A Yankee Rover, 1933; Sir Galahad and Other Rimes, 1936; New Sweden on the Delaware, 1938; Delaware Tercentenary Almanack, 1938; The Delaware Continentals, 1941. Contbr. to Saturday Rev. of Literature. Home: Bramshott, Greenville, Del. Office: 900 Market St., Wilmington, Del. Died Feb. 20, 1943.

WARD, Edward Joshua, social engr.; b. Buffalo, N.Y., Mar. 9, 1880; s. Henry (D.D.) and Basha (Barnes) W.; A.B., Hamilton Coll., 1902, A.M., 1905; grad. Auburn Theol. Sem., 1905; m. Laura E. Fairchild, June 4, 1909; 1 dau., Martha Fairchild. Dir. Broadway Recreation Field, Buffalo, 1899-1902; acting pastor Ch. of the Covenant, Washington, D.C., 1904; pastor First Presbyn. Ch., Silver Creek, N.Y., 1905-06 (gave demonstration of possibilities through opening manse as town club house, which caused first serious attempt to unite chs. in a small town so as to make some ch. bldg. available for pub., social and recreational purposes); asst. prof. history and English, Hamilton Coll., 1906-07; left ch. work and teaching to enter pub. service; supervisor Social Center Development, Rochester, N.Y., 1907-10; Wis. state adviser in civic and social center development under Extension Div., U. of Wis., 1910-15; in charge community organization work, U.S. Bur. Edn., Washington, 1916-21; teacher U.S. pub. sch. and supt. reindeer station, Wainwright, Alaska, 1921-22; sales mgr. for Va. of Keystone View Co., 1922-23; U.S. Immigration Service, immigrant inspr. at Buffalo, N.Y., 1924-26; technical adviser on immigration, U.S. Consulate, Hamburg, Germany, 1926-29; now sr. administrative asst. U.S. Dept. Justice. (The position in Rochester was first pub. position of its kind in any city; in Wis. the first of its kind in any state.) Sec. Social Center Assn. of America; chmn. Permanent Sch. Extension Com. Nat. Municipal League; dir. Playground and Pub. Recreation Assn. America; trustee Nat. Country Life Congress; mem. Am. Acad. Polit. and Social Science, Nat. Civic Secretaries' Com., Delta Upsilon; founder and sec. City Club, Rochester, 1908-10. Author: Story of the First Two Years of the Rochester Social Centers and Civic Clubs, 1909. Editor of Report of Sch. Extension Com., Nat. Municipal League, 1912; author and editor of numerous booklets and bulls. on social center development pub. by U. of Wis.; lecturer on popular and social subjects. Home: 1608 Upshur St. N. W. Address: U.S. Dept. of Justice, Washington, D.C. Died Dec. 22, 1943.

WARD, Freeman, geologist; b. Yankton, S.D., Aug. 9, 1879; s. Joseph and Sarah Frances (Wood) W.; Yankton Coll., 1898-1901, Sc.D., 1934; A.B., Yale U., 1903, Ph.D., 1908; m. Daisy Lee Eyerly, 1906; 1 dau., Sarah Wood. Asst. instr. and asst. prof. geology, Yale, 1903-15; prof. geology and head of dept., U. of S.D., also state geologist, 1915-26; prof. geology and head of dept., Lafayette Coll., since 1926. Field work Conn. State Survey, Pa. State Survey and U.S. Geol. Survey, various summers. Mem. A.A.A.S., Geol. Soc. America, Am. Assn. Petroleum Geologists, Am. Assn. Univ. Profs., Sigma Xi. Republican. Conglist. Home: 40 McCartney St., Easton, Pa. Died Sept. 14, 1943.

WARD, Gilbert Oakley, librarian, author; b. New York, N.Y., Feb. 21, 1880; s. Amasa Dwight and Mary Briggs (Oakley) W.; A.B., Columbia, 1902; grad. Pratt Inst. Library Sch., Brooklyn, N.Y., 1908; m. Gertrude Hamlin Sipher, Apr. 29, 1915; children—Wilfred Hamlin, Janet Oakley (dec.), Virginia Cranston. Asst., Pratt Inst. Free Library, 1908-09; librarian, East Tech. High Sch., Cleveland, 1909-10, supervisor high sch. branches Cleveland Pub. Library, 1911-13, tech. librarian, 1909-40, asst. to librarian since 1940. Mem. Am. Library Assn., Ohio Library Assn. (treas. 1921-23), Library Club of Cleveland and Vicinity, Cleveland Engring. Soc., Phi Beta Kappa Fraternity. Club: Professional Men's. Author: Practical Use of Books and Libraries, 1911; Suggestive Outlines and Methods for Teaching the Use of the Library, 1919; Publicity for Public Libraries, 1924. Contbr. to professional jours. and Book of the Rhymers' Club. Home: 3052 Albion Rd., Cleveland, O. Died Feb. 24, 1944.

WARD, Henry Baldwin, zoölogist; b. Troy, N.Y., Mar. 4, 1865; s. Richard Halsted and Charlotte Allen (Baldwin) W.; A.B., Williams Coll., 1885; post-grad. studies, univs. of Göttingen, Freiburg (Baden) Leipzig; A.M., Ph.D., Harvard, 1892; Sc.D., U. of Cincinnati, 1920, William Coll., 1921; LL.D., U. of Ore., 1932, U. of Neb., 1935; m. Harriet Blair, Sept. 11, 1894; children—Mrs. Cecilia Tanton, Charlotte Baldwin. Teacher of science, Troy High Sch., 1885-88; instr. morphology, U. of Mich., 1892-93; asso. prof. zoölogy, 1893-98, prof., 1899-1909, dean Coll. of Medicine, 1902-09, U. of Neb.; prof. zoölogy, U. of Ill., 1909-33, emeritus prof. of zoölogy since 1933; mem. Ill. State Bd. Mus. Advisers (sec. since 1937). In charge biol. work Mich. Fish Commn. on Lake Mich., 1894; asso. biol. survey Great Lakes, U.S. Fish Commn., since 1898; asso. editor Am. Naturalist, and of Reference Handbook of the Medical Sciences. Sec. Am. Micros. Soc., 1898-1904, pres. 1905; fellow A.A.A.S. (sec. sect. F, 1900, sec. council, 1901, gen. sec., 1902, v.p., 1905, permanent sec., 1933-37, del. to Brit. Assn. of Science Oxford, 1928); pres. Am. Soc. Zoölogists, 1912-14; pres. Am. Fisheries Soc., 1913; chmn. Nat. Wildlife Fed. Com. on Conservation Edn. since 1938; trustee Science Service, Inc., Washington; member American Med. Editors and Authors Assn., Zoöl. Soc. France, German Zoöl. Soc.; foreign mem. Imperial Soc. (Russian) for Acclimatization of Animals and Plants, Acad. Sciences of Czechoslovakia; foreign corr. mem. Venezuela Acad. Medicine; corr. mem. Royal Acad. Agr. Turin; pres. Neb. Acad. Science, 1901, Assn. Am. Med. Colls., 1908; first pres. Am. Soc. Parasitologists, 1925; mem. permanent com. on Internat. Zoöl. Congresses; gen. sec. Sigma Xi, 1895-1922, pres., 1922-24; nat. pres. Izaak Walton League America, 1928-30, mem. nat. exec. com. since 1925; mem. Delta Phi, Phi Beta Kappa, Sigma Xi, Alpha Omega Alpha. Clubs: University (Chicago); University (Urbana, Ill.); Cosmos (Washington, D.C.). Author: Quarter Century Record and History of Sigma Xi, 1913; Freshwater Biology, 1917; Parasites of the Human Eye, 1918; Introduction and Spread of the Fish Tapeworm in the United States, 1930; Foundations of Conservation Education, 1941; Medical Zoology in America's First Century, 1946. Contbr. of various monographs and papers on biol. subjects, especially animal parasites and relations of animals to disease; also articles on biology and stream pollution to Outdoor America, etc. Founder and editor Journal of Parasitology, 1914 (18 vols.). Address: Urbana, Ill. Died Nov. 30, 1945.

WARD, Henry Levi, naturalist; b. York, Livingston County, N.Y., Oct. 8, 1863; s. Henry Augustus and Phoebe Ann (Howell) W.; ed. pub. schs. and Free Acad., Rochester, N.Y., and U. of Rochester (spl.), 1883-84; m. Elva Mary Selby, Nov. 21, 1891; children—Margaret and Alice Greenleaf (twins, dec.), Marian Elizabeth (Mrs. Paul H. Gillan), Henry Selby. Collector of natural history specimens in West Indian Islands and S. America, 1879, on Calif. coast, 1883; anatomist Ward's Natural Science Establishment, Rochester, 1884-86; mem. Mexican govt. expdn. in search of the West Indian seal, 1886; osteologist of the Geog. and Exploring Commn., of the Mexican Govt., 1887-91; also mem. Mexican Commn. to Paris Expn., 1889; dir. and mgr., 1891-1902, v.p., 1901-02, Ward's Natural Science Establishment, Rochester; dir. Pub. Mus. of City of Milwaukee, 1902-20; rancher, Bellingham, Wash., 1921; dir. Kent Scientific Mus., Grand Rapids, Mich., 1922-32; dir. Neville Pub. Mus., Green Bay, Wis., 1933-41. Editor Ward's Natural Science Bulletin, 1884-86; contbr. to scientific press and publs. of various scientic assns.; pres., Wis. Acad. Sciences, Arts and Letters, 1916-18; past v.p. Wis. Nat. Hist. Soc.; charter mem. Am. Assn. Museums (pres. 1913); Wis. Archæol. Soc., Wis. Hist. Soc., Brown County Hist. Soc., Chi Psi; fellow A.A.A.S. Received silver and bronze medals as collaborator, Paris Expn., 1889; diploma as collaborator Chicago World's Fair, 1893; gold medal, Ill. Acad. Science, 1941. Home: 1345 C St., Lincoln, Neb.* Died Dec. 17, 1943.

WARD, John Chamberlain, bishop; b. Elmira, N.Y., Aug. 27, 1873; s. Hamilton and Mary Adelia (Chamberlain) W.; A.B., Harvard, 1896; B.D., Gen. Theol. Sem., 1899, S.T.D., 1923; D.D., Kenyon, 1924; unmarried. Deacon, 1899, priest, 1900, P.E. Ch. rector St. Stephen's Ch., Buffalo, 1899-1902, Grace Ch., Buffalo, 1902-21; consecrated bishop of Erie, Pa., September 22, 1921, retired June 1, 1943; member Special Committee on Budget and Program, P.E. Church. Mem. Pennsylvania State Commn. on Healing Arts, 1927; chmn. Citizens Relief Com., Erie, 1933. Chaplain 74th Inf., Nat. Guard N.Y., on Mexican border, 1916; chaplain same, local guard duty and Wadsworth, S.C., 1917; chaplain 105th Machine Gun Batt., 107th Inf., and 108th Inf., 27th Div., A.E.F., 1918, serving 9 mos. overseas; wounded in action; hon. disch. Mar. 1918, rank of capt.; later, lt. col. Reserves. Awarded D.S.C., Purple Heart (U.S.); M.C. (British). Mem. Am. Legion, Phi Beta Kappa. Republican. Clubs: Harvard, University. Home: 388 Delaware Av., Buffalo 2, N.Y. Died Feb. 15, 1949.

WARD, John William George, clergyman; b. Liverpool, Eng.; s. John George and Anne (Wilde) W.; prep. edn., Liverpool Sch. of Technology and Art; grad. with honors, Nottingham Congl. Coll., 1912; D.D. Congl. Coll. of Can., 1925; Litt.D., Olivet (Mich.) Coll., 1931; m. Alice Elsie Baskerville, July 5, 1905; children—Eileen Baskerville, Kenneth Beecher. Ordained Congl. ministry, 1911; pastor Emmanuel Ch., Bootle, Lanc., 1911-17, New Court, Tollington Park, London, 1917-24, Emmanuel Ch., Montreal, Can., 1924-28; First Ch., Detroit, Mich., 1928-32, First Presbyn. Ch., Oak Park, Ill., since Jan. 1, 1932. Spl. dramatic recitals, lecture and preaching work for Y.M.C.A., in France, 1916; hosp. orderly of British Red Cross, 1916-17; spl. preacher U.S and British Army of Occupation on Rhine; visiting preacher 3 yrs., Council of Interchange; moderator Congl. Chs. of Mich., 1931. Mem. Pi Gamma Mu (life). Club: Oak Park Rotary. Author: Problems That Perplex, 1919; Parables for Little People, 1921; Messages from Master Minds, 1922; The Master and the Twelve, 1924; Chats with Children, 1925; Cameos from Calvary, 1926; Treasure Trove for Little People, 1927; His Last Week, 1928; Portraits of the Prophets, 1930 (included in Vatican Library, Rome); The Beauty of the Beatitudes, 1931; The Rabbit and the Clock, 1932; The Tragedy and Triumph of Easter, 1933; Steering by the Stars, 1933; The Refiner's Fire, 1934; Special Day Sermons, 1935; The Glorious Galilean, 1936; Crowded Out, 1936; The God We Need, 1941; The Song of the Shepherd, 1942; More Parables for Little People, 1943. Wrote and produced Christmas pageants, Crowded Out, 1936 (which was translated into Chinese; produced in Pieping, 1940); A Syrian Romance, 1938; At Bethlehem's Inn, 1940. Known as orator and dramatic reader. Contbr. to mags.; staff writer Church Management. Writes under nom de plume, W. Hay Hardy, and his own name. Home: 1048 N. Euclid Av. Office: 931 Lake St., Oak Park, Ill. Died Sep. 29, 1945.

WARD, Lyman, educator; b. Hounsfield, Jefferson County, N.Y., Apr. 17, 1868; s. Lyman Trumbull and Freelove Stowell (Bates) W.; B.S., St. Lawrence U., 1892, D.D., 1926; m. Mary Louise, d. Hon. Geo. W. L. Smith, Oct. 5, 1898 (dec.); 1 dau., Mary Celina (Mrs. C. A. Rose). Ordained Universalist ministry, 1894; circuit rider northern N.Y., 1893-94; pastor Sawyer Memorial Ch., N.Y. City, 1895-97; founder, 1898, and prin. Southern Industrial Inst., Camp Hill. Ala., also pres. bd. trustees same; now emeritus. Rep. presidential elector, 1944; nominee for gov., 1946. Served for many yrs. as pres. Ala. state conv. of Universalists; mem. John Murray lectureship commn., serving U.S. and Can., 1920-24; apptd. by Gov. of Ala. on commn. to establish Southern Sociological Congress, 1914. Mem. Beta Theta Pi. Republican. Contbr. on ednl. and economic problems. Ala. legislature appropriated $50,000 (1927) for erection of fireproof bldg. for Southern Industrial Inst. (first time the state ever erected bldg. on pvt. property). Home: Camp Hill, Ala. Deceased.

WARDELL, Justus S. (wôr'dĕl); b. San Francisco, Calif., June 30, 1872; s. Benjamin Augustus and Pauline (Fliess) W.; ed. pub. schs.; m. Clara Louise Kellogg, July 9, 1895; children—Benjamin Augustus, Virginia Pauline. Began newspaper work in San Francisco, 1889; assumed management Daily Jour. of Commerce, 1897, owner, 1905-19; head of security business, San Francisco, many yrs. Mem. Calif. State Assembly, 1899-1901; delegate Democratic National Conv., 1904, 08; surveyor of customs, San Francisco, 1913-17; collector internal revenue, 1st Calif. Dist., 1917-20; Dem. candidate for gov. of Calif., 1926; del. at large to Dem. Nat. Conv., Houston, 1928, and chmn. Calif. delegation. Mem. Native Sons of the Golden West. Mason (Royal Arch). Clubs: Commercial, Commonwealth, Bohemian (San Francisco); Nat. Press, University (Washington, D.C.). Home: 2830 Broderick St., San Francisco, Calif. Address: Bohemian Club, San Francisco, Calif. Died Nov. 1945.

WARDLAW, Joseph Coachman, educator; b. Camilla, Mitchell County, Ga., Feb. 3, 1876; s. Joseph Pruitt and Anna Simmie (Coachman) W.; A.B., Emory U., 1895, A.M., 1895; student, U. of Chicago, 1897, 98, U. of Ga., 1903; m. Edna Roberta Powell, Dec. 20, 1899; children—Joseph Powell, Donald Coachman (dec.), Ralph Wilkinson (dec.), Roy Malcolm (dec.). Prof. English and Latin, Andrew College, Cuthbert, 1896, 97; asst. prin. pub. schs., Waynesboro, Ga., 1897-99; v.p. and prof. modern langs., Union Coll., Eufaula, Ala., 1899-1900; supt. pub. schs., Dublin, Ga., 1900-02, Thomasville, 1902-04, Albany, 1904-05, prof. Latin and history, Ga. State Coll. for Women, Milledgeville, Ga., 1905-07; prof. edn. and psychology, dir. normal dept. and supt.. Peabody School, same coll., 1908-12; prof. psychology and history of edn., U. of Georgia Summer Sch., 1912, asst. supt. same, 1915; head dept. of edn. and dir. training schs., State Teachers Coll., Athens, 1912-15, also dean, 1914-15; asst. supt. pub. schs. Atlanta, Ga., 1915-17, supt., 1917-18; mgr. 4th dist. Com. on Edn. and Special Training, War Dept., 1918-19; dist. vocational officer, Federal Bd. for Vocational Edn. (5th dist.), 1919; chief of vocational rehabilitation, U.S. Vet. Bur. (5th Dist.), Atlanta, 1921-22; chief vocational rehabilitation, dist. insp., exec. officer, and actg. dist. mgr. of U.S. Vet. Bur. (2d dist.), New York, 1922-25; supervisor New York Met. Dist. Near East Relief, 1925-27; dir. univ. extension, U. of Ga., 1928-32; dir. div. of gen. extension, Univ. System of Ga. since 1932; president Assn. of School Film Libraries; pres. Southern Conf. on Audio-Visual Education. Mem. N.E.A., Nat. Council of Edn., Am. Sociol. Soc., Nat. Econ. League (nat. council), The Source Research Council, Southern Edn. Council, Ga. Edn. Assn. (pres. 1915), Phi Beta Kappa, Phi Delta Theta, Pi Gamma Mu, Kappa Delta Pi. Democrat. Methodist. Scottish Rite Mason, K.T., Shriner, Odd Fellow, Kiwanian. Writer on ednl. topics. Traveled abroad, 1910, 13, 14. Home: Ivanhoe Apt. 1, 942 Ponce de León Av. N.E. Office: Univ. System of Georgia Extension Bldg., 223 Walton St. N.W., Atlanta, Ga. Died Jan. 24, 1947.

WARDLAW, Patterson, prof. edn.; b. Liberty Hill, S.C., Nov. 20, 1859; s. Andrew Bowie and Sarah Elizabeth (Thompson) W.; A.B., Erskine Coll., Due West, S.C., 1880, LL.D., 1906; student U. of Va., 1881-82, Princeton Theol. Sem., 1885-86, Clark U. and U. of Pa., summers; Litt.D., Presbyterian College, S.C., 1924; Ed. D., University of South Carolina; married Claudia M. Edwards, June 21, 1893 (died 1894); m. 2d, Mattie B. Lide, July 2, 1897 (died September 9, 1941); children—Joseph Patterson, Eliza Edwards, Laura (deceased), Andrew Bowie. Served as superintendent public schools, Darlington, S.C., 1889-94; prof. edn., U. of S.C., 1894-1939; also dean; dean emeritus since 1939. Chmn. bd. edn., Richland County, 1915-16; founding editor South Carolina Education, 1919. Mem. Phi Beta Kappa, State Teachers of S.C. (ex-pres.; hon. life mem.). Chmn. Illiteracy Commn. of S.C., 1917. Democrat. Presbyterian. Club: Kosmos, Rotary (Columbia). Contbr. on ednl. topics. Home: 831 Sumter St., Columbia 56, S.C. Died Jan. 18, 1948; buried Grove Hill Cemetery, Darlington, S.C.

WARE, Franklin B(ackus), architect; b. N.Y. City, July 12, 1873; s. James E. and Edith C. (Backus) W.; Ph.B., Columbia U. Sch. of Architecture, 1894; m. Grace M. Imlach, June 11, 1903. Began practice at N.Y. City, 1894; state architect, N.Y., 1907-12. Alderman, N.Y. City, 1901-05. Mem. N.G.N.Y., 1895-1903. Mem. Phi Delta Theta. Presbyterian. Clubs: National Republican, Columbia University. Home: 693 West End Av. Office: 1170 Broadway, New York, N.Y. Died May 3, 1945.

WARE, Norman Joseph, economics, sociology; b. Tilsonburg, Ont., Can., July 4, 1886; s. Henry and Sara (Joseph) W.; A.B., McMaster U., Toronto, Can., 1908; B.D., U. of Chicago, 1910, Ph.D., 1913; m. 2d, Katherine Walker, June 27, 1942. Came to U.S., 1919, naturalized citizen, 1924. Head of University Settlement, Toronto, 1913-14; with Khaki U., London, Eng., 1918-19; prof. sociology and economics, U. of Louisville, 1919-26; instr. New School for Social Research, New York, 1926-28, also arbitrator clothing industry, Rochester, N.Y.; asso. prof. economies and social science, Wesleyan U., Middletown, Conn., since Sept. 1928; sr. economist Bur. of Research and Statistics, Federal Social Security Bd., Washington, D.C., 1936-37; chmn. Conn. State Bd. of Mediation and Arbitration since 1941; chmn. Nat. War Labor Bd., Region I, Mar. 15, 1943; Industrial Relations Consultant since 1945; mem. National Railway Labor Board Panel since 1946. Member Canadian Expeditionary Force, 1915-19, World War I. Member Am. Econ. Assn., Am. Assn. Univ. Profs. Author: The Industrial Worker (1840-1860), 1924; The Labor Movement in the United States (1860-95), 1929; Labor in Modern Industrial Society, 1935; Labor in Canadian-American Relations; The History of Labor Interaction, (Relations of Canada and U.S. series), 1937. Regular corr. Am. Economic Rev., Jour. of Polit. Economy, Am. Hist. Review, Annals of Am. Acad. of Social and Polit. Science. Home: 32 Bartlett St., Portland, Conn. Died Dec. 27, 1949.

WAREING, Ernest Clyde (wâr'ing), pastor; b. Volga, Ind., May 29, 1872; s. James and Sarah (Wilson) W.; Ph.B., DePauw U., 1898, D.D., 1914; S.T.B., Boston U., 1901, Litt.D., Ohio Northern U., 1919; L.H.D., Evansville (Ind.) Coll., 1923; LL.D., McKendree Coll., 1928; m. Mary Alcinda Matlock, May 7, 1896; 1 son, Joel Matlock. Ordained M.E. ministry, 1901; pastor in Ind., at Plainfield, 1901-03, Williamsport, 1903-08, Plymouth, 1908-10, 1st Ch., Brazil, 1910-12; asso. editor, 1912-15, editor, 1916-32, Western Christian Advocate, Cincinnati; pastor Wayne St. Ch., Fort Wayne, Ind., 1932-33, First Church, Chattanooga, Tenn., 1933-36. Sec. Editorial Council of M.E. Church, 1915-32; pres. Editorial Council Religious Press of America, 1919-24; mem. Gen. Conf. M.E. Ch., 1916, 20; mem. bd. dirs. Lakeside Assembly and of Bible Conf. of the Assembly; bd. mgrs. Bd. of Edn. for Negroes; mem. Ecumenical Conf., London, 1921, Atlanta, Ga., 1932; mem. Gen. Conf. M.E. Ch., 1928, 32; trustee Chattanooga U., McKendree Coll., 1926; apptd. supt. Chattanooga District Holston Conf., 1936-39; pastor Red Bank Meth. Ch., since 1939. Dir. Bethesda Hosp., Cincinnati, O. Mem. Am. Acad. Polit. and Social Science, Sigma Nu, Pi Gamma Mu. Club: Authors'. Mason (32°). Author: Knights of the White Shield, 1906; The Building of a Great Sunday School, 1911; The Evangelism of Jesus, 1918; Critical Hours in the Preacher's Life; The Other Shepherd. Address: Patten Memorial Parish House, Chattanooga, Tenn. Died Feb. 4, 1944.

WARFIELD, C. Dorsey, pub. Baltimore News-Post and Baltimore Sunday American; b. Baltimore, Md., Mar. 16, 1898; s. Charles D. and Ella (Cox) W.; student Baltimore (Md.) City Coll., 1911-15; m. Florence Adler, Sept. 6, 1924. Business dept. Baltimore Sun, 1917-18, mech. supt., 1923-27, circulation dept., 1928, asst. business mgr., 1928-32; gen. mgr. Times-Herald, Washington, D.C., 1932-36; asst. pub. Washington Times, 1936-37, asso. pub., 1937; pub. Baltimore (Md.) News-Post and Baltimore Sunday Am. since 1937. Served in U.S. Navy, 1918-19. Episcopalian. Clubs: Baltimore Country, Merchants, Press (Baltimore); National Press (Washington, D.C.). Home: Warrington Apts. Office: Baltimore News-Post and Baltimore Sunday Am., Pratt & Commerce Sts., Baltimore, Md. Died March 22, 1947.

WARFIELD, William; b. Easton, Pa., Dec. 4, 1891, s. Ethelbert Dudley and Eleanor Frances (Tilton) W.; A.B., Lafayette Coll., 1911; post-grad. work, Princeton, 1911-13; Columbia Law Sch., 1913-14; m. Corinne Wendel, Jan. 29, 1920; 1 son, William; m. 2d, Marguerite Ruth, June 24, 1944. Made expeditions for scientific research and as consulting mining geologist to British Guiana and Trinidad, 1912, Mesopotamia and Arabia, 1913, India, 1912-13; mem. Am. expdn. to Sardes, Asia Minor, 1913, Serbian relief, 1914-15; attaché Am. Embassy, Petrograd, 1915-16; chargé d'affaires, Sofia, Bulgaria, 1916-17; dir. for Standard Oil Co. of N.J. in Argentina, Venezuela and Bolivia, 1920-26; pres. Trinidad Oil Fields, Inc., 1926-27; cons. petroleum engr., 1927-32; with Sperry Gyroscope Co., Inc., 1932-34, Am. Cyanamid Co., 1934-38, Davison Chemical Corp., Baltimore, 1938; dir. Standard Aircraft Products, Dayton, O., 1940-42; consultant to War Production Bd., Washington, D.C., 1942, Bd. of Economic Warfare, 1942-43. Commissioned captain, C.S.C., August 1917; transferred to Tank Corps, 1918; served in Meuse-Argonne offensive, 1918; promoted to maj. and lt. col., 1919. Dep. commr. of Am. Red Cross to Balkan States and commr. to Albania, 1919-20. Mem. Zeta Psi, Phi Beta Kappa; fellow Am. Geog. Soc., Am. Inst. Mining and Metall. Engrs. Several fgn. decorations. Clubs: University, Nat. Arts (New York); Royal Automobile (London). Author: The Gate of Asia, 1916. Address: National Arts Club, 15 Gramercy Park, New York. Died March 16, 1947; buried at Lexington, Ky.

WARNE, Frank Julian (wărn), economist; b. Parkersburg, W.Va., Mar. 16, 1874; s. William H. and Rosalie De Alberts (Warren) W.; A.M., 1899, Ph.D., 1902, sr. fellow in economics, 1902-03, research fellow, 1903-06, U. of Pa.; unmarried. Staff Philadelphia Public Ledger, 1896-1902; editor Railway World, 1903-06; studied in Paris, London, Edinburgh, Berlin, 1907; sec. N.Y. State Immigration Commn., 1908-09; spl. expert, U.S. Census, 1910; statistician, Federal Bd. of Arbitration, 1912; statistical representative Eastern conductors and trainmen in concerted wage movement, 1913; also in eight-hour day movement, 1916, and for firemen and enginemen on eastern, western and southern railroads, 1926-27. Was chief statistician Emergency Fleet Corp. and mgr. industrial relations and mem. bd. U.S. Housing Corp. Organizer and 1st dir. Sch. of Journalism of New York U. Apptd. by President Roosevelt, mem. Joint Congressional R.R. Investigation Commn. under R.R. Retirement Act. Mem. Beta Theta Pi. Author: The Slav Invasion and the Mine Workers, 1904; The Coal Mine Workers, 1905; The Immigrant Invasion, 1913; Railway Operation and Finance, 1913; Intercorporate Ownership and Interlocking Directorates of the Railroads of the U.S., 1914; The Tide of Immigration, 1916; Warne's Book of Charts, 1917; Warne's Elementary Course in Chartography, 1917; Industrial Relations, 1919; Chartography in Ten Lessons, 1919; The Workers at War, 1920; Ry. Employes' Reply to the Railroads, 1921. Also numerous pamphlets, editorials and articles on econ., social, polit. and industrial topics in various mags., rev., etc. Clubs: Authors' (London); Cosmos. Home: Cosmos Club. Office: Mills Building, Washington, D.C. Deceased.

WARNER, Ellsworth C(olonel), corp. official; b. Garden City, Minn., 1864; s. Amos and Aurelia (Dieley) W.; ed. pub. and high schs.; m. Mellie F. Bisbee, Jan. 15, 1890 (divorced 1922); children—Ellsworth B., Maurice A., Harold L., Wendell E.; m. 2d, Mrs. Roslyn C. Allen, Jan. 1930. Taught country sch.; state register of grain receipts, 1885-87; with Mankato Linseed Oil Co., 1887-89; purchased a linseed oil mill at La Crosse, Wis., 1889, and sold same to Nat. Linseed Oil Co. of which was made mgr. at La Crosse, Dubuque and St. Paul, continuing until 1897; in 1898 became pres. Midland Linseed Oil Co.; now dir. McGill-Warner-Bigelow Co., lithographing, bookbinding and printing; pres. E. C. Warner Co., Tuxedo Park Co.; v.p. Northwestern Fire & Marine Ins. Co.; dir. First Bank Stock Corp. (St. Paul), Twin City Fire Ins. Co., Title Ins. Co., First Nat. Bank (Minneapolis), Hanover Fire Ins. Co. and Fulton Fire Ins. Co. (both New York), Canadian Consol. Grain Co., Ltd. Clubs: Minneapolis, Minikahda, Lafayette, Woodhill Country (Minneapolis); Everglades, Old Guards Soc. of Palm Beach Golfers (Palm Beach, Fla.); Manitoba Club (Winnipeg, Can.). Home: 3030 W. Calhoun Blvd., Palm Beach, Fla. Office: Baker Bldg., Minneapolis, Minn.; (winter) First National Bank Bldg., Palm Beach, Fla. Died Jan. 5, 1942.

WARNER, Frank, surgeon; b. Ross County, O., August 2, 1855; s. Lewis B. and Cornelia Augusta (Forbes) W.; Ohio State U., 1876, 77; Columbus (O.) Med. Coll., 1878, 79; M.D., Bellevue Hosp. Med. Coll. (New York U.), 1883; Sc D., Denison, 1918; m. Carmen Adelaide Hambleton, Oct. 21, 1931. Practiced at Columbus since 1883; prof. operative and clin. surgery, Starling Med. Coll., 1889-1908; surgeon White Cross Hosp.; formerly surgeon to Grant Hosp., also to Children's Hosp.; mem. Ohio State Bd. Health, 1898-1913; mem. bd. Columbus Tuberculosis Soc., 1907-35. Trustee Columbus Pub. Library since 1909; mem. Columbus Gallery Fine Arts. Fellow Am. Coll. Surgeons; mem. A.M.A., Ohio State Med. Soc., Columbus Acad. Medicine, Ohio Hist. and Archæol. Soc., Optimist Club. Democrat. Methodist. Home: 177 Hubbard Av., Columbus O. Died Nov. 28, 1943.

WARNER, Harold, general attorney, Royal Insurance Company, Ltd., and Liverpool & London & Globe Ins. Co., Ltd.; U.S. fire mgr. British & Foreign Marine Ins. Co., Ltd.; atty. Thames & Mersey Marine Ins. Co.; pres. & dir. Newark Fire Ins. Co., Star Ins. Co., Federal Union Ins. Co., Queen Ins. Co., Seaboard Ins. Co.; Am. & Foreign Ins. Co.; v.p. and dir. Capital Fire Ins. Co., Prudential Ins. Co. of Gt. Britain located in New York, Hudson Ins. Co., Detroit Nat. Fire Insurance Co.; dir. Virginia Fire & Marine Insurance Co.; chmn. bd. Royal Indemnity Co., Eagle Indemnity Co., Globe Indemnity Co. Office: 150 William St., New York, N.Y. Died April 20, 1948.

WARNER, Henry Edward, editor; b. Elyria, O., Jan. 17, 1876; s. Rev. Thomas Corwin and Frances Rebecca (Laughlin) W.; ed. U. of Southern Calif. and U.S. Grant U.; m. Lydia Amo Lee, Oct. 27, 1897. With Knoxville Journal and Chattanooga Times and Press, 1890-96, Baltimore News, 1896-98; city editor Denver Times, 1898-1900; staff Baltimore News, 1900-03; mng. editor Binghamton Press, 1903; again with News, 1904; gen. press rep. Sarah Bernhardt and Shubert enterprises, 1906-07; spl. writer St. Paul Dispatch, 1908; with Baltimore Evening Sun, 1910; editor Sunday Sun, 1913, now circulation mgr. Started "Sidelights," verse and humor, Denver Times, 1908, continued same in Baltimore News, St. Paul Dispatch, Baltimore Evening Sun. Founder, 1903, and first pres. Am. Press Humorists. Club: City. Author: That House I Bought, 1912. Writer of music and songs since boyhood. Home: 3313 Bateman Av. Office: The Sun, Baltimore. Died Apr. 11, 1941.

WARNER, William Bishop, publisher, mfr.; b. Hannibal, Mo., Dec. 20, 1874; s. William Andrew and Maria Virginia (Bishop) W.; ed. pub. schs., Detroit, Mich.; m. Sibyl Moore, Apr. 17, 1909; children—Zoe Compton, Sibyl Virginia. Stock boy, later salesman, Edson, Moore Co., Detroit, 1891-98; salesman, Brown, Durrell Co., Chicago, 1898-1909; div. mdse. mgr. Wm. Filene's Sons Co., Boston, 1909-16, J. L. Hudson Co., Detroit, 1916-19; pres. McCall Corp., N.Y. City, since 1919; dir. Am. Woolen Co., Atlantic Mutual Ins. Co., Van Raalte Co., McCall Corp., Fiduciary Trust Co., W. T. Grant Co. Pres. BM News Co., Nat. Pubs. Assn. Mem. Nat. Assn. of Mfrs. (hon v.p., mem. bd. dirs.; exec. and finance com.); v.p. Am. Soc. Prevention Cruelty to Animals; dir. Jr. Achievement; chmn. bd., Tax Foundation; mem. bd. dirs., Citizens Nat. Com.; trustee, James Foundation. Republican. Presbyterian. Mason. Clubs: Union League, Blind Brook, Pelham Country, Lake Placid, Yaemans Hall (Charleston, S.C.). Home: 158 Elderwood Av., Pelham, N.Y. Office: 230 Park Avenue, New York, New York. Died May 4, 1946.

WARREN, Bentley Wirt, lawyer; b. Boston, Mass., Apr. 20, 1864; s. William Wirt and Mary (Adams) W.; A.B., Williams Coll., 1885, LL.D., 1935; studied law under Hon. Thomas P. Proctor and at Boston U.; married Ellen Hatch Windom, June 6, 1894; children—Mrs. Ellen Geer Sangster, Bentley W. Admitted to Suffolk bar, 1888, and since in practice at Boston; member Warren, Garfield, Whiteside & Lamson; pres., dir. and trustee, Boston & Providence R.R. Corp.; dir. Springfield Street Ry. Co., Mass. Hosp. Life Ins. Co., State Street Trust Co., Holyoke Water Power Co., Holyoke Power & Electric Co., North Texas Co., Union Freight R.R. Co.; trustee Consol. Investment Trust, Brighton Five Cents Savings Bank. Mem. Mass. House of Rep., 1891, 92, Mass. Civil Service Commn., 1903-05; legal adviser U.S. Fuel Adminstrn., 1917-19; trustee and ex-pres. Boston Symphony Orchestra; director Boston Municipal Research Bureau. Mem. Am. and Mass. bar assns., Bar Assn. City of Boston (mem. Council; ex-pres.), Am. Law Inst., Boston C. of C., Bostonian Soc., Mass. Hort. Soc., Colonial Soc. of Mass., New Eng. Historic Geneal. Soc.; Foreign Policy Assn.; fellow Am. Acad. of Arts and Sciences. Member and Ex-Pres. Dist. No. 1 chapter Assn. of Interstate Commerce Commission Practitioners. Trustee Williams College, Radcliffe College. Democrat. Episcopalian. Clubs: Somerset, Union (Boston); Williams (New York). Home: Williamstown, Mass.; (winter) 228 Beacon St., Boston. Office: 30 State St., Boston 9, Mass. Died Feb. 27 1947.

WARREN, Charles Elliott, banker; b. N.Y. City, Apr. 9, 1864; s. George William and Mary Elizabeth (Pease) W.; prep. edn., St. Paul's Sch., Garden City, N.Y.; student U. of Calif.; m. Anna Margaret Geissenhainer, Apr. 19, 1892. Began in banking business in N.Y. City, 1882; pres. Lincoln Nat. Bank, 1910-20; v.p. and chairman advisory board, Lincoln office of Irving Trust Co.; pres. Erie & Kalamazoo R.R. Co., Lake Shore & Mich. Southern R.R. Co., Lessee; pres. Nestor Mfg. Co.; treas., dir. Luth. Cemetery (New York). Vice-gov. War Credits Bd., Washington, 1917-18. Served in 7th Regt., later in 12th Regt., N.Y. Nat. Guard, beginning as pvt., advanced to lt. col. brigade and div. staff; major, 3d N.Y. inf. brigade, Spanish-Am. war; maj., lt. col. and col. Ordnance Corps, U.S. Army, World War I; col. 514th Coast Arty., U.S. Army; brig. gen., N.Y. Nat. Guard; comdt. Vet. Corps Arty., N.Y. City; col. Coast Arty., Reserve U.S. Army. Medal N.Y. Nat. Guard, also for Spanish-Am. war, State of N.Y. and Mexican Border service; Victory medal, Conspicuous Service Cross, D.S.M. (U.S.); Médaille de la Reconnaissance and Legion of Honor. Mem. N.Y. State Bankers Assn. (pres. 1915-16), Pilgrims, N.Y. Hist. Soc., Mayflower Soc., Soc. Colonial Wars, Colonial Order of the Acorn, S.R., Soc. of the Cincinnati, Soc. War of 1812, Loyal Legion, Army Ordnance Assn. (treas., dir.), Vets. of 7th Regt., N.Y. (107th U.S. Inf.), Am. Legion, Mil. Order Fgn. Wars, Soc. Am. Wars, N.Y. Soc. Mil. and Naval Officers World War, Mil. Order World Wars, Am. Tract Soc. (treas.), Order of the Runnemede. Republican. Episcopalian. Clubs: Military and Naval, Metropolitan, St. Nicholas Society (New York); Rockaway Hunting, Lawrence Beach. Home: Hewlett Neck Rd., Hewlett, L.I., N.Y. Office: 100 E. 42d St., New York, N.Y. Died Dec. 25, 1945.

WARREN, Edward Henry, prof. law; b. Worcester, Mass., Jan. 11, 1873; s. William Henry and Charlotte Elizabeth (Marsh) W.; A.B., Harvard, 1895; A.M., Columbia, 1896; post-grad. Harvard, 1896-97, LL.B., 1900; m. Elinor Foster, May 28, 1910; 1 dau., Elinor Foster Purdy (dec.). Practiced, New York, 1900-04; asst. prof. law, Harvard Law Sch., 1904-08, prof., 1908-13, Story prof. law, 1913-20, Weld prof. law, 1920-29, prof. of law, 1934-43, emeritus since 1943. Author: Cases on Corporation, 1909, 16; Cases on Property, 1915, 38; also exposition of the Rule Against Perpetuities in Cyclopædia of Law, 1905; treatise on Corporate Advantages Without Incorporation, 1929, lectures delivered at various English and Scottish universities, 1930-33; treatise on Margin Customers, 1941; Spartan Education, 1942. Home: Winter Park, Fla.* Died July 24, 1945.

WARREN, Edward Royal, naturalist; b. Waltham, Mass., Oct. 17, 1860; s. Royal Sibley and Susan Elizabeth (Bates) W.; S.B., Mass. Inst. Tech., 1881; Colorado Coll., 1881-83, D.Sc., 1939; m. Oct. 11, 1916, Maude Smith Bard; children—Ruth Elizabeth, Margaret Bates. Assaying and surveying, Gunnison County, Colo., 1882-92, surveying and mining engring., Cripple Creek, 1892-96; natural history work, specializing in mammalogy and ornithology, Colorado Springs, since 1902. Formerly hon. dir. Museum of Colorado Coll.; collaborator and field naturalist, Roosevelt Wild Life Expt. Sta., 1921-28. Mem. Am. Ornithologists Union, Cooper Ornithol. Club, Wilson Ornithol. Club, Colorado Audubon Soc., Biol. Soc. Washington, Am. Soc. Mammalogists; fellow of A.A.A.S. Unitarian. Author: The Mammals of Colorado, 1910; The Beaver—Its Work and Its Ways, 1927; also contbr. The Beaver in Yellowstone Nat. Park and Notes on the Beaver in Estes Park, in Roosevelt Wild Life Annals. Address: 1511 Wood Av., Colorado Springs, Colo. Died Apr. 20, 1942.

WARREN, Frederick Andrew, judge; b. Green Bay, Wis., Aug. 13, 1877; s. O. O. and Rasmini (Aaroy) W.; B.S., Fremont (Neb.) Coll., 1900; LL.B., U. of Neb., 1903; m. Clara J. Moen, May 31, 1906; children—Flora Clarene (Mrs. John J. Judd), Waldo Raymond, Stanford Winton, Eleanor Almeda, Dorothy Madelyn (Mrs. William Pond Chapin Jr.), Darrow Eldon. Admitted S.D. bar, 1903, in practice at Flandreau; city atty., 1907-09 and 1917-20; state's atty. Moody County, 1911-15; judge Supreme Court of S D. since 1931, presiding judge, 1935, 39, 44. City auditor, Flandreau, 1907-08, pres. bd. edn., 1927-30. Mem. Am. Bar Assn. (mem. exec. com. 1925), Am. Law Inst., S.D. Bar Assn. (pres. 1915), S.D. Hist. Soc. (mem. exec. com. since 1935), Flandreau Chamber of Commerce, Civil Legion, Phi Delta Phi. Democrat. Lutheran. Mason (K.T., Shriner), Odd Fellow, Elk, Woodman. Home: (legal) Flandreau, S.D. Address: State Capitol, Pierre, S.D. Died June 18, 1944.

WARREN, Frederick Emroy, livestock and wool grower; b. Cheyenne, Wyo., Jan. 20, 1884; s. Francis Emroy and Helen Mariah (Smith) W.; A.B., Harvard, 1905, A.M., 1906; LL.D., University of Wyoming, 1947; married Elizabeth L. Cook, December 28, 1910; children—Francis Emroy, Mary Helen. Entered livestock business with Warren Live Stock Co., 1905, mgr., 1914-29, pres. since 1929; pres. F. E. Warren Mercantile Co., Cheyenne Securities Co.; director American National Bank of Cheyenne. President Wyo. Live Stock and Sanitary Bd. Mem. Sigma Alpha Epsilon. Republican. Mason (Shriner). Home: 210 E. 17th St. Office: Box 858, Cheyenne, Wyo. Died May 26, 1949.

WARREN, James Thomas; b. Corinth, Miss., Dec. 5, 1884; s. John Thomas and Annie Lee (Skillman) W.; grad. Hall-Moody Junior Coll., Martin, Tenn., 1909; B.S., 1921, and A.M., 1926, George Peabody Coll. for Teachers, Nashville, Tenn.; LL.D., Georgetown (Ky.) Coll., 1929; m. Mattie Vincent, Dec. 26, 1912. V.p. Hall-Moody Junior Coll., 1911-15; supt. schs., Rockwood, Tenn., 1915-17; pres. Hall-Moody Junior Coll., 1917-26; v.p. Tenn. Coll. for Women, Murfreesboro, 1926-27; pres. Carson-Newman Coll. since 1927. Mem. Phi Delta Kappa, Pi Gamma Mu. Democrat. Baptist. Home: Jefferson City, Tenn. Died Jan. 16, 1948.

WARREN, Joseph, prof. law; b. Boston, Mass., Mar. 16, 1876; s. John Collins and Amy (Shaw) W.; A.B., Harvard, 1897, LL.B., 1900; m. Constance Martha Williams, June 19, 1905 (died May 1, 1935); children—Joseph, Richard, Howland Shaw, Mary Eleanor. Admitted to Mass. bar, 1900; sec. to Justice Gray, U.S. Supreme Court, 1900-01; prof. law, Harvard, 1913-19, Bussey prof., 1919-29, Weld prof. since 1929. Mem. Mass. Bar Assn., Bar Assn. City of Boston, Harvard Law Sch. Assn., Mass. Hist. Soc., Mass. Soc. of the Cincinnati (v.p.); fellow Am. Acad. Arts and Sciences. Republican. Unitarian. Clubs: Faculty Club of Harvard; Harvard (Boston); Harvard (New York); Country (Brookline). Home: 300 Dudley St., Brookline, Mass. Died Sep. 19, 1942.

WARREN, Minton M(achado), cons. engr.; b. Salem, Mass., Aug. 7, 1888; s. Minton and Salome A. (Machado) W.; desc. in 10th generation from Richard Warren of the Mayflower, 1620; prep. edn., Browne and Nichols Sch., Cambridge, Mass.; A.B cum laude, Harvard, 1910, M.C.E., 1912; m. Sarah Ripley Robbins, Sept. 17, 1927; children—Minton, William Bradford. Began engring. service under Hugh L. Cooper, on dam across Miss. River at Keokuk, Ia.; with Stone & Webster, constrn. engrs., 10 yrs., in design, constrn. and management; after World War I, served as chief engr. Technicolor Motion Picture Corp., also starting prodn. of several indsl. plants, in New England and Calif.; organized Aero Supply Co., mfrs. of hardware and fittings for airplane cos., in 1925; went to England, 1928, arranged for manufacture of the De Havilland Moth plane in the U.S. and was apptd. pres. of co. in U.S. and in charge of factory in Lowell, Mass.; v.p., mgr. and dir. Curtiss-Wright airplane mfg. plant at St. Louis, later sec. Curtiss-Wright Corp., Wright Aeronautical Corp., etc., until 1931; cons. practice N.Y. City and Boston since 1920; dir. research, Van Alstyne, Noel & Co., N.Y.; pres. and dir. Aeronautical Securities, Inc.; dir. Hercules Steel Products Corp. Commd. 1st lt. engrs., U.S. Army, Aug. 1917, capt., Aug. 1918; with 26th Div. in France; organized the first Am. topographical sect. participated in actions at Chemin-des-Dames, Chauteau Thierry, St. Mihiel, and Meuse-Argonne, at Verdun. Known for original research work in "water hammer," and discovery of formulas in hydraulics now largely adopted. Mem. Am. Soc. C.E., Harvard Engring. Soc. (pres. 1941-42), Soc. Mayflower Descendants. Republican. Episcopalian. Clubs: Harvard, City Midday Church Club (New York); Harvard (Boston). Home: 55 E. 86th St. Died Nov. 4, 1947.

WARREN, Robert B., economist; b. Prattsburg, N.Y., Mar. 15, 1891; s. George William and Claire Seymour (Beach) W.; A.B., Hamilton Coll., Clinton, N.Y., 1912; A.M., Harvard, 1916; m. Mildred Fisk, Dec. 31, 1921; children—Peter, Robert B., Eugenia. Instr. Robert Coll., Constantinople, Turkey, 1912-15; asso. editor, Am. City Mag., N.Y. City, 1920-21; economist, div. of research, Fed. Reserve Bd., Washington, 1922-26; economist, foreign dept., Fed. Reserve Bank of N.Y., 1926-27; economist and vice pres. Case, Pomeroy & Co., N.Y., 1928-38; prof. of economics, Inst. for Advanced Study, Princeton, N.J., since 1939. Consultant, U.S. Treasury, 1942-45. Captain, Infantry, U.S. Reserve, 1917-19. Author: The State in Society (with Henry Clay and Leo Wollman), 1939; The Search for Financial Security, 1940. Home: R.F.D. 2, Princeton, N.J. Died Mar. 23, 1950.

WARREN, Whitney, architect; pupil of Daumet and Girault, at École des Beaux Arts, Paris; hon. A.M., Harvard, 1913. Practicing architecture at New York. Awarded silver medal, Paris Expn., 1900. Mem. de l'Académie des Beaux Arts, Institut de France, 1905, Nat. Inst. Arts and Letters, Société Beaux Arts Architectes, Société Centrale des Architectes Français, Société des Architectes Diplomés par le Gouvernement Français, Société des Artistes Français, Royal Acad. of San Luc, Rome. Clubs: Knickerbocker, Racquet and Tennis. Architect for rebuilt Louvain Library. Address: 280 Park Av., New York, N.Y. Died Jan. 24, 1943.

WARREN, William Robinson, clergyman; b. Higginsville, Mo., Mar. 24, 1868; s. Rev. James L. and Ann C. (Watson) W.; A.B., Bethany (W.Va.) Coll., 1889, A.M., 1893; Litt.D., 1934; student U. of Chicago, 1897; m. Susan Alice Kemper, June 21, 1893; children—Kemper (dec.), Mary (dec.), Constance Louise (Mrs. Howard W. McCue), Julia Catherine (Mrs. Louis A. Harlan) (dec.), Edgar Lovett. Ordained to ministry Christian (Disciples) Ch., 1889; pastor Pinewood, Tenn., also prin. Pinewood Acad., 1889-90; pastor Dayton, O., 1890-92; prof. Latin, Bethany Coll. and pastor Bethany, W.Va., 1892-93; pastor Santa Barbara, Calif., 1893-96, Connellsville, Pa., 1897-1903; editor Christian Worker, Pittsburgh, Pa., 1903-05; sec. Centennial campaign and conv. of Disciples of Christ, Pittsburgh, 1905-09; gen. mgr. Christian Bd. of Publication and editor The Christian-Evangelist, St. Louis, Mo., 1910-12; sec. Bd. of Ministerial Relief, Indianapolis, Ind., 1912-18, pres., 1918-28; editor World Call, 1919-29; v.p. Pension Fund of Disciples of Christ, 1929-36, hon. v.p. since 1936; also editor in chief Survey of Service, same ch., 1928; dir. Christian Bd. of Publication, 1910-40; sec. United Christian Missionary Soc., 1920-29. Mem. Beta Theta Pi. Democrat. Author: Centennial Convention Report, 1910; The Life and Labors of Archibald McLean, 1923. Home: 317 Oak St., Sarasota, Fla. Died Sep. 15, 1947.

WARRINER, Eugene Clarence (wŏr'ĭn-ēr), coll. pres.; b. Earlville, Ill., Dec. 7, 1866; s. Remington and Sarah Ellen (Gilbert) W.; A.B., U. of Mich., 1891; grad. study, 1891-92, hon. A.M., 1912; grad. study Clark U., Harvard, Columbia; m. Ellen Wheeler, June 27, 1893; children—Paul (dec.), Mary Ellen, John. Teacher schs., Lee County, Ill., 1884-87; prin. high sch., Battle Creek, Mich., 1892-95; same, East Side, Saginaw, Mich., 1895-99, supt. schs., same, 1899-1917; pres. Central State Teachers Coll., Mt. Pleasant, Mich., 1918-39; retired June 30, 1939. Methodist. Rotarian. Wrote: The Teaching of Grammar School Classics, Geography of Michigan. Home: Mt. Pleasant, Mich. Died July 20, 1945.

WARRINER, Samuel Dexter, corp. officer; b. Lancaster, Pa., Feb. 24, 1867; s. Rev. Edward A. and Louisa (Voorhis) W.; A.B., Amherst, 1888; B.S., Lehigh U., 1890, E.M., 1890, hon. Eng.D., 1927; m. Stella Mercer Farnham, May 18, 1898; children—Farnham, Eloise (Mrs. Richard M. Ehret), R. Dexter, J. Dorrance. Pres. Lehigh Coal & Navigation Co. 1912, chmn. bd., since 1937; chmn. bd. and dir. Lehigh & New Eng. R.R. Co.; dir. Lehigh Navigation Coal Co., Inc., Allentown Terminal R.R. Co., Old Company's Lehigh, Inc.; dir. Cranberry Creek Coal Co., Admiralty Coal Corp., Alliance Ins. Co., Crab Orchard Improvement Co., Parkway Co., Pa. Salt Mfg. Co., Stonega Coke & Coal Co., Va. Coal and Iron Co., Westmoreland Coal Co., Westmoreland, Inc., Indemnity Ins. Co. of N. America, Ins. Co. of N. America, Phila. Fire & Marine Ins. Co., Pa. Co. for Insurances on Lives and Granting Annuities, Blue Ridge Real Estate Co., Del. Div. Canal Co. of Pa., Campbell Hall Connecting R.R. Co., Pochuck R.R. Co., Amboy Lehigh Coal Co., Monroe Water Supply Co., Nesquehoning Valley R.R. Co., Panther Valley Water Co., Summit Hill Water Co., Tresckow R.R. Co., Wilkes-Barre & Scranton Ry. Co., Greenwood Corp., 250 S. 18th St. Corp. Trustee Penn Mutual Life Insurance Co., Lehigh U. Mem. Am. Inst. of Mining and Metall. Engrs. Republican. Episcopalian. Clubs: Union League, Rittenhouse, Engineers, Midday, Philadelphia Country (Philadelphia, Pa.); Railroad-Machinery (New York, N.Y.); Westmoreland (Wilkes-Barre, Pa.); Boca Raton, Mahoning Valley Country, Montrose Country, North Mountain, Pohoqualine Fish Assn., Woodmont Rod and Gun, Newcomen Society. Home: "Fernheim," Montrose, Pa.; and 250 S. 18th St., Philadelphia, Pa. Office: 2001 Fidelity-Philadelphia Trust Bldg., Philadelphia. Died Apr. 3, 1942.

WARSHAW, Jacob, educator; b. London, Eng., Dec. 22, 1878; s. Lewis and Sophia (Burston) W.; A.B., Harvard, 1900; A.M., U. of N.C., 1902; certificate, U. of Paris, France, 1902; Ph.D., U. of Mo., 1912; m. Hazel Marie Williams, Aug. 3, 1920. Instr. modern langs., U. of N.C., 1900-01; teacher Porto

Rico, 1903-04; acting supt. schs., San Juan, P.R., 1904; dist. supt. schs. in P.R., 1904-07; prin. Central High Sch., San Juan, 1907; asso. editor, Porto Rican Rev., 1908; congress sec., Playground Assn. America, 1908; instr. Romance langs., U. of Mo., 1909-12, asst. prof., 1912-17, asso. prof., 1917-19; prof. modern langs., U. of Neb., 1919-24; prof. Romance langs., U. of Mo., 1924, chmn. dept., 1925, prof. Spanish and chmn. dept. Spanish since 1926. Visiting prof. U. of Colo., summers 1924, 29, 36. Decorated Knight Order Isabella the Catholic, 1933. Mem. Modern Lang. Assn. America, Nat. Federation Modern Lang. Teachers, Mo. State Teachers' Assn., Am. Assn. Teachers of Spanish (v.p. 1920 and 1934-36), Instituto de las Españas, Phi Beta Kappa, Sigma Delta Pi, Phi Sigma Iota, Order of Eastern Star of Mo.; corr. mem. Hispanic Soc. America, Instituto Cultural Argentino-Norteamericano, Ateneo Ibero-Americano, Buenos Aires, Academia Antioqueña de Historia, Colombia. Mason. Clubs: Discussion, Harvard (Columbia, Mo.). Author: Spanish-American Composition Book, 1917; The New Latin America, 1922; Elements of Spanish, 1924; Cosas, Cuentos y Chistes, 1931; Spanish Science and Invention (monograph), 1933; Santander Ateneo Prize translation of Pereda's La Leva, 1933; Spanish Verb Dial, 1939; also joint author of the Puerto Rican edition of Cornman and Gerson's Geography Primer. Editor of Albes' Viajando por Sud América, 1917; Galdós' La loca de la casa, 1924; Isaacs' María, 1926; Careta verde and El Señor Gobernador, 1928; also the literary series of the Univ. of Mo. Bulletin, 1917-19. Asso. editor, Hispania, 1938-40. Collaborator: List of Books for Junior College Libraries, 1937. Contbr. articles and verse in Modern Lang. Notes, Modern Language Review, Poet Lore, Drama, School and Society, etc. Address: 412 Stewart Rd., Columbia, Mo. Died Sept. 30, 1944; buried in Columbia Cemetery, Columbia, Mo.

WASH, Carlyle Hilton, army officer; b. Minneapolis, Minn., Oct. 15, 1889; s. James Alexander and Helen (Turnbull) W.; B.S., U.S. Mil. Acad., West Point, N.Y., 1913; m. Constance Rogers, May 14, 1919; 1 dau., Elizabeth Patricia (Mrs. Samuel Knox Eaton). Commd. 2d lt., Cav., 1913, advanced through ranks to brig. gen., 1940; with Pershing Expdn., Mexico, 1916; transferred to Air Corps, 1917; served in World War, 1917-18; comdg. gen., 2d Interceptor Command, since 1940. Clubs: Army and Navy (Washington, D.C.); Seattle Country (Seattle, Wash.); University (Tacoma, Wash.). Address: War Dept., Washington, D.C. Died Jan. 26, 1943.

WASHBURN, Frederic Augustus, physician; b. New Bedford, Mass., Nov. 22, 1869; s. Frederic Augustus and Mary Jane (Swan) W.; A.B., Amherst, 1892, M.A., 1928; M.D., Harvard, 1896; m. Amy Silsbee Appleton, Jan. 10, 1911; 1 dau., Amy (Mrs. Thomas Stewart Hamilton, Jr.). Asst. dir., Mass. Gen. Hosp., 1898-99 and 1903-08, dir., 1908-34, dir. emeritus since 1934; and dir. Mass. Eye and Ear Infirmary, 1915-34; commr. institutions, City of Boston, 1934-37; dir. Cambridge Hosp., 1937-40, cons. dir. 1940-47; director during World War II. Assistant surgeon and surg. U.S. Vols., 1898-1903; served in Puerto Rico, 1898, Philippines, 1899-1903; major comdg. Base Hosp. 6, A.E.F., in France, 1917; lt. col. Med. Corps, in charge hospitalization, Am. hosps. in Gt. Britain; col., chief surgeon, Base Sect. 3, A.E.F., London, Oct. 1918, Mar. 1919. Awarded D.S.M.; Companion Order St. Michael and St. George (British), award of merit and medal-American Hospital Association, 1941. Trustee Gardner State Hospital, 1923-38, chairman, 1923-35; ex-president Truro Neighborhood Association. Member A.M.A. (council med. edn. and hosps. 1932-38), Am. Hosp. Assn. (pres. 1912-13), Mass. Med. Soc., Mil. Order World War (comdr. Greater Boston Chapter 1923-24), Mass. Soc. Mayflower Descendants (gov. 1923-27). Club: Medical Superintendents (pres. 1921-33). Home: 190 Bay State Rd., Boston 15, Mass. Died Aug. 20, 1949.

WASHBURN, Frederic Baldwin, banker; b. Natick, Mass., July 19, 1871; s. Charles Watson and Elizabeth (Baldwin) W.; grad. high sch., Natick, Mass.; m. Jessie Bailey, Nov. 2, 1902 (dec.); children—Rodney, Elizabeth, Gordon B. Began with Natick Nat. Bank, 1888; with North Nat. Bank, Boston, 1891-94, U.S. Trust Co., Boston, 1894-97, Nat. Bank of Redemption, Boston, 1899-1900; pres. Worcester Five Cents Savings Bank, 1914-19, now trustee; pres. Mechanics Nat. Bank of Worcester, 1920-41; retired, 1941; pres. Franklin Savings Bank, Boston, 1919-20; dir. Merchants & Farmers Ins. Co. Asso. nat. bank examiner, Boston; bank commr., Mass. Trustee Clark U. Republican. Unitarian. Clubs: Worcester, Tatnuck Country (Worcester). Home: 8 Cedar St. Office: 303 Main St., Worcester. Mass. Died Oct. 23, 1944.

WASHBURN, Ives, publisher; b. New York, N.Y., May 24, 1887; s. William Ives and Carrie Woodruff (Fisher) W.; A.B., Amherst Coll., 1908; m. Elisabeth Crane, June 16, 1910; 1 son, John Henry. Began as reporter, New York Times, 1908; became editor, The Century Co., 1915; editor, George H. Doran Co., 1919; editor Romance Mag., The Butterick Co., 1921; mgr. London office The Century Co., 1923; pres. Ives Washburn, Inc., book publisher, New York, N.Y., since 1926. Served as pvt., sergt., 2d lt., Tank Corps, U.S. Army, 1918. Mem. New England Soc. (New York), Alpha Delta Phi. Clubs: Century, Players, P.E.N., Amherst (New York); Savage (London, Eng.). Home: 411 E. 57th St., New York 22. Office: 29 W. 57th St., New York 19, N.Y. Died Feb. 5, 1947.

WASHBURN, Robert, writer; b. Worcester, Mass., January 4, 1868; son Charles Francis and Mary Elizabeth (Whiton) W.; A.B., Harvard, 1890; student Harvard Law Sch., 1891-92; m. Martha Ross Clark, Aug. 15, 1916. Admitted to Mass. bar, 1892, and practiced at Worcester until 1916, at Boston, 1916-24; mem. Mass. Ho. of Rep., 1908-15; Mass. Senate, 1916; Rep. nominee for U.S. Senate, 1934. Mem. Harvard Law Assn., Inst. of 1770. Republican. Episcopalian. Clubs: The (T. R.) Roosevelt (founder, pres. and dir.). Author: Footprints, 1923; Calvin Coolidge—His First Biography, 1923; Smith's Barn, 1923; My Pen, 1940; The Nine Intimates, 1942. Campaign biographer of Calvin Coolidge, 1924; Ogden L. Mills, for governor, 1926; William M. Butler for U.S. Senate, 1930. Retired. Home: 31 Marlboro St., Boston, Mass. Died Feb. 26, 1946.

WASHBURNE, George Adrian, prof. of history; b. Chillicothe, O., Aug. 29, 1884; s. George Washington and Mary Catherine (Copeland) W.; A.B., Ohio State U., 1907; A.M., Columbia, 1913, Ph.D., 1923; unmarried. Teacher of history, North High Sch., Columbus, O., 1915-18; asst. prof. of history, Ohio State U., 1918-27, prof. since 1927, chmn. dept. of history since 1938; visiting prof. of history, U. of Tex., 1927, Ohio U., summer 1936. Mem. Am. Hist. Assn., English Speaking Union (pres. Columbus chapter 1938-42), Chi Phi. Conglist. Clubs: Columbus, Kit Kat (Columbus); Torch, Faculty. Author: Imperial Control of the Administration of Justice in the Thirteen American Colonies, 1923. Contbr. to professional and ednl. jours. Home: 65 W. 11th Av., Columbus, O. Died May 11, 1948; buried Sinking Springs, O.

WASSON, Thomas C(ampbell), foreign service officer; b. Great Falls, Mont., Feb. 8, 1896; s. Edmund Atwill and Mary (DeVeny) W.; ed. Newark (N.J.) grammar and high schs.; N.J. State Agrl. Coll., 1912-13; Cornell, 1913-14; pvt. tutors in Athens and Paris, 1914-16; Melbourne U., 1925-29; unmarried. Representative of mfg. co. in France, 1919; plantation mgr., 1920-24; clerk Am. consulate Melbourne, 1924, vice consul, 1925; vice consul, temp., at Adelaide, 1929; Puerto Cortes, 1930; Naples, 1933, consul, 1935; consul, Florence, 1936, Lagos, 1937; Vigo, 1939; Dakar, 1940; assigned to Dept. of State 1946-47; counsellor Am. Embassy, Athens, Greece, 1947-48; consul gen., Jerusalem, Palestine, Apr.-May 23, 1948. Served in U.S. Army, A.E.F., 1917-19. Home: 357 Parker St., Newark, N.J. Office: care State Dept., Washington, D.C. Died from sniper's bullet, May 23, 1948; buried in crypt of Washington Cathedral.

WATERFALL, Harry William, prof. mech. engring.; b. Boston, Mass., June 6, 1887; s. Harry and Helena (Hood) W.; S.B., Mass. Inst. Tech., 1911; m. Marie Ross Sinclair, Aug. 25, 1915. Asst. in mech. engring., Mass. Inst. Tech., 1911-12; asst. to chief engr. Cramp Shipbuilding Co., 1912-13; instr. in machine design U. of Ill., 1913-17; mech. engr. The Angus Co., Ltd., Calcutta, India, 1917-19; asst. prof. mech. engring. U. of Ill., 1919-20; asso. prof. mech. engring. Johns Hopkins U., 1920-29; sec. and mech. engr. Kwong Yuen & Co., Inc., New York, N.Y., 1929-35; special lecturer in engring. thermodynamics, New York U., 1935-36; asso. prof., later prof. and head dept. of mech. engring. Louisiana State U., since 1936. Awarded Franklin Medal (Boston), 1907; scholarship awards Mass. Inst. Tech., 1908, 1909, 1910. Mem. Am. Soc. M.E., American Soc. for Engring. Edn., La. Teachers Assn., La. Engring. Soc., Sigma Xi, Tau Beta Pi. Home: 416 E. State St., Baton Rouge 13, La. Died Mar. 1947.

WATERHOUSE, John, sugar factor; b. Honolulu, T.H., Nov. 20, 1873; s. John Thomas and Elizabeth Bourne (Pinder) W.; A.B., Princeton, 1896; m. Martha Alexander, Feb. 6, 1900. With J. T. Waterhouse, importer, Honolulu, 1896-99, Bishop & Co., bankers, 1899-1901, Alexander & Baldwin, sugar factors and commn. merchants, since 1901, pres. McBryde Sugar Co., Kahaku Plantation Co., Kauai Pineapple Co., Kauai Terminal, Ltd.; vice pres. Hawaiian Commercial & Sugar Co., Kahului R.R. Co., Maui Agrl. Co.; dir. Matson Navigation Co., Hawn Trust Co. Republican. Conglist. Clubs: Pacific, University, Commercial, Oahu Country, Hawaiian Polo and Racing. Home: Honolulu, T.H. Died Oct. 10, 1945.

WATERMAN, Herbert, prof.; b. Odessa, Russia, May 30, 1903; s. Joseph and Florence (Black) W.; came to U.S., 1920, naturalized 1927; B.S. cum laude, Coll. City of New York, 1930; B.S. in Engring., Columbia, 1930, Chem. E. (Illig medal), 1931, Ph.D., 1934; m. Beatrice Joy Rollin, June 2, 1933. Cons. engr. Colin G. Fink, New York, N.Y., 1931-32; chem. engr. Aerovox Corp., 1932-33, head research lab., 1933-34, dir. research and development, 1934-37, chief engr. and gen. mgr., 1937 to Feb. 1939, consultant to Sept. 1939; cons. engr. in chem., indsl. and electrochem. and electronic fields, Los Angeles, Calif., since 1939; lecturer in chem. engring. Univ. of Southern Calif., 1940-42, asst. prof., 1942-44, asso. prof., 1944-46, prof. since 1946, acting head dept. chem. engring., 1942-45, head since 1945. Licensed professional engr., New York State. Mem. Am. Inst. Chem. Engrs. (counsellor student chapter Univ. Southern Calif. since 1943), Am. Inst. Mining and Metall. Engrs., Am. Chem. Soc., Soc. Chem. Ind. (Great Britain), Electrochem. Soc., Los Angeles County Chamber of Commerce (tech. adviser smoke and fume com. since 1944, chmn. scientific com. since Mar. 1947), Phi Beta Kappa, Sigma Xi, Phi Lambda Upsilon, Epsilon Xi. Clubs: Chemists (New York); Engineers (San Francisco). Author: Graphs and Tables for Electroplaters, 1943; The Chemical Industry as Consumer of California Minerals (Bull. Calif. Div. of Mines), 1945. Contbr. numerous articles on capacitors and their applications in tech. pubs. Holder numerous patents in fields of electric capacitors, chem. manufacture and related fields. Home: 2100 Roselin Pl., Los Angeles 26, Calif. Died July 31, 1947.

WATERMAN, Julian Seesel, prof. law; b. Pine Bluff, Ark., Sept. 9, 1891; s. Gus and Rachel U. (Sessel) W.; A.B., Tulane, 1912; A.M., U. of Mich., 1913; J.D., U. of Chicago, 1923; m. Evangeline Pratt, Sept. 5, 1927. Instr. dept. economics and sociology, U. of Ark, 1914-17, asso. prof. and chmn. dept. economics, 1923-24, prof. law and dean law sch. since 1924, chmn. athletic council since 1933, vice president of the University since 1937. Member Ark. Exec. Tax Com., 1924-25, Ark. Commn. on Business Laws and Taxation, 1927-28. Entered U.S. Army, 1917; camp transportation officer, Camp Pike, Ark., 1918-19. Vice-pres. Southwest Athletic Conf., 1937-41, pres. 1941-43. Mem. Am. Assn. Univ. Profs., Ark. Bar Assn., Am. Bar Assn., Nat. Tax Assn. (exec. com. 1929-32), Scabbard and Blade, Tau Kappa Alpha, Order of Coif; hon. mem. Phi Alpha Delta, Phi Beta Kappa. Democrat. Home: Fayetteville, Ark. Died Sep. 18, 1943.

WATERMAN, Nixon, author; b. Newark, Ill., Nov. 12, 1859; s. Lyman and Elizabeth (Wakefield) W.; ed. country and town pub. schs., Valparaiso (Ind.) U.; m. Nellie Haskins, Mar. 14, 1883. On editorial staff Omaha World-Herald and Bee, 1887-90, Chicago Herald and Post, 1890-93; removed to Boston, 1905; mag. and book writer, since 1905; has given many public readings from own writings and occasional lectures on humorous lit., philos. topics. Clubs: Boston Authors' (pres. 1937-39), Puddingstone, Rimers; The Limerick (Orange Park, Fla.). Author: A Book of Verses, 1900; In Merry Mood, 1902; Boy Wanted, 1906; Sonnets of a Budding Bard, 1907; The Girl Wanted, 1909; Sunshine Verses, 1913; For You and Me (poems), 1913; A Rose to the Living and Other Poems, 1919, 29. Author and composer of nat. anthem, The United States of America, 1935; O Flag of Our Land (The New Star Spangled Banner), 1938. Editor: Ben King's Verse (for Chicago Press Club), 1894. Address: "Fair Acres," York Rd., Canton, Mass. Died Sept. 1, 1944.

WATERS, Lewis William, chemist; b. Orange, Mass., Oct. 3, 1888; s. William Wadsworth and Anna Amelia (Stone) W.; grad. Orange High Sch., 1906; B.S., Mass. Inst. Tech., 1910; m. Hazel E. Rugen, Apr. 4, 1915; children—Sally Eleanor, Lewis William. Instr. in food analysis, Mass. Inst. Tech., 1910-11; chemist Campbell Soup Co., 1911-14; asst. to Prof. W. T. Sedgwick, Mass. Inst. Tech., 1914; in charge research lab. United Fruit Co., Port Limon, Costa Rica, 1914-17; in charge biol. research dept. Expt. Sta., E. I. Du Pont de Nemours, Wilmington, Del., 1917-20; mgr. research dept., Minute Tapioca Co., 1920-27; asst. to exec. v.p. Gen. Foods Corp., 1927-30, v.p. in charge of research and development, 1930-43, v.p. in charge scientific relations since 1943. Lecturer N.Y. Univ. Consultant to scientific com. War Prodn. Bd.; mem. adv. com. on research and development Office of Q.M. Gen.; mem. tech. adv. com. Nutrition Foundation, Inc. Mem. A.A.A.S., Am. Chem. Soc. (councillor since 1937), Am. Pub. Health Assn., Nat. Assn. Mfrs. (com. scientific research 1939-41), Nat. Research Council, Inst. Food Technologists (councillor), Soc. Chem. Industry (councillor), Am. Acad. Sociol. and Polit. Sciences, Am. Inst of Chemists. Clubs: Chemists (N.Y.); Oriental (Mamaroneck, N.Y.). Contbr. to periodicals. Home: 80 Hartsdale Rd., White Plains, N.Y. Office: 250 Park Av., New York, N.Y. Died Mar. 31, 1944.

WATKINS, Edgar, lawyer; b. Campbell County, Ga., July 31, 1868; s. Moses Denman and Divine Howard (Word) W.; prep. edn., Hutchinson Inst., Whitesburg, Ga., LL.B., U. of Ga., 1889; LL.D., Ohio Northern U., 1922; m. Mary Belle Cameron, Mar. 1, 1894; children—Edgar, Robert Cameron, James Hogg, John Allan. Admitted to Ga. bar, 1889, and began practice at Carrollton; moved to Houston, Tex., 1896, Atlanta, Ga., 1907; county atty. Carroll County, Ga., 1892, 93; alderman, Houston, 1902, 03; pres. Bd. of Edn., Houston, 1904, 05; atty. Interstate Commerce Commn., Washington, D.C., 1914-17; alderman, Atlanta, 1922, 23; argued 25 cases before Supreme Court of U.S., appearing successfully against constitutionality of the Lever Food Control Act; atty. for 8 Southern States in interterritorial Commodity Rate Case; now mem. firm Watkins & Watkins; apptd. spl. asst. to Atty. Gen. to hear appeals of conscientious objectors under the Selective Service Act; Special Counsel State of Georgia, 1944-45. Dem. presidential elector, Georgia, 1928. President bd. trustees and chmn. exec. com. Oglethorpe U.; Am. trustee Yenching U., Peiping, China. Mem. Am., Ga. State and Atlanta bar assns., Am. Judicature Soc., Am. Law Inst., Internat. Law Assn., Nat. Council of Nat. Economic League, Phi Gamma Delta. Democrat. Presbyterian. Mason (K.T., 32°, Shriner). Clubs: City, Capital City (Atlanta); University (Washington, D.C.). Author: Watkins' Shippers and Carriers (4th edit.), 1930; Law and Business, 1925; Cases on Carriers, 1928; The Ordinary Man's Religion.

1933. Home: 3511 Piedmont Rd. N.E. Office: Citizens and Southern Nat. Bank Bldg., Atlanta, Ga. Died Aug. 22, 1945.

WATKINS, Henry Vaughan, lawyer; b. Hays Station, Miss., July 6, 1884; s. Thomas Henry and Julia (Brown) W.; LL.B., Millsaps Coll., 1903; student U. of Miss., 1904-05; m. Sadie Alice Sale, Nov. 14, 1907; children—Sadie Vee (Mrs. M. A. Lewis, Jr.), Janie H., Henry Vaughan, Betty (Mrs. Sidney Penn, Jr.), Archie Sale, Julia May, Amelia, Selby. Admitted to Miss. bar, 1905, and since in practice of law; pres. and atty. Miss Pub. Corp.; v.p. and atty. Plaza Investment Co., The Gammill Co.; atty. and dir. Magnolia State Bldg. & Loan Assn. Pres. Bd. of Trustees Hinds Jr. Coll.; pres. Community Welfare Assn. Pres. R. V. Powers Foundation, R. H. Green Foundation, Miss. Orphans Home. Mem. Kappa Alpha. Democrat. Methodist. Woodman, K.P., Odd Fellow. Home: 1409 N. State St. Office: Standard Life Bldg., Jackson, Miss. Died Jan. 6, 1944.

WATKINS, John Elfreth, newspaperman; b. Vincentown, N.J.; s. John Elfreth and Helen (Bryan) W.; grad. Central High Sch., Washington; m. Corinne C., d. Courtland C. Clements. Editor in chief of Review (published by four high schools of Washington) at age of 17; entered press galleries of Congress at 19 as assistant correspondent, Chicago Daily News and Indianapolis News. For 23 yrs. contributed to leading newspapers of the world a Washington column which became nucleus of the Watkins Syndicate which supplied news and feature matter to American and foreign press. Filled Washington assignments for and contributed Washington Column to Curtis Pub. Co. Organized for Cyrus H. K. Curtis, The Ledger Syndicate of Phila., beginning Dec. 1916, gen. mgr. Curtis' N.Y. Evening Post Syndicate; est. radio news service into Philadelphia directly from Europe, 1920. Created and developed many notable features for Curtis orgn.; after Curtis' death, re-established June 1935, Watkins Syndicate, Inc., of which is pres.; dir. distribution of London Times Cable Service, U.S. and Canada during World War I, subsequently the dispatches and columns of Raymond Gram Swing, Dorothy Thompson, Carl Ackerman, H. R. Knickerbocker, Geo. E. Sokolsky, Clinton W. Gilbert, Demaree Bess, Wythe Williams, Col. E. M. House, also commentaries of former pres. Taft, former pres. Poincaire, Glenn Babb, Nunnally Johnson, M. W. Fodor, Cardinal Mercier, Theodore Roosevelt, Jr., James W. Gerard. Developed Dorothy Dix into daily column. Directed press bur. Nat. Capital Centennial; chmn. com. on cables, Am. Publishers' Com. on Electrical Communications, 1920-21; mem. bd. govs. Assn. of Am. Newspaper Syndicates. Unitarian. Author of more than 100 mystery and detective stories, also numerous articles in mags.; author of screen features, "The Thread," "The Test." Address: 47 Llanfair Rd., Ardmore, Pa.; and Avalon, N.J. Died Feb. 13, 1946.

WATKINS, Raymond Edward, physician and surgeon; b. Fairdale, Ill., June 7, 1882; s. Myron F. and Isabelle Elizabeth (Crosby) W.; M.D., U. of Ill., 1909; student Chicago Grad. Sch. of Medicine, 1916, Harvard, 1918 and 1919; post grad. student Europe, 1936; m. Maud A. Stone, Oct. 31 1910; children—Elizabeth Jean (Mrs. Henry Irving Jorgensen), Nancy Rae. Engaged in practice of medicine since 1909; in general practice, Portland, Ore., 1911-22; practice limited to gynecology and obstetrics since 1922; prof. gynecology, Med. Sch., U. of Ore., 1929-31, prof. gynecology and obstetrics and head of dept. since 1931, chmn. com. on cancer study; chief of gynecologic and obstetrical service, teaching clinic, Multnomah Hosp. Served with orthopedic div., Med. Corps, U.S. Army, 1918-19. Diplomate Am. Bd. Gynecology and Obstetrics. Fellow Am. Coll. Surgeons; mem. Am. Gynecological Soc., Pacific Coast Surg. Soc., Pacific Coast Soc. of Obstetrics and Gynecology, Portland Acad. Medicine, Nu Sigma Nu, Alpha Omega Alpha (counselor since 1924). Mem. exec. faculty U. of Ore. Med. Sch. Club: University (Portland). Mem. editorial staff and advisory bd. Am. Jour. of Obstetrics and Gynecology. Contbr. chapter entitled "Retrodisplacement and Prolapse of the Uterus" in Textbook of Surgery by American Authors (Frederick Christopher), 1943; contbr. to treatise, Treatment of Cancer and Allied Diseases (Geo. T. Pack), 1941. Co-author: Obstetrics and Gynecology (Arthur Hale Curtis), 1933. Home: 2532 N.E. Alameda, Portland 12. Office: 833 S.W. 11th Av., Portland 5, Ore. Died Aug. 7, 1945.

WATSON, Adolphus Eugene, rear admiral; b. Norfolk, Va., Aug. 9, 1878; s. Rear Admiral Eugene Winslow and Virginia (Cruse) W.; grad. U.S. Naval Acad., 1899, Naval War Coll., 1925; m. Genevieve Gallagher, Jan. 10, 1907; 1 dau., Priscilla Winslow. Commd. ensign U.S. Navy, Feb. 1, 1901; promoted through grades to rank of rear adm., Sept. 1, 1932. Served on U.S.S. Montgomery, Spanish-Am. War and Philippine Campaign; exec. officer U.S.S. Florida with Grand Fleet in North Sea, World War; chief of staff Naval Mission to Brazil, 1927-29; chief of staff U.S. Battleship Fleet, 1931-32; mem. General Board U.S. Navy, 1932; comdr. of Destroyer Squadrons, Scouting Force, 1933-35; then pres. Naval Examining Board; comdr. Battleship Div. 2, 1937-39; comdt. 4th Naval Dist. and Navy Yard, Phila., 1939-42; retired, 1942. Recalled to active duty in Navy Dept., 1943-45. Awarded Navy Cross for services in World War I, Legion of Merit for services World War II. Clubs: Army and Navy (Washington); Loyal Legion (Phila.); Chevy Chase. Address: 2126 Connecticut Av., Washington. Died Oct. 3, 1949; buried in Arlington National Cemetery.

WATSON, Bruce Mervellon, educator, author; b. Windsor, N.Y., Feb. 28, 1860; s. Robert Bruce and Amanda R. (Porter) W.; grad. State Normal and Training Sch., Oswego, N.Y., 1885; studied Syracuse U.; m. Jennie E. Moore, June 28, 1894; children—Robert Bruce, Dorothy Moore (Mrs. D. H. Ecker), Helen Annette (Mrs. L. E. Steiner). Vice-prin. Pulaski (N.Y.) Acad., 1885-86; prin. Seymour Sch., Syracuse, 1887-1904; head of math. dept. Central High Sch., Syracuse, 1904-08; supt. schs., Spokane, Wash., 1908-16; mng. dir. Pub. Edn. and Child Labor Assn. of Pa., 1916-36. Admitted to New York bar, 1898. Pres. Inland Empire Teachers' Assn., 1912-13. Mem. Philadelphia Com. on Public Affairs. Mem. N.E.A. (mem. legislative commn. since 1931). Congregationalist. Mason. Charter mem. Phila. Torch Club. Author: Summary of Arithmetic, 1895; Heath Primary Arithmetic, 1901; Watson and White's Arithmetical Series (Charles Edward White), 3 books, 1907; Watson and White's Modern Arithmetics, 3 books, 1918; Watson's Simplified Arithmetics, 1924; Modern Practical Arithmetics, 1925; Junior High School Mathematics (3 vols.), 1931; The Mastery Mathematics, 3 vols. (with Bodley, Hayes and Gibson), 1935. Contbr. many articles on sch. adminstrn. and pedagogy. Editor: Pennsylvania's Children in School and at Work, semi-monthly, 1920-36. Home: 509 Woodland Court, Wayne, Pa. Died Jan. 26, 1943.

WATSON, Byron S., ins. exec.; b. Providence, R.I., May 26, 1876; s. Arthur Hamilton and Annie Potter (Sprague) W.; A.B., Brown U., 1897; m. Isabel Loomis, Oct. 31, 1899; children—Isabel Loomis (Mrs. Thomas W. Taylor), Annie Potter Sprague (Mrs. John E. Hurst), Hope (Mrs. George C. Davis). With Greene Anthony & Co., wholesale footwear, 1897-1903, partner, 1903-13, propr., 1913-32; dir. R.I. Ins. Co., since 1914, v.p. and chmn. bd., 1932-34, pres., 1934-41, chmn. bd. since 1941; pres. Belcher & Loomis Realty Co., Towne St. Inc.; director Union Trust Co., Nicholson File Co., American Screw Co., Narragansett Electric Co., Certain-teed Products Corp. Member Rhode Island National Guard, 1896-99; a.d.c. and col. on staff Gov. Kimball, 1901-03. Mem. Psi Upsilon. Republican. Episcopalian. Clubs: Hope, Agawam Hunt, Turks Head, Squantum (Providence); Dunes (Narragansett Pier); Point Judith Country. Home: 20 Benevolent St. Office: 31 Canal St., Providence 2, R.I. Died Sept. 9, 1947.

WATSON, Charles Roger, educationalist; b. Cairo, Egypt, July 17, 1873; s. Andrew and Margaret (McVickar) W.; A.B., Princeton, 1894, A.M., 1896, D.D., 1931; spl. student Princeton Theol. Sem., 1895-96, Allegheny Theol. Sem., 1897-98; grad. Princeton Theol. Sem., 1899; m. Maria Elizabeth Powell, Nov. 20, 1902; children—M. Elisabeth, Edward T. P., Margaret M., Charles R. Teacher Ohio State U., 1894-95, Princeton U., 1895-96, Lawrenceville Sch., 1896-97; in charge Mission Ch., Allegheny, Pa., 1899-1900; ordained U.P. ministry, July 26, 1900; pastor First Ch., St. Louis, 1900-02; corr. sec. Board of Foreign Missions, U.P. Ch. of North America, 1902-16, hon. corr. sec., 1916-22; sec. and pres.-elect Am. Univ., at Cairo, 1914-22, pres. 1922-1945; pres. emeritus since 1945. Mem. continuation com. World's Missionary Conf., Edinburgh, 1910. Spl. rep. of fgn. mission bds. of N. Am. at Paris Peace Conf., 1919. Mem. Internat. Missionary Council. Visited mission fields of India, Egypt and the Sudan, 1903-04, Egypt to study ednl and missionary problems, 1911-12, 15, 17; chmn. council com. for Western Asia and North Africa, 1924-26; mem. Jerusalem Conf., I.M.C., 1928. Apptd. mem. Nat. Commn. on Edn. in Egypt, 1931; mem. Near East Christian Council. Decorated by King Farouk I. of Egypt with Order of Ismail Second Class, 1945. Clubs: Princeton (New York); Gezirch Sporting Club, Rotary Internat. (Cairo; pres. 1941-42). Author of several books and numerous articles in mags. Home: 2933 Haverford Rd., Ardmore, Pa. Died Jan. 10, 1948; buried Princeton, N.J.

WATSON, Edward Minor, judge; b. Holly Springs, Miss., Dec. 20, 1874; s. Edward Minor and Lillie Perrin (Moore) W.; student Miss. Agrl. and Mech. Coll., 1890-91; LL.B., U. of Miss., 1897; m. Louisa Emily Bradley, June 1, 1905. Began practice at Oxford, Miss., 1897; removed to Honolulu, H.T., 1901; mem. commn. to draft county act, providing county system of govt. for Hawaii, 1904; del. to Dem. Nat. Conv., 1908, 12; justice Supreme Court of Hawaii, 1914-16; resigned to resume practice; judge First Circuit Court, Ty. of Hawaii, Div. of Domestic Relations, 1928-35, of U.S. Dist. Court since July, 1935. Mem. Delta Kappa Epsilon. Clubs: Pacific, University. Home: 1734 Anapuni St., Honolulu, T.H. Died Sept. 23, 1938.

WATSON, Edwin Martin, sec. to the President, army officer; b. Eufaula, Ala., Dec. 10, 1883; s. Peter Penn and Addie (Martin) W.; B.S., U.S. Mil. Acad., 1908; m. Frances Nash, Aug. 31, 1920. Commd. 2d lt., U.S. Army, 1908, and advanced through the grades to brig. gen., Apr. 1939, major-gen., Oct. 1940; served with 11th Inf., Ft. Russell, Wyo., 1908-10; aide-de-camp to Brig. Gen. Frederick A. Smith, Dept. of Mo., Omaha, Neb., 1910-12; with 24th Inf., Philippines, 1912-15; 1st lt. 28th Inf., Galveston, Tex., 1915; mil. aide to President Wilson, 1915-17; maj. 12th F.A., with A.E.F. at Toulon-Troyon, Aisne, Aisne-Marne and St. Mihiel campaigns, 1918; lt. col. St. Mihiel and Meuse-Argonne offensives, with 15th F.A., 77th Div., 1918; junior aide to President Wilson at Paris and U.S. and chief of Mil. Sect., Peace Conf., Paris, in charge of all functions at the President's official residence, Paris, and the arrangements of all the President's visits to foreign countries, including England, Italy, and Belgium, 1918-20; attended French arty. schs., 1920-22; student office F.A. Sch., Ft. Sill, Okla., 1923-24; exec. officer F.A. group, Organized Reserves, 2d Corps, New York, 1924-26, Command and Gen. Staff Sch., Ft. Leavenworth, 1926-27; mil. attaché, Am. Embassy, Brussels, 1927-31; mil. aide to President Roosevelt, 1933-41, sec. since Apr. 1939. Decorated Silver Star with oak leaf cluster (U.S.); Chevalier of Legion of Honor, Croix de Guerre with palm (France); Comdr. Order of Crown, Officer Order of Leopold (Belgium); Comdr. Nat. Order of Southern Cross (Brazil); Silver Cross (Sweden); Star of Abdon Calderon (Ecuador); Order of Danilo I (Montenegro). Clubs: University (New York); Apawamis (Rye, N.Y.); Metropolitan, Army and Navy, Chevy Chase (Washington, D.C.). Home: 3133 Connecticut Av. Office: The White House, Washington, D.C. Died Feb. 20, 1945.

WATSON, Hugh Hammond, consul gen.; b. Bradford, Vt., Nov. 10, 1885; s. John H. and Clara (Hammond) W.; A.B., U. of Vt., 1906; m. Eugenie Lillian Ellison, Apr. 23, 1923; children—John, Joan Claire, Hugh Robert, Betty Eugenie. Clerk Three Rivers Consulate, 1907-08; appointed vice and deputy consul, at Three Rivers, Dec. 28, 1907; vice and deputy consul, at Yarmouth, N.S., 1908-11, Belfast, Ireland, 1911-15; vice consul, at Liverpool, Eng., 1915-21; consul at Lille, France, 1921, at Lyons, 1922-32, Sydney, N.S., 1932-35; consul gen. at Halifax, N.S., 1935-37, Kingston, Jamaica, 1937-42, Glasgow, Scotland, since Feb. 1942. Address: Dept. of State, Washington, D.C.* Died May 23, 1947.

WATSON, James E., ex-senator; b. Winchester, Ind., Nov. 2, 1863; s. Enos L. W.; A.B., DePauw U., 1886, A.M., 1906; LL.D., Notre Dame Univ., 1910, Lincoln U., 1916; m. Flora Miller, Dec. 12, 1892; children—Edwin G., James E., Catherine, Joseph C. Admitted to Ind. bar, 1887, and began practice with father; removed to Rushville, Ind., 1893. Mem. 54th Congress (1895-97) and 56th to 60th Congresses (1899-1909), 6th Ind. Dist.; Rep. nominee for gov. of Ind., 1908; U.S. senator for unexpired term (1916-21) of Benjamin F. Shively, deceased; reëlected for term 1921-27 and 1927-33; majority leader, Senate, 1929-33; chmn. Com. Interstate Commerce. Del. to Rep. Nat. Conv., 1912, 20, 24, 32, 36; chmn. Com. on Resolutions, Republican Nat. Conv., 1920; Taft floor leader, 1912. Grand chancellor, Knights of Pythias, 1891-93. Address: Rushville, Ind. Died July 29, 1948.

WATSON, John Brown, educator; b. Smith County, Tex., 1872; s. Frank and Chrystial (Gary) W.; ed. Colgate U., 1900-01, Brown U., 1901-04, U. of Chicago, 1904-05, Cornell U., summer 1933; A.M., LL.D., Morehouse Coll.; m. Hattie Rutherford, Sept. 7, 1907. Reared on farm and became teacher in Smith County common and high schs., 1889-92; instr. in Morehouse Coll. (colored), Atlanta, Ga., 1904-09; sec. Nat. Com. Y.M.C.A., Atlanta, 1909-17; receiver of Atlanta State Savings Bank, Atlanta, Ga., 1921-23; pres. Leland Coll., Baton Rouge, La., 1923-28; pres. Agrl., Mech. and Normal Coll., Pine Bluff, Ark. (Arkansaw State Coll.), since 1928. Mem. Sigma Phi. Democrat. Baptist. Mem. Grand Order of Odd Fellows, Ancient and Accepted Masons. Club: Monday (Atlanta). Address: Agrl., Mechanical and Normal College, Pine Bluff, Ark. Died Dec. 6, 1942.

WATSON, Paul Barron, author; b. Morristown, N.J., Mar. 25, 1861; s. Barron Crowell and Julia (Willis) W.; A.B., Harvard U., 1881; m. Katharine H. Clarke, June 4, 1890; children—Paul Barron, Donald Clarke, John Whitman. Admitted to bar, 1885; practices in Boston. Treas. Wentworth Inst. Clubs: Union (Boston); University (N.Y.). Author: Bibliography of Pre-Columbian Discoveries of America, 1881; Marcus Aurelius Antoninus, 1884; The Swedish Revolution under Gustavus Vasa, 1889; Tales of Normandie, 1930; Some Women of France, 1936; Our Dollar, 1940; Our National Debt, 1940; Commodore James Barron, 1942; Our Constitution, 1946. Home: 79 Marlborough St. Office: 50 State St., Boston, Mass. Died Mar. 19, 1948.

WATSON, Robert, author; b. Glasgow, Scotland, May 28, 1882; s. James Rugland and Hester (Taylor) W.; ed. Pollok and Shawlands acads., Glasgow; m. Anna McNaught Johnstone, May 16, 1911; children—Doreen Hester (dec.), Hugh Douglas, Sheila Kathleen Nada. Went to Canada, 1908, came to U.S., 1933. Began as accountant William Sloan & Co., steamship owners, Glasgow; later with Hudson Bay Co., at Vernon, B.C., Saskatoon, Saskatchewan, Winnipeg. Traveled and lectured extensively. Fellow Royal Geog. Soc. (Eng.), Canadian Geog. Soc.; mem. Screen Writers Guild, Inc., Soc. of Authors, Playwrights and Composers, Canadian Authors Assn. (ex-v.p., ex-nat. treas.); formerly pres. United Scottish Socs., Manitoba. Mason. Author: (novels) My Brave and Gallant Gentleman, 1918; The Girl of O.K. Valley, 1919; Stronger Than His Sea, 1920; The Spoilers of the Valley, 1923; Gordon of the Lost Lagoon, 1925; Me and Peter, 1926; High Hazard, 1927; When Christmas Came to Fort Garry, 1935; Babes in Babylon, 1939; (non-fiction) Canada's Fur Bearers, 1925; Lower Fort Garry, 1928; Famous Forts of Manitoba, 1929; A Boy of the Great North West, 1930; Indians of Manitoba, 1931; (poetry) The Mad Minstrel, 1921; Dreams of Fort Garry (poetry), 1932; also screen plays: "Stop, Look and Love;" "Secret Patrol," "Tugboat Princess," "Gun Smoke," "Bob, Son of Battle." Editor of The Beaver Magazine (Hudson Bay Co.) 10 yrs.; associate editor of Hollywood Spectator, 1 yr. British correspondent, writer and tech. dir. numerous important screen plays. Home: 663 Anita St., Laguna Beach, Calif. Died Jan. 13, 1948; interred Melrose Abbey Mausoleum, Santa Ana, Calif.

WATSON, Robert Walker, life insurance exec.; b. Paris, Tex., Oct. 21, 1894; s. Robert Gill and Susan Jane (Westerman) W.; student U. of Tex., 1911-13; m. Ola M. Smith, May 14, 1921. With Am. Nat. Bank, Paris, Tex., 1913-17; foreign dept., Nat. City Bank of N.Y., 1919-20; with Morris Plan Ins. Soc., New York, since 1920; successively asst. treas., treas., v.p., now pres.; dir. and mem. exec. com. Morris Plan Corp. America, Puritan Corp.; dir. Morris Plan Industrial Bank of New York; dir. of Morris Plan banks in Richmond, Va., Knoxville, Tenn., Atlanta, Ga., and Cleveland, O. Served as 1st O.T.C., Leon Spring, Tex.; commd. officer, U.S. Army, 1917-19. Democrat. Clubs: Uptown (N.Y. City); Sleepy Hollow Country (Scarborough, N.Y.). Home: Old Post Road S., Croton-on-Hudson, N.Y. Office: 420 Lexington Av., New York, N.Y. Died Dec. 1, 1944.

WATSON, Samuel Newell, clergyman; b. Lyons, Ia., Feb. 27, 1861; s. George William and Hetty (Newell) W.; B.A., Trinity Coll., Conn., 1882, M.A., 1887; U. of the South, 1883-84; M.D., U. of Ia., 1893; (D.D., U. of Ia., 1889); m. Jeannette Grace Watkins, Jan. 7, 1885. Deacon, 1884, priest, 1885, P.E. Ch.; rector Trinity Ch., Iowa City, Ia., 1886-97, St. Paul's, Chillicothe, O., 1897-1903, St. Paul's, Akron, O., 1903-12; rector Am. Ch. in Paris, France, 1912-18, rector emeritus, 1918. Chaplain 3d Regt., Ia. Nat. Guard, 1886; relief work in France, World War, 1914-18. Pres. Council of Advice Am. Ch. in Europe. Decorated Officier Legion of Honor (French); Chevalier Order of Leopold (Belgium); Comdr. Order of St. Sava (Serbian). Mem. Alpha Delta Phi. Mason. Author: Those Paris Years, 1936. Home: 2321 State St. Address: P.O. Box 896, Santa Barbara, Calif. Died Mar. 27, 1942.

WATT, Homer Andrew (wŏt), prof. English; b. Wilkes-Barre, Pa., Sept. 11, 1884; s. Andrew Eton and Clara Susan (Woodruff) W.; A.B., Cornell U., 1906; M.A., U. of Wis., 1908, Ph.D., 1909; m. Effie Margaret Whyte, June 23, 1910; children—Harold Woodruff, William Whyte, Florence Jean. Mary M. Adams fellow U. of Wis., 1907-08, instr. English, 1909-16; asst. prof. English, New York Univ., 1916-20, asso. prof., 1920-22, prof. since 1922, head dept. since 1938; exchange prof. English, U. of Southern Calif., 1925-26; prof. English, U. of Va., summer 1928, U. of Colo., summer 1932. Mem. Modern Language Association of America, Medieval Academy of America, Modern Humanities Research Association, Nat. Council Teachers English, Shakespeare Assn. of Am., Bibliographical Soc. Am., N.Y. Acad. Pub. Edn., Phi Beta Kappa, Eta Sigma Phi. Awarded diploma decoration, Order of St. Sava IV (Yugoslavia). Republican. Congregationalist. Clubs: Andiron, New York University Faculty (pres., 1945-47) (New York). Author: Gorboduc, or Ferrex and Porrex, 1910; The Composition of Technical Papers, 1917, 25; (with J. B. Munn) Ideas and Forms in English and American Literature, 1925, 32; Highways in College Composition (with Oscar Cargill), 1930; Outlines of Shakespeare's plays (with K. J. Holzknecht and Raymond Ross), 1935, 38, 41; The Literature of England (with George B. Woods and George K. Anderson), 1936, 41, 47; Voices of Liberty (with F. M. K. Foster), 1941; New Highways in College Composition (with Oscar Cargill and William Charvat), 1943; Dictionary of English Literature (with W. W. Watt), 1945; College Reader (with Oscar Cargill), 1948. Editor: (with Prof. J. W. Cunliffe) Thackeray's English Humorists, 1911; Modern America Series of English Texts. Contbr. essays and tech. articles. Home: 19 Douglas Rd., Glen Ridge, N.J. Died Oct. 4, 1948.

WATT, Robert J., labor rep.; b. Scotland, July 16, 1894; s. Alexander and Helen (Robertson) W.; came to U.S., 1912, naturalized, 1919; m. Janet Learmonth, Apr. 28, 1917; children—Janet L., Robert A. Began as labor rep., 1915; pres. Lawrence (Mass.) Central Labor Union, 1925-30; v.p. Mass. State Fedn. of Labor, 1932-37, sec.-treas., 1929-37; labor member Mass. Unemployment Commn., 1936-38; Am. Workers del. to Geneva, 1936-40; mem. Pres. Roosevelt's Commn. to England and Sweden, 1938; internat. rep., Am. Fedn. of Labor, since 1936. Alternate mem. Nat. Defense Mediation Bd.; chmn. labor advisory com. Fed. Communications Commn.; mem. Fed. advisory board Vocational Edn. Labor del. to Internat. Labor Orgn. Conf., Paris, Oct. 1945. Served as pvt., inf., Canadian Army, 1917-19. Home: 1421 Massachusetts Av. N.W. Office: American Federation of Labor Bldg., Washington, D.C. Died July 23, 1947.

WATTS, Frank Overton, banker; b. Paducah, Ky., Nov. 14, 1867; s. Thomas Lacey and Ruth (Caldwell) W.; ed. pub. and prep. schs.; m. Helen Moore, Jan. 16, 1894; children—Lawson M., Mrs. Gentry Shelton, Jr., Frank O. Cashier First Nat. Bank, Union City, Tenn., 1888-97; cashier, 1897-1903, pres., 1903-12, First Nat. Bank, Nashville; v.p., 1912-13, pres., 1913-19, Third Nat. Bank, St. Louis; became pres. First Nat. Bank, 1919, now chmn. bd.; dir. Am. Central Ins. Co., C.&E.I. R.R. Co., Huttig Sash & Door Co., St. Louis Union Trust Co., Md. Casualty Co., Southwestern Bell Telephone Co. Mem. Federal Advisory Council from 8th Reserve dist. Federal Reserve System, 1915-22. Chmn. exec. com., 1908-09, v.p., 1909-10, pres., 1910-11, Am. Bankers Assn. Independent Democrat. Home: 33 Portland Pl. Office: First Nat. Bank in St. Louis, St. Louis, Mo. Died Nov. 5, 1946.

WATTS, Ralph L., horticulturist; b. Kerrmoor, Clearfield County, Pa., June 5, 1869; s. Martin Overholser and Marian Elizabeth (Hoyt) W.; B.S. in Agr., Pa. State Coll., 1890, M.S., 1899; D.Agr., Syracuse U., 1916; D.Sc.; R.I. State Coll., 1931; m. Hattie Searle, Jan. 1, 1895 (died 1940); children—Gilbert Searle, Curtis McClure, Grace Elizabeth; m. 2d, Bertha P. Myers, June 11, 1941. Horticulturist Tenn. Expt. Sta., 1890-99; lecturer farmers institutes, 1899-1908; prof. horticulture, Pa. State Coll., 1908-12, dean and dir. Sch. of Agr. and Expt. Sta., 1912-39, dean emeritus since Jan. 1, 1939. Mem. Soc. for Hort. Science, Vegetable Growers Assn. America (ex-pres.), A.A.A.S.; pres. Pa. State Conservation Council. Presbyterian. Mem. Phi Kappa Phi, Gamma Sigma Delta, Alpha Zeta, Delta Theta Sigma, Sigma Pi. Author: Vegetable Gardening (coll. textbook), 1912; The Vegetable Garden; Vegetable Forcing, 1917; Vegetable Growing Projects, 1921; Growing Vegetables, 1923; Rural Pennsylvania, 1925; The Vegetable Growing Business (with Gilbert S. Watts), 1939. Address: 225 E. Foster Av., State College, Pa. Died July 2, 1949.

WAUCHOPE, George Armstrong (wôk'ōp), univ. prof.; b. Natural Bridge, Va., May 26, 1862; s. Joseph W. and Jane (Armstrong) W.; A.B., Washington and Lee U., 1884, A.M., 1886, Ph.D., 1889, Litt.D., 1925; student in English, Harvard, 1898, in German, Berlin, 1889; traveled and studied in England, summer, 1908; m. Elizabeth Bostedo, Aug. 8, 1899; children—Virginia, Robert. Asst. prof. English, U. of Mo., 1891-95; prof. English, State U. of Ia., 1895-97; prof. English, U. of S.C., since 1898; supply prof. English lit., U. of Va., 1910; prof. English, U. of Va., summers, 1910-17, 19, Peabody Coll., 1918, 1921-29; lecturer Monteagle Assn., 1927. Fellow Washington and Lee U.; Poe centenary medalist, U. of Va., 1909; N.Y. Southern Soc. Medallion, 1935. Mem. Stage Soc., Drama League of America, Phi Beta Kappa, Modern Language Assn. of America, Omicron Delta Kappa, Kosmos Club. Author: From Generation to Generation, 1905; The Writers of South Carolina, 1910; Theories About Shakespeare, 1910; Henry Timrod: Poet and Man, 1912; Nineteenth Century Literature; The Spectre Ship; The Masque of the Woods; The New Irish Drama, 1920; Contemporary English Drama; Henry Arthur Jones and the Social Drama, 1921; Ideals of the English Speaking Peoples; Literary South Carolina, 1923. Editor: DeQuincey's Revolt of the Tartars, 1897; DeQuincey's Confessions of an Opium-Eater, 1898; George Eliot's Silas Marner, 1898; Essays of Charles Lamb, 1902; Longfellow's Courtship of Miles Standish, and Other Poems, 1902; Lamb's Essays of Elia, 1903; Spenser's Faerie Queene, Book I, 1903. Asst. editor The Critic, Baltimore Sun, Library of Southern Literature. Asso. editor Southern Literary Mag. Home: Columbia, S.C. Died June 6, 1943.

WAUGH, Frank Albert, landscape architect; b. Sheboygan Falls, Wis., July 8, 1869; s. Albert Freeman and Madeline (Biehler) W.; B.S., Kan. State Coll., 1891, M.S., 1893, also D.Sc.; grad. study, Cornell U., and in Germany and France; L.H.D., U. of Vt.; m. Alice Vail, Sept. 14, 1893; children—Dan F., Dorothy, Frederick V., Esther, Albert E., Sidney. In newspaper work in Topeka, Helena, Denver, 1891-93; prof. horticulture and landscape gardening, Mass. State Coll., Amherst, 1902-39, prof. of landscape architecture emeritus since 1939. Capt. Sanitary Corps, U.S. Army, 1918-19. Conglist. Author: Landscape Gardening, 1898; Plums and Plum Culture, 1899; Fruit Marketing, 1900; Systematic Pomology, 1903; Dwarf Fruit Trees, 1907; American Apple Orchard, 1908; The Landscape Beautiful, 1910; Kemp's Landscape Gardening, 1910; Beginner's Guide to Fruit Growing, 1912; American Peach Orchard, 1913; Rural Improvement, 1914; The Agricultural College, 1916; The Natural Style in Landscape Gardening, 1917; Outdoor Theatres, 1917; Downing's Landscape Gardening, 1921; Textbook of Landscape Gardening, 1922; Country Planning, 1924; Formal Design in Landscape Architecture, 1927; Hardy Shrubs, 1928; Everybody's Garden, 1930. Home: Amherst, Mass. Died Mar. 20, 1943.

WAXMAN, Percy, editor, writer, radio literary commentator; b. Australia; ed. Carlton Coll., Victoria, Australia; m. Constance Berry, Apr. 17, 1917. Came to U.S., 1905, naturalized, 1917. Copywriter, Barron Collier, Inc., N.Y. City, 1906-12; promotion dir. The Butterick Pub. Co., 1912-15; became mem. staff Pictorial Review, 1915, mng. editor, 1925-30, editor, 1930-32; asso. editor Cosmopolitan since 1935. Clubs: Players, Dutch Treat, American Yacht. Author: Versiflage (verse), 1922; The Black Napoleon (biography of Toussaint Louverture), 1931; What Price Mallorca, 1933. Collaborated with Cosmo Hamilton in musical comedy "Flora Bella"; with Eugene Lockhart in revue, "Bunk." Home: 40 W. 55th St. Office: Hearst Magazine Bldg., 8th Av. and 57th St., New York, N.Y. Died Jan. 12, 1948.

WAY, Cassius, veterinarian; b. Gilead, Conn., July 28, 1881; s. Charles Daniel and Katherine (Trumbull) W.; B.Agr., Conn. Agrl. Coll. (now U. of Conn.), 1899; A.B., Cornell U., 1906, D.V.M., 1907; m. Mary Barr Hamilton, Mar. 23, 1908. Pvt. practice as veterinarian, N.Y. City, 1907-08 and since 1919; milk sanitarian, Borden Co., N.Y. City, 1908-19, chief veterinarian, 1914-19. U.S. del. to 13th Internat. Congress of Veterinary Medicine, Zurich, Switzerland, 1938; mem. advisory com. on medicine and pub. health, N.Y. World's Fair, 1939-40. Mem. Am. Vet. Med. Assn. (pres., 1939-40), N.Y. City, N.Y. State vet. med. socs., Sigma Xi, Phi Zeta, Alpha Psi (Beta chapter), Omega Upsilon Phi, Gamma Alpha. Republican. Conglist. Mason (K.T., Shriner). Club: Cornell of New York (N.Y. City). Contbr. articles to vet. and scientific jours. Home: 13 Little John Pl., White Plains, N.Y. Office: 25 Vanderbilt Av., New York, N.Y. Died Aug. 5, 1948.

WAY, Luther B., judge U.S. Dist. Court, Eastern Dist. of Va., since 1931. Address: Federal Bldg., Norfolk, Va.* Died Oct. 23, 1942.

WAY, Sylvester Bedell, public utilities; b. Phila., Pa., Aug. 29, 1874; s. Wilson Bedell and Ellen Lord (Dewey) W.; graduated as special electric engineer, Drexel Institute, Philadelphia, 1896, Sc.D., hon., 1942; m. Lillie Elmyra Bauer, November 28, 1899; 1 dau., Helen Emma. Draftsman and erecting engr., Electric Storage Battery Co., Phila., 1896-98; chief electrician, Imperial Electric Light, Heat & Power Co., St. Louis, 1898, until its consolidation, 1902, with other cos., forming the Union Electric Light & Power Co., with which continued until 1911; with Milwaukee Electric Ry. & Light Co. (now Wis. Electric Power Co.) since 1911, first as asst. gen. mgr., and vice pres. and general manager, 1914-25, pres. since Oct. 23, 1925; chmn. bd. Milwaukee Electric Ry. & Transport Co. since 1938; pres. Wis. Gas & Electric Co. (Racine), Milwaukee Light, Heat & Traction Co., Wisconsin-Michigan Power Co.; dir. First Wisconsin National Bank, First Wisconsin Trust Co. Patentee various devices for equipment of electric and street ry. service. Fellow Am. Institute E.E. Republican. Baptist. Mason. Clubs: Milwaukee. Home: Hotel Schroeder. Office: Public Service Bldg., Milwaukee, Wis. Died Sep. 20, 1946.

WAY, Warren Wade, clergyman; b. Irvington, Ill., Mar. 18, 1869; s. Newton Edward and Lizzie Heaton (Erwin) W.; A.B., Hobart Coll., 1897 (class honors and Phi Beta Kappa), LL.D., 1932; Gen. Theol. Sem., New York, 1899; A.M., U. of Chicago, 1924; D.D., U. of the South, Sewanee, Tenn., 1929; m. Louisa Atkinson Smith, June 18, 1903; children—Evelyn Lee, Warren Wade, Roger Atkinson. Deacon, 1892, priest, 1899, P.E. Ch.; asst. minister All Angels' Ch., New York, 1898-99; missionary, Diocese of Springfield, 1900; rector Grace Ch., Cortland, N.Y., 1901-14, St. Luke's Ch., Salisbury, N.C., 1914-18, St. Mary's Sch.and Jr. Coll., Raleigh, N.C., 1918-32, St. James' Ch., Atlantic City, N.J., since 1932. Chmn. Salisbury Chapter A.R.C., July 1917-18. Club: Brigantine Country. Home: 105 S. North Carolina Av., Atlantic City, N.J. Died June 11, 1943.

WAYBURN, Ned (Edward Claudius), theatrical, radio and television producer; b. Pittsburgh, Pa., Mar. 30, 1874; s. Elbert Delos and Harriet Langdon (Beech) W.; student Chicago Manual Training Sch., Hart Conway's Chicago Sch. of Acting, Bryant and Stratton Business Coll.; m. Agnes Saye, Dec. 25, 1897; m. 2d, Helene Davis; 1 son, Edward Claudius (Ned); m. 3d, Marguerite Lee Kirby, Sept. 5, 1916. Began as archtl. draftsman; went on professional stage and toured with repertory cos.; in vaudeville as "The Man Who Invented Rag-time; did piano speciality with songs and also dancer, appearing in most cities in U.S. and Can.; became theatrical producer, mgr., dramatic coach, and dance stylist and creator, 1900; was exec. producing dir. Ziegfeld Follies, and asso. with Klaw & Erlanger, Messrs. Shubert, Florenz Ziegfeld, Charles Dillingham, etc.; produced in Europe; now pres. and mng. dir. all Ned Wayburn cos. and school. Home: 4501 Livingston Av., Fieldston, N.Y. Office: 5 W. 46th St., New York, N.Y. Died Sep. 3, 1942.

WAYNE, Joseph, Jr., banker; b. Phila., Pa., Sept. 26, 1873; s. Stephen Simmons and Isabella (Ross) W.; ed. pub. schools, Phila.; LL.D., U. of Pa., 1937; m. Laura B. Jayne, Apr. 16, 1902; children—Elizabeth B., Josephine, Laura J. Pres., 1914-26, Girard Nat. Bank, which was consolidated with Phila. Nat. Bank under title The Phila.-Girard Nat. Bank, which was consolidated with the Franklin-Fourth Street Nat. Bank in 1928 under title The Phila. Nat. Bank, of which he was pres. until Jan. 13, 1941, chmn. of bd. since 1941; dir. Phila. Saving Fund Soc., Provident Mut. Life Ins. Co., Pa. Fire Ins. Co., Ins. Co. of North America, Alliance Ins. Co., Indemnity Ins. Co. of North America, Midvale Co., Philadelphia Fire and Marine Ins. Co., Baldwin-Southwark Corp., Parkway Co., Pa. R.R. Co., Pa. Co. (Pa. R.R. lines west). Served as mem. exec. com. in charge of loan drives, 3d Federal Reserve Dist., World War I. Clubs: Union League, Rittenhouse, Racquet, Sunnybrook Golf, Germantown Cricket, Phila. Cricket. Home: 8200 St. Martins Lane, Chestnut Hill, Pa. Office: Philadelphia Nat. Bank, Philadelphia, Pa. Died May 26, 1942.

WEADOCK, Bernard Francis (wĕd'ŏk), lawyer; b. Saginaw, Mich., Mar. 24, 1881; s. George William and Elizabeth (Tarsney) W.; grad. high sch., Saginaw, 1902; student U. of Mich., 1902-03; LL.B., Detroit Coll. Law, 1905; m. Mary L. Dillon, June 26, 1912; children—Bernard F., Jane, Shirley, John Cullen. Began as messenger boy, corp. counsel's office, Detroit, 1904; admitted to Mich. bar, 1905, N.Y. bar, 1925; chief clk. and asst. corp. counsel, 1907-12; gen. atty., Detroit United Lines, 1912-20; in gen. practice,

Detroit, 1920-24; mem. firm J. C. & B. F. Weadock, 1924-29; mem. firm Weadock & Willkie, 1929-32; now practicing atty., Washington, D.C.; exec. dir. Nat. Electric Light Assn., 1932-33; v.p. and mng. dir., Edison Elec. Inst., 1933-39. Spl. counsel for Utility Assns. in investigation by Federal Trade Commn., 1928. Mem. Sigma Chi. Democrat. Catholic. Club: Chevy Chase Club (Md.). Home: 3052 P St. N.W. Office: 815 15th St. N.W., Washington, D.C. Died Oct. 26, 1947.

WEAGANT, Roy Alexander (wē'gănt), elec. engr., inventor; b. Morrisburg, Ont., Can., Mar. 29, 1881; s. William Henry and Annie Gouin (McMartin) W.; g.g.s. John Gunter Weagant, of Baltimore, Md., about 1794 or 95, who later moved to Can.; brought to Derby Line, Vt., 1884, and became citizen of U.S. by marriage of mother, after father's death, to native-born American; student Stanstead Coll., 2 yrs.; B.S., McGill, 1905; m. Isobel Louise Reichling, Dec. 8, 1906; 1 son, Carl Ludwig (dec.). Began with Montreal Light, Heat & Power Co., 1906, Westinghouse Electric & Mfg. Co., Pittsburgh, Pa., 1907, De Laval Steam Turbine Co., Trenton, N.J., 1908, Nat. Electric Signaling Co., 1908-13, chief engr. Marconi Wireless Telegraph Co., 1915-20, and cons. engr. of its successor, Radio Corp. of America, 1920-24; became v.p. and chief engr. De Forest Radio Co., 1924; now consultant, patent expert, Radio Corp. America. Perfected invention solving static problem in wireless telegraphy, 1919, reducing amount of power previously required by one-half and doing away with tall steel towers (awarded the Morris-Liebman prize for this work). Charter mem. and fellow Inst. Radio Engrs.; mem. New York Elec. Soc. Republican. Episcopalian. Home: Douglaston, N.Y. Died Aug. 23, 1942.

WEATHERBY, Charles Alfred, botanist; b. Hartford, Conn., Dec. 25, 1875; s. Charles Nathaniel and Grace Weld (Young) W.; A.B., 1897, A.M., 1898, Harvard U.; m. Una Lenora Foster, May 16, 1917. Associated with Gray Herbarium, Harvard U., since 1908, senator curator, 1937-40, research associate since 1940. Mem. Am. Acad., A.A.A.S., Bot. Soc. of Am., Am. Society Plant Taxonomists (president 1945), Am. Fern Soc. (sec., 1914-18; pres. 1943-44), Soc. Bibliography of Nat. Hist. (London), Brit. Pteridol. Soc. (hon.), New England Bot. Club, Conn. Bot. Soc. (v.p., 1910-29). Mem. Internat. Com. on Nomenclature of Vascular Plants since 1935; v.p. sect. on nomenclature of Internat. Congress, 1949. Editor Fern Journal, 1915-40; asso. editor Rhodora since 1929, Brittonia since 1943. Home: 27 Raymond St., Cambridge 40, Mass. Died June 21, 1949.

WEATHERBY, LeRoy Samuel, chemistry; b. Baldwin, Kan., Mar. 29, 1880; s. Samuel S. and Delia (Stearns) W.; A.B., U. of Kan., 1906, A.M., 1908; Ph.D., U. of Chicago, 1911; m. Frances Johnson, Sept. 6, 1911; 1 dau., Virginia. Began as teacher pub. schs., 1897; instr. physics and chemistry, Baker U., Baldwin, Kan., 1906-08; asst. prof. chemistry, Okla. Agrl. and Mech. Coll., 1908-09; teaching fellow and instr. in chemistry, U. of Chicago, 1909-11; with U. of Southern Calif. since 1911, prof. chemistry since 1913; exchange prof. Northwestern U., summers, 1924 and 1936; lecturer in chemistry, Columbia, 1st semester, 1924-25; exchange prof. U. of Wash., summer, 1927, George Washington U., summer, 1938, U. of Pittsburgh, summer, 1941. Mem. Am. Chem. Soc., Am. Inst. Food Tech., Sigma Xi, Phi Kappa Phi, Phi Lambda Upsilon, Alpha Epsilon Delta. Methodist. Contbr. on research in organic chemistry and nutrition. Home: 1299 W. 37th Drive. 7. Address: U. of So. Calif., Los Angeles, Calif. Died Oct. 21, 1946.

WEAVER, Arthur J., ex-gov., and orchardist; b. Falls City, Nebraska, Nov. 18, 1873; s. Archibald J. and Martha (Myers) W.; grad. Wyoming Sem., Kingston, Pa., 1892; A.B., U. of Neb., 1895, LL.B., 1896; m. Maude E. Hart, of White Pigeon, Mich., Sept. 2, 1908; children—Maude Harriet, Dorothy Jane, Arthur J., Ruth Jean, Phillip Hart, Josephine Miranda. Admitted to Neb. bar, 1896, and practiced at Falls City until 1904; engaged in fruit growing, grain and stock raising since 1905; pres. Weaver & Towle Orchards Co., Falls City Hotel Realty Co., Falls City Wholesale & Supply Co.; sec.-treas. Miles, Morehead & Weaver, Inc.; was dir. Omaha Br. of Federal Reserve Bank of Kansas City; governor of Nebraska, term 1929-31. Mem. Nebraska House of Representatives, 1899; city attorney Falls City, 1899-1901; county atty. Richardson County, 1901-03; mayor of Falls City, 1915; pres. Neb. Constl. Conv., 1920; chmn. Neb. Elector Coll., 1920; chmn. Rep. State Conv., 1924; delegate at large Rep. Nat. Convention, 1932; mem. Neb. State Bd. Agr. (v.p.), Neb. State Park Bd. (dir.). Pres. Miss. Valley Assn.; pres. Mo. River Navigation Assn., Nebraska State Hort. Soc. (ex-pres.), Nat. Econ. League, Native Sons and Daughters of Nebraska. Mason (32°), Odd Fellow, K.P., Woodman, Elk. Unanimously endorsed, 1925, for apptmt. as sec. of agr., by U.S. Senate and House delegation from Neb., also by gov. of Neb. and both branches of Neb. legislature. Home: Falls City, Neb.* Died Oct. 18, 1945.

WEAVER, Charles Clinton, clergyman; b. Ashe County, N.C., June 21, 1875; s. James Harvey and Jennie (Burkett) W.; A.B., Trinity (N.C.) Coll. 1895; Ph.D., Johns Hopkins U., 1900; D.D., Duke U., 1936; m. Florence Stacy, June 18, 1902; children—James Harvey, Lucius Stacy, Charles Clinton, Jennie, Philip Johnson. Pres. Rutherford Coll., 1900-03, Davenport Coll., 1903-10, Emory and Henry Coll., 1910-20, Martha Washington Coll., 1918-20; ordained ministry M.E. Ch., South, 1901; pastor at Monroe, N.C., 1920-24, Winston-Salem, 1924-33, Asheville, 1933-35; presiding elder Greensboro (N.C.) dist., 1935-36; pastor First M.E. Ch., Charlotte, N.C., 1936-40; supt. Winston-Salem District, N.C., 1940-44. Mem. Gen. Conf. M.E. Ch., South, 1918, 22, 30, 34, 38; mem. Uniting Conf., Meth. Ch., 1939, Gen. and Jurisdictional confs., 1940, 1944. Mem. Sigma Nu, Omicron Delta Kappa, Phi Beta Kappa. Mason. Supt. Chatham Memorial Hospital. Home: 142 Hawthorne Rd., Elkin, N.C. Died Mar. 19, 1946.

WEAVER, George Howitt, physician; b. Sussex, Wis., Oct. 22, 1866; s. William and Mary (Howitt) W.; ed. Carroll Coll., 1882-85, Univ. of Wooster, 1885-86; M.D., Rush Med. Coll., Chicago, 1889; m. Carolyn Earle, June 1901. Prof. pathology, Women's Med. Coll. of Northwestern Univ., 1893-97; asst. prof. pathology, Rush Med. Coll. (U. of Chicago), since 1899; asst. pathologist, Memorial Inst. for Infectious Diseases, Chicago, since 1902; attending physician children's and contagious diseases, Cook County (Ill.) Hosp., 1905-13; became attending physician Durand Hosp., 1913; became prof. pathology, Rush Med. Coll., now prof. emeritus. Mem. Assn. Am. Physicians, Am. Assn. Pathologists and Bacteriologists, A.M.A., Ill. and Chicago med. socs., Chicago Pathol. Soc. Home: Wilmette, Ill. Died Apr. 19, 1947.

WEAVER, Henry Grady, market research; b. Eatonton, Ga., Dec. 24, 1889; s. Dr. James David and Eliza Thomas (Carruth) W.; B.S., in Mech. Engring., Ga. Sch. of Tech., 1911; m. Claribel Jane Fraser, Feb. 27, 1923; children—Henry Grady, II, Mary Talbot. Prop. of garage, Eatonton, Ga., 1911-13; draftsman Haynes Automobile Co., Kokomo, Ind., 1913-16; asst. gen. mgr. Sun Motor Car Co., Elkhart, Ind., 1916-17; field research Hyatt Roller Bearing Co., Chicago, 1918-21; market and psychol. research Gen. Motors Corp., Detroit, Mich., since 1921, now dir. customer research staff. Received Harvard Research award (with $2000) for development of purchasing power indexes by counties. Mem. Economic Club of Detroit. Baptist. Mason (K.T., Shriner). Clubs: Automobile Old Timers, Recess, Players, Detroit, Adcraft (Detroit). Author: Mainspring, The Story of Human Progress and How Not to Prevent It; of numerous booklets on psychological research. Contributor to jours. Home: 1161 Chicago Blvd. Office: General Motors Corp., Detroit, Mich. Died Jan. 3, 1949.

WEAVER, Paul John, music dir.; b. Reedsburg, Wis., July 8, 1889; s. Isaiah and Kittie Belle (Stupfell) W.; B.A., U. of Wis., 1911; asso. Am. Guild of Organists, New York U., 1918; studied piano, voice, organ and theory under masters; m. Hazel V. Gantt, July 21, 1919; children—Paul John, Rachel Gantt. Dir. of music, Racine (Wis.) Coll., 1911-12; 1st asst. supervisor of music, pub. schs., St. Louis, Mo., 1915-19; prof. and dir. music, Univ. of N.C., 1919-29; prof. of music and chmn. of dept., Cornell U., since 1929; served as guest instr. Cornell U., U. of Calif., etc.; organist and choirmaster; dir. many choral orgns., especially U. of N.C. Glee Club. Dean N.C. Chapter Am. Guild Organists; organizer, 1922, and 1st pres. Southern Conf. for Music Edn.; Am. chmn. Internat. Music Conf. since 1928; mem. Nat. Research Council for Music Edn.; v.p., music supervisor Nat. Conf.; mem. Nat. Com. on People's Songs, Nat. Council on Reproducing Instruments; mem. advisory bd. sponsoring Nat. Broadcasting Co. mus. appreciation hour, Coll. Mus. Study and later Commn. on Music of Assn. of Am. Colls.; chmn. com. on music in higher edn., Music Educators Nat. Conf.; mem. Nat. Music Council. Mem. Alpha Tau Omega, Phi Mu Alpha. Served in U.S. Navy, World War. Editor of Music Supervisors' Journal, 1925-30. Home: 302 Wait Av., Ithaca, N.Y.* Died Oct. 14, 1946.

WEAVER, Rudolph, architect, educator; b. Roxbury Borough (now in Johnstown), Pa., Apr. 17, 1880; s. Henry and Sara Jane (Barnhart) W.; prep. edn. Pa. State Coll., 1902-03; Diploma in Architecture, Drexel Inst., 1905, B.S. in Engring., 1919; student architecture, Columbia, 1906-07; student Beaux-Arts Soc. Atelier Hornbostle, 1907, Harvard, summer 1927; travel in Europe, summer 1929, in Mexico, summer 1937; m. Alice Rossing Walden, Aug. 22, 1922. Apprentice to book binder, 1896, to printer, 1897; steel worker, 1898-1902; draftsman and designer, 1907-09; instr. in architecture, U. of Ill., 1909-11; coll. architect and head dept. architecture, State Coll. of Wash., 1911-23; univ. architect and head dept., U. of Ida., 1923-25; architect to Fla. State Bd. of Control, 1925; organized Sch. of Architecture, U. of Fla., 1925, and since dir.; archtl. consultant. Works include Science Hall and campus plan, U. of Ida.; coll. bldgs. for U. of Fla., State Coll. for Women, Sch. for the Deaf and Blind, Agr. and Mech. Coll., also campus plans; major bldgs. State Coll. of Wash.; State Rd. Dept. Bldg. Mem. Fla. State Bd. of Architecture, 1927-34 and 1941-45, pres. 1932-34; mem. City Plan Bd., Gainesville, Fla., since 1929, chmn. since 1932; mem. Civic Music Assn., pres., 1939-40; mem. Chamber of Commerce. Fellow Am. Inst. Architects (former mem. and chmn. judiciary com. nat. orgn.; pres. N. Fla. Chapter, 1928-29; nat. com. on edn. since 1942), mem. Soil Science Soc. of Florida, Florida Association Architects, A.A.A.S., Phi Kappa Phi, Sigma Tau, Mu Phi Alpha, Sigma Phi Epsilon, Sinfonia, Acacia. Club: Gainesville Kiwanis (pres. 1938). Home: 644 N. Bay St., Gainesville, Fla. Died Nov. 10, 1944.

WEAVER, Rufus Washington, clergyman; b. Greensboro, N.C., June 3, 1870; s. Preston De Kalb and Elizabeth Jane (Forbis) W.; B.A. and M.A., Wake Forest Coll., N.C., 1893, D.D., 1912, LL.D., 1918; Southern Bapt. Theol. Sem., 1896-99, Th.M., 1898, Th.D., 1899; studied, Johns Hopkins, 1905-06, U. of Cincinnati, 1906-07; D.D., Bethel College, Ky., 1912; LL.D., Baylor U., 1920; m. Mrs. Charlotte Mason Payne, Jan. 11, 1911. Ordained Bapt. ministry, 1893; pastor 1st Bapt. Ch., High Point, N.C., 1893-96, 1st Ch., Middletown, Ohio, 1899-1903, Brantly Ch., Baltimore, 1903-06, Mt. Auburn Ch., Cincinnati, 1906-08, Immanuel Ch., Nashville, Tenn., 1908-17; sec. Christian edn. of Tenn. Bapt. Conv., 1917-18; pres. Mercer U., Macon, Ga., 1918-27; corr. sec. Edn. Bd. Southern Bapt. Conv., 1927-28; chancellor Mercer U. system of colleges and secondary schools, 1920-25. Adj. prof. religious edn., Bibl. dept. Vanderbilt U., 1913-17; pres. edn. bd. of Tenn. Bapt. Conv., 1912-17; pres. Southern Bapt. Ednl. Assn., 1917-20; pres. Edn. Commn., 1919; trustee S.S. Bd., 1909-18, 1933-46; pastor First Ch., Washington, D.C., 1934-36; exec. sec. D.C. Bapt. Conv., 1934-43; exec. dir. Luther Rice Centennial Commn.; chmn. Com. on Army and Navy Chaplains, 1935-41; mem. Com. on Finance and Promotion, Northern Baptist Conv., 1934-43; Ministers Council 1935-43. Member Tenn. exec. com. Food Adminstrn., 1917-18. Mem. Ga. Illiteracy Commn., 1919-27; chmn. exec. com. Ga. Bapt. Conv., 1918-19; advisory com. Bapt. 75 million campaign; chmn. com. on univs. and theol. sems. of Southern Bapt. Conv., 1919-21. Mem. Ga. State Edn. Bd., 1922-25; dir. Ga. Edn. Assn., 1923-27; pres. Ga. Assn. Colls., 1923-26; mem. Com. on Edn. Nat. Council of Boy Scouts since 1922, Nat. Y.M.C.A. Constl. Conv., 1923; commn. on Negro Bapt. Theol. Sem., 1918-25; sec. and treas. Nat. Advisory Com. on Illiteracy, 1929-32; exec. dir. National Conf. on Religious Liberty. Mem. Theta Chi. Mason (32°; Grand Chaplain of Tenn., 1909-11). Clubs: Cosmos, Palaver, Inter-Church. Author: History of the Doctrine of Inspiration, 1899; The Christian Conversationalist, 1903; The Reconstruction of Religion, 1904; Religious Development of the Child, 1913; The Christian Faith at the Nation's Capitol, 1936; The Roumanian Crisis, 1938; The Vatican Envoy, 1940; The Forum of Freedom, 1940; Revolt Against God, 1944; Champions of Religious Liberty, 1946; numerous tracts and articles in religious press. Home: 3900 Connecticut Av. N.W., Washington, D.C. Died Jan. 31, 1947.

WEAVER, Walter Reed, army officer; b. Charleston, S.C., Feb. 23, 1885; s. Maj. Gen. Erasmus Morgan and Leize (Holmes) W.; educated Virginia Military Institute, 3 years; B.S., Military Academy, West Point, N.Y.; student Harvard, 1924, Army Industrial Coll., Washington, D.C., 1932-33; m. Elizabeth Ker Johnson, Sept. 30, 1911. Commd. 2d lt. U.S. Army, 1908, advanced through grades to maj. gen., 1941; assigned to 11th Inf. and served at Ft. D. A. Russell (now Francis E. Warren), Wyo., 1908; transferred to 28th Inf., Ft. Snelling, Minn., 1910; with 24th Inf., Philippines, 1912; with 15th Inf., Tientsin, China, Oct. 1914; recruiting at Columbus Barracks, O., 1915; with 22d Inf., Ft. Thomas, Ky., 1916; comdt. of flying cadets, Wilbur Wright Field, Dayton, O., 1917; organized U.S. Army Aviation Mech. Sch., St. Paul, Minn., 1917-18; chief of mech. training div., Supply Group, Office of Dir. of Air Service, Washington, D.C., 1919; received flying training, 1920; pilot, tech. observer, Kelly Field, Tex., 1921; chief of property requirements div., Supply Group, Office of Chief of Air Service, Washington, D.C., 1921; comdg. officer, Mitchel Field, N.Y., 1921-23; comdr., Boston Airport, 1923; comdr. air depot, Middletown, Pa., 1925-27; comdg. officer, Maxwell Field, Ala., 1927-31; chief of plans div., Office of Chief of Air Corps, 1932, chief of information div., 1933; rep. Air Corps Procurement Planning, N.Y. City, 1934-35; inspector, G.H.Q. Air Force, Langley Field, Va., 1935, post exec., Feb. 1936, comdg. officer 1st Air Base, June 1936; comdg. officer Langley Field, July 1937-39; comdt. Air Corps Tactical Sch., Maxwell Field, Ala., 1939; comdg. gen. Southeast Air Corps Training Center, Maxwell Field, Ala., 1940; acting chief of Air Corps, Washington, D.C., Dec. 1941-Mar. 1942; comdg. gen. of Army Air Forces Tech. Training Command, Knollwood Field, N.C., Mar. 1942-July 1943; retired, 1944; asst. to pres. for aviation, Aviation Corp. of Am. Received Distinguished Service Medal, 1943. Mem. Sigma Alpha Epsilon. Mason (Shriner). Clubs: Army and Navy (Washington); Metropolitan (New York); Kiwanis. Home: Fort Boykin, Smithfield, Va. Died Oct. 27, 1944; buried in Arlington National Cemetery.

WEAVER, Zebulon, ex-congressman; b. Weaverville, N.C., May 12, 1872; s. William Elbert and Hannah E. (Baird) W.; A.B., Weaver Coll., Weaverville, 1889; studied law, U. of N.C.; m. Anna Capers Hyman, Oct. 11, 1899; children—Mary D. (Mrs. C. H. Hites), Hannah Baird (Mrs. J. Frank Johnson), Theodore Hyman, Zebulon, Frances (Mrs. Walter Cuthrell). Admitted to N.C. bar, 1895; has specialized in corporation and real estate law; mem. N.C. Ho. of Rep., 1907, 09, Senate 1913-15; mem. 65th to 70th Congresses (1917-29) and 72d Congress (1931-33), 10th N.C. Dist., and 73d to 77th Congresses (1933-43), 11th N.C. Dist., 78th and 79th Congresses (1943-47), 12th N.C. Dist. Democrat. Methodist. Home: Asheville, N.C. Died Oct. 29, 1948.

WEBB, Alexander Stewart; b. N.Y. City, Feb. 5, 1870; s. Maj. Gen. Alexander Stewart and Anna (Remsen) W.; m. Mrs. Florence Sands Russell. Trustee Tuberculosis Preventorium for Children. Mem. St. Nicholas Soc., Soc. Colonial Wars, Soc. of the Cincinnati, Am. Soc. for Prevention of Cruelty to Animals (pres.). Home: Garden City, L.I. Office: 50 Madison Av., New York, N.Y. Died Jan. 12, 1948.

WEBB, Charles Aurelius, lawyer, publisher; b. Warrenton, N.C., Nov. 4, 1866; s. Alexander Smith and Annabell (Moore) W.; grad. Webb Sch., Tenn., 1885; A.B., U. of N.C., 1889; student law dept. same univ., 1891; m. Bell Bruce Banks, 1895 (dec.); m. 2d, Mrs. Jessie Close Shaw, Nov. 9, 1914; children—Charles Bruce, Robert Stanford, Julia Webb Woods, Mandeville Alexander. Began practice, Asheville, 1891; county atty. Buncombe County, N.C., 1901-12; mem. N.C. Senate, 1903-05, 1907 (pres. pro tem, 1905-07); chmn. State Hosp. Commn., 1907-11; chmn. Dem. State Exec. Com., 1912-14; U.S. marshal, Western Dist. of N.C., by apptmt. President Wilson, 1914-22. Pres. Asheville Citizen-Times Co., publishers of Asheville Citizen and Asheville Times. Director and president Asheville Colored Hospital. A pioneer in promotion of apple industry in Western N.C. and owner of one of largest orchards in the state. Mem. American Newspaper Publishers Assn. (formerly dir.), N.C. State Press Assn. (pres.), Southern Newspaper Pub. Assn. (dir.), Beta Theta Pi. Presbyn. Mason. K.P., Elk. Club: Rotary. Home: Asheville, N.C. Deceased.

WEBB, Charles Wallace, surgeon; b. Dallas, May 18, 1878; s. Charles Wheeler and Belle (Hamilton) W.; A.B., U. of Ark., 1905, LL.D. from same univ.; M.D., Johns Hopkins, 1909; m. Susan Bontecou, 1914; children—Marjory, Burton, Charles, Mary Louise, Susan. Resident Johns Hopkins, 1909-10, Clifton Springs (N.Y.) Sanitarium, 1910-11, U. of Leipzig, 1912-13; teacher anatomy Cornell U., 1913-16; chief surgeon Clifton Springs Sanitarium, 1916-36; mem. oral bd. examiners for surgery Strong Memorial Hosp., Rochester, N.Y., 1916-36; owner and chief surgeon Newark (N.J.) Hosp., 1936-48; surgeon Newark State Sch., 1936-48. Mem. Am., N.Y. and Wayne Co. med. assns., Phi Beta Kappa, Kappa Sigma. Democrat. Baptist. Mason. Home: Pleasant St., Clifton Springs, N.Y. Died July 6, 1949.

WEBB, Frank Elbridge, industrial engr., pub. works contractor; b. Calaveras County, Calif., Sept. 1, 1869; s. Elbridge and Annie E. (Settle); desc. of Mayflower ancestry; grad. Lincoln High Sch., San Francisco; studied law under John H. Dickinson, San Francisco; m. Elsa White Reid, Apr. 1928. Joined Nat. Guard of Calif., 1884; recruited regt. for Spanish-Am. War, but was sent on spl. mission around the world as confidential representative of President of U.S.; later served in Q.M. Dept. of the Army; engaged in handling gen. govt. supplies; with John A. Bensel, engr., 1906-16; made study of engring.; assisted in organization Plattsburg training camps; purchased supplies for French, English and Belgians in earlier years of World War, also assisted in organization for Am. defense; actively identified with construction of ships and loading plants on Eastern Seaboard, after U.S. entered World War; name carried on confidential list of War Dept. under rank of col.; connected with bridge building on Pacific Coast in Calif. since 1923; engr. for Chelsea docks and canals for State of N.Y. Mem. S.A.R. Decorated Knight Comdr. of the Holy Sepulchre; Knight Comdr. of Crown of Charlemagne. Candidate of Farmer-Labor Party for President of U.S., 1928; nominated for Presidency by same party in spring of 1932, declined; nominated for Presidency by Liberty Party, July 4, 1932. Presbyterian. Home: Washington, D.C.; also San Francisco, Calif. Address: 815 15th St. N.W., Washington, D.C. Died June 15, 1949.

WEBB, Gerald Bertram, physician; b. Cheltenham, Eng., Sept. 24, 1871; s. William John and Frances (Le Plastrier) W.; Guy's Hosp., London, 1890-93; M.D., U. of Denver, 1896; post-grad. work, Vienna and London, 1905-06; Sc.D., Colorado College 1936, University of Colorado, 1938; married Varina Howell Davis Hayes, July 30, 1904; children—Varina Margaret, Gerald Bertram (died), Frances Robine, Eleanor Constance Leila, Joel Addison Hayes. Came to the United States, 1893; in private practice at Colorado Springs since 1896; cons. physician Methodist, Sunnyrest, Glockner and St. Francis sanatoriums; chief of staff Union Printers Home; pres. Colo. Foundation for Research in Tuberculosis. Served as lt. col. Med. Corps U.S. Army, 1918; sr. consultant in tuberculosis, A.E.F., 1918-19. U.S. del. to Laennec-Centenary, Paris, Dec. 1926. Awarded Trudeau medal, Nat. Tuberculosis Assn., 1939. Fellow A.M.A., Am. Coll. Physicians, N.Y. Acad. of Medicine; mem. Assn. Am. Physicians (pres. 1939), Am. Clin. and Climatol. Assn. (pres. 1929-30), Am. Assn. Immunologists, Nat. Tuberculosis Assn. (pres. 1920; del. to Internat. Congress on Tuberculosis, Rome, 1912, Internat. Union Against Tuberculosis, Paris, 1920, London, 1921). Republican. Episcopalian. Club: Cheyenne Mountain Country. Author: (with C. T. Ryder) Overcoming Tuberculosis, 1927; Laennec—A Memoir, 1928; History of Tuberculosis, 1936; (with Desmond Powell) Henry Sewall, Physiologist and Physician. Home: 1222 N. Cascade Av. Office: Burns Bldg., Colorado Springs, Colo. Died Jan. 27, 1948.

WEBB, Robert Williams, banker; b. Richmond, Ind., Aug. 11, 1869; s. Benjamin and Sarah Terrell (Williams) W.; prep. edn., Earlham Coll., Richmond, Ind.; LL.B., U. of Minn., also LL.M.; m. Margaret McDonald, June 9, 1898; children—Harriet Libby, Robert Williams, John McDonald. With 1st Minneapolis Trust Co., 1894, pres., 1920-33; vice-pres. and dir. First National Bank of Minneapolis; director Title Insurance Company, Northwestern Fire & Marine Ins. Co., Twin City Fire Ins. Co. Trustee and v.p., Dunwoody Industrial Inst.; trustee Minneapolis Foundation. Mem. Phi Delta Phi. Republican. Quaker. Clubs: Minneapolis, Minikahda. Home: 124 Groveland Av., Minneapolis 4. Office: 115 S. 5th St., Minneapolis, Minn. Died Sept. 2, 1948.

WEBB, Ulysses Sigel, lawyer; b. Flemington, W.Va., Sept. 29, 1864; s. Cyrus and Elizabeth (Cather) W.; ed. pub. schs., Ft. Scott, Kan.; m. Grace Goodwin, Oct. 23, 1895. Settled at Quincy, 1888; admitted to Calif. bar, 1889; elected dist. atty. Plumas County, Calif., 1890 (resigned); became atty. gen. of Calif., 1902; resigned as atty. gen. 1939; now in pvt. practice. Republican. Home: 3865 Clay St. Office: Mills Tower, San Francisco, Calif.* Died July 31, 1947.

WEBB, William Alfred, ry. official; b. Eaton, O., May 16, 1878; s. Dr. William Porter W.; ed. high sch.; m. Alice Van Stone, 1907. Messenger Colo. Midland Ry., 1890, later various subordinate positions same road and on C. & S. Ry. at Denver, chief clk. to pres. and gen. mgr. same rd., 1903-05, and his asst., 1905-11; gen. mgr. Tex. Central R.R., 1911-12; gen. mgr., v.p. and chief operating officer, M.,K.&T. System, 1912-19; mem. Bd. of Adjustment No. 1, U.S. R.R. Adminstrn. at Washington, D.C., 1919-20; v.p. and gen. mgr. St. Louis S.W. Ry., 1920-21; pres. Cambria & Indiana R.R., at Phila., Pa., Mar.-Sept. 1922; chief commr. State Rys. of S. Australia since Sept. 1922. Presbyterian. Address: Adelaide, S. Australia. Died Aug. 9, 1936.

*WEBBER, Amos Richard, judge; b. Hinckley, O., Jan. 21, 1852; s. George Enoch and Jane Ann (Woodruff) W.; A.B., Baldwin U. (now Baldwin-Wallace Coll.), Berea, 1876, hon. LL.D., 1935; m. Ida E. Finch, May 6, 1875 (died 1906); children—Gilbert (dec.), Lawrence H. (dec.); m. 2d, Nettie Finch, Jan. 1, 1907 (died Feb. 28, 1931). Admitted to Ohio bar, 1876, and in practice at Elyria; pros. atty., 1888-94; judge Common Pleas Ct., 1901-04, and since 1922; mem. 58th and 59th Congresses (1903-07), 14th Ohio Dist.; offered in Congress while a member, and secured a hearing, on the first prohibition bill ever presented in that body to make the Dist. of Columbia dry; active worker for prohibition and woman suffrage for years; worked for enactment of 18th and 19th Constl. Amendments. Trustee Baldwin-Wallace Coll., Huron Rd. Hosp. (Cleveland). Republican. Mem. Ch. of Christ. Club: Elyria Round Table. Author: Biography of John Baldwin, 1925; Early History of Elyria and Her People, 1930; History of Hinckley, Ohio, 1933; also has written an autobiography. Received Centennial Merit Award given by Alumni Assn. Baldwin Wallace Coll., 1946. Home: Elyria, O. Deceased.

WEBER, Gustavus Adolphus, economist; b. St. Louis, Mo., Aug. 3, 1863; s. John George and Caroline (Becker) W.; ed. St. Louis U., Georgetown U.; LL.B., Howard U., Washington, 1897; m. Lillian Josephine Minch, Nov. 17, 1887; 1 son, Georges Minch. In charge U.S. Weather Bureau, St. Louis, and asst. dir. Mo. Weather Service, Washington U., 1884-89; spl. agt. U.S. Bur. of Labor, 1889-1902; also engaged in research work, asso. editor Bulletin of U.S. Bur. of Labor, and spent 3 yrs. (1889-92) in Europe investigating for the bur.; statis. experts in charge of Div. of Law and Research Work, 1902-09; gen. sec. Octavia Hill Association, Phila., and Phila. Housing Commn., 1909-10; asst. chief, Bur. Statistics, chief Div. of Internal Commerce, and comml. agent, Dept. Commerce and Labor, 1910-12; sec. Soc. for Betterment of Housing and Living Conditions, Richmond, Va., 1912-13; chief of cost of production div. Dept. of Commerce, 1913-16; mem. staff Inst. for Govt. Research of the Brookings Instn., 1916-18 and 1920-32. Research expert and statistician Council of Nat. Defense, 1918-20; statistician of President's Homes Commn., 1908. Vice pres. Washington Sanitary Improvement Co. Mem. Am. Econ. Assn., Pi Gamma Mu. Author of Housing and Living Conditions in the Neglected Sections of Richmond, Va.; Organized Efforts for the Improvement of Methods of Administration; and numerous service monographs on the history, activities and organization of U.S. Govt. bureaus. Home: 6 Wetherill Rd., Friendship Station, Washington, D.C. Died Dec. 7, 1942.

WEBBER, Herbert John, plant physiologist; b. Lawton, Mich., Dec. 27, 1865; s. John Milton and Rebecca Anna (Bradt) W.; B.S., U. of Neb., 1889, M.A., 1890; Ph.D., Washington U., 1901; hon. D.Agr., U. of Neb., 1913; hon. L.L.D., University of California, 1943; m. Lucene Anna Hardin, September 8, 1890; children—Mrs. Eugene Francis Morrison, Mrs. Fera Ellen Shear, Herbert Earl, John Milton. Instr. botany, U. of Neb., 1889-90; instr. botany, Shaw Sch. of Botany, Washington U., St. Louis, 1891-92; investigator of orange diseases in Fla. for U.S. Dept. Agr., 1893-97; investigator plant breeding, Washington, 1897-98; in charge of plant breeding investigations, U.S. Dept. Agr., 1899-1907; prof. exptl. plant biology, Cornell U., 1907-08; acting dir., 1909-10, prof. plant breeding, 1910-12, N.Y. State Coll. of Agr.; dir. Citrus Expt. Sta., dean Grad. Sch. of Tropical Agr. and prof. plant breeding, 1912-18, U. of Calif.; dir. Agrl. Expt. Sta. and prof. plant breeding, U. of Calif., 1919-20; gen. mgr., Pedigreed Seed Co., Hartsville, S.C., 1920-21; prof. subtropical horticulture and dir. citrus expt. sta., 1921-29, prof. subtropical horticulture, 1929-36, acting dean College Agr., 1923-24, U. of Calif., now prof. emeritus. Representative of U.S. Dept. of Agr. at Internat. Conf., London, on hybridization and cross-breeding, July 1899. Spl. commr. to study and report on citrus industry and organization of agricultural education and research dept. of agr., Union of South Africa, 1924-25. Medalist, Avocado Assn., 1938. Fellow and emeritus life mem. A.A.A.S.; mem. Am. Bot. Soc., American Genetic Assn., Ecol. Soc. America, Am. Soc. Hort. Science, Fla. State Horticultural Soc. (hon.), Nat. Council Boy Scouts of America, Sigma Xi, Alpha Zeta, Kappa Delta Rho. Mason. Contbr. to various reports, bulletins, and many other papers on plant breeding, anatomy, horticulture and diseases. Editor: The Citrus Industry: History, Botany and Breeding, Vol. I (U. of Calif. Press), 1943. Address: Citrus Experiment Sta., Riverside, Calif. Died Jan. 18, 1946.

WEBER, Joseph M., actor, mgr.; b. New York, Aug. 11, 1867; s. Abraham and Gertrude (Enoch) W.; ed. New York pub. sch.; m. Lillian Friedman, Jan. 3, 1897. Began stage career with Lewis M. Fields, 1877; mem. Weber & Fields, mgrs. several theatrical enterprises, 1885, and mgrs. Broadway Music Hall, 1895-1904; propr. and mgr. Weber's Theatre since 1904. Clubs: Lambs and Elks. Mason. Home: 212 N. Maple Drive, Beverly Hills, Calif. Died May 10, 1942.

WEBSTER, Cornelius Crosby, lawyer; b. Kennedy, N.Y., July 25, 1886; s. William Burton and Anna Makepeace (Crosby) W.; grad. Binghamton High Sch.; A.B. (magna cum laude), Harvard Coll., 1909; (Bowdoin lit. prize and medal); LL.B., Harvard Law Sch. (editor Harvard Law Review), 1912; m. Fannie Beecher Whitman, Oct. 11, 1913; children—Dorothy Whitman (Mrs. Thomas J. Murphy), Cornelius Crosby, Jane Beecher. Admitted to N.Y. bar and to practice before N.Y. Court of Appeals, 1912, also to U.S. Supreme Court; with Curtis, Mallet, Prevost, Colt & Mosle, N.Y. City, 1912-28; individual practice, N.Y. City, 1928-43; now with Hughes, Hubbard & Ewing; dir. and sec. Ferro-co Corp., Jones & Larson, Albert Carman, Inc.; dir. Coy Hunt & Co., 1935-40. Served as pvt., C.A.C., N.Y. Nat. Guard, 1915-18. Sec. exec. com. for Christian Science activities, N.Y. World's Fair, 1936-41. Trustee and chmn. First Church of Christ, Scientist, Flushing, N.Y., 1923-25, 1935-37, First Reader, 1938-40. Mem. Lambda Sigma. Republican. Clubs: Harvard, Harvard Law Sch., Harvard Downtown Lunch (New York). Author articles for Christian Science publs. Home: 45-28 Parsons Blvd., Flushing, N.Y. Died Jan. 7, 1947.

WEBSTER, John Clarence, surgeon; b. Shediac, N.B., Can., Oct. 21, 1863; s. James and Roslin Elizabeth (Chapman) W.; ed. Mt. Allison Coll., N.B., and univs. of Edinburgh, Leipzig, and Berlin; B.A., 1882, M.D., 1890 (Edinburgh), F.R.C.P.E., F.R.S.E., F.A.C.S.; D.Sc., LL.D., U. of Cincinnati; m. Alice, d. late Dr. William Lusk, of New York, 1899. First asst. dept. of midwifery and gynecology, Edinburgh, 1890-96; lecturer gynecology, McGill U., 1897-99; asst. gynecologist, Royal Victoria Hosp., Montreal, 1897-99; obstetrician and gynecologist, Presbyn. Hosp., Chicago, 1899-1920; prof. obstetrics and gynecology, Rush Med. Coll., Chicago, 1899-1920. Returned to Shediac, Can., 1920. Fellow Am. Coll. Surgeons, Am. Gynecol. Soc., corr. mem. Italian Obstet. and Gynecol. Soc., Royal Acad. Medicine, Palermo, Italy; fellow Royal Soc., Can. Author: Researches in Female Pelvic Anatomy, 1892; Tubo-Peritoneal Ectopic Gestation, 1892; Ectopic Gestation, 1895; Text Book of Diseases of Women, 1898; Human Placentation, 1902; and other med. monographs. Clubs: University (N.Y. and Montreal); Travellers (London) Home: Shediac, N.B., Can. Died March 16, 1950.

WEBSTER, Leslie Tillotson, med. research; b. New York, N.Y., July 23, 1894; s. Oliver C. and Florence A. (Tillotson) W.; B.A., Amherst, 1915, D.Sc., 1935; M.D., Johns Hopkins, 1919; m. Emily Johnston de Forest II, Jan. 5, 1924; children—Leslie Tillotson, Henry de Forest, John Crosby Brown, Emily Ann. Asst. resident pathologist, Johns Hopkins Hosp., and asst. in dept. of pathology, Johns Hopkins Med. Sch., 1919-20; with Rockefeller Institute for Medical Research since 1920, asso. mem., 1927-34, mem. since 1934. Mem. Soc. for Exptl. Biology and Medicine, Am. Soc. for Exptl. Pathology, Am. Epidemiol. Soc., Am. Assn. Pathologists and Bacteriologists, Soc. Am. Bacteriologists, Harvey Soc., A.A.A.S., Am. Pub. Health Assn., Alpha Delta Phi, Phi Beta Kappa, Alpha Omega Alpha fraternities. Congregationalist. Clubs: Cruising Club of America, Ausable Club. Author of papers treating of exptl. epidemiology, spread of epidemics, poliomyelitis, encephalitis, rabies, resistance to infectious diseases, etc. Home: 17 Dolma Rd., Scarsdale, N.Y. Address: Rockefeller Institute for Medical Research, 66th St. and York Av., New York, N.Y. Died July 12, 1943.

WEBSTER, William Reuben, engr.; b. Oyster Bay, N.Y., Apr. 30, 1868; s. William Reuben and Helen C. (Stephenson) W.; M.E., Cornell U., 1890; m. Susan W. Hinckley, Oct. 8, 1892; children—Eleanor (Mrs. Pendleton Marshall), William Reuben. Began as sales engr., Westinghouse, Church, Kerr & Co., 1890; engr., Aluminum Brass & Bronze Co., Bridgeport, Conn., 1892-93; supt. Bridgeport Copper Co., 1893-97; successively dept. supt., gen. supt., v.p., Bridgeport Brass Co., 1897-1936, dir. and chmn. bd. since 1930; trustee Bridgeport Peoples Savings Bank; dir. Bridgeport-City Trust Co. Mem. Bd. of Edn., Bridgeport, 1913-22. Fellow Am. Soc. Mech. Engrs., Am. Inst. Mining and Metall. Engrs., Am. Soc. for Testing Materials, Royal Society of Arts, Inst. of Metals (Gt. Britain), Theta Delta Chi, Soc. Colonial Wars. Republican. Episcopalian; sr. warden St. John's Ch. (Bridgeport). Clubs: University, Brooklawn Country (Bridgeport); Cornell Club of N.Y.; Lake Placid Club. Home: 208 Brooklawn Av. Office: Bridgeport Brass Co., Bridgeport, Conn. Died Apr. 28, 1945.

WEDDELL, Alexander Wilbourne, diplomatist; b. Richmond, Virginia, April 6, 1876; son of Rev. Alexander W. (D.D.) and Penelope Margaret (Wright) W.; student George Washington U., 1904-07, LL.B. from same univ.; student Univ. of Catania, Italy, and Univ. of Lausanne; Litt.D., Hampden-Sydney (Va.) College, 1930; LL.D., University of Richmond, 1937; LL.D., College of Wiliam and Mary, 1937; L.H.D., Rollins College, 1947; married Mrs. Virginia Chase Steedman, widow of James Harrison Steedman, May 31, 1923. In business, Richmond, until 1904; clerk Library of Congress, 1904-07; pvt. sec. to U.S. minister to Denmark, at Copenhagen, 1908-10; consul at Zanzibar, E. Africa, 1910-12, Catania, Italy, 1912-14; consul gen. at Athens, Greece, Apr. 24, 1914; apptd. consul gen. at Beirut, Syria, Dec. 1916; attached to Am. Diplomatic Agency, Cairo, Jan.-May 1917; consul gen. at Athens, 1917-20; commercial del. of U.S. on Interallied Bur. of Commercial Attachés, Athens, May 1917; del. of Am. War Trade Bd. at Athens, Jan. 1918; permanent U.S. del. on the Commn. Flancière Interalliée, and provsional del. on Commn. Militaire Interalliée, Athens, Feb. 1918, chargé d'affaires, Sept.-Oct. 1918; consul gen. Calcutta, India, 1920-24, Mexico City, 1924-28 (retired); ambassador to Argentina, 1933-39, to Spain, 1939-42, retired at own request because of ill-health, Oct. 31, 1942, since active in local civic affairs (by order of President Franklin Delano Roosevelt exempted from compulsory retirement at age 65 and age extended to 70, because "pub. interest requires this"); senior chmn. Am. delegation to Pan-Am. Commercial Conf., Buenos Aires, 1935; Am. representative Chaco war mediation group; U.S. delegate to the Pan-American Peace Conference, Buenos Aires, 1936; ambassador to Turkey on a special mission, 1946. Pres. Richmond Community Fund, 1932-33; Richmond Academy of Arts, 1930-35; a founder, with wife, of Va. Mus. of Fine Arts, pres. since 1942. Awarded Cross of Comdr. of George First (Greek), collar of Commendatore U.S. del. to 7th Pan-Am. Conf., Montevideo, 1933; della Corona d'Italia; medal of Solidaricdad (Panama); Order of Mercy (Serbia), for services World War I; Grand Cordon of Condor of the Andes, Bolivia, 1938. Mem. adv. bd. Confederate Memorial Lit. Soc., Writers Club of Richmond. Fellow Royal Geog. Soc., 1927; mem. Va. Hist. Soc. (exec. com.; pres. since 1944). Sons Confederate Vets., Soc. of the Cincinnati (standing Com., del. Triennial Conv.) S. R., Soc. Colonial Wars (dep. gov., 1946), Assn. for Preservation of Va. Antiquities (adv. bd.), Walpole Soc., English-Speaking Union (nat. v.p. since 1936; pres. Va. br., 1929-34), Kappa Alpha, Phi Beta Kappa. Episcopalian (pres. Found. St. John's Ch.; vestryman St. Paul's Ch.). Clubs: Century, Grolier (New York); Metropolitan (Washington); Commonwealth, Country (Richmond, Va.); St. James (London); Union Interalliée (Paris). Built Virginia House (from materials of the Old Priory at Warwick, Eng.) and with wife presented same to Va. Hist. Soc. Editor: Memorial Volume Virginia Historial Portraiture, 1930; Richmond, Virginia, in Old Prints, 1932; Introduction to Argentina, 1939; Portraiture in the Virginia Historical Society, 1945; A Description of Virginia House, 1947. Contbr. travel articles to mags. Address: Virginia House, Richmond 21, Va. Died Jan. 1, 1948; buried Hollywood Cemetery, Richmond, Va.

WEDDERBURN, Joseph Henry Maclagan, mathematician; b. Forfar, Scotland, Feb. 26, 1882; s. Alexander Stormonth Maclagan and Anne (Ogilvie) W.; M.A., Edinburgh U., 1903, D.Sc., 1908; studied Leipzig, Berlin and U. of Chicago; unmarried. Asst. in mathematics, Edinburgh U., 1905-09; asst. prof. mathematics, Princeton University, 1909-21, associate professor, 1921-28, professor, 1928-45, professor emeritus since 1945. Captain Seaforth Highlanders and capt. Royal Engrs., British Army, 1914-19. Fellow A.A.A.S., Royal Soc. (London), Royal Soc. (Edinburgh); mem. Am. Math. Soc., Circolo Matematico di Palermo. Presbyterian. Author: Lectures on Matrices, 1934. Contbr. on scientific topics. Home: 134 Mercer St., Princeton, N.J. Died Oct. 3, 1948.

WEE, Mons O. (wē), theologian; b. Norway, May 13, 1871; s. Ole Monsen and Marie M. W.; came to U.S., 1891, naturalized citizen, 1898; student Red Wing (Minn.) Seminary, 1892-98; U. of Edinburgh, summer, 1910; D.D., Luther College, Decorah, Ia., 1933; m. Mary Elizabeth Nelson, 1900; children—Ruth, Morris, Margaret, Luther. Ordained Norwegian Luth. ministry, 1898; pastor Dell Rapids, S. Dak., 1900-04, Jackson, Minn., 1905-08; prof. of theology, Red Wing (Minn.) Sem., 1908-17; prof. theology and librarian, Luth. Theol. Sem., St. Paul, Minn., since 1917. Editor Tidsskrift, 1912-17; editor Kurdistan Missionary (monthly), 1917-24, also Norsk Ungdom, monthly (Norwegian), 1922-25. Author: Haugeanism (book in English), 1918; Urgent Needs of Our Times, 1923; Hvem er Jesus (Who is Jesus), 1925; Moses, 1927; Shall I Live Forever, 1932; Men Who Knew God, 1933. Pres. Fedn. of Y.P. Socs. of Norse Young Peoples of America; v.p. Lutheran Orient Mission Soc.; tour of inspection to the mission field in Persia, 1899-1900. Author or editor various works in the Norwegian and English; editor-in-chief Fra Pioner Prestenes Saga. Pres. Minn. Leif Erikson Monument Assn. Address: Luther Theol. Seminary, St. Paul, Minn. Died Apr. 15, 1942.

WEED, Clarence Moores, naturalist; b. Toledo, O., Oct. 5, 1864; s. Jeremiah Evarts and Sarah J. (Moores) W.; B.S., Mich. Agrl. Coll., 1883, M.S., 1884; Sc.D., Ohio State U., 1890; m. Adah Lilian Aber, 1888; children—Helen Irene, Walter Aber, Margaret Aber. Entomologist and botanist, Ohio Expt. Sta., 1888-91; prof. zoölogy and entomology, 1891-1904, entomologist in Expt. Sta., 1891-1904, N.H. Coll. Agr. and Mech. Arts; instr., 1904-22, prin., 1922-32, pres. 1932-35, State Teachers Coll., Lowell, Mass.; secretary and manager Moses Greeley Parker Lectures, beginning 1922. Was regional dir. U.S. School Garden Army, 1918-20. Author: Insects and Insecticides, 1891; Fungi and Fungicides, 1894; Ten New England Blossoms and Their Insect Visitors, 1895; Spraying Corps, 1895; Life-Histories of American Insects, 1897; Stories of Insect Life, 1898; Seed-Travelers, 1898; Insect World, 1899; The Flower Beautiful, 1903; Birds in Their Relations to Man (with N. Dearborn), 1903; Laboratory Guide in Zoölogy (with C. W. Crossman), 1902; The Nature Calendar Series, 1902-03; Stories of Bird Life (compiler), 1903; Wild Flower Families, 1908; Our Trees—How to Know Them, 1908; The School Garden Book (with Philip Emerson), 1909; Farm Friends and Farm Foes, 1910; Seeing Nature First, 1913; Crop Production (with W. E. Riley), 1914; Butterflies Worth Knowing, 1917; Manual of School-Supervised Gardening, 1920; Over and Over Stories (with Margaret Weed), 1929; Insect Ways, 1930. Address: 854 Andover St., Lowell, Mass. Died July 20, 1947.

WEED, Frank Watkins, army officer; b. Baltimore, Md., Apr. 12, 1881; s. William Butler and Isabelle (Hall) W.; M.D., U. of Md., 1903; student Army Med. Sch., 1904-05; Army War Coll., 1928-29; m. Abigail S. Howell, Sept. 19, 1908; children—William Howell, Natalie Howell (Mrs. Robert Campbell Aloe). Served in the Med. Corps U.S. Army since 1904; editor in chief: The Medical Dept. of the U.S. Army in the World War (15 vols.), 1921-29. Promoted through grades to brig. gen., July 1942; surgeon, 1st Army, Governor's Island, N.Y., 1940-42; comdg. Letterman Gen. Hosp. since July 1942. Awarded Distinguished Service Medal (with Oak Leaf Cluster). Episcopalian. Address: Letterman General Hospital, San Francisco, Calif.* Died Oct. 1945.

WEED, Walter Harvey, geologist; b. St. Louis, May 1, 1862; s. Samuel Richards and Nellie S. (Jones) W.; E.M., Columbia Univ. Sch. of Mines, 1883; m. Helena C. Hill, 1896; children—Mrs. Eleanor Sharp, Walter Harvey, Mary Hill (Mrs. Mary W. Stephenson); m. 2d, Alma Stencel, 1913; 1 dau., Almita Patricia. Was on geol. survey of Yellowstone Park, 1883-89; discovered that colors of hot springs and geyser deposits are due to algae living in hot waters, and that the deposits are formed by algae life; discovered Death Gulch, Yellowstone Park, where elk, bears, etc., are killed by carbon dioxide gas of extinct hot spring. Also made valuable discoveries while engaged in gen. geol. exploration of Mont., 1889-98, mapping over 10,000 square miles, the results appearing as geologic folios of Geol. Survey of U.S.; in recent yrs. devoted mainly to economic geology, visiting mining centers of U.S., Can., Cuba, Hayti, Cent. Am. and Mexico; first to publish theory of secondary enrichment of ore deposits, 1899; spl. study and geologic exams. in Can. and British Columbia, 1906-07; with Adolph Lewisohn (Gen. Development Co.), 1906-09; in pvt. practice as Weed & Probert, 1910-12, since alone. Geologist U.S. Geol. Survey, 1883-1906; geologist N.C. Geol. Survey, 1901-06. Spl. commr. and expert on copper, and mem. Internat. Jury of Awards (mining), St. Louis Expn., 1904. Spl. editorial corr. Engineering and Mining Journal, New York, 1908; spl. corr. Mining and Scientific Press, San Francisco, 1910-12. Mem. Pan-Am. Scientific Congress, 1916. Fellow Geol. Soc. Am.; mem. Am. Inst. Mining Engrs. Club: Engineers' (New York). Author: Enrichment of Gold and Silver Veins, 1900; The Nature of Ore Deposits (Beck-Weed), 2 vols., 1905; Classification of Ore Deposits, 1906; Copper Mines of the World, 1907; Geology of Castle Mountain (U.S. Geol. Survey); Geology of Butte, Montana, 1914. Also in part, Genesis of Ore Deposits, 1901 (publ. Am. Inst. Mining Engrs.), and similar title, "Emmons" vol., 1913. Has written numerous papers on geol. subjects, particularly with reference to mineral deposits in U.S. and Mexico. Editor and pub. The Copper Handbook (Vols. XI-XVI), later The Mines Handbook (successor), until 1925. Home: Scarsdale, N.Y. Died Sept. 5, 1944.

WEEKS, Alanson, surgeon; b. Allegan, Mich., Sept. 15, 1877; s. Harrison S. and Julia (Shoemaker) W.; M.D., U. of Mich., 1899; m. Belle A. Harmes, June 7, 1905; 1 daughter, Leonie Belle. Became clinical professor of surgery, University of California Medical School, 1924, now emeritus; consultant in surgery St. Luke's Hosp., Children's, Marine and Emergency hosps.—all San Francisco. Served as maj. Med. Corps, U.S. Army, World War. Awarded D.S.M. (U.S.). Fellow Am. Coll. Surgeons; mem. Pacific Coast Surg. Assn., Am. Med. Assn., Calif. State and San Francisco County med. socs., Calif. Acad. of Medicine. Clubs: Pacific-Union, Family, Olympic (San Francisco); Country (Burlingame, Calif.); Country. Home: Pacific Union Club, San Francisco. Office: 384 Post St., San Francisco, Calif. Died Nov. 25, 1947.

WEEKS, John Eliakim, ex-congressman; b. Salisbury, Vt., June 14, 1853; s. E. H. and Elisabeth (Dyer) W.; ed. country and high schs.; m. Hattie J. Dyer, Oct. 14, 1879. Identified with banking in Vt. since 1882; pres. Addison County (Vt.) Trust Co., Columbus Smith Trust; dir. Brandon (Vt.) Nat. Bank. Gov. of Vt., 1927-31; mem. 72d Congress (1931-33), 1st Vt. Dist.; mem. State Institutions Commn. for Public Welfare for 28 years; chmn. Penol. Board, Vermont; trustee State Industrial School, Vt.; trustee Middlebury Coll.; pres. Grammar Sch. Bd., Middlebury. Republican. Conglist. Mason (K.T.). Rotarian. Home: Middlebury, Vt.* Died Sep. 10, 1949.

WEEKS, John Elmer, physician; b. Painesville, O., Aug. 9, 1853; s. Seth and Deborah A. (Blydenburgh) W.; M.D., University of Michigan, 1881, D.Sc. (hon.), 1912; LL.D., New York University, 1923; interne Almshouse and Workhouse Hospital, resident phys. Emigrant Hosp. and interne, Ophthalmic and Aural Inst., New York, 5½ yrs.; (hon. degree Sc.D., Univ. of Mich., 1912); m. Jennie Post Parker, Apr. 29, 1890. Chief of Vanderbilt Clinic, New York, 1888-90; lecturer diseases of the eye, Bellevue Hosp. Med. Coll., 1890-1900; prof. same, Univ. and Bellevue Hosp. Med. Coll. (New York U.), 1900-1920, now prof. emeritus; prof. diseases of the eye and ear, Woman's Med. Coll. of New York Infirmary for Women, 1893-99; cons. surgeon New York Eye and Ear Infirmary; 1st lt. U.S.A. Med. Res. Corps, 1911. Mem. A.M.A., N.Y. Acad. Med., etc. Clubs: Arlington, Waverly Country (Portland, Ore.). Republican. Presbyn. Author: Diseases of the Eye, 1910. Address: 20 E. 53d St., New York, N.Y., and Portland, Ore. Died Feb. 2, 1949.

WEEKS, Walter Scott, prof. mining; b. Chelsea, Mass., Oct. 1, 1882; s. Albert Poland and Mary Elizabeth (Day) W.; A.B., Harvard, 1906, S.B., 1907, M.E., 1909; m. Amabel Lee MacClure, Aug. 8, 1914; step-child, Amabel Lee MacClure (Mrs. John Eager Howard). Asst. in mining, Harvard, 1908-10, instr., 1910-15; asso. prof. of mining, U. of Calif., 1915-27, prof. since 1927; also engaged in consulting work in mining. Mem. Am. Inst. Mining and Metall. Engrs., Sigma Gamma Epsilon, Tau Beta Pi, Sigma Xi. Clubs: Harvard, Bohemian (San Francisco); Faculty (Berkeley). Author: Ventilation of Mines, 1926; also tech. papers. Home: 1429 Hawthorne Terrace, Berkeley, Calif. Died Aug. 9, 1946.

WEER, John Henry (wēr), Christian Science lecturer; b. Carlinville, Ill., Nov. 16, 1873; s. Henry Harrison and Katherine Lawrence (Grace) W.; ed. Carlinville pub. schs. and spl. courses Boston U.; m. Daisy A. Hewitt, Aug. 1903; m. 2d, Margaret C. Campbell, May 1919; m. 3d, Mrs. Lea Pemberton Kendall, Feb. 1925; 1 dau., Mrs. Mary Ellen Weer Hicks. Bank employee, Tacoma, 1889-96; with West Coast Grocery Co., Tacoma (advancing from clerk to vice-pres.), 1896-1922; Christian Science practitioner, Tacoma, 1923-26; mgr. Christian Science Benevolent Assn., Chestnut Hill, Mass., 1927-33; field rep. for The Mother Ch. (1st Ch. of Christ, Scientist), 1933-36; mem. Christian Science Bd. of Lectureship, 1936-40, now mgr. Camp Welfare Activities for The Mother Church (1st Ch. of Christ, Scientist). Republican. Club: Appalachian Mountain (Boston). Contbr. to Christian Science Jour. and Christian Science Sentinel. Home: Chestnut Hill, Mass. Office: 107 Falmouth St., Boston, Mass. Died Jan. 1942.

WEHRLE, Vincent (wēr'lē), bishop; b. Berg, Canton of St. Gall, Switzerland, Dec. 19, 1855; s. John Baptist and Elisabeth (Hafner) W.; classical studies, Diocesan Sem., St. Gall, 4 yrs., Einsiedeln, Switzerland, 2 yrs.; theol. and philos. studies at Einsiedeln. Entered Benedictine Order, 1875; ordained R.C. priest, 1882; came to U.S., 1882; missionary in Ark., 1882-85, Jasper, Ind., 1885-87, Stephan, S.D., 1887-88, Devils Lake, N.D., 1888-99, Richardton, N.D., 1899-1910; founder and first abbot of Assumption Abbey, Richardton, became abbot, 1903; consecrated bishop of Bismarck, April 19, 1910; resigned, 1939; apptd. titular bishop of Teos, Dec. 11, 1939. Address Bismarck, N.D. Died Nov. 1941; buried in St. Mary's Church, Richardton.

WEHRWEIN, George Simon (wēr'wīn), prof. economics; b. Newton, Manitowoc County, Wis., Jan. 31, 1883; s. Adam and Dorothea (Stoltenberg) W.; grad. State Normal Sch., Oshkosh, Wis., 1908; B.S. in Agr., U. of Wis., 1913, M.S., 1920, Ph.D., 1922; m. Anna Ruby Aug. 15, 1914; children—Austin Carl, Dorothea Magdalene, Annabel Ruby. Extension lecturer, U. of Tex., 1913-17; extension specialist Office of Farm Markets, State of Wash., 1917-18; asso. prof. of State Coll., Pa., 1918-19; research asso., Inst. for Research in Land Economics and Pub. Utilities, 1923-28; asso. prof. economics, U. of Wis., 1924-25, prof. economics, Northwestern U., 1925-28; prof. agrl. economics, U. of Wis., since 1928; mem. Wis. State Planning Board, 1935. Mem. Am. Econ. Assn., Am. Assn. Univ. Profs., Am. Farm Econ. Association (pres. 1942), Wisconsin State Historical Society, Am. Soc. of Planning Officials (vice-pres. 1944), Alpha Zeta. Congregationalist. Author: (with Richard T. Ely and Mary L. Shine) Outlines of Land Economics, 1922; (with Richard T. Ely) Land Economics, 1940. Home: 1809 Summit Av., Madison, Wis. Died Jan. 10, 1945.

WEIDMAN, Samuel, geologist; b. Reedsburg, Wis., Oct. 11, 1870; s. Alexander and Eleanor (McIlvaine) W.; desc. of Martin Weidman who emigrated from Germany and settled in Pa., 1733; B.S., U. of Wis., 1894; fellow in geology, same, 1895-96; fellow in geology, U. of Chicago, 1896-97; Ph.D., U. of Wis., 1898; m. Adda J. Westenhaver, Nov. 22, 1899; children—Samuel Henry, John McIlvaine, Robert Hulburt. Field asst. U.S. Geol. Survey in Lake Superior region, 1894-96; asst. geologist, 1897-99, geologist, 1899-1917, Wis. Geol. and Natural History Survey; prof. geology, University of Oklahoma, 1919-43, emeritus professor since September 1943. Democrat. Unitarian. Fellow Geol. Soc. America, A.A.A.S., Assn. American Geographers; mem. Am. Inst. Mining and Metall. Engrs., Am. Assn. Petroleum Geologists, Okla. Acad. of Science (pres. 1924), Sigma Xi. Author: Soils and Agriculture of North Central Wis., 1903, 2d edit., 1908; The Baraboo Iron-Bearing District, 1904; The Geology of North Central Wis., 1907; Soil Survey of Northwestern Wis., 1911; Soil Survey of Marinette County, Wis., 1911; The Water Supplies of Wisconsin, 1916; Miami-Picher Zinc-Lead District, 1932. Home: 512 Lahoma Av., Norman, Okla. Died Sept. 22, 1945.

WEILER, Royal William (wī'lẽr), newspaper pub.; b. Emaus, Pa., Sept. 7, 1880; s. John Wilson and Mary Elizabeth (Schmale) W.; ed. pub. schs.; m. Hester Estella Binder, Aug. 16, 1900; 1 son, Fred Wilson. Teacher pub. schs., Emaus, 1900-10; reporter, Allentown (Pa.) Democrat, 1910-13; gen. mgr. Allentown Democrat Pub. Co., 1913-19; pres. and mgr. Allentown Call Pub. Co. since 1919; pres. and mgr. Chronicle and News Publishing Co. since 1935; Call-Chronicle Newspapers, Inc., since 1946. Vice-president, Lehigh Valley Broadcasting Company. Member Allentown Police Pension Fund Commn. Rep. mem. Associated Press, Am. Newspaper Publishers Assn., Pa. Newspaper Pubs. Assn.; dir. Family Welfare Orgn., Lehigh County Hist. Soc., Lehigh County Humane Soc. Republican. Mason (33°), Shriner; mem. Tall Cedars of Lebanon, Odd Fellows, Elks, Eagles, Patriotic Order Sons of America, Maccabees, Chamber of Commerce, Internat. Circulation Managers Assn. Rotarian. Home: 1615 Linden St. Office: 101 N. 6th St., Allentown, Pa. Died Sept. 12, 1948.

WEINERT, Albert (wīn'ẽrt), sculptor; b. Leipzig, Germany, June 13, 1863; s. Edward Andréas and Augusta (Gerhard) W.; ed. Royal Acad., Leipzig; traveling scholarship, École des Beaux Arts, Brussels; came to U.S., 1886, naturalized citizen, 1903; m. Ann Eliza Nielsen, 1889. Prin. works: architectural sculptures in Congressional Library, Washington, D.C.; "Battle Monument" at Lake George, N.Y.; McKinley Monument, Toledo, O.; statue of Gov. Stevens T. Mason, Detroit, Mich.; statue of Lord Baltimore, at Baltimore, Md.; marble group, in Hall of Records, N.Y. City; bronze trophy for Submarine Div., U.S. Navy; decorative figures, San Francisco Expn., 1915. Mem. Nat. Sculpture Soc.; hon. mem. Washington (D.C.) Light Inf. Lutheran. Home: 1125 Grand Concourse, New York 52, N.Y. Died Nov. 29, 1947.

WEINSTEIN, Alexander (wīn'stīn), consulting industrial engr.; b. New York, N.Y. Oct. 8, 1891; s. David and Frieda (Chester) W.; student Columbia, 1922-28; unmarried. Industrial engr. Pacific Novelty Co. (Dupont Viscoloid Co.), 1918-20, Gem Safety Razor Co., 1924-26, Colombia Bank, 1920-24; cons. industrial engr. Hamersley Mfg. Co., 1926-34, Gilman Paper Co., 1934-35; apptd. by Federal Court as receiver Kelly Springfield Tire Co., 1935; apptd. by N.J. Chancery Court receiver Kelly Springfield Cos., 1935; sec. and treas. Kelly Springfield Tire Co., 1935; apptd. by Federal Court trustee Warner-Quinlan Co., 1936; cons. engr. for Preferred Stockholders Com. of Standard Gas & Electric Co., 1935-36. Served as lt. Sanitary Corps, U.S. Army, 1918-19. Rep. of industry on City Industrial Relations Bd.; mediator and arbitrator representing public on N.Y. St. Bd. of Mediation. Research asso., dept. of industrial engring., Columbia; dir. Hebrew Ednl. Soc. Fellow A.A.A.S.; mem. Am. Soc. Mech. Engrs., Nat. Soc. Professional Engrs., N.Y. State Soc. Professional Engrs., Tech. Assn. Paper and Pulp Industry, Acad. Polit. Science, Economic Research Round Table of Bankers Club, Soc. for Advancement of Management (advisory bd.), Soc. Industrial Engrs. (nat. treas.). Hebrew religion. Clubs: Bankers, Faculty of Columbia University, Economic, Sheepskin, Beethoven Soc., Philharmonic Soc. (New York); Inwood Country (L.I.). Contbr. to jours. Home: 1221 Hilldale Av., Los Angeles, Calif. Office: 120 Broadway, New York, N.Y. Died Feb. 19, 1947; buried in Mt. Zion Cemetery, Maspeth, L.I., N.Y.

WEIR, Irene, artist; b. St. Louis, Mo.; d. Walter and Annie Field (Andrews) Weir; g.d. Robert W. Weir of U.S. Mil. Acad.; B.F.A., Yale, 1906; student of J. Alden Weir; diplôme, l'Ecole des Beaux Arts Americaine, Fontainebleau, France, 1923-27; traveled and studied in Paris, Italy, Spain, Holland, England. Formerly dir. of art instrn., New Haven, Conn., and Brookline, Mass.; later dir. Slater Museum Sch. of Art, Norwich, Conn., and dir. of fine arts, dept. of Ethical Culture Sch., New York; founder and dir. sch. of Design and Liberal Arts, New York, 1917-29. Principal works: "Little Red Top," Museum of Fine Arts, Houston; portrait of Dr. Cyprian Willcox, Memorial Hall, U. of Ga.; portrait of Prof. Robert W. Weir, founder of art dept. U.S. Mil. Acad.; portrait of Maj. Gen. Irwin McDowell, West Point, N.Y.; portrait of Madame Curie, Memorial Hosp., N.Y.; murals "Baptism," "Crucifixion," "Adoring Saints," "New Life," "Mother and Babe with Jesus," Prison Chapel, New York; "Vision," St. Luke's, Katonah; "Garden of Hesperides," Women's University Club, New York; "Nativity," Julien Gallery, New York; "Portrait of My Mother," portrait "Old Man Praying"; portrait "An Old Fashioned Saint"; mural "St. Francis, Canticle of the Sun," Rollins Coll., Winter Park, Fla.; "Emigrants," "Steerage," Huntingdon Coll.; portrait of Arthur Fickenscher, dean of music department, "The Child Renewed," University of Virginia; portrait of Eleanor Josephthal. Member Association of Fine Arts (Yale), Art Alliance of America, Salons of America, Independent Artists of America, Nat. Assn. of Women Painters and Sculptors, Nat. Soc. of Etchers, Founder's Group of Museum of Fine Arts (Houston, Tex.). Clubs: Lyceum (London); Classical, Water Color, Women's University (New York). Author of "Greek Painter's Art." Author: Three Weirs; artists, Robert W. Weir (West Point), John F. Weir (Yale), J. Alden Weir (New York). Lecturer on art at Southern museums and universities. Address: Women's University Club, 40 Vanderbilt Av., New York, N.Y. (summers) Katonah, N.Y. Died Mar. 22, 1944.

WEIR, John M. (wẽr), army officer; b. Ind., Sept. 6, 1891; B.S. and LL.B., John B. Stetson U., 1914, A.M., 1917; grad. Inf. Sch., 1924. Commd. capt. Inf., O.R.C., 1917; active duty, 1917-20; 1st lt. Inf., 1920; transferred to Judge Advocate Gen. Dept., 1928, and advanced through the grades to brig. gen., Sept. 1943. Address: Judge Advocate General's Dept., War Dept., Washington, D.C.* Died Nov. 21, 1948.

WEIR, Samuel, univ. prof.; b. London, Ont., Can., Apr. 15, 1860; s. Robert and Martha (Sutton) W.; A.B., Northwestern U., 1880; B.D., Garrett Bibl. Inst., 1887; A.M., Ill. Wesleyan U., 1891; Ph.D., U. of Jena, 1895; m. Sarah Richards, June 2, 1897; children—Helen Irene (Mrs. Wm. C. Rempfer), Richard Sutton, Mary Frances (Mrs. Ed. J. Cooper). Prof. Latin and Greek, Southwest Kan. Coll., 1889-90; ordained M. E. ministry, 1884; pastor at Wichita, Kan., and Cheyenne, Wyo., 1889-92; instr. mathematics, Northwestern U., 1892-93; prof. ethics and history of edn., New York U., 1895-1901; lecturer on education, U. of Cincinnati, 1901-02; prin. Clarion (Pa.) State Normal Sch., 1902-04; v.p. and prof. of edn. and philosophy, Dak. Wesleyan U., 1905-11, dean Coll. of Liberal Arts, and prof. philosophy and psychology, 1911-14; prof. edn., Simpson Coll., Indianola, Ia., 1914-18; dean and acting pres., Ia. Wesleyan Coll., 1918-19, prof. edn., 1919-22; prof. edn. and psychology, Coll. of Puget Sound, 1922-38; prof. emeritus since 1938. Mem. N.E.A., Phi Beta Kappa, Phi Delta Kappa. Author: Christianity as a Factor in Civilization, 1893. Contbr. numerous articles on ednl. and philos. subjects. Home: 1109 N. Seventh St., Tacoma, Wash. Died Apr. 17, 1943.

WEISMAN, Russell (wīs'mȧn), coll. prof.; b. Van Wert, O., Feb. 7, 1890, s. Paul and Alice (Bauserman) W.; A.B., Adelbert Coll., 1912; A.M., Harvard, 1917; m. Blanche Watkins, Dec. 28, 1920; children—Russell, Anne, Paul. Prof. economics, Western Reserve U., since 1919; asso. editor Cleveland Plain Dealer since 1920, chief editorial writer since 1940. Mem. Phi Beta Kappa, Phi Gamma Delta. Republican. Baptist. Home: 3282 Chalfant Rd., Shaker Heights, O. Died Nov. 8, 1949.

WEISENBURGER, Walter Bertheau (wī'zĕn-bûrg-ẽr), exec. v.p. Nat. Assn. of Mfrs.; b. Barry, Ill., Feb. 6, 1888; s. John Edward and Nellie (Williams) W.; ed. high sch., Hannibal, Mo.; m. Gladys Marjorie Hofbauer, Feb. 27, 1911; children—Rex Montgomery, Marjorie Jane. Newspaper work, Monmouth, Ill., and Hannibal, 1905-08, 1913-17; asst. mng. editor Duluth (Minn.) Tribune, 1910-13; publicity dir., later asst. gen. sec. St. Louis Chamber Commerce, 1917-21; v.p. Nat. Bank Commerce, St. Louis, Mo., 1921-28; pres. St. Louis Chamber of Commerce, 1928-34; exec.-v.p. Nat. Assn. Mfrs., Washington, D.C., and New York, since Feb. 22, 1934. Served as exec.-v.p. Industrial Club of St. Louis, 1930-34, and as Mo. state dir. publicity United War Workers; originator of publicity for St. Louis 1st Liberty Loan Drive; campaign mgr. Community Fund Drive, 1927; former chmn. publicity com. Municipal Advertising Fund; was sec. St. Louis Roosevelt Memorial Drive, and sec. and dir. St. Louis Welcome Home for Soldiers. Mem. Christian (Disciples) Ch. Home: 26 Northway, Bronxville, N.Y.* Died June 23, 1947.

WEISS, William Erhard, chmn. of bd. Sterling Products, Inc.; b. Canton, O., Dec. 18, 1879; s. Erhard and Wilhelmina (Heil) W.; Ph.G., Phila. Coll. of Pharmacy and Science, 1896; m. Helena Schwertfeger, Oct. 16, 1901; children—Madelyn Elizabeth (Mrs. Henry Lane Kinnucan), William Erhard. Began as chemist and pharmacist, 1896; chmn. bd., gen. mgr. and dir. Sterling Products, also officer and dir. many subsidiary cos.; pres. and dir. Bayer-Samesan Co. Trustee Linsley Inst., Wheeling, W.Va. Democrat. Episcopalian. Mason (32°, K.T., Shriner), Elk. Clubs: Union League, The Terrace (New York); Detroit Club; Fort Henry, Wheeling Country, Cedar Rocks Golf (Wheeling, W.Va.); Boca Raton (Fla.); Everglades, Seminoles, Golf (Palm Beach), Fla.); Columbus Beach, Burt Lake Golf (Indian River, Mich.); Club de Peche Petit-Patos, Inc., Quebec, Can. Home: Elmwood, Wheeling W.Va. Office: 92-104 19th St., Wheeling, W.Va.; and 170 Varrick St., New York, N.Y. Died Sep. 3, 1942.

WELCH, Charles Whitefield, clergyman; b. White County, Tenn., Mar. 11, 1878; s. William and Georgia (McFarland) W.; student Ogden Coll., Bowling Green, Ky., 1900-01, hon. Litt.D., 1926; student Southwestern U., 1901-03, Presbyn. Theol. Sem., Chicago, 1908-11, Th.D., Southern Baptist Theol. Sem., Louisville, Ky., 1922; D.D., Cumberland U., 1925; LL.D., Centre Coll. of Ky., 1926; LL.D., Univ. of Kentucky, Lexington, Ky., 1942; m. Sarah Kennedy Burney, 1903 (died 1913); children—Robert Burney, Clara McFarland, Sarah Deborah; m. 2d, Evelyn B. Bridgement, 1916; 1 son, Charles Whitefield. Ordained to the ministry of Presbyn. Ch., 1902; pastor Park Av. Ch., New York, 1911-16; pastor Fourth Av. Ch., Louisville, Ky., since 1916. Elected moderator Presbyn. Ch., U.S.A., at 150th meeting of Gen. Assembly, Phila., 1938. Dir. Presbyn. Theol. Sem., Chicago, Louisville Presbyn. Theol. Sem., Centre Coll. of Ky.; Pikeville (Ky.) Coll. Awarded Algernon Sydney Sullivan medallion by U. of Ky. for service to State of Ky. during 1936. Mem. Theta Phi, Pi Kappa Alpha. Democrat. Mason (32°, K.T.). Clubs: Pendennis (Louisville). Home: 2346 Village Drive. Office: 318 W. Kentucky St., Louisville, Ky. Died Nov. 13, 1949; buried Resthaven Cemetery, Louisville, Ky.

WELCH, E(dward) Sohier, lawyer; b. Boston, Mass., Jan. 27, 1888; s. Francis Clarke and Edith (Thayer) W.; A.B., Harvard, 1909; LL.B., and J.B., Boston U., 1911; m. Barbara Hinkley, June 3, 1909 (divorced, 1926); children—Barbara, Francis Clarke, Edward Sohier, Holmes Hinkley; m. 2d, Margaret Pearmain (Bowditch), Sept. 1, 1926. Began in father's office, 1908, succeeding to his business upon his death, 1919; pres. Commercial Wharf Co., Lewis Wharf Co., Long Wharf Co., Metropolitan Storage Warehouse Co., Vermont & Mass. R.R. Co.; vice pres. Boston & Providence R.R. Co.; mng. trustee Bradlee & Francis, real estate trusts; trustee, South Terminal Trust, Boston Real Estate Trust, Tremont Building Trust; director Fifty Associates, Eastern Massachusetts Street Railway, Pepperell Mfg. Co., State Street Trust Co., Union Freight R.R. Co., State Street Exchange, United Elastic Corp.; mem. corp. Suffolk Savings Bank. Commd. lt. U.S.N.R.F., June 28, 1917; exec. and navigating officer U.S.S. Guinevere; attached to U.S. Naval Base, Brest, France, Oct. 16, 1917; resigned July 11, 1919. Clerk, proprs. of Louisburg Square. Trustee Masonic Edn. and Charity Trust, New Eng. Conservatory of Music, Soc. for Preservation of N.E. Antiquities, Member Boston and Massachusetts bar assns., Boston Real Estate Exchange, Bostonian Soc., Mass. Charitable Fire Society, A Republican Institution (treasurer), 250 Associates Harvard Business Sch., Mil. Order Fgn. Wars. Republican. Episcopalian. Mason (32°); mem. National Grange. Clubs: Somerset, Boston Press, Essex County, Manchester Yacht, Millwood Hunt, Wine and Food; Harvard Travellers. Home: 20 Louisburg Sq. Office: 73 Tremont St., Boston, Mass. Died June 27, 1948.

WELCH, Richard J., congressman. Member Calif. Senate, 1901-13 and of legislative body of City and County of San Francisco, 1916-26; elected to 69th Congress for unexpired term, and reëlected 70th to 80th Congresses (1927-49), 5th Calif. Dist. Republican. Home: 978 Guerrero St., San Francisco. Died Sept. 10, 1949.

WELCH, Stewart Henry, pediatrist; b. Uniontown, Ala., Dec. 23, 1881; s. John Carter and Caroline (Stewart) W.; A.B., Southern U., Greensboro, Ala., 1903; M.D., Cornell U., 1907; post-grad. work, New York Post Grad. Hosp., 1908-10; m. Virginia Scott Marks, June 6, 1917; children—Stewart Henry, Vernon Lee (Mrs. Richard H. Whitney), Lee (Mrs. Oliver Milton Cooper, Junior). Practiced at Birmingham, Alabama, since 1910, specializing in pediatrics since 1916. Fellow American Academy Pediatrics, A.M.A.; mem. Jefferson County Med. Soc. (past pres.), Southern Med. Assn. (chmn. pediatric div. 1946), Ala. State Med. Assn. (counselor). Chmn. Five Points Com. Y.M.C.A. Episcopalian (vestryman). Club: Country (Birmingham). Home: 1737 15th Av. S., Birmingham 5, Ala. Died Nov. 8, 1946.

WELCH, William Addams, park and cons. engr.; b. Cynthiana, Ky., Aug. 20, 1868; s. Ashbel Standard and Priscilla (Addams) W.; ed. high sch., Colorado Springs, Colo., Colorado Coll. (C.E. 1882), U. of Va. (M.E. 1886); m. Camille Beall, 1902; children—Jessie Elizabeth (Mrs. I. H. McAnally), William Addams. Engr. in railway location and constrn. in Eastern, Southern and Western states, Alaska, Mexico, and S. America; also engr. in reclamation, hydro-electric and harbor developments until 1900; gen. mgr. and chief engr. Palisades Interstate Park Commission, N.Y., since 1900; cons. engr. Bear Mountain Hudson River Bridge Corp. Served as chief engr. spruce production div., rank of maj., Air Service Production Div., U.S. Army, during World War; received commendation of chief of Air Service. Mem. Council Boy Scouts America (awarded the Silver Buffalo, also the Pugsley Medal, gold); dir. Nat. Council of State Parks; hon. pres. Appalachian Trail Conf. Mem. Am. Road Builders Assn., Am. Inst. Park Execs., Am. Soc. C.E., Adirondack Mountain Club, Audubon Soc., Nat. Park Soc., Am. Game and Protective Assn. Episcopalian. Clubs: Engineers, Camp Fire, Explorers (New York); Cosmos (Washington). Address: Bear Mountain, N.Y.* Died May 4, 1941.

WELD, Francis Minot, banker; b. New York, N.Y., Feb. 18, 1875; s. Francis Minot and Fanny E. (Bartholomew) W.; grad. Roxbury Latin Sch., Boston, 1893; A.B., Harvard, 1897, A.M., 1898; m. Margaret Low White, Nov. 7, 1903; m. 2d, Mrs. Julia Tiffany Parker, Aug. 17, 1930. Partner in banking firm of Moffat & White, 1905-10, White, Weld & Co., New York and Boston, since 1910; dir. Internat. Minerals and Chem. Corp., Atlas Assurance Co., Pilgrim Exploration Company. Trustee Met. Museum of Art of N.Y., French Inst. Served as captain and major inf., 77th Div., A.E.F. World War I. Received Silver Star and Purple Heart. For two years, 1942-1944, served in New York City Patrol Corps as Lt. Col. and then Colonel commanding the Manhattan Division. Mem. Phi Beta Kappa. Clubs: Brook, Century, University, Union, Harvard (pres. 1936-38), Down Town, Racquet-Tennis. Home: 660 Park Av. Office: 40 Wall St., New York, N.Y. Died Nov. 1, 1949.

WELLER, Ovington E., ex-senator; b. Reisterstown, Md., Jan. 23, 1862; grad. U.S. Naval Acad., 1881; LL.B., Nat. U., Washington, D.C., 1887, LL.M., 1888; married. Resigned from Navy, 1883; with Post Office Dept., Washington, 1883-87. Active in politics since 1903; chmn. State Roads Commn. of Md., 1912-15 (expending $16,000,000 on pub. roads); Rep. candidate for gov. of Md., 1915; del. at large and chmn. Md. delegations, Rep. Nat. Conv., 1916, 24, 36; elected treas. Nat. Senatorial Com., 1918; mem. U.S. Senate, 1921-27; chmn. Md. Pub. Service Commn. since 1935; mem. Rep. Nat. Com. from Md. Address: Tuscany Apt., Baltimore, Md.* Died Jan. 5, 1947.

WELLES, George Denison (wĕlz), lawyer; b. Toledo, O., Nov. 21, 1881; s. Gen. George E. and Julia E. (Smith) W.; LL.B., U. of Mich. Law Sch., 1921 (as of 1903); m. Mae Elizabeth Hunker, Sept. 11, 1907; children—George Denison, Margaret Virginia (Mrs. William C. Draper). Office boy, clerk and sec. of grain elevator, The Paddock-Hodge Co., 1898-1902; stenographer and law student with King & Tracy, law firm, 1902-03; attended U. of Mich. Law School, summer, 1903; admitted to Ohio bar, 1903, to practice before U.S. Supreme Court, 1919; in practice at Toledo, O. since 1903; atty. with King & Tracy, 1904-08; mem. firm King, Tracy, Chapman & Welles, 1908-14, Tracy, Chapman & Welles, 1914-35, Welles, Kelsey & Cobourn, 1935-37, Welles, Kelsey, Cobourn & Harrington since 1937; v.p. and dir. Securities, Inc., Toledo, since 1924; dir. and chmn. exec. com. Air-Way Electric Appliance Corp., Toledo, since 1937; dir. The Toledo Edison Co., Community Traction Co., The M. I. Wilcox Co. Mem. Toledo Charter Commn. and chmn. com. which drafted present Toledo charter, 1934. Mem. Toledo Mus. of Art. Mem. Toledo Chamber of Commerce (former dir.; pres. 1928-29), Toledo Bar Assn. (former trustee; pres. 1926-27), Am. and Ohio State bar assns., Am. Judicature Soc., Fedn. of Ins. Counsel, Fgn. Policy Assn., Chamber of Commerce of U.S.A., Ohio Chamber of Commerce, Alumni Assn. of U. of Mich., Ohio Soc. of N.Y., Hist. Soc. of Northwestern O. (a v.p. and trustee since 1936). Republican. Episcopalian. Clubs: Toledo, Country, University of Michigan (Toledo); Bankers of America (N.Y. City). Home: 2237 Collingwood Av. Office: Ohio Bldg., Toledo, O. Died Dec. 30, 1948.

WELLES, Henry Hunter, Jr.; b. Forty Fort, Luzerne County, Pa., Jan. 21, 1861; s. Henry Hunter (D.D.) and Ellen Susanna (Ladd) W.; A.B., Princeton, 1882, A.M., 1885; Columbia Coll. Law Sch., 1884-85; m. Caroline S. McMurtry, Oct. 4, 1892; children—Katharine Ryerson, Charlotte Rose, Henry H., III. Admitted to Pa. bar, 1885, and practiced about 1 yr.; mgr. family estate, 1886-1908, developing suburban real estate, 1886-1917; field rep. Board of Nat. Missions of Presbyn. Ch. in U.S.A., 1920-26; mem. staff Presbyn. Pension Fund Campaign, 1927. Republican. Elder First Presbyterian Ch., New York. Clubs: Westmoreland (Wilkes-Barre, Pa.); Princeton (New York). Home: 2 E. 86th St., New York, N.Y., and (summer) Glen Summit Springs, Mountain Top P.O., Pa. Died Jan. 7, 1943.

WELLING, Richard (Ward Greene), lawyer; b. North Kingstown, R.I., Aug. 27, 1858; s. Charles Hunt and Katharine Celia (Greene) W.; A.B., Harvard, 1880; student Harvard Law School, 1880-82; Pd.M., New York University, 1910; unmarried. Practiced in N.Y. City since 1883; treas. Tenement House Bldg. Co. Original mem. City Reform Club, 1882; an organizer City Club, Good Govt. Clubs, Nat. Municipal League; was sec. and treas. Commonwealth Club in ballot reform fight, in Low, Jerome, and Com. of 100 campaigns; active in every N.Y. City fusion campaign from Francis M. Scott, 1890, to LaGuardia; chmn., founder School Citizens' Com., 1904, now Nat. Self Govt. Com.; commr. Municipal Civil Service, 1910-13; ex-pres. George Jr. Republic; 1st chmn. joint application bd. Assn. for Improving Condition of the Poor; v.p. and sec. Am. Soc. Prevention Cruelty to Animals; pres. Civil Service Reform Assn.; v.p. and dir. Municipal Art Soc.; mem. council Nat. Sculpture Soc.; sec. Philharmonic Symphony Soc. of N.Y.; trustee City Club, George Jr. Republic; v.p., dir. Boys Brotherhood Republic; hon. v.p. Nat. Municipal League; advisory bd. Park Assn. N.Y. City. Mem. Squadron A, 1901-07; was mem. 1st Naval Battalion of New York, ensign U.S. Navy, on U.S. Glacier, Spanish-Am. War; lt. Fleet Naval Reserve, in comd. Montauk Pt. Naval Base, 1917-19, where he successfully applied "discipline by consent." Fellow Academy Political Science; member Progressive Education Association, N.E.A., National Society Study Edn., Soc. Colonial Wars. Clubs: City, Century, Harvard, West Side Tennis (former v.p.), Skating (New York). Episcopalian. Author: Self-Government Miscellanies, 1914; First Steps in Citizenship; The Merit System; My Classmate, Theodore Roosevelt; Military Self-Government—A War-Time Experience; Civics As It Should Be Taught; You and Your Politics; New Social Horizons; Responsibilities of Teachers in Civic Alertness; Student Self-Government; As the Twig Is Bent, 1942; Let's Teach Them To Govern Themselves. Home: Harvard Club. Office: 1 Wall St., New York 5. Died Dec. 17, 1946; buried Pojac, North Kingstown, R. I.

WELLIVER, Judson Churchill (wĕl'ĭ-vēr), corp. exec.; b. Aledo, Ill., Aug. 13, 1870; s. Morrison and Alpha (Harroun) W.; ed. pub. schs., Fort Dodge, Ia., Cornell Coll., Ia.; m. Jane Douglas Hutchins, July 3, 1899; children—Edward M., Allan J., Sarah H., Jane Douglas. Newspaper work, Sioux City Journal, Sioux City Tribune, Des Moines Leader; later polit. editor and editorial writer Washington Times, and Frank A. Munsey newspapers; sent to Europe by President Roosevelt, 1907, to report upon waterway systems of Europe and Great Britain, the companies' laws of Great Britain, and railroad situation in Europe, report pub. in Report Inland Waterways Commn., 1908; London corr. and European mgr. N.Y. Sun, 1917-18, in charge publicity at Harding hdqrs., Marion, O., during 1920 campaign, and attached to the White House organization after Mar. 4, 1921, occupying a confidential relation to Presidents Harding and Coolidge until Nov. 1, 1925, resigned; dir. public relations with Am. Petroleum Inst., 1925-27; editor The Herald, Washington, D.C., 1928; asst. to pres. of Pullman Co., 1928-31; dir. public relations Sun Oil Co., Phila. Clubs: Players (New York); Nat. Press (Washington); Pen and Pencil, Penn Athletic (Phila.). Contbr. to mags. Address: 1608 Walnut St., Philadelphia, Pa. Died Apr. 14, 1943.

WELLMAN, Arthur Holbrook, lawyer; b. E. Randolph (now Holbrook), Mass., Oct. 30, 1855; s. Joshua W. and Ellen M. (Holbrook) W.; 9th generation from William Bradford, of Plymouth Colony; A.B., Amherst Coll., 1878; A.M., 1881; Harvard Law Sch., 1880-81; LL.B., Boston U., 1882; m. Jennie L. Faulkner, Oct. 11, 1887; children—Sargent H., Katharine F. In law practice at Boston since 1882. Chmn. bd. of dir. Malden Trust Co. Mem. Common Council, 1885, and city solicitor, 1889-91, Malden; mem. sch. com., 1902-05 (chmn., 1904-05); mem. Mass. Ho. of Rep., 1892-94, Senate, 1895-96; mem. Prison Commission, 1898-1913. Republican. Instr., Boston U. Law Sch., 1886-91, prof. equity jurisprudence and equity pleading, 1891-1902. Pres. Mass. Bd. Ministerial Aid. Mem. Am. Bar Assn., Boston Bar Assn., Boston Congl. Club (pres. 1896), Topsfield Hist. Soc. (dir.; pres.), Phi Beta Kappa. Mason. Orator 250th Anniversary Malden Incorporation; del. Mass. Constl. Conv., 1917 (chmn. edn. com.). Pres. Soc. Alumni of Amherst Coll., 1896. Trustee Topsfield Pub. Library. Club: Union. Home: Topsfield, Mass. Office: 150 Congress St., Boston 10, Mass. Died Aug. 24, 1948.

WELLMAN, Francis L., lawyer; b. Brookline, Mass., July 29, 1854; s. William A. and Matilda Gouveneur (Ogden) W.; grad. Harvard U., 1876; m. Ethel Poole, Dec. 3, 1920. Admitted to Mass. bar, 1880, and began practice in Boston; removed to New York; asst. corp. counsel, City of New York, 8 yrs.; asst. dist. atty. 4 yrs.; now in gen. practice; mem. Wellman, Smyth & Lowenstein. Republican. Episcopalian. Clubs: University, Manhattan. Author: Art of Cross Examination, 1904, 4th edit., 1934; Day in Court, 1912; Gentlemen of the Jury, 1924. Home: 136 E. 67th St. Office: 25 Broad St., New York, N.Y.* Died June 8, 1942.

WELLS, Carolyn, author; b. Rahway, N.J.; d. William E. and Anna Wells; m. Hadwin Houghton, Apr. 2, 1918. Engaged in literary work since 1900. Clubs: Colony (New York); Lyceum (London). Author: At the Sign of the Sphinx, 1896; The Story of Betty, 1899; A Nonsense Anthology, 1902; The Gordon Elopement, 1904; A Parody Anthology, 1904; A Satire Anthology, 1905; A Whimsey Anthology, 1906; Emily Emmins Papers, 1907; Fluffy Ruffles, 1907; The Carolyn Wells Year Book, 1908; Seven Ages of Childhood, 1909; The Patty Books; The Marjorie Books; Dick and Dolly; The Gold Bag, 1911; A Chain of Evidence, 1912; The Lovers' Baedeker, 1912; Technique of the Mystery Story, 1915; The Book of Humorous Verse, 1920; The Outline of Humor, 1923; Book of Limericks, 1925; The Technical Mystery Story, 1929; The Cat in Verse, 1935; The Rest of My Life, 1937; The Importance of Being Murdered, 1939; Calling All Suspects, 1939; Crime Tears On, 1939; Murder Plus, 1940; Crime Incarnate, 1940; Devil's Work, 1941; Black Night Murders, 1941; Murder in the Casino, 1941; Who Killed Caldwell?, 1942; also many juvenile books and mystery stories. Home: 1 W. 67th St., New York, N.Y. Died Mar. 26, 1942.

WELLS, Chester, naval officer retired; b. Spring Hill, Pa., Oct. 15, 1870; s. Levi and Helen Louise (Jones) W.; student Pa. Normal Sch., Mansfield, 1885-86; B.S., U.S. Naval Acad., 1893; grad. U.S. Naval War Coll., 1921; m. Marion Leigh Dixson, Oct. 9, 1907; children—Christian Leigh, Helen Elizabeth. Entered U.S. Navy and promoted through grades to capt., 1917; retired in 1924 at own request after 36 years on active list; in Spanish-American War, Philippine Insurrection, North China Campaign, World War I. Pres. District Nat. Securities Corp.; mem. bd. dirs., chmn. trust com., Hamilton Nat. Bank (Washington). Awarded Sampson medal, 7 action clasps, Spanish-Am. War Medal, Philippine Insurrection medal, North China Campaign medal, Victory medal with convoy star, Navy Cross; Comdr. Order of Crown of Italy. Mem. Washington Nat. Monument Soc., Naval Hist. Foundation, Mil. Order of Carabao (past. comdr.), Naval and Mil. Order of Spanish-Am. War, Mil. Order of Dragon, (pres.), Am. Legion, Mil. Order Loyal Legion of U.S. Commandery of D.C. (past comdr.). Trustee, George Washington U.; pres. bd. dirs. Columbia Hosp.; past pres. Nat. Capital Area Council Boy Scouts America. Episcopalian. Republican. Clubs: Metropolitan, Army and Navy, Chevy Chase (Washington), N.Y. Yacht. Home: "Woodend," 9320 Jones Mill Rd., Chevy Chase, Md.; (summer) Welbec Farms, Wyalusing, Pa. Office: Colo. Bldg., 14th and G St. N.W., Washington, D.C. Died Sep. 17, 1948.

WELLS, H(arry) Edward, chemist; b. Hudson Falls, N.Y., Jan. 4, 1874; s. Thomas E. and Charlotte A. (Cornell) W.; B.S., Middlebury Coll., 1894, A.M., 1895; Ph.D., U. of Leipzig, 1897; m. Violet Harper, Apr. 2, 1910; children—Harry Edward, Durbin Harper, McDonald Harper. Food investigation, with W. O. Atwater, 1898-1900; instr. chemistry, Wesleyan U., Conn., 1899-1901; asso. prof. and prof. chemistry, Allegheny Coll., 1902-07; prof. chemistry, Washington and Jefferson Coll., 1907-18; instr. chemistry, Harvard, 1919-20; also atomic weight research; prof. chemistry, Smith Coll., since 1920; chemist Pratt & Whitney Div., United Aircraft, 1942-45. Captain C.W.S., 1918. Fellow A.A.A.S.; mem. Am. Chem. Soc., Delta Kappa Epsilon. Republican. Congregationalist. Home: 58 Paradise Road, Northampton, Mass. Died May 24, 1947; buried Sleepy Hollow Cemetery, Tarrytown, N.Y.

WELLS, H(arry) Gideon, pathologist; b. New Haven, Conn., July 21, 1875; s. Romanta and Emma Townsend (Tuttle) W.; Ph.B., Sheffield Scientific Sch. (Yale), 1895; A.M., Lake Forest (Ill.) U., 1897; M.D., Rush Med. Coll., Chicago, 1898; Ph.D., U. of Chicago, 1903; interne Cook County Hosp., 1898-99; studied in Berlin, 1904-05; A.M., Yale, 1912; m. Bertha Robbins, Apr. 2, 1902. Asso. in pathology, U. of Chicago, 1901-02, instr., 1903-04, asst. prof., 1904-09, asso. prof., 1909-13, prof. since 1913, professor emeritus since 1940, dean in medical work, 1904-14; director of medical research, Otho S. A. Sprague Memorial Institute, Chicago, since 1911. Member American Red Cross Commission to Rumania, 1917-19; commissioned lt. col. Mem. Assn. American Physicians, Cancer Research Soc., A.M.A., Chicago Pathol. Soc., Am. Assn. Pathologists and Bacteriologists, A.A.A.S., Soc. Biol. Chemistry, Nat. Acad. Sciences, 1925. Author: Chemical Pathology, 1907; Chemistry of Tuberculosis, 1923; Chemical Aspects of Immunity, 1925, 29. Contbr. numerous articles to med. and biol. jours. Address: University of Chicago, Chicago, Ill. Died Apr. 26, 1943.

WELLS, H(erbert) G(eorge), author; b. Bromley, Kent, Eng., Sept. 21, 1866; s. Joseph Wells (professional cricket player); ed. private sch. (Bromley), Midhurst Grammar Sch.; honorary D.Sc., honorary D.Litt., London University; married Isabel Mary Wells, 1891 (division 1894); m. 2d, Amy Catherine Robbins (died 1927); 2 sons. Began as apprentice in draper's establishment at age of 13; asst. master at Midhurst, 1882; later became univ. crammer. Author: The Wonderful Visit, 1895; The Time Machine, 1895; The Wheels of Chance, 1896; The Island of Doctor Moreau, 1896; The War of the Worlds, 1898; When the Sleeper Wakes, 1899; Love and Mr. Lewisham, 1900; Anticipations, 1901; The First Men in the Moon, 1901; The Discovery of the Future, 1902; The Sea Lady, 1902; Mankind in the Making, 1903; The Food of the Gods, 1904; Kipps, 1905; A Modern Utopia, 1905; In the Days of the Comet, 1906; The Future in America, 1906; The War in the Air, 1908; Tono Bungay, 1909; Ann Veronica, 1909; The History of Mr. Polly, 1910; The New Machiavelli, 1911; Floor Games for Children, 1911; Little Wars, 1913; The Wife of Sir Isaac Harman, 1914; The World Set Free, 1914; The Research Magnificent, 1915; Bealby, 1915; Mr. Britling Sees It Through, 1916; The Soul of a Bishop, 1917; Joan and Peter, 1918; The Undying Fire, 1919; The Outline of History, 1920; Russia in the Shadows, 1920; The Secret Places of the Heart, 1922; Men Like Gods, 1923; The Dream, 1924; The Story of a Great Schoolmaster, 1924; Christina Alberta's Father, 1925; The World of Wm. Clissold, 1926; Meanwhile, 1927; Mr. Blettsworthy on Rampole Island, 1928; The Science of Life (with Julian Huxley and G. P. Wells), 1929; Common Sense of World Peace (address delivered in the Reichstag), 1929; The Autocracy of Mr. Parham, 1930; The Work, Wealth and Happiness of Mankind, 1932; The Shape of Things to Come, 1933; The Bulpington of Blup, 1933; Experiment in Autobiography, 1934; The Croquet Player, 1937; Brynhild, 1937; Star Begotten, 1937; The Brothers, 1938; Apropos of Delores, 1938; World Brain, 1938; The Holy Terror, 1939; The New World Order, 1940; Babes in the Darkling Wood, 1940; All Aboard for Ararat, 1941; You Can't Be Too Careful, 1941; Crux Ansata: an Indictment of Roman Catholicism, 1943; Mind at the End of Its Tether, 1945; also numerous short stories in various collections, and considerable amount of political, religious and social controversy. Address: 13 Hanover Terrace, Regents Park, N.W. 1, London, Eng. Died Aug. 13, 1946.

WELLS, John Edwin, coll. prof.; b. Phila., Pa., Feb. 12, 1875; s. John Crouch and Sophie Katie (Roberts) W.; B.L., Swarthmore (Pa.) Coll., 1896, M.L., 1899; M.A., Columbia, 1900; Ph.D., Yale, 1915; m. Anna Coates Holmes, Feb. 12, 1904. Instr. French and English, Friends' Central Sch., Phila., 1896-99; prof. English and head dept. of English, Hiram (O.) Coll., 1901-11, Beloit (Wis.) Coll., 1911-17; prof. English and head dept., Conn. Coll. for Women, New London, since June 1917. Mem. Phi Beta Kappa. Republican. Baptist. Editor: The Owl and the Nightingale, 1907; Bible Selections Arranged for Many Uses, 1923; Thackeray's Roundabout Papers, 1925; Thackeray's Vanity Fair, 1928; etc. Author: A Manual of the Writings in Middle English, 1916, First Supplement, 1919, 2d Supplement, 1923, 3d Supplement, 1926, 4th Supplement, 1929, 5th Supplement, 1932, 6th Supplement, 1935, 7th Supplement, 1938; 8th Supplement, 1941; The Story of Wordsworth's Cintra, 1921; Practical Review Grammar, 1928, etc. Contbr. to mags. Home: 77 Vauxhall St., New London, Conn. Died June 23, 1943.

WELLS, John Miller, clergyman; b. Hinds County, Miss., July 16, 1870; s. William Calvin and Mary E.

(Miller) W.; M.A., Southwestern Presbyn. U., 1889; grad. Union Theol. Sem., Richmond, Va., 1893; Ph.D., Ill. Wesleyan U., 1897; D.D., Davidson, 1906, Washington and Lee, 1917; LL.D., Southwestern Presbyn. U., 1922; m. Saidee C. Maslin, Aug. 7, 1894; children—John M., Wm. Calvin, Thomas Maslin, Sarah Maslin (Mrs. William M. Blakely), Catherine Seymour. Ordained ministry Presbyterian Church in U.S., 1893; pastor Buena Vista, Va., 1893-96, Staunton, Va., 1896-1901; First Presbyn. Ch., Wilmington, N.C., 1901-21; president Columbia Theological Sem., 1921-24; pastor First Ch., Sumter, S.C., 1924-42, pastor emeritus since 1942. Moderator general Assembly Presbyterian. Church in the U.S., 1917; moderator Synod of N.C., 1908-09. Commr. to World Missionary Conf., Edinburgh, Scotland, 1910; chmn. Com. on Closer Relations Ref. Chs., 1917; commr. to World Presbyn. Alliance, Cardiff, Wales, 1925; rep. of Presbyn. Ch. in Council of Ref. Chs. and in Fed. Council; mem. Consensus Creed Com. of Alliance of Ref. Chs.; v.p. Fed. Council Chs. of Christ in America, Atlanta, 1927 (mem. administrative com. of the Council); v.p. Alliance of Ref. Chs. holding Presbyn. System, Boston, 1929, Belfast, Ireland, 1933; moderator Synod of S.C., 1932-33. Sprunt lecturer, Union Theol. Sem., 1936; chmn. Western sect. World Presbyterian Alliance, 1941-42. Mem. Pi Kappa Alpha. Democrat. Clubs: Rotary, Country. Author: Influences That Formed the Puritan Party, 1897; Southern Presbyterian Worthies, 1936. Apptd. chaplain U.S. Army for overseas service, 1918, but not commissioned because of Armistice. Home: Sumter, S.C. Died Jan. 2, 1947.

WELLS, Ralph Olney, lawyer; b. Hartford, Conn., Jan. 27, 1879; s. Daniel Halsey and Martha Ann (Breckenridge) W.; A.B., Yale, 1901; LL.B., Harvard, 1904; m. Mary Ida White, Nov. 27, 1908; children—Alfred White, Edward Spencer. Admitted to Conn. bar, 1904, and since practiced in Hartford; counsel for firm of Davis, Lee, Howard & Wright; Former mem. Court of Common Council, City Plan Commn., Bd. of Street Commrs. (all of Hartford). Mem. Am. and Conn. State bar assns., Internat. Assn. of Insurance Counsel, Phi Kappa Epsilon. Conglist. Club: University. Home: Andover, Conn. Office: 36 Pearl St., Hartford, Conn. Died Dec. 16, 1946.

WELLS, Roger Clark, chemist; b. Peterboro, N.Y., Oct. 24, 1877; s. Byron Wells and Lucy (Clark) W.; A.B., Harvard, 1901, Ph.D., 1904; m. Etta May Card, Feb. 24, 1914; children—Arthur Byron, Roger Clark. Asst. in chemistry, Harvard, 1902-04, working on atomic weights of sodium and chlorine with T. W. Richards, also instructor, 1904-05; instructor physical chemistry, Univ. of Pennsylvania, 1905-07; research chemist, Gen. Electric Co., 1907-08; physical chemist, U.S. Geol. Survey, 1908-30, mineral resource specialist on sodium compounds, 1917-20, chief chemist since 1930. Examined potash deposits in Chile, 1916; del. 1st Pan-Pacific Scientific Congress, Honolulu, 1920. Mem. Chem. Soc. of Washington (pres. 1921), Am. Chem. Soc., Washington Acad. Sciences, Geol. Soc. Washington (pres. 1937), Am. Inst. Mining and Metal. Engrs., Am. Geophys. Union, Sigma Xi, Phi Delta Theta; fellow Am. Mineral Soc., A.A.A.S., Geol. Soc. America. Clubs: Cosmos, Harvard. Author: Electric Activity in Ore Deposits, Analyses of Rock and Minerals (U.S. Geol. Survey); Determination of the Common and Rare Alkalis in Mineral Analysis (with R. E. Stevens); over 100 other govt. publs. and scientific papers. Home: 5607 Chevy Chase Parkway. Office: Geological Survey, Washington, D.C. Died Apr. 19, 1944.

WELLS, Rolla, ex-mayor; b. St. Louis, Mo., June 1, 1856; s. Erastus and Isabella Bowman (Henry) W.; student Washington and Princeton univs.; hon. A.M., Washington, 1915, Princeton, 1916; m. Jennie Howard Parker, Oct. 2, 1878 (died Apr. 9, 1917); m. 2d, Carlota Clark Church, Nov. 17, 1923. Employee, asst. supt. and gen. mgr., of a street railway corp., 1879-83; has been identified with various business enterprises; gov. Federal Reserve Bank of St. Louis, Oct. 28, 1914-Feb. 1, 1919; receiver United Rys. Co. of St. Louis, Mo., 1919-27. Mayor of St. Louis, 2 terms, 1901-09. Treas. Dem. Nat. Com., 1912-16. Clubs: University, Racquet, Country, Log Cabin, Commercial (St. Louis). Home: 25 Westmoreland Pl. Office: 509 Olive St., St. Louis, Mo.* Died Nov. 30, 1944.

WELLS, Thomas Bucklin, editor and pub.; born Painesville, O., Apr. 5, 1875; s. Thomas Bucklin and Anne Elizabeth (Jonas) W.; A.B., Yale, 1896; m. Harriet Sheldon, June 21, 1902. Chmn. bd. dirs. Harper & Brothers; editor Harper's Magazine. Mem. Delta Kappa Epsilon, Elihu Club and Elizabethan Club (all of Yale). Clubs: Centiry, Yale. Home: 29 Washington Sq. Address: Harper & Brothers, New York. Died 1941.

WELLS, Richard Harris, pres. Rotary Internat.; b. Salt Lake City, Utah, Oct. 21, 1896; s. Joseph S. and Anna (Scars) W.; ed. pub. schs. and high sch., Salt Lake City, and U. of Utah and Utah State Agrl. Coll.; m. Vilate Dunn, Sept. 21, 1921; children—Gail (Mrs. Keith Petty), Anne. Propr., Ida. Coal & Ice Co. since 1922; joint propr., Ida. Lumber & Hardware Co. since 1934; vice pres., Ida. Bank & Trust Co. since 1934 (all in Pocatello, Ida.). Pres. Pocatello Chamber of Commerce, 1926-27; chmn. bd. of edn., Pocatello, 1927-30. Dir. Ida. Mental Hosp., 1928-30. Founder and pres. Ida. Soc. for Crippled Children. Mem. Pocatello Selective Service Bd. Mem. Rotary Club since 1922 (pres. Pocatello Rotary, 1933-34; dist. gov., 1934-35; went to France as mem. aims and objects com., 1937; dir. Rotary Internat., 1938-39, pres. since 1944). Home: 248 S. 12th St. Office: 427 E. Center St., Pocatello, Ida. Died Jan. 6, 1947; buried, Pocatello, Ida.

WELLS, T(homas) Tileston, lawyer; b. N.Y. City, Sept. 12, 1865; s. John and Grace (Tileston) W.; student Columbia, 1883-87, LL.B., 1888; Harvard, 1888-89; Litt.D., Rutgers, 1912; m. Georgina Betts, Apr. 18, 1894; children—John, Rossiter Betts (dec.), Georgina Lawrence (Mrs. Cortlandt Schuyler Van Rensselaer). Admitted to N.Y. bar, 1890, and since practiced in N.Y. City. Hon. pres. Alliance Française of New York (pres. 6 yrs.); hon. pres. Alliance Française of New Brunswick, N.J.; consul gen. for Kingdom of Rumania, in New York, 1918-41. Mem. Delta Psi. Decorated Grand Officer of Order of Crown of Rumania; Knight Grand Comdr. Royal Order of St. Sava (Serbia); Officer Royal Greek Order of the Savior; Knight Legion of Honor; Officier d'Academie, France; Serbian Red Cross, 2d class; Grand Cross of Orthodox Order of the Holy Sepulchre; Grand Officer of Order of the Star (Rumania); Officer of the Civil and Military Order of Adolph of Nassau (Luxembourg). Club: Union. Home: 52 E. 76th St. Office: 36 W. 44th St., New York, N.Y.* Died Apr. 23, 1946.

WELSH, Robert Kaye, lawyer; b. Lisbon Twp., Waukesha County, Wis., Nov. 18, 1862; s. Thomas and Janet (Watson) W.; B.S., Beloit Coll., 1887, later LL.B.; m. Minerva Elma Prouty, July 20, 1889 (died Oct. 23, 1934); children—Carlton Kaye, Frank Alexander, Roger Thomas. High sch. teacher, Rockford, Ill., 1887-89; admitted to Ill. bar, 1889, and began practice at Rockford; judge Circuit Court, 17th Judicial Dist. of Ill., 1917-23 (resigned); resumed practice in Rockford; sr. mem. firm of Welsh & Welsh (father and three sons); has acted as gen. counsel and dir. of numerous corps.; served as city atty., corp. counsel, pres. Bd. of Edn. of Rockford, etc. Trustee Beloit Coll. Mem. Am. and Ill. State bar assns., Phi Kappa Psi, Phi Beta Kappa. Republican. Mem. Christian Union Ch. (non-denominational). Mason. Clubs: Midday, Rockford Country. Home: 1531 Harlem Blvd. Office: Rockford Nat. Bank Bldg., Rockford, Ill. Died Aug. 3, 1942.

WENDEL, Hugo Christian Martin, educator; b. Phila., Pa., Apr. 6, 1884; s. Hugo Rudolf and Louise (Freudenberger) W.; student Mt. Airy Sem., Phila., 1904-07; student philosophy and history, U. of Erlangen, 1907-08, U. of Leipzig, May-Aug. 1908; A.B., Princeton, 1910; Ph.D., U. of Pa., 1918; studied at Sorbonne, Paris, and L'Institut des Hautes Études Marocaines, Rabat, Morocco, 1925-26; m. Marie Theodora Petersen-Enge, Aug. 18, 1927; 1 dau., Marie Louise. Instr. in history Lankenau Sch. for Girls, Phila., 1910-14; Harrison fellow in history, U. of Pa., 1915-16, 1917-18, asst. in history, 1916-17; instr. in history, New York U., 1918-20, asst. prof., 1920-28, dir. Campus Concert Course, 1920-28; prof. history, chmn. Dept. History and Govt., L.I.U., since 1928; dir. summer schs., 1931-46; pres. Bronx Soc. Arts and Sciences, 1925-28. Vice pres. bd. education, United Lutheran Ch., 1926-32; mem. bd. edn., United Lutheran Synod, since 1944. Research and travel in Europe and North Africa, various periods. Mem. Internat. Law Seminar of Carnegie Endowment U. of Mich., summer 1936. Instr. in history S.A.T.C., New York U., 1918; later maj., staff specialist, U.S. Army Res. Mem. bd. dirs. Mt. Airy Sem., 1934-40. Mem. Am. Hist. Assn., Am. Philos. Assn., Foreign Policy Assn., Phi Beta Kappa, Delta Sigma Phi. Lutheran. Author: Democracy in the New German Constitution, 1920; The Evolution of Industrial Freedom, 1921; Mediterranean Menace, 1927; Proègé System in Morocco, 1930. Home: 5 Barry Pl., Fairlawn-Radburn, N.J. Address: Long Island University, Brooklyn, N.Y. Died Jan. 16, 1949.

WENDT, Julia Bracken, sculptor; b. Apple River, Ill., June 10, 1871; d. Andrew and Mary Bracken; removed with parents to Galena, Ill., 1876; began art studies in Art Inst. Chicago, 1887; assisted Lorado Taft in his studio, 1887-92; m. William Wendt, June 26, 1906. Assisted with decorations for Chicago Expn., 1892, besides assisting with decorations on grounds, carried out several independent commns., among them "The Statue of Illionis Welcoming the Nations," afterward presented to the State by the Ill. Woman's Expn. Bd.; took 1st sculpture prize offered in Chicago, 1898; apptd. on staff of sculptors, St. Louis Expn., 1904; took 1st prize for sculpture, Municipal Art League of Chicago, 1905; gold medal, San Diego Expn., 1915; Mrs. W. P. Harrison prize, Los Angeles, 1918. Modeled colossal group, Art, Science and History, in Mus. of Expn. Park, and statue of Lincoln, Lincoln Park, Los Angeles, Calif.; memorial tablet, Red Cross Ambulance Corps No. 1, Pasadena; memorial relief, Hollywood; portrait of John Steven McGroarty, for Calif. History and Landmark Soc.; portrait of Frank P. Flint, Flint Memorial; also represented in Vanderpoel Memorial Art Gallery, Chicago. Mem. Chicago Soc. Artists, Calif. Art Club, Am. Federation of Arts. Mem. Municipal Art Commn., Los Angeles, 3 yrs. Served as teacher of sculpture, Otis Art Inst., Los Angeles. Home: 2420 S. Coast Blvd., Laguna Beach, Calif.* Died June 22, 1942.

WENDT, William, artist; b. Germany, Feb. 20, 1865; pub. sch. edn.; self-taught in art; came to America, 1880; m. Julia Bracken, June 26, 1906. Painted in England and in America; exhibited in Salon, Paris, Royal Acad., London, and in leading Am. galleries. Awarded 2d Yerkes prize, Chicago Soc. Artists, 1893; Young Fortnightly prize, 1897; bronze medal, Buffalo Expn., 1901; silver medal, St. Louis, 1904; Cahn prize, Chicago, 1904; hon. mention Chicago Soc. of Artists, 1905; medal, Wednesday Club, St. Louis, 1910; hon. mention, Autumn Exhbn., Art. Inst. Chicago, 1911; fine arts prize, Soc. Western Artists, 1912; silver medal, Panama P.I. Expn., 1915; Grand Prize, San Diego Expn., 1915; Clarence S. Black prize, Calif. Art Club, 1917; Mrs. Keith Spaulding prize, Chicago Art Inst., 1922; 2d Balch purchase prize, Pan-American Exhbn.; Ranger Fund purchase prize, N.A.D., 1926; gold medal Pasadena Art Inst., 1930; 2d prize, Calif. State Fair, 1931, 1st prize in landscape class. Represented in permanent collections of Art Inst., Friends of Am. Art, Cliff Dwellers, Union League (Chicago); Athletic Club (Los Angeles); Cincinnati Mus.; Art Assn. (Indianapolis); William Preston Collection; Mus. of History, Science and Art, Los Angeles, University Club, Seattle, Wash., etc. A.N.A., 1913; mem. Am. Federation Arts, Laguna Beach Art Assn., Calif. Art Club. Club: Nat. Arts (New York). Home: 2420 S. Coast Blvd., Laguna Beach, Calif.* Died Dec. 29, 1946.

WENNER, William Ervin, educator; b. Pilgerheim, Pa., Aug. 27, 1872; s. George J. and Martha (Finley) W.; A.B., Westminster Coll., New Wilmington, Pa., 1897, Pd.D., 1936; m. Margie L. Rugh, Jan. 8, 1902; children—Thomas Bennett, Leland Carlos. Head of dept. of English, Slippery Rock (Pa.) State Normal Sch., 1905-07; asst. prin. Wooster Prep. Sch., 1907-09; supt. Harbor spl. schs., Ashtabula, O., since 1909; teacher Kent State Teachers Coll., summers 1926, 27, 28; lecturer on edni. and civic topics since 1914; mem. Ohio Ho. of Rep., 1918-22, Senate, 1922, 23; mem. Sherwood Eddy European Seminar and Inst. of Foreign Relations, summer 1931. Mem. N.E.A., Ohio State Teachers Assn. (pres. N.E. Sect. 1937); mem. Nat. Council Y.M.C.A., term 1924-28. Republican. Conglist. Mason (32°). Club: Nat. Exchange. Author: Outlines of American Literature, 1902. Home: Ashtabula, O. Died Jan. 13, 1949 buried Salem Lutheran Cemetery, Lamartine, Pa.

WENTWORTH, Catherine Denkman, artist, sculptor; b. Rock Island, Ill.; d. Frederick Carl A. and Anna Catherine (Bladel) Denkman; ed. Art Inst Chicago, later under Carl Marr (Munich) and Bouguereau and Ferrier (Paris); m. Edward S. Wentworth. First woman to win prize for full-length nude at Academie Julian, Paris; painted and modeled many noted persons in Europe and U.S. Represented in Museum of Clermont-Ferrand and Museum of Toulouse, France; Met. Museum of N.Y. City; The Palace of the Legion of Honor, San Francisco; also in numerous colleges and private collections. Officier d'Academie des Palms (Paris). Mem. New York Soc. of Painters. Presbyterian. Home: Santa Barbara, Calif. Address: 44 Fairway Road, Santa Barbara, Calif. Died Mar. 4, 1948.

WENTWORTH, Fred Wesley, architect. Mem. Am. Inst. Architects since 1901, fellow since 1926. Address: Wentworth and Vreeland, 630 E. 27th St., Paterson, N.J.* Deceased.

WENTZ, Louis Haines (Lew Wentz), oil producer; b. Tama City, Ia.; s. Louis and Adeline W.; moved with parents to Pittsburgh, Pa., at age of 6; unmarried. Settled at Ponca City, Okla., 1911, and became one of the principal oil and gas producers of the State, also mfr. of gasoline on large scale; mem. bd. dirs. Security Bank (Blackwell, Okla.). Founder of Lew Wentz Foundation of Okla. Univ., Okla. Agrl. and Mech. Coll., and other colleges of the state, for providing students with loans; organizer and treas. Okla. Soc. for Crippled Children; leader in movement for State Crippled Children's Law and construction of State Hosp. for Crippled Children; founder camp for boys' and girls' orgns. at Ponca City, also a wild game sanctuary near Ponca City. Mem. Okla. State Highway Commn. four yrs., chmn. two yrs. Del. at large Rep. Nat. Conv., 1928, 36, 40, 44, (chmn. del.). 1936-40; Rep. Nat. committeeman since 1940. Vice-chmn. Will Rogers Memorial Commn. of Okla.; 1st chmn. Okla. State Adv. Com. for sale of Defense Bonds. Hon. member Phi Beta Kappa, Beta Gamma Sigma, Acacia. Methodist. Mason (33°, K.T., Shriner). Clubs: Ponca City Country (Ponca City); City (Tulsa); City (Oklahoma City). Home: Ponca City, Okla. Died June 9, 1949; interred Ponca City Mausoleum.

WERFEL, Franz (vĕr'fĕl), playwright and novelist; b. Prague, Czechoslovakia, Sept. 10, 1890; s. Rudolph and Albine (Kussy) W.; ed. coll., Prague, univ., Leipzig, Germany; m. Alma Maria Mahler. Sergt. Austrian Army, World War I. Awarded Oesterre Tapferkeitsmedaille. Club: Pen (London, Eng.). Author: Verdi, 1924 (English translation 1925); Class Reunion, 1929; The Pure in Heart, 1931; Forty Days of Musa Dagh, 1934; The Man Who Conquered Death; Twilight of a World, 1937; Harken Unto the Voice, 1938; Embezzled Heaven, 1940; The Song of Bernadette, 1942; April in October; (plays), The Goat Song; The Mirror Man; Schweiger; Paulus Among the Jews; Juarez and Maxmilian; The Kingdom of God in Bohemia; The Eternal Road; In One Night; The Trojan Women; Jacobowsky and the Colonel (comedy); The Song of Bernadette; Star of Heaven. Address: 6900 Los Tilos Rd., Hollywood, Calif. Died Aug. 26, 1945.

WERLEIN, Elizabeth Thomas (Mrs. Philip Werlein III) (wĕr'lin); b. Bay City, Mich., Jan. 29, 1887; d. Henry and Marie Louise Felton (Smith) Thomas; ed. pub. schs. and pvt. tutors; voice culture under Jean de

Reszke, Paris; m. Philip Werlein III, Aug. 4, 1908 (died Feb. 22, 1917); children—Betty, Lorraine, Evelyn, Philip IV. Writer for newspapers since 1917; exec. head of public relations dept. of Saenger Theatres (over 200 motion picture theatres in 6 Southern states), 1924-30. Financial chmn. for Council Nat. Defense, New Orleans, 1917-20; chmn. Woman's Com., Liberty Loan Drives, 1917-20; organizer and comdt. Red Cross Canteen, New Orleans, 1919; chmn. Aeroplane Landing Fields for State La., 1917. Mem. Professional Women's Com. of Roosevelt Nat. Campaign Com.; mem. Democratic Victory Fund Nat. Com. Pres. Vieux Carré Property Owners Assn. Mem. bd. New Orleans Symphony Orchestra; mem. bd. New Orleans Spring Fiesta Assn. Democrat. Clubs: Quarante, Orleans (pres.), Petit Theatre, New Orleans Country. Given "Wings" at special ceremony N.Y. Aero Club, 1919. Asst. to Dr. Isaac Cline in restoring masterpieces to La. State Museum, 1934-36; now doing private commissions for museums. Hon. mem. Am. Inst. of Architects, awarded for preservation of Vieux Carre, New Orleans. Author of "Wrought Iron Railings of Vieux Carré." Home: 630 St. Ann, New Orleans, La.* Deceased.

WERTMAN, Floyd Rollan, vice-pres. S. S. Kresge Co.; b. Farm Mundy, Mich., Apr. 2, 1884; s. Jesse and Matilda (Leinbaugh) W.; ed. high sch., also some special studies; m. Fern V. Stouffer, 1912; children—John J. Robert D., William F. In wholesale dry goods business 3 yrs.; with S. S. Kresge Co. since 1906, now v.p. in charge of merchandising. Republican. Presbyterian. (Mason (32°). Clubs: Athletic, Golf, Rotary (Detroit). Home: 1686 Balmoral Drive. Office: 2727 2d St., Detroit, Mich. Died May 13, 1947.

WERTZ, Edwin Slusser, lawyer; b. Dalton, O., Aug. 7, 1875; s. William Henry Harrison and Carrie Virginia (Slusser) W.; student U. of Wooster, 1896; Ph.B., Ohio State U., 1899, LL.B., 1900; m. Elizabeth Johnson, July 11, 1906; children—Catharine Virginia, Caroline Slusser, William Henry Harrison, Elizabeth Johnson. Began practice at Wooster, 1905; mem. Ohio Ho. of Rep., from Wayne County, 1904-09; U.S. atty., Northern Dist. Ohio, appmt. Pres. Wilson, 1915-23; now practicing in Wooster. Mem. Battery H, 1st Ohio Vol. Light Arty., Spanish-Am. War, 1898. Presbyterian. Mem. Spanish War Vets. Mason (32°). Club: Cleveland Athletic. While mem. Ohio Gen. Assembly, was author of acts which created the Ohio Highway Dept., the Railroad Commn., abolished contract convict labor from Ohio prisons, drew the act defining the policy of Ohio regarding her state universities and declaring the intention of Ohio to build one great state univ. in Ohio State Univ., also the code amendment permitting the teaching of the elements of agriculture in the common schs. Home: 525 College Av. Office: 127½ E. Liberty St., Wooster, O. Died Nov. 7, 1943.

WESCOTT, Cassius Douglas (wĕs'kŏt), ophthalmologist; b. Salisbury Center, N.Y., May 25, 1861; s. Austin B. and C. Ermina (Byington) W.; M.D., Rush Med. Coll., 1883; m. Ada Virgil, Dec. 31, 1890; children—Virgil, Helen. Began teaching at Rush Med. Coll. as asst. in chem. laboratory, demonstrator of chemistry, 1883-84; resident physician, Ill. Eastern Hosp. for the Insane, Kankakee, 1884-86; gen. practice in Chicago, 1886-94; specialized in ophthalmology, since 1894; asst. surgeon, Ill. Charitable Eye and Ear Infirmary, 1887-88; apptd. surgeon to eye and ear dept., Central Free Dispensary, 1887; oculist to Cook County Hosp., 1891-93; lecturer on eye at Ill. Training Sch. for Nurses, 1891-1915; instr. ophthalmology, Rush Med. Coll., 1894-1900, asst. prof., 1900-07; ophthalmologist to C.,M.&St.P. Ry., 1894-1922; attending oculist, Washington Blvd. Hosp., 1900-22; asst. ophthalmologist, Presbyn. Hosp., Chicago, 1900-07; ophthalmologist, St. Luke's Hospital, 1907-15. Commd. 1st lt. Med. Res. Corps, Feb. 1911. Mem. Am. Ophthal. Soc. (pres. 1925), A.M.A., Am. Assn. Ry. Surgeons, Ill. State and Chicago med. socs., Chicago Ophthal. Soc. (pres. 1900), Chicago Pathol. Soc. (pres. 1893), C.,M.&St.P. Ry. Surgeons Assn., Chicago Inst. of Medicine (pres. 1924), Chicago Physicians Club. Trustee 3d Unitarian Ch., 1901-06. Clubs: University, City. Home: 526 8th St., Wilmette, Ill. Office: 30 N. Michigan Av., Chicago, Ill.* Died May 6, 1946.

WEST, Andrew Fleming, educator; b. Allegheny, Pa., May 17, 1853; s. Rev. Nathaniel and Mary (Fleming) W.; A.B., Princeton, 1874, Ph.D., 1883; LL.D., Lafayette Coll., 1897; D.Litt., Oxford U., 1902; m. Lucy Marshall Fitz Randolph, May 9, 1889. Prof. Latin, Princeton U., 1883-1928, dean Grad. Sch., 1901-28. Trustee Am. Acad. in Rome and chmn. Commn. on Sch. of Classical Studies. Writer on univ. edn. particularly classical edn. Hon. pres. Am. Classical League; past pres. Am. Philol. Assn.; v.p. Archeol. Inst. America. Planned Grad. Coll. of Princeton, opened 1913. Editor: Terence, 1888; The Philobiblon of Richard de Bury, 1889. Author: Alcuin and the Rise of the Christian Schools, 1893; Latin Grammar, 1902; The Proposed Graduate College of Princeton University, 1903; American Liberal Education, 1907; Education and the War, 1919; Presentations for Degrees, 1929; Stray Verses, 1931; American General Education, 1932. Home: Princeton, N.J. Died Dec. 27, 1943.

WEST, E. Lovette, pub. utilities exec., retired; b. Lakeville, N.Y., Sept. 19, 1875; s. Lovette P. and Harriet M. (Dimmock) W.; M.E., Cornell, 1899; M.M.E., Fellowship Sibley Coll., 1900; m. Bess Gail Palmer, July 11, 1903; 1 dau., Bernice Delmar. With J. G. White & Co., New York, 1900-02; supervising engr. fgn. utility work J. G. White & Co., Ltd., London, Eng., 1902-04; asst. engring. mgr. J. G. White & Co., New York, 1904-08; engr. and mgr. Colo. Power Co., Colo. Springs and Denver, Colo., 1908-12; gen. mgr. N.E. Power Co., Worcester, Mass., and Boston, 1912-14; engr. with Bonbright & Co., 1914; former pres. W. S. Barstow Management Assn. Reading Transit & Light Co., Met. Edison Co., Met. Power Co. (Reading); dir. Gen. Gas & Elec. Corp., 1917-29; resigned from all utilities, 1929. Mem. bd. of govs. Lawrence Hosp., 1934-39; dir. Community Welfare Fund, Bronxville, N.Y. Mem. Sigma Psi. Presbyterian. Club: Bankers (New York). Home: 120 Hampshire Rd., Bronxville, N.Y. Died March 6, 1944.

WEST, Egbert Watson, insurance exec.; b. Glens Falls, N.Y., May 1, 1863; s. William Henry and Susan (Miller) W.; ed. pub. schs.; m. Julia A. Parks, 1886; children—Mrs. Ruth W. Derby, Hewitt Seymour, Mrs. Dorothy W. Bowden, Mrs. Harriet W. Dyer. With the Glens Falls Ins. Co. since 1874, spl. agt., 1885, asst. sec., 1904, dir., 1907, v.p., 1915, became pres., 1920, now chmn. bd. and mem. bd. dirs.; chmn. bd. and mem. bd. dirs. Commerce Ins. Co., Glens Falls Indemnity Co.; mem. bd. dirs. Glens Falls Investing Corp. Republican. Presbyterian. Club: Glens Falls Country. Home: 266 Glen St., Glens Falls, N.Y. Died Aug. 13, 1944.

WEST, Elizabeth Howard, librarian; b. Pontotoc County, Miss., Mar. 27, 1873; d. James Durham (D.D.) and Mary Robertson (Waddel) West; B.A., Industrial Inst. and Coll. of Miss. (now Miss. State Coll. for Women), 1892; B.A., M.A., U. of Tex., 1901; library training U. of Tex., 1905-06. Teacher until 1906; asst., Library of Congress, Washington, D.C., 1906-11; archivist, Tex. State Library, 1911-15; librarian, Carnegie Library, San Antonio, 1915-18; state librarian, Tex., Aug. 31, 1918-Aug. 31, 1925 (1st woman ever commd. as head of a dept. in Tex. State Govt.); librarian Texas Tech. Coll., Lubbock, Texas, 1925-42, librarian emerita and hist. research specialist, September 1942-46; on leave 1930-32, to act as research asst. to Library of Congress European Historical Mission, in charge of its work in the Archivo General de Indias, Sevilla, Spain. Mem. Am. Library Assn., Tex. Library Assn. (pres. 1914-16), Southwestern Library Assn. (pres. 1922-24), Tex Congress of Parents and Teachers (life), D.A.R., Philosophical Soc. of Tex., Tex. State Hist. Assn. (fellow, life mem.), Fla. Hist. Society, Miss. Hist. Assn., Southwestern Com. on Latin-Am. Culture, Phi Beta Kappa, Delta Kappa Gamma. Democrat. Presbyterian. Author: Texas Historical Notebook, 1905. Compiler: Calendar of the Papers of Martin Van Buren, 1910; Calendar of the Papers of Mirabeau Buonaparte Lamar, 1914. Contbr. to Dictionary of Nat. Biography, Dictionary of Am. History and mags. Home: 1511 E. Brainard, Pensacola, Fla. Died Jan. 3, 1948.

WEST, George Henry, lawyer; b. Kansas City, Kan., Dec. 11, 1893; s. John William and Rose Ida (Arrighi) W.; ed. Christian Brothers Comml. Sch., 1905-08, De La Salle Acad., Kansas City, Mo., 1910-13; LL.B., Kansas City U., 1915; m. Adrienne Neild, Nov. 1, 1930; children—Constance Louise, George Henry, Jr. Admitted Mo. bar, 1915, Kan. bar, 1921; police judge Kansas City, Kan., 1921-23; admitted U.S. Dist. Court, 1924; chmn. Civil Service Commn., Kansas City, Kan., 1927-31, asso. city atty., 1931-33; county (Wyandotte) counsellor, 1933-42; admitted Superior Court of U.S., Jan. 1942; apptd. U.S. atty. for Dist. of Kan., July 8, 1942; v.p. and mem. bd. dirs. Bonds, Inc. Served as pvt. U.S. Marine Corps, World War I. Mem. Phi Alpha Delta. Club: Kansas City (Kansas City, Mo.). Home: 2235 Washington Blvd., Kansas City, Kansas. Address: Post Office Bldg., Topeka, Kan. Deceased.

WEST, James Edward; b. Washington, D.C., May 16, 1876; s. Robert and Mary (Tyree) W.; grad. Business High Sch., Washington, D.C., 1895; LL.B., LL.M., National U., 1901; LL.D., Kalamazoo Coll., 1928; M.H., Springfield Coll., 1928; LL.D., Hamilton Coll., 1941; m. Marion Speaks, June 19, 1907; children—Arthur, Marion, Helen, Robert. Admitted to bar, D.C., 1901. Apptd. by President Theodore Roosevelt mem. Board of Pension Appeals, later assistant atty. Dept. of Interior; also pvt. practice, Washington; admitted to bar Supreme Court of U.S., 1906. Organized Citizens' Com. and secured Juvenile Court for Washington, D.C.; promoted Washington Playground Assn.; organized and served as sec. Nat. Child Rescue League; conducted nat. campaign in behalf of dependent children; was sec. Pres. Roosevelt's White House Conf. on Care of Dependent Children; became executive officer Boy Scouts America, Jan. 1, 1911, later chief scout executive and was elected chief scout, 1943. Chmn. Sect. III G of President Hoover's White House Conference on Youth outside of the Home and School, 1930; chairman Committee of Character Building Agencies of President F. D. Roosevelt's Conf. on Mobilization for Human Needs, 1933; mem. White House Conf. on Children in a Democracy, 1939-40. Awarded: Silver Buffalo, for distinguished service to boyhood, Boy Scout America; Silver Wolf, Brit. Boy Scouts Assn.; Silver Carabao, Philippine Scout Assn.; Cross of Honor, United States Flag Assn.; gold medal, for distinguished service to humanity, Nat. Inst. Social Scis.; Parents' Mag. medal for outstanding services to children; citation Vets. Fgn. Wars; James E. West Award is annually presented in his honor by Ladies Auxiliary of Veterans Foreign Wars. Member board of directors Navy League of U.S., National Information Bureau; member board trustees Golden Rule Foundation. Member Recreation Commission, New Rochelle, N.Y. Mem. Internat. Scout Com. representing U.S.A. Presbyterian. Clubs: University (Washington, D.C.); Union League, Westchester Country (chairman board of governors). Author: Lone Scout of the Sky, 1928; Boys' Book of Honor (with Peter Lamb) 1931, He Who Sees in the Dark (with same), 1932; The Scout Jamboree (with William Hillcourt), 1934; Making the Most of Yourself, 1941; also pamphlets and articles on various phases of character education through scouting. Editor of Boys' Life, 1922-43. Home: 1338 North Av., New Rochelle, N.Y. Office: 6307 Chrysler Bldg., New York 17, N.Y. Died May 15, 1948.

WEST, Junius Edgar, b. nr. Waverly, Va., July 12, 1866; s. Henry Thomas and Susan Thomas (Cox) W.; student Suffolk (Va.) Collegiate Inst., 1880-82, Univ. of N.C., 1882-84, U. of Va., 1887, Washington and Lee U., 1887; m. Olive Beale, Jan. 17, 1903; 1 dau., Margaret (Mrs. Henry Bowen Frazier, Jr.). Began in ins. business, Waverly, 1888; mem. firms Harper & West, 1890-1906, West & Withers, gen. ins., Suffolk, since 1906; supt. schs., Sussex County, Va., July 1889-Nov. 1890; mem. Va. Ho. of Delegates, 1910-12; mem. Va. State Senate, 1912-22; lt. gov. of Va., 1922-30. Four-minute speaker, World War; chmn. United World War Work, Suffolk and Nansemond counties. Del. to Dem. Nat. Conv., 1896 and 1932; mem. Va. State Dem. Exec. Com., State Dem.-Central Com. and chmn. Dem. Co. Exec. Com. several yrs. Trustee Elon (N.C.) Coll. (sec. 20th Century Fund, 1901); formerly trustee State Teachers Coll., Farmville, Va. Chmn. Mission Bd. Southern Christian Conv. Mem. S.A.R. Rotarian. Pres. Suffolk Chamber of Commerce, 1937. Sponsored Men and Millions Movement of Southern Christian Conv., 1919. Mem. Va. Commn. of Fisheries since 1939. Home: 459 W. Washington St. Office: 117 N. Main St., Suffolk, Va. Died Jan. 1, 1947.

WEST, Milton H., congressman; b. near Gonzales, Tex., June 30, 1888; ed. West Tex. Mil. Acad., San Antonio; m. Temple Worley, 1914; 1 son, Milton Horace, Jr. Served with Tex. Rangers, 1911-12, studied law in office of James A. King and admitted to Tex. bar, 1915; practiced at Brownsville, Texas; dist. atty. 28th Jud. Dist of Tex., 1922-25, asst. dist. atty., 1927-30; mem. Tex. Legislature, 1930-33; elected, Apr. 1933, mem. 73d Congress (1933-35) to fill unexpired term of John N. Garner, and reelected to 74th to 80th Congresses (1935-49), 15th Tex. Dist. Democrat. Home: Brownsville, Texas. Died Oct. 28, 1948.

WESTCOTT, John Howell, univ. prof.; b. Phila., Pa., Aug. 3, 1858; s. John Howell and Mary (Dunton) W.; A.B., Princeton, 1877, A.M., 1880, Ph.D., 1887; studied Leipzig, 1877-78, Paris, 1878-79; law courses U. of Pa., 1879-81; m. Edith F. Sampson, July 9, 1895 (died Sept. 6, 1905); children—John Howell (dec.), Lilian Vaughan (Mrs. John Quincy Stewart), Mary Dunton (Mrs. H. T. Westbrook); m. 2d, Marian Bate, Mar. 25, 1908. Practiced law at Phila., 1881-85; tutor Latin, Princeton U., 1885-87, prof., 1889-1925, tutor Roman law, 1892-1925, prof. emeritus since 1925. Editor: (editions of Latin classics) Livy, Books 1, 21, 22, 1891, 1904; Livy Book 1, selections 21-30, 1924. Fifty Stories from Aulus Gellius, 1893; One Hundred and Twenty Epigrams from Martial, 1894; Selected Letters of Pliny the Younger, 1898; Ceasar's Gallic War, 1902; Suetonius—Julius and Augustus (with E. M. Rankin), 1918. Address: Princeton, N.J. Died May 19, 1942.

WESTERMAN, Harry James, cartoonist, painter; b. Parkersburg, W.Va., Aug. 8, 1876; s. Francis Meakin and Clara Ann (Tracey) W.; ed. pub. schs., Columbus Art Sch.; m. 2d, Grace G. Doyle, Feb. 11, 1931. With Ohio State Journal since 1897, cartoonist since 1901. Cartoonist McClure Syndicate. Member League Columbus Artists, Soc. Ind. Artists, New York, League Am. Artists. Republican. Methodist. Clubs: Pen and Pencil, Arion Music, Athletic, Faculty, Scioto Country. Mem. Am. Press Humorists. Author: Book of Cartoons, 1902; Young Lady Across the Way, 1913. Home: 4124 Riverside Drive. Address: Ohio State Journal, Columbus, O.* Died June 27, 1945.

WESTGATE, Lewis Gardner, geologist; b. Phenix, R.I., Oct. 8, 1868; s. George Lewis and Sarah Elizabeth (Gardner) W.; A.B., Wesleyan U., Conn., 1890; A.B., Harvard University, 1891, A.M., from same, 1892, Ph.D., from same, 1896; Sc.D., Wesleyan University, 1940; m. Martha Josephine Beach, Sept. 5, 1893. Asst. in geology, Harvard, 1891-92, Wesleyan U., 1892-93; teacher of science, Evanston Twp. (Ill.) High Sch., 1893-1900; prof. geology, Ohio Wesleyan U., 1900-39, emeritus since 1939; asst. geologist, U.S. Geol. Survey, 1912-19, asso. geologist, 1919-35. Fellow Geol. Soc. America (v.p. 1926), Mineral Soc. America, Ohio Acad. Science (pres. 1910-11); mem. Psi Upsilon, Omicron Delta Kappa, Phi Beta Kappa, Sigma Xi. Democrat. Methodist. Author of numerous geol. articles. Home: 124 Oak Hill Av., Delaware, O. Died March 30, 1948.

WESTHAFER, William Rader (wĕst'hā-fēr), coll. dean; b. Uhrichsville, O., July 8, 1879; s. Henry Washington and Elizabeth (Houk) W.; A.B., Ohio Wesleyan U., 1903, A.M., 1907, LL.D., 1934; A.M., Harvard, 1909; grad. study, U. of Chicago; m. Bessie Parrett, 1908; children—Robert Lewis, William James. Instr. in physics, Amherst Coll., 1909-12, asso. prof. physics, 1912-18; prof. and head dept. of physics, Coll. of Wooster (O.), 1918, dean of Coll.,

June 1929-June 1944 (resigned). Mem. Am. Physical Soc., Sigma Pi Sigma, Phi Beta Kappa. Republican. Presbyterian. Clubs: Rotary, Century. Author: Nine Thirty (talks to students), 1928. Contbr. popular articles on scientific and religious subjects. Home: 1149 Beall Av., Wooster, O. Died June 9, 1945.

WESTON, Charles Sidney, banker; b. Carbondale, Pa., Aug. 25, 1860; s. Edward W. and Susan Seeley (Moore) W.; student Granville Mil. Acad., 1876-78; C.E., Rensselaer Poly. Inst., 1882; m. Harriet Grace Storrs, Sept. 2, 1891. Engr. in employ Delaware & Hudson Co., 1882-85; asst. gen. real estate agt. and gen. real estate agt., same, 1885-1904; pres. Cherry River Paper Co., 1909-21; v.p. First Nat. Bank, Scranton, Pa., 1912-13, pres., 1913-36, chmn. bd., June 30, 1936-41; member board managers and member executive com. D.&H. Co., D.&H. R.R. Corp.; dir. Scranton-Lackawanna Trust Co., dir. First Nat. Bank, Scranton, Hudson Coal Co., Internat. Correspondence Schools, Internat. Ednl. Pub. Co., Internat. Textbook Co., Scranton Correspondence Schools, Everglades Cypress Co., Scranton Lace Co., Elk Lick Coal Co., Cherry River Broom and Lumber Co. Mem. Delta Phi Republican. Presbyterian. Clubs: Scranton, Country (Scranton); Waverly Country (Pennsylvania); Union League, New York Yacht, Bankers, Railroad (New York); Seigniory, Gatineau Rod and Gun (Quebec); Fox Hill Country (Pittston, Pa.); Oakmont Shooting (N.C.). Donor to City of Scranton of Weston Recreation Field and Community House. Home: 624 Monroe Av. Office: First Nat. Bank Bldg., Scranton, Pa. Died Oct. 14, 1947.

WESTON, Robert Spurr, cons. engr.; b. Concord, N.H., Aug. 1, 1869; s. Lon and Martha Burtch (Greenman) W.; B.Sc., Amherst Coll., 1891; A.M., 1894; student Mass. Inst. Tech., 1894-96. U. of Berlin (winter) 1896-97; m. Josephine Fitz-Randolph, Dec. 21, 1909; children—Elizabeth (died 1932), Joseph Fitz-Randolph. Asst. chemist, Louisville Water Co., 1895, 1896-98, Superior Water, Light & Power Co., 1898-99; with George W. Fuller, civil engr., New York, 1899; in private practice, 1899-1912; mem. Weston & Sampson since 1912; served states, cities, towns and corps. in connection with water supply, water purification, stream pollution, sewerage, sewage and industrial waste treatment; asst. prof. public health engring., Mass. Inst. Tech., 1913-16. Cons. engr. U.S. Shipping Bd., U.S. Housing Corp. and U.S. Army Engring. Corps. Mem. Am. Inst. Cons. Engrs. (former v.p.), Am. Soc. Civil Engrs., Am. Inst. Chem. Engrs., Am. Acad. Arts and Sciences, Boston Soc. Civil Engrs. (ex-pres.), Am. Water Works Assn. (hon. life mem.), New England Water Works (ex-pres. and hon. mem.), Am. Pub. Works Assn., Am. Chem. Soc., Am. Pub. Health Assn., Howard Benevolent Soc. (v.p.). Independent Republican. Congregationalist. Clubs: Boston City, Rotary (ex-pres.). Expert witness in important cases such as Chicago Drainage Canal, N.Y. vs. N.J., Delaware River Case, and Conn. vs. Mass. Author of tech. papers; joint author "Water Works Handbook." Home: 501 Boylston St., Brookline, Mass. Office: 14 Beacon St., Boston, Mass. Died July 29, 1943.

WETJEN, Albert Richard (wĕt'jĕn), author; b. London, Eng., Aug. 20, 1900; s. Daniel Dietrich and Lillian (Llyddon) W.; ed. Council School, London, 1904-13; m. Edith Cecelia Eisenbrandt, Apr. 12, 1923 (divorced 1942). Left school at 13; went to sea, 1914; twice shipwrecked; member of crew that took sultan of Zanzibar as prisoner of war to St. Helena; served in Manchester Regiment, British Army, 1918; sailed to Africa, 1919; emigrated to Canada, 1920; tramped into United States, 1921; correspondent for Oregon newspapers, 1922, then verse and stort story writer; traveled in Europe, 1924-25; editor Oregon Magazine, 1925-28; deckhand on freighter around S. America, 1928; worked in motion picture studios, 1930. Traveled Australia, New Zealand and South Seas, 1936. Mem. Authors' League America, Am. Legion, British Society of Authors and Composers. Socialist. Agnostic. Author: Captains All, 1924; Way for a Sailor!, 1928; Youth Walks on the Highway, 1930; Fiddlers' Green, 1931; Beyond Justice, 1936; Shark Gotch of the Islands, 1936; Chronicles of Shark Gotch, 1937 (English publication); Shark Gotch Shoots It Out, 1938; In the Wake of the Shark, 1939. Winner O. Henry Memorial award, 1926; holder British War Medal, Mercantile Marine War Medal. Naturalized Am. citizen since 1932. Mem. United Seamen's Service. Contbr. to nationally known mags. in U.S., Gt. Britain and Australia. Co-founder and editor The Outlander, a quarterly lit. rev., 1933. Address: care Brandt & Brandt, 101 Park Av., New York, N.Y. Died March 8, 1948.

WETMORE, Edward Ditmars, corp. official; b. Warren, Pa., Jan. 4, 1861; s. Lansing Ditmars and Maria Cynthia (Shattuck) W.; B.S., Lafayette Coll., 1882; LL.D., Columbia, 1884; m. Helen Davenport, July 9, 1888 (died 1906); children—Beatrice Davenport (Mrs. D. Bryant Turner, dec.), Rachel Weathrbee (dec.), Alice Cynthia (Mrs. Maurice R. Brann); m. 2d, Ella Leech, Oct. 1, 1907. Admitted to Pa. bar, 1885; mgr. Wetmore Lumber Co., 1885-1909; pres. Warren Trust Co., 1912-24; chmn. bd. Warren Bank & Trust Co., 1934-37; pres. Kinzua Lumber Co. since 1909, Kinzua Pine Mills Co. since 1927, Condon, Kinzua & Southern R.R. Co. since 1928, Wallowa Timber Co. since 1907; dir. and chairman executive committee Struthers Wells Corp., since 1938; v.p. Pa. Gas Co.; chmn. bd. of trustees Struthers Library Bldg.; mem. bd. Warren Gen. Hosp., Warren Library Assn. Clubs: Conewango and Conewango Valley Country (Warren, Pa.); Santa Barbara and Montecito Country (Santa Barbara, Calif.). Home: The Pines, Wetmore Farm, Warren. Office: 209 2d Av., Warren, Pa.* Died Jan. 20, 1946.

WETTEN, Emil C., lawyer; b. Chicago; ed. Lake Forest Univ.; LL.B., Univ. of Mich., 1895; m. Louise Walton, Jan. 19, 1910; 1 son, Walton. Admitted to bar, 1893; mem. of Wetten, Pegler & Dale; served as 1st asst. corp. counsel of Chicago. Mem. Am., Ill. State and Chicago bar assns., Delta Chi. Republican. Mason (32°, Shriner). Clubs: Hamilton (ex-pres.), Barrington Hills Country. Home: 200 E. Chestnut St. Office: 134 N. La Salle St., Chicago. Died March 11, 1947.

WETZEL, John Wesley, educator; b. Lena, Ill., Mar. 21, 1871; s. George and Eunice (Fowler) W.; ed. Simpson Coll., Indianola, Ia., 1887-90; Ph.B., Southwestern U., Winfield, Kan., 1894; grad. Cumnock Sch. Oratory, Northwestern U., 1897; m. Rena Belle Reed, Aug. 3, 1898. Dir. dept. of oratory, U. of Denver; and instr. Iliff Sch. of Theology, 1897-1900; instr. elocution, Yale Law Sch., since 1901; also instr. elocution and pulpit delivery, Hartford Theol. Sem., since 1905; asso. pastor, Asylum Hill Congl. Ch., Hartford, since 1918. Gives lectures and lecture recitals at chautauquas and under auspices ednl. and religious assns. Republican. Conglist. Home: 344 Farmington Av., Hartford, Conn. Died Oct. 28, 1945.

WEYERHAEUSER, Frederick Edward (wîr'hou-zẽr), lumberman; b. Rock Island, Ill., Nov. 4, 1872; s. Frederick and Elizabeth Sarah (Bloedel) W.; grad. Phillips Acad., Andover, 1892; A.B., Yale, 1896; m. Harriette Louise Davis, 1902; children—Virginia (dec.), Frederick, Charles Davis. In lumber business since beginning of active career. Pres. Weyerhaeuser Timber Co., Tacoma, Wash.; dir. Great Northern Ry. Co., First Nat. Bank of St. Paul. Mem. Delta Kappa Epsilon, Skull and Bones. Presbyterian. Home: 4?0 Grand Av. Office: First Nat. Bank Bldg., St. Paul, Minn. Died Oct. 18, 1945.

WEYERHAEUSER, Rudolph Michael, lumberman; b. Coal Valley, Ill., Mar. 11, 1868; s. Frederick and Elizabeth Sarah (Bloedel) W.; Ph.B., Yale, 1891; m. Louise Lindeke, Oct. 29, 1896; 1 dau., Margaret Louise. Began in lumber business at Rock Island, Ill., 1891; now pres. Northern Lumber Co., Edward Rutledge Timber Co., First Nat. Bank (Cloquet, Minn.), Potlatch Forests, Inc., Lewiston, Ida.; v.p. Wash., Idaho & Mont. Ry. Co.; dir. First Nat. Bank (St. Paul), N.P. Ry. Co. Republican. Presbyterian. Mason. Clubs: Minnesota, Somerset Country (St. Paul). Home: Cloquet, Minn.
Died July 12, 1946.

WEYMOUTH, Clarence Raymond (wā'mŭth), mechanical engr.; b. Oakland, Calif., Nov. 14, 1876; s. Tobias Delmont and Laura Nevada (Wells) W.; B.S., U. of Calif., 1898; unmarried. Asst. to prof. of mech. engring., U. of Calif., 1898-99; with Charles C. Moore & Co. Engrs., San Francisco, 1898-1925, serving as chief engr. and dir. (resigned). Chmn. com. on engring. and inventions, Calif. State Council of Defense, during latter part of World War I. Inventor of Moore automatic fuel oil system for controlling oil-fired boilers; designer of many steam-electric power plants in Inter-mountain and Pacific Coast states. Mem. Tau Beta Pi (hon. mem.), Sigma Psi; mem. Internat. Engring. Congress, 1915 (com. of management). Club: University. Contbr. papers on plant design, etc., to Trans. Am. Soc. Mech. Engrs. Home: Hotel Fairmont, San Francisco 6. Died Feb. 12, 1949.

WHALEY, George P., oil producer; b. Chesterfield, Ill., Sept. 25, 1870; s. George W. and Elizabeth (Adderly) W.; ed. high sch., Emporia, Kan.; unmarried. Began with Standard Oil Co., Pittsburgh, Pa., 1889; mem. lubricating sales com., Standard Oil Co. of N.J., 1895-1907; dir. Vacuum Oil Co., 1903-07, v.p., 1907-24, pres., 1924-30; retired from active business. Republican. Episcopalian. Clubs: Metropolitan, Recess, Lawyers, Church; Essex County (N. J.) Country; Short Hills (N.J.) Country; Rolling Rock Country (Ligonier, Pa.). Home: Short Hills, N.J. Died July 9, 1949.

WHAREY, James Blanton, prof. English; b. Cumberland County, Va., Mar. 4, 1872; s. James Morton and Mary Walker (Blanton) W.; A.B., Davidson (N.C.) Coll., 1892, M.A., 1895; grad. study, Johns Hopkins, 1896-99, Ph.D., 1904; grad. study, U. of Berlin, 1910-11; LL.D., Davidson College, North Carolina, 1934; m. Elizabeth Chapman, Mar. 14, 1906. Teacher, Cape Fear Acad., Wilmington, N.C., 1892-93; tutor, Davidson Coll., 1893-96; prof. English, Southwestern Presbyn. U., Clarksville, Tenn., 1899-1906, Peabody Coll. for Teachers, 1906-10; instr. in English, U. of Tex., 1912-13, adj. prof., 1914-18, asso. prof., 1919-23, prof. since 1924. Trustee Schreiner Inst., Kerrville, Tex. Mem. Modern Lang. Assn. America, Folk-Lore Soc. Tex., Phi Beta Kappa, Sigma Alpha Epsilon. Democrat. Presbyterian. Author: A Study of Bunyan's Allegories, 1904. Editor: Bunyan's Pilgrim's Progress, 1928. Contbr. articles to lang. publs. Home: 3006 Washington Sq., Austin, Tex. Died July 24, 1946.

WHARTON, James E., army officer; b. Elk, New Mexico, Dec. 2, 1894; commd. 2d lt. Inf., Officers Res. Corps, Aug. 1917, 2d lt. Regular Army, 1917, and advanced through the grades to brig. gen., Mar. 1942; on Civilian Corps Duty, Richmond, Mo., July 1933; at Fort Francis E. Warren, Wyoming, 1938; with Officers Branch Personnel Div., G-1, War Dept. Gen. Staff, Washington, D.C., June 1940; became chief of sect. Officers Branch, Sept. 1941; now attached to Hdqrs. Services of Supply, Washington, D.C.†* Died Aug. 12, 1944.

WHARTON, Lang, banker; b. Marlin, Tex., Oct. 14, 1880; s. John Newton and Annie (Lang) W.; student U. of Tex., 1902-03; m. Rebekah Phillips, Mar. 3, 1908; children—George Phillips, Rebekah (Mrs. Harry L. Robinson, Jr.). Began as clerk with Am. Nat. Bank, Dallas, Tex., then with City Nat. Bank, Dallas, until 1930; exec. v.p. First Nat. Bank, Dallas, since 1930; dir. C.,B.&Q. R.R. Co., C.,R.I.&P. Ry., Tex. Pacific Coal & Oil Co., Pioneer Air Lines, Inc. Mem. adv. com., chmn. exec. com. Dist. Agency Reconstruction Finance Corp., Washington. Mem. Phi Delta Theta. Presbyterian. Clubs: Petroleum, City, Brook Hollow Golf (Dallas); Southern Soc. (New York). Home: 4209 Lakeside Drive. Address: First National Bank, Dallas, Dallas, Tex. Died Jan. 9, 1949.

WHARTON, Theodore Finley, mfg. exec.; b. Noble County, Ohio, Apr. 16, 1870; s. Nathan B. and Amelia Ann (Johns) W.; student public schs., St. Cloud, Minn.; m. May Thompson, Sept. 9, 1896; children—Wayne Thompson, Russell Finley. Printer and bookkeeper St. Cloud (Minn.) Times, 1888-91; asso. with father-in-law office, Ashland, Wis., 1891-96; city clerk, Ashland, 1896-1902; accountant Haskins & Sells, St. Louis, Mo., 1902-11; partner and manager St. Louis office, 1906-11; comptroller Deere & Co., mfrs. agrl. equipment, 1911-42, treas. since 1942, sec. since 1912 and dir. since 1918; dir. Moline Nat. Bank. Mem. Moline Assn. Commerce, Farm Equipment Inst., Controllers Institute, Maroon and White Assn. (pres.); mem. Mo. State Board Accountancy, 1909-11. Republican. Conglist. Elk. Clubs: Rotary, After Dinner (Moline). Home: 2327 12th St. Office: 1325 3d Av., Moline, Ill.
Died Oct. 13, 1943.

WHEAT, Alfred Adams, judge; b. Nashua, N.H., June 13, 1867; s. George E. and Addie (Adams) W.; A.B., Dartmouth, 1889, LL.D., 1929; LL.B., Columbian (now George Washington U.), 1891; m. Gertrude Luther, Feb. 17, 1912. Admitted to D.C. bar, 1891, N.Y. bar, 1893; practiced at N.Y. City; apptd. spl. asst. to atty. gen. of U.S., 1922, and assigned to argument of govt. cases before Supreme Court of U.S.; represented U.S. in more than 100 cases; asso. justice Supreme Court of D.C., by apptmt. Pres. Hoover, 1929-30, chief justice since 1930, acting solicitor gen., Mar.-June 1929. Member Am. and N.Y. State bar assns., Assn. Bar City of New York, New York County Lawyers Assn., Phi Beta Kappa, Alpha Delta Phi, Casque and Gauntlet. Republican. Episcopalian. Clubs: Union League, Lawyers, Alpha Delta Phi, Dartmouth College (New York); Eastern Yacht (Marblehead, Mass.). Home: Mayflower Hotel. Address: District Court, Washington, D.C.
Died Mar. 11, 1943.

WHEAT, William Howard, congressman; b. Kahoka, Mo., Feb. 19, 1879; s. Thomas James (D.D.) and Sarah (Martin) W.; ed. Chaddock Coll. and Gem. City Business Coll., Quincy, Ill.; m. Mabel Williams, Sept. 17, 1902; 1 son, James Howard. Cashier Bank of Thomasboro (Ill.), 1900-06; cashier and v.p. First Nat. Bank of Thomasboro, 1906-20; pres. First Nat. Bank of Rantoul since 1909. Mem. 76th and 77th Congresses (1939-43), 19th Ill. Dist. Republican. Methodist. Mason (Shriner), Elk. Club: Champaign (Ill.) County Country. Home: Rantoul, Ill.
Died Jan. 16, 1944.

WHEELER, Candace Thurber, author, artist; born Delhi, N.Y.; d. Abner G. and Lucy (Dunham) Thurber; ed. Delaware Acad.; m. Thomas M. Wheeler, 1846. Founder of systems and first soc. of Decorative Arts; founder of Associated Artists; dir. Woman's Bldg., Chicago Expn., 1893; chmn. Woman's Art Com. Expn. Congress, 1893; mem. advisory com. Cooper Inst. Author: Double Darling and Other Fairy Tales, 1893; Household Art, 1894; Content in a Garden, 1900; Decorators and Decorating, 1900; Domestic Weavings, 1900. Contbr. on art and stories to mags. Address: 115 E. 23d St., New York. Died Aug. 5, 1923.

WHEELER, Charles Brewster, army officer; born Matteson, Ill., May 3, 1865; s. Christopher and Mary J. (Safford) W.; grad. U.S. Mil. Acad., 1887; m. Zella Lentilhon, Apr. 3, 1893. Commd. 2d lt. 5th Arty., June 12, 1887; 1st lt. ordnance, Dec. 15, 1890; capt. July 7, 1898; maj. June 25, 1906; lt. col., June 13, 1909; col., Nov. 3, 1914; brig. gen., Oct. 6, 1917. Duty in Office Chief of Ordnance, Washington, 1896-1906; chief ordnance officer, Philippine Div., also comdr. Manila Ordnance Depot, 1906-07; comd. Watertown (Mass.) Arsenal, 1908-17; assigned duty Office Chief of Ordnance, Mar. 4, 1917; apptd. acting chief of ordnance, Dec. 19, 1917; chief ordnance officer A.E.F., Apr. 1918; retired from army, Sept. 3, 1919, to go into business; now v.p. Eaton, Crane & Pike Co., Pittsfield, Mass. Comdr. Legion of Honor (France); Companion Order of the Bath (Eng.). Episcopalian. Clubs: Army and Navy, Metropolitan (Washington); St. Botolph (Boston); University (N.Y. City). Home: Pittsfield, Mass. Died Wayland, Mass., Apr. 11, 1946.

WHEELER, George Bourne, banker; b. Kennebunkport, Me., Aug. 1, 1853; s. John A. and Louise Moselle (Bourne) W.; grad. Me. Wesleyan Sem.,

Kents Hill, Me., 1871; A.B., Bowdoin, 1874; m. Laura Crawford, May 25, 1880; children—Helen Louise, Crawford. Editor Franklin (N.H.) Jour., 1876-80, Bloomington (Ill.) Leader, 1880-87; pub. San Diego (Calif.) Daily Bee, 1887-90; gen. mgr. Chippewa Valley (Wis.) Ry., Light & Power Co., 1891-1914; pres. Union Nat. Bank, Eau Claire, Wis., 1914-34, chmn. bd. dirs. since 1934; pres. Eau Claire Hotel Co.; dir. Wis. Bankshares Corp., Milwaukee. Pres. Eau Claire County Council of Defense during World War. Director Greater Wis. Assn., Masonic Temple Assn. Republican. Mason (33°); Past Grand Master of Masons of Wis.; Past Grand Comdr. K.T. of Wis.; Comdr. in Chief Eau Claire Consistory; active member Supreme Council, A.A.S.R. Clubs: Eau Claire, Kiwanis. Home: 704 Graham Av., Eau Claire, Wis. Died Jan. 22, 1943.

WHEELER, Homer Jay, agrl. chemist; b. Bolton, Mass., Sept. 2, 1861; s. Jesse Brown and Martha Ann (Sykes) W.; B.S., Mass. Agrl. Coll., also from Boston, Univ., 1883; A.M., Ph.D., U. of Göttingen, 1889; Sc.D., Brown Univ., 1911; D.Sc., Mass. State Coll., 1933; m. at Brooklyn, Frieda H. F. Ruprecht, May 15, 1891; children—Carl Otto Jordan, William Edwin, Roland Arthur. Asst. chemist, Mass. Agrl. Expt. Sta., 1883-87; chief chemist, R.I. Agrl. Expt. Sta., 1889-1905; dir. and agronomist, agrl. expt. sta., Sept. 1, 1901-12, acting pres., 1902-03, prof. geology, 1893-1912, and agrl. chemistry, 1903-07, R.I. State Coll.; resigned as dir. agrl. expt. sta., 1912; chief agronomist The Am. Agrl. Chem. Co., until Dec. 1931. Ex-pres. Assn. Official Agrl. Chemists U.S.; mem. Am. Chem. Soc., A.A.A.S., Am. Geog. Soc., Am. Soc. Agronomy (ex-pres.). Author: Manures and Fertilizers; Citrus Culture in Florida; Citrus Culture in California; also numerous bulletins, and reports of R.I. Agrl. Expt. Station, and miscellaneous publns. Chairman, during World War I, of sub-com. on soils and fertilizers of Nat. Research Council. Home: 386 N. Fullerton Av., Upper Montclair, N.J. Died Nov. 18, 1945.

WHEELER, Janet, portrait painter; b. Detroit, Mich.; d. Orlando B. and Amanda M. (Bennett) Wheeler; pupil Pa. Acad. Fine Arts; Julian Acad. and Courtois, Paris, France. Has exhibited at Salon, Paris, and in all principal Am. exhbns. Awarded 1st Toppan prize, and Mary Smith prize, both Pa. Acad. Fine Arts; gold medal, Art Club, Phila.; silver medal, St. Louis Expn., 1904. Mem. bd. dirs. Fellowship of Pa. Acad. Fine Arts; mem. Fedn. of Arts (Washington), Art Alliance (Phila.), Soc. of the History of Art (Paris). Clubs: Cosmopolitan (bd. govs.), Plastic of Phila. (v.p.); Lyceum, Am. Woman's (London), Home: The Barclay, E. Rittenhouse Sq., Philadelphia, Pa. Died Oct. 25, 1945.

WHEELER, John Brooks, surgeon; b. Stowe, Vt., Aug. 13, 1853; s. John Brooks and Eliza Jane (Hunt) W.; A.B., U. of Vermont, 1875, D.Sc., 1921; M.D., Harvard, 1879; m. Anna Griffin Sanford, Aug. 27, 1884; children—Mrs. Mary Sanford Stokes, Constance. Began practice at Burlington, Vt., 1881; instr. in surgery, Coll. of Medicine, U. of Vermont, 1881-90, prof. clin. and minor surgery, same, 1890-1900, prof. surgery, 1900-24, emeritus prof. surgery since 1924; attending surgeon Mary Fletcher Hosp., 1883-1924; now cons. surgeon; cons. surgeon to Bishop De Goesbriand Hosp.; cons. surgeon Fanny Allen Hosp. since 1895. Fellow Am. Coll. Surgeons; mem. New Eng. Surg. Soc., A.M.A., Am. Coll. Surgeons, Burlington and Chittenden County Clin. Soc. Club: Ethan Allen. Author: Memoirs of a Small-Town Surgeon. Home: 210 Pearl St., Burlington, Vt. Died May 1, 1942.

WHEELER, John Egbert, lumber mfr., pub.; b. Portville, N.Y., May 19, 1879; s. William Egbert and Allie (Mersereau) W.; student Phillips Acad., Andover, Mass., 3 yrs.; A.B., Yale, 1900; m. Margaret Culbertson, June 5, 1907; children—William Egbert, Mary Elizabeth, John Pogue, Margaret Knox. In lumber business at San Francisco since 1905; pres. Wheeler Timber Co. and Wheeler Pine Co., also officer in many lumber companies. Chmn. Pacific Coast advisory bd. of Associated Press, 1926. Republican. Presbyn. Clubs: University, Commonwealth (San Francisco); University, Press (Portland, Ore.). Home: 362 Georgetown Av., San Mateo, Calif. Office: Russ Bldg., San Francisco, Calif.* Died Sep. 6, 1943.

WHEELER, Ruth, physiol. chemist; b. Plains, Pa., Aug. 5, 1877; d. Jared Ward and Martha Jane (Evans) Wheeler; A.B., Vassar, 1899; Ph.D., Yale, 1913. Served as teacher science and German, high sch., Pa., and N.Y.; teacher chemistry, Pratt Inst., Brooklyn, 1905-11; instr. dietetics and nutrition, U. of Ill., 1912-13, asst. prof., 1913-15, asso. prof., 1915-16; dir. home economics dept., Goucher Coll., 1918-21; prof. and head dept. of nutrition, Coll. of Medicine, and chief dietitian, Univ. Hosps., State U. of Ia., 1921-26; professor nutrition and physiology, Vassar Coll., 1926-44; retired July 1944; prof. emeritus physiology, Vassar Coll., since 1944; also chmn. div. of euthenics and dir. summer Institute of Euthenics (Vassar), 1929-42; consultant in nutrition, department of medicine, Presbyterian Hospital (Columbia University, 1926-30. Chairman of Advisory committee on nutrition, American Red Cross, 1917-32; formerly member editorial bd. Jour. Home Economics, Am. Dietetic Assn. Fellow Am. Assn for the Advancement of Science; mem. Am. Dietetics Assn. (pres. 1924-26), Am. Soc. Biol. Chemists, Sigma Xi. Episcopalian. Author: (with Helen Wheeler) Talks to Nurses on Dietetics and Dietotherapy, 1926; American Red Cross Textbook on Food and Nutrition, 1927. Contbr. articles on nutrition and nutrition education. Address: Vassar College, Poughkeepsie, N.Y. Died Sept. 29, 1948.

WHEELOCK, Lucy, teacher, lecturer; b. Cambridge, Vt., Feb. 1, 1859; d. Edwin and Laura (Pierce) W.; Reading (Mass.) High Sch., Chauncy Hall Sch., Boston; grad. Mrs. Hatch's Training Sch., 1879; unmarried. Kindergartner in Chauncy Hall Sch., 1879-89; founder and head of Wheelock Kindergarten Training Sch., 1889. Pres. Internat. Kindergarten Union, 1895-99, chmn. Com. of 19, 1905-09, and chmn. com. on coöperation with N.E.A., 1914-19; chmn. Com. for Froebel Pilgrimage, 1911; 2d v.p. dept. superintendence N.E.A., 1916. Dir. House of Good Will, Roxbury Neighborhood House. Mem. Woman's Ednl. Industrial Union, Civic League, Mass. br. of Administrative Women, Mass. Child Welfare Com., Dept. of Superintendence N.E.A., Mass. State Kindergarten Assn.; mem. ednl. com. League of Nations, 1929. Conglist. Club: Woman's Republican. Author: Talks to Mothers, 1923. Editor: Pioneers of Kindergarten in America, 1923. Home: 100 Riverway, Boston. Died Oct. 2, 1946.

WHEELOCK, William Hawxhurst, realtor; b. New York, N.Y., Jan. 5, 1876; s. George G. and Alice (Townsend) W.; grad. Cutler Sch., New York; A.B., Harvard, 1898; m. Catharine Morgan Dix, Jan. 17, 1905; children—Alice (Mrs. Theodore E. Rath, Jr.), Morgan Dix. Began with Douglas Robinson & Co., New York, 1898, name changed to Brown, Wheelock, Harris, Stevens, Inc., of which is chmn. bd.; Am. dir. Liverpool & London & Globe Ins. Co., Star Ins. Co., Prudential Ins. Co. of Great Britain; dir. Globe Indemnity Co., Federal Union Ins. Co., Estate of Bradish Johnson, Henry William Corp., 720 Park Avenue Corp.; trustee of the Title Guarantee & Trust Co., Greenwich Savings Bank, Home Life Ins. Co. In charge Purchase, Storage and Traffic Div. of Gen. Staff, U.S. Army, Washington, D.C., World War. Trustee Children's Aid Soc., Northern Westchester Hosp. Republican. Presbyterian. Clubs: Union, Harvard, Down Town; Canadian Salmon. Home: 720 Park Av. Office: 67 Wall St., New York, N.Y. Died Feb. 16, 1942.

WHELAN, Charles A., merchant; b. Syracuse, N.Y., Mar. 28, 1863; s. Martin and Elizabeth (Keefe) W.; ed. pub. schs.; m. Sarah Louise Duplessis, June 4, 1890 (now dec.); children—Mrs. Clara Gray, Edward David, Eugene Francis, Albert Joseph, Mrs. Anne Kahn (dec.). Associate of Herbert S. Collins and George J. Whelan in wholesale cigar business, Syracuse, 1890; with latter, organized, 1901, the United Cigar Stores Co. of America, of which was pres. and chmn. bd.; chmn. bd. United Profit Sharing Co. Republican. Catholic. Died Dec. 9, 1941.

WHELAN, Ralph, lawyer; b. LeRoy, N.Y., Nov. 8, 1852; s. William B. and Lucy (Anderson) W.; B.A., U. of Rochester, 1874; LL.B., Albany Law Sch., 1877; unmarried. Admitted to N.Y. bar, 1877, Ill. bar, 1878, Minn. bar, 1886; in practice at Albany, N.Y., 1877-78, Rockford, Ill., 1878-83, Minneapolis, Minn., since 1886; mem. of firm of Koon, Whelan, Hempstead & Davis, and its predecessors, Minneapolis, since 1886. Mem. Am., N.Y. City, Minn. bar assns. Republican. Episcopalian. Clubs: Iroquois (Chicago); Minneapolis, Minikahda (Minneapolis); Lafayette (Minnetonka Beach, Minn.). Home: Hotel Plaza. Office: 539-545 Plymouth Bldg., Minneapolis, Minn. Died Dec. 26, 1942.

WHERRETT, Harry Scott (hwĕr'ĕt), plate glass mfr.; b. Connersville, Ind., Oct. 24, 1876; s. William Henry and Belle Jane (Scott) W.; grad. high sch., Kokomo, Ind., 1891; m. Mary Amy Sprague, Sept. 2, 1907. Began as jr. clk., Diamond Plate Glass Co., Kokomo, 1891; clk., sales dept. Pittsburgh Plate Glass Co., 1896-1901, asst. sales mgr., 1901-05, sales mgr., 1905-17, chmn. commercial dept., 1916-20, v.p., 1920-28, pres. 1928-41, vice chmn. bd., 1941-43, chmn. since Jan. 1, 1944; pres. Pittsburgh-Corning Corp.; chmn. bd. Thresher Varnish Co. (Dayton, O.); also officer or dir. many other cos. Mem. Optical Glass Com., World War I. Republican. Protestant. Clubs: Duquesne, Pittsburgh Athletic, Longue Vue Country (Pittsburgh); Rolling Rock (Ligonier, Pa.). Home: Park Mansions, Frew Av. Office: Grant Bldg., Pittsburgh, Pa. Died Aug. 13, 1944.

WHERRY, Arthur Cornelius (hwĕr'ĭ), dental surgeon; b. Edgerton, Kan., Aug. 27, 1880; s. Eli J. and Frances Ann (Weaver) W.; student Kansas City Dental Coll., 1899-1901; D.D.S., Lake Forest (Ill.) U., 1902; m. Daisy Brewer Smith, June 10, 1903 (died Sept. 12, 1943); children—Franklin Arthur (dec.), Theodore Edward, Frances Eleanor. Dentistry practice, Salt Lake City, since 1902. V.p. local Boy Scouts of America; ex-mem. bd. regents U. of Utah. Fellow Am. Coll. of Dentists; mem. Am. Dental Assn. (pres.), Council on Dental Edn., Omicron Kappa Upsilon, Delta Sigma Delta. Republican. Methodist. Mason (33°, Shriner), dir. Masonic Temple Assn. Rotarian. Clubs: Alta, Salt Lake Country. Home: 1426 Arlington Drive. Office: First Nat. Bank Bldg., Salt Lake City, Utah. Died Dec. 26, 1944.

WHETZEL, Herbert Hice (hwĕt'zĕl), plant pathologist; b. Avilla, Ind., Sept. 5, 1877; s. Joseph Conrad and Gertrude (Eckles) W.; B.A., Wabash Coll., 1902, M.A., 1906; Cornell Univ., 1902-06; hon. D.Sc., U. of Puerto Rico, in 1926; hon. D.Sc., Wabash College, 1931; m. Lucy Ethel Baker, May 17, 1904; children—Lucy Gertrude, Joseph Conrad; m. 2d, Bertha A. Baker, June 10, 1914. Assistant in botany, Cornell, 1902-04, instr., 1904-05; asst. prof. botany, 1906-07, asst. prof. plant pathology, 1907-09, prof. since 1909, N.Y. College Agr. (Cornell Univ.); also head of dept. plant pathology, Cornell U., 1906-22. Chmn. war emergency bd. of Am. Plant Pathologists, 1918. Mycol. explorations in Puerto Rico, Venezuela and Bermuda. Fellow A.A.A.S.; mem. Am. Phytopathol. Soc., Bot. Soc. America, Mycol. Soc. America, British Mycol. Soc., Canadian Phytopathol. Soc., Phi Delta Theta, Phi Beta Kappa, Gamma Alpha, Sigma Xi, Phi Kappa Phi, Alpha Zeta. Democrat. Club: Rotary. Author: Laboratory Outline in Plant Pathology, 1916, 25; (with L. R. Hesler) Manual of Fruit Diseases, 1917; An Outline of the History of Phytopathology, 1918. Home: Forest Home, Ithaca, N.Y. Died Nov. 30, 1944.

WHIPPLE, Wayne, author; b. nr. Meadville, Pa., Nov. 17, 1856; s. Andrew J. and H. Jane (Carr) W.; A.B., Allegheny Coll., 1877; m. Gertrude M. Kimball, Jan. 28, 1893; 1 son, Paul Kimball. Editor Kansas City (Mo.) Mail (now Star), 1877-79; editor with D. Lothrop Co., pubs., 1882-90; advt. mgr., 1890-1905; moved to Phila., 1905. Methodist. Mem. Phi Gamma Delta, Phi Beta Kappa. Author: Story-Life of Lincoln, 1908; Lincoln, Washington, Franklin and American Flag Story-Calendars, 1909, 10, 11; Stories of the White House, Liberty Bell, and American Flag (in Patriot Series), 1910; Story-Life of Washington, 1911; Story of Young Franklin, Young Washington, Young Lincoln, 1915; Story-Life of the Son of Man (stories from many sources), 1913; Story-Life of Napoleon, 1915; Young Andrew Jackson, Young U.S. Grant, Young Robert E. Lee, 1917- 18; The Heart of Lee, 1918; Hero Tales from History. Also motion picture scenarios and newspaper syndicate stories on Lincoln and other patriotic subjects, 1916-26. Designed, in 1908, arrangement of stars in the U.S. 'Flag of the Future,'' approved and awaiting formal adoption. Projected a new departure series of moving pictures involving colors and music, 1920-24; articles for mags. and newspaper syndicates in the spiritualizing of history and science, 1925-26; (3 series) Fifty New Lincoln Stories, New Light on Lincoln; also series on Spirit of Sport. Launched drives against war and devised the moving picture "Armageddon." Address: Care Century Co., New York. Died Oct. 22, 1942.

WHITACRE, Horace J. (hwĭt'ā-kēr), surgeon; b. 1869; B.S., Ohio State U., 1891; M.D., Coll. Phys. and Surg. (Columbia), 1894; hon. D.Sc., Coll. Puget Sound, 1932. Cons. surgeon U.S. Vets. Bur., 1919-41; pres. staff Tacoma (Wash.) Gen. Hosp., 1922-23; surgeon, U.S. Vets. Hosp.; pres. Pub. Health League of Wash., 1924-26; pres. Physicians and Dentists Business Bur., 1931-39. Campaign chmn. Tacoma Community Chest, 1922, now trustee; pres. Y.M.C.A., Tacoma, 1924-27. Governor Am. Coll. Surgeons; mem. A.M.A., Am. Soc. for Control of Cancer (Wash. State chmn.), Wash. State Med. Assn. (pres. 1931-32), North Pacific Surg. Assn. (pres. 1936), Pan-Pacific Surg. Congress, Tacoma Surg. Club (pres. 1929-30), Pierce County Med. Soc. (pres. 1940), Tacoma Chamber Commerce (pres. 1932). Clubs: Rotary (pres. 1919-21), University (pres. 1921-23). Office: Medical Arts Bldg., Tacoma. Wash.* Died Mar. 10, 1944.

WHITAKER, John Thompson, journalist, war corr.; b. Chattanooga, Tenn., Jan. 25, 1906; s. Lawson Spires and Thulie (Thompson) W.; A.B., U. of the South, Sewanee, Tenn., 1927; unmarried. Began as reporter Chattanooga News; later with New York Herald Tribune, as City Hall reporter, Albany and Washington, D.C., corr., and foreign corr. at League of Nations, Geneva; war corr. Ethiopian and Spanish Wars; was corr. for Chicago Daily News in Europe, Near East and South America, now on leave of absence. Serving as colonel, Army of U.S. Decorated Legion of Merit, Croce di Guerra (Italy). Mem. Phi Beta Kappa. Author: And Fear Came, 1936; Americas to the South, 1939; We Cannot Escape History, 1943. Lecturer. Home: 412 Georgia Av., Chattanooga 3, Tenn. Died Sep. 11, 1946.

WHITAKER, Robert, clergyman; b. Lancashire, Eng., Sept. 9, 1863; s. Robert and Agnes (Waddington) W.; ed. Lawrence Acad., Groton, Mass., 1 yr.; grad. Newton Theol. Instn., 1887; m. Ellen Jennie Longley, June 11, 1887 (died Apr. 26, 1901); m. 2d, Claire Esther Wall, Mar. 5, 1907. Missionary at Aguas Calientes, Mex., 1887-88; pastor Seattle, Wash., 1888-90, Salem, Ore., 1890-93, Oakland, Calif., 1893-98; gen. missionary and corr. sec. Gen. Bapt. Conv. of Calif., 1898-1901; pastor Palo Alto, Calif., 1901; teacher of ethics and public speaking, State U. of Nev., 1902-03; pastor Oakland, Calif., 1903-07; evangelist, and lecturer on social and ednl. lines, 1907-08; pastor Los Gatos, Calif., 1909-21, Seattle, Wash., 1922-23; ednl. work, San Diego, Calif., 1923-24; field sec. Am. Civil Liberties Union, and editor Open Forum, 1924-26; gen. ednl., literary and social publicity since 1927. Editorial writer for Pacific Baptist, 1891-99. Author: My Country and Other Verse; The Gospel at Work in Modern Life; Why Callest Thou Me Good?; One Woman's Worth; Laughter and Life, prize essay, 1915; Social Song, and Other Verse, 1936; The Call of the Human (verse), 1937; The World Community—The Way Out of World Chaos, 1940. Contbr. to many periodicals and mags., essays, stories, editorials, verse, etc. Home: 15 Lyndon Av., Los Gatos, Calif. Died June 30, 1944.

WHITCOMB, William Arthur, pres. Great Northern Paper Co.; b. Clinton, Ind., Jan. 18, 1873; s. John and Lydia Amelia (Parks) W.; Ph.B., De Pauw U., 1894; Ph.B., Sheffield Scientific Sch. (Yale), 1895;

m. Grace E. Merrall, Jan. 20, 1903; children—Merle, John Merrall, William Arthur. Mill supt. Glens Falls (N.Y.) Paper Mills Co., 1897-98; with Internat. Paper Co., N.Y. City, 1898-1910; with Great Northern Paper Co. since 1910, pres. since 1928. Republican. Club: Yale (New York). Home: Dedham, Mass. Office: 201 Devonshire St., Boston, Mass. Died June 10, 1946.

WHITE, Aaron Pancoast, coll. pres.; b. Frio Town, Tex., Dec. 13, 1882; s. Lycurgus Sobeski and Mary French (Pancoast) W.; B.A., Vanderbilt U., Nashville, Tenn., 1916, B.D., 1918; M.A., Peabody Coll. for Teachers, Nashville, 1933; m. Ada Ethel McBride, Oct. 23, 1918 (died Feb. 16, 1927); children—Mary Elizabeth, Ruth Elna; m. 2d, Kathreen Willis, July 3, 1935. Began as stenographer, 1906; teacher pub. schs., Blue River, Ore., 1910; shipping clk. in San Francisco, 1911-15; ordained ministry M.E. Ch., S., 1919; pastor Galt, Calif., 1919-21; teacher history and Bible, Morton-Elliott Jr. Coll., Elkton, Ky., 1921-22; pastor Big Clifty (Ky.) Circuit, 1922-23; dean Lindsey Wilson Jr. Coll., Columbia, 1923-32, became pres., 1932. Served as army Y.M.C.A. sec., at Camp Gordon, Ga., 1918-19, World War. Mem. Pi Gamma Mu. Awarded Shepherd prize in church history, Vanderbilt U., 1917. Democrat. Mason. Rotarian. Home: Columbia, Ky.* Died July 22, 1945.

WHITE, Alma, bishop Pillar of Fire Church; b. Lewis County, Ky., June 16, 1862; d. William Moncure and Mary-Ann (Harrison) Bridwell; Millersburg (Ky.) Female Coll., 3 yrs., A.B.; studied at U. of Denver; A.M. and D.D., Alma White College; m. Kent White, Meth. clergyman, Dec. 21, 1887; children—Arthur Kent, Ray Bridwell. Founder, 1901, and pres. Pillar of Fire Ch. (organized 1901); founder Alma White Coll., Alma Prep. School, Zarephath Bible Sem. (all Zarephath, N.J.), Belleview College and Alma Temple (Denver), Training Sch. (Los Angeles, Calif.), Eden Grove Acad. (Cincinnati, O.), Alma Bible College (London); pres. Pillar of Fire Corp. Bds. of N.J., Colo., N.Y., O; evangelist, 1893-1902; incorporated Pillar of Fire Ch., Colo., 1902, moved hdqrs. to Zarephath, N.J., 1908. Republican. Author: Looking Back from Beulah, 1902; Gems of Life (for children), 1907; Golden Sunbeams, 1909; The Chosen People, 1910; My Trip to the Orient, 1911; The New Testament Church, 1911; The Titanic Tragedy—God Speaking to the Nations, 1912; Truth Stranger than Fiction, 1913; Why I Do Not Eat Meat, 1915; Restoration of Israel, the Hope of the World, 1917; The Story of My Life and the Pillar of Fire (5 vols.), 1919-38; With God in the Yellowstone, 1920; The Ku Klux Klan in Prophecy, 1925; The Voice of Nature, 1927; Musings of the Past (verse), 1927; Hymns and Poems, 1931; Short Sermons, 1932; Radio Sermons and Lectures, 1936; Jerusalem, 1936; The Sword of the Spirit, 1937; Guardians of Liberty (3 vols.), 1943; Woman's Chains, 1943; Everlasting Life, 1944; The Bugle Call (hymnal), 1943; also more than 200 hymns. Preacher, lecturer, nature artist. Editor Pillar of Fire, Rocky Mountain Pillar of Fire, Occidental Pillar of Fire, London Pillar of Fire; The British Sentinel (London); The Dry Legion; founder radio sta. KPOF, Denver, 1927, WAWZ, Zarephath, N.J., 1931; founder Woman's Chains. Address: Zarephath, N.J.; also 1845 Champa St., Denver. Died June 26, 1946; buried Fairmont Cemetery, Denver.

WHITE, Alvan Newton, lawyer, educator; b. Fallbranch, Washington County, Tenn., May 8, 1869; s. Richard Jasper and Nancy Jane (Lady) W.; Greeneville and Tusculum Coll., Tusculum, Tenn.; A.B., Carson-Newman Coll., Jefferson City, Tenn., 1893; studied law and admitted to practice in Tenn., Okla. and N.M., and to U.S. Supreme Court, Mar. 9, 1916; m. Louise Dickinson, Oct. 24, 1899; children—Justine (dec.), Athington, Arneille. Removed to N.M., 1896; city atty., Silver City, N.M., 1897-98; county supt. schs., Grant County, N.M., 3 terms, 1901-07; defeated for legislature, 1898, Territorial Senate, 1906, for mem. N.M. Constl. Conv., 1910; 1st state supt. pub. instrn., 1912-16; resumed practice, Silver City, N.M., Jan. 1917; mem. N.M. Ho. of Rep. since 1926 (Dem. floor leader 1929; elected speaker of House 1931; again elected speaker of the House, by unanimous vote 1933, 35, 37; chmn. Dem. Central Com. for Grant County, 1926-27; mem. State Bar Commn., 1931-39; asst. dist. atty., 6th N.M. Jud. Dist., 1932. Federal dir. U.S. Employment Service for N.M., 1918. Mem. Am. Bar Assn. (mem. house of dels. 1937-39), N.M. Bar Assn. (pres. 1936-37). Democrat. Baptist. Am. incorporator Soc. for Preservation of Antiquities, N.M. Mason (32°, K.T., Shriner), Elk. Author: Geography of New Mexico, 1915; also published addresses, pamphlets, etc. Home: Silver City, N.M.* Deceased.

WHITE, Austin John, newspaper editor; b. Greenville, Pa., Aug. 18, 1892; s. Patrick John and Delia (O'Loughlin) W.; ed. pub. schs. of Conneaut, Ohio; m. Sarah Margaret Murphy, June 8, 1920. Reporter Conneaut (O.) News-Herald, 1908-17; editor Erie Dispatch, 1917-22; managing editor, Erie Dispatch-Herald, 1922-40, asso. editor since 1940. Sec. Pa. State Park and Harbor Commn., 1930-47. Served as chmn. selective service appeal bd. northwestern Pa. World War II. Trustee Thiel Coll., Greenville, Pa. Mem. Erie Chamber of Commerce (past dir.), Erie Y.M.C.A. (dir.), Erie Council of Chs. (vice pres.). Republican. Lutheran. Mason Scottish rite). Home: 3108 Maple St. Office: 20 E. 12th St., Erie, Pa. Died Jan. 13, 1949.

WHITE, Charles Harrison, business executive; b. Mansfield, O., Mar. 17, 1888; s. Frank H. and Aletha Ann (Rowland) W.; student pub. schs. of Mansfield and Cleveland, O.; m. Edna Ann Mills, Nov. 4, 1911; children—Jean Kathleen (Mrs. Harry A. Swigert), Robert Arthur. Employed in time, cost and traffic depts., Brown Hoisting Machinery Co. (now Indsl. Brownhoist Corp.), Cleveland, O., 1907-17; sales, Chicago, 1917-21, sales office, New Orleans, 1921-27, dist. mgr., Chicago, 1927-46, dir. sales entire U.S., south and west of Chicago, since 1946. Mem. Nat. Ry. Appliances Assn. (sec. since 1935, pres. 1936-37). Republican. Presbyterian (ruling elder). Clubs: Union League, Western Railway (Chicago); Westmoreland Country (Wilmette). Mason. Home: 3030 Isabella St., Evanston, Ill. Office: 208 S. LaSalle St., Chicago 4, Ill. Deceased.

WHITE, Clarence H.; b. Carleton, Neb., Aug. 26, 1874; s. Elisha and Laura A. (Blood) W.; B.Sc., Neb. Wesleyan Univ., 1902; m. Amy L. Steen, Apr. 15, 1903; children—Elma Lucile, Emma Jean, Josephine (dec.), Willard Steen, Clarence H. Publishing business, Toronto and Montreal, Can., Baltimore, Md., and Detroit, Mich., until 1908; moved to Ida. and engaged in land and irrigation projects; with J. R. Ellison organized Ellison-White Lyceum Bur., 1911 (changed to non-profit sharing, 1920). Trustee Willamette Univ. Mem. (ex-pres.), Internat. Lyceum and Chautauqua Assn.; established Australian Chautauqua Assn., 1921. Chmn. bd. Portland First Federal Savings and Loan Assn; pres. Asso. Realty Co., organized and inc. Jan. 1937. Delegate Gen. Conf. M.E. Ch. 1920; ex-mem. Unification Com., M.E. Chs., North and South. Mem. Phi Kappa Tau. Home: 3632 N.E. Davis St. Office: Studio Bldg., Portland, Ore. Died Jan. 31, 1945.

WHITE, David Stuart, veterinarian; b. W. New Brighton, Staten Island, N.Y., Sept. 28, 1869; s. William Henry and Catharine Ann (Elliott) W.; gen. course Ohio State U.; Dr. Vet. Medicine, same, 1890; post-grad. study in Germany and Austria, 1890-93; m. Nellie Eliza Smith, June 24, 1896 (dec.); m. 2d, Mabel Elizabeth Moran, Dec. 21, 1925. Asst. in veterinary medicine, Ohio State U., 1893-95, head dept. of veterinary medicine and dean College Veterinary Medicine, 1895-1929 (retired). Mem. Ohio N.G., 1887-90. Mem. advisory bd. Vet. Corps of Med. Dept., U.S. Army; commd. maj., Vet. Corps N.A., 1917, lt. col. and col., 1918; chief veterinarian A.E.F., France; hon. discharged, 1919; ranking colonel, Veterinary Res., U.S. Army, since 1921. Officer Legion of Honor (France), 1918; Comdr. St. Michael and St. George (Gt. Britain), 1919. Mem. Am. and Ohio Vet. Med. assns.; hon. mem. Pa. State Vet. Med. Assn.; hon. asso. mem. Royal Coll. Vet. Surgs. (Eng.), Sigma Xi, Alpha Psi. Clubs: Faculty (O.S.U.); Torch (Columbus). Translator: Malkmus' Physical Diagnostics, 1901. Author: Principles and Practice of Veterinary Medicine, 1917. Home: 1490 Cardiff Rd., Columbus, O. Died Jan. 7, 1944.

WHITE, Eliza Orne, author; b. Keene, N.H., Aug. 2, 1856; d. Rev. William Orne and Margaret Eliot (Harding) White; pub. and private schs.; Author: Miss Brooks, 1890; Winterborough, 1892; When Molly Was Six, 1894; The Coming of Theodora, 1895; A Little Girl of Long Ago, 1896; A Browning Courtship and Other Stories, 1897; A Lover of Truth, 1898; Ednah and Her Brothers, 1900; John Forsyth's Aunts, 1901; Lesley Chilton, 1903; An Only Child, 1905; A Borrowed Sister (sequel to An Only Child), 1906; After Noontide (selections by Margaret E. White), 1907; The Wares of Edgefield, 1909; Brothers in Fur, 1910; The Enchanted Mountain, 1911; The First Step, 1914; William Orne White, a Record of Ninety Years, 1917; The Blue Aunt, 1918; The Strange Year (sequel to The Blue Aunt), 1920; Peggy in Her Blue Frock, 1921; Tony, 1924; Joan Morse, 1926; Diana's Rose Bush, 1927; Adventures of Andrew, 1928; Sally in Her Fur Coat, 1929; The Green Door, 1930; When Abigail Was Seven, 1931; The Four Young Kendalls, 1932; Where is Adelaide?, 1933; Lending Mary, 1934; Ann Frances, 1935; Nancy Alden, 1936; The Farm Beyond the Town, 1937; Helen's Gift House, 1938; Patty Makes a Visit, 1939; The House Across the Way, 1940; I, the Autobiography of a Cat, 1941; Training Sylvia, 1942; When Esther Was a Little Girl, 1944. Home: 222 High St., Brookline, Mass.* Died Jan. 23, 1947.

WHITE, Edward Albert, prof. floriculture; born West Townsend, Mass., May 23, 1872; s. Edward and Susan Hartwell (Gates) W.; B.Sc., Mass. State Coll., 1895; m. Cora Crittenden, June 30, 1903; children—Emerson Edward, Kendall Crittenden, Barbara Crittenden. In charge of greenhouses, Mass. State Coll., 1895-97; florist, Arlington, Mass., 1897-1900; asst. prof. horticulture, Tex. Agrl. and Mech. Coll., 1900-02; prof. botany and forestry, Conn. Agrl. Coll., 1902-06; prof. floriculture, Mass. State Coll., 1906-13, head of dept. of floriculture and ornamental horticulture, Cornell U., 1913-39; prof. emeritus since 1939. Fellow Royal Hort. Soc. (Eng.); Hon. mem. Am. Orchid Soc., New York Florist Club; mem. A.A.A.S., Phi Kappa Phi, Kappa Sigma, Pi Alpha Xi. Republican. Presbyterian. Author: Principles of Floriculture, 1916; Principles of Flower Arrangement, 1923; American Orchid Culture, 1927, rev., 1939; American Chrysanthemum Culture, 1930; The Florist Business, 1933. Home: 316 The Parkway, Ithaca, N.Y. Died May 13, 1943.

WHITE, George Ared, army officer; b. Longbranch, Ill., July 18, 1881; s. Ared and Mary A. (Murray) W.; student All Hallows Coll., 1896-97; m. Henrietta Diana White, Feb. 22, 1905; children—Henrietta Marion (Mrs. J. A. Routh; now dec.), Dorothy Diana (Mrs. George E. Emich, Jr.). Enlisted U.S. Field Artillery, 1898; promoted through grades to maj. gen., 1929. Awarded Etoile Noir, French Legion of Honor. Dir. Nat. Rifle Assn. of Am. Mem. of original founders of Am. Legion in France. Republican. Methodist. Mason, Shrine. Club: University (Tacoma, Wash.). Founder and first editor-mgr., Am. Legion Mag., New York, 1919. Contbr. of articles to mags. Home: Clackamas, Ore. Address: Fort Lewis, Wash.* Deceased.

WHITE, George Edward, missionary; b. Marash, Turkey, Oct. 14, 1861; s. George Hills and Joanna (Fisher) W.; came to America in 1863; A.B. ("cyclone class"), Iowa Coll., 1882 (Phi Beta Kappa), A.M., 1887, D.D., 1906; Hartford Theol. Sem., 1885-86; B.D., Chicago Theol. Sem., 1887; student Oxford Univ., England, 1907; (hon.) LL.D., Anatolia College, Saloniki, 1936; m. Esther Burrill Robbins, June 29, 1887; children—Margaret Burrill, Mary Robbins, George Deforest, Esther King, Katherine Joanna. Teacher Latin and history, Hastings Coll., Neb., 1882-84; ordained Congl. ministry, 1887; pastor Waverly, Ia., 1887-90; missionary A.B.C.F.M. at Merzifun, Turkey; mem. faculty Anatolia Coll. and Merzifun Theol. Sem., 1890-1921; dean, Anatolia Coll., 1905-13, pres., 1913-33 (college relocated at Saloniki, 1923), pres. emeritus and field rep. of the college in America. Dir. Near East Relief, at Minneapolis, 1917-19, Merzifun, Turkey, 1919-21, Minneapolis, 1921-23. Samuel Ives Curtiss' fellow comparative religion, Chicago Theol. Sem., 1909-10. Mem. bd. dirs. Konia Apostolic Inst. Contbr. articles on religious and archæol. subjects and affairs in the Near East. Author: Charles Chapin Tracy, Missionary, Philanthropist, Educator, 1918; Adventuring with Anatolia College, 1940. Home: 928 High St., Grinnell, Ia. Address: Anatolia College, Saloniki, Greece; also 14 Beacon St., Boston. Died April 28, 1946; buried, Grinnell, Ia.

WHITE, Harry Dexter, economist; Ph.D., Harvard, 1930. Asst. dir. of research U.S. Treasury, 1934; became dir. monetary research U.S. Dept. of the Treasury, 1940, spl. asst. to sec. of treasury, 1942, asst. to sec., 1943-45, asst. sec., 1945-46; U.S. exec. dir. Internat. Monetary Fund, 1946-47. Office: 1818 H St. N.W., Washington, D.C. Died Aug. 16, 1948.

WHITE, Henry Seely, educator; b. Cazenovia, N.Y., May 20, 1861; s. Prof. Aaron and Isadore M. (Haight) W.; A.B., Wesleyan Univ., Conn., 1882; Ph.D., U. of Göttingen, 1891; LL.D., Northwestern U., 1915; Sc.D. from Wesleyan University, 1932; m. Mary Willard Gleason, Oct. 28, 1890; children—Charlotte Lucy, Martha Isadore (Mrs. E. Stuart Hubbard), Mary Willard (wife of Robert F. Perez, Jr., M.D.). Tutor in mathematics, Wesleyan U., 1884-87; asst. in mathematics, Clark U., 1890-92; prof. pure mathematics, 1892-1905, Northwestern U.; prof. mathematics, Vassar College, 1905-36, prof. emeritus since 1936. President Am. Math. Soc., 1907-08 (editor Trans., 1907-13); mem. Nat. Acad. Sciences, Phi Beta Kappa, Sigma Xi, Psi Upsilon. Author: Plane Curves of the Third Order, 1925. Contbr. to math. publs. Address: Vassar College, Poughkeepsie, N.Y. Died May 20, 1943.

WHITE, Herbert Judson, clergyman; b. Leominster, Mass., Aug. 27, 1864; s. Samuel Leander and Nancy Porter (Barker) W.; student Mass. Agrl. Coll., Amherst, 1883-86; Colgate, 1887; Newton Theol. Instn., 1898-99; D.D., McMinnville (now Linnfield) Coll., 1907; m. Annie Mabel Sprague, Dec. 11, 1888 (died 1925); children—Paul Judson, Burton Sprague, Harold Gordon; m. 2d, Florence Nellie Grove, Jan. 3, 1927. Ordained Bapt. ministry, 1890; pastor Joliet, Ill., 1890-95, Bethany Ch., Boston, 1895-99, Beverly, Mass., 1899-1905, Tacoma, Wash., 1905-09, 1st Ch., Hartford, Conn., 1909-23, Central Bapt. Ch., Hartford, 1923-26, First Ch., White Plains, N.Y., 1926-29, North Frankford Ch., Phila., 1929-37, Calvary Bapt. Ch., Torrington, Conn., 1941-43. Mason (K.T.). Clubs: Kiwanis, Lions, Exchange. Home: 408 Fourth St., Ocean City, N.J. Died Sept. 6, 1945; buried, Hartford, Conn.

WHITE, Horace, lawyer; b. Buffalo, N.Y., Oct. 7, 1865; s. Horace Keep and Marion (Strong) W.; A.B., Cornell, 1887; LL.B., Columbia, 1889; m. Jane L. Denison, Mar. 14, 1903. Practiced at Syracuse since 1890; sr. mem. White, Cheney, Shinaman & O'Neill. Mem. N.Y. Senate 6 terms, 1896-1908; lt.-gov. of N.Y., 1909, becoming gov. upon resignation of Gov. Hughes, Oct. 6, 1910, and served as such until Jan. 1, 1911. Episcopalian. Mem. Kappa Alpha. Clubs: Century, University, Citizens (Syracuse); University, Republican (New York). Home: 742 James St. Office: White Memorial Bldg., Syracuse, N.Y. Died Nov. 27, 1943.

WHITE, Horace Henry, lawyer; b. Opelousas, La., Feb. 7, 1864; s. Benjamin Franklin and Sallie Malone (Wynn) W.; B.A., Vanderbilt, 1886, LL.B., 1887; LL.D., Centenary Coll. of La., 1926; m. Fannie Andrews Blythe, Dec. 27, 1887; children—Richard Franklin, Ellen Blythe (wife of P. K. Rand, M.D.), Willie Wynn, Horace Manly, Julia Blythe, Ariail Culver, Manie Hatton (Mrs. P. J. Johnson), Robert McLin, Frances Margaret. Admitted to La. bar, 1887, and began practice at Alexandria; mem. White, Holloman & White; mem. La. State Constl. Conv., 1898, 1921; pres. State Bd. of Edn., La., 1927-41. Trustee Vanderbilt U. Pres. Legal Advisory Bd. of Rapides Parish, World War. Mem. Kappa Alpha (Southern; ex-chief officer). Mason, Odd Fellow. Democrat. Mem.

Unification Commn. M.E. Ch., S. Author: White's Analytical Index, 1907, 1912; White's Notarial Guide, 1924 (4 edits.); White's Louisiana Land Laws, 1926. Home: 1806 S. Lee St. Office: Guaranty Bank Bldg., Alexandria, La.* Died Oct. 13, 1946.

WHITE, Jacob Lee, clergyman; b. Forsyth County, N.C., Sept. 6, 1862; s. Jacob and Martha Ellen (Grubbs) W.; prep. edn. Shelby (N.C.) Acad.; A.M., Wake Forest (N.C.) Coll., 1886; D.D., Mercer U., 1898, Wake Forest, 1900; hon. LL.D., John B. Stetson Univ., 1934; m. Dovie Zulia Poston, Sept. 22, 1886; children—Lee McBride, Hubert Taylor, Sarah Mabel (dec.), William Royall, James Livingston, Charles Marion, Russell Conwell, Edward Poston, Martha Elizabeth (Mrs. R. E. Kunkel). Ordained ministry Bapt. Ch., 1884; pastor successively First Ch., Raleigh, Durham, Asheville, N.C., Macon, Ga., Greensboro, N.C., Central Ch., Memphis, Tenn., Tabernacle, Atlanta, Ga., until 1916, First Ch., Miami, Fla., 1916-Apr. 1936; has received into membership of First Ch. more than 4,000; accepted pastorate of First Bapt. Ch., Madison, Fla., March 1938; retired as honorary pastor, Nov. 1940; now conducting Bible Conferences; conductor of Southern Bible Conf., Miami, since 1918. Chaplain 2d Regiment, Georgia Vols., Spanish-American War; camp pastor, Miami, World War, also chmn. Home Service Committee Am. Red Cross. Trustee Mercer U., Bessie Tift Coll., Stetson U.; v.p. Foreign Mission Bd., Southern Bapt. Conv., 20 yrs.; mem. State Bd. Missions of Fla., 1916-27; pres. Fla. Bapt. State Conv., 1924-26. Democrat. Author of many published sermons and addresses; widely known as evangelist and orator. Home: 27 N.W. 47th St., Miami, Fla. Died Nov. 25, 1948.

WHITE, James A., anti-saloon leader; b. Bloomfield, Muskingum County, O., Oct. 13, 1872; Alexander H. and Christena (Hammond) W.; B.Pd., Muskingum (O.) Coll., 1898, B.S., 1905, M.S., 1906; LL.B., Ohio Northern U., Ada, O., 1906; LL.D., Muskingum Coll., 1921, Ohio Northern U., 1921; m. Myrtle Grow, Dec. 1, 1917; children—Thomas A., Mary Virginia (Mrs. R. W. Evans), Myrtle Jean, Marjorie Ruth. Law practice at Barnesville, O., 1900; mayor of Barnesville, 4 terms, 1898-1906, also justice of the peace, and mem. Bd. of Edn.; now U.S. referee in bankruptcy, Columbus Dist. Served 4 yrs., rank of capt., World War II. Pres. White Cross Hosp. Assn., Colored Rescue Mission (both Columbus); pres. bd. trustees Muskingum Coll., New Concord, Ohio. As mayor of Barnesville led attack with axes upon "blind tigers," and started the movement that later helped to place Ohio in the dry column; supt. Ohio Anti-Saloon League since 1915; leader in 5 state-wide elections to vote Ohio dry. Prosecuted about 250 saloon cases yearly for 10 yrs. up to 1919. Apptd. mem. Industrial Commn. of O., for 6 yr. term, Dec. 26, 1939. Republican. Lay del. to Gen. Conf. M.E. Ch. 4 times. Mason (32°, K.T., Shriner), K.P. Home: 44 12th Av. Office: 44 E. Broad St., Columbus, O. Died Mar. 14, 1949.

WHITE, James Gilbert, capitalist, engr., contractor; b. Milroy, Pa., Aug. 29, 1861; s. Rev. J. W. and Mary Miller (Beaver) W.; A.B., Pa. State College, 1882, A.M., 1884; Ph.D., Cornell Univ., 1885; m. Maud Mullon, Dec. 15, 1886; 1 son, James Dugald. Instr. physics in charge of dept., U. of Neb., 1885-87; pres. Western Engring Co., 1887-90; with Edison United Mfg. Co., 1890; in business as contractor, engr. and investment banker since 1890; established J. G. White & Co., Ltd., London, 1900. Mem. Am. Inst. E.E., Am. Soc. C.E., Pa. Soc., New York Elec. Soc., The Pilgrims, S.R. Home: Greenwich, Conn. Office: 37 Wall St., New York, N.Y. Died June 2, 1942.

WHITE, James Watson, ophthalmologist; b. Dutchess County, N.Y., July 3, 1876; s. Richard Watson and Sarah Celina (Myers) W.; prep. edn. Mt. Beacon Mil. Acad., Beacon, N.Y.; M.D., Albany Med. Coll., 1905; m. Margaret G. McClellan, Sept. 22, 1909; 1 dau., Betty. Teacher, Dutchess County, N.Y., 5 years; gen. practice of medicine, New York State, 1905-13, limited to ophthalmology since 1913; asso. prof. clin. ophthalmology, N.Y. Post Grad. Med. Sch. and Hosp., 1934-38, asso. prof. ophthalmology, 1938-39, prof. and dir. of service since 1939. Mem. N.Y. Acad. of Medicine, A.M.A., N.Y. State and County med. socs., Am. Ophthal. Soc., N.Y. Ophthal. Soc., Nu Sigma Nu. Presbyterian. Mason. Clubs: Montclair Golf. Home: 27 S. Fullerton Av., Montclair, N.J. Office: 15 Park Av., New York, N.Y. Died May 15, 1946.

WHITE, John Turner, judge; b. Greene County, Mo., Apr. 22, 1854; s. William and Margaret (Fry) W.; A.B., with highest honors, Drury Coll., Springfield, Mo., 1878, A.M., 1881, LL.D., 1918; m. Mary Hackney Jones, Oct. 11, 1883; children—Warren Lee, Mrs. Edith Margaret Reed, John Turner. Admitted to Mo. bar, 1882, and began practice at Springfield; mem. Thrasher, White & McCammon, 1887, until Thrasher retired, 1895; practiced with McCammon until 1902, then alone. Reporter St. Louis Court of Appeals, 1902-07; commr. Supreme Court of Mo., 1917-23; settled in Jefferson City, 1917; asso. justice Supreme Court of Mo., 1923-33; now retired. Trustee Drury Coll., 1908-19. Democrat. Mem. Christian (Disciples) Ch. Mason. Club: Country (Jefferson City). Wrote opinion on constitutionality of zoning ordinance of St. Louis which attracted wide attention, also The Cause of the Crime Wave, pub. by Mo. State Bar Assn. Home: 909 S. Fremont Av., Springfield, Mo. Deceased.

WHITE, Newman Ivey, educator; b. Statesville, N.C., Feb. 3, 1892; s. James Houston and Harriet Moore (Ivey) W.; A.B., Trinity Coll. (now Duke U.), 1913, A.M., 1914; A.M., Harvard, 1915, Ph.D., 1918; m. Marie Anne Updike, Aug. 10, 1922. Instr. of English, Ala. Poly. Inst., 1915-16, prof., 1916-17; instr. of English, Washington U., 1918-19; prof. of English, Trinity College (now Duke University) since 1919, chairman of the department since 1943. Established and conducted Durham (North Carolina) Labor and Materials Exchange for Unemployed, 1933. Mem. board dirs. English Inst., 1939-42. Member Modern Humanities Research Assn., Modern Lang. Assn. Am., American Folklore Society, Southeastern Folklore Association (secretary 1948), North Carolina Folklore Assn. (president 1948), Phi Beta Kappa, Omicron Delta Kappa, Sigma Upsilon. Compiler and editor: An Anthology of Verse by American Negroes (with W. C. Jackson), 1924; American Negro Folk-Songs, 1928; The Best of Shelley, 1932; The Unextinguished Hearth, 1938; Shelley, 2 vols., 1940. Portrait of Shelley, 1945. Contbr. to professional mags. Home: 1003 Lamond Av., Durham, N.C. Died Dec. 6, 1948.

WHITE, Newman Ivey, educator; b. Statesville, N.C., Feb. 3, 1892; s. James Houston and Harriet Moore (Ivey) W.; A.B., Trinity Coll. (now Duke U.), 1913, A.M., 1914; A.M., Harvard, 1915, Ph.D., 1918; m. Marie Anne Updike, Aug. 10, 1922. Instr. of English, Ala. Poly. Inst., 1915-16, prof., 1916-17; instr. of English, Washington U., 1918-19; prof. of English, Trinity Coll. (now Duke U.), since 1919. Established and conducted Durham (N.C.) Labor and Materials Exchange for Unemployed, 1933. Mem. board dirs. English Inst., 1939-42. Member Modern Humanities Research Assn., Modern Lang. Assn. Am., American Folklore Society, Phi Beta Kappa, Omicron Delta Kappa, Sigma Upsilon. Compiler and editor: An Anthology of Verse by American Negroes (with W. C. Jackson), 1924; American Negro Folk-Songs, 1928; The Best of Shelley, 1932; The Unextinguished Hearth, 1938; Shelley, 2 vols., 1940. Portrait of Shelley, 1945. Contbr. to professional mags. Home: 1003 Lamond Av., Durham, N.C. Died Dec. 6, 1948.

WHITE, Ray Bridwell, clergyman, educator; b. Morrison, Colo., Aug. 24, 1892; s. Kent and (Mollie) Alma (Bridwell) W.; A.B., Columbia, 1917; A.M., Princeton, 1921; D.D., Alma White College, 1928; student U. of Denver (leave of absence from Columbia Univ.), 1915-16; m. Grace Eaton Miller, Aug. 29, 1916. Ordained ministry Pillar of Fire Ch., 1913; nat. officer of the ch. since 1918, also a teacher, an editor of publications, v.pres. Pillar of Fire of New Jersey, v.pres. and sec. Pillar of Fire Corporation, Colo.; pres. Belleview Jr. (formerly Westminster) Coll. and Bible Sem., Colo., since 1921; pres. Zarephath Bible Sem.; co-mgr. and broadcaster radio stations WAWZ and KPOF. Founder Collegiate Legion of Honor. Republican. Author: The King's Message (sermons), 1916; The Doctrines and Discipline of the Pillar of Fire Church, 1918; A Challenge from the Pulpit (sermons), 1920; The Legend of Manitousa, Hank, Poems and Sketches, 1926; By What Authority, or Why the Pillar of Fire, 1928; The Truth Concerning Infallible Popes, 1929; The Trail of the Desert Sun, 1931; The Plaster of Paris Christ, 1933; (with Arthur K. White) A Toppling Idol—Evolution, 1933; The Book of God, 1935; Pulpit and Pen (sermons, lectures, essays), 1937; Eternal Security Insecure—or The Heresy of Once in Grace Always in Grace, 1939, rev. edit., 1940; The Acts of the Bolshevists versus the Acts of the Apostles (serial), 1944; The False Christ of Communism, 1946; Social Gospel, 1946. Address: 1845 Champa St., Denver, Colo.; and Zarephath, N.J. Died Nov. 5, 1946; buried Fairmont Cemetery, Denver.

WHITE, S(ebastian) Harrison, lawyer; b. Maries County, Mo., Dec. 24, 1864; s. Jonah W. and Cloa Ann (Reeder) W.; ed. pub. and pvt. schs. and Maironville (Mo.) Collegiate Inst.; m. Eva Dunbaugh, Dec. 25, 1893. Thrown upon own resources at age of 10; elected supt. pub. schs. Hickory County, Mo., 1887; admitted to bar, 1889; removed to Pueblo, Colo., 1889; city atty., Pueblo, 1897-99; pub. trustee of Pueblo County, 1900-03; dist. atty. 10th Jud. Dist., Colo., 1904-08; justice Supreme Court of Colo., 1909-19; elected mem. 70th Congress, 1st Colo. Dist., Nov. 15, 1927, to fill unexpired term of William N. Vaile, deceased. Democrat. Mem. Am. Bar Assn. Clubs: Elks, Knights of Pythias (Pueblo); Denver Athletic. Home: 1544 Race St. Office: Equitable Bldg., Denver, Colo.* Died Dec. 21, 1945.

WHITE, Stewart Edward, author; b. Grand Rapids, Mich., Mar. 12, 1873; s. T. Stewart and Mary E. (Daniell) W.; Ph.B., U. of Mich., 1895, M.A., 1903; Columbia Law Sch., 1896-97; m. Elizabeth Grant, Apr. 28, 1904. Maj., 144th F.A., 1917-18. Fellow Royal Geographical Soc. (London); mem. Nat. Inst. of Arts and Letters, Am. Acad. of Arts and Letters, A.A.A.S. Clubs: Bohemian, Burlingame. Author: The Westerners, 1901; Claim Jumpers, 1901; The Blazed Trail, 1902; Conjuror's House, 1903; The Forest, 1903; The Magic Forest, 1903; The Silent Places, 1904; The Mountains, 1904; Blazed Trail Stories, 1904; The Pass, 1906; (with Samuel Hopkins Adams) The Mystery, 1907; Arizona Nights, 1907; Camp and Trail, 1907; The Riverman, 1908; The Rules of the Game, 1909; The Cabin, 1910; The Adventures of Bobby Orde, 1911; The Land of Footprints, 1912; African Camp Fires, 1913; Gold, 1913; The Rediscovered Country, 1915; The Gray Dawn, 1915; The Leopard Woman, 1916; Simba, 1918; The Forty Niners, 1918; The Rose Dawn, 1920; Daniel Boone, 1922; On Tiptoe, 1922; The Glory Hole, 1924; Credo, 1925; Skookum Chuck, 1925; Lions in the Path, 1926; Back of Beyond, 1927; Why Be a Mudturtle, 1928; Dog Days, 1930; The Shepper-Newfounder, 1931; The Long Rifle, 1932; Ranchero, 1933; Folded Hills, 1934; Pole Star (with H. DeVighne); The Betty Book, 1937; Old California, 1937; Across the Unknown (with Harwood White), 1939; The Unobstructed Universe, 1940; The Story of California, 1940; Wild Geese Calling, 1940; Stampede, 1942; The Road I Know, 1942; Speaking for Myself, 1943; Anchors to Windward, 1943; The Stars Are Still There, 1946. Home: Burlingame, Calif. Died Sep. 18, 1946.

WHITE, Thomas Justin, newspaper exec.; b. Dublin, Ireland, Oct. 18, 1884; s. Peter and Annie (Mayne) W.; ed. Terenuse Coll., Dublin, Ireland, Armour Inst., Chicago, Chicago Business Coll.; m. Virginia Gillette, Aug. 7, 1915; children—Anne (Mrs. Clarence J. Dauphinot, Jr.), Carmel, Thomas Justin, Peter G., John Michael. Came to U.S., 1898, naturalized, 1918. Began with L. L. Summers Co., contractors, Albuquerque, N.M., 1900; successively sec. Summers Fibre Co., Port Huron, Mich., English rep. of Yale & Towne (machinery dept.), export dept. J. P. Morgan & Co., New York; sec. and treas. Mead, Patton & Co., New York; v.p. Newspaper & Magazine Paper Corp., New York, v.p. and gen. mgr. Internat. Mag. Co., New York, exec. v.p. Am. Newspapers, Inc.; pres. and gen. mgr. the Chicago Herald-American since 1939, and gen. mgr. New York Journal-American since 1940. Now supervisory dir. of the latter two properties. Catholic. Clubs: Metropolitan, Racquet and Tennis (New York); Chicago, Mid-Day (Chicago); Smithtown Country (Smithtown, L.I.); Old Field; Pittsburgh Club. Home: Smithtown, L.I., N.Y. Office: 326 W. Madison St., Chicago, Ill. Died July 9, 1948.

WHITE, Trumbull, writer, editor; b. Winterset, Ia., Aug. 12, 1868; s. John Trumbull and Frances (McCaughan) W.; student Amherst, 1886-88; m. Katherine Short, July 15, 1890; children—Laurence Trumbull (dec.), Owen Sheppard, Kenneth Sheldon. City editor Decatur (Ill.) Review, 1889; editor and pub. Evansville (Ind.) Call, 1889-90; with Chicago Morning News, Chicago Times and Chicago Record until 1901; canoe exploration northwestern Ontario, 1891; investigated Rainy Lake and Ontario gold fields, 1894; took steerage journeys across Atlantic to study immigration questions and conditions, 1894; inquiry industrial and financial conditions, Mexico, 1896; in charge Chicago Record's news service, Cuban Insurrection, 1897, Cuban, Porto Rican campaigns, etc., 1898, Hawaii, Samoa, New Zealand and Australian colonies, 1897-98; corr. for Record and syndicate from Central Asia, Caucasus and Siberia, 1899; on 1st experimental trip of line of steamers from Chicago via the Great Lakes and the St. Lawrence River to Europe and return, 1901; industrial investigations in Alaska for Morgan-Guggenheim interests, 1909. Editor The Red Book, 1903-06, Appleton's Magazine, 1906-09, Adventure, 1910-11, Everybody's, 1911-15; v.p. Leo L. Redding & Co., New York, 1919-29; editorial counsel since 1930; exec. sec. Council for Tariff Reduction since 1931. Author: Wizard of Wall Street, 1892; World's Columbian Exposition (with William Iglehart), 1893; Reuben and Cynthia at the World's Fair, 1893; War in the East, with history of China, Japan and Korea, 1895; Silver and Gold, or Both Sides of the Shield (edited), 1895; Free Silver in Mexico (with William E. Curtis), 1896; Our War with Spain, 1898; Our New Possessions, 1899; Round the World Tours, 1900; Martinique and the World's Great Disasters, 1902; San Francisco Earthquake (with R. Linthicum), 1906. Contbr. to Saturday Evening Post, New Outlook, Cosmopolitan, Everybody's, Outing, Appleton's, Metropolitan, etc. Honorary M.A., Amherst, 1910; member Amherst Chapter Delta Upsilon; hon. mem. Grinnell Chapter Sigma Delta Chi; charter mem. Dutch Treat Club. Home: 1950 Andrews Av., New York N.Y.; (summer) Cedar Brooks Farm, Petoskey, Mich. Office: 2 W. 45th St., New York. Died Dec. 13, 1941.

WHITE, Walter Porter, physical investigator; born Roxbury, Mass., Feb. 23, 1867; s. Frederick Oscar and Ruth Porter (Stockbridge) W.; A.B., Amherst, 1887; post-grad. work, Harvard, Mass. Inst. Tech., U. of Wis.; Ph.D., Cornell U., 1904; m. Christina I. Thomson, Aug. 14, 1901. Taught school, 1887-89, 1891-1901; engaged in investigations at Geophys. Lab., Washington, 1904-35. Member Philos. Society Washington (pres. 1923), Am. Physical Soc. Author: The Modern Calorimeter, 1928; also numerous scientific papers. Address: 3210 Newark St., Washington. Died Feb. 7, 1946.

WHITE, Wilbert Webster, clergyman; b. Ashland, O., Jan. 16, 1863; s. John M. and Martha Ann (Campbell) W.; A.B., U. of Wooster, 1881, A.M., 1884; grad. Xenia Theol. Sem., 1885; Ph.D., Yale, 1891; D.D., Muskingum Coll., 1896, New York U., 1913; m. Ella Henderson, Mar. 31, 1885; children—Helen Henderson, Wilbert, Wallace (dec.), Robert Campbell (dec.), Donald Murray. Ordained United Presbyn. ministry, 1885; pastor Peotone, Ill., 1885-86; prof. Hebrew and O.T. lit., Xenia Theol. Sem., 1890-95; teacher Moody Bible Inst., Chicago, 1895-97; in Bible work in India and Eng., 1897-1900; founder The Bible Seminary in New York and pres., 1900-40; hon. pres. since 1940; founder, 1925, Columbiona-on-Lake George, Silver Bay, New York. Mem. Soc. Bibl. Lit. and Exegesis, Nat. Soc. Bibl. Instructors, Ohio Soc.

of New York, Phi Beta Kappa. Presbyterian. Author: Thirty Studies in the Gospel by John, 1895; Thirty Studies in the Revelation, 1897; Inductive Studies in the Minor Prophets, 1894; Thirty Studies in Jeremiah, 1895; Studies in Old Testament Characters, 1900; Availing Prayer, 1900; Thirty Studies in the Gospel by Matthew, 1903; The Resurrection Body, 1923; How to Study, 1930. Home: Columbiona-on-Lake George, Silver Bay, N.Y.* Died Aug. 12, 1944.

WHITE, William Allen, newspaperman; b. Emporia, Kan., Feb. 10, 1868; s. Dr. Allen and Mary (Hatton) W.; ed. U. of Kan.; Ph D., Washburn, Oberlin, Beloit and Knox Colls. and Baker, Brown, Columbia and Harvard univs.; LL D., Northwestern U.; m. Sallie Lindsay, Apr. 27, 1893; children—William L., Mary (dec.). Proprietor and editor Emporia Daily and Weekly Gazette since 1895. Sent to France as an observer by Am. Red Cross, Aug. 1917; del. to Russian Conf. at Prinkipo, 1919. Mem. Rep. Nat. Conv. and mem. com. on resolutions, 1920, 28, 36. Trustee Coll. of Emporia, Kan. State U., Rockefeller Foundation, Roosevelt Memorial Assn. and Medal Com. Founder and chmn. Com. to Defend America by Aiding the Allies, 1940. Chmn. Kansas Com. to Sell Defense Bonds. Pres. Am. Soc. Newspaper Editors, 1937-38. Mem. Pulitzer Awards Com. Awarded gold medal for citizenship Theodore Roosevelt Memorial Assn., 1933. Member Nat. Inst. Arts and Letters. Clubs: Nat. Arts, Century (New York); Cosmos (Washington); University (Chicago). Author: The Real Issue and Other Stories, 1896; The Court of Boyville, 1899; Stratagems and Spoils, 1901; In Our Town, 1906; A Certain Rich Man, 1909; The Old Order Changeth, 1910; God's Puppets, 1916; In the Heart of a Fool, 1918; The Martial Adventures of Henry and Me, 1918; Life of Woodrow Wilson, 1924; Life of Calvin Coolidge, 1925; Masks in a Pageant, 1928; A Puritan in Babylon, 1933; The Changing West, 1939. Contbr. to mags. and newspapers. Mem. editorial bd. Yale Review. Address: Emporia, Kan. Died Jan. 29, 1944. Died Jan. 29, 1944.

WHITE, William Charles, physician; b. Woodstock, Ont., Sept. 3, 1874; s. James and Dorothy Jessie (MacLeod) W.; M.B., U. of Toronto, 1898, M.D., 1902; fellow Johns Hopkins Univ., 1899-1900; post-grad. work univs. of Leipzig and Heidelberg, 1901; m. Mary Ellen Cameron, Jan. 7, 1902; children—Dorothy Cameron (Mrs. H. T. Nicolson), Mary Veitch (Mrs. William C. Goodwyn). Professor of pathology, Central College of Physicians and Surgeons (later Ind. Med. Coll. Sch. of Medicine), Purdue U., Indianapolis, 1900-05; prof. neuro-anatomy and clin. psychiatry, Ind. U., 1905-07; asso. prof. medicine, U. of Pittsburgh, 1908-16; dir. Am. Red Cross Div. for relief and prevention of tuberculosis in France, 1917-18, in Italy, 1918-19; med. dir. Tuberculosis League of Pittsburgh, and dir. R. B. Mellon Research Lab., 1907-23; research, Nat. Inst. of Health, since 1923. Mem. A.A.A.S., Assn. Am. Physicians, Am. Climatol. Assn., Am. Sanatorium Assn., N.Y. Acad. Medicine, Tuberculosis Soc. of Scotland (hon.), Nat. Assn. Prevention Tuberculosis (dir.); Acad. of Medicine (Washington, D.C.), Am. Assn. History of Medicine, Alpha Omega Alpha, Sigma Xi, Phi Rho Sigma; chmn. med. research com., National Tuberculosis Assn.; chmn. Consultants on Hospitalization under sec. of U.S. Treasury; v. chmn., 1927-28; chmn., 1928-29; div. of med. sciences, Nat. Research Council, also served as chmn. Com. on Drug Addiction; chmn. Com. on Microbiology of Soil, and as scientific dir. Com. on Research in Syphilis; chmn. div. of ednl. relations of Nat. Research Council since 1933; pres. D.C. Assn. for Prevention of Tuberculosis, 1933-36; mem. adv. council, Henry Phipps Inst., Milbank Memorial Fund until 1937; del. and chmn. Conf. and Internat. Union Against Tuberculosis, Amsterdam, 1932; chmn. advisory com. to Health Dept., Washington, D.C. Awards: Commendatore Crown of Italy; Commandeur Order of St. Sava (Serbia); Trudeau Medal, 1940. Presbyterian. Clubs: Cosmos (pres. 1931-32). Author: A New Basis for Social Progress; Business of a City's Health; also various med. and social papers. Home: The Highlands, 1914 Conn. Av. Office: Washington 9, D.C. Died Aug. 10, 1947.

WHITE, William Monroe, hydraulic engr.; b. 1871; student Univ. of Ala.; M.E., Tulane U., 1899, hon. D.Sc., 1930; unmarried. Engr. with New Orleans Drainage Bd., 1899-1902; hydraulic engr. and chief engr., I. P. Morris Dept. of Wm. Cramp & Sons Ship and Engine Bldg. Co., Phila., 1902-11; was in charge hydraulic work of the co., including design and building of large hydro-electric installations in N. America, including those at Niagara Falls; chief engr. and mgr. hydraulic dept. Allis-Chalmers Mfg. Co., Milwaukee, Wis., 1911-43; cons. engr. since Jan. 1943; pres. Milwaukee Art Inst., 1941-46. Mem. Am. Soc. M.E., Nat. Electric Light Assn., Am. Inst. E.E., Sigma Xi, Tau Beta Pi. Contbr. numerous articles in tech. jours. of U.S., Europe and Japan. Received from Nat. Assn. of Mfrs., award of "Modern Pioneer," 1938. Home: 2963 N. Summit Av. Address: First Wisconsin Nat. Bank, Milwaukee, Wis. Died Feb. 9, 1949.

WHITE, William Parker, clergyman, educator; b. Davenport, Ia., Apr. 18, 1865; s. William and Mary Ann (Robinson) W.; A.B., Monmouth (Ill.) Coll., 1887, D.D., 1910; B.D., Xenia Theol. Sem., St. Louis, Mo., 1891; m. Mrs. Theressa Beckley, Sept. 2, 1925; 1 son, William C. Ordained ministry, U.P. Ch., 1890; pastor Albany, Ore., 1892-95; became pres. Bible Inst. of Los Angeles (Calif.), 1929; now holding Bible confs. in chs.; editor The King's Business, Regional dir. Moody Bible Inst. of Chicago. Moderator U.P. Synod of the Columbia two times, Presbytery of Ore. 4 times. Republican. Kiwanian. Author: Thinking Through the Scriptures, 1927; The Throne of David, 1928; also Three Reasons Why I Believe the Bible Is the Word of God; Is McPhersonism of the Lord? Address: 4230 McClung Drive, Los Angeles, Calif.* Deceased.

WHITE, William Wallace, lawyer; b. New York City, Mar. 4, 1862; s. William Wilson and Jane (Laing) W.; ed. pub. schs; grad. New York Law Sch., 1898; m. Reba Mundell Nicholson, July 19, 1891 (dec.); 1 son, Wallace (dec.); m. 2d, Florence Hogan Foster, Nov. 25, 1942. Admitted to New York bar, 1898; member Richards & Co., patents and trade marks, 1880-1906; alone, 1906-22; associated with son, 1922 until his death, 1933; mem. Wm. Wallace White & Scotti since 1934. Consul gen. of Paraguay; in charge Legation of Paraguay, 1919-24, and short period, 1942; del. of Paraguay to Am. Financial Conf., Washington, D.C., 1915; spl. rep. of Paraguay on governing bd. of the Pan American Union, 1924. Pres. Trade Activities, Inc. Trustee Village of Pelham, N.Y., 1927-28, mayor, 1929-31. Member Am. Bar Assn., Am. Soc. Internat. Law, New York Patent Law Assn., Am. Patent Law Assn., Pan-Am. Soc., Soc. of Foreign Consuls. Republican. Presbyterian. Home: Village of Pelham, N.Y. Office: 347 Madison Av., New York, N.Y. Died Nov. 29, 1944.

WHITEFORD, G(ilbert) H(ayes) (hwīt'fôrd), educator; b. Glen Morris, Md., October 17, 1876; s. John and Mary Jane (Yingling) W.; B.S., Md. Agrl. Coll., 1897; A.M., Columbia, 1912; Ph.D., Johns Hopkins, 1917; m. Florence Salabar, June 25, 1925. Teacher Gwynnbrook, Md., 1899-1901, Rome, Ga., 1901-02, Manchester, Md., 1902-03, Dawson, Ga., 1903, Baconton, Ga., 1904, Crockett, Va., 1904-05; instr. science, Anne Arundel Acad., Millersville, Md., 1905-07, Bellefonte (Pa.) Acad., 1907-09, business mgr. same, 1909-11; prof. chemistry, Albright Coll., Myerstown, Pa., 1911-15; asso. prof. chemistry, Colo. State Coll., 1917-18, prof. and head of dept. 1918-45, dean division of science and arts, 1934-45, dean emeritus since 1945. Fellow Am. Assn. for Advancement of Science, Chemical Society of London; mem. Am. Chem. Soc., Am. Assn. Univ. Profs., Am. Inst. Chemists, Colo. Schoolmasters Club, Soc. Chem. Industry (London), Colo., Wyo. Acad. of Science. Methodist. Author: Essentials of College Chemistry (with R. G. Coffin), 1937; Outline of Laboratory Work in Inorganic Chemistry (with R. G. Coffin and Elizabeth M. Wing), 1937. Home: 1612 S. College Av., Fort Collins, Colo. Died Nov. 13, 1947.

WHITEHEAD, Alfred North, philosophy; b. Ramsgate, England, Feb. 15, 1861; s. Canon Alfred W.; B.A., Trinity Coll., Cambridge, 1884, M.A., 1887, D.Sc., 1905; D.Sc., U. of Manchester, 1920; LL.D., St. Andrews, 1921; D.Sc., Harvard and U. of Wis., 1925, Yale, 1926, McGill U., Montreal, Can., 1931; m. Evelyn Willoughby Wade, Dec. 16, 1890; children—T. North, Jessie Marie. Lecturer and later sr. lecturer on mathematics, Trinity Coll., 1885-1911; lecturer on applied mathematics and mechanics and later reader in geometry, University Coll., U. of London, 1911-14; prof. applied mathematics and later chief prof. of mathematics, Imperial Coll. of Science and Technology of same univ., 1914-24, senator, 1919, dean of faculty of science, 1921; prof. philosophy, Harvard, 1924-36, now emeritus prof. Fellow Royal Soc., British Acad.; mem. Math. Soc., British Assn. Advancement Science. Tarner lecturer, Trinity Coll., 1919. Awarded James Scott prize, Royal Soc., Edinburgh, 1922; Sylvester medal, Royal Soc., London, 1925. Author: A Treatise on Universal Algebra, 1898; (with Bertrand Russell) Principia Mathematica, 1910; An Introduction to Mathematics, 1910; The Organization of Thought, 1916; The Principles of Natural Knowledge, 1919; The Concept of Nature, 1920; The Principle of Relativity, 1922; Science and the Modern World, 1925; Religion in the Making, 1926; Symbolism: Its Meaning and Effect, 1927; The Aims of Education, 1928; Process and Reality (Gifford Lectures), 1929; The Function of Reason, 1929; Adventures of Ideas, 1933; Nature and Life, 1934; Modes of Thought, 1938. Recipient British Order of Merit, 1945. Address: Harvard U., Cambridge, Mass. Died Dec. 30, 1947.

WHITESIDE, Walker, actor; b. Logansport, Ind., Mar. 16, 1869; s. Judge T. C. and Levinia J. W.; m Lelia Wolstan McCord, Oct. 19, 1893; 1 dau., Rosamond Walker. Made début as Richard III at the Grand Opera House, Chicago, 1884; New York début as Hamlet, in own company, at Union Sq. Theatre, Apr. 19, 1893, later as Richelieu; toured U.S. for many yrs. in Shakespearean and classical repertoire; appeared as David, in "The Melting Pot," 1908, as Tokeramo, in "The Typhoon," 1912; played in "Mr. Wu," 1914; appeared as David over 100 times at Queen's and Comedy theatres, London, 1914; leading character in "Mr. Jubilee Drax," season of 1917-18; played James Durie in "The Master of Ballantrae," season of 1919-20; in "The Hindoo," 1921-22, also in "The Arabian"; played title rôle in "Sakura"; prod. and played leading rôle in "The Royal Box," 1928; prod. The Chinese Bungalow, 1930-31; prod. Three Men and a Woman, Lyceum Theatre, New York, and on tour, 1931-32; coast-to-coast tour in revival of "The Master of Ballantrae," 1935-36. Clubs: The Lambs, Friars (New York). Home: Hastings-on-Hudson, N.Y. Died Aug. 1, 1942.

WHITFIELD, James Bryan (hwĭt'fēld), judge; b. in Wayne County, N.C., Nov. 8, 1860; s. Richard Allen and Mary W. (Croom) W.; ed. W. Fla. Sem., Tallahassee, Fla., B. L., Univ. of Virginia, 1886; LL.D., Univ. of Florida, 1945; m. Leila R. Nash, Nov. 25, 1896 (died Oct. 4, 1897); 1 son, John Nash; m. 2d, Margaret H. Randolph, June 12, 1901; children—Mary Croom, James Bryan, Julia Croom (Mrs. C. A. Neeley), Margaret Randolph (dec.), Randolph. Admitted to Fla. bar, 1886. Apptd. pvt. sec. Gov. Perry of Fla., Sept. 1888; county judge Leon County, Fla., 1888-89; clerk Supreme Court of Fla., 1889-97; state treas., Fla., 1897-1903; atty.-gen., Fla., 1903-04; justice Supreme Court of Fla. since 1904, chief justice, 1905, 1909, 1935, re-elected for term, 1937-43. Democrat. Episcopalian. Mem. Fla. Centennial Commn., 1944. Home: 409 S. Monroe St. Address: Supreme Court Bldg., Tallahassee, Fla. Died Aug. 20, 1948.

WHITIN, Ernest Stagg (hwĭt'ĭn), sociologist; b. Morristown, N.J., Mar. 14, 1881; s. Henry and Isabelle (Stagg) W.; A.B., Columbia, 1904, Ph.D., 1910; unmarried. Teacher and asst. in social legislation, Columbia, 1903-18; sec. New York Welfare Com., Nat. Civic Fedn., 1906-07; economist N.Y. State Dept. of Labor, 1907-08; chmn. exec. council Nat. Com. on Prisons and Prison Labor, since 1908. Mem. Prison Labor and Waste Reclamation sect. U.S. War Industries Bd., World War; asst. to Mayor John P. Michel of New York, 1913-14; adviser to labor sect., Am. Delegation to Peace Conf., Paris, 1919. Mem. Associates for Govt. Service (pres.), Soc. Colonial Wars. Episcopalian. Clubs: University (Washington); Lotos (New York), Faculty (Columbia U.). Author: Factory Legislation, State of Maine, 1908; Penal Servitude, 1912; Caged Man, 1913. Home: 110 W. 57th St. Office: 534 W. 114th St., New York, N.Y. Deceased.

WHITING, Lilian, author; b. Niagara Falls, N.Y., Oct. 3, 1859; d. Hon. Lorenzo Dow (Ill. state senator for 20 yrs.) and Lucia (Clement) Whiting; desc. of Cotton Mather and Rev. William Whiting, first minister at Concord, Mass.; privately educated. Lit. editor Boston Traveler, 1880-90; editor Boston Budget, 1890-93; since 1896 has passed part of every yr. in Europe, principally in Paris, Rome, Florence and London. Mem. Hellenic Society (London), Boston Soc. for Psychical Research, Authors' Club, Boston; hon. mem. Browning Socs., New York, Boston and California. Author: The World Beautiful (3 vols., 1st 2d and 3d series); From Dreamland Sent (poems); After Her Death, The Story of a Summer; A Study of the Life and Poetry of Elizabeth Barrett Browning; Kate Field—a Record; The Spiritual Significance, 1900; The World Beautiful in Books, 1901; Boston Days, 1902; The Life Radiant, 1903; The Florence of Landor, 1905; The Outlook Beautiful, 1905; The Joy That No Man Taketh from You, 1905; The Land of Enchantment, 1906; From Dream to Vision of Life, 1906; Italy, the Magic Land, 1907; Paris, the Beautiful, 1908; Louise Chandler Moulton, Poet and Friend, 1909; Life Transfigured, 1910; The Brownings—Their Life and Art, 1911; Athens, the Violet Crowned, 1913; The Lure of London, 1914; Women Who Have Ennobled Life, 1915; Canada the Spellbinder, 1917; The Adventure Beautiful, 1917; The Golden Road, 1918; They Who Understand, 1919. Address: The Brunswick, Boston, Mass.; (winter) Credito Italiano, Florence, Italy. Died Apr. 30, 1942.

WHITMAN, Roger B., author; b. New York, N.Y., June 22, 1875; s. Alfred and Sarah (Andrews) W.; student Columbia, 1894-95; m. Marian Curtis, Oct. 3, 1906; children—Roger C., Herbert S. Tech. dir. New York Sch. of Auto Engrs., 1905-08; sales manager, etc., Bosch Magneto Co., 1910-12; sec., dir. and mgr. Stromberg Motor Devices Co., 1913-14; architectural photographer, 1915-17. Commd. 1st lt. Photographic Div., Air Service, U.S. Army, Oct. 1917, capt., Apr. 1918. Asso. editor Country Life, 1920-25. Mem. N.Y. Naval Militia, 1897; voluntary sailor Spanish-Am. War, served aboard Yankee, Solace and Marblehead. Mem. Authors' League America, Phi Kappa Psi. Clubs: Dutch Treat and Players. Author: Motor Car Principles, fifth edition, 1915; Gas Engine Principles, 1912; Motor Cycle Principles and the Light Car, 1914; Tractor Principles, 1919; Beauty in Gardens, 1928; Home Owners' Fact Book, 1929; First Aid for the Ailing House, 1938. Contbr. articles on building to many mags. Editor of "Ailing House" column, daily in N.Y. Sun and in other newspapers through the Bell Syndicate. Writer and broadcaster under title "The House Detective." Home: 314 Nassau Blvd., Garden City, N.Y. Died July 21, 1942.

WHITING, William Henry, Jr., coll. prof.; b. Millwood, Va., July 24, 1862; s. W. Henry and Mary J. (Foote) W.; A.B., Hampden-Sydney Coll., 1880, A.M., 1882, LL.D., 1921; U. of Va., 1880-81; D.Litt., Austin College, 1923; m. Sarah Ray Currie, July 31, 1884. Asst. prof., 1881-85, prin., 1885-86, Prince Edward Acad., Va.; asst. prof., Univ. Sch., Nashville, 1886-88; prin. Clay Hill Acad., Va., 1888-1902; prof. Latin, 1902-05, 1906-39, acting pres., sessions 1904-05 and 1908-09, treas., 1911-14, dean of gen. faculty, 1919-20, Hampden-Sydney Coll.; now retired. Pres. Sch. Trustees' Assn. of Va., 1911-12; v.p. Classical Assn. of Middle West and South, 1911-13. Mem. Phi Gamma Delta, Sigma Upsilon, Phi Beta Kappa. Presbyterian. Democrat. Home: Hampden-Sydney, Virginia. Died March 28, 1949.

WHITLEY, Samuel Henry, coll. pres.; b. Cleburne, Tex., Sept. 1, 1878; s. Albert Handley and Mary Elizabeth W.; B.Litt., Trinity U., Waxahachie,

Tex., 1901, A.B., 1926, LL.D., 1929; Litt.D., Austin Coll., Sherman, Tex., 1925; A.M., Southern Meth. U., Dallas, Tex., 1926; m. Lucie Braden Love, Dec. 27, 1904; children—Robert Love (dec.), Albert Portlen, Mary Lou. Teacher, rural schs., Tex., 1901-06; prin. high sch., Mexia, Tex., 1906-09, Corsicana, Tex., 1909-14; asst. state supt. pub. instrn., Tex., 1914-19; dean E. Tex. State Teachers Coll., 1919-24, pres. since 1924. Pres. Tex. Soc. for Crippled Children. Pres. Southern Assn. Colls. and Secondary Schs., 1941, mem. commn. on Instns. of Higher Learning, 1940-43; mem. Am. Assn. Teachers College (pres. 1931-32), Kappa Delta Pi, Phi Delta Kappa, Pi Gamma Mu. Democrat. Presbyterian. Mason. Clubs: Rotary (gov. 48th Dist. Rotary Internat., 1929-30), Paidaeon. Home: Commerce, Tex. Died Oct. 2, 1946.

WHITLOCK, Herbert Percy, mineralogist; b. New York, 1868; s. Thomas and Caroline V. (Hull) W.; grad. Charlier Inst., New York, 1884; C.E., Columbia U. Sch. of Mines, 1889; m. Julia Jaques Gardner, 1904. Asst. in mineralogy, Columbia U., 1892-1901; asst. in mineralogy, N.Y. State Museum, 1901-04, mineralogist, 1904-16, state mineralogist, 1916-18; curator of mineralogy, Am. Museum Natural History, 1918-41, curator emeritus since 1941, dept. minerals and gems. Engaged in mineralogic and crystallographic research on mineral species, with special reference to calcite. Fellow Am. Acad. Arts and Sci., Mineral Soc. Am., Geological Soc. Am. N.Y. Acad. Science, hon. mem. N.Y. Mineralol. Club. Wrote Museum bulls.: Guide to Mineralogic Collection of the N.Y. State Museum, 1902; List of New York Mineral Localities, 1903; monograph on New York Calcite, 1910; List of New Crystal Forms of Minerals, 1910, 1922; The Story of the Minerals, 1925; The Story of the Gems, 1936; also many mineralogic contbns. Edited articles on minerals for Internat. Encyclopedia. Specialist on methods of public museum installation. Home: 103 Waverly Place. Office: Am. Museum of Natural History, New York, N.Y. Died Feb. 22, 1948.

WHITMAN, Charles Seymour, ex-governor; b. Hanover, Conn., Aug. 28, 1868; s. Rev. John Seymour and Lillie (Arne) W.; A.B., Amherst, 1890; LL.B., New York U., 1894; hon. M.A., Williams, 1904; LL.D., New York U., 1913, Amherst, 1913, Williams, 1914, and Hamilton, 1918; m. Olive Hitchcock, Dec. 22, 1908 (died May 29, 1926); children—Charles S., Olive (Mrs. J. J. Parsons). Assistant corp. counsel, New York, 1901-03; mem. and later pres., Bd. City Magistrates, New York, 1904-07; judge Ct. of Gen. Sessions, N.Y., by appmt. of Gov. Hughes, 1907; dist. atty. New York County, 1910-14; gov. of N.Y., terms Jan. 1, 1915-Dec. 31, 1918; resumed practice of law at N.Y. City, 1919; mem. Whitman, Ransom, Coulson & Goetz; commr. of Port Authority of New York. Republican. Presbyterian. Mason. Mem. Am. Bar Assn. (pres. 1926-27), N.Y. State Bar Assn., Bar Assn. City of New York, New York Chamber of Commerce, Soc. of the Cincinnati, S.R., Soc. Colonial Wars, S.A.R., St. Nicholas Soc., N.E. Soc. Alpha Delta Phi. Clubs: University, Metropolitan, Century, Down Town Assn., Union League, Piping Rock, Newport Country. Home: 1 W. 54th St. Office: 40 Wall St., New York, N.Y.* Died Mar. 29, 1947.

WHITMAN, Edward A., co-trustee, vice pres., Duluth, South Shore & Atlantic Ry.; co-trustee, Wisc. Central Ry. Office: 1417 First National-Soo Line Building, Minneapolis, Minn. Died Aug. 4, 1947.

WHITMAN, Ralph, naval officer; b. Boston, Mass., Apr. 7, 1880; s. Kilborn and Ella May (Wightman) W.; S.B., Mass. Inst. Tech., 1901; diploma, Naval War Coll., 1923; m. Frances Guyon Seabrook, Dec. 12, 1916; 1 dau., Frances Guyon. Civil engr., Engring. Dept., City of Boston, 1901-05, Isthmian Canal Commn. (studies for Panama Canal), 1905-07; commd. ensign, Civil Engr. Corps, U.S. Navy, 1907, and advanced through ranks to rear adm., 1939; stationed successively at Navy Yard, Phila.; Navy Dept., Washington; Naval Station, Guatanamo, Cuba; Naval Acad.; aide on staff of U.S. Mil. Gov., Santo Domingo, Dominican Republic; Naval Ordnance Plant, South Charleston, W.Va.; Naval War Coll.; Norfolk (Va.) Navy Yard; Mare Island (Calif.) Navy Yard; Naval Operating Base, Norfolk, Va.; stationed at Headquarters, 3d Naval District, New York City, from 1939, to April, 1944; retired, May 1, 1944. Awarded Marine Corps' Commemorative Expeditionary medal; Victory medal with West Indies clasp, special letter of commendation with silver star. Member American Soc., C.E., Boston Soc. C.E., Soc. of Am. Mil. Engrs., A.A.A.S., Internat. Assn. of Navigation Congresses, U.S. Naval Inst. Club: Army and Navy (Washington). Address: 30 Deer Hill Av., Danbury, Conn. Died Feb. 3, 1946.

WHITMAN, Royal, surgeon; b. Portland, Me., Oct. 24, 1857; s. Royal E. and Lucretia S.W.; M.D., Harvard, 1882; received diploma Royal Coll. Surgeons, Eng., 1889; m. Julia L. Armitage, Apr. 29, 1886. Specialist in surgery of deformities and diseases of the joints; has served as adj. prof. orthopaedic surgery, Coll. Phys. and Surg. (Columbia); prof. orthopaedic surgery, New York Polyclinic Med. Sch.; dir. mil. orthopaedic teaching; chmn. Advisory Board for Orthopaedics, etc.; surgeon Hosp. for Ruptured and Crippled; cons. to Hosp. St. John's Guild, St. Agnes' Hosp., St. Giles Hosp., Polyclinic Hosp., Shriners' Hosp. (Montreal), New York Home for Crippled Children, Darrach Home for Crippled Children, N.Y. State Board of Health, N.Y. Dept. of Labor. Pres. Am. Orthopaedic Assn., 1895; hon. fellow Royal Soc. of Medicine of London and Royal Coll. of Surgeons of England; fgn. mem. French Acad. of Surgery; mem. Kaiserlich Deutsche Academie der Natur Forcher; hon. mem. Am. British, French, Russian and Italian Orthopaedic assns. Clubs: Century (New York); Athenaeum (London). Author: A Treatise on Orthopaedic Surgery, 9th edit., 1930. Originator of "abduction treatment" for fracture of the neck of the femur; of operations for paralytic deformities, etc. Address: care Brown, Shipley & Co., 123 Pall Mall, London, England. Died Aug. 19, 1946.

WHITMAN, Russell, lawyer; b. Plymouth, Mass., Jan. 18, 1861; s. William H. and Helen (Russell) W.; A.B., Harvard, 1882; hon. LL.B., Chicago Law School, 1897; LL.D., Whitman Coll., 1934; m. Alice Mason Miller, Apr. 3, 1893 (dec.); children—Helen (Mrs. Manly S. Mumford), Sarah (Mrs. Howard Henderson), Winslow (dec.), John Russell. Teacher, Adams Acad., Quincy, Mass., 1882-84, Columbia Law Sch., 1884-85; admitted to Mass. bar, 1885, Ill. bar, 1886, and since practiced at Chicago; mem. Dent & Whitman, 1891-1906, then Whitman & Miller and now Whitman, Miller & Coon; judge Superior Court of Cook County, Sept.-Dec. 1935. Mem. Evanston Civil Service Commn., 1910, pres., 1920-24 and 1931-37; mem. Ill. State Bd. of Law Examiners, 1908-13; pres. Civil Service Reform Assn. of Chicago, 1913-16. Chmn. Draft Registration Bd., 1917. Mem. Chicago Bar Assn. (pres. 1925-26), Law Club (pres. 1906-07), Phi Beta Kappa, Delta Kappa Epsilon. Democrat. Unitarian. Author: Review and Quiz Book for Law Students, 1916. Home: 1334 Asbury Av., Evanston, Ill. Office: 30 N. La Salle St., Chicago. Died Dec. 23, 1949; buried Rose Hill Cemetery, Chicago.

WHITMORE, Frank Clifford, prof. organic chemistry; b. N. Attleboro, Mass., Oct. 1, 1887; s. Frank Hale and Lena Avilla (Thomas) W.; A.B., Harvard, 1911, A.M., 1912, Ph.D., in organic chemistry, 1914; (hon.) Sc.D., Franklin & Marshall Coll., 1937, U. of Delaware, 1937, Allegheny College, 1938, Philadelphia College of Osteopathy, 1943; married Marion Gertrude Mason, June 22, 1914; children—Frank C., Mason, Harry Edison, Marion Mason II, Patricia Joan (dec.). Instr. organic chemistry, Williams, 1916-17, Rice Inst., Houston, Tex., 1917-18; asst. prof. organic chemistry, U. of Minn., 1918-20; prof. organic chem., 1920, acting head chem. dept., 1924-25, head, 1925-29, Northwestern U., dean Sch. of Chem. and Physics, Pa. State Coll. since 1929; research prof. of organic chemistry since 1937. Mem. advisory com. Chemical Warfare Service U.S. Army 1934-40. Mem. Nat. Research Council (chmn. div. chemistry and chmn. technology, 1927-28 and central petroleum com., 1928-31; com. survey of research in industry, 1939-40); Nat. Defense Research Com. (chmn. sect. B-2, 1941-42 mem. sect. 16.3). Chemical consultant Office Prodn. Management, 1941, Office Q.M. Gen., U.S. Army, since 1942; mem. referee bd., Chem. Div., War Prodn. Board 1942-45. Mem. visiting com. chem. dept., Mass. Inst. Tech. since 1939. Fellow A.A.A.S. (v.p. 1932; chmn. Section C; council 1941-44); mem. American Academy, American Chemical Society (councilor 1926-28; director 1928-39; pres. 1938), Am. Inst. Chem. Engrs., Am. Inst. of N.Y., Nat. Inst. of Social Sciences, Nat. Pioneer Award Com., N.A.M., 1939-40, Pa. Job Mobilization Com., 1939-40, Pa. Chem. Soc. (pres. 1942-45), Com. Survey of Research in Industry, 1939-40, Chem. Soc. London, Deutsche Chemische Gesell., Army Ordnance Assn., U.S. Inf. Assn., Soc. for Advancement of Edn., American Philos. Society, Franklin Institute, Newcomen Society, Sigma Tau, Alpha Sigma, Sigma Xi, Alpha Chi Sigma, Phi Lambda Upsilon, Phi Kappa Phi, Sigma Pi Sigma, Alpha Epsilon Delta, Phi Beta Kappa, Phi Eta Sigma. Awarded Wm. H. Nichols Medal, 1937; Willard Gibbs medal, 1945. Clubs: Chemists (Chicago); Chemists (New York); Cosmos (Washington, D.C.); Center Hills Country (State College, Pa.). Author: Organic Compounds of Mercury, 1921; Organic Chemistry, 1937. Mem. editorial bd. Chemical Bulletin, 1923-28, Organic Synthesis, 1925—(editor in chief Vol. 7, 1927, Vol. 12, 1932). Home: State Coll., Pa. Died June 24, 1947.

WHITNALL, Harold Orville (hwit'nál), geologist; b. Morristown, N.J., Aug. 3, 1877; s. Thaddeus O. and Jessie (Minard) W.; Ph.B., Colgate, 1900, A.M., 1909; graduate study, Harvard, 1902-03; S.C.D., Bates College, 1939; S.C.D., Colgate Univ., 1944; m. Elizabeth Sherwood, Aug. 18, 1908; children—Thaddeus Orville, Helen S. (Mrs. Dale Gunn), Faith Esther. With Colgate University since 1903, instructor geology until 1909, assistant professor, 1909-12, asso. professor, 1912-21, prof. since 1921; also consulting practice; geologist for New York, Ontario & Western R.R. Asst. in geology, Harvard, summer 1908; field asst. N.Y. State Survey, 1905-07; consultant Dept. of Commerce, N.Y. State, since 1943. Rep. presdl. elector, 37th N.Y. Dist., 1924; mem. Assembly State of N.Y., 1927-29; chmn. Republican Com. of Madison County, N.Y., since 1940. Treas. Colgate Univ. Alumni Corp. since 1919; holder of Alumni award for distinguished service to Colgate U. Fellow A.A.A.S.; mem. Am. Inst. Mining and Metall. Engrs., Am. Assn. Mammalogists, Soc. Meteoric Research, N.Y. State Hist. Soc., Delta Kappa Epsilon, Phi Beta Kappa, Sigma Gamma Epsilon. Mason. Baptist. Author: Dawn of Mankind, 1924; Dinosaurs and Their World, 1924; A Parade of Ancient Animals, 1936; Hunter of The Caverns, 1939. Contbr. to mags. and newspapers. Home: Hamilton, N.Y. Died May 18, 1945.

WHITNEY, Alexander Fell (hwit'nê), president Brotherhood R.R. Trainmen; b. Cedar Falls, Ia., Apr. 12, 1873; s. Rev. Joseph Leonard and Martha Wallin (Batcheller) W.; ed. high sch., Cherokee, Ia.; m. Grace Elizabeth Marshman, Sept. 7, 1893 (died Mar. 7, 1923); children—Joseph Lafeton, Everett Alexander, Lydia Marie (Mrs. Richard J. Olson); m. 2d, Dorothy May Rowley, July 2, 1927. Began as r.r. news agt., 1888; brakeman successively with I.C. R.R., Fremont, Elkhorn & Mo. Valley R.R., U.P. R.R., C.&N.W. Ry., 1890-1901; chmn. gen. grievance com., Brotherhood R.R. Trainmen, 1901-07, member Board of Grand Trustees, 1905-07, vice-president, 1907-28, general secretary and treasurer, Feb.-July 1928, pres. since 1928. Chmn. Ry. Labor Execs. Assn., 1932-34; del. to Inter-Am. Conf. for the Maintenance of Peace, Buenos Aires, Argentina, Dec. 1936; mem. Com. on Unemployment Census, Sept. 1937; former chmn. Good Neighbor League of Northern Ohio; mem. exec. com. Ohio Safety Council; judge Pabst awards, 1944; grand. counsellor Ladies Auxiliary to Brotherhood R.R. Trainmen. Mem. Mont. Cowboys Assn., Los Angeles Breakfast Club; hon. mem. Air Pilots Assn. of Mont. Mason, Modern Woodman, Elk. Author: Main Street—not Wall Street, 1938. Contbr. various magazines. Home: 23012 W. Lake Rd., Bay Village, O. Office: 1370 Ontario St., Cleveland 13. Died July 9, 1949.

WHITNEY, Alfred Rutgers, constructing engr.; b. New York, N.Y., June 16, 1868; s. Alfred R. and Adeline Peers (Nesbitt) W.; M.E., Stevens Inst. Tech., 1890, E.D., 1921; unmarried. With Portage Iron Co., Duncansville, Pa., 1890-91; gen. mgr., later v.p. Puget Sound Wire Nail and Steel Co., Everett, Wash., 1891-94, also gen. mgr. and elec. engr. Everett R.R. and Electric Co. and cons. engr. Puget Sound Pulp and Paper Co., Everett & Monte Cristo R.R., 1891-94; rep. Carnegie Steel Co., in Japan, 1894; mem. firm A. R. Whitney, iron and steel mfrs. and contractors, New York, 1894-96; organizer, 1896, A. R. Whitney, Jr. & Co., Inc., 1899, as The Whitney Co., of which was pres. and treas. until 1926, chmn. bd., 1926-29; retired from active business, 1929. Company constructors of Great Am. Ins. Co. Bldg., W. R. Grace & Co. Bldg., Iron Age Bldg., New York; Masonic Temple and Central Branch Y.M.C.A., Brooklyn; Stock Exchange Bldg., Baltimore; Wentworth Inst., Boston; Amherst (Mass.) Coll. Library; International Trust Co. Bldg., Denver; Smith Building, Seattle, Wash., etc. War corr. in Ethiopia, 1930. Dir. Morristown Trust Co. Mem. Squadron A, cav., N.Y. Nat. Guard, 1897; maj. staff Gov. Frank W. Higgins, 1905, and of Gov. John Alden Dix, 1911; brevet maj., 1911, successively capt. and regtl. adj., maj. and brigade adj. gen., 1912-16; aide to rear admiral Nathaniel R. Usher, 1913-17; aide Bur. of Naval Intelligence, World War. Mem. Am. Soc. C.E., New Eng. Soc., Am. Geog. Soc., S.R., Delta Tau Delta. Republican. Episcopalian. Clubs: Union League, University, Downtown Assn., Metropolitan Opera, Piping Rock, New York Yacht, Seawanhaka-Corinthian Yacht, Cruising Club of America, Anglers' (New York); Traveler, Explorer, Angler, Yachtsman and Navigator. Writer on engring., travel, cruising, fishing, etc. Designer and builder of the "Ruffhouse," original of now universally accepted type of Fla. houseboat. Home: Morristown, N.J.; also 277 Park Av., New York 17, N.Y. Died Oct. 7, 1946.

WHITNEY, Gertrude Vanderbilt (Mrs. Harry Payne Whitney), sculptor; b. New York, N.Y.; d. Cornelius and Alice (Gwynne) Vanderbilt; Brearley Sch., N.Y.; studied sculpture under Hendrik C. Andersen and James E. Fraser, New York, and took a course at the Art Students' League, New York; studied under Andrew O'Connor, Paris; m. Harry Payne Whitney, Aug. 25, 1896. Prin. works: Aztec Fountain, in Pan-Am. Bldg., Washington, D.C., also Titanic Memorial, for same city; El Dorado Fountain, San Francisco; 2 panels for Triumphant Arch, New York; war memorial, erected at 168th St. and Broadway, New York; equestrian statue to Col. William F. Cody (Buffalo Bill); memorial, Peter Stuyvesant, N.Y. City; Columbus Memorial, Palos, Spain; St. Nazaire War Memorial, France, etc. Mem. Am. Federation Arts, Nat. Assn. of Women Artists, Inc., Nat. Institute Social Sciences, Internat. Hist. Soc., Nat. Arts Club. Clubs: Colony, Cosmopolitan. Home: 871 Fifth Av., New York, N.Y. Died Apr. 18, 1942.

WHITNEY, Henry Howard, officer U.S. Army; b. Glen Hope, Pa., Dec. 25, 1866; s. Rev. Walter R. and Eliza (Kegerreis) W.; grad. (with honors) Dickinson Sem., Williamsport, Pa., 1884; grad. U.S. Mil. Acad., 1892; m. Ellen Wadsworth, d. Henry Whitney Closson, Feb. 25, 1897; children—Julie Elizabeth (dec.) and Henry Wadsworth. Additional 2d lt. 4th Arty., June 11, 1892; 2d lt., Nov. 28, 1892; capt. asst. adj.-gen. vols., Hdqrs. of the Army, May 12, 1898-May 12, 1899; 1st lt., Mar. 2, 1899; capt. arty. corps, May 8, 1901, maj. Coast Arty. Corps, Apr. 14, 1909. Spl. duty mil. information div., War Dept., 1896-98; mil. attaché, Am. Legation, Buenos Aires, Apr. 12, 1898-Apr. 12, 1899; in May 1898, under orders Sec. of War, after visiting Cuba, incog. made mil. reconnaissance of Puerto Rico, disguised as an English sailor; furnished information which was basis of mil. campaign in P.R.; on Gen. Miles' staff during Spanish-Am. War; accompained Gen. Miles on his tour around the world, 1902-03, as lt. col. and a.d.c. chief staff; grad. Sch. of Submarine Defense, 1907; detailed in adj.-gen.'s dept., Oct. 3, 1910; in Philippine Islands, Jan. 31, 1911-14, as adj. gen. dept. of Mindanao; adj. Western Dept., at San Francisco, Jan. 13, 1914; comdg. Presidio of San Francisco, 1915; comdg. Coast Arty. at Ft. Winfield Scott, San Francisco, 1916; promoted lt. col., Coast Artillery Corps. June

1916; re-detailed adj. gen.'s dept. and ordered to Mexican border as adj. gen. El Paso Dist.; to San Francisco, as dept. adj., Western Dept., Apr. 1917; promoted col., July 1917; apptd. brig. gen. N.A., Aug. 5, 1917, and ordered to Camp Shelby, Miss.; apptd. comdr. 63d Field Arty. Brigade; apptd. mem. Gen. Staff A.E.F.; chief of staff, Dist. of Paris, France, 1918-19; retired June 30, 1920, at own request after more than 32 yrs.' service; brigadier general regular army, ret., June 21, 1930. Awarded D.S.C. and D.S.M.; Officier de la Legion d'Honneur (French); Commandeur de la Couronne de Roumanie avec Glaives (Rumanian); Commandeur de Danilo I (Montenegro). Mem. Loyal Legion, Am. Legion, Mil. Order World War, Mil. Order Foreign Wars; founder The Beloved Vagabonds, Inc., a society of wanderers and adventures. Mason (32°, Shriner). Clubs: St. Nicholas (New York); Racquet (Phila.); Bohemian (San Francisco); San Mateo Polo, California Yacht (Los Angeles); Pacific Coast (Long Beach); University (New York). Address: care War Dept., Washington, D.C. Died April 2, 1949.

WHITNEY, Marian Parker, coll. prof.; b. New Haven, Conn., February 1861; d. Prof William Dwight and Elizabeth W. (Baldwin) W.; ed. in private schools (of Yale University) U.S., Germany and France; graduate student Yale, and universities Paris and Zürich; Ph.D., Yale Univ., 1901; unmarried. Teacher modern languages, New Haven High School, 1891-1905; head dept. of German, Vassar Coll., 1905-29, also courses in comparative lit. (now emeritus prof.). Trustee 1928-42 (resigned), mem. exec. com. since 1932, Conn. Coll. for Women: examiner, Sarah Lawrence Coll., 1928-30. Mem. Modern Lang. Assn. America (1st v.p. 1918, 19), Internat. Council of Women (chmn. edn.), Internat. Fedn. Univ. Women, Am. Assn. Univ. Women (ex-pres. Conn. Fedn.), Am. Assn. Univ. Profs. (ex-chmn. com. research); mem. com. control Modern Lang. Study; mem. Nat. Research Council, 1931-34; mem. NRA Consumers Council of N.E., 1934. Clubs: Woman's Univ., Cosmopolitan (New York). Author: Advanced German Composition, 1910; Easy German Composition, 1912; (in collaboration) Geschichte der Deutschen Literatur, 1913. Editor several German and French grammars and text-books. Lecturer and writer on contemporary drama of Europe. Home: 186 Edwards St., New Haven, Conn. Died June 16, 1946.

WHITNEY, William Channing, architect; b. Harvard, Mass., Apr. 11, 1851; s. Benjamin Franklin and Louisa (Lawrence) W.; B.S., Mass. State Coll., 1872; m. Alma C. Walker, Oct. 6, 1881; children—Alice Lawrence Kingsbury (wife Lt. R. H. Spurway), Elinor Whitney Kingsbury (wife Lt. S. M. Carver), Richard Walker Kingsbury, Millicent Ames Kingsbury. General practice of architecture in Minneapolis, 1880-1940. Trustee Minneapolis Inst. Fine Arts. Fellow A.I.A. Clubs: Minneapolis, Skylight, Six O'Clock. Home: Hampshire Arms Hotel, Minneapolis.* Died Aug. 23, 1945.

WHITTIER, Clarke Butler, prof. law; b. St. Louis, July 24, 1872; s. Clarke and Eliza (Oliver) W.; A.B., Leland Stanford Jr. U., 1893; LL.B. (cum laude), Harvard, 1896; m. Clara Winifred Caldwell, Sept. 9, 1896; children—Howard Caldwell (dec.), Florence. Practiced law, Los Angeles, 1895-96; instr. law, 1897-99, asst. prof., 1899-1900, asso. prof., 1900-02, Leland Stanford Jr. U.; prof. law, U. of Chicago, 1902-14; prof. law, Leland Stanford Jr. U., 1915-37 (retired). Mem. Am. Bar Assn. Editor: Cases on Common Law Pleading. Address: Stanford University, Calif. Died Oct. 8, 1943.

WHITTY, Dame May, actress; b. England; d. Alfred and Mary L. (Ashton) Whitty; student private schs.; m. Ben Webster, Aug. 2, 1892; 1 dau., Margaret. Resident alien in U.S. intermittently since 1895. Actress at age of 16; played with many stars, including Mr. and Mrs. Kendal, Henry Irving and Ellen Terry, Richard Mansfield, Viola Allen, Grace George, Forbes Robertson; in pictures with Robert Montgomery, Greta Garbo and others. Dame Comdr. of British Empire, 1918. Mem. United Suffragists (worker in suffrage movement), Actress's Franchise League (chmn.); chmn. and v. pres. British Actors Equity; chmn. Theatrical Ladies Guild (London), Children's Country Holiday Fund (London). Address: care M.C.A., 9370 Burton Way, Beverly Hills, Calif. Died May 28, 1948.

WICKENDEN, William Elgin, engr., educator; b. Toledo, O., Dec. 24, 1882; s. Thomas Rogers and Ida (Consaul) W.; B.S., Denison U., 1904; U. of Wis., 1905-07; hon. Dr. Engr., Lafayette Coll., 1926, Worcester Poly. Inst., 1927, Case Sch. Applied Science, 1929, Rose Poly. Inst., 1936, Tulane U., 1939; hon. Sc.D., Dension Univ., 1928, Bucknell U., 1930; LL.D., Oberlin Coll., 1930, U. of Toledo, 1940; L.H.D., Otterbein U., 1933; m. Marion Susan Lamb, Sept. 2, 1908; children—Elizabeth, William Clarence. Instr., U. of Wis., 1905-09; asst. prof. elec. engring., Mass. Inst. Tech., 1909-14, asso. prof., 1914-18; personnel mgr. Western Electric Co., 1918-21; asst. v.p. Am. Telephone & Telegraph Co., 1921-23; dir. investigation, Soc. for Promotion Engring. Edn., 1923-29; pres. Case School of Applied Science since 1929. Regional supervisor personnel methods, S.A.T.C., 1918, World War. Chmn. Regional Labor Board for Northern Ohio, 1933, Ohio Highway Survey Commn., 1935-38. Chmn. Gen. Products Group, Office Production Management, 1941. Mem. Engrs. Council for Professional Development, 1933-38. Trustee Lake Erie Coll. Fellow A.A.A.S. (v.p., 1936), Am. Inst. E.E. (v.p. 1943); Am. Soc. M.E., Am. Acad. Polit. and Social Science, Soc. Promotion Engring. Edn. (pres. 1933; awarded Lamme medal 1935), Sigma Chi, Sigma Xi, Phi Beta Kappa, Tau Beta Pi, Theta Tau. Presbyterian. Author: Illumination and Photometry, 1909; Comparative Study of Engineering Education in the U.S. and in Europe, 1929. Home: 2530 Fairmount Blvd., Cleveland Heights, O. Address: Case School of Applied Science, Cleveland, O. Died Sep. 1, 1947.

WICKHEM, John Dunne (wĭk'ĕm), judge; b. Beloit, Wis., May 25, 1888; s. James George and Mary (Dunne) W.; A.B., Beloit Coll., 1910, LL.D., 1930; LL.B., U. of Wis., 1916, LL.D., 1940; m. Mary Luella Carroll, Sept. 11, 1920; children—John Carroll, Robert James. Instr. Beloit High Sch., 1910-14; mem. Lenicheck, Boesel & Wickhem, Milwaukee, 1917-30; asst. prof. law, U. of Wis., 1919-22, asso. prof., 1922-25, prof., 1925-30; justice Supreme Court of Wis. since 1930. Commr. on Uniform Laws, 1928-30. Chief editorial div. Bur. of War Trade Intelligence, 1918-19. Trustee of Beloit College (chmn.), Madison Y.M.C.A., St. Paul's U. Chapel. Mem. Am. Bar Assn., Wisconsin State, Dane County bar assns., Am. Law Inst. (council), Phi Beta Kappa, Am. Judicature Soc. (dir. 1939), Sigma Alpha Epsilon, Phi Delta Phi, Order of Coif. Democrat. Catholic. Clubs: Town and Gown, Gyro, Madison Literary, Madison, Professional. Home: 716 Edgewood Av., Madison, Wis. Died June 20, 1949.

WICKSER, Philip John, lawyer; b. Buffalo, N.Y., Apr. 4, 1887; s. John George and Katharine Anna (Houck) W.; A.B., Cornell U., 1908; LL.B., Harvard, 1911; m. Margaretta Melissa Fryer, Feb. 3, 1915; children—Robert Livingston, John Philip, Melissa (Mrs. Charles U. Banta). Admitted to N.Y. bar, 1912, Supreme Court of U.S., 1926; began practice at Buffalo with Kenefick, Cooke, Mitchell & Bass, 1912; mem. Palmer, Houck & Wickser, 1914-21 and since 1932, Palmer, Garono, Houck & Wickser 1921-32; chmn. bd. Buffalo Insurance Co.; dir. Marine Trust Co., Marine Safe Deposit Co., Dunlop Tire & Rubber Corp. (all Buffalo); sec., New York State Board of Law Examiners since 1921; mem. Board of Legal Examiners (Federal), 1941-43; chmn. National Conference Bar Examiners, 1931. Director Children's Aid, and Soc. for Prevention of Cruelty to Children of Erie County (pres. 1928-42); mem. N.Y. State Temporary Emergency Relief Administration, 1931-32 (chmn. 1932), vice chmn. Governor's Commn. on Unemployment Relief, N.Y., 1934-36; dir. Urban League, Memorial Center of Buffalo, Kleinhans Music Hall Management, Inc. (v.p.). Trustee, secretary treas., Grosvenor Library, Buffalo. Mem. Am. Bar Assn. (member board governors 1939-42; chairman conference bar association delegates 1931-32), Am. Law Institute, New York State Bar Association, American Judicature Soc. (dir.), Federation of Bar Assn. Western N.Y. (pres. 1928), Bar Assn. Erie County (pres. 1926), Assn. Bar City of New York, Buffalo Soc. Natural Sciences (dir.) Buffalo Fine Arts Acad. (dir.), Buffalo Hist. Soc. (v.p.), Pilgrims in U.S., Kappa Sigma, Phi Delta Phi, Pi Gamma Mu. Republican. Unitarian. Clubs; Buffalo, Automobile, Buffalo Country, Tennis and Squash, Saturn (Buffalo); Sankaty Head Golf (Nantucket); Harvard, Cornell, Century, Coffee House, Grolier (New York); Cosmos (Washington). Author articles on legal topics. Home: 245 Nottingham Terrace, Buffalo 16. Office: Buffalo Insurance Bldg., Buffalo 3, N.Y. Died Aug. 14, 1949.

WIDENER, Joseph E. (wĭd'nẽr), capitalist; grad. U. of Pa. Sch. of Architecture; m. Ella H. Pancoast (dec.). Dir. B.&O. R.R. Co., Land Title Bank and Trust Co., Reading Co. Interested in racing; maintains stud near Lexington, Ky., and Chantilly, France; prin. owner Belmont Park Racetrack, Hialeah Park Race Track of Miami Jockey Club. Owner of notable art collection, some 300 paintings, including 16 Rembrandts, Titians, Raphaels, Gainsboroughs, Van Dycks, Holbeins, Millets. Office: Land Title Bldg., Philadelphia, Pa. Died Oct. 26, 1943.

WIEGAND, Karl McKay (wē-gănd), botanist; b. Truxton, N.Y., June 2, 1873; s. John Christopher and Annie (McKay) W.; B.S., Cornell, 1894, Ph.D., 1898; m. Ella Maude Cipperly, Aug. 21, 1906. Asst. and instr. botany, Cornell U., 1894-1907; asso. prof. botany, Wellesley, 1907-13; prof. botany and head of dept., N.Y. State Coll. Agr., at Cornell U., 1913-41, prof. emeritus since Aug. 15, 1941. Fellow A.A.A.S.; mem. Bot. Soc. America, New Eng. Bot. Club, Sigma Xi, Phi Kappa Phi. Author of about 100 papers on bot. topics. Home: Upland Rd., Ithaca, N.Y. Died Mar. 12, 1942.

WIGGINS, Charles, 2d, headmaster; b. Cincinnati, O., Nov. 24, 1885; s. John and Elizabeth Arnold (Jewett) W.; prep. edn. Pomfret (Conn.) Sch.; A.B., Harvard, 1908; m. Laura Elizabeth Richards, Sept. 2, 1909. In architectural office of R. Clipston Sturgis, Boston, 1908-13; sr. master Pomfret Sch., 1914-20; headmaster Noble and Greenough Sch., Boston, since 1920. Republican. Episcopalian. Mason. Club: Tavern. Home: Dedham, Mass. Died Nov. 25, 1943.

WIESS, Harry Carothers (wīz), pres. Humble Oil & Refining Co.; b. Beaumont, Tex., July 30, 1887; s. William and Louise Elizabeth (Carothers) W.; student Lawrenceville (New Jersey) Sch., 1903-05; C.E., Princeton University, 1909; m. Olga Keith, Sept. 29, 1909; children—Elizabeth (Mrs. Lloyd Hilton Smith), Caroline (Mrs. William Howard Francis, Jr.), Margaret (Mrs. James Anderson Elkins, Jr.). With Paraffine Oil Company, Beaumont, Texas, 1910-17, president, 1912-17; one of organizers of the Humble Oil Co., Houston, Tex., 1917, v.p., 1917-33, exec. v.p., 1933-37, pres. since Feb. 8, 1937. Member National Petroleum Council. Chmn. Houston Community Chest, 1931-32; special term mem. of Corp. of the Mass. Inst. of Technology; charter trustee of Princeton U.; bd. trustees, Rice Inst. Mem. Am. Inst. Mining and Metall. Engrs. Dir. Am. Petroleum Inst. Democrat. Episcopalian. Clubs: Bayou, Texas Corinthian Yacht, Houston Country, Tejas (Houston); The Beach (Galveston); Cannon (Princeton Univ.); Eagle Lake Rod and Gun. Home: 2 Sunset Road. Office: Humble Bldg., Houston, Tex. Died Aug. 26, 1948.

WIEST, Howard, judge; b. Washington, Mich., Feb. 24, 1864; s. Jacob and Elizabeth W.; student law in offices of Atkinson & Atkinson, Detroit; m. Cora Newman, Dec. 19, 1888; children—Lucille, Theodosia. Admitted to bar, 1885, and began practice at Detroit; moved to Ingham County, Mich., 1890; circuit judge 30th Jud. Circuit, Jan. 1, 1900-Jan. 25, 1921; apptd. asso. justice Supreme Court of Mich. to fill vacancy, Jan. 25, 1921, elected later in yr. and reelected, 1923, 31 and 1939, present term expiring 1947. Republican. Address: Lansing, Mich.* Died Sep. 16, 1945.

WIGGINS, Sterling Pitts, clergyman; b. Harris County, Ga., Feb. 22, 1874; s. Robert Lemuel and Ann Elizabeth (Pitts) W.; grad. Emory U., 1894; m. Gussie Tigner, Dec. 14, 1897; 1 son, M. Tigner. Teacher pub. schs., Ga., 1894-97; ordained ministry M.E. Ch., S., 1897, pastor Pendleton, Ore., 1898-99, West Point, Ga., 1903-07, First Ch., Atlanta, 1910-12, St. John Ch., Augusta, 1913-15, Athens, Ga., 1916-20; presiding elder North Atlanta Dist., N. Ga. Conf., 1928-31; pastor Haygood Memorial Ch., Atlanta, since 1932. Mem. Alpha Tau Omega. Democrat. K.P. Home: 1270 Oxford Rd. N.E., Atlanta, Ga.* Died Apr. 15, 1945.

WIGGLESWORTH, Edward, gemologist; b. Boston, Mass., Nov. 3, 1885; s. Edward and Sarah (Willard) W.; A.B., Harvard, 1908, A.M., 1909, Ph.D., 1917; m. Sarah P. Rackemann, June 15, 1914; children—Edward, Thomas, Mary, Sarah, Jane, Anne. Asst. in geology, Harvard, 1910-16, also curator dept. of geology, 1909-17; curator mineralogy and geology, Boston Society Natural History, 1914-40, director, 1919-39, scientific director, 1939-40; hon. curator of gems since 1940; dir. Eastern Laboratory Gemological Inst. of America. Served as asst. to food administrator of Mass., World War. Mem. bd. dirs. and v.p. Farm and Trades Sch. Trustee Essex Agrl. Sch. Member Draft Appeal Bd., Essex County, A.A.A.S., Am. Mineral Soc., Am. Ornithologists Union, Am. Gem Society. Republican. Clubs: Union (Boston); Country of Brookline. Author: (with J. B. Woodworth) Geography and Geology of the Region, including Cape Cod, the Elizabeth Islands, Nantucket, Marthas Vineyard, No Man's Land and Block Island, 1934. Contributor to mags. Home: 7 Chestnut St. Address: 69 Newbury St., Boston, Mass.* Died May 6, 1945.

WIGHT, Francis Asa, clergyman; b. Andover, O., Feb. 16, 1854; s. John Norton and Susan Ann (West) W.; ed. Bible Coll., Transylvania U., Lexington, Ky.; m. Clara Marie Stone (grad. New Eng. Conservatory of Music), Sept. 27, 1886 (died 1904); children—Rev. Paul Stone, Francis Raymond. Ordained ministry Disciples of Christ, 1885; pastor Bedford, O., 1885-86, Miles Av. Ch., Cleveland, O., 1886-91, Central Ch., Los Angeles, Calif., 1892-94, Glendora, Calif., 1894-96; gen. evangelist, Andover, O., 1896-1903; pastor Erie, Pa., 1903-07, Pittsburgh, McKee's Rocks, Pa., 1909-16, St. James Street Christian Ch., Boston, 1916-18, Centre Street Baptist Ch., Boston, 1918-23; Duquesne, Pa., 1924-26, River Park, South Bend, Ind., 1927-31; evangelist, 1931-34. Republican. Author: The Kingdom of God, or The Reign of Heaven Among Men, 1923; Babylon, The Harlot, 1924; The Beast, Modernism and the Evangelical Faith, 1926; The Rapture or Translation of the Saints, 1929; God's Great Gift—The Holy Spirit, 1929; Revelation—Christ's Return, 1931; Heaven's Kingdom on Earth, 1935; Communism and Fascism Destroyed at Christ's Second Coming, 1937; America, God's Prepared Place, 1938; The Catching Up of Christ's True Church, 1939; The Gift of the Holy Spirit, 1940; The Time of the End, 1941; The Beast and the False Prophet and Hitler, 1941. Home: 547 Richmond Av., Buffalo, N.Y. Died Dec. 14, 1942.

WIGHT, William Drewin, architect; b. Halifax, N.S., Can., Jan. 22, 1882; s. Robert Adam and Emmaline (MacLean) W.; ed. high schools and architectural ateliers; studied in Europe for 1 year; m. Else Grant Symonds, June 16, 1910; children—Constance Symonds (Mrs. Donald Patterson), Jean MacLean. Came to U.S., 1900; naturalized, 1915. With McKim, Mead & White, N.Y. City, 1900-11; moved to Kansas City, Mo., 1911; mem. firm Wight & Wight. Among important buildings designed and supervised by firm: Mercy Hosp.; St. Mary's Chapel, Leavenworth; Clay County Court House; Pickwick Hotel and office building; Nettleton Home; Epperson Hall; Providence Hospital; Wyandotte County Court House; Southeast High School; Swope Memorial; Fountain, Frieze and Dedication Wall of Liberty Memorial; Swinney Gymnasium; William Rockhill Nelson Gallery of Art; Federal Courts Building; Municipal Courts and Police Building; Jackson County Court House (exterior design); City Hall of Kansas City; Greene Memorial Building and Administration Building of Wm. Jewell College; Asso. Architects Vet. Adminstrn. Hosp., Kansas City. Mem. Municipal Art Commn., 1924-40. Mem. Am.

Inst. Architects, Kansas City Art Inst. (bd. govs.), St. Andrews Soc. Episcopalian. Mason. Home: 1020 W. 56th St. Office: 923 Baltimore Av., Kansas City, Mo. Died Oct. 19, 1947; buried Mount Washington Cemetery.

WIGMORE, John Henry (wig'môr), prof. law; b. San Francisco, Calif., Mar. 4, 1863; s. John and Harriet (Joyner) W.; A.B., Harvard, 1883, A.M., LL.B., 1887; LL.D., U. of Wis., 1906, Harvard, 1909, Louvain, 1928, Northwestern, 1937, Lyon, 1939; m. Emma Hunt Vogl, Sept. 16, 1889. Practiced, Boston, 1887-89; prof. Anglo-American law, Keio Univ., Tokyo, 1889-92; prof. law since 1893, dean faculty of law, 1901-29 (emeritus), Northwestern U. Author: Digest of Decisions of the Massachusetts Railroad Commission, 1888; The Australian Ballot System, 1889; Notes on Land Tenure and Local Institutions in Old Japan, 1890; Materials for Study of Private Law in Old Japan, 1892, 1941; Treatise on Evidence (10 vols.), 1904-05, 1923, 1940; Pocket Code of Evidence, 1909, 1935, 1942; Principles of Judicial Proof, 1913, 1937; Student's Handbook of Evidence, 1935; Panorama of the World's Legal Systems, 1928, 36; Kaleidoscope of Justice, 1941. Editor: Greenleaf on Evidence (16th edit., Vol. 1), 1899; Compiled Examinations in Law, 1900; Cases on Torts (2 vols.), 1911; Cases on Evidence, 1913. Co-Editor: Select Essays in Anglo-American Legal History, 1907; Evolution of Law Series, 1915; Modern Criminal Science Series, 1910-1915; Modern Legal Philosophy Series, 1911-1921; Continental Legal History Series, 1912-1920. Also extensive contributor to legal publications and magazines. Pres. Am. Inst. Criminal Law and Criminology, 1909-10, Am. Assn. Univ. Profs., 1916. Commd. mem. staff of judge advocate gen. U.S. Army, with rank of maj., Aug. 1916; commd. lt. col. Feb. 1, 1918; col., June 9, 1918; hon. discharged, May 8, 1919. Awarded D.S.M. Mem. U.S. Sect. Inter-Am. High Commn., 1915-19. Hon. mem. Asiatic Soc. of Japan, 1914, Soc. of Teachers of Law (Eng.); corr. mem. Comité de Législation Etrangère (France); mem. Internat. Acad. of Comparative Law, League of Nations Com. on Intellectual Coöperation. Chevalier Legion of Honor (France), Aug. 1919; Order of Sacred Treasure (Japan), 1935; Am. Bar Assn. gold medal, 1932. Mem. Ill. Com. on Uniform State Laws, 1908-24 and since 1933. Home: 850 Lake Shore Drive. Address: 357 E. Chicago Av., Chicago, Ill. Died Apr. 20, 1943.

WILBUR, Ray Lyman, ex-secretary of the Interior, educator; b. Boonesboro, Ia., Apr. 13, 1875; s. Dwight Locke and Edna Maria (Lyman) W.; A.B., Stanford U., 1896, A.M., 1897; M.D., Cooper Med. Coll., San Francisco, 1899; student in medicine, Frankfurt-on-Main, and London, 1903-04, Univ. of Munich, 1909-10; LL.D., U. of Calif., 1919, U. of Ariz., 1919, U. of Pa., 1925, U. of N.M., 1928, U. of Chicago, U. of Pittsburgh, 1929, U. of Md., Duke U., Princeton, U. of Rochester, 1930, U. of Puerto Rico, New York U., Yale U., Univ. State of New York, Tusculum Coll., Univ. of So. Calif., 1931, Dartmouth, Ill. Wesleyan, 1932; Sc.D., Syracuse, 1924, Western Reserve, 1931; M.A. in Med., Hahnemann Med. Coll., Phila., 1930; m. Marguerite May Blake, Dec. 5, 1898; children—Mrs. Jessica Ely, Blake Colburn, Dwight Locke, Mrs. Lois Proctor Hopper, Ray Lyman. Instr. physiology, Stanford U., 1896-97; lecturer and demonstrator, physiology, Cooper Med. Coll., 1899-1900; asst. prof. physiology, Stanford U., 1900-03, prof. medicine, 1909-16, dean of Med. Sch., 1911-16, pres., Stanford, 1916-43; chancellor since 1943; on leave absence, 1929-33; sec. of Interior in cabinet of President Hoover, 1929-33. Chief, conservation div. U.S. Food Adminstrn., Washington, D.C., 1917; mem. Calif. State Council Defense (later War Council), 1917, and 1941-46; mem. Calif. State War Problems Bd., 1944-46; mem. citizens adv. com. Calif. State Reconstrn. and Reemployment Commn. and citizens adv. com. on Coordination of Research Facilities, 1944-46; mem. youth adv. com. U.S. Office Civilian Defense, 1943-46; chmn. Citizens Com. on Student Nurse Recruitment, 1944-46; consultant Navy Coll. Training Program since 1943; chmn. adv. com. Army Specialized Training Program since 1943. Pres. Calif. State Conf. Social Agencies, 1919, Council of Social and Health Agencies, San Francisco, 1922-25; v.p. San Francisco Community Chest, 1927-29, mem. bd. dirs., 1926-29, and since 1939; mem. Calif. State Park Commn., 1928-29; chmn. Fed. Oil Conservation Bd., 1929-33; mem. Migratory Bird Conservation Commn., and of Timber Conservation Bd., 1929-33; pres. Better Homes in America, 1929-35; chmn. White House Conf. on Child Health and Protection, 1929-31; chmn. Nat. Adv. Com. on Illiteracy, 1930-31. Trustee Rockefeller Foundation, 1923-40, Gen. Edn. Bd., 1930-40, Austin Riggs Foundation since 1944, Nutrition Foundation since 1942. Fellow A.A.A.S.; mem. Am. Acad. Medicine (pres. 1912-13), A.M.A. (pres. 1923-24; mem. council on med. edn. and hosps. 1920-23 and since 1925, chmn. 1929-46), Assn. Am. Med. Colls. (pres. 1924), Calif. Acad. Medicine (pres. 1917-18). Mem. med. adv. bd. Am. Leprosy Foundation since 1936; mem. med. council U.S. Vets. Bureau, 1924-41, chmn. 1924-29; pres. Calif. Soc. Promotion Med. Research, 1938; v.p. Research Council on Problems of Alcohol since 1944; chmn. Com. on Costs of Med. Care, 1927-35; pres. Calif. Physicians Service, 1939-45; mem. citizens planning com. Nat. Health Council Com. on Voluntary Health Agencies, 1946; pres. Am. Social Hygiene Assn. since 1936; mem. exec. bd. American Physiotherapy Assn. since 1944; chmn. Baruch Com. on Phys. Medicine since 1943. U.S. del. 6th Pan. Am. Conf., Havana, 1928; chmn. exec. com. Survey Race Relations on Pacific Coast, 1922-24; chmn. Inst. Pacific Relations, 1925-29 (chmn. Honolulu confs., 1925, 27; mem. Pacific Council and chmn. Am. Council, 1941; chmn. exec. com. San Francisco Bay Region Div. since 1936); chmn. control com. Bay Region Div. since 1936); chmn. central com. World Citizens Assn., 1938 40; pres. Pacific House, Inc., 1941; sponsor Japanese-Am. Citizens League since 1943; trustee Chinese Mass. Edn. Movement in U.S. since 1944; mem. Council Against Intolerance in America since 1943; mem. adv. council Students Internat. Union, Inc., since 1944; dir. Am. Soc. French Legion of Honor, 1944-45; adviser pub. welfare dept. Gen. Fedn. Womens Clubs since 1944; nat. pres. Motion Picture Research Council since 1935; v.p. nat. council Boy Scouts America since 1942, mem. nat. exec. bd., 1939-45, mem. adv. council since 1945; chmn. health com. Boys Clubs America since 1940; mem. bd. trustees Allied Youth since 1941. Charter Day speaker U. of Calif., 1941. Mem. Newcomen Soc., Phi Beta Kappa, Sigma Xi, Alpha Omega Alpha. Decorated Comdr. Order of Leopold II, Honor Cross of German Red Cross, Chevalier French Legion of Honor; recipient Dr. Wm. F. Snow medal for distinguished service to humanity, 1943. Clubs: Commonwealth, Bohemian, Pacific Union, Family (San Francisco); Cosmos, Nat. Press (Washington); Century (New York). Author: Annual Reports of the Secretary of the Interior, 1929, 30, 31, 32; Hoover Dam Contracts (with Northcutt Ely), 1933; Construction of Hoover Dam (with Elwood Mead), 1933; Conservation (with Wm. Atherton DuPuy), 1931; Stanford Horizons, 1936; Hoover Policies (with Arthur M. Hyde), 1937; March of Medicine, 1938; Human Hopes, 1940. Home: Stanford University, Calif. Died June 26, 1949.

WILBUR, Sibyl (Mrs. Sibyl Wilbur Stone), author, retired journalist; b. Elmira, N.Y., May 27, 1871; d. Dewitt Clinton and Anna Ballard (McKee) Wilbur; prep. edn., Minneapolis (Minn.) Acad.; student Hamline U.; m. John Stone Stone, Nov. 28, 1918. Formerly with Minneapolis Jour., Washington, New York, Chicago and Boston dailies, also contbr. to Woman's Home Companion and Collier's Mag. An organizer Woman's Suffrage Party, N.Y. City, and leader 14th Assembly Dist., 1911-12. Christian Scientist. Republican. Clubs: Nat. Arts (New York); Wednesday Club, University Women's (San Diego). Author: The Life of Mary Baker Eddy, 1908 (translated into French and German). Made a year's sojourn in Europe and Near East, 1928, and was presented at Egyptian Court in Cairo, to King Fuad, who gave a pvt. audience. Home: 3942 Alameda Drive, San Diego, Calif. Died July 21, 1946.

WILBUR, William Allen, univ. prof.; b. Mystic, Conn., Aug. 15, 1864; s. John Palmer and Elizabeth Jones (Gallup) W.; A.B., Brown, 1888, A.M., 1894, Litt.D., 1916; LL.D., George Washington U., 1931; m. Hannah, d. Rev. Samuel J. and Sabrina (Packer) Knapp, Dec. 18, 1889 (died Jan. 5, 1938); children—Elizabeth Sabrina (dec.), William Knapp; married 2d, Marian Lund, December 26, 1941. Teacher, Vermont Academy, 1888-89, Colby Acad., New London, N.H., 1889-90, Howard Sem., West Bridgewater, Mass., 1890-95; dean Columbian Acad. (now George Washington U.), 1895-97; prof. English, George Washington U., 1897-1935; dean Columbian Coll. (collegiate dept. George Washington U.), 1904-28; provost George Washington U., 1928-35, prof. emeritus, English, since 1935. Moderator Columbia Assn. Baptist Churches, 1913-16. Mem. Delta Kappa Epsilon, Phi Beta Kappa. Author: English, Rhetoric, 1913; Chronicles of Calvary Baptist Church in the City of Washington, 1913; History of the Columbia Association of Baptist Churches, 1928; The Ministry of Samuel Harrison Greene, 1936. Address: George Washington University, Washington, D.C.* Died Jan. 25, 1945.

WILCOX, John C., voice teacher; b. Sebewaing, Mich., May 5, 1870; s. William and Catherine (Edgcombe) W.; prep. edn., pub. schs.; musical edn., Mehan Sch. Vocal Art, Detroit, and under pvt. teachers, New York and Chicago; Mus.M., Denver (Colo.) Coll. Music, 1922; m. Caroline L. Fenton, Dec. 8, 1896; 1 dau., Martha. Began as baritone singer, Detroit, 1892; editor Song Journal (Detroit), 1894-95. The Concert-Goer (New York), 1896-1902; baritone soloist, chs., concerts and oratorios, also voice teacher, New York, 1903-06; condr. Wilcox Studios, Denver, 1907-27; dir. Denver Coll. Music, 1927-33; now teaching singing at Am. Conservatory of Music, and speech at the Meadville Theological School, Chicago. Director Denver Municipal Chorus, 1917-21. Regional song leader during the First World War. Member American Academy Teachers of Singing, Chicago Singing Teachers Guild, Music Teachers National Assn. (dir.), Nat. Assn. Teachers of Singing (past pres.), Pro Musica Soc., Sinfonia. Clubs: Rotary, Lakewood Country. Author: Vocal Guide for Song and Speech, 1925; The Living Voice, 1935; Voice Training for Speech and Choric Reading, 1938. Home: 116 E. San Rafael St., Colorado Springs, Colo. Died Nov. 20, 1947.

WILCOX, John Walter, Jr., naval officer; b. Milledgeville, Ga., Mar. 22, 1882; s. John Wesley and Anna Gray (Holmes) W.; ed. elementary and high sch., Macon, 1888-89; B.S., U.S. Naval Acad., 1905; grad. Naval War Coll., 1924; m. Caroline Manigault, Dec. 22, 1919; children—Arthur, Mary. Commd. ensign, U.S. Navy, 1905, and promoted through the grades to rear adm., 1938. Awarded special letter of Commendation by Navy Dept. for service in World War; decorated Mexican Campaign medal, World War medal with Silver Star, Am. Red Cross silver medal, Italian Croce Rossi silver medal. Mem. Sons of Confederate Vets. Episcopalian. Clubs: Army and Navy (Washington, D.C.); New York Yacht. Home: Kenwood, Chevy Chase, Md. Address: Navy Dept., Washington, D.C. Died Mar. 27, 1942.

WILCOX, Nelson James, retired atty., born in Eau Claire, Wisconsin, January 27, 1875; s. Nelson Chapman and Angeline Therese (Tewkesbury) W.; ed. pub. and high schs., Eau Claire; LL.B., U. of Wis., 1901; m. Mary R. McDonough, Sept. 30, 1903 (died 1916); children—Mary Petronilla (Mrs. A. Clayton Rector), Nelson J., Catherine Porter (Mrs. Fletcher C. Davis), Angeline Tewkesbury; m. 2d, Marion G. Richardson, Aug. 31, 1917; 1 son, Beverly Nelson. Admitted to bar, 1901; law clk. Isham, Lincoln & Beale, Chicago, 1901-02; atty. C.,St.P., M.&O. Ry. Co., at St. Paul, 1902-08; atty. C.,M.& St.P. Ry. Co., at Minneapolis, 1908-19; corp. atty. C.& N.W. Ry. Co., Chicago, 1919-20; asst. gen. solicitor same rd., 1920-1942., gen. solicitor same rd. and C.,St.P., M.&O. Ry. Co., 1942-45; retired from ry. service Feb. 1, 1945. Mem. Am. Bar Assn., S.A.R., Phi Delta Theta, Phi Delta Phi. Republican. Home: 1101 Ridge Av., Evanston, Ill. Died May 20, 1949; buried Lakewood Cemetery, Minneapolis.

WILCOX, Roy Porter, lawyer; b. Eau Claire, Wis., June 30, 1873; s. Nelson Chapman and Angeline (Tewkesbury) W.; LL.B., Cornell U. Law School, 1897; m. Luisa Maria de Freyre y Santander, June 17, 1903 (died Mar. 24, 1928); children—Luisa Maria, Francis John. Admitted to Wis. bar, 1896; practiced at Eau Claire since 1897; senior mem. Wilcox, Wilcox & Sullivan; gen. counsel Union Nat. Bank, and counsel or dir. various other corps.; mem. State Senate, Wis., 1917-20; as chmn. Joint Com. on Reconstruction of Wis. Legislature drafted "Reconstruction" program, 1918; mem. Legal Advisory Board under Selective Service Act. Republican candidate for gov. of Wis., 1918, 20, for U.S. Senate, 1925. Mem. advisory bd. Marquette U. Mem. Am. Law Inst., Am. Bar Assn., Wis. State Bar Assn. (pres. 1925-26), Nineteenth Circuit Bar Assn., Eau Claire County Bar Assn. (past pres.), S.A.R., Phi Delta Phi. Republican. K.C. (4th degree), Elk. Clubs: Cornell Savage, Masque, Glee, Elks, Eau Claire Rod and Gun, Eau Claire Country; University (Milwaukee). Contbr. on law and administrative topics. Home: 104 Wilcox Av. Office: Union National Bank Bldg., Eau Claire, Wis. Died May 20, 1946.

WILCOX, William Walter, mfr.; b. Middletown, Conn., Apr. 11, 1862; s. William Walter and Elizabeth (Crittenden) W.; B.A., Williams, 1885; m. Mary Root, Nov. 3, 1886; children—Pauline Root (Mrs. Julius B. Smith), William Walter (dec.). Now v.p. Wilcox, Crittenden & Co., mfrs. marine hardware (founded 1847); dir. Farmers & Mechanics Savings Bank; ex-mem. Conn. Ho. of Rep.; dir. Middletown Nat. Bank 25 yrs. Trustee and sec. bd. Conn. Hosp. for Insane 24 yrs. (resigned, 1931); trustee, chmn. bd. Long Lane Farm. Chmn. Middlesex County Red Cross, World War; mem. Conn. State Guard. Trustee Russell Library. Mem. Archeol. Soc. America. Republican. Conglist. Mem. Middlesex County Hist. Soc. (dir.), S.A.R., S.C.W., Williams-Conn. Alumni Assn. (pres.), Sigma Phi (Williams Coll. Chapter). Club: University (New York). Home: 271 Washington Terrace, Middletown, Conn. Died June 12, 1941.

WILDE, Arthur Herbert (wild), univ. pres.; b. Framingham, Mass., Apr. 29, 1865; s. Joseph and Susan Emily (French) W.; A.B., Boston U., 1887, S.T.B., 1891; Harvard Grad. Sch., 1898-1901, A.M., 1899, Ph.D., 1901; m. Sarah Frances Fellows, Sept. 6, 1892. Instr. Tilton (N.H.) Sem., 1887-89; instr. history, Acad. of Northwestern U., 1892-1901; instr. history, Northwestern U., 1893-1901; on leave of absence, 1898-1900; asst. prof. history, 1901-05, prof., 1905-11, Northwestern U.; prin. Evanston Acad. of Northwestern U., 1904-11; asst. to the pres., and sec. of the Univ. Council, same, 1909-11; pres. U. of Ariz., May 1911-Sept. 1914; prof. edn., 1914-35, dir., later dean Sch. of Edn., 1918-35, dean emeritus since 1935, Boston U. Republican. Conglist. Contbr. to mags. and revs. on culture of early middle ages and gen. ednl. matters. Home: 143 Fair Oaks Park, Needham, Mass.* Died Jan. 1944.

WILDER, Gerald Gardner, librarian; b. Pembroke, Me., Apr. 30, 1879; s. Albion and Arabella Libby (Gardner) W.; A.B., Bowdoin Coll., 1904, hon. A.M., 1929; m. Kathleen Eliot Hobart, July 16, 1908. Connected with Bowdoin Coll. Library since 1899, librarian since 1915. Mem. Me. Library Assn. (ex-pres.), Am. Hist. Assn., N.E. Historic-Geneal. Soc., Gen. Alumni Assn. Bowdoin (treas.), Phi Beta Kappa (ex-v.p. Bowdoin Chapter). Republican. Conglist. Home: Brunswick, Me.; (summer) Garnett's Head, Pembroke, Me. Died June 28, 1944.

WILDER, John Thomas, soldier; b. Hunter Village, N.Y., Jan. 31, 1830; s. Reuben and Mary (Merritt) W.; ed. pub. schs., N.Y.; m. Martha Stewart, May 18, 1858 (died 1892); 2d, Dora E. Lee, 1904. Served 7 yrs. apprenticeship at iron business, as draughtsman, machinist, pattern-maker and millwright until 1852; built and operated gen-machine and millwright works until Civil War; enlisted in Ind. as pvt. 1st Independent Battery Arty., April 21, 1861, and elected capt. same day; made lt.-col. 17th Ind. Inf., June 12 1861; col., Mar. 12, 1862; first in command brigade, Dec. 20, 1862; on June 24 cut his way through Confederate lines at Hoover's Gap, Tenn., against heavy odds, compelling Bragg to evacuate

Tennessee; led Rosecrans army to Chattanooga; shelled latter place 18 days and entered city Sept. 9, 1863; began great battle of Chickamauga Sept. 18, and brigade lines were not broken during the 3-days' battle; bvtd. brig.-gen. and brigade named "Wilder's Lightning Brigade" by gen. order. Organized, 1867, Roane Iron Works; built and operated 2 blast furnaces at Rockwood, Tenn. (first in South); built rail mill, Chattanooga, 1870; has been active in mineral development of Tennessee ever since. Gen. mgr. Roane Iron Co.; pres. and propr. Wilder Machine Works; v.p. C., C. & C. R.R.; pres. Roane Mountain Hotel Co.; gen. mgr. Fentress Coal & Coke Co.; v.p. and gen. mgr. Knoxville Power Co. Republican; U.S. Pension agt. at Knoxville, Tenn. Mem. Soc. Army of the Cumberland, Loyal Legion (Ohio), Nat. Geog. Soc., Iron and Steel Inst., Great Britain, Am. Inst. Mining Engrs. Address: Cherry Hill, Knoxville, Tenn. Died Oct. 20, 1917.

WILE, Ira Solomon, physician; b. Rochester, N.Y., Nov. 29, 1877; s. Solomon and Amelia (Meyer) W.; A.B. and B.S., U. of Rochester, 1898, M.S., 1908; M.D., U. of Pa., 1902; m. Saide E. Rigby, Sept. 27, 1905; children—Ira Rigby, Rigby, Alan Rigby, Mildred Rigby. Formerly lecturer in ednl. hygiene, New York U., and lecturer in dietetics and nutrition, dept. dental hygiene, Columbia; commr. of edn., N.Y. City, 1912-18. Mem. New York Milk Com.; a founder, N.Y. school lunch system, Manhattanville Nursery; founder Nat. Round Table for Speech Improvement, Assn. for Personality Training (pres. 1929-41); officer or dir. various philanthropic orgns. Editor Med. Review of Reviews, 1912-16; editor dept. surg. sociology, Am. Jour. Surgery, 1910-21; editor Med. Pickwick, 1921-22; asso. editor Am. Medicine, 1916-35; lecturer Am. Social Hygiene Assn., New School for Social Research, New York U., Coll. Phys. and Surg. (Columbia), Hunter Coll., Coll. City of New York, Brooklyn Coll.; asso. in pediatrics, Mt. Sinai Hosp. Mem. Nat. Com. for Mental Hygiene, Internat. Com. for Mental Hygiene. Fellow Am. Psychiatric Assn., Am. Pub. Health Assn., Am. Orthopsychiatric Assn. (pres. 1932), Am. Speech Correction Assn.; mem. A.A.A.S., Am., N.Y. State and County med. socs., Am. Acad. Polit. and Social Science, Am. Child Health Assn., Soc. for the Advancement of Education, Phi Beta Kappa. Republican. Jewish religion. Club: Civic (ex-pres.). Author: Blood Examinations in Surgery, 1908; Sex Education, 1912; The Challenge of Childhood, 1925; Marriage in the Modern Manner, 1929; Handedness—Right and Left; The Man Takes a Wife, 1937. Editor: Sex Life of the Unmarried Adult; Personality Development and Social Control in Terms of Constitution and Culture, 1939; The Challenge of Adolescence, 1939. Asso. editor Am. Jour. Orthopsychiatry; The Nervous Child. Home: 264 W. 73d St., New York, N.Y. Died Oct. 9, 1943.

WILES, Charles Peter (wilz), clergyman, editor; b. Lewistown, Md., Jan. 27, 1870; s. Americus G. P. and Sarah S. (Hummer) W.; ed. Millersville (Pa.) Normal Sch.; student Luth. Theol. Sem., Gettysburg, Pa., 1893-96; hon. A.M., Pa. Coll., Gettysburg, 1906; D.D., Carthage Coll., 1913; m. M. Alice Miller, June 10, 1896. Ordained Luth. ministry, 1896; pastor Rossville, Pa., 1896-1901, Pittsburgh, 1901-08, Washington, D.C., 1908-13; editor Lutheran Publ. Soc., Phila., 1913-18, United Luth. Publ. House, Phila., since 1918. Home: 259 Harvey St., Germantown. Office: Muhlenberg Bldg., Phila., Pa. Died Oct. 6, 1944.

WILES, Irving Ramsay, painter; b. Utica, N.Y., Apr. 8, 1861; s. Lemuel M. and Rachel (Ramsay) W.; ed. Sedgwick Inst., Great Barrington, Mass.; pupil in art of L. M. Wiles, Carroll Beckwith, William M. Chase and Carolus Duran; m. May Lee, 1887; 1 dau., Gladys Lee. Awarded third Hallgarten prize, Nat. Acad. Design; T. B. Clarke prize, same; hon. mention Paris Expn., 1889; medal, Chicago Expn., 1893; medal, Tennessee Centennial Expn.; prize, Soc. Washington Artists; gold medal, Buffalo Expn.; W. T. Evans prize, Am. Water Color Soc.; Shaw Fund, Soc. Am. Artists, 1900; medal, Paris Expn., 1900; gold medal, St. Louis Expn., 1904; silver medal, Appalachian Expn., 1910; gold medal, Exposicion Internacional de Arte, Buenos Aires, 1910; gold medal, Panama P.I. Expn., 1915, Palmer Prize, N.A.D., 1931, Proctor Prize, 1936; Medal of Honor, American Artists Professional League, 1943; 1st prize, Lotus Club, 1944. N.A., 1897; member National Institute Arts and Letters, American Water Color Soc., Nat. Acad. Design, Paris Soc. Am. Artists, Assn. Portrait Painters, Allied Artists America, Century Assn., Nat. Arts Club, Lotos Club. Home: Peconic, L.I., N.Y. Died July 29, 1948.

WILEY, Henry Ariosto, naval officer; b. Troy, Ala., Jan. 31, 1867; grad. U.S. Naval Acad., 1888. Ensign, July 1, 1890; promoted through grades to capt., Apr. 23, 1915. Served on Maple, Spanish-Am. War, 1898; comd. Standish, 1905; at U.S. Naval Acad., 1905-06; on Constellation, 1906-07; exec. officer, Kentucky, 1907-09; with Bur. of Navigation, Navy Dept., 1909-12; comd. Monterey, 1912, Saratoga, 1912-13; mem. Bd. Inspection and Survey Ships, Navy Dept., 1914-15; comd. New Jersey, 1916; apptd. comdr. Wyoming, June 17, 1916; served with 6th Battle Squadron Brit. Grand Fleet; temp. rear admiral, 1918; comdr. destroyers, Pacific Fleet, 1919-20; vice-admiral, 1923-25; Gen. Bd., 1925-27; comdr. U.S. Fleet with rank of admiral, 1927-29; retired Sept. 1929. Apptd. mem. Textile Labor Relations Bd., Sept. 1934; also mem. Steel Bd. Apptd. mem. U.S. Maritime Commn. 1936 for period of 4 yrs. Home: 1870 Wyoming Av. N.W., Washington, D.C. Died May 20, 1943.

WILGUS, William John, engr.; b. Buffalo, N.Y., Nov. 20, 1865; s. Frank Augustus and Margaret Ann (Woodcock) W.; grad. Buffalo Central High Sch., 1883; pupil in civ. engring., Buffalo, 1883-85; hon. D.E., Stevens Inst. Tech., 1921, U. of Vt., 1927; m. May Reed, Mar. 1, 1892 (died Oct. 2, 1918); m. 2d, Gertrude Bernadette Tobin, June 16, 1919. Rodman, draftsman, resident engr., div. engr., constrn. Minn. & Northwestern R.R. and its successor the C.,St.P.& K.C. Ry. (now C.G.W. Ry.), 1885-91; locating engr. Duluth & Winnipeg R.R., and Duluth & Iron Range R.R. extension to Mesabe range and resident engr. in charge constrn. Chicago Union Transfer Ry., 1890-93; with N.Y.C.&H.R. R.R. during rehabilitation, as assistant engineer Rome, Watertown & Ogdensburg div., 1893-97, chief engr. Terminal Ry. of Buffalo, 1895-98, resident engr., Eastern div., 1897, chief asst. engr., 1898, engr. maintenance of way, 1898-99, chief engr. constrn., and maintenance of way, enlargement of terminals, bridges, etc., including Grand Central Sta., New York and Weehawken terminals, 1899-1903, v.p. in gen. charge of constrn., including new extensions, change of motive power from steam to electricity and other improvements in New York electric zone, and inception and creation of new Grand Central Terminal, Feb. 1903-Sept. 1907; chairman Buffalo Union Station Committee, 1907; chmn. advisory bd. of engrs. for constrn. of tunnel under Detroit River, Detroit, connecting M.C. R.R. and Canada Southern Ry., 1905-10. Private consulting practice, 1908-20; chmn. bd. cons. engrs. for building interstate vehicular tunnel of States of N.Y. and N.J. beneath North River, New York, 1919-22; cons. engr. proposed railroad tunnel under The Narrows for City of New York, 1921-22; cons. engr. N.Y. Transit Commn., 1923-24; same to Regional Plan of New York and its Environs; cons. to rys., industries, states and Fed. Government. During World War mem. mil. ry. commn. to England and France; dir. mil. rys. and deputy dir. gen. transportation, A.E.F., rank col. U.S. Army. Awarded D.S.M. (U.S.), Officer Legion of Honor (France), Conspicuous Service Cross, State of N.Y. Mem. Art Commn. City of New York, 1922-24; director Work Relief, N.Y., 1934-35; War Dept. advisor, World War II, 1941-42. Hon. mem. Am. Society C.E. (Rowland prize, 1909; Wellington prize, 1942; past director, past pres., Metropolitan section); member American Railway Engring. Assn., Am. Ry. Guild, Engrs. Soc. of St. Paul, Vt. Soc. Engrs., Vt. Hist. Soc., N.E. Soc., Art Commn. Associates (New York), Am. Hist. Assn., Soc. Mayflower Descendants, S.A.R., Inst. C.E. Great Britain (Telford gold medal, 1911); hon. mem. Am. Inst. Architects. Clubs: Century (New York); University (Winter Park, Florida). Author: Transporting the A.E.F. in Western Europe, 1931; The Railway Interrelations of the United States and Canada, 1937; The Grand Central Terminal in Perspective, 1940; Life of Captain Stewart Degan, A Character of the American Revolution, 1942; The Role of Transportation in the Development of Vermont, 1945; also papers and articles on engring. subjects and public affairs. Home: 203 Broad St., Claremont, N.H. Died Oct. 24, 1949.

WILEY, William Foust, editor; b. Tarlton, Ohio, s. Ingham and Ella (Foust) W.; B.S., Heidelberg College, Tiffin, O., 1898; LL.D., Lincoln Memorial U., 1928; Litt.D., Heidelberg Coll., 1940; m. Flora Lorene Arnold, August 20, 1899; children—Donald Arnold, Andrew Foust, William Urner, Margaret Elinor. Began newspaper work at Washington, D.C., 1899; mng. editor Cincinnati Enquirer, 1901-18, gen. mgr., 1918-36, publisher since 1936; trustee Cincinnati Southern Ry. Mem. Ohio State Office Bldg. Commn.; chmn. State Commn. on Stream Pollution in Ohio River Valley. Chmn. bd. Cincinnati Chamber of Commerce; chmn. federal laws committee and chairman committee on wage and hours, American Newspaper Publishers Association. Clubs: Cuvier Press, Queen City, Cincinnati Club, Cincinnati Country, Cincinnati Golf, Camargo Country, Commercial. Home: 2750 Baker Pl., E. Walnut Hills. Office: 617 Vine St., Cincinnati, O. Died Aug. 24, 1944.

WILHELM, Donald, writer for magazines and lecturer; b. Defiance, O., Jan. 23, 1887; s. John and Agnes Navarre (Marantette) W.; ed. Hobart Coll., 1905-06, George Washington U., 1906-07, Harvard, 1908-12; m. Nina M. Warren, July 6, 1914; children—Donald, Warren, Jean. Mem. staff Buffalo (N.Y.) Courier and editor Lackawanna News, 1905; mem. staff of the Washington Post, and private secretary to congressman, 1906-07; mem. staff Boston Herald, 1907-08; editor the first aviation paper, Aero Daily News, Boston, 1908; corr. Summer Capital, Beverly, Mass., 1909; mem. staff U.S. Com. on Pub. Information, Washington, 1917-18; Washington corr. The Independent, 1918-22; was personal asst. to Secretary (later President) Hoover, 1922, 23, including six months' travel in Russia; Chautauqua lecturer, summer 1923; staff writer for World's Work, 1924-29; contbr. since 1911 articles to mags. including Liberty, Saturday Evening Post, Esquire, Harpers, Reader's Digest (including two in collaboration with Congressman Ross A. Collins, and "Radar, the greatest secret weapon of the war"), Country Gentleman, Collier's, etc., and of short stories to other magazines, and 150 studies of industry. Mem. Theta Delta Chi. Clubs: Correspondents', Harvard (N.Y.); Overseas, Cosmos (Washington, D.C.). Author: Theodore Roosevelt as an Undergraduate, 1910; The Story of Steel, 1915, revised edit., 1937; Writing for Profit, 1930; revised edit., 1937; The Book of Metals, 1931; Your Home and the Government, 1934; The Story of Iron and Steel, 1934; In the Steel Mill, etc. Correspondent for Reader's Digest, Liberty in England, 1942. Home: Riverside, Conn. Died Feb. 25, 1945.

WILKERSON, James Herbert, lawyer; b. Savannah, Mo., Dec. 11, 1869; s. John W. and Lydia (Austin) W.; A.B., DePauw U., Greencastle, Ind., 1889, LL.D., 1930; D.C.L., Ill. Wesleyan U., 1931; m. Mary Roth, Aug. 21, 1891; 1 son, Conrad D. Prin. high sch., Hastings, Neb., 1890-91; instr. DePauw U., 1891-93; practiced law at Chicago, 1893-1922; mem. firms Tenney, Coffeen, Harding & Wilkerson, and Wilkerson, Cassels & Potter. Mem. Ill. Ho. of Reps., 1902; county atty. Cook County, Ill., 1903-04; spl. asst. to atty. gen. of U.S., 1906-11; U.S. atty. Northern Dist. of Ill., 1911-14; chmn. Pub Utilities Commn. of Ill., 1919-21; U.S. dist. judge Northern Dist. of Ill., 1922-41. Mem. Phi Beta Kappa, Phi Delta Theta, Delta Chi. Clubs: Union League, University, Law, Skokie. Home: Glencoe, Ill. Address: 231 S. La Salle St., Chicago, Ill. Died Sept. 30, 1948.

WILKINS, Lawrence Augustus, educator; b. Des Moines, Ia., Nov. 11, 1878; s. Robert Henderson and Mary Frances (Guild) W.; Ph.B., Syracuse University, 1904; university scholar in Romance Languages, Columbia, 1905-07, A.M., 1907; m. Minnie Luella Roberts, Sept. 12, 1905 (died March 9, 1944); m. 2d, Opal Willard Gray, Oct. 7, 1944. Began teaching at Cheltenham Academy, Ogontz, Pa., 1907-14; teacher Spanish and French in high schools, New York City, 1907-14; head department of Spanish, DeWitt Clinton High Sch., N.Y. City, 1914-17; in charge modern langs., high schools, N.Y. City, 1917-19, dir. same, 1920-34, dir. of foreign languages, Jan. 1, 1935-Aug. 31, 1940; now retired; instr. in Spanish, extension teaching, Columbia, 1916-38; visiting prof. of Spanish, U. of Southern Calif., summer 1919; visiting prof. to Spain, Oct.-Dec. 1921, lecturing on modern lang. methodology, Junta para Ampliación de Estudios, Ministry of Public Instruction, Madrid, and in the universities of Valencia and Barcelona and in the Ateneo of Madrid; visiting prof. modern langs., U. of Wyo., summer 1928; head dept. Romance langs. and of Romance Lang. House, summer session, U. of Denver, 1931 and 1932. Chief founder and mem. Am. Assn. Teachers of Spanish (pres. 1918-20 and 1927; first v.p. 1923-26); one of founders and mem. gen. exec. council Instituto de las Españas; hon. mem. Société des Professeurs Français en Amérique; mem. Am. Assn. Teachers of French, Phi Beta Kappa, Pi Gamma Mu; corr. mem. Hispanic Society America. Comendador con Placa de la Real Orden de Isabel la Católica, by King Alfonso, 1921; Officier d'Académie (France), 1933; gold medalist Pan-American Society, 1937. Republican. Author: (with M. A. Luria) Lecturas Fáciles, 1916; Elementary Spanish Prose Book, 1917; (with Walter L. Hervey and others) Premier Secours—First Aid in Learning French, 1917; Unit Passages for Translation (into Spanish), 1918; Spanish in the High Schools—A Handbook of Methods, 1918; First Spanish Book, 1919; Second Spanish Book, 1920; Prognosis Test in Modern Languages, 1920; Beginners' Spanish Reader, 1921; Compendio de Gramática Española, 1920; Exercise Book in Spanish (with H. Alpern), 1921; La enseñanza de lenguas modernas en los Estados Unidos, 1922; First French Book, 1923; Spanish Reference Grammar, 1923; Antología de cuentos americanos, 1924; New First Spanish Book, 1925; (with Catharine R. Santelli) Beginners' Italian Reader, 1925; Achievement Tests in Spanish, 1925; New Second Spanish Book, 1926; New Spanish Reader for Beginners, 1930; Intermediate Spanish Reader, 1931; Primeros Pasos en Español, 1932; Segundos Pasos en Español, 1933; (with H. Alpern) Nuevos Ejercicios, 1933; (with A. L. Oller) Cuentecitos, 1934; Quinito, Explorador del Mundo, 1935; Quinito en España, 1940; Quinito en América, 1940. Editor: (with Mary E. Nash) Three One-Act Plays of Martinez Sierra, 1930; An Omnibus of Modern Spanish Prose, 1937. Editor of High Points (high schs. of N.Y. City), 1917-40. Home: "Miramontes," Estes Park, Colo. Died Dec. 24, 1945.

WILKINS, Thomas Russell, prof. physics; born Toronto, Ont., Can., June 6, 1891; s. Thomas and Annie (Cornell) W.; B.A., McMaster U. (Can.), 1912; Ph.D., U. of Chicago, 1921; grad. study, Cambridge (Eng.), 1925-26; m. Olive Cross, June 17, 1913. Science master Woodstock Coll. (Can.), 1913-14; instr. physics, U. of Chicago, 1916-17; prof. physics, Brandon (Can.) Coll., 1918-25, U. of Rochester since 1925; dir. Inst. of Optics, Rochester, since 1928. Served as master signal electrician, U.S. Signal Corps, 1917-18. Mem. Am. Phys. Soc., Optical Soc. Am., A.A.A.S., Am. Assn. Univ. Profs., Am. Assn. Physics Teachers, Sigma Xi, Alpha Chi. Baptist. Club: Fortnightly. Editor (with others) Orientation Course in Natural Science 1938. Contbr. tech. articles on radioactivity, atomic physics, photographic research. Secured photographic recordings of cosmic rays and of successive disintegrations of radium atoms. Home: Rochester, N.Y. Died Dec. 10, 1940.

WILKINSON, Howard Sargent, clergyman; b. Philadelphia, Pa.; s. Zimri and Emma Frances (Garwood) W.; A.B. and A.M., Dickinson Coll.; S.T.B., Boston U. Sch. of Theol., B.D., Episcopal Theol. Sch., Cambridge, Mass.; D.D., U. of Southern Calif. and Dickinson Coll.; m. Helen Adams Treadwell; 1 dau., Madeleine. Deacon P.E. Ch., 1912, priest, 1912; asst. rector, St. Paul Ch., New Haven, Conn., 1912, minister in charge, 1912-13; rector Emmanuel Ch., West Roxbury, Boston, Mass., 1913-31; asst. to the dean, Cathedral of the Incarnation, Garden

City, L.I., N.Y., 1931-36; rector St. Thomas' Ch., Washington, D.C., since Dec. 1936. Sec. of standing com., mem. exec. council, pres. of clericus and alternate deputy to Gen. Conv., all in Diocese of Washington. Served as captain, chaplain, U.S. Army, now maj., chaplain, O.R.C. Mason. Sojourner. Clubs: University, Torch, Cosmopolitan, Army and Navy Country Club. Contbr. to jours. Home: 1320 New Hampshire. Av. Office: 1772 Church St., Washington, D.C. Died Aug. 1, 1948.

WILKINSON, Theodore S., naval officer; b. Annapolis, Md., Dec. 22, 1888; s. Ernest and Gulielma Caroline (Bostick) W.; student St. Pauls School, Concord, N.H., 1902-05; B.S., U.S. Naval Acad., 1909; M.S., George Washington U., 1912; m. Catherine Dorsey Harlow, Dec. 17, 1918; children—Ann Harlow, Joan Susannah, Theodore S. Commd. ensign, U.S. Navy, 1911, and advanced through the grades to rear adm., Nov. 1941; served as experimental officer, Bureau of Ordnance, Navy Dept., World War I; sec. Navy General Board, 1931-34; chief of staff to comdt. Scouting Force and Hawaiian Detachment, 1939-41; comd. U.S.S. Mississippi, 1941; dir. of naval intelligence, Oct. 1941-July 1942, comdr. Battleship Div. Two, August 1942-Jan. 1943, deputy comdr. South Pacific, Jan. 1943-June 1943; comdr. Amphibious Force, South Pacific, July 15, 1943; comdr. 3d Amphibious Force, June 1944-Nov. 1945; mem. joint strategic Survey Com. Joint Chiefs of Staff, Jan.-Feb. 1946. Decorated Medal of Honor, D.S.M. (3); Companion of Bath (New Zealand). Sec. Navy letter of commendation for World War services. Mem. Am. Chem. Soc., Phi Sigma Kappa. Clubs: Metropolitan, Chevy Chase, Army and Navy, Army and Navy Country (Washington, D.C.); New York Yacht; Racquet (Phila.). Home: 3043 N. St., Washington. Died Feb. 21, 1946; buried in Arlington National Cemetery.

WILL, Arthur A., ex-mayor; born Louisville, May 22, 1871; s. Charles C. and Catherine K. (Kuebler) W.; ed. pub. schs. Louisville; m. Cora Goss, Nov. 13, 1901; children—Catherine Page (Mrs. P.E. Davis); Charles C. In bldg. contracting bus. since 1892; pres. Portland Federal Savings & Loan Assn., Louisville, dir. of Morris Plan Bank; elected mem. Bd. of Councilmen, 1908; mem. Bd. of Aldermen, 4 terms (pres. 1921-25); mayor of Louisville term 1925-27; chmn. Bd. of Pub. Safety, 1928-29; dir. of pub. works, 1930-33. Republican. Lutheran. Mason (K.T. Shriner), Odd Fellow, Redman, Woodman. Home: 2431 Montgomery St. Office: 2421 Cornwall St., Louisville. Died Oct. 8, 1940.

WILL, Theodore St. Clair, clergyman; b. Baltimore, Md., Dec. 22, 1886; s. William Russell and Mildred Florence (Sinclair) W.; student Deichmann Sch., 1902-06; A.B., Johns Hopkins U., 1910; B.D., Va. Theol. Sem., 1913; D.D., U. of the South, 1940; m. Eleanor Hardinge, Apr. 26, 1916; children—Theodore St. Clair, Jr., Austina Hardinge, Eleanor Caithness. Ordained deacon, P.E. Church, 1913, priest, 1914; curate, Christ Church, Baltimore, 1914-15; rector, Trinity Church, Elkridge, Md., 1916-19, St. John's Church, Kingsville, Md., 1920-28, Calvary, Ashland, Ky., 1928-32, Old St. John's, Hampton, Va., 1932-38; rector All Saints Church, Atlanta, Ga., since 1938. Examining chaplain Md., Lexington, and Southern Va. and Atlanta; archdeacon of Ashland; pres. standing com., Diocese of Lexington; del. to gen. convs. and provincial synods; active in Forward Movement. Mem. Atlanta Christian Council, Church Soc. for Coll. Work, Anglican Soc., Am. Retreat Assn. Mem. exec. com., Fed. Council Churches of Christ in Am. Decorated Order of Sangrael. Trustee Eggleston Memorial Hosp., Atlanta. Mason. Clubs: Friars', Piedmont Driving, Athletic (Atlanta). Author: The Rural Parish, 1926; The Episcopal Church, Heritage of American Christians, 1934; The Church of Our Fathers, 1936. Co-author: Presiding Bishop's Book for 1938. Home: 168 Peachtree Circle, N.E., Atlanta, Ga. Died Oct. 11, 1944.

WILLARD, Daniel, railway official; b. N. Hartland, Vt., Jan. 28, 1861; s. Daniel Spaulding and Mary Anna (Daniels) W.; student Mass. Agrl. Coll., 1878-79; LL.D., U. of Md., 1914, Dartmouth, 1915, U. of W.Va., 1919, Ohio U., 1927, Pa. Mil. Coll., 1928, U. of Pa., 1931, Middlebury Coll., 1931, Mass. State Coll., 1932, U. of Rochester, 1932, Oberlin Coll., 1934, University of Vermont, 1939; LL.D., Johns Hopkins Univ., 1941; Dr. Bus. Adminstrn., Syracuse Univ., 1927; m. Bertha Leone Elkins, Mar. 2, 1885; children—Harold Nelson (dec.), Daniel (dec.). Entered railway service 1879; in various duties on different rys. until 1899; asst. gen. mgr. B.&O. R.R., 1899-1901; asst. to the pres., later 3d v.p., and 1st v.p. and gen. mgr. Erie R.R., 1901-04; 2d v.p., C.,B.&Q. R.R., 1904-10; also pres. Colo. Midland Ry. Co., and v.p. C.&S. Ry. Co., 1909-10; pres. B.&O. R.R. Co., Jan. 15, 1910-June 1, 1941, chmn. of bd. since June 1, 1941; chmn. of board Buffalo, Rochester & Pittsburgh R.R., Reading Co., B.&O. Chicago Terminal R.R. Co.; dir. Am. Telephone & Telegraph Co., Richmond, Fredericksburg & Potomac R.R. Co., Richmond-Washington Co. Pres. Am. Ry. Assn., 1911-13. Mem. President's Orgn. on Unemployment Relief, 1931. Awarded gold medal, Nat. Inst. Social Sciences, 1939. Dir. Am. Arbitration Assn., Municipal Art Soc. (Baltimore); mem. Council on Foreign Relations, Phi Sigma Kappa Fraternity. Clubs: Chicago (Chicago); Maryland, Baltimore Country, Merchants' (Baltimore); Elkridge (Md.); Century, Recess (New York); Cosmos, Metropolitan (Washington). Mem. bd. trustees Johns Hopkins University, since 1914, pres. bd., 1926-41; trustee Johns Hopkins Hosp.; mem. board visitors U.S. Naval Acad., 1927. Apptd. mem. Advisory Commn. of Council Nat. Defense, Oct. 1916, and chmn., Mar. 1917; apptd. chmn. War Industries Bd., Nov. 17, 1917; resigned 1918. Commd. col. Engrs., U.S. Army, Nov. 2, 1918; hon. adviser to Army Industrial Coll. since 1925. Home: 206 Goodwood Gardens, Roland Park. Address: B.&O. R.R. Co., Baltimore, Md. Died July 6, 1942.

WILLARD, Frederic Wilson, pres. Nassau Smelting & Refining Co., Inc.; b. Houghton, N.Y., Apr. 16, 1881; s. Ephraim and Lucy Mae (Wilson) W.; A.B., U. of Mich., 1906, hon. A.M., 1929; m. Maude Myrtle Foote, Jan. 5, 1909; children—Harriet Aylene (Mrs. Robert Van Cleve Davies), Ruth Margaret. With Western Electric Co., 1906-31, analytical and research chemist, Chicago and New York, 1906-11, engr. mfg. methods, Chicago, 1913-15, asst. operating supt. Hawthorne Works, 1915-19, supt. Phila. instrument shop, 1919-21, div. supt. of installation, Phila., 1921-23, asst. engr. of mfg. Hawthorne Works, 1923-26, personnel dir., New York, 1926-29, asst. works mgr. Kearney Works, 1929-31; exec. v.p. Nassau Smelting & Refining Co., Inc., New York, 1931-37, pres. since 1937; dir. First Nat. Bank & Trust Co., Summit, since 1939, Summit Federal Savings & Loan Assn. since 1940. Mem. Zoning Bd. of Adjustment, Summit, 1932-34 and since 1941, also mem. Bd. Edn., 1934, 1937-38, pres., 1937. Mem. Nat. Research Council, chmn. div. chem. and chem. tech., 1933-36, mem. grants-in-aid bd., 1933-36, mem. exec. bd. since 1935; chmn. com. on Nat. Survey of Scientific Research in Industry, 1939-40 (survey completed, 1940); mem. War Metallurgy Com., 1941. Served as lt. col., Chem. Warfare Service, O.R.C., 1925-36. Mem. Am. Chem. Soc. (chmn. Chicago sect. 1920; chmn. coll. and univ. accrediting com. 1936; chmn. publ. com. 1944, mem. finance com. 1945), Am. Inst. Chem. Engrs. (dir. 6 yrs.), A.A.A.S., Mining and Metall. Soc. of America, Sigma Xi. Club: Chemists (New York). Editor Am. Chem. Soc. Monographs, 1943. Home: 12 Hawthorn Pl., Summit, N.J. Office: 170 Fulton St., New York 7, N.Y. Died Aug. 11, 1947.

WILLARD, Theodore A., inventor, mfr.; b. Castle Rock, Minn., Dec. 10, 1862; s. Robert R. and Ester (Day) W.; ed. country sch.; m. Florence V. Voorhees, Dec. 3, 1914. Learned trade of mech. engr.; spent over 30 yrs. in inventing devices for storage batteries; awarded 65 patents; inventor of the Willard Storage Battery and ex-pres. Willard Storage Battery Co., hdqrs. in Cleveland, O., branches in principal countries of the world. Methodist. Dir. Amateur Cinema League of New York City. Clubs: Bell Air Bay, Los Angeles, Los Angeles Country; The Racquet (Palm Springs, Calif.); Cleveland; Adventurers (Los Angeles). Author: The City of the Sacred Well, 1926; Wizard of Zacna, 1929; Bride of the Rain God, 1930; The Lost Empires of the Itzaes and Mayas, 1932; Kukulcan, The Bearded Conqueror, 1941. Home: 617 N. Linden Drive, Beverly Hills, Calif.; (winter) "Casa Maya," Palm Springs, Calif. Office: 246 131st St., Cleveland, O. Died Feb. 3, 1943.

WILLCOX, Walter Ross Baumes, prof. architecture; ed. Kalamazoo (Mich.) Coll., 3½ yrs., U. of Pa., 1893-94, and in Europe, 1907. Practiced Burlington, Vt., 1894-1906, Seattle (Wash.), 1908-22; mem. faculty U. of Ore. since 1922, also head of dept. of Arch.-Design Sch. Architecture and Allied Arts. Fellow Am. Inst. Architects. Address: Eugene, Ore.* Died Apr. 1947.

WILLET, Anne Lee (Mrs. William Willet), (wĭl'ĕt), artist, lecturer, teacher; b. at Bristol, Pa.; d. of Rev. Henry Flavel and Anne Townsend (Cooper) Lee; ed. Acad. of Fine Arts, Phila., also under pvt. teachers and abroad; m. William Willet (artist), June 30, 1896 (died 1921); children—Rachel W. (Mrs. Thomas Hopkins English), Henry Lee, Elizabeth L'Estrange (Mrs. Murray Forst Thompson). Exhibited at Metropolitan Museum, Architectural League, Edward McDowell Club, Hudson River Br. N.Y. Pub. Library (all New York); Pa. Acad. Fine Arts; Phila. Museum, Cosmopolitan Club, Art Alliance, Temple University (all Phila.); College of Denver (Colo.); Boston Acad. Fine Arts; Newport Art Assn.; Congressional Library and Smithsonian Museum, Washington; Boston Museum Art; Art Inst., Chicago; Carnegie Inst.; Architectural League, New Haven; High Museum, Atlanta, Ga.; Ney Museum of Art, Austin, Tex. Designer and maker with William Willet of all windows, U.S. Mil. Chapel, West Point, N.Y.; great west window, Grad. Coll., Princeton; sanctuary window, St. John's of Lattington, Locust Valley, L.I.; windows Holy Nativity Memorial Ch., Rockledge, Pa.; Greenwood Cemetery Chapel, Brooklyn; Harrison Memorial Holy Trinity Ch., Rittenhouse Sq., Phila.; Berry Memorial, Jefferson Av. Presbyn Ch., Detroit; Potter Memorial, Jamestown, R.I.; Pardee Memorial, Lake Placid, N.Y.; marble sanctuary, altar, mosaic, etc., Trinity P.E. Ch., Miami, Fla.; "Journeyings of the Pilgrims," Hilton Devotional Chapel, Chapel and Library, Chicago Theol. Sem.; du Pont Memorial sanctuary and façade, St. John's Cathedral, Wilmington, Del.; Harrison Memorial, Calvary P.E. Ch., Phila.; Patton Memorial, Ch. of the Savior, San Gabriel, Calif.; Chapel of the Mediator, Phila.; sanctuary, facade and transepts, First Presbyn. Ch. and Ch. of the Atonement, Chicago; windows Grace Church, Oak Park, Ill., Trowbridge Memorial, Santa Fe, N.M., Ch. of Blessed Sacrament, Detroit, Metropolitan M.E. Ch., Detroit; St. Andrew's Ch. (Elyria, O.), First Presbyn. Ch. (Kalamazoo, Mich.), All Saints' Ch. (Austin, Tex.), St. Aloysius Ch. (Detroit, Mich.), Grosse Pointe (Mich.) Memorial Ch., Ch. of the Resurrection (Rye, N.Y.). Mem. Am. Fedn. Arts, Acad. Fine Arts, The Edward MacDowell Assn. Founders and Patriots of America. Republican. Home-Studio: 2216 Rittenhouse Sq., Philadelphia, Pa. Died Jan. 18, 1943.

WILLETT, Herbert Lockwood, theologian; b. Ionia, Mich., May 5, 1864; s. Gordon A. and Mary E. (Yates) W.; A.B., Bethany Coll., W.Va., 1886, A.M., 1887; grad. student Yale, 1890-91; Ph.D., U. of Chicago, 1896; grad. student, U. of Berlin, 1898-99; m. Emma Augusta Price, Jan. 4, 1888; children—Herbert L., Robert Leslie, Paul Yates. Ordained Christian (Disciples) ministry, 1890; pastor Dayton, O., 1887-93; instr. Bible, Ann Arbor, Mich., 1893-95; acting dean and head of Disciples' Div. House, 1894-96, dean, 1896-1921; asst. in Semitic langs., U. of Chicago, 1896-97, instr., 1897-1900, asst. prof. Semitic langs. and lits., 1900-03, asso. prof., 1909-15, prof. Oriental langs. and literatures, 1915-29 (emeritus); minister Memorial Ch. of Christ, Chicago, 1908-20, Kenilworth (Ill.) Union Church since 1927. Pres. Chicago Church Fedn., 1916-20; Chicago rep. Federal Council Chs. of Christ in America, 1920-25, now chmn. mid-west com. Asso. editor Christian Century, Chicago; lecturer on Bible topics. Mem. Delta Tau Delta. Clubs: University, Quadrangle, City, Indian Hill, Shawnee (Chicago). Author: Life and Teachings of Jesus, 1898; Teachings of the Books, 1899; Prophets of Israel, 1899; The Ruling Quality, 1902; Plea for Union, 1901; Basic Truths of the Christian Faith, 1902; Studies in First Samuel, 1909; The Moral Leaders of Israel, 1916; The Call of the Christ, 1912; Our Bible—Its Origin, Character and Value, 1917; The Daily Altar; 1918; The Bible Through the Centuries, 1929; The Jew Through the Centuries, 1931. Home: Oak Crest Hotel, Evanston, Ill. Died Mar. 27, 1944.

WILLETT, Oscar Louis (wĭl'ĕt), lawyer; b. near Effingham, Ill., Mar. 11, 1881; s. Volney and Louisa (Wilborn) W.; B.S., Nat. Normal U., Lebanon, O., 1902, LL.B., 1902, Ph.B., 1903; grad. student U. of Chicago, 1902; m. Georgetta Pemberton, 1905 (died 1928); children—Madeline (Mrs. Burns, dec.), Oscar Louis (dec.), Beulah (Mrs. Harold C. Connal), Georgette (Mrs. Carl Schiff), Virginia Lou; m. 2d, Ethelga Beatty, Sept. 1929; children—Noelle Marie, Volney Louis, Ethelga Bea. Admitted to bars of Illinois, 1902, Wash., 1903, Calif., 1924; practiced in Seattle, Wash., 1903-23, in Calif. since 1923; in charge development of 16,000 acre residential community, Atascadero, Calif., 1925-31; chmn. Central Coast Highway Com., Calif. State Chamber of Commerce, 1926-33; apptd. by Federal Court to protect creditors in Palos Verdes Project, 1931; trustor and gen. mgr. Palos Verdes Trust since 1937; pres. Willett & Crane, Inc.; manager Palos Verde. Realty Co.; president South Bay Beach and Highway Association. Served with 9th Illinois Volunteers during Spanish-Am. War. Mem. California State Bar Assn., United Spanish War Vets., Vets. of Fgn. Wars; past pres. Southwest Dist. Highways Assn.; president Palos Verdes Estates Chamber of Commerce; mem. highway com. Harbor District Chambers of Commerce and California State Chamber of Commerce. Home: 628 Miramar Av., Hollywood Riviera, Calif. Office: 301 Palos Verdes Drive, Palos Verdes Estates, Calif. Died April 24, 1945.

WILLEY, Earle D., ex-congressman; b. Greenwood, Sussex County, Del., July 21, 1889; s. Jabez Turner and Fannie Amelia (Dukes) W.; Ph.B., Dickinson Coll. (Carlisle, Pa.), 1911, M.A., 1914; summer student U. of Pa., 1911-12; student George Washington U. Law Sch. 1916; m. Florence Agnes Gibson, Aug. 13, 1917. Prin. Greenwood (Del.) High Sch., 1911-15; sec. to Rep. Thomas W. Miller (Del.) at Washington, 1915-17; admitted to bar of Sussex County, 1920; state librarian, 1917-21; prosecuting attorney of Kent County, 1921-31; judge Court of Common Pleas, Kent County, 1931-39; judge Juvenile Ct. for Kent and Sussex counties, 1933-39; candidate for lt. gov., 1940; sec. state, del. 1941-42; mem. 78th Congress (1943-45), Del. at large. Trustee U. of Del., Elizabeth W. Murphy Sch. for Orphan Children, Dover. Mem. Del. State Bar, Kent Co. Bar Assn., Phi Kappa Psi, Nat. Grange, I.O.O.F. Club: Rotary (Dover). Address: State St., Dover, Del.* Died Mar. 17, 1950.

WILLEY, John Heston (wĭl'ē), clergyman; b. St. Michaels, Md.; s. Edward and Susanna (Hambleton) W.; B.D., Drew Theol. Sem., 1882; Ph.B., Ill. Wesleyan U., 1886; Ph.M., Syracuse U., 1887, Ph.D., 1888, S.T.D., 1908; studied Christ Ch. Coll. (Oxford U.), Eng., 1896; m. Ella M. Stickney, Apr. 27, 1892. Ordained ministry M.E. Ch., 1880; pastor successively Snow Hill, Md., Delaware City, Del., Milford, Del., Chestertown, Md., and College Church, Syracuse until 1896; pastor Nostrand Av. Ch., Brooklyn, 1898-1902, St. Mark's Ch., Brooklyn, 1902-10, Christ Ch., Pittsburgh, Pa., 1910-16, First Bapt. Ch., Montclair, N.J., since 1919. Pres. Lord's Day Alliance of the U.S. since 1930. Trustee Beaver Coll., Wilmington Acad., Syracuse U. Mem. N.Y. State Historical Soc., Art Collectors League N.J., S.A.R. (chaplain since 1920), Montclair Art Museum, Am. Inst. Sacred Lit., Audubon Soc., Optimist Internat. (lt. gov.), Phi Kappa Phi. Del. to Gen. Conf. M.E. Ch., 1916. Mason (32°, K.T. Prelate Commandery since 1930; asso. grand prelate state commandery, New Jersey, since 1938). Clubs: Authors Club America, Journalist, Clergy, Essex Fells Country. Author: Back to Bethlehem, 1905; John Chrysostom, 1906; Midsummer Nights with the Great Dreamer, 1908; Joshua the Warrior Prince, 1913; God's Age-Old

Purpose, 1918; Between Two Worlds, 1919; The World War and Tomorrow, 1920; Early Church Portraits, 1927; Humanity at Its Climax, 1928; Swords Bathed in Heaven, 1937. Home: 16 Upper Mountain Av., Montclair, N.J. Office: 156 5th Av., New York, N.Y. Died Nov. 8, 1942.

WILLHITE, Frank Vanatta (wil'hit), physician; b. Grant City, Mo., May 1, 1878; s. Robert Stone and Elizabeth Ellen (Vanatta) W.; student State Normal Sch., Kirksville, Mo., and U. of Mo.; M.D., U. of Ill., 1905; m. Nelle Zabel, Oct. 30, 1916; m. 2d, Mayble Hegge, July 9, 1927. Interne, Cook County (Ill.) Hosp., 1905-06; mem. med. staff, Yankton (S.D.) State Hosp., 1908-20, asst. supt., 1920-23; supt. State Sch. and Home for Feeble Minded, Redfield. Mem. Alpha Omega Alpha, Beta Theta Pi. Home: Redfield, S.D.* Died Oct. 1944.

WILLIAMS, Blanche Colton, writer; b. Attala County, Miss., Feb. 10, 1879; d. Millard F. and Ella (Colton) Williams; A.B., Miss. State Coll. for Women, 1898; A.M., Columbia, 1908, Ph.D., 1913. Instr. English, Stanton Coll., Natchez, Miss., 1898-1904, Grenada (Miss.) Coll., 1904-07; asst. in English, Teachers Coll. (Columbia), 1908-09, instr., 1909-10; instr. English, 1910, asst. prof., 1915, asso. prof., 1917, prof. and head dept., 1926-39; retired, Hunter Coll.; instr. in short story writing, extension dept. and summer session, Columbia, 1913-26. Awarded Scroll of the Grad. Schools of Columbia U., 1937. Mem. Modern Lang. Assn. of America, Shakespeare Assn. of America, Theta Sigma Phi, Delta Zeta. Clubs: Dixie, P.E.N. Author: Gnomic Poetry in Anglo-Saxon, 1914; A Handbook on Story Writing, 1917, rev. edit., 1930; How to Study "The Best Short Stories," 1919; Our Short Story Writers, 1920, 22; Studying the Short Story, 1926; Short Story Writing, 1930; Old English Handbook (with Marjorie Anderson), 1935; George Eliot—A Biography, 1936; Clara Barton—A Biography, 1941; Forever Young, A Life of John Keats, 1943. Editor: A Book of Short Stories, 1918; O. Henry Memorial Prize Stories, 1919-32 (14 vols.); Thrice Told Tales, 1924; Great Stories of All Nations (with Maxim Lieber), 1927; Poe's Tales, 1928; (with Maxim Lieber) A Panorama of the Short Story, 1929; Short Stories for College Classes, 1929; (with John Macy) Do You Know English Literature?, 1930; New Narratives, 1930; A Book of Essays, 1931; The Mystery and the Detective, 1938; American Edition of Wiliam Freeman's Plain English, 1939. Contbr. articles to Compton's Pictured Encyclopedia. Home: 200 W. 108th St., New York, N.Y. Died Aug. 9, 1944.

WILLIAMS, Carlos Grant, agrl. experimentation; b. Gustavus, O., Jan. 18, 1863; s. Carlos A. and Elmina (Moore) W.; ed. Gustavus Academy; hon. D.Sc., College of Wooster, O., 1931; m. Mayme A. Elder, Jan. 16, 1896; children—Margaret, Ruth, Robert. Agronomist, O. Agrl. Expt. Sta., 1903-21, dir. 1921-37; cons. agronomist since 1937. Contbg. editor Ohio Farmer since 1908; mem. Ohio Agrl. Commn., 1913-14; dir. Peoples Savings & Loan Co., Commercial Banking & Trust Co. (pres.). Mem. O. Council Defense, 1917-18; pres. Wayne County Red Cross, 1918. Fellow A.A.A.S. (vice-pres. 1931), Am. Soc. Agronomy (pres. 1925-26); mem. Soc. Promotion Agrl. Science, Grange. Conglist. Clubs: Century, Rotary. Originator 3 varieties of wheat. Author of 18 expt. sta. bulls. Contbr. to scientific jours. Home: 1004 N. Bever St., Wooster, Ohio. Died Oct. 4, 1946.

WILLIAMS, Charles Burgess, agronomist; b. Shiloh, N.C., Dec. 23, 1871; s. Robert Jones and Susan (Burgess) W.; B.S., N.C. Agricultural and Mech. Coll., 1893, M.S., 1896; Johns Hopkins, 1896-97; m. Margaret Williams Moring, July 5, 1900. Asst. state chemist of N.C., Raleigh, 1899-1907; head of dept. of agronomy, N.C. Expt. Sta., 1906-24, 1926-40, dir. of the station, 1907-12, vice-dir., 1913-32; dean of agriculture, N.C. State Coll., 1917-24, prof. emeritus of agronomy; agronomist, Dept. of Agronomy, N.C. Agrl. and Mech. Coll. Mem. A.A.A.S., Am. Soc. Agr., N.C. Acad. Science, Phi Kappa Phi. Democrat. Missionary Baptist. Home: 1405 Hillsboro St., Raleigh, N.C. Died June 25, 1947.

WILLIAMS, Clarence Russell, historian; b. Phila., Pa., Dec. 15, 1870; s. Rev. Moseley Hooker and Emma Virginia (Bockius) W.; A.B., U. of Pa., 1892; M.A., Princeton, 1895; graduate Princeton Theol. Sem., 1895; B.D., University of Chicago, 1901 (grad. work under President Harper); Ph.D., Yale, 1912; m. Gertrude Butler Hall, May 1, 1907 (died Mar. 23, 1945). Pastor Presbyterian Church, 1897-1900; lesson writer American S.S. Union, 1897-1913, Congl. Sunday Sch. and Pub. Soc., 1918-20; in A.L.A. War Service, Camps Upton and Merritt, 1918; prof. history, St. Stephen's Coll., 1919-21; acting asso. prof. Am. history, Rutgers Coll., 1921-22; grad. studies Columbia U., 1922-23; asso. prof., 1923, prof. history, 1924-27, U. of Vt.; prof. history U. of Puerto Rico, 1927-28; Library of Congress, 1928-36; historian with U.S. Constitution Sesquicentennial Commn., 1936-37; engaged in hist. research since 1937; visiting prof. summer, U. of New Hampshire, 1927, U. of Buffalo, 1929. Mem. Pi Gamma Mu. Author: The Appendices to the Gospel According to Mark, a Study in Textual Transmission. Contbr. to Dictionary of Am. Biography. Address: 44 W. Coulter St., Germantown, Philadelphia 44. Died Sept. 25, 1949.

WILLIAMS, Clark, banker; b. Canandaigua, N.Y., May 2, 1870; s. George N. and Abigail Stanley (Clark) W.; A.B., Williams Coll., 1892; LL.D., 1939; LL.D., The Citadel, 1933; m. Anna Plater, April 29, 1897. With Guaranty Trust Co., New York, 1892-94; clerk, asst. treas., treas. and v.p. U.S. Mortgage & Trust Co., 1894-1905; organizer, 1905, mng. v.p., 1905-07, Columbia Trust Co.; supt. of banks State of N.Y., 1907-09; comptroller state of N.Y., 1909-11; pres. Windsor Trust Co., New York, 1911-13; apptd. pres. Industrial Finance Corp. (owner "Morris Plan" of industrial loans and investments), June 1914. Apptd. Am. Red Cross rep. with 1st Div. A.E.F., Apr. 1918; dir. army field service, Am. Red Cross, with A.E.F., rank of major, 1919. Mem. firm Clark Williams & Co. (financial), N.Y., 1919-39; mem. firm Winthrop, Mitchell & Co. since 1939. Commd. lt. col. O.R.C., U.S. Army, 1925. Decorated Chevalier French Legion of Honor; recipient Algernon Sidney Sullivan award, 1938. Trustee emeritus of Williams Coll. Congregationalist. Mem. S.R., Loyal Legion, Kappa Alpha (Williams). Clubs: Union, University, Union League, Williams, Recess, Midday. Author: The Story of a Grateful Citizen (an autobiography in 2 vols.). Home: Field Point Park, Greenwich, Conn.* Died Dec. 18, 1946.

WILLIAMS, Clement Clarence, engr., educator; b. Bryant, Ill., Feb. 21, 1882; s. Isaac Greenbury and Martha Ann (Davis) W.; B.S., Southern Ia. Normal Sch., 1900; B.S. in C.E., U. of Ill., 1907; C.E., U. of Colo., 1909; LL.D., Lafayette, 1935; Eng.D., Northeastern U., 1936; Eng.D., Bucknell U., 1937, Case Sch. Applied Science, 1939; Sc.D., Hannemann Med. Coll., 1938, Muhlenberg Coll., 1940; LL.D., Rutgers, 1941, Moravian Coll., 1941; m. Grace Josephine Black, Aug. 31, 1910 (died Feb. 3, 1917); m. 2d, Ora Louella Webb, June 8, 1921; children—Ora Louise, Ellen Webb, Clement Webb. Formerly engaged in railway, bridge, municipal and highway engring. work; instr., asst. prof. and acting prof. civil engring., U. of Colo., 1907-14; prof. ry. engring., U. of Kan., 1914-18, prof. civ. engring., 1918-22; prof. civil engring. and head of dept., U. of Ill., 1922-26; dean Coll. of Engring., U. of Ia., 1926-35; pres. Lehigh U. 1935-44; cons. in engring. and indsl. education since 1944. Supervising engineer War Dept., in construction of explosive plants, 1918-19; trustee Carnegie Foundation for Advancement of Teaching. Mem. Am. Soc. C.E., Am. Ry. Engring. Assn., Wis. Acad. Science, Am. Soc. for Engring. Edn. (pres. 1934-35), Pa. Soc. Coll. Presidents (pres. 1940-41), Tau Beta Pi, Sigma Xi, Sigma Tau; fellow A.A.A.S. Republican. Congregationalist. Author: Design of Railway Location, 1917; Design of Masonry Structures and Foundations, 1921; Building and Engineering Career, 1934; Foundations, 1934; also various bulls. and articles in engring. mags. Licensed professional engineer. Home: 129 N. Prospect Av., Madison 5, Wis. Died. Feb. 20, 1947.

WILLIAMS, Curtis Chandler, lawyer; b. Hanover, O., Aug. 13, 1861; s. Richard Gilson and Elmira (Frost) W.; A.B., Mt. Union Coll., Alliance, O., 1883, hon. A.M., 1891; m. Margaret Mary Owen, July 5, 1893; children—Elmira Anne (Mrs. Arthur Seward Burket, dec.), Curtis Chandler, Margaret Iola, Marie Owen (dec.), Arthur Frost. Admitted to Ohio bar, 1886; began practice at Columbus; prosecuting atty. Franklin County, 1891-94; judge Court of Common Pleas, 1897-1903; in gen. practice of law, 1903-32; dir. of pub. safety, City of Columbus, Jan. 1932-May 1934; v.p. Federal Union Life Ins. Co., Dec. 1915-May 1932, pres. since May 1934. Del. to Dem. Nat. Conv., 1920, 24, 32. Mem. Am., Ohio State and Columbus bar assns., Internat. Law Assn., Ohio Archæol. and Hist. Soc., English-Speaking Union. Democrat. Presbyn. Mason (K.T., Shriner), K.P. (past grand chancellor), Odd Fellow. Club: Columbus. Home: 342 N. Remington Road, Bexley, Ohio. Died Apr. 2, 1942.

WILLIAMS, Cyrus Vance, prof. vocational edn.; b. Elmwood, Neb., Jan. 19, 1879; s. Matthew Bray and Mary Jane (Vance) W.; B.E., Neb. Teachers Coll., Peru, Neb., 1908; A.M., U. of Neb., 1910, B.S. in Agr., 1919, Ph.D., 1925; grad. study, Cornell Univ., summer, 1917, 20; m. Mary Lansing, Mar. 23, 1930; 1 dau., Joan Louise. Principal of schs., Stuart, Ia., 1902-04; supt. schs., Guthrie Center, Ia., 1904-08; prof. botany, Neb. Teachers Coll., 1908-09, Neb. Wesleyan U., 1910-13; supt. Neb. Sch. Agr., Curtis, Neb., 1913-18; spl. agent in agrl. edn., Federal Bd. for Vocational Edn., 1918-20; Kan. state dir. vocational edn., 1920-22; prof. vocational edn., Kan. State Agrl. Coll., since 1920. Mem. N.E.A., Am. Vocational Assn., Am. Assn. Advancement Agrl. Teaching, Kan. State Teachers Assn., Kan. Vocational Assn., Sigma Xi, Phi Kappa Phi, Alpha Zeta, Gamma Sigma Delta, Phi Delta Kappa, Alpha Phi Omega, Acacia. Republican. Mem. Christian (Disciples) Ch. Mason (32°, Shriner). Clubs: Kiwanis, Kansas Schoolmasters, Manhattan Country. Home: 1735 Fairview, Manhattan, Kan. Died Nov. 16, 1944.

WILLIAMS, Edward Huntington, physician; b. Durand, Ill., Nov. 1, 1868; s. Edward Jenner and Orilla N. (Webster) W.; brother of Henry Smith Williams; pub. sch. edn., Charles City, Ia.; M.D., State U. of Ia., 1892; m. 2d, Cora Young, Mar. 8, 1926. Asso. prof. pathology and bacteriology, State U. of Ia., 1892-93; asst. physician State Hosp. for Insane Criminals, Matteawan, N.Y., 1896-97; asst. physician Manhattan State Hosp., New York, 1897-99. Asso. editor 10th edit. Ency. Britannica (pub. in Eng.); asso. editor United Editors' Encyclopædia. Joint Author: (with Dr. Henry Smith Williams) A History of Science (5 vols.), 1904; Every-Day Science (11 vols.), 1910; The Wonders of Science in Modern Life (10 vols.), 1912; The Walled City—A Story of the Criminal Insane, 1913; Increasing Your Mental Efficiency, 1914; The Question of Alcohol, 1914; The Forest Pilot, 1915; Alcohol, Hygiene and Legislation, 1915; Mental Hygiene, 1919; Opiate Addiction—Its Handling and Treatment, 1922; Crime, Mental Abnormalities, and the Law (with Ernest Bryant Hoag, M.D.), 1922; Our Fear Complexes, 1923; Rest and Grow Strong, 1925; Red Plume, 1925; Larry of the North, 1926; How We Become Personalities, 1926; Red Plume Returns, 1927; Red Plume of the Royal Northwest Mounted, 1928; The Doctor in Court, 1929; Animal Autobiographies, 1930; The Insanity Plea, 1931; Drug Addicts are Human Beings, 1938. Home: 337 26th St., Santa Monica, Calif. Died June 24, 1944.

WILLIAMS, Edward Thomas, univ. prof.; b. Columbus, O., Oct. 17, 1854; s. William and Dinah Louisa (Hughes) W.; B.A., Bethany Coll., 1875, M.A., 1893, LL.D., 1915; m. Caroline D. Loos, Aug. 12, 1884; children—Edward Thrasher, Charles Louis Loos; m. 2d, Rose Sickler, Jan. 8, 1894; children—Alice Sickler, Gwladys Louise. Ordained ministry Disciples of Christ Ch., 1875; pastor Springfield, Ill., 1875-77, Denver, 1877-78, Brooklyn, 1878-81, Cincinnati, 1881-87; missionary in China, 1887-96; interpreter to Am. Consulate-Gen. at Shanghai, 1896-98; translator to Chinese Govt., Shanghai, 1898-1901; Chinese sec. Am. Legation at Peking, 1901-08; consul-gen. at Tientsin, Apr. 1908-Oct. 1909; asst. chief Div. of Far Eastern Affairs, Dept. of State, 1909-11; sec. Am. Legation, Peking, China, July 1911-13, chargé d'affaires, Aug.-Nov. 1911 and Feb.-Nov. 1913; chief Div. of Far Eastern Affairs, Dept. of State, 1914-18; Agassiz prof. Oriental langs. and lit., U. of Calif., 1918-27 (emeritus). Tech. del. to Peace Conf., Paris, 1919; special asst. to Dept. of State for the Conf. on Limitation of Armament and Pacific and Far Eastern Problems, 1921-22. Mem. Am. Oriental Soc., Royal Asiatic Soc. (life mem. China br.), Am. Anthrop. Assn., A.A.A.S., Am. Hist. Assn., Phi Kappa Psi; fellow Am. Geog. Soc. Decorated Chinese Order of the Golden Sheaf, 1918, Officer of same, 1919; Blue Ribbon Order of Jade, 1936. Democrat. Unitarian. Author: Recent Chinese Legislation, 1904; The State Religion of China Under the Manchus, 1913; China Yesterday and To-day, 1923; A Short History of China, 1928; also various monographs and reports. Home: 1410 Scenic Av., Berkeley, Calif. Died Jan. 27, 1944.

WILLIAMS, Ernest S., teacher, composer, conductor; b. Wayne Co., Ind., Sept. 27, 1881; s. Samuel E. and Ella (Hough) Williams; trained by father; student under music teachers New York City and Boston, Mass., 1900-07; Mus.D., Capitol College of Music, 1937; married Gladys A. Rice, July 8, 1944. Toured with bands Sousa, 1903; Pryor, 1915; Conway, 1916; Goldman, 1917-23, world tour, 1912-13; bandmaster Boston (Mass.) Cadet Band, 1904-07; dir. own band Lakeside Park, Denver, Colo., 1911; cond. Ithaca Coll. Symphony Orchestra, 1929-30; bandmaster Kismet Temple, 1920; 1st trumpet Phila. Orchestra under Stokowski, Victor Herbert, Richard Straus, George Enesco, Vincent D'Indy, Ossip Gabrilowitsch, 1917-23; dir. Ernest Williams School of Music, since 1922, teaching many noted artists; dir. symphonic band, N.Y. U., 1935-45; teacher trumpet, Juilliard School of Music, 1936-45; conductor Catskill Mountain Symphony Orchestra, summers since 1930; director Ernest Williams Music Camp, Saugerties, New York, summers since 1930. Served as bandmaster U.S. Army, 1898-1900. Composer: Symphony in C Minor for symphonic band (pub. 1938); Revolutionary Fantasy (pub. 1940); America-tone poem for band and orchestra with chorus (pub. 1941); Rip Van Winkle, Opera (not pub.); Method for Cornet and Trumpet (pub. 1936); Transposition Method for Trumpet (pub. 1938). Composer numerous tone poems, marches, solos, duets, trios, concertos for trumpet, cornet. Home and Office: R. 1, Saugerties, N.Y. Died Feb. 8, 1947.

WILLIAMS, Francis Churchill, editor; b. Phila., Apr. 23, 1869; s. Francis Howard and Mary B. (Houston) W.; B.A., U. of Pa., 1891; m. Grace Young, May 5, 1897 (died Oct. 12, 1920); 1 son, Francis Churchill; m. 2d, Marion Virginia Gormly, Apr. 4, 1923. Newspaper writer, corr. and editor, 1891-1900; literary adviser to J. B. Lippincott Co., pubs., 1902-06; associate editor Saturday Evening Post, 1907-27. Capt. Mil. Intelligence Div., Gen. Staff, 1918; grad. Army War Coll., G-2 course for the year 1923; maj., O.R.C., U.S.A., 1919, lt. col., 1924. Mem. Welcome Soc., Soc. of Colonial Wars, S.R., Hist. Soc. of Pa., Delta Phi. Clubs: Army and Navy. Author: J. Devlin, Boss, 1901; Stories of the College (co-author), 1902; The Captain, 1903. Contbr. biog., critical and hist. articles and fiction to mags. Home: Spring Meadown Farm, Burks County, Pa. Died Apr. 11, 1945.

WILLIAMS, Frank L., newspaperman; b. Granville, Delaware County, Ind., Dec. 29, 1866; s. Sampson H. and Sarah Catherine (Brackin) W.; ed. pub. schs. and Franklin (Neb.) Acad.; m. Mattie C. Crane, Apr. 8, 1889; children—Edith Blanche, Jesse Leonard, Jay Irvin. Began as printer on Franklin Echo, 1885; reporter Kearney Hub, 1889-95; publisher North Platte (Neb.) Daily Record, 1895-96; city editor of Kearney (Neb.) Hub, 1896-98; successively reporter, city editor, Neb. State Journal, Lincoln, 1898-1925, managing editor, 1925-27, editor since 1927. Member Lincoln City Library Board, Lincoln Chamber Commerce. Ind. Republican. Methodist. Mason (32°). Clubs: Layman's Interprofessional Institute. Home:

431 N. 16th St. Office: State Journal Bldg., Lincoln, Neb. Died Oct. 25, 1943.

WILLIAMS, George Bassett, govt. executive; b. Minneapolis, Minn., Sept. 20, 1878; s. Robert S. and Isabel S. (Cannon) W.; student Lehigh U., Bethlehem, Pa., 1895-97; B.S. in Architectural Engring., U. of Ill., 1899; m. Lora Wright, Sept. 23, 1908; children—Elizabeth West (Mrs. Thomas E. Covel), Robert Wright. Traverse man with U.S. Geological Survey, 1899; construction business until 1924; partner Lawrence Stern and Co., investment bankers, representing firm in Europe, particularly Germany, 1928-33; with R.F.C. since 1935; pres. and dir. The R.F.C. Mortgage Co., 1938-41; now exec. v.p. and dir., Defense Homes Corp. Mem. Sigma Chi. Episcopalian. Home: 2645 Fort Scott Drive, Arlington, Va. Office: Federal Loan Agency Bldg., Washington. Died June 18, 1946; buried Mount Hope Cemetery, Urbana, Ill.

WILLIAMS, George Van Siclen, lawyer; b. Rockland, Sullivan County, N.Y., June 6, 1869; s. Cornelius Crispell and Mary Jenette (Jocelyn) W.; ed. pub. schs.; LL.B., Albany Law Sch., 1890; m. Mae Louise Carll, Apr. 14, 1896; 1 son, George Carll. Practiced in New York, mem. Williams & Richardson, 1892-1920; counsel for Brooklyn City R.R. and Brooklyn Rapid Transit Co., 10 yrs.; chief counsel Conservation Commn. State of N.Y., 1911-12; pub. service commr. State of N.Y., Apr. 1, 1912-16. Pres. MacCoy Pub. & Masonic Supply Co. Formerly chmn. Dem. County Com. Kings County, and chmn. Law Com. Kings County Dem. Organization. Presbyterian. Home: Mountain Lakes, N.J. Office: 35 W. 32d St., New York, N.Y. Died Apr. 12, 1942.

WILLIAMS, Guinn, ex-congressman; b. Calhoun County, Miss., Apr. 22, 1871; ed. high sch.; m. Minnie Leatherwood, Nov. 14, 1893. In cattle and mule business for 30 yrs. County clk. Wise County, Tex., 1898-1902; mem. Tex. Senate, 1920-22 (resigned); elected to 67th Congress at spl. election, May 13, 1922, and reëlected 68th to 72d Congresses (1923-33), 13th Tex. Dist.; resigned as pres. of 5 banks after election. Democrat. Mem. M.E. Ch., S. Mason (32°). Home: Decatur, Tex. Died Jan. 9, 1948.

WILLIAMS, Henry Davison, patent lawyer; b. Brooklyn, N.Y., June 4, 1863; s. George Tappen and Elizabeth Ann (Davison) W.; B.S., Cooper Union, 1885, M.E., 1924; LL.B., Columbia, 1889; m. Euretta E. Gardner, June 21, 1892 (died Sept. 13, 1924); children—Edith Gardner, Gardner; m. 2d, Stella Howland Taylor Williams, Dec. 28, 1934. Mech. engr. and solicitor of patents, 1878-87; law clk. and office student, 1888-93; partner Redding & Kiddle, 1894; practiced alone, 1895-1917; partner firm Williams & Pritchard, 1917-25, Williams & Morse, 1925-28, Williams, Rich & Morse since 1928; chmn. of bd. Shreve & Adams, Inc. Mem. com. for securing adequate compensation for federal judiciary; organized campaign for funds for busts of John Marshall and Peter Cooper in Hall of Fame; active in promoting law for copyright registration of designs, for amendments to patent laws and trade mark laws, etc. Mem. Am. Bar Assn. (ex-vice-pres.), New York State Bar Assn., Bar Assn. City of New York, New York County Lawyers' Assn. (ex-dir.), Am. Patent Law Assn. (ex-v.p.), N.Y. Patent Law Assn. (ex-gov.), New York Law Inst., Chartered Instn. of Patent Agents (London), Inst. of Patent Attorneys (Australia), West End Assn. (pres.), Cooper Union Alumni Assn. (hon. pres.), Mchts. Assn. of N.Y. (com. on protection industrial property), Acad. Polit. Science, Internat. Assn. for Protection of Industrial Property (exec. com.; regional v.p.), Am. Acad. Air Law, Am. Arbitration Assn. (arbitrator), Com. on Foreign Patents and Trade Marks (advisory com.), Assn. for Preservation Va. Antiquities, Citizen's Guild of Washington's Boyhood Home. League of Nations Assn., Met. Museum, Am. Museum Natural History, Museum City of New York, Park Assn. N.Y. City, Merchants Assn. of New York, Charity Orgn. Soc., Citizens Union N.Y. City, S.R., etc. Republican. Club: City. Home: 308 W. 105th St. Office: 225 Broadway, New York, N.Y.* Deceased.

WILLIAMS, Henry Edison, journalist, radio broadcaster; b. North Ridgeway, N.Y., Sept. 15, 1886; s. Plynn Edward and Minnie (Ostrander) W.; desc. of Miles Standish and John Alden of the Mayflower; ed. pub. schs. and under pvt. tutors until 1918; spl. English and economics courses Lowell Institute (Harvard); m. Llora G. Champlin, Nov. 11, 1912; children—Prudence, Plynn Edison. Printer and free lance writer until 1930; rewrite man and feature writer Christian Science Monitor, Boston, 1931-33; broadcaster "The Monitor Views of the News," 1933-35; made survey of nat. parks and Indian reservations of U.S., 1932, contbg. series of articles to the Monitor; made political and industrial survey in Can., 1935; column, "Tower Views," in C.S. Monitor, 1936-37; lecturer on Am. Indians and fgn. news, also broadcaster over WBZ, WHDH, WMEX and WRUL; speaker on transcribed inspirational programs on 250 N.A. radio stations, since 1944; contbr. to C.S. publs. Member S.A.R., Handel and Hayden Soc. (Boston). Mason (32°). Club: University. Home: 86 Nonantum St., Newton, Mass. Address: 236 Huntington Av., Boston, Mass. Died Oct. 24, 1946.

WILLIAMS, Henry Morland, lawyer, trustee; b. Boston, Mass., Sept. 19, 1862; s. Henry Willard and Elizabeth Adeline (Low) W.; A.B., Harvard, 1885, LL.B., 1888; m. Eleanor Thaxter Dodd, Dec. 8, 1891; children—John Dodd, George Low, Sedric Whittemore, Henry Morland, Honor, Mansfield. Admitted to Mass. bar, 1888, and began practice at Boston; mem. Hayes & Williams, 1888-95, Williams & Fuller, 1915-31; dir. Towle Mfg. Co. (exec. com.); trustee realty and building trusts. Member Mass. Vol. Militia 11 years. President Harvard Housing Trust, Children's Mission to Children, Harvard Alumni Bulletin. Mem. of Bar Assn. of the City of Boston, Asso. Harvard Clubs (pres.), Harvard Alumni Assn. (dir.; mem. exec. com.), Am. Unitarian Assn. (treas.; dir.), Unitarian Service Pension Soc. (v.p.), Unitarian Laymen's League (one of founders), Harvard Class Secretaries' Assn. Republican. Unitarian. Clubs: Harvard (Boston); Faculty, Cambridge, Unitarian (pres. 1924-25). Editor, co-author annual reports Class of 1885, 1886-1940. Contbr. to Harvard Alumni Bull., Harvard Grads.' Mag., etc. Home: 100 Brattle St., Cambridge, Mass.; (summer) Cohasset, Mass. Office: 10 State St., Boston, Mass. Deceased.

WILLIAMS, Henry Smith, physician, author; b. Durand, Ill., Mar. 4, 1863; s. Edward Jenner and Orrilla N. (Webster) W.; brother of Edward Huntington W.; A.B., State U. of Iowa, 1887; M.D., Chicago Med. Coll., 1884; in univs., hosps. and libraries of Berlin, Paris, London, etc., 1898-1902; LL.D., Western Reserve, 1903; m. Florence Whitney, Nov. 9, 1889; m. 2d, Marina M. Gardner, Feb. 12, 1925. Practiced since 1884; specialist in nervous and mental diseases; asst. physician and pathologist State Hospital for Insane, Independence, 1887; asst. physician Manhattan State Hospital, 1888, Bloomingdale Asylum, 1889; medical supt. Randall's Island Hospital, 1892. Lecturer Hartford School of Sociology, 1891-92. Author: Check List of Iowa Birds (with C. L. Keys), 1887 (Davenport Acad. Science); The Story of Nineteenth Century Science, 1900; The History of Art of Writing, 1902; A History of Science (5 vols.), 1904 (with E. H. Williams, M.D.); The Effect of Alcohol, 1909; The Science of Happiness, 1909; Every Day Science (14 vols.), 1909-10 (with E. H. Williams, M.D.); The Conquest of Nature, 1911; Mental Obliquities, Science and Civilization, 1912; The Wonders of Science in Modern Life (10 vols.), 1912; Miracles of Science, 1913; Adding Years to Your Life, 1914; Luther Burbank—His Life and Work, 1915; The Proteal Treatment of Cancer and Allied Conditions, 1916; Proteal Therapy, 1917; The Proteomorphic Theory and the New Medicine, 1918; The Witness of the Sun, 1920; The Phantom Auto, 1921; Practical Radio, 1922; Story of Modern Science, 1923; The Great Astronomers, 1930; The Literary Digest Book of Marvels, 1931; The Biography of Mother Earth, 1931; Survival of the Fittest, 1932; Why Die Before Your Time?, 1933; Drugs Against Men, 1935; Wonder Book of World Progress (10 vols.), 1935; Your Glands and You, 1936; The Dope Ring, 1937; Drug Addicts Are Human Beings, 1938; The Private Lives of Birds, 1939; Etching Is the Ideal Hobby, 1941. Editor: Historians' History of the World (25 vols.), 1904; Works of Luther Burbank (12 vols.), 1915. Specialist in hæmatology; originator of the Proteomorphic Theory of Immunization, 1914, and one of the originators of nonspecific protein therapy and of the hypodermic use of vegetable proteins, or proteals, in treatment of conditions of disturbed metabolism. In recent years active as painter and etcher. More than 400 of his pictures are reproduced, many in full color, in mags. and books since 1930. Address: 200 N. Av. 66, Los Angeles, Calif. Died July 4, 1943.

WILLIAMS, Hugh, surgeon; b. Brookline, Mass., June 29, 1872; s. Moses and Martha C. (Fininley) W.; A.B., Harvard, 1894, M.D., 1898. Began practice, Boston, 1898; now retired from practice. Fellow Am. Coll. Surgeons; mem. A.M.A., Mass. Med. Soc., Suffolk Dist. Med. Soc. Unitarian. Clubs: Mass. Automobile, Boston Athletic Assn., Tennis and Racquet; Harvard (Boston and New York). Address: 301 Beacon St., Boston, Mass.* Died Feb. 22, 1945.

WILLIAMS, John Clark, clergyman, educator; b. Walnut Grove, O., May 6, 1877; s. Philander and Emily (Lawson) W.; B.A., Ohio State University, 1904; M.A., 1928; M.A., Kansas City (Kan.) Univ., 1905; (D.D., Adrian [Mich.] Coll., 1913); m. Nina Starr, Sept. 5, 1900 (died Jan. 2, 1910); m. 2d, Edith Obee, Jan. 1, 1912 (died Feb. 20, 1931); m. 3d, Marie Thompson, Sept. 16, 1933. Ordained M.P. ministry, 1907; pastor Whitehouse, O., 1904-06, Arlinton, O., 1906-09; prof. English lit., Kansas City U., 1909-12; pres. Westminster Coll., Tehuacana, Tex., 1912-21; chancellor Kansas City University, 1921-23; pres. Ohio Annual Conference, 1923-25, 1930-35; pastor Whitehouse, 1926-29, Middletown, 1929-30; Columbus since 1936. Pastor of University Meth. Church since 1936. Member Gen. Conf. M.P. Ch., 5 times to 1936, Meth. Uniting Conf., 1939. Member Commn. on Meth. Union. Mem. Pi Gamma Mu. K. of P. Author: The Man of God, 1916. Contbr. to Methodist Christian Advocate. Address: 140 12th Av., Columbus, O. Died Sep. 7, 1947.

WILLIAMS, John Edward, educator; b. Charlotte County, Va., Sept. 17, 1867; s. Albert Henry and Matilda Anne (Berkeley) W.; A.B., Hampden-Sydney Coll., 1892, LL.D., 1925; M.A., U. of Va., 1902, Ph.D., 1899; m. Sallie Taylor Patton, Aug. 28, 1905; children—William Patton, Anne Berkeley, Margaret French. Prin. high sch. Boydton, Va., 1892-94; asst. prin. Commerce Street Sch., Roanoke, Va., 1894-95; prin. pvt. sch., Boydton, 1895; licentiate instr. in mathematics, U. of Va., 1897-1903; adj. prof. mathematics, Va. Poly Inst., 1903, prof. since 1904, also dean since 1924. Mem. Va. State Bd of Edn., 1919-30; mem. Dem. State Central Com., Va.; mem. Bd. Trustees of Hampden-Sydney Coll. Mem. Am. Math. Soc., Math. Assn. America, Va. Acad. Science, Assn. Va. Colleges (pres. 1920), Phi Kappa Phi, Phi Beta Kappa; fellow A.A.A.S. Democrat. Presbyterian. Mason. Home: Blacksburg, Va. Died Apr. 10, 1940.

WILLIAMS, Joseph Vincent, lawyer; b. Sparta, Tenn., Mar. 1, 1872; s. Rev. James Tate and Matilda (Wallace) W.; student Doyle (Tenn.) Coll., 1887-1891; m. Annie Margaret Scholze, Feb. 5, 1902; children—Robert S., Joseph Vincent (officer, U.S. Naval Reserve), Gertrude (Mrs. Charles Marion Gaston), Margaret E. (Mrs. Frank M. Robbins, Jr.). Admitted to Tennessee bar, 1896, and since engaged in practice in Chattanooga; mem. Williams and Williams; U.S. commr. at Chattanooga, 1897-1905; county atty. Hamilton County, 1906-10, county judge, 1911-12. Chmn. Independent Judiciary Conv., 1910; chmn. State Dem. Conv. (nominated Senator R. L. Taylor for gov., 1910). Mem. Am. Bar Assn., Bar Assn. of Tenn. (pres. 1935-36), Chattanooga Bar Assn. (pres. 1933), Tenn. Society of S.A.R. (v.p. 1934-36). Democrat. Presbyterian. Club: Mountain City (Chattanooga). Author of James Tate Williams, His Family, and Recollections (family history, privately published), 1938. Home: 730 Dallas Rd. Office: Hamilton Nat. Bank Bldg., Chattanooga, Tenn. Died Aug. 31, 1947.

WILLIAMS, Lacey Kirk, clergyman; b. Eufaula, Ala.; s. Levi and Elizabeth W.; grad. divinity course, Bishop Coll., Marshall, Tex.; A.B., Ark. Bapt. Coll. (colored), Little Rock, Ark., 1913; D.D., Selma (Ala.) U.; LL.D., Bishop Coll., 1927; m. Georgia Lewis, Aug. 16, 1894; 1 son, Lacey Kirk. Ordained Bapt. ministry, 1894; pastorates at Marshall, Dallas and Fort Worth, Tex.; pastor Olivet Ch., Chicago, since 1916 (11,600 mems.). Pres. Bapt. Missionary and Ednl. Conv., Tex., 12 yrs.; dean theol. dept. I. and M. Coll., Fort Worth, 3 yrs., pres. 1 yr.; pres. Gen. Bapt. State Conv. of Ill.; pres. Nat. Baptist Conv., 1922; elected v.p. Bapt. World Alliance, 1928. Mem. Federal Council Chs. (3d vice chmn. exec. com.). Apptd. by Gov. Lowden mem. Chicago Interracial Commn.; apptd. by Gov Small, 1925, as mem. Council of Nat. Memorial Assn. for Ill. to erect memorial bldg. in Washington, to commemorate deeds of Negro soldiers and sailors of U.S.; head of com. that finished $650,000 bldg. at Nashville, Tenn., as hdqrs. Publishing House of Nat. Bapt. Conv. Lecturer. Received Harmon award "for outstanding work in the religious field," 1929. Led in reorganizing Victory Life Ins. Co., from receivership to successful business, and pres. Victory Mutual Life Ins. Co., 1934-40. Deceased 1940.

WILLIAMS, Leroy Blanchard, lawyer; b. Holland Patent, Oneida County, N.Y., June 5, 1867; s. John Henry and Sarah Jane (Blanchard) W.; A.B., Harvard, 1891; unmarried. Admitted to N.Y. bar, 1893, and since practiced in Syracuse; pres. Syracuse Savings Bank. Republican. Presbyterian. Home: 1524 S. Salina St. Office: Syracuse Savings Bank, Syracuse, N.Y. Died Aug. 13, 1945.

WILLIAMS, Mary Wilhelmine, historian; b. Stanislaus County, Calif., May 14, 1878; d. Charles and Caroline (Madsen) Williams; grad. State Normal Sch., San Jose, Calif., 1901; A.B., Stanford Univ., 1907, A.M., 1908, Ph.D., 1914; studied U. of Chicago. Teacher pub. schs. 6 yrs.; instr. history, Stanford, 1913, 14, Wellesley, 1914-15; asst. prof. history, Goucher Coll., 1915-19, asso. prof., 1919-20, prof., 1920-40, prof. emeritus since 1940. Special investigator for Honduras in connection with mediation by U.S. Dept. State of Honduranean-Guatemalan and Honduranean-Nicaraguan boundary disputes, 1918-19. Member Am. Hist. Assn. (exec. council 1922-26; sec. Latin-Am. Conf., 1923-34), com. on Latin-Am. Studies, U.S. Nat. Com. on Inter-Am. Intellectual Coöperation, Am. Assn. Univ. Women, Nat. Com. for Columbus Memorial Lighthouse, U.S. Dept. of State Sub-com. on Inter-Am. Fellowships and Professorships, 1938-40. Member Nat. Woman's Party, Pan-Am. League, Women's Internat. League for Peace and Freedom. (mem. Nat. Bd. 4 yrs.). Unitarian. Club: Stanford Women's. Author: Anglo-American Isthmian Diplomacy (1815-1915), 1914 (awarded Justin Winsor Prize by Am. Hist. Assn.); Cousin-Hunting in Scandinavia, 1916; Social Scandinavia in the Viking Age, 1920; The People and Politics of Latin America, 1930, 2d edit., 1938; Dom Pedro the Magnanimous, Second Emperor of Brazil, 1937; also Biography of John Middleton Clayton in American Secretaries of State and Their Diplomacy, 1928. Made spl. ednl. survey of Latin America for Am. Assn. Univ. Women, 1926-27. Contbr. to Dictionary of Am. Biography, Ency. of the Social Sciences, Dictionary of Am. History, also to mags. and ednl. and hist. reviews. Mem. bd. editors Hispanic-Am. Hist. Review, 1927-33, Equal Rights (Independent Feminist Weekly), 1935-36. Home: 752 Guinda St., Palo Alto, Calif. Died Mar. 10, 1944.

WILLIAMS, Richard Peters, Marine Corps officer (ret.); born Atlanta, Ga., June 20, 1879; s. Charles Wilson and Elizabeth (Overby) W.; ed. various pub. and pvt. schs. in U.S.; m. Agnes M. Miller, May 1909 (died Apr. 1913); m. 2d, Helen Strobhar, Oct. 21, 1921. Commd. 2d lt., U.S. Marine Corps, 1899, and advanced through the grades to brig. gen. 1934, retired Apr. 1, 1940; recalled to active duty Feb. 1, 1941, serving until Apr. 23, 1941 (retired); appointed secretary for defense, State of New Jersey, by Gov. Edison, June 3, 1941 (retired April 1, 1942). Served on various ships of United States Fleet and at shore stations in United States, P.I., China, Santo Domingo, Haiti; served as assistant chief of staff, G-3, attached to 6th Div. U.S. Army, in World War. Decorated Comdr. Order of Honor and Merit, Medaille Militaire and D.S.M. (Haiti); Naval D.S.M., Spanish-American War, Philippine Campaign, Cuban Pacification, Expeditionary (with 4 stars), Vera Cruz and Victory (with 2 bronze stars) medals (U.S.). Catholic. Clubs: Army and Navy (Washington, D.C.); University (Phila.); N.Y. Athletic (N.Y. City). Home: 1007 Whitaker St., Savannah, Ga. Died Mar. 14, 1950.

WILLIAMS, Robert, univ. pres.; b. Skipton, Yorkshire, Eng., Mar. 9, 1884; s. Thomas and Hannah (Fletcher) W.; A.B., Wesleyan U., Conn., 1911; D.D., Albion (Mich.) Coll., 1921; A.M., Boston U., 1927; grad. study, summers, Boston and Harvard; LL.D., Ohio Wesleyan, 1930, Boston U., 1941; m. Mabel Carolyn Howard, June 8, 1909; children—Milton Howard, Florence Ethel. Ordained ministry M.E. Ch., 1914; pastor Southbury, Conn., 1911-13; v.p. and registrar East Greenwich (R.I.) Acad., 1913-14; pastor Summerfield Ch., New Haven, Conn., 1914-18; dean of Dickinson Sem., Williamsport, Pa., 1918-21; dean and prof. philosophy, Albion Coll., 1921-29; pres. Ohio Northern U., 1929-43. Del. to General Conf. of Meth. Ch., 1940, Jurisdictional Conf. of Meth. Ch., Chicago, 1941. Member Delta Sigma Rho, Sigma Chi. Republican. Mason (Grand Chaplain of Grand Lodge F.&A.M., State of Ohio, 1940). Club: Rotary. Contbr. verse in Michigan Methodist Poetry, 1927, also articles in religious mags. Lecturer Rotary Internat., 1944. Home: Van Wert, O.* Died June 18, 1944.

WILLIAMS, Robert Gray, lawyer; b. Leesburg, Va., July 10, 1878; s. John James and Emilie (Gray) W.; prep. edn., Shenandoah Valley Acad., Winchester, Va.; student U. of Va., 1896-1900; LL.D., Roanoke Coll., Va., 1932; m. Elizabeth King, Dec. 1, 1900 (dec.); m. 2d, Hilda B. Dean, Sept. 4, 1940. Practiced at Winchester since 1900; city solicitor, Winchester, 12 yrs.; counsel Northern Va. Power Co., Va. Woolen Co., div. counsel B.&O. R.R. and local counsel Pa. R.R.; pres. and counsel Shenandoah Valley Nat. Bank; pres. Rockingham Pub. Co.; pres., counsel George Washington Hotel Corp.; dir. Chesapeake & Potomac Telephone Co. of Va. Trustee U. of Va. Alumni Fund, 1923; mem. Va. State Library Board; mem. board of visitors U. of Va., rector U. of Va. Mem. Am. Bar Assn., Va. State Bar Assn. (pres. 1926-27), Phi Beta Kappa, Delta Psi; mem. Commn. to Suggest Amendments to Va. Constn. Democrat. Episcopalian. Clubs: Winchester Golf; Colonnade (U. of Va.); Commonwealth (Richmond, Va.); Nat. Press (Washington, D.C.). Home: Winchester, Va. Died July 24, 1946.

WILLIAMS, Robert Lee, judge; b. Brundidge, Ala., Dec. 20, 1868; s. Jonathan and Sarah Julia (Paul) W.; M.A., Southern U. (now Birmingham-Southern Coll.), Greensboro, Ala., 1894, LL.D., 1913; LL.D., Tulsa U., 1934; unmarried. Admitted to bar, 1891, and began practice Troy, Ala.; went to Atoka, Indian Territory, 1896, and 6 months later to Durant; city atty., Durant; 1899; mem. Ind. Ty. Dem. Com., 1902-04; Dem. Nat. Com., 1904-08; mem. Okla. Constl. Conv., 1906-07; chief justice Supreme Ct. of Okla., 1907-08; reëlected for term 1909-15; resigned Mar. 10, 1914; gov. of Okla., term 1915-19; U.S. judge, Eastern Dist. of Okla., Feb. 19, 1919-37; became U.S. Circuit Judge Tenth Circuit, Apr. 26, 1937; retired Mar. 31, 1939, but continued to serve. Mem. Okla. State Hist. Soc. (pres.), Am. Bar Assn., Alpha Tau Omega (Ala. Beta Beta Chapter). Methodist. Mason (32°). Author: Constitution and Enabling Act of Okla., Annotated. Home: Durant, Okla. Died April 10, 1948.

WILLIAMS, Robert White, lawyer; b. E. Carroll Parish, La., Dec. 5, 1877; s. Robert Willoughby and Virginia (Sutton) W.; LL.B., Northern Ind. Law Sch., Valparaiso, 1898; m. Norma Stewart Cleneay, Nov. 11, 1920; children—Robert Willoughby, Elizabeth McCleneay. Practiced law with father at Tallahassee, Fla., 1898-1902; apptd. to Dept. of Agr., 1902; entered solicitor's office, 1907; apptd. law officer Forest Service, 1910, asst. solicitor, 1915, solicitor Dept. of Agr., 1920-29; dep. U.S. game conservation officer, 1929-31, asst. since July 11, 1931. Mem. Am. Ornithologists' Union, Washington Biologists' Field Club, Wilson Ornithol. Club, Cooper Ornithol. Club. Episcopalian. Author: Game Commissioners and Wardens, Their Appointment, Powers and Duties (U. S. Dept. Agr.), 1904; also articles on ornithology and wild life. Address: Biological Survey, U.S. Dept. Agriculture, Washington. Died Sept. 19, 1940.

WILLIAMS, Roy Hughes, judge; b. Milan, O., Sept. 1, 1874; s. Charles Ronald and Helen Hortense (Hughes) W.; student Oberlin Coll., 1890-92; LL.B., U. of Mich., 1897; m. Verna Lockwood, Dec. 7, 1898. Admitted to Ohio bar, 1897, and practiced in Sandusky; pros. atty. Erie County, 1901-07; judge Court of Common Pleas, Erie County, 1915-25; judge Court of Appeals, 6th Dist., 1925-34; judge Supreme Court of Ohio since Dec. 1, 1934. Served in Field arty., C.O.T.S., 44th Training Battery, Camp Zachary Taylor, Louisville, Ky., World War I. Mem. S.A.R. (ex-pres. Toledo Chapter). Republican. Presbyterian. Mason (32°), L.O.M. (Past Supreme Gov.). Home: 1415 Columbus Av., Sandusky, O.; (winter) 1015-16 Deshler-Wallick Hotel, Columbus 15, Ohio. Address: Supreme Court, Columbus, O. Died Dec. 18, 1946.

WILLIAMS, Roy T., clergyman; b. Many, La.; A.B., Peniel Coll., 1905, also B.D.; grad. student U. of Chicago; m. Eunice Harvey, 1906; children—Reginald, Roy T. Teacher Peniel Coll., 1907-11, pres., 1911-13; evangelist, 1913-15; gen. supt. Ch. of the Nazarene since 1915. Author: The Perfect Man; Temptation; Glimpses Abroad; Sanctification; Attitudes and Relations. Address: 2923 Troost Av., Kansas City, Mo.* Died Mar. 24, 1946.

WILSON, Rufus Rockwell, author; b. Troy, Pa., Mar. 15, 1865; s. Hiram and Mary (Rockwell) W.; ed. high sch.; m. Anna Otilie Erickson, June 2, 1934; children—Marion Elizabeth (dec.), Edward Strong. Journalist in Pittsburgh, Washington, New York, 1883-91; mag. writer and newspaper syndicate mgr., 1891-1906; on staff Brooklyn Eagle, 1906-08; editor and pub. Malden (Wash.) Herald, 1908-09; lit. and polit. reform work, 1911; sec. Seattle Comml. Club, 1911; sec. Humboldt Development Co., Eureka, Calif., 1912-13; community advt., New York, 1914-16; sec. Nat. Assn. Cotton Mfrs., 1917-21; organizer and gen. sec. First World Cotton Conf., New Orleans, 1919; engaged in mining, 1921-29; now pres. Primavera Press, Inc., Wilson Book Co. Author: Rambles in Colonial Byways, 1900; Washington, The Capital City, 1901; New York, Old and New, 1902; Lincoln in Caricature, 1903; New England in Letters, 1904; The Sea Rovers, 1906; A Noble Company of Adventurers, 1908; What Lincoln Read, 1932; Out of the West, 1932; Lincoln in Portraiture, 1936; Lincoln Among His Friends, 1942; Intimate Memories of Lincoln, 1945; Lincoln in Caricature (new edit.), 1946; New York in Literature, 1947. Editor: Burnaby's Travels Through North America, 1904; Heath's Memoirs of the American War, 1904; Moultrie's Memoirs of the American Revolution, 1905; The Golden Year, 1932; Across the Plains and Among the Diggings, 1936; Jedediah Smith: Trader and Trail Breaker, 1936; Lincoln's First Years in Illinois, 1946; Uncollected Works of Lincoln—A Supplement to Nicolay and Hay, 1947. Home: 610 W. Church St., Elmira, N.Y. Died Dec. 11, 1949.

WILLIAMS, Samuel Clay, lawyer; b. Mooresville, N.C., Sept. 24, 1884; s. Thomas Jefferson and Willie Ada (McCulloch) W.; A.B., Davidson (N.C.) Coll., 1905; LL.B., U. of Va., 1908; LL.D., Davidson Coll., 1941; m. LuTelle Sherrill, Nov. 23, 1910; children — Margaret Sherrill (Mrs. Thornton H. Brooks), Samuel Clay. Admitted to North Carolina bar, 1908, and began practice at Greensboro; member Sapp and Williams, 1910-14, Brooks, Sapp and Williams, 1914-17; moved to Winston-Salem, North Carolina, 1917; assistant general counsel R. J. Reynolds Tobacco Co., 1917-21, general counsel, 1921-25, v.p. and gen. counsel, 1925-31, pres., 1931-34, vice chmn. of bd., 1934-35, chmn. bd. since 1935; dir. Security Life & Trust Co., Am. Telephone & Telegraph Co. Dir. U.S. Chamber of Commerce, 1937-39; dir. and v.p. Nat. Assn. Mfrs., 1936-38. On leave of absence, served as chmn. for industry of Nat. Labor Bd., 1933-34, chmn. Nat. Industrial Recovery Bd., Sept. 1934-Mar. 1935; mem. business advisory council of Dept. of Commerce since 1933, chmn. 1934. Mem. bd. and exec. com., trustee Nat. Industrial Conf., chmn. bd., 1943-44. Trustee Davidson Coll.; trustee, mem. exec. com. Infantile Paralysis Found., 1936-46. Mem. Am. and N.C. State bar assns., Phi Beta Kappa, Omicron Delta Kappa, Delta Sigma Rho, Phi Delta Phi, Beta Theta Pi. Presbyterian. Clubs: Rotary, Twin City, Forsyth Country; Sedgefield Country; Congressional Country (Washington). Home: Robert E. Lee Hotel and Wilsherr Lodge. Office: R. J. Reynolds Tobacco Co., Winston-Salem, N.C. Died Feb. 25, 1949.

WILLIAMS, Samuel Cole, jurist; b. Gibson County, Tenn., Jan. 15, 1864; s. Thomas J. and Martha R. (Cole) W.; LL.B., Vanderbilt U., 1884; LL.D., Emory and Henry Coll.; L.H.D., Tusculum Coll.; m. Mary T. Mayne, July 20, 1892; children—Mayne (dec.), Gertrude (Mrs. R. R. Miller); m. 2d, Isabel Hayes Jan. 16, 1919; 1 dau., Martha Cole. Began practice, 1884; gen. counsel Ohio River & Charleston Ry., 1892-1903; chancellor of Tenn., by spl. appmt. of Gov. Hooper, 1912-13; apptd. asso. justice Supreme Court of Tenn., Feb. 12, 1913; elected for full term, Aug. 6, 1914; first dean Lamar School of Law, Emory U., 1920-25; chmn. Tenn. Code Commn. since 1929; chmn. Tenn Hist. Com. since 1941. Trustee Fort Loudoun Assn., and Hermitage Assn. Mem. Am. and Tenn. bar assns., Am. Law Inst., Am. Hist. Assn., Va. Hist. Soc., Tenn. Hist. Soc. (v.p.), E. Tenn. Hist. Soc. (pres.), Beta Theta Pi, Phi Delta Phi. Democrat. Methodist. Author: History Lost State of Franklin, 1924, rev. edit., 1933; Early Travels in the Tennessee Country, 1926, 28; Beginnings of West Tennessee, 1929; History of Codification in Tennessee, 1932; Gen. John T. Wilder, 1935; Dawn of Tennessee Valley and Tennessee History, 1937; Brig. Gen. Nathaniel Taylor, 1940; Phases of History of the Supreme Court of Tennessee, 1944; The Lincolns and Tennessee, 1942; Tennessee during the Revolutionary War, 1944; Admission of Tennessee into the Union, 1945; William Tatham, Wautagan, 1947. Editor: Timberlake's Memoirs, 1927; Adair's History of the American Indians, 1930; Williams' Annotated Code of Tenn., 8 vols. Home: "Aquone," Johnson City, Tenn. Died Dec. 14, 1947.

WILLIAMS, Thomas Frederick, clergyman; b. Gentryville, Ind., Nov. 5, 1876; s. Jacob Frederick M. and Arlevia Elizabeth (Bunton) W.; A.B., DePauw, 1907, D.D., 1925; S.T.B., Boston U., 1912; m. Edith Johnson, Aug. 3, 1910; 1 son, Thomas E. Teacher pub. schs., Ind., 1894-99; pastor Francisco Circuit, Ind., 1900-01; student pastor W. Washington Street Ch., Indianapolis, 1901-09, High Street Ch., Somersworth, N.H., 1909-12; ordained M.E. ministry, 1904; pastor Plainfield, Ind., 1912-16, Valparaiso, 1916-19, Trinity Ch., Lafayette, Ind., since May 1919. Dean, Battle Ground Epworth League Inst., 1925-34. Del. to Gen. Conf. M.E. Ch., Springfield, Mass., 1924, Kansas City, Mo., 1928, Atlantic City, N.J., 1932; mem. North Central Jurisdictional Conf. Methodist Ch., Chicago, 1940. President Preachers Aid Society Northwest Ind. Conf.; pres. bd. trustees Ind. Anti-Saloon League; mem. board dirs., Anti-Saloon League of America. Member North Central Jurisdictional Conf., Minneapolis, 1944. In Paebar's Anthology of Verse, and Who's Who In Poetry in America. Mem. Theta Phi, Delta Upsilon. Rotarian (del. Internat. Conv., Boston, 1933). Mason (York Rite; 32°). Home: 404 N. 6th St., Lafayette, Ind. Deceased.

WILLIAMS, Tyrrell, prof. law; b. Sandusky, O., July 17, 1875; s. Rev. Dr. Meade Creighton and Elizabeth Blaine (Riddle) W.: A.B., Princeton, 1898; LL.B., Washington University, St. Louis, 1900; m. Eleanor Niedringhaus, Aug. 17, 1907 (died Nov. 10, 1943); 1 son, Meade; m. 2d, Zoë Harrison Koerner, December 23, 1944. Practiced in St. Louis, 1900-13; professor law, and Madill professor contracts, Washington University, since February 1, 1913. Mem. American and St. Louis bar associations, Am. Law Inst. (charter mem., adviser on criminal procedure), Phi Beta Kappa, Phi Delta Phi. Republican. Presbyterian. Club: University. Author: (with G. A. Finkelnburg) Missouri Appellate Practice, 1905. Chief of enforcement div. U.S. Food Administration, at St. Louis, 1917-18; dir. Meyer Bros. Drug Co. Home: 443 Westgate Av., St. Louis 5, Mo. Died March 1, 1947.

WILLIAMS, W(alter) L(ong), veterinarian; b. Argenta, Ill., Feb. 26, 1856; s. Jackson and Lavina W.; U. of Ill., 1875-77; grad. Montreal Vet. Coll., 1879; m. Mary E. Wilkinson, Mar. 3, 1886; children Ethel May (Mrs. Samuel J. Plimpton), Paul, Walter Wilkinson, Luella, Mary Lavina (Mrs. Edward D. McDonald). Asst. state veterinarian of Ill., 1874-91; prof. vet. sci., Purdue Univ., 1891-93, Mont. Agrl. Coll., 1893-96; prof. vet. surgery, obstetrics, zoötechnics and jurisprudence, 1896-1915, prof. vet. obstetrics and research prof. diseases of breeding cattle, 1915-21, emeritus prof. since 1921, N.Y. State Veterinary College, at Cornell Univ. Asso. editor Am. Vet. Review, 1890-1912; editor for U.S. the Vet. Journal, London, 1906-08. Pres. Ill. State Vet. Med. Assn., 1888-91, Am. Vet. Med. Assn., 1893, N.Y. State Vet. Med. Soc., 1907-08; hon. member Ia. Vet. Med. Assn.; fgn. corr. mem. Société Centrale de Médicine Veterinaire of France; hon. mem. Central Vet. Soc. of England, Vet. Soc. of Sweden. Author Veterinary Obstetrics, Diseases of the Genital Organs of Domestic Animals, etc. Contbr. (article) Recollections of and Reflections upon Sixty-Five Years in the Veterinary Profession, in Cornell Veterinarian, Apr. and July 1945. Home: 209 White Park Rd., Ithaca, N.Y. Died Oct. 23, 1945; buried in Pleasant Grove Cemetery, Ithaca, N.Y.

WILLIAMS, Wayland Wells, writer, artist; b. New Haven, Conn., Aug. 16, 1888; s. Frederick Wells and Fanny Hapgood (Wayland) W.; B.A., Yale, 1910; studied U. of Munich, 1910-11; studied art in N.Y. City and at Yale Art Sch., 1929-34; unmarried. Reporter New York Evening Post, 1912-13; engaged in authorship until 1928; asst. state supervisor for Conn., Pub. Works of Art Project, 1934-35; Conn. State dir. art, Works Progress Adminstrn., 1935-1941; member Municipal Art Commn., New Haven. Exhibited art works at New Haven and Lime Rock, Conn., Stockbridge, Mass. Mem. New Haven Paint and Clay Club, Connecticut Academy of Fine Arts, Phi Beta Kappa, Psi Upsilon. Republican. Episcopalian. Clubs: University (New York); Graduate (New Haven). Author: The Whirligig of Time, 1916; Goshen Street, 1920; Family, 1923; I the King, 1924; The Seafarers (poems), 1924; Edited: Castle in Spain (poems by W. B. D. Henderson), 1942. Home: 155 Whitney Av., New Haven, Conn. Died May 6, 1945.

WILLIAMS, William; b. New London, Conn., June 2, 1862; s. Charles Augustus and Elizabeth H. W.; A.B., Yale, 1884 (A.M., 1906); LL.B., Harvard, 1888; A.M., Columbia, 1914. Practiced law at New York; U.S. commr. of immigration at New York, 1902-05, and May, 1909-July 1 1913; commr. water supply, gas and electricity, New York City, by apptmt. of Mayor Mitchel, since Feb., 1914. Asso. counsel for U.S. during Behring Sea arbitration with Great Britain, 1892. Maj. U.S.V. during Spanish-Am. War, 1898. Republican. Clubs: University, Metropolitan, Century, Down Town, Republican, Yale. Home: 1 W. 54th St. Office: Municipal Bldg., New York. Died Feb. 8, 1947.

WILLIAMS, William Clayton, Jr., mfg. exec.; b. Orange, Va., May 13, 1884; s. William Clayton and Evelyn (Johnson) W.; B.S., Va. Polytech. Inst., 1905; m. Sally Aiken, Mar. 20, 1914; children—Wyatt Aiken, Evelyn Johnson. Began as draftsman, 1906; with Interborough Rapid Transit Co., N.Y. City, 1906-11; asst. signal engr., Brooklyn Rapid Transit Co., 1911-17; plant engr., Chevrolet Motor Co., Tarrytown, N.Y., 1917, Fort Worth, Tex., 1917-21, mgr. plant, Oakland, Calif., 1921-26; in charge of all Chevrolet assembly plants, Detroit, 1926-37; with Gen. Motors Corporation, Detroit, since 1937, vice-pres. since 1940, and member administration committee. Episcopalian.

Home: "Yatton," Orange, Va. Office: General Motors Bldg., Detroit, Mich. Died Nov. 2, 1945.

WILLIAMSON, Frederick Ely, ry. official; b. Norwalk, O., June 14, 1876; s. James De Long and Edith (Ely) W.; grad. University Sch., Cleveland, O., 1894; A.B., Yale U., 1898, M.A., 1932; LL.D., Colgate U., 1035; hon. Dr.Engring., Rensselaer Poly. Inst., 1941; m. Hilda Raymond, October 11, 1905. With N.Y.C. R.R. Co., as clk., claim agt., freight agt., car accountant, asst. div. supt. and div. supt., 1898-1916; with U.S.R.R. Adminstrn., New York, 1917-18; gen. supt. and asst. to gen. mgr. N.Y.C. R.R. Co., 1918-25; v.p. in charge operation and maintenance N.P. Ry., 1925-28; exec. v.p. C.,B.&Q. R.R. and Colo. & Southern Ry., Sept., 1928-Jan. 1929, chmn. exec. com. and pres., 1929-32; pres. N.Y.C. R R. and its subsidiaries since 1932; dir. Central R R. of New Jersey, Cleveland-Cliffs Iron Company; director Federal Reserve Bank of New York. Associate Northwestern U. Lt. col. U.S. Army Res., retired. Dir. and mem. exec. com. Assn. of Am. Railroads; mem.' Am. Ry. Engring. Assn., Ohio Soc. of N.Y., Albany Soc. of N.Y., Pilgrims of U.S., Alpha Delta Phi. Clubs: Yale, Century Assn., Recess, The Links, Railroad (N.Y.); Southside Sportsmen's (L.I.); Chicago, Commercial (Chicago); Ft. Orange (Albany); Rolling Rock (Pittsburgh); Graduate (New Haven); University (Montreal); St. Maurice Game and Fish (La Tuque, P.Q.). Home: 1220 Park Av. Office: 230 Park Av., New York, N.Y. Died Sep. 29, 1944.

WILLIAMSON, Frederick Warren, lawyer; b. Mound City, Ill., Sept. 20, 1897; s. Albert Warren and Alma Inez (Culp) W.; A.B., Stanford U., 1919; LL.B., Harvard U., 1922; m. Ruth Chandler, June 26, 1924; children—Warren Brooks, Chandler, Susan, Norman Bruce. Admitted to Calif. bar, 1922, private practice of law since; asso. with Bauer, Wright and Macdonald, 1922-25; partner, Faries and Williamson, 1925-32; Faries, Williamson and Musick, 1932-34; Williamson, Ramsey & Hoge, 1934-36; Williamson, Hoge, Sargent, and Judson, 1936-38; Williamson, Hoge, and Judson since 1938. Dir. Yosemite Park and Curry Co., Serrano Corp., Rancho Santa Anita Inc. Served with coast arty., Officers Training Camp, Fortress Monroe, 1917-18. Vice-pres. Friends of Huntington Library; dir. Friends of Colleges at Claremont, trustee Pomona Coll.; trustee Calif. Inst. of Tech. Mem. Am., Calif. and Los Angeles County bar assns., Am. Judicature Soc., Calif. and Southern Calif. Hist. Socs., Calif. Inst. of Technology Associates, Va. Hist. Soc., Alpha Delta Phi. Republican. Conglist. Clubs: California, Sunset, Zamarano of Los Angeles (pres.); Bohemian, (San Francisco); Grolier (New York). Home: 1025 Arden Rd., Pasadena. Office: 810 Title & Insurance Bldg., Los Angeles, Calif. Died July 13, 1942.

WILLIAMSON, George, banker; b. Ora, Miss., Oct. 12, 1883; s. James and Charity (Rogers) W.; grad. high sch., and Soule's Business Coll., New Orleans, La., 1902; m. Fannie Askew, Jan. 11, 1911. Began career in small country bank; note clk. First Nat. Bank, Vicksburg, Miss., 1906, pres. since 1928; pres. Delta Ice Co. Democrat. Episcopalian. Home: Vicksburg, Miss. Died Nov. 1941.

WILLIAMSON, Jessie, Rep. nat. committeewoman for Calif. Home: 2816 Oak Knoll Terrace, Berkeley, Calif. Died July 22, 1948.

WILLIAMSON, Roy Elisha, clergyman, ch. exec.; b. Carterville, Ill., May 12, 1890; s. James Franklin and Valura Etta (Jones) W.; A.B., Shurtleff Coll., Alton, Ill., 1918, D.D., 1932; B.D., Rochester (N.Y.) Theol. Sem., 1922; m. Loueva Harrell, June 30, 1910; children—William Franklin, Marie Louise. Newspaper reporter, 1910-12; pastor rural chs., 1913-18; student pastor, 1919-22; ordained to ministry Bapt. Ch., 1915; pastor First Ch., Waterloo, Ia., 1922-26, Grand River Av. Ch., Detroit, Mich., 1926-36; exec. sec. Bapt. Missionary Conv. of State of N.Y. since 1936; mem. administrative com. Council on Finance and Promotion, Northern Bapt. Conv.; v.p. and mem. bd. of dirs. N.Y. State Council of Churches and Christian Edn.; mem. bd. of trustees Kenka Coll. and of Cook Acad. Served as 1st lt., chaplain, U.S. Army, with 4th Div. A.E.F., 1918-19. Mem. Ministerial Assn. of Syracuse, N.Y., Ministers Council of Northern Bapt. Conv. Republican. Mason. Club: Rotary. Editor of The Baptist New Yorker since 1936. Home: 826 Westcott St. Office: 433 S. Salina St., Syracuse, N.Y. Died Dec. 23, 1944.

WILLINGHAM, Henry J., educator; b. St. Clair County, Ala., Jan. 18, 1868; s. James Ezekiel and Mary Ann (Lewis) W.; A.B., Howard Coll., Ala., 1891; A.M., 1894, LL.D., same, 1911; also LL.D., from University of Ala., 1928; m. Sara Frances Nichols, Dec. 28, 1896; children—Henry Clay, Mary Clyde, Nell Nichols, Sara Frances. Pres. Lineville Coll., 1893-1900, Fifth Dist. Agrl. Sch., Ala., 1900-07; sec. State Bd. Examiners for Teachers, 1907-11; state supt. edn., Ala., term 1911-14; pres. State Teachers Coll., Florence, Ala., 1914-38, pres. emeritus since 1938; collector of internal revenue, Dist. of Ala., since Sept. 1, 1939. Ex-pres. Bapt. State Mission Bd.; trustee Howard Coll. Mem. Ala. Ednl. Assn. (pres. 1904-05), N.E.A. (v.p. supts.' div.). Mason, K.P., Odd Fellow. Mem. Kappa Delta Pi, Sigma Nu. Rotarian. Home: Florence, Ala. Died Dec. 4, 1948.

WILLINGHAM, William A.; chmn. bd. Universal Leaf Tobacco Co.; officer or dir. other cos. Home: "Robin Hill." 5101 Cary St. Office: Richmond Trust Bldg., Richmond, Va. Died May 29, 1945.

WILLIS, Bailey, geologist; b. Idlewild-on-Hudson, N.Y., May 31, 1857; s. Nathaniel Parker and Cornelia (Grinnell) W.; E.M., Columbia School Mines, 1878, C.E., 1879; hon. Ph.D., U. of Berlin, Germany, 1910; Sc.D., Columbia, 1929; m. Miss A. H. Grinnell, Mar. 4, 1882 (died 1896); 1 dau., Hope; m. 2d, Miss M. D. Baker, Apr. 21, 1898 (died March 21, 1941); children—Cornelius G., Robin, Margaret. Spl. expert iron ores, 10th Census, 1879-81; geologist Northern Transcontinental Survey, exploration for N.P. and allied cos., 1881-84; geologist U.S. Geol. Survey, 1884-1916; in charge Appalachian Div., New York to Ala., Cascade Range and Puget Sound Div., Wash., and editor Geologic Atlas of U.S.; asst. to dir. U.S. Geol. Survey, 1897-1902; geologist in charge of div. of areal and stratigraphic geology, 1900-02; geologist engaged in geol. explorations in China under auspices of Carnegie Instn. of Washington, 1903-04, gold medal, Société Géographique de France, 1910. Lecturer on geology, Johns Hopkins, 1895-1902, U. of Chicago, 1909; cons. geologist to minister pub. works, Argentina, 1911-15; prof. geology, Stanford U., Calif., 1915-22; emeritus, 1922. Chief of Latin Am. div. of Col. E. M. House "Inquiry," for Peace Conf., 1918. Seismologist, Carnegie Instn. of Washington expdns. to Chile, 1923, to Orient, Palestine, Cyprus, 1927, East Africa, 1929, to Japan, Philippines, India, 1937. Consulting geol. engineer since 1922. Decorated Commander Order of Leopold II, 1933; Belgian Legion of Honor, 1936. Mem. Geol. Society of Am. (pres. 1928), Society Am. Geographers, Am. Philos. Soc., Am. Acad. Arts and Sciences, Seismol. Soc. America (pres. 1921-26), Am. Inst. Mining and Metall. Engrs., Soc. Econ. Geologists, Nat. Acad. Sciences, etc.; hon. mem. Royal Geog. Soc. (London); Société Géologique de Belgique; foreign corr. Geol. Soc. London; Wissenschaftliche Gesellschaft (Munich), Gesellsch. z. Erdkunde (Berlin). Penrose medalist, 1944. Clubs: Engineers, Commonwealth (San Francisco); Cosmos (Washington). Author: Mechanics of Appalachian Structure; Research in China; Geologic Structures; Living Africa; African Plateaus and Rift Valleys; Northern Patagonia; Earthquake Conditions in Chile; Earthquakes in the Holy Land; A Yanqui in Patagonia; Geol. Map of N. America; also numerous sci. articles. Home: 539 Lasuen. Address: Box 1365, Stanford University, Calif. Died Feb. 19, 1949.

WILLKIE, Wendell Lewis (wĭl'kē), lawyer; b. Elwood, Ind., Feb. 18, 1892; s. Herman Francis and Henrietta (Trisch) W.; A.B., Indiana U., 1913, LL.B., 1916, LL.D., 1938; LL.D., Colgate U., 1939; Dartmouth Coll., 1941, Yale U., 1941, Bowdoin Coll., 1941, Rutgers University, 1941; Union Coll., 1942, Boston U., 1943, Oberlin Coll., 1943; Sc.D., Stevens Inst. of Technology, 1941; student Oberlin College, 1916; m. Edith Wilk, January 14, 1918; 1 son, Philip Herman. Admitted to Ind. bar, 1916, Ohio, 1919, N.Y., 1930; mem. law firm Willkie & Willkie, Elwood, 1916-19, Mather, Nesbitt & Willkie, Akron, O., 1919-29, Weadock & Willkie, N.Y. City, 1929-32; pres. Commonwealth & Southern Corp., 1933-40; mem. law firm Willkie, Owen, Otis, Farr & Gallagher; chmn. bd. 20th Century-Fox. Republican nominee for President of U.S., 1940. Trustee New York Hosp., Beekman Street Hosp., Hampton Inst. Enlisted as private, U S. Army, Apr. 6, 1917 (the day war was declared); served as 1st lt., 325th F.A., A E.F.; advanced to capt., 1918. Mem. Assn. of Bar City of New York. Republican. Episcopalian. Clubs: Century Assn., Lawyers Club, Downtown Assn. Author: One World, 1943. Home: 1010 5th Av. Office: 15 Broad St., New York, N.Y. Died Oct. 8, 1944.

WILLOUGHBY, Charles Clark, anthropologist; b. Winchendon, Mass., July 5, 1857; s. William Alonzo and Mehitable Edson (Clark) W.; Austin teaching fellow, Harvard, 1899-1901; hon. A.M., Bowdoin, 1915; m. Margaret Elizabeth Stanwood; children—Alice Stanwood, Ruth (died in infancy), Malcolm Francis. Asst. Dept. of Anthropology, Chicago Expn., 1892-93; chief asst. Peabody Museum of Archæology and Ethnology, Harvard, 1894-99, asst. curator, 1899-1913, asst. dir., 1913-15, dir. 1915-28, dir. emeritus since 1928. Fellow A.A.A.S.; mem. Am. Anthropol. Assn.; corr. mem. Swedish Soc. Anthropology and Geography. Writer on anthropol. subjects. Home: 291 School St., Watertown, Mass. Died Apr. 21, 1943.

WILLOUGHBY, Julius Edgar, civil engr.; b. Arkadelphia, Ala., Oct. 12, 1871; s. John P. and Mary Jane (Cosby) W; B.C.E, 1892, and C.E, U. of Ala.; m. Mary Alice Byars, Oct. 17, 1895; children—William (dec.), Mary, Ruth. Began with L.&N. R.R., 1892, asst. chief engr. constrn., 1900, engr. of constrn. and chief engr. of certain L.&N. subsidiary lines, 1901-11; chief engr. Caribbean Constrn. Co. and of Nat. Ry. of Hayti, 1912; with Atlantic Coast Line since 1913, asst. chief engr. until 1916, chief engr., 1916-42, consulting engineer since 1942; also chief engineer Tampa Southern R R. Company, Ft. Myers Southern R.R. Co., Charleston & Western Carolina Ry. Co. to 1942. Fellow A.A.A.S.; mem. Am. Soc. C.E., Am. Ry. Engring. Assn., N.C. Soc. Engrs. (hon.), Soc. Am. Mil. Engrs., Fla. Engr. Soc. Republican. Methodist. Club: Cape Fear. Has built and rebuilt more than 3,000 miles of ry. Address: Wilmington, N.C. Home: Blount Springs, Ala. Died Mar. 11, 1944.

WILLOUGHBY, Westel Woodbury, univ. prof.; b. Alexandria, Va., July 20, 1867; s. Westel and Jennie R. (Woodbury) W.; brother of William Franklin Willoughby; A.B., Johns Hopkins, 1888, Ph.D., 1891, (hon.) LL D., Johns Hopkins U., 1036; m. Grace Robinson, June 27, 1893; children—Westel Robinson, Laura Robinson (Mrs. John E. Rowe). Admitted to bar, 1891; practiced at Washington, 1891-97; acting asst. prof. polit. science, Leland Stanford Jr. U., 1894-95; prof. polit. science, Johns Hopkins, 1897-1933. Lecturer polit. science, George Washington U., 1927-03; lecturer political science, Princeton Univ., 1904-16; constl. adviser to Chinese Govt., 1916-17; chief tech. adviser to Chinese delegation, Washington Conf., 1921-22; counsellor and adviser to Chinese delegation Internat. Opium Conf., Geneva, 1924-25. Mem. Am. Polit. Science Assn. (ex-sec.-treas., ex-pres.), Am. Soc. Internat. Law. Author: The Supreme Court of the U S.—Its History and Administrative Importance, 1890; Government and Administration of the United States, 1891; The Nature of the State—A Study in Political Philosophy, 1896; The Rights and Duties of American Citizenship, 1898; Social Justice—A Critical Study, 1900; The Political Theories of the Ancient World, 1903; The American Constitutional System, 1904; Constitutional Law of the United States, 3 vols., 1929; Principles of the Constitutional Law of the United States; Prussian Political Philosophy, 1918; Foreign Rights and Interests in China, 1920, 27; Problem of Government (with Lindsay Rogers), 1921; China at the Conference, 1922; Fundamental Concepts of Public Law, 1924; Opium as an International Problem, 1925; The Ethical Basis of Political Authority, 1930; The Sino-Japanese Controversy and the League of Nations, 1935; Japan's Case Examined, 1940. Editor: The American State Series. Co-editor: Johns Hopkins University Studies in Historical and Political Science; mng. editor American Political Science Review, 1907-17. Home: 1921 Kalorama Road, Washington, D.C. Died Mar. 26, 1945.

WILLS, William Henry, ex-gov.; b. Chicago, Ill., Oct. 26, 1882; s. James Henry and Alzina Brown (Foster) W.; student common sch., Vergennes, Vt.; LL.D. (hon.) Norwich Univ., Univ. of Vermont, Middlebury College; m. Hazel McLeod, Aug. 19, 1914; 1 dau., Anne Kimball. Dry goods clk., 1900-15; ins., real estate agent since 1915; pres. William H. Wills Ins. Agency, Inc., Bennington, Vt., since 1928; v.p. County Nat. Bank. Mem. Vt. State Ho. of Rep., 1929-31, State Senate, 1931-35 (pres. pro tem. 1935-37); lt. gov., State of Vt., 1937-39, gov. 1941-45; mem. Fed. Communications Commn. since July 1945. Trustee Vt. Soldiers Home, Vt. Jr. Coll.; pres. bd. of trustees, Diocese of Vt. (Episcopalian); corporator H. W. Putnam Hosp.; dir. Goshen Camp for Crippled Children. Republican. Episcopalian (Jr. Warden, St. Peter's Ch., Bennington, Vt.). Mason (32°), Odd Fellow (past potentate, Cairo Temple), Elk. Club: Bennington Business Men's. Home: Bennington, Vt. Died Mar. 6, 1946.

WILLSON, Russell, naval officer; b. Fredonia, N.Y., Dec. 27, 1883; s. Sidney Louis and Lucy Fenton (Staats) W.; student Mass. Inst. Tech., 1901-02; B.S., U.S. Naval Acad., 1906; student U.S. Naval War Coll., 1923-24; m. Eunice Westcott, June 3, 1911; children—Eunice Russell, Mary Westcott, Russell, Jr. (lt. U.S.N. deceased, 1945). Commd. ensign, U.S. Navy, 1908, and advanced through the grades to rear admiral, 1939, vice admiral, 1942; served on U.S.S. New York at Vera Cruz, 1914, and later as flag lieut. to adm. Mayo, Atlantic Fleet; organized and developed Code Signal Sect., Navy Dept., World War I; with 6th Battle Squadron of Grand Fleet at end of War; comd. destroyers at Greenland in connection with Army's around-the-world flight; mem. Naval Mission to Brazil, 1927-30; naval attaché Am. Embassy, London, 1937-38; comdr. Battleship Div. One, U.S. Fleet, 1939-40; supt. U.S. Naval Acad., 1941; chief of staff U.S. Fleet, Jan. 1942; vice adm., Mar. 1942, and dep. comdr-in-chief U.S. Fleet, Oct. 1942; retired Jan. 1943; duty with Joint Chiefs of Staff, 1944-46; now associate editor, "World Report"; member U.S. delegation at Dumbarton Oaks; mil. advisor, San Francisco Conf. Decorated Navy Cross, Distinguished Service Medal (Navy), Distinguished Service Medal (Army). Episcopalian. Club: Chevy Chase. Address: 107 Hesketh St., Chevy Chase, Md. Died July 6, 1948; buried in U.S. Naval Academy Cemetery, Annapolis, Md.

WILLSON, Sidney Louis, former pres. Am. Writing Paper Co.; b. Dunkirk, N.Y., Aug. 3, 1867; s. Sidney Lewis and Elizabeth (Ruggles) W.; ed. pub. schs.; m. Louise Drolet Bulkley; 1 son (by 1st marriage), Sidney Louis (dec.). Admitted to Neb. bar, 1890; engaged in paper business since 1893; v.p. Graham Paper Co., St. Louis, 1914-23; began with Am. Writing Paper Co., Inc., Holyoke, 1923, v.p., general mgr., 1923, pres., 1923-37; retired, 1937, Chief of mfg. sect. of paper div. War Industries Bd., 1918. Pres. Am. Paper Pulp Assn., 1929-35. Republican. Episcopalian. Mason. Club: Rotary. Home: 1335 Bay Terrace, North Bay Island Miami Beach, Fla. Died Oct. 10, 1944.

WILMER, Frank J., banking; b. East Troy, Wis., Apr. 6, 1860; s. J. George and Elizabeth (Kresken) W.; grad. Whitewater (Wis.) State Normal Sch., 1882; m. Margaret Dwyer, Nov. 10, 1888; children—Marie (Mrs. Albert I. Kulzer), Marguerite, Frances (Mrs. Boyd B. Schlaefer), Eleanor (Mrs. N. Dan

Teters). School teacher, 1879-88; mcht., 1888-1904; in banking business since 1904; pres. Whitman County Nat. Bank since 1919, Pine City State Bank since 1929; pres. Rosalia Water Co.; sec. and treas. Meuli Land Co.; sec. Rosalia Telephone Co. Mem. Wash. State Senate, 1921-33; organizer North Pacific Grain Growers, Spokane, pres., 1930-31; dir. Farmers Nat. Grain Corp., 1930-32; mem. Nat. Wheat Advisory Com., 1930-32. Mem. bd. regents State Coll. of Wash.; pres. Wash. State Good Roads Assn. Republican. Catholic. Home: Rosalia, Wash. Died March 12, 1947.

WILMORE, John Jenkins (wĭl'môr), educator; b. Winchester, Ind., Oct. 15, 1864; s. James Willis and Hannah Ann (Jenkins) W.; B.M.E., Purdue U., 1888, M.E., same, 1891; honorary LL.D., Alabama Polytechnic Institute, 1935; married Moselle Rowena, June 11, 1891; children—Anna Estelle, Frank Whitaker. Began as instr. dept. mechanic arts, Ala. Poly. Inst., 1888, and has continued as acting dir., 1891-92, dir., 1892-94, prof. mech engring., 1894-1908, dean engring. and head prof. mech. engring. since 1908, chmn. administrative com. while instn. had no pres., 1932-36. Consultant in heat engring. Fellow A.A.A.S.; mem. Am. Soc. M.E., Soc. Promotion Engring. Edn., Newcomen Soc. of Eng., Phi Kappa Phi; hon. mem. Phi Kappa Phi, Tau Beta Pi, Pi Tau Sigma. Democrat. Home: Auburn, Ala. Died Apr. 11, 1943.

WILSON, Alexander Massey, prof. electrical engring.; b. Stranraer, Scotland, Aug. 31, 1876; s. James and Jane (Massey) W.; B.S., Purdue, 1901, M.E., 1903; m. Mary Keith Miles, Aug. 5, 1907 (died Aug. 1917); 1 son, Alexander Massey. Instr. in mech. engring., Purdue, 1901-04; asst. prof. elec. engring., U. of Ky., 1904, prof., 1904-11; prof. elec. engring., U. of Cincinnati, since 1911. Mem. Am. Inst. E.E. (v.p. 1933-35), Ill. Engring. Soc., Royal Soc. Arts (England). Republican. Clubs: Literary, University, Electric. Home: 519 Evanswood Pl., Clifton, Cincinnati, O.* Died Aug. 23, 1944.

WILSON, Alonzo Edes; b. Madison, Wis., Feb. 5, 1868; s. James V. and Charlotte (Plants) W.; ed. pub. and high schs., Chicago; m. Anna Marie Nelson, June 14, 1897; children—Grace Esther (Mrs. W. E. McLain), Virginia Hale (Mrs. Alfred Wallenstein), James Voorhis. Editor St. Paul Times, 1886, the Chicago Lever, 1890-95. Active in Prohibition Party; was sec. 6 state and 3 nat. convs.; sec.-treas., 1891-1902, chmn., 1902-11, Ill. Prohibition State Com. Prohibition candidate for sec. of State of Ill., 1896, for U.S. senator, 1916; elected mem. Ill. Ho. of Rep., 1904; pres. Nat. Lincoln Chautauqua System, 1906-18; dir. Speakers Bur., United War Work, 1917-18; nat. field sec. Meth. Centenary, 1918-19; commr. to Near East, 1922; nat. field dir. Near East Relief, 1921-29, nat. dir. Am. Business Men's Foundation since 1930. Methodist. Author: Prohibition, Hand Book, 1900; American Prohibition Year Book 1901-10. Home: 2123 Maple Av., Evanston, Ill. Office: 53 W. Jackson Blvd., Chicago, Ill. Died June 17, 1949.

WILSON, A(rthur) Orville, banker; b. Paoli, Orange County, Ind., May 16, 1869; s. James S. and Susan (Dunnington) W.; A.B., Tarkio (Mo.) Coll., 1888 (1st classical grad.); m. Mabel S. Penfield, Sept. 30, 1897. Began as bookkeeper First Nat. Bank, Tarkio, and became asst. cashier and dir., also was sec. to Hon. David Rankin, cattle feeder and banker; nat. bank examiner, 1901-06; made v.p. State Nat. Bank, St. Louis, 1906; now v.p. Mississippi Valley Trust Co. which absorbed the State Nat. Bank and Merchants Laclede Nat. Bank, July 1, 1929. Republican. Mem. United Presbyn. Ch. Club: Noonday. Home: 14 Windermere Pl. Office: Miss. Valley Trust Co., St. Louis, Mo. Died Sep. 5, 1942.

WILSON, Calvin Dill, clergyman, author; b. Baltimore, Md., July 12, 1857; s. Rev. Thomas Brown and Margaret (Saunders) W.; grad. Washington and Jefferson Coll., 1876; grad. Western Theol. Sem., Pittsburgh, Pa., 1879; D.D., Union Christian Coll., Merom, Ind., 1899; Litt.D., Washington and Jefferson Coll., 1938; m. Mary A. Webster, Oct. 23, 1889; 1 son, Maurice Webster. Licensed by Presbytery of Pittsburgh, Apr. 1878; ordained Presbyn. ministry, May 1880; pastor, Atglen, Pa., 1879-83, Churchville, Md., 1883-93, Franklin, O., 1893-1903, Glendale, O., 1903-32 (emeritus); now preacher-at-large. Mem. Glendale Co. of Cincinnati Home Guards, during war period; active worker in Liberty Loan campaigns for funds Am. Red Cross, Y.M.C.A. Mem. Sons of Revolution, Soc. Colonial Wars, Phi Gamma Delta and Phi Beta Kappa. Author: Bible Boys and Girls (with J. K. Reeve), 1896; The Child's Don Quixote, 1901; The Story of the Cid, for Young People, 1901; The Flight of the Hebrews (with J. K. Reeve), 1902; Making the Most of Ourselves, 1905, second series, 1909; Black Masters, 1905; The Faery Queene, for Young People, 1906; Chaucer, for Young People, 1906; Negroes Who Owned Slaves, 1911; Working One's Way Through College and University, 1912. Editor: Orations and Historical Addresses, by Samuel F. Hunt; Sword and Gown, by John R. Paxton; Glendale, the Beautiful (verse), 1931; Lines to a Gangster, 1934; Workless, 1934; Jew, 1935; Caesar (poem), 1937; Satan, Shell-Shocked (poem), 1937; Exiled Savants (poem), 1938; The Passing of Classical Allusions (prose), 1939; Turannoi (verse), 1939; Man in Power Searches His Soul (poem), 1940; An Apology to Christ (prose), 1940; Totalitarians (verse), 1940; Heroic Religion (poem), 1940; Visions and Thoughts Inside Church and Out (poem), 1941; Onward (poem), 1941; Lies (poem), 1942; One Octogenarian to Another (poem), 1943. Contbr. to various mags. and newspapers. Poems are quoted in Davis' Anthology of Newspaper Verses, The Singing Quill, The North American Book of Verse, and other anthologies. Home: Glendale, O. Died Apr. 28, 1946.

WILSON, Carroll Atwood, lawyer; b. Benton Falls, Me., May 12, 1886; s. Charles B. and L. Belle (Turner) W.; B.A., Williams, 1907, L.H.D., 1932; student Harvard, 1907; Rhodes scholar at Oxford U., 1908-11, B.C.L., Worcester Coll. (Oxford), 1911; hon. M.A., Wesleyan U., Middletown, Conn., 1935; LL.D., Colby College, 1940; m. Doris A. Janes, June 15, 1921 (div.); children—John Edward, Philo Calhoun, Bradford Janes; married 2d, Jean C. Shelly, May 29, 1943. In practice at Boston, 1911; member firm Hurlburt, Jones & Hall, 1916-19; gen. counsel Guggenheim Bros. and allied corps. since 1919; vice pres. and dir., American Smelting and Refining Company, 1945; trustee John Simon Guggenheim Memorial Foundation, Murry and Leonie Guggenheim Foundation. Mem. Phi Beta Kappa, Alpha Zeta Alpha (Williams College), Grolier Club, Council of Bibliographical Society of America (v.p. and chairman com. on publications). Author: Descriptive Catalogue of the Works of Thomas Hardy, 1940. Editor, first appearance in print of some four hundred familiar quotations, 1935. Home: 161 W. 16th St. Office: 120 Broadway, New York, N.Y. Died June 27, 1947.

WILSON, Carroll Louis, business management counsel; b. Minneapolis, Minn., March 16, 1900; s. Louis Blanchard and Mary Elizabeth (Stapleton) W.; A.B. cum laude, Harvard, 1920, A.B. in Mechanical Engineering, magna cum laude, 1922; m. Harriot Boynton Sawyer, June 20, 1923; children—Katherine, Constance Bird. Began as apprentice Westinghouse Electric Mfg. Co., 1922; heating engr. in sales dept. and later gen. engr., 1922-28; industrial analyst Investment Research Corp., Detroit, 1928-29; dir. research and mem. investment policy com. Scudder, Stevens & Clark, Boston, 1929-39; spl. asst. to U.S. Sec. of Commerce, 1939-40; exec. asst. to dir. Bur. of Fgn. and Domestic Commerce, 1939-40, asst. dir. Sept.-Dec. 1940, acting dir. Dec. 1940-Mar. 1941, dir Mar. 10, 1941-Aug. 1943; consultant to U.S. sec. Commerce since Aug. 1, 1943; consultant to Nat. Patent Planning Commn. since Nov. 1943; sec. Com. for Econ. Development, Sept. 15, 1942-Oct. 1, 1944. Served as mem. Harvard R.O.T.C., 1916-18, Harvard S.A.T.C., 1918. Mem. Tau Beta Pi, Am. Legion. Sec. Harvard Club of Mich., 1928. Episcopalian. Club: Harvard (Washington). Author of article on elec. furnaces in Mech. Engrs.' Handbook, 1930 edit. Home: 4400 Dexter St., N.W., Washington, D.C. Died June 27, 1947.

WILSON, Clifford Brittin, lawyer; b. Bridgeport, Conn., Dec. 2, 1879; s. James Albert and Mary Eliza (Wordin) W.; grad. Bridgeport High Sch., 1898; studied law in Probate Ct. while acting as asst. clerk, 1899-1903; m. Anastasia C. Dorsey, Nov. 10, 1914. Admitted to bar, 1902. President Bd. of Aldermen, Bridgeport, 1908-09; coroner Fairfield County, 1909-12; mayor of Bridgeport, 1911-21; lt. gov. of Conn., 1914-21. Mem. Coast Arty. Co., 1904-08, retiring as capt. 4th Co.; col. 4th Mil. Dist. Conn. State Guard, 1917-19. Republican. Baptist. Mason (K.T., 32°, Shriner), Odd Fellow, Elk. Home: Weston, Conn. Office: Liberty Bldg., Bridgeport, Conn. Died Jan. 1, 1943.

WILSON, David Roger, mfr.; b. Warren, O., Nov. 15, 1874; s. James Alfred and Isabella (Biggers) W.; student Akron (O.) High Sch.; m. Blanche F. Racer, Sept. 7, 1897; 1 son—Charles Elliott. Supt. Oldsmobile Co., 1902-07, Aero Car Co., Detroit, 1907-08; sales mgr. Ferro Machine & Foundry Co., 1908-14; v.p. and mgr. Wilson Foundry & Machine Co., Pontiac, Mich., 1914-21, pres. and gen. mgr. since 1921; pres. and receiver Willys-Overland Co., 1934-39. Mem. Soc. Automotive Engrs. Republican. Conglist. Mason, Elk. Club: Bloomfield Country (Bloomfield Center, Mich.). Home: 111 Oneida Rd. Office: Franklin Rd., Pontiac, Mich.* Died Mar. 11, 1949.

WILSON, Edward Clarkson, school prin.; born Solmesville, Ont., Can., July 11, 1870; s. Isaac and Ruth C. (Stickney) W.; B.S., Swarthmore (Pa.) Coll., 1891, M.A., 1921; m. Elizabeth West Twining, June 9, 1898. Teacher, 1891; prin. Friends Sch., Baltimore, 1903-27 (retired). Mem. Assn. Colls. and Prep. Schs., Ednl. Soc. Baltimore. Club: Baltimore Country. Home: Buck Hill Falls, Pa., and Highland Park Club, Lake Wales, Fla. Died Sept. 18, 1944.

WILSON, Francis Mairs Huntington, writer; b. Chicago, Ill., Dec. 15, 1875; s. Benjamin Mairs and Frances (Huntington) W.; A.B., Yale, 1897; m. Lucy Wortham James, Apr. 30, 1904; m. 2d, Hope Butler, Sept. 1, 1925. Sec. of Embassy, Japan, later 3d asst. sec. of state, and asst. sec. of state until 1913; ambassador on spl. mission to Turkey, 1910; mem. editorial staff Phila. Public Ledger, 1917-18, Phila. Evening Bulletin, 1921-22; with Nat. City Bank, N.Y., 1918-19; pres. M. & H. Mfg. Co., mfrs. signaling devices, Waterbury, Conn., 1927-35; dir. Commercial Museum, Phila., 1928-32. Engaged in writing since 1935. Mem. Soc. of the Cincinnati, Soc. Colonial Wars. Republican. Episcopalian. Author: Stultitia, 1914; The Peril of Hifalutin, 1918; Money and the Price Level, 1932. Memoirs of an Ex-Diplomat, 1945. Home: Hopelands, Woodbury, Conn. Died Dec. 31, 1946.

WILSON, Frank Elmer, bishop; b. Kittanning, Pa., Mar. 21, 1885; s. William White and Irene Mayhew (Ladd) W.; grad. Harvard Prep. Sch., Chicago, Ill., 1903; A.B., Hobart Coll., Geneva, N.Y., 1907, S.T.D., 1923; B.D., Gen. Theol. Sem., 1910; D.D., Nashotah House, 1929; S.T.D., Gen. Theol. Sem., 1929; m. Marie Louise Walker, Oct. 24, 1911 (died Nov. 1, 1924); 1 dau., Florence Harrington; m. 2d, Eleanor Lorinda Hall, 1929. Deacon, 1910, priest, 1910, P.E. Ch.; rector St. Ambrose Ch., Chicago Heights, Ill., 1910-13, St. Andrew's Ch., Chicago, 1913-15, St. Augustine's Ch., Wilmette, Ill., 1915-17, Christ Ch., Eau Claire, Wis., 1919-29; bishop, diocese of Eau Claire, since 1929. Served as chaplain A.E.F., 1917-18; maj., chaplain, U.S.R. Deputy, Gen. Conv. P.E. Ch., 1922, 25, 28. Pres. Trustees of Diocese of Eau Claire; trustee Nashotah House; trustee General Theological Seminary. Member Phi Beta Kappa, Sigma Phi fraternities. Decorated Italian Service Medal. Mason (33°). Club: Country. Author: Contrasts in the Character of Christ, 1916; What a Churchman Ought to Know, 1920; Common Sense Religion, 1922; The Divine Commission, 1927; Outline History of the Episcopal Church, 1932; Outline of Christian Symbolism, 1933; Outline of the Old Testament, 1935; Outline of the New Testament, 1935; Outline of the Prayer Book, 1936; Outline of Personal Prayer, 1937; Outline of the Sacraments, 1937; Faith and Practice, 1939; Outline of the English Reformation, 1940; Outline of the Christian Year, 1941. Asso. editor The Witness. Home: 145 Marston Av., Eau Claire, Wis. Died Feb. 16, 1944.

WILSON, George Henry, lawyer; b. Barry, Ill., Nov. 7, 1866; s. Rev. Henry and Mary Jane (Padgett) W.; A.B., Illinois Coll., 1888, A.M., 1891; LL.B., Northwestern U., 1891; m. Frances Wilkinson Hall, June 14, 1894 (died Mar. 15, 1928). Admitted to Ill. bar, 1891, and since practiced at Quincy; also mem. bar of Supreme Court of U.S.; mem. Wilson & Schmiedeskamp; dir. Mercantile Trust & Savings Bank. State's atty. Adams County, Ill., 1896-1900; corp. counsel, Quincy, 1907-09; mem. Ill. Ho. of Rep., 4 terms, 1909-15; spl. asst. to atty. gen. of U.S., Chicago, 1923. Past pres. bd. trustees Chaddock Boys Sch.; pres. Adams County Law Library. Mem. Am. Bar Assn., Illinois State Bar Assn. (pres. 1926-27), Adams County Bar Assn., Am. Judicature Soc., Am. Law Inst., S.A.R., Phi Delta Phi, Phi Beta Kappa. Republican. Methodist. Mason (32°). Club: Kiwanis. Home: 130 S. 24th St. Office: Mercantile Bldg., Quincy, Ill. Died Aug. 5, 1949.

WILSON, George Barry, naval officer; b. Norfolk, Va., Mar. 27, 1892; s. George Whitfield and Ada Maria (Maguire) W.; B.S., U.S. Naval Acad., 1914, student post grad. sch., 1919-20; M.S., Columbia, 1921; m. Mary Lawrence Stokes, Dec. 9, 1914; 1 dau., Mary Lawrence (Mrs. Desmond McTighe); m. 2d, Anna Ridout Tilghman, June 2, 1920; children—Anne Tilghman, George Barry, Ruth. Comd. ensign, U.S. Navy, 1914, advancing through the grades to rear adm., 1942; served in U.S.S. Delaware with British Grand Fleet during World War I; later assigned to Bureau of Aeronautics, then to U.S.S. Langley (first U.S. aircraft carrier); in destroyers of Battle Force (West Coast), 1923-25; aide to comdt. Navy Yard, Philadelphia, Pa., 1925-27; on staff of squadron comdr. of destroyers, Asiatic Sta., 1927-30; asst. inspector naval material, Philadelphia, Pa., 1930-32; gunnery officer, U.S.S. Mississippi, 1932-35; prodn. officer, Navy Yard, Pearl Harbor, 1935-38; exec. officer, U.S.S. Honolulu, 1938-40; various assignments Bureau of Naval Personnel, including dir. of officer personnel, 1940-42; comdg. officer, U.S.S. Alabama, 1942-43, chief of staff to comdr. U.S. Naval Forces in Europe, and naval attaché, London, Eng., since 1943. Home: 3420 39th St. N.W., Washington, D.C. Died Dec. 4, 1949.

WILSON, George W., dentist, dental educator; b. Green Bay, Wis., Feb. 28, 1890; s. William Andrew and Martha (Miller) W.; B.S., Marquette U., 1914, D.D.S., 1914; m. Blanche B. Clancy, July 11, 1916; children—Janet, Audrey, Patricia, Phyllis. Practicing dentist since 1914; part-time teacher, Marquette U., Milwaukee, Wis., 1914-27, full-time teacher since 1927, dir. of clin. dentistry since 1927, asst. dean 1940-43, dean since 1943. Mem. Am. Coll. Dentists (pres., 1940), Am. Dental Assn., Wis. State Dental Soc. (pres. 1939), Omicron Kappa Upsilon. Catholic. Co-editor Year Book of Dentistry since 1936. Home: 2359 N. Sherman Blvd. Office: 604 N. 16th St., Milwaukee, Wis. Died Nov. 11, 1947.

WILSON, George W.; dean Sch. of Commerce, St. Louis U. Address: 3674 Lindell Blvd., St. Louis, Mo.* Died June 5, 1945.

WILSON, Hugh Robert, diplomatic service; b. Evanston, Ill., Jan. 29, 1885; s. Hugh Robert and Alice (Tousey) W.; grad. The Hill Sch., Pottstown, Pa., 1902; B.A., Yale, 1906; studied Ecole Libre des Sciences Politiques, Paris; m. Katharine Bogle, Apr. 25, 1914; 1 son, Hugh Robert. With Wilson Bros., wholesale men's furnishers, Chicago, 1907-10; private sec. Am. minister, Lisbon, Portugal, 1911; sec. Legation, Guatemala, 1912; later served at Buenos Aires, Berlin, Vienna, Washington, D.C., Berne and Tokyo; chief Div. of Current Information, 1924-27, also chief of exec. com. Foreign Service Personnel Bd.; E.E. and M.P. to Switzerland, April 1927-Aug. 1937; apptd. asst. sec. of State Aug. 23, 1937; ambassador to Germany, 1938-39, advisor to Secretary of State, 1940; retired, Jan. 1, 1941. Secretary General Conference for Limitation of Naval Armaments, Geneva, 1927; adviser and del. Preparatory Commn. for Disarmament Conf.,

Geneva, 1928, 29, 30; Am. del. to Conf. for Abolition of Import and Export Prohibitions and Restrictions, Geneva, 1928, and to Commn. for Preparation of a Draft Conv. on the Private Mfr. of Arms and Ammunition and Implements of War, 1928-29; del. Red Cross and Prisoners of War Conf., Geneva, 1929; adviser London Naval Conf., 1930; rep. in consultative capacity Discussions on Armaments Truce, 3d (disarmament) Com. of Assembly of League of Nations, Geneva, 1931; del. Gen. Disarmament Conf., Geneva, 1932-37. Clubs: Metropolitan, Burning Tree (Washington); University (Chicago). Author: Education of a Diplomat, 1938; Diplomat Between Wars, 1941. Home: 2839 Woodland Dr., Washington, D.C.* Died Dec. 27, 1946.

Wilson, Irving Livingstone, merchant; b. Elwood, N.J., Aug. 16, 1866; s. John Henry and Helen Mar (Irving) W.; ed. pub. schs. of Elwood; m. Esther Mendenhall Sproul, Oct. 1908 (dec.). With Jacob Reed's Sons, Phila., Pa., since Feb. 25, 1881, as clerk 1881-85, dept. mgr., 1885-1905, v.p., 1905-06, pres. since 1906. Active in civic, business and political affairs. Sergt. at arms, Rep. Nat. Conv., 1896; presdl. elector, 1928. Dir. Ursinus Coll., Better Business Bureau, Nat. Assn. Retail Clothiers and Furnishers (ex-pres.); director Convention and Tourist Bureau of Phila., Philadelphia Merchants Association; trustee American Retail Federation. Former dir. and mem. exec. com. Phila. Chamber of Commerce; former v.p. and dir. Chestnut St. Bus. Mens Association, National Assn. Uniform Manufacturers. Served mem. 2d Troop Phila. City Cav., Pa. Nat. Guard, 1898-1904. Mem. Am. Acad. of Fine Arts, St. Andrews's Soc., N.J. Soc. in Pa. (dir.), Pa. Society Sons of Revolution, Franklin Inst. of Phila. Republican. Episcopalian. Mason. Clubs: Union League (former dir.), Phila. Country, Penn, Rotary (Phila.). Home: 3105 Midvale Av. Office: 1424 Chestnut St., Philadelphia, Pa. Died Mar. 21, 1946.

WILSON, J(ackson) Stitt, lecturer; b. Auburn, Ont., Can., Mar. 19, 1868; s. of William James and Sarah Ann (Stitt) W.; A.B., Northwestern U., 1897, A.M., 1901; studied Garrett Bibl. Inst.; m. Emma Agnew, Dec. 26, 1889. Ordained M.E. Ministry, 1897; pastor, Erie St. M.E. Ch., Chicago, 1898-97; resigned pulpit, 1897 and devoted himself to socialistic propaganda, addressing audiences in Eng., Wales, Can. and U.S.; Socialist candidate for gov. Calif., 1910; mayor of Berkeley, Calif., 1911-12, 1912-13; declined re-election. Author: The Impending Social Revolution, 1902; How I Became a Socialist, 1905; The Hebrew Prophets and the Social Revolution, 1907; The Harlots and the Pharisees, 1913; and other books and pamphlets. Social evangelist with Student Dept. of Y.M.C.A., past several yrs. Address: Berkeley, Calif. Died Aug. 28, 1942.

WILSON, James A., labor official; b. Erie, Pa., Apr. 23, 1876; s. James and Mary (Adair) W.; ed. pub. schs.; m. Elsie R. Schaeffer, June 21, 1905; children—James William, Robert Adair. Pres. Pattern Makers league of North America, 1902-34, vice-pres. metal trades dept.; vice-pres. Am. Fedn. of Labor, 1924-34; now labor counselor Internat. Labor Office, Geneva, Switzerland. Mem. Bd. of Labor Review, Pub. Works Adminstrn. Served as member two charter commn. of Cincinnati. Twice sent to Europe during World War as chmn. labor missions to influence labor orgns. of the allies to coöperate with their govts. in prosecution of the war. Del. A.F. of L. to British Trade Union Congress, 1906; labor adviser to World Monetary and Economic Conf., 1933. Mem. Cincinnati City Council, 1934-36; alternate mem. Nat. Defense Mediation Bd.; panel mem. War Labor Bd.; chmn. Selective Service Draft Appeal Bd. No. 1, Ohio. Mason, Elk, Moose. Clubs: Cuvier Press, Hyde Park Golf and Country. Home: 1547 Northwood Dr., Cincinnati, O. Office: 734 Jackson Pl., Washington, D.C.; and Internat. Labor Office, Geneva, Switzerland. Died Sept. 3, 1945.

WILSON, Jesse Everett, lawyer; b. Clay Twp., Owen County, Ind., Oct. 4, 1867; s. John W. and Piety Jane (Maners) W.; ed. pub. and high schs., Owen County, Ind.; LL.B., Ind. U., 1895; m. Gail C. Wasson, Dec. 14, 1904; children—Wasson J., Jane, Gail, Mary. Taught sch. 4 yrs.; admitted to Ind. bar, 1895; mem. 63d and 64th Gen. Assemblies, Ind., 1903-05; asst. sec. of the Interior, U.S., Sept. 1, 1905-Mar. 4, 1911; resumed law practice at Hammond, Ind. Pres. Lake County Bar Assn., 1924, 25, 26. Del. Progressive Nat. Conv., Chicago, 1912. Pres. Chamber of Commerce, Hammond, 1914-22; pres. Hammond chapter, Am. Red Cross, since 1922. Methodist. Home: 24 Highland St. Office: Calumet Bldg., Hammond, Ind. Died 1945.

WILSON, John Arthur, chemist; b. Chicago, Ill., Aug. 16, 1890; s. Ernest Clyde and Amy Florence (Christian) W.; student New York U., 1911-12, U. of Leeds, Eng., 1914-16; D.Sc., Lehigh U., 1929; m. Wynnaretta Cain, May 1, 1912; 1 dau., Wynnaretta. Began career as chemist, Edison Chem. Works, Silver Lake, N.J., 1911; chief chemist, A. F. Gallun & Sons Corp., Milwaukee, Wis., 1912-29; hon. research asst., Procter Internat. Research Lab., Leeds, Eng., 1915-16; cons. chemist, Milwaukee Sewerage Commn., 1920-30; spl. lecturer U. of Chicago, 1925, Columbia U., 1926; pres. Security Management Co., Milwaukee, 1926-29; pres. Internat. Security Management Co., Chicago, 1929-30; pres. Wis. Investment Co., 1930-38; pres. John Arthur Wilson, Inc., 1929-38; pres. Wilson Leather Co., Appleton, Milwaukee and N.Y. City, since 1933; tech. dir. Bona Allen, Inc., Buford, Ga., 1938-40; cons. chemist, N.Y. City since 1940. Noted for discoveries in tanning skins and treatment of leather and chemistry of leather manufacture; discovered system of chemically treating sewage sludges and disposal into fertilizer; invented process for making sheet leather; invented the new metaphosphate tannage; developed new concept of atomic structure. Coöperating expert Internat. Critical Tables; member Colloid Committee Nat. Research Council, 1920-26. Awarded Chandler medal, Columbia U., 1928, Nichols medal, N.Y. Sect. of Am. Chem. Soc., 1931. Dir. Procter Internat. Research Lab., U. of Leeds, Eng. Fellow A.A.A.S.; mem. Am. Chem. Soc. (v.p. 1921-27, chmn. Milwaukee sect., 1920, leather div., 1921-27), Am. Leather Chemists Assn. (pres. 1928-30), Internat. Society Leather Trades Chemists, Internationalen Vereines der Leder-Industrie-Chemiker, Société de Chimie Industrielle, Professional Men's Club of Milwaukee (pres. 1927-28), Sigma Xi. Republican. Episcopalian. Clubs: Athletic, Chemists Circle (pres. 1928), Ozaukee Country (pres. 1937-38), Yacht; Capital City (Atlanta). Author: The Chemistry of Leather Manufacture, 1923, 2d edit. Vol. I, 1928, Vol. II, 1929, Vol. III, 1941, also transl. into German, French and Russian; Viewing Leather Through the Eyes of Science, 1924; Colloid Chemistry as Applied to Activated Sludge, 1924; Sanitation, 1925; Analysis of Leather, 1931; Electronic Theory of Tanning, 1937; Modern Practice in Leather Manufacture, 1941; more than 200 articles in jours. of chem. and leather trades, etc. Home: 200 Cabrini Blvd. Address: 11 W. 42d St., New York, N.Y. Died Sep. 10, 1942.

WILSON, J(ohn) Gordon, physician; b. Edinburgh, Scotland, Dec. 10, 1866; s. of John and Grace (Glass) W.; M.A., Edinburgh U., 1885, M.B. and C.M., 1890; student univs. of Vienna and Berlin, 1890-91; m. Lilias Aimers, Sept. 8, 1900. Mem. faculty U. of Chicago, and instr. and asst. prof. anatomy, 1901-08; prof. otology and head of dept., 1908-20, prof. oto-laryngology and head of dept., 1920-45, professor emeritus since 1945, Northwestern University Medical School; consulting otolaryngologist, Passavant and Wesley hospitals, Chicago, Capt. Canadian Expeditionary Forces, World War I. Mem. Am. Laryngol. Assn., Am. Otol. Soc. (pres. 1929). Otol. Research Com. (sec. 1928-36, pres. 1937-38), Nat. Research Council, Inst. Medicine Chicago (pres. 1932), Am. Oto-Laryngol. Assn.; fellow A.A.A.S.; hon. mem. Harvey Soc. of New York. Club: University. Home: Old Bennington, Vt. Office: Medical School, 303 E. Chicago Av., Chicago 11, Ill. Died Aug. 13, 1948.

WILSON, John Reid, supt. schs.; b. Bloomfield, N.J., Apr. 30, 1874; s. Alexander S. and Anna F. (Hopwood) W.; student State Normal Sch., Trenton, N.J., 1890-93; student Columbia U., 1903-05, B.S., 1913. Teacher rural schs., villages and towns, 1893-1901; prin. graded schs., Paterson, N.J., 1901-06, supt. schs. since 1906. Trustee Paterson Pub. Library, Y.M.C.A. Mem. N.E.A., A.A.A.S., Society for Study of Edn., Am. Geog. Assn., N.J. State Teachers Assn., N.J. Council of Edn., N.J. Hist. Soc., N.J. and N.Y. Schoolmasters' Clubs. Episcopalian. Elk. Clubs: Hamilton, North Jersey Country. Home: 10 Manor Rd. Office: City Hall Annex, Paterson, N.J.* Died May 23, 1946.

WILSON, Louis Blanchard, pathologist; b. Pittsburgh, Pa., Dec. 22, 1866; s. Henry Harrison and Susan (Harbach) W.; M.D., U. of Minn., 1896, D.Sc., 1940; m. Mary Stapleton, Aug. 26, 1891 (died in 1920); children—Mrs. Alice Martin, Carroll Louis; m. 2d, Maud H. Mellish, Aug. 21, 1924 (died 1933); m. 3d, Grace G. McCormick, Jan. 2, 1935. Asst. prof. pathology and bacteriology, U. of Minn., 1896-1905; dir. Labs. of Mayo Clinic since 1905; prof. of pathology and dir. The Mayo Foundation for Medical Edn. and Research, U. of Minn., 1915-37; emeritus prof. pathology and dir., The Mayo Foundation, since 1937. Commd. Col. Medical R.C., U.S. Army, 1917. D.S.M. (U.S. Army), 1920. Mem. Assn. Am. Physicians, Am. Assn. Pathologists and Bacteriologists, Am. Anat. Soc., Am. Assn. Cancer Research, A.M.A. (council on edn. and hosps.), Assn. of American Med. Colleges (pres. 1931-33), Nat. Bd. of Med. Examiners, A.A.A.S., Adv. Bd. of Medical Specialties (pres. 1935-37), Minn. Hort. Society, Nat. Rifle Assn., Phi Beta Kappa, Sigma Xi (pres. 1932-33), Alpha Kappa Kappa, Alpha Omega Alpha. Unitarian. Clubs: University, Campus (Minneapolis); University, Commercial (Rochester). Contbr. various articles reprinted in "Collected Papers," by staff of Mayo Clinic, since 1910. Home: Rochester, Minn. Died Oct. 5, 1943.

WILSON, Lucius Edward; b. Anderson, Mich., July 16, 1878; s. Albert G. and Sarah (Bullis) W.; student Ferris Inst., Big Rapids, Mich., 1901-02, Detroit (Mich.) Coll. of Law, 1904-05; m. Lillie Grace Pope, July 19, 1905; children—Dorothy Pope, Mary, Lucius Edward, Jr. Asst. sec. Detroit Bd. of Commerce, 1905; exec. sec. Greater Des Moines Com., 1906-10; exec. sec. and reorganizer, Detroit Bd. of Commerce, 1911-12; dir. Dayton (O.) Citizens' Com., 1913, during which time govt. by city mgr. was adopted; organized movements for Chambers of Commerce or for new systems of city govts. in more than 450 cities, up to 1930; founder, 1914, and mng. dir. Am. City Bur. Summer Sch. for Commercial Secretaries; v.p. Am. City Bur., 1914-21; pres. General Organization Co., 1921-30; organized Am. Co-op. Assn., 1934; spl. asst., Census of Unemployment, Dept. of Commerce, Washington, D.C., 1937-38. Mem. Nat. Assn. Commercial Executives, Am. Civic Assn., Detroit Zoöl. Soc. Republican. Wrote: (brochure) Meaning of City Boosting, 1912; Community Leadership, 1919; Money, Credit and Debt, 1931. Home: Pinckney, Mich. Died Aug. 27, 1944.

WILSON, Margaret Barclay, coll. prof.; b. Dunfermline, Scotland, Aug. 28, 1863; d. Alexander and Margaret (Inglis) Wilson; came to U.S. at age of 7; A.B., Hunter Coll., 1901, D.Sc., 1945; M.Sc., New York U., 1902; M.D., Woman's Med. Coll. of N.Y. Infirmary, 1893. Instr. physiology, Normal Coll. (now Hunter Coll.), N.Y. City, 1893-1904, asso. prof. natural science, 1904-10, prof. physiology and hygiene, 1910-33, prof. emeritus since 1933, also hon. librarian, 1915-27. Fellow A.A.A.S., N.Y. Acad. Science, Am. Geog. Soc., N.Y. Acad. of Medicine; life mem. Am. Philol. Assn., Am. Classical League, Archeol. Inst. America; mem. History of Science Soc., Am. Pub. Health Assn., Am. Assn. of Univ. Women; hon. mem. of Classical Soc. of the Am. Acad. in Rome; asso. mem. Harvey Soc. Author: A Carnegie Anthology, 1915. Home: 2928 Upton St. N.W., Washington 8, D.C. Died Oct. 6, 1945.

WILSON, Margaret Woodrow, singer; b. Gainesville, Ga., Apr. 16, 1886; d. Woodrow (Pres. of U.S.) and Ellen (Axson) Wilson; student Goucher Coll., Baltimore, Md., 1903-05; studied voice and piano, Peabody Conservatory of Music, Baltimore, 1905-06; pupil in singing of Blanche Sylvana, Baltimore, 1906-07, of Vivian Edwards, Princeton, N.J., 1907-09, of Mrs. David Gillespie, of New York, 1909-12, of Ross David of New York, 1912-19, also studied with Mrs. MacDonald Sheridan, of New York. Professional début with Chicago Symphony Orchestra, Central N.Y. Music Festival, at Syracuse, N.Y., May 15, 1915; gave song recitals at Buffalo, Cleveland, and Erie, Pa., fall of 1915; made concert tour in behalf Am. Red Cross, in Middle West and South, Mar.-June 1917; soloist Me. Music Festival, Sept. 1917; concert tour through Southern States, for war relief, Oct.-Dec. 1917; sang for the soldiers at Southern camps, Feb.-June 1918, also at various naval stations; went to France, Oct. 1918, and sang in camps of armies of A.E.F., France, Belgium and England; returned to U.S., June 8, 1919. Democrat. Presbyterian. Club: Nat. Arts (New York). Home: White House, Washington. Died 1944.

WILSON, Morris Watson, pres. Royal Bank of Canada; b. Lunenburg, Nova Scotia, Mar. 1, 1883; s. J. H. and Helen (Young) W.; D.C.L., Bishop's Coll., 1939; LL.D., McGill U., 1943; m. Clara Leone Mason, 1914; 1 dau., Clara Leone Elizabeth. Gen. mgr. Royal Bank of Canada, Montreal, Can., 1929-31, vice pres., 1931-34, pres. and mng. dir., 1934. Vice pres. Montreal Trust Co.; dir. and mem. exec. com., Canadian Pacific Railway Co.; dir. Sun Life Assurance Co., Ogilvie Flour Mills Co., Ltd., Shawinigan Water and Power Co., Canada Cement Co.; cons. Mining and Smelting Co., Canadian Gen. Electric Co., Dominion Bridge Co.; Lord Beaverbrook's rep., British Ministry Aircraft Prodn., Canada and U.S., 1940; chmn. British Supply Council, Washington, 1941; Canadian rep., Combined Pulp and Paper Com., 1943; chancellor McGill U., since 1943. Decorated Companion St. Michael and St. George, 1944. Clubs: Mount Royal, Forest and Stream (Montreal); Mount Bruno Country (Mount Bruno); Rideau (Ottawa); Country (Havana, Cuba); York (Toronto); Laval-sur-le-Lac Golf; Seigniory, (Quebec). Home: 3471 Drummond St. Office: 360 St. James St. W., Montreal 1, Can. Died May 13, 1946.

WILSON, Percy, chmn. bd. Percy Wilson Mortgage & Finance Corp., b. Chicago, Ill., Oct. 30, 1890; s. Charles W. and Myra (Scheurmann) W.; ed. public schools of Gage, Okla., and law school, Chicago; m. Barbara Heggie, Jan. 1, 1918; children—Patricia (Mrs. John H. Rhoades, III), Theodore M., Robert H. Began with Frederick H. Bartlett Realty Co., Chicago, 1907, became treas. and mem. firm, 1923-25; founder and pres. Percy Wilson & Co., Chicago, 1926-36; founded Percy Wilson Mortgage and Finance Corp., 1935, now chmn. bd.; gen. mgr., real estate div., Marshall Field & Co., Chicago, 1936; mng. dir. Merchandise Mart, 1936-43; treas. Marshall Field & Co., 1937, v.p., 1938-Mar. 1943; pres. Realty Corp. (Chicago); mng. treas. Realty Security Trust. Regional dir. Fed. Housing Adminstrn., Ill., 1934-35. Past pres. Chicago Real Estate Bd.; treas. Nat. Assn. Real Estate Bds.; dir., past chmn. bd. govs., Merchants & Mfrs. Club, pres. Better Business Bureau, 1938-40, now dir. Trustee Lake Forest U., and Chicago Galleries Assn. Pres. Civic Fedn. of Chicago. Operator, Am. Protective League, World War I. Clubs: Ontwentsia (Lake Forest); Merchants and Manufacturers (Chicago). Home: 666 Sheridan Rd., Lake Forest, Ill. Office: 134 N. La Salle St., Chicago, Ill. Died Mar. 23, 1950.

WILSON, Riley Joseph, ex-congressman; b. Winn Parish, La., Nov. 12, 1871; grad. Iuka (Miss.) Male and Female Coll., 1894; m. Pearl Barnett, June 14, 1899; children—John B., Riley J., Saranell. Admitted to La. bar, 1898; mem. La. Constl. Conv., 1898; mem. La. Ho. of Rep., 1900-04; editor Catahoula News, 1898-1904; dist. atty., 8th Jud. Dist. of La., 1904-10 (resigned); elected judge same dist. for unexpired term, 1910, and reëlected for full term 1912 (resigned, 1914); mem. 64th to 74th Congresses (1915-37), 5th La. Dist. Democrat. Home: Ruston, La. Died Feb. 23, 1947.

WILSON, Robert, med. educator; b. Stateburg, S.C., Aug. 23, 1867; s. Robert and Nanna (Shand) W.; Coll. of Charleston, 1883-86; A.B., S.C. Coll., Columbia, S.C., 1887; M.D., Med. Coll. State of S.C., 1892; LL.D., Univ. of S.C., 1918, Coll. of Charleston, 1922; D.C.L. from U. of the South, 1926; m. Harriet Chisolm Cain, Nov. 27, 1895; children—Robert, Harriet Chisolm, James M. Instr. in bacteriology, 1893-1905, adj. prof. 1901-03, professor medicine, 1905-43, dean 1908-43, prof. medicine emeritus and spl. lecturer on med. history since 1943, dean emeritus since 1943, Med. Coll. State of South Carolina; chmn. S.C. State Bd. of Health, 1907-31. F. Am. Coll. Physicians; mem. A.M.A., Southern Med. Assn. (pres. 1915-16), S.C. Med. Assn. (pres. 1904-05), Nat. Assn. Study and Prevention Tuberculosis, Am. Climatol. and Clin. Assn., Tri-State Med. Assn. of the Carolinas and Va. (pres. 1927-28), Sigma Alpha Epsilon, etc. Democrat. Episcopalian. Home: 39 Legare St. Office: 165 Rutledge Av., Charleston, S.C. Died May 20, 1946.

WILSON, Robert Forrest, author; b. Warren, O., Jan. 20, 1883; s. James Forrest and Harriet Rose (Larned) W.; ed. Allegheny Coll. and Cambridge U.; m. Katherine Deniston Dewey, July 10, 1907; 1 dau., Denise. Newspaper reporter, Cleveland, O., 1905-07; editor News, North Battleford, Saskatchewan, 1906-07; newspaper reporter, Cleveland, 1907-10; rep. of Scripps and other newspapers at Washington, D.C., 1910-16; toured S. America, 1916, contbg. articles on trade conditions; condr. war service dept. St. Nicholas Mag., 1917-18; capt. Chem. W.S., 1918-20; served with asst. sec. of war in preparation of hist. data after armistice; European corr. McCall's Mag., 1923. Mem. Authors' League America, Phi Kappa Psi. Methodist. Club: Cosmos. Author: (with Benedict Crowell, asst. sec. of war) The Giant Hand, 1921; The Armies of Industry (2 vols.), 1921; The Road to France (2 vols.), 1921; Demobilization, 1921; The Pageant of the Nile, 1924; Paris on Parade, 1925. Home: 314 S. Clifton Terrace, Washington, D.C. Address: care Guaranty Trust Co., 1 rue des Italiens, Paris, France. Died May 9, 1942.

WILSON, Russell, pub. official, editor; b. Cincinnati, O., Nov. 10, 1876; s. Moses F. and Lucy (Thorpe) W.; student Princeton 1 yr.; LL.B., U. of Cincinnati, 1900; hon. A.M., Princeton U., 1936; LL.D., Marietta Coll., 1938; m. Elizabeth B. Smith, Sept. 20, 1923; children—Samuel Smith, Perkins. Dramatic editor Cincinnati Post, 1908-10; asso. editor Cincinnati Times-Star, 1913-30; non-partisan mayor of Cincinnati, 1930-38; councilman, 1938-46. Pres. Cincinnatus Assn., 1924-25; president Foreign Policy Assn., chmn. Cincinnati com. To Defend America by Aiding the Allies; mem. advisory com. Bundles for Britain; honorary director Cincinnati Red Cross; mem. of Ohio Com. of France Forever. Mem. Cincinnati Chapter Archeol. Inst. America, Sigma Chi, Phi Delta Phi, Sigma Sigma. Presbyterian. Mason. Clubs: Queen City, Cincinnati Club, Cincinnati Literary, Cincinnati Country, Commonwealth, Commercial; Union (Cleveland). Home: 2726 Johnstone Pl., Cincinnati, O.; (summer) Mt. Desert, Me.* Died Nov. 27, 1946.

WILSON, Samuel Mackay, lawyer; b. Louisville, Ky., Oct. 15, 1871; s. Samuel Ramsay and Mary Catherine (Bell) W.; ed. Centre Coll. Acad. (prep.), Danville, Ky., 1886-88, Centre Coll., 1888-91, Williams Coll., 1892-93, Law Sch. of Centre Coll., 1894-95 (no degree); LL.D., Transylvania College, 1924; LL.D., University of Kentucky, 1942; married Mary B. Shelby, Oct. 26, 1899. Admitted to Ky. bar, 1895; mem. Wilson & Harbison (later Wilson, Harbison, Hessinger, Lisle & Bush), since 1919. Teacher law, Transylvania U., 1908-10. Student Mil. Training Camp, Plattsburg, N.Y., Aug.-Sept. 1916, also May-Aug. 1917; commd. maj. judge advocate, Oct. 2, 1917; asst. judge advocate 77th Div., Nov. 1, 1917; went to France with 77th Div., Apr. 1918; div. judge advocate June 14, 1918-May 12, 1919 (hon. disch.); lt. col. J.A.G., O.R.C., Apr. 7, 1919, now lt. col. Res. Treas. and trustee Lexington Pub. Library. Mem. Am. Bar Assn., Am. Law Inst., Am. Antiquarian Soc., Virginia Hist. Soc., Ill. Hist. Soc., Am. Hist. Assn., Kansas Hist. Soc., Missouri Hist. Soc., Bibliog. Society of America, Southern Historical Assn., Grolier Club of New York, Mississippi Valley Hist. Assn., Maryland Hist. Soc., Hist. and Philos. Soc. of Ohio, Kentucky Acad. Science, Kentucky State Hist. Soc. (v.p.), John Bradford Club (pres.), Reserve Officers' Assn., Am. Legion, 77th Div. Assn., Mil. Order Foreign Wars, Mil. Order World War, Forty and Eight, Nat. Soc. Colonial Wars, Ky. Soc. S.R. (pres.), E. Tenn. Hist. Soc., Filson Club, Kappa Alpha, Omicron Delta Kappa. Pres. Henry Clay Memorial Foundation; president Pioneer National Monument Association; member Perry's Victory Memorial Commn. Democrat. Presbyterian. Clubs: Lexington Country; Pendennis, Arts (Louisville); Williams College (New York). Author: Early Bar of Fayette County, 1901; George Robertson (in Great American Lawyers), 1908; The Old Maysville Road, 1909; Year Book of Ky. Soc. S.R., 1913; Isaac Shelby and the Genet Mission, 1920; Susan Hart Shelby (memoir), 1923; The First Land Court of Kentucky, 1923; Kentucky Blue Grass, 1924; The Ohio Company of Virginia (1748-1798), 1926; Battle of the Blue Licks, 1927; History of Kentucky, 1928; also many newspaper and mag. articles, and memorial addresses, Algernon Sydney Sullivan award, U. of Ky., 1929; special master by appointment of Supreme Ct. of U.S. in disputed boundary suit between states of Kan. and Mo., 1941-44. Bequeathed personal library to U. of Ky. Home: 423 Fayette Park. Office: Security Trust Co. Bldg., Lexington, Ky. Died Oct. 10, 1946; buried at Lexington, Ky.

WILSON, Thomas Webber, judge; b. at Coldwater, Miss., Jan. 24, 1893; s. Joseph James (M.D.) and Lucy (Yancey) W.; A.B., LL.B., U. of Miss., 1913; married. Admitted to Miss. bar, Sept. 1913, and began practice at Laurel, Miss.; pros. atty. Jones County, Miss., 1915-19; dist. atty. 12th Jud. Dist. of Miss., 1919-23; mem. 68th to 70th Congresses (1923-29), 6th Miss. Dist.; federal judge of Virgin Islands, 1933-35; mem. Federal Bd. of Parole; chmn. U.S. Bd. of Parole, 1946-47; resigned and resumed practice of law. Democrat. Mem. Kappa Alpha. Presbyterian. Mason (32°, K.T.). Home: Coldwater, Miss. Died Jan. 31, 1948; buried Magnolia Cemetery, Coldwater, Miss.

WILSON, Thomas William, business executive; b. New York, N.Y., May 9, 1872; s. David and Frances Harriett (Crichton) W.; C.E., Lehigh University, 1894; m. Anna Beatrice Wilson, Sept. 1905. Engr. Pa. Steel Co., 1894-96; chief engr. Charleston City Ry. Co., 1896-98; chief engr. Internat. Ry. Co., 1898-1905, gen. mgr., 1905-12; v.p. and gen. mgr. Wilmington and Philadelphia Traction Co., 1912-27; pres. and dir. Delaware Coach Co., Delaware Power & Light Company, Delaware Bus Co., Southern Pennsyl. Bus. Co., 1927-43. Chmn. bd. and dir. Delaware Power & Light Co. since Oct. 1, 1943. Mem. Wilmington Savings Fund Soc.; dir. Wilmington C. of C., Delaware Safety Council. Trustee Group Hospital Service, Inc. Republican. Episcopalian. Clubs: Union League (Phila.); Wilmington, Vicmead Hunt, Rotary, Wilmington Country. Home: Hotel du Pont. Office: 600 Market St., Wilmington 99, Del. Died June 16, 1948.

WILSON, William B., biology; b. Jonesboro, Tenn., Mar. 7, 1866; s. George Washington and Elizabeth (Erwin) W.; B.S., Ottawa (Kan.) U., 1895, grad. study, 1896-97, M.S., 1898; grad. study, U. of Chicago, 1903, 07, 09, Puget Sound Marine Sta. (U. of Kan.), 1912; Sc.D., Hillsdale (Mich.) Coll., 1924; (hon.) LL.D., Ottawa Univ., Ottawa, Kan., 1937; m. Indie Clara Brinkerhoff, Apr. 11, 1893 (died Mar. 11, 1928); m. 2d, Alice Ida Gordon, Aug. 19, 1930. Prof. mathematics and natural science, Bacone (Okla.) Acad., 1895-96; prof. natural science, Bethel Coll., Russellville, Ky., 1897-1904; prof. biology, Ottawa U., since 1904, registrar, 1904-12, v.p., 1916-19, dean Coll. of Arts and Sciences, 1919-25, became dean and dir. summer sessions, 1924, and dean of men, 1934; prof. botany, summer sessions, Kansas U., 1915-19. Fellow A.A.A.S.; mem. Bot. Soc. America, Kan. Acad. Science (pres. 1929-30; exec. council 1930-31), Kan. Coll. Athletic Assn. (pres. 1923-30), Kan. Coll. Assn. (ex-pres.), Kan. State Teachers Assn. (chmn. coll. dept. 1926-28). Baptist. Clubs: Kiwanis, Schoolmasters, Country. Home: 748 Poplar St., Ottawa, Kan. Died Aug. 31, 1946.

WILSON, Willian Lyne, pres. Washington and Lee Univ.; b. Jefferson County, Va., May 3, 1843; ed. Charlestown, Va., Acad., 1851-58; grad. Columbian Univ., D.C., June, 1860; attended Univ. of Va., 1860-61; LL.D., Columbian, Hampden-Sidney Coll., Univ. of Miss., Tulane Univ., W.Va. Univ. and Central Coll., Mo.; m. Nannie Huntington, Aug. 6, 1868. Prof. Latin, Columbian Univ., 1865-71; lawyer, 1871-82; pres. W.Va. Univ., 1882-83; mem. Congress, 1883-95 (chmn. Com. Ways and Means, 1893-95); postmaster gen. of U.S., 1895-97; pres. Nat. Democratic Conv., 1892; regent, Smithsonian Instn.; pres. Washington and Lee Univ., 1897-1900. Address: Lexington, Va. Died October 17, 1900.

WILSON, William Otis, lawyer; b. Pardee, Kan., Jan. 14, 1870; s. William H. and Mary C. (Schriner) W.; grad. high sch., Bushnell, Ill., 1887; student Chicago (Ill.) Athenæum; Ph.B., U. of Chicago, 1897; LL.B., Chicago Coll. Law, 1899; m. Theodora Phelps, Oct. 30, 1902; children—Theodora (Mrs. Edward E. Murane), James Otis, William Phelps (dec.). Admitted to Ill. bar, 1899, and began practice at Chicago; moved to Casper, Wyo., 1907; atty. First Trust & Savings Bank of Casper (dir. 1915-26; v.p. 1918-28), Stockmen's Nat. Bank, 1915-26, Natrona County Abstract & Loan Co. (sec. 1914-26), Casper Mut. Bldg. & Loan Assn., 1918-26, Buffalo Basin Petroleum Company (sec. 1917-26; pres. 1926-28); city atty. Casper, Wyo., 1909-16; county and pros. atty. Natrona County, Wyo., 1910-14; atty. gen., Wyo., 1927-31; spl. lecturer U. of Wyo. Law Sch., 1935-36. Mem. exec. com. Legislative Voters League, Chicago, 1903-07, State Bd. Law Examiners, Wyo., 1920-28 (pres. 1926-28); mem. Commn. on Uniform State Laws, 1915. Mem. Sch. Bd., Natrona County High Sch., 1920-26, Dist. No. 2, Natrona County (Casper), 1910-26, Dist. No. 1, Laramie County (Cheyenne), 1937-46 (atty. for all three); mem. bd. dirs. Casper council Boy Scouts America, 1920-26 (pres. 1923); mem. Cheyenne Council same 1927-44; president, 1930-31; veteran scout 20 years; chmn. United Service Orgns. for Wyo. since 1942, National War Fund for Wyoming, 1943-44. President Kansas Society for Wyoming since 1943; chairman for Wyoming of Patriotic Volunteers of America; chairman Laramie County Americanization Association; appeal agent for Laramie County under National Defense Act. Mem. American Bar Association (v.p. for Wyo. 1921; chmn. its com. on observation of constitution week in Wyo., and com. on noteworthy changes in statute law, 1930-31; mem. council and house of dels. since 1935, mem. com. on hearings, 1945, member board of governors, since 1945; chairman Wyoming committee for improvement administration of justice and nat. defense; legal education and admission to bar; economic condition of bar; on membership; standing com. on State legislation; section on corp., banking and mercantile law. Mem. Wyo. State (ex-pres.) and Laramie County bar assns., American Judicature Soc. (Wyo. dir.), Assn. Attys. Gen. of U.S. (pres. 1930-31), Wyo. Children's Home Soc. (trustee 1927-31), Cheyenne C. of C. (pres. and dir. 1932-33), Cheyenne chapter War Dads (president, 1944-45, state president, 1945-46), S.A.R. (president Wyoming Society 1939-40), Phi Delta Theta, Phi Delta Phi. Republican. Mason (33°, K.T., Shriner), K.P.; grand master Masons of Wyoming, 1921-22. Clubs: Rotary (president Casper Club, 1925-26), Cheyenne Forum (pres. 1930), Cheyenne Country. Home: 2320 Capitol Av. Office: Majestic Bldg., Cheyenne, Wyo. Died Apr. 14, 1948.

WIMBERLY, Charles Franklin (wĭm'bēr-lĭ), clergyman; b. Jefferson County, Ill., Nov. 19, 1866; s. Thomas Jefferson and Martha M. (White) W.; student Ewing Coll., Ill., 1888-89, Southern Ill. Normal U., 1887; B.A., Kan. Normal Coll., Ft. Scott, 1892; student Vanderbilt U., bibl. dept., 1893-95 (D.D., Ky. Wesleyan Coll., 1916); m. Clara Maude Knott, Aug. 28, 1895; children—Cerise Bernice, Arthur Wesley (dec.), Mary Idris (dec.), Fred Newell (lt. col. inf. overseas), Paul Franklin (capt. ordn., overseas). Ordained ministry M.E. Ch., S., 1895; pastor in Missouri at Breckenridge, Maysville, St. Joseph, Shelbina Excelsior Springs, 1895-1905; office editor Pentecostal Herald, Louisville, Kentucky, 1905-06; pastor Lindsey Memorial Ch., Louisville, 1906-11, Madisonville, Ky., 1911-15, Franklin, Ky., 1915-17; conf. evangelist, 1917; formerly pastor Bethel Church, Charleston, S.C.; now retired from active ministry. Author: New Clothes for the Old Man, 1907; The Vulture's Claw, 1910; Cry in the Night, 1911; The Winepress, 1913; Is the Devil a Myth?, 1913; Behold the Morning, 1916; Living Themes Library (12 booklets), 1917; Who is the Beast? (co-author), 1918; Life and Labors of Dr. H. C. Morrison, 1919; Your Heart and Mine (co-author), 1921; Seven Seals of the Apocalypse, 1922. Also booklets issued by M.E. Ch., S.: Mastery of Manhood, 1924; Messages for the Times, 1926; Beacon Lights of Faith, 1927; Modern Apostles of Faith; Mills of the Gods; The Radio in Prophesy, 1931; Romance of the Itinerancy, Mysteries of the Kingdom; Fulfilled Prophecy, 1938; Wrath of God, and Other Sermons, 1939; World's Saturday Night, 1940; Lost Trail, 1941; also articles in religious and literary periodicals. On editorial staffs Pentecostal Herald, Louisville, Midnight Cry, Cincinnati, The Methodist, Altoona, Pa., God's Revivalist, Cincinnati. Home: 3020 Heyward St., Columbia, S.C. Died July 10, 1946.

WINANS, Edwin Baruch (wī'nănz), army officer; b. Hamburg, Mich., Oct. 31, 1869; s. late Hon. Edwin B. (gov. of Mich.) and Elizabeth (Galloway) W.; grad. U.S. Mil. Acad., 1891; m. Edith May, d. Brig. Gen. William Auman, U.S. Army, June 1, 1892; died Feb. 8, 1920; children—Katherine Auman (wife of Russell L. Maxwell, U.S. Army), Elizabeth Galloway (wife of W. R. Grove, Jr., U.S. Army); m. 2d, Esther Walker, Sept. 5, 1943. Commd. 2d lt. 5th Cav., June 12, 1891; 1st lt. 4th Cav., Apr. 30, 1898, maj. 34th Mich Inf., May 25, 1898; hon. mustered out vols., Nov. 26, 1898; capt. U.S. Army, Feb. 2, 1901; maj. of cav., Sept. 2, 1914; assigned to 7th Cav., Nov. 26, 1915; lt. col., Feb. 2, 1917; col. (temp.), Aug. 5, 1917; brig. gen. N.A., June 26, 1918; col. U.S. Army, Feb. 23, 1920; brig. gen., U.S. Army, Dec. 30, 1922. Served in Ind. Ty. and Tex., 1891-97; prof. mil. science and tactics, Mich. Mil. Acad., 1897-98; with regt. in Philippines, 1899-1900; with Punitive Expdn. in Mexico, 1916; apptd. comdr. 64th Brigade Inf., 32d Div., 1st Army Corps, A.E.F., 1918, and served therewith until close of war. Promoted col. cav., Feb. 23, 1920; brig. gen., Dec. 30, 1922; maj. gen., Oct. 18, 1927, and assigned as supt. U.S. Mil. Acad.; assigned as comdr. Hawaiian Div.; later in command 8th Corps Area. Ft. Sam Houston, Tex.; retired as maj. gen., Oct. 31, 1933. Mem. of League of Nations Commn. for the Government of Leticia, Jan. to July 1934. Awarded D.S.M. "for exceptionally distinguished and meritorious service" during three major offensives; Légion d'Honneur and Croix de Guerre with 2 palms, by French Govt. Address: Contemplation, Vienna, Va. Died Dec. 31, 1947; buried U.S. Military Academy Cemetery.

WINANT, John Gilbert (wī'nănt), diplomat; b. New York, N.Y., Feb. 23, 1889; s. Frederick and Jeanette L. (Gilbert) W.; prep. edn., St. Paul's Sch., Concord, N.H.; M.A., Princeton, 1925, Dartmouth, 1925; LL.D., U. of N.H., 1926; m. Constance Rivington Russell, Dec. 20, 1919; children—Constance, John G., Rivington Russell. Mem. N.H. Ho. of Rep., sessions 1917, 23, Senate, 1921; gov. of N.H., 1925-26, 1931-34; chmn. Textile Inquiry Bd., 1934; asst. dir. Internat. Labor Office, Geneva, 1935 and 1937-39, dir. since 1939; chmn. Social Security Bd., 1935-37, apptd. ambassador to Great Britain, 1941. Apptd. U.S. rep. on European Advisory Commn., 1943. Enlisted in Paris as pvt. A.E.F., 1917; with 1st Aero Squadron; comdr. 8th Observation Squadron; hon. discharged as capt., Apr. 1919. Mem. N.E. Council, Nat. Recreation Assn. (v.p.), N.H. Tuberculosis Assn. (pres.), Nat. Consumers League (pres.), Am. Assn. Labor Legislation (v.p.). Trustee Internat. Y.M.C.A. Coll. Republican. Episcopalian. Clubs: Wonolancet (Concord); Odd Volumes (Boston); Century, Racquet and Tennis (New York). Home: 274 Pleasant St., Concord, N.H. Address: American Embassy, London, England.* Died Nov. 3, 1947.

WINCHELL, Benjamin La Fon; b. Palmyra, Mo., July 8, 1858; s. Joseph Rice and Kate Anna (La Fon) W.; educated in ward and high schs., Hannibal, Mo., 1867-74; m. Jane Helm; 1 son, Benjamin La Fon. Was employed in Burlington ry. shops, Hannibal, later transferred to auditor's office, of the same line; served as chief clerk gen. freight office Atchison & Neb. R.R., Atchison, Kan., and then asst. gen pass agt., Kansas City, Ft. Scott & Memphis R.R., Kansas City, Mo.; gen. pass. agt. U.P., Denver & Gulf Ry., Denver, 1895; gen. pass. agt. St.L.&S.F. R.R., St. Louis, 1898; v.p. and traffic mgr. C.&S. Ry., Denver, Jan. 1899; pres. Kansas City, Ft. Scott & Memphis R.R., Oct. 15, 1900; v.p. and gen. mgr. "Frisco" System, Sept. 1901; 3d v.p. C.,R.I.&P. Ry., and 1st v.p. "Frisco" System, Oct. 1903; pres. C.,R.I.&P. Ry., 1904-09; vice chmn. exec. com. "Frisco" System, Apr. 14-Dec. 1, 1909, pres., Dec. 1, 1909-May 28, 1913, St.L.&S.F. R.R. Co. ("Frisco" System) and C.&E.I. R.R. Co.; apptd. receiver St.L.&S.F. Lines, May 28, 1913; resigned July 15, 1913, to become dir. of traffic, U.P. System; regional dir. railroads Southern Region, U.S. Ry. Administration, Atlanta, Ga., June 1918-Feb. 1920; v.p. Pierce Oil Corp., New York, since May 1920; chmn. and pres. Remington Typewriter Co., since June 1922; chmn. Remington, Rand, Inc., since 1927. Clubs: Metropolitan, Blind Brook, Recess, Cloud, Sleepy Hollow Country (New York); California (Los Angeles); Los Angeles Country (Beverly Hills, Calif.). Home: 4651 Fieldston Rd. Office: 315 Fourth Av., New York, N.Y. Died Mar. 16, 1942.

WINCHESTER, James Price, chmn. bd. Wilmington Trust Co.; mgr. Artisans Savings Bank. Address: Wilmington, Del. Died Jan. 27, 1943.

WINCHESTER, William Eugene, cotton-goods commn.; b. Providence, R.I., Nov. 4, 1877; s. Franklin Balch and Elizabeth Eudora (Jordan) W.; A.B., Brown U., 1898; student Phila. (Pa.) Textile Sch., 1899-1900; m. Frances Marye Beattie, June 14, 1905; 1 dau., Elizabeth Marye (Mrs. Randolph Brandt, Jr.). Teacher Latin, Providence Classical High Sch., 1898-99; instr. Phila. Textile Sch., 1900-03; dir. Miss. Textile Sch., 1903-05; cotton goods expert, Deering Milliken & Co., cotton goods commn. mchts., 1905-18, partner, 1918-22; v.p. Deering Milliken & Co. Inc., 1922-41; now pres. and dir. Lockwood Co. and dir. Deering Millikin & Co., Inc., Garner Print Works & Bleachery, Southern Worsted Corp., Dutchess Bleachery, Madison Woolen Co.; formerly pres., dir. Monarch Mills, Gainesville Cotton Mills, Whitney Mfg. Co., Lockhart Power Co., Lockhart R.R.; formerly v.p., dir. Darlington Mfg. Co. Mem. Phi Beta Kappa, Delta Upsilon. Republican. Episcopalian. Mason. Clubs: University, Merchants (pres. 1941), Brown University (New York). Author: (textbook) Principles and Processes of Cotton Yarn Manufacture, 1902. Home: 383 Park Av. Office: 383 Park Av., New York, N.Y. Died Jan. 14, 1943.

WINDET, Victor (wĭn-dĕt'), mech. engr.; b. Chicago, Ill., Aug. 12, 1867; s. Arthur W. and Eliza Vilette (Duncan) W.; B.Sc., Mass. Inst. Tech., 1889; m. Laura T. Barrett, Nov. 1894; children—Frances (dec.), Victor (dec.), Arthur, Charles B. Engr. with Chicago & Calumet Terminal R.R., 1889; mech., civ. and metall. engr., Ill. Steel Co., Chicago, 1889-1901; gen. contractor, heavy masonry, 1901-17; with Wellman Engring. Co., Cleveland, O., engr. gas producer div., 1917-27, mgr. div., 1928-32. Built two sulphuric acid plants in Wis. and steel furnaces at Watertown (Mass.) Arsenal for War Dept., World War; designed and built first concrete ore docks supported by submarine pilage and grillage, at South Chicago, for Ill. Steel Co. and Iroquois Iron Co. Republican. Presbyterian. Author: The Open Hearth, 1920; also engring., econ. and polit. contbns. to tech. and daily press. Home: 314 24th St. N., St. Petersburg, Fla. Died Apr. 10, 1945.

WINDHOLZ, Louis H. (wĭnd'hōlz), corp. official; b. Syracuse, N.Y., July 29, 1878; s. Louis and Louisa Marsh (Howe) W.; ed. pub. schs.; m. Adah Barker, Oct. 28, 1908. Pres. Pender Grocery Co., 1926-34; pres. Cavalier Hotel Corp.; v.p., dir. Norfolk Pier Corp.; dir. Nat. Marine Bank, S.A.L. Ry. Co., Norfolk Southern Bus Co., Princess Anne Power Co.; receiver Norfolk Southern Railroad; chairman Norfolk Housing Authority. Served as sergeant N.Y. Vols., Spanish-Am. War. Democrat. Episcopalian. Clubs: Princess Ann Country, Norfolk Country, Linkhorn Boat, Princess Ann Hunt, Cavalier Country, Virginia Club. Home: 542 Mowbray Arch, Norfolk (also Virginia Beach). Office: 423 Terminal Bldg., Norfolk, Va. Died July 24, 1942.

WINFIELD, George Freeman, clergyman; b. Gatesville, Tex., Jan. 10, 1879; s. John Milton and Sarah Elizabeth (Rye) W.; Ph.B., Polytechnic Coll., Ft. Worth, Tex., 1906; M.A., Southern Meth. U., Dallas, Tex., 1916; D.D. Centenary Coll., Shreveport, La., 1927; m. Harriett Preston Keller, June 28, 1906; children—Ruth Preston (Mrs. Joe Brown Love), Gerald Freeman. Ordained to ministry M.E. Church, South, 1901; pastor in Texas 12 years, building 6 churches and 2 parsonages; pres. Meridian (Tex.) Coll., 1911-19, Wesley Coll., Greenville, Tex., 1919-23, Lon Morris Coll., Jacksonville, Tex., 1923-28; pres. Whitworth Coll., 1928-38; pastor Broad Street Meth. Ch. 1938-40, Magnolia, Miss., Ch., 1940-42; Tylertown, Miss., Ch., 1942-43. Mem. Com. on Classification and Accrediting of Schs., of Tex., 1917-28. Mem. exec. com. Tex. State Teachers Assn., Am. Assn. Jr. Colleges (ex-pres.), Ednl. Assn. M.E. Ch., S. (ex-pres.). Democrat. Mason. Clubs: Kiwanis, Rotary. Home: 455 W. 4th St., Hattiesburg, Miss. Died Dec. 13, 1943.

WING, Charles Benjamin, civil engr.; b. Willow Brook (now Clinton Corners), N.Y., Jan. 18, 1864; s. Phineas Rice and Mary (Sands) W.; prep. edn. Poughkeepsie Mil. Inst.; C.E., Cornell U., 1886; fellow civ. engring., Cornell, 1886-87; m. Anna Maria Paddock, Sept. 18, 1888 (died Feb. 1905); children—Sumner Paddock, Winchester Paddock, Charles Benjamin, Robert Lewis; m. 2d, Mrs. Marian (Colt) Browne, Feb. 20, 1908; step children—Ashley Colt Browne, Mrs. Frances Browne Wenzel. Instr. civil engring., Cornell, 1886-90; asst. prof., 1890-91, prof. bridge and hydraulic engring., 1891-92, U. of Wis.; prof. structural engring., 1892-1929, emeritus since 1929, exec. head dept. civil engring., 1923-29, Stanford U.; vice chmn. and exec. officer Calif. State Redwood Park Commn., 1911-26; chief of Div. of Parks of State Dept. of Natural Resources of Calif., 1928-35; chief State Park Authority and engr. in charge of Federal coöperative projects in Calif. State Parks, 1935-36; cons. civil engr. since 1936. Major and lt. col. 23d Engineers, on ry. constrn. and highway work and with 1st Army in Argonne-Meuse, in France, April 1918-June 1919. Cons. engr. bridges, wireless towers and spl. structures, among which are the 1,000 ft. towers for the Shanghai, China, station of the Federal Telegraph Co. Councilman Palo Alto, 1909-29. Mem. Am. Soc. C.E., Pacific Assn. Cons. Engrs., Am. Soc. Testing Materials, Sigma Xi. Clubs: Commonwealth, Engineers (San Francisco). Author: Freehand Lettering for Working Drawings, 1893; Manual of Bridge Drafting (with C. H. Wright), 1896; also various papers in Trans. Am. Soc. C.E. and other tech. jours. Home and office: 345 Lincoln Av., Palo Alto, Calif. Died Aug. 22, 1945. Died Aug. 22, 1945.

WING, Leonard F., lawyer and banker; temporarily in U.S. Army; b. Vermont, Nov. 12, 1893; enlisted private Vt. N.G. 1917; inducted Federal Service with 43 Div., Feb. 24, 1941, as brig. gen.; placed in comd. 43d Inf. Div. Aug. 20, 1943; promoted maj. gen., U.S.A., Sept. 14, 1943; overseas since Sept. 23, 1942. Served in Northern and Southern Solomons, New Guinea, Luzon. Awarded Distinguished Service Medal. Home: 7 Kingsley Av., Rutland, Vt. Died Dec. 19, 1945.

WING, Wilson Gordon, banker; b. Valparaiso, Chile, Aug. 1, 1881; s. Wilson Dorr and Sarah (Flint) W.; brought to U.S., 1886; grad. Hotchkiss Sch., Lakeville, Conn., 1899; B.A., Yale, 1903; m. Marjorie Webster, May 10, 1919; children—Sally Ann, Wilson G. Engaged in agr., Calif., 1904-06; mfr., Providence, R.I., 1906-10; agriculturist, Tex., 1910-14; investments, Providence, 1914-22; pres., trustee Providence Institution for Savings since 1922; pres. Old Stone Safe Deposit & Trust Co.; dir. Providence Nat. Bank, Title Guarantee Co., Albany & Susquehanna R.R., R.I. Ins. Co. Pres. Nat. Assn. of Mutual Savings Banks, 1932-33; mem. Rhode Island Board of Parole, 1935-36. Trustee Providence Public Library, Rhode Island Hosp. Mem. Alpha Delta Phi. Unitarian. Clubs: Hope, Agawam Hunt, Jacobs Hill Hunt, Squantum, Providence Art; Knickerbocker, Leash, Yale (New York); Seminole Golf (Palm Beach, Fla.). Home: 30 Orchard Av. Address: Providence Institution for Savings, Providence, R.I. Died Feb. 3, 1944.

WINGATE, Charles Edgar Lewis (wĭn'gāt), newspaper editor; b. Exeter, N.H., Feb. 14, 1861; s. S. Dana and Oriana (Mitchell) W.; A.B., Harvard, 1883; m. Mabel Nickerson, Sept. 9, 1885; children—Mabel, Josephine, Dana Joseph Paine (dec.), Oriana. Gen. mgr. Boston Journal, 1898-1913; editor Boston Sunday Post to 1941. Chmn. Winchester School Committee, 1908-09. Dir. of Hotel & Railroad News Co., Metropolitan Sales Corp., Community Newsdealers Corp. Author: History of the Wingate Family, 1886; Playgoers' Year Book, 1888; Can Such Things Be?, 1888; Shakespeare's Heroines on the Stage, 1895; Shakespeare's Heroes on the Stage, 1896; A Captain of Youth, 1925; Life and Letters of Paine Wingate, 1930. Co-editor: Famous American Actors of To-Day, 1896. Asst. editor One Hundred Condensed Novels, 1919. Home: Winchester, Mass. Office: The Post, Boston, Mass. Died May 15, 1944; buried Wildwood Cemetery, Winchester, Mass.

WINGER, Otho, coll. pres.; b. Marion, Ind., Oct. 23, 1877; s. John M. and Mary (Smith) W.; prep. edn. Manchester Coll., North Manchester, Ind.; A.B., Ind. U., A.M., 1907; LL.D., Mount Morris Coll., 1918; m. Ida Miller, 1902; children—Robert, Paul. Ordained ministry Ch. of Brethren, 1897; prof. history and philosophy, Manchester Coll., 1907-11, pres., 1911-1941. Mem. Gen. Mission Bd., Ch. of Brethren, since 1912 (chmn. board, 1924-40); moderator Internat. Conf. Ch. of Brethren, 6 times to 1934. Author: Life of Elder R. H. Miller, 1909; History of the Church of the Brethren in Indiana, 1917; History and Doctrines of the Church of the Brethren, 1919; Letters from Foreign Lands, 1928; The Last of the Miamis, 1933; The Lost Sister Among the Miamis, 1936; The Potawatomi Indians, 1939; The Frances Slocum Trail, 1943. Home: North Manchester, Ind.*Died Aug. 13, 1946.

WINKELMANN, Christian H. (wĭng'kĕl-mȧn), bishop; b. Sept. 12, 1883. Ordained priest R.C. Ch., June 11, 1907; elected auxiliary bishop of St. Louis, Sept. 13, 1933, consecrated, Nov. 30, 1933; bishop of Wichita, Kan., since Dec. 27, 1939. Address: Wichita, Kan.*Died Nov. 18, 1946.

WINLOCK, Herbert Eustis, archeologist; b. Washington, D.C., Feb. 1, 1884; s. Wm. Crawford and Alice (Broom) W.; A.B., Harvard, 1906; hon. Litt.D., Yale, 1933, Princeton U., 1934; U. of Mich., 1936; Art D., Harvard, 1938; m. Helen Chandler, Oct. 26, 1912; children—Frances (dec.), William Crawford (dec.), Barbara. Engaged in archeol. excavations, 1900-31, at Lisht, Oasis of Kharga, and Luxor, Egypt, for Met. Museum of Art, dir. Egyptian Expdn., 1928-32, curator Egyptian dept., 1929-39; dir. Metropolitan Museum of Art, 1932-39; dir. emeritus since 1939. Served as capt., later maj. C.A.C., World War. Hon. fellow Am. Numismatic Soc.; mem. Am. Oriental Soc., Am. Assn. Museums (pres. 1936-38), Am. Philosophical Society of American Academy Arts and Sciences, Royal Asiatic Society (hon.), Society of the Cincinnati. Decorated Chevalier Legion of Honor (France), Orders of Leopold and of the Crown (Belgium). Clubs: Century, Round Table (New York). Author: (with A. C. Mace) The Tomb of Senebtisi, 1916; Basreliefs from the Temple of Rameses I at Abydos, 1921; (with W. E. Crum) The Monastery of Epiphanius, 1926; The Tomb of Meryet-Amun, 1932; The Treasure of Lahun, 1934; The Oasis of ed Dakhleh, 1936; The Temple of Rameses I at Abydos, 1937; The Temple of Hibis in el Khargeh Oasis, 1941; Materials Used in the Embalming of Tutankhamen, 1941; Excavation at Deir el Behri: 1911-31, 1942; The Slain Soldiers of Neb-Hepet Rē'Mentuhotpe, 1945; The Treasure of the Three Princesses, 1947; The Rise and Fall of the Middle Kingdom in Thebes, 1947. Contbr. to Bulletin of Metropolitan Museum Art, Met. Museum Studies, also Jour. Egyptian Archeology, Am. Jour. Semitic Languages, Am. Philosophical Soc., Scribner's Mag., Jour. Near Eastern Studies. Address: North Haven, Me. Died Jan. 26, 1950.

WINN, Charles V., Christian Science lecturer; b. Niles, Mich., Oct. 13, 1881; s. Peter John and Caroline (Crotty) W.; student Kalamazoo Coll., 1900-01, U. of Mich., 1906-07; m. Mrs. Marion Newman Brown, Jan. 30, 1913. Christian Science practitioner, Detroit, Mich., and Pasadena, Calif., 1908-29, lecturer since 1929, teacher since 1931. Contbr. articles to Christian Science jours. Home: 99 S. Raymond. Office: 626 Security Bldg., Pasadena, Calif. Deceased.

WINN, Robert Hiner, lawyer; b. Mt. Sterling, Ky., Feb. 23, 1871; s. William H. and Sarah Elizabeth (Grubbs) W.; A.B., Centre Coll., Danville, Ky., 1890; LL.D., State U. of Ky., 1912; m. Elizabeth Mannen Turney, June 1, 1904. Admitted to bar, 1894; judge Ky. Court of Appeals, 1911-13. Chmn. Rep. State Central Com., 1908-11. Pres. Ky. State Bar Assn., 1912-13; mem. Am. Law Inst. (an organizer), Phi Delta Theta. Del. to Rep. Nat. Conv., 1916; mem. Ky. State Bd. Control of Penal and Charitable Instns., 1920-24; mem. Ky. State Commn. for Admission to the Bar, 1920-23; permanent chmn. Rep. Gen. State Conv., Ky., 1931; apptd. by President Hoover, mem. Perry's Victory Memorial Commn. in charge of Put-In-Bay monument, 1932. Home: Mt. Sterling, Ky. Died May 17, 1946.

WINSER, Beatrice (wĭn'sẽr); b. Newark, N.J.; d. Henry and Edith (Cox) Winser; student Columbia, 1888. Joined staff Newark Pub. Library, 1889, asst. to city librarian, 1902, asst. dir. Newark Mus. (when founded), 1909, librarian, 1929, also dir. Newark Mus. Retired as librarian, 1942, as dir. Mus., 1947. First woman mem. Newark Bd. Edn. and first woman to serve on any governing bd., 1915. Mem. women's com. Coll. for Women est. as part of U. of N.J., 1918; dir. Northern N.J. sub-com. on employment of artists P.W.A.P., 1934; mem. com. directing Library Colony, Lake Placid, N.Y., 1930-31; chmn. Public Works of Art Projects Northern N.J., 1935; sec. Newark Art Commn., 1936; mem. N.J. Com. N.Y. World's Fair, 1938; chmn. Newark Victory Book Com., 1942, Wartime Council Newark Libraries, 1943, Com. on waste of consumer's interest of Newark Defense Council, 1941; mem. Citizens Adv. Com., Central Planning Bd. of Newark, 1945. Trustee Dana Coll., U. of Newark, N.J. Audubon Soc., 1939, Newark Mus. Assn., 1916. Fellow Am. Geog. Soc.; mem. A.L.A. (mem. council of 50, 1909 and 1930; 2d v.p. nat. assn., 1931), N.J. Library Assn. (charter mem., 1890; pres., 1907-08, 1921-22; hon. mem. 1930), Bach Soc. of N.J. (sec.), N.J. Art Edn. Council (hon. mem., 1944), A.R.C. (sponsoring com. Newark chapter), N.J. Mineralog. Soc. (corr. mem.), N.J. Hist. Soc. (mus. com.), Newark Mineralog. Soc. (hon.). Episcopalian. Home: 666 Highland Av., Newark, N.J. Died Sept. 14, 1947.

WINSHIP, Blanton, army officer, b. Macon, Ga., Nov. 23, 1869; A.B., Mercer U., 1889; LL.B., U. of Georgia, 1893; LL.D., Mercer U., 1932, also U. of Puerto Rico. Served as capt., 1st Ga. Inf., in Spanish-Am. War, 1898; as 1st lt. U.S. Army, Philippine Insurrection, 1899-1901; promoted through grades and appointed maj. gen., judge advocate general of United States Army, Mar. 1, 1931; retired. Recalled to active duty as coordinator Inter-Am. Defense Bd., Washington, D.C., Nov. 30, 1933. Assistant secretary of state and justice, and member of advisory commn. for revision of laws of Cuba, 1906-09; with Gen. Funston at Vera Cruz, Mex., as officer in charge civil affairs, 1912; served in France, 1917-23, with 42nd, 1st and 28th divs., on staff of 1st Corps and 1st Army at their organization; comd. 112th and 110th Inf. of 28th Div.; went to Switzerland on special mission, 1918; dir. gen. of service for settlement of all claims in Europe arising out of U.S. mil. operations and in one year settled over 100,000 claims, 1918-19; judge advocate Army of Occupation in Germany; served on different coms. of Reparations Commn. for execution of peace treaties, 1920-23. Mil. aide to Pres. of U.S., May 1927-Jan. 1928; legal adviser to gov. gen. P.I., 1928-30; represented Philippine govt. at confs. of commissioners on uniform state laws, 1930-31; mem. delegation representing U.S. at unveiling of statue of Henry Clay in Venezuela, 1930; spl. commr. to Liberia, 1933, and designated as Am. mem. Com. of League of Nations on Liberian Affairs; gov. of Puerto Rico, Jan. 1934-Sept. 1939. Awarded Silver Star Citation, D.S.M., D.S.C.; also decorated Officer Legion of Honor; received Pan-Am. Society's insignia, the "Gold Award," for service to the Pan-Am. Union. Home: Macon, Ga. Died Oct. 9, 1947.

WINSLOW, Carleton Monroe, architect; b. Damariscotta, Me., Dec. 27, 1876; s. Edwin Harvey and Clara Ariminta (Hunt) W.; student Art Inst., Chicago, Atélier Pascal and Atélier Chifflot Frères (Paris); m. Helen Hume, Sept. 3, 1910; 1 son, Carleton Monroe. Architect with San Diego Expn., 1911-16; practice in San Diego, 1911-17, in Los Angeles since 1917, branch office in Santa Barbara, 1918-42; architect for a number of churches, including St. Columba's Chapel at the Cathedral (Los Angeles), St. Luke's Ch. (Monrovia), Community Presbyterian Ch. (Beverly Hills, Calif.), Mary Star of the Sea Church (La Jolla, Calif.), Chapel of Bishop's Sch. (La Jolla), Fullerton High Sch., Santa Barbara Cottage Hosp., Valley Club (Montecito), residence W. H. Bliss (Santa Barbara). Member Diocesan Commn. on Architecture, Los Angeles; trustee Episcopalian Home for the Aged, Los Angeles; pres. Municipal Art Commn., Los Angeles, 1931-33; mem. advisory bd., Barlow Sanitorium, Los Angeles. Fellow Am. Inst. Architects. Mem. Santa Barbara Museum of Natural History (life), Mediæval Acad. of America, Soc. Colonial Wars (gov. 1930-31), California Soc., Sons of the Revolution (pres., 1939-40), Descendants of Knights of the Garter (Windsor, Eng.), Alpha Rho Chi. Republican. Episcopalian. Awarded gold medal in design, Architectural League of New York, 1905. Author: Architecture and the Gardens of the San Diego Exposition, 1916. Contbr. articles to archtl. jours. Home: 1943 Laughlin Park Dr., Los Angeles 27, Calif. Died Oct. 10, 1946.

WINSTON, Francis Donnell, judge; b. Windsor, N.C., Oct. 2, 1857; s. Patrick Henry and Martha Elizabeth (Byrd) W.; Cornell U.; A.B., U. of N.C., 1879, LL.D., 1920; student Dick & Dillard Law Sch., Greensboro, N.C.; m. Rosa Mary Kenney, May 30, 1889. Began practice, Windsor, 1882; mem. Winston, Matthews & Kenney till 1929; mem. N.C. Senate, 1887-88, House, 1889-1900, 1901-02, 1927; Democratic presidential elector, 2d District, 1896; at-large, 1912; judge Superior Court of N.C., 1901-02, 1916; pres. Dem. State Associated Clubs, 1902-06; lt.-gov. of N.C., 1905-09; pres. Dem. State Conv. of N.C., 1912; dist. atty., Eastern Dist. of N.C., by appointment of Pres. Wilson, 1914-16; judge of the Superior Court of N.C. many yrs., beginning 1916; judge Gen. County Court of Bertie County, N.C., since 1929. Mem. Dem. 2d Congressional Dist. Com. 15 yrs., Dem. State Exec. Com. 15 yrs. Dir. Bank of Windsor. Trustee U. of N.C. since 1887 (exec.; com.); dir. Southern Conservatory of Music, Durham, N.C. Mem. Am. Bar Assn., N.C. Bar Assn. (pres. 1911-12), State Hist. Soc., State Library Assn.; Folk-Lore Soc. Episcopalian. Grand Master of Masons of N.C., 1907-08; Elk. Home: Windsor, N.C. Died Jan. 28, 1941.

WINSTON, Gilmer; chmn. bd. Union Planters Nat. Bank. Address: Memphis, Tenn. Died Apr. 5, 1939.

WINSTON, Robert Watson, judge, author; b. Windsor, N.C., Sept. 12, 1860; s. Patrick Henry and Martha Elizabeth (Byrd) W.; A.B., U. of N.C., 1879, LL.B., 1881, LL.D., 1929; LL.D., Wake Forest Coll., 1915; D.Litt., Duke U., 1937; m. Sophronia Horner, Dec. 13, 1882 (died Feb. 1913); childrren—James Horner, Robt. W., Mrs. Gertrude Webb, Mrs. Amy W. Carr. Mem. Dem. State Com., 1885; mem. N.C. Senate, 1885; judge Superior Court of N.C., 1889-95 (resigned); chmn. Am. Red Cross for Wake County, N.C., World War. Pres. of Durham Chamber of Commerce, 1896; pres. N.C. Hist. Soc., 1897. Reëntered college at 60 to fit himself "to interpret the New South to the Nation and the Nation to the New South." Mem. Zeta Psi; hon. mem. Phi Beta Kappa, 1939. Author: Life of Andrew Johnson, 1928; High Stakes and Hair Trigger, the Life of Jefferson Davis, 1930; Robert E. Lee—A Biography, 1934; It's a Far Cry (autobiography), 1937; Horace Williams: Gadfly of Chapel Hill, 1942; Winston's Journal and Scrapbook, 1932-44 (4 vols.), 1944; also of the magazine articles, North Carolina, a Militant Mediocracy, Should the Color Line Go?, Untangling Europe, A Freshman Again at Sixty, How Free Is Free Speech?, The South Is Dead—Long Live the South. Centennial orator, hundredth anniversary of N.C. Supreme Court, 1920; addressed N.C. Bar Assn. on "A Garland for Ashes," outlining a program of progress for the South, 1934. Address: Durham, N.C. Died Oct. 14, 1944.

WINTER, Alice Ames, author, club woman, executive; born Albany, New York, November 25, 1865; daughter Reverend Charles G. and Julia Francis (Baker) Ames; A.B., Wellesley Coll., 1886, A.M., 1889; Litt.D., U. of Southern Calif., 1937; m. Thomas Gerald Winter, June 25, 1892. Pres. Minneapolis Woman's Club, 1907-15. Mem. Minnesota Child Labor Com., Minneapolis Visiting Nurses Assn., Minneapolis Playground Commn.; pres. Minneapolis Free Kindergarten Assn.; hon. mem. Minneapolis Civic and Commerce Assn.; sec. The Hostesses; chmn. woman's com. Minn. div. of Council Nat. Defense; dir. woman's auxiliary Minn. Commn. Public Safety; dir. Minneapolis Chapter Am. Red Cross. Author: The Prize to the Hardy, 1905; Jewel-Weed, 1907; The Business of Being a Club Woman, 1925; The Heritage of Woman, 1927. Editor: Charles Gordon Ames—A Spiritual Autobiography, 1913; contributing editor Ladies' Home Jour., 1924-28. Pres. Gen. Fedn. of Women's Clubs, 1920-24. Dir. Community Service Dept. of Motion Picture Producers and Distributors of America, 1929-43. Home: 1235 Solita Rd., Pasadena, Calif. Died Apr. 5, 1944.

WINTER, Charles Allan, artist; b. Cincinnati, O., Oct. 26, 1869; s. Alfred A. and Fannie A. (Ransley) W.; student Art Acad. of Cincinnati, 1884-94; awarded foreign scholarship and studied at Julian Acad., Paris, under Bouguereau and Gabriel Ferrier; spent 1 yr. in Italy, chiefly in art galleries of Rome; m. Alice M. Beach, Jan. 1, 1904. Teacher, St. Louis Sch. of Fine Arts, 1898-1901; moved to New York, 1901. Portrait and figure painter and illustrator, New York mags. Murals in Gloucester City Hall Auditorium, 1934, 36, 37, 38 and 39, Gloucester High School, 1935. Home-Studio: 134 Mt. Pleasant Av., East Gloucester, Mass. Died Sep. 23, 1942.

WINTER, Charles Edwin, ex-congressman; b. Muscatine, Ia., Sept. 13, 1870; s. William and Wilhelmina (Fiegenbaum) W.; Ph.B., Neb. Wesleyan, 1892; m. Augusta P. Hutchinson (died Apr. 29, 1913); children—major Stanley Thacher, M/Sergt. Warren Hutchinson, Franklin Charles (U.S. Marine Corps); m. 2d, Alice R. Maltby, Feb. 23, 1915. Admitted to Neb. bar, 1895, and practiced at Omaha; moved to Encampment, Wyo., 1902, to Casper, 1913. Judge 6th Jud. Dist., Wyo., 1913-19; mem. 68th to 70th Congresses (1923-29) at large; Republican candidate for U.S. Senate, 1928; attorney gen. and acting gov. of Puerto Rico, Mar. 1932-Oct. 21, 1933; again in practice of law since 1933. Republican candidate for rep. to Congress, 1934. Chmn. Liberty Loan Com. and Council of Defense, Casper, during World War I. Mem. Am. and Wyo. bar assns., Am. Law Inst. Republican. Mason (Shriner), K.P., Kiwanian, Elk, Moose. Author: Grandon of Sierra, 1907; Ben Warman (made into movie), 1917; 400,000,000 Acres—The Public Lands and Resources, 1931; Gold of Freedom (Wyoming historical novel), 1944. Wrote words of Wyo. State Song. Office: 217 Consolidated Royalty Bldg., Casper, Wyo. Died April 22, 1948.

WINTER, Ezra Augustus, mural painter; b. Manistee, Mich., Mar. 10, 1886; s. Augustus and Sarah (Bright) W.; student Olivet Coll., 1906-07, LL.D., 1924; studied art Chicago Acad. Fine Arts, 1908-09; winner of Am. Acad. in Rome scholarship, 1911, and studied and traveled in Europe. Mural paintings in Cunard Bldg. and New York Cotton Exchange, New York; Eastman Theatre, Rochester, N.Y.; Willard Straight Memorial, Cornell U.; Birmingham (Ala.) Pub. Library; Rochester (N.Y.) Savings Bank; George Rogers Clark Memorial, Vincennes, Ind.; Radio City Music Hall foyer, New York; Monroe High Sch. Auditorium, Rochester, N.Y.; decorative map, Federal Reserve Bd., and Reading Rooms, Library of Congress, Washington, D.C.; also many pvt. residences. Designed camouflage for U.S. Shipping Bd., World War. Awarded medal of honor in painting, Architectural League of New York, 1922; gold medal, New York Soc. Architects, 1923. Fellow Am. Acad. in Rome; mem. Nat. Soc. Mural Painters, Archtl. League of New York, Nat. Inst. Arts and Letters. N.A., 1928. Home: Falls Village, Conn. Died April 6, 1949.

WINTON, Andrew Lincoln, chemist; b. Westport, Conn., Jan. 26, 1864; s. Andrew Leavenworth and Mary Esther (Gorham) W.; Ph.B., Yale, 1884, Ph.D., 1904; U. of Graz, 1904; m. Kate G. Barber, Dec. 16, 1911. Chemist, Conn. Agrl. Expt. Sta., 1884-90, in charge Analytical Lab., 1890-1907, instr. organic analysis, Yale, 1902-06; chief of Chicago Food and Drug Lab., U.S. Dept. of Agr., 1907-14. Pres. Assn. Official Agrl. Chemists of U.S., 1898; mem. Am. Chem. Soc., Sigma Xi, Phi Lambda Upsilon; hon. mem. Phila. Coll. of Pharmacy. Author: Microscopy of Vegetable Foods; Course in Food Analysis; (with wife) Structure and Composition of Foods (4 vols), The Analysis of Foods. Collaborator: Moeller's Mikroskopie der Nahrungs—u. Genussmittel. Translator: Hanausek's Microscopy of Technical Products. Reviser: Leach's Food Inspection and Analysis. Contbr. papers on chem. and micros. analysis, adulteration of foods, etc., in Am. and foreign scientific jours. Home: Wilton, Conn. Died Oct. 17, 1946; buried Mountain Grove Cemetery, Bridgeport, Conn.

WINTHROP, Bronson, lawyer; b. Dec. 22, 1863; s. Egerton Leigh and Charlotte (Bronson) W.; A.B., Trinity Coll., Cambridge, Eng., 1886, A.M., 1889; LL.B., Columbia, 1891. Practiced at N.Y. City since 1891; mem. Winthrop, Stimson, Putnam & Roberts; dir. Bank of Manhattan Co.; trustee Am. Surety Co. Episcopalian. Clubs: Knickerbocker, Union, Century, Down Town, University, Grolier, Republican, Meadow Brook Golf, Piping Rock. Home: 39 E. 72d St. Office: 32 Liberty St., New York, N.Y. Died July 14, 1944.

WISE, Louise Waterman, social worker; b. New York, N.Y.; d. Julius and Justine (Mayer) Waterman; m. Rabbi Stephen S. Wise, Nov. 14, 1900; children—James Waterman and Justine Wise Polier. Began as artist, 1900; became social worker at Univ. Settlement; founder and pres. Visiting Nurse Assn., Portland, Ore.; founder and pres. since 1914 Child Adoption Com. of the Free Synagogue, N.Y. City (com. has placed over 3500 children); founder and pres. Women's Div., Am. Jewish Congress; founder and chmn. Congress Refugee Houses (have sheltered over 4,000 refugees of many lands and faiths); founder of Congress Defense Houses, which offered shelter for members of Armed Forces of United States and of the United Nations. Has exhibited paintings in Pennsylvania Academy and at Corcoran Gallery, Washington, D.C. Member Women Painters and Sculptors. Translator: The Unknown Sanctuary (by Aime Palliere); Why I Am a Jew (by Edmond Fleg); My Palestine (by same); The Land of Promise (by same). Democrat. Office: 7 Central Park West, New York, N.Y. Died Dec. 10, 1947.

WISE, Stephen Samuel, rabbi; b. Budapest, Hungary, Mar. 17, 1874; s. Aaron (rabbi) and Sabine de Fischer (Farkashasy) W.; Coll. City of New York, 1887-91; A.B., Columbia, 1892, Ph.D., 1901; hon. degrees Temple U., Syracuse U. Rollins Coll., Bates Coll., University of Oregon, Roanoke Coll., Hebrew Union College, Cincinnati; m. Louise, d. Julius and Justine Mayer Waterman, Nov. 14, 1900; children—James Waterman, Hon. Justine Wise Polier. Pastor Congregation of Madison Av. Synagogue, New York, 1893-1900, Beth Israel, Portland, Ore., 1900-06; founder, 1907, and since rabbi Free Synagogue of New York. Founder and 1st v.p. Ore. State Conf. Charities and Correction; founder, 1st sec. Fedn. of Am. Zionists; commr. child labor State of Ore.; chmn. in succession to Justice Brandeis, of Provisional Exec. Com. for Gen. Zionist Affairs; mem. com. on labor of Council Nat. Defense; chmn. commn. of Zionist Orgn. America and pres. delegation of Am. Jewish Congress at Peace Conf., Paris; pres. Am. Jewish Congress, World Jewish Congress; pres. Zionist Orgn. America, 1936-38. Chevalier Légion d'Honneur (France), 1919, Officer, 1937. Founder Eastern Council of Liberal Rabbis; trustee Nat. Child Labor Com. Founder and president Jewish Inst. of Religion (training of men for Jewish ministry); chmn. United Palestine Funds Appeal, 1925-26; founder and trustee Near East Relief; vice chmn. N.Y. City Affairs Com. chmn. War Emergency Zionist Com. Chmn. United Emergency Com. on European Jewish Affairs. Author: The Ethics of Solomon Ibn Gabirol, 1901; Beth Israel Pulpit (monthly sermon publ.), 3 vols.; Free Synagogue Pulpit (monthly sermon publ.), 10 vols.; How to Face Life; Child Versus Parent; The Great Betrayal (with Jacob de Haas); As I See It; Challenging Years (autobiography), 1949. Editor Opinion a Magazine of Jewish Life and Letters. Home: 502 Park Av., N.Y. City. Died April 19, 1949.

WISHARD, Luther Deloraine, religious worker; b. Danville, Ind., Apr. 6, 1854; s. Milton Morris and Mary Eleanor (Baker) W.; student, Ind. U. and Hanover (Ind.) Coll.; B.A., Princeton, 1877; post-grad. work in Athens, Edinburgh, and at Union and Princeton theol. sems.; m. Eva Fancher, Vernon, Ia., July 22, 1884. Sec. Am. Intercollegiate Y.M.C.A., 1877-88; student sec. World's Y.M.C.A., 1888-92; fgn. sec. Am. Y.M.C.A., 1892-99; founder and dir. Forward Missionary Movement, Presbyn. and Congl. denominations, 1898-1902; founder and chmn. Missionary Edn. Movement, 1901-03; was founder and editor The Intercollegian. Founder of financial movement for promoting the teaching of the Bible to school children by paid instrs. Mem. Commn. of War Council in France, World War; served on Shipping Bd. during closing months of war. Mem. Corp. Y.M.C.A. Training Sch., Springfield, Mass. Decorated by S.A.R. for war service, also by Commn. on Rehabilitation at Verdun. Mem. S.A.R., Beta Theta Pi. Republican. Presbyn. Clubs: Princeton (Chicago and New York). Author: A New Program of Missions, 1895; Students' Challenge to the Churches, 1899. Home: 541 Lexington Av., New York. Died Aug. 6, 1925.

WISHON, A. Emory (wĭsh-ŏn'), public utility exec.; b. St. James, Mo., July 10, 1882; s. Albert Graves and Henrietta Millicent (Emory) W.; M.E., Sch. of Mines and Metallurgy, U. of Missouri, 1908; m. Cora Hoen, July 30, 1906; children—Albert Graves (dec.), Martha (Mrs. Henry T. Jarrell), A. Emory. Promoted Coalinga Water & Electric Co. and introduced electricity in oil well operations; joined San Joaquin Light & Power Corp. as asst. gen. mgr. in charge southern div., 1910; made asst. gen. mgr. of all properties of the co., 1913, gen. mgr., 1920, pres., 1930-38, when co. properties were merged with Pacific Gas & Electric Co.; dir. Pacific Gas & Electric Co. since 1936, became corporate v.p. and asst. gen. mgr., 1938, vice pres. and gen. mgr., 1943; v.p. and dir. Valley Elec. Supply Co., dir. Yosemite Portland Cement Corp., Am. President Lines. Mem. Sigma Nu, Newcomen Soc. Mason (32°). Clubs: University Sequoia (Fresno); Claremont Country, Diablo Country (Oakland); Bohemian, Family, Pacific Union, (San Francisco); Sutter Club (Sacramento); California (Los Angeles). Home: 284 Mountain Av., Piedmont, Calif. Office: 245 Market St., San Francisco 6, Calif. Died Jan. 4, 1948.

WISNER, Oscar Francis, clergyman; b. Wilton Junction, Ia., Sept. 25, 1858; s. Charles Wesley and Sarah (Kunkle) W.; A.B., U. of Wooster, 1881, A.M., 1884; Western Theol. Sem., Pittsburgh, 2 yrs.; grad. Princeton Theol. Sem., 1885; D.D., Wooster, 1900; m. Sophie Gray Preston, July 29, 1889. Teacher, Wooster U., 1883-84; ordained Presbyn. ministry,

1885; went to Canton, China, as missionary and engaged as teacher, Presbyn. Acad., 1885-93; preached in Ia., 1894-95; pastor, Santa Monica, Calif., 1895-98; pres. Canton Christian Coll., Canton, China, 1898-1907; prof. of missions, U. of Wooster, 1908-12; field investigator Dept. Ch. and Country Life, Presbyn. Bd. of Home Missions, 1912-14; pastor Adrian Community Presbyn. Ch., Parma, Ida., 1915-16; Chinese interpreter U.S. Immigration Service, Angel Island, Calif., 1917-18; ednl. sec. Y.M.C.A., Camp Kearny, Calif., 1918-19; dir. Oilfields (Calif.) Indsl. Sch., since 1921. Author: Beginning English, 1900; Beginning Chinese, 1906. Home: Oilfields, Calif. Died March 1947.

WISSLER, Clark (wĭs'lẽr), anthropologist; born, Wayne County, Ind., Sept. 18, 1870; s. Benjamin Franklin and Sylvania (Needler) W.; A.B., Ind. U., 1897, A.M., 1899; Ph.D., Columbia University, 1901; LL.D. from Indiana University, 1929; m. Etta Viola Gebhart, June 14, 1899; children—Stanley Gebhart, Mary Viola. Instr. edn., New York U., 1901-02; asst. in anthropology, 1903-05; lecturer, 1905-09, Columbia; asst. in anthropology, 1903-06, curator, 1906-41, Am. Museum Natural History; professor anthropology, Yale, 1924-40. Division chmn. Nat. Research Council, 1920-21; consulting anthropologist Bishop Mus., Honolulu since 1920. Fellow N.Y. Acad. Sciences, Am. Ethnol. Soc., Am. Geog. Soc.; mem. Nat. Acad. Sciences, Sigma Xi, Phi Beta Kappa. Author: North American Indians of the Plains, 1912; Man and Culture, 1922; The Relation of Nature to Man in Aboriginal America, 1926; Social Anthropology, 1929; The American Indian, 1938; Indian Cavalcade, 1938; The Indian in the United States, 1940. Home: 15 W. 77th St., New York 24, N.Y. Died Aug. 25, 1947.

WITZEMANN, Edgar John (wĭts'ē-măn), chemist; b. Decatur, Ill., July 13, 1884; s. Albert C. and Eliza (Düring) W.; A.B., James Millikin Univ., Decatur, Ill., 1907; A.M., Ohio State U., 1909, Ph.D., 1912; m. Lulu L. Laughlin, Aug. 30, 1910; 1 dau., Margaret Elisa. Fellow in chemistry, Ohio State U., 1907-09, instr., 1909-12; mem. Otho S. A. Sprague Memorial Inst. (U. of Chicago), 1912-25; research chemist Mayo Foundation, Rochester, Minn., 1925-27; asst. prof. physiol. chemistry, U. of Wis., 1927-35, asso. prof., 1935-47, prof., 1947. Research chemist Chem. Warfare, Washington, D.C., 1918. Fellow A.A.A.S.; mem. Am. Chem. Soc., Am. Soc. Biol. Chemists, Soc. Exptl. Biology and Medicine, Deutsche Chemisches Gesellschaft, Sigma Xi. Republican. Conglist. Author numerous research repts. in Am. chem. periodicals. Home: 1913 Regent St., Madison, Wis. Died Nov. 30, 1947; buried Decatur, Ill.

WOERMANN, John William (wẽr'măn), engr.; b. St. Louis, Mo., Jan. 18, 1868; s. Henry William and Catherine M. (Schwiering) W.; C.E., Washington U., 1890; m. Elizabeth Graff Honens, Oct. 15, 1891; children—Elsie (Mrs. W. E. Kling), Lillian (Mrs. R. L. Ward). Surveys and improvements for U.S. Govt. on Rock River, Chicago River, Mo. River, and Ill. and Miss. Canal (Hennepin Canal), 1890-1902; in charge of surveys, plans and estimates for 14-ft. waterway from Chicago to St. Louis, 1902-05; pvt. practice on bridge construction and water power development, 1905-08; made plans and estimates for 1½-ft. waterway, St. Louis to Cairo, and for 9-ft. waterway, Chicago to St. Louis, 1908-09. U.S. asst. engr., Western Div. and Northwestern Div., U.S. Army, inspection of projects, plans, specifications, etc., for improvements on 35 rivers, harbors and canals in middle west, 1909-22; prin. asst. engr., Chicago District, 1922-29, senior and prin. engr. same office, 1929-39; now cons. engr. Mem. Am. Soc. C.E., Western Soc. of Engrs., Internat. Navigation Congress, Washington Univ. Assn.; pres. Alumni Assn. Washington U., 1916. Presbyterian. Mason. Clubs: Engineers (pres. 1915), City (St. Louis). Author of many papers and reports on lock and dam construction, navigation, water power, and flood control. Home: 1525 E. 65th St., Chicago, Ill. Died Dec. 9, 1942.

WOLCOTT, John Dorsey (wo͝ol'kŭt), librarian; b. Penn Yan, N.Y., May 17, 1871; s. John Dorsey and Caroline (Cornwell) W.; A.B., U. of Wis., 1895, A.M., 1896; A.M., Cornell, 1897; Ph.D., Yale, 1898; unmarried. Instr. and librarian, Classical Library, U. of Chicago, 1900-05; asst. Library of Congress, Washington, D.C., 1905-09; librarian and dir. library extension, U.S. Bur. Edn., 1909-28; curator of catalogs, Library of Congress, 1928-41 (retired 1941); edited Record of Current Ednl. Publs. (U.S. Bur. Edn.), and book review page in School Life, 1912-28; library specialist, U.S. Bur. Education survey of Rutgers U., 1926. Mem. Am. Assn. for Advancement of Science, Am. Library Assn., Bibliog. Soc. America, S.A.R. (historian D.C. Soc.), Society of the War of 1812 (historian D.C. Soc.), Phi Beta Kappa. Conglist. (del. to Internat. council, Bournemouth, Eng., 1930). Mason (32°). Author of many bulletins on Library Activities and contbr. chapters in repts. of commr. of edn. and articles in ednl. and library jours. and assn. proc. Home: 1314 Farragut St. Address: Library of Congress, Washington, D.C. Died Nov. 23, 1945.

WOLCOTT, Roger Henry, legal education; b. San Antonio, Tex., Jan. 12, 1885; s. Samuel Adams and Julia (Neal) W.; prep. edn., Norwich (Conn.) Acad.; A.B., Yale, 1905; LL.B., U. of Denver, 1907, B.C.S., 1914; m. Louise Webster Dugal, Oct. 28, 1907; children—Jonathan Adams former officer A.U.S., Sylvia Dugal (Mrs. Robert D. Henry). Admitted to Colorado bar, 1907, and practiced at Denver, 1907-27; associated with law orgn. of William V. Hodges, 1917-27; joined faculty U. of Denver Sch. of Law, 1927, dean of sch. Jan. 1928 to Sept. 1944, now dean emeritus; War Prodn. Bd., 1943 and 1944; elected co. judge, Denver, 1912. First treas. Denver Philharmonic Assn., 1912-13. Mem. Legal Adv. Bd., Denver, 1918, and appeal agt. during draft for World War; accepted for training in U.S. Naval Res. Flying Corps in fall of 1918. Mem. Bd. of Bar Examiners, Colo., 1925-27. Mem. Am. Colo. State and Denver bar assns., Beta Theta Pi (mem. Nat. bd. trustees 1910-14), Phi Delta Phi, Alpha Kappa Psi, Omicron Delta Kappa. Mason. Republican. Episcopalian. Clubs: Colorado Yale Assn. (ex-pres.), Cactus, Mile High (ex-pres.), City (ex-pres.), Law Club (ex-pres.). Home: 2233 Ash St., Denver 7, Colo. Died Oct. 30, 1948.

WOLD, Peter Irving (wōld), prof. physics; b. South Dakota, Nov. 27, 1881; s. Ivor Peterson and Gurine (Gimse) W.; B.S., U. of Ore., 1901, E.E., 1903; studied George Washington U.; Ph.D., Cornell U., 1915; m. Mary Helen Helff, June 30, 1909; children—Ivor Peterson, Mary Elizabeth, John Schiller. Instr. in physics, U. of Ore., 1900-03; examiner of patents, U.S. Patent Office, Washington, D.C., 1903-05, 1908-10; instr. in physics, Cornell U., 1905-08; adviser on patent matters, U.S. Signal Corps, 1910; prof. physics, Am. Indemnity Coll., Peking, China, 1911-14; Andrew D. White fellow in physics, Cornell U., 1914-15; physicist and asst. to chief engr., Western Electric Co., New York, 1915-20; prof. physics and head of dept., Union Coll., Schenectady, N.Y., since 1920, chmn. div. of science, same, since 1940; sometime consultant Gen. Electric Co. Research Lab.; visiting prof. of science (on leave of absence) in China for China Med. Bd. of Rockefeller Foundation, 1923-24; dir. Civil Aeronautics Administration at Union College, 1939-40; physicist on special research (on leave of absence) U.S. Navy at Pearl Harbor, Honolulu, 1940-41; Navy liaison office, Rudiatim Lab., Cambridge, Mass., 1943. Former mem. exec. com. of Div. Physical Sciences of Nat. Research Council; pres. Schenectady Council of Boy Scouts of America, 1931-35, mem. Nat. Council since 1938; pres. N.Y. State Sect. of Am. Physical Soc., 1938-40. Fellow Am. Physical Soc.; mem. A.A.A.S., Optical Soc. of America, Am. Assn. of Physics Teachers, Sigma Xi, Phi Beta Kappa, Eta Kappa Nu, Gamma Alpha, Rotary Club. Elder Presbyn. Ch. Inventor in elec. field. Lecturer on Chinese life, edn. and history. Author: Kimball-Wold College Physics. Contbr. on scientific subjects. Navy liaison office, Rudiatim Laboratory, Cambridge, Mass. Address: Union College, Schenectady, N.Y. Died June 17, 1945.

WOLD, Theodore, banker; b. Decorah, Ia., July 4, 1868; s. John S. and Elizabeth (Espeseth) W.; ed. pub. schs.; m. Belle E. Groves, Oct. 26, 1893; children—Mrs. Margaret Elizabeth Harland, Ernest Groves (killed in action at Château Thierry, France, Aug. 1, 1918). Clerk in gen. store, Decorah, Ia., 1885-89; bank clk., Elbow Lake, 1889-90; asst. cashier 1st Nat. Bank, Little Falls, Minn., 1890-96; cashier Merchants Bank, Winona, Minn., 1896-1910; pres. Scandinavian Am. Nat. Bank, Minneapolis, 1910-14; gov. Federal Reserve Bank, Minneapolis, 1914-20; became 1st v.p. Northwestern Nat. Bank, 1919, chmn. bd. since 1939; chmn. bd. Northwestern Nat. Bank & Trust Co.; dir. Northwestern Fire & Marine Ins. Co., Northwestern Nat. Life Ins. Co., Northwest Bancorporation. Conglist. Mason (32°), Elk. Clubs: Minneapolis, Minikahda Golf. Home: 1779 Emerson Av. S. Office: Northwestern Nat. Bank & Trust Co., Minneapolis, Minn.*

WOLF, Adolph Grant, judge; b. Washington, D.C., Jan. 11, 1869; s. Simon and Caroline (Hahn) W.; A.B., Johns Hopkins, 1890; student law and philosophy, U. of Berlin, 1890-91; LL.B., Columbian (now George Washington) U., 1892, M.L., 1893; m. Marian Sweet, Aug. 5, 1914. In practice at Washington, 1893-1904; mem. firm Wolf & Cohen, 1896-1904; asso. justice Supreme Court of Puerto Rico, July 1904-Nov. 15, 1941; retired; mem. Commn. on Uniform State Laws from Puerto Rico, 1918-30. Clubs: University (Washington); Union (San Juan); Lotos (New York). Address: San Juan, P.R. Died Nov. 3, 1947.

WOLF, Frank, pres. Commonwealth Bank; b. Centreville, Mich., 1867; s. Samuel J. and Emmaline I. (Ketcham) W. Pres. Commonwealth Bank, Detroit, Mich., First State Bank, Hendon, Mich., Wolf Bros. State Bank, Centreville, Mich.; v.p. Commercial Savings Bank, Constantine, Mich.; dir. Central Nat. Bank, Battle Creek, Mich. Home: Hotel Fort Shelby. Office: Dime Bldg., Detroit, Mich. Died Jan. 17, 1948.

WOLFE, Harry Preston, publisher; b. Cumberland, O., Apr. 26, 1872; s. Andrew J. and Nancy (Barton) W.; m. Maude Fowler, 1897; children—Robert Huston, Preston, Richard Stanton. President Columbus Evening Dispatch; v.p. Ohio State Journal; gen. mgr. and treas. The Wolfe Wearuwell Corp.; dir. Bancohio Corp. Dir. sale of war savings stamps for Ohio, World War. Presbyterian. Clubs: Athletic, Columbus Country, Scioto Country (Columbus). Address: Columbus Evening Dispatch, Columbus, O

Died Jan. 10, 1946.

WOLFENDEN, James (wo͝olf'ĕn-dĕn), congressman; b. Cardington, Delaware County, Pa., July 25, 1889; ed. pub. schs. and academy. Elected to 70th Congress, 1928, to fill vacancy caused by death of Thomas S. Butler, and reëlected to 71st to 78th Congresses (1929-45), 8th Pa. Dist. Republican. Home: Upper Darby, Pa.* Died Apr. 8, 1949.

WOLFSTEIN, David I. (wo͝olf'stēn), physician; b. Hannibal, Mo., Jan. 11, 1862; s. Isaac and Caroline (Levy) W.; M.D., Medical Coll. of Ohio, 1888; intern Cincinnati Hosp., 1888-89; post-grad. student Strassburg, Zürich, Prague, Vienna, Paris, and London, 1889-92, Paris, and London, 1898-99; m. Nettie F. Scheuer, June 4, 1894; children—Agnes (wife of Dr. Raphael Isaacs), Mrs. Robert P. Goldman, Mrs. A. J. Levin. In wholesale hardware business, 1880-85; in practice of gen. medicine, 1892-98; specialty in nervous and mental diseases since 1898. Trustee U. of Cincinnati, 1912-21, now fellow. Mem. A.M.A., Ohio State Med. Assn., Cincinnati Med. Soc., Am. Neurol. Assn. Clubs: City (ex-pres.). Awarded Fiske Fund prize, 1898. Retired, 1934. Home: 3560 Inwood, Clifton, Cincinnati, O. Died June 6, 1944.

WOLTERSDORF, Arthur Fred (wŏl'tẽrs-dôrf), architect; b. Chicago, Ill., Jan. 19, 1870; s. Louis and Emma (Haeger) W.; ed. high sch., Chicago; studied in architects' offices; spl. course in architecture, Mass. Inst. Tech.; traveled and studied in Europe, 1892-93; unmarried. Practiced, Chicago, since 1894; designed St. Paul's Evangelical Lutheran Church, Chicago; Mirador Office Bldg.; Hippach Memorial Chapel; Gordon Baking Co.'s Chicago plant; Advance Rumely Co.'s bldgs. in Kansas City, Wichita and Saskatoon, Can.; Woodlawn Branch, Chicago Public Library, etc. Fellow A.I.A. (ex-pres. Chicago chapter), Ill. Soc. Architects (ex-pres.). Lutheran. Clubs: University, Cliff Dwellers. Author: Living Architecture. Frequent contbr. to archtl. publs. Office: 520 N. Michigan Av., Chicago 11, Ill. Died March 3, 1948.

WONSON, Roy Warren (wŭn'sŭn), educator; b. Gloucester, Mass., Aug. 6, 1883; s. Charles Fred and Agnes Adele (Higgins) W.; student Summerville Acad., Augusta, Ga., 1896-98; B.S., Mil. Coll. of S.C., Charleston, 1902; m. Marie Augusta Hammond, June 5, 1913; 1 son, Charles Fred. Teacher pub. schs., Charleston, 1902-10; with Staunton Mil. Acad. since 1910, head of history dept., 1910-11, post adj., 1911-15, asst. headmaster, 1915-20, headmaster, 1920-39, headmaster emeritus since 1939. Mem. Naval and Mil. Order Spanish-Am. War. Mem. Southern Prep. Sch. Assn. (pres.), Va. Acad. Science; Colleague Am. Guild Organists. Episcopalian (choirmaster Trinity Ch. since 1910). Mason. Club: Beverley (pres.). Home: 214 N. Market St., Staunton, Va.

Died Oct. 11, 1942.

WOOD, Asa Butler, newspaper editor and pub.; b. Wapello County, Ia., Aug. 26, 1865; s. Claybourne and Jane (Warren) W.; grad. high sch., Agency, Ia., 1883; m. Maggie Claypool, Oct. 11, 1888; children—Bess Lucile (dec.), Jane Marie (Mrs. W. B. Sands), Sarah Dorothy (Mrs. J. W. Ponder), Marjorie Ellen (dec.), Alice Lynette (wife of Rev. H. R. Colbert), Warren Claypool. Printer, Ottumwa, Ia., 1882-86, Broken Bow, Neb., 1886; established Gering (Neb.) Courier, 1887 (Gering then 75 miles from a railroad), established newspaper at Torrington, Wyo., 1907, at Scottsbluff, Neb., 1912 (now Star-Herald, a daily). Mem. Neb. State Senate, 1924-30; del. Rep. Nat. Conv., 1892, 1916, 1940, postmaster Gering 17 yrs.; chairman of Park Board; secretary and manager Scotts Bluff County Fair Assn., 15 yrs.; charge of chautauqua and lyceum courses for 10 yrs.; chmn. Courthouse Bond Com.; organizer North Platte Valley Asso. Chambers of Commerce and successively held all offices; organizer Ore. Trail Days, an annual event; mem. Neb.-Ore. Trail Monument Com.; life mem. Nat. Ore. Trail Memorial Assn.; pres. Neb. Chapter Am. Pioneer Trails Assn., 1941. Served as chairman, Red Cross and secretary 3 Liberty Loan drives and Council of Defense during World War I. Member Nebraska State Historical Soc. (pres. 1937-40), Neb. State Irrigation Assn. (pres. 1922), Neb. Press Assn. (pres. 1911). Republican. Mem. Christian Ch. Mason (K.T., 32°, Shriner), O.E.S., Odd Fellow. Author: Pioneer Tales of the Nebraska Panhandle, 1938; Fifty Years of Yesterdays, 1944; also of pamphlet History of Christian Churches of North Platte Valley. Former contbr. Irrigation Age, Printers Ink, Inland Printer; contbr. features to newspapers. Home: 1925 12th St. Office: 1050 10th St., Gering, Neb. Died May 7, 1945.

WOOD, Casey Albert, opthalmologist; b. of Am. parents, Wellington, Ont., Can., Nov. 21, 1856; s. Orrin Cottier and Rosa Sophia (Leggo) W.; ed. pvt. English and French schs.; grad. Ottawa (Can.) Collegiate Inst., 1874; C.M., M.D., Univ. Bishop's Coll., 1877, D.C.L., 1903; M.D., McGill U. 1906, LL.D., 1921; M.C.P.S., Ont., 1878; student N.Y. Eye and Ear Infirmary and Post-Grad. Med. Sch., 1886, also at many European hosps., 1886-1914; m. Emma Shearer, Oct. 28, 1886. Clin. asst. Royal London Ophthal. Hosp. (Moorfields), 1888-89; asst. Wm. Lang Eye dept., Middlesex Hosp., London, 1889; house surgeon Central London Ophthal. Hosp., Gray's Inn Rd., 1889; asst. surgeon West London Ophthal. Hosp., 1889; went to Chicago, 1900; attending ophthal. surgeon Alexian Bros., Passavant Memorial and St. Luke's hosps. (later consultant); cons. surgeon (eye) Cook County and St. Anthony hosps.; prof. chemistry and pathology, Univ. Bishop's Coll., 1878-85; prof. opthalmology, Chicago Post-Grad. Med. Sch., 1890-97; prof. clin. ophthalmology, Coll. Physicians and Surgeons, Chicago, 1898-1906; head prof. opthalmology, Northwestern U., 1906-08, U. of Ill., 1909-13 (now emeritus). Hon. collaborator on birds, Smithsonian Instn., 1927; hon. lecturer on ornithology, Stanford U., 1928; research asso. Calif. Inst. Technology, 1932; retired from practice, 1917. Active service U.S. Army, as 1st lt., Nov. 1916-Feb.

1917, and later as maj.; head of exam. unit, at Chicago, of candidates for aviation and U.S. Signal Corps; in charge eye dept., Camp Sherman, O., Sept.-Dec. 1917; lt. col. on staff of surgeon gen., Washington, D.C., Dec. 1917-June 1919; now col. Med. Res. Corps, U.S. Army. Fellow Am. Acad. Medicine (pres. 1907), A.A.A.S., Mitglied d. ophthal. Gesellschaft (Germany), Am. Coll. Surgeons (foundation fellow), Acad. Medicine and of Medico-legal Soc. (Chicago), Am. Med. Assn. (chmn. sect. of ophthalmology 1889), Am. Acad. of Othalmology and Otology (pres. 1905-06), Am. Geog. Soc., Zoöl. Soc. of London (del. to Centenary); mem. Assn. Military Surgeons, Calif. Acad. Science, Am., British and Royal Austral. Ornithol. unions; hon. mem. Am. Numismatic Soc. (New York), N.Y. Charaka Club, Peregrine Club (Phila.); ex-pres. Chicago Ophthal. Soc. Editor in chief Annals of Ophthalmology, 1894-1901; chief editor Ophthal. Record, 1902-08; editorial staff Anales de Oftalmologia (Mexico), Med. Standard (Chicago) and Annals of Med. History (New York); editor Am. Journal of Ophthalmology, 1908-14; editor eye sect. Practical Med. Series, 1908-15; contbr. to various "systems" and textbooks, also author of many mag. articles on medical and natural history, including numerous transls. from German, French, Italian, Spanish, Latin and Arabic treatises. Traveled 15 yrs. in Europe, 1919-34, also in the Far East (3 yrs. in India and Ceylon), Oceania, S. America (with Dr. Wm. Beebe, 2 winters in British Guiana), and in West Indies for zoölogic and medico. hist.- research. Founder of Wood gold medal and of several spl. libraries at McGill Univ. Clubs: University (Chicago); Cosmos (Washington, D.C.); Authors (London); Athenæum (Pasadena, California). Author: Lessons in Diagnosis and Treatment of Eye Diseases, 1895; Toxic Amblyopias, 1896; Commoner Diseases of the Eye (3d edit., 1907, with T. A. Woodruff); Primary Sarcoma of the Iris (with Brown Pusey), 1908; A System of Ophthalmic Therapeutics, 1909; A System of Ophthalmic Operations, 2 vols., 1911; American Encyclopedia of Ophthalmology, 17 vols., 1908-12; Fundus Oculi of Birds, 1917; A Physician's Anthology (with Fielding Garrison), 1920; Birds of Fiji (with Alexander Wetmore), 1927-28; Introduction to the Study of Vertebrate Zoölogy (with annotated catalogue), 1931. Transl. (with notes) Benvenutus Grassus, De Oculis (A.D., 1474), 1930; transl. Tadhkirat, Arabic Note-Book of an Oculist (1000 A.D.), 1930; annotated transl. Notebook of a Tenth Century Oculist, 1936; transl. (with notes) of a Twelfth Century Codex, the De Arte Venandi cum Avibus by Emperor Frederick II (with Marjorie Fyfe), 1940. Home: Caltec, 551 S. Hill Av., Pasadena, Calif. Address: Hotel del Coronado, Coronado, Calif. Died Jan. 26, 1942.

WOOD, Charles, clergyman; b. Brooklyn, June 3, 1851; s. John J. and Mary (Lyon) W.; A.B., Haverford, 1870, A.M., 1873; grad. Princeton Theol. Sem., 1873; D.D., Princeton, 1885; LL.D., Coll. of Wooster, Ohio, 1923; m. Mary Hollingsworth Morris, Sept. 6, 1883 (died June 24, 1891); children—Morris, Marguerite (Mrs. W. Logan Mac Coy); m. 2d, Alice Cox, June 20, 1905. Ordained Presbyn. ministry, 1873; pastor Central Ch., Buffalo, 1873-78, Fourth Ch., Albany, 1881-86, First Ch., Germantown, Pa., 1886-97, Second Ch., Phila., 1897-1908, Ch. of The Covenant, Washington, 1908-28; pres. Nat. Presbyn. Ch., Washington. Author: Saunterings in Europe, 1882; Beginning Life, 1887; Friends and Foes of Youth, 1898; Some Moral and Religious Aspects of the War, 1915; The Living Christ and Some Problems of Today (William Belden Noble lectures at Harvard U.), 1919. Home: 1150 Connecticut Av., Washington. Died July 30, 1936.

WOOD, Charles Erskine Scott, writer; b. Erie, Pa., Feb. 20, 1852; s. William Maxwell and Rose (Carson) W.; Erie Acad., Baltimore City Coll.; grad. U.S. Mil. Acad., 1874; Ph.B., LL.B., Columbia U., 1883; m. Nannie Moale Smith, Nov. 26, 1878 (now dec.); m. 2d, Sara Bard Field. Served as 2d lt., later 1st lt. U.S.A., 1874-84; engaged in Nez Percé campaign, 1877, Banneck and Piute campaign, 1878. Admitted to bar, 1884, and practiced at Portland, Ore., until 1919. Mem. Bibliophile Soc., Boston. Club: Grolier (New York). Author: A Book of Tales, Being Myths of the North American Indians, 1901; A Masque of Love, 1904; The Poet in the Desert, 1915; Maia, 1916; Circe, 1919; Heavenly Discourse, 1927; Poems from the Ranges, 1929; Too Much Government, 1931. Home: Los Gatos, Calif. Died Jan. 21, 1944.

WOOD, Edith Elmer, author; b. Portsmouth, N.H., Sept. 24, 1871; d. Comdr. Horace (U.S. Navy) and Adele (Wiley) Elmer; B.L., Smith Coll., 1890, LL.D., 1940; A.M., Columbia, 1917, Ph.D., 1919; grad. N.Y. Sch. of Social Work, 1917; m. Lt. Albert Norton Wood, U.S. Navy, June 24, 1893; children—Horace Elmer (dec.), Thurston Elmer (dec.), Horace Elmer II, Albert Elmer. Writer since 1890. Founder, 1906, pres., 1906, 07, 09, hon. pres. since 1908, Anti-Tuberculosis League of Porto Rico; del. Internat. Congress Tuberculosis, 1908. Chmn. nat. com. on housing, Am. Assn. Univ. Women, 1917-29; in charge courses in housing, Columbia U. extension, 1926-30, Teachers College, summer sessions, 1925-32, 36, 37; consultant, housing div. Pub. Works Adminstr., 1933-37; consultant U.S. Housing Authority, 1938-42; mem. N.J. State Housing Authority, 1934-35; vice-pres. Nat. Pub. Housing Conf., 1932-36, dir., 1936-45; mem. exec. com. Internat. Housing Assn., 1931-37, Phi Beta Kappa. Author: Her Provincial Cousin, 1893; Shoulder Straps and Sunbonnets, 1901; The Spirit of the Service, 1903; An Oberland Châlet, 1910; The Housing of the Unskilled Wage Earner, 1919; Housing Progress in Western Europe, 1923; Recent Trends in American Housing, 1931; Slums and Blighted Areas in the United States (Housing Div. Bull.), 1935; Introduction to Housing Facts and Principles, 1939. Contbr. to mags. and periodicals. Home: Cape May Court House, N.J. Died Apr. 29, 1945; buried in U.S. Naval Academy Cemetery, Annapolis, Md.

WOOD, Frances Gilchrist, author; b. Hillsgrove, Ill., Nov. 25, 1859; d. Charles Allen and Lucy Ellen (Walker) G.; A.B., Carthage Coll., 1880, A.M., 1884, Litt.D., 1923; studied Sch. of Journalism, Columbia, 1917-19; m. Lansing Pruyn Wood, Dec. 11, 1893; children—Helen Pruyn, Emma Justine (Mrs. Aaron Polk). Auditor Ft. Madison & Northwestern Ry., later on editorial staff Appomattox (Dak.) Herald and Dallas (Tex.) News. Mem. O. Henry Memorial Award Com., 1921-32. Mem. Authors' League America, D.A.R. Republican. Episcopalian. Clubs: University, New York City Woman's. Author: Children's Pageant, 1913; Pageant of Ridgewood, N.J., 1915; Cartoons of Dress, 1917; Pageant Union School, 1919; Gospel Four Corners, 1930; Turkey Red, 1932. Contbr. short stories to leading mags. Home: 318 Edgewood Av., West Englewood, N.J. Died Dec. 21, 1944.

WOOD, Francis Asbury, philologist; b. Point Bluff, Wis., Jan. 17, 1859; s. Rev. Harvey Colcord and Ann Jane (Ellis) W.; A.B., Northwestern U., 1880, A.M., 1883; Ph.D., U. of Chicago, 1895; U. of Göttingen, Germany, 1888-90; L.H.D., Northwestern U., 1910; m. Rose H. Burt, Aug. 6, 1896. Prof. Greek and Latin, Chaddock Coll., Quincy, Ill., 1890-93; fellow in Germanic langs. and lits., U. of Chicago, 1893-95; asst. Medill High Sch., Chicago, 1895-97; prof. German, Cornell Coll., Ia., 1897-1903; instr., U. of Chicago, 1903-05, asst. prof. Germanic philology, 1905-09, asso. prof., 1909-14, prof., 1914-27, now emeritus. Mem. Modern Lang. Assn., Am. Linguistic Soc., Phi Beta Kappa. Author: Verner's Law in Gothic and the Reduplicating Verbs in Germanic, 1895; Color-Names and their Congeners, 1902; Indo-European "a: ai: au," A Study in Ablaut and in Word Formation, 1905; Elckerlijc-Everyman—the Question of Priority, 1910; Iteratives, Blends, and Streckformen, 1911; Kontaminationsbildungen und haplologische Mischformen, 1912; Some Parallel Formations in English, 1913; Post-Consonantal "W" in Indo-European, 1926. Contbr. numerous articles to philol. jours. of America and Germany. Home: La Jolla, Calif. Died June 19, 1948.

WOOD, Frederick Hill, lawyer; b. Lebanon, Me., Jan. 2, 1877; s. Frederick Ansel and Mary Calista (Hill) W.; A.B., U. of Kan., 1897, LL.B., 1899; m. Margery Pearson, July 11, 1914; 1 dau., Patricia. Admitted to Kan. and Mo. bars, 1899, N.Y., 1904; began practice in Lawrence, Kan.; practiced in Kansas City, Mo., 1899-1910; asst. prof. law, U. of Kan., 2 yrs.; gen. atty. St.L.&S.F. R.R. Co., at St. Louis, 1910-13; same for S.P. Co., N.Y. City, 1910-24; gen. practice as partner Cravath, Henderson & de Gersdorff, now Cravath, de Gersdorff, Swaine & Wood, since 1924; argued O'Fallon test case on principles of ry. rate valuation, Schechter case involving constitutionality of NRA Act, Carter case involving Guffey Bituminous Coal Conservation Act, and gold clause case before U.S. Supreme Court. Trustee Nightingale-Bamford Sch., N.Y. City; trustee Town Hall, Inc., N.Y. City; trustee Practicing Law Inst., N.Y. City. Mem. Am. and N.Y. State bar assns., Assn. Bar City of N.Y., N.Y. County Lawyers Assn., Phi Kappa Psi, Phi Delta Phi, Phi Beta Kappa. Republican. Clubs: University, Piping Rock, Manhattan, Broad St., Down Town Assn., Blind Brook, National Republican. Home: 550 Park Av. Office: 15 Broad St., New York, N.Y. Died Dec. 28, 1943.

WOOD, Frederick William, consulting engr.; b. Lowell, Mass., Mar. 16, 1857; s. William and Elizabeth French (Kidder) W.; B.S., Mass. Inst. Tech., 1877; m. Caroline Peabody Smith, Jan. 24, 1884; children—Frederick Brayton, Dorothy, Elizabeth (Mrs. Clarke Farwell Freeman), Helen, Caroline (Mrs. Carl Billings Willard), Richard Minot. Began with Pa. Steel Co. at Baldwin (now Steelton), Pa., 1877, gen. supt., 1884-89, gen. mgr., 1889-91, 2d v.p., 1893; pres. Md. Steel Co., 1891-1916; in charge of same after purchase by Bethlehem Steel Co., 1916-18; v.p. Am. Internat. Shipbuilding Corp., 1918-21; now chmn. bd. Eastern Rolling Mill Co.; dir. Consol. Gas, Electric Light & Power Co. of Baltimore, Savings Bank of Baltimore. Mem. Claims Commn. of U.S. Shipping Bd., Emergency Fleet Corp., 1921-23; term mem. of Corp. Mass. Inst. Tech., 1906-11; trustee Johns Hopkins U.; dir. Md. Inst. Mem. Am. Inst. Mining and Metall. Engrs., Am. Soc. M.E., Am. Soc. Naval Architects and Marine Engrs., Am. Iron and Steel Inst., A.A.A.S. Republican. Unitarian. Clubs: Maryland, Merchants (Baltimore); Engineers' (New York). Home: 2429 Keyworth Av., Baltimore, Md. Died Dec. 23, 1943.

WOOD, George Henry; b. Dayton, O., Nov. 3, 1867; s. Maj. Gen. Thomas J. (U.S. Army) and Caroline E. (Greer) W.; Ph.B., Yale, 1887; LL.B., Cincinnati Law Sch., 1889; m. Virginia Peirce, June 29, 1910; children—Thomas J., Peirce. Practiced law in Dayton, 1890-98; brokerage business, 1901-12. Enlisted as private, advanced to 2d lt., 3d Ohio Vol. Infantry, Spanish-Am. War, 1898; 1st lt. 28th U.S. Vol. Inf., Philippine Insurrection, 1899-1901; capt. and maj., Ohio Nat. Guard, 1901-12; adj. gen. of Ohio, 1913-15, 1917-19; in charge selective draft, State of Ohio. Recruited Ohio Nat. Guard from 8,000 to 25,000 men, making a complete div., which was drafted into the federal service as the 37th (Buckeye) Division. Commd. col. inf., June 24, 1918; joined 42d (Rainbow) Div. as comdr. of trains during 2d Battle of the Marne; served also at St. Mihiel and in the Argonne; mustered out, Jan. 18, 1919. Mem. Civ. Service Commn., Dayton, 1910-13; mil. comdr. Dayton, O., under martial law during great flood, 1913; sec. bd. mgrs. Nat. Home for Disabled Vol. Soldiers, Dayton, 1914-16, pres. since 1916; apptd. spl. rep. of administration covering Nat. Soldiers' Home activities, on consolidation of all veteran relief into Veterans' Administration, July 1, 1930; consultant to Administration of Veteran Affairs on Soldiers Home activities since July 1, 1933. Mem. nat. exec. com. of Am. Legion, 1919. Democrat. Presbyterian. Clubs: Buz Fuz, Dayton. Home: 25 Schantz Av., Dayton, Ohio.*

WOOD, George Willard, newspaper editor; b. Lewiston, Me., Aug. 31, 1854; s. James and Elizabeth (Blackwell) W.; A.B., Bates Coll., Lewiston, 1875; Ph.D., Yale, 1877; m. Laura N. Brackett, 1901 (dec.). Purchased Lewiston Daily Sun, 1898, and since editor-in-chief. Home: 112 Wood St. Office: 104 Park St., Lewiston, Me. Died Nov. 20, 1945.

WOOD, Henry, newspaper corr., b. Holland, Ia., Nov. 4, 1878; s. Charles Taylor and Josephine Sofia (Marks) W.; student U. of Missouri, 1901, 02, U. of Neb., 1904, 05; m. Noelle Juvet, Dec. 13, 1923; 1 son, Donald. Began with Omaha Daily News, 1901, later with Council Bluffs Nonpareil, Cleveland Press; connected with United Press Assn., 1910-34 and since 1936, successively mgr. Rome Bur., Paris, Bur., dir. United Press services with League of Nations, at Geneva, Switzerland; corr. during World War in France, Italy, Serbia and Turkey. Quit newspaper work, and returned to the U.S., 1934. Decorated Legion of Honor (French); Order of the Crown (Italian); Croix de Misèricorde (Serbian); Order of Prince Danilo I (Montenegrin); Order of the Crown (Belgian). Home: 359 Hyde St. Office: United Press, 814 Mission St., San Francisco, Calif.* Died Aug. 27, 1946.

WOOD, James Anderson, newspaperman; b. Portsmouth, O., Apr. 28, 1870; s. Oliver and Emily Hutte (Mytinger) W.; early yrs. spent on Indian reservations where father was agent; student Bishop Scott Acad., Portland, Ore., 1 yr.; m. Tuolumne Gooch Delaney, Aug. 5, 1912. Admitted Wash. bar, 1894; began newspaper work on Seattle Post-Intelligencer, 1896; city editor Seattle Times, 1904-07; dir. exploitation Alaska-Yukon-Pacific Expn., 1908-09; part owner and editor Seattle Town Crier, 1910-18; editor in chief Seattle Post-Intelligencer, 1918-21; editorial asso. Portland Oregonian, 1921-27; asso. editor Seattle Times since 1927. Mem. Am., Wash. State and Seattle bar assns., S.R., Mil. Order Loyal Legion. Rep. Episcopalian. Mason (32°). Clubs: Rainier, Cosmos, Washington Athletic, Washington State Press. Home: 3219 Cascadia Av. Office: Seattle Times, Seattle, Wash. Died Feb. 10, 1947.

WOOD, James Craven, gynecologist; b. Wood County, O., Jan. 11, 1858; s. Henry L. and Jane (Kunkle) W.; A.M., Ohio Wesleyan Univ.; M.D., U. of Mich. 1879; hon. A.M., Univ. of Michigan, 1914; m. Julia Kellogg Bulkley, December 28, 1883 (deceased); children—James L. (dec.), Edna Wood Williamson (dec.), Justin B. Practiced in Cleveland, O., since 1893; prof. obstetrics and diseases of women and children, U. of Mich. Homœ. Med. Coll., 1885-94; prof. gynecology, Cleveland-Pulte Med. College, 23 years; gynecologist, Huron Rd. Hosp.; mem. cons. staff Elyria Memorial Hosp. Pres. Am. Inst. Homœopathy, 1902; fellow A.M.A.; founder mem. Am. Coll. Surgeons (gov. 30 yrs.). Fellow Internat. Congress Gynecology and Obstetrics, hon. pres. Belgian session, 1892; ex-pres. Mich. and Ohio State Homœopathic medical socs. Author: A Text-book of Gynecology; Clinical Gynecology; Then and Now (play); The Reincarnation of Richard Warrington; The Value and Limitations of Homœopathy; Man and His Physician; An Old Doctor of the New School (autobiography), 1942; and more than 200 reprints and jour. articles. Club: Mid Day. Home: 2899 Brighton Rd., Shaker Heights, Ohio. Office: 816 Rose Bldg., Cleveland, O. Died Aug. 29, 1948.

WOOD, John Wilson, missionary exec.; b. New York, N.Y.; Aug. 4, 1866; s. John and Mary E. W.; B.S., Coll. of City of New York, 1886; D.C.L., U. of the South, 1915; m. Harriet R. Drom, 1891 (died 1931); m. 2d, Regina B. Lustgarten, 1939. In business life, 1886-90; gen. sec. Brotherhood of St. Andrew, 1890-1900; sec. Domestic and Foreign Missionary Soc. P.E. Ch., 1900-41; retired. Trustee Nat. Child Labor Com., also trustee Am. Church Inst. for Negroes, trustee Central China Coll.; trustee Fukien Christian U., Am. Church Bldg. Fund. Mem. Phi Beta Kappa. Made visitations of missions of P.E. Ch., Cuba, 1906, Puerto Rico, 1912, 29, 31, Alaska 1917, China, Japan, Philippines, Hawaii, 1918-19, 1923-24, 1927-28, 30, 33, South America, 1926, Haiti and Dominican Republic, 1931, Mexico, 1922. Editor, Spirit of Missions, 1900-14. Republican. Episcopalian (vestryman St. Peter's Ch., N.Y. City). Home: 402 W. 20th St., New York 11, N.Y. Died Aug. 7, 1947.

WOOD, Myron Ray, army officer; b. Salinas, Calif., Dec. 4, 1892; student U. of Colo.; enlisted as aviation cadet, 1918; commd. 2d lt. Aviation Sect. Signal Corps., Mar. 1918, 2d lt. Air Service, Regular Army,

1920, and advanced through the grades to brig. gen., June 1943; assigned to Wright Field, Dayton, O., as chief of Procurement Planning Br. Indsl. Planning Sect. Air Corps Material Div., June 1937; with Office of Chief of Air Corps, as asst. to the chief of Plans Div., Washington, D.C., July 1939; with Office of Asst. Sec. of War, Washington, D.C., Sept. 1939; became chief, Aircraft Div. Production Br. Office of Under Secretary of War, July 1940; named chief of Aircraft Sect. Production Br. Procurement and distribution Div., Hdqrs. Services of Supply (Army Service Forces), Washington, D.C., Apr. 1942; chief supply div. in charge Air Force Supply, European Theater of Operations since Sept. 1942. Rated command pilot, combat observer, aircraft observer.†* Died Oct. 29, 1946.

WOOD, Samuel Grosvenor, motion picture dir.; b. Phila., Pa., July 10, 1884; s. Wm. H. and Catherine (Corn) W.; ed. M. Hall Stanton Sch., Phila.; m. Clara L. Roush, Aug. 25, 1907; children—Jeane (Mrs. John Hallam Hiestand), Gloria, K. T. Stevens. Real estate and investing, Los Angeles, 1903-10, actor 1910-14; asst. to C. B. DeMille, 1914-16; motion picture dir. since 1916; has directed about 70 pictures, starring Wallace Reid, Gloria Swanson, Rudolph Valentino, Clark Gable, Marie Dressler, Joan Crawford, Jean Harlow, Norma Shearer and others; directed "Goodbye Mr. Chips," in England for Metro-Goldwyn-Mayer; recently produced and directed "For Whom the Bell Tolls"; now an independent producer and director; produced, directed Saratoga Trunk, Command Decision. Club: Bel Air Country. Home: 424 S. Irving Blvd. Office: M.G.M., Culver City, Calif. Died Sept. 22, 1949.

WOOD, Waddy Butler, architect; b. near St. Louis, Mo., June 19, 1869; s. Capt. Charles and Clara Forsyth (Hargraves) W.; Va. Poly. Inst., 1886-88; m. Elizabeth Lindsay Lomax, Oct. 1898; children—Mrs. Robert H. Hadow, Virginia Hargraves. Began as architect on own account, 1892; cons. architect Southern Ry. Co.; architect for remodeling State War and Navy Bldg., Washington; architect Southern Ry. Office Bldg., Potomac Electric Power Co. Office Bldg., Telephone Bldg. of C. & P. Telephone Co., 2 office buildings for Brookings Inst. and new building of Dept. of Interior. Designed temporary buildings in Washington, D.C., during World War, for practically all the different branches of U.S. Govt., covering about 60 acres of floor space. Fellow Am. Inst. Architects (past pres. Washington Chapter); mem. Columbia Hist. Soc., Va. Hist. Soc., Soc. of the Cincinnati (State of Va.). Episcopalian. Clubs: Metropolitan, Chevy Chase, Alfalfa (Washington). Home: 1909 23d St. N.W.; (summer) Warrenton. Va. Office: 1727 K St. N.W., Washington, D.C. Died Jan. 25, 1944.

WOOD, William Roscoe, agrl. editor; b. Malden, Mass., Aug. 17, 1874; s. William and Susan Maria (Whittle) W.; ed. pub. schs; m. Mabel Gertrude Lawhead, Aug. 21, 1895; children—Roscoe Edwin, Mayme Gertrude (Mrs. Lloyd L. Evans), George Everet, May Eleanor (Mrs. C. O. Gilmore). Jr. partner William Wood & Son, nurserymen, 1890-96; v.p. and mgr. Roeding & Wood Nursery Company, 1898-1914; farmer and fruit grower, 1914-23; asso. editor California Cultivator, 1922-23, mng. editor since 1923; sec.-treas. Cultivator Pub. Co. Republican. Mem. Christian (Disciples) Ch. Woodman. Club: Peter Pan Woodland. Home: 131 W. 6th St., San Dimas, Calif. Office: 317 Central Av., Los Angeles, Calif.* Died Oct. 25, 1941.

WOOD, William Thomas, army officer; b. Irving, Montgomery County, Ill., June 19, 1854; s. Preston and Jane K. W.; grad. U.S. Mil. Acad., 1877; m. Janet Judson Sanford, Sept. 27, 1877; 1 dau., Janet (wife of H. C. Pillsbury, U.S. Army). Commd. add. 2d lt. 4th Inf., June 15, 1877; promoted through grades to col., Mar. 12, 1910; retired on account of disability incurred in the line of duty, Apr. 3, 1913; brig. gen., June 21, 1930. Served at Ft. Clark, Tex., 1890-92, Fort Bliss, Tex., 1892-95; chief ordnance officer Dept. of Pacific, 1898-99; collector of customs, at Cebu, P.I., Mar.-Nov. 1899; treas. Philippine Archipelago and Island of Guam, 1899-1900; again in Philippines, 1905-07; insp. gen. Philippines Div., July-Aug. 1907; duty office of insp. gen., War Dept., 1907-09; insp. gen. Dept. of the East, Governors Island, N.Y., 1909-10; assigned 19th Inf., Mar. 12, 1910; comdg. 19th Inf. and post of Camp Jossman, P.I., 1910-11; comdg. recruit depot, Jefferson Bks., Mo., 1911-13; sec. U.S. Soldiers' Home, Washington, D.C., 1913-17; recalled to active service, May 16, 1917; brig. gen (temp.), Feb. 18, 1918; duty Office of Insp. Gen., War Dept., May 24, 1917-May 25, 1919; spl. inspection tour, Europe, May 27, 1919-July 5, 1919; assigned Office of Insp. Gen., July 5, 1919; sec. bd. Soldiers' Home, Washington, D.C., 1920-30. Awarded D.S.M. by Pres. Wilson, "for exceptionally meritorious and conspicuous service" as sr. asst. to the insp. gen. of the Army, which was presented by Gen. Pershing, at Paris, France, June 14, 1919; cited in War Dept. orders "for gallantry in action," near Manila, P.I., during Spanish-Am. War, and authorized to wear silver star on ribbon of Spanish-Am. war medal. Mem. Loyal Legion, Am. Legion. Episcopalian. Club: Army and Navy (Washington, D.C.). Address: War Dept., Washington, D.C. Died Dec. 19, 1943.

WOODARD, James Edward, banker; b. Omaha, Neb., Dec. 16, 1882; s. James Ira and Adeline (Barbeau) W.; A.B., Creighton U., Omaha; m. Judith Waite, Apr. 13, 1918; children—Joan, John Sloane. Treas. Anaconda Copper Mining Co.; dir. First Bank Stock Corp., Mont. Power Co., Mont. Flour Mills Co., Elec. Products Consolidated Co. Home: The Towers, Waldorf-Astoria Hotel. Office: 25 Broadway, New York 4, N.Y. Died Aug. 8, 1947.

WOODBRIDGE, Dwight Edwards, cons. engr.; b. Newton, Mass., July 19, 1865; s. Jonathan Edwards and Lydia (Judkins) W.; A.B., Carleton Coll., Northfield, Minn., 1887; m. Mary Munger, Oct. 6, 1890; children—Roger M., Mrs. Lydia W. Jamar. Began as mining engineer, Duluth Minn., 1898; late cons. engr. U.S. Bur. Mines in charge of all iron mining investigation. Pres. Ariz. Manganese Corp. Mem. Am. Inst. Mining and Metall. Engrs., Phi Kappa Psi. Mason (32°). Home: 1735 Wallace Av. Office: Sellwood Bldg., Duluth, Minn.*Died July 15, 1941.

WOODBURN, James Albert, univ. prof.; b. Bloomington, Ind., Nov. 30, 1856; s. James and Martha Jane (Hemphill) W.; A.B., Ind. U. 1876, A.M., 1885, LL.D., 1929; fellow and Ph.D., Johns Hopkins, 1890; LL.D., Colgate, 1909; Litt.D., Wabash Coll., 1923; m. Caroline Louise Gelston (A.B., U. of Mich.), Nov. 30, 1893; children—James Gelston, Janet McMillan (Mrs. Ernst H. Wiecking), Edward Albert (dec.) Prof. Am. History, Ind. U., 1890-1924, now emeritus prof. Mem. Ind. Hist. Commn., 1916-25. Mem. Ind. George Rogers Clark Memorial Commn., 1927-35; pres. Ind. Council on Foreign Relations, 1921-32. Life mem. Am. Hist. Assn., Miss. Valley Historical Society (pres. 1923), Ind. Hist. Soc. (pres. 1923-31; emeritus pres.); mem. Am. Polit. Science Assn., Indianapolis Literary Club, Phi Beta Kappa, Phi Gamma Delta. Author: Higher Education in Indiana, 1890; The American Republic and Its Government, 1903, revised 1914; Political Parties and Party Problems in the United States, 1903, rev. 1914 and 1922; Scotch-Irish Presbyterians in Monroe County, Indiana, 1910; Life of Thaddeus Stevens, 1913. Joint author with Prof. T. F. Moran and Prof. H. C. Hill, of textbook series on Am. history and civil govt., 1909-39; History of Indiana University, Vol. I, to 1901, 1940. Editor: Select Orations of Burke and Webster (with Prof. C. W. Hodgin), 1892; Johnston's Representative American Orations (4 vols.), 1895-97; Lecky's American Revolution (from Lecky's England in the Eighteenth Century), with bibliography and notes; Appleton's American Political History, from Prof. Alexander Johnston's articles in Lalor's Cyclopedia of Political Science and U.S. History (4 vols.). Regular contbr. to Am. Year Book on Am. polit. and party history, 1911-20; has also contbd. to Ency. Americana, Ency. Britannica, Cyclo. Am. Government, Dictionary of Am. Biography, hist. mags., etc. Presbyterian. Home: Bloomington. Ind.; also 12 Geddes Heights, Ann Arbor, Mich. Died Dec. 12, 1943.

WOODMAN, Raymond Huntington, organist, composer; b. Brooklyn, Jan. 18, 1861; s. Jonathan Call and Sarah Ann (Copeland) W.; ed. Coll. City of New York to jr. yr.; left to devote time to music; studied 4 yrs. under Dudley Buck; improvisation and composition under César Franck, Paris, 1888; Mus.D., N.Y. Coll. of Music and Grove City Coll., 1940; m. Ethel Field Righter, June 14, 1892; children—Winifred (M.D.), Jocelyn (M.D.). Alto St. George's Church, Flushing, L.I., where his father was organist and choirmaster; became asst. to his father, organist Christ Ch., Norwich, Conn., 1879-80; became organist and choirmaster, First Presbyn. Ch., Brooklyn, 1880, resigned June 1, 1941, after 61 years service; prof. music, Packer Collegiate Inst., resigned Jan. 1, 1941, after 46 years service; ex-warden and fellow of Am. Guild of Organists; mem. Am. Soc. Composers, Authors and Pubs. since 1925. Composer of many songs, cantatas, anthems, part-songs and compositions for piano and organ. Edited "Church Music" dept. New York Evangelist. 3 yrs. Address: 131 Hicks St., Brooklyn, N.Y. Died Dec. 25, 1943.

WOODROW, Samuel Hetherington, clergyman; b. Melbourne, Can. (father a citizen of U.S.), Mar. 23, 1862; s. Clark and Eliza (Spear) W.; A.B., Bates Coll., Me., 1888, D.D., 1903; grad. Yale Div. Sch., 1892; m. Minnie Clough, Nov. 6, 1888; children—Frank Clough, Christine Hetherington (dec.). Ordained Congl. ministry, 1892; pastor Westerly, R.I., 1892-95, Plymouth Ch., Providence, R.I., 1895-98, Hope Ch., Springfield, Mass., 1898-1907, First Ch., Washington, D.C., May 1, 1907-13, Pilgrim Ch., St. Louis, May 1, 1913-21, Newton Highlands, Mass., 1921-28. Delegate to missionary conv., Edinburgh, 1910; trustee Bates Coll., Hartford Sch. of Religious Pedagogy, Atlanta (Ga.) Theol. Sch., Drury Coll. Mem. Phi Beta Kappa. Republican. Author: Probability and Possibility of Miracles, 1899; Essential Truth, 1904. Has traveled extensively in U.S. and Europe. Clubs: Winthrop, Yale. Home: 906 N. State St., Jerseyville, Ill.* Died Sep. 5, 1943.

WOODRUFF, Caroline Salome (wood'rŭf), educator; b. West Burke, Vt.; d. George Washington and Octavia (Bemis) Woodruff; grad. St. Johnsbury Acad., State Normal Sch., Johnson Vt., Teachers Coll. of Columbia Univ.; hon. A.M., Middlebury Coll., 1926, Ed.D., Norwich U., 1933. Engaged as prin. and teacher Union Graded Sch., St. Johnsbury, Vt., until 1914; training teacher, State Dept. Edn., 1915-17; dist. supt. Essex County, 1917-18; prin. Jr. High Sch., State Normal Sch., Johnson, Vt., 1918-20; prin. State Normal Sch., Castleton, Vt., 1921-40. Pres. (1st woman pres.) Vt. Education Assn., 1914-15, chairman board of managers Vt. State Teachers Retirement Fund Assn.; pres. Vt. Women Teachers Club; v.p. Nat. Edn. Assn., 1928, 29, 34, dir., 1917-32, pres., 1937-38. Pres. Nat. Council of Administrative Women in Edn., 1927-29. Member Kappa Delta Pi (Kappa Chapter), Delta Kappa Gamma. Delegate to World Conf. of Edn. Assns., San Francisco, 1923, Edinburgh, 1925, Toronto, 1927, Geneva, 1929, Denver, 1931, Dublin, 1933, Tokio, 1937; mem. Jury of Award Children's Crusade, 1940. Democrat. Conglist. Author: My Trust and Other Verse, 1928. Address: Castleton, Vt. Died July 13, 1949.

WOODRUFF, Clinton Rogers, lawyer; b. Philadelphia, Pa., Dec. 17, 1868; s. Charles H. and Rachel A. (Pierce) W.; A.B., Central High Sch., Phila., 1886; Ph.B., U. of Pa., 1889, LL.B., 1892; m. Anna F. Miller, 1890; 1 dau., Mrs. Edwin S. Dixon, Jr.; m. 2d, Florence V. Stilwell, 1921. Chmn. joint com. on electoral reform in Pa.; spl. Indian commr. (with Charles J. Bonaparte), 1903-04, to investigate charges of fraud; sec. Phila. Municipal League, 1891-97, and counsel, 1897-1903; counsel Am. Acad. Polit. and Social Science; pres. Union Benevolent Assn.; chmn. Phila. Com. for Active Citizenship. Mem. Pa. legislature 2 terms; author of "personal registration" amendment to Pa. Constitution; pres. Bd. Personal Registration Commrs. for Phila., 1906-16 and 1919-20; pres. Civil Service Commission, Phila., 1920-24; became spl. asst. city solicitor, 1924; dir. of pub. welfare, City of Philadelphia, 1932-36. Pres. Am. Ch. Union, Christian Social Union, Churchmen's Alliance, Boys' Club of Phila. Chmn. Local Exemption Bd., 1917-18; mem. War Commn. Diocese of Pa., and of advisory com. Nat. Council Defense. Order Crown of King of Rumania, 1923. Mem. Am. Econ. Assn., Am. Polit. Science Assn., Nat. Civ. Service Reform League (council), Ednl. Club of Pa. (hon.), Am. Park and Outdoor Art Assn. (pres., 1902-04), Am. Civic Assn. (1st v.p., 1904-19; treas. 1920-24), Pa. Salary Survey Com. (chmn. bd.), Union Benevolent Assn., Public Charities Assn. (pres. and mem. exec. com.). Editor Proc. of Nat. Conf. for Good City Government, 1894-1911; sec. Nat. Municipal League, 1894-1920; hon. sec. since 1920, and editor Nat. Municipal Review. Chmn. diocesan social service com. and mem. joint commn. social service, P.E. Ch. Trustee Free Library, Phila.; trustee St. Stephen's Coll., Gen. Theol. Sem. of P.E. Ch. Author: City Government by Commission. Asso. Editor The Living Church. Editor the Nat. Municipal League Series; Municipal Encyclopædia; A New Municipal Program. Contbr. to reviews and mags. Home: 2219 Spruce St., Philadelphia, Pa. Deceased.

WOODRUFF, George, banker; b. Joliet, Ill., May 25, 1881; s. Frederick W. and Nellie (Davis) W.; ed. pub. schs., Joliet; student U. of Mich., 1900-01, Sheffield Scientific Sch. (Yale), 1901-03; LL.B., Yale U. Law Sch., 1903; studied banking in England, France and Germany. Asst. cashier First Nat. Bank, Joliet, 1904, v.p., 1906, elected pres., 1907; served as v.p., pres. and chmn. bd. Nat. Bank of Republic, Chicago, 1922-31; chmn. bd. First Nat. Bank of Joliet and Woodruff Securities Co. (Joliet). Inspected all Chinese and Siberian railroads for internat. banking group, 1909; made Am. preliminary survey for establishment of Am. branch banks in all countries of S. America, 1910; organized first amortization farm loan bank in America at Joliet, 1911; appointed by Taft adminstrn. mem. European Rural Credit Commn., 1913; a founder of Am. Acceptance Council, introducing acceptances to Am. business men; rep. of Ill. C. of C. at Commercial Conf., China, 1921. Asst. western mgr. Rep. Nat. Com., 1928. Pres. Ill. Bankers Assn., 1915-16; founder, and 1st pres. Ill. State C. of C., 1919-21. Presbyterian. Clubs: Union League, Mid-Day, University, Tavern, Attic, Racquet, Saddle and Cycle, Chicago Yacht (commodore 1927-29); Book and Gavel Club (Yale). Home: 1500 Lake Shore Drive. Office: 10 S. La Salle St., Chicago. Died July 24, 1946.

WOODRUFF, George Hobart, lawyer; b. Watertown, Conn., Feb. 25, 1873; s. John Frederick and Ellen (Atwood) W.; student lit. and law depts. Stanford U. (non-grad.); m. Nellie Brittan, Oct. 1901. Admitted to bar, 1902; city atty., Whittier, Calif., 1903-04; chief counsel Union Trust & Title Co., 1904-06; lecturer on real property, U. of Southern Calif., 1907-09; mem. firm Woodruff & Burr; owner Rancho de las Alturas, Rancho Mira Loma, and part owner Valley View Ranch, San Fernando Valley; v.p. Security Title Insurance & Guarantee Co., Los Angeles. Mem. Am., Calif. State and Los Angeles County bar assns., Los Angeles C. of C. Republican. Presbyterian. Mason (K.T., 32°, Shriner), Elk. Clubs: Jonathan, University, Stanford. Active in effecting legislation and reforms in behalf of delinquent boys. Home: Pasadena, Calif. Office: 530 W. 6th St., Los Angeles. Died Dec. 8, 1944.

WOODRUFF, John T., lawyer; born in Franklin County, Mo., Jan. 6, 1868; son of George W. and Susan (Rowland) W.; Steelville (Mo.) Normal Sch., 1889; studied law in office of Judge Ferdinand M. Jamison, Steelville; m. Lydia Brand, Oct. 29, 1901; children—Jessamine (wife of Dr. Carl O. Kohlbry), Susan (wife of Howard Pinkerton), John Thomas, David Brand. Admitted to Missouri bar, 1890, and began practice at Steelville; prosecuting attorney Crawford County, 1890-93; atty. for St. Louis-San Francisco Ry., 1894-1908; built Colonial Hotel, Frisco Office Bldg., Sansone Hotel, Woodruff Bldg., 1907-12, Ozarks Hotel, 1914, Kentwood Arms, 1926, Hickory Hill Golf Course, 1927, Pinebrook Inn, 1928; organizer Ash Grove Lime & Portland Cement Co.,

1906; organized Fireside Life Assn. (now Physicians Life and Casualty Co.), 1930, and since pres. First treas. State Teachers Coll., 1906-09; trustee and chmn. exec. com. Drury Coll., 1905-14; one of organizers and first pres. U.S. 66 Highway Assn. to promote highway Chicago to Los Angeles; one of organizers and chmn. bldg. com. Ozarks Empire Regional Fair; former pres. Springfield Chamber of Commerce. Democrat. Presbyterian. Mason. Home: 909 Walnut St. Office: Woodruff Bldg., Springfield, Mo. Died Jan. 31, 1949.

WOODRUFF, Lorande Loss, biologist; b. New York, N.Y., July 14, 1879; s. Charles Albert and Eloise Clara (Loss) W.; A.B., Columbia, 1901, A.M., 1902, Ph.D., 1905; (hon. M.A., Yale, 1915); m. Margaret Louise Mitchell, Dec. 21, 1905; children—Margaret Eloise (Mrs. T. C. Wilson), Dr. Lorande Mitchell. Asst. in biology, 1903-04, instr., 1904-07, Williams Coll.; instr. biology, 1907-09, asst. prof., 1909-15, prof., 1915-22, prof. of protozoölogy since 1922, Yale Univ.; dir. Osborn Zoöl. Lab., chmn. dept. of Zoölogy, and fellow of Branford Coll., Yale University, lecturer in zoölogy, 1905-07, embryology, 1907-14, Marine Biol. Lab., Woods Hole, Mass., trustee of same. Consulting physiologist, Chem. Warfare Service, U.S. Army, 1918. Chmn. of div. of biology and agr., Nat. Research Council, 1928-29; lecturer on protozoölogy, Univ. of Va., 1931, 36, 38, 40. Townsend Harris medal, Coll. City of N.Y., 1935. Fellow A.A.A.S.; mem. Nat. Acad. Sciences, Am. Soc. Zoölogists (sec.-treas., 1907-09, pres. 1942), Am. Physiol. Soc., Soc. for Exptl. Biology and Medicine, Am. Soc. Naturalists (v.p. 1923), Conn. Acad. Arts and Sciences, Am. Micros. Soc., Am. Assn. Univ. Profs. (chmn. Yale br. 1920-22), Sigma Xi (pres. Yale Chapter, 1915-16), Phi Beta Kappa, Alpha Delta Phi, Gamma Alpha; hon. mem. Sociedad Mexicana de Historia Natural. Republican. Conglist. Mason. Clubs: Graduate, Faculty. Author Foundations of Biology, 1922; 6th edition, 1941; Animal Biology, 1932, 2d edition, 1938; studies on life history of Protozoa, chiefly based on pedigreed race of Paramecium of over 20,000 generations; Endomixis, its significance in Infusoria, History of Biology. Contributing author: Evolution of the Earth and Its Inhabitants, 1918; Development of the Sciences, 1923, 2d series, 1941; Organic Adaptation to Environment, 1924; Earth and Man, 1929; Protozoa in Biological Research, 1941; Biological Symposia, 1940, 1941. Asso. editor Jour. of Morphology, 1922-24, and 1932-34. Home: 146 Cottage St., New Haven, Conn.; (summer) Woods Hole, Mass. Died June 23, 1947; buried Woods Hole, Mass.

WOODS, Albert Fred; b. Belvidere, Ill., Dec. 25, 1866; s. Fred M. and Eliza O. (Eddy) W.; B.Sc., U. of Neb., 1890, A.M., 1892, D.Agr., 1913; LL.D., St. John's College, Annapolis, Md., 1922; Sc.D., U. of Md., 1932; m. Bertha Gerneaux Davis, June 1, 1898; children—Charles Frederick (dec.), Albert Frederick (dec.), Mark Winton, Winton de Ruyter. Asst. botanist, U. of Neb., 1890-93; asst. chief and 1st assistant pathologist. Div. Vegetable Physiology and Pathology, U.S. Dept. Agr., 1893-1900, pathologist and physiologist and asst. chief Bur. of Plant Industry, 1900-10; dean Minn. State Agrl. Coll. and dir. of Expt. Sta., 1910-17; exec. officer Md. State Bd. of Agr. and pres. Maryland State College, July 1917-20; pres. U. of Md., 1920-26; dir. of scientific work, U.S. Dept. Agr., 1926-34; dir. Grad. School Department Agriculture, 1926-41, now director emeritus; educational adviser, 1941-47, retired 1947; principal pathologist Bureau Plant Industry, 1934-38. United States delegate International Institute of Agr., Rome, 1905, Internat. Bot. Congress, Vienna, 1905. Gen. chmn. coms. on food production and conservation Md. Council of Defense, 1917. Pres. First Inter-Am. Conf. on Agr., Forestry and Animal Husbandry, Washington, 1930. Fellow A.A.A.S. (mem. council), Botanical Society of America, American Society Naturalists, American Academy Political and Social Sci., Bot. Soc. Washington, Washington Acad. Sciences; mem. Nat. Research Council (chmn. com. on fertilizers, 1917-18; chmn. dir. of State Relations, 1923-24), Am. Hort. Soc. (ex-pres.), Land Grant Colleges Assn. of U.S. (pres. 1925), Silver Star Patrons of Husbandry. Gamma Sigma Delta, Sigma Xi, Alpha Zeta. Clubs: Cosmos, University (Washington). Wrote Plant Pathology in Ency. Americana, numerous reports and articles in publs. of Dept. of Agr. and scientific jours., etc. Home: 4001 Quintana St., Hyattsville, Md. Died April 12, 1948.

WOODS, Arthur, ex-police commr.; b. Boston, Mass., Jan. 29, 1870; s. Joseph Wheeler and Caroline Frances (Fitz) W.; A.B., Harvard, 1892; post-grad. work Harvard and U. of Berlin; hon. A.M., Harvard, 1916; LL.D., Trinity Coll., Conn., 1919; m. Helen Morgan Hamilton, June 10, 1916; children—John Pierpont, Leonard Hamilton, Alexander Hamilton, Caroline Frances. Schoolmaster, Groton (Mass.) Sch., 1895-1905; reporter New York Evening Sun, in lumber business in Mexico, and in cotton converting business, Boston, until 1907; dep. police commr., N.Y. City, 1907-09, and served as police commr., 1914-18. Apptd. asso. dir. of Committee on Pub. Information, for foreign propaganda, Feb. 1918; commd. lt. col. Aviation Sect., Mar. 1918; col. Aug. 1918; overseas, Sept.-Nov. 1918; apptd. asst. dir. of mil. aeronautics; hon. disch., Jan. 31, 1919; asst. to Sec. of War, in charge of efforts to help reëstablish service men in civil life, Mar.-Sept. 1919. Chmn. President's Com. for Employment, 1930-31. Formerly v.p. Colo. Fuel & Iron Co., dir. Bankers Trust Co., trustee Internat. Edn. Bd. and Rockefeller Foundation, chmn. and trustee Spelman Fund of N.Y., 1st chmn. Colonial Williamsburg, Williamsburg Restoration and Rockefeller Center; now chmn. Davison Fund. Awarded D.S.M. (U.S.); C.M.G. (British); Chevalier Legion of Honor (French), 1920. Republican. Episcopalian. Clubs: Harvard (Boston, Mass.); Chevy Chase, National Press (Washington, D.C.); Union Interalliée (Paris); American (London). Author: Crime Prevention, 1918; Policeman and Public, 1919; Dangerous Drugs, 1931. Home: 3014 N St. N.W., Washington. Died May 12, 1942; buried in Arlington National Cemetery.

WOODS, Homer Boughner, judge; b. near Harrisville, W.Va., July 16, 1869; s. Philip Axtel and Salina (Wells) W.; student Marietta (O.) Coll.; student W.Va. U. Law Sch., 1892; m. Winifred Davis, Sept. 10, 1891; children—Ralph Davis, Homer Boughner (dec.), Philip Wells (dec.), Miriam, Robert James, Samuel Thomas, Winifred. Teacher and prin. schs., in Ritchie County, W.Va., until 1895; county supt. schs., 2 terms; editor Ritchie Standard, 1896-98; pros. atty. Ritchie County, 2 terms, 1897-1904 inclusive; elected judge Circuit Court, 3d Jud. Circuit, 1904, for term of 8 yrs., and twice reëlected, last term to end 1928; resigned Dec. 31, 1924, to assume office as a judge of Supreme Court of Appeals, term 1925-36 inclusive; pres. Supreme Court, 1929, 34. Chmn. Ritchie Chapt. Am. Red Cross, World War; also chmn. of the 4 Liberty Loan drives and of the Y.M.C.A. drives. Mem. Am., W.Va. and Ritchie County bar assns. Republican. Baptist. Mason, Odd Fellow, Maccabee, Woodman, Kiwanian. Home: Harrisville, W.Va. Died March 4, 1941; buried Odd Fellows Cemetery, Harrisville, Ga.

WOODS, James Pleasant, ex-congressman; b. Roanoke, Va., Feb. 4, 1868; s. William and Sarah (Edington) W.; A.B., Roanoke Coll., 1892; studied law, U. of Va.; m. Susie K. Moon, July 20, 1904; children—Amine Elizabeth and Virginia Kathryn (twins), James Pleasant. Admitted to Va. bar, 1893, and since practiced at Roanoke; mayor of Roanoke, 1898; elected to vacancy in 65th Congress occasioned by resignation of Carter Glass, and elected to 66th and 67th Congresses (1919-23), 6th Va. Dist. Pres. bd. trustees Roanoke Coll.; mem. bd. Randolph-Macon Coll.; rector of bd. Va. Poly. Inst.—all of Virginia. Mem. Phi Beta Kappa (U. of Va.), Democrat. Methodist. Home: 1241 Clarke Av. Office: Boxley Bldg., Roanoke, Va. Died July 7, 1948.

WOODS, Thomas Francis, lawyer; b. Albany, N.Y., Jan. 17, 1882; s. Francis Henry and Rose (Murray) W.; student Williams College, 1904; LL.B., Union U. Law Sch., 1906; m. Mabel Eldred Shields, June 14, 1907; 1 son, Francis. Admitted to N.Y. bar, 1906, and since in practice at Albany, N.Y.; asso. counsel to Central Information Bur. of Canadian Liberal Party investigating war contracts, 1916; asst. N.Y. State dir. mil. census, 1917; spl. asst. atty. gen., N.Y., on gambling investigations, 1920; as amicus curiae, successfully challenged constitutionality of the NRA in N.Y. Court of Appeals in test case of Darweger v. Staats et al., 1935. Served as naval aviation observer and special liaison officer, with rank of ensign, U.S. Navy, World War. Awarded Silver Star (U.S. Navy); Conspicuous Service Cross (N.Y.); spl. citation Sec. of Navy. Mem. Poetry Soc. of America. Republican. Catholic. Clubs: University, Albany Country; Author's (London). Author: New York and Other Poems, 1931 (poems) Three Waters, 1933. Home: 115 S. Lake Av. Office: 93 State St., Albany, N.Y. Died Dec. 17, 1949.

WOODSIDE, John Thomas, cotton mfr.; b. on a farm, Woodville P.O., Greenville County, S.C., May 9, 1864; s. John Lawrence (M.D.) and Ellen Pamelia (Charles) W.; ed. dist. sch.; m. Lou A. Carpenter, Apr. 25, 1893. With Reedy River Mfg. Co. until 1892; in mercantile business at Pelzer, S.C., 1892-93, Greenville, 1893-1902; pres. Woodside Cotton Mills since its orgn., 1902 (said to be largest mill under one roof in America); formerly pres. Woodside Cotton Mills Co. (Woodside Cotton Mills, Simpsonville Cotton Mills and Fountain Inn Mfg. Co.); formerly pres. Myrtle Beach Estates, Inc., and v.p. Easley Cotton Mills; dir. Pioneer Life Ins. Co.; pres. Greenville Community Hotel Corp. Presbyterian. Home: Greenville, S.C. Died Jan. 5, 1946.

WOODSON, Walter Browne, naval officer; b. Lynchburg, Va., Oct. 18, 1881; s. Edgar Alonzo and Roberta Virginia (Browne) W.; B.S., U.S. Naval Acad., 1905; LL.B., with distinction, George Washington U., 1914; grad. naval War Coll., 1922-23; m. Ruth Halford, Sept. 9, 1911; children—Ruth Halford, Walter Browne, Jr., Halford. Commd. ensign, U.S. Navy, 1907, and advanced through the grades to rear adm., judge advocate gen., June 20, 1938; admitted to bars of Dist. Court and Court of Appeals of U.S. for Dist. of Columbia, and U.S. Supreme Court; dir. ship movements, Office of Chief Naval Operations, Navy Dept., 1918-19; asst. judge advocate gen., 1921-22; exec. officer, U.S.S. Colorado, 1923-24; comdr. Destroyer Div. 34, U.S. Fleet, 1924-25; chief of staff Destroyer Force, Atlantic Fleet, 1929-31; asst. judge advocate gen., 1931-34; comdg. officer, U.S.S. Houston, 1934-35; chief of staff, Asiatic Fleet, 1935-36; naval aide to President, 1937-38; judge advocate general 1938-43. Retired 1 Sept. 1943 for physical disability. Clubs: New York Yacht; Army and Navy (Washington, D.C.); Army and Navy Country (Arlington, Va.); Army and Navy (Manila, P.I.). Home: 536 A Av., Coronado, Calif. Died Apr. 23, 1948.

WOODWARD, Benjamin Duryea; b. Rutherford, N.J., Mar. 13, 1868; s. George E. and E. B. Deodata (Mortimer) W.; A.B., Columbia, 1888, A.M., 1889, Ph.D., 1891; Bachelier-ès-sciences, Sorbonne, Paris, 1885, Bachelier-ès-lettres, 1891. Tutor Romance langs. and lits., 1890-94, instr., 1894-1901, adj. prof., 1901-02, prof., 1902-08, Columbia. Asst. commr.-gen. for the U.S. to Paris Expn., 1898-1901, spl. commr., 1901-03. Clubs: University, Lawyers', Republican (New York), Travelers, Automobile (Paris, France). Author: Palatal Consonants in English, 1891; also biographies of French men of letters in Century Cyclopedia of Names. Editor (with intros. and English notes): Nanon (George Sand), 1893; Quatrevingt-treize (Victor Hugo), 1896; Iphigénie (Racine), 1896; Le Mariage de Gabrielle (Daniel Lesueur), 1897; Voltaire's Prose Extracts (in collaboration), 1897; Le Roman d'un jeune homme pauvre (Octave Feuillet), 1898. Address: University Club, New York. Died Apr 16, 1948.

WOODWARD, Charles Edgar, judge; b. New Salem, Fayette County, Pa., Dec. 1, 1876; s. Christopher and Sally Ann (Langley) W.; prep. edn., Lincoln (Ill.) U. (now Coll.); student Northwestern U., 1893-96, LL.D., 1931; m. Lura Hampson, June 7, 1899; children—Harold Christopher, Walter Hampson (dec.), Ila Margaret (Mrs. Thomas R. Willard). Began in the practice of law at Ottawa, Ill., 1899; mem. Stead, Woodward & Hibbs, 1913-18, Woodward & Hibbs since 1918. Asst. atty. gen. of Ill. under late William H. Stead, 1905-13; under supervision of Gov. Frank O. Lowden drafted civil administrative code of Ill., also drafted many other bills enacted into law by Gen. Assembly of Ill.; pres. Ill. Constl. Conv., 1920; judge U.S. Dist. Court, Northern Dist. of Ill., since 1929. Mem. Am. Bar Assn., Ill. State Bar Assn. Republican. Presbyterian. Mason, Odd Fellow. Home: 140 Blackstone Av., La Grange, Ill. Address: U.S. Court House, Chicago, Ill. Died May 15, 1942.

WOODWARD, Clifford Dewey, elec. and mech. engineer; b. Norwalk, O., Apr. 21, 1878; s. Dewey Amus and Agnes Helen (Tod) W.; ed. pub. schs., Norwalk, Cleveland and Lorain, O.; m. Anna Oswald, May 24, 1900; 1 dau., Claudia Helen. Electrician, Boston & Mont. Consolidated Copper & Silver Mining Co., Great Falls, Mont., 1898-1900; chief electrician Highland Boy Gold Mining Co., Murray, Utah, 1900-02; same, Boston & Mont. Reduction Works, Great Falls, 1902-10; asst. master mechanic same works, 1910-16; asst. chief engr. Anaconda Copper Mining Co. Reduction Works, Great Falls, 1916-18; chief elec. engr. Anaconda Copper Mining Co., Butte, 1918-27, chief engr. since 1927. Asso. mem. Am. Inst. E.E., S. AR Republican. Mason (Shriner). Club: Butte Country. Home: 1034 Caledonia St., Butte, Mont. Died Oct. 26, 1949; buried Mt. Moriah Cemetery, Butte.

WOODWARD, Edmund Lee, clergyman, physician, surgeon; b. Richmond, Va., Jan. 29, 1873; s. Warner Minor and Mary Eliza Kennedy (Stewart) W.; B.A., M.A., U. of Va., 1896, M.D., 1897; grad. Polyclinic Post-Grad. Sch., Phila., 1899; B.D., Theol. Sem. in Virginia, 1910, D.D., 1943; married Frances Peyton Gibson, d. late Bishop Robert A. Gibson, June 22, 1910 (died Aug. 27, 1945); children—David Stuart, John Minor. Missionary P.E. Ch., China, 1899-1914; founded St. James Hosp., Anking, 1900, dir. until 1907, also consultant until 1914; deacon, 1909, priest, 1910, P.E. Ch.; first dean Cathedral of Our Saviour, Anking, 1910-14; rector Grace Ch., The Plains, Va., 1914-21; dean Piedmont Convocation, Diocese of Va.; 1916-17, 1920-21; dean Richmond Convocation, 1922-23; dean Valley Convocation, 1935-37; dean, 1921-28, and charter trustee, since 1919, Ch. Schs. in Diocese of Va., Inc., P.E. Ch.; founder Cathedral Shrine of the Transfiguration, 1925, rector, 1925-41; founder and dir. Shrine Mont (center for devotion and fellowship), Orkney Springs, since 1928. Editor: The Virginia Churchman, 1922-28. Mem. Phi Theta Psi, Pi Mu. Democrat. Mason (K.T.). Author: The Mid-China Syllabary; The Peace of Jerusalem, memorial presented at Peace Conf., Versailles, 1918; The Cathedral Shrine of the Transfiguration, 1925. Home: Shrine Mont, Orkney Springs, Va. Died Feb. 2, 1948.

WOODWARD, Walter Carleton, church official; b. near Mooresville, Ind., Nov. 28, 1878; s. Ezra Hinshaw and Amanda (Maris) W.; grad. Friends Pacific Acad., Newberg, Ore., 1894; A.B., Pacific Coll., Newberg, 1898; B.L., Earlham Coll., Richmond, Ind., 1899; M.A., U. of Calif., 1908, Ph.D., 1910; m. Catherine Hartman, Sept. 10, 1912; children—Bernice Louise, Mary Ellen, Elisabeth. Asso. editor Newberg (Ore.) Graphic, 1900-06; prof. history and polit. science, Pacific Coll., 1906-07, Earlham Coll., 1910-15; dir. Ind. State Hist. Commn., 1915-16, in charge statewide centennial observance, ednl., hist. and patriotic; gen. sec. Five Years Meeting of Friends in America, 1917-28, now sec. exec. com.; editor The American Friend since 1917. Mem. exec. com. Federal Council Chs. of Christ in America; presiding clk. Perm. Bd. Ind. Yearly Meeting of Friends. Chmn. bd. trustees Earlham Coll.; mem. Corp. Haverford Coll. and Pacific Coll. Mem. Pi Gamma Mu. Clubs: Kiwanis, College Men's, Scribblers. Author: History of Political Parties in Oregon, 1913; Friendly Tales of Foreign Trails, 1923; Timothy Nicholson, Master Quaker, 1927. Home: 223 College Av. Office: 101 S. 8th St., Richmond, Ind. Died Apr. 14, 1942.

WOODWARD, William Creighton, physician; b. Washington, D.C., Dec. 11, 1867; s. Mark Rittenhouse and Martha Jane (Pursell) W.; M.D., Georgetown U., 1889 LL.M., 1900, LL.D., 1925; m. Ray Elliott,

Feb. 14, 1895; children—Paul Gilbert, Creighton Elliott (dec.), Doris (dec.), Mildred, Elinor. Admitted to Dist. of Columbia Court of Appeals, 1901, U.S. Supreme Court, 1917, Supreme Judicial Court of Mass., 1919, Ill. Supreme Court, 1924. Apptd. resident physician Central Dispensary and Emergency Hosp., 1892; physician to the poor, Dec. 7, 1892; coroner, D.C., 1893-94; prof. med. jurisprudence, Georgetown U., 1893-1936; health officer, D.C., 1894-1918; prof. state medicine, Georgetown U., 1894; prof. med. jurisprudence, med. dept., George Washington U., 1900-18; becoming same of law dept., Georgetown U., 1902-35; prof. of med. jurisprudence, med. dept. Howard U., 1916-18; prof. medical jurisprudence, Law Sch., Loyola U., 1925-31; professorial lecturer on medical jurisprudence, U. of Chicago Grad. Sch. of Medicine and Rush Med. College, 1930-39. Health commr., City of Boston, 1918-22; dir. Bur. of Legal Medicine and Legislation of American Medical Association, 1922-39. Mem. General Medical Board, Council National Defense, World War. Mem. Am. Pub. Health Assn. (ex-pres.), Conf. of State and Provincial Bds. of Health of N. America (ex-pres.), Am. Assn. Study and Prevention Infant Mortality (ex-pres.), A.M.A., Am. Bar Assn.; hon. mem. Am. Vet. Med. Assn., Internat. Assn. Milk Inspectors, Conf. State and Provincial Health Authorities of N. America. Home: 2701 Conn. Av. N.W., Washington 8, D.C. Died Dec. 22, 1949.

WOODY, Clifford, prof. edn.; b. Thorntown, Ind., June 2, 1884; s. Thomas N. and Susanna Beesley (Woody) W.; A.B., Ind. U., 1908, A.M., 1913; Ph.D., Columbia, 1916; m. Alice May Woody, Aug. 29, 1917. Teacher high sch. and supt. schs., Gaston, Ind., 1908-12; teacher high sch., Bloomington, Ind., fall of 1912; fellow Ind. U., 1913-14; scholarship, Columbia, 1914-15, fellow, 1915-16; asst. prof. edn., U. of Wash., 1916-18, asso. prof., 1919-20, professor, 1920-21; prof. education and dir., bureau education and research, U. of Mich., since 1921, serving as graduate adviser to Mich. Colleges of Edn. since 1938. Teacher summer term, U. of Ia., 1917, U. of Mich., 1920, U. of Chicago, 1921, U. of Washington, 1933, U. of Southern Calif., 1935. Fellow A.A.A.S., 1925; mem. N.E.A., Nat. Soc. for Study of Edn., Nat. Soc. Coll. Teachers of Edn. (mem. exec. com. 1928; sec.-treas. 1940-47), Mich. Acad. of Science, Am. Ednl. Research Asso. (pres. 1923-24), Phi Delta Kappa, Lambda Chi Alpha, Phi Kappa Phi, Pi Gamma Nu. Author: Measurements of Some Achievements in Arithmetic, 1916; Woody Arithmetic Scales—How to Use Them, 1920; Problems of Elementary School Instruction, 1923; Brown Woody Civics Test, 1925; Sangren Woody Reading Test, 1927; Administration of Testing Program (with P. V. Sangren), 1932; New Problems in Elementary School Instruction, 1932; Adventures in Dictionary Lands, Books I, II and III (with Lewis, Roemer and Mathews), 1932; Child Life Arithmetics (with Breed and Overman); Modern Life Speller (with Ayer and Oberholtzer); also numerous monographs, bulls. and articles. Editor: 18th Yearbook Nat. Soc. Coll. Teachers of Edn.; Quantitative Measurements in Institutions of Higher Learning, 1930. Editor 28th Yearbook, Nat. Soc. Coll. Teachers of Edn.: The Discipline of Practical Judgment in a Democratic Society, 1942; editor 29th Yearbook, N.S.C.T.E.: Adjustments in Edn. to Meet War and Postwar Needs, 1944. Mem. editorial bd. Jour. of Ednl. Research; mem. com. which prepared Sixth Yearbook of Dept. of Supervisors and Dirs. of Instruction. Home: Juniper Lane (Barton Hills), Ann Arbor, Mich. Died Nov. 19, 1948.

WOOLF, Samuel Johnson, artist; b. New York, N.Y., Feb. 12, 1880; s. Albert Edward and Rosamond (Wimpfheimer) W.; A.B., Coll. City of New York, 1899; studied Nat. Acad. Design and Art Students' League; m. Edith Truman, Mar. 1, 1904; children—Dorothy, Muriel. Represented in collections of Brook Club, Catholic Club, Coll. of City of New York, Normal Coll., Metropolitan Museum Art, N.Y. Public Library, etc.; exhibited at Nat. Acad. Design, Pa. Acad. Fine Arts, Carnegie Inst., Art Inst. Chicago, Corcoran Gallery. Awarded Hallgarten prize, Nat. Acad. Design, 1904; medal, Appalachian Expn., 1910; medal, St. Louis Expn., 1903; Medal International Expn., Paris, 1937; Townsend Harris Medal, College City of New York, 1944. Club: Dutch Treat. Mem. Bd. Higher Edn. of N.Y. Author: A Short History of Art, 1909; Drawn from Life, 1931; Here Am I, 1941; spl. corr. N.Y. Times; also contbr. to various mags. While a correspondent with the A.E.F., World War I, painted a series of portraits of the leading American generals, also a group of paintings and drawings of the troops at the front; also served as war correspondent in England and France for NEA, in 1944. Home: 299 Riverside Drive. Studio: 33 W. 67th St., New York, N.Y. Died Dec. 3, 1948.

WOOLLCOTT, Alexander (wool'kŭt), journalist; b. Phalanx, N.J., Jan. 19, 1887; s. Walter and Frances Grey (Bucklin) W.; A.B., Central High Sch., Phila., 1905; Ph.B., Hamilton Coll., 1909, L.H.D., 1924; post-grad. work Columbia, 1913; unmarried. Dramatic critic, N.Y. Times, 1914-22, N.Y. Herald, 1922, N.Y. World, 1925-28. Spent 2 yrs. as enlisted man in the A.E.F., including 1 yr. in the editorial council of "The Stars and Stripes." Mem. Theta Delta Chi. Author: Mrs. Fiske—Her Views on Acting, Actors and the Problems of the Stage, 1917; The Command Is Forward, 1919; Shouts and Murmurs; Mr. Dickens Goes to the Play, 1923; Enchanted Aisles, 1924; The Story of Irving Berlin, 1925; Going to Pieces, 1928; Two Gentlemen and a Lady, 1928; While Rome Burns, 1934; The Woollcott Reader, 1935; Woollcott's Second Reader, 1937. Contbr. to numerous periodicals. Appeared as Harold Sigrift in "Brief Moment" at Belasco Theatre, New York, 1931, as Binkie in "Wine of Choice," Guild Theatre, New York, 1938, and as Sheridan Whiteside in "The Man Who Came to Dinner," Santa Barbara, Calif., Feb. 9, 1940, as chorus in "The Yellow Jacket," Marblehead, Mass., Aug. 11, 1941. Broadcast as Town Crier on Am. networks and Brit. Broadcasting Co., 1929-42. Home: Bomoseen, Vt. Died Jan. 23, 1943.

WOOLLEN, Evans, banker; b. Indianapolis, Ind., Nov. 28, 1864; s. William Watson and Mary Allen Evans W.; B.A., Yale, 1886, M.A., 1889; LL.D., Wabash, 1928, Ind. U., 1929, Butler, 1929; m. Nancy Baker, June 9, 1896. Began practice of law at Indianapolis, 1888; pres. Fletcher Trust Co., 1912-34, chmn. since 1934; organizer Indianapolis Foundation, 1916. Mem. Psi Upsilon. Democrat. Presbyterian. Office: 108 N. Pennsylvania St., Indianapolis, Ind. Died May 20, 1942.

WOOLLEY, Alice Stone, physician; b. Yankton, S.D.; d. Miles and Ellen (Stone) Woolley; B.S., Columbia, 1923; M.D., U. of Maryland, 1930. Dir. physical education, Poughkeepsie (N.Y.) Y.W.C.A., 1908-25; interne, Gallinger Municipal Hosp., Washington, D.C., 1930-31, Childrens Hosp., Washington, D.C., 1931-32; in practice of medicine, Poughkeepsie, N.Y., since 1932; mem. courtesy staff Vassar Brothers Hosp., St. Francis Hosp., Northern Dutchess Health Center; med. consultant Bard Coll. Annandale-on-Hudson, N.Y., since 1944. Served in France, World War I, 1918-19. Awarded Medaille de la Reconnaissance Française (for 2 yrs. service), 1920. Mem. bd. Dutchess County chapter Am. Red Cross, Girl Scouts America, Poughkeepsie Womens City and County Civic Club; mem. Dutchess County Womens Republican Club. Fellow A.M.A.; mem. Am. Med. Womens Assn. (pres. 1944-45), Womens Med Soc. of N.Y. State (pres. 1940-41), Dutchess County Health Assn., N.Y. State and Dutchess County med. assns., Womens Med. Assn. of N.Y. City, Am. Assn. Univ. women, Mahwenawasigh Chapter D.A.R., Womens Overseas Service League. Clubs: Tuesday Literary (Poughkeepsie); Cosmopolitan (New York). Home: "Stoneridge," Cedarcliff Manor, Poughkeepsie, N.Y. Died Nov. 16, 1946.

WOOLLEY, Edward Mott, author; b. Milwaukee, Feb. 25, 1867; s. James T. and Mary A. (Shearman) W.; grad. high sch., Homer, Mich., 1883; m. Anna Lazelle Thayer, Dec. 20, 1898; children—Catherine, Marion. Engaged in mercantile business, 1883-93; entered newspaper and lit. work, 1893; reporter San Francisco Examiner, 1894; reporter and writer Chicago Herald and Times-Herald, 1895-1901; writer, lit. editor and editorial writer, Chicago Journal, 1901-04; editor Fuel, Chicago, 1905; editorial staff Chicago Post, 1906, System Mag., Chicago, 1907-09, since spl. writer for Saturday Evening Post, Collier's Weekly, McClure's Mag., Scribner's Magazine, World's Work, Everybody's, American, Good Housekeeping and other magazines special writer for newspaper syndicates. Noms de plume, "Robert Bracefield," "Richard Bracefield." Author: Pluck Will Win, 1903; Roland of Altenburg, 1904; A Minister of War, 1906; The Art of Selling Goods, 1907; The Castle of Gloom, 1908; Miss Huntington, 1908; The Real America in Romance (3 vols.), 1909-10; The Winning Ten, 1910; Donald Kirk Series, 1912-13; The Junior Partner, 1912; Addison Broadhurst, Master Merchant, 1913; The Cub Reporter, 1913; Free-Lancing for Forty Magazines, 1927; Writing for Real Money, 1928; The Curve, 1929; 100 Paths To a Living, 1931; also Romances of Small Business (500), serially in newspapers, 1923-25. Spl. research in occupational fields for syndicates; spl. war work for Com. Pub. on Information, etc. Home: 71 Park Av., Passaic, N.J. Died Mar. 31, 1947.

WOOLLEY, Mary Emma, coll. pres.; b. S. Norwalk, Conn., July 13, 1863; d. Rev. Joseph J. and Mary A. (Ferris) Woolley; A.B., Brown U., 1894, A.M., 1895, Litt.D., 1900; L.H.D., Amherst, 1900; LL.D., Smith Coll., 1910; A.M., Yale, 1914, LL.D., 1923; LL.D., Denison, 1931, Rollins Coll., 1933, Oberlin, 1933; LL.D., Lake Erie Coll., Painesville O., 1933, N.Y. U., 1935, Western Coll., 1936, Univ. of Chicago and Bucknell University, 1937; Ped.D., N.Y. State Teachers Coll., 1935; Litt.D., Wheaton Coll. (Mass.), 1934, Columbia U., 1937; LL.D., Mills Coll., 1938, Rockford College, 1940, College of Osteopathic Physicians and Surgeons, Los Angeles, 1940. Instr. Wheaton Sem., 1886-91; instr, 1895-96, asso. prof. Bibl. history, 1896-99, prof. and head dept. Bibl. history and lit., 1899-1900, Wellesley Coll.; pres. Mt. Holyoke Coll., 1900-37. Awarded Susan Rosenberger medal from Brown U., 1937; awarded Kassovo medal, Royal Red Cross of Yugoslavia, 1931; Monticello College Centenary medal, 1938; Cristobol Colon medal, 1940; "Daughter of the Regiment," 8th Conn. Volunteers (in Civil War); Women's Centennial Congress, 1940, honor to "Career Women"; scroll presented by Fedn. of Women's Clubs in recognition of outstanding service in the field of education, 1941. Apptd. by Pres. Hoover to Conf. for Reduction and Limitation of Armaments, Geneva, 1932, reappointed by Pres. Roosevelt, 1933. Mem. com. of direction Commn. on a Just and Durable Peace. Chairman U.S. Peoples Mandate for Inter-American Peace and Co-operation; Women's Co-operating Commn. of Federal Council of Chs. Hon. moderator Congregational-Christian Gen. Council, 1936. Senator Phi Beta Kappa, 1907, now life senator; chmn. Coll. Entrance Examination Bd., 1924-27, now life mem. Hon. mem. Nat. Bd. Y.W.C.A.; mem. Com. on Participation of Women in Post-War Planning, League of Nations Associations. American Association Univ. Women (pres. 1927-33; chmn. com. on international relations, 1933-39), R.I. br. Woman's Bd. of Missions, A.B.C.F.M. (corporate mem.), Bd. of Electors Hall of Fame, Nat. Council Congl. Chs. in the U.S., N.E. Woman's Press Assn., R.I. Soc. for Collegiate Edn. of Women, Salem Soc. for Higher Edn. for Women (hon.), World Alliance for Promoting Internat. Friendship through the Churches (dir.), Commn. on Internat. Justice and Goodwill Fed. Council Chs. of Christ in America, Am. Sch. Damascus, Inst. Pacific Relations, Honolulu (del. 1925, 27); trustee Chevy Chase Jr. Coll. (mem. bd. overseers), Rockford Coll., Barrington Sch., Santiago Coll. (Chile, S.A.), Lake Erie Coll., Inst. Internat. Edn. Member Pawtucket chapter D.A.R. Clubs: College (Boston); Cosmopolitan, Woman's University (New York); Nat. Club of Am. Assn. Univ. Women (Washington, D.C.). Author: (hist. monographs) Early History of the Colonial Post Office; Development of the Love of Romantic Scenery in America; History of the Passover Scandal; Internationalism and Disarmament; chapter in "Why Wars Must Cease"; chapter in "What I Owe to My Father"; "Women's Colleges in America," in Ency. Britannica; also numerous ednl. articles. Home: Westport, N.Y. Died Sept. 5, 1947.

WOOLLEY, Victor Baynard, judge; b. Wilmington, Del., Mar. 29, 1867; s. Augustus S. and Sarah (Baynard) W.; B.S., Delaware Coll., 1885, LL.D., 1913; student Harvard Law Sch., 1889-90; m. Mildred Clark, July 28, 1904; children—Victor Clark (dec.), John Augustus. Admitted to Del. bar, 1890; prothonotary, Superior Court, New Castle County, Del., 1895-1901; asso. judge, Supreme Court of Del., 1909-14; judge U.S. Circuit Court of Appeals for the 3d Circuit, by apptmt. of President Wilson, since Aug. 12, 1914. Lecturer on Delaware practice, U. of Pa. Law Dept. Trustee Univ. of Del.; mem. Soc. of Colonial Wars. Democrat. Episcopalian. Author: Woolley on Delaware Practice, 1906. Clubs: Wilmington, Wilmington Country. Home: Denbigh Hall, 14th and Broome Sts., Wilmington, Del. Died Feb. 22, 1945.

WOOLRYCH, Francis Humphry William, artist; b. Sydney, New South Wales, Australia, Feb. 1, 1864; s. Francis Benson William and Frances Emily (Sherrington) W.; ed. under private tutors; grad. Royal Acad. Fine Arts, Berlin, 1884; studied at École des Beaux Arts and Académie Colarossi, Paris, with Raphael Collin, Gustave Courtois and Puvis de Chavannes; m. Bertha, d. Orson Hewit, Oct. 1, 1887; children—Francis H. W., Edmund Hugh. Came to U.S., 1888, and settled in St. Louis; portrait, landscape and mural painter, oil and water color. Decoration: State Capitol, Jefferson City, Mo. Mem. Am. Fedn. Arts, St. Louis Artists' Guild. Club: Missouri Athletic. Home: 3855 Hartford St. Studio: Saum Studio Bldg., Grand and Franklin Avs., St. Louis, Mo.* Died Nov. 17, 1941.

WOOLSEY, John Munro, judge; b. Aiken, S.C., Jan. 3, 1877; s. William Walton and Katherine Buckingham (Convers) W.; prep. edn., pvt. sch., Englewood, N.J., and Phillips Acad., Andover, Mass.; A.B., Yale, 1898; LL.B., Columbia, 1901, LL.D., 1929; m. Alice Bradford Bacon, Nov. 14, 1911; 1 son, John Munro. Admitted to N.Y. bar, 1901; instr. in equity, Columbia Law Sch., 1905-06; mem. firm Kirlin, Woolsey, Campbell, Hickox & Keating, 1920-29; Am. asso. editor Revue de Droit Maritime Comparé, of Paris, 1922-29. Judge, U.S. Dist. Ct., Southern N.Y. Dist., 1929-43, retired Dec. 1943. Admiralty counsel to French High Commn., N.Y. City, World War. Founder, 1901, and 1st sec. Columbia Law Rev.; mem. advisory com. on research in internat. law, Harvard Law Sch., since 1928, and of visiting com. same, 1932-42; mem. visiting com. Harvard Forest since 1940; mem. bd. visitors Law Sch., Columbia Univ., since 1934, chmn., 1933-41; mem. advisory com., Harvey Sch., Hawthorne, N.Y., 1932-42, chmn. 1940-42. Mem. Art Com. of Addison Gallery, Andover, since 1937; chmn. of Addison Gallery Associates, 1939-42. Mem. Am. and N.Y. State bar assns., Assn. Bar City of N.Y. (sec. library com. 1926-29), Am. Law Inst., Am. Antiquarian Soc., Walpole Soc., Gen. Alumni Assn., Phillips Acad., Andover (pres. 1933-34), Alumni Assn. Law Sch. of Columbia (pres. 1934-36), New Eng. Soc. of New York (pres. 1937-38), Phi Beta Kappa, Phi Delta Phi, Alpha Delta Phi, Scroll and Key; asso. fellow Branford College (Yale) since 1934; mem. Phi Beta Kappa Associates. Republican. Episcopalian. Clubs: Century (2d v.p.), University (New York); Petersham (Mass.) Country. Home: 131 E. 66th St. Chambers: U.S. Court House, New York, N.Y. Died May 4, 1945.

WOOLSEY, Ross Arlington, surgeon; b. Knoxville, Ill., Dec. 23, 1877; s. Thomas Nelson and Mary Haskell (Fifield) W.; M.D., St. Louis U., 1904; m. Mary Ricaud Beck, Apr. 17, 1912; children—Anne Beck (Mrs. Eugene L. Pearce, Jr.), Ross Arlington. House surgeon Frisco Hosp., St. Louis, 1904-08, surgeon in charge, 1908-20; chief surgeon St.L.S.F. Ry. since 1920. Fellow Am. Coll. Surgeons; mem. A.M.A., Mo. State Med. Assn. (pres. 1937), Miss. Valley Med. Assn. (advisory com.), St. Louis Med. Soc., St. Louis Surg. Soc., St. Louis Clinics, Am. Bd. of Surgery, Southern Surg. Soc., Western Surg. Soc., Am. Soc. for Control of Cancer, Am. Assn. Ry. Surgeons, Southern Med. Soc. Republican. Episcopalian. Club: Bellerive Country (St. Louis). Contbr. to surg. jours. Office: 4960 Laclede Av., St. Louis, Mo. Died Feb. 23, 1942.

WOOLWORTH, Charles Sumner, merchant; b. Rodman, N.Y., Aug. 1, 1856; s. John Hubbell and Fanny (McBrier) W.; ed. pub. schs.; m. Anna E. Ryals, June 2, 1886 (died 1913); children—Ethel W., Fred E., Richard W. Began in five and ten cent stores on own account, at Scranton, Pa., 1880, later opening many branch stores in various parts of the country; business merged, 1912, with other concerns forming F. W. Woolworth Co., of which is now hon. chmn. bd.; v.p. U.S. Lumber Co., Miss. Central R.R. Co.; dir. First Nat. Bank (Scranton), Internat. Textbook Co., Scranton-Lackawanna Trust Co. Trustee Syracuse U., Wyoming (Pa.) Seminary, Scranton Y.M.C.A., Scranton Y.W.C.A., Mercy Hosp., Geisinger Memorial Hosp. (Danville, Pa.). Mem. advisory bd. Johnson's Manual Training Sch.; dir. Internat. Corr. Schs. Republican. Methodist. Clubs: Scranton, Country (Scranton); Everglades, Gulf Stream, Bath and Tennis (Palm Beach). Home: 520 Jefferson Av. Office: Scranton Life Bldg., Scranton, Pa. Died Jan. 7, 1947.

WOOTEN, Benjamin Allen (wōō'tĕn), prof. physics; b. Jefferson, Ala., July 29, 1891; s. Benjamin Allen and Louise (Danelly) W.; B.S. in E.E., Ala. Poly. Inst., 1911; E.E., 1912; M.A., Columbia, 1915, Ph.D., 1917; m. Mary Samford, June 1, 1916; 1 son, Benjamin Allen. Instr. in elec. engring., Ala. Poly. Inst., 1913-15, asst. prof. physics, 1915-16, prof. physics, 1919-21; instr. physics, Coll. of City of N.Y., 1917-19; McCormick prof. physics, Washington and Lee U., 1922-28; research work at Yerkes Obs., summers 1926 and 1934; head of physics dept., U. of Ala., since 1928; research asso., Underwater Sound Lab., Harvard, 1944. Fellow American Association for the Advancement of Science; mem. Am. Phys. Society, Am. Geophys. Union, Assn. Physics Teachers, Am. Phys. Soc. (1939-40), Phi Beta Kappa, Tau Beta Pi, Sigma Xi, Alpha Tau Omega. Democrat. Episcopalian. Mason. Contbr. to mags. Home: 1505 10th St., Tuscaloosa, Ala. Died July 9, 1947.

WOOTEN, Horace Oliver; b. Tyler, Tex., June 15, 1865; s. John Wesley and Sarah Angelina (Human) W.; student pub. schs., Tyler, Tex., 1871-77, Mahan's Commercial Coll., 1886-87; m. Lee Ella Hunt, Oct. 17, 1888; children—Enoch Oliver, Ina Dale (Mrs. Alvin T. Jones), Ona Snow (Mrs. Claude S. Lee), Horace Wesley, Stella Merle (Mrs. William S. Thomas), Sterling Hunt. Began as ranchman, 1888; grain dealer, 1890-98; in wholesale grocery business since 1898, now chmn. and pres. H. O. Wooten Grocery Co.; pres. Roscoe, Snyder & Pacific Ry. Co. since 1932; chmn. bd. Farmers & Mchts. Nat. Bank since 1928; pres. Wooten Investment Co.; owner Wooten Hotel, etc. Dir. Federal Reserve Bank of Dallas, 1915-23. Trustee McMurry Coll., Abilene, Tex. Democrat. Methodist. K.P. Club: Abilene City. Home: 242 Beach St. Office: North First and Walnut Sts., Abilene, Tex. Died Dec. 2, 1947.

WOOTTON, Bailey Peyton (wōōt'ŭn), lawyer; born Muhlenberg County, Ky., May 20, 1870; s. Joshua E. and Sarah J. (Taylor) W.; B.S., Lebanon (O.) U., 1890; LL.B., Southern U., 1898; m. Rebecca Boggs, July 1902; children—Thomas P., Sarah J. (dec.), Anita N. (dec.); m. 2d Clara Collins, Nov. 9, 1916; children—Kitty J., Alice R. Began as sch. teacher, 1887; edited country newspapers in Texas and Ky.; founded Hazard Weekly Herald, later daily; pres. Herald Pub. Co.; est. first bank in Hazard, the Hazard Bank; converted to First Nat. Bank and was its pres.; est. first telephone line into Hazard, also first Light & Power Company, Now Ky. & W. Va. Power Co.; admitted to Ky. bar, 1897; in practice at Hazard, 1900-31; represented L.&E., L.&N. and B.&O. railroads, numerous coal companies; title atty. for land holding companies abstracting, purchasing and developing over half million acres in Eastern Ky.; became atty. gen. State of Ky., 1932. Chmn. Dem. Com. of Perry County, Ky., 1904-16; mem. Dem. State Central Exec. Com. 1920-32, chmn. 1932-36; del. Dem. Conv., St. Louis, 1916. Pres. mem. Hazard Bd. Edn. 1908-28; mem. State Bd. Edn. 1932-36; supt. Ky. State Parks since 1936; pres. Hazard Chamber of Commerce, 6 yrs. Chmn. Selective Service Bd. during World War. Ky. del. to Southern Agr. Congress, Charleston, S.C., 1913; del. from Ky. to Nat. Good Roads Assn., Albuquerque, N.M., 1924; Ky. rep. to Nat. Assn. for the Prevention of Crime, Trenton, N.J., 1934. Mem. Hazard, Ky. and Am. bar assns., Future Farmers of America, Phi Beta Gamma, Mason. Club: Rotary. Home: 422 Ewing St., Frankfort, Ky. Office: Hazard, Ky. Died April 16, 1949; buried Frankfort Cemetery.

WORCESTER, David, coll. pres.; b. Boston, Mass., Oct. 4, 1907; s. Elwood and Blanche Stanley (Rulison) W.; A.B., Hobart, 1929; M.A., Harvard, 1930, Ph.D., 1934; LL.D., Hamilton Coll., 1946; m. Eloise Bond Bergland, 1940. Tutor and instr. Harvard English dept., 1934-42; head English dept. Michigan State Coll., 1942; pres. Hamilton Coll., Clinton, N.Y., since 1945. Served with U.S.N.R., 1942-45. Mem. Phi Beta Kappa, Sigma Phi. Episcopalian. Author: The Art of Satire, 1934. Home: College Hill, Clinton, N.Y. Died June 20, 1947.

WORCESTER, Joseph Ruggles (wōōs'tẽr), civil engr.; b. Waltham, Mass., May 9, 1860; s. Benjamin and Mary Clapp (Ruggles) W.; A.B., Harvard, 1882; m. Alice Jeannette Wheeler, Jan. 2, 1889; children—Alice M. (Mrs. C. D. Howe), Barbara (Mrs. C. T. Porter), Thomas, Ruth H. With Boston Bridge Works, most of time as chief engr., 1882-94; cons. practice, 1894-1906; sr. partner J. R. Worcester & Co., 1906-24. Trustee New Ch. Inst. Edn. Mem. Am. Soc. Civil Engrs., Am. Concrete Inst., Am. Soc. for Testing Materials, Am. Inst. Cons. Engrs., Am. Ry. Engring. Assn., Am. Acad. Arts and Sciences. Designed bridge over Connecticut River, at Bellows Falls, Vt.; bridge between Portland and South Portland, Me.; train shed of South Sta., Boston, etc. Swedenborgian. Home: Waltham. Mass. Office: 79 Milk St., Boston, Mass. Died May 9, 1943.

WORDEN, (J.) Perry (wûr'dĕn), author, lecturer; b. Hastings-on-Hudson, N.Y., May 25, 1866; s. of Amos Warren and Mary (Welch) W.; bro. Alice Graham Worden, educator (died 1929); A.B., Columbia, 1895; studied Germanics, Columbia, 1895-96; student philology and lit., univs. of Leyden and Halle-Saale, and at Sorbonne, 1896-1900; Ph.D., Halle, 1900; research, English and German univs., 1907-10; m. Effie Josephine Fussell, 1916. Reporter, spl. corr. N.Y. Sun and New York Tribune, 1888-92; sent to Europe as cycling tourist by Outing Magazine, 1892; since then, on repeated tours abroad, often with bicycle and camera; lecturer for New York Bd. of Edn. 5 yrs., for univ. extension, in America, Eng. and Germany, 12 yrs.; instr. in modern langs. various instns., 6 yrs.; in charge German dept., U. of Me., summer session, 1905; prof. modern langs., Kalamazoo (Mich.) Coll., 1905-07; Am. consul, Bristol, Eng., 1907-09; traveler, particularly in Western America, since 1911. Was for several yrs. Germanic reviewer for The Nation, and Berlin lit. corr. N.Y. Times' Saturday Book Rev. Republican. Episcopalian. Mem. Authors' League America. Club: Gamut. Author: Delft and Delft Ware, 1900; Schiller's Song of the Bell, 1900; Stories and Legends of the Rhine and the Neckar (Heidelberg), 1910; California of Yesterday, 1916; Visits and Chats with the Notable and Great, 1917; Second-hand Gossip, Men and Things, 1918; Memories of Mark Twain, 1938; Personal Recollections of Bret Harte, 1939. Advisory editor of Harris Newmark's Sixty Years in Southern California, 1915, also of 2d edit., 1926, and of 3d edition, 1930. Editor of the Temple-Workman family annals, covering one hundred years of California history. Founder and president and director Calif. Archives for Collection and Preservation of Calif. Hist. Data, now collecting and studying Californiana. Mem. Hist. Soc. So. Calif., and San Diego and Pasadena hist. socs. Has placed, at own expense, "Worden Memorial," Mount Hope (N.Y.) Cemetery, and numerous tablets and other lit., hist. memorials of Am.-European assns., in museums and libraries at Stratford-on-Avon, Bristol, London, Windsor, Heidelberg, Weimar, Berlin, Halle-Saale, Bonn, Leipzig, Vienna, New York, Boston and elsewhere, especially in Calif. Contbr. to Oxford English, Webster, and Standard dictionaries, and to mags. Author of "Agua Mansa" articles in Pasadena Star-News since 1929. Author: Admiral Worden at Monterey, 1847; Ella Housefield Lowe: In Memoriam. Active in reëstablishing Anglo-Am.-German friendly relations. Address: 952 Cornell Road, Oak Knoll, Pasadena, Calif. Died Mar. 20, 1945.

WORK, Hubert, ex-sec. of Interior; b. Marion Center, Pa., July 3, 1860; s. Moses Thompson and Tabitha Logan (Van Horn) W.; student Indiana (Pa.) State Normal Sch.; Med. Dept., U. of Mich., 1882-84; M.D., U. of Pa., 1885, LL.D., 1925; Sc.D., U. of Colo., 1925; LL.D., Lincoln Memorial U., 1923, U. of Calif., 1927; m. Laura M. Arbuckle, 1887 (died 1924); children—Philip (M.D.), Mrs. Dorcus Bissell, Robert V. H. (dec.); m. 2d, Ethel Reed Gano, Dec. 1933. Began practice, Greeley, Colo., 1885; removed to Pueblo, Colo.; founder, 1896, Woodcroft Hosp., for mental and nervous diseases. Del. at large Rep. Nat. Conv., 1908; chmn. Colo. Rep. State Central Com., 1912; was Colo. mem. Rep. Nat. Com.; 1st asst. postmaster gen. of U.S., Mar. 4, 1921-Mar. 4, 1922; postmaster general, Mar. 4, 1922-Mar. 4, 1923; sec. of the Interior, Mar. 5, 1923-July 24, 1928; chmn. Rep. Nat. Com., 1928-29. Mem. A.M.A. (ex-pres.), Colo. State Med. Soc. (ex-pres.), Am. Medico-Psychol. Assn. (pres. 1911). Was lt. col., M.C. U.S. Army. Presbyterian. Mason. Address: Englewood, Colo. Died Dec. 14, 1942.

WORK, Monroe Nathan, educator; b. Iredell County, N.C., Aug. 15, 1866; s. Alexander and Eliza (Hobbs) W.; grad. Chicago Theol. Sem., 1898; Ph.B., University of Chicago, 1902, A.M., 1903; D.Litt., Howard Univ., 1943; m. Florence Evelyn Hendrickson, Dec. 27, 1904. Professor pedagogy and history, Ga. State Industrial Coll., Savannah, 1903-08; dir. dept. of records and research, Tuskegee Inst. (colored), Ala., since 1908. Mem. Internat. Inst. of African Languages and Cultures, Am. Sociol. Soc., Am. Econ. Assn., Am. Acad. Polit. and Social Science, Assn. for Study of Negro Life and History, A.A.A.S., Southern Economic Association, Southern Historical Assn., Southern Sociol. Society. Methodist, Founder, 1912, and since editor of Negro Year Book; editor and compiler of Bibliography of the Negro in Africa and America, 1928; A Bibliography of European Colonization, and the Resulting Contacts of Peoples, Races, Nations and Culture (in preparation). Developed bureau of information relating to the Negro. Home: Tuskegee Institute, Ala. Died May 2, 1945.

WORK, William Roth, prof. elec. engineering; b. Steelton, Pa., May 4, 1881; s. Joseph Alexander and Alice Anna (Lupfer) W.; student Wittenberg Acad., Springfield, O., 1895-98; A.B., Wittenberg Coll., 1902, hon. D.Sc., 1920; M.E. in E.E., Ohio State U., 1905; m. Ola Frank Kautzman, June 27, 1907; children—Alice Myers (Mrs. Wilson McA. Kleibacker), William Worthington. With Carnegie Inst. of Tech. since 1906, head dept. electrical engring., 1921-44, asst. director, College of Engineering since 1942. Mem. Com. on Edn. and Special Training, General Staff, War Dept., 1918. Fellow A.A.A.S., Am. Inst. Elec. Engrs.; mem. Engrs. Soc. of Western Pa., Am. Soc. for Engring. Edn., Am. Assn. Univ. Profs., Beta Theta Pi, Sigma Xi, Tau Beta Pi, Eta Kappa Nu. Republican. Presbyterian. Home: 5702 Beacon St., Pittsburgh, Pa. Died Oct. 3, 1948.

WORKING, Daniel Webster, agricultural educator; b. Belle Plaine, Minn., May 9, 1862; s. Daniel Webster and Elizabeth (Gunderson) W.; B.Sc., Kan. State Agrl. Coll., 1888; A.M., U. of Denver, 1907; studied Grad. Sch. of Agr., Ithaca, N.Y., 1908, Ames, Ia., 1910; m. Ella Grace Booth, Nov. 9, 1892; children—Holbrook, Earl Booth, Elmer Joseph. Master Colo. State Grange, 1892-94; sec. Colo. Agrl. Coll., 1893-97; supt. schools, Arapahoe County, Colo., 1905-07; supt. agrl. extension work, W.Va. U., 1907-1911; with Office of Farm Management, U.S. Dept. Agr., 1911-14, Office of Extension Work, 1914-19; dean Coll. of Agr., U. of Ariz., 1919-22, dir. Agrl. Expt. Sta., 1919-21; spl. lecturer in agrl. economics, U. of Denver Sch. of Commerce, winter quarter, 1923. Fellow A.A.A.S.; mem. American Academy Political and Social Science. Republican. Conglist. Mason. Granger. Collaborating author of History of Agriculture in Colorado. Contbr. numerous articles in agrl. and hist. publs.; has served as editor or asso. editor various agrl. mags.; now columnist for National Grange Monthly. Home: 711 S. Forest St., Denver, Colo. Died Apr. 7, 1941.

WORRALL, David Elbridge (wôr'ăl), chemist; b. Westerley, R.I., Aug. 2, 1886; s. William Francis and Iona May (Paine) W.; B.S., R.I. State Coll., 1910; A.M., Harvard, 1911, Ph.D., 1919; grad. student U. of Graz, Austria, 1928; m. Harriet Taber Tucker, Nov. 28, 1914 (died Nov. 7, 1940); children—David Elbridge, Edward Tucker, Hilda. Chemist Guantanamo Sugar Co., Cuba, 1911-12; instr. chemistry, Smith Coll., 1914-17; asst. gas chemist Bur. of Mines, 1918-19; instr. chemistry, Harvard, 1919; asst. prof., chemistry, Tufts Coll., Medford, Mass., 1919-24, prof. since 1924; dir. of chem. laboratories since 1939; visiting lecturer, Radcliffe College, 1924-26. Served as 1st lt. Chem. Warfare Service, U.S. Army, 1918. Fellow A.A.A.S., Am. Acad. Arts and Sciences; mem. Am. Chem. Soc. (chmn. N.E. Sect. 1929-30); Am. Geog. Soc., Phi Beta Kappa (hon.), Alpha Chi Sigma, Theta Chi, Phi Kappa Phi. Unitarian. Republican. Author: Principles of Organic Chemistry, 1927. Contributor articles to Jour. Am. Chem. Soc. Home: 72 Badger Rd., Medford, Mass. Died Feb. 7, 1944.

WORTHING, Archie Garfield (wûr'thing), physicist; b. LeRoy, Wis., Feb. 6, 1881; s. Arthur James and Loella (McKnight) W.; grad. State Normal Sch., Oshkosh, Wis., 1900; B.A., U. of Wis., 1904; State U. of Ia., 1906-09; Ph.D., U. of Mich., 1911; m. Exie Lillian Witherbee, June 23, 1905; children—Marion Witherbee, Helen Witherbee, Robert Witherbee. Teacher grammar sch., Brandon, Wis., 1900-01; asst. in physics, U. of Wis., 1904-06; acting instr. physics, State U. of Ia., 1906-09; asso. physicist Physical Laboratory of National Lamp Works, Cleveland, Ohio, 1910-14; physicist Nela Research Laboratories, Cleveland, 1914-25; head of physics department Univ. of Pittsburgh, 1925-37, professor physics since 1925. Fellow Am. Phys. Soc.; mem. Optical Soc. Am. (vice-pres. 1939-41; pres. 1941-43), Am. Assn. Physics Teachers (vice-pres. 1940, pres. 1941), Am. Inst. Physics (member board govs. since 1941), Phi Beta Kappa, Sigma Xi, Sigma Pi Sigma. Unitarian. Co-author of books on scientific and tech. subjects and contbr. to scientific and tech. jours. Determined the true temperature scale of tungsten and other metals and their emissivities at incandescent temperatures. Home: 1372 N. Sheridan Av., Pittsburgh 6, Pa. Died July 30, 1949.

WORTHINGTON, Charles Campbell, mech. engr., retired; b. Booklyn, N.Y., Jan. 6, 1854; s. Henry Rossiter and Sara (Newton) W.; gen. engring. course, Columbia; m. Julia A. Hedden, 1879 (dec.); children—Julia Hedden (Mrs. Edmund Monroe Sawtelle), Henry Rossiter (dec.), Chas. Campbell (dec.), Edward Hedden, Reginald Stuart; m. 2d, Maude C. Rice, June 7, 1906; children—Sara Newton, Alice Rice. Owner and pres. Henry R. Worthington Corp., mfrs. steam pumps, 1875-1900 (retired); cons. and nominal pres. Worthington Mower Co., Stroudsburg, Pa. Inventor of Worthington high duty water works engine and hydraulic machinery now in use in principal countries of the world. Invented, 1913, and introduced the Worthington gang lawn mower, in general use on golf courses. Mem. Am. Soc. M.E. (ex-mem. council). Republican. Episcopalian. Clubs: Engineers', New York Athletic; Racquet and Tennis, Chevy Chase (Washington, D.C.). Home: Shawnee-on-Delaware, Pa. Died Oct. 21, 1944.

WORTHINGTON, William Alfred, railway official; b. Vallejo, Calif., June 18, 1872; s. J. A. and Kate W.; ed. pub. schs.; m. S. M. Breen, Apr. 27, 1905. Stenographer and clerk supt.'s office, S.P. Co., Sacramento, Calif., 1887-88; chief clerk to engr. maintenance of way, same road, San Francisco, 1888-93; statistician in gen. manager's office, 1893-95; chief clerk same office, 1895-1901; exec. sec. to asst. to pres., 1901-04; chief clerk in office of dir. maintenance and operation U.P. System and S.P. Co., Chicago, 1904-07; asst. to dir. maintenance and operation, 1907-12; asst. dir. maintenance and operation same roads, New York, 1912-13; same S.P Co., 1913-15; v.p. S.P. Co., Jan. 31, 1913-June 30, 1942, now retired; chmn. bd. Pacific Electric Ry. Co.; pres. Visalia Electric R.R.; v.p. Southern Pacific R.R. Co. of Mexico. Office: 65 Market St., San Francisco, California.* Died Dec. 24, 1945.

WOTHERSPOON, Marion Foster (wŏ'thėr-spoon), author; b. Northampton, Mass., Aug. 31, 1863; d. Richard Norman and Annie (Halsted) Foster; grad. high sch., Chicago, 1881, Chicago Froebel Assn. Training Sch., 1893; m. George Foote Washburne, M.D., June 22, 1886; children—Norman Foster Washburne (dec.), Carleton W. Washburne, Dorothea Washburne (widow of Prof. Herman J. Stegeman, U. of Ga.), John Noble Washburne; m. 2d, William Albert Wotherspoon, 1915 (died Oct. 19, 1933). Engaged as a newspaper and a magazine writer since 1894; conducted campaign as school editor Chicago Evening Post, which resulted in giving Chicago her present normal school; as delegate from Little Deaf Child's League was instrumental in securing passage of law providing pub. day sch. edn. for deaf children, the law since adopted in almost every state of the Union; state organizer Ill. Congress of Mothers, etc. Dem. nominee for Calif. Assembly, 1934; mem. Dem. State Central Com. of Calif. Mem. Am. Civil Liberties Union, League of Women Voters (Pasadena), Women's Civic League of Pasadena, Pasadena Cooperative Soc., Women's Internat. League for Peace and Freedom, Nat. Women's Party. Author: Success Library (Volume II), 1901; Every Day Essays, 1904; A Little Fountain of Life, 1904; Study of Child Life, 1907; Family Secrets, 1907; Mother's Year Book, 1908; The House on the North Shore, 1909; Old-Fashioned Fairy Tales, 1909; Indian Legends, 1910; A Search for a Happy Country, 1940. Home: 1655 Mt. Pleasant Rd., Winnetka, Ill. Died May 15, 1944.

WRIGHT, Arthur Davis, educator; b. Boston, Mass., Mar. 24, 1885; s. John and Margaret Ella (Snell) W.; prep. edn., McGuire's Sch., Richmond, Va., 1893-1900; A.B. and A.M., Coll. William and Mary, 1904; Ed. M., Harvard University, 1922; hon. A.M., Dartmouth College, 1927; married Mary Morris Rowe, Oct. 25, 1910; children—Mary Morris (Mrs. Josef A. Blair), Margaret Elizabeth. Teacher high sch., Hampton, Va., 1904-06; prin. Baker Sch., Richmond, 1906-09; supt. schs. Fredericksburg, Va., 1909-10, Henrico County, Va., 1910-15; state supervisor Negro schs., Va., 1915-20; asst. consultant in edn., 1st Corps Area, U.S. Army, 1920-21; asst. prof. edn., Dartmouth, 1921-27, prof., 1927-31; instr. in summer schs., U. of Rochester, 1922, Cornell U., 1923, George Washington U., 1924-28, U. of Mich., 1929-30. Mem. survey staff, Va. State Sch. Survey, 1919, Fla. State Sch. Survey, 1928; Pres. Anna T. Jeanes Negro Rural Sch. Fund and John F. Slater Fund, 1931-37; pres. Southern Edn. Foundation (consolidation of Jeanes and Slater Funds) since 1937; trustee Schofield N. and I. School, Aiken, S.C. Mem. N.E.A., Phi Beta Kappa, Kappa Phi Kappa (founder; nat. sec.), Theta Delta Chi, Phi Delta Kappa, Omicron Delta Kappa. Democrat. Episcopalian. Clubs: Harvard (New York); Cosmos (Washington). Wrote: (with J. G. Stevens) Readings in American College Education and Readings in the Principles of Vocational Guidance, 1924; The Negro Rural School Fund (Anna T. Jeanes Foundation), 1907-1933. Edited: (with G. E. Gardner) Hall's Lectures on School-Keeping, 1929. Address: 726 Jackson Pl. N.W., Washington 6, D.C. Died May 10, 1947.

WRIGHT, Arthur Mullin, surgeon; b. Lyndonville, N.Y., Sept. 30, 1879; s. Richard Brainard and Ella Agatha (Mullin) W.; A.B., Cornell, 1903, M.D., 1905; D.Sc. (honorary), New York University, 1947; married Alice Stanchfield, Apr. 27, 1912; children—Richard Stewart, Stanchfield. Practiced in N.Y. City since 1905; teacher surgery since 1907; George David Stewart prof. surgery, Univ. and Bellevue Hosp. Med. Coll., Grove Farm, Earleville, Md., 1933-47, emeritus prof. surgery since 1947; emeritus director surgery, French Hospital, New York City; consulting surgeon, Bellevue and St. Vincent's hospitals (both New York City), St. Francis Hosp. (Port Jervis, N.Y.), Mount Vernon Hosp. (Mt. Vernon), Jamaica Hosp. (Jamaica, L.I.), St. Luke's Hosp. (Newburgh), Southside Hosp. (Bayshore), St. Agnes' Hosp. (White Plains), Central Islip Hosp. (L.I.). Served as capt. Med. Corp, U.S. Army, 1917; maj. lt. col., 1918-19, in charge Base Hosp. No. 1, A.E.F.; col. Res. Corps. Fellow Am. Coll. Surgeons, A.M.A.; mem. Acad. Medicine, Am. Surg. Assn., N.Y. Surg. Soc.; Internat. Surgical Assn., Am. Bd. of Surgery. Decorated Chevalier Legion of Honor; Order of the Jade (Chinese); awarded meritorious citation for army service. Clubs: Cornell University. Contbr. surg. articles. Home: Earleville, Md. Died June 24, 1948.

WRIGHT, Bruce Simpson, clergyman; b. Eldred, Pa., Feb. 24, 1879; s. Albert Josiah and Bertha (Simpson) W.; A.B., Allegheny Coll., Meadville, Pa., 1905, D.D., 1920; m. Margarette Catherine Armstrong, Oct. 30, 1907; children—Harriet Esther, Elizabeth Anne, Robert Bruce. Pastor First M.E. Ch., Fredonia, N.Y., 1905-12, Simpson M.E. Ch., Erie, Pa., 1912-15, American Ch., Manila, P.I., 1915-18, Trinity M.E. Ch., Albany, N.Y., 1918-20, Asbury-Delaware M.E. Ch., Buffalo, N.Y., 1920-33, Old Stone M.E. Ch., Meadville, Pa., 1934-36, First Meth. Ch., Erie, Pa., since 1936. Chmn. Am. Defense Com., P.I., World War. Dean of Summer Grad. Sch. for Ministers, Silver Lake, N.Y. Exchange preacher to Brit. Isles, 1923-26. Mem. Commn. on World Peace of M.E. Ch. Trustee Allegheny Coll.; mem. advisory council Am. Brotherhood for the Blind. Pres. Erie Ministerial Assn., 1941. Mem. Y.M.C.A., Phi Delta Theta, Internat. Soc. Theta Phi. Republican. Mason (32°, K.T.). Clubs: University, Round Table, Rotary, Literary Union. Author: Americans Away, 1916; Moments of Devotion, 1921; The Life in the Spirit, 1927; God, the Greatest Poet—Man, His Greatest Poem, 1928, The House of Happiness, 1928; The Symphony of Faith, 1929; Pentecost Day by Day, 1930; Girded with Gladness, 1931; Steps Into the Sanctuary, 1932; Chancel Windows, 1933; Lenten Gallery, 1938. Contbr. to Christian Century, New York Christian Advocate, David C. Cook Publications, Meth. Church School Literature, Am. Tract Soc., etc. Home: 717 Sassafras St., Erie, Pa.; and "Wright-Wood," Kane, Pa. Study: 707 Sassafras St., Erie, Pa. Died Nov. 28, 1942.

WRIGHT, Charles Baker, coll. prof.; b. Cleveland, O., Oct. 5, 1859; s. Horton and Susan (Baker) W.; A.B., Buchtel Coll., Akron, O., 1880, A.M., 1885; student Johns Hopkins, 1882-85; grad. scholar same, 1884-85, apptd. fellow in English, 1885; hon. A.M., U. of Vt., 1904; L.H.D., Buchtel, 1905; Litt.D., Middlebury, 1915; m. Clara Wright Alexander, Sept. 2, 1885; children—John Alexander (dec.), Marjory Alexander (Mrs. Wm. Hazlett Upson). Prof. rhetoric and Eng. lit., 1885-1920, now emeritus, dean, 1913-18, acting pres., fall of 1918, Middlebury Coll. Conglist. Author: A Teacher's Avocations, 1925; Gleanings from Forefather's, 1926; The Making of Note-Books, 1928; Verses in Varying Mood, 1931; Aftermath, 1934. Home: Middlebury, Vt. Died Apr. 24, 1942.

WRIGHT, Daniel Thew, judge; b. Riverside, Hamilton Co., O., Sept. 24, 1864; s. D. Thew and Juliet Frances (Rogers) W.; grad. Hughes High Sch., Cincinnati, 1885; LL.B., Cincinnati Law Sch., 1887; married Alice Williams, October 26, 1887; children—Gladys Marie, Claire, Alice Liston, Daniel Thew III; m. 2d, Lou Price Hinton, Oct. 27, 1932. Admitted to bar, 1887; practiced at Cincinnati; specialist as trial lawyer; village solicitor of Riverside, 1888-90; mayor of Riverside, 1890-93; 2d asst., 1888-90, and 1st asst. pros. atty., Hamilton County, 1890-93; elected and served as judge Court of Common Pleas, Hamilton County, O., 1893-98; justice Supreme Court of D.C., Nov. 6, 1903-Nov. 1, 1914; resigned to resume practice of law. Republican. Home: Fenwick, Md. Died Nov. 18, 1943.

WRIGHT, Edward Richard, clergyman; b. Bellevue, O., Aug. 8, 1872; s. Alfred and Mary Ann (Megginson) W.; A.B., Western Reserve U., 1896, D.D., 1928; B.D., Union Theol. Sem., N.Y City, 1899; m. Marietta J. Crawford, June 7, 1899; 1 son, Crawford Kingsley. Ordained ministry Presbyn. Ch., 1899; pastor North Ch., Cleveland, 1899-1901, Willoughby, O., 1901-03, Collinwood br. Calvary Ch., Cleveland, 1903-08; religious editor Cleveland Leader, 1908-12; exec. sec. Federated Chs. of Cleveland, 1912-30; with Speakers Bur., New York Times, 1934; now religious editor Cleveland News. Republican. Home: 25901 Lake Shore Blvd., Cleveland, O. Died 1941.

WRIGHT, Frank Ayres, architect; b. Liberty, Sullivan County, N.Y., Nov. 19, 1854; s. A. B. and M. J. W.; A.B., Cornell, 1879; m. Elizabeth Hanford, Jan. 9, 1883; children—Mrs. Carile Hanford Middleditch, Mrs. Frances Hanford Poillon, Mrs. Elizabeth Juliette Slosson, Ehrick Hanford. In practice of architecture since 1879. One of founders and sec., 1885, Architectural League of New York; fellow Am. Inst. Architects. Trustee village S. Orange, N.J., 1887; dir. in various clubs. Mem. New Eng. Soc., Orange (N.J.) Architectural League. Clubs: Nat. Arts, Cornell (New York); Canoe Brook Country, Baltusrol Golf, Waterwitch. Author: Modern House Painting, 1880; Architectural Perspective for Beginners, 1882. Home: Summit, N.J. Died June 5, 1949.

WRIGHT, Frank C., ry. exec.; b. Owing's Mills, Md., July 13, 1871; s. John Atwood and Mary E. (Grimes) W.; ed. Baltimore Pub. Schs., Baltimore City Coll.; m. Carrie Butler, Oct. 3, 1893; children—Katharine Olive, Carol (Mrs. Edward Pennell Brooks), Charles Beverly (dec.), Marjorie, Frank C., John Matthew (dec.), David A. Messenger Md. Steamboat Company, Baltimore, 1886; vice-pres. Bangor & Aroostook Railroad Company since February 1920; pres. Lake Tankers Corp. since June 1927; chmn. of bd. Penn Anthracite Collieries, Scranton, Pa., since 1931; dir. div. of transportation loans, Federal Emergency Adminstrn. of Pub. Works, Washington, D.C., 1933-36; spl. asst. to board of dirs. R.F.C. since 1936; dir. Windsor Land Corporation, W.Va. Coal & Coke Corp., Lake Tankers Corp., Penn Anthracite Mining Co., Penn Anthracite Collieries Co., Southern Penn Anthracite Co., Elk Hill Coal & Iron Co., Ohio River Co., Erie R.R. Co., South Puerto Rico Sugar Co., Nat. Oil Transport Corp. Mem. Newcomen Soc. Democrat. Methodist. Mason. Clubs: India House (New York); Metropolitan (Washington, D.C.); Sleepy Hollow Country (Scarsboro-on-Hudson); Blind Brook (Port Chester, N.Y.). Home: Wilson Park, Tarrytown, N.Y. Office: 20 Exchange Pl., New York, N.Y.* Died May 29, 1946.

WRIGHT, Harold Bell, author; b. Rome, Oneida County, N.Y., May 4, 1872; s. William A. and Alma T. (Watson) W.; student prep. dept., Hiram Coll., O.; m. Frances E. Long, July 18, 1899; children—Gilbert Munger, Paul Williams (dec.), Norman Hall; m. 2d, Mrs. Winifred Mary Potter Duncan, Aug. 5, 1920. Painter and decorator, 1887-92; landscape painter, 1892-97; pastor Christian (Disciples) Ch., Pierce City, Mo., 1897-98, Pittsburg, Kan., 1898-1903, Forest Av. Ch., Kansas City, Mo., 1903-05, Lebanon, Mo., 1905-07, Redlands, Calif., 1907-08; retired from ministry 1908. Author: That Printer of Udell's, 1903; The Shepherd of the Hills, 1907; The Calling of Dan Matthews, 1909; The Uncrowned King, 1910; The Winning of Barbara Worth, 1911; Their Yesterdays, 1912; The Eyes of the World, 1914; When a Man's a Man, 1916; The Re-Creation of Brian Kent, 1919; Helen of the Old House, 1921; The Mine with the Iron Door, 1923; A Son of His Father, 1925; God and the Groceryman, 1927; Long Ago Told, 1929; Exit, 1930; Ma Cinderella, 1932; To My Sons, 1934; The Man Who Went Away, 1942. Home: Escondido, Calif. Died May 24, 1944; buried in Greenwood Memorial Park, San Diego, Calif.

WRIGHT, Herbert, international law; b. Washington, D.C., Mar. 28, 1892; s. Johnson Eliot and Susan Cecelia (Watson) W.; A.B., Georgetown U., 1911; A.M., Catholic U. of America, 1912, Ph.D., 1916; LL.D., Providence (R.I.) Coll., 1930; studied law, National U., 1937-40; m. Anna Cecelia Blakeney, Nov. 19, 1912; children—Margaret Frances, John Herbert (U.S. Navy), Thomas Blakeney. Instr. in Latin, Catholic U. of America, 1911-18; asst. to gen. editor Classics of Internat. Law, 1917-28; attached to Dept. of State, editing material on international law and related subjects, 1918-19; editor publs. of Carnegie Endowment for Internat. Peace, 1921-23; prof. polit. science, Georgetown U., 1923-30; managing editor Constl. Review, 1927-29; editor Internat. Conf. of Am. States on Conciliation and Arbitration, Washington, 1928-29; editor of Am. del. Internat. Conf. on Safety of Life at Sea, London, 1929, also of Internat. Tech. Cons. Com. on Radio Communications, The Hague, 1929; specialist in hist. research Latin Am. Affairs, Dept. of State, 1929-30; editor of Am. del. Naval Conf., London, 1930; apptd. editor Internat. Conf., Dept. of State, 1930 (resigned); lecturer internat. law and relations, Post-grad. Sch., U.S. Naval Acad., 1936-37; prof. internat. law and head of dept. of politics, Catholic U. of America since Sept. 1, 1930. Mem. Carnegie Internat. Law Conf., Paris, Brussels, The Hague and Geneva, 1926; apptd. by President Roosevelt mem. Internat. Com. U.S.-Latvia, 1939. Trustee Newman Sch. Mem. Am. Soc. Internat. Law, Internat. Law Assn. (mem. exec. com.), Am. Polit. Science Assn., Conf. of Teachers of Internat. Law and Related Subjects (sec. 1938-41), Vereeniging voor de Uitgave van Grotius. Catholic. Club: Cosmos. Author: Francisci de Victoria De Iure Belli Relectio, 1916; Some Less Known Works of Hugo Grotius, 1928; Biography of Philander Chase Knox, 1929; Francisco de Vitoria (addresses), 1932; Catholic Founders of International Law, 1934; I rapporti tra Stato e Chiesa secondo la Costituzione degli Stati Uniti, 1939; Memorandum in Support of the Retention of the Spanish Embargo, 1939; also biog. sketches of diplomats and statesmen in Dictionary of Am. Biography, 1928. Editor: Francisci de Victoria De Indis et De Iure Belli Relectiones (with others), 1916; The Constitutions of the States at War (1914-18), 1919; De Jure Belli ac Pacis Libri Tres, by Hugo Grotius (with others), 1925; Francisco Suarez (addresses), 1933; The Constitution of the United States (addresses), 1938. Address: Cosmos Club, Washington, D.C.* Died Apr. 12, 1945.

WRIGHT, Herbert E., clergyman; b. Branford, Conn., May 10, 1872; s. William Henry and Matilda Almira (Woodin) W.; grad. Wesleyan Acad., 1896; student Syracuse, 1900, D.C., 1922; m. Mary Esther Sexsmith, Dec. 19, 1900; 1 son, William Grange. Ordained ministry M.E. Ch., 1900; pastor Pilgrim Congl. Ch., Syracuse, 1898-1900, Fishkill, 1900-01, Elizabeth, 1902, Lee, Mass., 1902-04, Mt. Kisco, N.Y., 1905-07, Tarrytown, 1908-13, White Plains, 1914-18, Ossining, 1925; dist. supt., Newburgh Dist., 1919-24; pres. Drew Seminary for Young Women since 1925. Pres. Schoolmasters' Assn. of N.Y. City; mem. World Service Commn. of M.E. Ch. (exec. com. 1924-29). Pi Gamma Mu. Republican. Mason (32°). Clubs: Clergy, Town Hall (New York). Home: Carmel, N.Y. Died March 24, 1943.

WRIGHT, Herbert Perry, investment banker; b. Stockton, Ill., June 24, 1865; s. Burton and Hulda (Coon) W.; B.S., Northwestern U., 1887, M.S., 1890; m. Hattie Haw, Oct. 22, 1890 (died 1935); children—Herbert Edwin (dec.), Annie Lillien. Began in investment business, Kansas City, Mo., July 1, 1887; pres. Kansas Gas & Electric Co. from its organization, 1909 to 1933, chmn. bd. since 1933; a founder, 1901, and since dir. Kansas City Life Ins. Co., also mem. exec. com.; dir. Kansas City Power & Light Co., Safety Federal Savings & Loan Assn. For many years dir. St. Louis & San Francisco Ry., now also mem. exec. com.; largely instrumental in organizing the Sinclair Oil Co., Loose-Wiles Biscuit Co., Am. Power & Light Co., Cook Paint & Varnish Co., Sheffield Steel Co., Kansas Gas & Elec. Co., and other corps. Served as mem. exec. com. 10th Fed. Reserve Dist., in charge of sale of Liberty Bonds (always exceeding allotment in sale of bonds), World War, and mem. Capital Issues Bd., in same territory, for formation of new corps. A founder Investment Bankers Assn. of America and served as mem. bd. of dirs. and as v.p. (now barred from membership on account of retirement); mem. Chamber of Commerce, S.R. (past pres. Mo. Soc.), Sigma Chi. Former trustee Northwestern U. and Baker U. Clubs: Kansas City, University, Blue Hills Golf, Rotary. Home: The Walnuts. Office: Land Bank Bldg., Kansas City, Mo. Died Dec. 27, 1945.

WRIGHT, Isaac Miles, prof. education; b. Sclo, N.Y., Mar. 7, 1879; s. John S. and Belle E. (Saunders) W.; B.S., Alfred (N.Y.) U., 1904; Pd.M., New York U., 1914, Pd.D., 1916; m. Maude Goff Paul, June 24, 1909. Teacher rural sch., Belmont, N.Y., 1898-99; prin. grammar sch., Scio, N.Y., 1900-01; asst. in high sch., 1904-07; prin. high sch., Elliottville, 1907-10, Lawrence, 1910-13; teacher Dwight Sch., N.Y. City, 1913-17; prof. edn., Muhlenberg College, 1917-45, professor emeritus since 1945; director School of Education, and of Summer School of Muhlenberg College (increasing attendance at latter from 37 to 1,114 in 6 yrs.), Sept. 1917-June 1942. Member Allentown Board of Education since 1929, president, 1937-43. President Pennsylvania State Assn. Sch. Dirs., 1943-44. Mem. N.E.A., Am. Assn. of Sch. Adminstrs., Am. Assn. Univ. Profs., Nat. Council Geography Teachers, Nat. Soc. Coll. Teachers of Edn., Pa. Soc. S.R., Pa. State Teachers' Assn., Phi Kappa Tau (grand pres. 1928-30), Phi Delta Kappa, Kappa Phi Kappa, Omicron Delta Kappa. Republican. Episcopalian. Mason (K.T., Shriner). Clubs: Oakmont, Brookside, Rotary. Home: 2729 Gordon St., Allentown, Pa. Died Jan. 15, 1948.

WRIGHT, James Harris, fgn. service officer; b. Chillicothe, Mo., Feb. 21, 1907; s. Wade Hampton and Bertha (Nagle) W.; student U. of Mo., 1924-27; m. Mildred Beane, Jan. 28, 1930. Vice consul at Vera Cruz, Mexico, 1930; student Fgn. Service Sch., Dept. of State, 1930; vice consul, Cologne, Germany, 1930-37; vice consul and 3d sec., Bogota, Colombia, 1937-38, consul, 1938-40, 2d sec., 1940; assigned to Dept. of State, 1940; asst. to dir., Office Am. Republican Affairs, Dept. of State, 1943, chief Div. North and West Coast Affairs, 1944; liaison sec., United Nations Monetary and Financial Conf., Bretton Woods, N.H., 1944; polit. advisor, Second Council Meeting of U.N.R.R.A., Montreal, Can., 1944; temporary acting special asst. to asst. Sec. of State, 1945; alternate U.S. delegate, Inter-Am. Coffee Bd., 1945; counselor of U.S. Embassy, Havana, Cuba, 1945; special asst. to asst. sec. of state, 1946-47; dir. Office of Am. Republic Affairs, July 16, 1947. Mem. Am. Fgn. Service Assn. Clubs: Army and Navy (Washington). Home: 913 Cherry St., Chillicothe, Mo. Office: Dept. of State, Washington, D.C. Died Sept. 28, 1947.

WRIGHT, John Pilling, business exec.; b. Newark, Del., May 17, 1881; s. Samuel J. and Isabel (Pilling) W.; m. Elizabeth Johnson, Sept. 9, 1908. Pres. Continental Diamond Fibre Co. since 1929; pres. Delaware Rayon Co. (New Castle, Del.), New Bedford (Mass.) Rayon Co., Haveg Corp. (Marshalltown, Del.), Newark (Del.) Trust Co. Decorated Chevalier Legion of Honor (Fr.). Mem. bd. trustees, U. of Del. Club: Union League (Phila.). Office: S. Chapel St., Newark, Del. Died April 18, 1947.

WRIGHT, John Westley, ophthalmologist; b. Freeport, O., July 17, 1842; s. Benjamin and Lucinda (Rager) W.; M.Sc., New Market (later Scio, now Mt. Union) Coll., 1872, A.M., 1891; M.D., Cincinnati Coll. Medicine and Surgery, 1873; m. Elizabeth A. Hesket, Aug. 9, 1864 (died May 23, 1892); children—Frances Neva, Nellie Corina, John Hesket, Halstead Robert (dec.), Columbus Clinton (dec.), Anna Lucinda (dec.); m. 2d, Balzurah Conrow, July 25, 1893 (died Dec. 28, 1913). In practice as oculist at Columbus since 1880; prof. ophthalmology, Ohio Med. U. and Starling-Ohio Med. Coll., 1891-1910, emeritus prof. med. dept. Ohio State U., since 1910; ex-ophthalmologist Protestant Hosp.; one of incorporators of Ohio Med. U. and Protestant Hosp. Fellow A.M.A., Am. Acad. Medicine, Am. Acad. Ophthalmology and Oto-laryngology; mem. Ohio State Med. Assn., Columbus Acad. Medicine. Author: Text-book of Ophthalmology, 1896, 1900, 1909. Contbr. to proc. of med. socs. Home: 1686 Summit St, Office: 137 E. State St., Columbus, O. Died July 27, 1935.

WRIGHT, Leroy A., lawyer; b. New London, Ind., Feb. 10, 1863; s. Luna C. and Gulielma (Easterling) W.; student Kan. State College, 1881-84; m. Ida Heffleman, June 1, 1898; children—Lester A. (dec.), Evelyn (Mrs. Ivan Messenger). Began as publisher, 1885; editor Western Sch. Jour., 1883-85; city editor San Diego (Calif.) Union, 1888-89, San Diego Daily Sun, 1889-1900; admitted to Calif. bar, 1891, and since in practice of law at San Diego; formerly mem. Wright, Monroe, Harden & Thomas; sr. mem. Wright, Thomas & Dorman since 1940; pres. U. S. Grant Co., holding company, San Diego, since 1919; dir. U.S. Grant Hotel & Office Bldg. Co., Southern Title & Trust Co., Peoples Finance & Thrift Co. Mem. Calif. State Senate, 1907-15; pres. Bd. of Library Trustees, San Diego, 1904-09; dir. of Parks, San Diego, 1909-15. Pres. San Diego Hist. Soc., 1939-41. Republican. Elk. Club: Cuyamaca (San Diego). Home: 2470 B St. Office: Southern Title Bldg., 948 Third Av., San Diego, Calif.* Died Mar. 14, 1944.

WRIGHT, Merle St. Croix, Unitarian clergyman; b. Boston, Aug. 30, 1859; s. Edwin W.; grad. Harvard, 1881, A.M., 1884; grad. Harvard Divinity Sch., 1887; m. Louise Wilson, Mar. 20, 1895. Pastor church at Lenox Av. and 121st St., New York, since 1887. Home: 215 W. 126th St., New York. Deceased.

WRIGHT, Milton, author, editor; b. Pittsburgh, Pa., Dec. 30, 1887; s. William Charles and Mary Elizabeth (Jones) W.; LL.B., Brooklyn Law Sch. (St. Lawrence U.), 1910; student Wesleyan U., 1910-11; m. Leah Holmes Nathan, Mar. 10, 1913; children—Leah Mary (Mrs. George Taylor Conklin, Jr.), Helen Milton (Mrs. Richard Malcolm Blake), Barbara Milton. Admitted to N.Y. bar, 1911; reporter Brooklyn Daily Eagle, 1911-14; reporter and editor New York City News Assn., 1914-17; sec. Foreign Lang. Div., Liberty Loan Com., 1917-19; dir. Ukrainian Nat. Com., 1920-21; asso. editor Scientific Am., 1925-29; campaign publicity dir. various orgns., 1921-25, and since 1929; cons. expert U.S. Treasury Defense Savings Staff, 1941. Methodist. Mason. Author: Inventions, Patents and Trade Marks, 1927; How to Get Publicity, 1935; Getting Along with People, 1935; The Art of Conversation, 1936; Managing Yourself, 1938; Public Relations for Business, 1939; What's Funny and Why, 1939; Building Business for Your Bank, 1940. Editor-in-chief of Milton Wright's Library of Business Management (6 vols.), 1939. Contbr. to Your Life, Banking, etc.; lecturer on human nature and business. Died Dec. 29, 1941.

WRIGHT, Moorhead, banker; b. Little Rock, Ark., June 18, 1872; s. William Fulton and Louisa (Watkins) W.; grad. as cadet capt. Va. Mil. Inst., Lexington, Va., 1892; studied medicine, U. of Ark., 1 yr.; m. Hildegarde O. Penzel, Nov. 25, 1903; children—Charles Penzel, Moorhead, Fulton Watkins. Began as collector of rents, Cornish & England, Little Rock, 1893; became connected with S. J. Johnson & Co., bankers and brokers, 1894, and elected treas. upon incorporation, 1899; company developed into Union Trust Co., of which was made v.p. and treas., 1911, pres., 1915-28, chmn. bd., 1928-35; chmn. of bd. United Corp.; was dir. and chmn. bd. Little Rock Branch Federal Reserve Bank of St. Louis; v.p. of Southwest Joint Stock Land Bank; v.p. and dir. Commonwealth Federal Savings and Loan Assn. Served as 1st lt. and adjt. 2d Ark. Infantry Vols., Spanish-Am. War; mem. Ark. Council of Defense and state chmn. Nat. War Savings Com., World War. Pres. Little Rock Clearing House Assn., Little Rock Community Chest; mem. bd. govs. Little Rock Chamber Commerce. Mem. Am. Bankers Assn. (exec. council), Assn. Reserve City Bankers, Ark. Bankers Assn. (ex-pres.), Nat. Aeronautic Assn. (pres. Little Rock Chapter), Nat. Assn. Real Estate Exchanges, etc. Episcopalian. Clubs: Athletic Assn. (ex-pres.), Quapaw, Little Rock Country (ex-pres.), Spring Lake. Home: 2221 N. Palm St. Office: Union Nat. Bank Bldg., Little Rock, Ark. Died May 27, 1945.

WRIGHT, Orville, inventor; b. Dayton, O., Aug. 19, 1871; s. Milton and Susan Catharine (Koerner) W.; ed. pub. and high schs. to 1890; hon. B.S., Earlham Coll., Ind., 1909, LL.D., 1931; Dr. Tech. Sci., Royal Tech. Coll., Munich, 1909; LL.D., Oberlin, 1910, Harvard Univ., 1930, Huntington (Ind.) Coll., 1935; Sc.D., Trinity, 1915, Cincinnati, 1917, Ohio State U., 1930; M.A., Yale, 1919; Dr. Engring., Univ. of Michigan, 1924; D.Sc., Otterbein Coll., Westville, Ohio, 1947; Doctor of Engineering, University of Dayton, 1943; unmarried. With his late brother, Wilbur, was the first to fly with a heavier-than-air machine, Dec. 17, 1903, and with him the inventor of the system of control used in flying machines of today; dir. Wright Aeronautical Laboratory, Dayton, O. Awarded the Collier trophy, 1913, for development of the automatic stabilizer; gold medals: Aero Club of France, 1908; Aero Club of United Kingdom, 1908; Acad. of Sports of France, 1908; Aeronautical Soc. Gt. Britain, 1908; Congress of U.S., 1909; State of Ohio, 1909; City of Dayton, 1909; Aero Club America, 1909; French Acad. Sciences, 1909; Cross of Chevalier of Legion of Honor, French, 1909; Cross of Officer of Legion of Honor, 1924; Langley medal, Smithsonian Inst., 1910; Elliott Cresson medal, Franklin Inst., 1914; Albert medal, Royal Soc. Arts, 1917; The John Fritz medal, 1920; bronze medal, International Peace Society; The John Scott medal, 1925; Washington award, 1927; Distinguished Flying Cross awarded, Feb, 1929; Daniel Guggenheim medal, 1930; Franklin medal, 1933; Medal for Merit, 1947; hon. mem. Aero Club of Sarthe, France, Aeronautical Society, Great Britain, Aero Club of United Kingdom, Osterreichischen Flugtechnischen Vereines, Vienna, Verein Deutscher Flugtechniker, Berlin, American Society Mech. Engrs., Aeronautical Soc. America, Nat. Aeronautic Assn. (gov. at large, 1929-39), Nat. Exchange Club, Ohio Society of New York, Inst. of Aeronautical Science, 1932, Franklin Inst., Nat. Fedn. Post Office Clerks, Inst. of Mech. Engrs., London, Air Line Pilots Assn., Inc.; hon. fellow Royal Aeronautical Soc.; mem. Nat. Inventors Council, Nat. Acad. Sciences, Nat. Museum Engring. and Industry (v.p., 1924), Nat. Adv. Com. for Aeronautics, A.A. A.S., Franklin Inst., S.A.E., Engineers' Club of Dayton (hon. life); hon. scout Boy Scouts America. Mem. Daniel Guggenheim Fund for Promotion of Aeronautics; chmn. advisory com., Daniel Guggenheim Sch. of Aeronautics, New York Univ.; hon. Aircraft Pilot Certificate No. 1, issued by Civil Aeronautics Authority, 1940. Home: Park and Harmon Avs. Office: 15 N. Broadway, Dayton, O. Died Jan. 30, 1948; buried Woodlawn Cemetery, Dayton.

WRIGHT, Peter Clark, church official; b. Merton, Wis., Nov. 27, 1870; s. Charles and Phoebe Robinson (Mead) W.; grad. Wayland Acad., Beaver Dam, Wis., 1891; A.B., Brown U., 1895, D.D., 1917; B.D., Div. Sch., U. of Chicago, 1902; m. Alice Eugenia McIntyre, June 25, 1895 (died June 16, 1929); children—Charles Eugene, Burchard Updyke, Stuart Mead, Harmon McIntyre; m. 2d, Mrs. Cornelia Parish Updyke, Nov. 7, 1930 (dec. 1936); m. 3d, Irene M. Lamb, Sept. 24, 1937. Ordained Bapt. ministry, 1895; pastor successively Central Ch., Norwich, Conn., Gethsemane Ch., Phila., Asylum Av. Ch., Hartford, Conn., until 1920. Mem. bd. and exec. com. Conn. Bapt. Conv., 1902-13; mem. Ministers and Missionaries Benefit Bd., Northern Bapt. Conv., 1911-20, rec. sec., 1911-26, asso. sec., 1920-26, exec. sec., 1926-40; consultant sec. since 1940; clk. Northern Bapt. Conv., 1911-26; del. from Northern Bapt. Conv. to Federal Council of Chs. of Christ in America, 1928-40, chairman delegation, 1931-36; member Advisory Com. Federal Council Chs. of Christ in America, 1933-40; mem. Universal Christian Council for Life and Work, Am. Sect., 1932-40. Republican. Home: 19824 Carpenter Av., Hollis, N.Y. Office: 152 Madison Av., New York, N.Y. Died May 4, 1947.

WRIGHT, Richard Robert, educator, banker; b. Dalton, Ga., May 16, 1855; s. Robert Waddell and Harriet (Lynch) W.; A.B., Atlanta U., 1876, A.M., 1879; LL.D., Wilberforce, 1899; m. Lydia Elizabeth Howard, June 7, 1877; children—Richard Robert, Julia O., Mrs. Essie W. Thompson, Mrs. Lillian M. Clayton, Dr. Whittier H., Mrs. Edwina Mitchell, Emanuel C., Mrs. Harriet W. Lemon. Prin. Ware High Sch., 1880-91; pres. Ga. State Industrial Coll., 1891-1921; pres. Citizens & Southern Bank & Trust Co. of Phila. since 1921. Served in Spanish-Am. War as an additional paymaster with rank of major vols., Aug. 3-Dec. 1, 1898. Organizer and pres. Georgia State Agrl. and Industrial Assn.; anniversary speaker Am. Missionary Assn., 1907; trustee Atlanta Univ., 1880-98. Del. 4 Rep. nat. convs.; declined appointment E.E. and M.P. to Liberia, tendered by Pres. McKinley. Traveled extensively in Europe. Methodist. Mason (33°), Elk. Mem. Am. Acad. Polit. and Social Science. Pres. Nat. Assn. of Presidents of A. and M. Colleges for Negroes; pres. Nat. Assn. Teachers in Colored Schools, 1900-06; pres. Nat. Negro Bankers Assn., 1908-12. Secured passage of an act by U.S. Senate for appropriation of $250,000 to promote Semi-Centennial Emancipation Exhbn., 1913. Apptd. by gov. Ga. chmn. Colored Assn. Council of Food Production and Conservation; apptd. by gov. of Ga. as Negro historian of enlisted colored troops in France, and visited Eng., France and Belgium to collect hist. data for the archives of Ga. and for a book on the Negro in the Great War. Mem. Spanish-Am. War Veterans, Phila. Business League (pres.). Apptd. by Gov. J. S. Fisher of Pa. mem. commn. to erect a statue in memory of the colored soldiers in all Am. wars. Promoter of Youths' Thrift Clubs, 1933-35. Promoted Good-Will Airplane trip to Haiti, 1939. Author and inspirer of the idea of first U.S. postage stamp named for a Negro (Booker T. Washington postage stamp). Founder and organizer Nat. Freedom Day, 1941, celebrating anniversary of adoption of 13th Amendment. Received Muriel Dobbins Vocational School 1946 Pioneers of Industry Award for service to community by Bd. of Edn. Home: 554 N. 58th St. Office: 1849 South St., Philadelphia, Pa. Died July 2, 1947.

WRIGHT, R(obert) Charlton, retired publisher, editor and journalist; b. Guyton, Ga., Jan. 2, 1873; s. William Albion and Theodora (Patterson) W.; ed. pub. schs., Savannah and Waycross, Ga.; m. Anne Jane Yarnes, Sept. 28, 1902. Newspaper reporter, 1890-95; ry. advertising and transportation business, 1895-1905; with pub. utilities, Columbia, S.C., 1903-16; owner, pub. and editor Columbia Record, 1916-29 (retired). Mem. S.A.R., Sigma Delta Chi, Blue Key (U. of S.C.). Democrat. Episcopalian. Author: Plain Talks on the Constitution, 1935. Contbr. many articles and poems to mags. and newspapers. Lecturer and traveler. Home: Weirbluff, Weirsdale, Fla. Died Feb. 12, 1947.

WRIGHT, Roydon Vincent, editor; b. Red Wing, Minn., Oct. 8, 1876; s. Reuben Andrus and Louisa Anna (Schaefer) W.; prep. edn., high sch., St. Paul; M.E., U. of Minn., 1898; hon. Dr. Engring., Stevens Inst. Tech., 1931; m. Eliza Grumman Bratton, Oct. 7, 1901; children—Catharine Louisa (Mrs. William Claire Menninger), Dorothy Elizabeth (Mrs. Henry Edwards Sharpe), Esther McCay (dec.), Josephine Anne. Machinist apprentice, C.,M.&St.P. Ry., 1898-99; spl. apprentice, etc., C.G.W. Ry., 1899-1901; mech. engr., P.&L.E. R.R., 1901-04; asso. editor American Engineer and Railroad Journal, 1904-05, editor, 1905-10; mech. dept. editor Railway Age Gazette, 1910-11; mng. editor Railway Age, and editor Railway Mechanical Engineer, since Dec. 1911; v.p. and sec. Simmons-Boardman Pub. Corp.; also editor Locomotive Cyclopedia, Car Builders' Cyclopedia, Material Handling Cyclopedia; lecturer on citizenship, Newark Coll. of Engring. Dir. Ampere (N.J.) Bank & Trust Co. Pres. Nat. Conf. of Business Paper Editors, 1939-40; pres. Asso. Business Papers, Inc., 1940-41; trustee Am. Museum of Safety. Pres. John Fritz Medal Board, 1935; pres. United Engineering Soc., 1928-29. Hon. mem. and fellow Am. Soc. Mechanical Engineers (mem. bd. of public affairs and chairman com. on engineers civic responsibility; v.p. 1926-27, pres. 1931); member of New York Railroad Club (exec. com.), Silver Bay Association (pres.), Franklin Institute, Newcomen Society, Sigma Xi, Beta Theta Pi, Pi Tau Sigma (hon.). Vice-pres. Y.M.C.A. of Oranges; mem. transportation and program services committees Nat. Council Y.M.C.A.; chmn. Silver Bay Industrial Conf., 1936-37; mem. administration bd., Committee on Friendly Relations among Foreign Students; v.p. Nat. Safety Council, 1941-42. Mem. adv. bd. Dept. of Smoke Regulation, Hudson County, N.J.; freeholder, Essex County, N.J., 1935-37, State Senator, 1942 to 1947. Republican. (mem. State Com., 1940-43). Presbyterian. Clubs: Engineers, Railroad-Machinery. Co-author with Eliza G. Wright of "How to Be a Responsible Citizen." Author of a manual on citizenship (for Am. Soc. Mech. Engrs.). Contbr. to "Toward Civilization,"

1930. Home: 398 N. Walnut St., East Orange, N.J. Office: 30 Church St., New York. Died July 9, 1948.

WRIGHT, Walter Livingston, Jr., historian; born Lincoln Univ., Pa., May 15, 1900; s. Walter Livingston and Jean (Carr) W.; A.B., Princeton, 1921, Ph.D., 1928; A.M., Am. U. of Beirut, Syria, 1924; m. Katharine Hine Fenning, Sept. 10, 1928; children—Walter Livingston, Frederick Fenning. Instr. history and English, Am. U. of Beirut, 1921-25; grad. fellow in history, Princeton, 1925-30, resident research Turkish lang. and history, 1928-30; asst. prof. history, Princeton, 1930-35; pres. Am. Coll. for Girls, also Robert Coll., both Istanbul, Turkey, 1935-44; chief historian War Dept. Gen. Staff since Nov. 1943. sec. and expert on Turkish history and affairs, Hines-Kemmerer Econ. Mission to Turkey, 1934; chief Near East Sect., U.S. Office Coordinator of Information, Washington, D.C., Sept. 1941-Feb. 1942. Fellow in Near East Affairs, Library of Congress, 1943. Served in S.A.T.C., Princeton, 1918. Trustee Am. Coll. for Girls, Am. Hosp. of Istanbul. Mem. Am. Hist. Assn., Am. Oriental Soc., Am. Military Institute. Author: Ottoman Statecraft, 1935; also articles and reviews. Address: 3133 Connecticut Av. N.W., Washington 8, D.C. Died Jan. 17, 1946.

WRIGHT, Wilfred L., chmn. Savage Arms Corp.; b. Sioux City, Ia., May 18, 1877; s. Craig L. and Katherine (Van Dyke) W.; M.E., Cornell U., 1900; m. Margery White, Nov. 24, 1903; children—Craig, Hamilton. Pres. Savage Arms Corp., 1919-40, chmn. bd. since 1940; chmn. bd. Sipp-Eastwood Corp., Paterson, N.J. Clubs: University, Uptown (New York); Garden City Golf, Cherry Valley Golf (Garden City, L.I.). Home: Hempstead, L.I., N.Y. Office: 60 E. 42d St., New York, N.Y. Died Nov. 10, 1947.

WRIGHT, William Mason, army officer; b. Newark, N.J., Sept. 24, 1863; s. Edward H. and Dora M. W.; cadet U.S. Mil. Acad., July 1, 1882-Jan. 11, 1883; grad. Inf. and Cav. Sch., 1891; m. Marjorie Jerauld, June 1891; children—William Mason, Jerauld, Marjorie. Commd. 2d lt., 2d Inf., Jan. 19, 1885; 1st lt. 5th Inf., Dec. 17, 1891; trans. to 2d Inf., Feb. 9, 1892; capt. a.a.g. vols., May 20, 1898; hon. discharged vols., May 12, 1899; capt. U.S. Army, Mar. 2, 1899; promoted through grades to brig. gen. May 15, 1917; maj. gen. N.A., Aug. 5, 1917; maj. gen. regular army, Mar. 7, 1921. Participated in Santiago Campaign, 1898, later in subduing Philippine Insurrection; duty Gen. Staff, 1905-08; with Gen. Funston, at Vera Cruz, 1914; apptd. comdr. 35th Div., Sept. 1917; comd. 35th Div. with British, May 1-June 6, 1918, 3d, 5th and 7th corps A.E.F., in the Vosges, 89th Div. during the St. Mihiel and Meuse-Argonne offensives, and 1st Corps, Nov. 12, 1918-Mar. 22, 1919; dep. chief of staff, U.S. Army, Jan. 1920-July 1921; comdg. 9th Corps Area, July 1921; comdg. Philippine Dept., Feb.-Sept. 1922; retired Dec. 31, 1922. Awards: D.S.M., Knight Comdr. St. Michael and St. George, Comdr. Legion Honor, Grand Officier Order Leopold, Order Rising Sun, Croix de Guerre with Palm. Clubs: Union (New York); Metropolitan, Alibi (Washington). Address: War Dept., Washington, D.C. Died Aug. 16, 1943.

WROTH, Edward Pinkney, bishop; b. Darlington, Md., Jan. 11, 1889; s. Edward Worrell and Margaret Gilpin (Price) W.; A.B., Trinity Coll., 1915; B.D., Va. Theol. Sem., 1917, D.D. (hon.), 1944, Grove City Coll., 1945; m. Marjorie Virginia Hamill, May 24, 1920; children—Edward Pinkney, Ralph Lane, Mary Elizabeth. Ordained to ministry of Protestant Episcopal Ch., 1917; asso. rector Christ Ch., Baltimore, Md., 1917-18; rector Holy Trinity Ch., Baltimore, Md., 1918-19; asso. rector Ch. of The Ascension, Washington, 1919-20; rector St. Peter's Ch., Poolesville, Md. and Christ Ch., Barnesville, Md., 1920-22, St. Philip's Ch., Laurel, Md., 1922-25, Christ Ch., Georgetown, Washington, 1925-30, Trinity Memorial Ch., Warren Ch., 1930-43; bishop Diocese of Erie, since 1943. Chmn. Community Chest, Warren, Pa., Erie County Health and Tuberculosis Christmas Seal Sale (mem. bd. dirs.); sec. Library Bd., Warren, Pa., Crippled Children's Com., Warren County, Pa.; pres. Shakespeare Club, Warren, Pa.; mem. bd. dirs. Erie County Guidance Center, Council of Social Agencies, Erie, Pa.; mem. exec. council, Province Washington; mem. bd. trustees, The Soc. of the Protestant Episcopal Ch. for Advancement of Christianity in Pa. Pres. Mental Hygiene Soc. Northwestern Pa., vice pres. Erie Chapter Newcomen Soc., Washington Trail Council Boy Scouts Am. Address: 323 W. 6th St., Erie, Pa. Died June 22, 1946.

WULLING, Frederick John (wŭl'ĭng), pharmacologist; b. Brooklyn, N.Y., Dec. 24, 1866; s. John J. and Louise C. (Muns) W.; grad. business coll., 1884; grad. Columbia U. Coll. Pharmacy, 1887; Pharm.D., U. of Minn., 1894, LL.B., 1896, LL.M., 1898; hon. Pharm.M., Phila. Coll. Pharmacy, 1917, hon. Sc.D. Columbia U., 1929; ednl. trips to Eng., Germany, France, 1887, 89, 94, 97, 1911; m. Lucile Truth Gissel, 1897; 1 son, Emerson G. Prof. inorganic pharmaco-diagnosis, Brooklyn Coll. Pharmacy, 1891-92; dean of faculty and prof. pharmacology, Coll. of Pharmacy, 1892-1936, dir. medicinal plant garden, 1911-1936, U. of Minn. Retired with the title of Emeritus Dean, 1936. Asso. editor Pharm. Record, 1887-91. Trustee U.S. Pharmacopœial Conv., 1920-30. Pres. Am. Conf. Pharm. Faculties, 1914-15; pres. Am. Pharm. Assn., 1916-17; fellow A.A.A.S.; emeritus mem. Am. Chem. Soc.; mem. Minn. State Pharmaceutical Assn. (honorary life president since 1943), Minn. Academy Sciences (chairman 1910-30), Minneapolis Soc. Fine Arts (dir.); hon. mem. N.J. State Pharm. Assn., Phi Delta Chi, Gamma Mu, Rho Chi, etc. Clubs: Automobile, Campus, Country, Dinner, Art, Lafayette, etc. Author: Evolution of Botany, 1891; Medical and Pharmaceutical Chemistry, 1894; Chemistry of the Carbon Compounds, 1900; A Course in Law, 1908, The Pharmacist's Relation to the Public, 1931; Charles F. Chandler: A Retrospect, 1944; Peter Wendover Bedford: A Retrospect, 1945; The First Four Melendy Memorial Lectures, 1946. Contbr. to various tech. and other jours. Wulling Hall, U. of Minn. bldg., named in his honor, 1942. Home: 3305 2d Av. S., Minneapolis 8, Minn.; (summer) Felstow, Excelsior, Minn. Died Oct. 21, 1947.

WURLITZER, Rudolph H. (wûr'lĭt-zẽr), mfr. musical instruments; b. Cincinnati, Ohio, Dec. 30, 1873; s. Rudolph and Leonie (Farny) W.; ed. Woodward High Sch., Cincinnati; hon. Ph.D., U. of Berlin; m. Marie Richard, Jan. 31, 1900; children—Marianne (Mrs. J. M. Hutton, Jr.), Janet (Mrs. Sells Stites), Rembert, Natalie (Mrs. William E. Griess), Annette (Mrs. Frederic Barnes Knoop). Chmn. bd. Rudolph Wurlitzer Co., mfrs. musical instruments, Cincinnati. Violin expert; retired from private business to give full time to war work as exec. sec. Hamilton County (O.) Conservation Com. and coordinator for War Prodn. Bd., since June 1942. Home: 2147 Madison Rd. Office: 121 E. 4th St., Cincinnati, O. Died May 27, 1948.

WURTSMITH, Paul Bernard, army officer; b. Detroit, Mich., Aug. 9, 1906; s. Fred and Ella (Globensky) W.; student Holy Redeemer School; grad. Cass Tech. High Sch.; student U. of Detroit, 1925-27; m. Irene Catherine Gillespie Kloehr, June 6, 1933. Entered Army Air Corps, 1927; commd. 2d lt., 1928; promoted through grades to brig. gen., Feb. 1943; now maj. gen.; assigned to 50th Pursuit Group, Selfridge Field, Jan. 1941; assignment, Australia, Jan. 1942; returned to U.S., Aug. 1946; stationed MacDill Field, near Tampa, Fla. Decorated D.S.M. Home: 1318 Schley Av., San Antonio, Tex. Died Sept. 13, 1946; buried in Arlington National Cemetery.

WU TING-FANG, diplomatist; b. Hsin-hui dist., Kwangtung, China; ed. in Chinese literature and classics at Canton, in English at Hong Kong; studied English law and internat. law and other legal subjects, Lincoln's Inn, London, 1874; called to English bar; returned to China from England, 1877; LL.D., Univ. of Pa., 1900; married. Practiced as barrister at Hong Kong until 1882; apptd., 1882, by Li Hung Chang, Viceroy of Chihli, as legal adviser and dep. for fgn. affairs in Tientsin. Became promoter and chief dir. Kai Ping Ry. Co., and built first ry. in China; later apptd. by Imperial govt. co-dir. in Railway Bureau, constructing rys. in North China; apptd. chief dir. Tientsin Univ., on its establishment, 1895; first sec. of embassy of peace missions to Japan, 1895, and plenipotentiary for exchanging ratifications of peace treaty, effected at Chefoo; also assisted in negotiating, at Peking, Chino-Japanese treaty of Commerce and Navigation, ratified Oct., 1896; E.E. and M.P. of China to U.S., Spain and Peru, 1897-1902; reappointed E.E. and M.P. to U.S., 1907. Author numerous articles on China in Am. magazines. Address: Chinese Legation, Washington. Died June 23, 1922.

WYETH, Newell Convers, artist; b. Needham, Mass., Oct. 22, 1882; s. Andrew Newell and Henriette (Zirngiebel) W.; ed. Mechanics Art High Sch., Mass. Normal Art Sch., Eric Pape's Art Sch., all of Boston; studied with C.W. Reed and Howard Pyle; m. Carolyn Brenneman Bockius, Apr. 16, 1906; children—Henriette Zirngiebel, Carolyn Brenneman, Nathaniel Convers, Ann, Andrew. Principal works: Decorations of Grill room, Traymore Hotel, Atlantic City, N.J.; large panels, Mo. State Capitol, representing two battles of Civil War; two historic panels, Federal Reserve Bank and 5 large murals in New First Nat. Bank, Boston; triptych in dining room of Hotel Roosevelt, N.Y. City; 5 panels in Hubbard Memorial Bldg., Nat. Geographic Soc., Washington; large mural in Franklin Savings Bank, N.Y. City; mural panel, Penn. Mut. Life Ins. Co. Bldg., Phila.; triptych in the reredos of the Chapel of the Holy Spirit, Nat. Episcopal Cathedral, Washington, D.C.; a mural depicting the Builders of St. Andrew's School, St. Andrew's Episcopal School for Boys, Middletown, Del.; 10 mural paintings, Met. Life Ins. Bldg., N.Y. City. Awarded gold medal, San Francisco Expn., 1915; Beck prize, Pa. Acad. Fine Arts, 1910; 4th Clark prize, for painting, Corcoran Art Gallery, Washington, D.C., 1932. Has illustrated 20 juvenile classics. Mem. Nat. Acad. Republican. Unitarian. Home: Chadds Ford, Pa. Died Oct. 19, 1945.

WYMAN, Walter Scott, pub. utilities; b. Oakland, Me., May 6, 1874; s. Hiram and Ellen Augusta (Frizzell) W.; prep. edn., Coburn Classical Inst., Waterville, Me.; student Tuft's Coll., 1893-96; m. Alice Mabel Bartlett, Nov. 25, 1897; children—William Frizzell, Katherine Bartlett (Mrs. Howard Ingraham), Dorothy May (Mrs. Charles Hildreth), Margaret Ellen (Mrs. Robert P. Hazzard, Jr.). Asst. supt. Me. Water Co., 1896-99; gen. mgr. Waterville, Fairfield & Oakland Ry., 1899-1901; established, 1901, light and power business under title of the Messalonskee Electric Co., title changed, 1910, to Central Me. Power Co., of which was treas. and gen. mgr., pres. since 1924 (business grown from $1,500 a year to $7,000,000), pres. N.E. Pub. Service Co., owning stock of various pub. utilities in Me., N.H., Vt.; pres. Maine Seaboard Paper Co., Public Service Co. of N.H., Androscoggin Mills, Bates Mfg. Co. and Hill Mfg. Co. (Lewiston, Me.), Edwards Mfg. Co. (Augusta, Me.), York Mfg. Co. (Saco, Me.). Pres. Augusta Water Dist.; trustee Colby Coll. Fellow Am. Inst. Elec. Engrs. Republican. Mason. Shriner. Clubs: Abnaki, Augusta Country, Union League (New York); Cumberland (Portland, Me.). Home: 49 Western Av. Office: 9 Green St., Augusta, Me. Died Nov. 15, 1942.

WYNKOOP, Asa (wīn'kōōp), librarian; b. Saugerties, N.Y., Sept. 6, 1863; s. Mynderse and Mary Elizabeth (Schoonmaker) W.; A.B., Rutgers, 1887, A.M., 1907; student Sch. of Philosophy (Columbia), 1890-92; grad. Union Theol. Sem., 1892; studied U. of Marburg, 1902, grad. N.Y. State Library Sch., 1905; M.L.S., U. of the State of N.Y., 1919; D.L.S., Rutgers U., 1927; m. May Simpson Stratton, Nov. 19, 1904; 1 son, Stratton. Teacher Collegiate Grammar Sch., N.Y. City, 1887-89; fellow Columbia, 1892-94; ordained Presbyn. ministry, 1893; pastor Trinity Ch., South Orange, N.J., 1893-1901; apptd. state insp. pub. libraries, Albany, N.Y., 1905; founder, 1907, and editor "New York Libraries"; dir. Library Institutes, State of N.Y., also dir. Library Extension Div., 1926. Dir. library publicity in N.Y. for U.S. Food Adminstrn., 1917-19. Mem. N.Y. Library Assn. (pres. 1926-27), Phi Beta Kappa, Delta Upsilon. Republican. Presbyterian. Club: Valley Hunt (Pasadena). Author: Library Commns., State Aid and State Agencies, 1913. Compiler: Outlines for Library Insts. (Univ. State of N.Y.), 1914-27. Home: 480 Prospect Blvd., Pasadena, Calif. Died Oct. 21, 1942.

WYNNE, Shirley Wilmott, physician; b. New York City, Nov. 21, 1882; s. William Harmon and Julia T. (Hooper) W.; M.D., Coll. of Physicians and Surgeons, Columbia, 1904; D.P.H., New York U., 1919; m. Agnes G. Edwards, 1904; children—Shirley Wilmott, Ethel G., Harmon E. Intern City Hosp. and St. Francis Hosp., N.Y. City, 1904; began practice at N.Y. City, 1905; med. insp. Dept. of Health, City of New York, 1907-11, asst. registrar, 1911-15, chief of div. statis. research, 1915-20, asst. to commr., 1920-24, dir. of hosps., 1924-26, dep. commr., 1926-28, commr. of health, 1928-33; cons. physician Willard Parker Hosp., Midtown Hosp.; pres. Children's Welfare Fedn.; pres. Associated Health Foundation, Inc.; chmn. medical com. Boy Scout Foundation. Formerly prof. preventive medicine N.Y. Polyclinic Med. Sch. and Hosp.; formerly trustee N.Y. State Hosp. for Incipient Tuberculosis. Mem. Phi Kappa Sigma. Democrat. Catholic. Clubs: Columbia University, City (chmn. pub. health com.), Nat. Democratic. Home: Harmon-on-Hudson, N.Y. Office: 133 E. 58th St., New York, N.Y. Died Apr. 19, 1942.

Y

YANCEY, Edward Burbridge, industrialist; b. Harrisonburg, Va., Jan. 26, 1888; s. John Gibbon and Frances (Bradley) Y.; B.A., U. of Va., 1908, M.A., 1908; m. Jessie A. Willits, Oct. 25, 1913. With E. I. Du Pont de Nemours & Co. since 1908, chemist, conducting chem. research on T.N.T. and other explosives, 1908-17, asst. plant mgr. Repauno, N.J., 1919-23, mgr. similar explosives plants at Louviers, Colo., Joplin, Mo., and Birmingham, Ala., 5 yrs., became gen. mgr. explosives dept., 1935, elected to bd. dirs., 1938, vice pres. and mem. exec. com. since 1944. Mason (Shriner). Clubs: Country, Whist (Wilmington); Hickory Mt. (North Carolina); Delaware Turf. Home: Old Kennett Rd., R. 1, Wilmington. Office: DuPont Bldg., Wilmington, Del. Died Oct. 24, 1948.

YANTIS, George Franklin (yănt'ĭs), lawyer; b. Olympia, Wash., Oct. 28, 1885; s. John Vivian and Margaret (Hume) Y.; LL.B., U. of Wis., 1913; m. Ruth Louise Tower, June 21, 1913; children—George Franklin, Grace Louise (Mrs. William M. Lowry), Richard Tower. Admitted to Wash. bar, 1913, and since in private practice; prosecuting atty., Thurston County (Wash.), 1915-16; mem. Washington House of Representatives, 1931-37, 1945-47, speaker 1933-1945; chairman Northwest Regional Planning Commission, 1937-39; member Nat. Resources Planning Bd. since 1939. Dir. Am. Soc. Planning Officials; pres. Northwest Regional Council of Planning, Edn. and Pub. Adminstrn.; mem. Com. on Public Administration, Social Science Research Council, Wash. State Bar Assn. Democrat. Presbyn. Home: West Bay Drive. Office: First Nat. Bank Bldg., Olympia, Wash. Died Dec. 28, 1947.

YARD, Robert Sterling, editor, executive; b. Haverstraw, N.Y., Feb. 1, 1861; s. Robert Boyd and Sarah (Purdue) Y.; A.B., Princeton, 1883; m. Mary Belle Moffat, June 4, 1895. In shipping business with W. R. Grace & Co., 1884-87; reporter New York Sun, 1888-91; editor New York Herald, 1891-1900; mgr. book pub. business of R. H. Russell, 1900-01; mgr. book advertising Charles Scribner's Sons, 1901-05; editor The Lamp, 1903-05; editor in chief Moffat, Yard & Co., 1905-11; organizing sec. Nat. Citizens' League for Promotion of Sound Banking System, 1911-12; editor in chief, The Century Magazine, 1913-14; chief ednl. sect. Nat. Park Service, Dept. of Interior, 1914-19; organizer, 1919, and gen. sec. Nat. Parks Assn.

to 1934; editor National Park Bull., 1919-36, National Park News Service, 1926-36, news circulars, and other publications; sec. Joint Com. on Survey of Federal Lands, 1925-30; sec. Advisory Bd. on Educational and Inspirational Uses of Nat. Parks, 1927-32; founder, exec. sec. Wilderness Society, 1935-37, president and permanent secretary since 1937. Trustee and mgr. Robert Marshall Wilderness Trust since 1941. Fellow American Geographical Society, California Academy of Sciences. Club: Cosmos (Washington). Author: The Publisher, 1915; Glimpses of Our National Parks, 1916; The National Parks Portfolio, 1916; The Top of the Continent, 1917; The Book of the National Parks, 1919; Our Federal Lands, 1928; also monographs, mag. articles, etc. Editor Living Wilderness, Wilderness News. Home: 1840 Mintwood Place, Washington 9, D.C. Died May, 1945.

YATES, Charles Colt (yāts), shipping exec.; b. Binghamton, N.Y., Feb. 14, 1868; s. W. Lloyd and Charlotte (Colt) Y.; B.S. in Physics, Case Sch. Applied Science, Cleveland, 1890, M.S. in civ. engring., 1897; m. Lette Wise, Nov. 16, 1896 (died June 4, 1937); 1 son, Charles Forrest (dec.); m. 2d, Anne Louise McCrone, January 12, 1944. Entered field service U.S. Coast and Geodetic Survey, 1892, making the great trigonometrical survey in Rocky Mountains, hydrographic and geodetic surveys in Gulf of Mexico, Alaska, Canada, and New England; comdg. officer survey vessel Endeavor, 1898-99; investigation European hydrographic instns. including short cruises on British Navy Hydrographic Vessel "Research" and French Navy Hydrographic Vessel "Chemere," 1900; exec. officer survey vessel Pathfinder in Alaska and P.I., 1901-02; design and constrn. of the Fathomer, at Hongkong, and then comdg. officer in Philippines, 1903-05; triangulation Chesapeake Bay and rep. of Govt. on Md. and Del. oyster surveys, 1906-12; comdg. officer Bache, in hydrographic surveys and oceanographic cruise to Bermudas and W.I., 1913-14; in charge purchase and constrn. new survey vessels, 1915-16; entered U.S. Shipping Bd. as expert in marine affairs, Dec. 1916, and assisted Bernard N. Baker preparing plans orgn.; shipping mgr. and rep. U.S. Shipping Bd. at New York, 1917-19, operating at one time 128 ocean going ships with a personnel of 7,819 officers and crew afloat. Pres. Conn. Terminal Co. since 1919; consulting engr. with Harrison Williams on deep sea explorations, 1924-26. Mem. Am. Soc. C.E., Am. Geog. Soc., New York Geneal. and Biog. Soc. Episcopalian. Clubs: Cosmos (Washington, D.C.); Engineers', Produce Exchange Luncheon, Lake Placid (N.Y.); Hongkong (Hongkong). Author of reports, charts and technical papers on surveying and marine affairs. Home: Portsmouth Apts., Washington, D.C. Address: 26 Beaver St., New York, N.Y. Died Mar. 5, 1944.

YATES, Cullen, artist; b. Bryan, O., Jan. 24, 1866; s. Franklin B. and Lavinia A. (Punches) Y.; ed. under William M. Chase, Leonard Ochtman, etc., Acad. Design, N.Y., Acad. Julian, École des Beaux Arts, Paris; m. Mabel Taylor, May 27, 1911; children—Richard C., Lavinia. Specialty landscapes; represented in Phila. Art Club, Lotos Club, William T. Evans collection, Nat. Gallery, Washington, Montclair (N.J.) Gallery, Brooklyn Inst. Arts and Sciences, St. Louis Mus., Seattle Gallery, Nat. Arts Club (New York), Mus. of History, Science and Art (Los Angeles, Calif.), Youngstown (O.) Museum of Art, Phila. Art Club, Westfield (Mass.) Art Collection, Portland (Ore.) Art Galleries, Buck Hill (Pa.) Art Assn. (purchase prize), Newark (N.J.) Museum of Art, and many private collections. Bronze medal, St. Louis Exposition, 1904; George Inness, Jr., prize, Salmagundi Club; Joseph Isidor prize, same, 1921; Nat. Arts Club medal, 1932. A.N.A., 1908, N.A., 1919. Mem. New York Society of Painters, American Water Color Society, New York Water Color Club, Allied Artists America, Artists' Aid Soc. Clubs: Lotos, Salmagundi, Nat. Arts, Century Assn. (New York). Home: Shawnee on Delaware, Monroe County, Pa. Address: National Arts Club, 15 Gramercy Park, New York, N.Y.* Deceased.

YAW, Ellen Beach, opera singer; b. Boston, N.Y.; d. Ambrose Spencer and Mary Jane (Beach) Yaw; studied singing under Mme. Hevor Torpadie in New York, and under Marchesi in Paris, France; m. Vere Goldthwaite, 1907 (died 1912); m. 2d, Franklin Cannon, 1920 (divorced). Début, St. Paul, 1894; toured U.S.; sang in Paris, Rome, Naples, 1905-09, Met. Opera House, New York, 1908, in Lucia; in Europe, 1925-26; repertoire includes leading soprano roles in Romeo and Juliet, Rigoletto, Puritani, Magic Flute, Faust, La Traviata, Don Giovanni, etc. Sang in U.S., 1927, 28. Opened Lark Ellen Echo Bowl on Covina Estate for summer symphony orchestra concerts, 1934. Organized open-air studio of singing, 1939. Home: Covina, Calif. Died Sept. 10, 1947.

YAWKEY, Cyrus Carpenter, lumber mfr.; b. Chicago, Ill., Aug. 29, 1862; s. Samuel W. and Mary Uliaetta (Carpenter) Y.; grad. Mich. Mil. Acad., Orchard Lake, 1881; m. Alice M. Richardson, Oct. 13, 1887; 1 dau., Leigh (Mrs. Aytchmonde P. Woodson). Began as clk., hardware store, Saginaw, Mich., 1881; mem. firm Yawkey & Corbyn, hardware merchants, 1884-89, Yawkey & Lee Lumber Co., 1889-93; sec. and gen. mgr. Yawkey Lumber Co., 1893-1903, pres. since 1903; chmn. bd. Marathan Paper Mills Co.; pres. Montana-Dakota Utilities Co.; v.p. Alexander-Yawkey Timber Co., Yawkey-Alexander Lumber Co., Ontonagon Fibre Corp., Wausau Paper Mills Co., Yawkey-Bissell Lumber Co.; dir. McCloud River Lumber Co., Masonite Corp., Tomahawk Kraft Paper Co., B.C. Spruce Mills, Wis Box Co., Marathon Electric Mfg. Corp. Capt., 1888, maj., 1889, Mich. N.G.; capt., 1917, maj., 1918, col., 1919, Wisconsin State Guards. Chmn. County Bd., Oneida County, Wis., 1891-93; mem., Wisconsin Assembly, 1894-96; pres. Marathon County Park Commn. since 1920. Republican. Universalist. Mason (32°, K.T.). Clubs: Rotary, Wausau, Wausau Country. Home: 403 McIndoe St. Office: First Am. State Bank Bldg., Wausau, Wis.* Died May 18, 1943.

YENS, Karl (Karl Julius Heinrich Jens) (yĕns), artist; b. Hamburg, Germany, Jan. 11, 1868; s. Christian Karl and Ottilie (Paech) J.; apprentice mural and decorative arts, 1884-87; art student Koniglich Kunst Gewerbe Museum, Germany, 1887-89; m. Helene Grote, 1897 (died 1907); children—Anna (wife of Rev. Dan Huntington Fenn), Otto, Elizabeth; m. 2d, Kate Petry (dec.); m. 3d, Elsie (Wiesner) Manz, Sept. 1926. Came to U.S., 1901, naturalized, 1916. Mural, portrait, landscape, flower painter, N.E., 1901-05, Washington, 1905-06, N.Y. City, 1907-10, Pasadena and Los Angeles, 1910-18, Laguna Beach, Calif., since 1918. Murals or paintings in City Hall, Altona, Germany; Country Club, Brookline, Mass.; Duquesne Club, Pittsburgh; Astor Theater, N.Y. City. Represented in the Museum of History, Science and Art, and William Henry Russell Collection, Los Angeles; Fine Arts Gallery, San Diego; Vanderpoel Art Assn., Chicago; High School, San Pedro, California; Charles W. Bowers Memorial Museum, Santa Ana Orange Court, Golden Gate Internat. Exposition, Library of United States Naval Hospital, Corona, California. Awarded 1st prize at Calif. Water Color Soc., 1922, Painters and Sculptors Exhibit, Los Angeles, 1923, Fine Arts Gallery, San Diego, 1926, Internat. Bookplate Assn., Los Angeles, 1927; bronze medals at Biltmore Salon, Painters of the West, 1926, and Painters and Sculptors Club, Los Angeles, 1928; 1st gold medal, Pacific Southwest Expn., Long Beach, 1928; honorable mention at Ariz. State Fair, 1923, 27, 28, at Calif. State Fair, 1935, for water color at Anniversary Exhbn., Laguna Beach Art Assn., 1942; trophy at International Aeronautical Art Exhibit, 1937; several prizes from Laguna Beach Art Assn.; silver medal Scandinavian-Am. Art Soc., 1939, gold medal, 1940; Service Honor for art in national defense, March 1943. Honorary life member Los Angeles Art Association life mem. Laguna Beach Art Assn.; mem. Foundation of Western Art, Acad. Western Painters, Laguna Beach (Calif.) Art Assn., Scandinavian-Am. Art Soc. of the West (medal, 1939). Republican. Mem. Evangelical Lutheran Ch. Home: 2079 Coast Blvd. S., Laguna Beach, Calif. Died Apr. 13, 1945.

YOAKUM, Clarence Stone, psychologist; b. Leavenworth County, Kan., Jan. 11, 1879; s. Hedges Conger and Lydia Isabel (Stone) Y.; A.B., Campbell Coll., Kan., 1901; Ph.D., U. of Chicago, 1908; m. Louise Branch Storey, July 29, 1919; 1 dau., Margaret Isabel. Teacher pub. schools, 1898-1900; instr. psychology and edn., Campbell Coll., 1901-03; instr. science and mathematics, Hiawatha (Kan.) Acad., 1903-05; fellow in psychology, U. of Chicago, 1906-08; prof. and head dept. philosophy and psychology, U. of Tex., 1908-17; prof. of applied psychology, and dir. bur. personnel research, Carnegie Inst. Tech., Pittsburgh, 1919-24; apptd. prof. personnel management, U. of Mich., 1924, and dir. Bur. of Univ. Research, 1927; dean, Coll. Liberal Arts, Northwestern U., 1929-30; v.p. U. of Mich. since July 1930, dean of Grad. Sch. since January. 1935. First lt., capt. and maj. psychol. service, U.S. Army, 1917-19; served at Camp Lee, later in Office of Surgeon Gen. and as supervisor psychol. service in army camps. Mem. Am. Psychol. Assn., A.A.A.S., Inst. of Management American Assn., Univ. Profs., Sigma Xi, Gamma Alpha, Phi Gamma Delta, Phi Kappa Phi. Conglist. Clubs: Pittsburgh Athletic; City (New York). Author: Army Mental Tests (Yoakum and Yerkes), 1920; Selection and Training of Salesmen (Yoakum and Kenagy), 1925. Home: 2017 Hill St., Ann Arbor, Mich. Died Nov. 20, 1945.

YODER, Albert Henry, educator; b. near Nora Springs, Iowa, Feb. 15, 1866; s. William H. and Catherine Addie (Buskirk) Y.; grad. State Normal Sch., Madison, S.D., 1888; A.B., Ind. U., 1893; fellow in pedagogy, Clark U., 1893-94; course in psychology, U. of Chicago, 1895-96; spl. course in pediatrics, Northwestern U. Med. Sch., Chicago, 1896; m. Susan Norton Griggs, June 11, 1894; children—Leverett Griggs, Mrs. Miriam Lander, Mrs. Charlotte May Lust, Wm. Albert, Fdk. Griggs, Paul Buskirk. Teacher in common schs. 3 yrs.; supt. schs., Madison, S.D., 1888-91; instr. edn., Ind. U., 1893; prin. City Normal Sch., San Francisco, 1894-95; pres. Vincennes U., 1896-1900; prof. of edn., U. of Wash., 1901-06; supt. pub. schs., Tacoma, Wash., July 1, 1906-July 1910; staff lecturer on child sociology, New York Sch. of Philanthropy, Oct. 1, 1910-12; pres. State Normal Sch., Whitewater, Wis., 1912-19; dir. univ. extension, U. of N.D., 1919-34. V.p. Roosevelt Nat. Park Assn. Mem. Am. Numismatic Assn., S.A.R., Sigma Nu, Phi Delta Kappa. Club: Lions. Home: Seattle, Wash. Died Sept. 22, 1940.

YON, Pietro A., organist, composer; b. Settimo-Vittone, Italy, Aug. 8, 1886; s. Antonio and Margherita (Piazza) Y.; student Royal Conservatories of Milan and Turin; grad. Acad. of St. Cecilia, Rome, full honors in organ under R. Renzi, piano under A. Bustini and G. Sgambati, composition under C. de Sanctis; m. Francesca Pessagno, May 21, 1919 (now dec.); 1 son, Mario Charles. Came to U.S., 1907, naturalized, 1921. Made debut as substitute organist at the Vatican and the Royal Ch. of Rome, 1905-06; organist and choirmaster Ch. of St. Francis Xavier, New York, 1908-26; organist and musical director St. Patrick's Cathedral, New York, since 1926. Decorated Cavalier Order of Crown of Italy; hon. organist of the S.S. Basilica of St. Peter, Vatican, Rome. Composer: (choral works) "Jerusalem Surge," Missa "Regina Pacis"; (orchestral works) "Concerto Gregoriano," Missa "Melodica," "Solemnis," "Te Deum Laudamus," "Veni Creator"; (songs) "Gesu Bambino," "Christ Triumphant" and "O Faithful Cross"; also organ and piano works. Catholic. Home: 200 W. 58th St. Address: Carnegie Hall, New York, N.Y. Died Nov. 22, 1943.

YOST, Fielding Harris, dir. athletics; b. Fairview, W.Va., Apr. 30, 1871; s. Permenus Wesley and Elzena Jane (Ammons) Y.; ed. Fairmont (W.Va.) Normal Sch., Ohio Northern U.; LL.B., U. of W.Va., 1897; LL.D., Marshall Coll., 1928; m. Eunice Josephine Fite, Mar. 12, 1906. Promoted and developed hydro-electric plant, Tenn. Power Co., 1907-14; dir. Dixie Cement Co., Chattanooga, 1908-14, with Cumberland Valley Nat. Bank, Nashville, Tenn., 1912-19. Became dir. intercollegiate athletics, U. of Mich., July 1, 1921, also dir. four-yr. course in physical edn. and Summer Sch. for Athletic Coaching and Administration, and football coach, 1901-27. Fellow American Physical Education Association; member Phi Epsilon Kappa, Sigma Chi fraternities. Republican. Methodist. Clubs: Rotary, Barton Hills Country (Ann Arbor, Mich.); Detroit Athletic (hon. life). Author: Football for Player and Spectator, 1905; also many articles pertaining to athletics and youth. Silver Beaver award, 1932, and Silver Buffalo award, 1935, for service to youth from Boy Scouts of America. Home: 611 Stratford Drive, Ann Arbor, Mich. Died Aug. 20, 1946.

YOUNG, Art (Arthur Henry Young), cartoonist, author; b. near Orangeville, Stephenson County, Ill., Jan. 14, 1866; s. Daniel S. and Amanda (Wagner) Y.; student Acad. of Design, Chicago, 1884-86, Art Students League, N.Y. City, 1888-89, Academie Julian, Paris, 1889-90; Cooper Union, 1903-06; m. Elizabeth North, 1895; children—North, Donald Minot. News illustrator and cartoonist successively for Evening Mail, Daily News, Tribune, Inter-Ocean Chicago, 1884-94, for Denver Times, 1895; co-edito. The Masses, 1911-19; Washington corr. for Metropolitan Mag., 1912-17; editor and pub. Good Morning, N.Y. City, 1919-21; contbr. illustrations and cartoons to Life, Puck, Judge, Saturday Evening Post, Colliers, The Nation. Active in campaigns for woman suffrage, labor organization, racial equality, and abolition of child labor. Candidate of Socialist Party in N.Y. for State Assembly, 1913, State Senate, 1918. Mem. Am. Artists Congress. Socialist. Author: Trees at Night, 1927; On My Way, 1928; Art Young's Inferno, 1933; The Best of Art Young, 1936; Art Young, His Life and Times, 1939. Home: Bethel, Conn. Died Dec. 29, 1943.

YOUNG, Bert Edward, univ. prof.; b. Louisville, Ky., Jan. 2, 1875; s. Cyrus Harmon and Kate (Dunlap) Y.; B.S., Vanderbilt U., 1896, M.A., 1898; post-grad. study, U. of Chicago, 1898-99, 1901, U. of Paris and Grenoble, 1902-04; Dr. d'U., Grenoble, 1904; m. Ethel Barksdale Smith, 1903 (died July 21, 1918); m. 2d, Grace Maxwell Philputt, 1923. Head Dept. of Romance Langs., Vanderbilt, 1904-22 visiting prof., Columbia, 1915-16, summers 1912-16, and University of Chicago, 1917; prof. and head dept., Indiana U., since 1922. Dir. Modern Lang. Inst., Mil. Dept. of Southeast, 1918-19; mem. com. on colls., Council Nat. Defense, 1918-19. Served as sec., pres. and chmn. higher edn. com. of Southern Assn. Colls. and Secondary Schs., 1910-22; chmn. commn. on athletics, 1928 and 1929 and mem. com. on Latin-Am. cultural relations, Assn. Am. Colls., since 1940; sec. Central Div. Mod. Lang. Assn. and mem. exec. council and editorial com. of same, 1915-23; trustee Fed. Alliance Française since 1913; pres. 1942-45; mem. foreign study com. Inst. Internat. Edn., N.Y. since 1927; pres. Am. Assn. Teachers of French, 1930-32; pres. Modern Lang. Assn. Mid West and South, 1936-37; mem. exec. com. Nat. Fed. Modern Lang. Teachers, 1932-40; hon. mem. Soc. des Profs. de français en Amérique; del Internat. Conv. Rotary Clubs, Edinburgh, 1921, Ostende, 1927; del. World Fed. Edn. Assns., Denver 1931; apptd. by Department of State American delegate International Congress Modern Languages, Paris, 1937. Member Phi Beta Kappa, Kappa Alpha (S.). Episcopalian. Decorated Officier de l'Instruction publique (France), Médaille de la Reconnaissance française; Chevalier de la Légion d'Honneur. Holder half-mile record Southern Colls., 1894-95. Author: Michel Baron acteur et auteur dramatique élève de Molière, Paris, 1905. Editor Molière's Tartuffe, 1918 and Registre de La Grange. Mem. N.Y. War Fund Com. since 1944, Am. Library Com. for France, also Anne Morgan Com. for Caen, France. Home: 521 E. Kirkwood Av., Bloomington, Ind. Died Dec. 25, 1949.

YOUNG, C(lement) C(alhoun), ex-gov.; b. Lisbon, N.H., Apr. 28, 1869; s. Isaac E. and Mary R. (Calhoun) Y.; grad. high schs., San Jose and Santa Rosa, Calif.; B.L., U. of Calif., 1892; m. Lyla J. Vincent, Mar. 15, 1902; children—Barbara, Lucy. Teacher high sch., Santa Rosa, 1892-93; teacher and head English dept., Lowell High Sch., San Francisco, 1893-1906; with Mason-McDuffie Co., suburban development, Berkeley and San Francisco, 1906-44. Mem. Calif. Assembly, 1909-19 (speaker of House, 1913-19); del. to Rep. Nat. Conv., 1912; lt. gov. of Calif., 1919-27; Rep. presdl. elector, 1920 (chmn. Calif. Electoral Bd.); gov. of Calif., term, 1927-30 inclusive. Ex-officio regent, U. of Calif., 1913-30. Mem. Phi Beta Kappa, Phi Delta Theta. Republican. Conglist. Clubs: Commonwealth (San Francisco; pres., 1939-40). Author: (with Charles Mills Gayley) Principles and Progress of English Poetry, 1904. Home: 2?5 Alvarado Road. Office: 2101 Shattuck Av., Berkeley, Calif. Died Dec. 25, 1947.

YOUNG, Evan E.; b. Kenton, O., Aug. 17, 1878; s. Sutton E. and Emma (Stickney) Y.; student Hiram (O.) Coll., 1895-96, S.D. State Sch. Mines, 1897; LL.B., U. of Wis., 1903; m. Dawn Waite, Aug. 23, 1905 (died January 9, 1943). Second lieutenant Company M, 1st S.D. Volunteer Infantry, April 25, 1898; mustered out as captain and adjutant, 11th Cavalry, U.S.V., Mar. 13, 1901. Practiced law, Sioux Falls, S.D., 1903-05; Am. consul at Harput, Turkey, 1905-08, at Saloniki, 1908-09; chief, Div. Near Eastern Affairs, Dept. State, 1909-11; E.E. and M.P. to Ecuador, 1911-12; apptd. foreign trade adviser of Dept. of State, 1912; consul gen., at Halifax, N.S., 1913-19, at Constantinople, 1920; Am. commr. to Baltic provinces of Russia, 1920-22; ordered to Washington, 1922; detailed to Dept. of State, Feb. 15, 1923; chief Div. of Eastern European Affairs, 1923-25; apptd. foreign service officer Class 1, July 1, 1924; E.E. and M.P. to Dominican Republic, 1925-30, to Bolivia, Jan.-Feb. 1930 (resigned); vice pres. Pan-Am. Airways, Inc., 1930-44 (retired Aug. 17, 1944), and became mem. board dirs. Mem. Sigma Alpha Epsilon, Phi Delta Phi. Home: Turnerhame, Loudonville, N.Y. Died Jan. 13, 1946.

YOUNG, Gilbert Amos, mechanical engr.; b. Owosso, Mich., June 24, 1872; s. Amos G. and Mary (Alling) Y.; B.S. in M.E., S.D. State Coll., 1894; B.S. in M.E., Purdue U., 1899, M.E., 1903; M.M.E., Harvard, 1910; m. Berdella J. Keith, June 25, 1902; 1 son, Ronald Keith. Instr. practical mechanics, S.D. State Coll., 1894-98; asst. Purdue U., 1899-1901, instr. in mech. engring., 1901-03, successively asst., asso. and full prof. mech. engring., 1903-09, head Sch. of Mech. Engring. and dir. of Mech. Engring. Labs. since 1911. Republican. Presbyterian. Mem. Am. Soc. Mech. Engrs., Soc. Automotive Engrs., Soc. Promotion Engring. Edn., Pi Tau Sigma, Tau Beta Pi, Phi Gamma Delta, etc. Author: Text Notes, Steam Turbines, Gas Engines, Thermodynamics. Coauthor (with V. W. Young) Text book Elements of Thermodynamics. Writer on mech. engring. subjects. Home: Lafayette, Ind. Died June 27, 1943.

YOUNG, Helen Louise, prof. history; b. Marion, N.Y., July 20, 1877; d. Conway W. and Mary (Barnum) Y.; A.B., Cornell U., 1900; Ph.D., Yale, 1910; student Sorbonne, Paris, 1924-25. Asst. in dept. of history, Hunter Coll., 1910-16, prof. since 1916. Mem. Am. Hist. Assn., Am. Assn. Univ. Women. Women's University Club of New York. Address: Hunter College, New York. Died July 12, 1942.

YOUNG, Hugh Hampton, surgeon; b. San Antonio, Tex., Sept. 18, 1870; s. Gen. William Hugh and Frances Michie (Kemper) Y.; A.B., A.M., U. of Va., 1893, M.D., 1894; Johns Hopkins, 1894-95; D.Sc., Queen's U., Belfast, 1933; m. Bessy Mason Colston, June 4, 1901 (died May 21, 1928); children—Frances Kemper (Mrs. Wm. Francis Rienhoff), Frederick Colston, Helen Hampton (Mrs. Bennett Crain), Elizabeth Campbell (Mrs. Warren Russell Starr). Pathologist to Thomas Wilson Sanitarium, 1895; successively asst. resident surgeon, 1895-98, head of dept. urol. surgery, and asso. surgeon Johns Hopkins Hospital, and clinical professor of urology, Johns Hopkins U. Pres. Md. State Lunacy Commn. Pres. Am. Assn. Genito-Urinary Surgeons, 1909, Am. Urol. Assn., 1909, Medico-Chirurgical Faculty of Maryland, 1912; dir. urology A.E.F., 1917; sr. consultant in same, A.E.F., 1918; col. Med. Corps U.S. Army. Chmn. Bd. of Mental Hygiene for Md.; chmn. Md. Aviation Commn.; v.p. Baltimore Museum of Art; pres. Lyric Theatre; pres. Baltimore Opera Club; chmn. Md. Commn. for New York World's Fair, 1939. Awarded Keyes medal, for contributions to Urology, 1936; Francis Amory Septennial Prize for outstanding work on cancer of the prostate, 1941. Mem. Internat. Assn. Congres Internationale d'Urologie (pres. 1927); corr. mem. Association Française d'Urologie, Deutsche Gesellschaft für Urologie, Sociedad de Cirujia de Buenos Aires, Societa Italiana di Urologia, R. Romanae Medicorum Academie Praeses, Chi Phi and Nu Sigma Nu fraternities; fellow Royal College Surgeons of Ireland; honorary fellow Royal Society of Medicine; fellow American College of Surgeons. Clubs: Maryland, Elkridge, Gibson Island, Baltimore Country, Johns Hopkins, Bachelors Cotillon. Author: Studies in Urological Surgery (Vol. XIII, Johns Hopkins Hosp. Repts), 1906; Hypertrophy and Cancer of the Prostate (Vol. XIV, Johns Hopkins Reports), 1906; Young's Practice of Urology (2 vols); Urological Roentgenology; Genital Abnormalities, Hermaphroditism and Related Adrenal Diseases; Hugh Young, A Surgeon's Autobiography, 1940. Founder and editor Jour. of Urology. Has contributed over 350 papers to Am. and foreign med. jours. Home: 100 W. Cold Spring Lane, Baltimore, Md. Died Aug. 23, 1945.

YOUNG, Jacob William Albert, univ. prof.; b. York, Pa., Dec. 28, 1865; s. Rev. Jacob and Mary (Lentz) Y.; A.B., Bucknell U., 1887, A.M., 1890; U. of Berlin, 1888-89; Ph.D., Clark U., 1892; m. Louise van Hees Young, 1896. Instr. math., Bucknell, 1887-88; asso. in mathematics, U. of Chicago, 1892-94, instr., 1894-97, asst. prof., 1897-1908, asso. prof. pedagogy of mathematics, 1908-26, emeritus asso. prof. pedagogy of mathematics, 1926-48. Studied methods in pedagogy of mathematics, Ger., 1897-98, France, 1901, France and England, 1904-05, Austria, 1906, Italy, 1908; mem. Internat. Commn. on Teaching of Mathematics. Member American Math. Society, 1000 Men of Science, Phi Beta Kappa. Club: Quadrangle. Author: Differential and Integral Calculus (with C. E. Linebarger), 1900; The Teaching of Mathematics in Prussia, 1900; Arithmetic (with L. L. Jackson), Vols. I, II, 1904, Vol. III, 1905; The Teaching of Mathematics, 1907; Algebra (with same), 1908; The Appleton Arithmetics (with same), Vols. I, II, III, 1909; Second course in Algebra (with same), 1910; High School Algebra (with same), 1913. Editor and joint author of Monographs on Modern Mathematics, 1911. Contbr. to math. jours. Home: 5422 Blackstone Av., Chicago, Ill. Died Oct. 25, 1948.

YOUNG, Jeremiah Simeon, educator, author; b. Wellston, O., Sept. 9, 1866; s. William Riley and Rebecca (Woodrow) Y.; B.A., Kansas Coll., 1890; M.A., U. of Mich., 1898; Ph.D., U. of Chicago, 1902; m. Katherine Beegle, July 26, 1894; 1 dau., Elizabeth Maud. Prin. schs., Cheyenne Wells, Colo., 1891-92; asst. state supt. edn., Colo., 1893-94; teacher of history and govt., Colo. State Normal Sch., 1895-97; supt. schs., Fostoria, O., 1898-1900; acting prof. polit. and economic science, Lake Forest (Ill.) Coll., 1901-02; teacher history and polit. science, State Normal Sch., Mankato, Minn., 1902-08; asst. prof. economics and polit. science, 1909-10, of polit. science, 1910-12, asso. prof., 1913-15, prof., 1915-37, professor emeritus since 1937, former chmn. dept. polit. science, Univ. of Minn.; dir. Summer Sch. U. of Minnesota, 1915; visiting professor of government, Rollins Coll., Winter Park, Fla., 1937. Mem. advisory com. Minn. Minimum Wage Commn. Mem. Am. Polit. Science Assn. (exec. council), Minn. Acad. Social Sciences (sec. and editor Proc. vols. V, VI and VII), Minn. Ednl. Assn., Miss. Valley Hist. Assn. Author: The Government of Colorado, 1897; The Political and Constitutional History of the Cumberland Road, 1904; The Government of Minnesota, 1907; The State and the Government, 1916; Unified American Government (with E. Y. Wright), 1933; Growing in Citizenship (with E. M. Barton), 1939; Government of the American People (with J. I. Arnold and J. W. Manning), 1940; also numerous articles in polit. science, history and edn. Home: 152 Cortland Av. Winter Park, Fla. Died Dec. 30, 1947.

YOUNG, Karl, prof. English; b. Clinton, Ia., Nov. 2, 1879; s. George Billings and Frances Eliza (Hinman) Y.; A.B., U. of Mich., 1901; LL.D., 1937; A.M., Harvard, 1903, Ph.D., 1907; Litt.D., U. of Wis., 1934; m. Frances Campbell Berkeley, Aug. 10, 1911; children—George Berkeley, Karl. Successively asst. prof., asso. prof. and prof. English, U. of Wis., 1908-23; prof. Yale U. since 1923; now Sterling prof. and asso. fellow Jonathan Edwards Coll. Awarded Gollancz Memorial prize, Brit. Acad., 1941. Fellow A.A.A.S., Royal Soc. of Lit., Mediæval Acad. of America. Pres. Modern Language Assn. of America, 1940; mem. Phi Beta Kappa. Clubs: Elizabethan, Graduate (New Haven). Author: Origin and Development of the Story of Troilus and Criseyle, 1908; Ordo Rachelis, 1919; The Dramatic Association of the Easter Sepulchre, 1920; The Drama of the Medieval Church, 1933. Home: 195 Everit St., New Haven, Conn. Died Nov. 17, 1943.

YOUNG, Leon Decatur, clergyman; b. Highland, Kan., Dec. 2, 1872; s. John and Rachel F. (Nesbit) Y.; B.A., Highland Coll., 1897; student Princeton Theol. Sem., 1898-99; grad. McCormick Theol. Sem., 1900; D.D., Bellevue Coll., Omaha, Neb., 1910; LL.D., Hastings Coll., 1916; m. Dorothy Spriestersbach, May 6, 1902 (dec.); m. 2d, Mary B. Archibald, Aug. 2, 1938. Ordained Presbyterian ministry, 1900; pastor Charlestown, Ind., 1900-01, Washington, Ia., 1902-08, Beatrice, Neb., 1908-14, Lincoln, 1914-20, City Temple, Dallas, Tex., 1920-25. Abbey Presbyn. Ch., 1925-38, First Presbyn. Ch., Highland, Kan., 1939-41, pastor emeritus since Apr. 15, 1941. Trustee Highland Coll.; mem. Gen. Assembly Advisory Com. on Near East Relief; mem. Reorganization and Consolidation Com. of Gen. Assembly, 1920-23; vice moderator Gen. Assembly Presbyn. Church, U.S.A., 1932-33; Bible lecturer at Christian Workers Conferences, 1932-34; moderator Dallas Presbytery, Mar.-Sept. 1935; moderator Highland Presbytery, 1940; president United Forces Against the Liquor Traffic, Dallas County, Tex.; secretary United Texas Drys (State). Sec. Army Christian Commission, Camp Alger, Va., Spanish-Am. War; spl. preacher army camps, World War. Bible lecturer Mount Hermon Conf., 1934-37. Mem. Alpha Chi. Democrat. Clubs: Salesmanship, Dallas Writers, Lakewood, Kiwanis. Author: "Know Your Bible" Series (children's, students', young men's and adults' edits.). Organized "Know Your Bible" Club of America. Lectures: America for Me; Ten Certainties of Life Insurance; If I Were a Salesman. Author of single budget plan of ch. finance; originator of "Sin Board," which has received wide recognition. Address: Box 502, Highland, Kan. Died March 13, 1947.

YOUNG, Mary Vance, coll. prof.; b. Washington, Pa., May 22, 1866; d. John Seavers and Jane (Vance) Young; ed. Rome (Ga.) Coll., Shorter Coll., Rome, Ga., Albert Lea (Minn.) Coll.; Zürich, Paris, and Florence, 1894-99, Ph.D., U. of Zürich, 1899. Instr. Romance langs., Smith Coll., 1899-1901; prof. Romance langs., Mt. Holyoke Coll., 1901-28. Officier d Académie, French Govt., 1907. Mem. Modern Lang. Assn. Am., Modern Lang. Assn. N.E., Dante Soc. of Am., Dante Assn., Nat. Inst. Social Sciences, etc. Presbyterian. Author: Molière's Kunst Komoedien, 1899; Les Enseignements de Robert de Ho, 1902; Italian Grammar, 1904. Home: South Hadley, Mass. Died Apr. 1946.

YOUNG, Samuel Hall, clergyman; b. Butler, Pa., Sept. 12, 1847; s. Rev. Loyal Y. and Margaret (Johnston) Y.; A.B., U. of Wooster, 1875, D.D., 1899; studied Princeton Theol. Sem., 1875-76, Western Theol. Sem., Allegheny, Pa., 1876-78 (grad., 1878); m. Fannie E. Kellogg, Dec. 15, 1878; children—Abby G. (Mrs. B. E. Sanford), Margaret A. (Mrs. R. J. McCheeney), Fannie Louise. Teacher, Pa., Mich., and W.Va., 1866-70; ordained June 10, 1878, and went to Alaska as missionary to Ft. Wrangel, there as missionary and explorer, 1878-88; organized 1st Protestant ch. in Alaska, 1879; pastor Long Beach, Calif., 1888-90, Cabery, Ill., 1891, Cedar Falls, Ia., 1892-95, Wooster, O., 1895-97; sent to Klondike, 1877; organized 1st Presbyn. ch., Dawson, 1898; organized missions at Eagle and Rampart, Alaska, 1899, Nome and Teller, 1900; apptd. supt. of all Alaska Presbyn. missions, 1901; at Skagway, 1902-03, Council, 1903-04, Fairbanks, 1904-06, 1907-08, Teller, 1906-07, Cordova, 1908-10, Iditarod, 1911-12; spl. rep. of Presbyn. Nat. bd. of Missions, New York, 1913-21; gen. missionary for Alaska, 1922-25; spl. rep. since 1925. Visited all parts of Alaska and the Siberian Coast and Arctic Ocean by boat, traveling long distances in winter with dog-team. Author series of articles, The Gospel by Canoe, New York Evangelist, 1880-86; articles in Assembly Herald, Alaska and Mission Work, 1897-1901; many articles since in various magazines on adventures and experiences in Northwest; also poems. Author: Alaska Days with John Muir, 1915; Klondike Clan, 1916; Adventures in Alaska; and Kenowan, the Hyda Boy; 1919. Address: 250 E. Howe St., Seattle, Wash. Died Sept. 2, 1927.

YOUNG, Truman Post, lawyer; b. St. Louis, Mo., Sept. 19, 1877; s. Daniel Comstock and Clara Harrison (Post) Y.; student Smith and Rugby acads., St. Louis, 1885-95; A.B., Yale, 1899; LL.B., Washington U. Law Sch., St. Louis, 1901; m. Katharine Clifford, June 30, 1917 (died Jan. 8, 1919); m. 2d, Hilda Dunbar Jamieson, Nov. 25, 1922; children—Truman Post, Hilda Patterson, Anne Morrison, Frances Henshaw. Admitted to Mo. bar, 1901, and since practiced in St. Louis; first associated with uncle, T. A. Post, later with Nagel & Kirby; asst. U.S. atty., St. Louis, 1905-09; asso. city counselor, 1909-17; partner Fordyce, Halliday & White, 1917-19, Koerner, Fahey & Young, 1919-29, Thompson, Mitchell, Thompson & Young since 1929. Mem. Am., Mo. State and St. Louis bar assns., Zeta Psi, Phi Delta Phi. Republican. Conglist. Mason. Clubs: Noonday, University, Public Question, Mo. Athletic Assn. Home: 1 Harcourt Drive, Claverach Park. Office: 705 Olive St. St. Louis, Mo. Died June 18, 1942.

YOUNG, Walter Stevens, educator; b. Londonderry, N.H., Sept. 29, 1878; s. James Franklin and Elizabeth (Wilkins) Y.; B.S., Dartmouth Coll., 1901; hon. Ed.D., Clark U., 1938; m. Harriet Nute Young, June 25, 1910. Grad. asst., Dartmouth Coll., Hanover, N.H., 1901-03; teacher South High Sch., Worcester, Mass., 1903-12, asst. supt. schs., 1912-23, supt. schs., 1923-43; corporator Mechanics Savings Bank, Worcester. Pres. bd. trustees Pinkerton Acad., Derry, N.H.; trustee, Bancroft School, Worcester; chmn. advisory com. Salvation Army. Mem. N.E.A., N.E. Assn. Sch. Supts., Mass. Sch. Supts. Assn., Worcester County Teachers' Assn. (past pres.), Worcester Natural History Soc. (pres.), Worcester Safety Council (v.p.), S.A.R. Republican. Episcopalian (vestryman). Clubs: Economic (past pres.), Rotary (past pres.), Worcester. Home: 4 Marston Way. Office: City Hall, Worcester, Mass. Died Mar. 6, 1946.

YOUNGDAHL, Oscar Ferdinand (yŭng'däl), ex-congressman; b. Minneapolis, Minn., Oct. 13, 1893; s. John C. and Elizabeth (Johnson) Y.; B.A., Gustavus Adolphus Coll., St. Peter, Minn., 1916; spl. course U. of Chicago, 1918; LL.B., Minn. Coll. of Law, 1925; m. Mary C. Ribble, June 7, 1917; children—John Ribble, Mary Elizabeth, Janet Lou, Robert George. Prin. Ortonville (Minn.) High Sch. and instr. dramatics and pub. speaking, 1916-18; engaged in the sale of bonds and securities, 1919-25; studied law, nights, 1922-25; admitted to Minn. bar, 1925; jr. partner Tifft & Youngdahl since 1930. Candidate for atty. gen., 1936; mem. 76th and 77th Congresses (1939-43), 5th Minn. Dist. Enlisted in U.S. Navy, June 1918; hon. disch. Jan. 1919. Trustee Am. Legion Hosp. Assn. of Minn.; former dist. dir. Community Fund. Mem. Minn. State Bar Assn., Hennepin County Bar Assn., Phi Beta Gamma, Am. Legion (past dept. comdr.), 40 and 8. Republican. Lutheran. Mason (Shriner). Club: Athletic (Minneapolis). Home: 5104 Chowen Av. S. Office: Rand Tower, Minneapolis, Minn. Deceased.

YOUNGER, John, prof. industrial engring.; b. Glasgow, Scotland, Aug. 18, 1882; s. David and Sarah (Watts) Y.; grad. Allan Glen's Tech. Sch., 1899; B.S. in Engring., Glasgow U., 1903; m. Muriel E. Stoneham, July 31, 1907; children—David, Margot, Joan Isobel, Muriel Annette, Jack Stoneham. Came to U.S., 1910, naturalized citizen, 1917. Apprentice, Glasgow Locomotive Works, 1898-1903; works supervisor Woolwich (Eng.) Arsenal, 1903-05; chief tool engr. Arrol Johnson Motor Car Co., Eng., 1905-06; Asst. works mgr. Dennis Bros. Motor Co., Eng., 1906-10; chief engr. Pierce Arrow Motor Car Co., Cleveland, O., 1910-17; vice-pres. Standard Parts Co., Cleveland, 1919-23; asso. editor American Machinist, 1923-25; editor Automotive Abstracts, 1923-31. Prof. industrial engring., Ohio State U., since 1925. Served as cons. engr. to U.S. Govt. on motor transport, Mexican border troubles, 1916; chief of engring., U.S. Motor Transport Corps, 1917-19. Awarded D.S.M. (U.S.). Mem. Am. Soc. M.E., Am. Soc. Tool Engrs. (hon.). Clubs: Faculty, Triangle. Author: Work Routing, 1929. Contbr. to Transactions, Am. Soc. M.E., etc. Home: 1836 Chelsea Av., Columbus, O. Died Nov. 14, 1945.

YOUNGGREEN, Charles Clark, advertising; b. Topeka, Kan., Oct. 3, 1890; s. George and LaVinne (Dedrick) Y.; grad. high sch., Topeka, student U. of Kan.; m. Marjorie Eloise Martin, Aug. 13, 1918. Pub. Kansas Farmer, Topeka, 1916-18; advertising and sales mgr. J. I. Case Plow Works, Racine, Wis., 1918-22; advertising agency business, Milwaukee, 1922-30; now exec. vice-pres. Reincke-Ellis-Younggreen & Finn, Chicago. Served as 2d lt., later 1st lt. and capt. Aviation Corps, U.S. Army, World War; lt. Royal Flying Corps. Mem. Aviation Com., Milwaukee; gen. chmn. Milwaukee reception to Lts. Maitland and Hegenberger, Col. Lindbergh, the Bremen flyers, Capt. Koehl, Maj. Fitzmaurice and Baron Von Huenefeld; mem. Wis. State Aviation Com. Formerly dir. Internat. Dry Farming Congress, Kan. State Fair, Am. Assn. Adv. Agencies, Audit Bur. of Circulations; mem. Internat. Advertising Assn. (ex-pres.), Advertising Fedn. America (dir.; ex-pres.), Nat. Better Business Bur. (dir.), Chicago Assn. Commerce (advt. com.), Advertising Council of Chicago (exec. bd.), Nat. Aeronautical Assn., Phi Kappa Psi; former pres. Alpha Delta Sigma (nat. advt. frat.); pres. Chicago Advertising Agency Assn.; hon. mem. Advertising Assn., Mexico, British Advertising Assn., Continental Advertising Assn. Past comdr. Cudworth Post, Am. Legion; hon. mem. Advertising Men's Post No. 209, Am. Legion, N.Y.; former pres. Kan. Alumni Assn. of Chicago. Republican. Methodist. Mason (32°). Clubs: Advertising (ex-pres.; now hon. pres.), Mid-Day, Union League, Saddle and Cycle (Chicago); Advertising (New York). Ex-pres. Lions and Advertising clubs (Racine). Home: 1320 N. State St. Office: 520 N. Michigan Av., Chicago, Ill. Died Aug. 19, 1942.

YOUNT, Barton K(yle), army officer; b. Troy, O.; s. Noah and Ivy Caroline (Kyle) Y.; student Ohio State U., 1902-03; grad. U.S. Mil. Acad., 1907; m. Mildred Almy Parker, Sept. 29, 1914; 1 son, Barton Kyle. Commd. 2d lt., U.S. Army, 1907; and advanced through the grades to brig. gen., 1936; asst. chief of Air Corps, Washington, D. C.; promoted maj. gen. Oct. 1, 1940, lt. gen., 1943; comd. S.E. Air Dist., Tampa, Fla., Nov. 1940-July 1941; comd. W. Coast Air Corps Training Center, Moffett Field, Calif., July 1941-Jan. 1942; assigned to Office of Chief of Air Corps, Jan.-Mar. 1942; comdg. gen. Army Air Forces Flying Training Command, Fort Worth, Mar. 1942-July 1943; apptd. comdg. gen. Army Air Forces Training Command, July 1943; retired with rank of lt. gen., June 30, 1946. Pres. American Inst. for Fgn. Trade, Phoenix, Ariz., since July 1, 1946. Decorated: D.S.M. with Oak Leaf Cluster, Legion of Merit, Air Medal; Knight Comdr. Order of British Empire; Officer Legion of Honor (France); Officer, Order Crown of Italy; Grand Officer Order Orange-Nassau (with swords; Netherlands); Grand Officer Nat. Order Southern Cross (Brazil); Order of Merit (1st Class; Mexico); Cloud Banner Decoration (Chinese). Clubs: Army and Navy, Columbia Country (Washington, D.C.). Address: 514 W. Rose Lane, Phoenix, Ariz. Died July 11, 1949; buried Arlington National Cemetery.

YUST, William Frederick, librarian; b. Canton, Mo., Nov. 10, 1869; s. Fred and Dorothea (Kreie) Y.; B.A., Central Wesleyan Coll., Warrenton, Mo., 1893; Latin, Greek and modern langs., U. of Chicago, 1894-96; B.L.S., N.Y. State Library Sch., 1901; m. Florence Hosmer French, Jan. 17, 1906; children—Harlan French, William Frederick (dec.), Dorothea, Augusta Bowers. Tchr. pub. schs., 1893-94; asst. reference and circulation depts. U. of Chicago Library, 1896-99; asst. state insp. of libraries N.Y. State, 1901-04; librarian Louisville Free Pub. Library, Jan. 1, 1905-Mar. 31, 1912; librarian Public Library, Rochester, N.Y., 1912-32; librarian Rollins Coll., Winter Park, Fla., Nov. 1931-Apr.30, 1942; now librarian emeritus; librarian University Club of Winter Park, Florida, since Apr. 1942. Lecturer on library buildings, N.Y. State Library Sch., 1922-26. Awarded Rollins Decoration of Honor for eminent service, 1944. Pres. Ky. Library Assn., 1907-12, N.Y. State Library Assn., 1917-18, Fla. Library Assn., 1933-35; life mem. A.L.A., Ky. Library Association, N.Y. Library Assn., Fla. Library Assn., Rochester Hist. Soc. (sec. 1914-31); mem. Allied Arts Soc., Winter Park Chamber of Commerce, Florida Audubon Soc. Conglist. Clubs: University, Orlando Rotary (hon. mem. since 1941). Author: Fred Yust, Kansas Pioneer, 1937. Compiler Bibliography of Justin Winsor, 1902. Compiler: The Literary Colony of Winter Park, Fla., 1935-43, 5th edit., 1943, 6th edit. in preparation. Contbr. to library periodicals; wrote chapter on "Legislation" in Manual of Library Economy, pub. by A.L.A., 1912, 21, etc. Home: Winter Park, Fla.; (summer) Middlesex, N.Y. Died Nov. 16, 1947.

Z

ZACHER, Louis Edmund (zăk'ĕr), pres. Travelers Ins. Co.; b. Hartford, Conn., June 18, 1878; s. Louis H. Z.; M.A., Trinity Coll., 1939. With Farmers-Mechanics National Bank, Hartford, 1895-1904; sec. to pres. Travelers Ins. Co., 1904-10, asst. treas., 1910-12, treas., 1912-34, v.p., 1922-29, pres. since 1929; pres. Travelers Indemnity Co., Travelers Fire Ins., Charter Oak Fire Insurance Co.; U.S. trustee Scottish Union & Nat. Ins. Co.; dir. Travelers Bank & Trust Co., Conn. River Banking Co., Guaranty Trust Co. of N.Y., Am. Union Ins. Co., Central Union Insurance Co., Standard Screw Co.; trustee Hartford-Conn Trust Co., Soc. for Savings of Hartford; mem. advisory com. metropolitan br. of Chase Nat. Bank of New York. Republican. Episcopalian. Home: West Hartford. Office: Travelers Ins. Co., Hartford, Conn. Died June 28, 1945.

ZAVITZ, Edwin Cornell (zā'vĭts), headmaster; b. Ilderton, Ont., Can., July 4, 1892; s. Jonah Daniel and Emily (Cornell) Z.; brought to U.S., 1906; B.A., U. of Mich., 1914; M.A., Teachers Coll. (Columbia Univ.), 1931; m. Francis Marion John, Feb. 22, 1919; children—John James Cornell, Peter Kirk Cornell. Teacher Sidwells Friends Sch., Washington, D.C., 1914-20, Moraine Pk. Sch., Dayton, O., 1920-24; headmaster Antioch Sch., Yellow Springs, O., 1924-27; prof. edn., Antioch Coll., 1924-27; headmaster Chateau de Bures nr. Paris, France, 1928-30, Univ. Sch., Cincinnati, O., 1931-35, Baltimore Friends Sch., 1935-43, Sidwell Friends Sch., Washington, D.C., since July 1, 1943. With Am. Friends Service Com. and Am. Red Cross, in France, 1917-18. Dir. Foreign Policy Assn. of Cincinnati. Mem. N.E.A., Dept. of Superintendence, Progressive Edn. Assn., Phi Delta Kappa. Mem. Soc. of Friends. Clubs: Torch (Baltimore); Torch (Cincinnati); North Baltimore Kiwanis, Federal Schoolmen's. Home: 5803 Kirkside Dr., Chevy Chase 15, Md. Address: Sidwell Friends School, 3901 Wisconsin Av., Washington 16. Died Sept. 30, 1949.

ZEIDLER, Carl Frederick (zīd'lĕr), mayor, lawyer; b. Milwaukee, Wis., Jan. 4, 1908; s. Michael W. and Clara A. E. (Nitschke) Z.; Ph.B., Marquette U., 1929; J.D., Marquette U., 1931; unmarried. Admitted to Wis. bar, 1931, bar of U.S. Supreme Court, 1939. Asst. city atty of Milwaukee, 1936-40; elected mayor of Milwaukee, Apr. 3, 1940. Commissioned lt. (j.g.), U.S.N.R., 1942, and served as commander of gun crew aboard merchant ship. Received citizenship award, Vets. of Foreign Wars, 1939; national civic award, Nat. Civic League, 1939; Y's Men's Service award, Y.M.C.A., 1939; Distinguished Service award, Jr. Chamber of Commerce, 1939. Hon. life mem. Army and Navy Union, 1939; privileged mem. Milwaukee Press club, 1940; hon. Flying Cadet, 1941; hon. adm. of Flagship Fleet of American Airlines; hon. life mem. Wis. Civil Air Corps, 1941; hon. mem. National Aeronautics Association; chairman Milwaukee County Council of Defense; mem. of Salvation Army Advisory Board; hon. mem. Milwaukee Fire Dept. Post, Am. Legion; mem. Advisory Council of U.S. Conf. of Mayors; mem. Asociation de Amigos de Mexico; Milwaukee Junior Chamber of Commerce, Milwaukee Turners, Symphonic Male Chorus, Y.M.C.A., Y's Men's club, Delta Sigma Rho, Theta Rho and Delta Theta Phi frats. Lutheran. Mason, Eagle, Elk, Moose, K.P., Odd Fellows, O.E.S., White Shrine of Jerusalem. Mem. Milwaukee, State, and Nat. bar assns., Milwaukee Liederkranz, City Club, Arion Musical Club. Home: 504 N. 33d St. Office: City Hall, Milwaukee, Wis. Reported missing at sea by Navy Dept., Dec. 11, 1942.

ZEIGEN, Frederic (zī'gĕn); author, poet, financier; b. Saginaw, Mich., Apr. 18, 1874; s. Cass J. and Mary (von Weber) Z.; grad. Mich. State Normal Coll., 1901 (honor man, pres. class and class poet); studied law Nashville Coll. of Law; LL.D., 1903; m. Myrtle Annette Comer, Sept. 20, 1899; children—Gladys (dec.), Eola Valencia (Mrs. Fred Mengel), Phyllis Myrtle (Mrs. Harold Tanner). Supt. schs. Osceola County, Mich., 1901-02; established Zeigen Real Estate Exchange, Detroit, Mich., 1903; pres. Zeigen Constrn. Co. (Detroit), Investment Bankers Corp., Mich. Petroleum Co., Frederic Zeigen Properties, Chalfonte Apartments, Inc. Settled at Miami, Fla., 1919; founder, with William Jennings Bryan and W. E. Walsh and others, U. of Miami, managing regent and sec., 1924-29; regent Scudder Sch. for Girls, Miami; trustee, dir. U. of Peiping. Served as lt. vols. Spanish-American War; sec. State War Bd., Mich., 1917-18, World War. Mem. Authors' League America, Mich. Authors' Assn. (pres. 3 terms), Authors League Mich. (co-founder, pres. 4 terms, hon. pres.), Authors League Fla. (co-founder, 1st pres.), Methodist Laymen's Assn. of Mich. (pres. 4 terms), Art Founders Soc. of Detroit. Republican. Methodist. Mason (32°, Shriner). Clubs: Miami City, Biltmore Country, Detroit Athletic, Detroit Yacht; hon. life mem. Scarab Art Club. Author: Breezes from the Pines, 1898; Collected Poems, 1900; Therald Archer Knowlton, 1907; Star Dust and Dandelions, 1923; Lava, 1926; Black Christ, 1929; The Revolutionist (novel of German Revolution of 1848), 1931; Anthology of Better Poems; also (plays) Not His Daughter; The Clock Around. Composer over 40 published songs, etc. Address: 1632 S. Bay Shore Drive, Miami, Fla.; and 8655 Jefferson Av. E., Detroit, Mich. Office: 1118 Lafayette Bldg., Detroit, Mich. Died May 26, 1942.

ZELENY, Anthony (zĕl'ĕ-nĭ), physicist; b. Racine County, Wis., Apr. 20, 1870; s. Anthony Herbert and Josephine (Pítka) Z.; B.S., U. of Minn., 1892, M.S., 1893, Ph.D., 1907; U. of Chicago, 1900; Göttingen, 1912; Princeton, 1915-16; m. Mattie L. Day, June 8, 1897; children—Leslie Day, Lawrence. Instr. Physics, 1897-1906, asst. prof., 1906-09, prof., 1909-38, prof. emeritus since 1938, U. of Minn. Fellow A.A.A.S. (v.p. 1914), Am. Phys. Soc.; mem. Sigma Xi; foreign mem. Nat. Acad. Sciences of Czechoslovakia (Masarykova Akademie Práce). Author: A Manual of Physical Measurements (with H. A. Erikson), 1902; Elements of Electricity, 1930; also papers on elec. condensers, induction, galvanometers, thermocouples, low temperatures, etc. Home: 1933 E. River Terrace, Minneapolis 14, Minn. Died Dec. 15, 1947.

ZELIE, John Sheridan (zē'lē), clergyman; b. Princeton, Mass., May 3, 1866; s. Rev. John Sheridan and Caroline (Prescott) Z.; A.B., Williams, 1887, D.D., 1904; B.D., Yale, 1890; Litt.D., Western Reserve, 1921; L.H.D., Lake Forest Coll., 1930; m. Henrietta S. Campbell; children—John S., Frances C. Doux. Pastor Congl. Ch., Plymouth, Conn., 1890-94, Bolton Av. Presbyn. Ch., Cleveland, O., 1894-1900, First Reformed Ch., Schenectady, N.Y., 1900-03, Crescent Av. Presbyn. Ch., Plainfield, N.J., 1903-17, First Presbyn. Ch., Troy, N.Y., 1919-27. Served as chaplain of 2d, 28th and 79th divs. field hosps. and ambulances, and Base Hosp. 30, A.E.F., in France, 1918-19. On staff Am. Relief Administration, Russia, 1922. Mem. of Phi Beta Kappa, Delta Kappa Epsilon. Author: (with Carroll Perry) Bill Pratt, The Saw-Buck Philosopher, 1895; The Book of the Kindly Light (intimations from Cardinal Newman's hymn), 1909; Joseph Conrad the Man (with E. L. Adams), 1925; also articles in Atlantic Monthly, etc. Address: (summer) Cherryfield, Me.; (winter) Seabreeze, Daytona Beach, Fla. Died Nov. 9, 1942.

ZELLERBACH, Isadore, paper mfr.; chmn. exec. Zellerbach Paper Co.; chmn. exec. com. Crown-Zellerbach Corp.; also officer or dir. various other corps. Home: 3524 Jackson St. Office: 343 Sansome St., San Francisco. Died 1941.

ZERBE, Farran (zĕr-bē), numismatist; b. Tyrone, Pa., Apr. 16, 1871; s. James Albert and Bridget (McAvoy) Z.; ed. pub. and pvt. schs.; m. Gertrude Mahoney, Sept. 10, 1932. Mercantile business until 1900; chief numismatist, St. Louis Expn., 1904, Portland Expn., 1905-06; editor and pub. The Numismatist, 1909-10; exhibitor and lecturer, "Money of the World," 1907-14 and 1920-28; chief of numismatic dept. San Francisco Expn., 1915-16. Mem. U.S. Assay Com., 1909, 1923. Mem. Am. Numismatic Assn. (pres. 1907-09 and of Pacific Coast Soc., 1918-23), Am. Numismatic Soc. (New York), Numismatic Club (New York), Tyrone Club. Contbr. numerous articles on numismatics and finance. Collected over 50,000 specimens of mediums of exchange, ranging over 5,000 yrs., and of an extensive library on the subject; sold collection and library to Chase Nat. Bank, New York, 1928, and became curator and numismatist for the bank, emeritus since 1939. Address: 14 E. 28 St., New York, N.Y. Died Dec. 25, 1949.

ZETTLER, Emil Robert, sculptor; b. Karlsruhe, Baden, Germany, Mar. 30, 1878; s. August and Johanna (Ziller) Z.; brought to U.S., at age of 4; ed. pub. schs., Chicago; Art Inst. Chicago; Royal Acad., Berlin; Julian Acad., Paris; m. Mary Potter Jurey, Sept. 28, 1922 (died Jan. 19, 1927); m. 2d, Edythe Louise Flack, July 15, 1931; children—Gregory Flack, Roger Walford, Peter Emil. Exhibited in Salon, Paris, 1910. Pa. Acad. of Fine Arts, San Francisco Expn., 1915; Art Inst. Chicago. Hon. mention Art Inst. Chicago; awarded silver medal, Chicago Soc. Artists; bronze medal, San Francisco Expn.; Potter Palmer gold medal, Art Inst. Chicago, 1916, and Harry A. Frank prize, 1921; gold medal, Chicago Soc. Artists, 1923, and of Art Inst. Chicago Alumni Assn., 1925. Represented in Brooklyn Museum of Fine Arts, Municipal Art Collection, City of Chicago. Asso. instr. arch. sculpture and design, 1926-43; head Sch. Indsl. Art, Art Inst., Chicago, 1930-43. Sculpture mem. Municipal Art Commn. of Chicago, 1915-19. Club: Cliff Dwellers. Designer of official medal for Century of Progress Expn., Chicago, 1933. Received degree of Master of Fine Art, Art Inst. of Chicago, 1930. Home-studio: 521 Brierhill Lane, Deerfield, Ill. Died Jan. 10, 1946.

ZHDANOV, Andrei Alexandrovich (zhdá'nôf), govt. official; b. 1896. Sec. central com. Communist Party in charge propaganda until 1940; mem. exec. com. Communist Internat. to 1943; mem. Politburo since 1934; mem. Presidium Supreme Council of U.S.S.R.; party sec. Leningrad and N.W. Russia since 1934; pres. fgn. affairs com. of Soviet Union; mem. Mil. Council Leningrad Dist. Lt. gen., Feb. 1943; mem. Soviet Commn. on Nazi Crimes, U.S.S.R.; pres. Supreme Soviet of R.S.F.S.R.; signed Russo-Finnish Armistice, 1944; chmn. Control Commn. Finland, 1944; col. gen. since 1945. Awarded Order of Lenin, 1945, Order of Suvorov, 1944. Address: Helsinki Control Commission, Helsinki, Finland. Died Aug. 31, 1948.

ZIEGLER, Edward (zĕg'lĕr), music critic; b. Baltimore, Md., Mar. 25, 1870; s. Charles and Mary (Ohrenschall) Z.; ed. private schs., Baltimore; studied music in Baltimore and New York under Franz Xavier Arens; m. Suzanne Van Valkenberg; 1 dau.,

Suzanne (Mrs. Charles L. Gleaves). Music critic New York American, 1902, New York World, 1903-08; music and dramatic critic New York Herald, 1908-16; administrative sec. Met. Opera House, 1916-20, asst. gen. mgr. and consultant, since 1920. Contbr. to music periodicals. Author: Critique on Tristan and Isolde, 1909. Home: 570 Park Av. Office: Metropolitan Opera House, New York, N.Y. Died Oct. 25, 1947; buried Kent, Conn.

***ZIEGLER, Lloyd Hiram,** neurologist and psychiatrist; b. Bippus, Ind., June 1, 1892; s. Albert and Ellen (Schnitz) Z.; student Valparaizo (Ind.) U., 1909-12; A.B., Ind. Univ., 1914, A.M., 1916; M.B., U. of Minn., 1920, M.D., 1921; m. Grace Meredith Miller, June 8, 1918. Interne, St. Elizabeths Hosp., Washington, D.C., 1920; asst. surgeon and past asst. surgeon, U.S.P.H.S., stationed Hosp. No. 37, Waukesha, Wis., 1921-23; asst. resident in psychiatry, Henry Phipps Psychiatric Clinic, Johns Hopkins Hosp., 1923-24; fellow in medicine and neurology, Mayo Clinic, 1924-25; resident psychiatrist, Colo. Psychopathic Hosp., Denver, Colo., 1925-26; consultant on staff, Mayo Clinic, 1926-30; prof. neurology and psychiatry, Albany (N.Y.) Med. Coll., also neurologist in chief and psychiatrist in chief Albany Hosp., 1930-37; asso. med. dir., Milwaukee Sanitarium, Wauwatosa, Wis., 1937-42, med. dir. since 1942; lecturer in psychiatry, U. of Ill. Coll. of Medicine, Chicago, Ill., 1937-44. Served with U.S. Army, 1917-19; on reserve as med. student. Med. examiner Mil. Induction Center, Milwaukee, Wis., during World War II. Founder mem. Am. Bd. Psych. and Neurology (dir.). Dir. Visiting Nurses Assn., Milwaukee. Mem. A.M.A., Am. Psychiatric Assn., Am. Neurol. Assn., Central Neuropsychiatric Assn., N.Y. Psychiatric Soc., Assn. for Research in Nervous and Mental Diseases, Chicago Neurol. Soc., Ill. Psychiatric Soc., Phi Beta Kappa, Alpha Omega Alpha. Contbr. chapter on psychiatry in Nelson's Medical Specialties; also over 50 sci. papers to various publs. Home: 1220 Dewey Av. Office: Milwaukee Sanitarium, Wauwatosa, Wis. Died Jan. 8, 1945; buried Oakwood Cemetery, Rochester, Minn.

ZIESING, August, civil engr.; b. Peru, Ill., Feb. 19, 1858; s. Dr. Henry and Katherine (Brennemann) Z.; B.S., U. of Ill., 1878 (C.E., 1905); m. Alice A. Hanna, Feb. 27, 1884; children—Mabel (dec.), Henry Hanna, Mrs. Margarette Rector, Mrs. Gertrude Kemper, Mrs. Katherine Van Cleave. In bridge designing and constrn. work, 1878-81, ry. engring., 1881-83; mgr. and engr. Lassig Bridge Works, 1883-97; consulting engr., specialty railway structures, 1897-1901; v.p. and western manager, 1901-05, pres., Sept. 1905-1927, Am. Bridge Co.; retired from active bus., April 1, 1927. Mem. Am. Soc. C.E., Western Soc. Engrs., Am. Ry. Engring. Assn. Republican. Clubs: University, Union League, Engineers' (Chicago). Home: 125 Beach Rd., Glencoe, Ill. Died Feb. 16, 1942.

ZIMM, Bruno Louis, sculptor; b. New York, N.Y., Dec. 29, 1876; s. Louis and Olga (Shoreck) Z.; ed. Met. Art Sch., Met. Museum Art Students' League, New York; studied with Augustus St. Gaudens, and Karl Bitter; post-grad. work in Paris; m. Louise Seymour Hasbrouck, Oct. 29, 1919; 1 son, Bruno Hasbrouck. Awarded silver medal, Paris Expn., 1900; exhibited at St. Louis Expn., 1904, San Francisco Expn., 1915. Principal works: Memorial fountain, Riverside Drive and 116th St., New York; Slocum memorial, New York; Finnegan memorial, Houston, Tex.; Murdock memorial, Wichita, Kan.; bust of Robert E. Lee, Baylor Female Coll., Belton, Tex.; Sergt. York and Paul Revere, Seaboard Nat. Bank, New York; memorial tablet, 1st Nat. Bank, Jersey City, N.J.; Fathers of the Church and other statues in St. Pancras Ch., Brooklyn; Stations of the Cross, St. Clement's Ch., Phila.; etc. Mem. Nat. Sculpture Soc. Home: Woodstock, N.Y. Died Nov. 21, 1943.

ZIMMER, Verne A., official U.S. Dept. of Labor; b. Canaseraga, N.Y., Aug. 12, 1886; s. Adam and Katherine (Rohner) Z.; grad. Canaseraga High Sch., 1904; m. Harriet Burzynski, Feb. 21, 1919; children—James D., Patricia A. Factory insp., N.Y. Dept. of Labor, 1913-17; supt. N.Y. Public Employment Service, 1917-23; examiner in charge U.S. Employment Service, 1918-19; asst. industrial commr., N.Y. State, 1923-29; dir. Workmen's Compensation, N.Y., 1929-34; dir. Div. of Labor Standards, U.S. Dept. of Labor, since 1934; dir. U.S. Employment Service Mar.-July 1939; chmn. Nat. Com. for Conservation of Manpower in War Industries since 1940. Sec. treas. Internat. Assn. of Industrial Accident Bds. and Commns. since 1934. Govt. advisor to Internat. Labor Confs., Geneva, Switzerland, 1936-37. Democrat. Roman Catholic. Contbr. to publs. Home: 1745 Upshur St. N.W. Office: U.S. Dept. of Labor, Washington, D.C. Died Dec. 25, 1946; buried St. Mary's Cemetery, Canaseraga, N.Y.

ZIMMERLEY, Howard Henry, agrl. research; b. Erie, Pa., Feb. 26, 1890; s. Henry and Elizabeth (Petrie) Z.; B.S., Pa. State Coll., 1912; Ph.D., U. of Md., 1931; grad. study, U. of Md., part time, 1927-31; D.Sc., Clemson Agrl. Coll., 1937; m. Viola Olivet White, Dec. 21, 1916. Instr. horticulture, Pa. State Coll., 1912; horticulturist Kreg Pecan Co., Albany, Ga., 1913-14; asst horticulturist, Va. Truck Experiment Station, 1916; county agrl. agent, Del., 1917-19; horticulturist Va. Truck Expt. Station, 1918-31; sr. horticulturist U.S. Dept. Agr., 1931-32; dir. Va. Truck Expt. Station since 1932. Fellow Am. Assn. Agrl. Science; mem. Am. Soc. Hort. Sciences, Am. Soc. Plant Physiologists, Phi Kappa Phi, Sigma Psi. Democrat. Presbyterian. Mason. Club: Norfolk Rotary. Address: P O. Box 2160, Norfolk, Va. Died Oct. 15, 1944.

ZIMMERMAN, James Fulton, univ. pres.; b. Glen Allen, Mo., Sept. 11, 1887; s. James Madison and Emily Narcissus (McKelvey) Z.; student Marvin Collegiate Inst., Fredericktown, Mo., 1905-08; Vanderbilt, 1908-13, B.A., M.A.; grad. study, Columbia, 1919-23, Ph.D., 1925; m. Willia Adelia Tucker, Oct. 30, 1913; children—Elizabeth Adelia (Mrs. C. Sidney Cottle), Helen Emily (Mrs. R. Howard Brandenburg). Teacher public schools, Bollinger County, Mo., 1905-06; teacher of history, Duncan Preparatory School, Nashville, Tenn., 1913-15; acting prof. history and govt., West Tenn. Normal School, Memphis, Tenn., 1915; prin. high school, Paris, Tenn., 1916; instr. in economics and sociology, Vanderbilt U., 1917-19; asst. exec. sec. Inst. Social and Religious Research, N.Y. City, 1923-25; prof. polit. science, U. of N.M., 1925-27; pres. same univ. since 1927. Mem. Carnegie Endowment for Internat. Peace, European study group, summer 1931. Mem. Commn. on Institutions of Higher Edn., and vice-pres. North Central Assn. of Colleges and Secondary Schools, 1940-41; chmn. Commission on Cultural Relations with Latin America of Assn. of Am. Colleges; mem. Southwestern Polit. and Social Science Assn., Nat. Assn. State Univs. (pres. 1940-41), N.M. Ednl. Assn., A.A.A.S., Phi Beta Kappa, Phi Kappa Phi, Alpha Tau Omega, Sigma Upsilon, Pi Gamma Mu. Pres. Coronado Cuarto Centennial Commission, 1935-40. Mem. Bd. Sch. Am. Research; dir. Lab. of Anthropology; regent Museum of N.M. Rotarian. Author: The Impressment of Am. Seamen. Home: University Campus, Albuquerque, N.M. Died Oct. 20, 1944.

ZIMMERMAN, Orville, congressman; b. Glen Allen, Mo., Dec. 31, 1880; son of John Henry and Drucilla Caroline (McKelvey) Z.; graduate, Southeast Missouri State College, Cape Girardeau, Missouri, 1904; LL.B., University of Missouri, 1911; married Adah G. Hemphill, December 18, 1919; 1 son, Joe Adlai. Prin. Dexter (Mo.) High Sch., 1904-08; admitted to Mo. bar, 1911, and began practice at Kennett, Mo.; mem. Fort & Zimmerman, later Smith & Zimmerman; private practice since 1929; dir. and atty. Cotton Exchange Bank, Kennett; mem. Bd. of Edn., Kennett, 1928-36; mem. 74th to 80th Congress (1935-49), 10th Mo. Dist. Served as pvt. U.S. Army, World War; chmn. Legal Advisory Bd., Dunklin County, 1917-18. Mem. bd. regents Southeast Missouri State Coll., Cape Girardeau, Mo. Mem. Am., Mo. State and Dunklin County bar assns., Phi Alpha Delta, Delta Sigma Rho, Am. Legion. Democrat. Methodist. Mason (Shriner). Club: Lions. Home: Kennett, Mo. Died Apr. 7, 1948.

ZIMMERMANN, John Edward, mech. engr.; b. Buenos Aires, Argentine Republic, Jan. 31, 1874; s. John C. and Anna C. (MacKinley) Z.; B.A., Nat. Coll. of Buenos Aires, 1894; studied U. of Buenos Aires and U. of Pa.; m. Sarah Ann Frazier, June 5, 1900; children—Harriet F. (Mrs. Gerald W. Caner), Anna Cecilia (Mrs. Kennth Van Strum), Helena (Mrs. Reinhardt Wilbolz), Audrey (Mrs. Geo. Davis Gammon), Jean (Mrs. Edward L. Marshall). Served as private and interpreter with First City Troop of Phila., Puerto Rican campaign, Spanish-Am. War. Superintendent Am. Pulley Co., Phila., 1899-1901, sec., 1901-07; formerly mem. Dodge & Day, now Day & Zimmermann, Inc., pres. until 1929; pres. United Gas Improvement Co., 1929, chmn. of the board since Dec. 27, 1940; dir. Phila. Electric Co., Am. Pulley Co., United Gas Improvement Co., Conn. Gas & Coke Securities Co., Phila. Steam Co., Pa. R.R. Trustee U. of Pa. Mem. Am. Soc. Mech. Engrs., Franklin Inst. Clubs: Racquet, Philadelphia, Midday, Rittenhouse, Sunnybrook Golf, Boca Raton, Corinthian Yacht. Home: 25 E. Summit St., Chestnut Hill. Office: 1401 Arch St., Philadelphia, Pa. Died May 30, 1943.

ZINN, Alpha Alexander, life insurance; b. Clarksburg, W.Va., Sept. 12, 1880; s. Jasper Newton and Elizabeth Ann (Wolfe) Z.; ed. Kan. State Teachers Coll., Emporia; married Charlotte Shelton, October 30, 1907; children—Robert Shelton, Ruth Charlotte (Mrs. Robert Davy Eaglesfield), James Alexander. Vice president Maxwell Investment Company, Kansas City, Mo., 1917-24; v.p. Guaranty Trust Co. of Kansas City, 1919-24; then v.p. Southwest Trust Co.; v.p. Commerce Trust Co., 1925-32; now v.p. and dir. State Life Ins. Co. of Indianapolis. Member bd. govs. Mortgage Bankers Assn. of America (pres. 1929-30). Republican. Presbyterian. Club: Meridian Hills Country (Indianapolis). Pres. Trustees of Town of Meridian Hills. Home: 6463 N. Illinois St. Office: State Life Bldg., Indianapolis, Ind. Died June 18, 1947.

ZINSSER, August (zĭn'zẽr), banker; b. N.Y. City, Sept. 27, 1871; s. August and Marie (Schmidt) Z.; prep. edn., Dr. Sach's Sch., N.Y. City; A.B., Columbia, 1892; student Columbia Law Sch., 1893-94; m. Irene Van Buren, Aug. 25, 1915; children—Helen M., August; m. 2d, Mary Clayton, Apr. 1929. Admitted to New York bar, 1895, and practiced at N.Y. City until 1909; pres. Yorkville Bk., 1909-26; pres. Central Savings Bank, 1926-36, vice chmn., 1936-41; v.p. and treas. August Zinsser Realty Co.; trustee and mem. finance com. Guardian Life Ins. Co. Mem. Zeta Psi. Clubs: University, Columbia University. Home: Ridgefield, Conn. Died Sept. 26, 1948.

ZOELLNER, Joseph, Sr. (zĕl'nẽr), musician; b. Brooklyn, N.Y., Feb. 2, 1862; s. Johann and Kathrina Z.; studied violin with Lorenzen and Theodore Jacoby, New York, and with Ostermeyer and Hegner, at Aschaffenburg, Germany, and Henri Petri, Dresden; m. Helena Schneider, 1884; children—Joseph, Antoinette, Amandus. Musical dir. Niblo's Garden, New York, 1884; head of music schs., Brooklyn, 1882-1903, Stockton, Calif., 1903-06; toured in Russia, 1908-09; head of violin dept. École Communale, Etterbek, Brussels, Belgium, 1909-10; mem. Symphony Orchestra, Durant Brussels, 1910-12. Founder Zoellner String Quartette (father, daughter and two sons), 1904, which has given in America over 2,000 concerts since 1912; also played extensively in Europe, Paris, Brussels, London, Berlin, Cologne, Roubaix, Lille, Liège, etc. Founder (with his children) Zoellner Conservatory of Music, Los Angeles, Calif., 1922. Home: 1250 S. Windsor Blvd., Los Angeles 6, Calif. Died Jan. 24, 1950; buried Forest Lawn Cemetery, Glendale, Calif.

ZOLNAY, George Julian (zōl'nā), sculptor; b. July 4, 1863; honor grad. Royal Art Inst., Bucharest, and Imperial Acad. Fine Arts, Vienna, 1890; m. Abigail Rowan Gillim, 1902; children—Elizabeth (Mrs. Horace B. Smith), Margaret (Mrs. John Hone Auerbach). Lived in New York, 1892-1903; removed to St. Louis, 1903, in charge of sculpture division, Art Department, World's Fair, and instructor St. Louis School of Fine Arts (Washington University); resigned, 1909, to become director University City Art Academy; removed to Washington, D.C., 1913. Principal works: E. A. Poe and Tympanum, U. of Virginia; Jefferson Davis, Hayes and Winnie Davis memorials, Richmond, Va.; General McLaws and General Barton monuments, Savannah, Ga., Duncan Jacob memorial, Louisville; groups on U.S. Court House, San Francisco; Pierre Laclede monument, Colossal Lions, University City Gates, and Confederate monument, Forest Park, St. Louis; Sam Davis Confederate soldier monument, Parthenon frieze and Kiwanis war memorial, Nashville, Tenn.; Industrial monument, New Bedford, Mass.; Dr. Still monument, Kirksville, Mo.; "Education," frieze on new Central High Sch., Washington, statue of Sequoya, in Statuary Hall, etc. Portrait busts Emperor Francis Joseph, Victor Hugo, Gen. Stonewall Jackson, Gen. Fitzhugh Lee, Clara Hoffman, Maj. James S. Rollins, D.R. Francis, etc. Ex-pres. St. Louis Artists' Guild; sec. Internat. Sculpture Jury, World's Fair, St. Louis, 1904; chmn. Mo. Art Commn., Portland Expn., 1905. Mem. Union Internationale des Arts et Sciences (Paris), Soc. Washington Artists (ex-pres.); pres. Nat. Art Center. Decorated by King of Rumania Ordre Pour le Mérite, 1st class. Clubs: Cosmos, Arts (ex-pres.), Nat. Press (Washington); Nat. Arts (New York). Home: 161 E. 79th St. Studio: 15 Gramercy Park, New York, N.Y. Died May 1, 1949; buried Woodlawn Cemetery, New York.

ZORBAUGH, Charles Louis (zôr'baw), clergyman; b. Northfield, Des Moines County, Ia., Jan. 8, 1867; s. Conrad and Susannah (McClure) Z.; A.B., Parsons Coll., Fairfield, Ia., 1887, A.M., 1890; B.D., McCormick Theol. Sem., 1894; D.D., Buena Vista Coll., Storm Lake, Ia., 1905; m. Harriet C. Harvey, Sept. 5, 1894; children—Harvey Warren, Frederick McClure, Elizabeth Harvey. Teacher Neb. State Sch. for Deaf, Omaha, 1887-89, Kan. State Sch., Olathe, 1889-91; ordained Presbyn. ministry, 1894; organizer and pastor Windermere Ch., Cleveland, 1896-1911; supt. ch. extension (by election, Presbytery of Cleveland), 1911-24; exec. sec. Synod Ohio, 1924-37; ex-chmn. Comity Com. of Ohio Council of Chs.; founder-pres. Singing Quill, Presbyn. Poetry Soc. of Ohio, and Ohio Presbyn. Hist. Soc. Travel and writing abroad, 1937-38; interchange preacher in Great Britain, summer 1937. Mem. Western Reserve Hist. Soc., Am. Ch. History Soc. Clubs: City Club, Ohio Poetry Society (Cleveland); The Singing Quill, Verse Writers' Guild (Columbus); The Poets' Union; University (Winter Park, Fla.). Wrote: Vagabond Verse; The City Task of the Church; Ancestral Trails. Contbr. articles and verse. Home: 1877 Windemere St., East Cleveland, O. Died Aug. 17, 1943.

ZURLINDEN, Frank J.; b. Cleveland, O., July 7, 1877; s. Charles and Katherine (Grotenrath) Z., ed. St. Ignatius Coll.; business coll.; m. Frances Nisius, Oct. 23, 1901; children—Margaret Mary, Charles Francis, Helen Cecelia, Paul Robert. Rose from messenger to teller State Nat. Bank, Cleveland, 1895-1904; asst. loan teller to mgr. loan dept. First Nat. Bank, Cleveland, 1904-14; became mgr. loans, discounts and investment dept. Fed. Res. Bank of Cleveland, 1914, asst. cashier, 1917, asst. to gov., 1919, deputy gov., 1920, first v.p., 1936-43, retired June 30, 1943. Trustee Catholic Charities Corp. Mem. Parmadale advisory bd. K. of C. Club: Bankers (Pittsburgh). Home: 1026 Wilbert Rd., Lakewood, Ohio. Office: Federal Reserve Bank of Cleveland, Cleveland, O. Died Dec. 17, 1944.

ZWEIG, Stefan (tsvīk), author; b. Vienna, Austria, 1881. Entire career devoted to writing novels, short stories, novelettes, biographies, poems, dramas, essays and books of travel; literary and art critic. Upon German invasion of Austria, moved to England, then to South America. Author: Volpone (adaptation); Conflicts; Jeremiah; Joseph Fouche; Amok; Mental Healers; Letter from an Unknown Woman; Marie Antoinette; Kaleidoscope; Erasmus of Rotterdam; Mary, Queen of Scotland; The Right to Heresy; The Buried Candelabrum; Conqueror of the Seas; Beware of Pity; Master Builders; The Tide of Fortune, 1940, 12 hist. episodes revealing perfect historic process. Books have been translated into 22 languages including Chinese, Georgian, Japanese and Yiddish; plays performed in more than 20 countries. Address: Rosemount Lyncombe, Hill, Bath, Eng. Died Feb. 23, 1942.

ADDENDUM

(Deaths, or dates of death or other revisions, received after the main body of the volume [beginning on page 15] had gone to press.)

ABBOT, Everett (Vergnies), lawyer, author; b. Meadville, Pa., Feb. 3, 1862; s. Francis Ellingwood and Katherine Fearing (Loring) A.; A.B., Harvard, 1886, A.M., 1889; LL.B., Harvard Law Sch., 1889; m. Amy Hackes, Dec. 19, 1908. Practiced, New York, since 1890; mem. Keith & Abbot. Mem. Am., State, County and City Bar assns. Clubs: University, Reform. Author: Income Tax Law of 1894 (with Roger Foster), 1895; Justice and the Modern Law, 1913. Home: 160 E. 91st St. Office: 45 Cedar St., New York. Died Aug. 19, 1925.

ABBOTT, Clinton Gilbert, museum dir., ornithologist; b. Liverpool, Eng., Apr. 17, 1881 (parents U.S. citizens); s. Lewis Lowe and Grace (Van Dusen) A.; came to U.S. 1897; A.B. Columbia, 1903, student Cornell U., 1914-15; m. Dorothy Clarke, May 18, 1915; children—Dorothea Van Dusen (Mrs. Hal G. Evarts, Jr.), Lois Virginia (Mrs. Peter D. Whitney), Lucia Grace. Lecturer on ornithology and travel, Bd. of Edn., N.Y.; confidential sec. and editor, Conservation Comm., State of N.Y., 1918-21; in charge pub. edn., San Diego Natural History Museum, 1921-22, dir. since 1922. Trustee, The Bishop's Sch., La Jolla, Calif. Fellow San Diego Soc. Natural History (pres. 1923-25); mem. Linnaean Soc., N.Y. (sec. 1904-10, v.p. 1910-14), Am. Ornithologists' Union, Cooper Ornith. Club (pres. south. div. 1934), Am. Soc. Mammalogists, Western Soc. Naturalists, National Audubon Soc., Internat. Com. for Wildlife Protection, Alpha Delta Phi, Phi Beta Kappa. Clubs: Univ. (San Diego); La Jolla Beach and Tennis. Author: The Home Life of the Osprey, 1911. Contbr. to sci. journs. Home: 129 W. Palm St. Address: Natural History Museum, Balboa Park, San Diego, Calif. Died Mar. 5, 1946.

ABBOTT, Frank Danford, editor; b. Bethel, Vt., Jan. 29, 1853; s. Luther Barnett and Marian Elizabeth (Soper) A.; ed. in common schools, Owatonna, Minn.; grad. music and literature, Episcopal Coll., Faribault, Minn.; m. Eva Schugart, 187[illegible]. Began business with Geo. Woods & Co., Cambridgeport, Mass.; corr. various musical journals; founded The Presto (musical journ.), 1884, during the Chicago Expn. published daily edition of paper on the grounds of the expn. Author numerous musical papers and monographs. Official author of Awards Souvenir of Musical Instruments of the Chicago Expn. Hon. mem. various local and European musical and literary assns. Office: 440 S. Dearborn St., Chicago. Died Nov. 29, 1944.

ABBOTT, Keene, writer; b. Fremont, Neb.; s. Dr. Luther Jewett and Clara Frances (Culbertson) A.; ed. U. of Neb.; m. Mabel Avery Rundell, Aug. 29, 1905. Tutor English literature, U. of Ia., 1899; with brother, L. J. A., est. daily newspaper, The Lariat, Lawton, Okla., 1902; with World-Herald, Omaha, 1903-35, retired June 1935. Author: A Melody in Silver, 1911; Silent Battle; Indian Character Studies; Wine o' the Winds, 1920; Cinders; Tree of Life, 1927. Contbr. to mags. Address: 2461 St. Mary's Ave., Omaha. Died July 5, 1941.

ABBOTT, Wilbur Cortez, prof. history; b. Kokomo, Ind., Dec. 28, 1869; s. Thomas W. and Eleanor L. (Holliday) A.; A.B., Wabash Coll., 1892, A.M., 1904, D.Litt., 1922; Cornell, 1892-95; B.Litt., Oxford U., 1897; also studied on continent; hon. A.M., Yale, 1908; m. Margaret E. Smith, Sept. 6, 1899; children—Mary Eleanor, Charles Cortez. Fellow, 1892-93, instr., 1893-95, President White traveling fellow, 1895-96, Cornell; instr. history, U. of Mich., 1897-99; asst. prof. history, Dartmouth Coll., 1899-1902; prof. European history, U. of Kan., 1902-08; prof. history, Yale, 1908-20; prof. history, Harvard U., 1920-37. Research asso. in history, Yale, 1938-46; visiting prof., Columbia, 1939. Author: Colonel Blood, Crown Stealer, 1911; The Expansion of Europe, 1917; Colonel John Scott of Long Island, 1918; Conflicts with Oblivion, 1924; The New Barbarians, 1925; A Bibliography of Oliver Cromwell, 1929; New York in the American Revolution, 1929; Introduction to Documents relating to the International Status of Gibraltar, 1934; Adventures in Reputation, 1935; The Writings and Speeches of Oliver Cromwell, Vol. I, 1937, Vol. II, 1939, Vol. III, 1945, Vol. IV, 1946. Contbr. to periodicals. Home: Spring Farm, Pomfret Center, Conn., and 74 Sparks St., Cambridge, Mass. Died Feb. 3, 1947.

ABBOTT, William Rufus, telephone official; b. New York, N.Y., Sept. 18, 1869; s. William McKee and Hester (Beggs) A.; ed. pub. schs., New York; m. Mabel Rosalie Harland, June 1, 1892; children—Hester (Mrs. Louis E. Tilden), William Rufus. Clk. in auditor's office, Erie R.R. Co., New York, 1885-88; cashier, Westchester (N.Y.) Telephone Co., Feb. 1, 1888-May 19, 1890; clk. Metropolitan Telephone & Telegraph Co. (now N.Y. Telephone Co.), May 19, 1890-Feb. 18, 1893; with Ill. Bell Telephone Co. since Feb. 19, 1893, becoming gen. comml. supt., 1911, gen. mgr., 1914, v.p. and gen. mgr., Nov. 24, 1920, president, 1922, chairman board, 1930-34, retired; director, Illinois Bell Telephone Company. Mem. Chicago Zoölogy Soc., Wisconsin Soc. of Chicago (pres. 1923), Art Inst. Chicago, Am. Inst. Elec. Engrs., Western Soc. Engrs., Chicago Crime Commn. (exec. com. and sec., 1919-22), Chicago Plan Commn. (exec. com.), Employers' Assn. of Chicago (exec. com., 1920-22; v.p., 1923), First State Indsl. Wage Loan Soc. (responsible for eliminating the loan shark from Ill.; dir. and sec. from 1913 until it was merged with Morris Plan Bank, 1917), Am. Geog. Soc., Am. Forestry Assn., Field Mus. Natural History. Mem. Chicago Veteran Druggists' Assn., Chicago Assn. Commerce (dir.; chmn. exec. com., membership com., spl. coms.), Chamber Commerce U.S.A. (v.p. 1933). Republican. Presbyterian. Mason (K.T.). Clubs: Chicago Athletic (dir. 1906-08; vice-president 1909-10; (pres. 1911), Commercial (pres. 1926), Mid-Day, Glen View; Melbourne Golf and Country, Eau Gallie Yacht. Home: Melbourne, Fla. Died Mar. 2, 1950.

ACKERMAN, Frederick Lee, architect; b. Edmeston, N.Y., July 9, 1878; s. Samuel Bertrand and Anna L. (Reed) A.; B. Arch., Cornell, 1901; studied in Paris, 1904-05; m. Mary Eleanor Linton, Sept. 28, 1911. Mem. Trowbridge & Ackerman, 1906-20, since alone; firm architects Central Br. Y.M.C.A. Bldg., Brooklyn, residences of George D. Pratt (Glen Cove, L.I., Truman H. Newberry (Detroit), Balch Halls, Cornell Univ., Ithaca, etc. Formerly lecturer on architecture, Cornell and Columbia univs. Served as mem. N.Y. State Bd. for Registration of Architects, World War, also as chief of housing and town plan design of U.S. Shipping Bd. Emergency Fleet Corp.; tech. adviser City Plan Commn., Providence, R.I., and Housing Authority, N.Y. City; consultant housing div., Pub. Works Adminstrn., Washington, D.C.; consultant N.Y. State Div. of Housing. Fellow A.I.A.; mem. N.Y Assn Architects, Am Inst. of Planners, Nat. Housing Assn., Sigma Xi. Contbr. various articles on housing and town planning. Home: 25 East 83rd St. Office: 25 W. 44th St., New York, N.Y. Died Mar. 17, 1950.

ALEXANDER, Oakey Logan, corp. exec.; b. Parkersburg, W.Va., 1878; s. William Randolf and Isabella (Mann) A.; ed. Athens, W.Va.; m. Ethel Witherspoon, 1909. Began as salesman wholesale grocery Co.; now chmn. bd. Am. Enka Corp.; pres. and dir. Pocahontas Fuel Co., Pocahontas Steamship Company, Pocahontas Coal Corp., Pocahontas Light and Water Co., Pocahontas Corp.; dir. First Nat. Bank of Bluefield, Irving Trust Co., and various other companies. Home: 829 Park Av. Office: 1 Broadway, New York, N.Y. Died Jan. 21, 1950.

ALLEN, James Edward, college pres.; b. Hebron, Va., June 13, 1876; s. Peter Woodward (M.D.) and Fannie Blunt (Scott) A.; A.B., Hampden-Sydney, 1898, LL.D., 1923; studied U. of Va., summers 1902, 1903; grad. student in Latin, Johns Hopkins, 1903-05; m. Susan H. Garrott, June 18, 1910 (now dec.); children—Jas. Edward, Joseph Garrott, Robert Alfriend, Charles Garrott, Frances Blunt (dec.), Carter Randolph; m. 2d, Mrs. Parke D. Carter, June 11, 1927. Prin. schs., Phoebus, Va., 1900-01; v.prin. and instr. Latin, high sch., Newport News, 1901-03; instr. modern langs., Deichman Prep. Sch., Baltimore, 1904-05; instr. Latin, Notre Dame Coll., Md., 1905; prin. high sch. and instr. German, Newport News, 1905-06; prof. French and German, Davis and Elkins College, W.Va., 1906-09; pres. Davis and Elkins Coll., 1910-35; pres. Marshall Coll., Huntington, W.Va., 1935-42, emeritus since 1942., dir. Coll. Registration Service, N.Y. City, Apr.-July 1943. Member West Virginia Academy of Science, Randolph County (West Virginia) Historical Society (vice president 1932), Am. Geog. Soc., W.Va. State Planning Bd. for all Colls. and the Univ., Phi Beta Kappa, Kappa Delta Pi. Democrat. Presbyn.; mem. com. Christian Edn. Synod of W.Va., moderator of the Synod, 1934; mem. Southern Assn. of Presbyn. Colleges. Was "Four Minute Man," during the war. Clubs: Social, Literary, Educational, Rotary (pres. 1922-23). Contbr. on ednl. topics. Author of The Minimum Salary of a Rural Presbyterian Pastor, 1930. Home: 15 Holbrook Av., Danville, Va. Died Jan. 6, 1950.

ANGELL, William Robert, pres. Continental Aeronautic Corp.; b. Jesup, Ia., Feb. 10, 1877; s. William Henry and Catherine (Byers) A.; ed. pub. and high schs., Muskegon, Mich.; LL.B., Kent Coll. of Law, Chicago, 1898; m. Francie B. Savage, Sept. 12, 1899; children—William Robert and (adopted) Chester (1st lt. Air Corps; killed in action, March 16, 1944). Admitted to Ill. bar, 1899; chief clerk, Quigg & Bentley (later Bentley & Burling), attys., Chicago, 1898-1903; mem. Angell & Byers, 1903-04, Angell & Paddock, 1904-05; alone, 1905-17; sec. Continental Motors Corp., 1916-21, chmn. finance com., 1918-30, vice-pres., 1921-30, pres., 1930-39; pres. Continental Aeronautic Corp., Los Angeles; pres. and dir. Continental Aircraft Engine Co., 1930-34, Continental Divco Co., 1932-36; also pres. Home Finance Co. and Midland Corp.; dir. of Lakey Foundry & Machine Co., 1918-40. Trustee, Kalamazoo (Mich.) College. Charter mem. Aero Club of Mich. Mem. Mich. Nat. Guard 3 yrs. Fellow Am. Geog. Soc.; mem. Nat. Aeronautic Assn. of U.S. Army, Quartermaster Assn., Fathers Assn. of Culver Military Acad.; Order of Founders and Patriots of America. Republican. Presbyterian. Mason. Clubs: Detroit Golf, Detroit Athletic (Detroit); Wild Wing (Chicago). Address: Detroit-Leland Hotel, Detroit 26, Mich.; also North Manitou Island, Mich. Died Jan. 25, 1950.

ARCHER, Franklin Morse, banker; b. Camden, N.J., Nov. 27, 1873; s. Benjamin F. and Mary W. (Sloan) A.; grad. Episcopal Acad., Phila., 1890; A.B., Princeton U., 1894; LL.B., Harvard, 1897; m. Bessie M. Chandlee, June 14, 1900; children—Franklin Morse, Elizabeth C. (Mrs. Henry B. Guthrie, Jr.), Gertrude A. (Mrs. Richard L. Fitzwater, Jr.), Evan Chandlee. Admitted to N.J. bar, 1897, and practiced in Camden, 1897-1918; pres. Nat. Bank of Camden, 1918-22; pres. First Nat. State Bank of Camden, 1922-27; pres. First Camden Nat. Bank & Trust Co., 1927-47; chmn. bd. since 1947; dir. Camden Fire Ins. Co., Phila., Camden Ferry Co., Provident Mutual Life Ins. Co., West Jersey and Seashore R.R. Company, Esterbrook Pen Company, Camden, N.J. Member advisory com. 3d Fed. Reserve District of R.F.C. Director of the Cooper Hospital. Republican. Presbyterian. Clubs: Union League (Phila.); Nassau (Princeton); Tavistock Country (Haddonfield); City (Camden). Home: 570 Warwick Rd., Haddonfield, N.J. Office: Broadway and Cooper St., Camden, N.J. Died Feb. 2, 1950.

ARMSTRONG, Walter Preston, lawyer; b. Pittsboro, Miss., Oct. 26, 1884; s. George Wells and May (Cruthirds) A.; student Webb Sch., Bell Buckle, Tenn., 1898-1901, U. of Miss., 1901-02; A.B., Yale U., 1906, LL.B. magna cum laude, 1908; hon. LL.D., Boston University, 1942, Southwestern Coll., 1943; m. Irma Waddell, Nov. 12, 1912; 1 son, Walter Preston. Admitted to Tenn. bar, 1908, and began practice at Memphis; city atty., Memphis, 1920-24; special asst. to atty. general of U.S. under Selective Service Act; member Federal Board of Legal Examiners; mem. Armstrong, McCadden, Allen, Barden & Goodman. Mem. com. apptd. by sec. of war to suggest revision of court martial procedure. Member general council Am. Bar Assn., 1929-31, member House of Delegates since 1939, mem. exec. com., 1931-34, mem. bd. of editors Am. Bar Assn. Jour., 1934-41, and since 1943. Mem. Shelby County Bar Assn. (president 1932-33), Tennessee Bar Association (president 1936), Am. Bar Association (pres. 1941-42), Am. Law Inst. (mem. council), Acad. of Polit. and Social Science, Acad. Polit. Science, Assn. of Bar City of New York, Sigma Chi, Phi Delta Phi; honorary member Canadian Bar Association. Mem. Commrs. on Uniform State Laws for Tennessee. Independent Democrat. Methodist. Clubs: University, Memphis Country (Memphis); Lotos (New York). Contbr. to law jours. Home: 1219 East Parkway S. Office: Commerce Title Bldg., Memphis 3, Tenn. Died July 27, 1949. Buried Forest Hill Cemetery, Memphis, Tenn.

BABCOCK, Edward Vose, lumber; b. Fulton, N.Y., Jan. 31, 1864; s. Leaman B. and Harriet (Vose) B.; ed. pub. schs., Oswego County, N.Y.; m. 2d, Mary D. Arnold; children—Dorothy Arnold, Edward Vose, Fred Courtney. Entered lumber business as employe at Detroit; established E. V. Babcock & Co., lumber, Pittsburgh, Jan. 1, 1890; officer many lumber cos. Home: 5135 Ellsworth Av. Office: 908 Frick Bldg., Pittsburgh, Pa.* Died Sep. 2, 1948.

BACHELLER, Irving (Addison) (băch'ĕ-lĕr); b. Pierpont, N.Y., Sept. 26, 1859; s. Sanford Paul and Achsah Ann (Buckland) B.; B.S., St. Lawrence U., 1882, M.S., 1892, hon. A.M., 1901, L.H.D., 1911, A.B., 1912; Litt.D., Middlebury, 1910; LL.D., Rollins, 1940; m. Anna Detmar Schultz, Dec. 13, 1883. Actively connected with press of N.Y. for years, one of editors New York World, 1898-1900. Mem. Phi Beta Kappa, Soc. of Mayflower Descendants of N.Y., S.R., New England Soc. of N.Y. (pres.), Nat. Inst. Arts and Letters. Trustee St. Lawrence U. and Rollins Coll. Received the medal for art from the Grand Masonic Lodge of the State of New York in 1937. Author: The Master of Silence. 1890; The Still House of O'Darrow, 1894; Eben Holden, 1900; D'ri and I. 1901; Darrel of the Blessed Isles, 1903; Vergilius, 1904; Silas Strong, 1906; The Hand Made Gentleman, 1909; The Master, 1910; Keeping Up with Lizzie, 1911; Charge It, 1912; The Turning of Griggsby, 1913; Marryers, 1914; The Light in the Clearing, 1917; Keeping Up with William, 1918; A Man for the Ages, 1919; The Prodigal Village, 1920; In the Days of Poor Richard, 1922; The Scudders, 1923; Father Abraham, 1925; Dawn—A Lost Romance of the Time of Christ, 1927; Coming Up the Road—the story of a North Country Boyhood, 1928; The House of the Three Ganders, 1929; A Candle in the Wilderness, 1930; The Master of Chaos, 1931; Uncle Peel, 1933; The Harvesting, 1934; The Oxen of the Sun, 1935; A Boy for the Ages, 1937; From Stores of Memory, 1938; The Winds of God, 1941; Cricket Heron, (London), 1909; In Various Moods, 1910; The Opinion of a Cheerful Yankee, 1926. Address: care Mrs. Dora Bacheller Haines, Fairfax, Va. Died Feb. 24, 1950.

BARBER, William A., chmn. bd. Childs Co.; b. Chester County, S.C., 1869; s. Capt. Osmund and Mary (Westbrook B.; A.B., U. of S.C., 1889, LLB., LL.D; m. Melanie Wilmer Gordon, 1921; 1 son, Gordon. Admitted to practice before Supreme Ct. of S.C., 1891, U.S. Supreme Ct., 1895, Supreme Ct. of N.Y., 1899, later to various federal courts; elected atty. gen. of S.C., 1894; pres. Carolina & Northwestern Ry., 1900-17; v.p. and dir. Mogollon Mines, 1906-11; now sr. mem. Barber & Grunden. Chmn bd. and dir. of Childs Co., N.Y. City, since 1928, also Childs Dining Hall Co. and Childs Real Estate Co.; dir. N.Y. Trap Rock Corp. Mem. Assn. of the Bar of N.Y. Am. and N.Y. State bar assns., New York County Lawyers Assn., N.Y. Southern Soc., Phi Beta Kappa. Clubs: Metropolitan; Bankers. Home: 1030 Fifth Av. Office: 120 Broadway, N.Y. City.
Died Feb. 7, 1950.

BARRETT, Oliver Rogers, lawyer; b. Jacksonville, Ill., Oct. 14, 1873; s. Rev. George J. and Ellen (Watson) B.; LL.B. U. of Mich., 1896; LL.D., Lincoln Memorial U., 1929; m. Pauline S. Proctor, Dec. 25, 1911; 1 son, Roger Watson. Admitted to Ill. bar, 1896; practiced at Peoria, 1896-1905; removed to Chicago, 1905; mem. firm Daily, Dines, White & Fiedler. Mem. Am., Ill. State and Chicago bar associations, Society Trial Lawyers, American Historical Association, Midland Authors, Phi Beta Kappa. Republican. Clubs: Indian Hill; Caxton, Grolier (New York). Home: 623 Abbotsford Rd., Kenilworth, Ill. Office: 122 S. Michigan Av., Chicago 3, Ill. Died Mar. 5, 1950.

BLACKWELL, Alice Stone, journalist; b. East Orange, N.J., Sept. 14, 1857; d. Henry B. Blackwell and Lucy Stone; A.B., Boston U., 1881; Dr. Humanities (honorary) Boston Univ., 1945; unmarried. Assisted parents on Woman's Journal, Boston, asst. editor, 1883-1909, after their death, editor in chief till 1917, when the Woman's Journal, the Woman Voter, and the Headquarters News-Letter were consolidated as the Woman Citizen, of which was contbg. editor; editor paper called The Woman's Column, 1886-1905. Extensive writer on woman's suffrage. Served as sec. Nat. Am. Woman Suffrage Assn. about 20 yrs.; also served as pres. N.E. and Mass. Woman Suffrage assns. Hon. pres. Mass. League Women Voters; a presdl. elector for La Follette in 1924. Has taken deep interest in the Armenians and received Order of Melusine from Prince Guy de Lusignan; also deeply interested in the Jewish people and received Jewish Rose from the Jewish Advocate; awarded medal by Ford Hall Forum "for humanitarian service." Active in Am. Friends of Russian Freedom. Hon. trustee Boston U.; mem. Am. Assn. Univ. Women (past pres., Mass.); Phi Beta Kappa. Author: Lucy Stone, Pioneer of Woman's Rights, 1930. Editor: The Little Grandmother of the Russian Revolution—Catherine Breshkovsky's Own Story, 1917. Translator and Compiler: Armenian Poems, 1896, 1916; Songs of Russia, 1906; Songs of Grief and Gladness (from the Yiddish), 1908; Some Spanish-American Poets, 1929. Co-compiler: The Yellow Ribbon Speaker, 1911. Home: 1010 Massachusetts Av., Cambridge, Mass. Died Mar. 15, 1950.

BLAND, Schuyler Otis, congressman; b. Gloucester County, Va., May 4, 1872; s. Schuyler and Olivia James (Anderson) B.; student William and Mary Coll.; summer course in law, U. of Va.; m. Mary Crawford Putzel. Admitted to Va. bar, 1900; mem. Henley & Bland, Williamsburg and Newport News, Va., 1900-01; later associated in practice with Bickford & Stuart, and with R. G. Bickford; practiced alone since 1909; elected to 65th Congress, July 1918, to succeed William A. Jones, deceased, and reëlected 66th to 81st Congresses (1919-51), 1st Va. Dist. Mem. Va. State Bar Assn., Newport News Bar Assn., Phi Beta Kappa, Kappa Alpha (Southern). Democrat. Home: 3107 Chesapeake Av., Hampton, Va. Died Feb. 16, 1950; buried Greenlawn Cemetery, Newport News, Va.

BLUM, Leon (blōōm, lā-ōn), former premier of France; b. Paris, Apr. 9, 1872; student Lycée Charlemagne, Lycée Henri IV, l'Ecole Normale Supérieure. Began political career as mem. Council of State; published first writing in 1901; apptd. chief of Cabinet and minister of public works, 1914; deputy of Seine area (Paris) 1919. Pres. Socialist Party. Dir. of publ. "Le Populaire," since 1921. Dep. from Narbonne, 1928; became prime minister of France, 1936; resigned to be minister of state and v.p. of Council in the Chautemps Cabinet, 1937; again prime minister and finance minister in 1938. Blum had no official position in French govt. following its fall to the Nazis, but was arrested in 1940 with several other French statesmen and went on trial at Riom by Vichy govt. for responsibility of the French defeat in World War II; apptd. French ambassador extraordinary to negotiate economic agreements with the Allied countries. Author of books and discourses on govt., polit. science, social science, drama and other arts. Address: 25 Quai de Bourbon, Paris, France.* Died Mar. 30, 1950.

DOATNER, Victor Vincent, ry. exec.; b. Bethlehem, Miss., May 6, 1881; s. Franklin P. and Mary (Wills) B.; ed. Miss. Coll., Clinton, and Bowling Green (Ky.) Business U.; m. Ellen J. Kramer, 1946. With Yazo & Miss. Valley R.R. 1901, chief dispatcher and trainmaster, 1906-16, supt. New Orleans div., Vicksburg, Miss., July 1916-Aug. 1917, supt. Memphis (Tenn.) div., Aug. 1917-June 1921; pres. Peoria & Pekin Union Ry., 1921-29; pres. Chicago Great Western R.R., 1929-31; apptd. western regional dir. Fed. Coordinator of Transportation, July 1933, and dir. of regional coördination, June 15, 1934-June 15, 1936; railway consultant, also dir. and exec. rep. Gulf, Mobile and Ohio R.R., June 15, 1936-Jan. 1, 1942; dir. Chicago & Eastern Ill. R.R. since 1942; executive representative Norfolk. Southern Railway, 1942-47; director of railway transport, Office of Defense Transportation U.S.A., Washington, D.C., Jan. 1942-Apr. 1944, railway cons. since Apr. 1944. Mason (Shriner, Scottish Rite). Clubs: Old Elm, Chicago, Traffic (Chicago). Home: Ambassador Hotel. Office: Bankers Bldg., 105 W. Adams St., Chicago.
Died Feb. 11, 1950.

BOLES, Edgar Howard, insurance exec., lawyer; b. Phila., Pa., July 7, 1880; s. George Howard and Rhoda (Borden) B.; A.B., Haverford Coll., 1902; LL.B., U. of Pa., 1905; LL.D., Muhlenberg Coll., 1924; m. Blanche Huey, Oct. 18, 1905; children—Alan, Eloise, Laurence. Began law practice, Phila., 1905; asst. to gen. solicitor N.Y.C. R.R. Co., 1907-09; various official positions Lehigh Valley R.R. Co., becoming v.p. and gen. counsel until December 31, 1926; chmn. of bd., dir. Gen. Reinsurance Corp., 1926; pres., dir. Gen. Reinsurance Corp. and affiliates, Jan. 1927-Aug. 1946; chmn. bd., dir. North Star Reins. Corp.; dir. Herbert Clough, Inc.; dir. Lehigh Valley R.R. Co., Marine Midland Trust Co. of New York, Consol. Real Estate Co., Western Pacific R.R. Corp. Dir. Ins. Inst. of Am.; dir. Boys Clubs Am., Inc. Mem. The Pilgrims of U.S., Nat. Inst. Social Sciences. Republican. Clubs: University, St. Andrews Golf, Century. Home: 720 Park Av. Office: 120 Broadway, New York, N.Y. Died Feb. 4, 1950.

BOSWELL, Ira Mathews, clergyman, educator; b. Columbus, Miss., Apr. 28, 1866; s. Ira Mathews and Jane (Goodrich) B.; student Ky. (now Transylvania) U. and Coll. of the Bible, Lexington, Ky.; special studies under Dr. Clinton Lockhart; D.D., Cincinnati Bible Seminary, 1926; m. Lucie Cross Mimms, Dec. 30, 1899; children—Lady Louise (Mrs. Whitney Dunlap), Sarah Goodrich (Mrs. Jonathan Riddick Sanderlin). Ordained ministry Christian (Disciples) Ch., 1898; pastor Meridian, Miss., Selma, Ala., Port Gibson, Miss., 1899-1903, Chattanooga, 1903-16, Georgetown, Ky., 1916-35; prof. of Old Testaments, Christian doctrine and general apologetics, Cincinnati Bible Seminary, since 1939. Organized Juvenile Court, Chattanooga, an organizer of Chattanooga Bur. of Municipal Research. Chaplain S.C.V. of Tenn., rank of col.; has delivered addresses at nat. and internat. conventions of the Christian Church; selected by com. of Tenn. preachers to affirm the scripturalness of instrumental music in ch. worship in debate lasting 5 nights; mem. advisory com. of Christian Women's Benevolent Assn. of St. Louis, Yotsuya Missions, Japan; trustee Cincinnati Bible Sem.; dedicated the Dixie Highway, Cincinnati, Sept. 1921; dir. Dixie Highway Assn.; dir. Cincinnati Lookout Mt. Air-line Highway Assn.; mem. Pi Gamma Mu, Kappa Sigma. Awarded Faculty Key for distinguished services. Democrat. Mason (K.T., Shriner), K. of P., Woodman, Red Man. Author: Recollections of a Redheaded Man, 1915; God's Purpose Toward Us, 1927; Flaming Hearts, and Other Sermons, 1930. Home: 598 Sunset Rd., Louisville, Ky. Died Jan. 18, 1950.

BOWERS, Thomas Wilson, lawyer; b. Winona, Minn., Aug. 18, 1888; s. Lloyd W. and Louise (Wilson) B.; A.B. Yale, 1910; LL.B., Harvard, 1913; m. Louise Hellen, Oct. 31, 1914; children—Lloyd Wheaton, Thomas Wilson, Ellen. Admitted to bar, D.C., 1914, Ill., 1916, N.Y., 1922, also U.S. Supreme Ct.; examiner Interstate Commerce Commn., Washington, 1913-15; clerk Holt, Cutting & Sidley, Chicago, Ill., 1915-17, Cravath & Henderson, N.Y. City, 1919-22; asst. gen. counsel Federal Reserve Bank of N.Y. (City), 1922; v.p. Nat. Bank of Commerce, 1922-29, Bank of The Manhattan Co., 1930-42; dir. Universal Oil Products Co. (Chicago), Am. Export Lines, Inc., Ayrshire Colliers Corp., Sunray Oil Corp. of Del., Buda Co. (Harvey, Ill.), County Trust Co., White Plains, N.Y., Am. Overseas Airlines, Inc. Home: Washington, Conn. Office: 25 Broadway, N.Y. City 4. Died Mar. 16, 1950.

BOWMAN, Isaiah, univ. pres.; b. Waterloo, Ont., Can., Dec. 26, 1878; s. Samuel Cressman and Emily (Shantz) B.; grad. State Normal Coll., Ypsilanti, Mich., 1902; B.Sc., Harvard, 1905; Ph.D., Yale, 1909; hon. M.A., 1921; hon. M.Ed., Mich. State Coll., 1927; hon. Sc.D., Bowdoin Coll., 1931, Universities of Cuzco and Arequipa, Peru, 1941; Oxford Univ., 1918; LL.D., Dartmouth, Charleston, Dickinson and U. of Pa., 1935, U. of Wis. and Harvard, 1936, Queen's U. and U. of Western Ontario, 1937, Washington Coll., 1940, Johns Hopkins, 1949; hon. Litt.D., Marietta College, 1947; m. Cora Olive Goldthwait, June 28, 1909; children—Walter Parker, Robert Goldthwait, Olive. Asst. physiography Harvard 1904-05; instr. geography State Normal Coll., Ypsilanti, 1903-04; instr. geography Yale, 1905-09, asst. prof., 1909-15; dir. Am. Geography Soc., 1915-35; pres. Johns Hopkins, 1935-48, pres. emeritus, 1949. Leader first Yale South Am. Expdn., 1907; geographer and geologist Yale Peruvian Expdn., 1911; leader expdn. to Central Andes under auspices Am. Geography Soc., 1913. Chmn. Nat. Research Council, 1933-35, vice chmn. Sci. Adv. Bd., 1933-35. Chief territorial specialist Am. Commn. to Negotiate Peace, 1918-19; mem. various territorial commns. of the Peace Conf., Paris, 1919; physiographer U.S. Dept. Justice in Red River boundary dispute; Am. mem. Permanent Internat. Commn., China and U.S., since 1940; mem. London Mission of Dept. of State, 1944; chmn. territorial com. Dept. of State, 1942-43; vice-chmn. post-war adv. council Dept. of State, 1943-44; special adviser to Sec. of State, 1943-45; mem. American del. Dumbarton Oaks Conf., 1944; adviser to U.S. del. U.N. Conf., San Francisco, 1945; mem. Comm. on the Organization of the Exec. Branch of the Govt., 1948 (Hoover Commn.); mem. Pub. Adv. Com. on the China Program since 1948; cons. colonial development div. E.C.A., since 1949. Mem. bd. dirs. Am. Telephone & Telegraph Co., Council on Fgn. Relations, Woods Hole Oceanographic Inst., Am. Geog. Soc. of N.Y. (councilor, 1935); pres. Internat. Geog. Union, 1931-34. Fellow Am. Acad. Arts and Sciences; mem. Am. Philos. Soc. (council, 1935), Assn. American Geographers (pres., 1931), Nat. Acad. Sciences (v.p., 1941-45), A.A.A.S. (pres., 1943), Phi Beta Kappa; mem. bd. overseers Harvard Coll. since 1948; asso. mem. Nat. Acad. of Sciences, Peru, hon. corr. mem. Geogr. Society La Paz, Bolivia, Hispanic Soc. Am., Royal Geog. Soc., London, Swedish Soc. Anthropology and Geography (former mem., 1939), geog. socs. of Phila., Berlin, Finland, Jugoslavia, Rome, Colombia, etc.; corr. mem. Soc. Chilena de Hist. y Geogr.; recipient Livingstone gold medal Royal Scottish Geog. Soc., 1928; Bonaparte-Wyse Gold Medal of Geog. Soc. of Paris, 1917, for explorations in the publs. on S. America; Gold Medal Geog. Soc., Chicago, 1927; Cvijic Medal Geog. Soc. of Belgrade, 1935; Henry Grier Bryant Gold Medal Geog. Soc. of Phila., 1937; Patron's Medal Royal Geog. Soc. (London), 1941; Delgado Medal of the Geogr. Soc. of Lima, 1949; Explorers Club Medal awarded postumously, 1950. Clubs: Explorers (ex-sec. and ex-v.p.), Century (New York); Cosmos (Washington). Author: Fores Physiography, 1911; South America, 1915; The Andes of Southern Peru, 1916; The New World—Problems in Political Geography, 1921; Desert Trails of Atacama, 1928; An American Boundary Dispute, 1923; The Mohammedan World, 1924; International Relations, 1930; The Pioneer Fringe, 1931; Geography in Relation to the Social Sciences, 1934; Design for Scholarship, 1936; Graduate School in American Democracy, 1939. Co-editor and part author of Human Geography; editor and collaborator for Limits of Land Settlement, 1937. Home: The Warrington Apts., Baltimore 18. Office: The Johns Hopkins University, Baltimore 18, Md. Died Jan. 6, 1950.

BRANNON, Melvin Amos, educator; b. Lowell, Ind., Sept. 11, 1865; s. James and Eleanor (Foster) B.; A.B., Wabash Coll., 1889, A.M., 1890; Ph.D., Univ. of Chicago, 1912; LL.D., Whitman College, 1917; LL.D., Wabash, 1932, State U. Mont., 1936; D.Sc., U. of N.D., 1947; m. Lida Lowry, June 29, 1892 (died 1919); children—Eleanor Charlotte, Lida Converse; m. 2d, Mrs. Anna Lytle Tannahill, June 27, 1923 (died 1934); m. 3d, Yvonne Tissier, Oct. 20, 1938. Instr. in natural sciences, Ft. Wayne (Ind.) High Sch., 1890-94; prof. biology, U. of N.D., 1894-1914; organized Sch. of Medicine, U. of N.D., 1905, dean, 1905-11; dean Coll. of Liberal Arts, U. of N.D., 1911-14; pres. U. of Ida., 1914-17; pres. Beloit Coll., 1917-23; chancellor U. of Mont., 1923-33. Made federal survey of grasses and forage plants of N.D., 1895-96; organized biol. lab., Devils Lake, N.D., 1908, dir., 1908-14; organized public health lab. of N.D., 1909. Trustee Beloit Coll., 1917-23, hon. trustee since 1923. Mason. Fellow A.A.A.S.; mem. Am. Genetic Assn., Botanical Society of America, N.D. Acad. Science (pres. 1909), Ind. Acad. Sciences, Wis. Acad. Sciences, Arts and Letters (pres. 1922), Wis. Colls. Asso. (pres. 1919-21), Northwest Scientific Assn. (pres. 1925-26), National Assn. State Universities (pres. 1928), Phi Beta Kappa, Phi Kappa Phi, Sigma Xi, Phi Delta Theta, Sons of Am. Revolution. Clubs: Chicago Literary, Gainesville Rotary. Author papers on Marine algae, fresh water algae, The Influence of the Salton Sea upon Vegetable Tissues; The Influence of Heat upon the Maturation of Vegetables and Fruits; Some Biological Phenomena of a Dying Lake; Effect of Growth Substances on Green Algae; Some Myxophyceae of Florida. Home: Gainesville, Fla.
Died Mar. 26, 1950.

BROWN, Harry Sanford, business exec.; b. Tyler, Texas, Sept. 21, 1881; s. John A. and Emma A. Sanford; B.M.E. U. of Ark., 1901; M.E., Cornell U., 1904; m. Marjorie Carpenter. Mgr. Boston office, Power Specialty Co., 1904-18; v.p. Wheeler Condenser & Engineering Co., 1918-27; v.p. and dir. Foster Wheeler Corp., N.Y. City, 1927-35, pres., 1935-46, chmn. of bd. and pres., since 1946; chmn. of bd. and dir. Foster Wheeler, Ltd., Canada; dir. Liberty Mutual Insurance Co., also member N.Y. advisory bd. Clubs: Bankers, Baltusrol Golf, India House; Elizabeth Town and Country; Bay Head Yacht. Home: 511 Westminster Av., Elizabeth, N.J. Office: 165 Broadway, New York, N.Y. Died Feb. 18, 1950.

BROWN, Paul Goodwin, engineer; b. Red Oak, Ia., 1871; s. Isaac W. and Helen (Goodwin) B.; prep. edn., Wyoming Sem., Kingston, Pa.; student Cornell U., 1892-93; m. Antoinette Knapp, 1924. Formerly pres. Keystone State Corp. Mem. Am. Soc. C.E., Western Soc. Engrs., Delta Kappa Epsilon. Director and member executive committee Universal Pictures. Director St. Mary's Hospital, Civic Association, Four Arts, Community Chest (Palm Beach). Clubs: Racquet, Philadelphia, Engineers, Phila. Country (Phila.); Engineers, Links, Turf and Field, United Hunts, Cornell, Metropolitan (New York); Boca Raton (Fla.); Gulf Stream Golf (Delray Beach, Fla.); Old Guard Soc., Bath and Tennis, Everglades (Palm Beach). Home: 151 Hammon Av., Palm Beach, Fla. Office: 1321 Arch St., Philadelphia, Pa.

Died Mar. 24, 1950.

BUCK, Frank, wild animal authority, writer, explorer, motion picture producer; b. Gainesville, Texas, March 17, 1884; s. Howard D. and Ada (Sites) B.; educated public schools of Dallas, Texas; m. Muriel Reilly, 1928; 1 daughter, Barbara Muriel. Interested in wild animals, birds, reptiles since a boy; successively office boy, reporter, advertising agent, Chicago, 1901-11, made first expdn. to S.A., 1911; has made expdns. to Malaya, India, Borneo, New Guinea, Africa, etc.; pres. Frank Buck Enterprises, Inc.; pres. Jungleland, Inc. Motion pictures produced: Bring 'Em Back Alive, Jungle Menace, Wild Cargo, Fang and Claw. Author: (with E. Anthony) Bring 'Em Back Alive, 1931; Wild Cargo, 1932; (with F. L. Fraser) Fang and Claw, 1935; Tim Thompson in the Jungles, 1935; On Jungle Trails, 1937; Animals Are Like That, 1939; All in a Lifetime (autobiography), 1941. Contbr. to Collier's, Saturday Evening Post, etc. Home: 324 S. Bishop St., San Angelo, Tex.

Died Mar. 25, 1950.

BURROUGHS, Edgar Rice, author; b. Chicago, Ill., Sept. 1, 1875; s. Maj. George Tyler and Mary Evaline (Zieger) B.; ed. Harvard Sch., Chicago, Phillips Acad., Andover, Mass., and Mich. Mil. Acad., Orchard Lake, Mich.; m. Emma Centennia Hulbert, Jan. 31, 1900; children—Joan, Hulbert, John Coleman. Asst. comdt., Cav. Inst., Mich. Mil. Acad., 1895-96; served 7th U.S. Cav., Ft. Grant, Ariz., (discharged by favor); treas. Am. Battery Co., Chicago, 1899-1903; dept. mgr. Sears, Roebuck & Co., 1906-08; same, A. W. Shaw Co., pubs. of System, 1912-13; in interim was gold miner in Ore., storekeeper and cowboy in Ida., policeman in Salt Lake City, etc. Maj. 1st Batln. 2d Inf. Ill. Reserve Militia, Sept. 14, 1918-January 2, 1919; United Press correspondent, Sept. 22, 1942, until V-J Day. Member Loyal Legion. Club: Outrigger Canoe (Honolulu). Author: Tarzan of the Apes, 1914; The Return of Tarzan, 1915; The Beasts of Tarzan, 1916; The Son of Tarzan, 1917; A Princess of Mars, 1917; Tarzan and the Jewels of Opar, 1918; The Gods of Mars, 1918; Jungle Tales of Tarzan, 1919; The Warlord of Mars, 1919; Tarzan the Untamed, 1920; Thuvia, Maid of Mars, 1920; Tarzan the Terrible, 1921; The Mucker, 1921; The Chessmen of Mars, 1922; At the Earth's Core, 1922; Tarzan and the Golden Lion, 1923; Pellucidar, 1923; The Girl from Hollywood, 1923; The Land that Time Forgot, 1924; The Cave Girl, 1924; Tarzan and the Ant Men, 1925; The Bandit of Hell's Bend, 1925; The Eternal Lover, 1925; The Moon Maid, 1926; The Mad King, 1926; The Outlaw of Torn, 1927; The War Chief, 1927; The Tarzan Twins, 1927; The Master Mind of Mars, 1928; Tarzan, Lord of the Jungle, 1928; The Monster Men, 1929; Tarzan and The Lost Empire, 1929; Tanar of Pellucidar, 1930; Tarzan at the Earth's Core, 1930; A Fighting Man of Mars, 1931; Tarzan the Invincible, 1931; Jungle Girl, 1932; Tarzan Triumphant, 1932; Apache Devil, 1933; Tarzan and the City of Gold, 1933; Pirates of Venus, 1934; Tarzan and the Lion Man, 1934; Lost on Venus, 1935; Tarzan and the Leopard Men, 1935; Swords of Mars, 1936; Tarzan's Quest, 1936; The Oakdale Affair and the Rider, 1937; Back to the Stone Age, 1937; Thehad and the Lion, 1938; Tarzan and the Forbidden City, 1938; Carson of Venus, 1939; Tarzan the Magnificent, 1939; Synthetic Men of Mars, 1940; Deputy Sheriff of Comanche County, 1940; The Land of Terror, 1944; Escape on Venus, 1946; Tarzan and the Foreign Legion, 1947; Llana of Gathol, 1948; numerous novels and novelettes for mags. Home: 5465 Zelzah Av., Encino. Office: Tarzana, Calif. Died Mar. 19, 1950.

BUTTLES, John S., judge; b. Troy, N.Y., Jan. 20, 1877; s. Hiram S. and Sybil G. (Selleck) B.; grad. Brandon (Vt.) High Sch., 1893, U. of Vt., 1897, New York Law Sch., 1900; m. Marilla J. Whitcomb, May 28, 1901 (dec.); 1 son, Robert S.; m. 2d, Marion E. Seager, Nov. 14, 1914. In employ N.Y. Life Ins. Co. in N.Y. City, Dubuque, Ia., and Chicago, Ill., 1900-05; admitted to Vt. bar, 1906, and engaged in gen. practice of law at Rutland and Brandon, 1906-19; mem. Vt. Ho. of Rep., 1919; state commr. of industries, 1919-26; superior judge, 1926-37; asso. justice Vt. Supreme Ct. 1937-49, retired. Mem. Kappa Sigma, Phi Beta Kappa. Rep. Mason. (K.T., Shriner). Home: 61 Park St., Brandon, Vt.

Died May 18, 1949.

BYRON, Arthur William, pres. Actors' Equity Assn.; b. Brooklyn, N.Y., April 3, 1872; s. Oliver Doud and Mary Kate (Creban) B.; ed. St. Austin's Sch., S.D., and St. Paul's Sch., Garden City, L.I.; m. Lillian Hall, June 1898; m. 2d, Kathryn Keys. Has played leading parts with John Drew Co., Mary Mannering Co., Amelia Bingham Co., Sol Smith Russell Co., Maxine Elliott and Maude Adams. Now pres. Actors' Equity Assn. Address: 45 W. 47th St., New York, N.Y. Died July 16, 1943.

CARLSEN, Niels Christian, clergyman; b. Denmark, June 1, 1884; s. Carl Christian and Ane Christine (Jensen) C.; brought to U.S., 1894; grad. Preseminary of Dana Coll., Blair, Neb., 1907; grad. in theology, Trinity Sem., Blair, 1910; D.D., Capital U., Columbus, O., 1931; m. Martha Carolina Neve, June 15, 1910; children—Alvin Samuel, Viggo Immanuel, Verner Neve, Esther Marie, Rhoda Sarah, Raymond Christian, Lois Irene, Stanley Luther, Eunice Carla, Niels Christian. Ordained Luth. ministry, 1910; pastor Superior, Wis., and Duluth, Minn., 1910-14, Milltown, Wisconsin, 1914-19; Royal, Iowa, 1919-30. Decorated Knight of Dannebrog, 1936. Member Board of Elementary Christian Edn., United Evangelical Luth. Ch. in America, 1915-25; elected v.p. United Evangelical Lutheran Ch., 1921, pres. since 1925, full time pres. since 1930. Sec. Nat. Lutheran Council, 1928-33, v.p., 1933-37; del. to Lutheran World Conv., Copenhagen, Denmark, 1929, Paris, France, 1935; mem. exec. com. Am. Lutheran Conf. since 1930; pres. Eben-Ezer Mercy Inst., Brush, Colo., since 1930; vice-pres. Am-Denmark Relief since 1941; mem. exec. com. Nat. Lutheran Council. Home: Blair, Neb. Died Feb. 6, 1950; buried in Blair, Neb.

CHERRINGTON, Ernest Hurst, editor, temperance advocate; b. Hamden, O., Nov. 24, 1877; s. George and Elizabeth Ophelia (Paine) C.; ed. Ohio Wesleyan U., 1893-97; LL.D., 1921; Litt.D., Otterbein, 1922; m. Betty Clifford Denny, Mar. 17, 1903; children—Ernest Hurst, Ann Elizabeth (Mrs. Russell B. Driver). Became editor of Kingston (Ohio) Tribune, 1900; superintendent for Canton District, Ohio Anti-Saloon League, 1902; state asst. supt. Ohio Anti-Saloon League, Columbus, O., 1903-04; asso. editor The Pacific Issue, 1905; state supt. Anti-Saloon League of Wash., 1906-07; editor The Citizen, Seattle, 1906, 07; asso. editor, 1908, 09, editor since 1909, The American Issue, Chicago and Westerville, O.; editor The American Patriot, 1912-16, The National Daily, Westerville, O., 1915-16. Mng. dir. Richmond Virginian (daily), 1916-19. Sec. nat. exec. com., mem. nat. administrative com., and gen. mgr. pub. interests, Anti-Saloon League of America, 1915-36; also dir. The Temperance Education Foundation; gen. mgr. American Issue Pub. Co.; pres. chmn. exec. com. Scientific Temperance Federation; gen. sec. World League Against Alcoholism; sec. Nat. Temperance Council; pres. Intercollegiate Assn. for Study of Alcohol Problem, Columbus, O.; pres. Nat. Conf. of Orgns. Supporting 18th Amendment, 1930-31; chmn. Nat. Prohibition Bd. of Strategy, 1931-32. U.S. del. 13th Internat. Congress on Alcoholism, The Hague, 1911, 14th Congress, Milan, Italy, 1913 (elected mem. internat. permanent exec. com.), 16th Congress, Lausanne, Switzerland, 1921, 17th Congress, Copenhagen, 1923; sec. 15th Congress, Washington, D.C., and 16th Congress, Lausanne, Switzerland. Republican. Lay del. Gen. Conf. M.E. Ch., 8 times 1916-44; sec. Gen. Conf. Com. on Unification, 1920; mem. Joint Commn., 1920-28; member Commn. on Church Union of M.E. Church, 1920-36; mem. joint Commission which drafted plans for uniting Methodist Church, 1939; member Unifying Conf. of Three Methodisms, 1939; member executive committee M.E. Bd. of Home Missions, 1920-36; chmn. Cincinnati Area M.E. Centenary, 1919; mem. exec. com. Federal Council of Chs. in America, 1920-48; exec. sec. Bd. of Temperance of M.E. Ch., 1936-48; mem. Gen. Com. on Army and Navy Chaplains, since 1942; mem. Nat. Council of Service Men's Christian League, 1942. Mem. Phi Delta Theta. Mason (33°, K. T.). Author: History of the Anti-Saloon League, 1913; The Evolution of Prohibition in America, 1920; America and the World Liquor Problem, 1922; also numerous booklets, pamphlets and mag. articles. Compiler of the Anti-Saloon League Year Book, 1908-33. Editor in chief, Standard Encyclopedia of the Alcohol Problem. Editor The Voice since 1936. Home: 110 S. State St., Westerville, O. Died Mar. 13, 1950.

CHURCH, Ralph Edwin, lawyer, congressman; b. on farm near Catlin, Vermilion County, Ill., May 5, 1883; s. Henry George and Lola (Douglas) C.; A.B., U. of Mich., 1907; A.M., Northwestern U., 1909, LL.B., 1909; m. Marguerite Stitt, Dec. 21, 1918; children—Lt. Ralph Edwin, U.S.N.R., Lt. (j.g.) Wm. Stitt, U.S.N.R.; Marjory Williams. Admitted to bar, 1909, and since in practice at Chicago; asso. with Knapp & Campbell, 1909-16; sr. mem. Church & Traxler; State representative, 6th District Illinois, 1917-32; member 74th, 75th and 76th Congresses (1935-40), 78th to 80th Congresses (1943-48), 10th Illinois District, re-elected to 81st Congress, 1948, new 13th Illinois District; member Appropriations Merchant Marine and Fisheries, Naval Affairs, Patents, Revision of Laws, Elections No. 1, Expenditures in Executive Department, War Claims and Insular Affairs committees. Member Rep. Whip Orgn. Rep. candidate for U.S. Senate, 1940. During World War volunteered for mil. service, May 1917, and later was hon. discharged; mem. Ft. Sheridan Mil. Training Camp, 1915; exec. com. Central Dept. Citizens' Mil. Training Camp Assn., 1916; lt. comdr., U.S. Naval Res., 1938-41. Del. Inter-Parliamentary Conference, Oslo, Norway, 1939. Trustee Nat. Coll. of Edn. Mem. Am. Soc. Internat. Law, Am., Ill. State and Chicago bar associations, Chicago Association Commerce, Evanston Chamber of Commerce, Chicago Historical Society (life), Phi Kappa Psi, Delta Chi. Republican. Methodist. Mason (32°, Shriner). Clubs: Union League, Kiwanis, Executives, Evanston University, Navy, Sheridan Shore Yacht. Home: 300 Church St., Evanston, Ill. Office: 10 S. La Salle St., Chicago, Ill. Died Mar. 21, 1950.

CLARK, Walter Eli, ex-governor, journalist; b. Ashford, Conn., Jan. 7, 1869; s. Oren Andrus and Emily Janet (Jones) Clark; graduate Connecticut Normal School, New Britain, 1887; student Williston Seminary, 1891; B.Ph., Wesleyan University, Conn. 1895; Litt.D., 1945; married Lucy Harrison Norvell, June 15, 1898 (died 1928); married 2d, Juliet Staunton Clay, Aug. 13, 1929. Reporter Hartford Post, 1895; telegraph editor Washington Times, 1895-96, also editor Purple and Gold (Chi Psi mag.); Washington corr. N.Y. Commercial Advertiser, 1897; asst. to Washington corr. N.Y. Sun, 1897-1909; Washington corr. Seattle Post-Intelligencer, 1900-09, N.Y. Commercial and Toronto Globe, 1904-09, gov. of Alaska, Oct. 1, 1909-May 21, 1913; prospector and gold miner, Alaska, 1900. Editor and propr. Charleston (W.Va.) Daily Mail, since 1914. Republican. Presbyterian. Pres. Am. Rose Soc., 1928-29; mem. Chi Psi. Clubs: Metropolitan, Chevy Chase (Washington, D.C.); Edgewood, Kanawha (Charleston, W.Va.). Home: 1598 Virginia St. Office: Daily Mail, Charleston, W.Va.

Died Feb. 4, 1950.

CLOUD, Henry Roe, supt. of Haskell Institute; b. Thurston County, Nebr., Dec. 28, 1886, of Indian parents; A.B., Yale, 1910, A.M., 1912; B.D., Auburn Theol. Sem., 1913; D.D., Emporia (Kan.) Coll., 1932; m. Elizabeth Bender (Chippewa Indian), June 12, 1916; children—Elizabeth Marion, Anne Woisha, Lillian Alberta, Ramona Clark, Henry Roe. Ordained Presbyn. ministry, 1913; teacher, Wichita, 1916-28; editor The Indian Outlook; pres. Am. Indian Inst. since 1915; chmn. official delegation of Winnebagoes to the President, 1912-13; mem. Com. on Survey of Indian Schs. (Phelps Stokes Fund), 1914; mem. Com. of 100, apptd. by sec. of interior, 1925; mem. staff, survey of Indian affairs. Inst. for Govt. Research, 1926-27, 1929-30, co-author rept. to sec. of interior, 1928; spl. rep., U.S. Indian Service, 1931-33; apptd. by exec. order of President Roosevelt, supt. Haskell Inst., Aug. 16, 1933; apptd. supervisor Indian edn. at-large, Indian Bureau Service, Sept. 1, 1936; now supt. Umatilla Indian Agency. Mem. Beta Theta Pi, Elihu Club. Received Indian achievement award, 1935. Republican. Mason, Elk, Rotarian. Address: R. 1, Pendleton, Ore. Died Feb. 9, 1950.

COLE, Edward Smith, hydraulic engr.; b. Washington, D.C., Dec. 29, 1871; s. John Adams and Julia Mead (Alvord) C.; student U. of Ill., 1890-92; M.E., Cornell U., 1894; m. Mary Watkinson Rockwell, June 26, 1901; children—John Rockwell, Edward Shaw, Mary Watkinson (Mrs. William E. Jordan). Prin. asst. John A. Cole, cons. engr., Chicago, Ill., 1894-1903; active in development of pitometer and method for measurement of flow of water in pipes under pressure, 1896-98; in charge of studies with the pitometer for dept. of water supply, gas and electricity, City of N.Y., 1903-04; founder The Pitometer Company, New York City; formed British Pitometer Co. with Glenfield Kennedy, Limited, of Kilmarnock, Scotland and London, England, 1920. Fellow American Soc. Mech. Engineers (awarded Worcester Reed Warner Medal, Dec. 1948); mem. Montclair, N.J. Engrs. Soc., Am. Water Works Assn. (hon. mem.), Am. Soc. Civil Engrs. Republican. Conglist. Home: 133 Bellevue Av., Upper Montclair, N.J. Office: 50 Church St., New York 7; and 237 Lafayette St., New York, N.Y. Died Mar. 18, 1950.

CONNOR, Robert Digges Wimberly, univ. prof.; b. Wilson, N.C., Sept. 26, 1878; s. Henry Groves and Kate (Whitfield) C.; Ph. B., U. of North Carolina, 1899, LL.D., 1936; studied Columbia, 1920-21; LL.D., Duke, 1935; D.Litt., Lenoir-Rhyne Coll., 1936; m. Sadie Hanes, Dec. 23, 1902. Teacher and prin. schs. until 1904; sec. Edni. Campaign Com., office supt. pub. instrn., N.C., 1904-07; mem. and sec. N.C. Hist. Commn., 1903-07, sec., 1907-21, mem., 1932-34, mem. and chmn. since 1942; chmn. exec. bd., N.C. State Dept. Archives and History since 1943; mem. bd. trustees, Univ. of N.C., 1913-20; sec., 1914-20; Kenan prof. hist. and govt., U. of N.C., 1921-34; Craige prof. jurisprudence and history since 1941; archivist of the U.S., 1934-1941. Sec. North Carolina Teachers' Assembly, 1906-12; pres. N.C. Lit. and Hist. Assn., 1912 (sec. 1913-20); pres. Gen. Alumni Assn., U. of N.C., 1917-21, mem. Nat. Bd. for Historical Service, 1917. Member American Historical Assn., Soc. Am. Archivists, (pres. 1941-42), Southern Polit. Sci. Assn., Sigma Alpha Epsilon. Author: Cornelius Harnett, 1909; (with Clarence Poe) Life and Speeches of Charles B. Aycock, 1912; History of North Carolina (1585-1783), 1919; North Carolina—Rebuilding an Ancient Commonwealth, 1929. Mem. bd. editors N.C. Hist. Rev. Home. 404 Rosemary Lane, Chapel Hill, N.C. Died Feb. 25, 1950.

CONSTANT, Frank Henry, civil engr.; b. Cincinnati, O., July 25, 1869; s. Henry and Catherine (Ange) Constant; grad. Woodward High Sch., Cincinnati, 1887; C.E., with highest distinction, Cincinnati U., 1891, Sc.D., 1915; Sc.D., Lafayette, 1915; m. Annette G. Woodbridge, June 19, 1901; 1 son, Frank Woodbridge. Asst. engr. King Bridge Co., Cleveland, 1891-93; prin. asst. engr. Osborn Engring. Co., Cleveland, 1893-95; asst. prof. structural engring., 1895-97, prof. 1897-1914, U. of Minn.; prof. civ. engring. and head of dept., Princeton, 1914-37, prof. emeritus since 1937. Mem. Am. Soc. C.E., Soc. Promotion Engring. Edn., Phi Beta Kappa, Sigma Xi, Beta Theta Pi. Club: Princeton (N.Y. City). Home: 57 Battle Rd., Princeton, N.J. Died March 16, 1950.

CONWAY, John E(dward), writer; b. Boston, Mass., Oct 29, 1892; s. Edward Timothy and Bridget (Gallagher) C.; LL.B., Northeastern Univ., 1917; m. Evelyn Louise Canty, Nov. 14, 1921; children—John Edward, William Canty, Evelyn Carolyn, Edward Richard, Elizabeth Ann. Admitted to Mass. State bar, 1917, and practiced before U.S. Treasury Dept. and U.S. Tax cts. since 1933; feature articles (under name of Babe Ruth), Victory News Service, Inc., 1919-20; legal advisor to Jack Sharkey, 1921-48; articles on Jack Sharkey for King Features Syndicate, Inc., 1927-32; originator and writer, Mr. Boston column, Boston Am., 1927-42; sports dir., Boston American-Record-Sunday Advertiser, since 1934. Mass. State Racing Steward 1935-38; racing steward Rockingham Park 1939-45; dir. of racing Rockingham Park 1946; presiding steward Mass. Fair Circuit 1940-46. Mem. Am. Bar Assn., Fed. Bar Assn. Roman Catholic.

Author: Life of Archbishop Francis J. Spellman, 1940. Home: 310 Commonwealth Av., Chestnut Hill, Newton 67. Office: 5 Winthrop Square, Boston, Mass. Died Feb. 1, 1950.

CORBIN, Charles Russell, editor; b. Zanesville, O., Dec. 21, 1893; s. Charles William and Alice Josephine (Cashbaugh) C.; student Ohio State U., 1912-14; m. Maybelle Morgan, Oct. 4, 1916; 1 dau., Suzanne Joan. Reporter, Zanesville Signal, 1914-19; state editor Toledo (O.) Blade, 1919-21, news editor, 1921-25, asst. mng. editor, 1925-28, mng. editor, 1928-42; asst. to asst. dir. Press Div., Office of Censorship, Washington, D.C., 1942-43; assistant executive editor of the Minneapolis Star and Tribune, Minneapolis, Minn., since 1944. Served at Central O.T.C., Camp Gordon, Ga., World War, 1918. Mem. Am. Legion (past comdr.), Phi Delta Theta, Sigma Delta Chi, Alpha Phi Gamma. Episcopalian. Mason (32°, Shriner, K.T.). Clubs: Sojourners, Torch, National Press. Author: Why News Is News, 1928. Home: 224 W. Minnehaha Parkway. Office: Star and Tribune, Minneapolis, Minn. Died Feb. 19, 1950; buried Lakewood Cemetery, Minneapolis.

COX, Creed Fulton, army officer; b. Bridle Creek, Va., June 12, 1877; s. Melville B. and Martha (Fulton) C.; grad. U.S. Mil. Acad., 1901; m. Mrs. Margaret Kennedy Ross, Aug. 12, 1925 (died July 15, 1934). Commissioned 2d lt. cavalry, U.S. Army, Feb. 2, 1901; transferred to arty., promoted through successive grades to col. Served in Philippines, 1902-04; Cuba, 1906-07; assigned to Army Staff Coll., 1908-09; prof. mil. science and tactics, Shattuck Sch., Minn., 1909-12; instr. cav. various state nat. guards, 1914-17; instr. Sch. of Fire, Ft. Sill, Okla., 1917-18; with A.E.F. in France, May 1918-Jan. 1919; comdg. 13th F.A., Aisne-Marne, 77th F.A., St. Mihiel and Meuse-Argonne, barrage grouping 26th Div. and 4th Div.; gen. staff A.E.F., to war's close; War Dept. exec. staff, 1919; mil. observer S. Russia, Turkey, Bulgaria, 1920-21; mil. attaché Germany, Holland, Denmark, Norway, Sweden, 1921-24; pres. F.A. Bd., 1926-28; assigned to Army War Coll., 1929; asst. to chief Bur. Insular Affairs, 1929-32; comdg. 8th F.A. Regt., T.H., 1932-33; chief Bureau of Insular Affairs, with rank of brig. gen., May 1933-May 1937; retired, Sept. 30, 1937; adviser to President of P.I., 1938-39. Awarded D.S.M. (U.S.). Address: Independence, Va. Died Jan. 15, 1950.

CROCKER, William, botanist; b. Medina, O., Jan. 27, 1876; s. Charles David and Catherine C.; grad. Ill. State Normal U., Normal, Ill., 1898; A.B., U. of Illinois, 1902, A.M., 1903; Ph.D., University of Chicago, 1906; married Persis D. Smallwood, September 3, 1910 (she died July 2, 1948); children—Major John Smallwood, Lt. Colonel David Rockwell. Instr. biology, Northern Ill. State Normal Sch., 1903-04; asso. plant physiology, 1907-09, instr., 1909-11, asst. prof., later asso. prof., 1911-21, Univ. of Chicago; managing director Boyce Thompson Inst. for Plant Research, Yonkers, N.Y., since 1921; Walker-Ames visiting prof. U. of Wash., winter 1943; pres. Yonkers Board of Education, 1937-46. Fellow A.A.A.S. (vice chmn. Sect. G, 1925-26); member Botanical Society America (pres. 1924-25), Am. Chem. Soc., Am. Phytopathol. Soc., Phi Kappa Phi, Sigma Xi, Gamma Alpha. Mem. Nat. Research Council (chmn. div. of biology and agr., 1927-28); trustee Tropical Plant Research Foundation, 1927-43; acting dir. and gen. mgr., 1931-43; pres. T.I.B. Corp. Pres. Boyce Thompson Research Foundation; pres. Welfare Federation of Yonkers, N.Y., 1940. Research on delayed germination in seeds, effect of noxious gases on plants, plant hormones, etc. Mem. Am. Philos. Soc., Soc. of Arts and Sciences (medalist, 1931), Am. Inst. N.Y. (gold medal, 1938). Club: Hudson River Country. Author: Growth of Plants—Twenty Years' Research at Boyce Thompson Institute, 1948; (with Lela V. Barton) Twenty Years of Seed Research, 1948; (with Lela V. Barton) Seeds and Germination (in press). Home: 27 Arden Pl. Office: 1086 N. Broadway, Yonkers 3, N.Y. Died Feb. 11, 1950.

CURTIS, Arthur Melvin, lawyer; b. Wright County, Mo., Oct. 18, 1886; s. James Melvin and Rebecca (Barnett) C.; LL.B., U. of Mo., 1908; m. Jeanette Steele, Sept. 14, 1910; children—Jack Steele, E. C., Elizabeth Jeanette. Admitted to Mo. bar, 1908; partner Farrington & Curtis; pros. atty. Wright County, 1908-10; pres. Wright County Bank, Hartville, Mo., Springfield Packing Co.; mem. bd. dirs. Union Nat. Bank, Springfield, Mo.; dir. Springfield Grocer Co. Trustee Drury Coll., Springfield; chmn. Md. Rep. State Com., 1930-34; served as mem. Rep. Nat. Com., July 1935-June 1940; also dir. of organization for Com.; mem. bd. govs. Chamber of Commerce (former pres.). Methodist. Mason. Club: University: Home: 1016 E. Walnut St. Office: Landers Bldg., Springfield, Mo. Died Mar. 4, 1950.

DANGAIX, William Joseph (dăn'gā), capitalist; b. Phila., Pa., Sept. 16, 1864; s. Joseph and Mary (Lasserre) D.; student Sorbonne, Paris, and Inst. d'Études françaises de Touraine, Tours, France; studied Spanish 1 yr. in Spain; unmarried. Began at 18 as dept. clerk Superior Court, Brunswick, Ga.; in ins. and real estate business at Birmingham, Ala., many yrs.; gen. agt. for Southern States of Agrl. Ins. Co. of Watertown, N.Y., 10 yrs.; organizer and first pres. Birmingham Savings Bank, merged with Am. Trust & Savings Bank, of which was a dir. for many yrs.; bank merged into Am.-Traders Nat. Bank which was merged into First Nat. Bank of Birmingham; retired from active business, 1908, and has since spent most of time abroad, principally at Paris, but maintains legal citizenship at Birmingham. Under apptmt. as spl. asst. of Dept. of State, served, 1918-19, as foreign agt. of War Trade Bd., at Berne, Switzerland, and at Paris. Democrat. Catholic. Wrote booklets, How Latin America Affects Our Daily Life, 1917; How We Affect Latin America's Daily Life, 1919. Has traveled widely in Europe, Asia, Australasia, Africa and North, Central and South America. American Address: Care First National Bank, Birmingham, Ala. Foreign Address: Care Guaranty Trust Co., 4 Place de la Concorde, Paris, France. Died 1943.

DANIEL, John, physicist; b. Perry County, Ala., July 6, 1862; s. John and Susan Lee (Winfield) D.; A.B., U. of Ala., 1884, A.M., 1885, LL.D., 1914; Johns Hopkins, 1886-88; U. of Berlin, 1892; m. Grace Olive Knight, Sept. 2, 1896; children—Landon Garland, Ray Knight, John, Harben Winfield, Robert Bradley (dec.), Grace Olive. Asst. prof. psysics, U. of Ala., 1884-86; fellow, 1888, instr. physics, 1889, adjunct prof., 1890-93, prof., 1894-1939, prof. emeritus of physics since 1939, Vanderbilt U. Designed and installed the first electric dynamo at Vanderbilt Univ. (before commercial lighting); discovered depilatory and burning effect of X-Ray, describing same in Science for May, 1896; mem. Jury of Awards, Tennessee Centennial Expn., 1897. Fellow A.A.A.S.; charter mem. Tenn. Acad. Science. Mem. Phi Delta Theta, Phi Beta Kappa, Sigma Xi. Clubs: The Old Oak, The IV, The Faculty. Contbr. papers to Annales de Physique et Chimie, Philosophical Mag., Science, Physical Rev., etc. Home: 2500 Woodlawn Dr., Nashville, Tenn. Died Mar. 2, 1950.

DEMPSTER, Arthur Jeffrey, prof. physics; b. Toronto, Ont., Can., Aug. 14, 1886; s. James and Emily (Cheney) D.; A.B., U. of Toronto, 1909, A.M., 1910; grad. study univs. of Göttingen, 1911-12, Munich, 1912, Wurzburg, 1912-14, Chicago, 1914-16; 1851 Exhibition Scholar, 1912; Ph.D., U. of Chicago, 1916; Sc.D., U. of Toronto, 1937; married. Came to U.S., 1914, naturalized, 1918. Asst. prof. physics, U. of Chicago, 1919-23, asso. prof., 1923-27; prof. since 1927. Served as pvt. inf., U.S. Army, Nov. 1917-Mar. 1918, master signal electrician, Signal Corps, Mar.-Aug. 1918, 2d lt., in France, Oct. 1918-May 1919. Mem. Nat. Acad. Science, Am. Philos. Soc. Club: Quadrangle. Research in positive ray analysis of chem. elements, excitation of light and elec. discharges in gases. Home: 5757 Kenwood Av., Chicago, Ill. Died Mar. 11, 1950.

DILLON, John J., editor, pub.; b. Mongaup Valley, Sullivan County, N.Y., Nov. 7, 1856; s. John and Mary (Welsh) D.; ed. Liberty (N.Y.) Inst., and Albany (N.Y.) Coll.; m. Kate Maguire, June, 1891; children—Helene, Mary (Mrs. George Walsh); m. 2d, Mary C. May, Sept. 1, 1904; children—Catherine (Mrs. Edward J. McGratty, Jr.), Julia (Mrs. William F. Berghold), Virginia (Mrs. John F. Curry, Jr.). Began as school teacher, Sullivan County, 1874; writer and later asso. editor Orange County Farmer, 1884-90; with Rural New Yorker since 1890, as advt. mgr., 1890-92, editor and pub. since 1892; editor and pub. Rural Pub. Co.; pres., treas. and dir. Megonko Realty Co.; treas. and dir. Land Bank State of N.Y.; pres. and dir. Rural Savings & Loan Assn.; treas. and dir. Sherman Apt. Hotel. Pres. N.Y. State Agrl. Assn., 1915-16; commn. N.Y. State dept. foods and markets, 1915-16; mem. State commn. to organize the N.Y. State Land Bank, 1914. Mem. N.Y. State Grange. Roman Catholic. Author: Hind Sights, 1911; Organized Co-operation, 1923; Seven Decades of Milk, 1941. Home: Hotel Plaza, N.Y. City. Office: 333 W. 30th St., New York, N.Y. Died Mar. 1, 1950.

DOBYNS, A(shbel) Webster (dŏb'ĭns), lawyer; b. Austin, Tex., June 6, 1879; s. John Robert and Lilly (Webster) D.; B.A., Millsaps Coll., Jackson, Miss., 1899; M.A., Gallaudet Coll., Washington, D.C., 1900; LL.B., U. of Ark., 1908; m. Nancy McClerkin, Oct. 26, 1927. Teacher in schs. for deaf, Washington, Minnesota and N.Y. City, and later prin. Ark sch. for deaf, 1900-08; admitted to bar, Miss. and Ark., 1908; practiced law as mem. firm Riddick & Dobyns, Little Rock, Ark., 1908-19; asso. with Rose, Hemingway, Cantrell & Loughborough, 1919-23, mem. firm since 1923, firm name now Rose, Dobyns, Meek and House. Assistant adjutant general, Ark., 1918; capt. U.S. Army, and asst. adj., 97th Div., 1918; Judge Advocate General, Ark. Nat. Guard, and major, Judge Advocate General, U.S. Army Res., 1919-22. Mem. bd. trustees Southwest Legal Found., Dallas. Mem. and sec. of sub-com. which wrote constn. of Am. Legion at first conv., Minneapolis, Minn., 1919. Mem. Am. (house of dels., 1940-48; board govs., 1944-47), Arkansas (chairman exec. com., 1941-42), Little Rock (president 1925-26) bar assns., Am. Judicature Soc., Am. Law Inst., Newcomen Soc., Kappa Alpha (Southern), Phi Alpha Delta. Democrat. Presbyterian. Home: 1615 Battery St. Office: 314 W. Markham St., Little Rock, Ark. Died Mar. 26, 1950.

DUNCAN, George Brand, army officer; b. at Lexington, Ky., Oct. 10, 1861; s. late Henry T. and Lily (Brand) D.; grad. U.S. Mil. Acad., 1886; Army War Coll., 1912; m. Mary Kercheval, Oct. 23, 1895. Commd. 2d lt. 9th Inf., July 1, 1886; promoted through grades to brig. gen. N.A., 1917; maj. gen., 1918; brigadier gen. U.S. Army, 1920; promoted maj. gen. U.S. Army, Dec. 6, 1922; retired Oct. 10, 1925. Staff Major Gen. John M. Schofield, 1892-94; adjt. 4th Inf., 1894-98; adjt. gen. provisional div., Santiago, Cuba, July 1898, and provisional div. in P.R. and Dist. of Ponce, Aug.-Oct. 1898; in Philippines, 1899-1902, 1903-09 comdg. batn. Philippine scouts, 1905-09); Gen. Staff, 1914-17; with A.E.F. in France, June 1917-May 1919. Comd. 26th Inf., 1st Div., June-Sept. 1917; comd. 1st Brigade, 1st Div., Sept. 1917-May 1918; first Am. gen. officer comdg. a sector on the battle front, north of Toul, Jan. 1918 (brigade in battle north of Montdidier, Apr.-May, 1918); comd. 77th Div., May-Aug. 1918, in battle sector at Baccarat and in battle on the Vesle; comd. 82d Div. during Meuse-Argonne offensive, Oct. 1918, and until demobilization, May 1919; comdg. 7th Corps Area, Omaha, 1922-25. Awarded Croix de Guerre, Comdr. Legion of Honor (French) Companion of the Bath (British); D.S.M. (U.S.). Episcopalian. Clubs: Army and Navy (Washington, D.C.). Home: Lexington, Ky. Died Mar. 15, 1950.

EARP, Edwin Lee, sociologist; b. Illchester, Md., Oct. 26, 1867; s. Israel S. and Rachel Melcena (Barnette) E.; A.B., Dinckinson Coll., Pa. 1895; A.M., New York U., 1897; B.D., Drew Theol. Sem., 1898; Berlin, 1898-99; Ph.D., Leipzig, 1901; m. Lina Gibb Pearsall, of Ridgewood, N.J., May 1, 1901; children—Ruth, James Pearsall. Ordained M.E. ministry, 1900; pastor Newark and Plainfield, N.J., 1900-04; prof. sociology, Syracuse U., 1904-09, Drew Theological Seminary, Madison, N.J., 1909-38; retired June 1938. Member American Sociological Soc., National Civic Federation, Phi Delta Theta, Pi Gamma Mu., Phi Beta Kappa; mem. Nat. Council Y.M.C.A., terms 1924-30; pres. World's Conf. on Town and Country Work of World's Com. Y.M.C.A., Dassel, Germany, 1930. Mem. Madison Rotary Club. Author: Social Aspects of Religious Institutions, 1908; The Social Engineer, 1911; The Rural Church Movement, 1914; A Community Study, 1917; The Rural Church Serving the Community, 1918; Rural Social Organization, 1921; Biblical Backgrounds for Our Rural Message, 1922. Contbr. chapter to Socialized Church, 1909. Home: Basking Ridge, N.J. Died Feb. 4, 1950.

EASLEY, Gertrude Beeks (Mrs. Ralph M. Easley), (ēz'lē), sociologist; b. Greenville, Tenn., Jan. 16, 1867; d. James Crisfield and Sarah Jane (Brackenridge) Beeks; ed. pub. schools, Fort Wayne, Ind., and Chicago; m. Ralph M. Easley, Sept. 3, 1917 (dec.); 2 stepchildren. Asst. sec. Civic Fed. of Chicago; pres. Nat. Assn. Business Women, 1894-1901; head of Sociol. Dept., McCormick Harvesting Machine Co., Chicago, 1901-03; dir. Welfare Dept., The Nat. Civic Fed., since 1903. Investigator industrial enterprises, lecturer, writer and organizer. Dir. course in welfare work, New York U., 1913. Sent by Sec. of War William H. Taft to Panama to suggest improvements in conditions of employees, 1907, having received personal directions from President Theodore Roosevelt. Organized workmen's compensation, social ins., pension, profit sharing, industrial training depts. and minimum wage commn. of Nat. Civic Federation. Elected hon. mem. Stationary Firemen's Union, June 1, 1907. Apptd. by Samuel Gompers sec. exec. com. of Com. on Labor of Council of Nat. Defense, Apr. 2, 1917; initiated war risk ins. for soldiers and sailors and their dependents, housing for munition workers, and industrial training to increase war supplies, World War I; study Extent of Old Age Dependency, 1926. Organized dept. Patriotic Edn., 1940, Dept. Youth Edn., 1943. Mem. Women's Nat. Republican Club, Inc., Manhattan chapter Nat. Soc. of D.A.R., Andrew Jackson chapter (N.Y. County) Nat. Soc. Daughters of 1812. Home: Hotel Gregorian, N.Y. City; and Larchmont Hills, N.Y. Office: 42 W. 35th St., New York. Died Feb. 13, 1950.

EASTON, Burton Scott, clergyman, educator; b. Hartford, Conn., Dec. 4, 1877; s. Morton William and Maria Stille (Burton) E.; student U. of Göttingen, Germany, 1894; B.S., U. of Pa., 1898; Ph.D., 1901; B.D., Phila. Div. Sch., 1905, S.T.D., 1910; D.D., University of Glasgow, Scotland, 1935; m. Marian Pyott, Sept. 8, 1908. Deacon, 1905, priest, 1905, P.E. Ch.; instr. mathematics, U. of Ia., 1898-99, U. of Pa., 1901-05; prof. N.T., Nashotah (Wis.) House, 1905-11, Western Theol. Sem., Chicago, 1911-19; General Theol. Sem., 1919-49. Mem. Phi Beta Kappa, Sigma Xi, Alpha Chi Rho. Author: Constructive Development of the Group-Theory, 1902; The Teaching of St. Paul, 1919; Christ and His Teaching, 1922; The Gospel According to St. Luke, 1926; The Gospel Before the Gospels, 1928; The Real Jesus (with Bishop Charles Fiske), 1929; Christ in the Gospels, 1930; The Apostolic Tradition of Hippolytus, 1934; The Purpose of Acts, 1936; The Eternal Word in the Modern World (with H. C. Robbins), 1937; A Bond of Honour (with H. C. Robbins), 1938; What Jesus Taught, 1938; The Pastoral Epistles, 1947; also many theol. articles in revs., etc. Editor and contbr. Outline of Christianity, 1926; editor Anglican Theol. Rev. Home: 4 Chelsea Sq., New York 11, N.Y. Died Mar. 7, 1950.

EMBREE, Edwin Rogers; b. Osceola, Neb., July 31, 1883; s. William Norris and Laura (Fee) E.; early life and training in Wyo. and Ky.; B.A., Yale University, 1906; M.A., 1914; Litt.D., University of Hawaii, 1936; LL.D., U. of Ia., 1941, Howard U., 1948; m. Kate Scott Clark, July 16, 1907; children—John Fee, Edwina, Catherine. Reporter New York Sun, 1906-07; alumni editor Yale Alumni Weekly, 1907-11; alumni registrar, asst. sec., Yale, 1911-17, sec., 1917-23, dir. Div. of Studies, 1924-27, v.p., 1927, Rockefeller Found.; pres. Julius Rosenwald Fund, 1928-48; now president of the Librarian Found. Has specialized in study of races and of edn. in primitive cultures, also of Negro edn. and relations of negroes and whites; extended studies since 1921 of conditions in Far East and in Southern and Eastern Europe, especially in health, edn. and cultural clash. Chmn., Chicago Mayor's Committee on Race Relations, 1943-1948. Trustee of Roosevelt College of Chicago, since 1945. Trustee, Sarah Lawrence Coll. since 1944. Mem. Zeta Psi. Clubs: Cosmos (Wash.); Century (N.Y.); Tavern (Chgo.). Wrote Brown America, The Story of a New Race, 1931; Prospecting for Heaven—Science and the Good Life, 1932; Island India Goes to School, 1934; Indians of the Americas, 1939; American Negroes—A Handbook, 1942; Brown Americans: The Story of a Tenth of the Nation, 1943; Thirteen Against the Odds, 1944; also booklets—The Business of Giving Away Money, 1929; Religions by Contrary, 1929; A New

School for American Samoa, 1932; Samoa Offers an Exchange, 1933; Education for All the People, 1936; The Education of Teachers, 1938; Color and Democracy, 1942. Race Relations Balance Sheet, 1945. Co-Author: Human Biology and Racial Welfare, 1930; Our Children, 1932; The Collapse of Cotton Tenancy, 1935; Peoples of the Earth, 1948; Investment in People, The Story of the Julius Rosenwald Fund, 1949; Negroes in Am., 1949. Writer of mag. articles and monographs on edn., racial development and culture anthropology. Address: The Chatham Hotel, N.Y., N.Y. Died Feb. 21, 1950.

ERB, John Lawrence, organist, dir.; b. Berks County, Pa., Feb. 5, 1877; s. Milton Geist and Mary Katharine (Rhue) E.; ed. high sch., Pottstown, Pa., and The Hill Sch., Pottstown; Virgil Clavier Sch., N.Y. City, 1894-95; Met. Coll. of Music, N.Y., 1894-99, certificate in voice and organ, 1896; Doctor of Music, College of Wooster, 1921; m. Ethel Berenice Heydinger, Sept. 18, 1899; 1 son, Donald Milton. Organist St. James Ch., Pottstown, 1892-94, Broome St. Tabernacle, N.Y. City, 1895-1905; organist and dir. 2d Unitarian Ch., Brooklyn, 1897-1905; dir. music, Adelphi Coll., Brooklyn, 1896-97; dir. Conservatory of Music, Coll. of Wooster, O., 1905-13, also organist and dir. Westminster Presbyn. Ch., Wooster, 1905-13; organist and dir. 4th Presbyn. Ch., Chicago, 1913-14; dir. Sch. of Music and univ. organist, U. of Ill., 1914-21; organist and dir. McKinley Memorial Ch., Champaign, Ill., 1914-17; mng. dir. Am. Inst. Applied Music, N.Y. City, 1921-24; prof. music, Connecticut College, New London, Conn., 1923-42, prof. emeritus since 1942; organist, director First Congregational Ch., New London, 1925; organist, dir. United Congl. Ch., Norwich, 1926-29; dir. Norwich (Conn.) Choral Society, 1928-29; dir. New London (Conn.), Oratorio Society, 1941. President Ill. Fedn. Music Clubs, 1918, 1st v.p. 1919-21; mem. Music Teachers' Nat. Assn. (sec. 1913, 14, pres. 1915-19 and 1922), Nat. Assn. Organists (State pres. 1916), Am. Assn. Univ. Profs., Bohemians, St. Wilfrid, Phi Gamma Delta Frat., etc.; fellow Am. Guild of Organists, 1910. Lutheran. Author: Johannes Brahms (biography), 1905; Hymns and Church Music, 1910; The Elements of Harmony, 1911; Music Appreciation for the Student, 1925; Select Songs for the Assembly (with J. C. Kendel), 1931; Titans of Freedom (masque, with W. C. Langdon), prod. at U. of Ill., 1918; also booklet Elementary Theory, 1911. Composer of many organ and piano pieces, anthems; contbr. articles to mags. Home: 152 Rutland Rd., Brooklyn, N.Y. Died Mar. 17, 1950.

FAIRCHILD, Muir Stephen, air force officer; born in Bellingham, Washington, September 2, 1894; son of Harry Anson and Georgie Ann (Crockett) F.; student University of Washington, Seattle, Washington, 1913-17, Air Corps Engring. Sch., Dayton, O., 1928-29, Air Corps Tactical Sch., Montgomery, Ala., 1934-35, Army Industrial Coll., Washington, 1935-36, Army War Coll., Washington, 1936-37; m. Florence Alice Rossiter, Apr. 26, 1924; 1 dau., Betty Anne (Mrs. Ross Hamilton Calvert, Jr.). Commd. 2d lt., Aviation Sect., Signal Officers' Res. Corps, Jan. 1918; promoted through the grades to general, May 1948; mem. Joint Strategic Survey Com., Joint Chiefs of Staff, 1942-46; mem. U.S. del. Dumbarton Oaks Conf.; mil. advisor to U.S. del. San Francisco U.N. Conf.; became comdg. gen. The Air University, Maxwell Air Force Base, Alabama, January 1946; vice chief of staff United States Air Force, since May 1948. Awarded D.S.M., Legion of Merit, Distinguished Flying Cross, Purple Heart; Croix de Guerre (French); Italian War Medal; Order of Merit (Chile); Order of Condor of the Andes (Bolivia); Order of the Sun (Peru); Order of the Liberator (Venezuela). Mem. Kappa Sigma. Home: Fort Myer, Va. Address: Hdqrs. U.S. Air Force, Washington 25. Died Mar. 17, 1950.

FERGUSON, Samuel, pub. utility executive; B.S., Trinity Coll., Conn., 1896; E.E. and M.A., Columbia, 1899. Began with Gen. Electric Co., Schenectady, N.Y.; chmn. Hartford Electric Light Co.; chmn., pres. Connecticut Power Co.; dir. Arrow-Hart-Hegemon Co., Colt's Firearms Manufacturing Co., Hartford Accident & Indemnity Co., Hartford Fire Ins. Co., Hartford Steam Boiler Inspection & Ins. Co., Hartford Nat. Bank & Trust Co.; trustee Western Mass. Cos.; trustee Soc. for Savings. Trustee Trinity Coll. Mem. Am. Inst. E.E., Conn. Chamber Commerce (dir.). Home: 851 Prospect Av., West Hartford, Conn. Office: 266 Pearl St., Hartford, Conn. Died Feb. 10, 1950.

FRISCH, Hartvig, U.N. delegate; b. Hilleroed, Denmark, Jan. 17, 1893; s. Aage and Anna (Iversen) F.; Ph.D., Copenhagen U., 1941; m. Edith Lorentzen, December 25, 1931. Adj. teacher, Aarhus Kathedralskole, 1918-23; instr., Met. Sch., Copenhagen, 1923-41; pres., Studenter Samfundet, 1923-25; M.P., 1926; pres. Social-Dem. group, 1935-40; del., League of Nations, 1936; prof., 1941; del. U.N., 1945-47, minister of edn., 1947. Social-Democrat. Author: Europe's Kulturhistorie, 1928; Pest Over Europe, 1933; Cicero's Fight for the Republic, 1942, 46; Might and Right in Antiquity, 1944; Denmark Occupied and Liberated (Vols. I-III) 1945-48. other hist., social studies. Address: Hoesholm, Denmark. Died Feb. 11, 1950.

GARFIELD, James Rudolph, ex-secretary of the interior; b. Hiram, O., Oct. 17, 1865; s. James Abram (20th President of the U.S.) and Lucretia (Rudolph) G.; A.B., Williams Coll., 1885, LL.D., 1936; studied Columbia Law Sch.; LL.D., U. of Pittsburgh, 1909, Howard Univ., 1909; m. Helen Newell, Dec. 30, 1890. Admitted to bar, 1888; mem. Ohio Senate, 1896-99; mem. U.S. Civil Service Commn., 1902-03; commr. of corps., U.S. Dept. of Commerce and Labor, 1903-07; Sec. of the Interior, in cabinet of President Roosevelt, Mar. 4, 1907-Mar. 4, 1909; in law practice at Cleveland since 1909. Republican. Home: Mentor, Lake County, O. Office: 1425 Guardian Bldg., Cleveland 14, O. Died Mar. 24, 1950.

GARVER, Frederic Benjamin, prof. economics; b. Fairfield, Neb., Nov. 2, 1884; s. Daniel and Sarah (Epley) G.; B.A., U. of Neb., 1909; Ph.D., U. of Chicago, 1917; LL.D., U. of Neb., 1939; m. Blanche Davis, 1917; 1 dau., Margaret. Instr. in economics, U. of Chicago, 1912-14; instructor and asst. prof. economics, Stanford, 1914-19; asso. prof. and prof. economics, U. of Minn., since 1919. Author: Principles of Economics (with A. H. Hansen), 1928; 2d edit., 1937; 3d edit., 1947; (monographs) The Subvention in State Finances of Pennsylvania, 1919; The Location of Manufactures in the U.S. (with F. M. Boddy and A. J. Nixon), 1933. Home: 37 Arthur Av. S.E., Minneapolis, Minn. Died Feb. 1950.

GIMBEL, Ellis A., merchant; b. Vincennes, Ind., 1865; chmn. bd. and v.p. Gimbel Bros.; pres. Ninth Ward Realty Co., Gimbel Bros. Bank & Trust Co.; chmn. bd. Pa. Broadcasting Co. Home: 1900 Locust St. Office: Market and 9th Sts., Philadelphia, Pa.* Died Mar. 15, 1950.

GODDARD, Harold Clarke, coll. prof.; b. Worcester, Mass., Aug. 13, 1878; s. Lucius P. and Mary A. (Clarke) G.; A.B., Amherst Coll., 1900; A.M., Columbia, 1903, Ph.D., 1908; m. Fanny Whiting Reed, July 31, 1906; children—Eleanor (Mrs. Eugene Mark Worthen), Margaret (Mrs. Lee Elbert Holt). Instr. in mathematics, Amherst Coll., 1900-02; instr. English literature, Northwestern U., 1904-06, asst. prof., 1906-09; prof. English, Swarthmore Coll., 1909-46, prof. emeritus since 1946; prof. English, ad interim, Amherst Coll., second semester, 1946-47; visiting professor Columbia, summers 1916, 1920, 1924. Mem. Am. Assn. Univ. Profs., Modern Lang. Assn. of America. Author: Studies in New England Transcendentalism, 1908; Morale, 1919; W. H. Hudson: Bird-Man, 1928. Home: 915 Harvard Ave., Swarthmore, Pa. Died Feb. 27, 1950.

GOLDSBOROUGH, Laird S(hields) (gōldz'bûr-ō), editor; b. La Fayette, Ind., Mar. 6, 1902; s. Winder Elwell and Charlotte Poole (Wallace) G.; A.B., Yale, 1924; fellow Royal Univ. of Norway; m. Florence Maconaughy in Goldsborough, Eng., June 17, 1929. Asso. editor Fortune mag., 1929-34; foreign affairs editor of Time mag., 1925-40; became spl. asst. to chmn. bd. Time, Inc., 1941. Became co-ordinating officer in New York for Counter Espionage, U.S. Army Office of Strategic Services, 1943. Clubs: Union Interalliée (Paris); Yale (New York); Elizabethan (New Haven). Home: 1200 Fifth Av. Office: 9 Rockefeller Plaza, New York, N.Y. Died Feb. 1950.

HAM, Clifford Dudley; b. Detroit, Mich., Jan. 2, 1861; s. M. M. and Helen (Tucker) H.; A.B., Yale, 1883; m. Mary Barber, of Waterloo, Ia., June 28, 1892; children—Marian Barber, Clifford Dudley. Was sec. to gov. of Ia. and in newspaper work, Dubuque, Ia.; lt. col. 49th Ia. Vols., Spanish-Am. War, 1898-99; editor Dubuque Herald until 1903; in customs service, Philippine Islands, 1903-11, collector of customs, Iloilo, and surveyor of port, Manila; collector gen. of customs, Republic of Nicaragua, by appmt. of Pres. of Nicaragua, and fiscal agt. for bonded foreign loans of Nicaragua, since Dec. 1911. Episcopalian. Author of new tariff law, codification of Laws of Customs, Ports, Maritime Commerce and Vessels of Nicaragua, and map of Nicaragua. Address: Managua, Nicaragua, C. A.* Deceased.

HANSON, Michael Francis, newspaper pub.; b. Philadelphia, Pa., Feb. 16, 1867; s. Michael Henry and Delia (Ryan) H.; ed. Pierce Coll., Phila.; m. Sarah F. O'Neill, Philadelphia, August 23, 1893; children—Francis J. (dec.), Paul V., Sarah (Mrs. Paul Vanneman, Jr.), R. Kent, Rodman, Earle (dec.), Maurice, Marie Louise (Mrs. Robert F. Wilson), Wilmer. Began as reporter Philadelphia Record, 1890; became publisher Duluth (Minn.) Herald 1921; was also chmn. bd. The Herald Co.; now retired; v.p. Paul Block and associates. Home: 300 W. Willow Grove Ave., Chestnut Hill, Phila., Pa. Died Jan. 30, 1950.

HAUSMAN, William A., Jr., surgeon; b. Allentown, Pa., Nov. 18, 1878; s. William A. and Ida M. (Appel) H.; B.S., Muhlenberg Coll., Allentown, 1899, M.S., 1902, Sc.D., 1924; M.D., U. of Pa., 1902; m. Mary Repass, May 20, 1905; children—Mrs. Mary Frances Berkemeyer, Mrs. Dorothy Hancock Clewell, Mrs. Elizabeth Repass Watson. Interne Allentown Hospital, 1902-03, pathologist, same hospital, 1903-08; surgeon Sacred Heart Hospital, 1915-18, dean surgical department and chief of staff since 1918; dir. Second National Bank. Consulting surgeon Draft Bd. No. 1, Allentown, World War I. Trustee Muhlenberg Coll. Fellow Am. Coll. Surgeons; mem. Founders Group of Am. Bd. of Surgeons; mem. Am. and Pa. State med. assns., Lehigh County Med. Soc., Delta Theta, Phi Gamma Delta, Alpha Kappa Kappa (hon.). Democrat. Lutheran. Clubs: Livingston, Contemporary. Contbr. articles on surg. subjects. Home: College Drive, Park Ridge, Allentown. Office: 1116 Hamilton St., Allentown, Pa. Died Nov. 25, 1949.

HAWORTH, Sir (Walter) Norman, prof. chemistry; b. Chorley, Lancashire, Eng., Mar. 19, 1883; s. Thomas and Hannah (Crook) H.; D.Sc., U. of Manchester, 1911, LL.D. (hon.), 1947; Ph.D., U. of Gottingen, Germany, 1910; D.Sc. (hon.), Cambridge, Eng., 1939, Zurich, Switzerland, 1937, Oslo, Norway, 1946 Belfast, Ireland, 1947; married Violet Chilton Dobbie, August 15, 1922; children—James Chilton, Norman David. Senior demonstrator Imperial college of Science, London, 1911-12; lecturer and reader in chemistry, University of Saint Andrews, St. Andrews, Scotland, 1912-20; prof. chem., King's Coll., Newcastle-upon-Tyne, U. of Durham, 1920-25; prof. chem., U. of Birmingham, Eng., 1925-48, vice prin., 1947-48. Knighted, 1947. Awarded Longstaff medal, Chem. Soc., 1933, Davy medal, Royal Soc., 1934, Royal medal, Royal Soc., 1942; Nobel prize in chemistry, 1937. Fellow Royal Soc. of London (v.p. 1947-49). Mem. Chemical Soc. (pres. 1944-46); Johnson Soc., Lichfield, Eng. (pres. 1947-48); mem. (hon.) Acads. of Science, Bavaria, Brussels, Finland, Haarlem (Holland), Halle (Germany), Ireland, Vienna, Swiss Chem. Soc. Club: Athenaeum, London. Author numerous scientific papers on carbohydrates. Home: Thurcroft, Barnt Green, Nr. Birmingham, Eng. Died Mar. 1950.

HELLINGER, Ernst D(avid), univ. prof.; b. Striegau (then Germany), Sept. 30, 1883; s. Emil and Julie (Hellinger) H.; student U. of Heidelberg, U. of Breslau and U. of Goettingen; Ph.D., U. of Goettingen, 1907; unmarried. Came to U.S., 1939, naturalized, 1944. Privat docent, U. of Marburg, 1909-14; prof. mathematics U. of Frankfurt, 1914-35; lecturer Northwestern U., 1939-44, prof. of mathematics since 1944. Mem. Am. Math. Soc., Math. Assn. of Am., Sigma Xi. Home: 2215 Maple Av. Evanston, Ill. Died Mar. 28, 1950.

HOLLUMS, Ellis Clyde (hŏl'ŭmz), editor; b. Cherokee County, Ala., Oct. 18, 1893; s. Zachariah Ferrell and Lulu Ann (Wood) H.; ed. pub. schs. of Birmingham, Ala.; m. Rose Catherine Kirkier, Nov. 2, 1914; children—Ellis Clyde, Luther Ferrell, Daniel Harris. Copy boy Birmingham Ledger, 1907-09, classified advertisement salesman, 1909-12; sec. to editor Birmingham Age-Herald, 1913-15; reporter Birmingham Ledger, 1915-17, city editor, 1917-18, asst. mng. editor, 1918-20; chief clerk Ala. State Senate, 1920-21; city editor Jacksonville (Fla.) Journal, 1920-22; joined Miami (Fla.) Herald, 1922, exec. editor, 1938-Nov. 1, 1941; news dir. WQAM radio sta., 1941-43; exec. editor Columbus (Ga.) Ledger, 1943-45; telegraph editor Jacksonville Journal since 1946. Democrat. Baptist. Mason. Club: National Press. Home: 8100 Sycamore St., Jacksonville 6. Office: Journal Bldg., Jacksonville 2, Fla. Died Oct. 27, 1949.

HOPKINS, Arthur Melancthon, play producer; b. Cleveland, O., Oct. 4, 1878; s. David John and Mary (Jefferies) H.; ed. Western Reserve Acad.; m. Eva O'Brien, Nov. 4, 1915 (now deceased). Began career as producer in New York City, 1912; productions include: Steve; The Poor Little Rich Girl; Evangeline; We Are Seven; On Trial; The Deluge; The Happy Ending; Good Gracious, Annabelle; A Successful Calamity; The Rescuing Angel; Redemption; Be Calm, Camilla; A Gentile Wife; Wild Duck; Hedda Gabler; A Doll's House; The Jest; Richard III; Macbeth; Night Lodging; Daddy's Gone A-Hunting; The Claw; Anna Christie; The Hairy Ape; The Old Soak; Rose Bernd; Hamlet; Romeo and Juliet; The Laughing Lady; Launzi; A Royal Fandango; What Price Glory; The Second Mrs. Tanqueray; Close Harmony; First Flight; The Buccaneer; In a Garden; Deep River; Burlesque; House of Women; Paris Bound; Salvation; These Days; Machinal; Holiday; The Commodore Marries; Rebound; The Channel Road; This is New York; Torch Song; Roadside; The Passing Present; Rendezvous; Conquest; Lady Jane; The Petrified Forest; Paths of Glory; Bright Star; Star Spangled; Plumes in the Dust; Blow Ye Winds; The Joyous Season; The Magnificent Yankee; Hear that Trumpet. In April 1944 instituted radio series of hour versions of plays on the broadcast called "Arthur Hopkins Presents" with NBC. Gave series of 12 lectures at Fordham U. Summer Theatre session, July-Aug. 1947. Author: How's Your Second Act; The Glory Road; To a Lonely Boy; Remember This Day; Reference Point. Home: 45 Park Av. Office: Plymouth Theatre, New York, N.Y. Died Mar. 22, 1950.

HOWARD, Burton James, microscopist; b. Ionia, Mich., Sept. 17, 1872; s. William H. and Helen L. (Butler) H.; B.S., U. of Mich., 1897, post-grad. work, 1900-01; m. Gertrude Louise Peck, June 28, 1899; 1 dau., Bertha Helen. Asst. in chemistry, U. of Mich., 1895-96, asst. in pharmacognosy, 1901; microscopist in charge of Microchem. Lab., Bur. of Chemistry, U.S. Dept. of Agr., Washington, 1901-27; sr. microscopist, Bur. Chemistry and Soils, 1927-28; with Food, Drug and Insecticide Adminstrn., 1928-42, in charge Micro-analytical Lab., retired Sept. 1942. Prof. of microscopy, evenings, Nat. Coll. of Pharmacy, 1904-17. Mem. Am. Chem. Soc., A.A.A.S., Washington Bot. Soc. Republican. Methodist. Home: 1212 Decatur St. N.W., Washington, D.C.

Died Feb. 4. 1950.

HOWE, Percy Rogers, dental research; b. Providence, R.I., Sept. 30, 1864; s. James Albert and Elizabeth Rachel (Rogers) H.; grad. Nichols Latin Sch., Lewiston, Me., 1883; A.B., Bates Coll., 1887, Sc.D., 1927; D.D.S., Philadelphia Dental College, 1890; LL.D., Harvard University, 1941; m. Rose Alma Hilton, December 21, 1891 (died 1942); children—James Albert, John Farwell; m. 2d, Ruth Loring White, 1943. Began practice at Auburn, Maine, 1890; moved to Lewiston, 1891, to Boston, 1898; chief of research labs., Forsyth Dental Infirmary for Children, since 1915, dir. since 1927; asso. prof. dental research, Harvard, 1915-25, Thomas Alexander Forsyth prof. dental science; instr. in pathology, Harvard Medical School, 1925-40, now emeritus. Fellow dental surg., Royal Coll. Surgeons (Eng.); honorary fellow Internat. College Dentists, 1947. Member American Dental Association (pres. 1928-29), American Academy Arts and Sciences, Am. Acad. Dental Sci., Hist. Science Soc., New Eng. Pediatrics Soc., Norwegian Dental Soc., Acad. Internacional de odontologia, Fedn. Dentaire Internat., Sociedad Cubana de Odontologia Infantil, Sigma Xi, Phi Beta Kappa, Delta Sigma Delta. Awarded Jarvie medal by New York State Dental Society, 1926; Callahan medal, Columbus Dental Society, 1926; Newell Sill Jenkins medal, Conn. Dental Society, 1927; R.I. State Dental Soc. medal, 1929. Granted hon. award of American Dental Assn., 1945. Republican. Mason. Club: Harvard. Research in nutrition; originator of silver reduction treatment for infected dentine and septic roots, used extensively in the Army, World War; isolated group of bacteria from dental caries. Home: Belmont, Mass. Office: 140 The Fenway, Boston, Mass. Died Feb. 28, 1950.

HUME, William, lawyer; born Nashville, Tenn., Feb. 1, 1888; s. Leland and Louise (Trenholm) H.; ed. Branham and Hughes Prep. Sch., Spring Hill, Tenn., 1905, A.B. Vanderbilt U., 1909, LL.B., 1910; m. Sallie Phillips McKay, April 23, 1913. Senior partner, law firm, Hume, Howard and Davis since 1940. Trustee, mem. exec. com., George Peabody Coll. for Teachers; trustee, mem. exec. com. Fisk Univ.; mem. bd. of dirs., Southwestern at Memphis; mem. bd. of dirs., sec., Ward-Belmont Coll.; mem. joint univ. library bd., Vanderbilt, Peabody, Scarritt; mem. exec. com. foreign missions, Presbyterian Church in U.S., 1930-37; v.p. bd. of trustees, Monroe Harding Children's Home; mem. com. on ednl. institutions, Presbyterian Synod of Tenn.; pres. Nashville bd. of edn.; mem. bd. govs. Nashville C. of C.; mem. bd. park commr., Nashville Public library, Juvenile Aid Bur., Nashville chapter A.R.C., Travelers' Aid (Nashville), Nashville Anti-Tuberculosis Assn., Youth, Inc., Nashville. Mem. Nashville Bar Assn., Tenn. State Bar Assn., Delta Kappa Epsilon. Presbyterian. Club: Belle Meade Country. Home: 3625 W. End Av., Nashville 5. Office: American Trust Bldg., Nashville, Tenn. Died Jan. 10, 1950.

HUTT, Henry, illustrator; b. Chicago, Dec. 18, 1875; s. George Gottleib and Fredericka Dorothea (Will) H.; ed. pub. schs. and Art Inst. of Chicago; m. Edna Garfield Della Torre, of New York, Jan. 17, 1903. Engaged as illustrator, beginning at age of 14; now illustrator for mags. and periodicals. Died Jan. 19, 1950.

INGLIS, James (ing'glis), mfr.; b. Detroit, Mich., Aug. 15, 1864; s. Richard and Agnes (Lambie) I.; ed. pub. schs. and high sch., Detroit; m. Elizabeth Hughes, Oct. 21, 1903; children—Elizabeth A. (Mrs. William A. Scott), James H. Connected with Am. Blower Corp. since 1890, formerly pres., now chmn. bd.; formerly chmn. board Nat. Bank of Detroit 1, formerly director Federal Reserve Bank of Detroit, Mich.; dir. Am. Radiator & Standard Sanitary Corp., Detroit Lubricator Company, Michigan. Mutual Liability Company, Rome Cable Corporation. With War Industries Bd., Washington, D.C., World War. Pres. Detroit Bd. of Commerce, 1906. Republican. Clubs: Detroit, Detroit Athletic, Detroit Boat; Ann Arbor Golf and Outing. Home: 2301 Highland Rd., Ann Arbor, Mich. Office: care American Blower Corp., Detroit 32, Mich. Died Mar. 16, 1950.

JAFFE, Louis Isaac, newspaper editor; b. Detroit, Feb. 22, 1888; s. Philip and Lotta Maria (Kahn) J.; A.B., Trinity Coll. (now Duke U.), 1911; m. Margaret Stewart Davis, Dec. 8, 1920; 1 son, Christopher; m. 2d, Alice Cohn Rice, 1942; 1 son, Louis Isaac, Junior. Member staff Durham Sun, 1911; reporter and asst. city editor Richmond (Va.) Times-Dispatch, 1911-17; editor Virginian-Pilot, Norfolk, Va., since Nov. 1919; mem. board of dirs. Norfolk Newspapers, Inc. Student R.O.T.C., Fort Myer, Va.; commd. 2d lt. F.A., Nov. 1917; re-commd. Air Service, Kelly Field, Texas, December, 1917. Served in A.E.F., April 1918-March 1919; honorably discharged in France, Mar. 29, 1919; with Am. Red Cross Commn. to the Balkans, Apr.-July 1919; dir. Am. Red Cross News Service at Paris, July-Oct. 1919. Mem. Norfolk Council Com. on Higher Edn.; mem. adv. bd., Norfolk Div., Va. State Coll. for Negroes; dir. Norfolk General Hosp.; mem. bd. trustees Norfolk Museum of Arts and Sciences. Awarded Pulitzer prize for best newspaper editorial, 1929. Mem. Phi Beta Kappa, Omicron Delta Kappa. Democrat. Clubs: National Press (Washington), Virginia (Norfolk). Office: Norfolk Newspapers, Inc., 150 W. Brambleton Av., Norfolk, Va. Died Mar. 12, 1950.

JOHNSON, Emory Richard, univ. prof.; b. Waupun, Wis., Mar. 22, 1864; s. Eli and Angeline (Nichols) J.; B.L., U. of Wis., 1888, M.L., 1891; Ph.D., U. of Pa., 1893 (Sc.D., U. of Pa., 1913); m. Orra L. March, Sept. 5, 1894 (died 1923); m. 2d, Hedwig Anna Schroeder, Dec. 24, 1930. Instr. economics, Haverford College, 1893-96; instr. transportation and commerce, Univ. of Pennsylvania, 1893-96, asst. prof., 1896, prof. since 1902; dean Wharton School Finance and Commerce, 1919-33. Expert on transportation, U.S. Industrial Commn., 1899; mem. U.S. Isthmian Canal Commn., 1899-1904; expert on valuation of ry. property for U.S. Census Bur., 1904-05; expert on traffic, Nat. Waterways Commn., 1909; apptd., 1911, to report on Panama Canal traffic, tolls and measurement of vessels; mem. Pub. Service Commn. Pa., 1913-15; dir. Phila. Maritime Exch., 1907-28. Editor Annals of Am. Acad. Polit. and Social Science, 1901-14; arbitrator of dispute between S.P. Co. and Order of Railroad Telegraphers, 1907; mem. bd. that prepared an Economic History of the U.S., 1904-30. Asst. dir. Bur. of Transportation, War Trade Bd., 1917-18; rate expert U.S. Shipping Bd., 1918-19; transportation expert Chamber Commerce of U.S., 1919-21, 1923 and 1925. Chairman Research Council upon Operation and Effect of the Eighteenth Amendment, 1931. Chmn. Spl. Com. on Panama Tolls and Vessel Measurement Rules, 1936-37. Pres. National Institute Social Sciences, 1918-22; pres. Assn. of Collegiate Schs. of Business, 1920-21; mem. Am. Econ. Assn., Geog. Soc. Phila. (pres. 4 terms), Am. Philos. Soc., Sons of Revolution, S.A.R., Colonial Soc. of Pa., Nat. Institute Social Sciences (pres. 1918-22). Decorated by Emperor of Japan with medal of Order of the Rising Sun (3d rank), by Chinese Government, medal of Order of Chia-Ho (2d rank), 1926. Club: Print. Author: Inland Waterways, Their Relation to Transportation, 1893; American Railway Transportation, 1903; Ocean and Inland Water Transportation, 1906; Elements of Transportation, 1909; Railroad Traffic and Rates (with Prof. G. G. Huebner), 1911; Panama Canal Traffic and Tolls, 1912; Measurement of Vessels for the Panama Canal, 1913; History of Domestic and Foreign Commerce of the United States (with collaborators), 2 vols., 1915; The Panama Canal and Commerce, 1916; Principles of Railroad Transportation (with Prof. T. W. Van Metre), 1916; Principles of Ocean Transportation, 1918; The Ocean Freight Service (with Prof. G. G. Huebner), 1925; Interpretative Essays on China and England, 1927; Principles of Transportation (with collaborators), 1928; Transportation by Water (with Profs. G. G. Huebner and A. K. Henry), 1935; Government Regulation of Transportation, 1938; Transportation: Economic Principles and Practices (with G. G. Huebner and G. Lloyd Wilson), 1940; Life of a University Professor, An Autobiography, 1943; The Railroads and Public Welfare, 1944; Transport Facilities, Services and Policies, 1947; also author of papers on railways and economics, also Report to Isthmian Canal Commission on Industrial and Commercial Value of Isthmian Canal, 1901, to U.S. Shipping Bd. on Ocean Rates and Terminal Charges, 1919, to U.S. Tariff Commn. on Effect of Railroad Rates on Exports and Imports and Tariff Duties, 1922, to U.S. Bd. of Review on Traffic and Revenues of Proposed Trans-Florida Canal, 1934, and articles in econ. mags. and reports in bulls. of U.S. Dept. Labor and Bur. of the Census. Home: Hamilton Court, 39th and Chestnut Sts., Philadelphia, Pa.

Died Mar. 6, 1950.

JOHNSTONE, Edward Ransom, humanitarian; b. Galt, Ont., Can., Dec. 27, 1870; s. William and Jane (Ransom) J.; pub. schs., Cincinnati; hon. M.Sc. Princeton, 1923; hon. Litt.D., Rutgers, 1941; m. Olive Lehmann, June 16, 1898; children—Carol, Edward Lehmann, Earl Ransom, Douglas Davidson. Officer, Cincinnati House of Refuge (reformatory), 1889; teacher pub. schs., Hamilton County and Cincinnati, 1889-93; teacher and prin. Ind. Sch. for Feeble Minded Youth, 1893-98; asst. supt., 1898-1900, supt. 1900-22, exec. dir., 1922-44; dir. emeritus since 1944, Training School, Vineland, N.J. With army Edn. Corps of A.E.F., during World War I. Consultant N.J. State Dept. of Instns. and Agencies; mem. Am. Commn. to Serbia, 1919-20; chmn. com. on mental deficiency, White House Conf., 1930-31. Decorated Order of St. Sava of Serbia, 1920; awarded citation for distinguished service to agr., N.J. State Bd. of Agr., 1940; voted Vineland's outstanding citizen, 1939. Mem. Am. Assn. on Mental Deficiency (pres. 1902 and 1927), Nat. Conf. Social Work, N.J. State Conf. Social Welfare (pres. 1903), N.E.A., N.J. Council of Edn., Am. Prison Assn., State Prison and Parole Board (pres. since 1927), N.J. Crime Commn. (chmn. com. on edn., 1935), A.A.A.S., Eugenics Research Assn. Baptist. Mason, Elk. Club: Rotary. Editor The Training School Bulletin (monthly publ.). Dir. Tradesmen's Bank, Millville Utilities; pres. Electric Light Co. Vice-pres. Advisory Bd. N.J. Dairy Research Council. Home: Vineland, N.J.

Died Dec. 29, 1946.

JONES, Wallace Thaxter, business exec.; b. Brooklyn, N.Y., 1890; s. Wallace T. and Helen (Swift) J.; ed. Dartmouth, 1912; m. Josephine Traer. With Rockwood & Co. since 1912; now pres. and dir.; trustee, East Brooklyn Savings Bank. Dir. and mem. exec. and mfrs. coms., Brooklyn C. of C. Mem. Assn. of Cocoa and Chocolate Mfrs. of U.S. Clubs: University, Dartmouth Univ. Home: 455 E. 57th St., N.Y. City. Office: 88 Washington Av., Brooklyn, N.Y.* Died May 28, 1946.

KINGSFORD, Howard Nelson, pathologist; b. at Providence, R.I., Sept. 24, 1871; s. John C. and A. F. (Thatcher) K.; spl. student, chemistry, Brown, 1894-5; M.D., Dartmouth, 1896; grad. student, medicine, Harvard, 1898-9; (A.M., Dartmouth, 1907); m. Mabel P. Carpenter, Pawtucket, R.I., July 16, 1898. Instr. histology, bacteriology and pathology, 1898-1900, prof. pathology, 1906—, Dartmouth Med. Sch.; med. dir. Dartmouth Coll., 1902—; pathologist Mary Hitchcock Hosp.; state bacteriologist of N.H. Mem. Am. Assn. Pathologists and Bacteriologists, A.M.A., N.H. Med. Soc., N.H. Surg. Club, etc. Commd. capt., Med. R.C., 1917. Address: Hanover, N.H. Died Feb. 9, 1950.

KORZYBSKI, Alfred Habdank (Skarbek) (kôr-zib'ski), scientist, author; b. Warsaw, Poland, July 3, 1879; s. Ladislas Habdank K. and Countess Helena (Rzewuska) K.; ed. Warsaw Realschule and Warsaw Poly. Inst.; grad. study in Germany, Italy, U.S.; m. Mira Edgerly, Jan., 1919. Came to U.S. 1916, naturalized, 1940. Managed family estates in Poland; teacher of mathematics, physics, French and German in Warsaw, Poland; served with cav. and bodyguard heavy arty., also attached to Intelligence Dept., Russian Gen. Staff; sent to U.S. and Canada as artillery expert; sec. Polish-French Mil. Commn. in U.S., 1918; recruiting officer Polish-French Army, U.S. and Can., 1918; war lecturer for U.S. Govt.; sec. Polish Commn. (Labor Sect.), League of Nations, 1920; writer and lecturer; became pres. and dir. Inst. of General Semantics, Chicago, 1938, now Lakeville, Conn. Fellow American Assn. Advancement Sci.; member Am. Math. Soc., Chicago Soc. for Personality Study, Assn. for Symbolic Logic, N.Y. Acad. Sciences, Soc. for Applied Anthropology. Author: Manhood of Humanity—The Science and Art of Human Engineering, 1921; Science and Sanity, An Introduction to Non-aristotelian Systems and General Semantics, 1933, 3d edit., 1948; also many scientific papers. Address: Institute of General Semantics, Lakeville, Conn. Died Mar. 1, 1950.

LASKI, Harold Joseph, author, educator; b. Manchester, England, 1893; s. Nathan and Sarah (Frankenstein) L.; grad. U. of Oxford, 1914; m. Fridda Kerry, 1911; 1 dau., Diana. Lecturer McGill U., 1914-16, Harvard, 1916-20; prof. of polit. science, U. of London, since 1920. Mem. Industrial Court; mem. Lord Chancellors Com. on Ministers' Powers, 1930; mem. Departmental Com. on Local Govt., 1932, Com. on Legal Edn., 1933. Mem. Fabian Soc. Mem. Nat. exec. com. English Labor party. Author: A Grammar of Politics, 1926; Democracy in Crises, 1933; The State in Theory and Practice, 1935; Parliamentary Government in England, 1938; (essays) Danger of Being a Gentleman, 1940; Where Do We Go From Here, 1940; The American Presidency, 1940; Strategy of Freedom, 1941; Reflections on the Revolution of Our Time, 1943; Faith, Reason and Civilization, 1944; (with others) Road to Recovery, 1947; American Democracy, 1948; Liberty in the Modern State, 1949; numerous research bulls., pamphlets and mag. articles. Home: 5 Addison Bridge Place, London. Office: The London School of Economics and Political Science, London, England.* Died Mar. 24, 1950.

LEE, George Winthrop, librarian; b. Roxbury, Mass., Feb. 27, 1867; s. John Rose and Lucy Maria (Howard) L.; A.B., Harvard, 1889; m. Eleanor Selden Tucker, Sept. 24, 1907; children—St. George Tucker, Winthrop Howard. With Stone & Webster, engrs. and mgrs. pub. service corps., Boston, 1894-1929, librarian, 1900-29. Pres. Boston Esperanto Soc. since 1912; Boston delegate "Internacia Esperanto-Ligo", founder Emerson and Thoreau groups, Concord, Mass., 1936; initiator of interests associated with adult education and community centers. Episcopalian. Club: Engineers (Boston). Writer on business library interests and allied interests. Home: Concord, Mass. Died Oct. 2, 1948.

LEWIS, Vivian M., vice-chancellor; b. Paterson, N.J.; s. Isaac Arriston and Hannah (Davies) L.; LL.D., Lafayette Coll.; m. Sept. 27, 1916, Charlotte A. Jörgensen; children—Henry C., John C. Admitted N.J. bar, 1892; practiced in Paterson; judge advocate, 2d Regt. N.J.N.G., 1896-99, retired with rank of capt.; mem. Gen. Assembly, 1898-99, 1900; leader Rep. majority, 1900; city counsel, Paterson, 1904; counsel State Bd. Health, 1900-04; clerk in chancery, 1904-09; commr. of banking and ins., 1909-12; Rep. candidate for gov. of N.J., against Woodrow Wilson, 1910; vice-chancellor N.J. since Apr. 3, 1912 (declined apptmt. as chancellor 1919). Mem. N.J. Hist. Soc. Clubs: Hamilton, Arcola, Somerville, Pacific, Sankaty Head Golf. Home: Paterson, N.J.

Died Mar. 14, 1950.

LLOYD, Alice Crocker, univ. dean; b. Ann Arbor, Mich., Dec. 9, 1893; d. Alfred Henry and Margaret (Crocker) Lloyd; A.B., U. of Mich., 1916. Adviser of women, U. of Mich., 1926-30, dean of women since 1930. Mem. education council advisory to U.S. Navy on women's services. Mem. Phi Beta Kappa, Phi Kappa Phi, Mortar Board. Episcopalian. Home: 1735 Washtenaw Av., Ann Arbor, Mich.

Died Mar. 3, 1950.

MANTON, Martin Thomas, judge; b. N.Y. City, Aug. 2, 1880; s. Michael and Catherine (Mullen) M.; LL.B., Columbia, 1901; LL.D., Fordham U., Manhattan Coll., N.Y. Univ., U. of Vt.; m. Eva M. Morier, July 3, 1907. Judge U.S. Dist. Court, Southern Dist. of N.Y., Sept. 7, 1916; judge U.S. Circuit Court of Appeals, 2d Circuit, since 1918. Mem. Internat. Law Soc., N.Y. Bar Assn. Address: Federal Court House, New York. Died Nov. 17, 1946.

MAPLES, Harold E., business exec.; b. Oradell, N.J., 1890. Vice chmn. of bd. and gen. mgr. Albert Frank-Guenther Law, Inc. Dir. Upland Meadows, Inc., N.Y. City. Home: 85 Chestnut Av., Closter, N.J. Office: Albert Frank-Guenther Law, Inc., 131 Cedar St., New York, N.Y. Died Mar. 5, 1950.

MASTERS, Edgar Lee, author; b. Garnett, Kan., Aug. 23, 1869; s. Hardin Wallace and Emma J. (Dexter) M.; ed. high sch. and Knox Coll., Ill.; married Helen Jenkins, 1898 (div. 1923); married 2d, Ellen Coyne, 1926. Studied law in father's law office; admitted to bar, 1891. Democrat. Club: Jefferson (pres. 1904-05, 1907-08). Author: A Book of Verses, 1898; Songs and Sonnets, 1900; Maximilian (drama in blank verse), 1902; The New Star Chamber and Other Essays, 1904; Blood of the Prophets, 1905; Spoon River Anthology, 1915 (translated into Swedish, German, Norwegian, Flemish, Japanese); Songs and Satires, 1916; The Great Valley, 1916; Toward the Gulf (poems), 1918; Starved Rock (poems), 1919; Mitch Miller, 1920; Domesday Book, 1920; The Open Sea, 1921; Children of the Market Place, 1922; Skeeters Kirby, 1923; The Nuptial Flight, 1923; Mirage, 1924; The New Spoon River, 1924; Selected Poems, 1925; Lee, a Dramatic Poem, 1926; Kit O'Brien, 1927; Jack Kelso (a dramatic poem), 1928; The Fate of the Jury (poem), 1929; Gettysburg, Manila, Acoma, 1930; Lichee Nuts, 1930; Lincoln—

The Man, 1931; Godbey (A Dramatic Poem), 1931; The Serpent in the Wilderness, 1933; The Tale of Chicago, 1933; Dramatic Duologues, 1934; Richmond (dramatic poem), 1934; Andrew Jackson (drama), 1934; Invisible Landscapes (poems), 1935; Vachel Lindsay, a Biography, 1935; Poems of People, 1936; The Golden Fleece of California, 1936; Whitman, 1937; The New World (poem), 1937; The Tide of Time (novel), 1937; Mark Twain (biography), 1938; More People (poems), 1939; Emerson, 1940; Illinois Poems, 1941; Along the Illinois, 1942; The Sangamon, 1942. Awarded first $5000 fellowship granted by Acad. of Am. Poets, 1946. Address: Players Club, New York. Died Mar. 5, 1950.

MAXEY, George Wendell, chief justice of Pennsylvania; b. Forest City, Pa., Feb. 14, 1878; s. Benjamin and Margaret (Evans) M.; ed. Mansfield (Pa) State Normal School 1894-97; A.B., Univ. of Mich., 1902; LL.B., U. of Pa., 1906; married Lillian Danvers, Jan. 22, 1916; children—Mary D. (Mrs. George J. Schautz, Jr), Dorothy (Mrs. Lesley McCreath, Jr.), Lillian Louise. Admitted to Pa. bar, 1906; in practice at Scranton, 1906-20; dist. atty. Lackawanna County, 1914-20; judge 45th Dist., 1920-30; apptd. Nov. 24, 1930, justice Supreme Court of Pa., to fill vacancy for 6 weeks, elected, Nov. 4, 1930, for term, 1931-52, became chief justice, January 4, 1943 (term 9 years). Republican. Clubs: Scranton, Scranton Country; Rolling Rock (Ligonier Valley, Pa.). Home: 520 Monroe Av., Scranton. Office: First Nat. Bank Bldg., Scranton, Pa.; and 462 City Hall, Philadelphia, Pa.* Died Mar. 20, 1950.

McCAULEY, David Vincent (măk-kaw'lē), clergyman; b. New York, N.Y., Feb. 13, 1895; s. Richard Vincent and Mary Theresa (Gibson) McC.; ed. Fordham Prep. Sch., 1910-13, St. Andrew-on-Hudson, 1913-17; A.B., Woodstock (Md.) Coll., 1919, A.M., 1920; Ph.D., Gregorian U. (Rome), 1928. Entered Society of Jesus, 1913, ordained R.C. priest, 1927; instr. Canisius Coll., Buffalo, N.Y., 1920-22; asst. prof. biology Fordham U., 1922-23; prof. biology Holy Cross Coll., Worcester, Mass., 1923-24, Canisius Coll., 1928-30; prof. biology and psychology Woodstock (Md.) Coll., 1931-34; regent Schs. of Medicine and Dentistry, Georgetown U., Washington, D.C., 1934-46, dean Sch. of Medicine, 1935-46; rector Our Lady of Martyrs Tertianship; dir. Sacred Heart Retreat House since 1947. Mem. Am. Assn. Advancement Sci., Am. Assn. Jesuit Scientists, Nat. Conf. of Cath. Charities. Contbr. to professional and scientific jours. Address: Auriesville, N.Y. Died Mar. 2, 1950.

NEILSON, Harry Rosengarten, ins. brokerage; b. Phila., Dec. 6, 1893; s. Lewis and Clara Augusta (Rosengarten) N.; ed. Episcopal Acad., Phila., 1903-08, St. Paul's Sch., Concord, N.H., 1908-12; B.S., U. of Pa., 1916; m. Alberta P. Reath, Oct. 18, 1922 (dec.); children—Harry Rosengarten, Jr., Albert Pancoast, Benjamin Reath. Began as clk. with Powers-Weightman-Rosengarten Co., 1919; asst. sec., 1922-27; asst. sec. to successors, Merck & Co., Inc., 1927-28; asso. with W. H. Newbold, Son & Co., 1928-34; v.p. and sec. Higham-Neilson Co., ins. brokers, Phila., since 1934; dir. Merck & Co., Inc., Erie & Pittsburgh R.R. Co.; pres. Elmira & Williamsport R.R. Co. Served with First Troop Phila. City Cav. on Mexican border, 1916-17; 2d then 1st lt., U.S.N.A., 1917-18. Trustee Lankenau Hospital Mem. Delta Psi. Republican. Episcopalian. Clubs: Phila., Racquet, Gulph Mills Golf, St. Anthony, Loyal Legion (Phila.); St. Anthony (New York), Turf & Field, Thoroughbred Club of America, Maryland. Home: St. Davids, Pa. Office: Inquirer Bldg., Philadelphia 30. Died Sep. 27, 1949.

POTTER, Frank Maxson, business exec.; b. Newark, N.J., July 3, 1873; s. Frank Maxson and Mary L. (Williams) P.; B.S. in E.E. Lafayette College, 1896, hon. D.Sc., 1927; m. Sue Donaldson, May 17, 1899. Began as engr. N.Y. Independent Telephone Constrn. Co., 1896. Gen. supt. Newark (N.J.) Ind. Telephone Co., 1897-99; gen. supt. Syracuse Ind. Telephone Co., 1899-1903; gen. mgr., 1903-05; dist. mgr. Consol. Telephone Co., Inter Ocean-Long Dist. Telephone Co., 1903. Vice pres. and engr. Wire & Telephone Co. of America, 1905-09. Vice pres. and factory mgr. Rome Wire Co., 1909-18, 1919-27. Civil exec. dir. engine and plane maintenance, Div. of Mil. Aeronautics, Washington, D.C., 1918. Vice pres. and dir., chmn. research development and engring. patents, Gen. Cable Corp., 1928-39, now vice chmn. bd. dirs. and dir. Mem. Tau Beta Pi (hon.). Home: Turin Rd. Office: care General Cable Corp., Rome, N.Y. Died Mar. 18, 1950.

RAVNDAL, G(abriel) Bie, consul gen.; b. Norway, June 27, 1865; A.B., Royal U. of Norway, 1883, A.M., 1884; came to U.S., 1885; m. Dorothea Magelssen of Rushford, Minn., Sept. 14, 1893; children—Sarah Stockfleth, Inga Bie (Mrs. T. H. Keble), Christian Magelssen, Olaf, Eric. Newspaper pub. in Dak. 1889-98; 1st president Northwestern Scandinavian Singers Assn., 1891-93; mem. S.D. Ho. of Rep., 1892-94; consul at Beirut, Syria, 1898-1905, at Dawson, Yukon Ty., Can., 1905-06; consul-gen. at Beirut, 1906-10, at Constantinople, Dec. 1910; apptd. consul-gen., class II, Mar. 5, 1915; in charge consular interests at Constantinople of France, Great Britain, Russia, Italy, Belgium, Serbia, Montenegro, Switzerland, 1914-17; detailed to Consulate-Gen. at Paris, May 25, 1917; apptd. consul-gen. St. Nazaire, France, Nov. 5, 1917; at Nantes, France, Jan. 1, 1918; invited to appear before Am. Peace Mission, Paris, Feb. 1919; reassigned as consul-gen. at Constantinople, Mar. 8, 1919; apptd. U.S. commr. and consul-general at Constantinople, Apr. 20, 1919; resigned as commissioner, March 14, 1921; apptd. foreign service officer Class I, July 1, 1924; consul-gen. Zurich, Switzerland, Sept. 1925-28; consul-gen. Hamburg, 1928-29, Berlin, 1929-30; retired June 26, 1930. Pres. Beirut Relief Com. (agents of Am. Red Cross) during Cilician disturbance, 1909; founder and ex-president Beirut Chapter American Red Cross; founder and secretary Constantinople Chapter Am. Red Cross. Received December 23, 1909, the Am. Red Cross medal of merit in recognition of services in relief of suffering caused by massacres in Cilicia and Northern Syria. Mem. bd. Syrian Protestant Coll., 1898-1902; founder and hon. pres. Am. Chamber of Commerce for the Levant; U.S. del. 5th Internat. Congress of Chambers of Commerce, Boston, 1912. Founder and pres. Am. Club of Constantinople; v.p. Constantinople Golf Club. Author: Origin of the Capitulations and of the Consular Institution (U.S. Senate Document No. 34, 68th Congress, 1st session); Turkey, Commercial and Industrial Handbook, 1926; Scandinavian Pioneers in Dakota, Vol. XII, South Dakota Historical Collections. Home: Sioux Falls, S.D. Address: Dept. of State, Washington, D.C. Died March 24, 1950.

REYNOLDS, Isham E. (rĕn'oldz), music dir.; b. Birmingham, Ala., Sept. 27, 1879; s. William Pickney and Mary (Eastis) R.; student Mississippi Coll., Clinton, Miss., 1905-06, Moody Bible Inst., 1907-08; studied theory, composition, etc. under pvt. tutors; Mus.B., Univ. Extension Conservatory, Chicago, 1918; student Chicago Musical Coll., 1920; Mus.D., Southern Sch. of Fine Arts, Houston, Tex., 1942; m. Alice Velma Burns, July 18, 1900 (dec.); 1 dau. died in infancy; m. 2d, Lura Mae Hawk, July 17, 1912; 1 dau., Mary Lurames. Began as evangelist song leader, 1905; entered state evangelistic work, 1907; conducted campaigns as singer under Home Mission Bd. of Southern Bapt. Conv. for 5 yrs.; dir. sacred music, Southwest Bapt. Theol. Sem., 1915-45; retired, May 9, 1945, now dir. emeritus; Sch. of Sacred Music with $330,000 bldg., dedicated to sacred music; mem. exec. bd. Southwestern Press (songbook publishers). Resigned because of ill health, 1945; now doing field work, lecturing on Church Music. Mem. music com., Southern Bapt. Conv., since 1937. Mem. Music Teachers Nat. Assn.; mem. church music com., Music Educators Nat. Conf.; mem. Texas State Music Teachers Assn.; pres. Ft. Worth Music Teachers Assn. 1940-41. Democrat. Mason (Shriner). Author: Manual of Practical Church Music, 1924; Harmony Made Plain, 1923; rev. edit., 1943; Compositions as Applied to the Smaller Sacred Forms, 1923, rev. edit., 1943; The Church Choir Manual, 1925, rev. edit. under title The Choir, Its Personnel, Organization, Mission and Work, 1930; The Ministry of Music in Religion, 1929; Church Music, 1935 (Bapt. S. S. Bd. Study Course); The Choir in Non-Liturgical Churches; Music and the Scriptures; and Outlines of Church Music, 1940, rev. edit., 1942; also several cantatas, anthems and hymns, 1930-40; Ruth (sacred music drama), 1936. The Prodigal Son (sacred music drama), 1940; Music and the Scriptures, 1942. Joint author: Essentials in Notation, 1928. Joint compiler and editor: Kingdom Songs, 1922; Jehovah's Praise. 1925. Address: 1501 6th Av., Ft. Worth, Tex. Died May 10, 1949; buried Greenwood Cemetery, Ft. Worth, Tex.

SMITH, Sydney, judge; b. Lexington, Miss., Apr. 9, 1869; s. Thomas W. and Sarah Ann (West) S.; ed. pub. schs. Lexington and U. of Miss. Law Sch.; m. Matty Leigh Smith, Apr. 9, 1896 (dec.). Admitted to bar, 1893, practiced at Lexington; mem. firm Tackett & Smith, 1895-1906. Mem. Miss. Ho. of Rep., 2 terms, 1900-06; judge Circuit Court, 4th Jud. Dist., Sept. 1906-May 1909; asso. justice Supreme Court, Miss., 1909-12; chief justice since Aug. 1912. Democrat. Prof. law, Millsaps Coll. Law Sch., 1915-17. Mem. Council Am. Law Inst. since 1937. Baptist. Home: 855 N. Jefferson St. Address: State Capitol, Jackson, Miss.* Died July 24, 1948.

SPAIN, Charles Lyle, educator; b. South Bend, Ind., Mar. 3, 1869; s. David F. and Mary (Henkle) S.; B.A., U. of Mich., 1893, M.A., 1920; M.Pd., Ypsilanti (Mich.) Normal Sch., 1915; Ph.D., U. of Mich., 1923; LL.D., Wayne U., 1939; m. Annie Elliott, 1895. Teacher high sch., South Bend, 1889-90; grade prin. Central High Sch., Grand Rapids, Mich., 1893-98; prin. Madison Av. Sch., Grand Rapids, 1898-1901; v. prin. Washington Normal Sch., Detroit, Feb.-June 1901, prin., 1901-06; supervisor primary grades, pub. schs., Detroit, 1906-13, elementary schs., 1913-14; asst. supt. pub. schs., Detroit, 1914-19, deputy supt. schools, 1919-39, also exec. v.p. Wayne U., 1933-39, v.p. emeritus since 1939. Mem. Phi Delta Kappa. Republican. Episcopalian. Clubs: Univ. of Mich., Mich. Automobile, Michigan Union. Author: The Platoon Schools, 1920. Co-Author: Chadsey-Spain Readers; Public Elementary School Plant, 1930. Home: 201 E. Kirby Av., Detroit, Mich. Died Feb. 23, 1950.

SPECK, Frank Gouldsmith, anthropologist; b. Brooklyn, N.Y., Nov. 8, 1881; s. Frank G. and Hattie L. (Staniford) S.; A.B., Columbia, 1904, A.M., 1905; fellow U. of Pa., 1908; m. Florence Insley, Sept. 15, 1910. Asst. curator ethnology, Univ. Mus., U. of Pa., 1909-11; instr. anthropology, U. of Pa., 1909-11, asst. prof., 1911-25, prof. since 1925; lecturer in anthropology, Swarthmore Coll., 1923-27. Asst. editor Am. Anthropologist, 1920-37, Am. Journal Archæology, 1920-23; anthropologist with Nat. Research Council (exec. com. 1925). Hon. Curator Am. Ethnology, Peabody Mus., Salem, Mass., 1946. Mem. Am. Anthropol. Assn. (v.p., 1945), Am. Ethnol. Soc., Am. Folklore Soc. (pres. 1920-22), A.A.A.S., Anthropol. Soc. of Philadelphia (president 1920-22), Oriental Club Phila., Sigma Xi (pres. 1942), Sigma Phi Epsilon. Extensive field work among Indian tribes of Indian Ty., Okla., Southeastern and Northeastern U.S., Can., Newfoundland and Labrador peninsula. Author: Ethnology of Yuchi Indians, 1909; Ceremonial Songs of the Creek and Yuchi Indians, 1911; The Creek Indians of Taskigi Town, 1907; The Double Curve Motive in Northeastern Algonkian Art, 1914; Hunting Territories and Myths of the Temiskaming Algonquins, 1915; Social Life and Mythology of the Temagami Ojibwa, 1915; The Nanticoke Community of Delaware, 1915; Penobscot Shamanism, 1920; The Functions of Wampum Among the Northeastern Angonkian, 1919; Penobscot Transformer Texts, 1920; Boethuk and Micmac, 1922; The Rappahannock Indians of Virginia, 1925; The Penn Wampum Belts, 1925; Native Tribes and Dialects of Connecticut, 1926; Symbolism in Penobscot Art, 1927; also chapters in the Ethnology of the Powhatan Tribes of Virginia, 1928; Tribal Boundaries of Massachusetts and Wampanoag Indians, 1928; A Study of the Delaware Indian Big House Ceremony, 1931; Catawba Texts, 1935; Penobscot Tales and Religious Beliefs, 1935; Naskapi, Savage Hunters of the Labrador Peninsula, 1935; Oklahoma Delaware Ceremonies, Feasts and Dances, 1937; Montagnais Art in Birch-Bark, 1938; Penobscot Man, 1940; Gourds of the Southeastern Indians, 1941; Tutelo Spirit Adoption Ceremony, 1942; The Celestial Bear Comes Down to Earth, 1945; The Iroquois, 1946; Eastern Algonkian Block-Stamp Decoration, 1947. Home: Swarthmore, Pa. Died Feb. 6, 1950.

SPURR, Josiah Edward, geologist; b. Gloucester, Mass., Oct. 1, 1870; s. Alfred and Oratia E. (Snow) S.; A.B., Harvard, 1893, A.M., 1894; m. Sophie C. Burchard, Jan. 18, 1899; children—Edward Burchard, John Constantine, William Alfred, Robert Anton, Stephen Hopkins. Mining engr. and geologist to Sultan of Turkey, Apr. 1901-May 1902; geologist, U.S. Geol. Survey, 1902-06; chief geol. dept. Am. Smelting & Refining Co., Am. Smelters Securities Co., Guggenheim Exploration Co., 1906-08; Spurr & Cox (Inc.), cons. specialists in mining, 1908-11; v.p. in charge of mining, Tonopah Mining Co. of Nevada, 1911-17; mem. com. of mineral imports, U.S. Shipping and War Trade bds., 1917-18; exec. war minerals investigations, chief metal mining engineer, Bureau of Mines; chief engr., War Mineral Relief, 1918-19; editor Engineering and Mining Journal, 1919-27; prof. of geology, Rollins Coll., 1930-32. Mem. Mining and Metall. Soc. America (pres. 1921), Am. Inst. of Mining and Metall. Engineers, Soc. Econ. Geologists (pres. 1923), Geol. Soc. America, Am. Geog. Soc., Soc. Mayflower Descendants, Society of Colonial Wars. Author: The Iron-Bearing Rocks of the Mesabi Range in Minnesota (Minn. Geol. and Nat. Hist. Survey), 1894; Through the Yukon Gold Diggings, 1900; Geology Applied to Mining, 1904; The Ore Magmas, 1923; Geology Applied to Selenology, 1944; Features of the Moon, 1945; Lunar Catastrophic History, 1947; The Shrunken Moon, 1949; also various monographs and reports on economic geology, etc. Editor: Political and Commercial Geology, 1921. Mt. Spurr peak in Alaska named by U.S. Geol. Survey in honor of his explorations in Alaska, 1896, 98. Home: 324 Henkel Circle, Winter Park, Fla.; also Alstead, N.H. Died Jan. 12, 1950.

TROUT, Hugh Henry, Sr., surgeon; b. Staunton, Va., June 6, 1878; s. Philip H. and Olivia (Benson) T.; M.D., Univ. of Va., 1902; student in Europe, 1907-08; m. Leonora Cocke, 1910; children—Leonora (Mrs. Herman Bolster), Hugh Henry, Philip Cocke; m. 2d, Alice Green, 1926; children—Alice Green, Albert Henry. Intern Johns Hopkins Hosp., 1902-04; surgeon St. Joseph's German Hosp., Baltimore, 1904-05, Union Protestant Infirmary, 1905-08; pres. Jefferson Hosp., Roanoke, Va. Mem. bd. visitors U. of Va., Mary Washington Coll. Served as lt. col. Med. Corps, U.S. Army, 1918-19. Fellow Am. Coll. Surgeons; mem. A.M.A., Southern Med. Assn., Am. Surg. Assn., Southern Surg. Assn. (pres. 1931), Med. Soc. of Va. (pres., 1940), Internat. Surg. Assn., Alpha Omega Alpha, Phi Kappa Psi. Democrat. Episcopalian. Mason. Clubs: Rotary, Shenandoah (Roanoke, Va.). Home: 1301 Franklin Rd. Office: Jefferson Hosp., Roanoke, Va. Died Jan. 13, 1950.

WARNOW, Mark (war'nō), b. Monastrischt, Russia, Apr. 10, 1902; s. Joseph and Sara (Smollen) W.; brought to United States, 1907; educated public school and Eastern District High School, New York City; student Volpe Institute, 1919-22; married Helen D. McGowan, September 6, 1942 (div. 1949); 1 dau., Suzanne Helen. Received first violin lesson from father, 1909; later studied with Leopold Littenberg, Franz Kneisel, Mortimer Wilson, Arnold Volpe; while a student made concert tours with others, also became condr. of Salvation Army bands and amateur orchestras of Brooklyn Orchestra Soc.; acted as teacher of violin theory; condr. of grand opera for Marcel Opera Co., 1921; then condr. musical shows and player in symphony orchestras; with Columbia network since 1932; as concert maestro and arranger, has conducted for and helped develop such well known artists as Morton Downey, Kate Smith, Gertrude Neisen; created "Blue Velvet" music; work includes Westinghouse program with John Charles Thomas, March of Time, We, the People, Your Hit Parade (Saturday nights, coast to coast), All Time Hit Parade, Helen Hayes dramatic series; recently began musical direction of dramatic series with Victor Jory, Dangerously Yours. Produced and supervised musical comedy, What's Up, on legitimate stage, season, 1943-44. Office: 485 Madison Av., New York, N.Y. Died Oct. 17, 1949.

CORRIGENDA

Sketches to correct errors now brought to attention but not noted by either the biographees while alive, or survivors to whom proofs were mailed, and/or the proofreaders processing that printing; sketches omitted from the First Printing as a result of oversights or the lack of the notice of death; revisions (total or partial) requested by intimately interested and responsible sources; and/or dates of deaths, as well as other specific corrections necessary for reasons similar to the foregoing. Sketches of living biographees, erroneously listed in necrologies because of name similarities or other factors, and as a result included in this compilation, have been constructively expurgated by mechanically deleting the initial and last two lines on the printing plates.

ALLEE, Marjorie Hill, writer; Line 14: insert after "1942," "The House, 1944; Smoke Jumper, 1945."

BEARD, Charles Austin, author; Line 11: correct "Geto" to "Goto"; Line 22: insert after "1910," "(10th edition, 1949);" Line 39: insert after "1934," "Author."

CARROLL, Raymond G., writer; correct date of death to Dec. 12, 1943.

CARROLL, Robert Sproul, psychiatrist; b. Cooperstown, Pa., Feb. 18, 1869; s. Jonathan Edward and Margaret Jane (Sproul) C.; student Denison U., Granville, O., 1885-86; M.D., Marion Sims Coll. of Medicine (St. Louis U.) 1893; M.D., Rush Med. Coll. (U. of Chicago), 1897; m. 2d, Grace Stewart Potter (pianist), Feb. 28, 1918; children (1st marriage)—Mrs. Heloise Handcock, Donald Frederic (major in U.S. Army). Practiced medicine at Calvert, Tex., 1892-1902; associate superintendent Marysville (Ohio) Sanatorium, 1902-04; established Dr. Carroll's Sanitarium, Inc., Asheville, N.C., 1904, title changed 1912 to Highland Hosp., Inc. (hosp. donated to psychiatric dept. Duke U., 1939; retired as pres. and med. dir., 1946). Lecturer in psychiatry, Sch. Med., Duke U. Fellow Am. Psychiat. Assn., Assn. for Research in Nervous and Mental Disease, Assn. for Study of Internal Secretions, Southern Soc. Philosophy, Internat., Assn. Philosophy, A.A.A.S., Am. Eugenics Soc. Am. Ethnol. Soc., Eugenical Research Assn. Nat. Econ. League, Am. Museum Natural History, Assn. for Research in Human Heredity, N.Y. Acad. Sciences. Republican. Presbyn. Author: The Mastery of Nervousness, 1917; The Soul in Suffering, 1919; Our Nervous Friends, 1919; Old at 40 or Young at 60, 1920; The Grille Gate, 1922; Aseptic Meningitis in Combating the Praecox Problem, 1923; What Price Alcohol, 1941. Home: 400 Midland Drive, Asheville, N.C. Died July 26, 1949.

DU MOULIN, bishop; Line 1: add after "bishop", "b. Montreal, Can., July 9, 1870; s. John Philip (Bishop of Niagara, Ont.) and Francis Mary (Brough) Du M.;"

GAMMON, Robert William, clergyman; Line 6: Insert after "Quinn," "m. 2d, Sallie A. McDermott, Nov. 27, 1947."

GARDNER, Oliver Max, ex-governor; Line 17: insert after "1929-33", "apptd. under sec. of Treasury, Feb. 27, 1946; apptd. ambassador to Great Britain, Jan. 13, 1947;" Line 19: insert after "N.C.", "(father Consol. Univ. of N.C.)"; Line 20: insert after "1943", "; benefactor Gardner-Webb Coll., Birling Springs, N. C.;" Line 23: Add at end, "; buried in Sunset Cemetery, Shelby, N.C."

KELLOGG, John Harvey, surgeon; correct date of death to Dec. 14, 1943.

MILLER, Joseph Leggett, M.D.; b. Kewanee, Ill., Nov. 24, 1867; s. James and Jane (Leggett) M., reared on farm; B.S., U. of Mich., 1893; M.D. Northwestern U. Med. Sch., 1895; hon. D.Sc., M. of Mich., June 1933; married, 1901. Engaged in practice at Chicago, from 1895; formerly attending phys. Cook County Hosp.; now attending phys. St. Luke's Hosp.; prof. clin. medicine, U. of Chicago. Commd. maj. M.C., U.S.A. Sept. 1917; lt. col., Aug. 1918. Home: Chicago, Ill. Died Aug. 6, 1937.

PETTER, Rodolphe C., missionary; correct date of death to Jan. 6, 1947.

QUIRKE, Terence Thomas, prof. geology; correct date of death to Aug. 19, 1947.

ROOSEVELT Edith Kermit Carow; b. Norwich, Conn., Aug. 16, 1861; d. Charles and Gertrude Elizabeth (Tyler) Carow; ed. Miss Comstock's School; m. Theodore Roosevelt, 26th President of U.S., in London, Eng., Dec. 2, 1886; children—Theodore Jr., Kermit (dec.) Ethel Carow (Mrs. Richard Dethy), Archibald Bulloch, Quentin (dec.). Home: Oyster Bay. Died, Sept. 30, 1948.

ROOSEVELT, Franklin Delano; interred at Hyde Park, N.Y.

SACHS, Bernard, neurologist; correct date of death to Feb. 8, 1944.

SCHRUP Charles Joseph, ins. official; b. Dubuque, Ia., Jan. 17, 1886; s. Nicholas John and Mary Ann (Kransz) S.; ed. pub. and pvt. schs. of Dubuque; m. Mary Ethleen O'Rourke, Apr. 25, 1922; children—Eleanor Mary (Mrs. Robert G. Holscher), Charles Joseph, Nicholas John. Asst. treas. Dubuque Fire & Marine Ins. Co., 1911-13, treas., 1913-24, and 1938-43, also pres. since 1924; treas. Nat. Reserve Ins. Co., 1919-43, (merged with Dubuque Fire & Marine Ins. Co., pres. since 1924; pres. Am. Trust & Savings Bank, 1925-43, chmn. bd. since 1943; pres. and treas. Dubuque Securities Co.; dir. Western Ins. Bureau, Chicago. Mem. bd. regents, Loras Coll.) formerly Columbia Coll.), Dubuque. Mem. Chicago Athletic Assn. Catholic. Elk. Club: Golf. Home: 1380 Auburn St. Office: Roshek Bldg., Dubuque, Ia. Died Jan. 8, 1949.

SMART, E(dmund) Hodgson, artist; Line 5: insert after "1896", "m. 2d, Margaret Atkinson Murphy, Oct. 4, 1942."

SUTHERLAND, Howard, ex-senator; add date of death March 12, 1950.

TOWER, Edwin Briggs Hal, Jr., patent and copyright lawyer; b. Freehold, N.J., Aug. 2, 1879; s. Edwin Briggs Hale and Eleanor Hamilton (Bawden) T.; LL.B., Columbia University. (George Washington U.) 1902; m. Bessie Mather Applegate, May 4, 1909; children—(twin daus.) Jean (Mrs. William R. Rennie), Milbrey. Admitted to Courts: U.S. Supreme Court, 1921; Court of Appeals of D.C., 1908; Supreme Court of D.C., 1908; U.S. Circuit Court of Appeals for 7th Circuit, 1912; U.S. Court of Custom and Patent Appeals, 1931; Supreme Court of State of Wis., 1915; U. S. Dist. Courts for: Eastern Dist. of Wis., 1909; Northern Dist. of Ill., 1909; Western Dist. of N.Y., 1914; Northern Dist of O., Western Div. 1934; practice of patent, trademark and copyright causes, Milwaukee, Wis., 1908-47, New York, N.Y., 1909-28, and Chicago, Ill., 1909-16. Served in The Am. Protective League, received certificate of exceptional service as operative military intelligence staff, 1917-19. Author, Public Law 587, 79th Congress. Mem. Nat. Assn. Mfrs. (present mem. research and patents com., present chmn. spl. sub-com. on amending revised statutes to expedite recovery of damages in suits of infringement of patents). Wis. Mfrs. Assn., Am. Bar Assn., Assn. of Bar of City of New York, Am. Milwaukee (past pres.) patent law assns. Clubs; Chicago, University, Tavern, Post and Paddock (Chicago); Bankers of America (N.Y.) Mohawk (Schenectady, N.Y.); Milwaukee, Milwaukee Country (Milwaukee). Home: 2743 N. Lake Dr., Milwaukee 11. Office: First Wisconsin National Bank Bldg., Milwaukee 2. Died Mar. 27, 1948.